HARRAP'S
GIANT PAPERBACK

FRENCH
DICTIONARY

FRENCH-ENGLISH
ENGLISH-FRENCH

First published in Great Britain as
Harrap Concise French Dictionary 1997
by Chambers Harrap Publishers Ltd
7 Hopetoun Crescent, Edinburgh EH7 4AY

© Chambers Harrap Publishers 1998

ISBN 0-02-862376-2

Macmillan General Reference
A Simon and Schuster Macmillan Company
1633 Broadway
New York, NY 10019-6785

MACMILLAN is a registered trademark
of Macmillan Inc.

Printed in the United States of America

Editor-in-Chief/*Rédacteur en chef*
Patrick White

Editors/*Rédacteurs*
Stuart Fortey   Isabelle Elkaim
Anna Stevenson   Laurence Larroche
Georges Pilard

Contributors/*Collaborateurs*
Ruth Blackmore   Sophie Marin
Lynda Carey   Martine Pierquin
Lesley Johnston   Catherine Roux
Irene Lakhani   Cécile Vanwalleghem
Ruth Noble

Computing terminology/*Terminologie informatique*
Arnel Leyva   Annick Morel

Canadianisms/*Canadianismes*
Alain Garand

Data Management/*Informatique éditoriale*
Ilona Morison
Liam Rodger

Keyboarders/*Clavistes*
Sheena Cleland
Marian Shepherd

The Publisher would also like to thank the editorial teams that contributed to the various editions of the Harrap's *Shorter*, in particular the 1996 edition on which this book is largely based.

L'Éditeur aimerait également remercier les équipes de rédacteurs ayant collaboré aux diverses éditions du Harrap's *Shorter*, et notamment à l'édition de 1996, dont le présent ouvrage est largement inspiré.

iii

Trademarks

Words considered to be trademarks have been designated in this dictionary by the symbol ®. However, no judgement is implied concerning the legal status of any trademark by virtue of the presence or absence of such a symbol.

Marques déposées

Les termes considérés comme des marques déposées sont signalés dans ce dictionnaire par le symbole ®. Cependant, la présence ou l'absence de ce symbole ne constitue nullement une indication quant à la valeur juridique de ces termes.

Contents
Table des Matières

Preface

Harrap's Giant Paperback French Dictionary is a completely new book, based largely on the latest revision of the *Harrap's Shorter*. All entries and translations have been revised, and several new approaches have been applied by a team of British and French lexicographers working together in Harrap's Edinburgh offices. The English side has been enriched by neologisms collected as part of our sister company Chambers' Wordtrack programme to ensure that this dictionary is as up-to-date as possible. The result is an easy-to-use guide to modern English and French, with accurate, reliable translations.

As the dictionary will have a wide variety of users, and will find a place in school and workplace alike, it contains a broad range of vocabulary. In addition to good coverage of the French and English spoken today, including slang (an important feature of all Harrap dictionaries), technical terms from computing, finance, education, the media and business will be found alongside encyclopedic information such as proper and geographical names.

The growth of the Internet and the information superhighway is taking communication between the peoples of the world into a new era. Harrap has responded to the challenge this represents. Terms such as **Web site, browser, newsgroup**, and **naviguer sur l'Internet, cyperespace, internaute**, which are now commonplace, will all be found in these pages.

Patrick White
Edinburgh 1997

Préface

Ce dictionnaire *Harrap's Giant Paperback French Dictionary*, rédigé à partir du *Harrap's Shorter*, est un ouvrage entièrement nouveau. Chaque entrée, chaque traduction a été revue par une équipe de lexicographes français et britanniques basée à Édimbourg. Le côté anglais-français du dictionnaire s'est enrichi de néologismes extraits du corpus de Chambers (notre société-soeur), présentant ainsi un panorama aussi moderne que possible de la langue. Le *Harrap's Giant Paperback French Dictionary* est un ouvrage fiable et de consultation aisée, indispensable à quiconque s'intéresse au français et à l'anglais d'aujourd'hui.

Afin de satisfaire aux besoins des utilisateurs au collège et au lycée comme au bureau, cet ouvrage contient un très large éventail de vocabulaire. Le français et l'anglais parlés y sont traités en profondeur et l'argot (l'un des points forts des dictionnaires Harrap) y est bien représenté. On y trouvera également un abondant vocabulaire de spécialité (informatique, finance, enseignement, médias, commerce) ainsi que des noms propres et des noms de lieux.

L'expansion de l'Internet et de l'autoroute de l'information marque le début d'une ère nouvelle dans la communication entre les gens. Harrap a relevé le défi que cela représente. Des termes désormais d'usage courant tels que **Web site, browser, newsgroup** et **naviguer sur l'Internet, cyberespace, internaute** figurent dans ce dictionnaire.

Patrick White
Édimbourg 1997

Structure of Entries

Structure des Entrées

Indicateurs de champ sémantique pour les termes spécialisés
Field labels indicate senses belonging to a particular subject area

major ['meɪdʒə(r)] **1** *n* **(a)** *Mil* commandant *m*; **m. general** général *m* de division **(b)** *Am Univ* (subject) matière *f* principale
2 *adj* **(a)** *(important)* majeur(e); *(most important)* principal(e); *(accident, illness)* très grave; **of m. importance** de la plus haute importance **(b)** *Mus* majeur(e)
3 *vi Am Univ* **to m. in sth** se spécialiser en qch.

Anglais d'Amérique du Nord
American English senses indicated

Seule l'initiale du mot traité apparaît dans l'exemple
Headword abbreviated to first letter only

La phonétique complète est donnée pour chaque entrée
IPA shown in full for all headwords

management ['mænɪdʒmənt] *n* **(a)** *(activity)* (of company, project) gestion *f*, direction *f*; *(of economy, resources, shop, hotel)* gestion; **m. consultant** conseiller(ère) *m,f* en gestion; **m. studies** études *fpl* de gestion **(b)** *(managers, employers)* direction *f*; **under new m.** *(sign)* changement de propriétaire; **m. buyout** = rachat d'une société par la direction; **m. team** équipe *f* dirigeante

Les composés sont traités sous le premier élément et classés alphabétiquement
Compounds placed under first element; listed in alphabetical order

Chaque nouvelle catégorie grammaticale est traitée à la ligne et précédée d'un numéro en gras
New grammatical category introduced by bold numeral, placed on new line

managing director ['mænɪdʒɪŋ'daɪrektə(r)] *n* directeur(trice) *m,f* général(e)

Indique que la traduction fonctionne aussi au sens figuré
This label means that the translation also works in figurative contexts

melt [melt] **1** *vt also Fig* faire fondre
2 *vi* fondre; **to m. into thin air** s'évaporer, disparaître; **to m. into the crowd** se fondre dans la foule
►**melt away** *vi* (of snow) fondre; *(of clouds, vapour)* se dissiper; *(of crowd)* se disperser; *(of objections, opposition)* s'évanouir
►**melt down** *vt sep* (metal) fondre

Les verbes à particule sont précédés du signe ►
Phrasal verbs introduced by ►

Le genre des noms donnés en traduction est indiqué en italiques
Gender of noun translations shown in italic

Les homographes sont numérotés
Superscript number marks homographs

minute[1] ['mɪnɪt] **1** *n* **(a)** *(of time)* minute *f*; **ten minutes past/to three** trois heures dix/moins dix; **wait a m.!** attendez une minute!; **go downstairs this m.!** descends immédiatement!; **just a m.** une minute; **the m. my back was turned** dès que j'ai eu le dos tourné; **any m.** d'une minute à l'autre; **in a m.** dans une minute; **at the last m.** à la dernière minute; **m. hand** *(of watch)* grande aiguille *f*; **m. steak** steak *m* minute **(b)** *(note)* note *f*; **minutes** *(of meeting)* compte rendu *m*
2 *vt (make note of)* inscrire au procès-verbal
minute[2] [maɪ'njuːt] *adj* **(a)** *(small)* infime, minuscule **(b)** *(detailed)* minutieux(euse)

Les indicateurs sémantiques apparaissent en italiques et entre parenthèses
Sense indicators shown in italic in brackets

Le féminin est donné systématiquement
Feminine inflections shown consistently

La forme développée des abréviations est donnée systématiquement; chaque abréviation est traduite
Full form of abbreviation given consistently; all abbreviations have translations

MOD [eməʊ'diː] *n Br Pol* (abbr **Ministry of Defence**) ministère *m* de la Défense

mollusc, *Am* **mollusk** ['mɒləsk] *n* mollusque *m*

Les variantes orthographiques américaines sont données
American spelling variants shown

viii

académie [akademi] *nf* **(a)** *(des lettres, des sciences, d'art)* academy; **l'A. française** = learned society responsible for promoting the French language and imposing standards **(b)** *(école)* school, academy; **a. de musique/dessin** music/art school **(c)** *(dans l'Éducation nationale)* Br ≃ local education authority, Am ≃ school district

acquiescer [16] [akjese] *vi* to acquiesce **(à to)**; **a. d'un signe de tête** to nod in agreement

aider [ede] **1** *vt* to help; *(sujet: gouvernement)* to aid; **que puis-je faire pour vous a.?** how may I help you?; **je me suis fait a. par un ami** I got a friend to help me; **a. qn à faire qch** to help sb to do sth; **a. qn à monter/sortir** to help sb up/out; *Ironique* **tu veux que je t'aide?** stop that!; **elle n'aide jamais** she never helps (out) **- 2 aider à** *vt ind* to contribute towards; **a. à faire qch** to help to do sth **- 3 s'aider** *vpr* **(a)** *(soi-même)* **s'a. de qch** to use sth; **marcher en s'aidant d'une canne/de béquilles** to walk with the aid of a stick/crutches; *Prov* **aide-toi et le ciel t'aidera** God helps those who help themselves **(b)** *(l'un l'autre)* to help each other

amanché, -e [amãʃe] *adj Can* **mal a.** badly dressed

amnistier [66] [amnistje] *vt* to grant an amnesty to

arrière-plan *(pl* **arrière-plans)** [arjɛrplã] *nm aussi Fig* background; **à l'a.** in the background

arrière-saison *(pl* **arrière-saisons)** [arjɛrsɛzɔ̃] *nf Br* late autumn, *Am* late fall

arrière-train *(pl* **arrière-trains)** [arjɛrtrɛ̃] *nm (d'un animal)* (hind)quarters; *Fam (d'une personne)* rump, rear

artériosclérose [arterjoskleroz] *nf* hardening of the arteries, *Spéc* arteriosclerosis

athlétisme [atletism] *nm* athletics *(singulier)*; **épreuves d'a.** athletic events

avril [avril] *nm* April; **le premier a.** *(jour des farces)* April Fools' Day; *Prov* **en a., ne te découvre pas d'un fil** ne'er cast a clout till May is out; *voir aussi* **janvier**

English Phonetic Symbols

Symboles Phonétiques de l'Anglais

Consonnes/Consonants

[b] but [bʌt]
[d] dab [dæb]
[dʒ] jam [dʒæm]; gem [dʒem]
[f] fat [fæt]
[g] go [gəʊ]
[h] hat [hæt]
[j] yet [jet]
[k] cat [kæt]
[l] lad [læd]
[m] mat [mæt]
[n] no [nəʊ]
[ŋ] bang [bæŋ]
[p] pat [pæt]
[r] rat [ræt]
[(r)] *(seulement prononcé en cas de liaison avec le mot suivant)* far [fɑː(r)]
[s] sat [sæt]
[ʃ] sham [ʃæm]
[t] tap [tæp]
[tʃ] chat [tʃæt]
[θ] thatch [θætʃ]
[ð] that [ðæt]
[v] vat [væt]
[w] wall [wɔːl]
[z] zinc [zɪŋk]
[ʒ] pleasure [pleʒə(r)]
[χ] loch [lɒχ]

Voyelles/Vowels

[æ] bat [bæt]
[ɑː] art [ɑːt]
[e] bet [bet]
[ɜː] curl [kɜːl]
[ə] amend [ə'mend]
[iː] bee [biː]
[ɪ] bit [bɪt]
[ɒ] wad [wɒd]
[ɔː] all [ɔːl]
[ʊ] put [pʊt]
[uː] shoe [ʃuː]
[ʌ] cut [kʌt]

Diphtongues/Diphthongs

[aɪ] life [laɪf]
[aʊ] house [haʊs]
[eə] there [ðeə(r)]
[eɪ] date [deɪt]
[əʊ] low [ləʊ]
[ɪə] beer [bɪə(r)]
[ɔɪ] boil [bɔɪl]
[ʊə] poor [pʊə(r)]

Symboles Phonétiques du Français

French Phonetic Symbols

Consonants/Consonnes

[b] beau [bo]
[d] donner [dɔne]
[f] feu [fø]
[g] garde [gard]
[ʒ] gilet [ʒilɛ]
[k] camp [kɑ̃]
[l] lait [lɛ]
[m] mon [mɔ̃]
[n] né [ne]
[ŋ] parking [parkiŋ]
[ɲ] campagne [kɑ̃paɲ]
[p] pain [pɛ̃]
[r] rare [rar]
[s] six [sis]
[ʃ] chose [ʃoz]
[t] table [tabl]
[v] vie [vi]
[z] zéro [zero]

Vowels/Voyelles

[a] chat [ʃa]
[ɑ] âge [ɑʒ]
[e] été [ete]
[ə] le [lə]; devin [dəvɛ̃]
[ø] feu [fø]
[œ] seul [sœl]
[ɛ] père [pɛr]
[i] vite [vit]
[ɔ] donner [dɔne]
[o] chaud [ʃo]
[u] tout [tu]
[y] cru [kry]
[ɑ̃] enfant [ɑ̃fɑ̃]
[ɛ̃] vin [vɛ̃]
[ɔ̃] bon [bɔ̃]
[œ̃] un [œ̃]

Semi-vowels/Semi-voyelles

[w] noir [nwar]
[j] yoga [jɔga]; rail [raj]
[ɥ] huit [ɥit]

Abbreviations

Abréviations

gloss	=	glose
[introduces an explanation]		[introduit une explication]
cultural equivalent	≃	équivalent culturel
[introduces a translation which has a roughly equivalent status in the target language]		[introduit une traduction dont les connotations dans la langue cible sont comparables]
abbreviation	*abbr, abrév*	abréviation
adjective	*adj*	adjectif
adverb	*adv*	adverbe
agriculture	*Agr*	agriculture
American English	*Am*	anglais d'Amérique du Nord
anatomy	*Anat*	anatomie
architecture	*Archit*	architecture
article	*art*	article
astrology	*Astrol*	astrologie
astronomy	*Astron*	astronomie
cars	*Aut*	automobile
auxiliary	*aux*	auxiliaire
aviation	*Av*	aviation
Belgian French	*Belg*	belgicisme
botany	*Bot*	botanique
British English	*Br*	anglais britannique
Canadian French	*Can*	canadianisme
chemistry	*Chem, Chim*	chimie
cinema	*Cin*	cinéma
commerce	*Com*	commerce
computing	*Comptr*	informatique
conjunction	*conj*	conjonction
construction	*Constr*	construction
cooking	*Culin*	cuisine
economics	*Econ, Écon*	économie
electricity, electronics	*Elec, Él*	électricité, électronique
euphemism	*Euph*	euphémisme
exclamation	*exclam*	exclamation
feminine	*f*	féminin
familiar	*Fam*	familier
figurative	*Fig*	figuré
finance	*Fin*	finance
geography	*Geog, Géog*	géographie
geology	*Geol, Géol*	géologie
grammar	*Gram*	grammaire

history	*Hist*	histoire
humorous	*Hum*	humoristique
industry	*Ind*	industrie
invariable	*inv*	invariable
journalism	*Journ*	journalisme
law	*Jur*	droit
linguistics	*Ling*	linguistique
literary	*Lit, Litt*	littéraire
masculine	*m*	masculin
mathematics	*Math*	mathématiques
medicine	*Med, Méd*	médecine
weather	*Met, Météo*	météorologie
military	*Mil*	militaire
music	*Mus*	musique
noun	*n*	nom
shipping	*Naut*	nautisme
feminine noun	*nf*	nom féminin
feminine plural noun	*nfpl*	nom féminin pluriel
masculine noun	*nm*	nom masculin
masculine and feminine noun [same form for both genders]	*nmf*	nom masculin et féminin [formes identiques]
masculine and feminine noun [different form in the feminine]	*nm,f*	nom masculin et féminin [formes différentes]
masculine plural noun	*nmpl*	nom masculin pluriel
plural noun	*npl*	nom pluriel
proper noun	*npr*	nom propre
computing	*Ordinat*	informatique
parliament	*Parl*	parlement
pejorative	*Pej, Péj*	péjoratif
photography	*Phot*	photographie
physics	*Phys*	physique
plural	*pl*	pluriel
politics	*Pol*	politique
past participle	*pp*	participe passé
prefix	*pref, préf*	préfixe
preposition	*prep, prép*	préposition
pronoun	*pron*	pronom
proverb	*Prov*	proverbe
psychology, psychiatry	*Psy*	psychologie, psychiatrie
past tense	*pt*	prétérit
something	*qch*	quelque chose
somebody	*qn*	quelqu'un
registered trademark	®	marque déposée
radio	*Rad*	radio
rail	*Rail*	chemins de fer
religion	*Rel*	religion
somebody	*sb*	quelqu'un
school	*Sch, Scol*	domaine scolaire

Scottish English	*Scot*	anglais d'Écosse
sport	*Sp*	sport
something	*sth*	quelque chose
suffix	*suff*	suffixe
technical term	*Tech*	terme technique
telecommunications	*Tel, Tél*	télécommunications
textiles	*Tex*	textile
theatre	*Th*	théâtre
television	*TV*	télévision
typography, printing	*Typ*	typographie, imprimerie
university	*Univ*	domaine universitaire
verb	*v*	verbe
intransitive verb	*vi*	verbe intransitif
reflexive verb	*vpr*	verbe pronominal
transitive verb	*vt*	verbe transitif
transitive verb used with a preposition [e.g. **parvenir à** (to reach); ils sont **parvenus à** un accord (they reached an agreement)]	*vt ind*	verbe transitif indirect [par exemple: **parvenir à; ils sont parvenus à** un accord]
inseparable transitive verb [phrasal verb where the verb and the adverb or preposition cannot be separated, e.g. **look after**; he **looked after** the children]	*vt insep*	verbe transitif à particule inséparable [par exemple: **look after** (s'occuper de); he **looked after** the children (il s'occupait des enfants)]
separable transitive verb [phrasal verb where the verb and the adverb or preposition can be separated, e.g. **send back**; she **sent** the present **back** *or* she **sent back** the present]	*vt sep*	verbe transitif à particule séparable [par exemple: **send back** (rendre); she **sent** the present **back** *ou* she **sent back** the present (elle a rendu le cadeau)]
vulgar	*Vulg*	vulgaire
zoology	*Zool*	zoologie

All other labels are written in full.
Toutes les autres indications d'usage sont données en entier.

English-French
Anglais-Français

A

A, a¹ [eɪ] *n* (a) *(letter)* A, a *m inv*; **to get from A to B** aller d'un point à un autre; **from A to Z** de A à Z; **A bomb** bombe *f* A; *Br Sch* **A level** = diplôme de fin d'études secondaires sanctionnant une matière déterminée; *Br Sch* **A levels** ≃ baccalauréat *m*; *Br* **A road** ≃ (route *f*) nationale *f*; **A side** *(of record)* face *f* A; **A-Z** *(street guide)* index *m* des rues; **an A-Z of gardening** le jardinage de A à Z (b) *Sch (grade)* **to get an A** *(in exam)* avoir mention bien ou très bien; *(in homework, essay)* ≃ avoir entre 14 et 20 (c) *Mus* la *m inv*

a² [ə, *stressed* eɪ]

> a devient **an** [ən, *stressed* æn] devant voyelle ou h muet

indefinite art (a) *(in general)* un (une); **a man** un homme; **a woman** une femme; **an hour** une heure; **he's got a red nose** il a le nez rouge; **I haven't got a car** je n'ai pas de voiture; **what a day!** quelle journée!

(b) *(with professions, nationalities)* **he's an Englishman/ a father/a lawyer** il est anglais/père/avocat

(c) *(with prices, rates)* **30 pence a kilo** 30 pence le kilo; **three times a week** trois fois par semaine; **50 kilometres an hour** 50 kilomètres (à l')heure

(d) *(a certain)* **a Mr Watkins phoned** un certain M. Watkins a appelé

AA [eɪ'eɪ] *n* (a) *(abbr* **Automobile Association***)* = club automobile britannique offrant notamment des services de dépannage (b) *(abbr* **Alcoholics Anonymous***)* AA *mpl*

AAA *n* (a) [θriː'eɪz] *Br (abbr* **Amateur Athletics Association***)* = fédération britannique d'athlétisme (b) [eɪeɪ'eɪ] *Am (abbr* **American Automobile Association***)* = club automobile américain

AB [eɪ'biː] *n Am (abbr* **Artium Baccalaureus***) (diploma)* ≃ licence *f* de lettres; *(graduate)* ≃ licencié(e) *m,f* ès lettres

abaci ['æbəsaɪ] *pl of* abacus

aback [ə'bæk] *adv* **taken a. (by)** déconcerté(e) (par)

abacus ['æbəkəs] *(pl* **abaci** ['æbəsaɪ] *or* **abacuses** ['æbəkəsɪz]*) n* boulier *m*

abandon [ə'bændən] **1** *n* **with a. avec** abandon; **to drive with reckless a.** conduire avec insouciance **2** *vt* abandonner; *(match)* interrompre; **to a. ship** abandonner le navire

abase [ə'beɪs] *vt* **to a. oneself** s'abaisser, s'humilier

abashed [ə'bæʃt] *adj* honteux(euse) (at de)

abate [ə'beɪt] *vi (of storm, pain)* se calmer; *(of noise)* diminuer

abattoir ['æbətwɑː(r)] *n* abattoir *m*

abbess ['æbɪs] *n* abbesse *f*

abbey ['æbɪ] *(pl* **abbeys***) n* abbaye *f*

abbot ['æbət] *n* abbé *m*

abbreviate [ə'briːvɪeɪt] *vt* abréger

abbreviation [əbriːvɪ'eɪʃən] *n* abréviation *f*

ABC [eɪbiː'siː] *n* (a) *(alphabet)* alphabet *m*; **an ABC of gardening** un ABC du jardinage (b) *(abbr* **American Broadcasting Corporation***)* = chaîne de télévision américaine (c) *(abbr* **Australian Broadcasting Corporation***)* = chaîne de télévision australienne

abdicate ['æbdɪkeɪt] **1** *vt* **to a. the throne** abdiquer; **to a. responsibility** abdiquer devant ses responsabilités **2** *vi (of monarch)* abdiquer

abdication [æbdɪ'keɪʃən] *n (of throne)* abdication *f*; *(of responsibilities)* abandon *m*

abdomen ['æbdəmən] *n Anat & Zool* abdomen *m*

abdominal [əb'dɒmɪnl] *adj Anat* abdominal(e)

abduct [əb'dʌkt] *vt* enlever

abduction [əb'dʌkʃən] *n* enlèvement *m*

aberration [æbə'reɪʃən] *n* aberration *f*; **a mental a.** un moment de folie

abet [ə'bet] *(pt & pp* **abetted***) vt Law* **to aid and a. sb** être le complice de qn

abetting [ə'betɪŋ] *n Law* **aiding and a.** complicité *f*

abeyance [ə'beɪəns] *n* **in a.** *(of law, custom)* en désuétude

abhor [əb'hɔː(r)] *(pt & pp* **abhorred***) vt* détester, avoir horreur de

abhorrence [əb'hɒrəns] *n* horreur *f*

abhorrent [əb'hɒrənt] *adj* odieux(euse)

abide [ə'baɪd] *vt (tolerate)* **I can't a. him** je ne peux pas le supporter

▸abide by *vt insep (promise)* tenir; *(rule, decision)* se plier à, se soumettre à; **I a. by what I said** je maintiens ce que j'ai dit

abiding [ə'baɪdɪŋ] *adj (memory)* éternel(elle); *(impression)* durable

ability [ə'bɪlɪtɪ] *(pl* **abilities***) n* (a) *(talent, skill)* capacités *fpl* (in en), compétence *f* (in en) (b) *(capability)* capacité *f* (to à); *(to do)* **to the best of one's a.** de son mieux

abject ['æbdʒekt] *adj (miserable)* malheureux(euse); *(contemptible)* abject(e); **to make an a. apology** s'excuser platement; **a. poverty** misère *f* noire

ablaze [ə'bleɪz] *adj* en feu, en flammes; **to set sth a.** embraser qch; *Fig* **her eyes were a. with anger** ses yeux brillaient de colère

able ['eɪbl] *adj* (a) *(competent) (person, performance)* compétent(e) (b) **to be a. to do sth** *(be physically capable)* pouvoir faire qch; *(know how to)* savoir faire qch; **I won't be a. to come** je ne pourrai pas venir; **we waited all afternoon, but we weren't a. to see him** nous avons attendu tout l'après-midi mais nous n'avons pas réussi à le voir

able-bodied ['eɪbəl'bɒdɪd] *adj* robuste; *Naut* a. seaman matelot *m* de deuxième classe

abnormal [æb'nɔ:məl] *adj* anormal(e)

abnormality [æbnɔ:'mælɪt] (*pl* abnormalities) *n* (*irregularity*) anomalie *f*; (*physical*) malformation *f*

aboard [ə'bɔ:d] **1** *adv* (*on ship, aeroplane*) à bord; to go a. monter à bord

2 *prep* (*ship, aeroplane*) à bord de; (*bus, train*) dans

abode [ə'bəʊd] *n Lit* demeure *f*; *Law* of no fixed a. sans domicile fixe; *Law* right of a. droit *m* de séjour

abolish [ə'bɒlɪʃ] *vt* abolir; (*law*) abroger

abolition [æbə'lɪʃən] *n* abolition *f*; (*of law*) abrogation *f*

abominable [ə'bɒmɪnəbəl] *adj* abominable; the a. snowman l'abominable homme *m* des neiges

abomination [əbɒmɪ'neɪʃən] *n* abomination *f*

aborigine [æbə'rɪdʒɪnɪ] *n* aborigène *mf*

abort [ə'bɔ:t] **1** *vt* (a) *Med* (*woman*) avorter; the foetus was aborted la grossesse a été interrompue (b) (*project*) & *Comptr* abandonner

2 *vi Med* avorter, faire une fausse couche

abortion [ə'bɔ:ʃən] *n* avortement *m*, IVG *f*; to have an a. se faire avorter

abortive [ə'bɔ:tɪv] *adj* (*attempt, plan*) avorté(e)

abound [ə'baʊnd] *vi* abonder (in *or* with en)

about [ə'baʊt] **1** *prep* (a) (*regarding*) a book a. France un livre sur la France; the good/bad thing a. ... ce qu'il y a de bien/de mauvais dans ...; what's it a.? de quoi s'agit-il?; to talk a. sth parler de qch; to argue a. sth se disputer au sujet de qch; we must do something a. this problem il faut faire quelque chose à ce sujet

(b) (*in various parts of*) to walk a. the town se promener dans la ville; to look a. the room parcourir la pièce du regard

2 *adv* (a) (*in different directions, places*) to walk a. se promener; to run a. courir à droite et à gauche; to be lying a. traîner

(b) (*in the general area*) is Jack a.? est-ce que Jack est dans les environs *ou* parages?; there was nobody a. il n'y avait personne

(c) (*approximately*) environ, à peu près; a. thirty environ trente, une trentaine; a. ten years environ dix ans, une dizaine d'années; at a. one o'clock vers une heure; she's a. as tall as you elle est grande à peu près comme toi; I've just a. finished j'ai pratiquement terminé; a. time! ce n'est pas trop tôt!

(d) (*on the point of*) to be a. to do sth aller faire qch, être sur le point de faire qch; I'm not a. to ... (*have no intention of*) je n'ai pas l'intention de...

about-face [ə'baʊt'feɪs], **about-turn** [ə'baʊt'tɜ:n] *n* (*radical change*) revirement *m*

above [ə'bʌv] **1** *prep* (a) (*physically*) au-dessus de; the Seine a. Paris la Seine en amont de Paris

(b) (*with numbers*) plus de; the temperature didn't rise a. 10°C la température n'a pas dépassé 10°C

(c) (*in rank*) he is a. me il est mon supérieur

(d) (*not subject to*) to be a. suspicion être au-dessus de tout soupçon; her behaviour is a. criticism il n'y a rien à redire à son attitude

(e) (*superior to*) he thinks he's a. all that il se croit au-dessus de tout ça; she's not a. telling lies elle est capable de mentir; to get a. oneself se donner des airs

(f) a. all surtout; they value friendship a. all else ils font passer l'amitié avant tout le reste

2 *adv* (a) (*in general*) au-dessus; the tenants (of the flat)

a. les locataires du dessus; from a. (*from one's superiors*) d'en haut

(b) (*in book, document*) ci-dessus

above-board [ə'bʌvbɔ:d] *adj* (*honest*) franc (franche), honnête

above-mentioned [əbʌv'menʃənd], **above-named** [əbʌv'neɪmd] *adj* susdit(e), susnommé(e)

abrasion [ə'breɪʒən] *n* (*on skin*) écorchure *f*

abrasive [ə'breɪsɪv] **1** *n* (*substance*) abrasif *m*

2 *adj* (*surface, substance*) abrasif(ive); (*person, manner*) caustique

abreast [ə'brest] *adv* de front; to come a. of arriver à la hauteur de; to keep a. of (*events, progress*) se tenir au courant de

abridged [ə'brɪdʒd] *adj* abrégé(e)

abroad [ə'brɔ:d] *adv* à l'étranger; our colleagues from a. nos collègues étrangers; to get a. (*of news*) se répandre

abrupt [ə'brʌpt] *adj* (a) (*sudden*) brusque, soudain(e); the train came to an a. halt le train s'est brusquement *ou* soudainement arrêté (b) (*curt*) abrupt(e), brusque

abruptly [ə'brʌptlɪ] *adv* (a) (*suddenly*) brusquement, soudainement (b) (*curtly*) de façon abrupte, avec brusquerie

abscess ['æbses] *n* abcès *m*

abscond [əb'skɒnd] *vi Formal* s'enfuir, prendre la fuite

abseil ['æbseɪl] *vi* descendre en rappel; to a. down sth descendre qch en rappel

abseiling ['æbseɪlɪŋ] *n* rappel *m*, descente *f* en rappel; to go a. faire du rappel

absence ['æbsəns] *n* absence *f*; in the a. of (*person*) en l'absence de; (*thing*) faute de; *Law* sentenced in one's a. condamné(e) par contumace; *Prov* a. makes the heart grow fonder l'éloignement renforce l'affection

absent 1 *adj* ['æbsənt] (*pupil, expression*) absent(e); *Mil* a. without leave porté(e) manquant(e)

2 *vt* [æb'sent] to a. oneself (from) s'absenter (de)

absentee [æbsən'ti:] *n* absent(e) *m,f*; a. landlord propriétaire *m* absentéiste

absenteeism [æbsən'ti:ɪzm] *n* absentéisme *m*

absent-minded [æbsənt'maɪndɪd] *adj* distrait(e)

absent-mindedness [æbsənt'maɪndɪdnɪs] *n* distraction *f*

absolute ['æbsəlu:t] *adj* (a) (*total*) absolu(e); a. majority majorité *f* absolue; a. monarch monarque *m* absolu (b) (*emphatic*) he's an a. fool! il est complètement idiot!; a. rubbish! n'importe quoi!; an a. disgrace/disaster un véritable scandale/désastre

absolutely [æbsə'lu:tlɪ] *adv* absolument; you're a. right vous avez absolument *ou* tout à fait raison; do you support him? – a./a. not vous le soutenez? – absolument/absolument pas

absolution [æbsə'lu:ʃən] *n Rel* absolution *f*

absolve [əb'zɒlv] *vt Rel* absoudre (from *or* of de); (*from duty*) dispenser (from *or* of de); to be absolved from blame être innocenté(e)

absorb [əb'zɔ:b] *vt* (*liquid*) absorber; (*losses*) essuyer; to be absorbed in sth être absorbé(e) par qch

absorbent [əb'zɔ:bənt] *adj* absorbant(e)

absorbing [əb'zɔ:bɪŋ] *adj* (*work*) absorbant(e); (*book, question*) passionnant(e)

abstain [əb'steɪn] *vi* s'abstenir (from de)

abstemious [əb'sti:mɪəs] *adj* sobre

abstention [əb'sten∫ən] *n Pol* abstention *f*

abstinence ['æbstɪnəns] *n* abstinence *f*

abstract ['æbstrækt] **1** *n* (a) *(concept)* the a. l'abstrait *m* (b) *(of article)* résumé *m*
2 *adj* abstrait(e)
3 *vt* [æb'strækt] *Formal (remove)* extraire (**from** de)

abstraction [æb'stræk∫ən] *n* abstraction *f*

abstruse [əb'stru:s] *adj* obscur(e)

absurd [əb'sɜ:d] *adj* absurde

absurdity [əb'sɜ:dɪtɪ] (*pl* **absurdities**) *n* absurdité *f*

ABTA ['æbtə] *n* (*abbr* **Association of British Travel Agents**) = association d'agences de voyage britanniques

abundance [ə'bʌndəns] *n* abondance *f*; **an a. of talent** un grand talent; **in a.** en abondance

abundant [ə'bʌndənt] *adj* abondant(e); **to be a. in sth** abonder en qch

abundantly [ə'bʌndəntlɪ] *adv* en abondance; **a. clear** tout a fait clair(e)

abuse 1 *n* (a) *(of power)* abus *m* (b) *(insults)* injures *fpl*, insultes *fpl*; **term of a.** injure *f*, insulte *f* (c) *(cruelty)* mauvais traitements *mpl*, maltraitance *f*; *(sexual)* a. sévices *mpl* sexuels
2 *vt* [ə'bju:z] (a) *(misuse)* abuser de (b) *(insult)* injurier, insulter (c) *(ill-treat) (physically)* maltraiter; *(sexually)* faire subir des sévices sexuels à

abusive [ə'bju:sɪv] *adj (person, language)* grossier(ère)

abysmal [ə'bɪzməl] *adj (ignorance)* sans bornes; *(performance, quality)* épouvantable

abyss [ə'bɪs] *n also Fig* abîme *m*, gouffre *m*

AC ['eɪ'si:] *n Elec* (*abbr* **alternating current**) courant *m* alternatif

a/c *n* (*abbr* **account**) compte *m*

academic [ækə'demɪk] **1** *n (university teacher)* universitaire *mf*; *(intellectual)* intellectuel(elle) *m,f*
2 *adj* (a) *(of school)* scolaire; *(of university)* universitaire; **her a. achievements are impressive** elle a fait de brillantes études (b) *(intellectual)* intellectuel(elle) (c) *(theoretical)* théorique; **it's entirely a. whether he did it or not** qu'il l'ait fait ou non n'a aucune importance

academy [ə'kædəmɪ] (*pl* **academies**) *n* académie *f*; **a. of music** conservatoire *m* (de musique)

ACAS ['eɪkæs] *n* (*abbr* **Advisory, Conciliation and Arbitration Service**) = organisme britannique indépendant d'arbitrage des conflits du travail

accede [æk'si:d] *vi Formal* (a) **to a. to** *(request, demand)* accéder à; *(agreement, changes)* accepter (b) *(of monarch)* **to a. to the throne** accéder au trône

accelerate [ək'seləreɪt] **1** *vt (progress)* accélérer; *(downfall)* précipiter
2 *vi (of car, driver)* accélérer; *(of pace)* s'accélérer

acceleration [əkselə'reɪ∫ən] *n* accélération *f*

accelerator [ək'seləreɪtə(r)] *n* accélérateur *m*

accent ['æksənt] *n* accent *m*; **to put the a. on sth** *(emphasize)* mettre l'accent sur qch

accentuate [æk'sent∫ʊeɪt] *vt* accentuer

accept [ək'sept] *vt* (a) *(gift, apology, defeat)* accepter; *(responsibility)* assumer (**for** de); *(concede)* admettre; **to a. (that)...** admettre que... (b) *(into university)* admettre

acceptable [ək'septəbəl] *adj* acceptable; **to be a. to sb** *(suit)* convenir à qn

acceptance [ək'septəns] *n* (a) *(of invitation, apology, defeat)* acceptation *f*; **to find a.** être reconnu(e) (b) *(to university)* admission *f*; **a. speech** = discours prononcé par le lauréat d'un prix

access ['ækses] *n* accès *m* (**to** à); **to have a. to sth** avoir accès à qch; **to gain a. to** *(get inside)* s'introduire dans; *(reach)* accéder à; **a. road** route *f* d'accès; *(of motorway)* bretelle *f* d'accès; *Comptr* **a. code/time** code *m*/temps *m* d'accès
2 *vt Comptr* accéder à

accessible [ək'sesəbəl] *adj (place, explanation)* accessible; *(person)* joignable

accession [ək'se∫ən] *n (to power, throne)* accession *f*; *(library book)* acquisition *f*

accessory [ək'sesərɪ] (*pl* **accessories**) *n* (a) *(extra)* accessoire *m* (b) *Law* complice *mf* (**to** de)

accident ['æksɪdənt] *n* accident *m*; **by a.** par accident *ou* hasard; **to have an a.** avoir un accident; **a. insurance** assurance *f* accidents

accidental [æksɪ'dentəl] *adj* accidentel(elle); *Law* **a. death** mort *f* accidentelle

accidentally [æksɪ'dentəlɪ] *adv* accidentellement

accident-prone ['æksɪdəntprəʊn] *adj* prédisposé(e) aux accidents

acclaim [ə'kleɪm] **1** *n* louanges *fpl*; **to meet with great critical a.** être salué(e) par la critique
2 *vt (person)* acclamer; *(performance, film)* applaudir

acclamation [æklə'meɪ∫ən] *n (cheering)* acclamations *fpl*

acclimatize [ə'klaɪmətaɪz] *vi* s'acclimater (**to** à)

accolade ['ækəleɪd] *n* honneur *m*

accommodate [ə'kɒmədeɪt] *vt* (a) *(provide room for)* loger (b) *(satisfy)* satisfaire

accommodating [ə'kɒmədeɪtɪŋ] *adj (helpful)* obligeant(e); *(easy to please)* accommodant(e)

accommodation [əkɒmə'deɪ∫ən] *n* (a) *(lodging)* logement *m*; *(in hotel)* chambre *f* (d'hôtel) (b) *Formal (agreement)* compromis *m*

accompaniment [ə'kʌmpənɪmənt] *n Mus* accompagnement *m*; *Culin* garniture *f*

accompany [ə'kʌmpənɪ] (*pt & pp* **accompanied**) *vt* accompagner; **to be accompanied by sth** s'accompagner de qch

accomplice [ə'kʌmplɪs] *n* complice *mf*

accomplish [ə'kʌmplɪ∫] *vt (task)* accomplir; *(aim)* atteindre

accomplished [ə'kʌmplɪ∫t] *adj (performer)* accompli(e); *(performance)* très au point

accord [ə'kɔ:d] **1** *n* accord *m*; **in a. with** en accord avec; **with one a.** d'un commun accord; **of one's own a.** de son plein gré
2 *vt* accorder (**to** à)

▶**accord with** *vt insep* concorder avec

accordance [ə'kɔ:dəns] *n* **in a. with** en accord avec; **his statement is not in a. with the facts** sa déclaration ne concorde pas avec les faits

according to [ə'kɔ:dɪŋtu:] *prep* (a) *(depending on)* selon; **a. whether one is rich or poor** selon que l'on est riche ou pauvre; **a. which method you use** selon la méthode utilisée (b) *(in conformity with)* selon; **to go a. plan** se dérouler comme prévu (c) *(citing a source)* selon, d'après

accordingly [ə'kɔ:dɪŋlɪ] *adv* (a) *(appropriately)* en conséquence (b) *(therefore)* par conséquent

accordion [ə'kɔ:dɪən] *n* accordéon *m*

accost [əˈkɒst] vt accoster, aborder

account [əˈkaʊnt] n **(a)** (at bank) compte m; Com **accounts department** comptabilité f **(b)** (reckoning) to keep (an) a. of sth tenir un compte de qch; to take sth into a., to take a. of sth (consider) tenir compte de qch, prendre qch en compte; **taking everything into a.** (after all) au bout du compte; to call sb to a. demander des comptes à qn; to be brought to a. avoir des comptes à rendre **(c)** (importance) of no a. sans importance **(d)** on a. of (because of) à cause de; on no a., not on any a. en aucun cas, surtout pas; to set up in business on one's own a. s'installer à son compte; don't do it on my a.! ne le faites surtout pas pour moi! **(e)** (report) description f; Fig to give a good a. of oneself (in fight, contest) bien se défendre; by all accounts au dire de tous

►**account for** vt insep **(a)** (explain, justify) expliquer; five people have still not been accounted for (are still missing) cinq personnes n'ont toujours pas été retrouvées; there's no accounting for taste chacun ses goûts **(b)** (constitute) constituer

accountability [əˌkaʊntəˈbɪlɪti] n responsabilité f (to envers)

accountable [əˈkaʊntəbəl] adj responsable (to sb envers qn; for sth de qch); (for sum of money) redevable (for de); to hold sb a. tenir qn pour responsable

accountancy [əˈkaʊntənsi] n comptabilité f

accountant [əˈkaʊntənt] n comptable mf

accounting [əˈkaʊntɪŋ] n comptabilité f; a. period période f comptable

accrue [əˈkruː] vi Fin (of interest) s'accumuler; to a. to sb (of interest, benefits) revenir à qn

accumulate [əˈkjuːmjʊleɪt] **1** vt accumuler **2** vi s'accumuler

accumulation [əˌkjuːmjʊˈleɪʃən] n accumulation f

accuracy [ˈækjʊrəsi] n (of calculation, translation) exactitude f, précision f; (of firearm, shot) précision; (of portrayal) fidélité f

accurate [ˈækjʊrət] adj (calculation, translation) exact(e), précis(e); (firearm, shot) précis(e); (portrayal) fidèle

accurately [ˈækjʊrətli] adv (calculate, translate) avec exactitude ou précision; (aim) avec précision; (portray) fidèlement

accusation [ˌækjʊˈzeɪʃən] n accusation f; to make an a. (against sb) porter ou lancer une accusation (contre qn)

accuse [əˈkjuːz] vt to a. sb (of sth/of doing sth) accuser qn (de qch/de faire qch)

accused [əˈkjuːzd] (pl accused) n Law the a. l'inculpé(e) m,f

accuser [əˈkjuːzə(r)] n accusateur(trice) m,f

accusing [əˈkjuːzɪŋ] adj (look, tone) accusateur(trice)

accustom [əˈkʌstəm] vt accoutumer, habituer; to be accustomed to sth/to doing sth être habitué à qch/à faire qch; to get ou grow accustomed to sth/to doing sth s'accoutumer ou s'habituer à qch/à faire qch

AC/DC [ˈeɪsiːˈdiːsiː] n Elec (abbr **alternating current/direct current**) courant alternatif/courant continu

ace [eɪs] **1** n **(a)** (in cards) as m; a. of spades as de pique; Fig to have an a. up one's sleeve avoir un atout en réserve; to come within an a. of doing sth être à deux doigts de faire qch **(b)** (tennis) ace m **(c)** Fam (expert) as m; flying a. as de l'aviation **2** adj Fam (very good) super inv

acerbic [əˈsɜːbɪk] adj acerbe

acetate [ˈæsɪteɪt] n Chem acétate m

acetic acid [əˈsiːtɪkˈæsɪd] n acide m acétique

ache [eɪk] **1** n douleur f; aches and pains douleurs fpl **2** vi (of person) avoir mal; my head aches j'ai mal à la tête; my leg aches j'ai mal à la jambe, ma jambe me fait mal; Fig to be aching to do sth mourir d'envie de faire qch

achieve [əˈtʃiːv] vt (aim) atteindre, parvenir à; to a. success réussir; to a. a lot faire beaucoup de chemin

achievement [əˈtʃiːvmənt] n (action) réalisation f; (thing achieved) réussite f

acid [ˈæsɪd] **1** n **(a)** (chemical) acide m **(b)** Fam (LSD) acide m; a. house (music) acid house m **2** adj (chemical, taste) acide; a. rain pluies fpl acides; Fig a. test test m décisif **(b)** (tone, remark) aigre

acidic [əˈsɪdɪk] adj acide; (tone, remark) aigre

acidity [əˈsɪdɪti] n (of chemical, taste) acidité f; (of tone, remark) aigreur f

acknowledge [əkˈnɒlɪdʒ] vt (mistake, debt, truth) admettre, reconnaître; to a. (receipt of) a letter accuser réception d'une lettre; this restaurant is acknowledged to be the best in the city ce restaurant est considéré comme le meilleur de la ville; they didn't a. me or my presence elle m'a ignoré

acknowledg(e)ment [əkˈnɒlɪdʒmənt] n (of mistake, debt, truth) reconnaissance f; in a. of (service, achievement) en reconnaissance de; (letter) en réponse à; acknowledgements (in book) remerciements mpl; a. slip (for letter) accusé m de réception

ACLU [ˈeɪsiːeljuː] n (abbr **American Civil Liberties Union**) = organisme américain qui milite pour les droits civiques

acne [ˈækni] n acné f

acolyte [ˈækəlaɪt] n disciple mf

acorn [ˈeɪkɔːn] n gland m

acoustic [əˈkuːstɪk] adj acoustique; a. guitar guitare f acoustique

acoustics [əˈkuːstɪks] npl acoustique f

acquaint [əˈkweɪnt] vt **(a)** (with person) to be acquainted with sb connaître qn; to become ou get acquainted (with) faire ou lier connaissance (avec) **(b)** (with facts, situation) to be acquainted with sth connaître qch; to a. sb with sth mettre qn au courant de qch; to a. oneself with sth se familiariser avec qch

acquaintance [əˈkweɪntəns] n **(a)** (person) connaissance f **(b)** (familiarity) (with person, facts) familiarité f; to make sb's a. faire la connaissance de qn

acquiesce [ˌækwɪˈes] vi consentir (in à)

acquiescence [ˌækwɪˈesəns] n consentement m (in à)

acquiescent [ˌækwɪˈesənt] adj consentant(e)

acquire [əˈkwaɪə(r)] vt (knowledge, reputation, property) acquérir; (habit, accent, air) prendre; to a. a taste for sth prendre goût à qch; it's an acquired taste c'est quelque chose que l'on apprend à aimer

acquisition [ˌækwɪˈzɪʃən] n acquisition f

acquisitive [əˈkwɪzɪtɪv] adj matérialiste

acquit [əˈkwɪt] (pt & pp acquitted) vt **(a)** Law acquitter **(b)** to a. oneself well/badly s'en sortir ou s'en tirer bien/mal

acquittal [əˈkwɪtəl] n Law acquittement m

acre ['eɪkə(r)] *n* = 4047 m², ≃ demi-hectare *m*; **acres of forest** des hectares de forêt; *Fam* **acres of space** plein de place

acrid ['ækrɪd] *adj* âcre

acrimonious [ækrɪ'məʊnɪəs] *adj* (*person, remark*) hargneux(euse); (*discussion*) virulent(e)

acrimony ['ækrɪmənɪ] *n* acrimonie *f*, hargne *f*

acrobat ['ækrəbæt] *n* acrobate *mf*

acrobatic [ækrə'bætɪk] *adj* acrobatique

acrobatics [ækrə'bætɪks] 1 *n* acrobatie *f*
2 *npl Fig* **mental a.** gymnastique *f* intellectuelle

acronym ['ækrənɪm] *n* sigle *m*

across [ə'krɒs] 1 *prep* (a) (*from one side to the other of*) **to go a. sth** traverser qch; **to run a. the road** traverser la route en courant; **to swim a. a river** traverser une rivière à la nage; **the bridge a. the river** le pont sur la rivière; **she threw it a. the room** elle l'a lancé à l'autre bout de la pièce
(b) (*on the other side of*) de l'autre côté de; **she lives a. the road** elle habite en face; **the woman (from) a. the road** la femme d'en face
(c) (*throughout*) dans tout le pays; **a. the political spectrum** dans l'ensemble de la classe politique
2 *adv* (a) (*from one side to the other*) **to run/swim a.** traverser en courant/à la nage; **go a. and see her** traverse et va la voir
(b) (*with distance*) **it's 10 cm/2 km a.** ça fait 10 cm/2 km de large
(c) **a. from me/my house** en face de moi/de chez moi
(d) (*in crosswords*) horizontalement

acrylic [ə'krɪlɪk] 1 *n* (*fabric*) acrylique *m*
2 *adj* (*paint, fibre*) acrylique; (*garment*) en acrylique

act [ækt] 1 *n* (a) (*thing done*) acte *m*; **to be in the a. of doing sth** être en train de faire qch; **to catch sb in the a. of doing sth** surprendre qn en train de faire qch; **to catch sb in the a.** prendre qn sur le fait *ou* en flagrant délit; *Fam* **to get in on the a.** (*get involved*) se mettre dans le coup; **a. of war** acte *m* de guerre; *Law* **a. of God** catastrophe *f* naturelle
(b) (*of play*) acte *m*; (*in cabaret, circus*) numéro *m*; *Fig* **to put on an a.** faire semblant; *Fig* **to get one's a. together** se secouer; *Fig* **it's all an a.** c'est du cinéma
(c) *Law* **a.** (*of parliament*) loi *f*
2 *vt* (*character*) jouer (le rôle de), tenir le rôle de; (*play*) jouer; *Fig* **to a. the part** se conduire comme il convient
(b) (*behave like*) **to a. the fool** *or* **the goat** faire l'imbécile; *Fam* **a. your age (not your shoe size!)** arrête de faire l'enfant!
3 *vi* (a) (*take action*) agir; **to a. for sb** (*of lawyer*) représenter qn; **to a. as secretary/chairperson** remplir les fonctions de secrétaire/président; **to a. as a warning** servir d'avertissement; **to a. as an incentive** être une motivation
(b) (*behave*) agir, se comporter; **to a. stupid** faire l'idiot
(c) (*of actor*) jouer; **I always wanted to a.** j'ai toujours voulu être acteur

▸**act out** *vt sep* (*fantasy*) vivre; (*scene*) jouer

▸**act up** *vi* (*of car, child, injury*) faire des siennes

acting ['æktɪŋ] 1 *n* (*performance*) jeu *m*; (*profession*) métier *m* d'acteur
2 *adj* (*temporary*) par intérim

action ['ækʃən] *n* (a) (*individual act*) acte *m*, action *f*; *Prov* **actions speak louder than words** les actes en disent plus long que les paroles (b) (*activity*) action *f*; **to take a.** prendre des mesures; **to go into a.** passer à l'action; **to be out of a.** (*machine, car*) être en panne; (*person*) être hors service; *Fam* **where's the a. round here?** où est-ce que ça bouge par ici?; *Com* **a. plan** objectifs *mpl* (c) *Mil* combats *mpl*; **to see a.** combattre; **missing in a.** porté(e) disparu(e) (d) (*of film, novel*) action *f*; *TV* **a. replay** = répétition d'une séquence précédente (e) *Law* action *f*, procès *m*; **to bring an a. against sb** intenter un procès à qn

activate ['æktɪveɪt] *vt* déclencher

active ['æktɪv] *adj* (*person, mind, imagination*) actif(ive); (*interest, dislike*) vif (vive); (*volcano*) en activité; **to be a. in doing sth** s'employer activement à faire qch; *Mil* **on a. service** en service actif (b) *Gram* actif(ive)

actively ['æktɪvlɪ] *adv* activement; **to a. dislike sb** détester cordialement qn

activist ['æktɪvɪst] *n Pol* militant(e) *m,f*

activity [æk'tɪvɪtɪ] (*pl* **activities**) *n* activité *f*; (*in street*) animation *f*

actor ['æktə(r)] *n* acteur *m*

actress ['æktrɪs] *n* actrice *f*

actual ['æktʃʊəl] *adj* (a) (*real*) réel(elle); (*example*) concret(ète); **in a. fact** en fait (b) (*specific*) I **can't remember her a. words** je ne me rappelle pas ses paroles exactes; **although the garden is big, the a. house is small** le jardin est grand, mais la maison elle-même est petite

actually ['æktʃʊəlɪ] *adv* (a) (*really*) réellement, vraiment; **what a. happened?** qu'est-ce qui s'est passé au juste?; **what she a. means is...** en réalité, ce qu'elle veut dire c'est... (b) (*in fact*) en fait; **I'm not sure, a.** en fait, je ne suis pas sûr

actuary ['æktʃʊərɪ] (*pl* **actuaries**) *n* actuaire *mf*

acumen ['ækjʊmən] *n* flair *m*; **business a.** sens *m* des affaires

acupuncture ['ækjʊpʌŋktʃə(r)] *n* acuponcture *f*

acute [ə'kju:t] *adj* (a) (*pain*) aigu(ë); (*remorse, embarrassment*) vif (vive); (*problem, shortage*) grave (b) (*eyesight*) perçant(e); (*accent, angle*) aigu(ë)

acutely [ə'kju:tlɪ] *adv* (*painful, embarrassing*) extrêmement; (*aware*) profondément

AD [eɪ'di:] *adv* (*abbr* **Anno Domini**) apr. J.-C.

ad [æd] *n Fam* (*classified*) petite annonce *f*; (*on radio, TV*) pub *f*

Adam ['ædəm] *n Fam* I **wouldn't know him from A.** je ne le connais ni d'Ève ni d'Adam; **A.'s apple** pomme *f* d'Adam

adamant ['ædəmənt] *adj* formel(elle), catégorique (*about* sur); **to be a. that...** soutenir que...

adapt [ə'dæpt] 1 *vt* adapter; **to a. oneself to sth** s'adapter à qch
2 *vi* s'adapter

adaptable [ə'dæptəbəl] *adj* (*instrument, tool*) adaptable; (*person*) souple

adaptation [ædəp'teɪʃən] *n* (*of book, play*) adaptation *f*; (*of machine, design*) modification *f*

adapter [ə'dæptə(r)] *n* (*for several plugs*) prise *f* multiple; (*for foreign plugs*) adaptateur *m*

ADC [eɪdi:'si:] *n Mil* (*abbr* **aide-de-camp**) aide *m* de camp

add [æd] *vt* ajouter (**to** à); *(figures)* additionner; **this book adds little to the debate** ce livre n'apporte pas grand-chose au débat

▶**add up 1** *vt sep (figures)* additionner

2 *vi (give correct total)* être juste *ou* exact(e); *(make sense)* tenir debout

▶**add up to** *vt insep (amount to)* **it adds up to £126** ça fait 126 livres au total *ou* en tout; **it all adds up to an enjoyable day out** tout cela fera de cette excursion un moment bien agréable; **it doesn't a. up to much** ça ne fait pas grand-chose au bout du compte

adder ['ædə(r)] *n (snake)* vipère *f*

addict ['ædɪkt] *n* (**drug**) a. toxicomane *mf*; **heroin a.** héroïnomane *mf*; **to be a TV a.** être accro à la télé

addicted [ə'dɪktɪd] *adj* **to be a. to sth** *(drugs)* être dépendant(e) de qch; *(TV programme)* être accro à qch

addiction [ə'dɪkʃən] *n (to drugs)* dépendance *f* (**to** à), accoutumance *f* (**to** à); *(to chocolate, films)* passion *f* (**to** pour)

addictive [ə'dɪktɪv] *adj (substance)* qui crée une dépendance ou accoutumance; **soap operas are very a. on** devient vite accro aux feuilletons

Addis Ababa ['ædɪs'æbəbə] *n* Addis-Abeba

addition [ə'dɪʃən] *n (action)* addition *f*; *(thing added)* ajout *m* (**to** à); *(person)* nouveau venu (nouvelle venue) *m,f*; **she's the latest a. to the team** c'est la dernière arrivée dans l'équipe; **in a. (to)** en plus (de)

additional [ə'dɪʃənəl] *adj* supplémentaire

additive ['ædɪtɪv] *n* additif *m*

addled ['ædəld] *adj (egg)* pourri(e); *(brain)* confus(e)

add-on ['ædɒn] *n* Comptr produit *m* supplémentaire *ou* complémentaire

address [ə'dres] **1** *n* (**a**) *(of person, letter)* adresse *f*; **a. book** carnet *m* d'adresses (**b**) *(speech)* discours *m*, allocution *f*

2 *vt* (**a**) *(letter, remarks, criticism)* adresser (**to** à) (**b**) *(speak to)* (person, crowd) s'adresser à; **he addressed her as "Your Majesty"** il l'a appelée "Votre Majesté" (**c**) *(question, problem)* aborder; **to a. oneself to sth** *(problem)* aborder qch; *(task)* entreprendre qch

adenoids ['ædɪnɔɪdz] *npl* Anat végétations *fpl*

adept [ə'dept] *adj* habile (**at** à); **to be a. at doing sth** être habile à faire qch

adequate ['ædɪkwət] *adj (enough)* suffisant(e); *(satisfactory)* satisfaisant(e), adéquat(e); **you were given a. warning** on vous a prévenu suffisamment à l'avance

adhere [əd'hɪə(r)] *vi (stick)* adhérer (**to** à); **to a. to** *(rule)* observer; *(belief)* adhérer à; *(plan)* se conformer à

adherence [əd'hɪərəns] *n (to rule)* observation *f* (**to** de); *(to belief, plan)* adhésion *f* (**to** à)

adherent [əd'hɪərənt] *n* adhérent(e) *m,f*

adhesion [əd'hi:ʒən] *n* (**a**) *(stickiness)* adhérence *f* (**b**) *(to belief, plan)* adhésion *f* (**to** à)

adhesive [əd'hi:sɪv] **1** *n* adhésif *m*, colle *f*

2 *adj* adhésif(ive), collant(e); **a. tape** ruban *m* adhésif

ad hoc ['æd'hɒk] *adj (measure)* ad hoc *inv*; *(arrangement)* temporaire; **a. committee** comité *m* spécial *ou* ad hoc; **on an a. basis** au coup par coup

ad infinitum ['ædɪnfɪ'naɪtəm] *adv* à l'infini; **and so on a.** et ainsi de suite à n'en plus finir

adjacent [ə'dʒeɪsənt] *adj* adjacent(e); *(street)* voisin(e); *(room)* contigu(ë)

adjective ['ædʒɪktɪv] *n* adjectif *m*

adjoin [ə'dʒɔɪn] *vt* être contigu(ë) *ou* attenant(e) à

adjoining [ə'dʒɔɪnɪŋ] *adj* attenant(e)

adjourn [ə'dʒɜ:n] **1** *vt (meeting, trial)* ajourner, remettre à plus tard

2 *vi (of meeting, trial)* être ajourné(e); **to a. to another room** passer dans une autre pièce

adjournment [ə'dʒɜ:nmənt] *n* ajournement *m*

adjudge [ə'dʒʌdʒ] *vt* **to a. sb guilty/the winner** déclarer qn coupable/vainqueur

adjudicate [ə'dʒu:dɪkeɪt] *vt* juger

adjudication [ədʒu:dɪ'keɪʃən] *n* jugement *m*, décision *f*

adjudicator [ə'dʒu:dɪkeɪtə(r)] *n (in dispute)* arbitre *m*; *(in competition)* juge *m*

adjunct ['ædʒʌŋkt] *n (thing)* accessoire *m*

adjust [ə'dʒʌst] **1** *vt (machine, mechanism)* régler, ajuster; *(pay, figures)* ajuster; *(clothes)* rajuster; **to a. oneself to sth** s'adapter à qch

2 *vi (of person)* s'adapter (**to** à)

adjustable [ə'dʒʌstəbəl] *adj* ajustable, réglable; **a. spanner** clé *f* à molette

adjustment [ə'dʒʌstmənt] *n (of machine, mechanism)* réglage *m*; *(to pay, figures)* réajustement *m*; **to make an a. to sth** régler qch; **a period of a.** une période d'adaptation

ad-lib ['æd'lɪb] **1** *adv* en improvisant, de manière improvisée

2 *vi (pt & pp ad-libbed)* improviser

ad-man ['ædmæn] *n Fam* publicitaire *m*

admin ['ædmɪn] *n Fam (work)* travail *m* administratif; *(department)* administration *f*

administer [əd'mɪnɪstə(r)] *vt* (**a**) *(estate, funds)* administrer, gérer; *(territory)* administrer (**b**) *(give)* *(punishment, medication)* administrer; *(blow)* donner

administration [ədmɪnɪ'streɪʃən] *n* (**a**) *(work)* administration *f* (**b**) *(government)* gouvernement *m*

administrative [əd'mɪnɪstrətɪv] *adj* administratif(ive)

administrator [əd'mɪnɪstreɪtə(r)] *n* administrateur(trice) *m,f*

admirable ['ædmərəbəl] *adj* admirable

admiral ['ædmərəl] *n* amiral *m*

Admiralty ['ædmərəltɪ] *n* **the A.** ≃ le ministère de la Marine

admiration [ædmə'reɪʃən] *n* admiration *f* (**for** pour)

admire [əd'maɪə(r)] *vt* admirer

admirer [əd'maɪərə(r)] *n* admirateur(trice) *m,f*

admiring [əd'maɪrɪŋ] *adj (look, glance)* admiratif(ive)

admissible [əd'mɪsɪbəl] *adj (behaviour, error)* admissible, acceptable; Law recevable

admission [əd'mɪʃən] *n* (**a**) *(entry)* (**to school, hospital**) admission *f*; *(to museum, exhibition)* entrée *f*; *(price)* (prix *m* d')entrée *f*; **no a.** *(sign)* entrée interdite (**b**) *(acknowledgement)* (of guilt) aveu *m*; (of crime) confession *f*; **by his own a.** de son propre aveu

admit [əd'mɪt] *(pt & pp admitted)* **1** *vt* (**a**) *(allow to enter)* laisser entrer; *(to hospital, college)* admettre; **to be admitted to hospital** être admis(e) à l'hôpital; **children not admitted** *(sign)* les enfants ne sont pas admis; **a. on ticket** entrée valable pour une personne (**b**) *(acknowledge)* (fact, mistake, guilt) admettre, reconnaître; *(crime)* avouer; **I must a. you're right** je dois reconnaître que vous avez raison; **to a. defeat** s'avouer vaincu(e)

2 *vi* **to a. to** *(mistake)* reconnaître; **I a. to being in a bad**

mood yesterday je dois admettre que j'étais de mauvaise humeur hier

admittance [əd'mɪtəns] n (entry) accès m; **to gain a.** parvenir à entrer; **to refuse sb a.** refuser de laisser entrer qn; **no a.** (sign) entrée interdite

admittedly [əd'mɪtɪdlɪ] adv de l'aveu général; **a., it was dark when I saw him** je dois convenir qu'il faisait sombre quand je l'ai vu

admonish [əd'mɒnɪʃ] vt (reprimand) admonester, faire des remontrances à (**for** pour)

ad nauseam [æd'nɔ:sɪæm] adv à n'en plus finir

adobe [ə'dəʊbɪ] n (clay) adobe m

adolescence [ædə'lesəns] n adolescence f

adolescent [ædə'lesənt] n adolescent(e) m,f

adopt [ə'dɒpt] vt (child, custom, approach, measures) adopter; (career, candidate) choisir; (tone, attitude) prendre

adopted [ə'dɒptɪd] adj (child) adopté(e); (son, daughter) adoptif(ive); **my a. country** mon pays d'adoption

adoption [ə'dɒpʃən] n adoption f

adorable [ə'dɔːrəbəl] adj adorable

adoration [ædə'reɪʃən] n adoration f

adore [ə'dɔː(r)] vt adorer

adorn [ə'dɔːn] vt orner, parer (**with** de)

adornment [ə'dɔːnmənt] n (decorations) ornements mpl, parure f

ADP [eɪdiː'piː] n Comptr (abbr **automatic data processing**) traitement m automatique des données

adrenalin(e) [ə'drenəlɪn] n adrénaline f

Adriatic [eɪdrɪ'ætɪk] n the A. (Sea) la mer Adriatique, l'Adriatique f

adrift [ə'drɪft] adv & adj to be a. (of boat) aller à la dérive; **to go a.** (of plan) tomber à l'eau; **to come a.** (come apart) se défaire

adroit [ə'drɔɪt] adj habile (**at doing sth** à faire qch)

adulation [ædjʊ'leɪʃən] n adulation f

adult ['ædʌlt, ə'dʌlt] **1** n adulte mf

2 adj adulte; (film) pour adultes; **a. education** enseignement m pour adultes

adulterate [ə'dʌltəreɪt] vt (food) empoisonner; (wine) frelater; (language) corrompre

adulteration [ədʌltə'reɪʃən] n (of food) empoisonnement m; (of wine) frelatage m

adulterer [ə'dʌltərə(r)] n adultère mf

adulterous [ə'dʌltərəs] adj adultère

adultery [ə'dʌltərɪ] n adultère m; **to commit a.** commettre l'adultère

adulthood ['ædʌlthʊd] n âge m adulte

advance [əd'vɑːns] **1** n (a) (forward movement) avance f; (progress) progrès m; **to make advances to sb** faire des avances à qn; **in a.** (book, apply, inform) à l'avance; (pay) d'avance; **six weeks in a.** six semaines à l'avance; **a. booking** réservation f à l'avance; **a. notice** or **warning** préavis m (b) (loan) avance f

2 vt (move forward) faire avancer; (chess piece) avancer; (science, knowledge) faire progresser, faire avancer (b) (idea, opinion) avancer, mettre en avant (c) (loan) avancer

3 vi (move forward) s'avancer (**towards** vers); (make progress) avancer

advanced [əd'vɑːnst] adj avancé(e); **she's very a. for her age** elle est très en avance pour son âge

advantage [əd'vɑːntɪdʒ] n avantage m (**over** sur); **to take a.** of profiter de; **to turn a situation to one's a.** tourner une situation à son avantage; **it would be to your a.** il serait dans votre intérêt de...; **a. Sampras** (in tennis) avantage Sampras

advantageous [ædvən'teɪdʒəs] adj avantageux(euse) (**to** pour)

advent ['ædvənt] n (arrival) arrivée f; Rel A. l'Avent m

adventure [əd'ventʃə(r)] n aventure f; **a. playground** terrain m de jeux (spécialement aménagé); **a. story** récit m d'aventures; (novel) roman m d'aventure(s)

adventurer [əd'ventʃərə(r)] n aventurier(ère) m,f

adventurous [əd'ventʃərəs] adj (person) aventureux(euse); (plan) audacieux(euse)

adverb ['ædvɜːb] n adverbe m

adversary ['ædvəsərɪ] (pl adversaries) n adversaire mf

adverse ['ædvɜːs] adj défavorable

adversely ['ædvɜːslɪ] adv **to influence sb a.** exercer une influence défavorable sur qn; **a. affected** affecté(e)

adversity [əd'vɜːsɪtɪ] n adversité f; **in a.** dans l'adversité

advert ['ædvɜːt] n (for product) pub f; (for job, event) annonce f

advertise ['ædvətaɪz] **1** vt (a) (product, service) faire de la réclame ou de la publicité pour; (job) mettre une annonce pour; **advertised on TV** vu(e) à la télé (b) (call attention to) he didn't want to a. his presence il ne voulait pas se faire remarquer

2 vi (for job) mettre une annonce; (to sell product) faire de la publicité ou de la réclame; **to a. for sb** passer une annonce pour trouver qn

advertisement [əd'vɜːtɪsmənt] n (for product, service) publicité f, réclame f; (for job, event) annonce f; Fig **you're not a good a. for your school** vous ne faites pas honneur à votre école

advertiser ['ædvətaɪzə(r)] n annonceur(euse) m,f

advertising ['ædvətaɪzɪŋ] n publicité f; **a. agency** agence f de publicité; **a. campaign** campagne f de publicité

advice [əd'vaɪs] n conseil(s) m(pl) (**on** sur); **a piece of a.** un conseil; **that's good a.** c'est un bon conseil; **to give sb a.** donner des conseils à qn; **to ask sb's a.** demander conseil à qn; **to take sb's a.** suivre le conseil ou les conseils de qn

advisable [əd'vaɪzəbəl] adj recommandé(e)

advise [əd'vaɪz] vt (a) (give advice to) conseiller; **to a. sb to do sth** conseiller à qn de faire qch; **to a. sb against doing sth** déconseiller à qn de faire qch; **I wouldn't a.** je ne le conseillerais ou recommanderais pas (b) (inform) **to a. sb that...** aviser qn que...

adviser, advisor [əd'vaɪzə(r)] n conseiller(ère) m,f

advisory [əd'vaɪzərɪ] adj consultatif(ive); **in an a. capacity** en tant que conseiller

advocate 1 n ['ædvəkət] (a) Scot Law avocat(e) m,f; **the Lord A.** ≃ le procureur général (b) (of cause, doctrine) partisan(e) m,f

2 vt ['ædvəkeɪt] (policy, plan) préconiser, conseiller

AEA [eɪi:'eɪ] n Br (abbr **Atomic Energy Authority**) ≃ Commissariat m à l'énergie atomique

AEC [eɪi:'si:] n Am (abbr **Atomic Energy Commission**) ≃ Commissariat m à l'énergie atomique

Aegean [ɪ'dʒi:ən] n the A. (Sea) la mer Égée

aegis ['i:dʒɪs] n **under the a. of...** sous l'égide de...

aeon, Am **eon** ['iːən] n Fig éternité f; **aeons ago** il y a une éternité

aerate ['eəreɪt] vt (water) gazéifier

aerial ['eərɪəl] **1** n (of radio, TV) antenne f
  2 adj aérien(enne)

aerobics [eəˈrəʊbɪks] n aérobic m

aerodrome ['eərədrəʊm] n aérodrome m

aerodynamic [eərəʊdaɪˈnæmɪk] adj aérodynamique

aerogram(me) ['eərəɡræm] n aérogramme m

aeronautic(al) [eərəˈnɔːtɪk(əl)] adj aéronautique

aeroplane ['eərəpleɪn] n avion m

aerosol ['eərəsɒl] n aérosol m; **a. spray** atomiseur m

aesthetic, Am **esthetic** [ɪsˈθetɪk] adj esthétique

afar [əˈfɑː(r)] adv Lit **from a.** de loin

affable ['æfəbəl] adj affable, courtois(e)

affair [əˈfeə(r)] n **(a)** (matter, concern) affaire f; **that's my a.!** c'est mes affaires!; **to put one's affairs in order** mettre de l'ordre dans ses affaires; **current affairs** les questions fpl d'actualité; **foreign affairs** les affaires étrangères; **affairs of state** les affaires de l'État; **in the present state of affairs** dans l'état actuel des choses **(b)** (sexual) liaison f; **to have an a. with sb** avoir une liaison avec qn **(c)** (event) affaire f; **the wedding was a quiet a.** le mariage fut célébré dans l'intimité; **what kind of a. was it?** c'était comment?

affect¹ [əˈfekt] vt **(a)** (have effect on) (person, organ, health) affecter; (decision) influencer; (of issue, law) concerner **(b)** (move emotionally) affecter, toucher; **to be deeply affected by sth** être très affecté(e) par qch

affect² vt (indifference, interest) affecter, feindre; **to a. an accent** prendre un accent

affectation [æfekˈteɪʃən] n affectation f

affected [əˈfektɪd] adj (unnatural) affecté(e), maniéré(e)

affection [əˈfekʃən] n affection f

affectionate [əˈfekʃənət] adj affectueux(euse) (towards avec ou envers)

affidavit [æfɪˈdeɪvɪt] n Law déclaration f par écrit et sous serment

affiliate 1 n [əˈfɪlɪət] (person) affilié(e) m,f
  2 vt [əˈfɪlɪeɪt] affilier (to ou with à); **affiliated company** filiale f

affiliation [əfɪlɪˈeɪʃən] n affiliation f

affinity [əˈfɪnɪti] (pl affinities) n **(a)** (liking, attraction) affinité f (for ou with/between avec/entre); **to have an a. with sb/sb** avoir des affinités avec qn/qn **(b)** (relationship, connection) lien m (between/with entre/avec)

affirm [əˈfɜːm] vt **(a)** (state) affirmer **(b)** (confirm) confirmer

affirmation [æfəˈmeɪʃən] n **(a)** (statement) affirmation f, assertion f **(b)** (confirmation) confirmation f

affirmative [əˈfɜːmətɪv] **1** n **to answer in the a.** répondre affirmativement ou par l'affirmative
  2 adj affirmatif(ive)

affix 1 n ['æfɪks] Ling affixe m
  2 vt [əˈfɪks] attacher (to à); (notice, poster) fixer (to à)

afflict [əˈflɪkt] vt affliger; **afflicted with rheumatism** affligé(e) de rhumatismes

affliction [əˈflɪkʃən] n (illness) affection f; (misfortune) malheur m

affluent ['æfluənt] adj riche; **the a. society** la société d'abondance

afford [əˈfɔːd] vt **(a)** (financially) **to be able to a. sth** avoir les moyens d'acheter qch; **I can't a. it** mes moyens ne me le permettent pas; **we can't a. a new car** nous ne pouvons pas nous offrir une nouvelle voiture; **she can a. to eat out twice a week** elle peut se permettre d'aller au restaurant deux fois par semaine **(b)** (non-financial use) **I can't a. to wait** je ne peux pas attendre; **can you a. the time?** est-ce que vous avez le temps?; **I can't a. not to** je n'ai pas le choix; **we can't a. another mistake** nous ne pouvons pas nous permettre une nouvelle erreur **(c)** Formal (give) offrir, procurer

affordable [əˈfɔːdəbəl] adj (price, purchase) abordable; (house) (d'un prix) abordable

affray [əˈfreɪ] n rixe f

affront [əˈfrʌnt] **1** n affront m, offense f
  2 vt offenser, faire (un) affront à; **to be/feel affronted** être/se sentir offensé(e)

Afghan ['æfɡæn] **1** n **(a)** (person) Afghan(e) m,f **(b)** (dog) lévrier m afghan
  2 adj afghan(e); **A. hound** lévrier m afghan

Afghanistan [æfˈɡænɪstɑːn] n l'Afghanistan m

afield [əˈfiːld] adv **further a.** plus loin

AFL/CIO [eɪefelsiaɪˈəʊ] n (abbr American Federation of Labor and Congress of Industrial Organizations) = confédération syndicale américaine

afloat [əˈfləʊt] adv & adj à flot; **to stay a.** (of boat, company) se maintenir à flot

afoot [əˈfʊt] adv **there's something a.** il se prépare ou se trame quelque chose

aforementioned [əˈfɔːmenʃənd] adj susmentionné(e)

afraid [əˈfreɪd] adj **(a)** (scared) **to be a.** (of) avoir peur (de); **that's (exactly) what I was a. of!** c'est bien ce que je craignais!; **I was a. there would be an accident** je craignais un accident **(b)** (sorry) **I'm a. so/not** je crains que oui/que non; **I'm a. she's out** je regrette, mais elle est sortie; **I'm a. I can't help you** j'ai bien peur de ne pouvoir vous aider

afresh [əˈfreʃ] adv de nouveau, à nouveau; **to start a.** recommencer

Africa ['æfrɪkə] n l'Afrique f

African ['æfrɪkən] **1** n Africain(e) m,f; **A. American** Noir(e) m,f américain(e)
  2 adj africain(e)

Afrikaans [æfrɪˈkɑːnz] n afrikaans m

aft [ɑːft] adv Naut à l'arrière

after ['ɑːftə(r)] **1** prep **(a)** (with time) après; **a. dinner** après dîner; **a. three days** au bout de trois jours; **the day a. the battle** le lendemain de la bataille; **it's a. five** il est cinq heures passées; Am **it's twenty a. six** il est six heures vingt; **a. all** (all things considered) après tout; (despite everything) finalement
  (b) (with motion) après; **to run a. sb** courir après qn; **close the door a. you** fermez la porte derrière vous; **a. you!** après vous!
  (c) (in search of) **to be a. sb/sth** chercher qn/qch
  (d) (expressing sequence) après; **a. her, he is the best** après elle, c'est lui le meilleur
  (e) (expressing repetition) après; **day a. day** jour après jour; **year a. year** d'une année sur l'autre, tous les ans; **time a. time** cent fois; **it's one thing a. another** j'ai/nous avons/etc des problèmes à n'en plus finir
  (f) (in honour of) **to name sb/sth a. sb** donner le nom de qn à qn/qch
  2 adv après; **soon/long a.** peu/longtemps après; **the**

week a. la semaine d'après; **the day** a. le lendemain

3 *conj (when subject changes)* après que + *indicative* ou *Fam subjunctive; (when subject stays the same)* après + *infinitive*; **I came** a. **he left** je suis arrivé après qu'il est ou *Fam* soit parti; a. **I saw him I went out** je suis sorti après l'avoir vu; a. **doing sth** après avoir fait qch

afterbirth ['ɑːftəbɜːθ] *n* placenta *m*

aftercare ['ɑːftəkeə(r)] *n (after operation)* soins *m* postopératoires; *(of convalescent, delinquent)* surveillance *f*

after-effect ['ɑːftərəfekt] *n (of drug)* effet *m* secondaire; *Fig (of event)* répercussion *f*, contrecoup *m*

after-life ['ɑːftəlaɪf] *n* vie *f* après la mort

aftermath ['ɑːftəmæθ] *n* suites *fpl*, conséquences *fpl*

afternoon [ɑːftə'nuːn] *n* après-midi *m inv* ou *f inv*; **in the** a. *(pendant)* l'après-midi; **at two o'clock in the** a. à deux heures de l'après-midi; **good** a.! bonjour!

aftersales service ['ɑːftəseɪlz'sɜːvɪs] *n Com* service *m* après-vente

aftershave ['ɑːftəʃeɪv] *n* a. **(lotion)** (lotion *f*) après-rasage *m*

aftertaste ['ɑːftəteɪst] *n also Fig* arrière-goût *m*

afterthought ['ɑːftəθɔːt] *n* réflexion *f* après coup; **as an** a. après coup

afterwards ['ɑːftəwədz] *adv* après; **I regretted it** a. par la suite, je l'ai regretté

again [ə'gen] *adv* (a) *(in general)* de nouveau, encore; **to begin** a. recommencer; **he never came back** a. il n'est plus jamais revenu; **don't do it** a.! ne recommence pas!; **not you** a.! encore toi!; **once** a. encore une fois, une fois de plus; **a. and** a. à maintes reprises; **now and** a. de temps en temps, de temps à autre; **half as much** a. moitié plus; **I'd like half as much** a. je voudrais encore la moitié de ça; **what did you say** a.? qu'avez-vous dit déjà? (b) *(besides)* en outre; *(then)* a. *(on the other hand)* d'un autre côté; a., **I may have imagined it** cela dit, il se peut aussi que je l'aie imaginé

against [ə'genst] *prep* (a) *(in opposition to)* contre; **to be** a. **sb/sth** être contre qn/qch, être opposé(e) à qn ou qch; **to have something/nothing** a. **sb/sth** avoir quelque chose/ne rien avoir contre qn/qch; a. **the law** contraire à la loi, illégal(e)

(b) *(as protection from)* contre; **to warn sb** a. **sb/sth** mettre qn en garde contre qn/qch

(c) *(in contact with)* contre; **to lean** a. **sth** s'appuyer contre qch

(d) *(in comparison with)* contre; **three deaths this year (as)** a. **thirty in 1990** trois morts cette année contre trente en 1990; **the pound rose/fell** a. **the dollar** la livre a augmenté/chuté par rapport au dollar

age [eɪdʒ] **1** *n* (a) *(of person)* âge *m*; **to be twenty years of** a. avoir vingt ans, être âgé(e) de vingt ans; **what** a. **is she?, what's her** a.? quel âge a-t-elle?; **he doesn't look his** a. il ne fait pas son âge; **people of all ages** des gens de tout âge; a. **group** tranche d'âge; a. **of consent =** âge légal où on peut avoir des rapports sexuels; a. **limit** limite *f* d'âge

(b) *(old)* a. vieillesse *f*

(c) *(adulthood)* **to come of** a. atteindre sa majorité; **to be under** a. *Law* être mineur(e); *(not old enough to buy alcohol etc)* ne pas avoir l'âge

(d) *(era)* âge *m*, époque *f*

(e) *Fam (long time)* **it's ages since I saw him** il y a une éternité que je ne l'ai pas vu; **I've been waiting (for) ages** ça fait une éternité que j'attends

2 *vt & vi (continuous* **aging** *or* **ageing)** vieillir

aged *adj* (a) [eɪdʒd] *(of the age of)* a. **twenty** âgé(e) de vingt ans (b) ['eɪdʒɪd] *(old)* âgé(e), vieux (vieille)

ageing ['eɪdʒɪŋ] **1** *n (of person, wine)* vieillissement *m*; a. **process** processus *m* de vieillissement

2 *adj (becoming older)* vieillissant(e); *(old)* vieux (vieille)

ageism ['eɪdʒɪzəm] *n* âgisme *m*

agency ['eɪdʒənsɪ] *n* (a) *Com* agence *f*; **advertising/travel** a. agence de publicité/de voyages (b) **through the** a. **of** par l'entremise ou l'intermédiaire de

agenda [ə'dʒendə] *n (of meeting)* ordre *m* du jour; *Fig* programme *m*

agent ['eɪdʒənt] *n* (a) *(representative, spy)* agent *m* (b) *(instrument)* agent *m*; **to be the** a. **of sth** être l'instrument de qch

age-old ['eɪdʒəʊld] *adj* séculaire

aggravate ['ægrəveɪt] *vt* (a) *(worsen)* aggraver (b) *Fam (annoy)* agacer, exaspérer

aggravating ['ægrəveɪtɪŋ] *adj* (a) *Law* aggravant(e) (b) *Fam (annoying)* agaçant(e), exaspérant(e)

aggravation [ægrə'veɪʃən] *n* (a) *(worsening)* aggravation *f* (b) *Fam (annoyance)* embêtements *mpl*

aggregate ['ægrɪgət] **1** *n* total *m*, ensemble *m*; **on** a. au total

2 *adj* collectif(ive); a. **scores** résultats *mpl* globaux

aggression [ə'greʃən] *n* agressivité *f*; **an act of** a. une agression

aggressive [ə'gresɪv] *adj* agressif(ive)

aggressively [ə'gresɪvlɪ] *adv (violently)* d'une manière agressive; *(speak)* d'un ton agressif; *(vigorously)* énergiquement, avec dynamisme

aggressor [ə'gresə(r)] *n* agresseur *m*

aggrieved [ə'griːvd] *adj (expression, tone)* vexé(e); **to be or feel** a. se sentir lésé(e)

aggro ['ægrəʊ] *n Fam (violence)* grabuge *m*, bagarre(s) *f[pl]*; *(trouble)* enquiquinement *m*

aghast [ə'gɑːst] *adj* horrifié(e) **(at** par)

agile ['ædʒaɪl] *adj* agile

agility [ə'dʒɪlɪtɪ] *n* agilité *f*

agitate ['ædʒɪteɪt] **1** *vt (liquid, person)* agiter

2 *vi* **to** a. **for/against sth** mener une campagne en faveur de/contre qch

agitated ['ædʒɪteɪtɪd] *adj (person)* agité(e)

agitation [ædʒɪ'teɪʃən] *n* agitation *f*

agitator ['ædʒɪteɪtə(r)] *n Pol* agitateur(trice) *m,f*

aglow [ə'gləʊ] *adj (sky)* embrasé(e); **to be** a. **with** *(of person)* rayonner de

AGM [eɪdʒi:'em] *n Com (abbr* **annual general meeting)** AGA *f*

agnostic [æg'nɒstɪk] *n & adj* agnostique *mf*

ago [ə'gəʊ] *adv* **ten years** a. il y a dix ans; **long** a. il y a longtemps; **not long** a. il n'y a pas longtemps; **as long** a. **as 1840** déjà en 1840, dès 1840; **a short time** a., **a little while** a. il y a peu de temps, tout à l'heure; **how long** a. **was that?** c'était il y a combien de temps?

agog [ə'gɒg] *adj (in émoi)*; **he was** a. **to hear the latest news** il brûlait d'apprendre les dernières nouvelles

agonize ['ægənaɪz] *vi* se ronger les sangs, se tourmenter **(over** à propos de)

agonizing ['ægənaɪzɪŋ] *adj (pain, death)* atroce; *(silence, wait)* angoissant(e); *(decision, dilemma)* pénible, déchirant(e)

agony ['ægənɪ] (*pl* **agonies**) *n (physical pain)* douleur *f* atroce; *(mental pain)* angoisse *f*; **to be in a.** être au supplice *ou* au martyre; **it's a. walking in these shoes!** c'est un véritable supplice de marcher avec ces chaussures!; **a. aunt** *(in newspaper)* = responsable de la rubrique courrier du cœur; **a. column** *(in newspaper)* courrier *m* du cœur

agoraphobia [ægərə'fəʊbɪə] *n* agoraphobie *f*

agrarian [ə'greərɪən] *adj* agraire

agree [ə'gri:] **1** *vt* (a) *(reach agreement on) (price, time, conditions)* se mettre d'accord sur; **to a. to do sth** convenir de faire qch; **(are we) agreed?** (nous sommes) d'accord?
(b) *(concur)* **to a.** (that)… s'accorder à dire que…; **I a. that's expensive, but…** c'est cher, j'en conviens, mais…; **everyone agrees (that) he's the best** tout le monde s'accorde à dire qu'il est le meilleur
(c) *(consent)* **to a. to do sth** accepter de faire qch, consentir à faire qch; **we'll have to a. to differ on that** je crois qu'ici il va nous falloir accepter nos différences d'opinion; **it is generally agreed that…** il est généralement admis que…

2 *vi* (a) *(be of same opinion, concur)* être d'accord *(with sur/avec)*; *(after discussion)* se mettre d'accord; **I quite or entirely a.** je suis entièrement d'accord; **I'm afraid I can't a.** j'ai bien peur de ne pas être du même avis; **I couldn't a. more!** ça c'est bien dit!; **I don't a. with all this violence on television** je n'approuve pas toute cette violence à la télévision
(b) *(match) (of statements, facts, opinions)* concorder, coïncider *(with avec)*; *Gram* s'accorder *(with avec)*
(c) *(accept) (condition)* **to a.** à) **to a. to a condition/proposal** accepter une condition/une proposition

▸**agree on** *vt insep* être d'accord sur; *(after discussion)* se mettre d'accord sur

▸**agree with** *vt insep (of food)* réussir à

agreeable [ə'gri:əbəl] *adj* (a) *(pleasant)* agréable; *(person)* aimable (b) *(acceptable)* **if that is a. to you** si cela vous convient

agreed [ə'gri:d] *adj (price, time)* convenu(e)

agreement [ə'gri:mənt] *n* (a) *(contract, assent) & Gram* accord *m* (**on** *or* **about** sur); **to come to an a.** tomber *ou* se mettre d'accord; **by mutual a.** d'un commun accord; **the proposal met with unanimous a.** la proposition a été reçue à l'unanimité; **to be in a. with sb** être d'accord avec qn; **to be in a. with a decision** approuver une décision (b) *(of facts, account)* **to be in a. with** concorder avec

agricultural [ægrɪ'kʌltʃərəl] *adj* agricole; **a. college** = école supérieure d'agriculture et d'agronomie; **a. labourer** ouvrier *m* agricole

agriculture ['ægrɪkʌltʃə(r)] *n* agriculture *f*

agronomy [ə'grɒnəmɪ] *n* agronomie *f*

aground [ə'graʊnd] *adv* **to run a.** *(of ship)* s'échouer; *(of project, government)* échouer

ahead [ə'hed] *adv* (a) *(in space)* devant; **to go on a.** partir devant; **the road a. was clear** devant nous/moi/etc la route était libre; **a. of** devant (b) *(winning)* **to be a.** être en tête; **to get a.** *(in career)* avancer; **to get a. of sb** dépasser qn (c) *(in time)* **to plan a.** faire des projets; **in the years a.** dans les années à venir; **a. of** *(prior to)* avant; **a. of schedule** *(flight, train)* en avance sur l'horaire; *(project)* en avance sur ses prévisions; **to be a. of one's time** être en avance sur son temps

ahoy [ə'hɔɪ] *exclam* **a. there!** oh(é)!; **ship a.!** ohé du bateau!

AI [eɪ'aɪ] *n* (a) *Comptr (abbr* **artificial intelligence**) IA *f* (b) *Biol (abbr* **artificial insemination**) insémination *f* artificielle (c) *Pol (abbr* **Amnesty International**) Amnesty International *f*

aid [eɪd] **1** *n* (a) *(help, for disaster relief)* aide *f*, secours *m*; **with the a. of sb** avec l'aide de qn; **with the a. of sth** à l'aide de qch; **to go to sb's a.** aller *ou* se porter au secours de qn; **in a. of** *(fund-raising event)* au profit de; *Fam* **what's (all) this in a. of?** c'est en quel honneur? (b) *(device)* outil *m*; **teaching aids** matériel *m* pédagogique
2 *vt* aider; *Law* **to a. and abet sb** être le complice de qn

aide [eɪd] *n* assistant(e) *m,f*, conseiller(ère) *m,f*

aide-de-camp ['eɪd'dəkɒŋ] *(pl* **aides-de-camp**) *n Mil* aide *m* de camp

aiding ['eɪdɪŋ] *n Law* **a. and abetting** complicité *f*

AIDS [eɪdz] *n* sida *m*; **A. clinic** = clinique spécialisée dans le traitement du sida; **A. sufferer** sidéen(enne) *m,f*, malade *mf* du sida; **A. virus** virus *m* du sida

ailing ['eɪlɪŋ] *adj (person)* souffrant(e); *(company, economy)* qui bat de l'aile

ailment ['eɪlmənt] *n* mal *m*

aim [eɪm] **1** *n* (a) *(at target)* **to take a. (at)** viser; **her a. was good** elle visait bien (b) *(goal)* but *m*, dessein *m*; **with the a. of doing sth** dans le but ou dessein de faire qch
2 *vt* (a) *(stone)* lancer (at à); *(camera)* braquer (at sur); **to a. a gun at sb/sth** mettre qn/qch en joue; **to a. a blow at sb** chercher à frapper qn; **to be aimed at sb** *(of remarks, TV programme)* être destiné(e) à qn
3 *vi* **to a.** *(with gun)* viser; **to a. to do sth** *(intend)* avoir l'intention de faire qch

aimless ['eɪmlɪs] *adj (existence, remark)* sans but

ain't [eɪnt] *very Fam* (a) **= is not, am not, are not** (b) **= has not, have not**

air [eə(r)] **1** *n* (a) *(in general)* air *m*; **by a.** par avion; **to be on the a.** *(of person)* être à l'antenne; *(of programme)* être diffusé(e); **to throw sth (up) in the a.** lancer qch en l'air; **our plans are up in the a.** *(undecided)* nos projets n'ont toujours pas de forme précise; *(of rumour)* circuler; *(of feeling, idea)* être dans l'air; **a. bag** sac *m* gonflable de sécurité; **a. bed** matelas *m* pneumatique; **a. filter** filtre *m* à air; **the A. Force** l'Armée *f* de l'air; **a. freight** fret *m* aérien; **a. freshener** désodorisant *m*; **a. hostess** hôtesse *f* de l'air; **a. raid** raid *m* aérien; **a. rifle** fusil *m* à air comprimé; **a. show** salon *m* de l'aéronautique; **a. steward** steward *m*; **a. stewardess** hôtesse *f* de l'air; **a. terminal** aérogare *f*; **a. traffic control** contrôle *m* aérien; **a. traffic controller** contrôleur *m* aérien, aiguilleur *m* du ciel (b) *(melody)* air *m* (c) *(look) air m*, apparence *f*; **he has a certain a. about him** c'est quelqu'un qui en impose; **to give oneself or to put on airs** se donner des airs
2 *vt* (a) *(room, clothing, bedding)* aérer (b) *(opinions, grievances)* exposer

airborne ['eəbɔ:n] *adj (seeds, particles)* en suspension dans l'air; *(troops)* aéroporté(e); **once we are a.** une fois que nous aurons décollé

air-conditioned ['eəkən'dɪʃənd] *adj* climatisé(e), à air conditionné

air-conditioning ['eəkən'dɪʃənɪŋ] *n* climatisation *f*

air-cooled ['eəku:ld] *adj* refroidi(e) par air

aircraft ['eəkrɑ:ft] *(pl* **aircraft**) *n* avion *m*; **a. carrier** porte-avions *m inv*

air-crew ['eəkru:] *n Av* équipage *m*

airfield ['eəfi:ld] *n* champ *m ou* terrain *m* d'aviation

airing ['eərɪŋ] *n* to give sth an a. *(room, clothes, bedding)* aérer qch; *(opinions, grievances)* exposer; **a. cupboard** = placard où se trouve le chauffe-eau

airless ['eəlɪs] *adj (room)* qui sent le renfermé; *(evening, atmosphere)* lourd(e)

airlift ['eəlɪft] **1** *n* pont *m* aérien
2 *vt (supplies, troops)* transporter par avion; *(refugees)* évacuer par avion

airline ['eəlaɪn] *n* ligne *f* ou compagnie *f* aérienne; **a. pilot** pilote *m* de ligne

airlock ['eəlɒk] *n* **(a)** *(in submarine, spacecraft)* sas *m* **(b)** *(in pipe)* poche *f* d'air

airmail ['eəmeɪl] **1** *n (service)* poste *f* aérienne; **a. letter** aérogramme *m*
2 *adv* **to send sth a.** envoyer qch par avion
3 *vt (letter)* envoyer par avion

airplane ['eəpleɪn] *n Am* avion *m*

airport ['eəpɔːt] *n* aéroport *m*

air-sea rescue ['eəsiː'reskjuː] *n* sauvetage *m* aérien en mer

airship ['eəʃɪp] *n* dirigeable *m*

airsick ['eəsɪk] *adj* to be a. avoir le mal de l'air

airspace ['eəspeɪs] *n* espace *m* aérien

airstrip ['eəstrɪp] *n* piste *f* d'atterrissage

airtight ['eətaɪt] *adj* hermétique

airtime ['eətaɪm] *n Rad & TV* temps *m* d'antenne

airwaves ['eəweɪvz] *npl* ondes *fpl* (hertziennes)

airworthy ['eəwɜːðɪ] *adj (aircraft)* en état de voler

airy ['eərɪ] *adj* **(a)** *(room, house)* bien aéré(e) **(b)** *(person, attitude)* insouciant(e), désinvolte

airy-fairy ['eərɪ'feərɪ] *adj Fam (idea, scheme)* farfelu(e)

aisle [aɪl] *n (in supermarket, cinema)* allée *f*; *(in church) (at side)* bas-côté *m*; *(central)* allée; *(in plane, bus)* couloir *m*; *Fam* **she had them rolling in the aisles** *(of comedian)* elle a fait mourir le public de rire; **a. seat** *(in plane)* place *f* côté couloir

ajar [ə'dʒɑː(r)] *adv & adj* entrouvert(e)

aka [eɪkeɪ'eɪ] *adv (abbr* **also known as)** alias

akin [ə'kɪn] *adv & adj* **to be a.** to être apparenté(e) à

alabaster ['æləbæstə(r)] *n* albâtre *m*

alacrity [ə'lækrɪtɪ] *n* empressement *m*

alarm [ə'lɑːm] **1** *n* **(a)** *(signal, device)* alarme *f*; **to raise** *or* **give the a.** donner l'alarme; **a. clock** réveil *m*, réveille-matin *m inv*; **a. signal** signal *m* d'alarme **(b)** *(fright, anxiety)* alarme *f*, frayeur *f*; **there's no cause for a.** il n'y a aucune raison de s'alarmer
2 *vt* effrayer, alarmer; **to be alarmed at sth** s'alarmer *ou* s'effrayer de qch

alarming [ə'lɑːmɪŋ] *adj* alarmant(e), inquiétant(e)

alarmist [ə'lɑːmɪst] *n & adj* alarmiste *mf*

alas [ə'læs] *exclam* hélas!

Albania [æl'beɪnɪə] *n* l'Albanie *f*

Albanian [æl'beɪnɪən] **1** *n* **(a)** *(person)* Albanais(e) *m,f* **(b)** *(language)* albanais *m*
2 *adj* albanais(e)

albatross ['ælbətrɒs] *n* albatros *m*

albeit [ɔːl'biːɪt] *conj* quoique, bien que

albino [æl'biːnəʊ] *(pl* **albinos)** *n* albinos *mf*

album ['ælbəm] *n (record, for photos, stamps)* album *m*

albumen ['ælbjʊmɪn] *n* **(a)** *(in egg)* albumen *m* **(b)** *(in blood)* albumine *f*

alchemy ['ælkəmɪ] *n* alchimie *f*

alcohol ['ælkəhɒl] *n* alcool *m*

alcoholic [ælkə'hɒlɪk] **1** *n (person)* alcoolique *mf*
2 *adj* alcoolique; *(drink)* alcoolisé(e)

alcoholism ['ælkəhɒlɪzəm] *n* alcoolisme *m*

alcove ['ælkəʊv] *n (in wall)* niche *f*; *(larger)* renfoncement *m*

alder ['ɔːldə(r)] *n* au(l)ne *m*

ale [eɪl] *n* = bière anglaise au malt

alert [ə'lɜːt] **1** *n* alerte *f*; **to be on the a.** être en état d'alerte, être sur le qui-vive
2 *adj (watchful)* éveillé(e); *(lively)* vif (vive); **to be a. to sth** *(aware of)* être conscient(e) de qch
3 *vt* alerter; **to a. sb to a danger** alerter *ou* avertir qn d'un danger

Aleutian Islands [æl'uːʃən'aɪləndz] *npl* **the A.** les îles *fpl* Aléoutiennes

Alexandria [ælɪg'zɑːndrɪə] *n* Alexandrie *f*

alfalfa [æl'fælfə] *n* luzerne *f*

alfresco [æl'freskəʊ] *adv & adj* en plein air

algae ['ældʒiː] *npl* algues *fpl*

algebra ['ældʒɪbrə] *n* algèbre *f*

Algeria [æl'dʒɪərɪə] *n* l'Algérie *f*

Algerian [æl'dʒɪərɪən] **1** *n* Algérien(enne) *m,f*
2 *adj* algérien(enne)

Algiers [æl'dʒɪəz] *n* Alger *m*

algorithm ['ælgərɪðəm] *n Comptr* algorithme *m*

alias ['eɪlɪəs] *(pl* **aliases) 1** *n* nom *m* d'emprunt, faux nom
2 *adv* alias

alibi ['ælɪbaɪ] *n Law* alibi *m*

alien ['eɪlɪən] **1** *n* **(a)** *Formal (foreigner)* étranger(ère) *m,f* **(b)** *(from outer space)* extraterrestre *mf*
2 *adj* **(a)** *(strange)* étranger(ère) **(b)** *(from outer space)* extraterrestre

alienate ['eɪlɪəneɪt] *vt (supporters, readers)* s'aliéner; **they feel alienated from society** ils se sentent mis à l'écart de la société

alight¹ [ə'laɪt] *adj (burning)* en flammes, en feu; **to set sth a.** mettre le feu à qch

alight² [ə'laɪt] *pt & pp of* **alighted** *or* **alit** [ə'lɪt]) *vi* **(a)** *Formal (from train, car)* descendre **(b)** *(of bird, eyes, glance)* se poser **(on** sur)

align [ə'laɪn] *vt* aligner; **to a. oneself with sb** s'aligner sur qn

alignment [ə'laɪnmənt] *n* alignement *m*; **out of a.** désaligné(e); **in a. (with)** aligné(e) (sur)

alike [ə'laɪk] **1** *adj* semblable, pareil(eille); **to look a.** se ressembler
2 *adv (dress, think)* de la même façon; **old and young a.** les vieux comme les jeunes

alimentary canal [ælɪ'mentərɪkə'næl] *n Anat* tube *m* digestif

alimony ['ælɪmənɪ] *n Law* pension *f* alimentaire

alit [ə'lɪt] *pt & pp of* **alight**

alive [ə'laɪv] *adj* **(a)** *(living)* to be a. être vivant(e); to keep sb a. maintenir qn en vie; **to keep a memory/custom a.** entretenir un souvenir/une tradition; **to stay a.** survivre; **to be a. and well** se bien porter; **the oldest woman a.** la doyenne du monde **(b)** *(aware)* **to be a. to sth** avoir parfaitement conscience de qch **(c)** *(full of vitality)* **I've never felt so a.** je ne me suis jamais senti aussi bien de ma vie; **to come a.** s'animer (d) *(teeming)* **to be a. with sth** grouiller de qch

alkali ['ælkəlaɪ] *n* alcali *m*

alkaline ['ælkəlaɪn] *adj* alcalin(e)

all [ɔːl] 1 *adj* (a) *(every one of)* tous (toutes); **a. men** tous les hommes; **a. the girls** toutes les filles; **a. the others** tous les autres; **a. four of them** tous les quatre; **at a. hours** à des heures impossibles

(b) *(the whole of)* tout(e); **a. the wine** tout le vin; **a. day** toute la journée; **a. her life** toute sa vie; **a. the time** tout le temps

(c) *(for emphasis)* **a. sorts of things** toutes sortes de choses; **what's a. that noise?** c'est quoi, tout ce bruit?; **in a. honesty** en toute honnêteté; **for a. his wealth...** il a beau être riche...; **it's not a. that easy** ce n'est pas si facile (que ça); **you, of a. people, should understand** si quelqu'un doit comprendre ça, c'est bien toi; **of a. the stupid things to say!** ce n'est vraiment pas malin de dire un truc pareil!

2 *pron* (a) *(everyone)* tous (toutes) *mpl, fpl*; **a. of us** nous tous; **a. of them say that...,** **they a. say that...** ils disent tous que...; **a. together** tous ensemble

(b) *(everything)* tout *m*; **that's a.** c'est tout; **he ate a. of it,** he ate it a. il a tout mangé; **a. I said was...** tout ce que j'ai dit, c'est...; **I did a.** I could j'ai fait tout ce que j'ai pu; **it was a. I could do not to laugh** j'ai bien failli rire; **best/worst of a.,** ... le mieux/le pire, c'est que...; **I like this best of a.** c'est ça que je préfère; **most of a.** surtout; **when a. is said and done** au bout du compte; **it's a. the same to me** ça m'est égal; **thirty men in a.** trente hommes en tout *ou* au total; **a. in a.** dans l'ensemble; **it cost £260, a. in a.** ça a coûté 260 livres tout compris; *Ironic* **it cost a. of £2** ça a coûté la coquette somme de 2 livres

3 *adv* (a) *(entirely)* tout; **a. alone** tout(e) seul(e); **to be a. in black** être tout en noir; **to be a. for sth** être pour qch; **a. ears/smiles** tout ouïe/sourire; **I forgot a. about it** j'ai complètement oublié; **he's not a. bad** il n'a pas que de mauvais côtés; **a. over Spain/the world** dans toute l'Espagne/le monde entier; **a. over (the place)** partout; **a. too soon** trop tôt; **a. along** depuis le début; **a. but** *(almost)* presque, pratiquement; **it's/he's a. yours** il est à vous; *Fam* **a. in** *(exhausted)* crevé(e)

(b) **at a.** *(in the slightest)* du tout; **do you know her at a.?** tu la connais?; **if it's at a. possible** si c'était possible; **not at a.** pas du tout; *(when thanked)* je t'en prie

(c) *(with comparatives)* **a. the better/worse** d'autant mieux/plus mal; **a. the easier/faster** d'autant plus facile/rapide

(d) *(in games)* **2 a. 2** partout; **4 (games) a.** *(in tennis)* 4 jeux partout; **15 a.** *(in tennis)* 15 partout

4 *n* **to give one's a.** se donner à fond

Allah ['ælə] *n* Allah

allay [ə'leɪ] *vt (doubts, suspicions)* dissiper; *(fear, pain)* soulager

all-clear ['ɔːl'klɪə(r)] *n (after air-raid)* (signal *m* de) fin *f* d'alerte; *Fig (for project)* feu *m* vert

allegation [ælɪ'geɪʃən] *n* allégation *f*

allege [ə'ledʒ] *vt* alléguer, prétendre; **it is alleged that...** on prétend que...

alleged [ə'ledʒd] *adj (thief, culprit)* présumé(e)

allegedly [ə'ledʒdlɪ] *adv* prétendument; **he a. stole £500** il aurait volé 500 livres

allegiance [ə'liːdʒəns] *n (to party, cause)* fidélité *f*; *(to king)* allégeance *f*

allegory ['ælɪɡərɪ] *(pl* **allegories)** *n* allégorie *f*

all-embracing [ɔːlɪm'breɪsɪŋ] *adj (term, category)* large

allergic [ə'lɜːdʒɪk] *adj* allergique **(to** à)

allergy ['ælədʒɪ] *(pl* **allergies)** *n* allergie *f* **(to** à)

alleviate [ə'liːvɪeɪt] *vt* soulager, calmer

alley ['ælɪ] *(pl* **alleys)** *n (street)* ruelle *f*; **a. cat** chat *m* de gouttière

alleyway ['ælɪweɪ] *n (street)* ruelle *f*

alliance [ə'laɪəns] *n* alliance *f*; **to enter into an a. with sb** former une alliance avec qn

allied ['ælaɪd] *adj (countries)* allié(e); *(issues, phenomena)* lié(e)

alligator ['ælɪɡeɪtə(r)] *n* alligator *m*; **a. shoes/handbag** chaussures *fpl*/sac *m* en crocodile

all-important ['ɔːlɪm'pɔːtənt] *adj* essentiel(elle), capital(e)

all-in ['ɔːlɪn] *adj (price)* tout compris; **a. wrestling** lutte *f* libre, catch *m*

alliteration [əlɪtə'reɪʃən] *n* allitération *f*

all-night ['ɔːlnaɪt] *adj (party, session)* qui dure toute la nuit

allocate ['æləkeɪt] *vt (resources, money)* affecter, attribuer **(to** à); *(duties)* assigner **(to** à); *(time)* prévoir **(to** pour)

allocation [ælə'keɪʃən] *n (distribution)* affectation *f*; *(share)* part *f*

allot [ə'lɒt] *(pt & pp* **allotted)** *vt (resources, money)* attribuer **(to** à); *(duties, job)* assigner **(to** à); **in the allotted time** dans le temps imparti

allotment [ə'lɒtmənt] *n* (a) *(land)* jardin *m* ouvrier (b) *(distribution)* (of money) affectation *f*; *(share)* part *f*

all-out ['ɔː'laʊt] *adj (resistance, effort)* acharné(e); *(strike, war)* total(e)

allow [ə'laʊ] *vt* (a) *(permit)* permettre; **to a. sb to do sth** permettre à qn de faire qch; **a. me!** *(offering help)* permettez(-moi)!; **smoking is not allowed** il est interdit de fumer; **I'm not allowed to do it** je n'ai pas l'autorisation de le faire; **to a. oneself to be deceived/persuaded** se laisser abuser/convaincre (b) *(allocate, grant)* accorder; *(time)* compter, prévoir

▶**allow for** *vt insep* tenir compte de; **add another hour to a. for delays** il faut prévoir une heure de plus au cas où il y aurait des retards

allowable [ə'laʊəbəl] *adj (error, delay)* admissible

allowance [ə'laʊəns] *n* (a) *(money given)* rente *f*, pension *f*; *(pocket money)* argent *m* de poche; **travel a.** indemnité *f* de transport (b) **to make a. for sth** tenir compte de qch; **I'm tired of making allowances for him** j'en ai assez de lui trouver des excuses

alloy ['ælɔɪ] *n* alliage *m*

all-powerful ['ɔːl'paʊəfʊl] *adj* tout-puissant (toute-puissante)

all-purpose ['ɔːl'pɜːpəs] *adj* universel(elle); **a. cleaner/adhesive** détachant *m*/colle *f* tous usages

all right [ɔːl'raɪt] 1 *adj* **are you a.?** ça va?; **he was in a car crash but he's a.** il a eu un accident de voiture mais il n'a rien; **it's a.** *(acceptable)* ce n'est pas mal; *(not a problem)* ce n'est pas grave; **to be a. for money** avoir suffisamment d'argent; **to be a. at maths/French** se débrouiller en maths/français; *Fam* **she's a bit of a.!** elle est bien foutue!

2 *adv* (yes) oui; **is it a. if I smoke?** ça ne vous dérange pas si je fume?; **a., let's get started** bon, commençons

all-round ['ɔːl'raʊnd] *adj (education, improvement)* général(e); **an a. athlete** un athlète complet

all-rounder ['ɔːl'raʊndə(r)] *n* **she's a good a.** elle est bonne en tout

allspice ['ɔːlspaɪs] *n* poivre *m* de la Jamaïque

all-star ['ɔːl'stɑː(r)] *adj* **an a. cast** une distribution prestigieuse

all-time ['ɔːl'taɪm] *adj (record)* absolu(e); **unemployment has reached an a. high/low** le chômage n'a jamais été aussi élevé/bas

allude [ə'luːd] *vi* **to a.** to faire allusion à

allure [ə'lʊə(r)] *n* attrait *m*

allusion [ə'luːʒən] *n* allusion *f*; **to make an a. to sth** faire allusion à qch

ally 1 *n* ['ælaɪ] *(pl* **allies**) allié(e) *m,f*
2 *vt* [ə'laɪ] *(pt & pp* **allied**) **to a. oneself with** s'allier à *ou* avec

almanac ['ɔːlmənæk] *n* almanach *m*

almighty [ɔːl'maɪtɪ] **1** *n* **the A.** le Tout-Puissant
2 *adj Fam (fuss, row)* terrible

almond ['ɑːmənd] *n* amande *f*; **a. tree** amandier *m*

almost ['ɔːlməʊst] *adv* presque; **it's a. six o'clock** il est presque six heures; **we're a. there** *(in journey)* nous sommes presque arrivés; *(in task)* nous avons presque fini; **she a. missed the bus** elle a failli rater l'autobus

alms [ɑːmz] *npl* aumône *f*

aloft [ə'lɒft] *adv* en l'air

alone [ə'ləʊn] *adv & adj* seul(e); **to leave sb a.** laisser qn tranquille; **to leave sth a.** ne pas toucher à qch; **I did it a.** je l'ai fait tout seul; **to go it a.** faire cavalier seul; **we are not a. in thinking that...** nous ne sommes pas les seuls à penser que...; **you a. can help me** vous seul pouvez m'aider; **I can't afford a bicycle, let a. a car!** je n'ai pas assez d'argent pour m'acheter une bicyclette, encore moins une voiture!

along [ə'lɒŋ] **1** *prep* le long de; **to walk a. the shore** marcher le long de la côte; **to sail a. the coast** longer la côte; **I was walking a. the street** je marchais dans la rue; *Fig* **somewhere a. the way** à un moment donné
2 *adv* **to move a.** avancer; **she'll be a. in ten minutes** elle sera là dans dix minutes; **to bring sth a.** apporter qch; **to bring sb a.** amener qn; **he knew all a.** il le savait depuis le début; **a. with** *(as well as)* ainsi que

alongside [ə'lɒŋ'saɪd] *prep (next to)* à côté de; *(along)* le long de; *Naut* **to come a. a ship/quay** accoster un bateau/quai

aloof [ə'luːf] **1** *adj* distant(e)
2 *adv* **to remain a.** *(from sth)* rester à l'écart (de qch)

aloud [ə'laʊd] *adv* à haute voix; **I was thinking a.** je pensais tout haut

alpha ['ælfə] *n* alpha *m*; *Phys* **a. rays** rayons *mpl* alpha

alphabet ['ælfəbet] *n* alphabet *m*

alphabetical [ælfə'betɪkəl] *adj* alphabétique; **in a. order** dans l'ordre alphabétique

alphabetically [ælfə'betɪklɪ] *adv* alphabétiquement

Alpine ['ælpaɪn] *adj* alpin(e); **an A. village** un village des Alpes

Alps [ælps] *npl* **the A.** les Alpes *fpl*

already [ɔːl'redɪ] *adv* déjà; **have you finished a.?** vous avez déjà fini?

alright [ɔːl'raɪt] = **all right**

Alsatian [æl'seɪʃən] **1** *n (dog)* berger *m* allemand; *(person from Alsace)* Alsacien(enne) *m,f*
2 *adj* alsacien(enne)

also ['ɔːlsəʊ] *adv* aussi; **not only...but a....** non seulement... mais en plus...

also-ran ['ɔːlsəʊræn] *n (in horse race)* cheval *m* non classé; *Fig (person)* perdant(e) *m,f*

altar ['ɔːltə(r)] *n* autel *m*; **a. boy** enfant *m* de chœur

alter ['ɔːltə(r)] **1** *vt* changer; *(garment)* faire des retouches à; **he altered his opinion later** il a changé d'avis plus tard; **that doesn't a. the fact that...** cela ne change rien au fait que...
2 *vi* changer

alteration [ɔːltə'reɪʃən] *n (to design, plan)* modification *f*, changement *m*; *(to timetable)* changement; *(to garment)* retouche *f*

altercation [ɔːltə'keɪʃən] *n* altercation *f*

alter ego ['æltə'riːgəʊ] *n* alter ego *m*

alternate 1 *adj* ['ɔːltənət] **1** *adj* [ɔːl'tɜːnət] alterné(e); **on a. days** un jour sur deux
2 *vt* employer tour à tour
3 *vi* alterner **(with** avec)

alternately [ɔːl'tɜːnɪtlɪ] *adv* tour à tour, alternativement

alternating ['ɔːltəneɪtɪŋ] *adj* alterné(e); *Elec* **a. current** courant *m* alternatif

alternative [ɔːl'tɜːnətɪv] **1** *n (choice)* choix *m*, solution *f*; **there is no a.** il n'y a pas le choix; **she had no a. but to obey** elle n'a pu faire autrement que d'obéir
2 *adj* **(a)** *(plan, route)* de remplacement; **an a. proposal** une contre-proposition **(b)** *(music, comedy)* alternatif(ive); **a. energy** énergies *fpl* de substitution; **a. medicine** médecine *f* douce

alternatively [ɔːl'tɜːnətɪvlɪ] *adv (on the other hand)* ou bien

alternator ['ɔːltəneɪtə(r)] *n* alternateur *m*

although [ɔːl'ðəʊ] *conj* bien que + *subjunctive*; **a. it's late** bien qu'il soit tard

altitude ['æltɪtjuːd] *n* altitude *f*

alto ['æltəʊ] *(pl* **altos**) *n (male voice)* haute-contre *f*; *(female voice)* contralto *m*; **a. clef** clef *f* d'ut; **a. saxophone** saxophone *m* alto

altogether [ɔːltə'geðə(r)] **1** *adv* **(a)** *(entirely)* complètement; **I was not a. pleased** je n'étais pas ravi **(b)** *(in total)* en tout; **a. the bill came to £63** en tout l'addition s'élevait à 63 livres
2 *n Fam* **in the a.** *(naked)* nu(e) comme un ver

altruism ['æltrʊɪzəm] *n* altruisme *m*

altruistic [æltrʊ'ɪstɪk] *adj* altruiste

aluminium [æljʊ'mɪnɪəm], *Am* **aluminum** [ə'luː-mɪnəm] *n* aluminium *m*; **a. foil** papier *m* d'aluminium

always ['ɔːlweɪz] *adv* toujours; **I can a. try** je peux toujours essayer

AM ['eɪ'em] *n Rad (abbr* **amplitude modulation)** AM

am [æm] *1st pers singular of* **be**

a.m. ['eɪ'em] *adv (abbr* **ante meridiem)** du matin; **five a.m.** cinq heures du matin

amalgam [ə'mælgəm] *n* amalgame *m*

amalgamate [ə'mælgəmeɪt] **1** *vt (metals, ideas)* amalgamer; *(companies)* fusionner
2 *vi (of companies)* fusionner

amass [ə'mæs] *vt* amasser, accumuler

amateur ['æmətə(r)] 1 *n* amateur *m*
2 *adj (painter, musician)* amateur; *Pej (work, performance)* d'amateur

amateurish [æmə'tɜːrɪʃ] *adj Pej* d'amateur

amaze [ə'meɪz] *vt* stupéfier; **I was amazed by his courage** son courage m'a stupéfié

amazement [ə'meɪzmənt] *n* stupéfaction *f*, stupeur *f*; **in a.** avec stupéfaction *ou* stupeur

amazing [ə'meɪzɪŋ] *adj* (a) *(surprising)* stupéfiant(e); **it's a. that no one helped her** il est incroyable que personne ne lui soit venu en aide (b) *(excellent)* formidable

Amazon ['æməzən] *n* (a) **the A.** *(river)* l'Amazone *f*; *(region)* l'Amazonie *f* (b) *(female warrior)* Amazone *f*

ambassador [æm'bæsədə(r)] *n* ambassadeur(drice) *m,f*

amber ['æmbə(r)] 1 *n (colour, stone)* ambre *m*; *(of traffic light)* orange *m*
2 *adj (jewellery)* d'ambre; *(colour)* couleur d'ambre, ambré(e)

ambience, ambiance ['æmbɪəns] *n* ambiance *f*

ambiguity [æmbɪ'gjuːɪtɪ] *(pl* **ambiguities**) *n* ambiguïté *f*

ambiguous [æm'bɪgjʊəs] *adj* ambigu(ë)

ambition [æm'bɪʃən] *n* ambition *f*

ambitious [æm'bɪʃəs] *adj* ambitieux(euse)

ambivalent [æm'bɪvələnt] *adj* ambivalent(e)

amble ['æmbəl] *vi* marcher d'un pas tranquille

ambulance ['æmbjʊləns] *n* ambulance *f*; **a. man** ambulancier *m*; **a. woman** ambulancière *f*

ambush ['æmbʊʃ] 1 *n also Fig* embuscade *f*
2 *vt also Fig* tendre une embuscade à; **to be ambushed** tomber dans une embuscade

ameba *Am* = **amoeba**

amen ['ɑː'men] *exclam* amen!, ainsi soit-il!

amenable [ə'miːnəbəl] *adj* souple; **to prove a. to a suggestion** approuver une proposition

amend [ə'mend] *vt (text, law)* modifier, amender; *(error)* corriger

amendment [ə'mendmənt] *n (to law, proposal)* amendement *m*

amends [ə'mendz] *npl* **to make a. (for sth)** faire amende honorable (pour qch); **to make a. to sb for sth** dédommager qn de qch

amenities [ə'miːnɪtɪz] *npl (shops)* commerces *mpl*; *(facilities)* équipements *mpl* collectifs

America [ə'merɪkə] *n* l'Amérique *f*

American [ə'merɪkən] 1 *n* Américain(e) *m,f*
2 *adj* américain(e); **the A. Civil War** la guerre de Sécession; **A. football** football *m* américain; **A. Indian** Indien(enne) *m,f* d'Amérique

amethyst ['æmɪθɪst] *n* améthyste *f*

amiable ['eɪmɪəbəl] *adj* aimable

amicable ['æmɪkəbəl] *adj* amical(e); **an a. agreement** un arrangement à l'amiable

amid [ə'mɪd], **amidst** [ə'mɪdst] *prep* au milieu de

amino acid [æ'miːnəʊ'æsɪd] *n* acide *m* aminé

amiss [ə'mɪs] *adv & adj* **there's something a.** il y a quelque chose qui ne va pas; **to take sth a.** prendre qch de travers, mal prendre qch; **a cup of coffee wouldn't go a.** une tasse de café serait bienvenue

ammeter ['æmiːtə(r)] *n Elec* ampèremètre *m*

ammonia [ə'məʊnɪə] *n* ammoniac *m*

ammunition [æmjʊ'nɪʃən] *n (for guns)* munitions *fpl*; *Fig (in debate, argument)* arguments *mpl*

amnesia [æm'niːzɪə] *n* amnésie *f*

amnesty ['æmnɪstɪ] *(pl* **amnesties**) *n* amnistie *f*

amoeba, *Am* **ameba** [ə'miːbə] *n* amibe *f*

amok [ə'mɒk] *adv* **to run a.** être pris(e) de folie furieuse

among [ə'mʌŋ], **amongst** [ə'mʌŋst] *prep* parmi; **a. the crowd** au milieu de la foule; **we are a. friends** nous sommes entre amis; **they quarrel a. themselves** ils se disputent entre eux; **the money was divided a. them** l'argent a été divisé entre eux; **a. the best** parmi les meilleurs; **a. other things** entre autres choses

amoral [eɪ'mɒrəl] *adj* amoral(e)

amorphous [ə'mɔːfəs] *adj (mass, lump)* informe; *(ideas, beliefs)* confus(e)

amount [ə'maʊnt] *n* (a) *(sum of money)* somme *f* (b) *(quantity)* quantité *f*; **a large a. of time/effort** beaucoup de temps/d'énergie; **a certain a. of discomfort** un certain manque de confort; **in large amounts** en grande quantité; **in small amounts** en petites quantités

▸**amount to** *vt insep* (a) *(add up to)* s'élever à; **her debts a. to £700** ses dettes s'élèvent à 700 livres (b) *(mean)* **it amounts to the same thing** cela revient au même; *Fig* **he'll never a. to much** il n'arrivera jamais à rien

amp [æmp] *n* (a) *Elec (unit)* ampère *m*; **a 13-a. plug** une prise de 13 ampères (b) *Fam (amplifier)* ampli *m*

ampere ['æmpeə(r)] *n Elec* ampère *m*

ampersand ['æmpəsænd] *n* esperluette *f*

amphetamine [æm'fetəmɪn] *n* amphétamine *f*

amphibian [æm'fɪbɪən] 1 *n* amphibie *m*
2 *adj* amphibie

amphibious [æm'fɪbɪəs] *adj* amphibie

amphitheatre, *Am* **amphitheater** ['æmfɪθɪətə(r)] *n* amphithéâtre *m*

ample ['æmpəl] *adj* (a) *(large) (woman, bosom)* fort(e) (b) *(plentiful)* abondant(e); **to have a. time to do sth** avoir largement le temps de faire qch; **to have a. opportunity to do sth** avoir tout loisir de faire qch; **this will be a. ce** sera largement suffisant

amplifier ['æmplɪfaɪə(r)] *n* amplificateur *m*

amplify ['æmplɪfaɪ] *(pt & pp* **amplified**) *vt (essay, remarks)* développer; *(current, volume)* amplifier

amputate ['æmpjʊteɪt] *vt* amputer

amputation [æmpjʊ'teɪʃən] *n* amputation *f*

Amsterdam [æmstə'dæm] *n* Amsterdam

amuck [ə'mʌk] = **amok**

amulet ['æmjʊlet] *n* amulette *f*

amuse [ə'mjuːz] *vt* (a) *(make laugh)* amuser (b) *(occupy)* occuper; **a. oneself by doing sth** se distraire en faisant qch; **to keep sb amused** distraire qn

amusement [ə'mjuːzmənt] *n* (a) *(enjoyment)* amusement *m*; **much to everyone's a.** au grand amusement de tous (b) *(pastime)* distraction *f*; **a. arcade** galerie *f* de jeux; **a. park** parc *m* d'attractions

amusing [ə'mjuːzɪŋ] *adj* amusant(e)

an [ən, *stressed* æn] *see* **a²**

anabolic steroid [ænə'bɒlɪk'stɪərɔɪd] *n* stéroïde *m* anabolisant

anachronism [ə'nækrənɪzəm] *n* anachronisme *m*

anaconda [ænə'kɒndə] *n* anaconda *m*

anaemia, *Am* **anemia** [ə'niːmɪə] *n* anémie *f*

anaemic, *Am* **anemic** [ə'ni:mɪk] *adj* anémique

anaesthetic, *Am* **anesthetic** [ænəs'θetɪk] *n* *(substance)* anesthésique *m*; *(process)* anesthésie *f*; **under a.** sous anesthésie; **local/general a.** anesthésie locale/générale

anaesthetist, *Am* **anesthetist** [ə'ni:sθətɪst] *n* anesthésiste *mf*

anaesthetize, *Am* **anesthetize** [ə'ni:sθətaɪz] *vt* anesthésier

anagram ['ænəgræm] *n* anagramme *f*

anal ['eɪnəl] *adj* anal(e)

analgesic [ænəl'dʒi:zɪk] **1** *n* analgésique *m*
 2 *adj* analgésique

analog *Am* = **analogue**

analogous [ə'næləgəs] *adj* analogue (**to** à)

analogue, *Am* **analog** ['ænəlɒg] *n* analogue *m*; **a. clock** horloge *f* à affichage analogique

analogy [ə'nælədʒɪ] *(pl* **analogies***)* *n* analogie *f*

analyse, *Am* **analyze** ['ænəlaɪz] *vt* analyser; *Psy* psychanalyser

analysis [ə'næləsɪs] *(pl* **analyses** [ə'næləsi:z]*)* *n* analyse *f*; *Psy* psychanalyse *f*; *Fig* **in the final a.** en fin de compte, au bout du compte

analyst ['ænəlɪst] *n* analyste *mf*; *Psy* (psych)analyste *mf*

analytic(al) [ænə'lɪtɪk(əl)] *adj* analytique

analyze *Am* = **analyse**

anarchist ['ænəkɪst] *n* anarchiste *mf*

anarchy ['ænəkɪ] *n* anarchie *f*

anathema [ə'næθəmə] *n* **(a)** *Rel* anathème *m* **(b)** *(repellent)* **the very idea was a. to her** l'idée même lui faisait horreur

anatomical [ænə'tɒmɪkəl] *adj* anatomique

anatomy [ə'nætəmɪ] *n* anatomie *f*

ANC [eɪen'si:] *n* *(abbr* **African National Congress***)* ANC *m*

ancestor ['ænsestə(r)] *n* ancêtre *mf*

ancestral [æn'sestrəl] *adj* ancestral(e); **a. home** demeure *f* ancestrale

ancestry ['ænsestrɪ] *n* *(descent)* ascendance *f*

anchor ['æŋkə(r)] **1** *n* *Naut* ancre *f*; *Fig* planche *f* de salut; **at a.** au mouillage; **to drop a.** jeter l'ancre; **to weigh a.** lever l'ancre
 2 *vt* **(a)** *Naut* ancrer **(b)** *(fix securely)* ancrer (**to** à) **(c)** *(radio, TV programme)* présenter
 3 *vi* *Naut* jeter l'ancre

anchorman ['æŋkəmən] *n* *(of radio, TV programme)* présentateur *m* principal

anchorwoman ['æŋkəwʊmən] *n* *(of radio, TV programme)* présentatrice *f* principale

anchovy ['æntʃəvɪ] *(pl* **anchovies***)* *n* anchois *m*

ancient ['eɪnʃənt] *adj* ancien(enne); *Fig* *(person, car)* très vieux (vieille); **a. history** histoire *f* ancienne; **A. Rome** la Rome antique
 2 *n* **the ancients** les anciens *mpl*

ancillary [æn'sɪlərɪ] *adj* auxiliaire

and [ænd, *unstressed* ənd, ən] *conj* **(a)** *(in general)* et; **she can read a. write** elle sait lire et écrire; **my mother a. father** mon père et ma mère; **chicken a. chips** du poulet-frites; **a vodka a. orange** une vodka orange; **do that again a. I'll hit you!** si tu recommences, je te frappe!; **wait a. see** tu verras bien; **nice a. warm** bien chaud(e)

(b) *(to)* **go a. look for it** va le chercher; **come a. see me** viens me voir; **try a. help me** essaie de m'aider

(c) *(in numbers)* **two hundred a. two** deux cent deux; **four a. a half** quatre et demi; **an hour a. twenty minutes** une heure vingt; **a. five make nine** quatre et *ou* plus cinq font neuf

(d) *(expressing repetition)* **hours a. hours** pendant des heures et des heures; **better a. better** de mieux en mieux; **smaller a. smaller** de plus en plus petit(e); **she talked a. talked** elle n'arrêtait pas de parler

(e) **a. so on a. so forth** et ainsi de suite

Andalusia [ændə'lu:sɪə] *n* l'Andalousie *f*

Andes ['ændi:z] *npl* **the A.** les Andes *fpl*

Andorra [æn'dɔ:rə] *n* l'Andorre *f*

Andorran [æn'dɔ:rən] **1** *n* Andorran(e) *m,f*
 2 *adj* andorran(e)

anecdotal [ænɪk'dəʊtəl] *adj* anecdotique

anecdote ['ænɪkdəʊt] *n* anecdote *f*

anemia, anemic *Am* = **anaemia, anaemic**

anemone [ə'nemənɪ] *n* *(flower)* anémone *f*; **sea a.** anémone de mer

anesthetic, anesthetist *etc Am* = **anaesthetic, anaesthetist** *etc*

anew [ə'nju:] *adv* encore, de nouveau; **to start a.** recommencer

angel ['eɪndʒəl] *n* ange *m*; *Fam* **you're an a.!** tu es un ange!

Angeleno [ændʒə'li:nəʊ] *(pl* **Angelenos***)* *n* = personne née à *ou* habitant Los Angeles

angelic [æn'dʒelɪk] *adj* angélique

anger ['æŋgə(r)] **1** *n* colère *f*; **a fit of a.** un accès de colère; **to speak in a.** parler sous le coup de la colère
 2 *vt* mettre en colère
 3 *vi* **to be slow/quick to a.** ne pas se mettre facilement/se mettre facilement en colère

angina [æn'dʒaɪnə] *n* angine *f* de poitrine

angle ['æŋgəl] **1** *n* **(a)** *Math* angle *m* **(b)** *(viewpoint)* point *m* de vue; **seen from this a.** vu sous cet angle
 2 *vi* **(a)** *(fish)* pêcher à la ligne **(b)** *Fam* **to a. for an invitation** chercher à se faire inviter

angler ['æŋglə(r)] *n* *(person)* pêcheur(euse) *m,f* à la ligne; **a. fish** baudroie *f*, lotte *f* de mer

Anglican ['æŋglɪkən] *n* & *adj* anglican(e) *m,f*

angling ['æŋglɪŋ] *n* *(fishing)* pêche *f* à la ligne

Anglo-American ['æŋgləʊə'merɪkən] *adj* anglo-américain(e)

Anglo-Saxon ['æŋgləʊ'sæksən] **1** *n* **(a)** *(person)* Anglo-Saxon(onne) *m,f* **(b)** *(language)* anglo-saxon *m*
 2 *adj* anglo-saxon(onne)

Angola [æŋ'gəʊlə] *n* l'Angola *m*

Angolan [æŋ'gəʊlən] **1** *n* Angolais(e) *m,f*
 2 *adj* angolais(e)

angora [æŋ'gɔ:rə] *n* angora *m*; **a. jumper** pull *m* en angora

angrily ['æŋgrɪlɪ] *adv* avec colère

angry ['æŋgrɪ] *adj* *(person)* en colère, fâché(e); *(voice, speech, letter)* furieux(euse); **to get a. (with)** se fâcher (contre), se mettre en colère (contre); **to make sb a.** mettre qn en colère

anguish ['æŋgwɪʃ] *n* angoisse *f*

anguished ['æŋgwɪʃt] *adj* *(look, cry)* d'angoisse

angular ['æŋgjʊlə(r)] *adj* anguleux(euse)

animal ['ænɪməl] n animal m; **the a. kingdom** le règne animal; **a. rights** les droits mpl des animaux; **he's an a.** (uncivilized person) c'est une brute

animate 1 adj ['ænɪmɪt] animé(e)
2 vt ['ænɪmeɪt] animer

animated ['ænɪmeɪtɪd] adj (expression, discussion) animé(e); **to become a.** s'animer; **a. cartoon** dessin m animé

animation [ænɪ'meɪʃən] n animation f

animator ['ænɪmeɪtə(r)] n Cin animateur(trice) m,f

animism ['ænɪmɪzəm] n animisme m

animosity [ænɪ'mɒsɪtɪ] n animosité f

aniseed ['ænɪsiːd] n (flavour) anis m; (seed) graine f d'anis

Ankara ['æŋkərə] n Ankara

ankle ['æŋkəl] n cheville f; **a. boots** chaussures fpl montantes; **a. socks** socquettes fpl

anklet ['æŋklɪt] n (ankle bracelet) bracelet m de cheville

annals ['ænəlz] npl annales fpl

annex 1 vt [æ'neks] annexer
2 n ['æneks] Am = **annexe**

annexation [ænek'seɪʃən] n annexion f

annexe, Am **annex** ['æneks] n (of building, document) annexe f

annihilate [ə'naɪəleɪt] vt anéantir

annihilation [ənaɪə'leɪʃən] n anéantissement m

anniversary [ænɪ'vɜːsərɪ] (pl **anniversaries**) n anniversaire m; **wedding a.** anniversaire de mariage

anno Domini ['ænəʊ'dɒmɪnaɪ] adv en l'an de grâce

annotate ['ænəteɪt] vt annoter

announce [ə'naʊns] vt annoncer

announcement [ə'naʊnsmənt] n (of news) annonce f; (formal statement) avis m

announcer [ə'naʊnsə(r)] n (on radio, TV programme) annonceur(euse) m,f, speaker (speakerine) m,f

annoy [ə'nɔɪ] vt agacer; **to get annoyed** se mettre en colère, se fâcher; **to be annoyed with sb** être en colère contre qn

annoyance [ə'nɔɪəns] n (feeling) agacement m; (annoying thing) ennui m

annoying [ə'nɔɪɪŋ] adj agaçant(e), ennuyeux(euse); **how a.!** comme c'est ennuyeux!

annual ['ænjʊəl] **1** n (a) (plant) plante f annuelle (b) (book) publication f annuelle; (for children) album m (publié une fois par an)
2 adj annuel(elle); **a. general meeting** assemblée f générale annuelle

annually ['ænjʊəlɪ] adv (every year) tous les ans; (per year) par an

annul [ə'nʌl] (pt & pp **annulled**) vt Law (contract, marriage) annuler

anode ['ænəʊd] n anode f

anodyne ['ænədaɪn] adj (bland) anodin(e)

anoint [ə'nɔɪnt] vt oindre (**with** de)

anomalous [ə'nɒmələs] adj anormal(e)

anomaly [ə'nɒməlɪ] (pl **anomalies**) n anomalie f

anon¹ [ə'nɒn] adv Lit (soon) bientôt

anon² adj (abbr **anonymous**) anonyme

anonymity [ænə'nɪmɪtɪ] n anonymat m

anonymous [ə'nɒnɪməs] adj anonyme; **to remain a.** garder l'anonymat

anorak ['ænəræk] n anorak m

anorexia [ænə'reksɪə] n anorexie f; **a. nervosa** anorexie mentale

anorexic [ænə'reksɪk] adj anorexique

another [ə'nʌðə(r)] adj & pron (a) (additional) un (une) autre m,f; **a. cup of tea** une autre tasse de thé; **in a. ten years** dans dix ans; **don't say a. word** plus un mot; **a. Picasso/Vietnam** un nouveau Picasso/Việt Nam
(b) (different) un (une) autre m,f; **that's quite a. matter** c'est une toute autre affaire; **a. time, perhaps** (declining invitation) une autre fois, peut-être; **what with one thing and a., I forgot** avec tout ce qui s'est passé, j'ai oublié; **one way or a.** d'une façon ou d'une autre
(c) (reciprocal) **they saw one a.** ils se sont vus

answer ['ɑːnsə(r)] **1** n (to question, letter) réponse f; (to problem) solution f; **I knocked but there was no a.** j'ai frappé mais personne n'a répondu; **there's no a.** (on telephone) ça ne répond pas; **he has an a. to everything** il a réponse à tout; Formal **in a. to your letter** en réponse à votre lettre
2 vt répondre à; **"I'll do it tomorrow," he answered** "je le ferai demain", a-t-il répondu; **to a. the telephone** répondre au téléphone; **to a. the door** ouvrir (la porte)
3 vi (of person) répondre
▶**answer back** vi (be impertinent) répondre
▶**answer for** vt insep répondre de; **he has a lot to a. for** il a beaucoup de comptes à rendre
▶**answer to** vt insep (a) (be accountable to) **to a. to sb** être responsable devant qn; **she answers to no one** elle n'a de comptes à rendre à personne (b) (correspond to) (description) répondre à (c) **the dog answers to the name of Rover** le chien répond au nom de Rover

answerable ['ɑːnsərəbəl] adj **to be a. to sb** être responsable devant qn; **he is a. to nobody** il n'a de comptes à rendre à personne

answering machine ['ɑːnsərɪŋ'məʃiːn], **answer-phone** ['ɑːnsəfəʊn] n répondeur m (téléphonique)

ant [ænt] n fourmi f; **a. hill** fourmilière f

antagonism [æn'tægənɪzəm] n antagonisme m

antagonist [æn'tægənɪst] n antagoniste mf

antagonize [æn'tægənaɪz] vt rendre hostile

Antarctica [æn'tɑːktɪkə] n l'Antarctique m

ante ['æntɪ] n Fam **to up the a.** (in gambling, conflict) augmenter la mise

anteater ['æntiːtə(r)] n fourmilier m

antecedents [æntɪ'siːdəns] npl antécédents mpl

antelope ['æntɪləʊp] n antilope f

antenatal [æntɪ'neɪtəl] adj prénatal(e); **a. clinic** cours m de préparation à l'accouchement

antenna [æn'tenə] n (a) (pl **antennae** [æn'teniː]) (of insect, snail) antenne f (b) (pl **antennas**) (of radio, TV) antenne f

anteroom ['æntɪruːm] n antichambre f

anthem ['ænθəm] n hymne m; **national a.** hymne national

anthology [æn'θɒlədʒɪ] (pl **anthologies**) n anthologie f

anthracite ['ænθrəsaɪt] n anthracite m

anthrax ['ænθræks] n (disease) anthrax m

anthropologist [ænθrə'pɒlədʒɪst] n anthropologue m

anthropology [ænθrə'pɒlədʒɪ] n anthropologie f

anti- ['æntɪ] pref anti-; **a.-American** antiaméricain(e)

anti-aircraft ['æntɪ'eəkrɑːft] *adj (gun, defences)* antiaérien(enne)

antibiotic [æntɪbaɪ'ɒtɪk] *n* antibiotique *m*

antibody ['æntɪbɒdɪ] (*pl* **antibodies**) *n Med* anticorps *m*

Antichrist ['æntɪkraɪst] *n* Antéchrist *m*

anticipate [æn'tɪsɪpeɪt] *vt* **(a)** *(expect)* prévoir, s'attendre à; *(foresee)* anticiper; **we hadn't anticipated such stiff resistance** nous ne nous attendions pas à une telle résistance; **as anticipated, there was trouble** comme on s'y attendait, il y eut des problèmes **(b)** *(foreshadow)* préfigurer, annoncer

anticipation [æntɪsɪ'peɪʃən] *n* **(a)** *(foresight)* prévoyance *f*; **in a. of trouble** en prévision de troubles; **thanking you in a.** en vous remerciant d'avance, avec mes remerciements anticipés **(b)** *(eagerness)* impatience *f*

anticlimax [æntɪ'klaɪmæks] *n* déception *f*

anti-clockwise [æntɪ'klɒkwaɪz], *Am* **counter-clockwise** ['kaʊntə'klɒkwaɪz] **1** *adj* **in an a. direction** dans le sens inverse des aiguilles d'une montre
2 *adv* dans le sens inverse des aiguilles d'une montre

antics ['æntɪks] *npl* **he's been up to his usual a.** il a encore fait des siennes

anticyclone [æntɪ'saɪkləʊn] *n Met* anticyclone *m*

antidepressant [æntɪdɪ'presənt] *n* antidépresseur *m*

antidote ['æntɪdəʊt] *n also Fig* antidote *m* (**to** contre)

antifreeze ['æntɪfriːz] *n* antigel *m*

Antigua and Barbuda [æn'tiːgəːbɑː'bjuːdə] *n* Antigua-et-Barbuda

antipathy [æn'tɪpəθɪ] *n* antipathie *f* (**towards** pour)

antiperspirant [æntɪ'pɜːspɪrənt] *n* déodorant *m*

Antipodes [æn'tɪpədiːz] *npl* **the A.** l'Australie *f* et la Nouvelle-Zélande

antiquarian [æntɪ'kweərɪən] **1** *n (dealer)* antiquaire *mf*; *(collector)* collectionneur(euse) *m, f* d'antiquités
2 *adj (book)* ancien(enne); **a. bookshop** = librairie spécialisée dans les livres anciens

antiquated ['æntɪkweɪtɪd] *adj* vieillot(otte)

antique [æn'tiːk] **1** *n* antiquité *f*; **a. dealer** antiquaire *mf*; **a. shop** magasin *m* d'antiquités
2 *adj* antique; **a. furniture** meubles *mpl* anciens

antiquity [æn'tɪkwɪtɪ] *n* (*pl* **antiquities**) *n (historical period, ruin)* antiquité *f*

antiracist [æntɪ'reɪsɪst] *adj* antiraciste

anti-Semitic [æntɪsɪ'mɪtɪk] *adj* antisémite

antiseptic [æntɪ'septɪk] **1** *n* antiseptique *m*
2 *adj* **(a)** *(anti-bacterial)* antiseptique **(b)** *Fig (lacking character or warmth) (place)* aseptisé(e); *(person)* froid(e)

antisocial [æntɪ'səʊʃəl] *adj* **(a)** *(disruptive)* asocial(e) **(b)** *(unsociable)* peu sociable

antithesis [æn'tɪθɪsɪs] (*pl* **antitheses** [æn'tɪθɪsiːz]) *n (opposite)* opposé *m*

antlers ['æntləz] *npl* bois *mpl*

antonym ['æntənɪm] *n* antonyme *m*

Antwerp ['æntwɜːp] *n* Anvers

anus ['eɪnəs] *n* anus *m*

anvil ['ænvɪl] *n* enclume *f*

anxiety [æn'zaɪətɪ] (*pl* **anxieties**) *n* **(a)** *(worry, concern)* inquiétude *f*; *(stronger)* anxiété *f*; **my main a. is...** mon principal souci est...; **there is no cause for a.** il n'y a pas de quoi s'inquiéter; **to feel a.** être anxieux(euse) **(b)**

(eagerness) désir *m*, souci *m*; **in her a. to help** dans son désir ou souci de se rendre utile

anxious ['æŋkʃəs] *adj* **(a)** *(worried)* inquiet(ète); *(stronger)* anxieux(euse); **to be a. for sb** être inquiet ou s'inquiéter pour qn; **to be a. about sth** être inquiet ou s'inquiéter pour qch **(b)** *(worrying) (moment)* d'angoisse; *(period)* angoissant(e) **(c)** **to be a. to do sth** *(impatient)* être impatient(e) de faire qch; *(eager)* tenir à faire qch

anxiously ['æŋkʃəslɪ] *adv* **(a)** *(worriedly)* avec inquiétude; *(stronger)* anxieusement **(b)** *(with impatience)* impatiemment, avec impatience

any ['enɪ] **1** *pron* **(a)** *(some)* **have you got a.?** en avez-vous?; **is/are there a. left?** en reste-t-il?; **can a. of them speak English?** y en a-t-il parmi eux qui parlent anglais?
(b) *(in negatives)* **I haven't got a.** je n'en ai pas; **there was nothing in a. of the boxes** il n'y avait rien dans aucune des boîtes; **few, if a., can read** aucun, ou presque aucun, ne sait lire
(c) *(no particular one)* n'importe lequel (laquelle) *m, f*; **a. of us** n'importe lequel d'entre nous
(d) *(every one)* tous ceux (toutes celles) *mpl, fpl*; **keep a. you find** garde tous ceux que tu trouveras
2 *adj* **(a)** *(some) (singular)* du (de la); *(plural)* des; **have you a. milk/flour/apples?** avez-vous du lait/de la farine/des pommes?
(b) *(in negatives)* **he hasn't got a. money** il n'a pas d'argent; **without a. doubt** sans aucun doute; **that won't do a. good** ça ne servira à rien
(c) *(no particular)* n'importe quel (quelle); **come a. day** venez n'importe quel jour; **a. minute now** d'une minute à l'autre
(d) *(every)* tout(e); **a. pupil who forgets his books will be punished** tout élève qui oubliera ses livres sera puni; **at a. rate, in a. case** en tout cas
3 *adv* **(a)** *(with comparative)* **I'm not a. better** je ne vais pas mieux; **does that make it a. easier?** est-ce que c'est plus facile comme ça?; **we don't see them a. longer** or **more** nous ne les voyons plus; **do you want a. more tea?** veux-tu encore du thé?; **I don't like her a. more than you do** je ne l'aime pas plus que toi
(b) *Fam* **a. old how** n'importe comment; **that didn't help us a.** ça ne nous a été d'aucun secours

anybody ['enɪbɒdɪ] *pron* **(a)** *(indeterminate)* quelqu'un; **would a. like some more cake?** quelqu'un veut-il encore du gâteau?; **she'll know if a. does** si quelqu'un doit le savoir, c'est bien elle
(b) *(in negatives)* **not a. ne... personne; there isn't a. here** il n'y a personne ici; **there was hardly a.** il n'y avait presque personne
(c) *(no matter who)* n'importe qui; **a. will tell you so** n'importe qui *ou* tout le monde vous le dira; **bring along a. you like** amenez qui vous voudrez; **a. else** or **but her would have refused** tout autre qu'elle aurait refusé; **it's a.'s guess** Dieu seul le sait; **he's not just a.!** ce n'est pas n'importe qui!
(d) *(person with status)* **he'll never be a.** il ne fera jamais rien dans la vie

anyhow ['enɪhaʊ] *adv* **(a)** *(however)* de toute façon *ou* manière; **a., let's get back to what we were saying** bref, revenons à ce que nous disions; **I don't care, I'm going a.** ça m'est égal, j'y vais quand même **(b)** *Fam (carelessly)* n'importe comment

anyone ['enɪwʌn] = **anybody**

anyplace ['enɪpleɪs] *Am* = **anywhere**

anything ['enɪθɪŋ] **1** *pron* (a) *(indeterminate)* quelque chose; **is there a. I can do?** est-ce que je peux faire quelque chose?; **have you a. to write with?** as-tu de quoi écrire?; **will there be a. else?** *(in shop)* et avec ça?; **have you a. smaller?** avez-vous quelque chose de plus petit?; *(money)* vous n'avez pas quelque chose de plus petit?; **if a. should happen to me** s'il m'arrivait quelque chose *ou* quoi que ce soit; **is (there) a. the matter?** il y a quelque chose qui ne va pas?

(b) *(in negatives)* **not a.** ne... rien; **he earns; he doesn't do a.** il ne fait rien; **hardly a.** presque rien

(c) *(no matter what)* n'importe quoi; **he eats a.** il mange de tout; **I love a. French** j'aime tout ce qui est français; **she would do a. for me** elle ferait n'importe quoi pour moi; **he was a. but friendly** il était tout sauf amical; **are you angry? - a. but** tu es fâché? - non, loin de là

2 *adv* **is it a. like the other one?** est-ce qu'il lui ressemble un peu à l'autre ou pas du tout?; **she doesn't look a. like her sister** elle ne ressemble pas du tout à sa sœur; **the food wasn't a. like as bad as they said** la nourriture était loin d'être aussi mauvaise que ce qu'on m'avait dit; *Fam* **as funny/strong as a.** drôle/fort(e) comme tout; *Fam* **to work like a.** travailler comme un fou (une folle); *Fam* **it's not that you're wrong or a.** ce n'est pas que tu aies tort

anyway ['enɪweɪ] = **anyhow**

anywhere ['enɪweə(r)] *adv* (a) *(in questions)* quelque part; **did you go a. yesterday?** êtes-vous allé quelque part hier?; **can you see it a.?** tu le vois?

(b) *(in negatives)* **not a.** ne... nulle part; **I can't find it a.** je ne le trouve nulle part; **we're not getting a.** nous n'avançons pas; **he isn't a. near as clever as her** il est loin d'être aussi intelligent qu'elle

(c) *(no matter where)* n'importe où; **put it a.** mets-le n'importe où; **I'd know her a.** je la reconnaîtrais entre mille; **it's miles from a.** c'est loin de tout; **a. else** n'importe où

AO(C)B [eɪəʊ(siː)'biː] *(abbr* **any other (competent) business)** divers

aorta [eɪ'ɔːtə] *n* aorte *f*

apart [ə'pɑːt] *adv* (a) *(at a distance)* à l'écart **(from** de); **to stand a.** *(of person)* se tenir à l'écart; **the garage stands a. from the house** le garage est séparé de la maison

(b) *(separated)* **they are far a.** ils sont éloignés l'un de l'autre; **the two towns are 10 kilometres a.** les deux villes sont à 10 kilomètres l'une de l'autre; **they're never a.** ils ne se séparent jamais; **with one's legs a.** les jambes écartées; **two years a.** à deux ans d'intervalle; **to set sth a. for sth** réserver qch à qch; **to live a.** vivre séparément; **it's difficult to tell them a.** il est difficile de les distinguer l'un de l'autre; **joking a., ...** blague à part, ...

(c) *(to pieces)* **to take sth a.** *(machine)* démonter qch; **to come a.** *(of garment)* se découdre

(d) *(excepting)* **a. from** à part; **a. from the fact that...** indépendamment du fait que...

apartheid [ə'pɑːtaɪt] *n* apartheid *m*

apartment [ə'pɑːtmənt] *n Am* appartement *m*; **a. building** immeuble *m* d'habitation

apathetic [æpə'θetɪk] *adj* qui manque d'enthousiasme; **to be a. about sth** être indifférent(e) à qch

apathy ['æpəθɪ] *n* manque *m* d'enthousiasme

ape [eɪp] **1** *n (animal)* grand singe *m*; *Fam* **to go a.** piquer une crise

2 *vt (imitate)* singer

aperitif [əperɪ'tiːf] *n* apéritif *m*

aperture ['æpətjʊə(r)] *n* ouverture *f*

APEX ['eɪpeks] *adj* **A. ticket** = billet d'avion ou de train à tarif réduit, soumis à certaines restrictions

apex ['eɪpeks] *n* sommet *m*

aphasia [ə'feɪzɪə] *n Med* aphasie *f*

aphid ['eɪfɪd] *n* puceron *m*

aphorism ['æfərɪzəm] *n* aphorisme *m*

aphrodisiac [æfrəʊ'dɪzɪæk] **1** *n* aphrodisiaque *m*
2 *adj* aphrodisiaque

apiece [ə'piːs] *adv* chacun(e); **they cost £3 a.** ils valent 3 livres pièce *ou* chacun

aplenty [ə'plentɪ] *adv* en abondance

aplomb [ə'plɒm] *n* sang-froid *m*

apocalypse [ə'pɒkəlɪps] *n* apocalypse *f*

apocalyptic [əpɒkə'lɪptɪk] *adj* apocalyptique

apolitical [eɪpə'lɪtɪkəl] *adj* apolitique

apologetic [əpɒlə'dʒetɪk] *adj (tone, smile)* désolé(e); **to be a. about sth** s'excuser de qch; **she was quite a. about it** elle s'est répandue en excuses

apologize [ə'pɒlədʒaɪz] *vi* s'excuser; **to a. to sb for sth** s'excuser de qch auprès de qn, présenter ses excuses à qn pour qch; **she apologized for being late/for not telling him earlier** elle s'est excusée d'être en retard/de ne pas le lui avoir dit plus tôt

apology [ə'pɒlədʒɪ] *(pl* **apologies)** *n* excuses *fpl*; **to make/offer an a.** faire/présenter des excuses; **I owe you an a.** je vous dois des excuses; *Pej* **an a. for a dinner** un semblant de dîner

apoplectic [æpə'plektɪk] *adj Fig (angry)* furieux(euse); **to be a. with rage** s'étrangler de rage

apoplexy ['æpəpleksɪ] *n Med* apoplexie *f*; *Fig (anger)* rage *f*

apostle [ə'pɒsəl] *n* apôtre *m*

apostolic(al) [æpɒs'tɒlɪk(əl)] *adj* apostolique

apostrophe [ə'pɒstrəfɪ] *n* apostrophe *f*

appal, *Am* **appall** [ə'pɔːl] *(pt & pp* **appalled)** *vt (shock)* choquer, scandaliser; *(fill with horror)* horrifier; **to be appalled at** *or* **by sth** être choqué(e)/horrifié(e) par qch; **it appals me to think that...** je suis horrifié(e) à la pensée que...

appalling [ə'pɔːlɪŋ] *adj (behaviour)* scandaleux(euse); *(conditions, smell, weather, film)* épouvantable

apparatus [æpə'reɪtəs] *n (machine)* appareil *m*; *(set of machines, in laboratory)* équipement *m*; *(in gym)* agrès *mpl*; **a piece of a.** un appareil

apparel [ə'pærəl] *n* mise *f*

apparent [ə'pærənt] *adj* (a) *(obvious)* clair(e), évident(e); **it soon became a. that...** il est vite devenu évident que...
(b) *(seeming)* apparent(e)

apparently [ə'pærəntlɪ] *adv* apparemment; **a. he's going to Venice** il paraît qu'il va à Venise

apparition [æpə'rɪʃən] *n* apparition *f*

appeal [ə'piːl] **1** *n* (a) *(call)* appel *m* **(for** à); **to make an a. for help** lancer un appel à l'aide; **charity a.** = appel aux dons lancé par une organisation caritative (b) *Law* appel *m*; **on a.** en seconde instance; **A. Court, Court of A.** cour *f* d'appel (c) *(attraction)* attrait *m*; **to have great a.** *(of idea)* être très attrayant(e); *(of person)* avoir beaucoup de charme; **their music has a wide a.** leur musique attire un public très varié

2 *vt Am Law* **to a. a decision** faire appel d'une décision

3 *vi* (a) *(make a plea)* **to a. (to sb) for help/money**

demander de l'aide/de l'argent (à qn); **to a. to sb's generosity** faire appel à la générosité de qn **(b) to a. to sb** (attract) attirer qn **(c)** Law se pourvoir en appel; **to a. against a decision** faire appel d'une décision

appealing [ə'piːlɪŋ] adj (idea) séduisant(e); (person, manner) sympathique

appear [ə'pɪə(r)] vi **(a)** (come into view) apparaître; (of publication) paraître; **where did you a. from?** d'où sors-tu?; **to a. on TV** passer à la télé **(b)** Law comparaître **(c)** (look, seem) sembler; **to a. to be lost** avoir l'air d'être perdu(e); **there appears to be a mistake** il semble qu'il y ait une erreur; **so it would a.** c'est ce qu'on dirait

appearance [ə'pɪərəns] n **(a)** (arrival) apparition f, arrivée f; **to put in an a.** faire acte de présence **(b)** (of actor) to make a television a. passer à la télévision **(c)** (of publication) parution f **(d)** Law (in court) comparution f **(e)** (looks, demeanour) apparence f; **it's wrong to judge by appearances** il ne faut pas se fier aux apparences; **appearances can be deceptive** les apparences peuvent être trompeuses; **to keep up appearances** sauver les apparences

appease [ə'piːz] vt (anger, person) apaiser, calmer; Pol composer avec

appeasement [ə'piːzmənt] n (of person, anger) apaisement m; Pol conciliation f

append [ə'pend] vt (list, document) joindre (to à); (one's signature) apposer (to à)

appendage [ə'pendɪdʒ] n appendice m; **she was tired of being treated as her husband's a.** elle en avait assez de n'être traitée que comme la femme de son mari

appendicitis [əpendɪ'saɪtɪs] n appendicite f

appendix [ə'pendɪks] (pl **appendices** [ə'pendɪsiːz]) n **(a)** Anat appendice m; **to have one's a. (taken) out** se faire opérer de l'appendicite **(b)** (of book) appendice m

appetite ['æpɪtaɪt] n **(a)** (for food) appétit m; **to have a good a.** avoir bon appétit; **to spoil sb's a.** couper l'appétit à qn; **to give sb an a.** donner faim à qn; (of fresh air, walk) creuser qn **(b)** (enthusiasm) (for knowledge, travel) soif f (for de); (for music, cinema) goût m (for pour)

appetizer ['æpɪtaɪzə(r)] n also Fig amuse-gueule m

appetizing ['æpɪtaɪzɪŋ] adj appétissant(e)

applaud [ə'plɔːd] vt & vi applaudir

applause [ə'plɔːz] n (clapping) applaudissements mpl; (approval) approbation f

apple ['æpəl] n pomme f; **he was the a. of her eye** (her favourite) elle tenait à lui comme à la prunelle de ses yeux; **a. core** trognon m de pomme; **a. juice** jus m de pomme; **a. pie** (without top crust) tarte f aux pommes; (with top crust) tourte f aux pommes; **as American as a. pie** typiquement américain(e); **a. tart** tarte f aux pommes; **a. tree** pommier m

applecart ['æpəlkɑːt] n **to upset the a.** (spoil plan) tout chambouler

apple-pie ['æpəlpaɪ] adj **in a. order** parfaitement en ordre

appliance [ə'plaɪəns] n appareil m; **electrical/domestic a.** appareil électrique/ménager

applicable [ə'plɪkəbəl] adj applicable; **the rule is a. to everybody** la règle s'applique à tous; **delete where not a.** (on form) rayer les mentions inutiles

applicant ['æplɪkənt] n (for job) candidat(e) m,f (for à)

application [æplɪ'keɪʃən] n **(a)** (for job) candidature f (for à); (for passport, patent) demande f (for de); **a. form** (for job) formulaire m de candidature **(b)** (of rule, theory, paint) application f **(c)** (effort) application f, assiduité f

applied [ə'plaɪd] adj (maths, physics) appliqué(e)

apply [ə'plaɪ] (pt & pp **applied**) **1** vt **(a)** (put on) appliquer (to sur) **(b)** (use) (system, theory) appliquer **(c)** (to job) **one's mind to sth** concentrer ses efforts sur qch; **to a. oneself (to one's work)** s'appliquer

2 vi **(a) to a. to sb for sth** s'adresser à qn pour obtenir qch; **to a. for a job** poser sa candidature pour un poste; **to a. for a grant** faire une demande de bourse **(b)** (of law, rule) s'appliquer (to à)

appoint [ə'pɔɪnt] vt (person) nommer; (committee) constituer; **to a. sb to a post** nommer qn à un poste; **to a. sb (as) manager** nommer qn directeur(trice)

appointed [ə'pɔɪntɪd] adj Formal (agreed) (place, hour) convenu(e), dit(e)

appointment [ə'pɔɪntmənt] n **(a)** (meeting, with doctor) rendez-vous m; **to make a. with sb** prendre rendez-vous avec qn; (with dentist, doctor) prendre rendez-vous chez qn **(b)** (to job) nomination f; (of committee) constitution f; **to make an a.** pourvoir un poste; Com **by a. to His/Her Majesty** (sign) fournisseur de la Couronne; **appointments** (in newspaper) offres d'emploi

apportion [ə'pɔːʃən] vt répartir

appraisal [ə'preɪzəl] n (of standards, personnel) évaluation f

appraise [ə'preɪz] vt (performance, situation) évaluer; (value) estimer

appreciable [ə'priːʃəbəl] adj (change, difference) appréciable, sensible

appreciate [ə'priːʃɪeɪt] **1** vt **(a)** (be grateful for) (help) reconnaître de; (kindness) être sensible à; **I a. your helping me** je vous suis reconnaissant de m'avoir aidé **(b)** (grasp, understand) être conscient(e) de; **he doesn't a. how lucky he is** il ne se rend pas compte de la chance qu'il a **(c)** (acknowledge) apprécier

2 vi (of goods, investment) prendre de la valeur; (of value) augmenter

appreciation [əpriːʃɪ'eɪʃən] n **(a)** (gratitude) gratitude f, reconnaissance f; **in a. of** en reconnaissance de **(b)** (understanding) conscience f; **she has no a. of what is involved** elle ne se rend pas compte de ce que cela implique **(c)** (review, assessment) critique f; **a musical/wine a. society** une société d'amateurs de musique/de vin **(d)** Fin **a. of assets** plus-value f d'actif

appreciative [ə'priːʃɪətɪv] adj (grateful) reconnaissant(e); **to be a. of sb's help/efforts** être reconnaissant à qn de son aide/des ses efforts **(b)** (review) élogieux(euse); (response) favorable; **the audience were very a.** le public a beaucoup aimé; **to be a. of sth** apprécier qch

apprehend [æprɪ'hend] vt **(a)** Law (arrest) appréhender **(b)** Formal (understand) comprendre

apprehension [æprɪ'henʃən] n **(a)** (fear) appréhension f **(b)** Law (arrest) arrestation f

apprehensive [æprɪ'hensɪv] adj inquiet(ète); **to be a. about sth/doing sth** appréhender qch/de faire qch

apprentice [ə'prentɪs] **1** n apprenti(e) m,f

2 vt **to a. sb to sb** placer qn en apprentissage chez qn

apprenticeship [ə'prentɪʃɪp] n also Fig apprentissage m; **to serve one's a.** faire ses premières armes

approach [əˈprəʊtʃ] **1** n (a) *(coming) (of person, season)* approche f; **to make an a. to sb** *(proposal)* faire une proposition à qn (b) *(method)* approche f (to de); **let's try a different a.** essayons d'aborder le problème différemment (c) *(route of access)* voie f d'accès; **the approaches to a town** les abords mpl d'une ville; **a. road** voie d'accès

2 vt (a) *(get nearer to)* approcher de; **I'm approaching forty-five** je vais sur mes quarante-cinq ans (b) *(go up to)* aborder; *(organization)* approcher; **to be easy/difficult to a.** être d'un abord facile/difficile (c) *(problem)* aborder

3 vi approcher

approachable [əˈprəʊtʃəbəl] adj *(person)* d'un abord facile

approaching [əˈprəʊtʃɪŋ] adj *(holiday, season)* qui approche; *(car)* qui vient en sens inverse

appropriate[1] [əˈprəʊprɪət] adj *(suitable)* approprié(e) (**to** à); *(moment)* opportun(e)

appropriate[2] [əˈprəʊprɪeɪt] vt (a) *(take, steal)* s'approprier (b) *(set aside) (money, funds)* affecter (**to** à)

appropriately [əˈprəʊprɪətlɪ] adv *(suitably)* de manière appropriée; *(properly)* convenablement

appropriation [əprəʊprɪˈeɪʃən] n *(of funds)* affectation f

approval [əˈpruːvəl] n approbation f; **to meet with sb's a.** obtenir l'approbation de qn; *Com* **on a.** à l'essai

approve [əˈpruːv] vt *(action, proposal)* approuver; *(treaty)* ratifier

▸**approve of** vt insep approuver; **I don't a. of your friends** tes amis ne me plaisent pas; **she doesn't a. of them smoking** elle n'aime pas qu'ils fument

approving [əˈpruːvɪŋ] adj approbateur(trice)

approx *(abbr* **approximately)** env.

approximate 1 adj [əˈprɒksɪmɪt] approximatif(ive)

2 vi [əˈprɒksɪmeɪt] **to a. to sth** se rapprocher de qch

approximately [əˈprɒksɪmətlɪ] adv approximativement, environ

approximation [əprɒksɪˈmeɪʃən] n approximation f

Apr *(abbr* **April)** avril

APR [eɪpiːˈɑːr] n Fin *(abbr* **annual percentage rate)** TEG m

apricot [ˈeɪprɪkɒt] n *(fruit)* abricot m; **a. tree** abricotier m

April [ˈeɪprɪl] n avril m; **A. showers** ≃ giboulées fpl de mars; **A. Fool's Day** le premier avril; *see also* **May**

apron [ˈeɪprən] n (a) *(clothing)* tablier m; **he's still tied to his mother's a. strings** *(dependent on her)* il est toujours pendu aux jupes de sa mère (b) Av aire f de stationnement

apt [æpt] adj (a) *(word, description)* juste (b) *(likely)* **to be a. to do sth** avoir tendance à faire qch

aptitude [ˈæptɪtjuːd] n aptitude f, don m; **to have an a. for sth** avoir une aptitude ou un don pour qch; **a. test** test m d'aptitude

aptly [ˈæptlɪ] adv *(described)* justement; *(chosen)* bien

aquamarine [ˈækwəməˈriːn] **1** n *(gem)* aigue-marine f

2 adj *(colour)* bleu vert inv

aquarium [əˈkweərɪəm] n aquarium m

Aquarius [əˈkweərɪəs] n le Verseau; **to be (an) A.** être (du) Verseau

aquatic [əˈkwætɪk] adj aquatique

aqueduct [ˈækwɪdʌkt] n aqueduc m

aquiline [ˈækwɪlaɪn] adj aquilin(e)

Arab [ˈærəb] **1** n Arabe mf

2 adj arabe

Arabia [əˈreɪbɪə] n l'Arabie f

Arabian [əˈreɪbɪən] adj arabe; **the A. Sea** la mer d'Oman

Arabic [ˈærəbɪk] **1** n *(language)* arabe m

2 adj arabe; **A. numerals** chiffres mpl arabes

arable [ˈærəbəl] adj arable

arachnid [əˈræknɪd] n Zool arachnide m

arbiter [ˈɑːbɪtə(r)] n *(in dispute)* arbitre m; **the a. of taste** l'arbitre des élégances

arbitrary [ˈɑːbɪtrərɪ] adj arbitraire

arbitrate [ˈɑːbɪtreɪt] **1** vt arbitrer

2 vi servir d'arbitre (**between** entre)

arbitration [ɑːbɪˈtreɪʃən] n arbitrage m; **to go to a.** *(of parties)* avoir recours à l'arbitrage

arbitrator [ˈɑːbɪtreɪtə(r)] n médiateur(trice) m,f

arc [ɑːk] n arc m; **a. lamp** lampe f à arc

arcade [ɑːˈkeɪd] n (a) *(for shopping)* galerie f marchande (b) Archit galerie f

arch[1] [ɑːtʃ] **1** n (a) Archit arche f (b) *(of foot)* voûte f plantaire; **to have fallen arches** avoir les pieds plats

2 vt **to a. one's back** *(inwards)* se cambrer; *(outwards)* se voûter

arch[2] adj **a. enemy** ennemi(e) m,f juré(e)

arch[3] adj *(mischievous)* espiègle

archaeological, Am **archeological** [ɑːkɪəˈlɒdʒɪkəl] adj archéologique

archaeologist, Am **archeologist** [ɑːkɪˈɒlədʒɪst] n archéologue mf

archaeology, Am **archeology** [ɑːkɪˈɒlədʒɪ] adj archéologie f

archaic [ɑːˈkeɪɪk] adj archaïque

archangel [ˈɑːkeɪndʒəl] n archange m

archbishop [ɑːtʃˈbɪʃəp] n archevêque m

archduke [ɑːtʃˈdjuːk] n archiduc m

archeological, archeologist etc Am = **archaeological, archaeologist** etc

archer [ˈɑːtʃə(r)] n archer m

archery [ˈɑːtʃərɪ] n tir m à l'arc

archetypal [ɑːkɪˈtaɪpəl] adj **the a. English village** l'archétype m du village anglais

archetype [ˈɑːkɪtaɪp] n archétype m

Archimedes [ɑːkɪˈmiːdiːz] n Archimède f

archipelago [ɑːkɪˈpeləgəʊ] n *(pl* **archipelagoes** or **archipelagos**) n archipel m

architect [ˈɑːkɪtekt] n architecte mf; **he was the a. of his own downfall** il a été l'artisan de sa propre ruine

architecture [ˈɑːkɪtektʃə(r)] n architecture f

archives [ˈɑːkaɪvz] npl archives fpl

archway [ˈɑːtʃweɪ] n arche f

arctic [ˈɑːktɪk] **1** n **the A.** l'Arctique m; **the A. Circle** le cercle (polaire) arctique; **the A. Ocean** l'océan m Arctique

2 adj (a) *(climate)* arctique (b) Fam *(very cold)* **a spell of a. weather** un froid polaire

ardent [ˈɑːdənt] adj *(desire, love)* ardent(e); *(admirer, believer)* fervent(e)

ardour [ˈɑːdə(r)] n *(of desire, love)* ardeur f; *(religious)* ferveur f

arduous [ˈɑːdjʊəs] adj ardu(e), pénible

are [ɑː(r)] plural and 2nd pers singular of **be**

area ['eərɪə] n (a) (surface) superficie f, surface f; **the room is 24 square metres in a**. la pièce a une surface de 24 mètres carrés (b) (region) région f; (of countryside, forest) zone f; (in building) partie f; (of town, city) quartier m; (of knowledge) domaine m; **the London a.** la région de Londres; **an a. of agreement** un terrain d'entente; Am Tel **a. code** indicatif m; Com **a. manager** directeur(trice) m,f régional(e)

arena [ə'ri:nə] n (a) (Roman) arène f; (stadium) stade m (b) (area of activity) (economic, international) scène f

aren't [ɑ:nt] (a) = **are not** (b) **a. I?** = **am I not?**

Argentina [ɑ:dʒən'ti:nə] n l'Argentine f

Argentine ['ɑ:dʒəntaɪn] **1** n (person) Argentin(e) m,f; Old-fashioned **the A.** (country) l'Argentine f
2 adj argentin(e)

Argentinian [ɑ:dʒən'tɪnɪən] **1** n Argentin(e) m,f
2 adj argentin(e)

arguable ['ɑ:gjʊəbl] adj (a) (questionable) discutable; **it is a. whether it would have made any difference** on peut se demander si ça aurait changé quoi que ce soit (b) (conceivable) défendable; **it is a. that...** on pourrait soutenir que...

arguably ['ɑ:gjʊəblɪ] adv **it's a. the city's best restaurant** on peut dire que c'est le meilleur restaurant de la ville

argue ['ɑ:gju:] **1** vt (position) défendre; **to a. the case for sth** plaider en faveur de qch; **to a. that...** soutenir que...
2 vi (quarrel) se disputer (about à propos de); **to a. for sth** plaider en faveur de qch; **to a. against sb/sth** s'opposer à qn/qch; **don't a.!** ne discute pas!, pas de discussion!

argument ['ɑ:gjʊmənt] n (a) (quarrel) dispute f; (debate) discussion f; **to have an a. about sth** (quarrel) se disputer à propos de qch; (debate) discuter de qch; **to get into an a.** se disputer; **and I don't want any arguments!** et pas de discussion! (b) (reason) an **a. for/against doing sth** une raison de faire/de ne pas faire qch (c) (point) argument m (for/against en faveur de/contre); **for a.'s sake** à titre d'exemple

argumentative [ɑ:gjʊ'mentətɪv] adj (person) qui a l'esprit de contradiction; (tone) agressif(ive)

aria ['ɑ:rɪə] n aria f

arid ['ærɪd] adj aride

Aries ['eəri:z] n le Bélier; **to be (an) A.** être (du) Bélier

arise [ə'raɪz] (pt arose [ə'rəʊz], pp arisen [ə'rɪzən]) vi (of problem, possibility) surgir; (of situation) naître; (of question) se poser; (of storm) se lever; **if the need arises** si le besoin s'en fait sentir

aristocracy [ærɪs'tɒkrəsɪ] n aristocratie f

aristocrat ['ærɪstəkræt] n aristocrate mf

aristocratic [ærɪstə'krætɪk] adj aristocratique

Aristotle ['ærɪstɒtl] n Aristote

arithmetic [ə'rɪθmətɪk] n (calculations) calculs mpl; (subject) calcul m, arithmétique f

arithmetical [ærɪθ'metɪkəl] adj arithmétique; **an a. error** une erreur de calcul

ark [ɑ:k] n arche f

arm [ɑ:m] **1** n (a) (of person, chair, garment) bras m; **to carry sb/sth in one's arms** porter qn/qch dans ses bras; **to take sb's a.** prendre qn par le bras; **a. in a.** bras dessus bras dessous; **to receive sb with open arms** (warmly welcome) recevoir qn à bras ouverts; Fig **to keep sb at a.'s length** tenir qn à distance (b) **arms** (weapons) armement m; **arms race** course f aux armements (c) (in heraldry) (coat of) **arms** armoiries fpl
2 vt (person, country) armer; **to a. oneself with the facts** s'armer de faits

armadillo [ɑ:mə'dɪləʊ] (pl armadillos) n tatou m

Armageddon [ɑ:mə'gedən] n l'Apocalypse f; Fig apocalypse f

armaments ['ɑ:məmənts] npl armement m, armes fpl

armband ['ɑ:mbænd] n (at funeral, for swimming) brassard m

armchair ['ɑ:mtʃeə(r)] n fauteuil m; **an a. sportsman** un sportif en chambre

armed [ɑ:md] adj armé(e) (with de); **a. forces** forces fpl armées; **a. robbery** vol m à main armée

Armenia [ɑ:'mi:nɪə] n l'Arménie f

Armenian [ɑ:'mi:nɪən] **1** n Arménien(enne) m,f
2 adj arménien(enne)

armhole ['ɑ:mhəʊl] n emmanchure f

armistice ['ɑ:mɪstɪs] n armistice m; **A. day** l'Armistice m

armour ['ɑ:mə(r)] n (a) (of knight) armure f; **suit of a.** armure complète (b) Mil (of tank) blindage m; (tanks) blindés mpl

armoured car ['ɑ:məd'kɑ:] n voiture f blindée

armoury ['ɑ:mərɪ] (pl armouries) n (store) arsenal m

armpit ['ɑ:mpɪt] n aisselle f

army ['ɑ:mɪ] (pl armies) n armée f; (land forces) armée f de terre; **to be in the a.** être dans l'armée, être militaire

aroma [ə'rəʊmə] n arôme m

aromatic [ærəʊ'mætɪk] adj aromatique

arose [ə'rəʊz] pt of **arise**

around [ə'raʊnd] **1** prep (a) (position) autour de; **a. the table** autour de la table; **there were hills all a. the town** il y avait des collines tout autour de la ville; **there were posters all a. the walls** il y avait des posters partout sur les murs; **a. here** par ici
(b) (motion) autour de; **to look a. a room** jeter un coup d'œil à une pièce; **to travel a. the world** faire le tour du monde; **to walk a. the town/the streets** se promener en ville/dans les rues
2 adv (a) (surrounding) autour; **a garden with a fence a.** un jardin avec une clôture autour; **all a.** tout autour; **for miles a.** à des kilomètres à la ronde
(b) (in different directions) **to walk a.** se promener; **there were books lying all a.** il y avait des livres qui traînaient partout
(c) (in the general area) dans le coin; **is Jack a.?** est-ce que Jack est dans le coin?; **there was nobody a.** il n'y avait personne
(d) (approximately) environ; **at a. one o'clock** vers une heure

arousal [ə'raʊzəl] n (sexual) excitation f; (of interest, suspicion) éveil m

arouse [ə'raʊz] vt (sleeping person) réveiller; (emotion, desire, suspicion) éveiller; (enthusiasm, opposition) soulever; (sexually) exciter

arraign [ə'reɪn] vt Law traduire en justice

arraignment [əˈreinmənt] n Law lecture f de l'acte d'accusation

arrange [əˈreindʒ] 1 vt (a) (put in order) arranger; (classify) ranger (b) (organize) (wedding, meeting) arranger; (time, date) fixer; (accommodation) s'occuper de; (outing) organiser; (one's affairs) mettre en ordre; **to a. where to go/what to do** prévoir où aller/quoi faire; **it was arranged that...** il a été prévu que...; **an arranged marriage** un mariage arrangé

2 vi **to a. to do sth** s'arranger pour faire qch; (with someone else) convenir ou prévoir de faire qch; **they arranged for a taxi to meet me** ils se sont arrangés pour qu'un taxi vienne me chercher

arrangement [əˈreindʒmənt] n (a) (of objects, furniture) disposition f (b) (plan) arrangement m; **to make arrangements** prendre des dispositions, faire le nécessaire; **I've made all the arrangements** j'ai tout arrangé (c) (agreement) arrangement m; **the a. was that...** il avait été convenu que...; **viewing by a.** (sign) visites sur rendez-vous; **to come to an a. with sb** parvenir à un arrangement avec qn (d) Mus arrangement m

array [əˈrei] n (collection) collection f, éventail m

arrears [əˈriəz] npl arriéré m; **to be two months in a. with the rent** devoir deux mois de loyer; **to be in a. with one's work** avoir du travail en retard; **to be paid monthly in a.** être payé(e) à la fin du mois

arrest [əˈrest] 1 n arrestation f; **to be under a.** être en état d'arrestation; **to make an a.** procéder à une arrestation

2 vt (capture, stop) arrêter; (attention) attirer

arresting [əˈrestɪŋ] adj (striking) saisissant(e)

arrival [əˈraivəl] n arrivée f; **on a.** à l'arrivée; **a new a.** (at work, in club) un nouveau venu (une nouvelle venue); (baby) un nouveau-né (une nouveau-née)

arrive [əˈraiv] vi (a) (at place) arriver; **to a. at** (solution, decision) arriver à, parvenir à (b) Fam (attain success) réussir, arriver

arrogance [ˈærəgəns] n arrogance f

arrogant [ˈærəgənt] adj arrogant(e)

arrow [ˈærəʊ] n flèche f

arrowhead [ˈærəʊhed] n pointe f de flèche

arrowroot [ˈærəʊruːt] n Culin arrow-root m

arse [ɑːs] n Br Vulg (a) (buttocks) cul m; **to make an a. of sth** saloper qch (b) (stupid person) connard (connasse) m,f; **to make an a. of oneself** se couvrir de ridicule

▸**arse about, arse around** vi Vulg déconner

arsehole [ˈɑːshəʊl] n Vulg (a) (anus) trou m du cul (b) (stupid person) connard (connasse) m,f; **don't be such an a.!** ne fais pas le salaud (la salope)!

arsenal [ˈɑːsənəl] n arsenal m; (of devices, arguments) panoplie f

arsenic [ˈɑːsənɪk] n arsenic m

arson [ˈɑːsən] n incendie m criminel ou volontaire

arsonist [ˈɑːsənɪst] n incendiaire mf

art [ɑːt] n (a) (in general) art m; (school subject) arts mpl plastiques; (college course) beaux-arts mpl; **the arts in Great Britain** la création artistique en Grande-Bretagne; **arts and crafts** artisanat m; **a. gallery** (museum) musée m d'art; (shop) galerie f d'art; **a. school** école f des beaux-arts, beaux-arts mpl (b) Univ arts lettres fpl (c) (technique) art m; **there's an a. to making pastry** la pâtisserie, c'est tout un art

artefact [ˈɑːtɪfækt] n (manufactured object) objet m

arteriosclerosis [ɑːˌtɪəriəʊskləˈrəʊsɪs] n Med artériosclérose f

artery [ˈɑːtəri] (pl arteries) n artère f

artful [ˈɑːtfʊl] adj (a) (skilful) (person) habile; (solution, reply) astucieux(euse) (b) (cunning) malin(igne)

arthritic [ɑːˈθrɪtɪk] adj arthritique

arthritis [ɑːˈθraɪtɪs] n arthrite f

arthropod [ˈɑːθrəpɒd] n Zool arthropode m

arthrosis [ɑːˈθrəʊsɪs] n Med arthrose f

artichoke [ˈɑːtɪtʃəʊk] n (globe) a. artichaut m

article [ˈɑːtɪkəl] 1 n article m; **a. of clothing** vêtement m; Gram **definite/indefinite a.** article défini/indéfini 2 vt Law mettre en apprentissage (to chez)

articulate¹ [ɑːˈtɪkjʊlət] adj (person) qui s'exprime avec facilité; (account) clair(e)

articulate² [ɑːˈtɪkjʊleit] vt (a) (word) articuler; **to a. one's words** articuler (b) (idea, feeling) exprimer

articulated lorry [ɑːˈtɪkjʊleitɪdˈlɒri] n semi-remorque m

articulation [ɑːˌtɪkjʊˈleiʃən] n articulation f

artificial [ɑːtɪˈfɪʃəl] adj artificiel(elle); **a. insemination** insémination f artificielle; Comptr **a. intelligence** intelligence f artificielle; **a. respiration** respiration f artificielle

artificially [ɑːtɪˈfɪʃəli] adv artificiellement

artillery [ɑːˈtɪləri] n artillerie f

artisan [ɑːtɪˈzæn] n artisan m

artist [ˈɑːtɪst] n artiste mf

artistic [ɑːˈtɪstɪk] adj artistique; (temperament, person) artiste

artistry [ˈɑːtɪstri] n (of painting, game) qualité f artistique; (of painter, footballer) art m

artless [ˈɑːtlɪs] adj (simple) naturel(elle); (clumsy) maladroit(e)

artwork [ˈɑːtwɜːk] n (in book, magazine) illustrations fpl

arty [ˈɑːti] adj Fam (person) prétentieux(euse) (et passionné d'art)

Aryan [ˈeəriən] 1 n Aryen(enne) m,f 2 adj aryen(enne)

as [əz, stressed æz] 1 adv (a) (with manner) **as promised/planned** comme promis/prévu; **A as in Anne** A comme Anne

(b) (in comparisons) **as tall as me** aussi grand(e) que moi; **as white as a sheet** blanc (blanche) comme un linge; **twice as big as** deux fois plus grand que; **I came as fast as I could** je suis venu aussi vite que j'ai pu; **as much money/many people as** autant d'argent/de gens que; **as much/many as you want** autant que tu veux; **as soon as possible** dès que possible; **as recently as last week** pas plus tard que la semaine dernière

(c) **as if** comme si; **it isn't as if** or **though it's difficult** ce n'est pourtant pas compliqué; **she looked as if** or **though she was angry** elle avait l'air fâché; **it looks as if** or **though he's already left** on dirait qu'il est déjà parti

(d) **as well** aussi, également; **he has two cars as well as a motorbike** il a une moto et aussi deux voitures

(e) **as for** quant à

2 conj (a) (with time) **he went out as I came in** il sortit au moment où j'entrais; **as the day went on** à mesure que la journée passait; **we'll see as we go along** nous verrons au fur et à mesure; **as you get older** en vieillissant, avec l'âge; **as always** comme toujours

(b) (with manner) comme; **as I was saying** comme je

disais; **do as you're told** fais ce qu'on te dit; **as often happens,...** comme c'est souvent le cas,...; **it's hard/far enough as it is** c'est assez difficile/loin comme ça; **as it were** pour ainsi dire

(c) *(concessive)* **late as it was,...** bien qu'il fût tard,...; **try as she might,...** elle avait beau essayer,...; **strange as it may seem,...** aussi étrange que cela puisse paraître,...; **much as I like her,...** je l'aime bien, mais...

(d) *(because)* puisque, comme

(e) *(in addition)* **mother is well, as are the children** maman va bien, et les enfants aussi

3 *prep* comme; **to work as a team** travailler en équipe; **to regard sb as a friend** considérer qn comme un ami; **I meant it as a compliment** c'était un compliment; **she used it as a bandage** elle s'en est servi comme d'un bandage; **as a woman, I think that...** en tant que femme, je pense que...

asap [eɪeser'piː] *adv (abbr* **as soon as possible)** dès que possible

asbestos [æs'bestəs] *n* amiante *f*

asbestosis [æsbes'təʊsɪs] *n Med* asbestose *f*

ascend [ə'send] **1** *vt (mountain)* gravir, faire l'ascension de; *(throne)* accéder à; *(stairs)* gravir
2 *vi* monter

ascendancy, ascendency [ə'sendənsɪ] *n* ascendant *m*

ascendant, ascendent [ə'sendənt] *n* **to be in the a.** prospérer

Ascension [ə'senʃən] *n Rel* l'Ascension *f*

ascent [ə'sent] *n also Fig* ascension *f*

ascertain [æsə'teɪn] *vt* établir

ascetic [ə'setɪk] **1** *n* ascète *mf*
2 *adj* ascétique

ASCII [æskɪ] *n (abbr* **American Standard Code for Information Interchange)** ASCII *m*

ascribe [ə'skraɪb] *vt* attribuer (**to** à)

ASEAN [æzɪæn] *n (abbr* **Association of South-East Asian Nations)** ANASE *f*

aseptic [er'septɪk] *adj* aseptique

asexual [er'seksjʊəl] *adj* asexué(e)

ash¹ [æʃ] *n (tree)* frêne *m*

ash² *n (from fire, cigarette)* cendre *f; Rel* **A. Wednesday** mercredi *m* des Cendres

ashamed [ə'ʃeɪmd] *adj* honteux(euse); **to feel a.** avoir honte; **to be a.** of avoir honte de; **I am a. to say that...** j'avoue à ma grande honte que...; **there is nothing to be a.** of il n'y a pas de quoi avoir honte; **you ought to be a. of yourself!** tu devrais avoir honte!

ashen ['æʃən] *adj* blême

ashore [ə'ʃɔː(r)] *adv (on land)* à terre; **to go a.** débarquer

ashtray ['æʃtreɪ] *n* cendrier *m*

Asia ['eɪʒə] *n* l'Asie *f;* **A. Minor** l'Asie mineure

Asian ['eɪʒən] **1** *n* Asiatique *mf; Br (from Indian sub-continent)* = personne originaire du sous-continent indien
2 *adj* asiatique; *Br (from Indian sub-continent)* du sous-continent indien; *Am* **A. American** Américain(e) *m,f* d'origine asiatique

Asiatic [eɪʒɪ'ætɪk] **1** *n* Asiatique *mf*
2 *adj* asiatique

aside [ə'saɪd] **1** *adv* **to stand a.** s'écarter; **to take sb a.** prendre qn à part; **to put** *or* **set sth a.** *(reserve)* mettre qch de côté; **politics a.,...** toute question de politique mise à part,...; **a. from** à part
2 *n* aparté *m*

asinine ['æsɪnaɪn] *adj* stupide

ask [ɑːsk] **1** *vt* (a) *(enquire about)* demander; **to a. (sb) a question** poser une question (à qn); **to a. sth** demander qch à qn; **to a. sb the time** demander l'heure à qn; **to a. sb the way** demander son chemin à qn; **don't a. me!** je n'en ai pas la moindre idée! (b) *(request)* demander; **to a. sb for sth** demander qch à qn; **to a. to do sth** demander à faire qch; **to a. sb to do sth** demander à qn de faire qch; **to a. a favour of sb, to a. sb a favour** demander un service à qn; **if it isn't asking too much** si ce n'est pas trop demander; **to a. sb's permission to do sth** demander à qn la permission de faire qch (c) *(invite)* inviter; **to a. sb to lunch** inviter qn à déjeuner

2 *vi* (a) *(enquire)* se renseigner (**about** sur) (b) *(request)* demander; **you only have to a.!** il n'y a qu'à demander!; **to a. for sth** demander qch; *Fam* **he was asking for it** il l'a cherché

▶**ask after** *vt insep* demander des nouvelles de

askance [ə'skæns] *adv* **to look a. at sb** regarder qn de travers

askew [ə'skjuː] *adv* de travers

asking [ɑːskɪŋ] *n* **it's yours for the a.** il suffit de le demander pour l'obtenir; **a. price** prix *m* demandé

ASL [eɪes'el] *n (abbr* **American Sign Language)** = langage par signes d'origine américaine

asleep [ə'sliːp] *adj* **to be a.** dormir; **to fall a.** s'endormir; **to be fast** *or* **sound a.** dormir profondément

asocial [er'səʊʃəl] *adj* asocial(e)

asparagus [ə'spærəgəs] *n* asperge *f*

aspect ['æspekt] *n* (a) *(of problem, subject)* aspect *m* (b) *(of building)* exposition *f*

asperity [æ'sperɪtɪ] *n (of character, voice)* rudesse *f*

aspersions [ə'spɑːʃənz] *npl* **to cast a. on sth** mettre qch en doute; **to cast a. on sb's honour** porter atteinte à l'honneur de qn

asphalt ['æsfælt] *n* asphalte *m*

asphyxiate [æs'fɪksɪeɪt] *vt* asphyxier

asphyxiation [æsfɪksɪ'eɪʃən] *n* asphyxie *f*

aspic ['æspɪk] *n Culin* gelée *f;* **it was as if the house had been preserved in a.** la maison donnait l'impression de n'avoir pas subi le passage du temps

aspirate ['æspərət] *adj Ling* aspiré(e)

aspiration [æspɪ'reɪʃən] *n (ambition)* aspiration *f*

aspire [ə'spaɪə(r)] *vi* **to a. to do sth** aspirer à faire qch

aspirin ['æsprɪn] *n* aspirine *f*

aspiring [ə'spaɪərɪŋ] *adj* **to be an a.** actor/writer aspirer à devenir acteur/écrivain

ass¹ [æs] *n* (a) *(animal)* âne *m* (b) *Fam (idiot)* imbécile *mf;* **to make an a. of oneself** se ridiculiser

ass² *n Am very Fam* cul *m*

assail [ə'seɪl] *vt* (a) *(attack)* attaquer (b) **to a. sb with questions** assaillir qn de questions; **assailed by doubts** en proie au doute

assailant [ə'seɪlənt] *n* agresseur *m*

assassin [ə'sæsɪn] *n* assassin *m*

assassinate [ə'sæsɪneɪt] *vt* assassiner

assassination [əsæsɪ'neɪʃən] *n* assassinat *m*

assault [ə'sɔːlt] **1** *n* Mil assaut *m* (**on** de); Law agression *f* (**on** contre); (criticism) attaque *f* (**on** contre); Mil **a. course** parcours *m* du combattant
2 *vt* Law agresser; **to be sexually assaulted** être victime d'une agression sexuelle

assemble [ə'sembəl] **1** *vt* (people) rassembler, réunir; (facts, objects) rassembler; (machine, furniture) assembler, monter
2 *vi* (of people) se rassembler, se réunir

assembly [ə'semblɪ] (*pl* **assemblies**) *n* (**a**) (gathering) assemblée *f*; Br Sch = rassemblement des élèves d'une école avant d'entrer en classe; **a. hall** (in school) = salle où se réunissent les élèves d'une école (**b**) (of machine, furniture) assemblage *m*, montage *m*; **a. instructions** instructions *fpl* de montage; Ind **a. line** chaîne *f* de montage

assent [ə'sent] **1** *n* assentiment *m*
2 *vi* donner son assentiment (**to** à)

assert [ə'sɜːt] *vt* (one's rights, point of view) faire valoir; **to a. one's authority** asseoir son autorité; **to a. oneself** s'imposer; **to a. that...** affirmer que...

assertion [ə'sɜːʃən] *n* (statement) déclaration *f*; (of right) revendication *f*

assertive [ə'sɜːtɪv] *adj* assuré(e)

assertiveness [ə'sɜːtɪvnɪs] *n* assurance *f*; **a. training** = cours pour adultes visant à améliorer la confiance en soi des participants

assess [ə'ses] *vt* (**a**) (value, damage) estimer; **to a. sb's income** (for tax purposes) évaluer les revenus de qn (**b**) (situation, impact) étudier, analyser; (performance, ability, quality) évaluer

assessment [ə'sesmənt] *n* (**a**) (of value) estimation *f*; (for insurance or tax purposes) évaluation *f*; (of situation) étude *f*, analyse *f*; (of performance, ability, quality) évaluation *f*

assessor [ə'sesə(r)] *n* Fin contrôleur *m*

asset ['æset] *n* atout *m*; **she is a great a. to the firm** c'est quelqu'un de très précieux pour l'entreprise; Fin **assets** avoir *m*; Fin **a. stripper** = personne qui rachète une société pour profiter de la réalisation de l'actif; Fin **a. stripping** démembrement *m* (suite au rachat d'une société)

assiduous [ə'sɪdjʊəs] *adj* assidu(e)

assign [ə'saɪn] *vt* (task) assigner (**to** à); (funds) affecter (**to** à); (importance) attacher (**to** à); **to a. sb to do sth** charger qn de faire qch

assignation [æsɪg'neɪʃən] *n* Formal or Hum (meeting) rendez-vous *m*

assignment [ə'saɪnmənt] *n* (**a**) (of funds) affectation *f*; (of tasks) distribution *f* (**b**) (task) Sch devoir *m*; Journ reportage *m*; (of soldier, politician) mission *f*

assimilate [ə'sɪmɪleɪt] **1** *vt* assimiler
2 *vi* (of immigrants) s'assimiler, s'intégrer

assimilation [əsɪmɪ'leɪʃən] *n* assimilation *f*

assist [ə'sɪst] **1** *vt* (person) aider, assister; (process, development) faciliter; **to a. sb in doing** or **to do sth** aider qn à faire qch
2 *vi* aider

assistance [ə'sɪstəns] *n* aide *f*, secours *m*; **to come to sb's a.** venir en aide à qn; **can I be of any a.?** puis-je être utile à quelque chose?

assistant [ə'sɪstənt] *n* assistant(e) *m,f*; (shop) **a.** vendeur(euse) *m,f*; **a. manager** sous-directeur(trice) *m,f*

assizes [ə'saɪzɪz] *npl* Law assises *fpl*

associate 1 *n* [ə'səʊsɪət] (in business) associé(e) *m,f*; (in crime) complice *mf*
2 *adj* (company) associé(e)
3 *vt* [ə'səʊsɪeɪt] (**a**) (mentally) associer (**with** à) (**b**) **to be associated with** avoir des liens avec
4 *vi* **to a. with sb** fréquenter qn

associated [ə'səʊsɪeɪtɪd] *adj* associé(e); **a. company** société *f* affiliée

association [əsəʊsɪ'eɪʃən] *n* association *f*; **the name has unfortunate associations for her** ce nom lui évoque des souvenirs désagréables; **in a. with** en association avec

assorted [ə'sɔːtɪd] *adj* (colours, flavours) variés(ées); (biscuits, sweets) assortis(ies)

assortment [ə'sɔːtmənt] *n* assortiment *m*

assuage [ə'sweɪdʒ] *vt* Lit apaiser

assume [ə'sjuːm] *vt* (**a**) (suppose) supposer; **I a. he'll come** je suppose qu'il viendra; **he was assumed to be rich** on le supposait riche; **let us a. that...** supposons ou mettons que... (**b**) (power, control) prendre; (name) adopter; **to a. responsibility for sth** devenir responsable de qch; **an assumed name** un nom d'emprunt (**c**) (appearance, shape) prendre

assumption [ə'sʌmpʃən] *n* (**a**) (supposition) supposition *f*; **to work on the a. that...** se fonder sur l'hypothèse que... (**b**) (of power) prise *f* (**c**) Rel **the A.** l'Assomption *f*

assurance [ə'ʃʊərəns] *n* (**a**) (guarantee) assurance *f*; **he gave me his a.** il me l'a assuré (**b**) (confidence) assurance *f* (**c**) Br (insurance) assurance *f*

assure [ə'ʃʊə(r)] *vt* assurer; **to a. sb of sth** assurer qn de qch

assured [ə'ʃʊəd] *adj* (victory, success) assuré(e), certain(e); (person, performance) plein(e) d'assurance

assuredly [ə'ʃʊərɪdlɪ] *adv* assurément

asterisk ['æstərɪsk] *n* astérisque *m*

asteroid ['æstərɔɪd] *n* astéroïde *m*

asthma ['æsmə] *n* asthme *m*

asthmatic [æs'mætɪk] *n & adj* asthmatique *mf*

astonish [ə'stɒnɪʃ] *vt* étonner; **to be astonished at** or **by sth** être étonné(e) par qch

astonishing [ə'stɒnɪʃɪŋ] *adj* (amazing) incroyable; (performance) extraordinaire; **I find it a. that...** je m'étonne que... + subjunctive

astonishment [ə'stɒnɪʃmənt] *n* étonnement *m*; **to my a.** à mon grand étonnement

astound [ə'staʊnd] *vt* stupéfier

astounding [ə'staʊndɪŋ] *adj* stupéfiant(e), incroyable

astral ['æstrəl] *adj* astral(e)

astray [ə'streɪ] *adv* **to go a.** (become lost) s'égarer; **to lead sb a.** (morally) détourner qn du droit chemin

astride [ə'straɪd] *prep* à cheval sur, à califourchon sur

astringent [ə'strɪndʒənt] **1** *n* Med astringent *m*
2 *adj* Med astringent(e); Fig (person, voice) caustique

astrologer [ə'strɒlədʒə(r)] *n* astrologue *mf*

astrological [æstrə'lɒdʒɪkəl] *adj* astrologique

astrology [ə'strɒlədʒɪ] *n* astrologie *f*

astronaut ['æstrənɔːt] *n* astronaute *mf*

astronomer [ə'strɒnəmə(r)] *n* astronome *mf*

astronomic(al) [æstrə'nɒmɪk(əl)] *adj* astronomique

astronomy [ə'strɒnəmɪ] *n* astronomie *f*

astrophysics [æstrəʊ'fɪzɪks] *n* astrophysique *f*

Astroturf® [ˈæstrəʊtɜːf] n gazon m artificiel

astute [əˈstjuːt] adj astucieux(euse)

astutely [əˈstjuːtlɪ] adv astucieusement

asunder [əˈsʌndə(r)] adv Lit to tear sth a. mettre qch en pièces

asylum [əˈsaɪləm] n asile m; (mental) a. asile m d'aliénés

asymmetric(al) [eɪsɪˈmetrɪk(əl)] adj asymétrique

asymmetry [eɪˈsɪmɪtrɪ] n asymétrie f

at [æt, unstressed ət] prep (a) (with place) à; **at the office** au bureau; **at university** à l'université; **at the station** à la gare; **at the top/bottom (of)** en haut/bas (de); **at John's (house)** chez John; **at home** chez soi, à la maison (b) (with time) à; **at six o'clock** à six heures; **at night** la nuit; **at Christmas** à Noël; **at the beginning** au début; **at (the age of) twenty** à (l'âge de) vingt ans (c) (with price, speed) à; **at 60 mph** ≃ à 90 km/h; **at 50p a pound** à 50 pence la livre (d) (with direction) **to look at sb/sth** regarder qn/qch; **to shout at sb** crier après qn; **to throw sth at sb** jeter qch à qn (e) (with cause) **to be angry at sb** être fâché(e) contre qn; **to be surprised at sth** être surpris(e) de ou par qch; **to be shocked at sth** être choqué(e) par qch (f) (with activity) **to be at work/lunch** être en train de travailler/déjeuner; **she's been at it all weekend** elle n'a pas arrêté du week-end; **while you're at it** tant que tu y es; **to be good/bad at sth** (subject) être bon (bonne)/mauvais(e) en qch; **to be good/bad at doing sth** être/ne pas être doué(e) pour faire qch

atavistic [ætəˈvɪstɪk] adj atavique

ate [eɪt] pt of **eat**

atheism [ˈeɪθɪɪzəm] n athéisme m

atheist [ˈeɪθɪɪst] n athée mf

Athens [ˈæθənz] n Athènes

athlete [ˈæθliːt] n athlète mf; **a.'s foot** mycose f

athletic [æθˈletɪk] adj (fit) athlétique

athletics [æθˈletɪks] npl athlétisme m

Atlantic [ətˈlæntɪk] 1 n the A. l'Atlantique m
2 adj (coast) atlantique; (island) de l'Atlantique; **the A. Ocean** l'océan Atlantique

atlas [ˈætləs] n atlas m

ATM [eɪtiːˈem] n Fin (abbr **automated teller machine**) DAB m

atmosphere [ˈætməsfɪə(r)] n atmosphère f; Fig atmosphère, ambiance f

atmospheric [ætməsˈferɪk] adj (pressure) atmosphérique; Fig (music, lighting) d'ambiance

atoll [ˈætɒl] n Geog atoll m

atom [ˈætəm] n atome m; **a. bomb** bombe f atomique

atomic [əˈtɒmɪk] adj atomique; **a. bomb** bombe f atomique; **a. energy** énergie f atomique; **a. warfare** guerre f atomique ou nucléaire

▸**atone for** [əˈtəʊn] vt insep (sin, crime) expier; (mistake) racheter, réparer

atonement [əˈtəʊnmənt] n (for sin, crime) expiation f; (for mistake, behaviour) réparation f

atrocious [əˈtrəʊʃəs] adj (crime) atroce; (behaviour) ignoble; (meal) infect(e); (decision, joke) très mauvais(e); (weather, conditions, journey) épouvantable

atrocity [əˈtrɒsɪtɪ] n (pl atrocities) n atrocité f

atrophy [ˈætrəfɪ] (pt & pp atrophied) vi s'atrophier

attach [əˈtætʃ] vt (label, importance) attacher (to à); (blame, responsibility) imputer (to à); (document) joindre (to à); (employee) détacher (to à); **to a. oneself to sb** ne pas lâcher qn d'une semelle; **to be attached to** (like) être attaché(e) à

attachment [əˈtætʃmənt] n (a) (device) accessoire m (b) (secondment) détachement m (c) (fondness) attachement m; **to form an a. to sb** s'attacher à qn

attack [əˈtæk] 1 n (a) attaque f; **to be** ou **come under a.** être attaqué(e); **to launch an a. on** attaquer; **an a. of nerves** une crise de nerfs; **to have an a. of doubt** être assailli(e) par le doute
2 vt attaquer; (rights) porter atteinte à; (problem, task) s'attaquer à; **to be attacked** se faire attaquer

attacker [əˈtækə(r)] n (assailant) agresseur m; (in sport) attaquant(e) m,f

attain [əˈteɪn] vt (goal, ambition) réaliser; (rank, age) atteindre

attainable [əˈteɪnəbəl] adj (goal, ambition) réalisable

attainment [əˈteɪnmənt] n (of goal, ambition) réalisation f

attempt [əˈtempt] 1 n tentative f; **to make an a. at doing sth** or **to do sth** essayer ou tâcher de faire qch; **they made no a. to help** ils n'ont pas essayé d'aider; **to make an a. on sb's life** attenter à la vie de qn; **at the first a.** du premier coup
2 vt to a. to do sth essayer ou tenter de faire qch; **to a. a smile** essayer de sourire; Law **attempted murder** tentative f d'assassinat

attend [əˈtend] 1 vt (meeting) assister à; (school) aller à; (of doctor) suivre
2 vi (be present) être présent(e)

▸**attend to** vt insep (matter, problem, customer) s'occuper de

attendance [əˈtendəns] n (presence) présence f; **to be in a. on sb** s'occuper de qn; **there was a good/poor a.** il y avait beaucoup de/peu de monde; **a. register** registre m des présences

attendant [əˈtendənt] n (in museum, car park) gardien(enne) m,f; (in cloakroom) préposé(e) m,f; (at petrol pump) pompiste mf

attention [əˈtenʃən] n (a) (in general) attention f; **to pay a.** (listen to) écouter attentivement; (watch) regarder attentivement; **to pay a. to detail** faire attention aux détails; **to give sb/sth one's full a.** consacrer toute son attention à qn/qch; **to attract** or **catch sb's a.** attirer l'attention de qn; **to draw a. to oneself** se faire remarquer; **your a. please, ladies and gentlemen** mesdames et messieurs, votre attention s'il vous plaît; **for the a. of Mr Harvey** (in letter) à l'attention de M. Harvey (b) (repairs) **the engine needs some a.** le moteur a besoin d'être réparé (c) Mil **a.!** garde-à-vous!; **to stand at** or **to a.** être au garde-à-vous

attentive [əˈtentɪv] adj (paying attention) attentif(ive); (considerate) attentionné(e) (**to** pour)

attentively [əˈtentɪvlɪ] adv attentivement

attest [əˈtest] 1 vt attester
2 vi to a. to témoigner de

attic [ˈætɪk] n grenier m

attire [əˈtaɪə(r)] n tenue f

attitude [ˈætɪtjuːd] n (a) (behaviour) attitude f (b) (opinion) opinion f; **what's your a. to abortion?** quelle est votre position sur l'avortement?; **to take the a. that...** considérer que...; Com **a. survey** enquête f (c) (pose) pose f; **to strike an a.** prendre une pose affectée

attn Com (abbr **for the attention of**) à l'attention de

attorney [ə'tɜːnɪ] (pl **attorneys**) n Am (lawyer) avocat(e) m,f

attract [ə'trækt] vt attirer; **I'm extremely attracted to her** elle me plaît énormément; **the thought of working for him doesn't a. me** la perspective de travailler pour lui ne m'attire guère

attraction [ə'trækʃən] n (a) (power) attirance f; **the prospect holds little a. for me** cette perspective ne m'attire guère (b) (attractive aspect) attrait m

attractive [ə'træktɪv] adj (person, offer) séduisant(e); (prospect) attrayant(e); **do you find her a.?** est-ce qu'elle te plaît?

attribute 1 n ['ætrɪbjuːt] attribut m
2 vt [ə'trɪbjuːt] attribuer (**to** à)

attrition [ə'trɪʃən] n usure f; **war of a.** guerre f d'usure

attuned [ə'tjuːnd] adj **to be a. to sth** être accoutumé(e) à qch

atypical [eɪ'tɪpɪkəl] adj atypique

aubergine ['əʊbəʒiːn] n Br aubergine f

auburn ['ɔːbən] adj (hair) auburn inv

auction ['ɔːkʃən] **1** n vente f aux enchères; **to put sth up for a.** mettre qch aux enchères; **a. room** salle f des ventes
2 vt vendre aux enchères

▸**auction off** vt sep vendre aux enchères

auctioneer [ɔːkʃə'nɪə(r)] n commissaire-priseur m

audacious [ɔː'deɪʃəs] adj audacieux(euse)

audacity [ɔː'dæsɪtɪ] n audace f

audible ['ɔːdɪbəl] adj audible

audience ['ɔːdɪəns] n (a) (spectators, listeners) public m; **a. participation** participation f du public (b) (meeting with monarch, Pope) audience f; **to grant sb an a.** accorder une audience à qn

audio ['ɔːdɪəʊ] adj **a. cassette** cassette f audio; **a. equipment** équipement m sonore

audiotypist ['ɔːdɪəʊˌtaɪpɪst] n audiotypiste mf

audiovisual [ɔːdɪəʊ'vɪzjʊəl] adj audiovisuel(elle)

audit ['ɔːdɪt] Fin **1** n audit m
2 vt vérifier

audition [ɔː'dɪʃən] **1** n audition f
2 vt & vi auditionner

auditor ['ɔːdɪtə(r)] n Fin commissaire m aux comptes

auditorium [ɔːdɪ'tɔːrɪəm] n (of theatre, concert hall) salle f; (lecture theatre) amphithéâtre m

auditory ['ɔːdɪtrɪ] adj auditif(ive)

Aug (abbr **August**) août

augment [ɔːg'ment] vt augmenter, accroître

augur ['ɔːgə(r)] vi **to a. well/badly** être de bon/mauvais augure

August ['ɔːgəst] n août m; see also **May**

august [ɔː'gʌst] adj Lit (distinguished) auguste

aunt [ɑːnt] n tante f

auntie, aunty ['ɑːntɪ] (pl **aunties**) n Fam tata f, tantine f

au pair [əʊ'peə(r)] n (jeune fille f) au pair f

aura ['ɔːrə] n aura f; (of place) atmosphère f

aural ['ɔːrəl] adj auditif(ive)

auspices ['ɔːspɪsɪz] npl **under the a. of** sous l'égide de

auspicious [ɔː'spɪʃəs] adj prometteur(euse)

Aussie ['ɒzɪ] n Fam Australien(enne) m,f

austere [ɒ'stɪə(r)] adj austère

austerity [ɒ'sterɪtɪ] n austérité f

Australasia [ɒstrə'leɪʒə] n l'Australasie f

Australasian [ɒstrə'leɪʒən] adj d'Australasie

Australia [ɒ'streɪlɪə] n l'Australie f

Australian [ɒ'streɪlɪən] **1** n Australien(enne) m,f
2 adj australien(enne)

Austria ['ɒstrɪə] n l'Autriche f

Austrian ['ɒstrɪən] **1** n Autrichien(enne) m,f
2 adj autrichien(enne)

autarchy ['ɔːtɑːkɪ] n autocratie f

authentic [ɔː'θentɪk] adj authentique

authenticate [ɔː'θentɪkeɪt] vt authentifier

authenticity [ɔːθen'tɪsɪtɪ] n authenticité f

author ['ɔːθə(r)] n auteur m

authoritarian [ɔːθɒrɪ'teərɪən] adj autoritaire

authoritative [ɔː'θɒrɪtətɪv] adj (a) (voice, manner) autoritaire (b) (work, document) qui fait autorité

authority [ɔː'θɒrɪtɪ] (pl **authorities**) n (a) (power) autorité f; **the authorities** les autorités fpl; **I'd like to speak to someone in a.** je voudrais parler à un responsable (b) (authorization) autorisation f; **to give sb a. to do sth** autoriser qn à faire qch; **on one's own a.** de son propre chef (c) (expert) **to be an a. on sth** faire autorité en matière de qch; **to have sth on good a.** tenir qch de source sûre

authorization [ɔːθəraɪ'zeɪʃən] n autorisation f

authorize ['ɔːθəraɪz] vt autoriser; **to a. sb to do sth** autoriser qn à faire qch

autism ['ɔːtɪzəm] n autisme m

autistic [ɔː'tɪstɪk] adj autiste

auto ['ɔːtəʊ] (pl **autos**) n Am auto(mobile) f, voiture f

auto- ['ɔːtəʊ] pref auto-

autobiographical [ɔːtəʊbaɪə'græfɪkəl] adj autobiographique

autobiography [ɔːtəʊbaɪ'ɒgrəfɪ] (pl **auto-biographies**) n autobiographie f

autocrat ['ɔːtəkræt] n autocrate m

autocratic [ɔːtə'krætɪk] adj autocratique

Autocue® ['ɔːtəkjuː] n téléprompteur m

autograph ['ɔːtəgrɑːf] **1** n autographe m; **a. album** album m d'autographes
2 vt signer, dédicacer

automat ['ɔːtəmæt] n Am = cafétéria équipée de distributeurs automatiques

automate ['ɔːtəmeɪt] vt automatiser

automatic [ɔːtə'mætɪk] **1** n (car) (voiture f) automatique f; (pistol) (pistolet m) automatique m; (washing machine) machine f à laver automatique
2 adj automatique; Comptr **a. data processing** traitement m automatique des données; Av **a. pilot** pilote m automatique; Fig **to be on a. pilot** marcher au radar

automatically [ɔːtə'mætɪklɪ] adv automatiquement

automation [ɔːtə'meɪʃən] n automatisation f

automaton [ɔː'tɒmətən] n automate m

automobile ['ɔːtəməʊbiːl] n Am auto(mobile) f, voiture f

autonomous [ɔː'tɒnəməs] adj autonome

autonomy [ɔː'tɒnəmɪ] n autonomie f

autopsy ['ɔːtɒpsɪ] (pl **autopsies**) n autopsie f

autumn ['ɔːtəm] n automne m; **(in) (the) a.** en automne

autumnal [ɔːˈtʌmnəl] *adj* automnal(e)

auxiliary [ɔːɡˈzɪlɪərɪ] **1** *n* (*pl* **auxiliaries**) (*person*) auxiliaire *mf*; *Ling* auxiliaire *m*
2 *adj* auxiliaire

avail [əˈveɪl] **1** *n* of no a. (*not effective*) inutile; **to no a.** (*in vain*) en vain
2 *vt* to a. oneself of sth profiter de qch

availability [əveɪləˈbɪlɪtɪ] *n* disponibilité *f*

available [əˈveɪləbəl] *adj* disponible; **tickets are still a.** il reste des tickets; **this model is a. in black and in green** ce modèle existe en noir et en vert

avalanche [ˈævəlɑːnʃ] *n also Fig* avalanche *f*

avant-garde [ævɒŋˈɡɑːd] *adj* d'avant-garde, avant-gardiste

avarice [ˈævərɪs] *n* avarice *f*

Ave (*abbr* **avenue**) av.

avenge [əˈvendʒ] *vt* venger; **to a. oneself on sb** se venger sur qn

avenue [ˈævɪnjuː] *n* avenue *f*; *Fig* possibilité *f*

aver [əˈvɜː(r)] (*pt & pp* **averred**) *vt Lit* déclarer, affirmer

average [ˈævərɪdʒ] **1** *n* moyenne *f*; **on a.** en moyenne; **above/below a.** supérieur(e)/inférieur(e) à la moyenne
2 *adj* moyen(enne)
3 *vt* atteindre la moyenne de; **to a. eight hours' work a day** travailler en moyenne huit heures par jour

▸**average out** *vi* it'll a. out over a month sur un mois ça s'équilibrera

▸**average out at** *vt insep* my expenses a. out at £400 per month mes dépenses s'élèvent en moyenne à 400 livres par mois

averse [əˈvɜːs] *adj* opposé(e) (to à) ; he is not a. to a glass of wine il prend volontiers un verre de vin

aversion [əˈvɜːʃən] *n* aversion *f*; **to have an a. to sb/sth** avoir qn/qch en aversion

avert [əˈvɜːt] *vt* (a) (*turn away*) (*eyes, thoughts*) détourner (**from** de) (b) (*prevent*) (*misfortune, accident*) éviter, prévenir

aviary [ˈeɪvɪərɪ] (*pl* **aviaries**) *n* volière *f*

aviation [eɪvɪˈeɪʃən] *n* aviation *f*

avid [ˈævɪd] *adj* avide (**for** de)

avidly [ˈævɪdlɪ] *adv* avidement, avec avidité

avocado [ævəˈkɑːdəʊ] (*pl* **avocados**) *n* a. (**pear**) avocat *m*

avoid [əˈvɔɪd] *vt* éviter; (*question*) esquiver; **to a. doing sth** éviter de faire qch; **to a. sb/sth like the plague** fuir qn/qch comme la peste

avoidable [əˈvɔɪdəbəl] *adj* évitable

avowed [əˈvaʊd] *adj* déclaré(e)

AWACS [ˈeɪwæks] *n Mil* (*abbr* **Airborne Warning and Control System**) AWACS *m*

await [əˈweɪt] *vt* attendre; *Law* to be awaiting trial être en instance de jugement

awake [əˈweɪk] **1** *adj* éveillé(e); he lay a. for hours worrying il s'inquiétude l'a tenu éveillé pendant des heures; *Fig* he was a. to the danger il avait conscience du danger
2 *vt* (*pt* awoke [əˈwəʊk], *pp* awoken [əˈwəʊkən]) réveiller
3 *vi* s'éveiller, se réveiller; *Fig* to a. to a danger prendre conscience d'un danger

awaken [əˈweɪkən] (*pt* awakened [əˈweɪkənd], *pp* awakened *or* awoken [əˈwəʊkən]) **1** *vt* réveiller
2 *vi* s'éveiller, se réveiller

awakening [əˈweɪkənɪŋ] *n* réveil *m*

award [əˈwɔːd] **1** *n* (*prize*) prix *m*; *Law* dommages-intérêts *mpl*
2 *vt* (*prize, contract*) décerner; (*damages*) accorder; **to a. sb sth** décerner qch à qn

award-winning [əˈwɔːdwɪnɪŋ] *adj* (*film, book*) primé(e); (*writer, author*) lauréat(e)

aware [əˈweə(r)] *adj* to be a. of sth avoir conscience de qch; **to be a. that...** savoir que...; not that I am a. of pas que je sache; **as far as I'm a.** autant que je sache; **to become a. of sth** se rendre compte de qch; **politically a.** politisé(e)

awareness [əˈweənɪs] *n* conscience *f*

awash [əˈwɒʃ] *adj* (*flooded*) inondé(e)

away [əˈweɪ] *adv* (a) (*in space*) a long way a. très loin; far a. dans le lointain, au loin; it's 10 kilometres a. c'est à 10 kilomètres (d'ici); **to keep a. from** ne pas s'approcher de; **to go a.** partir, s'en aller; **go a.!** va-t'en!; **to put sth a.** ranger qch; **to take sth a. from sb** retirer qch à qn; **to stand a. from sth** se tenir à l'écart de qch; **to turn a.** se détourner
(b) (*not at school, work*) **to be a.** être absent(e)
(c) (*in time*) Christmas is only two weeks a. nous ne sommes qu'à deux semaines de Noël; **right a.** tout de suite

awe [ɔː] *n* crainte *f* mêlée de respect; **to be in a. of sb/sth** éprouver pour qn/qch une crainte mêlée de respect

awe-inspiring [ˈɔːmspaɪərɪŋ] *adj* imposant(e)

awesome [ˈɔːsəm] *adj* (a) (*incredible*) impressionnant(e) (b) *Am Fam* (*wonderful*) super *inv*

awful [ˈɔːfʊl] *adj* horrible, affreux(euse); **an a. lot of people** plein de monde; it cost an a. lot ça a coûté beaucoup d'argent

awfully [ˈɔːflɪ] *adv* (a) (*very badly*) terriblement mal (b) (*very*) très; I'm a. sorry je regrette infiniment *ou* énormément; I'm a. glad je suis rudement content

awhile [əˈwaɪl] *adv* wait a. attendez un moment *ou* un peu

awkward [ˈɔːkwəd] *adj* (a) (*clumsy*) gauche, maladroit(e) (b) (*inconvenient*) (*situation, silence*) embarrassant(e); (*location*) peu pratique; **don't be so a.** arrête de nous ennuyer; **to arrive at an a. moment** arriver au mauvais moment; *Fam* he's an a. customer il n'est pas commode

awl [ɔːl] *n* alêne *f*, poinçon *m*

awning [ˈɔːnɪŋ] *n* (*of shop*) store *m*

awoke [əˈwəʊk] *pt of* awake

awoken [əˈwəʊkən] *pp of* awake, awaken

AWOL [ˈeɪwɒl] *adj* (*abbr* **absent without leave**) to go A. s'absenter sans permission; *Fig* disparaître

awry [əˈraɪ] *adv* to go a. aller de travers

axe, *Am* **ax** [æks] **1** *n* hache *f*; *Fig* to have an a. to grind agir dans un but intéressé; *Fam* two hospitals have been given the a. on va fermer deux hôpitaux
2 *vt Fam* (*jobs*) supprimer; (*costs*) réduire

axes [ˈæksiːz] *pl of* axis

axiom [ˈæksɪəm] *n* axiome *m*

axiomatic [æksɪəˈmætɪk] *adj* (*evident*) évident(e)

axis [ˈæksɪs] (*pl* axes [ˈæksiːz]) *n Math* axe *m*; *Hist* the A. powers les puissances *fpl* de l'Axe

axle [ˈæksəl] *n* (*of vehicle*) essieu *m*

azalea [əˈzeɪlɪə] *n* azalée *f*

Azerbaijan [æzəbaɪˈdʒɑːn] *n* l'Azerbaïdjan *m*

Azerbaijani [æzəbɑɪˈdʒuːnɪ], **Azeri** [əˈrɛəz] **1** *n* Azerbaïdjanais(e) *m,f*, Azéri(e) *m,f* **2** *adj* azerbaïdjanais(e), azéri(e)

Azores [əˈzɔːz] *npl* the A. les Açores *fpl*

Aztec [ˈæztek] **1** *n* Aztèque *mf* **2** *adj* aztèque

azure [ˈæʒə(r)] **1** *n* azur *m* **2** *adj* d'azur, azuré(e)

B

B, b [biː] *n* (a) *(letter)* B, b *m inv;* **B-movie** série B *f; Br* **B road** route *f* secondaire (b) *Mus* si *m* (c) *Sch (grade)* **to get a B** *(in exam)* avoir mention assez bien; *(in homework, essay)* ≃ avoir 12 ou 13 sur 20

b *(abbr* **born)** né(e)

BA [biːˈeɪ] *n (abbr* **Bachelor of Arts) to have a BA in history** ≃ avoir une licence en histoire; **John Smith BA** ≃ John Smith, licencié ès lettres/en histoire/*etc*

baa [baː] **1** *exclam* bêê!
2 *vi (pt & pp* **baaed** *or* **baa'd** [baːd]) bêler

babble [ˈbæbəl] **1** *vi* (a) *(of baby)* babiller; *(of adult)* bafouiller; **what are you babbling on about?** qu'est-ce que tu baragouines? (b) *(of water)* murmurer
2 *n* murmure *m*

babe [beɪb] *n* (a) *Lit (baby)* **b. (in arms)** bébé *m* (b) *Fam (woman)* belle nana *f*

baboon [bəˈbuːn] *n* babouin *m*

baby [ˈbeɪbɪ] **1** *n (pl* **babies)** (a) *(child)* bébé *m;* **b. brother** petit frère *m;* **b. sister** petite sœur *f;* **b. boom** baby-boom *m; Am* **b. carriage** landau *m;* **b. grand** *(piano)* demi-queue *m;* **b. talk** langage *m* enfantin (b) *(idioms)* **to throw the b. out with the bathwater** jeter le bébé avec l'eau du bain; **to leave sb holding the b.** refiler le bébé à qn
2 *vt (pt & pp* **babied)** materner

baby-faced [ˈbeɪbɪfeɪst] *adj* au visage poupin

babyhood [ˈbeɪbɪhʊd] *n* petite enfance *f*

babyish [ˈbeɪbɪɪʃ] *adj Pej* de bébé

baby-minder [ˈbeɪbɪmaɪndə(r)] *n* nourrice *f*

baby-sit [ˈbeɪbɪsɪt] *(pt & pp* **baby-sat** [ˈbeɪbɪsæt]) *vi* faire du baby-sitting; **to b. for sb** garder les enfants de qn

baby-sitter [ˈbeɪbɪsɪtə(r)] *n* baby-sitter *mf*

baby-walker [ˈbeɪbɪwɔːkə(r)] *n* trotteur *m*

bachelor [ˈbætʃələ(r)] *n* célibataire *m;* **b. flat** garçonnière *f; Univ* **B. of Arts** *(qualification)* ≃ licence *f* ès lettres/en histoire/*etc; (person)* ≃ licencié(e) *m,f* ès lettres/en histoire/*etc; Univ* **B. of Science** *(qualification)* ≃ licence *f* ès sciences; *(person)* ≃ licencié(e) *m,f* ès sciences

bacillus [bəˈsɪləs] *(pl* **bacilli** [bəˈsɪlaɪ]) *n Biol* bacille *m*

back [bæk] **1** *n* (a) *(of person, animal)* dos *m; also Fig* **to turn one's b. on sb** tourner le dos à qn; **to sit/stand with one's b. to sb** tourner le dos à qn; **b. pain** mal *m* de dos; **to have b. problems** avoir des problèmes de dos; **b. slapping** *(self-congratulatory)* félicitations *fpl* excessives
(b) *(of hand, book)* dos *m; (of page)* dos, verso *m; (of chair)* dossier *m; (of car)* arrière *m; (of throat)* fond *m;* **at the b. (of),** *Am* **in the b. (of)** *(behind)* derrière; *(at far end of)* au fond (de); **the dress fastens at the b.** cette robe s'attache dans le dos; **at the b. of the book** à la fin du livre; **the b. of the neck** la nuque; **he knows London like the b. of his hand** il connaît Londres comme sa poche; *Fam* **in**

the b. of beyond au diable; **b. to front** devant derrière, à l'envers
(c) *(in sport)* arrière *mf*
(d) *(idioms)* **to do sth behind sb's b.** faire qch derrière le dos de qn; **I'll be glad to see the b. of him** je serai content d'en être débarrassé; **with one's b. to the wall** *(in desperate situation)* le dos au mur; **put your b. into it!** il faut t'y mettre!; **to break the b. of the work** faire le plus gros du travail; *Euph* **passage** rectum *m;* Fig; *Fam* **the boss was on my b. all day** *Fam* j'ai eu le patron sur le dos toute la journée; *Fam* **get off my b.!** fiche-moi la paix!; *Fam* **to put** *or* **get sb's b. up** braquer qn
2 *adj* (a) *(in space) (part, wheel)* arrière *inv; Fig* **to put sth on the b. burner** remettre qch à plus tard; **b. door** porte *f* de derrière; **b. garden** jardin *m* de derrière; *Fig* **he got it through the b. door** il a magouillé pour l'avoir; **the b. road** petite route *f;* **b. room** chambre *f* du fond; *Fig* **to take a b. seat** rester discret(ète); **b. yard** *Br (enclosed area)* arrière-cour *f; Am (garden)* jardin *m* de derrière
(b) *(in time)* **b. number** *(of magazine, newspaper)* vieux numéro *m;* **b. pay** rappel *m* de salaire; **b. rent** arriéré(s) *m(pl)* de loyer
3 *adv* (a) *(in space)* en arrière; **to stand** *or* **step b.** reculer; **to jump b.** faire un bond en arrière; **we passed it 3 kilometres b.** nous l'avons dépassé à 3 kilomètres d'ici
(b) *(in return, retaliation)* **to hit sb b.** rendre son coup à qn; **to call sb b.** rappeler qn; **if you kick me I'll kick you b.** si tu me donnes un coup de pied, je te le rendrai; **to get one's own b. (on sb)** prendre sa revanche (sur qn); **to get b. at sb** prendre sa revanche sur qn
(c) *(to original starting point)* **to come b.** revenir; **to go b.** retourner; **when will she be b.?** quand sera-t-elle de retour?; **b. in Britain** en Grande-Bretagne; **a few pages b.** quelques pages plus haut
(d) *(in time)* **a few years b.** il y a quelques années; **b. when...** à l'époque où...; **b. in 1982** en 1982; **as far b. as 1914** dès 1914
4 *vt* (a) *(support)* soutenir, appuyer; *(financially)* financer
(b) *(bet on)* parier *ou* miser sur
(c) *(move backwards)* **to b. one's car into the garage** entrer au garage en marche arrière; **to b. one's car into a lamppost** rentrer dans un lampadaire en faisant marche arrière
5 *vi (move backwards)* reculer; *(in car)* faire marche arrière

▶**back away** *vi* reculer **(from** devant)

▶**back down** *vi (in argument)* céder; *(in conflict)* faire marche arrière

▶**back off** *vi* reculer

▶**back on to** *vt insep* donner sur

▶**back out** *vi* (a) *(move backwards)* sortir à reculons; *(in car)* sortir en marche arrière (b) *(from agreement)* se dédire

▶**back up** *vt sep* (a) *(support)* soutenir, appuyer; *(story, account)* étayer (b) *Comptr (data, file)* sauvegarder

2 vi **(a)** *(move backwards)* reculer; *(in car)* faire marche arrière **(b)** *Compt* sauvegarder

backache ['bækeɪk] *n* mal *m* au dos

backbencher ['bæk'bentʃə(r)] *n Br Parl* député *m* de base

backbiting ['bækbaɪtɪŋ] *n Fam* médisance *f*

backbone ['bækbəʊn] *n* épine *f* dorsale, colonne *f* vertébrale; *Fig* **he's got no b.** il n'a rien dans le ventre

backbreaking ['bækbreɪkɪŋ] *adj (work)* éreintant(e)

backchat ['bæktʃæt], *Am* **backtalk** ['bæktɔːk] *n Fam* impertinence *f*

backcloth ['bækklɒθ] *Br* = **backdrop**

backdate ['bækdeɪt] *vt* antidater

backdrop ['bækdrɒp] *n Th* toile *f* de fond; *Fig* **against a b. of continuing violence** avec, comme toile de fond, un climat de violence permanente

backer ['bækə(r)] *n (of political party)* partisan *m; (for project)* commanditaire *m*

backfire [bæk'faɪə(r)] *vi (of car)* pétarader; *Fig* **the plan backfired on them** leur plan s'est retourné contre eux

backgammon ['bækgæmən] *n* backgammon *m*

background ['bækgraʊnd] *n* **(a)** *(of scene)* arrière-plan *m*, fond *m*; **in the b.** à l'arrière-plan, dans le fond; *Fig* **to stay in the b.** rester dans l'ombre; **b. music** *(in restaurant)* musique *f* d'ambiance; **she likes b. music when she's working** elle aime travailler avec un fond sonore; **b. noise** bruit *m* de fond **(b)** *(social)* origines *fpl; (educational)* formation *f; (professional)* expérience *f;* **from a disadvantaged b.** d'un milieu défavorisé; **we need someone with a b. in computers** il nous faut quelqu'un qui s'y connaisse en informatique **(c)** *(circumstances)* contexte *m;* **against a b. of discord** dans un climat de mécontentement; **can you give me some b. information?** pouvez-vous me donner quelques renseignements?; **I need a bit more b.** il me faut plus de données

backhand ['bækhænd] *n (in tennis)* revers *m*

backhanded [bæk'hændɪd] *adj (compliment)* équivoque

backhander ['bækhændə(r)] *n Fam (bribe)* pot-de-vin *m*

backing ['bækɪŋ] *n (support)* soutien *m;* **financial b.** financement *m*

backlash ['bæklæʃ] *n (reaction)* contrecoup *m (against* à); *(political)* réaction *f (against* à)

backlit ['bæklɪt] *adj Compt* rétro-éclairé(e)

backlog ['bæklɒg] *n* retard *m;* **to have a b. of work** avoir du travail en retard

backpack ['bækpæk] **1** *n* sac *m* à dos

2 *vi* faire de la randonnée; **she backpacked around Europe** elle a fait toute l'Europe, sac à dos

backpacker ['bækpækə(r)] *n* routard(e) *m,f*

back-pedal ['bæk'pedəl] *(pt & pp* **back-pedalled**, *Am* **back-pedaled)** *vi Fig* faire marche arrière

backrest ['bækrest] *n* dossier *m*

back-seat ['bæksiːt] *adj Fam* **b. driver** = personne qui donne des conseils au conducteur; **I don't want any b. driving** je n'ai besoin des conseils de personne quand je conduis

backside [bæk'saɪd] *n Fam* derrière *m*, postérieur *m*

backslash ['bækslæʃ] *n Compt* barre *f* oblique inversée

backsliding ['bækslaɪdɪŋ] *n Fam* rechute *f;* **she was on the lookout for any signs of b.** elle nous surveillait pour voir si nous nous relâchions

backspace ['bækspeɪs] *n Compt* retour *m* en arrière

backstage [bæk'steɪdʒ] *adv also Fig* dans les coulisses

backstairs [bæk'steəz] *n* escalier *m* de service

backstitch ['bækstɪtʃ] *n (in sewing)* point *m* de piqûre

backstreet ['bækstriːt] *n* petite rue *f;* **b. abortion** avortement *m* clandestin

backstroke ['bækstrəʊk] *n (in swimming)* dos *m* crawlé

backtalk ['bæktɔːk] *Am* = **backchat**

back-to-back [bæktə'bæk] **1** *adj (victories, meetings)* consécutifs(ives)

2 *adv* **(a)** *(physically)* dos à dos **(b)** *(consecutively)* de suite

backtrack ['bæktræk] *vi* **(a)** *(retrace one's steps)* revenir sur ses pas **(b)** *(renege)* faire marche arrière; **to b. on a promise/decision** revenir sur une promesse/une décision

backup ['bækʌp] *n (support)* soutien *m*, appui *m; Mil* renforts *mpl; Compt* **b. copy/file** copie *f*/fichier *m* de sauvegarde; **b. system** système *m* de sauvegarde; **b. team** *(providing support)* équipe *f* technique; *(on standby)* équipe *f* de remplacement

backward ['bækwəd] **1** *adj (a) (direction)* en arrière; **she left without a b. glance** elle est partie sans se retourner **(b)** *(retarded) (child)* retardé(e), attardé(e); *(country)* en retard; *Br Fam* **he isn't b. in coming forward** il n'a pas peur de se mettre en avant

2 *adv* = **backwards**

backwardness ['bækwədnɪs] *n (of child)* arriération *f* mentale; *(of country)* retard *m*

backwards ['bækwədz] *adv* en arrière; *(walk)* à reculons; *(fall)* à la renverse; *(read)* à l'envers; **to walk b. and forwards** aller et venir; *Fig* **to know sth b.** connaître qch à fond

backwash ['bækwɒʃ] *n (of boat)* ....s *m; Fig* conséquences *fpl* néfastes

backwater ['bækwɔːtə(r)] *n (a) (of river)* bras *m* ....; *(isolated place)* trou *m* perdu

bacon ['beɪkən] *n (a) (food)* bacon *m* **(b)** *(idioms) Fam* **to save sb's b.** sauver la peau de qn; *Fam* **to bring home the b.** *(earn wages)* faire bouillir la marmite; *(succeed)* réussir

bacteria [bæk'tɪərɪə] *npl* bactéries *fpl*

bacterial [bæk'tɪərɪəl] *adj* bactérien(enne)

bacteriological [bæktɪərɪə'lɒdʒɪkəl] *adj* bactériologique

bacteriology [bæktɪərɪ'ɒlədʒɪ] *n* bactériologie *f*

bad [bæd] *(comparative* **worse** [wɜːs], *superlative* **worst** [wɜːst]) *adj (a) (of poor quality, unpleasant)* mauvais(e); **it's not b.** *(fair)* ce n'est pas mal; *(good)* ce n'est pas mal du tout; **to be b. at maths** être mauvais en maths; **to be b. at cooking** être mauvais(e) cuisinier(ère); **things are going from b. to worse** c'est de pire en pire ou de mal en pis; **it was a b. time to leave** ce n'était pas le moment de partir; **to have a b. time** passer un mauvais moment; **there's b. blood between them** il y a de la rancune entre eux; **to get into sb's b. books** se faire prendre en grippe par qn; **b. cheque** chèque *m* sans provision; *Fin* **b. debts** créances *fpl* douteuses; **in b. faith** de mauvaise foi; **b. feeling** animosité *f;* **I gave it up as a b. job** j'ai fini par laisser tomber; **to be a b. loser** être mauvais(e) perdant(e); **b. luck** malchance *f;* **b. manners** mauvaises manières *fpl;* **in a b. mood** de mauvaise humeur; *Fig* **she's b. news** elle ne t'/lui/*etc* apportera que des ennuis **(b)** *(unfortunate)* **it's (really) too b.!, that's too b.!** c'est vraiment dommage!; **to have a b. effect on sth** nuire à qch; **he'll come to a b. end** il finira mal

(c) *(not healthy)* **to have a b. back/heart** avoir le dos/cœur fragile; **smoking is b. for you** fumer est mauvais pour la santé; **to be in a b. way** aller mal

(d) *(wicked)* *(person, behaviour)* méchant(e); **to use b. language** dire des gros mots

(e) *(serious)* *(mistake, accident)* grave; *(pain)* fort(e); **I've got a really b. headache** j'ai vraiment très mal à la tête; **to have a b. cold** avoir un gros rhume

(f) *(rotten)* mauvais(e); **to go b.** *(of fruit)* se gâter, pourrir; *(of milk)* tourner; *Fig* **a b. apple** une brebis galeuse

(g) *(guilty)* **to feel b. about sth** s'en vouloir de qch

baddie, baddy ['bædɪ] *(pl* **baddies)** *n Fam* méchant(e) *m,f*

badge [bædʒ] *n* *(of company, organization)* badge *m*; *(fashion accessory)* pin's *m*; *Mil* insigne *m*

badger ['bædʒə(r)] **1** *n* *(animal)* blaireau *m*
2 *vt* harceler; **to b. sb into doing sth** harceler qn jusqu'à ce qu'il fasse qch

bad-looking [bæd'lʊkɪŋ] *adj* **not b.** pas mal

badly ['bædlɪ] *adv* *(comparative* **worse** [wɜːs], *superlative* **worst** [wɜːst])* **(a)** *(not well)* mal; **to do b.** *(in exam, competition)* avoir un mauvais résultat; **he didn't do b.** il ne s'en est pas mal tiré; **she took it very b.** elle a très mal pris la chose; **to be b. off** être mal; **to be b. off for sth** *(lacking)* manquer de qch; **to be b. off for money** avoir des problèmes d'argent; **to get on b. (with sb)** ne pas s'entendre (avec qn) **(b)** *(seriously)* *(damaged, broken)* gravement; **to be b. beaten** *(physically)* être roué(e) de coups; *(in match, competition)* être battu(e) à plates coutures; **b. wounded** gravement ou grièvement blessé(e) **(c)** *(greatly)* **to want sth b.** avoir très envie de qch; **to be b. in need of sth** avoir grand besoin de qch

bad-mannered [bæd'mænəd] *adj* mal élevé(e)

badminton ['bædmɪntən] *n* badminton *m*

bad-mouth ['bædmaʊθ] *vt Am Fam* dire du mal de

badness ['bædnɪs] *n* **(a)** *(poor quality)* mauvaise qualité *f* **(b)** *(wickedness)* méchanceté *f*

bad-tempered [bæd'tempəd] *adj* *(person)* grincheux(euse); *(remark)* désagréable

BAF [biːeɪ'ef] *n (abbr* **British Athletics Federation)** = fédération britannique d'athlétisme

baffle ['bæfəl] *vt* *(confuse)* laisser perplexe; **to be baffled** être perplexe; **I'm baffled as to why she did it** je ne comprends vraiment pas pourquoi elle a fait cela **(b)** *(foil)* *(plot, attempt)* déjouer

baffling ['bæflɪŋ] *adj* déconcertant(e)

BAFTA ['bæftə] *n (abbr* **British Academy of Film and Television Arts)** = organisation qui décerne chaque année des récompenses aux personnalités du cinéma et de la télévision britanniques

bag [bæg] **1** *n* *(of paper, plastic)* sac *m*; *(handbag)* sac à main; **bags under the eyes** des poches sous les yeux; *Fam* **to be a b. of bones** être un sac d'os; *Fig* **it's in the b.** *(of deal, victory)* c'est dans la poche **(b)** *Fam* **bags of** *(lots)* des masses de; **we've bags of time** nous avons tout le temps; **there's bags of room** il y a plein de place **(c)** *Br very Fam Pej (woman)* **old b.** vieille toupie *f*
2 *vt (pt & pp* **bagged)** **(a)** *(put in bags)* mettre en sac **(b)** *(in hunting)* abattre, tuer **(c)** *Fam (claim)* accaparer

bagel ['beɪgəl] *n* = petite couronne de pain

baggage ['bægɪdʒ] *n* bagages *mpl*; *Av* **b. allowance** franchise *f* de bagages; *Av* **b. handler** bagagiste *mf*; *Av* **b. reclaim** retrait *m* des bagages

baggy ['bægɪ] *adj (garment) (by design)* large; *(out of shape)* déformé(e)

Baghdad [bæg'dæd] *n* Bagdad

bagpipes ['bægpaɪps] *npl* cornemuse *f*

bah [bɑː] *exclam* bah!

Bahamas [bə'hɑːməz] *npl* **the B.** les Bahamas *fpl*

Bahrain [bɑː'reɪn] *n* Bahreïn

Bahraini [bɑː'reɪnɪ] **1** *n* Bahreïni(e) *m,f*
2 *adj* bahreïni(e)

bail [beɪl] *n* *Law (guarantee)* caution *f*; **on b.** sous caution; **to grant sb b.** libérer qn sous caution; **to stand b. for sb** se porter garant(e) de qn

▶**bail out** *vt sep* **to b. sb out** *Law* se porter garant(e) de qn; *Fig* tirer qn d'affaire; *Fig* **to b. a company out** renflouer une entreprise

bailiff ['beɪlɪf] *n* **(a)** *Law* huissier *m* **(b)** *(on estate)* régisseur *m*

bait [beɪt] **1** *n also Fig* appât *m*; *Fig* **to rise to the b.** mordre à l'hameçon; *Fig* **to swallow** *or* **take the b.** mordre à l'hameçon
2 *vt* **(a)** *(torment)* harceler **(b)** *(attach bait to)* mettre l'appât à

baize [beɪz] *n* feutre *m*

bake [beɪk] **1** *vt* *(food)* (faire) cuire au four; *(clay)* cuire
2 *vi* **(a)** *(of food)* cuire **(b)** *Fam* **I'm baking** je crève de chaleur

baked [beɪkt] *adj* **b. beans** haricots *mpl* blancs à la tomate; **b. potato** pomme *f* de terre au four

baker ['beɪkə(r)] *n* boulanger(ère) *m,f*; **b.'s (shop)** boulangerie *f*; **b.'s dozen** treize à la douzaine

bakery ['beɪkərɪ] *(pl* **bakeries)** *n* boulangerie *f*

baking ['beɪkɪŋ] **1** *n* **to do some b.** *(bread)* faire du pain; *(cakes)* faire de la pâtisserie; **b. powder** levure *f* chimique; **b. sheet** *or* **tray** plaque *f* (du four); **b. soda** bicarbonate *m* de soude; **b. tin** *(for meat)* plat *m* à rôtir; *(for cakes)* moule *m* à gâteau
2 *adj Fam* **it's b.** *(hot)* on crève de chaleur

balaclava [bælə'klɑːvə] *n* passe-montagne *m*

balance ['bæləns] **1** *n* **(a)** *(equilibrium)* équilibre *m*; **to keep/lose one's b.** garder/perdre son équilibre; **to throw sb off b.** faire perdre son équilibre à qn; *Fig* **to catch sb off b.** prendre qn au dépourvu; **the b. of power** l'équilibre des pouvoirs; **on b.** tout compte fait; **to strike a b.** trouver le juste milieu
(b) *(of bank account)* solde *m*; *(in accounting)* bilan *m*; *Econ* **b. of trade/payments** balance *f* commerciale/des paiements; **b. sheet** bilan
(c) *(for weighing)* balance *f*; *Fig* **to hang** *or* **be in the b.** *(of decision, result)* être en jeu
2 *vt* *(object)* maintenir en équilibre; **he sought to b. the claims of the two parties** il a tenté de contenter les deux partis; **they b. each other well** *(of people)* ils sont complémentaires; *Fin* **to b. the books** arrêter les comptes
3 *vi* **(a)** *(physically)* tenir en équilibre
(b) **she couldn't get the accounts to b.** elle n'arrivait pas à équilibrer les comptes

balanced ['bælənst] *adj (account, reporting)* objectif(ive); *(judgement)* pondéré(e); **b. diet** alimentation *f* équilibrée

balancing act ['bælənsɪŋ'ækt] *n Fig* **to do a b.** faire des acrobaties

balcony ['bælkənɪ] (*pl* **balconies**) *n* (*in house, theatre*) balcon *m*

bald [bɔːld] *adj* (**a**) (*person*) chauve; (*tyre*) lisse; **to go b.** devenir chauve, perdre ses cheveux; *Fam* **as b. as a coot** chauve comme un œuf; **b. eagle** aigle *m* à tête blanche; **b. patch** tonsure *f* (**b**) (*plain*) **the b. truth** la vérité toute nue; **a b. statement of the facts** une simple exposition des faits

balderdash ['bɔːldədæʃ] *n Fam* bêtises *fpl*, balivernes *fpl*

balding ['bɔːldɪŋ] *adj* qui commence à perdre ses cheveux; **a b. man** un homme à la calvitie naissante

baldly ['bɔːldlɪ] *adv* (*reply*) sèchement

baldness ['bɔːldnɪs] *n* (**a**) (*of person*) calvitie *f* (**b**) (*of statement, demand*) sécheresse *f*

bale [beɪl] *n* (*of cloth, paper*) balle *f*; (*of hay*) botte *f*

▶**bale out** *vi* (*of pilot*) s'éjecter; *Fig* (*from difficult situation*) s'éclipser

Balearic [bælɪ'ærɪk] *n & adj* the Balearics, the B. Islands les (îles *fpl*) Baléares *fpl*

baleful ['beɪlfʊl] *adj* sinistre, maléfique; **she gave me a b. look** elle m'a lancé un regard noir

Bali ['bɑːlɪ] *n* Bali

Balinese [bɑːlɪ'niːz] *adj* balinais(e)

balk [bɔːk] *vi* **1** (*runner, racehorse*) empêcher de passer **2** *vi* reculer (**at** devant)

Balkan ['bɔːlkən] **1** *n* **the Balkans** les Balkans *fpl* **2** *adj* balkanique

ball¹ [bɔːl] *n* (**a**) (*in game*) (*for football, rugby, basketball*) ballon *m*; (*for cricket, tennis, golf*) balle *f*; (*for billiards*) bille *f*, boule *f*; (*of paper, of fire*) boule; (*of wool*) pelote *f*; **to roll sth (up) into a b.** mettre qch en boule; **b. bearing** (*ball*) bille; (*device*) roulement *m* à billes; **b. boy/girl** (*in tennis*) ramasseur(euse) *m,f* de balles; **b. game** (*in general*) jeu *m* de balle; *Am* (*baseball match*) match *m* de baseball; *Fig* **that's a whole new b. game** (*irrelevant*) ça n'a rien à voir; (*different situation*) c'est une autre paire de manches (**b**) (*of foot*) plante *f*; (*of hand*) paume *f* (**c**) *Vulg* **balls** (*testicles*) couilles *fpl*; (*nonsense*) conneries *fpl*; *Fig* **to have a lot of balls** avoir des couilles (**d**) (*idioms*) **to be on the b.** (*alert*) avoir de la présence d'esprit; (*knowledgeable*) connaître son affaire; **to start the b. rolling** faire démarrer les choses; **the b. is in your court** la balle est dans votre camp; **to play b.** (*co-operate*) jouer le jeu

ball² *n* (*party*) bal *m*; *Fam* **to have a b.** s'éclater; **b. dress** *or* **gown** robe *f* de bal

ballad ['bæləd] *n* ballade *f*

ball-and-socket joint [bɔːlən(d)'sɒkɪt'dʒɔɪnt] *n Anat* articulation *f* à emboîtement; *Tech* joint *m* à rotule

ballast ['bæləst] *n* (**a**) *Naut* lest *m* (**b**) *Rail* ballast *m*

ballcock ['bɔːlkɒk] *n* soupape *f* à flotteur

ballerina [bælə'riːnə] *n* ballerine *f*; **prima b.** danseuse *f* étoile

ballet ['bæleɪ] *n* danse *f* classique; (*work*) ballet *m*; **b. dancer** danseur(euse) *m,f* classique; **b. shoe** chausson *m* de danse

ballistic [bə'lɪstɪk] *adj* (*missile*) balistique; *Fam Fig* **to go b.** piquer une crise

ballistics [bə'lɪstɪks] *npl* balistique *f*

balloon [bə'luːn] **1** *n* (**a**) (*for party, travel*) ballon *m*; *Fam Fig* **when the b. goes up** quand il va y avoir du grabuge (**b**) (*in cartoon*) bulle *f* **2** *vi* (*swell*) gonfler

ballooning [bə'luːnɪŋ] *n* **to go b.** faire du ballon

balloonist [bə'luːnɪst] *n* aérostier *m*

ballot ['bælət] **1** *n* (*process*) tour *m* de scrutin; (*vote*) scrutin *m*, vote *m*; **to hold a b.** organiser des élections; **to put sth to a b.** soumettre qch à un vote; **b. box** urne *f*; **this matter should be decided at the b. box** c'est aux urnes que doit se décider cette question; **b. paper** bulletin *m* de vote; **b. rigging** fraude *f* électorale **2** *vt* consulter

ballpark ['bɔːlpɑːk] *Am* **1** *n* terrain *m* de base-ball **2** *adj* **a b. figure** une estimation

ballpoint ['bɔːlpɔɪnt] *n* **b. (pen)** stylo *m* (à) bille

ballroom ['bɔːlruːm] *n* salle *f* de bal; **b. dancing** danses *fpl* de salon

▶**balls up** *vt sep Br very Fam* foirer

balls-up ['bɔːlzʌp] *n Br very Fam* merdier *m*; **to make a b. of sth** foirer qch

ballyhoo [bælɪ'huː] *n Fam* battage *m* publicitaire

balm [bɑːm] *n* baume *m*

balmy ['bɑːmɪ] *adj* (*weather*) doux (douce)

baloney [bə'ləʊnɪ] *n Fam* (*nonsense*) bêtises *fpl*

balsa ['bɔːlsə] *n* balsa *m*

balsam ['bɔːlsəm] *n* balsam *m*

Baltic ['bɔːltɪk] **1** *n* **the B.** la Baltique **2** *adj* (*state*) balte; **the B. Sea** la mer Baltique

balustrade [bælə'streɪd] *n* balustrade *f*

bamboo [bæm'buː] *n* bambou *m*; **b. shoots** pousses *fpl* de bambou

bamboozle [bæm'buːzəl] *vt Fam* embobiner

ban [bæn] **1** *n* interdiction *f*; **to impose a b. on sth** interdire qch **2** *vt* (*pt & pp* **banned**) interdire; **to b. sb from doing sth** interdire à qn de faire qch

banal [bə'næl] *adj* banal(e)

banality [bə'nælɪtɪ] (*pl* **banalities**) *n* banalité *f*

banana [bə'nɑːnə] *n* banane *f*; **b. tree** bananier *m*; *Fam* **to be/go bananas** (*mad*) être/devenir cinglé(e); *Fam* **b. republic** république *f* bananière; *also Fig* **b. skin** peau *f* de banane; **b. split** banana split *m inv*

band¹ [bænd] *n* (**a**) (*of metal*) bande *f*, bague *f*; (*around hat*) ruban *m*; (*around cigar*) bague; (*of colour*) bande, raie *f* (**b**) *Rad* bande *f* de fréquence (**c**) (*of ages, tax*) tranche *f*; (*of salaries*) catégorie *f*

band² *n* (*of friends*) groupe *m*, cercle *m*; (*of robbers*) bande *f*; (*of musicians*) (*rock*) groupe; (*jazz*) orchestre *m*, groupe

▶**band together** *vi* se liguer (**against** contre)

bandage ['bændɪdʒ] **1** *n* bandage *m*; (*for support*) bande *f* **2** *vt* bander; **to b. sb's arm** bander le bras à qn

▶**bandage up** *vt sep* bander

Band-Aid® ['bændeɪd] *n Am* sparadrap *m*

B & B [biːən'biː] *n Br* (*abbr* **bed and breakfast**) (*service*) ≃ chambre *f* avec petit déjeuner; **to stay at a B & B** ≃ prendre une chambre d'hôte

bandit ['bændɪt] *n* bandit *m*

bandmaster ['bændmɑːstə(r)] *n* chef *m* de musique

bandsman ['bændzmən] *n* musicien *m*

bandstand ['bændstænd] *n* kiosque *m* à musique

b & w *n Phot & Cin* (*abbr* **black and white**) noir et blanc *inv*

bandwagon ['bændwægən] *n Fam* **to jump on the b.** prendre le train en marche

bandy¹ ['bændɪ] *adj* to have b. legs avoir les jambes arquées

bandy² (*pt & pp* bandied) *vt* (*words, insults*) échanger; her name was being bandied about as a possible candidate son nom est revenu plusieurs fois parmi ceux des candidats possibles

bandy-legged [bændɪ'leg(ɪ)d] *adj* aux jambes arquées

bane [beɪn] *n* plaie *f*; he's the b. of my life il m'empoisonne l'existence

bang [bæŋ] 1 *n* (a) (*noise*) claquement *m*; (*explosion*) détonation *f*; the door shut with a b. la porte s'est refermée en claquant; *Fig* to go with a b. (*of party, event*) être un grand succès (b) (*blow*) coup *m* violent; to get a b. on the head recevoir un coup sur la tête

2 *adv* (a) *Fam* b. went my hopes of a quiet weekend pour le week-end tranquille, c'était loupé (b) *Fam* (*exactly*) b. in the middle en plein milieu; b. on time pile à l'heure

3 *exclam* (*sound of gun*) pan!; (*explosion*) boum!

4 *vt* (*hit*) frapper (violemment); to b. one's head se cogner la tête

5 *vi* (*of door, window*) claquer, battre; the door banged shut la porte se ferma en claquant; to b. at *or* on the door frapper à la porte à coups violents; to b. into sth se cogner à qch

▶**bang about, bang around** *vi* (*make noise*) faire du potin

▶**bang on** *vi Fam* he's always banging on about it il n'arrête pas de bassiner tout le monde avec cela

▶**bang up** *vt sep Br very Fam* (*imprison*) boucler

banger ['bæŋə(r)] *n Br* (a) *Fam* (*sausage*) saucisse *f* (b) (*firework*) pétard *m* (c) *Fam* (*car*) old b. vieille guimbarde *f*

Bangkok [bæŋ'kɒk] *n* Bangkok

Bangladesh [bæŋglə'deʃ] *n* le Bangladesh

Bangladeshi [bæŋglə'deʃɪ] 1 *n* Bangladeshi *mf*, Bangladais(e) *m,f*

2 *adj* bangladeshi, bangladais(e)

bangle ['bæŋgəl] *n* bracelet *m*

bangs [bæŋz] *npl Am* frange *f*

banish ['bænɪʃ] *vt* (*exile*) bannir (**from** de); *Fig* (*thought, fear*) chasser

banishment ['bænɪʃmənt] *n* bannissement *m*

banister ['bænɪstə(r)] *n* rampe *f* d'escalier

banjo ['bændʒəʊ] (*pl* banjos *or* banjoes) *n* banjo *m*

bank¹ [bæŋk] 1 *n* (a) (*of river*) berge *f*, bord *m*; (*of earth*) talus *m*; (*of clouds, fog*) banc *m*; (*of lights, switches*) rangée *f*

2 *vt* the road is banked by trees la route est bordée d'arbres

3 *vi* (a) (*of clouds, snow*) s'amonceler (b) (*of plane*) virer

bank² 1 *n* (a) (*financial institution*) banque *f*; b. account compte *m* en banque; b. balance solde *m*; b. charges frais *mpl* bancaires; b. clerk employé(e) *m,f* de banque; b. draft traite *f* bancaire; *Br* b. holiday jour *m* férié; b. loan prêt *m* bancaire; b. manager directeur(trice) *m,f* d'agence; *Fin* b. rate taux *m* de l'escompte; b. statement relevé *m* de banque (b) (*in gambling*) banque *f*; to break the b. faire sauter la banque; *Fig* it won't break the b. ça ne me/te/le/*etc* ruinera pas (c) (*store*) blood b. banque *f* du sang; data b. banque de données

2 *vt* (*funds*) mettre *ou* déposer à la banque

3 *vi* to b. with sb avoir un compte chez qn; who do you b. with? à quelle banque êtes-vous?

▶**bank on** *vt insep* (*outcome, success*) compter sur

bankbook ['bæŋkbʊk] *n* livret *m ou* carnet *m* de compte

banker ['bæŋkə(r)] *n Fin* banquier(ère) *m,f*; b.'s draft traite *f* bancaire

banking ['bæŋkɪŋ] *n* (*business*) opérations *fpl* bancaires; she's in b. elle travaille dans la banque

banknote ['bæŋknəʊt] *n* billet *m* de banque

bankroll ['bæŋkrəʊl] *vt Am* (*finance*) financer

bankrupt ['bæŋkrʌpt] 1 *n Fin* failli(e) *m,f*

2 *adj* failli(e); to be b. être en faillite; to go b. faire faillite; *Fig* to be morally b. avoir perdu toute crédibilité

3 *vt Law* mettre en faillite; *Fig* (*make poor*) ruiner

bankruptcy ['bæŋkrʌptsɪ] *n Law* faillite *f*; *Fig* (*poverty*) ruine *f*

banner ['bænə(r)] *n* bannière *f*; the Star-Spangled B. la bannière étoilée; b. headline manchette *f*

bannister ['bænɪstə(r)] = **banister**

banns [bænz] *npl* bans *mpl*

banquet ['bæŋkwɪt] *n* banquet *m*

bantam ['bæntəm] *n* poulet de petite taille

bantamweight ['bæntəmweɪt] *n* (*in boxing*) poids *m* coq

banter ['bæntə(r)] 1 *n* taquineries *fpl*

2 *vi* plaisanter

bap [bæp] *n* petit pain *m* rond

baptism ['bæptɪzəm] *n* baptême *m*; *Fig* a b. of fire un baptême du feu

baptismal [bæp'tɪzməl] *adj* (*certificate*) de baptême; b. font fonts *mpl* baptismaux

Baptist ['bæptɪst] *n* baptiste *m,f*

baptize [bæp'taɪz] *vt* baptiser

bar [bɑ:(r)] 1 *n* (a) (*of metal*) barre *f*; (*of gold*) lingot *m*; (*of chocolate*) (*large*) tablette *f*; (*smaller*) barre; (*on window*) barreau *m*; (*of electric fire*) résistance *f*; b. of soap savonnette *f*, morceau *m* de savon; to be behind bars être derrière les barreaux; b. chart histogramme *m*; *Comptr* b. code code-barres *m*

(b) (*obstacle*) obstacle *m*; to be a b. to sth faire obstacle à qch; to impose a b. on sth interdire qch

(c) *Law* the B. ≃ l'Ordre *m* des avocats, le barreau; to be called to the B. s'inscrire au barreau; to read for the B. faire son droit; the prisoner at the b. l'accusé(e) *m,f*

(d) (*pub, in hotel*) bar *m*; (*pub counter*) comptoir *m*, bar

(e) *Mus* mesure *f*

2 *vt* (*pt & pp* barred) (a) (*door*) barrer; to b. sb's way barrer le passage à qn

(b) (*ban*) (*from club, pub*) exclure; to b. sb from doing sth interdire à qn de faire qch

3 *prep* sauf, à l'exception de; the finest b. none sans conteste le (la) meilleur(e)

barb [bɑ:b] *n* (a) (*on hook, arrow*) barbillon *m* (b) (*remark*) pique *f*

Barbadian [bɑ:'beɪdɪən] 1 *n* = personne née à ou habitant la Barbade

2 *adj* de la Barbade

Barbados [bɑ:'beɪdɒs] *n* la Barbade

barbarian [bɑ:'beərɪən] *n & adj* barbare *mf*

barbaric [bɑ:'bærɪk] *adj* barbare; (*manners, behaviour*) de barbare

barbarism ['bɑ:bərɪzəm] *n* barbarie *f*

barbarity [bɑ:'bærɪtɪ] *n* (*pl* barbarities) *n* (*cruelty*) barbarie *f*; (*act*) atrocité *f*

barbarous ['bɑ:bərəs] *adj* barbare

barbecue ['bɑːbɪkjuː] **1** *n* barbecue *m*; **to have a b.** faire un barbecue; **b. sauce** sauce *f* barbecue
2 *vt* cuire au barbecue

barbed [bɑːbd] *adj* (a) *(hook)* barbelé(e); **b. wire** (fil *m* de fer) barbelé *m* (b) *(remark, comment)* acerbe

barber ['bɑːbə(r)] *n* coiffeur *m* pour hommes; *(old-fashioned)* barbier *m*; **to go to the b.'s** aller chez le coiffeur/barbier

barbershop ['bɑːbəʃɒp] *n Am* salon *m* de coiffure *(pour hommes)*; **b. quartet** = quatuor chantant en harmonie

barbiturate [bɑːˈbɪtjʊrət] *n* barbiturique *m*

bard [bɑːd] *n Lit (poet)* barde *m*; **the B.** Shakespeare

bare [beə(r)] **1** *adj* (a) *(not covered)* nu(e); *(countryside)* nu, dénudé(e); *(in one's feet)* (les) pieds nus; **to lay sth b.** mettre qch à nu, exposer qch (b) *(empty) (room, cupboard)* vide; **to strip a house b.** tout enlever dans une maison (c) *(just sufficient)* **the b. minimum** le strict minimum; **the b. bones of the case** les grandes lignes de l'affaire; **the b. necessities** *(of life)* le strict nécessaire; **a b. majority** une petite *ou* faible majorité
2 *vt* mettre à nu, découvrir; **to b. one's teeth** montrer les dents; **to b. one's heart** *or* **soul to sb** ouvrir son cœur à qn

bareback ['beəbæk] **1** *adj* **b. rider** cavalier(ère) *m,f* qui monte à cru
2 *adv* **to ride b.** monter à cru

barefaced ['beəfeɪst] *adj (impudence, lie, liar)* éhonté(e)

barefoot(ed) ['beəfʊt(ɪd)] **1** *adj* (aux) pieds nus
2 *adv* nu-pieds, (les) pieds nus

bareheaded [beəˈhedɪd] **1** *adj* nu-tête *inv*, à la tête nue
2 *adv* nu-tête, (la) tête nue

bare-legged [beəˈleg(ɪ)d] **1** *adj* aux jambes nues
2 *adv* (les) jambes nues

barely ['beəlɪ] *adv* (a) *(scarcely)* à peine; **b. enough** tout juste assez (b) *(sparsely)* **b. furnished** avec très peu de meubles

barf [bɑːf] *vi Am Fam* vomir

bargain ['bɑːgɪn] **1** *n* (a) *(agreement)* marché *m*, affaire *f*; **to make** *or* **strike a b.** with sb conclure un marché avec qn; **you haven't kept your side** *or* **part of the b.** vous n'avez pas tenu votre part du marché; **to drive a hard b.** ne pas faire de cadeaux; **into the b.** *(in addition)* par-dessus le marché, en plus (b) *(good buy)* affaire *f*, occasion *f*; **b. hunter** acheteur(euse) *m,f* à la recherche de bonnes affaires; **b. price** prix *m* exceptionnel
2 *vi* **to b. with sb** négocier avec qn
▸**bargain away** *vt sep (rights, privileges)* brader
▸**bargain for** *vi insep (reaction, question)* s'attendre à ; **I didn't b. for that** je ne m'y attendais pas; **he got more than he bargained for** il ne s'attendait pas à cela
▸**bargain on** *vt insep* **I didn't b. on that** je ne m'y attendais pas

barge [bɑːdʒ] *n* péniche *f*
▸**barge in** *vi (enter)* faire irruption

bargepole ['bɑːdʒpəʊl] *n* gaffe *f*; **I wouldn't touch it with a b.** *(it's disgusting)* ça me dégoûte d'y toucher; *(it's risky for you)* si j'étais vous, je ne m'en mêlerais pas

baritone ['bærɪtəʊn] *n* baryton *m*

barium ['beərɪəm] *n Chem* baryum *m*; *Med* **b. meal** (bouillie *f* de) sulfate *m* de baryum

bark¹ [bɑːk] **1** *n (of tree)* écorce *f*
2 *vt* **to b. one's shins** s'écorcher les jambes

bark² **1** *n (of dog)* aboiement *m*; *Fig* **his b. is worse than his bite** il n'est pas si méchant qu'il y paraît
2 *vt (order)* aboyer
3 *vi* aboyer (at après); *(of person)* crier (at sur); *Fam Fig* **you're barking up the wrong tree** tu fais fausse route

barkeeper ['bɑːkiːpə(r)] *n Am* barman *m*

barley ['bɑːlɪ] *n* orge *m*; **b. sugar** sucre *m* d'orge

barmaid ['bɑːmeɪd] *n Br* serveuse *f* (de bar)

barman ['bɑːmən] *n Br* serveur *m*, barman *m*

barmy ['bɑːmɪ] *adj Br Fam* toqué(e), cinglé(e)

barn [bɑːn] *n* grange *f*; *(for cows)* étable *f*; *(for horses)* écurie *f*; **b. dance** bal *m* folklorique; **b. owl** effraie *f*

barnacle ['bɑːnəkəl] *n* bernacle *f*

barnstorming ['bɑːnstɔːmɪŋ] *adj (speech, performance)* plein(e) de brio

barnyard ['bɑːnjɑːd] *n* cour *f* de ferme

barometer [bəˈrɒmɪtə(r)] *n* baromètre *m*

baron ['bærən] *n* baron *m*; *Fig* **press/oil b.** magnat *m* de la presse/du pétrole

baroness ['bærənɪs] *n* baronne *f*

baronet ['bærənɪt] *n* baronnet *m*

baroque [bəˈrɒk] **1** *n* baroque *m*
2 *adj* baroque

barrack ['bærək] *vt (heckle)* chahuter

barracks ['bærəks] *npl* caserne *f*; **to be confined to b.** être consigné(e)

barracuda [bærəˈkjuːdə] *n* barracuda *m*

barrage ['bærɑːʒ] **1** *n* (a) *(dam)* barrage *m* (b) *Mil* tir *m* de barrage; *Fig (of questions, abuse)* flot *m*
2 *vt* **to b. sb with** *(questions)* assaillir qn de; *(criticism)* accabler qn de

barrel ['bærəl] *n* (a) *(container)* tonneau *m*, fût *m*; *(of oil)* baril *m*; *Fam* **to have sb over a b.** tenir qn à sa merci; *Fam* **the party wasn't exactly a b. of laughs** cette soirée, ça n'a pas été une partie de rigolade; **b. organ** orgue *m* de Barbarie (b) *(of gun)* canon *m*

barren ['bærən] *adj (woman, land, discussion)* stérile; *(landscape)* désolé(e)

barrenness ['bærənnɪs] *n (of land, discussion)* stérilité *f*

barrette [bəˈret] *n Am* barrette *f*

barricade ['bærɪkeɪd] **1** *n* barricade *f*
2 *vt* barricader; **to b. oneself** se barricader

barrier ['bærɪə(r)] *n also Fig* barrière *f*; **the Great B. Reef** la Grande Barrière

barring ['bɑːrɪŋ] *prep* sauf; **b. accidents** sauf imprévu; **b. a miracle** à moins d'un miracle

barrister ['bærɪstə(r)] *n Br Law* ≃ avocat(e) *m,f*

barrow ['bærəʊ] *n (wheelbarrow)* brouette *f*

bartender ['bɑːtendə(r)] *n Am* serveur(euse) *m,f* (de bar)

barter ['bɑːtə(r)] **1** *n* troc *m*
2 *vt* troquer (for contre)
3 *vi* marchander

basalt ['bæsɔːlt] *n* basalte *m*

base [beɪs] **1** *n* (a) *(of cliff, column)* pied *m*; *(of lamp, statue)* socle *m*; *(of spine)* bas *m*; *(of jug)* cul *m*; *(of triangle, structure)* base *f*; *Fin* **b. rate** taux *m* de base (b) *(for expedition, campaign)* base *f*; *(for tourism)* point *m* de départ; **b. camp** camp *m* de base (c) *(in baseball)* base *f*; *Fig* **we didn't get past first b.** nous ne sommes pas arrivés à grand-chose; **to touch b.** *(with sb)* entrer en contact (avec qn)
2 *adj* (a) *Formal (motive, conduct)* bas (basse), vil(e) (b) **b. metals** métaux *mpl* vils

3 *vt (hopes, opinion)* fonder (**on** sur); **to be based on** *(of calculation, film)* être basé(e) sur; **to be based in** *(of job, troops, company)* être basé à

baseball ['beɪsbɔːl] *n* base-ball *m*; **b. cap** casquette *f*; **b. mitt** gant *m* de baseball

Basel ['bɑːzəl] *n* Bâle

baseless ['beɪslɪs] *adj* sans fondement

baseline ['beɪslaɪm] *n (in tennis)* ligne *f* de fond

basement ['beɪsmənt] *n* sous-sol *m*; **b. flat** = appartement en partie en sous-sol

bases ['beɪsiːz] *pl of* basis

bash [bæʃ] *Fam* **1** *n* (**a**) *(blow)* coup *m*; *(with fist)* coup de poing; *Br* **to have a b. at sth/doing sth** essayer qch/de faire qch (**b**) *(party)* fête *f*
2 *vt* **to b. one's head** se cogner la tête
▶**bash in** *vt sep Br Fam (door, headlight)* enfoncer; **I'll b. your face in!** je vais te défoncer la tête!
▶**bash up** *vt sep Br Fam (person)* tabasser; *(car)* esquinter

bashful ['bæʃfʊl] *adj* timide; *(modest)* modeste

bashfulness ['bæʃfʊlnɪs] *n* timidité *f*; *(modesty)* modestie *f*

BASIC ['beɪsɪk] *n Comptr (abbr* **Beginners' All-purpose Symbolic Instruction Code)** basic *m*

basic ['beɪsɪk] **1** *n* **the basics** l'essentiel *m*; *(of language, science)* les rudiments *mpl*; **let's get down to basics** venons-en à l'essentiel; **to get back to basics** *(traditional values)* retrouver les vraies valeurs
2 *adj (principle, problem, vocabulary)* de base; *(accommodation, understanding)* rudimentaire; **I get the b. idea** je vois en gros de quoi il s'agit; **to be b. to sth** être essentiel(elle) à qch; **b. pay** salaire *m* de base

basically ['beɪsɪklɪ] *adv* (**a**) *(on the whole)* en gros; *(in fact)* en fait (**b**) *(fundamentally)* fondamentalement

basil ['bæzəl] *n* basilic *m*

basilica [bə'zɪlɪkə] *n* basilique *f*

basin ['beɪsən] *n* (**a**) *(for cooking)* bol *m*; *(for washing hands)* lavabo *m*; *(plastic, for washing up)* bassine *f*, cuvette *f* (**b**) *Geog* bassin *m*

basis ['beɪsɪs] *(pl* **bases** [beɪsiːz]*) n (for discussion)* base *f*; *(for opinion, accusation)* fondement *m*; **to be paid on a weekly/monthly b.** être payé à la semaine/au mois; **on an informal b.** à titre non officiel; **to have a b. in fact** être fondé(e); **on the b. of what you've told me** d'après ce que tu m'as dit

bask [bɑːsk] *vi* **to b. in the sun** se chauffer au soleil; **he basked in her approval** il se délectait à l'idée qu'il avait son approbation

basket ['bɑːskɪt] *n (of fruit, for washing)* corbeille *f*; *(for shopping, in basketball)* panier *m*; *Fam* **he's a real b. case** il est complètement cinglé

basketball ['bɑːskɪtbɔːl] *n* basket(-ball) *m*; **b. player** basketteur(euse) *m,f*

basketful ['bɑːskɪtfʊl] *n* (plein) panier *m*

Basle [bɑːl] *n* Bâle

Basque [bɑːsk] **1** *n* (**a**) *(person)* Basque *mf* (**b**) *(language)* basque *m*
2 *adj* basque; **the B. Country** le Pays basque

bas-relief [bɑːrɪ'liːf] *n* bas-relief *m*

bass¹ [bæs] *n (seawater)* bar *m*; *(freshwater)* perche *f*

bass² [beɪs] **1** *n (voice, singer, guitar)* basse *f*; *(on amplifier)* basses *fpl*; *(double-bass)* contrebasse *f*
2 *adj (voice)* de basse; *(guitar, clarinet)* bas (basse); **b. clef** clef *f* de fa; **b. drum** grosse caisse *f*

basset ['bæsɪt] *n* **b. (hound)** basset *m*

bassist ['beɪsɪst] *n* bassiste *mf*

bassoon [bə'suːn] *n* basson *m*

bastard ['bɑːstəd] **1** *n* (**a**) *(illegitimate child)* bâtard(e) *m,f* (**b**) *Vulg (unpleasant man)* salaud *m*; **you lucky b.!** sacré veinard!; **a b. of a job** une vraie galère
2 *adj (child)* bâtard(e)

baste [beɪst] *vt (meat)* arroser de son jus

bastion ['bæstɪən] *n also Fig* bastion *m*

bat¹ [bæt] *n (animal)* chauve-souris *f*; *Fam* **like a b. out of hell** comme un fou (une folle)

bat² **1** *n (for cricket, baseball)* batte *f*; *(for table tennis)* raquette *f*; *Fam* **to do sth off one's own b.** faire qch de sa propre initiative
2 *vt (pt & pp* **batted)** **she didn't b. an eyelid** elle n'a pas sourcillé ou bronché
3 *vi (in cricket, baseball)* manier la batte

batch [bætʃ] *n (of bread)* fournée *f*; *(of people)* groupe *m*; *(of goods)* lot *m*; *Comptr* **b. file** fichier *m* séquentiel; *Comptr* **b. processing** traitement *m* par lots

bated ['beɪtɪd] *adj* **with b. breath** en retenant son souffle

bath [bɑːθ] **1** *n* (**a**) *(action)* bain *m*; **to take** *or* **have a b.** prendre un bain; **to give sb a b.** baigner qn; *Br (swimming)* **baths** piscine *f*; **b. mat** tapis *m* de bain; **b. salts** sels *mpl* de bain; **b. towel** drap *m* de bain (**b**) *(object)* baignoire *f*
2 *vt* baigner
3 *vi* se baigner

bathe [beɪð] **1** *n Old-fashioned* **to go for a b.** (aller) se baigner
2 *vt (wound)* laver; **bathed in tears/sweat** baigné(e) de larmes/de sueur
3 *vi Old-fashioned (swim)* se baigner

bather ['beɪðə(r)] *n* baigneur(euse) *m,f*

bathing ['beɪðɪŋ] *n* **b. is prohibited** *(sign)* la baignade est interdite; **b. cap** bonnet *m* de bain; **b. costume** maillot *m* de bain; **b. trunks** slip *m* de bain

bathos ['beɪθɒs] *n* chute *f* du sublime au ridicule

bathrobe ['bɑːθrəʊb] *n* peignoir *m* de bain

bathroom ['bɑːθruːm] *n* salle *f* de bains; *Am (toilet)* toilettes *fpl*; **b. scales** pèse-personne *m*

bathtub ['bɑːθtʌb] *n* baignoire *f*

batik [bə'tiːk] *n* batik *m*

batman ['bætmən] *n Mil* ordonnance *f*

baton ['bætən] *n (in relay race)* témoin *m*; *(of conductor)* baguette *f*; *Br (of policeman)* matraque *f*; **b. charge** charge *f* à la matraque

batsman ['bætsmən] *n* batteur *m*

battalion [bə'tæljən] *n* bataillon *m*

▶**batten down** ['bætn] *vt insep* **to b. down the hatches** condamner les panneaux; *Fig* se tenir prêt(e)

batter¹ ['bætə(r)] *n (in baseball)* batteur *m*

batter² *n (in cooking)* pâte *f* à frire

batter³ *vt (beat)* cogner sur; *(person)* battre

battered ['bætəd] *adj* (**a**) **b. women** femmes *fpl* battues; **b. child** enfant *m* martyr (**b**) *(hat, saucepan, car)* cabossé(e); *(furniture, house)* délabré(e)

battering ram ['bætərɪŋræm] *n* bélier *m*

battery ['bætərɪ] (*pl* **batteries**) *n* (a) (*of radio, clock*) pile *f*; (*of car*) batterie *f*; **to be b. operated** *or* **powered** fonctionner sur piles; **b. charger** chargeur *m* de piles/batteries (b) *Mil* batterie *f*; *Fig* (*of criticism, complaints*) déluge *m* (c) **a b. of tests** une batterie de tests (d) **b. farming** élevage *m* en batterie; **b. hen** poule *f* de batterie

battle ['bætəl] 1 *n* bataille *f*; *Fig* combat *m*, lutte *f*; **it was a b. of wits between them** ils ont joué au plus fin; **to do b. with sb** être en conflit avec qn; **that's half the b.** la partie est à moitié gagnée; **b. cry** cri *m* de guerre; **a b. royal** une violente empoignade

2 *vi* se battre, lutter

battleaxe ['bætəlæks] *n* hache *f* d'armes; *Fam Pej* (*woman*) virago *f*

battledress ['bætəldres] *n* tenue *f* de combat

battlefield ['bætəlfi:ld], **battleground** ['bætəlgraʊnd] *n also Fig* champ *m* de bataille

battle-hardened ['bætəl'hɑ:dənd] *adj* aguerri(e)

battlements ['bætəlmənts] *npl* remparts *mpl*

battle-scarred ['bætəl'skɑ:d] *adj* marqué(e) par la guerre

battleship ['bætəlʃɪp] *n* cuirassé *m*

batty ['bætɪ] *adj Fam* dingue

bauble ['bɔ:bəl] *n* (*on Christmas tree*) boule *f*; (*worthless thing*) babiole *f*

baud [bɔ:d] *n Comptr* baud *m*; **b. rate** débit *m* en bauds

baulk [bɔ:lk] = **balk**

bauxite ['bɔ:ksaɪt] *n* bauxite *f*

Bavaria [bə'veərɪə] *n* la Bavière

Bavarian [bə'veərɪən] 1 *n* Bavarois(e) *m,f*

2 *adj* bavarois(e)

bawdy ['bɔ:dɪ] *adj* grivois(e), paillard(e)

bawl [bɔ:l] 1 *vt* brailler

2 *vi* brailler; **to b. at sb** hurler après qn

▶**bawl out** *vt sep* (a) (*shout*) hurler (b) (*reprimand*) passer un savon à

bay¹ [beɪ] *n* (*shrub*) laurier *m*; **b. leaf** feuille *f* de laurier

bay² [beɪ] 1 *n* (a) (*on coastline*) baie *f*; **the B. of Bengal** le golfe du Bengale; **the B. of Biscay** le golfe de Gascogne (b) *Archit* travée *f*; **loading b.** aire *f* de chargement; **parking b.** place *f* de parking; **b. window** bow-window *m* (c) **to keep** *or* **hold sb at b.** tenir qn à distance; **to keep** *or* **hold sth at b.** se préserver de qch

2 *vi* (*of dog, wolf*) hurler

bayonet ['beɪənɪt] 1 *n* baïonnette *f*

2 *vt* **to b. sb** passer qn à la baïonnette

bazaar [bə'zɑ:(r)] *n* (a) (*in Middle East*) bazar *m* (b) (*in aid of charity*) vente *f* de charité

bazooka [bə'zu:kə] *n* bazooka *m*

BBC [bi:bi:'si:] *n* (*abbr* **British Broadcasting Corporation**) BBC *f*

BC [bi:'si:] *adv* (*abbr* **before Christ**) av. J.-C.

be [bi:]

À l'oral et dans un style familier à l'écrit, le verbe **be** peut être contracté: **I am** devient **I'm, he/she/it is** deviennent **he's/she's/it's** et **you/we/they are** deviennent **you're/we're/they're**. Les formes négatives **is not/are not/was not** et **were not** se contractent respectivement en **isn't/aren't/wasn't** et **weren't**.

1 *vi* (*present* I **am**, you/we/they **are**, he/she/it **is**; *pt* **were** [wɜ:(r)]; *1st and 3rd person singular* **was** [wɒz]; *pp* **been** [bi:n]) (a) (*with state, condition*) être; **she's clever/pretty** elle est intelligente/jolie; **I'm a doctor/lawyer** je suis médecin/avocat; **they're English/Spanish** ils sont anglais/espagnols; **to be hungry/thirsty** avoir faim/soif; **to be cold/hot** (*of person*) avoir froid/chaud; (*of thing*) être froid(e)/chaud(e); **it's cold/hot** (*weather*) il fait froid/chaud; **to be 2 metres long/wide** faire 2 mètres de long/de large; **three and two are five** trois et deux font cinq

(b) (*with location*) être; **where is the station?** où est *ou* se trouve la gare?; **here I am** me voici; **there you are!** te voilà!; **where was I?** (*after digression*) où en étais-je?

(c) (*with time, date*) **it's six o'clock** il est six heures; **what day is it today?** quel jour sommes-nous?; **today's Friday/the tenth** c'est vendredi/le dix; **when is the concert?** quand a lieu le concert?; **it's a fortnight since I saw him** je l'ai vu il y a quinze jours

(d) (*with age*) **to be twenty (years old)** avoir vingt ans; **how old is he?** quel âge a-t-il?

(e) (*with cost*) coûter, valoir; **how much is it?** combien ça coûte?; **the tickets are £5 each** les billets valent 5 livres

(f) (*with health*) aller; **how are you?** comment vas-tu?; **I'm fine** ça va; **he's better/worse** il va mieux/plus mal

(g) (*with imperatives*) **be good!** sois sage!; **don't be stupid!** ne sois pas ridicule!; **let's be reasonable!** soyons raisonnables!

(h) (*with question tags*) **she's beautiful, isn't she?** elle est belle, n'est-ce pas *ou* non?; **they're big, aren't they?** ils sont grands, n'est-ce pas *ou* non?; **he isn't English, is he?** il n'est pas anglais, si?

(i) (*as past participle of* go) **I've been to London/to the museum** je suis allé à Londres/au musée; **where have you been?** où étais-tu passé?

2 *vaux* (a) (*in continuous tenses*) **to be doing sth** faire qch; **I was reading when the phone rang** j'étais en train de lire quand le téléphone a sonné; **she is/was laughing** elle rit/riait; **I'm leaving tomorrow** je pars demain; **it's raining** il pleut; **I've been waiting for hours** ça fait des heures que j'attends

(b) (*with passives*) **he was killed** il a été tué; **he wasn't allowed** to go on ne l'a pas autorisé à y aller

(c) (*followed by infinitive*) **the house is to be sold** la maison doit être vendue; **there is to be an election** des élections sont prévues; **she was never to see them again** elle ne devait jamais les revoir; **you are not to mention this to anyone** tu ne dois en parler à personne

beach [bi:tʃ] 1 *n* plage *f*; **b. ball** gros ballon *m* en plastique; **b. hut** cabine *f* sur la plage

2 *vt* (*boat, ship*) échouer

beachcomber ['bi:tʃkəʊmə(r)] *n* = personne qui ramasse des objets échoués ou abandonnés sur la plage

beachhead ['bi:tʃhed] *n* tête *f* de pont

beacon ['bi:kən] *n* (*signal, buoy*) balise *f*; (*lighthouse*) phare *m*; (*bonfire*) feu *m* d'alarme; *Fig* **a b. of hope** une source d'espoir

bead [bi:d] *n* perle *f*; **a string of beads** un collier

beady ['bi:dɪ] *adj* **to have one's b. eyes on sb/sth** surveiller qn/qch de près

beagle ['bi:gəl] *n* beagle *m*

beak [bi:k] *n* (a) (*of bird*) bec *m*; *Fam* (*nose*) nez *m* crochu (b) *Br Fam* (*magistrate*) juge *m*

beaker ['bi:kə(r)] *n* gobelet *m*

be-all and end-all ['biːɔːləˈnendɔːl] n Fam **winning isn't the b.** gagner n'est pas tout

beam [biːm] **1** n (a) (in building, in gymnastics) poutre f (b) (of sun, moon) rayon m; (of torch, headlamp) faisceau m lumineux; Phys faisceau (c) (idioms) Fam **to be off b.** être à côté de la plaque; Fam **broad in the b.** (of person) large de hanches
2 vt (programme, information) transmettre
3 vi (shine) (of sun, moon) briller; **to b. with pride/pleasure** rayonner de fierté/de plaisir

bean [biːn] n (a) (vegetable) haricot m; (of coffee) grain m; **b. curd** pâte f de soja (b) (idioms) Fam **to be full of beans** être plein(e) d'énergie; Fam **it isn't worth a b.** ça ne vaut pas un radis; Fam **he hasn't a b.** il n'a pas un radis

beanbag ['biːnbæg] n (for juggling) balle f lestée; (for sitting on) fauteuil m poire

beanfeast ['biːnfiːst] n Br Hum grande fête f

beanpole ['biːnpəʊl] n (a) (stick) rame f (b) Fam (thin person) asperge f

beansprout ['biːnspraʊt] n germe m de soja

beanstalk ['biːnstɔːk] n tige f de haricot

bear¹ [beə(r)] n (animal) ours m; (female) ourse f; **b. cub** ourson m; **to give sb a b. hug** serrer qn très fort dans ses bras; Fin **b. market** marché m à la baisse

bear² [pt **bore** [bɔː(r)], pp **borne** [bɔːn]] **1** vt (a) (carry) porter; (weight, load) supporter; (bring) apporter; **to b. sth away** emporter qch; **to b. sth in mind** (remember) se souvenir de qch; (take into account) tenir compte de qch; **it bears no relation to...** cela n'a aucun rapport avec...; **to b. the responsibility for sth** assumer la responsabilité de qch
(b) (endure) supporter; **I can't b. him** je ne peux pas le supporter; **I couldn't b. it any longer** je n'en pouvais plus; **he can't b. losing** il ne supporte pas de perdre; **it doesn't b. thinking about** l'idée même en est insupportable
(c) (produce) (child) donner naissance à; Fin (interest) rapporter; **she bore him three children** elle lui a donné trois enfants; **to b. fruit** (of tree) porter des fruits; (of effort, plan) porter ses fruits
2 vi (move) **to b. (to the) right/left** tourner à droite/gauche
▸**bear down (up)on** vt insep foncer sur
▸**bear out** vt sep confirmer, corroborer
▸**bear up** vi tenir le coup; **b. up!** courage!
▸**bear with** vt insep supporter; **if you could b. with me** si vous voulez bien patienter

bearable ['beərəbəl] adj supportable

beard [bɪəd] n barbe f; **to have a b.** porter la barbe

bearded ['bɪədɪd] adj barbu(e)

bearer ['beərə(r)] n (of news, cheque) porteur(euse) m,f; (of passport) titulaire mf

bearing ['beərɪŋ] n (a) (comportment) port m (b) (in mechanism, engine) palier m (c) (orientation) **to find** or **get one's bearings** s'orienter; Fig s'y retrouver; **to lose one's bearings** être désorienté(e) (d) (relevance) rapport m (on avec)

beast [biːst] n (a) (animal) bête f; **b. of burden** bête de somme (b) Fam (unpleasant person) peau f de vache; (cruel person) brute f; **a b. of a job** un travail pénible

beastly ['biːstlɪ] adj Fam (unpleasant) horrible

beat [biːt] **1** n (a) (of heart) battement m; (in bar, of music) temps m; (rhythm) rythme m (b) Br (of policeman) ronde f; **to be on the b.** faire sa ronde
2 adj Fam (exhausted) crevé(e); **dead b.** complètement crevé
3 vt (pt **beat**, pp **beaten** ['biːtən]) (a) (person, eggs) battre; **to b. a drum** battre du tambour; **to b. its wings** (of bird) battre des ailes; **to b. a path through the crowd** se frayer un chemin à travers la foule; Fam **b. it!** dégage! (b) (defeat) battre; **that will take some beating** c'est difficile de faire mieux; **I left early to b. the traffic** je suis parti tôt pour éviter les embouteillages; **he beat me to it** il a été plus rapide que moi; **you can't b. a good book** rien de tel qu'un bon livre; Prov **if you can't b. them, join them** il faut savoir hurler avec les loups; Fam **that beats everything!** ça c'est le meilleur!; Fam **it beats me why he did it** je ne pige vraiment pas pourquoi il a fait ça; Fam **it beats me!** ça me dépasse!
4 vi (a) (of heart) battre (b) **to b. about** or **around the bush** tourner autour du pot
▸**beat back** vt sep repousser
▸**beat down 1** vt sep (price) faire baisser; **I b. her down to £40** je lui ai fait baisser son prix à 40 livres
2 vi (of rain) tomber à verse; (of sun) taper
▸**beat off** vt sep repousser
▸**beat out** vt sep (fire, flames) étouffer
▸**beat up** vt sep (assault) tabasser

beaten ['biːtən] **1** adj **b. earth** terre f battue; Fig **off the b. track** à l'écart
2 pp of **beat**

beater ['biːtə(r)] n (a) (in hunting) rabatteur m (b) (in cookery) fouet m

beatification [biːætɪfɪˈkeɪʃən] n béatification f

beating ['biːtɪŋ] n (punishment) correction f; (in fight) raclée f; (defeat) défaite f; **to give sb a b.** (as punishment) donner une correction à qn; (beat up) flanquer une raclée à qn

beat-up ['biːtʌp] adj Fam (car) tout(e) déglingué(e)

beaut [bjuːt] n Fam **what a b.!** quelle merveille!

beautician [bjuːˈtɪʃən] n esthéticien(enne) m,f

beautiful ['bjuːtɪfʊl] adj (person, weather, music) (très) beau (belle); (smell, taste) très bon (bonne)

beautifully ['bjuːtɪfʊlɪ] adv merveilleusement bien

beautify ['bjuːtɪfaɪ] (pt & pp **beautified**) vt embellir

beauty ['bjuːtɪ] n (pl **beauties**) n (attribute, person) beauté f; (object) bijou m; **that's the b. of it** c'est ça qui est bien; **b. contest** concours m de beauté; **b. parlour** or **salon** institut m de beauté; **b. queen** reine f de beauté; **b. spot** (on face) grain m de beauté; (in country) site m remarquable

beaver ['biːvə(r)] n castor m
▸**beaver away** vi travailler d'arrache-pied (at à)

becalmed [bɪˈkɑːmd] adj encalminé(e)

became [bɪˈkeɪm] pt of **become**

because [bɪˈkɒz] conj parce que; **why? – (just) b.** pourquoi? – parce que; **b. of** à cause de

beck [bek] n **to be at sb's b. and call** être aux ordres de qn

beckon ['bekən] **1** vt faire signe à; **to b. sb in** faire signe à qn d'entrer
2 vi (of prospect) être attirant(e); **to b. to sb** faire signe à qn; **fame beckons for him** la gloire l'attend

become [br'kʌm] (*pt* became [br'keɪm], *pp* become) **1** *vt Formal* (*of behaviour*) être digne de; (*of clothes, colour*) aller bien à

2 *vi* (a) (*come to be*) devenir; **to b. old** vieillir; **to b. thin** maigrir; **to b. known** (*of truth*) être révélé(e) (b) **what will b. of him?** que va-t-il devenir?; **I don't know what has become of her** je ne sais pas ce qu'elle est devenue

becoming [br'kʌmɪŋ] *adj* (*behaviour*) convenable; (*clothes, colour*) seyant(e)

BEd [bi:'ed] *n Univ* (*abbr* **Bachelor of Education**) (*qualification*) = diplôme universitaire d'aptitude à l'enseignement; (*person*) = titulaire d'un BEd

bed [bed] **1** *n* (a) (*for sleeping*) lit *m*; **to be in b.** être au lit; **to go to b.** aller au lit; **to put a child to b.** coucher un enfant; **to go to b. with sb** coucher avec qn; *Fam* **to get out of b. on the wrong side** se lever du pied gauche; **b. and breakfast** (*accommodation*) chambre *f* avec petit déjeuner; **to stay in a b. and breakfast** ≃ prendre une chambre d'hôte; **b. linen** draps *mpl* (*et taies d'oreiller etc*) (b) (*of river*) lit *m* (c) (*of flowers*) parterre *m*; (*of vegetables*) carré *m* (d) *Culin* **lit m; on a b. of rice** garni(e) de riz (e) *Geol* couche *f*

2 *vt* (*pt & pp* bedded) *Fam Old-fashioned* coucher avec

▶**bed down** *vi* **to b. down (for the night)** s'installer (pour la nuit)

bedbug ['bedbʌg] *n* punaise *f*

bedclothes ['bedkləʊðz] *npl* draps *mpl* et couvertures *fpl*

bedding ['bedɪŋ] *n* draps *mpl* et couvertures *fpl*

bedevil [br'devəl] (*pt & pp* bedevilled, *Am* bedeviled) *vt* **to be bedevilled by sth** (*complaints*) être assailli(e) de qch; (*problems*) être accablé(e) de qch; (*of project*) être sapé(e) par qch

bedfellow ['bedfeləʊ] *n Fig* **they make strange bedfellows** ils forment une drôle de paire

bedlam ['bedləm] *n* (*chaos*) bazar *m*

Bedouin ['beduɪn] **1** *n* Bédouin(e) *m,f*

2 *adj* bédouin(e)

bedpan ['bedpæn] *n* bassin *m*

bedpost ['bedpəʊst] *n* colonne *f* de lit

bedraggled [br'drægəld] *adj* trempé(e) et crotté(e)

bedridden ['bedrɪdən] *adj* alité(e); (*permanently*) grabataire

bedrock ['bedrɒk] *n Geol* substrat *m* rocheux; *Fig* (*of beliefs, faith*) fondement *m*

bed-roll ['bedrəʊl] *n* matériel *m* de couchage

bedroom ['bedru:m] *n* chambre *f* (à coucher)

bedside ['bedsaɪd] *n* chevet *m*; **b. lamp** lampe *f* de chevet; **to have a good b. manner** (*of doctor*) savoir s'y prendre avec les malades; **b. table** table *f* de nuit *ou* de chevet

bedsit ['bedsɪt] *n Br* chambre *f* meublée

bedsock ['bedsɒk] *n* chaussette *f* pour le lit

bedsore ['bedsɔ:(r)] *n* escarre *f*

bedspread ['bedspred] *n* dessus-de-lit *m inv*

bedstead ['bedsted] *n* châlit *m*

bedtime ['bedtaɪm] *n* **b.!** c'est l'heure d'aller au lit!; **it's past my b.** je devrais déjà être couché; **b. story** histoire *f* (*pour endormir un enfant*)

bed-wetting ['bedwetɪŋ] *n* énurésie *f* nocturne

bee [bi:] *n* abeille *f*; *Fam* **he's got a b. in his bonnet about it** c'est son idée fixe; *Br Fam* **she thinks she's the b.'s knees** elle ne se prend pas pour n'importe qui

beech [bi:tʃ] *n* hêtre *m*

beechnut ['bi:tʃnʌt] *n* faîne *f*

beef [bi:f] **1** *n* (a) (*meat*) bœuf *m*; **b. stew** ragoût *m* de bœuf (b) *Fam* (*strength*) **to have plenty of b.** avoir du muscle; **give it some b.!** allez, du nerf! (c) *Fam* (*complaint*) **what's your b.?** c'est quoi ton problème?

2 *vi Fam* (*complain*) rouspéter (**about** contre)

▶**beef up** *vt sep Fam* (*text, resources*) étoffer

beefburger ['bi:fbɜ:gə(r)] *n* hamburger *m*

beefeater ['bi:fi:tə(r)] *n* = garde de la Tour de Londres

beefsteak ['bi:fsteɪk] *n* bifteck *m*

beefy ['bi:fɪ] *adj Fam* (*muscular*) costaud(e)

beehive ['bi:haɪv] *n* (*for bees*) ruche *f*

beekeeper ['bi:ki:pə(r)] *n* apiculteur(trice) *m,f*

beeline ['bi:laɪn] *n Fam* **to make a b. for** foncer droit sur

been [bi:n] *pp* of **be**

beep [bi:p] **1** *n* (*of computer, alarm clock*) bip *m*; (*of car*) coup *m* de Klaxon®; (*device*) bip

2 *vt* biper

3 *vi* (*of computer, alarm clock*) faire bip; (*of car*) klaxonner

beer [bɪə(r)] *n* bière *f*; **b. garden** = jardin ou terrasse où les clients d'un pub peuvent consommer; **b. glass** verre *m* à bière

beery ['bɪərɪ] *adj* (*smell, taste*) de bière; (*breath*) qui sent la bière

beeswax ['bi:zwæks] *n* cire *f* d'abeille

beet [bi:t] *n* betterave *f*; *Am* = **beetroot**

beetle ['bi:təl] *n* scarabée *m*

beetroot ['bi:tru:t] *n* betterave *f* (rouge); *Fam* **to go b.** devenir rouge comme une tomate

befall [br'fɔ:l] (*pt* befell [br'fel], *pp* befallen [br'fɔ:lən]) *vt Lit* arriver à

befit [br'fɪt] (*pt & pp* befitted) *vt Formal* convenir à

befitting [br'fɪtɪŋ] *adj* convenable

before [br'fɔ:(r)] **1** *prep* (a) (*with time*) avant; **I got here b. you** je suis arrivé avant toi; **the day b. the battle** la veille de la bataille; **b. that,...** avant,...

(b) (*with place*) devant; **b. my very eyes** sous mes propres yeux

(c) (*in importance*) avant; **she puts her family b. everything else** pour elle, la famille passe avant tout le reste

2 *adv* (a) (*with time*) avant; **two days b.** deux jours avant; **the day b.** le jour précédent, la veille; **the year b.** l'année précédente; **I've seen her b.** je l'ai déjà vue; **I've told you b.** je te l'ai déjà dit

(b) (*in space*) **this page and the one b.** cette page et celle d'avant *ou* et la précédente

3 *conj* **b. doing sth** avant de faire qch; **come and see me b. you leave** venez me voir avant de partir; **give it to her b. she cries** donne-le-lui avant qu'elle (ne) se mette à pleurer

beforehand [br'fɔ:hænd] *adv* à l'avance; **check b.** vérifiez au préalable

befriend [br'frend] *vt* **to b. sb** se prendre d'amitié pour qn

befuddled [br'fʌdəld] *adj* (*person*) perdu(e); (*mind*) embrouillé(e); **b. with drink** abruti(e) par l'alcool

beg [beg] (*pt & pp* **begged**) **1** *vt* to b. sb to do sth supplier qn de faire qch; **he begged a favour of me** il m'a supplié de lui rendre un service; **to b. sb's forgiveness** implorer le pardon de qn; **I b. your pardon** (*I apologize*) (je vous demande) pardon; (*what did you say?*) pardon?; **I b. to differ** je me permets d'être d'un autre avis; **this begs the question why** on peut se demander pourquoi

2 *vi* (*for money*) mendier; **I b. of you!** je vous en supplie!; **to b. for sth** (*money*) mendier qch; (*help*) implorer qch; **to b. for mercy** demander grâce; **there are still a few tickets going begging** il reste encore quelques billets

began [bɪ'gæn] *pt of* **begin**

beggar ['begə(r)] **1** *n* mendiant(e) *m,f*; *Br Fam* **poor b.!** pauvre diable!; *Br Fam* **lucky b.!** veinard!; *Prov* **beggars can't be choosers** nécessité fait loi

2 *vt* **to b. belief** être incroyable; **to b. description** être indescriptible

begin [bɪ'gɪn] (*pt* **began** [bɪ'gæn], *pp* **begun** [bɪ'gʌn]) **1** *vt* commencer; (*piece of work, new chapter*) commencer, entamer; **to b. to do sth, to b. doing sth** commencer à faire qch; **he began laughing** il s'est mis à rire; **I couldn't (even) b. to explain** je ne peux (vraiment) pas expliquer

2 *vi* commencer; **to b. by doing sth** commencer par faire qch; **to b. again** recommencer; **to b. with,...** pour commencer,...

beginner [bɪ'gɪnə(r)] *n* débutant(e) *m,f*

beginning [bɪ'gɪnɪŋ] *n* début *m*, commencement *m*; **in** *or* **at the b.** au début, au commencement; **at the b. of the year/month** au début de l'année/du mois; **I knew from the b. something was wrong** j'ai su dès le début que quelque chose n'allait pas; **to start from the b.** commencer au commencement; **from b. to end** (*read*) du début à la fin

begonia [bɪ'gəʊnɪə] *n* bégonia *m*

begrudge [bɪ'grʌdʒ] *vt* (**a**) (*resent*) **to b. doing sth** faire qch à contrecœur, rechigner à faire qch (**b**) (*envy*) **to b. sb sth** envier qch à qn

beguile [bɪ'gaɪl] *vt* (**a**) (*enchant*) envoûter (**b**) (*deceive*) enjôler; **to b. sb into doing sth** faire faire qch à qn en le séduisant

beguiling [bɪ'gaɪlɪŋ] *adj* enjôleur(euse)

begun [bɪ'gʌn] *pp of* **begin**

behalf [bɪ'hɑːf] *n* **on b. of sb, on sb's b.** au nom de qn, de la part de qn; **don't worry on my b.** ne vous inquiétez pas pour moi

behave [bɪ'heɪv] *vi* (*of person*) se conduire, se comporter; (*be good*) bien se tenir; (*of car, machine*) marcher, fonctionner; **b. yourself!** tiens-toi bien!; (*to child*) sois sage!

behavior, behavioral *etc Am* = **behaviour, behavioural** *etc*

behaviour, *Am* **behavior** [bɪ'heɪvjə(r)] *n* comportement *m*, conduite *f*; **to be on one's best b.** se tenir particulièrement bien

behavioural, *Am* **behavioral** [bɪ'heɪvjərəl] *adj* de comportement

behaviourism, *Am* **behaviorism** [bɪ'heɪvjərɪzəm] *n Psy* behaviorisme *m*

behead [bɪ'hed] *vt* décapiter

beheld [bɪ'held] *pt & pp of* **behold**

behest [bɪ'hest] *n* **at sb's b., at the b. of sb** sur ordre de qn

behind [bɪ'haɪnd] **1** *prep* derrière; **he hid b. it** il s'est caché derrière; **to be b. sb** (*support*) être avec qn; **to be b. schedule** avoir du retard; **to put sth b. one** (*forget*) ne plus penser à qch; **she's ten minutes b. them** elle a dix minutes de retard sur eux; **to be b. the times** (*old-fashioned*) retarder sur son temps; **the reasons b. sth** les raisons de qch; **what's b. all this?** qu'est-ce que ça cache?

2 *adv* derrière; **from b.** (*viewed*) de derrière; (*attacked*) par-derrière; **to stay** *or* **remain b.** (*not leave*) rester; **to be b. with one's work** être en retard dans son travail; **to be b. with the rent** être en retard pour payer le loyer; **they are only three points b.** (*in contest*) ils ne sont qu'à trois points

3 *n Fam* (*buttocks*) derrière *m*

behindhand [bɪ'haɪndhænd] *adv* en retard; **to be b. with the rent** être en retard pour payer le loyer; **to be b. with one's work** avoir du travail en retard

behold [bɪ'həʊld] (*pt & pp* **beheld** [bɪ'held]) *vt Lit* voir; **a sight to b.** un spectacle

beholden [bɪ'həʊldən] *adj Formal* **to be b. to sb** être redevable à qn

beholder [bɪ'həʊldə(r)] *n Prov* **beauty is in the eye of the b.** l'amour est aveugle

beige [beɪʒ] **1** *n* beige *m*

2 *adj* beige

Beijing [beɪ'ʒɪŋ] *n* Pékin, Beijing

being ['biːŋ] *n* (**a**) (*creature*) être *m* (**b**) (*existence*) **to come into b.** naître; **to be in b.** exister

Beirut [beɪ'ruːt] *n* Beyrouth

Belarus [belə'ruːs] *n* la Biélorussie

belated [bɪ'leɪtɪd] *adj* tardif(ive); **wishing you a b. happy birthday** je te souhaite un bon anniversaire avec un peu de retard

belch [beltʃ] **1** *n* (*burp*) rot *m*; **to give a (loud) b.** roter (bruyamment)

2 *vt* **to b. smoke/flames** (*of fire, chimney*) cracher de la fumée/des flammes

3 *vi* (*of person*) roter

beleaguered [bɪ'liːgəd] *adj* (*city, army*) assiégé(e); (*government*) assailli(e) de toutes parts; (*person*) accablé(e)

Belfast [bel'fɑːst] *n* Belfast

belfry ['belfrɪ] (*pl* **belfries**) *n* beffroi *m*, clocher *m*

Belgian ['beldʒən] **1** *n* Belge *mf*

2 *adj* belge

Belgium ['beldʒəm] *n* la Belgique

Belgrade [bel'greɪd] *n* Belgrade

belie [bɪ'laɪ] *vt* (*feelings, background*) ne pas refléter

belief [bɪ'liːf] *n* (**a**) (*conviction*) conviction *f*; (*religious*) croyance *f*; **in the b. that...** étant convaincu(e) que...; **it is my b. that...** je suis convaincu(e) que... (**b**) (*confidence*) foi *f* (**in** en)

believable [bɪ'liːvəbəl] *adj* crédible, plausible

believe [bɪ'liːv] **1** *vt* croire; **I b. (that) I'm right** je crois que j'ai raison; **I b. him to be alive** je crois qu'il est vivant; **she is believed to be in hiding** on pense qu'elle se cache; **I don't b. a word of it** je n'en crois pas un mot; **I could scarcely b. my eyes** j'en croyais à peine mes yeux; **I don't b. it!** c'est pas vrai!

2 *vi* (**a**) **to b. in sth** (*have faith in*) croire à qch; **to b. in God** croire en Dieu; **to b. in sb** (*have confidence in*) avoir foi en qn; **to b. in oneself** avoir confiance en soi (**b**) **to believe in sth** (*be in favour of*) croire à qch; **I don't b. in making promises** je n'aime pas faire de promesses (**c**) *(think, suppose)* croire; **I b. not** je ne crois pas, je crois que non; **I b. so** je crois (que oui)

believer [bɪ'liːvə(r)] *n* (a) *(religious person)* croyant(e) *m,f*; **to be a b.** être croyant(e) (b) *(supporter)* **to be a b. in sth** croire à qch

belittle [bɪ'lɪtəl] *vt* rabaisser; **to b. oneself** se rabaisser

Belize [be'liːz] *n* le Belize

bell [bel] *n (of church)* cloche *f*; *(handbell, on cat)* clochette *f*; *(on door, bicycle)* sonnette *f*; **to ring the b.** *(on door)* sonner; *Br Fam* **to give sb a b.** passer un coup de fil à qn; **b. jar** cloche; **b. tower** clocher *m*

belladonna [belə'dɒnə] *n* belladone *f*

bell-bottoms ['belbɒtəmz] *npl* pantalon *m* (à) pattes d'éléphant

bell-boy ['belbɔɪ] *n Am Fam* groom *m*

belle [bel] *n* beauté *f*; **the b. of the ball** la reine du bal

bellhop ['belhɒp] *n Am Fam* groom *m*

bellicose ['belɪkəʊs] *adj* belliqueux(euse)

belligerence [be'lɪdʒərəns] *n* agressivité *f*

belligerent [be'lɪdʒərənt] **1** *n (in war)* belligérant(e) *m,f*; *(in dispute)* partie *f*

2 *adj (aggressive)* agressif(ive), belliqueux(euse); *(at war)* belligérant(e)

bellow ['beləʊ] **1** *n (of bull)* beuglement *m*, mugissement *m*; *(of person)* braillement *m*

2 *vi (of bull)* beugler, mugir; *(of person)* brailler

bellows ['beləʊz] *npl (pair of)* **b.** soufflet *m*

bell-ringer ['belrɪŋə(r)] *n* carillonneur(euse) *m,f*

belly ['belɪ] *(pl* **bellies***) n* ventre *m*; **to have a full/an empty b.** avoir le ventre plein/vide; **b. dance** danse *f* du ventre; **b. laugh** gros rire *m*

bellyache ['belɪeɪk] *Fam* **1** *n* mal *m* au ventre

2 *vi (complain)* rouspéter, râler *(about sb/about sth* après qn/au sujet de qch)

belly-button ['belɪbʌtən] *n Fam* nombril *m*

belly-flop ['belɪflɒp] **1** *n* plat *m*

2 *vi (pt & pp* **belly-flopped***)* faire un plat

bellyful ['belɪfʊl] *n Fam* **to have had a b. of sb/sth** en avoir marre/ras le bol de qn/qch

belong [bɪ'lɒŋ] *vi* (a) **to b. to** *(be property of)* appartenir à; **that book belongs to me** ce livre m'appartient ou est à moi (b) **to b. to** *(club, party)* être membre de; *(category)* appartenir à (c) *(have a proper place)* **to put sth back where it belongs** remettre qch à sa place; **the saucepans don't b. in that cupboard** les casseroles ne vont pas ou ne se rangent pas dans ce placard; **I feel I b. here** je me sens à ma place ici

belonging [bɪ'lɒŋɪŋ] *n* **to have a sense of b.** se sentir à sa place

belongings [bɪ'lɒŋɪŋz] *npl* affaires *fpl*

beloved **1** *n* [bɪ'lʌvɪd] *Lit* bien-aimé(e) *m,f*

2 *adj* [bɪ'lʌvd] bien-aimé(e)

below [bɪ'ləʊ] **1** *prep* (a) *(line, age, temperature)* au-dessous de; *(bridge, ground)* sous (b) *(with numbers)* moins de

2 *adv* au-dessous, en bas; *(in text)* ci-dessous; **on the floor b.** à l'étage du dessous; **it's 10 degrees b.** il fait moins dix

belt [belt] **1** *n* (a) *(for trousers)* ceinture *f*; *Fig* **to tighten one's b.** se serrer la ceinture; *Fig* **to have sth under one's b.** *(driving licence, degree)* avoir qch en poche; *(experience)* avoir qch à son actif; *Fig* **that was a bit below the b.** *(of remark, criticism)* c'était un coup bas (b) *(of machine)* courroie (c) *(of land)* région *f*, zone *f* (d) *Fam (blow)* coup *m*; **to give sb a b.** flanquer un gnon à qn

2 *vt (hit) (ball)* cogner dans; *(person)* flanquer un gnon à

3 *vi Fam (move quickly)* **to b. along** foncer; **she belted down the stairs** elle a descendu les escaliers quatre à quatre

▶**belt out** *vt sep Fam (song)* brailler

▶**belt up** *vi Br very Fam (be quiet)* la fermer; **b. up!** la ferme!

bemoan [bɪ'məʊn] *vt (loss, somebody's death)* pleurer; *(one's fate)* se lamenter sur

bemused [bɪ'mjuːzd] *adj* perplexe

bench [bentʃ] *n (seat) & Pol* banc *m*; *(worktable)* établi *m*; *Br Law* **the b.** *(magistrates)* la magistrature; *(court)* la cour; **to be on the b.** *(in football)* être remplaçant(e)

benchmark ['bentʃmɑːk] *n (for comparison)* référence *f*

bend [bend] **1** *n* (a) *(of road)* virage *m*, tournant *m*; *(of river)* méandre *m*; *(of pipe)* coude *m*; *Fam* **round the b.** dingue (b) **the bends** *(decompression sickness)* la maladie des caissons

2 *vt (pt & pp* **bent** [bent]*) (leg, arm, wire)* plier; *(head)* baisser; *(light)* réfracter; **do not b.** *(on envelope)* ne pas plier; **on bended knee** à genoux; **to b. the rules** faire une entorse au règlement; *Br Fam* **to b. sb's ear** tenir la jambe à qn

3 *vi (of road)* tourner; *(of river)* faire un coude; *(of branch)* plier

▶**bend down** *vi* se pencher

▶**bend over** *vi* se pencher; *Fig* **to b. over backwards to do sth** se décarcasser pour faire qch

bender ['bendə(r)] *n Fam* beuverie *f*; **to go on a b.** prendre une cuite

beneath [bɪ'niːθ] **1** *prep* (a) *(physically)* sous (b) *(unworthy of)* **to marry b. one** faire une mésalliance; **she thinks it's b. her to work** elle pense que travailler est indigne d'elle; **b. contempt** parfaitement méprisable

2 *adv* dessous, au-dessous; **from b.** de dessous

Benedictine [benɪ'dɪktɪn] *adj Rel* bénédictin(e)

benediction [benɪ'dɪkʃən] *n Rel* bénédiction *f*

benefactor ['benɪfæktə(r)] *n* bienfaiteur *m*

benefactress ['benɪfæktrɪs] *n* bienfaitrice *f*

beneficent [bɪ'nefɪsənt] *adj (system)* bienfaisant(e); *(person)* bon (bonne)

beneficial [benɪ'fɪʃəl] *adj* bénéfique (**to** pour)

beneficiary [benɪ'fɪʃərɪ] *(pl* **beneficiaries***) n* bénéficiaire *mf*

benefit ['benɪfɪt] **1** *n* (a) *(advantage)* profit *m*; **to have the b. of sth** pouvoir profiter de qch; **for sb's b.,** **for the b. of sb** à l'intention de qn; **that remark was for my b.** cette remarque m'était destinée; **to give sb the b. of the doubt** accorder à qn le bénéfice du doute (b) *(charity event)* spectacle *m* de bienfaisance; **b. match** match *m* de bienfaisance (c) *(state payment)* allocation *f*; **to be on b.** toucher une aide de l'État; **social security benefits** prestations *fpl* sociales

2 *vt (person, country)* profiter à; *(trade)* favoriser

3 *vi* **to b. from sth** tirer profit de qch; **you'll b. from a holiday** ça te fera du bien d'aller en vacances; **who stands to b. most?** à qui cela profitera-t-il le plus?

Benelux ['benɪlʌks] *n* Benelux *m*; **the B. countries** les pays du Benelux

benevolence [bɪ'nevələns] *n* bienveillance *f*

benevolent [bɪ'nevələnt] *adj* bienveillant(e); **b. society** association *f* de bienfaisance

Bengal [beŋ'gɔːl] *n* le Bengale

Bengali [beŋ'gɔːlɪ] **1** *n* (a) *(person)* Bengali *mf* (b) *(language)* bengali *m*
2 *adj* bengali

benign [bɪ'naɪn] *adj (attitude)* bienveillant(e); *(climate)* doux (douce); *(tumour)* bénin(igne)

Benin [be'niːn] *n* le Bénin

bent [bent] **1** *n (taste)* penchant *m*, inclination *f*; *(aptitude)* dispositions *fpl*; **to have a musical b.** avoir des dispositions pour la musique
2 *adj* (a) *(curved)* tordu(e); *(out of shape)* plié(e); *(person, back)* voûté(e) (b) *Fam (dishonest)* pourri(e); **b. copper** (flic *m*) ripou *m* (c) *very Fam (homosexual)* pédé, = terme injurieux qualifiant un homosexuel (d) **to be b. on doing sth** *(determined)* être résolu(e) à faire qch; **to be b. on sth** vouloir à tout prix qch
3 *pt & pp of* **bend**

benzene ['benziːn] *n Chem* benzène *m*

benzine ['benziːn] *n Chem* benzine *f*

bequeath [bɪ'kwiːð] *vt Formal* léguer (**to** à)

bequest [bɪ'kwest] *n Formal* legs *m*

berate [bɪ'reɪt] *vt* réprimander

Berber ['bɜːbə(r)] **1** *n* Berbère *mf*
2 *adj* berbère

bereaved [bɪ'riːvd] **1** *npl* **the b.** la famille du défunt (de la défunte)
2 *adj* en deuil; **recently b.** qui vient de perdre un être cher

bereavement [bɪ'riːvmənt] *n* deuil *m*; **b. counselling** = aide psychologique aux personnes en deuil

bereft [bɪ'reft] *adj* **to be b. of sth** être privé(e) de qch; **to feel b.** se sentir totalement seul(e)

beret ['bereɪ] *n* béret *m*

bergamot ['bɜːgəmɒt] *n* bergamote *f*

berk [bɜːk] *n Br Fam* andouille *f*; **to feel a right b.** se sentir idiot(e)

Berlin [bɜː'lɪn] *n* Berlin; **the B. Wall** le mur de Berlin

Berliner [bɜː'lɪnə(r)] *n* Berlinois(e) *m,f*

Bermuda [bə'mjuːdə] *n les* Bermudes *fpl*; **B. shorts** bermuda *m*

Bern(e) [bɜːn] *n* Berne

berry ['berɪ] (*pl* **berries**) *n* baie *f*

berserk [bə'zɜːk] *adj Fam* **to go b.** devenir fou furieux (folle furieuse)

berth [bɜːθ] **1** *n* (a) *(on train, ship)* couchette *f* (b) *(in harbour)* poste *m* à quai; *Fig* **to give sb a wide b.** éviter qn
2 *vt (boat)* amarrer à quai
3 *vi (of boat)* aborder *ou* se ranger à quai

beseech [bɪ'siːtʃ] (*pt & pp* **besought** [bɪ'sɔːt]) *vt Lit* supplier

beseeching [bɪ'siːtʃɪŋ] *adj* suppliant(e)

beset [bɪ'set] (*pt & pp* **beset**) *vt* assaillir; **to be beset by doubts** être assailli(e) par le doute; **to be beset with dangers/difficulties** être en proie à toutes sortes de dangers/difficultés

beside [bɪ'saɪd] *prep* (a) *(next to)* à côté de; *(sea, lake)* au bord de; **that's b. the point** cela n'a rien à voir; **to be b. oneself with joy/anger** être fou (folle) de joie/de colère (b) *(compared to)* à côté de, par rapport à

besides [bɪ'saɪdz] **1** *prep* à part; **other people b. ourselves** d'autres gens que nous; **what else can you do b. type?** à part taper, que savez-vous faire?; **b. being an excellent singer, she also plays the violin** non seulement elle chante très bien, mais en plus elle joue du violon; **b. which she was unwell** sans compter qu'elle ne se sentait pas bien
2 *adv* en plus; **many more b.** bien d'autres encore

besiege [bɪ'siːdʒ] *vt (castle, town)* assiéger; *Fig* **to b. sb with complaints/requests** assaillir qn de plaintes/demandes

besmirch [bɪ'smɜːtʃ] *vt Lit* souiller

besotted [bɪ'sɒtɪd] *adj* **to be b. with** *(person, car)* s'être entiché(e) de; *(idea)* être obsédé(e) par

besought [bɪ'sɔːt] *pt & pp of* **beseech**

bespatter [bɪ'spætə(r)] *vt* éclabousser (**with** de)

bespectacled [bɪ'spektəkəld] *adj* qui porte des lunettes, à lunettes

bespoke [bɪ'spəʊk] *adj* (fait(e)) sur mesure; **b. tailor** tailleur *m* à façon

best [best] (*superlative of* **good, well**) **1** *n* **the b.** *(the best thing)* ce qu'il y a de mieux; **that's the b. I could find** c'est ce que j'ai trouvé de mieux; **at b.** au mieux; **the b. of it is...** le plus beau, c'est...; **at the b. of times** en temps normal; **to do one's b.** faire de son mieux (**to** pour); **to look one's b.** être à son avantage; **to be at one's b.** être au mieux de sa forme; **to bring out the b. in sb** révéler les qualités de qn; **to get the b. of the bargain** faire une bonne affaire; **to get the b. out of sth** tirer le meilleur parti de qch; **to make the b. of sth** s'accommoder de qch; **we are the b. of friends** nous sommes les meilleurs amis du monde; **to be in the b. of health** se porter à merveille; **to the b. of my knowledge** autant que je sache; **to the b. of one's ability** de son mieux; **he can sing with the b. of them** il chante aussi bien que n'importe qui; **to hope for the b.** avoir espoir; **to have** *or* **get the b. of both worlds** gagner sur les deux tableaux; *Fam* **all the b.!** bonne chance!; **my brother sends his b.** mon frère vous fait ses amitiés
2 *adj* meilleur(e); **my b. dress** ma plus belle robe; **she is b. at French** *(of group of people)* c'est la meilleure en français; **to put one's b. foot forward** faire de son mieux; **the b. part of a year** pratiquement un an; **I'm acting in your b. interests** j'agis au mieux de vos intérêts; **it is b. to...** le mieux, c'est de...; *Com* **b. before date** date *f* limite de consommation; **the b. case scenario** le scénario le plus optimiste; **b. man** *(at wedding)* garçon *m* d'honneur; **may the b. man win** *(in contest)* que le meilleur gagne
3 *adv* le mieux; **as b. I could** du mieux que j'ai pu, de mon mieux; **you know b.** c'est vous qui êtes le mieux placé pour savoir; **do as you think b.** fais comme bon te semblera; **the b. dressed man** l'homme le mieux habillé; **she came off b.** *(in argument)* elle a eu le dessus
4 *vt (in contest, argument)* l'emporter sur

bestial ['bestɪəl] *adj* bestial(e)

bestiality [bestɪ'ælɪtɪ] *n* bestialité *f*

bestow [bɪ'stəʊ] *vt* accorder (**on** à)

bestseller [best'selə(r)] *n* best-seller *m*

bestselling [best'selɪŋ] *adj (book, author)* à succès

bet [bet] **1** *n* pari *m*; **to make** *or* **place a b.** parier; *Fig* **my b. is that he'll come** je parie qu'il viendra; *Fig* **your best**

b. would be to... ce que tu as de mieux à faire, c'est de...; *Fig* **it's a safe b.** il y a gros à parier

2 *vt* (*pt & pp* **betted** *or* **betted**) *also Fig* parier; *Fam* **I b. you she'll win** je te parie qu'elle va gagner; *Fam Fig* **b. you I will!** chiche (que je le fais)!

3 *vi* parier (**on** sur); **to b. on a horse** miser sur un cheval; *Fig* **I wouldn't b. on it!** je n'y compterais pas trop!; *Fam* **you b.!** et comment!; *Fam* **John says he's sorry – I b. (he does)!** John dit qu'il regrette – tu parles!

betel ['biːtəl] *n* bétel *m*; **b. nut** noix *f* d'arec

Bethlehem ['beθlɪhem] *n* Bethléem

betide [bɪ'taɪd] *vt Lit* **woe b. him/you!** malheur à lui/à toi!

betray [bɪ'treɪ] *vt also Fig* trahir; **to b. sb to the enemy** livrer qn à l'ennemi

betrayal [bɪ'treɪəl] *n* (a) (*of person, country*) trahison *f*; **b. of trust** abus *m* de confiance (b) (*of emotion*) indice *m*

betrothal [bɪ'trəʊðəl] *n Lit* fiançailles *fpl*

betrothed [bɪ'trəʊðd] *n & adj Lit* fiancé(e) *m,f*

better ['betə(r)] (*comparative of* **good, well**) **1** *I expected b. of you* j'attendais mieux de ta part; **you should respect your (elders and) betters** il faut respecter ses aînés; **to change for the b.** (*of person*) changer en bien; (*of situation*) s'améliorer; **to get the b. of sb** avoir le dessus sur qn; **her shyness got the b. of her** sa timidité a été trop forte; **the sooner/faster the b.** le plus tôt/vite possible sera le mieux

2 *adj* meilleur(e); **to be b.** (*after illness*) aller mieux; **to get b.** (*of person, wound*) aller mieux; (*of situation, weather*) s'arranger; **he's b. at maths/running than his brother** il est meilleur en maths/à la course que son frère; **it would be b. for you to go** il vaudrait mieux que vous y alliez; **that's b.!** voilà qui est mieux!; **b. luck next time!** tu feras mieux la prochaine fois!; **the b. part of a week** pratiquement une semaine; *Br Fam* **my b. half** ma moitié

3 *adv* mieux; **to look b.** (*of ill person*) avoir meilleure mine; **b. and b.** de mieux en mieux; **so much the b., all the b.** d'autant mieux; **for b. or for worse** pour le meilleur et pour le pire; **you had b. not stay** tu ferais mieux de ne pas rester; **to think b. of it** se raviser; **to be b. off** (*financially*) être plus à l'aise; (*in situation*) être mieux

4 *vt* (*improve*) améliorer; (*surpass*) faire mieux que; **to b. oneself** améliorer sa situation

betterment ['betəmənt] *n* amélioration *f*; (*of mankind*) progrès *m*

betting ['betɪŋ] *n* (*bets*) paris *mpl*; *Fam Fig* **the b. is that...** il y a fort à parier que...; **what's the b. that...?** combien tu paries que...?; **b. slip** bulletin *m* de pari; **b. shop** ≃ PMU *m*

between [bɪ'twiːn] **1** *prep* entre; **(in) b. now and Monday** d'ici lundi; **we bought it b. us** nous l'avons acheté à nous deux/trois/*etc*; **this is strictly b. you and me** que cela reste entre nous; **b. you, me and the gatepost** (soit dit) entre nous

2 *adv* **(in) b.** au milieu

bevel ['bevəl] **1** *n* biseau *m*

2 *vt* (*pt & pp* **bevelled**, *Am* **beveled**) biseauter

beverage ['bevərɪdʒ] *n* boisson *f*

bevvied ['bevɪd] *adj Br Fam* (*drunk*) bourré(e)

bevvy ['bevɪ] (*pl* **bevvies**) *n Br Fam* (*drink*) alcool *m*

bevy ['bevɪ] (*pl* **bevies**) *n* (*group*) nuée *f*

bewail [bɪ'weɪl] *vt* (*loss*) pleurer; (*one's fate*) se lamenter sur

beware [bɪ'weə(r)] *vi* se méfier (**of** de); **b.! attention!**; **b. of the dog** (*sign*) chien méchant

bewilder [bɪ'wɪldə(r)] *vt* dérouter, laisser perplexe

bewildered [bɪ'wɪldəd] *adj* dérouté(e), perplexe

bewildering [bɪ'wɪldərɪŋ] *adj* déroutant(e)

bewilderment [bɪ'wɪldəmənt] *n* perplexité *f*; **to his b.** à son grand étonnement

bewitch [bɪ'wɪtʃ] *vt* ensorceler

bewitching [bɪ'wɪtʃɪŋ] *adj* (*smile, beauty*) enchanteur(eresse)

beyond [bɪ'jɒnd] **1** *prep* (a) (*in space, time*) au-delà de; **the house is b. the church** la maison est après l'église (b) (*surpassing*) **to live b. one's means** vivre au-dessus de ses moyens; **it's b. me** (how they can do it) ça me dépasse (qu'ils puissent faire ça); **due to circumstances b. our control** en raison de circonstances indépendantes de notre volonté; **it's b. my power** ça n'est pas en mon pouvoir; **I'm b. caring** ça m'est complètement égal; **it's b. doubt** cela ne fait aucun doute; **it's b. question** c'est incontestable; **it's b. a joke** ce n'est plus drôle; **b. belief** incroyable; **b. reach** hors de portée; **b. repair** irréparable (c) (*except*) à part

2 *adv* au-delà

3 *n* **the b.** l'au-delà *m*

Bhutan [buː'tɑːn] *n* le Bhoutan

bias ['baɪəs] **1** *n* (a) (*inclination*) préjugé *m*, parti *m* pris (**against/towards** contre/en faveur de) (b) (*in sewing*) biais *m*

2 *vt* (*pt & pp* **bias(s)ed**) influencer (**against/towards** contre/en faveur de)

bias(s)ed ['baɪəst] *adj* (*article, account*) partial(e); (*person*) de parti pris; (*opinion*) préconçu(e); **to be b. in sb's favour** avoir un préjugé en faveur de qn

bib [bɪb] *n* (*for baby*) bavoir *m*, bavette *f*; (*of apron, dungarees*) bavette *f*

bible ['baɪbəl] *n also Fig* bible *f*; **the B.** la Bible; *Fam* **b. basher** grenouille *f* de bénitier; *Am* **the B. Belt** = ensemble des États du sud des États-Unis où le fondamentalisme chrétien est très répandu

biblical ['bɪblɪkəl] *adj* biblique; *Fam Hum* **to know sb in the b. sense** connaître qn au sens biblique du terme

bibliography [bɪblɪ'ɒgrəfɪ] (*pl* **bibliographies**) *n* bibliographie *f*

bibliophile ['bɪblɪəfaɪl] *n* bibliophile *mf*

bicameral [baɪ'kæmərəl] *adj Pol* bicaméral(e)

bicarbonate [baɪ'kɑːbənət] *n* bicarbonate *m*; **b. of soda** bicarbonate de soude

bicentenary [baɪsen'tiːnərɪ], *Am* **bicentennial** [baɪsen'tenɪəl] **1** *n* bicentenaire *m*

2 *adj* bicentenaire

biceps ['baɪseps] (*pl* **biceps**) *n Anat* biceps *m*

bicker ['bɪkə(r)] *vi* se chamailler

bickering ['bɪkərɪŋ] *n* chamailleries *fpl*

bicycle ['baɪsɪkəl] *n* bicyclette *f*, vélo *m*; **to ride a b.** faire de la bicyclette *ou* du vélo; **b. clip** pince *f* à vélo; **b. kick** (*in football*) retourné *m* bicyclette

bid¹ [bɪd] **1** *n* (**a**) *(offer)* offre *f*; *(at auction)* enchère *f*; **to make a b.** *(for sth)* faire une offre (pour qch); *(at auction)* faire une enchère (sur qch) (**b**) *(attempt)* tentative *f* (**for sth/to do sth** de qch/pour faire qch); **a rescue/suicide b.** une tentative de sauvetage/de suicide; **to make a b. for power** *(legally)* faire une offre pour le pouvoir; *(illegally)* faire une tentative de coup d'État

2 *vt* (*pt & pp* **bid**) *(offer)* offrir; *(at auction)* faire une enchère de; **what am I bid for this table?** que m'offrirez-vous pour cette table?

3 *vi* **to b. for sth** faire une offre pour qch; *(at auction)* faire une enchère sur qch

bid² [*pt* **bade** [bæd, beɪd] *or* **bid**, *pp* **bidden** [ˈbɪdən] *or* **bid**] *vt Lit* **to b. sb welcome** souhaiter la bienvenue à qn; **to b. sb goodbye** faire ses adieux à qn

bidder [ˈbɪdə(r)] *n (at auction)* enchérisseur(euse) *m,f*; **the highest b.** le plus offrant

bidding¹ [ˈbɪdɪŋ] *n (at auction)* enchères *fpl*

bidding² *n Lit (command)* **at sb's b.** sur l'ordre de qn

bide [baɪd] *vt* **to b. one's time** attendre le bon moment

bidet [ˈbiːdeɪ] *n* bidet *m*

biennial [baɪˈenɪəl] **1** *n (plant)* plante *f* bisannuelle

2 *adj* bisannuel(elle)

bier [bɪə(r)] *n* brancards *mpl*

biff [bɪf] *Fam* **1** *n* gnon *m*

2 *vt* flanquer un gnon à

bifocal [baɪˈfəʊkəl] **1** *n* **bifocals** lunettes *fpl* à double foyer

2 *adj* à double foyer

big [bɪg] **1** *adj* (**a**) *(tall, large)* grand(e); *(fat)* gros (grosse); *(drop, increase)* fort(e); *(fashionable)* à la mode; **to get big(ger)** *(taller)* grandir; *(fatter)* grossir; **my b. brother** mon grand frère; **a b. problem** un gros problème; **to be a b. eater** être un gros mangeur (une grosse mangeuse); **a b. hand for our guest!** on applaudit bien fort notre invité!; **the B. Apple** = surnom de New York; **b. business** les milieux d'affaires; **Aut b. end** tête *f* de bielle; **b. game** *(in hunting)* gros gibier *m*; **b. spender** panier *m* percé; **b. toe** gros orteil *m*; **b. top** *(of circus)* chapiteau *m*; **b. wheel** *(at fair)* grande roue *f*

(**b**) *(idioms)* **it's her b. day tomorrow** demain c'est son grand jour; **to have b. ideas** avoir de grands projets; **don't get any b. ideas!** ne t'excite pas trop!; *Fam* **what's the b. idea?** c'est quoi cette histoire?; **to earn b. money** gagner beaucoup d'argent; **to make it b.** réussir; **to go in for sth in a b. way** adorer qch; *Ironic* **that's b. of you!** tu es trop bon!; **to be too b. for one's boots** ne plus se sentir; **to be b. on sth** tenir à qch; **to have a b. mouth** *(be indiscreet)* parler trop; *Fam* **b. gun** gros bonnet *m*; *Fig* **a b. name** un grand nom; *Fam* **b. shot** *or* **noise** gros bonnet *m*; **the b. time** le succès

2 *adv* **to talk b.** faire l'important; **to think b.** voir grand

bigamist [ˈbɪgəmɪst] *n* bigame *mf*

bigamous [ˈbɪgəməs] *adj* bigame

bigamy [ˈbɪgəmɪ] *n* bigamie *f*

biggie, biggy [ˈbɪgɪ] (*pl* **biggies**) *n Fam* **it's going to be a b.** *(storm, new film)* ça va faire mal

bighead [ˈbɪghed] *n Fam* crâneur(euse) *m,f*

bigheaded [bɪgˈhedɪd] *adj* crâneur(euse); **to get b.** commencer à avoir la grosse tête

big-hearted [bɪgˈhɑːtɪd] *adj* **to be b.** avoir le cœur sur la main

bigot [ˈbɪgət] *n* sectaire *mf*

bigoted [ˈbɪgətɪd] *adj* sectaire (**against** à l'égard de)

bigotry [ˈbɪgətrɪ] *n* sectarisme *m*

bigwig [ˈbɪgwɪg] *n Fam* gros bonnet *m*

bike [baɪk] *n* vélo *m*; *(motorcycle)* moto *f*; *Br Fam* **on your b.!** (**a**) *(go away)* dégage!; *(don't talk nonsense)* à d'autres!; **b. shed** remise *f* à vélos

biker [ˈbaɪkə(r)] *n Fam* motard(e) *m,f*

bikini [bɪˈkiːnɪ] *n* bikini® *m*; **b. bottom** bas *m* de maillot; **b. top** haut *m* de maillot

bilateral [baɪˈlætərəl] *adj* bilatéral(e)

bilberry [ˈbɪlbərɪ] (*pl* **bilberries**) *n* myrtille *f*

bile [baɪl] *n* bile *f*; *Fig (bitterness)* hargne *f*

bilge [bɪldʒ] *n Fam (nonsense)* bêtises *fpl*

bilingual [baɪˈlɪŋgwəl] *adj* bilingue

bilious [ˈbɪlɪəs] *adj* (**a**) *(nauseous)* nauséeux(euse); **b. attack** crise *f* de foie; **b. yellow** jaunâtre (**b**) *(bad-tempered)* hargneux(euse)

Bill [bɪl] *n Br Fam* **the (Old) B.** *(the police)* les flics *mpl*

bill¹ [bɪl] *n (of bird)* bec *m*

2 *vi Fam* **to b. and coo** roucouler

bill² **1** *n* (**a**) *(in restaurant)* addition *f*; *(for goods, services)* facture *f*; *(in hotel)* note *f*; *Fin* **b. of exchange** lettre *f* de change (**b**) *Am (banknote)* billet *m* (**c**) *(notice)* affiche *f*; **(stick) no bills** *(sign)* défense d'afficher; *Th* **to head** *or* **top the b.** être en tête d'affiche (**d**) *(list)* **b. of fare** menu *m*; **to give sb a clean b. of health** trouver qn en parfaite santé; *Fam* **to fit the b.** faire l'affaire (**e**) *Pol (proposed law)* projet *m* de loi; **B. of Rights** = les dix premiers amendements à la Constitution américaine

2 *vt* (**a**) *(give invoice to)* envoyer la facture à (**b**) *(publicize)* annoncer

billboard [ˈbɪlbɔːd] *n* panneau *m* d'affichage

billet [ˈbɪlɪt] *Mil* **1** *n* cantonnement *m*

2 *vt* cantonner

billfold [ˈbɪlfəʊld] *n Am* portefeuille *m*

billiard [ˈbɪljəd] *n* **billiards** billard *m*; **b. ball/table** boule *f*/table *f* de billard

billion [ˈbɪljən] *n* milliard *m*; *Old-fashioned* billion *m*; *Fam* **I've got billions of things to do!** j'ai des tonnes de choses à faire!

billionaire [bɪljəˈneə(r)] *n* milliardaire *mf*

billow [ˈbɪləʊ] **1** *n (of smoke)* nuage *m*

2 *vi* ondoyer

billowy [ˈbɪləʊɪ] *adj* ondoyant(e); *(sea)* houleux(euse)

billposter [ˈbɪlpəʊstə(r)] *n* **billposters will be prosecuted** *(sign)* ≃ défense d'afficher

billy-can [ˈbɪlɪkæn] *n* gamelle *f*

billy-goat [ˈbɪlɪgəʊt] *n* bouc *m*

bimbo [ˈbɪmbəʊ] (*pl* **bimbos**) *n Fam Pej* minette *f*

bin [bɪn] **1** *n* poubelle *f*

2 *vt* (*pt & pp* **binned**) *Fam* mettre à la poubelle

binary [ˈbaɪnərɪ] *adj Math & Comptr* binaire; **b. code/number** code *m*/nombre *m* binaire

bind [baɪnd] **1** *n Fam* plaie *f*; **to be in a b.** avoir un embêtement

2 *vt* (*pt & pp* **bound** [baʊnd]) (**a**) *(tie)* attacher; **to be bound hand and foot** être pieds et poings liés; **they are bound together by ties of friendship** ils sont unis par les liens de l'amitié

(**b**) *(bandage)* bander

(**c**) *(book)* relier

(**d**) *(cause to stick)* lier

(**e**) *(oblige)* **to be bound by sth** être lié(e) par qch; **she**

bound me to secrecy elle m'a fait jurer de garder le secret; **you are bound to report any change in your income** vous êtes tenu de signaler tout changement dans vos revenus

▸**bind over** *vt sep Law* sommer

▸**bind up** *vt sep* (a) *(cut, wound)* bander (b) **to be bound up with sth** *(involved)* être lié(e) à qch

binder ['baɪndə(r)] *n* (a) *(for papers)* classeur *m* (b) *(bookbinder)* relieur(euse) *m,f* (c) *(farm machinery)* lieuse *f*

binding ['baɪndɪŋ] **1** *n* reliure *f*
2 *adj (contract, promise)* qui engage ou lie

binge [bɪndʒ] *Fam* **1** *n (drinking spree)* beuverie *f*; **to go on a b.** prendre une cuite; **to go on a shopping b.** aller claquer du fric dans les magasins; **to have a chocolate b.** faire une orgie de chocolat
2 *vi* **to b. on sth** *(drink)* s'enfiler des litres de qch; *(food)* s'empiffrer de qch

bingo ['bɪŋgəʊ] **1** *n* ≃ loto *m*; **b. hall** ≃ salle où l'on joue au "bingo"
2 *exclam* et voilà!

binman ['bɪnmæn] *n Br* éboueur *m*

binoculars [bɪ'nɒkjʊləz] *npl* jumelles *fpl*

bint [bɪnt] *n very Fam* pétasse *f*

biochemical [baɪəʊ'kemɪkəl] *adj* biochimique

biochemist [baɪəʊ'kemɪst] *n* biochimiste *mf*

biochemistry [baɪəʊ'kemɪstrɪ] *n* biochimie *f*

biodegradable [baɪəʊdɪ'greɪdəbəl] *adj* biodégradable

biodiversity [baɪəʊdaɪ'vɜːsɪtɪ] *n* biodiversité *f*

biographer [baɪ'ɒgrəfə(r)] *n* biographe *mf*

biographic(al) [baɪə'græfɪk(əl)] *adj* biographique

biography [baɪ'ɒgrəfɪ] *(pl* **biographies***) n* biographie *f*

biological [baɪə'lɒdʒɪkəl] *adj* biologique; **b. warfare** guerre *f* bactériologique; **b. washing powder** lessive *f* aux enzymes

biologist [baɪ'ɒlədʒɪst] *n* biologiste *mf*

biology [baɪ'ɒlədʒɪ] *n* biologie *f*

biopsy ['baɪɒpsɪ] *(pl* **biopsies***) n Med* biopsie *f*

biorhythm ['baɪəʊrɪðəm] *n* rythme *m* biologique

biosphere ['baɪəsfɪə(r)] *n* biosphère *f*

biotechnology [baɪəʊtek'nɒlədʒɪ] *n* biotechnologie *f*

bipartisan [baɪpɑː'tɪzæn] *adj Pol* bipartite

biped ['baɪped] *n* bipède *m*

biplane ['baɪpleɪn] *n* biplan *m*

birch [bɜːtʃ] *n* (a) *(tree)* bouleau *m*; **to give sb the b.** fouetter qn
2 *vt (beat)* fouetter

bird [bɜːd] *n* (a) *(in general)* oiseau *m*; *(poultry)* volaille *f*; **b. of paradise** oiseau de paradis; **b. of prey** oiseau de proie, rapace *m*; **b. sanctuary** réserve *f* ornithologique; **b. table** mangeoire *f* pour oiseaux (b) *Br Fam (woman)* nana *f* (c) *(idioms) Fam* **a little b. told me** c'est mon petit doigt qui me l'a dit; **the b. has flown** l'oiseau s'est envolé; *Prov* **a b. in the hand is worth two in the bush** un tiens vaut mieux que deux tu l'auras; *Prov* **birds of a feather flock together** qui se ressemble s'assemble; **to kill two birds with one stone** faire d'une pierre deux coups; *Euph* **it's time you told him about the birds and the bees** il serait temps de lui expliquer que les bébés ne naissent pas dans les choux

birdbath ['bɜːdbɑːθ] *n* vasque *f* pour les oiseaux

bird-brained ['bɜːdbreɪnd] *adj Fam (idea)* extravagant(e); **to be b.** *(of person)* avoir une cervelle d'oiseau

birdcage ['bɜːdkeɪdʒ] *n* cage *f* à oiseaux; *(in zoo)* volière *f*

birdie ['bɜːdɪ] *n* (a) *Fam (bird)* petit oiseau *m*; *Fig* **watch the b.!** *(when taking photo)* attention, le petit oiseau va sortir! (b) *(in golf)* birdie *m*

birdseed ['bɜːdsiːd] *n* graines *fpl* pour oiseaux

bird's-eye view ['bɜːdzaɪ'vjuː] *n* vue *f* d'ensemble

birdwatcher ['bɜːdwɒtʃə(r)] *n* ornithologue *mf* amateur

bird-watching ['bɜːdwɒtʃɪŋ] *n* **to go b.** aller observer les oiseaux

Birmingham ['bɜːmɪŋəm] *n* Birmingham

Biro® ['baɪrəʊ] *(pl* **Biros***) n Br* stylo *m* (à) bille

birth [bɜːθ] *n* naissance *f*; **to give b. (to)** accoucher (de); **at b.** à la naissance; **by b.** de naissance; **from b.** *(blind, deaf)* de naissance; **b. certificate** acte *m* de naissance; **b. control** contrôle *m* des naissances; *Fig* **b. pangs** accouchement *m* douloureux; **b. rate** taux *m* de natalité

birthday ['bɜːθdeɪ] *n* anniversaire *m*; *Fam* **to be in one's b. suit** *(of man)* être en costume d'Adam; *(of woman)* être en costume d'Ève; **b. card/present** carte *f*/cadeau *m* d'anniversaire

birthmark ['bɜːθmɑːk] *n* tache *f* de naissance, envie *f*

birthplace ['bɜːθpleɪs] *n* lieu *m* de naissance

birthright ['bɜːθraɪt] *n* droit *m* acquis à la naissance; *Fig* droit élémentaire

Biscay ['bɪskeɪ] *n see* **bay**

biscuit ['bɪskɪt] *n* biscuit *m*; *Fam* **that really takes the b.!** ça, c'est le bouquet!

bisect [baɪ'sekt] *vt* couper en deux

bisexual [baɪ'seksjʊəl] *n & adj* bisexuel(elle) *m,f*

bishop ['bɪʃəp] *n* évêque *m*; *(in chess)* fou *m*

bishopric ['bɪʃəprɪk] *n* évêché *m*

bison ['baɪsən] *n* bison *m*

bistro ['biːstrəʊ] *(pl* **bistros***) n* petit restaurant *m*

bit¹ [bɪt] *n* (a) *(in horseriding)* mors *m*; *Fig* **to get the b. between one's teeth** prendre le mors aux dents (b) *(for drill)* mèche *f*

bit² *n* (a) *(piece)* bout *m*; *(of film, book)* passage *m*; **a b. of news** une nouvelle; **to take sth to bits** démonter qch; **to tear sth to bits** déchirer qch en petits morceaux; **to smash sth to bits** briser qch en mille morceaux; **he has eaten every b.** il a mangé jusqu'à la dernière miette; **to do one's b.** participer; *Fam* **she's a b. of all right** elle est pas mal; *Fam* **to have a b. on the side** *(have male lover)* avoir un amant; *(have female lover)* avoir une maîtresse; **bits and pieces** *(personal belongings)* affaires *fpl*; *(small items)* trucs *mpl*

(b) **a b. (of)** *(expressing degree)* un peu (de); **a b. late/ heavy/tired** un peu en retard/lourd(e)/fatigué(e); **we had a b. of difficulty in finding him** nous avons eu quelque difficulté à le trouver; **he's a b. of a know-all** il a un côté je-sais-tout; **b. by b.** petit à petit; **not a b. of it!** pas du tout!; **wait a b.!** attends une minute!; **it takes a b. of getting used to** il faut un moment pour s'y habituer; **a good b. older** nettement plus âgé(e); **a little b. (of)** un tout petit peu (de); **every b. as good/interesting as** tout aussi bon (bonne)/intéressant(e) que; *Fam* **that's a b. much!** ça c'est un peu fort!; **b. part** *(in play, film)* petit rôle *m*

(c) *Comptr* bit *m*

(d) *Fam (coin)* pièce *f*; *Am* **two bits** vingt-cinq cents *mpl*

bit³ *pt of* **bite**

bitch [bɪtʃ] **1** n (a) (female dog) chienne f (b) very Fam Pej (woman) garce f; **I've had a b. of a day!** j'ai eu une putain de journée!; **life's a b.!** chienne de vie!
2 vi Fam (complain) râler, rouspéter (about après)

bitchy ['bɪtʃɪ] adj Fam vache

bite [baɪt] **1** n (a) (of person) coup m de dent; (of dog) morsure f; (of insect) piqûre f; (of snake) morsure, piqûre (b) (mouthful) bouchée f; **to take a b. out of sth** mordre dans qch; **I haven't had a b. to eat all day** je n'ai rien mangé de la journée
(c) Fig (of speech, article) mordant m; (of sauce) piquant m
2 vt (pt **bit** [bɪt], pp **bitten** ['bɪtən]) (a) (of person, dog) mordre; (of insect) piquer; (of snake) mordre, piquer; **the dog bit him in the leg** le chien l'a mordu à la jambe; **to b. one's nails** se ronger les ongles
(b) (idioms) **to b. one's tongue** (stay silent) se mordre la langue; Fam **to b. the bullet** faire contre mauvaise fortune bon cœur; Fam **to b. the dust** (of scheme, plan) tomber à l'eau; **to b. the hand that feeds you** cracher dans la soupe; Prov **once bitten twice shy** chat échaudé craint l'eau froide
3 vi (a) (of person, dog) mordre; (of insect) piquer; (of snake) mordre, piquer; **to b. into sth** mordre dans qch
(b) Fig (be felt) se faire sentir
▸**bite off** vt sep couper d'un coup de dent; Fig **to b. off more than one can chew** avoir les yeux plus gros que le ventre; Fam Fig **to b. sb's head off** rembarrer qn

biting ['baɪtɪŋ] adj (wind, satire) cinglant(e)

bit-mapped ['bɪtmæpt] adj Comptr pixélisé(e)

bitten ['bɪtən] pp of **bite**

bitter ['bɪtə(r)] **1** n Br (beer) = bière anglaise brune faite avec beaucoup de houblon
2 adj (a) (taste) amer(ère); Fig **it was a b. pill to swallow** la pilule était amère, c'était dur à avaler (b) (harsh) (wind, cold) glacial(e); (weather) rigoureux(euse); (opposition, resistance) âpre; (struggle) implacable; (tears, disappointment) amer(ère); **to go on to the b. end** aller jusqu'au bout (c) (resentful) amer(ère); (words) acerbe; **to feel** or **be b. about sth** éprouver de l'amertume à propos de qch

bitterly ['bɪtəlɪ] adv (a) (extremely) extrêmement; (opposed) résolument, farouchement; **to b. regret doing sth** regretter amèrement d'avoir fait qch; **it was b. cold** il faisait un froid de canard (b) (resentfully) avec amertume

bitterness ['bɪtənɪs] n amertume f

bittersweet ['bɪtəswiːt] adj also Fig doux-amer (douce-amère)

bitty ['bɪtɪ] adj Fam (patchy) décousu(e)

bitumen ['bɪtjʊmɪn] n bitume m

bivouac ['bɪvʊæk] **1** n bivouac m
2 vi (pt & pp **bivouacked**) bivouaquer

bi-weekly [baɪ'wiːklɪ] **1** adj (fortnightly) bimensuel(elle); (twice weekly) bihebdomadaire
2 adv (fortnightly) deux fois par mois; (twice weekly) deux fois par semaine

bizarre [bɪ'zɑː(r)] adj bizarre

blab [blæb] (pt & pp **blabbed**) Fam **1** vt dire
2 vi (chatter) bavarder; (betray secret) vendre la mèche; **don't go blabbing to everybody** ne va pas le dire à tout le monde

black [blæk] **1** n (a) (colour) noir m; **b. doesn't suit her** le noir ne lui va pas
(b) (person) Noir(e) m,f
(c) **in the b.** (person) solvable; (account) créditeur(trice)
(d) (idioms) **it says here in b. and white** c'est écrit noir sur blanc; **he sees everything in b. and white** avec lui, c'est ou tout l'un ou tout l'autre
2 adj (a) (colour) noir(e); **a b. man** un Noir; **a b. woman** une Noire; **to be b. and blue** (bruised) être couvert(e) de bleus; **b. belt** (in martial arts) ceinture f noire; **b. box** (flight recorder) boîte f noire; **b. coffee** café m noir; **b. eye** œil m poché; Astron **b. hole** trou m noir; **b. humour** humour m noir; **b. ice** verglas m; **b. pudding** boudin m noir; **b. sheep** brebis f galeuse
(b) (evil, unfavourable) noir(e); **to give sb a b. look** jeter à qn un regard noir; **the future is looking b.** l'avenir est sombre; **b. magic** magie f noire; **it was a b. mark against him** c'était un mauvais point pour lui; **b. spot** (for accidents) point m noir
(c) (unofficial) **b. economy** économie f souterraine; **b. market** marché m noir
(d) (in proper names) **the B. Country** = la région de Birmingham (qui est particulièrement industrielle); **the B. Death** la peste noire; **the B. Forest** la Forêt-Noire; **B. Forest gateau** forêt-noire f; Br **B. Maria** panier m à salade; **the B. Sea** la mer Noire
3 vt (a) (blacken) noircir; **to b. one's face** se noircir le visage
(b) (boycott) mettre à l'index, boycotter
▸**black out** vt sep (a) (censor) rayer (d'un gros trait noir) (b) (city) plonger dans l'obscurité (c) (TV programme) interrompre
2 vi (faint) perdre connaissance, s'évanouir

black-and-white [blækən'waɪt] adj (film, photograph) (en) noir et blanc inv; (TV) noir et blanc inv

blackball ['blækbɔːl] vt blackbouler

blackberry ['blækbərɪ] (pl **blackberries**) n mûre f

blackbird ['blækbɜːd] n merle m noir

blackboard ['blækbɔːd] n tableau m (noir)

blackcurrant ['blækkʌrənt] n cassis m

blacken ['blækən] vt noircir; Fig **to b. sb's character** calomnier qn

blackguard ['blægɑːd] n Old-fashioned fripouille f

blackhead ['blækhed] n point m noir

blackjack ['blækdʒæk] n (a) Am (truncheon) nerf m de bœuf (b) (card game) black jack m, ≃ vingt-et-un m

blackleg ['blækleg] n Fam (strikebreaker) jaune m

blacklist ['blæklɪst] **1** n liste f noire
2 vt mettre sur la liste noire

blackmail ['blækmeɪl] **1** n chantage m; **emotional b.** chantage aux sentiments
2 vt faire chanter

blackness ['blæknɪs] n noirceur f

blackout ['blækaʊt] n (a) (during air-raid) black-out m inv; Fig **to impose a news b.** empêcher la divulgation d'une information (b) (fainting fit) évanouissement m

blacksmith ['blæksmɪθ] n forgeron m; (who shoes horses) maréchal-ferrant m

bladder ['blædə(r)] n vessie f

blade [bleɪd] n (of knife, sword) lame f; (of propeller, oar) pale f; (of grass) brin m

blame [bleɪm] **1** n responsabilité f, faute f; **to put the b. (for sth) on sb** faire porter à qn la responsabilité (de qch); **to take the b. for sth** endosser la responsabilité de qch

2 vt rendre responsable, faire porter la responsabilité à (for de); **to b. sb for doing sth** reprocher à qn d'avoir fait qch; **I am to b.** je suis fautif, c'est de ma faute; **the bad weather was to b.** c'était à cause du mauvais temps; **I b. myself for what happened** je m'en veux pour ce qui est arrivé; **I don't b. you for wanting to leave** je ne te reproche pas de vouloir partir; **she has nobody to b. but herself** elle n'a de reproche à faire qu'à elle-même

blameless ['bleɪmlɪs] adj irréprochable

blameworthy ['bleɪmwɜːðɪ] adj (person) coupable, blâmable; (conduct) répréhensible

blanch [blɑːntʃ] **1** vt Culin blanchir

2 vi (go pale) blêmir, pâlir

blancmange [bləˈmɒnʒ] n blanc-manger m

bland [blænd] adj (person, appearance) terne; (food) insipide, fade; (music) sans intérêt; (promise) vain(e); **despite her b. assurances...** malgré ses protestations de politesse...

blandishments ['blændɪʃmənts] npl cajoleries fpl; **to resist sb's b.** ne pas se laisser amadouer par qn

blandly ['blændlɪ] adv (speak, reply) mielleusement

blank [blæŋk] **1** n (a) (space) blanc m; **my mind is a b.** j'ai un trou; **Fig to draw a b.** faire chou blanc (b) (rifle cartridge) cartouche f à blanc; **to fire blanks** tirer à blanc; **Fam Fig** être stérile

2 adj (paper, screen) blanc (blanche), vierge; (face) sans expression; **with a b. expression on his face** le visage sans expression; **to look b.** avoir l'air déconcerté ou ahuri; **my mind went b.** j'ai eu un trou; **b. cassette** cassette f vierge; **b. cheque** chèque m en blanc; **Fig to give sb a b. cheque** donner carte blanche à qn; **b. verse** vers mpl blancs

▶**blank out** vt sep also Fig effacer

blanket ['blæŋkɪt] **1** n couverture f; **Fig (of fog, cloud)** manteau m

2 adj (general) général(e), global(e); **the government imposed a b. ban on demonstrations** le gouvernement a interdit toutes les manifestations; **b. term** terme m général

blankly ['blæŋklɪ] adv (without expression) sans expression; (without understanding) l'air déconcerté; **she stared b. into space** elle avait le regard perdu dans le vide

blare ['bleə(r)] **1** n beuglements mpl

2 vi (of TV, radio) beugler

▶**blare out 1** vt sep beugler

2 vi beugler; **the music was blaring out** la musique était à fond

blarney ['blɑːnɪ] n Fam boniments mpl

blasé ['blɑːzeɪ] adj blasé(e); **she was very b. about the accident** l'accident ne lui avait fait ni chaud ni froid

blaspheme [blæsˈfiːm] vi blasphémer

blasphemous ['blæsfəməs] adj blasphématoire

blasphemy ['blæsfəmɪ] n blasphème m

blast [blɑːst] **1** n (a) (of wind) coup m, rafale f; (of heat) bouffée f; (of steam) jet m; (of whistle, horn) coup m; **at full b. (radio, TV, heater)** à fond; **b. furnace** haut-fourneau m (b) (explosion) explosion f; (shock wave) souffle m d'une explosion; **Fam meeting her/hearing that song was a real b. from the past!** la rencontrer/cette chanson m'a ramené des années en arrière (c) **Am Fam (good time) it was a b.** c'était génial; **we had a b.** on s'est super marrés

2 vt (a) (hole, tunnel) creuser (en dynamitant); **the building had been blasted by a bomb** le bâtiment avait été détruit par une bombe; **Fam to b. sb's head off** faire sauter la tête à qn (b) **Fam (criticize)** démolir (c) **Fam (it)!** zut alors!

▶**blast off** vi (of space rocket) décoller

blast-off ['blɑːstɒf] n (of space rocket) lancement m

blatant ['bleɪtənt] adj flagrant(e), manifeste; (lie) éhonté(e)

blatantly ['bleɪtəntlɪ] adv de façon flagrante; **b. obvious** tout à fait évident(e)

blather ['blæðə(r)] vi Am Fam parler à tort et à travers

blaze [bleɪz] **1** n (a) (fire) feu m; **many people died in the b.** beaucoup de gens ont péri dans les flammes (b) (of colour, light) éclat m; **the film was released in a b. of publicity** ils ont fait une publicité monstre pour la sortie du film; **to go out in a b. of glory** s'en aller plein(e) de gloire (c) **Fam what the blazes does he want?** mais qu'est-ce qu'il veut, bon sang?

2 vt Fig **to b. a trail** ouvrir la voie

3 vi (of fire, sun) flamboyer; (of light) être éclatant(e); **the house was blazing with lights** la maison était tout illuminée; **to b. with anger (of person)** fulminer; (of eyes) lancer des éclairs de colère

blazer ['bleɪzə(r)] n blazer m

blazing ['bleɪzɪŋ] adj (burning) en feu, enflammé(e); **Fig a b. row** une violente dispute

bleach [bliːtʃ] **1** n (eau f de) Javel f

2 vt (clothes) passer à l'eau de Javel ou à la Javel; (hair) décolorer

bleak [bliːk] adj (landscape, weather) morne, triste; (outlook) lugubre; (prospect) peu encourageant(e)

bleary ['blɪərɪ] adj (eyes) rouge

bleary-eyed [blɪərˈaɪd] adj **to be b. (from lack of sleep)** avoir de petits yeux; (from hay fever, crying) avoir les yeux rouges

bleat [bliːt] **1** n (of sheep) bêlement m

2 vi (of sheep) bêler; **Fig (complain)** ronchonner (about à propos de)

bleed [bliːd] (pt & pp bled [bled]) **1** vt Med saigner; (radiator) purger; **Fig to b. sb dry** saigner qn à blanc

2 vi saigner; **her nose is bleeding** elle saigne du nez; **to b. to death** saigner à mort

bleeder ['bliːdə(r)] n Br very Fam salaud m

bleeding ['bliːdɪŋ] **1** n saignement m; **has the b. stopped?** est-ce que tu saignes/est-ce qu'il saigne/etc toujours?

2 adj (a) (wound) qui saigne (b) Br very Fam (for emphasis) **you b. liar!** sale menteur!; **you b. idiot!** espèce de con!

3 adv Br very Fam (for emphasis) foutrement; **that was b. stupid!** c'était vraiment con!

bleep [bliːp] **1** n bip m

2 vi faire bip

bleeper ['bliːpə(r)] n (pager) bip m

blemish ['blemɪʃ] **1** n (mark) marque f; **Fig it left a b. on her reputation** cela a entaché sa réputation

2 vt Fig (reputation) entacher

blench [blentʃ] vi avoir un mouvement de recul

blend [blend] **1** n mélange m

2 vt mélanger (with à ou avec)

3 vi se mélanger, se mêler; **the colours b. together well** ces couleurs se marient bien ou vont bien ensemble

▶**blend in** vi (with surroundings) se fondre (**with** dans)

▶**blend into** vt insep (surroundings) se fondre dans; **to b. into the background** se fondre dans le décor

blender ['blendə(r)] n mixer m, mixeur m

bless [bles] (pt & pp **blessed** or **blest** [blest]) vt (a) (say blessing for) bénir; **God b. you!** que Dieu te bénisse!; **b. you!** (when somebody sneezes) à tes souhaits! (b) **to be blessed with sth** (talent, beauty) être doté(e) de qch; **they have been blessed with two fine children** ils ont deux beaux enfants

blessed ['blesɪd] adj (a) (holy) béni(e) (b) Fam (for emphasis) **the whole b. day** toute la sainte journée; **the whole b. lot** tout le bazar, tout le bataclan; **it's a b. nuisance having to...** quelle barbe d'avoir à...; **I can't see a b. thing!** je n'y vois absolument rien!

blessing ['blesɪŋ] n (a) (religious) bénédiction f; Fig to **give sb/sth one's b.** donner à qn/qch sa bénédiction (b) (benefit, advantage) bienfait m; **it was a b. in disguise** finalement, ça a été une bonne chose; **it was a mixed b.** il y avait du bon et du mauvais; **to count one's blessings** s'estimer heureux de ce qu'on a

blest [blest] pt & pp of **bless**

blether ['bleðə(r)] vi Fam parler à tort et à travers; Scot papoter

blew [blu:] pt of **blow**

blight [blaɪt] 1 n (on cereals) rouille f; (on potatoes) brunissure f; Fig to **cast a b. over sth** jeter un froid sur qch
2 vt Fig assombrir; (hopes) anéantir

blighter ['blaɪtə(r)] n Br Fam Old-fashioned type m, gars m; **lucky b.** veinard m

blimey ['blaɪmɪ] exclam Br Fam zut alors!

blind¹ [blaɪnd] 1 npl the b. les aveugles mpl; **school for the b.** école f pour aveugles; **they don't know what they're doing, it's like the b. leading the b.** ils ne savent pas ce qu'ils font, ils sont aussi nuls l'un que l'autre
2 adj (a) also Fig aveugle; **a b. man** un aveugle; **a b. woman** une aveugle; **b. in one eye** borgne, aveugle d'un œil; **as b. as a bat** myope comme une taupe; **to be b. to sth** ne pas voir qch; **to turn a b. eye to sth** fermer les yeux sur qch; **b. with fury** aveuglé(e) par la colère; also Fig **b. alley** impasse f; **b. date** = rencontre arrangée avec quelqu'un que l'on ne connaît pas; **b. man's buff** (jeu m de) colin-maillard m; **b. spot** (for driver) angle m mort; Fig **to have a b. spot for maths** être nul (nulle) en maths (b) Fam (for emphasis) **he didn't take a b. bit of notice** il n'y a pas prêté la moindre attention; **it didn't make a b. bit of difference** ça n'a pas fait la moindre différence
3 adv **b. drunk** ivre mort(e)
4 vt aveugler; Fig **love blinded her to his faults** aveuglée par l'amour, elle n'a pas vu ses défauts

blind² n Br (for windows) store m

blindfold ['blaɪndfəʊld] 1 n bandeau m
2 vt to **b. sb** mettre un bandeau à qn; **to be blindfolded** avoir les yeux bandés

blinding ['blaɪndɪŋ] adj (a) (light) aveuglant(e); Fig (intensity, realization) affolant(e) (b) Br Fam (excellent) génial(e)

blindly ['blaɪndlɪ] adv Fig aveuglément

blindness ['blaɪndnɪs] n cécité f; Fig aveuglement m

blink [blɪŋk] 1 n (a) (of eyes) clignement m de paupières (b) Br Fam **to be on the b.** (of TV, machine) faire des siennes
2 vt to **b. one's eyes** cligner des yeux
3 vi (of person) cligner des yeux; (of light) clignoter

blinkered ['blɪŋkəd] adj (approach, attitude) borné(e); **to be b.** (of person) avoir des œillères

blinkers ['blɪŋkəz] npl (a) (for horse) œillères fpl; Fig **to be wearing b.** avoir des œillères (b) Fam (indicators) clignotants mpl

blinking ['blɪŋkɪŋ] adj (a) (light) clignotant(e) (b) Br Fam (for emphasis) sacré(e); **what a b. nuisance!** quelle barbe!; **you b. idiot!** espèce d'imbécile!

blip [blɪp] n (on radar screen) spot m; Fam (temporary problem) hic m inv, os m

bliss [blɪs] n bonheur m, béatitude f; **breakfast in bed, what b.!** le petit déjeuner au lit, quel bonheur!

blissful ['blɪsfʊl] adj (person) (bien)heureux(euse); (holiday) plein(e) de bonheur; **I'd rather remain in b. ignorance** j'aime autant ne pas savoir

blissfully ['blɪsfʊlɪ] adv merveilleusement; **b. happy** au comble du bonheur; **to be b. unaware that...** ne pas se douter le moins du monde que...

blister ['blɪstə(r)] 1 n (on skin) ampoule f, cloque f; (on paint) cloque f
2 vt (skin) provoquer des ampoules sur; (paint) faire des cloques sur
3 vi (of skin) se couvrir d'ampoules; (of paint) cloquer

blistering ['blɪstərɪŋ] adj (sun, heat) brûlant(e); (criticism, attack) virulent(e)

blithe [blaɪð] adj (attitude, disregard) désinvolte; Lit (person) joyeux(euse), allègre

blithely ['blaɪðlɪ] adv (ignore, disregard) avec une complète désinvolture; Lit (happily) joyeusement, allègrement

blithering ['blɪðərɪŋ] adj **a b. idiot** un(e) sombre idiot(e)

blitz [blɪts] n (air bombardment) blitz m, bombardement m aérien; Hist **the B.** le Blitz; Fam **to have a b. on sth** s'attaquer à qch

blizzard ['blɪzəd] n tempête f de neige

bloated ['bləʊtɪd] adj (stomach, face) gonflé(e); (ego) énorme

blob [blɒb] n (a) (of cream, jam, paint) tache f; (of ink) pâté m (b) (indistinct shape) silhouette f

bloc [blɒk] n Pol bloc m

block [blɒk] 1 n (a) (of wood, stone) bloc m; (for execution, of butcher) billot m; Fam **I'll knock your b. off!** je vais te casser la gueule!; **b. and tackle** (for lifting) palan m; **b. capitals** majuscules fpl en caractères d'imprimerie; **b. diagram** (flow chart) schéma m fonctionnel (b) Br (building) immeuble m; Am (group of buildings) pâté m de maisons; Br **b. of flats** immeuble m (c) (of shares) paquet m; **b. of seats** bloc-sièges m inv; **b. booking** réservation f ou location f de groupe; **b. vote** vote m groupé
2 vt (a) (pipe, road, proposal) bloquer; (view) cacher; **to b. sb's way** barrer ou bloquer le passage à qn; Fin **to b. a cheque** faire opposition à un chèque (b) Comptr (text) sélectionner

▶**block off** vt sep (road, exit) barrer

▶**block out** vt sep (light) empêcher d'entrer ou de passer; (a memory) refouler; (music, noise) faire abstraction de

▶**block up** *vt sep (tunnel, passageway)* boucher; *(door, window)* murer; **to have a blocked-up nose** avoir le nez bouché

blockade [blɔ'keɪd] **1** *n* blocus *m* (**on** à)
2 *vt* bloquer, faire le blocus de

blockage ['blɒkɪdʒ] *n* obstruction *f*

blockbuster ['blɒkbʌstə(r)] *n (film)* film *m* à grand spectacle; *(novel)* best-seller *m*

blockhead ['blɒkhed] *n Fam* lourdaud *m*

bloke [bləʊk] *n Br Fam* type *m*

blonde [blɒnd] *n & adj* blond(e) *m,f*

blood [blʌd] **1** *n* (a) sang *m*; **to give b.** donner du sang; **b. bank** banque *f* du sang; **b. cell** globule *m* sanguin; **b. clot** caillot *m*; **b. count** numération *f* globulaire; **b. donor** donneur(euse) *m,f* de sang; **b. group** groupe *m* sanguin; **b. poisoning** septicémie *f*, toxémie *f*; **b. pressure** tension *f (artérielle)*; **to have low/high b. pressure** avoir la tension basse/de la tension; **b. relation** parent(e) *m,f*; **b. sports** la chasse; **b. test** prise *f* de sang; **b. transfusion** transfusion *f* sanguine; **b. vessel** vaisseau *m* sanguin (b) *(idioms)* **to have b. on one's hands** avoir du sang sur les mains; **it makes my b. boil** ça me fait bouillir; **it makes my b. run cold** ça me glace le sang; **in cold b.** de sang-froid; **he's after your b.** il en a après toi; **to have sth in one's b.** avoir qch dans le sang; **it's like trying to get b. out of a stone** c'est comme si on se heurtait à un mur; *Prov* **b. is thicker than water** la famille passe avant tout
2 *vt (initiate)* initier

bloodbath ['blʌdbɑːθ] *n* bain *m* de sang

bloodcurdling ['blʌdkɜːdlɪŋ] *adj* à vous tourner les sangs

bloodhound ['blʌdhaʊnd] *n* limier *m*

bloodless ['blʌdlɪs] *adj* (a) *(without bloodshed)* **it was a b. coup** le coup d'État s'est déroulé sans effusion de sang (b) *(pale)* exsangue

bloodletting ['blʌdletɪŋ] *n* (a) *Med* saignée *f* (b) *(slaughter, feud)* effusion *f* de sang

bloodshed ['blʌdʃed] *n* effusion *f* de sang; **without b.** sans verser le sang

bloodshot ['blʌdʃɒt] *adj (eyes)* injecté(e) de sang

bloodstain ['blʌdsteɪn] *n* tache *f* de sang

bloodstained ['blʌdsteɪnd] *adj* taché(e) de sang

bloodstream ['blʌdstriːm] *n* sang *m*

bloodsucker ['blʌdsʌkə(r)] *n also Fig* sangsue *f*

bloodthirsty ['blʌdθɜːstɪ] *adj (person)* sanguinaire; *(film)* sanglant(e)

bloody ['blʌdɪ] **1** *adj* (a) *(bleeding, bloodstained)* ensanglanté(e); *(battle, revolution)* sanglant(e); *Fig* **to give sb a b. nose** mettre une raclée à qn (b) *Br very Fam* foutu(e); **you b. fool!** connard!; **b. hell!** merde!
2 *adv Br very Fam* **it's b. hot!** il fait une putain de chaleur!; **I'm b. tired** putain, qu'est-ce que je suis crevé; **not b. likely!** putain, il n'y a pas de danger!; **he can b. well do it himself!** il peut parfaitement se démerder tout seul!

bloody-minded [blʌdɪ'maɪndɪd] *adj Br* **to be b.** être un(e) emmerdeur(euse); **don't be so b.!** arrête d'emmerder le monde!

bloom [bluːm] **1** *n* fleur *f*; **in (full) b.** *(tree)* en fleur(s); *(flower)* éclos(e); **in the b. of youth** à ou dans la fleur de l'âge
2 *vi (of garden, flower, talent)* fleurir; *Fig* **to be blooming with health** être resplendissant(e) *ou* éclatant(e) de santé

bloomer ['bluːmə(r)] *n* (a) *Fam (mistake)* bourde *f* (b) *(bread)* ≃ bâtard *m* court

bloomers ['bluːməz] *npl* culotte *f* bouffante

blooming ['bluːmɪŋ] *Br Fam (for emphasis)* **1** *adj* sacré(e); **you b. idiot!** espèce d'idiot!
2 *adv* **b. good** sacrément bon (bonne); **b. awful** carrément horrible; **he's b. useless!** il est totalement nul!

blossom ['blɒsəm] **1** *n* fleur *f*; **in b.** en fleur(s)
2 *vi* fleurir; *Fig* s'épanouir; *Fig* **she had blossomed into a charming young woman** elle était devenue une charmante jeune femme

blot [blɒt] **1** *n (of ink)* pâté *m*; *Fig* **a b. on sb's reputation** une tache faite à la réputation de qn; *Fig* **to be a b. on the landscape** gâcher le paysage
2 *vt (pt & pp blotted) (stain)* tacher; *(with ink)* faire un pâté/des pâtés sur; **to b. one's lipstick** fixer son rouge à lèvres *(en pressant les lèvres sur un mouchoir en papier)*; *Fig* **to b. one's copybook** ternir sa réputation

▶**blot out** *vt sep (sun, light)* masquer; *(memory)* effacer

blotch [blɒtʃ] *n (on skin)* tache *f*

blotchy ['blɒtʃɪ] *adj (skin)* couvert(e) de taches

blotter ['blɒtə(r)] *n* buvard *m*

blotting paper ['blɒtɪŋpeɪpə(r)] *n* buvard *m*; **a sheet of b.** un buvard

blotto ['blɒtəʊ] *adj Br Fam (drunk)* bourré(e)

blouse [blaʊz] *n* chemisier *m*, corsage *m*

blow[1] [bləʊ] *n* (a) *(hit)* coup *m*; **to come to blows (over sth)** en venir aux mains (pour *ou* au sujet de qch); *Fig* **to strike a b. for sth** remporter une victoire pour qch; *Fig* **to soften the b.** atténuer le choc (b) *(setback)* coup *m*; **this news was a b. to us** cette nouvelle a été pour nous un coup rude; **it was a b. to her pride** son orgueil en a pris un coup

blow[2] [*pt* blew [bluː], *pp* blown [bləʊn]] **1** *vt* (a) *(of wind, person)* **the wind blew down the fence** le vent a renversé la barrière; **the wind blew the door open** le vent a fait s'ouvrir la porte; **to b. glass** souffler le verre; **to b. the horn** klaxonner; **to b. a whistle** donner un coup de sifflet; **to b. the whistle on sb/sth** dénoncer qn/qch; **to b. the dust off sth** souffler sur qch pour en enlever la poussière; **to b. sb a kiss** envoyer un baiser à qn; **to b. bubbles** faire des bulles; **to b. one's nose** se moucher; *Fig* **to b. one's own trumpet** chanter ses propres louanges
(b) *Elec* **to b. a fuse** faire sauter un plomb; *Fig (of person)* disjoncter; *Fam Fig* **the Grand Canyon blew my mind!** quel pied, le Grand Canyon!; *Fam Fig* **the prices blew my mind!** j'ai été affolé par les prix!
(c) *Fam (waste) (chance)* gâcher; **that's blown it!** ça a tout gâché!, ça a fait tout louper!
(d) *Fam (money)* claquer (**on sth** pour s'acheter qch)
2 *vi* (a) *(of wind, person)* souffler; **to b. down** *ou* **over** *(of fence, tree)* se renverser; **the door blew open/shut** le vent a ouvert/fermé la porte; **to b. on one's fingers** se souffler sur les doigts; *Fig* **to b. hot and cold** souffler le chaud et le froid
(b) *Elec (of fuse)* sauter

▶**blow away 1** *vt sep* **to b. sth away** *(of wind)* faire s'envoler qch; *Fam Fig* **to b. sb away** *(shoot dead)* descendre qn; *Fam Fig* **his latest film blew me away!** son dernier film, c'est le pied!

2 *vi (of paper, hat)* s'envoler

▶**blow off 1** *vt sep (of wind)* emporter; *Fam Fig* **to b. sb's head off** faire sauter la cervelle à qn

2 *vi (of hat)* s'envoler

▶**blow out** *vt sep (of wind)* éteindre; *(candle, match)* souffler

▶**blow over** *vi (of storm, argument)* se calmer; **the scandal soon blew over** le scandale fut vite oublié

▶**blow up 1** *vt sep* **(a)** *(balloon, tyre)* gonfler **(b)** *(explode)* faire sauter **(c)** *(enlarge) (photograph)* agrandir; *Fig* **the incident was blown up out of all proportion** on a fait une histoire incroyable autour de ce petit incident

2 *vi (of bomb)* exploser, sauter; *Fig (lose one's temper)* piquer une colère; **to b. up at sb/sth** se mettre en colère contre qn/qch

blow-by-blow [bləʊbaɪˈbləʊ] *adj (account)* minutieux(euse), détaillé(e)

blow-dry [ˈbləʊdraɪ] **1** *n* brushing *m*

2 *vt* **to b. sb's hair** faire un brushing à qn

blower [ˈbləʊə(r)] *n Br Fam (telephone)* bigophone *m*

blowhole [ˈbləʊhəʊl] *n (of whale)* évent *m*

blowjob [ˈbləʊdʒɒb] *n Vulg* pipe *f*; **to give sb a b.** tailler une pipe à qn

blowlamp [ˈbləʊlæmp] = **blowtorch**

blown [bləʊn] *pp of* **blow**

blow-out [ˈbləʊaʊt] *n* **(a)** *(of tyre)* éclatement *m* **(b)** *Fam (big meal)* gueuleton *m*

blowpipe [ˈbləʊpaɪp] *n* sarbacane *f*

blowtorch [ˈbləʊtɔːtʃ] *n (for welding)* chalumeau *m*, lampe *f* à souder; *(for removing paint)* brûloir *m*

blowzy [ˈblaʊzɪ] *adj* négligé(e)

blub [blʌb] *(pt & pp* **blubbed**) *vi Fam* pleurer comme une madeleine

blubber [ˈblʌbə(r)] **1** *n (fat)* graisse *f*

2 *vi Fam (cry)* pleurer comme une madeleine

bludgeon [ˈblʌdʒən] *vt* matraquer; *Fig* **to b. sb into doing sth** obliger brutalement qn à faire qch

blue [bluː] **1** *n* **(a)** *(colour)* bleu *m*; **Fig out of the b.** à l'improviste; **her resignation came out of the b.** sa démission nous a pris par surprise **(b)** **the blues** *(music)* le blues; *Fam* **to have the blues** *(be depressed)* avoir le cafard

2 *adj* **(a)** *(colour)* bleu(e); **b. with cold** bleu de froid; *Fam* **she can complain until she's b. in the face** elle peut se plaindre autant qu'elle veut; **once in a b. moon** tous les trente-six du mois; *Fam* **to scream b. murder** crier comme un putois; **b. blood** sang *m* bleu; **b. cheese** bleu *m*; **b. whale** baleine *f* bleue **(b)** *Fam (sad)* **to feel b.** avoir le cafard **(c)** *Fam (obscene) (joke)* grivois(e), paillard(e); *(film)* porno; **to tell b. stories** en raconter des vertes et de pas mûres

bluebell [ˈbluːbel] *n* jacinthe *f* des bois

blueberry [ˈbluːbərɪ] *(pl* **blueberries**) *n Am* airelle *f*, myrtille *f*

bluebird [ˈbluːbɜːd] *n* rouge-gorge *m* bleu

bluebottle [ˈbluːbɒtl] *n* mouche *f* de la viande

blue-chip [ˈbluːtʃɪp] *adj Fin* **b. shares** valeurs *fpl* de père de famille; **b. company** affaire *f* de premier ordre

blue-collar [ˈbluːkɒlə] *adj* **b. worker** col *m* bleu

blue-eyed [ˈbluːaɪd] *adj* aux yeux bleus; *Br Fam* **his mother's b. boy** le petit chéri de sa maman

blueprint [ˈbluːprɪnt] *n Archit & Ind* plan *m*; *Fig* projet *m*; **a b. for success** une garantie de succès

bluff¹ [blʌf] **1** *n (deception)* bluff *m*; **to call sb's b.** *(at cards)* inviter qn à mettre les cartes sur la table; *(in negotiation)* prendre qn au mot

2 *vt* **you're bluffing me** tu bluffes

3 *vi* bluffer

bluff² *n (cliff)* à-pic *m inv*

bluff³ *adj (manner)* direct(e)

blunder [ˈblʌndə(r)] **1** *n* gaffe *f*

2 *vi (make mistake)* faire une gaffe; **to b. along** *(move clumsily)* avancer d'un pas maladroit; **to b. against** *or* **into sb/sth** heurter qn/à qch

blunderbuss [ˈblʌndəbʌs] *n* tromblon *m*

blunt [blʌnt] **1** *adj (a) (blade)* émoussé(e); *(pencil)* mal taillé(e) **(b)** *(manner)* brutal(e); *(question, statement)* direct(e); *(refusal)* net (nette); *(person)* brusque; **to be b.,** ... pour parler franchement, ...

2 *vt (blade)* émousser; *(pencil)* épointer; *Fig (anger, enthusiasm)* émousser, atténuer

bluntly [ˈblʌntlɪ] *adv (frankly)* franchement; **I told him b. that...** je lui ai dit tout net que...

bluntness [ˈblʌntnɪs] *n* **(a)** *(of blade)* manque *m* de tranchant **(b)** *(of manner, statement)* rudesse *f*; *(of person)* franchise *f*

blur [blɜː] **1** *n (vague shape)* forme *f* vague; *(unclear memory)* vague souvenir *m*; **without my glasses, everything is a b.** sans mes lunettes, je suis complètement dans le brouillard; **to go by in a b.** *(of time)* passer à toute vitesse

2 *vt (pt & pp* **blurred**) brouiller, troubler

3 *vi* se brouiller; *(of memories)* s'estomper

blurb [blɜːb] *n (on book cover)* notice *f* publicitaire

blurred [blɜːd] *adj (ink)* qui a bavé; *(writing)* flou(e); *(vision)* trouble

▶**blurt out** [blɜːt] *vt sep* laisser échapper; **"I love him!" she blurted out** "je l'aime!" lâcha-t-elle

blush [blʌʃ] **1** *n* rougeur *f*; **to spare sb's blushes** éviter à qn un embarras

2 *vi* rougir; **to b. with shame** rougir de honte; **to b. at the thought of sth** rougir en pensant à qch; **I b. to admit it** j'ai honte de l'admettre

blusher [ˈblʌʃə(r)] *n* blush *m*, fard *m* à joues

bluster [ˈblʌstə(r)] **1** *n* protestations *fpl* véhémentes

2 *vi* protester avec véhémence

blustery [ˈblʌstərɪ] *adj (day)* venteux(euse), de grand vent; *(wind)* violent(e)

BMA [biːemˈeɪ] *n (abbr* **British Medical Association**) ≃ ordre *m* des médecins

BO [biːˈəʊ] *n Fam (abbr* **body odour**) odeur *f* corporelle; **to have BO** sentir mauvais

boa [ˈbəʊə] *n* **b.** **(constrictor)** boa *m* (constricteur); **(feather) b.** boa *m*

boar [bɔː(r)] *n (male pig)* verrat *m*; *(wild pig)* sanglier *m*

board [bɔːd] **1** *n* **(a)** *(piece of wood)* planche *f*; *(for notices)* panneau *m*; *(for chess)* échiquier *m*; *(for draughts)* damier *m*; *(for Monopoly® etc)* tableau *m*; *(blackboard)* tableau; **to go by the b.** *(of plan, system)* être abandonné(e); **across the b.** globalement; **b. game** jeu *m* de société *(avec des pions etc)*

(b) *(of company)* conseil *m*, comité *m*; **b. (of directors)** conseil d'administration; **b. of enquiry** commission *f* d'enquête; **b. of examiners** jury *m* d'examen; *Br* **B. of**

Trade ≃ ministère *m* du Commerce; **b. meeting** réunion *f* du conseil

(c) *(meals)* **half b.** demi-pension *f*; **full b.** pension *f* complète, **b. and lodging** *(in hotel)* pension complète

(d) **on b.** à bord; **to go on b.** monter à bord; *Fig* **to take sth on b.** *(idea, proposal)* prendre qch en considération; *(problem)* tenir compte de qch

2 *vt (ship, plane)* embarquer; *(train, bus)* monter dans **3** *vi* (a) *(lodge)* être en pension (**with** chez); *(at school)* aller en pension

(b) *Av* **flight 123 is now boarding** l'embarquement du vol 123 a commencé

▶**board up** *vt sep (house, window)* condamner

boarder ['bɔːdə(r)] *n (lodger)* pensionnaire *mf*; *(at school)* interne *mf*, pensionnaire

boarding ['bɔːdɪŋ] *n* (a) **b. card** *or* **pass** carte *f* d'embarquement; (b) **b. house** pension *f* de famille; **b. school** pensionnat *m*

boardroom ['bɔːdruːm] *n* salle *f* de réunion *(du conseil d'administration)*

boardwalk ['bɔːdwɔːk] *n Am* = passage en bois sur la plage

boast [bəʊst] **1** *n* vantardise *f*

2 *vt* **the school boasts a fine library** l'école est fière de posséder une belle bibliothèque

3 *vi* se vanter (**about** de); **it's nothing to b. about!** il n'y a pas de quoi se vanter!

boastful ['bəʊstfʊl] *adj* vantard(e), fanfaron(onne)

boasting ['bəʊstɪŋ] *n* vantardise *f*, fanfaronnade *f*

boat [bəʊt] *n* bateau *m*; *(small)* canot *m*, embarcation *f*; **to come by b.** venir en bateau, prendre le bateau; *Fig* **we're all in the same b.** nous sommes tous dans le même cas; *Fig* **to push the b. out** *(celebrate lavishly)* faire des frais; **the B. Race** = traditionnelle course d'aviron qui oppose chaque année sur la Tamise une équipe d'Oxford à une équipe de Cambridge

boat-builder ['bəʊtbɪldə(r)] *n* constructeur *m* de bateaux

boater ['bəʊtə(r)] *n (hat)* canotier *m*

boathouse ['bəʊthaʊs] *n* hangar *m* pour bateaux

boating ['bəʊtɪŋ] *n* canotage *m*; **to go b.** faire du canotage

boat-load ['bəʊtləʊd] *n* cargaison *f*; *Fig* **by the b.** par bateaux entiers

boatswain ['bəʊsən] *n Naut* maître *m* d'équipage

boatyard ['bəʊtjɑːd] *n* chantier *m* de construction pour canots et bateaux de plaisance

Bob [bɒb] *n Fam* **and B.'s your uncle!** et voilà le travail!

bob¹ [bɒb] *n* (a) *(curtsey)* petite révérence *f*; (b) *(hairstyle)* (coupe *f* au) carré *m* (c) *(bobsleigh)* bobsleigh *m*

2 *vt (pt & pp bobbed)* (a) **to b. one's head** hocher la tête (b) **to have one's hair bobbed** se faire faire un carré

3 *vi* **to b. up and down** s'agiter; **to b. about** *(on water)* se balancer

bob² *(pl bob)* *n Br Fam Old-fashioned (shilling)* shilling *m*; **that must cost a few b.** à mon avis, ce n'est pas donné; **he's not short of a b. or two** il a de quoi

bobbin ['bɒbɪn] *n* bobine *f*

bobble ['bɒbəl] *n (on hat)* pompon *m*

bobby ['bɒbɪ] *(pl bobbies)* *n Br Fam (policeman)* flic *m*

bobsled ['bɒbsled], **bobsleigh** ['bɒbsleɪ] *n* bobsleigh *m*

bod [bɒd] *n Fam* (a) *Br (man)* type *m*; *(woman)* femme *f* (b) *(body)* corps *m*; **he's got a nice b.** il est bien foutu

bode [bəʊd] *vi* **to b. well/ill (for)** être de bon/mauvais augure (pour)

bodice ['bɒdɪs] *n* corsage *m*

bodily ['bɒdɪlɪ] **1** *adj* corporel(elle), physique; **b. functions** fonctions *fpl* corporelles; **b. needs** besoins *mpl* physiques

2 *adv (grab)* à bras-le-corps; **he was carried b. to the door** on l'a saisi à bras-le-corps et puis on l'a transporté jusqu'à la porte

body ['bɒdɪ] *(pl bodies)* *n* (a) *(of person, animal)* corps *m*; *(dead)* cadavre *m*, corps *m*; **to have enough to keep b. and soul together** avoir juste de quoi vivre; *Fam* **over my dead b.!** plutôt crever!; **b. bag** = sac servant au transport des dépouilles mortelles; *Fig* **to deliver a b. blow (to)** porter un coup terrible (à); **b. builder** culturiste *mf*; **b. building** culturisme *m*; **b. count** *(of casualties)* comptage *m* des morts; *(of those present)* comptage des présents; **b. language** langage *m* corporel; **b. odour** odeur *f* corporelle; **b. stocking** *(without legs)* body *m*; *(with legs)* combinaison *f* collante; **b. warmer** petit gilet *m* chaud

(b) *(of wine)* corps *m*; *(of hair)* volume *m*

(c) *(group)* corps *m*; **a large b. of people** une foule nombreuse; **b. of evidence** ensemble *m* de preuves; **b. of water** masse *f* d'eau; **public b.** organisme *m* public; **the b. politic** le corps politique

(d) *(main part)* *(of car)* carrosserie *f*; *(of letter)* corps *m*; *(of argument)* essentiel *m*; **b. shop** atelier *m* de carrosserie

(e) *(garment)* body *m*

bodyguard ['bɒdɪgɑːd] *n (person)* garde *m* du corps; *(group)* gardes *mpl* du corps

bodywork ['bɒdɪwɜːk] *n (of car)* carrosserie *f*

Boer ['bəʊə(r)] *n* Boer *mf*; **the B. War** la guerre des Boers

boffin ['bɒfɪn] *n Br Fam Hum (scientist)* savant *m*

bog [bɒg] *n* (a) *(marsh)* marécage *m* (b) *Br* very *Fam (toilet)* chiottes *fpl*; **b. roll** *or* **paper** PQ *m*

▶**bog down** *(pt & pp bogged)* *vt sep* **to get bogged down (in)** *(mud)* s'enliser (dans), s'embourber (dans); *(details)* se perdre (dans)

bogey ['bəʊgɪ] *(pl bogeys)* *n* (a) *(cause of fear)* hantise *f* (b) *Fam (from nose)* crotte *f* de nez

bogeyman ['bəʊgɪmæn] *n* **the b.** le croque-mitaine, le Père fouettard

boggle ['bɒgəl] *vi Fam* **to b. at doing sth** rechigner à faire qch; **the mind boggles!** ça laisse rêveur!

Bogotá [bɒgə'tɑː] *n* Bogotá

bogus ['bəʊgəs] *adj* faux (fausse); *Fam* **he's completely b.** c'est vraiment un faux jeton

Bohemian [bəʊ'hiːmɪən] **1** *n (native of Bohemia)* Bohémien(enne) *m,f*; *(artistic person)* bohème *mf*

2 *adj (person, lifestyle)* bohème; *(from Bohemia)* bohémien(enne)

boil¹ [bɔɪl] *n (on skin)* furoncle *m*

boil² [bɔɪl] **1** *n* **to come to the b.** arriver à ébullition; **to bring sth to the b.** amener qch à ébullition; *Fig* **to go off the b.** ne plus marcher très fort

2 *vt* faire bouillir; **to b. the kettle** mettre de l'eau à chauffer

3 *vi* bouillir; **the kettle's boiling** la bouilloire siffle; **the saucepan has boiled dry** l'eau de la casserole s'est complètement évaporée; **to b. with rage** bouillir (de colère)

▶**boil down to** *vt insep Fam* **it all boils down to...** ça revient à...

▶**boil over** *vi (of milk, soup)* déborder; *Fig (of situation)* empirer, s'aggraver

▶**boil up** *vt sep (water, milk)* faire bouillir

boiler ['bɔɪlə(r)] *n* chaudière *f*; **b. maker** chaudronnier *m*; **b. room** salle *f* des chaudières, chaufferie *f*; **b. suit** bleu *m* de chauffe

boiling ['bɔɪlɪŋ] **1** *adj* bouillant(e); *Fam* **I'm b.!** je crève de chaleur!; **b. point** point *m* d'ébullition; *Fig* **the situation has reached b. point** la situation est explosive
2 *adv* **it's b. hot** il fait une chaleur à crever

boisterous ['bɔɪstərəs] *adj* bruyant(e)

bold [bəʊld] *adj* (a) *(brave)* hardi(e), intrépide (b) *(shameless)* **as b. as brass** culotté(e) (c) *(striking) (colour)* vif (vive); *(handwriting)* vigoureux(euse); *Typ* **b. type** caractères *mpl* gras

boldly ['bəʊldlɪ] *adv (bravely)* hardiment

boldness ['bəʊldnɪs] *n (bravery)* hardiesse *f*

Bolivia [bə'lɪvɪə] *n* la Bolivie

Bolivian [bə'lɪvɪən] **1** *n* Bolivien(enne) *m,f*
2 *adj* bolivien(enne)

bollard ['bɒləd] *n Naut* bollard *m*; *Br (traffic barrier)* borne *f*

bollocking ['bɒləkɪŋ] *n very Fam* **to give sb a b.** engueuler qn

bollocks ['bɒləks] *npl Vulg (testicles)* couilles *fpl*; **b.!** *(nonsense)* c'est des conneries!

Bolshevik ['bɒlʃəvɪk] *n & adj* bolchevique *mf*

Bolshevism ['bɒlʃəvɪzəm] *n* bolchevisme *m*

bolshie, bolshy ['bɒlʃɪ] *adj Fam* râleur(euse)

bolster ['bəʊlstə(r)] **1** *n (pillow)* traversin *m*
2 *vt (confidence, pride)* renforcer, consolider

bolt [bəʊlt] **1** *n* (a) *(on door)* verrou *m*; *(metal fastening)* boulon *m*; *Fam* **he has shot his b.** il a échoué après avoir joué sa dernière carte (b) *Fam (dash)* **to make a b. for it** se sauver à toutes jambes; **she made a b. for the door** elle s'est précipitée vers la porte; **b. hole** refuge *m* (c) **b. of lightning** foudre *f*; *Fig* **it came like a b. from the blue** ça a été comme un coup de tonnerre
2 *adv* **b. upright** droit(e) comme un i
3 *vt* (a) *(lock)* verrouiller; *(fasten with bolts)* boulonner (b) *(food)* engloutir
4 *vi (of horse)* s'emballer; *(of person)* décamper, déguerpir

▶**bolt down** *vt sep (food)* engloutir

bomb [bɒm] **1** *n* bombe *f*; *Br Fam* **to go like a b.** foncer; *Fam* **to cost a b.** coûter les yeux de la tête; **b. disposal expert** démineur *m*; **b. scare** alerte *f* à la bombe
2 *vt* bombarder
3 *vi Am (fail)* faire un bide

▶**bomb along** *vi Fam (go quickly)* foncer

bombard [bɒm'bɑːd] *vt* bombarder; *Fig* **to b. sb with questions** bombarder *ou* assaillir qn de questions

bombardment [bɒm'bɑːdmənt] *n* bombardement *m*

bombast ['bɒmbæst] *n* emphase *f*

bombastic [bɒm'bæstɪk] *adj* ampoulé(e), emphatique

bomber ['bɒmə(r)] *n (aircraft)* bombardier *m*; *(person)* poseur(euse) *m,f* de bombe; **b. jacket** blouson *m* d'aviateur

bombing ['bɒmɪŋ] *n (aerial)* bombardement *m*; *(by terrorists)* attentat *m* à la bombe

bombshell ['bɒmʃel] *n* obus *m*; *Fig* **to drop a b.** faire une révélation fracassante; *Fam Fig* **a blonde b.** une magnifique blonde

bombsite ['bɒmsaɪt] *n* zone *f* bombardée; *Fig* **your bedroom is (like) a b.!** quel capharnaüm, ta chambre!

bona fide ['bəʊnə'faɪdɪ] *adj* véritable

bonanza [bə'nænzə] *n* aubaine *f*; **a b. year** une année exceptionnelle

bonbon ['bɒnbɒn] *n* bonbon *m*

bonce [bɒns] *n Fam (head)* caboche *f*

bond [bɒnd] **1** *n* (a) *(attachment)* lien *m*; **to feel a b. with sb** se sentir lié(e) à qn (b) *Fin* obligation *f* (c) *Law* caution *f*; *Formal* **my word is my b.** je n'ai qu'une parole (d) *Com* **in b.** en dépôt
2 *vt* (a) *(stick)* coller (b) *Fig (unite)* **to b. together** créer des liens entre
3 *vi* (a) *(stick)* adhérer (b) *Fig (form attachment)* créer des liens affectifs **(with sb** avec qn)

bondage ['bɒndɪdʒ] *n* (a) *(slavery)* esclavage *m* (b) *(sexual)* = pratique sexuelle où l'un des partenaires est attaché

bonding ['bɒndɪŋ] *n (emotional attachment)* liens *mpl* affectifs; **male b.** activités *fpl* que l'on fait entre hommes; *Fam Hum* **they're doing some male b. in the pub** ils sont en train de célébrer leur amitié au pub

bone [bəʊn] **1** *n* (a) *(of person, animal)* os *m*; *(of fish)* arête *f*; **b. china** porcelaine *f* tendre; **b. meal** engrais *m (de cendre d'os)* (b) *(idioms)* **to work one's fingers to the b.** se tuer au travail; **b. idle** *or* **lazy** paresseux(euse) comme une couleuvre; **I feel it in my bones** je le sens; **b. of contention** sujet *m* de dispute; *Fam* **to have a b. to pick with sb** avoir un compte à régler avec qn; **she made no bones about it** elle ne l'a pas caché; **close to the b.** *(tactless, risqué)* limite
2 *vt (chicken, meat)* désosser; *(fish)* ôter les arêtes de

▶**bone up on** *vt insep Fam* potasser

bone-dry ['bəʊn'draɪ] *adj* complètement sec (sèche)

bonfire ['bɒnfaɪə(r)] *n (for burning rubbish)* feu *m*; *(for celebration)* feu de joie; *Br* **B. Night** = soirée du 5 novembre, célébration de la tentative de Guy Fawkes de faire sauter le Parlement en 1605

bong [bɒŋ] *n (sound)* bong *m*

bonhomie ['bɒnəmi:] *n* bonhomie *f*

bonk¹ [bɒŋk] *vt Fam (hit)* frapper

bonk² *Br very Fam* **1** *n* **to have a b.** s'envoyer en l'air
2 *vt* s'envoyer en l'air
3 *vi* s'envoyer en l'air avec

bonkers ['bɒŋkəz] *adj Br Fam (mad)* dingue

Bonn [bɒn] *n* Bonn

bonnet ['bɒnɪt] *n* (a) *(hat)* bonnet *m* (b) *Br (of car)* capot *m*

bonny ['bɒnɪ] *adj Scot* joli(e)

bonsai ['bɒnzaɪ] *n* bonsaï *m*

bonus ['bəʊnəs] *n (pl* **bonuses)** (a) *(money)* prime *f*; **b. scheme** système *m* de primes de rendement (b) *(advantage)* avantage *m*; **b. number** *(in lottery)* numéro *m* supplémentaire

bony ['bəʊnɪ] *adj (person, limb)* maigre, décharné(e); *(fish)* plein(e) d'arêtes

boo [bu:] **1** *n (pl* **boos)** huée *f*
2 *vt (pt & pp* **booed)** huer
3 *exclam* hou!; **he wouldn't say b. to a goose** c'est un grand timide

boob [bu:b] *Br Fam* **1** *n* (a) *(mistake)* gaffe *f*; **to make a b.** faire une gaffe (b) *(breast)* nichon *m*; **b. tube** *(garment)* bustier *m*

2 *vi (make mistake)* faire une gaffe

booby-prize ['bu:bɪpraɪz] *n* prix *m* décerné au dernier *(en guise de plaisanterie)*

booby-trap ['bu:bɪtræp] **1** *n* *(explosive device)* objet *m* piégé; *(practical joke)* piège *m*

2 *vt (pt & pp booby-trapped)* piéger *(en guise de farce)*

book [bʊk] *n* **1** (a) *(in general)* livre *m*; *(of stamps)* carnet *m*; *(of matches)* pochette *f*; *Fin* **the books** *(of company)* les comptes *mpl*; **b. club** club *m* du livre; **b. end** serre-livres *m inv*; **b. token** chèque-cadeau *m* pour des livres (b) *(idioms)* **physics is a closed b. to me** je ne comprends absolument rien à la physique; **in my b.** à mon avis; **to be in sb's good books** être dans les petits papiers de qn, être bien vu(e) par qn; **to be in sb's bad books** être mal vu(e) par qn; **to bring sb to b.** forcer qn à rendre des comptes; **by** *or* **according to the b.** selon la procédure; **to throw the b. at sb** infliger la peine maximale à qn

2 *vt* (a) *(seat, room, table, ticket)* réserver; *(performer)* engager; **to b. sb on a flight** réserver une place pour qn sur un vol; **fully booked** *(hotel, flight)* complet(ète) (b) *(for traffic offence)* dresser une contravention à; *(in football match)* donner un carton jaune à

▶**book in 1** *vt sep* **to b. sb in** *(to hotel)* réserver une chambre à qn

2 *vi (take a room)* prendre une chambre; *(register)* inscrire son nom dans le registre d'un hôtel

▶**book up 1** *vt sep* **the hotel is fully booked up** l'hôtel est complet; **I'm booked up for this evening** je suis pris toute la soirée

2 *vi (make reservation)* réserver

bookable ['bʊkəbəl] *adj (seat, flight)* qui peut être réservé(e)

bookbinder ['bʊkbaɪndə(r)] *n* relieur(euse) *m,f*

bookbinding ['bʊkbaɪndɪŋ] *n* reliure *f*

bookcase ['bʊkkeɪs] *n* bibliothèque *f*

bookie ['bʊkɪ] *n Fam (bookmaker)* bookmaker *m*

booking ['bʊkɪŋ] *n* (a) *(reservation)* réservation *f*; **to make a b.** effectuer une réservation; **b. office** bureau *m* de location (b) *(in football)* **to receive a b.** recevoir un carton jaune

bookish ['bʊkɪʃ] *adj (person)* studieux(euse); *Pej (approach, style)* livresque

bookkeeping ['bʊkki:pɪŋ] *n Fin* comptabilité *f*

booklet ['bʊklɪt] *n* brochure *f*

bookmaker ['bʊkmeɪkə(r)] *n (in betting)* bookmaker *m*

bookmark(er) ['bʊkmɑ:k(ə(r))] *n* marque-page *m inv*

bookseller ['bʊkselə(r)] *n* libraire *mf*

bookshelf ['bʊkʃelf] (*pl* **bookshelves** ['bʊkʃelvz]) *n* étagère *f*; **bookshelves** *(furniture)* bibliothèque *f*

bookshop ['bʊkʃɒp] *n* librairie *f*

bookstall ['bʊkstɔ:l] *n (in railway station, airport)* kiosque *m* à journaux; *(selling second-hand books)* étalage *m* de bouquiniste

bookstore ['bʊkstɔ:(r)] *n Am* librairie *f*

bookworm ['bʊkwɜ:m] *n Fig* passionné(e) *m,f* de lecture

boom¹ [bu:m] *n* (a) *(barrier)* estacade *f*; *(for sail)* bôme *f* (b) *Cin & TV* perche *f*

boom² **1** *n (economic)* boom *m*; **b. town** ville *f* en plein essor économique

2 *vi (of business, trade)* être florissant(e)

boom³ **1** *n (sound)* détonation *f*

2 *vi (of thunder, gun)* gronder; *(of person)* tonitruer

boomerang ['bu:məræŋ] *n* boomerang *m*

booming ['bu:mɪŋ] *adj (voice)* tonitruant(e)

boon [bu:n] *n* bénédiction *f*, aubaine *f*

boor ['bʊə(r)] *n* rustaud(e) *m,f*

boorish ['bʊərɪʃ] *adj* rustre, grossier(ère)

boost [bu:st] **1** *n* **to give sth a b.** *(production, economy)* relancer qch; **to give sb's confidence a b.** redonner confiance à qn; **to give sb's morale a b.** remonter le moral à qn

2 *vt Tel (signal)* régénérer; *(production, economy)* relancer; **to b. sb's hopes** redonner espoir à qn

booster ['bu:stə(r)] *n* (a) **b. (rocket)** fusée *f* de démarrage (b) *Elec* survolteur *m* (c) *Med (injection)* rappel *m*

boot [bu:t] **1** *n* (a) *(footwear)* (*for walking*) brodequin *m*; *(for sport)* chaussure *f*; *(ankle-length)* bottine *f*; *(knee-length)* botte *f* (b) *Br (of car)* coffre *m* (c) *(idioms)* **the b. is on the other foot** les rôles sont inversés; *Fam* **to give sb the b.** mettre qn à la porte; *Fam* **to get the b.** se faire mettre à la porte; *Fam* **they put** *or* **stuck the b. into him** *(kicked)* ils l'ont roué de coups de pied; *(criticized)* ils lui ont passé un savon; **he's a liar and a thief to b.** c'est un menteur et par-dessus le marché c'est un voleur

2 *vt* (a) *Fam (kick)* donner un coup de pied dans; **to b. sb out** mettre qn à la porte (b) *Comptr* amorcer

3 *vi Comptr* **to b. (up)** s'amorcer

bootee [bu:'ti:] *n* chausson *m* *(de bébé)*

booth [bu:ð] *n* (a) *(at fair)* baraque *f*, stand *m*; *(for telephone)* cabine *f*; *(in voting)* isoloir *m*; *(in restaurant)* alcôve *f*

bootlace ['bu:tleɪs] *n* lacet *m (de botte)*

bootleg ['bu:tleg] *adj (alcohol)* de contrebande; *(recording)* pirate

bootstrap ['bu:tstræp] *n* (a) tirant *m* de botte; *Fig* **to pull oneself up by one's bootstraps** se faire tout(e) seul(e) (b) *Comptr* routine *f* d'amorçage

booty ['bu:tɪ] *n (loot)* butin *m*

booze [bu:z] *Fam* **1** *n (alcohol)* alcool *m*

2 *vi* picoler

boozer ['bu:zə(r)] *n Fam (person)* poivrot(e) *m,f*; *Br (pub)* pub *m*

booze-up ['bu:zʌp] *n Br Fam* beuverie *f*; **to have a b.** prendre une cuite

boozy ['bu:zɪ] *adj Fam (voice, breath)* aviné(e)

bop¹ [bɒp] *Fam* **1** *n (dance)* danse *f*

2 *vi (pt & pp bopped)* danser

bop² *Fam* **1** *n (blow)* léger coup *m*

2 *vt (pt & pp bopped)* (*hit*) donner un léger coup à

boracic [bə'ræsɪk] *n Chem* borique

border ['bɔ:də(r)] **1** *n* (a) *(edge)* bord *m*; *(in garden)* plate-bande *f* (b) *(frontier)* frontière *f*; **the Borders** = région vallonnée du sud-est de l'Écosse; **b. guard** garde-frontière *m*; **b. town** ville *f* frontière *ou* frontalière

2 *vt (country)* avoir une frontière commune avec; *(road)* border

▶**border on** *vt insep (of country)* avoir une frontière commune avec; *Fig* **to b. on insanity/the ridiculous** friser la folie/le ridicule

borderland ['bɔ:dəlænd] *n* zone *f* frontalière

borderline ['bɔ:dəlaɪn] *n* frontière *f*, ligne *f* de démarcation; **a b. case** un cas limite

bore[1] ['bɔː(r)] 1 *n* (*person*) raseur(euse) *m,f*; (*thing*) chose *f* ennuyeuse; **what a b.!** quelle barbe!

2 *vt* ennuyer

bore[2] 1 *n* (*calibre*) calibre *m*

2 *vt* (*with drill*) forer; **to b. a hole in sth** percer un trou dans qch

bore[3] *pt of* **bear**[2]

bored [bɔːd] *adj* (*sigh, look*) d'ennui; **to be b.** s'ennuyer; *Fam* **to be b. stiff** s'ennuyer à mourir

boredom ['bɔːdəm] *n* ennui *m*

boring ['bɔːrɪŋ] *adj* ennuyeux(euse)

born [bɔːn] 1 *adj* **to be a b. writer/leader** être un écrivain/leader né

2 (*pp of* **bear**) **to be b.** naître; **I was b. in London/in 1975** je suis né à Londres/en 1975; *Fam* **I wasn't b. yesterday** je ne suis pas né de la dernière pluie

born-again ['bɔːnəgen] *adj* **b. Christian** chrétien(enne) *m,f* régénéré(e)

borne [bɔːn] *pp of* **bear**[2]

Borneo ['bɔːnɪəʊ] *n* Bornéo

borough ['bʌrə] *n Br* circonscription *f* électorale urbaine

borrow ['bɒrəʊ] *vt* emprunter (**from sb** à qn); **to be living on borrowed time** (*of ill person, government*) ne plus en avoir pour longtemps

2 *vi* emprunter (**from sb** à qn)

borrower ['bɒrəʊə(r)] *n* emprunteur(euse) *m,f*

borstal ['bɔːstəl] *n Br Formerly* maison *f* de redressement

bosh [bɒʃ] *Fam* **1** *n* sottises *fpl*

2 *exclam* n'importe quoi!

Bosnia(-Herzegovina) ['bɒznɪə('hɜːtsəgə'viːnə)] *n* la Bosnie(-Herzégovine)

Bosnian ['bɒznɪən] **1** *n* Bosniaque *mf*

2 *adj* bosniaque; **B. Croat/Muslim/Serb** Croate *mf*/ Musulman(e) *m,f*/Serbe *mf* de Bosnie

bosom ['bʊzəm] **1** *n* (*of woman*) poitrine *f*; *Fig* **in the b. of one's family** au sein de la famille

2 *adj* **b. friend** ami(e) *m,f* intime

Bosphorus ['bɒsfərəs] *n* **the B.** le Bosphore

boss[1] [bɒs] *n* (*on shield*) ombon *m*, ombo *m*

boss[2] *Fam* **1** *n* (*at work*) patron(onne) *m,f*; **to be one's own b.** être son propre patron; **to show sb who's the b.** montrer à qn qui commande

2 *vt* **to b. sb** (*about or around*) donner des ordres à qn

bossy ['bɒsɪ] *adj* autoritaire; *Fam* **a b. boots** un petit chef, un tyran

bosun ['bəʊsən] *n Naut* maître *m* d'équipage

botanic(al) [bə'tænɪk(əl)] *adj* botanique; **b. garden(s)** jardin *m* botanique

botanist ['bɒtənɪst] *n* botaniste *mf*

botany ['bɒtənɪ] *n* botanique *f*

botch [bɒtʃ] *Fam* **1** *n* travail *m* salopé; **to make a b. of sth** (*job*) saloper qch; (*interview, exam*) rater qch complètement

2 *vt* **to b. sth** (**up**) (*job*) saloper qch; (*interview, exam*) rater complètement

botched [bɒtʃt] *adj Fam* raté(e); **a b. job** un travail de sagouin

both [bəʊθ] **1** *pron* les deux; **b. (of them) are dead** ils sont morts tous les deux; **b. of us saw it** nous l'avons vu tous les deux

2 *adj* les deux; **b. (the) brothers** les deux frères; **b. my parents** mes deux parents; **on b. sides** des deux côtés; **you can't have it b. ways** on ne peut pas tout avoir

3 *adv* **b. in Britain and in France** aussi bien en Grande-Bretagne qu'en France; **she is b. intelligent and beautiful** elle est à la fois intelligente et belle

bother ['bɒðə(r)] **1** *n* (*trouble*) ennui *m*; **if it's not too much b.** si cela ne vous dérange pas trop; **to go to the b. of doing sth** prendre la peine de faire qch

2 *vt* (*a*) (*annoy*) déranger; **my back's still bothering me** j'ai toujours des problèmes de dos; **I hate to b. you but…** je suis désolé de vous déranger mais… (*b*) (*care*) **to be bothered about sth** s'inquiéter de qch; *Fam* **I can't be bothered** ça ne me dit rien; *Fam* **I'm not bothered** ça m'est égal

3 *vi* (*care*) s'inquiéter (**about de**); **he didn't even b. to apologize** il n'a même pas pris la peine de s'excuser; **don't b.!** ce n'est pas la peine!

4 *exclam* zut!

bothersome ['bɒðəsəm] *adj* ennuyeux(euse), gênant(e)

Botswana [bɒt'swɑːnə] *n* le Botswana

bottle ['bɒtəl] **1** *n* (*a*) (*container*) bouteille *f*; (*for perfume*) flacon *m*; (*for baby*) biberon *m*; *Fam* **to take to or hit the b.** se mettre à picoler; **b. bank** conteneur *m* pour la récupération du verre usagé; **b. green** vert bouteille *inv*; **b. opener** ouvre-bouteilles *m inv*; décapsuleur *m*; **b. party** = soirée où chacun apporte une bouteille (*b*) *Br Fam* (*courage*) cran *m*

2 *vt* mettre en bouteille

▸**bottle out** *vi Br very Fam* se dégonfler; **he bottled out of the fight** il a eu peur de se battre

▸**bottle up** *vt sep* (*emotions, anger*) refouler, ravaler

bottled ['bɒtəld] *adj* en bouteille; **b. water** eau *f* minérale

bottle-feed ['bɒtəlfiːd] (*pt & pp* **bottle-fed** ['bɒtəlfed]) *vt* nourrir au biberon

bottleneck ['bɒtəlnek] *n* (*in road*) rétrécissement *m* de la chaussée; (*in traffic*) embouteillage *m* (*dû à un rétrécissement de la chaussée*); (*in production*) goulot *m* d'étranglement

bottom ['bɒtəm] **1** *n* (*a*) (*lowest part*) (*of well, box, sea*) fond *m*; (*of street*) bout *m*; (*of stairs, mountain, page*) bas *m*; (*of ship*) carène *f*, fond *m*; **from the b. of one's heart** du fond du cœur; **to be at the b. of the class** être le (la) dernier(ère) de la classe; **to touch b.** (*of boat*) toucher le fond (*b*) (*buttocks*) derrière *m*; (*idioms*) **to be at the b. of sth** être à l'origine de qch; **to get to the b. of sth** aller au fond des choses; **at b.** au fond; **the b. has fallen out of the market** le marché s'est effondré; *Fam* **bottoms up!** cul sec!

2 *adj* du bas; **b. deck** (*on bus*) niveau *m* inférieur; **b. floor** rez-de-chaussée *m inv*; *Fam* **you can bet your b. dollar that…** vous pouvez être sûr que…; **b. gear** en première; **b. line** (*financially*) le solde final; *Fig* **the b. line is that he is unsuited to the job** le fait est qu'il n'est pas fait pour ce travail

▸**bottom out** *vi* (*of recession, slump*) atteindre son maximum; (*of price*) atteindre son minimum

bottomless ['bɒtəmlɪs] *adj* (*abyss*) sans fond; (*reserve*) inépuisable; *Fig* **a b. pit** un gouffre

bottommost ['bɒtəmməʊst] *adj* le (la) plus bas (basse)

botulism ['bɒtjʊlɪzəm] *n* botulisme *m*

boudoir ['bu:dwɑː(r)] *n* boudoir *m*

bouffant ['bu:fɒn] *adj* gonflant(e)

bough [bau] *n* branche *f*

bought [bɔːt] *pt & pp of* **buy**

boulder ['bəʊldə(r)] *n* gros bloc *m* de roche

boulevard ['bu:ləvɑːd] *n* boulevard *m*

bounce [baʊns] **1** *n* (a) (of ball) rebond *m* (b) Fig (energy) entrain *m*
2 *vt* (a) (ball) faire rebondir; Fig **to b. an idea off sb** soumettre une idée à qn (de manière informelle) (b) Fam (cheque) refuser d'honorer
3 *vi* (a) (of ball) rebondir (off contre); **to b. into/out of a room** (of person) entrer/sortir d'une pièce en sautillant (b) Fam **the cheque bounced** le chèque a été refusé (parce qu'il était sans provision)

▸**bounce back** *vi* (after illness, disappointment) se remettre rapidement

bouncer ['baʊnsə(r)] *n* Fam (doorman) videur *m*

bouncing ['baʊnsɪŋ] *adj* **a b. baby** un bébé en pleine santé

bouncy ['baʊnsɪ] *adj* (a) (ball) qui rebondit bien; (mattress) élastique (b) Fig (person) plein(e) d'entrain

bound[1] [baʊnd] **1** *n* (leap) bond *m*; **at one b.** d'un bond
2 *vi* (leap) bondir

bound[2] *adj* (a) (destined) **b. for** en route pour (b) (in predictions) **he's b. to come** il ne peut pas manquer de venir; **it was b. to happen** ça devait arriver

bound[3] *pt & pp of* **bind**

boundary ['baʊndərɪ] (*pl* **boundaries**) *n* limite *f*

bounder ['baʊndə(r)] *n* Fam Old-fashioned goujat *m*

boundless ['baʊndlɪs] *adj* illimité(e), sans bornes

bounds [baʊndz] *npl* (limit) limites *fpl*; **out of b.** interdit(e); **it is not beyond the b. of possibility** c'est dans le domaine du possible; **to know no b.** (of anger, ambition) être sans bornes

bountiful ['baʊntɪfʊl] *adj* abondant(e)

bounty ['baʊntɪ] (*pl* **bounties**) *n* (a) (reward) récompense *f*; **b. hunter** chasseur *m* de primes (b) (generosity) générosité *f*

bouquet [bu:'keɪ] *n* (of flowers, wine) bouquet *m*

bourbon ['bɜːbən] *n* (whisky) bourbon *m*

bourgeois ['bʊəʒwɑː] *adj* bourgeois(e)

bourgeoisie [bʊəʒwɑː'zi:] *n* bourgeoisie *f*

bout [baʊt] *n* (a) (of illness) accès *m*; (of work, activity) période *f* (b) (boxing match) combat *m*

boutique [bu:'ti:k] *n* boutique *f*

bovine ['bəʊvaɪn] *adj* bovin(e)

bow[1] [bəʊ] *n* (a) (weapon) arc *m*; (for violin) archet *m* (b) (in hair, on dress) nœud *m*; **b. tie** nœud papillon

bow[2] [baʊ] *n* (of ship) proue *f*, avant *m*

bow[3] **1** *n* salut *m*; **to take a b.** saluer
2 *vt* **to b. one's head** baisser la tête
3 *vi* (a) (as greeting, sign of respect) saluer; Fig **to b. down before sb** s'incliner devant qn (b) Fig (yield) **to b. to sb/sth** s'incliner devant qn/qch

▸**bow out** *vi* (resign) tirer sa révérence

bowdlerize ['baʊdləraɪz] *vt* expurger

bowed [baʊd] *adj* (back) voûté(e); (head) baissé(e); **b. with age** courbé(e) par le fardeau des ans

bowel ['baʊəl] *n* intestin *m*; Lit **the bowels of the earth** les entrailles *fpl* de la terre; **b. complaint** affection *f* intestinale

bower ['baʊə(r)] *n* tonnelle *f*

bowl[1] [bəʊl] *n* (a) (small dish) bol *m*; (for salad) saladier *m*; (for soup) assiette *f* creuse (b) (of toilet) cuvette *f*

bowl[2] **1** *n* **bowls** (game) boules *fpl*
2 *vi* (in cricket) lancer la balle

▸**bowl along** *vi* (of car, bicycle) rouler à toute vitesse

▸**bowl over** *vt sep* (knock down) renverser; Fig (astound) **to be bowled over by sth** être stupéfié(e) par qch

bow-legged [bəʊ'legɪd] *adj* aux jambes arquées

bowler ['bəʊlə(r)] *n* (a) (hat) chapeau *m* melon (b) (in cricket) lanceur *m*

bowling ['bəʊlɪŋ] *n* (game) jeu *m* de boules; **b. alley** piste *f* de bowling; (building) bowling *m*; **b. green** terrain *m* de boules (gazonné)

box [bɒks] **1** *n* (a) (container) boîte *f*; (larger) caisse *f*; (postal) boîte postale; **b. camera** appareil *m* photo compact (b) (on form) case *f*; (containing text) encadré *m*; (penalty) **b.** (in football) surface *f* de réparation (c) Br Fam **the b.** (television) la télé (d) (in theatre) loge *f*
2 *vt* (a) (place in box) mettre en boîte/en caisse (b) **to b. sb's ears** gifler qn
3 *vi* (fight) boxer

boxer ['bɒksə(r)] *n* (a) (fighter) boxeur *m*; **b. shorts, boxers** (underwear) caleçon *m* (b) (dog) boxer *m*

boxing ['bɒksɪŋ] *n* boxe *f*; **b. glove/match** gant *m*/match *m* de boxe; **b. ring** ring *m*

Boxing Day ['bɒksɪŋ'deɪ] *n* Br le lendemain de Noël

box-office ['bɒksɒfɪs] *n* bureau *m* de location; **a b. success** un succès au box-office

boxroom ['bɒksru:m] *n* petite chambre *f*

boy [bɔɪ] *n* garçon *m*; **a night out with the boys** une soirée avec les copains; Fam **oh b.!** ça alors!; Fam **boys will be boys** il faut bien que jeunesse se passe; **B. Scout** scout *m*

boycott ['bɔɪkɒt] **1** *n* boycott *m*
2 *vt* boycotter

boyfriend ['bɔɪfrend] *n* petit ami *m*

boyhood ['bɔɪhʊd] *n* enfance *f*

boyish ['bɔɪɪʃ] *adj* (of man) (looks, behaviour) de garçon; (of woman) (looks) de garçon; (behaviour) de garçon manqué

BR [bi:'ɑ:(r)] *n* (abbr **British Rail**) ≃ la SNCF

bra [brɑ:] *n* soutien-gorge *m*

brace [breɪs] **1** *n* (a) (on teeth) appareil *m* dentaire *ou* orthodontique (b) Br **braces** (for trousers) bretelles *fpl* (c) (pair) (of birds, pistols) paire *f* (d) **b. and bit** (tool) vilebrequin *m* (avec mèche)
2 *vt* **to b. oneself** (for impact) s'accrocher; Fig **to b. oneself (for sth)** se préparer (à qch) (b) (reinforce) consolider

bracelet ['breɪslɪt] *n* bracelet *m*

bracing ['breɪsɪŋ] *adj* (wind, weather) vivifiant(e)

bracken ['brækən] *n* fougère *f*

bracket ['brækɪt] **1** *n* (a) (for shelves) équerre *f* (b) (in writing) parenthèse *f*; **in brackets** entre parenthèses (c) (category) (of tax) tranche *f*; (of salaries) fourchette *f*; **the fifteen to twenty age b.** les quinze à vingt ans
2 *vt* (word, phrase) mettre entre parenthèses (b) (classify) associer; **to b. together** mettre dans la même catégorie

brackish ['brækɪʃ] *adj* saumâtre

brag [bræg] (*pt & pp* **bragged**) *vi* se vanter (**about** de)

braggart ['brægət] *n* vantard(e) *m,f*

braid [breɪd] **1** *n* (*of hair*) tresse *f*, natte *f*; (*of cloth*) galon *m*
2 *vt* (*hair, thread*) tresser

Braille [breɪl] *n* braille *m*

brain [breɪn] *n* cerveau *m*; **brains** (*as food*) cervelle *f*; *Fam* **to have brains** être intelligent(e); *Fam* **she's the brains of the business** c'est elle le cerveau de l'entreprise; *Fam* **to have money/sex on the b.** être obsédé(e) par l'argent/le sexe; **b. damage** lésions *fpl* cérébrales; **b. dead** dans un coma dépassé; **the b. drain** la fuite des cerveaux; **b. surgeon** neurochirurgien(enne) *m,f*; **b. tumour** tumeur *f* au cerveau; *Fam* **b. wave** (*brilliant idea*) idée *f* de génie
2 *vt Fam* (*hit*) assommer

brainbox ['breɪnbɒks] *n Fam* cerveau *m*

brainchild ['breɪntʃaɪld] *n* (*idea, project*) idée *f*, trouvaille *f*

brainless ['breɪnlɪs] *adj* stupide

brainpower ['breɪnpaʊə(r)] *n* intelligence *f*

brainstorm ['breɪnstɔːm] *n Fam* (**a**) *Br* (*mental confusion*) moment *m* d'égarement (**b**) *Am* (*brilliant idea*) idée *f* de génie

brainstorming ['breɪnstɔːmɪŋ] *n* brainstorming *m*, remue-méninges *m*

brainwash ['breɪnwɒʃ] *vt* faire un lavage de cerveau à; **to b. sb into doing sth** faire faire qch à qn à force d'endoctrinement

brainy ['breɪnɪ] *adj Fam* intelligent(e)

braise [breɪz] *vt* braiser

brake [breɪk] **1** *n* frein *m*; **to apply the brake(s)** freiner; *Fig* **to put the brakes on a project** ralentir l'exécution d'un projet; **b. fluid** liquide *m* de freins; **b. lights** feux *mpl* de stop; **b. pedal** pédale *f* de frein
2 *vi* freiner

braking distance ['breɪkɪŋ'dɪstəns] *n* distance *f* de freinage

bramble ['bræmbəl] *n* ronce *f*

bran [bræn] *n* son *m*

branch [brɑːntʃ] **1** *n* (**a**) (*of tree, family, subject*) branche *f*; (*of river*) bras *m*; (*of railway, road*) embranchement *m*; **b. line** (*of railway*) ligne *f* secondaire (**b**) (*of shop*) succursale *f*; (*of bank*) agence *f*
2 *vi* bifurquer

▶**branch off** *vi* (*of discussion*) bifurquer (**into** vers)

▶**branch out** *vi* se diversifier; **to b. out into** étendre ses activités à

brand [brænd] **1** (**a**) (*of product*) marque *f*; *Fig* **she has her own b. of humour** elle a un sens de l'humour particulier; **b. image** image *f* de marque; **b. leader** marque la plus vendue; **b. name** marque (**b**) (*on cattle*) marque *f* (*au fer rouge*)
2 *vt* (*cattle*) marquer au fer rouge; *Fig* **the image was branded on her memory** l'image était gravée dans sa mémoire; *Fig* **to b. sb (as) a liar/coward** coller à qn l'étiquette de menteur(euse)/lâche

brandish ['brændɪʃ] *vt* brandir

brand-new ['bræn(d)'njuː] *adj* flambant neuf (neuve)

brandy ['brændɪ] (*pl* **brandies**) *n* (*cognac*) cognac *m*; (*more generally*) eau-de-vie *f*; **cherry b.** cherry *m*

brash [bræʃ] *adj* exubérant(e)

brass [brɑːs] *n* (**a**) (*metal*) laiton *m*; *Br Fam* **it's not worth a b. farthing** ça ne vaut pas un clou; **to get down to b. tacks** en venir aux faits; *Br Fam* **it's b. monkey weather** il fait un froid de canard (**b**) *Mus* (*brass instruments*) cuivres *mpl*; **b. band** fanfare *f* (**c**) *Br Fam* (*money*) oseille *f*, pognon *m* (**d**) *Br Fam* (*cheek, nerve*) culot *m*; **to have a b. neck** avoir du culot, être culotté(e)

▶**brass off** *vt sep Br Fam* **to be brassed off (with)** en avoir marre (de)

brassière ['bræzɪə(r)] *n* soutien-gorge *m*

brassy ['brɑːsɪ] *adj Fam* (*person, manner*) exubérant(e)

brat [bræt] *n Pej* morveux(euse) *m,f*

bravado [brə'vɑːdəʊ] *n* bravade *f*

brave [breɪv] **1** *n* (*native American*) brave *m*
2 *adj* courageux(euse); **a b. effort** un bel effort; **a b. new world** un paradis; *Pej & Ironic* **un monde utopique; to put a b. face on it** faire bonne contenance
3 *vt* braver

bravely ['breɪvlɪ] *adv* courageusement

bravery ['breɪvərɪ] *n* courage *m*

bravo [brɑː'vəʊ] *exclam* bravo!

brawl [brɔːl] **1** *n* bagarre *f*; **a drunken b.** une querelle d'ivrognes
2 *vi* se bagarrer

brawn [brɔːn] *n Fam* (*strength*) muscle *m*; **he's all b. and no brain** il a du muscle mais rien dans la tête

brawny ['brɔːnɪ] *adj* musclé(e)

bray [breɪ] **1** *n* (*of donkey*) braiement *m*; *Fig* (*of person*) braillement *m*
2 *vi* (*of donkey*) braire; *Fig* (*of person*) brailler

brazen ['breɪzən] *adj* effronté(e), impudent(e); (*lie*) éhonté(e)

▶**brazen out** *vt sep* **to b. it out** s'en tirer au culot

brazier ['breɪzɪə(r)] *n* brasero *m*

Brazil [brə'zɪl] *n* le Brésil

brazil [brə'zɪl] *n* **b. (nut)** noix *f* du Brésil

Brazilian [brə'zɪlɪən] **1** *n* Brésilien(enne) *m,f*
2 *adj* brésilien(enne)

breach [briːtʃ] **1** *n* (**a**) (*in wall*) brèche *f*; *Fig* **to step into the b.** (*in emergency*) intervenir au pied levé (**b**) (*of agreement*) rupture *f* (**of** de); (*of trust*) abus *m* (**of** de); (*of discipline*) manquement *m* (**of** à); (*of rules*) infraction *f* (**of** à); *Law* **b. of the peace** atteinte *f* à l'ordre public (**c**) (*in relationship*) **it caused a b. in their relationship** cela les a conduits à se brouiller
2 *vt* (**a**) (*defences*) ouvrir une brèche dans (**b**) (*contract, agreement*) rompre; (*rules*) enfreindre

bread [bred] *n* (**a**) (*food*) pain *m*; **a loaf of b.** un pain; **b. and butter** du pain beurré; *Fig* gagne-pain *f*; *Fig* **he knows which side his b. is buttered on** il sait où est son intérêt; **b. bin** boîte *f* à pain; **b. knife** couteau *m* à pain (**b**) *very Fam* (*money*) blé *m*, pognon *m*

bread-and-butter [bredən'bʌtə(r)] *adj Fam* **b. issues** questions *fpl* essentielles

breadbasket ['bredbɑːskɪt] *n* corbeille *f* à pain

breadboard ['bredbɔːd] *n* planche *f* à pain

breadcrumb ['bredkrʌm] *n* miette *f* de pain; **breadcrumbs** (*in recipe*) chapelure *f*; **fried in breadcrumbs** pané(e)

breadline ['bredlaɪn] *n* **on the b.** indigent(e), sans ressources

breadth [bredθ] *n* (a) *(width)* largeur *f* (b) *(of mind, opinions)* largeur *f* (c) *(of outlook, understanding)* ampleur *f*

breadwinner ['bredwɪnə(r)] *n* to be the b. faire bouillir la marmite

break [breɪk] **1** *n* (a) *(in bone)* fracture *f*; *(in wall, fence)* brèche *f*; *(in clouds)* trouée *f*; *(in electric circuit)* rupture *f*; **at b. of day** au point du jour; *Elec* **b. switch** disjoncteur *m*
(b) *(interval, rest)* pause *f*; *(holidays)* vacances *fpl*; **(commercial) b.** *(on TV, radio)* page *f* de publicité; **without a b.** sans interruption; **a b. in the weather** un changement de temps; *Fam* **give me a b.!** fiche-moi la paix deux minutes!
(c) *Fam (escape)* évasion *f*; **to make a b. for it** se faire la belle; **to make a b. for the exit** se précipiter vers la sortie
(d) *Fam (chance)* chance *f*; **to have a lucky b.** avoir de la veine; **this could be your big b.** ça pourrait être la chance de ta vie

2 *vt (pt* **broke** [brəʊk], *pp* **broken** ['brəʊkən]) (a) *(in general)* casser; **to b. one's arm** se casser le bras; **to b. sth into pieces** mettre qch en morceaux; **to b. the sound barrier** franchir le mur du son; *Fig* **to b. the ice** briser la glace; **to b. one's journey** s'arrêter en route; *Fig* **b. a leg!** *(good luck!)* bonne chance!
(b) *(cushion) (fall, force)* amortir
(c) *(destroy) (person, resistance, strike)* briser; *(health)* ruiner; **to b. sb's heart** briser le cœur à qn; **to b. sb's serve** *(in tennis)* prendre le service de qn
(d) *(infringe) (agreement, promise)* rompre; *(rule, speed limit)* enfreindre
(e) *(news, story)* annoncer *(to* à*)*

3 *vi* (a) *(of glass, machine, bone)* se casser; *(of weather)* changer; *(of day)* se lever; *(of waves)* se briser; *(of voice) (with emotion)* se briser; *(at puberty)* muer; **to b. in two** se casser en deux; **to b. loose** se détacher
(b) *(of news, story)* éclater

▶**break away** *vi* (a) *(escape)* **to b. away from** *(person)* échapper à; *(place)* s'évader de (b) **to b. away from** *(cut ties with) (party, country)* quitter; *(family)* couper les ponts avec

▶**break down 1** *vt sep* (a) *(destroy) (resistance)* briser (b) *(analyze) (argument, figures)* décomposer **(into** en*)*
2 *vi* (a) *(of car, machine)* tomber en panne; *(of talks)* échouer; *(of argument)* s'effondrer; *(of person under pressure)* craquer; **to b. down (in tears)** fondre en larmes (b) *(change chemically)* se décomposer **(into** en*)*

▶**break even** *vi* rentrer dans ses frais

▶**break in 1** *vt sep (horse)* dresser; *(new shoes)* faire; *(new recruit)* former; **to b. oneself in to sth** se faire à qch
2 *vi (of burglar)* entrer par effraction

▶**break into** *vt insep* (a) *(of burglar)* entrer par effraction dans (b) *(begin suddenly)* **to b. into laughter** éclater de rire; **to b. into song/a run** se mettre à chanter/courir (c) *(showbusiness)* percer dans; *(market)* percer sur

▶**break off 1** *vt sep* (a) *(detach) (twig, handle)* casser (b) *(terminate) (relations, engagement)* rompre
2 *vi* (a) *(become detached)* se casser (b) *(stop talking, working)* s'interrompre

▶**break open 1** *vt sep (door)* enfoncer; *(lock, safe)* forcer
2 *vi* s'ouvrir

▶**break out** *vi* (a) *(escape)* s'évader **(of** de*)* (b) *(of argument)* éclater; *(of disease)* se déclarer; **to b. out in a sweat** se mettre à transpirer; **to b. out in a rash** avoir une éruption de boutons

▶**break through 1** *vt insep (wall)* faire une brèche dans; *(barrier)* forcer; *Fig (someone's reserve, shyness)* vaincre
2 *vi (of sun)* percer les nuages

▶**break up 1** *vt sep* (a) *(reduce to pieces)* couper en morceaux (b) *(estate, company)* morceler; *(machine)* démonter (c) *(fight, quarrel)* faire cesser
2 *vi* (a) *(disintegrate)* se disloquer (b) *(end) (of talks)* cesser; *(of meeting, school term)* se terminer; *(of school)* fermer; *(of pupils)* être en vacances; **to b. up with sb** *(end relationship)* rompre avec qn

▶**break with** *vt insep* rompre avec

breakable ['breɪkəbəl] **1** *n* **breakables** objets *mpl* fragiles
2 *adj* fragile

breakage ['breɪkɪdʒ] *n* **were there any breakages?** est-ce qu'il y a eu de la casse?; **all breakages must be paid for** *(sign)* tout article cassé doit être payé

breakaway ['breɪkəweɪ] *adj* dissident(e)

breakdown ['breɪkdaʊn] *n* (a) *(of car, machine, computer)* panne *f*; *(of talks, in communication)* rupture *f*; **(nervous) breakdown** dépression *f* (nerveuse); **to have a b.** *(of motorist)* tomber en panne; *(of person under pressure)* faire une dépression; **b. truck** dépanneuse *f*, camion *m* de dépannage (b) *(analysis) (of figures, costs)* détail *m*

breaker ['breɪkə(r)] *n (wave)* déferlante *f*

break-even point [breɪk'iːvənpɔɪnt] *n Fin* seuil *m* de rentabilité

breakfast ['brekfəst] **1** *n* petit déjeuner *m*; **to have b.** prendre son petit déjeuner, déjeuner; **b. cereal** céréales *fpl*; **b. television** émissions *fpl* (télévisées) du matin
2 *vi* prendre son petit déjeuner, déjeuner; **to b. on sth** manger qch au petit déjeuner

break-in ['breɪkɪn] *n* cambriolage *m*

breaking ['breɪkɪŋ] *n* (a) *Law* **b. and entering** entrée *f* par effraction (b) **b. point** *(of patience)* limite *f*; **to reach b. point** *(of person)* être à bout; *(of marriage)* être au bord de la rupture

breakneck ['breɪknek] *adj* **at b. speed** à toute allure

break-out ['breɪkaʊt] *n (from prison)* évasion *f*

breakthrough ['breɪkθruː] *n (discovery)* découverte *f* majeure; **there has been a b. in talks** un pas décisif a été franchi dans les négociations; **to make a b.** *(discovery)* faire une découverte majeure; *(in talks)* faire un pas décisif

breakwater ['breɪkwɔːtə(r)] *n* brise-lames *m inv*

bream [briːm] *n (pl* **bream)** *n* brème *f*

breast [brest] *n (of woman) & Lit (of man)* sein *m*; *(of chicken)* blanc *m*; **to make a clean b. of it** tout avouer; **b. cancer** cancer *m* du sein; **b. pocket** poche *f* de poitrine

breastbone ['brestbəʊn] *n* sternum *m*

breast-feed ['brestfiːd] *(pt & pp* **breast-fed** ['brestfed]) *vt & vi* allaiter

breastplate ['brestpleɪt] *n* plastron *m (de cuirasse)*

breaststroke ['brest(t)strəʊk] *n* brasse *f*

breath [breθ] *n* souffle *m*; **to take a deep b.** inspirer profondément; **to pause for b.** s'arrêter pour reprendre sa respiration; **bad b.** mauvaise haleine *f*; **they are not to be mentioned in the same b.** on ne saurait les comparer; **in the next b.** aussitôt après; *also Fig* **to hold one's b.** retenir son souffle; *Fam* **don't hold your b.!** c'est pas demain la veille!; **to waste one's b.** gaspiller sa salive; **out of b.** à bout de souffle, hors d'haleine; **to get short of b.** s'essouffler; **to get one's b. back** reprendre haleine, reprendre son souffle; **under one's b.** à voix basse; *Fig* to take sb's b. away couper le souffle à qn; a b. of wind/of air un souffle de vent/d'air; to go out for a b. of fresh air sortir prendre l'air; *Fig* she's a real b. of fresh air elle apporte une bouffée d'air frais; b. test Alcotest®

breathalyse, breathalyze ['breθəlaɪz] *vt* faire passer l'Alcotest® à

breathalyser, breathalyzer ['breθəlaɪzə(r)] *n* Alcotest®

breathe [briːð] 1 *vt* (a) (*inhale*) respirer (b) (*idioms*) to b. a sigh of relief pousser un soupir de soulagement; *Lit* to b. one's last rendre son dernier soupir; don't b. a word (of it)! pas un mot!; to b. fire (*in anger*) jeter feu et flammes; to b. new life into sth (*project, scheme*) insuffler une force nouvelle à qch
2 *vi* respirer; (*exhale*) souffler; to b. heavily (*noisily*) respirer bruyamment; (*with difficulty*) respirer avec difficulté; *Fig* to b. easily again respirer; *Fig* to b. down sb's neck (*follow*) talonner qn; (*nag*) être tout le temps sur le dos de qn

▸**breathe in** *vt* inhaler
2 *vi* inspirer

▸**breathe out** *vi* expirer

breather ['briːðə(r)] *n Fam* (*rest*) pause *f*; to take a b. faire une pause

breathing ['briːðɪŋ] *n* respiration *f*; b. apparatus bouteille *f* d'oxygène et masque; *Fig* to give sb some b. space laisser respirer qn

breathless ['breθlɪs] *adj* (*person*) hors d'haleine; (*calm*) plat(e); (*silence*) profond(e)

breathtaking ['breθteɪkɪŋ] *adj* (*beauty, scenery*) à couper le souffle; (*speed*) vertigineux(euse); (*audacity*) sidérant(e)

breathy ['breθɪ] *adj* (*voice*) haletant(e)

bred [bred] *pt & pp of* **breed**

breech [briːtʃ] *n* (a) *Med* b. delivery *or* birth (accouchement *m* par le) siège *m* (b) (*of gun*) culasse *f*

breeches ['brɪtʃɪz] *npl* (pair of) b. culotte *f*

breed [briːd] 1 *n also Fig* race *f*
2 *vt* (*pt & pp* bred [bred]) (*animals*) élever; *Fig* (*discontent*) engendrer
3 *vi* se reproduire

breeder ['briːdə(r)] *n* (*of animals*) éleveur(euse) *m,f*; *Phys* b. reactor surgénérateur *m*

breeding ['briːdɪŋ] *n* (a) (*of animals*) élevage *m*; b. ground lieu *m* de reproduction; *Fig* (*of discontent, revolution*) foyer *m* (b) (*of person*) (good) b. éducation *f*, manières *fpl*

breeze [briːz] 1 *n* brise *f*; *Am Fam* it was a b. c'était du gâteau
2 *vi* to b. in/out (*quickly*) entrer/sortir en coup de vent; (*casually*) entrer/sortir avec désinvolture

breeze-block ['briːzblɒk] *n Br* parpaing *m*

breezy ['briːzɪ] *adj* (a) (*weather*) venteux(euse) (b) (*casual*) désinvolte

brethren ['breðrən] *npl Rel* frères *mpl*

Breton ['bretən] 1 *n* Breton(onne) *m,f*
2 *adj* breton(onne)

breviary ['briːvɪərɪ] *n* (*pl* breviaries) *n Rel* bréviaire *m*

brevity ['brevɪtɪ] *n* brièveté *f*

brew [bruː] 1 *n* (*beer*) bière *f*; (*tea*) thé *m*; *Fig* (*mixture*) mélange *m*
2 *vt* (*beer*) brasser; (*tea*) faire infuser, préparer
3 *vi* (*of beer*) fermenter; (*of tea*) infuser; there's a storm brewing il y a de l'orage dans l'air; *Fig* there's something brewing il se trame quelque chose; there's trouble brewing il va y avoir du grabuge

▸**brew up** *vi Br Fam* faire du thé

brewer ['bruːə(r)] *n* brasseur *m*

brewery ['bruːərɪ] (*pl* breweries) *n* brasserie *f* (*fabrique*)

briar ['braɪə(r)] *n* (*plant*) bruyère *f*; (*pipe*) pipe *f* de bruyère; b. rose églantine *f*

bribe [braɪb] 1 *n* pot-de-vin *m*
2 *vt* acheter; to b. sb into doing sth acheter qn pour qu'il fasse qch

bribery ['braɪbərɪ] *n* corruption *f*

bric-à-brac ['brɪkəbræk] *n* bric-à-brac *m*

brick [brɪk] *n* (a) (*for building*) brique *f*; *Fig* to drop a b. faire une gaffe; b. wall mur *m* en briques; you're banging your head against a b. wall tu perds ton temps (b) *Br Fam Old-fashioned* (*kind man*) chic type *m*; (*kind woman*) chic fille *f*

▸**brick up** *vt sep* murer

brickie ['brɪkɪ] *n Br Fam* maçon *m*

bricklayer ['brɪkleɪə(r)] *n* maçon *m*

brickwork ['brɪkwɜːk] *n* briquetage *m*

bridal ['braɪdəl] *adj* nuptial(e); b. dress *or* gown robe *f* de mariée; b. suite suite *f* nuptiale

bride [braɪd] *n* mariée *f*; the b. and groom les mariés *mpl*

bridegroom ['braɪdgruːm] *n* marié *m*

bridesmaid ['braɪdzmeɪd] *n* demoiselle *f* d'honneur

bridge[1] ['brɪdʒ] *n* (*over river*) pont *m*; (*on ship*) passerelle *f*; (*on teeth*) bridge *m*; (*of nose*) arête *f*; *Fig* we'll cross that b. when we come to it chaque chose en son temps; *Fig* b. building réconciliation *f*
2 *vt* (*river*) construire un pont sur; to b. a gap (*in knowledge*) combler une lacune; to b. the gap between rich and poor combler le fossé entre les riches et les pauvres

bridge[2] *n* (*card game*) bridge *m*

bridgehead ['brɪdʒhed] *n Mil* tête *f* de pont

bridging loan ['brɪdʒɪŋləʊn] *n Fin* prêt-relais *m*

bridle ['braɪdəl] 1 *n* bride *f*; b. path piste *f* cavalière
2 *vt* (*horse*) brider
3 *vi* (*with anger*) s'indigner (at de)

brief [briːf] 1 *n Law* dossier *m*; (*instructions*) consignes *fpl*
2 *adj* bref (brève); (*garment*) court(e); in b.,..., to be b.,... en bref,...
3 *vt* (*inform*) mettre au courant (on de)

briefcase ['briːfkeɪs] *n* serviette *f*

briefing ['briːfɪŋ] *n* (*meeting*) briefing *m*; (*information*) instructions *fpl*

briefly ['briːflɪ] *adv* brièvement; (*hesitate, smile*) pendant un court instant; (put) b.,... en bref,...

briefs [briːfs] *npl* (*underwear*) slip *m*

brier ['braɪə(r)] = **briar**

brigade [brɪ'geɪd] *n* brigade *f*

brigadier [brɪgə'dɪə(r)] *n* général *m* de brigade

brigand ['brɪgənd] *n Lit* brigand *m*

bright [braɪt] **1** adj (a) (sun, light) brillant(e); (day) clair(e); (colour) vif (vive); **to go b. red** (blush) devenir rouge comme une tomate (b) (hopeful) **the future looks b.** l'avenir s'annonce bien; **the situation is looking a bit brighter** la situation commence à s'améliorer; *Fig* **the only b. spot is...** la seule chose positive est...; **to look on the b. side (of things)** prendre les choses du bon côté (c) (cheerful) vif (vive) (d) (clever) (person) intelligent(e); (idea) lumineux(euse); **to be b. at sth** être doué(e) en qch
2 adv **b. and early** de bon matin

brighten ['braɪtən] **1** vt (room, mood) égayer
2 vi (of weather, sky) s'éclaircir; (of face, eyes) s'éclairer; (of prospects) s'améliorer

▸**brighten up 1** vt sep (room) égayer
2 vi (of person) devenir plus gai(e); (of weather, sky) s'éclaircir; (of face) s'éclairer; (of prospects) s'améliorer

bright-eyed ['braɪtaɪd] adj aux yeux brillants; *Fig* (eager) enthousiaste; *Fam* **b. and bushy-tailed** frais (fraîche) et dispos(e)

brightly ['braɪtlɪ] adv (say) gaiement; (lit, coloured) vivement; **the sun was shining b.** il faisait un soleil radieux; **to smile b.** faire un sourire radieux

brightness ['braɪtnɪs] n (of light, sun, colour) éclat m; (of lighting) intensité f; (on TV) luminosité f

brilliance ['brɪljəns] n (a) (of light, colour) éclat m (b) (of person) intelligence f; (of idea) ingéniosité f

brilliant ['brɪljənt] adj (a) (light) éclatant(e); (sun, smile) radieux(euse) (b) (scientist, career, pupil) brillant(e) (c) (excellent) formidable

brilliantly ['brɪljəntlɪ] adv (a) (coloured, lit) vivement (b) (acted, played) brillamment

brim [brɪm] **1** n (of cup, glass, hat) bord m; **to be full to the b. (with)** être plein(e) à ras bord (de)
2 vi (pt & pp **brimmed**) **to be brimming with sth** (liquid) être rempli(e) à ras bord de qch; (enthusiasm, ideas) déborder de qch; **eyes brimming with tears** yeux noyés de larmes

▸**brim over** vi also *Fig* déborder (**with** de)

brimful ['brɪmfʊl] adj plein(e) à ras bord; *Fig* **b. of health/life** débordant(e) de santé/vie

brimstone ['brɪmstəʊn] n *Fig* **to preach fire and b.** menacer les fidèles des feux de l'enfer

brine [braɪn] n saumure f

bring [brɪŋ] (pt & pp **brought** [brɔːt]) vt (a) (cause to come) (object, letter, news) apporter; (person, animal) amener; **to b. sth to sb's attention** signaler qch à l'attention de qn; **what brings you to London?** qu'est-ce qui vous amène à Londres?; **to b. sth out of sth** (box, bag) sortir qch de qch; **to b. a child into the world** mettre un enfant au monde; *Law* **to b. an action against sb** intenter un procès à qn
(b) (cause) provoquer; **it has brought me great happiness** cela m'a procuré un grand bonheur; **to b. sb (good) luck/bad luck** porter bonheur/malheur à qn; **to b. new hope to sb** redonner de l'espoir à qn; **to b. tears to sb's eyes** faire venir les larmes aux yeux de qn
(c) (to a particular condition) **to b. sth into disrepute** discréditer qch; **to b. sth into question** remettre qch en question; **to b. sth to an end** mettre fin à qch; **to b. sth to light** (crime, secret) révéler qch; **to b. sth to mind** faire penser à qch; **I couldn't bring myself to do it** je n'ai pas pu me décider ou me résoudre à le faire
(d) (be sold for) rapporter

▸**bring about** vt sep (cause) entraîner, provoquer

▸**bring along** vt sep (person) amener; (object) apporter

▸**bring back** vt sep (a) (person) ramener; (gift) rapporter; **to b. sb back to life** ramener qn à la vie; **to b. sb back to health** rendre la santé à qn (b) (memory) rappeler (c) (law, practice) rétablir

▸**bring down** vt sep (a) (from shelf, attic) descendre (b) (soldier, plane) abattre; (government) faire tomber, renverser; *Fam* **her performance brought the house down** son interprétation lui a valu des applaudissements enthousiastes (c) (lower) (price, temperature) faire baisser

▸**bring forward** vt sep (a) (proposal) émettre; (plan) proposer; (reasons, evidence) avancer (b) (advance time of) avancer (c) *Com* (in bookkeeping) reporter

▸**bring in** vt sep (a) (expert, consultant) faire appel à; **the police brought him in for questioning** la police l'a emmené au poste pour l'interroger (b) (earn) (of person) gagner; (of investment, sale) rapporter (c) (law, act) introduire (d) *Law* (verdict) rendre

▸**bring off** vt sep (accomplish) réussir

▸**bring on** vt sep (cause) provoquer; **you've brought it on yourself** tu l'as cherché

▸**bring out** vt sep (a) (publish) sortir (b) (cause to appear) **to b. out the best/the worst in sb** faire ressortir les qualités/les défauts de qn; **strawberries b. her out in a rash** les fraises lui donnent de l'urticaire; **to b. sb out of their shell** faire sortir qn de sa coquille

▸**bring round** vt sep (a) (revive) ranimer, faire revenir à soi (b) (persuade) convaincre; **she brought him round to her point of view** elle l'a rallié à son point de vue (c) (conversation) amener (**to** sur)

▸**bring to** vt sep (revive) ranimer, faire revenir à soi

▸**bring together** vt sep réunir

▸**bring up** vt sep (a) (subject) soulever (b) (child) élever; **I was brought up to be polite** on m'a appris à être poli (c) (vomit) vomir

bring-and-buy ['brɪŋən'baɪ] n *Br* (sale) vente f de charité

brink [brɪŋk] n also *Fig* bord m; *Fig* **to be on the b. of sth** (war, ruin, disaster) être au bord de qch; (death, success) être à deux doigts de qch; **to be on the b. of doing sth** être à deux doigts de faire qch

brinkmanship ['brɪŋkmənʃɪp] n politique f de la corde raide

brisk [brɪsk] adj (a) (weather) frais (fraîche); (wind) vivifiant(e) (b) (person) (efficient) énergique; (dismissive) vif (vive) (c) (rapid) **at a b. pace** (work) rapidement; (walk) d'un pas vif; **to go for a b. walk** se promener d'un pas vif; **business is b.** les affaires marchent bien

briskly ['brɪsklɪ] adv (a) (efficiently) énergiquement; (dismissively) vivement (b) (rapidly) (walk) d'un pas vif

bristle ['brɪsəl] **1** n (a) (of plant, brush, face) poil m; (of pig) soie f
2 vi (a) (of animal, animal's fur) se hérisser; **to b. (with anger) (at)** se hérisser (à) (b) **to be bristling with** (people) grouiller de; (difficulties) être hérissé(e) de

Brit [brɪt] n *Fam* Britannique mf

Britain ['brɪtən] n la Grande-Bretagne

British ['brɪtɪʃ] **1** npl **the B.** les Britanniques mpl
2 adj britannique; **B. Columbia** la Colombie-Britannique; **the B. Isles** les îles fpl Britanniques; **B. Summer Time** heure f d'été (en Grande-Bretagne)

Briton ['brɪtən] n Britannique mf; *Hist* **ancient B.** Breton(onne) m,f (de la Grande-Bretagne)

Brittany ['brɪtənɪ] n la Bretagne

brittle ['brɪtəl] adj (object, hair, voice) cassant(e); (bones) friable

broach [brəʊtʃ] vt (subject) aborder

broad¹ [brɔːd] adj (road, smile, sense, mind) large; (accent) fort(e), prononcé(e); (humour) grossier(ère); (hint) appuyé(e); **in b. daylight** en plein jour; Fig **au grand jour**; **to be in b. agreement** être d'accord sur l'essentiel; Fig **to be a b. church** admettre de nombreuses tendances; **a b. outline** les grandes lignes fpl; **b. bean** fève f

broad² n Am Fam (woman) gonzesse f

broadcast ['brɔːdkɑːst] 1 n émission f
2 vt (pt & pp **broadcast**) diffuser; Fam **don't b. it!** ne va pas le crier sur les toits!
3 vi (of station) émettre

broadcaster ['brɔːdkɑːstə(r)] n (person) (on TV, radio) présentateur(trice) m,f; (TV station) chaîne f de télévision; (radio station) station f de radio

broadcasting ['brɔːdkɑːstɪŋ] n (action) diffusion f; **he works in b.** (radio) il travaille à la radio; (TV) il travaille à la télé

broaden ['brɔːdən] 1 vt élargir; **to b. one's horizons** élargir son horizon
2 vi **to b. (out)** s'élargir

broadly ['brɔːdlɪ] adv (generally) en gros; **to smile b.** faire un large sourire; **b. speaking** en gros

broad-minded [brɔːd'maɪndɪd] adj (person) large d'esprit; (attitude) ouvert(e)

broadsheet ['brɔːdʃiːt] n journal m grand format (synonyme de qualité)

broad-shouldered [brɔːd'ʃəʊldəd] adj large d'épaules; Fig **to be b.** bien encaisser

broadside ['brɔːdsaɪd] n Naut **to fire a b.** tirer une bordée; Fig **to fire a b. at sb/sth** attaquer violemment qn/qch

brocade [brəʊ'keɪd] n brocart m

broccoli ['brɒkəlɪ] n brocolis mpl

brochure ['brəʊʃə(r)] n brochure f

brogue [brəʊg] n (accent) accent m

brogues [brəʊgz] npl (shoes) = chaussures solides souvent ornées de petits trous

broil [brɔɪl] vt & vi Am griller

broke [brəʊk] 1 adj Fam fauché(e); **to go for b.** jouer le tout pour le tout
2 pt of **break**

broken ['brəʊkən] 1 adj (object, bone) cassé(e); (promise) rompu(e); (marriage, heart, person) brisé(e); (ground, surface) irrégulier(ère); **to speak b. English** parler un mauvais anglais; **b. home** famille f désunie
2 pp of **break**

brokenhearted [brəʊkən'hɑːtɪd] adj **to be b.** avoir le cœur brisé

broker ['brəʊkə(r)] n Fin (for shares, currency) agent m de change; Com (for goods, insurance) courtier m

brolly ['brɒlɪ] n (pl **brollies**) n Br Fam pépin m, pébroc m

bromide ['brəʊmaɪd] n Chem bromure m; Fig banalité f

bronchial ['brɒŋkɪəl] adj Anat bronchique; **b. pneumonia** broncho-pneumonie f; **b. tubes** bronches fpl

bronchitic [brɒŋ'kɪtɪk] adj bronchitique

bronchitis [brɒŋ'kaɪtɪs] n bronchite f; **to have b.** avoir une bronchite

bronze [brɒnz] 1 n bronze m; **to win a b.** (medal) remporter une médaille de bronze; **the B. Age** l'âge m du bronze
2 adj (material) de ou en bronze; (colour) couleur bronze inv

bronzed [brɒnzd] adj bronzé(e)

brooch [brəʊtʃ] n broche f

brood [bruːd] 1 n (of birds) couvée f; Hum (of children) progéniture f
2 vi (of hen) couver; Fig **to b. (over or about sth)** ruminer (qch)

broody ['bruːdɪ] adj (hen) couveuse; Fig (woman) en mal d'enfant

brook¹ [brʊk] n (stream) ruisseau m

brook² vt Formal (tolerate) tolérer

broom [bruːm] n (a) (plant) genêt m (b) (for cleaning) balai m; Fig **a new b.** = un nouvel arrivant qui veut tout changer

broomstick ['bruːmstɪk] n manche m à balai

Bros npl Com (abbr **Brothers**) Richardson B. Richardson frères

broth [brɒθ] n (soup) (thin) bouillon m; (thick) potage m

brothel ['brɒθəl] n maison f close

brother ['brʌðə(r)] n frère m

brotherhood ['brʌðəhʊd] n fraternité f; Rel confrérie f; **the b. of man** la fraternité humaine

brother-in-law ['brʌðərɪnlɔː] n (pl **brothers-in-law**) n beau-frère m

brought [brɔːt] pt & pp of **bring**

brow [braʊ] n (a) (forehead) front m; (eyebrow) sourcil m (b) (of hill) sommet m

browbeat ['braʊbiːt] (pt **browbeat**, pp **browbeaten** ['braʊbiːtən]) vt intimider; **to b. sb into doing sth** forcer qn à faire qch en usant d'intimidation

brown [braʊn] 1 n marron m
2 adj marron inv; (hair) brun(e); (skin) mat(e); (tanned) bronzé(e); (bread, flour, rice) complet(ète); **b. paper** papier m kraft; **b. sugar** sucre m roux, cassonade f
3 vt (in cooking) faire dorer
4 vi (in cooking) dorer

browned-off [braʊnd'ɒf] adj Br Fam **to be b. (with)** en avoir marre (de); **to be b. with doing sth** en avoir marre de faire qch

Brownie ['braʊnɪ] n ≃ jeannette f; Fig **to win or get b. points** se faire bien voir

brownie ['braʊnɪ] n Am (cake) = petit gâteau au chocolat et aux noix

brown-nose ['braʊnnəʊz] vi Vulg faire le lèche-cul

browse [braʊz] 1 n **to have a b.** (in shop) regarder; **to have a b. through sth** (collection, shelves) jeter un œil sur qch; (magazine) feuilleter qch
2 vt Comptr **to b. the Web** naviguer sur le Web
3 vi (a) (in shop) regarder; **to b. through sth** (collection, shelves) jeter un œil sur qch; (magazine) feuilleter qch (b) (of animal) brouter

browser ['braʊzə(r)] n Comptr logiciel m de navigation sur le Web

bruise [bruːz] 1 n (on body) bleu m; (on fruit) meurtrissure f
2 vt (person) faire un bleu à; Fig (feelings, pride) blesser; **to b. one's arm** se faire un bleu au bras
3 vi (of person) se faire des bleus; (of fruit) s'abîmer

bruiser ['bruːzə(r)] *n Fam* grosse brute *f*

bruising ['bruːzɪŋ] **1** *n (bruises)* bleus *mpl*
  2 *adj (encounter, experience)* douloureux(euse)

Brummie ['brʌmɪ] *n Fam* = personne née à ou habitant Birmingham

brunch [brʌntʃ] *n Fam* brunch *m*

Brunei [bruː'naɪ] *n* le Brunei

brunette [bruː'net] *n* brune *f*

brunt [brʌnt] *n* **to bear** or **take the b. of sth** *(attack)* essuyer le plus fort de qch; *(anger)* faire les frais de qch

brush [brʌʃ] **1** *n* **(a)** *(for clothes, hair)* brosse *f*; *(for sweeping)* balai *m*; *(for painting)* pinceau *m* **(b)** *(action)* **to give sth a b.** donner un coup de brosse à qch; **to give the floor a b.** donner un coup de balai; **to give one's hair a b.** se donner un coup de brosse **(c)** *(light touch)* effleurement *m*; *Fam* **to have a b. with the law** avoir des démêlés avec la justice **(d)** *(of fox)* queue *f* **(e)** *(undergrowth)* broussailles *fpl*
  2 *vt* **(a)** *(clothes, shoes)* brosser; **to b. one's hair/teeth** se brosser les cheveux/les dents; **to b. the floor** balayer **(b)** *(touch lightly)* effleurer
  3 *vi* **to b. against sb/sth** effleurer qn/qch; **to brush past sb/sth** effleurer qn/qch en passant

▸**brush aside** *vt sep (objection, obstacle)* balayer; *(opponent)* écarter

▸**brush off** *vt sep* **(a)** *(from clothes, shoes)* enlever d'un coup de brosse **(b)** *(person)* envoyer promener; *(insult, incident)* ignorer

▸**brush up** *vt sep* **(a)** *(leaves, crumbs)* balayer **(b)** *Fam (subject, language)* **to b. up (on)** se remettre à

brushed [brʌʃt] *adj (cotton, nylon)* gratté(e)

brush-off ['brʌʃɒf] *n Fam* **to give sb the b.** envoyer promener qn

brush-up ['brʌʃʌp] *n* **to have a wash and b.** faire un brin de toilette

brushwood ['brʌʃwʊd] *n (as fuel)* petit bois *m*; *(undergrowth)* broussailles *fpl*

brushwork ['brʌʃwɜːk] *n Art* touche *f*

brusque [bruːsk] *adj* brusque

brusquely ['bruːsklɪ] *adv (behave)* avec brusquerie; *(say)* d'un ton brusque

Brussels ['brʌsəlz] *n* Bruxelles; **B. sprout** chou *m* de Bruxelles

brutal ['bruːtəl] *adj* brutal(e); *(attack, crime)* sauvage

brutality [bruː'tælɪtɪ] *n* brutalité *f*; *(of attack, crime)* sauvagerie *f*

brutalize ['bruːtəlaɪz] *vt (ill-treat)* brutaliser; *(make insensitive)* rendre insensible

brutally ['bruːtəlɪ] *adv* avec brutalité; *(beat, attack)* sauvagement

brute [bruːt] **1** *n (animal)* bête *f*; *(person)* brute *f*
  2 *adj* **b. force** or **strength** force *f* brutale

brutish [bruːtɪʃ] *adj* bestial(e)

BSc [biːes'siː] *n (abbr* **Bachelor of Science)** **to have a B. in computer science/physics** avoir une licence d'informatique/de physique; **John Smith B.** John Smith, licencié en chimie/informatique/*etc*

BSE [biːes'iː] *n (abbr* **bovine spongiform encephalopathy)** EBS *f*, maladie *f* de la vache folle

BSI [biːes'aɪ] *n (abbr* **British Standards Institution)** = association britannique de normalisation

BST [biːes'tiː] *n (abbr* **British Summer Time)** heure *f* d'été *(en Grande-Bretagne)*

bubble ['bʌbəl] **1** *n (of air, soap)* bulle *f*; *Fig* **the b. has burst** le rêve est terminé; **b. bath** bain *m* moussant; **b. gum** chewing-gum *m*; *Comptr* **b. jet printer** imprimante *f* à bulles
  2 *vi (form bubbles)* bouillonner

▸**bubble over** *vi (of liquid)* déborder; *Fig* **to b. over with joy** ne plus se tenir de joie

bubbly ['bʌblɪ] **1** *n Fam (champagne)* champ *m*
  2 *adj* **(a)** *(liquid)* plein(e) de bulles **(b)** *(person)* débordant(e) de vitalité

bubonic [bjuː'bɒnɪk] *adj* **b. plague** peste *f* bubonique

buccaneer [bʌkə'nɪə(r)] *n* boucanier *m*

Bucharest [buːkə'rest] *n* Bucarest

buck [bʌk] **1** *n* **(a)** *Am Fam (dollar)* dollar *m*; **to make a fast** or **quick b.** faire du fric **(b)** *(of deer, rabbit)* mâle *m* **(c)** *Fam (responsibility)* **to pass the b.** refiler le bébé; **the b. stops here** en fin de compte c'est moi le responsable
  2 *vt* **to b. the system/a trend** aller à l'encontre de l'ordre établi/d'une tendance
  3 *vi (of horse)* faire le saut de mouton

▸**buck up** *Fam* **1** *vt sep (encourage)* remonter le moral à; **to b. one's ideas up** se prendre en main
  2 *vi Fam (cheer up)* reprendre courage; *(hurry)* se grouiller

bucket ['bʌkɪt] **1** *n* seau *m*; *Br Fam* **it's raining buckets** il tombe des cordes; *Fam* **to cry buckets** pleurer comme une madeleine; *Fam* **b. shop** *(for air tickets)* agence *f* de voyages à prix réduits
  2 *vi Br Fam* **it's bucketing (down)** il tombe des cordes

buckle ['bʌkəl] **1** *n* boucle *f*
  2 *vt* **(a)** *(fasten)* boucler **(b)** *(deform)* déformer; *(wheel)* voiler
  3 *vi (deform)* se déformer; *(of wheel)* se voiler; *(of knees)* flancher; **she buckled at the knees** ses jambes ont cédé sous elle

▸**buckle down** *vi* s'y mettre; **to b. down to a task** s'atteler à une tâche

buckshot ['bʌkʃɒt] *n* chevrotine *f*

buckskin ['bʌkskɪn] *n* daim *m (peau)*

buckteeth [bʌk'tiːθ] *npl* dents *fpl* de lapin

bucktoothed [bʌk'tuːθt] *adj* **to be b.** avoir des dents de lapin

buckwheat ['bʌkwiːt] *n* sarrasin *m*

bucolic [bjuː'kɒlɪk] *adj Lit* bucolique

bud [bʌd] **1** *n (of leaf, branch)* bourgeon *m*; *(of flower)* bouton *m*
  2 *vi (pt & pp* **budded)** *(of tree)* bourgeonner; *(of flowers)* être en boutons

Budapest ['buːdəpest] *n* Budapest

Buddha ['bʊdə] *n* Bouddha

Buddhist ['bʊdɪst] **1** *n* bouddhiste *mf*
  2 *adj (priest, doctrine)* bouddhiste; *(art, temple)* bouddhique

budding ['bʌdɪŋ] *adj (genius, actor)* en herbe; *(talent)* naissant(e)

buddy ['bʌdɪ] *(pl* **buddies)** *n Fam (friend)* pote *m*; **hey, b.!** dis donc, mec!

budge [bʌdʒ] **1** *vt (move)* bouger; *Fig (convince)* faire changer d'avis
  2 *vi (move)* bouger; *Fig (yield)* céder

budgerigar ['bʌdʒərɪgɑː(r)] *n* perruche *f*

budget ['bʌdʒɪt] **1** *n* budget *m*; *Br Pol* **the B.** le budget; **to go over b.** dépasser le budget; **to be within b.** être dans les limites du budget; **b. deficit/surplus** déficit *m*/ excédent *m* budgétaire

2 *vt* (*time, money*) gérer

3 *vi* **to b. for sth** prévoir qch

budgetary ['bʌdʒɪtərɪ] *adj Fin* budgétaire

budgie ['bʌdʒɪ] *n Fam* perruche *f*

Buenos Aires ['bwenɒs'aɪrɪz] *n* Buenos Aires

buff [bʌf] **1** *n* (**a**) (*colour*) couleur *f* chamois (**b**) *Fam* **in the b.** (*naked*) à poil (**c**) (*enthusiast*) mordu(e) *m,f*; **film b.** cinéphile *mf*

2 *adj* (*couleur*) chamois *inv*; (*envelope*) en papier kraft

3 *vt* (*polish*) lustrer

buffalo ['bʌfələʊ] (*pl* buffalo *or* buffaloes) *n* buffle *m*

buffer[1] ['bʌfə(r)] *n* (*on railway track*) butoir *m*; *Comptr* mémoire *f* tampon; **to act as a b.** faire tampon; **b. state** État *m* tampon; **b. zone** zone *f* tampon

buffer[2] *n Br Fam* **old b.** vieux schnock *m*

buffet[1] ['bʌfɪt] *n* (*of wind*) secouer; *Fig* **to be buffeted by events** être ballotté(e) par les événements

buffet[2] ['bʊfeɪ] *n* (**a**) (*sideboard*) buffet *m* (**b**) (*meal*) buffet *m*; **b. lunch/dinner** buffet (**c**) (*in station*) buffet *m*; **b.** (*car*) wagon-restaurant *m*, voiture-restaurant *f*

buffeting ['bʌfɪtɪŋ] *n* **to take a b.** (*of ship*) être violemment ballotté(e); *Fig* (*of person*) être fortement ébranlé(e)

buffoon [bə'fu:n] *n* bouffon *m*; **to play the b.** faire le pitre

bug [bʌg] **1** *n* (**a**) (*insect*) insecte *m*; (*bed bug*) punaise *f* (**b**) *Fam* (*illness*) virus *m*, microbe *m*; **a stomach b.** un embarras gastrique; **there's a b. going round** il y a un virus qui traîne; *Fig* **the travel b.** le virus des voyages (**c**) *Comptr* bug *m*, bogue *m* (**d**) (*listening device*) micro *m*

2 *vt* (*pt & pp* bugged) (**a**) (*telephone*) mettre sur écoute; (*building, room*) cacher des micros dans (**b**) *Fam* (*annoy*) taper sur les nerfs à; (*nag*) embêter; **stop bugging me about it!** arrête de m'embêter avec ça!

bugbear ['bʌgbeə(r)] *n Fam* cauchemar *m*

bug-eyed [bʌg'aɪd] *adj* aux yeux exorbités

bug-free [bʌg'fri:] *adj Comptr* sans bug

bugger ['bʌgə(r)] **1** *n very Fam* (*unpleasant person*) connard(asse) *m,f*; **you silly b.!** espèce d'andouille!; **the poor b.!** le pauvre!; **it's a b. of a job** c'est une vraie galère; **b. all** que dalle; **he knows b. all about it** il y connaît que dalle

2 *vt* (**a**) (*sodomize*) sodomiser (**b**) *very Fam* **b. (it)!** merde!; **I'll be buggered if I'm going to do it!** tu peux toujours courir pour que je le fasse!; **I'm buggered if I know** je ne sais foutre rien; **that's really buggered it!** ça a tout foutu en l'air!

▶**bugger about, bugger around** *very Fam* **1** *vt sep* **to b. sb about** se foutre de la gueule de qn

2 *vi* glander

▶**bugger off** *vi very Fam* se casser, foutre le camp

▶**bugger up** *vt sep very Fam* (*plan*) foutre en l'air; (*TV, machine*) bousiller

buggered ['bʌgəd] *adj very Fam* (*broken*) foutu(e); (*exhausted*) nase

buggery ['bʌgərɪ] *n* (**a**) *Law* sodomie *f* (**b**) *very Fam* **to run like b.** prendre ses jambes à son cou

buggy ['bʌgɪ] *n* (*pl* buggies) *n* (**a**) *Br* (*pushchair*) poussette *f*; *Am* (*pram*) landau *m* (**b**) (*carriage*) boghei *m*, buggy *m*

bugle ['bju:gəl] *n* clairon *m*

bugler ['bju:glə(r)] *n* (*sonneur m de*) clairon *m*

build [bɪld] **1** *n* carrure *f*

2 *vt* (*pt & pp* built [bɪlt]) construire; **to be built (out) of sth** être construit(e) en qch; **to b. sth into sth** (*include*) inclure qch dans qch; **to b. one's hopes on sth** fonder ses espoirs sur qch

▶**build on 1** *vt sep* (*add*) ajouter

2 *vt insep* (*success*) tirer parti de

▶**build up 1** *vt sep* (**a**) (*resources*) accumuler; **to b. up speed/one's strength** prendre de la vitesse/des forces; **don't b. your hopes up** ne te fais pas d'illusions (**b**) (*custom*) se constituer; (*reputation*) se faire; (*company*) développer; **to b. up an immunity (to sth)** s'immuniser (contre qch) (**c**) (*hype*) faire du battage autour de

2 *vi* (*of clouds*) s'amasser; (*of hurricane, storm*) se préparer; (*of tension, pressure*) s'accumuler

builder ['bɪldə(r)] *n* maçon *m*; (*business owner*) entrepreneur *m* (dans le bâtiment)

building ['bɪldɪŋ] *n* (**a**) (*structure*) bâtiment *m*; immeuble *m* (**b**) (*action*) construction *f*; **the b. trade** le bâtiment; **b. block** cube *m*; *Fig* élément *m* essentiel; **b. site** chantier *m* (de construction); *Br* **b. society** ≃ société *f* de crédit immobilier

build-up ['bɪldʌp] *n* (*of tension, forces*) accumulation *f*; (*hype*) battage *m*; **the b. to Christmas/the match** la période précédant Noël/le match

built [bɪlt] *pt & pp of* build

built-in ['bɪl'tɪn] *adj* (*cupboard*) encastré(e); (*included*) compris(e); **b. obsolescence** obsolescence *f* programmée

built-up ['bɪl'tʌp] *adj* **b. area** agglomération *f* urbaine

bulb [bʌlb] *n* (**a**) (*of plant*) bulbe *m* (**b**) (*light bulb*) ampoule *f*

bulbous ['bʌlbəs] *adj* bulbeux(euse); **a b. nose** un gros nez

Bulgaria [bʌl'geərɪə] *n* la Bulgarie

Bulgarian [bʌl'geərɪən] **1** *n* (**a**) (*person*) Bulgare *mf* (**b**) (*language*) bulgare *m*

2 *adj* bulgare

bulge [bʌldʒ] **1** *n* renflement *m*

2 *vi* (*of stomach*) être gonflé(e); (*of bag, pocket*) être bourré(e) (**with** de)

bulimia [bə'lɪmɪə] *n* boulimie *f*

bulk [bʌlk] **1** *n* (**a**) (*mass*) masse *f*; **the b. (of sth)** la majeure partie (de qch) (**b**) *Com* **in b.** en gros; **b. purchase** achat *m* en gros

2 *vi* **to b. sth out** étoffer qch

3 *vi* **to b. large** (*of problem*) occuper une place importante

bulkhead ['bʌlkhed] *n Naut* cloison *f*

bulky ['bʌlkɪ] *adj* volumineux(euse), encombrant(e)

bull[1] [bʊl] *n* (**a**) (*animal*) taureau *m*; **b. elephant** éléphant *m* mâle; *Fin* **b. market** marché *m* à la hausse (**b**) *Fam* (*nonsense*) conneries *fpl* (**c**) (*idioms*) **to take the b. by the horns** prendre le taureau par les cornes; **like a b. in a china shop** comme un éléphant dans un magasin de porcelaine

bull[2] *n Rel* bulle *f*

bulldog ['bʊldɒg] *n* bouledogue *m*; **b. clip** pince *f* à dessin

bulldoze ['buldəʊz] vt (land) aplanir au bulldozer; (building) démolir au bulldozer; Fig to b. sb into doing sth forcer qn à faire qch

bulldozer ['buldəʊzə(r)] n bulldozer m

bullet ['bʊlɪt] n balle f; b. hole impact m de balle; b. wound blessure f par balle

bulletin ['bʊlɪtɪn] n bulletin m; b. board Am (noticeboard) panneau m d'affichage; Comptr serveur m télématique

bulletproof ['bʊlɪtpruːf] adj (car, glass) blindé(e); b. vest gilet m pare-balles

bullfight ['bʊlfaɪt] n corrida f, course f de taureaux; (art) tauromachie f

bullfighter ['bʊlfaɪtə(r)] n torero m

bullfighting ['bʊlfaɪtɪŋ] n (bullfights) courses fpl de taureaux; (art) tauromachie f

bullfinch ['bʊlfɪntʃ] n bouvreuil m

bullfrog ['bʊlfrɒg] n grenouille-taureau f

bullion ['bʊljən] n gold b. lingots mpl d'or

bullish ['bʊlɪʃ] adj Fin (market) à la hausse; Fig (optimistic) optimiste

bullock ['bʊlək] n bœuf m

bullring ['bʊlrɪŋ] n arène f

bull's-eye ['bʊlzaɪ] n mille m; also Fig to hit the b. mettre dans le mille

bullshit ['bʊlʃɪt] Vulg 1 n (nonsense) conneries fpl
2 exclam c'est des conneries tout ça!
3 vt (pt & pp bullshitted) to b. sb raconter des conneries à qn; she bullshitted her way into the job elle a bluffé pour avoir le poste
4 vi (talk nonsense) dire des conneries

bully ['bʊlɪ] 1 n (pl bullies) (child) terreur f; (adult) tyran m; don't be such a b. ne sois pas si tyrannique
2 vt (pt & pp bullied) maltraiter; to b. sb into doing sth forcer qn à faire qch
3 exclam Ironic b. for you! bravo!

bully-boy ['bʊlɪbɔɪ] n voyou m; b. tactics manœuvres fpl d'intimidation

bullying ['bʊlɪɪŋ] 1 n brimades fpl
2 adj brutal(e)

bulrush ['bʊlrʌʃ] n jonc m

bulwark ['bʊlwəːk] n also Fig rempart m (against contre)

bum [bʌm] Fam 1 n (a) Br (buttocks) derrière m (b) Am (tramp) clochard(e) m,f
2 adj (of poor quality) minable; to get a b. deal se faire avoir
3 vt (pt & pp bummed) to b. a cigarette from or off sb taxer une cigarette à qn; to b. a ride se faire prendre en stop
▶**bum around** vi Fam (be idle) glander; (travel) vadrouiller

bumblebee ['bʌmblbiː] n bourdon m

bumbling ['bʌmblɪŋ] adj b. fool or idiot imbécile m

bumf [bʌmf] n Fam paperasse f

bummer ['bʌmə(r)] n Fam what a b.! quelle poisse!

bump [bʌmp] 1 n (a) (jolt) secousse f; to land with a b. tomber violemment par terre; Fig to come back down to earth with a b. redescendre brusquement sur terre (b) (lump) bosse f
2 vt upon s.o.'s head se cogner la tête
▶**bump into** vt insep (collide with) rentrer dans; Fam (meet by chance) tomber sur

▶**bump off** vt sep Fam (kill) liquider
▶**bump up** vt sep Fam (price) gonfler, augmenter

bumper ['bʌmpə(r)] 1 n Br (of car) pare-chocs m inv; b. car (at fairground) auto f tamponneuse
2 adj b. crop récolte f exceptionnelle; b. issue numéro m exceptionnel

bumpkin ['bʌmpkɪn] n (country) b. péquenaud(e) m,f

bump-start ['bʌmpstɑːt] vt to b. a car pousser une voiture pour la faire démarrer

bumptious ['bʌmpʃəs] adj suffisant(e)

bumpy ['bʌmpɪ] adj (road) cahoteux(euse); (journey) agité(e); (landing) violent(e); Fam Fig to give sb/sth a b. ride malmener qn/qch

bun [bʌn] n (a) (sweet) petit gâteau m brioché; (for burger, petit pain m rond (b) (hairstyle) chignon m

bunch [bʌntʃ] n (of flowers) bouquet m; (of bananas) régime m; (of grapes) grappe f; (of keys) trousseau m; (of people) bande f; (of cyclists) peloton m; bunches (hairstyle) couettes fpl; he's the best of a bad b. c'est le moins mauvais du lot; she's the best or the pick of the b. c'est la meilleure du lot; a whole b. of things to do tout un tas de choses à faire
▶**bunch together** vi (of people) se serrer

bundle ['bʌndəl] 1 n (of clothes) paquet m; (of banknotes, papers) liasse f; (of straw) botte f; Fam I don't go a b. on horror films je ne suis pas un fana de films d'horreur; Fam Ironic you're a b. of laughs! c'est fou ce que tu as l'air gai; Fam she's a b. of nerves c'est un paquet de nerfs
2 vt to b. sb out of the door mettre qn dehors sans ménagement; to b. sb into a car embarquer qn dans une voiture
▶**bundle off** vt sep Fam (send) expédier

bung [bʌŋ] 1 n (a) (plug) bonde f (b) Br Fam (bribe) bakchich m
2 vt Br Fam (put) mettre; (throw) balancer; b. it there mets-le là; b. me over an orange balance-moi une orange
▶**bung up** vt sep Fam boucher; my nose is bunged up j'ai le nez bouché

bungalow ['bʌŋgələʊ] n pavillon m de plain-pied

bungee jumping ['bʌndʒiːdʒʌmpɪŋ] n saut m à l'élastique

bunghole ['bʌŋhəʊl] n bonde f

bungle ['bʌŋgəl] 1 vt (attempt) rater; (job) gâcher
2 vi se tromper

bunion ['bʌnjən] n oignon m (au pied)

bunk[1] [bʌŋk] n (bed) lit m; (in train, ship) couchette f; b. beds lits superposés

bunk[2] n Br Fam to do a b. (run away) se faire la malle
▶**bunk off** vi Br Fam (from school) sécher (les cours)

bunker ['bʌŋkə(r)] n (a) (for coal) coffre m à charbon (b) Mil bunker m, blockhaus m; nuclear b. abri m antiatomique (c) Br (on golf course) bunker m

bunkum ['bʌŋkəm] n Fam âneries fpl

bunny ['bʌnɪ] n (pl bunnies) n Fam b. (rabbit) petit lapin m

Bunsen burner ['bʌnsən'bɜːnə(r)] n bec m Bunsen

bunting ['bʌntɪŋ] n (decorations) guirlandes fpl de fanions

buoy [bɔɪ] n bouée f
▶**buoy up** vt sep (person, prices) soutenir

buoyancy ['bɔɪənsɪ] n (in water) flottabilité f; Fig (of market) stabilité f

buoyant ['bɔɪənt] *adj* (*in water*) qui flotte; *Fig* (*economy, prices*) stable; *Fig* (*person, mood*) plein(e) d'allant

burble ['bɜːbəl] *vi* (*of stream*) murmurer; (*of person*) marmonner

burden ['bɜːdən] **1** *n also Fig* fardeau *m*; **b. of taxation** pression *f* fiscale; *Law* **b. of proof** charge *f* de la preuve **2** *vt Fig* accabler (**with** de)

burdensome ['bɜːdənsəm] *adj* lourd(e)

bureau ['bjʊərəʊ] (*pl* **bureaux** ['bjʊərəʊz]) *n* (**a**) (*desk*) bureau *m*, secrétaire *m*; *Am* (*chest of drawers*) commode *f* (**b**) (*office*) bureau *m*; *Am* (*government department*) service *m*

bureaucracy [bjʊə'rɒkrəsɪ] *n* bureaucratie *f*

bureaucrat ['bjʊərəkræt] *n* bureaucrate *mf*

bureaucratic [bjʊərə'krætɪk] *adj* bureaucratique

bureaux ['bjʊərəʊz] *pl of* **bureau**

burgeon ['bɜːdʒən] *vi* (*of trade*) se développer; (*of crime*) augmenter; (*of relationship*) s'épanouir; **a burgeoning talent** un talent qui s'affirme

burger ['bɜːgə(r)] *n* hamburger *m*

burglar ['bɜːglə(r)] *n* cambrioleur(euse) *m,f*; **b. alarm** alarme *f* (de sécurité)

burglarize ['bɜːgləraɪz] *vt Am* cambrioler

burglar-proof ['bɜːgləpruːf] *adj* inviolable

burglary ['bɜːglərɪ] (*pl* **burglaries**) *n* cambriolage *m*

burgle ['bɜːgəl] *vt* cambrioler

Burgundy ['bɜːgəndɪ] *n* la Bourgogne

burgundy ['bɜːgəndɪ] *adj* (*colour*) bordeaux *inv*

burial ['berɪəl] *n* enterrement *m*; **b. ground** cimetière *m*

Burkina-Faso [bɜː'kiːnə'fæsəʊ] *n* le Burkina

burlesque [bɜː'lesk] **1** *n* (*caricature*) parodie *f*; (*style*) burlesque *m* **2** *adj* burlesque

burly ['bɜːlɪ] *adj* bien bâti(e)

Burma ['bɜːmə] *n Formerly* la Birmanie

Burmese [bɜː'miːz] **1** *npl* the B. les Birmans *mpl* **2** *n* (**a**) (*person*) Birman(e), *m,f* (**b**) (*language*) birman *m* **3** *adj* birman(e)

burn¹ [bɜːn] **1** *n* brûlure *f* **2** *vt* (*pt & pp* **burnt** [bɜːnt] *or* **burned**) (**a**) (*fuel, building*) brûler; **to b. one's hand/one's finger** se brûler la main/le doigt; **to b. a hole in sth** faire un trou dans qch (**b**) (*idioms*) **to have money to b.** avoir de l'argent à ne plus savoir quoi en faire; **to b. one's boats** *or* **one's bridges** brûler ses vaisseaux; **to b. the candle at both ends** brûler la chandelle par les deux bouts; **to b. the midnight oil** travailler tard **3** *vi* brûler; (*of light*) briller; **the fire is burning low** le feu baisse; *Fig* **to b. with desire** brûler de désir; **to b. with anger** bouillonner de colère; **to b. with enthusiasm** déborder d'enthousiasme

▶**burn down 1** *vt sep* incendier **2** *vi* être détruit(e) par le feu

▶**burn out 1** *vt sep* **to b. itself out** (*of fire*) s'éteindre; *Fig* **to b. oneself out** (*become exhausted*) s'épuiser **2** *vi* (*of fire*) s'éteindre

▶**burn up 1** *vt sep* (*energy*) dépenser **2** *vi* (*of rocket*) se désintégrer

burn² *n Scot* (*stream*) ruisseau *m*

burner ['bɜːnə(r)] *n* brûleur *m*

burning ['bɜːnɪŋ] *adj* (*on fire*) en feu; (*very hot*) brûlant(e); (*passion, ambition*) dévorant(e); **a b. issue** une question brûlante

burnish ['bɜːnɪʃ] *vt* polir, brunir

burnt [bɜːnt] **1** *adj* brûlé(e) **2** *pt & pp of* **burn¹**

burnt-out ['bɜːnt'aʊt] *adj* (*building, car*) calciné(e); *Fig* (*person*) usé(e)

burp [bɜːp] **1** *n* rot *m* **2** *vi* roter

burr¹ [bɜː(r)] *n* (*of plant*) = petite boule renfermant des graines et pourvue de piquants qui, en se détachant, s'accroche aux vêtements

burr² *n* **to speak with a b.** grasseyer

burrow ['bʌrəʊ] **1** *n* (*of animal*) terrier *m* **2** *vi* (*of animal*) creuser la terre

bursar ['bɜːsə(r)] *n Univ* intendant(e) *m,f*

bursary ['bɜːsərɪ] (*pl* **bursaries**) *n* (*grant*) bourse *f* (d'études)

burst [bɜːst] **1** *n* (*of laughter*) éclat *m*; (*of enthusiasm*) élan *m*; **a b. of activity** une poussée d'activité; **a b. of applause** une salve d'applaudissements; **a b. of gunfire** une rafale; **a b. of speed** une pointe de vitesse **2** *vt* (*pt & pp* **burst**) (*balloon, tyre*) faire éclater; **to b. its banks** (*of river*) déborder, sortir de son lit **3** *vi* (*of balloon, bubble, tyre, pipe*) éclater; *Fig* **to be bursting with pride** déborder de fierté; **to be bursting with impatience** bouillir d'impatience; **to be bursting to do sth** mourir d'envie de faire qch; **to be bursting (for the toilet)** avoir un besoin pressant; *Fig* **to be bursting at the seams** (*of room*) être plein(e) à craquer

▶**burst into** *vt insep* (**a**) (*enter*) faire irruption dans (**b**) (*suddenly start*) **to b. into flames** prendre feu; **to b. into song** se mettre à chanter; **to b. into laughter/tears** éclater de rire/en sanglots

▶**burst open** *vi* (*of door*) s'ouvrir brusquement; (*of packet*) éclater

▶**burst out** *vi* **to b. out laughing** éclater de rire; **to b. out crying** éclater en sanglots

Burundi [bə'rʊndɪ] *n* le Burundi

bury ['berɪ] (*pt & pp* **buried**) *vt* (*body, treasure*) enterrer; (*of avalanche, mudslide*) *and Fig* (*hide*) ensevelir; **to b. oneself in one's work** se plonger dans son travail; **to b. one's face in one's hands** enfouir son visage dans ses mains; **to b. the hatchet** enterrer la hache de guerre

bus [bʌs] **1** *n* (*pl* **buses** *or* **busses**) (**a**) (*vehicle*) bus *m*, autobus *m*; **by b.** en bus; **b. conductor/driver** receveur *m*/chauffeur *m* de bus; **b. lane** couloir *m* de bus; **b. route** ligne *f* de bus; **b. shelter** Abribus® *m*; **b. station** gare *f* routière; **b. stop** arrêt *m* d'autobus (**b**) *Comptr* bus *m* **2** *vt* (*pt & pp* **bused** *or* **bussed**) transporter en autobus

bush [bʊʃ] *n* (*plant*) buisson *m*; **the b.** (*in Africa, Australia*) la brousse; *Fam* **b. telegraph** téléphone *m* arabe

bushed [bʊʃt] *adj Fam* (*exhausted*) vanné(e), claqué(e)

bushel ['bʊʃəl] *n* boisseau *m*; *Fig* **don't hide your light under a b.** ne cache pas ton talent

bushfire ['bʊʃfaɪə(r)] *n* feu *m* de brousse

bushy ['bʊʃɪ] *adj* touffu(e)

busily ['bɪzɪlɪ] *adv* **to be b. doing sth** être très occupé(e) à faire qch

business ['bɪznɪs] n (a) (task, concern) affaire f; **it's none of your b.** cela ne te regarde pas, ce ne sont pas tes affaires; **it's/it's not my b. to...** c'est/ce n'est pas à moi de...; **mind your own b.!** occupe-toi de tes affaires ou de ce qui te regarde!; **to make it one's b. to do sth** prendre sur soi de faire qch; **to go about one's b.** vaquer à ses occupations; **to get down to b.** se mettre au travail; **to mean b.** ne pas plaisanter; **I'm sick of the whole b.** j'en ai assez de toute cette histoire; **he was working like nobody's b.** il travaillait très dur; **she can tell jokes like nobody's b.** elle raconte très bien les histoires drôles; *Br Fam* **it's the b.** *(excellent)* c'est génial

(b) *(individual company)* affaire f, entreprise f; *(commercial activity)* affaires; **to be in the entertainment b.** être dans le spectacle; **I'm not in the b. of making compromises** ce n'est pas mon genre de faire des compromis; **to be in b.** être dans les affaires; **to go into b.** s'installer; **to go into b. with sb** monter une affaire avec qn; **to go out of b.** fermer; **to go to London on b.** aller à Londres pour affaires; **how's b.?** comment vont les affaires?; **it's good/bad for b.** c'est bon/mauvais pour les affaires; **to talk b.** parler affaires; **to do b. with sb** traiter avec qn; *Fin* **b. account** compte m professionnel; **b. card** carte f de visite; **b. class** *(on plane)* classe f affaires; **b. hours** *(of shop)* heures fpl d'ouverture; *(of office)* heures de bureau; **b. lunch** déjeuner m d'affaires; **b. management** gestion f d'entreprise; **b. park** parc m d'activités; **b. school** école f de commerce; **b. studies** études fpl commerciales ou de commerce; **b. trip** voyage m d'affaires

businesslike ['bɪznɪslaɪk] adj professionnel(elle)

businessman ['bɪznɪsmæn] n homme m d'affaires; **to be a good b.** avoir le sens des affaires

businesswoman ['bɪznɪswʊmən] n femme f d'affaires; **to be a good b.** avoir le sens des affaires

busk [bʌsk] vi Br jouer de la musique *(dans les rues ou le métro)*

busker ['bʌskə(r)] n Br musicien(enne) m,f *(dans les rues ou le métro)*

busman ['bʌsmən] n Fam **a b.'s holiday** = vacances pendant lesquelles on fait la même chose qu'à son travail

bust¹ [bʌst] n (a) *(of woman)* poitrine f; **b. measurement** tour m de poitrine (b) *(statue)* buste m

bust² Fam 1 adj (a) *(broken)* fichu(e) (b) **to go b.** *(bankrupt)* faire faillite

2 vt *(pt & pp busted or bust)* (a) *(break)* bousiller (b) *(arrest)* coffrer

▶**bust out** vi Fam *(escape)* se tirer *(of de)*

▶**bust up** vt sep Fam *(disrupt) (event)* interrompre; *(relationship)* ficher en l'air

bustle ['bʌsəl] 1 n *(commotion)* animation f

2 vi **to b. (about)** s'activer, s'affairer

bust-up ['bʌstʌp] n Fam *(dispute)* engueulade f; *(of relationship)* fin f; **to have a b.** *(argue)* s'engueuler

busy ['bɪzi] 1 adj (a) *(person)* occupé(e); *(day, week)* chargé(e); *(road)* à grande circulation; **to keep sb b.** occuper qn; **to keep oneself b.** s'occuper; **to be b. doing sth** être occupé à faire qch; **the train was very b.** il y avait beaucoup de monde dans le train (b) Am *(telephone line)* occupé(e); **I keep getting the b. signal** ça sonne toujours occupé

2 vt *(pt & pp busied)* **to b. oneself with sth** s'occuper à qch

busybody ['bɪzibɒdi] *(pl busybodies)* n Fam fouineur(euse) m,f

but [bʌt] 1 prep *(except)* sauf, à part; **any day b. tomorrow** n'importe quand sauf demain; **it's nothing b. prejudice** ce ne sont rien que des préjugés; **she is anything b. stupid** elle est loin d'être bête; **b. for sars; the last b. one** l'avant-dernier(ère) m,f; **the next b. one** le (la) deuxième

2 adv Formal seulement; **he is b. a child** ce n'est qu'un enfant; **had I b. known!** si (seulement) j'avais su!; **one can b. try** on peut toujours essayer

3 conj mais; **not once b. twice** pas une fois, mais deux!; **I told her to do it b. she refused** je lui ai dit de le faire mais elle a refusé; **b. I tell you I saw it!** mais puisque je te dis que je l'ai vu!; **I had no choice b. to go** je n'ai pas pu faire autrement que d'y aller; **what could I do b. invite him?** comment pouvais-je faire autrement que de l'inviter?

4 n **no buts!** il n'y a pas de 'mais' qui tienne!

butane ['bjuːteɪn] n butane m

butch [bʊtʃ] adj Fam hommasse

butcher ['bʊtʃə(r)] 1 n also Fig boucher(ère) m,f; **b.'s (shop)** boucherie f; **to go to the b.'s** aller chez le boucher ou à la boucherie

2 vt *(animal)* abattre; Fig *(person, song)* massacrer

butchery ['bʊtʃəri] n also Fig boucherie f

butler ['bʌtlə(r)] n maître m d'hôtel

butt [bʌt] 1 n (a) *(of rifle)* crosse f; *(of cigarette)* mégot m; Fig **to be the b. of a joke** être la cible d'une plaisanterie (b) Am Fam *(buttocks)* fesses fpl

2 vt *(hit with head)* donner un coup de tête à

▶**butt in** vi *(interrupt)* intervenir

butter ['bʌtə(r)] 1 n beurre m; **she looks as if b. wouldn't melt in her mouth** on lui donnerait le bon Dieu sans confession; **b. bean** = gros haricot blanc; **b. dish** beurrier m; **b. knife** couteau m à beurre; **b. mountain** montagne f de beurre

2 vt beurrer

▶**butter up** vt sep Fam *(flatter)* passer de la pommade à

buttercup ['bʌtəkʌp] n bouton m d'or

butterfingers ['bʌtəfɪŋgəz] n Fam empoté(e) m,f

butterfly ['bʌtəflaɪ] *(pl butterflies)* n papillon m; Fig **to have butterflies (in one's stomach)** avoir l'estomac noué; **b. (stroke)** *(in swimming)* (brasse f) papillon m

buttermilk ['bʌtəmɪlk] n babeurre m

butterscotch ['bʌtəskɒtʃ] n caramel m dur au beurre

buttock ['bʌtək] n fesse f

button ['bʌtən] 1 n (a) *(on shirt, machine)* bouton m; **b. mushroom** petit champignon m de Paris (b) Am *(badge)* badge m

2 vt *(shirt, dress)* boutonner; Fam **b. it!** la ferme!

▶**button up** vt sep *(shirt, dress)* boutonner

buttonhole ['bʌtənhəʊl] 1 n boutonnière f

2 vt *(detain)* coincer

buttress ['bʌtrɪs] 1 n Archit contrefort m; Fig pilier m

2 vt Fig *(support)* renforcer

buxom ['bʌksəm] adj *(plump)* planureux(euse); *(full-bosomed)* à la poitrine généreuse

buy [baɪ] 1 n **a good/bad b.** une bonne/mauvaise affaire

2 vt *(pt & pp bought* [bɔːt]) (a) *(purchase)* acheter; **to b. sth, to b. sth for sb** acheter qch à qn; **to b. sth from sb** acheter qch à qn; Fig **to b. time** gagner du temps; **he's bought it** *(has died)* il a passé l'arme à gauche (b) Fam *(believe)* avaler

▶**buy in** vt sep *(supplies)* faire des stocks de

▶**buy into** vt insep (company, scheme) acheter des parts de

▶**buy off** vt sep Fam acheter

▶**buy out** vt sep Com racheter la part de

▶**buy up** vt sep (land, shares) acheter; (supplies) faire des stocks de

buyer ['baɪə(r)] n acheteur(euse) m,f; **b.'s market** marché m demandeur

buy-out ['baɪaʊt] n Com rachat m

buzz [bʌz] 1 n (a) (noise) bourdonnement m; (of plane) vrombissement m; Fam **b. word** mot m à la mode (b) Fam (phone call) to give sb a b. passer un coup de fil à qn (c) Fam (thrill) to get a b. out of doing sth prendre son pied à faire qch
2 vt Fam (on intercom) appeler à l'Interphone®; (on pager) biper
3 vi (make noise) bourdonner; Fig to b. with excitement (of town) bourdonner d'excitation; my head was buzzing j'avais la tête lourde; Fam now we're buzzing! maintenant on est lancés!

▶**buzz off** vi Br Fam se tirer

buzzard ['bʌzəd] n buse f

buzzer ['bʌzə(r)] n (on intercom) bouton m de l'Interphone®; (on clock, oven) sonnerie f

buzzing ['bʌzɪŋ] n bourdonnement m

by [baɪ] prep 1 (a) (agent) par; **he was arrested by the police** il a été arrêté par la police, la police l'a arrêté; **made by hand** fait(e) à la main; **a play by Shakespeare** une pièce de Shakespeare
(b) (with manner, means) **by train/car/plane** en train/voiture/avion; **by doing sth** en faisant qch; **to pay by credit card** payer par carte de crédit; **to have a child by sb** avoir un enfant de qn; **to take sb by the hand/arm** prendre qn par la main/le bras; **to know sb by name/sight** connaître qn de nom/de vue; **to earn one's living by teaching** gagner sa vie en enseignant
(c) (close to) près de; **by the fire** près du feu; **by the sea** au bord de la mer; **by the side of the road** sur le bord de la route
(d) (via) par; **by land/sea** par terre/mer
(e) (past) **to walk by sb/sth** passer devant qn/qch; **to drive by sb/sth** passer devant qn/qch (en voiture)
(f) (at or before) **she should be here by now** elle devrait être ici à l'heure qu'il est; **it'll be ready by tomorrow** ce

sera prêt pour demain; **by 1980 they were all dead** en 1980 ils étaient déjà tous morts; **by then it was too late** il était déjà trop tard
(g) (during) **by day/night** de jour/nuit
(h) (with measurements, quantities, numbers) **to divide/multiply by three** diviser/multiplier par trois; **3 metres by 2** 3 mètres sur 2; **to sell sth by weight** vendre qch au poids; **one by one** un par un
(i) (according to) **to go by appearances** se fier aux apparences; **to call sb by their first name** appeler qn par son prénom; **what do you mean by that?** qu'est-ce que tu entends par là?
(j) (with reflexive pronouns) **by oneself** tout(e) seul(e)
(k) (as a result of) **by accident/chance/mistake** par accident/hasard/erreur
2 adv (a) **by and large** dans l'ensemble; **by the way,...** au fait,...
(b) (past) **to go/walk by** passer; **to drive by** passer (en voiture)

bye [baɪ] exclam Fam au revoir!, salut!; **b. for now!** à bientôt!

bye-bye ['baɪbaɪ] exclam Fam au revoir!, salut!

by-election ['baɪɪlekʃən] n Pol élection f partielle

Byelorussia [bɪeləʊ'rʌʃə] = Belarus

Byelorussian [bɪeləʊ'rʌʃən] 1 n Biélorusse mf
2 adj biélorusse

bygone ['baɪgɒn] 1 n **let bygones be bygones** oublions le passé
2 adj révolu(e); **in b. days** autrefois

by-line ['baɪlaɪn] n (in newspaper) signature f

bypass ['baɪpɑːs] 1 n (a) (road) rocade f (b) (heart operation) pontage m
2 vt (of road) also Fig contourner; (middleman) court-circuiter

by-product ['baɪprɒdʌkt] n sous-produit m, dérivé m; Fig conséquence f indirecte

bystander ['baɪstændə(r)] n passant(e) m,f

byte [baɪt] n Comptr octet m

byway ['baɪweɪ] n (road) petite route f

byword ['baɪwɜːd] n **to be a b. for** être synonyme de

Byzantine [bɪ'zæntaɪn] adj also Fig byzantin(e)

C

C, c [siː] n (a) (letter) C, c m inv (b) Mus do m, ut m (c) Sch (grade) **to get a C** (in exam) avoir mention passable; (in homework, essay) ≃ avoir 10 ou 11 sur 20

C (a) (abbr **centigrade**) C (b) (abbr **century**) s.; C.16 XVIᵉ s.

c, ca (abbr **circa**) (approximately) env.; (with dates) vers

CAB [siːeɪˈbiː] n (abbr **Citizens' Advice Bureau**) = organisme bénévole britannique de conseil, notamment en matière juridique et sociale

cab [kæb] n (a) (taxi) taxi m; **c. driver** chauffeur m de taxi (b) (of train, lorry) cabine f

cabaret [ˈkæbəreɪ] n cabaret m; **c. artist** artiste mf de cabaret

cabbage [ˈkæbɪdʒ] n chou m; **red c.** chou rouge; **c. white** (butterfly) piéride f du chou

cabbie, cabby [ˈkæbɪ] (pl **cabbies**) n Fam (chauffeur m de) taxi m

cabin [ˈkæbɪn] n (of ship, plane) cabine f; (hut) cabane f; **c. boy** (on ship) mousse m; **c. crew** (on plane) équipage m

cabinet [ˈkæbɪnɪt] n (a) (piece of furniture) meuble m (à tiroirs); (with glass front) vitrine f (b) Pol cabinet m; **c. meeting** ≃ Conseil m des ministres; **c. minister** ministre m, membre m du cabinet

cabinet-maker [ˈkæbɪnɪtmeɪkə(r)] n ébéniste mf

cable [ˈkeɪbl] 1 n (electrical) & Tel câble m; **c. car** téléphérique m; **c. (television)** (télévision f par) câble 2 vt (message) câbler; **to c. sb** envoyer un câble à qn

caboodle [kəˈbuːdl] n Fam **the whole (kit and) c.** tout le bazar ou bataclan

cacao [kəˈkɑːəʊ] n (plant) cacaotier m, cacaoyer m; **c. bean** fève f de cacao

cache [kæʃ] n (a) (of drugs, arms) cache f (b) Comptr mémoire-cache f

cack-handed [kækˈhændɪd] adj Fam maladroit(e)

cackle [ˈkækl] 1 n (a) (of hen) caquet m (b) Fam (talking) caquetage m; (laugh) gloussement m; **cut the c.!** arrête de jacasser! 2 vi (a) (of hen) caqueter (b) Fam (laugh) glousser

cacophonous [kəˈkɒfənəs] adj cacophonique

cactus [ˈkæktəs] (pl **cacti** [ˈkæktaɪ] or **cactuses**) n cactus m

CAD [siːeɪˈdiː] n Comptr (abbr **computer-aided design**) CAO f

cad [kæd] n Br Fam Old-fashioned mufle m

cadaver [kəˈdævə(r)] n cadavre m

cadaverous [kəˈdævərəs] adj cadavérique

caddie [ˈkædɪ] n (in golf) caddie m

caddy [ˈkædɪ] (pl **caddies**) n (tea) c. boîte f à thé

cadence [ˈkeɪdəns] n cadence f, rythme m

cadet [kəˈdet] n Mil élève m officier; **c. corps** peloton m de préparation militaire

cadge [kædʒ] vt Fam quémander (from or off à); **to c. a meal off** or **from sb** se faire inviter à manger par qn; **can I c. a lift from you?** tu me déposes?

cadmium [ˈkædmɪəm] n Chem cadmium m

Caesarean, Caesarian [sɪˈzeərɪən] n **C. (section)** césarienne f

café, cafe [ˈkæfeɪ] n café m

cafeteria [kæfɪˈtɪərɪə] n cafétéria f

caff [kæf] n Br Fam bistro m

caffeine [ˈkæfiːn] n caféine f; **c. free** décaféiné(e)

cage [keɪdʒ] 1 n (for bird, animal) cage f; (of lift) cabine f 2 vt mettre en cage; **to feel caged in** se sentir prisonnier (ère)

cagey [ˈkeɪdʒɪ] adj (evasive) évasif(ive) (**about** sur); (cautious) prudent(e)

cagoule [kəˈguːl] n K-way® m inv

cahoots [kəˈhuːts] npl Fam **to be in c. (with sb)** être de mèche (avec qn)

CAI [siːeɪˈaɪ] n Comptr (abbr **computer-aided instruction**) EAO m

cairn [keən] n cairn m

Cairo [ˈkaɪrəʊ] n Le Caire

cajole [kəˈdʒəʊl] vt enjôler; **to c. sb into doing sth** persuader qn de faire qch

cake [keɪk] 1 n (a) (food) gâteau m; (pastry) petit gâteau; **c. shop** pâtisserie f; **c. tin** moule m à gâteau (b) (of soap) pain m (c) (idioms) **it's a piece of c.** c'est du gâteau; Prov **you can't have your c. and eat it** on ne peut pas avoir le beurre et l'argent du beurre 2 vt **her shoes were caked with mud** ses chaussures étaient couvertes de boue

CAL [kæl] n Comptr (abbr **computer-aided learning**) EAO m

calamity [kəˈlæmɪtɪ] (pl **calamities**) n calamité f

calcium [ˈkælsɪəm] n calcium m

calculate [ˈkælkjʊleɪt] 1 vt calculer; (consequences, risk) évaluer; **his remark was calculated to shock** sa remarque était destinée à choquer 2 vi **to c. on sth** compter sur qch; **to c. on doing sth** compter faire qch

calculated [ˈkælkjʊleɪtɪd] adj (risk) calculé(e); (crime) prémédité(e)

calculating [ˈkælkjʊleɪtɪŋ] adj calculateur(trice)

calculation [kælkjʊˈleɪʃən] n calcul m

calculator [ˈkælkjʊleɪtə(r)] n calculatrice f

calculus [ˈkælkjʊləs] n Math calcul m

calendar ['kælɪndə(r)] n calendrier m; **c. month** mois m civil; **c. year** année f civile

calf¹ [kɑːf] (pl **calves** [kɑːvz]) n (animal) veau m; the cow is in or with c. la vache est pleine; Fig **to kill the fatted c.** tuer le veau gras

calf² (pl **calves** [kɑːvz]) n (of leg) mollet m

calfskin ['kɑːfskɪn] n veau m

caliber Am = **calibre**

calibrate ['kælɪbreɪt] vt étalonner, calibrer

calibre, Am caliber ['kælɪbə(r)] n also Fig calibre m

calico ['kælɪkəʊ] n calicot m

California [kælɪ'fɔːnɪə] n la Californie

call [kɔːl] **1** n (a) (shout) appel m, cri m
(b) (appeal) appel m (for à); **a c. to arms** un appel aux armes
(c) (on phone) appel m, coup m de téléphone; **to give sb a c.** passer un coup de téléphone à qn; **to make a c.** passer un coup de téléphone ou de fil; **to return sb's c.** rappeler qn; **c. girl** call-girl f
(d) (visit) visite f; **to pay a c. on sb** rendre visite à qn
(e) (demand) demande f; **there are a lot of calls on my time** je suis très pris; **there's not much c. for it** il n'y a pas beaucoup de demande; **there's no c. for that kind of language!** inutile d'être impoli!; **to be on c.** (of doctor) être de garde

2 vt (a) (shout to) appeler
(b) (summon) appeler; **he's been called away** il a dû s'absenter; **he called me over to show me something** il m'a appelé pour que je vienne voir quelque chose; **to c. a meeting** décider d'organiser une réunion; **to c. a strike** appeler à la grève; **to c. sb's attention to sth** attirer l'attention de qn sur qch
(c) (on phone) appeler, téléphoner; (taxi) appeler
(d) (name) appeler; **she's called Katy** elle s'appelle Katy; **to c. sb names** injurier qn; **to c. sb a liar/a thief** traiter qn de menteur/de voleur; **c. yourself a computer expert!** et moi qui te croyais si bon en informatique!; **let's c. it £10** disons (que ce sera) 10 livres; **do you c. that clean?** tu trouves vraiment que c'est propre?; **let's c. it a day** assez pour aujourd'hui

3 vi (a) (shout) appeler; **to c. to sb** appeler qn; **to c. for help** appeler au secours ou à l'aide
(b) (on phone) appeler, téléphoner; **to c. for an ambulance** appeler une ambulance; **who's calling?** qui est à l'appareil?
(c) (visit) passer; **this train will c. at York and Peterborough** ce train s'arrêtera à York et Peterborough

▶**call back** vt sep & vi rappeler

▶**call for** vt insep (a) (require) nécessiter; **this calls for a celebration!** il faut fêter ça!; **that wasn't called for!** c'était parfaitement déplacé! (b) (demand) réclamer

▶**call in 1** vt sep (doctor, police) appeler, faire venir; (expert) faire appel à
2 vi (visit) passer (on sb chez qn)

▶**call off** vt sep (match, holiday) annuler; (search, strike) mettre fin à; (engagement) rompre

▶**call on** vt insep (a) (request) **to c. on sb to do sth** (urgently) demander instamment à qn de faire qch; (politely) inviter qn à faire qch (b) (visit) rendre visite à

▶**call out 1** vt sep (a) (doctor, plumber, troops) appeler; **to c. sb out on strike** donner l'ordre de grève à qn (b) (shout) appeler
2 vi (shout) crier

▶**call up** vt sep (a) (on phone) appeler, téléphoner à (b) (memory, image) évoquer (c) Mil appeler (sous les drapeaux)

callbox ['kɔːlbɒks] n cabine f téléphonique

caller [kɔːlə(r)] n (visitor) visiteur(euse) m,f; (on phone) correspondant(e) m,f; **next c., please** appel suivant, s'il vous plaît

calligraphy [kə'lɪgrəfɪ] n calligraphie f

calling ['kɔːlɪŋ] n (vocation) vocation f

callipers ['kælɪpəz] npl (a) (for legs) attelles fpl (b) (measuring device) compas m

callisthenics [kælɪs'θenɪks] n gymnastique f rythmique

callous ['kæləs] adj dur(e)

call-up ['kɔːlʌp] n Mil appel m (sous les drapeaux); **c. papers** ordre m d'incorporation

callus ['kæləs] n cal m

calm [kɑːm] **1** n calme m; also Fig **a dead c.** un calme plat; also Fig **the c. before the storm** le calme qui précède la tempête
2 adj calme, tranquille; (sea) calme; **to keep c.** rester calme; **to grow calmer** se calmer
3 vt calmer, apaiser; **to c. one's nerves** se calmer

▶**calm down 1** vt sep calmer
2 vi se calmer

calmly ['kɑːmlɪ] adv calmement

Calor Gas® ['kælə'gæs] n butane m

calorie ['kælərɪ] n calorie f

calumny ['kæləmnɪ] (pl **calumnies**) n calomnie f

calve [kɑːv] vi (of cow) vêler

calves [kɑːvz] pl of **calf**

calypso [kə'lɪpsəʊ] (pl **calypsos**) n Mus calypso m

CAM [siːeɪem] n Comptr (abbr **computer-aided manufacture**) FAO f

cam [kæm] n Tech came f

Cambodia [kæm'bəʊdɪə] n le Cambodge

Cambodian [kæm'bəʊdɪən] **1** n Cambodgien(enne) m,f
2 adj cambodgien(enne)

camcorder ['kæmkɔːdə(r)] n Caméscope® m

came [keɪm] pt of **come**

camel ['kæməl] n chameau m; (female) chamelle f; **c. coat** manteau m en poil de chameau; **c. driver** chamelier m

camelhair ['kæməlheə(r)] n poil m de chameau

camellia [kə'miːlɪə] n camélia m

cameo ['kæmɪəʊ] (pl **cameos**) n (a) (jewellery) camée m; **c. brooch** camée m (b) (in film) n. (c) (role) brève apparition f (d'un acteur connu)

camera ['kæmərə] n (a) (photographic) appareil photo m; TV & Cin caméra f; TV **off c.** hors champ; **on c.** à l'écran; **c. crew** équipe f de prise de vue (b) Law **in c.** à huis clos

cameraman ['kæmərəmən] n cameraman m

Cameroon [kæmə'ruːn] n le Cameroun

camisole ['kæmɪsəʊl] n caraco m

camomile ['kæməmaɪl] n camomille f; **c. tea** camomille f

camouflage ['kæməflɑːʒ] **1** n also Fig camouflage m
2 vt also Fig camoufler

camp¹ [kæmp] **1** n camp m, campement m; **c. bed** lit m de camp; **c. site** (establishment) (terrain m de) camping m; (in general) campement
2 vi to c. (out) camper

camp² adj Fam (effeminate) efféminé(e)

campaign [kæm'peɪn] **1** n campagne f
2 vi faire campagne (**for/against** pour/contre)
campaigner [kæm'peɪnə(r)] n militant(e) m,f; **to be a c. for/against sth** faire campagne pour/contre qch
camper ['kæmpə(r)] n (person) campeur(euse) m,f; (vehicle) camping-car m
campfire ['kæmpfaɪə(r)] n feu m de camp
camphor ['kæmfə(r)] n camphre m
camping ['kæmpɪŋ] n camping m; **to go c.** faire du camping; **c. site** (terrain m de) camping
campus ['kæmpəs] n campus m
camshaft ['kæmʃɑːft] n Aut arbre m à cames
can¹ [kæn] **1** n (a) (of food) boîte f; (of drink) can(n)ette f; (for petrol) bidon m; (of paint) pot m; Fig **let's not open up that c. of worms** ne commençons pas avec cette série de problèmes; **c. opener** ouvre-boîte m (b) Am very Fam (toilet) chiottes fpl; (prison) taule f, tôle f
2 vt (pt & pp **canned**) (a) (fruit, meat) mettre en boîte ou en conserve; Fig **canned laughter** (on radio, TV) rires mpl préenregistrés (b) Am Fam **c. it!** (keep quiet) la ferme!

can² [kæn, stressed kæn]

> Le verbe **can** n'a ni infinitif, ni gérondif, ni participe. Pour exprimer l'infinitif ou le participe on aura recours à la forme correspondante de **be able to** (he wanted to be able to speak English; she has always been able to swim). La forme négative est **can't**, qui s'écrit **cannot** dans la langue soutenue.

modal aux v (a) (be able to) pouvoir; **I c. go** je peux y aller; **I c. see/hear them** je les vois/entends; **we can't possibly do it** nous ne pouvons en aucun cas le faire; **he'll do what he c.** il fera ce qu'il pourra; **how c. you tell?** à quoi vois-tu ça?; **it can't be done** c'est impossible à faire
(b) (know how to) savoir; **I c. swim** je sais nager; **c. you speak English?** parles-tu anglais?
(c) (indicating possibility) pouvoir; **it c. get very hot here** il peut faire très chaud ici; **it can't have been easy for her** ça n'a pas dû être facile pour elle; **you CAN'T be serious!** tu n'es pas sérieux!; **what c. it be?** qu'est-ce que ça peut bien être?
(d) (with requests, permission) pouvoir; **c. I ask you something?** je peux vous demander quelque chose?; **you can't smoke in here** on ne peut pas fumer ici
Canada ['kænədə] n le Canada
Canadian [kə'neɪdɪən] **1** n Canadien(enne) m,f
2 adj canadien(enne)
canal [kə'næl] n canal m
Canary [kə'neərɪ] n **the C. Islands, the Canaries** les (îles fpl) Canaries fpl
canary [kə'neərɪ] n (pl **canaries**) n canari m; **c. yellow** jaune canari inv
cancel ['kænsəl] (pt & pp **cancelled**, Am **canceled**) **1** vt annuler; (cheque) faire opposition à
2 vi se décommander
▶**cancel out** vt sep annuler; **to c. each other out** s'annuler
cancellation [kænsə'leɪʃən] n annulation f; **c. fee** frais mpl d'annulation
Cancer ['kænsə(r)] n (sign of zodiac) le Cancer; **to be (a) C.** être (du) Cancer; Geog **the Tropic of C.** le tropique du Cancer
cancer ['kænsə(r)] n (disease) cancer m; **lung/skin c.** cancer du poumon/de la peau; **c. research** cancérologie f

cancerous ['kænsərəs] adj Med cancéreux(euse)
candelabra [kændɪ'lɑːbrə] n candélabre m
candid ['kændɪd] adj franc (franche)
candidacy ['kændɪdəsɪ] n candidature f
candidate ['kændɪdeɪt] n candidat(e) m,f (**for** à); **to stand as a c.** poser sa candidature, se présenter
candidature ['kændɪdətʃə(r)] = **candidacy**
candidly ['kændɪdlɪ] adv franchement
candied ['kændɪd] adj glacé(e), confit(e); **c. peel** zeste m confit
candle ['kændəl] n bougie f; **he can't hold a c. to you** il ne t'arrive pas à la cheville; **it's not worth the c.** le jeu n'en vaut pas la chandelle
candlelight ['kændəllaɪt] n lumière f d'une bougie; **by c.** à la chandelle ou bougie
candlelit ['kændəllɪt] adj aux chandelles
candlestick ['kændəlstɪk] n bougeoir m; (taller) chandelier m
candour ['kændə(r)] n franchise f
candy ['kændɪ] (pl **candies**) n Am (sweet) bonbon m; (sweets) bonbons m; **c. store** confiserie f
candyfloss ['kændɪflɒs] n Br barbe f à papa
cane [keɪn] **1** n (of sugar, bamboo) canne f, tige f; (walking stick) canne; (for punishment) verge f, baguette f; **to get the c.** recevoir des coups de verge ou de baguette; **c. furniture** meubles mpl en rotin; **c. sugar** sucre m de canne
2 vt (beat) frapper avec une verge ou une baguette
canine ['keɪnaɪn] **1** n (tooth) canine f
2 adj canin(e)
canister ['kænɪstə(r)] n boîte f (en métal); (of gas) bonbonne f
canker ['kæŋkə(r)] n also Fig chancre m
cannabis ['kænəbɪs] n cannabis m
cannery ['kænərɪ] n (pl **canneries**) n conserverie f
cannibal ['kænɪbəl] n cannibale mf
cannibalize ['kænɪbəlaɪz] vt cannibaliser
cannon ['kænən] (pl **cannons** or **cannon**) n canon m; **c. fodder** chair f à canon
cannonball ['kænənbɔːl] n boulet m de canon
cannot ['kænɒt] = **can not**
canny ['kænɪ] adj rusé(e)
canoe [kə'nuː] n canoë m
canoeing [kə'nuːɪŋ] n canoë-kayak m; **to go c.** faire du canoë-kayak
canoeist [kə'nuːɪst] n canoëiste mf
canon ['kænən] n (a) (religious decree) & Fig canon m; **c. law** droit m canon (b) (priest) chanoine m
canonize ['kænənaɪz] vt Rel canoniser
canoodle [kə'nuːdəl] n Hum se faire des mamours
canopy ['kænəpɪ] (pl **canopies**) n (above bed) baldaquin m; (outside shop) auvent m; (parachute) parachute m; (of tree branches) canopée f
cant [kænt] n (hypocrisy) langage m hypocrite
can't [kɑːnt] = **can not**
cantaloup(e) ['kæntəluːp] n melon m (cantaloup)
cantankerous [kæn'tæŋkərəs] adj revêche, acariâtre
canteen [kæn'tiːn] n (a) (restaurant) cantine f (b) (water bottle) gourde f (c) (of cutlery) ménagère f

canter ['kæntə(r)] **1** n (on horse) petit galop m
2 vi (of horse) aller au petit galop; Fig **to c. through a speech** expédier un discours; Fig **to c. through an exam** réussir un examen haut la main

cantilever ['kæntɪli:və(r)] n Tech poutre f en porte-à-faux; **c. bridge** pont m cantilever

Cantonese [kæntə'ni:z] **1** n (language) cantonais m
2 adj cantonais(e)

canvas ['kænvəs] n (a) (cloth) (grosse) toile f; **under c.** (in tent) sous la tente; Naut sous voiles (b) Art toile f

canvass ['kænvəs] **1** vt (a) Pol **to c. sb** faire campagne auprès de qn (b) Com (consumers) sonder; Fig **to c. opinion** sonder l'opinion
2 vi (a) Pol faire du porte-à-porte (dans le cadre d'une campagne électorale) (b) Com faire du démarchage

canvasser ['kænvəsə(r)] n Pol = personne qui fait du porte-à-porte dans le cadre d'une campagne électorale

canyon ['kænjən] n canyon m, canon m

CAP [si:eɪ'pi:] n (abbr **Common Agricultural Policy**) PAC f

cap [kæp] **1** n (a) (hat) (without peak) bonnet m; (with peak) casquette f; Sp **to win a c.** être sélectionné(e) dans l'équipe nationale; Fig **to go c. in hand to sb** se présenter chapeau bas devant qn; Prov **if the c. fits (wear it)** qui se sent morveux se mouche
(b) (cover) (of bottle) capsule f; (of pen) capuchon m
(c) (for toy gun) amorce f
(d) (contraceptive) diaphragme m
2 vt (pt & pp capped) (a) (cover) recouvrir (with de)
(b) **to have a tooth capped** se faire refaire l'émail d'une dent
(c) (surpass, do better than) surpasser; **that caps the lot!** c'est le bouquet!; **to c. it all,...** pour couronner le tout,...
(d) Sp **to be capped for England** être sélectionné(e) dans l'équipe d'Angleterre
(e) (spending) limiter

capability [keɪpə'bɪlɪtɪ] (pl capabilities) n capacité f (to do sth de faire qch); **it is beyond our capabilities** c'est au-dessus de nos moyens

capable ['keɪpəbəl] adj capable; **to be c. of doing sth** être capable de faire qch; **the business is in c. hands** l'affaire est entre de bonnes mains

capably ['keɪpəblɪ] adv avec compétence

capacious [kə'peɪʃəs] adj vaste, spacieux(euse)

capacitor [kə'pæsɪtə(r)] n Elec condensateur m

capacity [kə'pæsɪtɪ] (pl capacities) n (a) (of container, bus, theatre) & Elec capacité f; **the stadium has a c. of 50,000** le stade peut accueillir 50 000 spectateurs; **full to c.** plein(e); **there was a c. crowd at the match** le stade était bondé pour le match (b) (aptitude) **to have a c. for sth** être capable de qch; **to be beyond sb's c.** dépasser les compétences de qn; **to be within sb's c.** être dans les possibilités de qn; **c. for work** capacité f de travail (c) (output) capacité f; **at full c.** à plein (d) (role) **in my c. as...** en ma qualité de...

cape¹ [keɪp] n (cloak) pèlerine f, cape f

cape² n Geog cap m; **the C. of Good Hope** le cap de Bonne-Espérance; **C. Town** Le Cap

caper¹ ['keɪpə(r)] n Culin câpre f

caper² **1** n (prank) cabriole f; **what a c.!** (fuss) quel cirque!
2 vi **to c. (about)** faire des cabrioles

Cape Verde [keɪp'vɜ:d] n le Cap-Vert

capillary [kə'pɪlərɪ] **1** (pl capillaries) n capillaire m
2 adj capillaire

capital ['kæpɪtəl] **1** n (a) (letter) majuscule f, capitale f (b) **c. (city)** capitale f (c) Fin capital m; Fig **to make c. out of sth** tirer parti de qch; **c. assets** actif m immobilisé; **c. expenditure** dépenses fpl en capital; **c. gains tax** impôt m sur les plus-values (en capital); **c. goods** biens mpl d'équipement; **c. investment** investissement m de capitaux
2 adj (a) (letter) majuscule; **c. T** T majuscule; **he's rich with a c. R** il est vraiment très riche (b) Law **c. crime or offence** crime m capital ou puni de mort; **c. punishment** peine f capitale (c) (important) capital(e); **of c. importance** d'une importance capitale (d) Br Old-fashioned (splendid) extra inv

capitalism ['kæpɪtəlɪzəm] n capitalisme m

capitalist ['kæpɪtəlɪst] n & adj capitaliste mf

capitalization [kæpɪtəlaɪ'zeɪʃən] n Fin capitalisation f

capitalize ['kæpɪtəlaɪz] vt (a) Fin capitaliser (b) (initial letter) écrire avec une majuscule; (whole word) écrire en majuscules

▸**capitalize on** vt insep profiter de, tirer parti de

Capitol ['kæpɪtəl] n Am Pol **the C.** le Capitole

capitulate [kə'pɪtjʊleɪt] vi capituler (to devant)

capon ['keɪpɒn] n Culin chapon m

caprice [kə'pri:s] n caprice m

capricious [kə'prɪʃəs] adj capricieux(euse)

Capricorn ['kæprɪkɔ:n] n (sign of zodiac) le Capricorne; **to be a** (C.) être (du) Capricorne; Geog **the Tropic of C.** le tropique du Capricorne

capsicum ['kæpsɪkəm] n Culin poivron m

capsize [kæp'saɪz] **1** vt faire chavirer
2 vi chavirer

capstan ['kæpstən] n Naut cabestan m

capsule ['kæpsju:l] n (of medicine) gélule f; (space) **c.** capsule f spatiale

Capt (abbr **Captain**) Capt

captain ['kæptɪn] **1** n capitaine m
2 vt être le capitaine de; **he captained them to victory** il les a conduits à la victoire

captaincy ['kæptɪnsɪ] n (in sport) **during her c.** pendant qu'elle était capitaine

caption ['kæpʃən] n légende f

captivate ['kæptɪveɪt] vt fasciner

captivating ['kæptɪveɪtɪŋ] adj fascinant(e)

captive ['kæptɪv] n & adj captif(ive) m,f; **to be taken c.** être fait(e) prisonnier(ère); **he had a c. audience** son auditoire était forcé de l'écouter

captivity [kæp'trɪvɪtɪ] n captivité f; **in c.** en captivité

captor ['kæptə(r)] n ravisseur(euse) m,f

capture ['kæptʃə(r)] **1** n capture f; (of town, enemy, position) prise f
2 vt (person, animal) capturer; (town, enemy, position) prendre (from à); (in chess) prendre; Fig (mood) rendre; **to c. sb's imagination** parler à l'imagination de qn; **to c. the moment** saisir l'instant

car [kɑː(r)] *n* (**a**) *(automobile)* voiture *f*, automobile *f*; **by c.** en voiture; **c. bomb** voiture piégée; **c. boot sale** = vente à la brocante où les vendeurs exposent leurs marchandises à l'arrière de leur voiture; **c. crash** accident *m* de voiture; **c. door** portière *f* de voiture; *Br* **c. hire**, *Am* **c. rental** location *f* de voitures; **c. industry** industrie *f* automobile; *Br* **c. park** parc *m* de stationnement, parking *m*; **c. phone** téléphone *m* de voiture; **c. pool** = groupe de personnes effectuant régulièrement un trajet dans la même voiture; **c. radio** autoradio *m* (**b**) *Am (rail wagon)* voiture *f*, wagon *m*

carafe [kəˈræf] *n* carafe *f*

caramel [ˈkærəməl] *n* caramel *m*

carat [ˈkærət] *n* carat *m*; **18-c. gold** or (*m* à) 18 carats

caravan [ˈkærəvæn] *n* caravane *f*; *(pulled by horse)* roulotte *f*; **c. holiday** vacances *fpl* en caravane; **c. site** camping *m* (pour caravanes)

caraway [ˈkærəweɪ] *n* carvi *m*, cumin *m* des prés; **c. seeds** graines *fpl* de carvi

carbohydrate [kɑːbəʊˈhaɪdreɪt] *n* hydrate *m* de carbone; *(in food)* glucide *m*; **low-/high-c. diet** régime *m* hypoglucidique/hyperglucidique

carbolic [kɑːˈbɒlɪk] *adj Chem* **c. acid** phénol *m*; **c. soap** ≃ savon *m* de Marseille

carbon [ˈkɑːbən] *n* carbone *m*; **c. copy** copie *f* (au carbone); *Fig* **she is a c. copy of her mother** c'est la copie conforme de sa mère; **c. dioxide** dioxyde *m* de carbone, gaz *m* carbonique; **c. fibre** fibre *f* de carbone; **c. monoxide** monoxyde *m* de carbone; **c. paper** (papier *m*) carbone

carbonated [ˈkɑːbəneɪtɪd] *adj* gazéifié(e); *(naturally)* gazeux(euse)

carbonize [ˈkɑːbənaɪz] *vt* carboniser

carbuncle [ˈkɑːbʌŋkəl] *n Med* furoncle *m*

carburettor, *Am* **carburetor** [ˈkɑːbjʊretə(r)] *n* carburateur *m*

carcase, carcass [ˈkɑːkəs] *n (of animal)* carcasse *f*

carcinogenic [kɑːsɪnəˈdʒenɪk] *adj Med* carcinogène

card [kɑːd] *n* (**a**) *(for card game)* carte *f*; **to play cards** jouer aux cartes; **c. game** jeu *m* de cartes; **c. table** table *f* de jeux; **c. trick** tour *m* de cartes (**b**) *(with printed information)* carte *f*; *(postcard)* carte (postale); *Pol* **c. vote** = scrutin où chaque délégué muni d'une carte vote pour la totalité des membres qu'il représente; **c. index** *or* **file** fichier *m* (**c**) *(plastic)* carte *f* (**d**) *(cardboard)* carton *m* (fin) (**e**) *Comptr* carte *f* (**f**) *(idioms)* **play your cards right and you could get promoted** si tu mènes bien ton jeu, tu seras peut-être promu; **to put one's cards on the table** jouer cartes sur table; **to have a c. up one's sleeve** avoir un atout dans son jeu; **it is** *Br* **on** *or Am* **in the cards that...** il est bien possible que...; *Br Fam* **to get one's cards** se faire virer

cardamom [ˈkɑːdəməm] *n* cardamome *f*

cardboard [ˈkɑːdbɔːd] *n* carton *m*; **c. box** (boîte *f* en) carton; **c. city** = campement où les sans-abri vivent dans des cartons; *Fig & Pej* **c. characters** personnages *mpl* sans aucune profondeur

card-carrying [ˈkɑːdkærɪŋ] *adj* **c. member** adhérent(e) *m,f*

cardiac [ˈkɑːdɪæk] *adj* cardiaque; **c. arrest** arrêt *m* cardiaque

cardigan [ˈkɑːdɪɡən] *n* cardigan *m*

cardinal [ˈkɑːdɪnəl] **1** *n Rel* cardinal *m*
2 *adj* cardinal(e); *Fig* **it's a c. sin** c'est impardonnable

cardiograph [ˈkɑːdɪəʊɡræf] *n* cardiographe *m*

cardiologist [kɑːdɪˈɒlədʒɪst] *n* cardiologue *mf*

cardiology [kɑːdɪˈɒlədʒɪ] *n* cardiologie *f*

cardiovascular [kɑːdɪəʊˈvæskjʊlə(r)] *adj* cardio-vasculaire

cardphone [ˈkɑːdfəʊn] *n* téléphone *m* à carte

cardsharp(er) [ˈkɑːdʃɑːp(ə(r))] *n* tricheur(euse) *m,f* professionnel(elle)

care [keə(r)] **1** *n* (**a**) *(worry)* souci *m*; **she doesn't have a c. in the world** elle n'a pas le moindre souci
(**b**) *(attention)* soin *m*; *(medical treatment)* soins médicaux; **to put a lot of c. into sth** apporter beaucoup de soin à qch; **to drive without due c.** conduire imprudemment; **to take c. of** s'occuper de; **to take c. of oneself** savoir se débrouiller tout(e) seul(e); *(healthwise)* prendre soin de sa santé; **to take c. to do sth** faire bien attention à faire qch; **take c.!** *(goodbye)* fais attention!
(**c**) *(protection)* soins *mpl*; *(of clothes, machine)* entretien *m*; **to put a child in c.** mettre un enfant à l'Assistance publique; **to be in** *or* **under sb's c.** avoir été confié(e) à qn; **write to me c. of Mrs Wallace** écrivez-moi chez Mme Wallace *ou* aux bons soins de Mme Wallace
2 *vt* (**a**) *(mind)* **I don't c. what he says** peu m'importe ce qu'il en dit; **I don't c. whether he likes it or not** peu m'importe que cela lui plaise ou non
(**b**) *(like)* **would you c. to come with me?** aimeriez-vous m'accompagner?
3 *vi* (**a**) *(be concerned)* se préoccuper, se soucier *(about* de); **that's all he cares about** c'est tout ce qui l'intéresse; **to c. about sb** *(be fond of)* aimer qn
(**b**) *(mind)* **I don't c. ;ça m'est égal; who cares?** qu'est-ce que ça peut faire?; **I could be dead for all they c.!** ils se moquent éperdument de ce qui peut m'arriver!; **I couldn't c. less** je m'en moque éperdument

▸**care for** *vt insep* (**a**) *(look after)* soigner (**b**) *(like)* aimer

career [kəˈrɪə(r)] **1** *n* carrière *f*; **it's a good/bad c. move** c'est bon/mauvais pour ma/ta/*etc* carrière; **careers officer** conseiller(ère) *m,f* d'orientation; **careers service** service *m* d'orientation professionnelle
2 *vi* **to c. (along)** aller à vive allure; **the car careered off the road** la voiture a quitté la route à vive allure

careerist [kəˈrɪərɪst] *n Pej* carriériste *mf*

carefree [ˈkeəfriː] *adj* insouciant(e)

careful [ˈkeəfəl] *adj* (**a**) *(cautious)* prudent(e); **be c. of that step** fais attention à la marche; (**b**) **c.!** fais attention!; **to be c. to do sth** faire bien attention à faire qch; **she was c. not to mention his name** elle a bien fait attention à ne pas mentionner son nom; **be c. what you say** fais attention à ce que tu dis; **you can't be too c. these days** on n'est jamais trop prudent de nos jours (**b**) *(thorough)* *(work, inspection)* minutieux(euse); **after c. consideration** après mûre réflexion

carefully [ˈkeəfəlɪ] *adv* (**a**) *(cautiously)* prudemment (**b**) *(thoroughly)* soigneusement, avec soin; *(listen)* attentivement; **c. worded** aux termes choisis (avec soin)

careless [ˈkeəlɪs] *adj* (**a**) *(negligent)* négligent(e); *(work)* négligé(e); **to be c. about one's appearance** être négligé(e); **a c. mistake** une faute d'inattention, une étourderie; **a c. remark** une remarque inconsidérée (**b**) *(unconcerned)* insouciant(e)

carelessly [ˈkeəlɪslɪ] *adv (negligently)* négligemment

carelessness [ˈkeəlɪsnɪs] *n (negligence)* négligence *f*

carer ['keərə(r)] n (professional) aide mf à domicile; (relative) = personne s'occupant d'un parent malade ou âgé

caress [kə'res] 1 n caresse f
2 vt caresser

caretaker ['keəteikə(r)] n concierge mf, gardien(enne) m,f; c. government gouvernement m intérimaire

careworn ['keəwɔːn] adj usé(e) par les soucis

cargo ['kɑːgəʊ] (pl cargoes or cargos) n cargaison f; c. boat or ship cargo m; c. plane avion-cargo m

Caribbean [kærɪ'biːən, Am kə'rɪbɪən] 1 n the C. (Sea) la mer des Caraïbes; the C. (region) la Caraïbe
2 adj caraïbe

caribou ['kærɪbuː] n caribou m

caricature ['kærɪkətjʊə(r)] 1 n caricature f
2 vt caricaturer

caricaturist ['kærɪkə'tjʊərɪst] n caricaturiste mf

caries ['keəriːz] n Med carie f

caring ['keərɪŋ] adj (society, personality) humain(e); (parent) aimant(e); (atmosphere) chaleureux(euse); the c. professions les professions fpl médicales et paramédicales

carnage ['kɑːnɪdʒ] n carnage m

carnal ['kɑːnəl] adj charnel(elle)

carnation [kɑː'neɪʃən] n œillet m

carnival ['kɑːnɪvəl] n (celebration) carnaval m; (funfair) fête f foraine

carnivore ['kɑːnɪvɔː(r)] n carnivore m

carnivorous [kɑː'nɪvərəs] adj carnivore

carob ['kærəb] n (fruit) caroube f; (tree) caroubier m

carol ['kærəl] n (Christmas) c. chant m de Noël

carouse [kə'raʊz] vi faire la fête

carousel [kærə'sel] n (a) Am (at funfair) chevaux mpl de bois, manège m (b) (at airport) carrousel m (pour bagages) (c) (for slides) magasin m

carp¹ [kɑːp] (pl carp) n (fish) carpe f

carp² n se plaindre (at de)

Carpathians [kɑː'peɪθɪənz] npl the C. les Carpates fpl

carpenter ['kɑːpɪntə(r)] n menuisier m; (on building site) charpentier m

carpentry ['kɑːpɪntrɪ] n menuiserie f; (on building site) charpenterie f

carpet ['kɑːpɪt] 1 n (a) (rug) & Fig (of flowers, snow) tapis m; (fitted) moquette f; c. bombing bombardement m intensif; c. slippers pantoufles fpl (b) (idioms) to pull the c. out from under sb faire un tour de cochon à qn
2 vt (a) (with rug) recouvrir d'un tapis; (with fitted carpet) moquetter; (with snow) recouvrir d'un tapis; (with fitted carpet) recouvert(e) de neige (b) Fam (tell off) sermonner

carpet-sweeper ['kɑːpɪtswiːpə(r)] n balai m mécanique

carport ['kɑːpɔːt] n abri m pour voiture

carriage ['kærɪdʒ] n (a) (vehicle) voiture f (b) (of train) voiture f, wagon m; Br (of typewriter) chariot m; c. return retour-chariot m (d) Com (transport) transport m; (cost) frais mpl de port; c. forward (en) port m dû; c. free franco de port; c. paid (en) port m payé (e) (bearing) (of person) port m

carriageway ['kærɪdʒweɪ] n chaussée f

carrier ['kærɪə(r)] n (a) (of disease, germs) porteur(euse) m,f (b) Com (company, airline) transporteur m; (on bicycle) porte-bagages m inv (c) c. (bag) sac m (en papier ou en plastique)

carrion ['kærɪən] n charogne f

carrot ['kærət] n also Fig carotte f; a c. and stick approach la carotte et le bâton

carry ['kærɪ] (pt & pp carried) 1 vt (a) (transport, convey) porter; (goods, passengers) transporter; (electricity, fuel) acheminer; (gun, money) avoir sur soi; (a scar) avoir; (disease) être porteur(euse) de; the current carried the raft out to sea le courant a emporté le radeau au large; to c. an image in one's head avoir une image en tête; to be carrying sb's child (be pregnant) porter l'enfant de qn; Fig to c. the can porter le chapeau; Fig she refused to c. the can for their mistake elle refusa qu'ils lui fassent porter la responsabilité de leur erreur
(b) (involve) (risk) comporter; to c. a fine/penalty être passible d'une amende/d'une peine; to c. weight/authority avoir du poids/de l'autorité
(c) (develop) to c. sth too far pousser qch trop loin; to c. an argument to its logical conclusion aller au bout d'un raisonnement
(d) (capture, win) to c. all before one (be successful) remporter tous les prix; (win support, approval) vaincre toutes les résistances; his argument carried the day son argument l'a emporté
(e) (proposal, motion) voter
(f) (of newspaper, news programme) (story) faire état de; (advertisement) contenir
(g) Com (keep in stock) vendre
(h) to c. oneself (behave) se conduire
(i) Math c. two et je retiens deux
2 vi (of sound) porter; her voice carries well elle a une voix qui porte bien

▶**carry away** vt sep (a) (take away) emporter (b) to get carried away (excited) s'emballer

▶**carry forward** vt sep Fin reporter; carried forward report, à reporter

▶**carry off** vt sep (a) (take away) emporter; (prize) remporter (b) (do successfully) she carried it off (well) elle s'en est bien sortie

▶**carry on** 1 vt sep (tradition) perpétuer; (business, trade) exercer; (correspondence) entretenir; (conversation) poursuivre
2 vi (a) (continue) continuer, poursuivre; to c. on doing sth continuer de ou à faire qch (b) Fam (behave badly) mal se conduire; I don't like the way she carries on je n'aime pas ses façons (c) Fam (have an affair) avoir une liaison (with avec) (d) (talk) parler sans cesse (about de)

▶**carry out** vt sep (plan, threat, decision) mettre à exécution; (experiment, test) faire, effectuer; (instructions) exécuter

carrycot ['kærɪkɒt] n porte-bébé m inv

carry-on ['kærɪɒn] n Fam ramdam m; what a c.! quel cirque!

carry-out ['kærɪaʊt] n Am & Scot (meal) repas m à emporter; (restaurant) = boutique qui fait des plats à emporter

carsick ['kɑːsɪk] adj to be c. avoir mal au cœur en voiture

cart [kɑːt] 1 n (vehicle) charrette f; (trolley) chariot m; Fig to put the c. before the horse mettre la charrue avant les bœufs
2 vt Fam (carry) trimballer

▶**cart off** vt sep Fam to c. sb off emmener qn

cart² n (abbr **cartridge**) cassette f

carte blanche [kɑːt'blɑːʃ] n to give sb c. (to do sth) donner carte blanche à qn (pour faire qch)

cartel [kɑː'tel] *n Econ* cartel *m*

carthorse ['kɑːthɔːs] *n* cheval *m* de trait; *Fig* lourdaud *m*

cartilage ['kɑːtɪlɪdʒ] *n* cartilage *m*

cartographer [kɑː'tɒgrəfə(r)] *n* cartographe *mf*

cartography [kɑː'tɒgrəfɪ] *n* cartographie *f*

carton ['kɑːtən] *n (of yoghurt, cream)* pot *m*; *(of milk, fruit juice)* brique *f*; *(of cigarettes)* cartouche *f*

cartoon [kɑː'tuːn] *n (drawing)* dessin *m* humoristique; *(film)* dessin animé; **c. (strip)** bande *f* dessinée

cartoonist [kɑː'tuːnɪst] *n* dessinateur(trice) *m,f*

cartridge ['kɑːtrɪdʒ] *n (a) (for gun, pen, of film)* cartouche *f*; **c. belt** cartouchière *f* **(b)** **c. paper** papier *m* à cartouche

cartwheel ['kɑːtwiːl] *n* roue *f* de charrette; **to turn cartwheels** faire la roue

carve [kɑːv] *vt (wood, stone, statue)* sculpter; *(name)* graver; *(meat)* découper

▶**carve out** *vt sep* to c. out a career for oneself faire carrière, the company carved out a niche for itself la société s'est taillé une place sur le marché

▶**carve up** *vt sep Fig (territory)* découper

carving ['kɑːvɪŋ] *n (a) Art* sculpture *f* **(b)** **c. knife** *(for meat)* couteau *m* à découper

carwash ['kɑːwɒʃ] *n* = station de lavage automatique pour autos; *(sign)* lavage automatique

cascade [kæs'keɪd] **1** *n* cascade *f*
2 *vi* tomber en cascade

case¹ [keɪs] *n (a) (instance, situation) & Med* cas *m*; **a c. in point** un cas d'espèce; **in c. of emergency/accident** en cas d'urgence/accident; **in c. he isn't there** au cas où il ne serait pas là; **I'll take it just in c.** je vais le prendre au cas où; **just in c. it rains** au cas où il pleuvrait; **in any c.** *(besides)* de toute façon; **in that c.** dans ce cas; **in such a c.** en pareil cas; **as the c. may be** suivant le cas; **if that's the c.** dans ce cas(-là), s'il en est ainsi; *Med* **c. history** antécédents *mpl*; **c. study** étude *f* de cas
(b) *Law* affaire *f*; **the c. will be heard on 5 January** l'audience aura lieu le 5 janvier; **the c. for the defence** la défense; **the c. for the prosecution** l'accusation *f*; *Fig* **the c. for sb/sth** les arguments *mpl* en faveur de qn/qch; *Fig* **she has a good c.** elle a de bons arguments; **c. law** droit *m* jurisprudentiel

case² [keɪs] *n (a) (container) (for spectacles, cigarettes, musical instrument)* étui *m*; *(for jewellery)* écrin *m*; *(packing)* c. caisse *f*; **a c. of wine** une caisse de vin; **(display** *or* **glass) c.** vitrine *f* **(b)** *(suitcase)* valise *f*; *(briefcase)* porte-documents *m inv* **(c)** *Typ* **lower/upper c.** bas *m*/haut *m* de casse

casement ['keɪsmənt] *n* **c. (window)** fenêtre *f* à deux battants

cash [kæʃ] **1** *n (coins, banknotes)* liquide *m*; *Fam (money in general)* sous *mpl*; **to pay (in) c.** payer en liquide *ou* en espèces; **c. on delivery** paiement *m* à la livraison; **c. and carry** *(shop)* magasin *m* de demi-gros; **c. in hand** fonds *m ou* argent *m* en caisse; **c. box** caisse *f*; **c. card** carte *f* de retrait; **c. crop** culture *f* commerciale; **c. desk** caisse *f*; **c. dispenser** *or* **machine** distributeur *m* automatique de billets; *Fin* **c. flow** trésorerie *f*; **c. price** prix *m* au comptant; **c. register** caisse enregistreuse
2 *vt (cheque, postal order)* encaisser

▶**cash in on** *vt insep Fam* profiter de, tirer profit de

cash-book ['kæʃbʊk] *n* livre *m ou* journal *m* de caisse

cashew ['kæʃuː] *n* **c. (nut)** noix *f* de cajou

cashier [kæ'ʃɪə(r)] *n* caissier(ère) *m,f*

cashmere ['kæʃmɪə(r)] *n* cachemire *m*

cashpoint ['kæʃpɔɪnt] *n* distributeur *m* automatique de billets

casing ['keɪsɪŋ] *n Tech* boîtier *m*; *(of sausage)* boyau *m*

casino [kə'siːnəʊ] *(pl* **casinos)** *n* casino *m*

cask [kɑːsk] *n* fût *m*, tonneau *m*

casket ['kɑːskɪt] *n (a) (for jewellery)* coffret *m* **(b)** *(coffin)* cercueil *m*

Caspian Sea ['kæspɪənsiː] *n* **the C.** la mer Caspienne

cassava [kə'sɑːvə] *n* manioc *m*

casserole ['kæsərəʊl] *n (pot)* cocotte *f*; *(food)* ragoût *m*

cassette [kæ'set] *n* cassette *f*; **c. player** lecteur *m* de cassettes; **c. recorder** magnétophone *m* à cassettes

cassock ['kæsək] *n* soutane *f*

cast [kɑːst] **1** *n (a) (of play, film)* acteurs *mpl*; *(list)* distribution *f* **(b)** *(moulded object)* moulage *m*; *Med* **(plaster)** c. plâtre *m*; *Fig* **c. of mind** tournure *f* d'esprit **(c)** **to have a c. in one's eye** *(squint)* avoir une coquetterie dans l'œil
2 *n (pt & pp* **cast**) **(a)** *(throw) (stone)* jeter, lancer; *(shadow, net, line)* jeter; **to c. one's eyes over sth** parcourir qch des yeux; **to c. doubt on sth** jeter un doute sur qch, faire planer un doute sur qch; *Fig* **to c. light on sth** permettre de comprendre qch; **to c. one's mind back to sth** revenir sur qch, se rappeler qch; **to c. its skin** *(of reptile)* muer; **to c. a spell over sb** envoûter qn *Br* **to c. one's vote (for)** voter (pour) **(c)** *(film, play)* faire la distribution de; **she was cast as or in the role of Desdemona** on l'a choisie pour le rôle de Desdémone **(d)** *(metal, statue)* couler; **c. iron** fonte *f*

▶**cast about, cast around** *vi* to c. about *or* around for sth chercher qch

▶**cast aside** *vt sep (idea, prejudice)* se défaire de

▶**cast away** *vt sep* to be cast away faire naufrage

▶**cast down** *vt sep* to be cast down être abattu(e) *ou* découragé(e)

▶**cast off** **1** *vt sep (clothes, chains)* rejeter, enlever; *(chains)* se libérer de
2 *vi (a) Naut* larguer les amarres **(b)** *(in knitting)* arrêter les mailles

▶**cast on** *vi (in knitting)* monter les mailles

castanets [kæstə'nets] *npl* castagnettes *fpl*

castaway ['kɑːstəweɪ] *n* naufragé(e) *m,f*

caste [kɑːst] *n (social rank)* caste *f*

caster sugar ['kɑːstə(r)ʃʊgə(r)] *n* sucre *m* en poudre

castigate ['kæstɪgeɪt] *vt Formal* critiquer sévèrement

casting ['kɑːstɪŋ] **1** *n (of play, film)* distribution *f*, casting *m*
2 *adj* **c. vote** voix *f* prépondérante

cast-iron ['kɑːst'aɪən] *adj* en *ou* de fonte; *Fig (alibi, guarantee)* en béton

castle ['kɑːsəl] **1** *n* château *m*; *(in chess)* tour *f*; *Fig* **to build castles in the air** bâtir des châteaux en Espagne
2 *vi (in chess)* roquer

cast-off ['kɑːstɒf] **1** *n (garment)* vieux vêtement *m*; *(person)* laissé-pour-compte (laissée-pour-compte) *m,f*
2 *adj* **c. clothing** vieux vêtements *mpl*

castor ['kɑːstə(r)] *n (on furniture)* roulette *f*

castor oil [kɑːstə'rɔɪl] *n* huile *f* de ricin

castrate [kæs'treɪt] *vt* châtrer, castrer

castration [kæs'treɪʃən] *n* castration *f*

casual ['kæʒjʊəl] *adj* (a) *(offhand)* *(remark, glance)* en passant (b) *(relaxed, informal)* décontracté(e); *(conversation)* à bâtons rompus; *(clothes)* sport *inv* (c) *(careless)* désinvolte (d) *(meeting)* fortuit(e) (e) *(employment, worker)* temporaire

casually ['kæʒjʊəlɪ] *adv* (a) *(remark, glance)* en passant (b) *(informally)* avec décontraction; *(dress)* sport (c) *(carelessly)* avec désinvolture (d) *(meet)* par hasard

casualty ['kæʒjʊəltɪ] (*pl* **casualties**) *n* victime *f*; **c. department** *(service in hosp)* urgences *fpl*

cat [kæt] *n* (a) *(animal)* chat *m*; *(female)* chatte *f*; **the big cats** les grands fauves *mpl*; **c. burglar** monte-en-l'air *m inv*; **c.'s eye®** *(on road)* catadioptre *m*; **c. flap** chatière *f*; **c. litter** litière *f* pour chats (b) *(idioms)* **to play a c.-and-mouse game with sb** jouer au chat et à la souris avec qn; *Fam* **to be like a c. on a hot tin roof** *or* **on hot bricks** ne pas tenir en place; **to let the c. out of the bag** vendre la mèche; **to fight like a c. and dog** être comme chien et chat; **to set the c. among the pigeons** jeter un pavé dans la mare; *Fam* **there isn't enough room to swing a c.** il n'y a même pas la place de se retourner; *Fam* **he thinks he's the cat's whiskers** il se croit sorti de la cuisse de Jupiter

cataclysm ['kætəklɪzm] *n* cataclysme *m*

Catalan ['kætələn] **1** *n* (a) *(person)* Catalan(e) *m,f* (b) *(language)* catalan *m*
2 *adj* catalan(e)

catalogue, *Am* **catalog** ['kætəlɒg] **1** *n* catalogue *m*
2 *vt* inventorier

Catalonia [kætə'ləʊnɪə] *n* la Catalogne

catalyst ['kætəlɪst] *n also Fig* catalyseur *m*

catamaran [kætəmə'ræn] *n* catamaran *m*

catapult ['kætəpʌlt] **1** *n* *(hand-held)* fronde *f*, lance-pierre *m*; *(on aircraft carrier)* & *Hist (weapon)* catapulte *f*
2 *vt* catapulter; **to c. sb to stardom** propulser qn vers la gloire

cataract ['kætərækt] *n* *(in river)* & *Med* cataracte *f*

catarrh [kə'tɑː(r)] *n* inflammation *f* des muqueuses respiratoires

catastrophe [kə'tæstrəfɪ] *n* catastrophe *f*

catastrophic [kætə'strɒfɪk] *adj* catastrophique

catatonic [kætə'tɒnɪk] *adj Med* catatonique

catcall ['kætkɔːl] *n* sifflet *m*

catch [kætʃ] **1** *n* (a) *(of ball)* prise *f* au vol; **good c.!** bien attrapé!
(b) *(in fishing)* prise *f*; *(of a whole day)* pêche *f*
(c) *(fastening)* *(of door)* loquet *m*; *(of window)* loqueteau *m*; *(of bracelet)* fermoir *m*
(d) *(disadvantage)* **where's the c.?** c'est quoi le truc *ou* le piège?; **it's a c.-22 situation** c'est un cercle vicieux
2 *vt* (*pt & pp* **caught** [kɔːt]) (a) *(ball, thief)* attraper; *(fish)* prendre; **caught you!** je t'y prends!; **to c. sb doing sth** surprendre qn en train de *ou* à faire qch; **you won't c. me doing that again** on ne m'y reprendra plus; **to be caught in a storm** être surpris(e) par un orage; **to c. the sun** *(of room, garden)* être ensoleillé(e); *(of person)* prendre des couleurs
(b) *(bus, train)* prendre; *(film)* voir
(c) *(hear)* saisir
(d) *(manage to find)* trouver; **you've caught me at a bad time** tu arrives/me téléphones au mauvais moment; **I'll c. you later!** on se voit plus tard!
(e) *(clothes)* accrocher (**on** à); **to c. one's fingers in the door** se prendre *ou* se coincer les doigts dans la porte

3 *vi* (a) *(of fire)* prendre
(b) *(in door)* se prendre, se coincer; *(on a nail)* s'accrocher
(c) *(of person)* **to c. at sth** s'accrocher à qch

▶**catch on** *vi* (a) *(of fashion)* prendre (b) *Fam (understand)* piger

▶**catch out** *vt sep* *(of difficult question)* piéger; *(of situation)* surprendre

▶**catch up 1** *vt sep* (a) *(reach)* rattraper (b) **to get caught up in sth** *(discussion)* être entraîné(e) dans qch; *(book, film)* être absorbé(e) par qch; *(traffic jam)* être pris(e) dans qch
2 *vi* *(close gap, get closer)* **to c. up with sb** rattraper qn; **to c. up with sth** *(news, gossip)* se mettre au courant de qch; **to c. up with one's work** se mettre à jour dans son travail; **his past caught up with him** son passé a resurgi

catch-all ['kætʃɔːl] *adj Fam* fourre-tout *inv*

catching ['kætʃɪŋ] *adj (disease, habit)* contagieux(euse)

catchment area ['kætʃmənteərɪə] *n* *(of school)* = zone desservie par une école; *(of hospital)* = zone desservie par un hôpital

catchphrase ['kætʃfreɪz] *n* *(political)* slogan *m*; *(of comedian)* formule *f* favorite

catchy ['kætʃɪ] *adj (tune, slogan)* facile à retenir

catechism ['kætəkɪzəm] *n* catéchisme *m*

categorical [kætɪ'gɒrɪkəl] *adj* *(denial, refusal)* catégorique; *(evidence)* formel(elle)

categorize ['kætɪgəraɪz] *vt* étiqueter (**as** comme)

category ['kætɪgərɪ] (*pl* **categories**) *n* catégorie *f*

cater ['keɪtə(r)] *vi* (a) *(provide food)* s'occuper de la nourriture; **to c. for** *(guests)* fournir le repas pour; *(event)* fournir le(s) repas de (b) **to c. for** *(needs, tastes)* satisfaire; **parties catered for** *(sign in restaurant)* noces et banquets

caterer ['keɪtərə(r)] *n* traiteur *m*

catering ['keɪtərɪŋ] *n* *(trade)* restauration *f*; **to do the c.** fournir les repas; **c. school** école *f* hôtelière

caterpillar ['kætəpɪlə(r)] *n* chenille *f*; **c. track** *(on tank, tractor)* chenille

catfish ['kætfɪʃ] *n* poisson-chat *m*

cathartic [kə'θɑːtɪk] *adj* cathartique

cathedral [kə'θiːdrəl] *n* cathédrale *f*; **c. city** ville *f* épiscopale, évêché *m*

catheter ['kæθɪtə(r)] *n Med* cathéter *m*

cathode ['kæθəʊd] *n Elec* cathode *f*; **c. ray tube** tube *m* cathodique

Catholic ['kæθlɪk] *Rel* **1** *n* catholique *mf*; **to be a C.** être catholique
2 *adj* catholique

catholic ['kæθlɪk] *adj (wide-ranging)* éclectique

Catholicism [kə'θɒlɪsɪzəm] *n* catholicisme *m*

catkin ['kætkɪn] *n* chaton *m* *(d'arbre)*

catnap ['kætnæp] *n Fam* petit somme *m*

catsuit ['kætsuːt] *n* combinaison *f* collante

cattle ['kætəl] *npl* bétail *m*; **c. breeding** élevage *m* de bétail; **c. grid** = grille recouvrant une fosse et empêchant le passage du bétail; *also Fig* **c. market** marché *m* ou foire *f* aux bestiaux; **c. truck** bétaillère *f*

catty ['kætɪ] *adj Fam* vache; **c. remark** vacherie *f*

catwalk ['kætwɔ:k] *n* podium *m*

Caucasian [kɔ:'keɪʒən] **1** *n* (*white person*) Blanc (Blanche) *m,f* (*de type européen*)
2 *adj* (*in ethnology*) blanc (blanche) (*de type européen*)

Caucasus ['kɔ:kəsəs] *n* **the C.** le Caucase

caucus ['kɔ:kəs] *n Pol Br* = comité à l'intérieur d'un parti politique; *Am* caucus *m*

caught [kɔ:t] *pt & pp of* **catch**

cauldron ['kɔ:ldrən] *n* chaudron *m*

cauliflower ['kɒlɪflaʊə(r)] *n* chou-fleur *m*; **c. cheese** chou-fleur au gratin; *Fam* **c. ear** oreille *f* en chou-fleur

cause [kɔ:z] **1** *n* **(a)** (*origin*) cause *f*; **c. and effect** la cause et l'effet **(b)** (*reason*) raison *f*, motif *m*; **to have good c. for doing sth** avoir de bonnes raisons de faire qch; **and with good c.** et pour cause; **to give c. for complaint** donner lieu à des plaintes; **to give c. for concern** être inquiétant(e) **(c)** (*purpose, mission*) cause *f*; **to make common c. (with sb)** faire cause commune (avec qn); **it's all in a good c.** (*for charity*) c'est pour une bonne cause; *Fig* c'est pour la bonne cause
2 *vt* provoquer; (*trouble*) causer; **to c. sb grief** faire de la peine à qn; **to c. sb to do sth** faire faire qch à qn; **he caused the plan to fail** il a fait échouer le plan

causeway ['kɔ:zweɪ] *n* chaussée *f* (*sur un marécage*)

caustic ['kɔ:stɪk] *adj also Fig* caustique; **c. soda** soude *f* caustique

cauterize ['kɔ:təraɪz] *vt Med* cautériser

caution ['kɔ:ʃən] **1** *n* **(a)** (*prudence*) prudence *f*; **c.!** (*sign*) attention!; **to exercise c.** être prudent(e); **to throw c. to the wind(s)** abandonner toute prudence **(b)** (*warning*) avertissement *m*
2 *vt* **(a)** (*warn*) mettre en garde (**against sth** contre qch); **to c. sb against doing sth** déconseiller à qn de faire qch **(b)** *Br* donner un avertissement à **(c)** *Law* **to c. sb** (*on arrest*) informer qn de ses droits; (*instead of prosecuting*) donner un avertissement à qn

cautionary ['kɔ:ʃənərɪ] *adj* **a c. tale** une histoire édifiante

cautious ['kɔ:ʃəs] *adj* prudent(e)

cautiously ['kɔ:ʃəslɪ] *adv* prudemment, avec prudence

cautiousness ['kɔ:ʃəsnɪs] *n* prudence *f*

cavalier [kævə'lɪə(r)] *adj* cavalier(ère)

cavalry ['kævəlrɪ] *n* cavalerie *f*

cave [keɪv] *n* grotte *f*; **c. dweller** (*contemporary*) troglodyte *m*; (*prehistoric*) homme *m* des cavernes; **c. paintings** peintures *fpl* rupestres
►**cave in** *vi* (*of ground, structure*) s'affaisser; *Fig* (*stop resisting*) céder (**to** à)

caveman ['keɪvmæn] *n* homme *m* des cavernes

cavern ['kævən] *n* caverne *f*

cavernous ['kævənəs] *adj* immense

caviar(e) ['kævɪɑ:(r)] *n* caviar *m*

cavity ['kævɪtɪ] (*pl* **cavities**) *n* cavité *f*; **c. wall insulation** isolation *f* des murs creux

cavort [kə'vɔ:t] *vi* faire des cabrioles; *Fig* batifoler

caw [kɔ:] **1** *n* croassement *m*
2 *vi* croasser

cayenne [keɪ'en] *n* **c.** (**pepper**) (poivre *m* de) Cayenne *m*

CB [si:'bi:] *n* (*abbr* **Citizens' Band**) CB *f*

CBE [si:bi:'i:] *n* (*abbr* **Commander of the (Order of the) British Empire**) = distinction honorifique britannique

CBI [si:bi:'aɪ] *n Br* (*abbr* **Confederation of British Industry**) = confédération du patronat britannique

cc [si:'si:] *n* (*abbr* **cubic centimetre(s)**) cm³

CD [si:'di:] *n* **(a)** (*abbr* **compact disc**) CD *m*, compact *m*; **CD player** lecteur *m* laser ou de CD **(b)** (*abbr* **Corps Diplomatique**) CD

CDI [si:di:'aɪ] *n Comptr* (*abbr* **compact disc interactive**) CD-I *m inv*

Cdr *n* (*abbr* **Commander**) commandant

Cdre *n* (*abbr* **Commodore**) contre-amiral

CD-ROM [si:di:'rɒm] *n Comptr* (*abbr* **compact disc read-only memory**) CD-ROM *m inv*

cease [si:s] **1** *vt* cesser; **to c. doing sth** cesser de faire qch; **to c. fire** cesser le feu
2 *vi* cesser (**from doing sth** *or* **to do sth** de faire qch); **it never ceases to amaze me** ça ne me laisse jamais de m'étonner

cease-fire ['si:sfaɪə(r)] *n* cessez-le-feu *m inv*

ceaseless ['si:slɪs] *adj* incessant(e), continuel(elle)

ceaselessly ['si:slɪslɪ] *adv* sans cesse, continuellement

cedar ['si:də(r)] *n* (*tree, wood*) cèdre *m*

cede [si:d] *vt Law* (*territory, property*) céder; **to c. a point** concéder un point

cedilla [sɪ'dɪlə] *n* cédille *f*

Ceefax® ['si:fæks] *n Br* = télétexte de la BBC

ceilidh ['keɪlɪ] *n* = bal folklorique écossais ou irlandais

ceiling ['si:lɪŋ] *n* (*of room*) & *Fig* (*limit*) plafond *m*; *Fig* **to hit the c.** piquer une crise; **c. price** prix *m* plafond

celebrant ['selɪbrənt] *n Rel* officiant *m*

celebrate ['selɪbreɪt] **1** *vt* (*anniversary, win, occasion*) fêter, célébrer; (*mass*) célébrer
2 *vi* faire la fête

celebrated ['selɪbreɪtɪd] *adj* célèbre

celebration [selɪ'breɪʃən] *n* célébration *f*; **celebrations** (*festivities*) festivités *fpl*; **in c. of sth** pour célébrer *ou* fêter qch; **this calls for a c.!** il faut fêter *ou* arroser ça!

celebrity [sɪ'lebrɪtɪ] (*pl* **celebrities**) *n* (*person, fame*) célébrité *f*

celery ['selərɪ] *n* céleri *m*

celestial [sɪ'lestɪəl] *adj* céleste

celibacy ['selɪbəsɪ] *n* (*chastity*) absence *f* de rapports sexuels; (*by choice*) chasteté *f*; *Rel* célibat *m*

celibate ['selɪbət] *adj* **to be c.** ne pas avoir de rapports sexuels; (*by choice*) être chaste; *Rel* être célibataire

cell [sel] *n* cellule *f*

cellar ['selə(r)] *n* cave *f*

cellist ['tʃelɪst] *n* violoncelliste *mf*

cello ['tʃeləʊ] (*pl* **cellos**) *n* violoncelle *m*

cellophane® ['seləfeɪn] *n Br* Cellophane® *f*

cellular ['seljʊlə(r)] *adj* cellulaire; **c. phone** téléphone *m* cellulaire

cellulite ['seljʊlaɪt] *n* cellulite *f*

celluloid® ['seljʊlɔɪd] *n* Celluloïd® *m*

cellulose ['seljʊləʊs] *n* cellulose *f*

Celsius ['selsɪəs] *adj* Celsius; **10 degrees C.** 10 degrés Celsius

Celt [kelt] *n* Celte *mf*

Celtic ['keltɪk] *adj* celte, celtique

cement [sɪ'ment] **1** *n* ciment *m*; **c. mixer** bétonnière *f*
2 *vt also Fig* cimenter

cemetery ['semətrɪ] (*pl* **cemeteries**) *n* cimetière *m*

cenotaph ['senətɑːf] *n* cénotaphe *m*

censor ['sensə(r)] **1** *n* censeur *m*; **the censors banned the film** la censure a interdit le film
2 *vt* censurer

censorious [sen'sɔːrɪəs] *adj* sévère (**of** vis-à-vis de)

censorship ['sensəʃɪp] *n* censure *f*

censure ['senʃə(r)] **1** *n* critique *f*; *Pol* **vote of c.** motion *f* de censure
2 *vt* blâmer; (*officially*) donner un blâme à

census ['sensəs] *n* recensement *m*

cent [sent] *n* cent *m*; *Am Fam* **I haven't got a c.** je n'ai pas un rond

centaur ['sentɔː(r)] *n* centaure *m*

centenarian [sentɪ'neərɪən] *n* centenaire *mf*

centenary [sen'tiːnərɪ], *Am* **centennial** [sen'tenɪəl] **1** *n* centenaire *m*
2 *adj* centenaire

center *Am* = **centre**

centigrade ['sentɪgreɪd] *adj* centigrade; **10 degrees c.** 10 degrés centigrades

centigram(me) ['sentɪgræm] *n* centigramme *m*

centilitre, *Am* **centiliter** ['sentɪliːtə(r)] *n* centilitre *m*

centime ['sɒntiːm] *n* centime *m*

centimetre, *Am* **centimeter** ['sentɪmiːtə(r)] *n* centimètre *m*

centipede ['sentɪpiːd] *n* mille-pattes *m inv*

central ['sentrəl] *adj* central(e); **C. London** le centre de Londres; **our hotel is quite c.** notre hôtel est dans le centre; **of c. importance** d'une importance capitale; **C. America** l'Amérique *f* centrale; **C. American** d'Amérique centrale; **c. bank** banque *f* centrale; **C. Europe** l'Europe *f* centrale; **C. European** d'Europe centrale; **C. European Time** heure *f* de l'Europe centrale; **c. government** gouvernement *m* central; **c. heating** chauffage *m* central; *Aut* **c. locking** verrouillage *m* centralisé; **c. nervous system** système *m* nerveux central; *Comptr* **c. processing unit** unité *f* centrale; **c. reservation** (*on motorway*) terre-plein *m* central; *Am* **C. Standard Time** heure *f* du centre de l'Amérique du Nord

Central African Republic ['sentrəl'æfrɪkənrɪ'pʌblɪk] *n* République *f* centrafricaine

centralize ['sentrəlaɪz] *vt* centraliser

centrally ['sentrəlɪ] *adv* (*funded, administered*) de façon centralisée; **c. located** central(e); **the flat is c. heated** l'appartement a le chauffage central

centre, *Am* **center** ['sentə(r)] **1** *n* centre *m*; **in the c.** au centre; *Pol* **left/right of c.** du centre gauche/droit; **c. of gravity** centre de gravité; **c. of attention** centre d'attraction; **c. forward** (*in football*) avant-centre *m*
2 *vt* (*attention, interest*) concentrer (**on** sur)

centrefold, *Am* **centerfold** ['sentəfəʊld] *n* (*in magazine*) double page *f* centrale détachable; (*nude photo*) photo *f* de pin-up

centrepiece, *Am* **centerpiece** ['sentəpiːs] *n* (*on table*) centre *m* de table; (*main attraction*) pièce *f* de résistance

centrifugal [sentrɪ'fjuːgəl] *adj* centrifuge

century ['sentʃərɪ] (*pl* **centuries**) *n* siècle *m*; **the 19th c.** le 19ᵉ siècle

CEO [siːiː'əʊ] *n Com* (*abbr* **Chief Executive Officer**) D.G. *m*; **President and C.** président(e)-directeur(trice) *m,f* général(e), P.-D.G. *m,f*

ceramic [sə'ræmɪk] **1** *n* (*material*) céramique *f*; **ceramics** (*art*) céramique; (*objects*) céramiques *fpl*
2 *adj* en céramique

cereal ['sɪərɪəl] *n* céréale *f*; **(breakfast) c.** céréales

cerebellum [serɪ'beləm] *n Anat* cervelet *m*

cerebral ['serɪbrəl] *adj* (*intellectual*) & *Anat* cérébral(e); *Med* **c. palsy** paralysie *f* cérébrale

cerebrum [serɪ'brəm] *n Anat* cerveau *m*

ceremonial [serɪ'məʊnɪəl] **1** *n* cérémonial *m*
2 *adj* de cérémonie

ceremonious [serɪ'məʊnɪəs] *adj* cérémonieux(euse)

ceremony ['serɪmənɪ] (*pl* **ceremonies**) *n* cérémonie *f*; **without c.** sans cérémonies; **to stand on c.** faire des cérémonies

cert [sɜːt] *n Fam* **it's a (dead) c.** c'est garanti

certain ['sɜːtən] *adj* **(a)** (*sure*) (*failure, victory*) certain(e), assuré(e); (*cure, solution*) infaillible; **I can't say for c.** je ne peux pas l'affirmer; **I'll tell you next week for c.** je vous le dirai la semaine prochaine sans faute; **to know sth for c.** être certain(e) de qch; **to be c. of sth** être sûr(e) ou certain(e) de qch; **they're c. of winning** ils sont assurés de gagner; **to make c. of sth** (*find out*) s'assurer de qch; (*be sure to get*) s'assurer qch; **he is c. to come** il viendra à coup sûr **(b)** (*particular*) certain(e); **a c. Philip Thomas** un certain Philip Thomas

certainly ['sɜːtənlɪ] *adv* certainement; **c. not!** certainement pas!; **she's c. very clever, but...** certes elle est très intelligente, mais...

certainty ['sɜːtəntɪ] (*pl* **certainties**) *n* (*strong likelihood*) certitude *f*; (*conviction*) conviction *f*; **there is no c. that we will win** il n'est pas certain que nous gagnions; **to know sth for a c.** être certain(e) de qch

certifiable ['sɜːtɪfaɪəbəl] *adj Fam* (*mad*) bon (bonne) pour l'asile

certificate [sə'tɪfɪkət] *n* certificat *m*; (*in education*) diplôme *m*

certify ['sɜːtɪfaɪ] (*pt & pp* **certified**) *vt* **(a)** (*confirm*) certifier; **this is to c. that...** nous certifions par la présente que...; **to c. sb (insane)** déclarer que l'état de santé de qn nécessite l'internement psychiatrique **(b)** (*give certificate to*) délivrer un certificat à

certitude ['sɜːtɪtjuːd] *n* certitude *f*

cervical ['sɜːvɪkəl, sə'vaɪkəl] *adj* **c. cancer** cancer *m* du col de l'utérus; **c. smear** frottis *m* vaginal

cervix ['sɜːvɪks] (*pl* **cervices** ['sɜːvɪsiːz]) *n Anat* col *m* de l'utérus

cessation [se'seɪʃən] *n* cessation *f*

cesspit ['sespɪt], **cesspool** ['sespuːl] *n* fosse *f* d'aisances; *Fig* cloaque *m*

Ceylon [sɪ'lɒn] *n Formerly* Ceylan

cf [siː'ef] (*abbr* **confer, compare**) cf

CFC [siːef'siː] (*pl* **CFCs**) *n* (*abbr* **chlorofluorocarbon**) CFC *m*

Chad [tʃæd] *n* le Tchad

chafe [tʃeɪf] **1** *vt (skin)* irriter; *(of shoes)* blesser
2 *vi (of skin)* être irrité(e); *(of shoes)* frotter **(against** contre); *Fig* **to c. at or against sth** *(resent)* s'irriter de qch

chaff [tʃɑːf] **1** *n* balle *f*; *Fig* **to separate the wheat from the c.** séparer le bon grain de l'ivraie
2 *vt (tease)* taquiner

chaffinch ['tʃæfɪntʃ] *n* pinson *m*

chagrin ['ʃægrɪn] *n* dépit *m*

chain [tʃeɪn] **1** *n* chaîne *f*; *(for medallion)* chaînette *f*; **in chains** enchaîné(e); **to pull the c.** *(in toilet)* tirer la chasse (d'eau); **c. gang** chaîne de forçats; **c. letter** = lettre faisant partie d'une chaîne; **c. mail** cotte *f* de mailles; **c. reaction** réaction *f* en chaîne; **c. saw** tronçonneuse *f*; **c. store** magasin *m* à succursales multiples
2 *vt (prisoner)* enchaîner; *(dog, bicycle)* attacher avec une chaîne **(to** à)

▶**chain up** *vt sep (prisoner)* enchaîner; *(dog, bicycle)* attacher avec une chaîne **(to** à)

chain-smoke ['tʃeɪnsməʊk] *vi* fumer cigarette sur cigarette

chair [tʃeə(r)] **1** *n* **(a)** *(seat)* chaise *f*; *(armchair)* fauteuil *m* **(b)** *(chairperson)* président(e) *m,f*; **to be in the c.** présider **(c)** *Univ (of professor)* chaire *f*
2 *vt (meeting)* présider

chairlift ['tʃeəlɪft] *n* télésiège *m*

chairman ['tʃeəmən] *n (of meeting, political party)* président *m*; *(of company)* président-directeur *m* général, P.D.G. *f*

chairmanship ['tʃeəmənʃɪp] *n* présidence *f*

chairperson ['tʃeəpɜːsən] *n* président(e) *m,f*

chairwoman ['tʃeəwʊmən] *n* présidente *f*

chalet ['ʃæleɪ] *n* chalet *m*

chalice ['tʃælɪs] *n Rel* calice *m*

chalk [tʃɔːk] **1** *n* craie *f*; **they are like c. and cheese** c'est le jour et la nuit; *Fam* **not by a long c.** loin s'en faut
2 *vt (mark)* marquer à la craie; *(write)* écrire à la craie

▶**chalk up** *vt sep (victory)* remporter

chalkboard ['tʃɔːkbɔːd] *n Am* tableau *m* (noir)

chalky ['tʃɔːkɪ] *adj (soil, complexion)* crayeux(euse); *(taste, texture)* plâtreux(euse)

challenge ['tʃælɪndʒ] **1** *n* défi *m* **(to** à); **to launch a leadership c.** chercher à conquérir la direction du parti; **the job presents a real c.** ce travail est très stimulant
2 *vt* **(a)** *(of job)* être stimulant(e) pour; **to c. sb to do sth** défier qn de faire qch; **he challenged me to a fight** il m'a défié de me battre contre lui **(b)** *(statement, authority)* contester **(c)** *Mil* interpeller

challenger ['tʃælɪndʒə(r)] *n Sp* challenger *m*

challenging ['tʃælɪndʒɪŋ] *adj (job)* stimulant(e)

chamber ['tʃeɪmbə(r)] *n* **(a)** *(hall)* chambre *f*; *Pol* **Lower/ Upper C.** Chambre basse/haute; **C. of Commerce** Chambre de commerce; **c. music** musique *f* de chambre; **c. pot** pot *m* de chambre **(b)** *Law* **chambers** *(of barrister, judge)* cabinet *m* *(au tribunal)* **(c)** *(of heart)* cavité *f*; *(of revolver)* chambre *f*

chambermaid ['tʃeɪmbəmeɪd] *n* femme *f* de chambre

chameleon [kə'miːlɪən] *n* caméléon *m*

chamois *n* **(a)** ['ʃæmɪ] **c. (leather)** peau *f* de chamois **(b)** ['ʃæmwɑː] *(deer)* chamois *m*

champ[1] [tʃæmp] *n Fam* champion(onne) *m,f*

champ[2] *vi Fig* **to c. at the bit** ronger son frein

champagne [ʃæm'peɪn] *n* champagne *m*

champion ['tʃæmpɪən] **1** *n (in sport, of cause)* champion(onne) *m,f*; **world/European c.** champion(onne) du monde/d'Europe
2 *vt* défendre

championship ['tʃæmpɪənʃɪp] *n* championnat *m*

chance [tʃɑːns] **1** *n* **(a)** *(luck)* hasard *m*; **by c.** par hasard; **to leave nothing to c.** ne rien laisser au hasard; **by any c.** par hasard; *Fam* **c. would be a fine thing!** ça ne risque pas! **(b)** *(opportunity)* occasion *f*; **to give sb a c.** donner une chance à qn; **she was trying to apologize but you didn't give her a c.** elle essayait de s'excuser mais tu ne lui en as pas laissé l'occasion; **now's your c.!** à toi de jouer!; **it's your last c.** c'est ta dernière chance; **to have an eye to the main c.** chercher à tirer profit de toutes les occasions **(c)** *(likelihood)* chance *f* **(of** de); **to have** *or* **stand a c. of doing sth** avoir des chances de faire qch; **there's no c. of that happening** il n'y a aucune chance que cela se produise; **(the) chances are (that)...** il y a fort à parier que... **(d)** *(risk)* risque *m*; **to take a c.** prendre un risque
2 *adj (discovery)* accidentel(elle); *(meeting)* fortuit(e)
3 *vt* **to c. doing sth** prendre le risque de faire qch; *Fam* **to c. one's arm** tenter le coup
4 *vi* **to c. to do sth** faire qch par hasard

▶**chance on, chance upon** *vt insep* tomber (par hasard) sur

chancellor ['tʃɑːnsələ(r)] *n* **(a)** *Univ Br* président(e) *m,f* honoraire; *Am* président(e) *m,f* **(b)** *Pol (in Austria, Germany)* chancelier *m*; *Br* **C. of the Exchequer**) Chancelier de l'Échiquier, ≃ ministre *m* des Finances

chancy ['tʃɑːnsɪ] *adj Fam (risky)* risqué(e)

chandelier [ʃændə'lɪə(r)] *n* lustre *m*

change [tʃeɪndʒ] **1** *n* **(a)** *(alteration)* changement *m*; **a c. for the better/worse** une amélioration/détérioration; **a c. of address** un changement d'adresse; **a c. of clothes** des vêtements *mpl* de rechange; **to have a c. of heart** changer d'avis; **for a c.** pour une fois; *Ironic* pour changer; **that makes a c.** ça change un peu; **the c. (of life)** *(menopause)* le retour d'âge
(b) *(money)* monnaie *f*; **small** *or* **loose c.** petite ou menue monnaie; **have you got c. for a £10 note?** avez-vous la monnaie de 10 livres ou sur un billet de 10 livres?
2 *vt* **(a)** *(alter)* changer; *(transform)* transformer **(into** en); **to c. one's mind** changer d'avis; **to c. the subject** changer de sujet
(b) *(exchange)* changer **(for** pour ou contre); **to c. hands** *(of money, car)* changer de mains; **to c. trains** changer de train; **to c. places with sb** changer de place avec qn; *Fig* **I wouldn't like to c. places with him** je ne voudrais pas être à sa place
(c) *(money)* changer; **to c. dollars into francs** changer des dollars en francs
(d) **to get changed** *(put on other clothes)* se changer
3 *vi* **(a)** *(alter)* changer; **to c. into sth** se transformer en qch
(b) *(put on other clothes)* se changer
(c) *(of passenger)* changer

▶**change over** *vi* changer; **to c. over from sth to sth** passer de qch à qch; **to c. over to another channel** changer de chaîne

changeable ['tʃeɪndʒəbəl] *adj (person, mood)* changeant(e); *(weather)* variable

changeless ['tʃeɪndʒlɪs] *adj* immuable

changeover ['tʃeɪndʒəʊvə(r)] *n (to new system, currency)* passage *m (to* à); *(after election, appointment)* transition *f*

changing ['tʃeɪndʒɪŋ] *adj* changeant(e)

changing room ['tʃeɪndʒɪŋruːm] *n* vestiaire *m; (in shop)* cabine *f* d'essayage

channel ['tʃænəl] **1** *n (a) (waterway)* chenal *m; (of communication, distribution)* canal *m;* **to go through the proper channels** suivre la filière officielle **(b)** *TV* chaîne *f; Rad* bande *f* de fréquences **(c) the (English) C.** la Manche; **the C. Islands** les îles *fpl* Anglo-Normandes; **the C. Tunnel** le tunnel sous la Manche
2 *vt (pt & pp* **channelled,** *Am* **channeled)** canaliser (**to** vers)

chant [tʃɑːnt] **1** *n (a) (of demonstrators)* slogan *m* **(b)** *Rel* psalmodie *f*
2 *vt* scander
3 *vi (of demonstrators)* scander des slogans; *Rel* psalmodier

chaos ['keɪɒs] *n* chaos *m;* **our plans were thrown into c.** nos projets ont été bouleversés; **c. theory** théorie *f* du chaos

chaotic [keɪ'ɒtɪk] *adj* chaotique

chap [tʃæp] *n Fam (man)* bonhomme *m,* type *m;* **a good c.** un brave type

chapel ['tʃæpəl] *n* chapelle *f*

chaperone ['ʃæpərəʊn] **1** *n* chaperon *m*
2 *vt* chaperonner

chaplain ['tʃæplɪn] *n Rel* aumônier *m*

chaplaincy ['tʃæplɪnsɪ] *n* aumônerie *f*

chapped [tʃæpt] *adj (lips, skin)* gercé(e)

chapter ['tʃæptə(r)] *n* chapitre *m;* **a c. of accidents** série noire; *Fig* **to quote c. and verse for sth** donner les références exactes de qch

char¹ [tʃɑː(r)] *(pt & pp* **charred)** *vt (burn)* carboniser

char² *Br Fam* **1** *n (cleaning lady)* femme *f* de ménage
2 *vi (pt & pp* **charred)** *(clean)* faire des ménages

char³ *n Br Fam (tea)* thé *m*

character ['kærɪktə(r)] *n (a) (in novel, film, play)* personnage *m;* **c. actor/actress** acteur(trice) *m,f* de composition **(b)** *(personality)* caractère *m;* **his remark was in/out of c.** ça lui ressemble bien/ça ne lui ressemble pas d'avoir fait une remarque pareille; **to have/lack c.** avoir du/manquer de caractère; **a person of good c.** une personne honorable; **c. assassination** diffamation *f;* **c. reference** *(when applying for job)* références *fpl; Law* **c. witness** témoin *m* de moralité **(c)** *(person)* individu *m;* **he's quite a c.!** c'est quelqu'un! **(d)** *(letter)* caractère *m; Comptr* **c. set** jeu *m* de caractères

characteristic [kærɪktə'rɪstɪk] **1** *n* caractéristique *f*
2 *adj* caractéristique; **it's c. of him** ça lui ressemble bien, c'est bien de lui

characterization [kærɪktəraɪ'zeɪʃən] *n (of problem, situation)* description *f; (in novel)* psychologie *f* des personnages

characterize ['kærɪktəraɪz] *vt (describe)* décrire; *(be characteristic of)* caractériser

charade [ʃə'rɑːd] *n (farce)* mascarade *f;* **charades** *(party game)* charades *fpl* mimées

charcoal ['tʃɑːkəʊl] *n* charbon *m* de bois; *Art* fusain *m;* **c. drawing** (dessin *m* au) fusain; **c. grey** anthracite *inv*

charge [tʃɑːdʒ] **1** *n (a) (cost)* frais *mpl;* **free of c.** gratuitement; **c. account** compte *m* clients; **c. card** carte *f* de paiement *(de grand magasin)* **(b)** *Law* chef *m* d'accusation; **to be arrested on a c. of...** être arrêté(e) pour...; **to bring a c. against sb** accuser qn; **c. sheet** ≃ procès-verbal *m* **(c)** *(responsibility)* **to take c. of sth** prendre qch en charge; **to be in c. of** être responsable de; **I'm in c. here!** c'est moi le chef ici! **(d)** *(of explosive)* charge *f*
2 *vt (a) (price)* faire payer, demander; **to c. sb £10** faire payer £10 à qn; **c. it to my account** mettez ça sur mon compte **(b)** *Law* inculper **(with de) (c)** *(attack)* attaquer **(d)** *Elec* charger; *Fig* **a highly charged atmosphere** une atmosphère très tendue
3 *vi (rush)* charger; **to c. in/out** entrer/sortir en trombe

chariot ['tʃærɪət] *n* char *m*

charisma [kə'rɪzmə] *n* charisme *m*

charismatic [kærɪz'mætɪk] *adj* charismatique

charitable ['tʃærɪtəbəl] *adj (person, action)* charitable; *(organization)* caritatif(ive); *(work)* pour une association caritative

charity ['tʃærɪtɪ] *(pl* **charities)** *n (a) (quality)* charité *f; Prov* **c. begins at home** charité bien ordonnée commence par soi-même **(b)** *(organization)* association *f* caritative

charlady ['tʃɑːleɪdɪ] *(pl* **charladies)** *n Br* femme *f* de ménage

charlatan ['ʃɑːlətən] *n* charlatan *m*

Charlie ['tʃɑːlɪ] *n Br Fam* **to feel a right or proper C.** se sentir vraiment bête

charm [tʃɑːm] **1** *n (a) (attractiveness)* charme *m;* **to turn on the c.** faire le charmeur/la charmeuse **(b)** *(spell)* charme *m;* **it worked like a c.** ça a marché comme sur des roulettes **(c)** *(lucky)* **c.** amulette *f*
2 *vt* charmer; **she charmed the money out of him** elle lui a extorqué son argent en lui faisant du charme; **to lead a charmed life** être né(e) sous une bonne étoile

charmer ['tʃɑːmə(r)] *n* charmeur(euse) *m,f*

charming ['tʃɑːmɪŋ] *adj also Ironic* charmant(e)

charred [tʃɑːd] *adj* carbonisé(e)

chart [tʃɑːt] **1** *n (graph)* diagramme *m,* graphique *m; (map)* carte *f;* **the charts** *(pop music)* le hit-parade
2 *vt (a) (on map)* porter sur une carte **(b)** *Fig (progress, rise)* retracer

charter ['tʃɑːtə(r)] **1** *n (of town)* charte *f; (of university)* statuts *mpl;* **c. flight** (vol *m*) charter *m*
2 *vt (plane, ship)* affréter

chartered accountant ['tʃɑːtədə'kaʊntənt] *n* expert-comptable *m*

charwoman ['tʃɑːwʊmən] *n Br* femme *f* de ménage

chary ['tʃeərɪ] *adj* circonspect(e); **to be c. of doing sth** hésiter à faire qch

chase [tʃeɪs] **1** *n (pursuit)* poursuite *f;* **to give c. to sb** donner la chasse à qn
2 *vt (pursue)* poursuivre, donner la chasse à; *(sexually)* courir après
3 *vi* **to c. after sb** *(pursue)* poursuivre qn, donner la chasse à qn; *(sexually)* courir après qn

▶**chase up** *vt sep (person)* relancer; *(letter)* retrouver la trace de

chaser ['tʃeɪsə(r)] *n* = alcool bu après une bière ou vice versa

chasm ['kæzəm] *n also Fig* gouffre *m,* abîme *m*

chassis ['ʃæsɪ] *n (of car)* châssis *m*

chaste [tʃeɪst] *adj* chaste

chasten [ˈtʃeɪsən] *vt* rendre plus humble

chastise [tʃæsˈtaɪz] *vt* châtier; *(criticize)* fustiger

chastisement [tʃæsˈtaɪzmənt] *n* châtiment *m*; *(criticism)* fustigation *f*

chastity [ˈtʃæstɪtɪ] *n* chasteté *f*; **c. belt** ceinture *f* de chasteté

chat [tʃæt] **1** *n* discussion *f*; **to have a c. (with sb)** discuter *ou* bavarder (avec qn); **c. show** *(on TV)* talk-show *m*
2 *vi (pt & pp chatted)* bavarder; **to c. about sth** discuter de qch

▸**chat up** *vt sep Br Fam* draguer

chattel [ˈtʃætəl] *n Law* bien *m* meuble

chatter [ˈtʃætə(r)] **1** *n* bavardage *m*, papotage *m*
2 *vi (talk)* bavarder, papoter; **my teeth were chattering** je claquais des dents

chatterbox [ˈtʃætəbɒks] *n Fam* pie *f*

chatty [ˈtʃætɪ] *adj (person)* bavard(e); *(letter)* plein(e) de détails

chauffeur [ˈʃəʊfə(r)] **1** *n* chauffeur *m*
2 *vt* conduire

chauvinism [ˈʃəʊvɪnɪzəm] *n (patriotism)* chauvinisme *m*; *(male)* c. machisme *m*

chauvinist [ˈʃəʊvɪnɪst] *n & adj (patriotic)* chauvin(e) *m,f*; *(male)* c. *(sexist)* macho *m*

chauvinistic [ʃəʊvɪˈnɪstɪk] *adj (patriotic)* chauvin(e); *(sexist)* macho

cheap [tʃiːp] **1** *n* **to do sth on the c.** faire qch à peu de frais *ou* pour pas cher
2 *adj* **(a)** *(inexpensive)* bon marché *inv*, pas cher (chère); **cheaper** meilleur marché *inv*, moins cher (chère); **c. rate** tarif *m* réduit **(b)** *(of little value)* de peu de valeur; *(vulgar)* de mauvais goût; **to feel c.** *(of person)* se sentir minable; **it's c. and nasty** c'est de la camelote
3 *adv Fam* **it was going c.** c'était bon marché

cheapen [ˈtʃiːpən] *vt (degrade)* gâcher; **to c. oneself** s'abaisser

cheaply [ˈtʃiːplɪ] *adv (buy)* (à) bon marché, à bas prix; *(live, travel)* à peu de frais, pour pas cher

cheapskate [ˈtʃiːpskeɪt] *n Fam* radin(e) *m,f*

cheat [tʃiːt] **1** *n (dishonest person)* escroc *m*; *(at games)* tricheur(euse) *m,f*; *(deception, trick)* tricherie *f*, triche *f*
2 *vt* duper, rouler; *(financially)* escroquer; **to c. sb out of sth** *(money)* escroquer qch à qn; *(chance)* priver qn de qch
3 *vi* tricher

▸**cheat on** *vt insep (be unfaithful to)* tromper

cheating [ˈtʃiːtɪŋ] *n* tricherie *f*, triche *f*; **that's c.!** c'est de la triche!

check¹ [tʃek] **1** *n* **(a)** *(inspection)* vérification *f*, contrôle *m* (on de); **to run a c. on sb** enquêter sur qn **(b)** *(restraint)* **to keep sb in c.** tenir qn en échec; **to keep sth in c.** *(emotion, enemy advance)* contenir qch; *Pol* **checks and balances** équilibre *m* des pouvoirs **(c)** *(in chess)* échec *m*; **in c.** en échec **(d)** *Am (cheque)* chèque *m*; *(restaurant bill)* addition *f*
2 *vt* **(a)** *(verify, examine) (information, statement)* vérifier; *(passport, ticket)* contrôler; **to c. that...** vérifier *ou* s'assurer que... **(b)** *(restrain) (inflation)* enrayer; *(emotion, impulse, enemy advance)* contenir
3 *vi* vérifier; **to c. on sth** vérifier qch; **to c. on sb** surveiller qn; **you'd better c. with her** vous feriez mieux de lui demander

▸**check in 1** *vt sep (baggage)* enregistrer
2 *vi (at hotel)* remplir le registre; *(at airport)* se présenter à l'enregistrement

▸**check out 1** *vt sep* **(a)** *(investigate) (person)* se renseigner sur; *(information)* vérifier **(b)** *Fam (look at)* viser
2 *vi (leave hotel)* quitter l'hôtel

▸**check up** *vi* vérifier; **to c. up on sb** surveiller qn

check² **1** *n (pattern)* carreaux *mpl*
2 *adj* à carreaux

checkers [ˈtʃekəz] *npl Am* jeu *m* de dames

check-in [ˈtʃekɪn] *n Av* **c. (desk)** (comptoir *m* d')enregistrement *m*

checkmate [ˈtʃekmeɪt] **1** *n (in chess)* échec *m* et mat
2 *vt (in chess)* faire échec et mat à; *Fig (opponent)* faire échec à

checkout [ˈtʃekaʊt] *n (in supermarket)* caisse *f*

checkpoint [ˈtʃekpɔɪnt] *n (poste m de) contrôle *m*

checkup [ˈtʃekʌp] *n Med* bilan *m* complet

cheek [tʃiːk] **1** *n* **(a)** *(of face)* joue *f*; **to dance c. to c.** danser joue contre joue; **c. by jowl (with sb)** coude à coude (avec qn); *Fig* **to turn the other c.** tendre l'autre joue **(b)** *(buttock)* fesse *f* **(c)** *Fam (impudence)* toupet *m*, culot *m*; **he's got a c.!** il est culotté *ou* gonflé!
2 *vt Fam (be impudent to)* être insolent(e) avec

cheekbone [ˈtʃiːkbəʊn] *n* pommette *f*

cheeky [ˈtʃiːkɪ] *adj Fam* effronté(e)

cheep [tʃiːp] *vi (of bird)* piailler

cheer [tʃɪə(r)] **1** *n* **(a)** *(shout)* hourra *m*; **cheers** acclamations *fpl*, bravos *mpl*; **three cheers for Mary!** un ban pour Mary! **(b)** *Fam* **cheers!** *(when drinking)* (à votre) santé!; *(goodbye)* à bientôt!; *(thanks)* merci! **(c)** *Lit (good spirits)* **to be of good c.** être de bonne humeur
2 *vt* **(a)** *(applaud)* acclamer **(b)** *(make happier)* remonter le moral à
3 *vi (shout)* pousser des hourras *ou* des acclamations

▸**cheer on** *vt sep (support)* encourager

▸**cheer up 1** *vt sep (person)* remonter le moral à; *(room)* égayer
2 *vi (of person)* reprendre courage; **c. up!** courage!

cheerful [ˈtʃɪəfʊl] *adj (person)* gai(e), de bonne humeur; *(room, music, mood)* gai; *(conversation)* enjoué(e)

cheerfully [ˈtʃɪəfʊlɪ] *adv* gaiement, avec entrain; *Fam* **I could c. strangle him!** je l'étranglerais volontiers!

cheerily [ˈtʃɪərɪlɪ] *adv* gaiement

cheerio [tʃɪərɪˈəʊ] *exclam* salut!

cheerleader [ˈtʃɪəliːdə(r)] *n* = majorette qui encourage les supporters d'une équipe sportive à manifester leur enthousiasme

cheerless [ˈtʃɪəlɪs] *adj* morne; *(room)* triste

cheery [ˈtʃɪərɪ] *adj* joyeux(euse), gai(e)

cheese [tʃiːz] *n* fromage *m*; *Fam (say)* **c.!** *(for photograph)* souriez!; **c. sandwich/omelette** sandwich *m*/omelette *f* au fromage

▸**cheese off** *vt sep Fam* **to be cheesed off (with)** en avoir marre (de)

cheeseboard [ˈtʃiːzbɔːd] *n (selection)* plateau *m* de fromages

cheeseburger [ˈtʃiːzbɜːgə(r)] *n* cheeseburger *m*

cheesecake [ˈtʃiːzkeɪk] *n* gâteau *m* au fromage blanc

cheetah [ˈtʃiːtə] *n* guépard *m*

chef [ʃef] *n* chef *m (cuisinier)*

chemical ['kemɪkəl] **1** *n* produit *m* chimique
2 *adj* chimique; **c. warfare** guerre *f* chimique; **c. weapons** armes *fpl* chimiques

chemist ['kemɪst] *n* (a) *Br (pharmacist)* pharmacien(enne) *m,f*; **c.'s (shop)** pharmacie *f* (b) *(scientist)* chimiste *mf*

chemistry ['kemɪstrɪ] *n* chimie *f*; *Fig* **there was a certain c. between them** il y avait une certaine affinité entre eux

chemotherapy [kiːməʊˈθerəpɪ] *n Med* chimiothérapie *f*

cheque [tʃek] *n Fin* chèque *m*; **to make out** *or* **write a c. (to sb)** faire un chèque (à l'ordre de qn); **a c. for £10** un chèque de 10 livres; **c. card** carte *f* bancaire *(sans laquelle un chéquier n'est pas valable)*

chequebook ['tʃekbʊk] *n* carnet *m* de chèques, chéquier *m*

chequered ['tʃekəd] *adj (patterned)* à carreaux; *Fig* **she's had a c. career** elle a eu une carrière en dents de scie

cherish ['tʃerɪʃ] *vt (memory, person)* chérir; *(hopes)* caresser, nourrir

cherry ['tʃerɪ] *(pl* **cherries**) *n (fruit)* cerise *f*; **c. (tree)** cerisier *m*; **c. orchard** cerisaie *f*

cherub ['tʃerəb] *(pl* **cherubs** *or* **cherubim** ['tʃerəbɪm]) *n* chérubin *m*

chess [tʃes] *n* échecs *mpl*; **a game of c.** une partie d'échecs; **c. player** joueur(euse) *m,f* d'échecs

chessboard ['tʃesbɔːd] *n* échiquier *m*

chessman ['tʃesmæn], **chesspiece** ['tʃespiːs] *n* pièce *f* (de jeu d'échecs)

chest [tʃest] *n* (a) *(of person)* poitrine *f*; *Fig* **to get it off one's c.** dire ce qu'on a sur le cœur (b) *(box)* coffre *m*, caisse *f*; **c. of drawers** commode *f*

chestnut ['tʃesnʌt] **1** *n (nut)* châtaigne *f*; *(tree, wood)* châtaignier *m*; **(horse)** *c.* marron *m* d'Inde; *Fam* **an old c.** une plaisanterie usée
2 *adj (hair)* châtain; *(horse)* alezan(e)

chew [tʃuː] *vt* mâcher, mastiquer; *(cigar, end of pen)* mâchonner; **to c. one's nails** se ronger les ongles

▶**chew over** *vt sep Fam* réfléchir à, cogiter sur

chewing gum ['tʃuːɪŋɡʌm] *n* chewing-gum *m*

chewy ['tʃuːɪ] *adj (meat)* caoutchouteux(euse); *(sweet)* mou (molle)

chic [ʃiːk] *adj* élégant(e), chic

chick [tʃɪk] *n* (a) *(young bird)* oisillon *m*; *(young chicken)* poussin *m* (b) *Fam (woman)* nana *f*

chicken ['tʃɪkɪn] **1** *n* (a) *(bird)* poulet *m*; *Prov* **don't count your chickens (before they are hatched)** il ne faut pas vendre la peau de l'ours avant de l'avoir tué; **c. feed** *(food)* nourriture *f* pour volaille; *Fam Fig* **that's c. feed!** c'est une misère! (b) *Fam (coward)* lâche *mf*, froussard(e) *m,f*
2 *adj Fam (cowardly)* froussard(e)

▶**chicken out** *vi Fam* se dégonfler

chickenpox ['tʃɪkɪnpɒks] *n* varicelle *f*

chickpea ['tʃɪkpiː] *n* pois *m* chiche

chicory ['tʃɪkərɪ] *n* endive *f*

chide [tʃaɪd] *(pt* **chided** *or* **chid** [tʃɪd], *pp* **chided** *or* **chidden** ['tʃɪdən]) *vt Lit* réprimander

chief [tʃiːf] **1** *n (of tribe)* chef *m*; *Fam* **the c. (boss)** le patron; *Mil* **c. of staff** chef d'état-major; **(White House) c. of staff** secrétaire *m* de la Maison-Blanche
2 *adj (most important)* principal(e); **c. assistant** principal(e) collaborateur(trice) *m,f*; *Com* **c. executive** directeur(trice) *m,f* général(e); *Am* **c. executive officer** directeur(trice) *m,f* général(e)

chiefly ['tʃiːflɪ] *adv* principalement, surtout

chieftain ['tʃiːftən] *n (of clan)* chef *m*

chiffon ['ʃɪfɒn] *n* mousseline *f* de soie

chilblain ['tʃɪlbleɪn] *n* engelure *f*

child [tʃaɪld] *(pl* **children** ['tʃɪldrən]) *n* enfant *m*; **it's c.'s play** c'est un jeu d'enfant; **children's literature** littérature *f* enfantine *ou* pour enfants; **c. abuse** mauvais traitements *mpl* à enfant; *(sexual)* sévices *mpl* sexuels infligés à un enfant; **c. benefit** ≃ allocations *fpl* familiales; **c. labour** travail *m* des enfants; **c. minder** nourrice *f*

child-bearing ['tʃaɪldbeərɪŋ] *n* maternité *f*; **of c. age** en âge d'avoir des enfants

childbirth ['tʃaɪldbɜːθ] *n* accouchement *m*; **to die in c.** mourir en couches

childhood ['tʃaɪldhʊd] *n* enfance *f*

childish ['tʃaɪldɪʃ] *adj Pej* puéril(e); **don't be so c.!** ne faites pas l'enfant!

childless ['tʃaɪldlɪs] *adj* sans enfant(s)

childlike ['tʃaɪldlaɪk] *adj* enfantin(e)

childproof ['tʃaɪldpruːf] *adj* **c. lock** *(in car)* = serrure de sécurité pour enfants; **c. bottle** = bouteille pourvue d'une capsule de sécurité

children ['tʃɪldrən] *pl of* **child**

Chile ['tʃɪlɪ] *n* le Chili

Chilean ['tʃɪlɪən] **1** *n* Chilien(enne) *m,f*
2 *adj* chilien(enne)

chill [tʃɪl] **1** *n* coup *m* de froid; **to catch a c.** prendre froid; **a c. of fear** un frisson de peur; **there's a c. in the air** le fond de l'air est frais
2 *adj* froid(e), glacé(e)
3 *vt (wine, food)* mettre au frais; *(of wind)* glacer; **serve chilled** *(on product)* servir frais

▶**chill out** *vi Fam* se détendre; **c. out!** on se calme!

chilli ['tʃɪlɪ] *(pl* **chillis** *or* **chillies**) *n (dish)* chili *m* con carne; **c. (pepper)** piment *m* (rouge); **c. powder** piment *m* en poudre

chilling ['tʃɪlɪŋ] *adj (frightening)* à vous donner le frisson

chilly ['tʃɪlɪ] *adj also Fig* froid(e)

chime [tʃaɪm] **1** *n (of bells)* carillon *m*
2 *vt* **the clock chimed nine o'clock** le carillon de l'horloge sonna neuf heures
3 *vi (of clock, bells)* carillonner

▶**chime in** *vi Fam (in conversation)* intervenir

chimney ['tʃɪmnɪ] *(pl* **chimneys**) *n* cheminée *f*; *Fam* **to smoke like a c.** *(of person)* fumer comme un pompier; **c. sweep** ramoneur *m*

chimneypot ['tʃɪmnɪpɒt] *n* mitre *f*

chimpanzee [tʃɪmpæn'ziː], *Fam* **chimp** [tʃɪmp] *n* chimpanzé *m*

chin [tʃɪn] *n* menton *m*; *Fig* **to keep one's c. up** tenir bon, tenir le coup

China ['tʃaɪnə] *n* la Chine

china ['tʃaɪnə] *n* porcelaine *f*; **c. clay** kaolin *m*

Chinese [tʃaɪˈniːz] **1** *npl* the C. *(people)* les Chinois *mpl*
2 *n* (**a**) *(person)* Chinois(e) *m,f* (**b**) *(language)* chinois *m*
3 *adj* chinois(e)

Chink [tʃɪŋk] *n Fam* Chinetoque *mf*, = terme raciste désignant un Chinois

chink[1] [tʃɪŋk] *n (gap)* fente *f*, lézarde *f*; *Fig* to find a c. in sb's armour trouver le talon d'Achille de qn

chink[2] **1** *n (sound)* tintement *m*
2 *vt (coins, glasses)* faire tinter
3 *vi* tinter

chintz [tʃɪnts] *n* chintz *m*

chinwag [ˈtʃɪnwæg] *n Fam* to have a c. tailler une bavette

chip [tʃɪp] **1** *n* (**a**) *(of wood, glass)* éclat *m*; *(in plate, cup)* ébréchure *f*; this cup has a c. in it cette tasse est ébréchée (**b**) chips *Br (French fries)* frites *fpl*; *Am (crisps)* (pommes *fpl*) chips *mpl*; *Br* c. shop = petite boutique où l'on vend du poisson pané et frit, accompagné de frites (**c**) *(in gambling)* jeton *m* (**d**) *Comptr* puce *f* (**e**) *(idioms)* he's a c. off the old block c'est son père tout craché; to have a c. on one's shoulder en vouloir à tout le monde; *Fam* when the chips are down dans les moments critiques; *Fam* he's had his chips *(it's too late for him)* il est cuit *ou* fichu
2 *vt (pt & pp* chipped) (**a**) *(cut at) (stone, wood)* tailler; *(damage) (knife, plate)* ébrécher; *(furniture)* écorner; to c. one's tooth se casser un petit bout de dent (**b**) *(in sport)* to c. the ball frapper la balle par en dessous
3 *vi (of plate, cup)* s'ébrécher

▶**chip in** *vi Fam (give money)* participer; to c. in with a suggestion intervenir pour faire une suggestion

chipboard [ˈtʃɪpbɔːd] *n* aggloméré *m*

chipmunk [ˈtʃɪpmʌŋk] *n* tamia *m* rayé

chiropodist [kɪˈrɒpədɪst] *n* pédicure *mf*

chiropody [kɪˈrɒpədɪ] *n* pédicurie *f*

chirp [tʃɜːp] **1** *n (of birds)* gazouillis *m*, pépiement *m*; *(of grasshopper)* chant *m*
2 *vt & vi (of bird)* gazouiller, pépier; *(of grasshopper)* chanter

chirpy [ˈtʃɜːpɪ] *adj* d'humeur joyeuse

chirrup [ˈtʃɪrəp] = **chirp**

chisel [ˈtʃɪzəl] **1** *n (tool)* ciseau *m*; *(for sculpture)* burin *m*
2 *vt (pt & pp* chiselled, *Am* chiseled) (**a**) *(in woodwork, sculpture)* ciseler (**b**) *very Fam (cheat)* rouler

chit [tʃɪt] *n* bon *m*

chitchat [ˈtʃɪttʃæt] *n Fam* bavardage *m*, papotage *m*

chivalrous [ˈʃɪvəlrəs] *adj* chevaleresque; *(towards women)* galant(e)

chivalry [ˈʃɪvəlrɪ] *n (courteous behaviour)* courtoisie *f*; *(towards women)* galanterie *f*; *Hist* chevalerie *f*

chives [tʃaɪvz] *npl* ciboulette *f*

chiv(v)y [ˈtʃɪvɪ] *(pt & pp* chiv(v)ied) *vt Br Fam* harceler; to c. sb into doing sth harceler qn jusqu'à ce qu'il fasse qch; to c. sb along faire se presser qn

chloride [ˈklɔːraɪd] *n Chem* chlorure *m*

chlorinate [ˈklɔːrɪneɪt] *vt* chlorer

chlorine [ˈklɔːriːn] *n Chem* chlore *m*

chloroform [ˈklɒrəfɔːm] *n Chem* chloroforme *m*

chlorophyll(l) [ˈklɒrəfɪl] *n Biol* chlorophylle *f*

choc-ice [ˈtʃɒkaɪs] *n* = glace individuelle rectangulaire enrobée de chocolat

chock [tʃɒk] *n (for wheel of car, plane)* cale *f*

chock-a-block [ˈtʃɒkəˈblɒk] *adj Fam* plein(e) à craquer

chocolate [ˈtʃɒklət] **1** *n* chocolat *m*; hot c. chocolat chaud
2 *adj (made of chocolate)* en chocolat; *(chocolate-flavoured)* au chocolat; c. (coloured) chocolat *inv*

choice [tʃɔɪs] **1** *n* choix *m*; you have no c. vous n'avez pas le choix; there isn't much c. il n'y a pas grand choix; available in a wide c. of colours disponible dans une large gamme de coloris
2 *adj* (**a**) *(well chosen)* choisi(e); she used some c. language *(offensive)* elle a juré comme un charretier (**b**) *(food)* de choix; *(wine)* fin(e)

choir [ˈkwaɪə(r)] *n* chœur *m*

choirboy [ˈkwaɪəbɔɪ] *n* jeune choriste *m*

choke [tʃəʊk] **1** *n (of car)* starter *m*
2 *vt* (**a**) *(strangle)* étrangler (**b**) *(block) (sink, road)* boucher
3 *vi* s'étrangler; to c. with anger s'étrangler de colère; she choked on a fishbone elle a failli s'étouffer en avalant une arête

▶**choke back** *vt sep (tears, words, anger)* ravaler

cholera [ˈkɒlərə] *n* choléra *m*

cholesterol [kəˈlestərɒl] *n* cholestérol *m*

choose [tʃuːz] *(pt* chose [tʃəʊz], *pp* chosen [ˈtʃəʊzən]) **1** *vt* choisir; to c. to do sth choisir de faire qch; there's not much to c. between them ils se valent
2 *vi* choisir *(between* entre); I'll do as I c. je ferai comme il me plaît

choosy [ˈtʃuːzɪ] *adj Fam* difficile

chop [tʃɒp] **1** *n* (**a**) *(with axe)* coup *m*; *Fam* to get the c. *(get sacked)* se faire saquer (**b**) *(of lamb, pork)* côtelette *f*
2 *vt (pt & pp* chopped) *(wood)* couper; *(meat, vegetables)* couper en morceaux; *(finely)* hacher
3 *vi* to c. and change changer sans cesse; he's always chopping and changing il change d'avis comme de chemise

▶**chop down** *vt sep (tree)* abattre

▶**chop off** *vt sep* trancher, couper; to c. sb's head off couper la tête à qn

chopper [ˈtʃɒpə(r)] *n* (**a**) *(cleaver)* couperet *m*; *(axe)* hachette *f* (**b**) *Fam (helicopter)* hélico *m*

chopping [ˈtʃɒpɪŋ] *n* c. block *(of butcher)* billot *m*; c. board planche *f* (à découper)

choppy [ˈtʃɒpɪ] *adj (sea, lake)* agité(e)

chopsticks [ˈtʃɒpstɪks] *npl* baguettes *fpl*

choral [ˈkɔːrəl] *adj* choral(e); c. society chorale *f*

chord [kɔːd] *n* (**a**) *Mus* accord *m*; *Fig* her speech struck a c. with the electorate son discours a trouvé un écho auprès des électeurs (**b**) *Math (of arc)* corde *f*

chore [tʃɔː(r)] *n* (**a**) chores *(in household)* travaux *mpl* ménagers (**b**) *(unwelcome task)* corvée *f*

choreograph [ˈkɒrɪəɡrɑːf] *vt* faire la chorégraphie de; *Fig* orchestrer

choreography [kɒrɪˈɒɡrəfɪ] *n* chorégraphie *f*

chorister [ˈkɒrɪstə(r)] *n* choriste *mf*

chortle [ˈtʃɔːtəl] **1** *n* gloussement *m* (de joie)
2 *vi* glousser (de joie)

chorus [ˈkɔːrəs] **1** *n* (**a**) *(of song)* refrain *m* (**b**) *(group of singers, actors)* chœur *m*; *Fig* a c. of protest un concert de protestations; c. girl danseuse *f* de revue
2 *vt* dire en chœur

chose [tʃəʊz] *pt of* **choose**

chosen ['tʃəʊzən] **1** *adj* choisi(e); **the c. few** les heureux élus *mpl*
2 *pp of* **choose**

Christ [kraɪst] **1** *n* le Christ *m*, Jésus-Christ *m*
2 *exclam very Fam* bon Dieu!; **C. Almighty!** nom de Dieu!

christen ['krɪsən] *vt (name)* baptiser

christening ['krɪsənɪŋ] *n* baptême *m*

Christian ['krɪstʃən] **1** *n* chrétien(enne) *m,f*; **to be a C.** être chrétien
2 *adj* chrétien(enne); **C. name** prénom *m*

Christianity [krɪstrˈænɪtɪ] *n* christianisme *m*

Christmas ['krɪsməs] *n* Noël *m*; **at C.** à Noël; **Merry or Happy C.!** joyeux Noël; **C. cake** gâteau *m* de Noël *(aux fruits secs)*; **C. card** carte *f* de Noël; **C. carol** chant *m* de Noël; **C. Day** jour *m* de Noël; **C. Eve** veille *f* de Noël; **C. pudding** pudding *m* (de Noël); **C. tree** sapin *m* de Noël

chrome [krəʊm] *adj* chromé(e)

chromium ['krəʊmɪəm] *n Chem* chrome *m*

chromosome ['krəʊməsəʊm] *n Biol* chromosome *m*

chronic ['krɒnɪk] *adj* **(a)** *(invalid, illness, unemployment)* chronique **(b)** *Fam (bad)* atroce

chronicle ['krɒnɪkəl] **1** *n* chronique *f*; *Fig (of disasters)* suite *f*
2 *vt* faire la chronique de

chronological [krɒnəˈlɒdʒɪkəl] *adj* chronologique

chronology [krəˈnɒlədʒɪ] *n* chronologie *f*

chrysalis ['krɪsəlɪs] *n Zool* chrysalide *f*

chrysanthemum [krɪˈsænθəməm] *n* chrysanthème *m*

chubby ['tʃʌbɪ] *adj* potelé(e), dodu(e); *(face)* joufflu(e); **c.-cheeked** joufflu

chuck [tʃʌk] *vt Fam* **(a)** *(throw)* lancer, balancer **(b)** *(boyfriend, girlfriend)* plaquer; **to get chucked** se faire plaquer

▸**chuck away** *vt sep Fam* balancer; *Fig (opportunity)* foutre en l'air

▸**chuck out** *vt sep Fam (throw away)* balancer; *(from house, school, club)* vider

chuckle ['tʃʌkəl] **1** *n* petit rire *m*
2 *vi* rire tout bas

chuffed [tʃʌft] *adj Fam* tout(e) content(e) **(about de)**

chug [tʃʌg] *(pt & pp* **chugged***) vi (train)* haleter; *Fam* **he's still chugging along in the same job** il a toujours le même boulot pépère

chum [tʃʌm] *n Fam* copain (copine) *m,f*

chummy ['tʃʌmɪ] *adj Fam* copain (copine); **to be a bit too c.** être un peu trop familier(ère)

chump [tʃʌmp] *n Fam* **(a)** *(foolish person)* idiot(e) *m,f* **(b) to be off one's c.** être timbré(e)

chunk [tʃʌŋk] *n* gros morceau *m*; *(of bread)* quignon *m*; *(of time)* partie *f*

chunky ['tʃʌŋkɪ] *adj Fam (well-built)* bien bâti(e); *(fat)* grassouillet(ette); *(pullover)* gros (grosse)

church [tʃɜːtʃ] *n* **(a)** *(building)* église *f*; *(French Protestant)* temple *m*; **to go to c.** aller à l'église/au temple; **c. hall** salle *f* paroissiale **(b)** *(institution)* **the C. of England** l'Église *f* anglicane; **the C. of Scotland** l'Église d'Écosse

churchgoer ['tʃɜːtʃɡəʊə(r)] *n* pratiquant(e) *m,f*

churchyard ['tʃɜːtʃjɑːd] *n* cimetière *m*

churlish ['tʃɜːlɪʃ] *adj (rude)* grossier(ère); *(surly)* revêche

churn [tʃɜːn] **1** *n (for making butter)* baratte *f*; *(for milk)* bidon *m* à lait
2 *vt (butter)* battre; **the propeller churned up the water** l'eau bouillonnait sous l'action des hélices
3 *vi* **my stomach's churning** *(because of nervousness)* j'ai l'estomac noué

▸**churn out** *vt sep Fam (books)* pondre (en série); *(goods)* produire en série

chute [ʃuːt] *n* **(a)** *(for parcels)* glissière *f*; *(rubbish)* c. vide-ordures *m inv* **(b)** *(in swimming pool, playground)* toboggan *m* **(c)** *Fam (parachute)* parachute *m*

chutney ['tʃʌtnɪ] *n* chutney *m*

CIA [siːaɪˈeɪ] *n Am (abbr* **Central Intelligence Agency)** CIA *f*

cicada [sɪˈkɑːdə] *n* cigale *f*

CID [siːaɪˈdiː] *n Br (abbr* **Criminal Investigation Department)** ≃ P.J.

cider ['saɪdə(r)] *n* cidre *m*; **c. apple** pomme *f* à cidre; **c. vinegar** vinaigre *m* de cidre

cigar [sɪˈɡɑː(r)] *n* cigare *m*

cigarette [sɪɡəˈret] *n* cigarette *f*; **c. ash** cendre *f* de cigarette; **c. butt** *or* **end** mégot *m*; **c. case** étui *m* à cigarettes; **c. holder** fume-cigarette *m inv*; **c. lighter** briquet *m*; *(in car)* allume-cigare *m*; **c. machine** distributeur *m* automatique de cigarettes; **c. packet** paquet *m* de cigarettes; **c. paper** papier *m* à cigarettes

C-in-C [siːɪnˈsiː] *n Mil & Naut (abbr* **Commander-in-Chief)** commandant *m* en chef

cinch [sɪntʃ] *n Fam* **it's a c.** c'est un jeu d'enfant

cinder ['sɪndə(r)] *n* cendre *f*; **cinders** cendres *fpl*; **burnt to a c.** complètement carbonisé(e)

Cinderella [sɪndəˈrelə] *n* Cendrillon *f*

cine ['sɪnɪ] *pref* **c. camera** caméra *f*; **c. film** pellicule *f*

cinema ['sɪnəmə] *n* cinéma *m*; **to go to the c.** aller au cinéma

cinnamon ['sɪnəmən] *n* cannelle *f*

cipher ['saɪfə(r)] *n (code)* chiffre *m*, code *m*; *Fig* **he's a mere c.** c'est un zéro

circa ['sɜːkə] *prep (of time)* aux alentours de; *(of amount)* environ

circle ['sɜːkəl] **1** *n* **(a)** *(shape)* cercle *m*; **to sit in a c.** s'asseoir en cercle; *Fig* **to go round in circles** tourner en rond **(b)** *(movement)* **to come full c.** revenir à son point de départ **(c)** *(in theatre)* balcon *m*; **lower/upper c.** premier/deuxième balcon **(d)** *(group)* cercle *m*, groupe *m*; **in certain circles** dans certains milieux
2 *vt* **(a)** *(go round)* tourner autour de **(b)** *(surround)* entourer **(with de)**
3 *vi (of plane, birds)* tourner, décrire des cercles

circuit ['sɜːkɪt] *n* **(a)** *(electric)* circuit *m*; **c. breaker** disjoncteur *m* **(b)** *(in motor racing) (course)* circuit *m*; *(lap)* tour *m*

circuitous [sɜːˈkjuːɪtəs] *adj (route)* détourné(e); *(reasoning)* alambiqué(e)

circular ['sɜːkjʊlə(r)] **1** *n (letter)* circulaire *f*; *(advertisement)* prospectus *m*
2 *adj (movement, argument)* circulaire

circulate ['sɜːkjʊleɪt] **1** *vt* faire circuler
2 *vi* circuler

circulation [sɜːkjʊˈleɪʃən] *n (of air, blood, money)* circulation *f*; *(of newspaper)* tirage *m*; **for internal c. only** *(document)* à usage interne uniquement; *Fig* **to be out of c.** *(of person)* disparaître de la circulation

circumcise ['sɜːkəmsaɪz] *vt (boy)* circoncire; *(girl)* exciser

circumcision [sɜːkəm'sɪʒən] *n* circoncision *f;* **female c.** excision *f*

circumference [sə'kʌmfərəns] *n* circonférence *f*

circumflex ['sɜːkəmfleks] *n* accent *m* circonflexe

circumlocution [sɜːkəmlə'kjuːʃən] *n* circonlocution *f,* périphrase *f*

circumnavigate [sɜːkəm'nævɪgeɪt] *vt* **to c. sth** faire le tour de qch en bateau

circumscribe ['sɜːkəmskraɪb] *vt (limit)* limiter

circumspect ['sɜːkəmspekt] *adj* circonspect(e)

circumstances ['sɜːkəmstənsɪz] *npl* circonstances *fpl;* **in** *or* **under the c.** étant donné les circonstances; **in** *or* **under no c.** en aucun cas, sous aucun prétexte; **due to c. beyond our control** en raison de circonstances indépendantes de notre volonté

circumstantial [sɜːkəm'stænʃəl] *adj* **c. evidence** preuves *fpl* indirectes

circumvent [sɜːkəm'vent] *vt (law, rule)* contourner

circus ['sɜːkəs] *n* cirque *m*

cirrhosis [sɪ'rəʊsɪs] *n Med* cirrhose *f*

cissy ['sɪsɪ] *(pl* **cissies)** *n Fam* poule *f* mouillée

cistern ['sɪstən] *n* citerne *f; (in lavatory)* réservoir *m* de chasse d'eau

citadel ['sɪtədel] *n* citadelle *f*

citation [saɪ'teɪʃən] *n* citation *f*

cite [saɪt] *vt* citer

citizen ['sɪtɪzən] *n* citoyen(enne) *m,f; (of city)* habitant(e) *m,f;* **c.'s band (radio)** citizen band *f*

citizenship ['sɪtɪzənʃɪp] *n* citoyenneté *f*

citric acid ['sɪtrɪk'æsɪd] *n* acide *m* citrique

citrus fruit ['sɪtrəsfruːt] *n* agrumes *mpl;* **a c.** un agrume

city ['sɪtɪ] *(pl* **cities)** *n (grande)* ville *f; Br* **the C.** la City *(quartier des affaires de Londres);* **c. centre** centre-ville *m*

civic ['sɪvɪk] *adj (duty, pride)* civique; *(building, authorities)* municipal(e); **c. centre** salle *f* municipale

civil ['sɪvəl] *adj (of society)* civil(e); **c. aviation** aviation *f* civile; **c. defence** protection *f* civile; **c. disobedience** résistance *f* passive; **c. engineering** génie *m* civil; **c. law** *(subject)* droit *m* civil; *Law* **c. rights** droits civils; **c. servant** fonctionnaire *mf;* **the c. service** la fonction publique; **c. war** guerre *f* civile **(b)** *(polite)* poli(e)

civilian [sɪ'vɪljən] **1** *n* civil *m*
2 *adj* civil(e)

civility [sɪ'vɪlɪtɪ] *(pl* **civilities)** *n* politesse *f*

civilization [sɪvɪlaɪ'zeɪʃən] *n* civilisation *f*

civilize ['sɪvɪlaɪz] *vt* civiliser

civilized ['sɪvɪlaɪzd] *adj* civilisé(e); **their divorce was very c.** leur divorce s'est passé sans heurts

cl *(abbr* **centilitre)** cl

clad [klæd] *adj* **c. in** vêtu(e) de

claim [kleɪm] *n* **(a)** *(demand) (for damages, compensation)* demande *f* d'indemnisation; *(as a right)* revendication *f;* **to lay c. to sth** revendiquer qch; **I have many claims on my time** je suis très pris; **it's his only c. to fame** c'est la seule façon dont il se soit distingué; **the town's only c. to fame** la seule chose pour laquelle cette ville soit connue **(b)** *(assertion)* déclaration *f;* **she makes no c. to originality** elle ne prétend pas être originale
2 *vt* **(a)** *(as a right)* revendiquer; **to c. damages (from sb)** réclamer des dommages et intérêts (à qn); **to c.**

responsibility for sth revendiquer qch **(b)** *(assert)* **to c. that...** affirmer que...; **he claims to be an expert** il prétend être un expert **(c)** *(lost property)* réclamer **(d)** *(life)* **the epidemic has claimed thousands of lives** l'épidémie a fait des milliers de victimes

claimant ['kleɪmənt] *n (to throne)* prétendant(e) *m,f; Law (for social security, insurance)* demandeur(eresse) *m,f*

clairvoyant [kleə'vɔɪənt] **1** *n* voyant(e) *m,f*
2 *adj* extralucide

clam [klæm] *n* palourde *f*

▶**clam up** *(pt & pp* **clammed)** *vi Fam* se fermer comme une huître

clamber ['klæmbə(r)] *vi* **to c. up sth** escalader qch

clammy ['klæmɪ] *adj* moite

clamorous ['klæmərəs] *adj* bruyant(e)

clamour ['klæmə(r)] **1** *n (noise)* clameur *f; (protest)* tollé *m*
2 *vi* **to c. for sth** réclamer qch à grands cris

clamp [klæmp] **1** *n (tool)* serre-joint *m; (fixed to bench)* étau *m; Med* clamp *m; (wheel)* c. sabot *m* (de Denver)
2 *vt (fasten)* fixer; *(car)* mettre un sabot à

▶**clamp down on** *vt insep* faire la chasse à

clampdown ['klæmpdaʊn] *n* répression *f* (on de)

clan [klæn] *n also Fig* clan *m*

clandestine [klæn'destɪn] *adj* clandestin(e)

clang [klæŋ] **1** *n* bruit *m* métallique
2 *vi (of bell)* retentir; **the gate clanged shut** le portail se ferma avec un bruit métallique

clanger ['klæŋə(r)] *n Fam* gaffe *f;* **to drop a c.** faire une gaffe

clank [klæŋk] **1** *n* bruit *m* métallique
2 *vi* cliqueter

clap [klæp] **1** *n* **(a)** *(with hands)* **to give sb a c.** applaudir qn; **a c. of thunder** un coup de tonnerre **(b)** *very Fam* **the c.** la chaude-pisse
2 *vt (pt & pp* **clapped)** **(a)** *(applaud)* applaudir; **to c. one's hands** applaudir; *(once)* frapper dans ses mains; **to c. sb on the back** donner une tape sur le dos à qn **(b)** *(put)* **he clapped his hat on** il enfonça son chapeau sur sa tête; *Fam* **to c. sb in prison** coller qn en prison; *Fam* **to c. eyes on sb/sth** voir qn/qch
3 *vi (applaud)* applaudir

clapped-out ['klæpt'aʊt] *adj Fam (car, machine)* déglingué(e)

clapper ['klæpə(r)] *n (of bell)* battant *m; Fam* **to run like the clappers** courir à toutes jambes

clapping ['klæpɪŋ] *n (applause)* applaudissements *mpl*

claptrap ['klæptræp] *n Fam* bêtises *fpl*

claret ['klærət] *n* bordeaux *m* (rouge)

clarification [klærɪfɪ'keɪʃən] *n* clarification *f,* éclaircissement *m*

clarify ['klærɪfaɪ] *(pt & pp* **clarified)** *vt* clarifier, éclaircir

clarinet [klærɪ'net] *n* clarinette *f*

clarity ['klærɪtɪ] *n* clarté *f*

clash [klæʃ] **1** *n* **(a)** *(of opinions, interests)* conflit *m; (between people, armies)* affrontement *m* **(b)** *(of metal objects)* fracas *m*
2 *vi* **(a)** *(come into conflict)* s'affronter; **to c. with sb** affronter qn; **police clashed with protesters** il y a eu des heurts entre la police et les manifestants **(b)** *(of evidence, explanations)* ne pas correspondre; *(of colours)* jurer **(c)** *(of events)* **to c. with** tomber en même temps que **(d)** *(of metal objects)* s'entrechoquer

clasp [klɑːsp] **1** *n* (*on necklace, handbag*) fermoir *m*; **c. knife** canif *m*
2 *vt* (*grip*) serrer; (*embrace*) étreindre; **to c. sb's hand** serrer la main à qn

class [klɑːs] **1** *n* (*in school, category, social group*) classe *f*; **to be in a c. of one's own** être insurpassable; **c. struggle** lutte *f* des classes
2 *vt* (*classify*) classer (**as** parmi)

classic ['klæsɪk] **1** *n* (**a**) (*book*) classique *m* (**b**) *Sch & Univ* **classics** lettres *fpl* classiques
2 *adj* classique

classical ['klæsɪkəl] *adj* classique; **c. music** musique *f* classique

classification [klæsɪfɪ'keɪʃən] *n* classification *f*; (*of students*) classement *m*

classified ['klæsɪfaɪd] **1** *n* **the classifieds** (*in newspaper*) les petites annonces *fpl*
2 *adj* (**a**) (*secret*) confidentiel(elle) (**b**) **c. advertisements** (*in newspaper*) petites annonces *fpl*

classify ['klæsɪfaɪ] (*pt & pp* **classified**) *vt* classer

classmate ['klɑːsmeɪt] *n* camarade *mf* de classe

classroom ['klɑːsruːm] *n* (salle *f* de) classe *f*

classy ['klɑːsɪ] *adj Fam* qui a de la classe; (*bar*) chic

clatter ['klætə(r)] **1** *n* (*of shoes*) claquement *m*; (*of dishes*) fracas *m*
2 *vi* **the car clattered along the road** la voiture descendit la rue dans un bruit de ferraille; **to c. about** (*of person*) s'activer bruyamment

clause [klɔːz] *n* (*of contract*) clause *f*; *Gram* proposition *f*

claustrophobia [klɔːstrə'fəʊbɪə] *n* claustrophobie *f*

claustrophobic [klɔːstrə'fəʊbɪk] *adj* (*person*) claustrophobe

clavicle ['klævɪkəl] *n* clavicule *f*

claw [klɔː] **1** *n* (*of animal*) griffe *f*; (*of bird of prey*) serre *f*; (*of crab, lobster*) pince *f*; **c. hammer** marteau-arrache-clou *m*
2 *vt* (*scratch*) griffer; *Fig* **to c. one's way to the top** parvenir au sommet à force de travail

▶**claw back** *vt* (*money*) récupérer

clay [kleɪ] *n* argile *f*; (*terre f*) glaise *f*; **c. court** (*for tennis*) court *m* en terre battue; **c. pigeon** pigeon *m* d'argile; **c. pigeon shooting** ball-trap *m*

clean [kliːn] **1** *n* **to give sth a c.** nettoyer qch
2 *adj* (**a**) (*not dirty*) propre; (*piece of paper*) blanc (blanche); **a c. game/fight** un jeu/une bataille dans les règles; **c. living** vie *f* saine; **to have a c. driving licence** avoir tous ses points sur son permis de conduire (**b**) (*not obscene*) décent(e); **it's good c. fun** c'est innocent (**c**) (*clear*) (*shape, outline*) net (nette); **to make a c. break** (*of couple*) rompre une bonne fois pour toutes
3 *adv* (**a**) (*completely*) **to cut c. through sth** couper qch net; *Fam* **I c. forgot** j'ai complètement oublié (**b**) *Fam* **to come c.** dire la vérité
4 *vt* nettoyer; **to c. one's teeth/hands** se laver les dents/mains

▶**clean out** *vt sep* (**a**) (*cupboard, room*) nettoyer à fond (**b**) *Fam* (*leave without money*) nettoyer, plumer

▶**clean up 1** *vt sep* nettoyer
2 *vi* (**a**) (*tidy up*) nettoyer; (*wash oneself*) se laver (**b**) *Fam* (*win money*) toucher un gros paquet

clean-cut [kliːn'kʌt] *adj* (*features*) net (nette), bien dessiné(e)

cleaner ['kliːnə(r)] *n* (*person*) agent *m* de service; (*substance*) produit *m* de nettoyage; **c.'s** (*shop*) pressing *m*; *Fam* **to take sb to the c.'s** (*cheat*) nettoyer ou plumer qn

cleaning ['kliːnɪŋ] *n* nettoyage *m*; (*housework*) ménage *m*; **c. lady** femme *f* de ménage

cleanliness ['klenlɪnɪs] *n* (*of place, person*) propreté *f*

cleanly ['kliːnlɪ] *adv* proprement; (*fight*) dans les règles

cleanse [klenz] *vt* nettoyer; (*skin*) démaquiller

cleanser ['klenzə(r)] *n* (*for skin*) démaquillant *m*

clean-shaven [kliːn'ʃeɪvən] *adj* rasé(e) de près

cleansing lotion ['klenzɪŋləʊʃən] *n* lait *m* démaquillant

clear [klɪə(r)] **1** **to be in the c.** (*not under suspicion*) être lavé(e) de tout soupçon; (*out of danger*) être hors de danger
2 *adj* (**a**) (*liquid, image, directions*) clair(e); (*picture*) net (nette); (*glass*) transparent(e); (*skin*) net; **on a c. day** par temps clair; **all c.!** la voie est libre!; **to have a c. conscience** avoir la conscience tranquille; **as c. as a bell** (*of voice, sound*) cristallin(e); **c. profit** bénéfice *m* net; **c. winner** vainqueur *m* incontesté
(**b**) (*obvious*) clair(e), évident(e); **to make it c. to sb that...** bien faire comprendre à qn que...; **it is c. that...** il est clair ou évident que...; **to make oneself c.** se faire comprendre; **I wasn't c. what she meant** je n'étais pas sûr d'avoir parfaitement compris ce qu'elle voulait dire
(**c**) (*space, road, passageway*) libre
(**d**) **to be c. of sth** (*rid of*) être débarrassé(e) de qch
3 *adv* **to steer c. of** éviter; **stand c. of the doors!** attention à la fermeture automatique des portières!
4 *vt* (**a**) (*road, area*) dégager; **the police cleared the square of demonstrators** la police a forcé les manifestants à évacuer la place; **to c. one's throat** se racler la gorge; **to c. the table** débarrasser la table; **to c. a debt** s'acquitter d'une dette; *Fig* **to c. the decks** déblayer le terrain; *Fig* **to c. the way for sth** ouvrir la voie à qch; *Fig* **to c. the air** mettre les choses au point
(**b**) (*exonerate*) disculper, innocenter; **to c. sb of blame** disculper qn; **to c. sb's name** blanchir (le nom de) qn
(**c**) (*jump over*) sauter, franchir
(**d**) (*authorize*) (*proposal, request*) approuver; **I'll need to c. it with the boss** il faut que j'obtienne la permission du patron
5 *vi* (**a**) (*weather*) s'éclaircir; (*of sky*) se dégager; (*of fog*) se lever
(**b**) (*of cheque*) **the cheque hasn't cleared yet** le chèque n'a pas encore été viré

▶**clear away** *vt sep* (*dishes*) ranger; (*obstruction*) enlever

▶**clear off** *vi Br Fam* (*leave*) filer, se tirer

▶**clear out 1** *vt sep* (*cupboard*) vider; (*garage, shed*) débarrasser
2 *vi Fam* (*leave*) filer, se tirer

▶**clear up 1** *vt sep* (**a**) (*room*) ranger (**b**) (*doubt, misunderstanding*) dissiper; **to c. up a matter** tirer une affaire au clair
2 *vi* (*of weather*) s'éclaircir

clearance ['klɪərəns] *n* (**a**) *Com* **c. sale** liquidation *f* (**b**) (*authorization*) autorisation *f* (**c**) (*space*) espace *m* (libre)

clear-cut ['klɪə'kʌt] *adj* (*division, outline, feature*) net (nette); (*opinion*) tranché(e); **it's not as c. as that** ce n'est pas aussi simple que ça

clear-headed ['klɪə'hedɪd] *adj* lucide

clearing ['klɪərɪŋ] *n* (*in forest*) clairière *f*

clearing house ['klɪərɪŋhaʊs] *n Fin* chambre *f* de compensation

clearly ['klɪəlɪ] adv (a) (explain, write) clairement; (see) bien (b) (obviously) évidemment; **he is c. wrong** il est évident qu'il a tort

clearness ['klɪənɪs] n clarté f; (of image) netteté f

clearout ['klɪəraʊt] n **to have a c.** faire le nettoyage par le vide

clear-sighted ['klɪə'saɪtɪd] adj (perceptive) clairvoyant(e)

cleavage ['kliːvɪdʒ] n (of woman) décolleté m

cleave [kliːv] (pt cleaved or cleft [kleft] or clove [kləʊv], pp cleaved or cleft or cloven ['kləʊvən]) vt Lit fendre
▶**cleave to** (pt & pp cleaved) vt insep Formal être fidèle à

cleaver ['kliːvə(r)] n hachoir m

clef [klef] n Mus clé f, clef f

cleft [kleft] 1 n fissure f
2 adj fendu(e); **c. palate** division f palatine; **to be caught in a c. stick** (in awkward situation) être entre le marteau et l'enclume
3 pt & pp of **cleave**

clemency ['klemənsɪ] n clémence f

clementine ['klementiːn] n clémentine f

clench [klentʃ] vt **to c. one's fist/teeth** serrer le poing/les dents

Cleopatra ['kliːəʊ'pætrə] n Cléopâtre

clergy ['klɜːdʒɪ] n clergé m

clergyman ['klɜːdʒmən] n ecclésiastique m; (Protestant) pasteur m; (Catholic) prêtre m

cleric ['klerɪk] n Rel ecclésiastique m

clerical ['klerɪkəl] adj (a) (administrative) **c. assistant** employé(e) m, f de bureau; **c. work** travail m de bureau (b) Rel clérical(e)

clerk [klɑːk, Am klɜːrk] n (a) (office worker) employé(e) m, f de bureau (b) Am (in shop) vendeur(euse) m, f

clever ['klevə(r)] adj (intelligent) intelligent(e); (plan, idea) ingénieux(euse); **to be c. with one's hands** être adroit(e) de ses mains; Fam **to be too c. by half** être trop malin(igne); Fam **a c. Dick** un petit malin

cleverly ['klevəlɪ] adv (intelligently) intelligemment; (planned) ingénieusement

cleverness ['klevənɪs] n (intelligence) intelligence f; (of plan) ingéniosité f; (skill) adresse f

cliché ['kliːʃeɪ] n cliché m

click [klɪk] 1 n (sound) petit bruit m sec
2 vt **to c. one's heels** claquer les talons; **to c. one's tongue** faire claquer sa langue
3 vi (a) (make a sound) faire un petit bruit sec (b) Fam (become obvious) faire tilt (c) Fam (of people) **we clicked straight away** ça a accroché tout de suite entre nous

client ['klaɪənt] n client(e) m, f

clientele [kliːən'tel] n clientèle f

cliff [klɪf] n falaise f

cliffhanger ['klɪfhæŋə(r)] n **it was a real c.** il y a eu du suspense jusqu'au bout

climactic [klaɪ'mæktɪk] adj qui constitue le point culminant

climate ['klaɪmət] n climat m

climatic [klaɪ'mætɪk] adj climatique

climax ['klaɪmæks] 1 n (of series of events) paroxysme m; (of reign, career) apogée m; (of film, book) point m culminant; (sexual) orgasme m
2 vi (of series of events) atteindre son paroxysme; (of reign, career) atteindre son apogée; (of film, book) atteindre son point culminant; (sexually) atteindre l'orgasme

climb [klaɪm] 1 n montée f, ascension f
2 vt (tree) grimper à; (mountain) faire l'ascension de; (rock face) escalader; (stairs) monter
3 vi (of road, prices) grimper; (of plane) prendre de l'altitude, monter; **to c. over sth** passer par-dessus qch
▶**climb down** vt insep (descend) descendre
2 vi (a) (descend) descendre (b) Fig (in argument) revenir sur sa décision

climber ['klaɪmə(r)] n (a) (mountaineer) alpiniste mf (b) (plant) plante f grimpante

climbing ['klaɪmɪŋ] 1 n (hill-walking) randonnée f en montagne; (of rockface) escalade f; (mountaineering) alpinisme m; **c. frame** cage f à poules
2 adj (plant) grimpant(e)

clinch [klɪntʃ] 1 n (of fighters) corps à corps m; (of lovers) étreinte f
2 vt (settle) (deal) conclure; (argument) résoudre; **that clinches it!** voilà qui règle le problème une fois pour toutes!

cling [klɪŋ] (pt & pp clung [klʌŋ]) vi **to c. to** (rope, person) s'accrocher à; Fig (opinion) persister dans; (faith) se raccrocher à

clingfilm ['klɪŋfɪlm] n film m alimentaire

clinic ['klɪnɪk] n (part of hospital) service m; Br (private hospital) clinique f

clinical ['klɪnɪkəl] adj (a) Med clinique (b) (unemotional) froid(e)

clink [klɪŋk] 1 n (sound) tintement m
2 vt faire tinter; **to c. glasses with sb** trinquer avec qn
3 vi (of glasses) tinter

clink² n very Fam (prison) taule f

clip¹ [klɪp] 1 n (for paper) trombone m; (for hair) barrette f
2 vt (pt & pp clipped) (paper) attacher (avec un trombone) (to à)
3 vt **to c. together** s'emboîter

clip² 1 n (a) Fam (blow) **to give sb a c. round the ear** flanquer une taloche à qn (b) (of film, programme) extrait m
2 vt (pt & pp clipped) vt (a) (hit) **to c. sb round the ear** flanquer une taloche à qn (b) (hedge) tailler; (ticket) poinçonner; (dog) couper les poils à; (hair, nails) couper; Fig **to c. sb's wings** réduire la marge de manœuvre de qn

clipboard ['klɪpbɔːd] n planchette f porte-papiers (à pince)

clip-on ['klɪpɒn] adj **c. earring** clip m; **c. microphone** micro-cravate m; **c. sunglasses** = verres teintés que l'on fixe à une autre paire de lunettes

clipped [klɪpt] adj (speech, tone) saccadé(e)

clipper ['klɪpə(r)] n (ship) clipper m

clippers ['klɪpəz] npl (for hair) tondeuse f; (for nails) coupe-ongles m inv; (for hedge) cisaille f

clipping ['klɪpɪŋ] n (from newspaper) coupure f

clique [kliːk] n clique f

clitoris ['klɪtərɪs] n clitoris m

cloak [kləʊk] 1 n cape f; Fig **under the c. of darkness** sous le couvert de la nuit
2 vt Fig **cloaked in secrecy** enveloppé(e) de mystère

cloak-and-dagger [kləʊkən'dægə(r)] *adj (film, book)* d'espionnage; *Fig (mysterious)* mystérieux(euse)

cloakroom ['kləʊkruːm] *n* vestiaire *m*

clobber¹ ['klɒbə(r)] *n Br Fam (clothes)* frusques *fpl*, fringues *fpl*; *(belongings)* barda *m*

clobber² *vt Fam (hit)* tabasser; *(defeat)* battre à plate couture

clock [klɒk] 1 *n* (a) *(large)* horloge *f*; *(small)* pendule *f*; **round the c.** vingt-quatre heures sur vingt-quatre; **a race against the c.** une course contre la montre; **to put the clocks forward/back** *(in spring, autumn)* avancer/retarder les pendules; *Fig* **to turn the c. back** revenir en arrière; **c. radio** radio-réveil *m* (b) *Fam (mileometer)* compteur *m* kilométrique
2 *vt (measure speed of)* chronométrer; *(reach speed of)* atteindre

▸**clock in** *vi* pointer *(en arrivant sur son lieu de travail)*

▸**clock off** *vi* pointer *(en quittant son lieu de travail)*

▸**clock on** = clock in

▸**clock out** = clock off

▸**clock up** *vt sep (profits)* réaliser; *(votes)* totaliser; **this car has clocked up 10,000 miles** cette voiture a 10 000 miles au compteur

clockmaker ['klɒkmeɪkə(r)] *n* horloger(ère) *m,f*

clockwise ['klɒkwaɪz] *adv* dans le sens des aiguilles d'une montre

clockwork ['klɒkwɜːk] 1 *n* **to go like c.** *(of interview, ceremony)* marcher comme sur des roulettes; **to run like c.** *(of office, system)* être réglé(e) comme du papier à musique
2 *adj (toy)* mécanique

clod [klɒd] *n (of earth)* motte *f*

clog [klɒg] 1 *n (shoe)* sabot *m*
2 *vt (pt & pp* **clogged***) (block)* boucher
3 *vi* se boucher

▸**clog up** *vt sep* boucher
2 *vi* se boucher

cloister ['klɔɪstə(r)] *n* cloître *m*

cloistered ['klɔɪstəd] *adj* **to lead a c. life** mener une vie de reclus(e)

clone [kləʊn] 1 *n also Fig* clone *m*
2 *vt Biol* cloner

close¹ [kləʊs] 1 *adj* (a) *(in distance, time, relationship)* proche; **to be in c. contact with sb** être en contact étroit avec qn; **a c. friend** un ami intime; **a c. relative** un proche parent; **that was a c. call** on s'en est fallu de peu; **at c. quarters** de près; **at c. range** de près; **c. combat** corps à corps *m* (b) *(inspection)* minutieux(euse); *(attention)* soutenu(e); **to keep a c. watch on sb/sth** surveiller qn/qch de près (c) *(weather)* lourd(e); *(room)* qui sent le renfermé (d) *(contest, election)* serré(e)
2 *n (cul-de-sac)* impasse *f*
3 *adv (near)* près; **to hold sb c.** serrer qn; **c. to** près de; **c. to tears** au bord des larmes; **c. to victory** proche de la victoire; **to come c. to death** frôler la mort; **to be c. to sb** *(emotionally)* être proche de qn; **c. at hand** à proximité; **to follow c. behind sb** suivre qn de près; **to be c. on fifty** friser la cinquantaine; **c. up** de près

close² [kləʊz] 1 *n (end)* fin *f*; **to draw to a c.** tirer à sa fin; **to bring sth to a c.** clore qch
2 *vt* (a) *(door, eyes, book, road)* fermer; *Fig* **to c. ranks around sb** former bloc autour de qn; *(meeting, debate)* clore; *(account)* fermer; *(deal)* conclure (b) *(business, shop)* fermer
3 *vi (of shop, business)* fermer; *(of door)* se fermer

▸**close down** 1 *vt (production, operations)* cesser; *(business, factory)* fermer
2 *vi (of business, factory)* fermer; **Channel 6 closes down at midnight** les émissions sur Channel 6 se terminent à minuit

▸**close in** *vi (of night)* tomber; **to c. in on sb** se rapprocher de qn

▸**close up** 1 *vt sep (shop)* fermer
2 *vi* (a) *(of wound, hole)* se refermer (b) *(of shopkeeper)* fermer

close-cropped ['kləʊs'krɒpt] *adj (hair)* coupé(e) ras

closed [kləʊzd] *adj* fermé(e); **c. circuit television** f en circuit fermé; **behind c. doors** à huis clos; *Ind* **c. shop** = usine ou société qui n'embauche que des travailleurs syndiqués

close-fitting ['kləʊs'fɪtɪŋ] *adj* bien ajusté(e)

close-knit ['kləʊs'nɪt] *adj (community, group)* très soudé(e)

closely ['kləʊslɪ] *adv* (a) *(examine, listen, watch)* attentivement; *(resemble)* beaucoup; **to be c. related** *(of concepts)* être étroitement lié(es); *(of people)* être proches parents; **c. contested** très serré(e) (b) *(populated)* densément; **c. packed** très serré(e)

closeness ['kləʊsnɪs] *n (physical proximity)* proximité *f*; *(of relationship, contact)* intimité *f*

close-run ['kləʊs'rʌn] *adj (election, race)* serré(e)

close-set ['kləʊs'set] *adj (eyes)* rapproché(e)

closet ['klɒzɪt] 1 *n* placard *m*; *Fig* **to come out of the c.** révéler son homosexualité
2 *adj* **c. homosexual** = personne qui cache son homosexualité; *Hum* **he's a c. Gary Glitter fan** il n'ose pas avouer qu'il aime Gary Glitter
3 *vt* enfermer; **to c. oneself away** s'enfermer, s'isoler

close-up ['kləʊsʌp] *n* gros plan *m*; **in c.** en gros plan

closing ['kləʊzɪŋ] *n* fermeture *f*; **c. date** date *f* limite; **c. prices** cours *mpl* de clôture; **c. speech** discours *m* de clôture; **c. time** heure *f* de fermeture

closure ['kləʊʒə(r)] *n (of company, shop)* fermeture *f* *(définitive)*

clot [klɒt] 1 *n* (a) *(of blood)* caillot *m* (b) *Fam (stupid person)* andouille *f*
2 *vi (pt & pp* **clotted***) (of blood)* (se) coaguler

cloth [klɒθ] *n* (a) *(material)* tissu *m*; **a man of the c.** un membre du clergé (b) *(duster)* chiffon *m*

clothe [kləʊð] *(pt & pp* **clad** [klæd] *or* **clothed***) vt* vêtir, habiller

clothes [kləʊðz] *npl* vêtements *mpl*; **to put one's c. on** s'habiller; **to take one's c. off** se déshabiller; **c. brush** brosse *f* à habits; **c. hanger** cintre *m*; **c. horse** séchoir *m* *(à linge)*; **c. line** corde *f* à linge; **c. peg** pince *f* à linge

clothing ['kləʊðɪŋ] *n (clothes)* vêtements *mpl*; **an article of c.** un vêtement; **the c. industry** l'industrie *f* du vêtement

clotted cream ['klɒtɪd'kriːm] *n* = crème fraîche très épaisse, typique du sud-ouest de l'Angleterre

cloud [klaʊd] 1 *n* (a) *(in sky)* nuage *m*; *Fig (of insects)* nuée *f* (b) *(idioms)* **to be under a c.** être en disgrâce; **to have one's head in the clouds** être dans les nuages; *Fam* **to be on c. nine** être aux anges
2 *vt* (a) *(mirror)* embuer (b) *(happiness)* jeter une ombre sur; *(judgement)* affecter; **to c. the issue** embrouiller la question

▸**cloud over** *vi (of sky)* se couvrir

cloudburst ['klaʊdbɜːst] n averse f

cloudless ['klaʊdlɪs] adj sans nuages

cloudy ['klaʊdɪ] adj (a) (sky, day) nuageux(euse) (b) (liquid) trouble

clout [klaʊt] Fam 1 n (a) (blow) coup m; to give sb a c. (with sth) frapper qn (avec qch) (b) (power, influence) influence f; to have a lot of c. avoir le bras long
2 vt (hit) flanquer une taloche à

clove[1] [kləʊv] n (of garlic) gousse f

clove[2] (spice) clou m de girofle

clove[3] pt of cleave

cloven ['kləʊvən] 1 adj c. hoof sabot m fendu
2 pp of cleave

clover ['kləʊvə(r)] n trèfle m; Fig to be in c. être comme un coq en pâte

clown [klaʊn] 1 n clown m; to act the c. faire le clown
2 vi to c. about or around faire le clown

cloying ['klɔɪɪŋ] adj (taste, smell) écœurant(e)

club [klʌb] 1 n (a) (society) club m; Fam Fig join the c.! tu n'es pas le seul/la seule! (b) (nightclub) boîte f (de nuit) (c) (weapon) massue f, gourdin m; (in golf) club m (d) clubs (in cards) trèfle m; ace of clubs as m de trèfle
2 vt (pt & pp clubbed) (hit) frapper avec une massue
3 vi to go clubbing aller en boîte

▸**club together** vi se cotiser (to buy pour acheter)

clubhouse ['klʌbhaʊs] n pavillon m

cluck [klʌk] 1 n gloussement m
2 vi glousser

clue [kluː] n (in crime, mystery) indice m; (in crossword) définition f; to give sb a c. donner un indice à qn, mettre qn sur la voie; Fam he hasn't a c. il est vraiment nul

▸**clue up** vt sep Fam to be clued up (on sth) être très calé(e) (en qch)

clueless ['kluːlɪs] adj Fam nul (nulle)

clump [klʌmp] 1 n (a) (of bushes) massif m; (of people) groupe m (b) (sound) bruit m bref et sourd
2 vi to c. about marcher d'un pas lourd

clumsiness ['klʌmzɪnɪs] n (of person, movement) maladresse f

clumsy ['klʌmzɪ] adj (person, movement) maladroit(e)

clung [klʌŋ] pt & pp of cling

cluster ['klʌstə(r)] 1 n (of grapes) grappe f; (of people, islands, houses) groupe m
2 vi to c. round sb/sth se grouper autour de qn/qch

clutch[1] [klʌtʃ] 1 n (in car) embrayage m; to let the c. in/out embrayer/débrayer; c. pedal pédale f d'embrayage (b) (grasp) to fall into sb's clutches tomber entre les griffes de qn
2 vt tenir fermement
3 vi to c. at sth s'agripper à qch; Fig to c. at straws se raccrocher à n'importe quoi

clutch[2] n (of eggs) couvée f

clutter ['klʌtə(r)] 1 n désordre m; in a c. en désordre
2 vt encombrer; to be cluttered (up) with sth être encombré(e) de qch

cluttered ['klʌtəd] adj encombré(e)

cm n (abbr centimetre(s)) cm

CNAA [siːenerˈeɪ] n Br (abbr Council for National Academic Awards) = organisme chargé de délivrer les diplômes dans les établissements d'enseignement supérieur non universitaires

CND [siːenˈdiː] n Br (abbr Campaign for Nuclear Disarmament) = mouvement prônant le désarmement nucléaire

CO [siːˈəʊ] n Mil (abbr Commanding Officer) chef m de corps

Co, co [kəʊ] n (abbr company) Cie; Fig Jane and co Jane et compagnie

c/o [siːˈəʊ] (abbr care of) chez, aux bons soins de

coach [kəʊtʃ] 1 n (a) Br (bus) car m; (horse-drawn carriage) carrosse m; (section of train) voiture f, wagon m; c. party excursionnistes mpl (voyageant en car); c. trip excursion f en car (b) (of athlete, team) entraîneur(euse) m,f
2 vt (athlete, team) entraîner; to c. sb for an exam donner des leçons particulières à qn en préparation à un examen

coachbuilder ['kəʊtʃbɪldə(r)] n Aut carrossier m

coagulant [kəʊˈægjʊlənt] n Med coagulant m

coagulate [kəʊˈægjʊleɪt] vi coaguler

coal [kəʊl] n (a) charbon m; c. bunker coffre m à charbon; c. merchant négociant m en charbon; c. mine mine f de charbon; c. miner mineur m; c. mining extraction f du charbon; c. tar goudron m de houille (b) (idioms) to carry coals to Newcastle porter de l'eau à la rivière; to haul sb over the coals réprimander qn vertement

coalesce [kəʊəˈles] vi s'unir

coalfield ['kəʊlfiːld] n bassin m houiller

coalition [kəʊəˈlɪʃən] n coalition f

coalman ['kəʊlmæn] n charbonnier m

coarse [kɔːs] adj (a) (person, language) grossier(ère), vulgaire (b) (surface, texture) grossier(ère); to have c. hair avoir le cheveu épais et rêche

coarsely ['kɔːslɪ] adv (a) (vulgarly) vulgairement (b) (roughly) c. chopped/ground haché(e)/moulu(e) grossièrement

coarseness ['kɔːsnɪs] n (a) (of person, language) grossièreté f, vulgarité f (b) (of surface, texture) grossièreté f

coast [kəʊst] 1 n côte f; Fig the c. is clear la voie est libre
2 vi (in car, on bicycle) avancer en roue libre; Fig she coasted through her exams elle a eu ses examens haut la main

coastal ['kəʊstəl] adj côtier(ère)

coaster ['kəʊstə(r)] n (a) (for glass) dessous m de verre (b) (ship) caboteur m

coastguard ['kəʊstgɑːd] n garde-côte m

coastline ['kəʊstlaɪn] n littoral m

coat [kəʊt] 1 n (a) (garment) manteau m; c. hanger cintre m; c. hook patère f; (of horse) robe f; (of dog) pelage m (c) (of snow, paint) couche f (d) (in heraldry) c. of arms armoiries fpl
2 vt (with mud, paint) couvrir (with de); (with chocolate, sugar) enrober (with de)

coating ['kəʊtɪŋ] n (of paint, dust) couche f; (of chocolate) enrobage m

co-author [kəʊˈɔːθə(r)] 1 n coauteur m
2 vt to c. a book with sb écrire un livre en collaboration avec qn

coax [kəʊks] vt enjôler; to c. sb to do or into doing sth amener qn à faire qch par des cajoleries; to c. sth out of sb obtenir qch de qn par des cajoleries

cob [kɒb] n (a) (horse) cob m (b) (of corn) épi m

cobalt ['kəʊbɒlt] n cobalt m; c. blue bleu m de cobalt

cobble ['kɒbəl] **1** n pavé m
2 vt paver

▶**cobble together** vt sep bricoler

cobbled ['kɒbəld] adj (path, street) pavé(e)

cobbler ['kɒblə(r)] n cordonnier m

cobblers ['kɒbləz] npl Br (a) very Fam (nonsense) conneries fpl (b) Vulg (testicles) couilles fpl

COBOL ['kəʊbɒl] n Comptr (abbr **Common Business Oriented Language**) Cobol m

cobra ['kəʊbrə] n cobra m

cobweb ['kɒbweb] n toile f d'araignée; Fig **to brush the cobwebs off sth** ressortir qch

cocaine [kə'keɪn] n cocaïne f

cock [kɒk] **1** n (**a**) (male fowl) coq m; **c. sparrow** moineau m mâle (**b**) Vulg (penis) bi(t)te f
2 vt (gun) armer; **to c. a snook at sb** faire la nique à qn; **to c. its ears** (of horse, dog) dresser les oreilles

▶**cock up** vt sep Br very Fam (plan, arrangement) faire foirer; (exam) se planter à

cockade [kɒ'keɪd] n cocarde f

cock-a-doodle-doo ['kɒkədu:dəl'du:] exclam cocorico!

cock-a-hoop ['kɒkə'hu:p] adj enchanté(e)

cockatoo [kɒkə'tu:] n cacatoès m

cocked [kɒkt] adj **to knock sb into a c. hat** (outclass) surpasser qn

cockerel ['kɒkərəl] n jeune coq m

cocker spaniel [kɒkə'spænjəl] n cocker m

cockeyed ['kɒkaɪd] adj Fam (decision, plan) farfelu(e)

cockfight ['kɒkfaɪt] n combat m de coqs

cockle ['kɒkəl] n (**a**) (shellfish) coque f (**b**) Fam **it warmed the cockles of his heart** ça lui a réchauffé le cœur

Cockney ['kɒknɪ] **1** n (**a**) (person) cockney mf (**b**) (dialect) cockney m
2 adj cockney

cockpit ['kɒkpɪt] n cabine f de pilotage, cockpit m

cockroach ['kɒkrəʊtʃ] n cafard m

cocksure [kɒk'ʃʊə(r)] adj (person, manner) présomptueux(euse)

cocktail ['kɒkteɪl] n also Fig cocktail m; **c. dress** robe f de cocktail; **c. lounge** bar m confortable (dans un pub, un hôtel); **c. party** cocktail; **c. shaker** shaker m; **c. stick** pique f

cocky ['kɒkɪ] adj Fam culotté(e)

cocoa ['kəʊkəʊ] n (powder, drink) cacao m; **c. butter** beurre m de cacao

coconut ['kəʊkənət] n noix f de coco; **c. milk** lait m de coco; **c. palm** cocotier m

cocoon [kə'ku:n] **1** n also Fig cocon m
2 vt Fig (protect) couver

COD [si:əʊ'di:] n Com (abbr **cash on delivery**) paiement m à la livraison

cod [kɒd] n morue f; **c. liver oil** huile f de foie de morue

coddle ['kɒdəl] vt (child) dorloter

code [kəʊd] **1** n (**a**) (cipher) code m; **in c.** codé(e); **c. book**; **c. name** nom m de code; **c. number** numéro m de code (**b**) (rules) code m; **c. of conduct** déontologie f, code de conduite
2 vt (message) coder

codeine ['kəʊdi:n] n codéine f

codify ['kəʊdɪfaɪ] (pt & pp **codified**) vt codifier

codswallop ['kɒdzwɒləp] n Fam foutaises fpl

coeducational [kəʊedjʊ'keɪʃənəl] adj (school) mixte

coefficient [kəʊɪ'fɪʃənt] n Math coefficient m

coerce [kəʊ'ɜːs] vt forcer, contraindre; **to c. sb into doing sth** contraindre qn à faire qch

coercion [kəʊ'ɜːʃən] n coercition f

coexist [kəʊɪg'zɪst] vi coexister

coexistence [kəʊɪg'zɪstəns] n coexistence f

C of E [si:əv'i:] adj Rel (abbr **Church of England**) anglican(e)

coffee ['kɒfɪ] n café m; **c. bar** café m; **c. bean** grain m de café; **c. break** pause-café f; **c. cup** tasse f à café; **c. grinder** moulin m à café; **c. grounds** marc m de café; **c. machine** (in café) percolateur m; (vending machine) machine f à café; (in home) cafetière f électrique; **c. mill** moulin m à café; **c. pot** cafetière; **c. spoon** cuillère f à café; **c. table** table f basse; **c. table book** grand livre m illustré

coffer ['kɒfə(r)] n (chest) coffre m; Fig **the coffers** (of company, country) les caisses fpl

coffin ['kɒfɪn] n cercueil m

cog [kɒg] n (tooth on gearwheel) dent f; (gearwheel) roue f dentée, rouage m; Fig **a c. in the machinery** un rouage dans la machine

cogent ['kəʊdʒənt] adj convaincant(e)

cogitate ['kɒdʒɪteɪt] vi Formal méditer, réfléchir

cognac ['kɒnjæk] n cognac m

cognition [kɒg'nɪʃən] n cognition f

cohabit [kəʊ'hæbɪt] vi vivre en concubinage (**with** avec)

cohabitation [kəʊhæbɪ'teɪʃən] n concubinage m

coherence [kəʊ'hɪərəns] n cohérence f

coherent [kəʊ'hɪərənt] adj cohérent(e)

cohesion [kəʊ'hi:ʒən] n cohésion f

cohesive [kəʊ'hi:sɪv] adj cohésif(ive)

coiffure [kwɑ:'fjʊə(r)] n coiffure f

coil [kɔɪl] **1** n (**a**) (of rope, wire) rouleau m; (electrical) bobine f; (contraceptive device) stérilet m (**b**) (single loop) anneau m
2 vt enrouler (**around** autour de)

▶**coil up** vi (of snake) se lover

coin [kɔɪn] **1** n pièce f (de monnaie); Fig **the other side of the c.** le revers de la médaille
2 vt (phrase, word) inventer; **to c. money** battre monnaie; Fam **he's coining it** il se fait un fric fou; Hum & Ironic **..., to c. a phrase ...**, comme on dit

coinage ['kɔɪnɪdʒ] n (**a**) (coins) monnaie f (**b**) (word) mot m nouveau, néologisme m; (phrase) expression f nouvelle

coincide [kəʊɪn'saɪd] vi coïncider (**with** avec)

coincidence [kəʊ'ɪnsɪdəns] n coïncidence f

coincidental [kəʊɪnsɪ'dentəl] adj fortuit(e)

coin-operated ['kɔɪnɒpəreɪtɪd] adj (machine) à pièces

coitus ['kɔɪtəs] n Formal coït m; **c. interruptus** coït interrompu

coke [kəʊk] n (**a**) (fuel) coke m (**b**) Fam (cocaine) coke f

col (abbr **column**) col

colander ['kɒləndə(r)] n passoire f

cold [kəʊld] **1** *n* **(a)** *(low temperature)* froid *m*; **to feel the c.** être frileux(euse); *Fig* **to be left out in the c.** rester sur la touche **(b)** *(illness)* rhume *m*; **to have a c.** avoir un rhume; **to catch a c.** attraper un rhume
2 *adj also Fig* froid(e); **I'm c.** j'ai froid; **it's c.** *(weather)* il fait froid; **to get c.** *(of food)* refroidir; *(of weather)* se refroidir; *also Fig* **to be in a c. sweat** avoir des sueurs froides; *Fam* **that leaves me c.** ça me laisse froid; **that's c. comfort** c'est une maigre consolation; *Fig* **to get c. feet (about sth)** hésiter (à faire qch) à la dernière minute; **to give sb the c. shoulder** snober qn; **c. cream** cold-cream *m*; *Met* **c. front** front *m* froid; **c. meats** viandes *fpl* froides; **c. sore** bouton *m* de fièvre; **c. start** *(of car)* démarrage *m* à froid; **c. storage** conservation *f* par le froid; **c. war** guerre *f* froide
3 *adv* **to do sth c.** faire qch à froid; *Fam Fig* **to be out c.** être sans connaissance

cold-blooded ['kəʊld'blʌdɪd] *adj (animal)* à sang froid; *Fig (person)* froid(e), insensible; **c. murder** meurtre *m* commis de sang-froid

cold-hearted ['kəʊld'hɑːtɪd] *adj (person, decision)* impitoyable

coldly ['kəʊldlɪ] *adv* froidement

coldness ['kəʊldnɪs] *n* froideur *f*

cold-shoulder ['kəʊld'ʃəʊldə(r)] *vt* snober

coleslaw ['kəʊlslɔː] *n* = salade de chou blanc à la mayonnaise

colic ['kɒlɪk] *n* colique *f*

collaborate [kə'læbəreɪt] *vi also Pej* collaborer (**with** avec)

collaboration [kəlæbə'reɪʃən] *n also Pej* collaboration *f*

collaborator [kə'læbəreɪtə(r)] *n also Pej* collaborateur(trice) *m,f*

collage ['kɒlɑːʒ] *n* collage *m*

collapse [kə'læps] **1** *n (of building, prices)* effondrement *m*
2 *vi (of person, building, prices)* s'effondrer, s'écrouler

collapsible [kə'læpsəbəl] *adj (table, bed)* pliant(e)

collar ['kɒlə(r)] **1** *n (of shirt)* col *m*; *(for dog)* collier *m*
2 *vt Fam (seize)* pincer

collarbone ['kɒləbəʊn] *n* clavicule *f*

collate [kə'leɪt] *vt* rassembler

collateral [kə'lætərəl] **1** *n Fin* nantissement *m*
2 *adj Mil* **c. damage** victimes *fpl* civiles

colleague ['kɒliːg] *n* collègue *mf*

collect [kə'lekt] **1** *adv Am* **to call sb c.** appeler qn en PCV
2 *vt* **(a)** *(stamps, paintings)* collectionner, faire collection de **(b)** *(gather) (belongings)* rassembler; *(information, news)* recueillir; *(rubbish)* ramasser; *(taxes)* lever; **to c. the dust** *(of ornament)* prendre la poussière; **to c. sb** *(pick up)* passer prendre qn **(c)** *(compose)* **to c. one's thoughts** se concentrer; **to c. oneself** se calmer
3 *vi (of people)* se rassembler; *(of things)* s'amasser; *(of dust)* s'accumuler

collected [kə'lektɪd] *adj* **(a)** *(calm)* calme **(b)** **c. works** œuvres *fpl* complètes

collection [kə'lekʃən] *n* **(a)** *(of stamps, paintings)* collection *f* **(b)** *(act of collecting) (of money)* recouvrement *m*; *(of rubbish)* ramassage *m*; *(of taxes)* levée *f*; **to take a c.** *(for charity)* faire une collecte; **c. plate** *(in church)* plat *m* de quête

collective [kə'lektɪv] **1** *n (group)* collectif *m*; *(farm)* coopérative *f* agricole
2 *adj* collectif(ive); **c. bargaining** = négociations afin d'établir une convention collective; **c. noun** collectif *m*

collectively [kə'lektɪvlɪ] *adv* collectivement

collectivize [kə'lektɪvaɪz] *vt* collectiviser

collector [kə'lektə(r)] *n* **(a)** *(of stamps, paintings)* collectionneur(euse) *m,f*; **c.'s item** pièce *f* de collection **(b)** **c. of taxes** percepteur *m*

college ['kɒlɪdʒ] *n Br (of further education)* établissement *m* d'enseignement supérieur; *Br (part of university)* = association d'enseignants et d'étudiants au sein de certaines universités, disposant d'une semi-autonomie administrative; *Am (university)* université *f*; **to be at c.** être étudiant(e); **c. of education** ≃ école *f* normale

collide [kə'laɪd] *vi* entrer en collision (**with** avec)

collie ['kɒlɪ] *n* colley *m*

colliery ['kɒlɪərɪ] *n (pl* **collieries)** *n* houillère *f*, mine *f* de charbon

collision [kə'lɪʒən] *n* collision *f*; *Fig* **to be on a c. course** aller droit au conflit

colloquial [kə'ləʊkwəl] *adj* familier(ère)

colloquialism [kə'ləʊkwəlɪzəm] *n* expression *f* familière

collude [kə'luːd] *vi* être de connivence (**with** avec)

collusion [kə'luːʒən] *n* collusion *f*; **to be in c. with sb** être de connivence avec qn

collywobbles ['kɒlɪwɒbəlz] *npl Fam* **to have the c.** avoir la trouille

cologne [kə'ləʊn] *n* eau *f* de Cologne

Colombia [kə'lʌmbɪə] *n* la Colombie

Colombian [kə'lʌmbɪən] **1** *n* Colombien(enne) *m,f*
2 *adj* colombien(enne)

colon ['kəʊlən] *n* **(a)** *Anat* côlon *m* **(b)** *(punctuation mark)* deux-points *m*

colonel ['kɜːnəl] *n* colonel *m*

colonial [kə'ləʊnɪəl] *adj* colonial(e)

colonialism [kə'ləʊnɪəlɪzəm] *n* colonialisme *m*

colonist ['kɒlənɪst] *n* colon *m*

colonize ['kɒlənaɪz] *vt*-coloniser

colonnade [kɒlə'neɪd] *n Archit* colonnade *f*

colony ['kɒlənɪ] *n (pl* **colonies)** *n* colonie *f*

color, colored *etc Am* = **colour, coloured** *etc*

colossal [kə'lɒsəl] *adj* colossal(e)

colour ['kʌlə(r)] **1** *n* **(a)** *(of chemical, dye)* couleur *f*; **what c. is it?** de quelle couleur est-ce?; **c. bar** *(racial discrimination)* discrimination *f* raciale; **c. scheme** coloris *mpl*, couleurs *fpl*; **c. supplement** *(of newspaper)* supplément *m* en couleurs; **c. television** télévision *f* couleur *(b) (idioms)* **to be off c.** *(of person)* ne pas être dans son assiette; **to give c. to a story** rendre un récit plus vivant; **let's see the c. of your money** voyons la couleur de ton argent; **to pass with flying colours** être reçu(e) brillamment ou haut la main; **to show one's true colours** se montrer sous son vrai jour; **to nail one's colours to the mast** afficher ses opinions
2 *vt* **(a)** *(of chemical, dye)* colorer; *(with felt-tips, crayons)* colorier; **to c. one's hair** se faire une couleur *(b) Fig (judgement, view)* fausser
3 *vi (blush)* rougir

▶**colour in** *vt sep* colorier

colour-blind ['kʌləblaɪnd] *adj* daltonien(enne)

colour-coded [ˈkʌləkəʊdɪd] *adj* différencié(e) par des couleurs

coloured [ˈkʌləd] *adj* (a) *(illustration)* en couleurs; *(pen, ink)* de couleur; *(person)* de couleur; Fig **a highly c. narrative** un récit haut en couleurs (b) *(person)* de couleur

colourful [ˈkʌləfʊl] *adj* coloré(e); *(vivid)* coloré, pittoresque; **a c. character** un personnage haut en couleurs

colouring [ˈkʌlərɪŋ] *n* (a) *(in food)* colorants *mpl* (b) *(complexion)* teint *m*; **to have dark/fair c.** avoir le teint mat/clair (c) **c. book** album *m* à colorier

colourless [ˈkʌləlɪs] *adj* (a) *(clear)* incolore (b) Fig *(dull)* insipide, fade

colt [kəʊlt] *n* poulain *m*

Columbus [kəˈlʌmbəs] *n* **Christopher C.** Christophe Colomb

column [ˈkɒləm] *n (of troops, text, in building)* colonne *f*; *(newspaper feature)* rubrique *f*

columnist [ˈkɒləmɪst] *n (for newspaper, magazine)* chroniqueur(euse) *m,f*

coma [ˈkəʊmə] *n* coma *m*; **to go into a c.** tomber dans le coma; **to be in a c.** être dans le coma

comatose [ˈkəʊmətəʊs] *adj also Fig* comateux(euse)

comb [kəʊm] **1** *n* (a) *(for hair)* peigne *m*; **to give one's hair a c.** se donner un coup de peigne (b) *(of cock)* crête *f*
2 *vt* (a) *(hair)* peigner; **to c. one's hair** se peigner (b) *(search)* ratisser, passer au peigne fin

combat [ˈkɒmbæt] **1** *n* combat *m*; **c. jacket** veste *f* de treillis; **c. zone** zone *f* de combat
2 *vt (disease, prejudice, crime)* combattre

combatant [ˈkɒmbətənt] *n & adj* combattant(e) *m,f*

combination [kɒmbɪˈneɪʃən] *n* combinaison *f*; **c. of circumstances** un concours de circonstances; **c. lock** serrure *f* à combinaison

combine [kəmˈbaɪn] **1** *n* [ˈkɒmbaɪn] (a) **c. (harvester)** moissonneuse-batteuse *f* (b) Econ cartel *m*
2 *vt* combiner, allier; **to c. business with pleasure** joindre l'utile à l'agréable
3 *vi (of people)* s'associer; *(of companies)* fusionner; *(of chemical elements)* se combiner

combustible [kəmˈbʌstɪbəl] *adj* combustible

combustion [kəmˈbʌstʃən] *n* combustion *f*; **c. chamber** chambre *f* de combustion

come [kʌm] *(pt* came [keɪm]*, pp* come*) vi* (a) *(move)* venir *(from* de*); (arrive)* arriver; **to c. from France/Edinburgh** venir de France/d'Édimbourg; **to c. to the end of sth** arriver à la fin de qch; **here he comes!** le voilà!; **coming!** j'arrive!; **c., c.!** allons, allons!; **she always comes to me for help** elle s'adresse toujours à moi quand elle a besoin d'aide; **she came running towards us** elle vint vers nous en courant, elle courut vers nous; **the rain came pouring down** il s'est mis à tomber des cordes; **nothing comes between her and her work** son travail passe avant tout; Fig **she has come a long way since then** elle a fait du chemin depuis; Fam **I don't know whether I'm coming or going!** je ne sais plus où j'en suis!
(b) *(in time)* **c.** January en janvier; **c. next summer** l'été prochain; **in the days/years to c.** dans les jours/années à venir; **it came as a shock/surprise to me** ça m'a fait un choc/une surprise; Fam **he had it coming (to him)** ça lui pendait au nez
(c) *(happen)* **to c. to do sth** finir par faire qch; **c. to**

think of it maintenant que j'y pense; **to take things as they c.** prendre les choses comme elles viennent; **c. what may** quoi qu'il arrive; **how c....?** comment se fait-il que...? + *subjunctive*
(d) *(in sequence)* **to c. first/last** *(in race, competition)* finir premier/dernier; **October comes before November** octobre vient avant novembre; **what comes next?** qu'est-ce qui vient après?
(e) *(exist, be available)* **to c. in three sizes/colours** exister en trois tailles/couleurs; **work of that quality doesn't c. cheap** du travail de cette qualité, ça se paie; **he's as tough as they c.** il n'y a pas plus dur que lui
(f) *(become)* **to c. loose** se défaire; **to c. true** se réaliser; **to c. open** s'ouvrir; **to c. of age** devenir majeur(e)
(g) *(reach)* **to c. up/down to** arriver (jusqu')à
(h) *very Fam (reach orgasm)* jouir

▶**come about** *vi* se produire, arriver

▶**come across 1** *vt insep (find)* tomber sur
2 *vi (make an impression)* **to c. across well/badly** bien/mal passer; **he comes across as a nice person** il a l'air gentil

▶**come after** *vt insep (chase)* poursuivre

▶**come along** *vi* (a) **c. along!** allons, pressons! (b) *(make progress) (of project, work)* avancer; **his French is coming along well** il fait des progrès en français (c) *(arrive)* venir

▶**come at** *vt insep (attack)* attaquer

▶**come away** *vi (become detached)* se détacher

▶**come back** *vi* revenir; **it's all coming back to me** ça me revient; **to c. back to what I was saying...** pour revenir à ce que je disais...

▶**come by 1** *vt insep (acquire)* obtenir, trouver
2 *vi (visit)* passer

▶**come down** *vi* (a) *(descend)* descendre; *(of temperature, prices)* baisser; Fig **to c. down in the world** déchoir; **to c. down with the flu** attraper la grippe (b) *(decide)* **to c. down in favour of sb/sth** décider en faveur de qn/qch (c) **to c. down to** *(be a matter of)* se ramener à, se résumer à; **it comes down to the fact that...** le fait est que...

▶**come down on** *vt insep (reprimand)* passer un savon à

▶**come forward** *vi* se présenter; **no one has come forward with any suggestions** personne n'a fait de suggestions

▶**come in** *vi* (a) *(of person)* entrer; *(of tide)* monter; **c. in!** entrez!; **to c. in first/second** arriver premier/deuxième (b) *(have a role)* intervenir; **and where do I c. in?** et moi, qu'est-ce que je fais?; **to c. in useful** être utile

▶**come in for** *vt insep* **to c. in for criticism** faire l'objet de critiques

▶**come into** *vt insep* (a) *(room, city)* entrer dans; **to c. into the world** venir au monde; **to c. into existence** être créé(e); **to c. into force or effect** *(of law, ruling)* entrer en vigueur; **to c. into power** arriver au pouvoir; **luck didn't c. into it** la chance n'a rien à voir là-dedans (b) *(inherit)* hériter de

▶**come of** *vi (result from)* **no good will c. of it** cela n'amènera rien de bon; **that's what comes of being too ambitious** c'est ce qui arrive lorsqu'on est trop ambitieux

▶**come off 1** *vt insep* (a) *(fall from)* horse, bicycle) tomber de (b) **c. off it!** arrête ton char!
2 *vi* (a) *(be removed) (of button)* se détacher; *(of paint)* s'écailler; *(of stain)* partir (b) *(succeed)* réussir; **to c. off well/badly** *(in contest)* bien/mal s'en tirer

▶**come on** vi (a) **c. on!** allez! (b) *(make progress) (of project, work)* avancer; **his chess is coming on** il fait des progrès aux échecs; **I feel a cold coming on** je sens que je suis en train de m'enrhumer (c) *(of lights)* s'allumer; *(of heating)* se mettre en route

▶**come out** vi (a) *(of person, magazine, film)* sortir; *(of sun)* paraître; *(of truth)* se faire jour; **to c. out on strike** se mettre en grève; **to c. out in a rash** se couvrir de boutons; **to c. out in favour of/against sth** se prononcer pour/contre qch; **he came out of the deal well/badly** il a fait une bonne/mauvaise affaire; **to c. out with** *(remark, opinion)* sortir (b) *(of tooth, hair)* tomber; *(of screw)* se dévisser; *(of stain)* partir (c) *(as gay or lesbian)* déclarer son homosexualité

▶**come over 1** vt insep *(affect)* a strange feeling came over me j'ai eu une sensation étrange; **what's come over you?** qu'est-ce qui te prend?
   2 vi (a) *(visit)* passer (b) *(make impression)* **to c. over well/badly** bien/mal passer (c) *(feel)* **to c. over all funny** se sentir tout(e) drôle; **to c. over all dizzy** être pris(e) de vertiges

▶**come round** vi (a) *(visit)* passer (b) *(regain consciousness)* reprendre connaissance (c) *(accept)* accepter; **to c. round to sb's way of thinking** se rallier à l'opinion de qn

▶**come through 1** vi *(of message, news)* arriver
   2 vt insep *(survive) (war, crisis, illness)* survivre à

▶**come to 1** vt insep (a) *(amount to)* s'élever à; **the scheme never came to anything** le projet n'a jamais abouti (b) *(reach)* **to c. to the point** en venir au fait; **to c. to a conclusion** arriver à une conclusion; **what is the world coming to?** où va-t-on? (c) *(be a matter of)* **when it comes to...** pour ce qui est de...; **if it comes to that...** à ce compte-là...
   2 vi *(regain consciousness)* reprendre connaissance

▶**come together** vi *(gather)* se rassembler

▶**come up 1** vt insep *(stairs, hill)* monter
   2 vi (a) *(of sun)* se lever; *(of opportunity, question, problem)* se présenter; **to c. up against a problem** rencontrer un problème; **there are some interesting films coming up on television** il y a quelques films intéressants qui vont bientôt passer à la télévision; **I'll let you know if anything comes up** je te préviendrai si quelque chose se présente; **the case comes up (for trial) tomorrow** le procès commence demain (b) **to c. up with** *(funding, solution)* trouver; *(idea, theory)* proposer

▶**come upon** vt insep *(find)* tomber sur

▶**come up to** vt insep (a) *(approach)* s'approcher de (b) *(equal)* **the film didn't c. up to my expectations** le film n'était pas à la hauteur de mes espérances

comeback [ˈkʌmbæk] n **to make a c.** *(of fashion)* revenir; *(of actor, sportsperson)* faire un come-back

COMECON [ˈkɒmɪkɒn] n Formerly *(abbr* **Council for Mutual Economic Assistance)** COMECON m

comedian [kəˈmiːdɪən] n comique mf; Fig *(practical joker)* farceur(euse) m,f

comedienne [kəmiːdɪˈen] n comique f

comedown [ˈkʌmdaʊn] n Fam régression f

comedy [ˈkɒmɪdɪ] n *(pl* **comedies)** *(play, film)* comédie f; *(of situation)* comique m; *(situation comedy)* sitcom m; **c. show** *(on TV)* spectacle m comique

come-on [ˈkʌmɒn] n Fam *(enticement)* appât m; **to give sb the c.** *(sexually)* faire du gringue à qn

comer [ˈkʌmə(r)] n **open to all comers** ouvert(e) à tous

comet [ˈkɒmɪt] n comète f

comeuppance [kʌmˈʌpəns] n Fam **to get one's c.** avoir ce qu'on mérite

comfort [ˈkʌmfət] **1** n (a) *(ease)* confort m; *(financial)* aisance f; **to do sth in the c. of one's own home** faire qch confortablement chez soi; **comforts** *(luxuries)* commodités fpl; **I like my home comforts** j'aime mon petit confort; **the bullets were too close for c.** les balles passaient un peu trop près à mon goût; Am **c. station** toilettes fpl publiques (b) *(consolation)* réconfort m, consolation f; **if it's any c.,...** si ça peut vous consoler,...; **to take c. from** or **in sth** trouver du réconfort dans qch
   2 vt *(console)* réconforter, consoler

comfortable [ˈkʌmftəbl] adj (a) *(place, bed, chair)* confortable; *(person)* bien in, à l'aise; **to be c.** *(of patient)* ne pas souffrir; **to make oneself c.** se mettre à l'aise ou à son aise; **I wouldn't feel c. accepting that money** ça me mettrait mal à l'aise d'accepter cet argent (b) *(majority, income)* confortable; **to be in c. circumstances** mener une vie aisée

comfortably [ˈkʌmftəblɪ] adv (a) *(sit)* confortablement; **to be c. off** *(financially)* être à l'aise financièrement; **to live c.** *(easily)* facilement; **to win c.** gagner avec une avance confortable

comforter [ˈkʌmfətə(r)] n Am *(quilt)* édredon m

comforting [ˈkʌmfətɪŋ] adj réconfortant(e)

comfy [ˈkʌmfɪ] adj Fam *(place, bed, chair)* confortable; *(person)* bien in, à l'aise

comic [ˈkɒmɪk] **1** n (a) *(performer)* comique mf (b) **c.** *(book)* bande f dessinée, BD f
   2 adj comique; **c. opera** opéra-comique m; **to provide some c. relief** détendre l'atmosphère; **c. strip** bande f dessinée, BD f

comical [ˈkɒmɪkəl] adj comique

coming [ˈkʌmɪŋ] **1** n (a) *(of person)* venue f, arrivée f; *(of night)* approche f; **comings and goings** allées fpl et venues
   2 adj *(year, week)* prochain(e); *(elections, difficulties)* à venir

comma [ˈkɒmə] n virgule f

command [kəˈmɑːnd] **1** n (a) *(order)* ordre m; Comptr commande f; Comptr **c. language** langage m de commandes (b) *(authority, control)* commandement m; **to be in c. (of sth)** *(army, ship)* commander (qch); **to be in c. of the situation** maîtriser la situation, être au commandement; **to have sth at one's c.** avoir qch à sa disposition; **she has a good c. of English** elle a une bonne maîtrise de l'anglais; **c. economy** économie f planifiée
   2 vt (a) *(give order to)* **to c. sb to do sth** ordonner ou commander à qn de faire qch (b) *(ship, regiment)* commander (c) *(have at one's disposal)* avoir à sa disposition (d) *(respect, admiration, attention)* forcer; **to c. a high price** se vendre cher

commandant [ˈkɒməndænt] n Mil commandant m

commandeer [kɒmənˈdɪə(r)] vt réquisitionner

commander [kəˈmɑːndə(r)] n Mil commandant m; Naut capitaine m de frégate; **c.-in-chief** commandant en chef

commanding [kəˈmɑːndɪŋ] adj (a) Mil **c. officer** chef m de corps (b) *(voice)* de commandement; *(appearance)* qui en impose; *(position)* dominant(e); *(lead)* considérable

commandment [kəˈmɑːndmənt] n Rel commandement m

commando [kə'mɑːndəʊ] (pl **commandos** or **commandoes**) n Mil (soldier, unit) commando m

commemorate [kə'meməreɪt] vt commémorer

commemoration [kəmemə'reɪʃən] n commémoration f

commemorative [kə'memərətɪv] adj commémoratif(ive)

commence [kə'mens] vt & vi Formal commencer; **to c. doing sth** commencer à faire qch

commencement [kə'mensmənt] n (a) Formal (beginning) commencement m, début m (b) Am Univ remise f des diplômes

commend [kə'mend] vt (a) (praise) louer, féliciter; **to c. sb for bravery** louer qn pour sa bravoure (b) (recommend) recommander; **the train journey has little to c. it** je ne vous recommande pas le voyage en train (c) Lit (entrust) recommander (**to** à)

commendable [kə'mendəbəl] adj louable

commendation [komen'deɪʃən] n (praise) éloges mpl; (in competition) mention f spéciale; Mil citation f

commensurate [kə'menʃərət] adj Formal proportionnel(elle) (**with** à)

comment ['koment] **1** n commentaire m, observation f (**on** sur); **no c.!** sans commentaire!
2 vt **to c. that…** faire remarquer ou observer que…; **"how interesting"**, **he commented** "comme c'est intéressant", remarqua-t-il ou observa-t-il
3 vi faire des commentaires (**on** sur)

commentary ['koməntərɪ] (pl **commentaries**) n commentaire m

commentate ['koməntert] vi faire le commentaire; **to c. on sth** commenter qch

commentator ['koməntertə(r)] n commentateur(trice) m,f

commerce ['komɜːs] n commerce m

commercial [kə'mɜːʃəl] **1** n (advertisement) publicité f, pub f
2 adj also Pej commercial(e); **c. artist** graphiste mf; Fin **c. bank** banque f commerciale; **c. break** page f de publicité; **c. law** droit m commercial; **c. traveller** voyageur m de commerce; **c. value** valeur f marchande; **c. vehicle** véhicule m de commerce

commercialism [kə'mɜːʃəlɪzəm] n Pej mercantilisme m

commercialized [kə'mɜːʃəlaɪzd] adj Pej commercial(e)

commercially [kə'mɜːʃəlɪ] adv commercialement; **c. available** disponible dans le commerce

commie ['komɪ] n & adj Fam Pej coco mf

commiserate [kə'mɪzəreɪt] vi **to c. with sb** être désolé(e) pour qn

commiseration [kəmɪzə'reɪʃən] n commisération f; **you have my commiserations** je suis désolé pour vous

commission [kə'mɪʃən] **1** n (a) Com (payment) commission f (b) (of work, painting) commande f (c) (investigating body) commission f (d) Naut **in c.** armé(e); **out of c.** désarmé(e) (e) Mil brevet m d'officier
2 vt (a) (order) (work, painting) commander; **to c. sb to do sth** charger qn de faire qch (b) Mil **to be commissioned** être nommé(e) officier

commissionaire [kəmɪʃə'neə(r)] n portier m

commissioner [kə'mɪʃənə(r)] n membre m d'une commission; **c. of police** ≃ commissaire m de police; Law **c. for oaths** = homme de loi habilité à recevoir des déclarations sous serment

commit [kə'mɪt] (pt & pp **committed**) vt (a) (error, crime) commettre; **to c. suicide** se suicider (b) **to c. oneself** (promise) s'engager; **to c. oneself to (doing) sth** s'engager à (faire) qch; **to c. sth to sth** (resources, troops) engager qch dans qch (c) (entrust) confier (**to** à); **to c. sth to writing** coucher qch par écrit; **to c. sth to memory** apprendre qch par cœur (d) (confine) **to c. sb (to prison)** incarcérer qn; **to c. sb (to mental institution)** interner qn (e) Law **to c. sb for trial** mettre qn en accusation

commitment [kə'mɪtmənt] n (a) (obligation) engagement m; **family/business commitments** obligations fpl familiales/professionnelles (b) (dedication) dévouement m (**to** à); **to make a c.** s'engager; **she lacks c.** elle ne s'investit pas assez

committed [kə'mɪtɪd] adj dévoué(e) (**to** à); (Christian, socialist) convaincu(e); **to be c. (to one's work)** beaucoup s'impliquer (dans son travail)

committee [kə'mɪtɪ] n comité m, commission f

commode [kə'məʊd] n (a) (chest of drawers) commode f (b) (toilet) chaise f percée

commodious [kə'məʊdɪəs] adj spacieux(euse)

commodity [kə'modɪtɪ] (pl **commodities**) n Econ marchandise f, produit m; Fin matière f première; **to be a rare c.** être une denrée rare; **commodities market** marché m des matières premières

commodore ['komədɔː(r)] n Naut ≃ contre-amiral m

common ['komən] **1** n (a) **to have sth in c. (with)** avoir qch en commun (avec); **in c. with** (similar to) de même que (b) (land) terrain m communal
2 adj (a) (frequent) commun(e), courant(e); **in c. use** d'usage courant (b) (shared) commun(e); **it is by c. consent the best** de l'avis de tous, c'est le meilleur; **C. Agricultural Policy** politique f agricole commune; Fin **c. currency** monnaie f unique; also Fig **c. denominator** dénominateur m commun; **the c. good** le bien commun; Fig **c. ground** terrain m d'entente; **it's c. knowledge (that)…** tout le monde sait que…; **the C. Market** le Marché commun; Sch **c. room** (for pupils) salle f commune; (for teachers) salle des professeurs (c) (average) **c. or garden** ordinaire, standard inv; **the c. cold** le rhume; **the c. man** l'homme m de la rue; **the c. people** les gens mpl ordinaires (d) Pej (vulgar) vulgaire

commoner ['komənə(r)] n roturier(ère) m,f

common-law ['komənlɔː] adj **c. husband** concubin m; **c. marriage** concubinage m; **c. wife** concubine f

commonly ['komənlɪ] adv communément

commonplace ['komənpleɪs] **1** n lieu m commun
2 adj courant(e)

Commons ['komənz] npl **the (House of) C.** la Chambre des communes

Commonwealth ['komənwelθ] n **the C.** le Commonwealth

commotion [kə'məʊʃən] n (noise) vacarme m; (disruption) agitation f

communal ['komjunəl] adj (bathroom, resource) commun(e); (life) communautaire

commune 1 ['komjuːn] (collective) communauté f
2 vi [kə'mjuːn] **to c. with nature** communier avec la nature

communicable [kə'mju:nɪkəbəl] *adj (disease)* transmissible

communicant [kə'mju:nɪkənt] *n Rel* communiant(e) *m,f*

communicate [kə'mju:nɪkeɪt] **1** *vt* communiquer; *(illness)* transmettre
2 *vi* communiquer (**with** avec)

communication [kəmju:nɪ'keɪʃən] *n* communication *f*; **to be in c. with sb** être en contact avec qn; **c. cord** sonnette *f* d'alarme

communicative [kə'mju:nɪkətɪv] *adj* communicatif(ive)

communion [kə'mju:njən] *n Rel* communion *f*; **to take C.** communier

communism ['kɒmjʊnɪzəm] *n* communisme *m*

communist ['kɒmjʊnɪst] *n & adj* communiste *mf*

community [kə'mju:nɪtɪ] *(pl* **communities)** *n* communauté *f*; **the business c.** le milieu des affaires; **c. centre** foyer *m* municipal; *Formerly* **c. charge** = en Grande-Bretagne, impôt regroupant taxe d'habitation et impôts locaux; **c. service** travail *m* d'intérêt général; **c. spirit** esprit *m* communautaire

commute [kə'mju:t] **1** *vt Law* commuer (**to** en)
2 *vi* to **c. (to work)** faire la navette entre son domicile et son travail

commuter [kə'mju:tə(r)] *n* banlieusard(e) *m,f (qui fait la navette entre son domicile et son travail)*; **c. train** train *m* de banlieue

Comoros ['kɒmərɒs] *n* the **C. (Islands)** les Comores *fpl*

compact [kəm'pækt] **1** *n* ['kɒmpækt] **(a)** *(for powder)* poudrier *m* **(b)** *(treaty)* accord *m* **(c)** *Am (car)* petite voiture *f*
2 *adj* compact(e); **c. disc** disque *m* compact; **c. disc player** lecteur *m* de disques compacts
3 *vt* compacter

companion [kəm'pænjən] *n* **(a)** *(friend)* compagnon (compagne) *m,f*; *(of elderly woman)* dame *f* de compagnie; **travelling c.** compagnon de voyage **(b)** *(guidebook)* guide *m*

companionable [kəm'pænjənəbəl] *adj (person)* sociable; *(manner)* amical(e)

companionship [kəm'pænjənʃɪp] *n* compagnie *f*

company ['kʌmpənɪ] *(pl* **companies)** *n* **(a)** *(companionship)* compagnie *f*; **in his c.** en sa compagnie; **to keep sb c.** tenir compagnie à qn; **to be good c.** être de bonne compagnie; **to part c. with sb** *(split up)* se séparer de qn; *(disagree)* ne plus être d'accord avec qn; **to get into bad c.** avoir de mauvaises fréquentations; **to do sth in c.** *(in public)* faire qch en public; **to be expecting c.** *(guests)* attendre de la visite **(b)** *(business)* société *f*; **publishing c.** maison *f* d'édition; **Hobbs and C.** Hobbs et Compagnie; **c. car** voiture *f* de fonction; **c. policy** politique *f* de la société; *Com* **c. secretary** secrétaire *mf* général(e) **(c)** *(army unit, theatre group)* compagnie *f*

comparable ['kɒmpərəbəl] *adj* comparable (**to** à)

comparative [kəm'pærətɪv] **1** *n Gram* comparatif *m*
2 *adj* **(a)** *(relative)* *(cost, comfort, wealth)* relatif(ive) **(b)** *(study, research)* comparatif(ive); *(psychology, literature)* comparé(e)

compare [kəm'peə(r)] **1** *vt* comparer (**with** *or* **to** avec *ou*

à); **compared with** *or* **to** par rapport à, à côté de; *Fig* **to c. notes** échanger ses impressions
2 *vi* être comparable (**with** à); **to c. favourably with sth** ne le céder en rien à qch
3 *n Lit* **beyond c.** sans pareil(eille)

comparison [kəm'pærɪsən] *n* comparaison *f*; **in** *or* **by c. (with)** en comparaison (avec); **there is no c.** il n'y a pas de comparaison; **to draw** *or* **make a c. between sth and sth** faire la comparaison entre qch et qch

compartment [kəm'pɑ:tmənt] *n* compartiment *m*

compass ['kʌmpəs] *n* **(a)** *(for finding direction)* boussole *f*; *(of boat)* compas *m* **(b)** *Math* **(pair of) compasses** compas *m* **(c)** *(scope) (of mind)* portée *f*; *(of powers)* étendue *f*

compassion [kəm'pæʃən] *n* compassion *f*

compassionate [kəm'pæʃənət] *adj (person, attitude)* compatissant(e); *(by nature)* humain(e); **to be c. towards sb** éprouver de la compassion pour qn; **on c. grounds** pour raisons personnelles; **c. leave** congé *m* exceptionnel pour raisons personnelles

compatibility [kəmpætə'bɪlɪtɪ] *n* compatibilité *f*

compatible [kəm'pætəbəl] *adj* compatible (**with** avec)

compatriot [kəm'pætrɪət] *n* compatriote *m*

compel [kəm'pel] *(pt & pp* **compelled)** *vt* forcer, obliger; **to c. sb to do sth** forcer *ou* obliger qn à faire qch; **to c. admiration/respect** forcer l'admiration/le respect

compelling [kəm'pelɪŋ] *adj (film, performance)* captivant(e); *(argument)* convaincant(e); *(urge)* irrésistible

compendium [kəm'pendɪəm] *n (book)* précis *m*; *(of games)* sélection *f*

compensate ['kɒmpenseɪt] **1** *vt* dédommager (**for** de)
2 *vi* to **c. for sth** compenser qch

compensation [kɒmpen'seɪʃən] *n* compensation *f*; *(money)* dédommagement *m*, indemnité *f*

compensatory [kɒmpen'seɪtərɪ] *adj* compensatoire

compere ['kɒmpeə(r)] **1** *n* animateur(trice) *m,f*, présentateur(trice) *m,f*
2 *vt* animer, présenter

compete [kəm'pi:t] *vi* **(a)** *(contend)* rivaliser (**with** avec); *(of company)* être en concurrence (**with** avec); **to c. for sth** se disputer qch **(b)** *(in race, competition)* concourir (**for** pour)

competence ['kɒmpɪtəns] *n* **(a)** *(ability)* compétence *f*, compétences *fpl* **(b)** *Law* compétence *f*

competent ['kɒmpɪtənt] *adj (person)* compétent(e); **a c. piece of work** du bon travail

competition [kɒmpɪ'tɪʃən] *n* **(a)** *(contest)* concours *m*; *(in sport)* compétition *f* **(b)** *(rivalry)* rivalité *f*; *(between companies, candidates)* concurrence *f*; **to be in c. with sb** être en concurrence avec qn; **the c.** *(opponents)* *(in sport)* les adversaires *mpl*; *(in business)* la concurrence; **there's no c.!** il n'y a aucune comparaison!

competitive [kəm'petɪtɪv] *adj (person)* qui a l'esprit de compétition; *(atmosphere)* de compétition; *(price, company)* compétitif(ive); **c. sports** sports *mpl* de compétition; *Com* **c. tendering** appel *m* d'offres

competitor [kəm'petɪtə(r)] *n* concurrent(e) *m,f*

compilation [kɒmpɪ'leɪʃən] *n* compilation *f*

compile [kəm'paɪl] *vt (list)* dresser

complacency [kəm'pleɪsənsɪ] *n* autosatisfaction *f*

complacent [kəm'pleɪsənt] *adj* content(e) de soi; **to be c. about sth** faire de l'autosatisfaction à propos de qch

complain [kəm'pleɪn] *vi* se plaindre (**about** de); **to c. of** *(illness)* se plaindre de; **I can't c. about the service** je n'ai pas à me plaindre du service; **how are things? – can't c.** comment ça va? – je n'ai pas à me plaindre

complaint [kəm'pleɪnt] *n* (a) *(grievance)* récrimination *f*; *(official)* plainte *f*, réclamation *f*; **to have cause** *or* **grounds for c.** avoir des raisons de se plaindre; **to lodge** *or* **make a c. against sb** porter plainte contre qn (b) *(illness)* maladie *f*

complement 1 *n* ['kɒmpləmənt] (a) *Gram* complément *m* (b) *Naut & Fig* **the full c.** l'effectif *m* complet
2 *vt* ['kɒmplɪment] compléter

complementary [kɒmplɪ'mentərɪ] *adj* complémentaire; **c. medicine** médecines *fpl* alternatives *ou* parallèles

complete [kəm'pliːt] **1** *adj* (a) *(whole)* complet(ète); *(utter)* total(e); **he is a c. fool** il est complètement idiot (b) *(finished)* achevé(e)
2 *vt* (a) *(whole)* achever; *(fill in)* *(form)* compléter (b) *(make whole)* compléter

completely [kəm'pliːtlɪ] *adv* complètement

completion [kəm'pliːʃən] *n* achèvement *m*; **on c.** *(of work)* à l'achèvement; **to near c.** toucher à sa fin

complex ['kɒmpleks] **1** *n* (*of buildings, psychological*) complexe *m*; **to have a c. about sth** être complexé(e) par qch
2 *adj* complexe

complexion [kəm'plekʃən] *n* teint *m*; **to have a fair c.** avoir le teint clair; *Fig* **that puts a different c. on things** voilà qui change tout

complexity [kəm'pleksɪtɪ] (*pl* **complexities**) *n* complexité *f*

compliance [kəm'plaɪəns] *n* observation *f* (**with** de); **in c. with** conformément à

compliant [kəm'plaɪənt] *adj* complaisant(e), accommodant(e)

complicate ['kɒmplɪkeɪt] *vt* compliquer

complicated ['kɒmplɪkeɪtɪd] *adj* compliqué(e)

complication [kɒmplɪ'keɪʃən] *n* complication *f*

complicity [kəm'plɪsɪtɪ] *n* complicité *f* (**in** dans)

compliment 1 ['kɒmplɪmənt] *n* compliment *m*; **to pay sb a c.** faire un compliment à qn; **with compliments** avec nos compliments; **compliments of the season** meilleurs vœux; **compliments slip** papillon *m* à en-tête *(portant la mention 'avec les compliments de...')*
2 *vt* ['kɒmplɪment] **to c. sb on sth** *(bravery, command of language)* féliciter qn pour qch; *(dress, haircut)* faire des compliments à qn sur qch

complimentary [kɒmplɪ'mentərɪ] *adj* (a) *(praising)* élogieux(euse) (**about** à l'égard de) (b) *(free)* gratuit(e); **c. ticket** billet *m* de faveur

comply [kəm'plaɪ] (*pt* & *pp* **complied**) *vi* **to c. with** *(rule)* se conformer à, se plier à; *(order)* obéir à; *(request)* accéder à

component [kəm'pəʊnənt] **1** *n* *(electrical, chemical)* composant *m*; *Fig* composante *f*
2 *adj* **c. part** pièce *f* détachée; *Fig* composante *f*

compose [kəm'pəʊz] *vt* (a) *(music, poetry)* composer (b) *(constitute)* **to be composed of** être composé(e) de, se composer de (c) *(calm)* **to c. oneself** se ressaisir

composed [kəm'pəʊzd] *adj* calme

composer [kəm'pəʊzə(r)] *n* compositeur(trice) *m,f*

composite ['kɒmpəzɪt] *adj* *(photograph)* composite

composition [kɒmpə'zɪʃən] *n* composition *f*; *(essay)* rédaction *f*

compositor [kəm'pɒzɪtə(r)] *n* *Typ* compositeur(trice) *m,f*

compost ['kɒmpɒst] *n* compost *m*; **c. heap** tas *m* de compost

composure [kəm'pəʊʒə(r)] *n* sang-froid *m*

compound[1] ['kɒmpaʊnd] **1** *n* *Chem & Gram* composé *m*
2 *adj* composé(e); *Med* **c. fracture** fracture *f* compliquée; *Fin* **c. interest** intérêts *mpl* composés
3 *vt* [kəm'paʊnd] *(problem)* aggraver

compound[2] ['kɒmpaʊnd] *n* *(enclosure)* enceinte *f*

comprehend [kɒmprɪ'hend] *vt* comprendre

comprehensible [kɒmprɪ'hensəbəl] *adj* compréhensible

comprehension [kɒmprɪ'henʃən] *n* compréhension *f*; **it is beyond my c.** cela dépasse mon entendement

comprehensive [kɒmprɪ'hensɪv] *adj* *(answer, programme)* complet(ète); *(study)* exhaustif(ive); *(view)* d'ensemble; *(defeat, victory)* écrasant(e); *Fin* **c. insurance** assurance *f* tous risques; *Br* **c. (school)** établissement *m* secondaire *(n'opérant pas de sélection à l'entrée)*

compress 1 *n* ['kɒmpres] *Med* compresse *f*
2 *vt* [kəm'pres] *(air, gas)* comprimer; *Fig* *(text)* condenser

compression [kəm'preʃən] *n* *(of air, gas)* compression *f*; *Fig* raccourcissement *m*

compressor [kəm'presə(r)] *n* compresseur *m*

comprise [kəm'praɪz] *vt* comprendre, se composer de; **to be comprised of** comprendre, se composer de

compromise ['kɒmprəmaɪz] **1** *n* compromis *m*; **c. solution** solution *f* de compromis
2 *vt* *(person, security)* compromettre; *(principles)* transiger sur; **to c. oneself** se compromettre
3 *vi* transiger (**on** sur)

compromising ['kɒmprəmaɪzɪŋ] *adj* compromettant(e)

compulsion [kəm'pʌlʃən] *n* *(urge)* besoin *m*; *(obligation)* contrainte *f*; **under c.** sous la contrainte; **to be under no c. to do sth** ne pas être obligé(e) de faire qch

compulsive [kəm'pʌlsɪv] *adj* *(smoker, gambler, liar)* invétéré(e); **c. eating** boulimie *f*; **it's c. viewing** c'est captivant

compulsory [kəm'pʌlsərɪ] *adj* obligatoire; **c. redundancy** ≃ licenciement *m* sec; **c. retirement** mise *f* à la retraite d'office

compunction [kəm'pʌŋkʃən] *n* remords *m*, scrupules *mpl*

computation [kɒmpjʊ'teɪʃən] *n* calcul *m*

compute [kəm'pjuːt] *vt* calculer

computer [kəm'pjuːtə(r)] *n* ordinateur *m*; **c. game** jeu *m* électronique; **to be c. literate** avoir des connaissances en informatique; **c. printout** impression *f*; **c. program** programme *m* informatique; **c. programmer** programmeur(euse) *m,f*; **c. programming** programmation *f*; **c. science** informatique *f*; **c. scientist** informaticien(enne) *m,f*; **c. simulation** simulation *f* par ordinateur

computerization [kəmpjuːtəraɪ'zeɪʃən] *n* informatisation *f*

computerize [kəm'pjuːtəraɪz] *vt* informatiser

computing [kəm'pjuːtɪŋ] *n* informatique *f*

comrade ['kɒmreɪd] *n* camarade *mf*

comradeship ['kɒmreɪdʃɪp] n camaraderie f

con¹ [kɒn] Fam **1** n (swindle) arnaque f; **c. man** arnaqueur m

2 vt (pt & pp **conned**) (swindle) arnaquer; **to c. sth out of sb** arnaquer qn de qch; **to c. sb into doing sth** persuader qn de faire qch par la ruse

con² n Fam (convict) taulard(e) m,f

con³ n (disadvantage) see **pro**

concave [kɒn'keɪv] adj concave

conceal [kən'siːl] vt cacher, dissimuler (from à)

concealer [kən'siːlə(r)] n (make-up) camoufleur m

concede [kən'siːd] **1** vt concéder; **to c. defeat** s'avouer vaincu(e); **to c. that...** admettre que...

2 vi s'incliner

conceit [kən'siːt] n (vanity) vanité f, suffisance f

conceited [kən'siːtɪd] adj vaniteux(euse), suffisant(e)

conceivable [kən'siːvəbəl] adj concevable, imaginable; **it is c. that...** il est concevable que... + subjunctive

conceivably [kən'siːvəblɪ] adv **we might c. get there by six** il se peut que nous soyons arrivés pour six heures; **she couldn't c. have done it** il est inconcevable qu'elle ait fait ça

conceive [kən'siːv] **1** vt **(a)** (child, idea) concevoir **(b)** (understand) concevoir

2 vi **to c. of** concevoir qch

concentrate ['kɒnsəntreɪt] **1** n concentré m

2 vt concentrer (on sur)

3 vi se concentrer (on sur); **to c. on doing sth** s'appliquer à faire qch

concentration [kɒnsən'treɪʃən] n concentration f; **c. camp** camp m de concentration; **to have a short c. span** ne pas avoir une grande capacité de concentration

concentric [kən'sentrɪk] adj Math concentrique

concept ['kɒnsept] n concept m

conception [kən'sepʃən] n **(a)** (of child, idea) conception f **(b)** (understanding) **to have no c. of sth** n'avoir aucune idée ou notion de qch

conceptual [kən'septjʊəl] adj conceptuel(elle)

conceptualize [kən'septjʊəlaɪz] vt conceptualiser

concern [kən'sɜːn] **1** n **(a)** (interest) **it's no c. of mine/yours** cela ne me/vous regarde pas; **this is a matter of public c.** c'est une affaire qui nous concerne tous **(b)** (worry, compassion) inquiétude f, souci m; **to give cause for c.** être un sujet d'inquiétude; **there is no cause for c.** il n'y a pas de raison de s'inquiéter; **to show c.** se montrer inquiet(ète) **(c)** (company) entreprise f

2 vt **(a)** (affect) concerner; **to c. oneself with sth** se préoccuper ou se soucier de qch; **as far as I'm concerned,...** pour moi,..., en ce qui me concerne,...; **to whom it may c.** à qui de droit **(b)** (worry) inquiéter **(c)** (be about) (of book) traiter de; **it concerns your request for a transfer** c'est au sujet de votre demande de transfert

concerned [kən'sɜːnd] adj (worried) inquiet(ète) (about au sujet de)

concerning [kən'sɜːnɪŋ] prep au sujet de

concert ['kɒnsət] n **(a)** (musical) concert m; **c. hall** salle f de concert; **c. pianist** concertiste mf **(b)** (cooperation) **in c. (with)** de concert (avec)

concerted [kən'sɜːtɪd] adj concerté(e)

concertina [kɒnsə'tiːnə] n concertina m

concerto [kən'tʃɜːtəʊ] (pl **concertos**) n concerto m

concession [kən'seʃən] n **(a)** (compromise, giving up) concession f **(b)** (discount) tarif m réduit

concessionary [kən'seʃənərɪ] adj (fare) réduit(e)

conciliate [kən'sɪlɪeɪt] vt apaiser

conciliation [kənsɪlɪ'eɪʃən] n conciliation f; (in dispute) conciliation, arbitrage m; **the dispute went to c.** le conflit a été soumis à l'arbitrage

conciliatory [kən'sɪlɪətərɪ] adj conciliant(e)

concise [kən'saɪs] adj concis(e)

conclude [kən'kluːd] **1** vt **(a)** (speech, book, treaty) conclure; (conference, festival) clore **(b)** (deduce) **to c. that...** conclure que...

2 vi (of speaker) conclure (with sur); (of conference, festival) se clore (with sur)

concluding [kən'kluːdɪŋ] adj final(e)

conclusion [kən'kluːʒən] n **(a)** (inference) conclusion f; **to come to** or **reach a c.** arriver à une conclusion **(b)** (end) conclusion f; **in c.** pour conclure, en conclusion

conclusive [kən'kluːsɪv] adj concluant(e)

concoct [kən'kɒkt] vt also Fig concocter

concoction [kən'kɒkʃən] n (drink, dish) mixture f

concord ['kɒŋkɔːd] n (harmony) entente f

concordance [kən'kɔːdəns] n (agreement) accord m; **to be in c. with sth** être en accord avec qch

concourse ['kɒŋkɔːs] n (in airport, railway station) hall m

concrete ['kɒŋkriːt] **1** n béton m; **c. jungle** forêt f de béton; **c. mixer** bétonnière f

2 adj en béton; Fig (definite) concret(ète)

concubine ['kɒŋkjʊbaɪn] n concubine f

concur [kən'kɜː(r)] (pt & pp **concurred**) vi (of person) être d'accord (with avec); (of findings, results) concorder (with avec)

concurrent [kən'kʌrənt] adj simultané(e), concordant(e)

concurrently [kən'kʌrəntlɪ] adv simultanément

concussed [kən'kʌst] adj commotionné(e)

concussion [kən'kʌʃən] n commotion f cérébrale

condemn [kən'dem] vt **(a)** (disapprove of) condamner **(b)** Law (sentence) condamner (to à); **condemned cell** cellule de condamné à mort **(c)** (building) déclarer inhabitable

condemnation [kɒndem'neɪʃən] n condamnation f

condensation [kɒnden'seɪʃən] n **(a)** (moisture) (on glass) buée f; (on walls) condensation f **(b)** (process) condensation f

condense [kən'dens] **1** vt condenser; **condensed milk** lait m condensé

2 vi se condenser

condenser [kən'densə(r)] n Tech condensateur m

condescend [kɒndɪ'send] vi **to c. to do sth** condescendre à faire qch; **to c. towards sb** se montrer condescendant(e) envers qn

condescending [kɒndɪ'sendɪŋ] adj condescendant(e)

condescension [kɒndɪ'senʃən] n condescendance f

condiment ['kɒndɪmənt] n condiment m

condition [kən'dɪʃən] **1** n **(a)** (state) état m; (of person) forme f; **in good/bad c.** (of machine, road) en bon/mauvais état; **you're in no c. to drive** tu n'es pas en état de conduire; **to be in good c./out of c.** (of person) être/ne pas être en forme

(b) conditions (circumstances) conditions fpl; **working conditions** conditions de travail; **driving conditions** état m des routes; Law **conditions of employment**

contrat *m* de travail

(c) *(requirement)* condition *f*; **on the c. that...** à (la) condition que... + *subjunctive*; **on no c.** sous aucun prétexte, en aucun cas

(d) *(disease)* maladie *f*; **heart c.** maladie du cœur

2 *vt* **(a)** *(influence)* conditionner; **to be conditioned by** *(depend on)* dépendre de; **we have been conditioned to believe that...** on nous a appris à croire que...; *Psy* **conditioned reflex** réflexe *m* conditionné

(b) *(hair)* mettre de l'après-shampo(o)ing sur

conditional [kən'dɪʃənəl] 1 *n Gram* **the c.** le conditionnel

2 *adj* conditionnel(elle); **to be c. on** dépendre de; *Law* **c. discharge** liberté *f* conditionnelle

conditionally [kən'dɪʃənəlɪ] *adv (accept, grant)* sous certaines conditions

conditioner [kən'dɪʃənə(r)] *n (for hair)* après-shampo(o)ing *m*

conditioning [kən'dɪʃənɪŋ] *n (psychological)* conditionnement *m*

condo ['kɒndəʊ] *n (pl* **condos)** *n Am Fam (abbr* **condominium)** appartement *m* en copropriété

condolences [kən'dəʊlənsɪz] *npl* condoléances *fpl*

condom ['kɒndəm] *n* préservatif *m*

condominium [kɒndə'mɪnɪəm] *n Am (apartment)* appartement *m* en copropriété

condone [kən'dəʊn] *vt* excuser

condor ['kɒndɔ:(r)] *n* condor *m*

conducive [kən'dju:sɪv] *adj* **to be c. to** être favorable *ou* propice à

conduct [kən'dʌkt] 1 *n* ['kɒndʌkt] *(behaviour)* conduite *f*
2 *vt* **(a)** *(business, orchestra)* diriger; *(campaign, inquiry, experiment)* mener; **to c. oneself** se conduire **(b)** *(guide)* guider; **we were conducted round the factory** on nous a fait visiter l'usine; **a conducted tour** une visite guidée **(c)** *(heat, electricity)* conduire
3 *vi Mus* diriger

conductivity [kɒndʌk'tɪvɪtɪ] *n Phys* conductivité *f*

conductor [kən'dʌktə(r)] *n* **(a)** *Br (on bus)* receveur *m* **(b)** *(of orchestra)* chef *m* d'orchestre **(c)** *Phys* conducteur *m*

conductress [kən'dʌktrɪs] *n Br (on bus)* receveuse *f*

conduit ['kɒndɪt] *n* conduit *m*

cone [kəʊn] *n* **(a)** *(shape)* cône *m* **(b)** *(of pine)* pomme *f* de pin **(c)** *(for ice cream)* cornet *m* **(d)** *(for traffic)* cône *m* de signalisation

cone-shaped ['kəʊnʃeɪpt] *adj* conique

confab ['kɒnfæb] *n Fam* **to have a c. about sth** discuter de qch

confectioner [kən'fekʃənə(r)] *n* confiseur(euse) *m,f*; *Culin* **c.'s custard** crème *f* pâtissière; **c.'s (shop)** confiserie *f*

confectionery [kən'fekʃənərɪ] *n (sweets)* confiserie *f*

confederacy [kən'fedərəsɪ] *n* confédération *f*

confederate [kən'fedərət] 1 *n (accomplice)* complice *m*
2 *adj Pol* confédéré(e)

confederation [kənfedə'reɪʃən] *n* confédération *f*

confer [kən'fɜ:(r)] *(pt & pp* **conferred)** 1 *vt (title, degree, powers)* octroyer (**on** à)
2 *vi (discuss) (of several people)* se consulter; **to c. with sb about sth** discuter de qch avec qn

conference ['kɒnfərəns] *n* conférence *f*, congrès *m*; *Com* **to be in c.** être en conférence

confess [kən'fes] 1 *vt (crime, mistake)* confesser, avouer; *(feeling)* avouer; *Rel* confesser; **to c. that...** confesser *ou* avouer que...
2 *vi* avouer; *Rel* se confesser; **to c. to sth** *(crime, mistake)* confesser *ou* avouer qch; *(feeling)* avouer qch

confession [kən'feʃən] *n* confession *f*, aveu *m*; *Rel* confession; **to go to c.** aller se confesser

confessional [kən'feʃənəl] *n Rel* confessionnal *m*

confessor [kən'fesə(r)] *n Rel* confesseur *m*

confetti [kən'fetɪ] *n* confettis *mpl*

confidante [kɒnfɪ'dænt] *n* confident(e) *m,f*

confide [kən'faɪd] 1 *vt* **to c. sth to sb** confier qch à qn
2 *vi* **to c. in sb** se confier à qn

confidence ['kɒnfɪdəns] *n* **(a)** *(trust)* confiance *f* (**in** en); **I have every c. that...** je ne doute pas un instant que...; **to take sb into one's c.** se confier à qn; **c. trick** escroquerie *f* **(b)** *(self-assurance)* confiance *f* en soi **(c)** *(secret)* confidence *f*; **in c.** en confidence

confident ['kɒnfɪdənt] *adj* **(a)** *(self-assured) (person)* sûr(e) de soi; *(smile, exterior)* confiant(e) **(b)** *(certain)* certain(e); **to be c. of doing sth** être certain de faire qch

confidential [kɒnfɪ'denʃəl] *adj* confidentiel(elle)

confidentiality [kɒnfɪdenʃɪ'ælɪtɪ] *n* confidentialité *f*

confidentially [kɒnfɪ'denʃəlɪ] *adv* confidentiellement, en confidence

confidently ['kɒnfɪdəntlɪ] *adv* **(a)** *(with self-assurance)* avec assurance **(b)** *(with certainty)* avec confiance

configuration [kənfɪgjʊ'reɪʃən] *n* configuration *f*

confine [kən'faɪn] *vt* **(a)** *(imprison)* enfermer; **to be confined to bed** être alité(e); **to be confined to barracks** être consigné(e); **confined space** espace *m* restreint **(b)** *(limit)* **to c. oneself to (doing) sth** se limiter *ou* s'en tenir à (faire) qch

confinement [kən'faɪnmənt] *n* **(a)** *(in prison)* emprisonnement *m* **(b)** *Old-fashioned Med (labour)* couches *fpl*

confines ['kɒnfaɪnz] *npl (of town)* confins *mpl*; *Fig (limits)* limites *fpl*; **within the c. of** dans les limites de

confirm [kən'fɜ:m] *vt* confirmer; *(power, position)* consolider, renforcer

confirmation [kɒnfə'meɪʃən] *n also Rel* confirmation *f*

confirmed [kən'fɜ:md] *adj (smoker, liar)* invétéré(e); *(bachelor)* endurci

confiscate ['kɒnfɪskeɪt] *vt* confisquer (**from** à)

confiscation [kɒnfɪs'keɪʃən] *n* confiscation *f*

conflict 1 *n* ['kɒnflɪkt] conflit *m*; **to come into c. with** entrer en conflit avec
2 *vi* [kən'flɪkt] être en contradiction (**with** avec)

conflicting [kən'flɪktɪŋ] *adj (opinions)* opposé(e); *(reports, evidence)* contradictoire

confluence ['kɒnfluəns] *n (of rivers)* confluent *m*

conform [kən'fɔ:m] *vi* se plier aux règles; **to c. to** *(rules)* obéir à, se plier à; *(standards)* être en conformité avec; **to c. with** être conforme à

conformist [kən'fɔ:mɪst] *n & adj* conformiste *mf*

conformity [kən'fɔ:mɪtɪ] *n* conformité *f*; **in c. with** conformité *ou* en accord avec

confound [kən'faʊnd] *vt* **(a)** *(puzzle)* laisser perplexe **(b)** *(frustrate) (plans)* faire échouer **(c)** *(surprise)* confondre **(d)** *Fam (damn)* **c. it!** quelle barbe!; **c. him!** le diable l'emporte!

confront [kən'frʌnt] vt affronter, faire face à; **to be confronted by sth** être confronté(e) à qch; **to c. sb with sth** confronter qn à qch

confrontation [kɒnfrʌn'teɪʃən] n affrontement m

confuse [kən'fjuːz] vt (bewilder) embrouiller; (mix up) confondre (**with** avec)

confused [kən'fjuːzd] adj (person) perdu(e); (instructions, account, mind) confus(e); **I'm c.** je m'y perds; **to get c.** s'embrouiller

confusing [kən'fjuːzɪŋ] adj (bewildering) déroutant(e); (muddled) confus(e)

confusion [kən'fjuːʒən] n (bewilderment) perplexité f; (disorder, lack of clarity) confusion f; **to throw sth into c.** chambouler qch

congeal [kən'dʒiːl] vi (of blood) (se) coaguler

congenial [kən'dʒiːnɪəl] adj agréable

congenital [kən'dʒenɪtəl] adj congénital(e); Fig **he's a c. liar** il ment tout le temps, c'est congénital

conger [ˈkɒŋɡə(r)] n **c. (eel)** congre m

congested [kən'dʒestɪd] adj (street, city, lungs) congestionné(e); (nose) bouché(e)

congestion [kən'dʒestʃən] n (of traffic) encombrements mpl; (of lungs) congestion f

conglomerate [kən'ɡlɒmərət] n conglomérat m

Congo [ˈkɒŋɡəʊ] n **the C.** (country) le Congo

Congolese [kɒŋɡə'liːz] **1** n Congolais(e) m,f
2 adj congolais(e)

congratulate [kən'grætjʊleɪt] vt féliciter (**on** de); **to c. oneself on having done sth** se féliciter d'avoir fait qch

congratulations [kəngrætjʊ'leɪʃənz] npl félicitations fpl; **c. on your promotion/passing your exams** félicitations pour votre promotion/vos examens

congratulatory [kən'grætjʊleɪtəri] adj de félicitations

congregate [ˈkɒŋɡrɪɡeɪt] vi se rassembler, s'assembler

congregation [kɒŋɡrɪ'ɡeɪʃən] n (of church) assemblée f des fidèles

congress [ˈkɒŋɡres] n (conference) congrès m; Am Pol **C.** le Congrès (assemblée législative américaine)

Congressman [ˈkɒŋɡresmən] n Am Pol membre m du Congrès

Congresswoman [ˈkɒŋɡreswʊmən] n Am Pol membre m du Congrès

conical [ˈkɒnɪkəl] adj conique

conifer [ˈkɒnɪfə(r)] n conifère m

coniferous [kə'nɪfərəs] adj (forest) de conifères; **c. tree** conifère m

conjecture [kən'dʒektʃə(r)] **1** n conjecture f; **it's sheer c.** ce ne sont que des suppositions
2 vt supposer
3 vi faire des conjectures

conjugal [ˈkɒndʒʊɡəl] adj conjugal(e)

conjugate [ˈkɒndʒʊɡeɪt] Gram **1** vt conjuguer
2 vi se conjuguer

conjugation [kɒndʒʊ'ɡeɪʃən] n Gram conjugaison f

conjunction [kən'dʒʌŋkʃən] n conjonction f; **in c. with** conjointement avec

conjunctivitis [kəndʒʌŋktɪ'vaɪtɪs] n conjonctivite f

conjure [ˈkʌndʒə(r)] vi (do magic) faire des tours de passe-passe; Fig **a name to c. with** un nom prestigieux

►**conjure up** vt sep (a) (produce) faire apparaître; **she conjured up a meal** elle s'est débrouillée pour préparer un repas en un rien de temps; **to c. sth up out of nowhere** faire apparaître qch comme par magie (b) (call to mind) évoquer

conjurer [ˈkʌndʒərə(r)] n prestidigitateur m, illusionniste mf

conjuring [ˈkʌndʒərɪŋ] n prestidigitation f; **c. trick** tour m de prestidigitation ou de passe-passe

conjuror [ˈkʌndʒərə(r)] = **conjurer**

conk [kɒŋk] n Fam (nose) blair m, pif m

►**conk out** vi Fam (a) (stop working) (of machine, TV) flancher; **the car conked out on me** la voiture m'a claqué entre les doigts (b) (fall asleep) se mettre à pioncer

conker [ˈkɒŋkə(r)] n Fam (chestnut) marron m d'Inde; Br **conkers** (game) = jeu qui consiste à faire éclater le marron que son adversaire tient au bout d'une ficelle

conman [ˈkɒnmæn] n escroc m

connect [kə'nekt] **1** vt (pipes, wires, circuits) relier (**to** à); **to c. sth to the mains** brancher qch sur secteur (b) (link, associate) **to c. sb/sth to sb/sth** établir un lien entre qn/qch et qn/qch; **there is nothing to c. the two crimes** il n'y a aucun lien entre les deux crimes; **to be connected with** avoir un lien ou un rapport avec; **the two issues are not connected** les deux questions n'ont aucun rapport; **are they connected?** (of people) sont-ils parents?; **to be well connected** (of person) avoir des relations (c) Tel mettre en ligne ou en communication (**with** avec); **can you c. me with lost property?** pourriez-vous me passer les objets trouvés?

2 vi (a) (of pipes, wires, roads) être relié(e) (**with** avec); (of rooms) communiquer (**with** avec) (b) (of train, plane) assurer la correspondance (**with** avec) (c) (of blow) atteindre son but; **the blow connected with his knee** le coup l'a atteint au genou

►**connect up** vt sep (pipes, wires) raccorder

connection [kə'nekʃən] n (a) (link, association) lien m, rapport m; **in c. with** à propos de; **in this c.** à ce propos (b) (acquaintance) relation f; **to have important connections** avoir des relations en haut lieu (c) (of pipes, wires) raccordement m (d) (train, plane) correspondance f

connivance [kə'naɪvəns] n connivence f

connive [kə'naɪv] vi (a) (conspire) comploter; **to c. with sb** être de connivence avec qn (b) **to c. at sth** (let happen) laisser faire qch

conniving [kə'naɪvɪŋ] adj intrigant(e)

connoisseur [kɒnə'sɜː(r)] n connaisseur(euse) m,f (**of** en)

connotation [kɒnə'teɪʃən] n connotation f

conquer [ˈkɒŋkə(r)] vt (country, someone's heart) conquérir; (difficulty, fears) vaincre

conquering [ˈkɒŋkərɪŋ] adj victorieux(euse)

conqueror [ˈkɒŋkərə(r)] n vainqueur m

conquest [ˈkɒŋkwest] n conquête f; **to make a c. of sb** faire la conquête de qn

conscience [ˈkɒnʃəns] n conscience f; **to have a clear c.** avoir la conscience tranquille; **to have a guilty c.** avoir mauvaise conscience; **to have sth on one's c.** avoir qch sur la conscience; **to have no c. about doing sth** ne pas avoir de scrupules à faire qch; **in all c.** raisonnablement

conscientious [kɒnʃɪ'enʃəs] adj consciencieux(euse); **c. objector** objecteur m de conscience

conscious ['kɒnʃəs] *adj* (a) *(awake)* conscient(e) (b) *(aware)* to be c. of sth conscient(e) de qch/ que...; to become c. of sth prendre conscience de qch, s'apercevoir de qch; *Psy* the c. mind la conscience (c) *(intentional)* conscient(e); to make a c. effort to do sth faire un effort particulier pour faire qch; to make a c. decision to do sth prendre délibérément à faire qch

consciousness ['kɒnʃəsnɪs] *n* (a) *(wakefulness)* conscience *f*; to lose/regain c. perdre/reprendre connaissance (b) *(awareness)* conscience *f* (of de); to raise people's c. of sth sensibiliser les gens à qch

conscript 1 ['kɒnskrɪpt] *conscrit m*
2 *vt* [kən'skrɪpt] enrôler; to be conscripted être appelé(e) (sous les drapeaux)

conscription [kən'skrɪpʃən] *n* conscription *f*

consecrate ['kɒnsɪkreɪt] *vt Rel & Fig* consacrer

consecration [kɒnsɪ'kreɪʃən] *n* consécration *f*

consecutive [kən'sekjʊtɪv] *adj* consécutif(ive); on three c. days trois jours consécutifs, trois jours de suite

consensus [kən'sensəs] *n* consensus *m*

consent 1 [kən'sent] *n* consentement *m*, assentiment *m*
2 *vi* to c. to sth/to do sth consentir à qch/à faire qch

consequence ['kɒnsɪkwəns] *n* (a) *(result)* conséquence *f*; as a c., in c. par conséquent; to take the consequences subir les conséquences (b) *(importance)* importance *f*; of little c. de peu d'importance; of no c. sans importance

consequent ['kɒnsɪkwənt] *adj* résultant(e); c. upon sth qui résulte de qch; the war and its c. loss of life la guerre et les pertes en vies humaines qui en résultent

consequently ['kɒnsɪkwəntlɪ] *adv* par conséquent

conservation [kɒnsə'veɪʃən] *n* (of environment) protection *f*; (of energy) économies *fpl*; c. area (of town, city) quartier *m* préservé; (nature reserve) réserve *f* naturelle

conservationist [kɒnsə'veɪʃənɪst] *n* défenseur *m* de l'environnement

Conservative [kən'sɜːvətɪv] *Br Pol* **1** *n* conservateur(trice) *m,f*
2 *adj* conservateur(trice); the C. Party le Parti conservateur

conservative [kən'sɜːvətɪv] **1** *n* conservateur(trice) *m,f*
2 *adj* conservateur(trice); (conventional) classique; at a c. estimate au bas mot

conservatory [kən'sɜːvətərɪ] (*pl* conservatories) *n* (a) *(room)* véranda *f* (b) *Mus* conservatoire *m*

conserve [kən'sɜːv] **1** ['kɒnsɜːv] (jam) confiture *f*
2 *vt* [kən'sɜːv] (monument, language, tradition) préserver; (water, energy) faire des économies de

consider [kən'sɪdə(r)] *vt* (a) *(think over)* considérer; (offer, matter) étudier; he was considering whether to go out when... il était en train de se demander s'il allait sortir lorsque...; to c. doing sth envisager de faire qch; to c. sb for a job envisager qn pour un poste (b) *(take into account)* penser, réfléchir à; (possibility) envisager; (person's feelings) tenir compte de; all things considered tout bien considéré (c) *(regard)* considérer; I c. her a friend je la considère comme une amie; c. it done considère que c'est déjà fait; c. yourself dismissed considère-toi comme renvoyé

considerable [kən'sɪdərəbəl] *adj* considérable; after c. difficulty après bien des difficultés

considerate [kən'sɪdərət] *adj* prévenant(e) (towards envers); that wasn't very c. of you ce n'était pas très aimable de ta part

consideration [kənsɪdə'reɪʃən] *n* (a) *(deliberation)* to be under c. être à l'étude; after due c. après mûre réflexion; to take sth into c. prendre qch en considération (b) *(factor)* facteur *m* (c) *(respect)* considération *f*; show some c.! tu pourrais faire preuve d'un peu de considération!; out of c. for par égard pour (d) *(payment)* contribution *f*; for a small c. en échange d'une modique somme

considering [kən'sɪdərɪŋ] **1** *prep* étant donné, vu
2 *conj* étant donné que; c. (that) he is so young étant donné son jeune âge
3 *adv (after all)* not bad c. pas mal après tout

consign [kən'saɪn] *vt* (a) *(dispose of)* reléguer (to à); she was consigned to a life of loneliness elle fut condamnée à une existence solitaire (b) *(entrust)* confier (to à) (c) *(send)* expédier (to à)

consignment [kən'saɪnmənt] *n* (of goods) envoi *m*, expédition *f*

▶**consist of** [kən'sɪst] *vt insep* consister en, se composer de

consistency [kən'sɪstənsɪ] *n* (a) *(of substance, liquid)* consistance *f* (b) *(of arguments, ideas)* cohérence *f*; (of behaviour, person) logique *f*; (of performer, results) régularité *f*

consistent [kən'sɪstənt] *adj* (arguments, ideas) cohérent(e); (behaviour, person) logique; (quality, standard) constant(e); (performer, results) régulier(ère); (refusal, failure) persistant(e); to be c. with concorder avec

consistently [kən'sɪstəntlɪ] *adv* (play, perform) avec régularité; (fail, deny, oppose) toujours

consolation [kɒnsə'leɪʃən] *n* consolation *f*; if it's any c. si ça peut te consoler; c. prize prix *m* de consolation

console¹ ['kɒnsəʊl] *n* (control panel) console *f*

console² [kən'səʊl] *vt* consoler (for de)

consolidate [kən'sɒlɪdeɪt] **1** *vt also Fig* consolider; (position) renforcer; (power) asseoir
2 *vi* se consolider

consolidation [kənsɒlɪ'deɪʃən] *n also Fig* consolidation *f*; (of position, power) renforcement *m*

consonant ['kɒnsənənt] **1** *n* consonne *f*
2 *adj Formal* c. with en accord avec

consort ['kɒnsɔːt] *n* (spouse of monarch) époux (épouse) *m,f*; (prince) c. prince *m* consort

▶**consort with** [kən'sɔːt] *vt insep* frayer avec, fréquenter

consortium [kən'sɔːtɪəm] (*pl* consortiums *or* consortia [kən'sɔːtɪə]) *n Com* consortium *m*

conspicuous [kən'spɪkjʊəs] *adj* (easily visible) bien visible; (bravery) remarquable; to look c. ne pas passer inaperçu(e); to make oneself c. se faire remarquer; in a c. position bien en évidence; to be c. by one's absence briller par son absence; c. consumption consommation *f* ostentatoire

conspiracy [kən'spɪrəsɪ] (*pl* conspiracies) *n* conspiration *f*; c. theory = théorie postulant l'existence d'un complot pour expliquer des événements demeurés mystérieux

conspirator [kən'spɪrətə(r)] *n* conspirateur(trice) *m,f*

conspiratorial [kənspɪrə'tɔːrɪəl] *adj* de conspirateur; a c. wink un coup d'œil complice

conspire [kən'spaɪə(r)] *vi* (of person) se liguer (against/ with contre/avec); (for political reasons) conspirer (against/with contre/avec); circumstances conspired against me les circonstances se sont liguées contre moi

constable ['kʌnstəbəl] *n Br* agent *m* de police; *(rural)* gendarme *m*; **chief c.** = commissaire *m* de police divisionnaire

constabulary [kən'stæbjʊlər] *(pl* **constabularies)** *n* police *f*

constant ['kɒnstənt] **1** *n Math & Phys* constante *f* **2** *adj* **(a)** *(unchanging) (price, temperature)* constant(e); *(friend)* fidèle **(b)** *(continual) (attention, noise, care)* continuel(elle); *(questions, complaints)* incessant(e); **a c. stream of insults** un flot d'injures ininterrompu

constellation [kɒnstə'leɪʃən] *n* constellation *f*

consternation [kɒnstə'neɪʃən] *n* consternation *f*

constipated ['kɒnstɪpeɪtɪd] *adj also Fig* constipé(e)

constipation [kɒnstɪ'peɪʃən] *n* constipation *f*

constituency [kən'stɪtjʊənsɪ] *(pl* **constituencies)** *n* circonscription *f* (électorale)

constituent [kən'stɪtjʊənt] **1** *n* **(a)** *Pol* électeur(trice) *m,f* **(b)** *(part)* élément *m* constitutif **2** *adj* constitutif(ive); *c. part* élément *m* constitutif

constitute ['kɒnstɪtjuːt] *vt* constituer

constitution [kɒnstɪ'tjuːʃən] *n* **(a)** *(of state, organization)* constitution *f* **(b)** *(of person)* constitution *f*; **to have a strong c.** avoir une santé de fer; **to have a weak c.** être de santé fragile

constitutional [kɒnstɪ'tjuːʃənəl] **1** *n (walk)* (courte) promenade *f* **2** *adj (reform, decision, monarchy)* constitutionnel(elle)

constrain [kən'streɪn] *vt* contraindre, obliger **(to do à faire); to feel constrained to do sth** se sentir obligé(e) de faire qch

constraint [kən'streɪnt] *n* contrainte *f*; **to place constraints upon** imposer des contraintes à; **under c.** sous la contrainte

constrict [kən'strɪkt] *vt (blood vessel)* resserrer; *(movement)* gêner; **to feel constricted** se sentir à l'étroit

constriction [kən'strɪkʃən] *n (of blood vessel)* constriction *f*; *(of person)* gêne *f*

construct 1 *n* ['kɒnstrʌkt] *(idea)* concept *m* **2** *vt* [kən'strʌkt] construire

construction [kən'strʌkʃən] *n* **(a)** *(building) & Gram* construction *f*; **under c.** en construction; **the c. industry** l'industrie *f* du bâtiment, le bâtiment; *c. site* chantier *m* (de construction); *c. worker* ouvrier *m* du bâtiment **(b)** *(interpretation)* **to put a favourable/an unfavourable c. on sth** bien/mal interpréter qch

constructive [kən'strʌktɪv] *adj* constructif(ive)

construe [kən'struː] *vt* interpréter

consul ['kɒnsəl] *n* consul *m*

consular ['kɒnsjʊlə(r)] *adj* consulaire

consulate ['kɒnsjʊlət] *n* consulat *m*

consult [kən'sʌlt] **1** *vt* consulter **(on sur** *ou* **à propos de) 2** *vi* consulter **(with sb/about sth** qn/à propos de qch)

consultancy [kən'sʌltənsɪ] *(pl* **consultancies)** *n* **(a)** *(of doctor)* poste *m* de spécialiste *(haut placé dans la hiérarchie hospitalière)* **(b)** *Com* conseil *m*; **to do c. work** être consultant(e)

consultant [kən'sʌltənt] *n* **(a)** *(doctor)* spécialiste *mf (pratiquant à l'hôpital)* **(b)** *(adviser)* consultant(e) *m,f*

consultation [kɒnsəl'teɪʃən] *n (reference)* consultation *f*; *(discussion)* délibération *f*; **to hold a c. with sb** s'entretenir avec qn; **in c. with sb** en consultation avec qn

consume [kən'sjuːm] *vt (food, fuel, power)* consommer; **to be consumed with jealousy/desire** brûler de jalousie/désir

consumer [kən'sjuːmə(r)] *n (of product)* consommateur(trice) *m,f*; **c. durables** biens *mpl* de consommation durables; **c. goods** biens de consommation; *Econ* **c. price index** indice *m* des prix de détails; **c. protection** la défense du consommateur; **c. society** société *f* de consommation

consumerism [kən'sjuːmərɪzəm] *n* consumérisme *m*

consummate 1 *adj* [kən'sʌmɪt] *(linguist, cook)* de premier ordre; *(snob, hypocrite)* parfait(e) **2** *vt* ['kɒnsəmeɪt] *(marriage, relationship)* consommer

consumption [kən'sʌmpʃən] *n* **(a)** *(of goods, resources)* consommation *f*; **unfit for human c.** impropre à la consommation **(b)** *Old-fashioned (tuberculosis)* consomption *f*

contact ['kɒntækt] **1** *n* **(a)** *(act of touching)* contact *m*; **to be in/come into c. with** être en/entrer en contact avec; **to make c. with sb** prendre contact avec qn; **to lose c. with sb** perdre contact avec qn; **to get in c. with sb** contacter qn; *c.* **lenses**, *Fam* **contacts** lentilles *fpl* (de contact) **(b)** *(acquaintance)* relation *f*; **he has lots of contacts** il connaît beaucoup de monde **2** *vt* se mettre en rapport avec, contacter

contagious [kən'teɪdʒəs] *adj (disease)* contagieux(euse); *(laughter)* communicatif(ive)

contain [kən'teɪn] *vt* **(a)** *(hold)* contenir, renfermer; *(include)* contenir **(b)** *(control)* contenir; **to c. oneself** se contenir; **he was unable to c. his laughter** il ne put s'empêcher de rire

container [kən'teɪnə(r)] *n (for storage)* récipient *m*; *(for transport)* conteneur *m*; *c.* **lorry** camion *m* adapté au transport des conteneurs; *c.* **ship** (navire *m*) porte-conteneurs *m inv*; *c.* **terminal** terminal *m* à conteneurs

contaminate [kən'tæmɪneɪt] *vt also Fig* contaminer

contamination [kəntæmɪ'neɪʃən] *n* contamination *f*

contd *(abbr* **continued)** **c. on page 14** suite (à la) page 14

contemplate ['kɒntəmpleɪt] **1** *vt (look at)* contempler; *(consider)* réfléchir à; **to c. doing sth** envisager de *ou* songer à faire qch **2** *vi (consider)* méditer

contemplation [kɒntəm'pleɪʃən] *n* contemplation *f*

contemplative [kən'templətɪv] *adj* contemplatif(ive)

contemporary [kən'tempərərɪ] *(pl* **contemporaries)** *n & adj* contempo-rain(e) *m,f*

contempt [kən'tempt] *n* mépris *m*; **to hold sb/sth in c.** avoir du mépris pour qn/qch, mépriser qn/qch; **to be beneath c.** être des plus méprisables; *Law* **c. of court** outrage *m* au tribunal

contemptible [kən'temptəbəl] *adj* méprisable

contemptuous [kən'temptjʊəs] *adj* méprisant (e); **to be c. of sth** mépriser qch

contend [kən'tend] **1** *vt (maintain)* **to c. that...** prétendre *ou* soutenir que... **2** *vi* **(a)** *(struggle)* **to c. with sth** lutter contre qch; *(difficulties)* affronter qch; **they still had the chairman to c. with** il leur restait à régler le problème du P.D.G. **(b)** *(compete)* **to c. for sth** se battre pour qch; *(for job, contract)* être en concurrence pour qch

contender [kən'tendə(r)] *n (in sport)* concurrent(e) *m,f*; *(in election, for job)* candidat(e) *m,f*

content¹ ['kɒntent] n (a) *(quantity)* teneur f; *(of book, speech, essay)* fond m; *(of)* protein/fibre c. teneur en protéines/fibres (b) contents *(of pockets, drawer, house)* contenu m; contents page *(of book)* table f des matières

content² [kən'tent] 1 adj *(happy)* content(e), satisfait(e) (with de); to be c. with one's lot se contenter de son sort

2 vt contenter; to c. oneself with sth/with doing sth se contenter de qch/de faire qch

contented [kən'tentɪd] adj *(person)* content(e), satisfait(e) (with de); *(smile, sigh)* de satisfaction

contention [kən'tenʃən] n (a) *(dispute)* dispute f (b) *(competition)* to be in c. (for sth) être en compétition (pour qch) (c) *(opinion)* affirmation f; it is my c. that... j'affirme que...

contentious [kən'tenʃəs] adj *(issue, views)* controversé(e); *(person)* querelleur(euse)

contentment [kən'tentmənt] n contentement m

contest 1 n ['kɒntest] *(competition)* concours m; *(for job, presidency)* lutte f; *(in boxing)* combat m

2 vt [kən'test] *(right, ability, will)* contester; to c. a seat se porter candidat(e); a fiercely contested election une élection très disputée

contestant [kən'testənt] n *(in competition, game)* concurrent(e) m,f; *(in election)* candidat(e) m,f

context ['kɒntekst] n contexte m; in/out of c. en/hors contexte; to put sth into c. replacer qch dans son contexte

continent¹ ['kɒntɪnənt] n *(land mass)* continent m; the C. l'Europe f (continentale)

continent² adj Med continent(e)

continental [kɒntɪ'nentəl] adj (a) *(in geography)* continental(e); c. drift dérive f des continents; c. shelf plate-forme f continentale (b) *(European)* européen(enne); c. breakfast = petit déjeuner se composant de tartines et d'une boisson chaude; c. quilt couette f

contingency [kən'tɪndʒənsɪ] n *(pl* contingencies) éventualité f; to allow for every c. parer à toute éventualité; c. fund caisse f ou fond m de prévoyance; c. plan plan m d'urgence

continual [kən'tɪnjʊəl] adj continuel(elle), incessant(e)

continuation [kəntɪnjʊ'eɪʃən] n *(of story)* suite f; *(of action, work)* prolongation f; *(of road)* prolongement m

continue [kən'tɪnju:] 1 vt *(activity, journey)* continuer, poursuivre; *(after interruption)* reprendre, continuer; *(tradition)* perpétuer; to c. to do or doing sth continuer à ou de faire qch; to be continued à suivre; continued on page 30 suite (à la) page 30

2 vi *(of situation)* se prolonger; to c. on one's way continuer ou poursuivre son chemin; she will c. as director until December elle continuera d'assumer ses fonctions de directrice jusqu'en décembre; the situation cannot c. cette situation ne peut pas durer

continuity [kɒntɪ'nju:ɪtɪ] n continuité f; c. announcer *(on TV, radio)* speaker(ine) m,f; c. girl scripte f

continuous [kən'tɪnjʊəs] adj continu(e); Sch & Univ c. assessment contrôle m continu; Comptr c. paper or stationery papier m (en) continu; Cin c. performance cinéma m permanent

contort [kən'tɔ:t] 1 vt tordre

2 vi se tordre (with de)

contortion [kən'tɔ:ʃən] n *(of features)* crispation f; *(of body)* contorsion f

contour ['kɒntʊə(r)] n contour m; c. (line) courbe f de niveau; c. map carte f en courbes de niveau

contraband ['kɒntrəbænd] n contrebande f; c. goods marchandises fpl de contrebande

contraception [kɒntrə'sepʃən] n contraception f

contraceptive [kɒntrə'septɪv] 1 n contraceptif m
2 adj c. pill pilule f contraceptive

contract [kən'trækt] 1 n ['kɒntrækt] contrat m; to be under c. être sous contrat; to enter into a c. passer un contrat; to take out a c. on sb *(hire assassin)* engager un tueur à gages pour assassiner qn; c. killer tueur m à gages

2 vt *(illness, debt)* contracter; to c. to do sth s'engager (par contrat) à faire qch

3 vi *(shrink)* se contracter

▶**contract out** 1 vt sep *(work)* sous-traiter

2 vi Com *(of insurance policy, pension plan)* arrêter de souscrire (of à)

contraction [kən'trækʃən] n contraction f

contractor [kən'træktə(r)] n *(businessman)* entrepreneur m *(en bâtiment)*; *(worker)* ouvrier m *(en bâtiment)*

contractual [kən'træktjʊəl] adj contractuel(elle)

contradict [kɒntrə'dɪkt] vt *(disagree with)* contredire; *(deny)* démentir; to c. oneself se contredire

contradiction [kɒntrə'dɪkʃən] n contradiction f; it's a c. in terms c'est parfaitement contradictoire

contradictory [kɒntrə'dɪktərɪ] adj contradictoire

contraflow ['kɒntrəfləʊ] n c. (system) *(on motorway)* = circulation sur une voie unique, lors de travaux routiers

contralto [kən'træltəʊ] *(pl* contraltos) n contralto mf

contraption [kən'træpʃən] n Fam machin m, truc m

contrary ['kɒntrərɪ] 1 n contraire m; on the c. au contraire; unless you hear to the c. sauf avis contraire; there was no evidence to the c. il n'y avait pas de preuve du contraire

2 adj (a) *(opposite)* contraire (to à); *(ideas, interests)* opposé(e) (to à); c. to my expectations contre mon attente; c. to popular belief contrairement à ce que croient la plupart des gens (b) [kən'treərɪ] *(awkward)* contrariant(e)

contrast [kən'trɑ:st] 1 n ['kɒntrɑ:st] contraste m *(between* entre); in c. with or to par opposition à; by c. par contraste

2 vt mettre en contraste (with avec)

3 vi faire contraste (with avec)

contravene [kɒntrə'vi:n] vt enfreindre

contravention [kɒntrə'venʃən] n *(of law)* infraction f (of à); in c. of a treaty en violation d'un traité

contribute [kən'trɪbju:t] 1 vt *(money)* verser; *(time, clothes)* donner; to c. an article to a newspaper écrire un article pour un journal; he didn't c. anything to the discussion il n'a pas pris part à la discussion

2 vi contribuer (to à); *(to charity)* donner (to à); *(to newspaper)* collaborer (to à); to c. to a discussion prendre part à une discussion

contribution [kɒntrɪ'bju:ʃən] n contribution f (to à); the chocolate mousse was David's c. c'est David qu'il faut remercier pour la mousse au chocolat

contributor [kən'trɪbjʊtə(r)] n *(to charity)* donateur(trice) m,f; *(to newspaper)* collaborateur(trice) m,f (to de)

contributory [kən'trɪbjʊtərɪ] adj *(cause, factor)* concourant(e); to be a c. factor in sth concourir à qch; Law c. negligence manque m de précautions

contrite [ˈkɒntraɪt] *adj* contrit(e)

contrition [kənˈtrɪʃən] *n* contrition *f*

contrivance [kənˈtraɪvəns] *n* (*device*) appareil *m*; (*scheme, plan*) système *m*

contrive [kənˈtraɪv] *vt* inventer; **to c. to do sth** trouver le moyen de faire qch

contrived [kənˈtraɪvd] *adj* forcé(e), qui manque de naturel

control [kənˈtrəʊl] **1** *n* (**a**) (*power, restriction*) contrôle *m*; **to impose controls on prices** imposer le contrôle des prix; **to take c.** (*of the situation*) prendre les choses en main; **to have c. over** (*power*) contrôler; (*authority*) avoir de l'autorité sur; **to be in c. of sth** contrôler qch; **to be back in c.** avoir repris le contrôle; **to get out of c.** devenir incontrôlable; **to let sth get out of c.** perdre le contrôle de qch; **to bring a fire under c.** maîtriser un incendie; **to keep one's feelings under c.** maîtriser ses émotions; **reality is under c.** je domine/nous dominons/*etc* la situation; **to lose c.** (*of oneself*) ne plus être maître de soi; **to regain c.** (*of oneself*) se ressaisir; **c. group** groupe *m* témoin; **c. tower** (*at airport*) tour *f* de contrôle (**b**) (*device*) **the controls** les commandes *fpl*; **to be at the controls** être aux commandes; **c. panel** tableau *m* de bord

2 *vt* (*pt & pp* **controlled**) (*production, expenditure, prices*) contrôler; (*business*) diriger; (*child, pupils*) avoir de l'autorité sur; (*disease*) maintenir à un niveau raisonnable, (*vehicle*) garder le contrôle de; **to c. oneself** se maîtriser; **to c. one's anger** maîtriser sa colère

controlled [kənˈtrəʊld] *adj* (*person*) maître de soi, posé(e); (*experiment, explosion*) contrôlé(e)

controlling interest [kənˈtrəʊlɪŋˈɪntrest] *n Fin* participation *f* majoritaire

controversial [kɒntrəˈvɜːʃəl] *adj* **to be c.** (*of film, decision*) être controversé(e); (*of person*) être provocateur(trice)

controversy [ˈkɒntrəvɜːsɪ, kənˈtrɒvəsɪ] *n* (*pl* **controversies**) *n* controverse *f*

conundrum [kəˈnʌndrəm] *n* (*riddle*) devinette *f*; (*mystery*) énigme *f*

conurbation [kɒnɜːˈbeɪʃən] *n* conurbation *f*

convalesce [kɒnvəˈles] *vi* être en convalescence

convalescence [kɒnvəˈlesəns] *n* convalescence *f*

convalescent [kɒnvəˈlesənt] *adj* (*patient*) convalescent(e); **c. home** maison *f* de repos

convection [kənˈvekʃən] *n* convection *f*; **c. heater** convecteur *m*

convene [kənˈviːn] **1** *vt* (*meeting*) convoquer

2 *vi* (*of meeting, committee*) se réunir

convenience [kənˈviːnɪəns] *n* commodité *f*; **at your c.** dès que possible; *Formal* **at your earliest c.** dans les meilleurs délais; (*public*) **c.** (*toilet*) toilettes *fpl* publiques; **c. food** aliments *mpl* tout prêts

convenient [kənˈviːnɪənt] *adj* (*arrangement, method*) commode, pratique; **to be c.** (*for sb*) (*of arrangement*) être commode *ou* pratique (pour qn); (*of time*) convenir (à qn)

convent [ˈkɒnvənt] *n Rel* couvent *m*; **c. school** école *f* tenue par des sœurs

convention [kənˈvenʃən] *n* (**a**) (*conference*) convention *f*, congrès *m* (**b**) (*agreement*) convention *f* (**c**) (*established practice*) usage *m*; **the c. is that...** l'usage veut que...

conventional [kənˈvenʃənəl] *adj* conventionnel(elle); **c. warfare** guerre *f* conventionnelle; **c. weapon** arme *f* conventionnelle; **c. wisdom** sagesse *f* populaire

converge [kənˈvɜːdʒ] *vi* converger (**on** sur)

conversant [kənˈvɜːsənt] *adj* **to be c. with sth** s'y connaître en qch; (*with events, developments*) être au courant de qch

conversation [kɒnvəˈseɪʃən] *n* conversation *f*; **to have a c. with sb** avoir une conversation avec qn; **to make c.** faire la conversation; **the vase is quite a c. piece** le vase alimente bien des conversations; *Fam* **to be a c. stopper** *or* **killer** arrêter net la conversation

conversational [kɒnvəˈseɪʃənəl] *adj* (*style*) de la conversation; *Comptr* (*mode*) dialogue; **in a c. tone** sur le ton de la conversation

conversationalist [kɒnvəˈseɪʃənəlɪst] *n* **to be a good c.** avoir de la conversation; **I'm not much of a c.** je ne suis pas brillant causeur

converse¹ [kənˈvɜːs] *vi* (*talk*) converser (**about** sur), s'entretenir (**about** de)

converse² [ˈkɒnvɜːs] *n* (*opposite*) **the c.** le contraire

conversion [kənˈvɜːʃən] *n* (**a**) (*transformation*) conversion *f*; (*of building*) aménagement *m*; **c. table** (*for measurements*) table *f* de conversion (**b**) (*in rugby*) transformation *f*

convert [kənˈvɜːt] **1** *n* [ˈkɒnvɜːt] *Rel & Fig* converti(e) *m,f* (**to** à)

2 *vt* (**a**) *Rel & Fig* convertir (**to** à); (*building*) aménager (**into** en) (**b**) (*in rugby*) **to c. a try** transformer un essai

3 *vi Rel & Fig* se convertir (**to** à)

convertible [kənˈvɜːtəbl] **1** *n* (*car*) décapotable *f*

2 *adj* (*sofa*) convertible; (*car*) décapotable; **c. currency** monnaie *f ou* devise *f* convertible

convex [kɒnˈveks] *adj* convexe

convey [kənˈveɪ] *vt* (**a**) (*communicate*) transmettre; **to c. one's meaning** communiquer sa pensée (**b**) (*transport*) transporter

conveyancing [kənˈveɪənsɪŋ] *n Law* procédure *f* translative de propriété

conveyor belt [kənˈveɪəbelt] *n* convoyeur *m*, tapis *m* roulant

convict 1 *n* [ˈkɒnvɪkt] détenu(e) *m,f*

2 *vt* [kənˈvɪkt] **to c. sb** (**of**) déclarer qn coupable (**de**)

conviction [kənˈvɪkʃən] *n* (**a**) *Law* condamnation *f*; **to have no previous convictions** n'avoir jamais été condamné(e) (**b**) (*belief*) conviction *f*; **to lack c.** manquer de conviction

convince [kənˈvɪns] *vt* convaincre (**of/that** de/que); **I was convinced I was right** j'étais convaincu d'avoir raison

convincing [kənˈvɪnsɪŋ] *adj* convaincant(e); (*defeat*) décisif(ive)

convivial [kənˈvɪvɪəl] *adj* (*person*) chaleureux(euse); (*atmosphere*) joyeux(euse)

convoluted [ˈkɒnvəluːtɪd] *adj* (*argument, explanation*) compliqué(e)

convoy [ˈkɒnvɔɪ] *n* convoi *m*

convulse [kənˈvʌls] *vt* secouer; **to be convulsed with laughter/pain** se tordre de rire/de douleur

convulsions [kənˈvʌlʃənz] *npl Med* convulsions *fpl*; *Fig* **to be in c.** (*of laughter*) se tordre

coo [kuː] (*pt & pp* **cooed**) *vi* (*of dove*) roucouler; *Fam* **to c. over sb/sth** s'extasier devant qn/qch

cook [kʊk] **1** n cuisinier(ère) m,f; Prov **too many cooks spoil the broth** on n'arrive jamais à rien quand tout le monde met son grain de sel
2 vt (meal) préparer; (food) (faire) cuire; Fig **to c. the books** falsifier les comptes
3 vi (of food) cuire; (of person) faire la cuisine; Fam **what's cooking?** qu'est-ce qui se passe?
▶**cook up** vt sep (excuse, story) inventer

cookbook ['kʊkbʊk] n Am livre m de cuisine

cooker ['kʊkə(r)] n (stove) cuisinière f

cookery ['kʊkərɪ] n cuisine f; **c. book** livre m de cuisine

cookie ['kʊkɪ] n (a) (Am (biscuit) biscuit m; Fam **that's the way the c. crumbles!** c'est la vie!, (que veux-tu!) (b) (person) **a tough c.** un(e) dur(e) à cuire; **a smart c.** un(e) malin(igne)

cooking ['kʊkɪŋ] n (process) cuisson f; (activity) cuisine f; **to do the c.** faire la cuisine; **c. apple** pomme f à cuire; **c. chocolate** chocolat m à cuire; **c. foil** papier m alu; **c. time** temps m de cuisson; **c. utensils** ustensiles mpl de cuisine

cool [kuːl] **1** n (a) (coldness) fraîcheur f (b) (calm) **to keep/lose one's c.** garder/perdre son sang-froid
2 adj (a) (wind, weather, drink) frais (fraîche); (coffee, bathwater) tiède; **it's c. outside** il fait frais dehors; Fam **I lost a c. thousand** j'ai bien perdu mille livres/dollars/etc (b) (calm) calme; (unfriendly) froid(e); **c. as a cucumber** parfaitement calme; **keep c.!** ne t'angoisse pas!; **to keep a c. head** garder la tête froide; **to be a c. customer** être culotté(e) (c) Fam (good) cool inv; (trendy) branché(e)
3 adv Fam **to play it c.** rester calme
4 vt rafraîchir, refroidir; Fam **c. it!** on se calme!; Fam **to c. one's heels** poireauter
5 vi (of liquid) refroidir; (of anger) passer; (of passion, enthusiasm) se refroidir
▶**cool down 1** vt sep (a) (of cold drink) rafraîchir (b) (make calm) calmer
2 vi (a) (of weather) se rafraîchir; (of liquid) refroidir (b) (become calm) se calmer
▶**cool off** vi (a) (of person) se rafraîchir (b) (of passion, enthusiasm) se refroidir; (of angry person) se calmer

coolant ['kuːlənt] n liquide m de refroidissement

cool-headed [kuːl'hedɪd] adj calme; **to remain c.** garder la tête froide

cooling ['kuːlɪŋ] adj (drink) rafraîchissant(e); (agent) réfrigérant(e); Ind & Com **c. off period** période f de réflexion; **c. tower** tour f de réfrigération

coop [kuːp] n (for chickens) poulailler m
▶**coop up** vt sep **to keep sb cooped up** tenir qn enfermé(e); **to feel cooped up** se sentir à l'étroit

co-op ['kəʊɒp] n coopérative f

cooperate [kəʊ'ɒpəreɪt] vi coopérer (with avec)

cooperation [kəʊɒpə'reɪʃən] n coopération f

cooperative [kəʊ'ɒpərətɪv] **1** n coopérative f
2 adj coopératif(ive)

coopt [kəʊ'ɒpt] vt coopter (onto à)

coordinate 1 [kəʊ'ɔːdɪnət] (a) Math coordonnée f (b) **coordinates** (clothes) coordonnés mpl
2 vt [kəʊ'ɔːdɪneɪt] coordonner

coordination [kəʊɔːdɪ'neɪʃən] n coordination f

coordinator [kəʊ'ɔːdɪneɪtə(r)] n coordinateur(trice) m,f

co-owner ['kəʊ'əʊnə(r)] n copropriétaire mf

cop [kɒp] **1** n Fam (a) (policeman) flic m; **to play cops and robbers** jouer aux gendarmes et aux voleurs (b) **it's not much c.** ça ne vaut pas grand-chose
2 vt (pt & pp copped) **to c. it** (be punished) se faire pincer; (die) clamser
▶**cop out** vi Fam (avoid responsibility) se défiler; (choose easy solution) choisir la solution de facilité; **to c. out of doing sth** ne pas avoir le cran de faire qch

cope [kəʊp] vi se débrouiller, s'en tirer; **to c. with** (demand) faire face à; **I just can't c.** je n'y arrive pas; **he can't c. with his job** il ne s'en sort pas dans son travail

Copenhagen [kəʊpən'heɪgən] n Copenhague

copier ['kɒpɪə(r)] n (photocopier) (photo)copieuse f

copilot ['kəʊpaɪlət] n copilote m

copious ['kəʊpɪəs] adj copieux(euse); (tears, notes, amounts) abondant(e)

cop-out ['kɒpaʊt] n Fam solution f de facilité

copper ['kɒpə(r)] **1** n (a) (metal) cuivre m; Fam **coppers** (coins) petite monnaie f (b) Fam (policeman) flic m
2 adj **c.(-coloured)** (couleur) cuivre inv, cuivré(e)

copperplate ['kɒpəpleɪt] n **c. (writing)** écriture f moulée

coppice ['kɒpɪs] n taillis m

coproduction [kəʊprə'dʌkʃən] n Cin coproduction f

copse [kɒps] n taillis m

copulate ['kɒpjʊleɪt] vi copuler

copulation [kɒpjʊ'leɪʃən] n copulation f

copy ['kɒpɪ] **1** (pl copies) n (a) (reproduction) copie f (b) (of letter, document) copie f, double m; **c. typist** dactylo mf (c) (of book) exemplaire m; (of newspaper) numéro m (d) Journ (written material) copie f; **the story made good c.** ça a fait un bon sujet d'article; **c. editor** (in journalism) secrétaire mf de rédaction; (in publishing) réviseur m
2 vt (pt & pp copied) (painting, document, text) copier
3 vi (in exam) copier

copybook ['kɒpɪbʊk] n cahier m d'écriture; **c. example** exemple m classique

copycat ['kɒpɪkæt] Fam **1** n copieur(euse) m,f
2 **c. crime/murder** délit m/meurtre m inspiré par un autre

copyright ['kɒpɪraɪt] **1** n droit m d'auteur, copyright m; **to be out of c.** être tombé(e) dans le domaine public
2 adj protégé(e) par le droit d'auteur

copywriter ['kɒpɪraɪtə(r)] n rédacteur(trice) m,f publicitaire

coquette [kɒ'ket] n Lit coquette f

coral ['kɒrəl] n corail m; **c. island** île f corallienne; **c. reef** récif m corallien; **the C. Sea** la mer de Corail

cord [kɔːd] n (a) (string) grosse ficelle f; (for curtains, pyjamas) cordon m (b) (corduroy) velours m côtelé; **a c. jacket** une veste en velours côtelé; **cords** pantalon m en velours côtelé

cordial ['kɔːdɪəl] **1** n (drink) sirop m
2 adj (friendly) cordial(e)

cordless ['kɔːdlɪs] adj sans fil

cordon ['kɔːdən] n cordon m
▶**cordon off** vt sep (road) barrer; (area) boucler

corduroy ['kɔːdərɔɪ] n velours m côtelé; **c. trousers** pantalon m en velours côtelé

core [kɔ:(r)] **1** *n* (*of apple*) trognon *m*; (*of earth, magnet*) noyau *m*; (*of nuclear reactor*) centre *m*; (*of argument, problem*) cœur *m*; **hard c.** noyau dur; **he's rotten to the c.** il est pourri jusqu'à la moelle; *Sch* **c. curriculum** tronc *m* commun

2 *vt* (*apple*) évider

Corfu [kɔ:'fu:] *n* Corfou

coriander [kɒrɪ'ændə(r)] *n* coriandre *f*

cork [kɔ:k] **1** *n* (*material*) liège *m*; (*stopper*) bouchon *m* (en liège)

2 *vt* (*bottle*) boucher

corked [kɔ:kt] *adj* (*wine*) bouchonné(e)

corkscrew ['kɔ:kskru:] *n* tire-bouchon *m*

cormorant ['kɔ:mərənt] *n* cormoran *m*

corn¹ [kɔ:n] *n* (**a**) *Br* (*wheat*) blé *m* (**b**) *Am* (*maize*) maïs *m*; **c. on the cob** maïs en épi; **c. bread** pain *m* à la farine de maïs; **c. meal** farine *f* de maïs; **c. oil** huile *f* de maïs

corn² *n* (*on foot*) cor *m*; **c. plaster** pansement *m* pour cors

cornea ['kɔ:nɪə] *n* Anat cornée *f*

corned beef ['kɔ:nd'bi:f] *n* corned-beef *m*

corner ['kɔ:nə(r)] **1** *n* (**a**) (*of room, street, page, screen*) coin *m*; **out of the c. of one's eye** du coin de l'œil; **it's just round the c.** c'est juste au coin; **Christmas is just round the c.** on est tout près de Noël; **to turn the c.** tourner au coin de la rue; *Fig* (*of economy, company*) passer la période critique; **c. shop** magasin *m* de quartier (**b**) (*bend in road*) tournant *m*; *Fig* **to cut corners** (*with time*) faire les choses à la va-vite; (*with materials, money*) faire les choses à l'économie (**c**) (*in football*) **c. (kick)** corner *m*; **to take a c.** tirer un corner

2 *vt* (**a**) (*person, animal*) acculer (**b**) (*market*) accaparer

3 *vi* (*of car, driver*) prendre un virage

cornerstone ['kɔ:nəstəʊn] *n* also Fig pierre *f* angulaire

cornet ['kɔ:nɪt] *n* (**a**) (*musical instrument*) cornet *m* à pistons (**b**) (*ice-cream*) **c.** cornet *m*

cornfield ['kɔ:nfi:ld] *n* (*of wheat*) champ *m* de blé; (*of maize*) champ de maïs

cornflakes ['kɔ:nfleɪks] *npl* corn flakes *mpl*

cornflour ['kɔ:nflaʊə(r)] *n* Br farine *f* de maïs

cornflower ['kɔ:nflaʊə(r)] *n* (*plant*) bleuet *m*; **c. blue** bleu barbeau *inv*

cornice ['kɔ:nɪs] *n* corniche *f*

Cornish ['kɔ:nɪʃ] **1** *npl* **the C.** (*people*) les Cornouaillais *mpl*

2 *n* (*language*) cornique *m*

3 *adj* cornouaillais(e); *Br* **C. pasty** feuilleté *m* à la viande

Cornwall ['kɔ:nwəl] *n* Cornouailles *f*

corny ['kɔ:nɪ] *adj Fam* (*joke*) nul (nulle); (*film, novel*) tarte

corollary [kə'rɒlərɪ] (*pl* **corollaries**) *n* corollaire *m*

coronary ['kɒrənərɪ] Med **1** (*pl* **coronaries**) *n* infarctus *m* (du myocarde)

2 *adj* coronarien(enne); **c. thrombosis** infarctus *m* du myocarde

coronation [kɒrə'neɪʃən] *n* couronnement *m*; **c. chicken** = morceaux de poulet préparés avec de la mayonnaise au curry

coroner ['kɒrənə(r)] *n* Law coroner *m*

corporal¹ ['kɔ:pərəl] *adj* corporel(elle); **c. punishment** châtiment *m* corporel

corporal² *n* Mil (*in infantry*) caporal *m*; (*in cavalry, artillery*) brigadier *m*

corporate ['kɔ:pərət] *adj* Com d'entreprise; **c. culture** culture *f* d'entreprise; **c. image** image *f* de marque de l'entreprise

corporation [kɔ:pə'reɪʃən] *n* (**a**) Com société *f*; **c. tax** impôt *m* sur les sociétés (**b**) (*council*) conseil *m* municipal

corps [kɔ:(r)] (*pl* **corps** [kɔ:z]) *n* Mil corps *m*

corpse [kɔ:ps] *n* cadavre *m*; **a lifeless c.** un corps inerte

corpulent ['kɔ:pjʊlənt] *adj* corpulent(e)

corpuscle ['kɔ:pʌsəl] *n* Anat corpuscule *m*; **red/white (blood) corpuscles** globules *mpl* rouges/blancs

corral [kɒ'rɑ:l] *n* Am corral *m*

correct [kə'rekt] *adj* **1** (**a**) (*accurate*) exact(e); **to prove c.** se vérifier, s'avérer juste; **if my memory is c.** si j'ai bonne mémoire; **he is c.** (*right*) il a raison; **that's c.** c'est exact (**b**) (*person, behaviour*) correct(e), convenable; **it wasn't the c. thing to say/do** ce n'était pas la chose à dire/faire

2 *vt* (*homework, proofs, error*) corriger; (*misunderstanding*) dissiper; **c. me if I'm wrong, but...** reprenez-moi si je me trompe, mais...; **I stand corrected** j'avais tort

correction [kə'rekʃən] *n* correction *f*

correlate ['kɒrɪleɪt] **1** *vt* mettre en rapport *ou* en corrélation (**with** avec); **they are closely correlated** ils sont étroitement liés

2 *vi* être en rapport *ou* en corrélation (**with** avec)

correlation [kɒrɪ'leɪʃən] *n* corrélation *f*

correspond [kɒrɪ'spɒnd] *vi* (**a**) (*be in accordance*) correspondre (**with** *or* **to** à) (**b**) (*be equivalent*) correspondre (**to** à), être l'équivalent (**to** de) (**c**) (*write letters*) correspondre (**with** avec)

correspondence [kɒrɪ'spɒndəns] *n* (**a**) (*relationship*) rapport *m* (**between** entre) (**b**) (*letter-writing*) correspondance *f*; **I don't get much c.** je ne reçois pas beaucoup de courrier; **c. course** cours *m* par correspondance

correspondent [kɒrɪ'spɒndənt] *n* correspondant(e) *m,f*

corresponding [kɒrɪ'spɒndɪŋ] *adj* correspondant(e)

corridor ['kɒrɪdɔ:(r)] *n* couloir *m*, corridor *m*; *Fig* **the corridors of power** les hautes sphères *fpl* du pouvoir

corroborate [kə'rɒbəreɪt] *vt* corroborer, confirmer

corroboration [kərɒbə'reɪʃən] *n* corroboration *f*, confirmation *f*

corrode [kə'rəʊd] **1** *vt* (*metal*) corroder, attaquer; *Fig* (*society*) miner; (*optimism, friendship*) entamer

2 *vi* (*of metal*) se corroder

corrosion [kə'rəʊʒən] *n* corrosion *f*

corrosive [kə'rəʊsɪv] **1** *n* corrosif *m*

2 *adj* corrosif(ive)

corrugated ['kɒrəgeɪtɪd] *adj* (*cardboard*) ondulé(e); **c. iron** tôle *f* ondulée

corrupt [kə'rʌpt] **1** *adj* (*dishonest*) corrompu(e)

2 *vt* corrompre; Comptr altérer; **to c. sb's morals** dépraver qn

corruption [kə'rʌpʃən] *n* corruption *f*

corset ['kɔ:sɪt] *n* corset *m*

Corsica ['kɔ:sɪkə] *n* la Corse

Corsican ['kɔ:sɪkən] **1** *n* Corse *mf*

2 *adj* corse

cortege [kɔ:'teʒ] *n* cortège *m*

cortex ['kɔ:teks] (*pl* **cortices** ['kɔ:tɪsi:z]) *n* cortex *m*

cortisone ['kɔ:tɪzəʊn] *n* cortisone *f*

cos¹ [kɒz] *conj* Br Fam parce que

cos² [kɒs] *n* c. (lettuce) romaine *f*

cosh [kɒʃ] *Br* **1** *n* matraque *f*
 2 *vt* matraquer

cosmetic [kɒz'metɪk] **1** *n* cosmétique *m*, produit *m* de beauté; **to wear a lot of cosmetics** se maquiller beaucoup
 2 *adj Fig (superficial)* superficiel(elle); **c. surgery** chirurgie *f* esthétique

cosmic ['kɒzmɪk] *adj* cosmique; *Fig* prodigieux(euse)

cosmonaut ['kɒzmənɔːt] *n* cosmonaute *mf*

cosmopolitan [kɒzmə'pɒlɪtən] *adj* cosmopolite

cosmos ['kɒzmɒs] *n* cosmos *m*

cosset ['kɒsɪt] *vt* couver, choyer

cost [kɒst] **1** *n* (a) *(price)* coût *m*; *Law* **costs** dépens *mpl*; *also Fig* **at little/great c.** à peu de/à grands frais; **at great c. to his health** au prix de sa santé; *Econ* **c. of living** coût de la vie; *Com* **c. of production** coût de production; *Fin* **c. accounting** comptabilité *f* analytique; *Econ* **c. benefit analysis** analyse *f* coûts-bénéfices; *Com* **c. price** prix *m* coûtant (b) *(idioms)* **to count the c. of sth** tirer la leçon de qch; **at all costs** à tout prix; **as I found out to my c.** comme je l'ai appris à mes dépens
 2 *vt* (a) *(pt & pp cost) also Fig* coûter; **how much does it c.?** combien ça coûte?; **it costs £25** ça coûte *ou* c'est 25 livres; **whatever it costs** quel qu'en soit le prix; *Fam* **to c. a fortune** *or* **the earth** coûter les yeux de la tête; **the attempt cost him his life** cette tentative lui a coûté la vie (b) *(pt & pp costed) Com (budget)* évaluer le coût de

co-star ['kəʊstɑː(r)] **1** *n (in film)* partenaire *mf* à l'écran
 2 *vt (pt & pp* **co-starred)** **the film co-stars Harvey Keitel** Harvey Keitel joue aussi dans ce film; **co-starring Ewan McGregor** avec Ewan McGregor
 3 *vi* jouer dans un des rôles principaux

Costa Rica ['kɒstə'riːkə] *n* le Costa Rica

Costa Rican ['kɒstə'riːkən] **1** *n* Costaricien(enne) *m,f*
 2 *adj* costaricien(enne)

cost-effective [kɒstɪ'fektɪv] *adj* rentable

costing ['kɒstɪŋ] *n Com (of job)* évaluation *f* du coût; *(of article)* évaluation *f* du prix de revient

costly ['kɒstlɪ] *adj* cher (chère), coûteux(euse); **it was a c. mistake** c'est une erreur qui a coûté cher

costume ['kɒstjuːm] *n* costume *m*; **(swimming) c.** maillot *m* de bain; **c. drama** film *m*/pièce *f* en costumes d'époque; **c. jewellery** bijoux *mpl* fantaisie

cosy ['kəʊzɪ] *adj (room, armchair, pub)* confortable; **to feel c.** *(in room)* être confortablement installé(e); *Fig & Pej* **they have a c. relationship** ils sont un peu trop copain-copain

cot [kɒt] *n Br (for child)* lit *m* d'enfant, petit lit; *Am (folding bed)* lit pliant; **c. death** mort *f* subite du nourrisson

cottage ['kɒtɪdʒ] *n* ≃ petite maison, généralement à la campagne; **c. cheese** fromage *m* blanc (égoutté); **c. hospital** = hôpital de médecine générale en zone rurale; **c. industry** industrie *f* artisanale; *(at home)* industrie familiale; **c. pie** hachis *m* Parmentier

cotton ['kɒtən] *n* coton *m*; **a c. shirt** une chemise en coton; **c. bud** Coton-Tige® *m*; *Am* **c. candy** barbe *f* à papa; **c. wool** ouate *f*, coton hydrophile

▸**cotton on** *vi Fam* piger; **c. on to sth** piger qch

couch [kaʊtʃ] **1** *n* divan *m*, canapé *m*; *(at doctor's)* lit *m*; *Fam* **to be a c. potato** passer sa vie devant la télé
 2 *vt (express)* formuler

cougar ['kuːgə(r)] *n* couguar *m*, puma *m*

cough [kɒf] **1** *n* toux *f*; **to have a c.** tousser; **c. pastille** *f* pour la toux; **c. mixture** sirop *m* pour la toux
 2 *vi* tousser

▸**cough up** **1** *vt sep (phlegm, blood)* cracher; *Fam (money)* allonger
 2 *vi Fam (pay)* allonger

could [kʊd]

> La forme négative est **couldn't**. Dans les contextes où il est nécessaire d'utiliser une langue plus soignée, on écrit **could not**.

modal aux v (a) *(was able to)* **we couldn't do it** nous n'avons pas pu le faire; **he did what he c.** il a fait ce qu'il pouvait; **I c. hear them talking** je les entendais parler; **I c. have tried harder** j'aurais pu faire plus d'efforts; **he couldn't have been kinder** il a été on ne peut plus aimable; **how could you!** comment as-tu pu faire ça!; **I c. have hit him!** *(I was so angry)* je l'aurais battu!
 (b) *(knew how to)* **I c. swim well at that age** à cet âge-là je savais déjà bien nager; **c. you speak French then?** tu parlais français à cette époque-là?
 (c) *(indicating possibility)* **it c. be weeks before he's better** il pourrait se passer des semaines avant qu'il ne rétablisse; **it c. have been worse** ça aurait pu être pire
 (d) *(with requests)* **c. you get me some water?** est-ce que tu pourrais m'apporter de l'eau?
 (e) *(in conditional, suggestions)* **it c. be** peut-être; **if I had more money I c. buy a new car** si j'avais plus d'argent je pourrais acheter une nouvelle voiture; **we c. always telephone** on pourrait toujours téléphoner

couldn't ['kʊdənt] = **could not**

couldn't-care-less ['kʊdəntkeə'les] *adj* **c. attitude** je-m'en-foutisme *m*

council ['kaʊnsəl] *n* (a) *(assembly)* conseil *m*; **C. of Europe** Conseil de l'Europe (b) *(local government)* municipalité *f*; **to be on the c.** être au conseil municipal; *Br* **c. house** ≃ habitation *f* à loyer modéré, H.L.M. *f*; **c. tax** = en Grande-Bretagne, impôt regroupant taxe d'habitation et impôts locaux

councillor ['kaʊnsələ(r)] *n* conseiller(ère) *m,f*, membre *m* du conseil

counsel ['kaʊnsəl] **1** *n* (a) *(advice)* conseil *m*, avis *m*; **to keep one's own c.** *(about plans)* garder ses projets pour soi; *(about opinions)* garder ses opinions pour soi (b) *Br (lawyer)* avocat(e) *m,f*; **c. for the defence** avocat *m* de la défense; **c. for the prosecution** procureur *m*; **King's/Queen's C.** = membre haut placé du barreau
 2 *vt (pt & pp* **counselled,** *Am* **counseled)** *(caution, patience)* conseiller; **to c. sb** *(advise)* conseiller qn; *(give psychological help to)* apporter une aide psychologique à qn; **to c. sb to do sth** conseiller à qn de faire qch

counselling ['kaʊnsəlɪŋ] *n* assistance *f* psychosociale

counsellor ['kaʊnsələ(r)] *n* (a) *(adviser, therapist)* conseiller(ère) *m,f* (b) *Am Law* avocat(e) *m,f*

count¹ [kaʊnt] *n (nobleman)* comte *m*

count² **1** *n* (a) *(calculation)* compte *m*, comptage *m*; **at the last c.** au dernier comptage; **to keep a c. of sth** tenir le compte de qch; **to lose c.** se perdre dans ses calculs; **I've lost c. of how many times I've asked you to...** je t'ai demandé je ne sais combien de fois de... (b) *(in boxing) & Fig* **to be out for the c.** être K.-O. (c) *Law* chef *m* d'accusation; *Fig* **on a number of counts** à plusieurs égards
 2 *vt* (a) *(enumerate)* compter; **there were four of us counting/not counting the dog** nous étions quatre en comptant/sans compter le chien (b) *(consider)* considérer

(as comme); **c. yourself lucky you weren't killed** estime-toi heureux de n'avoir pas été tué

3 vi **(a)** (add up) compter; **to c. (up) to ten** compter jusqu'à dix **(b)** (be important, valid) compter; **that doesn't c. ça** ne compte pas; **it counts as one of my worst experiences** ça a été une de mes pires expériences

▶**count against** vt insep jouer contre

▶**count down** vi faire le compte à rebours

▶**count in** vt sep (include) compter; **c. me in!** j'en suis!

▶**count on** vt insep compter sur; **to c. on sb to do sth** compter sur qn pour faire qch

▶**count out** vt sep **(a)** (money) compter **(b)** (exclude) **c. me out!** ne comptez pas sur moi! **(c)** (in boxing) **to be counted out** être (mis(e)) K.-O.

▶**count up** vt sep compter

countable ['kaʊntəbəl] adj comptable

countdown ['kaʊntdaʊn] n compte m à rebours

countenance ['kaʊntɪnəns] Formal **1** n **(a)** (face) visage m **(b)** (support) **to give c. to** (rumours) accréditer; (plans) approuver

2 vt (support) approuver

counter¹ ['kaʊntə(r)] n **(a)** (in shop) comptoir m; (in supermarket) rayon m; (in bank) guichet m; **available over the c.** (medicine) en vente libre; **to buy/sell sth under the c.** acheter/vendre qch au noir **(b)** (token in game) jeton m **(c)** (counting device) compteur m

counter² **1** adv **c. to** contrairement à; **to run c. to** aller à l'encontre de

2 vt contrer; **to c. that...** riposter que...

3 vi riposter

counteract [kaʊntə'rækt] vt (influence) contrecarrer; (rumours, effects) neutraliser

counterattack ['kaʊntərətæk] **1** n contre-attaque f

2 n & vi contre-attaquer

counter-clockwise ['kaʊntə'klɒkwaɪz] Am **1** adj in a **c. direction** dans le sens inverse des aiguilles d'une montre

2 adv dans le sens inverse des aiguilles d'une montre

counterfeit ['kaʊntəfɪt] **1** n faux m

2 adj faux (fausse)

3 vt contrefaire

counterfoil ['kaʊntəfɔɪl] n talon m, souche f

counterintelligence [kaʊntərɪn'telɪdʒəns] n contre-espionnage m

countermand ['kaʊntəmɑːnd] vt annuler

countermeasure ['kaʊntəmeʒə(r)] n contre-mesure f

counteroffensive ['kaʊntərə'fensɪv] n contre-offensive f

counterpane ['kaʊntəpeɪn] n couvre-lit m

counterpart ['kaʊntəpɑːt] n (person) homologue mf; (system) équivalent m

counterpoint ['kaʊntəpɔɪnt] n Mus contrepoint m

counterproductive ['kaʊntəprə'dʌktɪv] adj contre-productif(ive)

counterproposal ['kaʊntəprə'pəʊzəl] n contre-proposition f

counter-revolution ['kaʊntərevə'luːʃən] n contre-révolution f

counter-revolutionary ['kaʊntərevə'luːʃənərɪ] n & adj contre-révolutionnaire mf

countersign ['kaʊntəsaɪn] vt contresigner, viser

counterweight ['kaʊntəweɪt] n contrepoids m

countess ['kaʊntɪs] n comtesse f

countless ['kaʊntlɪs] adj innombrable; **on c. occasions** à maintes occasions; **c. times** un nombre incalculable de fois

country ['kʌntrɪ] (pl countries) n **(a)** (political entity) pays m; **to go to the c.** (call elections) appeler le pays aux urnes **(b)** (as opposed to town) campagne f; **in the c.** à la campagne; **c. and western music** country m ou f

countryside ['kʌntrɪsaɪd] n campagne f

county ['kaʊntɪ] (pl counties) n comté m; **c. council** ≃ conseil m général; **c. town** chef-lieu m de comté

coup [kuː] n (surprising achievement) (beau) coup m; Pol **c. (d'état)** coup m d'État

couple ['kʌpəl] **1** n **(a)** (of things) **a c. of** (two) deux; (a few) quelques **(b)** (people) couple m; **the happy c.** les heureux époux mpl

2 vt **(a)** (associate) associer (**with** à) **(b)** (combine) allier (**with** à)

couplet ['kʌplɪt] n distique m

coupon ['kuːpɒn] n (form) coupon m; (money-off) **c.** (for discount) bon m de réduction

courage ['kʌrɪdʒ] n courage m; **to have the c. to do sth** avoir le courage de faire qch; **to have the c. of one's convictions** avoir le courage de ses opinions

courageous [kə'reɪdʒəs] adj courageux(euse)

courageously [kə'reɪdʒəslɪ] adv courageusement, avec courage

courgette [kʊə'ʒet] n Br courgette f

courier ['kʊrɪə(r)] n (messenger) messager m, coursier m; (in tourism) guide m; (drug smuggler) passeur(euse) m,f

course [kɔːs] n **(a)** (of river, time, events) cours m; **to be on c.** Naut suivre le cap; Fig être en bonne voie; Naut **to be off c.** dévier de son cap; **in the c. of time** (gradually) à la longue; (eventually) finalement; **in the c. of the evening** au cours de la soirée; **c. of action** ligne f de conduite; **to be in the c. of doing sth** être en train de faire qch; **in the normal c. of events** en temps normal; **to let things take** or **run their c.** laisser les choses suivre leur cours normal **(b)** (naturellement, bien sûr; **of c. not** bien sûr que non **(c)** (at college, university) cours m (**in** de); **c. of lectures** série f de conférences **(d)** Med **c. of treatment** traitement m **(e)** (of meal) plat m **(f)** (for race) parcours m; (for horseracing) champ m de courses; (for golf) terrain m

2 vi (of liquid) couler

court [kɔːt] **1** n **(a)** Law cour f, tribunal m; **to go to c.** aller en justice; **to take sb to c.** faire un procès à qn; **to settle a case out of c.** arranger une affaire à l'amiable; **c. of appeal** cour d'appel; **c. of inquiry** commission f d'enquête; **c. of law** cour, tribunal; **c. appearance** comparution f en justice; Mil **c. martial** cour martiale **(b)** (for tennis, squash) court m **(c)** (royal) cour f; **to hold c.** tenir des discours à un entourage admiratif; **c. shoe** escarpin m

2 vt **(a)** Old-fashioned (woo) courtiser **(b)** (seek) (friendship, favour) rechercher; (death) braver; (disaster, danger) aller au-devant de

3 vi Old-fashioned **to be courting** (of couple) se fréquenter

courteous ['kɜːtɪəs] adj courtois(e), poli(e)

courtesy ['kɜːtɪsɪ] (pl courtesies) n courtoisie f, politesse f; **by c. of...** avec l'aimable autorisation de...; **to exchange courtesies** se faire des politesses; **c. call** visite f de politesse; **c. car** = voiture mise à la disposition d'un client par un hôtel ou un garage

courthouse ['kɔːthaʊs] n Am palais m de justice, tribunal m

courtier ['kɔːtɪə(r)] n (man) courtisan m; (woman) dame f de la cour

court-martial ['kɔːt'mɑːʃəl] (pt & pp court-martialled, Am court-martialed) vt faire passer en cour martiale; **to be court-martialled** passer en cour martiale

courtroom ['kɔːtruːm] n Law salle f d'audience

courtship ['kɔːtʃɪp] n (of people) cour f; (of animals) parade f nuptiale

courtyard ['kɔːtjɑːd] n cour f

cousin ['kʌzən] n cousin(e) m,f

cove [kəʊv] n crique f

covenant ['kʌvənənt] Law 1 n convention f, contrat m
2 vt promettre par contrat

Coventry ['kʌvəntrɪ, 'kɒvəntrɪ] n Fig **to send sb to C.** mettre qn en quarantaine

cover ['kʌvə(r)] 1 n (a) (lid) couvercle m
(b) (soft covering) housse f; **covers** (blankets) couvertures fpl
(c) (of book, magazine) couverture f; **from c. to c.** de la première à la dernière page; **c. price** prix m de vente
(d) (shelter) **to take c.** s'abriter; **to break c.** sortir à découvert; Fig **to manifester publiquement; under c. of darkness** à la faveur de la nuit
(e) Fin (in insurance) couverture f
(f) (song) **c. (version)** reprise f
2 vt (a) (person, object) couvrir (**with/in** de); **to c. one's eyes** se couvrir les yeux; **to c. a wall with paint** recouvrir un mur de peinture; **to c. oneself with glory** se couvrir de gloire; **to c. one's costs** couvrir ses frais; **to c. a song** (of musician) reprendre une chanson
(b) (hide) (one's embarrassment, confusion) dissimuler; **to c. one's tracks** brouiller les pistes
(c) (travel over) parcourir; **we covered 100 km in one day** nous avons fait ou parcouru 100 km en un jour; Fig **to c. a lot of ground** traiter de nombreux problèmes
(d) (include, deal with) (of book, lecture) traiter de; **to c. a story** (of journalist) couvrir un sujet
(e) Fin (with insurance) couvrir (**for or against** contre); Fig **to c. oneself** (take precautions) se couvrir
▶**cover for** vt insep (replace) remplacer; (provide excuses for) couvrir
▶**cover up** 1 vt sep (a) (corruption, mistakes) dissimuler; (scandal) étouffer (b) (put cover on) recouvrir
2 vi (conceal the truth) cacher la vérité (**for sb** pour protéger qn)

coverage ['kʌvərɪdʒ] n (on TV, in newspapers) couverture f médiatique

covering ['kʌvərɪŋ] n (on furniture) housse f; (of snow, dust) couche f; (of chocolate) nappage m

coverlet ['kʌvəlɪt] n dessus-de-lit m inv

covert ['kʌvət] adj (operation) secret(ète), clandestin(e); (look) furtif(ive)

cover-up ['kʌvərʌp] n **there was a c.** l'affaire a été étouffée

covet ['kʌvɪt] vt convoiter

covetous ['kʌvɪtəs] adj envieux(euse); **to be c. of sth** convoiter qch

cow¹ [kaʊ] n (a) (animal) vache f; (female elephant, whale) femelle f; **till the cows come home** (wait) jusqu'à la saint-glinglin; (argue, talk) à n'en plus finir (b) very Fam Pej (woman) peau f de vache

cow² vt intimider; **to look cowed** avoir un air de chien battu

coward ['kaʊəd] n lâche mf, poltron(onne) m,f

cowardice ['kaʊədɪs], **cowardliness** ['kaʊədlɪnəs] n lâcheté f, poltronnerie f

cowardly ['kaʊədlɪ] adj lâche

cowboy ['kaʊbɔɪ] n (a) (cattle handler, in westerns) cowboy m (b) Br Fam Pej (workman) filou m

cower ['kaʊə(r)] vi se tapir; **to c. before sb** trembler devant qn

cowhide ['kaʊhaɪd] n peau f de vache

cowl [kaʊl] n (on monk's habit, on chimney) capuchon m; **c. neck** col m boule

coworker ['kəʊwɜːkə(r)] n Am collègue mf

cowshed ['kaʊʃed] n étable f

cox [kɒks] 1 n (in rowing) barreur(euse) m,f
2 vt & vi barrer

coy [kɔɪ] adj (shy) timide; Pej (affectedly shy) (faussement) timide (**about** à propos de)

coyote [kɔɪ'əʊtɪ] n coyote m

CPU [siːpiː'juː] n Comptr (abbr **central processing unit**) unité f centrale

crab [kræb] n (a) (crustacean) crabe m (b) Fam (pubic louse) morpion m (c) **c. apple** pomme f sauvage

crabbed ['kræbɪd] adj (writing) en pattes de mouche

crabby ['kræbɪ] adj Fam maussade, grincheux(euse)

crack [kræk] 1 n (a) (in glass, porcelain) fêlure f; (in wood) fente f; (in wall) lézarde f; (in ice, rock) fissure f; **at the c. of dawn** à la pointe du jour
(b) (sound) (of branches, ice) craquement m; (of whip) claquement m; (of gunfire) détonation f; Fig **to give sb a fair c. of the whip** donner toutes ses chances à qn; Fig **to have a c. at sth** tenter sa chance à qch
(c) (blow) coup m (**on** sur)
(d) Fam (joke, insult) plaisanterie f
(e) (drug) crack m
2 adj Fam (team, regiment) d'élite; **c. shot** fin tireur m
3 vt (a) (glass, porcelain) fêler; (wood) fendre; (wall) lézarder; (ice, rock) fissurer
(b) (make sound with) (whip) faire claquer; (fingers) faire craquer
(c) Fam (hit) **to c. sb over the head** assommer qn; **she cracked her head against the wall** elle s'est cogné la tête contre le mur
(d) (solve) (problem) résoudre; (code) décrypter
(e) (break into) (safe) percer; (nut) casser
(f) Fam (joke) raconter
4 vi (a) (of glass, porcelain) se fêler; (of wood) se fendre; (of wall) se lézarder; (of ice, rock) se fissurer; (of paint) se craqueler
(b) (of voice) se casser
(c) (of person under pressure) craquer
(d) (make sound) (of branches, ice) craquer; (of whip) claquer; (of gunfire) retentir; Fam Fig **to get cracking** se grouiller
▶**crack down** vi **to c. down (on)** prendre des mesures énergiques (en matière de)
▶**crack up** Fam 1 vt sep **it's not all it's cracked up to be** ce n'est pas aussi bien qu'on le dit
2 vi (go mad) craquer

crackbrained ['krækbreɪnd] adj Fam dingue

crackdown ['krækdaʊn] n mesures fpl énergiques (**on** en matière de)

cracked [krækt] *adj Fam (mad)* dingue, cinglé(e)

cracker ['krækə(r)] *n* (a) *(biscuit)* biscuit *m* salé, cracker *m* (b) *(firework)* pétard *m*; *(at Christmas)* diablotin *m* (c) *Fam (excellent thing, person)* pure merveille *f*; **she's a c.** *(very attractive)* elle est canon

crackers ['krækəz] *adj Fam* dingue, cinglé(e)

crackle ['krækəl] 1 *n (of twigs)* craquement *m*; *(of shots, fire)* crépitement *m*; *(of frying)* grésillement *m*; *(of radio)* crachotement *m*
2 *vi (baby)* bercer *(dans ses bras)*; *(object)* tenir délicatement

crackling ['kræklɪŋ] *n* (a) *(of fire)* crépitement *m*; *(on radio)* crachotement *m* (b) *(pork skin)* couenne *f* grillée

crackpot ['krækpɒt] *Fam* 1 *n (person)* fêlé(e) *m,f*, cinglé(e) *m,f*
2 *adj (plan)* dingue

cradle ['kreɪdəl] 1 *n* (a) *(of child, civilization)* berceau *m*; **from the c. to the grave** du berceau à la tombe (b) *(for cleaning windows)* nacelle *f*
2 *vt (baby)* bercer *(dans ses bras)*; *(object)* tenir délicatement

craft[1] [krɑːft] *n* (a) *(skill)* habileté *f*; *(professional)* métier *m* (b) *(cunning)* ruse *f*

craft[2] *(pl* **craft)** *n (boat)* (petite) embarcation *f*

craftsman ['krɑːftsmən] *n* artisan *m*; **this is the work of a real c.** c'est l'œuvre d'un spécialiste

craftsmanship ['krɑːftsmənʃɪp] *n* habileté *f* (manuelle); **a wonderful piece of c.** un pur chef-d'œuvre; **the c. is magnificent** c'est vraiment du beau travail

crafty ['krɑːftɪ] *adj* malin(igne)

crag [kræg] *n* rocher *m* à pic

craggy ['krægɪ] *adj (rocky)* rocheux(euse); *(features)* anguleux(euse)

cram [kræm] *(pt & pp* **crammed)** 1 *vt* fourrer, entasser **(into** dans); **to c. food into one's mouth** se gaver, s'empiffrer; **to be crammed (with)** être bourré(e) (de)
2 *vi* (a) s'entasser **(into** dans) (b) *Fam (study)* bûcher

cramp [kræmp] 1 *n* crampe *f*
2 *vt (restrict)* gêner; *Fam* **to c. sb's style** priver qn de ses moyens

cramped [kræmpt] *adj (surroundings)* exigu(ë); **to be c. for space** être à l'étroit

cranberry ['krænbərɪ] *n (pl* **cranberries)** *n* canneberge *f*; **c. sauce** sauce *f* à la canneberge

crane [kreɪn] 1 *n (lifting device, bird)* grue *f*; **c. fly** *(insect)* tipule *f*
2 *vt* **to c. one's neck** tendre le cou
3 *vi* **to c. forward** tendre le cou

cranium ['kreɪnɪəm] *(pl* **crania** ['kreɪnɪə]) *n Anat* boîte *f* crânienne

crank[1] [kræŋk] *n (gear mechanism)* manivelle *f*

crank[2] [kræŋk] *n Fam (eccentric)* excentrique *mf*; **a religious c.** un fanatique religieux

crankshaft ['kræŋkʃɑːft] *n Aut* vilebrequin *m*

cranky ['kræŋkɪ] *adj Fam (eccentric)* excentrique

crap [kræp] 1 *n* (a) *Vulg (excrement)* merde *f*; **to have or take a c.** chier (b) *very Fam (junk)* saloperies *fpl*; *(nonsense)* conneries *fpl*; *(disgusting substance)* saloperie *f*; **don't talk c.!** ne dis pas de conneries!
2 *adj very Fam (bad)* nul (nulle)

crash [kræʃ] 1 *n* (a) *(noise)* fracas *m* (b) *(accident)* accident *m*; *(in train, plane)* catastrophe *f*; **c. barrier** glissière *f* de sécurité; **c. helmet** casque *m*; **c. landing** atterrissage *m* en catastrophe (c) *(financial)* krach *m*
2 *adj* **c. course** cours *m* intensif; **c. diet** régime *m* amaigrissant intensif
3 *vt* (a) **to c. one's car** avoir un accident de voiture (b) *Fam* **to c. a party** = aller à une fête sans y être invité
4 *vi* (a) *(make noise)* s'écraser avec fracas; **to c. to the ground** s'écrouler avec fracas; **he was crashing around in the kitchen** il s'agitait bruyamment dans la cuisine (b) *(of cars)* se percuter; **to c. into** rentrer dans (c) *(of business)* faire faillite; *(of economy)* s'effondrer et être au *Comptr* tomber en panne (e) *Fam (go to sleep)* s'écrouler

▶**crash out** *vi Fam (go to sleep)* s'écrouler, **he was crashed out on the sofa** il roupillait sur le divan

crashing ['kræʃɪŋ] *adj* **a c. bore** *(person)* une personne assommante; *(task)* une besogne assommante

crash-land ['kræʃlænd] *vi* atterrir en catastrophe

crass [kræs] *adj* grossier(ère); **c. ignorance** ignorance *f* crasse; **c. stupidity** immense bêtise *f*

crate [kreɪt] *n (box)* caisse *f*; *(for fruit)* cageot *m*; *(for bottles)* casier *m*

crater ['kreɪtə(r)] *n* cratère *m*

cravat [krə'væt] *n* foulard *m*

crave [kreɪv] 1 *vt (cigarette)* avoir très envie de; *(affection)* être en manque de
2 *vi* **to be craving for sth** *(cigarette)* avoir très envie de qch; *(affection)* être en manque de qch; *(opportunity)* attendre qch avec impatience

craving ['kreɪvɪŋ] *n* envie *f*; **to have a c. for sth** *(cigarette)* avoir très envie de qch; *(affection)* être en manque de qch

crawl [krɔːl] 1 *n* (a) *(slow pace)* **to move at a c.** *(of car, driver)* rouler au pas; *(of person)* piétiner sur place (b) *(swimming stroke)* crawl *m*
2 *vi* (a) *(of person)* ramper; *(of baby)* marcher à quatre pattes; *(of car)* rouler au pas (b) *Fam (be infested)* **to be crawling with** grouiller de; **to make sb's skin c.** flanquer des boutons à qn (c) *Fam (be obsequious)* faire le lèche-bottes; **to c. to sb** lécher les bottes à qn

crawler ['krɔːlə(r)] *n Fam (obsequious person)* lèche-bottes *mf inv*

crayfish ['kreɪfɪʃ] *n* écrevisse *f*

crayon ['kreɪɒn] *n (wax)* crayon *m* gras; *(pencil)* crayon *m* de couleur

craze [kreɪz] *n* engouement *m* **(for** pour)

crazed [kreɪzd] *adj (look, person)* fou (folle)

crazy ['kreɪzɪ] *adj* fou (folle); **to go c.** devenir fou; **to drive sb c.** rendre qn fou; **to be c. about sb/sth** être fou de qn/qch; **like c.** *(run, work)* comme un fou (une folle); **c. paving** dallage *m* irrégulier en pierres plates

creak [kriːk] 1 *n (of hinge)* grincement *m*; *(of floor, shoes)* craquement *m*
2 *vi (of hinge)* grincer; *(of floor, shoes)* craquer

creaky ['kriːkɪ] *adj (hinge)* grinçant(e); *(floor)* qui craque; *Fig (plot, dialogue)* boiteux(euse)

cream [kriːm] 1 *n* (a) *(of milk)* crème *f*; **c. of tomato/chicken soup** crème de tomates/volaille; **c. cake** gâteau *m* à la crème; **c. cheese** fromage *m* frais à tartiner (b) *Fig* **the c.** *(best part)* la crème (de la crème); **c.** *(lotion)* crème *f* (d) *(colour)* crème *m*
2 *adj* **c.(-coloured)** *(de couleur)* crème *inv*
3 *vt Culin (butter)* battre en crème

▶**cream off** vt sep Fig (money, profits) écrémer; **the universities c. off the best students** les universités sélectionnent les meilleurs étudiants

creamy ['kri:mɪ] adj (taste, consistency) crémeux(euse); (skin) laiteux(euse)

crease [kri:s] 1 n (in skin, fabric) pli m
2 vt (fabric) froisser; **to c. one's brow** plisser le front
3 vi (of fabric) se froisser; (of face, brow) se plisser

▶**crease up** vi Fam (laugh) se tordre (de rire)

create [kri:'eɪt] 1 vt créer; **to c. a sensation/a good impression** faire sensation/bonne impression
2 vi Fam (get angry) faire une scène

creation [kri:'eɪʃən] n création f

creative [kri:'eɪtɪv] adj (person, activity) créatif(ive); (process, imagination) créateur(trice); Fin **c. accounting** manipulations fpl comptables; **c. writing** techniques fpl de l'écriture

creator [kri:'eɪtə(r)] n créateur(trice), m,f; Rel **the C.** le Créateur

creature ['kri:tʃə(r)] n (person) créature f, être m; (animal) bête f; **to be a c. of habit** avoir ses petites habitudes; **c. comforts** confort m matériel; **to like one's c. comforts** aimer son confort

crèche [kreʃ] n (nursery) crèche f; (in shopping centre) halte-garderie f

credence ['kri:dəns] n **to give c. to sth** ajouter foi à qch

credentials [krɪ'denʃəlz] npl (a) (proof of identity) pièces fpl justificatives d'identité; (of ambassador) lettres fpl de créance (b) (proof of ability) références fpl; Fig **to establish one's c.** faire ses preuves

credibility [kredɪ'bɪlɪtɪ] n crédibilité f

credible ['kredɪbəl] adj crédible; **it is hardly c. that...** il est difficile de croire que...

credit ['kredɪt] 1 n (a) (financial) crédit m; **to be in c.** (of person) avoir un compte créditeur; (of account) être créditeur(trice); **to give sb c.** faire crédit à qn; **to buy/sell sth on c.** acheter/vendre qch à crédit; **c. card** carte f de crédit; Econ **c. control** encadrement m du crédit; **c. limit** plafond m de crédit; **c. note** crédit m; Fin **c. rating** degré m de solvabilité; Econ **c. squeeze** restrictions fpl de crédit; **c. transfer** transfert m, virement m
(b) (belief) **to give c. to sth** ajouter foi à qch; **to gain c.** (of theory) être accepté(e)
(c) (recognition) mérite m; **you have to give him c. for his honesty** tu es bien forcé de reconnaître qu'il est honnête; **to take the c. for sth** s'attribuer le mérite de qch; **to do sb c.** faire honneur à qn; **it does you c.** c'est tout à ton honneur; **c. where c.'s due** il faut rendre à César ce qui est à César; **to her c. she refused** c'est tout à son honneur d'avoir refusé; **she is a c. to the school** elle fait honneur à l'école
(d) **credits** (of film) générique m
2 vt (a) (money) virer (**to an account** sur un compte)
(b) (attribute) **to c. sb with sth** attribuer qch à qn
(c) (believe) croire; **would you c. it?** tu te rends compte?

creditable ['kredɪtəbəl] adj (praiseworthy) honorable; (efforts, attempt) louable

creditor ['kredɪtə(r)] n Fin créditeur(trice) m,f

credulity [krɪ'dju:lɪtɪ] n crédulité f

credulous ['kredjʊləs] adj crédule

creed [kri:d] n also Fig principes mpl; **political c.** credo m politique

creek [kri:k] n (small bay) crique f; (stream) ruisseau m; Fam Fig **to be up the c. (without a paddle)** être dans le pétrin

creep [kri:p] 1 n Fam (a) (unpleasant man) type m répugnant; (obsequious person) lèche-bottes mf inv (b) **to give sb the creeps** faire froid dans le dos à qn
2 vi (pt & pp crept [krept]) (of animal, person) ramper; (of plants) ramper; (vertically) grimper; **to c. in/out** entrer/sortir à pas de loup; **to c. into bed** se glisser sous les draps; **old age has crept up on me** je me fais vieux; Fam **it makes my flesh c.** ça me flanque des boutons

creeper ['kri:pə(r)] n (plant) plante f rampante; (climbing) plante grimpante

creeping ['kri:pɪŋ] adj (gradual) progressif(ive)

creepy ['kri:pɪ] adj Fam sinistre

creepy-crawly ['kri:pɪ'krɔ:lɪ] (pl **creepy-crawlies**) n Fam bestiole f rampante

cremate [krɪ'meɪt] vt incinérer

cremation [krɪ'meɪʃən] n incinération f

crematorium [kremə'tɔ:rɪəm] (pl **crematoria** [kremə'tɔ:rɪə]) n crématorium m

creole ['kri:əʊl] 1 n (a) (person) Créole mf (b) (language) créole m
2 adj créole

creosote ['kri:əsəʊt] n créosote f

crêpe [kreɪp, krep] n (a) (textile) crêpe m; **c. bandage** bande f Velpeau®; **c. paper** papier m crépon; **c. (-rubber) soles** semelles fpl de crêpe (b) (pancake) crêpe f

crept [krept] pt & pp of **creep**

crescendo [krɪ'ʃendəʊ] (pl **crescendos**) n Mus & Fig crescendo m inv; **to rise to a c.** (of music, complaints) aller crescendo

crescent ['kresənt] 1 n (shape) croissant m; (street) rue f en croissant
2 adj **c.(-shaped)** en forme de croissant ou de demi-lune; **c. moon** croissant m de lune

cress [kres] n cresson m

crest [krest] n (of bird, wave, helmet) crête f; (of hill) sommet m; (coat of arms) armoiries fpl; Fig **to be on the c. of a wave** être dans une période faste

crestfallen ['krestfɔ:lən] adj abattu(e), découragé(e)

Cretan ['kri:tən] 1 n Crétois(e) m,f
2 adj crétois(e)

Crete [kri:t] n la Crète

cretin ['kretɪn] n Fam crétin(e) m,f

crevice ['krevɪs] n (in rock) crevasse f, fissure f; (in wall) lézarde f

crew [kru:] 1 n (of ship, plane) équipage m; (of ambulance) équipe f; Fam (gang, group) bande f; **c. cut** (hairstyle) brosse f, cheveux mpl (coupés) en brosse
2 vt (ship) **the ship was crewed by** le bateau avait un équipage de

crib [krɪb] 1 n (a) (cradle) berceau m; (Nativity scene) crèche f (b) Fam **c. (sheet)** (in exam) antisèche f
2 vt (pt & pp cribbed) Fam (copy) pomper

crick [krɪk] 1 n **to have a c. in one's neck** avoir un torticolis
2 vt **to c. one's neck** attraper un torticolis

cricket¹ ['krɪkɪt] n (insect) grillon m

cricket² n (sport) cricket m; Fig **that's not c.!** ce n'est pas du jeu!; **c. ball** balle f de cricket; **c. bat** batte f de cricket; **c. pitch** terrain m de cricket

crikey ['kraɪkɪ] *exclam Fam* mince alors!

crime [kraɪm] *n* crime *m*; *Law* délit *m*; **c. is on the increase** la criminalité augmente; *Fig* **it's a c. to waste money like that** c'est un crime de gaspiller de l'argent de cette façon; **c. wave** vague *f* de criminalité; **c. writer** auteur *m* de romans policiers

Crimea [kraɪ'mɪə] *n* la Crimée

Crimean [kraɪ'mɪən] *adj* de Crimée; **the C. War** la guerre de Crimée

criminal ['krɪmɪnəl] **1** *n* criminel(elle) *m,f*
2 *adj* criminel(elle); *Fig* **it's c. to knock down that building** c'est un crime de démolir ce bâtiment; **to go to c. court** être jugé(e) au pénal; **c. law** droit *m* pénal; **c. lawyer** avocat *m* au pénal; **c. offence** délit *m*; *(more serious)* crime *m*; **c. record** casier *m* judiciaire

criminalize ['krɪmɪnəlaɪz] *vt* criminaliser

criminology [krɪmɪ'nɒlədʒɪ] *n* criminologie *f*

crimp [krɪmp] *vt (hair)* friser; *(pastry)* pincer

crimson ['krɪmzən] **1** *n* pourpre *m*
2 *adj* pourpre; **to go c. with rage** devenir rouge de colère

cringe [krɪndʒ] *vi* **(a)** *(show fear)* avoir un mouvement de recul **(b)** *(be embarrassed)* avoir envie de rentrer sous terre; **it makes me c.** ça me donne envie de rentrer sous terre

cringing ['krɪndʒɪŋ] *adj (afraid)* craintif(ive); *(servile)* servile

crinkle ['krɪŋkəl] **1** *n (in paper, fabric)* pli *m*
2 *vt (paper, fabric)* froisser; **to c. one's nose** froncer le nez
3 *vi (of brow, nose)* se froncer; *(of face)* se rider

crinkly ['krɪŋklɪ] *adj (skin)* ridé(e); *(paper, fabric)* froissé(e)

cripple ['krɪpəl] **1** *n* estropié(e) *m,f*
2 *vt* estropier; *Fig (industry, system)* paralyser

crippling ['krɪplɪŋ] *adj (illness)* invalidant(e) **(b)** *(effect, strike)* paralysant(e); *(taxes)* écrasant(e)

crisis ['kraɪsɪs] *(pl* **crises** ['kraɪsiːz]*) n* crise *f*; **to be in c.** être en (pleine) crise; **c. management** habileté *f* à gérer les situations de crise; **c. point** point *m* critique

crisp [krɪsp] **1** *Br* **(potato) crisps** (pommes *fpl*) chips *fpl*; **a c.** une chips
2 *adj (apple, vegetable)* croquant(e); *(pastry)* croustillant(e); *(bank note)* neuf (neuve); *(sheets)* frais (fraîche); *(snow)* qui crisse sous les pas; *(air, breeze)* vif (vive); *(style)* vif (vive) et précis(e); *(tone)* brusque, tranchant(e)

crispbread ['krɪspbred] *n* pain *m* suédois

crisply ['krɪsplɪ] *adv (say)* d'un ton brusque *ou* tranchant; *(write)* dans un style vif et précis

crispy ['krɪspɪ] *adj* croustillant(e)

criss-cross ['krɪskrɒs] **1** *vt* entrecroiser
2 *vi* s'entrecroiser

criterion [kraɪ'tɪərɪən] *(pl* **criteria** [kraɪ'tɪərɪə]*) n* critère *m*

critic ['krɪtɪk] *n (reviewer)* critique *mf*; *(opponent)* détracteur(trice) *m,f*

critical ['krɪtɪkəl] *adj* **(a)** *(judgemental)* critique *(of* à l'égard de*)*; **to be c. of sb/sth** critiquer qn/qch **(b)** *(essay, study)* critique; **to be a c. success** être acclamé(e) par la critique **(c)** *(decisive)* crucial; **the next few days will be c.** les prochains jours seront décisifs; **in a c. condition** *(of patient)* dans un état critique

criticism ['krɪtɪsɪzəm] *n* critique *f*

criticize ['krɪtɪsaɪz] **1** *vt* critiquer; **to c. sb for sth** reprocher qch à qn; **to c. sb for doing sth** reprocher à qn de faire/d'avoir fait qch
2 *vi* critiquer

critique [krɪ'tiːk] *n* critique *f*

croak [krəʊk] **1** *n (of frog)* coassement *m*; *(of raven)* croassement *m*
2 *vi* **(a)** *(of frog)* coasser; *(of raven)* croasser; *(of person)* parler d'une voix rauque **(b)** *very Fam (die)* claquer

Croat ['krəʊæt] **1** *n (person)* Croate *mf*
2 *adj* croate

Croatia [krəʊ'eɪʃə] *n* la Croatie

Croatian [krəʊ'eɪʃən] = **Croat**

crochet ['krəʊʃeɪ] **1** *n (travail m au)* crochet *m*; **c. hook** crochet
2 *vt (shawl, blanket)* faire au crochet
3 *vi* faire du crochet

crock [krɒk] *n* **(a)** *(pot)* pot *m* de terre **(b)** *Fam* **old c.** *(person)* croulant(e) *m,f*

crockery ['krɒkərɪ] *n* vaisselle *f*

crocodile ['krɒkədaɪl] *n* **(a)** *(animal)* crocodile *m*; **c. tears** larmes *fpl* de crocodile **(b)** *(line of people)* **to walk in a c.** marcher en rangs par deux

crocus ['krəʊkəs] *n* crocus *m*

croft [krɒft] *n* petite ferme *f*

crone [krəʊn] *n Pej* vieille bique *f*

crony ['krəʊnɪ] *(pl* **cronies**) *n* copain (copine) *m,f*

crook [krʊk] **1** *n* **(a)** *(criminal)* escroc *m* **(b)** *(of shepherd)* houlette *f*; *(of bishop)* crosse *f* **(c)** *(curve)* coude *m*; **in the c. of one's arm** au creux du bras
2 *vt (finger, arm)* plier

crooked ['krʊkɪd] *adj* **(a)** *(not straight)* de travers; *(nose)* tordu(e); **a c. smile** un sourire en coin **(b)** *(dishonest, illegal)* malhonnête

croon [kruːn] *vt & vi* chantonner, fredonner

crop [krɒp] **1** *n* **(a)** *(of fruit, vegetables)* récolte *f*; *(of cereals)* moisson *f*; *Fig* **this year's c. of films** la production cinématographique de cette année **(b)** *(handle of whip)* **(riding)** cravache *f* **(c)** *(of bird)* jabot *m* **(d)** *(short haircut)* coupe *f* très courte
2 *vt (pt & pp* **cropped**) **(a)** *(cut)* couper; *(hair)* couper ras **(b)** *(of cattle)* brouter

▸**crop up** *vi (of issue, question)* surgir; *(of problem, opportunity)* se présenter; *(of name)* être mentionné(e)

cropper ['krɒpə(r)] *n Fam* **to come a c.** se prendre une gamelle

croquet ['krəʊkeɪ] *n* croquet *m*

croquette [krə'ket] *n Culin* croquette *f*

cross [krɒs] **1** *n* **(a)** *(sign, shape)* croix *f*; **to make the sign of the c.** faire le signe de croix
(b) *(hybrid) & Fig* croisement *m* **(between** entre*)*
(c) *(in boxing)* coup *m* croisé; *(in football)* centre *m*
2 *adj (annoyed)* fâché(e); **to get c. (with sb)** se fâcher (contre qn); **to be c. with oneself** s'en vouloir; **we've never had a c. word** nous n'avons jamais eu un mot plus haut que l'autre
3 *vt* **(a)** *(river, road)* traverser; **to c. sb's path** se trouver sur le chemin de qn; **it crossed my mind that...** il m'est venu à l'esprit que...
(b) *(make into shape of cross)* croiser; **to c. oneself** se signer; **to c. one's legs/arms** croiser les jambes/bras; **to keep one's fingers crossed** croiser les doigts; **to c. one's eyes** loucher; *Fig* **to c. swords (with sb)** croiser

le fer (avec qn); *Fig* we must have got our wires crossed nous avons dû mal nous comprendre; *Fam* c. my heart (and hope to die) croix de bois, croix de fer

(c) *(oppose)* contrecarrer

(d) *(animals, plants)* croiser (with avec)

(e) *(in writing)* to c. a cheque barrer un chèque; to c. one's t's mettre une barre à ses t

4 *vi* (a) to c. se croiser; our letters crossed in the post nos lettres se sont croisées

(b) *(go across)* traverser; to c. from Dover to Calais faire la traversée de Douvres à Calais

▶cross off, cross out *vt sep* barrer, rayer

crossbar ['krɒsbɑ:(r)] *n (on bike)* barre *f; (of goalposts)* barre transversale

crossbow ['krɒsbəʊ] *n* arbalète *f*

crossbreed ['krɒsbri:d] *n (of animals)* croisement *m; (of plants)* hybride *m*

cross-Channel ['krɒs'tʃænəl] *adj* transmanche *inv*

crosscheck ['krɒs'tʃek] 1 *n* vérification *f* (par recoupement)

2 *vt* vérifier par recoupement

cross-country ['krɒs'kʌntrɪ] *adj* c. runner coureur(euse) *m,f* de fond; c. running cross *m*

cross-examination ['krɒsɪgzæmɪ'neɪʃən] *n Law* contre-interrogatoire *m; Fig* interrogatoire *m* serré

cross-examine ['krɒsɪg'zæmɪn] *vt Law* soumettre à un contre-interrogatoire; *Fig* soumettre à un interrogatoire serré; to c. sb about sth interroger qn en détail sur qch

cross-eyed ['krɒsaɪd] *adj* to be c. loucher

crossfire ['krɒsfaɪə(r)] *n* feu *m* croisé; *Fig* to be caught in the c. être pris(e) entre deux feux

crossing ['krɒsɪŋ] *n* (a) *(of sea, river)* traversée *f* (b) *(in street)* passage *m* (pour) piétons, passage clouté

cross-legged ['krɒs'legɪd] *adv* to sit c. être assis(e) en tailleur

cross-platform [krɒs'plætfɔ:m] *adj Comptr* multi-plateforme

cross-purposes ['krɒs'pɜ:pəsɪz] *npl* to be at c. ne pas parler de la même chose

cross-reference ['krɒs'refərəns] *n* renvoi *m*

crossroads ['krɒsrəʊdz] *(pl* crossroads) *n* carrefour *m*, croisement *m; Fig (decisive moment)* point *m* crucial

cross-section ['krɒs'sekʃən] *n* coupe *f* ou section *f* transversale; *Fig (of population)* échantillon *m* représentatif

crosswind ['krɒswɪnd] *n* vent *m* de travers

crossword ['krɒswɜ:d] *n* c. (puzzle) mots *mpl* croisés

crotch [krɒtʃ] *n* entrejambe *m*

crotchet ['krɒtʃɪt] *n Mus* noire *f*

crotchety ['krɒtʃɪtɪ] *adj Fam* grognon

crouch [kraʊtʃ] *vi (of animal)* se tapir; *(of person)* s'accroupir

croupier ['kru:pɪə(r)] *n* croupier *m*

crow [krəʊ] 1 *n (bird)* corbeau *m*; as the c. flies à vol d'oiseau; c.'s feet *(on face)* pattes *fpl* d'oie; c.'s nest *(on ship)* nid-de-pie *m*

2 *vi* (a) *(of cock)* chanter (b) *(exult)* se vanter (about de)

crowbar ['krəʊbɑ:(r)] *n* levier *m*

crowd [kraʊd] 1 *n* (a) *(large number of people)* foule *f; (at sporting event)* public *m;* there was a c. at the cinema il y avait beaucoup de monde au cinéma; *Fig* to stand out from the c. se distinguer de la masse; *Fig* to follow the c. suivre le mouvement; to be a c. puller attirer les foules

(b) *Fam (group)* bande *f*

2 *vt (people, objects)* entasser; *(streets, square)* envahir; don't c. me! laisse-moi respirer!

3 *vi* to c. (together) s'entasser; to c. round sb se presser autour de qn

▶crowd out *vt sep (of deal, market)* exclure (of de)

crowded ['kraʊdɪd] *adj (place)* bondé(e); *(day, schedule)* chargé(e)

crown [kraʊn] 1 *n* (a) *(of monarch)* couronne *f;* the C. *(the monarchy)* la Couronne; *Br Law* c. court ≃ assises *fpl*, Cour *f* d'assises; c. jewels joyaux *mpl* de la Couronne; c. prince prince *m* héritier (b) *(top) (of head)* sommet *m* de la tête; *(of hat)* haut *m; (of hill)* sommet; *(of tooth)* couronne *f*

2 *vt also Fig* couronner; *Fam* I'll c. you! *(hit on the head)* je vais te flanquer une calotte!; and to c. it all... et pour couronner le tout...

crowning ['kraʊnɪŋ] *adj (achievement)* suprême; c. glory couronnement *m*

crucial ['kru:ʃəl] *adj* (a) *(very important)* crucial(e) (b) *very Fam (very good)* d'enfer

crucible ['kru:sɪbəl] *n* creuset *m; Fig (test)* épreuve *f*

crucifix ['kru:sɪfɪks] *n* crucifix *m*

crucifixion [kru:sɪ'fɪkʃən] *n* crucifixion *f*

crucify ['kru:sɪfaɪ] *(pt & pp* crucified) *vt* crucifier; *Fig (criticize)* descendre en flammes; *(defeat)* écraser

crude [kru:d] *adj* (a) *(unsophisticated, unrefined)* grossier(ère); c. (oil) pétrole *m* brut (b) *(rude, vulgar)* vulgaire

cruel ['kruəl] *adj* cruel(elle); *(winter)* rude; you have to be c. to be kind qui aime bien châtie bien

cruelty ['kruəltɪ] *n* cruauté *f*

cruet ['kru:ɪt] *n Culin* c. (stand or set) service *m* à condiments

cruise [kru:z] 1 *n (on ship)* croisière *f;* to go on a c. faire une croisière; c. missile missile *m* de croisière

2 *vi (of passengers)* être en croisière; *(of taxi)* être en maraude; *(of car)* rouler; *Fam (look for sexual partner)* draguer; cruising speed *(of ship, plane)* vitesse *f* de croisière

cruiser ['kru:zə(r)] *n (ship)* (battle) c. croiseur *m; (cabin)* c. yacht *m* de croisière

crumb [krʌm] *n also Fig* miette *f;* my only c. of comfort is... mon seul petit réconfort est...

crumble ['krʌmbəl] 1 *n (dessert)* = dessert aux fruits recouvert de pâte sablée

2 *vt (bread, cake)* émietter

3 *vi (of stone)* s'effriter; *(of bread)* s'émietter; *Fig (of empire, hopes)* s'effondrer

crumbly ['krʌmblɪ] *adj* friable

crumpet ['krʌmpɪt] *n* (a) *(teacake)* = petite crêpe épaisse mangée avec du beurre, de la confiture etc (b) *very Fam (women)* nanas *fpl;* a nice bit of c. une belle nana

crumple ['krʌmpəl] 1 *vt (material, dress)* froisser, chiffonner; to c. sth into a ball mettre qch en boule

2 *vi (of material, dress)* se froisser, se chiffonner; *Fig (of face)* se crisper

crunch [krʌntʃ] **1** n (sound) craquement m; (of snow, gravel) crissement m; Fig **when it comes to the c.** au moment crucial; Fig **if it comes to the c.** au pire
2 vt (with teeth) croquer (dans)
3 vi (of snow, gravel) crisser; **to c. on sth** (with teeth) croquer (dans) qch

crunchy ['krʌntʃɪ] adj croquant(e); (snow, gravel) qui crisse sous les pas

crusade [kru:'seɪd] **1** n also Fig croisade f
2 vi **to c. for/against sth** se battre pour/contre qch

crusader [kru:'seɪdə(r)] n Hist croisé m; Fig militant(e) m,f (**for/against** pour/contre)

crush [krʌʃ] **1** n (a) (crowd) foule f; (confusion) bousculade f; **c. barrier** barrière f de sécurité (b) (drink) **orange/lemon c.** = boisson gazeuse à l'orange/au citron (c) Fam (infatuation) béguin m; **to have a c. on sb** avoir le béguin ou en pincer pour qn
2 vt écraser; (grapes) presser; (ice) piler; (in a drawer, suitcase) entasser; Fig (opponent) écraser; (revolt) étouffer, mater; (hopes, person) anéantir
3 vi (be crammed) s'entasser; (crease) se froisser

crushing ['krʌʃɪŋ] adj (defeat) écrasant(e); (blow) terrible; (remark) cinglant(e)

crust [krʌst] n (of bread, pie, the earth) croûte f; Fam **to earn a c.** gagner sa croûte

crustacean [krʌs'teɪʃən] n crustacé m

crusty ['krʌstɪ] adj (a) (bread, roll) croustillant(e) (b) (person) acariâtre

crutch [krʌtʃ] n (a) (for walking) béquille f; Fig (support) soutien m; **to be on crutches** marcher avec des béquilles (b) (crotch) entrejambe m

crux [krʌks] n (of matter, problem) cœur m

cruzado [cru:'za:dəʊ] n (pl cruzados) n cruzado m

cry [kraɪ] n (pl **cries**) (a) (call) (of person, animal) cri m; (in demonstration) slogan m; **to give a c.** pousser un cri; **a c. for help** un appel au secours; **to be a far c. from sth** n'avoir rien à voir avec qch (b) (weeping) **to have a good c.** pleurer un bon coup
2 vt (pt & pp cried) [kraɪd] (a) (exclaim) crier (b) (weep) **to c. oneself to sleep** s'endormir en pleurant
3 vi (a) (weep) pleurer; **to c. over sth** se lamenter sur qch; Prov **it's no use crying over spilt milk** ce qui est fait est fait (b) (shout, call) crier; **to c. for help** appeler à l'aide ou au secours

►**cry off** vi (from invitation) se décommander

►**cry out 1** vt sep (a) (shout) crier (b) (weep) **to c. one's eyes** ou **heart out** pleurer toutes les larmes de son corps
2 vi (shout) pousser un cri; Fam **for crying out loud!** mais bon sang!; Fam **that wall is crying out for a coat of paint** ce mur aurait grand besoin d'une couche de peinture

crybaby ['kraɪbeɪbɪ] (pl **crybabies**) n Fam pleurnicheur(euse) m,f

crying ['kraɪɪŋ] **1** n (weeping) pleurs mpl
2 adj (need) urgent(e); **it's a c. shame that...** il est scandaleux que... + subjunctive

crypt [krɪpt] n crypte f

cryptic ['krɪptɪk] adj énigmatique; **c. crossword** = mots croisés dont les définitions sont des énigmes

crystal ['krɪstəl] **1** n cristal m; **c. ball** boule f de cristal; **c. vase** vase m de ou en cristal
2 adj (clear) cristallin(e), limpide

crystal-clear ['krɪstəl'klɪə(r)] adj (water) limpide; (explanation) clair(e) comme de l'eau de roche

crystallize ['krɪstəlaɪz] **1** vt Chem cristalliser; **crystallized fruit** fruits mpl confits
2 vi Chem & Fig se cristalliser

CSE [si:es'i:] n Br Formerly (abbr **Certificate of Secondary Education**) = diplôme de fin d'études du premier cycle de l'enseignement secondaire

CST [si:es'ti:] n Am (abbr **Central Standard Time**) = heure du centre de l'Amérique du Nord

cub [kʌb] n (of fox) renardeau m; (of bear) ourson m; (of lion) lionceau m; (of wolf) louveteau m; **C.** (Scout) louveteau m

Cuba ['kju:bə] n Cuba m

Cuban ['kju:bən] **1** n Cubain(e) m,f
2 adj cubain(e)

cubbyhole ['kʌbɪhəʊl] n cagibi m

cube [kju:b] **1** n (shape) cube m; (of sugar) morceau m; Math **c. root** racine f cubique
2 vt Math élever au cube

cubic ['kju:bɪk] adj cubique; **c. capacity** volume m; **c. metre** mètre m cube

cubicle ['kju:bɪkəl] n (in hospital, dormitory) box m; (in swimming pool) cabine f; (in public toilet) W.-C. m

cubism ['kju:bɪzəm] n Art cubisme m

cuckold ['kʌkəld] **1** n cocu m
2 vt cocufier, faire cocu

cuckoo ['kʊku:] **1** n (bird) coucou m; **c. clock** coucou m
2 adj Fam (mad) dingue

cucumber ['kju:kʌmbə(r)] n concombre m

cud [kʌd] n **to chew the c.** ruminer

cuddle ['kʌdəl] **1** n câlin m; **to give sb a c.** faire un câlin à qn
2 vt câliner, faire des câlins à
3 vi se câliner, se faire des câlins; **to c. up to sb** se pelotonner ou se blottir contre qn

cuddly ['kʌdlɪ] adj Fam (child, animal) mignon(onne) à croquer; Euph (plump) rond(e); **c. toy** peluche f

cudgel ['kʌdʒəl] **1** n gourdin m, trique f; Fig **to take up the cudgels on sb's behalf** prendre fait et cause pour qn
2 vt (pt & pp cudgelled, Am cudgeled) donner des coups de gourdin ou de trique à; **to c. one's brains** se creuser la cervelle

cue¹ [kju:] n (of actor) réplique f; Fig (signal) signal m; Fig **to take one's c. from sb** prendre exemple sur qn; **c. card** (for public speaker) aide-mémoire m inv

cue² n (in billiards, pool) queue f; **c. ball** boule f blanche

cuff¹ [kʌf] n (of shirt) poignet m; (handcuffs) **cuffs** menottes fpl; Fam **off the c.** au pied levé; **c. links** boutons mpl de manchette

cuff² ¹ n (blow) calotte f
2 vt (hit) donner une calotte à

cuisine [kwi'zi:n] n cuisine f

cul-de-sac ['kʌldəsæk] n also Fig impasse f

culinary ['kʌlɪnərɪ] adj culinaire

cull [kʌl] **1** n (of seals, deer) abattage m
2 vt (a) (herd) réduire la taille de; (animal) abattre (b) (select) sélectionner (**from** parmi)

culminate ['kʌlmɪneɪt] vi **to c. in sth** aboutir à qch

culmination [kʌlmɪ'neɪʃən] n point m culminant

culottes [ku:'lɒts] npl jupe-culotte f

culpable ['kʌlpəbəl] adj coupable (**of** de); Scot Law **c. homicide** homicide m involontaire

culprit ['kʌlprɪt] n coupable mf

cult [kʌlt] n culte m; (sect) secte f; **c. figure** personnage m culte; **c. film** film m culte

cultivate ['kʌltɪveɪt] vt also Fig cultiver

cultivated ['kʌltɪveɪtɪd] adj cultivé(e)

cultivation [kʌltɪ'veɪʃən] n culture f

cultivator ['kʌltɪveɪtə(r)] n (for farm) cultivateur m; (for garden) motoculteur m; (person) cultivateur(trice) m,f

cultural ['kʌltʃərəl] adj culturel(elle)

culture ['kʌltʃə(r)] n (a) (artistic activity, refinement) culture f; Hum **c. vulture** fou (folle) m,f de culture (b) (society) culture f; **c. shock** choc m culturel (c) Biol culture f

cultured ['kʌltʃəd] adj (educated) cultivé(e); **c. pearl** perle f de culture

cumbersome ['kʌmbəsəm] adj (luggage, furniture) encombrant(e); (procedure, style) lourd(e)

cumin ['kʌmɪn] n cumin m

cumulative ['kjuːmjʊlətɪv] adj cumulatif(ive)

cunning ['kʌnɪŋ] 1 n (deviousness) ruse f; (ingenuity) astuce f, ingéniosité f
2 adj (devious) rusé(e); (ingenious) astucieux(euse), ingénieux(euse)

cunt [kʌnt] n Vulg (vagina) chatte f; (as insult) enculé(e) m,f

cup [kʌp] 1 n (a) (for drinking, measurement) tasse f; (plastic, paper) gobelet m; Fam Fig **it's not my c. of tea** ce n'est pas ma tasse de thé; **it's not everyone's c. of tea** tout le monde n'aime pas (b) (trophy) coupe f; **c. final** finale f de coupe; **c. tie** match m éliminatoire de coupe (c) (of bra) bonnet m
2 vt (pt & pp cupped) **to c. one's hands round one's mouth** mettre ses mains en porte-voix; **to c. one's hand behind one's ear** mettre sa main en cornet

cupboard ['kʌbəd] n placard m; Fam **c. love** amour m intéressé; **c. space** rangements mpl

cupcake ['kʌpkeɪk] n = sorte de madeleine

Cupid ['kjuːpɪd] n Cupidon

cuppa ['kʌpə] n Fam tasse f de thé

curable ['kjʊərəbəl] adj guérissable

curate ['kjʊərət] n Rel vicaire m; **this book is a bit of a c.'s egg** il y a du bon et du mauvais dans ce livre

curator [kjʊə'reɪtə(r)] n conservateur m

curb [kɜːb] 1 n (a) (limit) **to put a c. on sth** mettre un frein à qch (b) Am (of road) bordure f de trottoir
2 vt (spending) réduire; (emotions) réfréner

curd [kɜːd] n **curd(s)** lait m caillé; **c. cheese** fromage m blanc battu

curdle ['kɜːdəl] 1 vt cailler
2 vi (se) cailler

cure [kjʊə(r)] 1 n remède m (for contre); **there is no known c.** on n'a pas encore trouvé de remède; **beyond c.** (person) incurable; (situation) irrémédiable
2 vt (a) (person) guérir (of de); (b) (preserve, by salting) saler; (by smoking) fumer; (by drying) sécher; (hides) traiter

cure-all ['kjʊərɔːl] n panacée f

curfew ['kɜːfjuː] n couvre-feu m

curio ['kjʊərɪəʊ] n (pl curios) n curiosité f

curiosity [kjʊərɪ'ɒsɪtɪ] n (pl curiosities) n curiosité f; Prov **c. killed the cat** la curiosité est un vilain défaut

curious ['kjʊərɪəs] adj (inquisitive, strange) curieux(euse); **to be c. to see/know** vouloir voir/savoir par curiosité

curl [kɜːl] 1 n (of hair) boucle f; (of smoke) volute f
2 vt (hair) boucler; (tightly) friser; **to c. one's lip** faire une moue dédaigneuse; **to c. oneself into a ball** se rouler en boule
3 vi (of hair) boucler; (tightly) friser; (of paper, leaves) se recroqueviller; (of smoke) s'élever en volutes
▶**curl up** vi (a) (make oneself comfortable) se pelotonner (b) (protect oneself) se rouler en boule (c) (of paper, leaves) se recroqueviller

curler ['kɜːlə(r)] n (for hair) bigoudi m

curlew ['kɜːljuː] n courlis m

curling ['kɜːlɪŋ] n (a) (sport) curling m (b) **c. tongs** fer m à friser

curly ['kɜːlɪ] adj (hair) bouclé(e); (tightly) frisé(e)

currant ['kʌrənt] n raisin m de Corinthe; **c. bun** petit pain m aux raisins

currency ['kʌrənsɪ] n (pl currencies) n (a) (money) monnaie f; (foreign) devise f; **c. market** marché m monétaire (b) (acceptance) **to gain c.** (of theory) être accrédité(e); (of idea, belief) se répandre; **to give c. to a rumour** faire courir un bruit

current ['kʌrənt] 1 n (of river, electricity) & Fig (trend) courant m; Fig **to swim against the c.** aller à contre-courant
2 adj (existing, present) actuel(elle); **c. affairs** actualité f; **c. issue** (of magazine) dernier numéro m (b) Br Fin **c. account** compte m courant; **c. assets** actif m de roulement; **c. expenditure** dépenses fpl courantes; **c. liabilities** passif m exigible (c) (common) courant(e)

currently ['kʌrəntlɪ] adv actuellement

curriculum [kə'rɪkjʊləm] n (pl curricula [kə'rɪkjʊlə]) n Sch programme m; **c. vitae** curriculum vitae m inv

curry[1] ['kʌrɪ] 1 n (pl curries) curry m; **c. powder** curry m
2 vt (pt & pp curried) curried chicken/lamb poulet m/agneau m au curry

curry[2] vt **to c. favour with sb** s'insinuer dans les bonnes grâces de qn

curse [kɜːs] 1 n (a) (jinx, affliction) malédiction f, mauvais sort m; (swearword) juron m; **to put a c. on sb** jeter un sort à qn (b) (scourge) fléau m
2 vt maudire; **to be cursed with sth** être affligé(e) de qch
3 vi jurer

cursor ['kɜːsə(r)] n Comptr curseur m; **c. key** touche f de déplacement

cursory ['kɜːsərɪ] adj superficiel(elle)

curt [kɜːt] adj sec (sèche)

curtail [kɜː'teɪl] vt (shorten) abréger, écourter; (limit) réduire

curtain ['kɜːtən] n rideau m; **to draw the curtains** (open) ouvrir les rideaux; (close) fermer ou tirer les rideaux; Fam Fig **it's curtains for her** elle est fichue; Th **c. call** rappel m; **c. raiser** Th lever m de rideau; Fig prélude m (to à); **c. ring** anneau m de rideau; **c. rail** or **rod** tringle f à rideau
▶**curtain off** vt sep séparer par un rideau

curts(e)y ['kɜːtsɪ] 1 n (pl curtsies or curtseys) révérence f
2 vi (pt & pp curtsied or curtseyed) faire la révérence (to à)

curvaceous [kɜː'veɪʃəs] adj pulpeux(euse)

curvature ['kɜːvətʃə(r)] n courbure f; **c. of the spine** scoliose f

curve [kɜːv] **1** n courbe f; (in road) tournant m, virage m; (in river) méandre m

2 vi (of spine) se courber; (of road) faire une courbe; (of river) serpenter

curved [kɜːvd] adj (line) courbe; (spine) courbé(e)

cushion ['kʊʃən] **1** n (on chair, of air) coussin m; (on billiard table) bande f

2 vt (blow, impact) amortir; **to c. sb against sth** protéger qn contre qch

cushy ['kʊʃɪ] adj Fam pépère, peinard(e); **a c. number** une bonne planque

custard ['kʌstəd] n crème f anglaise; **c. pie** (in slapstick comedy) tarte f à la crème; **c. powder** préparation f instantanée pour crème anglaise

custodial [kʌsˈtəʊdɪəl] adj Law **c. sentence** peine f de prison

custodian [kʌsˈtəʊdɪən] n gardien(enne) m,f

custody ['kʌstədɪ] n (a) (of children, important papers) garde f; **to have c. of sb** avoir la garde de qn; **in safe c.** sous bonne garde (b) Law garde f à vue; **to take sb into c.** placer qn en garde à vue

custom ['kʌstəm] n (a) (tradition, practice) coutume f; **it was his c. to rise early** il avait l'habitude de se lever tôt (b) Com clientèle f; **to take one's c. elsewhere** aller se fournir ailleurs

customary ['kʌstəmərɪ] adj (usual) habituel(elle); (traditional) traditionnel(elle); **it is c. to...** il est d'usage de...

custom-built ['kʌstəmbɪlt] adj (car, offices) construit(e) sur mesure; (kitchen units) fabriqué(e) sur mesure

customer ['kʌstəmə(r)] n client(e) m,f; Fam Fig **he's an awkward c.** c'est un type pas commode; Com **c. services** (department) service m clientèle

customize ['kʌstəmaɪz] vt (vehicle) customiser; (kitchen, computer) personnaliser

custom-made ['kʌstəm'meɪd] adj (fait(e)) sur mesure

customs ['kʌstəmz] npl douane f; **to go through c.** passer la douane; **c. declaration** déclaration f en douane; **c. duty** droits mpl de douane; **c. officer** douanier(ère) m,f

cut [kʌt] **1** n (a) (in flesh, text, film) coupure f; (in wood, cloth) entaille f; **c. of meat** morceau m (de viande); Fam **to be a c. above sb/sth** être un cran au-dessus de qn/qch
(b) (in wages, prices) réduction f
(c) (blow) coup m; **the c. and thrust of debate** les joutes fpl oratoires
(d) Fam (share) part f
(e) (style) (of clothes, hair) coupe f

2 adj Fig **c. and dried** (clear) simple; (decided) décidé(e); **c. flowers** fleurs fpl coupées; **c. glass** cristal m taillé

3 vt (pt & pp **cut**) (a) (in general) couper; (into slices) trancher, découper; **to c. one's finger/nails** se couper le doigt/les ongles; **to c. sb's hair** couper les cheveux à qn; **to have one's hair cut** se faire couper les cheveux; **to c. sth in two or in half** couper qch en deux; **to c. sth to pieces** couper qch en morceaux; **to c. oneself loose or free** se dégager, se libérer; **to c. a record** enregistrer un disque
(b) (wages, prices) réduire
(c) (idioms) **to c. one's losses** limiter les dégâts; **to c. one's teeth on sth** se faire les dents sur qch; **it's cutting it or things (a bit) fine** ça tait (un peu) juste; **to c. sb short** couper la parole à qn; **to c. sth short** écourter qch; **to c. a long story short...** bref...

4 vi (a) (of knife, scissors) couper; (of wind) être cinglant(e);

Cin **c.!** coupez!
(b) (idioms) **that's an argument that cuts both ways** c'est un argument à double tranchant; Fam **to c. and run** décamper

▸**cut across** vt insep (a) (field) couper à travers (b) (transcend) transcender

▸**cut back 1** vt sep (a) (bush, tree) tailler (b) (costs, production) réduire
2 vi **to c. back on sth** (spending, time) réduire qch; **to c. back on smoking/drinking** fumer/boire moins

▸**cut down 1** vt sep (a) (tree, soldier) abattre; **to be c. down in one's prime** être fauché(e) à la fleur de l'âge (b) (speech, text) abréger; (spending, time) réduire; Fig **to c. sb down to size** rabattre son caquet à qn
2 vi = **cut back**

▸**cut in** vi (a) (interrupt conversation) intervenir (b) (in car) **to c. in in front of sb** faire une queue de poisson à qn

▸**cut into** vt insep (with knife) entamer; (of rope, handle) blesser

▸**cut off** vt sep (a) (remove) couper; **to c. off sb's head** trancher la tête à qn, décapiter qn; Fig **that would be cutting off your nose to spite your face** ça va te retomber sur le nez (b) (disconnect) couper; **we've been cut off** (had electricity disconnected) on nous a coupé l'électricité; **I've been cut off** (during phone conversation) j'ai été coupé (c) (isolate) isoler; **to be cut off from** être coupé(e) de

▸**cut out 1** vt sep (a) (picture, article) découper; (tumour) enlever; Fam **to have got one's work c. out** avoir du pain sur la planche; **to be cut out for sth** être fait(e) pour qch (b) (stop) supprimer; **to c. out smoking/puddings** arrêter de fumer/de manger des desserts; Fam **c. it out!** ça va maintenant! (c) (exclude) **to c. sb out of one's will** déshériter qn; **to c. sb out of a deal** évincer qn
2 vi (of engine) caler; (of machine) s'arrêter

▸**cut up 1** vt sep (a) (food, paper) couper; (into slices) découper (b) Fam (upset) **to be very cut up (about sth)** être complètement chamboulé(e) (par qch)
2 vi Fam **to c. up rough** (of person) devenir agressif(ive)

cutback ['kʌtbæk] n réduction f

cute [kjuːt] adj mignon(onne)

cuticle ['kjuːtɪkəl] n cuticule f

cutlery ['kʌtlərɪ] n couverts mpl; Com argenterie f

cutlet ['kʌtlɪt] n côtelette f

cutoff ['kʌtɒf] n **c. date** date f limite; **c. point** limite f; (for tax) seuil m

cutout ['kʌtaʊt] n (a) (shape) silhouette f (b) Elec disjoncteur m

cut-price ['kʌt'praɪs] adj (goods) à prix réduit; (rate) réduit(e)

cutthroat ['kʌtθrəʊt] **1** n assassin m
2 adj (competition) acharné(e); **c. razor** coupe-choux m inv

cutting ['kʌtɪŋ] **1** n (a) (of plant) bouture f (b) (newspaper) **c.** coupure f de journal ou de presse (c) (railway) **c.** voie f en déblai
2 adj (wind, remark) cinglant(e); **c. edge** tranchant m; Fig **to be at the c. edge of technology** être à la pointe du progrès

cuttlefish ['kʌtəlfɪʃ] n seiche f

CV [siːˈviː] n (abbr **curriculum vitae**) CV m

cyanide ['saɪənaɪd] n Chem cyanure m

cybercafé ['saɪbəˈkæfeɪ] n cybercafé m

cybernetics [saɪbə'netɪks] *n Comptr* cybernétique *f*

cyberspace ['saɪbəspeɪs] *n Comptr* cyberespace *m*

cyclamen ['sɪkləmən] (*pl* **cyclamen**) *n* cyclamen *m*

cycle ['saɪkəl] **1** *n* (a) *(pattern)* cycle *m* (b) *(bicycle)* bicyclette *f*, vélo *m*; **c. lane** voie *f* réservée aux vélos; **c. path** piste *f* cyclable; **c. racing** course *f* cycliste
2 *vi* aller à bicyclette *ou* à vélo

cyclic(al) ['saɪklɪk(əl)] *adj* cyclique

cycling ['saɪklɪŋ] *n* cyclisme *m*; **to go on a c. holiday** faire du cyclotourisme; **c. track** piste *f* cycliste

cyclist ['saɪklɪst] *n* cycliste *mf*

cyclone ['saɪkləʊn] *n Met* cyclone *m*

cygnet ['sɪgnɪt] *n* jeune cygne *m*

cylinder ['sɪlɪndə(r)] *n* (*shape*) cylindre *m*; (*gas container*) bouteille *f*; **four-/eight-c. engine** moteur *m* à quatre/huit cylindres; **c. block** bloc-cylindres *m*; **c. head** culasse *f*

cylindrical [sɪ'lɪndrɪkəl] *adj* cylindrique

cymbal ['sɪmbəl] *n* cymbale *f*

cynic ['sɪnɪk] *n* cynique *mf*

cynical ['sɪnɪkəl] *adj* cynique (**about** sur)

cypress ['saɪprəs] *n* cyprès *m*

Cypriot ['sɪprɪət] **1** *n* Chypriote *mf*, Cypriote *mf*
2 *adj* chypriote, cypriote

Cyprus ['saɪprəs] *n* Chypre

cyst [sɪst] *n Med* kyste *m*

cystitis [sɪs'taɪtɪs] *n Med* cystite *f*

czar [zɑ:(r)] *n* tsar *m*, czar *m*

Czech [tʃek] **1** *n* (a) *(person)* Tchèque *mf* (b) *(language)* tchèque *m*
2 *adj* tchèque; **the C. Republic** la République tchèque

Czechoslovakia [tʃekəʊslə'vækɪə] *n Formerly* la Tchécoslovaquie

D

D, d [diː] n (**a**) (letter) D, d m inv (**b**) Mus ré m (**c**) Sch (grade) **to get a D** avoir entre 8 et 10 sur 20

D Am Pol (abbr **Democrat**) démocrate

DA [diːeɪ] n Am Law (abbr **district attorney**) ≃ procureur m de la République

dab [dæb] **1** n (of paint) petit coup m; (of glue) point m; (of perfume) goutte f; Br Fam **dabs** (fingerprints) empreintes fpl (digitales)
2 adj **to be a d. hand at sth** être doué(e) pour qch
3 vt (pt & pp **dabbed**) (paint) passer; (eyes, wound) tamponner

dabble ['dæbəl] **1** vt **to d. one's feet in the water** balancer ses pieds dans l'eau
2 vi **to d. in politics/journalism** faire vaguement de la politique/du journalisme

dabbler ['dæblə(r)] n amateur(trice) m,f

dachshund ['dækshʊnd] n teckel m

dad [dæd] n Fam papa m

daddy ['dædɪ] (pl **daddies**) n Fam papa m

daddy-longlegs [dædɪ'lɒŋlegz] (pl **daddy-longlegs**) n Fam tipule f

daffodil ['dæfədɪl] n jonquille f

daft [dɑːft] adj Br idiot(e); **to be d. about sb/sth** être fou (folle) de qn/qch

dagger ['dægə(r)] n (**a**) (weapon) dague f (**b**) (idioms) **to be at daggers drawn** (with sb) être à couteaux tirés (avec qn); **to look daggers at sb** foudroyer qn du regard

dago ['deɪgəʊ] (pl **dagoes** or **dagos**) n very Fam = terme injurieux désignant un Espagnol, un Portugais, un Italien ou un Latino-Américain

dahlia ['deɪlɪə] n dahlia m

daily ['deɪlɪ] **1** n (pl **dailies**) (newspaper) quotidien m
2 adj quotidien(enne); **on a d. basis** (paid, calculated) à la journée; (used) quotidiennement; Fam **the d. grind** le train-train quotidien; **d. paper** quotidien m
3 adv tous les jours, quotidiennement; **twice d.** deux fois par jour

dainty ['deɪntɪ] adj délicat(e)

dairy ['deərɪ] (pl **dairies**) n (shop) crémerie f; (factory) laiterie f; **d. cow** vache f laitière; **d. farm** = ferme spécialisée dans la production laitière; **d. farming** élevage m de vaches laitières; **d. produce** produits mpl laitiers

dais ['deɪs] n estrade f

daisy ['deɪzɪ] (pl **daisies**) n pâquerette f; (bigger) marguerite f; Fam **to push up the daisies** manger les pissenlits par la racine; **d. chain** guirlande f de pâquerettes

daisywheel ['deɪzɪwiːl] n (on printer) marguerite f

dale [deɪl] n vallée f

dalliance ['dælɪəns] n Lit badinage m

dally ['dælɪ] (pt & pp **dallied**) vi (dawdle) traîner, lambiner; **to d. over a decision** mettre du temps à se décider; **to d. with sb** flirter avec qn

Dalmatian [dæl'meɪʃən] n (dog) dalmatien m

dam [dæm] **1** n barrage m
2 vt (pt & pp **dammed**) (river, lake) construire un barrage sur
▶ **dam up** vt sep (river, lake) construire un barrage sur

damage ['dæmɪdʒ] **1** n (**a**) (to machine, building) dégâts mpl; (to health, reputation) mal m; **to do** or **cause d. to** (building) faire des dégâts dans; (health, reputation) nuire à; Fig **the d. is done** le mal est fait; Br Fam **what's the d.?** ça fait combien?; **we have to do some d. limitation** il faut limiter les dégâts (**b**) **damages** (compensation) dommages-intérêts mpl
2 vt (machine, building) abîmer, endommager; (health, reputation) nuire à; (chances) compromettre; (person) faire du tort à

damaging ['dæmɪdʒɪŋ] adj préjudiciable (**to** à)

Damascus [də'mæskəs] n Damas

damask ['dæməsk] n damas m

dame [deɪm] n (**a**) Am Fam (woman) pépée f; Br (in pantomime) = dans la pantomime, personnage comique de vieille dame tenu par un homme (**b**) Br (title) = titre donné à une femme ayant reçu une distinction honorifique

damn [dæm] **1** n very Fam **I don't give a d.** j'en ai rien à fiche; **it's not worth a d.** ça ne vaut pas un clou
2 adj very Fam fichu(e); **you d. fool!** espèce d'idiot(e)!; **he's a d. nuisance!** qu'est-ce qu'il peut être casse-pieds!
3 adv very Fam **d. all!** que dalle; **you know d. well what I mean!** tu sais fichtrement bien ce que je veux dire!
4 exclam very Fam **d.!** zut!, mince!
5 vt (**a**) (criticize severely) éreinter (**b**) very Fam **d. the expense!** au diable l'avarice!; **d. it!** zut!, mince!; **well I'll be damned!** ben mince alors!

damnation [dæm'neɪʃən] **1** n Rel damnation f
2 exclam Fam **d.!** bon sang!

damned [dæmd] **1** npl Rel **the d.** les damnés mpl
2 adj & adv very Fam = **damn**

damning ['dæmɪŋ] adj (admission, revelation) accablant(e)

damp [dæmp] **1** n humidité f
2 adj humide; (skin) moite; **d. course** isolant m contre l'humidité; Fig **d. squib** déception f
3 vt (make wet) humecter; **to d. down a fire** couvrir un feu

dampen ['dæmpən] vt (make wet) humecter; Fig **to d. sb's spirits** décourager qn

damper ['dæmpə(r)] n Mus étouffoir m; Fig **to put a d. on sth** jeter un froid sur qch

damsel ['dæmzəl] *n Lit* damoiselle *f*; *Hum* **a d. in distress** une belle éplorée

damson ['dæmzən] *n (fruit)* prune *f* de Damas; *(tree)* prunier *m* de Damas

dance [dɑ:ns] **1** *n* danse *f*; *(event)* soirée *f* dansante; *(for young people)* boum *f*; *(formal)* bal *m*; *Fam* **to lead sb a (merry) d.** donner du fil à retordre à qn; **d. band** orchestre *m* de danse; **d. floor** piste *f* de danse; **d. hall** salle *f* de bal; **d. music** *(in clubs)* dance (music) *f*
2 *vt (waltz, tango)* danser
3 *vi* danser; **they danced down the road** ils ont descendu la rue en dansant

dancer ['dɑ:nsə(r)] *n* danseur(euse) *m,f*

dancing ['dɑ:nsɪŋ] *n* danse *f*; **d. shoes** chaussons *mpl* de danse

dandelion ['dændɪlaɪən] *n* pissenlit *m*

dander ['dændə(r)] *n Fam* **to get sb's d. up** hérisser qn

dandruff ['dændrəf] *n* pellicules *fpl*

dandy ['dændɪ] **1** *n (pl* **dandies***)* dandy *m*
2 *adj Fam* génial(e); **everything's just (fine and) d.** tout marche comme sur des roulettes

Dane [deɪn] *n* Danois(e) *m,f*

danger ['deɪndʒə(r)] *n* danger *m*; **in d.** en danger; **out of d.** hors de danger; **to be in d. of doing sth** risquer de faire qch; **there's no d. that...** il n'y a pas de danger que... + *subjunctive*; **to be on the d. list** *(of patient)* être dans un état critique; **to be off the d. list** *(of patient)* être hors de danger; **d. money** prime *f* de risque; *Fig* **d. sign** signal *m* d'alarme

dangerous ['deɪndʒərəs] *adj* dangereux(euse)

dangerously ['deɪndʒərəslɪ] *adv* dangereusement; **they came d. close to losing** ils ont bien failli perdre

dangle ['dæŋɡəl] **1** *vt* balancer; *Fig* **to d. sth in front of sb** faire miroiter qch à qn
2 *vi (of legs)* pendre; *(from rope, chain)* se balancer; *Fig* **to keep sb dangling** laisser qn dans l'incertitude

Danish ['deɪnɪʃ] **1** *n (language)* danois *m*
2 *adj* danois(e); **D. (pastry)** = sorte de chausson fourré aux fruits

dank [dæŋk] *adj* humide et froid(e)

Danube ['dænju:b] *n* **the D.** le Danube

dapper ['dæpə(r)] *adj* soigné(e)

dappled ['dæpəld] *adj* tacheté(e); *(horse)* pommelé(e)

dare ['deə(r)] **1** *n* défi *m*; **to do sth for a d.** faire qch par défi
2 *vt* **to d. to do sth** oser faire qch; **to d. sb to do sth** défier qn de faire qch; **I d. you!** chiche!; **don't you d. (do that)!** ne t'avise pas de faire ça!; **how d. you!** comment oses-tu!; **I d. say** sans doute, c'est bien possible

daredevil ['deədevəl] **1** *n* casse-cou *mf inv*
2 *adj (person)* casse-cou *inv*; *(stunt, escape)* auda-cieux(euse)

daring ['deərɪŋ] **1** *n* audace *f*
2 *adj* audacieux(euse)

dark [dɑ:k] **1** *n* **(a)** *(darkness)* obscurité *f*; **before/after d.** avant/après la tombée de la nuit; **in the d.** dans le noir **(b)** *(idioms)* **to be in the d. (about)** ne pas être au courant (de)
2 *adj* **(a)** *(not light)* sombre; *(skin, hair)* foncé(e); **it's d. by six o'clock** il fait nuit à six heures; **it's getting d.** il commence à faire nuit; **d. glasses** lunettes *fpl* noires; *Fig* **d. horse** *(competitor)* outsider *m*; *(in politics)* candidat(e) *m,f* surprise; *(secretive person)* personne *f* pleine de mystère **(b)**

Fig (thought) sombre, morose; *(period)* sombre; *(look)* noir(e); *Hist* **the D. Ages** le Haut Moyen Âge; *Fig* **to be in the D. Ages** être encore au Moyen Âge

darken ['dɑ:kən] **1** *vt (sky, colour)* assombrir; **never d. my door again!** ne remettez plus les pieds chez moi!
2 *vi (of sky, colour, thoughts)* s'assombrir

darkness ['dɑ:knɪs] *n* obscurité *f*; **in d.** dans l'obscurité

darkroom ['dɑ:kru:m] *n* chambre *f* noire

dark-skinned [dɑ:k'skɪnd] *adj* à la peau mate

darling ['dɑ:lɪŋ] *n (term of address) (to woman)* chérie *f*; *(to man)* chéri *m*; **she's the d. of the press** c'est la coqueluche des journaux
2 *adj (dear)* cher (chère); *(charming)* adorable

darn[1] [dɑ:n] *vt (mend)* repriser

darn[2] *Fam* **1** *adj* sacré(e); **it's a d. nuisance!** c'est vachement embêtant!
2 *exclam* **d. (it)!** zut!

darning ['dɑ:nɪŋ] *n* reprisage *m*; **d. needle** aiguille *f* à repriser

dart [dɑ:t] **1** *n* **(a)** *(missile)* flèche *f*; **darts** *(game)* fléchettes *fpl* **(b)** *(movement)* **to make a d. for sth** se ruer vers qch
2 *vt* **to d. a glance at sb** jeter un regard à qn
3 *vi* **to d. in/out** entrer/sortir comme une flèche

dartboard ['dɑ:tbɔ:d] *n* cible *f (de jeu de fléchettes)*

dash [dæʃ] **1** *n* **(a)** *(of liquid)* goutte *f*; *(of humour, colour)* touche *f* **(b)** *(hyphen, in Morse code)* tiret *m* **(c)** *(run)* course *f* effrénée; **to make a d. for sth** se ruer vers qch; **to make a d. for it** s'enfuir **(d)** *(style)* panache *m*; **to cut a d.** avoir fière allure **(e)** *(of car)* tableau *m* de bord
2 *vt* **(a)** *(throw)* jeter; **to d. sth to the ground** jeter qch par terre **(b)** *(destroy) (hopes)* réduire à néant; *Fam* **d. (it)!** zut!
3 *vi* **to d. in/out** entrer/sortir comme une flèche; **I dashed about** *or* **around all day** j'ai couru toute la journée; *Fam* **I must d.** il faut que je file
▸**dash off 1** *vt sep (letter)* écrire en vitesse
2 *vi (leave)* filer

dashboard ['dæʃbɔ:d] *n (of car)* tableau *m* de bord

dashing ['dæʃɪŋ] *adj (person)* fringant(e); *(appearance)* élégant(e)

DAT [di:eɪ'ti:] *n (abbr* **digital audio tape***)* cassette *f* numérique

data ['deɪtə] *n* informations *fpl*; *Comptr* données *fpl*; **an item** *or* **piece of d.** une information/donnée; **d. bank** banque *f* de données; *Comptr* **d. processing** traitement *m* de l'information; **d. protection** protection *f* de l'information

database ['deɪtəbeɪs] *n Comptr* base *f* de données

date[1] [deɪt] *n (fruit)* datte *f*; **d. palm** palmier *m* dattier

date[2] **1** *n (a) (day)* date *f*; **d. of birth** date de naissance; **what's the d. (today)?** le combien sommes-nous (aujourd'hui)?; **to d.** à ce jour; **up to d.** *(with work)* à jour; *(with events, news)* au courant; *(in fashion)* à la mode; **out of d.** périmé(e); **d. stamp** tampon *m ou* timbre *m* à date **(b)** *(with girlfriend, boyfriend)* rendez-vous *m*; **d. rape** = viol commis par une connaissance de la victime **(c)** *Am (girlfriend, boyfriend)* ami(e) *m,f*
2 *n (a) (letter, ticket)* dater **(b)** *Am (go out with)* sortir avec
3 *vi* **(a)** **to d. from** *or* **back to** *(of custom, practice)* remonter à; *(of building)* dater de **(b)** *(go out of fashion)* dater

dateline ['deɪtlaɪn] *n* date *f* et lieu de rédaction

dating agency ['deɪtɪŋeɪdʒənsɪ] *n* agence *f* matrimoniale

dative ['deɪtɪv] n Gram datif m

daub [dɔːb] vt barbouiller (**with** de)

daughter ['dɔːtə(r)] n fille f

daughter-in-law ['dɔːtərɪnlɔː] (pl **daughters-in-law**) n belle-fille f

daunt [dɔːnt] vt intimider; **nothing daunted** sans se décourager

daunting ['dɔːntɪŋ] adj intimidant(e)

dawdle ['dɔːdəl] vi traînasser, lambiner

dawn [dɔːn] **1** n also Fig aube f; **at d.** à l'aube; **from d. to dusk** du lever au coucher du soleil; **the d. chorus** le chant des oiseaux à l'aube
2 vi (of day) se lever; Fig (of life, civilization) naître
▶**dawn on** vt insep the truth finally dawned on her la vérité a fini par lui apparaître; **it dawned on me that...** je me suis rendu compte que...

day [deɪ] n (a) (period of daylight, twenty-four hours) jour m; (referring to duration) journée f; **once/twice a d.** une fois/deux fois par jour; **the d. before yesterday** avant-hier; **the d. after tomorrow** après-demain; **all d.** toute la journée; **d. after d.** jour après jour; **to change from d. to d.** changer d'un jour sur l'autre; **to live from d. to d.** vivre au jour le jour; **one d., one of these days** un de ces jours; **any d. now** d'un jour à l'autre; **the other d.** l'autre jour; **every other d.** tous les deux jours, un jour sur deux; **a year ago to the d.** il y a un an jour pour jour; **from d. one** dès le début; **to take a d. off** prendre un jour de congé; **to be paid by the d.** être payé(e) à la journée; **to work d. and night** travailler jour et nuit; Fam **he's sixty if he's a d.** il a soixante ans bien sonnés; **d. nursery** crèche f; **d. pupil** externe mf; **d. release** formation f continue en alternance; **d. return** (train ticket) aller et retour m valable pour la journée; **d. school** externat m; **d. shift** (in factory) équipe f de jour; **d. trip** excursion f d'une journée
(b) (era) **in my d.** de mon temps; **in this d. and age** à notre époque; **this government/TV has had its d.** ce gouvernement/cette télé a fait son temps; **in the days of...** du temps de...; **these days** de nos jours; **in those days** en ce temps-là; **those were the days!** c'était le bon temps!; **in days to come** à l'avenir
(c) (idioms) **it's all in a d.'s work** c'est la routine; **to make sb's d.** mettre qn de bonne humeur; Fam **let's call it a d.** ça suffit pour aujourd'hui; Fam **that'll be the d.!** c'est pas demain la veille!; **to name the d.** (of wedding) choisir la date de son mariage; **to carry** or **win the d.** l'emporter

daybreak ['deɪbreɪk] n lever m du jour; **at d.** au lever du jour

daydream ['deɪdriːm] **1** n rêverie f; Pej rêvasserie f
2 vi rêver (**about** à); Pej rêvasser

daylight ['deɪlaɪt] n jour m, lumière f; **it was still d.** il faisait encore jour; Fig **it's d. robbery!** c'est du vol pur et simple!

daytime ['deɪtaɪm] n jour m, journée f; **in the d.** pendant la journée; **d. TV** = émissions de télévision diffusées pendant la journée

day-to-day ['deɪtə'deɪ] adj courant(e), quotidien(enne); **on a d. basis** au jour le jour

daze [deɪz] **1** n **in a d.** (from news) abasourdi(e); (from drug, blow) étourdi(e)
2 vt (of news) abasourdir; (of drug, blow) étourdir

dazed [deɪzd] adj (by news) abasourdi(e); (by drug, blow) étourdi(e)

dazzle ['dæzəl] vt also Fig éblouir

dazzling ['dæzlɪŋ] adj also Fig éblouissant(e)

DC [diː'siː] n (a) Elec (abbr **direct current**) courant m continu (b) (abbr **District of Columbia**) DC

deacon ['diːkən] n Rel diacre m

deaconess [diːkə'nes] n Rel diaconesse f

dead [ded] **1** adj (a) (not alive) mort(e); **a d. man** un mort; **a d. woman** une morte; Fig **to be d. to the world** dormir d'un sommeil profond; Fam **over my d. body!** moi vivant, jamais!; Fam **I wouldn't be seen d. in that dress!** je ne porterais cette robe pour rien au monde!; Fam **as d. as a doornail** or **a dodo** mort et bien mort; Fig **d. and buried** mort et enterré; Fam **if Dad finds out, you're for d.** si Papa l'apprend, il va te tuer; **the D. Sea** la mer Morte
(b) (numb) (limb) engourdi(e); **to go d.** s'engourdir
(c) (voice, eyes) éteint(e); (phone) sans tonalité; (battery) mort(e); **this place is d. in winter** cet endroit est mort en hiver; **d. ball** (in football) ballon m mort; also Fig **d. end** cul-de-sac m; Fig **d. weight** poids m mort
(d) (absolute) **calm** calme m plat; **d. heat** (in race) arrivée f ex aequo; Fam **it was a d. loss** ça n'a servi à rien; **he's a d. loss** c'est un bon à rien; Fam **to be a d. ringer for sb** être le sosie de qn
2 adv (a) (completely) **to be d. set against sth** être totalement opposé(e) à qch; **to stop d.** s'arrêter net; Fam **d. beat** or **tired** crevé(e); **d. slow** (sign) roulez au pas
(b) Fam (very) vachement
(c) (exactly) **on six o'clock** à six heures précises; **d. on time** exactement à l'heure
3 n **at d. of night** au plus profond de la nuit; **in the d. of winter** au cœur de l'hiver
4 npl **the d.** les morts mpl; **to rise from the d.** ressusciter d'entre les morts

deadbeat ['dedbiːt] n Fam feignant(e) m,f

deaden ['dedən] vt (blow, sound) amortir; (pain) calmer; **to become deadened to sth** devenir insensible à qch

deadline ['dedlaɪn] n (day) date f limite; (time) heure f limite; **to work to a d.** avoir un délai à respecter

deadlock ['dedlɒk] **1** n impasse f
2 vt **to be deadlocked** (of talks, negotiations) être au point mort

deadly ['dedlɪ] **1** adj (a) (poison, blow, enemy) mortel(elle); (weapon) meurtrier(ère); (silence) de mort; **d. nightshade** belladone f (b) Fam (boring) mortel(elle)
2 adv (very) **d. accurate** extrêmement précis(e); **d. boring** d'un ennui mortel; **to be d. serious** être on ne peut plus sérieux(euse)

deadpan ['dedpæn] adj (expression) figé(e); (humour) pince-sans-rire inv

deadwood ['dedwʊd] n Fig personnes fpl inutiles

deaf [def] **1** adj sourd(e); **d. and dumb** sourd-muet, sourde-muette; **to go d.** devenir sourd; **as d. as a post** sourd comme un pot; **to turn a d. ear to sb/sth** faire la sourde oreille à qn/qch; **the appeal fell on d. ears** l'appel n'a pas été entendu
2 npl **the d.** les sourds mpl

deaf-aid ['defeɪd] n appareil m acoustique

deafen ['defən] vt (make deaf) rendre sourd(e); (temporarily) assourdir

deafening ['defənɪŋ] adj assourdissant(e)

deafness ['defnəs] n surdité f

deal¹ [diːl] n (wood) planche f

deal² 1 *n* (a) *(agreement)* affaire *f*, marché *m*; **to do a d.** conclure un marché; **it's a d.!** marché conclu!; **to get a good/bad d.** faire une bonne/mauvaise affaire; **he's had a raw d.** on ne lui a jamais fait de cadeaux; *Fam Ironic* **big d.!** la belle affaire! **it's no big d.** ce n'est pas bien grave (b) *(amount)* **a good or great d.** beaucoup; **not a great d.** peu; **to have a great d. to do** avoir beaucoup à faire; **a good or great d. of my time** une grande partie de mon temps; **a good d. quicker/easier** beaucoup plus rapide/facile (c) *(in cards)* **whose d. is it?** c'est à qui de donner?; **your d.!** à vous de donner!

2 *vt (pt & pp dealt* [delt]) (a) *(cards)* donner, distribuer; **to d. sb/sth a blow** donner un coup à qn/qch (c) *(drugs)* vendre

3 *vi* (a) *(in card game)* donner, distribuer (b) *(trade)* **to d. in** leather faire le commerce des cuirs

▶**deal out** *vt sep (cards)* distribuer; **to d. out justice** rendre la justice

▶**deal with** *vt insep (subject)* traiter de; *(problem)* s'occuper de; **I know how to d. with him** je sais m'y prendre avec lui

dealer ['diːlə(r)] *n* (a) *(in card game)* donneur(euse) *m,f* (b) *Com* marchand(e) *m,f*; *(in cars)* concessionnaire *m*; *(in drugs)* dealer *m*, revendeur(euse) *m,f*

dealings ['diːlɪŋz] *npl* rapports *mpl*, relations *fpl*; **to have d. with sb** traiter avec qn

dealt [delt] *pt & pp* de **deal**

dean [diːn] *n Rel & Univ* doyen *m*

dear [dɪə(r)] 1 *n* **my d.** *(to man)* chéri; *(to woman)* chérie; **poor d.** mon pauvre/ma pauvre; **be a d. and...** sois un amour et...; *Fam* **an old d.** une grand-mère

2 *adj* (a) *(loved)* cher (chère); **to hold sb/sth d.** tenir à qn/qch; **a friend** un bon ami/une bonne amie; **a place d. to the hearts of...** un endroit cher à...; *Fam* **to run for d. life** se sauver à toutes jambes (b) *(in letter)* **D.** Sir Monsieur; **D. Madam** Madame; **D. Sir or Madam, D. Sir/Madam** Monsieur, Madame; **D. Mr Thomas** Cher M. Thomas; **D. Andrew** Cher Andrew; **My dearest Gertrude** Ma chère Gertrude (c) *(expensive)* cher (chère)

3 *adv (buy, sell)* cher; *Fig* **it cost me d.** ça m'a coûté cher

4 *exclam* **oh d.!** mon Dieu!

dearly ['dɪəlɪ] *adv (very much)* **to love sb d.** aimer qn de tout son cœur; **I would d. love to know** j'aimerais vraiment savoir; *Fig* **she paid d. for her mistake** elle a payé très cher son erreur

dearth [dɜːθ] *n* pénurie *f* (of de)

death [deθ] *n* (a) *(end of life)* mort *f*; **to put sb to d.** mettre qn à mort, exécuter qn; **a fight to the d.** une lutte à mort; **d. camp** camp *m* de la mort; **d. certificate** acte *m* de décès; **d. mask** masque *m* mortuaire; **d. penalty** peine *f* de mort; **d. rate** taux *m* de mortalité; *Am* **d. row** = quartier d'une prison où les condamnés attendent leur exécution; **d. sentence** condamnation *f* à mort; **d. squad** escadron *m* de la mort; **d. throes** agonie *f*; **d. toll** nombre *m* de morts; **D. Valley** la Vallée de la Mort; **d. warrant** ordre *m* d'exécution

(b) *(idioms)* **to look like d. (warmed up)** avoir l'air d'un déterré/d'une déterrée; **to be sick to d. of sth** en avoir marre de qch; **to be scared to d.** être mort(e) de peur; **those children will be the d. of me!** ces enfants finiront par me tuer!; **you'll catch your d. (of cold!)** tu vas attraper la crève!; **to be at d.'s door** être à l'article de la mort; **to sound the d. knell for sth** sonner le glas de qch

deathbed ['deθbed] *n* lit *m* de mort

deathly ['deθlɪ] *adj (pallor)* mortel(elle); *(silence)* de mort

deathtrap ['deθtræp] *n* **this house/car is a d.** cette maison/voiture est très dangereuse

deathwatch beetle ['deθwɒt∫'biːtəl] *n* vrillette *f*

debacle [deɪ'bɑːkəl] *n* débâcle *f*

debar [dɪ'bɑː(r)] *(pt & pp debarred) vt (from club)* exclure; **to d. sb from doing sth** interdire à qn de faire qch

debase [dɪ'beɪs] *vt (person)* rabaisser; *(reputation)* ternir; *(currency)* déprécier; **to d. oneself** se déprécier

debasement [dɪ'beɪsmənt] *n (of person)* rabaissement *m*; *(of currency)* dépréciation *f*

debatable [dɪ'beɪtəbəl] *adj* discutable

debate [dɪ'beɪt] 1 *n* discussion *f*; *(organized)* débat *m*; **after much d.** après bien des discussions

2 *vt (issue)* débattre de, discuter de; **he debated whether to do it** il se demandait s'il le ferait ou non

3 *vi* participer à des débats

debating society [dɪ'beɪtɪŋsəsaɪətɪ] *n* = société qui organise des débats

debauched [dɪ'bɔːt∫t] *adj* débauché(e)

debauchery [dɪ'bɔːt∫ərɪ] *n* débauche *f*

debilitate [dɪ'bɪlɪteɪt] *vt* débiliter

debilitating [dɪ'bɪlɪteɪtɪŋ] *adj* débilitant(e)

debility [dɪ'bɪlɪtɪ] *n* débilité *f*

debit ['debɪt] 1 *n* débit *m*; *Fig* **on the d. side,...** l'inconvénient, c'est que...

2 *vt (person, account)* débiter (**with** de)

debonair [debə'neə(r)] *adj* élégant(e) et raffiné(e)

debrief [diː'briːf] *vt* faire faire un compte rendu de fin de mission à

debriefing [diː'briːfɪŋ] *n* compte *m* rendu de fin de mission

debris ['debriː] *n (of building)* décombres *mpl*; *(of plane, car)* débris *mpl*

debt [det] *n* dette *f*; **to be in d.** avoir des dettes; *Fig* **I shall always be in your d.** je vous serai toujours redevable; **to owe sb a d. of gratitude** être redevable à qn; **d. collector** agent *m* de recouvrement

debtor ['detə(r)] *n* débiteur(trice) *m,f*

debug [diː'bʌg] *(pt & pp debugged) vt Comptr (program)* déboguer

debunk [diː'bʌŋk] *vt Fam (theory)* discréditer; *(myth)* détruire

debut ['deɪbjuː] *n* début *m*; **to make one's d.** faire ses débuts

Dec *(abbr December)* décembre

decade ['dekeɪd] *n* décennie *f*

decadence ['dekədəns] *n* décadence *f*

decadent ['dekədənt] *adj* décadent(e)

decaffeinated [diː'kæfɪneɪtɪd] *adj* décaféiné(e)

decant [dɪ'kænt] *vt* décanter

decanter [dɪ'kæntə(r)] *n* carafe *f*

decapitate [dɪ'kæpɪteɪt] *vt* décapiter

decathlon [dɪ'kæθlɒn] *n* décathlon *m*

decay [dɪ'keɪ] 1 *n* (a) *(of wood)* pourriture *f*; *(of teeth)* carie *f* (b) *(of civilization)* déclin *m*; *(of building)* délabrement *m*

2 *vi* (a) *(of wood)* pourrir; *(of teeth)* se carier (b) *(of civilization)* péricliter; *(of building)* se délabrer

decease [dɪ'siːs] *n Formal* décès *m*

deceased [dɪ'si:st] *Formal* **1** *n* **the d.** le défunt (la défunte)
 2 *adj* décédé(e)

deceit [dɪ'si:t] *n* tromperie *f*, supercherie *f*

deceitful [dɪ'si:tful] *adj (person)* fourbe; *(behaviour)* malhonnête

deceive [dɪ'si:v] *vt* tromper, abuser; **to be deceived by appearances** se laisser abuser par les apparences; **to d. oneself** se mentir à soi-même; **to d. sb into doing sth** faire faire qch à qn en le manipulant; **I thought my eyes were deceiving me** je n'en croyais pas mes yeux

decelerate [di:'seləreɪt] *vi* ralentir

December [dɪ'sembə(r)] *n* décembre *m*; *see also* **May**

decency ['di:sənsɪ] *n (respectability)* décence *f*; **to have the common d. to do sth** avoir la décence de faire qch; **he didn't even have the d. to tell us first** il n'a même pas eu la politesse de nous avertir avant

decent ['di:sənt] *adj* **(a)** *(respectable)* respectable; *Fam* **are you d.?** es-tu visible? **(b)** *(of acceptable quality, size)* convenable, correct(e) **(c)** *(kind)* gentil(ille)

decently ['di:səntlɪ] *adv* **(a)** *(respectably)* convenablement; **to dress d.** s'habiller décemment **(b)** *(to an acceptable degree)* convenablement, correctement **(c)** *(kindly)* gentiment

decentralization [di:sentrəlaɪ'zeɪʃən] *n* décentralisation *f*

decentralize [di:'sentrəlaɪz] *vt* décentraliser

deception [dɪ'sepʃən] *n* tromperie *f*, supercherie *f*

deceptive [dɪ'septɪv] *adj* trompeur(euse)

deceptively [dɪ'septɪvlɪ] *adv* **it looks d. easy** c'est moins facile que ça en a l'air; **she looks d. shy** c'est une fausse timide

decibel ['desɪbel] *n* décibel *m*

decide [dɪ'saɪd] **1** *vt (outcome, match, future)* décider de; **d. to do sth** décider de faire qch; **it was decided to wait for her reply** il fut décidé d'attendre sa réponse; **that was what decided me** c'est ce qui m'a décidé; **that decides the matter** ça règle la question
 2 *vi* décider; **to d. on sth** choisir qch; **to d. against doing sth** décider de ne pas faire qch; **they decided against going out** ils décidèrent de ne pas sortir; **to d. in favour of doing sth** décider de faire qch

decided [dɪ'saɪdɪd] *adj* **(a)** *(person)* décidé(e); *(opinion)* ferme **(b)** *(difference, preference, improvement)* net (nette)

decidedly [dɪ'saɪdɪdlɪ] *adv* **(a)** *(answer, say)* d'un ton résolu **(b)** *(very)* franchement; **he was d. unhelpful** il n'a pas été serviable du tout

decider [dɪ'saɪdə(r)] *n (goal)* but *m* décisif; *(match)* match *m* décisif

deciding [dɪ'saɪdɪŋ] *adj* décisif(ive)

deciduous [dɪ'sɪdjʊəs] *adj* à feuilles caduques

decimal ['desɪml] **1** *n* décimale *f*
 2 *adj* décimal(e); **d. point** virgule *f*; **correct to five d. places** exact(e) jusqu'à la cinquième décimale

decimalization [desɪməlaɪ'zeɪʃən] *n* décimalisation *f*

decimate ['desɪmeɪt] *vt* décimer

decipher [dɪ'saɪfə(r)] *vt* déchiffrer

decision [dɪ'sɪʒən] *n (a)* *(of question)* décision *f* **(b)** *(resolve)* fermeté *f*, résolution *f*

decision-making [dɪ'sɪʒənmeɪkɪŋ] *n* prise *f* de décision

decisive [dɪ'saɪsɪv] *adj* **(a)** *(person, manner)* résolu(e) **(b)** *(action, event)* décisif(ive)

deck [dek] **1** *n* **(a)** *(of ship)* pont *m*; *(of bus)* niveau *m*, étage *m*; **on d.** sur le pont; **d. chair** transat *m* **(b)** **d.** *(of cards)* jeu *m* (de cartes)
 2 *vt* **to d. oneself out in one's Sunday best** se mettre sur son trente et un

declaim [dɪ'kleɪm] *vt & vi* déclamer

declamatory [dɪ'klæmətərɪ] *adj* déclamatoire

declaration [deklə'reɪʃən] *n* déclaration *f*; **the D. of Independence** la Déclaration d'indépendance

declare [dɪ'kleə(r)] **1** *vt* déclarer; **to d. war (on)** déclarer la guerre (à); **have you anything to d.?** *(at customs)* avez-vous quelque chose à déclarer?
 2 *vi* **to d. for/against sth** se déclarer en faveur de/contre qch; *Old-fashioned* **I do d.!** ça alors!

declassify [di:'klæsɪfaɪ] *(pt & pp* **declassified)** *vt (document)* ne plus considérer comme confidentiel

declension [dɪ'klenʃən] *n Gram* déclinaison *f*

decline [dɪ'klaɪn] **1** *n* déclin *m*; **to go into d.** *(of person, company, industry)* dépérir; *(of economy)* perdre de sa vigueur; *(of health)* se détériorer; **to be on the d.** *(of inflation, crime)* être en baisse
 2 *vt* **(a)** *(offer, invitation)* décliner; **to d. to do sth** refuser de faire qch **(b)** *Gram* décliner
 3 *vi* **(a)** *(refuse)* refuser **(b)** *(of health, influence)* décliner, baisser; **to d. in importance** perdre de son importance

declining [dɪ'klaɪnɪŋ] *adj (decreasing)* en baisse; *(deteriorating)* déclinant(e)

decode [di:'kəʊd] *vt* décoder

decompose [di:kəm'pəʊz] *vi* se décomposer

decomposition [di:kɒmpə'zɪʃən] *n* décomposition *f*

decompression [di:kəm'preʃən] *n* décompression *f*; **d. chamber** chambre *f* de décompression; **d. sickness** maladie *f* des caissons

decongestant [di:kən'dʒestənt] *n Med* décongestionnant *m*

decontaminate [di:kən'tæmɪneɪt] *vt* décontaminer

decor ['deɪkɔ:(r)] *n* décor *m*

decorate ['dekəreɪt] *vt* **(a)** *(with decorations)* décorer (**with** de) **(b)** *(with paint)* peindre; *(with wallpaper)* tapisser **(c)** *(with medal)* décorer

decoration [dekə'reɪʃən] *n* **(a)** *(of room, cake)* décoration *f* **(b)** *(medal)* décoration *f*, médaille *f*

decorative ['dekərətɪv] *adj* décoratif(ive)

decorator ['dekəreɪtə(r)] *n* **(painter and) d.** (peintre *m*) décorateur *m*

decorous ['dekərəs] *adj Formal* bienséant(e)

decorum [dɪ'kɔ:rəm] *n* convenances *fpl*, décorum *m*

decoy 1 *n* ['di:kɔɪ] *also Fig* leurre *m*
 2 *vt* [dɪ'kɔɪ] leurrer

decrease 1 *n* ['di:kri:s] diminution *f*, baisse *f* (**in** de); **to be on the d.** être en diminution
 2 *vt* [di:'kri:s] réduire, baisser
 3 *vi* diminuer, baisser

decreasing [di:'kri:sɪŋ] *adj* décroissant(e), en baisse

decree [dɪ'kri:] **1** *n* décret *m*; *Law* **d. absolute** jugement irrévocable; **d. nisi** jugement *m* provisoire
 2 *vt* décréter

decrepit [dɪ'krepɪt] *adj (person)* décrépit(e); *(thing)* délabré(e)

decriminalize [di:'krɪmɪnəlaɪz] *vt* dépénaliser

decry [dɪ'kraɪ] *(pt & pp* **decried)** *vt* décrier

dedicate ['dedɪkeɪt] *vt (book, song)* dédier (**to** à); **to d. oneself to sth** se consacrer à qch; **she dedicated her life to helping the poor** elle a consacré sa vie aux pauvres

dedicated ['dedɪkeɪtɪd] *adj* **(a)** *(committed)* consciencieux(euse); **to be d. to sth** se consacrer à qch; **she is d. to helping the poor** elle se consacre aux pauvres; **he is d. to his family** il est entièrement dévoué à sa famille **(b)** *Comptr* spécialisé(e); **d. word processor** machine f servant uniquement au traitement de texte

dedication [dedɪ'keɪʃən] *n* **(a)** *(of book, song)* dédicace f **(b)** *(devotion)* dévouement m

deduce [dɪ'dʒuːs] *vt* déduire (**from** de)

deduct [dɪ'dʌkt] *vt* déduire (**from** de)

deductible [dɪ'dʌktəbəl] *adj* déductible; *Fin* **d. for tax purposes** déductible des impôts

deduction [dɪ'dʌkʃən] *n* **(a)** *(subtraction)* déduction f; **after deductions** une fois les prélèvements effectués **(b)** *(conclusion)* déduction f; **by a process of d.** par déduction

deed [diːd] *n* **(a)** *(action)* acte m, action f; **to do one's good d. for the day** faire sa bonne action de la journée **(b)** *Law (document)* acte m notarié; **d. of covenant** = document par lequel on s'engage à verser régulièrement une somme à un organisme; **to change one's name by d. poll** changer légalement son nom

deem [diːm] *vt Formal* juger, estimer

deep [diːp] **1** *n Lit* **the d.** l'océan m
2 *adj* **(a)** *(water, sleep, thinker, cut)* profond(e); **to be 10 metres d.** faire 10 mètres de profondeur; **two/four d.** sur deux/quatre rangs; *Fig* **to be in d. water** être dans le pétrin; **d. in debt** criblé(e) de dettes; **d. in thought** plongé(e) dans ses pensées; **d. end** *(of swimming pool)* côté m le plus profond; *Fig* **to go off the d. end** (at sb) s'emporter (contre qn); *Fig* **to be thrown in at the d. end** être mis(e) dans le bain; **the D. South** *(of United States)* le Sud profond **(b)** *(colour)* foncé(e), sombre; *(sound)* grave
3 *adv* profondément; **to walk d. into the forest** pénétrer profondément dans la forêt; **to look d. into sb's eyes** pénétrer qn du regard; **to work d. into the night** travailler tard dans la nuit; **d. down he's very kind** au fond il est très gentil; **to run d.** *(of emotions, prejudice, mistrust)* être profond(e)

deepen ['diːpən] **1** *vt (well, ditch)* approfondir; *(sorrow, interest)* augmenter; *Fig* **to d. sb's understanding of sth** permettre à qn de mieux comprendre qch
2 *vi* **(a)** *(of river, silence)* devenir plus profond(e); *(of conviction, belief)* augmenter; *(of mystery)* s'épaissir **(b)** *(of sound, voice)* devenir plus grave

deep-freeze ['diːp'friːz] *n* congélateur m

deep-fry ['diːp'fraɪ] *vt* faire cuire dans la friture

deep-fryer ['diːp'fraɪə(r)] *n* friteuse f

deep-rooted [diːp'ruːtɪd] *adj* profondément enraciné(e)

deep-sea ['diːp'siː] *adj* **d. diver** plongeur m sousmarin; **d. fishing** pêche f hauturière

deep-seated ['diːp'siːtɪd] *adj* profond(e)

deer ['dɪə(r)] *(pl* **deer)** *n (male)* daim m; *(female)* biche f

deerstalker ['dɪəstɔːkə(r)] *n (hat)* chapeau m de chasse *(à la Sherlock Holmes)*

deface [dɪ'feɪs] *vt (monument, statue)* dégrader; *(poster, wall)* barbouiller

de facto [deɪ'fæktəʊ] *adj & adv* de facto

defamation [defə'meɪʃən] *n* diffamation f

defamatory [dɪ'fæmətərɪ] *adj* diffamatoire

defame [dɪ'feɪm] *vt* diffamer

default [dɪ'fɔːlt] **1** *n* **(a)** *Law (failure to appear in court)* défaut m; *Fig* **by d.** par défaut **(b)** *Comptr* **d. drive** lecteur m par défaut; **d. font** police f par défaut
2 *vi Law* **(a)** *(fail to appear in court)* ne pas comparaître **(b)** *(fail to pay)* **to d. on alimony payments** manquer au versement de la pension alimentaire

defaulter [dɪ'fɔːltə(r)] *n Law* contumace mf; *(debtor)* débiteur(trice) m,f défaillant(e)

defeat [dɪ'fiːt] **1** *n* défaite f
2 *vt (army, opponent)* vaincre; *(government)* mettre en minorité; **that defeats the object or purpose** ça va à l'encontre du but recherché

defeatism [dɪ'fiːtɪzəm] *n* défaitisme m

defeatist [dɪ'fiːtɪst] *n & adj* défaitiste mf

defecate ['defəkeɪt] *vi* déféquer

defect 1 ['diːfekt] *n* défaut m
2 *vi* [dɪ'fekt] **to d. to the enemy** passer à l'ennemi

defection [dɪ'fekʃən] *n* défection f

defective [dɪ'fektɪv] *adj (machine, reasoning)* défectueux(euse); *(hearing)* déficient(e)

defector [dɪ'fektə(r)] *n* transfuge mf

defence, *Am* **defense** [dɪ'fens] *n* défense f; **to come to sb's d.** venir à l'aide de qn; **she said in her d. that...** elle a dit à sa décharge que...; *Law* **d. counsel** avocat m de la défense; **d. mechanism** *(psychological)* mécanisme m de défense; *Law* **witness for the d.** témoin m à décharge

defenceless, *Am* **defenseless** [dɪ'fensləs] *adj* sans défense

defend [dɪ'fend] **1** *vt* défendre (**from** *or* **against** contre)
2 *vi (in sport)* défendre

defendant [dɪ'fendənt] *n Law* défendeur(eresse) m,f

defender [dɪ'fendə(r)] *n* défenseur m

defending [dɪ'fendɪŋ] *adj* **d. champion** champion(onne) m,f en titre

defense, defenseless *Am* = **defence, defenceless**

defensible [dɪ'fensəbəl] *adj* défendable

defensive [dɪ'fensɪv] **1** *n* **on the d.** sur la défensive
2 *adj* défensif(ive); **to be/get d.** être/se mettre sur la défensive

defer [dɪ'fɜː(r)] *(pt & pp* **deferred) 1** *vt (postpone)* différer, remettre
2 *vi* **to d. to** s'en remettre à

deference ['defərəns] *n* déférence f; **out of** *or* **in d. to** par déférence pour

deferential [defə'renʃəl] *adj* déférent(e)

deferment [dɪ'fɜːmənt] *n* ajournement m, report m

defiance [dɪ'faɪəns] *n* défi m; **in d. of** au mépris de

defiant [dɪ'faɪənt] *adj (gesture, look)* de défi; *(person)* provocant(e)

deficiency [dɪ'fɪʃənsɪ] *(pl* **deficiencies)** *n* **(a)** *(lack) (of resources)* manque m; *(of vitamins, minerals)* carence f **(b)** *(flaw)* défaut m

deficient [dɪ'fɪʃənt] *adj* insuffisant(e); **to be d. in** manquer de

deficit ['defɪsɪt] *n Fin* déficit m

defile [dɪ'faɪl] *vt (memory)* salir; *(sacred place, tomb)* profaner

definable [dɪ'faɪnəbəl] *adj* définissable

define [dɪ'faɪn] *vt* définir

definite ['defɪnɪt] *adj* (a) *(precise)* *(views, plan, date, answer)* précis(e); *(decision)* définitif(ive) (b) *(noticeable)* *(advantage, improvement)* net *(nette)* (c) *(certain)* certain(e); *(insistent)* catégorique; **I can't be d.** je n'en suis pas sûr (d) *Gram* **d. article** article *m* défini

definitely ['defɪnɪtlɪ] *adv* (a) *(certainly)* sans aucun doute; **I'll d. be there** c'est sûr que j'y serai; **are you going? – d.!** est-ce que vous y allez? – absolument!; **d. not!** certainement pas! **he told me very d. that he didn't want to go** il m'a dit très clairement qu'il ne voulait pas y aller (b) *(noticeably)* *(improved, superior)* nettement

definition [defɪ'nɪʃən] *n* (a) *(of word)* définition *f*; **by d.** par définition (b) *(of image)* définition *f*; *(of binoculars)* netteté *f*

definitive [dɪ'fɪnɪtɪv] *adj* *(book)* qui fait autorité; *(version)* définitif(ive); **she was the d. Juliet** elle était la Juliette idéale

deflate [dɪ'fleɪt] 1 *vt* (a) *(ball, tyre)* dégonfler (b) *Econ* **to d. the economy** pratiquer une politique déflationniste (c) *(person)* démonter
2 *vi (of tyre)* se dégonfler

deflated [dɪ'fleɪtɪd] *adj (person)* déprimé(e)

deflation [dɪ'fleɪʃən] *n Econ* déflation *f*

deflationary [dɪ'fleɪʃənərɪ] *adj Econ* déflationniste

deflect [dɪ'flekt] 1 *vt (ball, bullet)* (faire) dévier; *(sound)* renvoyer; *(criticism)* détourner; *Fig (person)* détourner *(from de)*
2 *vi (of ball, bullet)* dévier

deflection [dɪ'flekʃən] *n (of ball, bullet)* déviation *f*

deforestation [diːfɒrɪ'steɪʃən] *n* déboisement *m*

deform [dɪ'fɔːm] *vt* déformer

deformation [diːfɔː'meɪʃən] *n* déformation *f*

deformity [dɪ'fɔːmɪtɪ] *(pl* **deformities***) n* difformité *f*

defraud [dɪ'frɔːd] *vt (tax office)* frauder; *(employer)* escroquer; **to d. sb of sth** escroquer qch à qn

defray [dɪ'freɪ] *vt Formal* **to d. sb's expenses** défrayer qn; **to d. the cost of sth** rembourser les frais de qch

defrost [diː'frɒst] 1 *vt (fridge)* dégivrer; *(food)* décongeler
2 *vi (of fridge)* se dégivrer; *(of food)* se décongeler

deft [deft] *adj* adroit(e), habile

defunct [dɪ'fʌŋkt] *adj (person)* défunt(e); *(organization)* dissous(oute); *(law)* abandonné(e)

defuse [diː'fjuːz] *vt also Fig* désamorcer

defy [dɪ'faɪ] *(pt & pp* **defied***) vt (authority, law)* braver; *(logic, analysis)* défier; **to d. description** défier toute description; **to d. sb to do sth** mettre qn au défi de faire qch

degenerate 1 *n & adj* [dɪ'dʒenərət] dégénéré(e) *m,f*
2 *vi* [dɪ'dʒenəreɪt] dégénérer *(into* en*)*

degeneration [dɪdʒenə'reɪʃən] *n* dégénérescence *f*

degradation [degrə'deɪʃən] *n* avilissement *m*; *(squalor)* misère *f*

degrade [dɪ'greɪd] *vt* avilir; **I won't d. myself by answering that** je ne m'abaisserai pas à répondre à cela

degrading [dɪ'greɪdɪŋ] *adj* dégradant(e)

degree [dɪ'griː] *n* (a) *(extent)* degré *m*, point *m*; **to a d.**, **to some d.** jusqu'à un certain point; **to such a d. that...** à *(un)* tel point que...; **by degrees** petit à petit; **a d. of risk** un certain risque; **a d. of truth** une part de vérité (b) *(of temperature, in geometry)* degré *m*; **it's 25 degrees** *(of temperature)* il fait 25 degrés (c) *(at university)* diplôme *m* universitaire; *(bachelor's)* ≃ licence *f*; *(master's)* ≃ maîtrise *f*; *(PhD)* doctorat *m*; **to take** *or* **do a d.** préparer un diplôme

dehumanize [diː'hjuːmənaɪz] *vt* déshumaniser

dehumidifier [diːhjuː'mɪdɪfaɪə(r)] *n* déshumidificateur *m*

dehydrated [diːhaɪ'dreɪtɪd] *adj* déshydraté(e); **to get d.** se déshydrater

dehydration [diːhaɪ'dreɪʃən] *n* déshydratation *f*

de-icer [diː'aɪsə(r)] *n* dégivreur *m*

deify ['diːɪfaɪ] *(pt & pp* **deified***) vt* déifier

deign [deɪn] *vt* **to d. to do sth** condescendre à *ou* daigner faire qch

deindustrialization [diːɪndʌstrɪəlaɪ'zeɪʃən] *n* désindustrialisation *f*

deity ['diːɪtɪ] *(pl* **deities***) n* divinité *f*, dieu *(déesse) m,f*

dejected [dɪ'dʒektɪd] *adj* abattu(e), découragé(e)

dejection [dɪ'dʒekʃən] *n* abattement *m*, découragement *m*

delay [dɪ'leɪ] 1 *n* retard *m*; **without d.** sans délai; **an hour's d.** une heure de retard; **all flights are subject to d.** tous les vols risquent d'avoir du retard
2 *vt* (a) *(project, decision, act)* retarder; *(traffic)* ralentir; **to be delayed** *(of train, plane)* avoir du retard; **delaying tactics** manœuvres *fpl* dilatoires (b) *(put off)* *(decision, publication)* différer; **we can't d. telling her any longer** on ne peut plus attendre davantage, nous devons le lui dire
3 *vi* tarder; **don't d.!** faites vite!

delayed-action [dɪleɪd'ækʃən] *adj (drug, fuse, shutter)* à retardement

delectable [dɪ'lektəbəl] *adj* délicieux(euse)

delegate 1 *n* ['delɪgət] délégué(e) *m,f*
2 *vt* ['delɪgeɪt] *(power, responsibility)* déléguer *(to* à*)*; **to d. sb to do sth** déléguer qn pour faire qch
3 *vi* déléguer

delegation [delɪ'geɪʃən] *n* délégation *f*

delete [dɪ'liːt] *vt* supprimer; **d. where inapplicable** rayer les mentions inutiles

deleterious [delɪ'tɪərɪəs] *adj Formal* délétère

deletion [dɪ'liːʃən] *n* suppression *f*

deli ['delɪ] *n Fam (shop)* épicerie *f* fine; *(café)* restaurant-traiteur *m*

deliberate 1 *adj* [dɪ'lɪbərət] (a) *(intentional)* délibéré(e); **it wasn't d.** ça n'était pas voulu (b) *(unhurried)* *(movement)* mesuré(e); *(person)* méticuleux(euse)
2 *vi* [dɪ'lɪbəreɪt] *(think)* réfléchir *(on* sur*)*; *(discuss)* délibérer *(on* sur*)*

deliberately [dɪ'lɪbərətlɪ] *adv* (a) *(intentionally)* délibérément; **she did it d.** elle l'a fait exprès (b) *(unhurriedly)* de façon mesurée

deliberation [dɪlɪbə'reɪʃən] *n* (a) *(thought)* réflexion *f*; *(discussion)* délibération *f*, débat *m* (b) *(unhurriedness)* mesure *f*; **with d.** posément

delicacy ['delɪkəsɪ] *(pl* **delicacies***) n* (a) *(quality)* délicatesse *f* (b) *(food)* mets *m* délicat

delicate ['delɪkət] *adj* délicat(e)

delicately ['delɪkətlɪ] *adv* (a) *(finely)* délicatement (b) *(tactfully)* avec délicatesse

delicatessen [delɪkə'tesən] *n (shop)* épicerie *f* fine; *(café)* restaurant-traiteur *m*

delicious [dɪ'lɪʃəs] *adj* délicieux(euse)

delight [dɪ'laɪt] 1 *n* plaisir *m*, joie *f*; **to my/her d.** à mon/son grand plaisir; **to take d. in sth** se réjouir de qch; **the car is a d. to drive** conduire cette voiture est un plaisir; **the delights of camping** les joies du camping; **the delights of Blackpool** les charmes de Blackpool
2 *vt* ravir, réjouir
3 *vi* **to d. in doing sth** prendre plaisir à faire qch; *Hum* **he delights in the name of Fergus Fotherington** il répond au joli nom de Fergus Fotherington

delighted [dɪ'laɪtɪd] *adj* ravi(e), enchanté(e) **(with** de)

delightful [dɪ'laɪtfʊl] *adj (person, smile)* charmant(e); *(meal, evening)* délicieux(euse)

delightfully [dɪ'laɪtfʊlɪ] *adv (sing, write)* merveilleusement

delimit [di:'lɪmɪt] *vt* délimiter

delineate [dɪ'lɪnɪeɪt] *vt (plan, proposal)* définir

delinquency [dɪ'lɪŋkwənsɪ] *n* délinquance *f*

delinquent [dɪ'lɪŋkwənt] *n & adj* délinquant(e) *m,f*

delirious [dɪ'lɪrɪəs] *adj also Fig* délirant(e); **to be d.** délirer

deliriously [dɪ'lɪrɪəslɪ] *adv* follement; **d. happy** fou (folle) de joie

delirium [dɪ'lɪrɪəm] *n also Fig* délire *m*; *Med* **d. tremens** delirium tremens *m*

deliver [dɪ'lɪvə(r)] 1 *vt* **a** *(letter, parcel)* remettre, distribuer **(to** à); *(water, electricity, gas)* distribuer; *(goods)* livrer; **to have sth delivered** faire livrer qch; *Fig* **to d. the goods** tenir ses engagements **(b)** *(blow)* donner; *Sp (pass)* faire; *(speech, verdict)* prononcer; *(ultimatum)* poser; **to d. a service** proposer un service **(c)** *(baby)* mettre au monde
2 *vi* livrer; *Fig (keep one's promise)* tenir ses engagements; *Com* **we d.** nous livrons à domicile

deliverance [dɪ'lɪvərəns] *n Formal* délivrance *f* **(from** de)

delivery [dɪ'lɪvərɪ] *n (pl* **deliveries)** *n* **(a)** *(of letter, parcel)* distribution *f*, remise *f*; *(of goods)* livraison *f*; **to take d. of sth** prendre livraison de qch; **d. date** date *f* de livraison; **d. man** livreur *m*; **d. van** camion *m* de livraison **(b)** *(way of speaking)* diction *f* **(c)** *(of baby)* accouchement *m*

delta ['deltə] *n (of river, Greek letter)* delta *m inv*; **d. wing** *(of plane)* aile *f* delta

delude [dɪ'lu:d] *vt* tromper; **to d. oneself** se faire des illusions

deluge ['delju:dʒ] 1 *n also Fig* déluge *m*
2 *vt* inonder **(with** de)

delusion [dɪ'lu:ʒən] *n* illusion *f*; **to be under a d.** se faire des illusions; **delusions of grandeur** mégalomanie *f*

de luxe [dɪ'lʌks] *adj* de luxe, haut de gamme *inv*

delve [delv] *vi also Fig* **to d. into** fouiller dans

demagogue ['deməgɒg] *n* démagogue *mf*

demand [dɪ'mɑ:nd] 1 *n* **(a)** *(request)* demande *f*; exigence *f*; **to make demands on sb** exiger beaucoup de qn **(b)** *(for goods)* demande *f* **(for** de); **to be in d.** être demandé(e) ou recherché(e)
2 *vt* exiger, réclamer

demanding [dɪ'mɑ:ndɪŋ] *adj (person)* exigeant(e); *(job)* astreignant(e)

demarcation [di:mɑ:'keɪʃən] *n* démarcation *f*; *Ind* **d. dispute** conflit *m* d'attributions; **d. line** ligne *f* de démarcation

demean [dɪ'mi:n] *vt* humilier; **to d. oneself** s'abaisser

demeanour, *Am* **demeanor** [dɪ'mi:nə(r)] *n* comportement *m*

demented [dɪ'mentɪd] *adj* fou (folle)

dementia [dɪ'menʃɪə] *n* démence *f*

demerara sugar [demə'reərə'ʃʊgə(r)] *n* cassonade *f*

demigod ['demɪgɒd] *n* demi-dieu *m*

demilitarize [di:'mɪlɪtəraɪz] *vt* démilitariser

demise [dɪ'maɪz] *n also Fig* disparition *f*

demister [di:'mɪstə(r)] *n Br Aut* dispositif *m* antibuée

demo ['deməʊ] *(pl* **demos)** *n Fam* **(a)** *(protest)* manif *f* **(b)** **d. (tape)** maquette *f*

demob [di:'mɒb] *(pt & pp* **demobbed)** *vt Br Fam* démobiliser

demobilize [di:'məʊbɪlaɪz] *vt* démobiliser

democracy [dɪ'mɒkrəsɪ] *(pl* **democracies)** *n* démocratie *f*

Democrat ['deməkræt] *n (US politician)* démocrate *mf*

democrat ['deməkræt] *n* démocrate *mf*

democratic [demə'krætɪk] *adj* démocratique

democratically [demə'krætɪklɪ] *adv* démocratiquement

demographic [demə'græfɪk] *adj* démographique

demolish [dɪ'mɒlɪʃ] *vt (building, theory)* démolir; *Fam (eat)* engloutir; *(in game)* écraser

demolition [demə'lɪʃən] *n* démolition *f*

demon ['di:mən] *n* démon *m*; *Fam* **he's a d. tennis player** c'est un as du tennis

demonic [dɪ'mɒnɪk] *adj* démoniaque

demonstrable [dɪ'mɒnstrəbəl] *adj* démontrable

demonstrate ['demənstreɪt] 1 *vt (fact, theory)* démontrer; **to d. how sth works** montrer comment qch fonctionne
2 *vi (protest)* manifester **(for/against** pour/contre)

demonstration [demən'streɪʃən] *n* **(a)** *(of fact, theory)* démonstration *f* **(b)** *(political)* manifestation *f*

demonstrative [dɪ'mɒnstrətɪv] *adj also Gram* démonstratif(ive)

demonstrator ['demənstreɪtə(r)] *n* **(a)** *(protester)* manifestant(e) *m,f* **(b)** *(of machine)* démonstrateur(trice) *m,f*

demoralize [dɪ'mɒrəlaɪz] *vt* démoraliser

demoralizing [dɪ'mɒrəlaɪzɪŋ] *adj* démoralisant(e)

demote [dɪ'məʊt] *vt* rétrograder

demotion [dɪ'məʊʃən] *n* rétrogradation *f*

demur [dɪ'mɜ:(r)] *(pt & pp* **demurred)** *vi* soulever une objection

demure [dɪ'mjʊə(r)] *adj* réservé(e)

demystify [di:'mɪstɪfaɪ] *(pt & pp* **demystified)** *vt* démystifier

den [den] *n* **(a)** *(of lion, fox, bear)* antre *m*, tanière *f*; *Fig* **a d. of iniquity** un lieu de perdition; **a d. of thieves** un repaire de voleurs **(b)** *(room)* bureau *m*

denationalize [di:'næʃənəlaɪz] *vt* dénationaliser

denature [di:'neɪtʃə(r)] *vt* dénaturer

denial [dɪ'naɪəl] n (a) *(of request)* refus m; *(of right)* atteinte f; **d. of justice** déni m de justice (b) *(of accusation, rumour, guilt)* démenti m (c) *(psychological)* dénégation f

denigrate ['denɪgreɪt] vt dénigrer

denim ['denɪm] n (toile f de) jean m, denim m; **denims** *(jeans)* un jean; **d. skirt/shirt** jupe f/chemise f en jean

Denmark ['denmɑːk] n le Danemark

denomination [dɪnɒmɪ'neɪʃən] n (a) *(religious)* confession f (b) *Fin* valeur f

denominator [dɪ'nɒmɪneɪtə(r)] n *Math* dénominateur m

denote [dɪ'nəʊt] vt indiquer

dénouement [deɪ'nuːmɒŋ] n dénouement m

denounce [dɪ'naʊns] vt dénoncer

dense [dens] adj (a) *(smoke, fog, jungle, crowd)* dense (b) *Fam (stupid)* bouché(e)

densely ['denslɪ] adv **d. populated** fortement peuplé(e); **d. wooded** très boisé(e)

density ['densɪtɪ] n densité f

dent [dent] 1 n bosse f; *Fig* **the wedding put a d. in his savings** le mariage a fait un trou dans ses économies 2 vt cabosser; *Fig (confidence)* entamer

dental ['dentəl] adj dentaire; **d. appointment** rendez-vous m chez le dentiste; **d. floss** fil m dentaire; **d. hygiene** hygiène f dentaire; **d. nurse** assistant(e) m,f dentaire; **d. surgeon** chirurgien-dentiste m

dentist ['dentɪst] n dentiste mf; **to go to the d.'s** aller chez le dentiste

dentistry ['dentɪstrɪ] n dentisterie f

dentures ['dentʃəz] npl *(set of)* **d.** dentier m

denude [dɪ'njuːd] vt dénuder; **to be denuded of sth** être dépourvu(e) de qch

denunciation [dɪnʌnsɪ'eɪʃən] n dénonciation f

deny [dɪ'naɪ] *(pt & pp denied)* vt (a) *(request)* refuser; **to d. sb his rights** priver qn de ses droits; **to d. oneself sth** se priver de qch (b) *(fact)* nier; *(rumour)* démentir; **to d. responsibility for sth** nier être responsable de qch; **to d. doing sth** nier avoir fait qch; **there's no denying that…** il est indéniable que…; **to d. all knowledge of sth** nier avoir connaissance de qch

deodorant [diː'əʊdərənt] n déodorant m; *(for room)* désodorisant m

depart [dɪ'pɑːt] vi *(leave)* partir *(from* de); **to d. from** *(tradition, subject, truth)* s'écarter de

department [dɪ'pɑːtmənt] n *(in company)* service m; *(in shop)* rayon m; *Univ* département m; *(of government)* ministère m; *Fig* **that's my d.** c'est mon rayon; **d. store** grand magasin m

departmental [diːpɑːt'mentəl] adj *(manager)* de service; *Univ* **d. head** chef m de département

departure [dɪ'pɑːtʃə(r)] n *(from place)* départ m; *(from tradition)* écart m; *(from plan)* modification f; **a new d.** un nouveau départ; **d. lounge** *(in airport)* salle f d'embarquement; **d. time** heure f de départ

depend [dɪ'pend] vi **to d. on** dépendre de; **that depends, it all depends** ça dépend; **to d. on sb** *(rely on)* compter sur qn; *(financially)* être à la charge de qn; **you can d. on it** tu peux compter là-dessus; **it depends on how much money I have** cela dépend de l'argent que j'ai; *Ironic* **you can d. on him to be late** tu peux compter sur lui pour être en retard

dependable [dɪ'pendəbəl] adj *(person, machine)* fiable; *(information)* sûr(e)

dependant [dɪ'pendənt] n personne f à charge

dependence [dɪ'pendəns] n *(reliance)* dépendance f *(on* à)

dependency [dɪ'pendənsɪ] *(pl dependencies)* n dépendance f

dependent [dɪ'pendənt] adj *(child)* à charge; **to be d. on** dépendre de; **to be d. on sb** *(financially)* être à la charge de qn

depict [dɪ'pɪkt] vt *(of painting)* représenter; *(of film, book)* décrire

depiction [dɪ'pɪkʃən] n *(in painting)* représentation f; *(in film, book)* description f

depilatory [dɪ'pɪlətərɪ] adj dépilatoire

deplete [dɪ'pliːt] vt réduire, diminuer

depletion [dɪ'pliːʃən] n réduction f, diminution f

deplorable [dɪ'plɔːrəbəl] adj déplorable

deplore [dɪ'plɔː(r)] vt déplorer

deploy [dɪ'plɔɪ] vt déployer

deployment [dɪ'plɔɪmənt] n déploiement m

depopulate [diː'pɒpjʊleɪt] vt dépeupler

depopulation [diːpɒpjʊ'leɪʃən] n dépeuplement m

deport [dɪ'pɔːt] vt *(criminal)* déporter; *(immigrant)* expulser

deportation [diːpɔː'teɪʃən] n *(of criminal)* déportation f; *(of immigrant)* expulsion f

deportment [dɪ'pɔːtmənt] n (a) *(posture)* maintien m (b) *(behaviour)* comportement m

depose [dɪ'pəʊz] vt déposer

deposit [dɪ'pɒzɪt] 1 n (a) *(in bank)* dépôt m; *Br* **d. account** compte m de dépôt (b) *(returnable)* caution f; *(first payment)* acompte m, arrhes fpl; **to put down a d. on sth** verser un acompte pour qch (c) *(of minerals)* gisement m; *(of wine)* dépôt m (d) *Br Pol* **to lose one's d.** perdre son cautionnement 2 vt déposer

deposition [diːpə'zɪʃən] n *Law* déposition f

depositor [dɪ'pɒzɪtə(r)] n *Fin* déposant(e) m,f

depot ['depəʊ] n *Mil & Com* dépôt m; *Am (bus station)* gare f routière

depravation [deprə'veɪʃən] n dépravation f

depraved [dɪ'preɪvd] adj dépravé(e)

depravity [dɪ'prævɪtɪ] n dépravation f

deprecate ['deprɪkeɪt] vt dévaloriser

deprecating ['deprɪkeɪtɪŋ], **deprecatory** ['deprɪkeɪtərɪ] adj désapprobateur(trice); **to be d. about sb/sth** dévaloriser qn/qch

depreciate [dɪ'priːʃɪeɪt] vi *(in value)* se déprécier

depreciation [dɪpriːʃɪ'eɪʃən] n *(in value)* dépréciation f

depress [dɪ'pres] vt (a) *(person)* déprimer; *Fig (prices)* faire baisser; *(economy, market)* affaiblir (b) *(press) (button, lever)* appuyer sur

depressed [dɪ'prest] adj *(person)* déprimé(e); *Fig (economy, market, region)* touché(e) par la crise; **to make sb d.** déprimer qn

depressing [dɪ'presɪŋ] adj déprimant(e)

depression [dɪ'preʃən] n (a) *(of person, economy)* dépression f (b) *Met* dépression f (c) *(hollow)* creux m; *(in landscape)* dépression f

deprivation [deprɪ'veɪʃən] n *(hardship)* privations fpl; **emotional d.** carence f affective

deprive [dɪ'praɪv] vt **to d. sb of sth** priver qn de qch

deprived [dɪ'praɪvd] *adj* défavorisé(e); *(childhood)* malheureux(euse)

dept *(abbr* **department)** dép.

depth [depθ] *n* profondeur *f*; **in d.** *(investigate, discuss)* en profondeur; **to be out of one's d.** *(of swimmer)* ne plus avoir pied; *Fig* ne pas être à la hauteur; **in the depths of winter** au cœur de l'hiver; **in the depths of despair** au plus profond du désespoir; *Naut* **d. charge** grenade *f* sous-marine; *Phot* **d. of field** profondeur de champ

deputation [depjʊ'teɪʃən] *n* délégation *f*

depute [dɪ'pjuːt] *vt* **to d. sb to do sth** charger qn de faire qch

deputize ['depjʊtaɪz] *vi* **to d. for sb** remplacer qn

deputy ['depjʊtɪ] *(pl* **deputies)** *n (second-in-command)* adjoint(e) *m,f*; *(replacement)* remplaçant(e) *m,f*; *(political representative)* député *m*; *Am (policeman)* shérif *m* adjoint; **d. head** *(of school)* directeur(trice) *m,f* adjoint(e); **d. manager** directeur(trice) *m,f* adjoint(e); **d. prime minister** vice-Premier ministre *m*

derail [dɪ'reɪl] **1** *vt Fig (project, plan)* faire avorter; **to be derailed** *(of train)* dérailler
2 *vi (of train)* dérailler

derailment [dɪ'reɪlmənt] *n* déraillement *m*

deranged [dɪ'reɪndʒd] *adj* dérangé(e)

derby [*Br* 'dɑːbɪ, *Am* 'dɜːbɪ] *(pl* **derbies)** *n* **(a)** *(football match)* derby *m* **(b)** *Am (hat)* chapeau *m* melon

deregulate [diː'regjʊleɪt] *vt (economy, market)* déréguler; *(prices)* libérer; *(industry)* déréglementer

deregulation [diː,regjʊ'leɪʃən] *n (of economy, market)* dérégulation *f*; *(of industry)* déréglementation *f*

derelict ['derɪlɪkt] *adj* abandonné(e); *(ruined)* en ruines

dereliction [derɪ'lɪkʃən] *n* abandon *m*; **d. of duty** manquement *m* au devoir

deride [dɪ'raɪd] *vt* ridiculiser

derision [dɪ'rɪʒən] *n* dérision *f*

derisive [dɪ'raɪsɪv] *adj* moqueur(euse)

derisory [dɪ'raɪsərɪ] *adj* dérisoire

derivation [derɪ'veɪʃən] *n (source)* origine *f*

derivative [dɪ'rɪvətɪv] **1** *n Chem & Gram* dérivé *m*
2 *adj* banal(e), sans originalité

derive [dɪ'raɪv] **1** *vt* dériver, provenir **(from** de); **to d. pleasure from sth** prendre plaisir à qch; **to be derived from** provenir de
2 *vi* **to d. from** provenir de

dermatitis [dɜːmə'taɪtɪs] *n Med* dermite *f*, dermatite *f*

dermatology [dɜːmə'tɒlədʒɪ] *n Med* dermatologie *f*

derogatory [dɪ'rɒgətərɪ] *adj* désobligeant(e)

derrick ['derɪk] *n* derrick *m*

derv [dɜːv] *n Br (fuel)* gas-oil *m*, gazole *m*

desalination [diːˌsælɪ'neɪʃən] *n* dessalement *m*

descend [dɪ'send] **1** *vt (hill, stairs)* descendre
2 *vi (go down)* descendre; *(of darkness, dusk)* tomber; **in descending order** en ordre décroissant; **every summer tourists d. on the town** chaque été les touristes débarquent en ville; *Fig* **to d. to sb's level** s'abaisser au niveau de qn **(b)** **to d. or be descended from sb** *(be related to)* descendre de qn

descent [dɪ'sent] *n* **(a)** *(of plane, from mountain)* descente *f* **(b)** *(ancestry)* **to be of Norman d.** être d'origine normande

describe [dɪs'kraɪb] *vt* décrire

description [dɪs'krɪpʃən] *n* description *f*; *(issued by police)* signalement *m*; **to answer** *or* **fit the d.** répondre au signalement; **beyond d.** indescriptible; **birds of all descriptions** des oiseaux de toutes sortes; **he's a journalist of some d.** il travaille dans le journalisme

descriptive [dɪs'krɪptɪv] *adj* descriptif(ive)

desecrate ['desɪkreɪt] *vt* profaner

desecration [desɪ'kreɪʃən] *n* profanation *f*

desegregation [diːsegrɪ'geɪʃən] *n* déségrégation *f*

desert[1] ['dezət] *n* désert *m*; **d. island** île *f* déserte

desert[2] [dɪ'zɜːt] **1** *vt* abandonner; **to d. one's post** *(of soldier)* déserter son poste
2 *vi (from army)* déserter

deserted [dɪ'zɜːtɪd] *adj* désert(e)

deserter [dɪ'zɜːtə(r)] *n* déserteur *m*

desertion [dɪ'zɜːʃən] *n Law* abandon *m* du domicile conjugal; *Mil* désertion *f*

deserts [dɪ'zɜːts] *npl* **he got his just d.** il a eu ce qu'il méritait

deserve [dɪ'zɜːv] *vt* mériter; **to d. to do sth** mériter de faire qch; **she deserves to be punished** elle mérite une punition

deserving [dɪ'zɜːvɪŋ] *adj (person)* méritant(e); *(action, cause)* méritoire; **to be d. of praise** être digne d'éloge

design [dɪ'zaɪn] **1** *n* **(a)** *(pattern)* *(on fabric, wallpaper)* motif *m* **(b)** *(style)* *(of car, furniture)* modèle *m*; *(of clothes)* coupe *f* **(c)** *(drawing)* *(of building, machine)* plan *m* **(d)** *(subject)* design *m*, stylisme *m* **(e)** *(planning)* *(of product, machine)* conception *f* **(f)** *(intention)* dessein *m*; **by d.** à dessein; **to have designs on** avoir des vues sur
2 *vt (building, vehicle)* concevoir; *(clothes, furniture)* créer; **to be designed for sth/to do sth** *(intended)* être destiné(e) à qch/à faire qch

designate ['dezɪgneɪt] **1** *vt* désigner; **to d. sb to do sth** désigner qn pour faire qch; **this area has been designated a national park** cette zone a été classée parc national
2 *adj* désigné(e)

designation [dezɪg'neɪʃən] *n* **(a)** *(appointment)* nomination *f*; *(of funds)* affectation *f* **(b)** *(title)* désignation *f*

designer [dɪ'zaɪnə(r)] *n* concepteur(trice) *m,f*; *(of building)* architecte *m,f*; *(of clothes)* styliste *m,f* (de mode); *(of theatre set)* décorateur(trice) *m,f*; **d. clothes** vêtements *mpl* de marque; **d. drugs** drogues *fpl* de synthèse

desirable [dɪ'zaɪərəbəl] *adj* souhaitable; *(job, location)* attrayant(e); *(sexually)* désirable; **a d. residence** une belle résidence

desire [dɪ'zaɪə(r)] **1** *n* désir *m*, envie *f*; **I have no d. to go** je n'ai aucune envie d'y aller
2 *vt* désirer; **to d. to do sth** désirer faire qch, avoir envie de faire qch; **it leaves a lot to be desired** ça laisse beaucoup à désirer

desirous [dɪ'zaɪərəs] *adj Formal* désireux(euse) **(of** de)

desist [dɪ'zɪst] *vi Formal* cesser; **to d. from doing sth** cesser de faire qch

desk [desk] *n (in school)* table *f*; *(with lid)* pupitre *m*; *(in office, home)* bureau *m*; *(hotel reception)* réception *f*; **d. diary** agenda *m*; **a d. job** un travail de bureau; **d. lamp** lampe *f* de bureau

desktop ['desktɒp] *n Comptr* **d. computer** ordinateur *m* de bureau; **d. publishing** publication *f* assistée par ordinateur

desolate ['desələt] *adj (place)* désolé(e); *(future, prospect)* sombre; *(person)* abattu(e), affligé(e)

desolation [desə'leɪʃən] *n* désolation *f*; *(of person)* affliction *f*

despair [dɪs'peə(r)] **1** *n* désespoir *m*; **to be in d.** être désespéré(e); **to drive sb to d.** désespérer qn

2 *vi* désespérer; **I d. of you** tu me désespères

despairing [dɪ'speərɪŋ] *adj* désespéré(e)

despatch [dɪ'spætʃ] = **dispatch**

desperate ['despərət] *adj* désespéré(e); **to be in d. need of sth** avoir désespérément besoin de qch; **to be d. to do sth** vouloir à tout prix faire qch; **to be d. for sth** avoir désespérément besoin de qch

desperately ['despərətlɪ] *adv* désespérément; *(ill)* très gravement; **to be in love** être éperdument amoureux(euse); **to be d. sorry about sth** être affreusement désolé(e) de qch

desperation [despə'reɪʃən] *n* désespoir *m*; **in d.** par désespoir

despicable [dɪ'spɪkəbəl] *adj* méprisable

despise [dɪ'spaɪz] *vt* mépriser

despite [dɪs'paɪt] *prep* malgré

despondency [dɪs'pɒndənsɪ] *n* abattement *m*

despondent [dɪ'spɒndənt] *adj* abattu(e)

despot ['despɒt] *n* despote *m*

despotic [dɪs'pɒtɪk] *adj* despotique

despotism ['despətɪzəm] *n* despotisme *m*

dessert [dɪ'zɜːt] *n* dessert *m*; **d. wine** vin *m* doux

dessertspoon [dɪ'zɜːtspuːn] *n* cuillère *f* à dessert

destabilize [diː'steɪbəlaɪz] *vt* déstabiliser

destination [destɪ'neɪʃən] *n* destination *f*; **to reach one's d.** arriver à destination; *Comptr* **d. disk/drive** disquette *f*/lecteur *m* cible

destine ['destɪn] *vt* destiner

destined ['destɪnd] *adj* (a) *(meant)* destiné(e); **to be d. to do sth** être destiné à faire qch; **he was d. to become famous** *(by fate)* il était destiné à devenir célèbre; *(reporting a fact)* il devait plus tard devenir célèbre (b) *(of plane, ship)* **d. for** à destination de

destiny ['destɪnɪ] *(pl* **destinies)** *n* destin *m*, destinée *f*

destitute ['destɪtjuːt] *adj* sans ressources; **to be utterly d.** être dans la misère

destroy [dɪs'trɔɪ] *vt* (a) *(damage, ruin)* détruire (b) *(animal)* abattre; *(vermin)* éliminer

destroyer [dɪs'trɔɪə(r)] *n (ship)* contre-torpilleur *m*

destruction [dɪs'trʌkʃən] *n* destruction *f*; *(damage)* ravages *mpl*

destructive [dɪs'trʌktɪv] *adj* destructeur(trice)

desultory ['desəltərɪ] *adj (conversation)* décousu(e); *(attempt)* peu convaincant(e)

detach [dɪ'tætʃ] *vt* détacher **(from** de); **to d. oneself (from)** s'éloigner (de)

detachable [dɪ'tætʃəbəl] *adj* amovible

detached [dɪ'tætʃt] *adj* (a) *(separate)* détaché(e), séparé(e); **to become** *or* **get d. from sth** se détacher de qch; **d. house** maison *f* individuelle, pavillon *m*; *Med* **d. retina** décollement *m* de la rétine (b) *(disinterested)* *(tone)* détaché(e); **he's rather d.** il sait garder ses distances

detachment [dɪ'tætʃmənt] *n* (a) *(military unit)* détachement *m* (b) *(objectivity)* détachement *m*

detail ['diːteɪl] **1** *n* (a) *(item of information)* détail *m*; **to pay attention to d.** être minutieux(euse); **to go into detail(s)** entrer dans les détails; **in d.** en détail; **details** *(information)* renseignements *mpl*; *(address and phone number)* coordonnées *fpl* (b) *Mil* détachement *m*

2 *vt* (a) *(describe)* détailler (b) *Mil* **to d. sb to do sth** donner l'ordre à qn de faire qch

detailed ['diːteɪld] *adj (account, description)* détaillé(e); *(work)* minutieux(euse)

detain [dɪ'teɪn] *vt (in prison)* placer en détention; *(in hospital)* garder; *(delay)* retenir; **such details need not d. us** ne nous laissons pas arrêter par de tels détails

detainee [diːteɪ'niː] *n* détenu(e) *m,f*

detect [dɪ'tekt] *vt* détecter

detection [dɪ'tekʃən] *n* travail *m* de détective; **to escape d.** *(of mistake, change)* passer inaperçu(e); *(of burglar)* ne pas être découvert(e)

detective [dɪ'tektɪv] *n (private)* détective *m*; *(police officer)* ≃ inspecteur(trice) *m,f* de police; **d. story** roman *m* policier; **d. work** enquêtes *fpl*

detector [dɪ'tektə(r)] *n* détecteur *m*

détente [deɪ'tɒnt] *n* détente *f*

detention [dɪ'tenʃən] *n* (a) *Law* détention *f*; *Law* **d. centre** = centre de détention pour mineurs (b) *Sch* retenue *f*

deter [dɪ'tɜː(r)] *(pt & pp* **deterred)** *vt* dissuader; **to d. sb from doing sth** dissuader qn de faire qch

detergent [dɪ'tɜːdʒənt] *n (for cleaning)* produit *m* de nettoyage

deteriorate [dɪ'tɪərɪəreɪt] *vi* se détériorer

deterioration [dɪtɪərɪə'reɪʃən] *n* détérioration *f*

determination [dɪtɜːmɪ'neɪʃən] *n* détermination *f*

determine [dɪ'tɜːmɪn] *vt* (a) *(decide)* **to d. to do sth** décider de faire qch; **to d. that...** décider que... (b) *(cause, date)* déterminer

determined [dɪ'tɜːmɪnd] *adj* déterminé(e), résolu(e); **to be d. to do sth** être déterminé *ou* résolu à faire qch; **I'm d. that we'll succeed** je suis déterminé à ce que nous réussissions

deterrent [dɪ'terənt] **1** *n* moyen *m* de dissuasion; **to act as a d.** avoir un effet dissuasif

2 *adj (effect)* dissuasif(ive)

detest [dɪ'test] *vt* détester

dethrone [diː'θrəʊn] *vt* détrôner

detonate ['detəneɪt] **1** *vt* faire exploser

2 *vi* exploser

detonation [detə'neɪʃən] *n* explosion *f*, détonation *f*

detonator ['detəneɪtə(r)] *n* détonateur *m*

detour ['diːtʊə(r)] *n* détour *m*

detoxification [diːtɒksɪfɪ'keɪʃən], *Fam* **detox** ['diːtɒks] *n* désintoxication *f*; **d. centre/programme** centre *m*/cure *f* de désintoxication

▸**detract from** [dɪ'trækt] *vt insep* diminuer; **I don't want to d. from her achievement, but...** je ne veux pas minimiser ce qu'elle a accompli, mais...

detractor [dɪ'træktə(r)] *n* détracteur(trice) *m,f*

detriment ['detrɪmənt] *n* **to the d. of** au détriment de; **without d. to** sans porter préjudice à

detrimental [detrɪ'mentəl] *adj* préjudiciable **(to** à); **to have a d. effect on** nuire à

detritus [dɪ'traɪtəs] *n* détritus *mpl*

deuce [djuːs] *n (in tennis)* égalité *f*

Deutschmark ['dɔɪt∫maːk] n (deutsche) mark m

devaluation [diːvæljuˈeɪ∫ən] n (a) (of currency) dévaluation f (b) (of person, achievement) dévalorisation f

devalue [diːˈvæljuː] vt (a) (currency) dévaluer (b) (person, achievement) dévaloriser

devastate ['devəsteɪt] vt (crops, village) dévaster; (person) anéantir; **I was devastated by the news** la nouvelle m'a anéanti

devastating ['devəsteɪtɪŋ] adj (storm, bombardment) dévastateur(trice); (news, findings, argument) accablant(e); (criticism) cinglant(e); (charm, beauty) irrésistible

devastation [devəsˈteɪ∫ən] n dévastation f

develop [dɪˈveləp] 1 vt (a) (skills, theory, argument) développer; (product) mettre au point (b) (region) développer; (site) aménager; **developed countries** pays mpl développés (c) (acquire) (infection, illness) attraper; (habit) prendre; **to d. a liking** or **taste for sth** se mettre à aimer qch (d) (film) développer

2 vi (a) (grow) se développer; **to d. into** devenir (b) (become apparent) apparaître

developer [dɪˈveləpə(r)] n (a) (of land) promoteur m (b) Phot révélateur m

developing [dɪˈveləpɪŋ] adj (region, country) en (voie de) développement; (crisis) en évolution

development [dɪˈveləpmənt] n (a) (growth) développement m; (of idea) évolution f; **d. aid** aide f au développement; Br **d. area** = zone à fort taux de chômage où l'État incite les industries à venir s'installer (b) (progress, change) développement m; **there have been some interesting developments** il y a eu quelques faits nouveaux intéressants; **the latest developments in medical research** les dernières découvertes médicales

deviant ['diːvɪənt] adj déviant(e)

deviate ['diːvɪeɪt] vi dévier (**from** de); Fig s'écarter (**from** de)

deviation [diːvɪˈeɪ∫ən] n déviation f (**from** par rapport à); Fig écart m (**from** par rapport à)

device [dɪˈvaɪs] n (a) (mechanism) dispositif m; (gadget) appareil m; (**explosive**) **d.** engin m explosif (b) (method, scheme) stratagème m; **to leave sb to their own devices** laisser qn se débrouiller

devil ['devəl] n (a) (evil spirit) diable m; **the D.** le Diable (b) Fam (person) **poor d.!** pauvre diable!; **you little d.!** (to child) petit diable!; **you lucky d.!** veinard! (c) Fam (for emphasis) **what the d. are you doing?** mais qu'est-ce que tu fabriques?; **how the d....?** comment diable...?; **we had a d. of a job moving it** nous avons eu un mal de chien à le déplacer (d) (idioms) **he's a bit of a d.** il est un peu obsédé; **go on, be a d.!** allez, laisse-toi tenter!; **to work like the d.** travailler comme un(e) fou (folle); **to be (caught) between the d. and the deep blue sea** avoir à choisir entre la peste et le choléra; **talk of the d.!** quand on parle du loup!; Prov **better the d. you know (than the d. you don't)** on sait ce qu'on perd, on ne sait pas ce qu'on trouve; **to play d.'s advocate** se faire l'avocat du diable

devilish ['devəlɪ∫] adj diabolique

devil-may-care ['devəlmeɪˈkeə(r)] adj insouciant(e)

devious ['diːvɪəs] adj (person, mind) retors(e); (scheme, route) tortueux(euse); (means) détourné(e)

devise [dɪˈvaɪz] vt imaginer, élaborer

devoid [dɪˈvɔɪd] adj dénué(e), dépourvu(e) (**of** de)

devolution [diːvəˈluː∫ən] n Pol décentralisation f

devolve [dɪˈvɒlv] 1 vt déléguer

2 vi **to d. on** incomber à; **power devolves on the regional assembly** le pouvoir appartient à l'assemblée régionale

devote [dɪˈvəut] vt consacrer (**to** à); **to d. oneself to** se consacrer à

devoted [dɪˈvəutɪd] adj (parent) dévoué(e); (admirer) fervent(e); **years of d. service** des années de bons et loyaux services; **they are d. to each other** ils sont très attachés l'un à l'autre

devotee [devəˈtiː] n (of writer, artist) admirateur(trice) m,f; (of idea) partisan m; (of sport, music) passionné(e) m,f

devotion [dɪˈvəu∫ən] n (to cause, friend, family) dévouement m; (to god, saint) dévotion f; **devotions** (prayers) prières fpl

devour [dɪˈvauə(r)] vt also Fig dévorer

devout [dɪˈvaut] adj (person) dévot(e); (wish) fervent(e)

dew [djuː] n rosée f

dewy-eyed [djuːˈaɪd] adj (loving) ému(e); (naive) ingénu(e)

dexterity [deksˈterɪtɪ] n dextérité f

dext(e)rous ['dekstrəs] adj adroit(e), habile

diabetes [daɪəˈbiːtiːz] n diabète m

diabetic [daɪəˈbetɪk] n & adj diabétique mf; **d. chocolate** chocolat m pour diabétiques

diabolical [daɪəˈbɒlɪkəl] adj (a) (evil) diabolique (b) Fam (very bad) épouvantable

diadem ['daɪədem] n diadème m

diagnose ['daɪəgnəuz] vt also Fig diagnostiquer

diagnosis [daɪəgˈnəusɪs] (pl diagnoses [daɪəgˈnəusiːz]) n also Fig diagnostic m

diagnostic [daɪəgˈnɒstɪk] adj diagnostique

diagonal [daɪˈægənəl] 1 n diagonale f

2 adj diagonal(e)

diagram ['daɪəgræm] n schéma m

dial ['daɪəl] 1 n (of clock, phone) cadran m; (control knob) bouton m

2 vt (pt & pp dialled, Am dialed) (phone number) composer; (operator, country) appeler

dialect ['daɪəlekt] n dialecte m

dialectic(al) [daɪəˈlektɪk(əl)] adj dialectique

dialling ['daɪəlɪŋ] n Br **d. code** indicatif m; **d. tone** tonalité f

dialogue, Am **dialog** ['daɪəlɒg] n dialogue m; Comptr **d. box** boîte f de dialogue

dialysis [daɪˈælɪsɪs] n Med dialyse f

diameter [daɪˈæmɪtə(r)] n diamètre m; **the wheel is 60 cm in d.** la roue a un diamètre de 60 cm

diametrically [daɪəˈmetrɪklɪ] adv diamétralement

diamond ['daɪəmənd] n (gem) diamant m; (shape) losange m; **diamonds** (card suit) carreau m; **d. jubilee** soixantième anniversaire m; **d. necklace/ring** collier m/bague f de ou en diamants

diaper ['daɪəpə(r)] n Am couche f

diaphanous [daɪˈæfənəs] adj diaphane

diaphragm ['daɪəfræm] n diaphragme m

diarrhoea, Am **diarrhea** [daɪəˈrɪə] n diarrhée f

diary ['daɪərɪ] (pl diaries) n (personal) journal m (intime); (for appointments) agenda m

diatribe ['daɪətraɪb] n diatribe f (**against** contre)

dice [daɪs] **1** *n* (*pl* **dice**) dé *m*; **to play d.** jouer aux dés **2** *vt* (*food*) couper en dés **3** *vi* **to d. with death** jouer avec sa vie

dicey ['daɪsɪ] *adj Fam* risqué(e)

dichotomy [daɪ'kɒtəmɪ] (*pl* **dichotomies**) *n* dichotomie *f*

dick [dɪk] *n* (a) *Vulg* (*penis*) bite *f* (b) *Am Fam* (*detective*) privé *m*

dickens ['dɪkɪnz] *n Br Fam* **who/what/why the dick....?** qui/que/pourquoi diable...?

dickhead ['dɪkhed] *n Br Vulg* (*idiot*) tête *f* de nœud

dicky ['dɪkɪ] *adj Br Fam* **to have a d. heart** avoir le cœur fragile

dictate 1 *n* ['dɪkteɪt] ordre *m*; **she followed the dictates of her conscience** elle fit ce que lui dictait sa conscience
2 *vt* [dɪk'teɪt] (a) (*letter, passage, conditions*) dicter (b) (*determine*) imposer; (*choice*) dicter
3 *vi* (a) (*dictate text*) dicter (b) (*give orders*) **to d. to sb** donner des ordres à qn; **I won't be dictated to!** je n'ai pas d'ordres à recevoir!

dictation [dɪk'teɪʃən] *n* dictée *f*; **to take d.** écrire sous la dictée

dictator [dɪk'teɪtə(r)] *n* dictateur *m*

dictatorial [dɪktə'tɔːrɪəl] *adj* (*power, regime*) dictatorial(e); (*manner, tone*) autoritaire

dictatorship [dɪk'teɪtəʃɪp] *n* dictature *f*

diction ['dɪkʃən] *n* (*pronunciation*) diction *f*; (*choice of words*) style *m*

dictionary ['dɪkʃənərɪ] (*pl* **dictionaries**) *n* dictionnaire *m*

did [dɪd] *pt of* **do**

didactic [dɪ'dæktɪk] *adj* didactique

diddle ['dɪdəl] *vt Fam* rouler; **he diddled me out of £500** il m'a escroqué 500 livres

didn't ['dɪdənt] = **did not**

die¹ [daɪ] *n* (a) (*pl* **dice** [daɪs]) (*in games*) dé *m*; **the d. is cast** les dés sont jetés (b) (*pl* **dies** [daɪz]) (*mould*) matrice *f*

die² [daɪ] (*pt & pp* **died**, *continuous* **dying**) **1** *vi* mourir (**from** or of de); **she is dying** elle est mourante; **to d. hard** (*of habit, rumour*) avoir la vie dure; *Fam* **never say d.!** il ne faut jamais désespérer!; *Fam* **I nearly died of shame** j'ai cru mourir de honte; *Fam* **to be dying to do sth** mourir d'envie de faire qch; *Fam* **I'm dying for a cigarette** je meurs d'envie de fumer une cigarette; **the engine died on me/us** le moteur a calé
2 *vt* **to d. a natural/violent death** mourir de mort naturelle/violente; *Fig* **to d. a death** (*of proposal*) tomber à l'eau; (*of performer*) faire une bide

▶**die away** *vi* (*of sound, voice*) s'affaiblir

▶**die down** *vi* (*of fire*) baisser; (*of wind*) tomber; (*of sound*) s'affaiblir; (*of excitement, scandal*) se calmer

▶**die off** *vi* mourir

▶**die out** *vi* (*of family, species*) s'éteindre

die-hard ['daɪhɑːd] **1** *n* réactionnaire *mf*
2 *adj* pur(e) et dur(e)

diesel ['diːzəl] **1** *n* (*fuel*) gas-oil *m*, gazole *m*; (*car, railway engine*) diesel *m*
2 *adj* (*engine, train*) diesel; **d. oil** or **fuel** gas-oil *m*, gazole *m*

diet ['daɪət] **1** *n* (*usual food*) alimentation *f*; (*restricted food*) régime *m*; **to be/go on a d.** être/se mettre au régime
2 *vi* être au régime

dietary ['daɪətərɪ] *adj* alimentaire; **d. fibre** fibres *fpl* (alimentaires)

dietician [daɪə'tɪʃən] *n* diététicien(enne). *m, f*

differ ['dɪfə(r)] *vi* (a) (*be different*) différer (**from** de); **to d. in size/colour** être de taille/couleur différente (b) (*disagree*) ne pas être d'accord; **to d. with sb** ne pas être d'accord avec qn; **I beg to d.** permettez-moi d'être d'un autre avis; **to agree to d.** garder chacun son opinion

difference ['dɪfərəns] *n* (a) (*disparity*) différence *f* (**between/in** entre/de); **that doesn't make any d.** ça ne fait aucune différence; **it makes no d. to me** cela m'est égal; **that makes all the d.** voilà qui change tout; **a car with a d.** une voiture pas comme les autres (b) (*disagreement*) désaccord *m*, différend *m*; **d. of opinion** divergence *f* d'opinion; **we have to settle our differences** il faut nous mettre d'accord

different ['dɪfərənt] *adj* (a) (*not the same*) différent(e) (**from** de); **that's quite a d. matter** ça, c'est une autre affaire; **she feels a d. person** elle ne se sent plus la même; **he just wants to be d.** il veut se singulariser (b) (*various*) différents(es), divers(es)

differential [dɪfə'renʃəl] **1** *n* (*in wages, prices*) écart *m*; *Math* **d. calculus** calcul *m* différentiel; *Aut* **d. (gear)** différentiel *m*
2 *adj* différentiel(elle)

differentiate [dɪfə'renʃɪeɪt] **1** *vt* différencier (**from** de)
2 *vi* faire la différence (**between** entre)

differently ['dɪfərəntlɪ] *adv* différemment

difficult ['dɪfɪkəlt] *adj* difficile; **to find it d. to do sth** avoir du mal à faire qch; **he's d. to get on with** il n'est pas commode; **you're just being d.** tu le fais exprès pour embêter le monde; **to make life d. for sb** compliquer la vie à qn

difficulty ['dɪfɪkəltɪ] (*pl* **difficulties**) *n* difficulté *f*; **to have d. in doing sth** avoir des difficultés *ou* du mal à faire qch; **to make difficulties for sb** créer des difficultés à qn

diffidence ['dɪfɪdəns] *n* manque *m* de confiance en soi

diffident ['dɪfɪdənt] *adj* peu sûr(e) de soi; **to be d. about doing sth** hésiter à faire qch

diffuse 1 *adj* [dɪ'fjuːs] diffus(e)
2 *vt* [dɪ'fjuːz] diffuser, répandre
3 *vi* se diffuser, se répandre

dig [dɪg] **1** *n* (a) (*in archaeology*) fouilles *fpl* (b) (*poke*) **a d. in the ribs** un coup de coude dans les côtes (c) (*remark*) pique *f*; **to have a d. at sb** lancer une pique à qn
2 *vt* (*pt & pp* **dug** [dʌg]) (a) (*hole, grave, ditch*) creuser; (*garden*) bêcher; *Fig* **she is digging her own grave** elle est en train de creuser sa propre tombe (b) (*thrust*) **to d. sth into sth** planter qch dans qch (c) *very Fam* (*like*) **she really digs that kind of music** ce genre de musique, ça la botte (d) *very Fam* (*look at*) mater; **d. that guy over there** mate un peu le mec, là-bas (e) *very Fam* (*understand*) piger; **you d.?** tu piges?
3 *vi* (*of person, animal*) creuser; (*in archaeology*) faire des fouilles; **to d. for sth** creuser pour trouver qch

▶**dig in 1** *vt sep Fig* **to d. one's heels in** s'entêter
2 *vi* (a) (*of soldiers*) se retrancher (b) *Fam* (*eat*) attaquer

▶**dig out** *vt sep* (a) (*bullet, splinter*) extraire; (*person from ruins, snow drift*) dégager (b) *Fam* (*find*) (*information*) dénicher

▶**dig up** *vt sep* (a) (*plant*) arracher; (*treasure, body*) déterrer; (*road*) excaver (b) *Fam* (*find*) (*information, person*) dénicher

digest 1 n ['daɪdʒest] *(summary)* condensé m
2 vt [dɪ'dʒest] *also Fig* digérer

digestible [dɪ'dʒestəbəl] *adj* digeste

digestion [dɪ'dʒestʃən] n digestion f

digestive [dɪ'dʒestɪv] *adj* digestif(ive); **d.** **(biscuit)** = sorte de sablé; **d. system/tract** système m/tube m digestif

digger ['dɪgə(r)] n *(machine)* excavateur m

digit ['dɪdʒɪt] n **(a)** *(finger)* doigt m; *(toe)* orteil m **(b)** *(number)* chiffre m

digital ['dɪdʒɪtəl] *adj* numérique; **d. recording** enregistrement m numérique

dignified ['dɪgnɪfaɪd] *adj* digne

dignify ['dɪgnɪfaɪ] *(pt & pp dignified)* vt donner de la dignité à; **I won't d. that remark with a response!** je ne m'abaisserai pas à répondre à cette remarque!

dignitary ['dɪgnɪtərɪ] *(pl dignitaries)* n dignitaire m

dignity ['dɪgnɪtɪ] n dignité f; **she considered it beneath her d. to respond** elle estimait indigne d'elle de répondre

digress [daɪ'gres] vi faire une digression; **to d. from** s'écarter de; **...,** **but I d. ...,** mais je m'égare

digression [daɪ'greʃən] n digression f

digs [dɪgz] npl Br Fam chambre f meublée

dike [daɪk] = **dyke**

dilapidated [dɪ'læpɪdeɪtɪd] *adj* délabré(e)

dilapidation [dɪlæpɪ'deɪʃən] n délabrement m

dilate [daɪ'leɪt] **1** vt dilater
2 vi se dilater

dilation [daɪ'leɪʃən] n dilatation f

dilatory ['dɪlətərɪ] *adj Formal (reply)* dilatoire; **to be d. in doing sth** tarder à faire qch

dilemma [daɪ'lemə] n dilemme m; **to be in a d.** être placé(e) devant un dilemme

dilettante [dɪlɪ'tæntɪ] n dilettante mf

diligence ['dɪlɪdʒəns] n application f, zèle m

diligent ['dɪlɪdʒənt] *adj* consciencieux(euse)

dill [dɪl] n aneth m

dilly-dally ['dɪlɪ'dælɪ] *(pt & pp dilly-dallied)* vi Fam *(loiter)* traînasser; *(hesitate)* tergiverser

dilute [daɪ'lu:t] **1** *adj* dilué(e)
2 vt *(liquid)* diluer; Fig *(policy, proposal)* édulcorer

dilution [daɪ'lu:ʃən] n Fig *(of policy, proposal)* édulcoration f

dim [dɪm] **1** *adj* **(a)** *(light, chance, hope)* faible; *(outline, memory)* vague; *(eyesight)* faible, trouble; *(future)* sombre; **to take a d. view of sth** avoir une piètre opinion de qch **(b)** *(stupid)* bête
2 vt *(pt & pp dimmed)* *(light)* baisser, atténuer
3 vi *(of light)* baisser

dime [daɪm] n Am *(pièce f de)* 10 cents mpl; Fam **it's not worth a d.** ça ne vaut pas un clou; Fam **they're a d. a dozen** il y en a à la pelle

dimension [daɪ'menʃən] n *also Fig* dimension f

diminish [dɪ'mɪnɪʃ] vt & vi diminuer; Law **diminished responsibility** responsabilité f atténuée

diminishing [dɪ'mɪnɪʃɪŋ] *adj* décroissant(e); **the law of d. returns** la loi des rendements décroissants

diminutive [dɪ'mɪnjʊtɪv] **1** n Gram diminutif m
2 *adj* minuscule

dimly ['dɪmlɪ] *adv (lit)* faiblement; *(remember, see)* vaguement

dimmer ['dɪmə(r)] n **d. (switch)** variateur m

dimple ['dɪmpəl] n fossette f

dimwit ['dɪmwɪt] n Fam andouille f

din [dɪn] n vacarme m

dine [daɪn] vi dîner

▶**dine out** vi dîner dehors; **to d. out on a story** rabâcher une histoire

diner ['daɪnə(r)] n **(a)** *(person)* dîneur(euse) m,f **(b)** Am *(restaurant)* petit restaurant m

ding-dong ['dɪŋ'dɒŋ] **1** n **(a)** *(sound)* ding dong m **(b)** Fam *(fight)* bagarre f
2 *adj* Fam *(argument, contest)* acharné(e)

dinghy ['dɪŋ(g)ɪ] *(pl dinghies)* n **(rubber) d.** canot m pneumatique; **(sailing) d.** dériveur m

dingo ['dɪŋgəʊ] *(pl dingoes)* n dingo m

dingy ['dɪndʒɪ] *adj (room, street)* miteux(euse); *(colour)* terne

dining ['daɪnɪŋ] n **d. car** *(on train)* wagon-restaurant m; **d. hall** *(in school)* réfectoire m; Form salle f à manger; **d. table** table f de salle à manger

dinner ['dɪnə(r)] n *(evening meal)* dîner m; *(lunch)* déjeuner m; **what's for d.?** qu'est-ce qu'on mange?; **to have d.** *(in evening)* dîner; *(at midday)* déjeuner; **d. hour** *(at school)* heure f du déjeuner; **d. jacket** smoking m; **d. lady** = femme de service dans une cantine scolaire; **d. party** dîner; **d. service** service m de table; **d. time** *(in evening)* heure du dîner; *(lunchtime)* heure du déjeuner

dinosaur ['daɪnəsɔ:(r)] n *also Fig* dinosaure m

dint [dɪnt] n Formal **by d. of** à force de; **by d. of her efforts** grâce à ses efforts

diocese ['daɪəsɪs] n Rel diocèse m

diode ['daɪəʊd] n Elec diode f

dioxide [daɪ'ɒksaɪd] n Chem dioxyde m

dip [dɪp] **1** n **(a)** *(slope)* descente f; *(hollow)* dépression f; *(in prices, figures)* baisse f **(b)** Fam *(swim)* baignade f; **to go for a d.** faire trempette **(c)** *(sauce)* = sauce dans laquelle on trempe des crudités, des biscuits salés etc
2 vt *(pt & pp dipped)* **(a)** *(immerse)* plonger **(b)** *(lower)* baisser; Br **to d. one's headlights** se mettre en codes *(quand on est en pleins phares)*
3 vi *(of ground)* descendre; *(of prices, temperature)* baisser; **the sun dipped below the horizon** le soleil descendit derrière l'horizon

▶**dip into** vt insep *(savings, capital)* puiser dans; *(book)* feuilleter

DipEd [dɪp'ed] n Br *(abbr Diploma in Education)* ≃ CAPES m

diphtheria [dɪf'θɪərɪə] n Med diphtérie f

diphthong ['dɪfθɒŋ] n Ling diphtongue f

diploma [dɪ'pləʊmə] n diplôme m

diplomacy [dɪ'pləʊməsɪ] n *also Fig* diplomatie f

diplomat ['dɪpləmæt] n diplomate mf

diplomatic [dɪplə'mætɪk] *adj* diplomatique; Fig *(person)* diplomate; **d. bag** valise f diplomatique; **d. corps** corps m diplomatique; **d. immunity** immunité f diplomatique

dipper ['dɪpə(r)] n *(ladle)* louche f; **the Big D.** *(constellation)* la Grande Ourse; **big d.** *(at fairground)* montagnes fpl russes

dipsomaniac [dɪpsə'meɪnɪæk] n dipsomane mf

dipstick ['dɪpstɪk] n (a) Aut jauge f de niveau d'huile (b) Fam (idiot) abruti(e) m,f

dire ['daɪə(r)] adj (consequences) tragique; Fam (bad) épouvantable; **to be in d. need of sth** avoir un besoin urgent de qch; **to be in d. straits** être dans une mauvaise passe

direct [dɪ'rekt, daɪ'rekt] 1 adj direct(e); (refusal, denial) catégorique; **the d. opposite** l'exact opposé; **to be a d. descendant of sb** descendre de qn en ligne directe; Elec **d. current** courant m continu; Fin **d. debit** prélèvement m automatique; **d. hit** coup m au but; **d. mail** publipostage m; Gram **d. object** complément m d'objet direct; Pol **d. rule** administration f centrale; Com **d. selling** vente f directe; Gram **d. speech** discours m direct; Fin **d. taxation** contributions fpl directes
2 adv directement; (broadcast) en direct (from de)
3 vt (a) (remark) adresser (at à); (gaze, light) diriger (at sur); (funds, effort) consacrer (towards à); **can you d. me to the station?** pouvez-vous m'indiquer le chemin de la gare?
(b) (company, actors) diriger; (traffic) régler; (play) mettre en scène; (film) réaliser
(c) (instruct) **to d. sb to do sth** ordonner à qn de faire qch; **as directed** selon les instructions

direction [dɪ'rekʃən] n (a) (way) direction f, sens m; **in the d. of** en direction de; **they ran off in all directions** ils sont partis en courant dans toutes les directions; **the town was surrounded by hills in all directions** la ville était entourée de tous côtés par des collines
(b) (management) (of project) direction f; (of play) mise f en scène; (of film) réalisation f; **under the d. of** (orchestra) sous la direction de
(c) **directions** (to place) indications fpl; (for use) instructions fpl; **to ask for directions** demander son chemin

directly [dɪ'rektlɪ, daɪ'rektlɪ] 1 adv (a) (go, write) directement; **to be d. descended from sb** descendre de qn en ligne directe
(b) (exactly) juste; **d. opposite** juste en face de
(c) (frankly) (answer, speak) ouvertement
(d) (soon) immédiatement; **I'll be there d.** j'arrive tout de suite
2 conj aussitôt que, dès que; **I'll come d. I've finished** je viendrai dès que j'aurai fini

director [dɪ'rektə(r)] n (manager) directeur(trice) m,f; (board member) administrateur(trice) m,f; (of film) réalisateur(trice) m,f; (of play) metteur m en scène; Br Law **D. of Public Prosecutions** = magistrat dont le rôle recouvre à la fois celui du procureur général et celui du procureur de la République

directorate [dɪ'rektər(e)ɪt] n (board) conseil m d'administration

directorship [dɪ'rektəʃɪp] n direction f

directory [dɪ'rektərɪ] n (pl directories) n (of phone numbers) annuaire m; Comptr répertoire m; (street) **d. index m** (des rues); Br **d. enquiries** renseignements mpl (téléphoniques)

dirge [dɜːdʒ] n chant m funèbre; Fam Fig chanson f lugubre

dirham ['dɪˈræm] n dirham m

dirt [dɜːt] n (a) (on clothes, body) saleté f; (mud) boue f; (soil) terre f; **to treat sb like a d.** traiter qn comme un chien; Fam **dog d.** crotte f de chien; **d. road** chemin m de terre
(b) Fam (scandal) cancans mpl, ragots mpl

dirt-cheap ['dɜːt'tʃiːp] Fam 1 adj donné(e)
2 adv pour trois fois rien

dirty ['dɜːtɪ] 1 adj (a) (unclean) (person, hands, clothes) sale; (with mud) crotté(e); **to get d.** se salir; also Fig **to get one's hands d.** se salir les mains; Fig **to wash one's d. linen in public** laver son linge sale en public (b) Fig (unpleasant, unsavoury) **it's a d. business** c'est une activité peu reluisante; **to give sb a d. look** regarder qn d'un sale œil; **d. work** sale boulot m (c) (book, film, joke) cochon(onne); (language, word) grossier(ère); **d. old man** vieux cochon m; **d. weekend** week-end m coquin; **"communism" is a d. word nowadays** "communisme" est un mot tabou de nos jours
2 adv (a) (fight) déloyalement (b) (obscenely) **to talk d.** dire des cochonneries (c) Fam (for emphasis) vachement; **a d. big hole** un sacré grand trou
3 vt (pt & pp dirtied) salir
4 Br Fam **to do the d. on sb** jouer un sale tour à qn

disability [dɪsə'bɪlɪtɪ] (pl disabilities) n handicap m, infirmité f; **d. allowance** pension f d'invalidité

disable [dɪs'eɪbəl] vt (person) rendre infirme; (ship) désemparer; (alarm system) désactiver

disabled [dɪs'eɪbəld] 1 adj **the d.** les handicapés mpl
2 adj handicapé(e); **d. toilet** toilettes fpl pour handicapés

disabuse [dɪsə'bjuːz] vt Formal **to d. sb (of an idea)** détromper qn

disadvantage [dɪsəd'vɑːntɪdʒ] 1 n désavantage m, inconvénient m; **to be at a d.** être désavantagé(e); **to put sb at a d.** désavantager qn
2 vt désavantager

disadvantaged [dɪsəd'vɑːntɪdʒd] adj défavorisé(e)

disaffected [dɪsə'fektɪd] adj mécontent(e); (stronger) révolté(e)

disaffection [dɪsə'fekʃən] n désaffection f

disagree [dɪsə'griː] vi (a) (quarrel) ne pas être d'accord; **to d. with sb (about)** ne pas être d'accord avec qn (sur) (b) (of reports, figures) ne pas concorder (c) (of climate, food) **to d. with sb** ne pas réussir à qn

disagreeable [dɪsə'griːəbəl] adj désagréable

disagreement [dɪsə'griːmənt] n (a) (failure to agree) désaccord m; **to be in d. with sb** être en désaccord avec qn (b) (quarrel) différend m (c) (discrepancy) différence f

disallow [dɪsə'laʊ] vt Formal (objection, claim) rejeter; (goal, try) refuser

disappear [dɪsə'pɪə(r)] vi disparaître

disappearance [dɪsə'pɪərəns] n disparition f

disappoint [dɪsə'pɔɪnt] vt décevoir

disappointed [dɪsə'pɔɪntɪd] adj déçu(e) (in or with par)

disappointing [dɪsə'pɔɪntɪŋ] adj décevant(e)

disappointment [dɪsə'pɔɪntmənt] n déception f; **to be a d.** être décevant(e)

disapproval [dɪsə'pruːvəl] n désapprobation f

disapprove [dɪsə'pruːv] vi désapprouver; **to d. of sth** désapprouver qch; **he disapproves of them** ils ne lui plaisent pas

disapproving [dɪsə'pruːvɪŋ] adj (tone, look) désapprobateur(trice); **to be d. of sth** désapprouver qch

disarm [dɪs'ɑːm] vt & vi désarmer

disarmament [dɪs'ɑːməmənt] n désarmement m; **d. talks** conférence f sur le désarmement

disarming [dɪs'ɑːmɪŋ] adj (smile, honesty) désarmant(e)

disarray [dɪsə'reɪ] n désordre m; **in d.** en désordre

disaster [dɪ'zɑːstə(r)] n désastre m; (earthquake, fire, crash) catastrophe f; **d. area** région f sinistrée; Fam Fig (person) maladroit(e) m,f; **d. movie** film m catastrophe

disastrous [dɪ'zɑːstrəs] adj désastreux(euse)

disband [dɪs'bænd] **1** vt (regiment) supprimer; (organization) dissoudre
2 vi (of organization) se dissoudre; (of regiment) être supprimé(e)

disbelief [dɪsbɪ'liːf] n incrédulité f; **in d.** (listen, watch) avec incrédulité

disbelieve [dɪsbɪ'liːv] vt ne pas croire

disburse [dɪs'bɜːs] vt Formal débourser

disc, Am **disk** [dɪsk] n disque m; Aut **d. brake** frein m à disque; **d. jockey** disc-jockey m

discard [dɪs'kɑːd] vt (person) laisser tomber; (plan, proposal) abandonner; (object) se débarrasser de

discern [dɪ'sɜːn] vt (shape, object) discerner; (sound, difference) percevoir

discernible [dɪ'sɜːnɪbəl] adj (shape, object) discernable; (sound, difference) perceptible

discerning [dɪ'sɜːnɪŋ] adj (person) perspicace; (taste) fin(e)

discharge 1 [dɪst'ʃɑːdʒ] **(a)** (of patient) sortie f; (authorization) autorisation f de sortie; (of prisoner) mise en liberté, libération f; (of soldier) libération; (for unfitness) réforme f **(b)** (of firearm) décharge f **(c)** (of gas, chemical) dégagement m; (of pus, fluid) écoulement m
2 vt [dɪs'tʃɑːdʒ] **(a)** (patient) laisser sortir; (prisoner) libérer; (employee) congédier, renvoyer; (soldier) libérer; (for unfitness) réformer **(b)** (firearm) décharger **(c)** (gas, chemical) dégager; (fluid) déverser; **to d. pus** suppurer **(d)** (duty, debt) s'acquitter de; (fine) payer

disciple [dɪ'saɪpəl] n disciple mf

disciplinary ['dɪsɪplɪnərɪ] adj disciplinaire

discipline ['dɪsɪplɪn] **1** n discipline f
2 vt (punish) punir; **to d. oneself** se discipliner

disclaim [dɪs'kleɪm] vt (renounce) renoncer à; (deny) démentir

disclaimer [dɪs'kleɪmə(r)] n démenti m

disclose [dɪs'kləʊz] vt révéler

disclosure [dɪs'kləʊʒə(r)] n révélation f

disco ['dɪskəʊ] (pl **discos**) n discothèque f, boîte f (de nuit)

discolour, Am **discolor** [dɪs'kʌlə(r)] vt (fade) décolorer; (stain) (with age) jaunir; (with smoke) noircir; **to become discoloured** se décolorer

discomfiture [dɪs'kʌmfɪtʃə(r)] n embarras m

discomfort [dɪs'kʌmfət] n (lack of comfort) inconfort m; (pain) légère douleur f; **to be in some d.** éprouver une légère douleur

disconcerting [dɪskən'sɜːtɪŋ] adj déconcertant(e)

disconnect [dɪskə'nekt] vt (gas, electricity, phone) couper; (machine, appliance) débrancher

disconsolate [dɪs'kɒnsələt] adj désespéré(e)(at par)

discontent [dɪskən'tent] n mécontentement m

discontented [dɪskən'tentɪd] adj mécontent(e) (with de)

discontinue [dɪskən'tɪnjuː] vt interrompre; Com **discontinued line** fin f de série

discord ['dɪskɔːd] n discorde f

discordant [dɪs'kɔːdənt] adj (opinions, sound) discordant(e)

discotheque ['dɪskətek] n discothèque f, boîte f (de nuit)

discount 1 ['dɪskaʊnt] n remise f; **at a d.** au rabais
2 vt (a) ['dɪskaʊnt] (price) baisser; (goods) solder **(b)** [dɪs'kaʊnt] (suggestion, rumours) ignorer, ne pas tenir compte de; (possibility, fact) écarter

discourage [dɪs'kʌrɪdʒ] vt (a) (dishearten) décourager **(b)** (dissuade) **to d. sb from doing sth** dissuader qn de faire qch

discouragement [dɪs'kʌrɪdʒmənt] n (a) (loss of enthusiasm) découragement m **(b)** (dissuasion) **to act as** or **be a d. (to sth)** avoir un effet dissuasif (sur qch)

discouraging [dɪs'kʌrɪdʒɪŋ] adj décourageant(e)

discourse Formal **1** n ['dɪskɔːs] (speech) discours m; (conversation) conversation f
2 vi [dɪs'kɔːs] **to d. (up)on sth** discourir sur qch

discourteous [dɪs'kɜːtɪəs] adj discourtois(e)

discourtesy [dɪs'kɜːtəsɪ] n impolitesse f

discover [dɪs'kʌvə(r)] vt découvrir

discovery [dɪs'kʌvərɪ] (pl **discoveries**) n découverte f

discredit [dɪs'kredɪt] **1** n discrédit m; **to be a d. to sb/sth** déshonorer qn/qch; **much to their d., they didn't even apologize** ils ne se sont même pas excusés, ce qui ne leur fait pas honneur
2 vt (person, theory) discréditer

discreet [dɪs'kriːt] adj discret(ète)

discrepancy [dɪs'krepənsɪ] (pl **discrepancies**) n décalage m (between entre)

discretion [dɪs'kreʃən] n (a) (tact) discrétion f **(b)** (judgement) jugement m; **at the manager's d.** à la discrétion du directeur; **to use one's own d.** juger par soi-même

discretionary [dɪs'kreʃənərɪ] adj discrétionnaire

discriminate [dɪs'krɪmɪneɪt] **1** vt distinguer (from de)
2 vi **to d. between** faire la différence entre; **to d. against** faire de la discrimination envers; **to be discriminated against** être victime de discrimination; **to d. in favour of** favoriser

discriminating [dɪs'krɪmɪneɪtɪŋ] adj perspicace

discrimination [dɪskrɪmɪ'neɪʃən] n (a) (bias) discrimination f **(b)** (taste) discernement m **(c)** (differentiation) différenciation f

discriminatory [dɪs'krɪmɪnətərɪ] adj discriminatoire

discursive [dɪs'kɜːsɪv] adj discursif(ive)

discus ['dɪskəs] n disque m

discuss [dɪs'kʌs] vt discuter de

discussion [dɪs'kʌʃən] n discussion f; **under d.** en discussion

disdain [dɪs'deɪn] **1** n dédain m
2 vt dédaigner; **to d. to do sth** dédaigner de faire qch

disdainful [dɪs'deɪnfʊl] adj dédaigneux(euse)

disease [dɪ'ziːz] n maladie f

diseased [dɪ'ziːzd] adj malade

disembark [dɪsɪm'bɑːk] vt & vi débarquer

disembodied [dɪsɪm'bɒdɪd] adj désincarné(e)

disenchanted [dɪsɪn'tʃɑːntɪd] adj désenchanté(e); **to be d. with sth** être déçu(e) par qch

disenchantment [dɪsɪn'tʃɑːntmənt] n désenchantement m

disengage [dɪsɪn'geɪdʒ] **1** vt dégager (from de); **to d. oneself from sth** se retirer de qch
2 vi se retirer (from de); Mil cesser le combat

disentangle [dɪsɪn'tæŋgəl] *vt* démêler

disfavour, *Am* **disfavor** [dɪs'feɪvə(r)] *n* to be in d. être en défaveur; **to fall into d. (with sb)** tomber en disgrâce (auprès de qn)

disfigure [dɪs'fɪgə(r)] *vt* défigurer

disfigurement [dɪs'fɪgəmənt] *n* défigurement *m*

disgrace [dɪs'greɪs] **1** *n (shame)* honte *f*; to be in d. **(with sb)** être en disgrâce (auprès de qn); **to be a d. to one's family/country** déshonorer sa famille/son pays; **it's a d.!** c'est une honte!
2 *vt* déshonorer, couvrir de honte; **to d. oneself** se déshonorer

disgraceful [dɪs'greɪsfʊl] *adj* honteux(euse); **it's a d.!** c'est honteux *ou* scandaleux!

disgracefully [dɪs'greɪsfʊlɪ] *adv* scandaleusement, honteusement

disgruntled [dɪs'grʌntəld] *adj* mécontent(e)

disguise [dɪs'gaɪz] **1** *n (costume)* déguisement *m*; **in d.** déguisé(e)
2 *vt* déguiser; **to d. oneself as** se déguiser en; **there is no disguising the fact that...** on ne peut pas cacher le fait que...

disgust [dɪs'gʌst] **1** *n* dégoût *m*; **to fill sb with d.** remplir qn de dégoût, écœurer qn; **in d.** dégoûté(e), écœuré(e)
2 *vt* dégoûter; **to be disgusted with oneself** se dégoûter

disgusting [dɪs'gʌstɪŋ] *adj* répugnant(e)

dish [dɪʃ] **1** *n (bowl, food)* plat *m*; **d. of the day** plat du jour; **dishes** *(crockery)* vaisselle *f*; **to do the dishes** faire la vaisselle
2 *vt Fam* **to d. the dirt** tout raconter
▸**dish out** *vt sep (food)* servir; *(money, advice)* distribuer
▸**dish up** *vt sep (meal)* servir

disharmony [dɪs'hɑːmənɪ] *n* désaccord *m*

dishcloth ['dɪʃklɒθ] *n (for washing)* lavette *f*; *(for drying)* torchon *m*

disheartening [dɪs'hɑːtənɪŋ] *adj* décourageant(e)

dishevelled [dɪ'ʃevəld] *adj (person, appearance)* débraillé(e); *(hair)* ébouriffé(e); *(clothes)* en désordre

dishonest [dɪs'ɒnɪst] *adj* malhonnête

dishonesty [dɪs'ɒnɪstɪ] *n* malhonnêteté *f*

dishonour, *Am* **dishonor** [dɪs'ɒnə(r)] **1** *n* déshonneur *m*
2 *vt* déshonorer

dishonourable, *Am* **dishonorable** [dɪs'ɒnərəbəl] *adj* déshonorant(e)

dishtowel ['dɪʃtaʊəl] *n* torchon *m*

dishwasher ['dɪʃwɒʃə(r)] *n (person)* plongeur(euse) *m,f*; *(machine)* lave-vaisselle *m inv*

dishwater ['dɪʃwɔːtə(r)] *n also Fig* eau *f* de vaisselle

dishy ['dɪʃɪ] *adj Br Fam* mignon(onne)

disillusioned [dɪsɪ'luːʒənd] *adj* désillusionné(e); to be d. **with sb/sth** être déçu(e) par qn/qch; **to become d.** perdre ses illusions

disincentive [dɪsɪn'sentɪv] *n* to be a d. **(to sth)** avoir un effet dissuasif (sur qch)

disinclination [dɪsɪŋklɪ'neɪʃən] *n* manque *m* d'enthousiasme **(to do sth** à faire qch)

disinclined [dɪsɪn'klaɪnd] *adj* to be d. **to do sth** être peu disposé(e) à faire qch

disinfect [dɪsɪn'fekt] *vt* désinfecter

disinfectant [dɪsɪn'fektənt] *n* désinfectant *m*

disinformation [dɪsɪnfɔː'meɪʃən] *n* désinformation *f*

disingenuous [dɪsɪn'dʒenjʊəs] *adj (person, answer)* peu sincère; *(manner, smile)* faux (fausse)

disinherit [dɪsɪn'herɪt] *vt* déshériter

disintegrate [dɪs'ɪntɪgreɪt] *vi* se désintégrer; *(of confidence)* s'effriter; *(of marriage, relationship)* se désagréger

disintegration [dɪsɪntɪ'greɪʃən] *n* désintégration *f*; *(of marriage, relationship)* désagrégation *f*

disinterest [dɪs'ɪntərɪst] *n (impartiality)* impartialité *f*; *(lack of interest)* désintérêt *m*, indifférence *f*

disinterested [dɪs'ɪntərɪstɪd] *adj (unbiased)* impartial(e); *(uninterested)* indifférent(e)

disinvestment [dɪsɪn'vestmənt] *n Fin* désinvestissement *m*

disjointed [dɪs'dʒɔɪntɪd] *adj (style, speech)* décousu(e); *(movements)* saccadé(e)

disk [dɪsk] *n* **(a)** *Comptr* disque *m*; *(floppy)* disquette *f*; **d. drive** unité *f* de disques **(b)** *Am* = **disc**

diskette [dɪs'ket] *n Comptr* disquette *f*

dislike [dɪs'laɪk] **1** *n* aversion *f* (**of** *ou* **for** pour); **we have the same likes and dislikes** nous avons les mêmes goûts; **to take a d. to sb/sth** prendre qn/qch en grippe
2 *vt* ne pas aimer; **I don't d. him** il ne me déplaît pas

dislocate ['dɪsləkeɪt] *vt* **(a)** *(shoulder, hip)* déboîter; **to d. one's shoulder** se déboîter l'épaule **(b)** *(plan, timetable)* perturber

dislocation [dɪslə'keɪʃən] *n* **(a)** *(of shoulder, hip)* déboîtement *m* **(b)** *(of plan, timetable)* perturbation *f*

dislodge [dɪs'lɒdʒ] *vt (opponent, President)* déloger **(from** de); *(brick, slate)* arracher; *(obstacle)* déplacer; *(something stuck)* décoincer

disloyal [dɪs'lɔɪəl] *adj* déloyal(e)

disloyalty [dɪs'lɔɪəltɪ] *n* déloyauté *f*

dismal ['dɪzməl] *adj (face, countryside)* lugubre; *(failure, performance)* lamentable; *(future)* sombre

dismantle [dɪs'mæntəl] *vt (empire, network)* démanteler; *(machine)* démonter

dismay [dɪs'meɪ] **1** *n* consternation *f*; **in d.** consterné(e); **(much) to my d.** à ma grande consternation
2 *vt* consterner

dismember [dɪs'membə(r)] *vt also Fig* démembrer

dismiss [dɪs'mɪs] *vt* **(a)** *(from job)* renvoyer **(b)** *(send away)* congédier; *(pupils)* libérer; *Mil* **d.1** rompez! **(c)** *(thought, theory)* rejeter; *(proposal, suggestion)* écarter; *(danger, threat)* ignorer; **she is dismissed as an airhead** elle est considérée comme une évaporée **(d)** *Law (case)* classer; *(appeal, charge)* rejeter

dismissal [dɪs'mɪsəl] *n* **(a)** *(of employee)* renvoi *m*, licenciement *m* **(b)** *Law (of case)* fin *f* de non-recevoir; *(of appeal, charge)* rejet *m*

dismissive [dɪs'mɪsɪv] *adj* dédaigneux(euse); **to be d. of sb/sth** faire peu de cas de qn/qch

dismount [dɪs'maʊnt] *vi (from horse, bicycle)* descendre, mettre pied à terre

disobedience [dɪsə'biːdɪəns] *n* désobéissance *f*

disobedient [dɪsə'biːdɪənt] *adj* désobéissant(e); **to be d. to sb** désobéir à qn

disobey [dɪsə'beɪ] *vt (person, order)* désobéir à; *(law)* enfreindre

disorder [dɪs'ɔːdə(r)] n (a) (confusion, unrest) désordre m; **in d.** en désordre (b) Med troubles mpl; **a nervous d.** des troubles nerveux

disordered [dɪs'ɔːdəd] adj désordonné(e)

disorderly [dɪs'ɔːdəlɪ] adj (untidy, unruly) désordonné(e); (crowd) agité(e); Law **d. conduct** atteinte f à l'ordre public

disorganization [dɪsɔːgənaɪ'zeɪʃən] n désorganisation f

disorganized [dɪs'ɔːgənaɪzd] adj désorganisé(e)

disorientate [dɪs'ɔːrɪənteɪt], **disorient** [dɪs'ɔːrɪənt] vt désorienter

disown [dɪs'əʊn] vt désavouer, renier

disparage [dɪs'pærɪdʒ] vt dénigrer

disparaging [dɪs'pærɪdʒɪŋ] adj méprisant(e)

disparate ['dɪspərət] adj disparate

disparity [dɪs'pærɪtɪ] (pl **disparities**) n disparité f

dispassionate [dɪs'pæʃənət] adj (calm) calme; (impartial) impartial(e)

dispatch [dɪs'pætʃ] 1 n (a) (of letter, parcel) expédition f, envoi m (b) (message) dépêche f; Mil **to be mentioned in dispatches** être cité(e) à l'ordre du jour; **d. rider** Mil estafette f; (courier) coursier(ère) m,f (c) Formal (promptness) promptitude f; **with d.** promptement
2 vt (a) (send) envoyer (b) (kill) liquider

dispel [dɪs'pel] (pt & pp **dispelled**) vt dissiper

dispensable [dɪs'pensəbəl] adj dont on peut se passer

dispensary [dɪs'pensərɪ] (pl **dispensaries**) n Med (in pharmacy) officine f; (in hospital) pharmacie f

dispensation [dɪspen'seɪʃən] n Law & Rel (exemption) dispense f (**from** de)

dispense [dɪs'pens] vt (justice) rendre; (advice) prodiguer; (medication) préparer; (of vending machine) distribuer

▶**dispense with** vt insep se passer de; **to d. with the need for sth** rendre qch superflu(e)

dispensing chemist [dɪs'pensɪŋ'kemɪst] n pharmacien(enne) m,f

dispersal [dɪs'pɜːsəl] n dispersion f

disperse [dɪs'pɜːs] 1 vt (seeds, people) disperser; (knowledge, information) propager
2 vi (of crowd) se disperser; (of darkness, mist, clouds) se dissiper

dispirited [dɪs'pɪrɪtɪd] adj découragé(e), abattu(e)

displace [dɪs'pleɪs] vt (a) (shift) déplacer; **displaced persons** personnes fpl déplacées (b) (supplant) remplacer, supplanter

displacement [dɪs'pleɪsmənt] n (a) (of water, people) déplacement m (b) (substitution) remplacement m

display [dɪs'pleɪ] 1 n (a) (of goods) étalage m; (of handicrafts, paintings) exposition f; **on d.** à l'étalage; (sign, notice) affiché(e); **d. cabinet** vitrine f; **d. copy** (of book) exemplaire m de démonstration; **d. window** vitrine f (b) (demonstration) démonstration f (c) Comptr écran m
2 vt (a) (goods) exposer; (sign, notice) afficher (b) (emotion) manifester; (talent, concern, ignorance) faire preuve de

displease [dɪs'pliːz] vt mécontenter, contrarier; **to be displeased with sb/sth** ne pas être satisfait(e) de qn/qch

displeasure [dɪs'pleʒə(r)] n déplaisir m, mécontentement m

disposable [dɪs'pəʊzəbəl] adj (a) (nappy, lighter) jetable (b) (funds, income) disponible

disposal [dɪs'pəʊzəl] n (a) (getting rid) enlèvement m, élimination f (b) (of property) cession f, vente f (c) (availability) **to have sth at one's d.** avoir qch à sa disposition

dispose [dɪs'pəʊz] vt Formal (arrange) disposer

▶**dispose of** vt insep (a) (rubbish) jeter, se débarrasser de; (problem) régler (b) (kill) se débarrasser de

disposed [dɪs'pəʊzd] adj (willing) **to be d. to do sth** être disposé(e) à faire qch

disposition [dɪspə'zɪʃən] n (a) (temperament) tempérament m, nature f (b) (inclination) tendance f; **to have a d. to do sth** avoir tendance à faire qch (c) Formal (arrangement) disposition f

dispossess [dɪspə'zes] vt déposséder (**of** de)

disproportionate [dɪsprə'pɔːʃənət] adj disproportionné(e) (**to** à)

disprove [dɪs'pruːv] (pp **disproved**, Law **disproven** [dɪs'prəʊvən]) vt réfuter

dispute [dɪs'pjuːt] 1 n (debate) controverse f; (argument) dispute f; **the matter in d.** l'objet de la controverse; **it's beyond d.** c'est incontestable; **it's open to d.** c'est contestable; (industrial) **d.** conflit m social
2 vt (discuss) discuter; (call into question) contester
3 vi se quereller (**with/about** avec/à propos de)

disqualification [dɪskwɒlɪfɪ'keɪʃən] n (from competition) disqualification f; **d. from driving** retrait m de permis

disqualify [dɪs'kwɒlɪfaɪ] (pt & pp **disqualified**) vt (from competition) disqualifier (**from** de); **to d. sb from driving** retirer le permis de conduire à qn

disquiet [dɪs'kwaɪət] n inquiétude f

disregard [dɪsrɪ'gɑːd] 1 n mépris m
2 vt ignorer, ne tenir aucun compte de

disrepair [dɪsrɪ'peə(r)] n délabrement m; **in (a state of) d.** délabré(e); **to fall into d.** se délabrer

disreputable [dɪs'repjʊtəbəl] adj (person) peu recommandable; (behaviour) peu honorable; (neighbourhood, pub) mal famé(e)

disrepute [dɪsrɪ'pjuːt] n discrédit m; **to bring sb/sth into d.** discréditer qn/qch; **to fall into d.** tomber en discrédit

disrespect [dɪsrɪ'spekt] n irrespect m; **to treat sb with d.** manquer de respect à qn; **I meant no d.** je ne voulais pas être irrespectueux

disrespectful [dɪsrɪ'spektfʊl] adj irrespectueux(euse); **to be d. to sb** manquer de respect à qn

disrupt [dɪs'rʌpt] vt perturber

disruption [dɪs'rʌpʃən] n (of traffic, life, routine) perturbation f; (of meeting) interruption f

disruptive [dɪs'rʌptɪv] adj perturbateur(trice); **to be d.** faire du chahut

dissatisfaction [dɪsætɪs'fækʃən] n mécontentement m (**with** envers)

dissatisfied [dɪ'sætɪsfaɪd] adj mécontent(e) (**with** de)

dissect [dɪ'sekt] vt also Fig disséquer

dissemble [dɪ'sembəl] vt & vi dissimuler

disseminate [dɪ'semɪneɪt] 1 vt propager, répandre
2 vi se propager, se répandre

dissension [dɪ'senʃən] n dissension f

dissent [dɪ'sent] 1 n désaccord m
2 vi être en désaccord (**from** avec)

dissenter [dɪ'sentə(r)] n Pol dissident(e) m,f

dissenting [dɪ'sentɪŋ] adj dissident(e)

dissertation [dɪsəˈteɪʃən] n mémoire m

disservice [dɪˈsɜːvɪs] n to do sb/sth a d. rendre un mauvais service à qn/qch

dissident [ˈdɪsɪdənt] n & adj dissident(e) m,f

dissimilar [dɪˈsɪmɪlə(r)] adj différent(e) (to de)

dissipate [ˈdɪsɪpeɪt] 1 vt (fears, doubts) dissiper; (money, energy) gaspiller
2 vi (of mist, doubts) se dissiper

dissipation [dɪsɪˈpeɪʃən] n (debauchery) débauche f

dissociate [dɪˈsəʊsɪeɪt] vt dissocier (from de); to d. oneself from sb/sth se dissocier ou se désolidariser de qn/qch

dissolute [ˈdɪsəluːt] adj dissolu(e)

dissolve [dɪˈzɒlv] 1 vt dissoudre
2 vi se dissoudre; to d. into tears fondre en larmes

dissuade [dɪˈsweɪd] vt to d. sb from doing sth dissuader qn de faire qch

distance [ˈdɪstəns] 1 n distance f; from a d. de loin; in the d. au loin; within five minutes' walking d. à cinq minutes de marche; a short d. away tout près; some d. away assez loin; to keep one's d. garder ses distances; to keep sb at a d. tenir qn à distance; Sp & Fig to go the d. tenir la distance; d. learning enseignement m à distance
2 vt to d. oneself from sb/sth prendre ses distances vis-à-vis de qn/qch

distant [ˈdɪstənt] adj (a) (far-off) lointain(e); in the d. past il y a très longtemps; in the d. future dans un avenir lointain; 3 kilometres d. à 3 kilomètres de distance (b) (reserved) distant(e) (c) (distracted) distrait(e); she had a d. look son regard était perdu dans le vague

distantly [ˈdɪstəntlɪ] adv (a) to be d. related to sb être un parent éloigné de qn (b) (distractedly) distraitement

distaste [dɪsˈteɪst] n dégoût m (for pour)

distasteful [dɪsˈteɪstfʊl] adj déplaisant(e)

distemper[1] [dɪsˈtempə(r)] n (animal disease) maladie f de Carré

distemper[2] n (paint) détrempe f

distend [dɪsˈtend] 1 vt distendre
2 vi se distendre

distil, Am **distill** [dɪsˈtɪl] (pt & pp distilled) vt distiller

distillery [dɪsˈtɪlərɪ] (pl distilleries) n distillerie f

distinct [dɪsˈtɪŋkt] adj (a) (different) distinct(e) (from de); as d. from par opposition à (b) (clear) clair(e); (preference, improvement, difference) net (nette); it's a d. possibility c'est fort possible

distinction [dɪsˈtɪŋkʃən] n (a) (difference) distinction f; to draw a d. between faire une distinction entre (b) (honour, excellence) distinction f; Ironic I had the d. of coming last j'ai eu l'honneur de venir en dernier; a writer/scientist of d. un écrivain/scientifique réputé; with d. (perform, serve) brillamment (c) (in exam) mention f bien

distinctive [dɪsˈtɪŋktɪv] adj distinctif(ive)

distinctly [dɪsˈtɪŋktlɪ] adv (a) (clearly) (speak, hear) distinctement; (remember) très bien; I d. told you not to do it je t'ai clairement dit de ne pas le faire (b) (decidedly) (better, easier) nettement; (stupid, ill-mannered) vraiment

distinguish [dɪsˈtɪŋgwɪʃ] 1 vt (a) (recognize) distinguer (b) (characterize, differentiate) distinguer (from de); distinguishing marks (on passport) signes mpl particuliers (c) to d. oneself (by sth/by doing sth) se distinguer (par qch/en faisant qch)
2 vi to d. between faire la distinction entre

distinguished [dɪsˈtɪŋgwɪʃt] adj (performance, career) brillant(e); (person, air) distingué(e)

distort [dɪsˈtɔːt] vt also Fig déformer

distorted [dɪsˈtɔːtɪd] adj also Fig déformé(e)

distortion [dɪsˈtɔːʃən] n also Fig distorsion f, déformation f

distract [dɪsˈtrækt] vt distraire; to d. sb's attention détourner l'attention de qn; to be easily distracted se laisser facilement distraire

distracted [dɪsˈtræktɪd] adj préoccupé(e)

distracting [dɪsˈtræktɪŋ] adj gênant(e), qui distrait

distraction [dɪsˈtrækʃən] n (a) (interruption, amusement) distraction f (b) (madness) to drive sb to d. rendre qn fou (folle)

distraught [dɪsˈtrɔːt] adj angoissé(e); d. with grief fou (folle) de douleur

distress [dɪsˈtres] 1 n (mental) désarroi m; (physical) douleur f; to be in d. (mentally) être bouleversé(e); (physically) souffrir; (of ship) être en détresse; d. signal signal m de détresse
2 vt (upset) bouleverser

distressed [dɪsˈtrest] adj bouleversé(e)

distressing [dɪsˈtresɪŋ] adj bouleversant(e)

distribute [dɪsˈtrɪbjuːt] vt (give out) & Com (supply) distribuer; (spread out) répartir

distribution [dɪstrɪˈbjuːʃən] n (giving out) & Com (supplying) distribution f; (spreading out) répartition f; d. of wealth distribution des richesses; Com d. cost coût m de distribution; d. rights droits mpl de distribution

distributor [dɪsˈtrɪbjʊtə(r)] n (a) (person, company) distributeur(trice) m,f; (of cars) concessionnaire mf (b) Aut distributeur m

district [ˈdɪstrɪkt] n (of country) région f; (of town, city) quartier m; (administrative) district m; Am d. attorney ≃ procureur m de la République; Br d. council conseil m municipal; d. nurse infirmière f visiteuse

distrust [dɪsˈtrʌst] 1 n méfiance f (of à l'égard de)
2 vt se méfier de

distrustful [dɪsˈtrʌstfʊl] adj méfiant(e); to be d. of se méfier de

disturb [dɪsˈtɜːb] vt (a) (interrupt) déranger; (criminal) surprendre; (someone's sleep) troubler; Law to d. the peace troubler l'ordre public (b) (worry) perturber (c) (disarrange) (papers, room) déranger; (surface of water) agiter; (ground) remuer

disturbance [dɪsˈtɜːbəns] n (a) (nuisance) dérangement m (b) (atmospheric, emotional) perturbation f (c) (fight) bagarre f; (riot) émeute f; to cause or create a d. semer le désordre; Law troubler l'ordre public

disturbed [dɪsˈtɜːbd] adj (night, sleep) agité(e); (mentally, emotionally) perturbé(e)

disturbing [dɪsˈtɜːbɪŋ] adj perturbant(e)

disunity [dɪsˈjuːnɪtɪ] n désunion f

disuse [dɪsˈjuːs] n to fall into d. tomber en désuétude

ditch [dɪtʃ] **1** n (at roadside) fossé m; (as defence) douve f; (for drainage) rigole f

2 vt Fam (get rid of) (thing) se débarrasser de; (plan, idea) abandonner; (boyfriend, girlfriend) plaquer

dither ['dɪðə(r)] Fam **1** n to be in a d. être dans tous ses états

2 vi hésiter, tergiverser; **stop dithering!** décide-toi!

ditto ['dɪtəʊ] adv idem; Fam **I'm hungry – d.** j'ai faim – itou ou moi aussi

ditty ['dɪtɪ] (pl ditties) n Fam chansonnette f

divan [dɪ'væn] n divan m; **d. bed** divan-lit m

dive [daɪv] **1** n (a) (of swimmer) plongeon m; (of submarine, diver) plongée f; **to make a d. for sth** (rush) se précipiter vers qch; **to go into a d.** (of plane) piquer du nez (b) Fam Pej (place) bouge m

2 vi (Am pt dove [dəʊv]) plonger; (of plane) piquer; **to d. for cover** plonger à couvert; **to d. for the exit/into the pub** se précipiter vers la sortie/au pub

diver ['daɪvə(r)] n plongeur(euse) m,f; (deep sea) scaphandrier m

diverge [daɪ'vɜːdʒ] vi (of rays, opinions) diverger; (of roads) se séparer; (of people) avoir des opinions divergentes

divergence [daɪ'vɜːdʒəns] n divergence f

divergent [daɪ'vɜːdʒənt], **diverging** [daɪ'vɜːdʒɪŋ] adj divergent(e)

diverse [daɪ'vɜːs] adj divers(e)

diversification [daɪvɜːsɪfɪ'keɪʃən] n diversification f

diversify [daɪ'vɜːsɪfaɪ] (pt & pp diversified) **1** vt diversifier

2 vi se diversifier

diversion [daɪ'vɜːʃən] n (a) (of traffic) déviation f; (of plane, funds) détournement m; **to create a d.** faire diversion (b) (amusement) distraction f

diversity [daɪ'vɜːsɪtɪ] n diversité f

divert [daɪ'vɜːt, dɪ'vɜːt] vt (a) (traffic) dévier; (plane, funds, attention) détourner (b) (amuse) to **d. oneself** se distraire

divest [daɪ'vest] vt Formal to **d. sb of sth** (authority) priver qn de qch; (possession) débarrasser qn de qch

divide [dɪ'vaɪd] **1** vt (a) (money, food) partager (between; among entre); **to d. sth in two/three** diviser qch en deux/trois (b) Math diviser (by par) (c) (separate) séparer (from de)

2 vi (of road) bifurquer; (of group) se diviser; **to d. and rule** diviser pour régner

3 n fossé m

▶**divide up** vt sep partager

divided [dɪ'vaɪdɪd] adj divisé(e)

dividend ['dɪvɪdend] n dividende m; Fig **to pay dividends** porter ses fruits

dividers [dɪ'vaɪdəz] npl (mathematical instrument) compas m à pointe sèche

dividing [dɪ'vaɪdɪŋ] adj **d. line** ligne f de démarcation; **d. wall** mur m de séparation

divine [dɪ'vaɪn] **1** adj also Fig divin(e)

2 vt deviner

diving ['daɪvɪŋ] n (in swimming pool) plongeon m; (sub-aqua) plongée f; **d. bell** cloche f à plongeur; **d. board** plongeoir m; **d. suit** scaphandre m

divinity [dɪ'vɪnɪtɪ] (pl divinities) n (a) (divine nature, god) divinité f (b) (subject) théologie f; (in school) instruction f religieuse

divisible [dɪ'vɪzɪbəl] adj divisible

division [dɪ'vɪʒən] n (a) (separation) partage m (b) (distribution) répartition f, partage m; **d. of labour** division f du travail (c) (discord) division f (d) (unit) division f; **first/second d.** (in sporting league) première/deuxième division

divisive [dɪ'vaɪsɪv] adj qui crée des divisions

divorce [dɪ'vɔːs] **1** n divorce m; **d. proceedings** procédure f de divorce

2 vt (husband, wife) divorcer de; **to get divorced (from sb)** divorcer (de qn) (b) Fig séparer (**from** de)

3 vi divorcer

divorcee [dɪvɔː'siː] n divorcé(e) m,f

divulge [daɪ'vʌldʒ] vt divulguer

DIY [diːaɪ'waɪ] n (abbr **do-it-yourself**) bricolage m

dizzy ['dɪzɪ] adj (a) (unsteady) étourdi(e); **to feel d.** avoir le vertige; Fig **to reach the d. heights of...** atteindre les hauteurs vertigineuses de...; **d. spell** étourdissement m (b) Fam (frivolous) écervelé(e); **a d. blonde** une blonde évaporée

DJ ['diːdʒeɪ] n (a) (abbr **disc jockey**) DJ m (b) Fam (abbr **dinner jacket**) smoking m

Djibouti [dʒɪ'buːtɪ] n Djibouti

DNA [diːen'eɪ] n (abbr **deoxyribonucleic acid**) ADN m

do¹ [dəʊ] n Mus do m

do² [duː]

> Les formes négatives sont **don't/doesn't** et **didn't**, qui deviennent **do not/does not** et **did not** à l'écrit, dans un style plus soutenu.

1 v aux (3rd person singular **does** [dʌz], pt **did** [dɪd], pp **done** [dʌn]) (a) (in negatives) **I don't speak French** je ne parle pas français; **I didn't see him** je ne l'ai pas vu

(b) (in questions) **do you speak French?** (est-ce que) tu parles français?; **did you see him?** (est-ce que) tu l'as vu?; **don't you speak French?** tu ne parles pas français?; **didn't you see him?** tu ne l'as pas vu?

(c) (for emphasis) **he DOES speak French!** mais oui, il parle français!; **I DIDN'T see him!** mais non, je ne l'ai pas vu!; **it doesn't matter – it DOES matter!** ce n'est pas grave – si, c'est grave!

(d) (as substitute for main verb) **she writes better than I do** elle écrit mieux que moi; **if you want to speak to her, do it now** si tu veux lui parler, fais-le tout de suite; **do you speak French? – yes, I do/no, I don't** parlez-vous français? – oui/non; **I like Paris – so do I** j'aime Paris – moi aussi; **you left the door unlocked – so I did** tu as laissé la porte ouverte – effectivement; **you said you would go – no, I didn't** tu as dit que tu irais – non, ce n'est pas vrai

(e) (in tag questions) **you speak French, don't you?** vous parlez français, n'est-ce pas ou non?; **John doesn't live there, does he?** John n'habite pas là, si?; **they said they'd come, didn't they?** ils ont bien dit qu'ils viendraient, non?; **you didn't see her, did you?** est-ce que tu l'as vue ou pas?

2 vt (a) (in general) faire; **what do you do?** (what's your job?) que faites-vous dans la vie?; **don't do that again!** ne refais jamais ça!; **what are you going to do about it?** qu'est-ce que tu vas faire?

(b) (activity) faire; **to do the housework/the dishes** faire le ménage/la vaisselle; **to do one's hair** se coiffer; **to do one's teeth** se brosser les dents; Fam **to do drugs** se droguer; **they do good food here** ils font de la bonne cuisine ici; **it just isn't done!** ça ne se fait pas, c'est tout!; Fam **let's do lunch!** on se fait une bouffe?

(c) *(have effect on)* **to do sb good** faire du bien à qn; **that hairstyle does nothing/does a lot for her** cette coiffure ne la flatte pas/la flatte; **this music does nothing for me** cette musique ne me plaît pas tellement (d) *(be enough for)* **will £10 do you?** est-ce que 10 livres te suffiront?; **that'll do me** ça m'ira (e) *(study)* faire; **to do French/physics** faire du français/de la physique (f) *(with speed, distance)* **the car was doing 100 (miles per hour)** ≃ la voiture faisait du 160 (à l'heure); **we did 500 km on the first day** nous avons fait 500 km le premier jour (g) *Fam (cheat)* avoir; **I've been done!** je me suis fait avoir! (h) *Fam (prosecute)* avoir; **to get done for speeding** se faire pincer pour excès de vitesse

3 *vi* (a) *(act)* **to do well/badly** bien/mal se débrouiller; **do as you're told** fais ce qu'on te dit; **you would do well to accept** tu ferais bien d'accepter; **how do you do?** enchanté(e); **how are you doing?** (comment) ça va? (b) *(be enough)* **two bottles of wine will do** deux bouteilles de vin suffiront; **that'll do** *(is satisfactory)* ça ira; *(stop it)* ça suffit maintenant!

4 *n* (a) **the do's and don'ts** les choses *fpl* à faire et à ne pas faire (b) *(pl* **dos**) *Fam (party)* fête *f*

▸**do away with** *vt insep* (a) *(abolish)* supprimer (b) *Fam (kill)* zigouiller

▸**do down** *vt sep* rabaisser; **to do oneself down** se rabaisser

▸**do for** *vt insep Fam* **to be done for** être fichu(e)

▸**do in** *vt sep Fam* (a) *(murder)* zigouiller (b) *(exhaust)* **to be done in** être complètement crevé(e) (c) *(injure)* **to do one's back/knee in** se bousiller le dos/genou

▸**do out of** *vt insep Fam* **to do sb out of sth** *(job)* priver qn de qch; *(money)* faire perdre qch à qn

▸**do over** *vt sep Fam* **to d. sb over** tabasser qn

▸**do up 1** *vt sep* (a) *(fasten)* fermer; *(shoelaces)* attacher (b) *(wrap)* envelopper (c) *(improve appearance of)* restaurer; *(room, house)* rénover; *Fam* **to do oneself up** *(dress smartly)* se faire beau (belle)

2 *vi (of clothes)* se fermer

▸**do with** *vt insep* (a) *(benefit from)* **I could do with a cup of tea** je prendrais bien une tasse de thé; **you could do with a haircut** tu aurais bien besoin de te faire couper les cheveux (b) *(be connected with)* **to have nothing to do with sb/sth** *(be unconnected to)* n'avoir rien à voir avec qn/qch; *(not get involved with)* n'avoir rien à faire avec qn/qch; **I had nothing to do with it** je n'ai rien à voir là-dedans; **it's nothing to do with you** *(not your business)* ça ne te regarde pas (c) *(finish using)* **to have done with sth** avoir fini avec qch; **have you done with the scissors yet?** est-ce que tu as fini avec les ciseaux?; **it's all over and done with** c'est du passé

▸**do without 1** *vt insep* se passer de

2 *vi* se priver

doc [dɒk] *n Fam (doctor)* toubib *m*

docile ['dəʊsaɪl] *adj* docile

dock¹ [dɒk] **1** *n (for ships)* dock *m*; **d. workers** dockers *mpl*

2 *vi (of ship)* accoster; *(of two spacecraft)* s'arrimer

dock² *n Law* banc *m* des accusés

dock³ *vt* (a) *(tail)* couper (b) *(wages)* faire une retenue sur

docker ['dɒkə(r)] *n* docker *m*

dockyard ['dɒkjɑːd] *n* chantier *m* naval

doctor ['dɒktə(r)] **1** *n* (a) *(medical)* docteur *m*, médecin *m*; **to go to the d.('s)** aller chez le médecin; *Fam Fig* **just what the d. ordered** exactement ce qu'il me fallait (b) *Univ* docteur *m*; **D. of Science** docteur ès sciences

2 *vt* (a) *Fam (accounts, evidence)* falsifier (b) *(cat)* castrer

doctorate ['dɒktərɪt] *n Univ* doctorat *m* (**in** en)

doctrinaire [dɒktrɪ'neə(r)] *adj* doctrinaire

doctrinal [dɒk'traɪnəl] *adj* doctrinal(e)

doctrine ['dɒktrɪn] *n* doctrine *f*

document 1 *n* ['dɒkjʊmənt] document *m*; *Comptr* **d. reader** lecteur *m* de documents

2 *vt* ['dɒkjʊment] (a) *(show in detail)* présenter (b) *(support)* étayer; **the first documented case** le premier cas établi

documentary [dɒkjʊ'mentərɪ] **1** *n (pl* **documentaries)** *(TV programme)* documentaire *m*

2 *adj (film)* documentaire; *(proof)* littéral(e)

documentation [dɒkjʊmen'teɪʃən] *n* documentation *f*

dodder ['dɒdə(r)] *vi* marcher d'un pas hésitant

doddering ['dɒdərɪŋ] *adj (walk)* hésitant(e); **a d. old fool** un vieux gâteux (une vieille gâteuse)

doddle ['dɒdəl] *n Fam* **it's a d.** c'est simple comme bonjour

dodge [dɒdʒ] **1** *n* (a) *Fam (trick)* truc *m*, combine *f*; **tax d.** combine pour payer moins d'impôts (b) *(movement)* écart *m*

2 *vt (blow, responsibility, question)* esquiver; *(person)* éviter; *(police)* échapper à

3 *vi* **to d.** *(out of the way)* faire un bond de côté

dodgems ['dɒdʒəmz] *npl* autos *fpl* tamponneuses

dodgy ['dɒdʒɪ] *adj Br Fam (suspect)* louche; *(not working properly)* en mauvais état; *(risky)* risqué(e); *(milk, meat)* douteux(euse)

dodo ['dəʊdəʊ] *(pl* **dodoes** *or* **dodos**) *n* dodo *m*, dronte *m*; **(as) dead as a d.** mort(e) et enterré(e)

DOE [di:əʊ'i:] *n Br (abbr* **Department of the Environment)** ≃ ministère *m* de l'Environnement

doe [dəʊ] *n (deer)* biche *f*; *(rabbit)* lapine *f*

does [dʌz] *3rd person singular of* **do**

doesn't ['dʌzənt] = **does not**

doff [dɒf] *vt* **to d. one's cap to sb** se découvrir devant qn

dog [dɒg] **1** *n* (a) *(animal)* chien *m*; **d. biscuit** biscuit *m* pour chien; **d. collar** collier *m* de chien; *Fam (of cleric)* col blanc *(d'un religieux)*; **d. food** nourriture *f* pour chien; **d. handler** maître-chien *m*; *Br* **d. licence** ≃ permis nécessaire pour posséder un chien; **to do the d. paddle** nager comme un petit chien; **d. racing** courses *fpl* de lévriers; **d. tag** plaque *f* d'identité (b) *Fam (person)* **you lucky d.!** sacré veinard!; **dirty d.** sale type *m* (c) *Fam Pej (ugly woman)* laideron *m* (d) *Am (hot dog)* hot dog *m* (e) *(idioms)* *Fam* **to lead a d.'s life** avoir une vie de chien; *Fam* **to make a d.'s breakfast** *or* **dinner of sth** gâcher qch; *Fam* **it's a d.-eat-d. world** c'est un monde sans pitié; *Fam* **to go to the dogs** *(of place)* aller à vau-l'eau; *(of person)* filer un mauvais coton; *Fam* **to be a d. in the manger** être un empêcheur de tourner en rond; *Fam* **you can't teach an old d. new tricks** les vieilles habitudes ont la vie dure; *Prov* **every d. has his day** tout le monde a son heure de gloire

2 *vt (pt & pp* **dogged)** *(follow)* suivre de près; **to d. sb's**

footsteps être sur les talons de qn; **to be dogged by misfortune** être poursuivi(e) par la malchance

dog-eared ['dɒgɪəd] *adj (page)* corné(e); *(book)* aux pages cornées

dogfight ['dɒgfaɪt] *n (between planes)* combat *m* aérien; *(between people)* bagarre *f*

dogfish ['dɒgfɪʃ] *n* roussette *f*

dogged ['dɒgɪd] *adj* tenace

doggerel ['dɒgərəl] *n (comical)* poésie *f* burlesque; *(bad)* vers *mpl* de mirliton

doggy ['dɒgɪ] *(pl doggies) n Fam* toutou *m*; **d. bag** = petit sac fourni par certains restaurants pour que les clients puissent emporter les restes

doghouse ['dɒghaʊs] *n Fam* **to be in the d.** ne pas être en odeur de sainteté

dogma ['dɒgmə] *n* dogme *m*

dogmatic [dɒg'mætɪk] *adj* dogmatique

do-gooder ['duː'gʊdə(r)] *n Fam Pej* âme *f* charitable

dogsbody ['dɒgzbɒdɪ] *(pl dogsbodies) n Br Fam* factotum *m*

dog-tired ['dɒg'taɪəd] *adj Fam* claqué(e), crevé(e)

dogwood ['dɒgwʊd] *n* cornouiller *m*

doh [dəʊ] *n Mus* do *m*

doily ['dɔɪlɪ] *(pl doilies) n* napperon *m*

doing ['duːɪŋ] *n* (a) **this is his d.** c'est son œuvre; **it was none of my d.** je n'y étais pour rien; **that takes some d.** il faut le faire (b) **doings** faits *mpl* et gestes *mpl*

do-it-yourself [duːɪtjɔː'self] *n* bricolage *m*; **a d. enthusiast** un(e) adepte du bricolage

doldrums ['dɒldrəmz] *npl* **to be in the d.** *(of person)* broyer du noir; *(of economy)* être en plein marasme

dole [dəʊl] *n Br Fam* (indemnités *fpl* de) chômage *m*; **to be on the d.** être au chômage; *Fig* **to join the d. queue** se retrouver au chômage

▸**dole out** *vt sep Fam* distribuer

doleful ['dəʊlfʊl] *adj* triste

doll [dɒl] *n* poupée *f*; **d.'s house** maison *f* de poupée

▸**doll up** *vt sep Fam* **to d. oneself up** se pomponner

dollar ['dɒlə(r)] *n* dollar *m*; **d. bill** billet *m* de un dollar

dollop ['dɒləp] *n Fam (of cream, mashed potato)* bonne cuillerée *f*; *(of mud, clay)* tas *m*

dolly ['dɒlɪ] *(pl dollies) n* (a) *Fam (toy)* poupée *f* (b) *(for camera)* chariot *m*

dolphin ['dɒlfɪn] *n* dauphin *m*

dolt [dəʊlt] *n Fam* andouille *f*

domain [də'meɪn] *n also Fig* domaine *m*

dome [dəʊm] *n* dôme *m*

domestic [də'mestɪk] *adj* (a) *(appliance, use, tasks)* ménager(ère); *(animal)* domestique; **d. bliss** bonheur *m* familial; *Br* **d. science** *(school subject)* cours *mpl* de couture et de cuisine; **d. servant** domestique *mf* (b) *(policy, flight, affairs)* intérieur(e); *(economy, currency)* national(e)

domesticate [də'mestɪkeɪt] *vt (animal)* domestiquer; *Hum* **to be domesticated** *(of person)* se débrouiller plutôt bien avec les travaux ménagers

domicile ['dɒmɪsaɪl] *n Law* domicile *m*

dominance ['dɒmɪnəns] *n (of disease, gene)* dominance *f*; *(of race, political party)* prédominance *f*; *(of person)* supériorité *f*

dominant ['dɒmɪnənt] *adj* dominant(e); *(person, character)* dominateur(trice)

dominate ['dɒmɪneɪt] *vt & vi* dominer

domination [dɒmɪ'neɪʃən] *n* domination *f*

domineering [dɒmɪ'nɪərɪŋ] *adj* dominateur(trice)

Dominica [də'mɪnɪkə] *n* la Dominique

Dominican [də'mɪnɪkən] **1** *n* Dominicain(e) *m,f*
2 *adj* dominicain(e); **the D. Republic** la République Dominicaine

dominion [də'mɪnjən] *n* domination *f*

domino ['dɒmɪnəʊ] *(pl dominoes) n* domino *m*; *Pol & Fig* **d. effect** effet *m* d'entraînement

don¹ [dɒn] *n Br Univ* professeur *m* d'université *(surtout à Oxford et Cambridge)*

don² *(pt & pp donned) vt Formal (clothing)* mettre, revêtir

donate [də'neɪt] *vt* faire don de; **to d. blood** donner son sang

donation [də'neɪʃən] *n* donation *f*; don *m*

done [dʌn] *pp of* **do**

donkey ['dɒŋkɪ] *(pl donkeys) n (animal) & Fam (person)* âne *m*; *Fam* **I haven't seen her for d.'s years** je ne l'ai pas vue depuis une éternité; *Fam* **to talk the hind legs off a d.** avoir la langue bien pendue; **d. jacket** ≃ caban *m*; *Fam* **d. work** travail *m* pénible

donor ['dəʊnə(r)] *n* donneur(euse) *m,f*; **d. card** carte *f* de donneur d'organe

don't [dəʊnt] = **do not**

donut ['dəʊnʌt] *n Am* beignet *m*

doodle ['duːdəl] **1** *n* gribouillis *m*, gribouillage *m*
2 *vi* gribouiller

doom [duːm] **1** *n* destin *m (funeste)*; **to be all d. and gloom** voir tout en noir
2 *vt* **to be doomed** *(of person) (unlucky)* être marqué(e) par le destin; *(about to die)* être perdu(e); **to be doomed (to failure)** *(of project)* être voué(e) à l'échec; **to be doomed to do sth** être condamné(e) à faire qch

doom-laden ['duːmleɪdən] *adj* funeste, sinistre

doomsday ['duːmzdeɪ] *n* jour *m* du Jugement dernier; **till d.** indéfiniment

door [dɔː(r)] *n* porte *f*; *(of train, car)* portière *f*; **to answer the d.** aller ouvrir (la porte); **to see sb to the d.** raccompagner qn à la porte; **to show sb to the d.** mettre qn à la porte; **to shut the d. in sb's face** fermer la porte au nez de qn; **she lives two doors away** elle habite deux portes plus loin; *Fig* **to lay sth at sb's d.** imputer qch à qn; **out of doors** dehors, en plein air; **d. handle** *f* de porte; **d. knocker** heurtoir *m*

doorbell ['dɔːbel] *n* sonnette *f*

doorkeeper ['dɔːkiːpə(r)] *n* portier *m*

doorknob ['dɔːnɒb] *n* bouton *m* de porte

doorman ['dɔːmən] *n (in hotel)* portier *m*; *(in block of flats)* concierge *m*

doormat ['dɔːmæt] *n* paillasson *m*; *Fig* **to treat sb like a d.** traiter qn comme un moins que rien

doorpost ['dɔːpəʊst] *n* montant *m* de porte

doorstep ['dɔːstep] *n* pas *m* de la porte, seuil *m*; *Fig* **on one's d.** à deux pas

doorstop ['dɔːstɒp] *n (fixed)* butoir *m*; *(wedge)* cale-porte *m*

door-to-door ['dɔːtə'dɔː(r)] *adj* **d. canvassing** porte-à-porte *m* électoral; **d. salesman** démarcheur *m*

doorway ['dɔːweɪ] *n* porte *f*; **in the d.** dans l'embrasure de la porte

dope [dəup] **1** n (**a**) very Fam (cannabis) shit m; Fam d. test (for athlete) contrôle m antidopage (**b**) Fam (idiot) andouille f **2** vt (person, horse) (to make faster) doper; (to make slower) droguer; (food, drink) mettre une drogue dans

dopey ['dəupɪ] adj Fam idiot(e)

dorm [dɔ:m] n Fam (dormitory) dortoir m

dormant ['dɔ:mənt] **1** adj (volcano) en sommeil; (conflict, emotion) latent(e); (idea) qui sommeille **2** adv to lie d. être en sommeil

dormitory ['dɔ:mɪtərɪ] n (pl dormitories) n (**a**) dortoir m; d. town cité-dortoir f (**b**) Am Univ résidence f universitaire

dormouse ['dɔ:maus] n (pl dormice ['dɔ:maɪs]) n loir m

dorsal ['dɔ:səl] adj dorsal(e)

DOS [dɒs] n Comptr (abbr **disk operating system**) DOS m

dose [dəus] **1** n (amount) dose f; a bad d. of (the) flu une bonne grippe; to have a d. of measles avoir la rougeole **2** vt Fam bourrer (with de); to d. oneself (up) with pills se bourrer de médicaments

dosh [dɒʃ] n Br Fam (money) fric m

doss [dɒs] vi very Fam to d. (down) crécher

dosser ['dɒsə(r)] n Br very Fam (tramp) clodo mf

doss-house ['dɒshaus] n Br Fam asile m de nuit

dossier ['dɒsɪeɪ] n dossier m

dot [dɒt] **1** n point m; on the d. à l'heure pile; at three o'clock on the d. à trois heures pile; Comptr d. matrix printer imprimante f matricielle **2** vt (pt & pp dotted) parsemer (with de); to d. an i/a j mettre un point sur un i/un j; dotted line pointillé m; to sign on the dotted line ≃ signer à l'endroit indiqué; Fig donner son consentement; Fig to d. the i's (and cross the t's) peaufiner les détails

dotage ['dəutɪdʒ] n to be in one's d. être gâteux(euse)

▶**dote on, dote upon** [dəut] vt insep adorer

dotty ['dɒtɪ] adj Fam (person, idea) toqué(e); to be d. about sb être fou (folle) de qn

double ['dʌbəl] **1** n (**a**) (of person) double m, sosie m (**b**) (hotel room) chambre f pour deux personnes (**c**) doubles (in tennis) double m; a doubles match un double (**d**) at or on the d. à l'instant (**e**) (measure of drink) double m **2** adj double; d. m (when spelling) deux m; a d. whisky un double whisky; d. agent agent m double; d. bass contrebasse f; d. bed grand lit m, lit à deux personnes; d. bill (at cinema) double programme m; d. chin menton m; d. cream ≃ crème f fraîche épaisse; Br to talk d. Dutch parler chinois; d. fault (in tennis) double faute f; to be in d. figures (of statistic) avoir atteint plus de dix; inflation is now in d. figures l'inflation a passé la barre des 10%; to lead a d. life mener une double vie; d. meaning double sens m; d. room chambre f pour deux personnes; to have d. standards faire deux poids, deux mesures; to do a d. take marquer un temps d'arrêt; Br d. yellow line = double ligne jaune indiquant une zone de stationnement interdit **3** adv to see d. voir double; to fold sth d. plier qch en deux; to be bent d. être plié(e) en deux **4** vt (a) (multiply by two) doubler (b) (fold) plier en deux **5** vi (a) (increase twofold) doubler (b) to d. as sth servir aussi de qch

▶**double back** vi rebrousser chemin

▶**double up** vi (bend) se plier en deux (with de)

double-barrelled ['dʌbəl'bærəld] adj (shotgun) à deux coups; (surname) à rallonge

double-breasted ['dʌbəl'brestɪd] adj (jacket, suit) croisé(e)

double-check ['dʌbəl'tʃek] vt & vi bien vérifier

double-cross ['dʌbəl'krɒs] vt trahir, doubler

double-dealing ['dʌbəl'di:lɪŋ] n fourberie f

double-decker ['dʌbəl'dekə(r)] n Br (bus) autobus m à impériale ou à étage

double-edged ['dʌbəl'edʒd] adj also Fig à double tranchant

double-glazing ['dʌbəl'gleɪzɪŋ] n double vitrage m

double-jointed ['dʌbəl'dʒɔɪntɪd] adj désarticulé(e)

double-lock ['dʌbəl'lɒk] vt fermer à double tour

double-park ['dʌbəl'pɑ:k] vi se garer en double file

double-quick ['dʌbəl'kwɪk] adv en vitesse

doubly ['dʌblɪ] adv doublement; to make d. sure of sth bien vérifier qch; d. difficult deux fois plus difficile; to be d. careful redoubler de prudence

doubt [daut] **1** n doute m; to have doubts about sth avoir des doutes sur qch; to be in d. (of person) douter (about de); (of outcome) être incertain(e); when in d. en cas de doute, dans le doute; beyond d. sans le moindre doute; no d. sans doute; there is no d. that... il ne fait aucun doute que...; there is no d. about her guilt sa culpabilité ne fait aucun doute; there is some d. about... il y a des doutes quant à... **2** vt douter de; I d. it j'en doute

doubtful ['dautful] adj (**a**) (uncertain) (person) dubitatif(ive); (outcome) incertain(e); to be d. about sth avoir des doutes sur qch (**b**) (questionable) douteux(euse)

dough [dəu] n (**a**) (for bread) pâte f (**b**) Fam (money) fric m

doughnut ['dəunʌt] n beignet m

dour [duə(r)] adj austère

douse [daus] vt (**a**) (soak) arroser (**b**) (extinguish) éteindre

dove¹ [dʌv] n colombe f

dove² [dəuv] Am pt of **dive**

dovecot(e) ['dʌvkɒt] n colombier m

Dover ['dəuvər] n Douvres

dovetail ['dʌvteɪl] vi (fit closely) concorder, cadrer (with avec)

dowager ['dauədʒə(r)] n douairière f

dowdy ['daudɪ] adj (person) inélégant(e); (clothes, image) démodé(e)

dowel ['dauəl] n cheville f

down¹ [daun] n (feathers) duvet m

down² [daun] **1** prep to go d. the stairs/the street descendre les escaliers/la rue; to run d. the stairs/the street descendre les escaliers/la rue en courant; to fall d. the stairs dégringoler les escaliers; the tears ran d. her cheeks les larmes coulaient sur ses joues **2** adv (**a**) (with motion) to come/go d. descendre; to fall d. tomber; to bend d. se pencher; petrol has come or gone d. in price le prix de l'essence a baissé; I'll be d. in a minute je descends tout de suite; d. with traitors! à bas les traîtres! (**b**) (with position) en bas; d. here/there ici/là en bas; further d. plus bas; petrol is d. in price le prix de l'essence a baissé; one d., two to go! et d'un! encore deux et c'est fini!; everyone from the boss d. tout le monde, même le chef

(c) *(in crosswords)* verticalement

(d) *(idioms)* **to be d. on sb/sth** avoir une dent contre qn/qch; **it's d. to her** *(her decision)* c'est à elle de décider; *(her achievement)* c'est grâce à elle; **I'm d. to my last pound/cigarette** il ne me reste plus qu'une livre/une cigarette

3 *n Fam* **to have a d. on sb/sth** avoir une dent contre qn/qch

4 *adj* **(a)** *(depressed)* déprimé(e) **(b)** **to be d.** *(of computer, telephones)* être en panne

5 *vt* **(a)** *(aircraft)* abattre **(b)** *(drink)* descendre; **to d. tools** *(of workers)* se mettre en grève

down-and-out ['daʊnən'aʊt] *Fam* **1** *n (tramp)* clochard(e) *m,f*
  2 *adj* sans le sou

downbeat ['daʊnbiːt] *adj* **(a)** *(gloomy, pessimistic)* triste, pessimiste **(b)** *(restrained)* réservé(e) **(about** sur)

downcast ['daʊnkɑːst] *adj (eyes)* baissé(e); *(person)* abattu(e), découragé(e)

downer ['daʊnə(r)] *n Fam* **(a)** *(drug)* tranquillisant *m* **(b)** *(depressing situation)* situation *f* déprimante; *(depressing event)* événement *m* déprimant

downfall ['daʊnfɔːl] *n (of government)* chute *f*; *(of person)* ruine *f*

downgrade ['daʊngreɪd] *vt* rétrograder

downhearted [daʊn'hɑːtɪd] *adj* découragé(e)

downhill ['daʊn'hɪl] **1** *adj (slope)* en pente; **d. skiing** ski *m* alpin ou de descente
  2 *adv* **to go d.** *(of road, car)* descendre; *Fig (of person, career)* être sur le déclin

download [daʊn'ləʊd] *vt Comptr* télécharger

down-market [daʊn'mɑːkɪt] *adj (product)* bas de gamme *inv*; *(area, place)* populaire

down payment [daʊn'peɪmənt] *n* acompte *m*

downpour ['daʊnpɔː(r)] *n* averse *f*

downright ['daʊnraɪt] **1** *adj (stupidity, dishonesty)* véritable; **it's a d. lie!** c'est un mensonge flagrant!
  2 *adv (stupid, untrue)* carrément

downsizing ['daʊnsaɪzɪŋ] *n* réduction *f* d'effectifs

Down's syndrome ['daʊnz'sɪmdrəʊm] *n* trisomie *f* 21

downstairs 1 *adj* ['daʊnsteəz] *(on a lower floor)* de l'étage du dessous; *(on ground floor)* du rez-de-chaussée; **the d. flat** l'appartement du dessous; **the d. bathroom** la salle de bains du bas
  2 *adv* [daʊn'steəz] en bas; **to come/go d.** descendre; **he lives d.** il habite à l'étage au-dessous

downstream [daʊn'striːm] *adv* en aval; *(with movement)* vers l'aval

downswing ['daʊnswɪŋ] *n Econ* tendance *f* à la baisse

down-to-earth ['daʊntə'з:θ] *adj* terre à terre *inv*

downtown ['daʊn'taʊn] *Am* **1** *n (city centre)* centre-ville *m*
  2 *adj* du centre-ville; **d. New York** le centre de New York
  3 *adv* au centre-ville

downtrodden ['daʊntrɒdən] *adj* opprimé(e)

downturn ['daʊntɜːn] *n (economic)* baisse *f*

down under ['daʊn'ʌndə(r)] *adv Fam (in Australia)* en Australie; *(in New Zealand)* en Nouvelle-Zélande

downward ['daʊnwəd] *adj* vers le bas; **a d. trend** une tendance à la baisse

downwards ['daʊnwədz] *adv* vers le bas

dowry ['daʊrɪ] *n (pl* **dowries)** *n* dot *f*

doze [dəʊz] **1** *n* somme *m*; **to have a d.** faire un somme
  2 *vi* somnoler

▸**doze off** *vi* s'assoupir

dozen ['dʌzn] *n* douzaine *f*; **half a d./a d. eggs** une demi-douzaine/une douzaine d'œufs; *Fam* **dozens of times/people** des dizaines de fois/gens

dozy ['dəʊzɪ] *adj* **(a)** *(sleepy)* **to feel d.** avoir envie de dormir **(b)** *Fam (stupid)* abruti(e)

Dr *(abbr* **Doctor)** Dr

drab [dræb] *adj (person, colour)* terne; *(atmosphere, city)* morne

drachma ['drækmə] *n* drachme *f*

draconian [drə'kəʊnɪən] *adj* draconien(enne)

draft[1] [drɑːft] **1** *n* **(a)** *(of letter)* brouillon *m*; *(of law, proposal)* avant-projet *m*; *(of novel)* jet *m* **(b)** *Fin* traite *f* **(c)** *Am (conscription)* conscription *f*; **d. dodger** insoumis *m*
  2 *vt* **(a)** *(letter)* faire le brouillon de; *(proposal)* rédiger; *(law, bill)* préparer **(b)** *(recruit)* **to d. sb in** détacher qn

draft[2] *Am =* **draught**

draftsman *Am =* **draughtsman**

drafty *Am =* **draughty**

drag [dræg] **1** *n* **(a)** *(air resistance)* traînée *f*; **d. racing** courses *fpl* de dragsters **(b)** *Fam (person)* raseur(euse) *m,f*; *(task)* corvée *f*; **the party was a real d.** la soirée était vraiment rasante **(c)** *Fam (on cigarette)* taffe *f*; **to take** *or* **have a d. on a cigarette** tirer une taffe sur une cigarette **(d)** *Fam (women's clothing worn by man)* **to be in d.** être travesti; **d. artist** travesti *m*; **d. queen** travelo *m*
  2 *vt (pt & pp* **dragged)** **(a)** *(pull)* traîner; *Fig* **to d. one's feet** traîner les pieds; *Fig* **to d. oneself away from sth** s'arracher à qch **(b)** *(pond, canal)* draguer
  3 *vi (of film, day)* traîner en longueur; *(of conversation)* languir

▸**drag on** *vi (of meeting, film)* traîner en longueur, s'éterniser

▸**drag out** *vt sep (meeting, speech)* faire traîner

▸**drag up** *vt sep (refer to)* ressortir

dragnet ['drægnet] *n (in deep-sea fishing)* seine *f*, senne *f*; *Fig (to catch criminals)* rafle *f*

dragon ['drægən] *n also Fig* dragon *m*

dragonfly ['drægənflaɪ] *n (pl* **dragonflies)** *n* libellule *f*

dragoon [drə'guːn] **1** *n (soldier)* dragon *m*
  2 *vt* **to d. sb into doing sth** forcer qn à faire qch

drain [dreɪn] **1** *n* **(a)** *(for water, sewage)* égout *m*; *Fig* **to throw money down the d.** jeter l'argent par les fenêtres; **that's five years' work down the d.** voilà cinq années de travail perdues; **that's my holiday down the d.** ce sont mes vacances qui tombent à l'eau **(b)** *(on resources)* ponction *f* **(on** sur); *(on strength)* perte *f* **(on** de)

  2 *vt (liquid)* vider; *(vegetables)* égoutter; **to d. one's glass** finir son verre; *Fig* **to feel drained** être épuisé(e) ou vidé(e)

  3 *vi (of liquid)* s'écouler; *(of dishes)* égoutter; *(of sink, washing machine)* se vider; *(of river)* se jeter; **the colour drained from her face** elle est devenue blême

▸**drain away** *vi (of liquid)* s'écouler; *Fig (of strength, enthusiasm)* s'épuiser; *(of fear, tension)* s'apaiser

drainage ['dreɪnɪdʒ] *n* drainage *m*

drainpipe ['dreɪnpaɪp] *n* tuyau *m* d'écoulement; **d. trousers, drainpipes** pantalon *m* cigarette

drake [dreɪk] *n* canard *m* (mâle)

dram [dræm] *n (of whisky)* goutte *f*

drama ['drɑːmə] n (a) (art form) théâtre m; (play) drame m; Fig **to make a d. out of sth** faire un drame de qch; **d. school** école f d'art dramatique (b) (excitement) action f

dramatic [drə'mætɪk] adj (a) (work) dramatique; (actor) de théâtre (b) (significant) spectaculaire (c) (theatrical) théâtral(e)

dramatist ['dræmətɪst] n auteur m dramatique, dramaturge mf

dramatize ['dræmətaɪz] vt (a) (adapt) (for stage) adapter pour la scène; (for screen) adapter pour l'écran (b) (exaggerate) dramatiser

drank [dræŋk] pt of **drink**

drape [dreɪp] 1 npl Am **drapes** (curtains) rideaux mpl
2 vt (table, coffin) draper (**with** de); **to d. sth over sth** draper qch sur qch

drastic ['dræstɪk] adj (solution, change) radical(e); (improvement, decline) spectaculaire; (action) énergique; (shortage, difficulty) dramatique

drat [dræt] exclam Fam **d. (it)!** nom de nom!

draught, Am **draft** [drɑːft] n (a) (wind) courant m d'air; **d. excluder** bourrelet m (b) (of air) gorgée f; (of air) bouffée f (c) **on d.** (beer) à la pression; **d. beer** bière f pression

draughtboard ['drɑːftbɔːd] n damier m

draughts [drɑːfts] n (game) (jeu m de) dames fpl

draughtsman, Am **draftsman** ['drɑːftsmən] n dessinateur(trice) m,f

draughty, Am **drafty** ['drɑːftɪ] adj plein(e) de courants d'air

draw [drɔː] 1 n (a) (in match, argument) match m nul (b) (lottery) loterie f, tombola f; (for sporting competition) tirage m au sort (c) (attraction) attraction f
2 vt (pt drew [druː], pp drawn [drɔːn]) (a) (picture, diagram, map) dessiner; (circle, line) tracer; **to d. sb's picture** faire le portrait de qn (b) (pull) (cart) tirer; (person) attirer (**towards** vers); **to d. the curtains** (open or shut) tirer les rideaux; **to d. breath** souffler (c) (extract) retirer; (pistol, sword) dégainer; (water, wine) tirer; Fig (strength, comfort) retirer, puiser (**from** de); **to d. a knife on sb** menacer qn d'un couteau; **to d. a salary** toucher un salaire; **to d. blood** (of dog) mordre jusqu'au sang; (of cat) griffer jusqu'au sang; **to d. lots for sth** tirer qch au sort; **to d. a conclusion from sth** tirer une conclusion de qch; **she refused to be drawn on the issue** elle refusa de se laisser entraîner sur ce sujet; **they were drawn against the champions** (in competition) le tirage au sort a décidé qu'ils joueraient contre les champions (d) (attract) attirer; **to d. a crowd** (of incident) créer un attroupement; (of play) attirer le public; **to feel drawn to sb/sth** se sentir attiré(e) par qn/qch; Fig **to d. sb's fire** s'attirer les foudres de qn
3 vi (a) (make picture) dessiner (b) (in game) faire match nul (**with** avec) (c) (move) **to d. ahead of sb** devancer qn; **to d. level with sb** rattraper qn; **to d. to an end** or **a close** tirer ou toucher à sa fin; **to d. near** (s')approcher; **to d. to a halt** s'arrêter

▶**draw back 1** vt sep (sheet, veil) retirer
2 vi reculer; **to d. back from doing sth** hésiter à faire qch

▶**draw in** vi (of night) raccourcir

▶**draw on 1** vt insep (resources, savings) tirer sur; (experience) se servir de
2 vi (of evening) approcher

▶**draw out** vt sep (a) (encourage to talk) faire parler (b) (prolong) faire durer

▶**draw up 1** vt sep (a) (chair) approcher; **she drew herself up to her full height** elle s'est dressée de toute sa hauteur (b) (plan, document) dresser; (will) rédiger
2 vi (of vehicle) s'arrêter

drawback ['drɔːbæk] n inconvénient m

drawbridge ['drɔːbrɪdʒ] n pont-levis m

drawer [drɔː(r)] n tiroir m

drawers [drɔːz] npl Old-fashioned (for women) culotte f; (for men) caleçon m

drawing ['drɔːɪŋ] n dessin m; **d. board** planche f à dessin; Fig **it's back to the d. board!** retour à la case départ!; **d. paper** papier m à dessin; **d. pin** punaise f; **d. room** salon m

drawl [drɔːl] 1 n voix f traînante
2 vi parler d'une voix traînante

drawn [drɔːn] 1 adj (face) blême; (features) tiré(e); **to look d.** avoir les traits tirés
2 pp of **draw**

drawstring ['drɔːstrɪŋ] n cordon m

dread [dred] 1 n terreur f; **to have a d. of sth** avoir la hantise de qch
2 vt **to d. sth/doing sth** appréhender ou redouter qch/de faire qch; **I d. to think!** je n'ose pas imaginer!

dreaded ['dredɪd] adj redouté(e)

dreadful ['dredfʊl] adj (a) (terrible) épouvantable, affreux(euse); **to feel d.** se sentir vraiment mal; **I feel really d. about it!** quand j'y pense, je suis horriblement gêné! (b) Fam (for emphasis) terrible; **it's a d. bore/shame!** c'est vraiment rasant/dommage!

dreadfully ['dredfʊlɪ] adv (a) (very badly) affreusement (b) Fam (extremely) terriblement, horriblement

dreadlocks ['dredlɒks] npl petites nattes fpl (des nastas)

dream [driːm] 1 n rêve m; **to have a d. (about)** rêver (de); **to have a bad d.** faire un mauvais rêve; **a d. come true** un rêve devenu réalité; **it worked like a d.** ça a marché à merveille
2 adj de rêve; **my d. house** la maison de mes rêves; **d. world** monde m imaginaire; Fig **to live in a d. world** vivre en pleine utopie
3 vi (pt & pp dreamt [dremt] or dreamed) **to d. that...** rêver que...; Fig **I never dreamt you would take me seriously** je n'aurais jamais pensé que tu me prendrais au sérieux
4 vt rêver (**of** or **about** de); Fam **I wouldn't d. of it!** je n'y songerais même pas!

▶**dream up** vt sep (scheme, excuse) imaginer, inventer

dreamer ['driːmə(r)] n rêveur(euse) m,f

dreamt [dremt] pt & pp of **dream**

dreamy ['driːmɪ] adj rêveur(euse)

dreary ['drɪərɪ] adj morne

dredge [dredʒ] vt (canal, harbour) draguer; Fig **to d. one's memory** fouiller dans ses souvenirs

▶**dredge up** vt sep (body, object) repêcher; Fig (scandal, memory) déterrer

dredger ['dredʒə(r)] n (boat) dragueur m

dregs [dregz] npl (of wine) lie f; (of coffee) marc m; (in cup) fond m de tasse; Fig **the d. of society** les bas-fonds mpl de la société

drench [drentʃ] *vt* tremper (**with** *or* **in** de); **drenched to the skin** trempé(e) jusqu'aux os

dress [dres] **1** *n* (**a**) *(for woman)* robe *f* (**b**) *(clothing)* tenue *f*; **to have good d. sense/no d. sense** savoir/ne pas savoir s'habiller; *d.* **circle** premier balcon *m*; **d. rehearsal** (répétition *f*) générale *f*; **d. shirt** chemise *f* de soirée

2 *vt* (**a**) *(person)* habiller, vêtir; **to d. oneself, to get dressed** s'habiller; **to be dressed in black/in rags** être vêtu(e) de noir/de haillons; **well/badly dressed** bien/mal habillé(e) (**b**) *(wound)* panser (**c**) *(salad)* assaisonner; **dressed crab** chair *f* de crabe

3 *vi* s'habiller

▶**dress up** *vi* *(elegantly)* se faire beau (belle), s'habiller; *(in fancy dress)* se déguiser (**as** en)

dresser ['dresə(r)] *n* (**a**) *(in kitchen)* vaisselier *m* (**b**) *Am (dressing table)* coiffeuse *f* (**c**) *Th (person)* habilleur(euse) *m,f*

dressing ['dresɪŋ] *n* (**a**) **d. gown** robe *f* de chambre; **d. room** *(in theatre)* loge *f*; *(in gym, sports centre)* vestiaire *m*; *(in home)* cabinet *m* de toilette; **d. table** coiffeuse *f* (**b**) *(for wound)* pansement *m* (**c**) *(for salad)* assaisonnement *m*

dressing down ['dresɪŋ'daʊn] *n Fam* savon *m*; **to give sb a d.** passer un savon à qn

dressmaker ['dresmeɪkə(r)] *n* couturier(ère) *m,f*

dressmaking ['dresmeɪkɪŋ] *n* couture *f*

dressy ['dresɪ] *adj (clothes, party)* habillé(e)

drew [dru:] *pt* of **draw**

drib [drɪb] *n* **in dribs and drabs** petit à petit

dribble ['drɪbəl] **1** *n (saliva)* bave *f*; *(of blood, oil)* filet *m* **2** *vi* (**a**) *(of person)* baver (**b**) *(of liquid)* dégouliner; *Fig* **to d. in/out** *(of people)* entrer/sortir au compte-gouttes (**c**) *(of footballer)* dribbler

drier ['draɪə(r)] *n (for clothes)* séchoir *m*; *(for hair) (on stand)* casque *m*; *(hand-held)* sèche-cheveux *m inv*

drift [drɪft] **1** *n* (**a**) *(of current)* direction *f*, sens *m*; *(of events)* cours *m*; **the d. towards home ownership** la tendance actuelle à l'accession à la propriété; **d. net** *(for fishing)* filet *m* dérivant (**b**) *(meaning)* sens *m* général; *Fam* **I get the d.** j'ai compris (**c**) *(of snow)* congère *f*, *(of leaves)* amoncellement *m*; *(of fog, mist)* traînée *f*

2 *vi* (**a**) *(of boat)* dériver, aller à la dérive; *(of smoke)* flotter; *(of events)* tendre (**towards** vers); *(of person)* se laisser porter par les événements; **people drifted in and out** les gens entraient et sortaient nonchalamment; **to d. apart** *(of friends)* se perdre de vue; *(of couple)* devenir des étrangers l'un pour l'autre; **to d. into war/crime** être entraîné(e) vers la guerre/le crime (**b**) *(of sand, snow)* s'amonceler, s'entasser

drifter ['drɪftə(r)] *n (person)* **she's a bit of a d.** elle n'a pas vraiment de but dans la vie

driftwood ['drɪftwʊd] *n (in sea)* bois *m* flottant *ou* flotté; *(on shore)* bois rejeté par la mer

drill [drɪl] **1** *n* (**a**) *(tool)* foret *m*, mèche *f*; *(electric)* perceuse *f*; *(of dentist)* fraise *f*, roulette *f*; *(pneumatic)* marteau *m* piqueur; **d. bit** foret (**b**) *(training)* exercice *m* **2** *vt* (**a**) *(well)* forer; *(hole)* percer (**b**) *(train)* *(soldiers)* entraîner; *Fam* **to d. sth into sb** enfoncer qch dans la tête de qn

3 *vi* (**a**) *(for oil)* forer (**for** pour trouver); *(in wall, rock)* percer (**into** dans) (**b**) *(of troops)* faire l'exercice

drink [drɪŋk] **1** *n* boisson *f*; **to have a d.** prendre un verre, boire quelque chose; **to go for a d.** aller prendre un verre; **to pay for the drinks** payer les consommations; *Fam* **the d.** *(sea)* la baille; **to take to d.** se mettre à boire; **to have a d. problem** (trop) boire; **drinks machine** distributeur *m* automatique de boissons

2 *vt* *(pt* **drank** [dræŋk], *pp* **drunk** [drʌŋk]) boire; **she drank us all under the table** nous avions tous roulé sous la table depuis longtemps qu'elle était encore debout

3 *vi* boire; **to d. like a fish** boire comme un trou; **to d. to sb** *or* **to sb's health** boire à la santé de qn; *Fig* **to d. to sth** arroser qch; **to d. in the atmosphere** se pénétrer de l'atmosphère

▶**drink up 1** *vt sep* finir (de boire)
2 *vi* vider son verre

drinkable ['drɪŋkəbəl] *adj (water)* potable; *(wine, beer)* buvable

drink-driving ['drɪŋk'draɪvɪŋ] *n* conduite *f* en état d'ivresse

drinker ['drɪŋkə(r)] *n* buveur(euse) *m,f*; **to be a heavy d.** boire beaucoup

drinking ['drɪŋkɪŋ] *n* **d. is bad for you** l'alcool est mauvais pour la santé; **d. chocolate** chocolat *m* en poudre; **d. fountain** fontaine *f* publique; **d. straw** paille *f*; **d. water** eau *f* potable

drip [drɪp] **1** *n* (**a**) *(drop)* goutte *f*; *(sound)* bruit *m* de l'eau qui goutte (**b**) *(in hospital)* goutte-à-goutte *m inv*; **to be on a d.** être sous perfusion (**c**) *Fam (weak person)* mou (molle) *m,f*

2 *vt* *(pt & pp* **dripped**) laisser tomber goutte à goutte; **you're dripping water everywhere!** tu mets de l'eau partout!; **to be dripping with sweat/blood** ruisseler de sueur/sang; *Fig* **to be dripping with jewels** être couvert(e) de bijoux

3 *vi* *(of liquid)* tomber goutte à goutte, goutter; *(of tap)* fuir

drip-dry ['drɪp'draɪ] *adj (shirt, fabric)* ne nécessitant aucun repassage

dripping ['drɪpɪŋ] **1** *n* graisse *f* de rôti
2 *adj (tap)* qui fuit
3 *adv* **d. wet** trempé(e)

drive [draɪv] **1** *n* (**a**) *(trip)* promenade *f* en voiture; **it's an hour's d. away** c'est à une heure en voiture; **to go for** *or* **take a d.** aller faire une promenade en voiture

(**b**) *(of car)* **left-hand d.** conduite *f* à gauche; **four-wheel d.** *(car)* quatre-quatre *m inv*; *(system)* propulsion *f* à quatre roues motrices; **front-wheel d.** *(car, system)* traction *f* avant; **rear-wheel d.** *(car, system)* traction *f* arrière

(**c**) *Comptr* lecteur *m*, unité *f*

(**d**) *(in golf, tennis)* drive *m*

(**e**) *(initiative)* énergie *f*, dynamisme *m*

(**f**) *(of house)* allée *f*

(**g**) *(campaign)* **sales/membership d.** campagne *f* pour attirer les acheteurs/de nouveaux membres

2 *vt* *(pt* **drove** [drəʊv], *pp* **driven** ['drɪvən]) (**a**) *(car, train)* conduire; **to d. sb somewhere** conduire qn en voiture quelque part

(**b**) *(direct, guide) (cattle)* mener, conduire; *(people)* chasser (**c**) *(push)* **to d. sb to sth/to do sth** pousser qn à qch/à faire qch; **to d. sb mad** rendre qn fou (folle); **to d. oneself too hard** trop exiger de soi-même; **to d. a hard bargain** ne pas faire de cadeau; **to d. prices up/down** faire monter/baisser les prix

(**d**) *(machine)* actionner, faire marcher; **to be driven by electricity** marcher à l'électricité

3 *vi* (*in car*) conduire; **can you d.?** savez-vous conduire?; **I don't d.** je n'ai pas mon permis; **to d. to work** aller au travail en voiture

►**drive at** *vt insep* **what are you driving at?** où voulez-vous en venir?

►**drive away 1** *vt sep* (**a**) (*in car*) emmener en voiture (**b**) (*force to leave*) chasser
2 *vi* (*in car*) s'en aller en voiture

►**drive off 1** *vt sep* (*repel*) (*attackers*) chasser
2 *vi* (*in car*) s'en aller en voiture

►**drive on** *vi* (*in car*) continuer (sa route)

drive-in ['draɪvɪn] *n* (*cinema*) drive-in *m*, ciné-parc *m*; (*restaurant*) = restaurant où on est servi dans sa voiture

drivel ['drɪvəl] *n Fam* bêtises *fpl*, balivernes *fpl*; **to talk (a load of) d.** dire n'importe quoi

driven ['drɪvən] *pp of* **drive**

driver ['draɪvə(r)] *n* (**a**) (*of car, bus*) conducteur(trice) *m,f*; (*of lorry, taxi*) chauffeur(euse) *m,f*; (*of train*) mécanicien(enne) *m,f*; *Am* **d.'s license** permis *m* de conduire (**b**) (*golf club*) driver *m*

driveway ['draɪvweɪ] *n* allée *f*

driving ['draɪvɪŋ] **1** *n* (*in car*) conduite *f*; *Fig* **to be in the d. seat** être aux commandes; **d. instructor** moniteur(trice) *m,f* d'auto-école; **d. lessons** leçons *fpl* de conduite; *Br* **d. licence** permis *m* de conduire; **d. school** auto-école *f*; **d. test** (*examen m du*) permis de conduire
2 *adj* (*rain*) battant(e); *Fig* **d. force** moteur *m*

drizzle ['drɪzəl] **1** *n* crachin *m*
2 *vi* bruiner

droll [drəʊl] *adj* drôle, comique; *Ironic* **oh, very d.!** très drôle!

dromedary ['drɒmədərɪ] (*pl* **dromedaries**) *n* dromadaire *m*

drone [drəʊn] **1** *n* (**a**) (*bee*) faux-bourdon *m* (**b**) (*of conversation, traffic, plane*) bourdonnement *m*
2 *vi* (**a**) (*of bee*) bourdonner (**b**) (*of person*) parler d'un ton monotone

►**drone on** *vi* parler ad nauseam (*d'une voix monotone*) (*about the*)

drool [druːl] *vi* (*dribble*) baver; *Fig* **to d. over sb/sth** baver d'admiration devant qn/qch; *Fig* **she was drooling at the idea** elle en salivait d'avance

droop [druːp] *vi* (*of head*) pencher; (*of shoulders*) tomber; (*of flower*) pencher la tête; *Fig* (*of person*) perdre ses forces

drop [drɒp] **1** *n* (**a**) (*of liquid*) goutte *f*; **drops** (*for eyes, nose*) gouttes; **you've had a d. too much** (*to drink*) tu as bu un coup de trop; *Fig* **it's only a d. in the ocean** ce n'est qu'une goutte d'eau dans l'océan
(**b**) (*fall*) (*in prices, numbers*) chute *f*, baisse *f* (**in** de); (*by parachute*) parachutage *m*; **a d. of 10 metres** un à-pic *ou* escarpement de 10 mètres; *Fig* **at the d. of a hat** sans la moindre hésitation
2 *vt* (*pt & pp* **dropped**) (**a**) (*allow to fall*) laisser tomber; (*bomb*) lâcher; **to d. sb a line/a card** envoyer *ou* écrire un mot/une carte à qn; **I'll d. you at the station** (*in car*) je te déposerai à la gare
(**b**) (*lower*) (*prices, one's eyes*) baisser
(**c**) (*abandon*) (*subject, idea, plan*) abandonner; **to d. sb** (*as friend*) laisser tomber qn; (*from team*) écarter qn; **to d. maths/French** (*of student*) arrêter les maths/le français; *Law* **to d. the charges** abandonner les poursuites
(**d**) (*omit*) (*letter, syllable*) omettre, supprimer; (*when speaking*) ne pas prononcer
(**e**) (*lose*) (*points*) perdre

3 *vi* (**a**) (*of object*) tomber; (*of ground*) s'affaisser; **he dropped to sixth place** il est descendu à la sixième place; *Fam* **I'm ready to d.** (*with fatigue*) je tombe de fatigue; *Fam* **people are dropping like flies** les gens tombent comme des mouches; **to d. dead** tomber raide mort(e); *Fam* **d. dead!** va te faire voir!; *Fam* **let it d.!** laisse tomber!
(**b**) (*of prices, temperature, voice*) baisser; (*of wind*) tomber; (*of speed*) diminuer

►**drop by** *vi* (*visit*) passer

►**drop in** *vi* passer (**on sb** chez qn)

►**drop off 1** *vt sep* (*person from car*) déposer
2 *vi* (**a**) **to d. off (to sleep)** s'assoupir, s'endormir (**b**) (*of membership, attendance*) diminuer

►**drop out** *vi* (**a**) (*of object*) (*from pocket, bag*) tomber (**b**) (*of person*) (*from contest*) se retirer; (*from society*) devenir un(e) marginal(e); (*from university*) abandonner ses études

►**drop round 1** *vt sep* (*deliver*) déposer
2 *vi* (*visit*) passer

droplet ['drɒplɪt] *n* gouttelette *f*

dropout ['drɒpaʊt] *n Fam* (*from society*) marginal(e) *m,f*; (*from university*) étudiant(e) *m,f* qui abandonne ses études

dropper ['drɒpə(r)] *n* (*for medicine*) compte-gouttes *m inv*

droppings ['drɒpɪŋz] *npl* (*of birds*) fiente *f*; (*of animals*) crottes *fpl*

dross [drɒs] *n Fam* (*rubbish*) rebut *m*; **I've never heard such d. in all my life** j'ai rarement entendu de telles bêtises

drought [draʊt] *n* sécheresse *f*

drove [drəʊv] **1** *n* **to arrive in droves** arriver en foule
2 *pt of* **drive**

drown [draʊn] **1** *vt* (**a**) (*in water*) noyer; **to d. oneself** se noyer; **to d. one's sorrows** noyer son chagrin dans l'alcool (**b**) (*sound*) couvrir
2 *vi* (*die*) se noyer

►**drown out** *vt sep* (*sound*) couvrir; (*person*) couvrir la voix de

drowse [draʊz] *vi* somnoler

drowsy ['draʊzɪ] *adj* **to be** *ou* **feel d.** avoir envie de dormir

drudge [drʌdʒ] *n* (*man*) homme *m* de peine; (*woman*) bonne *f* à tout faire

drudgery ['drʌdʒərɪ] *n* travail *m* pénible *ou* ingrat

drug [drʌɡ] **1** *n* (*medicine*) médicament *m*; (*narcotic*) drogue *f*; **hard/soft drugs** drogues dures/douces; **to take drugs** se droguer; **d. abuse** usage *m* de stupéfiants; **d. addict** drogué(e) *m,f*; **d. dealer** (*large-scale*) trafiquant *m* de drogue; (*small-scale*) petit trafiquant de drogue, dealer *m*; **d. squad** brigade *f* des stupéfiants
2 *vt* (*pt & pp* **drugged**) droguer

druggist ['drʌɡɪst] *n Am* pharmacien(enne) *m,f*

drugstore ['drʌɡstɔː(r)] *n Am* drugstore *m*

druid ['druːɪd] *n* druide *m*

drum [drʌm] **1** *n* (**a**) (*musical instrument*) tambour *m*; **d. kit, drums** batterie *f* (**b**) (*container*) fût *m*; (*for oil*) bidon *m*
2 *vt* (*pt & pp* **drummed**) **to d. one's fingers** tambouriner de ses doigts; **to d. sth into sb** enfoncer qch dans la tête de qn
3 *vi* (*play drums*) jouer de la batterie; **the rain was drumming on the window panes** la pluie tambourinait contre les vitres

►**drum up** *vt* (*support, enthusiasm*) rechercher

drummer ['drʌmə(r)] n (in pop band) batteur(euse) m,f; (in military band) tambour m

drumstick ['drʌmstɪk] n (a) (for playing drums) baguette f de tambour (b) (chicken leg) pilon m

drunk [drʌŋk] 1 n (man) homme m soûl; (woman) femme f soûle; (habitual) ivrogne mf
2 adj ivre, soûl(e); to get d. se soûler; Law d. and disorderly = en état d'ivresse sur la voie publique; Fig d. with joy/power ivre de joie/puissance
3 pp of drink

drunkard ['drʌŋkəd] n ivrogne mf

drunken ['drʌŋkən] adj (person) ivre; (party) bien arrosé(e); in a d. stupor hébété(e) par l'alcool; d. brawl querelle d'ivrognes

dry [draɪ] 1 adj (a) (weather, clothing, skin, hair, wine) sec (sèche); (day) sans pluie; to run or go d. (of river) s'assécher; (of spring) se tarir, s'épuiser; d. as a bone complètement sec; Naut d. dock cale f sèche; d. ice neige f carbonique; d. land terre f ferme; d. rot pourriture f sèche; d. run coup m d'essai, test m (b) (boring) (style, person) ennuyeux(euse) (c) (humour) teinté(e) d'ironie
2 vt (pt & pp dried) sécher; (clothes) faire sécher; (skin) dessécher; (dishes) essuyer; to d. oneself se sécher; to d. one's hair se sécher les cheveux
3 vi sécher

▸**dry out** vi (a) (of alcoholic) se faire désintoxiquer (b) (of wood, ground) sécher; (of skin) se dessécher

▸**dry up** vi (a) (of well, pool) se dessécher, tarir (b) (of funds, conversation) tarir; (of inspiration) se tarir (c) (forget one's lines) oublier son texte; (have nothing more to say) ne plus rien avoir à dire

dry-clean ['draɪ'kliːn] vt nettoyer à sec

dry-cleaner's ['draɪ'kliːnəz] n teinturerie f, pressing m

dry-cleaning ['draɪ'kliːnɪŋ] n (a) (process) nettoyage m à sec (b) (clothes) vêtements mpl laissés chez le teinturier

dryer ['draɪə(r)] = drier

DSS [diː'es] n Br (abbr **Department of Social Security**) ≃ Sécurité f sociale

DTI [diːtiː'aɪ] n Br (abbr **Department of Trade and Industry**) ≃ ministère m du Commerce et de l'Industrie

DTP [diːtiː'piː] n Comptr (abbr **desktop publishing**) PAO f

DTs [diː'tiːz] npl (abbr **delirium tremens**) the D. le delirium tremens

dual ['djuːəl] adj double; d. carriageway (road) route f à deux chaussées; d. nationality double nationalité f; d. ownership copropriété f

dual-purpose ['djuːəl'pɜːpəs] adj à double emploi

dub [dʌb] (pt & pp dubbed) vt (a) (film) doubler (into en) (b) (nickname) surnommer

dubbing ['dʌbɪŋ] n (of film) doublage m

dubious ['djuːbɪəs] adj (a) (uncertain) incertain(e); to be d. (about) avoir quelques doutes (au sujet de) (b) (questionable) douteux(euse)

Dublin ['dʌblɪn] n Dublin

Dubliner ['dʌblɪnə(r)] n = personne née ou habitant à Dublin

duchess ['dʌtʃɪs] n duchesse f

duchy ['dʌtʃɪ] (pl duchies) n duché m

duck [dʌk] 1 n canard m; (female) cane f; to take to sth like a d. to water faire qch comme si on l'avait fait toute sa vie; criticism runs off him like water off a d.'s back les critiques glissent sur lui; d. pond mare f aux canards
2 vt (a) (head) baisser subitement; to d. sb (under water) faire faire le plongeon à qn (b) (avoid) (obligations) se dérober à; to d. the issue/question se dérober
3 vi (lower head) baisser la tête, se baisser; (under water) plonger sous l'eau; to d. behind a tree se cacher derrière un arbre

▸**duck out of** vt insep to d. out of doing sth éviter de faire qch; he ducked out of the meeting il s'est débrouillé pour ne pas assister à la réunion

duck-billed platypus ['dʌkbɪld'plætɪpəs] n ornithorynque m

duckling ['dʌklɪŋ] n (male) caneton m; (female) canette f

duct [dʌkt] n conduit m

dud [dʌd] Fam 1 n (person) incapable mf; (shell) obus m qui n'a pas éclaté; (banknote) faux m
2 adj (shell) qui n'a pas éclaté; (banknote) faux (fausse); (cheque) en bois

dude [duːd] n Am type m

due [djuː] 1 n (a) (what is owed) dû m; to give her her d., she did apologize pour lui rendre justice, il faut reconnaître qu'elle s'est excusée
(b) dues (membership fees) cotisation f
2 adj (a) (owed) dû (due); to fall d. échoir, arriver à échéance; are you d. any money from her? vous doit-elle de l'argent?; you're d. an apology je vous dois/il vous doit/etc une excuse; d. to par la suite de, en raison de; what is it d. to? c'est dû à quoi?; Fin d. date échéance f
(b) (merited, proper) dû (due), mérité(e); to give sb d. warning avertir qn dans les formes; after d. consideration après mûre réflexion; with all d. respect,... avec tout le respect que je vous dois,...; in d. course (when appropriate) en temps voulu; (eventually) le moment venu
(c) (expected) the train is d. (in or to arrive) le train doit arriver d'un moment à l'autre; when is he due (in or to arrive)? quand doit-il arriver?; when is the baby d.? pour quand la naissance est-elle prévue?; she's d. back any minute elle doit revenir d'un moment à l'autre; the film/book is d. out soon le film/livre va sortir sous peu
3 adv d. north/south plein nord/sud

duel ['djuːəl] 1 n duel m; to fight a d. se battre en duel
2 vi (pt & pp duelled, Am dueled) se battre en duel

duet [djuː'et] n duo m; (for piano) morceau m à quatre mains

duff [dʌf] adj Fam nul (nulle)

▸**duff up** vt sep Fam rosser, tabasser

duffel ['dʌfəl] = duffle

duffer ['dʌfə(r)] n Fam (incompetent person) nul (nulle) m,f

duffle ['dʌfəl] n d. (coat) duffle-coat m; d. bag sac m (de) marin

dug [dʌg] pt & pp of dig

dugout ['dʌgaʊt] n (a) (canoe) pirogue f (b) (shelter) Mil tranchée-abri f; Sp banc m de touche

duke [djuːk] n duc m

dull [dʌl] **1** *adj* (a) *(boring)* ennuyeux(euse), terne; **as d. as ditchwater** ennuyeux comme la pluie (b) *(un-intelligent)* lent(e) (c) *(not sharp)* *(pain, sound)* sourd(e); *(blade, senses)* émoussé(e) (d) *(not bright)* *(colour, surface)* terne; *(eyes)* sans éclat; *(weather, sky)* sombre, maussade

2 *vt* (a) *(pleasure)* rendre moins vif (vive); *(pain)* endormir, calmer; *(sound)* amortir, assourdir; *(blade, senses)* émousser (b) *(make less bright)* ternir

duly ['dju:lɪ] *adv* (a) *(properly)* dûment (b) *(as expected)* comme prévu

dumb [dʌm] *adj* (a) *(unable to speak)* muet(ette); **to be struck d.** *(with astonishment)* en rester muet; **d. animal** bête f; **d. insolence** silence m insolent (b) *Fam (stupid)* bête; **d. blonde** blonde f évaporée

dumbbell ['dʌmbel] *n* haltère m

dumbfounded [dʌm'faʊndɪd], **dumbstruck** ['dʌmstrʌk] *adj* abasourdi(e), ébahi(e)

dumbwaiter ['dʌmweɪtə(r)] *n (lift)* monte-plats m inv

dummy ['dʌmɪ] **1** *n* (pl **dummies**) (a) *(in shop window)* mannequin m; *(of ventriloquist)* marionnette f; *(model, fake)* objet m factice (b) *(for baby)* tétine f (c) *Fam (idiot)* abruti(e) m,f

2 *adj (fake)* factice; **d. run** coup m d'essai

dump [dʌmp] **1** *n* (a) *(for refuse)* décharge f; *Fam Pej (town)* bled m paumé; *(house)* dépotoir m; **d. truck** tombereau m, dumper m (b) *Mil (store)* dépôt m (c) *Comptr* vidage m

2 *vt* (a) *(put down)* déposer (b) *(dispose of)* se débarrasser de; *(waste)* déverser; *Fam (boyfriend, girlfriend)* plaquer (c) *Comptr (memory)* vider

dumper ['dʌmpə(r)] *n* **d. (truck)** tombereau m, dumper m

dumping ['dʌmpɪŋ] *n* (a) **no d.** *(sign)* décharge interdite; **d. ground** décharge f; *Fig* dépotoir m (b) *Econ* dumping m

dumpling ['dʌmplɪŋ] *n (in stew)* boulette f de pâte; *Scot* = sorte de plum-pudding écossais

dumps [dʌmps] *npl Fam* **to be down in the d.** broyer du noir, avoir le cafard

dumpy ['dʌmpɪ] *adj Fam (person, appearance)* boulot(otte)

dunce [dʌns] *n (at school)* âne m, cancre m; **d.'s cap** bonnet m d'âne

dune [dju:n] *n* dune f

dung [dʌŋ] *n (of cow)* bouse f; *(of horse)* crottin m; *(of wild animal)* fumées fpl

dungarees [dʌŋgə'ri:z] *npl (a pair of)* **d.** une salopette f; *(of workman)* un bleu de travail

dungeon ['dʌndʒən] *n (underground)* cachot m; *Hist (tower)* donjon m

dunghill ['dʌŋhɪl] *n* tas m de fumier

dunk [dʌŋk] *vt* tremper

Dunkirk [dʌn'kɜ:k] *n* Dunkerque f

duo ['dju:əʊ] (pl **duos**) *n (in music)* duo m; *(two people)* couple m

duodenal [dju:əʊ'di:nəl] *adj (ulcer)* duodénal(e)

dupe [dju:p] **1** *n* dupe f

2 *vt* duper, tromper; **to d. sb into doing sth** faire faire qch à qn en le dupant

duplicate **1** ['dju:plɪkət] *n (of key)* double m; *(of letter, receipt)* double m, duplicata m; **in d.** en double, en deux exemplaires

2 *adj* **d. key** un double de la clé; **a d. copy** un duplicata

3 *vt* ['dju:plɪkeɪt] *(copy)* faire un double/duplicata de; *(on photocopier)* faire une photocopie de (b) *(do again)* refaire

duplication [dju:plɪ'keɪʃən] *n* (a) *(copying)* reproduction f (b) *(repetition)* répétition f

duplicity [dju:'plɪsɪtɪ] *n* duplicité f

durability [djʊərə'bɪlɪtɪ] *n (of material)* résistance f; *(of friendship)* durabilité f

durable ['djʊərəbəl] **1** *n (consumer)* **durables** biens mpl durables

2 *adj (material)* résistant(e); *(friendship)* durable

duration [djʊ'reɪʃən] *n* durée f; **for the d.** pour longtemps

duress [djʊ'res] *n* **under d.** sous la contrainte

during ['djʊərɪŋ] *prep* pendant, durant; *(in the course of)* au cours de

dusk [dʌsk] *n* crépuscule m; **at d.** au crépuscule, à la tombée de la nuit

dust [dʌst] **1** *n* (a) *(dirt, powder)* poussière f; **d. cover** *(for furniture)* housse f; **d. cover** or **jacket** *(for book)* chemise f, jaquette f (b) *(action)* **to give sth a d.** passer un coup de chiffon sur qch (c) *(idioms)* **once the d. has settled** une fois que les choses se seront calmées; *Fam* **you won't see me for d.!** vous ne me reverrez pas de sitôt!

2 *vt* (a) *(clean)* dépoussiérer, épousseter (b) *(sprinkle)* *(with flour, sugar)* saupoudrer (**with** de)

3 *vi (clean)* épousseter

▶ **dust down, dust off** *vt sep (furniture)* épousseter; *Fig (legislation)* dépoussiérer; *(one's French)* se remettre à

dustbin ['dʌstbɪn] *n* poubelle f

dustcart ['dʌstkɑ:t] *n* benne f à ordures

duster ['dʌstə(r)] *n (cloth)* chiffon m (à poussière); *(for blackboard)* brosse f

dustman ['dʌstmən] *n* éboueur m

dustpan ['dʌstpæn] *n* pelle f (à poussière)

dustsheet ['dʌstʃi:t] *n* housse f

dust-up ['dʌstʌp] *n Fam (brawl)* bagarre f; **to have a d. with sb** se bagarrer avec qn

dusty ['dʌstɪ] *adj* poussiéreux(euse), couvert(e) de poussière; **to get d.** se couvrir de poussière

Dutch [dʌtʃ] **1** *npl* **the D.** *(people)* les Hollandais mpl

2 *n (language)* hollandais m

3 *adj* hollandais(e); *Fam* **I need some D. courage** j'ai besoin d'un verre pour me donner du courage; **D. cap** *(contraceptive)* diaphragme m

4 *adv Fam* **to go D.** payer chacun sa part

Dutchman ['dʌtʃmən] *n* Hollandais m, Néerlandais m; *Fam* **if that's a real diamond, (then) I'm a D.** si ça c'est un vrai diamant, alors je mange mon chapeau

Dutchwoman ['dʌtʃwʊmən] *n* Hollandaise f, Néerlandaise f

dutiful ['dju:tɪfʊl] *adj (obedient)* obéissant(e)

duty ['dju:tɪ] (pl **duties**) *n* (a) *(obligation)* devoir m (**to** envers); **to do one's d.** faire son devoir; **to fail in one's d.** manquer à son devoir; **to make it one's d. to...** se faire un devoir de...; **it's your d. to...** il est de votre devoir de...

(b) *(task)* **duties** fonctions fpl; **to take up** or **assume one's duties** entrer en fonctions; **to carry out** or **perform one's duties** exercer ses fonctions

(c) *(of soldier, employee)* **to be on/off d.** être/ne pas être de service; **d. roster** tableau m de service

(d) *Fin (tax)* droit m; **to pay d. on sth** payer une taxe sur qch

duty-free ['dju:tɪ'fri:] *adj (cigarettes, wine, perfume)* hors taxe; **d. shop** magasin m hors taxe

duvet ['du:veɪ] *n* couette *f*; **d. cover** housse *f* de couette

dwarf [dwɔːf] (*pl* **dwarfs** *or* **dwarves** [dwɔːvz]) **1** *n & adj* nain(e) *m,f*

2 *vt* (*be taller than*) écraser; *Fig* (*achievements, success*) éclipser

dwell [dwel] (*pt & pp* **dwelled** *or* **dwelt** [dwelt]) *vi Lit* (*live*) demeurer

▶**dwell on, dwell upon** *vt insep* remâcher, ressasser; **let's not d. on it** n'y pensons plus

dwelling ['dwelɪŋ] *n Lit* **d. (place)** demeure *f*, résidence *f*; **d. house** maison *f* d'habitation

dwelt [dwelt] *pt & pp of* **dwell**

dwindle ['dwɪndəl] *vi* diminuer; **to d. (away) to nothing** se réduire à rien

dwindling ['dwɪndəlɪŋ] *adj* (*funds, membership*) en baisse; (*enthusiasm*) faiblissant(e)

dye [daɪ] **1** *n* (*for clothes, hair*) teinture *f*

2 *vt* teindre; **to d. sth black/red** teindre qch en noir/rouge; **to d. one's hair** se teindre les cheveux

dyed-in-the-wool ['daɪdɪnðə'wʊl] *adj* (*conservative, Englishman*) bon teint *inv*

dying ['daɪɪŋ] **1** *npl* **the d.** les mourants *mpl*, les moribonds *mpl*

2 *adj* (*person*) mourant(e), agonisant(e); (*industry, tradition*) moribond(e); **to my d. day** jusqu'à ma mort; **d. wish** dernières volontés *fpl*; **d. words** dernières paroles *fpl*

dyke [daɪk] *n* (**a**) (*barrier*) digue *f* (**b**) *very Fam* (*lesbian*) gouine *f*, = terme injurieux désignant une lesbienne

dynamic [daɪ'næmɪk] **1** *n* (*driving force*) dynamique *f*

2 *adj also Fig* dynamique

dynamics [daɪ'næmɪks] *npl* dynamique *f*

dynamism ['daɪnəmɪzəm] *n* (*of person, society*) dynamisme *m*

dynamite ['daɪnəmaɪt] **1** *n also Fig* dynamite *f*; *Fam* **it's d.!** (*marvellous*) c'est du tonnerre!

2 *vt* dynamiter

dynamo ['daɪnəməʊ] (*pl* **dynamos**) *n* dynamo *f*

dynastic [dɪ'næstɪk] *adj* dynastique

dynasty ['dɪnəstɪ] (*pl* **dynasties**) *n* dynastie *f*

dysentery ['dɪsəntrɪ] *n* dysenterie *f*

dysfunctional [dɪs'fʌŋkʃənəl] *adj* **a d. family** une famille à problèmes

dyslexia [dɪs'leksɪə] *n* dyslexie *f*

dyslexic [dɪs'leksɪk] *adj* dyslexique

dystrophy ['dɪstrəfɪ] *n Med* dystrophie *f*

E

E, e [iː] *n* (a) *(letter)* E, e *m inv* (b) *Mus* mi *m* (c) *(abbr east)* E (d) *(abbr ecstasy)* X *m*, exta *m*

each [iːtʃ] **1** *adj* chaque; **e. one of us** chacun(e) de nous ou d'entre nous

2 *pron* (a) *(both, all)* chacun(e) *m,f*; **e. of us** chacun(e) de nous ou d'entre nous; **we e. earn £300** nous gagnons chacun 300 livres; **peaches at 25 pence e.** pêches à 25 pence chacune ou 25 pence pièce; **a little of e.** un peu de chaque (b) *(reciprocal)* **e. other** *(two)* l'un l'autre (l'une l'autre); *(more than two)* les uns les autres (les unes les autres); **separated from e. other** séparé l'un de l'autre; **they hate e. other** ils se haïssent; **we write to e. other** nous nous écrivons

eager ['iːgə(r)] *adj* (a) *(look, voice)* avide; *(supporter)* fervent(e); *(desire, hope)* ardent(e), vif (vive); **to be e. for sth/to do sth** désirer vivement qch/faire qch; **to be e. to please** être désireux(euse) de plaire; *Fam* **to be an e. beaver** être zélé(e)

eagerly ['iːgəlɪ] *adv* *(listen)* avidement; *(work, talk)* avec enthousiasme; **e. awaited** attendu(e) avec impatience

eagerness ['iːgənɪs] *n* impatience *f*; *(to learn, please)* vif désir *m*; **to show e. in doing sth** montrer un intérêt très vif à faire qch

eagle ['iːgəl] *n* aigle *m*

eagle-eyed [iːgə'laɪd] *adj* aux yeux d'aigle

ear [ˈɪə(r)] *n* (a) *(organ)* oreille *f*; **to have an e. for music** avoir l'oreille musicale; **to have an e. for languages** avoir une bonne oreille pour les langues; *Med* **e., nose and throat specialist** oto-rhino-laryngologiste *mf*; **e. lobe** lobe *m* de l'oreille (b) *(of wheat)* épi *m* (c) *(idioms)* **to play it by e.** *(improvise)* improviser; **to have sb's e.** avoir l'oreille de qn; **to keep one's e. to the ground** être sur le qui-vive; **to go in one e. and out the other** *(of words, information)* entrer par une oreille et sortir par l'autre; *Fam* **to be up to one's ears in debt** être endetté(e) jusqu'au cou; *Fam* **to be up to one's ears in work** être accablé(e) de travail; *Fam* **to be thrown out on one's e.** se faire jeter dehors ou sur le pavé; **I'm all ears** je suis tout ouïe; **my ears were burning** j'avais les oreilles qui sifflaient; **the house was falling down around their ears** la maison s'écroulait tout autour d'eux

earache ['ɪəreɪk] *n* mal *m* d'oreille(s); **to have e.** avoir mal à l'oreille/aux oreilles

eardrum ['ɪədrʌm] *n* tympan *m*

earful ['ɪəfʊl] *n Fam* **to give sb an e.** passer un savon à qn; **to get an e.** se faire passer un savon

earl [ɜːl] *n* comte *m*

earlier ['ɜːlɪə(r)] **1** *adj (previous)* plus ancien(enne); **I caught an e. train** j'ai pris un train qui partait plus tôt; **her e. novels** ses romans précédents

2 *adv* **e. (on)** avant; **a few days e.** quelques jours plus tôt; **no e. than tomorrow** pas avant demain; **as we saw e.** comme nous l'avons vu auparavant

earliest ['ɜːlɪəst] **1** *n* **at the e.** au plus tôt; **the e. I can be there is four o'clock** je pourrai être là à quatre heures au plus tôt

2 *adj (opportunity, memory)* premier(ère); **from the e. times** depuis les temps les plus reculés; **at the e. possible moment** le plus tôt possible, dans les plus brefs délais

early ['ɜːlɪ] **1** *adj* (a) *(in the day)* matinal(e); **to have an e. night** se coucher tôt; **to be an e. riser** être matinal, se lever de bon matin; *Prov* **the e. bird catches the worm** l'avenir appartient à ceux qui se lèvent tôt

(b) *(at beginning of period of time)* **in (the) e. summer** au début de l'été; **at an e. age** tout jeune; **in the e. 1980s** au début des années 80; **an e. example of...** un des premiers exemples de...

(c) *(ahead of time)* en avance; **half an hour e.** en avance d'une demi-heure

(d) *(premature) (death)* prématuré(e); **e. retirement** préretraite *f*; *Mil* **e. warning system** système *m* radar de préalerte

(e) *(in future)* **at an e. date** prochainement

2 *adv* (a) *(in the day)* de bonne heure, tôt; **e. in the morning** de bon matin de bonne heure; **e. in the evening** tôt dans la soirée; **as e. as possible** le plus tôt possible

(b) *(at beginning of period of time)* **e. in the year** au début de l'année; **e. on** dès l'abord; **e. in one's life** dans sa jeunesse; **e. in one's career** au début de sa carrière

(c) *(ahead of time)* **too e.** trop tôt

(d) *(prematurely) (die)* prématurément; **to retire e.** prendre une retraite anticipée

earmark ['ɪəmɑːk] *vt (funds)* assigner, affecter *(for* à); **the building is earmarked for closure** il est prévu que ce bâtiment soit fermé

earn [ɜːn] *vt (money)* gagner; *(rest, respect)* mériter; **to e. sb's love** gagner le cœur de qn; **to e. sb's praise** valoir des éloges à qn; **to e. one's living** gagner sa vie

earner ['ɜːnə(r)] *n (wage)* salarié(e) *m,f*; **to be a big/small e.** gagner beaucoup/peu; *Fam* **a nice little e.** une bonne petite affaire

earnest ['ɜːnɪst] **1** *n* **in e.** sérieusement; **things have started in e.** les choses ont vraiment commencé

2 *adj (person, effort, discussion)* sérieux(euse); *(expression)* pénétré(e), grave; *(voice)* pressant(e); *(desire)* profond(e)

earnestly ['ɜːnɪstlɪ] *adv* sérieusement; *(desire)* profondément; *(hope, believe)* sincèrement

earning power ['ɜːnɪŋ'paʊə(r)] *n* revenu *m* potentiel

earnings ['ɜːnɪŋz] *npl (of person)* salaire *m*; *(of company)* bénéfices *mpl*; **e. related** *(pensions, benefits)* proportionnel(elle) au salaire

earphones ['ɪəfəʊnz] *npl* écouteurs *mpl*

earpiece ['ɪəpiːs] *n (of telephone)* écouteur *m*

earplug ['ɪəplʌg] *n* boule *f* Quiès®

earring ['ɪərɪŋ] *n* boucle *f* d'oreille

earshot ['ɪəʃɒt] *n* within/out of e. à portée/hors de portée de voix

ear-splitting ['ɪəsplɪtɪŋ] *adj* à vous déchirer *ou* crever les tympans

earth [ɜːθ] **1** *n* (a) *(planet)* the E. la Terre; *Fam* **where/why on e....?** où/pourquoi diable...?; **to cost the e.** coûter les yeux de la tête; **to promise sb the e.** promettre la lune à qn (b) *(ground)* sol *m*; *(soil)* terre *f*; *Fig* **to come back to e.** revenir (brutalement) sur terre; *Fig* **to go to e.** *(of fugitive)* se terrer (c) *Br Elec* terre *f*, masse *f*
2 *vt Br Elec* mettre à la terre

earthenware ['ɜːθənweə(r)] **1** *n* poterie *f* (de terre)
2 *adj* en ou de terre cuite

earthling ['ɜːθlɪŋ] *n* terrien(enne) *m,f*

earthly ['ɜːθlɪ] *adj* (a) *(life, existence)* terrestre (b) *Fam (for emphasis)* **there's no e. reason why...** il n'y a absolument aucune raison pour que...; **she hasn't got an e.** *(chance)* elle n'a pas la moindre chance

earthquake ['ɜːθkweɪk] *n* tremblement *m* de terre, séisme *m*

earth-shattering ['ɜːθʃætərɪŋ] *adj Fam* stupéfiant(e)

earthworks ['ɜːθwɜːks] *n* travaux *mpl* de terrassement; *Mil* fortifications *fpl* en terre

earthworm ['ɜːθwɜːm] *n* ver *m* de terre

earthy ['ɜːθɪ] *adj* (a) *(of or like earth)* terreux(euse); **to have an e. smell** sentir la terre (b) *(coarse)* truculent(e); *(uninhibited)* direct(e)

earwax ['ɪəwæks] *n* cérumen *m*, cire *f*

earwig ['ɪəwɪg] *n (insect)* perce-oreille *m*

ease [iːz] **1** *n* (a) *(facility)* facilité *f*, aisance *f*; **with e.** avec facilité *ou* aisance (b) *(comfort)* tranquillité *f*, bien-être *m*; **at e.** à l'aise; **to put sb at (their) e.** mettre qn à l'aise; **to put** *or* **set sb's mind at e.** rassurer qn; **a life of e.** une vie d'oisiveté
2 *vt* (a) *(alleviate) (pain)* calmer, soulager; **to e. sb's mind** rassurer qn (b) *(relax) (pressure)* soulager; *(tension)* réduire; *(restrictions)* assouplir (c) *(move carefully, slowly)* déplacer doucement
3 *vi (of pain, pressure)* s'atténuer; *(of wind, rain)* se calmer; *(of situation)* se détendre

▶**ease off, ease up** *vi (of pain, rain)* se calmer

easel ['iːzəl] *n* chevalet *m*

easily ['iːzɪlɪ] *adv* (a) *(without difficulty)* facilement, sans difficulté; **that's e. said** c'est facile à dire (b) *(undoubtedly)* **e. the best** de loin le meilleur/la meilleure; **he is e. forty** il a au moins quarante ans (c) *(comfortably)* à son aise

easiness ['iːzɪnɪs] *n* (a) *(of task)* facilité *f* (b) *(of manner)* décontraction *f*

east [iːst] **1** *n* est *m*; **to the e. (of)** à l'est (de); **the E.** *(the Orient)* l'Orient *m*; *(Eastern Europe)* l'Est *m*
2 *adj (coast, side)* est *inv*; *(wind)* d'est; **E. Africa** l'Afrique *f* orientale; **the E. End** = les quartiers pauvres et populeux de l'Est de Londres ou Glasgow; *Formerly* **E. Germany** l'Allemagne *f* de l'Est; *Old-fashioned* **the E. Indies** les Indes *fpl* orientales; **the E. Side** = les quartiers est de New York
3 *adv* à l'est; *(travel)* vers l'est; **e. of the Rhine** à l'est du Rhin; **to face e.** être orienté(e) à l'est

eastbound ['iːstbaʊnd] *adj (train, traffic)* en direction de l'est

Easter ['iːstə(r)] *n* Pâques *fpl*; **at E.** à Pâques; **E. egg** œuf *m* de Pâques; **E. Island** l'île *f* de Pâques; **E. Sunday** dimanche *m ou* jour *m* de Pâques; **E. week** *(following Easter)* semaine *f* de Pâques; *(Holy Week)* semaine sainte

easterly ['iːstəlɪ] **1** *n (wind)* vent *m* d'est
2 *adj (point)* à l'est; *(wind)* d'est, qui vient de l'est; **in an e. direction** vers l'est

eastern ['iːstən] *adj* est *inv*; *(of Far East)* oriental(e); **e. France** l'est *m* de la France; **E. Europe** l'Europe *f* de l'Est; *Am* **E. Standard Time** heure *f* de la côte est de l'Amérique du Nord

eastward ['iːstwəd] **1** *adj (in the east)* à l'est, dans l'est
2 *adv* = **eastwards**

eastwards ['iːstwədz] *adv (face, point)* à l'est; *(go, travel)* vers l'est

easy ['iːzɪ] **1** *adj* (a) *(not difficult)* facile; *(solution)* simple; **to be e. to please** ne pas être difficile; **to get on with** facile à vivre; *Fam* **as e. as ABC** *or* **as pie** facile comme tout, simple comme bonjour; **the e. way out** la solution de facilité; *Fam* **e. money** argent *m* facile; **e. on the eye** agréable à regarder; *Com* **by e. payments, on e. terms** avec facilités de paiement; *Fam* **I'm e.** *(I don't mind)* ça m'est égal (b) *(comfortable, relaxed) (pace, life)* tranquille; *(manners)* libre, dégagé(e); *(style)* facile, naturel(elle); *Fam* **to be on e. street** ne pas avoir de problèmes financiers; **to have an e. time (of it)** avoir la vie facile; **e. chair** fauteuil *m*
2 *adv* **to go e. on sb/sth** y aller doucement avec qn/qch; **to take things** *or* **it e.** *(lead a life of ease)* mener une vie tranquille; *(not overdo things)* ralentir; **take it e.!** *(calm down)* t'en fais pas!; **that's easier said than done** c'est plus facile à dire qu'à faire; **e. come, e. go** ça va, ça vient

easy-going ['iːzɪ'gəʊɪŋ] *adj (tolerant)* coulant(e), accommodant(e); *(calm)* décontracté(e)

eat [iːt] *(pt* ate [et, eɪt], *pp* eaten ['iːtən]) **1** *vt* (a) manger; **to e. one's breakfast** prendre son petit déjeuner (b) *(idioms)* **to e. sb out of house and home** ruiner qn en nourriture; *Fam* **I could e. a horse!** j'ai une faim de loup!; *Fam* **he won't e. you!** il ne va pas te manger!; *Fam* **what's eating you?** qu'est-ce qui te tracasse?; **to e. one's words** se rétracter; *Fam* **if it works, I'll e. my hat** si ça réussit, je mange mon chapeau
2 *vi* manger; *Fig* **you'll have them eating out of your hand** ils te mangeront dans la main

▶**eat away** *vt insep (erode) (rocks, self-confidence)* éroder, miner; *(foundations)* saper

▶**eat into** *vt insep (erode)* ronger; *Fig (time, savings)* entamer

▶**eat out** *vi* manger dehors, manger au restaurant

▶**eat up 1** *vt sep* (a) *(food)* manger jusqu'à la dernière miette, finir (b) *(petrol, money)* consommer beaucoup de
2 *vi* finir son assiette; **e. up!** mange!

eaten ['iːtən] *pp of* **eat**

eater ['iːtə(r)] *n* mangeur(euse) *m,f*

eatery ['iːtərɪ] *(pl* eateries) *n Am* (café-)restaurant *m*

eats [iːts] *npl Fam* bouffe *f*

eau de Cologne ['əʊdəkə'ləʊn] *n* eau *f* de Cologne

eaves [iːvz] *npl* avant-toit *m*

eavesdrop ['iːvzdrɒp] *(pt & pp* eavesdropped) *vi* **to e. (on sb/sth)** écouter avec indiscrétion (qn/qch); **she was eavesdropping outside the door** elle écoutait à la porte

ebb [eb] 1 *n* (*of tide*) reflux *m*; **e. tide** marée *f* descendante; *Fig* the **e. and flow** (*of events*) les fluctuations *fpl*; *Fig* to be at a low e. (*of person, spirits*) être déprimé(e)
2 *vi* (*of tide*) baisser

▶**ebb away** *vi* (*of water*) s'écouler; (*of strength, enthusiasm*) faiblir, baisser

ebony ['ebənɪ] *n* ébène *f*

ebullience [ɪ'bʌlɪəns] *n* bouillonnement *m*, effervescence *f*

ebullient [ɪ'bʌlɪənt] *adj* bouillant(e), exubérant(e)

EC [i:'si:] *n* (*abbr* **European Community**) CE *f*

eccentric [ek'sentrɪk] *n & adj* excentrique *mf*

eccentricity [eksən'trɪsɪtɪ] *n* excentricité *f*

ecclesiastic [ɪkli:zɪ'æstɪk] 1 *n* ecclésiastique *m*
2 *adj* ecclésiastique

ECG [i:si:'dʒi:] *n Med* (*abbr* **electrocardiograph**) électrocardiographe *m*

echelon ['eʃəlɒn] *n* échelon *m*

echo ['ekəʊ] 1 *n* (*pl* **echoes**) *also Fig* écho *m*
2 *vt* (*pt & pp* **echoed**) (*words*) répéter; (*opinion*) se faire l'écho de
3 *vi* résonner (**with** de)

eclair [er'kleə(r)] *n* (*pastry*) éclair *m*; **chocolate e.** éclair au chocolat

eclectic [ə'klektɪk] *adj* (*tastes, style*) éclectique; (*blend*) hétérogène

eclipse [ɪ'klɪps] 1 *n* *also Fig* éclipse *f*
2 *vt* *also Fig* éclipser

eco-friendly ['i:kəʊfrendlɪ] *adj* (*product*) écologique, vert(e); (*lifestyle, person*) qui respecte l'environnement

ecological [i:kə'lɒdʒɪkəl] *adj* (*damage, balance*) écologique; (*campaign, activist*) écologiste

ecologist [ɪ'kɒlədʒɪst] *n* écologiste *mf*

ecology [ɪ'kɒlədʒɪ] *n* écologie *f*

economic [i:kə'nɒmɪk] *adj* (a) *Econ* économique (b) (*profitable*) rentable; **to make sth e.** rentabiliser qch

economical [i:kə'nɒmɪkəl] *adj* (*cost-effective*) économique; (*style*) concis(e); **to be e. with the truth** ne dire la vérité qu'à moitié

economically [i:kə'nɒmɪklɪ] *adv* économiquement; (*written*) dans un style concis

economics [i:kə'nɒmɪks] 1 *n* économie *f*
2 *npl* (*financial aspects*) aspects *mpl* financiers

economist [ɪ'kɒnəmɪst] *n* économiste *mf*

economize [ɪ'kɒnəmaɪz] *vi* économiser (**on** sur)

economy [ɪ'kɒnəmɪ] (*pl* **economies**) *n* économie *f*; **economies of scale** économies d'échelle; *Av* **e. class** classe *f* économique; **e. drive** politique *f* de réduction des dépenses; **e. measure** mesure *f* d'économie; **e. size** (*of packet*) taille *f* économique

ecstasy ['ekstəsɪ] (*pl* **ecstasies**) *n* (*emotional state*) extase *f*; (*drug*) ecstasy *f*; **to go into ecstasies over sth** s'extasier devant qch

ecstatic [ek'stætɪk] *adj* fou (folle) de joie; **he was e. about** *or* **over the news** la nouvelle l'a rendu fou de joie

ECT [i:si:'ti:] *n Med* (*abbr* **electroconvulsive therapy**) traitement *m* par électrochocs

ECU, ecu ['ekju:, 'i:kju:] *n* (*abbr* **European Currency Unit**) ÉCU *m*, écu *m*

Ecuador ['ekwədɔ:(r)] *n* l'Équateur *m*

ecumenical [i:kjʊ'menɪkəl] *adj* *Rel* œcuménique

eczema ['eksɪmə] *n* eczéma *m*; **to have e.** avoir de l'eczéma

ed [ed] (a) (*abbr* **edition**) éd(it) *f* (b) (*abbr* **editor**) dir.

eddy ['edɪ] 1 *n* (*pl* **eddies**) tourbillon *m*
2 *vi* (*pt & pp* **eddied**) (*of water*) faire des remous; (*of wind, snow*) tourbillonner

Eden ['i:dən] *n* l'Éden *m*

edge [edʒ] 1 *n* (a) (*of table, road, river*) bord *m*; (*of wood*) lisière *f*; (*of book*) tranche *f*; **at the water's e.** au bord de l'eau; **to be on the e. of** (*new age*) être au seuil de; (*war*) être au bord de; *Fig* **to be on the e. of one's seat** retenir son souffle
(b) (*of blade, tool*) tranchant *m*; (*of stone*) arête *f*; **to take the e. off** (*blade, appetite*) émousser; (*enjoyment*) gâter; *Fig* **to be on e.** être énervé(e); *Fig* **to set sb on e.** énerver qn
(c) (*advantage*) **to have the e. (over sb)** être avantagé(e) (par rapport à qn)
2 *vt* (*in sewing*) border (**with** de)
3 *vi* (*move slowly*) **to e. past sb** passer lentement devant qn; **to e. towards** avancer lentement vers

▶**edge out** *vt sep* (*supplant*) évincer (**of** de)

edgeways ['edʒweɪz], **edgewise** ['edʒwaɪz] *adv* (*on its edge*) de chant; (*from side*) de côté; *Fam* **I can't get a word in e.** je ne peux pas en placer une

edgy ['edʒɪ] *adj* nerveux(euse); **to get e.** s'énerver

edible ['edɪbəl] *adj* (*safe to eat*) comestible; (*fit to eat*) mangeable

edict ['i:dɪkt] *n Formal* édit *m*

edification [edɪfɪ'keɪʃən] *n* édification *f*

edifice ['edɪfɪs] *n* *also Fig* édifice *m*

edify ['edɪfaɪ] (*pt & pp* **edified**) *vt* édifier

edifying ['edɪfaɪɪŋ] *adj* édifiant(e)

Edinburgh ['edɪnbrə] *n* Édimbourg

edit ['edɪt] *vt* (a) (*correct*) réviser; (*prepare for publication*) préparer pour la publication; **edited by** (*coordinated by*) sous la direction de (b) (*film*) monter (c) (*manage*) (*newspaper, magazine*) diriger (d) *Comptr* éditer

▶**edit out** *vt sep* (*scene*) couper

editing ['edɪtɪŋ] *n Cin* montage *m*

edition [ɪ'dɪʃən] *n* (*of book, newspaper*) édition *f*; **in Tuesday's e. of the programme** dans l'émission de mardi

editor ['edɪtə(r)] *n* (a) (*of published work*) (*author*) rédacteur(trice) *m,f*; (*in charge*) directeur(trice) *m,f* (b) (*of film*) monteur(euse) *m,f* (c) (*of newspaper, magazine*) rédacteur(trice) *m,f* en chef; (*of section*) rédacteur(trice) (d) *Comptr* (*software*) éditeur *m*

editorial [edɪ'tɔ:rɪəl] 1 *n* éditorial *m*
2 *adj* de rédaction

EDP [i:di:'pi:] *n Comptr* (*abbr* **electronic data processing**) informatique *f*

educate ['edjʊkeɪt] *vt* éduquer, instruire; **he was educated at Oxford** il a fait ses études à Oxford

educated ['edjʊkeɪtɪd] *adj* instruit(e); **I made an e. guess** j'ai émis une hypothèse, mais je ne risquais guère de me tromper

education [edjʊ'keɪʃən] *n* (*process of learning, knowledge*) éducation *f*; (*process of teaching*) enseignement *m*; **to get (oneself) an e.** faire des études; **to complete one's e.** terminer ses études; *Fig* **it was an e. working over there** c'était instructif de travailler là-bas

educational [edjʊˈkeɪʃənəl] *adj (system)* éducatif(ive); *(establishment, publisher)* scolaire; *(qualification)* d'enseignement; *(experience, visit)* instructif(ive)

Edwardian [edˈwɔːdɪən] *adj (architecture, furniture)* de l'époque d'Édouard VII

EEC [iːiːˈsiː] *n Formerly (abbr* **European Economic Community***)* CEE *f*

eel [iːl] *n* anguille *f*

eerie [ˈɪərɪ] *adj (atmosphere, cry)* sinistre; *(silence)* de mort; *(feeling)* étrange

eerily [ˈɪərɪlɪ] *adv* étrangement

eff [ef] *vi Fam Euph* **to e. and blind** débiter des grossièretés

efface [ɪˈfeɪs] *vt* effacer

effect [ɪˈfekt] **1** *n* **(a)** *(result)* effet *m* (**on** sur); **to take e.** *(of drug, medicine)* faire effet, agir; *(of law)* prendre effet; **to put sth into e.** mettre qch en application; **in e.** en fait; **or words to that e.** ou quelque chose d'approchant **(b)** *(impression)* effet *m*; **for e.** pour faire de l'effet **(C)** *Formal* **personal effects** effets *mpl* personnels

2 *vt (cause) (change, rescue)* effectuer; *(saving, wish; solution)* apporter (**to** à)

effective [ɪˈfektɪv] *adj* **(a)** *(efficient, successful)* efficace; *(argument, speech)* convaincant(e) **(b)** *(actual, real) (profit, value)* réel(elle); **she will assume e. control of the business** c'est elle qui dirigera concrètement l'entreprise **(C)** *Law (in force)* **to be e.** prendre effet

effectively [ɪˈfektɪvlɪ] *adv* **(a)** *(efficiently)* avec efficacité; *(speak)* de façon convaincante **(b)** *(really)* en fait, en réalité; **they are e. the same** en fait, ils sont identiques

effectiveness [ɪˈfektɪvnɪs] *n* efficacité *f*

effeminate [ɪˈfemɪnət] *adj* efféminé(e)

effervescent [efəˈvesənt] *adj also Fig* effervescent(e)

effete [ɪˈfiːt] *adj (person)* veule; *(gesture)* efféminé(e)

efficacious [efɪˈkeɪʃəs] *adj Formal* efficace

efficacy [ˈefɪkəsɪ] *n Formal* efficacité *f*

efficiency [ɪˈfɪʃənsɪ] *n* efficacité *f*; *(output, productivity)* rendement *m*

efficient [ɪˈfɪʃənt] *adj* efficace; *(productive)* performant(e); **to be e. at sth** faire qch avec compétence

efficiently [ɪˈfɪʃəntlɪ] *adv* efficacement

effigy [ˈefɪdʒɪ] *n (pl* **effigies***)* effigie *f*

effing [ˈefɪŋ] *adj Fam Euph* fichu(e)

effluent [ˈefluənt] *n* effluents *mpl*

effort [ˈefət] *n* **(a)** *(exertion)* effort *m*; **to make an e. (to do sth)** faire un effort (pour faire qch); **put some e. into it!** fais un effort!; **to be worth the e.** valoir la peine **(b)** *(attempt)* tentative *f* (**at doing sth** pour faire qch); **a good e.** un bel effort; **a poor e.** un effort insuffisant

effortless [ˈefətlɪs] *adj (victory, success)* facile; *(skill, grace)* naturel(elle)

effortlessly [ˈefətlɪslɪ] *adv* sans effort

effrontery [ɪˈfrʌntərɪ] *n* effronterie *f*

effusive [ɪˈfjuːsɪv] *adj (person)* démonstratif(ive), expansif(ive); *(welcome)* enthousiaste

effusively [ɪˈfjuːsɪvlɪ] *adv (praise, welcome)* avec un enthousiasme débordant; *(thank)* avec effusion

EFL [iːefˈel] *n (abbr* **English as a Foreign Language***)* anglais *m* langue étrangère

EFT [iːefˈtiː] *n Comptr (abbr* **electronic funds transfer***)* transfert *m* de fonds électronique

EFTA [ˈeftə] *n (abbr* **European Free Trade Association***)* AELE *f*

EFTPOS [ˈeftpɒs] *n Comptr (abbr* **electronic funds transfer at point of sale***)* transfert *m* de fonds électronique sur point de vente

eg [iːˈdʒiː] *abbr* p. ex.

egalitarian [ɪɡælɪˈteərɪən] **1** *n* égalitariste *mf*

2 *adj (society)* égalitaire

egalitarianism [ɪɡælɪˈteərɪənɪzəm] *n* égalitarisme *m*

egg [eɡ] *n* **(a)** œuf *m*; **e. cup** coquetier *m*; **e. timer** sablier *m*; **e. white** blanc *m* d'œuf; **e. yolk** jaune *m* d'œuf **(b)** *(idioms)* **a good e. (man)** un brave type; *(woman)* une brave fille; **a bad e.** *(man)* une sale type; *(woman)* une sale bonne femme; **to have e. on one's face** être ridicule; *Prov* **Don't put all your eggs in one basket** il ne faut pas mettre tous ses œufs dans le même panier

▶**egg on** *vt sep* encourager (**to do sth** à faire qch)

egghead [ˈeɡhed] *n Hum or Pej* intello *mf*

eggplant [ˈeɡplɑːnt] *n Am* aubergine *f*

eggshell [ˈeɡʃel] *n* coquille *f* d'œuf

eggwhisk [ˈeɡwɪsk] *n* fouet *m*

egis [ˈiːɡɪs] *Am* = **aegis**

ego [ˈiːɡəʊ] *(pl* **egos***)* *n* ego *m*; **to give sb's e. a boost** flatter l'ego de qn; *Fam* **he's on an e. trip** il fait ça uniquement parce que ça flatte son ego

egocentric [iːɡəʊˈsentrɪk] *adj* égocentrique

egoist [ˈiːɡəʊɪst] *n* égoïste *mf*

egotism [ˈiːɡəʊtɪzəm] *n* égocentrisme *m*

egotist [ˈiːɡəʊtɪst] *n* égocentrique *mf*

egotistic(al) [iːɡəʊˈtɪstɪk(əl)] *adj* égocentrique

Egypt [ˈiːdʒɪpt] *n* l'Égypte *f*

Egyptian [ɪˈdʒɪpʃən] **1** *n* Égyptien(enne) *m,f*

2 *adj* égyptien(enne)

eiderdown [ˈaɪdədaʊn] *n* édredon *m*

eight [eɪt] **1** *n* huit *m inv*; **come at e.** venez à huit heures; **e. and e. are sixteen** huit et huit font seize; **there were e. of us** nous étions huit; **all e. of them left** tous les huit sont partis, ils sont partis tous les huit; **the e. of hearts** *(in cards)* le huit de cœur

2 *adj* huit; **e. cars** huit voitures; **e. pounds** huit livres; **on page e.** (à la) page huit; **to be e. (years old)** avoir huit ans; **they live at number e.** ils habitent au numéro huit; **e. o'clock** huit heures; **it's e. minutes to five** il est cinq heures moins huit

eighteen [eɪˈtiːn] **1** *n* dix-huit *m inv*

2 *adj* dix-huit; *see also* **eight**

eighteenth [eɪˈtiːnθ] **1** *n* **(a)** *(fraction)* dix-huitième *m*; *(in series)* dix-huitième *mf* **(b)** *(of month)* dix-huit *m inv*

2 *adj* dix-huitième; *see also* **eighth**

eighth [eɪtθ] **1** *n* **(a)** *(fraction)* huitième *m*; *(in series)* huitième *mf*; **Edward the E.** Édouard Huit **(b)** *(of month)* huit *m inv*; **(on) the e. of May** le huit mai; **we're leaving on the e.** nous partons le huit

2 *adj* huitième

eightieth [ˈeɪtɪəθ] **1** *n (fraction)* quatre-vingtième *m*; *(in series)* quatre-vingtième *mf*

2 *adj* quatre-vingtième

eighty [ˈeɪtɪ] **1** *n* quatre-vingts *m inv*; **he was doing e.** *(in car)* il faisait du quatre-vingt (à l'heure); **in the eighties** *(decade)* dans les années quatre-vingt; **to be in one's eighties** avoir quatre-vingts ans passés; **the temperature was in the eighties** il faisait dans les vingt-cinq degrés

2 *adj* quatre-vingts; **e. cars/passengers** quatre-vingts voitures/passagers; **e. percent** quatre-vingt pour cent; **she's about e. (years old)** elle a dans les quatre-vingts ans

Eire ['eərə] *n* l'Eire *f*

either ['aiðə(r), 'i:ðə(r)] **1** *adj* **(a)** *(one or the other)* l'un (l'une) ou l'autre; **I didn't like e. book** je n'ai aimé ni l'un ni l'autre de ces livres; **e. candidate may win** les deux candidats ont des chances de gagner **(b)** *(both)* les deux; on **e. side** des deux côtés; **in e. case** dans les deux cas

2 *pron* *(one or the other)* l'un (l'une) *m,f* ou l'autre; **e. (of them) will do** l'un ou l'autre fera l'affaire; **I don't want e. (of them)** je ne veux ni l'un ni l'autre; **I don't believe e. of you** je ne vous crois ni l'un ni l'autre

3 *conj* **e... or...** ou... ou..., soit... soit...; **e. you or your brother** ou toi ou ton frère, soit toi soit ton frère; **she doesn't eat e. meat or fish** elle ne mange ni viande ni poisson; **e. come in or go out!** ou tu rentres ou tu sors!

4 *adv* **if you don't go, I won't go e.** si tu n'y vas pas, moi non plus; **I don't like him – I don't e.** je ne l'aime pas – moi non plus

either-or ['aiðɔ:r)] *adj* **it's an e. situation** c'est soit l'un soit l'autre

ejaculate [i'dʒækjʊleit] *vi* éjaculer

ejaculation [idʒækjʊ'leiʃən] *n* **(a)** *(of semen)* éjaculation *f* **(b)** *Old-fashioned (exclamation)* exclamation *f*

eject [i'dʒekt] **1** *vt* *(cassette)* éjecter; *(troublemaker)* expulser

2 *vi* *(from plane)* s'éjecter

ejection [i'dʒekʃən] *n* *(of cassette, from plane)* éjection *f*; *(of troublemaker)* expulsion *f*

ejector seat [i'dʒektə(r)si:t] *n* siège *m* éjectable

▶**eke out** [i:k] *vt sep (money)* dépenser avec parcimonie; *(nations, supplies)* consommer avec parcimonie; **to e. out a living** gagner péniblement sa vie

elaborate 1 *adj* [i'læbərət] *(meal)* élaboré(e); *(drawing, description)* détaillé(e); *(excuse, scheme)* compliqué(e)

2 *vt* [i'læbəreit] *(formulate)* élaborer; *(flesh out)* développer

3 *vi* être plus précis; **to e. on sth** donner plus de détails sur qch

elan [er'lɑ:n] *n Lit* impétuosité *f*

elapse [i'læps] *vi* s'écouler

elastic [i'læstik] **1** *n* élastique *m*

2 *adj also Fig* élastique; **e. band** élastique *m*, bracelet *m* en caoutchouc

elasticated [i'læstikeitid] *adj* *(garment, material)* extensible; *(waist)* élastique

elasticity [i:læs'tisiti] *n also Fig* élasticité *f*

Elastoplast® [i'læstəplɑ:st] *n* Élastoplast® *m*

elated [i'leitid] *adj* transporté(e) (de joie)

elation [i'leiʃən] *n* exaltation *f*

elbow ['elbəʊ] **1** *n* coude *m*; **out at the elbows** *(of pullover, jacket)* troué(e) aux coudes; *Fig* **to give sb the e.** *(of employer)* se débarrasser de qn; *(of lover)* plaquer qn; *Fig* **to use some e. grease** mettre de l'huile de coude

2 *vt* **to e. sb (in the ribs)** donner un coup de coude (dans les côtes) à qn; **to e. sb aside** écarter qn d'un coup de coude; *Fig* jouer des coudes pour évincer qn; **to e. one's way through** se frayer un passage en jouant des coudes

elbowroom ['elbəʊrʊm] *n Fam Fig* **to have enough e.** avoir assez de liberté

elder¹ ['eldə(r)] **1** *n* **(a)** *(older person)* aîné(e) *m,f*; **young people should respect their elders** les jeunes doivent le respect à leurs aînés **(b)** *(of tribe)* ancien(enne) *m,f*; *(of church)* = membre d'une congrégation protestante chargé de seconder le ministre dans certaines tâches

2 *adj* *(brother, sister)* aîné(e); **e. statesman** grand homme *m* politique

elder² *n (tree)* sureau *m*

elderberry ['eldəberi] *n* *(pl* **elderberries***)* baie *f* de sureau

elderly ['eldəli] **1** *npl* **the e.** les personnes *fpl* âgées

2 *adj* âgé(e)

eldest ['eldist] **1** *n* **the e.** l'aîné(e) *m,f*

2 *adj* aîné(e)

elect [i'lekt] **1** *adj* élu(e)

2 *vt* **(a)** *(councillor, MP)* élire **(b)** *Formal (choose)* **to e. to do sth** choisir de faire qch

election [i'lekʃən] *n* élection *f*; **to hold an e.** procéder à une élection; **to stand for e.** se présenter aux élections; **e. campaign** campagne *f* électorale

electioneering [ilekʃə'nɪərɪŋ] *n* propagande *f* électorale

elective [i'lektiv] **1** *n Univ (course)* option *f*

2 *adj* *(assembly)* électoral(e); *Univ (course)* optionnel(elle)

elector [i'lektə(r)] *n* électeur(trice) *m,f*

electoral [i'lektərəl] *adj* électoral(e); **e. reform** réforme *f* du mode de scrutin; **e. roll** liste *f* électorale

electorate [i'lektərət] *n* électorat *m*

electric [i'lektrik] *adj* électrique; *Fig (atmosphere)* chargé(e) d'électricité; **e. blanket** couverture *f* chauffante; **e. chair** chaise *f* électrique; **e. cooker** cuisinière *f* électrique; **e. shock** décharge *f* électrique; *Med* électrochoc *m*

electrical [i'lektrikəl] *adj* électrique; **e. engineering** électrotechnique *f*

electrically [i'lektrikəli] *adv* **e. powered/operated** qui fonctionne à l'électricité; **e. charged** chargé(e) d'électricité

electrician [ilek'triʃən] *n* électricien(enne) *m,f*

electricity [ilek'trisiti] *n* électricité *f*

electrification [ilektrifi'keiʃən] *n* électrification *f*

electrify [i'lektrifai] *(pt & pp* **electrified***)* *vt* électrifier; *Fig (excite)* électriser

electrifying [i'lektrifaiiŋ] *adj Fig* électrisant(e)

electrocardiogram [ilektrəʊ'kɑ:diəʊgræm] *n Med* électrocardiogramme *m*

electrocardiograph [ilektrəʊ'kɑ:diəʊgræf] *n Med* électrocardiographe *m*

electrocute [i'lektrəkju:t] *vt* électrocuter; **to e. oneself** s'électrocuter

electrocution [ilektrə'kju:ʃən] *n* électrocution *f*

electrode [i'lektrəʊd] *n* électrode *f*

electrolysis [ilek'trolisis] *n* électrolyse *f*

electromagnet [ilektrəʊ'mægnit] *n* électroaimant *m*

electron [i'lektron] *n* électron *m*; **e. microscope** microscope *m* électronique

electronic [ilek'tronik] *adj* électronique; *Fin* **e. banking** bancatique *f*; *Comptr* **e. mail** courrier *m* électronique; *Comptr* **e. office** bureau *m* informatisé

electronically [ilek'tronikli] *adv* électroniquement

electronics [ilek'troniks] **1** *n (subject)* électronique *f*; **e. company** société *f* d'électronique; **the e. industry**

l'industrie f (de l')électronique
 2 *npl* **the e.** *(of machine)* le système électronique

electroplated [ɪ'lektrəplettɪd] *adj* plaqué(e) *(par électrodéposition)*

electroshock [ɪlektrəʊ'ʃɒk] *adj* **e. therapy** or **treatment** traitement *m* par électrochocs

elegance ['eligəns] *n* élégance *f*

elegant ['eligənt] *adj (appearance, movement)* élégant(e); *(reasoning)* clair(e) et simple

elegantly ['eligəntlɪ] *adv* avec élégance; **e. proportioned** aux proportions élégantes

elegy ['elɪdʒɪ] *(pl* **elegies)** *n* élégie *f*

element ['elɪmənt] *n* **(a)** *(constituent part)* part *f*; **an e. of danger/chance** une part de danger/chance; **this film has all the elements of a hit movie** ce film réunit tous les ingrédients d'un grand succès
 (b) *(factor)* **the e. of surprise** l'effet *m* de surprise; **the human/time e.** le facteur humain/temps
 (c) *(in society)* élément *m*; **the hooligan e.** la frange constituée par les hooligans
 (d) *Chem* élément *m*
 (e) *(of kettle, electric fire)* résistance *f*
 (f) *(force of nature)* **the four elements** les quatre éléments; *Fig* **to brave the elements** braver les éléments; **to be in one's e.** être dans son élément

elemental [elɪ'mental] *adj (basic)* fondamental(e)

elementary [elɪ'mentərɪ] *adj* élémentaire; *Am (education)* primaire; **my Arabic is rather e.** je parle un arabe assez rudimentaire; *Am* **e. school** école *f* primaire

elephant ['elɪfənt] *n* éléphant *m*

elephantine [elɪ'fæntaɪn] *adj (movements)* lourd(e) et gauche; *(proportions)* éléphantesque

elevate ['elɪveɪt] *vt* élever **(to** à); **to e. sb to the peerage** élever qn à la pairie

elevated ['elɪveɪtɪd] *adj (position, rank)* élevé(e); *(thoughts, discussion)* qui vole haut; *(language)* soutenu(e); **e. railway** métro *m* aérien

elevation [elɪ'veɪʃən] *n* **(a)** *(height)* altitude *f* **(b)** *(promotion)* élévation *f* **(to** à) **(c)** *Archit* élévation *f*

elevator ['elɪveɪtə(r)] *n* **(a)** *Am (lift)* ascenseur *m* **(b)** *(for goods)* élévateur *m* **(c)** *(on aeroplane wing)* gouvernail *m* de profondeur

eleven [ɪ'levən] **1** *n* onze *m inv*; **the French e.** *(football team)* le onze de France
 2 *adj* onze; *see also* **eight**

elevenses [ɪ'levənzɪz] *npl Br Fam* casse-croûte *m inv (vers onze heures du matin)*

eleventh [ɪ'levənθ] **1** *n* **(a)** *(fraction)* onzième *m*; *(in series)* onzième *mf* **(b)** *(of month)* onze *m inv*
 2 *adj* onzième; **at the e. hour** à la dernière minute; *see also* **eighth**

elf [elf] *(pl* **elves** [elvz]) *n* elfe *m*

elicit [ɪ'lɪsɪt] *vt (information, smile)* tirer **(from** de); *(reaction, response)* susciter **(from** de la part de)

eligibility [elɪdʒɪ'bɪlɪtɪ] *n (for grant, benefit)* droit *m* **(for** à)

eligible ['elɪdʒɪbəl] *adj* **to be e. for sth** avoir droit à qch; **e. bachelor** bon parti *m*

eliminate [ɪ'lɪmɪneɪt] *vt* éliminer

elimination [ɪlɪmɪ'neɪʃən] *n* élimination *f*; **by a process of e.** (en procédant) par élimination

elite [eɪ'liːt] **1** *n* élite *f*
 2 *adj* d'élite

elitism [eɪ'liːtɪzəm] *n* élitisme *m*

elitist [eɪ'liːtɪst] *n & adj* élitiste *mf*

elixir [ɪ'lɪksə(r)] *n Lit* élixir *m*

Elizabethan [ɪlɪzə'biːθən] **1** *n* = Anglais vivant sous le règne d'Élisabeth 1ère
 2 *adj* élisabéthain(e)

elk [elk] *n* élan *m*

ellipse [ɪ'lɪps] *n Math* ellipse *f*

ellipsis [ɪ'lɪpsɪs] *(pl* **ellipses** [ɪ'lɪpsiːz]) *n Gram* ellipse *f*

elm [elm] *n* orme *m*

elocution [elə'kjuːʃən] *n* élocution *f*, diction *f*

elongate ['iːlɒŋgeɪt] *vt* allonger

elope [ɪ'ləʊp] *vi* s'enfuir (pour se marier)

eloquence ['eləkwəns] *n* éloquence *f*

eloquent ['eləkwənt] *adj* éloquent(e)

else [els] *adv* **anyone e.** n'importe qui; *(in negative sentences)* personne d'autre; **is anyone e. interested?** quelqu'un d'autre est-il intéressé?; **someone e.** quelqu'un d'autre; **everyone e.** tous les autres; **no one e.** personne d'autre; **anything e.** n'importe quoi d'autre; *(in negative sentences)* rien d'autre; **have you anything e. to do?** as-tu autre chose à faire?; **something e.** autre chose, quelque chose d'autre; **everything e.** tout le reste; **nothing e.** rien d'autre; **somewhere e.** autre part, ailleurs; **anywhere e.** (n'importe où) ailleurs; *(in negative sentences)* nulle part ailleurs; **everywhere e.** partout ailleurs; **nowhere e.** nulle part ailleurs; **who e. was there?** qui d'autre était là?; **who broke it? – Peter, who e.?** qui l'a cassé? – Peter, qui d'autre veux-tu que ce soit!; **what e.?** quoi d'autre?; **when e.?** à quel autre moment/quelle autre date?; **where e. did you go?** où êtes-vous allés ailleurs?; **how e.?** de quelle autre manière?; **why e.?** pour quelle autre raison?; **little e.** pas grand-chose d'autre; **there isn't much e.** we can do nous ne pouvons pas faire grand-chose d'autre; **or e.** *(otherwise)* sinon; **do what I tell you or e.!** fais ce que je te dis ou sinon...!

elsewhere ['elsweə(r)] *adv* ailleurs, autre part

ELT [iːel'tiː] *n (abbr* **English Language Teaching)** anglais *m* langue étrangère

elucidate [ɪ'luːsɪdeɪt] *vt (mystery)* élucider; *(reasons)* expliquer

elude [ɪ'luːd] *vt* échapper à

elusive [ɪ'luːsɪv] *adj (person)* insaisissable; *(concept)* difficile à saisir

elver ['elvə(r)] *n* civelle *f*

elves [elvz] *pl of* **elf**

emaciated [ɪ'meɪsɪeɪtɪd] *adj* émacié(e)

e-mail ['iːmeɪl] **1** *n* courrier *m* électronique
 2 *vt* envoyer un courrier électronique à

emanate ['emənet] **1** *vt* dégager
 2 *vi* émaner **(from** de)

emancipate [ɪ'mænsɪpeɪt] *vt* émanciper

emancipated [ɪ'mænsɪpeɪtɪd] *adj* émancipé(e)

emancipation [ɪmænsɪ'peɪʃən] *n* émancipation *f*

emasculate [ɪ'mæskjʊleɪt] *vt Fig* amputer

embalm [ɪm'bɑːm] *vt* embaumer

embankment [ɪm'bæŋkmənt] *n (beside railway)* talus *m*; *(beside river)* berge *f*, quai *m*

embargo [em'bɑːgəʊ] *(pl* **embargoes)** **1** *n* embargo *m*; **to put an e. on** mettre un embargo sur
 2 *vt* mettre un embargo sur

embark [ɪm'bɑːk] *vi* embarquer; *Fig* to e. (up)on sth s'embarquer dans qch

embarrass [ɪm'bærəs] *vt* embarrasser, gêner; *(make ashamed)* faire honte à

embarrassed [ɪm'bærəst] *adj (ashamed, uncomfortable)* embarrassé(e), gêné(e); *(financially)* gêné(e) (financièrement)

embarrassing [ɪm'bærəsɪŋ] *adj* embarrassant(e), gênant(e); **how e.!** comme ça a dû être/c'est embarrassant!

embarrassment [ɪm'bærəsmənt] *n* embarras *m*, gêne *f*; **much to my e.** à mon grand embarras; **to be an e. to sb** être une source d'embarras pour qn

embassy ['embəsɪ] *(pl* **embassies***)* *n* ambassade *f*; **the French E.** l'ambassade de France

embattled [ɪm'bætəld] *adj* assiégé(e) de toutes parts

embed [ɪm'bed] *(pt & pp* **embedded***)* *vt* **(a)** to be embedded in sth être fiché(e) dans qch; *(with cement)* être scellé(e) dans qch; *Fig* to be embedded in sb's memory être gravé(e) dans la mémoire de qn **(b)** *Comptr* intégrer

embellish [ɪm'belɪʃ] *vt (room)* embellir **(with** de); *(account)* enjoliver

embers ['embəz] *npl* braises *fpl*

embezzle [ɪm'bezəl] *vt* détourner **(from** de)

embezzlement [ɪm'bezəlmənt] *n* e. **(of funds)** détournement *m* de fonds

embezzler [ɪm'bezlə(r)] *n* escroc *m*

embitter [ɪm'bɪtə(r)] *vt (person)* aigrir, remplir d'amertume

embittered [ɪm'bɪtəd] *adj (person)* aigri(e)

emblazon [ɪm'bleɪzən] *vt (shield)* orner **(with** de); *Fig (name, headline)* étaler

emblem ['embləm] *n* emblème *m*

embodiment [ɪm'bɒdɪmənt] *n* incarnation *f*

embody [ɪm'bɒdɪ] *(pt & pp* **embodied***)* *vt* incarner

embolden [ɪm'bəʊldən] *vt* enhardir; to e. sb to do sth donner à qn le courage de faire qch

embolism ['embəlɪzəm] *n Med* embolie *f*

embossed [ɪm'bɒst] *adj (metal, leather)* repoussé(e); *(letter, wallpaper, design)* en relief

embrace [ɪm'breɪs] **1** *n* étreinte *f*
2 *vt* **(a)** *(person)* étreindre; *Fig (belief, religion)* embrasser **(b)** *(include)* couvrir
3 *vi* s'étreindre

embroider [ɪm'brɔɪdə(r)] *vt (cloth)* broder; *Fig (account, report)* enjoliver

embroidery [ɪm'brɔɪdərɪ] *n* broderie *f*

embroil [ɪm'brɔɪl] *vt* entraîner **(in** dans); to get embroiled in sth se laisser entraîner dans qch

embryo ['embrɪəʊ] *(pl* **embryos***)* *n* embryon *m*; *Fig* in e. *(plan, idea)* à l'état embryonnaire

embryonic [embrɪ'ɒnɪk] *adj Biol* embryonnaire; *(plan, idea)* à l'état embryonnaire

emend [ɪ'mend] *vt* corriger

emendation [iːmen'deɪʃən] *n* correction *f*

emerald ['emərəld] *n* émeraude *f*; **an e. necklace** un collier d'émeraudes; **e. (green)** (vert *m*) émeraude *m*; **the E. Isle** la verte Érin

emerge [ɪ'mɜːdʒ] *vi (of person, truth)* émerger **(from** de); **it later emerged that...** il est apparu par la suite que...

emergence [ɪ'mɜːdʒəns] *n (from hiding)* apparition *f*; *(of truth)* révélation *f*; *(of new state, new leader)* émergence *f*

emergency [ɪ'mɜːdʒənsɪ] *(pl* **emergencies***)* *n* urgence *f*; **in an e., in case of e.** en cas d'urgence; **e. exit** sortie *f* de secours; **e. landing** atterrissage *m* forcé; **e. services** services *mpl* d'urgence; **e. stop** arrêt *m* d'urgence

emergent [ɪ'mɜːdʒənt] *adj (talent, ability)* naissant(e); *(nation)* en voie de développement

emery ['emərɪ] *n* émeri *m*; **e. board** lime *f* à ongles *(en papier émeri)*; **e. paper** papier *m* émeri

emetic [ɪ'metɪk] **1** *n* émétique *m*
2 *adj* émétique

emigrant ['emɪɡrənt] **1** *n* émigrant(e) *m,f*; *(when settled)* émigré(e) *m,f*
2 *adj* migrant(e); *(when settled)* émigré(e)

emigrate ['emɪɡreɪt] *vi* émigrer

emigration [emɪ'ɡreɪʃən] *n* émigration *f*

émigré ['emɪɡreɪ] *n* émigré(e) *m,f*

eminence ['emɪnəns] *n* **(a)** *(importance)* position *f* éminente; *(of post)* distinction *f* **(b)** *(title of cardinal)* **Your E.** Votre Éminence

eminent ['emɪnənt] *adj* éminent(e)

eminently ['emɪnəntlɪ] *adv* éminemment

emirate ['emɪreɪt] *n* émirat *m*

emissary ['emɪsərɪ] *(pl* **emissaries***)* *n* émissaire *m*

emission [ɪ'mɪʃən] *n (of gas, light, bank notes)* émission *f*

emit [ɪ'mɪt] *(pt & pp* **emitted***)* *vt (heat, signal, sound)* émettre; *(smell)* dégager; *(sigh, cry)* pousser

emotion [ɪ'məʊʃən] *n (strength of feeling)* émotion *f*; *(individual feeling)* sentiment *m*

emotional [ɪ'məʊʃənəl] *adj (person, reaction)* émotif(ive); *(problem, shock)* émotionnel(elle); *(film, farewell)* émouvant(e); **to get e.** être ému(e)

emotionally [ɪ'məʊʃənəlɪ] *adv (thank, welcome)* avec effusion; **to be e. involved with sb** avoir une relation intime avec qn; **to get e. involved (with sb)** s'attacher (à qn); **e. deprived** en manque d'affection

emotive [ɪ'məʊtɪv] *adj (issue)* sensible; *(argument, words)* qui fait vibrer la corde sensible

empathize ['empəθaɪz] *vi* to e. **with** *(person)* comprendre; *(plight, problems)* compatir à

empathy ['empəθɪ] *n* compassion *f*

emperor ['empərə(r)] *n* empereur *m*

emphasis ['emfəsɪs] *(pl* **emphases** ['emfəsiːz]*)* *n* accent *m*; **to lay** or **place e. on sth** *(point, fact)* mettre l'accent sur qch; *(word, syllable)* appuyer sur qch

emphasize ['emfəsaɪz] *vt (point, fact)* insister sur; *(word, syllable)* appuyer sur

emphatic [ɪm'fætɪk] *adj (denial, response, person)* catégorique; *(gesture, tone)* énergique

emphatically [ɪm'fætɪkəlɪ] *adv (say)* énergiquement; *(refuse, deny)* catégoriquement; **most e.!** absolument!

empire ['empaɪə(r)] *n also Fig* empire *m*

empirical [em'pɪrɪkəl] *adj* empirique

empiricism [em'pɪrɪsɪzəm] *n* empirisme *m*

employ [ɪm'plɔɪ] **1** *n Formal* to be in sb's e. être employé(e) par qn
2 *vt (workers, force, skills)* employer; *(tool, means)* utiliser

employee [em'plɔɪiː] *n* employé(e) *m,f*; **employees** *(staff)* personnel *m*, salariés *mpl*

employer [ɪm'plɔɪə(r)] *n* employeur(euse) *m,f*

employment [ɪm'plɔɪmənt] n (a) (work) emploi m; to be in e. avoir un emploi; to be without e. être sans emploi; to give e. to sb employer qn; e. agency or bureau bureau m ou agence f de placement (b) (use) (of money, force) emploi m; (of tool) utilisation f

empower [ɪm'paʊə(r)] vt to e. sb to do sth habiliter qn à faire qch

empress ['emprɪs] n impératrice f

emptiness ['emptɪnɪs] n vide m

empty ['emptɪ] **1** (a (bottle) bouteille f vide
2 adj (container, existence) vide; (promise, threat, words) en l'air; **on an e. stomach** l'estomac vide, à jeun
3 vt vider
4 vi se vider

▶**empty out** vt sep (pockets) vider

empty-handed ['emptɪ'hændɪd] adv les mains vides, bredouille

empty-headed ['emptɪ'hedɪd] adj sans cervelle; **to be e.** n'avoir rien dans la tête

EMS [i:em'es] n (abbr **European Monetary System**) SME m

EMU [i:em'ju:] n (abbr **Economic and Monetary Union**) union f économique et monétaire

emu ['i:mju:] n émeu m

emulate ['emjʊleɪt] vt imiter

emulsion [ɪ'mʌlʃən] n émulsion f

enable [ɪ'neɪbl] vt (a) (allow) to e. sb to do sth permettre à qn de faire qch (b) Comptr (function, device) mettre en service

enact [ɪ'nækt] vt (tragedy, play) jouer; (law) promulguer

enamel [ɪ'næml] **1** n émail m
2 vt (pt & pp **enamelled**, Am **enameled**) émailler

enamoured, Am **enamored** [ɪ'næməd] adj to be e. of être entiché(e) de; **I'm not exactly e. of the idea** je ne peux pas dire que cette idée me ravisse

encampment [ɪn'kæmpmənt] n Mil camp m, campement m

encapsulate [ɪn'kæpsjʊleɪt] vt résumer

encase [ɪn'keɪs] vt envelopper; (in concrete) noyer

enchant [ɪn'tʃɑːnt] vt (a) (charm) enchanter, ravir (b) (put under a spell) ensorceler

enchanting [ɪn'tʃɑːntɪŋ] adj (idea) très séduisant(e); (voice, person, smile) charmant(e), ravissant(e)

enchantment [ɪn'tʃɑːntmənt] n enchantement m

enchantress [ɪn'tʃɑːntrɪs] n enchanteresse f

encircle [ɪn'sɜːkəl] vt (of road, walls) entourer; (of army, police) encercler, cerner

enclave ['enkleɪv] n enclave f

enclose [ɪn'kləʊz] vt (a) (surround) entourer; **an enclosed space** un espace clos (b) (include in letter) joindre (**in** à); **enclosed please find..., please find enclosed...** veuillez trouver ci-joint ou ci-inclus...

enclosure [ɪn'kləʊʒə(r)] n (a) (area) enceinte f; (for animals) enclos m; (in horseracing) paddock m (b) (in letter) pièce f jointe

encode [en'kəʊd] vt coder, chiffrer; Comptr encoder

encompass [ɪn'kʌmpəs] vt englober, couvrir

encore ['ɒŋkɔ:(r)] n = chanson, morceau etc exécutés à la suite d'un rappel; **to call for an e.** bisser; **e.!** bis!

encounter [ɪn'kaʊntə(r)] **1** n rencontre f
2 vt (person, difficulty) rencontrer; (enemy) affronter

encourage [ɪn'kʌrɪdʒ] vt encourager; **to e. sb to do sth** encourager qn à faire qch

encouragement [ɪn'kʌrɪdʒmənt] n encouragement m; **to give sb e.** encourager qn

encouraging [ɪn'kʌrɪdʒɪŋ] adj encourageant(e); (smile) d'encouragement

▶**encroach on, encroach upon** [ɪn'krəʊtʃ] vt insep empiéter sur; **the sea is encroaching on the land** la mer gagne du terrain

encrusted [ɪn'krʌstɪd] adj e. **with** (jewels) incrusté(e) de; (mud) couvert(e) de

encumber [ɪn'kʌmbə(r)] vt to be encumbered **with** être encombré(e) de

encumbrance [ɪn'kʌmbrəns] n gêne f, embarras m (**to** pour)

encyclical [ɪn'sɪklɪkəl] n Rel encyclique f

encyclop(a)edia [ɪnsaɪklə'piːdɪə] n encyclopédie f

encyclop(a)edic [ɪnsaɪklə'piːdɪk] adj encyclopédique

end [end] **1** n (a) (extremity) bout m, extrémité f; **from one e. to the other** d'un bout à l'autre; **e. to e.** bout à bout; **to stand sth on e.** mettre qch debout; **his hair was standing on e.** ses cheveux se dressaient sur sa tête; Fig **to come to the e. of the road** or **line** être en fin de parcours
(b) (of month, book, meeting) fin f; **for days on e.** pendant des jours entiers; **to put an e. to sth** mettre fin à qch; **to come to an e.** prendre fin; Fig **at the e. of the day** au bout du compte; **in the e.** à la longue; **she gave me the money back in the e.** elle a fini par me rembourser; **it's not the e. of the world** ce n'est pas la fin du monde; Fam **no e. of** énormément de; **e. product** produit m fini; Fig résultat m
(c) (aim, purpose) fin f, but m; **an e. in itself** une fin en soi; **to what e.?** à quelle fin?, dans quel but?; **the e. justifies the means** la fin justifie les moyens
(d) (idioms) Fam **to keep one's e. up** ne pas se laisser abattre; Fam **to make ends meet** joindre les deux bouts; Fam **this job will be the e. of me!** ce boulot, j'y laisserai ma peau!; Fam **to get hold of the wrong e. of the stick** mal comprendre; **we shall never hear the e. of it!** on n'a pas fini d'en entendre parler!
2 vt finir, terminer; (argument, uncertainty) mettre fin à; Fam **to e. it all** (commit suicide) en finir
3 vi finir, se terminer; (of road, path) s'arrêter; **it ended in a fight/a divorce** ça a fini en bagarre/par un divorce

▶**end up** vi finir; (in particular place) se retrouver; **to e. up doing sth** finir par faire qch

endanger [ɪn'deɪndʒə(r)] vt (person, life) mettre en danger; (chances, future, health) compromettre; **an endangered species** une espèce menacée

endear [ɪn'dɪə(r)] vt to e. oneself to sb se rendre sympathique aux yeux de qn

endearing [ɪn'dɪərɪŋ] adj (person, personality) attachant(e); (smile, habit) charmant(e)

endearment [ɪn'dɪəmənt] n terms of e. mots mpl tendres

endeavour, Am **endeavor** [ɪn'devə(r)] **1** n effort m
2 vi to e. to do sth s'efforcer de faire qch

endemic [en'demɪk] adj endémique; Fig e. **to** propre à

ending ['endɪŋ] n (of story) fin f; (of word) terminaison f

endive ['endaɪv] n (a) (curly) e. (chicorée f) frisée f (b) Am (chicory) endive f

endless ['endlɪs] adj (desert, number, possibilities) infini(e); (list, wait, task) interminable

endocrine ['endəʊkraɪn] *adj Med* e. gland glande *f* endocrine

endocrinology [endəʊkrɪ'nɒlədʒɪ] *n* endocrinologie *f*

endorse [ɪn'dɔːs] *vt* (a) *(document, cheque)* endosser; *Br (driving licence)* décompter des points sur (b) *(approve) (action)* approuver; *(opinion)* souscrire *ou* adhérer à; *(candidature)* appuyer

endorsement [ɪn'dɔːsmənt] *n* (a) *(on document, cheque)* endos *m*; *Br (on driving licence)* = mention portée sur le permis de conduire à la suite d'une infraction (b) *(approval) (of action)* approbation *f* (of de); *(of opinion)* adhésion *f* (of à); *(of candidature)* appui *m* (of à)

endow [ɪn'daʊ] *vt* doter (with de)

endowment [ɪn'daʊmənt] *n* (a) *Fin* dotation *f*; e. mortgage (b) *(talent)* don *m*, talent *m*   assurance-vie (b) *(talent)* don *m*, talent *m*

endurable [ɪn'djʊərəbəl] *adj* supportable

endurance [ɪn'djʊərəns] *n* endurance *f*; beyond e. au-delà des limites du supportable; e. test épreuve *f* d'endurance; *Fig* this is a real e. test ma patience est mise à rude épreuve

endure [ɪn'djʊə(r)] 1 *vt (violence, hardship)* endurer; *(person, insults)* supporter
2 *vi (last)* survivre

enduring [ɪn'djʊərɪŋ] *adj* durable

enema ['enəmə] *n* lavement *m*

enemy ['enəmɪ] 1 *n (pl* enemies) ennemi(e) *m,f*; to be one's own worst e. se desservir soi-même
2 *adj (army, ship)* ennemi(e)

energetic [enə'dʒetɪk] *adj* énergique

energetically [enə'dʒetɪklɪ] *adv* énergiquement

energy ['enədʒɪ] *n* énergie *f*; to save e. faire des économies d'énergie; e. crisis crise *f* de l'énergie

energy-saving ['enədʒɪseɪvɪŋ] *adj* qui économise l'énergie

enervating ['enəveɪtɪŋ] *adj* débilitant(e)

enfeeble [ɪn'fiːbəl] *vt* affaiblir

enfold [ɪn'fəʊld] *vt* envelopper (in dans); to e. sb in one's arms serrer qn dans ses bras

enforce [ɪn'fɔːs] *vt (regulation)* mettre en vigueur; *(rights)* faire valoir; to e. the law faire respecter la loi

enforcement [ɪn'fɔːsmənt] *n (of a law)* mise *f* en vigueur

enfranchise [ɪn'fræntʃaɪz] *vt* accorder le droit de vote à

engage [ɪn'geɪdʒ] 1 *vt* (a) *(employ)* engager; *(workmen)* embaucher (b) *(occupy) (person)* occuper; *(attention)* fixer; to e. sb in conversation engager la conversation avec qn; to be engaged in doing sth être occupé(e) à faire qch (c) *Mil (enemy)* attaquer (d) *(cog, gear)* mettre en prise; to e. the clutch embrayer
2 *vi* (a) to e. in *(activity, sport)* s'adonner à (b) *(of cog wheel)* (s')engager

engaged [ɪn'geɪdʒd] *adj* (a) *(to be married)* fiancé(e) (b) *(busy)* occupé(e) (in à); *Br (phone, public toilet)* occupé; to be otherwise e. avoir d'autres engagements

engagement [ɪn'geɪdʒmənt] *n* (a) *(to be married)* fiançailles *fpl*; e. ring bague *f* de fiançailles (b) *(appointment)* rendez-vous *m* (c) *(military action)* combat *m*, engagement *m*

engaging [ɪn'geɪdʒɪŋ] *adj* engageant(e), attrayant(e)

engender [ɪn'dʒendə(r)] *vt* faire naître, engendrer

engine ['endʒɪn] *n (of car, plane, ship)* moteur *m*; e. room salle *f* des machines; e. trouble panne *f* de moteur

(b) *(of train)* locomotive *f*; e. driver conducteur *m*, mécanicien *m*

engineer [endʒɪ'nɪə(r)] 1 *n (technical specialist)* ingénieur *m*; *(mechanic)* dépanneur *m*; *(on ship)* mécanicien *m*
2 *vt (cause) (plan, downfall, defeat)* machiner, manigancer; *(situation)* manigancer

engineering [endʒɪ'nɪərɪŋ] *n* ingénierie *f*

England ['ɪŋglənd] *n* l'Angleterre *f*

English ['ɪŋglɪʃ] 1 *n (language)* anglais *m*; E. class/teacher cours *m*/professeur *m* d'anglais
2 *npl* the E. les Anglais *mpl*
3 *adj* anglais(e); the E. Channel la Manche

Englishman ['ɪŋglɪʃmən] *n* Anglais *m*

Englishwoman ['ɪŋglɪʃwʊmən] *n* Anglaise *f*

engrave [ɪn'greɪv] *vt* graver

engraver [ɪn'greɪvə(r)] *n* graveur *m*

engraving [ɪn'greɪvɪŋ] *n* gravure *f*

engrossed [ɪn'grəʊst] *adj* plongé(e) (in dans), absorbé(e) (in par)

engrossing [ɪn'grəʊsɪŋ] *adj* absorbant(e), captivant(e)

engulf [ɪn'gʌlf] *vt (of waves, flames)* engloutir; *(of feeling)* s'emparer de

enhance [ɪn'hɑːns] *vt (quality of life, chances)* améliorer; *(beauty, colour)* rehausser, mettre en valeur; *(ability, effect)* renforcer; *(reputation, pleasure)* accroître; *(value)* augmenter

enigma [ɪ'nɪgmə] *n* énigme *f*

enigmatic [enɪg'mætɪk] *adj* énigmatique

enjoy [ɪn'dʒɔɪ] *vt* (a) *(take pleasure from)* prendre plaisir à; *(film, book, concert)* aimer; *(food, drink)* savourer; to e. doing sth aimer faire qch; to e. oneself s'amuser (b) *(benefit from)* jouir de

enjoyable [ɪn'dʒɔɪəbəl] *adj* agréable

enjoyment [ɪn'dʒɔɪmənt] *n* plaisir *m*; to get e. out of sth retirer du plaisir de qch; to get e. out of doing sth prendre plaisir à faire qch

enlarge [ɪn'lɑːdʒ] 1 *vt* agrandir; *(hole)* élargir
2 *vi* s'agrandir; to e. (up)on sth s'étendre sur qch

enlargement [ɪn'lɑːdʒmənt] *n* agrandissement *m*; *(of hole)* élargissement *m*

enlighten [ɪn'laɪtən] *vt* éclairer (on sur)

enlightened [ɪn'laɪtənd] *adj* éclairé(e)

enlightenment [ɪn'laɪtənmənt] *n (clarification)* éclaircissement *m*; for your e. pour votre édification; *Hist* the E. le Siècle des Lumières

enlist [ɪn'lɪst] 1 *vt (support, help)* s'assurer; *(soldier)* enrôler, engager
2 *vi (of soldier)* s'engager

enliven [ɪn'laɪvən] *vt* animer; *(party)* égayer, animer

en masse ['ɒn'mæs] *adv* en masse, tous ensemble

enmesh [ɪn'meʃ] *vt* to be enmeshed in sth être empêtré(e) dans qch

enmity ['enmɪtɪ] *n* inimitié *f*, hostilité *f*

enormity [ɪ'nɔːmɪtɪ] *n* énormité *f*

enormous [ɪ'nɔːməs] *adj (in physical size)* énorme; *(patience, gratitude, power, intelligence)* immense; *(strength)* colossal(e)

enormously [ɪ'nɔːməslɪ] *adv* énormément

enough [ɪ'nʌf] 1 *adj* assez de; e. money/wine assez d'argent/de vin; more than e. food plus de nourriture qu'il n'en faut
2 *pron* assez; to be e. suffire; more than e. plus qu'il

n'en faut; **that's e.!** ça suffit!; **e. is e.** il ne faut pas exagérer; **to have e. to live on** avoir de quoi vivre; **e. said!** je vois!; **to have had e. of sb/sth** en avoir assez de qn/qch

3 *adv* **(a)** *(sufficiently)* assez; **good e.** assez bon (bonne); **he didn't try hard e.** il n'a pas vraiment essayé **(b)** *(reasonably)* assez; **she's a nice e. girl** c'est une fille assez sympa; **oddly** *or* **strangely e.,**.... chose curieuse,...

enquire [ɪn'kwaɪə(r)] = **inquire**

enquiry [ɪn'kwaɪrɪ] = **inquiry**

enrage [ɪn'reɪdʒ] *vt* rendre furieux(euse)

enrapture [ɪn'ræptʃə(r)] *vt* éblouir, émerveiller

enraptured [ɪn'ræptʃəd] *adj* ébloui(e), émerveillé(e)

enrich [ɪn'rɪtʃ] *vt* enrichir

enrol, *Am* **enroll** [ɪn'rəʊl] *(pt & pp* **enrolled) 1** *vt* *(soldier)* enrôler; *(student)* immatriculer; *(worker)* embaucher

2 *vi (of soldier)* s'enrôler; *(of students)* s'inscrire

enrolment, *Am* **enrollment** [ɪn'rəʊlmənt] *n (of soldier)* enrôlement *m*; *(of student)* immatriculation *f*; *(of worker)* embauche *f*

ensconce [ɪn'skɒns] *vt* **to e. oneself** s'installer confortablement **(in** place)

ensemble [ɒn'sɒmbl] *n* ensemble *m*

enshrine [ɪn'ʃraɪn] *vt* **to be enshrined in sth** *(of belief, principle)* être enraciné(e) dans qch

ensign ['ensaɪn] *n* **(a)** *(flag)* drapeau *m*; *Naut* pavillon *m* national **(b)** *Am (naval officer)* enseigne *m (de vaisseau de deuxième classe)*

enslave [ɪn'sleɪv] *vt* réduire à l'esclavage, asservir

ensnare [ɪn'sneə(r)] *vt* *(animal, criminal)* prendre au piège; *Fig (lover)* attirer dans ses filets

ensue [ɪn'sjuː] *vi* s'ensuivre

ensuing [ɪn'sjuːɪŋ] *adj (in the past)* qui a suivi; *(in the future)* qui suivra

en suite ['ɒn'swiːt] *adj* **e. bathroom** *(in hotel)* salle de bain *f* particulière; *(in house)* salle de bain *f* attenante

ensure [ɪn'ʃʊə(r)] *vt* assurer; **to e. that...** faire en sorte que... + *subjunctive*

ENT [iːen'tiː] *n (abbr* **Ear, Nose and Throat)** ORL *f*; **E. specialist** ORL *mf*

entail [en'teɪl] *vt* **(a)** *(involve)* entraîner, occasionner; *(difficulties)* comporter; **what does the e.?** en quoi le travail consiste-t-il? **(b)** *Law* **to e. an estate** substituer un bien

entangle [ɪn'tæŋgl] *vt* **to get** *or* **become entangled in sth** *(of person, animal)* s'empêtrer dans qch; *(of hair, string, wires)* s'emmêler dans qch; *Fig* **to be entangled with sb** *(emotionally)* avoir une histoire avec qn

entanglement [ɪn'tæŋgəlmənt] *n* enchevêtrement *m*; **emotional entanglements** complications *fpl* sentimentales

enter ['entə(r)] **1** *vt* **(a)** *(house, country, army)* entrer dans; *(university)* entrer à; *(race, exam, competition)* participer à; **to e. sb for an exam** inscrire qn à un examen; **to e. sb for a race** inscrire qn au nombre des participants d'une course; **it never entered my head that...** il ne m'est jamais venu à l'esprit que...; **to e. a protest** protester formellement **(b)** *Comptr (data)* entrer, introduire

2 *vi (go in)* entrer; **to e. for a race** se faire inscrire pour une course

▶**enter into** *vt insep (a) (begin) (service, relationship)* entrer en; *(dispute)* entrer dans; *(negotiations)* entamer, engager;

to e. into partnership with sb s'associer avec qn; **to e. into conversation with sb** engager une conversation avec qn **(b)** *(have a part in)* **money doesn't e. into it** l'argent n'entre pas en ligne de compte

enterprise ['entəpraɪz] *n* **(a)** *(undertaking, company)* entreprise *f* **(b)** *(initiative)* initiative *f*

enterprising ['entəpraɪzɪŋ] *adj* entreprenant(e); *(imaginative)* plein(e) d'imagination; *(solution)* ingénieux(euse)

entertain [entə'teɪn] **1** *vt* **(a)** *(amuse)* divertir, amuser; **to e. guests** recevoir (des invités) **(b)** *(consider) (idea)* considérer; *(hope)* nourrir; *(fear, suspicion)* éprouver

2 *vi (receive guests)* recevoir

entertainer [entə'teɪnə(r)] *n* fantaisiste *mf*; *(comedian)* comique *mf*

entertaining [entə'teɪnɪŋ] **1** *n (of guests)* **to do a lot of e.** recevoir beaucoup

2 *adj (amusing)* divertissant(e), amusant(e)

entertainment [entə'teɪnmənt] *n* **(a)** *(amusement)* divertissement *m*, amusement *m*; *Com* **e. allowance** indemnité *f* de représentation **(b)** *(performances)* spectacle *m*, divertissement *m*; **the e. business** l'industrie *f* du spectacle; **entertainments guide** guide *m* des spectacles

enthral, *Am* **enthrall** [ɪn'θrɔːl] *(pt & pp* **enthralled)** *vt* captiver, passionner; *(of object, beauty)* fasciner; *(of prospect, idea)* enthousiasmer

enthralling [ɪn'θrɔːlɪŋ] *adj* captivant(e), passionnant(e); *(object, beauty)* fascinant(e); *(prospect, idea)* enthousiasmant(e)

enthuse [ɪn'θjuːz] **1** *vt* enthousiasmer

2 *vi* s'enthousiasmer *(about* or *over* pour)

enthusiasm [ɪn'θjuːzɪæzəm] *n* enthousiasme *m*

enthusiast [ɪn'θjuːzɪæst] *n* passionné(e) *m,f*; **a golf e.** un passionné de golf

enthusiastic [ɪnθjuːzɪ'æstɪk] *adj* enthousiaste

enthusiastically [ɪnθjuːzɪ'æstɪklɪ] *adv* avec enthousiasme

entice [ɪn'taɪs] *vt* attirer, séduire; **to e. sb to do sth** inciter qn à faire qch; **to e. sb away from sb/sth** appâter qn pour qu'il quitte qn/qch

enticing [ɪn'taɪsɪŋ] *adj (offer, idea)* séduisant(e), tentant(e); *(dish)* alléchant(e); *(smile)* charmeur(euse)

entire [ɪn'taɪə(r)] *adj* **(a)** *(whole)* entier(ère), tout(e); **the e. day** toute la journée, la journée entière **(b)** *(intact)* intact(e)

entirely [ɪn'taɪəlɪ] *adv* entièrement, complètement

entirety [ɪn'taɪərətɪ] *n* intégralité *f*; **in its e.** dans son intégralité, intégralement

entitle [ɪn'taɪtl] *vt* **(a)** *(allow)* **to e. sb to sth** donner à qn droit à qch; **to e. sb to do sth** permettre à qn de faire qch; **to be entitled to sth** avoir droit à qch; **to be entitled to do sth** avoir le droit de faire qch **(b)** *(book, chapter, song)* intituler

entitlement [ɪn'taɪtlmənt] *n* = ce qui revient de droit à quelqu'un

entity ['entɪtɪ] *n (pl* **entities)** *n* entité *f*

entomologist [entə'mɒlədʒɪst] *n* entomologiste *mf*

entomology [entə'mɒlədʒɪ] *n* entomologie *f*

entourage ['ɒntuːrɑːʒ] *n* entourage *m*

entrails ['entreɪlz] *npl* entrailles *fpl*

entrance¹ ['entrəns] *n* **(a)** *(way in, act of entering)* entrée *f*; **to make one's e.** faire son entrée; **to gain e. to** s'introduire *ou* pénétrer dans **(b)** *(admission) (to club)* admission *f*; *(to cinema)* entrée *f*; **e. examination** examen *m* d'entrée

entrance² [ɪn'trɑːns] *vt (charm)* ravir, transporter

entrancing [ɪn'trɑːnsɪŋ] *adj* ravissant(e), enchanteur(eresse)

entrant ['entrənt] *n (in race, competition)* inscrit(e) *m,f*; *(in examination)* candidat(e) *m,f*

entreat [ɪn'triːt] *vt* **to e. sb to do sth** implorer qn de faire qch

entreaty [ɪn'triːtɪ] *(pl* **entreaties)** *n* prière *f*, supplication *f*

entrée ['ɒntreɪ] *n (dish before main course)* entrée *f*; *Am (main course)* plat *m* de résistance

entrenched [ɪn'trentʃd] *adj (views, ideas)* arrêté(e); *(customs)* enraciné(e)

entrepreneur [ɒntrəprə'nɜː(r)] *n* entrepreneur *m*

entrepreneurial [ɒntrəprə'nɜːrɪəl] *adj (person)* qui a l'esprit d'entreprise; *(skill, talents)* d'entrepreneur

entrust [ɪn'trʌst] *vt* **to e. sb with sth, to e. sth to sb** confier qch à qn

entry ['entrɪ] *(pl* **entries)** *n* **(a)** *(way in, act of entering)* entrée *f*; **to make one's e.** faire son entrée; **to gain e. to** s'introduire *ou* pénétrer dans **(b)** *(of competitor)* inscription *f*; **e. form** feuille *f* d'inscription **(c)** *(in encyclopedia)* article *m*; *(in dictionary)* entrée *f*; *(in diary)* note *f*

entryphone ['entrɪfəʊn] *n* Interphone® *m*

entwine [ɪn'twaɪn] **1** *vt* entrelacer
2 *vi* s'entrelacer

enumerate [ɪ'njuːməreɪt] *vt* énumérer, détailler

enunciate [ɪ'nʌnsɪeɪt] *vt (sound, word)* prononcer, articuler; *(opinion, view)* énoncer

envelop [ɪn'veləp] *vt* envelopper **(in** dans)

envelope ['envələʊp, 'ɒnvələʊp] *n* enveloppe *f*

enviable ['envɪəbəl] *adj* enviable

envious ['envɪəs] *adj* envieux(euse); **to be e. of sb** envier qn

enviously ['envɪəslɪ] *adv* avec envie

environment [ɪn'vaɪrənmənt] *n* **(a)** *(surroundings)* milieu *m* **(b)** *(nature)* **the e.** l'environnement *m*; **Department** *or* **Ministry of the E.** ministère *m* de l'Environnement

environmental [ɪnvaɪrən'mentəl] *adj* **e. damage** dégâts *mpl* causés à l'environnement; **e. disaster** désastre *m* écologique; **e. policy** politique *f* de l'environnement

environmentalist [ɪnvaɪrən'mentəlɪst] *n* écologiste *mf*

environs [ɪn'vaɪrənz] *npl* environs *mpl*, alentours *mpl*

envisage [ɪn'vɪzɪdʒ], *Am* **envision** [en'vɪʒən] *vt* envisager

envoy ['envɔɪ] *n* envoyé(e) *m,f*

envy ['envɪ] **1** *n* envie *f*, jalousie *f*; **to be the e. of sb** être un objet d'envie pour qn
2 *vt (pt & pp* **envied)** envier; **to e. sb sth** envier qch à qn

enzyme ['enzaɪm] *n* enzyme *f*

EOC [iːəʊ'siː] *Br (abbr* **Equal Opportunities Commission)** = organisme gouvernemental qui veille à l'égalité des chances sur le lieu de travail

eon *Am* = **aeon**

epaulette, *Am* **epaulet** ['epəlet] *n* épaulette *f*

ephemeral [ɪ'femərəl] *adj* éphémère

epic ['epɪk] **1** *n (poem, novel)* épopée *f*; *(film)* film *m* à grand spectacle
2 *adj* épique

epicentre, *Am* **epicenter** ['episentə(r)] *n* épicentre *m*

epicurean [epɪkjʊ'rɪən] *n & adj* épicurien(enne) *m,f*

epidemic [epɪ'demɪk] *also Fig* **1** *n* épidémie *f*
2 *adj* épidémique

epidermis [epɪ'dɜːmɪs] *n Anat* épiderme *m*

epidural [epɪ'djʊərəl] *n Med* péridurale *f*

epigram ['epɪgræm] *n* épigramme *f*

epilepsy ['epɪlepsɪ] *n* épilepsie *f*

epileptic [epɪ'leptɪk] **1** *n* épileptique *mf*
2 *adj* épileptique; **e. fit** crise *f* d'épilepsie

epilogue ['epɪlɒg] *n* épilogue *m*

Epiphany [ɪ'pɪfənɪ] *n* Épiphanie *f*

episcopal [ɪ'pɪskəpəl] *adj* épiscopal(e); **e. palace** évêché *m*

episcopalian [ɪpɪskə'peɪlɪən] *n & adj* épiscopalien(enne) *m,f*

episode ['epɪsəʊd] *n (part of story)* épisode *m*; *(incident)* incident *m*

epistle [ɪ'pɪsəl] *n also Hum* épître *f*

epitaph ['epɪtɑːf] *n* épitaphe *f*

epithet ['epɪθet] *n* épithète *f*

epitome [ɪ'pɪtəmɪ] *n* **to be the e. of sth** être l'exemple même de qch

epitomize [ɪ'pɪtəmaɪz] *vt* incarner

epoch ['iːpɒk] *n* époque *f*

epoch-making ['iːpɒkmeɪkɪŋ] *adj* qui fait date

eponymous [ɪ'pɒnɪməs] *adj* éponyme

EPS [iːpiː'es] *n (abbr* **earnings per share)** BPA *m*

equable ['ekwəbəl] *adj* constant(e); *(person)* à l'humeur égale

equal ['iːkwəl] **1** *n* égal(e) *m,f*; **to treat sb as an e.** traiter qn d'égal à égal
2 *adj* **(a)** *(identical)* égal(e) **(to** à); **all things being e.** en principe; **in e. measure** en quantité égale; **on e. terms** sur un pied d'égalité; **e. opportunities** égalité *f* des chances; **e. pay** égalité des salaires; **e. rights** égalité des droits **(b)** *(good enough)* **to be e. to sth** être à la hauteur de qch
3 *vt (pt & pp* **equalled,** *Am* **equaled)** égaler

equality [ɪ'kwɒlɪtɪ] *n* égalité *f*

equalize ['iːkwəlaɪz] **1** *vt* égaliser; *(chances, forces)* équilibrer
2 *vi (in sport)* égaliser

equalizer ['iːkwəlaɪzə(r)] *n* **(a)** *(in sport)* but *m* égalisateur **(b)** *Elec* égaliseur *m* de potentiel

equally ['iːkwəlɪ] *adv* **(a)** *(to an equal degree)* tout aussi **(b)** *(in equal amounts)* (share, divide) en parts égales **(c)** *(likewise)* tout aussi bien

equanimity [ekwə'nɪmɪtɪ] *n* sérénité *f*

equate [ɪ'kweɪt] *vt* assimiler **(with** avec)

equation [ɪ'kweɪʒən] *n* équation *f*

equator [ɪ'kweɪtə(r)] *n* équateur *m*

equatorial [ekwə'tɔːrɪəl] *adj* équatorial(e); **E. Guinea** la Guinée équatoriale

equestrian [ɪ'kwestrɪən] **1** *n* cavalier(ère) *m,f*; *(in circus)* écuyer(ère) *m,f*
2 *adj (sport, ability)* équestre

equidistant [ekwɪ'dɪstənt] *adj* équidistant(e)

equilateral [ekwɪ'lætərəl] *adj* équilatéral(e)

equilibrium [ekwɪ'lɪbrɪəm] *n* équilibre *m*

equinox ['ekwɪnɒks] *n* équinoxe *m*

equip [ɪ'kwɪp] (*pt & pp* **equipped**) *vt* (a) (*provide with equipment*) équiper (**with** de) (b) (*prepare*) préparer (**for** pour)

equipment [ɪ'kwɪpmənt] *n* équipement *m*; (*in factory*) installations *fpl*, matériel *m*; **e. allowance** subvention *f* pour l'achat de matériel

equitable ['ekwɪtəbəl] *adj* équitable

Equity ['ekwɪtɪ] *n* = syndicat des artistes de théâtre et de télévision

equity ['ekwɪtɪ] (*pl* **equities**) *n* (a) (*fairness*) équité *f* (b) *Fin* (*of shareholders*) fonds *mpl* ou capitaux *mpl* propres; (*of company*) capital *m* actions; **equities** actions *fpl* ordinaires

equivalent [ɪ'kwɪvələnt] **1** *n* équivalent *m*
2 *adj* équivalent(e) (**to** à)

equivocal [ɪ'kwɪvəkəl] *adj* équivoque, ambigu(ë)

equivocate [ɪ'kwɪvəkeɪt] *vi* user d'équivoques *ou* de faux-fuyants

equivocation [ɪkwɪvə'keɪʃən] *n* paroles *fpl* équivoques, faux-fuyants *mpl*

ER [iː'ɑː(r)] *n* (a) *Br* (*abbr* **Elizabeth Regina**) la Reine Elizabeth (b) *Am* (*abbr* **Emergency Room**) urgences *fpl*

era ['ɪərə] *n* ère *f*

eradicate [ɪ'rædɪkeɪt] *vt* éradiquer

erase [ɪ'reɪz] *vt* effacer; (*with eraser*) gommer

eraser [ɪ'reɪzə(r)] *n* gomme *f*

erect [ɪ'rekt] **1** *adj* droit(e), debout; (*penis, nipples*) en érection
2 *vt* (*building*) ériger; (*statue*) élever, ériger; (*scaffolding*) dresser

erection [ɪ'rekʃən] *n* (a) (*of building, statue*) construction *f*, érection *f* (b) (*erect penis*) érection *f*

ergonomic [ɜːgə'nɒmɪk] *adj* ergonomique

ergonomics [ɜːgə'nɒmɪks] *n* ergonomie *f*

Eritrea [erɪ'treɪə] *n* l'Érythrée *f*

Eritrean [erɪ'treɪən] **1** *n* Érythréen(enne) *m,f*
2 *adj* érythréen(enne)

ERM [iːɑː'rem] *n* (*abbr* **Exchange Rate Mechanism**) mécanisme *m* de change

ermine ['ɜːmɪn] *n* hermine *f*

erode [ɪ'rəʊd] **1** *vt* (*rock, soil*) éroder; (*metal*) corroder, ronger; *Fig* (*confidence, power*) miner
2 *vi* (*of rock, soil*) s'éroder; (*of metal*) se corroder; *Fig* (*of confidence, power*) s'éroder peu à peu

erogenous [ɪ'rɒdʒɪnəs] *adj* érogène; **e. zone** zone *f* érogène

Eros ['ɪərɒs] *n* Éros

erosion [ɪ'rəʊʒən] *n* (*of rock, soil*) & *Fig* (*of confidence, power*) érosion *f*; (*of metal*) corrosion *f*

erotic [ɪ'rɒtɪk] *adj* érotique

eroticism [ɪ'rɒtɪsɪzəm] *n* érotisme *m*

err [ɜː(r)] *vi* (*make mistake*) faire erreur; **to e. on the side of caution** pécher par excès de prudence; *Prov* **to e. is human** l'erreur est humaine

errand ['erənd] *n* commission *f*, course *f*; **to run errands for sb** (aller) faire des commissions *ou* des courses pour qn; **e. boy** garçon *m* de courses

erratic [ɪ'rætɪk] *adj* (*service, results, pulse*) irrégulier(ère); (*playing, performance*) inégal(e); (*behaviour*) imprévisible; (*person*) lunatique; (*driving*) mal assuré(e)

erroneous [ɪ'rəʊnɪəs] *adj* erroné(e)

error ['erə(r)] *n* (*mistake*) erreur *f*, faute *f*; **to make an e.** faire une erreur; **in e.** par erreur; **an e. of judgement** une erreur de jugement; **to see the e. of one's ways** reconnaître ses erreurs

ersatz ['ɜːzæts] *adj* **e. coffee** un succédané de café

erstwhile ['ɜːstwaɪl] *adj Lit* ancien(enne)

erudite ['erʊdaɪt] *adj* érudit(e)

erudition [erʊ'dɪʃən] *n* érudition *f*

erupt [ɪ'rʌpt] *vi* (*of volcano*) entrer en éruption; (*of person*) exploser; (*of anger, violence*) éclater; (*of spot*) sortir

eruption [ɪ'rʌpʃən] *n* éruption *f*

escalate ['eskəleɪt] *vi* (*of prices*) monter en flèche; (*of conflict*) s'intensifier, s'aggraver

escalation [eskə'leɪʃən] *n* (*of prices*) montée *f* en flèche; (*of conflict*) escalade *f*

escalator ['eskəleɪtə(r)] *n* escalier *m* roulant, Escalator® *m*

escalope ['eskəlɒp] *n* escalope *f*

escapade ['eskəpeɪd] *n* fredaine *f*, frasque *f*

escape [ɪs'keɪp] **1** *n* (*of person*) évasion *f*; (*of gas, water*) fuite *f*; **to make one's e.** s'échapper; *Com* **e. clause** clause *f* échappatoire; **e. route** (*from fire*) itinéraire *m* de sortie de secours; (*of criminal*) itinéraire emprunté pour s'échapper
2 *vt* (*danger, punishment*) échapper à; **to e. sb's notice** échapper à l'attention de qn; **her name escapes me** son nom m'échappe
3 *vi* (*of person, gas, water*) s'échapper (**from** de); (*from prison*) s'évader (**from** de); **to e. unhurt** s'en tirer indemne; **to e. from reality** s'évader de la réalité

escapee [eskeɪ'piː] *n* évadé(e) *m,f*

escapism [ɪs'keɪpɪzəm] *n* évasion *f* (hors de la réalité)

escapist [ɪs'keɪpɪst] **1** *n* personne *f* qui cherche à s'évader de la réalité
2 *adj* d'évasion

escapologist [eskə'pɒlədʒɪst] *n* prestidigitateur *m* spécialiste de l'évasion

escarpment [ɪs'kɑːpmənt] *n* escarpement *m*

eschew [ɪs'tʃuː] *vt* éviter; **to e. sb's company** fuir *ou* éviter qn

escort **1** *n* ['eskɔːt] (*for convoy*) escorte *f*; (*for tourists*) guide *m*; (*from agency*) hôtesse *f*; (*ship*) bâtiment *m* d'escorte; **under e.** sous escorte; **e. agency** agence *f* d'hôtesses; *Mil* **e. duty** service *m* d'escorte
2 *vt* [ɪs'kɔːt] escorter; (*prisoner*) conduire sous escorte

escudo [e'skuːdəʊ] (*pl* **escudos**) *n* escudo *m*

Eskimo ['eskɪməʊ] **1** *n* (*pl* **Eskimos**) Esquimau(aude) *m,f*
2 *adj* esquimau(aude), eskimo *inv*

esophagus [iː'sɒfəgəs] (*pl* **esophagi** [iː'sɒfəgaɪ]) *Am* = **oesophagus**

esoteric [esəʊ'terɪk] *adj* ésotérique

ESP [iːes'piː] *n* (*abbr* **extrasensory perception**) perception *f* extra-sensorielle

especially [ɪs'peʃəlɪ] *adv* (a) (*in particular*) surtout (b) (*more than normally*) particulièrement; **we were e. lucky with the weather** le temps nous a été particulièrement favorable (c) *(expressly)* (tout) spécialement, exprès; **I did it e. for you** je l'ai fait spécialement *ou* exprès pour vous

Esperanto [espə'ræntəʊ] *n* l'Espéranto *m*

espionage ['espɪɒnɑːʒ] *n* espionnage *m*

esplanade [esplə'neɪd] *n* esplanade *f*

espouse [ɪs'paʊz] *vt* épouser

espresso [es'presəʊ] *(pl* **espressos)** *n* expresso *m*

Esq *(abbr* **Esquire)** **Derek Wilson, E.** = **Monsieur Derek Wilson**

essay ['eseɪ] *n (at school)* composition *f; (for younger pupils)* rédaction *f; (at university)* dissertation *f*

essayist ['eseɪɪst] *n* essayiste *mf*

essence ['esəns] *n* (a) *(most important part or quality)* essence *f; (of speech)* essentiel *m; (of question)* fond *m;* **in e.** essentiellement, surtout; **the very e. of bravery** le courage même; **time is of the e.** le temps est le facteur prioritaire (b) *Culin (extract)* extrait *m*

essential [ɪ'senʃəl] **1** *npl* **essentials** *(basic foodstuffs)* produits *mpl* de première nécessité; *(basic issues)* essentiel *m;* **just pack a few essentials** ne prends que l'essentiel **2** *adj* (a) *(basic)* essentiel(elle); **e. oil** huile *f* essentielle (b) *(indispensable)* essentiel(elle), indispensable (**to or for** à); **it is e. that...** il est essentiel que... + *subjunctive*

essentially [ɪ'senʃəlɪ] *adv* essentiellement

EST [iːes'tiː] *n Am (abbr* **Eastern Standard Time)** heure *f* de la côte est de l'Amérique du Nord

establish [ɪs'tæblɪʃ] *vt* (a) *(set up) (company)* fonder; *(custom)* instaurer; *(system, organization)* établir; **to e. oneself in business** s'établir dans les affaires; **to e. a reputation** se faire une réputation; **the film established her as an important director** avec ce film, elle s'est affirmée comme un metteur en scène important (b) *(prove)* établir

established [ɪs'tæblɪʃt] *adj* établi(e); *(fact)* acquis(e)

establishment [ɪs'tæblɪʃmənt] *n* (a) **the E.** *(dominant group)* l'establishment *m; (prevailing values)* l'ordre *m* établi (b) *(hotel, restaurant)* établissement *m; (of company, organization)* constitution *f; (of fact)* constatation *f*

estate [ɪs'teɪt] *n* (a) *Law (possessions)* biens *mpl* (b) *(land)* terre *f,* propriété *f; Br (housing)* **e.** lotissement *m; (with council houses)* cité *f* H.L.M.; *Br* **e. agency** agence *f* immobilière; *Br* **e. agent** agent *m* immobilier (c) *Br* **e. (car)** break *m*

esteem [ɪs'tiːm] **1** *n* estime *f,* considération *f;* **to hold sb in high e.** avoir qn en haute estime; **to hold sb in low e.** avoir peu d'estime pour qn **2** *vt* (a) *(person)* estimer; *(thing)* priser (b) *Formal (consider)* considérer; **she esteemed it a great honour to be invited** elle se sentit fort honorée d'avoir été invitée

esthetic *Am* = **aesthetic**

estimate 1 *n* ['estɪmət] *(calculation)* évaluation *f,* calcul *m; Com* devis *m;* **at a rough e.** à vue de nez **2** *vt* ['estɪmeɪt] estimer, évaluer; *(value)* estimer

estimation [estɪ'meɪʃən] *n* (a) *(calculation)* estimation *f,* évaluation *f* (b) *(judgement)* jugement *m,* opinion *f;* **in my e.** à mon avis; **to go up/down in sb's e.** monter/ descendre dans l'estime de qn

Estonia [es'təʊnɪə] *n* l'Estonie *f*

Estonian [es'təʊnɪən] **1** *n* (a) *(person)* Estonien(enne) *m,f* (b) *(language)* estonien *m* **2** *adj* estonien(enne)

estranged [ɪs'treɪndʒd] *adj (couple)* séparé(e); **her e. husband** son mari, dont elle est séparée; **their e. son** leur fils, avec qui ils sont brouillés

estrogen ['iːstrədʒən] *Am* = **oestrogen**

estuary ['estjʊərɪ] *(pl* **estuaries)** *n* estuaire *m*

ETA [iːtiː'eɪ] *n (abbr* **estimated time of arrival)** heure *f* d'arrivée prévue

et al [et'æl] *(abbr* **et alii)** et autres

etc [et'setrə] *adv (abbr* **et cetera)** etc

etch [etʃ] *vt* graver à l'eau-forte; *Fig* **to be etched in sb's memory** être gravé(e) dans la mémoire de qn

etching ['etʃɪŋ] *n (gravure f* à l')eau-forte *f*

eternal [ɪ'tɜːnəl] *adj* éternel(elle); *Fig (continual)* continuel(elle), sans fin

eternally [ɪ'tɜːnəlɪ] *adv* éternellement

eternity [ɪ'tɜːnɪtɪ] *n* éternité *f; Fam* **to wait/last an e.** attendre/durer une éternité; **e. ring** = bague entièrement sertie de pierres symbolisant l'éternité du mariage

ether ['iːθə(r)] *n* éther *m*

ethereal [ɪ'θɪərɪəl] *adj* éthéré(e); *(fragile)* léger(ère), impalpable

ethical ['eθɪkəl] *adj* éthique, moral(e)

ethically ['eθɪklɪ] *adv* sur le plan éthique; **to behave e.** suivre la déontologie

ethics ['eθɪks] *npl* éthique *f,* morale *f; (of profession)* déontologie *f*

Ethiopia [iːθɪ'əʊpɪə] *n* l'Éthiopie *f*

Ethiopian [iːθɪ'əʊpɪən] **1** *n (person)* Éthiopien(enne) *m,f* **2** *adj* éthiopien(enne)

ethnic ['eθnɪk] *adj* ethnique; **e. cleansing** purification *f* ethnique; **e. minority** minorité *f* ethnique

ethnically ['eθnɪklɪ] *adv* du point de vue ethnique

ethnocentric [eθnəʊ'sentrɪk] *adj* ethnocentrique

ethnography [eθ'nɒgrəfɪ] *n* ethnographie *f*

ethnology [eθ'nɒlədʒɪ] *n* ethnologie *f*

ethos ['iːθɒs] *n (of people)* génie *m; (of class)* culture *f*

etiquette ['etɪket] *n* étiquette *f;* **professional e.** usages *mpl* professionnels

Etruscan [ɪ'trʌskən] **1** *n* (a) *(person)* Étrusque *mf* (b) *(language)* étrusque *m* **2** *adj* étrusque

etymological [etɪmə'lɒdʒɪkəl] *adj* étymologique

etymology [etɪ'mɒlədʒɪ] *n* étymologie *f*

EU [iː'juː] *n (abbr* **European Union)** UE *f*

eucalyptus [juːkə'lɪptəs] *n* eucalyptus *m*

Eucharist ['juːkərɪst] *n* **the E.** l'eucharistie *f*

eulogize ['juːlədʒaɪz] *vt* faire l'éloge de

eulogy ['juːlədʒɪ] *(pl* **eulogies)** *n* éloge *m*

eunuch ['juːnək] *n* eunuque *m*

euphemism ['juːfɪmɪzəm] *n* euphémisme *m*

euphemistic [juːfɪ'mɪstɪk] *adj* euphémique

euphoria [juː'fɔːrɪə] *n* euphorie *f*

euphoric [juː'fɒrɪk] *adj* euphorique

Eurasian [jʊə'reɪʒən] **1** *n* Eurasien(enne) *m,f* **2** *adj* eurasien(enne); *(continent)* eurasiatique

EURATOM [jʊə'rætəm] *n (abbr* **European Atomic Energy Community)** CEEA *f,* EURATOM *f*

eureka [jʊə'riːkə] *exclam* eureka!

Euro, euro ['jʊərəʊ] *(pl* **Euros, euros)** *n (European currency)* euro *m*

Eurocheque ['jʊərəʊtʃek] n Eurocheque m

Eurodollar ['jʊərəʊdɒlə(r)] n eurodollar m

Euro-MP ['jʊərəʊempiː] n député(e) m,f européen(enne)

Europe ['jʊərəp] n l'Europe f

European [jʊərə'piːən] 1 n Européen(enne) m,f
2 adj européen(enne); **E. Commission** Commission f européenne; **E. Community** Communauté f européenne; **E. Court of Human Rights** Cour f européenne des droits de l'homme; **E. Court of Justice** Cour de justice européenne; **E. Currency Unit** unité f monétaire européenne; **E. Economic Community** Communauté f économique européenne; **E. Free Trade Association** Association f européenne de libre-échange; **E. Monetary System** Système m monétaire européen; **E. Parliament** Parlement m européen; **E. Union** Union f européenne

Eurosceptic [jʊərəʊ'skeptɪk] n eurosceptique mf

Eustachian tube [juːˈsteɪʃən'tjuːb] n Anat trompe f d'Eustache

euthanasia [juːθə'neɪzɪə] n euthanasie f

evacuate [ɪ'vækjʊeɪt] vt évacuer

evacuation [ɪvækjʊ'eɪʃən] n évacuation f

evacuee [ɪvækjʊ'iː] n évacué(e) m,f

evade [ɪ'veɪd] vt (blow) esquiver, éviter; (question) éluder; (pursuer) échapper à; (responsibilities) se soustraire à, se dérober à; **to e. tax** frauder le fisc

evaluate [ɪ'væljʊeɪt] vt évaluer

evaluation [ɪvæljʊ'eɪʃən] n évaluation f

evangelical [iːvæn'dʒelɪkəl] 1 n protestant(e) m,f évangélique
2 adj évangélique

evangelism [ɪ'vændʒɪlɪzəm] n évangélisme m

evangelist [ɪ'vændʒɪlɪst] n évangéliste m

evangelize [ɪ'vændʒɪlaɪz] 1 vt évangéliser; (person) prêcher l'Évangile à
2 vi prêcher l'Évangile

evaporate [ɪ'væpəreɪt] 1 vt faire évaporer; **evaporated milk** lait m condensé
2 vi (of liquid) s'évaporer; Fig (of enthusiasm, hope) s'envoler

evaporation [ɪvæpə'reɪʃən] n évaporation f

evasion [ɪ'veɪʒən] n (escape) évasion f, fuite f; (of pursuer, responsibilities, question) dérobade f; (tax) e. fraude f fiscale

evasive [ɪ'veɪsɪv] adj (person, reply) évasif(ive); **to take e. action** faire une manœuvre d'évitement

eve [iːv] n (day before) veille f; **on the e. of** à la veille de

even ['iːvən] 1 adj (a) (flat) égal(e); (smooth) uni(e) (b) (regular) (breathing, pace) régulier(ère), égal(e); (temperature) constant(e); **to have an e. temper** être d'humeur égale; **e. number** nombre m pair (c) (equal) **to have an e. chance (of doing sth)** avoir une chance sur deux (de faire qch); Fig **to get e. with sb** prendre sa revanche sur qn
2 adv (a) même; (with comparatives) encore; **without e. speaking** sans même dire un mot; **I never e. saw it** je ne l'ai même pas vu; **e. bigger/more interesting** encore plus gros (grosse)/intéressant(e); **e. as I speak** au moment même où je parle (b) (in phrases) **e. if** même si; **e. now** même maintenant, aujourd'hui encore; **e. so** cependant, quand même; **e. then** (already) déjà (à cette époque); (all the same) même dans ces conditions; **e. though** bien que + subjunctive
3 vt (make equal) rendre égal(e); **to e. the odds** égaliser les chances

▸**even out 1** vt sep (differences) niveler; (workload) répartir plus également; (inequalities) réduire; **to e. things out** rendre les choses équitables
2 vi (of differences) se niveler; (of workload) être réparti(e) plus également; (of inequalities) se réduire

▸**even up** vt sep (differences); **to e. things up** équilibrer les choses

even-handed [iːvən'hændɪd] adj juste, équitable

evening ['iːvnɪŋ] n soir m; (referring to duration) soirée f; **tomorrow e.** demain soir; **yesterday e.** hier soir; **good e.!,** Fam **e.!** bonsoir!; **in the e.** le soir; **a musical/cultural e.** une soirée musicale/culturelle; **e. class** cours m du soir; **e. dress** (for men) tenue f de soirée; (for women) robe f du soir; **e. paper** journal m du soir; **e. performance** (of play) représentation f en soirée

evenly ['iːvənlɪ] adv (a) (uniformly) uniformément (b) (regularly) (breathe) régulièrement, de façon régulière; (speak) calmement (c) (equally) (divide, distribute) également, de façon égale; **e. matched** (in size) de grandeur égale; (in strength) de force égale

evensong ['iːvənsɒŋ] n Rel office m du soir

event [ɪ'vent] n (a) (occurrence) événement m; **in any e.** en tout cas; **in the e. of fire** en cas d'incendie; **in the e. of her refusing** au cas où elle refuserait; **after the e.** après coup (b) (in athletics) épreuve f

even-tempered [iːvən'tempəd] adj d'humeur égale

eventful [ɪ'ventfʊl] adj (day, life) mouvementé(e), riche en événements

eventual [ɪ'ventjʊəl] adj final(e), définitif(ive)

eventuality [ɪventjʊ'ælɪtɪ] (pl **eventualities**) n éventualité f; **in that e.** dans cette éventualité

eventually [ɪ'ventjʊəlɪ] adv (in the end) finalement, en fin de compte; (at a future date) par la suite; **they e. reached the castle** ils ont fini par arriver au château; **he'll do it e.** il le fera tôt ou tard

ever ['evə(r)] adv (a) (at any time) **have you e. been to Spain?** es-tu déjà allé en Espagne?; **do you e. see Alan these days?** ça t'arrive de voir Alan?; **the worst/best e.** le pire/meilleur que soit; **more than e.** plus que jamais; **she's a liar/fool if e. there was one** c'est une menteuse/idiote de première
(b) (always) **e. since (then)/1960** depuis (lors)/1960; **all she e. does is criticize** elle ne fait que critiquer; **she was as friendly as e.** elle était toujours aussi aimable; **e. the gentleman, he opened the door for her** toujours galant, il lui ouvrit la porte; **for e.** pour toujours
(c) (with negative sense) **not e.** jamais; **hardly e.** presque jamais; **nothing e. happens** il ne se passe jamais rien; **I don't think I'll e. see him again** je ne pense pas que je le reverrai; **I seldom if e. see her** je la vois peu ou pas du tout
(d) (for emphasis) **e. so pretty** si joli(e); **e. so much** or **such a lot of money** tant d'argent; **e. so slightly** très légèrement; **e. such a nice girl** une fille si sympathique

evergreen ['evəgriːn] 1 n (tree) arbre m à feuilles persistantes; (bush) arbuste m à feuilles persistantes
2 adj à feuilles persistantes; Fig **e. topic** question f toujours d'actualité

everlasting [evə'lɑːstɪŋ] adj (eternal) éternel(elle); (continual) continuel(elle), sans fin

evermore [evə'mɔː(r)] adv Formal toujours; **for e.** à jamais

every ['evrɪ] adj (a) (each) chaque; **children of e. age** des enfants de tous âges; **at e. opportunity** à la moindre occasion; **from e. side** de tous côtés; **e. one of us** chacun(e) d'entre nous; **e. man for himself!** chacun pour soi!

(b) *(indicating regular occurrence)* **e. week** chaque semaine, toutes les semaines; **e. ten years** tous les dix ans; **e. other** *or* **second day** tous les deux jours, un jour sur deux; **e. other line** une ligne sur deux; **e. so often, e. now and again** de temps en temps

(c) *(for emphasis)* **you have e. right to be angry** vous avez tout lieu d'être mécontent; **e. bit as good/ intelligent as...** tout aussi bon (bonne)/intelligent(e) que...; **she has e. chance of winning** elle a de très fortes chances de gagner

everybody ['evrɪbɒdɪ] *pron* tout le monde, chacun(e) *m,f*; **e. I know was there** tous ceux que je connais se trouvaient là; **e. else** tous les autres; **e. who is anybody** les gens qui comptent

everyday ['evrɪdeɪ] *adj* **(a)** *(daily)* journalier(ère), quotidien(enne); **it's an e. occurrence** ça se produit tous les jours **(b)** *(used every day)* de tous les jours; **for e. wear/use** à porter/utiliser tous les jours; **e. expression** expression *f* courante **(c)** *(ordinary)* usuel(elle), ordinaire

everyone ['evrɪwʌn] = **everybody**

everything ['evrɪθɪŋ] *pron* tout; **e. I did seemed to go wrong** tout ce que je faisais semblait voué à l'échec; **he did e. possible** il a fait tout son possible; **money isn't e.** l'argent n'est pas tout

everywhere ['evrɪweə(r)] *adv* partout; **to look e.** regarder partout; **e. you go** où que vous alliez, partout où vous allez; **e. you look there is poverty** de quelque côté que l'on se tourne, on voit la misère

evict [ɪ'vɪkt] *vt* expulser

eviction [ɪ'vɪkʃən] *n* expulsion *f*; **e. order** avis *m* d'expulsion

evidence ['evɪdəns] **1** *n* **(a)** *(reason for belief)* évidence *f*; *(indication)* marque *f*, signe *m*; **to be in e.** être en évidence; **to show e. of** donner des signes de; **there was no e. of his stay in the house** rien ne montrait qu'il eût séjourné dans la maison **(b)** *(in court case)* preuve *f*; *(testimony)* témoignage *m*; **to give e.** témoigner; **to call sb in e.** appeler qn à la barre des témoins; **to turn** *Br* **King's** *or* **Queen's** *or Am* **State's e.** témoigner contre ses complices *(sous promesse de pardon)*

2 *vt Formal* **as evidenced by...** comme en témoigne...

evident ['evɪdənt] *adj* évident(e), manifeste

evidently ['evɪdəntlɪ] *adv* **(a)** *(clearly)* manifestement, à l'évidence; **there have e. been some problems** il est clair *ou* évident qu'il y a eu des problèmes **(b)** *(apparently)* apparemment; **so she won't be coming? – e. not** alors elle ne vient pas? – il semble bien que non

evil ['iːvəl] **1** *n* mal *m*

2 *adj (person, look)* mauvais(e), malveillant(e); *(influence, effect)* maléfique; *(spirit)* malfaisant(e), malin(igne); *(temper)* coléreux(euse)

evildoer ['iːvəlduːə(r)] *n Lit* homme (femme) *m,f* méchant(e)

evil-looking ['iːvəlˌlʊkɪŋ] *adj* à l'aspect malfaisant

evil-minded ['iːvəlˈmaɪndɪd] *adj* malintentionné(e)

evil-smelling ['iːvəlˈsmelɪŋ] *adj* nauséabond(e)

evince [ɪ'vɪns] *vt Formal* faire montre de

evocation [evə'keɪʃən] *n* évocation *f*

evocative [ɪ'vɒkətɪv] *adj* évocateur(trice) **(of** de)

evoke [ɪ'vəʊk] *vt* **(a)** *(conjure up)* évoquer **(b)** *(provoke)* provoquer, susciter

evolution [iːvə'luːʃən] *n* évolution *f*, développement *m*

evolutionary [iːvə'luːʃənərɪ] *adj* évolutif(ive)

evolve [ɪ'vɒlv] **1** *vt (theory, plan)* élaborer, mettre au point

2 *vi (of species, situation)* évoluer, se développer

ewe [juː] *n* brebis *f*

ex [eks] *n Fam (former husband, wife, girlfriend, boyfriend)* ex *mf*

ex- [eks] *pref (former)* ex-; **ex-minister/teacher** ancien ministre *m*/professeur *m*

exacerbate [eg'zæsəbeɪt] *vt* aggraver

exact [ɪg'zækt] **1** *adj* exact(e), précis(e); **at the e. moment when...** juste au moment où..., au moment précis où...; **those were her e. words** c'est ce qu'elle a dit mot pour mot; **the e. opposite** exactement le contraire; **on January 5th, to be e.** le 5 janvier, pour être précis

2 *vt (obedience, tax)* exiger **(from** de); *(promise)* extorquer **(from** à)

exacting [ɪg'zæktɪŋ] *adj* exigeant(e)

exactitude [ɪg'zæktɪtjuːd] *n Formal* exactitude *f*

exactly [ɪg'zæktlɪ] *adv* exactement; **not e.** pas tout à fait; *Ironic* pas vraiment

exaggerate [ɪg'zædʒəreɪt] *vt & vi* exagérer

exaggerated [ɪg'zædʒəreɪtɪd] *adj* exagéré(e)

exaggeration [ɪgzædʒə'reɪʃən] *n* exagération *f*

exalt [ɪg'zɔːlt] *vt Formal* exalter

exalted [ɪg'zɔːltɪd] *adj* **(a)** *(high) (rank)* élevé(e); *(person)* haut placé(e) **(b)** *Formal (joyful)* exalté(e)

exam [ɪg'zæm] *n* examen *m*; **to take** *or* **sit an e.** passer un examen; **e. result** résultat *m* d'examen

examination [ɪgzæmɪ'neɪʃən] *n* examen *m*; **to take** *or* **sit an e.** passer un examen; **e. board** ≃ académie *f* *(division administrative de l'enseignement)*; **e. result** résultat *m* d'examen

examine [ɪg'zæmɪn] *vt (evidence, patient, question)* examiner; *(student)* faire passer un examen à; **to e. one's conscience** faire son examen de conscience

examinee [ɪgzæmɪ'niː] *n* candidat(e) *m,f*

examiner [ɪg'zæmɪnə(r)] *n* examinateur(trice) *m,f*

example [ɪg'zɑːmpl] *n* exemple *m*; **for e.** par exemple; **to set an e. (to sb)** donner l'exemple (à qn); **to make an e. of sb** faire un exemple de qn; **to follow sb's e.** suivre l'exemple de qn; **to lead by e.** montrer l'exemple

exasperate [ɪg'zɑːspəreɪt] *vt* exaspérer; **to get exasperated** s'irriter

exasperating [ɪg'zɑːspəreɪtɪŋ] *adj* exaspérant(e)

exasperation [ɪgzɑːspə'reɪʃən] *n* exaspération *f*

excavate ['ekskəveɪt] *vt (hole, tunnel)* creuser; *(remains)* déterrer, exhumer; *(site)* faire des fouilles dans

excavation [ekskə'veɪʃən] *n* excavation *f*

excavator ['ekskəveɪtə(r)] *n (machine)* excavatrice *f*

exceed [ɪk'siːd] *vt* **(a)** *(limits)* excéder, dépasser; *(hopes, fears)* dépasser; *(one's authority)* outrepasser **(b)** *(number, amount)* dépasser

exceedingly [ɪk'siːdɪŋlɪ] *adv* extrêmement

excel [ɪk'sel] *(pt & pp* **excelled***)* **1** *vt also Ironic* **to e. oneself** se surpasser

2 *vi* exceller **(at** *or* **in** à *ou* en)

excellence ['eksələns] *n* excellence *f*

excellency ['eksələnsɪ] *n* **Your/His E.** Votre/Son Excellence *f*

excellent ['eksələnt] *adj* excellent(e)

except [ɪk'sept] **1** *prep* sauf, à l'exception de; **nobody e.** **him** personne excepté *ou* sauf lui; **I would go, e. I'm** **busy** j'irais bien, mais je suis occupé; **e. for** à part; **e. that** excepté que, si ce n'est que; **e. when** sauf *ou* à part quand
2 *vt* excepter, exclure (**from** de); **present company** **excepted** les personnes présentes exceptées; **not** **excepting...** sans excepter...

exception [ɪk'sepʃən] *n* **(a)** (*thing excepted*) exception *f*; **to make an e. of sth/for sb** faire une exception pour qch/qn; **with the e. of...** à l'exception de..., exception faite de...; **without e.** sans exception; **the e. proves the** **rule** c'est l'exception qui confirme la règle **(b)** **to take e.** **to sth** (*be offended*) se formaliser *ou* s'offenser de qch; (*object*) trouver à redire à qch

exceptionable [ɪk'sepʃənəbəl] *adj Formal* critiquable, (*offensive*) offensant(e)

exceptional [ɪk'sepʃənəl] *adj* exceptionnel(elle)

exceptionally [ɪk'sepʃənlɪ] *adv* exceptionnellement; (*in exceptional cases*) à titre exceptionnel

excerpt ['eksɜːpt] *n* extrait *m* (**from** de)

excess [ɪk'ses] *n* **(a)** **to do sth to e.** faire qch à l'excès; **to pay the e.** (*on ticket*) payer un supplément; **e.** **baggage** excédent *m* de bagages

excessive [ɪk'sesɪv] *adj* excessif(ive)

excessively [ɪk'sesɪvlɪ] *adv* extrêmement; (*eat, drink*) à l'excès

exchange [ɪks'tʃeɪndʒ] **1** *n* **(a)** (*of prisoners, ideas*) échange *m*; **in e.** (**for**) en échange (de); **a heated e.** un échange de paroles assez vives; **e. visit** échange **(b)** *Fin* (*of currency*) change *m*; **e. controls** contrôle *m* des changes; **e.** **rate** taux *m* de change; **e. rate mechanism** mécanisme *m* de change **(c)** (*Stock*) **E.** Bourse *f* (*des valeurs*) **(d)** (*telephone*) e. central *m* téléphonique
2 *vt* échanger; **to e. sth for sth** échanger qch contre qch

exchangeable [ɪks'tʃeɪndʒəbəl] *adj* échangeable (**for** contre)

exchequer [eks'tʃekə(r)] *n Br* **the E.** ≃ le Trésor Public; **the Chancellor of the E.** le Ministre des Finances

excise ['eksaɪz] *n* (*duties*) droits *mpl* d'accise
2 *vt* [ɪk'saɪz] (*remove*) (*tumour*) exciser; (*piece of text*) couper

excitable [ɪk'saɪtəbəl] *adj* nerveux(euse)

excite [ɪk'saɪt] *vt* **(a)** (*get worked up*) énerver, surexciter; (*arouse enthusiasm in*) enthousiasmer; (*stimulate*) exciter **(b)** (*give rise to*) (*admiration, desire*) provoquer; (*envy, interest*) susciter; (*curiosity*) piquer

excited [ɪk'saɪtɪd] *adj* (*worked up*) énervé(e), excité(e); (*enthusiastic*) enthousiaste; **to get e. (about)** s'exciter (pour); (*angry*) s'énerver (contre)

excitedly [ɪk'saɪtɪdlɪ] *adv* (*speak, laugh*) avec animation; (*wait*) avec une impatience fébrile

excitement [ɪk'saɪtmənt] *n* (*agitation*) agitation *f*; (*enthusiasm*) animation *f*, enthousiasme *m*; **to cause** **great e.** faire sensation

exciting [ɪk'saɪtɪŋ] *adj* passionnant(e); (*idea, prospect*) enthousiasmant(e)

exclaim [ɪks'kleɪm] **1** *vt* **"leave me alone,"** **he** **exclaimed** "laissez-moi", s'est-il écrié
2 *vi* s'exclamer, s'écrier

exclamation [eksklə'meɪʃən] *n* exclamation *f*; *Br* **e.** **mark**, *Am* **e. point** point *m* d'exclamation

exclamatory [eks'klæmətərɪ] *adj* exclamatif(ive)

exclude [ɪks'kluːd] *vt* exclure (**from** de); (*doubt, suspicion*) écarter; **excluding...** à l'exclusion de...

exclusion [ɪks'kluːʒən] *n* exclusion *f* (**from** de); **to the** **e. of...** à l'exclusion de...

exclusive [ɪks'kluːsɪv] **1** *n* (*in newspaper, on TV*) exclusivité *f*
2 *adj* **(a)** (*right, article, interview*) exclusif(ive) **(b)** (*chic*) huppé(e), (*club social circle*) très fermé(e); (*clothing, jewellery*) de grande marque **(c)** (*only*) seul(e), unique
3 *adv* **e. of delivery** frais de livraison non compris; **e. of** **tax** hors taxes

exclusively [ɪks'kluːsɪvlɪ] *adv* exclusivement; (*in* *newspaper, on TV*) en exclusivité

excommunicate [ekskə'mjuːnɪkeɪt] *vt* excommunier

excommunication [ekskəmjuːnɪ'keɪʃən] *n* excommunication *f*

excrement ['ekskrɪmənt] *n* excrément *m*

excrescence [eks'kresəns] *n* excroissance *f*

excrete [ɪks'kriːt] *vt Formal* excréter

excruciating [ɪks'kruːʃɪeɪtɪŋ] *adj* (*pain, embarrassment*) atroce; **the whole evening was e.** (*embarrassing*) on a été gênés toute la soirée; (*boring*) on s'est horriblement ennuyés toute la soirée

excruciatingly [ɪks'kruːʃɪeɪtɪŋlɪ] *adv* (*painful, embarrassing*) atrocement; *Fam* **e. funny** tordant(e)

excursion [ɪks'kɜːʃən] *n* excursion *f*

excuse 1 *n* [ɪks'kjuːs] excuse *f*; **to be a poor e. for** être nul (nulle) comme
2 *vt* [ɪks'kjuːz] **(a)** (*forgive*) excuser, pardonner; **e. me!** pardon!, excusez-moi!; **e. me?** (*what did you say?*) pardon? **(b)** (*exempt*) exempter, dispenser (**from** de) **(c)** **to e. oneself** s'excuser

ex-directory [eksdɪ'rektərɪ] *adj Br* **to be e.** (*of person,* *number*) être sur la liste rouge

execrable ['eksɪkrəbəl] *adj* exécrable, abominable

execute ['eksɪkjuːt] *vt* (*prisoner, order*) exécuter; (*plan,* *operation*) mettre à exécution

execution [eksɪ'kjuːʃən] *n* (*of prisoner, order*) exécution *f*; **in the e. of one's duty** dans l'exercice de ses fonctions

executioner [eksɪ'kjuːʃənə(r)] *n* bourreau *m*

executive [ɪg'zekjʊtɪv] **1** *n* (*businessman*) cadre *m*; (*committee*) bureau *m*, comité *m* central
2 *adj* (*post*) de cadre; (*car, suite*) de luxe; *Br* **e. director** directeur *m* administratif

executor [ɪg'zekjʊtə(r)] *n Law* exécuteur(trice) *m,f* testamentaire

exemplary [ɪg'zemplərɪ] *adj* exemplaire

exemplify [ɪg'zemplɪfaɪ] (*pt & pp* **exemplified**) *vt* illustrer

exempt [ɪg'zempt] **1** *adj* exempté(e), dispensé(e) (**from** de)
2 *vt* exempter, dispenser (**from** de)

exemption [ɪg'zem(p)ʃən] *n* exemption *f*, dispense *f* (**from** de)

exercise ['eksəsaɪz] **1** *n* exercice *m*; **to take e.** faire de l'exercice; **e. bike** vélo *m* d'appartement; **e. book** cahier *m*
2 *vt* **(a)** (*body, mind*) exercer **(b)** (*right, influence*) exercer; (*caution, restraint*) user de
3 *vi* faire de l'exercice; (*train*) s'entraîner

exert [ɪg'zɜːt] *vt* (*pressure, influence*) exercer; (*force*) faire usage de; **to e. oneself** se remuer, se donner du mal

exertion [ɪg'zɜːʃən] *n* (*of force*) usage *m*, emploi *m*; (*effort*) effort *m*

exhale [eks'heɪl] *vi* expirer

exhaust [ɪg'zɔːst] **1** n (on car) échappement m; e. **(fumes)** gaz mpl d'échappement; **e. pipe** tuyau m d'échappement
2 vt (person, resources) épuiser

exhausted [ɪg'zɔːstɪd] adj épuisé(e)

exhausting [ɪg'zɔːstɪŋ] adj épuisant(e)

exhaustion [ɪg'zɔːstʃən] n épuisement m

exhaustive [ɪg'zɔːstɪv] adj (list) exhaustif(ive); (analysis, description) détaillé(e), minutieux(euse); (enquiry, search) approfondi(e)

exhibit [ɪg'zɪbɪt] **1** n (in art exhibition) objet m exposé; (in court case) pièce f à conviction
2 vt (a) (object, goods) exhiber, montrer (b) (painting in exhibition) exposer (c) (show) (courage, judgement) faire preuve de; **to e. signs of stress/wear** donner des signes de tension/d'usure

exhibition [eksɪ'bɪʃən] n (a) (of paintings) exposition f; Fam Fig **to make an e. of oneself** se donner en spectacle (b) (of courage, bad manners) démonstration f; **it was a disgraceful e.** ce fut un spectacle honteux

exhibitionist [eksɪ'bɪʃənɪst] n (a) personne f qui aime se faire remarquer (b) Psy exhibitionniste m

exhibitor [ɪg'zɪbɪtə(r)] n exposant(e) m,f

exhilarated [ɪg'zɪləreɪtɪd] adj grisé(e)

exhilarating [ɪg'zɪləreɪtɪŋ] adj (air, walk) vivifiant(e); (experience) grisant(e); (news) enthousiasmant(e)

exhort [ɪg'zɔːt] vt exhorter, encourager (**to do sth** à faire qch)

exhortation [ɪgzɔː'teɪʃən] n exhortation f

exhume [eks'hjuːm] vt exhumer, déterrer

exigent ['eksɪdʒənt] adj (a) (urgent) urgent(e), pressant(e) (b) (demanding) exigeant(e)

exile ['eksaɪl] **1** n (a) (banishment) exil m, bannissement m; **in e.** en exil (b) (exiled person) exilé(e) m,f
2 vt exiler

exist [ɪg'zɪst] vi (a) (be in existence) exister; (of conditions) régner (b) (survive) se maintenir en vie, survivre (**on** avec)

existence [ɪg'zɪstəns] n existence f; **in e.** existant(e), qui existe; **to come into e.** naître; **to go out of e.** disparaître, cesser d'exister

existential [egzɪs'tenʃəl] adj existentiel(elle)

existentialism [egzɪs'tenʃəlɪzəm] n existentialisme m

existentialist [egzɪs'tenʃəlɪst] n & adj existentialiste m

existing [ɪg'zɪstɪŋ] adj (situation) actuel(elle)

exit ['eksɪt] **1** n sortie f; **to make an e.** sortir; Pol **e. poll** = sondage effectué auprès des électeurs immédiatement après qu'ils ont voté; **e. visa** visa m de sortie
2 vi (leave) & Comptr sortir

exodus ['eksədəs] n exode m

ex officio [eksə'fɪʃɪəʊ] adj (member) de droit

exonerate [ɪg'zɒnəreɪt] vt (absolve) disculper, innocenter (**from** or of de)

exorbitant [ɪg'zɔːbɪtənt] adj exorbitant(e)

exorcism ['eksɔːsɪzəm] n exorcisme m

exorcist ['eksɔːsɪst] n exorciste mf

exorcize ['eksɔːsaɪz] vt exorciser

exotic [ɪg'zɒtɪk] adj exotique

expand [ɪks'pænd] **1** vt (production, output) accroître; (empire) agrandir; (mind, circle of friends) élargir; (range, idea) développer
2 vi (of solid, gas) se dilater; (of company) s'agrandir

▶**expand on, expand upon** vt insep développer

expanded [ɪks'pændɪd] adj étendu(e); Comptr (memory) expansé(e); **e. polystyrene** polystyrène m expansé

expanding [ɪks'pændɪŋ] adj (market, company) en expansion, qui se développe; (universe) en expansion

expanse [eks'pæns] n étendue f

expansion [ɪks'pænʃən] n expansion f; (of gas) dilatation f; Comptr **e. card** carte f d'extension

expansive [ɪks'pænsɪv] adj (gas) dilatable; (person) expansif(ive); **in an e. mood** d'humeur expansive

expat [eks'pæt] n & adj Br Fam expatrié(e) m,f

expatriate 1 [eks'pætrɪət] expatrié(e) m,f
2 vt [eks'pætrɪeɪt] expatrier

expect [ɪks'pekt] **1** vt (a) (anticipate) s'attendre à; **to e. to do sth** compter ou espérer faire qch; **to e. sb to do sth** s'attendre à ce que qn fasse qch; **I expected as much** je m'y attendais; **to e. the worst** s'attendre au pire; **to be expecting a baby** attendre un bébé
(b) (require) to e. sth **to e. sb to do sth** attendre de qn qu'il/elle fasse qch; **to e. sth from sb** attendre qch de qn; **I know what is expected of me** je sais ce qu'on attend de moi; **to e. too much from sb/sth** trop attendre de qn/qch (c) (suppose) **to e. (that)...** penser que...; **I e. so/not** je crois bien que oui/non
2 vi (be pregnant) **to be expecting** attendre un bébé

expectancy [ɪks'pektənsɪ] n attente f; **an air of e.** l'air d'attendre quelque chose

expectant [ɪks'pektənt] adj impatient(e); **e. mother** future maman f

expectation [ekspek'teɪʃən] n espérance f; **in (the) e. of sth** dans l'attente de qch; **to have high expectations of sb/sth** attendre beaucoup de qn/qch; **to come up to expectations** se montrer à la hauteur; **to fall short of (sb's) expectations** décevoir (qn); **contrary to all expectations** contre toute attente

expected [ɪks'pektɪd] adj attendu(e); (hoped for) espéré(e)

expectorant [ɪks'pektərənt] **1** n Med expectorant m
2 adj expectorant(e)

expediency [ɪks'piːdɪənsɪ] n opportunité f; Pej (opportunism) opportunisme m

expedient [ɪks'piːdɪənt] **1** n expédient m
2 adj opportun(e), expédient(e)

expedite ['ekspɪdaɪt] vt Formal activer, accélérer

expedition [ekspə'dɪʃən] n expédition f; Fam **a shopping e.** une séance de shopping

expeditionary [ekspə'dɪʃənərɪ] adj Mil **e. force/corps** force f/corps m expéditionnaire

expel [ɪks'pel] (pt & pp expelled) vt expulser; (from school) renvoyer

expendable [ɪks'pendəbl] adj (person) qui n'est pas irremplaçable; (troops) que l'on peut sacrifier

expenditure [ɪks'pendɪtʃə(r)] n (of money, energy) dépense f

expense [ɪks'pens] n (a) (cost) dépense f, frais mpl; **to go to great e. (to do sth)** faire de grosses dépenses (pour faire qch); **no e. was spared** on n'a pas regardé à la dépense; **at the e. of one's health/sanity** aux dépens de sa santé/santé mentale; **to make a joke at sb's e.** faire une plaisanterie aux dépens de qn (b) Com **expenses** frais mpl, dépenses fpl; **it's on expenses** ça va sur la note de frais; **all expenses paid** tous frais payés; **e. account** note f de frais

expensive [iks'pensıv] *adj (object, shop, restaurant)* cher (chère); *(procedure, habit)* couteux(euse); *(tastes)* de luxe; *(mistake)* qui coûte cher

experience [iks'pıərıəns] **1** *n* expérience *f*; **to learn from e.** tirer les leçons d'une expérience; **in my e.** d'après mon expérience

2 *vt (emotions, pain)* ressentir; *(hunger, success)* connaître, faire l'expérience de; *(difficulties, problems)* avoir

experienced [iks'pıərıənst] *adj* expérimenté(e); **to be e. in sth** avoir de l'expérience en qch; *(observer)* averti(e)

experiment [iks'perımənt] **1** *n* expérience *f*; **as an e.** à titre d'essai

2 *vi* expérimenter **(on** sur); **to e. with** *(technique, drugs)* essayer

experimental [iksperı'mentəl] *adj* expérimental(e)

expert ['ekspə:t] **1** *n* expert *m*, spécialiste *mf*

2 *adj* expert(e), habile; *(advice, opinion)* d'un expert; **to be e. in** *or* **at sth** être expert en qch; *Comptr* **e. system** système *m* expert; *Law* **e. witness** expert *m* cité comme témoin

expertise [ekspə:'ti:z] *n (technical, financial)* compétence *f*, connaissances *fpl*; *(as cook, carpenter)* savoir-faire *m*

expertly ['ekspə:tlı] *adv* de manière experte

expiate ['ekspıeıt] *vt Formal* expier

expire [iks'paıə(r)] *vi* **(a)** *(of law, deadline, passport)* expirer **(b)** *Lit (die)* expirer

expiry [iks'paıərı] *n* expiration *f*, fin *f*; **e. date** *(date f d')*échéance *f*, date d'expiration

explain [iks'pleın] **1** *vt* expliquer; **to e. oneself** *(make oneself clear)* s'expliquer; *(justify oneself)* se justifier

2 *vi* donner des explications, expliquer; *(make oneself clear)* s'expliquer

▸explain away *vt sep (give explanation for)* donner une explication satisfaisante à; *(justify)* justifier

explanation [eksplə'neıʃən] *n* explication *f*; **to give an e. of sth** *(make clear)* expliquer qch; *(justify)* justifier qch

explanatory [iks'plænətərı] *adj* explicatif(ive)

expletive [iks'pli:tıv] *n* juron *m*

explicable [eks'plıkəbəl] *adj* explicable

explicit [eks'plısıt] *adj* explicite

explicitly [eks'plısıtlı] *adv* de manière explicite

explode [iks'pləʊd] **1** *vt (bomb)* faire exploser; *Fig (idea, theory)* démontrer la fausseté de

2 *vi (of bomb)* & *Fig (with anger)* exploser; *(of mine)* sauter; **to e. with laughter** éclater de rire

exploit 1 *n* ['eksplɔıt] exploit *m*

2 *vt* [iks'plɔıt] **(a)** *(take unfair advantage of)* exploiter **(b)** *(use)* *(resources, scandal)* exploiter; *(talents)* mettre à profit

exploitation [eksplɔı'teıʃən] *n* exploitation *f*

exploration [eksplə'reıʃən] *n* exploration *f*

exploratory [iks'plɒrətərı] *adj (trip)* d'exploration; *(surgery, discussions, talks)* exploratoire

explore [iks'plɔ:(r)] **1** *vt (area, countryside)* explorer; *(possibility, idea)* étudier

2 *vi* partir en exploration

explorer [iks'plɔ:rə(r)] *n* explorateur(trice) *m,f*

explosion [iks'pləʊʒən] *n also Fig* explosion *f*

explosive [iks'pləʊsıv] **1** *n* explosif *m*

2 *adj also Fig* explosif(ive)

exponent [iks'pəʊnənt] *n* **(a)** *(of theory, idea)* avocat(e) *m,f*; *(of piece of music)* interprète *mf* **(b)** *Math* exposant *m*

exponential [ekspəʊ'nenʃəl] *adj* exponentiel(elle)

export 1 *n* ['ekspɔ:t] **(a)** *(product)* article *m* d'exportation; **exports** *(of country)* exportations *fpl* **(b)** *(activity)* exportation *f*; **e. duty** droit(s) *m(pl)* de sortie; **e. licence** licence *f* d'exportation; **e. trade** exportations *fpl*

2 *vt* [eks'pɔ:t] *also Comptr* exporter

exportation [ekspɔ:'teıʃən] *n* exportation *f*

exporter [eks'pɔ:tə(r)] *n* exportateur(trice) *m,f*

expose [iks'pəʊz] *vt* **(a)** *(to air, cold, danger)* & *Phot* exposer **(to** à); *(wire)* mettre à jour; **to e. oneself to danger** s'exposer au danger **(b)** *(reveal)* *(secret)* éventer; *(crime)* dévoiler; *(criminal)* démasquer; *(feelings)* afficher; **to e. sb as a traitor/criminal** révéler que qn est un traître/ criminel; **to e. oneself** *(of flasher)* s'exhiber

exposé [eks'pəʊzeı] *n (article, book)* exposé *m*; *(of scandal, corruption)* révélations *fpl*

exposed [iks'pəʊzd] *adj* exposé(e) **(to** à)

exposition [ekspə'zıʃən] *n (explanation)* exposition *f*, exposé *m*

expostulate [iks'pɒstjʊleıt] *vi Formal* vitupérer

exposure [iks'pəʊʒə(r)] *n* **(a)** *(to air, cold, danger)* exposition *f*; **to die of e.** mourir de froid **(b)** *(publicity)* couverture *f*; **to get a lot of e.** faire l'objet d'une importante couverture médiatique **(c)** *(of crime)* révélation *f*; *(of criminal, scandal)* dénonciation *f* **(d)** *Phot* pose *f*; **e. meter** posemètre *m*

expound [iks'paʊnd] *vt Formal* exposer

express [iks'pres] **1** *n (train)* express *m*, rapide *m*

2 *adj* **(a)** *(clear)* *(purpose, instruction)* exprès(esse); *(order)* formel(elle) **(b)** *(rapid)* *(letter, delivery)* exprès *inv*; *(train)* express *inv*

3 *adv* **to send sth e.** envoyer qch en exprès

4 *vt* exprimer; **to e. oneself** s'exprimer

expression [iks'preʃən] *n* expression *f*

expressionism [iks'preʃənızəm] *n* expressionnisme *m*

expressionist [iks'preʃənıst] *n* & *adj* expressionniste *mf*

expressionless [iks'preʃənləs] *adj* sans expression

expressive [iks'presıv] *adj* expressif(ive); *(gesture, silence)* éloquent(e)

expressly [iks'preslı] *adv* expressément

expropriate [eks'prəʊprıeıt] *vt* exproprier

expropriation [eksprəʊprı'eıʃən] *n* expropriation *f*

expulsion [iks'pʌlʃən] *n* expulsion *f*; *(from school)* renvoi *m*

expunge [iks'pʌndʒ] *vt* effacer

expurgate ['ekspə:geıt] *vt* expurger

exquisite ['ekskwızıt] *adj* exquis(e); *(pleasure)* vif (vive)

exquisitely [eks'kwızıtlı] *adv* d'une manière exquise

extant [eks'tænt] *adj* qui existe encore

extempore [iks'tempərı] **1** *adj (speech)* impromptu(e)

2 *adv* **to speak e.** improviser

extemporize [iks'tempəraız] *vi* improviser

extend [iks'tend] **1** *vt* **(a)** *(in space)* étendre, allonger; *(knowledge)* accroître; *(frontiers)* faire reculer; *(house)* agrandir **(b)** *(in time)* prolonger **(c)** *(give, offer)* *(one's hand)* tendre; *(thanks)* présenter; *(support)* offrir; *Fin* **to e. credit to sb** accorder un crédit à qn

2 *vi* **(a)** *(in space)* s'étendre **(b)** *(in time)* se prolonger, continuer

extended family [iks'tendıd'fæmılı] *n* famille *f* au sens large

extension [ɪks'tenʃən] n (a) (to building) annexe f (b) (in time) prolongation f; (for essay) délai m supplémentaire (c) (for telephone) poste m (d) e. (cable) rallonge f

extensive [ɪks'tensɪv] adj (area, knowledge) vaste, étendu(e); (damage, repairs) important(e); to make e. use of sth faire un usage considérable de qch

extensively [ɪks'tensɪvlɪ] adv (travel, read) énormément; (revised, rewritten) entièrement; (damaged) gravement; to use sth e. se servir beaucoup de qch

extent [ɪks'tent] n (a) (of land, damage, knowledge) étendue f (b) (degree) to an e., to a certain e., to some e. jusqu'à un certain point, dans une certaine mesure; to a large e. en grande partie, dans une large mesure; to such an e. that... à tel point que...; to what e.? jusqu'à quel point?

extenuating circumstances [ɪks'tenjʊeɪtɪŋ'sɜːkəmstənsɪz] npl circonstances fpl atténuantes

exterior [ɪks'tɪərɪə(r)] 1 n (of building, car) extérieur m; (of person) extérieur, dehors mpl
2 adj extérieur(e)

exterminate [ɪks'tɜːmɪneɪt] vt exterminer; (disease) éradiquer

extermination [ɪkstɜːmɪ'neɪʃən] n extermination f; (of disease) éradication f

external [ɪks'tɜːnəl] adj (events, trade, debt) extérieur(e); (angle, damage, wall) externe; Univ (examiner) de l'extérieur; Pol e. affairs affaires fpl étrangères ou extérieures; for e. use only (on medicine) à usage externe

extinct [ɪks'tɪŋkt] adj (animal, species) disparu(e), qui n'existe plus; (volcano) éteint(e)

extinction [ɪks'tɪŋkʃən] n extinction f

extinguish [ɪks'tɪŋgwɪʃ] vt (fire) éteindre; (hope) anéantir

extinguisher [ɪks'tɪŋgwɪʃə(r)] n extincteur m

extirpate [ɪkstə'peɪt] vt Formal extirper

extol, Am **extoll** [ɪks'təʊl] (pt & pp extolled) vt (virtues, merits) exalter, vanter; (beauty) célébrer, chanter

extort [ɪks'tɔːt] vt (money) extorquer (from à); (promise) arracher (from à)

extortion [ɪks'tɔːʃən] n extorsion f

extortionate [ɪks'tɔːʃənət] adj exorbitant(e)

extra ['ekstrə] 1 n (in film) figurant(e) m,f; (on bill) supplément m
2 adj (a) (additional) supplémentaire, de plus; no e. charge sans supplément de prix; e. time (in sporting contest) prolongation f (b) (spare) de réserve, de rechange
3 adv (a) (more than usual) extrêmement; to be e. careful faire particulièrement attention; e. large (clothing) grand patron; e. special très spécial(e) (b) (charge, pay) en plus, en sus

extract 1 n ['ekstrækt] (a) (concentrate) extrait m, concentré m (b) (from book, film) extrait m
2 vt [ɪks'trækt] (tooth, raw material) extraire (from de); (confession, information) soutirer (from à)

extraction [ɪks'trækʃən] n (a) (removal) extraction f (b) (origin) (social) extraction f; (geographical) origine f; she is of Danish e. elle est d'origine danoise

extractor fan [ɪks'træktə(r)] n aérateur m

extracurricular ['ekstrəkə'rɪkjʊlə(r)] adj Sch extrascolaire

extradite ['ekstrədaɪt] vt extrader

extradition [ekstrə'dɪʃən] n extradition f

extrajudicial ['ekstrədʒuː'dɪʃəl] adj extrajudiciaire

extramarital ['ekstrə'mærɪtəl] adj extraconjugal(e)

extramural ['ekstrə'mjʊərəl] adj Univ de formation continue

extraneous [ɪks'treɪnɪəs] adj Formal (details) sans rapport; (considerations) en dehors de la question

extraordinarily [ɪks'trɔː'dənərɪlɪ] adv extraordinairement

extraordinary [ɪks'trɔːdənɪ] adj extraordinaire; e. powers pouvoirs mpl extraordinaires; e. general meeting assemblée f générale extraordinaire

extrapolate [ɪk'stræpəleɪt] vt & vi extrapoler (from à partir de)

extrapolation [ɪkstræpə'leɪʃən] n extrapolation f

extrasensory perception ['ekstrə'sensərɪpə'sep-ʃən] n perception f extrasensorielle

extraterrestrial ['ekstrətɪ'restrɪəl] n & adj extraterrestre mf

extravagance [ɪks'trævəgəns] n (a) (excessive spending) gaspillage m (b) (extravagant purchase) folie f

extravagant [ɪks'trævəgənt] adj (person) dépensier(ère); (tastes) dispendieux(euse); (object) hors de prix

extravaganza [ekstrævə'gænzə] n grand spectacle m

extreme [ɪks'triːm] 1 n extrême m; in the e. à l'extrême; to go from one e. to the other passer d'un extrême à l'autre; to go to extremes pousser les choses à l'extrême
2 adj extrême; Pol the e. left l'extrême gauche

extremely [ɪks'triːmlɪ] adv extrêmement

extremism [ɪks'triːmɪzəm] n extrémisme m

extremist [ɪks'triːmɪst] n & adj extrémiste mf

extremity [ɪks'tremɪtɪ] (pl extremities) n (a) (end) extrémité f (b) extremities (of body) extrémités fpl (c) (extreme situation) situation f extrême; (extreme measure) mesure f extrême

extricate ['ekstrɪkeɪt] vt dégager, tirer; to e. oneself from (danger, difficulties) se tirer de

extrovert ['ekstrəvɜːt] n & adj extraverti(e) m,f

exuberance [ɪg'zjuːbərəns] n exubérance f

exuberant [ɪg'zjuːbərənt] adj exubérant(e)

exude [ɪg'zjuːd] vt (sweat, odour) exsuder; (health, confidence) déborder de

exult [ɪg'zʌlt] vi exulter, se réjouir (in de)

exultant [ɪg'zʌltənt] adj (mood) joyeux(euse); (cry) de triomphe

eye [aɪ] 1 n (a) (of person, storm) œil m; (of needle) chas m; to open/close one's eyes ouvrir/fermer les yeux; to look sb straight in the e. regarder qn droit dans les yeux; as far as the e. can see à perte de vue; to make e. contact with sb regarder qn (droit) dans les yeux; e. drops (medicine) gouttes fpl pour les yeux; at e. level à la hauteur des yeux; e. shadow ombre f à paupières; e. test examen m de la vue
(b) (idioms) in the eye(s) of the law aux yeux de la loi; to be in the public e. occuper une position en vue; to have an e. for a bargain savoir reconnaître une bonne affaire; to have an e. for detail/colour avoir l'œil pour les détails/les couleurs; to look at sth with a critical e. regarder qch d'un œil critique; to see e. to e. with sb voir les choses du même œil que qn; for your eyes only confidentiel(elle); to keep one's eyes and ears open rester en éveil; to keep one's eyes peeled or skinned ouvrir l'œil; to open sb's eyes to sth ouvrir ou dessiller les yeux à qn sur qch; to shut or close one's eyes to sth fermer les yeux sur qch; to do sth with one's eyes

open faire qch en connaissance de cause; **to catch sb's e.** attirer l'attention de qn; **to have eyes in** *or* **at the back of one's head** avoir des yeux derrière la tête; **he only has eyes for her** il n'a d'yeux que pour elle; **to set** *or* **lay eyes on sth** poser les yeux sur qch; **I saw it with my own eyes** je l'ai vu de mes propres yeux; **to run** *or* **cast one's e. over sth** jeter un coup d'œil sur qch; **to keep an e. on sb/sth** surveiller qn/qch; **to keep an e. out for sth** être à l'affût de qch; **to have one's e. on sb/sth** *(be watching)* avoir qn/qch à l'œil; *(have in mind)* avoir l'œil sur qn/qch; **to make eyes at sb** faire de l'œil à qn; **with an e. to...** en vue de...; **to be up to one's eyes in work** avoir du travail par-dessus la tête; **to be up to one's eyes in debt** être endetté(e) jusqu'au cou; *Fam* **that's one in the e. for him!** ça lui fera les pieds!; **an e. for an e., a tooth for a tooth** œil pour œil, dent pour dent

2 *vt* regarder, observer

▶**eye up** *vt sep* reluquer

eyeball ['aɪbɔːl] *n* globe *m* oculaire

eyebrow ['aɪbraʊ] *n* sourcil *m*; *Fig* **to raise one's eyebrows** *(in surprise)* lever les sourcils

eye-catching ['aɪkætʃɪŋ] *adj* accrocheur(euse)

eyeful ['aɪfʊl] *n Fam* **to get an e. of sb/sth** *(look at)* reluquer qn/qch

eyeglass ['aɪglɑːs] *n* monocle *m*

eyeglasses ['aɪglɑːsɪz] *npl Am (spectacles)* lunettes *fpl*

eyelash ['aɪlæʃ] *n* cil *m*

eyelid ['aɪlɪd] *n* paupière *f*; *Fig* **she didn't bat an e.** elle n'a pas sourcillé

eyeliner ['aɪlaɪnə(r)] *n* eye-liner *m*

eye-opener ['aɪəʊpənə(r)] *n* révélation *f*; **it was an e. for him** ça lui a ouvert les yeux

eyepatch ['aɪpætʃ] *n* cache *m* (sur l'œil)

eyeshade ['aɪʃeɪd] *n* visière *f*

eyesight ['aɪsaɪt] *n* vue *f*

eyesore ['aɪsɔː(r)] *n* horreur *f*

eyestrain ['aɪstreɪn] *n* fatigue *f* oculaire

eyetooth ['aɪtuːθ] *(pl* **eyeteeth** ['aɪtiːθ]*)* *n* canine *f*; **I'd give my eyeteeth to go with them** je donnerais n'importe quoi pour aller avec eux

eyewash ['aɪwɒʃ] *n (for eye)* collyre *m*; *Fig (nonsense)* boniment *m*, poudre *f* aux yeux

eyewitness ['aɪwɪtnɪs] *n* témoin *m* oculaire

eyrie ['ɪərɪ] *n* aire *f*

F, f [ef] *n* (a) *(letter)* F, f *m inv*; *Br Euph* the **F word** = euphémisme désignant le mot "fuck" (b) *Mus* fa *m*

fa [fɑː] *n Mus* fa *m*

FA [eˈfeɪ] *n (abbr* **Football Association***)* = fédération anglaise de football

fab [fæb] *adj Br Fam* sensass

fable [ˈfeɪbəl] *n* fable *f*

fabled [ˈfeɪbəld] *adj* légendaire; *Fig* fabuleux(euse)

fabric [ˈfæbrɪk] *n (cloth)* tissu *m*, étoffe *f*; *(of building)* structure *f*; *Fig* the **f. of society** le tissu social

fabricate [ˈfæbrɪkeɪt] *vt (news, story, alibi)* forger, fabriquer; *(make)* fabriquer

fabulous [ˈfæbjʊləs] *adj* fabuleux(euse)

fabulously [ˈfæbjʊləslɪ] *adv (rich)* fabuleusement

façade [fəˈsɑːd] *n also Fig* façade *f*

face [feɪs] **1** *n* (a) *(of person)* visage *m*, figure *f*; *very Fam* **shut your f.!** ferme-la!, la ferme!; **I told him to his f.** je le lui ai dit en face; **I shall never be able to look her in the f. again** je ne pourrai plus jamais la regarder en face; **to show one's f.** se montrer; **to set one's f. against sth** se braquer contre qch; **in the f. of** *(danger, threat, enemy)* devant, face à; *Fam* **in your f.** *(music, campaign)* percutant(e); **f. cloth** ≃ gant *m* de toilette; **f. cream** crème *f* pour le visage; **f. pack** masque *m*; **f. powder** poudre *f*

(b) *(expression)* mine *f*; **to make** *or* **pull faces** faire des grimaces; **to keep a straight f.** garder son sérieux; **to put a good f. on it** garder le sourire

(c) *(appearance)* **on the f. of it** à première vue; **to save f.** sauver la face; **to lose f.** perdre la face; **the changing f. of Britain** le visage changeant de la Grande-Bretagne; **to take sth at f. value** prendre qch au pied de la lettre

(d) *(surface) (of the earth)* surface *f*; *(of clock)* cadran *m*; *(of coin, cliff)* face *f*; **to disappear off the f. of the earth** se volatiliser; **f. down** *(person)* sur le ventre; *(document)* face imprimée dessous; *(playing card)* à l'envers; **f. up** *(person)* sur le dos; *(document)* face imprimée dessus; *(playing card)* à l'endroit

2 *vt* (a) *(confront) (difficulty, danger)* affronter, faire face à; **to be faced with sth** être confronté(e) à qch; **to f. facts** regarder les choses en face, se rendre à l'évidence; **he faces six months in prison** il risque six mois de prison; **I can't f. going to work today** je n'ai pas le courage d'aller travailler aujourd'hui; **let's f. it** soyons réalistes; *Fig* **to f. the music** *(deal with situation)* faire front; *(accept consequences)* assumer ses responsabilités

(b) *(look towards)* faire face à; **to f. the front** regarder devant soi

3 *vi* **to f. north/south** *(of house)* être orienté(e) au nord/sud; **to f. towards** *(of person)* se tourner vers

▶**face up to** *vt insep (person)* tenir tête à; *(reality, fears)* affronter

faceless [ˈfeɪslɪs] *adj* anonyme

face-lift [ˈfeɪslɪft] *n (plastic surgery)* lifting *m*; *Fig (of building)* restauration *f*; **to have a f.** se faire faire un lifting

face-saving [ˈfeɪseɪvɪŋ] *adj* qui permet de sauver la face

facet [ˈfæsɪt] *n (of gem, character)* facette *f*; *(of problem, situation)* dimension *f*

facetious [fəˈsiːʃəs] *adj* facétieux(euse); **don't be f.!** ne plaisante pas!

face-to-face [ˈfeɪstəˈfeɪs] **1** *adj* **a f. meeting** un face à face

2 *adv (meet)* face à face

facial [ˈfeɪʃəl] **1** *n* soin *m* du visage; **to have a f.** se faire faire un soin du visage

2 *adj* facial(e); *(expression, hair)* du visage

facile [ˈfæsaɪl] *adj Pej* facile

facilitate [fəˈsɪlɪteɪt] *vt* faciliter

facility [fəˈsɪlɪtɪ] *(pl* **facilities***) n* (a) *(ease)* facilité *f* (b) *(skill)* **to have a f. for sth** avoir un don pour qch (c) **facilities** *(for cooking, washing)* équipement *m*; *(for sport)* installations *fpl*; **shopping facilities** magasins *mpl*; **transport facilities** moyens *mpl* de transport (d) *(building)* **a detention f.** un établissement pénitentiaire (e) *(feature) (of computer, stereo)* option *f*

facsimile [fækˈsɪmɪlɪ] *n (copy)* fac-similé *m*; *(fax)* télécopie *f*

fact [fækt] *n* fait *m*; **in f.** en fait; **to distinguish f. from fiction** discerner la fiction de la réalité; **the f. is (that)...** le fait est que...; **it's a f. that...** c'est un fait que...; **to know for a f. (that)...** savoir pertinemment que...; **it's a f. of life** c'est une réalité; **to tell sb the facts of life** expliquer à qn comment on fait les enfants

fact-finding [ˈfæktfaɪndɪŋ] *adj* d'enquête

faction [ˈfækʃən] *n* faction *f*

factor [ˈfæktə(r)] *n (aspect, in maths)* facteur *m*

factory [ˈfæktərɪ] *(pl* **factories***) n* usine *f*; *(small)* fabrique *f*; *Am* **the f.** *(teaching staff)* le personnel enseignant

factual [ˈfæktʃʊəl] *adj* basé(e) sur les faits

faculty [ˈfækəltɪ] *(pl* **faculties***) n (of mind, in university)* faculté *f*; *Am* **the f.** *(teaching staff)* le personnel enseignant

fad [fæd] *n* mode *f* *(for* de)

fade [feɪd] **1** *vt* faner

2 *vi (of flower, material, colour)* se faner; *(of light)* baisser; *(of memory)* s'éteindre; *(of hope)* s'amenuiser; **to f. from memory** s'effacer de la mémoire

▶**fade away** *vi (of sound)* s'éteindre; *Fig (of person)* s'éteindre peu à peu

▶**fade out** **1** *vt sep Cin* fermer en fondu; *(music)* terminer par un fondu

2 *vi* se terminer en fondu

faded ['feɪdɪd] *adj (flower, colour)* fané(e); *(photograph, garment)* décoloré(e)

fading ['feɪdɪŋ] *adj (light)* pâlissant(e)

faeces ['fiːsiːz] *npl* fèces *fpl*

▶**faff about, faff around** [fæf] *vi Br Fam* perdre son temps

fag [fæg] *n* (a) *Br Fam (cigarette)* clope *m* or *f* (b) *Br Fam (unpleasant job)* corvée *f* (c) *Am very Fam (homosexual)* pédé *m,* = terme injurieux désignant un homosexuel

faggot ['fægət] *n* (a) *(firewood)* fagot *m* (b) *Br (meatball)* boulette *f* de viande (c) *Am very Fam (homosexual)* pédé *m,* = terme injurieux désignant un homosexuel

Fahrenheit ['færənhaɪt] *adj* Fahrenheit *inv*

fail [feɪl] 1 *n* (a) *(in exam)* échec *m*; **without f.** sans faute

2 *vt (exam, test)* échouer à, rater; *(candidate)* recaler; **to f. a drugs test** être positif(ive) au contrôle anti-dopage; **words f. me** les mots me manquent; **his nerve failed him** le courage lui a fait défaut; **I won't f. you** vous pouvez compter sur moi

3 *vi (of person, plan)* échouer; *(of business)* faire faillite; *(of engine)* caler; *(of memory, eyesight, light)* baisser; *(of brakes)* lâcher; **to f. to do sth** *(not succeed)* ne pas arriver à faire qch; *(forget)* négliger de faire qch; **I f. to see what the problem is** je ne vois pas où est le problème; **if all else fails** en désespoir de cause; **to f. in one's duty** manquer à son devoir; **it never fails** *(of strategy, excuse)* ça marche à tous les coups

failed [feɪld] *adj (artist, politician)* raté(e)

failing ['feɪlɪŋ] 1 *n (fault)* faiblesse *f*, défaut *m*
2 *adj (sight, strength)* qui baisse
3 *prep* à défaut de; **f. that** à défaut; **f. all else** en désespoir de cause

fail-safe ['feɪlseɪf] *adj (mechanism)* à sûreté intégrée

failure ['feɪljə(r)] *n (of plan, attempt)* échec *m*; *(person)* raté(e) *m,f*; *(of machine)* panne *f*; *(of company)* faillite *f*; **to be a f.** *(of show, film)* faire un bide; **f. to keep a promise** manquement *m* à une promesse; **f. to pay a bill** défaut *m* de paiement d'une facture

faint [feɪnt] 1 *n* **to fall down in a f.** s'évanouir
2 *adj (hope, smell)* faible; *(mark, writing)* à peine visible; *(colour)* pâle; *(idea)* vague; **I haven't got the faintest idea** je n'en ai pas la moindre idée; **to feel** or **be f.** *(of person)* se sentir mal
3 *vi (lose consciousness)* s'évanouir

faint-hearted ['feɪnt'hɑːtɪd] *adj* timoré(e)

faintly ['feɪntlɪ] *adv* (a) *(remember, hear, see)* vaguement; *(shine)* faiblement (b) *(slightly) (uneasy, ridiculous)* légèrement

fair¹ ['feə(r)] *n* (a) *Br (funfair)* fête *f* foraine (b) *(trade fair)* foire *f*

fair² 1 *adj* (a) *(just)* juste, équitable; *(price)* raisonnable; *(fight)* loyal(e); **it's not f.** ce n'est pas juste; **fair's f.!** ce n'est que justice!; **f. enough!** *(OK)* d'accord!; **(rightly so)** ça se comprend!; **it is f. to say (that)...** on peut dire que...; **to be f.,...** pour être honnête,...; **by f. means or foul** par tous les moyens; *Prov* **all's f. in love and war** tous les moyens sont bons; *Fam* **to give sb a f. crack of the whip** donner sa chance à qn; **to be f. game** être une proie facile; **f. play** fair-play *m*; **to get one's f. share** recevoir son dû; **we've had our f. share of problems** nous avons eu notre lot de problèmes
(b) *(quite good)* assez bon (bonne); **a f. idea** une assez bonne idée; **at a f. pace** à une allure assez rapide; **a f. amount of** pas mal de; **f. to middling** comme ci comme ça
(c) *(weather)* beau (belle)
(d) *(light-coloured) (hair)* blond(e); *(skin)* pâle
(e) *(attractive)* beau (belle); *Old-fashioned* **the f.** or **fairer sex** le beau sexe

2 *adv (act, fight)* loyalement; *(play)* jouer franc jeu; **you can't say fairer than that** il n'y a pas plus équitable; **to beat sb f. and square** battre qn à plates coutures

fairground ['feəɡraʊnd] *n* parc *m* d'attractions

fair-haired ['feə'heəd] *adj* blond(e)

fairly ['feəlɪ] *adv* (a) *(quite)* assez; **it is f. certain (that)...** il est à peu près certain que... (b) *(justly)* équitablement; *(play, fight)* loyalement; *(describe)* objectivement (c) *(for emphasis)* **we f. raced home** nous sommes rentrés ventre à terre

fair-minded ['feə'maɪndɪd] *adj* équitable

fairness ['feənɪs] *n (of person, decision)* impartialité *f*; **in all f.** en toute justice (b) *(of hair)* blondeur *f*; *(of skin)* pâleur *f*

fair-sized ['feə'saɪzd] *adj* assez grand(e)

fairway ['feəweɪ] *n* fairway *m*

fair-weather friend ['feəweðə'frend] *n* = ami qui n'est là que quand tout va bien

fairy ['feərɪ] *(pl* **fairies)** *n* (a) *(magical being)* fée *f*; **f. godmother** bonne fée *f*; **f. lights** guirlande *f* lumineuse *(pour sapin de Noël)* (b) *very Fam (homosexual)* tapette *f,* = terme injurieux désignant un homosexuel

fairytale ['feərɪteɪl] *n* conte *m* de fées; **a f. ending** une fin digne d'un conte de fées

faith [feɪθ] *n* foi *f*; **to have f. in sb** avoir foi en qn; **to be of the Catholic/Jewish f.** être de religion catholique/ juive; **to keep f. with sb** tenir ses engagements envers qn; **in good f.** en toute bonne foi; **f. healer** guérisseur(euse) *m,f*

faithful ['feɪθfʊl] 1 *npl* **the f.** les fidèles *mpl*
2 *adj* fidèle

faithfully ['feɪθfʊlɪ] *adv* fidèlement; **yours f.** *(in formal letter)* recevez l'expression de mes/nos sentiments distingués

fake [feɪk] 1 *n (object)* faux *m*; *(person)* bluffeur *m*
2 *adj* faux (fausse)
3 *vt (signature)* contrefaire; *(result)* truquer; **to f. an illness** feindre d'être malade

falcon ['fɔːlkən] *n* faucon *m*

falconry ['fɔːlkənrɪ] *n* fauconnerie *f*

Falkland ['fɔːlkənd] *n* **the F. Islands, the Falklands** les Malouines *fpl*, les Falkland *fpl*

fall [fɔːl] 1 *n* (a) *(of person, prices, besieged city, snow)* chute *f*; **to have a f.** tomber, faire une chute; *Fig* **to be heading for a f.** courir à sa perte; *Am Fam* **f. guy** *(scapegoat)* bouc *m* émissaire
(b) *Am (autumn)* automne *m*
(c) *(waterfall)* chutes *fpl*

2 *vi (pt* **fell** [fel], *pp* **fallen** ['fɔːlən]) (a) *(drop, fall over)* tomber; **to f. down a hole** tomber dans un trou; **to f. off a bicycle/chair** tomber d'un vélo/d'une chaise; *Fig* **to f. into a trap** tomber dans un piège; *also Fig* **to f. flat** tomber à plat; **to f. to pieces** *(of object)* tomber en morceaux; *Fig (of person)* craquer; **to f. short of doing sth** ne pas réussir à faire qch
(b) *(decrease) (of price, temperature, standards)* chuter, baisser
(c) *(of government, city, soldier)* tomber

(d) *(of silence, darkness, light)* tomber; **the responsibility falls on you** c'est à vous qu'en incombe la responsabilité; *Formal* **it falls to me to introduce...** j'ai l'honneur de vous présenter...

(e) *(become)* **to f. asleep** s'endormir; **to f. ill** tomber malade; **to f. in love (with)** tomber amoureux(euse) (de); **to f. silent** se taire; **to f. victim to an epidemic** être victime d'une épidémie; **the match fell victim to the weather** le match a dû être annulé en raison du mauvais temps

(f) *(be classified)* se classer; **to f. into two categories** se diviser en deux catégories; **suddenly everything fell into place** soudain tout est devenu clair

(g) *(occur)* **Christmas Day falls on a Thursday** Noël tombe un jeudi

▶**fall away** *vi (of ground)* descendre; *(of attendance)* diminuer

▶**fall back on** *vt insep (resort to)* se rabattre sur

▶**fall behind** *vi (in race)* se faire distancer; **to f. behind with the rent** être en retard pour payer son loyer

▶**fall down** *vi (of person)* tomber; *(of building)* s'écrouler, s'effondrer; **that's where your argument falls down** c'est par là que pèche ton raisonnement

▶**fall for** *vt insep Fam* (a) *(fall in love with)* tomber amoureux(euse) de (b) *(trick)* se laisser prendre à; **to f. for it** s'y laisser prendre

▶**fall in** *vi* (a) *(of roof)* s'écrouler, s'effondrer (b) *Mil (of troops)* former les rangs

▶**fall off** *vi* (a) *(of object)* tomber (b) *(of profits, attendance)* diminuer

▶**fall out** *vi* (a) *(quarrel)* se brouiller, se fâcher (with avec) (b) *Mil* rompre les rangs

▶**fall over 1** *vi* tomber (par terre)
2 *vt insep (stumble on)* trébucher sur; *Fig* **to be falling over oneself to do sth** *(be very keen)* se mettre en quatre pour faire qch

▶**fall through** *vi (of plan, deal)* tomber à l'eau

fallacious [fə'leɪʃəs] *adj* erroné(e)

fallacy ['fæləsɪ] *(pl* **fallacies)** *n* erreur *f*

fallen ['fɔːlən] **1** *npl* **the f.** les soldats *mpl* tombés au combat
2 *adj (angel)* déchu(e); *(woman)* perdu(e)
3 *pp of* **fall**

fallible ['fælɪbəl] *adj* faillible

Fallopian tube [fə'ləʊpɪən'tjuːb] *n Anat* trompe *f* de Fallope

fallout ['fɔːlaʊt] *n (nuclear)* retombées *fpl* radioactives; *Fig (from scandal)* retombées *fpl*; **f. shelter** abri *m* antiatomique

fallow ['fæləʊ] *adj* en jachère; **to lie f.** être en jachère; *Fig* **a f. period** un passage à vide

false [fɔːls] *adj* faux (fausse); **f. alarm** fausse alerte *f*; **f. dawn** faux espoir *m*; **f. economy** fausse économie *f*; **f. friend** *(in foreign language)* faux ami *m*; **f. modesty** fausse modestie *f*; *Fig* **to strike a f. note** *(in film)* sonner faux; *(of person)* faire une gaffe; **under f. pretences** *(illegally)* par des moyens frauduleux; *(by lying)* sous des prétextes fallacieux; **f. start** *(in race)* faux départ *m*; **f. teeth** dentier *m*; **to bear f. witness** faire un faux témoignage

falsehood ['fɔːlshʊd] *n* mensonge *m*

falsely ['fɔːlslɪ] *adv (described)* faussement; *(accused)* à tort; *(smile)* avec fausseté

falsetto [fɔːl'setəʊ] *(pl* **falsettos)** *n Mus* voix *f* de fausset

falsify ['fɔːlsɪfaɪ] *(pt & pp* **falsified)** *vt* (a) *(forge) (records, document)* falsifier (b) *(disprove) (theory)* prouver la fausseté de

falter ['fɔːltə(r)] *vi also Fig* vaciller; *(of voice)* hésiter

fame [feɪm] *n* renom *m*, renommée *f*; **to seek f. and fortune** rechercher la gloire et la fortune

famed [feɪmd] *adj* célèbre (for pour)

familiar [fə'mɪlɪə(r)] *adj* (a) *(well-known)* familier(ère) (to à) (b) *(intimate)* familier(ère), intime; **to be on f. terms with sb** avoir des rapports amicaux avec qn; **to get too f. with sb** se permettre trop de familiarités avec qn (c) *(acquainted)* **to be f. with sb/sth** bien connaître qn/qch

familiarity [fəmɪlɪ'ærɪtɪ] *n* (a) *(intimacy)* familiarité *f*; **f. breeds contempt** avec l'habitude vient la lassitude (b) *(acquaintance)* connaissance *f* (with de)

familiarize [fə'mɪlɪəraɪz] *vt* **to f. sb with sth** familiariser qn avec qch; **to f. oneself with sth** se familiariser avec qch

family ['fæmɪlɪ] *(pl* **families)** *n* famille *f*; **it runs in the f.** c'est de famille, ça tient de famille; **to start a f.** fonder une famille; **to treat sb as one of the f.** traiter qn comme un membre de la famille; *Fam* **to be in the f. way** être enceinte; **f. allowance** allocations *fpl* familiales; **f. business** entreprise *f* familiale; **f. doctor/life** docteur *m*/vie *f* de famille; **f. man** homme *m* attaché à sa famille; **f. planning** planning *m* familial; **f. planning clinic** (centre *m* de) planning familial; **f. resemblance** air *m* de famille; **f. tree** arbre *m* généalogique

famine ['fæmɪn] *n* famine *f*; **f. relief** aide *f* aux victimes d'une famine

famished ['fæmɪʃd] *adj* affamé(e)

famous ['feɪməs] *adj* célèbre (for pour)

famously ['feɪməslɪ] *adv Fam* **to get on f.** *(with sb)* s'entendre à merveille (avec qn)

fan¹ [fæn] **1** *n (cooling device) (hand-held)* éventail *m*; *(mechanical)* ventilateur *m*; **f. belt** *(of car)* courroie *f* de ventilateur; **f. heater** radiateur *m* soufflant
2 *vt (pt & pp* **fanned)** (a) *(face, person)* éventer; **to f. oneself** s'éventer (b) *(fire, passions)* attiser

▶**fan out** *vi* se déployer en éventail

fan² *n (enthusiast)* fan *m/f*; *(of sports team)* supporter *m*; *Fig* **I'm not a f. of electric cookers** je n'aime pas trop les cuisinières électriques; **f. club** fan-club *m*; **f. mail** courrier *m* des admirateurs

fanatic [fə'nætɪk] *n & adj* fanatique *m/f*

fanatical [fə'nætɪkəl] *adj* fanatique

fanciful ['fænsɪfʊl] *adj* (a) *(unrealistic) (idea, project)* chimérique; *(person)* qui se fait des idées (b) *(design, style)* plein(e) de fantaisie

fancy ['fænsɪ] **1** *(pl* **fancies)** *n* (a) *(imagination)* imagination *f*
(b) *(whim)* fantaisie *f*, caprice *m*
(c) *(liking)* **to take a f. to sb** prendre qn en affection; *(sexually)* s'enticher de qn; **to take a f. to sth** s'enticher de qch; **the house didn't take her f.** la maison ne lui a pas plu
2 *adj (jewels, gadget, hat)* fantaisie *inv*; *(party, hotel)* chic *inv*; *(food, decoration)* recherché(e); **f. dress** déguisement *m*; **f. dress party** soirée *f* déguisée
3 *vt (pt & pp* **fancied)** (a) *Fam (want)* **I didn't f. the idea** ça ne me tentait pas; **do you f. a drink?** ça te dit de boire un verre?
(b) *Br (be attracted to)* **he fancies her** elle lui plaît
(c) *(imagine)* **to f. (that)...** croire *ou* penser que...; **I f.**

I've seen her before j'ai l'impression de l'avoir déjà vue; *Fam* **f. that!** ça alors!; **f. meeting you here!** si je m'attendais à te/vous rencontrer ici!

(d) *(have good opinion of)* to f. sb to win penser que qn va gagner; *Pej* **he fancies himself** il ne se prend pas pour n'importe qui; to f. oneself as a writer/musician se prendre pour un écrivain/musicien; **I don't f. his chances of getting the job** je crois qu'il a peu de chances d'obtenir le poste

fanfare ['fænfeə(r)] *n* fanfare *f*

fang [fæŋ] *n (of dog)* croc *m*; *(of snake)* crochet *m*

fanny ['fænɪ] *(pl* **fannies***) n* (a) *Br Vulg (vagina)* chatte *f* (b) *Am Fam (buttocks)* derrière *m*, fesses *fpl*; **f. pack** banane *f*

fantasize ['fæntəsaɪz] *vi* fantasmer *(about* sur)

fantastic [fæn'tæstɪk] *adj* (a) *Fam (excellent)* formidable, fantastique (b) *(enormous) (price)* astronomique; *(wealth, size)* prodigieux(euse) (c) *(unbelievable) (claim, story)* grotesque, absurde (d) *(strange) (creature)* fantastique; *(design)* plein(e) de fantaisie

fantasy ['fæntəzɪ] *(pl* **fantasies***) n* (a) *(unrealistic idea)* chimère *f*; *(sexual)* fantasme *m* (b) *(imagination)* fantaisie *f* (c) *(literature)* littérature *f* fantastique

FAO [efeɪ'əʊ] *n (abbr* **Food and Agriculture Organization)** FAO *f*

far [fɑː(r)] *(comparative* **farther** ['fɑːðə(r)] *or* **further** ['fɜːðə(r)], *superlative* **farthest** ['fɑːðɪst] *or* **furthest** ['fɜːðɪst]) **1** *adj* **in f. distance** au loin, dans le lointain; **the f. end** l'autre bout; *Pol* **the f. left/right** l'extrême gauche *f*/droite *f*; **the F. East** l'Extrême-Orient *m*; **it's a f. cry from** ça n'a rien à voir avec

2 *adv* (a) *(in distance)* loin; **how f. is it to Toulouse?** combien y a-t-il jusqu'à Toulouse?; **f. away (from)** loin (de); **f. below/above** loin au-dessous/au-dessus; **as f. as** jusqu'à; *also Fig* **to go f.** aller loin; *Fig* **to go so f. as to do sth** aller jusqu'à faire qch; *Fig* **to go too f.** aller trop loin; *also Fig* **f. from…** loin de…; *Fig* **f. from it** loin de là; *Fig* **f. be it from me to…** loin de moi l'idée de…; **f. and wide** partout; *Fig* **as f. as I can see** pour autant que je puisse en juger; **as f. as I know** (pour) autant que je sache; **as f. as I'm concerned** en ce qui me concerne; *Fig* **as f. as possible** autant que possible

(b) *(in time)* **so f.** jusqu'ici, jusqu'à présent; **so f. so good** jusqu'ici tout va bien; **for as f. back as I can remember** d'aussi loin que je me souvienne; **to work f. into the night** travailler jusqu'à une heure avancée de la nuit

(c) *(much)* beaucoup; **f. better/bigger** beaucoup mieux/plus grand; **by f.** de loin; **f. and away the best** de loin le meilleur/la/le meilleure

faraway ['fɑːrəweɪ] *adj* lointain(e); *(look)* perdu(e) dans le vague

farce [fɑːs] *n* farce *f*; *Fig* **it's a f.!** c'est grotesque!

farcical ['fɑːsɪkəl] *adj* grotesque

fare [feə(r)] **1** *n* (a) *(for journey)* tarif *m*; **to pay one's f.** acheter son billet (b) *(taxi passenger)* client(e) *m*,*f* (c) *Formal (food)* chère *f*

2 *vi* se débrouiller

farewell [feə'wel] *n* adieu *m*; **to say** *or* **make one's farewells** faire ses adieux; **f. dinner** dîner *m* d'adieu

far-fetched ['fɑː'fetʃt] *adj (idea, plan)* tiré(e) par les cheveux

far-flung ['fɑː'flʌŋ] *adj* lointain(e)

farm [fɑːm] **1** *n* ferme *f*; **f. animals** animaux *mpl* de ferme; **f. labourer** ouvrier *m* agricole

2 *vt (land)* cultiver, exploiter

3 *vi* être cultivateur(trice)

▶**farm out** *vt sep (work)* confier en sous-traitance *(to* à); *(child)* confier *(to* à)

farmer ['fɑːmə(r)] *n* fermier(ère) *m*,*f*, agriculteur(trice) *m*,*f*

farmhouse ['fɑːmhaʊs] *n (corps* *m* de) ferme *f*

farming ['fɑːmɪŋ] *n (business)* agriculture *f*

farmland ['fɑːmlænd] *n* terres *fpl* arables

farmyard ['fɑːmjɑːd] *n* cour *f* de ferme

Faroe ['feərəʊ] *n* **the F. Islands, the Faroes** les îles *fpl* Féroé

far-off ['fɑːrɒf] *adj (country, time)* lointain(e); *(place)* éloigné(e)

far-out ['fɑːraʊt] *adj Fam (strange)* farfelu(e); *(avant-garde)* avant-gardiste; **f.!** *(fantastic)* génial!

far-reaching ['fɑː'riːtʃɪŋ] *adj (decision, change)* de grande envergure; *(consequences)* d'une grande portée

Farsi ['fɑːsiː] *n* farsi *m*

far-sighted ['fɑː'saɪtɪd] *adj* (a) *(forward-looking) (person)* prévoyant(e); *(decision)* avisé(e) (b) *Am (longsighted)* presbyte

fart [fɑːt] *Fam* **1** *n* pet *m*

2 *vi* péter

▶**fart about** *vi Fam (waste time)* glander

farther ['fɑːðə(r)] *comparative of* **far**

farthest ['fɑːðɪst] *superlative of* **far**

farthing ['fɑːðɪŋ] *n Br Hist* quart *m* de penny; *Fam* **he hasn't a (brass) f.** il n'a pas le sou

fascinate ['fæsɪneɪt] *vt* fasciner

fascinating ['fæsɪneɪtɪŋ] *adj* fascinant(e)

fascination [fæsɪ'neɪʃən] *n* fascination *f*

fascism ['fæʃɪzəm] *n* fascisme *m*

fascist ['fæʃɪst] *n & adj* fasciste *mf*

fashion ['fæʃən] **1** *n* (a) *(in clothes)* mode *f*; **in f.** à la mode; **out of f.** démodé(e), passé(e) de mode; **f. designer** styliste *mf*; *(big name)* couturier *m*; **f. house** maison *f* de couture; **f. show** défilé *m* de mode; *Pej* **f. victim** esclave *mf* de la mode (b) *(manner)* manière *f*; **after a f.** tant bien que mal

2 *vt (form)* façonner; *(make)* confectionner

fashionable ['fæʃənəbəl] *adj* à la mode

fast¹ [fɑːst] **1** *adj* (a) *(rapid)* rapide; *Fam* **he pulled a f. one on me** il m'a joué un mauvais tour; **f. food** restauration *f* rapide; **f. food restaurant** fast-food *m*; **the f. lane** *(of motorway)* la voie rapide; *Fig* **to live life in the f. lane** vivre à cent à l'heure (b) *(clock, watch)* **my watch is (five minutes)** f. ma montre avance (de cinq minutes) (c) *(secure) (grip)* ferme, solide; *(door, lid)* bien fermé(e); *(colour)* résistant(e)

2 *adv* (a) *(rapidly)* vite, rapidement; **not so f.!** pas si vite!; **to play f. and loose with the facts** truquer les faits; **to play f. and loose with sb's emotions** jouer avec les sentiments de qn (b) *(securely)* solidement; **to hold f.** tenir bon; **f. asleep** profondément endormi(e)

fast² [fɑːst] **1** *n (lack of food)* jeûne *m*; *Rel* **f. day** jour *m* de jeûne

2 *vi* jeûner; *Med* être à la diète

fasten ['fɑːsən] **1** *vt (door, window)* fermer; *(belt, buttons)* attacher; *Fig* **to f. one's eyes on sth** fixer son regard sur qch

2 *vi (garment)* s'attacher

fastener ['fɑːsənə(r)] n (of garment) (hook) agrafe f; (press stud) bouton-pression m; (of bag, jewellery) fermoir m

fast-forward ['fɑːst'fɔːwəd] **1** n avance f rapide

2 vt (cassette) mettre en avance rapide

fastidious [fæ'stɪdɪəs] adj difficile; (about manners, hygiene, details) pointilleux(euse) (about sur)

fast-moving ['fɑːst'muːvɪŋ] adj rapide

fat [fæt] **1** n (a) (flesh) graisse f; (of cooked meat) gras m; (for cooking) matière grasse f; **f. content** teneur f en graisse ou en lipides (b) (idioms) Fam **the f.'s in the fire!** ça va chauffer!; **to live off the f. of the land** vivre comme un coq en pâte; **to chew the f. (with sb)** tailler le bout de gras (avec qn)

2 adj (person) gros (grosse); Fam (cheque, profit, salary) gros; **to get f.** grossir; Fig **to grow f. at the expense of others** (become rich) s'engraisser aux dépens des autres; Fam **a f. lot of good that'll do you!** ça te fera une belle jambe!; Fig **f. cat** (person) gros salaire m; Fam **f. chance!** tu parles!

fatal ['feɪtəl] adj mortel(elle)

fatalistic [feɪtə'lɪstɪk] adj fataliste

fatality [fə'tælɪtɪ] (pl **fatalities**) n (a) (person killed) mort m (b) (fate) fatalité f

fatally ['feɪtəlɪ] adv (wounded) mortellement; **f. ill** condamné(e); **to be f. damaging to sth** causer un tort irréparable à qch

fate [feɪt] n destin m, sort m; **to suffer** or **share the same f.** avoir le même sort; **it's a f. worse than death** c'est ce qu'on peut imaginer de pire

fated ['feɪtɪd] adj **to be f. to do sth** être destiné(e) à faire qch

fateful ['feɪtfʊl] adj (words, day) fatidique

father ['fɑːðə(r)] **1** n (parent, priest) père m; **from f. to son** de père en fils; **he was like a f. to me** il était comme un père pour moi; **like f., like son** tel père, tel fils; **Our F. (God)** Notre Père; **F. Christmas** le Père Noël; **F.'s Day** la fête des pères; **to be a f. figure to sb** jouer le rôle du père pour qn

2 vt (child) engendrer

fatherhood ['fɑːðəhʊd] n paternité f

father-in-law ['fɑːðərɪnlɔː] n beau-père m

fatherly ['fɑːðəlɪ] adj paternel(elle)

fathom ['fæðəm] **1** n (unit of measurement) = 1,8 m, brasse f

2 vt (understand) comprendre

▶**fathom out** vt sep (understand) comprendre

fatigue [fə'tiːg] **1** n (a) (tiredness) fatigue f; **metal f.** fatigue des métaux (b) Mil **f.** (duty) corvée f; **fatigues** (clothes) treillis m

2 vt (person) fatiguer

fatso ['fætsəʊ] (pl **fatsos** or **fatsoes**) n very Fam (man) gros lard m; (woman) grosse vache f

▶**fatten up** vt sep faire grossir, engraisser

fatty ['fætɪ] **1** (pl **fatties**) n Fam gros (grosse) m,f; **hey f.!** eh, bouboule!

2 adj (food, meat) gras (grasse); (tissue) adipeux(euse); **f. acid** acide m gras

fatuous ['fætjʊəs] adj idiot(e)

faucet ['fɔːsɪt] n Am robinet m

fault [fɔːlt] **1** n (a) (flaw) défaut m; (in mechanism, on phone line) problème m; **to find f. with** trouver à redire à; **to be generous to a f.** être généreux(euse) à l'excès (b) (guilt) faute f; **to be at f.** être en faute; **whose f. is**

it? à qui la faute?; **it's my f.** c'est (de) ma faute; **through no f. of mine** sans que ce soit de ma faute (c) (in tennis, squash) faute f (d) (geological) faille f

2 vt (person) prendre en défaut; (logic) trouver une faille dans; **her attitude can't be faulted** il n'y a rien à redire à sa conduite

faultless ['fɔːltlɪs] adj impeccable

faulty ['fɔːltɪ] adj défectueux(euse)

faun [fɔːn] n faune m

fauna ['fɔːnə] n faune f

favor, favorable etc Am = **favour, favourable** etc

favour, Am favor ['feɪvə(r)] **1** n (a) (approval) **to be in/out of f.** (of person) être bien/mal vu(e); (of method) être/ne plus être en faveur; **to look on sth/sb with f.** être bien disposé(e) envers qch/qn; **to find f. with sb** trouver grâce aux yeux de qn

(b) (act of kindness) service m; **to do sb a f.** rendre service à qn; Br Fam **do me a f. and shut up!** ferme-la, tu veux?; **to ask sb a f., to ask a f. of sb** demander un service à qn

(c) (advantage) **that's a point in her f.** c'est un élément en sa faveur; Fin **balance in your f.** solde m en votre faveur

(d) **in f. of** (in preference to) en faveur de; **to be in f. of sth** être partisan(e) de qch/être favorable à qch

2 vt (a) (prefer) être pour, être partisan(e) de; **to f. sb** (be biased towards) favoriser qn

(b) (honour) **to f. sb with sth** gratifier qn de qch

favourable, Am favorable ['feɪvərəbəl] adj favorable; (terms) avantageux(euse); **in a f. light** sous un jour favorable

favourite, Am favorite ['feɪvərɪt] **1** n favori(ite) m,f, préféré(e) m,f; (in betting) favori

2 adj favori(ite), préféré(e)

favouritism, Am favoritism ['feɪvərɪtɪzəm] n favoritisme m

fawn¹ [fɔːn] n (a) (deer) faon m (b) (colour) fauve m

2 adj (colour) fauve

fawn² vi **to f. on sb** ramper devant qn

fax [fæks] **1** n (machine) fax m, télécopieur m; (message) fax m, télécopie f; **f. number** numéro m de fax

2 vt (message, document) faxer, envoyer par fax; (person) envoyer un fax à

faze [feɪz] vt Fam déconcerter

FBI [efbiː'aɪ] n Am (abbr **Federal Bureau of Investigation**) FBI m

fear [fɪə(r)] **1** n peur f; (worry) crainte f; **to be** or **go in f. of** avoir peur de, redouter; **to go in f. of one's life** craindre pour sa vie; Fam **to put the f. of God into sb** faire une peur bleue à qn; **he didn't tell her for f. of her reaction** il ne lui a rien dit par peur de sa réaction; **for f. of doing sth** de peur de faire qch; **I didn't tell him, for f. that he'd be angry** je ne lui ai rien dit, de peur qu'il ne se mette en colère; Fam **no f.!** pas de danger!

2 vt craindre, redouter; **I f. there's been a misunderstanding** je crains qu'il (n')y ait eu un malentendu; **I f. so/not** je crains que oui/non; **to f. the worst** craindre le pire

3 vi **to f. for** craindre pour; **never f.!** ne crains rien!

fearful ['fɪəfʊl] adj (a) (pain, consequence, noise) épouvantable (b) (person) apeuré(e); **to be f. of doing sth** avoir peur de faire qch

fearless ['fɪəlɪs] adj intrépide

fearlessly ['fɪəlɪslɪ] adv avec intrépidité

fearsome ['fɪəsəm] adj effrayant(e)

feasibility [fi:zə'bɪlɪtɪ] n possibilité f; (of plan) faisabilité f; **f. study** étude f de faisabilité

feasible ['fi:zəbəl] adj faisable

feast [fi:st] 1 n festin m, banquet m; Rel **f. day** (jour m de) fête f
2 vt **to f. one's eyes on sth** repaître ses yeux de qch
3 vi **to f. on** se régaler de

feat [fi:t] n exploit m; **a f. of skill** un tour de force

feather ['feðə(r)] 1 n plume f; **you could have knocked me down with a f.** je n'en revenais pas; Fig **that's a f. in her cap** elle peut en être fière; **f. bed** lit m de plumes
2 vt Fig **to f. one's nest** faire son beurre

featherweight ['feðəweɪt] n (in boxing) poids m plume

feathery ['feðərɪ] adj doux (douce) et léger(ère) comme de la plume

feature ['fi:tʃə(r)] 1 n (a) (of face) trait m (b) (characteristic) caractéristique f (c) **f.** (film) long métrage m (d) (in newspaper) article m de fond; (on television, radio) reportage m; **f. writer** éditorialiste mf
2 vt (of magazine, exhibition) présenter; **a film featuring...** un film ayant pour vedette...
3 vi (appear) figurer

featureless ['fi:tʃəlɪs] adj sans caractéristiques marquées

Feb (abbr February) février

febrile ['fi:braɪl] adj fébrile

February ['februərɪ] n février m; see also **May**

feckless ['feklɪs] adj (a) (irresponsible) irresponsable (b) (ineffectual) incapable

fed [fed] pt & pp of **feed**

federal ['fedərəl] adj fédéral(e)

federalism ['fedərəlɪzəm] n fédéralisme m

federalist ['fedərəlɪst] n & adj fédéraliste mf

federation [fedə'reɪʃən] n fédération f

fed up ['fedʌp] adj Fam **to be f. (with)** en avoir ras le bol (de), en avoir marre (de)

fee [fi:] n (of lawyer, doctor) honoraires mpl; (for entrance) droit m d'entrée; (for membership) cotisation f; **school fees** droits mpl d'inscription; **a f.-paying school** une école privée

feeble ['fi:bəl] adj faible; (attempt) peu convaincant(e)

feeble-minded ['fi:bəl'maɪndɪd] adj faible d'esprit

feebly ['fi:blɪ] adv faiblement; (protest, reprimand) mollement

feed [fi:d] 1 n (a) (animal food) nourriture f (b) (for baby) (from breast) tétée f; (from bottle) biberon m
2 vt (pt & pp fed [fed]) (a) (give food to) donner à manger à; (baby) (from breast) donner la tétée à; (from bottle) donner son biberon à; (plant) mettre de l'engrais à; **we were well fed** nous étions bien nourris; **to f. one's family** nourrir sa famille (b) (supply) **to f. a fire** alimenter un feu; **to f. coins into a machine** mettre des pièces dans une machine; **to f. sb with information** fournir des informations à qn
3 vi (survive) **to f. on** se nourrir de

feedback ['fi:dbæk] n Elec effet m Larsen; Fig (response) écho m, réactions fpl

feel [fi:l] 1 n (a) (sensation) toucher m; **the f. of silk against her skin** le contact de la soie contre sa peau; **the film has an authentic f. to it** le film dégage une impression d'authenticité
(b) (knack) **to have a f. for translation/music** avoir

un sens inné de la traduction/musique; **to get the f. of sth** s'habituer à qch
2 vt (pt & pp felt [felt]) (a) (touch) toucher; (investigate) tâter; **to f. one's way** (in darkness) avancer à tâtons; Fig (in new situation) essayer de s'habituer
(b) (be physically aware of) sentir; **I felt the floor tremble or trembling** j'ai senti le sol trembler
(c) (experience) (relief, pain, despair) ressentir, éprouver; **I f. it in my bones** (have intuition) je le sens
(d) (believe) **to f. (that)...** penser que...
3 vi (a) (physically) **to f. tired** se sentir fatigué(e); **to f. ill** ne pas se sentir bien; **to f. hot/cold/hungry/thirsty** avoir chaud/froid/faim/soif; **my foot feels better** j'ai moins mal au pied; **how are you feeling?** comment ça va ou te sens-tu?; **I don't f. myself** je ne suis pas dans mon assiette; **to f. up to doing sth** (well enough) se sentir assez bien pour faire qch; (competent enough) se sentir de taille à faire qch; **to f. (like) a new man/woman** se sentir comme neuf/neuve
(b) (emotionally) se sentir; **to f. strongly about sth** avoir des idées très arrêtées sur qch; **I f. bad about leaving her** cela m'ennuie de la quitter; **how would you f. if...?** comment vous sentiriez-vous...?; **it feels strange** c'est étrange; **I felt as if I'd seen him before** j'avais l'impression de l'avoir déjà vu; **to f. like doing sth** avoir envie de faire qch; **I f. like a cup of tea** (would like) j'ai envie d'une tasse de thé
(c) (have sympathy) **to f. for sb** plaindre qn
(d) (of things) **to f. hard/hot** être dur(e)/chaud(e); **it feels like (it's going to) rain** on dirait qu'il va pleuvoir
(e) (search) **to f. in one's pockets for sth** chercher qch dans ses poches; **he felt on the ground for the key** il cherchait à tâtons la clé sur le sol

feeler ['fi:lə(r)] n (of insect) antenne f; (of snail) corne f; Fig **to put out feelers** tâter le terrain

feeling ['fi:lɪŋ] n (a) (sense of) f. toucher m; **to have no f. in one's arm** avoir le bras mort (b) (sensation) (of cold, pain) sensation f (c) (emotion, impression) sentiment m; **a f. of joy/anger** de la joie/colère; **to speak with f.** (emotionally) parler avec émotion; (warmly) parler avec chaleur; **I know the f.!** je sais ce que c'est!; **I had a f. I might find you here** je pensais bien vous trouver ici; **to hurt sb's feelings** blesser qn; **to have no feelings** n'avoir aucun cœur; **feelings were running high** les esprits étaient très échauffés; **no hard feelings!** sans rancune! (d) (sensitivity) sensibilité f; **to have a f. for sth** (music, art) être sensible à qch

feet [fi:t] pl of **foot**

feign [feɪn] vt (anger, surprise) feindre; **to f. illness/sleep** feindre d'être malade/de dormir

feint [feɪnt] 1 n (in combat sports) feinte f
2 vi (in combat sports) faire une feinte

felicitous [fɪ'lɪsɪtəs] adj heureux(euse)

feline ['fi:laɪn] 1 n félin m
2 adj félin(e)

fell[1] [fel] pt of **fall**

fell[2] vt (tree) abattre, couper; (opponent) terrasser

fell[3] adj **at one f. swoop** d'un seul coup

fell[4] n (hill) colline f

fellow ['feləʊ] n (a) (comrade) camarade mf; **f. citizen** concitoyen(enne) m,f; **f. countryman/countrywoman** compatriote mf; **f. passenger** compagnon m de voyage; **f. worker** collègue mf; **f. student** camarade d'études; **f. feeling** sympathie f; Fig **f. traveller** (in politics) compagnon m de route (b) (teacher) professeur m titulaire; *(student)* boursier(ère) *m,f*; *(of academy, society)* membre *m* (C) *Fam (man)* gars *m*

fellowship ['feləʊʃɪp] *n* (a) *(friendship)* camaraderie *f* (b) *(association)* association *f*, corporation *f* (C) *(at university)* bourse *f* de recherche

felon ['felən] *n Law* criminel(elle) *m,f*

felony ['feləni] *(pl* **felonies)** *n Law* crime *m*

felt[1] [felt] *n (fabric)* feutre *m*; *(thinner)* feutrine *f*

felt[2] *pt & pp of* **feel**

felt-tip ['felttɪp] *n f.* **(pen)** (crayon *m*) feutre *m*

female ['fi:meɪl] **1** *n (person)* femme *f*; *(animal, plant)* femelle *f*

 2 *adj (person)* féminin(e); *(animal, plant)* femelle

feminine ['femɪnɪn] **1** *n Gram* féminin *m*; **in the f.** au féminin

 2 *adj* féminin(e)

femininity [femɪ'nɪnɪtɪ] *n* féminité *f*

feminism ['femɪnɪzəm] *n* féminisme *m*

feminist ['femɪnɪst] *n & adj* féministe *mf*

femur ['fi:mə(r)] *n Anat* fémur *m*

fen [fen] *n (marshy land)* marais *m*; **the Fens** = plaines marécageuses à l'est de l'Angleterre

fence [fens] **1** *n* (a) *(barrier)* clôture *f*; *(more solid)* barrière *f*; *Fig* **to sit on the f.** ménager la chèvre et le chou; *Fig* **to get off the f.** se prononcer (b) *Fam (receiver of stolen property)* receleur(euse) *m,f*

 2 *vi (as sport)* faire de l'escrime

▸**fence off** *vt sep* séparer par une clôture

fencing ['fensɪŋ] *n (sport)* escrime *f*

fend [fend] *vi* **to f. for oneself** se débrouiller (tout(e) seul(e))

▸**fend off** *vt sep (attack, blow)* parer; *(question)* éluder

fender ['fendə(r)] *n* (a) *Am (of car)* aile *f* (b) *(for fireplace)* garde-feu *m inv*

fennel ['fenəl] *n* fenouil *m*

ferment 1 *n* ['fɜ:ment] *(commotion)* agitation *f*; **in a (state of) f.** en effervescence

 2 *vi* [fə'ment] *(of alcoholic drink)* fermenter

fermentation [fɜ:men'teɪʃən] *n* fermentation *f*

fern [fɜ:n] *n* fougère *f*

ferocious [fə'rəʊʃəs] *adj* féroce

ferocity [fə'rɒstɪ] *n* férocité *f*

ferret ['ferɪt] **1** *n* furet *m*

 2 *vi* **to f. (about) for sth** fouiller à la recherche de qch

▸**ferret out** *vt sep (object, information)* dénicher

ferris wheel ['ferɪs'wi:l] *n* grande roue *f*

ferrous ['ferəs] *adj* ferreux(euse)

ferry ['ferɪ] **1** *n (pl* **ferries)** bac *m*; *(larger)* ferry *m*

 2 *vt (pt & pp* **ferried)** transporter

 3 *vi* **to f. back and forth** faire la navette

ferryman ['ferɪmæn] *n* passeur *m*

fertile ['fɜ:taɪl] *adj also Fig* fertile

fertility [fə'tɪlɪtɪ] *n also Fig* fertilité *f*; **f. treatment** traitement *m* de la stérilité

fertilize ['fɜ:tɪlaɪz] *vt (egg, plant)* féconder; *(soil)* fertiliser

fertilizer ['fɜ:tɪlaɪzə(r)] *n* engrais *m*

fervent ['fɜ:vənt] *adj (admirer, nationalist)* fervent(e); *(belief, desire)* ardent(e)

fervour, *Am* **fervor** ['fɜ:və(r)] *n* ferveur *f*

fester ['festə(r)] *vi (of wound)* s'infecter; *Fig (of situation)* s'envenimer; *(of dislike, resentment)* s'aviver

festival ['festɪvəl] *n* festival *m*; *(religious)* fête *f*

festive ['festɪv] *adj* de fête; **in f. mood** d'humeur festive; **the f. season** *(Christmas)* les fêtes (de fin d'année)

festivity [fes'tɪvɪtɪ] *(pl* **festivities)** *n (merriness)* gaieté *f*; **the festivities** *(celebrations)* les festivités *fpl*

festoon [fes'tu:n] *vt* orner **(with** de)

fetal ['fi:təl] *Am =* **foetal**

fetch [fetʃ] *vt* (a) *(bring)* aller chercher (b) *(be sold for)* rapporter

▸**fetch up** *vi (end up) (of people)* se retrouver

fetching ['fetʃɪŋ] *adj (person, hat, smile)* ravissant(e)

fête [feɪt] **1** *n* fête *f*

 2 *vt* fêter

fetid ['fetɪd] *adj* fétide

fetish ['fetɪʃ] *n (object)* fétiche *m*; **to have a f. for sth** faire une fixation sur qch

fetter ['fetə(r)] **1** *n* **fetters** *(on slave, prisoner)* fers *mpl*; *(on rights, freedom)* entraves *fpl*

 2 *vt (slave, prisoner)* enchaîner; *Fig (union, women)* entraver la liberté de

fettle ['fetəl] *n* **in good** *or* **fine f.** en condition

fetus ['fi:təs] *Am =* **foetus**

feud [fju:d] **1** *n* querelle *f*

 2 *vi* se quereller **(with** avec)

feudal ['fju:dəl] *adj* féodal(e); *Fig (approach, attitude)* moyenâgeux(euse)

feudalism ['fju:dəlɪzəm] *n* le système féodal

fever ['fi:və(r)] *n also Fig* fièvre *f*; **to have a f.** avoir de la fièvre; **excitement had risen to f. pitch** l'excitation était à son comble

feverish ['fi:vərɪʃ] *adj* fiévreux(euse); *Fig (atmosphere)* de fièvre

few [fju:] **1** *adj* (a) *(not many)* peu de; **f. friends** peu d'amis; **too f.** trop peu de; **f. and far between** rarissime; **every f. minutes** toutes les deux ou trois minutes; **as f. as a dozen** finished the race seuls une douzaine d'entre eux ont terminé la course (b) *(some)* **a f.** quelques; **a f. friends** quelques amis; **a good f., quite a f.** pas mal de; **in the next f. days** dans les jours qui suivent/suivirent

 2 *pron* (a) *(not many)* peu; **there are too f. of us** nous sommes trop peu nombreux; **f. of them** peu d'entre eux; **f., if any** **children** aucun enfant ou presque (b) *(some)* **a f.** quelques-uns (quelques-unes) *mpl,fpl*; **a f. of the survivors** quelques-uns des survivants; **a f. of them** quelques-uns d'entre eux

 3 *n* **the f. who came** les rares personnes *fpl* qui sont venues

fewer ['fju:ə(r)] *(comparative of* **few) 1** *adj* moins de; **f. friends** moins d'amis; **no f. than thirty** pas moins de trente; **the houses became f.** les maisons devenaient plus rares; **f. and f. people** de moins en moins de gens

 2 *pron* moins; **there are f.** *(of them)* **than I thought** il y en a moins que je ne pensais

fewest ['fju:ɪst] *(superlative of* **few) 1** *adj* le moins de

 2 *pron* le moins

fiasco [fɪ'æskəʊ] *(pl* **fiascos)** *n* fiasco *m*

fib [fɪb] *Fam* **1** *n* bobard *m*

 2 *vi (pt & pp* **fibbed)** raconter des bobards

fibber ['fɪbə(r)] *n Fam* menteur(euse) *m,f*

fibre, *Am* **fiber** ['faɪbə(r)] *n* fibre *f*; *(in diet)* fibres *fpl*; **f. optics** technologie *f* des fibres optiques

fibreglass, *Am* **fiberglass** ['faɪbəɡlɑːs] *n* fibre *f* de verre

fibrous ['faɪbrəs] *adj* fibreux(euse)

fickle ['fɪkəl] *adj (person)* lunatique; *(weather)* changeant(e)

fiction ['fɪkʃən] *n (genre)* fiction *f; (books)* livres *mpl* de fiction; *(lie)* invention *f*

fictional ['fɪkʃənəl] *adj* fictif(ive)

fictitious [fɪk'tɪʃəs] *adj* fictif(ive)

fiddle ['fɪdəl] **1** *n* (a) *(violin)* violon *m* (b) *Br Fam (swindle)* combine *f;* **to be on the f.** traficoter
2 *vt Br Fam (cheat)* combiner; **to f. the accounts** truquer les comptes
3 *vi* (a) *(play violin)* jouer du violon (b) *(fidget)* **to f.** *(about or around)* **with sth** tripoter qch

fiddler ['fɪdlə(r)] *n* violoniste *mf*

fiddlesticks ['fɪdəlstɪks] *exclam Old-fashioned (nonsense)* balivernes!; *(expressing annoyance)* zut de zut!

fiddly ['fɪdəlɪ] *adj Fam* minutieux(euse)

fidelity [fɪ'delɪtɪ] *n* fidélité *f*

fidget ['fɪdʒɪt] **1** *n* **to be a f.** ne pas tenir en place
2 *vi* ne pas tenir en place; **stop fidgeting!** tiens-toi tranquille!

fidgety ['fɪdʒɪtɪ] *adj* agité(e)

field [fiːld] **1** *n* (a) *(of farm) & Comptr* champ *m; (for sport)* terrain *m; (of oil, coal)* gisement *m;* **to work in the f.** *(not in office)* travailler sur le terrain; **f. of vision** champ visuel; **f. events** *(in athletics)* le saut et le lancer; *Am* **f. hockey** hockey *m* sur gazon; **f. study** étude *f* sur le terrain; *Sch & Univ* **f. trip** voyage *m* d'étude; **f. work** *(scientific)* recherches *fpl* sur le terrain (b) *Mil* **in the f.** en campagne; *Fig* **to have a f. day** s'en donner à cœur joie; **f. glasses** jumelles *fpl;* **f. gun** canon *m* (de campagne); **f. hospital** antenne *f* chirurgicale; **f. marshal** ≃ maréchal *m* de France (c) *(of knowledge)* domaine *m (in race, contest)* partants *mpl;* **to lead the f.** *Sp* mener le peloton; *Fig* occuper la première place
2 *vt* (a) *(team)* composer; *(candidates)* présenter (b) *(question)* répondre à

fieldmouse ['fiːldmaʊs] *(pl* **fieldmice** ['fiːldmaɪs]*) n* mulot *m*

fiend [fiːnd] *n (cruel person)* monstre *m; (demon)* démon *m;* **sex f.** obsédé(e) *m,f* sexuel(elle); **jazz f.** fanatique *mf* de jazz

fiendish ['fiːndɪʃ] *adj (scheme, question)* diabolique; *(weather, temper)* abominable

fiendishly ['fiːndɪʃlɪ] *adv (difficult)* horriblement

fierce [fɪəs] *adj (animal, look)* féroce; *(appearance, person)* redoutable; *(wind, storm, criticism)* violent(e); *(heat)* torride; *(contest)* acharné(e)

fiercely ['fɪəslɪ] *adv (look)* d'un œil féroce; *(fight)* avec acharnement; *(criticize)* violemment

fiery ['faɪərɪ] *adj (red)* ardent(e); *(sky)* enflammé(e); *(taste)* très épicé(e); *(person, character)* fougueux(euse)

FIFA ['fiːfə] *n (abbr* **Fédération Internationale de Football Association)** FIFA *f*

fifteen [fɪf'tiːn] **1** *n* (a) *(number)* quinze *m inv* (b) *Sp (rugby team)* quinze *m*
2 *adj* quinze; *see also* **eight**

fifteenth [fɪf'tiːnθ] **1** *n* (a) *(fraction)* quinzième *m* (b) *(in series)* quinzième *mf* (c) *(of month)* quinze *m inv*
2 *adj* quinzième; *see also* **eighth**

fifth [fɪfθ] **1** *n* (a) *(fraction)* cinquième *m* (b) *(in series)* cinquième *mf* (c) *(of month)* cinq *m inv*
2 *adj* cinquième; *Pol* **f. column** cinquième colonne *f; see also* **eighth**

fiftieth ['fɪftɪəθ] **1** *n* (a) *(fraction)* cinquantième *m* (b) *(in series)* cinquantième *mf*
2 *adj* cinquantième

fifty ['fɪftɪ] **1** *n* cinquante *m inv*
2 *adj* cinquante; *see also* **eighty**

fig[1] [fɪɡ] *n (fruit)* figue *f; Fam* **she doesn't give or care a f.** elle s'en fiche éperdument; **f. leaf** feuille *f* de figuier; *(in paintings)* feuille de vigne; *Fig* **it's just a f. leaf** ce n'est qu'une couverture; **f. tree** figuier *m*

fig[2] *(abbr* **figure)** fig

fight [faɪt] **1** *n* (a) *(physical)* bagarre *f; (verbal)* dispute *f; (boxing match)* combat *m;* **to get into a f. with sb** *(physical)* se battre avec qn; *(verbal)* se disputer avec qn; **to start a f. (with sb)** provoquer une bagarre (avec qn); **to put up a good f.** bien se défendre (b) *(spirit)* **to show some f.** résister; **there was no f. left in him** il n'avait plus le cœur à se battre (c) *(struggle)* lutte *f (for/against* pour/contre)
2 *vt (pt & pp* **fought** [fɔːt])* *(person)* se battre contre; *(decision, enemy)* combattre; *(disease, fire, temptation)* lutter contre; *(election)* participer à; **to f. a war** être en guerre; *Law* **to f. a case** *(of lawyer)* défendre une cause; *(of defendant)* être en procès; *Fig* **I'm not going to f. your battles for you** c'est à vous de vous débrouiller; **to f. one's way through a crowd** se frayer un chemin à travers une foule
3 *vi* (a) *(physically)* se battre **(against** contre); *(verbally)* se disputer; **to f. shy of doing sth** éviter à tout prix de faire qch (b) *(struggle)* lutter **(for/against** pour/contre); **to f. for breath** suffoquer

▶ **fight back 1** *vt sep (tears)* retenir; *(anger)* réprimer
2 *vi (retaliate)* se défendre

▶ **fight off** *vt sep (attacker)* repousser; *(illness)* combattre

▶ **fight out** *vt sep* **f. it out amongst yourselves** réglez ça entre vous

fighter ['faɪtə(r)] *n (in fight)* combattant(e) *m,f; (for cause)* lutteur(euse) *m,f;* **she's a real f.** *(determined)* c'est une battante; **f. (plane)** avion *m* de chasse; **f. squadron/pilot** escadron *m*/pilote *m* de chasse

fighting ['faɪtɪŋ] **1** *n (scuffles)* bagarres *fpl; Mil* combat *m*
2 *adj* **to have a f. chance** avoir de bonnes chances; **to be f. fit** être dans une forme éblouissante

figment ['fɪɡmənt] *n* **it's a f. of your imagination** c'est le fruit de ton imagination

figurative ['fɪɡərətɪv] *adj (sense)* figuré(e); *(art)* figuratif(ive)

figuratively ['fɪɡərətɪvlɪ] *adv* **f. speaking** métaphoriquement parlant

figure ['fɪɡə(r)] **1** *n* (a) *(number)* chiffre *m;* **to be good at figures** être bon (bonne) en calcul; **to reach double/three figures** atteindre la dizaine/centaine (b) *(body shape)* silhouette *f; (of woman)* avoir une jolie silhouette; **to have a good f.** *(of woman)* avoir une jolie silhouette; **a fine f. of a man** un bel homme; **to cut a sorry f.** avoir l'air pitoyable (c) *(person, character)* personnage *m;* **a distinguished f.** une personnalité (d) *(illustration, geometric shape)* figure *f* (e) *(expression)* **f. of speech** figure *f* de rhétorique; **it's just a f. of speech** c'est une façon de parler
2 *vt* **to f. (that)...** *(think)* penser que...; *(estimate)* supposer que...

3 vi (a) (appear) (in list, book) figurer (b) Fam (make sense) that figures! ça se tient!

▶**figure on** vt insep to f. on doing sth compter faire qch

▶**figure out** vt sep (amount) calculer; (solution) trouver; (problem, person) arriver à comprendre

figurehead ['fɪgəhed] n (on ship) figure f de proue; Fig & Pej (of country, party) homme m de paille

Fiji ['fiːdʒiː] n les (îles fpl) Fidji fpl

Fijian [fiː'dʒiːən] **1** n Fidjien(enne) m,f
2 adj fidjien(enne)

filament ['fɪləmənt] n Elec filament m

filch [fɪltʃ] vt Fam faucher (**from sb** à qn)

file[1] [faɪl] **1** n (tool) lime f
2 vt (metal) limer; **to f. one's nails** se limer les ongles

file[2] **1** n (a) (folder) chemise f; (ring-bound) classeur m; (documents) dossier m (**on** sur); **to have sth on f.** avoir qch dans ses dossiers (b) Comptr fichier m; **f. manager** gestionnaire m de fichiers; **f. server** serveur m de fichiers
2 vt (a) (documents, letters) classer (b) (complaint, claim, request) déposer
3 vi **to f. for divorce** demander le divorce

file[3] **1** n (line) file f; **in single f.** en file indienne
2 vi **to f. past sb/sth** défiler devant qn/qch; **to f. in/out** entrer/sortir l'un(e) après l'autre

filial ['fɪlɪəl] adj filial(e)

filigree ['fɪlɪgriː] n filigrane m

Filipino [fɪlɪ'piːnəʊ] **1** n (pl **Filipinos**) Philippin(e) m,f
2 adj philippin(e)

fill [fɪl] **1** n **to eat one's f.** manger à sa faim; Fig **to have had one's f. of sth** en avoir assez de qch
2 vt (a) (container) remplir (**with** de); **to be filled with admiration/hope** être plein(e) d'admiration/d'espoir; **to have a tooth filled** se faire plomber une dent (b) (occupy) (time) occuper; **to f. a vacancy** (of employer) pourvoir à un poste vacant
3 vi se remplir (**with** de)

▶**fill in** vt sep (a) (hole) combler, boucher; (form) remplir; **to f. in time** occuper son temps (b) Fam (inform) **to f. sb in** (**on** sth) mettre qn au courant (de qch)
2 vi **to f. in for sb** remplacer qn

▶**fill out** vt sep (form, application) remplir
2 vi (get fatter) grossir

▶**fill up 1** vt sep (glass) remplir jusqu'au bord; Fam **f. her up!** (with petrol) le plein!
2 vi (a) (of tank, container) se remplir (b) (buy petrol) faire le plein

fillet ['fɪlɪt] **1** n (of fish, beef) filet m; **f. steak** filet de bœuf
2 vt (fish) découper en filets

filling ['fɪlɪŋ] **1** n (a) (in tooth) plombage m; (in sandwich, pie) garniture f (b) **f. station** station-service f
2 adj (food, meal) nourrissant(e)

filly ['fɪlɪ] (pl **fillies**) n (horse) pouliche f

film [fɪlm] **1** n (movie) film m; (layer, for camera) pellicule f; (a roll of) f. une pellicule, un rouleau de pellicule; **f. actor/ actress** acteur m/actrice f de cinéma; **f. critic** critique mf de cinéma; **f. director** réalisateur(trice) m,f; **the f. industry** l'industrie f cinématographique; **f. library** cinémathèque f; **f. maker** cinéaste mf; **f. script** scénario m, script m; **f. star** vedette f de cinéma, star f; **f. studio** studio m de cinéma
2 vt & vi filmer

filter ['fɪltə(r)] **1** n filtre m; **f. coffee** café m filtre; **f. paper** papier m filtre; Aut **f. lane** = voie réservée aux véhicules qui tournent; Aut **f. signal** (on traffic light) flèche f de dégagement
2 vt filtrer
3 vi (a) (move slowly) **to f. in/out** entrer/sortir lentement (b) Aut (of traffic) **to f. to the right/left** dégager à droite/ gauche pour tourner

▶**filter out** vt sep also Fig éliminer

▶**filter through 1** vt insep (of liquid, light) passer à travers
2 vi (of information) filtrer

filth [fɪlθ] n (dirt) crasse f; (in street) immondices fpl; (obscene words) obscénités fpl; **it's f.** (of book, film) c'est dégoûtant

filthy ['fɪlθɪ] **1** adj (a) (very dirty) dégoûtant(e) (b) (very bad) **in a f. temper** d'une humeur massacrante; **to give sb a f. look** regarder qn d'un sale œil; Br **f. weather** temps m de chien (c) (obscene) dégoûtant(e), obscène
2 adv Fam **f. rich** pourri(e) de fric

fin [fɪn] n (of fish) nageoire f; (of aeroplane) empennage m; (of swimmer) palme f

final ['faɪnəl] **1** n (a) (of competition) **the f.** la finale (b) Univ **finals** Br examens mpl de dernière année; Am examens mpl finaux
2 adj (a) (last) dernier(ère); **f. demand** dernier avis m; **f. warning** dernier avertissement m (b) (definitive) final(e); **the umpire's decision is f.** la décision de l'arbitre est sans appel; **and that's f.!** un point, c'est tout!

finale [fɪ'nɑːlɪ] n finale m

finalist ['faɪnəlɪst] n finaliste mf

finalize ['faɪnəlaɪz] vt (details, plans) mettre au point; (deal) conclure

finally ['faɪnəlɪ] adv (a) (lastly) finalement (b) (at last) enfin; **she had f. met him** elle l'avait enfin rencontré (c) (irrevocably) définitivement; **it hasn't been f. decided yet** aucune décision définitive n'a encore été prise

finance [faɪ'næns, 'fɪ'næns] **1** n (a) (subject) finance f; **f. company** or **house** société f financière (b) **finances** (funds) finances fpl
2 vt financer

financial [faɪ'nænʃəl, fɪ'nænʃəl] adj financier(ère); **it was not a f. success** cela n'a pas rapporté beaucoup d'argent; **f. adviser** conseiller m financier; **f. market** marché m financier; **f. statement** bilan m financier; Br **f. year** exercice m comptable

financially [faɪ'nænʃəlɪ, fɪ'nænʃəlɪ] adv financièrement

financier [faɪ'nænsɪə(r)] n financier m

finch [fɪntʃ] n fringillidé m

find [faɪnd] **1** n découverte f; **it's quite a f.** c'est une fameuse trouvaille
2 vt (pt & pp **found** [faʊnd]) (a) (discover) trouver; **to try to f. sth** chercher qch; **she was nowhere to be found** elle était introuvable; **I found her waiting in the hall** je l'ai trouvée qui attendait dans le vestibule; **this flower is commonly found in England** on trouve couramment cette fleur en Angleterre; **I found myself back where I'd started** je me suis retrouvé à mon point de départ; **you will f. that I'm right** tu verras que j'ai raison; **I was surprised to f. that...** j'ai découvert avec surprise que...; **he couldn't f. it in his heart to tell her** il n'avait pas le cœur à le lui dire; **to f. one's way** trouver son chemin; **to f. a way to do sth** trouver moyen de faire qch; **to f. oneself** (spiritually) se trouver

(b) *(experience)* trouver; **they will f. it easy/difficult** cela leur sera facile/difficile; **to f. it necessary to do sth** se trouver dans la nécessité de faire qch; **she found it impossible to understand him** elle avait beaucoup de mal à le comprendre; **how did you f. the meal?** le repas vous a-t-il plu?; **I found myself agreeing with her** il s'est trouvé que j'étais d'accord avec elle

(c) *Law* **to f. sb guilty/not guilty** déclarer qn coupable/ non coupable

3 *vi Law* **to f. for/against sb** rendre un verdict en faveur de/contre qn

▶**find out 1** *vt sep* (a) *(discover)* découvrir (b) *(person)* prendre en défaut

2 *vi* **to f. out about sth** apprendre qch

finder ['faɪndə(r)] *n* **the f. of the money** la personne qui trouva/trouvera l'argent; *Fam* **finders keepers (losers weepers)** celui qui le trouve le garde

findings ['faɪndɪŋz] *npl* conclusions *fpl*; *Law (of jury, court)* verdict *m*

fine[1] [faɪn] **1** *n (penalty)* amende *f*

2 *vt* condamner à une amende; **to f. sb £10** infliger une amende de 10 livres à qn

fine[2] **1** *adj* (a) *(excellent)* excellent(e); *(foods, wine)* fin(e); *(weather)* beau; **to appeal to sb's finer feelings** faire appel aux bons sentiments de qn; **she's a f. woman** c'est une femme admirable; **f. art, the f. arts** les beaux-arts *mpl*; **she's got it down to a f. art** elle fait ça à la perfection

(b) *(satisfactory)* bien *inv*; **she's/everything's f.** elle/tout va bien; **that's f. by me** je n'y vois aucune objection

(c) *Ironic* **you're a f. one to talk!** tu peux bien parler!; **this is another f. mess you've got us into!** tu nous a encore mis dans un beau pétrin!

(d) *(thin)* (hair, rain, line) fin(e)

(e) *(subtle) (distinction)* subtil(e); **not to put too f. a point on it** pour parler carrément; **there's a f. line between eccentricity and madness** il n'y a qu'un pas de l'excentricité à la folie

2 *adv* très bien; **they get on f.** ils s'entendent (très) bien

finely ['faɪnlɪ] *adv* (a) *(judged)* soigneusement; *(written, painted)* admirablement; *Fig* **f. balanced** équilibré(e) (b) *(chopped, ground, grated)* finement

finery ['faɪnərɪ] *n* parure *f*; **she was dressed in all her f.** elle était habillée avec élégance

finesse [fɪ'nes] *n* finesse *f*

finger ['fɪŋgə(r)] **1** *n* (a) *(of hand, glove)* doigt *m*; **to keep one's fingers crossed** croiser les doigts; **f. bowl** rince-doigts *m inv*; **f. food** *(snacks)* amuse-gueule *mpl* (b) *(measure)* **a f. of brandy** un doigt de cognac (c) *Av* passerelle *f* (d) *(idioms)* **he's got them (wrapped) round his little f.** il fait d'eux ce qu'il veut; **to have a f. in every pie** être mêlé(e) à tout; **don't you dare lay a f. on him** je vous défends de le toucher; **she never lifts a f. to help me** elle ne lève jamais le petit doigt pour m'aider; **I can't quite put my f. on it** je n'arrive pas à mettre le doigt dessus; **to get one's fingers burnt** se brûler les doigts; *Br very Fam* **get or pull your f. out!** remue-toi!

2 *vt* (a) *(feel)* tâter (b) *very Fam (inform on)* balancer

fingernail ['fɪŋgəneɪl] *n* ongle *m*

fingerprint ['fɪŋgəprɪnt] *n* empreinte *f* digitale

fingertip ['fɪŋgətɪp] *n* bout *m* du doigt; **to have sth at one's fingertips** savoir qch sur le bout des doigts

finicky ['fɪnɪkɪ] *adj (person)* tatillon(onne); *(job, device)* compliqué(e)

finish ['fɪnɪʃ] **1** *n* (a) *(end) (of day, meeting)* fin *f*; *(of race)* arrivée *f* (b) *(surface) (of fabric, leather)* apprêt *m*; **paint with a gloss/matt f.** peinture *f* vernie/mate (c) *(workmanship)* finition *f*

2 *vt* (a) *(end)* finir, terminer; **to f. doing sth** finir *ou* terminer de faire qch (b) *(kill) (person)* achever; *Fam* **he's finished!** il est fini!

3 *vi* finir, se terminer; **to f. fourth** *(in race, contest)* finir *ou* terminer quatrième

▶**finish off 1** *vt sep* (a) *(complete, use up)* finir, terminer (b) *(kill)* achever; *(ruin) (chances, hopes)* anéantir

2 *vi* finir, terminer

▶**finish up 1** *vt sep (use up)* finir

2 *vi (end up)* se retrouver; **to f. up doing sth** finir par faire qch

▶**finish with** *vt insep* (a) *(stop using)* **to f. with sth** finir de se servir de qch (b) *(boyfriend, girlfriend)* laisser tomber

finished ['fɪnɪʃt] *adj* (a) *(completed)* fini(e); *(supplies)* épuisé(e) (b) *(performance)* soigné(e)

finishing ['fɪnɪʃɪŋ] *adj* **to put the f. touches to sth** mettre la dernière main à qch; **f. line** ligne *f* d'arrivée; **f. school** = école d'arts d'agrément pour les jeunes filles

finite ['faɪnaɪt] *adj* limité(e); *Gram (verb)* conjugué(e)

Finland ['fɪnlənd] *n* la Finlande

Finn [fɪn] *n (person)* Finlandais(e) *m,f*, Finnois(e) *m,f*

Finnish ['fɪnɪʃ] **1** *n (language)* finlandais *m*, finnois *m*

2 *adj* finlandais(e), finnois(e)

fir [fɜː(r)] *n* **f. (tree)** sapin *m*; **f. cone** pomme *f* de pin

fire ['faɪə(r)] **1** *n* (a) *(in hearth)* feu *m*; *(large, destructive)* incendie *m*; *(heater)* appareil *m* de chauffage; **electric/gas f.** radiateur *m* électrique/au gaz; **on f.** en feu; **to catch f.** prendre feu; **to set f. to sth, to set sth on f.** mettre le feu à qch; **f.!** au feu!; *Fig* **to play with f.** jouer avec le feu; **to fight f. with f.** combattre le feu par le feu; **f. alarm** sirène *f* d'incendie; *Br* **f. brigade,** *Am* **f. department** sapeurs-pompiers *mpl*, pompiers *mpl*; **f. door** porte *f* coupe-feu; **f. drill** exercice *m* d'évacuation en cas d'incendie; **f. engine** voiture *f* de pompiers; **f. escape** escalier *m* de secours; **f. extinguisher** extincteur *m*; **f. fighter** pompier *m*; **to be a f. hazard** constituer un risque d'incendie; **f. hydrant** bouche *f* d'incendie; **f. insurance** assurance *f* contre l'incendie; **f. regulations** *(laws)* normes *fpl* de protection contre les incendies; *(instructions)* consignes *fpl* en cas d'incendie; **f. sale** = vente d'objets endommagés dans un incendie; **f. station** caserne *f* de pompiers (b) *(of artillery)* tirs *mpl*; **to open f.** ouvrir le feu; **to hold one's f.** ne pas tirer; **to come under f.** être exposé(e) aux tirs; *Fig (be criticized)* être exposé à de sévères critiques; **f. power** puissance *f* de tir (c) *Fig (enthusiasm)* fougue *f*, ardeur *f*

2 *vt* (a) *(shoot) (missile, flare)* lancer; **to f. a gun (at)** tirer un coup de fusil (sur); *Fig* **to f. a question at sb** poser une question à qn à brûle-pourpoint (b) *(dismiss)* virer (c) *Fig* **to f. sb's imagination** enflammer l'imagination de qn (d) *(pottery)* cuire

3 *vi* (a) *(with gun)* tirer **(at** sur); *Fam Fig* **f. away!** *(to questioner)* allez-y! (b) *(of engine)* tourner

firearm ['faɪərɑːm] *n* arme *f* à feu

firebrand ['faɪəbrænd] *n (torch)* tison *m*, brandon *m*; *Fig (person)* brandon de discorde

firecracker ['faɪəkrækə(r)] *n* pétard *m*

firefly ['faɪəflaɪ] *(pl* fireflies) *n* luciole *f*

fireguard ['faɪəgɑːd] *n* garde-feu *m inv*

firelight ['faɪəlaɪt] n lumière f du feu

firelighter ['faɪəlaɪtə(r)] n allume-feu m inv

fireman ['faɪəmən] n pompier m

fireplace ['faɪəpleɪs] n cheminée f

fireproof ['faɪə'pru:f] adj ignifugé(e)

fireside ['faɪəsaɪd] n **by the f.** au coin du feu

firewall ['faɪəwɔ:l] n Comptr firewall m, contrôle m d'accès

firewood ['faɪəwʊd] n bois m de chauffage

firework ['faɪəwɜ:k] n pièce f d'artifice; **fireworks** (display) feu m d'artifice; Fig **there'll be fireworks** il va y avoir du grabuge; **f. display** feu d'artifice

firing ['faɪərɪŋ] n tir m; Fig **to be in the f. line** être l'objet de violentes critiques; **f. squad** peloton m d'exécution

firm¹ [fɜ:m] n (company) entreprise f, firme f

firm² [fɜ:m] 1 adj (a) (fruit, body, mattress, handshake) ferme; Fig (foundations, friendship) solide; **the f. favourite** le/la grand(e) favori(ite); **it's my f. belief (that)...** j'ai la ferme conviction que... (b) (strict) ferme (c) (definite) (decision) ferme; (date) précis(e); (evidence) sérieux(euse)

2 adv **to stand f.** tenir bon ou ferme; **to hold f. to one's principles/beliefs** être fidèle à ses principes/croyances

firmly ['fɜ:mlɪ] adv (a) (securely) solidement; **I f. believe (that)...** j'ai la ferme conviction que... (b) (strictly) fermement

first [fɜ:st] 1 n (a) (in series) premier(ère) m,f; **we were the f. to arrive** nous étions les premiers arrivés; **it's the f. I've heard of it** c'est la première fois que j'en entends parler, première nouvelle; **Edward the F.** Edward Premier
(b) (of month) premier m; **we're leaving on the f.** nous partons le premier
(c) (beginning) **from f. to last** du début jusqu'à la fin; **from the f.** dès le début; **at f.** d'abord
(d) Br Univ **to get a f.** (in degree) ≃ avoir sa licence avec mention bien ou très bien
(e) (first gear) première f
(f) (unique event) première f

2 adv (a) (firstly) d'abord; **f. time** pour la première fois; **at f. hand** de première main; **f. things f.!** commençons par le commencement; **I don't know the f. thing about motorbikes** je ne connais absolument rien aux motos; **f. thing (in the morning)** dès le matin; **at f. light** aux premières lueurs du jour; **at f. sight** à première vue; **in the f. place** d'abord; **the F. World War** la Première Guerre mondiale; **f. aid** (skill) secourisme m; (treatment) premiers soins mpl; **f. cousin** cousin(e) m,f, germain(e); **f. edition** édition f originale; **f. gear** première f (vitesse f); Am **the f. lady** la première dame des États-Unis (épouse du président); Naut **f. mate** second m; **f. name** prénom m; **f. night** (of play) première f; Law **f. offender** ≃ personne qui commet un délit pour la première fois

3 adv (a) (firstly) d'abord; **f. and foremost** avant toute chose; **f. of all** en premier lieu, d'abord
(b) (for the first time) pour la première fois; **I f. met her in London** je l'ai rencontrée pour la première fois à Londres
(c) (before others) le premier, la première; **you go f.!** (in queue) passez devant!; **to come f.** (in race) arriver premier(ère); (in exam) être reçu(e) premier(ère); **my family comes f.** ma famille passe avant le reste; **f. come, f. served** les premiers arrivés sont les premiers servis; **ladies f.!** les femmes d'abord!; **I won't do it, I'd resign f.** plutôt démissionner que de faire ça

first-aid [fɜ:st'eɪd] adj **f. certificate** brevet m de secourisme; **f. kit** trousse f de secours

first-born [fɜ:stbɔ:n] n Lit (boy) premier-né m; (girl) première-née f

first-class [fɜ:stklɑ:s] 1 adj (a) (compartment, ticket) de première classe (b) **f. stamp** timbre m au tarif normal (c) Univ **f. honours (degree)** ≃ licence f avec mention bien ou très bien (d) (excellent) excellent(e)
2 adv (a) (travel) en première classe (b) (post) au tarif normal

first-degree [fɜ:stdɪ'gri:] adj (a) Med (burns) au premier degré (b) Am Law **f. murder** assassinat m

first-hand [fɜ:sthænd] adj & adv de première main

firstly ['fɜ:stlɪ] adv premièrement, en premier lieu

first-past-the-post [fɜ:stpɑ:stðə'pəʊst] adj Pol **f. system** scrutin m à un tour

first-rate [fɜ:streɪt] adj excellent(e)

first-time buyer [fɜ:st'taɪm'baɪə(r)] n = personne achetant une propriété pour la première fois

fiscal ['fɪskəl] adj fiscal(e); **f. policy** politique f budgétaire; **f. year** exercice m comptable

fish [fɪʃ] 1 n (pl fish or fishes) (a) poisson m; Br **f. and chips** poisson frit avec des frites; **f.-and-chip shop** = magasin où l'on vend du poisson frit et des frites ainsi que d'autres produits cuits dans la friture; **f. cake** croquette f de poisson; **f. farm** établissement m piscicole; Br **f. fingers**, Am **f. sticks** bâtonnets mpl de poisson; **f. knife** couteau m à poisson; **f. slice** pelle f à poisson; **f. tank** aquarium m (b) (idioms) **there are plenty more f. in the sea** un de perdu, dix de retrouvés; **to have other f. to fry** avoir d'autres chats à fouetter; **to feel like a f. out of water** ne pas se sentir dans son élément; **to be neither f. nor fowl** n'être ni chair ni poisson

2 vt (river) pêcher dans; **to f. sth out of somewhere** sortir qn/qch de quelque part

3 vi pêcher; Fig **to f. for compliments** rechercher les compliments; **she fished around in her pocket for some change** elle a fouillé dans sa poche pour trouver de la monnaie

fisherman ['fɪʃəmən] n pêcheur m

fish-hook ['fɪʃhʊk] n hameçon m

fishing ['fɪʃɪŋ] n pêche f; **to go f.** aller à la pêche; **f. boat** bateau m de pêche; **f. grounds** lieux mpl de pêche; **f. line** ligne f; **f. net** filet m de pêche (f); **f. port** port m de pêche; **f. rod** canne f à pêche

fishmonger ['fɪʃmʌŋgə(r)] n poissonnier(ère) m,f; **f.'s (shop)** poissonnerie f

fishnet ['fɪʃnet] adj (stockings, tights) résille inv

fishy ['fɪʃɪ] adj (a) (smell, taste) de poisson (b) Fam (suspicious) louche

fission ['fɪʃən] n fission f

fissure ['fɪʃə(r)] n (in mountain, rock) fissure f; Med scissure f

fist [fɪst] n poing m; Fig **she made a good f. of it** elle s'en est plutôt bien sortie

fistful ['fɪstfʊl] n poignée f

fisticuffs ['fɪstɪkʌfs] npl Hum coups mpl de poing

fit¹ [fɪt] n (seizure) attaque f; **to have a f.** avoir une attaque; Fam Fig **to have** or **throw a f.** piquer une crise; **in a f. of temper** dans un accès de colère; **a f. of coughing** une quinte de toux; **a f. of crying** une crise de larmes; **to be in fits** (of laughter) se tordre de rire; **in fits and starts** par à-coups

fit² **1** *n* **the jacket is a good f.** cette veste me/te/*etc* va bien; **comfortable/tight f.** coupe *f* confortable/ajustée

2 *adj* **(a)** *(appropriate)* **f. to eat** mangeable; **f. to drink** buvable; **f. for the bin** bon (bonne) à jeter; **f. for human consumption** propre à la consommation; **a meal f. for a king** un repas digne d'un *ou* de roi; **do as you see *or* think f.** faites comme bon vous semblera; **to see f. to do sth** juger bon de faire qch; **that's all he's f. for** il n'est bon qu'à cela; **to be f. to do sth** *(worthy of)* être digne de faire qch; **to be f. to drop** tomber de fatigue

(b) *(healthy)* en forme; **to get f.** retrouver la forme; **to keep f.** se maintenir en forme; **to be f. to do sth** *(healthy enough)* être en état de faire qch; *Fam* **to be as f. as a fiddle** péter la forme

(c) *Fam (attractive)* canon *inv*

3 *vt (pt & pp* **fitted)** **(a)** *(match)* correspondre à; **to make the punishment f. the crime** proportionner la peine au délit

(b) *(be the right size for)* aller à; **to f. sb** aller à qn; **this key fits the lock** cette clé rentre dans la serrure

(c) *(install)* adapter **(to/on** à/sur); **to f. a carpet** poser de la moquette; **to f. sth with sth** équiper *ou* pourvoir qch de qch

(d) *(insert)* **to f. sth into/onto sth** faire rentrer qch dans/sur qch; **we can f. another two people inside** il y a encore de la place pour deux personnes

4 *vi* **(a)** *(be the right size) (of lid, key, plug)* aller; **to f. together** s'adapter; **to f. into sth** rentrer dans qch

(b) *(of clothes)* **it fits perfectly** ça me/te/*etc* va parfaitement

▸**fit in 1** *vt sep (in timetable)* caser

2 *vi* **(a)** *(go into place)* aller **(b)** *(of person)* être à sa place

▸**fit up** *vt sep very Fam (frame)* **to be fitted up** être victime d'un coup monté

fitful ['fɪtfʊl] *adj (sleep)* agité(e); **to make f. progress** progresser par à-coups

fitness ['fɪtnɪs] *n* **(a)** *(health)* forme *f* **(b)** *(suitability)* aptitude *f* (**for** à)

fitted ['fɪtɪd] *adj* **(a)** *(jacket, dress)* ajusté(e); **f. carpet** moquette *f*; **f. sheet** drap-housse *m* **(b)** *(kitchen)* intégré(e); *(wardrobe)* encastré(e)

fitting ['fɪtɪŋ] **1** *n* **(a)** *(of clothes)* essayage *m*; **f. room** cabine *f* d'essayage **(b)** **fittings** *(in office)* installations *fpl*; *(in house)* accessoires *mpl*

2 *adj* approprié(e) (**to** à)

five [faɪv] **1** *n* cinq *m inv*

2 *adj* cinq; **f. o'clock shadow** barbe *f* d'un jour; *see also* **eight**

fiver ['faɪvə(r)] *n Br Fam (sum)* 5 livres *fpl*; *(note)* billet *m* de 5 livres

fix [fɪks] **1** *n* **(a)** *Fam (difficulty)* **to be in a f.** être dans le pétrin; **to get into a f.** se fourrer dans le pétrin **(b)** *very Fam (of drug)* dose *f*; *Fig* **she needs her daily f. of chocolate** il lui faut sa dose quotidienne de chocolat **(c)** *Fam* **to be a f.** *(of election, contest)* être truqué(e)

2 *vt* **(a)** *(attach securely)* fixer (**to** à); **to f. sth in one's memory** graver qch dans sa mémoire; **to f. one's attention on sth** fixer son attention sur qch; **to f. one's eyes on sb/sth** fixer qn/qch (**b)** *(decide) (limit, price)* fixer **(c)** *(repair)* arranger, réparer **(d)** *(arrange) (meeting)* arranger; **to f. one's hair** se coiffer; *Fam* **I'll f. him!** je vais lui faire son affaire! **(e)** *Fam (election, contest)* truquer

▸**fix up** *vt sep* **(a)** *(arrange)* arranger **(b)** *(provide)* **to f. sb up with a job/flat** trouver un emploi/appartement à qn; **I've fixed you up with a date** je t'ai arrangé un rendez-vous galant

fixation [fɪk'seɪʃən] *n* fixation *f*; **to have a f. about sth** faire une fixation sur qch

fixed [fɪkst] *adj* **(a)** *(price, costs, income)* fixe; **f. assets** immobilisations *fpl* **(b)** *(definite) (ideas)* bien arrêté(e); *(plans)* précis(e) **(c)** *Fam* **how are you f. for money/ time?** tu as de l'argent/le temps? **(d)** *Fam (election, contest)* truqué(e)

fixer ['fɪksə(r)] *n Fam* combinard(e) *m,f*

fixture ['fɪkstʃə(r)] *n* **(a)** **fixtures** *(in house, office)* éléments *mpl* fixes; **bathroom fixtures** sanitaires *mpl*; *Fam* **to be a f.** *(of person)* faire partie des meubles **(b)** *Br (in sport)* rencontre *f*

fizz [fɪz] **1** *n* **(a)** *(sound)* pétillement *m*; *(bubbles)* gaz *m* **(b)** *Fam (soft drink)* boisson *f* gazeuse; *(champagne)* champ *m*

2 *vi (of champagne)* pétiller

▸**fizzle out** ['fɪzl] *vi Fam (of plan)* tomber à l'eau; *(of enthusiasm, interest)* retomber; *(of relationship)* partir en eau de boudin

fizzy ['fɪzɪ] *adj (wine)* mousseux(euse); *(soft drink)* gazeux(euse)

fjord [fjɔːd] *n* fjord *m*

flab [flæb] *n Fam (fat)* graisse *f*

flabbergasted ['flæbəgɑːstɪd] *adj Fam* abasourdi(e)

flabby ['flæbɪ] *adj (person, features)* bouffi(e); *(limbs)* mou (molle); *Fig (argument, reasoning)* qui manque de rigueur

flaccid ['flæsɪd] *adj* flasque

flag [flæg] **1** *n* drapeau *m*; *Naut* pavillon *m*; **F. Day** *(in United States)* = le 14 juin, fête commémorant l'adoption du drapeau américain; **f. day** *(for charity)* = jour où une association caritative organise une collecte en vendant des macarons, des insignes etc

2 *vt (pt & pp* **flagged)** *(mark)* marquer; *(mark)* signaler; **to f.** **(down) a taxi** héler un taxi

3 *vi (of person, conversation, interest)* faiblir; *(of strength, spirits)* baisser

flagellate ['flædʒəleɪt] *vt* flageller

flagpole ['flægpəʊl] *n* mât *m (de drapeau)*

flagrant ['fleɪgrənt] *adj* flagrant(e)

flagrantly ['fleɪgrəntlɪ] *adv* de façon flagrante; **dishonest** d'une malhonnêteté flagrante

flagship ['flægʃɪp] *n (of fleet)* navire *m* amiral; *Fig (of range of products, party)* fleuron *m*

flagstone ['flægstəʊn] *n* dalle *f*

flail [fleɪl] **1** *n (tool)* fléau *m*

2 *vt* agiter

3 *vi (of rope, cable)* se balancer; *(of arms, legs)* s'agiter dans tous les sens

▸**flail about, flail around** *vi (of arms, legs)* s'agiter dans tous les sens; *(of person)* se débattre

flair ['fleə(r)] *n* don *m* (**for** pour); **to do sth with f.** faire qch avec style; **to have a f. for business** avoir le sens des affaires; **to have a f. for doing sth** avoir le don de faire qch

flak [flæk] *n* tir *m* antiaérien *ou* de DCA; *Fig* critiques *fpl*; **she got a lot of f. for her decision** sa décision a été très critiquée; **f. jacket** gilet *m* pare-balles

flake [fleɪk] **1** *n (of snow, cereal)* flocon *m*; *(of paint)* écaille *f*; *(of soap)* paillette *f*; **a f. of skin** un bout de peau morte

2 *vi (of paint)* s'écailler; **my skin is flaking** je pèle

▸**flake out** *vi Fam* s'effondrer de fatigue

flaky ['fleɪkɪ] *adj* **(a)** *(paint)* écaillé(e); *(pastry)* feuilleté(e) **(b)** *Am (eccentric)* loufoque

flamboyant [flãm'bɔɪənt] *adj (person)* extraverti(e); *(gesture)* théâtral(e); *(clothes, colours)* voyant(e)

flame [fleɪm] **1** *n* flamme *f*; **to go up in flames** prendre feu; *Fig (of hopes, chances)* partir en fumée; **to burst into flames** s'enflammer; *Fam* **an old f. (man)** un ancien amoureux; *(woman)* une ancienne amoureuse
2 *vi (of fire)* flamber

flameproof ['fleɪmpruːf] *adj* ignifugé(e); *(dish)* qui va sur le feu

flamethrower ['fleɪmθrəʊə(r)] *n* lance-flammes *m inv*

flaming ['fleɪmɪŋ] **1** *adj* **(a)** *(burning)* enflammé(e); *Fig (sunset)* flamboyant(e); **a f. temper** une colère noire **(b)** *Br Fam (for emphasis)* sacré(e)
2 *adv Br Fam* vachement; **don't be so f. stupid!** ne sois pas si bête, merde!

flamingo [flə'mɪŋɡəʊ] *(pl* **flamingos)** *n* flamant *m*

flammable ['flæməbəl] *adj* inflammable

flan [flæn] *n* tarte *f*

Flanders ['flɑːndəz] *n* les Flandres *fpl*, la Flandre

flank [flæŋk] **1** *n* flanc *m*; *(of beef, mutton)* flanchet *m*
2 *vt* flanquer **(with** *or* **by** de)

flannel ['flænəl] *n* **(a)** *(fabric)* flanelle *f*; **(pair of) flannels** pantalon *m* en flanelle **(b)** *Br (face-cloth)* ≃ gant *m* de toilette **(c)** *Br Fam (evasive words, flattery)* blabla *m*

flap [flæp] **1** *n* **(a)** *(of envelope, book cover, tent)* rabat *m*; *(of aeroplane)* volet *m* **(b)** *Fam (panic)* **to be in a f.** être affolé(e), paniquer
2 *vt (pt & pp* **flapped)** **to f. its wings** *(of bird)* battre des ailes; **to f. one's arms** agiter les bras
3 *vi* **(a)** *(of wings, flag)* battre **(b)** *Fam (panic)* s'affoler, paniquer

flapjack ['flæpdʒæk] *n* **(a)** *Br (biscuit)* = biscuit épais à l'avoine **(b)** *Am (pancake)* = petite crêpe épaisse

flare [fleə(r)] **1** *n* **(a)** *(signal)* signal *m* lumineux; *(rocket)* fusée *f* éclairante **(b)** **(pair of) flares** pantalon *m* (à) pattes d'éléphant
2 *vt (nostrils)* dilater
3 *vi (of fire)* flamboyer; **tempers flared at the meeting** le ton est monté à la réunion

▸**flare up** *vi (of fire)* s'embraser; *(of medical condition)* se déclencher; *(of anger, trouble)* éclater

flash [flæʃ] **1** *n* **(a)** *(of light)* éclair *m*; **a f. of lightning** un éclair; **f. of wit** trait *m* d'esprit; **f. of inspiration** éclair de génie; **in a f.** *(very quickly)* en un clin d'œil; *Fig* **a f. in the pan** un feu de paille; **f. flood** crue *f* subite; **f. point** *(of situation)* point *m* de rupture; *(region)* point chaud *m* **(b)** *(in photography)* flash *m*; **f. photography** photographie *f* au flash
2 *adj Br Fam (showy) (clothes, car, jewellery)* tape-à-l'œil *inv*; *(person)* aux goûts tapageurs
3 *vt (smile, look)* lancer **(at** à); *(card, badge)* montrer rapidement **(at** à); **to f. one's headlights at sb** faire un appel de phares à qn
4 *vi* **(a)** *(of diamond)* briller; *(of light)* clignoter **(b)** *(move quickly)* **to f. past** passer comme un éclair; **my life flashed before me** ma vie a défilé devant mes yeux **(c)** *Fam (expose oneself)* s'exhiber (at devant)

flashback ['flæʃbæk] *n (in novel, film)* flash-back *m inv*, retour *m* en arrière

flasher ['flæʃə(r)] *n Br Fam* **(a)** *(man exposing himself)* exhibitionniste *m* **(b)** *(car indicator)* clignotant *m*

flashing ['flæʃɪŋ] *adj (light)* clignotant(e)

flashlight ['flæʃlaɪt] *n* torche *f* électrique

flashy ['flæʃɪ] *adj Fam (clothes, car, jewellery)* tape-à-l'œil *inv*; *(person)* aux goûts tapageurs

flask [flɑːsk] *n (for alcohol)* flasque *f*; *(in chemistry)* fiole *f*; **(Thermos®) f.** *(bouteille f)* Thermos® *f*

flat [flæt] **1** *n* **(a)** *Br (apartment)* appartement *m* **(b)** *Fam (flat tyre)* pneu *m* à plat; *(punctured)* pneu crevé
2 *adj (surface)* plat(e); *(nose)* camus; **as f. as a pancake** plat comme une galette; *Fam (flat-chested)* plate comme une limande; **f. cap** casquette *f*; **f. racing** plat *m*; **f. rate** tarif *m* unique; **f. tyre** pneu *m* à plat; *(punctured)* pneu crevé **(b)** *(refusal)* **to give a f. refusal** refuser net **(c)** *(existence)* monotone; *(voice)* terne; *(battery)* à plat; *(drink)* éventé(e) **(d)** *(in music)* (a semitone lower) bémol; *(out of tune)* en dessous du ton; **B f.** si *m inv* bémol
3 *adv* **(a)** *(level)* à plat; **to fall f. on one's face** tomber à plat ventre; *Fig* se casser le nez; *Fig* **to fall f.** *(of joke)* tomber à plat; **he pressed himself f. against the wall** il s'est plaqué contre le mur **(b)** *(completely)* **to turn sb down f.** opposer un refus catégorique à qn; **in twenty seconds f.** en vingt secondes pile; **to work f. out** travailler d'arrache-pied; *Fam* **to be f. broke** être complètement fauché(e)

flat-chested [flæt'tʃestɪd] *adj* **to be f.** avoir peu de poitrine

flatfish ['flætfɪʃ] *n* poisson *m* plat

flat-footed [flæt'fʊtɪd] *adj* **to be f.** avoir les pieds plats

flatly ['flætlɪ] *adv (refuse, deny)* catégoriquement

flatmate ['flætmeɪt] *n Br* colocataire *mf*; **we used to be flatmates** nous partagions un appartement

flatten ['flætən] *vt* aplatir; **to f. oneself against a wall** s'aplatir contre un mur; *Fam* **to f. sb** casser la tête à qn

flatter ['flætə(r)] *vt (of person, clothes)* flatter; *Fam* **don't f. yourself!** ne te fais pas trop d'illusions!

flattering ['flætərɪŋ] *adj (words, photo)* flatteur(euse); *(clothes, colour)* qui avantage

flattery ['flætərɪ] *n* flatterie *f*

flatulence ['flætjʊləns] *n Med* flatulence *f*

flaunt [flɔːnt] *vt (knowledge, wealth)* étaler; *(jewels)* exhiber; *Fig (ignorance, bad manners)* étaler sans complexes

flavour, *Am* **flavor** ['fleɪvə(r)] **1** *n* **(a)** *(of food)* goût *m*; *(of ice cream, yoghurt)* parfum *m* **(b)** *(characteristic)* note *f*; **her stories have a Provençal f.** ses histoires fleurent bon la Provence
2 *vt (savoury food)* relever **(with** de); *(sweet food)* parfumer **(with** à); **vanilla flavoured** parfumé(e) à la vanille

flavouring, *Am* **flavoring** ['fleɪvərɪŋ] *n* parfum *m*; **artificial f.** arôme *m* artificiel

flavourless, *Am* **flavorless** ['fleɪvəlɪs] *adj Br* sans saveur, insipide

flaw [flɔː] *n* défaut *m*; *(in plan, argument)* faille *f*

flawed [flɔːd] *adj* qui a un défaut/des défauts; *(plan, argument)* bancal(e)

flawless ['flɔːlɪs] *adj* parfait(e)

flax [flæks] *n* lin *m*

flay [fleɪ] *vt (flog)* fouetter; *Fig (criticize)* éreinter

flea [fliː] *n* puce *f*; *Fam* **to send sb away with a f. in his ear** envoyer promener qn; **f. market** *(marché m* aux) puces *fpl*

fleabite ['fliːbaɪt] *n* piqûre *f* de puce

flea-bitten ['fliːbɪtən] *adj (person, animal)* plein(e) de puces; *Fam (shabby)* miteux(euse)

fleck [flek] **1** *n (of colour, light)* petite tache *f*; *(of dust)* grain *m*

2 *vt* tacheter (**with** de); **hair flecked with grey** cheveux *mpl* grisonnants

fled [fled] *pt & pp of* **flee**

fledgling ['fledʒlɪŋ] **1** *n (young bird)* oisillon *m*
2 *adj Fig (person)* novice, débutant(e); *(company, state)* naissant(e)

flee [fliː] *(pt & pp* **fled** [fled]) *vi* fuir, s'enfuir; **to f. from persecution** fuir la persécution

fleece [fliːs] **1** *n* (**a**) *(of sheep)* toison *f* (**b**) *(garment)* fourrure *f* polaire
2 *vt Fam (cheat)* estamper

fleecy ['fliːsɪ] *adj* duveteux(euse)

fleet [fliːt] *n (of ships)* flotte *f; (of taxis, buses)* parc *m; Fig (convoy)* file *f*

fleet-footed ['fliːt'fʊtɪd] *adj Lit* au pied léger

fleeting ['fliːtɪŋ] *adj (moment, happiness, glance)* fugace; *(beauty)* éphémère; *(visit)* court(e), rapide; **to catch a f. glimpse of sth/sb** entrevoir qn/qch

Flemish ['flemɪʃ] **1** *n (language)* flamand *m*
2 *adj* flamand(e)

flesh [fleʃ] *n* chair *f;* **in the f.** en chair et en os; **to make sb's f. creep or crawl** donner la chair de poule à qn; **his own f. and blood** *(children)* la chair de sa chair; *(close family)* les siens *mpl;* **f. wound** blessure *f* superficielle

▶**flesh out** *vt sep (plan, remarks)* étoffer

fleshy ['fleʃɪ] *adj* charnu(e)

flew [fluː] *pt of* **fly**

flex [fleks] **1** *n Br (cable)* cordon *m*
2 *vt (arms, knees)* fléchir; *(muscles)* faire jouer; *Fig* **they're just flexing their muscles** ce n'est qu'une démonstration d'autorité de leur part

flexible ['fleksəbəl] *adj* flexible

flexitime ['fleksɪtaɪm] *n* horaires *mpl* flexibles *ou* à la carte

flick [flɪk] **1** *n* (**a**) *(with finger)* pichenette *f; (of whip, tail)* petit coup *m;* **at the f. of a switch** en appuyant juste sur un bouton; **f. knife** couteau *m* à cran d'arrêt (**b**) *Br Fam Old-fashioned* **the flicks** *(cinema)* le ciné, le cinoche
2 *vt (with finger)* donner une chiquenaude à; **he flicked the cigarette ash onto the carpet** il fit tomber la cendre de sa cigarette sur le tapis; **to f. the hair out of one's eyes** écarter les cheveux de ses yeux

▶**flick through** *vt insep (book, magazine)* feuilleter; *(photographs)* passer rapidement en revue

flicker ['flɪkə(r)] **1** *n (of flame)* vacillement *m; Fig (of hope)* lueur *f; (of interest, annoyance)* pointe *f;* **a f. of light** une lueur vacillante
2 *vi (of flame, light)* vaciller

flier ['flaɪə(r)] *n* (**a**) *(passenger)* = personne qui voyage en avion (**b**) *(leaflet)* prospectus *m*

flight [flaɪt] *n* (**a**) *(act of flying, specific trip)* vol *m;* **it's two hours' f. from Edinburgh** c'est à deux heures de vol d'Édimbourg; *Fig* **f. of fancy** lubie *f;* **f. attendant** *(male)* steward *m; (female)* hôtesse *f* de l'air; **f. deck** *(of aircraft)* poste *m ou* cabine *f* de pilotage; **f. path** trajectoire *f* de vol; **f. recorder** enregistreur *m* de vol; **f. simulator** simulateur *m* de vol (**b**) *(group of birds)* vol *m,* volée *f; Fig* **in the top f.** parmi les tout premiers (**c**) **f.** *(of stairs)* escalier *m;* **two flights up from me** deux étages au-dessus de chez moi (**d**) *(escape)* fuite *f;* **to put sb to f.** mettre qn en fuite

flightless ['flaɪtlɪs] *adj* coureur(euse)

flighty ['flaɪtɪ] *adj (fickle)* volage

flimsy ['flɪmzɪ] *adj (structure, fence)* peu solide; *(dress, excuse, plot)* léger(ère); *(evidence)* ténu(e)

flinch [flɪntʃ] *vi (with pain)* tressaillir; *(at an idea)* frémir; **to do sth without flinching** faire qch sans broncher; **to f. from doing sth** hésiter à faire qch

fling [flɪŋ] **1** *n Fam (affair)* aventure *f*
2 *vt (pt & pp* **flung** [flʌŋ]) jeter; *(ball)* lancer; **to f. oneself into an armchair** se jeter dans un fauteuil; **to f. one's arms around sb** ptendre qn dans ses bras; *Fig* **to f. oneself into a task** se lancer dans une tâche

▶**fling out** *vt sep (object)* jeter; *(person)* mettre à la porte; *(proposal, case)* rejeter

flint [flɪnt] *n (stone)* silex *m; (of lighter)* pierre *f* (à briquet)

flip [flɪp] **1** *n Fam* **the f. side** *(of record)* la face B; *Fig (of situation)* le revers de la médaille
2 *vt (pt & pp* **flipped**) *(record, pancake, card)* retourner; **to f. the switch** appuyer sur l'interrupteur; **to f. a coin** jouer à pile ou face; *Fam* **to f. one's lid** *(get angry)* piquer une crise; *(go mad)* perdre la boule
3 *vi Fam (get angry)* piquer une crise; *(go mad)* perdre la boule

▶**flip through** *vt insep (book, magazine)* feuilleter; *(photos, samples)* jeter un coup d'œil à

flip-flops ['flɪpflɒps] *npl* (**a pair of**) **f.** des tongs *fpl*

flippant ['flɪpənt] *adj* désinvolte, cavalier(ère)

flipper ['flɪpə(r)] *n (of animal)* nageoire *f; (of diver)* palme *f*

flirt [flɜːt] **1** *n* charmeur(euse) *m,f*
2 *vi* flirter (**with** avec); *Fig* **to f. with an idea** caresser une idée

flirtatious [flɜː'teɪʃəs] *adj (look, smile)* charmeur(euse); **to be f.** aimer flirter; **to be f. with sb** flirter avec qn

flit [flɪt] **1** *n Br Fam* **to do a moonlight f.** déménager à la cloche de bois
2 *vi (pt & pp* **flitted**) **to f. about** *(of bird)* voleter; *Fig* **to f. from one thing to another** *(of person)* s'éparpiller

float [fləʊt] **1** *n* (**a**) *(on fishing line)* bouchon *m; (for swimming, on net)* flotteur *m* (**b**) *(in procession)* char *m* (**c**) *(money)* fonds *m* de caisse
2 *vt* (**a**) *(ship)* mettre à flot (**b**) *(idea, proposal)* émettre; *(company)* introduire en Bourse
3 *vi* flotter; **to f. to the surface** remonter à la surface; *Fam Fig* **he's floating around somewhere** il traîne par là

floating ['fləʊtɪŋ] *adj* flottant(e); *(population)* fluctuant(e); **f. voter** électeur(trice) *m,f* indécis(e)

flock [flɒk] **1** *n (of sheep)* troupeau *m; (of birds)* vol *m,* volée *f; Rel (congregation)* ouailles *fpl; Fig (of people)* foule *f*
2 *vi (gather)* **to f. around sb** s'attrouper autour de qn; **people are flocking to the exhibition** les gens vont en masse *ou* en foule voir l'exposition

flog [flɒg] *(pt & pp* **flogged**) *vt* (**a**) *(beat)* fouetter; *Fam* **to be flogging a dead horse** se dépenser en pure perte; *Fam* **to f. a subject to death** s'étendre indéfiniment sur un sujet (**b**) *Br Fam (sell)* vendre

flood [flʌd] **1** *n* inondation *f; (of light)* flot *m;* **the F.** *(in the Bible)* le Déluge; **to be in floods (of tears)** verser des torrents de larmes
2 *vt (land, bathroom)* inonder; **to be flooded with light** être inondé(e) de lumière; **the river flooded its banks** la rivière a débordé *ou* est sortie de son lit; **to f. the market (with sth)** inonder le marché (de qch); **to be flooded with complaints/telephone calls** être submergé(e) de réclamations/de coups de fil
3 *vi (of river)* déborder; **the sun's rays came flooding**

through the window les rayons du soleil entraient à flots par la fenêtre; **letters came flooding in** nous avons/ils ont/*etc* été submergés de lettres; **it all came flooding back** tout m'/lui/*etc* est revenu d'un coup

floodgates ['flʌdgeɪts] *n Fig* **to open the floodgates to sth** laisser la porte ouverte à qch

flooding ['flʌdɪŋ] *n* inondation(s) *f(pl)*

floodlight ['flʌdlaɪt] **1** *n* projecteur *m*; **by f.** à la lumière des projecteurs

floodlit ['flʌdlɪt] *adj (stadium, match)* éclairé(e) aux projecteurs; *(building)* illuminé(e)

floor [flɔː(r)] **1** *n* **(a)** *(of room, forest)* sol *m*; *(of Stock Exchange)* parquet *m*; *(of ocean)* fond *m*; **f. show** spectacle *m* de cabaret **(b)** *(at meeting, debate)* **to give sb the f.** donner la parole à qn; **to take the f.** prendre la parole; **questions from the f.** questions *fpl* du public **(c)** *(storey)* étage *m*; **to live ten floors up** habiter au dixième étage
2 *vt (knock down)* envoyer au tapis; *Fig (of question, criticism)* désarçonner

floorboard ['flɔːbɔːd] *n* latte *f* de plancher

floozie, floozy ['fluːzɪ] *(pl* **floozies)** *n very Fam* pouffiasse *f*

flop [flɒp] **1** *n (failure)* fiasco *m*, bide *m*; **to be a f.** *(of film)* faire un bide; *(of party)* être un bide
2 *vi (pt & pp* **flopped) (a)** *(fall) (into water)* tomber; *(onto seat)* s'affaler **(b)** *(fail)* échouer; *(of film)* faire un bide; *(of party)* être un bide

floppy ['flɒpɪ] **1** *(pl* **floppies)** *Comptr* disquette *f*
2 *adj (ears)* pendant(e); *(garment)* flottant(e); *(hat)* mou (molle); *Comptr* **f. disk** disquette *f*

flora ['flɔːrə] *n (plant life)* flore *f*

floral ['flɔːrəl] *adj* floral(e); **f. tribute** *(at funeral)* couronne *f* de fleurs

Florence ['flɒrəns] *n* Florence

florid ['flɒrɪd] *adj (style)* fleuri(e); *(complexion)* rubicond(e)

Florida ['flɒrɪdə] *n* la Floride

florist ['flɒrɪst] *n* fleuriste *mf*; **f.'s (shop)** fleuriste *m*

floss [flɒs] **1** *n (dental)* **f.** fil *m* dentaire
2 *vt* nettoyer avec du fil dentaire

flotation [fləʊ'teɪʃən] *n Com (of company)* lancement *m*

flotsam ['flɒtsəm] *n* **f. (and jetsam)** débris *mpl* refoulés par la mer; *Fig* **the f. of society** les laissés-pour-compte *mpl* de la société

flounce [flaʊns] **1** *n (in sewing)* volant *m*
2 *vi* **to f. in/out** entrer/sortir de façon théâtrale

flounder ['flaʊndə(r)] **1** *n (fish)* flet *m*
2 *vi (in water, mud)* patauger; *(in job, course, speech)* perdre pied

flour ['flaʊə(r)] **1** *n* farine *f*
2 *vt* fariner

flourish ['flʌrɪʃ] **1** *n (gesture)* grand geste *m* théâtral; *(musical, in writing)* fioriture *f*
2 *vt (brandish)* brandir
3 *vi (of plant, person)* prospérer; *(of business, arts)* être florissant(e)

flourishing ['flʌrɪʃɪŋ] *adj (plant)* qui prospère; *(business)* florissant(e)

flout [flaʊt] *vt (rule, instruction)* faire fi de; *(person)* défier l'autorité de; *(authority)* défier

flow [fləʊ] **1** *n (of liquid)* écoulement *m*; *(of electrical current, information)* circulation *f*; *(of tide, capital)* flux *m*; **f. of traffic** circulation; *Fig* **in full f.** en plein discours; **to follow the f. of an argument** suivre (le fil d')un raisonnement; *Fig* **to go with the f.** suivre le mouvement; **f. chart** organigramme *m*
2 *vi* **(a)** *(of liquid)* couler; *(of electrical current)* circuler; *(of traffic)* s'écouler; *Fig (of writing)* couler bien; *(of ideas)* affluer; **to f. into the sea** *(of river)* se jeter dans la mer **(b)** **to f. from** *(result from)* découler de

flower ['flaʊə(r)] **1** *n* fleur *f*; **to be in f.** être en fleur(s); *Fig* **in the first f. of youth** dans la fleur de l'âge; **f. arranging** art *m* floral; **f. garden** jardin *m* d'agrément; **f. girl** = jeune demoiselle d'honneur; **f. show** exposition *f* florale
2 *vi* fleurir

flowerbed ['flaʊəbed] *n* parterre *m* de fleurs

flowerpot ['flaʊəpɒt] *n* pot *m* de fleurs

flowing ['fləʊɪŋ] *adj (hair)* flottant(e); *(movement, style)* fluide

flown [fləʊn] *pp of* **fly**

flu [fluː] *n* grippe *f*; **a dose** *or* **bout of (the) f.** une grippe; **to have (the) f.** avoir la grippe

fluctuate ['flʌktjʊeɪt] *vi (of prices)* fluctuer; *(of pulse, temperature)* varier

fluctuation [flʌktjʊ'eɪʃən] *n (of prices)* fluctuation *f*; *(of pulse, temperature)* variation *f*

flue [fluː] *n (of heater, chimney)* tuyau *m*

fluency ['fluːənsɪ] *n* aisance *f* **(of/in** de/en)

fluent ['fluːənt] *adj (speech, style)* fluide; **he is f. in French, he speaks f. French** il parle couramment français

fluently ['fluːəntlɪ] *adv (express oneself)* avec facilité *ou* aisance; *(speak language)* couramment

fluff [flʌf] **1** *n* peluche *f*; **a bit of f.** une peluche
2 *vt* **(a) to f. sth (up)** *(pillow, duvet)* remettre qch en forme *(en le secouant)* **(b)** *Fam (botch)* rater

fluffy ['flʌfɪ] *adj* duveteux(euse); *(clouds)* cotonneux(euse)

fluid ['fluːɪd] **1** *n* fluide *m*, liquide *m*; **bodily fluids** sécrétions *fpl*
2 *adj (substance)* fluide, liquide; *(style, movement)* fluide; *(situation, plans)* mal défini(e); **f. ounce** = 0,031

fluidity [fluː'ɪdɪtɪ] *n (of style, movement)* fluidité *f*; *(of situation, plans)* imprécision *f*

fluke [fluːk] *n Fam (stroke of luck)* coup *m* de veine *ou* de bol; **by a f.** par hasard; **his success was a pure f.** c'est un hasard qu'il ait réussi

fluk(e)y ['fluːkɪ] *adj Fam (person)* veinard(e)

flummox ['flʌməks] *vt Fam* scier

flung [flʌŋ] *pt & pp of* **fling**

flunk [flʌŋk] *Fam* **1** *vt (exam)* rater; *(student)* recaler, coller
2 *vi (in exam)* être recalé(e) *ou* collé(e)

flunkey ['flʌŋkɪ] *n (pl* **flunkeys)** *n Fam Pej* larbin *m*

fluorescent [flʊə'resənt] *adj* fluorescent(e)

fluoride ['flʊəraɪd] *n* fluorure *m*; **f. toothpaste** dentifrice *m* au fluor

flurry ['flʌrɪ] *n (of snow)* bourrasque *f*; **a f. of activity/excitement** une soudaine activité/excitation

flush [flʌʃ] **1** *n* **(a)** *(beginning)* **in the f. of youth** dans tout l'éclat de sa jeunesse **(b)** *(in cards)* flush *m* **(c)** *(in toilet)* chasse *f* (d'eau)
2 *adj* **(a)** *(even)* de niveau **(with** avec) **(b)** *Fam (rich)* plein(e) aux as
3 *vt* **to f. the toilet** tirer la chasse (d'eau)
4 *vi* **(a)** *(of person)* rougir **(with** de) **(b)** *(of toilet)* **the toilet**

isn't **flushing properly** la chasse d'eau ne fonctionne pas bien

►**flush out** vt sep (force to emerge) déloger

flushed [flʌʃd] adj (person, face) rouge (**with** de)

fluster ['flʌstə(r)] vt démonter; **to get flustered** se démonter

flute [fluːt] n flûte f traversière

flutter ['flʌtə(r)] 1 n (a) (of wings, eyelashes, heart) battement m; Fig **to be in a f.** (of excitement) être en émoi (b) Br Fam (bet) petit pari m; **to have a f.** parier ou jouer une petite somme (**on** sur)
2 vt **to f. its wings** (of bird) battre des ailes; **to f. one's eyelashes at sb** regarder qn en battant des cils
3 vi (of birds, insects) voleter; (of heart) battre; (of flag) flotter

flux [flʌks] n **to be in a state of f.** changer perpétuellement

fly[1] [flaɪ] n (a) f., **flies** (of trousers) braguette f (b) **f. sheet** (of tent) auvent m

fly[2] Br Fam 1 n **to do sth on the f.** (spontaneously) faire qch sur le coup
2 adj (cunning) malin(igne)

fly[3] (pl **flies**) n (insect) mouche f; **he wouldn't hurt a f.** il ne ferait pas de mal à une mouche; **they were dropping like flies** ils tombaient comme des mouches; Fig **a f. in the ointment** un os; Fam Fig **there are no flies on her** elle est loin d'être bête; **I wish I could be a f. on the wall** (at interview, meeting) si je pouvais être une petite souris

fly[4] (pt **flew** [fluː], pp **flown** [fləʊn]) 1 vt (a) (plane) piloter; (goods) transporter en avion; (route) emprunter; **to f. Air India** voyager avec Air India (b) (kite) faire voler; **to f. a flag** (of ship) arborer un pavillon; Fig **to f. the flag** (for one's country) défendre les couleurs de son pays; (flee) s'enfuir de; Fig **to f. the nest** (of child) quitter le nid
2 vi (a) (of bird, plane) voler; (of passenger) voyager en avion, prendre l'avion; **Fam to send sb/sth flying** envoyer rouler qn/qch; **to f. over London** survoler Londres; **to f. across the Atlantic** traverser l'Atlantique en avion (b) (of flag, hair) flotter (c) (move quickly) **I must f.** il faut que je file; **to f. to sb's help** voler au secours de qn; **how time flies!** comme le temps passe! **the door flew open** la porte s'est ouverte brusquement; **to f. into a rage** sortir de ses gonds; **Fam to send sb/sth flying** envoyer rouler qn/qch; **to f. in the face of reason/logic** défier la raison/toute logique

►**fly away** vi (of bird, papers) s'envoler

►**fly in 1** vt sep (troops, rescuers) transporter en avion
2 vi (of passenger) arriver en avion

►**fly out 1** vt sep (survivors) transporter en avion
2 vi (of passenger) partir en avion

fly-by-night ['flaɪbaɪnaɪt] adj Fam Pej (company) véreux(euse)

flyer ['flaɪə(r)] = **flier**

flying ['flaɪŋ] 1 n (as pilot) pilotage m; (as passenger) voyages mpl en avion; **she loves f.** (as pilot) elle adore piloter; (as passenger) elle adore prendre l'avion; **f. club** aéro-club m; **f. lessons** leçons fpl de pilotage; **f. time** heures fpl de vol
2 adj (bird, fish) volant(e); **they were hurt by f. glass** ils ont été blessés par des éclats de verre; **to pass with f. colours** réussir haut la main; **f. boat** hydravion m; **f. doctor** médecin m volant; **f. saucer** soucoupe f volante (b) (rapid) **a f. visit** une visite éclair; **to get off to a f. start** très bien démarrer

flyleaf ['flaɪliːf] (pl **flyleaves** ['flaɪliːvz]) n page f de garde

flyover ['flaɪəʊvə(r)] n Br Aut pont m routier

flypaper ['flaɪpeɪpə(r)] n papier m tue-mouches

fly-past ['flaɪpɑːst] n Av défilé m aérien

flyweight ['flaɪweɪt] n (in boxing) poids m mouche

FM [e'fem] n (abbr **frequency modulation**) FM f

FO [e'fəʊ] n Br (abbr **Foreign Office**) (ministère m des) Affaires fpl étrangères

foal [fəʊl] 1 n (horse) poulain m; (female) pouliche f
2 vi pouliner

foam [fəʊm] 1 n (on sea) écume f; (on beer, bath) mousse f; **f. rubber** caoutchouc m Mousse®
2 vi (of sea) écumer; (of beer, bath) mousser; **to f. at the mouth** baver; Fig écumer de rage

foamy ['fəʊmɪ] adj (sea) écumeux(euse); (beer) moussant(e)

fob [fɒb] n chaîne f (de montre); **f. watch** montre f de gousset

►**fob off** vt (pt & pp **fobbed**) vt sep Fam **to f. sb off with an excuse** se débarrasser de qn en lui racontant des salades; **to f. sth off on sb** refiler ou fourguer qch à qn

focal ['fəʊkəl] adj focal(e); **f. point** foyer m; Fig (of discussion) point m central

focus ['fəʊkəs] 1 n (pl **focuses** or **foci** ['fəʊkaɪ]) (of lens) foyer m; Fig (of discontent) cible f; (of interest, attention) centre m; **f. group** (of customers) groupe m témoin; **to be in f.** être au point; **to be out of f.** ne pas être au point
2 vt (lens, camera) mettre au point; (rays, attention, energy) concentrer (**on** sur); **all eyes were focused on him** tous les regards étaient tournés vers lui
3 vi **to f. on sth** (with camera) faire la mise au point sur qch; (with eyes) fixer qch; Fig (of debate, speaker) se concentrer sur qch

fodder ['fɒdə(r)] n fourrage m

foe [fəʊ] n ennemi m

foetal, Am **fetal** ['fiːtəl] adj fœtal(e); **in the f. position** en position fœtale

foetus, Am **fetus** ['fiːtəs] n fœtus m

fog [fɒg] n brouillard m; Fig **to be in a f.** (confused) être dans le brouillard; **f. lamp** or **light** (on car) (phare m) antibrouillard m

►**fog up** (pt & pp **fogged**) vi (of windows, glasses) s'embuer

fogbound ['fɒgbaʊnd] adj (port, airport) bloqué(e) en raison du brouillard

fogey ['fəʊgɪ] (pl **fogeys**) n Fam **old f.** vieux (vieille) schnock m,f

foggy ['fɒgɪ] adj brumeux(euse); **it's f.** il y a du brouillard; Fam **I haven't (got) the foggiest (idea)!** je n'en ai pas la moindre idée!

foghorn ['fɒghɔːn] n (on ship) corne f de brume; Fam **a voice like a f.** une voix de stentor

fogy ['fəʊgɪ] (pl **fogies**) = **fogey**

foible ['fɔɪbəl] n (habit) manie f; (weakness) point m faible

foil [fɔɪl] 1 n (a) (metal sheet) feuille f; (cooking or kitchen) **f.** papier m alu(minium) (b) (complement) **to act as a f. (to or for)** servir de repoussoir (à) (c) (sword) fleuret m
2 vt (plan, ambitions) contrecarrer; (attempt, coup) faire échouer

foist [fɔɪst] vt refiler (**on** à); (ideas) imposer (**on** à)

fold[1] [fəʊld] n (sheep) **f.** parc m à moutons

fold² 1 *n* pli *m*; *(of fat)* bourrelet *m*

2 *vt* (a) plier; **to f. sth in two** *or* **in half** plier qch en deux; **to f. one's arms** croiser les bras (b) *(in cooking)* mélanger délicatement

3 *vi* (a) *(of chair, table)* se plier, se replier (b) *Fam (of business)* plier boutique

▶**fold up** 1 *vt sep* plier, replier

2 *vi* *(of map, chair)* se plier, se replier

foldaway ['fəʊldəweɪ] *adj (table, bed)* pliant(e)

folder ['fəʊldə(r)] *n (file, document wallet)* chemise *f*; *(ring binder)* classeur *m*; *Comptr* répertoire *m*

folding ['fəʊldɪŋ] *adj (chair, table)* pliant(e); **f. doors** porte *f* en accordéon

foliage ['fəʊlɪdʒ] *n* feuillage *m*

folio ['fəʊlɪəʊ] *(pl* **folios**) *n* folio *m*

folk [fəʊk] 1 *npl Fam (people)* gens *mpl*; **my/your folks** *(family)* ma/ta famille

2 *adj (national)* folklorique; **f. (music)** *(musique f)* folk *m*; **f. singer** chanteur(euse) *m,f* folk; **f. song** chanson *f* folk

folklore ['fəʊklɔ:(r)] *n* folklore *m*

follow ['fɒləʊ] 1 *vt* suivre; *(act, performance)* passer après; *(career)* poursuivre; **the road follows the coast** la route longe la côte; **to f. one's nose** *(go straight ahead)* aller tout droit; *(act instinctively)* y aller à l'instinct

2 *vi* (a) *(come after)* suivre; **proceed as follows** procéder comme suit (b) *(result)* s'ensuivre; **it follows that...** il s'ensuit que... (c) *(understand)* suivre

▶**follow on** *vi* (a) *(go after)* **you go ahead, we'll f. on** pars devant, nous te suivons (b) *(continue)* **to f. on from sth** découler de qch

▶**follow through** 1 *vt sep (project, plan)* mener à son terme

2 *vi* **he's full of ideas but he seldom follows through** il a beaucoup d'idées, mais il les met rarement à exécution

▶**follow up** *vt sep (advantage, success)* exploiter; *(opportunity)* saisir; *(contact)* garder; *(clue)* suivre

follower ['fɒləʊə(r)] *n (of team)* supporter *m*; *(of ideas, politician)* partisan(e) *m,f*; *(of philosopher)* disciple *m*

following ['fɒləʊɪŋ] 1 *n (supporters) (of team)* supporters *mpl*; *(of ideas, politician)* partisans *mpl*; *(of programme)* public *m*

2 *pron* **the f.** *(things, points)* ce qui suit; *(people)* les personnes *fpl* suivantes

3 *adj* suivant(e); **(on) the f. day** le jour suivant, le lendemain

4 *prep* après

follow-up ['fɒləʊʌp] *n Com (of orders)* suivi *m*

folly ['fɒlɪ] *n* folie *f*; **an act of f.** une folie

foment [fə'ment] *vt Lit* fomenter

fond [fɒnd] *adj* (a) **to be f. of sb/sth** aimer bien qn/qch; **to become f. of sb** s'attacher à qn; **to become f. of sth** prendre goût à qch; **to be f. of doing sth** aimer bien faire qch (b) *(loving)* tendre, affectueux(euse); **f. memories (of)** de bons souvenirs (de) (c) *(hope)* naïf(ïve)

fondle ['fɒndəl] *vt* caresser

fondly ['fɒndlɪ] *adv* (a) *(lovingly)* tendrement, affectueusement (b) *(naïvely)* naïvement

fondness ['fɒndnɪs] *n* (a) *(affection)* tendresse *f*, affection *f* *(for pour)* (b) *(liking)* penchant *m* *(for pour)*

font [fɒnt] *n* (a) *Rel* fonts *mpl* baptismaux (b) *Typ & Comptr* police *f* de caractères, fonte *f*

food [fu:d] *n* nourriture *f*; **Chinese/Mexican f.** la cuisine chinoise/mexicaine; **to be off one's f.** ne pas avoir d'appétit; **to give sb f. for thought** donner à penser *ou* à réfléchir à qn; *Biol* **f. chain** chaîne *f* alimentaire; **f. industry** industrie *f* alimentaire; **f. poisoning** intoxication *f* alimentaire; **f. processor** robot *m* de cuisine

foodstuffs ['fu:dstʌfs] *npl* produits *mpl* alimentaires

fool [fu:l] 1 *n (stupid person)* imbécile *mf*, idiot(e) *m,f*; *(jester)* fou *m*; **you'd be a f. to buy it** tu serais bien bête de l'acheter; **any f. knows that** le premier imbécile venu sait ça; **a f. of a doctor** un imbécile de docteur; **to play** *or* **the f.** faire l'idiot; **to make a f. of sb** *(make look ridiculous)* ridiculiser qn; *(tease)* se moquer de qn; **to make a f. of oneself** se couvrir de ridicule; **the more f. you!** tu es vraiment bête!; **I felt such a f.** je me suis senti vraiment bête; **she's no** *or* **nobody's f.** on ne la lui fait pas, elle est maligne; **to live in a f.'s paradise** se bercer d'illusions; *Fam* **there's no f. like an old f.** il n'y a pire fou qu'un vieux fou

2 *vt (deceive)* avoir, duper; **you can't f. me** on ne m'a pas comme ça; **to let oneself be fooled by sth** se laisser avoir par qch; **you could have fooled me!** je ne l'aurais pas cru!

▶**fool about, fool around** *vi* (a) *(act foolishly)* faire l'imbécile; **to f. about** *or* **around with sth** *(clumsily, for fun)* jouer avec qch; *(fiddle)* tripoter qch (b) *(waste time)* perdre son temps (c) *(have affair(s))* avoir une aventure/des aventures

foolhardy ['fu:lhɑ:dɪ] *adj* téméraire, imprudent(e)

foolish ['fu:lɪʃ] *adj (stupid)* idiot(e); *(imprudent)* insensé(e); **to look sb look f.** ridiculiser qn

foolishly ['fu:lɪʃlɪ] *adv (stupidly)* bêtement; *(imprudently)* imprudemment

foolproof ['fu:lpru:f] *adj (method, plan)* infaillible; *(device)* indétraquable

foot [fʊt] *(pl* **feet** [fi:t]) 1 *n* (a) *(of person, horse, chair)* pied *m*; *(of other animal)* patte *f*; **to put one's feet up** *(have a rest)* se reposer; **to set f. on** poser le pied sur; **I shall never set f. in his house again** je ne remettrai jamais plus les pieds chez lui; **to be on one's feet all day** être debout du matin au soir; **to be on one's feet again** *(after illness)* être de nouveau sur pied; **on f.** à pied; **under f.** sous les pieds; *Mil* **f. patrol** patrouille *f* à pied; **f. pump** pompe *f* à pied; **f. soldier** fantassin *m*, soldat *m* d'infanterie

(b) *(of mountain, stairs)* pied *m*; *(of page)* bas *m*; *(of bed, table)* bout *m*

(c) *(in poetry)* pied *m*

(d) *(unit of measurement)* = 0,3048 m, pied *m* (anglais); **three f.** *or* **feet six (inches)** trois pieds six pouces

(e) *(idioms)* **to have one's feet firmly on the ground** avoir les pieds sur terre; **to have one f. in the grave** avoir un pied dans la tombe; **she hasn't put a f. wrong** elle n'a pas commis la moindre erreur; **to put one's f. down** *(be firm)* faire preuve de fermeté; *(refuse)* mettre le holà; *Fam* **to put one's f. in it** faire une gaffe; **to find one's feet** s'adapter; **to get a f. in the door** avoir un pied dans la place; *Fam* **my f.!** mon œil!

2 *vt* **to f. the bill** payer la note

footage ['fʊtɪdʒ] *n Cin* séquences *fpl*, images *fpl*

foot-and-mouth disease [fʊtən'maʊθdɪ'zi:z] *n* fièvre *f* aphteuse

football ['fʊtbɔ:l] *n (soccer)* football *m*; *(American)* football américain; *(ball)* ballon *m* (de football); **f. club**

club *m* de foot(ball); f. **fan** supporter *m* d'une équipe de football; f. **ground** terrain *m* de football; f. **hooligan** hooligan *m*; f. **pitch** terrain de football; f. **player** footballeur(euse) *m,f*; *Br* f. **pools** ≃ loto *m* sportif; f. **supporter** supporter *mf* d'une équipe de football

footballer ['fʊtbɔ:lə(r)] *n* footballeur(euse) *m,f*

footbridge ['fʊtbrɪdʒ] *n* passerelle *f*

foothills ['fʊthɪlz] *npl* contreforts *mpl*

foothold ['fʊthəʊld] *n* prise *f* (pour le pied); *Fig* **to gain a f.** (of theory, feeling) se propager

footing ['fʊtɪŋ] *n* (a) (balance) **to lose one's f.** perdre l'équilibre (b) (level) **on an equal f.** sur un pied d'égalité; **to be on a friendly f. with sb** avoir des rapports amicaux avec qn

footlights ['fʊtlaɪts] *npl Th* rampe *f*

footloose ['fʊtlu:s] *adj* libre; **to be f. and fancy-free** être libre comme l'air

footman ['fʊtmən] *n* valet *m* de pied

footnote ['fʊtnəʊt] *n* note *f* de bas de page; *Fig* détail *m*

footpath ['fʊtpɑ:θ] *n* sentier *m*

footprint ['fʊtprɪnt] *n* trace *f* de pas; (of bare foot) empreinte *f* de pied

footrest ['fʊtrest] *n* repose-pieds *m inv*

footsie ['fʊtsɪ] *n Fam* **to play f. with sb** faire du pied à qn

footsore ['fʊtsɔ:(r)] *adj* **to be f.** avoir mal aux pieds

footstep ['fʊtstep] *n* pas *m*; *Fig* **to follow in sb's footsteps** suivre les traces de qn

footwear ['fʊtweə(r)] *n* chaussures *fpl*

footwork ['fʊtwɜ:k] *n* jeu *m* de jambes; *Fig* **it required some rather fancy f.** il a fallu faire des pieds et des mains

fop [fɒp] *n* dandy *m*

foppish ['fɒpɪʃ] *adj* de dandy

for [fɔ:(r), unstressed fə(r)] **1** *prep* (a) (expressing purpose, destination) pour; **to leave f. France** partir pour la France; **there's no time f. that** il n'y a pas de temps pour ça; **what's it f.?** c'est pour quoi faire?; **can you give me something f. the pain?** pouvez-vous me donner quelque chose contre la douleur?
(b) (because of) pour, en raison de; **she couldn't sleep f. the pain** elle ne pouvait pas dormir à cause de la douleur
(c) (expressing cost, amount) **I bought it f. £10** je l'ai acheté 10 livres; **a cheque f. £50** un chèque de 50 livres
(d) (considering) pour; **he is big f. his age** il est grand pour son âge; **f. all the good it will do you** pour ce que ça changera; **f. all his wealth, he was still unhappy** en dépit de toutes ses richesses, il était toujours malheureux
(e) (representing) **A f. Anne** A comme Anne; **what's the French f. "book"?** comment dit-on "book" en français?
(f) (duration) **I was there f. a month** je suis resté là-bas (pendant) un mois; **I've been here f. a month** il y a un mois que je suis ici, je suis ici depuis un mois; **I will be here f. a month** je serai ici pendant un mois; **I haven't been there f. a month** je n'y suis pas allé depuis un mois; **I'm going away f. a fortnight** je pars pour quinze jours; **we have enough food f. two days** nous avons suffisamment à manger pour deux jours
(g) (with point in time) **f. the first/last time** pour la première/dernière fois; **I need it f. Friday** j'en ai besoin pour vendredi
(h) (as compared to) pour; **they sell ten red bikes f. every black one** ils vendent dix vélos rouges pour un noir
(i) (in favour of) **to be f. sth** être pour qch, être favorable à

qch; *Fam* **I'm all f. it!** je suis tout à fait pour!
(j) (introducing an infinitive clause) **it is too early f. me to decide** il est trop tôt pour que je prenne une décision; **it will be difficult f. her to come** il lui sera difficile de venir; **it took an hour f. us to get there** il nous a fallu une heure pour arriver là-bas
(k) (idioms) **f. all I know** pour ce que j'en sais; **that's men f. you!** c'est bien les hommes!; *Fam* **he's f. it!** qu'est-ce qu'il va prendre!

2 *conj Lit* (because) car

forage ['fɒrɪdʒ] **1** *n* (animal food) fourrage *m*; *Mil* **f. cap** calot *m*
2 *vi* **to f. for sth** fouiller pour trouver qch

foray ['fɒreɪ] *n* incursion *f* (into dans)

forbear [fɔ:'beə(r)] (pt forbore [fɔ:'bɔ:(r)], pp forborne [fɔ:'bɔ:n]) *vi Formal* **to f. to do sth** s'abstenir de faire qch

forbearance [fɔ:'beərəns] *n Formal* patience *f*

forbid [fə'bɪd] (pt forbade [fə'bæd, fə'beɪd], pp forbidden [fə'bɪdən]) *vt* interdire; **to f. sb to do sth** interdire à qn de faire qch; **smoking is forbidden** il est interdit de fumer; **God f.!** Dieu m'en/nous en préserve!

forbidding [fə'bɪdɪŋ] *adj* (appearance, look, landscape) sinistre; (task) rébarbatif(ive)

force [fɔ:s] **1** *n* (a) (strength, power, influence) force *f*; **by sheer or brute f.** par la force; **by f. of circumstance(s)** par la force des circonstances; **f. of habit** la force de l'habitude; **several forces conspired to bring about his downfall** plusieurs facteurs ont contribué à provoquer sa chute (b) *Mil* **the (armed) forces** les forces *fpl* armées; **to join forces (to do sth)** joindre ses efforts (pour faire qch); **they turned out in (full) f.** ils sont venus en masse (c) (effect) **to come into f.** entrer en vigueur

2 *vt* (a) (compel) **to f. sb to do sth** or **into doing sth** forcer ou obliger qn à faire qch; **to f. sth on sb** imposer qch à qn; **they forced the enemy back** ils ont repoussé l'ennemi (par la force); **to f. the issue** précipiter les choses; **to f. sb's hand** forcer la main à qn; **to f. one's way through a crowd** se frayer un passage à travers la foule; **to f. oneself on sb** (sexually) essayer d'abuser de qn physiquement

▸**force down** *vt sep* (a) (aircraft) obliger à atterrir (b) (food) se forcer à avaler

▸**force open** *vt sep* (door, window, lock) forcer

forced [fɔ:st] *adj* (manner, laugh) forcé(e), artificiel(elle); **f. labour** travail *m* forcé; *Av* **f. landing** atterrissage *m* forcé; *Mil* **f. march** marche *f* forcée

force-feed ['fɔ:s'fi:d] (pt & pp force-fed ['fɔ:s'fed]) *vt* (person) nourrir de force; (livestock) gaver

forceful ['fɔ:sfəl] *adj* (person, language) énergique; (argument) puissant(e)

forceps ['fɔ:seps] *npl* forceps *mpl*; **f. delivery** accouchement *m* aux forceps

forcible ['fɔ:səbəl] *adj* (a) *Law* **f. entry** entrée *f* par effraction (b) (argument) puissant(e); (reminder) brutal(e)

forcibly ['fɔ:sɪblɪ] *adv* (a) (by force) de force (b) (argue) vigoureusement

ford [fɔ:d] **1** *n* gué *m*
2 *vt* traverser à gué

fore [fɔ:(r)] **1** *n* **to come to the f.** (of person) commencer à être connu(e); (of issue) être mis(e) en évidence
2 *adj Naut* à l'avant

forearm ['fɔ:rɑ:m] *n* avant-bras *m inv*

forebear ['fɔ:beə(r)] *n* ancêtre *mf*

foreboding [fɔːˈbəʊdɪŋ] n (mauvais) pressentiment m

forecast [ˈfɔːkɑːst] **1** n prévisions fpl; (in horseracing) pronostics mpl (of the courses); **(weather) f.** prévisions météorologiques, météo f
2 vt (pt & pp **forecast(ed))** prévoir; (in horseracing) pronostiquer

foreclose [fɔːˈkləʊz] vt Fin **to f. a mortgage** saisir un immeuble hypothéqué

forecourt [ˈfɔːkɔːt] n (of petrol station) devant m

forefathers [ˈfɔːfɑːðəz] npl aïeux mpl

forefinger [ˈfɔːfɪŋgə(r)] n index m

forefront [ˈfɔːfrʌnt] n **to be in the f. of** être au premier plan de

forego [fɔːˈgəʊ] (pt **forewent** [fɔːˈwent], pp **foregone** [fɔːˈgɒn]) vt renoncer à

foregone [ˈfɔːgɒn] **to be a f. conclusion** être couru(e) d'avance

foreground [ˈfɔːgraʊnd] **1** n premier plan m; **in the f.** au premier plan
2 vt mettre au premier plan

forehand [ˈfɔːhænd] n (in tennis) coup m droit; **f. volley** volée f de face

forehead [ˈfɒrɪd, ˈfɔːhed] n front m

foreign [ˈfɒrɪn] adj étranger(ère); **f. affairs** les affaires fpl étrangères; **f. aid** aide f aux pays étrangers; (from point of view of recipient) aide de l'étranger; Med **f. body** corps m étranger; Journ **f. correspondent** correspondant(e) m,f à l'étranger; **f. currency** devises fpl étrangères; **f. legion** légion f étrangère; Pol **F. Minister**, Br **F. Secretary** ministre m des Affaires étrangères; Br Pol **F. Office** ministère m des Affaires étrangères; **f. trade** commerce m extérieur

foreigner [ˈfɒrɪnə(r)] n étranger(ère) m,f

foreleg [ˈfɔːleg] n patte f de devant; (of horse) membre m antérieur

foreman [ˈfɔːmən] n (of workers) contremaître m; (of jury) président m

foremost [ˈfɔːməʊst] adj le (la) plus important(e)

forename [ˈfɔːneɪm] n prénom m

forensic [fəˈrensɪk] adj Law légal(e); **f. evidence** résultats mpl des expertises médico-légales; **f. medicine** médecine f légale; **f. scientist** médecin m légiste

foreplay [ˈfɔːpleɪ] n préliminaires mpl amoureux

forerunner [ˈfɔːrʌnə(r)] n **(a)** (person) précurseur m (of de) **(b)** (sign) signe m précurseur (of de)

foresee [fɔːˈsiː] (pt **foresaw** [fɔːˈsɔː], pp **foreseen** [fɔːˈsiːn]) vt prévoir

foreseeable [fɔːˈsiːəbəl] adj prévisible; **in the f. future** dans un avenir proche; **for the f. future** dans l'immédiat

foreshadow [fɔːˈʃædəʊ] vt annoncer

foresight [ˈfɔːsaɪt] n prévoyance f

foreskin [ˈfɔːskɪn] n Anat prépuce m

forest [ˈfɒrɪst] n forêt f; **f. fire** incendie m de forêt

forestall [fɔːˈstɔːl] vt devancer

forester [ˈfɒrɪstə(r)] n (garde m) forestier m

forestry [ˈfɒrɪstrɪ] n sylviculture f; **the F. Commission** ≃ Les Eaux et Forêts fpl; **f. worker** (forester) forestier m; (lumberjack) bûcheron m

foretaste [ˈfɔːteɪst] n avant-goût m (of de)

foretell [fɔːˈtel] (pt & pp **foretold** [fɔːˈtəʊld]) vt prédire

forethought [ˈfɔːθɔːt] n prévoyance f

forever [fəˈrevə(r)] adv **(a)** (eternally) pour toujours; **nothing lasts f.** tout a une fin; **the journey seemed to last f.** il semblait que le voyage ne finirait jamais **(b)** (repeatedly) sans cesse; **he was f. changing his mind** il changeait sans cesse ou constamment d'avis **(c)** Fam (a long time) une éternité; **to take f. (to do sth)** mettre un temps infini (à faire qch)

forewarn [fɔːˈwɔːn] vt prévenir, avertir; Prov **forewarned is forearmed** un homme averti en vaut deux

forewent [fɔːˈwent] pt of **forego**

foreword [ˈfɔːwɜːd] n avant-propos m inv, préface f

forfeit [ˈfɔːfɪt] n **1** (in game) gage m; Law amende f
2 vt (rights) être déchu(e) de; (property) se faire confisquer; (someone's respect) perdre

forgave [fəˈgeɪv] pt of **forgive**

forge [fɔːdʒ] **1** n forge f
2 vt **(a)** (metal, alliance) forger **(b)** (cheque, signature, banknote) contrefaire; **to f. a document/passport** faire un faux document/passeport

▶ **forge ahead** vi **(a)** (make progress) faire des progrès; (of company) aller de l'avant **(b)** (outstrip competitors) prendre de l'avance (**of** sur)

forged [fɔːdʒd] adj faux (fausse)

forgery [ˈfɔːdʒərɪ] (pl **forgeries**) n **(a)** (activity) contrefaçon f; (of document, banknote) falsification f **(b)** (thing forged) faux (fausse) m,f

forget [fəˈget] (pt **forgot** [fəˈgɒt], pp **forgotten** [fəˈgɒtən]) **1** vt oublier; **to f. to do sth** oublier de faire qch; **to f. how to do sth** oublier comment on fait qch, ne plus savoir faire qch; **to be forgotten** tomber dans l'oubli; **f. it!** (in reply to apology, thanks) il n'y a pas de quoi!; (stop talking about it) laisse tomber!
2 vi oublier; **to f. about sb/sth** oublier qn/qch; **you can f. about going to London!** tu peux faire une croix sur ton voyage à Londres! **let's f. about it** n'y pensons plus

forgetful [fəˈgetfʊl] adj **to be f.** avoir mauvaise mémoire

forget-me-not [fəˈgetmɪnɒt] n myosotis m

forgivable [fəˈgɪvəbəl] adj excusable, pardonnable

forgive [fəˈgɪv] (pt **forgave** [fəˈgeɪv], pp **forgiven** [fəˈgɪvən]) **1** vt pardonner; **to f. sb for sth** pardonner qch à qn; **if you'll f. the pun** pardonnez-moi ce jeu de mots; **f. me for interrupting** pardonnez-moi de vous interrompre
2 vi pardonner; **to f. and forget** oublier sa rancune

forgiveness [fəˈgɪvnɪs] n pardon m

forgiving [fəˈgɪvɪŋ] adj indulgent(e)

forgo [fɔːˈgəʊ] = **forego**

forgot [fəˈgɒt] pt of **forget**

forgotten [fəˈgɒtən] pp of **forget**

fork [fɔːk] **1** n **(a)** (for food) fourchette f **(b)** (for gardening) fourche f **(c)** (in road, path) bifurcation f
2 vi (of road, path) bifurquer

▶ **fork out** Fam **1** vt sep allonger
2 vi casquer (**for** pour)

forked [fɔːkt] adj (stick, tongue) fourchu(e); **f. lightning** éclairs mpl

fork-lift truck [ˈfɔːklɪft ˈtrʌk] n chariot m (élévateur) à fourche

forlorn [fəˈlɔːn] adj (person, look) triste, malheureux(euse); (hope, attempt) désespéré(e)

form [fɔːm] **1** n **(a)** *(shape) (of object, animal)* forme f; *(of person)* silhouette f; **to take the f. of sth** prendre la forme de qch **(b)** *(type)* forme f; **in the f. of** sous forme de; **f. of address** titre m de politesse **(c)** *(politeness)* **as a matter of f., for f.'s sake** pour la forme, par pure formalité; **it's good/bad f. to...** cela se fait/ne se fait pas de... **(d)** *(for applications, orders)* formulaire m **(e)** *(condition, performance)* forme f; *(in horseracing)* performances fpl; **to be in** or **on good f.** être en forme; **on present f.** si l'on en juge par la situation actuelle **(f)** Br Sch *(class, year)* classe f

2 vt *(government, character)* former; *(idea)* avoir; *(opinion)* se faire, se former; *(relationship, friendship)* nouer; *(organization, obstacle)* constituer; **to f. a plan to do sth** projeter de faire qch; **to f. part of sth** faire partie de qch

3 vi se former

formal [ˈfɔːməl] adj *(manner)* cérémonieux(euse); *(offer, occasion, invitation)* officiel(elle); *(language)* soutenu(e); **f. dress** tenue f de soirée

formality [fɔːˈmælɪtɪ] *(pl* **formalities***)* n *(procedure)* formalité f

formalize [ˈfɔːməlaɪz] vt officialiser

formally [ˈfɔːmalɪ] adv *(behave)* de façon cérémonieuse; *(invite, announce)* officiellement; **to dress f.** porter une tenue de soirée

format [ˈfɔːmæt] **1** n format m

2 vt *(pt & pp* **formatted***)* Comptr formater

formation [fɔːˈmeɪʃən] n *(act, arrangement)* formation f; *(of idea, plan)* élaboration f

formative [ˈfɔːmətɪv] adj formateur(trice); **the f. years** les années fpl de formation

former [ˈfɔːmə(r)] **1** pron **the f.** celui-là (celle-la); *(plural)* ceux-là (celles-là)

2 adj *(pupil, colleague, job)* ancien(enne) *(before noun)*; **in f. times** autrefois; **in a f. life** dans une vie antérieure

formerly [ˈfɔːməlɪ] adv autrefois; **Mrs Connelly, f. Miss Paton** Mme Connelly, née Paton; **Zambia, f. Northern Rhodesia** la Zambie, ancienne Rhodésie du Nord

formidable [ˈfɔːmɪdəbəl] adj *(opponent, difficulty)* redoutable; *(performance, talent)* formidable

formula [ˈfɔːmjʊlə] *(pl* **formulas** or **formulae** [ˈfɔːmjʊliː]*)* n **(a)** *(scheme, in maths, chemistry)* formule f; **the f. for success** la clé de la réussite; **a peace f.** une solution en faveur de la paix; Aut Fl. **1** formule 1 **(b)** Am *(baby food)* lait m en poudre

formulate [ˈfɔːmjʊleɪt] vt *(plan, proposal)* élaborer; *(thought, opinion)* formuler

fornication [fɔːnɪˈkeɪʃən] n Formal fornication f

forsake [fəˈseɪk] *(pt* **forsook** [fəˈsʊk], *pp* **forsaken** [fəˈseɪkən]*)* vt Lit *(abandon)* abandonner **(b)** *(renounce)* renoncer à

forswear [fɔːˈsweə(r)] *(pt* **forswore** [fɔːˈswɔː(r)], *pp* **forsworn** [fɔːˈswɔːn]*)* vt Lit renoncer à

fort [fɔːt] n fort m, forteresse f; Fig **to hold the f.** monter la garde

forte [ˈfɔːtɪ] n fort m

forth [fɔːθ] adv en avant; **to go f.** avancer; **to walk back and f.** marcher de long en large, faire les cent pas; **from that day f.** à dater de ce jour; **and so f.** et cetera, et ainsi de suite

forthcoming [fɔːθˈkʌmɪŋ] adj **(a)** *(election)* prochain(e); *(book, film)* qui sortira bientôt **(b)** *(available)* **no money was f.** l'argent n'est pas arrivé **(c)** *(informative)* expansif(ive) *(about* sur)

forthright [ˈfɔːθraɪt] adj franc (franche)

forthwith [fɔːθˈwɪθ] adv Formal immédiatement, sur-le-champ

fortieth [ˈfɔːtɪəθ] **1** n **(a)** *(fraction)* quarantième m **(b)** *(in series)* quarantième mf

2 adj quarantième

fortification [fɔːtɪfɪˈkeɪʃən] n fortification f

fortified [ˈfɔːtɪfaɪd] adj **(a)** *(town)* fortifié(e) **(b)** **f. wine** vin m viné

fortify [ˈfɔːtɪfaɪ] *(pt & pp* **fortified***)* vt Mil fortifier; **to f. oneself** se prémunir

fortitude [ˈfɔːtɪtjuːd] n force f morale

fortnight [ˈfɔːtnaɪt] n Br quinzaine f, quinze jours mpl; **a f. today** aujourd'hui en quinze; **a f.'s holiday** quinze jours ou deux semaines fpl de vacances

fortnightly [ˈfɔːtnaɪtlɪ] Br **1** adj bimensuel(elle)

2 adv tous les quinze jours, bimensuellement

fortress [ˈfɔːtrɪs] n forteresse f

fortuitous [fɔːˈtjuːɪtəs] adj fortuit(e)

fortunate [ˈfɔːtʃənət] adj heureux(euse); **to be f.** avoir de la chance; **to be f. enough to do sth** avoir la chance de faire qch

fortunately [ˈfɔːtʃənətlɪ] adv heureusement, par bonheur

fortune [ˈfɔːtʃən] n **(a)** *(riches)* fortune f; **to make a** or **one's f.** faire fortune; **to cost a f.** coûter une fortune ou les yeux de la tête **(b)** *(luck)* chance f; **good f.** chance; **bad f.** malchance f; **to tell sb's f.** dire la bonne aventure à qn

fortune-teller [ˈfɔːtʃəntelə(r)] n diseur(euse) m,f de bonne aventure

forty [ˈfɔːtɪ] **1** n quarante m inv

2 adj quarante; Fam **to have f. winks** piquer ou faire un petit somme; see also **eighty**

forum [ˈfɔːrəm] n forum m; Comptr *(on Internet)* groupe m de discussions; **a f. for debate** un lieu de débat

forward [ˈfɔːwəd] **1** n *(in sport)* avant m

2 adj **(a)** *(position)* avant inv; *(movement)* en avant, vers l'avant; **f. planning** planification f; Fin **f. market** marché m à terme **(b)** *(impudent, bold)* effronté(e), hardi(e)

3 adv **(a)** *(of time)* **from this/that day f.** à partir d'aujourd'hui/de ce jour-là; **to put the clocks f.** avancer les pendules **(b)** *(of direction)* en avant; **to walk f.** avancer **(c)** *(of position)* à l'avant; **we're sitting too far f.** *(in cinema, theatre)* nous sommes assis trop près; **the seat is too far f.** le siège est trop avancé

4 vt **(a)** *(letter)* faire suivre; *(complaint, query)* faire passer *(to* à) **(b)** *(one's career, interests)* favoriser

forwarding agent [ˈfɔːwədɪŋˈeɪdʒənt] n Com *(agent m)* transitaire m

forward-looking [ˈfɔːwədlʊkɪŋ] adj progressiste

forwards [ˈfɔːwədz] adv = **forward**

fossil [ˈfɒsəl] n fossile m; Fam **an old f.** *(man)* un vieux croûton; *(woman)* une vieille bique; **f. fuel** combustible m fossile

fossilized [ˈfɒsɪlaɪzd] adj fossilisé(e); Fig sclérosé(e)

foster [ˈfɒstə(r)] **1** adj **f. child** = enfant placé dans une famille d'accueil; **f. parents** famille f d'accueil, parents mpl nourriciers

2 vt **(a)** *(child)* prendre en famille d'accueil **(b)** *(idea, hope)* nourrir, entretenir; *(friendship)* stimuler

fought [fɔːt] pt & pp of **fight**

foul [faʊl] **1** n (in sport) faute f
2 adj (a) (disgusting) (smell, taste) infect(e), nauséabond(e); (weather) sale; (air) vicié(e); (language) ordurier(ère); **to be in a f. mood** être d'une humeur massacrante (b) (illegal) **f. play** Sp jeu m irrégulier; Law acte m criminel
3 adv (a) **to smell f.** puer; **to taste f.** avoir un goût infect (b) **to fall f. of the law** avoir des démêlés avec la justice
4 vt (a) (pollute) salir (b) (entangle) s'enchevêtrer autour de (c) (in sport) commettre une faute contre
▶ **foul up** vt sep Fam (ruin) gâcher

foul-mouthed [faʊl'maʊðd] adj au langage ordurier ou grossier

found[1] [faʊnd] vt (a) (city, organization) fonder; (company) créer; (empire) établir (b) (base) baser, fonder (**on** sur)

found[2] pt & pp of **find**

foundation [faʊn'deɪʃən] n (a) (of city, organization) fondation f; (of company) création f (b) (basis) fondement m, base f; **to be without f.** être dénué(e) de fondement (c) **foundations** (of building, society) fondations fpl (d) (make-up) **f. (cream)** fond m de teint

founder[1] ['faʊndə(r)] n (of hospital, school) fondateur(trice) m,f; **f. member** membre m fondateur

founder[2] vi (of ship) s'échouer; Fig (of project, talks) avorter

founding father ['faʊndɪŋ'fɑ:ðə(r)] n père m fondateur

foundling ['faʊndlɪŋ] n Old-fashioned enfant mf trouvé(e)

foundry ['faʊndrɪ] n (pl **foundries**) fonderie f

fount [faʊnt] n Lit & Fig source f

fountain ['faʊntɪn] n fontaine f; **f. pen** stylo m (à) plume

four [fɔː(r)] **1** n quatre m inv; **on all fours** à quatre pattes
2 adj quatre; **to the f. corners of the earth** aux quatre coins du monde; see also **eight**

four-eyes [fɔː'raɪz] n Fam binoclard(e) m,f

four-figure ['fɔː'fɪgə(r)] adj **a f. sum** un montant de quatre chiffres

fourfold ['fɔːfəʊld] **1** adj **a f. increase** une augmentation au quadruple
2 adv **to increase f.** quadrupler

four-legged ['fɔː'legɪd] adj quadrupède; Hum **f. friend** ami m à quatre pattes

four-letter word ['fɔːletə'wɜːd] n gros mot m

four-poster ['fɔː'pəʊstə(r)] n **f. (bed)** lit m à baldaquin

foursome ['fɔːsəm] n groupe m de quatre personnes

fourteen [fɔː'tiːn] **1** n quatorze m inv
2 adj quatorze; see also **eight**

fourteenth [fɔː'tiːnθ] **1** n (a) (fraction) quatorzième m (b) (in series) quatorzième mf (c) (of month) quatorze m inv
2 adj quatorzième; see also **eighth**

fourth [fɔːθ] **1** n (a) (fraction) quatrième m (b) (in series) quatrième mf (c) (of month) quatre m inv
2 adj quatrième; see also **eighth**

fourthly ['fɔːθlɪ] adv quatrièmement

fowl [faʊl] n (pl **fowl**) volaille f

fox [fɒks] **1** n renard m; Fig **a sly old f.** (cunning person) un vieux renard; **f. cub** renardeau m; **f. hunt** chasse f au renard
2 vt (perplex) laisser perplexe; (deceive) duper

foxglove ['fɒksglʌv] n digitale f (pourprée)

fox-hunting ['fɒkshʌntɪŋ] n chasse f au renard

foxtrot ['fɒkstrɒt] n fox-trot m inv

foxy ['fɒksɪ] adj (a) Fam (sly) rusé(e) (b) Am Fam sexy inv

foyer ['fɔɪeɪ] n (in theatre) foyer m; (in cinema, hotel) hall m

fraction ['frækʃən] n (in maths) fraction f; Fig (small part) petite partie f; **a f. too small/large** un tout petit peu trop petit(e)/grand(e)

fractional ['frækʃənəl] adj (very small) infime

fractious ['frækʃəs] adj (adult) de mauvaise humeur; (baby) pleurnicheur(euse); (tone, expression) irrité(e)

fracture ['fræktʃə(r)] **1** n fracture f
2 vt (bone) fracturer; (pipe) fendre
3 vi (of bone) se fracturer; (of pipe) se fendre

fragile ['frædʒaɪl] adj fragile; Fam **I'm feeling a bit f. this morning** (after drinking) j'ai un peu la gueule de bois ce matin

fragility [frə'dʒɪlɪtɪ] n fragilité f

fragment 1 n ['frægmənt] fragment m; **I only heard a f. of what was said** je n'ai entendu que des bribes de la conversation
2 vi [fræg'ment] (of object) se fragmenter; (of organization) éclater

fragrance ['freɪgrəns] n parfum m

fragrant ['freɪgrənt] adj odorant(e), parfumé(e)

frail [freɪl] adj (person) frêle; (object) fragile

frailty ['freɪltɪ] n faiblesse f

frame [freɪm] **1** n (a) (of picture) cadre m, encadrement m; (of door, window) encadrement (b) (of person, animal) ossature f; (of building, bridge) charpente f; (of bicycle) cadre m; (of spectacles) monture f (c) **f. of mind** état m d'esprit; **f. of reference** système m de référence
2 vt (a) (surround) encadrer (b) (compose) (answer) formuler; (law) rédiger (c) Fam (falsely incriminate) monter un coup contre

franc [fræŋk] n (currency) franc m; **Belgian/French/Swiss f.** franc belge/français/suisse

France [frɑːns] n la France

franchise ['fræntʃaɪz] **1** n (a) Com franchise f (b) Pol droit m de vote
2 vt Com franchiser

francophile ['fræŋkəʊfaɪl] n & adj francophile mf

francophone ['fræŋkəʊfəʊn] n & adj francophone mf

frank [fræŋk] **1** adj franc (franche); **to be f....** pour être franc...
2 vt (letter) affranchir

Frankfurt ['fræŋkfɜːt] n Francfort

frankfurter ['fræŋkfɜːtə(r)] n saucisse f de Francfort

frankincense ['fræŋkɪnsens] n encens m

frankly ['fræŋklɪ] adv franchement

frantic ['fræntɪk] adj (rush, pace) frénétique; (attempt, effort) désespéré(e); **f. with worry** fou (folle) d'inquiétude

frantically ['fræntɪklɪ] adv frénétiquement; (work, write) avec frénésie; (try) désespérément

fraternal [frə'tɜːnəl] adj fraternel(elle)

fraternity [frə'tɜːnɪtɪ] n (pl **fraternities**) n (a) (brotherliness) fraternité f (b) (group) confrérie f; **the banking/medical f.** la confrérie des banquiers/médecins (c) Am Univ = organisation d'étudiants; **f. house** = maison communautaire (d'étudiants d'une même organisation)

fraternize ['frætənaɪz] vi fraterniser (**with** avec)

fraud [frɔːd] n (a) (person) imposteur m (b) (deception) supercherie f; (crime) fraude f; **the F. Squad** ≃ (le service de) la Répression des Fraudes

fraudulent ['frɔ:djʊlənt] *adj (charge, accusation, feelings)* faux (fausse); *(claim, transaction)* frauduleux(euse)

fraught [frɔ:t] *adj (person, situation)* tendu(e); *(day)* éprouvant(e); **f. with danger** rempli(e) d'embûches; **f. with emotion** chargé(e) d'émotion

fray¹ [freɪ] *n (brawl)* bagarre *f*; **to enter the f.** entrer dans l'arène

fray² 1 *vt (material)* user
2 *vi (of material)* s'user; *(of tempers)* s'échauffer; *(of nerves)* craquer

frazzle ['fræzəl] *n* **to be burnt to a f.** *(of food)* être carbonisé(e); *(of person)* être brûlé(e) par le soleil

frazzled ['fræzəld] *adj Fam (person)* lessivé(e), épuisé(e); *(nerves)* à plat

freak [fri:k] *n* **(a)** *(strange being)* monstre *m*, phénomène *m*; **f. show** exhibition *f* de monstres **(b)** *(strange event)* **by a f. of fortune** par un coup de chance; **f. accident** accident *m* imprévisible; **f. storm** orage *m* inattendu **(c)** *(enthusiast)* fana *mf*; **jazz/film f.** fana de jazz/cinéma
2 *vi* = **freak out**

▶**freak out** *Fam* 1 *vt sep (shock, scare)* faire flipper
2 *vi (panic)* paniquer; *(become angry)* piquer une crise

freckle ['frekəl] *n* tache *f* de rousseur

free [fri:] 1 *adj* **(a)** *(unrestricted)* libre (**from** *or* de); *(movement)* dégagé(e); **to be f. of sb** être débarrassé(e) de qn; **f. from worry** sans souci; **to be f. to do sth** être libre de faire qch; **to set sb f.** rendre sa liberté à qn; **f. and easy** décontracté(e); *Fam* **feel f. to borrow the car** n'hésitez pas à emprunter la voiture; (**as**) **f. as a bird** libre comme l'air; **to be a f. agent** être libre (de ses mouvements); *Fig* **to have a f. hand** avoir pleine liberté d'action; *Econ* **f. enterprise** libre entreprise *f*; **f. fall** *(of parachutist, economy)* chute *f* libre; **f. kick** *(in football)* coup *m* franc; *Econ* **f. market** économie *f* de marché; **f. speech** liberté *f* d'expression; **f. throw** *(in basketball)* lancer *m* franc; **f. trade** libre-échange *m*; **f. verse** vers *mpl* libres; **f. will** libre arbitre *m*; **to do sth of one's own f. will** faire qch de son plein gré
(b) *(unoccupied)* *(person, seat, table, time)* libre
(c) *(without charge)* gratuit(e); **f. gift** cadeau *m*
(d) *(generous)* **to be f. with one's advice** être prodigue en conseils
2 *adv (without charge)* gratuitement; **to do sth for f.** faire qch gratuitement
3 *vt (pt & pp* **freed** [fri:d]) *(prisoner, time, place)* libérer (**from** de); *(something stuck)* dégager (**from** de); **to f. oneself from** *or* **of sth** se libérer de qch

freedom ['fri:dəm] *n* liberté *f*; **to have the f. to do sth** être libre de faire qch; **f. of information** libre accès *m* à l'information; **f. of speech/worship** liberté d'expression/de culte; **to give sb the f. of the city** nommer qn citoyen(enne) *m,f* d'honneur de la ville; **f. fighter** guérillero *m*, révolutionnaire *mf*

free-for-all ['fri:fərɔ:l] *n* mêlée *f*, bagarre *f*

freehold ['fri:həʊld] *n Law* propriété *f* foncière perpétuelle et libre

freeholder ['fri:həʊldə(r)] *n* propriétaire *m* foncier (à perpétuité)

freelance ['fri:lɑ:ns] 1 *n* travailleur(euse) *m,f* indépendant(e)
2 *adj* indépendant(e), free-lance *inv*
3 *adv* **to work f.** travailler en indépendant(e) *ou* en free-lance
4 *vi* travailler en indépendant(e) *ou* en free-lance

freeloader ['fri:ləʊdə(r)] *n Fam* pique-assiette *mf inv*, parasite *m*

freely ['fri:lɪ] *adv (give)* sans compter; *(speak)* en toute liberté; *(spend)* libéralement; **f. available** *(for sale)* en vente libre; *(easy to get hold of)* qu'on peut se procurer facilement

freemason ['fri:meɪsən] *n* franc-maçon *m*

freemasonry ['fri:meɪsənrɪ] *n* franc-maçonnerie *f*

Freepost® ['fri:pəʊst] *n Br* ≃ correspondance-réponse *f*

free-range ['fri:'reɪndʒ] *adj* de ferme

freestyle ['fri:staɪl] *n (in swimming)* nage *f* libre

freethinker ['fri:θɪŋkə(r)] *n* libre-penseur(euse) *m,f*

freeway ['fri:weɪ] *n Am* autoroute *f*

freewheel ['fri:wi:l] *vi (on bicycle)* être en roue libre; *(in car)* rouler au point mort

freeze [fri:z] 1 *n (in weather)* gel *m*, gelée *f*; **price/wage f.** gel des prix/salaires
2 *vt (pt* **froze** [frəʊz], *pp* **frozen** ['frəʊzən]) *(food)* congeler; *(prices, assets)* geler; **to be frozen to death** être mort(e) de froid
3 *vi* **(a)** *(of weather)* **it's freezing** *(below zero)* il gèle; *Fig (very cold)* on gèle **(b)** *(of liquid, food)* geler; **to f. to death** mourir de froid; *Fam* **I'm freezing** je suis gelé **(c)** *(stand still)* s'arrêter net, se figer; **f.!** ne bougez plus!

▶**freeze out** *vt sep Fam* **to f. sb out** *(of conversation, deal)* exclure qn; *Com* **to f. out the competition** évincer les concurrents

▶**freeze over** *vi (of pond, river)* geler

▶**freeze up** *vi (of mechanism)* geler

freeze-dried ['fri:z'draɪd] *adj (coffee, herbs)* lyophilisé(e)

freeze-frame ['fri:z'freɪm] *n Cin* arrêt *m* sur image

freezer ['fri:zə(r)] *n* congélateur *m*; *(ice-box)* freezer *m*

freezing ['fri:zɪŋ] **f. (cold)** *(room, weather, temperature)* glacial(e); *(water)* glacé(e); **it's f. cold in here** on meurt de froid ici

freight [freɪt] *Com* 1 *n (transport)* fret *m*, transport *m* de marchandises; *(goods)* cargaison *f*; *(price)* prix *m* de transport; **f. train** train *m* de marchandises
2 *vt (goods)* transporter

freighter ['freɪtə(r)] *n (ship)* cargo *m*

French [frentʃ] 1 *n (language)* français *m*; *Hum* **pardon my F.** *(after swearing)* excusez mon langage; **F. class/teacher** classe *f*/professeur *m* de français
2 *npl* **the F.** *(people)* les Français *mpl*
3 *adj* français(e); **F. fries** frites *fpl*; **F. horn** cor *m* d'harmonie; **F. kiss** baiser *m* avec la langue; *Br Old-fashioned* **F. letter** capote *f* anglaise; **F. loaf** *or* **stick** baguette *f*; **F. Polynesia** la Polynésie Française; **F. window** porte-fenêtre *f*

Frenchman ['frentʃmən] *n* Français *m*

French-speaking ['frentʃ'spi:kɪŋ] *adj* francophone

Frenchwoman ['frentʃwʊmən] *n* Française *f*

frenetic [frə'netɪk] *adj* frénétique

frenzied ['frenzɪd] *adj (person)* affolé(e); *(attack)* déchaîné(e); *(activity)* frénétique; **f. with rage/worry** fou (folle) de rage/d'inquiétude

frenzy ['frenzɪ] *(pl* **frenzies**) *n* frénésie *f*, folie *f*; **to work oneself into a f.** se mettre dans tous ses états

frequency ['fri:kwənsɪ] *(pl* **frequencies**) *n* fréquence *f*; **f. band** bande *f* de fréquences

frequent 1 *adj* ['fri:kwənt] fréquent(e); **it's a f. occurrence** cela se produit souvent
2 *vt* [frɪ'kwent] fréquenter

frequently ['fri:kwəntlɪ] *adv* fréquemment, souvent

fresco ['freskəʊ] (*pl* **frescos** *or* **frescoes**) *n* fresque *f*

fresh [freʃ] 1 *adj* (a) (*food, news*) frais (fraîche); to smell f. sentir bon le frais; to get some f. air s'aérer; f. water (*not salty*) eau *f* douce; it's still f. in my mind c'est encore frais dans ma mémoire; as f. as a daisy frais et dispos *inv* (b) (*page, attempt, drink*) nouveau(elle) (*before noun*); to make a f. start recommencer à zéro (c) (*original*) (*approach, writing*) nouveau(elle), original(e) (d) *Am Fam* (*cheeky*) insolent(e); to get f. with sb (*sexually*) faire des avances à qn

2 *adv* f. from (*school, university*) frais émoulu(e) de; we're f. out of lemons nous n'avons plus de citrons

freshen ['freʃən] *vi* (*of wind, weather*) rafraîchir

▶**freshen up** *vi* (*wash*) faire un brin de toilette

fresher ['freʃə(r)] *n Br Univ* étudiant(e) *m,f* de première année; **freshers' week** = semaine d'orientation précédant la rentrée universitaire pour les nouveaux étudiants

freshly ['freʃlɪ] *adv* fraîchement; f. baked sortant du four; f. made qui vient d'être fait

freshman ['freʃmən] *n Am Univ* étudiant(e) *m,f* de première année

freshness ['freʃnɪs] *n* (a) (*of food*) fraîcheur *f* (b) (*originality*) nouveauté *f*, originalité *f*

freshwater ['freʃwɔːtə(r)] *adj* (*fish*) d'eau douce

fret [fret] (*pt & pp* **fretted**) *vi* (*worry*) s'inquiéter, se tourmenter

fretful ['fretfʊl] *adj* inquiet(ète)

Freudian ['frɔɪdɪən] *adj* freudien(enne); **F. slip** lapsus *m*

FRG [efɑː'dʒiː] *n* (*abbr* **Federal Republic of Germany**) RFA *f*

Fri (*abbr* **Friday**) vendredi

friar ['fraɪə(r)] *n* religieux *m*, moine *m*

fricassee [frɪkə'siː] *n* fricassée *f*

friction ['frɪkʃən] *n also Fig* friction *f*

Friday ['fraɪdɪ] *n* vendredi *m*; *see also* **Saturday**

fridge [frɪdʒ] *n* frigo *m*

fridge-freezer ['frɪdʒ'friːzə(r)] *n* frigo *m* avec congélateur

fried [fraɪd] *adj* frit(e)

friend [frend] *n* ami(e) *m,f*; to be friends with sb être ami avec qn; to make friends with sb devenir ami avec qn; that's what friends are for c'est à ça que servent les amis; we're just good friends nous sommes bons amis, c'est tout; he's no f. of mine ce n'est pas un ami; to have friends in high places avoir des amis bien placés; to be a f. of the arts être un défenseur des beaux-arts; *Prov* a f. in need is a f. indeed c'est dans le besoin que l'on connaît ses amis

friendless ['frendlɪs] *adj* (*person*) sans amis; (*childhood*) solitaire

friendly ['frendlɪ] 1 *n Sp* match *m* amical

2 *adj* amical(e); f. advice conseils *mpl* d'ami; a f. nation un pays ami; to be f. with sb être ami(e) avec qn; to be on f. terms with sb être en bons termes avec qn; *Mil* f. fire tirs *mpl* provenant de son propre camp

friendship ['frendʃɪp] *n* amitié *f*

fries [fraɪz] *npl* (**French**) f. frites *fpl*

frieze [friːz] *n Art & Archit* frise *f*

frigate ['frɪgət] *n* frégate *f*

fright [fraɪt] *n* peur *f*, effroi *m*; to take f. prendre peur; to get a f. avoir peur; to give sb a f. faire peur à qn; *Fam* to look a f. être à faire peur

frighten ['fraɪtən] *vt* effrayer, faire peur à; to f. sb into doing sth faire peur à qn jusqu'à ce qu'il fasse qch; *Fam* to f. the life *or* the wits out of sb rendre qn fou (folle) de peur

2 *vi* I don't f. easily je ne me laisse pas effrayer facilement

frightened ['fraɪtənd] *adj* apeuré(e); to be f. (of) avoir peur (de); to be f. to do sth avoir peur de faire qch

frightening ['fraɪtənɪŋ] *adj* effrayant(e)

frightful ['fraɪtfʊl] *adj* épouvantable, affreux(euse)

frightfully ['fraɪtfʊlɪ] *adv* terriblement

frigid ['frɪdʒɪd] *adj* (*sexually*) frigide; (*smile, atmosphere*) glacial(e)

frill [frɪl] *n* volant *m*; *Fig* with no frills (*ceremony*) sans chichis; (*holiday*) rudimentaire

frilly ['frɪlɪ] *adj* à volants

fringe [frɪndʒ] *n* (a) (*of hair, on clothes, lampshade*) frange *f* (b) (*edge*) (*of forest*) lisière *f*; (*of town*) abords *mpl*; on the fringes of society en marge de la société; f. benefits avantages *mpl* divers; *Pol* f. group groupuscule *m*; f. theatre théâtre *m* alternatif

frisk [frɪsk] 1 *vt* (*search*) fouiller

2 *vi* to f. about gambader

frisky ['frɪskɪ] *adj* (*person*) plein(e) d'entrain; (*horse*) nerveux(euse)

fritter ['frɪtə(r)] *n Culin* beignet *m*

▶**fritter away** *vt sep* gaspiller

frivolity [frɪ'vɒlɪtɪ] (*pl* **frivolities**) *n* frivolité *f*

frivolous ['frɪvələs] *adj* frivole; (*remark*) futile

frizzy ['frɪzɪ] *adj* crépu(e)

fro [frəʊ] *adv* to go to and f. aller et venir

frock [frɒk] *n* (*dress*) robe *f*; f. coat redingote *f*

frog [frɒg] *n* (a) (*animal*) grenouille *f*; *Fam* to have a f. in one's throat avoir un chat dans la gorge (b) *Br Fam* (*French person*) = terme xénophobe, souvent humoristique, désignant un Français

frogman ['frɒgmən] *n* homme-grenouille *m*

frogmarch ['frɒgmɑːtʃ] *vt* emmener de force

frogspawn ['frɒgspɔːn] *n* œufs *mpl* de grenouille

frolic ['frɒlɪk] (*pt & pp* **frolicked**) *vi* s'ébattre

from [frɒm, *unstressed* frəm] *prep* (a) (*expressing place of origin*) de; where are you f.?, where do you come f.? d'où êtes-vous?, d'où venez-vous?; she's f. Portugal elle vient du Portugal; f. Edinburgh to Paris d'Édimbourg à Paris; the train f. Manchester le train de Manchester; 10 km f. Paris à 10 km de Paris

(b) (*expressing time*) à partir de, f. tomorrow à partir de demain; f. then (on) depuis ce jour-là; f. the beginning dès le début; f. six to seven o'clock de six heures à sept heures; f. morning to *or* till night du matin au soir; five years f. now dans cinq ans; blind f. birth aveugle de naissance

(c) (*expressing range, change*) f.... to... de... à...; children f. seven to nine years les enfants de sept à neuf ans; wine f. £4 a bottle du vin à partir de 4 livres la bouteille

(d) (*expressing source*) de; to buy sth f. sb acheter qch à qn; to drink f. a cup boire dans une tasse; a quotation f. the Bible une citation tirée de la Bible; made f. rubber en caoutchouc

(e) (*expressing removal*) de; to take sth f. sb prendre qch à

qn; **he was banned f. the club** il a été exclu du club
(**f**) (on the basis of) **f. what I heard/saw…** d'après ce que
j'ai entendu/vu…

frond [frɒnd] n (of fern) fronde f; (of palm) feuille f

front [frʌnt] **1** n (**a**) (not back) devant m; (of car, plane, boat)
avant m; (of building) façade f; **on the f. of the book** sur la
couverture du livre; **at the f. of the book** au début du
livre; **I sat in the f.** (of car) j'étais assis devant; Br **the f.**
(at seaside) le front de mer, la promenade
(**b**) (outward appearance) **his kindness is only a f.** sa
gentillesse n'est qu'une façade; **the company is a f. for
their arms dealing** l'entreprise sert de couverture à leur
trafic d'armes; **f. man** (of TV, radio programme) présentateur
m; (of pop group, organization) leader m
(**c**) Mil, Pol & Met front m; **on all fronts** sur tous les
fronts; Met **warm/cold f.** front chaud/froid
(**d**) **in f.** devant; (in race, contest) en tête; **in f. of** devant
(**e**) Fam **to pay up f.** payer d'avance; **to be up f. about
sth** être franc (franche) au sujet de qch
2 adj de devant; Br Pol **f. bench** = le banc des ministres et
celui du cabinet fantôme; **f. door** porte f d'entrée; Mil **f.
line** front m; **f. cover** couverture f; **f. page** (of newspaper)
première page f; **f. room** (lounge) salon m; **f. row** premier
rang m; **to have a f.-row seat** (in theatre) être (assis(e)) au
premier rang; Fig être aux premières loges; **f. seat** (in car)
siège m avant; **f. teeth** dents fpl de devant; **f. view** vue f de
face
3 vt (organization, pop group) être à la tête de; (government)
diriger; (TV programme) présenter
4 vi (of building) **the house fronts onto the river** la
maison donne sur le fleuve

frontage [ˈfrʌntɪdʒ] n (of building) façade f; (of shop)
devanture f

frontal [ˈfrʌntəl] adj Anat frontal(e); Mil (attack) de front

frontier [ˈfrʌntɪə(r)] n frontière f; **the frontiers** (of
knowledge, science) les limites fpl; **f. guard** garde-frontière
m; **f. town** ville f frontalière

frontispiece [ˈfrʌntɪspiːs] n frontispice m

frontrunner [ˈfrʌntrʌnə(r)] n favori(ite) m,f

frost [frɒst] n gel m; Fig **there was a f.** il a gelé

▶**frost over, frost up** vi (of window) se couvrir de
givre

frostbite [ˈfrɒstbaɪt] n gelure f

frostbitten [ˈfrɒstbɪtən] adj gelé(e)

frosted [ˈfrɒstɪd] adj (glass) dépoli(e)

frosting [ˈfrɒstɪŋ] n Am (on cake) glaçage m

frosty [ˈfrɒstɪ] adj (night, air) glacé(e); Fig (welcome, smile)
glacial(e)

froth [frɒθ] **1** n (on beer, cappuccino) mousse f; (on waves)
écume f
2 vi (of liquid) mousser; **he was frothing at the mouth**
il bavait; (with anger) il écumait de rage

frothy [ˈfrɒθɪ] adj (beer, cappuccino) mousseux(euse)

frown [fraʊn] **1** n froncement m de sourcils
2 vi froncer les sourcils; **to f. at sb** regarder qn en
fronçant les sourcils

▶**frown on, frown upon** vt insep (disapprove of)
désapprouver

froze [frəʊz] pt of **freeze**

frozen [ˈfrəʊzən] **1** adj (food) congelé(e), surgelé(e); (lake,
hands) gelé(e)
2 pp of **freeze**

fructose [ˈfrʌktəʊs] n fructose m

frugal [ˈfruːgəl] adj frugal(e)

fruit [fruːt] n fruit m; **some f.** (several pieces) des fruits;
(one piece) un fruit; Fig **to bear f.** (of plan, investment) porter
ses fruits; **fruits of the forest** fruits des bois; **f. bowl**
coupe f à fruits; **f. juice** jus m de fruit; Br **f. machine**
machine f à sous; **f. salad** salade f de fruits; **f. tree** arbre m
fruitier

fruitcake [ˈfruːtkeɪk] n cake m; Fam (mad person) fou
(folle) m,f

fruitful [ˈfruːtfʊl] adj (discussion) fructueux(euse)

fruition [fruːˈɪʃən] n **to come to f.** (of plan, effort) porter
ses fruits

fruitless [ˈfruːtlɪs] adj (attempt, search, trip)
infructueux(euse)

fruity [ˈfruːtɪ] adj (taste) fruité(e); Fam (voice) étoffé(e)

frump [frʌmp] n Fam **she's a f.** elle fait mémère

frumpish [ˈfrʌmpɪʃ], **frumpy** [ˈfrʌmpɪ] adj Fam **to be
f.** faire mémère

frustrate [frʌsˈtreɪt] vt (person) décevoir, frustrer; (plan)
contrarier

frustrated [frʌsˈtreɪtɪd] adj frustré(e)

frustrating [frʌsˈtreɪtɪŋ] adj frustrant(e)

frustration [frʌsˈtreɪʃən] n frustration f

fry [fraɪ] (pt & pp **fried**) **1** vt faire frire
2 vi frire

frying pan [ˈfraɪɪŋpæn] n poêle f (à frire); **to jump out
of the f. into the fire** tomber de Charybde en Scylla

ft (abbr **foot** or **feet**) p., pd.

FTP [eftiːˈpiː] n Comptr (abbr **File Transfer Protocol**)
FTP

fuchsia [ˈfjuːʃə] n fuchsia m

fuck [fʌk] Vulg **1** n (intercourse) baise f; **to have a f.** baiser;
I don't give a f. j'en ai rien à foutre; **what the f. do you
think you're doing?** putain, mais qu'est-ce que tu fous?;
f. knows why he came! mais pourquoi il est venu,
bordel!; **f.! bordel!, merde!
2 vt baiser; **f. it!** et merde!; **f. you!** va te faire foutre!
3 vi baiser

▶**fuck about, fuck around** vi Vulg (play the fool)
déconner; (waste time) glander

▶**fuck off** vi Vulg (go away) se casser; **f. off!** va te faire
foutre!

fuck-all [ˈfʌkˈɔːl] n Vulg **he's done f. this week** il a fait
que dalle cette semaine; **she knows f. about it** elle en
sait que dalle

fucked [ˈfʌkt] adj Vulg (broken) foutu(e)

fucking [ˈfʌkɪŋ] Vulg **1** adj **he's a f. idiot!** c'est un
connard!; **where's the f. car?** où est cette putain de
voiture?
2 adv (cold, brilliant, stupid) foutrement

fuddy-duddy [ˈfʌdɪdʌdɪ] (pl **fuddy-duddies**) n **an
old f.** (man) un vieux schnock; (woman) une vieille
mémère

fudge [fʌdʒ] **1** n (sweet) caramel m mou
2 vt **to f. an issue** éluder une question

fuel [ˈfjʊəl] **1** n combustible m; (for engine) carburant m;
Fig **to add f. to the flames** jeter de l'huile sur le feu; **f.
consumption** (of car) consommation f (d'essence); **f.
gauge** jauge f de carburant; **f. injection** injection f de
carburant; **f. pump** pompe f d'alimentation; **f. tank**
réservoir m
2 vt (pt & pp **fuelled**, Am **fueled**) Fig (hatred) attiser;
(speculation) nourrir

fug [fʌg] n Br Fam odeur f de renfermé; (in smoke-filled room) atmosphère f enfumée

fugitive ['fju:dʒɪtɪv] n fugitif(ive) m,f

fugue [fju:g] n Mus fugue f

fulcrum ['fʌlkrəm] n pivot m

fulfil, Am **fulfill** [fol'fɪl] (pt & pp **fulfilled**) vt (plan, ambition) réaliser; (condition, duty) remplir; (need) répondre à; **to feel fulfilled** (of person) se sentir épanoui(e)

fulfilment, Am **fulfillment** [fol'fɪlmənt] n (of plan, condition,) réalisation f; (satisfaction) épanouissement m; **to find** or **achieve f.** s'épanouir

full [fol] **1** adj **(a)** (container) plein(e) (**of** de); (hotel, bus, car park) complet(ète); (day) chargé(e); **to be f. of praise for sb** ne pas tarir d'éloges sur qn; **to be f. of oneself** être imbu(e) de soi-même; **f. to the brim** plein à ras bords; **don't speak with your mouth f.!** ne parle pas la bouche pleine!; **to be f. (up)** (of person) être rassasié(e); **on a f. stomach** le ventre plein

(b) (complete; amount) intégral(e); (explanation, recovery) complet(ète); (support) total(e); **to take f. responsibility for sth** assumer l'entière responsabilité de qch; **she gave me the f. story** elle m'a raconté toute l'histoire; **the f. horror** toute l'horreur; **to lead a f. life** avoir une vie bien remplie; **I waited two f. hours** or **a f. two hours** j'ai attendu deux bonnes heures; **in f. flow** (speaker) en plein discours; **to be in f. swing** (of party, sales) battre son plein; **in f. view of** sous les yeux de; **f. board** pension f complète; Phot **in f. colour** en couleur; **f. fare** plein tarif m; **f. house** (in theatre) salle f comble; (in cards) main f pleine; **f. moon** pleine lune f; **f. name** nom m et prénom m; **f. price** plein tarif; **f. stop** (punctuation) point m final; **f. time** (in sport) fin f de match

(c) (maximum) at **f. speed** à toute vitesse; **at f. stretch** (work) à plein rendement; **to get f. marks** (in exam) avoir tous les points (

(d) (skirt, sleeve) bouffant(e); **a f. figure** (of woman) un corps épanoui; **f. lips** lèvres fpl pleines

2 adv **you know f. well that...** tu sais parfaitement que...; **it hit him f. in the face** il a reçu le coup en pleine figure

3 n **to pay in f.** payer intégralement; **name in f.** nom et prénoms; **to live life to the f.** vivre pleinement

fullback ['folbæk] n (in football, rugby) arrière m

full-blown [fol'bləʊn] adj (row) vrai(e); (crisis) de grande envergure; **to have f. AIDS** avoir le sida

full-bodied ['fol'bodɪd] adj (wine) corsé(e)

full-grown ['fol'grəʊn] adj adulte

full-length ['fol'leŋθ] adj (portrait, mirror) en pied; (dress) long (longue); **f. film** long métrage m

fullness ['folnɪs] n **in the f. of time** avec le temps

full-page ['fol'peɪdʒ] adj (advert, illustration) pleine page

full-scale ['fol'skeɪl] adj **(a)** (model) grandeur nature inv **(b)** (search) de grande envergure; **f. war** guerre f généralisée

full-time ['fol'taɪm] adj & adv à temps complet, à plein temps; Fig **looking after the baby is a f. job** s'occuper du bébé ne laisse pas une minute de libre; **to be in f. employment** travailler à plein temps

full-timer ['fol'taɪmə(r)] n travailleur(euse) m,f à temps complet ou à plein temps

fully ['folɪ] adv **(a)** (completely) complètement, entièrement; (understand, be aware) parfaitement, tout à fait; **f. booked** complet(ète); **f. grown** adulte **(b)** (at least) **it takes f. two hours** cela prend au moins deux heures

fully-fledged ['folɪ'fledʒd] adj Br Fig qualifié(e)

fulminate ['fʌlmɪneɪt] vi fulminer (**against** contre)

fulness [fʌlnɪs] = **fullness**

fulsome ['folsəm] adj enthousiaste; **to be f. in one's praise of sb/sth** porter qn/qch aux nues

fumble ['fʌmbəl] **1** vt (ball) mal attraper

2 vi fouiller; **to f. for sth** fouiller pour trouver qch; (in dark) tâtonner pour trouver qch; **to f. for words** chercher ses mots; **he fumbled with the switch** il a essayé maladroitement de faire fonctionner l'interrupteur

fume [fju:m] **1** npl **fumes** émanations fpl; (from car exhaust) gaz mpl d'échappement; **petrol fumes** vapeurs fpl d'essence

2 vi **(a)** (give off fumes) fumer **(b)** (be angry) **to be fuming** rager

fumigate ['fju:mɪgeɪt] vt désinfecter par fumigation

fun [fʌn] n plaisir m; **to have f.** s'amuser; **it's/he's great f.** c'est/il est très amusant; **there'll be f. and games** (trouble) il va y avoir du grabuge; **it's no f. having to stay at home** ce n'est pas drôle de devoir rester à la maison; **to make f. of** se moquer de; **to say sth in f.** dire qch pour rire ou en plaisantant; **to do sth for f.** or **for the f. of it** faire qch pour s'amuser; Ironic **what f.!** c'est drôle!

function ['fʌŋkʃən] **1** n **(a)** (role) & Math fonction f; Comptr **f. key** touche f de fonction **(b)** (party) réception f; (public) cérémonie f

2 vi fonctionner; **to f. as** jouer le rôle de, faire fonction de

functional ['fʌŋkʃənəl] adj **(a)** (practical) fonctionnel(elle) **(b)** (operational) opérationnel(elle)

functionary ['fʌŋkʃənərɪ] (pl **functionaries**) n fonctionnaire mf

fund [fʌnd] **1** n **(a)** (of money) fonds m; **funds** fonds mpl, capitaux mpl; **to be in funds** être en fonds; Fin **f. manager** gestionnaire mf de fonds **(b)** (of information) mine f

2 vt financer

fundamental [fʌndə'mentəl] **1** n **fundamentals** principes mpl, fondements mpl

2 adj fondamental(e), essentiel(elle); **her f. honesty** sa profonde honnêteté

fundamentalist [fʌndə'mentəlɪst] n & adj (religious) intégriste mf, fondamentaliste mf

fundamentally [fʌndə'mentəlɪ] adv fondamentalement

funding ['fʌndɪŋ] n financement m

fund-raiser ['fʌndreɪzə(r)] n (person) collecteur(trice) m,f de fonds; (event) = manifestation organisée au profit d'une œuvre de bienfaisance

funeral ['fju:nərəl] n enterrement m; (formal) funérailles fpl, obsèques fpl; Fam **that's your f.!** c'est ton problème!; **f. director** entrepreneur m de pompes funèbres; Mus **f. march** marche f funèbre; **f. parlour** établissement m de pompes funèbres; **f. procession** cortège m funèbre; **f. service** service m funèbre

funfair ['fʌnfeə(r)] n fête f foraine

fungal ['fʌŋɡəl] adj **f. infection** mycose f

fungus ['fʌŋɡəs] (pl **fungi** ['fʌŋɡaɪ]) n (mushroom, toadstool) champignon m; (on walls) moisissure f; Med fongus m

funk [fʌŋk] n **(a)** Fam Old-fashioned (fright) **to be in a f.** avoir une peur bleue **(b)** (music) funk m

funky ['fʌŋkɪ] adj very Fam (clothing, suggestion, music) cool inv

funnel ['fʌnəl] **1** *n* (a) (of locomotive, steamship) cheminée f (b) (for filling) entonnoir *m*
2 *vt* (*pt & pp* **funnelled**, *Am* **funneled**) (direct) (funds) acheminer (**to** vers); **to f. liquid into sth** verser un liquide dans qch

funnily ['fʌnɪlɪ] *adv* (strangely) bizarrement; **f. enough,...** bizarrement,...

funny ['fʌnɪ] *adj* (a) (amusing) drôle, amusant(e); **are you trying to be f.?** tu te crois drôle?; *Ironic* **v. funny!** très drôle; *Fam* **f. bone** petit juif *m* (b) (strange) bizarre, drôle; **I feel a bit f.** (ill) je me sens un peu bizarre; **to taste/smell f.** avoir un drôle de goût/une drôle d'odeur; **f., I thought I'd locked the door** c'est curieux, je croyais avoir fermé la porte à clé; **(it's) f. you should say that** c'est drôle que tu dises ça; *Fam* **he's a bit f. in the head** il est un peu bizarre; *Fam* **I don't want any f. business!** et pas de blagues!; *Fam* **f. farm** maison f de fous

fur [fɜː(r)] *n* (a) (hair) poils *mpl*; (animal skin) fourrure f; *Fig* **the f. was flying** ça chauffait; **f. coat** manteau *m* de fourrure; **f. trade** commerce *m* de fourrures (b) (in kettle, boiler) tartre *m*

furious ['fjʊərɪəs] *adj* (person) furieux(euse) (**with** contre); (quarrel, storm) violent(e); **to be f. with oneself** être en colère contre soi-même; **at a f. speed** à une vitesse folle

furiously ['fjʊərɪəslɪ] *adv* furieusement; (work, write) frénétiquement

furlong ['fɜːlɒŋ] *n* = 201 m, furlong *m*

furnace ['fɜːnɪs] *n* fourneau *m*; *Fig* **it's like a f. in here!** quelle fournaise!

furnish ['fɜːnɪʃ] *vt* (a) (house, flat) meubler (b) *Formal* (provide) fournir; **to f. sb with sth** fournir qch à qn

furnished ['fɜːnɪʃd] *adj* (flat, room) meublé(e); **f. accommodation** *n* meublé *m*

furnishings ['fɜːnɪʃɪŋz] *npl* ameublement *m*

furniture ['fɜːnɪtʃə(r)] *n* meubles *mpl*, mobilier *m*; **a piece of f.** un meuble; **f. polish** encaustique f pour les meubles; **f. remover** déménageur *m*; **f. shop** magasin *m* de meubles *ou* d'ameublement; **f. van** camion *m* de déménagement

furore, *Am* **furor** ['fjʊərɔː(r)] *n* (uproar) scandale *m*

furrow ['fʌrəʊ] **1** *n* (in field) sillon *m*; (on face) ride f profonde
2 *vt Lit* **his brow was furrowed with worry** son front était plissé par l'inquiétude

furry ['fɜːrɪ] *adj* (animal) à poil; **f. toy** peluche f; **to have a f. tongue** avoir la langue chargée

further ['fɜːðə(r)] (comparative of **far**) **1** *adj* (a) (more distant) plus loin (b) (additional) supplémentaire; **upon f. consideration** après plus ample réflexion; **until f. notice** jusqu'à nouvel ordre; **without f. delay** sans plus attendre; *Br* **f. education** = enseignement supérieur dispensé par un établissement autre qu'une université
2 *adv* (a) (in general) plus loin; **this mustn't go any f.** (don't tell anyone else) il faut que cela reste entre nous; **I didn't question him any f.** je ne l'ai pas interrogé davantage; **that doesn't get us much f.** ça ne nous avance pas beaucoup; **f. back** (in space) plus loin en arrière; (in time) plus loin dans le temps; **f. on** (in space) plus loin; (in time) plus tard (b) *Formal* (moreover) de plus; **f. to your letter...** suite à votre lettre...
3 *vt* (cause, career) faire avancer

furthermore [fɜːðə'mɔː(r)] *adv Formal* en outre, de plus

furthermost ['fɜːðəməʊst] *adj Lit* le (la) plus reculé(e)

furthest ['fɜːðɪst] (superlative of **far**) **1** *adj* le (la) plus éloigné(e)
2 *adv* le plus loin

furtive ['fɜːtɪv] *adj* sournois(e)

fury ['fjʊərɪ] *n* (of person, storm) fureur f; **to be in a f.** (of person) être furieux(euse); *Fam* **to work like f.** travailler avec acharnement

fuse, *Am* **fuze** [fjuːz] **1** *n* (a) (for plug) fusible f; **f. box** boîte f à fusibles; **f. wire** fusible *m* (b) (for dynamite) détonateur *m*; (in bomb) amorce f; *Fam Fig* **to have a short f.** (be short-tempered) se mettre facilement en colère
2 *vt* (metal) fondre; (join) fusionner
3 *vi* (a) (of metals) fondre; **to f. together** fusionner (b) (of organizations, parties) fusionner (c) *Br Elec* **the lights have fused** les plombs ont sauté

fused [fjuːzd] *adj Elec* (plug, appliance) muni(e) d'un fusible

fuselage ['fjuːzəlɑːʒ] *n* fuselage *m*

fusillade [fjuːzɪ'leɪd] *n* (of bullets) fusillade f; *Fig* (of criticism, questions) avalanche f

fusion ['fjuːʒən] *n* fusion f

fuss [fʌs] **1** *n* histoires *fpl*; **what's all the f. about?** qu'est-ce que c'est que toutes ces histoires?; **I don't want any f.** pas de cérémonie; **a lot of f. about** *or* **over nothing** beaucoup d'histoires pour pas grand-chose; **I don't see what all the f. is about** je ne vois pas pourquoi on en fait un tel cas; **to kick up** *or* **make a f.** faire des histoires; **to make a f. of sb** être aux petits soins pour qn
2 *vt Fam* **I'm not fussed** ça m'est égal
3 *vi* faire des histoires; **to f. about** s'activer

fusspot ['fʌspɒt] *n Fam* chichiteux(euse) *m,f*

fussy ['fʌsɪ] *adj* (a) (person) difficile, exigeant(e); **I'm not f.** (I don't mind) ça m'est égal (b) (dress, décor) surchargé(e)

futile ['fjuːtaɪl] *adj* (attempt, protest) vain(e); (remark, suggestion) futile

futility [fjuː'tɪlɪtɪ] *n* futilité f

futon ['fuːtɒn] *n* futon *m*

future ['fjuːtʃə(r)] **1** *n* (a) (in time) avenir *m*; **in (the) f.** à l'avenir; **in the near/distant f.** dans un avenir proche/lointain; **she's got a job with a (good) f.** elle a une situation pleine d'avenir (b) *Fin* **futures** opérations *fpl* à terme (c) *Gram* futur *m*; **the f. perfect** le futur antérieur
2 *adj* futur(e); **at some f. date** à une date ultérieure; **for f. reference** à titre d'information

futuristic ['fjuːtʃə'rɪstɪk] *adj* futuriste

fuze *Am* = **fuse**

fuzz [fʌz] *n* (a) (on fabric) peluches *fpl*; (on peach, skin) duvet *m* (b) *Fam* **the f.** (police) les flics *mpl*

fuzzy ['fʌzɪ] *adj* (outline, photo) flou(e); (idea) vague; (hair) crépu(e); **f. logic** logique f floue

G

G, g [dʒiː] n (a) (letter) G, g m inv (b) Mus sol m

g (abbr **gramme**) gr

gab [gæb] (pt & pp **gabbed**) vi Fam (talk) papoter; (gossip) jaser

gabardine [gæbəˈdiːn] n gabardine f

gabble [ˈgæbəl] **1** n a g. of conversation un bruit de conversation
2 vi (incoherently) bredouiller; **to g. on** papoter

gable [ˈgeɪbəl] n pignon m; **g. end** (wall) pignon m

Gabon [ˈgæbən] n le Gabon

Gabonese [gæbəˈniːz] **1** n Gabonais(e) m,f
2 adj gabonais(e)

▶**gad about** [gæd] (pt & pp **gadded**) vi Fam être en vadrouille

gadfly [ˈgædflaɪ] (pl **gadflies**) n (insect) taon m; Fig (person) casse-pieds mf inv

gadget [ˈgædʒɪt] n gadget m

Gaelic [ˈgeɪlɪk, Scot ˈgælɪk] **1** n gaélique m
2 adj gaélique; **G. football** = jeu de balle irlandais à quinze où il est autorisé de taper dans le ballon avec la main

Gaels [geɪlz] npl the G. les Gaëls mpl

gaff [gæf] n (a) (in fishing) gaffe f (b) Br Fam (home) piaule f (c) Fam **to blow the g. (on)** vendre la mèche (à propos de)

gaffe [gæf] n (blunder) gaffe f

gaffer [ˈgæfə(r)] n Br Fam (boss) chef m

gag [gæg] **1** n (a) (on mouth) bâillon m (b) Fam (joke) blague f
2 vt (pt & pp **gagged**) (person) bâillonner; Fig (media, opposition) museler
3 vi (retch) avoir des haut-le-cœur

gaga [ˈgɑːgɑː] adj Fam gâteux(euse), gaga inv

gage Am = **gauge**

gaggle [ˈgægəl] n also Fig troupeau m

gaiety [ˈgeɪətɪ] n gaieté f

gaily [ˈgeɪlɪ] adv (happily) joyeusement; (laugh) de bon cœur; **g. coloured** aux couleurs gaies

gain [geɪn] **1** n (a) (profit) gain m, profit m; **for personal g.** par intérêt personnel (b) (increase) augmentation f (in de); Fin (on stock market) hausse f; **to make gains** (progress) progresser; Fin (of shares) augmenter
2 vt (a) (advantage, degree) obtenir; (victory, prize) remporter; (reputation, experience) acquérir; (sympathy, respect) gagner; **to g. entrance (to)** entrer (dans); (of burglar) s'introduire (dans) (b) (increase) **to g. weight/speed** prendre du poids/de la vitesse; also Fig **to g. ground on** gagner du terrain sur; **to g. time** gagner du temps
3 vi (a) (benefit) **to g. by sth** bénéficier de qch (b)

(increase) **to g. in confidence** gagner de l'assurance; **to g. in popularity** devenir populaire (c) (of clock) avancer

▶**gain on** vt insep valso Fig gagner du terrain sur

gainful [ˈgeɪnfʊl] adj **g. employment** un emploi rémunéré

gainfully [ˈgeɪnfʊlɪ] adv **to be g. employed** avoir un emploi rémunéré

gainsay [geɪnˈseɪ] (pt & pp **gainsaid** [geɪnˈsed]) vt Formal contredire; **there's no gainsaying her ability** son talent est indéniable

gait [geɪt] n démarche f

gal [gæl] n Fam Old-fashioned fille f

gala [ˈgɑːlə] n gala m; **swimming g.** compétition f de natation; **g. evening/performance** soirée f/ représentation f de gala

galactic [gəˈlæktɪk] adj galactique

Galapagos [gəˈlæpəgəs] npl **the G. (Islands)** les (îles fpl) Galapagos fpl

galaxy [ˈgæləksɪ] (pl **galaxies**) n galaxie f; Fig **a g. of stars** une pléiade de vedettes

gale [geɪl] n (strong wind) vent m violent; Fig **a g. of laughter** un éclat de rire

gall [gɔːl] **1** n (a) Med bile f; **g. bladder** vésicule f biliaire (b) (impudence) culot m
2 vt (annoy) irriter, exaspérer

gallant [ˈgælənt] adj (brave) brave, vaillant(e); (polite) galant(e)

gallantry [ˈgæləntrɪ] n (bravery) bravoure f; (politeness) galanterie f

galleon [ˈgælɪən] n galion m

gallery [ˈgælərɪ] (pl **galleries**) n (a) (art) **g. (for sale)** galerie f d'art; (for exhibition) musée m (b) (in theatre) galerie f; Fig **to play to the g.** (of politician) chercher à épater la galerie

galley [ˈgælɪ] (pl **galleys**) n (a) (ship) galère f; **g. slave** galérien m (b) (ship's kitchen) cuisine f (c) Typ **g. (proof)** placard m

Gallic [ˈgælɪk] adj (French) français(e); Hist (of Gaul) gaulois(e)

galling [ˈgɔːlɪŋ] adj humiliant(e)

▶**gallivant about, gallivant around** [ˈgælɪvænt] vi être en vadrouille

gallon [ˈgælən] n (in UK) = 4,54 l, gallon m; (in US) = 3,78 l, gallon

gallop [ˈgæləp] **1** n galop m; **at a g.** au galop
2 vi galoper; Fig **to g. through one's work** expédier son travail

gallows [ˈgæləʊz] n potence f, gibet m; **g. humour** humour m noir

gallstone ['gɔ:lstəʊn] n calcul m biliaire

galore [gə'lɔ:(r)] adv Fam à profusion, à gogo

galvanize ['gælvənaɪz] vt also Fig galvaniser; **to g. sb into action** pousser qn à agir

galvanized ['gælvənaɪzd] adj galvanisé(e)

Gambia ['gæmbɪə] n the G. la Gambie

Gambian ['gæmbɪən] 1 n Gambien(enne) m,f
2 adj gambien(enne)

gambit ['gæmbɪt] n (in chess) gambit m; (in negotiation, diplomacy) tactique f; **opening g.** (in negotiation, diplomacy) manœuvre f d'approche

gamble ['gæmbəl] 1 n (risk) risque m; **to take a g.** prendre un risque
2 vi (money) jouer, parier
3 vi jouer (de l'argent); **to g. on the horses** jouer aux courses; **she gambled on nobody noticing** elle comptait sur le fait que personne ne s'en apercevrait

gambler ['gæmblə(r)] n joueur(euse) m,f

gambling ['gæmblɪŋ] n jeux mpl d'argent; **g. debts** dettes fpl de jeu; **g. den** tripot m

gambol ['gæmbəl] (pt & pp gambolled, Am gamboled) vi gambader

game [geɪm] 1 n (a) (activity, sport) jeu m; (of cards, pool, chess) partie f; (match) match m; **to have a g. of tennis/football** faire une partie de tennis/foot(ball); **g., set and match** (in tennis) jeu, set et match; **games** Br (school subject) sports mpl de plein air; (sporting event) jeux mpl; **politics is just a g. to them** pour eux, la politique n'est qu'un jeu; **g. show** jeu m télévisé
(b) (skill) jeu m
(c) (animals, food) gibier m; **g. reserve** réserve f de gibier
(d) (idioms) **to play the g.** jouer le jeu; **two can play at that g.** on peut jouer à deux à ce petit jeu-là; **to beat sb at his own g.** battre qn à sa propre jeu; **to play games with sb** jouer avec qn; **to give the g. away** vendre la mèche; **what's his g.?** où veut-il en venir?; **I know what your g. is!** je sais bien où vous voulez en venir!; **the g.'s up for him** c'est fichu pour lui; **I've been in this g. a long time** ça fait longtemps que je suis de la partie; Br Fam **to be on the g.** (of prostitute) faire le trottoir
2 adj (a) (brave) courageux(euse); **to be g. (to do sth)** (willing) être partant(e) (pour faire qch)
(b) Fam **a g. leg** une patte folle

gamekeeper ['geɪmki:pə(r)] n garde-chasse m

gamely ['geɪmlɪ] adv courageusement

gamma ['gæmə] n gamma m; Phys **g. rays** rayons mpl gamma

gammon ['gæmən] n jambon m; **g. steak** = tranche épaisse de jambon (à servir grillée)

gammy ['gæmɪ] adj Fam **a g. leg** une patte folle

gamut ['gæmət] n gamme f; **to run the g. of** (emotions) passer par toute la gamme de

gamy ['geɪmɪ] adj (flavour) faisandé(e)

gander ['gændə(r)] n (a) (male goose) jars m (b) Br very Fam **to take a g.** (at) (look) jeter un coup d'œil (à)

gang [gæŋ] n (of criminals, children, friends) bande f; (of workers) équipe f

▶**gang up** vi to **g. up on sb** se liguer contre qn; **to g. up with sb** s'allier avec qn

gangbang ['gæŋbæŋ] n very Fam (group rape) viol m collectif

Ganges ['gændʒi:z] n the G. le Gange

gangland ['gæŋlænd] n (underworld) milieu m, pègre f; **g. boss/killer** caïd m/tueur m du milieu; **g. killing** règlement m de compte (entre gangsters)

gangling ['gæŋglɪŋ] adj dégingandé(e)

ganglion ['gæŋglɪən] (pl ganglia ['gæŋglɪə]) n ganglion m

gangplank ['gæŋplæŋk] n passerelle f

gangrene ['gæŋgri:n] n gangrène f; **to have g.** avoir la gangrène

gangrenous ['gæŋgrɪnəs] adj gangreneux(euse)

gangster ['gæŋstə(r)] n gangster m; **g. film** film m de gangsters

gangway ['gæŋweɪ] n (in theatre) allée f; (in plane, train) couloir m; (on ship) passerelle f; **g.!** dégagez, s'il vous plaît!

gannet ['gænɪt] n (bird) fou m de Bassan; Fig (greedy person) goinfre mf

gantry ['gæntrɪ] (pl gantries) n (for crane, over railway) portique m; (for rocket) tour f de lancement

gaol [dʒeɪl] Br = **jail**

gap [gæp] n (a) (space) espace m; (narrower) interstice m; (in wall) brèche f; (in text) blanc m (b) (difference) (in age, ability) écart m; **the g. between rich and poor** le fossé entre les riches et les pauvres (c) (in knowledge) lacune f; **his death leaves a g. in all our lives** sa mort nous laisse un vide; Com **a g. in the market** un créneau (d) (in time) intervalle m (e) (mountain pass) col m

gape [geɪp] vi (a) (stare) rester bouche bée; **to g. at sb/sth** regarder qn/qch bouche bée (b) **to g. (open)** (of door, blouse) s'ouvrir tout(e) grand(e); (of wound, hole) être béant(e)

gaping ['geɪpɪŋ] adj béant(e)

garage ['gæra:ʒ, 'gærɪdʒ] n (for storing or repairing car) garage m; (petrol station) station-service f

garb [gɑ:b] n Lit costume m

garbage ['gɑ:bɪdʒ] n (a) Am (rubbish) ordures fpl; **g. can** poubelle f; **g. heap** tas m d'ordures; **g. man** éboueur m (b) (nonsense) âneries fpl; **to talk g.** dire n'importe quoi

garbled ['gɑ:bəld] adj confus(e)

garden ['gɑ:dən] 1 n jardin m; Fig **to lead sb up the g. path** faire marcher qn; **g. centre** jardinerie f; **g. flat** appartement m en rez-de-chaussée avec jardin; **g. furniture** meubles mpl de jardin; **g. party** réception f en plein air, garden-party f
2 vi jardiner, faire du jardinage

gardener ['gɑ:dnə(r)] n jardinier(ère) m,f

gardening [gɑ:dnɪŋ] n jardinage m; **to do the g.** s'occuper du jardin

gargantuan [gɑ:'gæntjʊən] adj gargantuesque

gargle ['gɑ:gəl] vi se gargariser (**with** avec)

gargoyle ['gɑ:gɔɪl] n gargouille f

garish ['geərɪʃ] adj (clothes) voyant(e); (taste) vulgaire; (colours) criard(e); (light) cru(e)

garland ['gɑ:lənd] 1 n guirlande f
2 vt enguirlander (**with** de)

garlic ['gɑ:lɪk] n ail m; **g. bread** = pain chaud au beurre d'ail; **g. butter** beurre m d'ail; **g. sausage** saucisson m à l'ail

garment ['gɑ:mənt] n vêtement m

garnet ['gɑ:nɪt] n grenat m

garnish ['gɑ:nɪʃ] 1 n garniture f
2 vt garnir (**with** avec)

garret ['gærət] n mansarde f

garrison ['gærɪsən] **1** *n* garnison *f*; **g. duty** service *m* de garnison; **g. town** ville *f* de garnison
2 *vt (troops)* mettre en garnison

garrotte [gə'rɒt] **1** *n* garrot *m*
2 *vt* exécuter au garrot

garrulous ['gærʊləs] *adj (person)* loquace, bavard(e); *(account, letter)* verbeux(euse)

garter ['gɑːtə(r)] *n* jarretière *f*; *Br* **the Order of the G.** l'Ordre *m* de la Jarretière; *Am* **g. belt** porte-jarretelles *m inv*; **g. snake** couleuvre *f*

gas [gæs] **1** *n* (a) gaz *m inv*; *Med (gaz)* anesthétique *m*; **g. bill** note *f* de gaz; **g. chamber** chambre *f* à gaz; **g. cooker** cuisinière *f* à gaz; **g. cylinder** bouteille *f* de gaz; **g. fire** radiateur *m* à gaz; **g. lamp** lampe *f* à gaz; **g. mask** masque *m* à gaz **(b)** *Am (gasoline)* essence *f*; *Fam* **to step on the g.** appuyer sur le champignon; **g. station** station-service *f*; **g. tank** réservoir *m* **(c)** *Fam (amusing situation)* **to have a g.** rigoler; **what a g.!** quelle rigolade!
2 *vt (pt & pp gassed) (person)* asphyxier; *(deliberately)* gazer; **to g. oneself** se suicider au gaz
3 *vi Fam (chat)* jacasser

gasbag ['gæsbæg] *n Fam (chatterbox)* bavard(e) *m,f*; *(boaster)* vantard(e) *m,f*

gaseous ['gæsɪəs, 'geɪsɪəs] *adj* gazeux(euse)

gash [gæʃ] **1** *n (in skin, wood)* entaille *f*; *(in metal)* fente *f*
2 *vt* entailler

gasket ['gæskɪt] *n (in engine)* joint *m* de culasse; *Fam* **to blow a g.** piquer une colère

gasoline ['gæsəliːn] *n Am* essence *f*

gasometer [gæ'sɒmɪtə(r)] *n* gazomètre *m*

gasp [gɑːsp] **1** *n (of surprise)* sursaut *m*; **to be at one's last g.** être sur le point de rendre son dernier soupir
2 *vi* avoir le souffle coupé **(with** *or* **in** de); **to make sb g.** couper le souffle à qn; **to g. for breath** *or* **for air** haleter, suffoquer; *Fam* **to be gasping for a cigarette/a drink** mourir d'envie de fumer une cigarette/de boire un verre

gassy ['gæsɪ] *adj* gazeux(euse)

gastric ['gæstrɪk] *adj* gastrique; **g. flu** grippe *f* gastro-intestinale; **g. juices** sucs *mpl* gastriques; **g. ulcer** ulcère *m* à l'estomac

gastritis [gæs'traɪtɪs] *n* gastrite *f*; **to have g.** avoir une gastrite

gastro-enteritis [gæstrəʊentə'raɪtɪs] *n* gastro-entérite *f*; **to have g.** avoir une gastro-entérite

gastronomic [gæstrə'nɒmɪk] *adj* gastronomique

gastronomy [gæs'trɒnəmɪ] *n* gastronomie *f*

gasworks ['gæswɜːks] *n* usine *f* à gaz

gate [geɪt] *n* (a) *(in garden, field)* barrière *f*; *(of city, in airport)* porte *f* **(b)** *Sp (spectators)* nombre *m* de spectateurs; *(takings)* recette *f*

gâteau ['gætəʊ] *(pl* **gâteaux** ['gætəʊz]) *n* gros gâteau *m* à la crème

gatecrash ['geɪtkræʃ] *vt Fam* **to g. a party** aller à une fête sans y être invité(e)

gatecrasher ['geɪtkræʃə(r)] *n Fam* intrus(e) *m,f*

gatehouse ['geɪthaʊs] *n* loge *f*

gatekeeper ['geɪtkiːpə(r)] *n* gardien(enne) *m,f*

gatepost ['geɪtpəʊst] *n* montant *m* (de porte); *Fam* **between you, me and the g.** entre nous

gateway ['geɪtweɪ] *n* entrée *f*; *Fig* **the g. to the East** la porte de l'Orient; **the g. to success** la voie de la réussite

gather ['gæðə(r)] **1** *vt* **(a)** *(collect) (people, belongings)* rassembler; *(information)* recueillir; *(wood, papers)* ramasser; *(fruit, flowers)* cueillir; *(harvest)* rentrer; **to g. one's thoughts** rassembler ses idées; **to g. sb in one's arms** serrer qn dans ses bras **(b)** *(accumulate)* **to g. dirt** s'encrasser; *also Fig* **to g. dust** ramasser de la poussière; **to g. speed** prendre de la vitesse **(c)** *(conclude, understand)* **to g. that...** croire comprendre que...; **as you may already have gathered,...** comme vous avez déjà dû le deviner,...
2 *vi (of people)* se rassembler; *(of things)* s'accumuler; *(of storm)* se préparer

▶**gather round 1** *vt insep* se rassembler autour de
2 *vi* se rassembler

▶**gather together 1** *vt sep (belongings)* rassembler; *(evidence)* recueillir
2 *vi (of people)* se rassembler

▶**gather up** *vt sep* ramasser

gathering ['gæðərɪŋ] **1** *n (group)* attroupement *m*; *(meeting)* réunion *f*
2 *adj (darkness, speed)* croissant(e); *also Fig* **the g. storm** l'orage qui se prépare

GATT [gæt] *n (abbr* **General Agreement on Tariffs and Trade)** GATT *m*

gauche [gəʊʃ] *adj* gauche, maladroit(e)

gaudily ['gɔːdɪlɪ] *adv* de façon criarde

gaudy ['gɔːdɪ] *adj* tape-à-l'œil *inv*; *(colours)* criard(e)

gauge [geɪdʒ] **1** *n* **(a)** *(size) (of screw, wire, gun)* calibre *m*; *(of railway track)* écartement *m* **(b)** *(measuring device)* jauge *f* **(c)** *Fig (indicator)* signe *m*, indicateur *m* (**of** de)
2 *vt* évaluer

Gaul [gɔːl] *n Hist (region)* la Gaule; *(inhabitant)* Gaulois(oise) *m,f*

gaunt [gɔːnt] *adj* décharné(e)

gauntlet ['gɔːntlɪt] *n (glove)* gant *m* à manchette; *Hist* gantelet *m*; *Fig* **to throw** *or* **fling down the g. (to sb)** jeter le gant (à qn); *Fig* **to take up the g.** relever le gant; *Fig* **to run the g. of sth** s'exposer à qch

gauze [gɔːz] *n* gaze *f*

gave [geɪv] *pt of* **give**

gavel ['gævəl] *n* marteau *m*

gawk [gɔːk] *vi Fam* rester bouche bée; **to g. at sb/sth** rester bouche bée à regarder qn/qch

gawky ['gɔːkɪ] *adj Fam* gauche, empoté(e)

gawp [gɔːp] *vi Fam* rester bouche bée; **to g. at sb/sth** rester bouche bée à regarder qn/qch

gay [geɪ] **1** *n (homosexual)* homosexuel(elle) *m,f*
2 *adj* **(a)** *(homosexual)* homosexuel(elle), gay *inv*; **g. rights** les droits *mpl* des homosexuels **(b)** *Old-fashioned (happy)* gai(e); **with g. abandon** avec insouciance

Gaza ['gɑːzə] *n* Gaza; **the G. Strip** la Bande de Gaza

gaze [geɪz] **1** *n* regard *m*; **to meet** *or* **return sb's g.** regarder qn dans les yeux
2 *vi* **to g. at sb/sth** regarder fixement qn/qch; **to g. into space** regarder dans le vague

gazelle [gə'zel] *n* gazelle *f*

gazette [gə'zet] *n* journal *m* officiel

gazetteer [gæzə'tɪə(r)] *n* index *m* géographique

gazump [gə'zʌmp] *vt Br Fam* = revenir sur une promesse de vente de maison pour accepter l'offre plus élevée d'une tierce personne

GB ['dʒiː'biː] *n (abbr* **Great Britain)** GB

GBH [dʒi:bi:'eɪtʃ] n Law (abbr **grievous bodily harm**) coups mpl et blessures fpl

GCE [dʒi:si:'i:] n Br Formerly (abbr **General Certificate of Education**) = diplôme de fin d'études secondaires

GCHQ. [dʒi:si:eɪtʃ'kju:] n Br (abbr **Government Communications Headquarters**) = service de renseignement et d'écoute du gouvernement britannique

GCSE [dʒi:si:es'i:] n Br (abbr **General Certificate of Secondary Education**) = diplôme de fin de premier cycle de l'enseignement secondaire, sanctionnant une matière déterminée

GDP [dʒi:di:'pi:] n Econ (abbr **gross domestic product**) PIB m

GDR [dʒi:di:'ɑ:(r)] n Formerly (abbr **German Democratic Republic**) the G. la RDA

gear [gɪə(r)] n (a) (on car, bicycle) vitesse f; Fig to put sb's plans out of g. perturber les projets de qn; **first/second** g. première f/seconde f (vitesse); Br g. **lever** changement m de vitesse (b) Fam (equipment) attirail m; (belongings) affaires fpl (c) Fam (clothes) fringues fpl

▶**gear to** vt sep to g. sth to sth adapter qch à qch

▶**gear towards** vt sep to be geared towards sb/sth s'adresser à qn/qch

gearbox [gɪəbɒks] n boîte f (de changement) de vitesses

gearstick [gɪəstɪk] n changement m de vitesses

gee [dʒi:] exclam (a) (to horse) g. up! hue! (b) Am g. (whizz)! mince alors!

gee-gee [dʒi:dʒi:] n Fam (in children's language) dada m

geese [gi:s] pl of **goose**

geezer [ˈgi:zə(r)] n Br very Fam type m; **old g.** vieux bonhomme m

Geiger counter [ˈgaɪgəˈkaʊntə(r)] n compteur m Geiger

gel [dʒel] **1** n gel m

2 vi (of liquid) se gélifier; Fig (of ideas, plans) prendre forme; (of team) se souder

gelatine [dʒeləti:n] n gélatine f

gelatinous [dʒɪˈlætɪnəs] adj gélatineux(euse)

gelding [ˈgeldɪŋ] n hongre m

gelignite [ˈdʒelɪgnaɪt] n gélignite f

gem [dʒem] n (precious stone) pierre f précieuse; Fig (person) perle f; (film, joke, goal) pure merveille f

Gemini [ˈdʒemɪnaɪ] n (sign of zodiac) les Gémeaux mpl; to be (a) G. être (des) Gémeaux

gemstone [ˈdʒemstəʊn] n pierre f gemme

gen [dʒen] n Br Fam (information) tuyaux mpl

gender [ˈdʒendə(r)] n (a) Gram genre m (b) (sex) sexe m

gene [dʒi:n] n Biol gène m; Fig it's in his genes (of talent, characteristic) c'est héréditaire

genealogy [dʒi:nɪˈælədʒɪ] n généalogie f

genera [ˈdʒenərə] pl of **genus**

general [ˈdʒenərəl] **1** n (a) in g. en général (b) Mil général m

2 adj général(e); **as a g. rule** en règle générale; **in g. terms** en termes généraux; g. **anaesthetic** anesthésie f générale; **G. Assembly** (of United Nations) Assemblée f générale; g. **election** élections fpl générales; g. **knowledge** culture f générale; g. **manager** directeur(trice) m/f général(e); g. **meeting** assemblée f générale; g. **practice** (in medicine) médecine f générale; g. **practitioner** (doctor) médecin m généraliste; the g.

public le grand public; g. **store** bazar m; g. **strike** grève f générale

generality [dʒenəˈrælɪtɪ] (pl **generalities**) n généralité f

generalization [dʒenərəlaɪˈzeɪʃən] n généralisation f

generalize [ˈdʒenərəlaɪz] **1** vt to become generalized (of practice, belief) se généraliser
2 vi généraliser

generally [ˈdʒenərəlɪ] adv (taken overall) dans l'ensemble; (as a general rule) généralement, en général; g. **speaking** d'une manière générale

generate [ˈdʒenəreɪt] vt (electricity, heat) produire; (income) créer; (reaction, response) provoquer; (interest, ideas) faire naître

generation [dʒenəˈreɪʃən] n (a) (of people, products) génération f; from g. to g. de génération en génération; **the younger/older g.** la jeune/l'ancienne génération; **the g. gap** le fossé entre les générations (b) (of electricity) production f

generator [ˈdʒenəreɪtə(r)] n Elec générateur m

generic [dʒɪˈnerɪk] adj générique

generosity [dʒenəˈrɒsɪtɪ] n générosité f

generous [ˈdʒenərəs] adj généreux(euse)

generously [ˈdʒenərəslɪ] adv généreusement

genesis [ˈdʒenɪsɪs] n genèse f; (the Book of) G. la Genèse

genetic [dʒɪˈnetɪk] adj génétique; g. **code** code m génétique; g. **engineering** génie m génétique; g. **fingerprinting** empreinte f génétique

genetically [dʒɪˈnetɪklɪ] adv génétiquement

genetics [dʒɪˈnetɪks] n génétique f

Geneva [dʒɪˈni:və] n Genève; **Lake G.** le Lac de Genève, le Lac Léman; **the G. Convention** la Convention de Genève

genial [ˈdʒi:nɪəl] adj cordial(e)

geniality [dʒi:nɪˈælɪtɪ] n cordialité f

genially [ˈdʒi:nɪəlɪ] adv cordialement

genie [ˈdʒi:nɪ] (pl **genii** [ˈdʒi:nɪaɪ]) n génie m

genital [ˈdʒenɪtəl] **1** npl **genitals** organes mpl génitaux
2 adj génital(e)

genitive [ˈdʒenɪtɪv] Gram **1** n génitif m; **in the g.** au génitif
2 adj génitif(ive)

genius [ˈdʒi:nɪəs] n génie m; Ironic **to have a g. for sth/doing sth** avoir le génie de qch/de faire qch; **man/work of g.** homme m/œuvre f de génie

Genoa [ˈdʒenəʊə] n Gênes f

genocide [ˈdʒenəsaɪd] n génocide m

genre [ˈʒɒnrə] n (of film, novel) genre m

gent [dʒent] n Br Fam (a) (well-bred man) gentleman m (b) (man) homme m; **gents' footwear** chaussures fpl pour hommes; **gents** (toilets) toilettes fpl des hommes; (sign) messieurs

genteel [dʒenˈti:l] adj (refined) distingué(e); (respectable) comme il faut; Pej (affected) maniéré(e)

Gentile [ˈdʒentaɪl] n gentil m

gentle [ˈdʒentəl] adj (person, manner) doux (douce); (push, breeze, rise, slope) léger(ère); (hint) discret(ète); (exercise) modéré(e); **to be g. with sb** être doux avec qn; **to be g. with sth** faire attention à qch; Fam **a g. giant** un agneau sous des airs de brute

gentleman [ˈdʒentəlmən] n (a) (well-bred man) gentleman m; **g.'s agreement** gentleman's agreement m

(b) *(man)* homme *m*; **Ladies and Gentlemen!** mesdames et messieurs!

gentlemanly ['dʒentəlmənlɪ] *adj* bien élevé(e)

gentleness ['dʒentəlnɪs] *n* douceur *f*

gently ['dʒentlɪ] *adv* *(speak, remind)* gentiment; *(slope)* en pente douce; **g. (does it)!** allez-y doucement!

gentrification [dʒentrɪfɪ'keɪʃən] *n Br* embourgeoisement *m*

gentry ['dʒentrɪ] *n* petite noblesse *f*

genuflect ['dʒenjʊflekt] *vi Formal* faire une génuflexion

genuine ['dʒenjʊm] *adj* **(a)** *(manuscript, painting)* authentique; *(gold, leather)* véritable; *(excuse)* valable; *(offer)* sérieux(euse) **(b)** *(sincere)* sincère; **it was a g. mistake** ce n'était pas intentionnel

genuinely ['dʒenjʊmlɪ] *adv* *(sincerely)* sincèrement, vraiment

genus ['dʒiːnəs] *(pl* **genera** ['dʒenərə]*) n Biol* genre *m*

geo- ['dʒiːəʊ] *pref* géo-

geographer [dʒɪ'ɒɡrəfə(r)] *n* géographe *mf*

geographic(al) [dʒɪə'ɡræfɪk(əl)] *adj* géographique

geography [dʒɪ'ɒɡrəfɪ] *n* géographie *f*

geologic(al) [dʒɪə'lɒdʒɪk(əl)] *adj* géologique

geologist [dʒɪ'ɒlədʒɪst] *n* géologue *mf*

geology [dʒɪ'ɒlədʒɪ] *n* géologie *f*

geometric(al) [dʒɪə'metrɪk(əl)] *adj* géométrique

geometry [dʒɪ'ɒmɪtrɪ] *n* géométrie *f*

geophysics [dʒɪəʊ'fɪzɪks] *n* géophysique *f*

geopolitics [dʒɪəʊ'pɒlɪtɪks] *n* géopolitique *f*

Geordie ['dʒɔːdɪ] *n Br Fam* = personne née à ou habitant Tyneside

Georgia ['dʒɔːdʒə] *n (country, US state)* la Géorgie

Georgian ['dʒɔːdʒən] **1** *n* **(a)** *(person)* Géorgien(enne) *m,f* **(b)** *(language)* géorgien *m*
2 *adj* géorgien(enne)

geothermal [dʒiːəʊ'θɜːməl] *adj* géothermique

geranium [dʒə'remjəm] *n* géranium *m*

gerbil ['dʒɜːbɪl] *n* gerbille *f*

geriatric [dʒerɪ'ætrɪk] **1** *n* malade *mf* gériatrique; *Fam Pej (old person)* gâteux(euse) *m,f*
2 *adj* *(hospital)* gériatrique; *(care)* aux vieillards; **g. medicine** gériatrie *f*

geriatrics [dʒerɪ'ætrɪks] *n* gériatrie *f*

germ [dʒɜːm] *n* **(a)** *(causing disease)* microbe *m*; **g. warfare** guerre *f* bactériologique **(b)** *(of seed)* & *Fig (of idea)* germe *m*

German ['dʒɜːmən] **1** *n* **(a)** *(person)* Allemand(e) *m,f* **(b)** *(language)* allemand *m*; **G. class/teacher** cours *m*/ professeur *m* d'allemand
2 *adj* allemand(e); **G. measles** rubéole *f*; **G. shepherd** berger *m* allemand

germane [dʒɜː'mem] *adj Formal* approprié(e); **to be g. to sth** avoir rapport à qch

Germanic [dʒɜː'mænɪk] *adj* germanique

Germany ['dʒɜːmənɪ] *n* l'Allemagne *f*

germinate ['dʒɜːmmeɪt] *vi* germer

germination [dʒɜːmɪ'neɪʃən] *n* germination *f*

gerrymandering ['dʒerɪmændərɪŋ] *n Pol* charcutage *m* électoral

gerund ['dʒerənd] *n Gram* gérondif *m*

gestation [dʒes'teɪʃən] *n also Fig* gestation *f*; **g. period** période *f* de gestation

gesticulate [dʒes'tɪkjʊleɪt] *vi* gesticuler

gesture ['dʒestʃə(r)] **1** *n also Fig* geste *m*; *Fig* **as a g. of friendship** en témoignage d'amitié
2 *vi (single action)* faire un geste; *(repeatedly)* faire des gestes; **to g. to sb** faire signe à qn; **to g. towards sb/sth** désigner qn/qch d'un geste

get [get] *(pt & pp* **got** [gɒt]*, Am pp* **gotten** ['gɒtən]*)* **1** *vt* **(a)** *(obtain)* obtenir; *(job)* trouver; **to g. sth for sb** obtenir qch pour qn; **I got the idea from a book** j'ai trouvé l'idée dans un livre; **to g. the right answer** trouver la solution; **to g. the wrong answer** se tromper
(b) *(buy)* acheter; **to g. sth for sb** acheter qch à qn
(c) *(receive) (present, reply)* recevoir; *(surprise, shock)* avoir; **we can't g. Radio 4 here** on ne reçoit pas Radio 4 ici; **to g. £15,000 a year** gagner 15 000 livres par an; **we don't g. many visitors here** nous ne recevons pas beaucoup de visites ici
(d) *(catch) (person, disease)* attraper; *(train, bus)* prendre; *Fam* **I'll g. you for that** je t'aurai
(e) *(fetch)* aller chercher; **to g. sth for sb** aller chercher qch pour qn; **can I g. you anything?** je te rapporte quelque chose?
(f) *Fam (annoy)* énerver
(g) *Fam (understand)* piger; **do you g. my meaning?** tu vois ce que je veux dire?; **to g. the point** piger; **to g. a joke** saisir une blague
(h) *(send)* **to g. sth to sb** faire parvenir qch à qn
(i) *(cause to be in a certain state)* **to g. sth dry/wet** sécher/ mouiller qch; **to g. sth clean/dirty** nettoyer/salir qch; **you've got him worried** tu l'as fait s'inquiéter; **to g. sb pregnant** mettre qn enceinte; **to g. the children to bed** envoyer les enfants au lit
(j) *(cause to be done)* **to g. sth done** faire faire qch; **to g. the house painted** faire peindre la maison; **she got her work finished** elle a terminé son travail
(k) *(cause to do)* **to g. sb to do sth** faire faire qch à qn; **she got me to help her** elle m'a persuadé de l'aider; **you can g. them to wrap it for you** tu peux leur demander de te l'emballer
(l) *(do gradually)* **to g. to know sb** apprendre à connaître qn; **you'll g. to like him** tu finiras par l'apprécier; **she soon got to thinking that...** elle se mit bientôt à penser que...
(m) *(have opportunity)* **to g. to do sth** avoir l'occasion de faire qch
(n) *(possess) (with have)* **she hasn't got a car** elle n'a pas de voiture; **she's got measles/AIDS** elle a la rougeole/le sida; **what's that got to do with it?** qu'est-ce que ça a à voir?
(o) *(must) (with have)* **I've got to go** il faut que j'y aille; **it's got to be done** il faut que ce soit fait
2 *vi* **(a)** *(arrive)* arriver; **to g. home** arriver chez soi; **to g. back** arriver; **how do you g. there?** comment fait-on pour y aller?; **he got as far as chapter five** il est allé jusqu'au chapitre cinq; **to g. to the point where...** ça en est arrivé à un point où...
(b) *(move)* & *Fig* **to g. in sb's way** se mettre sur le chemin de qn; **where has he got to?** où est-il passé?; **we're getting nowhere** on n'avance pas
(c) *(become)* **to g. angry** se mettre en colère; **to g. better** s'améliorer; **to g. drunk** se soûler; **to g. old** vieillir
(d) *(with past participle)* **to g. broken** se casser(e); **to g. stolen** être volé(e); **to g. killed** se faire tuer; **to g. dressed** s'habiller; **to g. married** se marier
(e) *(start)* **to g. going** *(leave)* se mettre en route; *(start*

working) se mettre au travail; **to g. talking with sb** entrer en conversation avec qn

▸**get about** *vi (of person)* se déplacer; *(of news, rumour)* circuler

▸**get across** *vt sep (ideas, message)* faire passer

▸**get ahead** *vi* avancer

▸**get along** *vi* (a) *(leave)* s'en aller, partir (b) *(progress)* **how are you getting along in your new job?** comment ça va, votre nouveau travail?; **we can g. along without them** nous pouvons très bien nous passer d'eux (c) *(have good relationship)* s'entendre

▸**get around 1** *vt insep (problem, difficulty)* contourner; **there's no getting around it, we'll have to tell her** on n'a pas le choix, il va falloir lui dire

  2 *vi* = **get about**

▸**get around to** *vt insep* **to g. around to doing sth** trouver le temps de faire qch

▸**get at** *vt insep* (a) *(have access to)* accéder à; *(reach)* atteindre; **to g. at the truth** découvrir la vérité (b) *(imply)* **what are you getting at?** où veux-tu en venir? (c) *Fam (criticize)* s'en prendre à

▸**get away** *vi (escape, leave)* se sauver; *(have a holiday)* s'échapper; *Fam* **g. away!** *(expressing disbelief)* sans blague!

▸**get away with** *vt insep* (a) *(fine, warning)* s'en tirer avec (b) *(crime)* **he stole the money and got away with it** il a volé l'argent et il ne s'est pas fait prendre; *Fig* **that child gets away with murder** on lui passe tout à ce gosse

▸**get back 1** *vt sep (recover)* récupérer; *(strength)* reprendre

  2 *vi (return)* revenir

▸**get back at** *vt insep* **to g. back at sb (for sth)** se venger de qn (pour qch)

▸**get behind** *vt insep (support)* soutenir

  2 *vi (become delayed)* prendre du retard **(with** *or* **in** dans)

▸**get by** *vi (manage)* se débrouiller, s'en tirer **(on/in** avec/ **en)**

▸**get down 1** *vt sep* (a) *(reduce) (weight)* perdre; *(costs, temperature)* faire baisser (b) *(depress)* déprimer (c) *(fetch)* descendre

  2 *vi (descend)* descendre **(from** de)

▸**get down to** *vt insep* se mettre à; **to g. down to the facts** en venir aux faits

▸**get in 1** *vt sep* (a) *(bring inside)* rentrer (b) *(insert)* **I couldn't g. a word in** je n'ai pas pu en placer une (c) *(stock up with)* faire provision de

  2 *vi* (a) *(gain entrance)* entrer (b) *(arrive)* arriver (c) *(be elected)* être élu(e)

▸**get into** *vt insep* (a) *(house)* entrer dans; *(car)* monter dans; **to g. into Parliament** être élu(e) *or* député; **to g. into trouble** s'attirer des ennuis; *Fam* **I don't know what's got into her** je ne sais pas ce qui lui prend (b) *(clothes, boots)* enfiler; **I can't g. into my dress any more** je n'entre plus dans ma robe (c) *Fam (become interested in) (activity)* commencer à s'intéresser à; *(book)* rentrer dans

▸**get in with** *vt insep (group of people)* se mettre bien avec

▸**get off 1** *vt sep* (a) **to g. sb off** *(save from punishment)* tirer qn de là (b) *(send)* **to g. the children off to school** envoyer les enfants à l'école

  2 *vt insep (train, bus)* descendre de

  3 *vi* (a) *(from train, bus)* descendre; *Fig* **I told him where to g. off** je l'ai envoyé promener (b) *(go unpunished)* s'en tirer (c) *(begin)* **to g. off to sleep** s'endormir; **to g. off to a good/bad start** commencer bien/mal

▸**get off on** *vt insep very Fam* **to g. off on sth** être excité(e) par qch; **to g. off on doing sth** prendre son pied à faire qch

▸**get off with** *vt insep Br Fam* lever

▸**get on 1** *vt sep (clothes)* mettre, enfiler

  2 *vt insep (train, bus, plane)* monter dans

  3 *vi* (a) *(enter train, bus)* monter (b) *(progress)* réussir; **to g. on in life** *or* **in the world** réussir dans la vie; **how are you getting on?** *(how are you?)* comment ça va?; **how did you g. on?** *(in exam, at meeting)* comment ça s'est passé? (c) *(have good relationship)* s'entendre; **to g. on well/badly with sb** s'entendre bien/mal avec qn (d) *(age)* **to be getting on (in years)** se faire vieux (vieille)

▸**get on for** *vt insep (approach)* **he must be getting on for fifty now** il doit approcher la cinquantaine; **it was getting on for midnight** il était presque minuit; **there were getting on for 200 people there** on approchait les 200 personnes

▸**get onto** *vt insep* (a) *(contact)* se mettre en rapport avec (b) *(move onto subject of)* en arriver à; **they eventually got onto the subject of money** ils en vinrent finalement à parler d'argent

▸**get out 1** *vt sep* (a) *(bring out)* sortir (b) *(remove) (nail, splinter)* retirer; *(stain)* faire partir

  2 *vi* (a) *(leave)* sortir (b) *(of secret, news)* transpirer

▸**get out of** *vt insep (vehicle)* sortir de; **to g. out of the way** s'écarter; **g. out of here!** *(go away)* va-t-en!; *Fam (I don't believe you)* arrête de dire des bêtises!; **to g. out of doing sth** s'arranger pour ne pas faire qch

▸**get over 1** *vt sep (idea, information)* faire passer; *(facts)* expliquer

  2 *vt insep* (a) *(road, river)* traverser, franchir; *(wall, fence)* passer par-dessus (b) *(illness, trauma)* se remettre de

▸**get over with** *vt sep* **to g. sth over with** en finir avec qch

▸**get round 1** *vt insep* = **get around**

  2 *vi* = **get about**

▸**get round to** *vt insep* = **get around to**

▸**get through 1** *vt insep (communicate)* **to g. sth through to sb** faire comprendre qch à qn

  2 *vt insep* (a) *(pass through) (hole, roof)* passer à travers (b) *(survive) (test, interview)* survivre à; *(period of time)* tenir (c) *(finish)* achever (d) *(consume) (food, drink)* consommer; *(money)* dépenser

  3 *vi* (a) *(arrive) (of news)* parvenir; *(of messenger)* arriver (b) **to g. through to sb** *(on telephone)* obtenir la communication avec qn; *Fig (make understand)* se faire comprendre par qn

▸**get together 1** *vt sep (money)* réunir; *(belongings, ideas)* rassembler

  2 *vi (of people)* se réunir

▸**get up 1** *vt sep* (a) *(out of bed)* faire lever (b) *(dress up)* **he got himself up in his best clothes** il a mis ses plus beaux vêtements (c) *very Fam (achieve erection)* **he couldn't g. it up** il n'a pas réussi à bander

  2 *vt insep Fig* **to g. up sb's nose** taper sur les nerfs à qn

  3 *vi (rise)* se lever

▸**get up to** *vt insep (do)* **what have you been getting up to recently?** qu'est-ce que tu as fait ces derniers temps?; **to g. up to mischief** faire des bêtises; **he's been getting up to his old tricks** il a encore fait des siennes

getaway ['getəweɪ] *n* fuite *f*; **to make one's g.** prendre la fuite; **g. car** = voiture utilisée pour prendre la fuite

get-rich-quick ['get'rɪtʃ'kwɪk] *adj Fam* **a g. scheme** un moyen de devenir riche rapidement

get-together ['gettəgeðə(r)] *n Fam* réunion *f* (entre amis)

get-up ['getʌp] *n Fam (clothes)* accoutrement *m; (fancy dress)* déguisement *m*

get-up-and-go ['getʌpənd'gəʊ] *n Fam* énergie *f*

get-well card ['get'wel'kɑːd] *n* carte *f* de prompt rétablissement

geyser ['giːzə(r)] *n* **(a)** *(spring)* geyser *m* **(b)** *Br (water heater)* chauffe-eau *m inv*

Ghana ['gɑːnə] *n* le Ghana

Ghanaian [gɑː'neɪən] **1** *n* Ghanéen(enne) *m,f*
2 *adj* ghanéen(enne)

ghastly ['gɑːstlɪ] *adj (terrible)* horrible, épouvantable; *(mistake)* monstrueux(euse)

Ghent [gent] *n* Gand

gherkin ['gɜːkɪn] *n* cornichon *m*

ghetto ['getəʊ] *(pl* **ghettoes** *or* **ghettos)** *n* ghetto *m; Fam* **g. blaster** radiocassette *f*

ghost [gəʊst] **1** *n* fantôme *m;* **you look as though you've seen a g.** on dirait que tu as vu un revenant; **not the g. of a chance** pas la moindre chance; **to give up the g.** *(of person, machine)* rendre l'âme; **g. story** histoire *f* de fantôme; **g. town** ville *f* fantôme
2 *vt* **to g. a book** servir de nègre pour un livre

ghostly ['gəʊstlɪ] *adj* spectral(e)

ghostwrite ['gəʊstraɪt] *vt* **to g. a book** servir de nègre pour un livre

ghostwriter ['gəʊstraɪtə(r)] *n* nègre *m*

ghoul [guːl] *n (evil spirit)* goule *f; Fig (morbid person)* personne *f* morbide

ghoulish ['guːlɪʃ] *adj (humour, remark)* morbide; *(scene)* macabre

GHQ [dʒiːeɪtʃ'kjuː] *n Mil (abbr* **General Head-quarters)** QG *m inv*

GI [dʒiː'aɪ] *n Am Fam* GI *m inv*

giant ['dʒaɪənt] **1** *n* géant(e) *m,f;* **g. killer** *(in sport)* vainqueur *m* surprise
2 *adj* géant(e)

gibber ['dʒɪbə(r)] *vi* baragouiner

gibbering ['dʒɪbərɪŋ] *adj* au discours incohérent; *Fam* **a g. idiot** un(e) pauvre idiot(e)

gibberish ['dʒɪbərɪʃ] *n* charabia *m;* **to talk g.** dire n'importe quoi

gibbet ['dʒɪbɪt] *n* gibet *m,* potence *f*

gibbon ['gɪbən] *n* gibbon *m*

gibe [dʒaɪb] **1** *n* moquerie *f*
2 *vi* **to g. at sb** se moquer de qn

giblets ['dʒɪblɪts] *npl* abats *mpl*

Gibraltar [dʒɪ'brɔːltə(r)] *n* Gibraltar

giddiness ['gɪdɪnɪs] *n* étourdissement *m,* vertige *m*

giddy ['gɪdɪ] *adj* **to be** *or* **feel g.** avoir le vertige; **it makes me (feel) g.** ça me donne le vertige; *Fig* **the g. heights** les hautes sphères *fpl*

GIF [dʒɪf] *n Comptr (abbr* **Graphic Information Format)** GIF *m*

gift [gɪft] *n* **(a)** *(present)* cadeau *m; Prov* **never look a g. horse in the mouth** à cheval donné on ne regarde pas la bouche; **g. shop** boutique *f* de cadeaux; **g. token** chèque-cadeau *m* **(b)** *(talent)* don *m;* **to have a g. for sth** être

doué(e) pour qch; **to have the g. of the gab** *(be talkative)* avoir la langue bien pendue; *(speak persuasively)* avoir du bagout

gifted ['gɪftɪd] *adj* doué(e); *(artist, musician)* de talent

gift-wrapped ['gɪftræpt] *adj* sous paquet-cadeau

gig [gɪg] *n* **(a)** *(carriage)* cabriolet *m* **(b)** *Fam (pop concert)* concert *m*

gigabyte ['dʒɪgəbaɪt] *n Comptr* gigaoctet *m*

gigantic [dʒaɪ'gæntɪk] *adj* colossal(e), gigantesque

giggle ['gɪgəl] **1** *n* **(a)** *(laugh)* petit rire *m* idiot; **to have (a fit of) the giggles** avoir le fou rire *m; Fam (amusement)* **what a g.!** quelle rigolade!; **to do sth for a g.** faire qch pour rigoler
2 *vi* rire (nerveusement)

giggly ['gɪgəlɪ] *adj* **to be g.** pouffer de rire

gigolo ['dʒɪgələʊ] *(pl* **gigolos)** *n* gigolo *m*

gild [gɪld] *(pt & pp* **gilded** *or* **gilt** [gɪlt]) *vt* dorer; *Fig* **to g. the lily** surcharger

gill [dʒɪl] *n (liquid measure)* = 0,142 l, quart *m* de pinte

gills [gɪlz] *npl (of fish)* ouïes *fpl,* branchies *fpl; Fig* **to be green about the g.** avoir le teint verdâtre

gilt [gɪlt] **1** *n* dorure *f; Fin* **gilts** titres *mpl ou* fonds *mpl* d'État
2 *adj* doré(e)
3 *pt & pp of* **gild**

gilt-edged ['gɪltedʒd] *adj Fin* **g. securities** *or* **stocks** titres *mpl ou* fonds *mpl* d'État

gimlet ['gɪmlɪt] *n (tool)* vrille *f; Fig* **g. eyes** yeux *mpl* perçants

gimme ['gɪmi] *very Fam =* **give me**

gimmick ['gɪmɪk] *n* truc *m,* astuce *f*

gimmicky ['gɪmɪkɪ] *adj* artificiel(elle)

gin [dʒɪn] *n* gin *m;* **g. and tonic** un gin tonic

ginger ['dʒɪndʒə(r)] **1** *n* gingembre *m;* **g. ale** = boisson gazeuse au gingembre pouvant servir à couper un alcool; **g. beer** limonade *f* au gingembre
2 *adj (hair)* roux (rousse)

▸**ginger up** *vt sep Fam (person, group)* stimuler; *(film, story)* donner du punch à

gingerbread ['dʒɪndʒəbred] *n* pain *m* d'épice; **g. man** = bonhomme en biscuit parfumé au gingembre

gingerly ['dʒɪndʒəlɪ] *adv* avec précaution

gingham ['gɪŋəm] *n* vichy *m*

gingivitis [dʒɪndʒɪ'vaɪtɪs] *n Med* gingivite *f*

ginormous [dʒaɪ'nɔːməs] *adj Fam* gigantesque, énorme

ginseng ['dʒɪnseŋ] *n* ginseng *m*

gipsy ['dʒɪpsɪ] *(pl* **gipsies)** *n (Eastern European)* tzigane *mf; (Spanish)* gitan(e) *m,f;* **g. caravan** roulotte *f*

giraffe [dʒɪ'rɑːf] *n* girafe *f*

gird [gɜːd] *(pt & pp* **girded** *or* **girt** [gɜːt]) *vt Lit* **to g. one's loins** se ceindre les reins

girder ['gɜːdə(r)] *n* poutre *f* (métallique)

girdle ['gɜːdəl] **1** *n (corset)* gaine *f*
2 *vt Lit (surround)* ceindre, entourer

girl [gɜːl] *n* fille *f;* **a French g.** une (jeune) Française; *Br* **G. Guide** éclaireuse *f*

girlfriend ['gɜːlfrend] *n (lover)* petite amie *f; (friend)* amie *f*

girlhood ['gɜːlhʊd] *n* enfance *f,* jeunesse *f*

girlie ['gɜːlɪ] *n Fam* **g. mag** magazine *m* érotique

girlish ['gɜːlɪʃ] *adj* (*of girl*) de fille; (*of woman, effeminate man*) de jeune fille; **g. laughter** rire *m* de jeune fille

giro ['dʒaɪrəʊ] (*pl* **giros**) *n* Br (**a**) Fin **g. account** compte *m* chèque postal, CCP *m* (**b**) Fam (*unemployment cheque*) allocation *f* (de) chômage

girt [gɜːt] *pt & pp* of **gird**

girth [gɜːθ] *n* (*of tree*) circonférence *f*; (*of person*) corpulence *f*

gist [dʒɪst] *n* essentiel *m*; **to get the g.** saisir l'essentiel

git [gɪt] *n* Br very Fam con (conne) *m,f*

give [gɪv] **1** *vt* (*pt* **gave** [geɪv], *pp* **given** ['gɪvən]) (**a**) (*in general*) donner; (*as present*) offrir; **to g. sth to sb, to g. sb sth** donner qch à qn; (*as present*) offrir qch à qn; **to g. sb a dirty look** lancer un regard noir à qn; **he was given ten years/a fine** il a été condamné à dix ans de prison/à une amende; **g. her my love** embrasse-la pour moi; **she gave her age as twenty** elle a déclaré qu'elle avait vingt ans; **she gave me to understand that...** elle m'a fait comprendre que...; **g. or take a few minutes/pence** à quelques minutes/pence près

(**b**) (*with noun to form verbal expressions*) **to g. a laugh** partir d'un éclat de rire; **to g. a sigh** pousser un soupir; **to g. sb a smile** sourire à qn; **to g. sb a fright** faire peur à qn; **to g. sb a kiss** embrasser qn; **he gave his face a wash** il s'est lavé le visage; **she gave the soup a stir** elle a remué la soupe

2 *vi* (**a**) (*donate*) donner; **please g. generously** soyez généreux, s'il vous plaît; **to g. of one's time** donner de son temps

(**b**) (*yield, break*) (*of cloth, shoes*) se faire; (*of rope*) lâcher; (*of support, door*) céder

(**c**) Am Fam **what gives?** quoi de neuf?

3 *n* (*of fabric*) élasticité *f*

▶**give away** *vt sep* (**a**) (*give for nothing*) donner (**b**) (*prize*) distribuer; **to g. the bride away** conduire la mariée à l'autel (**c**) (*reveal*) trahir

▶**give back** *vt sep* rendre

▶**give in 1** *vt sep* (*hand over*) remettre
 2 *vi* (*surrender*) céder (**to** à); (*admit defeat*) abandonner

▶**give off** *vt sep* (*smell, heat*) dégager

▶**give onto** *vt insep* **the house gives directly onto the street** la maison donne directement sur la rue

▶**give out 1** *vt sep* (**a**) (*money, food*) distribuer; (*information*) donner (**b**) (*noise*) émettre; (*heat*) répandre
 2 *vi* (*of supplies, patience*) s'épuiser; (*of luck*) tourner

▶**give over 1** *vt sep* (*money, objects*) remettre; (*devote*) consacrer (**to** à)
 2 *vi* Fam **g. up on sb, will you?** arrête, d'accord?

▶**give up 1** *vt sep* (*possessions*) renoncer à; (*activity, hope*) abandonner; **to g. up smoking** arrêter de fumer; **to g. up one's job** quitter son emploi; **to g. sb up for dead** considérer qn comme mort(e)
 2 *vi* abandonner; **to g. up on sb** perdre tout espoir en qn; (*of doctors*) perdre tout espoir en ce qui concerne qn; **to g. up on sth** laisser tomber qch

▶**give way** *vi* (**a**) (*collapse*) (*of support*) céder; (*of floor, ceiling*) s'effondrer; (*of rope, legs*) lâcher; (*of ground*) se dérober (**b**) (*yield*) (*in argument*) céder (**to** à); (*in car*) céder le passage (**to** à); **her tears gave way to laughter** ses larmes ont cédé la place au rire

give-and-take ['gɪvən'teɪk] *n* concessions *fpl* (mutuelles); **there has to be some g.** il faut que chacun y mette du sien

giveaway ['gɪvəweɪ] *n* Fam (**a**) (*revelation*) **what she said about the night before was the g.** ce qu'elle a dit sur la soirée précédente l'a trahie; **it was a dead g.** cela en disait long (**b**) (*free gift*) cadeau *m*; **g. price** prix *m* imbattable

given ['gɪvən] **1** *adj* (**a**) (*specific*) (*time, place*) donné(e); **at a g. point** à un moment donné; **g. name** prénom *m* (**b**) (*apt, likely*) **to be g. to doing sth** avoir tendance à faire qch
 2 *conj* (**a**) (*considering*) étant donné; **g. that...** étant donné que...; **g. the nature of the case** étant donné la nature de l'affaire (**b**) **g. the chance again** si l'occasion se représentait
 3 *pp* of **give**

gizmo ['gɪzməʊ] (*pl* **gizmos**) *n* Fam truc *m*, machin *m*

gizzard ['gɪzəd] *n* gésier *m*

glacé cherry ['glæsɪ'tʃerɪ] *n* cerise *f* confite

glacial ['gleɪsɪəl] *adj* glaciaire; Fig glacial(e)

glacier ['glæsɪə(r)] *n* glacier *m*

glad [glæd] *adj* heureux(euse), content(e) (**about** de); **I would be g. to assist you** je serais ravi de pouvoir vous aider; **to be g. of sth** (*grateful for*) être heureux d'avoir qch; Fam **to put on one's g. rags** se mettre sur son trente et un

gladden ['glædən] *vt* réjouir

glade [gleɪd] *n* Lit clairière *f*

gladiator ['glædɪeɪtə(r)] *n* gladiateur *m*

gladiolus [glædɪ'əʊləs] (*pl* **gladioli** [glædɪ'əʊlaɪ]) *n* glaïeul *m*

gladly ['glædlɪ] *adv* avec plaisir, volontiers

glamorize ['glæməraɪz] *vt* rendre séduisant(e) *ou* attrayant(e)

glamorous ['glæmərəs] *adj* (*person*) élégant(e); (*place, job, image*) prestigieux(euse); (*dress*) magnifique

glamour, *Am* **glamor** ['glæmə(r)] *n* (*of person*) séduction *f*; (*of job, lifestyle*) prestige *m*; Fam **g. girl** belle fille *f*, pin-up *f*

glance [glɑːns] **1** *n* coup *m* d'œil; **to have a g. at sth** jeter un coup d'œil à qch; **at a g.** d'un coup d'œil; **at first g.** au premier coup d'œil
 2 *vi* **to g. at** regarder brièvement, jeter un coup d'œil à; **to g. through sth** parcourir qch rapidement

▶**glance off** *vt insep* (*of blow, missile*) ricocher sur

glancing ['glɑːnsɪŋ] *adj* (*blow*) oblique

gland [glænd] *n* glande *f*

glandular ['glændjʊlə(r)] *adj* glandulaire; **g. fever** mononucléose *f* infectieuse

glare [gleə(r)] **1** *n* (**a**) (*angry stare*) regard *m* furieux (**b**) (*bright light*) éclat *m*, lumière *f* éblouissante; Fig **in the full g. of publicity** sous les feux de médias
 2 *vi* (*stare angrily*) **to g. at sb/sth** fixer qn/qch d'un air furieux

glaringly ['gleərɪŋlɪ] *adv* **it's g. obvious** ça saute aux yeux

Glasgow ['glɑːzgəʊ] *n* Glasgow

glass [glɑːs] *n* verre *m*; (*glassware*) verrerie *f*; **a g. of wine** un verre de vin; **g. bottle** bouteille *f* en verre; **g. case** vitrine *f*; **g. door** porte *f* vitrée; **g. eye** œil *m* de verre; **g. wool** laine *f* de verre

glass-blowing ['glɑːsbləʊɪŋ] *n* soufflage *m* du verre

glasses ['glɑːsɪz] *npl* (*spectacles*) lunettes *fpl*

glassful ['glɑːsfʊl] *n* verre *m*

glasshouse ['glɑːshaʊs] *n Br* serre *f*; *Prov* **people who live in glasshouses shouldn't throw stones** il faut être sans défauts pour critiquer autrui

glasspaper ['glɑːspeɪpə(r)] *n* papier *m* de verre

glassware ['glɑːsweə(r)] *n* verrerie *f*

glassworks ['glɑːswɜːks] *n* verrerie *f*; *(for crystal)* cristallerie *f*

glassy ['glɑːsɪ] *adj (eyes, look)* vitreux(euse); *(water)* immobile

Glaswegian [glæz'wiːdʒən] **1** *n* = personne née à ou habitant Glasgow
2 *adj* de Glasgow

glaucoma [glɔː'kəʊmə] *n* glaucome *m*; **to have g.** avoir un glaucome

glaze [gleɪz] **1** *n (on pottery)* vernis *m*; *(on pastry)* glaçage *m*
2 *vt* **(a)** *(window)* vitrer **(b)** *(pottery)* vernisser; *(pastry)* glacer
▸**glaze over** *vi (of eyes)* devenir vitreux(euse)

glazed [gleɪzd] *adj* **(a)** *(roof, door)* vitré(e) **(b)** *(pottery)* vernissé(e)

glazier ['gleɪzɪə(r)] *n* vitrier *m*

gleam [gliːm] **1** *n (of light)* rayon *m*; *Fig* **a g. of hope** une lueur d'espoir
2 *vi* luire, briller; *(of water)* miroiter

gleaming ['gliːmɪŋ] *adj* étincelant(e)

glean [gliːn] *vt* glaner

glee [gliː] *n (delight)* joie *f*; *(malicious pleasure)* jubilation *f*

gleeful ['gliːfʊl] *adj (happy)* joyeux(euse); **to be g.** *(maliciously)* jubiler

glen [glen] *n Scot* vallée *f*

glib [glɪb] *adj (person, excuse)* désinvolte; *(reply)* spécieux(euse)

glibly ['glɪblɪ] *adv (reply)* de façon désinvolte; *(speak)* avec aisance

glide [glaɪd] *vi (move smoothly)* glisser; *(of aircraft, bird)* planer

glider ['glaɪdə(r)] *n (aircraft)* planeur *m*

gliding ['glaɪdɪŋ] *n (sport)* vol *m* à voile

glimmer ['glɪmə(r)] **1** *n* faible lueur *f*; *(of water)* reflet *m*; *Fig* **a g. of hope** une lueur d'espoir
2 *vi (of light)* luire; *(of water)* miroiter; *(of metal)* étinceler

glimpse [glɪmps] **1** *n* **to catch a g. of** entrevoir; **a g. of the future** un aperçu de (ce que sera) l'avenir
2 *vt* entrevoir

glint [glɪnt] **1** *n (of light) (flash)* éclat *m*; *(continuous)* scintillement *m*; *(of water)* reflet *m*; **with a g. in her eye** avec une lueur dans le regard
2 *vi (of light, eye)* briller; *(of water, metal)* scintiller

glisten ['glɪsən] *vi (of water, metal)* scintiller; **his forehead glistened with sweat** la sueur perlait sur son front

glitter ['glɪtə(r)] **1** *n (sparkle)* scintillement *m*; *Fig (of occasion)* éclat *m*, faste *m*
2 *vi* scintiller; *Prov* **all that glitters is not gold** tout ce qui brille n'est pas d'or

glittering ['glɪtərɪŋ] *adj (jewels)* scintillant(e); *Fig (occasion, career)* brillant(e)

glitz [glɪts] *n* clinquant *m*, tape-à-l'œil *m*

glitzy ['glɪtsɪ] *adj Fam* tape-à-l'œil *inv*

gloat [gləʊt] *vi (at one's own success)* jubiler (**at** à l'idée de); *(about somebody else's misfortune)* se réjouir (**about** *or* **over**

de); **I don't like to g., but...** ce n'est pas que ça me réjouisse, mais...

global ['gləʊbəl] *adj (comprehensive)* global(e); *(worldwide)* mondial(e); **g. village** village *m* planétaire; **g. warming** réchauffement *m* de la planète

globally ['gləʊbəlɪ] *adv (comprehensive)* globalement; *(worldwide)* mondialement

globe [gləʊb] *n (sphere)* globe *m*; *(with map)* globe *m* terrestre; **the g.** *(the earth)* le globe terrestre; **to travel the g.** voyager dans le monde entier

globetrotter ['gləʊbtrɒtə(r)] *n Fam* globe-trotter *mf*

globule ['glɒbjuːl] *n* gouttelette *f*

gloom [gluːm] *n* **(a)** *(darkness)* obscurité *f* **(b)** *(sadness)* morosité *f*

gloomily ['gluːmɪlɪ] *adv (sadly)* sombrement

gloomy ['gluːmɪ] *adj* **(a)** *(dark)* sombre; *(weather)* morose **(b)** *(sad)* triste **(c)** *(pessimistic)* pessimiste; **g. thoughts** idées *fpl* noires

glorified ['glɔːrɪfaɪd] *adj* **she's just a g. secretary** elle n'est rien de plus qu'une secrétaire

glorify ['glɔːrɪfaɪ] *(pt & pp* **glorified**) *vt* **(a)** *(extol)* célébrer; *Rel* **to g. God** rendre gloire à Dieu **(b)** *(war, violence)* glorifier

glorious ['glɔːrɪəs] *adj* **(a)** *(reign, victory)* glorieux(euse) **(b)** *(view, sunshine)* magnifique

gloriously ['glɔːrɪəslɪ] *adv* **(a)** *(die, reign)* avec gloire **(b)** *(beautifully)* superbement; **it was g. sunny** il faisait un soleil splendide

glory ['glɔːrɪ] *n* **(a)** *(honour)* gloire *f* **(b)** *(splendour)* splendeur *f*
▸**glory in** *vt insep* se glorifier de

gloss¹ [glɒs] *n (in text)* glose *f*

gloss² [glɒs] *n (shine)* lustre *m*; *Fig* vernis *m*; *Fig* **to take the g. off sth** gâcher qch; **g. paint** peinture *f* brillante
▸**gloss over** *vt insep* passer sur

glossary ['glɒsərɪ] *(pl* **glossaries**) *n* glossaire *m*

glossy ['glɒsɪ] *adj* brillant(e); **g. brochure** brochure *f* luxueuse; **g. magazine** magazine *m* de luxe; **g. paper** papier *m* glacé

glottal stop ['glɒtəl'stɒp] *n* coup *m* de glotte

glove [glʌv] *n* gant *m*; *Fig* **the gloves are off** tous les coups sont permis; **g. compartment** *(in car)* boîte *f* à gants; **g. puppet** marionnette *f* à gaine

glow [gləʊ] **1** *n (light)* lueur *f*; *(on cheeks)* couleurs *fpl*; **the g. of the setting sun** l'embrasement du couchant; *Fig* **a g. of pride/satisfaction** un vif sentiment de fierté/ satisfaction
2 *vi (of light, fire)* rougeoyer; *Fig* **to be glowing with health** être resplendissant(e) de santé; *Fig* **to g. with pride/pleasure** rayonner de fierté/plaisir

glower ['glaʊə(r)] *vi* **to g. at sb** lancer des regards noirs à qn

glowing ['gləʊɪŋ] *adj (cigarette, coal)* incandescent(e); *(metal)* chauffé(e) au rouge; *Fig (praise, words)* chaleureux(euse); *(description, report)* enthousiaste; *Fig* **to paint sth in g. colours** présenter qch sous un jour très favorable

glow-worm ['gləʊwɜːm] *n* ver *m* luisant

glucose ['gluːkəʊs] *n* glucose *m*

glue [gluː] **1** *n* colle *f*
2 *vt* coller (**to** à); *Fig* **to be glued to the television** être cloué(e) devant la télévision

glue-sniffing ['glu:snɪfɪŋ] *n* inhalation *f* de colle

glum [glʌm] *adj* maussade

glut [glʌt] 1 *n (of goods)* encombrement *m*
2 *vt (pt & pp* **glutted**) (a) *(market, economy)* encombrer, inonder (b) to g. **oneself (on)** se gaver (de)

glutinous ['glu:tɪnəs] *adj* gluant(e)

glutton ['glʌtən] *n (greedy person)* goinfre *mf*, glouton(onne) *m,f*; *Fig* to be a g. **for punishment** être masochiste

gluttony ['glʌtənɪ] *n* goinfrerie *f*, gloutonnerie *f*

glycerin ['glɪsərɪn], **glycerine** ['glɪsəri:n], **glycerol** ['glɪsərɒl] *n* glycérine *f*

GMT [dʒi:em'ti:] *n (abbr* **Greenwich Mean Time)** GMT *m*

gnarled [nɑ:ld] *adj* noueux(euse)

gnash [næʃ] *vt* to g. **one's teeth** grincer des dents

gnat [næt] *n* moucheron *m*

gnaw [nɔ:] 1 *vt (of rodent)* ronger
2 *vi* (a) *(of rodent)* to g. **through sth** ronger qch (b) *Fig (of doubt, guilt)* to g. **away at sb** ronger qn

gnome [nəʊm] *n* gnome *m*

GNP [dʒi:en'pi:] *n Econ (abbr* **Gross National Product)** PNB *m*

gnu [nu:] *n* gnou *m*

go [gəʊ] 1 *vi* (*3rd person singular* **goes** [gəʊz], *pt went* [went], *pp* **gone** [gɒn]) (a) *(move)* aller; to go **to France** aller en France; to go **to the doctor** aller chez le docteur; to go **home** rentrer chez soi; to go **swimming/skiing** (aller) nager/skier; **the proceeds will go to charity** l'argent recueilli sera versé à des œuvres de charité; *Fig* **where do we go from here?** et maintenant, qu'est-ce qu'on fait?
(b) *(leave)* partir, s'en aller; **I've got to go** il faut que j'y aille; **let's go!** allons-y!
(c) *(function)* marcher; *(of bell)* sonner; to **keep the conversation going** entretenir la conversation
(d) *(progress)* aller; to go **well/badly** bien/mal se passer; *Fam* **how's it going?** comment ça va?; **how does the tune/story go?** c'est quoi, l'air/l'histoire, déjà?
(e) *(of time)* passer; **the time went quickly/slowly** le temps a passé vite/lentement; **it has just gone eight** il est huit heures à peine passées; **there are only five minutes to go** il ne reste que cinq minutes
(f) *(disappear, deteriorate)* disparaître; *(of light bulb)* griller; *(of fuse)* sauter; *(of batteries)* s'user; **her sight/voice is going** elle est en train de perdre la vue/la voix; **most of my money goes on food** l'essentiel de mon argent passe dans la nourriture
(g) *(forming future)* to be **going to do sth** aller faire qch; **I was going to walk** j'allais y aller à pied; **it's going to rain** il va pleuvoir
(h) *(match)* aller (**with** avec); **these colours go/don't go** ces couleurs vont bien/ne vont pas ensemble
(i) *(be available)* **there's a job going at the factory** il y a une place à l'usine; **is there any wine going?** est-ce qu'il y a du vin?; **it went for £12** on l'a vendu 12 livres
(j) *(fit)* entrer; **the piano won't go through the door** le piano ne passera pas par la porte; **four into three won't go** trois n'est pas divisible par quatre
(k) *(belong)* aller; **the cups go on that shelf** les tasses vont sur cette étagère
(l) *(become)* devenir; to go **crazy** devenir fou (folle); to go **red** rougir; to go **cold** refroidir
(m) *(be the rule)* **what she says goes** c'est elle qui commande
(n) *Fam (urinate)* aller aux toilettes
(o) *Am* **two burgers to go** *(to take away)* deux hamburgers à emporter
2 *vt* (a) *(make sound)* & *Fam (say)* faire; **cows go moo la vache fait meuh**; to go **bang/plop** faire paf/plouf
(b) *(idioms)* to go **it alone** se lancer en solo; to go **one better than sb** faire mieux que qn, surenchérir sur qn; *Fam* **I could really go a beer!** je me ferais bien une bière!
3 *n (pl* **goes**) (a) *(expressing activity)* to be **on the go** ne pas arrêter; **she had three boyfriends on the go at the same time** elle avait trois copains en même temps; **it's all go** ça n'arrête pas; **from the word go** dès le début
(b) *(energy)* to be **full of go** être dynamique
(c) *(success)* to **make a go of sth** réussir qch
(d) *(turn)* tour *m*; **(it's) your go!** *(in game)* c'est ton tour!, c'est à toi!; to **have a g.** *(in game)* c'est ton tour!, c'est à toi!; to **have a g. at doing sth** essayer de faire qch; *Fam* **let's have a go!** allons-y!; *(let me try)* laisse-moi essayer!; **at one go** d'un coup; **£1 a go** par/allez/1 livre le tour
(e) *(idioms)* to **have a go at sb** incendier qn

▶**go about** 1 *vi (circulate)* (*of person)* se promener; (*of rumour)* circuler; **you can't go about saying things like that!** il ne faut pas raconter des choses pareilles!; **there's a bug going about** il y a un microbe qui se promène
2 *vt insep (travel) (country)* parcourir (b) *(tackle) (task)* vaquer à; to go **about doing sth** s'y prendre pour faire qch; **how do I go about getting a licence?** que dois-je faire pour obtenir un permis?

▶**go across** *vt insep & vi* traverser

▶**go after** *vt insep (pursue)* to go **after sb** courir après qn; to go **after sth** essayer d'obtenir qch

▶**go against** *vt insep* (a) *(contradict) (principles, instincts)* aller à l'encontre de (b) *(be unfavourable to)* **the decision went against him** la décision lui a été défavorable

▶**go ahead** *vi* (a) *(take place)* avoir lieu; to go **ahead with sth** commencer ou entreprendre qch; **may I say something?** – go ahead puis-je dire quelque chose? – allez-y (b) *(go in front)* passer devant; to go **ahead of sb** devancer qn

▶**go along** *vi (proceed)* se dérouler; **as we go along** en chemin; to **do sth as one goes along** faire qch au fur et à mesure

▶**go along with** *vt insep (suggestion, plan)* approuver, être d'accord avec

▶**go at** *vt insep (person, task)* s'attaquer à

▶**go away** *vi (leave)* partir; *(disappear)* disparaître; **go away!** allez-vous-en!; to go **away on business/for the weekend** partir en voyage d'affaires/en week-end

▶**go back** *vi* (a) *(return)* revenir; to go **back to doing sth** se remettre à faire qch; to go **back to sleep** se rendormir; to go **back to one's old ways** reprendre ses anciennes habitudes (b) *(in time)* to go **back to** remonter à; *Fam* **we go back a long way** ça fait longtemps qu'on se connaît

▶**go back on** *vt insep (promise)* revenir sur

▶**go before** 1 *vi (precede)* précéder
2 *vt insep* to go **before the court** *(of defendant, case)* passer au tribunal

▶**go by** 1 *vi* (a) *(pass)* passer; to **watch the world go by** regarder passer les gens (b) *(of time)* s'écouler
2 *vt insep* (a) *(be guided by)* to go **by appearances** juger d'après les apparences; to go **by the rules** respecter les règles (b) *(be known by)* to go **by the name of** être connu(e) sous le nom de

▸**go down 1** *vt insep (descend)* descendre

2 *vi* (a) *(descend)* descendre; *(of sun)* se coucher; *(of ship)* sombrer; **to go down on one's knees** s'agenouiller; *Fig* se mettre à genoux; **to go down with an illness** tomber malade (b) *(be defeated)* être vaincu(e); **I'm not going to go down without a fight** je me battrai jusqu'au bout (c) *(of level, temperature, prices)* baisser; *(of tyre, balloon)* se dégonfler (d) *(be received)* **to go down well/badly** être bien/mal reçu(e); **he has gone down in history as a tyrant** l'histoire a retenu de lui l'image d'un tyran

▸**go for** *vt insep* (a) *(attack)* attaquer; **if you really want the job, go for it!** si tu veux vraiment le poste, bats-toi!; *Fam* **go for it!** vas-y! (b) *(like)* avoir un faible pour (c) *(choose)* prendre (d) **he has got a lot going for him** il a bien des atouts (e) *(apply to)* s'appliquer à; **the same goes for you** ça vaut aussi pour toi

▸**go in** *vi (enter)* entrer; *(fit)* rentrer; *(of sun)* se cacher

▸**go in for** *vt insep* (a) *(competition)* s'inscrire à (b) *(like)* **she doesn't go in for cooking/sports** elle n'est pas très portée sur la cuisine/les sports

▸**go into** *vt insep* (a) *(enter)* entrer dans (b) *(examine)* examiner

▸**go off 1** *vi* (a) *(leave)* partir *(with* avec*)* (b) *(of meat, fish)* s'avarier; *(of milk)* tourner (c) *(of bomb)* exploser; *(of alarm)* se déclencher; **the gun went off** le coup est parti (d) *(of event)* **to go off well or smoothly** se dérouler bien (e) *(stop working)* **the power went off** l'électricité a été coupée; **the light went off** la lumière s'est éteinte

2 *vt insep (lose liking for)* ne plus aimer, se lasser de; **I've gone off the idea** l'idée ne me séduit plus

▸**go on 1** *vi* (a) *(continue)* continuer; **to go on doing sth** continuer à faire qch; **as time went on** avec le temps (b) *(proceed)* **to go on to sth** passer à qch; **to go on to do sth** poursuivre en faisant qch (c) *(talk excessively)* **don't go on about it!** arrête de parler de ça!; **he does go on a bit** il est un peu soûlant; **to go on at sb** s'en prendre à qn (d) *(happen)* se passer; **what's going on here?** qu'est-ce qui se passe ici? (e) *(of electricity, light, heating)* s'allumer

2 *vt insep* (a) *(be guided by)* se fonder sur; **the police have nothing to go on** la police n'a rien sur quoi se fonder (b) *(approach)* **she's two going on three** elle va sur ses trois ans

▸**go out** *vi* (a) *(leave)* sortir; **to go out for a meal** aller au restaurant; **to go out on strike** se mettre en grève (b) *(date)* sortir ensemble; **to go out with sb** sortir avec qn (c) *(of fire, light)* s'éteindre (d) *(become unfashionable)* passer de mode (e) *(be eliminated)* être éliminé(e) (f) *(of TV, radio programme)* être diffusé(e)

▸**go over 1** *vi* (a) *(cross)* **to go over to sb** aller vers qn (b) *(switch)* **to go over to sth** passer à qch (c) *(of suggestion, joke)* **to go over well/badly** être bien/mal reçu(e)

2 *vt insep* (a) *(bridge)* passer; *(road)* traverser; **the ball went over the wall** la balle est passée par-dessus le mur (b) *(examine)* passer en revue; *(figures, accounts)* vérifier; **to go over sth in one's mind** repasser qch dans son esprit

▸**go round** *vt insep* **to go round town** faire un tour en ville; **to go round the shops** faire les magasins

2 *vi* (a) *(visit)* **I said I'd go round (and see her)** j'ai dit que j'irai la voir; **she's gone round to a friend's** elle est allée voir un ami (b) *(circulate)* *(of rumour)* circuler; *(of cold, flu)* se promener (c) *(be enough)* **there was enough food/drink to go round** il y avait assez à manger/ boire pour tout le monde

▸**go through 1** *vt insep* (a) *(penetrate)* traverser (b) *(suffer)* subir (c) *(complete)* *(formalities)* accomplir (d) *(examine)* passer en revue; *(one's notes, speech)* revoir; *(suitcase, house)* fouiller; **to go through sb's pockets** fouiller les poches de qn (e) *(use up)* *(money)* dépenser; *(food)* consommer; **we've gone through six bottles of milk** nous avons bu six bouteilles de lait

2 *vi (be completed)* *(of deal)* être conclu(e); *(of bill)* passer; *(of divorce)* être prononcé(e)

▸**go through with** *vt insep* aller jusqu'au bout de; **I can't go through with the wedding** finalement, je ne me marie plus; **I can't go through with it** je ne peux pas le faire

▸**go under** *vi (of ship)* couler; *Fig (of firm)* faire faillite

▸**go up 1** *vt insep* monter

2 *vi* (a) *(climb, rise)* monter; *(of theatre curtain)* se lever; **to go up to bed** monter se coucher; **a shout went up from the crowd** un cri s'éleva de la foule; *Fig* **to go up in the world** *(socially)* faire son chemin (b) *(of prices, temperature)* monter, grimper; **to go up in sb's estimation** monter dans l'estime de qn (c) *(explode)* sauter

▸**go up to** *vt insep* (a) *(approach)* se diriger vers (b) *(reach)* aller jusqu'à

▸**go with** *vt insep* (a) *(accompany)* aller (de pair) avec; **a company car goes with the job** le poste donne droit à une voiture de fonction (b) *(harmonize)* aller avec

▸**go without 1** *vi* se priver; **I'd rather go without** je préfère m'en passer

2 *vt insep* se passer de

goad [gəʊd] **1** *n Fig (remark, criticism)* aiguillon *m*

2 *vt Fig (person)* provoquer; **to g. sb into doing sth** harceler qn jusqu'à ce qu'il fasse qch

▸**goad on** *vt sep* aiguillonner

go-ahead [gəʊəhed] **1** *n* **to give sb/sth the g.** donner le feu vert à qn/qch

2 *adj (enterprising)* entreprenant(e), dynamique

goal [gəʊl] *n* (a) *(aim)* but *m*, objectif *m* (b) *(in football, hockey)* but *m*; **g. kick** coup *m* de pied de but; **g. line** ligne *f* de but; **g. scorer** buteur(euse) *m,f*

goalkeeper ['gəʊlkiːpə(r)], *Fam* **goalie** ['gəʊli] *n* gardien *m* de but, goal *m*

goalless ['gəʊllɪs] *adj* **g. draw** match *m* nul

goalmouth ['gəʊlmaʊθ] *n (in football)* (entrée *f* du) but *m*

goalpost ['gəʊlpəʊst] *n* poteau *m* de but; **the goalposts** les buts *mpl*; *Fig* **to move or shift the goalposts** changer les règles du jeu

goat [gəʊt] *n* chèvre *f*; **g.'s milk** lait *m* de chèvre; *Fam* **it really gets my g.!** ça me tape vraiment sur les nerfs!; *Fam* **to act or play the g.** faire l'idiot(e)

goatherd ['gəʊthɜːd] *n* chevrier(ère) *m,f*

goatskin ['gəʊtskɪn] *n* peau *f* de chèvre

gob [gɒb] *Br very Fam* **1** *n (mouth)* gueule *f*; **shut your g.!** (ferme) ta gueule!

2 *vi (pt & pp gobbed) (spit)* mollarder

gobble ['gɒbl] **1** *vt (eat)* engloutir

2 *vi (of turkey)* glouglouter

▸**gobble up** *vt sep also Fig* engloutir

gobbledygook ['gɒbldɪguːk] *n Fam* charabia *m*

go-between ['gəʊbɪtwiːn] *n* intermédiaire *mf*

goblet ['gɒblɪt] *n* verre *m* à pied; *(in medieval times)* coupe *f*

goblin ['gɒblɪn] *n* lutin *m*

gobsmacked ['gɒbsmækt] *adj Br very Fam* **to be g.** en rester estomaqué(e)

go-cart ['gəʊkɑːt] = **go-kart**

god [gɒd] n (a) (divine being) dieu m; **G.** Dieu m; **G. forbid!** Dieu m'en garde!; **G. willing** si Dieu le veut; **I wish to G.** I hadn't told him si seulement je ne lui avais rien dit; **in G.'s name** au nom du Ciel; Fam **(oh) my G.!** mon Dieu!; Fam **for G.'s sake!** pour l'amour du ciel!; Fam **G. knows** Dieu seul le sait; Fam **he thinks he's G.'s gift to women** il s'imagine que toutes les femmes sont folles de lui (b) Fam **the gods** (in theatre) le poulailler

godchild ['gɒdtʃaɪld] n filleul(e) m,f

goddaughter ['gɒddɔːtə(r)] n filleule f

goddess ['gɒdɪs] n déesse f

godfather ['gɒdfɑːðə(r)] n parrain m

god-fearing ['gɒdfɪərɪŋ] adj pieux(euse)

godforsaken ['gɒdfəseɪkən] adj perdu(e)

godless ['gɒdlɪs] adj impie

godmother ['gɒdmʌðə(r)] n marraine f

godparent ['gɒdpeərənt] n (godfather) parrain m; (godmother) marraine f; **my godparents** mon parrain et ma marraine

godsend ['gɒdsend] n aubaine f

godson ['gɒdsʌn] n filleul m

go-getter [gəʊ'getə(r)] n Fam battant(e) m,f

goggle ['gɒgəl] vi ouvrir des yeux ronds; **to g. at sb/sth** regarder qn/qch avec des yeux ronds

goggle-eyed ['gɒgəlaɪd] adj Fam avec des yeux ronds

goggles ['gɒgəlz] npl (for swimming) lunettes fpl de plongée; (for skiing) lunettes de ski; (for worker) lunettes protectrices

go-go dancer ['gəʊgəʊ'dɑːnsə(r)] n danseuse f de boîte de nuit

going ['gəʊɪŋ] 1 n (a) (progress) **that's very good g.!** voilà qui n'est pas mal du tout!; **it's slow g.** (at work) ça n'avance pas vite (b) (condition of ground) terrain m; Fig **the book/film was pretty heavy g.** le livre/film était plutôt indigeste; Fig **to get out while the g. is good** se retirer tant que la chance nous/leur/etc est favorable
2 adj (a) (successful) **a g. concern** une affaire qui tourne (b) (current) (price, rate) courant(e), actuel(elle)

going-away ['gəʊɪŋə'weɪ] adj **g. outfit** = tenue de voyage de noces; **g. party/present** fête f/cadeau m d'adieu

going-over ['gəʊɪŋ'əʊvə(r)] n Fam **to give sb a g.** (beating) tabasser qn; (criticism) sonner les cloches à qn

goings-on ['gəʊɪŋzɒn] npl Fam (activities) activités fpl; (events) événements mpl

goitre, Am **goiter** ['gɒɪtə(r)] n goitre m

go-kart ['gəʊkɑːt] n (child's toy) petit chariot m; (with engine) kart m; **g. racing** karting m

gold [gəʊld] 1 n or m; **g. bullion** or en barre; **g. dust** poussière f d'or; **tickets are like g. dust** les billets valent de l'or; **g. leaf** or **foil** feuille f d'or; **g. medal** médaille f d'or; also Fig **g. mine** mine f d'or; **g. plate** orfèvrerie f; Fin **g. reserves** réserves fpl d'or
2 adj (made of gold) en or; (gold-coloured) doré(e)

gold-digger ['gəʊld'dɪgə(r)] n Fam Pej (woman) croqueuse f de diamants

golden ['gəʊldən] adj (made of gold) en or; (gold-coloured) doré(e); **a g. opportunity** une occasion en or; **the g. age** l'âge m d'or; **g. boy** enfant m chéri; **g. eagle** aigle m royal; **g. girl** enfant f chérie; **g. handshake** (retirement bonus) indemnité f de départ; **g. jubilee** jubilé m; **g. rule** règle f d'or; Fin **g. share** action f privilégiée; **g. wedding** noces fpl d'or

goldfinch ['gəʊldfɪntʃ] n chardonneret m

goldfish ['gəʊldfɪʃ] (pl goldfish) n poisson m rouge; **g. bowl** bocal m à poissons rouges; **it's like living in a g. bowl** c'est comme vivre en vitrine

gold-plated ['gəʊld'pleɪtɪd] adj plaqué(e) or

goldsmith ['gəʊldsmɪθ] n orfèvre m

golf [gɒlf] n golf m; **g. ball** balle f de golf; **g. club** (stick, association) club m de golf; **g. course** terrain m de golf

golfer ['gɒlfə(r)] n joueur(euse) m,f de golf

golfing ['gɒlfɪŋ] n golf m; **g. umbrella** grand parapluie m (de golf)

golly ['gɒlɪ] exclam Fam Old-fashioned fichtre!

gondola ['gɒndələ] n (a) (boat) gondole f (b) (cable car) cabine f de téléphérique

gondolier [gɒndə'lɪə(r)] n gondolier m

gone [gɒn] 1 adj (a) (past) **it's g. nine o'clock** il est neuf heures passées (b) Fam **to be six months g.** (pregnant) être enceinte de six mois; Fam **to be pretty far g.** (drunk) être complètement bourré(e); Fam **to be g. on sb** (infatuated) avoir le béguin pour qn
2 pp of **go**

goner ['gɒnə(r)] n Fam **I thought she was a g.** (would die) j'ai cru qu'elle allait y passer; **I'm a g. if she finds out** si elle l'apprend, je suis mort

gong [gɒŋ] n gong m; Br Fam (medal) breloque f

gonna ['gɒnə] Fam = **going to**

gonorrhoea, Am **gonorrhea** [gɒnə'rɪə] n blennorragie f; **to have g.** avoir une blennorragie

goo [guː] n Fam (a) (sticky substance) substance f visqueuse (b) (sentimentality) guimauve f

good [gʊd] 1 n (a) bien m; **to do g.** faire le bien; **he's up to no g.** il prépare un mauvais coup; **to see the g. in sb/sth** voir les bons côtés de qn/qch
(b) (benefit) **I did it for your own g.** je l'ai fait pour ton bien; **it was all to the g.** c'était tout bénéfice; **we were £100 to the g.** nous avons fait 100 livres de bénéfice; **for the g. of one's health** pour sa santé; **for the common g.** dans l'intérêt général; **it will do you g.** cela te fera du bien; **it won't do any g.** cela ne servira à rien; **what's the g. of that?** à quoi bon?; **it's no g.** ça ne sert à rien; **it's no g. complaining** cela ne sert à rien de se plaindre; **he's no g.** (incompetent) il est nul; (morally bad) il ne vaut pas grand-chose
(c) **for g.** (permanently) pour toujours; **she is gone for g.** elle est partie pour de bon
2 adj (comparative **better** ['betə(r)], superlative **best** [best]) (a) (in quality) bon (bonne); (weather, handwriting) beau (belle); **she looks g. in that hat** ce chapeau lui va bien, elle est bien avec ce chapeau; **to taste g.** avoir bon goût; **(that) sounds g.!** bonne idée!; **g. to eat** comestible; **it's g. to see you** ça fait plaisir de vous voir; Fam **that's a g. one!** (of story, joke) elle est bien bonne!; **he thinks he's too g.** for us il se croit trop bien pour nous; **to earn g. money** bien gagner sa vie; **you've got a g. chance** tu as tes chances; **to be on to a g. thing** être sur un bon filon; **to have a g. time** s'amuser; **to show sb a g. time** faire passer un bon moment à qn; **all in g. time** chaque chose en son temps; **too g. to be true** trop beau pour être vrai; **as g. as new** comme neuf (neuve); **he as g. as called** me a liar pour un peu, il m'aurait traité de menteur; **the g. old days** le bon vieux temps; **g. afternoon!** bonjour!; **the G. Book** la sainte Bible; **he's a g. friend** c'est un ami;

G. Friday le Vendredi Saint; *Fam* g. grief! fichtre!; the g. life la belle vie; *Fam* g. Lord!, g. heavens!, g. gracious! bon sang!; g. morning! bonjour!; g. night! bonne nuit!; the G. Samaritan le bon Samaritain

(b) *(advantageous)* a g. opportunity une bonne occasion; to be in a g. position to do sth être bien placé(e) pour faire qch; it's looking g. ça se présente bien

(c) *(beneficial)* bon (bonne); he doesn't know what's g. for him il n'a pas un sou de bon sens; to be g. for business être bon pour les affaires; it's a g. thing we were here heureusement que nous étions là; g. riddance! bon débarras!

(d) *(skilful)* bon (bonne) (at en); to be g. with one's hands être habile de ses mains; to be g. with children savoir y faire avec les enfants; to be g. in bed bien faire l'amour

(e) *(well-behaved)* sage; be g.! *(to child)* sois sage!; to be as g. as gold être sage comme une image; to lead a g. life mener une vie respectable; g. conduct *or* behaviour bonne conduite *f*

(f) *(kind)* gentil(ille); that's very g. of you c'est très aimable *ou* très gentil de votre part; he was very g. about it il s'est montré très compréhensif; to do sb a g. turn rendre un service à qn

(g) *(valid)* bon (bonne); a g. reason une bonne raison, une raison valable; he's g. for £25,000 *(has in credit)* il dispose de 25 000 livres

(h) *(for emphasis)* bon (bonne); a g. two hours deux bonnes heures; a g. deal of, a g. many beaucoup de; to have a g. look at sb/sth bien regarder qn/qch; to have a g. cry pleurer un bon coup; a g. long time un bien long moment

(i) to make g. *(of person)* faire son chemin; to make g. one's losses compenser ses pertes; to make g. one's promise tenir sa promesse; he made g. his escape il a réussi son évasion

3 *adv* (a) I'll do it when I'm g. and ready je le ferai quand ça me chantera

(b) *(as comment, answer)* bien; I feel better today – g. je me sens mieux aujourd'hui – tant mieux

goodbye [gʊd'baɪ] *n* au revoir *m*; g.! au revoir!; to say g. to sb dire au revoir à qn; he can say g. to his hopes of winning il peut dire adieu à ses espoirs de victoire

good-for-nothing ['gʊdfənʌθɪŋ] *n* bon (bonne) à rien *m,f*

good-humoured, *Am* **good-humored** [gʊd-'hju:məd] *adj (debate, meeting)* détendu(e); to be g. *(of person)* avoir un caractère enjoué

good-looking ['gʊdlʊkɪŋ] *adj* beau (belle)

good-natured [gʊd'neɪtʃəd] *adj (person)* d'un caractère agréable; *(remarks, laugh)* bon enfant *inv*

goodness ['gʊdnɪs] *n* (a) *(of person)* bonté *f* (b) *(of food)* qualités *fpl* nutritives (c) *(in exclamations)* g. (me)! mon Dieu!; thank g.! Dieu merci!; for g. sake! pour l'amour de Dieu!

goods [gʊdz] *npl* (a) *Law* biens *mpl* (b) *(articles)* articles *mpl*, marchandises *fpl*; *Fig* to deliver the g. remplir ses engagements; *Fig* to come up with the g. faire le nécessaire; g. train/depot train *m*/dépôt *m* de marchandises

good-tempered [gʊd'tempəd] *adj (person)* d'un caractère facile; *(discussion)* aimable

goodwill [gʊd'wɪl] *n* (a) *(benevolence)* bienveillance *f*; *(willingness)* bonne volonté *f*; *Com* fonds *m* de commerce

goody ['gʊdɪ] *n* (a) *(pl* goodies*)* *Fam* (a) *(person)* bon *m*; the goodies and the baddies les bons *mpl* et les méchants *mpl* (b) goodies *(nice food)* bonnes choses *fpl*; *(nice things)* petits cadeaux *mpl*

2 *exclam* chouette!

goody-goody ['gʊdɪgʊdɪ] *Fam Pej* 1 *n* (*pl* goody-goodies*)* fayot *m*

2 *adj* fayot

gooey [gu:ɪ] *adj Fam* (a) *(sticky)* gluant(e) (b) *(sentimental)* à la guimauve

goof [gu:f] *Am Fam* 1 *n* (a) *(blunder)* gaffe *f*, bourde *f* (b) *(idiot)* cave *m*

2 *vi* faire une gaffe *ou* une bourde

▶**goof about**, **goof around** *vi Am Fam* faire l'idiot(e)

▶**goof off** *Am Fam* 1 *vt insep* to g. off work ne pas aller bosser

2 *vi* flemmarder, glandouiller

goofy ['gu:fɪ] *adj Fam* (a) *(stupid)* loufoque (b) *Br (buck-toothed)* qui a les dents en avant

goolies ['gu:lɪz] *npl Br very Fam (testicles)* couilles *fpl*

goon [gu:n] *n Fam* (a) *Br (stupid person)* imbécile *mf* (b) *Am (thug)* gorille *m*

goose [gu:s] *(pl* geese [gi:s]*)* *n* oie *f*; *Fig* his g. is cooked il est fichu; to kill the g. that lays the golden egg tuer la poule aux œufs d'or; *Br* g. pimples, *Am* g. bumps chair *f* de poule

gooseberry ['gʊzbərɪ] *(pl* gooseberries*)* *n* groseille *f* à maquereau; *Br Fam* to play g. tenir la chandelle; g. bush groseillier *m*

gooseflesh ['gu:sfleʃ] *n* chair *f* de poule

goose-step ['gu:sstep] 1 *n* pas *m* de l'oie

2 *vi (pt & pp* goose-stepped*)* marcher au pas de l'oie

gopher ['gəʊfə(r)] *n (animal)* spermophile *m*

gore [gɔ:(r)] 1 *n (blood)* sang *m* (versé)

2 *vt (of bull)* encorner; to be gored to death être tué(e) à coups de corne

gorge [gɔ:dʒ] 1 *n (valley)* gorge *f*, défilé *m*

2 *vt* to g. oneself se gorger, se gaver (on de)

3 *vi* se gorger, se gaver (on de)

gorgeous ['gɔ:dʒəs] *adj* magnifique; *(meal, food)* excellent(e)

gorilla [gə'rɪlə] *n* gorille *m*

gormless ['gɔ:mlɪs] *adj Br Fam* balourd(e)

gorse [gɔ:s] *n* ajoncs *mpl*

gory ['gɔ:rɪ] *adj (film, crime, war)* sanglant(e); *(covered in blood)* ensanglanté(e); *Fig & Hum* in g. detail avec tous les détails

gosh [gɒʃ] *exclam Fam* ça alors!

goshawk ['gɒshɔ:k] *n* autour *m*

gosling ['gɒzlɪŋ] *n* oison *m*

go-slow [gəʊ'sləʊ] *n Br* grève *f* du zèle

gospel ['gɒspəl] *n* évangile *m*; to take sth as g. accepter qch comme parole d'évangile; g. (music) gospel *m*; g. singer chanteur(euse) *m,f* de gospel

gossamer ['gɒsəmə(r)] *n* (a) *(spider's web)* fils *mpl* de la Vierge (b) *(fabric)* gaze *f* légère

gossip ['gɒsɪp] 1 *n* (a) *(person)* bavard(e) *m,f*, *(ill-natured)* commère *f* (b) *(talk)* bavardages *mpl*; *(ill-natured)* commérage(s) *m(pl)*; have you heard the latest g.? tu sais la nouvelle?; to have a g. *(about)* bavarder (à propos de); g. column *(in newspaper)* chronique *f* mondaine

2 *vi* bavarder; *(ill-naturedly)* colporter des commérages

gossipy ['gɒsɪpɪ] *adj (person)* bavard(e); *(ill-natured)* cancanier(ère); *(letter, conversation)* plein(e) de petits potins

got [gɒt] *pt & pp of* **get**

Gothic ['gɒθɪk] **1** *n (artistic style, language)* gothique *m* **2** *adj* gothique

gotta ['gɒtə] *very Fam* = **got to**

gotten ['gɒtən] *Am pp of* **get**

▶**gouge out** [gaʊdʒ] *vt sep (hole, path)* creuser; **to g. sb's eye out** arracher l'œil à qn

goulash ['guːlæʃ] *n* goulasch *m*

gourd [gʊəd] *n* gourde *f*

gourmet ['gʊəmeɪ] *n* gourmet *m*, gastronome *mf*; **g. restaurant** restaurant *m* gastronomique

gout [gaʊt] *n (disease)* goutte *f*

Gov (a) *(abbr* **government**) gouvernement *m* (b) *(abbr* **governor**) gouverneur *m*

govern ['gʌvən] *vt* (a) *(state, country)* gouverner (b) *(of scientific law)* régir (c) *(emotions)* maîtriser, contenir

governess ['gʌvənɪs] *n* gouvernante *f*

governing ['gʌvənɪŋ] *adj (party, coalition)* au pouvoir; *(concept, principle)* directeur(trice); **g. body** conseil *m* d'administration

government ['gʌvənmənt] *n* gouvernement *m*; **g. intervention** intervention *f* du gouvernement

governmental [gʌvən'mentl] *adj* gouvernemental(e)

governor ['gʌvənə(r)] *n (of colony, bank, US state)* gouverneur *m*; *(of prison)* directeur *m*; *(of school)* = fonctionnaire gestionnaire d'une école; *Br Fam* **the g.** *(boss)* le patron; **g. general** gouverneur *m* général

governorship ['gʌvənəʃɪp] *n (post)* poste *m* de gouverneur; *(function)* fonctions *fpl* de gouverneur

Govt *(abbr* **government**) gouvernement *m*

gown [gaʊn] *n (of woman)* robe *f*; *(of magistrate, academic)* robe, toge *f*; *(of surgeon)* blouse *f*

GP [dʒiː'piː] *n Br (abbr* **general practitioner**) (médecin *m*) généraliste *mf*

GPO [dʒiːpiː'əʊ] *n Br Formerly (abbr* **General Post Office**) ≃ PTT *fpl*

gr *(abbr* **gramme(s)**) g

grab [græb] **1** *n* to make a g. at *or* for sth essayer d'attraper qch; *Fam* to be up for grabs être à qui veut le prendre; *(be for sale)* être à qui veut l'acheter

2 *vt (pt & pp* **grabbed**) (a) *(seize)* to g. (hold of) sb/sth saisir qn/qch; *(more tightly)* empoigner qn/qch; I'll g. a sandwich later j'avalerai un sandwich plus tard (b) *Fam (attract)* the idea doesn't g. me ça ne me dit rien; how does that g. you? ça te dit?

3 *vi* to g. at sb essayer de s'agripper à qn; to g. at sth essayer d'attraper qch

grace [greɪs] **1** *n* (a) *(of movement, dancer, manners)* grâce *f*; to do sth with (a) good/bad g. faire qch de bonne/mauvaise grâce; to have the (good) g. to do sth avoir la grâce de faire qch (b) *(favour)* to be in sb's good graces être dans les bonnes grâces de qn; *Rel* in a state of g. en état de grâce; to fall from g. perdre la grâce; *Fig* tomber en disgrâce; **there, but for the g. of God, go I** je remercie le ciel de m'avoir épargné (d) *(for payment of a bill)* seven days' g. sept jours de délai ou de grâce (e) *(prayer before meal)* bénédicité *m* (f) *(form of address)* Your G. *(to bishop)* Monseigneur; *(to duke)* Monsieur le duc; *(to duchess)* Madame la duchesse

2 *vt* (a) *(honour)* honorer (with de) (b) *(decorate)* embellir, enjoliver

graceful ['greɪsfʊl] *adj (person, movement)* gracieux(euse); *(speech, style)* élégant(e)

gracefully ['greɪsfʊlɪ] *adv* avec grâce, gracieusement

graceless ['greɪslɪs] *adj* (a) *(inelegant)* disgracieux(euse) (b) *(rude)* effronté(e)

gracious ['greɪʃəs] **1** *adj* (a) *(kind, polite)* poli(e), affable; *(in victory)* courtois(e) (b) *(elegant)* pleine(e) de raffinement **2** *exclam* g. (me)!, goodness g.! mon Dieu!

graciously ['greɪʃəslɪ] *adv* avec grâce; *(accept, invite)* de bonne grâce

gradation [grə'deɪʃən] *n (of colours)* gradation *f*; *(on thermometer)* degré *m*; *(of meaning)* nuance *f*

grade [greɪd] **1** *n* (a) *(rank)* grade *m*, rang *m*; *(in profession)* échelon *m* (b) *(quality)* qualité *f*; *(of vegetable, fruit)* calibre *m*; *Fig* to make the g. se montrer à la hauteur (c) *Am Sch (mark)* note *f* (d) *Am (year at school)* classe *f*; **g. school** ≃ école *f* primaire

2 *vt* (a) *(classify)* classer; *(fruit, vegetables)* calibrer (b) *Am (essay, exercise)* noter

gradient ['greɪdɪənt] *n* (a) *(of slope)* dénivellation *f* (b) *(of temperature)* gradient *m*

gradual ['grædjʊəl] *adj* graduel(elle), progressif(ive)

gradualism ['grædjʊəlɪzm] *n* gradualisme *m*

gradually ['grædjʊəlɪ] *adv* graduellement, progressivement

graduate 1 ['grædjʊət] *n* (a) *Br (from university)* ≃ licencié(e) *m,f*; *Am (from high school)* bachelier(ère) *m,f*

2 *adj Am (postgraduate)* **g. studies** études *fpl* de troisième cycle

3 *vi* ['grædjʊeɪt] (a) *Br (from university)* obtenir sa licence; *Am (from high school)* avoir son bac (b) *(progress)* to g. from sth to sth passer de qch à qch

graduated ['grædjʊeɪtɪd] *adj (thermometer)* gradué(e); *(pay rise)* progressif(ive)

graduation [grædjʊ'eɪʃən] *n (from school, university)* remise *f* des diplômes; **g. ceremony** cérémonie *f* de remise des diplômes

graffiti [grə'fiːtiː] *n* graffiti *mpl*; **a piece of g.** un graffiti

graft¹ [grɑːft] **1** *n (technique)* greffe *f*; *(thing grafted)* greffon *m*

2 *vt* greffer (onto sur)

graft² *Fam* **1** *n* (a) *Am (bribe)* pot-de-vin *m* (b) *Br (work)* (hard) **g.** boulot *m*

2 *vi Br (work hard)* bosser dur

grafter ['grɑːftə(r)] *n Br Fam* bosseur(euse) *m,f*

grain [greɪn] *n* (a) *(of wheat, salt, sand)* grain *m*; **a g. of truth** une once de vérité (b) *(in photo, wood)* grain *m*; *(in meat, material)* fil *m*; *Fig* it goes against the g. for me to do it ce n'est pas dans ma nature de le faire (c) *(cereals)* céréales *fpl*

grainy ['greɪnɪ] *adj* granuleux(euse)

gram [græm] *n* gramme *m*

grammar ['græmə(r)] *n* grammaire *f*; **g. (book)** (livre *m* de) grammaire; *Br* **g. school** ≃ lycée *m*

grammarian [grə'meərɪən] *n* grammairien(enne) *m,f*

grammatical [grə'mætɪkəl] *adj* grammatical(e)

grammatically [grə'mætɪklɪ] *adv* grammaticalement

gramme [græm] *n* gramme *m*

gramophone ['græməfəʊn] *n Br Old-fashioned* gramophone *m*

gran [græn] *n Br Fam (grandmother)* grand-mère *f*; *(term of address)* mamie *f*, mémé *f*

granary ['grænəri] (*pl* **granaries**) *n* grenier *m*; *Br* g. **bread** = sorte de pain complet

grand [grænd] **1** *adj* (a) (*imposing*) grandiose, imposant(e); **to do things on a g. scale** faire les choses en grand; *Mus & Fig* g. **finale** apothéose *f*; *Am* g. **jury** = jury qui décide si une affaire doit être portée ou non devant les tribunaux; g. **master** (*in chess*) grand maître *m*; **the G. National** = steeple-chase la plus célèbre d'Angleterre; g. **piano** piano *m* à queue; g. **slam** grand chelem *m*; g. **total** somme *f* totale (b) *Fam* (*excellent*) excellent(e)
2 *n* (*pl* **grand**) *Fam* (*thousand pounds*) mille livres *fpl*; (*thousand dollars*) mille dollars *mpl*

grandchild ['græntʃaɪld] (*pl* **grandchildren** ['græntʃɪldrən]) *n* (*boy*) petit-fils *m*; (*girl*) petite fille *f*; **grandchildren** petits-enfants *mpl*

gran(d)dad ['grændæd] *n Fam* (a) (*grandfather*) grand-père *m*; (*term of address*) papi *m*, pépé *m* (b) *Pej* (*old man*) pépé *m*

grandaddy ['grændædi] (*pl* **grandaddies**) *n Fam* grand-père *m*; (*term of address*) papi *m*, pépé *m*

granddaughter ['grændɔ:tə(r)] *n* petite fille *f*

grandeur ['grændʒə(r)] *n* (*of person*) grandeur *f*, noblesse *f*; (*of building, surroundings*) splendeur *f*, magnificence *f*

grandfather ['grænfɑ:ðə(r)] *n* grand-père *m*; g. **clock** horloge *f* comtoise

grandiloquent [græn'dɪləkwənt] *adj* grandiloquent(e)

grandiose ['grændɪəʊs] *adj* (*building*) monumental(e); (*term, title*) pompeux(euse); (*idea, scheme*) démesuré(e)

grandly ['grændlɪ] *adv* (*impressively*) de façon grandiose; (*pompously*) de façon pompeuse

grandma ['grænmɑː] *n Fam* grand-mère *f*; (*term of address*) mamie *f*, mémé *f*

grandmother ['grænmʌðə(r)] *n* grand-mère *f*

grandpa ['grænpɑː] *n Fam* grand-père *m*; (*term of address*) papi *m*, pépé *m*

grandparent ['grænpeərənt] *n* grand-parent *m*

grandson ['grænsʌn] *n* petit-fils *m*

grandstand ['grændstænd] *n* tribune *f* d'honneur; *Fig* **to have a g. view of sth** être bien placé(e) pour voir qch

granite ['grænɪt] *n* granit *m*

granny ['grænɪ] (*pl* **grannies**) *n Fam* grand-mère *f*; (*term of address*) mamie *f*, mémé *f*; g. **flat** = partie d'une maison aménagée indépendamment pour héberger un parent âgé; g. **knot** double nœud *m*

grant [grɑːnt] **1** *n* (*financial aid*) subvention *f*; (*for student*) bourse *f* (d'études)
2 *vt* (a) (*allow*) (*permission*) donner; (*interview, request*) accorder; **to take sth for granted** considérer qch comme allant de soi ou comme étant dû; **to take sb for granted** croire que qn sera toujours là (b) (*award*) (*money, subsidy*) accorder, allouer (c) (*admit*) admettre; **I g. that he's talented** je reconnais qu'il a du talent

granular ['grænjʊlə(r)] *adj* granuleux(euse)

granulated sugar ['grænjʊleɪtɪd'ʃʊgə(r)] *n* sucre *m* semoule

granule ['grænjʊl] *n* (*of salt, sand*) grain *m*; (*of coffee*) granule *m*

grape [greɪp] *n* grain *m* de raisin; **some grapes** du raisin; g. **harvest** vendange(s) *f(pl)*; g. **juice** jus *m* de raisin; g. **picker** vendangeur(euse) *m,f*

grapefruit ['greɪpfruːt] *n* pamplemousse *m*; g. **juice** jus *m* de pamplemousse

grapevine ['greɪpvaɪn] *n* vigne *f*; (*climbing*) treille *f*; *Fam* **I heard on the g. that...** j'ai entendu par le téléphone arabe que...

graph [grɑːf] *n* graphique *m*, diagramme *m*; g. **paper** papier *m* millimétré

graphic ['græfɪk] *adj* (a) (*vivid*) très détaillé(e); (*language*) cru(e); **in g. detail** de façon très détaillée (b) g. **artist** graphiste *m,f*; g. **arts** arts *mpl* graphiques; g. **designer** graphiste; g. **equalizer** égalisateur *m* graphique; g. **novel** bande *f* dessinée (pour adultes)

graphically ['græfɪklɪ] *adv* (*describe*) de façon très détaillée

graphics ['græfɪks] **1** *n* (*art*) arts *mpl* graphiques
2 *npl Comptr* graphismes *mpl*, graphiques *mpl*

graphite ['græfaɪt] *n* graphite *m*, mine *f* de plomb

graphology [græ'fɒlədʒɪ] *n* graphologie *f*

grapnel ['græpnəl] *n Naut* grappin *m*

grapple ['græpəl] *vi* (*fight*) lutter corps à corps (**with** avec); *Fig* (*with problem*) se débattre (**with** avec)

grappling hook ['græplɪŋ'hʊk], **grappling iron** ['græplɪŋ'aɪən] *n Naut* grappin *m*

grasp [grɑːsp] **1** *n* (a) (*hold*) prise *f*; *Fig* **to have sth within one's g.** avoir qch à sa portée (b) (*understanding*) compréhension *f* (**of** de)
2 *vt* (a) (*hold firmly*) saisir; (*more tightly*) empoigner; **to g. sb's arm** saisir qn par le bras; *Fig* **to g. the opportunity** saisir l'occasion (b) (*understand*) saisir, comprendre

grasping ['grɑːspɪŋ] *adj* (*mean*) avide, cupide

grass [grɑːs] **1** *n* (a) (*plant*) herbe *f*; *Fig* **she doesn't let the g. grow under her feet** elle ne perd pas de temps; *Fig* g. **roots** (*of organization*) base *f*; g. **roots support/opposition** soutien *m*/opposition *f* de la base; g. **snake** couleuvre *f* (à collier); g. **widow** = femme dont le mari est souvent en déplacement (b) (*lawn*) pelouse *f*, gazon *m*; **keep off the g.** (*sign*) pelouse interdite; g. **court** (*in tennis*) court *m* en gazon (c) (*pasture*) herbage *m*; *Fig* **to put sb out to g.** mettre qn à la retraite (d) *Fam* (*marijuana*) herbe *f* (e) *Br very Fam* (*informer*) balance *f*, indic *m*
2 *vi Br very Fam* (*inform*) moucharder; **to g. on sb** balancer qn

grasshopper ['grɑːshɒpə(r)] *n* sauterelle *f*

grassland ['grɑːslænd] *n* prairie *f*, pré *m*

grassy ['grɑːsɪ] *adj* herbu(e), herbeux(euse)

grate[1] [greɪt] *n* (*of hearth*) grille *f*; (*fireplace*) foyer *m*

grate[2] *vt* (*cheese, nutmeg*) râper
2 *vi* (*of machinery*) grincer; **to g. on the ear** (*of voice*) écorcher les oreilles; (*of sound*) faire mal aux oreilles; **it really grates on me** or **on my nerves** ça me tape vraiment sur les nerfs

grateful ['greɪtfʊl] *adj* reconnaissant(e) (**for** de); **I would be g. if you could let me know** je vous serais reconnaissant de m'en informer

gratefully ['greɪtfʊlɪ] *adv* avec reconnaissance

grater ['greɪtə(r)] *n* râpe *f*

gratification [grætɪfɪ'keɪʃən] *n* satisfaction *f*

gratified ['grætɪfaɪd] *adj* satisfait(e), content(e)

gratify ['grætɪfaɪ] (*pt & pp* **gratified**) *vt* (*person*) faire plaisir à; (*wish, desire*) satisfaire

gratifying ['grætɪfaɪɪŋ] *adj* satisfaisant(e)

grating[1] ['greɪtɪŋ] *adj* (*noise*) grinçant(e); (*voice*) éraillé(e)

grating[2] *n* (*grille*) grille *f*

gratis ['grɑːtɪs] *adv* gratis

gratitude ['grætɪtjuːd] n gratitude f, reconnaissance f

gratuitous [grə'tjuːɪtəs] adj gratuit(e)

gratuitously [grə'tjuːɪtəslɪ] adv gratuitement, sans raison

gratuity [grə'tjuːɪtɪ] (pl gratuities) n Formal (tip) pourboire m

grave [greɪv] 1 n tombe f; Fig **it would make him turn in his g.** ça le ferait se retourner dans sa tombe; **to have one foot in the g.** avoir un pied dans la tombe
2 adj (manner, voice) solennel(elle); (situation) grave; **to make a g. mistake** se tromper lourdement

gravedigger ['greɪvdɪgə(r)] n fossoyeur m

gravel ['grævəl] n gravier m; **g. path** allée f de gravier; **g. pit** carrière f de gravier

gravelly ['grævəlɪ] adj (sand, soil) graveleux(euse); (voice) râpeux(euse)

gravely ['greɪvlɪ] adv gravement

graven ['greɪvən] adj **g. image** idole f

graveside ['greɪvsaɪd] n **at the g.** près de la tombe

gravestone ['greɪvstəʊn] n pierre f tombale

graveyard ['greɪvjɑːd] n cimetière m

gravitate ['grævɪteɪt] vi **to g. towards sth** (of person) être attiré(e) par qch; **most of the guests had gravitated towards the bar** la plupart des invités s'étaient rapprochés du bar

gravitational [grævɪ'teɪʃənəl] adj gravitationnel(elle); **g. pull** gravitation f

gravity ['grævɪtɪ] n (a) (physical force) gravité f, pesanteur f (b) (seriousness) gravité f

gravy ['greɪvɪ] n = sauce f à base de jus de viande; **g. boat** saucière f; Fam **to get on the g. train** trouver un filon

gray Am = grey

graze¹ [greɪz] 1 vt (of farmer) (cattle) faire paître
2 vi (of cattle) paître

graze² 1 n écorchure f; (less serious) égratignure f
2 vt écorcher; (less seriously) égratigner

grease [griːs] 1 n graisse f; **g. gun** pistolet m graisseur
2 vt (machine) graisser, lubrifier; (cake tin) beurrer; **to g. back one's hair** se gominer les cheveux; Fam Fig **to g. sb's palm** graisser la patte à qn; Fam **like greased lightning** en quatrième vitesse

greasepaint ['griːspeɪnt] n maquillage m de théâtre

greaseproof paper ['griːspruːf'peɪpə(r)] n papier m sulfurisé

greasy ['griːsɪ] adj (a) (covered in grease) graisseux(euse); (hair, skin, food) gras (grasse) (b) Fam (manner) mielleux(euse)

great [greɪt] 1 n grand nom m
2 adj a (large, important) grand(e); **a g. many people** beaucoup de monde; **to reach a g. age** parvenir à un âge avancé; **to take g. care (of)** prendre grand soin de; **they are g. friends** ce sont de grands amis
(b) (in proper names) **G. Britain** la Grande-Bretagne; **G. Dane** danois m; **the G. Lakes** les Grands Lacs mpl; **Greater London** Londres et son agglomération; Hist **the G. War** la Grande Guerre
(c) Fam (very good) formidable, génial(e); **to have a g. time** bien s'amuser
(d) (enthusiastic) **to be a g. knitter/reader** adorer tricoter/la lecture; **to be a g. believer in doing sth** être partisan(e) de faire qch; Fam **she's a g. one for having everything planned in advance** avec elle, on peut être sûr que tout sera préparé à l'avance

3 adv Fam (a) (well) très bien; **to feel g.** se sentir en super forme
(b) (for emphasis) **a g. big dog** un chien énorme; **you g. fat slob!** espèce de gros tas!

great-aunt ['greɪtɑːnt] n grand-tante f

greatcoat ['greɪtkəʊt] n pardessus m

great-grandchild ['greɪt'grænʧaɪld] (pl **great-grandchildren** ['greɪt'grænʧɪldrən]) n (boy) arrière-petit-fils m; (girl) arrière-petite-fille f; **great-grandchildren** arrière-petits-enfants mpl

great-granddaughter ['greɪt'grændɔːtə(r)] n arrière-petite-fille f

great-grandfather ['greɪt'grænfɑːðə(r)] n arrière-grand-père m

great-grandmother ['greɪt'grænmʌðə(r)] n arrière-grand-mère f

great-grandparents ['greɪt'grænpeərənts] npl arrière-grands-parents mpl

great-grandson ['greɪt'grænsʌn] n arrière-petit-fils m

greatly ['greɪtlɪ] adv très

greatness ['greɪtnɪs] n (a) (of person, action) grandeur f; **to achieve g.** rejoindre les plus grands (b) (of thing, problem) importance f

great-uncle ['greɪtʌŋkəl] n grand-oncle m

grebe [griːb] n grèbe m

Grecian ['griːʃən] adj grec (grecque)

Greece [griːs] n la Grèce

greed [griːd] n (for food) gourmandise f; (for money) avidité f, cupidité f; (for fame, power) recherche f avide (for de)

greedily ['griːdɪlɪ] adv (eat) goulûment; (look, say) avec gourmandise

greediness ['griːdɪnɪs] = greed

greedy ['griːdɪ] adj (for food) gourmand(e); (for money, fame, power) avide; Fam **g. guts** goinfre mf

Greek [griːk] 1 n (a) (person) Grec (Grecque), m,f (b) (language) grec m; **modern G.** le grec moderne; Fam **it's all G. to me** c'est de l'hébreu pour moi
2 adj grec (grecque)

green [griːn] 1 n 1 (a) (colour) vert m (b) **greens** (vegetables) légumes mpl verts (c) (grassy area) pelouse f, gazon m; (in golf) green m (d) (environmentalist) écologiste mf
2 adj (a) (colour) vert(e); **to go or turn g.** (of traffic lights) passer au vert; (of person, fields) verdir; **to be g. with envy** être vert de jalousie; Fig **to give sb the g. light** (to do sth) donner le feu vert à qn (pour faire qch); **to have g. fingers** avoir la main verte; **g. beans** haricots mpl verts; **g. belt** zone f verte; Am **g. card** = permis m de travail; **g. salad** salade f verte (b) (young, inexperienced) jeune, inexpérimenté(e); (naive) naïf (naïve) (c) (environmentalist) écologiste; **the G. Party** le parti écologiste

greenback ['griːnbæk] n Am Fam billet m vert

greenery ['griːnərɪ] n verdure f

green-eyed ['griːnaɪd] adj aux yeux verts; **the g. monster** la jalousie

greenfield ['griːnfiːld] n **g. site** (for factory) terrain m non-bâti

greenfly ['griːnflaɪ] (pl **greenflies**) n puceron m

greengage ['griːngeɪdʒ] n reine-claude f

greengrocer ['griːngrəʊsə(r)] n Br marchand(e) m,f de fruits et légumes; **g.'s (shop)** magasin m de fruits et légumes

greenhouse ['gri:nhaʊs] *n* serre *f*; **g. effect** effet *m* de serre

Greenland ['gri:nlənd] *n* le Groenland

Greenlander ['gri:nləndə(r)] *n* Groenlandais(e) *m,f*

Greenwich Mean Time ['grenɪtʃ'mi:ntaɪm] *n* temps *m* universel

greet [gri:t] *vt (say hello to)* saluer; *(welcome) (person, idea)* accueillir

greeting ['gri:tɪŋ] *n* salut *m*; *(more formal)* salutation *f*; **New Year greetings** vœux *mpl* de bonne année; **greetings card** carte *f* de vœux

gregarious [grɪ'georɪəs] *adj* sociable

gremlin ['gremlɪn] *n Fam* diablotin *m*

Grenada [grə'neɪdə] *n* la Grenade

grenade [grə'neɪd] *n* grenade *f*

grenadier [grenə'dɪə(r)] *n* grenadier *m*

grenadine ['grenədi:n] *n* grenadine *f*

grew [gru:] *pt of* **grow**

grey, *Am* **gray** [greɪ] **1** *n (colour)* gris *m*
2 *adj* gris(e); *Fig (dull)* morne; **to go g.** *(grey-haired)* grisonner; *Fig* **a g. area** une zone d'ombre; **g. matter** *(brain)* matière *f* grise
3 *vi (of hair)* grisonner

grey-haired ['greɪheəd] *adj* aux cheveux gris

greyhound ['greɪhaʊnd] *n* lévrier *m*; **g. stadium** cynodrome *m*

greying ['greɪŋ] *adj (hair)* grisonnant(e)

grid [grɪd] *n* (a) *(bars)* grille *f*, grillage *m* (b) *(on map)* quadrillage *m*; **g. layout** *(of town)* quadrillage, damier *m*; **g. reference** coordonnées *fpl* (c) *(for electricity)* réseau *m* électrique

griddle ['grɪdəl] *n (for cooking)* tôle *f*

gridiron ['grɪdaɪən] *n* (a) *(for cooking)* gril *m* (b) *Am (American football)* football *m* américain; *(playing field)* terrain *m* de football

gridlock ['grɪdlɒk] *n* embouteillage monstre

grief [gri:f] *n* (a) *(pain)* chagrin *m*; **to come to g.** échouer; *Fam* **good g.!** mon Dieu! (b) *Fam (hassle)* **to give sb g.** embêter qn

grief-stricken ['gri:fstrɪkən] *adj* accablé(e) de douleur *ou* de chagrin

grievance ['gri:vəns] *n* (a) *(resentment)* grief *m* (b) *(complaint)* doléance *f*; **to air one's grievances** exprimer ses doléances; *Ind* **g. procedure** procédure *f* pour porter plainte

grieve [gri:v] **1** *vt* chagriner, affliger
2 *vi* **to g. for sb/over sth** pleurer qn/qch

grieving ['gri:vɪŋ] *adj* éploré(e)

grievous ['gri:vəs] *adj Formal* grave; *Law* **g. bodily harm** coups *mpl* et blessures *fpl*

grievously ['gri:vəslɪ] *adv (seriously)* gravement; **you are g. mistaken** vous commettez une grave erreur

griffin ['grɪfɪn] *n* griffon *m*

grill [grɪl] **1** *n Br (for cooking)* gril *m*; *(food)* grillade *f*; **a mixed g.** un assortiment de grillades
2 *vt* (a) *Br (cook)* griller (b) *Fam (interrogate)* cuisiner

grille [grɪl] *n (bars)* grille *f*; **(radiator) g.** *(on car)* calandre *f*

grilling ['grɪlɪŋ] *n Fam (interrogation)* **to give sb a g.** cuisiner qn

grim [grɪm] *adj* (a) *(stern)* sinistre; **to hang on like g. death** se cramponner; **to look g.** *(of person) (serious)* avoir un air sinistre; *(ill)* avoir très mauvaise mine (b) *Fam (bad)* lamentable; **how do you feel? – pretty g.!** comment te sens-tu? – pas terrible!

grimace ['grɪməs] **1** *n* grimace *f*
2 *vi* grimacer, faire la grimace

grime [graɪm] *n* saleté *f*

grimly ['grɪmlɪ] *adv (fight, hold on)* avec acharnement

grimy ['graɪmɪ] *adj* encrassé(e)

grin [grɪn] **1** *n* grand sourire *m*
2 *vi (pt & pp* **grinned**) faire un grand sourire (**at** à); *Fig* **to g. and bear it** tâcher de garder le sourire

grind [graɪnd] **1** *n Fam (work)* corvée *f*; **the daily g.** le train-train quotidien
2 *vt (pt & pp* **ground** [graʊnd]) (a) *(grain, coffee)* moudre; **to g. one's teeth** grincer des dents (b) *(glass, gems)* dépolir
3 *vi (of wheels, gears)* grisser; **to g. to a halt** *(of car, machine)* s'immobiliser; *(of project, economy)* s'arrêter

▶**grind down** *vt sep Fig* venir à bout de

▶**grind on** *vi (proceed relentlessly)* ne pas en finir

▶**grind out** *vt sep (article, novel)* pondre

grinder ['graɪndə(r)] *n* (for coffee, pepper) moulin *m*; *(for polishing)* polissoire *f*; *(for sharpening)* meule *f*

grinding ['graɪndɪŋ] *adj (poverty)* extrême; **to come to a g. halt** *(of car, machine)* s'immobiliser; *(of project, economy)* s'arrêter

grindstone ['graɪndstəʊn] *n* meule *f*; *Fig* **to keep one's nose to the g.** travailler dur

gringo ['grɪŋgəʊ] *(pl* **gringos**) *n Am Fam* gringo *m*

grip [grɪp] **1** *n* (a) *(hold, grasp)* prise *f*; **to have a strong g.** avoir une bonne poigne; **to get a g. on sth** avoir prise sur qch; *Fig* **to get to grips with sth** s'attaquer à qch; *Fig* **to get a g. on oneself** se ressaisir; *Fig* **get a g.!** reprends-toi, ressaisis-toi!; *Fig* **to have a firm g. on a situation** avoir une situation bien en main; **to lose one's g.** lâcher prise; **to lose one's g. on sth** lâcher qch; *Fig* **to lose one's g. on reality** perdre pied avec la réalité; *Fig* **to be in the g. of a disease/a crisis** être en proie à une maladie/une crise (b) *(handle)* poignée *f* (c) *(hair)* **g. pince** *f* (à cheveux) (d) *Am (bag)* mallette *f*
2 *vt (pt & pp* **gripped**) (a) *(seize)* saisir, prendre; *(hold)* empoigner, agripper; *(of tyres)* adhérer à; *Fig* **to be gripped by panic** être pris(e) de panique; *Fig* **the audience was gripped by the play** la pièce a captivé les spectateurs
3 *vi (of tyre)* adhérer

gripe [graɪp] **1** *n* (a) *Fam (complaint)* **to have a g. about sth** avoir à se plaindre de qch; **what's your g.?** de quoi te plains-tu? (b) *(pain)* **gripes** coliques *fpl*; **g. water** = médicament pour coliques infantiles
2 *vi Fam (complain)* ronchonner, râler (**about** à propos de)

gripping ['grɪpɪŋ] *adj* passionnant(e)

grisly ['grɪzlɪ] *adj* macabre, sinistre

grist [grɪst] *n* **it's all g. to the mill** cela apporte de l'eau à mon/ton/*etc* moulin

gristle ['grɪsəl] *n* nerfs *mpl*

gristly ['grɪslɪ] *adj* nerveux(euse)

grit [grɪt] **1** *n* (a) *(gravel)* gravillons *mpl*; *(in eye)* poussière *f*; *(for icy roads)* sable *m* (b) *(courage, determination)* cran *m*
2 *vt (pt & pp* **gritted**) (a) *(road)* sabler (b) *(clench)* **to g. one's teeth** grincer des dents; *Fig* serrer les dents

gritter ['grɪtə(r)] n Br camion m de sablage

gritty ['grɪtɪ] adj (a) (soil, road) plein(e) de gravillons (b) (determined) qui a du cran, résolu(e) (c) **g. realism** réalisme m cru

grizzle ['grɪzəl] vi (complain) ronchonner, râler (about à propos de)

grizzled ['grɪzəld] adj (hair, person) grisonnant(e)

grizzly ['grɪzlɪ] 1 n (pl grizzlies) **g. (bear)** grizzly m
2 adj (hair, person) grisonnant(e)

groan [grəʊn] 1 n (of pain) gémissement m; (of disappointment, dismay) grognement m; (of chair, floor) grincement m
2 vi (in pain) gémir, pousser un gémissement; (in disappointment, dismay) grogner, pousser un grognement; **to g. under the weight of sth** (of shelf, chair) se creuser sous le poids de qch

grocer ['grəʊsə(r)] n épicier(ère) m,f; **g.'s (shop)** épicerie f

groceries ['grəʊsərɪz] npl (provisions) provisions fpl

grocery ['grəʊsərɪ] (pl groceries) n (shop) épicerie f

grog [grɒg] n Fam grog m

groggy ['grɒgɪ] adj Fam groggy inv

groin [grɔɪn] n aine f

groom [gruːm] 1 n (a) (of horse) palefrenier m (b) (at wedding) marié m
2 vt (horse) panser; (dog) toiletter; Fig (candidate) préparer

groove [gruːv] n (in wood, metal) rainure f; (in record) sillon m; Fig to get stuck in a g. s'encroûter

groovy ['gruːvɪ] adj Fam chouette

grope [grəʊp] 1 vt (a) **to g. one's way forward** avancer à tâtons (b) Fam (sexually) peloter, tripoter
2 vi **to g. (about) for sth** chercher qch à tâtons

gross [grəʊs] 1 n (pl gross) (quantity) grosse f, douze douzaines fpl
2 adj (a) (fat) obèse (b) (blatant) (error) grossier(ère); (ignorance) crasse; (abuse) choquant(e); (injustice) flagrant(e); Law **g. negligence** négligence f coupable (c) (vulgar) grossier(ère) (d) (profit, income, weight) brut(e); Econ **g. domestic product** produit m intérieur brut; **g. national product** produit national brut (e) Fam (disgusting) répugnant(e)
3 vt (profit) gagner brut; **to g. £40,000 a year** gagner brut 40 000 livres par an

grossly ['grəʊslɪ] adv (exaggerated) grossièrement; (negligent) extrêmement; (unfair) vraiment; **g. overweight** obèse

grotesque [grəʊ'tesk] adj grotesque

grotto ['grɒtəʊ] (pl grottoes or grottos) n grotte f

grotty ['grɒtɪ] adj Br Fam minable; **to feel g.** se sentir vaseux(euse)

grouch [graʊtʃ] Fam 1 n (a) (person) râleur(euse) m,f (b) (complaint) plainte f
2 vi râler, ronchonner (about à propos de)

grouchy ['graʊtʃɪ] adj Fam râleur(euse), ronchon(onne)

ground [graʊnd] 1 n (a) (earth) sol m, terre f; **to sit on the g.** s'asseoir par terre; **above g.** en surface; **below g.** sous terre; **burnt to the g.** entièrement brûlé(e); Fig to get off the g. (of project) démarrer; Fig **to work oneself into the g.** se tuer au travail; **to go to g.** se cacher; **to run sb to g.** traquer qn; **g. control** contrôle m au sol; **g. crew** personnel m au sol; Br **g. floor** rez-de-chaussée m; Mil **g. forces** forces fpl au sol; **g. frost** gelée f blanche; **at g. level** au rez-de-chaussée; **g. rules** règles fpl de base; **g.**

staff = personnel responsable de l'entretien d'un terrain de sport
(b) (land) terrain m; Fig **to find common g. for negotiations** trouver un terrain d'entente en vue de négociations; **to be sure of one's g.** être sûr(e) de son fait; Fig **to be on shaky g.** être en terrain miné; Fig **to change** or **shift one's g.** changer de tactique; Fig **to break new g.** faire œuvre de pionnier; Fig **to cover a lot of g.** (of book, lecture) couvrir de très nombreux domaines; Fig **to gain** or **g. on sb** gagner du terrain sur qn; Fig **to lose g. to sb** perdre du terrain sur qn; Fig **to stand** or **hold one's g.** tenir bon
(c) **grounds** (of school, hospital, country house) parc m
(d) **grounds** (reasons) raisons fpl, motifs mpl; **to have (good) grounds for doing sth** avoir de bonnes raisons de faire qch; **on grounds of ill-health** pour raisons de santé; Law **grounds for divorce** motif m de divorce
2 adj (coffee, pepper) moulu(e); Am **g. meat** viande f hachée
3 vt (a) (base) baser, appuyer (on sur)
(b) (educate) **to g. sb in sth** former qn à qch
(c) Am (electrical current) mettre à la masse
(d) (aeroplane) interdire de vol
(e) (prevent from going out) priver de sortie
4 pt & pp of **grind**

groundhog ['graʊndhɒg] n marmotte f d'Amérique

grounding ['graʊndɪŋ] n (a) (basis) fondement m (b) (basic knowledge) bases fpl (in de ou en)

groundless ['graʊndlɪs] adj sans fondement

groundnut ['graʊndnʌt] n Br arachide f; **g. oil** huile f d'arachide

groundsheet ['graʊndʃiːt] n tapis m de sol

groundsman ['graʊndzmən] n = responsable de l'entretien d'un terrain de sport

groundswell ['graʊndswel] n **a g. of support** un raz-de-marée

groundwork ['graʊndwɜːk] n travail m préparatoire; **to do** or **lay the g. (for sth)** préparer le terrain (pour qch)

group [gruːp] 1 n groupe m; **g. decision** décision f collective; **g. dynamics** dynamique f de groupe; **g. photograph** photographie f de groupe; **g. therapy** thérapie f de groupe
2 vt grouper
3 vi se grouper

groupie ['gruːpɪ] n Fam groupie f

grouping ['gruːpɪŋ] n (of people) groupe m

grouse[1] [graʊs] (pl grouse) n (bird) tétras m, grouse f

grouse[2] Fam 1 n (complaint) **to have a g. (about sth)** avoir des raisons de se plaindre (de qch)
2 vi ronchonner, grogner (about au sujet de)

grout [graʊt] n mastic m

grove [grəʊv] n bosquet m

grovel ['grɒvəl] (pt & pp grovelled, Am groveled) vi (on ground) être à quatre pattes; **to g. to sb** ramper ou s'aplatir devant qn

grovelling, Am **groveling** ['grɒvəlɪŋ] adj obséquieux(euse)

grow [grəʊ] (pt grew [gruː], pp grown [grəʊn]) 1 vt (a) (vegetables) cultiver; (flowers) faire pousser; **to g. a beard** se laisser pousser la barbe; **to g. one's hair** se laisser pousser les cheveux (b) Com (company) développer
2 vi (increase in size) (plant) pousser; (person, animal) grandir; (problem) s'aggraver; (economy, feeling) croître; Fam **it'll g. on you** (of music, book) tu finiras par t'y intéresser

(b) *(become)* devenir; **to g. old** vieillir; **to g. angry** se fâcher **(c)** *(come eventually)* **to g. to like sth** finir par aimer qch

▶**grow apart** *vi (of people)* s'éloigner

▶**grow out of** *vt insep* **(a)** *(become too big for)* **he's grown out of his shoes** ses chaussures sont maintenant trop petites pour lui **(b)** *(become too old for)* **she grew out of her dolls** elle a passé l'âge de jouer à la poupée; **most children g. out of such behaviour** la plupart des enfants cessent de se conduire ainsi en grandissant

▶**grow up** *vi (become adult)* grandir; **when I g. up** quand je serai grand; **when I was growing up** quand j'étais petit; *Fam* **g. up!** ne fais pas l'enfant!

grower ['grəʊə(r)] *n (person)* cultivateur(trice) m,f; *(of trees, flowers)* horticulteur(trice) m,f

growing ['grəʊɪŋ] *adj (child)* en pleine croissance; *(town, population)* en pleine expansion; *(debt)* qui augmente, qui va croissant; *(discontent)* croissant(e); **there was a g. fear that...** on craignait de plus en plus que...; **g. pains** *(of child)* douleurs *fpl* de croissance; *Fig (of firm, country)* difficultés *fpl* de croissance

growl [graʊl] **1** *n (of dog)* grondement *m*
2 *vi (of dog)* gronder; *(of person)* grogner, grommeler *(at* contre)

growling ['graʊlɪŋ] *n (of dog)* grondement *m*

grown [grəʊn] **1** *adj* grand(e); **a g. woman** une adulte; **to be fully g.** avoir atteint sa taille adulte
2 *pp of* **grow**

grown-up 1 *n* ['grəʊnʌp] grand(e) m,f, grande personne f; **the grown-ups** les grands, les grandes personnes
2 *adj* [grəʊn'ʌp] *(person, topic)* adulte; **he was very g. about it** il a fait preuve de beaucoup de maturité

growth [grəʊθ] *n* **(a)** *(of person, plant, economy)* croissance f; *(of population, demand)* augmentation f; **a week's g. of beard** une barbe d'une semaine; **g. area** secteur *m* en expansion; **g. industry** industrie f en expansion **(b)** *(tumour)* grosseur f

grub [grʌb] *n* **(a)** *(larva)* larve f **(b)** *Fam (food)* bouffe f; **g.'s up!** à la bouffe!

▶**grub about, grub around** *(pt & pp grubbed) vi Fam* farfouiller **(for sth** pour trouver qch)

grubby ['grʌbɪ] *adj* crasseux(euse)

grudge [grʌdʒ] **1** *n* rancune f; **to bear sb a g.** en vouloir à qn
2 *vt* **(a)** *(give unwillingly)* **to g. sb sth** donner qch à qn à contrecœur **(b)** *(resent)* **to g. doing sth** faire qch à contrecœur; **she grudges him his success** elle lui en veut parce qu'il a réussi

grudging ['grʌdʒɪŋ] *adj* accordé(e) à contrecœur; **to be g. in one's praise** être avare de compliments

grudgingly ['grʌdʒɪŋlɪ] *adv* à contrecœur, à regret

gruel ['gruːəl] *n* gruau *m*

gruelling, *Am* **grueling** ['gruːəlɪŋ] *adj (journey, experience)* épuisant(e)

gruesome ['gruːsəm] *adj* abominable, horrible; **to relate sth in g. detail** raconter qch jusqu'aux détails les plus horribles

gruesomely ['gruːsəmlɪ] *adv* abominablement

gruff [grʌf] *adj (tone, manner)* bourru(e); *(voice)* gros (grosse)

gruffly ['grʌflɪ] *adv* d'un ton bourru

grumble ['grʌmbəl] **1** *n* grommellement *m*, grognement *m*; **she obeyed without so much as a g.** elle a obéi sans la moindre protestation
2 *vi (of person)* grommeler; *(of stomach)* gargouiller; **to g. about sth** rouspéter contre qch; **(I) mustn't g.** il ne faut pas se plaindre

grumbler ['grʌmblə(r)] *n* grincheux(euse) m,f

grumbling ['grʌmblɪŋ] **1** *n* ronchonnements *mpl*
2 *adj* grognon(onne); **g. appendix** appendicite f chronique

grump [grʌmp] *n Fam* grincheux(euse) m,f

grumpily ['grʌmpɪlɪ] *adv* en ronchonnant

grumpy ['grʌmpɪ] *adj* grognon(onne)

grunge [grʌndʒ] *n (music, fashion)* grunge *m*

grunt [grʌnt] **1** *n (of pig, person)* grognement *m*; **to give a g.** pousser un grognement
2 *vi (of pig, person)* grogner

Guadeloupe [gwɑːdə'luːp] *n* la Guadeloupe

guarantee [gærən'tiː] **1** *n (spoken, written)* garantie f; **she gave me her g.** that it wouldn't happen again elle m'a assuré que cela ne se reproduirait plus; **there's no g. that she'll come** ce n'est pas sûr qu'elle vienne; *Com* **under g.** sous garantie
2 *vt* garantir; **I can't g. that she'll come** je ne garantis pas qu'elle viendra; **the watch is guaranteed for two years** cette montre est garantie deux ans; *Fin* **to g. sb against loss** garantir qn contre les pertes

guaranteed [gærən'tiːd] *adj* garanti(e)

guarantor [gærən'tɔː(r)] *n* garant(e) m,f

guard [gɑːd] **1** *n* **(a)** *(defences)* **to be on one's g.** être sur ses gardes; **to put sb on his g.** mettre qn en garde; **to put sb off his g.** déjouer la vigilance de qn; **to catch sb off his g.** prendre qn au dépourvu; **his g. was down** il ne se méfiait pas **(b)** *(supervision)* garde f; **to keep sb under g.** garder qn sous surveillance; **to be on g. duty** être de garde; **g. dog** chien *m* de garde **(c)** *(sentry)* garde *m*; *(on train)* chef *m* de train; *Am (in prison)* gardien *m*; *Mil (group of sentries)* garde f; **g. of honour** garde f d'honneur; *Br* **g.'s van** *(on train)* fourgon *m* du chef de train **(d)** *(device) (on machine)* protection f **(e)** *(in basketball)* défenseur *m*
2 *vt* garder; **to g. sb from danger** protéger qn d'un danger

▶**guard against** *vt insep* se prémunir contre; **he was keen to g. against any further mistakes** il prenait garde de ne pas commettre de nouvelles erreurs

guarded ['gɑːdɪd] *adj* prudent(e)

guardedly ['gɑːdɪdlɪ] *adv* avec circonspection, avec prudence

guardhouse ['gɑːdhaʊs] *n Mil* poste *m* de garde; *(prison)* prison f

guardian ['gɑːdɪən] *n (of standards)* gardien(enne) m,f; *Law (of minor)* tuteur(trice) m,f; **g. angel** ange *m* gardien

guardianship ['gɑːdɪənʃɪp] *n Law (of minor)* tutelle f

guardrail ['gɑːdreɪl] *n* garde-fou *m*, parapet *m*; *(on ship)* bastingage *m*

guardroom ['gɑːdruːm] *n* corps *m* de garde

guardsman ['gɑːdzmən] *n* garde *m (de la garde royale)*

Guatemala [gwætɪ'mɑːlə] *n* le Guatemala

Guatemalan [gwætɪ'mɑːlən] **1** *n* Guatémaltèque *mf*
2 *adj* guatémaltèque

guava ['gwɑːvə] *n* goyave f; **g. tree** goyavier *m*

guerrilla [gə'rɪlə] *n* guérillero *m*; **g. warfare** guérilla f

guess [ges] **1** n estimation f; **to have** or **make a g.** deviner; Ironic **I'll give you three guesses!** devine!; **at a g., (I'd say) three hundred** je dirais environ trois cents; **your g. is as good as mine** j'en ai pas la moindre idée; **it's anybody's g.** qui sait?

2 vt **(a)** (attempt to answer) deviner; **g. who I saw!** devine qui j'ai vu!; **g. what!** tu sais quoi?; **you've guessed it!** tu as deviné! **(b)** (suppose) supposer, croire; **I g. you're right** tu dois avoir raison

3 vi deviner; **to g. right** deviner juste; **to g. wrong** se tromper; **to keep sb guessing** laisser qn dans l'ignorance; **to g. at sth** essayer de deviner qch

guessing game ['gesɪŋgeɪm] n jeu m de devinettes; Fig **it's a bit of a g.** on ne peut que spéculer

guesstimate ['gestɪmɪt] n Fam calcul m au pif

guesswork ['gesws:k] n conjecture f; **it's pure** or **sheer g.** c'est de la pure conjecture

guest [gest] n (at home, party, on TV programme) invité(e) m,f; (at hotel) client(e) m,f; **be my g.!** je t'en prie!; **to make a g. appearance** (on TV programme) passer en invité vedette; (in film) participer à titre exceptionnel; **g. artist** invité vedette; **g. room** chambre f d'amis; **g. speaker** conférencier(ère) m,f

guesthouse ['gesthaʊs] n pension f de famille

guff [gʌf] n Fam âneries fpl

guffaw [gʌ'fɔ:] **1** n gros rire m
2 vi s'esclaffer

GUI ['gu:i] n Comptr (abbr **Graphical User Interface**) interface f utilisateur graphique

Guiana [gaɪ'ɑ:nə] n la Guyane

guidance ['gaɪdəns] n direction f; **under the g. of** sous la direction de; **for your g.** à titre d'information

guide [gaɪd] **1** n **(a)** (person) guide m; **(Girl) G.** éclaireuse f; **g. dog** chien m d'aveugle **(b)** (book) guide m **(to g.) (c)** (indication) indication f (**to** sur); **as a g.** à titre indicatif
2 vt guider; **to be guided by sth** suivre qch

guidebook ['gaɪdbʊk] n guide m

guided ['gaɪdɪd] adj **g. missile** missile m guidé; **g. tour** visite f guidée

guideline ['gaɪdlaɪn] n (indication) indication f; **guidelines** directives fpl; **as a general g.** en règle générale

guiding ['gaɪdɪŋ] adj (principle, concept) directeur(trice)

guild [gɪld] n (association) association f

guilder ['gɪldə] n florin m

guile [gaɪl] n ruse f

guileless ['gaɪlɪs] adj candide

guillemot ['gɪlɪmɒt] n guillemot m

guillotine ['gɪləti:n] **1** n (for execution) guillotine f; (for cutting paper) massicot m; Br Pol **to put a g. on a bill** = imposer une limite de temps aux débats précédant un vote
2 vt (execute) guillotiner

guilt [gɪlt] n culpabilité f; **to feel g.** se sentir coupable; **g. complex** complexe m de culpabilité

guiltily ['gɪltɪlɪ] adv d'un air coupable

guiltless ['gɪltlɪs] adj innocent(e)

guilty ['gɪltɪ] adj coupable; **to find sb g./not g.** déclarer qn coupable/non coupable; **to feel g.** se sentir coupable; **to have a g. conscience** avoir mauvaise conscience; **g. secret** secret m inavouable

Guinea ['gɪnɪ] n la Guinée

guinea ['gɪnɪ] n **(a)** Br (coin) guinée f **(b) g. fowl** pintade f; **g. pig** cobaye m, cochon m d'Inde; Fig **to be a g. pig** servir de cobaye

Guinea-Bissau ['gɪnɪbɪ'saʊ] n la Guinée-Bissau

Guinean ['gɪneɪən] **1** n Guinéen(enne) m,f
2 adj guinéen(enne)

guise [gaɪz] n apparence f; **in** or **under the g. of** sous l'apparence de; **in a different g.** sous une autre forme

guitar [gɪ'tɑ:(r)] n guitare f

guitarist [gɪ'tɑ:rɪst] n guitariste mf

gulch [gʌltʃ] n Am ravin m

gulf [gʌlf] n **(a)** (bay) golfe m; **the (Persian) G.** le golfe Persique; **the G. of Mexico** le golfe du Mexique; **the G. Stream** le Gulf Stream; **the G. War** la guerre du Golfe **(b)** (between people, ideas) abîme m, gouffre m (**between** entre)

gull [gʌl] n mouette f, goéland m

gullet ['gʌlɪt] n gosier m

gullibility [gʌlɪ'bɪlɪtɪ] n crédulité f

gullible ['gʌlɪbəl] adj crédule

gully ['gʌlɪ] (pl gullies) n petit ravin m

gulp [gʌlp] **1** n **(a)** (of food) bouchée f; (of drink) gorgée f; **in** or **at one g.** d'un coup **(b)** (of surprise) serrement m de gorge
2 vt (food, drink) engloutir
3 vi (with surprise) avoir un serrement de gorge

▶**gulp down** vt sep (food, drink) engloutir

gum [gʌm] **1** n **(a)** (in mouth) gencive f; **g. disease** gingivite f **(b)** (adhesive) colle f **(c) (chewing) g.** chewing gum m **(d)** (resin) **g. arabic** gomme f arabique; **g. tree** gommier m; Fig **to be up a g. tree** être dans le pétrin
2 vt (pt & pp gummed) (stick) coller

▶**gum up** vt sep (mechanism) enrayer; (eyes) coller

gumboot ['gʌmbu:t] n botte f de caoutchouc

gummed [gʌmd] adj gommé(e)

gummy ['gʌmɪ] adj collant(e)

gumption ['gʌmʃən] n Fam (common sense) jugeote f; (courage) cran m

gumshield ['gʌmʃi:ld] n protège-dents m inv

gun [gʌn] **1** n **(a)** (pistol) pistolet m; (rifle) fusil m; (artillery piece) canon m; **g. carriage** affût m de canon; **g. dog** chien m d'arrêt; **g. laws** législation f sur les armes à feu; **g. licence** permis m de port d'armes **(b)** (idioms) Fam **big g.** huile f; Fam **to be going great guns** marcher très fort; **to stick to one's guns** tenir bon; **to jump the g.** s'emballer
2 vt (pt & pp gunned) (engine) accélérer

▶**gun down** vt sep abattre

▶**gun for** vt insep **to be gunning for sb** en avoir après qn; **she's gunning for his job** elle fait tout ce qu'elle peut pour lui prendre son poste

gunboat ['gʌnbəʊt] n canonnière f; **g. diplomacy** politique f de la canonnière

gunfight ['gʌnfaɪt] n fusillade f

gunfire ['gʌnfaɪə(r)] n (of artillery) tirs mpl d'artillerie; (of smaller guns) coups mpl de feu

gunge [gʌndʒ] n Fam matière f gluante

gung-ho [gʌŋ'həʊ] adj **(a)** (overly enthusiastic) d'un enthousiasme irritant **(b)** (keen for war) va-t-en-guerre inv

gunk [gʌŋk] n Fam matière f gluante

gunman ['gʌnmən] n homme m armé

gunner ['gʌnə(r)] n artilleur m

gunpoint ['gʌnpɔint] n **at g.** sous la menace d'une arme à feu

gunpowder ['gʌnpaʊdə(r)] n poudre f (à canon)

gunrunner ['gʌnrʌnə(r)] n trafiquant(e) m,f d'armes

gunrunning ['gʌnrʌnɪŋ] n trafic m d'armes

gunship ['gʌnʃɪp] n (**helicopter**) **g.** hélicoptère m de combat

gunshot ['gʌnʃɒt] n coup m de feu; **g. wound** blessure f par balle

gunsmith ['gʌnsmɪθ] n armurier m

gunwale ['gʌnəl] n Naut plat-bord m

gurgle ['gɜːgəl] 1 n (of liquid) gargouillement m; (of baby) gazouillis m

  2 vi (of liquid) gargouiller; (of baby) gazouiller

guru ['guːruː] n gourou m

gush [gʌʃ] 1 n (of water) jaillissement m; Fig (of words) flot m

  2 vi (a) (of water) jaillir; **tears gushed from her eyes** elle pleurait à chaudes larmes (b) Pej (talk effusively) s'extasier (**over** or **about** devant)

gushing ['gʌʃɪŋ] adj Pej (person, praise) exubérant(e)

gusset ['gʌsɪt] n soufflet m

gust [gʌst] 1 n (of wind) rafale f; (of hot air) bouffée f

  2 vi (of wind) souffler par rafales

gusto ['gʌstəʊ] n enthousiasme m

gusty ['gʌstɪ] adj (wind) qui souffle par rafales; (day, weather) de grand vent

gut [gʌt] 1 n (a) (intestine) intestin m; Fam **guts** (of person, machine) entrailles fpl; Fam **to sweat** or **work one's guts out** se tuer à la tâche; Fam **to hate sb's guts** ne pas pouvoir sentir qn; Fam **I'll have his guts for garters** je vais le massacrer; **a g. feeling** une intuition; **g. reaction** réaction f viscérale (b) Fam **guts** (courage) cran m; **I didn't have the guts to tell them** je n'ai pas eu le courage de le leur dire

  2 vt (pt & pp **gutted**) (a) (fish) vider (b) (building) (of fire) ravager; (of builder) vider entièrement

gutless ['gʌtlɪs] adj Fam lâche

gutsy ['gʌtsɪ] adj Fam courageux(euse)

gutted ['gʌtɪd] adj Br Fam (disappointed) effondré(e)

gutter ['gʌtə(r)] 1 n (in street) caniveau m; (on roof) gouttière f; Fig **to end up in the g.** finir sous les ponts; Fig **to drag oneself out of the g.** se sortir de la misère; Fam Pej **g. press** presse f à scandales

  2 vi (of candle) vaciller

guttural ['gʌtərəl] adj guttural(e)

guy¹ [gaɪ] n Fam (a) (man) type m, mec m; **a tough g.** un dur (b) (person) **hi guys!** salut la compagnie!

guy² n g. (rope) (for tent) tendeur m

Guyana [gaɪ'ænə] n le Guyana

Guyanese [gaɪə'niːz] 1 n Guyanais(e) m,f

  2 adj guyanais(e)

Guy Fawkes Night ['gaɪ'fɔːks'naɪt] n Br = soirée du 5 novembre, célébration de la tentative de Guy Fawkes de faire sauter le Parlement en 1605

guzzle ['gʌzəl] vt Fam (food) engloutir; (drink) siffler

gym [dʒɪm] n (gymnasium) gymnase m; (gymnastics) gym f; **g. shoes** chaussures fpl de gym

gymkhana [dʒɪm'kɑːnə] n concours m hippique

gymnasium [dʒɪm'neɪzɪəm] n gymnase m

gymnast ['dʒɪmnæst] n gymnaste mf

gymnastic [dʒɪm'næstɪk] adj gymnastique

gymnastics [dʒɪm'næstɪks] 1 n gymnastique f

  2 npl Fig **mental/verbal g.** gymnastique f intellectuelle/verbale

gynaecological, Am **gynecological** [gaɪnɪkə'lɒdʒɪkəl] adj gynécologique

gynaecologist, Am **gynecologist** [gaɪnɪ'kɒlədʒɪst] n gynécologue mf

gynaecology, Am **gynecology** [gaɪnɪ'kɒlədʒɪ] n gynécologie f

gyp [dʒɪp] n Br Fam **to give sb g.** faire souffrir qn

gypsum ['dʒɪpsəm] n gypse m

gypsy ['dʒɪpsɪ] = gipsy

gyrate [dʒaɪ'reɪt] vi (of planet, sphere) tourner; (of dancer) tournoyer

gyration [dʒaɪ'reɪʃən] n giration f

gyroscope ['dʒaɪrəskəʊp] n gyroscope m

H, h [eɪtʃ] *n (letter)* H, h *m inv*; **H bomb** bombe *f* H

haberdashery ['hæbədæʃərɪ] *(pl* **haberdasheries)** *n* **(a)** *Br (sewing items, shop)* mercerie *f* **(b)** *Am (men's clothes, shop)* chemiserie *f*

habit ['hæbɪt] *n* **(a)** *(custom, practice)* habitude *f*; **to be in the h. of doing sth** avoir l'habitude de faire qch; **to get into the h. of doing sth** prendre l'habitude de faire qch; **to get out of the h. of doing sth** perdre l'habitude de faire qch; **don't make a h. of it!** que cela ne devienne pas une habitude!; **from force of h.** par habitude **(b)** *Fam (addiction to drugs)* accoutumance *f*; **to kick the h.** décrocher **(c)** *(of monk, nun)* habit *m*

habitable ['hæbɪtəbəl] *adj* habitable

habitat ['hæbɪtæt] *n* habitat *m*

habitation [hæbɪ'teɪʃən] *n* habitation *f*; **there were no signs of h.** l'endroit semblait inhabité; **fit for h.** habitable; **unfit for h.** inhabitable

habitual [hə'bɪtjʊəl] *adj (generosity, rudeness)* habituel(elle); *(liar, drunk)* invétéré(e)

habitually [hə'bɪtjʊəlɪ] *adv* habituellement

habituate [hə'bɪtjʊeɪt] *vt* habituer (**to** à); **to become habituated to sth** s'habituer à qch

hack¹ [hæk] **1** *vt* **(a)** *(cut)* tailler, taillader; **to h. sb/sth to pieces** tailler qn/qch en pièces; **to h. one's way through the jungle** se frayer un chemin dans la jungle à la machette **(b)** *very Fam (cope with)* **he can't h. it** il ne s'en sort pas

2 *vi* **(a)** *(cut)* **to h. at sth** taillader qch **(b)** *(cough)* tousser d'une toux sèche **(c)** *Comptr* **to h. into sth** entrer dans qch par effraction

▸**hack down** *vt sep* abattre

▸**hack off** *vt sep* **(a)** *(branch, limb)* couper **(b)** *Fam* **to be hacked off (with sb/sth)** en avoir marre (de qn/qch)

hack² *n* **(a)** *Fam Pej (journalist)* journaliste *mf* besogneux(euse); *(political activist)* militant(e) *m,f* **(b)** *(horseride)* **to go for a h.** aller faire une promenade à cheval **(c)** *Am Fam (taxi)* taxi *m*

hacker ['hækə(r)] *n Comptr* pirate *m* informatique

hacking jacket ['hækɪŋ'dʒækɪt] *n* veste *f* d'équitation

hackles ['hækəlz] *npl (of dog)* poils *mpl* du cou; *(of bird)* plumes *fpl* du cou; *Fig* **to make sb's h. rise** hérisser qn

hackney cab ['hæknɪkæb], **hackney carriage** ['hæknɪ'kærɪdʒ] *n Formal (taxi)* fiacre *m*

hackneyed ['hæknɪd] *adj (argument)* rebattu(e); *(language)* banal(e); **h. expression** lieu *m* commun

hacksaw ['hæksɔː] *n* scie *f* à métaux

had [hæd] *pt & pp of* **have**

haddock ['hædək] *(pl* **haddock** *or* **haddocks)** *n* églefin *m*

hadn't ['hædənt] = **had not**

haemoglobin, *Am* **hemoglobin** [hiːməʊ'gləʊbɪn] *n* hémoglobine *f*

haemophilia, *Am* **hemophilia** [hiːməʊ'fɪlɪə] *n* hémophilie *f*

haemophiliac, *Am* **hemophiliac** [hiːməʊ'fɪlɪæk] *n* hémophile *mf*

haemorrhage, *Am* **hemorrhage** ['hemərɪdʒ] **1** *n also Fig* hémorragie *f*

2 *vi Med* faire une hémorragie; *Fig (of support, funds)* diminuer

haemorrhoids, *Am* **hemorrhoids** ['hemərɔɪdz] *npl Med* hémorroïdes *fpl*

hag [hæg] *n Pej* vieille taupe *f*

haggard ['hægəd] *adj* hâve

haggis ['hægɪs] *n* = panse de brebis farcie *(plat national écossais)*

haggle ['hægəl] *vi* marchander (**with** sb avec qn); **to h. over sth** marchander qch; **to h. about** *or* **over the price of sth** chicaner sur le prix de qch

hagiography [hægɪ'ɒgrəfɪ] *n* hagiographie *f*

Hague [heɪg] *n* **the H.** La Haye

hail¹ [heɪl] **1** *n* grêle *f*; *Fig* **a h. of bullets/insults** une pluie de balles/d'injures; **a h. of blows** une volée de coups

2 *vi* **it's hailing** il grêle

hail² *vt* **(a)** *(attract attention of)* héler **(b)** *(acclaim)* saluer **(as** comme)

▸**hail from** *vt insep* être originaire de

hailstone ['heɪlstəʊn] *n* grêlon *m*

hailstorm ['heɪlstɔːm] *n* averse *f* de grêle

hair [heə(r)] *n* **(on head)** cheveux *mpl*; *(on body, animal)* poils *mpl*; *(single hair)* *(on head)* cheveu *m*; *(on body, animal)* poil *m*; **to have fair/long h.** avoir les cheveux clairs/longs; **to do one's h.** se coiffer; **to comb one's h.** se peigner; **to brush one's h.** se brosser les cheveux; **to have** *or* **get one's h. cut** se faire couper les cheveux; **if you harm** *or* **touch a h. on that child's head...** si tu touches à un cheveu de la tête de cet enfant...; **to make sb's h. stand on end** faire dresser les cheveux sur la tête à qn; *Fam* **keep your h. on!** calmez-vous!; *Fam* **to get in sb's h.** enquiquiner qn; *Fig* **to let one's h. down** se laisser aller; *Fam* **h. of the dog** *(for hangover)* = verre d'alcool pris pour calmer la gueule de bois; **h. gel** gel *m* pour les cheveux; *Br* **h. slide** barrette *f*

hairband ['heəbænd] *n* bandeau *m*

hairbrush ['heəbrʌʃ] *n* brosse *f* à cheveux

haircut ['heəkʌt] *n* coupe *f* de cheveux; **to have a h.** se faire couper les cheveux

hairdo ['heəduː] *(pl* **hairdos)** *n Fam* coiffure *f*

hairdresser ['heədresə(r)] n coiffeur(euse) m,f; **to go to the h.'s** aller chez le coiffeur

hairdressing ['heədresɪŋ] n coiffure f; **h. salon** salon m de coiffure

hairdryer ['heədraɪə(r)] n sèche-cheveux m inv

hairgrip ['heəgrɪp] n pince f à cheveux

hairless ['heəlɪs] adj (face) glabre; (puppy) sans poils

hairline ['heəlaɪn] n (a) (of person) naissance f des cheveux; **to have a receding h.** avoir le front qui se dégarnit (b) **h. crack** (in pipe, wall) légère fêlure f; **h. fracture** (of bone) fêlure f

hairnet ['heənet] n résille f, filet m à cheveux

hairpiece ['heəpi:s] n postiche m

hairpin ['heəpɪn] n épingle f à cheveux; **h. bend** (on road) virage m en épingle à cheveux

hair-raising ['heəreɪzɪŋ] adj à faire dresser les cheveux sur la tête

hair's-breadth ['heəzbredθ] n **by a h.** (win, lose) de justesse; **the car missed him by a h.** la voiture l'a frôlé; **to be within a h. of** être à deux doigts de

hairspray ['heəspreɪ] n laque f

hairstyle ['heəstaɪl] n coiffure f

hairy ['heərɪ] adj (a) (covered in hair) velu(e), poilu(e) (b) Fam (scary) effrayant(e)

Haiti ['heɪtɪ] n Haïti

Haitian ['heɪʃən] 1 n Haïtien(enne) m,f
2 adj haïtien(enne)

hake [heɪk] (pl hake or hakes) n merlu m, colin m

halcyon days ['hælsɪən deɪz] npl Lit jours mpl heureux

hale [heɪl] adj vigoureux(euse); **to be h. and hearty** être en pleine forme

half [hɑ:f] 1 n (pl halves [hɑ:vz]) (a) (in general) moitié f; **h. an hour** une demi-heure; **h. past ten** dix heures et demie; **it's h. past** il est la demie; **to fold/cut sth in h.** plier/couper qch en deux; **h. a dozen** une demi-douzaine; **h. of them** la moitié d'entre eux; **to have h. a mind to do sth** avoir bien envie de faire qch; Hum **my better** or **other h.** ma moitié; **she is too clever by h.** elle est beaucoup trop maligne; **she doesn't do things by halves** elle ne fait pas les choses à moitié; **to go halves with sb** partager avec qn; Fam **you don't know the h. of it!** tu ne sais pas tout!
(b) (fraction) demie f, moitié f; **three and a h.** trois et demi
(c) first/second **h.** (in match) première/deuxième mi-temps f
(d) (ticket) billet m demi-tarif
(e) Br (half pint) demi m
2 adj demi(e); **h. board** demi-pension f; **h. day** demi-journée f; **h. hour** demi-heure f; **every h. hour** toutes les demi-heures; **h. price** demi-tarif m; **at h. price** à moitié prix
3 adv à moitié; **to h. do sth** faire qch à moitié; **h. full/empty** à moitié plein(e)/vide; **you're h. right** tu n'as pas tout à fait tort; Br Fam **not h.!** plutôt!; Br Fam **it isn't h. cold!** il fait rudement froid!

half- [hɑ:f] pref **h.-asleep** à moitié endormi(e); **h.-dead** à moitié mort(e); **h.-naked** à moitié nu(e)

half-baked [hɑ:f'beɪkt] adj Fam bancal(e)

halfbreed ['hɑ:fbri:d] n métis(isse) m,f

half-brother ['hɑ:fbrʌðə(r)] n demi-frère m

half-caste ['hɑ:fkɑ:st] n métis(isse) m,f

half-cock ['hɑ:f'kɒk] n Fam Fig **to go off at h.** (of plan, event) avorter, échouer

half-hearted ['hɑ:f'hɑ:tɪd] adj (effort, performance) timide, hésitant(e); (belief, support) peu enthousiaste

half-heartedly ['hɑ:f'hɑ:tɪdlɪ] adv sans grand enthousiasme, sans conviction

half-hourly [hɑ:f'aʊəlɪ] adv toutes les demi-heures

half-life ['hɑ:flaɪf] n Phys demi-vie f

half-mast ['hɑ:f'mɑ:st] n Br **at h.** (flag) en berne; Fam (socks) en accordéon

half-sister ['hɑ:f'sɪstə(r)] n demi-sœur f

half-size ['hɑ:f'saɪz] n (in shoes) demi-pointure f

half-term ['hɑ:f'tɜ:m] n Br **h. (holiday)** = congé de milieu de trimestre

half time ['hɑ:f'taɪm] n (in match) mi-temps f

half-truth ['hɑ:f'tru:θ] n demi-vérité f

halfway [hɑ:f'weɪ] 1 adj **at the h. point** (in space) à mi-chemin; (in time) à la moitié; **h. line** (on sports pitch) ligne f médiane
2 adv à mi-chemin; Fig **to meet sb h.** faire un compromis avec qn

halfwit ['hɑ:fwɪt] n simple mf d'esprit

halfwitted [hɑ:f'wɪtɪd] adj stupide

half-yearly ['hɑ:f'jɪəlɪ] adj semestriel(elle)

halibut ['hælɪbət] (pl halibut or halibuts) n flétan m

halitosis [hælɪ'təʊsɪs] n mauvaise haleine f

hall [hɔ:l] n (a) (entrance room) entrée f; (corridor) couloir m (b) (for concerts, meetings) salle f (c) Br Univ **h. of residence** résidence f universitaire

hallmark ['hɔ:lmɑ:k] n (on metal) poinçon m; Fig (typical quality) signe m

hallo [hə'ləʊ] = **hello**

hallowed ['hæləʊd] adj saint(e), béni(e)

Hallowe'en [hæləʊ'i:n] n = veille de la Toussaint durant laquelle les enfants se déguisent en fantôme ou en sorcière

hallucinate [hə'lu:sɪneɪt] vi avoir des hallucinations

hallucination [həlu:sɪ'neɪʃən] n hallucination f

hallucinatory [hə'lu:sɪnətərɪ] adj hallucinatoire

hallucinogenic [həlu:sɪnəʊ'dʒenɪk] adj hallucinogène

hallway ['hɔ:lweɪ] n (entrance room) entrée f; (corridor) couloir m

halo ['heɪləʊ] (pl haloes or halos) n auréole f

halt [hɔ:lt] 1 n halte f, arrêt m; **to come to a h.** s'arrêter; **to bring sth to a h.** interrompre ou faire cesser qch; **to call a h. to sth** mettre fin à qch
2 vt interrompre
3 vi s'arrêter

halter ['hɔ:ltə(r)] n (for horse) licou m

halterneck ['hɔ:ltənek] adj (dress, top) dos-nu inv

halting ['hɔ:ltɪŋ] adj (voice, progress) hésitant(e)

halve [hɑ:v] vt (a) (divide in two) diviser en deux; (cake, fruit) couper en deux (b) (reduce by half) réduire de moitié

halves [hɑ:vz] pl of **half**

ham [hæm] 1 n (a) (meat) jambon m (b) Fam (actor) cabotin(e) m,f; **h. acting** cabotinage m
2 vt (pt & pp hammed) Fam (of actor) **to h. it up** en faire trop

Hamburg ['hæmbɜ:g] n Hambourg

hamburger ['hæmbɜ:gə(r)] n hamburger m

ham-fisted ['hæm'fɪstɪd] adj Fam maladroit(e)

hamlet ['hæmlɪt] *n* hameau *m*

hammer ['hæmə(r)] **1** *n* marteau *m*; **to come under the h.** *(be auctioned)* être mis(e) aux enchères; *Fam* **to go at it h. and tongs** mettre le paquet; **the h. and sickle** la faucille et le marteau

2 *vt* (a) *(hit with hammer) (nail)* enfoncer (**into** dans); *(wall)* taper à coups de marteau; *Fig* **to h. one's point home** insister lourdement (b) *(hit with fist) (object)* frapper du poing; *(person)* frapper à coups de poing (c) *Fam (defeat)* écraser

▸**hammer away at** *vt insep Fig (problem)* travailler avec acharnement sur

▸**hammer out** *vt sep Fig (plan, compromise)* mettre au point

hammering ['hæmərɪŋ] *n* (a) *(noise)* martèlement *m* (b) *Fam (defeat)* raclée *f*; **they gave us a real h.** ils nous ont mis une vraie raclée

hammock ['hæmək] *n* hamac *m*

hamper ['hæmpə(r)] **1** *n (for food)* panier *m*; **(Christmas) h.** = panier garni de gourmandises offert à Noël

2 *vt (hinder)* gêner, entraver

hamster ['hæmstə(r)] *n* hamster *m*

hamstring ['hæmstrɪŋ] **1** *n* tendon *m* du jarret

2 *vt (pt & pp* **hamstrung** ['hæmstrʌŋ]) *(incapacitate)* paralyser

hand [hænd] **1** *n* (a) *(part of body)* main *f*; *(of clock, watch)* aiguille *f*; **to hold hands** se tenir par la main; **h. in h.** la main dans la main; **to hold sth in one's h.** tenir qch à la main; **to take sb by the h.** prendre qn par la main; **on one's hands and knees** à quatre pattes; **by h.** *(make, wash)* à la main; *(on envelope)* en ville, E.V.; **hands off!** pas touche!; **hands up!** haut les mains!; **h. basin** lavabo *m*; **h. cream** crème *f* pour les mains; **h. grenade** grenade *f*; **h. luggage** bagages *mpl* à main

(b) *(worker)* ouvrier(ère) *m,f*; *(sailor)* matelot *m*; **to be an old h. at sth** avoir une expérience considérable de qch

(c) *(handwriting)* **in his own h.** de sa main

(d) *(in cards)* main *f*, jeu *m*; *Fig* **to show one's h.** dévoiler son jeu

(e) *(idioms)* **at** or **on h.** disponible; **to have sth to h.** avoir qch sous la main; **to ask for sb's h. (in marriage)** demander la main de qn; **to be in good hands** être en de bonnes mains; **to fall into the wrong hands** tomber en de mauvaises mains; **it's out of my hands** ça ne dépend plus de moi; **to change hands** *(of money, car)* changer de mains; **to have a h. in sth** être impliqué(e) dans qch; **to go h. in h. with sth** aller de pair avec qch; **to try one's h. at sth** s'essayer à qch; **to turn one's h. to sth** s'essayer à qch; **to lend sb a h.** donner un coup de main à qn; **to give sb a big h.** *(applaud)* applaudir qn bien fort; **to suffer at sb's hands** souffrir aux mains de qn; **on (the) one h.** d'une part; **on the other h.** d'autre part; **to have time on one's hands** avoir du temps à soi; **to have a situation in h.** contrôler une situation; **to take sb in h.** prendre qn en main; **to get out of h.** devenir incontrôlable; **to dismiss a suggestion out of h.** rejeter une proposition sur-le-champ; **to have one's hands full** être débordé(e); **to have one's hands tied** avoir les mains liées; **to be h. in glove with sb** être de mèche avec qn; **to live from h. to mouth** mener une existence précaire; **to lose money h. over fist** perdre des sommes considérables; **to make money h. over fist** gagner une fortune; **to win hands down** gagner haut la main

2 *vt* donner, passer; **he handed her the letter to read**

il lui a passé la lettre pour qu'elle la lise; *Fig* **to h. sth to sb on a plate** apporter qch à qn sur un plateau; *Fig* **you've got to h. it to him** c'est une qualité qu'il faut lui reconnaître

▸**hand back** *vt sep* rendre, repasser

▸**hand down** *vt sep* (a) *(jewellery, tradition, skill)* transmettre (b) *(give)* passer

▸**hand in** *vt sep* remettre; **to h. in one's resignation** donner sa démission

▸**hand on** *vt sep* transmettre

▸**hand out** *vt sep* distribuer

▸**hand over** *vt sep* donner

▸**hand round** *vt sep* faire circuler

handbag ['hændbæg] *n* sac *m* à main

handball ['hændbɔːl] *n* (a) *(game)* handball *m* (b) *(offence)* main *f*

handbook ['hændbʊk] *n* guide *m*, manuel *m*

handbrake ['hændbreɪk] *n* frein *m* à main

handclap ['hændklæp] *n* **to give sb the slow h.** = applaudir qn très lentement pour signifier son dédain

handcuff ['hændkʌf] *vt* passer les menottes à

handcuffs ['hændkʌfs] *npl* menottes *fpl*

handful ['hændfʊl] *n (of sand, rice, people)* poignée *f*; *Fig* **that child is a real h.** cet enfant n'est pas facile

handgun ['hændɡʌn] *n* revolver *m*, pistolet *m*

handicap ['hændɪkæp] **1** *n* handicap *m*

2 *vt (pt & pp* **handicapped**) handicaper

handicapped ['hændɪkæpt] **1** *npl* **the h.** les handicapés *mpl*

2 *adj* handicapé(e)

handicraft ['hændɪkrɑːft] *n (skill)* artisanat *m*; *(object)* objet *m* artisanal

handiwork ['hændɪwɜːk] *n* travail *m* manuel; *Hum* **this looks like Jane's h.** ça, c'est signé Jane!

handkerchief ['hæŋkətʃɪf] *n* mouchoir *m*

handle ['hændəl] **1** *n (of broom, knife, saucepan)* manche *m*; *(of suitcase, door)* poignée *f*; *(of cup)* anse *f*; *Fig* **to fly off the h.** piquer une colère; *Fig* **to get a h. on sth** piger qch

2 *vt* (a) *(touch, hold)* manipuler, toucher à; **h. with care** *(on panel)* ≃ fragile; **to h. the ball** *(in football)* toucher le ballon avec la main (b) *Fam (cope with) (situation, crisis)* faire face à (c) *Com (business, contract, client)* s'occuper de

3 *vi (of car, boat)* **to h. well** être maniable

handlebars ['hændlbɑː(r)z] *npl* guidon *m*

handmade ['hænd'meɪd] *adj* fait(e) à la main

hand-me-downs ['hændmɪdaʊnz] *npl Fam* **I wear my brother's h.** je mets les vieilles frusques de mon frère

handout ['hændaʊt] *n* (a) *(donation)* don *m* (b) *(leaflet)* prospectus *m*

hand-picked ['hænd'pɪkd] *adj (person, team)* trié(e) sur le volet

handrail ['hændreɪl] *n* rampe *f*

handset ['hændset] *n (of telephone)* combiné *m*

handshake ['hændʃeɪk] *n* poignée *f* de main

hands-off ['hæn'zɒf] *adj (approach, style)* non-interventionniste

handsome ['hænsəm] *adj* (a) *(physically attractive)* beau (belle) (b) *(praise)* sincère; *(price, profit)* considérable; *(reward)* beau (belle)

handsomely ['hænsəmlɪ] *adv* (a) *(dressed, furnished)* élégamment (b) *(rewarded, paid)* généreusement

hands-on ['hæn'zɒn] *adj* **the director has a h. style of management** le directeur n'a pas peur de mettre la main à la pâte; **h. training** formation *f* pratique

handstand ['hændstænd] *n* **to do a h.** faire un équilibre sur les mains

hand-to-hand ['hæntə'hænd] *adj (combat)* au corps à corps

hand-to-mouth ['hæntə'maʊθ] **1** *adj (existence)* précaire
2 *adv* **to live h.** tirer le diable par la queue

handwriting ['hændraɪtɪŋ] *n* écriture *f*

handwritten ['hændrɪtən] *adj* manuscrit(e)

handy ['hændɪ] *adj* **(a)** *(useful)* pratique; **to come in h.** être utile **(b)** *(convenient)* commode; **the flat is very h. for the shops** l'appartement est tout près des commerces **(c)** *(within reach)* à portée de la main; **have you got a pen h.?** est-ce que tu as un stylo à portée de la main? **(d)** *(skilful)* bricoleur(euse); **he's very h. in the kitchen** il est bon cuisinier

handyman ['hændɪmæn] *n* homme *m* à tout faire

hang [hæŋ] **1** *n Fam* **to get the h. of sth** piger qch
2 *vt (pt & pp hung* [hʌŋ]*)* **(a)** *(suspend) (from ceiling)* pendre, suspendre; *(on wall)* accrocher **(b) to h. one's head** baisser la tête; **he hung his head in shame** il baissa la tête sous l'effet de la honte **(c)** *(pt & pp hanged) (criminal)* pendre
3 *vi* **(a)** *(be suspended) (from ceiling)* être suspendu(e); *(on wall)* être accroché(e); *Fig* **she hung on his every word** elle était pendue à ses lèvres **(b)** *(be executed)* être pendu(e) **(c)** *(of clothes)* tomber
▸**hang about, hang around** *vi Fam (wait)* poireauter; **to keep sb hanging about** *or* **around** faire poireauter qn
▸**hang back** *vi* hésiter
▸**hang in** *vi Fam* **h. in there!** accroche-toi!, tiens bon!
▸**hang on** *vi* **(a)** *Fam (wait)* patienter, attendre **(b)** *(survive)* tenir le coup
2 *vt insep (depend on)* dépendre de
▸**hang on to** *vt insep* garder
▸**hang out 1** *vt sep (washing)* étendre
2 *vi* **(a)** *(from pocket, box)* dépasser **(b)** *Fam (spend time)* traîner
▸**hang together** *vi (of argument, statements)* se tenir
▸**hang up 1** *vt sep (hat, picture)* accrocher
2 *vi (on telephone)* raccrocher; **to h. up on sb** raccrocher au nez de qn

hangar ['hæŋə(r)] *n* hangar *m*

hangdog ['hæŋdɒg] *adj (look, expression)* de chien battu

hanger ['hæŋə(r)] *n (for clothes)* cintre *m*

hanger-on ['hæŋə'rɒn] *(pl* hangers-on*)* *n* parasite *m*, pique-assiette *m inv*

hang-glider ['hæŋglaɪdə(r)] *n* deltaplane *m*

hang-gliding ['hæŋglaɪdɪŋ] *n* deltaplane *m*; **to go h.** faire du deltaplane

hanging ['hæŋɪŋ] *n (execution)* pendaison *f*

hangman ['hæŋmən] *n* bourreau *m*

hangnail ['hæŋneɪl] *n* envie *f*

hang-out ['hæŋaʊt] *n Fam* repaire *m*

hangover ['hæŋəʊvə(r)] *n* **(a)** *(from drinking)* gueule *f* de bois **(b)** *(practice, belief)* reste *m*, vestige *m*

hang-up ['hæŋʌp] *n Fam* complexe *m*; **to have a h. about sth** être complexé(e) à propos de qch

hanker ['hæŋkə(r)] *vi* **to h. after** *or* **for sth** avoir très envie de qch

hankering ['hæŋkərɪŋ] *n* **to have a h. for sth** avoir très envie de qch

hankie, hanky ['hæŋkɪ] *(pl* hankies*)* *n Fam* mouchoir *m*

hanky-panky ['hæŋkɪ'pæŋkɪ] *n Fam* **(a)** *(sexual activity)* galipettes *fpl* **(b)** *(underhand behaviour)* entourloupettes *fpl*

Hanover ['hænəʊvə(r)] *n* Hanovre

haphazard [hæp'hæzəd] *adj (choice, decision)* pris(e) au hasard; *(attempt)* mal organisé(e)

haphazardly [hæp'hæzədlɪ] *adv* n'importe comment

hapless ['hæplɪs] *adj* infortuné(e)

happen ['hæpən] *vi* arriver, se produire; **it happened ten years ago** c'est arrivé il y a dix ans; **what happened?** que s'est-il passé?; **to h. again** se reproduire; **it so happens (that)...** il se trouve justement que...; **as if nothing had happened** comme si de rien n'était; **as it happens,...** justement...; **what has happened to him?** que lui est-il arrivé?; **to h. to meet sb** rencontrer qn par hasard; **I h. to know (that)...** il se trouve que je sais que...; **do you h. to know whether...?** savez-vous par hasard si...?
▸**happen on, happen upon** *vt insep* tomber sur

happening ['hæpənɪŋ] **1** *n* événement *m*
2 *adj Fam (town)* dynamique

happily ['hæpɪlɪ] *adv* **(a)** *(play)* gentiment; *(chat)* tranquillement; **a h. married couple** un ménage heureux; **they lived h. ever after** ≃ ils vécurent heureux et eurent beaucoup d'enfants **(b)** *(fortunately)* heureusement, par bonheur **(c)** *(willingly)* volontiers

happiness ['hæpɪnɪs] *n* bonheur *m*

happy ['hæpɪ] *adj* **(a)** *(content, cheerful)* heureux(euse); **to be h. with sth** être satisfait(e) de qch; **to make sb h.** rendre qn heureux; **to keep sb h.** satisfaire qn; **a story with a h. ending** une histoire qui finit bien; **a h. medium** le juste milieu; **h. birthday/Christmas!** joyeux anniversaire/Noël!; **h. New Year!** bonne année! **(b)** *(fortunate) (choice, phrase)* heureux(euse) **(c)** *(willing)* **to be h. to do sth** être heureux(euse) de faire qch

happy-go-lucky ['hæpɪgəʊ'lʌkɪ] *adj* insouciant(e)

harangue [hə'ræŋ] **1** *n* harangue *f*
2 *vt* haranguer; *(about)* au sujet de)

harass [hə'ræs, 'hærəs] *vt* harceler

harassed [hə'ræst, 'hærəst] *adj* stressé(e)

harassment [hə'ræsmənt, 'hærəsmənt] *n* harcèlement *m*; **police h.** harcèlement policier

harbour, *Am* **harbor** ['hɑːbə(r)] **1** *n* port *m*
2 *vt (fugitive)* cacher; *(hope, suspicion)* nourrir; **to h. a grudge against sb** garder rancune à qn

hard [hɑːd] **1** *adj* **(a)** *(substance)* dur(e); *(fact, evidence)* tangible; **Fig to be as h. as nails** être dur; **in h. cash** en liquide; *Comptr* **h. copy** copie *f* sur papier; **h. core** *(of group)* noyau *m* dur; *Ten* **h. court** *(for tennis)* court *m* en dur; *Comptr* **h. disk** disque *m* dur; **h. drugs** drogues *fpl* dures; *Pol* **h. left/right** extrême gauche *f*/droite *f*; *Comptr* **h. return** retour *m* chariot obligatoire; *Br* **h. shoulder** *(on motorway)* bande *f* d'arrêt d'urgence
(b) *(difficult) (strenuous)* pénible; **it was h. work persuading him to come** ça n'a pas été facile de le convaincre de venir; **it's h. to say...** il est difficile de dire...; **to be h. to please** être difficile (à satisfaire); **to learn sth the h. way** apprendre qch à ses dépens; **to do things the h. way** se compliquer la vie; **h. of hearing** dur(e)

d'oreille

(c) *(harsh) (person, conditions, life)* dur(e); **to have a h. time (of it)** en baver; **to be h. on sb** être dur avec qn; **to give sb a h. time** mener la vie dure à qn; **a h. winter** un hiver rigoureux; **no h. feelings?** sans rancune?; **to take a h. line on sth** prendre une position très ferme sur qch; **h. luck!**, *Fam* **h. cheese!** pas de chance!

(d) *(intense)* **to be a h. worker** travailler dur; *Law* **h. labour** travaux *mpl* forcés; *Com* **to give sb the h. sell** essayer de convaincre qn d'acheter à toute force

(e) *(water)* calcaire

2 *adv* **(a)** *(work)* dur; *(push, hit)* fort; **to try h.** faire de son mieux; **to look h. at sb/sth** regarder qn/qch fixement; **to think h.** bien réfléchir; **to be h. at work** être en plein travail; **it's raining h.** il pleut à verse; **to feel h. done by** se sentir brimé(e); *Fam* **h. up** *(broke)* fauché(e)

(b) *(near)* **h. by** tout près de; **to follow h. upon sb/sth** suivre qn/qch de près

hard-and-fast [ˈhɑːdənˈfɑːst] *adj (rule)* absolu(e)

hardback [ˈhɑːdbæk] *n* livre *m* relié

hard-bitten [ˈhɑːdˈbɪtən] *adj* endurci(e)

hardboard [ˈhɑːdbɔːd] *n* aggloméré *m*

hard-boiled [ˈhɑːdˈbɔɪld] *adj (egg)* dur(e); *Fig (person)* dur à cuire

hard-core [ˈhɑːdkɔː(r)] *adj (supporter)* inconditionnel(elle); *(pornography)* hard *inv*; *(punk)* hard-core *inv*

hard-earned [ˈhɑːdˈɜːnd] *adj* durement gagné(e)

harden [ˈhɑːdən] **1** *vt* endurcir; **to h. oneself to sth** s'endurcir à qch

2 *vi (of substance, attitude)* durcir

hardened [ˈhɑːdənd] *adj (steel)* trempé(e); *(drinker)* invétéré(e); *(criminal)* endurci(e)

hard-fought [ˈhɑːdˈfɔːt] *adj (election, contest)* âprement disputé(e)

hard-headed [ˈhɑːdˈhedɪd] *adj (attitude, person)* réaliste

hard-hearted [ˈhɑːdˈhɑːtɪd] *adj* dur(e)

hard-hitting [ˈhɑːdˈhɪtɪŋ] *adj (criticism, report)* sans indulgence

hardliner [ˈhɑːdˈlaɪnə(r)] *n (politician, activist)* jusqu'au-boutiste *mf*

hardly [ˈhɑːdlɪ] *adv (scarcely)* à peine; **h. had I arrived when...** j'étais à peine arrivé que...; **you can h. expect me to do that** vous ne vous attendez tout de même pas à ce que je fasse ça; **I can h. believe it** j'ai du mal à y croire; *also Ironic* **I can h. wait** j'ai hâte d'y être; **h. ever** presque jamais; **h. anyone/anything** presque personne/rien

hardness [ˈhɑːdnɪs] *n* **(a)** *(of substance)* dureté *f* **(b)** *(of problem)* difficulté *f*

hard-on [ˈhɑːdɒn] *n Vulg* **to have/get a h.** bander

hard-pressed [ˈhɑːdˈprest], **hard-pushed** [ˈhɑːdˈpʊʃt] *adj on sth; to be h. for time/money* manquer de temps/d'argent; **to be h. to do sth** avoir du mal à faire qch

hardship [ˈhɑːdʃɪp] *n* épreuve *f*; **to live in h.** vivre dans la misère

hardware [ˈhɑːdweə(r)] *n* **(a)** *(tools)* matériel *m*; **(military) h.** *(weapons)* matériel militaire, armement *m*; **h. store** quincaillerie *f* **(b)** *Comptr* matériel *m*, hardware *m*

hard-wearing [ˈhɑːdˈweərɪŋ] *adj* résistant(e)

hard-won [ˈhɑːdˈwʌn] *adj* durement acquis(e)

hard-working [ˈhɑːdˈwɜːkɪŋ] *adj* travailleur(euse)

hardy [ˈhɑːdɪ] *adj* résistant(e), robuste

hare [heə(r)] **1** *n* lièvre *m*

2 *vi* **to h. off** partir en trombe

harebrained [ˈheəbreɪnd] *adj* écervelé(e)

harelip [ˈheəlɪp] *n* bec-de-lièvre *m*

harem [hɑːˈriːm] *n* harem *m*

haricot [ˈhærɪkəʊ] *n* **h. (bean)** haricot *m* blanc

hark [hɑːk] *exclam Lit* écoutez!; *Fam* **h. at him!** comme il y va!

►**hark back** *vi* **to h. back to sth** évoquer qch; **he's always harking back to that mistake I made** il revient toujours sur l'erreur que j'ai faite

harlot [ˈhɑːlət] *n Lit* prostituée *f*

harm [hɑːm] **1** *n* mal *m*; *(to reputation)* tort *m*; **to do sb h.** faire du mal à qn; **to do oneself h.** se faire du tort; **it will do more h. than good** cela va faire plus de mal que de bien; **I can't see any h. in it** je ne vois pas de mal à ça; **there's no h. in trying** ça ne coûte rien d'essayer; **you will come to no h.** il ne t'arrivera rien (de mal); **out of h.'s way** en sûreté, en lieu sûr

2 *vt (physically)* faire du mal à; *(health, reputation, cause)* nuire à; *(skin, fabric)* abîmer

harmful [ˈhɑːmfʊl] *adj (influence, activity)* néfaste; *(substance, ray)* nocif(ive)

harmless [ˈhɑːmlɪs] *adj (person, animal)* inoffensif(ive); *(joke)* innocent(e); **it's just a bit of h. fun** ça ne fait de mal à personne

harmonica [hɑːˈmɒnɪkə] *n* harmonica *m*

harmonious [hɑːˈməʊnɪəs] *adj* harmonieux(euse)

harmonization [hɑːmənaɪˈzeɪʃən] *n* harmonisation *f*

harmonize [ˈhɑːmənaɪz] **1** *vt* harmoniser

2 *vi* s'harmoniser **(with** avec**)**

harmony [ˈhɑːmənɪ] *(pl* **harmonies***)* *n also Fig* harmonie *f*; **in h. with** en harmonie ou en accord avec; **to live in h. (with)** vivre en harmonie (avec)

harness [ˈhɑːnɪs] **1** *n* **(a)** *(for horse, baby, of parachute)* harnais *m*; *(for climber)* baudrier *m* **(b)** *(idioms)* **to work in h. (with)** travailler en équipe (avec); **to die in h.** mourir à la tâche

2 *vt (horse)* harnacher; *(to a cart)* atteler; *(resources)* exploiter

harp [hɑːp] *n* harpe *f*

►**harp on** *vi* **to h. on about sth** revenir sans arrêt sur qch

harpist [ˈhɑːpɪst] *n* harpiste *mf*

harpoon [hɑːˈpuːn] **1** *n* harpon *m*

2 *vt* harponner

harpsichord [ˈhɑːpsɪkɔːd] *n* clavecin *m*

harpy [ˈhɑːpɪ] *(pl* **harpies***)* *n* harpie *f*

harrow [ˈhærəʊ] *n* herse *f*

harrowing [ˈhærəʊɪŋ] *adj (experience, sight)* pénible; *(account, image)* déchirant(e)

harry [ˈhærɪ] *(pt & pp* **harried***)* *vt* harceler

harsh [hɑːʃ] *adj (voice, sound)* strident(e); *(climate)* rude; *(treatment, person)* dur(e)

harshly [ˈhɑːʃlɪ] *adv (answer, speak, treat)* durement

harvest [ˈhɑːvɪst] **1** *n (of fruit)* récolte *f*; *(of crops)* moisson *f*; *(of grapes)* vendange *f*; **h. festival** = fête religieuse pour célébrer la fin de la moisson

2 *vt (fruit)* récolter; *(crops)* moissonner; *(grapes)* vendanger; *Fig (information)* récolter

has [hæz] *3rd pers singular of* **have**

has-been [ˈhæzbiːn] *n Fam Pej* has been *mf inv*

hash [hæʃ] *n* (a) *(stew)* hachis *m*; *Am* **h. browns** = pommes de terre sautées (b) *very Fam (hashish)* hasch *m* (c) *(idioms) Fam* **to make a h. of sth** faire un beau gâchis de qch

hashish [ˈhæʃiːʃ] *n* haschich *m*

hasn't [ˈhæznt] = **has not**

hassle [ˈhæsəl] *Fam* **1** *n* embêtements *mpl*; **it's too much h.** c'est trop de tintouin; **it's a real h.** buying a house l'achat d'une maison est un vrai casse-tête; **to give sb h.** faire des histoires à qn
2 *vt* embêter, harceler; **don't h. me!** arrête de m'embêter!

haste [heɪst] *n* hâte *f*; **in h.** en hâte, à la hâte; **to make h.** se dépêcher, se hâter; *Prov* **more h. less speed** hâtez-vous lentement

hasten [ˈheɪsən] **1** *vt (accelerate)* précipiter; **to h. sb's departure** avancer *ou* hâter le départ de qn
2 *vi* se presser; **I h. to add...** je m'empresse d'ajouter...

hastily [ˈheɪstɪlɪ] *adv (write, prepare)* hâtivement; *(say, eat)* précipitamment; **too h.** trop vite

hasty [ˈheɪstɪ] *adj (departure, removal)* précipité(e); *(meal)* rapide; *(reply, decision)* irréfléchi(e); **to jump to a h. conclusion** conclure à la légère

hat [hæt] *n* chapeau *m*; *also Fig* **to take one's h. off to sb** tirer son chapeau à qn; *Fig* **to pass the h. round** *(collect money)* faire la quête; *Fig* **to throw one's h. in the ring** *(enter contest)* se porter candidat(e); *Fam Fig* **to keep sth under one's h.** garder qch pour soi; *Fig* **I'm speaking with my lawyer's h. on** je parle en ma qualité de juriste; **h. stand** portemanteau *m*; **h. trick** *(of goals)* = trois buts marqués par le même joueur; *(of victories)* triplé *m*

hatch[1] [hætʃ] *n (of ship)* écoutille *f*; *Fam* **down the h.!** cul sec!; *(serving)* **h.** passe-plat *m*

hatch[2] [hætʃ] **1** *vt (egg)* faire éclore; *Fig (scheme, plot)* tramer
2 *vi (of egg)* éclore

hatchback [ˈhætʃbæk] *n (car) (three-door)* voiture *f* à trois portes, trois-portes *f inv*; *(five-door)* voiture *f* à cinq portes, cinq-portes *f inv*

hatchet [ˈhætʃɪt] *n* hachette *f*; *Fam* **to do a h. job on sb/sth** *(of critic, reviewer)* démolir qn/qch; *Fam* **h. man** homme *m* de main

hate [heɪt] **1** *n* haine *f*; **h. mail** lettres *fpl* d'injures
2 *vt* détester, haïr; **to h. doing sth** détester faire qch, avoir horreur de faire qch; **she hates to be contradicted** elle a horreur qu'on la contredise; *Fam* **I h. to tell you, but you've missed your train** ça m'ennuie de te le dire, mais je pense que tu as raté ton train

hateful [ˈheɪtfʊl] *adj* odieux(euse)

hatpin [ˈhætpɪn] *n* épingle *f* à chapeau

hatred [ˈheɪtrɪd] *n* haine *f (of/for* de/pour)

haughty [ˈhɔːtɪ] *adj* hautain(e)

haul [hɔːl] **1** *n* (a) *(fish caught)* prise *f*; *(loot)* butin *m*; *(of drugs, stolen goods)* saisie *f* (b) *Fam (journey)* parcours *m*, trajet *m*; **it's a long h.** la route est longue; *Fig* c'est un travail de longue haleine
2 *vt* (a) *(pull)* tirer; *(tow)* remorquer; *Fam* **he was hauled in for questioning** on l'a emmené pour l'interroger; *Fam Fig* **to h. sb over the coals** *(reprimand)* passer un savon à qn; **she was hauled up before the headmaster** elle a été convoquée chez le proviseur (b) *(transport)* transporter par camion

haulage [ˈhɔːlɪdʒ] *n (transportation)* transport *m* (routier); *(costs)* (frais *mpl* de) transport; **h. firm** entreprise *f* de transports routiers

haulier [ˈhɔːlɪə(r)], *Am* **hauler** [ˈhɔːlə(r)] *n (company)* entreprise *f* de transports routiers

haunch [hɔːntʃ] *n (of person)* hanche *f*; *(of venison)* cuissot *m*; **to sit** *or* **squat on one's haunches** être accroupi(e)

haunt [hɔːnt] **1** *n (of criminals)* repaire *m*; *(of group of people)* (lieu *m* de) rendez-vous *m*; **it's one of his favourite haunts** *(favourite places)* c'est un des endroits qu'il fréquente habituellement
2 *vt also Fig* hanter

haunted [ˈhɔːntɪd] *adj (castle, room)* hanté(e); *Fig* **he has a h. look** il a l'air égaré

haunting [ˈhɔːntɪŋ] *adj* obsédant(e)

Havana [həˈvænə] *n* la Havane; **H. (cigar)** havane *m*

have [hæv]

Les formes négatives, **haven't** et **hasn't**, s'écrivent **have not** et **has not** dans un style plus soutenu.

---

1 *vt (pt & pp had)* (a) *(own)* avoir; **they've (got) a big house** ils ont une grande maison; **she doesn't h.** *or* **hasn't got a car** elle n'a pas de voiture; **I've (got) things to do** j'ai des choses à faire; **you can h. it back tomorrow** je te le rendrai demain; **to h. sb in one's power** tenir qn à sa merci; **to h. it on good authority that...** tenir de source sûre que...

(b) *(with noun to denote activity)* **to h. a swim** se baigner; **to h. a shave** se raser; **to h. a bath** prendre un bain; **to h. lunch** déjeuner; **to h. a cigarette** fumer une cigarette; **to h. a drink** prendre un verre; **to h. a good/bad time** passer un bon/mauvais moment

(c) *(with illnesses)* **to h. a cold** être enrhumé(e); **to h. flu/cancer** avoir la grippe/un cancer

(d) *(cause to do, to be done)* **to h. sb do sth** faire faire qch à qn; **to h. sth done** faire faire qch; **to h. one's hair cut** se faire couper les cheveux; **h. him call me** dis-lui de m'appeler; **I'll h. you know that...!** je vous signale que...!

(e) *(in passive constructions)* **I had my watch stolen** on m'a volé ma montre; **three houses had their windows broken** il y a des fenêtres brisées dans trois maisons

(f) *(allow)* **I won't h. it!** je n'accepte pas ça!; **I won't h. you causing trouble!** pas question que tu fasses des histoires!

(g) *(be compelled)* **to h. (got) to do sth** devoir faire qch; **I h.** *or* **I've got to go** je dois y aller; **you don't h. to come with me** tu n'es pas obligé de venir avec moi; **do you h.** *or* **h. you got to work?** est-ce qu'il faut vraiment que tu travailles?; **it has** *or* **it's got to be done** il faut que ce soit fait

(h) *Fam (idioms)* **to be had** *(cheated)* se faire avoir; **to h. had it** être fichu(e); **to h. had it with sb/sth** en avoir marre de qn/qch; **he had it coming** ça lui pendait au nez

2 *v aux* avoir/être

Most French verbs will conjugate with **avoir** to form the perfect tense. However, all reflexive verbs and many intransitive verbs – mainly of motion – will conjugate with **être**.

---

to h. seen avoir vu; **to h. left** être parti(e); **to h. hurt oneself** s'être blessé(e); **I've worked here for three years** je travaille ici depuis trois ans; **we've seen this film before – no we haven't!** nous avons déjà vu ce film – mais non!; **you haven't done the dishes – yes, I h.!** tu n'as pas fait la vaisselle – si, je l'ai faite!; **you h. told him, haven't you?** tu le lui as dit, n'est-ce pas *ou* non?; **you haven't forgotten, h. you?** tu n'as pas oublié, n'est-ce pas *ou* hein?

3 *n* **the haves and the have-nots** les riches *mpl* et les pauvres

▶**have in** *vt sep Fam* **to h. it in for sb** en avoir après qn

▶**have off** *vt sep Br very Fam* **to h. it off (with sb)** *(have sexual intercourse)* s'envoyer en l'air (avec qn)

▶**have on** *vt sep* **(a)** *(be wearing)* porter; **to h. nothing on** *(be naked)* être nu(e) **(b)** *Fam (fool)* **to h. sb on** faire marcher qn **(c)** *(have arranged)* **to h. a lot on** avoir beaucoup à faire; **to h. nothing on** n'avoir rien de prévu **(d)** **to h. sth on sb** disposer d'informations compromettantes pour qn

▶**have out** *vt sep* **(a)** *(have removed)* **to h. a tooth out** se faire arracher une dent; **to h. one's appendix out** se faire opérer de l'appendicite **(b)** *(resolve)* **to h. it out with sb** s'expliquer avec qn

▶**have up** *vt sep* **to be had up (for sth)** être jugé(e) (pour qch)

haven ['heɪvən] *n* refuge *m*

haven't ['hævnt] = **have not**

haversack ['hævəsæk] *n* sac *m* à dos

havoc ['hævək] *n* **(a)** *(damage)* ravages *mpl*, dégâts *mpl*; **to cause** *or* **wreak h.** faire des ravages **(b)** *(confusion)* pagaille *f*; **to play h. with sth** *(plans)* chambouler qch

Hawaii [hə'waɪi] *n* Hawaii

Hawaiian [hə'waɪən] **1** *n* Hawaiien(enne) *m,f*
2 *adj* hawaiien(enne)

hawk[1] [hɔ:k] *n also Fig* faucon *m*; **to watch sb/sth like a h.** regarder qn/qch d'un œil perçant

hawk[2] *vt* **to h. one's wares** *(in market, street)* vendre ses marchandises à la criée; *(from door to door)* faire du porte-à-porte

hawk-eyed ['hɔ:kaɪd] *adj* **to be h.** avoir des yeux de lynx

hawkish ['hɔ:kɪʃ] *adj Pol* belliciste

hawser ['hɔ:zə(r)] *n* aussière *f*

hawthorn ['hɔ:θɔ:n] *n* aubépine *f*

hay [heɪ] **1** *n* foin *m*; **to make h.** faire les foins; *Fig* **to make h. while the sun shines** en profiter tant que ça dure

hayfever ['heɪfi:və(r)] *n* rhume *m* des foins

hayloft ['heɪlɒft] *n* fenil *m*

haystack ['heɪstæk] *n* meule *f* de foin

haywire ['heɪwaɪə(r)] *adv Fam* **to go h.** *(of plan)* mal tourner; *(of mechanism)* se détraquer

hazard ['hæzəd] **1** *n* *(danger)* danger *m*, risque *m*; **a fire h.** un risque d'incendie; **a health h.** un danger pour la santé; **h. lights** feux *mpl* de détresse
2 *vt* *(one's life, fortune)* risquer; *(opinion)* hasarder; **to h. a guess** essayer de deviner

hazardous ['hæzədəs] *adj* dangereux(euse); *(financial venture)* hasardeux(euse)

haze [heɪz] *n* *(mist)* brume *f*; *(of doubt, confusion)* atmosphère *f*; **my mind was in a h.** j'avais l'esprit embrouillé

hazel ['heɪzəl] *n* *(colour)* (couleur *f*) noisette *f*; **h. (tree)** noisetier *m*

hazelnut ['heɪzəlnʌt] *n* noisette *f*

hazily ['heɪzɪlɪ] *adv* vaguement

hazy ['heɪzɪ] *adj* *(weather)* brumeux(euse); *(image, memory)* flou(e), vague; **to be h. about sth** *(remember vaguely)* n'avoir qu'un vague souvenir de qch

he [hi:] **1** *pron* **(a)** *(unstressed)* il; **he's Scottish** il est écossais; HE **hasn't got it!** ce n'est pas lui qui l'a!
2 *n* **it's a he** *(of animal)* c'est un mâle

head [hed] **1** *n* **(a)** *(of person)* tête *f*; **a fine h. of hair** une belle chevelure; **from h. to foot** *or* **toe** de la tête aux pieds; **to stand on one's h.** faire le poirier; *Fig* **to stand sth on its h.** retourner qch; **to win by a h.** *(of horse)* gagner d'une tête; *Fig* **she's h. and shoulders above the other candidates** les autres candidats ne lui arrivent pas à la cheville; **h. cold** rhume *m* de cerveau; **h. start** *(advantage)* avantage *m*; *(in race)* avance *f*
(b) *(intellect, mind)* tête *f*; **to do sums in one's h.** calculer de tête; **to have a good h. on one's shoulders** avoir la tête sur les épaules; **to have a good h. for business** avoir le sens des affaires; **to have a good h. for figures** être à l'aise avec les chiffres; **to have a (good) h. for heights** ne pas avoir le vertige; **to take it into one's h. to do sth** se mettre en tête de faire qch; **to take it into one's h. that...** se mettre dans la tête que...; **it never entered my h. that...** il ne m'est jamais venu à l'esprit que...; **to put ideas into sb's h.** donner des idées à qn; *Fam* **he's not right in the h.** il a un grain
(c) *(of pin, hammer, list, bed)* tête *f*; *(of arrow)* pointe *f*; *(of page, stairs)* haut *m*; *(of table)* bout *m*; *(on beer)* mousse *f*; *(on tape recorder)* tête *f*; **a h. of lettuce/cabbage** un pied de laitue/chou; **heads or tails?** *(when tossing coin)* pile ou face?; **to build up a h. of steam** *(of campaign)* s'intensifier; *(of person)* progresser rapidement; **to come to a h.** *(of conflict, crisis)* atteindre un paroxysme
(d) *(person in charge)* *(of family, the Church, business)* chef *m*; **h. of state** chef d'État; *Br Sch* **h. (teacher)** directeur(trice) *m,f*; *Br Sch* **h. boy/girl** = élève choisi parmi les grands pour maintenir la discipline et représenter son école; **h. office** siège *m* (social); **h. waiter** maître *m* d'hôtel
(e) *(unit)* **£10 per h.** *or* **a h.** 10 livres par personne; **six h. of cattle** six têtes de bétail
(f) *(idioms)* **we put our heads together** nous nous sommes tous mis; **they'll have your h. (on a plate) for this** cela te coûtera la tête; **to bury** *or* **have one's h. in the sand** se mettre la tête dans le sable; **to give sb his h.** lâcher la bride à qn; **on your own h. be it** à tes risques et périls; **to go over sb's h.** *(appeal to higher authority)* ne pas consulter qn *(en suivant la voie hiérarchique)*; *Fam* **to shout one's h. off** crier à tue-tête; **the wine/praise went to his h.** le vin/compliment lui est monté à la tête; *Prov* **two heads are better than one** deux avis valent mieux qu'un; **off the top of one's h.** au hasard; **it was** *or* **went over my h.** ça m'a dépassé; **I can't make h. nor tail of this** ça n'a ni queue ni tête; *Fam* **to lose one's h.** *(panic)* perdre la tête; *(get angry)* perdre son calme; *Fam* **to keep one's h.** garder son calme; *Fam* **to be off one's h.** avoir perdu la boule
2 *vt* **(a)** *(lead)* *(organization, campaign)* diriger; *(list)* venir en tête de
(b) *(steer)* diriger; **one of the locals headed me in the right direction** un des habitants m'a indiqué la bonne direction
(c) *(put a title on)* *(page, chapter)* intituler
(d) *(in football)* **to h. the ball** faire une tête
3 *vi* *(move)* se diriger; **they were heading out of town** ils sortaient de la ville

▶**head for** *vt insep* se diriger vers; **you're heading for disaster** tu vas droit au désastre; **you're heading for trouble** tu vas avoir des ennuis

▶**head off 1** *vt sep (divert)* éviter
2 *vi (depart)* partir

headache ['hedeɪk] *n* mal *m* de tête; *Fig (problem)* casse-tête *m inv*; **to have a h.** avoir mal à la tête

headband ['hedbænd] *n* bandeau *m*

headboard ['hedbɔːd] n tête f de lit

headbutt ['hedbʌt] vt donner un coup de tête à

headcase ['hedkeɪs] n Fam cinglé(e) m,f

headdress ['heddres] n coiffure f

headed ['hedɪd] adj h. (note)paper papier m à en-tête

header ['hedə(r)] n (a) Typ en-tête m (b) (in football) (coup m de) tête f

headfirst ['hed'fɜːst] adv la tête la première

headgear ['hedgɪə(r)] n couvre-chef m

head-hunt ['hed'hʌnt] vt Com to be head-hunted être recruté(e) par un chasseur de têtes

head-hunter ['hedhʌntə(r)] n Com chasseur m de têtes

heading ['hedɪŋ] n (of chapter, article) titre m; (of letter) en-tête m; it comes or falls under the h. of... c'est à mettre sous la rubrique de...

headlamp ['hedlæmp] n (on car) phare m

headland ['hedlənd] n cap m, pointe f

headlight ['hedlaɪt] n (on car) phare m

headline ['hedlaɪn] 1 n (of TV news) titre m; (of newspaper) (gros) titre; to hit the headlines faire la une des journaux; to be h. news faire la une des journaux
2 vt (article, section) intituler

headlong ['hedlɒŋ] 1 adj there was a h. rush for the bar tout le monde s'est rué vers le bar
2 adv (fall) la tête la première; (rush) tête baissée

headmaster [hed'mɑːstə(r)] n directeur m

headmistress [hed'mɪstrəs] n directrice f

head-on ['hed'ɒn] adj & adv de front; to meet sb h. aborder qn de front; a h. collision une collision frontale

headphones ['hedfəʊnz] npl écouteurs mpl

headquarters [hed'kwɔːtəz] npl (of organization) siège m (social); Mil quartier m général

headrest ['hedrest] n appui-tête m

headroom ['hedruːm] n (under bridge, inside car) hauteur f

headscarf ['hedskɑːf] (pl headscarves ['hedskɑːvz]) n foulard m

headset ['hedset] n écouteurs mpl

headstone ['hedstəʊn] n (on grave) pierre f tombale

headstrong ['hedstrɒŋ] adj têtu(e), entêté(e)

headway ['hedweɪ] n to make h. avancer, faire des progrès

headwind ['hedwɪnd] n vent m contraire; Naut vent debout

heady ['hedɪ] adj (atmosphere) enivrant(e); (wine, perfume) capiteux(euse); (heights, days) grisant(e)

heal [hiːl] 1 vt (wound, person) guérir; (disagreement) régler; Fig wounds which only time would h. des blessures que seul le temps cicatriserait
2 vi (of wound) to h. (up or over) cicatriser

health [helθ] n santé f; to be in good/poor h. être en bonne/mauvaise santé; Fig the economy is in good h. l'économie se porte bien; the Department of H. ≃ le ministère de la Santé; to drink (to) sb's h. boire à la santé de qn; h. care soins mpl médicaux; Br h. centre dispensaire m; h. cover (insurance) assurance f médicale; h. farm centre m de remise en forme; h. food produits mpl biologiques; h. hazard or risk risque m pour la santé; h. insurance assurance maladie; h. resort station f climatique; (by sea) station balnéaire; the H. Service ≃ la Sécurité f sociale; h. visitor = infirmière effectuant des visites de contrôle à domicile

healthy ['helθɪ] adj (person) en bonne santé; (climate) salubre; (food, habit, economy) sain(e); a h. appetite un bon appétit; it is a h. sign that... c'est bon signe que...; he has a h. respect for his opponents il apprécie ses adversaires à leur juste valeur

heap [hiːp] 1 n tas m; Fig people at the top/bottom of the h. ceux qui sont en haut/bas de l'échelle sociale; Fam she's got heaps of money elle a plein d'argent; Fam we've got heaps of time on a largement le temps
2 vt entasser; his plate was heaped with food son assiette était remplie de nourriture; to h. sth with remplir qch de; a heaped spoonful (in recipe) une cuillerée bien pleine; to h. riches/praise on sb couvrir qn de richesses/d'éloges; to h. insults on sb abreuver qn d'injures

hear [hɪə(r)] (pt & pp heard [hɜːd]) 1 vt (a) (perceive) entendre; to h. sb speak entendre qn parler; I can hardly h. myself think! on ne s'entend plus ici!; to make oneself heard se faire entendre; let's h. it for... applaudissons bien fort...; have you heard the one about...? est-ce que tu connais celle de...? (b) (listen to) écouter; h., h.! (at meeting) bravo!; Law to h. a case juger une affaire (c) (find out) entendre (dire), apprendre; have you heard the news? tu connais la nouvelle?; I h. you're getting married j'ai entendu dire que tu te maries
2 vi entendre; I can't h. properly je n'entends pas bien; to h. from sb avoir des nouvelles de qn; you'll be hearing from my lawyer! vous allez entendre parler de mon avocat!; to h. of or about sth entendre parler de qch; I won't h. of it! je ne veux pas en entendre parler!

▸**hear out** vt sep to h. sb out écouter qn jusqu'au bout

hearing ['hɪərɪŋ] n (a) (sense) ouïe f, audition f; h. aid audiophone m (b) (earshot) to be within/out of h. être à portée/hors de portée de voix (c) (chance to explain) to give sb a fair h. laisser parler qn, laisser qn s'expliquer (d) Law (inquiry) audition f

hearsay ['hɪəseɪ] n ouï-dire m inv, on-dit m inv; Law h. evidence déposition f sur la foi d'autrui

hearse [hɜːs] n corbillard m

heart [hɑːt] n (a) (organ) cœur m; to have h. trouble to have a weak or bad h. être cardiaque; h. attack crise f cardiaque; h. disease maladie f cardiaque; h. failure arrêt m cardiaque; h. surgery chirurgie f cardiaque; h. transplant transplantation f cardiaque
(b) (seat of the emotions) cœur m; to have a big h. avoir bon cœur; a h. of gold un cœur d'or; a h. of stone un cœur de pierre; have a h.! ayez un peu de cœur!; her h.'s in the right place elle a bon cœur; with a heavy h. le cœur gros; my h. sank j'ai été très déçu; to have one's h. in one's mouth avoir le cœur serré(e); to break sb's h. briser le cœur à qn; to wear one's h. on one's sleeve ne pas cacher ses sentiments; affairs or matters of the h. affaires fpl de cœur; Ironic my h. bleeds for you ça me fait de la peine pour toi; in my h. of hearts au fond de mon cœur; from the bottom of one's h. du fond du cœur; he loved her with all his h. il l'aimait de toute son âme; at h. au fond; to have sb's welfare/interests at h. avoir le bien-être/les intérêts de qn à cœur; to take sth to h. prendre qch à cœur; to set one's h. on sth vouloir qch à tout prix; he's a man after my own h. il est comme moi; to one's h.'s content tout son soûl
(c) (enthusiasm, courage) to take h. reprendre courage; to lose h. se décourager; he tried to convince them but his h. wasn't in it il a essayé de les convaincre mais le cœur n'y était pas; I didn't have the h. to tell him je n'ai

pas eu le cœur de lui dire
 (d) by h. *(know)* par cœur
 (e) *(centre) (of city, forest)* cœur *m*; **the h. of the matter** le fond du problème
 (f) *(in cards)* **hearts** cœur *m*

heartache ['hɑːteɪk] *n* chagrin *m*, peine *f*

heartbeat ['hɑːtbiːt] *n* *(rhythm)* pouls *m*; *(single beat)* battement *m* de cœur

heartbreaking ['hɑːtbreɪkɪŋ] *adj* déchirant(e), navrant(e)

heartbroken ['hɑːtbrəʊkən] *adj* **to be h.** avoir le cœur brisé

heartburn ['hɑːtbɜːn] *n* *(indigestion)* brûlures *fpl* d'estomac

hearten ['hɑːtən] *vt* encourager

heartening ['hɑːtənɪŋ] *adj* encourageant(e)

heartfelt ['hɑːtfelt] *adj* sincère, qui vient du cœur

hearth [hɑːθ] *n* *(fireplace, home)* foyer *m*

heartily ['hɑːtɪlɪ] *adv* *(welcome, applaud)* chaleureusement; *(agree)* de tout cœur; *(eat)* avec appétit; **to be h. sick of sth** être profondément dégoûté(e) de qch

heartlands ['hɑːtlændz] *npl* centre *m*, cœur *m*

heartless ['hɑːtlɪs] *adj* sans cœur, cruel(elle)

heart-rending ['hɑːtrendɪŋ] *adj* déchirant(e), navrant(e)

heart-searching ['hɑːtsɜːtʃɪŋ] *n* **after much h.** après avoir longuement réfléchi

heartstrings ['hɑːtstrɪŋz] *npl* **to tug at sb's h.** jouer sur la corde sensible de qn

heart-throb ['hɑːtθrɒb] *n* *Fam* idole *f*

heart-to-heart ['hɑːtə'hɑːt] *n* **to have a h. with sb** avoir une conversation à cœur ouvert avec qn

heart-warming ['hɑːtwɔːmɪŋ] *adj* réconfortant(e), qui réchauffe le cœur

hearty ['hɑːtɪ] *adj* **(a)** *(person, laugh)* jovial(e); *(approval, welcome)* chaleureux(euse); **to have a h. dislike of sth** avoir une sainte horreur de qch; **my heartiest congratulations** mes plus sincères félicitations **(b)** *(substantial) (meal, appetite)* solide

heat [hiːt] **1** *n* **(a)** *(high temperature)* chaleur *f*; **to give out h.** dégager de la chaleur; **to cook at a moderate/low h.** faire cuire à feu moyen/doux; **h. exhaustion** coup *m* de chaleur; **h. haze** brume *f* de chaleur; **h. loss** déperdition *f* de chaleur; **h. rash** boutons *mpl* de chaleur; *Med* **h. treatment** thermothérapie *f* **(b)** *(passion)* feu *m*; **in the h. of the moment/argument** dans le feu de l'action/de la discussion **(c)** *Fam (pressure)* **to turn up the h.** mettre la pression; **the h. is on** la tension est à son comble **(d)** *(of female animal)* **in** or **on h.** en chaleur **(e)** *(in sport)* éliminatoire *f*
 2 *vt (food, water)* faire chauffer; *(room, building)* chauffer
 ▶**heat up 1** *vt* se réchauffer
 2 *vi (of water)* chauffer; *(of room)* se réchauffer; *Fig (of argument, contest)* s'animer

heated ['hiːtɪd] *adj* **(a)** *(room, building, swimming pool)* chauffé(e) **(b)** *(argument)* animé(e); **to become h.** *(of person)* s'échauffer

heater ['hiːtə(r)] *n* radiateur *m*

heath [hiːθ] *n* lande *f*

heathen ['hiːðən] *n* *Rel* païen(enne) *m,f*; *Hum* barbare *mf*

heather ['heðə(r)] *n* bruyère *f*

heating ['hiːtɪŋ] *n* chauffage *m*

heatproof ['hiːtpruːf] *adj* résistant(e) à la chaleur; *(clothing)* isolant(e)

heatstroke ['hiːtstrəʊk] *n* coup *m* de chaleur

heatwave ['hiːtweɪv] *n* vague *f* de chaleur

heave [hiːv] **1** *n* effort *m*
 2 *vt* **(a)** *(pull)* tirer fort; *(push)* pousser fortement; *(lift)* soulever avec effort; **she heaved herself out of her chair** elle s'extirpa de sa chaise; **to h. a sigh of relief** pousser un soupir de soulagement **(b)** *Fam (throw)* balancer
 3 *vi* **(a)** *(pull)* **they heaved on the rope** ils tirèrent sur la corde fortement **(b)** *(of deck, ground)* tanguer, se soulever; *(of bosom)* se soulever **(c)** *(retch)* avoir des haut-le-cœur; *(vomit)* vomir **(d)** *(pt & pp* hove [həʊv]*) also Fig* **to h. into view** paraître à l'horizon
 ▶**heave to** *(pt & pp* hove [həʊv]*) vi Naut* se mettre en panne.

heaven ['hevən] *n* paradis *m*, ciel *m*; **in h.** au paradis, au ciel; *Fig (overjoyed)* aux anges; **this is h.!** c'est le paradis!, **to move h. and earth to do sth** remuer ciel et terre pour faire qch; **the heavens opened** il s'est mis à pleuvoir à torrents; *Fam* **it stinks to high h.** ça pue; **(good) heavens!, heavens above!** juste ciel!, mon Dieu!; **thank h. (for that)!** Dieu merci!; **h. knows why...** Dieu seul sait pourquoi...; **for h.'s sake!** pour l'amour du ciel!; **h. forbid!** que le ciel nous en préserve!

heavenly ['hevənlɪ] *adj* **(a)** **h. body** corps *m* céleste **(b)** *Fam (weather, food)* divin(e)

heaven-sent ['hevənsent] *adj* providentiel(elle)

heavily ['hevɪlɪ] *adv* *(fall, walk, tax)* lourdement; *(sleep)* profondément; *(breathe)* bruyamment; **to drink/smoke h.** boire/fumer beaucoup; **it was raining h.** il pleuvait à torrents; **to rely** or **depend h.** on dépendre beaucoup de; **h. built** solidement charpenté(e); **to be h. defeated** subir une lourde défaite

heavy ['hevɪ] **1** *n (pl* heavies*) Fam (tough guy)* dur *m*
 2 *adj* **(a)** *(in weight, food)* lourd(e); **how h. is it?** combien est-ce que ça pèse?; **a h. blow** un coup violent; *Fig* un coup rude; **h. goods vehicle** poids *m* lourd; **h. industry** industrie *f* lourde; **h. metal** *Chem* métal *m* lourd; *(music)* heavy metal *m*
 (b) *(large, thick) (coat, shoes)* gros (grosse); **h. losses** lourdes pertes *fpl*
 (c) *(intense) (fighting)* violent(e); *(rain, showers)* fort(e); *(drinker, smoker)* gros (grosse); **a h. cold** un gros rhume; **there was h. traffic** il y avait beaucoup de circulation; **to be a h. sleeper** avoir le sommeil lourd; **to come under h. fire** essuyer un feu nourri
 (d) *(oppressive) (smell)* fort(e); *(sky, fine, sentence)* lourd(e); **h. responsibility** lourde responsabilité *f*
 (e) *(hard) (work, day, breathing)* pénible; **it was h. going** c'était difficile ou ardu; **h. seas** grosse mer *f*
 (f) *Fam (threatening) (situation)* difficile, pénible; **to get h. with sb** être agressif(ive) avec qn
 (g) *Fam (serious) (book, article)* indigeste

heavy-duty ['hevɪ'djuːtɪ] *adj* *(machine)* à usage industriel; *(clothing, boots)* résistant(e)

heavy-handed ['hevɪ'hændɪd] *adj* *(clumsy)* maladroit(e); *(government, policy)* autoritaire; **the police responded in a h. way** la police est intervenue de façon très agressive

heavyweight ['hevɪweɪt] *n (in boxing)* poids *m* lourd; *Fig* **a political h.** un grand ponte de la politique; **an intellectual h.** un grand intellectuel

Hebrew ['hiːbruː] **1** *n (language)* hébreu *m*
 2 *adj* hébraïque

Hebrides ['hebrɪdiːz] *npl* the H. les (îles *fpl*) Hébrides *fpl*

heck [hek] *n Fam* h.! zut!; **what the h. are you doing here?** qu'est-ce que tu fiches là?; **what the h.!** et puis flûte!; **a h. of a lot** des masses

heckle ['hekəl] 1 *vt* interpeller, interrompre
2 *vi* chahuter

heckler ['heklə(r)] *n* chahuteur(euse) *m,f*

heckling ['hekəlɪŋ] *n* chahut *m*

hectare ['hektɑː(r)] *n* hectare *m*

hectic ['hektɪk] *adj (busy)* agité(e); *(eventful)* mouvementé(e); **a h. life** une vie trépidante

hector ['hektə(r)] *vt* rudoyer

hectoring ['hektərɪŋ] *adj* autoritaire

he'd [hiːd] = **he had, he would**

hedge [hedʒ] 1 *n* (a) *(in field, garden)* haie *f* (b) *(barrier)* a **h. against inflation** une protection contre l'inflation
2 *vt* (a) *(field)* entourer d'une haie (b) to h. **one's bets** se couvrir
3 *vi (in discussion)* ne pas se mouiller

hedgehog ['hedʒhɒg] *n* hérisson *m*

hedgerow ['hedʒrəʊ] *n* haie *f*

hedonism ['hedənɪzəm] *n* hédonisme *m*

heed [hiːd] 1 *n* to pay (no) h. to, to take (no) h. of (ne pas) tenir compte de
2 *vt (warning, advice)* tenir compte de

heedless ['hiːdlɪs] *adj* to be h. of ne pas tenir compte de

heel [hiːl] 1 *n (of foot, shoe, sock)* talon *m*; high heels talons hauts; **he had the police at his heels** il avait la police sur les talons *ou* à ses trousses; to take to one's heels prendre ses jambes à son cou; **to turn on one's h.** tourner les talons; *Fam* to cool *or* kick one's heels *(wait)* poireauter; *Fig* to bring sb to h. *(bring under control)* mettre qn au pas
2 *vt (shoe)* réparer le talon de

hefty ['heftɪ] *adj Fam (person)* costaud(e); *(suitcase, box)* lourd(e); *(blow)* puissant(e); *(bill, fine)* gros (grosse)

heifer ['hefə(r)] *n* génisse *f*

height [haɪt] *n (of building, tree)* hauteur *f*; *(of mountain)* altitude *f*; *(of person)* taille *f*; **what h. are you?** combien mesurez-vous?; to gain/lose h. *(of plane)* prendre/perdre de l'altitude; **to be afraid of heights** avoir le vertige; **she's at the h. of her powers** elle est au maximum de ses capacités; **she's at the h. of her career** elle est à l'apogée de sa carrière; **the h. of fashion** la dernière mode; **it's the h. of madness!** c'est de la folie pure!; at **the h. of the storm** au plus fort de l'orage; **the season is at its h.** la saison bat son plein

heighten ['haɪtən] *vt (sensation)* intensifier; *(tension)* augmenter; **to h. public awareness** sensibiliser l'opinion

heinous ['heɪnəs] *adj Formal (crime)* abominable, atroce

heir [eə(r)] *n* héritier(ère) *m,f*; **to be h. to sth** être l'héritier de qch; **h. apparent** héritier présomptif

heiress ['eərɪs] *n* héritière *f*

heirloom ['eəluːm] *n* a family h. un objet de famille

held [held] *pt & pp of* **hold**

helicopter ['helɪkɒptə(r)] *n* hélicoptère *m*

heliport ['helɪpɔːt] *n* héliport *m*

helium ['hiːlɪəm] *n* hélium *m*

hell [hel] *n (a) Rel* enfer *m*; *Fam* h.! zut alors!
(b) *Fam (for emphasis)* a h. of a price un prix salé; **what**

the h. do you think you're doing? qu'est-ce que tu fous?; **who the h. are you?** qui diable êtes-vous?; **she put up a h. of a fight** elle s'est bien défendue; **to have a h. of a time** *(good)* s'éclater; *(bad)* en baver; a h. of a lot of... énormément de...; **he's one** *or* a h. of a guy c'est un brave type
(c) *Fam (idioms)* it was h. c'était l'enfer; **to feel like h.** se sentir horriblement mal; **to make sb's life h.** faire de la vie de qn un enfer; **these shoes are giving me h.** ces chaussures me font un mal de chien; **all h. was let** *or* **broke loose** ce fut le chaos; **there'll be h. to pay if...** ça va barder si...; go to h.! va te faire voir!; **to run like h.** courir comme un dératé; **like h. (I will)!** certainement pas!; **until h. freezes over** jusqu'à la saint-glinglin; **come h. or high water** quoi qu'il arrive; **to run h. for leather** courir ventre à terre; **to do sth for the h. of it** faire qch sans raison particulière

he'll [hiːl] = **he will, he shall**

hellbent ['helbent] *adj Fam* to be h. on doing sth vouloir à tout prix faire qch

hellhole ['helhəʊl] *n Fam (bar, club)* bouge *m*; *(prison)* enfer *m*

hellish ['helɪʃ] *adj Fam* infernal(e)

hello [he'ləʊ] *exclam* bonjour!; *(on phone)* allô!; to say h. to sb dire bonjour à qn; h., **what's this?** *(indicating surprise)* tiens, qu'est-ce que c'est que ça?

hell-raiser ['helreɪzə(r)] *n Fam* perturbateur(trice) *m,f*

helm [helm] *n (of ship)* barre *f*; *also Fig* to be at the h. être à la barre

helmet ['helmɪt] *n* casque *m*

helmsman ['helmzmən] *n* timonier *m*

help [help] 1 *n* (a) *(aid)* aide *f*; to shout for h. crier à l'aide; h.! à l'aide!, au secours!; to be of h. to sb aider qn; thank you, you've been a great h. merci beaucoup de votre aide; **there was no h. for it** il n'y avait rien à faire; **with the h. of sb** avec l'aide de qn; **with the h. of sth** *(implement)* à l'aide de qch (b) *(cleaning woman)* femme *f* de ménage
2 *vt* (a) *(aid)* aider; to h. sb to do sth aider qn à faire qch; to h. sb to their feet aider qn à se mettre debout; to h. sb on/off with his coat aider qn à mettre/enlever son manteau; to h. one another s'entraider; to h. oneself to sth se servir en *ou* de qch; h. yourself! servez-vous! (b) *(prevent)* I can't h. it je ne peux pas m'en empêcher; it can't be helped on n'y peut rien; I couldn't h. laughing/overhearing je ne pouvais pas m'empêcher de rire/d'écouter; **he can't h. being bald** ce n'est pas de sa faute s'il est chauve; not if I can h. it! pas si je peux l'éviter!
3 *vi* aider; can I h.? puis-je vous aider?; that doesn't h. very much cela ne nous avance pas beaucoup

▶**help out** *vt sep & vi* aider

helper ['helpə(r)] *n* aide *mf*, assistant(e) *m,f*

helpful ['helpfʊl] *adj (person)* serviable; *(advice, device, book)* utile; **to be h.** *(of person)* se rendre utile, aider

helpfully ['helpfʊlɪ] *adv* obligeamment

helping ['helpɪŋ] 1 *n (portion)* part *f*, portion *f*; I had a second h. of spaghetti je me suis resservi des spaghettis
2 *adj* to lend a h. hand donner un coup de main

helpless ['helplɪs] *adj (powerless)* impuissant(e); *(invalid)* impotent(e); **we were h. to prevent it** nous n'avons pas pu l'empêcher; **to be h. with laughter** être plié(e) de rire

helplessly ['helplɪslɪ] *adv (watch)* sans pouvoir agir; *(struggle)* en vain

helpline ['helplaɪn] n service m d'assistance téléphonique

Helsinki [hel'sɪŋkɪ] n Helsinki

helter-skelter ['heltə'skeltə(r)] **1** n (at fairground) toboggan m
2 adv **to run h.** courir comme un(e) fou (folle); **to fall h.** faire une chute spectaculaire

hem [hem] **1** n ourlet m
2 vt (pt & pp **hemmed**) ourler

▸**hem in** vt sep (surround) cerner

he-man ['hiːmæn] n Fam homme m viril

hemisphere ['hemɪsfɪə(r)] n hémisphère m

hemline ['hemlaɪn] n ourlet m

hemlock ['hemlɒk] n ciguë f

hemoglobin, hemophilia etc Am = **haemoglobin, haemophilia** etc

hemorrhage, hemorrhoids Am = **haemorrhage, haemorrhoids**

hemp [hemp] n chanvre m

hen [hen] n poule f; Fam **h. party** = soirée organisée entre amies avant le mariage de l'une d'entre elles

hence [hens] adv (a) (thus) d'où; **h. his anger** d'où sa colère (b) (from now) d'ici; **five years h.** d'ici cinq ans

henceforth [hens'fɔːθ] adv Formal dès lors, désormais

henchman ['hentʃmən] n Pej acolyte m

hencoop ['henkuːp] n cage f à poules

henhouse ['henhaʊs] n poulailler m

henna ['henə] n henné m

henpecked ['henpekt] adj mené(e) par le bout du nez

hepatitis [hepə'taɪtɪs] n hépatite f

her [unstressed hə(r), stressed haː(r)] **1** pron (**a**) (direct object) la; **I hate h.** je la déteste; **I love h.** je l'aime; **I can understand her son but not HER** je comprends son fils, mais elle, je ne la comprends pas (**b**) (indirect object) lui; **I gave h. the book** je lui ai donné le livre; **I gave it to h.** je le lui ai donné (**c**) (after preposition) elle; **I'm thinking of h.** je pense à elle (**d**) (as complement of verb to be) elle; **it's h.!** c'est elle!; **it was h. who did it** c'est elle qui l'a fait
2 possessive adj son (sa); (plural) ses; **h. husband** son mari; **h. family** sa famille; **h. parents** ses parents; **it wasn't HER idea!** ce n'est pas elle qui en a eu l'idée! (**b**) (for parts of body) **she hit h. head** elle s'est cogné la tête

herald ['herəld] **1** n (messenger) héraut m; Fig (sign) signe m avant-coureur
2 vt annoncer

heraldry ['herəldrɪ] n héraldique f

herb [haːb] n herbe f aromatique

herbal ['haːbəl] adj à base de plantes; **h. tea** tisane f

herbalist ['haːbəlɪst] n herboriste mf

herbicide ['haːbɪsaɪd] n herbicide m

herbivorous [haː'bɪvərəs] adj herbivore

herd [haːd] **1** n (of cattle, sheep, elephants) troupeau m; (of horses) troupe f; (of people) groupe m; Pej troupeau; **the h. instinct** l'instinct grégaire
2 vt (cattle, people) rassembler

herdsman ['haːdzmən] n gardien m de troupeau

here [hɪə(r)] **1** adv (**a**) ici; **over h.** par ici; **h. it/he is** le voilà; **h.!** (at roll call) présent!; **come h.!** viens ici!; **h., come and look at this!** eh! viens voir ça!; **she's not h.** elle n'est pas là; **h. she comes** la voilà; **h. and now** immédiatement; **h. and there** çà et là; Fig **that's neither h. nor there** ça n'a aucun rapport; **what have**

we h.? qu'est-ce que c'est que ça?; **h.'s what you have to do** voilà ce que tu as à faire; **h. goes!** allons-y!; **h.'s to the future!** à l'avenir!
2 n **the h. and now** le présent

hereafter [hɪər'aːftə(r)] **1** n Lit **the h.** l'au-delà m
2 adv Formal (below) ci-après; (in the future) dorénavant

hereby [hɪə'baɪ] adv Formal (in writing) par la présente; (in speech) solennellement

hereditary [hɪ'redɪtərɪ] adj héréditaire

heredity [hɪ'redɪtɪ] n hérédité f

heresy ['herəsɪ] (pl **heresies**) n hérésie f

heretic ['herətɪk] n hérétique mf

heretical [hɪ'retɪkəl] adj hérétique

heritage ['herɪtɪdʒ] n patrimoine m

hermaphrodite [haː'mæfrədaɪt] n & adj hermaphrodite mf

hermetic [haː'metɪk] adj hermétique

hermetically [haː'metɪklɪ] adv hermétiquement

hermit ['haːmɪt] n ermite m; **h. crab** bernard-l'ermite m inv

hernia ['haːnɪə] n hernie f

hero ['hɪərəʊ] (pl **heroes**) n héros m; **h. worship** adulation f, idolâtrie f

heroic [hɪ'rəʊɪk] adj héroïque

heroically [hɪ'rəʊɪklɪ] adv héroïquement

heroics [hɪ'rəʊɪks] npl coup m d'éclat

heroin ['herəʊɪn] n (drug) héroïne f; **h. addict** héroïnomane mf

heroine ['herəʊɪn] n (female hero) héroïne f

heroism ['herəʊɪzəm] n héroïsme m

heron ['herən] n héron m

hero-worship ['hɪərəʊwaːʃɪp] (pt & pp **hero-worshipped**) vt idolâtrer

herpes ['haːpiːz] n herpès m

herring ['herɪŋ] (pl **herring** or **herrings**) n hareng m

hers [haːz] possessive pron (**a**) (singular) le sien (la sienne) m,f; (plural) les siens (les siennes) mpl, fpl; **my house is big, but h. is bigger** j'ai une grande maison, mais la sienne est plus grande encore (**b**) (used attributively) **this book is h.** ce livre est à elle; **a friend of h.** un ami à elle; **where's that brother of h.?** où son frère a-t-il bien pu passer?

herself [haː'self] pron (**a**) (reflexive) **she spoils h.** elle se gâte; **she hurt h.** elle s'est blessée (**b**) (emphatic) elle-même; **she h. has never...** elle-même n'a jamais...; **she told me h.** elle me l'a dit elle-même; **she's not h. today** elle n'est pas dans son état normal aujourd'hui (**c**) (after preposition) **she lives by h.** elle vit seule; **she bought it for h.** elle se l'est acheté; **she talks to h.** elle parle toute seule

he's [hiːz] = **he is, he has**

hesitancy ['hezɪtənsɪ] n hésitation f

hesitant ['hezɪtənt] adj hésitant(e); **to be h. about doing sth** hésiter à faire qch

hesitate ['hezɪteɪt] vi hésiter

hesitation [hezɪ'teɪʃən] n hésitation f; **without h.** sans hésitation, sans hésiter

heterogeneous [hetərə'dʒiːnɪəs] adj hétérogène

heterosexual [hetərəʊ'seksjʊəl] n & adj hétérosexuel(elle) m,f

het up ['hetʌp] *adj Br Fam* énervé(e); **to get h. (about sth)** se mettre dans tous ses états (pour qch)

heuristics [hjuː'rɪstɪks] *npl* heuristique *f*

hew [hjuː] (*pp* **hewn** [hjuːn] *or* **hewed**) *vt* (*wood*) couper; (*rock*) tailler

hexagon ['heksəgən] *n* hexagone *m*

hexagonal [hek'sægənəl] *adj* hexagonal(e)

hey [heɪ] *exclam* eh!; **h. presto!** le tour est joué!

heyday ['heɪdeɪ] *n* apogée *m*; **in its h.** à son apogée; **in his h.** au sommet de sa gloire

HGV [eɪtʃdʒiː'viː] *n Br* (*abbr* **heavy goods vehicle**) PL *m*; **H. licence** permis *m* PL

hi [haɪ] *exclam Fam* salut!

hiatus [haɪ'eɪtəs] *n* (*interruption*) interruption *f*; (*in conversation*) silence *m*; (*in manuscript, records*) lacune *f*

hibernate ['haɪbəneɪt] *vi* hiberner

hibernation [haɪbə'neɪʃən] *n* hibernation *f*; **to go into h.** entrer en hibernation

hiccup ['hɪkʌp] **1** *n* hoquet *m*; *Fig* (*in plan*) accroc *m*; **to have (the) hiccups** avoir le hoquet
2 *vi* avoir le hoquet; (*once*) avoir un hoquet

hick [hɪk] *n Am Fam* péquenaud(e) *m,f*

hickory ['hɪkərɪ] (*pl* **hickories**) *n* (*tree, wood*) hickory *m*, noyer *m* blanc d'Amérique

hid [hɪd] *pt of* **hide**

hidden ['hɪdən] **1** *adj* caché(e); **h. agenda** programme *m* secret
2 *pp of* **hide**

hide¹ [haɪd] **1** *n* (*for birdwatching*) affût *m*
2 *vt* (*pt* **hid** [hɪd], *pp* **hidden** ['hɪdən]) cacher (**from** à); **to have nothing to h.** n'avoir rien à cacher; **to be hidden from sight** être caché(e); **to h. oneself** se cacher
3 *vi* se cacher (**from** de)

hide² *n* (*skin*) peau *f*; *Fig* **to save one's h.** sauver sa peau; **I haven't seen h. nor hair of her** je ne l'ai pas vue du tout

hide-and-seek [haɪdən'siːk] *n* cache-cache *m*; **to play h.** jouer à cache-cache

hidebound ['haɪdbaʊnd] *adj* rigide

hideous ['hɪdɪəs] *adj* (*ugly*) hideux(euse); (*horrific*) horrible

hideously ['hɪdɪəslɪ] *adv* horriblement, affreusement

hide-out ['haɪdaʊt] *n* cachette *f*

hiding¹ ['haɪdɪŋ] *n* (*concealment*) **to be in h.** se cacher; **to go into h.** se cacher; **to come out of h.** sortir de sa cachette; (*after war*) sortir de la clandestinité; **h. place** cachette *f*

hiding² *n Fam* (*beating*) raclée *f*; **to give sb a h.** donner une raclée à qn; *Fig* **to be on a h. to nothing** n'avoir aucune chance

hierarchical [haɪə'rɑːkɪkəl] *adj* hiérarchique

hierarchy ['haɪərɑːkɪ] (*pl* **hierarchies**) *n* hiérarchie *f*

hieroglyphics [haɪərə'glɪfɪks] *npl* hiéroglyphes *mpl*

hi-fi ['haɪfaɪ] *n* hi-fi *f inv*; (*stereo system*) chaîne *f* hi-fi

higgledy-piggledy ['hɪgəldɪ'pɪgəldɪ] *Fam* **1** *adj* en désordre
2 *adv* pêle-mêle

high [haɪ] **1** *n* (a) (*peak*) (*in career, performance*) sommet *m*; (*in quantity, degree*) maximum *m*; **unemployment has reached a new h.** le chômage a atteint un nouveau record; **to be on a h.** (*from drugs*) planer; (*from success*) être sur un petit nuage; **the highs and lows** les hauts *mpl* et

les bas *mpl*
(b) (*weather front*) anticyclone *m*
2 *adj* (a) (*mountain, building*) haut(e), élevé(e); **to be 2 metres h.** faire 2 mètres de haut; *Fam* **to be left h. and dry** être laissé(e) en plan; **h. jump** saut *m* en hauteur; *Fam Fig* **you'll be for the h. jump** tu vas te faire engueuler; **h. jumper** sauteur(euse) *m,f* en hauteur; **h. tide** marée *f* haute; **h. wire** corde *f* raide
(b) (*price, speed, standards*) élevé(e); (*quality*) premier(ère); **to have a h. opinion of sb** avoir une haute opinion de qn; **h. explosive** explosif *m* puissant; **h. point** point *m* culminant; **in h. spirits** plein(e) d'entrain; *Law* **h. treason** haute trahison *f*; **h. winds** vents *mpl* forts
(c) (*rank, position*) haut(e); **to act all h. and mighty** agir avec beaucoup d'arrogance; *Mil* **h. command** haut commandement *m*; **H. Commission** haut-commissariat *m*; **H. Court** ≃ tribunal *m* de grande instance; **H. Mass** grand-messe *f*; **h. school** = école secondaire qui accueille les élèves de 11 à 18 ans; **h. society** haute société *f*
(d) (*in tone, pitch*) aigu(ë); *Fig* **h. note** (*of career, performance*) point *m* culminant
(e) (*with time*) **it's h. time you got yourself a job** il est grand temps que tu trouves un travail; **h. noon** plein midi; **h. summer** plein été; *Br* **h. tea** = dîner pris assez tôt dans la soirée
(f) (*meat*) avancé(e)
(g) *Fam* **to be h.** (*on drugs*) planer; *Fig* (*on success, excitement*) être euphorique
3 *adv* (*aim, jump*) haut; **to hunt h. and low for sth** remuer ciel et terre pour trouver qch; **feelings were running h.** la tension montait

highbrow ['haɪbraʊ] *adj* intellectuel(elle)

highchair ['haɪtʃeə(r)] *n* chaise *f* haute

Higher ['haɪər] *n Scot* = diplôme de fin d'études secondaires sanctionnant une matière déterminée

higher education ['haɪəredjʊ'keɪʃən] *n* enseignement *m* supérieur

high-flier, high-flyer ['haɪ'flaɪə(r)] *n* (*person*) battant(e) *m,f*; (*company*) société *f* qui va de l'avant

high-flying ['haɪ'flaɪŋ] *adj* ambitieux(euse)

high-frequency ['haɪ'friːkwənsɪ] *adj* (à) haute fréquence *inv*

high-handed ['haɪ'hændɪd] *adj* autoritaire, despotique

high-heeled ['haɪ'hiːld] *adj* à talons hauts

Highland ['haɪlənd] *adj* (*from Scottish Highlands*) des Highlands; **H. cattle** vaches *fpl* des Highlands

Highlander ['haɪləndə(r)] *n* (*of Scotland*) habitant(e) *m,f* des Highlands

Highlands ['haɪləndz] *npl* **the H.** (*of Scotland*) les Highlands *fpl*

high-level ['haɪlevəl] *adj* (*talks*) à haut niveau; (*delegation*) de haut niveau

highlight ['haɪlaɪt] **1** *n* (a) (*of performance, career*) point *m* culminant; **highlights** (*of match, event*) moments *mpl* forts
(b) **highlights** (*in hair*) (*artificial*) mèches *fpl*; (*natural*) reflets *mpl*
2 *vt* (a) (*problem, difference*) mettre en évidence, souligner
(b) (*with highlighter*) surligner; *Comptr* (*block of text*) sélectionner

highlighter ['haɪlaɪtə(r)] *n* (*pen*) surligneur *m*

highly ['haɪlɪ] *adv* (a) (*very*) très, extrêmement; **h. paid** très bien payé(e); **h. seasoned** fortement assaisonné(e); **h. strung** hypersensible (b) (*favourably*) **to think h. of**

sb avoir une haute opinion de qn; **to speak h. of sb** parler de qn en termes élogieux

high-minded ['haɪ'maɪndɪd] *adj (sentiments, behaviour)* noble; *(person)* qui a des principes

Highness ['haɪnɪs] *n* His/Her Royal H. Son Altesse *f*

high-pitched ['haɪpɪtʃt] *adj* aigu(ë)

high-powered ['haɪ'paʊəd] *adj (engine, car, telescope)* très puissant(e); *(job)* à hautes responsabilités; *(person)* qui occupe un poste à hautes responsabilités

high-pressure ['haɪ'preʃə(r)] *adj* (a) *(cylinder, gas, machine)* à haute pression (b) *(salesman)* agressif(ive)

high-profile ['haɪ'prəʊfaɪl] *adj (person)* très en vue; *(campaign)* de grande envergure

high-rise ['haɪ'raɪz] **1** *n (block of flats)* tour *f*
2 *adj* **h. building** tour *f*

high-risk ['haɪrɪsk] *adj (strategy, investment)* à haut risque

highroad ['haɪrəʊd] *n Old-fashioned* grand-route *f*; *Fig* **the h. to success** la voie du succès

high-speed ['haɪ'spiːd] *adj* ultrarapide; *(train)* à grande vitesse

high-spirited ['haɪ'spɪrɪtɪd] *adj* plein(e) d'entrain

high-tech ['haɪ'tek] *adj (appliance)* perfectionné(e); *(industry)* de pointe; *(approach, solution)* qui a recours à une technologie de pointe **h. approach, solution**

high-up ['haɪʌp] *adj Fam (important)* haut placé(e)

highway ['haɪweɪ] *n (main road)* route *f* nationale *f*; *(motorway)* autoroute *f*; **H. Code** code *m* de la route

highwayman ['haɪweɪmən] *n* bandit *m* de grand chemin

hijack ['haɪdʒæk] *vt (plane)* détourner; *(car, lorry)* s'emparer de force de; *(idea)* s'approprier

hijacker ['haɪdʒækə(r)] *n (of plane)* pirate *m* de l'air

hike [haɪk] **1** *n* (a) *(walk)* randonnée *f*; **to go on** *or* **for a h.** faire une randonnée; *Fam Fig* **go take a h.!** lâche-moi les baskets! (b) *(in prices)* hausse *f*
2 *vt (prices)* augmenter
3 *vi (walk)* faire de la randonnée

hiker ['haɪkə(r)] *n* randonneur(euse) *m,f*

hiking ['haɪkɪŋ] *n* randonnée *f*; **to go h.** faire de la randonnée; **h. boots** chaussures *fpl* de marche

hilarious [hɪ'leərɪəs] *adj* hilarant(e)

hilariously [hɪ'leərəslɪ] *adv* **h. funny** à se tordre de rire; **to laugh h.** se tordre de rire

hilarity [hɪ'lerɪtɪ] *n* hilarité *f*; **his suggestion was greeted with much h.** sa suggestion déclencha l'hilarité générale

hill [hɪl] *n* (a) *(small mountain)* colline *f*; *Fig* **to be over the h.** commencer à se faire vieux (vieille) (b) *(slope)* côte *f*, pente *f*; **to go down/up the h.** descendre/monter la côte

hillbilly ['hɪlbɪlɪ] *(pl* **hillbillies***) n Am* péquenaud(e) *m,f*

hillock ['hɪlək] *n* butte *f*

hillside ['hɪlsaɪd] *n* coteau *m*

hilltop ['hɪltɒp] *n* sommet *m* de la colline

hillwalker ['hɪlwɔːkə(r)] *n* randonneur(euse) *m,f*

hill-walking ['hɪlwɔːkɪŋ] *n* randonnée *f* en basse montagne

hilly ['hɪlɪ] *adj* vallonné(e)

hilt [hɪlt] *n (of sword)* poignée *f*; *(of knife, dagger)* manche *m*; *Fig* **to back sb to the h.** soutenir qn sans réserve

him [hɪm] *pron* (a) *(direct object)* le; **I hate h.** je le déteste; **I love h.** je l'aime; **I can understand his son but not** HIM je comprends son fils, mais lui, je ne le comprends pas

(b) *(indirect object)* lui; **I gave h. the book** je lui ai donné le livre; **I gave it to h.** je le lui ai donné (c) *(after preposition)* lui; **I'm thinking of h.** je pense à lui (d) *(as complement of verb to be)* lui; **it's h.!** c'est lui!; **it was h. who did it** c'est lui qui l'a fait

Himalayan [hɪmə'leɪən] *adj* himalayen(enne)

Himalayas [hɪmə'leɪəz] *npl* **the H.** l'Himalaya *m*

himself [hɪm'self] *pron* (a) *(reflexive)* se; **he spoils h.** il se gâte; **he hurt h.** il s'est blessé (b) *(emphatic)* lui-même; **he h. has never...** lui-même n'a jamais...; **he told me h.** il me l'a dit lui-même (c) *(after preposition)* **he lives by h.** il vit seul; **he bought it for h.** il se l'est acheté; **he talks to h.** il parle tout seul

hind[1] [haɪnd] *adj (back)* de derrière; **h. legs** pattes *fpl* de derrière

hind[2] *n (female deer)* daim *m* femelle

hinder ['hɪndə(r)] *vt (impede)* gêner; *(delay)* retarder; **to h. sb from doing sth** empêcher qn de faire qch

Hindi ['hɪndɪ] *n (language)* hindi *m*

hindquarters ['haɪndkwɔːtəz] *npl* arrière-train *m*

hindrance ['hɪndrəns] *n* entrave *f*, obstacle *m*

hindsight ['haɪndsaɪt] *n* recul *m*; **with (the benefit of) h.** avec le recul

Hindu ['hɪnduː] **1** *n* Hindou(e) *m,f*
2 *adj* hindou(e)

Hinduism ['hɪnduːɪzəm] *n* hindouisme *m*

hinge [hɪndʒ] *n* charnière *f*, gond *m*; **to come off its hinges** sortir de ses gonds
▶**hinge on, hinge upon** *vt insep (depend on)* dépendre de

hint [hɪnt] **1** *n* (a) *(allusion)* allusion *f*; *(clue)* indice *m*; **to drop sb a h.** faire une allusion à l'intention de qn; **to take the h.** comprendre l'allusion; **he can't take a h.** il faut lui mettre les points sur les i (b) *(sign)* signe *m* (c) *(small amount)* soupçon *m* (d) *(piece of advice)* truc *m*, conseil *m*
2 *vt* **to h. that...** insinuer ou laisser entendre que...
▶**hint at** *vt insep* faire allusion à

hinterland ['hɪntəlænd] *n* arrière-pays *m inv*

hip[1] [hɪp] *n (part of body)* hanche *f*; **h. flask** flasque *f*; **h. joint** articulation *f* de la hanche; **h. pocket** poche *f* revolver

hip[2] *adj Fam (trendy)* branché(e)

hippo ['hɪpəʊ] *(pl* **hippos***) n Fam* hippopotame *m*

hippopotamus [hɪpə'pɒtəməs] *(pl* **hippopotami** [hɪpə'pɒtəmaɪ]*) n* hippopotame *m*

hippy ['hɪpɪ] *(pl* **hippies***) n* hippie *mf*

hire [haɪə(r)] **1** *n Br (of car, equipment)* location *f*; **for h.** à louer; *(taxi)* libre; **h. car** voiture *f* de location
2 *vt* (a) *(car, equipment)* louer (b) *(lawyer, worker)* engager
▶**hire out** *vt sep Br (boat, bicycle)* louer; *(one's services)* offrir

hired ['haɪəd] *adj (car, suit)* de location; **h. hand** *(on farm)* ouvrier(ère) *m,f* agricole

hire purchase ['haɪə'pɜːtʃɪs] *n Com* achat *m* à crédit; **h. agreement** contrat *m* de vente à tempérament

hirsute ['hɜːsjuːt] *adj Lit* velu(e)

his [hɪz] **1** *possessive adj* (a) *(singular)* son (sa); *(plural)* ses; **h. job** son travail; **h. wife** sa femme; **h. parents** ses parents; **it wasn't** HIS **idea!** ce n'est pas lui qui en a eu l'idée! (b) *(for parts of body)* **he hit h. head** il s'est cogné la tête
2 *possessive pron* (a) *(singular)* le sien (la sienne) *m,f*;

(plural) les siens (les siennes) *mpl, fpl*; **my house is big, but h. is bigger** j'ai une grande maison, mais la sienne est plus grande encore **(b)** *(used attributively)* **this book is h.** ce livre est à lui; **a friend of h.** un de ses amis; **where's that brother of h.?** où son frère a-t-il bien pu passer?

Hispanic [hɪsˈpænɪk] **1** *Am* Latino-Américain(e) *m,f*
 2 *adj* hispanique

hiss [hɪs] **1** *n (sound)* sifflement *m*; *(to express disapproval)* sifflet *m*
 2 *vt & vi* siffler

histogram [ˈhɪstəgræm] *n* histogramme *m*

historian [hɪsˈtɔːrɪən] *n* historien(enne) *m,f*

historic [hɪsˈtɒrɪk] *adj* historique

historical [hɪsˈtɒrɪkəl] *adj* historique

historically [hɪsˈtɒrɪklɪ] *adv* historiquement

history [ˈhɪstərɪ] *(pl* **histories)** *n* histoire *f*; **to go down in h.**, **to make h.** *(of event)* faire date; *(of person)* entrer dans l'histoire; *Fig* **that's (ancient) h.** c'est de l'histoire ancienne; **h. book/teacher** livre *m*/professeur *m* d'histoire **(b)** *(medical record)* antécédents *mpl*; **there is a h. of diabetes in his family** il y a des cas de diabète dans sa famille

histrionic [hɪstrɪˈɒnɪk] *adj Pej* théâtral(e)

histrionics [hɪstrɪˈɒnɪks] *npl Pej* scène *f*; **to have h.** faire une scène

hit [hɪt] **1** *n (a) (blow)* coup *m*; *(in shooting)* tir *m* réussi; **to score a direct h.** taper dans le mille; **h. list** *(of targets)* liste *f* noire; **h. man** tueur *m* à gages **(b)** *(success)* succès *m*; **to be a h. with sb** avoir beaucoup de succès auprès de qn; **h. (record)** hit *m*
 2 *adj (film, play)* à succès
 3 *vt (pt & pp* **hit)** **(a)** *(of person)* frapper; *(of bullet)* atteindre; *(of car)* percuter; *Comptr (key)* frapper, appuyer sur; **to h. one's head (on sth)** se cogner la tête (contre qch); *Fig* **it suddenly hit me that...** j'ai réalisé tout d'un coup que...; *Fig* **he didn't know what had hit him** il n'a pas eu le temps de se rendre compte de ce qui lui arrivait **(b)** *(reach) (barrier, difficulty)* se heurter à; **to h. a note** atteindre une note; **to h. 90 (miles an hour)** ≃ faire du 140 (à l'heure); **to h. an all-time low** *(of investment, relationship)* être au plus bas; **the circus hits town tomorrow** le cirque arrive en ville demain; **it hits the shops next week** c'est en vente la semaine prochaine; *Fam* **to h. the road** *(leave)* se mettre en route **(c)** *(affect)* toucher; **to be hard hit by sth** être durement touché(e) par qch
 4 *vi* frapper

▸**hit back 1** *vt sep* **to h. sb back** rendre un coup à qn
 2 *vi also Fig* riposter (**at** à)

▸**hit off** *vt sep Fam* **to h. it off** accrocher

▸**hit on, hit upon** *vt insep (idea, solution)* trouver

▸**hit out** *vi* **to h. out at sb** *(physically)* frapper qn; *(verbally)* s'en prendre à qn

hit-and-run [ˈhɪtənˈrʌn] *adj* **h. accident** = accident à la suite duquel l'automobiliste prend la fuite

hitch [hɪtʃ] **1** *n (a) (difficulty)* problème *m*; **without a h.** sans anicroche **(b)** *(knot)* nœud *m*
 2 *vt (a) (attach)* attacher (**to** à); *Fam Fig* **to get hitched** *(married)* passer devant Monsieur le Maire **(b)** *Fam* **to h. a lift** faire du stop
 3 *vi Fam* faire du stop; **to h. to Paris** aller à Paris en stop

▸**hitch up** *vt sep (trousers, skirt)* remonter

hitchhike [ˈhɪtʃhaɪk] *vi* faire de l'auto-stop; **to h. to Paris** aller à Paris en auto-stop

hitchhiker [ˈhɪtʃhaɪkə(r)] *n* auto-stoppeur(euse) *m,f*

hi-tech [ˈhaɪˈtek] = **high-tech**

hither [ˈhɪðə(r)] *adv Lit* ici; **h. and thither** çà et là

hitherto [ˈhɪðəˈtuː] *adv* jusqu'ici, jusqu'à présent

hit-or-miss [ˈhɪtɔːˈmɪs] *adj* aléatoire, approximatif(ive)

HIV [eɪtʃaɪˈviː] *n (abbr* **human immunodeficiency virus)** VIH *m*; **to be H. positive/negative** être séropositif(ive)/séronégatif(ive)

hive [haɪv] *n* ruche *f*; *Fig* **a h. of activity** une véritable ruche

▸**hive off** *vt sep (money, profits)* séparer

HMG [eɪtʃemˈdʒiː] *n Br (abbr* **Her/His Majesty's Government)** = le gouvernement de sa majesté *(expression utilisée sur les documents officiels)*

HMI [eɪtʃemˈaɪ] *n Br (abbr* **Her/His Majesty's Inspectorate)** ≃ Inspection *f* académique; *(abbr* **Her/His Majesty's Inspector)** ≃ inspecteur(trice) *m,f* de l'éducation nationale

HMS [eɪtʃemˈes] *n (abbr* **Her/His Majesty's Ship)** = abréviation précédant le nom des navires de la marine britannique

HMSO [eɪtʃemesˈəʊ] *n (abbr* **Her/His Majesty's Stationery Office)** ≃ Imprimerie *f* nationale

HNC [eɪtʃenˈsiː] *n Br (abbr* **Higher National Certificate)** = diplôme technique préparé en un an

HND [eɪtʃenˈdiː] *n Br (abbr* **Higher National Diploma)** = diplôme technique préparé en deux ans

hoard [hɔːd] **1** *n (of food)* réserve *f*, provisions *fpl*; *(of money)* trésor *m*
 2 *vt (food)* amasser, stocker; *(money)* amasser, thésauriser

hoarder [ˈhɔːdə(r)] *n* personne *f* qui fait des réserves; **she's a real h.** elle ne jette rien

hoarding [ˈhɔːdɪŋ] *n (a) (of food)* stockage *m* **(b)** *(for poster)* panneau *m* d'affichage

hoarfrost [ˈhɔːfrɒst] *n* givre *m*, gelée *f* blanche

hoarse [hɔːs] *adj* enroué(e); **to shout oneself h.** s'enrouer à force de crier

hoary [ˈhɔːrɪ] *adj (story)* vieux (vieille); *(joke)* éculé(e)

hoax [həʊks] **1** *n* canular *m*; **to play a h. on sb** faire un canular à qn; **h. caller** auteur *m* de canular(s) téléphonique(s)
 2 *vt* faire un canular à

hob [hɒb] *n (on electric cooker)* table *f* de cuisson; *(on hearth)* plaque *f*

hobble [ˈhɒbəl] *vi* boitiller

hobby [ˈhɒbɪ] *(pl* **hobbies)** *n* passe-temps *m inv*, hobby *m*

hobbyhorse [ˈhɒbɪhɔːs] *n (toy)* cheval *m* de bois *(tête emmanchée sur un bâton)*; *Fig (favourite subject)* dada *m*

hobnail boot [ˈhɒbneɪlˈbuːt] *n* chaussure *f* ferrée

hobnob [ˈhɒbnɒb] *(pt & pp* **hobnobbed)** *vi Fam* **to h. with sb** frayer avec qn

hock[1] [hɒk] *n (wine)* vin *m* du Rhin

hock[2] *Fam* **1** *n* **to be in h.** *(of object)* être au clou; *(of person)* être endetté(e)
 2 *vt* mettre au clou

hockey [ˈhɒkɪ] *n Br (on grass)* hockey *m* (sur gazon); *Am (on ice)* hockey *m* (sur glace); **h. stick** crosse *f* de hockey

hocus-pocus [ˈhəʊkəsˈpəʊkəs] *n (trickery)* tromperie *f*, supercherie *f*; *(talk)* paroles *fpl* trompeuses

hoe [həʊ] **1** *n* houe *f*, binette *f*
 2 *vt (pt & pp* **hoed)** biner, sarcler

hog [hɒg] **1** n (a) (pig) porc m châtré; Fam **to go the whole h.** aller jusqu'au bout (b) (glutton) glouton(onne) m,f, goinfre mf
2 vt (pt & pp **hogged**) Fam (monopolize) monopoliser; **to h. the limelight** monopoliser l'attention

Hogmanay [ˈhɒgməˈneɪ] n Scot la Saint-Sylvestre

hogwash [ˈhɒgwɒʃ] n Fam âneries fpl

hoist [hɔɪst] **1** n (device) appareil m de levage
2 vt hisser; Fig **to be hoist with one's own petard** se faire prendre à son propre piège

hoity-toity [ˈhɔɪtɪˈtɔɪtɪ] adj **to be h.** se donner de grands airs

hold [həʊld] **1** n (a) (grip) prise f; **to have h. of sb/sth** tenir qn/qch; **to catch** or **take h. of sth** saisir qch; Fig **to get h. of sb** (find) trouver qn; (on phone) joindre qn; Fig **to get h. of sth** se procurer qch; **to let go one's h.** relâcher son étreinte, lâcher prise; **to lose one's h. on reality** perdre le sens des réalités; Fig **to have a h. on** or **over sb** avoir de l'emprise sur qn
(b) (in wrestling) prise f; Fig **no holds barred** tous les coups sont permis
(c) **to be on h.** (of project) être en suspens; (of telephone caller) être en attente; **to put sth on h.** mettre qch en suspens; **to put sb on h.** (on telephone) mettre qn en attentes
(d) (of ship) cale f; (of plane) soute f
2 vt (pt & pp **held** [held]) (a) (grip) tenir; **to h. sb/sth tight** tenir qn/qch serré(e), serrer qn/qch; **to h. hands** se tenir (par) la main; **to h. sth in position** maintenir qch en place; **to h. sb prisoner** retenir qn prisonnier(ère); **the police are holding him for questioning** il a été placé en garde à vue; **to h. sb's interest/attention** retenir l'intérêt/l'attention de qn; **to h. sb to his promise** obliger qn à tenir sa promesse; **to h. one's breath** retenir sa respiration ou son souffle; Fig **don't h. your breath!** ce n'est pas pour demain! **there's no holding her** il n'y a pas moyen de l'arrêter; **h. your tongue!** tais-toi!; Fam **h. it!, h. your horses!** attendez!, minute!; **to h. a note** (of singer) tenir une note; **h. the line!** (on telephone) ne quittez pas!
(b) (keep) (town, position) tenir; (ticket, room) réserver; **to h. one's ground** tenir bon; **to h. one's own** se défendre
(c) (carry) **to h. one's head high** garder la tête haute; **to h. oneself well** se tenir bien
(d) (contain) contenir; Fig **to h. water** (of theory, story) tenir la route; **nobody knows what the future holds** personne ne sait ce que l'avenir nous réserve; **it holds no interest for me** ça ne présente aucun intérêt pour moi
(e) (conduct) (negotiations) mener; (meeting) organiser; (conversation) avoir
(f) (possess) (title, rank, opinion) avoir; (job, position) occuper; (record) détenir; **to h. office** être en fonction
(g) (consider) **to h. sb responsible** tenir qn pour responsable; **to h. sb in respect** respecter qn; **to h. that...** soutenir que...
3 vi (of rope) tenir; **h. tight!** tiens bon!
(b) (of agreement, weather) durer; (of luck) persister; **the same holds (true) for you** cela vaut aussi pour toi

▸**hold against** vt sep **to h. sth against sb** reprocher qch à qn

▸**hold back 1** vt sep (a) (restrain) (person, emotion) retenir; (progress, project) ralentir, freiner (b) (conceal) cacher
2 vi (refrain) se retenir (**from doing** de faire)

▸**hold down** vt sep (a) (restrain) (person) immobiliser; (taxes, prices) bloquer (b) (job) (occupy) avoir; (keep) garder

▸**hold forth** vi disserter, pérorer (**about** or **on** sur)

▸**hold off 1** vt sep (a) (keep at bay) tenir à distance (b) (delay) remettre à plus tard, repousser; **to h. off making a decision** remettre une décision à plus tard
2 vi (delay) attendre

▸**hold on** vi (a) (last) tenir (b) (wait) patienter; **h. on!** attendez!; (on telephone) ne quittez pas! (c) (not let go) s'accrocher

▸**hold on to** vt insep (a) (rope, handle) s'agripper à; Fig (idea, hope) s'accrocher à (b) (keep) garder

▸**hold out 1** vt sep (one's hand) tendre; (hope, opportunity) offrir
2 vi (a) (resist) tenir (le coup) (b) (wait) **to h. out for a better offer** attendre une meilleure offre (c) (last) durer

▸**hold over** vt sep remettre, reporter

▸**hold together 1** vt sep **to h. sth together** faire tenir qch; **to be held together with sth** tenir avec qch
2 vi (of party, group of people) rester uni(e); (of marriage, relationship) tenir

▸**hold up 1** vt sep (a) (support) soutenir (b) (raise) lever; Fig **to h. sb/sth up as an example** montrer ou citer qn/qch en exemple; Fig **to h. sb/sth up to ridicule** tourner qn/qch en ridicule (c) (delay) retarder (d) (rob) attaquer
2 vi (of theory, alibi) (se) tenir; (of good weather) se maintenir; **she's holding up well under the pressure** elle tient bien le coup

▸**hold with** vt insep (agree with) être d'accord avec; (approve of) approuver

holdall [ˈhəʊldɔːl] n fourre-tout m inv

holder [ˈhəʊldə(r)] n (a) (of licence, ticket, record, trophy) détenteur(trice) m,f; (of passport, degree) titulaire mf; (of belief, opinion) tenant m (b) (device) support m

holding [ˈhəʊldɪŋ] n (a) (property) propriété f (b) (of shares) participation f; Com **h. company** holding m (c) Fig **h. operation** opération f destinée à gagner du temps

hold-up [ˈhəʊldʌp] n (a) (delay) (in plan) retard m; (of traffic) ralentissement m (b) (armed robbery) hold-up m inv, attaque f à main armée (c) (hold-ups) (stockings) bas mpl jarretière

hole [həʊl] **1** n (a) (opening) trou m; (of rabbit, fox) terrier m; also Fig **to make a h. in sth** faire un trou dans qch; Fig **to pick holes in sth** relever les failles de qch; Fig **a h. in the law** un vide juridique; **to get a h. in one** (in golf) faire un trou en un; Fam Fig **to be in a h.** (in difficulty) être dans le pétrin (b) Fam Pej (room, house) taudis m; (town) trou m
2 vt (ship) faire une brèche dans; (in golf) **to h. a putt** faire le trou

▸**hole up** vi Fam (hide) se terrer

holiday [ˈhɒlɪdeɪ] **1** n (a) Br (vacation) vacances fpl; **a month's h.** un mois de vacances; **to be on h.** être en vacances; **to go on h.** aller ou partir en vacances; **h. camp** camp m de vacances; Fig **it was no h. camp** ce n'était pas une partie de plaisir; **h. home** résidence f secondaire; **h. season** saison f touristique (b) (day off) (jour m de) congé m (c) (public) jour m férié
2 vi Br passer les vacances; (in summer) passer les vacances d'été

holidaymaker [ˈhɒlɪdeɪmeɪkə(r)] n Br vacancier(ère) m,f; (in summer) estivant(e) m,f

holiness [ˈhəʊlɪnɪs] n sainteté f; **Your H.** Votre Sainteté

holistic [həʊˈlɪstɪk] adj holistique

Holland [ˈhɒlənd] n la Hollande

holler [ˈhɒlə(r)] vi Fam brailler

hollow [ˈhɒləʊ] **1** n creux m
2 adj (a) (container, cheeks) creux(euse); (eyes) cave (b)

(sound) creux(euse); *(voice)* blanc (blanche); *(laugh)* forcé(e) **(c)** *(promise, guarantee)* vain(e); *(victory)* sans signification **3** *adv* **(a) to sound h.** sonner creux **(b)** *Fam* **to beat sb h.** battre qn à plate(s) couture(s)

▶**hollow out** *vt sep* évider

holly ['hɒlɪ] *n* houx *m*

hollyhock ['hɒlɪhɒk] *n* rose *f* trémière

holocaust ['hɒləkɔːst] *n* holocauste *m*

hologram ['hɒləgræm] *n* hologramme *m*

holster ['həʊlstə(r)] *n* étui *m* de revolver

holy ['həʊlɪ] *adj* saint(e); *Fam* **h. cow** *or* **smoke** *or* **mackerel!** ça alors!; **the H. Bible** la Sainte Bible; **H. Communion** communion *f*; **the H. Father** le saint-père; **the H. Ghost** *or* **Spirit** le Saint-Esprit; *Fam* **H. Joe** grenouille *f* de bénitier; **the H. Land** la Terre Sainte; **h. orders** ordres *mpl*; **h. war** guerre *f* sainte; **h. water** eau *f* bénite; **H. Week** la semaine sainte

homage ['hɒmɪdʒ] *n* hommage *m*; **to pay h. to sb** rendre hommage à qn

home [həʊm] **1** *n* **(a)** *(house)* maison *f*; *(of animal, plant)* habitat *m*; **at h.** à la maison, chez soi; **to feel at h.** se sentir chez soi; **make yourself at h.** faites comme chez vous; **to leave h.** *(in the morning)* partir de chez soi; *(one's parents' home)* partir de chez ses parents; **to be away from h.** être en déplacement; **to be a h. from h.** être un second chez-soi; **to make one's h. in France** s'établir en France; **old people's h.** maison *f* de retraite; **children's h.** foyer *m* pour enfants; **h. address** adresse *f* personnelle, domicile *m*; **h. banking** banque *f* à domicile; **h. brew** bière *f* maison; **h. cooking** cuisine *f* familiale; *Br* **the H. Counties** = les comtés limitrophes de Londres; **h. economics** *(school subject)* arts *mpl* ménagers; **h. help** aide *f* ménagère; **h. life** vie *f* de famille; *Fin* **h. loan** prêt *m* immobilier; **h. movie** film *m* amateur; **h. owner** propriétaire *mf*; *Am* **Sch h. room** salle *f* où l'on fait l'appel; **h. run** *(in baseball)* tour *m* complet; **h. straight** *(in athletics)* la dernière ligne droite; **h. town** ville *f* natale; **to tell sb a few h. truths** dire ses quatre vérités à qn

(b) *(country, region)* patrie *f*; **at h. and abroad** dans notre pays et à l'étranger; **an example nearer h.** un exemple qui nous concerne plus; **Milan, the h. of fashion** Milan, capitale de la mode; **h. front** arrière *m*; **h. news** nouvelles *fpl* nationales; *Br Pol* **H. Office** ≃ ministère *m* de l'Intérieur; *Pol* **h. rule** régime *m* d'autonomie politique; *Br Pol* **the H. Secretary** ≃ le ministre de l'Intérieur

2 *adv* **(a)** *(to or at one's house)* à la maison, chez soi; *Fig* **to bring sth h. to sb** faire comprendre qch à qn; **to send sb h.** *(to house)* renvoyer qn chez soi; *(to home country)* rapatrier qn

(b) *(all the way)* **he hammered the nail h.** il enfonça complètement le clou; **the bolt slid h.** le verrou se ferma

▶**home in on** *vt insep (target)* se diriger vers; *(mistake, evidence)* relever

homecoming ['həʊmkʌmɪŋ] *n (to one's house)* retour *m* (au foyer); *(to one's country)* retour au pays

home-grown ['həʊm'grəʊn] *adj (vegetables)* du jardin; *Fig (not imported)* national(e)

homeland ['həʊmlænd] *n* patrie *f*, pays *m* (d'origine)

homeless ['həʊmlɪs] **1** *npl* **the h.** les sans-abri *mpl* **2** *adj* sans abri

homely ['həʊmlɪ] *adj* **(a)** *Br (person, atmosphere, decor)* agréable et sans prétention **(b)** *Am (plain)* sans charme

home-made ['həʊm'meɪd] *adj* fait(e) maison

homeopath ['həʊmɪəʊpæθ] *n* homéopathe *mf*

homeopathic ['həʊmɪəʊ'pæθɪk] *adj* homéopathique

homeopathy ['həʊmɪ'ɒpəθɪ] *n* homéopathie *f*

homesick ['həʊmsɪk] *adj* **to be** *or* **feel h.** avoir le mal du pays; *(of child)* s'ennuyer de ses parents; **to be h. for sth** avoir la nostalgie de qch

homesickness ['həʊmsɪknɪs] *n* mal *m* du pays

homespun ['həʊmspʌn] *adj Fig (wisdom, advice)* simple

homestead ['həʊmsted] *n* propriété *f*; *(farm)* ferme *f*

homeward ['həʊmwəd] **1** *adj* de retour **2** *adv (to one's house)* vers sa maison; *(to one's own country)* vers son pays; **to be h.-bound** être sur le chemin du retour

homewards ['həʊmwədz] *adv* = **homeward**

homework ['həʊmwɜːk] *n Sch* devoirs *mpl*; **to do one's h.** faire ses devoirs; *Fig* faire des recherches

homicidal [hɒmɪ'saɪdəl] *adj* meurtrier(ère)

homicide ['hɒmɪsaɪd] *n* homicide *m*

homily ['hɒmɪlɪ] *n (pl* **homilies)** homélie *f*, sermon *m*

homing ['həʊmɪŋ] *adj* **h. device** mécanisme *m* d'autoguidage; **h. pigeon** pigeon *m* voyageur

homogeneous [həʊmə'dʒiːnɪəs, hə'mɒdʒɪnəs] *adj* homogène

homogenize [hə'mɒdʒənaɪz] *vt* homogénéiser

homonym ['hɒmənɪm] *n* homonyme *m*

homophobia [həʊmə'fəʊbɪə] *n* intolérance *f* à l'égard des homosexuels

homosexual [həʊmə'seksjʊəl] *n & adj* homosexuel(elle) *m,f*

homosexuality [həʊməseksjʊ'ælɪtɪ] *n* homosexualité *f*

Hon *adj Br Parl (abbr* **Honourable) the H. member for** Monsieur/Madame le député de

honcho ['hɒntʃəʊ] *n (pl* **honchos)** *n Fam* **the head h.** le boss

Honduras [hɒn'djʊərəs] *n* le Honduras

hone [həʊn] *vt (skill)* peaufiner

honest ['ɒnɪst] *adj* honnête **(with** avec); **she has an h. face** elle a un visage franc; **the h. truth** la vérité vraie; **to be h., I don't know** honnêtement *ou* à dire vrai, je ne sais pas; **to earn an h. living** gagner honnêtement sa vie; *Hum* **to make an h. woman of sb** *(marry)* faire de qn une honnête femme

honestly ['ɒnɪstlɪ] *adv* **(a)** *(legitimately, sincerely)* honnêtement; **to obtain sth h.** obtenir qch par des moyens honnêtes; **I can h. say that…** honnêtement, je peux dire que… **(b)** *(expressing indignation)* **well h.!** franchement!; **h.! some people!** il y a des gens, je te jure!

honesty ['ɒnɪstɪ] *n* honnêteté *f*; **in all h.** en toute honnêteté; *Prov* **h. is the best policy** l'honnêteté est toujours récompensée

honey ['hʌnɪ] *n* **(a)** *(food)* miel *m* **(b)** *Am Fam (term of endearment)* chéri(e) *m,f*

honeycomb ['hʌnɪkəʊm] **1** *n* rayon *m* de miel **2** *vt* **the mountain is honeycombed with tunnels** la montagne est truffée de tunnels

honeymoon ['hʌnɪmuːn] **1** *n* voyage *m* de noces; *Fig* **the h. is over** l'état de grâce est terminé **2** *vi* partir en voyage de noces

honeysuckle ['hʌnɪsʌkəl] *n* chèvrefeuille *m*

Hong Kong ['hɒŋ'kɒŋ] *n* Hongkong

honk [hɒŋk] **1** n (of goose) cri m; (of car horn) coup m de Klaxon®
2 vi (of goose) cacarder; (of car driver) klaxonner

honky ['hɒŋkɪ] (pl honkies) n Am very Fam sale Blanc (Blanche) m,f, = terme injurieux désignant un Blanc

honor, honorable etc Am = honour, honourable etc

honorary ['ɒnərərɪ] adj (member) honoraire; (title) honorifique; Univ h. degree grade m honoris causa

honour, Am **honor** ['ɒnə(r)] **1** n (a) (respect) honneur m; **in h. of** en l'honneur de; **in h. of** the occasion pour l'occasion; **to have the h. of doing sth** avoir l'honneur de faire qch; Hum **to what do I owe this h.?** qu'est-ce qui me vaut cet honneur?; **Your H.** (judge) Votre Honneur
(b) (good name) honneur m; **to feel h. bound to do sth** se sentir tenu(e) par l'honneur de faire qch; **on my (word of) h.!** parole d'honneur!; Prov **(there is) h. among thieves** les loups ne se mangent pas entre eux
(c) (award, distinction) **honours list** = liste de distinctions honorifiques accordées par le souverain britannique; **honours degree** diplôme m universitaire; **he was buried with full military honours** il a été enterré avec tous les honneurs militaires; Hum **to do the honours** (serve food or drink) faire les honneurs; (make introductions) faire les présentations
2 vt honorer; **I felt honoured that they had invited me** je me suis senti honoré par leur invitation

honourable, Am **honorable** ['ɒnərəbəl] adj honorable; Br Parl **the H. member for** Monsieur/Madame le député de; **h. mention** mention f spéciale

honourably, Am **honorably** ['ɒnərəblɪ] adv honorablement

hooch [huːtʃ] n Am Fam (liquor) gnôle f

hood [hʊd] n (a) (of coat, cloak) capuche f; (with eye-holes) cagoule f; Br (of car, pram) capote f; Am (car bonnet) capot m; (over cooker, fireplace) hotte f (b) Am Fam (gangster) truand m

hoodlum ['huːdləm] n Fam voyou m

hoodwink ['hʊdwɪŋk] vt Fam embobiner; **to h. sb into doing sth** embobiner qn pour qu'il fasse qch

hoof [huːf] **1** n (pl hooves [huːvz]) sabot m
2 vt Fam **to h. it** aller à pinces

hoo-ha ['huːhɑː] n Fam (fuss) tintouin m

hook [hʊk] n (a) (for hanging) (in general) crochet m; (for coats) patère f; (for meat) croc m; (on clothes) agrafe f; (on fishing) hameçon m; **to leave the phone off the h.** (on purpose) laisser le téléphone décroché; (accidentally) mal raccrocher son téléphone; Fam Fig **to get** or **let sb off the h.** tirer qn d'affaire; Fam **he swallowed it h., line and sinker** (believed it) il a tout gobé; Fam **by h. or by crook** coûte que coûte (b) (in boxing) crochet m
2 vt accrocher; **to h. a fish** attraper un poisson

▶**hook up 1** vt sep Comptr connecter (**to** à)
2 vi (a) (of dress) s'agrafer (b) Comptr se connecter; TV **to h. up with** faire une émission en duplex avec

hooked [hʊkt] adj (a) **h. nose** nez m crochu (b) Fam (addicted) **to be h.** (on) être accro (à); (on cinema, jazz) être mordu(e) (de)

hooker [hʊkər] n (a) Br (in rugby) talonneur m (b) Am Fam (prostitute) pute f

hooky ['hʊkɪ] n Am Fam **to play h.** sécher les cours

hooligan ['huːlɪgən] n hooligan m, vandale m

hooliganism ['huːlɪgənɪzəm] n hooliganisme m, vandalisme m

hoop [huːp] n cerceau m; (in croquet) arceau m; Fig **to put sb through the hoops** mettre qn à l'épreuve

hooray [hʊˈreɪ] exclam hourra!

hoot [huːt] **1** n (a) (of owl) hululement m; (of horn) coup m de Klaxon®; (of ship, factory whistle) mugissement m; **hoots of laughter** éclats mpl de rire; Fam Fig **I don't give a h.** or **two hoots** je m'en fiche comme de l'an quarante (b) Fam **she's a h.!** elle est tordante!; **it was a h.!** c'était tordant!
2 vt (person) huer; **he was hooted off the stage** il a quitté la scène sous les huées
3 vi (of owl) hululer; (of train) siffler; (of car) klaxonner; **to h. with laughter** hurler de rire

hooter ['huːtə(r)] n Br (of ship, factory) sirène f; (of car) Klaxon® m (b) Fam (nose) pif m

hoover® ['huːvə(r)] **1** n aspirateur m
2 vt (room) passer l'aspirateur dans; (carpet) passer l'aspirateur sur

hooves [huːvz] pl of hoof

hop [hɒp] **1** n (jump) saut m; Fam (dance) bal m; **a short h.** (journey) un petit voyage; Fam Fig **to catch sb on the h.** prendre qn de court ou au dépourvu
2 vt (pt & pp hopped) Fam **h. it!** fiche le camp!
3 vi (jump) sautiller; (on one leg) sauter à cloche-pied; Fam **h. in!** (to car) allez, grimpe!; **he hopped onto the first train** il a sauté dans le premier train

▶**hop off** vi Fam ficher le camp

hope [həʊp] **1** n espoir m; **in the h. of doing sth** dans l'espoir de faire qch; **in the h. that...** dans l'espoir que...; **to have little h. of doing sth** avoir peu de chances de faire qch; **to have hopes of doing sth** avoir l'espoir de faire qch; **don't get your hopes up** n'espère pas trop; **to raise hopes of sth** faire naître l'espoir de qch; **she hasn't got a h. of winning** elle n'a aucune chance de gagner; Ironic **some h.!** tu peux toujours rêver!; Fam **we live in h.!** l'espoir fait vivre!
2 vt **to h. to do sth** espérer faire qch; **to h. (that)...** espérer que...; **I h. you're right** j'espère que tu as raison; **I h. and pray that...** je prie le ciel que...; **I h. so** j'espère (bien); **I h. not** j'espère que non
3 vi espérer; **to h. for sth** espérer qch; **don't h. for too much** n'en attends pas trop; **we'll just have to h. for the best** espérons que tout se passe bien; **to h. against h.** espérer malgré tout

hopeful ['həʊpfəl] **1** n Fam **a young h.** un jeune espoir
2 adj (situation) encourageant(e); (person) optimiste; **to be h. that...** avoir bon espoir que...

hopefully ['həʊpfəlɪ] adv (a) (with luck) avec un peu de chance; **h. not** espérons que non (b) (in a hopeful manner) **to do sth h.** faire qch plein(e) d'espoir

hopeless ['həʊplɪs] adj (a) (without hope) (person, cause, situation) désespéré(e); **it's h.!** ça ne sert à rien! (b) Fam (very bad) nul (nulle) (at en)

hopelessly ['həʊplɪslɪ] adv (a) (inconsolably) avec désespoir (b) (completely) complètement; **he was h. in love with her** il était éperdument amoureux d'elle

hopping ['hɒpɪŋ] adv Fam **to be h. mad** être fou (folle) de rage

hops [hɒps] npl (for making beer) houblon m

hopscotch ['hɒpskɒtʃ] n marelle f

horde [hɔːd] n horde f

horizon [həˈraɪzən] n horizon m; **on the h.** à l'horizon; Fig en vue

horizontal [hɒrɪˈzɒntəl] **1** n horizontale f
2 adj horizontal(e)

horizontally [ˌhɒrɪˈzɒntəlɪ] adv horizontalement

hormonal [hɔːˈməʊnəl] adj hormonal(e)

hormone [ˈhɔːməʊn] n hormone f; **h. replacement therapy** hormonothérapie f de substitution

horn [hɔːn] n (a) (of animal) corne f; (of insect) antenne f (b) (musical instrument) cor m; (on car) Klaxon® m; **to sound one's h.** klaxonner (c) (idioms) **to be on the horns of a dilemma** être en proie à un dilemme

horned [hɔːnd] adj à cornes

hornet [ˈhɔːnɪt] n frelon m; Fig **to stir up a h.'s nest** mettre le feu aux poudres

hornpipe [ˈhɔːnpaɪp] n matelote f

horn-rimmed [ˈhɔːnrɪmd] adj **h. spectacles or glasses** lunettes fpl à monture d'écaille

horny [ˈhɔːnɪ] adj (a) (hands) calleux(euse) (b) very Fam (sexually aroused) excité(e); (sexually attractive) bandant(e)

horoscope [ˈhɒrəskəʊp] n horoscope m

horrendous [hɒˈrendəs] adj horrible, affreux(euse)

horrendously [hɒˈrendəslɪ] adv horriblement, affreusement

horrible [ˈhɒrəbəl] adj (a) (unpleasant) horrible, affreux(euse); **how h.!** quelle horreur! (b) (unkind) méchant(e) (to avec)

horribly [ˈhɒrɪblɪ] adv horriblement; **to behave h.** se conduire horriblement mal

horrid [ˈhɒrɪd] adj (a) (unpleasant) affreux(euse) (b) (unkind) méchant(e) (to avec)

horrific [hɒˈrɪfɪk] adj horrible

horrify [ˈhɒrɪfaɪ] (pt & pp horrified) vt horrifier

horrifying [ˈhɒrɪfaɪɪŋ] adj horrifiant(e)

horror [ˈhɒrə(r)] n horreur f; **to my h.,...** à ma grande horreur,...; **to have a h. of sth** avoir horreur de qch; **it gives me the horrors** ça me donne le frisson; Fam **that child's a little h.** cet enfant est un petit monstre; **h. film** film m d'horreur; Fig **h. story** histoire f épouvantable

horror-stricken [ˈhɒrəstrɪkən], **horror-struck** [ˈhɒrəstrʌk] adj frappé(e) d'horreur

horse [hɔːs] n (a) (animal) cheval m; **h. chestnut** (tree) marronnier m; (fruit) marron m; **h. racing** courses fpl de chevaux; **h. riding** équitation f; **h. trading** (in negotiation) maquignonnage m (b) (in gymnastics) cheval m d'arçons (c) (idioms) **to get on one's high h.** monter sur ses grands chevaux; **to eat like a h.** manger comme quatre; **to hear sth from the h.'s mouth** entendre qch de la bouche de l'intéressé

▸**horse about, horse around** vi chahuter

horseback [ˈhɔːsbæk] n **on h.** à cheval

horsebox [ˈhɔːsbɒks] n van m

horse-drawn [ˈhɔːsdrɔːn] adj tiré(e) par des chevaux

horsefly [ˈhɔːsflaɪ] (pl horseflies) n taon m

horsehair [ˈhɔːsheə(r)] n crin m (de cheval)

horseman [ˈhɔːsmən] n cavalier

horsemanship [ˈhɔːsmənʃɪp] n (skill) talent m de cavalier

horseplay [ˈhɔːspleɪ] n chahut m

horsepower [ˈhɔːspaʊə(r)] n puissance f (en chevaux); (unit) cheval-vapeur m

horseradish [ˈhɔːsrædɪʃ] n raifort m

horseshoe [ˈhɔːsʃuː] n fer m à cheval

horsewhip [ˈhɔːswɪp] **1** n cravache f **2** vt (pt & pp horsewhipped) cravacher

horsewoman [ˈhɔːswʊmən] n cavalière f

hors(e)y [ˈhɔːsɪ] adj (a) (horse-like) chevalin(e) (b) (keen on horses) passionné(e) de chevaux (c) Br Fam (upper-class) = typique de la noblesse de campagne britannique, élégant et féru d'équitation

horticultural [ˌhɔːtɪˈkʌltʃərəl] adj horticole

horticulture [ˈhɔːtɪkʌltʃə(r)] n horticulture f

hose [həʊz] **1** n (pipe) tuyau m **2** vt arroser (au jet d'eau)

▸**hose down** vt sep laver au jet

hosepipe [ˈhəʊzpaɪp] n tuyau m d'arrosage

hosiery [ˈhəʊzɪərɪ] n bonneterie f

hospice [ˈhɒspɪs] n (hospital) = établissement pour malades en phase terminale

hospitable [hɒsˈpɪtəbəl] adj hospitalier(ère)

hospitably [hɒsˈpɪtəblɪ] adv avec hospitalité

hospital [ˈhɒspɪtəl] n hôpital m; **in h.** à l'hôpital; **h. bed/food** lit m/nourriture f d'hôpital; **h. care** soins mpl hospitaliers

hospitality [ˌhɒspɪˈtælɪtɪ] n hospitalité f

hospitalize [ˈhɒspɪtəlaɪz] vt **to be hospitalized** être hospitalisé(e)

host¹ [həʊst] **1** n (a) (at home, party) hôte m; (on TV, radio) animateur(trice) m,f; **h. city/country** ville f/pays m d'accueil; Biol (of parasite) hôte m **2** vt (party) donner, organiser; (TV, radio show) animer

host² n (great number) **a (whole) h. of** (toute) une foule de

host³ n Rel hostie f

hostage [ˈhɒstɪdʒ] n otage m; **to take/hold sb h.** prendre/garder qn en otage; **to offer a h. to fortune** hypothéquer l'avenir

hostel [ˈhɒstəl] n (for homeless people, students) foyer m; (youth hostel) auberge f de jeunesse

hostess [ˈhɒstɪs] n (at home, party) hôtesse f; (on TV, radio) animatrice f; (on plane) hôtesse (de l'air); **h. trolley** desserte f

hostile [ˈhɒstaɪl, Am ˈhɒstəl] adj hostile (to à)

hostility [hɒsˈtɪlɪtɪ] n (pl hostilities) n hostilité f (towards envers); **hostilities** (fighting) hostilités fpl

hot [hɒt] adj (a) (having high temperature) chaud(e); **to get h.** (of person) commencer à avoir chaud; **to be h.** (of person) avoir chaud; (of thing) être chaud(e); **it's h.** (of weather) il fait chaud; Med **h. flushes** bouffées fpl de chaleur; Am **h. tub** Jacuzzi®

(b) (spicy) (food) épicé(e); (pepper, mustard) fort(e)

(c) (close) **you're getting h.** (in guessing game) tu brûles; **to be h. on sb's trail** être aux trousses de qn

(d) Fam (good) **to be h. on sth** (be knowledgeable about) être calé(e) en qch; (attach importance to) être très à cheval sur qch; **it wasn't such a h. idea** l'idée n'était pas si géniale; **how are you? – not so h.** comment ça va? – pas terrible; **to be h. stuff (at)** être un as (en)

(e) Fam (sexy) sexy inv

(f) Fam (stolen) chouré(e)

(g) (idioms) **h. off the press** (of news) de dernière minute; (of book) qui vient juste de paraître; **too h. to handle** (issue) brûlant(e); **to have a h. temper** s'emporter facilement; **to get h. under the collar** se mettre en colère; **h. favourite** (in race) grand favori; **that's h. air** tout ça, c'est du vent; **they're selling like h. cakes** ils se vendent comme des petits pains; **the h. gossip** les derniers potins; **h. line** (telephone number) permanence f téléphonique; **h. news** les toutes dernières nouvelles; *Fam* **h. potato** *(controversial issue)* sujet *m* brûlant; **to be in the h. seat** *(of politician, manager)* avoir toutes les responsabilités; **h. spot** *(trouble spot)* point *m* chaud; *Fam* **to get into h. water** *(in difficult situation)* s'attirer des ennuis

▸**hot up** *(pt & pp hotted)* vi *Fam (of situation, conflict)* s'envenimer; *(of race, debate, contest)* s'animer

hot-air balloon ['hɒteəbə'lu:n] *n* montgolfière f

hotbed ['hɒtbed] *n* **a h. of rebellion/intrigue** un foyer de rébellion/d'intrigue

hot-blooded ['hɒt'blʌdɪd] *adj* au sang chaud, passionné(e)

hotchpotch ['hɒtʃpɒtʃ] *n Fam* mélange *m*

hotdog ['hɒtdɒg] *n* hot dog *m*

hotel [həʊ'tel] *n* hôtel *m*; **h. room/manager** chambre f/gérant *m* d'hôtel; **the h. trade** l'industrie f hôtelière

hotelier [həʊ'teljeɪ] *n* hôtelier(ère) *m,f*

hotfoot ['hɒt'fʊt] *Fam* **1** *adv* en vitesse
2 vt **to h. it** aller à toute vitesse

hothead ['hɒthed] *n* tête f brûlée

hot-headed ['hɒt'hedɪd] *adj* exalté(e)

hothouse ['hɒthaʊs] *n* serre f (chaude)

hotly ['hɒtlɪ] *adv (reply, protest)* vivement; **h. contested** âprement disputé(e)

hotplate ['hɒtpleɪt] *n (on cooker)* plaque f (chauffante); *(for keeping food warm)* chauffe-plat *m*

hotpot ['hɒtpɒt] *n (stew)* ragoût *m*

hots ['hɒts] *npl very Fam* **to have the h. for sb** *(of man)* bander pour qn; *(of woman)* mouiller pour qn

hotshot ['hɒtʃɒt] *n Fam (expert)* as *m*, crack *m*

hot-tempered ['hɒt'tempəd] *adj* colérique, coléreux(euse)

hot-water [hɒt'wɔ:tə(r)] *adj* d'eau chaude; **h. bottle** bouillotte f

hound [haʊnd] **1** *n (dog)* chien *m* de chasse
2 vt *(persecute)* traquer, pourchasser

hour ['aʊə(r)] *n* heure f; **an h. and a half** une heure et demie; **half an h.** une demi-heure; **to pay sb by the h.** payer qn à l'heure; **to take hours over sth** mettre des heures à faire qch; **we've been waiting for hours** ça fait des heures que nous attendons; **to work long hours** faire de longues journées (de travail); **to keep late hours** *(of person)* se coucher tard; **till all hours** jusqu'à très tard; **where were you in my h. of need?** où étais-tu quand j'avais besoin de toi?; **h. hand** *(of watch, clock)* petite aiguille f

hourglass ['aʊəglɑ:s] *n* sablier *m*; **an h. figure** une taille de guêpe

hourly ['aʊəlɪ] **1** *adj* **at h. intervals** toutes les heures; **h. rate** taux *m* horaire
2 *adv (every hour)* toutes les heures; *(at any time)* d'un moment à l'autre

house 1 *n* [haʊs] **(a)** *(dwelling)* maison f; **to stay at sb's h.** loger chez qn; **from h. to h.** de porte à porte; **they keep open h.** leur maison est toujours ouverte; *Fig* **to put one's h. in order** balayer devant sa porte; **to get on like a h. on fire** *(very well)* s'entendre comme larrons en foire; **the H. of Commons/Lords** la Chambre des communes/lords; **the Houses of Parliament** le Parlement; **the H. of Representatives** la Chambre des représentants; *Law* **to be under h. arrest** être assigné(e) à résidence; **h. guest** invité(e) *m,f*; **h. martin** hirondelle f

de fenêtre; **h. painter** peintre *m* en bâtiment; **h. party** partie f de campagne; **h. plant** plante f d'intérieur *ou* d'appartement; **h. spider** araignée f commune
(b) *Com (company)* maison f; **h. style** style *m* de la maison
(c) *(restaurant)* **on the h.** aux frais de la maison; **h. wine** vin *m* de la maison
(d) *Th* **an empty/good h.** une salle vide/pleine
(e) **h. (music)** house music f
(f) *Br Sch* = groupe d'élèves d'une école secondaire qui disputent ensemble des compétitions sportives etc
2 vt [haʊz] *(person)* loger; *(collection, mechanism)* contenir, recevoir

houseboat ['haʊsbəʊt] *n* péniche f aménagée

housebound ['haʊsbaʊnd] *adj* confiné(e) chez soi

housebreaker ['haʊsbreɪkə(r)] *n* cambrioleur(euse) *m,f*

housebreaking ['haʊsbreɪkɪŋ] *n* cambriolage *m*

housecoat ['haʊskəʊt] *n* robe f d'intérieur

housefly ['haʊsflaɪ] *(pl* **houseflies)** *n* mouche f domestique

household ['haʊshəʊld] *n* ménage *m*; **h. appliance** appareil *m* électroménager; **h. chores** tâches *fpl* ménagères; **he's a h. name** tout le monde connaît son nom

householder ['haʊshəʊldə(r)] *n (owner)* propriétaire *mf*; *(tenant)* locataire *mf*

househusband ['haʊs'hazbənd] *n* homme *m* au foyer

housekeeper ['haʊski:pə(r)] *n (private)* gouvernante f; *(in institution)* intendante f

housekeeping ['haʊski:pɪŋ] *n* **h. (money)** argent *m* du ménage

housemaid ['haʊsmeɪd] *n* femme f de chambre; **h.'s knee** *(inflammation)* inflammation f du genou

houseman ['haʊsmən] *n Br Med* interne *m*

housemaster ['haʊsmɑ:stə(r)] *n Br Sch* = dans une école privée, professeur chargé d'un "house"

housemistress ['haʊsmɪstrɪs] *n Br Sch* = dans une école privée, professeur chargée d'un "house"

house-proud ['haʊspraʊd] *adj* **she's very h.** elle prend grand soin de son intérieur

houseroom ['haʊsru:m] *n* **I wouldn't give it h.** *(theory, suggestion)* je ne perdrais pas mon temps avec ça

house-to-house ['haʊstə'haʊs] *adj* **to make a h. search** fouiller chaque maison

house-trained ['haʊstreɪnd] *adj (dog)* propre; *Hum (husband, partner)* bien dressé(e)

house-warming ['haʊswɔ:mɪŋ] *n* **h. (party)** pendaison f de crémaillère; **to have a h. party** pendre la crémaillère

housewife ['haʊswaɪf] *(pl* **housewives** ['haʊswaɪvz]) *n* femme f au foyer

housework ['haʊswɜ:k] *n* ménage *m*

housing ['haʊzɪŋ] *n (accommodation)* logement *m*; *Br* **h. association** = organisme d'aide au logement; *Br* **h. benefit** ≃ allocation f logement; *Br* **h. estate** *(council-owned)* cité f HLM; *(private)* lotissement *m*; **the h. market** le marché de l'immobilier; *Am* **h. project** cité f HLM

hove [həʊv] *pt & pp of* **heave**

hovel ['hɒvəl] *n* taudis *m*

hover ['hɒvə(r)] *vi* **(a)** *(of bird)* planer; *(of helicopter)* effectuer un vol stationnaire **(b)** *(of person)* **to h. near sb** être derrière le dos de qn

hovercraft ['hɒvəkrɑ:ft] *n* hovercraft *m*, aéroglisseur *m*

how [haʊ] *adv* (**a**) (*in what way, by what means*) comment; **h. did they find out?** comment l'ont-ils appris?; **h. do you spell this word?** comment s'écrit ce mot?; *Fam* **h. come?** comment ça se fait?; *Fam* and **h.!** et comment!

(**b**) (*to what extent*) **h. much money?** combien d'argent?; **h. many people?** combien de gens?; **h. old are you?** quel âge as-tu?; **h. big is it?** c'est grand comment?; **h. long have you been here?** depuis combien de temps êtes-vous ici?; **h. often do you see him?** tu le vois tous les combien?; **you know h. difficult it is** tu sais à quel point c'est difficile; **h. useful will it be?** est-ce que ce sera très utile?

(**c**) (*greetings, enquiries after health*) **h. are you?** comment vas-tu?; *Fam* **h. are things?** ça va?; **h.'s business?** comment vont les affaires?

(**d**) (*in exclamations*) que, comme; **h. pretty she is!** qu'elle est jolie!, comme elle est jolie!; **h. disgusting!** c'est vraiment dégoûtant!; **h. true!** c'est bien vrai!; **h. she's changed!** comme elle a changé!

(**e**) (*in suggestions*) **h. about a game of cards?** et si on faisait une partie de cartes?; **h. about going out for a meal?** et si on allait manger quelque part?; **h. about it?** ça te dirait?; **h. about you?** et toi?

however [haʊˈevə(r)] **1** *adv* (**a**) (*in whatever degree*) si... que + *subjunctive*; **h. clever she is** si intelligente qu'elle soit; **h. hard she tried**, she couldn't do it elle avait beau essayer, elle n'y arrivait pas (**b**) (*in whatever way*) **h. you look at it...** de quelque façon qu'on envisage la chose... (**c**) (*in what way*) comment; **h. did she find out?** comment a-t-elle bien pu l'apprendre?

2 *conj* pourtant, cependant; **h., this does not explain why she...** ceci n'explique pourtant pas pourquoi elle...

howl [haʊl] **1** *n* (*of animal, person*) hurlement *m*; **howls of derision** des huées *fpl*

2 *vi* (*of animal, person*) hurler; **to h. with laughter** hurler de rire

▶**howl down** *vt sep* huer

howler ['haʊlə(r)] *n Fam* (*mistake*) bourde *f*

howling ['haʊlɪŋ] **1** *n* (*of wind, wolf*) hurlement *m*; (*of baby*) hurlements

2 *adj* (*wolf*) qui hurle; (*gale, wind*) furieux(euse); *Fam* **it wasn't exactly a h. success** ça n'a pas vraiment eu un succès fou

HP, hp [eɪtʃˈpi:] *n* (*a*) (*abbr* **horsepower**) CV *m* (**b**) (*abbr* **hire purchase**) achat *m* à crédit

HQ [eɪtʃˈkju:] *n* (*abbr* **headquarters**) QG *m*

hr (*abbr* **hour**) h

HRH [eɪtʃɑːˈreɪtʃ] *n Br* (*abbr* **Her/His Royal Highness**) SAR *f*

HRT [eɪtʃɑːˈtiː] *n Med* (*abbr* **hormone replacement therapy**) hormonothérapie *f* de substitution

HTML [eɪtʃtiːemˈel] *n Comptr* (*abbr* **Hyper Text Markup Language**) HTML

HTTP [eɪtʃtiːtiːˈpiː] *n Comptr* (*abbr* **Hyper Text Transfer Protocol**) HTTP

hub [hʌb] *n* (**a**) (*of wheel*) moyeu *m* (**b**) (*of community*) centre *m*

hubbub ['hʌbʌb] *n* brouhaha *m*

hubby ['hʌbɪ] (*pl* **hubbies**) *n Fam* petit mari *m*

hubcap ['hʌbkæp] *n* (*of wheel*) enjoliveur *m*

huddle ['hʌdəl] **1** *n* (*of people*) petit groupe *m*; (*of things*) tas *m*

2 *vi* se blottir

▶**huddle together** *vi* se blottir les uns contre les autres

▶**huddle up** *vi* se blottir les uns contre les autres

Hudson Bay [hʌdsənˈbeɪ] *n* la baie d'Hudson

hue[1] [hjuː] *n* (*colour*) teinte *f*

hue[2] *n* **h. and cry** tollé *m*; **to raise a h. and cry about sth** crier haro sur qch

huff [hʌf] **1** *n Fam* **to be in a h.** faire la tête

2 *vi* **to h. and puff** (*blow*) souffler; *Fig* (*show annoyance*) maugréer

huffy ['hʌfɪ] *adj Fam* (*sulky*) susceptible

hug [hʌg] **1** *n* étreinte *f*; **to give sb a h.** serrer qn (dans ses bras)

2 *vt* (*pt & pp* **hugged**) (**a**) (*embrace*) serrer (dans ses bras) (**b**) *Fig* (*shore, kerb*) serrer; (*ground*) raser

huge [hjuːdʒ] *adj* (*very big*) énorme; (*very tall, long*) immense

hugely ['hjuːdʒlɪ] *adv* énormément, extrêmement

hulk [hʌlk] *n* (**a**) (*of ship*) épave *f* (**b**) (*person*) mastodonte *m*

hulking ['hʌlkɪŋ] *adj Fam* **a h. great man** une armoire à glace

hull [hʌl] **1** *n* (**a**) (*of ship*) coque *f* (**b**) (*of pea*) cosse *f*

2 *vt* (*peas*) écosser

hullabaloo [hʌləbəˈluː] *n* (*pl* **hullabaloos**) *n Fam* raffut *m*

hullo [hʌˈləʊ] = **hello**

hum [hʌm] **1** *n* bourdonnement *m*

2 *vt* (*pt & pp* **hummed**) (*tune*) fredonner

3 *vi* (**a**) (*of person*) fredonner; (*of insect, computer*) bourdonner; (*of engine, fridge*) ronronner; **to h. and haw** hésiter; **to h. with activity** bourdonner d'activité (**b**) *Fam* (*smell*) chlinguer

human ['hjuːmən] **1** *n* (*être m*) humain *m*

2 *adj* humain(e); **h. being** être *m* humain; **h. error** erreur *f* humaine; **h. nature** la nature humaine; **h. resources** ressources *fpl* humaines; **h. rights** droits *mpl* de l'homme

humane [hjuːˈmeɪn] *adj* humain(e)

humanely [hjuːˈmeɪnlɪ] *adv* humainement

humanism ['hjuːmənɪzəm] *n* humanisme *m*

humanistic [hjuːməˈnɪstɪk] *adj* humaniste

humanitarian [hjuːmænɪˈteərɪən] **1** *n* philanthrope *mf*

2 *adj* humanitaire

humanity [hjuːˈmænɪtɪ] *n* humanité *f*; *Univ* **humanities** lettres *fpl*

humanize ['hjuːmənaɪz] *vt* humaniser

humankind [hjuːmənˈkaɪnd] *n* humanité *f*

humanly ['hjuːmənlɪ] *adv* **to do everything h. possible** faire tout ce qui est humainement possible

humble ['hʌmbəl] **1** *adj* (*meek*) humble; (*unpretentious*) modeste; **in my h. opinion** à mon humble avis; *Fig* **to eat h. pie** reconnaître qu'on a tort

2 *vt* humilier

humbling ['hʌmbəlɪŋ] *adj* humiliant(e)

humbly ['hʌmbəlɪ] *adv* (*meekly*) humblement; (*modestly*) modestement

humbug ['hʌmbʌg] *n* (**a**) (*nonsense*) balivernes *fpl* (**b**) (*hypocrite*) charlatan *m* (**c**) *Br* (*sweet*) berlingot *m*

humdinger ['hʌmdɪŋə(r)] *n Fam* **a h. of a film/book** un film/livre extra

humdrum ['hʌmdrʌm] *adj* monotone

humerus ['hjuːmərəs] (*pl* **humeri** ['hjuːməraɪ]) *n Anat* humérus *m*

humid ['hju:mɪd] *adj* humide

humidifier [hju:'mɪdɪfaɪə(r)] *n* humidificateur *m*

humidity [hju:'mɪdɪtɪ] *n* humidité *f*

humiliate [hju:'mɪlɪeɪt] *vt* humilier

humiliating [hju:'mɪlɪeɪtɪŋ] *adj* humiliant(e)

humiliation [hjʊmɪlɪ'eɪʃən] *n* humiliation *f*

humility [hju:'mɪlɪtɪ] *n* humilité *f*

hummingbird ['hʌmɪŋbɜ:d] *n* colibri *m*

humor, humorless *Am* = **humour, humourless**

humorous ['hju:mərəs] *adj (situation)* drôle, comique; *(writer, drawing, remark)* humoristique

humorously ['hju:mərəslɪ] *adv* avec humour

humour, humor *Am* ['hju:mə(r)] 1 *n* (a) *(fun)* humour *m* (b) *Formal (mood)* humeur *f*
  2 *vt (indulge)* faire plaisir à

humourless, Am humorless ['hju:məlɪs] *adj* dépourvu(e) d'humour

hump [hʌmp] 1 *n (on back, road)* bosse *f*
  2 *vt* (a) *Fam (carry)* trimbaler (b) *Vulg (have sex with)* sauter

humpback ['hʌmpbæk] *n* **h. bridge** pont *m* en dos d'âne; **h. whale** baleine *f* à bosse

humus ['hju:məs] *n* humus *m*

hunch [hʌntʃ] 1 *n (intuition)* intuition *f*; **to have a h. that...** avoir l'intuition que...
  2 *vt* **to h. one's shoulders** rentrer les épaules

hunchback ['hʌntʃbæk] *n* bossu(e) *m,f*

hundred ['hʌndrəd] 1 *n* cent *m*; **one or a h.** cent; **a h. and twenty-five pages** cent vingt-cinq pages; **two h. pages** deux cents pages; **I've told you hundreds of times** je te l'ai dit des centaines de fois; **to live to be a h.** vivre jusqu'à cent ans
  2 *adj* cent; **a h. kilometres an hour** cent kilomètres à l'heure; **one or a h. per cent** cent pour cent; **to be a h. per cent certain** être sûr(e) à cent pour cent; **I'm not feeling a h. per cent** je ne me sens pas au mieux de ma forme; **the h. metres** *(in athletics)* le cent mètres

hundredfold ['hʌndrədfəʊld] *adv* **to increase a h.** centupler

hundredth ['hʌndrədθ] 1 *n* (a) *(fraction)* centième *m* (b) *(in series)* centième *mf*
  2 *adj* centième; *Fam* **for the h. time, no!** pour la centième fois, non!; *see also* **eighth**

hundredweight ['hʌndrədweɪt] *n Br* = 50,8 kg, (poids *m* de) 112 livres *fpl*; *Am* = 45,36 kg, (poids de) 100 livres

hung [hʌŋ] 1 *adj* **h. jury/parliament** jury *m*/parlement *m* sans majorité
  2 *pt & pp of* **hang**

Hungarian [hʌŋ'geərɪən] 1 *n* (a) *(person)* Hongrois(e) *m,f* (b) *(language)* hongrois *m*
  2 *adj* hongrois(e)

Hungary ['hʌŋgərɪ] *n* la Hongrie

hunger ['hʌŋgə(r)] *n* faim *f*; *Fig (for power)* soif *f* (**for** de); **h. strike** grève *f* de la faim

▸**hunger after, hunger for** *vt insep Fig* avoir soif de

hungrily ['hʌŋgrɪlɪ] *adv* avec *Fig* avidement

hungry ['hʌŋgrɪ] *adj* **to be h.** avoir faim; **to be h. for knowledge** être avide de connaissances

hunk [hʌŋk] *n* (a) *(of bread, meat)* gros morceau *m* (b) *Fam (attractive man)* beau mec *m*

hunky ['hʌŋkɪ] *adj Fam (man)* bien foutu

hunt [hʌnt] 1 *n (for animals)* chasse *f*; *(for person, work)* recherche *f*

  2 *vt (animal)* chasser; *(criminal)* pourchasser
  3 *vi* (a) *(search)* **to h. for** rechercher (b) *(kill animals)* chasser

▸**hunt down** *vt sep (animal, person)* traquer; *(information)* dénicher

▸**hunt out** *vt sep (find)* *(person)* retrouver; *(thing)* dénicher

hunted ['hʌntɪd] *adj (look)* hagard(e)

hunter ['hʌntə(r)] *n* chasseur *m*

hunting ['hʌntɪŋ] *n* chasse *f*; **to go h.** aller à la chasse; **h. ground** terrain *m* de chasse; **h. lodge** pavillon *m* de chasse

huntsman ['hʌntsmən] *n* chasseur *m*

hurdle ['hɜ:dəl] 1 *n (in race)* haie *f*; *Fig (obstacle)* obstacle *m*
  2 *vi (jump over)* sauter, franchir

hurdler ['hɜ:dlə(r)] *n Sp* coureur(euse) *m,f* de haies

hurdling ['hɜ:dlɪŋ] *n Sp* course *f* de haies

hurl [hɜ:l] 1 *vt* jeter, lancer (**at** sur); *(insults)* lancer (**at** à); **to h. oneself at sb** se jeter ou se ruer sur qn
  2 *vi Fam (vomit)* dégobiller

hurling ['hɜ:lɪŋ] *n* = version irlandaise du hockey sur gazon qui oppose deux équipes de quinze joueurs

hurly-burly ['hɜ:lɪ'bɜ:lɪ] *n Fam* tohu-bohu *m inv*

hurrah [hʊ'rɑ:], **hurray** [hʊ'reɪ] *exclam* hourra!

hurricane ['hʌrɪkən, *Am* 'hʌrɪkeɪn] *n* ouragan *m*; **h. lamp** lampe *f* tempête

hurried ['hʌrɪd] *adj (gesture, conversation, meal)* rapide; *(departure)* précipité(e); *(work)* fait(e) à la hâte; *(decision, choice)* pris(e) à la hâte

hurriedly ['hʌrɪdlɪ] *adv* précipitamment

hurry ['hʌrɪ] 1 *n* hâte *f*; **to be in a h. (to do sth)** être pressé(e) (de faire qch); **to do sth in a h.** faire qch à la hâte; **to leave in a h.** partir à la hâte; **I won't do that again in a h.** je ne suis pas prêt de recommencer; **there's no h.** rien ne presse; **what's the h.?** qu'est-ce qui presse?
  2 *vt (pt & pp hurried) (person)* presser; *(work)* hâter; **he was hurried to hospital** on l'a transporté d'urgence à l'hôpital
  3 *vi* se dépêcher, se presser; **to h. to do sth** se dépêcher *ou* se presser de faire qch; **to h. into/out of a room** se précipiter dans une/hors d'une pièce

▸**hurry along** 1 *vt sep (person)* faire se dépêcher; *(work)* accélérer
  2 *vi* se presser

▸**hurry back** *vi* se dépêcher de revenir

▸**hurry on** 1 *vt sep (person)* faire circuler; *(work)* faire accélérer
  2 *vi (leave)* partir en hâte

▸**hurry up** 1 *vt sep* faire accélérer
  2 *vi* se dépêcher; **h. up!** vite!, dépêche-toi!

hurt [hɜ:t] 1 *n (emotional)* blessure *f*
  2 *adj* blessé(e)
  3 *vt (pt & pp hurt)* (a) *(physically)* faire mal à; *(reputation, chances)* nuire à; **to h. oneself** se faire mal; **to h. one's foot** se faire mal au pied; **to get h.** se blesser; *Fig* **it won't h. him to have to wait** ça ne lui fera pas de mal d'attendre un peu (b) *(emotionally)* faire du mal *ou* de la peine à; **to h. sb's feelings** blesser qn
  4 *vi* (a) *(cause pain)* faire mal; **where does it h.?** où est-ce que ça fait mal?; **my foot hurts** j'ai mal au pied, mon pied me fait mal (b) *(emotionally)* faire mal

hurtful ['hɜ:tfʊl] *adj* blessant(e)

hurtle ['hɜːtəl] vi **to h. along** avancer à toute vitesse; **to h. down the street** dévaler la rue; **to h. towards** foncer sur

husband ['hʌzbənd] 1 n mari m

2 vt Formal (one's resources) ménager

husbandry ['hʌzbəndrɪ] n agriculture f; **animal h.** élevage m

hush [hʌʃ] 1 n (quiet) silence m; **h.!** chut!

2 vt calmer

▸**hush up** vt sep (scandal) étouffer

hushed [hʌʃt] adj (conversation) étouffé(e); (silence) profond(e); **to talk in h. tones** parler à voix basse

hush-hush ['hʌʃhʌʃ] adj Fam top secret inv

husk [hʌsk] 1 n (of seed) enveloppe f; (of pea) cosse f; (of nut) brou m

2 vt (grain) décortiquer

husky¹ ['hʌskɪ] adj (voice) rauque

husky² (pl **huskies**) n (dog) husky m

hussar [hʊ'zɑː(r)] n Mil hussard m

hussy ['hʌsɪ] (pl **hussies**) n Old-fashioned or Hum gourgandine f

hustings ['hʌstɪŋz] npl **on the h.** en campagne

hustle ['hʌsəl] 1 n **h. (and bustle)** effervescence f

2 vt (shove, push) **to h. sb away** emmener qn de force; **I was hustled into a small room** on m'a poussé dans une petite pièce

hustler ['hʌslə(r)] n Am Fam (swindler) arnaqueur(euse) m,f

hut [hʌt] n (shed) cabane f; (dwelling) hutte f

hutch [hʌtʃ] n (for rabbit) clapier m

hyacinth ['haɪəsɪnθ] n jacinthe f

hybrid ['haɪbrɪd] 1 n hybride m

2 adj hybride

hydrangea [haɪ'dreɪndʒə] n hortensia m

hydrant ['haɪdrənt] n prise f d'eau; **fire h.** bouche f d'incendie

hydraulic [haɪ'drɔːlɪk] adj hydraulique; **h. engineering** hydraulique f

hydraulics [haɪ'drɔːlɪks] n hydraulique f

hydrocarbon [haɪdrəʊ'kɑːbən] n hydrocarbure m

hydrochloric acid [haɪdrəʊ'klɒrɪk'æsɪd] n acide m chlorhydrique

hydroelectric [haɪdrəʊɪ'lektrɪk] adj hydroélectrique

hydroelectricity [haɪdrəʊɪlek'trɪsɪtɪ] n hydroélectricité f

hydrofoil ['haɪdrəfɔɪl] n hydrofoil m, hydroptère m

hydrogen ['haɪdrədʒən] n hydrogène m; **h. bomb** bombe f à hydrogène

hydrolysis [haɪ'drɒlɪsɪs] n hydrolyse f

hydrophobia [haɪdrə'fəʊbɪə] n Med (rabies) rage f

hydroplane ['haɪdrəpleɪn] n (boat) hydroglisseur m; (seaplane) hydravion m

hydroxide [haɪ'drɒksaɪd] n hydroxyde m

hyena [haɪ'iːnə] n hyène f

hygiene ['haɪdʒiːn] n hygiène f

hygienic [haɪ'dʒiːnɪk] adj hygiénique

hymen ['haɪmen] n hymen m

hymn [hɪm] n cantique m; **h. book** livre m de cantiques

hymnal ['hɪmnəl] n livre m de cantiques

hype [haɪp] Fam 1 n (publicity) battage m publicitaire

2 vt (publicize) faire du battage publicitaire pour

▸**hype up** vt sep Fam (a) (publicize) faire du battage publicitaire pour (b) **to be hyped up** (excited) être surexcité(e)

hyper ['haɪpə(r)] adj Fam (overexcited) surexcité(e)

hyperactive [haɪpə'ræktɪv] adj hyperactif(ive)

hyperbola [haɪ'pɜːbələ] n Math hyperbole f

hyperbole [haɪ'pɜːbəlɪ] n hyperbole f

hypercritical [haɪpə'krɪtɪkəl] adj hypercritique

hypermarket ['haɪpəmɑːkɪt] n hypermarché m

hypersensitive [haɪpə'sensɪtɪv] adj hypersensible

hypertension [haɪpə'tenʃən] n Med hypertension f

hypertext ['haɪpətekst] n Comptr hypertexte m; **h. link** lien m hypertexte

hyphen ['haɪfən] n trait m d'union

hyphenate ['haɪfəneɪt] vt (word) mettre un trait d'union à; **a hyphenated word** un mot à trait d'union

hypnosis [hɪp'nəʊsɪs] n hypnose f

hypnotic [hɪp'nɒtɪk] adj hypnotique

hypnotism ['hɪpnətɪzəm] n hypnotisme m

hypnotist ['hɪpnətɪst] n hypnotiseur(euse) m,f

hypnotize ['hɪpnətaɪz] vt hypnotiser

hypoallergenic [haɪpəʊælə'dʒenɪk] adj hypoallergénique

hypochondria [haɪpə'kɒndrɪə] n hypocondrie f

hypochondriac [haɪpə'kɒndrɪæk] n hypocondriaque mf

hypocrisy [hɪ'pɒkrɪsɪ] n hypocrisie f

hypocrite ['hɪpəkrɪt] n hypocrite mf

hypocritical [hɪpə'krɪtɪkəl] adj hypocrite

hypodermic [haɪpə'dɜːmɪk] 1 n seringue f hypodermique

2 adj hypodermique

hypotenuse [haɪ'pɒtənjuːz] n Math hypoténuse f

hypothermia [haɪpə'θɜːmɪə] n hypothermie f; **to have h.** faire de l'hypothermie

hypothesis [haɪ'pɒθəsɪs] (pl **hypotheses** [haɪ-'pɒθəsiːz]) n hypothèse f

hypothesize [haɪ'pɒθəsaɪz] 1 vt **to h. that...** émettre l'hypothèse que...

2 vi faire des hypothèses

hypothetical [haɪpə'θetɪkəl] adj hypothétique

hysterectomy [hɪstə'rektəmɪ] (pl **hysterectomies**) n hystérectomie f; **to have a h.** subir une hystérectomie

hysteria [hɪs'tɪərɪə] n (a) (panic) hystérie f (b) (laughter) fou rire m

hysterical [hɪs'terɪkəl] adj (a) (uncontrolled) hystérique; **to be h.** faire une crise de nerfs; **h. laughter** fou rire m (b) (very funny) tordant(e)

hysterically [hɪs'terɪklɪ] adv (a) (uncontrolledly) sans pouvoir se contrôler; **to laugh h.** avoir le fou rire (b) **h. funny** tordant(e)

hysterics [hɪs'terɪks] npl (a) (panic) crise f de nerfs; **to go into** or **have h.** avoir une crise de nerfs (b) (laughter) fou rire m; **to be in h.** avoir le fou rire

I

I¹, i [aɪ] *n (letter)* I, i *m inv*

I² *pron* je; **I'm Scottish** je suis écossais; **I haven't got it!** ce n'est pas moi qui l'ai!

IAEA [aɪeɪiːˈeɪ] *n (abbr International Atomic Energy Agency)* AIEA *f*

IBA [aɪbiːˈeɪ] *n (abbr Independent Broadcasting Authority)* ≃ CSA *m (organisme qui contrôle les chaînes de télévision et de stations de radio privées britanniques)*

Iberian [aɪˈbɪːrɪən] *adj* ibérique; **the I. Peninsula** la péninsule Ibérique

ibex [ˈaɪbeks] *n* bouquetin *m*

ibid [ˈɪbɪd] *adv (abbr ibidem)* ibid

IBM [aɪbiːˈem] *n (abbr intercontinental ballistic missile)* MBI *m*

IBRD [aɪbiːɑːˈdiː] *n (abbr International Bank for Reconstruction and Development)* BIRD *f*

IBS [aɪbiːˈes] *n (abbr irritable bowel syndrome)* colopathie *f* fonctionnelle

ice [aɪs] **1** *n* **(a)** *(frozen water, ice-cream)* glace *f*; *(on road)* verglas *m*; **i. age** période *f* glaciaire; **i. cube** glaçon *m*; **i. floe** banquise *f*; **i. hockey** hockey *m* sur glace; **i. lolly** glace *f* à l'eau; **i. pack** sachet *m* de glace; **i. pick** pic *m* à glace; **i. rink** patinoire *f* **(b)** *(idioms)* **to put a project on i.** geler un projet; **to break the i.** rompre la glace; **to be skating on thin i.** avancer sur un terrain glissant; **that cuts no i. with me** ça ne marche pas avec moi

2 *vt (cake)* glacer

▶**ice over** *vi* geler

▶**ice up** *vi* se givrer

iceberg [ˈaɪsbɜːɡ] *n* iceberg *m*; *Fig* **that's just the tip of the i.** ce n'est que la partie visible de l'iceberg; **i. lettuce** = variété croquante de laitue de serre

icebound [ˈaɪsbaʊnd] *adj* bloqué(e) par les glaces

icebox [ˈaɪsbɒks] *n Br (in fridge)* freezer *m*; *Am (fridge)* réfrigérateur *m*

icebreaker [ˈaɪsbreɪkə(r)] *n (ship)* brise-glace *m inv*; *Fig (at party, in conversation)* **it's a good i.** c'est un bon moyen de briser la glace

icecap [ˈaɪskæp] *n* calotte *f* glaciaire

ice-cold [ˈaɪsˈkəʊld] *adj* glacé(e); *(wind)* glacial(e)

iced [aɪst] *adj* **(a)** *(water)* avec des glaçons **(b)** *(cake)* glacé(e)

Iceland [ˈaɪslənd] *n* l'Islande *f*

Icelander [ˈaɪsləndə(r)] *n* Islandais(e) *m,f*

Icelandic [aɪsˈlændɪk] **1** *n (language)* islandais *m*
2 *adj* islandais(e)

ice-skate [ˈaɪsskeɪt] **1** *n* patin *m* à glace
2 *vi* faire du patin à glace

ice-skating [ˈaɪsskeɪtɪŋ] *n* patinage *m (sur glace)*

icicle [ˈaɪsɪkəl] *n* glaçon *m (qui pend d'une gouttière etc)*

icing [ˈaɪsɪŋ] *n (on cake)* glaçage *m*; *Fig* **the i. on the cake** la cerise sur le gâteau; **i. sugar** sucre *m* glace

icon [ˈaɪkɒn] *n also Fig* icône *f*

iconoclastic [aɪkɒnəʊˈklæstɪk] *adj* iconoclaste

icy [ˈaɪsɪ] *adj* **(a)** *(road)* verglacé(e); *(ground)* gelé(e); *(water, hands)* glacé(e); *(wind)* glacial(e) **(b)** *Fig (expression, reply)* glacial(e)

ID [aɪˈdiː] *n (abbr identification)* papiers *mpl* (d'identité); **ID card** carte *f* d'identité

I'd [aɪd] = **I had, I would**

idea [aɪˈdɪə] *n* **(a)** *(individual notion)* idée *f*; **to put an i. into sb's head** mettre une idée dans la tête de qn; **the very i.!** quelle idée!; *Fam* **what's the big i.?** qu'est-ce qui te prend? **(b)** *(concept)* conception *f*; **to have an i. that...** avoir l'impression que...; **that's not my i. of fun** ce n'est pas vraiment conforme à ce que je m'amuserais; **it's her i. of a joke** elle trouve ça drôle; **I have no i.** je n'ai aucune idée; **I had no i. that...** je ne savais pas que...; **I thought the i. was for them to come here** je croyais qu'il était prévu qu'ils viennent ici; **the general i. is to...** l'idée est de...

ideal [aɪˈdiːəl] **1** *n* idéal *m*
2 *adj* idéal(e) *(for* pour)

idealism [aɪˈdɪəlɪzəm] *n* idéalisme *m*

idealist [aɪˈdɪəlɪst] *n* idéaliste *mf*

idealistic [aɪdɪəˈlɪstɪk] *adj* idéaliste

idealize [aɪˈdɪəlaɪz] *vt* idéaliser

ideally [aɪˈdiːəlɪ] *adv* **(a)** *(extremely well)* idéalement; **they're i. matched** ils vont parfaitement bien ensemble **(b)** *(in an ideal situation)* dans l'idéal

identical [aɪˈdentɪkəl] *adj* identique; **i. twins** *(boys)* vrais jumeaux *mpl*; *(girls)* vraies jumelles *fpl*

identification [aɪdentɪfɪˈkeɪʃən] *n* **(a)** *(of body, criminal)* identification *f* **(b)** *(documents)* papiers *mpl* (d'identité)

identify [aɪˈdentɪfaɪ] *(pt & pp* identified) **1** *vt* **(a)** *(recognize)* identifier **(b)** *(associate)* **to i. sth with sth** identifier qch à qch
2 *vi* s'identifier *(with sb* à qn); **I can't i. with his problems** j'ai du mal à comprendre ses problèmes

identifying mark [aɪˈdentɪfaɪɪŋˈmɑːk] *n* signe *m* particulier

Identikit® [aɪˈdentɪkɪt] *n* **I. (picture)** portrait-robot *m*

identity [aɪˈdentɪtɪ] *(pl* identities) *n* identité *f*; **it was a case of mistaken i.** il y a eu erreur sur la personne; **i. card** carte *f* d'identité; **i. crisis** crise *f* d'identité; **i. parade** séance *f* d'identification

ideological [aɪdɪəˈlɒdʒɪkəl] *adj* idéologique

ideology [aɪdɪˈɒlədʒɪ] *(pl* ideologies) *n* idéologie *f*

idiocy [ˈɪdɪəsɪ] *n* idiotie *f*

idiom ['ɪdɪəm] n (expression) expression f, locution f; (dialect) idiome m

idiomatic [ɪdɪə'mætɪk] adj idiomatique

idiosyncrasy [ɪdɪəʊ'sɪŋkrəsɪ] (pl **idiosyncracies**) n particularité f; (foible) petite manie f

idiosyncratic [ɪdɪəʊsɪŋ'krætɪk] adj particulier(ère)

idiot ['ɪdɪət] n idiot(e) m,f

idiotic [ɪdɪ'ɒtɪk] adj idiot(e)

idle ['aɪdəl] **1** adj (a) (unoccupied) (factory, machine) arrêté(e); (person) désœuvré(e); **an i. moment** un moment libre (b) (lazy) oisif(ive) (c) (futile) (threat, boast) vain(e); (gossip, rumour) pour passer le temps; (curiosity) simple

2 vi (of engine) tourner au ralenti

▶**idle away** vt sep (time) **we idled the afternoon away chatting** nous avons passé l'après-midi à bavarder

idleness ['aɪdəlnɪs] n (a) (inaction) inactivité f (b) (laziness) oisiveté f

idler ['aɪdlə(r)] n (lazy person) paresseux(euse) m,f

idly ['aɪdlɪ] adv (a) (inactively) sans rien faire (b) (casually) négligemment

idol ['aɪdəl] n idole f

idolatry [aɪ'dɒlətrɪ] n idolâtrie f

idolize ['aɪdəlaɪz] vt idolâtrer

idyll ['ɪdɪl] n (situation) situation f idyllique; (place) endroit m idyllique

idyllic [ɪ'dɪlɪk] adj idyllique

ie ['aɪ'iː] (abbr **id est**) c.-à-d.

if [ɪf] **1** conj (a) (conditional) si; **if I were rich...** si j'étais riche...; **if I were you...** si j'étais toi..., à ta place...
(b) (conceding) **the film was good, if rather long** le film était un peu long, mais bien; **if anything it's better** c'est presque mieux
(c) (whether) si; **I asked if it was true** j'ai demandé si c'était vrai
(d) (in phrases) **if not** sinon; **there were hundreds, if not thousands, of people** il y avait des centaines de gens, voire des milliers; **if so** si c'est le cas; **if only I had more money...** si seulement j'avais plus d'argent...; **if and when they arrive...** quand ils arriveront, s'ils arrivent...; **she sees them rarely, if at all** or **if ever** elle ne les voit jamais, ou alors très rarement

2 n **ifs and buts** restrictions fpl; **it's a big if** c'est un grand point d'interrogation

iffy ['ɪfɪ] adj Fam (doubtful) incertain(e); (suspect) louche

igloo ['ɪgluː] (pl **igloos**) n igloo m

ignite [ɪg'naɪt] **1** vt (fire) allumer; (paper) enflammer; Fig (conflict) déclencher

2 vi (of fire) prendre; (of paper) s'enflammer; Fig (of conflict) se déclencher

ignition [ɪg'nɪʃən] n (of car) allumage m; **to switch on/off the i.** mettre/couper le contact; **i. key** clé f de contact

ignoble [ɪg'nəʊbəl] adj ignoble

ignominious [ɪgnə'mɪnɪəs] adj ignominieux(euse)

ignoramus [ɪgnə'reɪməs] n ignorant(e) m,f, ignare mf

ignorance ['ɪgnərəns] n (a) (lack of knowledge) ignorance f; **out of** or **through i.** par ignorance (b) (ill manners) manque m d'éducation

ignorant ['ɪgnərənt] adj (a) (lacking knowledge) (person) ignorant(e); (remark) d'ignorant; **to be i. of sth** ignorer qch (b) (ill-mannered) mal élevé(e)

ignore [ɪg'nɔː(r)] vt ignorer; **just i. him!** ne fais pas attention à lui!

iguana [ɪg'wɑːnə] n iguane m

ilk [ɪlk] n **of that i.** de ce genre

ill¹ [ɪl] **1** npl **ills** maux mpl
2 adj (a) (unwell) malade; **to feel i.** ne pas se sentir bien; **to fall** or **be taken i.** tomber malade (b) (bad, poor) **ill effects** effets mpl néfastes; **i. feeling** animosité f; **i. fortune** malchance f; **to be in i. health** être en mauvaise santé; **i. at ease** mal à l'aise; **of i. repute** mal famé(e); **i. will** malveillance f
3 adv mal; **I can i. afford it** je peux difficilement me le permettre; **to speak/think i. of sb** dire/penser du mal de qn

ill² (abbr **illustration**) ill

I'll [aɪl] = **I will, I shall**

ill-advised ['ɪləd'vaɪzd] adj (person) malavisé(e); (decision comment) peu judicieux(euse); **to be i. to do sth** être malavisé de faire qch

ill-bred ['ɪl'bred] adj mal élevé(e)

ill-concealed ['ɪlkən'siːld] adj mal dissimulé(e)

ill-considered ['ɪlkən'sɪdəd] adj irréfléchi(e)

ill-disposed ['ɪldɪs'pəʊzd] adj **to be i. towards sb/sth** être mal disposé(e) envers qn/qch

illegal [ɪ'liːgəl] adj illégal(e); (immigrant) clandestin(e)

illegality [ɪlɪ'gælɪtɪ] n illégalité f

illegible [ɪ'ledʒəbəl] adj illisible

illegitimate [ɪlɪ'dʒɪtɪmət] adj illégitime

ill-equipped ['ɪlɪ'kwɪpd] adj mal équipé(e); Fig **to be i. to do sth** ne pas être apte à faire qch

ill-fated [ɪl'feɪtd] adj (day, occasion) fatal(e); (person, enterprise) malheureux(euse)

ill-founded ['ɪl'faʊndɪd] adj sans fondement

ill-gotten gains ['ɪlgɒtn'ɡaɪnz] npl biens mpl mal acquis

illiberal [ɪ'lɪbərəl] adj (person) intolérant(e); (measure) restrictif(ive)

illicit [ɪ'lɪsɪt] adj illicite

ill-informed [ɪlɪn'fɔːmd] adj mal informé(e); (idea) inexact(e)

ill-intentioned ['ɪlɪn'tenʃənd] adj malintentionné(e)

illiteracy [ɪ'lɪtərəsɪ] n analphabétisme m

illiterate [ɪ'lɪtərət] **1** n analphabète mf
2 adj analphabète

ill-mannered [ɪl'mænəd] adj grossier(ère)

ill-natured [ɪl'neɪtʃəd] adj désagréable

illness ['ɪlnɪs] n maladie f

illogical [ɪ'lɒdʒɪkəl] adj illogique

ill-suited ['ɪl'suːtɪd] adj inapproprié(e) (**to** à); (person) inapte (**to** à)

ill-tempered ['ɪl'tempəd] adj (person) qui a mauvais caractère; (remark) désagréable

ill-timed ['ɪl'taɪmd] adj inopportun(e)

ill-treat [ɪl'triːt] vt maltraiter

illuminate [ɪ'luːmɪneɪt] vt (a) (light up) (room) éclairer; (building) illuminer (b) (clarify) éclairer

illuminating [ɪ'luːmɪneɪtɪŋ] adj éclairant(e)

illumination [ɪluːmɪ'neɪʃən] n (a) (lighting) éclairage m; **illuminations** (decorative lights) illuminations fpl (b) (clarification) éclaircissements mpl

ill-use 1 *n* ['ɪl'ju:s] mauvais traitement *m*
2 *vt* ['ɪl'ju:z] maltraiter

illusion [ɪ'lu:ʒən] *n* illusion *f*; to be under the i. that... s'imaginer que...; **to be under** *or* **have no illusions about sb/sth** ne se faire aucune illusion sur qn/qch

illusory [ɪ'lu:sərɪ] *adj* illusoire

illustrate ['ɪləstreɪt] *vt* illustrer

illustration [ɪləs'treɪʃən] *n* illustration *f*

illustrator ['ɪləstreɪtə(r)] *n* illustrateur(trice) *m,f*

illustrious [ɪ'lʌstrɪəs] *adj* illustre

ILO [aɪe'ləʊ] *n* (*abbr* **International Labour Organization**) OIT *f*

I'm [aɪm] = **I am**

image ['ɪmɪdʒ] *n* image *f*; to be the i. of sb être le portrait de qn

imagery ['ɪmɪdʒərɪ] *n* imagerie *f*, images *fpl*

imaginary [ɪ'mædʒɪnərɪ] *adj* imaginaire

imagination [ɪmædʒɪ'neɪʃən] *n* imagination *f*; **it's (all in) your i.** tu te fais des idées

imaginative [ɪ'mædʒɪnətɪv] *adj* (*person*) imaginatif(ive); (*excuse, solution*) original(e)

imagine [ɪ'mædʒɪn] *vt* imaginer; to i. doing sth s'imaginer faire qch; **to i. sb doing sth** imaginer qn faisant qch; **I can't why...** je n'arrive pas à comprendre pourquoi...; **you're imagining things** tu te fais des idées; **you must have imagined it** tu as dû rêver

imbalance [ɪm'bæləns] *n* déséquilibre *m*

imbecile ['ɪmbɪsi:l] *n* imbécile *mf*

imbibe [ɪm'baɪb] *vt Formal* (*drink*) absorber; *Fig* (*knowledge, ideas*) absorber, assimiler

imbue [ɪm'bju:] *vt Formal* **to i. sb with sth** imprégner qn de qch; **to be imbued with scorn/fervour** (*of speech, book*) être empreint(e) de mépris/ferveur

IMF [aɪe'mef] *n* (*abbr* **International Monetary Fund**) FMI *m*

imitate ['ɪmɪteɪt] *vt* imiter

imitation [ɪmɪ'teɪʃən] *n* (*action, copy*) imitation *f*; **in i. of** à l'imitation de; **i. jewellery** faux bijoux *mpl*; **i. leather** similicuir *m*, imitation cuir

imitative ['ɪmɪtətɪv] *adj* imitatif(ive)

imitator ['ɪmɪteɪtə(r)] *n* imitateur(trice) *m,f*

immaculate [ɪ'mækjʊlət] *adj* impeccable; *Rel* the I. Conception l'Immaculée Conception *f*

immaterial [ɪmə'tɪərɪəl] *adj* sans importance

immature [ɪmə'tjʊə(r)] *adj* immature

immaturity [ɪmə'tjʊərɪtɪ] *n* immaturité *f*

immeasurable [ɪ'meʒərəbəl] *adj* incommensurable

immediacy [ɪ'mi:dɪəsɪ] *n* immédiateté *f*; (*of danger, disaster*) imminence *f*

immediate [ɪ'mi:dɪət] *adj* (**a**) (*instant*) immédiat(e); (*danger*) imminent(e) (**b**) (*nearest, vicinity*) proche; (*future*) immédiat(e); **the i. family** les proches parents *mpl*

immediately [ɪ'mi:dɪətlɪ] **1** *adv* immédiatement, tout de suite
2 *conj* dès que

immemorial [ɪmɪ'mɔ:rɪəl] *adj* from time i. depuis des temps immémoriaux

immense [ɪ'mens] *adj* immense

immensely [ɪ'menslɪ] *adv* (*interesting, painful*) extrêmement; (*rich*) immensément; (*enjoy oneself*) énormément

immensity [ɪ'mensɪtɪ] *n* immensité *f*; (*of problem, task*) énormité *f*

immerse [ɪ'mɜːs] *vt also Fig* plonger (in dans); to i. oneself in sth se plonger dans qch

immigrant ['ɪmɪgrənt] *n & adj* immigré(e) *m,f*

immigrate ['ɪmɪgreɪt] *vi* immigrer

immigration [ɪmɪ'greɪʃən] *n* immigration *f*; to go through i. passer (à) l'immigration; i. control contrôle *m* de l'immigration; **i. officer** agent *m* des services de l'immigration

imminent ['ɪmɪnənt] *adj* imminent(e)

immobile [ɪ'məʊbaɪl] *adj* immobile

immobilize [ɪ'məʊbɪlaɪz] *vt* immobiliser

immoderate [ɪ'mɒdərət] *adj* immodéré(e)

immodest [ɪ'mɒdɪst] *adj* (*vain*) présomptueux(euse); (*indecent*) impudique

immoral [ɪ'mɒrəl] *adj* immoral(e); **i. earnings** gains *mpl* du proxénétisme

immorality [ɪmə'rælɪtɪ] *n* immoralité *f*

immortal [ɪ'mɔ:təl] **1** *n* immortel(elle) *m,f*
2 *adj* immortel(elle); (*memory*) impérissable

immortality [ɪmɔ:'tælɪtɪ] *n* immortalité *f*

immovable [ɪ'mu:vəbəl] *adj* (*object*) fixe; *Fig* (*person, opposition*) inébranlable

immune [ɪ'mju:n] *adj* (*to disease*) immunisé(e) (to contre); *Fig* (*to criticism*) imperméable (to à); **i. from taxation** exonéré(e) d'impôts; *Med* **i. system** système *m* immunitaire

immunity [ɪ'mju:nɪtɪ] *n* (*to disease*) immunité *f*; (*from taxation*) exonération *f*; *Law* **i. (from prosecution)** immunité

immunization [ɪmjʊnaɪ'zeɪʃən] *n* immunisation *f*

immunize ['ɪmjʊnaɪz] *vt* immuniser (**against** contre)

immutable [ɪ'mju:təbəl] *adj* immuable

imp [ɪmp] *n* (*sprite*) lutin *m*; *Fig* (*mischievous child*) garnement *m*

impact 1 [ɪm'pækt] *n* impact *m*; to make an i. on sb/sth avoir un impact sur qn/qch; on i. au moment de l'impact
2 *vt* [ɪm'pækt] (*collide with*) heurter; (*influence*) avoir un impact sur

impacted [ɪm'pæktɪd] *adj* (*tooth*) inclus(e)

impair [ɪm'peə(r)] *vt* (*sight, hearing*) affaiblir; (*relations, chances*) compromettre

impale [ɪm'peɪl] *vt* empaler (**on** sur)

impart [ɪm'pɑ:t] *vt Formal* (*heat, light, quality*) donner; (*knowledge, news*) transmettre

impartial [ɪm'pɑ:ʃəl] *adj* impartial(e)

impartiality [ɪmpɑ:ʃɪ'ælɪtɪ] *n* impartialité *f*

impassable [ɪm'pɑ:səbəl] *adj* (*river, barrier*) infranchissable; (*road*) impraticable

impasse ['æmpɑ:s] *n* impasse *f*; to have reached an i. être dans une impasse

impassioned [ɪm'pæʃənd] *adj* passionné(e)

impassive [ɪm'pæsɪv] *adj* impassible

impassively [ɪm'pæsɪvlɪ] *adv* impassiblement

impatience [ɪm'peɪʃəns] *n* impatience *f*

impatient [ɪm'peɪʃənt] *adj* impatient(e); to be i. to do sth être impatient de faire qch; to be i. for sth avoir soif de qch; to get i. (with sb) s'impatienter (contre qn)

impatiently [ɪm'peɪʃəntlɪ] *adv* avec impatience

impeach [ɪm'piːtʃ] vt Am Law mettre en accusation (selon la procédure qui vise les hauts fonctionnaires américains)

impeccable [ɪm'pekəbəl] adj impeccable

impede [ɪm'piːd] vt gêner

impediment [ɪm'pedɪmənt] n (a) (obstacle) obstacle m (b) (disability) handicap m

impel [ɪm'pel] (pt & pp impelled) vt (a) (oblige) obliger; (incite) pousser (b) (push) propulser

impending [ɪm'pendɪŋ] adj imminent(e)

impenetrable [ɪm'penɪtrəbəl] adj (defences, mystery) impénétrable; (jargon) incompréhensible

imperative [ɪm'perətɪv] 1 n Gram impératif m; in the i. à l'impératif
2 adj impératif(ive); it is i. that he should come il faut impérativement qu'il vienne

imperceptible [ɪmpə'septɪbəl] adj imperceptible

imperfect [ɪm'pɜːfɪkt] 1 n Gram the i. l'imparfait m; in the i. à l'imparfait
2 adj (not perfect) imparfait(e); Gram de l'imparfait; i. tense imparfait m

imperfection [ɪmpə'fekʃən] n imperfection f

imperial [ɪm'pɪərɪəl] adj (a) (of empire) impérial(e) (b) (weights and measures) = relatif au système de mesure anglo-saxon utilisant les miles, les pints etc

imperialism [ɪm'pɪərɪəlɪzəm] n impérialisme m

imperialist [ɪm'pɪərɪəlɪst] n & adj impérialiste mf

imperil [ɪm'perɪl] (pt & pp imperilled, Am imperiled) vt mettre en péril

imperious [ɪm'pɪərɪəs] adj impérieux(euse)

impermanent [ɪm'pɜːmənənt] adj temporaire

impersonal [ɪm'pɜːsənəl] adj impersonnel(elle)

impersonate [ɪm'pɜːsəneɪt] vt (pretend to be) se faire passer pour; (imitate) imiter

impersonation [ɪmpɜːsə'neɪʃən] n (pretence of being) usurpation f d'identité; (imitation) imitation f

impersonator [ɪm'pɜːsəneɪtə(r)] n (impostor) imposteur m; (mimic) imitateur(trice) m,f

impertinence [ɪm'pɜːtɪnəns] n impertinence f

impertinent [ɪm'pɜːtɪnənt] adj impertinent(e)

imperturbable [ɪmpə'tɜːbəbəl] adj imperturbable

impervious [ɪm'pɜːvɪəs] adj also Fig imperméable (to à)

impetuous [ɪm'petjʊəs] adj impétueux(euse)

impetus ['ɪmpɪtəs] n élan m

▸**impinge on** [ɪm'pɪndʒ] vt insep affecter, avoir un effet sur

impious ['ɪmpɪəs] adj impie

impish ['ɪmpɪʃ] adj espiègle

implacable [ɪm'plækəbəl] adj implacable

implant 1 n ['ɪmplɑːnt] Med implant m
2 vt [ɪm'plɑːnt] (a) Med implanter (b) (opinion, belief) inculquer

implausible [ɪm'plɔːzɪbəl] adj peu plausible, invraisemblable

implement 1 n ['ɪmplɪmənt] instrument m; (for cooking) ustensile m; (for gardening, DIY) outil m
2 vt ['ɪmplɪment] (plan, agreement) mettre en application

implementation [ɪmplɪmen'teɪʃən] n (of plan, agreement) mise f en œuvre, application f

implicate ['ɪmplɪkeɪt] vt impliquer

implication [ɪmplɪ'keɪʃən] n implication f; by i. implicitement

implicit [ɪm'plɪsɪt] adj (a) (implied) implicite; it was i. in her remarks c'était impliqué dans ses remarques (b) (absolute) absolu(e); i. faith confiance f aveugle

implied [ɪm'plaɪd] adj implicite

implore [ɪm'plɔː(r)] vt implorer; to i. sb to do sth implorer qn de faire qch

imploring [ɪm'plɔːrɪŋ] adj implorant(e)

imply [ɪm'plaɪ] (pt & pp implied) vt (a) (insinuate) insinuer, sous-entendre (b) (involve) impliquer; (presuppose) supposer

impolite [ɪmpə'laɪt] adj impoli(e)

impoliteness [ɪmpə'laɪtnɪs] n impolitesse f

imponderable [ɪm'pɒndərəbəl] 1 n impondérable m
2 adj impondérable

import 1 n ['ɪmpɔːt] (a) (item, activity) importation f; i. duty droit m de douane à l'importation (b) Formal (importance) importance f
2 vt [ɪm'pɔːt] also Comptr importer

importance [ɪm'pɔːtəns] n importance f; of the utmost i. de la plus haute importance; it is of no great i. ça n'a pas grande importance; to attach i. to sth attacher de l'importance à qch; to be full of one's own i. être imbu(e) de sa personne

important [ɪm'pɔːtənt] adj important(e); to be i. to sb être important pour qn; to become more i. prendre de l'importance; it's not i. c'est sans importance

importantly [ɪm'pɔːtəntlɪ] adv (speak) d'un air important; but, more i.... mais, plus important...

importation [ɪmpɔː'teɪʃən] n importation f

importer [ɪm'pɔːtə(r)] n importateur(trice) m,f

import-export ['ɪmpɔːt'ekspɔːt] n i. (trade) import-export m

importune [ɪm'pɔːtjuːn] vt Formal importuner

impose [ɪm'pəʊz] 1 vt (silence, one's will, restrictions) imposer (on à); to i. a tax on sth taxer qch; to i. a fine on sb condamner qn à (payer) une amende
2 vi (take advantage) s'imposer

▸**impose on, impose upon** vt insep (take advantage of) abuser de; to i. on or upon sb abuser de la gentillesse de qn

imposing [ɪm'pəʊzɪŋ] adj imposant(e)

imposition [ɪmpə'zɪʃən] n (a) (of tax, fine) imposition f (b) (unfair demand) it was a bit of an i. il y avait de l'abus

impossibility [ɪmpɒsɪ'bɪlɪtɪ] (pl impossibilities) n impossibilité f; it's a physical i. c'est matériellement impossible

impossible [ɪm'pɒsɪbəl] 1 n the i. l'impossible m; to do/achieve the i. faire/réussir l'impossible
2 adj impossible; to make it i. for sb to do sth mettre qn dans l'impossibilité de faire qch

impossibly [ɪm'pɒsɪblɪ] adv (extremely) incroyablement

impostor [ɪm'pɒstə(r)] n imposteur m

impotence ['ɪmpɒtəns] n impuissance f

impotent ['ɪmpɒtənt] adj impuissant(e)

impound [ɪm'paʊnd] vt Law saisir; (car) mettre à la fourrière

impoverish [ɪm'pɒvərɪʃ] vt appauvrir

impoverished [ɪm'pɒvərɪʃd] adj appauvri(e)

impracticable [ɪm'præktɪkəbəl] adj impraticable, irréalisable

impractical [ɪm'præktɪkəl] adj (suggestion) irréaliste; (person) qui manque de sens pratique

imprecise [ɪmprɪˈsaɪs] *adj* imprécis(e)

imprecision [ɪmprɪˈsɪʒən] *n* imprécision *f*

impregnable [ɪmˈpregnəbəl] *adj (fortress)* imprenable; *Fig (argument)* irréfutable, inattaquable

impregnate [ˈɪmpregneɪt] *vt* **(a)** *(fertilize)* féconder **(b)** *(soak)* imprégner **(with de)**

impresario [ɪmprəˈsɑːrɪəʊ] (*pl* **impresarios** or **impresari** [ɪmprəˈsɑːriː]) *n* imprésario *m*

impress [ɪmˈpres] *vt* **(a)** *(make an impression on)* impressionner; **to be impressed with** or **by sb/sth** être impressionné(e) par qn/qch; **to i. sb favourably/ unfavourably** faire une impression favorable/ défavorable à qn/qch; **to i. sth on sb** faire comprendre qch à qn **(c)** *(imprint)* **to i. sth on sth** imprimer qch sur qch

impression [ɪmˈpreʃən] *n* **(a)** *(effect)* impression *f*; **to make an i. on sb** marquer qn; **to make an i. on sth** avoir un impact sur qch; **to make a good/bad i. (on sb)** faire bonne/mauvaise impression (à qn); **to create a false i.** donner une fausse impression; **to be under the i. that...** avoir l'impression que...; **to give the i. that...** donner l'impression que...
(b) *(imprint) (in wax, snow)* empreinte *f*
(c) *(of book)* réimpression *f*
(d) *(imitation)* imitation *f*; **to do impressions** faire des imitations; **to do an i. of sb** imiter qn

impressionable [ɪmˈpreʃənəbəl] *adj* impressionnable

impressionism [ɪmˈpreʃənɪzəm] *n* Art impressionnisme *m*

impressionist [ɪmˈpreʃənɪst] **1** *n* **(a)** Art impressionniste *mf* **(b)** *(mimic)* imitateur(trice) *m,f*
2 *adj* Art impressionniste

impressionistic [ɪmˌpreʃəˈnɪstɪk] *adj* vague

impressive [ɪmˈpresɪv] *adj* impressionnant(e)

imprint¹ *n* [ˈɪmprɪnt] empreinte *f*
2 *vt* [ɪmˈprɪnt] imprimer **(on** sur**); her words are imprinted on my memory** ses mots restent gravés dans ma mémoire

imprison [ɪmˈprɪzən] *vt* emprisonner

imprisonment [ɪmˈprɪzənmənt] *n* emprisonnement *m*

improbability [ɪmprɒbəˈbɪlɪtɪ] (*pl* **improbabilities**) *n* improbabilité *f*

improbable [ɪmˈprɒbəbəl] *adj (unlikely)* improbable; *(unbelievable)* invraisemblable

impromptu [ɪmˈprɒmptjuː] **1** *adj (speech, party)* improvisé(e)
2 *adv (unexpectedly)* à l'improviste; *(ad lib)* au pied levé

improper [ɪmˈprɒpə(r)] *adj* **(a)** *(use, purpose)* mauvais(e); *(behaviour)* déplacé(e); Law **i. practices** pratiques *fpl* malhonnêtes **(b)** *(lewd)* indécent(e)

impropriety [ɪmprəˈpraɪətɪ] *n* inconvenance *f*; *(of language)* impropriété *f*

improve [ɪmˈpruːv] **1** *vt* améliorer; *(invention, technique)* perfectionner; **to i. one's mind** se cultiver
2 *vi* s'améliorer; *(of business)* reprendre

▸**improve on**, **improve upon** *vt insep* améliorer; **to i. on a bid** surenchérir

improved [ɪmˈpruːvd] *adj (system, design)* perfectionné(e)

improvement [ɪmˈpruːvmənt] *n* amélioration *f* (**in** de); *(of invention, technique)* perfectionnement *m*; **to be an i. on** être meilleur(e) que; **there's room for i.** on peut faire

mieux; **to make improvements (to a house)** faire des travaux d'aménagement (dans une maison)

improvident [ɪmˈprɒvɪdənt] *adj* Formal *(person)* imprévoyant(e)

improvisation [ɪmprəvaɪˈzeɪʃən] *n* improvisation *f*

improvise [ˈɪmprəvaɪz] *vt & vi* improviser

imprudent [ɪmˈpruːdənt] *adj* imprudent(e)

impudence [ˈɪmpjʊdəns] *n* impudence *f*, insolence *f*

impudent [ˈɪmpjʊdənt] *adj* impudent(e), insolent(e)

impugn [ɪmˈpjuːn] *vt* Formal mettre en doute

impulse [ˈɪmpʌls] *n* impulsion *f*; **to feel an i. to do sth** avoir une soudaine envie de faire qch; **on i.** sur un coup de tête; **i. buying** achat *m* d'impulsion

impulsive [ɪmˈpʌlsɪv] *adj* impulsif(ive)

impunity [ɪmˈpjuːnɪtɪ] *n* impunité *f*; **with i.** en toute impunité

impure [ɪmˈpjʊə(r)] *adj* impur(e)

impurity [ɪmˈpjʊərɪtɪ] (*pl* **impurities**) *n* impureté *f*

impute [ɪmˈpjuːt] *vt* Formal **to i. sth to sb** imputer *ou* attribuer qch à qn

in [ɪn] **1** *prep* **(a)** *(with place)* dans; **in the garden** dans le jardin; **in France** en France; **in Japan** au Japon; **in the USA** aux États-Unis; **in Paris** à Paris; **in hospital** à l'hôpital; **in town** en ville; **in bed** au lit; **in here** ici; **in there** là
(b) *(with expressions of time)* **in 1927/April** en 1927/avril; **in (the) spring** au printemps; **in (the) summer** en été; **in the afternoon** l'après-midi; **in the 70s** dans les années 70
(c) *(expressing manner)* **in French** en français; **to write in pen** écrire au stylo; **in a loud voice** d'une voix forte; **in this way** ainsi, de cette façon
(d) *(within, during)* **she did it in three hours** elle l'a fait en trois heures; **he'll be here in three hours** il sera ici dans trois heures; **I haven't seen him in years** ça fait des années que je ne l'ai pas vu
(e) *(with situation, arrangement)* **in the rain** sous la pluie; **in the sun** au soleil; **dressed in white** habillé(e) en blanc; **in danger** en danger; **in twos** deux par deux; **in a circle/line** en rond/rang
(f) *(with numbers, quantities, ratios)* **one in ten** un sur dix; **in small/large quantities** en petite/grande quantité; **2 metres in length/height/width** 2 mètres de long/de haut/de large; **she's in her sixties** elle a la soixantaine; **the temperature was in the nineties** ≃ il faisait dans les trente degrés
(g) *(with gerund)* **to have no difficulty in doing sth** ne pas avoir de mal à faire qch; **in saying this...** en disant cela...
(h) *(with field of activity)* **to be in insurance/publishing** être dans les assurances/l'édition
(i) *(idioms)* **I didn't think she had it in her to...** je ne l'aurais pas crue capable de...

2 *adv* **(a)** *(inside)* dedans; **to go in** entrer, rentrer
(b) *(not out)* **is your mother in?** est-ce que ta mère est là?; **to stay in** *(at home)* rester à la maison
(c) **to be in** *(of plane, train)* être arrivé(e)
(d) *(fashionable)* à la mode
(e) **in that...** puisque..., vu que...
(f) *(idioms)* **to have it in for sb** en vouloir à qn; **she's in for a shock/surprise** elle va avoir un choc/une surprise; **to be in on a plan/secret** être dans le coup; **he's in for it** ça va être sa fête

3 *adj* **the in crowd** les branchés *mpl*

4 *n* **the ins and outs** *(of question)* les tenants *mpl* et les aboutissants; *(of plot)* les subtilités *fpl*

inability [mə'bılıtı] *n* incapacité *f* **(to do sth** à faire qch)

inaccessibility [mækses'bılıtı] *n* inaccessibilité *f*

inaccessible [mæk'sesıbəl] *adj* inaccessible **(to** à)

inaccuracy [m'ækjorəsı] *(pl* **inaccuracies)** *n (of estimate, translation, report)* inexactitude *f*; *(of rifle, instrument)* manque *m* de précision

inaccurate [m'ækjorət] *adj (estimate, translation, report)* inexact(e); *(rifle, instrument)* qui manque de précision

inaction [m'ækʃən] *n* inaction *f*

inactive [m'æktıv] *adj* inactif(ive)

inactivity [mæk'tıvıtı] *n* inactivité *f*

inadequacy [m'ædıkwəsı] *(pl* **inadequacies)** *n* insuffisance *f*; **a feeling of i.** un complexe d'infériorité

inadequate [m'ædıkwət] *adj* insuffisant(e); **to feel i.** ne pas se sentir à la hauteur

inadmissible [məd'mısıbəl] *adj Law (evidence)* irrecevable

inadvertent [məd'vɜ:tənt] *adj* involontaire

inadvertently [məd'vɜ:təntlı] *adv* par inadvertance

inadvisable [məd'vaızəbəl] *adj* déconseillé(e)

inalienable [m'eılıənəbəl] *adj Formal* inaliénable

inane [ı'neın] *adj* idiot(e), stupide

inanimate [m'ænımət] *adj* inanimé(e)

inanity [ı'nænıtı] *n* ineptie *f*

inapplicable [m'æplıkəbəl] *adj* inapplicable **(to** à); **delete where i.** *(sign)* rayer la mention inutile

inappropriate [mə'prəoprıət] *adj (behaviour, remark)* déplacé(e); *(dress)* peu approprié(e) **(to** à); *(time)* inopportun(e)

inapt [m'æpt] *adj* peu approprié(e)

inarticulate [mɑ:'tıkjolıt] *adj (sound)* inarticulé(e); **to be i.** *(of person)* avoir du mal à s'exprimer; **to be i. with rage** bégayer de rage

inasmuch as [məz'mʌtʃəz] *conj Formal* dans la mesure où

inattention [mə'tenʃən] *n* inattention *f*

inattentive [mə'tentıv] *adj* inattentif(ive) **(to** à)

inaudible [m'ɔ:dıbəl] *adj* inaudible

inaugural [ı'nɔ:gjorəl] *adj* inaugural(e)

inaugurate [ı'nɔ:gjorert] *vt (building, exhibition)* inaugurer; *(president)* investir

inauguration [mɔ:gjo'reıʃən] *n (of building, exhibition)* inauguration *f*; *(of president)* cérémonie *f* de prise de fonctions

inauspicious [mɔ:s'pıʃəs] *adj* peu propice; **to get off to an i. start** mal commencer

inauthentic [mɔ:'θentık] *adj* inauthentique

in-between [mbı'twi:n] *adj* intermédiaire

inborn ['mbɔ:n] *adj* inné(e)

inbred ['mbred] *adj (person)* de parents consanguins; *(distrust, confidence)* inné(e)

in-built ['mbılt] *adj (trait)* inhérent(e); **his height gives him an i. advantage** sa taille lui donne un avantage dès le départ

Inc [mk] *adj (abbr* **Incorporated**) ≃ SARL

Inca ['mkə] **1** *n* Inca *mf*
2 *adj* inca

incalculable [m'kælkjoləbəl] *adj (consequences, damage)* incalculable; *(help, value)* inestimable

incandescent [mkæn'desənt] *adj* incandescent(e); *Fig* **i. with rage** fou (folle) de rage

incantation [mkæn'teıʃən] *n* incantation *f*

incapable [m'keıpəbəl] *adj* incapable **(of** de); *(through illness)* impotent(e); *(through drink)* ivre mort(e); **to be i. of doing sth** être incapable de faire qch

incapacitate [mkə'pæsıtert] *vt* rendre impotent(e); **to be incapacitated for work** être inapte au travail

incapacity [mkə'pæsıtı] *n* incapacité *f*; **i. to do sth** incapacité à faire qch

incarcerate [m'kɑ:sərert] *vt Formal* incarcérer

incarceration [mkɑ:sə'reıʃən] *n Formal* incarcération *f*

incarnate [m'kɑ:neıt] *adj* incarné(e)

incarnation [mkɑ:'neıʃən] *n* incarnation *f*; **in a previous i.** dans une vie antérieure

incautious [m'kɔ:ʃəs] *adj* imprudent(e)

incendiary [m'sendıərı] **1** *n (pl* **incendiaries)** *(arsonist)* incendiaire *mf*; *(bomb)* bombe *f* incendiaire
2 *adj also Fig* incendiaire

incense¹ ['msens] *n* encens *m*

incense² [m'sens] *vt (anger)* rendre furieux(euse)

incentive [m'sentıv] *n (stimulus)* motivation *f*; *(payment)* prime *f*; **there is no i. for students to work hard** il n'y a rien qui encourage les étudiants à travailler dur; **i. scheme** *(for workers)* système *m* de primes

inception [m'sepʃən] *n* début *m*

incessant [m'sesənt] *adj* incessant(e)

incest ['msest] *n* inceste *m*

incestuous [m'sestjoəs] *adj* incestueux(euse); *Fig (environment, group)* très fermé(e)

inch [mtʃ] *n* **(a)** *(unit of measurement)* = 2,54 cm, pouce *m*; **i. by i.** petit à petit, peu à peu **(b)** *(idioms)* **I know every i. of this town** je connais cette ville comme ma poche; **he's every i. the gentleman** c'est le parfait gentleman; **to miss sth by inches** manquer qch d'un cheveu; **to be within an i. of doing sth** être à deux doigts de faire qch; **she won't give an i.** elle ne cédera pas d'un pouce; **give her an i. and she'll take a mile** tu lui en donnes jusqu'au coude, elle en demande long comme le bras

▸**inch along, inch forward** *vi* avancer tout doucement

incidence ['msıdəns] *n (frequency)* taux *m*; *(of disease)* incidence *f*

incident ['msıdənt] *n* incident *m*; *(in book, film)* scène *f*; **full of i.** riche en incidents

incidental [msı'dentəl] *adj (minor)* accessoire **(to** par rapport à); **i. expenses** faux frais *mpl*; **i. music** *(in film)* musique *f*

incidentally [msı'dentəlı] *adv (by the way)* au fait

incinerate [m'sınərert] *vt* incinérer; *Fig* carboniser

incineration [msınə'reıʃən] *n* incinération *f*

incinerator [m'sınərertə(r)] *n* incinérateur *m*

incipient [m'sıpıənt] *adj Formal* naissant(e)

incision [m'sıʒən] *n* incision *f*

incisive [m'saısıv] *adj* incisif(ive)

incisor [m'saızə(r)] *n* incisive *f*

incite [m'saıt] *vt (violence, unrest)* inciter à; **to i. sb to do sth** inciter qn à faire qch

incitement [m'saıtmənt] *n* incitation *f* **(to** à)

incivility [ɪnsɪ'vɪlɪtɪ] (*pl* **incivilities**) *n Formal* incivilité *f*

inclement [ɪn'klemənt] *adj Formal* (*weather*) inclément(e)

inclination [ɪnklɪ'neɪʃən] *n* (a) (*liking*) inclination *f*, penchant *m* (**for** pour); (*desire*) envie *f*; **to have an i. to do sth** avoir envie de faire qch (b) (*tendency*) tendance *f* (**towards** à); **to have an i. to do sth** avoir tendance à faire qch; **by i.** de *ou* par nature (c) (*angle*) inclinaison *f*

incline 1 *n* ['ɪnklaɪn] (*slope*) pente *f*
2 *vt* [ɪn'klaɪn] (a) (*cause*) **to i. sb to do sth** inciter qn à faire qch (b) (*lean*) incliner; **to i. one's head** incliner la tête (c) **to be inclined to do sth** (*tend*) avoir tendance à faire qch; **I'm inclined to agree** j'aurais tendance à être d'accord
3 *vi* (*lean*) s'incliner; (*tend*) **to i. to** *ou* **towards** pencher pour; **to i. to the belief that...** être porté(e) à croire que...

include [ɪn'kluːd] *vt* inclure, comprendre; (*in letter*) joindre; **the price does not i. accommodation** le logement n'est pas compris dans le prix

including [ɪn'kluːdɪŋ] *prep* y compris; **seven not i. the children** sept sans compter les enfants

inclusion [ɪn'kluːʒən] *n* inclusion *f*

inclusive [ɪn'kluːsɪv] *adj* (*price, sum*) net, nette; **to be i. of** comprendre; **i. of VAT** TVA comprise; **from the 4th to the 12th February i.** du 4 au 12 février inclus

incognito [ɪnkɒg'niːtəʊ] *adv* incognito

incoherence [ɪnkəʊ'hɪərəns] *n* incohérence *f*

incoherent [ɪnkəʊ'hɪərənt] *adj* incohérent(e)

income ['ɪnkʌm] *n* revenu *m*; *Br* **i. support** ≃ RMI *m*; **i. tax** impôt *m* sur le revenu

incoming ['ɪnkʌmɪŋ] *adj* (*government, president*) nouveau(elle); (*plane, train, mail*) à l'arrivée; montant(e); (*phone call*) de l'extérieur; (*tide*) montant(e)

incommensurate [ɪnkə'menʃərɪt] *adj* **to be i. with** ne pas être proportionnel(le) à

incommunicado [ɪnkəmjuːnɪ'kɑːdəʊ] *adj* (*uncontactable*) injoignable

in-company ['ɪnkʌmpənɪ] *adj* **i. training** formation *f* sur le lieu de travail

incomparable [ɪn'kɒmpərəbəl] *adj* incomparable

incompatible [ɪnkəm'pætɪbəl] *adj* incompatible (**with** avec)

incompetence [ɪn'kɒmpɪtəns] *n* incompétence *f*

incompetent [ɪn'kɒmpɪtənt] *adj* incompétent(e)

incomplete [ɪnkəm'pliːt] *adj* (a) (*not whole*) incomplet(ète) (b) (*not finished*) inachevé(e)

incomprehensible [ɪnkɒmprɪ'hensɪbəl] *adj* incompréhensible

incomprehension [ɪnkɒmprɪ'henʃən] *n* incompréhension *f*

inconceivable [ɪnkən'siːvəbəl] *adj* inconcevable

inconclusive [ɪnkən'kluːsɪv] *adj* (*evidence, results*) peu concluant(e); **the meeting/investigation was i.** la réunion/l'enquête n'a abouti à rien

incongruity [ɪnkɒŋ'gruːɪtɪ] (*pl* **incongruities**) *n* incongruité *f*

incongruous [ɪn'kɒŋgrʊəs] *adj* incongru(e)

inconsequential [ɪnkɒnsɪ'kwenʃəl] *adj* insignifiant(e), sans importance

inconsiderate [ɪnkən'sɪdərɪt] *adj* (*person*) sans égards pour les autres; (*remark*) déplacé(e); **it was i. of you not**

to invite her ce n'est pas gentil de ta part de ne pas l'avoir invitée

inconsistency [ɪnkən'sɪstənsɪ] (*pl* **inconsistencies**) *n* (*in argument*) incohérence *f*; (*between reports, descriptions*) contradiction *f*; (*uneven quality*) irrégularité *f*

inconsistent [ɪnkən'sɪstənt] *adj* (*person*) incohérent(e); (*uneven*) irrégulier(ère); **to be i. with** ne pas concorder *ou* cadrer avec

inconsolable [ɪnkən'səʊləbəl] *adj* inconsolable

inconspicuous [ɪnkən'spɪkjʊəs] *adj* qui passe inaperçu(e)

incontestable [ɪnkən'testəbəl] *adj* incontestable

incontinence [ɪn'kɒntɪnəns] *n* incontinence *f*

incontinent [ɪn'kɒntɪnənt] *adj* incontinent(e)

incontrovertible [ɪnkɒntrə'vɜːtɪbəl] *adj Formal* incontestable

inconvenience [ɪnkən'viːnjəns] **1** *n* désagrément *m*; **to be an i. to sb** déranger qn
2 *vt* déranger

inconvenient [ɪnkən'viːnjənt] *adj* (*time*) mauvais(e); (*place, arrangement*) peu commode; **it's a bit i. just now** ça ne tombe pas très bien en ce moment

incorporate [ɪn'kɔːpəreɪt] *vt* incorporer; (*have as quality*) comprendre

incorrect [ɪnkə'rekt] *adj* incorrect(e)

incorrigible [ɪn'kɒrɪdʒɪbəl] *adj* incorrigible

incorruptible [ɪnkə'rʌptɪbəl] *adj* incorruptible

increase 1 *n* ['ɪnkriːs] (*in price, rate, sales*) augmentation *f*, hausse *f* (**in** de); (*in salary*) augmentation (de salaire); (*in pain, population*) accroissement *m* (**in** de); **to be on the i.** être en hausse
2 *vt* [ɪn'kriːs] augmenter; **to i. one's efforts** redoubler d'efforts; **to i. one's speed** accélérer
3 *vi* augmenter; **to i. in price** augmenter; **to i. in value** prendre de la valeur

increasing [ɪn'kriːsɪŋ] *adj* croissant(e)

increasingly [ɪn'kriːsɪŋlɪ] *adv* de plus en plus

incredible [ɪn'kredɪbəl] *adj* (a) (*unbelievable*) incroyable (b) *Fam* (*excellent*) génial(e)

incredibly [ɪn'kredɪblɪ] *adv* (a) (*extremely*) incroyablement; *Fam* **i. good** génial(e) (b) (*unbelievably*) i., **no one was hurt** aussi incroyable que cela puisse paraître, personne n'a été blessé

incredulous [ɪn'kredjʊləs] *adj* incrédule

increment ['ɪnkrɪmənt] *n* augmentation *f*

incriminate [ɪn'krɪmɪneɪt] *vt* incriminer, mettre en cause

incriminating [ɪn'krɪmɪneɪtɪŋ] *adj* compromettant(e)

incubate ['ɪnkjʊbeɪt] *vt* (*of bird*) couver; (*baby*) mettre en couveuse

incubation [ɪnkjʊ'beɪʃən] *n* incubation *f*; *Med* **i. period** (*of infection*) durée *f* d'incubation

incubator ['ɪnkjʊbeɪtə(r)] *n* (*for babies*) couveuse *f*; (*for eggs*) incubateur *m*

inculcate ['ɪnkʌlkeɪt] *vt Formal* **to i. sth in sb, to i. sb with sth** inculquer qch à qn

incumbent [ɪn'kʌmbənt] **1** *n* **the present i. (of the presidency)** le président en exercice
2 *adj* **it is i. on sb to do sth** il incombe *ou* appartient à qn de faire qch

incur [ɪn'kɜː(r)] (*pt & pp* **incurred**) *vt* (*blame, expense*) encourir; (*loss*) subir; (*risk*) courir; (*person's anger*) s'attirer; (*debt*) contracter

incurable [ɪn'kjʊərəbəl] *adj also Fig* incurable

incurious [ɪn'kjʊərɪəs] *adj* peu curieux(euse)

incursion [ɪn'kɜ:ʃən] *n Formal* incursion *f*

indebted [ɪn'detɪd] *adj (financially)* endetté(e); *(for help, advice)* redevable (**to** à); **I am i. to my family for all their support** je suis reconnaissant à ma famille pour son soutien

indebtedness [ɪn'detɪdnɪs] *n (financial)* endettement *m*; *(for help, advice)* dette *f* (**to** envers)

indecency [ɪn'di:sənsɪ] *n* indécence *f*; *Law* attentat *m* à la pudeur

indecent [ɪn'di:sənt] *adj* indécent(e); **to do sth with i. haste** mettre un empressement déplacé à faire qch; *Law* **i. assault** attentat *m* à la pudeur; *Law* **i. exposure** outrage *m* public à la pudeur

indecipherable [ɪndɪ'saɪfərəbəl] *adj* indéchiffrable

indecision [ɪndɪ'sɪʒən] *n* indécision *f*

indecisive [ɪndɪ'saɪsɪv] *adj (person)* indécis(e); *(battle, election)* à l'issue peu claire

indecorous [ɪn'dekərəs] *adj Formal* peu digne

indeed [ɪn'di:d] *adv* (a) *(used with 'very')* vraiment; **very big i.** vraiment très grand; **thank you very much i.** merci mille fois
(b) *(in confirmation)* en effet, effectivement; *(certainly)* certainement
(c) *(what's more)* en fait, et même; **I think so, i. I'm sure of it** je pense que oui, en fait j'en suis sûr
(d) *(expressing ironic surprise)* **have you i.?** vraiment?

indefatigable [ɪndɪ'fætɪgəbəl] *adj Formal* infatigable

indefensible [ɪndɪ'fensɪbəl] *adj (behaviour, attitude)* injustifiable, impardonnable; *(theory)* indéfendable

indefinable [ɪndɪ'faməbəl] *adj* indéfinissable

indefinite [ɪn'defɪnɪt] *adj* (a) *(period of time, number)* indéterminé(e) (b) *(idea, plan)* mal défini(e) (c) *Gram* indéfini(e)

indefinitely [ɪn'defɪnɪtlɪ] *adv* indéfiniment

indelible [ɪn'delɪbəl] *adj also Fig* indélébile

indelicate [ɪn'delɪkət] *adj* indélicat(e)

indemnify [ɪn'demnɪfaɪ] *(pt & pp indemnified)* vt **to i. sb for sth** *(compensate)* indemniser *ou* dédommager qn de qch; **to i. sb against sth** *(give security)* assurer qn contre qch

indemnity [ɪn'demnɪtɪ] *(pl indemnities)* *n (guarantee)* garantie *f*, assurance *f*; *(money)* indemnité *f*, dédommagement *m*

indent *Typ* **1** *n* ['ɪndent] alinéa *m*
2 *vt* [ɪn'dent] mettre en retrait

indentation [ɪnden'teɪʃən] *n (mark)* trace *f*, empreinte *f*; *(in coastline)* découpure *f*; *Typ* alinéa *m*

independence [ɪndɪ'pendəns] *n* indépendance *f* (**from** par rapport à)

independent [ɪndɪ'pendənt] *adj* indépendant(e) (**of** de); *Br* **i. school** école *f* privée

independently [ɪndɪ'pendəntlɪ] *adv* indépendamment; **i. of** indépendamment de; **to live i.** être indépendant(e)

in-depth ['ɪndepθ] *adj* approfondi(e), en profondeur

indescribable [ɪndɪs'kraɪbəbəl] *adj* indescriptible

indestructible [ɪndɪs'trʌktəbəl] *adj* indestructible

indeterminate [ɪndɪ'tɜ:mɪnət] *adj* indéterminé(e)

index ['ɪndeks] *n (of book)* index *m*; *(in library)* fichier *m*; **i. finger** index

2 *vt* (a) *(book)* dresser l'index de (b) *Fin (wages)* indexer (**to** sur)

index-linked ['ɪndeks'lɪŋkt] *adj Fin* indexé(e)

India ['ɪndɪə] *n* l'Inde *f*

Indian ['ɪndɪən] **1** *n* Indien(enne) *m,f*
2 *adj* indien(enne); **I. elephant** éléphant *m* d'Asie; **in I. file** en file indienne; **the I. Ocean** l'océan *m* Indien; **I. summer** été *m* indien

indicate ['ɪndɪkeɪt] **1** *vt* (a) *(point to, show)* indiquer (b) *(intention, opposition, willingness)* signaler
2 *vi (of car driver)* mettre son clignotant

indication [ɪndɪ'keɪʃən] *n (sign)* signe *m*; *(information)* indication *f*; **she gave no i. of her feelings** elle n'a rien laissé voir de ses sentiments; **there is every i. that...**, **all the indications are that...** tout porte à croire que...

indicative [ɪn'dɪkətɪv] **1** *n Gram* indicatif *m*; **in the i.** à l'indicatif
2 *adj* **to be i. of** être symptomatique de

indicator ['ɪndɪkeɪtə(r)] *n* (a) *(sign)* indice *m*; **economic indicators** indicateurs *mpl* économiques (b) *Br (of car)* clignotant *m*

indict [ɪn'daɪt] *vt Law* inculper (**for** de)

indictable [ɪn'daɪtəbəl] *adj Law* **i. offence** délit *m*

indictment [ɪn'daɪtmənt] *n Law* inculpation *f*; *Fig* **it is an i. of our society** c'est une preuve accablante de l'état de notre société

indie ['ɪndɪ] *adj Br (music, band)* indépendant(e)

indifference [ɪn'dɪfərəns] *n* indifférence *f* (**to** pour); **it's a matter of complete i. to me** cela m'est complètement indifférent

indifferent [ɪn'dɪfərənt] *adj* (a) *(not interested)* indifférent(e) (**to** à); **I am** *or* **feel i. about him** il m'est indifférent (b) *(mediocre)* médiocre

indigenous [ɪn'dɪdʒɪnəs] *adj* indigène

indigestible [ɪndɪ'dʒestɪbəl] *adj also Fig* indigeste

indigestion [ɪndɪ'dʒestʃən] *n* troubles *mpl* digestifs; **to have an attack of i.** avoir des troubles digestifs

indignant [ɪn'dɪgnənt] *adj* indigné(e); **to get i. about sth** s'indigner de qch

indignation [ɪndɪg'neɪʃən] *n* indignation *f*

indignity [ɪn'dɪgnɪtɪ] *n* indignité *f*

indigo ['ɪndɪgəʊ] **1** *n* indigo *m*
2 *adj* indigo *inv*

indirect [ɪndɪ'rekt] *adj* indirect(e); *(person)* pas direct(e); *Com* **i. costs** frais *mpl* indirects; *Gram* **i. object** complément *m* d'objet indirect; *Gram* **i. speech** discours *m* indirect

indirectly [ɪndɪ'rektlɪ] *adv* indirectement

indiscernible [ɪndɪ'sɜ:nɪbəl] *adj (reason)* obscur(e); *(difference)* imperceptible

indiscipline [ɪn'dɪsɪplɪn] *n* indiscipline *f*

indiscreet [ɪndɪs'kri:t] *adj* indiscret(ète)

indiscretion [ɪndɪs'kreʃən] *n* indiscrétion *f*

indiscriminate [ɪndɪs'krɪmɪnɪt] *adj* (a) **i. killing** tuerie *f* générale; **to be i. in one's praise** distribuer les compliments à tort et à travers

indispensable [ɪndɪs'pensəbəl] *adj* indispensable

indisposed [ɪndɪs'pəʊzd] *adj Formal (ill)* indisposé(e)

indisputable [ɪndɪs'pju:təbəl] *adj (evidence, argument)* incontestable; *(leader)* incontesté(e)

indissoluble [ɪndɪ'sɒljʊbəl] *adj Formal* indissoluble

indistinct [ɪndɪs'tɪŋkt] *adj* indistinct(e)

indistinguishable [ɪndɪs'tɪŋgwɪʃəbəl] *adj* impossible à distinguer **(from** de)

individual [ɪndɪ'vɪdjʊəl] **1** *n (person)* individu *m*; **a private i.** un particulier
  2 *adj* **(a)** *(of or for one person)* individuel(elle); *(bathroom)* privé(e); **i. tuition** cours *mpl* particuliers **(b)** *(characteristic)* personnel(elle)

individualist [ɪndɪ'vɪdjʊəlɪst] *n* individualiste *mf*

individuality [ɪndɪvɪdjʊ'ælɪtɪ] *n* individualité *f*

individually [ɪndɪ'vɪdjʊəlɪ] *adv* individuellement

indivisible [ɪndɪ'vɪzɪbəl] *adj* indivisible

Indochina [ɪndəʊ'tʃaɪnə] *n* l'Indochine *f*

indoctrinate [ɪn'dɒktrɪneɪt] *vt* endoctriner; **to i. sb with an idea** inculquer une idée à qn

indoctrination [ɪndɒktrɪ'neɪʃən] *n* endoctrinement *m*

indolent ['ɪndələnt] *adj Formal* paresseux(euse)

indomitable [ɪn'dɒmɪtəbəl] *adj* indomptable

Indonesia [ɪndəʊ'niːzɪə] *n* l'Indonésie *f*

Indonesian [ɪndəʊ'niːʒən] **1** *n* **(a)** *(person)* Indonésien(enne) *m,f* **(b)** *(language)* indonésien *m*
  2 *adj* indonésien(enne)

indoor ['ɪndɔː(r)] *adj (swimming pool, tennis court)* couvert(e); *(plant)* d'appartement; *(photography)* d'intérieur; **i. athletics** athlétisme *m* en salle

indoors [ɪn'dɔːz] *adv* à l'intérieur; **to go i.** rentrer; **I've been i. all day** je suis resté enfermé toute la journée

induce [ɪn'djuːs] *vt* **(a)** *(persuade)* **to i. sb to do sth** persuader qn de faire qch **(b)** *(cause)* provoquer **(c)** *Med* **to i. labour** provoquer l'accouchement; **she's had to be induced** il a fallu provoquer l'accouchement

inducement [ɪn'djuːsmənt] *n (incentive)* incitation *f*; *(financial)* avantage *m* financier

induction [ɪn'dʌkʃən] *n* **(a)** *(into job)* période *f* d'introduction; **i. course** stage *m* de formation **(b)** *Med (of labour)* déclenchement *m* **(c)** *Elec* induction *f*

inductive [ɪn'dʌktɪv] *adj (reasoning)* inductif(ive)

indulge [ɪn'dʌldʒ] **1** *vt (child)* gâter; *(passion)* donner libre cours à; **they indulged his every whim** ils lui passaient tous ses caprices; **to i. oneself** se faire plaisir; **go on, i. me!** allez, fais-moi plaisir!
  2 *vi* **to i. in sth** *(as a habit)* se livrer à qch; *(as a treat)* s'offrir qch

indulgence [ɪn'dʌldʒəns] *n* **(a)** *(leniency)* indulgence *f* **(b)** *(treat)* gâterie *f*

indulgent [ɪn'dʌldʒənt] *adj* indulgent(e) **(to** avec)

industrial [ɪn'dʌstrɪəl] *adj* industriel(elle); **i. action** grève *f*; **to take i. action** faire grève; **i. disease** maladie *f* professionnelle; **i. dispute** conflit *m* entre la direction et les travailleurs; **i. espionage** espionnage *m* industriel; *Br* **i. estate** zone *f* industrielle; **i. injury** accident *m* du travail; **i. park** zone *f* industrielle; **i. relations** relations *fpl* entre les travailleurs et le patronat; **the I. Revolution** la révolution industrielle; **i. tribunal** ≃ conseil *m* de prud'hommes; **i. unrest** conflits *mpl* sociaux; **i. waste** déchets *mpl* industriels

industrialist [ɪn'dʌstrɪəlɪst] *n* industriel *m*

industrialize [ɪn'dʌstrɪəlaɪz] *vt* industrialiser

industrious [ɪn'dʌstrɪəs] *adj* travailleur(euse)

industry ['ɪndəstrɪ] *(pl* **industries)** *n* **(a)** *(economic sector)* industrie *f*; **heavy/light i.** l'industrie lourde/légère; **the aircraft/mining i.** l'industrie aéronautique/minière;

the tourist/entertainment i. l'industrie du tourisme/du spectacle **(b)** *(hard work)* assiduité *f*

inebriated [ɪn'iːbrɪeɪtɪd] *adj Formal or Hum* ivre

inedible [ɪn'edɪbəl] *adj (plant, mushroom)* non comestible; *(food)* immangeable

ineffable [ɪn'efəbəl] *adj Formal* ineffable

ineffective [ɪnɪ'fektɪv] *adj* inefficace

ineffectual [ɪnɪ'fektjʊəl] *adj* inefficace

inefficiency [ɪnɪ'fɪʃənsɪ] *n* inefficacité *f*, manque *m* d'efficacité

inefficient [ɪnɪ'fɪʃənt] *adj* inefficace

inelegant [ɪn'elɪgənt] *adj* inélégant(e)

ineligible [ɪn'elɪdʒɪbəl] *adj* **to be i. for sth** ne pas avoir droit à qch; **to be i. to do sth** ne pas avoir le droit de faire qch

inept [ɪn'ept] *adj (person)* incompétent(e); *(remark)* inepte

ineptitude [ɪn'eptɪtjuːd] *n* incompétence *f*

inequality [ɪnɪ'kwɒlɪtɪ] *(pl* **inequalities)** *n* inégalité *f*

inequitable [ɪn'ekwɪtəbəl] *adj Formal* inéquitable

inert [ɪ'nɜːt] *adj* inerte

inertia [ɪ'nɜːʃɪə] *n* inertie *f*

inescapable [ɪnɪ'skeɪpəbəl] *adj (conclusion)* incontournable; *(resemblance)* indéniable; **it's an i. fact that...** il est indéniable que...

inessential [ɪnɪ'senʃəl] *adj* non essentiel(elle)

inestimable [ɪn'estɪməbəl] *adj* inestimable

inevitability [ɪnevɪtə'bɪlɪtɪ] *n* caractère *m* inévitable

inevitable [ɪn'evɪtəbəl] **1** *n* **the i.** l'inévitable *m*
  2 *adj* inévitable; *(conclusion)* incontournable

inevitably [ɪn'evɪtəblɪ] *adv* inévitablement

inexact [ɪnɪg'zækt] *adj (memory, estimate)* imprécis(e)

inexcusable [ɪnɪks'kjuːzəbəl] *adj* inexcusable

inexhaustible [ɪnɪg'zɔːstɪbəl] *adj* inépuisable

inexorable [ɪn'eksərəbəl] *adj* inexorable

inexpensive [ɪnɪks'pensɪv] *adj* pas cher (chère), bon marché *inv*

inexperience [ɪnɪks'pɪərɪəns] *n* inexpérience *f*

inexperienced [ɪnɪks'pɪərɪənst] *adj* inexpérimenté(e); **to be i. in doing sth** ne pas avoir l'habitude de faire qch

inexplicable [ɪnɪks'plɪkəbəl] *adj* inexplicable

inexpressible [ɪnɪks'presɪbəl] *adj* inexprimable

inexpressive [ɪnɪks'presɪv] *adj* inexpressif(ive)

inextricably [ɪneks'trɪkəblɪ] *adv* inextricablement

infallibility [ɪnfælɪ'bɪlɪtɪ] *n* infaillibilité *f*

infallible [ɪn'fælɪbəl] *adj* infaillible

infamous ['ɪnfəməs] *adj (well-known)* tristement célèbre; *(crime, rumour)* infâme

infamy ['ɪnfəmɪ] *n Formal* infamie *f*

infancy ['ɪnfənsɪ] *n (childhood)* petite enfance *f*; *Fig* **when medicine was still in its i.** alors que la médecine en était encore à ses balbutiements

infant ['ɪnfənt] *n* bébé *m*; **i. mortality** mortalité *f* infantile; **i. school** = école primaire pour enfants de 5 à 7 ans

infanticide [ɪn'fæntɪsaɪd] *n* infanticide *m*

infantile ['ɪnfəntaɪl] *adj Pej* infantile, puéril(e)

infantry ['ɪnfəntrɪ] *n* infanterie *f*

infantryman ['ɪnfəntrɪmən] *n* soldat *m* d'infanterie, fantassin *m*

infatuated [ɪnˈfætjʊeɪtɪd] *adj* to be i. with sb être entiché(e) de qn

infatuation [ɪnfætjʊˈeɪʃən] *n (with person)* tocade *f*, passade *f* (with pour)

infect [ɪnˈfekt] *vt (water, food)* contaminer; *(with prejudice)* corrompre; **to become infected** *(of wound)* s'infecter; **to i. sb with sth** transmettre qch à qn; **her enthusiasm infected us all** elle nous a communiqué son enthousiasme

infection [ɪnˈfekʃən] *n* infection *f*

infectious [ɪnˈfekʃəs] *adj* (a) *(disease)* infectieux(euse); *(person)* contagieux(euse) (b) *(laughter, enthusiasm)* communicatif(ive)

infer [ɪnˈfɜː(r)] *(pt & pp inferred) vt* déduire *(from de)*

inference [ˈɪnfərəns] *n* conclusion *f*; **by i.** par déduction

inferior [ɪnˈfɪərɪə(r)] **1** *n* inférieur(e) *m,f*; **to be sb's i.** être inférieur à qn
2 *adj* inférieur(e) *(to à)*

inferiority [ɪnfɪərɪˈɒrɪtɪ] *n* infériorité *f*; **i. complex** complexe *m* d'infériorité

infernal [ɪnˈfɜːnəl] *adj* (a) *(diabolical)* infernal(e), diabolique (b) *Fam (for emphasis)* **it's an i. nuisance** c'est diablement imbêtant; **that i. idiot!** cette espèce d'idiot!

inferno [ɪnˈfɜːnəʊ] *(pl infernos) n (hell)* enfer *m*; *(blaze)* brasier *m*

infertile [ɪnˈfɜːtaɪl] *adj* stérile

infertility [ɪnfəˈtɪlɪtɪ] *n* stérilité *f*

infest [ɪnˈfest] *vt* **to be infested with** *or* **by sth** être infesté(e) de qch

infidelity [ɪnfɪˈdelɪtɪ] *n* infidélité *f*

infighting [ˈɪnfaɪtɪŋ] *n* querelles *fpl* intestines

infiltrate [ˈɪnfɪltreɪt] **1** *vt* infiltrer
2 *vi* s'infiltrer

infiltration [ɪnfɪlˈtreɪʃən] *n* infiltration *f*

infinite [ˈɪnfɪnɪt] **1** *n* **the i.** l'infini *m*
2 *adj* infini(e); *Rel & Hum* **in her i. wisdom** dans son infinie sagesse

infinitely [ˈɪnfɪnɪtlɪ] *adv* infiniment

infinitesimal [ɪnfɪnɪˈtesɪmal] *adj* infinitésimal(e)

infinitive [ɪnˈfɪnɪtɪv] *n Gram* infinitif *m*; **in the i.** à l'infinitif

infinity [ɪnˈfɪnɪtɪ] *n* infinité *f*; *Math* infini *m*

infirm [ɪnˈfɜːm] *adj* infirme

infirmary [ɪnˈfɜːmərɪ] *(pl infirmaries) n (hospital)* hôpital *m*; *(in school, prison)* infirmerie *f*

infirmity [ɪnˈfɜːmɪtɪ] *(pl infirmities) n (weakness)* infirmité *f*

inflame [ɪnˈfleɪm] *vt* (a) *(desire)* allumer; *(curiosity)* attiser; *(crowd)* enflammer (b) **to become inflamed** *(of wound)* s'enflammer

inflammable [ɪnˈflæməbəl] *adj (substance)* inflammable; *Fig (situation)* explosif(ive)

inflammation [ɪnfləˈmeɪʃən] *n* inflammation *f*

inflammatory [ɪnˈflæmətrɪ] *adj* incendiaire

inflatable [ɪnˈfleɪtəbəl] **1** *n (rubber dinghy)* canot *m* pneumatique
2 *adj* gonflable

inflate [ɪnˈfleɪt] **1** *vt* (a) *(tyre, lifejacket)* gonfler (b) *(prices)* faire monter
2 *vi* se gonfler

inflated [ɪnˈfleɪtɪd] *adj (tyre, lifejacket)* gonflé(e); **to have an i. opinion of oneself** avoir une opinion trop flatteuse de soi-même

inflation [ɪnˈfleɪʃən] *n Econ* inflation *f*

inflationary [ɪnˈfleɪʃənrɪ] *adj Econ* inflationniste

inflect [ɪnˈflekt] **1** *vt* (a) *(voice)* moduler (b) *Gram* ajouter la désinence de
2 *vi Gram* prendre une désinence

inflexibility [ɪnfleksɪˈbɪlɪtɪ] *n* rigidité *f*

inflexible [ɪnˈfleksɪbəl] *adj* rigide

inflict [ɪnˈflɪkt] *vt (suffering, punishment, defeat)* infliger *(on à)*; *(damage)* causer *(on à)*; **to i. oneself on sb** infliger sa présence à qn

in-flight [ˈɪnflaɪt] *adj* **i. entertainment** distractions *fpl* en vol; **i. meal** repas *m* servi pendant le vol

influence [ˈɪnflʊəns] **1** *n* influence *f* *(on sur)*; **to be a good/bad i. (on sb)** avoir une bonne/mauvaise influence *(sur qn)*; **to have i. over sb** avoir de l'influence sur qn; **under the i. of drink** sous l'empire de la boisson
2 *vt* influencer; **to be easily influenced** être influençable

influential [ɪnflʊˈenʃəl] *adj* influent(e)

influenza [ɪnflʊˈenzə] *n* grippe *f*

influx [ˈɪnflʌks] *n* afflux *m*

info [ˈɪnfəʊ] *n Fam* renseignements *mpl*

inform [ɪnˈfɔːm] **1** *vt* informer *(of or about* de); **to keep sb informed of sth** tenir qn au courant de qch
2 *vi* **to i. on sb** dénoncer qn

informal [ɪnˈfɔːməl] *adj* (a) *(unaffected)* simple (b) *(casual)* décontracté(e); *(word, language)* familier(ère) (c) *(unofficial) (meeting, talks)* officieux(euse)

informality [ɪnfɔːˈmælɪtɪ] *n* (a) *(unaffectedness)* simplicité *f* (b) *(casualness)* décontraction *f* (c) *(of talks)* caractère *m* officieux

informally [ɪnˈfɔːməlɪ] *adv* (a) *(unaffectedly)* avec simplicité (b) *(casually)* avec décontraction (c) *(hold talks)* officieusement

informant [ɪnˈfɔːmənt] *n* informateur(trice) *m,f*

information [ɪnfəˈmeɪʃən] *n* (a) *(news, facts)* renseignements *mpl*; **a piece of i.** un renseignement; **for further i.** pour de plus amples renseignements; **i. bureau** bureau *m* des renseignements (b) *Comptr* **i. processing** traitement *m* de l'information; **i. retrieval** recherche *f* documentaire; **i. science** informatique *f*; **the i. superhighway** l'autoroute *f* de l'information; **i. technology** informatique

informative [ɪnˈfɔːmətɪv] *adj* instructif(ive); **she was very i.** elle nous a appris beaucoup de choses

informed [ɪnˈfɔːmd] *adj (person)* bien renseigné(e), bien informé(e); **my i. guess is that...** en me basant sur ce que je sais, je dirais que...; **an i. decision** une décision prise en connaissance de cause

informer [ɪnˈfɔːmə(r)] *n* indicateur *m*

infra dig [ˈɪnfrəˈdɪg] *adj Fam* rabaissant(e), dégradant(e)

infrared [ɪnfrəˈred] *adj* infrarouge

infrastructure [ˈɪnfrəstrʌktʃə(r)] *n* infrastructure *f*

infrequent [ɪnˈfriːkwənt] *adj* rare, peu fréquent(e)

infringe [ɪnˈfrɪndʒ] *vt (rule, law)* enfreindre; *(right)* empiéter sur
▸**infringe on** *vt insep* empiéter sur

infringement [ɪnˈfrɪndʒmənt] *n (of rule, law)* infraction *f* *(of* à); *(of right)* atteinte *f* *(of* à)

infuriate [ɪnˈfjuːrɪeɪt] vt exaspérer

infuriating [ɪnˈfjuːrɪeɪtɪŋ] adj exaspérant(e)

infuse [ɪnˈfjuːz] 1 vt (a) (energy, hope) insuffler (into à) (b) (tea) faire infuser

2 vi (of tea) infuser

infusion [ɪnˈfjuːʒən] n (drink) infusion f

ingenious [ɪnˈdʒiːnɪəs] adj ingénieux(euse)

ingenuity [ɪndʒɪˈnjuːɪtɪ] n ingéniosité f

ingenuous [ɪnˈdʒenuəs] adj (naive) ingénu(e); (frank) franc (franche)

inglorious [ɪnˈɡlɔːrɪəs] adj déshonorant(e), honteux(euse)

ingot [ˈɪŋɡət] n lingot m

ingrained [ɪnˈɡreɪnd] adj (prejudice, habit) enraciné(e); i. dirt crasse f

ingratiate [ɪnˈɡreɪʃɪeɪt] vt to i. oneself (with sb) se faire bien voir (de ou par qn)

ingratiating [ɪnˈɡreɪʃɪeɪtɪŋ] adj doucereux(euse)

ingratitude [ɪnˈɡrætɪtjuːd] n ingratitude f

ingredient [ɪnˈɡriːdɪənt] n also Fig ingrédient m; Fig the missing i. l'élément m manquant

ingrowing [ˈɪnɡrəʊɪŋ], **ingrown** [ˈɪnɡrəʊn] adj i. toenail ongle m incarné

inhabit [ɪnˈhæbɪt] vt habiter

inhabitable [ɪnˈhæbɪtəbəl] adj habitable

inhabitant [ɪnˈhæbɪtənt] n habitant(e) m,f

inhabited [ɪnˈhæbɪtɪd] adj habité(e) (by par)

inhale [ɪnˈheɪl] 1 vt (gas, fumes) inhaler; (cigarette smoke) avaler

2 vi inspirer; (in smoking) avaler la fumée

inhaler [ɪnˈheɪlə(r)] n (for asthmatics) inhalateur m

inherent [ɪnˈheərənt] adj inhérent(e) (in à)

inherit [ɪnˈherɪt] vt hériter (from de)

inheritance [ɪnˈherɪtəns] n héritage m; i. tax droits mpl de succession

inhibit [ɪnˈhɪbɪt] vt (progress, growth) entraver; (person) inhiber

inhibited [ɪnˈhɪbɪtɪd] adj (person) inhibé(e)

inhibition [ɪnɪˈbɪʃən] n inhibition f; to have no inhibitions about doing sth n'avoir aucune honte à faire qch

inhospitable [ɪnhɒˈspɪtəbəl] adj inhospitalier(ère)

in-house [ˈɪnˈhaʊs] 1 adj (training) interne; (staff) qui travaille sur place

2 adv sur place

inhuman [ɪnˈhjuːmən] adj inhumain(e)

inhumane [ɪnhjuːˈmeɪn] adj inhumain(e)

inhumanity [ɪnhjuːˈmænɪtɪ] n inhumanité f, cruauté f

inimical [ɪˈnɪmɪkəl] adj (people) ennemi(e), hostile; (conditions) contraire (to à)

inimitable [ɪˈnɪmɪtəbəl] adj inimitable

iniquitous [ɪˈnɪkwɪtəs] adj inique

iniquity [ɪˈnɪkwɪtɪ] n (pl iniquities) n iniquité f

initial [ɪˈnɪʃəl] 1 n initiale f; initials (signature) paraphe m

2 adj initial(e), premier(ère); in the i. stages of sth au stade initial de qch

3 vt (pt & pp initialled, Am initialed) parapher

initially [ɪˈnɪʃəlɪ] adv au début

initiate [ɪˈnɪʃɪeɪt] vt (a) (negotiations) amorcer; (rumour, project) lancer; Law to i. proceedings (against sb)

entamer des poursuites (contre qn) (b) to i. sb into a secret society/gang faire subir à qn les épreuves initiatiques d'une société secrète/d'un gang

initiation [ɪnɪʃɪˈeɪʃən] n (a) (beginning) commencement m, début(s) m(pl) (b) (induction) initiation f; i. ceremony rite m d'initiation

initiative [ɪˈnɪʃətɪv] n initiative f; to take the i. (in doing sth) prendre l'initiative (de faire qch); to use one's i. faire preuve d'initiative; on one's own i. de sa propre initiative

inject [ɪnˈdʒekt] vt (drug, money) injecter; (enthusiasm) communiquer; to i. new life into sth donner un nouvel essor à qch

injection [ɪnˈdʒekʃən] n injection f, piqûre f; Fig polio i. vaccin m contre la polio; to give sb an i. faire une piqûre à qn

injudicious [ɪndʒuːˈdɪʃəs] adj peu judicieux(euse), malavisé(e)

injunction [ɪnˈdʒʌŋkʃən] n Law arrêt m, jugement m

injure [ˈɪndʒə(r)] vt (person) blesser; (reputation, interests) nuire à; to i. oneself se blesser; to i. one's leg se blesser à la jambe; her pride is injured elle est blessée dans son orgueil

injured [ˈɪndʒəd] 1 n the i. les blessés mpl

2 adj blessé(e); (look, voice) offensé(e); Law the i. party la partie lésée

injurious [ɪnˈdʒʊərɪəs] adj nuisible, préjudiciable (to à)

injury [ˈɪndʒərɪ] n (pl injuries) n (physical) blessure f; to do oneself an i. se blesser; i. time (in football match) arrêts mpl de jeu

injustice [ɪnˈdʒʌstɪs] n injustice f; to do sb an i. être injuste envers qn

ink [ɪŋk] n encre f; i. pad tampon m (encreur)

ink-jet [ˈɪŋkdʒet] adj Comptr i. (printer) imprimante f à jet d'encre

inkling [ˈɪŋklɪŋ] n soupçon m; to have an i. of sth se douter de qch

inkwell [ˈɪŋkwel] n encrier m (de pupitre)

inky [ˈɪŋkɪ] adj (a) (stained with ink) taché(e) d'encre (b) i. (black) noir(e) comme (de) l'encre

inlaid [ɪnˈleɪd] adj (with wood) marqueté(e); (with jewels) incrusté(e) (with de)

inland 1 adj [ˈɪnlənd] intérieur(e); the I. Revenue ≃ le fisc

2 adv [ɪnˈlænd] (travel) vers l'intérieur; (live) dans les terres

in-laws [ˈɪnlɔːz] npl (spouse's parents) beaux-parents mpl; (spouse's family) belle-famille f

inlet [ˈɪnlet] n (a) (of sea) petit bras m de mer (b) (of pipe, machine) (orifice m d') entrée f

inmate [ˈɪnmeɪt] n (in prison) détenu(e) m,f; (in mental hospital) interné(e) m,f

inn [ɪn] n auberge f

innards [ˈɪnədz] npl entrailles fpl

innate [ɪˈneɪt] adj inné(e)

inner [ˈɪnə(r)] adj (a) (chamber, lining) intérieur(e); i. circle (of party, association) initiés mpl; i. city quartiers mpl déshérités du centre-ville; i. ear oreille f interne; i. tube chambre f à air (b) (thought, feeling) intime; (peace) intérieur(e)

innermost [ˈɪnəməʊst] adj (part) le (la) plus profond(e); (thoughts, feelings) le (la) plus secret(ète)

innings ['ɪnɪŋz] *n (in cricket)* tournée *f*, tour *m* de batte; *Fig* **she had a good i.** elle a bien profité de la vie

innkeeper ['ɪnkiːpə(r)] *n* aubergiste *mf*

innocence ['ɪnəsəns] *n* innocence *f*

innocent ['ɪnəsənt] **1** *n* innocent(e) *m,f*; **to act the i.** faire l'innocent

2 *adj* innocent(e)

innocuous [ɪ'nɒkjʊəs] *adj* inoffensif(ive); *(remark)* anodin(e)

innovate ['ɪnəveɪt] *vi* innover

innovation [ɪnə'veɪʃən] *n* innovation *f*

innovative ['ɪnəveɪtɪv] *adj* (in)novateur(trice)

innovator ['ɪnəveɪtə(r)] *n* (in)novateur(trice) *m,f*

innuendo [ɪnjʊ'endəʊ] *(pl* **innuendos** *or* **innuendoes)** *n (insinuation)* insinuation *f*; *(in jokes)* allusion *f* grivoise

innumerable [ɪ'njuːmərəbəl] *adj* innombrable

inoculate [ɪ'nɒkjʊleɪt] *vt* vacciner; **to i. sb with sth** inoculer qch à qn; **to i. sb against sth** vacciner qn contre qch

inoculation [ɪnɒkjʊ'leɪʃən] *n* inoculation *f*

inoffensive [ɪnə'fensɪv] *adj (animal, person)* inoffensif(ive); *(remark, humour)* qui n'a rien d'offensant; *(odour)* qui n'a rien de désagréable

inoperable [ɪn'ɒpərəbəl] *adj* inopérable

inoperative [ɪn'ɒpərətɪv] *adj (rule)* inopérant(e); *(machine)* arrêté(e)

inopportune [ɪn'ɒpətjuːn] *adj* inopportun(e)

inordinate [ɪn'ɔːdɪnət] *adj* démesuré(e)

inorganic [ɪnɔː'gænɪk] *adj* inorganique

in-patient ['ɪnpeɪʃənt] *n* patient(e) *m,f* hospitalisé(e)

input ['ɪnpʊt] **1** *n* **(a)** *Elec* puissance *f* d'alimentation; *(terminal)* entrée *f*; *Comptr* entrée *f*, introduction *f* **(b)** *(contribution)* contribution *f*

2 *vt (pt & pp* **input)** *Comptr (data)* entrer

inquest ['ɪnkwest] *n Law* enquête *f*; *Fig (in politics, business)* analyse *f*; **to hold an i.** *Law (of coroner)* mener une enquête **(into** sur); *(in politics, business)* faire une analyse **(into** de)

inquire [ɪn'kwaɪə(r)] **1** *vt* demander

2 *vi* se renseigner *(about* sur); **i. within** *(sign)* s'adresser ici

▸**inquire after** *vt insep* demander des nouvelles de

▸**inquire into** *vt insep* faire des recherches sur

inquiring [ɪn'kwaɪrɪŋ] *adj (mind)* curieux(euse); *(look, voice)* interrogateur(trice)

inquiry [ɪn'kwaɪrɪ] *(pl* **inquiries)** *n* **(a)** *(official investigation)* enquête *f*; **to hold an i. (into** sth**)** faire une enquête (sur qch) **(b)** *(request for information)* demande *f* de renseignements; **to make inquiries (about** sth**)** se renseigner (sur qch); **i. desk** bureau *m* de(s) renseignements

Inquisition [ɪnkwɪ'zɪʃən] *n* **the I.** l'Inquisition *f*

inquisitive [ɪn'kwɪzɪtɪv] *adj (person, mind)* curieux(euse); *(look)* interrogateur(trice)

inroads ['ɪnrəʊdz] *npl* **to make i. into** *(capital, savings)* entamer; *(market)* pénétrer

insane [ɪn'seɪn] *adj (person)* dément(e); *Fam (desire, scheme)* fou (folle); **to go i.** devenir fou, perdre la raison; **to be i. with grief/jealousy** être fou de douleur/jalousie

insanely [ɪn'seɪnlɪ] *adv* comme un fou (une folle); **i. jealous** d'une jalousie maladive

insanitary [ɪn'sænɪtrɪ] *adj* insalubre, malsain(e)

insanity [ɪn'sænɪtɪ] *n (of person)* démence *f*; *Fam (of desire, scheme)* folie *f*

insatiable [ɪn'seɪʃəbəl] *adj* insatiable

inscribe [ɪn'skraɪb] *vt (write)* écrire; *(engrave)* inscrire, graver

inscription [ɪn'skrɪpʃən] *n (on stone, coin)* inscription *f*; *(in book)* dédicace *f*

inscrutable [ɪn'skruːtəbəl] *adj (look, face)* impénétrable; *(remark)* énigmatique

insect ['ɪnsekt] *n* insecte *m*; **i. bite** piqûre *f* d'insecte; **i. repellent** anti-moustiques *m inv*

insecticide [ɪn'sektɪsaɪd] *n* insecticide *m*

insecure [ɪnsɪ'kjʊə(r)] *adj* **(a)** *(person)* angoissé(e) **(b)** *(government)* fragile; *(job, future)* précaire; **to be financially i.** être dans une situation financière précaire

insecurity [ɪnsɪ'kjʊərɪtɪ] *n* **(a)** *(of person)* angoisse *f* **(b)** *(of job, future)* précarité *f*

insemination [ɪnsemɪ'neɪʃən] *n* insémination *f*

insensible [ɪn'sensɪbəl] *adj (unaware, unconscious)* inconscient(e) *(to* de)

insensitive [ɪn'sensɪtɪv] *adj (person)* insensible *(to* à); *(remark)* indélicat(e)

insensitivity [ɪnsensɪ'tɪvɪtɪ] *n* insensibilité *f*

inseparable [ɪn'sepərəbəl] *adj* inséparable

insert 1 *n* ['ɪnsɜːt] *(in magazine)* encart *m*

2 *vt* [ɪn'sɜːt] *(key, finger)* introduire **(into** dans); *(clause)* insérer **(in** dans); *(advertisement)* mettre **(in** dans)

insertion [ɪn'sɜːʃən] *n* insertion *f*

inset ['ɪnset] *n (in map, picture)* médaillon *m*

inshore [ɪn'ʃɔː(r)] **1** *adj (navigation, fishing)* côtier(ère)

2 *adv (be situated)* sur la côte; *(travel)* vers la côte, vers les terres

inside 1 *n* [ɪn'saɪd] **(a)** *(of house)* intérieur *m*; **on/from the i.** à/de l'intérieur; **to overtake on the i.** *(in Britain)* doubler par la gauche; *(in Europe, USA)* doubler par la droite **(b)** *Fam* **insides** *(internal organs)* entrailles *fpl* **(c)** *(in phrases)* **i. out** *(clothes)* à l'envers; *Fig* **to know sth i. out** connaître qch comme sa poche

2 *vi* ['ɪnsaɪd] intérieur(e); **to have i. information** avoir des informations de première main; *Fam* **it's an i. job** c'est quelqu'un de la maison qui a fait ça; **i. lane** *(in Britain)* voie *f* de gauche; *(in Europe, USA)* voie *f* de droite; **i. left** *(in football)* intérieur *m* gauche; **to know the i. story** connaître les dessous de l'affaire

3 *adv* [ɪn'saɪd] **(a)** *(indoors)* à l'intérieur; **come i.!** entrez! **(b)** *(within oneself)* en son for intérieur **(c)** *Fam (in prison)* en taule

4 *prep* [ɪn'saɪd] **(a)** *(place)* à l'intérieur de, dans **(b)** *(with time)* **i. (of)** a week/an hour** en moins d'une semaine/heure

insider [ɪn'saɪdə(r)] *n* initié(e) *m,f*; *Fin* **i. dealing, i. trading** délit *m* d'initié

insidious [ɪn'sɪdɪəs] *adj* insidieux(euse)

insight ['ɪnsaɪt] *n* **(a)** *(perspicacity)* perspicacité *f* **(b)** *(understanding)* aperçu *m*; **to get an i. into sth** avoir un aperçu de qch

insignia [ɪn'sɪgnɪə] *n* insigne *m*

insignificance [ɪnsɪg'nɪfɪkəns] *n* insignifiance *f*; **to pale into i. (beside** sth**)** sembler totalement insignifiant(e) (à côté de qch)

insignificant [ɪnsɪg'nɪfɪkənt] *adj* insignifiant(e)

insincere [ɪnsɪn'sɪə(r)] *adj* peu sincère, faux (fausse)

insincerity [ɪnsɪn'serɪtɪ] *n* manque *m* de sincérité, fausseté *f*

insinuate [ɪn'sɪnjʊeɪt] *vt* insinuer; **to i. oneself into sb's favour** s'insinuer dans les bonnes grâces de qn

insinuation [ɪnsɪnjʊ'eɪʃən] *n* insinuation *f*

insipid [ɪn'sɪpɪd] *adj* insipide

insist [ɪn'sɪst] **1** *vt* **(a)** *(maintain)* **to i. that...** soutenir *ou* maintenir que... **(b)** *(demand)* **to i. (that) sb does sth** insister pour que qn fasse qch
2 *vi* insister; **to i. on sth** exiger qch; **to i. on doing sth** tenir à faire qch

insistence [ɪn'sɪstəns] *n* insistance *f* (**on** à); **I stayed at her i.** elle insista, et je restai

insistent [ɪn'sɪstənt] *adj* (*person, demand*) pressant(e); **to be i.** se montrer pressant; **to be i. about sth** insister sur qch

insofar as [ɪnsəʊ'fɑːrəz] *adv* dans la mesure où

insole [ɪnsəʊl] *n* semelle *f* intérieure

insolence ['ɪnsələns] *n* insolence *f* (**to** envers)

insolent ['ɪnsələnt] *adj* insolent(e) (**to** envers)

insoluble [ɪn'sɒljʊbəl] *adj* insoluble

insolvency [ɪn'sɒlvənsɪ] *n Fin* (*of person*) insolvabilité *f*; (*of company*) faillite *f*

insolvent [ɪn'sɒlvənt] *adj Fin* (*person*) insolvable; (*company*) en faillite

insomnia [ɪn'sɒmnɪə] *n* insomnie *f*

insomniac [ɪn'sɒmnɪæk] *n* insomniaque *mf*

inspect [ɪn'spekt] *vt* (*passport, luggage, picture*) examiner; (*school, factory*) inspecter; (*troops*) passer en revue

inspection [ɪn'spekʃən] *n* (*of passport, luggage, picture*) examen *m*; (*of school, factory*) visite *f* d'inspection *f*; (*of troops*) revue *f*; **on closer i.** en y regardant de plus près

inspector [ɪn'spektə(r)] *n* (*of schools, factories*) inspecteur *m*(trice) *f*; *Br* (*on train, bus*) contrôleur(euse) *m,f*; *Br* (**police**) **i.** inspecteur *m* de police

inspiration [ɪnspɪ'reɪʃən] *n* inspiration *f*; **to be an i. to sb** inspirer qn

inspire [ɪn'spaɪə(r)] *vt* inspirer; **to i. sb to do sth** pousser qn à faire qch; **to i. sth in sb, to i. sb with sth** inspirer qch à qn

inspired [ɪn'spaɪəd] *adj* inspiré(e)

inspiring [ɪn'spaɪərɪŋ] *adj* exaltant(e)

instability [ɪnstə'bɪlɪtɪ] *n* instabilité *f*

install, *Am* **instal** [ɪn'stɔːl] *vt* installer; **to i. sb in a post** mettre qn à un poste; **to i. oneself in an armchair** s'installer dans un fauteuil

installation [ɪnstə'leɪʃən] *n* installation *f*

instalment, *Am* **installment** [ɪn'stɔːlmənt] *n* **(a)** (*part payment*) versement *m*; **to pay by instalments** payer par versements échelonnés **(b)** (*of radio, TV programme*) épisode *m*

instance ['ɪnstəns] *n* (*example*) cas *m*; **for i.** par exemple; **in the first i.** en (tout) premier lieu

instant ['ɪnstənt] **1** *n* (*moment*) instant *m*, moment *m*; **this i.** immédiatement; **not an i. too soon** juste à temps; **the i. I saw her** dès que je l'ai vue
2 *adj* (*reply, success, dislike*) immédiat(e); (*solution*) instantané(e); *TV* **i. replay** reprise *f* de l'action **(b)** (*coffee, soup*) instantané(e)

instantaneous [ɪnstən'teɪnɪəs] *adj* instantané(e)

instantly ['ɪnstəntlɪ] *adv* instantanément

instead [ɪn'sted] *adv* (*in place of sth*) à la place; (*in place of sb*) à ma/sa/*etc* place; **i. of** (*thing*) au lieu de; (*person*) à la place de; **i. of doing sth** au lieu de faire qch

instep ['ɪnstep] *n* (*of foot*) cou-de-pied *m*; (*of shoe*) cambrure *f*

instigate ['ɪnstɪgeɪt] *vt* être à l'origine de

instigation ['ɪnstɪgeɪʃən] *n* instigation *f*; **at sb's i.** à l'instigation de qn

instigator ['ɪnstɪgeɪtə(r)] *n* instigateur(trice) *m,f*

instil, *Am* **instill** [ɪn'stɪl] (*pt & pp* **instilled**) *vt* (*courage, pride*) inspirer (**in** à); (*doubt, jealousy*) instiller (**in** à); (*idea*) inculquer (**into** à)

instinct ['ɪnstɪŋkt] *n* instinct *m*; **he has an i. for the game** ce jeu, chez lui, c'est instinctif

instinctive [ɪn'stɪŋktɪv] *adj* instinctif(ive)

institute ['ɪnstɪtjuːt] **1** *n* institut *m*
2 *vt* (*system, procedure*) établir, instituer; (*search*) lancer; *Law* (*enquiry*) ordonner; **to i. proceedings (against sb)** entamer *ou* engager des poursuites (**contre qn**)

institution [ɪnstɪ'tjuːʃən] *n* (*organization*) institution *f*; (*public, financial*) établissement *m*; (*for old people*) hospice *m*; (*for mental patients*) asile *m*; *Fig* **to become a national i.** (*of event, TV programme*) devenir une institution nationale

institutional [ɪnstɪ'tjuːʃənəl] *adj* institutionnel(elle)

institutionalize [ɪnstɪ'tjuːʃənəlaɪz] *vt* **(a)** (*put in a home*) placer dans un établissement spécialisé; **to become institutionalized** (*of prisoner, patient*) devenir complètement dépendant(e) **(b)** (*turn into an institution*) institutionnaliser

instruct [ɪn'strʌkt] *vt* **(a)** (*teach*) enseigner; **to i. sb in sth** enseigner qch à qn **(b)** (*command*) ordonner; **to i. sb to do sth** ordonner à qn de faire qch

instruction [ɪn'strʌkʃən] *n* **(a)** (*training*) instruction *f*, enseignement *m* **(b) instructions** (*orders*) instructions *fpl*, directives *fpl* **(c) instructions** (*for use*) notice *f* (d'emploi); **i. manual** manuel *m* d'entretien

instructive [ɪn'strʌktɪv] *adj* instructif(ive)

instructor [ɪn'strʌktə(r)] *n* **(a)** (*of sporting activity, driving*) moniteur(trice) *m,f* **(b)** *Am* (*university lecturer*) professeur *m*

instrument ['ɪnstrəmənt] *n* instrument *m*; **i. board** *or* **panel** (*in plane, car*) tableau *m* de bord

instrumental [ɪnstrə'mentəl] **1** *n* (*music without words*) instrumental *m*
2 *adj* **(a)** (*contributory*) **to be i. in sth** jouer un rôle décisif dans qch **(b)** (*in music*) instrumental(e)

instrumentalist [ɪnstrə'mentəlɪst] *n* instrumentiste *mf*

instrumentation [ɪnstrəmen'teɪʃən] *n* instrumentation *f*

insubordinate [ɪnsə'bɔːdɪnət] *adj* insubordonné(e)

insubordination [ɪnsəbɔːdɪ'neɪʃən] *n* insubordination *f*

insubstantial [ɪnsəb'stænʃəl] *adj* (*structure, argument*) peu solide; (*meal*) frugal(e); (*book*) creux(euse), qui manque de substance

insufferable [ɪn'sʌfrəbəl] *adj* insupportable, intolérable

insufficient [ɪnsə'fɪʃənt] *adj* insuffisant(e)

insular ['ɪnsjʊlə(r)] *adj* borné(e); (*climate*) insulaire

insulate ['ɪnsjʊleɪt] *vt* isoler; *Fig* **to be insulated from sth** être protégé(e) de qch

insulating tape ['ɪnsjʊleɪtɪŋ'teɪp] *n* chatterton *m*

insulation [ɪnsjʊ'leɪʃən] *n* isolation *f*

insulin [ɪnsjʊlɪn] *n* insuline *f*

insult 1 *n* ['ɪnsʌlt] *(words, action)* insulte *f*; **to add i. to injury** aggraver les choses
2 *vt* [ɪn'sʌlt] insulter

insulting [ɪn'sʌltɪŋ] *adj* insultant(e)

insuperable [ɪn'suːpərəbəl] *adj* insurmontable

insurance [ɪn'ʃʊərəns] *n* assurance *f*; **to take out i.** prendre une assurance; **i. broker** courtier *m* en assurances; **i. claim** demande *f* d'indemnité; *(for more serious damage)* déclaration *f* de sinistre; **i. company** compagnie *f* d'assurances; **i. policy** police *f* d'assurance; **i. premium** prime *f* d'assurance

insure [ɪn'ʃʊə(r)] *vt* assurer (**against** contre); **to i. one's life** s'assurer sur la vie

insured [ɪn'ʃʊəd] *adj* assuré(e) (**against** contre); **i. value** valeur *f* assurée

insurer [ɪn'ʃʊərə(r)] *n* assureur *m*

insurgent [ɪn'sɜːdʒənt] *n* insurgé(e) *m,f*

insurmountable [ɪnsə'maʊntəbəl] *adj* insurmontable

insurrection [ɪnsə'rekʃən] *n* insurrection *f*

intact [ɪn'tækt] *adj* intact(e)

intake ['ɪnteɪk] *n* **(a)** *(of alcohol, food)* consommation *f*; *(of calories)* absorption *f* **(b)** *(pupils)* élèves *mpl*; *(recruits)* contingent *m* **(c)** *Tech* admission *f*

intangible [ɪn'tændʒɪbəl] *adj* impalpable

integer ['ɪntɪdʒə(r)] *n Math* nombre *m* entier

integral ['ɪntɪgrəl] *adj (essential)* indispensable; **to be an i. part of sth** faire partie intégrante de qch; *Math* **i. calculus** calcul *m* intégral

integrate ['ɪntɪgreɪt] **1** *vt* intégrer (**into** à)
2 *vi* s'intégrer (**into** à)

integrated ['ɪntɪgreɪtɪd] *adj* intégré(e); *(school)* qui pratique la déségrégation raciale

integration [ɪntɪ'greɪʃən] *n* intégration *f*

integrity [ɪn'tegrɪtɪ] *n* intégrité *f*

intellect ['ɪntɪlekt] *n* intellect *m*, intelligence *f*

intellectual [ɪntɪ'lektjʊəl] **1** *n* intellectuel(elle) *m,f*
2 *adj* intellectuel(elle)

intelligence [ɪn'telɪdʒəns] *n* **(a)** *(faculty)* intelligence *f*; *Psy* **i. quotient** quotient *m* intellectuel; **i. test** test *m* d'intelligence **(b)** *(secret service)* services *mpl* secrets; **i. officer** agent *m* de renseignements; **i. service** services secrets

intelligent [ɪn'telɪdʒənt] *adj* intelligent(e)

intelligentsia [ɪntelɪ'dʒentsɪə] *n* intelligentsia *f*

intelligible [ɪn'telɪdʒɪbəl] *adj* intelligible

intemperate [ɪn'tempərət] *adj (climate)* rude; *(person, behaviour)* intempérant(e)

intend [ɪn'tend] *vt* **to i. to do sth** avoir l'intention de faire qch; **to i. sth for sb** destiner qch à qn; **was that intended?** était-ce intentionnel?; **it was intended as a compliment/a joke** c'était un compliment/pour plaisanter; **I didn't i. her to see it yet** il n'était pas dans mes intentions qu'elle le voie si tôt

intended [ɪn'tendɪd] **1** *n Old-fashioned or Hum (future spouse)* futur(e) *m,f*
2 *adj (consequence, outcome)* prévu(e); *(effect)* escompté(e); *(insult, mistake)* voulu(e)

intense [ɪn'tens] *adj* intense; *(interest, anger)* vif (vive); *(person)* passionné(e)

intensely [ɪn'tenslɪ] *adv* **(a)** *(amusing, boring)* extrêmement **(b)** *(look at, speak)* intensément, avec intensité

intensify [ɪn'tensɪfaɪ] *(pt & pp* intensified*)* **1** *vt (search, effort)* intensifier; *(pressure)* augmenter
2 *vi* s'intensifier

intensity [ɪn'tensɪtɪ] *n* intensité *f*

intensive [ɪn'tensɪv] *adj* intensif(ive); *Med* **i. care** soins *mpl* intensifs

intent [ɪn'tent] **1** *n* intention *f*; **to all intents and purposes** quasiment
2 *adj (look)* intense; **to be i. on doing sth** être résolu(e) ou déterminé(e) à faire qch

intention [ɪn'tenʃən] *n* intention *f*; **to have every i. of doing sth** avoir la ferme intention de faire qch; **to have no i. of doing sth** n'avoir nullement l'intention de faire qch

intentional [ɪn'tenʃənəl] *adj* intentionnel(elle), voulu(e)

intentionally [ɪn'tenʃənəlɪ] *adv* intentionnellement; **I didn't do it i.** je ne l'ai pas fait exprès

intently [ɪn'tentlɪ] *adv (listen, look at)* attentivement

inter [ɪn'tɜː(r)] *(pt & pp* interred*)* *vt* inhumer, enterrer

interact [ɪntə'rækt] *vi* **(a)** *(of person)* communiquer (**with** avec); *(of two or more people)* communiquer entre eux (elles) **(b)** *(of chemical)* réagir (**with** avec); *(of two or more chemicals)* réagir entre elles (eux)

interaction [ɪntə'rækʃən] *n* interaction *f*

interactive [ɪntə'ræktɪv] *adj* interactif(ive)

intercede [ɪntə'siːd] *vi* intercéder (**with/for** auprès de/ en faveur de)

intercept [ɪntə'sept] *vt* intercepter

interception [ɪntə'sepʃən] *n* interception *f*

intercession [ɪntə'seʃən] *n* intercession *f*

interchange 1 *n* ['ɪntətʃeɪndʒ] *(exchange)* échange *m*; *(on motorway)* échangeur *m*
2 *vt* [ɪntə'tʃeɪndʒ] *(exchange)* échanger; *(transpose)* intervertir

interchangeable [ɪntə'tʃeɪndʒəbəl] *adj* interchangeable

intercom ['ɪntəkɒm] *n* Interphone® *m*

interconnect [ɪntəkə'nekt] *vt* interconnecter

intercontinental [ɪntəkɒntɪ'nentəl] *adj* intercontinental(e); **i. ballistic missile** missile *m* balistique intercontinental

intercourse ['ɪntəkɔːs] *n* **(a)** *(sexual)* **i.** rapports *mpl* (sexuels) **(b)** *Formal (dealings)* commerce *m*, relations *fpl*

interdependent ['ɪntədɪ'pendənt] *adj* inter-dépendant(e)

interest 1 *n* ['ɪntrest] **(a)** *(curiosity)* intérêt *m*; *(hobby)* centre *m* d'intérêt; **of i.** intéressant(e); **of historical i.** intéressant du point de vue historique; **to be of i. to sb** intéresser qn; **to take an i. in sth** s'intéresser à qch; **to lose i. (in sth)** se désintéresser (de qch)
(b) *(stake)* intérêt *m*; **to have a financial i. in sth** avoir investi financièrement dans qch
(c) *(benefit)* intérêt *m*; **to act in sb's interests** agir dans l'intérêt de qn; **the public i.** l'intérêt public; **it's in my i. to do it** j'ai tout intérêt à le faire; **in the interests of...** dans l'intérêt de...
(d) *(on loan, investment)* intérêt(s) *m(pl)*
2 *vt* intéresser; **to i. sb in sth** intéresser qn à qch; **can I i. you in a drink?** je peux vous offrir un verre?

interested [ɪn'trestɪd] *adj* intéressé(e); **to be interested in sth** s'intéresser à qch; **he seemed i. in the proposal** il a semblé intéressé par cette proposition

interest-free ['ɪntrest'friː] *adj (loan)* sans intérêt; *(credit)* gratuit(e)

interesting ['ɪntrestɪŋ] *adj* intéressant(e)

interface ['ɪntəfeɪs] *n Comptr* interface *f*

interfere [ɪntə'fɪə(r)] *vi* (a) *(meddle)* se mêler (**in** de); **he's always interfering** il est toujours à se mêler de ce qui ne le regarde pas; **don't i. with my papers** ne touche pas à mes papiers; *Euph* **to i. with sb** *(sexually)* abuser de qn (b) **to i. with sth** *(hinder)* gêner qch

interference [ɪntə'fɪərəns] *n* (a) *(meddling)* ingérence *f* (b) *Rad & TV* interférences *fpl*

interfering [ɪntə'fɪərɪŋ] *adj* importun(e)

interim ['ɪntərɪm] **1** *n* **in the i.** entre-temps
2 *adj (agreement, report)* provisoire

interior [ɪn'tɪərɪə(r)] **1** *n* intérieur *m*
2 *adj* intérieur(e); **i. decorator** décorateur(trice) *m,f* (d'intérieurs); **i. designer** architecte *mf* d'intérieur

interject [ɪntə'dʒekt] *vt (remark)* lancer; *(protest)* émettre

interjection [ɪntə'dʒekʃən] *n* interjection *f*

interlocking [ɪntə'lɒkɪŋ] *adj (parts)* emboîtable; *(gears)* qui s'enclenchent

interlocutor [ɪntə'lɒkjutə(r)] *n Formal* interlocuteur (trice) *m,f*

interloper ['ɪntələʊpə(r)] *n* intrus(e) *m,f*

interlude ['ɪntəluːd] *n also Fig* intermède *m*

intermarriage [ɪntə'mærɪdʒ] *n (within a family)* mariage *m* consanguin; *(with member of another group)* mariage

intermarry [ɪntə'mærɪ] *(pt & pp* **intermarried***) vi* se marier *(au sein de la même famille)*

intermediary [ɪntə'miːdɪərɪ] *(pl* **intermediaries***) n* intermédiaire *mf*

intermediate [ɪntə'miːdɪət] *adj* intermédiaire; *(student)* de niveau moyen

interminable [ɪn'tɜːmɪnəbəl] *adj* interminable

intermingle [ɪntə'mɪŋgəl] **1** *vt* mélanger (**with** avec)
2 *vi* se mêler (**with** à), se mélanger (**with** avec)

intermission [ɪntə'mɪʃən] *n* entracte *m*

intermittent [ɪntə'mɪtənt] *adj* intermittent(e)

intern 1 *n* ['ɪntɜːn] *Am Med* interne *mf*
2 *vt* [ɪn'tɜːn] interner

internal [ɪn'tɜːnəl] *adj* interne; *(flight)* intérieur(e); **i. combustion engine** moteur *m* à combustion interne

internalize [ɪn'tɜːnəlaɪz] *vt* intérioriser

internally [ɪn'tɜːnəlɪ] *adv* intérieurement; **not to be taken i.** *(on medicine container)* à usage externe

international [ɪntə'næʃənəl] **1** *n (in sport) (player)* international(e) *m,f*; *(match)* match *m* international
2 *adj* international(e); **I. Date Line** ligne *f* de changement de date; *Fin* **I. Monetary Fund** Fonds *m* monétaire international

internee [ɪntɜː'niː] *n* interné(e) *m,f*

Internet ['ɪntənet] *n Comptr* **the I.** l'Internet *m*

internment [ɪn'tɜːnmənt] *n* internement *m*

interpersonal [ɪntə'pɜːsənəl] *adj* interpersonnel(elle)

interplay ['ɪntəpleɪ] *n* interaction *f* (**of** or **between** entre)

Interpol ['ɪntəpɒl] *n* Interpol

interpolate [ɪn'tɜːpəleɪt] *vt (remark, question)* glisser; *(word, passage)* intercaler

interpose [ɪntə'pəʊz] *vt* interposer (**between** entre)

interpret [ɪn'tɜːprɪt] **1** *vt* interpréter
2 *vi* faire l'interprète

interpretation [ɪntɜːprɪ'teɪʃən] *n* interprétation *f*

interpreter [ɪn'tɜːprɪtə(r)] *n* interprète *mf*

interracial [ɪntə'reɪʃəl] *adj* interracial(e)

interrelated [ɪntərɪ'leɪtɪd] *adj* lié(e)

interrogate [ɪn'terəgeɪt] *vt* interroger

interrogation [ɪnterə'geɪʃən] *n* interrogatoire *m*

interrogative [ɪntə'rɒgətɪv] **1** *n Gram* interrogatif *m*; *(question mark)* point *m* d'interrogation
2 *adj (look, tone)* interrogateur(trice); *Gram* interrogatif(ive)

interrogator [ɪn'terəgeɪtə(r)] *n* interrogateur(trice) *m,f*

interrupt [ɪntə'rʌpt] **1** *vt* interrompre
2 *vi* **it's rude to i.** ce n'est pas poli d'interrompre les gens; **I'm sorry to i.** je suis désolé de vous interrompre

interruption [ɪntə'rʌpʃən] *n* interruption *f*

intersect [ɪntə'sekt] **1** *vt* couper
2 *vi* se couper

intersection [ɪntə'sekʃən] *n (of roads)* carrefour *m*

intersperse [ɪntə'spɜːs] *vt* **to be interspersed with sth** être parsemé(e) de qch; **sunshine interspersed with showers** temps ensoleillé entrecoupé d'averses

intertwine [ɪntə'twaɪn] **1** *vt* entremêler (**with** de); **to be intertwined** *(of two things)* être entrelacés(ées)
2 *vi* s'entrelacer

interval ['ɪntəvəl] *n* intervalle *m*; *(at theatre)* entracte *m*; **at regular intervals** à intervalles réguliers; **at weekly intervals** toutes les semaines; **sunny intervals** éclaircies *fpl*

intervene [ɪntə'viːn] *vi (of person)* intervenir (**in** dans); *(of event)* survenir

intervening [ɪntə'viːnɪŋ] *adj* intermédiaire; **in the i. period** entre-temps, dans l'intervalle

intervention [ɪntə'venʃən] *n* intervention *f*

interview ['ɪntəvjuː] **1** *n (for job)* entretien *m*; *TV & Journ* interview *f*
2 *vt (for job)* faire passer un entretien à; *TV & Journ* interviewer

interviewee [ɪntəvjuː'iː] *n (for job)* candidat(e) *m,f (à qui l'on fait passer un entretien)*; *TV & Journ* personne *f* interviewée

interviewer ['ɪntəvjuːə(r)] *n (for job)* = personne qui fait passer un entretien; *TV & Journ* interviewer(euse) *m,f*

intestate [ɪn'testeɪt] *adj Law* **to die i.** mourir intestat

intestinal [ɪntes'taɪnəl] *adj* intestinal(e)

intestine [ɪn'testɪn] *n* intestin *m*; **large i.** gros intestin; **small i.** intestin grêle

intimacy ['ɪntɪməsɪ] *n (of relationship, atmosphere)* intimité *f*; *Euph (sexual)* relations *fpl* intimes

intimate ['ɪntɪmət] **1** *n* intime *mf*
2 *adj (friend, restaurant)* intime; *(knowledge)* approfondi(e); *Euph* **to be i. with sb** *(sexually)* avoir des relations intimes avec qn
3 *vt* ['ɪntɪmeɪt] *Formal (hint at)* faire comprendre; *(make known)* signifier

intimately ['ɪntɪmətlɪ] *adv* intimement

intimidate [ɪn'tɪmɪdeɪt] *vt* intimider; **to i. sb into doing sth** forcer qn à faire qch en usant d'intimidation

intimidation [ɪntɪmɪ'deɪʃən] *n* intimidation *f*

into ['ɪntʊ] *prep* (a) *(with motion, direction)* dans; **to go i. a house** entrer dans une maison; **to get i. bed** se mettre au lit; **to crash i. sth** rentrer dans qch

(b) *(expressing change)* en; **to change i. sth** se changer en qch; **to translate sth i. English** traduire qch en anglais; **to break sth i. pieces** mettre qch en morceaux

(c) *(in division)* **three i. six goes twice** six divisé par trois donne deux

(d) *Fam (keen on)* **to be i.** jazz être branché(e) jazz; **he's really i. my sister** il en pince vraiment pour ma sœur

intolerable [ɪn'tɒlərəbəl] *adj* intolérable

intolerance [ɪn'tɒlərəns] *n* intolérance *f*

intolerant [ɪn'tɒlərənt] *adj* **to be i. of sb** être intolérant(e) à l'égard de qn; **to be i. of sth** ne pas tolérer qch

intonation [ɪntə'neɪʃən] *n* intonation *f*

intone [ɪn'təʊn] *vt (speak)* débiter; *(of preacher)* psalmodier

intoxicated [ɪn'tɒksɪkeɪtɪd] *adj (drunk)* ivre; *Fig* **i. with power/fame** ivre de puissance/gloire

intoxication [ɪntɒksɪ'keɪʃən] *n also Fig* ivresse *f*

intractable [ɪn'træktəbəl] *adj (person)* intraitable; *(problem)* très délicat(e)

intransigence [ɪn'trænzɪdʒəns] *n Formal* intransigeance *f* (over sur)

intransigent [ɪn'trænzɪdʒənt] *adj Formal* intransigeant(e) (over sur)

intransitive [ɪn'trænzɪtɪv] *adj Gram* intransitif(ive)

intrauterine device ['ɪntrə'juːtəramdɪ'vaɪs] *n Med* stérilet *m*

intravenous ['ɪntrə'viːnəs] *adj Med (drip)* veineux(euse); **i. injection** intraveineuse *f*

in-tray ['ɪntreɪ] *n* bac *m* du courrier à traiter

intrepid [ɪn'trepɪd] *adj* intrépide

intricacy ['ɪntrɪkəsɪ] *(pl* **intricacies***) n* complexité *f*; **the intricacies of the law** les subtilités du droit

intricate ['ɪntrɪkət] *adj* compliqué(e)

intrigue 1 *n* ['ɪntriːg] intrigue *f*
2 *vt* [ɪn'triːg] *(interest)* intriguer

intrinsic [ɪn'trɪnsɪk] *adj* intrinsèque

introduce [ɪntrə'djuːs] *vt* **(a)** *(person)* présenter (**to** à); **to i. oneself** se présenter; **to i. sb to sth** initier qn à qch **(b)** *(reform, practice)* introduire

introduction [ɪntrə'dʌkʃən] *n* **(a)** *(of person)* présentation *f*; **to make the introductions** faire les présentations **(b)** *(to book)* avant-propos *m inv*, introduction *f* **(c)** *(of reform, practice)* introduction *f* **(d)** *(first experience)* initiation *f* (**to** à)

introductory [ɪntrə'dʌktərɪ] *adj* d'introduction; *(price, offer)* de lancement

introspection [ɪntrə'spekʃən] *n* introspection *f*

introspective [ɪntrə'spektɪv] *adj (person)* introverti(e); *(mood)* introspectif(ive)

introvert ['ɪntrəvɜːt] *n* introverti(e) *m,f*

introverted ['ɪntrəvɜːtɪd] *adj* introverti(e)

intrude [ɪn'truːd] *vi* **(a)** *(impose oneself)* déranger **(b)** *(interfere)* **her work intrudes on her family life** son travail empiète sur sa vie de famille; **to i. on sb's privacy** s'immiscer dans la vie privée de qn

intruder [ɪn'truːdə(r)] *n* intrus(e) *m,f*

intrusion [ɪn'truːʒən] *n* intrusion *f*

intrusive [ɪn'truːsɪv] *adj* importun(e)

intuition [ɪntjuː'ɪʃən] *n* intuition *f*

intuitive [ɪn'tjuːɪtɪv] *adj* intuitif(ive)

Inuit ['ɪnuːɪt] **1** *n* Inuit *mf*
2 *adj* inuit

inundate ['ɪnʌndeɪt] *vt* inonder (**with** de); *Fig (with phone calls, letters)* submerger (**with** de)

invade [ɪn'veɪd] *vt* envahir; **to i. sb's privacy** s'immiscer dans la vie privée de qn

invader [ɪn'veɪdə(r)] *n* envahisseur(euse) *m,f*

invalid¹ [ɪn'vælɪd] *adj (document, argument)* non valable; *(marriage)* non valide

invalid² ['ɪnvəlɪd] *n (disabled person)* invalide *mf*, infirme *mf*; *(ill person)* malade *mf*

invalidate [ɪn'vælɪdeɪt] *vt (theory)* infirmer; *(document, contract)* invalider

invaluable [ɪn'væljʊəbəl] *adj* précieux(euse)

invariable [ɪn'veərɪəbəl] *adj* invariable

invariably [ɪn'veərɪəblɪ] *adv* invariablement

invasion [ɪn'veɪʒən] *n* invasion *f*

invective [ɪn'vektɪv] *n* invectives *fpl*

inveigh [ɪn'veɪ] *vi Formal* **to i. against** invectiver contre

inveigle [ɪn'veɪgəl] *vt* **to i. sb into doing sth** entortiller qn pour qu'il fasse qch

invent [ɪn'vent] *vt* inventer

invention [ɪn'venʃən] *n* **(a)** *(action, thing invented)* invention *f* **(b)** *(creativity)* inventivité *f*

inventive [ɪn'ventɪv] *adj* inventif(ive)

inventiveness [ɪn'ventɪvnəs] *n* inventivité *f*

inventor [ɪn'ventə(r)] *n* inventeur(trice) *m,f*

inventory ['ɪnventərɪ] *(pl* **inventories***) n (list)* inventaire *m*; *(stock)* stock(s) *m(pl)*

inverse ['ɪnvɜːs] *adj* inverse

invert [ɪn'vɜːt] *vt (turn upside down)* renverser; *(reverse)* inverser, intervertir

invertebrate [ɪn'vɜːtɪbrɪt] **1** *n* invertébré *m*
2 *adj* invertébré(e)

inverted [ɪn'vɜːtɪd] *adj (upside down)* renversé(e); *(reversed)* inversé(e); **i. commas** guillemets *mpl*; **to be an i. snob** faire du snobisme à l'envers

invest [ɪn'vest] **1** *vt* **(a)** *(money, time)* investir (**in** dans) **(b)** *(right, power)* investir (**with** de)
2 *vi* investir (**in** dans)

investigate [ɪn'vestɪgeɪt] *vt (crime)* enquêter sur; *(question)* examiner

investigation [ɪnvestɪ'geɪʃən] *n* enquête *f*

investigative [ɪn'vestɪgətɪv] *adj (journalism)* d'investigation

investigator [ɪn'vestɪgeɪtə(r)] *n* enquêteur(euse) *m,f*

investment [ɪn'vestmənt] *n* investissement *m*; **i. account** compte *m* d'investissement; **i. analyst** analyste *mf* en placements; **i. bank** banque *f* d'affaires; **i. income** revenu *m* provenant d'investissements; **i. trust** société *f* de placement

investor [ɪn'vestə(r)] *n* investisseur *m*

inveterate [ɪn'vetərət] *adj (gambler, drunkard, liar)* invétéré(e); *(critic)* acharné(e)

invidious [ɪn'vɪdɪəs] *adj (choice, comparison)* inéquitable; *(position, task)* peu enviable

invigilate [ɪn'vɪdʒɪleɪt] **1** *vt Br (exam)* surveiller
2 *vi* surveiller les candidats *(à un examen)*

invigilator [ɪn'vɪdʒɪleɪtə(r)] *n Br (in exam)* surveillant(e) *m,f (des candidats à un examen)*

invigorating [ɪnˈvɪgəreɪt] *adj* vivifiant(e)

invincible [ɪnˈvɪnsɪbəl] *adj* invincible

inviolable [ɪnˈvaɪələbəl] *adj Formal* inviolable

inviolate [ɪnˈvaɪələt] *adj Formal* inviolé(e)

invisible [ɪnˈvɪzɪbəl] *adj* invisible (to à); **i. earnings** invisibles *mpl*; **i. ink** encre *f* sympathique

invitation [ɪnvɪˈteɪʃən] *n* invitation *f*

invite 1 *n* [ˈɪnvaɪt] *Fam* invit' *f*
   2 *vt* [ɪnˈvaɪt] **(a)** *(guest)* inviter; **to i. sb in/up** inviter qn à entrer/monter; **to i. sb to do sth** inviter qn à faire qch; **applications are invited for the post of...** ≃ nous recrutons un... **(b)** *(trouble, criticism) (of person)* aller au-devant de

inviting [ɪnˈvaɪtɪŋ] *adj* attrayant(e); *(food)* appétissant(e)

in vitro fertilization [ɪnˈviːtrəʊfɜːtɪlaɪˈzeɪʃən] *n* fécondation *f* in vitro

invoice [ˈɪnvɔɪs] *Com* **1** *n* facture *f*; **to make out an i.** établir une facture
   2 *vt (goods)* facturer; *(person, company)* envoyer la facture à

invoke [ɪnˈvəʊk] *vt Formal (God, law)* invoquer; *(spirit, feeling)* évoquer; **to i. sb's aid** appeler qn à son secours

involuntary [ɪnˈvɒləntərɪ] *adj* involontaire

involve [ɪnˈvɒlv] *vt* **(a)** *(implicate)* **to be/get i. in sth** impliquer qn dans qch; **this doesn't i. you** ça ne te concerne pas **(b)** *(entail) (work, expense)* impliquer, entraîner; **my job involves a lot of travel** je suis amené à voyager pour mon travail

involved [ɪnˈvɒlvd] *adj* **(a)** *(implicated)* **to be/get i. in sth** *(crime, affaire)* être impliqué(e) dans qch; **to be i. in an accident** avoir un accident; **to be i. in teaching/banking** être dans l'enseignement/la banque; **50 people were i. in the project** 50 personnes ont pris part au projet; **the police became i.** la police est intervenue; **don't get i.!** ne te mêle pas de ça!; **how much money is i.?** de combien d'argent s'agit-il?
   (b) *(emotionally)* **to be/get i. with sb** sortir avec qn; **I don't want to get i.** je ne veux pas m'engager
   (c) *(engrossed)* **to be i. in a book/film** s'absorber dans un livre/film; **I'm getting really i. in this job** je commence à trouver ce travail vraiment intéressant
   (d) *(complicated)* compliqué(e)

involvement [ɪnˈvɒlvmənt] *n* **(a)** *(participation)* participation *f* **(in à)** **(b)** *(commitment)* engagement *m* **(in dans)**

invulnerable [ɪnˈvʌlnərəbəl] *adj* invulnérable **(to à)**

inward [ˈɪnwəd] *adj* **(a)** *(thoughts, feelings)* intime **(b)** *(movement)* vers l'intérieur; *Econ* **i. investment** investissements *mpl* étrangers

inward-looking [ɪnwədˈlʊkɪŋ] *adj* replié(e) sur soi-même

inwards [ˈɪnwədz] *adv* vers l'intérieur

iodine [ˈaɪədiːn] *n Chem* iode *m*; *(antiseptic)* teinture *f* d'iode

ion [ˈaɪən] *n* ion *m*

Ionian [aɪˈəʊnɪən] *n* **the I. (Sea)** la mer Ionienne

ionize [ˈaɪənaɪz] *vt* ioniser

iota [aɪˈəʊtə] *n* iota *m*; **she hadn't changed one i.** elle n'avait pas du tout changé; **not an i. of truth** pas une once de vérité

IOU [aɪəʊˈjuː] *n* (= *I owe you*) reconnaissance *f* de dette

IP [aɪˈpiː] *n Comptr (abbr* **Internet Protocol)** IP **address** adresse *f* IP

IPA [aɪpiːˈeɪ] *n (abbr* **International Phonetic Alphabet)** API *m*

IQ [aɪˈkjuː] *n (abbr* **intelligence quotient)** QI *m*

IRA [aɪɑːˈreɪ] *n (abbr* **Irish Republican Army)** IRA *f*

Iran [ɪˈrɑːn] *n* l'Iran *m*

Iranian [ɪˈreɪnɪən] **1** *n* **(a)** *(person)* Iranien(enne) *m,f* **(b)** *(language)* iranien *m*
   2 *adj* iranien(enne)

Iraq [ɪˈrɑːk] *n* l'Irak *m*

Iraqi [ɪˈrɑːkɪ] **1** *n* Irakien(enne) *m,f*, Iraquien(enne) *m,f*
   2 *adj* irakien(enne), iraquien(enne)

irascible [ɪˈræsɪbəl] *adj (person)* irascible; *(temperament)* colérique

irate [aɪˈreɪt] *adj* furieux(euse)

ire [ˈaɪə(r)] *n Lit* courroux *m*

Ireland [ˈaɪələnd] *n* l'Irlande *f*

iris [ˈaɪrɪs] *n* iris *m*

Irish [ˈaɪrɪʃ] **1** *npl (people)* **the I.** les Irlandais *mpl*
   2 *n (language)* irlandais *m*
   3 *adj* irlandais(e); **I. coffee** Irish coffee *m*; **the I. Sea** la mer d'Irlande; **I. stew** = ragoût de mouton, aux pommes de terre et aux oignons

Irishman [ˈaɪrɪʃmən] *n* Irlandais *m*

Irishwoman [ˈaɪrɪʃwʊmən] *n* Irlandaise *f*

irk [ɜːk] *vt* agacer

irksome [ˈɜːksəm] *adj* agaçant(e)

iron [ˈaɪən] **1** *n* **(a)** *(metal, golf club)* fer *m*; **made of i.** en fer; **to have an i. constitution** avoir une santé de fer; **an i. will** une volonté de fer; **i. discipline** discipline *f* de fer; **the I. Age** l'âge *m* de fer; **the I. Curtain** le rideau de fer; **i. lung** poumon *m* d'acier; **i. ore** minerai *m* de fer **(b)** *(for clothes)* fer *m* (à repasser); *Fig* **to have several irons in the fire** avoir plusieurs fers au feu
   2 *vt & vi (clothes)* repasser

▸**iron out** *vt sep (difficulty)* aplanir; *(problem)* résoudre

ironic(al) [aɪˈrɒnɪk(əl)] *adj* ironique

ironing [ˈaɪənɪŋ] *n* repassage *m*; **to do the i.** repasser, faire le repassage; **i. board** planche *f* ou table *f* à repasser

ironmonger [ˈaɪənmʌŋgə(r)] *n Br* quincaillier(ère) *m,f*; **i.'s (shop)** quincaillerie *f*

irony [ˈaɪrənɪ] *n (pl* **ironies)** *n* ironie *f*; **the i. is that...** ce qu'il y a d'ironique, c'est que...

irrational [ɪˈræʃənəl] *adj* irrationnel(elle)

irreconcilable [ɪrekənˈsaɪləbəl] *adj (enemy)* irréconciliable; *(hatred)* implacable; *(belief, idea)* incompatible, inconciliable

irredeemable [ɪrɪˈdiːməbəl] *adj (fault)* irréparable; *(situation)* irrémédiable

irrefutable [ɪrɪˈfjuːtəbəl] *adj* irréfutable

irregular [ɪˈregjʊlə(r)] *adj* irrégulier(ère)

irregularity [ɪregjʊˈlærɪtɪ] *n (pl* **irregularities)** *n* irrégularité *f*

irrelevance [ɪˈreləvəns], **irrelevancy** [ɪˈreləvənsɪ] *n (of remark, advice)* manque *m* d'à-propos

irrelevant [ɪˈreləvənt] *adj (remark, advice)* hors de propos; **that's i.** cela n'a rien à voir (avec la question)

irreligious [ɪrɪˈlɪdʒəs] *adj* irréligieux(euse)

irremediable [ɪrɪˈmiːdɪəbəl] *adj Formal (situation, loss)* irrémédiable; *(mistake)* irréparable

irreparable [ɪˈrepərəbəl] *adj* irréparable

irreplaceable [ɪrɪˈpleɪsəbəl] *adj* irremplaçable

irrepressible [ɪrɪ'presɪbəl] *adj* (*urge*) irrépressible; (*good humour*) à toute épreuve; **he's i.** rien n'entame sa bonne humeur

irreproachable [ɪrɪ'prəʊtʃəbəl] *adj* irréprochable

irresistible [ɪrɪ'zɪstəbəl] *adj* irrésistible

irresolute [ɪ'rezəluːt] *adj* irrésolu(e), indécis(e)

irrespective of [ɪrɪ'spektɪvəv] *prep* indépendamment de, sans tenir compte de

irresponsible [ɪrɪ'spɒnsɪbəl] *adj* irresponsable

irretrievable [ɪrɪ'triːvəbəl] *adj* (*loss*) irrémédiable; (*money*) irrécupérable; (*mistake, situation*) irréparable

irreverent [ɪ'revərənt] *adj* irrévérencieux(euse)

irreversible [ɪrɪ'vɜːsəbəl] *adj* (*decision, process*) irréversible

irrevocable [ɪ'revəkəbəl] *adj* irrévocable

irrigate ['ɪrɪgeɪt] *vt* irriguer

irrigation [ɪrɪ'geɪʃən] *n* irrigation *f*; **i. canal** *or* **ditch** canal *m* d'irrigation

irritable ['ɪrɪtəbəl] *adj* irritable; **i. bowel syndrome** colopathie *f* fonctionnelle

irritant ['ɪrɪtənt] *n* (*to eyes, skin*) irritant *m*; (*to person, government*) empêcheur(euse) *m,f* de tourner en rond

irritate ['ɪrɪteɪt] *vt* (*annoy*) agacer, irriter; *Med* irriter

irritating ['ɪrɪteɪtɪŋ] *adj* agaçant(e), irritant(e)

irritation [ɪrɪ'teɪʃən] *n* agacement *m*, irritation *f*; *Med* irritation *f*

IRS [aɪɑː'res] *n Am* (*abbr* **Internal Revenue Service**) **the I.** le fisc

is [ɪz] *3rd pers singular of* **be**

ISBN [aɪes biː'en] *n* (*abbr* **International Standard Book Number**) ISBN *m*

Islam ['ɪzlɑːm] *n* l'Islam *m*

Islamic [ɪz'læmɪk] *adj* islamique

island ['aɪlənd] *n* île *f*; (*small*) îlot *m*; (*in road*) refuge *m*

islander ['aɪləndə(r)] *n* (*in general*) insulaire *mf*; (*of specific island*) habitant(e) *m,f* de l'île

isle [aɪl] *n* île *f*; **the I. of Man** l'île de Man; **the I. of Wight** l'île de Wight

isn't ['ɪzənt] = **is not**

ISO [aɪes'əʊ] *n* (*abbr* **International Standards Organization**) ISO *f*

isobar ['aɪsəʊbɑː(r)] *n* isobare *f*

isolate ['aɪsəleɪt] *vt* isoler (**from** de)

isolated ['aɪsəleɪtɪd] *adj* isolé(e)

isolation [aɪsə'leɪʃən] *n* isolement *m*; **in i.** (**from**) isolément (de); **i. ward** salle *f* des contagieux

isotope ['aɪsəʊtəʊp] *n Phys* isotope *m*

Israel ['ɪzreɪl] *n* Israël *m*

Israeli [ɪz'reɪlɪ] **1** *n* Israélien(enne) *m,f*
2 *adj* israélien(enne)

Israelite ['ɪzrəlaɪt] *n Hist* Israélite *mf*

issue ['ɪsjuː, 'ɪʃuː] **1** *n* (a) (*topic*) problème *m*, question *f*; **the issues of the day** les questions du jour; **that's not the i.** ce n'est pas (là) le problème; **to avoid the i.** esquiver le problème; **to confuse the i.** compliquer les choses; **to make an i. of sth** faire toute une affaire de qch; **at i.** en cause; **to take i. with sb** exprimer son désaccord avec qn (b) (*of banknotes, stamps*) émission *f* (c) (*of magazine*) numéro *m*
2 *vt* (*banknote, stamp*) émettre; (*order*) donner; **to i. sb with sth** délivrer qch à qn; **to i. a statement** faire une déclaration; *Law* **to i. a summons** notifier une citation

3 *vi Formal* (*of blood, smoke, water*) s'échapper (**from** de); (*of noise*) provenir (**from** de)

Istanbul [ɪstæn'bʊl] *n* Istanbul

isthmus ['ɪsməs] *n* isthme *m*

IT [aɪ'tiː] *n Comptr* (*abbr* **information technology**) l'informatique *f*

it [ɪt] *pron* (a) (*subject*) il (elle) *m,f*; **where's the book? – it's on the shelf** où est le livre? – il est sur l'étagère; **put the TV on – it's not working** allume la télé – elle est en panne; **it's a big house** c'est une grande maison; **it's the best film I've ever seen** c'est le meilleur film que j'aie jamais vu
(b) (*direct object*) le (la) *m,f*; **I can do it** je peux le/la faire; **I saw it** je l'ai vu
(c) (*indirect object*) lui; **give it something to eat** donne-lui à manger
(d) (*prepositional object*) **on it** dessus; **under it** dessous; **beside it** à côté; **I forgot about it** j'ai oublié
(e) (*as impersonal subject*) **it's raining** il pleut; **it's ten o'clock** il est dix heures; **it's cold today** il fait froid aujourd'hui; **it's impossible to work in this heat** il est impossible de travailler avec cette chaleur; **it's me** c'est moi
(f) (*as complement of verb to be*) **that's it** (*that's all*) c'est tout

Italian [ɪ'tæljən] **1** *n* (a) (*person*) Italien(enne) *m,f* (b) (*language*) italien *m*; **I. class/teacher** classe *f*/professeur *m* d'italien
2 *adj* italien(enne)

italic [ɪ'tælɪk] *Typ* **1** *n* italic(s) italique *m*
2 *adj* italique

Italy ['ɪtəlɪ] *n* l'Italie *f*

itch [ɪtʃ] **1** *n* démangeaison *f*; *Fig* **to have an i. to do sth** brûler d'envie de faire qch
2 *vi* (*of person*) éprouver des démangeaisons; **my hand itches** j'ai la main qui me démange; *Fig* **to be itching to do sth** brûler d'envie de faire qch

itchy ['ɪtʃɪ] *adj* **I've got an i. hand, my hand's i.** j'ai la main qui me démange; *Fig* **to have i. feet** avoir la bougeotte

it'd ['ɪtəd] = **it would, it had**

item ['aɪtəm] *n* (*in collection, list*) article *m*; (*in news*) entrefilet *m*; (*longer*) article *m*; **an i. of clothing** un vêtement; **personal items** objets *mpl* personnels; *Fam* **they're an i.** ils sortent ensemble

itemize ['aɪtəmaɪz] *vt* détailler

iterative ['ɪtərətɪv] *adj Comptr* itératif(ive)

itinerant [ɪ'tɪnərənt] *adj* (*preacher*) itinérant(e); (*salesman, musician*) ambulant(e)

itinerary [aɪ'tɪnərərɪ] (*pl* **itineraries**) *n* itinéraire *m*

it'll ['ɪtəl] = **it will**

ITN [aɪtiː'en] *n Br* (*abbr* **Independent Television News**) = service produisant le journal télévisé d'ITV

its [ɪts] *possessive adj* (a) (*singular*) son (sa); (*plural*) ses; **i. bone** son os; **i. litter** sa litière; **i. kittens** ses châtons (b) (*for parts of body*) **the bear hurt i. paw** l'ours s'est blessé à la patte

it's [ɪts] = **it is, it has**

itself [ɪt'self] *pron* (a) (*reflexive*) **the dog hurt i.** le chien s'est blessé (b) (*emphatic*) **this method is simplicity i.** cette méthode est la simplicité même; **the town i. isn't very interesting** la ville (elle-)même n'est pas d'un grand intérêt (c) (*after preposition*) **by i.** tout(e) seul(e); **in i.** en soi

ITV [aɪtiːˈviː] n Br (abbr **Independent Television**) = chaîne de télévision privée britannique

IUD [aɪjuːˈdiː] n Med (abbr **intra-uterine device**) stérilet m

I've [aɪv] = I have

IVF [aɪviːˈef] n Med (abbr **in vitro fertilization**) FIV f

ivory [ˈaɪvərɪ] n ivoire m; **the I. Coast** la Côte d'Ivoire; Fig **i. tower** tour f d'ivoire

ivy [ˈaɪvɪ] n (plant) lierre m; Am **I. League** = ensemble des huit universités les plus prestigieuses du nord-est des États-Unis

J

J, j [dʒeɪ] *n (letter)* J, j *m inv*

jab [dʒæb] **1** *n (a) (with elbow, finger)* coup *m; (in boxing)* direct *m* **(b)** *Br Fam (injection)* piqûre *f*
2 *vt (pt & pp jabbed)* he jabbed her in the leg with a pencil il lui a enfoncé un crayon dans la jambe; **to j. a finger at sb** agiter son doigt sous le nez de qn

jabber ['dʒæbə(r)] *vi Fam (talk unclearly)* marmonner; *(chatter)* jacasser

Jack [dʒæk] *n* **J. Frost** le Bonhomme Hiver; *Br Fam* **I'm all right, J.** moi, ça va, merci

jack [dʒæk] *n* **(a)** *(person)* **every man j. of them** absolument tout le monde; **j. of all trades** touche-à-tout *mf* **(b)** *(for car)* cric *m* **(c)** *(in cards)* valet *m* **(d)** *(electric plug)* prise *f ou* fiche *f* mâle

▸**jack in** *vt sep Br Fam* plaquer
▸**jack up** *vt sep Fam (price, salaries)* augmenter

jackal ['dʒækəl] *n* chacal *m*

jackass ['dʒækæs] *n also Fig* âne *m*

jackboot ['dʒækbuːt] *n* botte *f* de cavalier; *Fig* **under the j. of** sous la botte de

jackdaw ['dʒækdɔː] *n* choucas *m*

jacket ['dʒækɪt] *n (coat)* veste *f; (of book)* jaquette *f; (of boiler)* chemise *f*, enveloppe *f*; **j. potatoes** pommes de terre *fpl* en robe des champs *ou* en robe de chambre

jackhammer ['dʒækhæmə(r)] *n* marteau-piqueur *m*

jack-in-the-box ['dʒækɪnðəbɒks] *n* diable *m* à ressort

jackknife ['dʒæknaɪf] **1** *n (pl* **jackknives)** couteau *m* de poche
2 *vi (of articulated lorry)* **the lorry jackknifed** la remorque du camion s'est soudain mise en travers de la route

jack-o'-lantern ['dʒækə'læntən] *n Am* = lanterne faite dans une citrouille sur laquelle on a creusé un visage

jackpot ['dʒækpɒt] *n (in lottery)* gros lot *m*; **to hit** *ou* **win the j.** gagner le gros lot

jack rabbit *n* = gros lièvre commun en Amérique du Nord

Jacobean [dʒækə'bɪən] *adj* = de l'époque de Jacques 1er (1603-1625)

Jacobite ['dʒækəbaɪt] *n & adj* jacobite *mf*

Jacuzzi® [dʒə'kuːzi] *n* Jacuzzi®*m*

jade [dʒeɪd] **1** *n (stone, colour)* jade *m*
2 *adj (colour)* **j.(-green)** vert jade

jaded ['dʒeɪdɪd] *adj (tired)* las *(lasse);* *(bored)* blasé(e); **to be j. with sth** être las de qch; **to have a j. palate** avoir le palais blasé

jag [dʒæg] *n Fam* **(a) to go on a (drinking) j.** prendre une cuite; **to have a crying j.** avoir une crise de larmes **(b)** *Scot (injection)* piqûre *f*

jagged ['dʒægɪd] *adj (coastline, mountain top)* déchiqueté(e), découpé(e); *(blade)* ébréché(e)

jaguar [*Br* 'dʒægjʊə(r), *Am* 'dʒægwɑː(r)] *n* jaguar *m*

jail [dʒeɪl] **1** *n* prison *f*; **to be in j.** être en prison; **to go to j.** aller en prison
2 *vt* emprisonner, mettre en prison

jailbird ['dʒeɪlbɜːd] *n Fam (in prison)* taulard(e) *m,f; (recidivist)* cheval *m* de retour

jailbreak ['dʒeɪlbreɪk] *n* évasion *f*

jailer ['dʒeɪlə(r)] *n* geôlier(ère) *m,f*

jailhouse ['dʒeɪlhaʊs] *n Am* prison *f*

jailor ['dʒeɪlə(r)] *n* = **jailer**

Jakarta [dʒə'kɑːtə] *n* Djakarta

jalop(p)y ['dʒælɒpɪ] *(pl* **jalop(p)ies)** *n Fam* vieille guimbarde *f*, vieux tacot *m*

jam¹ [dʒæm] **1** *n (a) (crowd) (of people)* foule *f; (of traffic)* encombrement *m* **(b)** *Fam (difficult situation)* **to be in/get into a (bit of a) j.** être/se fourrer dans le pétrin **(c)** *(improvised performance)* **j. (session)** jam-session *f*, bœuf *m*
2 *vt (pt & pp jammed)* **(a)** *(pack tightly) (objects)* entasser **(into dans);** *(container)* bourrer **(with de); people/cars jammed the street** la rue était noire de monde/embouteillée **(b)** *(immobilize) (drawer, mechanism)* coincer, bloquer; *(radio broadcast, station)* brouiller; *(switchboard)* saturer
3 *vi (a) (of drawer, mechanism)* se coincer, se bloquer **(b)** *(of crowd)* s'entasser **(into dans) (c)** *(of musicians)* improviser

▸**jam on** *vt sep* **to j. on the brakes** écraser la pédale de frein

jam² [dʒæm] *n (fruit preserve)* confiture *f*; **j. tart** tarte *f* à la confiture

Jamaica [dʒə'meɪkə] *n* la Jamaïque

Jamaican [dʒə'meɪkən] **1** *n* Jamaïcain(e) *m,f*
2 *adj* jamaïcain(e)

jamb [dʒæm] *n* montant *m*

jamboree [dʒæmbə'riː] *n (scouts' meeting)* jamboree *m; Fam (celebration)* fête *f*

jamming ['dʒæmɪŋ] *n (of radio broadcast, station)* brouillage *m*

jammy ['dʒæmɪ] *adj* **(a)** *(covered with jam)* plein(e) de confiture **(b)** *Br Fam (lucky)* verni(e)

jam-packed ['dʒæm'pækd] *adj* plein(e) à craquer; *(street)* noir(e) de monde, bondé(e)

Jan *(abbr* **January)** janvier

jangle ['dʒæŋgəl] **1** *n* cliquetis *m*
2 *vt* faire cliqueter
3 *vi* cliqueter; *Fig* **her voice made his nerves j.** sa voix lui mettait les nerfs en pelote

janitor ['dʒænɪtə(r)] *n Am & Scot (caretaker)* concierge *mf*

January ['dʒænjʊəri] *n* janvier *m*; *see also* **May**

Jap [dʒæp] *n very Fam* Jap *mf*, = terme raciste désignant un Japonais

Japan [dʒə'pæn] *n* le Japon

Japanese [dʒæpə'niːz] *1 npl (people)* **the J.** les Japonais *mpl*
2 *n* **(a)** *(person)* Japonais(e) *m,f* **(b)** *(language)* japonais *m*; **J. class/teacher** classe *f*/professeur *m* de japonais
3 *adj* japonais(e)

jape [dʒeɪp] *n* blague *f*

jar¹ [dʒɑː(r)] *1 n (jolt)* choc *m*, secousse *f*
2 *vt (pt & pp* **jarred)** *also Fig* secouer; **someone jarred my elbow** quelqu'un m'a cogné le coude
3 *vi* **(a)** *(make unpleasant sound)* rendre un son discordant; **to j. on the ears** écorcher les oreilles; **to j. on the nerves** taper sur les nerfs **(b)** *(of colours)* jurer; *(of ideas)* être en contradiction

jar² *n (container)* pot *m*; *(earthenware)* jarre *f*; *Br Fam* **to have a j.** prendre un pot

jargon ['dʒɑːɡən] *n Pej* jargon *m*

jarring ['dʒɑːrɪŋ] *adj (noise, voice)* discordant(e); *(blow)* qui ébranle tout le corps

jasmine ['dʒæzmɪn] *n* jasmin *m*

jaundice ['dʒɔːndɪs] *n* jaunisse *f*

jaundiced ['dʒɔːndɪst] *adj Fig (attitude, view)* aigu(ë), amer(ère)

jaunt [dʒɔːnt] *n* excursion *f*, sortie *f*

jauntiness ['dʒɔːntɪnɪs] *n (cheerfulness)* enjouement *m*; *(carefreeness)* insouciance *f*

jaunty ['dʒɔːntɪ] *adj (cheerful)* enjoué(e); *(carefree)* insouciant(e)

Java ['dʒɑːvə] *n* Java

javelin ['dʒævlɪn] *n* javelot *m*

jaw [dʒɔː] *1 n* mâchoire *f*; **jaws** *(of animal)* gueule *f*; **the jaws of death** les griffes *fpl* de la mort
2 *vi Fam (chat)* papoter

jawbone ['dʒɔːbəʊn] *n* maxillaire *m*

jawbreaker ['dʒɔːbreɪkə(r)] *n Fam (word)* mot *m* imprononçable; *(name)* nom *m* à coucher dehors

jay [dʒeɪ] *n* geai *m*

jaywalker ['dʒeɪwɔːkə(r)] *n* = piéton qui traverse en dehors des passages cloutés

jaywalking ['dʒeɪwɔːkɪŋ] *n* = fait de traverser en dehors des passages cloutés

jazz [dʒæz] *n* jazz *m*; *Fam* **and all that j.** et tout le tremblement *ou* le bazar

▸**jazz up** *vt sep Fam (enliven) (clothes, room, style)* égayer; *(party)* animer; *(taste)* relever

jazzy ['dʒæzɪ] *adj (tune)* jazzy *inv*; *(clothes, pattern)* aux couleurs vives

jealous ['dʒeləs] *adj* jaloux(ouse); **to be j. of sb** être jaloux de qn

jealously ['dʒeləslɪ] *adv* jalousement; **to guard sth j.** veiller jalousement sur qch

jealousy ['dʒeləsɪ] *n* jalousie *f*

jeans [dʒiːnz] *npl* jeans *m*

Jeep® [dʒiːp] *n* Jeep® *f*

jeer [dʒɪə(r)] *1 n (mocking)* moquerie *f*; **the jeers of the crowd** *(booing)* les huées *fpl* de la foule
2 *vt (boo)* huer; *(mock)* se moquer de
3 *vi* **to j. at sb/sth** *(boo)* huer qn/qch; *(mock)* se moquer de qn/qch

jeering ['dʒɪərɪŋ] *1 n (booing)* huées *fpl*; *(mocking)* moqueries *fpl*
2 *adj* railleur(euse), moqueur(euse)

jeez [dʒiːz] *exclam Fam* mince alors!

Jehovah [dʒɪ'həʊvə] *n* Jéhovah; **J.'s Witness** témoin *m* de Jéhovah

jell [dʒel] *vi (of liquid)* se gélifier; *Fig (of ideas, plans)* prendre forme; *Fig (of team)* constituer un ensemble cohérent

jelly ['dʒelɪ] *(pl* **jellies)** *n (dessert, jam)* gelée *f*; *Br* **j. baby** = bonbon à base de gelatine, en forme de petit bonhomme

jellybean ['dʒelɪbiːn] *n* = bonbon couvert de sucre, en forme de haricot

jellyfish ['dʒelɪfɪʃ] *n* méduse *f*

jemmy ['dʒemɪ] *(pl* **jemmies)** *n Br* pince-monseigneur *f*

jeopardize ['dʒepədaɪz] *vt* compromettre; *(life)* mettre en danger

jeopardy ['dʒepədɪ] *n* **in j.** en danger, en péril; **to put sb/sth in j.** mettre qn/qch en danger *ou* en péril

jerk¹ [dʒɜːk] *1 n (sudden pull)* secousse *f*, coup *m* sec; **to give sth a j.** tirer sur qch d'un coup sec
2 *vt (pull)* tirer brusquement; *(in order to move)* déplacer par à-coups
3 *vi* **to j. forward** *(of car)* faire un bond en avant; *(of head)* partir en avant; **to j. to a halt** s'arrêter avec des soubresauts

jerk² *n Fam (person)* abruti(e) *m,f*

▸**jerk off** *vi Vulg (masturbate)* se branler

jerkily ['dʒɜːkɪlɪ] *adv* de manière saccadée

jerky ['dʒɜːkɪ] *adj (movement)* saccadé(e); *(style)* hâché(e)

jerrican ['dʒerɪkæn] *n* jerrican *m*

jerry-built ['dʒerɪbɪlt] *adj* construit(e) à la va-vite

Jersey ['dʒɜːzɪ] *n (island)* Jersey; **J. (cow)** jersiaise *f*

jersey ['dʒɜːzɪ] *(pl* **jerseys)** *n (garment)* pull(-over) *m*, tricot *m*

Jerusalem [dʒə'ruːsələm] *n* Jérusalem; **J. artichoke** topinambour *m*

jest [dʒest] *1 n* plaisanterie *f*; **in j.** pour plaisanter
2 *vi* plaisanter

jester ['dʒestə(r)] *n* farceur(euse) *m,f*; *Hist* **(court) j.** fou *m* (du roi)

jesting ['dʒestɪŋ] *adj (remark)* pour rire; *(tone)* de la plaisanterie

Jesuit ['dʒezjʊɪt] *n* jésuite *m*

Jesuitical [dʒezjʊ'ɪtɪkəl] *adj Pej (argument, reasoning)* de jésuite

Jesus ['dʒiːzəs] *1 n* Jésus *m*; **J. Christ** Jésus-Christ
2 *exclam Fam* **J. (Christ)!** nom de Dieu!

jet¹ [dʒet] *1 n* **(a)** *(plane)* jet *m*, avion *m* à réaction; **j. engine** réacteur *m*, moteur *m* à réaction; **j. fighter** chasseur *m* à réaction; **j. lag** fatigue *f* due au décalage horaire; **j. propulsion** propulsion *f* par réaction; **the j. set** la jet-set *f*; *(nozzle, of liquid)* jet *m*
2 *vi (pt & pp* **jetted)** *Fam (travel by plane)* **to j. in** venir en avion; **to j. off** s'envoler; **to j. around the world** passer son temps dans les avions

jet² *1 n (stone)* jais *m*
2 *adj* **j. (black)** de jais

jet-lagged ['dʒetlægd] *adj* fatigué(e) par le décalage horaire

jet-powered [dʒet'paʊəd], **jet-propelled** [dʒetprə-'peld] *adj* à réaction

jettison ['dʒetɪsən] vt (cargo) jeter à la mer ou par-dessus bord; (plan, tradition) abandonner

jetty ['dʒetɪ] (pl **jetties**) n jetée f; (for landing) embarcadère m

Jew [dʒuː] n Juif (Juive) m,f

jewel ['dʒuːəl] n (gem, piece of jewellery) bijou m; Fig (person) perle f

jeweller, Am **jeweler** ['dʒuːələ(r)] n bijoutier(ère) m,f; **j.'s (shop)** bijouterie f

jewellery, Am **jewelry** ['dʒuːəlrɪ] n bijoux mpl; **a piece of j.** un bijou

Jewess ['dʒuːɪs] n Old-fashioned Juive f

Jewish ['dʒuːɪʃ] adj juif (juive)

Jewry ['dʒuːərɪ] n **the J.** la communauté juive

jib¹ [dʒɪb] n (a) (sail) foc m (b) (of crane) flèche f

jib² (pt & pp **jibbed**) vi **to j. at sth/at doing sth** rechigner à qch/à faire qch

jibe [dʒaɪb] **1** n moquerie f
2 vi **to j. at sb** se moquer de qn

jiffy ['dʒɪfɪ] n Fam **in a j.** dans un instant, tout de suite

jig [dʒɪg] **1** n (dance, music) gigue f
2 vi (pt & pp **jigged**) (dance) danser la gigue

jigger ['dʒɪgə(r)] vt Fam (TV, microwave) bousiller; **to j. one's back/knee** s'esquinter le dos/genou

jiggered ['dʒɪgəd] adj Fam (TV, microwave) bousillé(e); (back, knee) esquinté(e)

jiggery-pokery ['dʒɪgərɪ'pəʊkərɪ] n Br Fam micmac m

jiggle ['dʒɪgəl] **1** vt secouer rapidement
2 vi remuer dans tous les sens

▸**jiggle about, jiggle around** = jiggle

jigsaw ['dʒɪgsɔː] n (a) (saw) scie f sauteuse (b) (game) **j. (puzzle)** puzzle m

jihad [dʒɪ'hæd] n djihad m

jilt [dʒɪlt] vt (lover) plaquer

jingle ['dʒɪŋgəl] **1** n (a) (of bells, coins) tintement m; (of keys) cliquetis m (b) (catchy tune) jingle m
2 vt (bells, coins) faire tinter; (keys) faire cliqueter
3 vi (of bells, coins) tinter; (of keys) cliqueter

jingoism ['dʒɪŋgəʊɪzəm] n Pej chauvinisme m

jingoistic [dʒɪŋgəʊ'ɪstɪk] adj Pej chauvin(e)

jinx [dʒɪŋks] Fam **1** n (spell, curse) (mauvais) sort m; **to put a j. on sb/sth** jeter un sort à qn/qch
2 vt **to be jinxed** être maudit(e)

JIT [dʒɪt] adj Com (abbr **just in time**) juste à temps

jitters ['dʒɪtəz] npl Fam **to have** or **get the j.** être à cran

jittery ['dʒɪtərɪ] adj Fam à cran

jive [dʒaɪv] **1** n (music, dance) swing m
2 vi (dance) danser le swing

Jnr (abbr **Junior**) **Thomas Smith, J.** Thomas Smith fils

job [dʒɒb] n (a) (employment, post) travail m, emploi m; **to be out of a j.** être sans travail ou emploi; Br Fam **it's jobs for the boys** on place d'abord les petits copains; **j. creation** création f d'emploi; **j. description** description f de poste; **to go j. hunting** chercher du travail; **j. losses** suppressions fpl d'emplois; **j. offer** offre f d'emploi; **j. opportunities** débouchés mpl; **j. satisfaction** satisfaction f dans le travail; **j. security** sécurité f de l'emploi; **j. sharing** partage m de poste; **j. title** fonction f
(b) (piece of work, task) tâche f; **to do a good j.** faire du beau travail; Fig **to do the j.** (serve purpose) convenir, faire l'affaire; **it was quite a j. getting her to come** la

convaincre de venir n'a pas été une mince affaire; Com **j. lot** lot m

(c) (responsibility, duty) travail m; **to have the j. of doing sth** être chargé(e) de faire qch

(d) Fam (crime) coup m

(e) (idioms) Br **it's a good j. (that)...!** heureusement que...!; **that's just the j.!** c'est juste ce qu'il faut!

jobbing ['dʒɒbɪŋ] adj Br (carpenter, electrician) à la tâche ou pièce

Jobcentre ['dʒɒbsentə(r)] n Br ≃ agence f nationale pour l'emploi, ANPE f

jobless ['dʒɒblɪs] **1** npl **the j.** les sans-emploi mpl
2 adj sans emploi

job-share ['dʒɒbʃeə(r)] **1** n poste m partagé
2 vi partager un poste

jockey ['dʒɒkɪ] **1** n (pl **jockeys**) jockey m
2 vi **to j. for position** jouer des coudes

jockstrap ['dʒɒkstræp] n slip m à coquille

jocular ['dʒɒkjʊlə(r)] adj enjoué(e)

jodhpurs ['dʒɒdpəz] npl jodhpurs mpl

Joe [dʒəʊ] n Am Fam **he's an ordinary J.** c'est un mec ordinaire; Br **J. Bloggs, J. Public** Monsieur Tout-le-monde

jog [dʒɒg] **1** n (a) (push) secousse f; (with elbow) coup m de coude; **to give sb's memory a j.** rafraîchir la mémoire de qn (b) (run) course f (à petites foulées); **to break into a j.** se mettre à courir (à petites foulées); **to go for a j.** aller faire un jogging
2 vt (pt & pp **jogged**) (push) pousser; **to j. sb's elbow** donner un coup de coude à qn; **to j. sb's memory** rafraîchir la mémoire à qn
3 vi (run) faire du jogging; **to go jogging** aller faire un jogging

▸**jog along** vi (run) courir à petites foulées; Fig (in job, life) aller son petit bonhomme de chemin

jogger ['dʒɒgə(r)] n joggeur(euse) m,f

jogging ['dʒɒgɪŋ] n jogging m; **j. bottoms** pantalon m de jogging; **j. suit** tenue f de jogging

joggle ['dʒɒgəl] vt secouer légèrement

Johannesburg [dʒəʊ'hænɪzbɜːg] n Johannesburg

john [dʒɒn] n Am Fam (lavatory) petit coin m

John Bull ['dʒɒn'bʊl] n (Englishman) l'Anglais m moyen; (England) l'Angleterre f

join [dʒɔɪn] **1** n raccord m; (in fabric) couture f
2 vt (a) (unite, connect) relier; (planks) joindre; **to j. two things together** relier une chose à une autre; **to j. battle** engager le combat; **to j. forces (with sb)** s'unir (à qn)
(b) (club, political party) adhérer à; (army) s'engager dans; (discussion, game) se joindre à; **to j. a union** se syndiquer; **to j. the queue** se mettre dans la queue; Fam Fig **j. the queue!** tu n'es pas le seul (la seule)!
(c) (meet with) rejoindre; **may I j. you?** (to sb at table) puis-je me joindre à vous?
(d) (of river, road) rejoindre; **where the river joins the sea** où le fleuve se jette dans la mer
3 vi (a) (of pipes, roads, rivers) se rejoindre
(b) (in club, political party) adhérer; (in union) devenir membre

▸**join in 1** vt insep participer à, prendre part à
2 vi participer

▸**join up** vi Mil s'engager

joiner ['dʒɔɪnə(r)] n Br (carpenter) menuisier m

joint [dʒɔɪnt] **1** n (a) (in body) articulation f; **out of j.** déboîté(e); Br Fig **to put sb's nose out of j.** dépiter qn
(b) (in woodwork) assemblage m; (in metalwork) joint m
(c) (of beef) rôti m; (of lamb) gigot m
(d) Fam (nightclub) boîte f; (restaurant) resto m
(e) Fam (cannabis cigarette) joint m
2 adj commun(e); (effort) conjugué(e); **j. account** compte m joint; **j. custody** garde f jointe; **j. ownership** copropriété f; **j. stock company** société f par actions; **j. venture** entreprise f commune
3 vt (chicken) découper

jointly ['dʒɔɪntlɪ] adv conjointement

joist [dʒɔɪst] n solive f

joke [dʒəʊk] **1** n (a) (remark) plaisanterie f, blague f; (prank, trick) tour m, farce f; **to tell** or **crack a j. (about sth)** raconter une blague (sur qch); **to make a j. (about sth)** faire une plaisanterie (sur qch); **to make a j. of sth** rire de qch; **to say/do sth for a j.** dire/faire qch pour rire; **the j. was on him** la plaisanterie s'est retournée contre lui; **she can't take a j.** elle n'aime pas la plaisanterie; **it's no j.** ce n'est pas une mince affaire!; **it's no j. waiting for hours** ce n'est pas drôle d'attendre pendant des heures; **it's getting beyond a j.** ça n'est plus drôle, la plaisanterie a assez duré; **to play a j. on sb** jouer un tour à qn (b) Fam **to be a j.** (ridiculous) être lamentable
2 vi plaisanter; **to j. about sth** plaisanter sur qch; **I was only joking** je plaisantais; **you're joking!, you must be joking!** tu plaisantes!, tu veux rire!; **joking apart...** blague à part...

joker ['dʒəʊkə(r)] n (a) (clown) farceur(euse) m,f; (incompetent person) plaisantin m (b) (in cards) joker m; Fig **the j. in the pack** la grande inconnue

jokily ['dʒəʊkɪlɪ] adv en plaisantant

jokingly ['dʒəʊkɪŋlɪ] adv en plaisantant

joky ['dʒəʊkɪ] adj (person) blagueur(euse); (mood, conversation) jovial(e); (remark, comment) moqueur(euse)

jolly ['dʒɒlɪ] **1** adj (cheerful) joyeux(euse), gai(e); **the J. Roger** le pavillon noir
2 adv Br Fam (very) rudement, drôlement; **j. good!** super!; **it serves him j. well right!** c'est vraiment bien fait pour lui!
3 vt (pt & pp jollied) **to j. sb into doing sth** amadouer qn pour qu'il fasse qch; **to j. sb along** amadouer qn

jolt [dʒəʊlt] **1** n (a) (shake) secousse f (b) (shock, surprise) choc m, coup m; **to give sb a j.** faire un choc ou un coup à qn
2 vt (shake) secouer; (shock, surprise) ébranler; **to j. sb into action** secouer les puces à qn; **to j. sb out of a depression** faire sortir qn de son état dépressif
3 vi (shake) secouer; **to j. along** (of vehicle) cahoter; **to j. to a stop** (of vehicle) s'arrêter avec des à-coups; **his head jolted forward/back** sa tête est partie en avant/en arrière

Jordan ['dʒɔːdən] n (country) la Jordanie; **the (River) J.** le Jourdain

Jordanian [dʒɔː'deɪnɪən] **1** n Jordanien(enne) m,f
2 adj jordanien(enne)

josh [dʒɒʃ] vt Fam mettre en boîte

joss stick ['dʒɒsstɪk] n bâton m d'encens

jostle ['dʒɒsəl] **1** vt bousculer; **to j. sb out of the way** écarter qn en jouant des coudes
2 vi (push) se bousculer; **to j. for position** (in contest, job) jouer des coudes

jot [dʒɒt] n **he doesn't care a j.** il s'en fiche complètement; **there isn't a j. of truth in what you**

say il n'y a pas une once de vérité dans ce que vous dites; **it doesn't make a j. of difference** ça ne fait pas la moindre différence

▶**jot down** (pt & pp jotted) vt sep noter

jotter ['dʒɒtə(r)] n cahier m

jottings ['dʒɒtɪŋz] npl notes fpl

joule [dʒuːl] n Phys joule m

journal ['dʒɜːnəl] n (publication) revue f; (diary) journal m; **to keep a j.** tenir un journal

journalese [dʒɜːnə'liːz] n Fam Pej jargon m journalistique

journalism ['dʒɜːnəlɪzəm] n journalisme m

journalist ['dʒɜːnəlɪst] n journaliste mf

journalistic [dʒɜːnə'lɪstɪk] adj journalistique

journey ['dʒɜːnɪ] **1** n (pl journeys) voyage m; (short) trajet m; **a train j.** un voyage en train; **to make a j.** faire un voyage; **to go (away) on a j.** partir en voyage; **to get to** or **reach the end of one's j.** arriver à destination
2 vi voyager

joust [dʒaʊst] vi Hist jouter; Fig (compete) se chamailler

jovial ['dʒəʊvɪəl] adj jovial(e), enjoué(e)

jovially ['dʒəʊvɪəlɪ] adv jovialement

jowl [dʒaʊl] n (jaw) mâchoire f; (cheek) bajoue f

joy [dʒɔɪ] n (a) (happiness) joie f (b) (pleasure) plaisir m; **she's a j. to be with** c'est un plaisir d'être avec elle (c) Br Fam (success) **did you have** or **get) any j.?** ça a marché?

joyful ['dʒɔɪfʊl] adj (occasion, news) heureux(euse); (person, party) joyeux(euse)

joyfully ['dʒɔɪfəlɪ] adv joyeusement

joyless ['dʒɔɪlɪs] adj triste

joyous ['dʒɔɪəs] adj (occasion, news) heureux(euse); (person, party) joyeux(euse)

joyride ['dʒɔɪraɪd] n (in stolen car) = virée dans une voiture volée; **to go for a j.** = faire une virée dans une voiture volée

joyrider ['dʒɔɪraɪdə(r)] n = chauffard qui conduit une voiture volée

joystick ['dʒɔɪstɪk] n (in aircraft) manche m à balai; (for computer) manette f

JP [dʒeɪ'piː] n Law (abbr **Justice of the Peace**) juge m de paix

Jr (abbr **Junior**) Thomas Smith, Jr Thomas Smith fils

jubilant ['dʒuːbɪlənt] adj (shouts) de joie; (expression) réjoui(e); (person) exultant(e); (celebration) joyeux(euse); **to be j.** (at or about sth) être transporté(e) de joie (par qch)

jubilation [dʒuːbɪ'leɪʃən] n (grande) joie f, jubilation f

jubilee ['dʒuːbɪliː] n (golden) **j.** cinquantième anniversaire m, jubilé m; **silver/diamond j.** vingt-cinquième/soixantième anniversaire

Judaic [dʒuː'deɪɪk] adj judaïque

Judaism ['dʒuːdeɪɪzəm] n judaïsme m

Judas ['dʒuːdəs] n (traitor) Judas m

judder ['dʒʌdə(r)] vi Br être agité(e) de secousses; **to j. to a halt** s'arrêter avec des secousses

judge [dʒʌdʒ] **1** n (a) (in law, sport) juge m; (in competition) membre m du jury (b) (expert) **to be a good/poor j. of sth** s'y connaître/ne pas s'y connaître en qch; **I will be the j. of that** c'est moi qui (en) jugerai
2 vt (a) (in law, sport) juger (b) (assess critically) juger; **to j. sb by** or **on sth** juger qn sur ou d'après qch; **to j. sb/sth a success/failure** considérer que qn/qch a réussi/échoué; **to j. it necessary to do sth** estimer ou juger nécessaire

de faire qch; **don't j. a book by its cover** l'habit ne fait pas le moine (**c**) *(estimate)* estimer, évaluer

3 *vi* juger; **to j. by appearances** juger d'après les apparences; **to j. for oneself** juger par soi-même; **judging by...** à en juger par...

judg(e)ment, *Am* **judgment** ['dʒʌdʒmənt] *n* (**a**) *(decision)* jugement *m*; **to sit in j.** *(of judge, court)* siéger; **to pass j.** *(of judge, court)* rendre un jugement; **Fig to sit in or pass j. on sb** porter des jugements sur qn, juger qn; *Rel* **J. Day** le (jour du) Jugement dernier (**b**) *(opinion)* avis *m*, opinion *f*; **to form a j.** se faire un avis *ou* une opinion (**c**) *(discernment)* jugement *m*; **to have good j.** faire preuve de jugement; **to have poor j.** manquer de jugement; **to trust sb's j.** s'en remettre au jugement de qn; **in my j.** à mon sens; **against my better j.** en sachant que c'est/c'était une erreur

judg(e)mental [dʒʌdʒ'mentl] *adj* critique

judicial [dʒu:'dɪʃl] *adj* judiciaire

judiciary [dʒu:'dɪʃərɪ] *n (judges)* magistrature *f*; *(branch of government)* pouvoir *m* judiciaire

judicious [dʒu:'dɪʃəs] *adj* judicieux(euse)

judiciously [dʒu:'dɪʃəslɪ] *adv* judicieusement

judiciousness [dʒu:'dɪʃəsnɪs] *n* bon sens *m*

judo ['dʒu:dəʊ] *n* judo *m*

jug [dʒʌg] *n* (**a**) *(for wine, water)* pichet *m*; *(for cream, milk)* pot *m* (**b**) *very Fam (prison)* en taule

juggernaut ['dʒʌgənɔ:t] *n Br* poids *m* lourd

juggle ['dʒʌgl] **1** *vt also Fig* jongler avec

2 *vi also Fig* jongler (**with** avec)

juggler ['dʒʌglə(r)] *n* jongleur(euse) *m,f*

jugular ['dʒʌgjʊlə(r)] **1** *n* jugulaire *f*; *Fig* **to go for the j.** frapper au point sensible

2 *adj* jugulaire

juice [dʒu:s] *n* (**a**) *(of fruit, meat)* jus *m*; *(of plant)* suc *m* (**b**) *Fam (petrol)* jus *m*

juicy ['dʒu:sɪ] *adj* (**a**) *(fruit)* juteux(euse); *(meat)* qui rend du jus (**b**) *Fig (contract, deal)* juteux(euse); *(story)* croustillant(e)

jukebox ['dʒu:kbɒks] *n* juke-box *m*

Jul *(abbr* **July)** juillet

July [dʒu:'laɪ] *n* juillet *m*; *see also* **May**

jumble ['dʒʌmbl] **1** *n (of things)* tas *m*; *(of ideas, words)* fatras *m*; **in a j.** *(things)* en désordre, en pagaïe; *(ideas, words)* embrouillé(e); *Br* **j. sale** vente *f* de charité

2 *vt (things)* mélanger; *(ideas, words)* embrouiller

jumbo ['dʒʌmbəʊ] *adj* (**a**) *(sized)* énorme, géant(e); **j. jet** jumbo jet *m*, gros-porteur *m*

jump [dʒʌmp] **1** *n* (**a**) *(leap)* saut *m*; *Fig* **go take a j.!** va te faire voir ailleurs!; *Fig* **to be one j. ahead** avoir une longueur d'avance; **j. jet** ADAV*m*; *Br* **j. leads** câbles *mpl* de démarrage; **j. suit** combinaison *f*

(**b**) *(rise)* hausse *f* soudaine (**in** de)

(**c**) *(on racecourse)* obstacle *m*

2 *vt (hedge, ditch)* sauter; *Fam* **to j. sb** attaquer qn; **to j. bail** se dérober à la justice *(alors qu'on est en liberté provisoire)*; **to j. the gun** *(in race)* faire un faux départ; *Fig* anticiper, agir prématurément; **to j. the lights** *(in car)* brûler un feu rouge; *Br* **to j. the queue** passer avant son tour; **to j. ship** déserter le navire

3 *vi* (**a**) *(leap)* sauter; **to j. to one's feet** se lever d'un bond; **to j. for joy** sauter de joie; **to j. onto a train** sauter dans un train; **to j. out of the window** sauter par la fenêtre; **to j. to conclusions** tirer des conclusions

hâtives; *Fig* **let's wait and see which way she jumps** attendons de voir ce qu'elle va faire; *Fam* **to j. down sb's throat** rabrouer qn; *Fig* **to j. out at sb** *(of mistake, surprising detail)* sauter aux yeux de qn

(**b**) *(go directly)* **to j. from one subject to another** *or* **to the next** sauter d'un sujet à l'autre; **the film then jumps to the present** le film passe d'un seul coup au présent

(**c**) *(of unemployment, inflation)* faire un bond

(**d**) *(make a sudden movement)* *(of person)* sursauter; *(of heart)* faire un bond; *(of record player needle)* sauter; **we nearly jumped out of our skins** ça nous a fichu un coup

▶**jump at** *vt insep (offer, chance)* sauter sur

▶**jump on** *vt insep Fam (reprimand)* sauter sur (**for doing** d'avoir fait)

jumped-up [dʒʌmp'tʌp] *adj Br Fam Pej* prétentieux(euse)

jumper ['dʒʌmpə(r)] *n Br (sweater)* pull(-over) *m*; *Am (sleeveless dress)* robe-chasuble *f*

jumping-off place ['dʒʌmpɪŋ'ɒf pleɪs], **jumping-off point** ['dʒʌmpɪŋ'ɒf pɔɪnt] *n* point *m* de départ; *Fig* tremplin *m*

jump-start ['dʒʌmpstɑ:t] *vt* faire démarrer avec des câbles de démarrage

jumpy ['dʒʌmpɪ] *adj* nerveux(euse)

Jun *(abbr* **June)** juin

junction ['dʒʌŋkʃən] *n (of roads, railway lines)* embranchement *m*; *Elec* **j. box** boîte *f* de dérivation

juncture ['dʒʌŋktʃə(r)] *n Formal* **at this j.** à ce moment(-là)

June [dʒu:n] *n* juin *m*; *see also* **May**

jungle ['dʒʌŋgl] *n also Fig* jungle *f*

junior ['dʒu:nɪə(r)] **1** *n* (**a**) *(in age)* **to be sb's j.** être plus jeune que qn; **he's three years my j.** il a trois ans de moins que moi (**b**) *(in rank)* subalterne *mf*

2 *adj* (**a**) *(in age)* **to be j. to sb** être plus jeune que qn; **Thomas Smith, J.** Thomas Smith fils; *Am* **j. high (school)** *(between 11 and 15)* ≃ collège *m* d'enseignement secondaire; *Br* **j. school** *(between 7 and 11)* = classes primaires du cours élémentaire au cours moyen (**b**) *(in rank)* subalterne; **to be j. to sb** être au-dessous de qn; **j. teacher/executive** jeune professeur *m*/cadre *m*; *Br Univ* **j. common room** salle *f* des étudiants de premier cycle et de licence; *Br Parl* **j. minister** secrétaire *m* d'État

juniper ['dʒu:nɪpə(r)] *n* **j. (tree)** genévrier *m*, genièvre *m*; **j. berry** baie *f* de genièvre

junk¹ [dʒʌŋk] **1** *n (unwanted objects)* bric-à-brac *m*; *(inferior goods)* camelote *f*; *Fin* **j. bond** obligation *f*; **j. food** cochonneries *fpl*; **j. mail** prospectus *mpl*; **j. shop** brocante *f*

2 *vt Fam (discard) (objects)* bazarder; *(plan)* laisser tomber

junk² *n (boat)* jonque *f*

junket ['dʒʌŋkɪt] *n* (**a**) *(food)* lait *m* caillé (**b**) *Pej (trip by public official)* voyage *m* aux frais du contribuable

junkie, junky ['dʒʌŋkɪ] *(pl* junkies) *n Fam (drug addict)* drogué(e) *m,f*; **a fast-food/game-show j.** un accro des fast-food/jeux télévisés

junkyard ['dʒʌŋkjɑ:d] *n (for metal)* ferraille *f*

junta ['dʒʌntə] *n* junte *f*

Jupiter ['dʒu:pɪtə(r)] *n (planet)* Jupiter

jurisdiction [dʒʊərɪs'dɪkʃən] *n* juridiction *f*; **to have j. over sb** avoir autorité sur qn; **to come within** *or* **under the j. of...** être sous la juridiction de...

jurisprudence [dʒʊərɪs'pruːdəns] *n* jurisprudence *f*

jurist ['dʒʊərɪst] *n* (*legal expert*) juriste *mf*

juror ['dʒʊərə(r)] *n Law* juré(e) *m,f*

jury ['dʒʊərɪ] (*pl* **juries**) *n Law* jury *m*; **to be** or **serve on the j.** être membre *ou* faire partie du jury; **to be on j. duty** or **service** être convoqué(e) pour faire partie d'un jury; *Fig* **the j. is still out on that one** ça reste à voir; **j. box** banc *m* des jurés

just [dʒʌst] **1** *adj* (*fair*) juste; **it's only j. that...** c'est normal que... + *subjunctive*; **to get one's j. deserts** n'avoir que ce que l'on mérite

2 *adv* (**a**) (*exactly*) exactement; **that's j. what I told her** c'est exactement ce que je lui ai dit; **j. how many are there?** combien y en a-t-il au juste?; **that's j. the point!** justement!, précisément!; **j. my luck!** c'est bien ma chance!; **it's j. as good/difficult as...** c'est tout aussi bon/difficile que...; **j. then** juste à ce moment-là; **j. now** en ce moment; **j. as I was leaving...** juste au moment où je partais...; **I can j. see her as a doctor** je la vois très bien médecin

(**b**) (*only*) juste; **she's j. a baby** ce n'est qu'un bébé; **it costs j. $10** ça coûte juste 10 dollars

(**c**) (*barely*) juste; **j. before/after** juste avant/après; **j. over/under £50** à peine plus/moins de 50 livres; **j. in time** juste à temps; **it's only j. big enough** c'est tout juste assez grand; **they j. caught the train** ils ont eu le train de justesse; **they j. missed the train** ils ont raté le train d'un cheveu

(**d**) (*recently*) **to have j. done sth** venir de faire qch; **j. yesterday/last year** pas plus tard qu'hier/que l'année dernière

(**e**) (*simply*) **it was j. wonderful/dreadful!** c'était tout simplement merveilleux/affreux!; **he j. refuses to listen!** il refuse carrément d'écouter!; **j. ask if you need money** si tu as besoin d'argent, tu n'as qu'à demander

(**f**) (*in threats, exhortations*) **j. (you) try/wait!** essaie/ attends un peu pour voir!; **(that's) j. as well!** heureusement!

(**g**) **j. about** (*almost*) à peu près; **they're j. about the same** ils se valent; **I can j. about manage** j'y arrive tout juste; **to be j. about to do sth** être sur le point de faire qch

justice ['dʒʌstɪs] *n* (**a**) (*power of law*) justice *f*; **to bring sb to j.** traduire qn en justice (**b**) (*fairness*) légitimité *f*; **this photograph doesn't do him j.** cette photo ne le met pas en valeur; **to do j. to a meal** faire honneur à un repas; **to do oneself j.** se montrer sous son meilleur jour (**c**) (*judge*) juge *m*; *Br* **J. of the Peace** juge de paix

justifiable ['dʒʌstɪfaɪəbəl] *adj* justifié(e), légitime; **j. homicide** légitime défense *f*

justifiably ['dʒʌstɪfaɪəblɪ] *adv* à juste titre

justification [dʒʌstɪfɪ'keɪʃən] *n* justification *f*; **in j. of sth** pour justifier qch

justify ['dʒʌstɪfaɪ] (*pt & pp* **justified**) *vt* justifier; **to be justified in doing sth** avoir de bonnes raisons de faire qch

justly ['dʒʌstlɪ] *adv* (*fairly*) avec justice; (*deservedly*) à juste titre

▶**jut out** [dʒʌt] (*pt & pp* **jutted**) **1** *vt sep* (*chin*) avancer

2 *vi* (*of balcony, rock*) faire saillie; **to j. out over sth** surplomber qch; **to j. out into the sea** s'avancer dans la mer

jute [dʒuːt] *n* jute *m*

juvenile ['dʒuːvnaɪl] **1** *n Law* mineur(e) *m,f*

2 *adj* (**a**) *Law* (*crime, delinquency*) juvénile; **j. court** tribunal *m* pour enfants; **j. delinquent** jeune délinquant(e) *m,f* (**b**) *Pej* (*childish*) puéril(e)

juxtapose [dʒʌkstə'pəʊz] *vt* mettre en juxtaposition (**with** avec)

juxtaposition [dʒʌkstəpə'zɪʃən] *n* juxtaposition *f*

K

K, k [keɪ] *n* (a) *(letter)* K, k *m inv* (b) *(abbr* **thousand, thousand pounds)** he earns **30K** il gagne 30 000 livres sterling (c) Compt *(abbr* **kilobyte)** KO

Kabul ['kɑːbʊl] *n* Kaboul

Kaffir ['kæfə(r)] *n very Fam* nègre (négresse) *m,f,* = terme raciste désignant un(e) Noir(e) d'Afrique du Sud

kaftan ['kæftæn] *n* caf(e)tan *m*

kale [keɪl] *n* chou *m* frisé

kaleidoscope [kə'laɪdəskəʊp] *n* kaléidoscope *m*

kamikaze [kæmɪ'kɑːzɪ] 1 *n also Fig* kamikaze *m*
2 *adj* kamikaze

Kampuchea [kæmpʊ'tʃɪə] *n Formerly* le Kampuchéa

kangaroo [kæŋgə'ruː] *n* kangourou *m;* **k. court** tribunal *m* irrégulier

kaput [kə'pʊt] *adj Fam* kaput *inv*

karate [kə'rɑːtɪ] *n* karaté *m;* **k. chop** coup *m* de karaté

Kashmir [kæʃ'mɪə(r)] *n* Cachemire

Kashmiri [kæʃ'mɪərɪ] 1 *n* (a) *(person)* Cachemirien (enne) *m,f* (b) *(language)* cachemirien *m*
2 *adj* cachemirien(enne)

Katmandu [kætmæn'duː] *n* Katmandou

kayak ['kaɪæk] *n* kayak *m*

Kazak(h)stan [kæzæk'stɑːn] *n* Kazakhstan *m*

kebab [kə'bæb] *n* brochette *f;* **shish k.** chiche-kébab *m;* **doner k.** sandwich *m* grec

kedgeree [kedʒə'riː] *n* = riz pilaf au poisson fumé et aux œufs durs

keel [kiːl] *n (of ship)* quille *f; Fig* **to be on an even k.** être stable

▶**keel over** *vi (of boat)* chavirer; *Fam (of person)* s'écrouler

keen [kiːn] *adj* (a) *(enthusiastic)* enthousiaste; *(student)* assidu(e); **to be k. on sb** avoir un faible pour qn; **to be k. on doing sth** *(habitually)* adorer faire qch; *(want to do)* avoir très envie de faire qch; **to be k. to do sth** avoir très envie de faire qch; **to be k. for sth to happen** tenir beaucoup à ce que qch arrive; *Fam* **to be as k. as mustard** déborder d'enthousiasme; **to take a k. interest in sth** s'intéresser de très près à qch
(b) *(eye, mind, look)* vif (vive); *(price)* compétitif(ive); **to have a k. eye for detail** remarquer jusqu'au moindre détail
(c) *(intense)* vif (vive); *(remorse)* cuisant(e); *(competition)* intense

keenly ['kiːnlɪ] *adv* (a) *(enthusiastically)* avec enthousiasme (b) *(intensely)* profondément; **to be k. aware of sth** avoir une conscience aiguë de qch; **k. contested** âprement disputé(e)

keep [kiːp] 1 *n* (a) **to pay for one's k.** payer sa pension; **to earn one's k.** *(make a living)* gagner sa vie; *(pay one's way)* payer sa pension

(b) *(of castle)* donjon *m*
(c) *Fam* **for keeps** pour de bon

2 *vt (pt & pp* kept [kept]*)* (a) *(retain)* garder; *(store)* ranger; **to k. sth from sb** dissimuler qch à qn; **to k. its shape/colour** *(of garment)* ne pas se déformer/déteindre; **to k. sb's attention** retenir l'attention de qn; **k. the change** gardez la monnaie
(b) *(maintain)* **to k. a diary** tenir un journal; **to k. order** maintenir l'ordre; **to k. a record of sth** garder une trace écrite de qch; **to k. a secret** garder un secret
(c) *(maintain in a certain condition)* **to k. sth secret** garder qch secret; **to k. sb awake** empêcher qn de (s'en)dormir; **to k. sb waiting** faire attendre qn; **she keeps her flat clean** son appartement est toujours bien tenu
(d) *(look after)* *(poultry, cows)* élever; *(shop)* tenir; *(family, mistress)* entretenir; **a kept woman** une femme entretenue
(e) *(detain)* retenir; **what kept you?** pourquoi ce retard?
(f) *(observe)* respecter; *(promise)* tenir; **to k. late hours** se coucher tard; **to k. one's word** tenir parole

3 *vi* (a) *(remain)* rester; **to k. well** rester en bonne santé; **to k. quiet** se tenir tranquille; **how are you keeping?** comment allez-vous?
(b) *(continue)* **to k. straight on** continuer tout droit; **k. (to the) left/right** serrez à gauche/à droite; **to k. doing sth** ne pas arrêter de faire qch; **to k. smiling** garder le sourire; **to k. going** tenir le coup
(c) *(of food)* se conserver; *Fig* **it will k.** *(of problem)* ça peut attendre

▶**keep away** 1 *vt sep* **to k. sb away (from sb/sth)** empêcher qn de s'approcher (de qn/qch)
2 *vi* **to k. away from sb/sth** ne pas s'approcher de qn/qch

▶**keep back** 1 *vt sep* (a) *(crowd, tears)* retenir; **to k. sth back from sb** cacher qch à qn (b) *(delay)* retarder
2 *vi (not approach)* ne pas s'approcher

▶**keep down** 1 *vt sep* (a) *(head)* baisser; **to k. one's voice down** parler moins fort; **to k. the noise down** faire moins de bruit; *Fig* **to k. one's head down** ne pas se faire remarquer; **I can't k. my food down** je vomis tout ce que je mange (b) *(repress)* *(people)* opprimer; *(prices)* empêcher d'augmenter
2 *vi (not stand up)* se tapir

▶**keep from** *vt sep* **to k. sb from doing sth** empêcher qn de faire qch; **to k. sb from his work** empêcher qn de travailler

▶**keep in** *vt sep (pupil)* garder en retenue; **to k. sb in overnight** *(in hospital)* garder qn pour la nuit

▶**keep in with** *vt insep Fam* **to k. in with sb** rester en bons termes avec qn

▶**keep off** 1 *vt sep* **to k. one's hands off sb/sth** ne pas toucher à qn/qch

2 vt insep **k. off the grass** (sign) Pelouse interdite

3 vi (stay away) ne pas intervenir

▸**keep on** 1 vt sep (clothing, employee) garder; (lights, TV) laisser allumé(e); Fam **k. your hair on!** on se calme!

2 vi continuer; **to k. on doing sth** continuer de faire qch; **to keep on about sth** insister constamment sur qch

▸**keep on at** vt insep Fam **to k. on at sb** (to do sth) être toujours sur le dos de qn (pour qu'il fasse qch)

▸**keep out** 1 vt sep (not allow to enter) empêcher d'entrer

2 vi (stay away from) **to keep out of sth** éviter qch; **to k. out of sb's way** éviter qn; **to k. out of danger** rester à l'abri du danger; **to k. out of trouble** ne pas s'attirer d'ennuis; **to k. out of an argument** rester en dehors d'une dispute; **k. out** (sign) défense d'entrer

▸**keep to** 1 vt sep (a) (hold) **to k. sb to a promise** faire tenir une promesse à qn; **to k. sth to a minimum** minimiser qch (b) (not reveal) **to k. sth to oneself** garder qch pour soi; **to k. oneself to oneself** rester à l'écart

2 vt insep (promise) tenir; (contract, agreement) respecter; (subject) s'en tenir à; **to k. to one's bed** garder le lit

▸**keep up** 1 vt sep (a) (custom) conserver; **to k. up the payments** continuer à payer; **to k. it up** (continue to do well) continuer comme ça; **k. up the good work!** continuez à bien travailler!; **to k. up appearances** sauver les apparences (b) (keep awake) empêcher de dormir

2 vi (a) (of rain, snow) continuer (b) (remain level) tenir le rythme; **to k. up with sb** aller à la même allure que qn; **to k. up with the Joneses** rivaliser de standing avec ses voisins; **to k. up with events** se tenir informé(e) de l'actualité; **to k. up with the times** être à la page

keeper ['kiːpə(r)] n (in zoo, park, museum) gardien(enne) m,f; (gamekeeper) garde-chasse m; Fam (goalkeeper) goal m

keep-fit ['kiːp'fɪt] n gymnastique f; **to do k.** faire de la gymnastique; **k. class** cours m de gymnastique

keeping ['kiːpɪŋ] n (a) (care) garde f; **to have sb/sth in one's k.** avoir qn/qch sous sa garde (b) (conformity) **in k. with** conformément à; **out of k. with** en désaccord avec

keepsake ['kiːpseɪk] n souvenir m

keg [keg] n baril m

ken [ken] n **to be beyond sb's k.** être en dehors des compétences de qn

kennel ['kenəl] n (for guard dog) niche f; (for hunting dogs) chenil m; **to put a dog into kennels** mettre un chien en pension

Kenya ['kenjə, 'kiːnjə] n Kenya m

Kenyan ['kenjən] 1 n Kenyan(e) m,f

2 adj kenyan(e)

kept [kept] pt & pp de **keep**

kerb [kɜːb] n Br bordure f de trottoir

kerbcrawler ['kɜːbkrɔːlə(r)] n = personne au volant qui accoste les prostituées

kerbcrawling ['kɜːbkrɔːlɪŋ] n = fait d'accoster des prostituées tout en restant dans sa voiture

kerbstone ['kɜːbstəʊn] n Br bordure f de trottoir

kerfuffle [kə'fʌfəl] n Fam (fuss) histoires fpl; (noise, excitement) remue-ménage m

kernel ['kɜːnəl] n (of nut) amande f; (of grain) grain m; Fig (of problem) fond m, essentiel m

kerosene ['kerəsiːn] n (a) Am pétrole m (lampant); **k. lamp** lampe f à pétrole (b) (aircraft fuel) kérosène m

kestrel ['kestrəl] n faucon m crécerelle

ketchup ['ketʃəp] n (tomato) **k.** ketchup m

kettle ['ketəl] n bouilloire f; **to put the k. on** mettre l'eau à chauffer; Fam **a different k. of fish** une autre affaire

kettledrum ['ketəldrʌm] n timbale f

key [kiː] 1 n (a) (of door, clock, toy) clé f; (of piano, typewriter) touche f; Fig **the k. to happiness/success** la clé du bonheur/de la réussite (b) (to map) légende f; (to exercise) solutions fpl (c) (in music) ton m; **in the k. of C** en ut; **to be off k.** (of singer) chanter faux; (of musician) jouer faux

2 adj (role, factor, figure) clé; (influence, consideration) capital(e); **k. person** pivot m

▸**key in** vt sep (data) saisir

keyboard ['kiːbɔːd] n (of piano, computer) clavier m

keyhole ['kiːhəʊl] n trou m de serrure; **k. surgery** chirurgie f à incision minimale

keynote ['kiːnəʊt] 1 n tonique f; Fig (of speech, approach) point m essentiel

2 adj (speech) programme; (speaker) principal(e)

keypad ['kiːpæd] n Comptr pavé m

keyring ['kiːrɪŋ] n porte-clés m inv

keystone ['kiːstəʊn] n Archit & Fig clef f de voûte

keystroke ['kiːstrəʊk] n Comptr touche f

kg (abbr **kilogram**) kg

KGB [keɪdʒiː'biː] n Formerly KGB m

khaki ['kɑːkɪ] 1 n kaki m

2 adj kaki inv

Khartoum [kɑː'tuːm] n Khartoum

kHz (abbr **kilohertz**) kHz

kibbutz [kɪ'bʊts] (pl **kibbutzim** [kɪbʊt'siːm]) n kibboutz m

kibosh ['kaɪbɒʃ] n Fam **to put the k. on sth** faire tomber qch à l'eau

kick [kɪk] 1 n (a) (with foot) coup m de pied; (of horse) ruade f; (of gun) recul m; **to give sb/sth a k.** donner un coup de pied à qn/dans qch; Fam Fig **she needs a k. up the backside** elle a besoin d'un bon coup de pied au derrière; Fig **that was a k. in the teeth for him** ça a été une gifle pour lui; **that drink has a real k. to it!** cette boisson est vraiment traître!; (b) Fam (thrill) **to get a k. out of doing sth** prendre son pied à faire qch; **to do sth for kicks** faire qch pour s'amuser

2 vt donner un coup/des coups de pied à; (football) taper dans; **to get kicked** recevoir un coup/des coups de pied; Fam **k. the bucket** casser sa pipe; Fig **to k. a man when he's down** s'acharner sur qn qui a perdu ses moyens; **I could have kicked myself** je me serais donné des gifles; **to k. the habit** (stop taking drugs) arrêter (la drogue)

3 vi donner un coup/des coups de pied; (of horse) ruer; (of gun) reculer; Fam Fig **to k. against sth** regimber contre qch

▸**kick about, kick around** 1 vt sep (ball) taper dans; Fam (idea) tester; **don't let them k. you around** tu ne devrais pas les laisser te traiter comme ça

2 vi Fam (hang around) traîner; **there are plenty of people like that kicking around** des gens comme ça, ce n'est pas ça qui manque

▸**kick in** vt sep (door) enfoncer à coups de pied; Fam **to k. sb's head in** casser la tête à qn

▸**kick off** vi (in football) donner le coup d'envoi; Fam Fig (in meeting, debate) démarrer

▸**kick out** vt sep Fam mettre à la porte

▶**kick up** *vt sep Fam* to k. up a fuss faire tout un plat *ou* toute une histoire; to k. up a row *or* a racket faire du boucan

kickback ['kɪkbæk] *n Fam (payment)* pot-de-vin *m*

kickoff ['kɪkɒf] *n (in football)* coup *m* d'envoi; *Fam Fig* for a k. *(to start with)* pour commencer

kick-start ['kɪkstɑːt] 1 *n (on motorbike)* kick *m*
2 *vt (motorbike)* démarrer au kick; *Fig (economy)* donner un sérieux coup de pouce à

kid [kɪd] 1 *n* (a) *Fam (child)* gamin(e) *m,f*, gosse *mf*; my k. brother mon petit frère; it's k.'s stuff *(easy)* c'est un jeu d'enfant; *(childish)* c'est bon pour les gosses (b) *(young goat)* chevreau *m*; *(female)* chevrette *f*; *(skin)* chevreau; k. gloves gants *mpl* en chevreau; *Fig* to handle sb with k. gloves prendre des gants avec qn
2 *vt (pt & pp kidded) Fam (fool)* faire marcher; to k. oneself se faire des illusions
3 *vi* to be kidding plaisanter; no kidding! sans blague!

kidnap ['kɪdnæp] *(pt & pp kidnapped, Am kidnaped)* *vt* kidnapper, enlever

kidnapper ['kɪdnæpə(r)] *n* ravisseur(euse) *m,f*, kidnappeur(euse) *m,f*

kidnapping ['kɪdnæpɪŋ] *n* enlèvement *m*, kidnapping *m*

kidney ['kɪdnɪ] *(pl kidneys) n (of person)* rein *m*; *(for food)* rognon *m*; k. bean haricot *m* rouge; k. donor donneur(euse) *f* de rein; k. machine rein artificiel

kill [kɪl] 1 *n (in hunting) (action)* mise *f* à mort; *(animals killed)* tableau *m* de chasse; to be in at the k. assister à la mise à mort; *Fig* assister au dénouement
2 *vt (person, animal)* tuer; to k. oneself se tuer; *Fam* to k. oneself laughing mourir de rire; *Ironic* don't k. yourself! surtout, ne te surmène pas!; *Fam* this one'll k. you *(of joke)* ça va te faire mourir de rire; to k. two birds with one stone faire d'une pierre deux coups; *Fam* my feet/these shoes are killing me mes pieds/ces chaussures me font un mal de chien (b) *Fig (friendship)* détruire; *(sound)* amortir; *(pain)* calmer; *(chances)* anéantir; *Journ* to k. a story retirer une information; to k. time tuer le temps

▶**kill off** *vt sep (people)* tuer; *(character in film, novel)* faire mourir; *Fig (hope)* anéantir

killer ['kɪlə(r)] *n* tueur(euse) *m,f*; he knew his k. il connaissait son meurtrier; *Fam Fig* those steps were a k.! ces escaliers m'ont tué!; *Fam Fig* this one's a k. *(joke)* celle-ci est à mourir de rire; k. (disease) maladie *f* meurtrière; *Fig* to have the k. instinct être impitoyable; k. whale épaulard *m*

killing ['kɪlɪŋ] 1 *n (of person)* meurtre *m*; *(of animals)* destruction *f*; *Fam* to make a k. faire un bénéfice énorme
2 *adj Fam (exhausting)* tuant(e); *(very amusing)* tordant(e)

killjoy ['kɪldʒɔɪ] *n* rabat-joie *m inv*

kiln [kɪln] *n* four *m*

kilo ['kiːləʊ] *(pl kilos) n* kilo *m*

kilobyte ['kɪləbaɪt] *n Comptr* kilo-octet *m*

kilogram(me) ['kɪləɡræm] *n* kilogramme *m*

kilohertz ['kɪləʊhɜːts] *(pl kilohertz) n* kilohertz *m*

kilometre, *Am* **kilometer** ['kɪləmiːtə(r), kɪ'lɒmɪtə(r)] *n* kilomètre *m*

kilowatt ['kɪləwɒt] *n* kilowatt *m*; k.-hour kilowatt-heure *m*

kilt [kɪlt] *n* kilt *m*

kilter ['kɪltə(r)] *n Fam* out of k. *(of machine part)* déréglé(e) *(with* par rapport à); *(of budget)* déséquilibré(e)

kimono [kɪ'məʊnəʊ] *(pl kimonos) n* kimono *m*

kin [kɪn] *n Formal* parents *mpl*

kind¹ [kaɪnd] *n* (a) *(sort)* genre *m*, espèce *f*; all kinds of... toutes sortes de...; something of the k. quelque chose comme ça, quelque chose de ce genre; I said nothing of the k.! je n'ai jamais dit ça!; she's really boring – she's nothing of the k.! elle est vraiment ennuyeuse – mais pas du tout! in a k. of way d'une certaine manière; well, it's coffee of a k. I suppose je suppose qu'on peut appeler ça du café; we're two of a k. nous sommes pareils; it's the only one of its k. c'est le seul de ce genre; he's that k. of person il est comme ça; this is my k. of party! voilà le genre de soirée que j'aime! this k. of thing ce genre de chose
(b) in k. *(payment)* en nature
(c) *Fam* you look k. of tired tu as l'air un peu fatigué; I k. of expected this je m'y attendais un peu; do you like it? – k. of ça te plaît? – oui, plus ou moins; it was a k. of saucer-shaped thing c'était quelque chose qui ressemblait à une soucoupe

kind² *adj* gentil(ille); to be k. to sb être gentil avec qn; *Formal* would you be k. enough to *or* so k. as to...? auriez-vous la bonté de...?; k. to the skin *(of detergent, soap)* qui n'irrite pas la peau; by k. permission of... with the kind authorisation de...

kinda ['kaɪndə] *very Fam* = kind of

kindergarten ['kɪndəɡɑːtən] *n* jardin *m* d'enfants

kind-hearted ['kaɪnd'hɑːtɪd] *adj (person)* qui a bon cœur; *(action)* généreux(euse)

kindle ['kɪndəl] *vt (flame)* allumer; *Fig (emotions)* éveiller

kindling ['kɪndlɪŋ] *n* petit bois *m*

kindly ['kaɪndlɪ] 1 *adv* gentiment; to speak k. of sb dire du bien de qn; *Formal* (would you) k. be quiet! voudriez-vous avoir la bonté de vous taire!; she didn't take k. to being criticized elle n'a pas apprécié qu'on la critique
2 *adj (person)* gentil(ille); *(tone, advice)* bienveillant(e)

kindness ['kaɪndnɪs] *n* gentillesse *f*; to do sth out of the k. of one's heart faire qch par bonté d'âme; to do sb a k. rendre service à qn

kindred ['kɪndrɪd] *adj* du même genre, de la même nature; we are k. spirits c'est mon alter ego

kinetic [kɪ'netɪk] *adj* cinétique

king [kɪŋ] *n* roi *m*; the three kings *(in the Bible)* les Rois mages; the k. of the beasts le roi des animaux

kingdom ['kɪŋdəm] *n* royaume *m*; the k. of heaven le royaume des cieux; the animal/plant k. le règne animal/végétal; *Fam* until *or* till k. come jusqu'à la saint-glinglin; *Fam* to send sb to k. come envoyer qn ad patres

kingfisher ['kɪŋfɪʃə(r)] *n* martin-pêcheur *m*

kingpin ['kɪŋpɪn] *n Fig (of organization, company)* cheville *f* ouvrière

king-size(d) ['kɪŋsaɪz(d)] *adj* (a) *(cigarette)* long (longue); a k. bed un lit d'1 m 95 de large (b) *Fam (headache, problem)* sacré(e)

kink [kɪŋk] *n (in wire, rope)* boucle *f*; *(in hair)* frisette *f (in character)* bizarrerie *f*

kinky ['kɪŋkɪ] *adj* (a) *(hair)* frisotté(e) (b) *Fam (person) (sexually)* qui a des goûts sexuels bizarres; *(eccentric)* extravagant(e); *(garment)* sexy *inv*; *(behaviour, practice)* pervers(e)

kinship ['kɪnʃɪp] *n* parenté *f*

kinsman ['kɪnzmən] n Lit parent m

kinswoman ['kɪnzwʊmən] n Lit parente f

kiosk ['ki:ɒsk] n kiosque m

kip [kɪp] Fam 1 n Br (sleep) **to have a k.** piquer un roupillon; **to get some k.** roupiller
2 vi (pt & pp **kipped**) Br (sleep) roupiller

kipper ['kɪpə(r)] n hareng m salé et fumé

Kirg(h)izia [kɜ:'gɪzɪə], **Kirg(h)izstan** [kɜ:gɪz'stæn] n le Kirghizistan

kirk [kɜ:k] n Scot église f; **the K.** l'Église (presbytérienne) d'Écosse

kiss [kɪs] 1 n baiser m; **to give sb a k.** donner un baiser à qn; **to give sb the k. of life** faire du bouche-à-bouche à qn; Fig **to be the k. of death for sth** porter un coup fatal à qch; **k. curl** accroche-cœur m
2 vt embrasser; **to k. sb goodbye** dire au revoir à qn en l'embrassant; Fig **you can k. your promotion goodbye** tu peux dire adieu à ta promotion
3 vi s'embrasser; **to k. and make up** se réconcilier; **to k. and tell** dévoiler à la presse ses secrets d'alcôve (impliquant généralement une personne célèbre)

kissogram ['kɪsəgræm] n = service permettant de faire délivrer un message, un poème, une chanson etc, souvent grivois, accompagnés d'un baiser, pour une occasion particulière

kit [kɪt] n (a) (equipment) équipement m, matériel m (b) (sports clothes) tenue f (c) (for assembly) (model) k. maquette f; **to make sth from a k.** faire qch à partir de pièces détachées; **in k. form** en kit

▶**kit out** (pt & pp **kitted**) vt sep équiper (**with** de)

kitbag ['kɪtbæg] n sac m de marin; Mil sac à paquetage

kitchen ['kɪtʃɪn] n cuisine f; **k. knife** couteau m de cuisine; **k. roll** essuie-tout m inv, Sopalin® m; **k. sink** évier m; Fam **to take everything but the k. sink** emporter des tonnes de choses; (of thief) ne laisser que les murs; **k. unit** élément m de cuisine

kitchenette [kɪtʃɪ'net] n coin-cuisine m, kitchenette f

kitchenware ['kɪtʃɪnweə(r)] n vaisselle f et ustensiles mpl de cuisine

kite [kaɪt] n (a) (toy) cerf-volant m; **to fly a k.** faire voler un cerf-volant; Fig lancer un ballon d'essai; Fam **go fly a k.!** va voir là-bas si j'y suis!; Fam **as high as a k.** excité(e) comme une puce (b) (bird) milan m

kith [kɪθ] n Lit **k. and kin** parents mpl et amis mpl

kitsch [kɪtʃ] n kitsch m

kitten ['kɪtən] n chaton m; Fig **to have kittens** être dans tous ses états

kitty ['kɪtɪ] n (a) Fam (cat) minou m (b) (for bills, in cards) cagnotte f

kiwi ['ki:wi:] n (a) (bird) kiwi m; **k. fruit** kiwi (b) Fam K. (New Zealander) Néo-Zélandais(e) m,f

kleptomania [kleptə'meɪnɪə] n kleptomanie f

kleptomaniac [kleptə'meɪnɪæk] n kleptomane mf

km (abbr **kilometre**) km

kmph (abbr **kilometres per hour**) km/h

knack [næk] n talent m; (for manual activity) tour m de main; **to have the k. of** or **a k. for doing sth** avoir un don pour faire qch; Ironic avoir le don de faire qch; **to get the k. (of doing sth)** attraper le tour de main (pour faire qch)

knacker ['nækə(r)] n équarrisseur m; **k.'s yard** chantier m d'équarrissage

knackered ['nækəd] adj Br very Fam (tired) crevé(e); (broken, damaged) foutu(e)

knapsack ['næpsæk] n sac m à dos

knave [neɪv] n (a) (in cards) valet m (b) Lit (scoundrel) coquin m, fripon m

knead [ni:d] vt (dough) pétrir; (muscles) masser

knee [ni:] 1 n genou m; **to go down on one's knees** s'agenouiller; Fig **to bring sb to his knees** obliger qn à capituler
2 vt (hit with knee) donner un coup de genou à

kneecap ['ni:kæp] 1 n rotule f
2 vt (pt & pp **kneecapped**) tirer dans les rotules à

knee-deep ['ni:di:p] adj **to be k. in sth** (in water, snow) être enfoncé(e) jusqu'aux genoux dans qch; Fig (in problems) avoir qch jusqu'au cou; (in work) être débordé(e) de qch

knee-high ['ni:haɪ] adj **to be k.** (of water, snow) arriver à hauteur du genou; Fam **when I was k. to a grasshopper** quand j'étais haut comme trois pommes

kneejerk ['ni:dʒɜ:k] adj (reaction, response) instinctif(ive)

kneel [ni:l] (pt & pp **knelt** [nelt]) vi s'agenouiller, se mettre à genoux; **to k. down** se mettre à genoux

knee-length ['ni:leŋθ] adj (skirt) qui descend jusqu'aux genoux; (boots, socks) qui monte jusqu'aux genoux

knees-up ['ni:zʌp] n Br Fam **to have a k.** faire la fête

knell [nel] n Lit glas m; **to toll the k. for sb** signer l'arrêt de mort de qn; **to toll the k. for sth** sonner le glas de qch

knelt [nelt] pt & pp of **kneel**

knew [nju:] pt of **know**

knickerbockers ['nɪkəbɒkəz] npl knickers mpl

knickers ['nɪkəz] npl (a) (underwear) culotte f, slip m; Br Fam **to get one's k. in a twist** perdre les pédales (b) Am (breeches) knickers mpl

knick-knack ['nɪknæk] n Fam babiole f

knife [naɪf] 1 n (pl **knives** [naɪvz]) couteau m; **k. and fork** couvert m; Fig **to get** or **have one's k. into sb** en vouloir à qn; **k. sharpener** aiguisoir m
2 vt (stab) donner un coup de couteau à, poignarder

knife-edge ['naɪfedʒ] n Fig **to be on a k.** (of person) être sur les nerfs; **to be balanced on a k.** (of situation, game) ne tenir qu'à un fil

knife-point ['naɪfpɔɪnt] n **at k.** sous la menace d'un couteau

knifing ['naɪfɪŋ] n agression f au couteau

knight [naɪt] 1 n chevalier m; (in chess) cavalier m
2 vt faire chevalier

knighthood ['naɪthʊd] n (title) **to be given a k.** être fait chevalier

knit [nɪt] (pt & pp **knitted** or **knit**) 1 vt (sweater) tricoter; **to k. one's brows** froncer les sourcils
2 vi tricoter, faire du tricot

▶**knit together** vi (of broken bones) se ressouder

knitted ['nɪtɪd] adj tricoté(e)

knitting ['nɪtɪŋ] n (item produced) tricot m; **to do some k.** tricoter; **k. machine** machine f à tricoter; **k. needle** aiguille f à tricoter

knitwear ['nɪtweə(r)] n lainages mpl

knives [naɪvz] pl of **knife**

knob [nɒb] n (on cane) pommeau m; (on banisters) pomme f; (on drawer, door) poignée f; (on radio) bouton m; **a k. of butter** une noix de beurre

knobbly ['nɒblɪ] *adj* couvert(e) de bosses; *(tree)* noueux(euse); **k. knees** genoux *mpl* cagneux

knock [nɒk] **1** *n (blow)* coup *m*; **there was a k. at the door** on frappa à la porte

2 *vt* **(a)** *(hit)* frapper, heurter; **to k. sb to the ground** faire tomber qn en le frappant; **to k. sb unconscious** assommer qn; **to k. one's head against sth** se cogner la tête contre qch; **to k. a hole in sth** faire un trou dans qch; **to k. holes in an argument** démolir un argument; **to k. some sense into sb** apprendre à vivre à qn; *Fig* **to k. sb into shape** mettre qn au pas **(b)** *Fam (criticize)* débiner; **don't k. it until you've tried it** il faut essayer avant de critiquer

3 *vi* **(a)** *(hit)* frapper; **to k. at the door** frapper à la porte; **to k. against sth** heurter qch; **his knees were knocking** ses genoux s'entrechoquaient **(b)** *(of engine)* cogner

▸**knock about, knock around 1** *vt sep* **(a)** malmener; *(beat up)* battre **(b)** *Fam (idea, suggestion)* discuter de

2 *vi Fam (hang around)* traîner; **to k. about with sb** fréquenter qn

3 *vt insep Fam (spend time in)* **to k. about the world** rouler sa bosse; **she's been knocking about Glasgow for years** elle traîne à Glasgow depuis des lustres

▸**knock back** *vt sep Fam* **(a)** *(drink)* s'envoyer **(b)** *(reject)* envoyer bouler

▸**knock down** *vt sep* **(a)** *(pedestrian)* renverser **(b)** *(building)* abattre **(c)** *(price)* baisser

▸**knock off 1** *vt sep* **(a)** *(cause to fall off)* faire tomber; **he was knocked off his bike by a car** une voiture a heurté son vélo et il est tombé; *Fam* **to k. sb's head or block off** casser la figure à qn; *Fam* **to k. sth off the price** baisser un peu le prix **(b)** *very Fam (steal)* piquer, faucher **(c)** *Fam (kill)* zigouiller **(d)** *Fam* **k. it off!** *(stop it)* ça suffit!, arrête! **(e)** *Fam (produce quickly)* expédier

2 *vi (finish work)* finir

▸**knock out** *vt sep* **(a)** *(make unconscious)* mettre K.-O.; *Fam* **to k. sb's brains or teeth out** arranger le portrait à qn **(b)** *(eliminate from competition)* éliminer

▸**knock over** *vt sep* faire tomber

▸**knock up** *vt sep* **(a)** *(make hastily)* construire en vitesse; *(meal)* préparer en vitesse **(b)** *very Fam (make pregnant)* mettre en cloque

knockdown price ['nɒkdaʊn'praɪs] *n Fam* **at a k.** à très bas prix

knocker ['nɒkə(r)] *n* **(a)** *(on door)* heurtoir *m* **(b)** *very Fam* **knockers** *(breasts)* nichons *mpl*

knocking ['nɒkɪŋ] *n (at door)* coups *mpl*; *(of engine)* cognement *m*

knock-kneed ['nɒk'ni:d] *adj* **to be k.** avoir les genoux en dedans

knock-on effect ['nɒkɒnɪ'fekt] *n* répercussions *fpl* en chaîne

knockout ['nɒkaʊt] **1** *n* **(a)** *(in boxing)* knock-out *m inv*; *Fig* coup *m* de grâce **(b)** *Fam* **he's/she's a k.** *(attractive)* il/elle est canon

2 *adj* **(a) k. blow** *(in boxing)* coup *m* qui provoque un K.-O.; *Fig* coup *m* de grâce; *Fig* **to deliver the k. blow** donner le coup de grâce **(b) k. competition** compétition *f* avec épreuves éliminatoires

knot [nɒt] **1** *n* **(a)** *(in general)* nœud *m*; **to tie/untie a k.** faire/défaire un nœud; *Fam Fig* **to tie the k.** *(get married)* se marier **(b)** *Naut (unit of speed)* nœud *m*; *Fam Fig* **at a rate of knots** à toute allure **(c)** *(group of people)* petit groupe *m*

2 *vt (pt & pp* **knotted)** *(rope, string)* nouer; *very Fam* **get knotted!** va te faire voir!

knotty ['nɒtɪ] *adj (problem)* épineux(euse)

know [nəʊ] **1** *n Fam* **to be in the k.** être au courant

2 *vt (pt* **knew** [nju:], *pp* **known** [nəʊn]**)** **(a)** *(be acquainted with)* connaître; **to get to k. sb** apprendre à connaître qn; **when I first knew her** quand j'ai fait sa connaissance; **I've never known anything like it** je n'ai jamais rien vu de tel; **I k. her to say hello to** nous nous saluons, c'est tout; **knowing him...** le connaissant...

(b) *(have knowledge of)* savoir; **she thinks she knows all the answers** elle croit avoir réponse à tout; **to k. Spanish** connaître l'espagnol; **to k. a lot/a little about sth** bien s'y connaître/s'y connaître un peu en qch; **she knows what she is talking about** elle sait de quoi elle parle; **to k. how to do sth** savoir faire qch; *Fam* **to k. a thing or two** être malin(igne); **to k. one's own mind** savoir ce que l'on veut; **heaven or God knows!** Dieu seul le sait!

(c) *(recognize)* reconnaître *(by* à*)*; *(distinguish)* distinguer *(from* de*)*; **to k. right from wrong** savoir faire la distinction entre le bien et le mal

3 *vi* savoir; **to k. about sth** être au courant de qch; **to get to k. of sth** apprendre qch; **as far as I k.** *(pour)* autant que je sache; **how should I k.?** comment le saurais-je?; **you never k.** on ne sait jamais; **not that I k.** of pas que je sache; **to k. better than to do sth** savoir qu'il ne faut pas faire qch; **you k.**... tu sais...

know-all ['nəʊ:l] *n Fam* monsieur *m*/madame *f* je-sais-tout

know-how ['nəʊhaʊ] *n Fam* savoir-faire *m*; *(technical)* know-how *m*

knowing ['nəʊɪŋ] **1** *n* **there's no k.** c'est impossible de savoir

2 *adj (look, smile)* entendu(e)

knowledge ['nɒlɪdʒ] *n* **(a)** *(of fact)* connaissance *f*; **(not) to my k.** (pas) à ma connaissance; **to have no k. of sth** ignorer qch; **to have full k. of sth** avoir pleine connaissance de qch; **it is common k. that...** c'est un fait notoire que...; *Formal* **it has recently come to our k. that...** il a été récemment porté à notre connaissance que... **(b)** *(learning)* savoir *m*, connaissances *fpl*; *Prov* **k. is power** savoir c'est pouvoir; *Comptr* **k.-based system** système *m* basé sur les connaissances

knowledgeable ['nɒlɪdʒəbl] *adj* savant(e); **to be k. about sth** bien s'y connaître en qch

known [nəʊn] **1** *adj* connu(e); *(notorious)* notoire

2 *pp of* **know**

knuckle ['nʌkəl] *n* articulation *f* ou jointure *f* (du doigt)

▸**knuckle down** *vi Fam* se mettre au boulot; **to k. down to sth** se mettre à qch

▸**knuckle under** *vi Fam* mettre les pouces

knuckle-duster ['nʌkəldʌstə(r)] *n* coup-de-poing *m* américain

KO ['keɪ'əʊ] *Fam* **1** *n (pl* **KO's** ['keɪ'əʊz]*) (in boxing)* K.-O. *m*

2 *vt (pt & pp* **KO'd** ['keɪ'əʊd]*) (in boxing)* mettre K.-O.

koala [kəʊ'ɑːlə] *n* **k. (bear)** koala *m*

kopeck ['kəʊpek] *n* kopeck *m*

Koran [kə'rɑːn] *n* **the K.** le Coran

Koranic [kə'rænɪk] *adj* coranique

Korea [kə'rɪə] *n* la Corée; **North/South K.** la Corée du Nord/du Sud

Korean [kə'rɪən] **1** *n* (a) *(person)* Coréen(enne) *m,f* (b) *(language)* coréen *m*
 2 *adj* coréen(enne); **the K. War** la guerre de Corée

kosher ['kəʊʃə(r)] *adj* (a) *(in Judaism)* casher *inv,* kasher *inv* (b) *Fam (legitimate)* régio *inv*

kowtow [kaʊ'taʊ] *vi* **to k. to sb** faire des courbettes devant qn

Kraut [kraʊt] *n very Fam* Boche *mf,* = terme injurieux désignant un Allemand

krona ['krəʊnə] *(pl* **kronor** ['krəʊnɔ:(r)]) *n* couronne *f*

krone ['krəʊnə] *(pl* **kroner** ['krəʊnə(r)]) *n* couronne *f*

kudos ['kju:dɒs] *n (prestige)* prestige *m; (fame)* célébrité *f*

Kurd [kɜ:d] **1** *n* Kurde *mf*
 2 *adj* kurde

Kurdish ['kɜ:dɪʃ] **1** *n (language)* kurde *m*
 2 *adj* kurde

Kurdistan [kɜ:dɪ'stæn] *n* le Kurdistan

Kuwait [kʊ'weɪt] *n* le Koweït

Kuwaiti [kʊ'weɪtɪ] **1** *n* Koweïtien(enne) *m,f*
 2 *adj* koweïtien(enne)

kW *(abbr* **kilowatt)** kW

L

L, l [el] *n* (a) *(letter)* L, l *m inv* (b) *Br* **L-plate** = plaque apposée sur une voiture pour signaler que le conducteur est en conduite accompagnée

LA [el'eɪ] *n (abbr* **Los Angeles)** Los Angeles

Lab *Br Pol (abbr* **Labour)** les travaillistes *mpl*

lab [læb] *n Fam (abbr* **laboratory)** labo *m*

label ['leɪbəl] **1** *n* (a) *also Fig* étiquette *f* (b) *(of record company)* label *m*
2 *vt (pt & pp* **labelled,** *Am* **labeled)** *also Fig* étiqueter; *Fig* **to l. sb a liar** qualifier qn de menteur(euse)

labor, labored *etc Am* = **labour, laboured** *etc*

laboratory [lə'bɒrətrɪ] *(pl* **laboratories)** *n* laboratoire *m*; **l. assistant** laborantin(e) *m,f*

laborious [lə'bɔːrɪəs] *adj (work)* pénible, fatigant(e); *(explanation)* laborieux(euse)

laboriously [lə'bɔːrɪəslɪ] *adv* laborieusement

labour, *Am* **labor** ['leɪbə(r)] **1** *n* (a) *(work)* labeur *m*; **l. camp** camp *m* de travail
(b) *(workers)* main-d'œuvre *f*; **l. costs** coût *m* de la main-d'œuvre; **l. dispute** conflit *m* du travail; *Br Formerly* **L. Exchange** bureau *m* de placement; **l. force** effectifs *mpl*; **l. market** marché *m* du travail; **l. shortage** pénurie *f* de main-d'œuvre
(c) *Br Pol* **L., the L. Party** le parti travailliste, les travaillistes *mpl*
(d) *(task)* effort *m*; **to do sth as a l. of love** faire qch pour le plaisir
(e) *(childbirth)* travail *m*; **to be in l.** être en travail; **l. pains** douleurs *fpl* de l'accouchement
2 *vt* **to l. a point** s'étendre sur un sujet
3 *vi* (a) *(of person)* peiner *(over* sur); **to l. in vain** s'échiner en vain; **to be labouring under a misapprehension** être dans l'erreur
(b) *(of engine)* peiner

laboured, *Am* **labored** ['leɪbəd] *adj* laborieux(euse)

labourer, *Am* **laborer** ['leɪbərə(r)] *n* manœuvre *m*; *(on farm)* ouvrier(ère) *m,f* agricole

labouring, *Am* **laboring** ['leɪbərɪŋ] *adj* **a l. job** du travail *m* de manœuvre

labour-intensive, *Am* **labor-intensive** [leɪbərɪn'tensɪv] *adj* qui demande une main-d'œuvre importante

labour-saving, *Am* **labor-saving** ['leɪbəseɪvɪŋ] *adj* qui simplifie la tâche

labrador ['læbrədɔː(r)] *n* labrador *m*

laburnum [lə'bɜːnəm] *n* cytise *m*

labyrinth ['læbərɪnθ] *n* labyrinthe *m*

labyrinthine [læbə'rɪnθaɪn] *adj Archit* en labyrinthe; *Fig* labyrinthique

lace [leɪs] **1** *n* (a) *(cloth)* dentelle *f*; **l. curtain** rideau *m* en ou de dentelle (b) *(of shoe)* lacet *m*
2 *vt* (a) *(shoes)* **to l. (up)** lacer (b) *(drink)* ajouter de l'alcool à; *Fig (story)* entremêler *(with* de); **to l. a drink with sth** ajouter qch dans une boisson

lacerate ['læsəreɪt] *vt* lacérer

laceration [læsə'reɪʃən] *n* lacération *f*

lace-up ['leɪsʌp] **1** *n (shoe)* chaussure *f* à lacets
2 *adj (shoe)* à lacets

lachrymose ['lækrɪməʊs] *adj Lit* larmoyant(e)

lack [læk] **1** *n* manque *m (of* de); **for l. of...** faute de...
2 *vt* manquer de
3 *vi* **to be lacking in sth** manquer de qch

lackadaisical [lækə'deɪzɪkəl] *adj* désinvolte

lackey ['lækɪ] *(pl* **lackeys)** *n Pej* larbin *m*

lacklustre, *Am* **lackluster** ['læklʌstə(r)] *adj* terne

laconic [lə'kɒnɪk] *adj* laconique

lacquer ['lækə(r)] **1** *n* laque *f*
2 *vt* laquer

lacrosse [lə'krɒs] *n Sp* crosse *f*

lacuna [lə'kjuːnə] *(pl* **lacunae** [lə'kjuːniː] *or* **lacunas)** *n* lacune *f*

lad [læd] *n Fam* (a) *(young man)* jeune gars *m*; *(boy)* garçon *m*; **he's a big l.** c'est un grand gaillard; **he's a bit of a l.** or **quite a l.** c'est un sacré fêtard (b) **lads** *(friends)* **he's gone out with the lads** il est sorti avec les copains; **come on, lads!** allez les mecs!

ladder ['lædə(r)] **1** *n (for climbing, in tights)* échelle *f*; **the social l.** l'échelle sociale; *Fig* **to get one's foot on the l.** mettre un pied à l'étrier; *Fig* **to reach the top of the l.** atteindre le sommet de l'échelle
2 *vt (tights)* filer
3 *vi (of tights)* filer

laden ['leɪdən] *adj* chargé(e) *(with* de)

ladle ['leɪdəl] **1** *n* louche *f*
2 *vt* **to l. (out)** *(soup)* servir (à la louche)
3 *vi Fig* **to l. out advice/praise** distribuer les conseils/les compliments

lady ['leɪdɪ] *(pl* **ladies)** *n* (a) dame *f*; **a young l.** *(unmarried)* une jeune fille; *(married)* une jeune dame; **the l. of the house** la maîtresse de maison; **ladies and gentlemen!** mesdames et messieurs!; **ladies' man** homme *m* à femmes; **ladies' (room)** toilettes *fpl* *(des dames)*; **l. friend** amie *f* (b) **Our L.** Notre-Dame *f* (c) *(title)* **L.** Browne lady Browne *(titre de noblesse féminin)*; **L. Luck** la chance; *Fam* **to act like L. Muck** jouer à la grande dame

ladybird ['leɪdɪbɜːd] *n* coccinelle *f*

lady-in-waiting ['leɪdɪn'weɪtɪŋ] *(pl* **ladies-in-waiting)** *n* dame *f* d'honneur

lady-killer ['leɪdɪkɪlə(r)] *n Fam* bourreau *m* des cœurs

ladylike ['leɪdɪlaɪk] *adj (woman)* comme il faut; *(air, behaviour)* distingué(e)

ladyship ['leɪdɪʃɪp] *n also Ironic* Her/Your L. madame

lag [læg] **1** *n* (a) *(gap)* décalage *m* (b) *very Fam (prisoner)* old l. repris *m* de justice

2 *vt & vi pp* **lagged**) *(pipes, boiler)* isoler

3 *vi (of person, economy)* to l. behind être à la traîne; to l. behind sb/sth être à la traîne derrière qn/qch

lager ['lɑːgə(r)] *n* bière *f* blonde; *Fam* l. lout voyou *m* imbibé de bière

laggard ['lægəd] *n* traînard(e) *m,f*

lagoon [lə'guːn] *n* lagune *f*; *(of atoll)* lagon *m*

laid [leɪd] *pt & pp of* **lay**

laid-back [leɪd'bæk] *adj Fam* cool *inv*, relax *inv*

lain [leɪn] *pp of* **lie**²

lair [leə(r)] *n* repaire *m*

laird [leəd] *n Scot* propriétaire *m* foncier

laisser-faire [leɪser'feə(r)] **1** *n* laisser-faire *m*

2 *adj* de laisser-faire

laity ['leɪtɪ] *n* the l. les laïques *mpl*

lake [leɪk] *n* lac *m*; L. Geneva le lac de Genève, le lac Léman; the L. District, the Lakes la région des lacs *(dans le nord-ouest de l'Angleterre)*

lamb [læm] *n* agneau *m*; poor l.! pauvre biquet!; like lambs to the slaughter comme des veaux que l'on mène à l'abattoir; l. chop côtelette *f* d'agneau

lambast ['læm'bæst] *vt* fustiger

lambing ['læmɪŋ] *n* agnelage *m*

lambskin ['læmskɪn] *n* peau *f* d'agneau

lambswool ['læmswʊl] **1** *n* lambswool *m*

2 *adj* en lambswool

lame [leɪm] **1** *adj also Fig* boiteux(euse); to be l. boiter; to go l. se mettre à boiter; *Fig* l. duck canard *m* boiteux

2 *vt* rendre boiteux(euse)

lamé ['lɑːmeɪ] *n* lamé *m*; a l. dress une robe en lamé

lamely ['leɪmlɪ] *adv* maladroitement

lament [lə'ment] **1** *n* lamentation *f*; *Mus* complainte *f*

2 *vt* se lamenter sur; the late lamented Mr Jones le regretté M. Jones

3 *vi* se lamenter (over *sur*)

lamentable ['læməntəbəl] *adj* lamentable; *(decision, loss)* déplorable

lamentably ['læməntəblɪ] *adv* lamentablement

lamentation [læmən'teɪʃən] *n* lamentation *f*

laminate ['læmɪneɪt] *n* stratifié *m*

laminated ['læmɪneɪtɪd] *adj* (a) *(glass)* feuilleté(e); *(wood, plastic)* stratifié(e) (b) *(paper, identity card)* plastifié(e)

lamp [læmp] *n* lampe *f*

lamplight ['læmplaɪt] *n* by l. à la lumière d'une lampe

lampoon [læm'puːn] **1** *n* pamphlet *m*

2 *vt* brocarder

lamppost ['læmppəʊst] *n* réverbère *m*

lamprey ['læmprɪ] *(pl* **lampreys)** *n* lamproie *f*

lampshade ['læmpʃeɪd] *n* abat-jour *m inv*

lampstand ['læmpstænd] *n* pied *m* de lampe

LAN [elen'en] *n Comptr (abbr* **local area network)** réseau *m* local

lance [lɑːns] **1** *n (weapon)* lance *f*

2 *vt (abscess)* percer, inciser

lance corporal ['lɑːns'kɔːpərəl] *n* ≃ caporal *m*

lancer ['lɑːnsə(r)] *n (soldier)* lancier *m*

lancet ['lɑːnsɪt] *n* lancette *f*

land [lænd] **1** *n* (a) *(ground, nation)* terre *f*; on l. sur terre; to live off the l. vivre du produit de la terre; to be in the l. of the living être toujours de ce monde; *Mil* l. forces armée *f* de terre; l. reclamation mise *f* en valeur des sols; l. reform réforme *f* agraire

(b) *(property)* terres *fpl*

2 *vt* (a) *(passengers, cargo)* débarquer

(b) *(plane)* poser

(c) *(fish)* sortir de l'eau

(d) *Fam (job, prize)* décrocher

(e) *Fam (put)* to l. sb in prison/court mener qn en prison/au tribunal; to l. sb in trouble attirer des ennuis à qn

(f) *Fam* to be landed with sth rester avec qch sur les bras; I got landed with doing the dishes c'est moi qui ai dû me taper à la vaisselle

(g) *Fam (hit)* to l. sb one en coller une à qn

3 *vi* atterrir; *(of gymnast)* se réceptionner; *Fig* to l. on one's feet retomber sur ses pieds

▸**land up** *vi* atterrir

landed ['lændɪd] *adj* l. gentry noblesse *f* terrienne; l. proprietor propriétaire *mf* terrien(enne)

landfall ['lændfɔːl] *n Naut* to make l. arriver en vue des côtes

landfill site ['lændfɪl'saɪt] *n* décharge *f* publique

landing ['lændɪŋ] *n* (a) *(of cargo, troops)* débarquement *m*; l. card carte *f* de débarquement; l. craft navire *m* de débarquement; l. stage débarcadère *m* (b) *(of aircraft)* atterrissage *m*; l. gear train *m* d'atterrissage; l. lights phares *mpl* d'atterrissage; l. strip piste *f* d'atterrissage (c) *(of staircase)* palier *m*

landlady ['lændleɪdɪ] *(pl* **landladies)** *n* (a) *(of rented accommodation)* propriétaire *f* (b) *(of small hotel)* logeuse *f*; *(of pub)* patronne *f*

landlocked ['lændlɒkt] *adj* sans accès à la mer

landlord ['lændlɔːd] *n* (a) *(of rented accommodation)* propriétaire *m* (b) *(of pub)* patron *m*

landmark ['lændmɑːk] *n (distinctive feature)* point *m* de repère; *Fig (important event)* événement *m* marquant

landmass ['lændmæs] *n* masse *f* continentale

landmine ['lændmaɪn] *n* mine *f* terrestre

landowner ['lændəʊnə(r)] *n* propriétaire *mf* foncier(ère)

landowning ['lændəʊnɪŋ] *adj* the l. classes la propriété foncière

landscape ['lændskeɪp] **1** *n* paysage *m*; l. design aménagement *m* d'espaces verts; l. gardener jardinier(ère) *m,f* paysagiste; *Comptr* l. (orientation) format *m* paysage; l. painter paysagiste *mf*

2 *vt* aménager en espaces verts

landslide ['lændslaɪd] *n* (a) *(of land)* glissement *m* de terrain (b) *(election victory)* raz *m inv* de marée électoral; to win by a l. gagner avec une majorité écrasante

landslip ['lændslɪp] *n* glissement *m* de terrain

landward ['lændwəd] **1** *adj (wind)* marin(e); on the l. side du côté des terres

2 *adv* vers la terre

lane [leɪn] *n* (a) *(in country)* chemin *m*; *(in town)* ruelle *f*, passage *m* (b) *(on road)* voie *f*, file *f*; get in l. = panneau indiquant aux automobilistes de se placer dans la file appropriée (c) *(for runner, swimmer)* couloir *m*

language ['læŋgwɪdʒ] n (a) (of a people) langue f; Fam Fig **we don't talk the same l.** nous ne parlons pas la même langue; **l. laboratory** laboratoire m de langues; **l. learning/teaching** apprentissage m/enseignement m des langues (b) (style of speech or writing) langage m

languid ['læŋgwɪd] adj alangui(e)

languidly ['læŋgwɪdlɪ] adv paresseusement

languish ['læŋgwɪʃ] vi languir (**for** après); **to l. in prison** moisir en prison

languor ['læŋgə(r)] n langueur f

languorous ['læŋgərəs] adj alangui(e)

lank [læŋk] adj (hair) terne

lanky ['læŋkɪ] adj dégingandé(e)

lanolin(e) ['lænəlɪn] n lanoline f

lantern ['læntən] n lanterne f

Laos [laʊs] n le Laos

Laotian ['laʊʃən] **1** n Laotien(enne) m,f
2 adj laotien(enne)

lap¹ [læp] n (a) genoux mpl; **to sit on sb's l.** s'asseoir sur les genoux de qn (b) (idioms) **it's in the l. of the gods** on ne peut que s'en remettre au sort; **she expects everything to fall into her l.** elle s'attend à ce que tout lui tombe tout cuit dans le bec; **to live in the l. of luxury** vivre dans le luxe

lap² 1 n (in race) tour m; **l. of honour** tour d'honneur
2 vt (pt & pp **lapped**) (overtake) prendre un tour d'avance sur

lap³ (pt & pp **lapped**) vi (of animal) laper; **to l. against sth** (of waves) clapoter contre qch
▶**lap up** vt sep (drink) laper; Fam Fig (enjoy indiscriminately) se délecter de; (believe) gober, avaler

lapdog ['læpdɒg] n chien m d'appartement; Fig toutou m

lapel [lə'pel] n revers m

Lapland ['læplænd] n la Laponie

Laplander ['læplændə(r)] n Lapon(one) m,f

Lapp [læp] **1** n (a) (person) Lapon(one) m,f (b) (language) lapon m
2 adj lapon(one)

lapse [læps] **1** n (a) (of time) laps m de temps (b) (in standards, concentration) baisse f (**in** de); (in behaviour) écart m (**in** de)
2 vi (of concentration, standards) baisser; (of person) retomber dans un travers; **to l. into silence** se taire (b) (of permit, membership) expirer

lapsed [læpst] adj (Catholic) qui ne pratique plus

laptop ['læptɒp] n Comptr portable m

lapwing ['læpwɪŋ] n vanneau m

larceny ['lɑːsənɪ] n Law vol m

larch [lɑːtʃ] n mélèze m

lard [lɑːd] **1** n (fat) saindoux m
2 vt Fam Fig **to l. one's writings with quotations** truffer ses écrits de citations

larder ['lɑːdə(r)] n garde-manger m inv

large [lɑːdʒ] **1** n **to be at l.** être en liberté; **people at l., the public at l.** le grand public
2 adj (a) (big) grand(e); (fat, bulky) gros (grosse); (audience) nombreux(euse); **to grow** or **get larger** s'agrandir; (of person) grossir; **to make sth larger** agrandir qch; **as l. as life** en chair et en os; **larger than life** haut(e) en couleur (b) (extensive, significant) **to a l. extent** en grande partie; **a l. part of** une grande partie de
3 adv **by and l.** dans l'ensemble

largely ['lɑːdʒlɪ] adv en grande partie

large-scale ['lɑːdʒˈskeɪl] adj (map) à grande échelle; (undertaking) ambitieux(euse); (disaster) immense

largesse [lɑːˈʒes] n largesse f

lark¹ [lɑːk] n (bird) alouette f; **to rise with the l.** se lever au chant du coq

lark² n (joke) rigolade f; **to do sth for a l.** faire qch pour rire; **I don't like this fancy dress l.** je n'aime pas du tout cette histoire de bal masqué
▶**lark about, lark around** vi faire le fou (la folle)

larva ['lɑːvə] (pl **larvae** ['lɑːviː]) n larve f

laryngitis [lærɪnˈdʒaɪtɪs] n laryngite f; **to have l.** avoir une laryngite

larynx ['lærɪŋks] n larynx m

lasagne [ləˈzænjə] n lasagnes fpl

lascivious [ləˈsɪvɪəs] adj lascif(ive)

laser ['leɪzə(r)] n laser m; **l. beam** rayon m laser; **l. printer** imprimante f laser; **l. surgery** chirurgie f au laser

lash [læʃ] **1** n (a) (eyelash) cil m (b) (of whip) coup m de fouet
2 vt (a) (with whip) cingler; (of rain, waves) fouetter (b) (tie) lier, attacher
3 vi **the rain** or **it was lashing down** il pleuvait dru
▶**lash out** vi (a) **to l. out at sb** (physically) donner un coup/des coups à qn; (verbally) s'en prendre violemment à qn (b) Fam (spend extravagantly) claquer un fric fou (**on** pour)

lashings ['læʃɪŋz] npl Fam (lots) des tas; **l. of cream/ jam** une tonne de crème/confiture

less [læs] n jeune fille f

lassitude ['læsɪtjuːd] n (weariness) lassitude f; (laziness) paresse f

lasso [læ'suː] **1** n (pl **lassoes** or **lassos**) lasso m
2 vt (pt & pp **lassoed**) attraper au lasso

last¹ [lɑːst] **1** n **the l.** le dernier (la dernière) m,f; **the l. but one** l'avant-dernier(ère) m,f; **we'll never hear the l. of it** on n'a pas fini d'en entendre parler; **I don't think we've heard the l. of him** je crois que nous n'en sommes pas encore débarrassés; **that's the l. I saw of her** je ne l'ai pas revue depuis; **that's the l. of the wine** on a fini le vin; **to** or **till the l.** jusqu'à la fin; **at (long) l.** enfin
2 adj (a) (final) dernier(ère); **you are my l. hope** vous êtes mon dernier espoir; **to have the l. word** avoir le dernier mot; **the l. word in comfort/style** le summum du confort/de l'élégance; **at the l. moment** au dernier moment, à la dernière minute; **l. thing at night** avant de se coucher; **to be on one's l. legs** être au bout du rouleau; **he's the l. person I'd ask to help me** c'est (bien) la dernière personne à qui je demanderais de m'aider; **that's the l. thing I'd do** c'est (bien) la dernière chose que je ferais; **as a l. resort** en dernier recours; **the L. Judgement** le Jugement dernier; **l. name** nom m de famille; **l. rites** derniers sacrements mpl; Fig **the l. straw** la goutte d'eau qui a fait déborder le vase
(b) (most recent) dernier(ère); **the l. time I saw him** la dernière fois que je l'ai vu; **l. January** en janvier (dernier); **l. night** (during the night) la nuit dernière; (in the evening) hier (au) soir; **l. Tuesday** mardi dernier; **l. week** la semaine dernière
3 adv **to arrive/finish l.** arriver/finir dernier; **when I l. saw him** la dernière fois que je l'ai vu; **l. but not least** enfin

last² n (for shoe) forme f (à chaussure)

last³ 1 *vt* it will l. me a lifetime j'en ai pour la vie; it **has lasted him well** ça lui a fait de l'usage

2 *vi* durer; **it's too good to l.** c'est trop beau pour durer; **the supplies won't l. two months** les provisions ne seront pas suffisantes pour deux mois; **he won't l. long in that job** il ne tiendra pas très longtemps à ce poste; **she won't l.** the night elle ne passera pas la nuit

▸**last out** 1 *vt sep* to l. the year out *(of person)* survivre jusqu'à la fin de l'année; *(of supplies)* suffire pour l'année

2 *vi (of person)* tenir le coup; *(of supplies)* suffire

last-ditch ['lɑ:st'dɪtʃ] *adj* ultime

lasting ['lɑ:stɪŋ] *adj* durable

lastly ['lɑ:stlɪ] *adv* pour finir, en dernier lieu

last-minute ['lɑ:st'mɪnɪt] *adj* de dernière minute

latch [lætʃ] *n* loquet *m*

▸**latch onto** *vt insep Fam* **(a)** *(attach oneself to)* to l. onto sb/sth s'accrocher à qn/qch **(b)** *(understand)* to l. onto sth piger qch

latchkey ['lætʃki:] *n (pl* **latchkeys)** *n* clef *f* de la porte d'entrée; **l. child** = enfant dont les parents travaillent et qui doit rentrer seul après l'école

late [leɪt] 1 *adj* **(a)** *(not on time)* en retard; **to be l. (for sth)** être en retard (pour qch); **to be ten minutes l.** avoir dix minutes de retard **(b)** *(far on in time)* tard; **it's getting l.** il se fait tard; **to keep l. hours** se coucher tard; **in the l. afternoon** en fin d'après-midi; **in l. summer** vers la fin de l'été; **to be in one's l. thirties** approcher de la quarantaine; **in the l. eighties** vers la fin des années 80; *Fig* **it's a bit l. in the day to...** il est un peu tard pour... **(c)** *(dead)* feu(e); **my l. husband** feu mon mari

2 *adv* **(a)** *(in general)* tard; **to work l.** travailler tard; **l. into the night** jusqu'à une heure avancée de la nuit; **l. in the year** vers la fin de l'année; **l. in life** sur le tard; *Prov* **better l. than never** mieux vaut tard que jamais **(b)** *(recently)* as **l. as last week** pas plus tard que la semaine dernière; **of l.** récemment

latecomer ['leɪtkʌmə(r)] *n* retardataire *mf*

lately ['leɪtlɪ] *adv* dernièrement, récemment; **until l.** jusqu'à ces derniers temps

lateness ['leɪtnɪs] *n (of person, train)* retard *m*; **the l. of the hour** l'heure *f* tardive

latent ['leɪtənt] *adj (disease, tendency)* latent(e); *(period)* de latence

later ['leɪtə(r)] 1 *adj* ultérieur(e); **I caught a l. train** j'ai pris un train qui partait plus tard; **l. events proved that...** la suite des événements a prouvé que...; **her l. novels** ses derniers romans; **in l. life** avec l'âge

2 *adv* **l. (on)** plus tard; **a few days l.** quelques jours plus tard; **no l. than tomorrow** demain au plus tard; **as we shall see l.** comme nous le verrons par la suite; *Fam* **see you l.!** à plus tard!

lateral ['lætərəl] *adj* latéral(e); **l. thinking** approche *f* originale

latest ['leɪtɪst] 1 *n* at the l. au plus tard; **the l. I can stay is four o'clock** je peux rester jusqu'à quatre heures au plus tard; **have you heard the l.?** vous savez la dernière?

2 *adj (most recent)* dernier(ère)

latex ['leɪteks] *n* latex *m*

lathe [leɪð] *n* tour *m*

lather ['lɑ:ðə(r)] 1 *n* mousse *f*; *Fam* to work oneself or **get into a l. (about sth)** se mettre dans tous ses états (à propos de qch)

2 *vt* savonner

Latin ['lætɪn] 1 *n* **(a)** *(person) (European)* Latin(e) *m,f*; *(Latin American)* Latino-Américain(e) *m,f* **(b)** *(language)* latin *m*

2 *adj* latin(e); **L. America** l'Amérique *f* latine; **L. American** latino-américain(e)

latitude ['lætɪtju:d] *n also Fig* latitude *f*

latrine [lə'tri:n] *n* latrines *fpl*

latter ['lætə(r)] 1 *n (of two)* the l. le second (la seconde)

2 *adj* **(a)** *(of two)* second(e) **(b)** *(last)* dernier(ère); **the l. half or part of June** la deuxième moitié de juin

latter-day ['lætə'deɪ] *adj* moderne; *Rel* the **L. Saints** les mormons *mpl*

latterly ['lætəlɪ] *adv (recently)* dernièrement, récemment; *(towards the end of a period)* vers la fin

lattice ['lætɪs] *n* treillis *m*; **l. window** fenêtre *f* à croisillons de plomb

latticework ['lætɪswɜːk] *n* treillis *m*

Latvia ['lætvɪə] *n* la Lettonie

Latvian ['lætvɪən] 1 *n* **(a)** *(person)* Letton(onne) *m,f* **(b)** *(language)* letton *m*

2 *adj* letton(onne)

laudable ['lɔːdəbəl] *adj* louable, digne de louanges

laudanum ['lɔːdənəm] *n* laudanum *m*

laugh [lɑːf] 1 *n* rire *m*; *Fam* **to have a good l.** bien se marrer; *Fam* **to do sth for a l.** faire qch pour rire; *Ironic* **that's a l.!** la bonne blague!; *Fam* **he's a good l.** on se marre avec lui; **to have the last l.** être bien vengé(e)

2 *vi* rire (at de); *Fam* **don't make me l.!** laisse-moi rire!; *Fam* **to l. one's head off** être mort(e) de rire; *Fam* **if you get that job, you'll be laughing** si tu obtiens le poste, ça sera super; **he'll be laughing on the other side of his face when...** il rira jeune quand...; *Fam* **to l. all the way to the bank** s'en mettre plein les poches; *Prov* **he who laughs last laughs longest** rira bien qui rira le dernier

3 *vt* **to l. oneself silly** se tordre de rire; **you'll be laughed out of court** vous vous couvrirez de ridicule

▸**laugh off** *vt sep* tourner en plaisanterie

laughable ['lɑːfəbəl] *adj* ridicule

laughing ['lɑːfɪŋ] 1 *n* rires *mpl*

2 *adj* rieur(euse); **it's no l. matter** ce n'est pas à prendre à la légère; **she was in no l. mood** elle n'était pas d'humeur à rire; **l. gas** gaz *m* hilarant; **l. stock** risée *f*; **to make sb a l. stock** faire de qn un sujet de plaisanterie

laughter ['lɑːftə(r)] *n* rires *mpl*

launch [lɔːntʃ] 1 *n* **(a)** *(boat)* chaloupe *f*; **(motor) l.** vedette *f* **(b)** *(of ship, rocket, product)* lancement *m*; **l. pad** plate-forme *f* de lancement

2 *vt (ship, rocket, product)* lancer; *(enquiry)* ouvrir; **to l. sb on a career** *(of event)* marquer le début de la carrière de qn

▸**launch into** *vt insep (attack, story, complaint)* se lancer dans

launching ['lɔːntʃɪŋ] *n (of ship, rocket, product)* lancement *m*; *(of enquiry)* ouverture *f*; **l. pad** plate-forme *f* de lancement

launder ['lɔːndə(r)] *vt also Fig* blanchir

launderette [lɔːn'dret] *n Br* laverie *f* automatique

laundry ['lɔːndrɪ] *n* linge *m*; **to do the l.** faire la lessive; **l. basket** panier *m* à linge

laurel ['lɒrəl] *n* laurier *m*; *Fig* **to rest on one's laurels** se reposer sur ses lauriers; **l. wreath** couronne *f* de lauriers

lava ['lɑːvə] *n* lave *f*

lavatory ['lævətrɪ] (*pl* **lavatories**) *n* toilettes *fpl*; **to go to the l.** aller aux toilettes; **l. paper** papier *m* hygiénique

lavender ['lævɪndə(r)] **1** *n* (*shrub*) lavande *f*; **l. water** (eau *f* de Cologne à la) lavande
2 *adj* (*colour*) bleu lavande *inv*

lavish ['lævɪʃ] **1** *adj* (a) (*person*) prodigue (**with/in** de) (b) (*gift, meal, décor*) somptueux(euse); (*spending*) extravagant(e); (*portion*) généreux(euse)
2 *vt* **to l. sth on sb** couvrir qn de qch

lavishly ['lævɪʃlɪ] *adv* somptueusement; **to spend l.** dépenser sans compter; **to praise sb l.** couvrir qn d'éloges

law [lɔ:] *n* (a) (*rule*) loi *f*; **there's no l. against it** aucune loi ne l'interdit; **the laws of gravity** les lois de la pesanteur; **to be a l. unto oneself** n'en faire qu'à sa tête (b) (*set of rules*) loi *f*; **to break the l.** enfreindre la loi; **to be above the l.** être au-dessus des lois; **to take the l. into one's own hands** se faire justice soi-même; **l. and order** l'ordre *m* public; **l. enforcement** le respect de la loi; **l. firm** cabinet *m* d'avocats (c) (*system of justice, subject*) droit *m*; **to practise l.** exercer une profession juridique (d) **Fam the l.** (*police*) les flics *mpl*

law-abiding ['lɔ:əbaɪdɪŋ] *adj* respectueux(euse) des lois
lawbreaker ['lɔ:breɪkə(r)] *n* personne *f* qui transgresse la loi
lawcourt ['lɔ:kɔ:t] *n* cour *f* de justice
lawful ['lɔ:fʊl] *adj* (*legal*) légal(e); (*rightful*) légitime
lawless ['lɔ:lɪs] *adj* (*country, society*) livré(e) à l'anarchie; (*mob*) sans foi ni loi
lawlessness ['lɔ:lɪsnɪs] *n* anarchie *f*
lawmaker ['lɔ:meɪkə(r)] *n* législateur(trice) *m,f*
lawn [lɔ:n] *n* pelouse *f*, gazon *m*; **l. tennis** tennis *m*
lawnmower ['lɔ:nməʊə(r)] *n* tondeuse *f* (à gazon)
lawsuit ['lɔ:su:t] *n* action *f* en justice; **to bring a l. against sb** intenter une action en justice contre qn
lawyer ['lɔ:jə(r)] *n* avocat(e) *m,f*; (*for wills, conveyancing*) notaire *m*; (*in company*) conseiller(ère) *m,f* juridique
lax [læks] *adj* (*discipline, principles, conduct*) relâché(e); (*person*) laxiste
laxative ['læksətɪv] **1** *n* laxatif *m*
2 *adj* laxatif(ive)
laxity ['læksɪtɪ], **laxness** ['læksnɪs] *n* (*of discipline, principles, conduct*) relâchement *m*; (*of person*) laxisme *m*
lay¹ [leɪ] *adj* **Rel** laïque; **l. preacher** prédicateur *m* laïque
lay² [leɪ] *vt* (*pt & pp* **laid** [leɪd]) (a) (*place*) mettre, poser; **to l. sb flat** coucher *ou* étendre qn; **to l. sth flat** poser *ou* coucher qch à plat; **to l. sb to rest** inhumer qn; **to l. one's hands on sth** mettre la main sur qch; **she reads everything she can l. her hands on** elle lit tout ce qui lui tombe sous la main; **if you l. a finger on her...** si tu touches à un seul cheveu de sa tête...; **to have nowhere to l. one's head** n'avoir nulle part où dormir; **to l. eyes on sb/sth** poser les yeux sur qn/qch; **to l. emphasis on sth** insister sur qch; **to l. the facts before sb** exposer les faits à qn; **to l. claim to sth** prétendre à qch; **to l. the blame on sb** faire porter la responsabilité à qn; **to l. sth bare** mettre qch à nu; **to l. oneself open to criticism** s'exposer à la critique; **to l. sb's fears to rest** apaiser les craintes de qn (b) (*foundations, carpet, trap, cable*) poser; *Br* **to l. the table** mettre la table (c) (*egg*) pondre (d) **to l. a bet** parier (**on** sur)

(e) *very Fam* **to get laid** s'envoyer en l'air
2 *vi* (*of bird*) pondre
3 *pt of* **lie²**

▶**lay aside** *vt sep* (a) (*money*) mettre de côté (b) (*prejudices, doubt*) oublier

▶**lay by** *vt sep* (*money*) mettre de côté

▶**lay down** *vt sep* (a) **to l. down one's arms** rendre *ou* déposer les armes; **to l. down one's life** sacrifier sa vie (b) (*principle, rule*) établir, poser; **to l. down the law** dicter sa loi

▶**lay in** *vt sep* (*supplies, food*) stocker

▶**lay into** *vt insep* **Fam** (*physically*) rosser; (*verbally*) voler dans les plumes à

▶**lay off** *vt sep* (*make redundant*) licencier; (*temporarily*) mettre en chômage technique
2 *vt insep* **Fam** (a) (*abstain from*) arrêter; **to l. off drink** arrêter de boire (b) (*leave alone*) ficher la paix à
3 *vi* **Fam** (*desist*) arrêter

▶**lay on** *vt sep* (*food, drink*) fournir; (*party, entertainment*) organiser

▶**lay out** *vt sep* (a) (*arrange, display*) arranger, disposer; (*dead body*) faire la toilette de (b) (*house, town*) concevoir

layabout ['leɪəbaʊt] *n* **Fam** bon (bonne) *m,f* à rien
lay-by ['leɪbaɪ] (*pl* **lay-bys**) *n* aire *f* de stationnement
layer ['leɪə(r)] **1** *n* couche *f*
2 *vt* (*hair*) dégrader; **to have one's hair layered** se faire faire un dégradé
layman ['leɪmən] *n* **Rel** laïque *m*; (*non-specialist*) profane *m*
lay-off ['leɪɒf] *n* licenciement *m*; (*temporary*) mise *f* en chômage technique
layout ['leɪaʊt] *n* (*of town*) plan *m*; (*of building*) agencement *m*; (*of text*) mise *f* en page
laywoman ['leɪwʊmən] *n* **Rel** laïque *f*; (*non-specialist*) profane *f*
laze [leɪz] *vi* **to l.** (**about** *or* **around**) paresser, fainéanter
laziness ['leɪzɪnɪs] *n* paresse *f*, fainéantise *f*
lazy ['leɪzɪ] *adj* (*person*) paresseux(euse), fainéant(e); (*afternoon*) passé(e) à ne rien faire
lazybones ['leɪzɪbəʊnz] (*pl* **lazybones**) *n* **Fam** flemmard(e) *m,f*
lb (*abbr* **pound**) livre *f*
LCD [elsi:'di:] *n* (*abbr* **liquid crystal display**) affichage *m* à cristaux liquides
LDC [eldi:'si:] *n* **Econ** (*abbr* **less developed country**) PVD *m*
LEA [eli:'eɪ] *n* (*abbr* **local education authority**) = organisme chargé de l'enseignement au niveau régional
lead¹ [led] *n* (a) (*metal*) plomb *m*; **l. poisoning** saturnisme *m* (b) (*for pencil*) mine *f* (c) (*idioms*) **to go down like a l. balloon** tomber à plat; *Fam* **to fill sb full of l.** truffer qn de plomb; *Fam* **to swing the l.** tirer au flanc
lead² [li:d] **1** *n* (a) (*advantage*) avance *f*; **to be in l.** être en tête; **to take** *ou* **go into the l.** prendre la tête; **lnd l. time** (*for production*) délai *m* de production; (*for delivery*) délai de livraison (b) (*example*) exemple *m*; **to give sb the l.** donner l'exemple à qn; **to follow sb's l.** suivre l'exemple de qn (c) (*clue*) indice *m* (d) (*in card game*) **it's your l.** à vous de jouer (e) (*in film, play*) premier rôle *m*, rôle principal (f) (*for dog*) laisse *f* (g) (*cable*) câble *m* *ou* fil *m* (électrique)

2 vt (pt & pp **led** [led]) **(a)** (guide) mener, conduire; **you l. the way** montre-nous le chemin; **to l. the conversation away from a subject** détourner la conversation; **to be easily led** être très influençable; **that leads me to believe that...** cela m'amène à penser que...

(b) **to l. a happy/sad life** mener une vie heureuse/triste **(c)** (be leader of) mener **(d)** (be ahead of) **to l. the field** mener; Fig **to l. the field in sth** être en tête dans le domaine de qch; **to l. sb by 8 points** avoir une avance de 8 points sur qn

3 vi **(a)** (of road) mener, conduire (**to** à) **(b)** **l. to sth** (cause) mener à qch **(c)** (in competition, race) mener; (in card game) jouer le premier; **you l. and I'll follow** vas-y, je te suis

▶**lead away** vt sep emmener

▶**lead off** vi **(a)** (road, corridor) partir (**from** de) **(b)** (in discussion) commencer

▶**lead on** vt sep (deceive) tromper, duper

▶**lead up to** vt insep (of person) en venir à; (of event) précéder; **what are you leading up to?** où veux-tu en venir?

leaded ['ledɪd] adj **l. window** fenêtre f à croisillons de plomb; **l. petrol** essence f au plomb

leaden ['ledən] adj (heavy) lourd(e)

leader ['liːdə(r)] n **(a)** (of group) chef m; (of riot) meneur(euse) m,f; (in race) premier(ère) m,f; **to be a born l.** être fait(e) pour commander **(b)** (in newspaper) éditorial m

leadership ['liːdəʃɪp] n (people in charge) dirigeants mpl; (position) direction f; (quality) qualités fpl d'encadrement

lead-free [led'friː] adj (petrol, paint) sans plomb

lead-in ['liːdɪn] n TV & Rad introduction f

leading ['liːdɪŋ] adj **(a)** (best, most important) principal(e); **l. article** (in newspaper) éditorial m; **l. lady** (in film, play) premier rôle m féminin; Fig **l. light** personnalité f de premier plan; **l. man** (in film, play) premier rôle masculin; **l. role** (in film, play) premier rôle **(b)** (team, runner) de tête **(c)** **l. question** question f tendancieuse

leaf [liːf] n (pl **leaves** [liːvz]) n **(a)** (of plant) feuille f; (of book) feuillet m; Fig **to turn over a new l.** s'acheter une conduite; Fig **to take a l. out of sb's book** prendre exemple sur qn **(b)** (of table) (inserted) rallonge f; (hinged) battant m

▶**leaf through** vt insep (book, magazine) feuilleter

leaflet ['liːflɪt] **1** n prospectus m; (political) tract m; (folded) dépliant m

2 vt (area) distribuer des prospectus dans

leafy ['liːfɪ] adj (tree) feuillu(e); (street) ombragé(e); **a l. suburb** une banlieue verte

league [liːg] n ligue f; (in sport) championnat m; **to be in l. with sb** être de mèche avec qn; Fig **to be in a different l.** être hors classe; **l. champions** vainqueurs mpl du championnat

leak [liːk] **1** n also Fig fuite f; (in boat) voie f d'eau; Fam **to take or have a l.** pisser un coup

2 vt (information) divulguer (**to** à); **the pipe was leaking gas/water** du gaz/de l'eau fuyait du tuyau

3 vi fuir; (of shoe) prendre l'eau; (of boat) faire eau; **the roof is leaking** il y a une fuite dans le toit

leakage ['liːkɪdʒ] n fuite f

leaky ['liːkɪ] adj (bucket, pipe, tap) qui fuit; (roof) qui a une fuite; (shoe) qui prend l'eau; (boat) qui fait eau

lean¹ [liːn] adj **(a)** (person, face) mince; (meat) maigre **(b)** (harvest) maigre; (year) de vaches maigres

lean² (pt & pp **leant** [lent] or **leaned**) **1** vt **to l. sth on/against sth** appuyer qch sur/contre qch

2 vi (of building) pencher; **to l. on/against sth** s'appuyer sur/contre qch; Fig **to l. on sb** (rely on) s'appuyer sur qn; (pressurize) faire pression sur qn; **the Leaning Tower of Pisa** la tour de Pise; **to l. out of the window** se pencher à la fenêtre

▶**lean back** vi se pencher en arrière

▶**lean over 1** vt insep **to l. over sb/sth** se pencher par-dessus qn/qch

2 vi se pencher

leaning ['liːnɪŋ] n (tendency) inclination f, penchant m (**towards** pour); **to have artistic leanings** avoir des dispositions artistiques

leant [lent] pt & pp of **lean**

lean-to ['liːntuː] n (pl **lean-tos**) n appentis m

leap [liːp] **1** n saut m, bond m; Fig **to take a l. in the dark** faire un saut dans l'inconnu; Fig **to advance by leaps and bounds** avancer à pas de géant; **l. year** année f bissextile

2 vt (pt & pp **leapt** [lept] or **leaped**) franchir d'un bond ou d'un saut

3 vi sauter, bondir; **to l. to one's feet** se lever d'un bond; **to l. at the chance** sauter sur l'occasion; **to l. for joy** sauter de joie

leapfrog ['liːpfrɒg] **1** n saute-mouton m; **to play l.** jouer à saute-mouton

2 vt (pt & pp **leapfrogged**) Fig passer avant

leapt [lept] pt & pp of **leap**

learn [lɜːn] (pt & pp **learnt** [lɜːnt] or **learned**) **1** vt apprendre

2 vi apprendre; **to l. of or about sth** apprendre qch; **to l. from one's mistakes** tirer un enseignement de ses erreurs

learned ['lɜːnɪd] adj savant(e), érudit(e); Br Law **my l. friend** mon éminent confrère

learner ['lɜːnə(r)] n (beginner) débutant(e) m,f; (student) étudiant(e) m,f; **to be a quick/slow l.** apprendre vite/lentement; **l. (driver)** apprenti(e) m,f conducteur(trice)

learning ['lɜːnɪŋ] n (act of learning) apprentissage m; (knowledge) savoir m, connaissances fpl; **l. curve** courbe f d'assimilation

learnt [lɜːnt] pt & pp of **learn**

lease [liːs] **1** n bail m; Fig **to give sb a new l. of life** redonner à qn goût à la vie

2 vt louer (**from/to** à)

leasehold ['liːshəʊld] n (contract) bail m; (property) location f à bail

leaseholder ['liːshəʊldə(r)] n locataire mf

leash [liːʃ] n (for dog) laisse f; Fig **to keep sb on a tight l.** tenir la bride haute à qn

leasing ['liːsɪŋ] n Com location-vente f

least [liːst] **1** n **the l.** le moins; ..., **to say the l.** le moins qu'on puisse dire, c'est que...; **it's the l. I can do** c'est la moindre des choses; **that's the l. of my worries** c'est le cadet de mes soucis; **at l.** au moins; **he's leaving, at l. that's what I've heard** il part, du moins c'est ce que j'ai entendu dire; **at l. as old as...** au moins aussi vieux que...; **at the very l. they should pay your expenses** ce serait vraiment le moindre des choses qu'ils te remboursent tes frais; **not in the l.** pas du tout; **it doesn't matter in the l.** cela n'a pas la moindre importance

2 *adj* (*superlative of* **little**) (*smallest*) moindre; **the l. thing annoys her** un rien l'agace

3 *adv* **the l. difficult** le (la) moins difficile; **l. of all her** elle encore moins que les autres; **when I was l. expecting it** au moment où je m'y attendais le moins

leather ['leðə(r)] **1** *n* cuir *m*

2 *vt Fam* (*beat*) tanner le cuir à

leather-bound ['leðəbaʊnd] *adj* (*book*) relié(e) en cuir

leathery ['leðərɪ] *adj* (*face, skin*) tanné(e); (*meat*) coriace

leave [liːv] **1** *n* (**a**) (*permission*) permission *f*, autorisation *f*; **to ask l. to do sth** demander la permission *ou* l'autorisation de faire qch; **to grant** *or* **give sb l. to do sth** accorder *ou* donner à qn l'autorisation de faire qch

(**b**) (*holiday*) congé *m*; **to be on l.** (*from work*) être en congé; (*from army*) être en permission; **l. of absence** (*from work*) congé exceptionnel; (*from army*) permission *f* exceptionnelle

(**c**) (*farewell*) **to take one's l.** (*of sb*) prendre congé (de qn); **to take l. of one's senses** perdre l'esprit

2 *vt* (*pt & pp* **left** [left]) (**a**) (*depart from*) quitter; **to l. the table** se lever de table; **the car left the road** la voiture a quitté la route

(**b**) (*put, deposit*) **to l. sth somewhere** (*on purpose*) laisser qch quelque part; (*accidentally*) oublier qch quelque part; **take it or l. it** c'est à prendre ou à laisser; **to l. a message for sb** laisser un message pour qn

(**c**) (*allow to remain*) laisser; **to l. the door open** laisser la porte ouverte; **to l. oneself open to criticism** laisser la porte ouverte aux critiques; **to l. sth unfinished** laisser qch inachevé(e); **to l. sb to do sth** laisser qn faire qch; **l. it to me** laisse-moi faire; **to l. much** *or* **a lot to be desired** laisser beaucoup à désirer; **let's l. it at that** restons-en là; **to l. well alone** ne pas s'en mêler; **l. me alone!** fiche-moi la paix!

(**d**) (*bequeath*) laisser (**to** à); **he leaves a wife and three children** (*after dying*) il laisse une femme et trois enfants

(**e**) **to be left** (*remain*) rester; **there are a few chocolates left** il reste quelques chocolats; **three from seven leaves four** sept moins trois égale quatre

3 *vi* (*depart*) partir

▸**leave behind** *vt sep* **to l. sth behind** (*on purpose*) laisser qch; (*accidentally*) oublier qch; **to l. sb behind** partir sans qn

▸**leave off** *vt insep Fam* **to l. off doing sth** arrêter de faire qch; **to l. off work** cesser le travail

2 *vi* s'arrêter

▸**leave on** *vt sep* (*light, TV*) laisser allumé(e)

▸**leave out** *vt sep* (**a**) (*omit*) omettre (**b**) (*not involve*) **to l. sb out of sth** laisser qn en dehors de qch; **to feel left out** se sentir exclu(e) (**c**) (*leave ready, available*) **I'll l. your dinner out on the table for you** je te laisserai ton dîner sur la table; **l. the disks out where I can see them** laisse les disquettes en évidence (**d**) (*leave outside*) laisser dehors; **who left the milk out?** qui a oublié de mettre le lait au frigo? (**e**) *Fam* **l. it out!** (*stop it*) arrête!

▸**leave over** *vt sep* **to be left over** (*of food, money*) rester; **there's some lasagne left over** il reste des lasagnes

leaven ['levən] *n* levain *m*

leaves [liːvz] *pl of* **leaf**

leave-taking ['liːvteɪkɪŋ] *n* adieux *mpl*

Lebanese [lebə'niːz] **1** *npl* (*people*) **the L.** les Libanais *mpl*

2 *n* (*pl* **Lebanese**) (*person*) Libanais(e) *m,f*

3 *adj* libanais(e)

Lebanon ['lebənən] *n* le Liban

lecher ['letʃə(r)] *n* obsédé *m*

lecherous ['letʃərəs] *adj* lubrique

lechery ['letʃərɪ] *n* lubricité *f*

lectern ['lektən] *n* lutrin *m*

lecture ['lektʃə(r)] **1** *n* (**a**) (*talk*) conférence *f*; (*at university*) cours *m* magistral; **l. theatre** amphithéâtre *m* (**b**) *Fam* (*reprimand*) sermon *m*; **to give sb a l.** faire la morale à qn

2 *vt Fam* (*reprimand*) faire la morale à

3 *vi* (*give public lectures*) donner une conférence/des conférences; (*at university*) donner un cours magistral/des cours magistraux

lecturer ['lektʃərə(r)] *n Univ* enseignant(e) *m,f* (*d'université*)

LED [eliː'diː] *n Elec* (*abbr* **light-emitting diode**) LED *f*

led [led] *pt & pp of* **lead**

ledge [ledʒ] *n* (*on cliff*) corniche *f*; (*of window, on building*) rebord *m*

ledger ['ledʒə(r)] *n* grand livre *m*

leech [liːtʃ] *n also Fig* sangsue *f*; **to cling to sb like a l.** se cramponner à qn comme une sangsue

leek [liːk] *n* poireau *m*

leer ['lɪə(r)] **1** *n* (*lustful*) regard *m* lubrique; (*cruel*) regard sadique

2 *vi* **to l. at sb** (*lustfully*) regarder qn d'un air lubrique; (*cruelly*) regarder qn d'un air sadique

lees [liːz] *npl* (*of wine*) lie *f*

leeward ['liːwəd] *n* côté *m* sous le vent

2 *adj* sous le vent; **the L. Islands** les îles *fpl* Sous-le-Vent

leeway ['liːweɪ] *n* marge *f* de manœuvre

left¹ [left] **1** *n* gauche *f*; **on** *or* **to the l.** à gauche; **on my l.** à ma gauche

2 *adj* gauche; **the l. wing** (*of party*) l'aile *f* gauche

3 *adv* à gauche

left² *pt & pp of* **leave**

left-field ['left'fiːld] *adj Am Fam* (*bizarre*) bizarroïde

left-hand ['left'hænd] *adj* de gauche; (*corner, side*) gauche; **l. drive** conduite *f* à gauche; **on the l. side** à gauche

left-handed [left'hændɪd] **1** *adj* gaucher(ère)

2 *adv* de la main gauche

left-hander [left'hændə(r)] *n* (*person*) gaucher(ère) *m,f*

left luggage (office) ['left'lʌgɪdʒ('ɒfɪs)] *n* consigne *f*

leftover ['leftəʊvə(r)] **1** *adj* **l. food/paint** un reste de nourriture/de peinture

2 *n* **leftovers** restes *mpl*

left-wing ['leftwɪŋ] *adj* de gauche

left-winger ['left'wɪŋə(r)] *n* homme (femme) *m,f* de gauche

leg [leg] **1** *n* (**a**) (*of person, trousers*) jambe *f*; (*of animal*) patte *f*; (*of table, chair*) pied *m* (**b**) *Culin* (*of lamb*) gigot *m*; (*of chicken*) cuisse *f*; (*of pork*) rôti *m* (**c**) (*of journey, race*) étape *f* (**d**) (*idioms*) **to pull sb's l.** faire marcher qn; **to show a l.** se lever; **to shake a l.** se remuer; **you don't have a l. to stand on** tu n'as rien sur quoi t'appuyer; **to give sb a l. up** donner un coup de pouce à qn; *very Fam* **to get one's l. over** baiser

2 *vt* (*pt & pp* **legged**) *Fam* **to l. it** jouer des gambettes

legacy ['legəsɪ] *n* (*pl* **legacies**) *n also Fig* legs *m*; **to come into a l.** faire un héritage

legal ['liːgəl] *adj* légal(e); **to take l. action (against sb)** intenter une action (contre qn); **to take l. advice** consulter un avocat; **l. aid** aide *f* juridique; **the l. profession** les professions *fpl* juridiques; **to be l. tender** avoir cours (légal)

legality [liːˈgælɪti] *n* légalité *f*

legalization [liːgəlaɪˈzeɪʃən] *n* légalisation *f*

legalize ['liːgəlaɪz] *vt* légaliser

legally ['liːgəlɪ] *adv* légalement

legate ['legɪt] *n Rel* légat *m*

legation [lɪˈgeɪʃən] *n* légation *f*

legend ['ledʒənd] *n* légende *f*; **to be a l. in one's own lifetime** être une légende vivante

legendary ['ledʒəndərɪ] *adj* légendaire

leggings ['legɪŋz] *npl (of woman)* caleçon *m*; *(of cowboy)* jambières *fpl*

leggy ['legɪ] *adj (person)* tout en jambes

legible ['ledʒɪbəl] *adj* lisible

legion ['liːdʒən] *n* légion *f*

legionary ['liːdʒənərɪ] *(pl* **legionaries)** *n* légionnaire *m*

legionnaire [liːdʒəˈneə(r)] *n* légionnaire *m*; **l.'s disease** maladie *f* du légionnaire

legislate ['ledʒɪsleɪt] *vi* légiférer **(against** contre)

legislation [ledʒɪsˈleɪʃən] *n (laws)* législation *f*; *(action)* élaboration *f* des lois

legislative ['ledʒɪslətɪv] *adj* législatif(ive)

legislator ['ledʒɪsleɪtə(r)] *n* législateur(trice) *m,f*

legislature ['ledʒɪslətʃə(r)] *n* corps *m* législatif

legitimacy [lɪˈdʒɪtɪməsɪ] *n* légitimité *f*

legitimate 1 *adj* [lɪˈdʒɪtɪmət] légitime
2 *vt* [lɪˈdʒɪtɪmeɪt] légitimer

legitimately [lɪˈdʒɪtɪmətlɪ] *adv* légitimement

legless ['legləs] *adj Fam (drunk)* complètement bourré(e)

legroom ['legruːm] *n* place *f* pour les jambes

legume ['legjuːm] *n Bot* légumineuse *f*

legwarmers ['legwɔːməz] *npl* jambières *fpl*

leisure ['leʒə(r), *Am* 'liːʒər] *n* loisirs *mpl*; **to do sth at one's l.** faire qch à son rythme; **a life of l.** une vie de loisirs; **l. activities** activités *fpl* de loisirs; **l. centre** centre *m* de loisirs

leisurely ['leʒəlɪ, *Am* 'liːʒərlɪ] *adj (weekend)* relax *inv*; **at a l. pace** sans se presser; **to make l. progress** avancer à son rythme; **to go for a l. stroll** se promener tranquillement

lemming ['lemɪŋ] *n* lemming *m*; **to follow sb like lemmings** suivre qn comme des moutons

lemon ['lemən] **1** *n (fruit, colour)* citron *m*; *Fam* **I felt like a real l.** j'ai vraiment eu l'air malin; **l. curd** = pâte à tartiner au citron; **l. sole** limande-sole *f*; **l. squeezer** presse-citron *m*; **l. tea** thé *m* au citron; **l. tree** citronnier *m*
2 *adj* **l. (coloured)** jaune citron *inv*

lemonade [leməˈneɪd] *n (carbonated)* limonade *f*; *(freshly squeezed)* citronnade *f*

lemur ['liːmə(r)] *n* maki *m*

lend [lend] *(pt & pp* **lent** [lent]) *vt (money, book, pen)* prêter; *(support)* apporter **(to à); to l. credibility to sth** rendre qch crédible; **to l. sb a (helping) hand** donner un coup de main à qn; **to l. an ear** or **one's ear to...** prêter l'oreille à...; **her work doesn't l. itself to dramatization** son œuvre ne se prête pas à une adaptation théâtrale

lender ['lendə(r)] *n* prêteur(euse) *m,f*

lending ['lendɪŋ] *n* prêt *m*; **l. library** bibliothèque *f* de prêt; **l. rate** taux *m* (d'un prêt)

length [leŋθ] *n* **(a)** *(in space)* longueur *f*; **it's 4.50 m in l.** ça fait 4,50 m de long; **the l. and breadth of the country** dans tout le pays
(b) *(in time)* durée *f*; **at (great) l.** longuement; **a great l. of time** longtemps; **l. of service** ancienneté *f*
(c) **to go to the l. of doing sth** aller jusqu'à faire qch; **to go to great lengths to do sth** se donner beaucoup de mal pour faire qch; **he would go to any lengths (to do sth)** il ne reculerait devant rien (pour faire qch)
(d) *(of wood, string)* morceau *m*

lengthen ['leŋθən] **1** *vt* allonger, rallonger
2 *vi (of days)* allonger, rallonger; *(of shadows)* s'allonger

lengthily ['leŋθɪlɪ] *adv* longuement

lengthways ['leŋθweɪz], **lengthwise** ['leŋθwaɪz] *adv* dans le sens de la longueur

lengthy ['leŋθɪ] *adj* long (longue)

lenient ['liːnɪənt] *adj* indulgent(e)

Leningrad ['lenɪngræd] *n Formerly* Leningrad

lens [lenz] *(pl* **lenses)** *n (of spectacles)* verre *m*; *(of camera)* objectif *m*; *(of eye)* cristallin *m*; **(contact) l.** lentille *f* (de contact); **l. cap** capuchon *m* d'objectif

Lent [lent] *n Rel* carême *m*; **to keep L.** faire carême

lent [lent] *pt & pp of* **lend**

lentil ['lentɪl] *n* lentille *f*

Leo ['liːəʊ] *(pl* **Leos)** *n (sign of zodiac)* le Lion; **to be (a) L.** être (du) Lion

leopard ['lepəd] *n* léopard *m*

leotard ['liːətɑːd] *n* justaucorps *m*

leper ['lepə(r)] *n* lépreux(euse) *m,f*; **l. colony** léproserie *f*

leprechaun ['leprəkɔːn] *n* lutin *m*, farfadet *m*

leprosy ['leprəsɪ] *n* lèpre *f*; **to have l.** avoir la lèpre

lesbian ['lezbɪən] **1** *n* lesbienne *f*
2 *adj* lesbien(enne)

lesion ['liːʒən] *n* lésion *f*

Lesotho [lɪˈsuːtuː] *n* le Lesotho

less [les] **1** *adj (comparative of little)* moins de; **it's l. than a week's work** cela représente moins d'une semaine de travail; **the distance is l. than I thought** c'est moins loin que je ne pensais
2 *prep* moins; **a year l. two days** un an moins deux jours; *Fin* **you've got £50, l. what I spent on the train ticket** j'ai 50 livres, moins ce que j'ai dépensé pour le billet de train
3 *pron* moins; **I don't think any (the) l. of you** tu n'as pas baissé dans mon estime; **I see l. of her nowadays** je la vois moins ces temps-ci; **in l. than an hour** en moins d'une heure; **the l. said about it the better** moins on en parle mieux c'est; *Fam* **l. of that!** ça suffit!
4 *adv* moins; **l. and l.** de moins en moins; **no more, no l.** ni plus ni moins; **still l., even l.** encore moins; **nothing l. than total obedience** rien moins que une obéissance totale; **she was driving a Rolls, no l.!** elle conduisait une Rolls, rien que ça!; **I expected no l. from you** je n'en attendais pas moins de vous; **they haven't got a fridge, much l. a freezer** ils n'ont pas de réfrigérateur et encore moins de congélateur

lessen ['lesən] **1** *vt (importance, cost)* diminuer, réduire; *(noise)* atténuer; *(enthusiasm, pain)* calmer
2 *vi (of pain, anger)* se calmer; *(of noise)* s'atténuer

lesser ['lesə(r)] *adj* (*in size*) plus petit(e); (*in importance*) moindre; **the l. of two evils** un moindre mal; **to a l. extent** *or* **degree** dans une moindre mesure

lesson ['lesən] *n* leçon *f*; *Fig* **he has learnt his l.** ça lui a servi de leçon; *Fig* **to teach sb a l.** (*of person*) donner une bonne leçon à qn; (*of event, experience*) servir de leçon à qn

lest [lest] *conj Formal* de peur ou de crainte que + *subjunctive*; **l. we forget** (*on war memorial*) pour ne pas oublier

let¹ [let] *n* (*in tennis*) let *m*

let² **1** *n* (*of property*) location *f*; **short/long l.** location *f* de courte/longue durée
2 *vt* (*pt & pp* **let**) (*rent out*) louer; (*house*) **to l.** (maison) à louer

let³ (*pt & pp* **let**) *vt* **(a)** (*allow*) **to l. sb do sth** laisser qn faire qch, permettre à qn de faire qch; **l. me see** voyons un peu; (*show me*) fais(-moi) voir; **to l. sb know** sth faire savoir qch à qn; **to l. sth pass** laisser passer qch; **to l. sth go** lâcher qch; **to l. oneself go** se laisser aller; **to l. sb go** laisser partir qn; (*make redundant*) se séparer de qn; **don't l. it get you down/get to you** ne te laisse pas abattre/ affecter par ça; **don't l. me see you here again!** que je ne vous retrouve plus ici!; **can you l. me have it back tomorrow?** pouvez-vous me le rendre demain?; *Math* **l. AB be equal to CD** soit AB égal à CD
  (b) (*with suggestions*) **l.'s go!** allons-y!; **l.'s hurry!** dépêchons-nous!; **l.'s not have an argument about it!** on ne va pas se disputer pour ça!; **now, don't l.'s have any nonsense!** allons, pas de bêtises!

▶**let by** *vt sep* (*allow to pass*) laisser passer

▶**let down** *vt sep* **(a)** (*hem*) rallonger; (*tyre*) dégonfler; *Fig* **to l. one's hair down** se défouler **(b)** *Fam* (*disappoint, fail*) laisser tomber; **the car l. us down again** la voiture nous a encore lâchés

▶**let in** *vt sep* **(a)** (*allow to enter*) laisser entrer; **to l. oneself in** (*to house*) entrer; **to l. in the light** laisser entrer *ou* passer la lumière; (*of shoes*) **to l. in water** (*of shoes*) prendre l'eau **(b)** **to l. sb in on a plan** mettre qn au courant d'un projet; **to l. sb in on a secret** mettre qn dans le secret **(c)** *Fam* **to l. oneself in for a hard time** aller au-devant de grandes difficultés; **what are you letting yourself in for?** est-ce que tu sais à quoi tu t'exposes?

▶**let into** *vt sep* **to l. sb into the house** faire entrer qn; **to l. sb into a secret** mettre qn dans le secret

▶**let off** *vt sep* **(a)** (*bomb*) lâcher; (*firework*) tirer; *Fig* **to l. off steam** se défouler **(b)** (*excuse*) ne pas sanctionner; **I'll l. you off this time** ça va pour cette fois; **they l. him off with a fine** il s'en est tiré avec une amende

▶**let on** *vt sep Fam* **(a)** (*tell*) dire; **don't l. on that I was there** n'allez pas dire que j'y étais **(b)** (*claim*) prétendre; **he wasn't as ill as he l. on** il n'était pas aussi malade qu'il le prétendait

▶**let out** *vt sep* **(a)** (*release*) laisser sortir; (*prisoner*) libérer; (*air, yell*) laisser échapper; (*secret*) divulguer **(b)** (*jacket, trousers*) élargir **(c)** (*rent out*) louer

▶**let up** *vi* (*lessen*) diminuer; (*stop*) cesser; **once he's started, he never lets up** une fois lancé, il ne s'arrête plus

let-down ['letdaʊn] *n Fam* déception *f*

lethal ['liːθəl] *adj* mortel(elle); *Fam* **that vodka's l.!** elle est meurtrière, cette vodka!; **l. dose** dose *f* létale *ou* mortelle; **l. weapon** arme *f* meurtrière

lethargic [lɪ'θɑːdʒɪk] *adj* mou (molle)

lethargy ['leθədʒɪ] *n* mollesse *f*

let-out ['letaʊt] *n Fam* (*from obligation*) excuse *f*, prétexte *m*

letter ['letə(r)] *n* lettre *f*; **the l. of the law** la lettre de la loi; **to do sth to the l.** faire qch à la lettre; *Com* **l. of credit/exchange** lettre de crédit/de change; **l. of acknowledgement** accusé *m* de réception; **l. bomb** lettre piégée; **l. box** boîte *f* aux lettres; **l. opener** coupe-papier *m inv*

letterhead ['letəhed] *n* en-tête *m*; (*paper*) papier *m* à en-tête

lettuce ['letɪs] *n* salade *f* (verte)

let-up ['letʌp] *n Fam* (*in conflict*) trêve *f*; (*in weather*) accalmie *f*; (*in pressure*) relâchement *m*; **to work fifteen hours without a l.** travailler quinze heures sans répit

leukaemia, *Am* **leukemia** [luː'kiːmɪə] *n* leucémie *f*

level ['levəl] **1** *n* niveau *m*; **at eye l.** à (la) hauteur des yeux; **to be on a l. with sb** être sur un pied d'égalité avec qn; *Fam* **on the l.** régulier(ère); **to come down to sb's l.** se mettre à la portée de qn; **to sink to sb's l.** tomber au niveau de qn; **at ministerial/international l.** à l'échelon ministériel/international
2 *adj* **(a)** (*not sloping*) plat(e); *Fig* **a l. playing field** une situation qui ne défavorise personne
  (b) **to be l. with sb/sth** (*physically*) être au niveau de qn/qch; (*in race, ability, progress*) être au même niveau que qn/qch; **to draw l. with** (*in race, match*) rattraper; **to do one's l. best** faire tout son possible; **l. crossing** passage *m* à niveau; **l. pegging** à égalité; **l. spoonful** cuillerée *f* rase
  (c) (*voice, tone*) égal(e); **to keep a l. head** garder son sang-froid
3 *(pt & pp* **levelled,** *Am* **leveled**) **(a)** (*make level*) niveler, égaliser; (*building*) raser
  (b) (*aim*) (*blow*) porter (**at** à); (*criticism*) adresser (**at** à); (*accusation*) porter (**at** contre)
4 *vi Fam* **to l. with sb** parler franchement à qn

▶**level off, level out** *vi* (*of ground*) s'aplanir; (*of prices, demand*) se stabiliser; (*of aircraft*) se redresser

level-headed ['levəl'hedɪd] *adj* pondéré(e)

lever ['liːvə(r), *Am* 'levə(r)] **1** *n also Fig* levier *m*
2 *vt* **to l. sth open** ouvrir qch au moyen d'un levier

leverage ['liːvərɪdʒ] *n* (*power*) effet *m* de levier; *Fig* (*influence*) pression *f*

leveraged buyout ['liːvərɪdʒd'baɪaʊt] *n Fin* OPA *f* à crédit

levitate ['levɪteɪt] *vi* léviter

levitation [levɪ'teɪʃən] *n* lévitation *f*

levity ['levɪtɪ] *n* légèreté *f*

levy ['levɪ] **1** *n* (*pl* **levies**) taxe *f* (**on** sur)
2 *vt* (*pt & pp* **levied**) lever, percevoir (**on** sur)

lewd [luːd] *adj* obscène

lexical ['leksɪkəl] *adj* lexical(e)

lexicographer [leksɪ'kɒɡrəfə(r)] *n* lexicographe *mf*

liability [laɪə'bɪlɪtɪ] *n* **(a)** *Law* **liabilities** (*a*) *Law* (*responsibility*) responsabilité *f* (**for** de); *Fin* **liabilities** passif *m* **(b)** (*disadvantage*) handicap *m* (**to** pour)

liable ['laɪəbəl] *adj* **(a)** *Law* (*responsible*) responsable (**for** de) **(b)** (*to tax*) assujetti(e) (**to** à); (*to fine*) passible (**to** de) **(c)** (*likely*) **to be l. to do sth** risquer de faire qch

liaise [liː'eɪz] *vi* **to l. with sb** (*be in contact with*) assurer la liaison avec qn; (*work together with*) collaborer avec qn

liaison [lɪ'eɪzɒn] n (a) (contact) liaison f; (co-operation) collaboration f; Mil **l. officer** officier m de liaison (b) (love affair) liaison f

liar ['laɪə(r)] n menteur(euse) m,f

libel ['laɪbəl] Law1 n diffamation f; **l. action** procès m en diffamation; **l. laws** lois fpl contre la diffamation

2 vt (pt & pp libelled, Am libeled) diffamer (par écrit)

libellous, Am **libelous** ['laɪbələs] adj diffamatoire

liberal ['lɪbərəl] **1** n Pol **L.** libéral(e) m,f

2 adj (a) (tolerant) libéral(e) (b) (generous, abundant) généreux(euse); **to be l. with one's praise/advice** ne pas être avare de compliments/de conseils (c) Pol **L.** libéral(e)

liberalism ['lɪbərəlɪzəm] n libéralisme m

liberalize ['lɪbərəlaɪz] vt libéraliser; (law) assouplir

liberally ['lɪbərəlɪ] adv libéralement, généreusement

liberate ['lɪbəreɪt] vt libérer

liberated ['lɪbəreɪtɪd] adj (person) libéré(e); (views, ideas) progressiste

liberation [lɪbə'reɪʃən] n libération f; **l. movement** mouvement m de libération

liberator ['lɪbəreɪtə(r)] n libérateur(trice) m,f

Liberia [laɪ'bɪərɪə] n le Liberia

Liberian [laɪ'bɪərɪən] **1** n Libérien(enne) m,f

2 adj libérien(enne)

libertarian [lɪbə'teərɪən] n & adj libertaire mf

liberty ['lɪbətɪ] (pl **liberties**) n liberté f; **at l.** en liberté; **to be at l. to do sth** être libre de faire qch; **to take the l. of doing sth** prendre la liberté de faire qch; **to take liberties with sb/sth** prendre des libertés avec qn/qch; Fam **what a l.!** quel culot!

libido [lɪ'biːdəʊ] n libido f

Libra ['liːbrə] n (sign of zodiac) la Balance; **to be (a) L.** être (de la) Balance

librarian [laɪ'breərɪən] n bibliothécaire mf

library ['laɪbrərɪ] (pl **libraries**) n bibliothèque f; **l. book** livre m de bibliothèque; **l. card** carte f de bibliothèque

libretto [lɪ'bretəʊ] (pl **librettos** or **libretti** [lɪ'bretiː]) n Mus livret m

Libya ['lɪbɪə] n la Libye

Libyan ['lɪbɪən] **1** n Libyen(enne) m,f

2 adj libyen(enne)

lice [laɪs] pl of **louse**

licence, Am **license¹** ['laɪsəns] n (a) (permit) permis m; Com **under l.** sous licence; (driving) **l.** permis de conduire; (TV) **l.** redevance f (télé); **l. number** (of car) numéro m d'immatriculation; **l. plate** plaque f d'immatriculation (b) (freedom) liberté f; (excessive freedom) licence f

license² vt Com accorder une licence à; **to be licensed to carry a gun** avoir un permis de port d'armes

licensed ['laɪsənst] adj **l. premises** débit m de boissons; **l. restaurant** = restaurant possédant une licence de débit de boissons

licensing ['laɪsənsɪŋ] n **l. hours** (of pub) heures fpl d'ouverture; **l. laws** lois fpl relatives aux débits de boissons

licentious [laɪ'senʃəs] adj licencieux(euse)

lichen ['laɪkən] n lichen m

lick [lɪk] **1** n (a) (with tongue) coup m de langue; (b) Fam **at a great l., at full l.** à toute allure

2 vt (a) (with tongue) lécher; **to l. one's lips** se lécher les lèvres; Fig se (pour)lécher les babines; Fig **to l. one's wounds** panser ses blessures; Fam Fig **to l. sb's boots** lécher les bottes à qn; Vulg **to l. sb's arse** faire du lèche-cul à qn; Fam **to l. sb into shape** dresser qn (b) Fam (defeat) mettre une raclée à

licorice ['lɪkərɪs] = **liquorice**

lid [lɪd] n (a) (of pot, jar) couvercle m (b) (idioms) **to take the l. off sth** exposer qch au grand jour; **to keep its on sth** étouffer qch

lie¹ [laɪ] **1** n mensonge m; **to tell a l.** dire un mensonge; **to give the l. to sth** démentir qch; **l. detector** détecteur m de mensonges

2 vi mentir; **to l. through one's teeth** mentir effrontément

lie² **1** n **to find out the l. of the land** (in politics, business) tâter le terrain

2 vi (pt lay [leɪ], pp lain [leɪn]) (a) (of person, animal) (be in a lying position) être couché(e) ou allongé(e); (get down) se coucher, s'allonger; **here lies...** (on gravestone) ci-gît...; **to l. in bed** rester au lit; **I lay awake all night** je n'ai pas dormi de la nuit; Fig **to l. low** garder un profil bas; Fig **to l. in wait for sb** guetter l'arrivée de qn

(b) (of object) être, se trouver; **snow lay on the hills** il y avait de la neige sur les collines; **to l. in ruins** (of building) être en ruines; (of career, hopes) être détruit(e)

(c) (of abstract thing) **the responsibility lies with the author** la responsabilité incombe à l'auteur; **to know where one's interests l.** savoir où se trouve son intérêt; **the difference lies in that...** la différence réside dans le fait que...; **a brilliant future lies before her** un brillant avenir s'ouvre devant elle; **what lies behind this uncharacteristic generosity?** que cache cette générosité inhabituelle?

▸**lie about** vi traîner

▸**lie back** vi s'allonger

▸**lie down** vi se coucher, s'étendre; Fig **to take criticism/an insult lying down** se laisser critiquer/insulter sans réagir; **I'm not going to take this lying down** je ne vais pas me laisser faire

▸**lie in** vi faire la grasse matinée

Liechtenstein ['lɪktənstaɪn] n le Liechtenstein

lie-down ['laɪdaʊn] n **to have a l.** faire une sieste

lie-in ['laɪ'ɪn] n **to have a l.** faire la grasse matinée

lieu [ljuː, luː] n **in l.** à la place; **in l. of** au lieu de

lieutenant [Br lef'tenənt, Am luː'tenənt] n Mil lieutenant m; Naut lieutenant de vaisseau; Am (police officer) inspecteur m de police; Fig (helper) lieutenant; **l. colonel** lieutenant-colonel m

life [laɪf] (pl **lives** [laɪvz]) n (a) (existence) vie f; **to take sb's l.** tuer qn; **to take one's own l.** se suicider; **to bring sb back to l.** ramener qn à la vie; **a matter of l. and death** une question de vie ou de mort; **l. after death** la vie après la mort; **to risk one's l.** risquer sa vie; **l. and limb** risquer sa vie ou sa peau; **to escape with one's l.** avoir la vie sauve; **to lose one's l.** perdre la vie; **no lives were lost** on ne déplore aucune victime; **he held on to the rope for dear l.** il s'accrochait au cordage avec l'énergie du désespoir; **run for your lives!** sauve qui peut!; Fam **not on your l.!** jamais de la vie!; Fam **I couldn't for the l. of me remember** je n'arrivais absolument pas à me rappeler; **from l.** (to draw, paint) d'après nature; **bird l.** oiseaux mpl; **plant l.** végétaux mpl; **l. belt** ceinture f de sauvetage; **l. cycle** cycle m de vie; **l. force** force f vitale; **l. form** forme f de vie; **l. jacket** gilet m de sauvetage; **l.**

sciences sciences *fpl* de la vie **(b)** *(period of existence)* vie *f*; **she had worked all her l.** elle avait travaillé toute sa vie; **never in (all) my l.** jamais de ma vie; **a l. of Tolstoy** une biographie de Tolstoï; *Fam* **to get l.** en prendre pour perpète; **l. annuity** rente *f* viagère; **l. expectancy** espérance *f* de vie; **l. imprisonment** emprisonnement *m* à vie; **l. insurance** assurance-vie *f*; **l. member** membre *m* à vie; *Br* **l. peer** pair *m* à vie; **l. pension** pension *f* à vie; **l. sentence** condamnation *f* à perpétuité; **l. span** *(of person, animal)* espérance *f* de vie; *(of machine)* durée *f* de vie; **to write one's l. story** écrire son autobiographie

(c) *(mode of existence)* vie *f*; *Fam* **to live** *or* **lead the l. of Riley** se la couler douce; **to make a new l. for oneself** refaire sa vie; **way of l.** style *m* de vie; **he makes her l. a misery** il lui rend la vie insupportable; **to make l. worth living** donner un sens à l'existence; *Fam* **how's l.?** comment ça va?; **what a l.!** quelle vie!; **such is** *or* **that's l.!** c'est la vie!; **this is the l.!** voilà ce que j'appelle vivre!; *Fam* **get a l.!** t'es vraiment nul!

(d) *(liveliness)* **to come to l.** s'animer; **to bring sb to l.** *(of book, author)* donner vie à qn; **the l. and soul of the party** le boute-en-train de la soirée; **there's l. in the old dog yet** il n'a pas encore dit son dernier mot, le vieux

lifeblood ['laɪfblʌd] *n (of person)* souffle *m* vital; *Fig (of economy, society)* moteur *m*

lifeboat ['laɪfbəʊt] *n* canot *m* de sauvetage

life-giving ['laɪfɡɪvɪŋ] *adj (sun, water)* nourricier(ère); *(aid)* vital(e)

lifeguard ['laɪfɡɑːd] *n (at the seaside)* surveillant(e) *m,f* de baignade; *(at swimming pool)* maître *m* nageur

lifeless ['laɪflɪs] *adj* sans vie; *(performance, style)* qui manque de vie

lifelessly ['laɪflɪslɪ] *adv* sans vie

lifelike ['laɪflaɪk] *adj (portrait)* très ressemblant(e)

lifeline ['laɪflaɪn] *n Fig* planche *f* (de salut); **to throw sb a l.** offrir *ou* tendre à qn une planche (de salut)

lifelong ['laɪflɒŋ] *adj* de toujours

lifer ['laɪfə(r)] *n Fam (prisoner)* condamné(e) *m,f* à perpète

life-saver ['laɪfseɪvə(r)] *n Fam* **seatbelts can be life-savers** le port de la ceinture de sécurité peut sauver des vies; *Fig* **you're a l.!** tu me sauves la vie!

life-saving ['laɪfseɪvɪŋ] *adj* salvateur(trice); *(equipment)* de réanimation; **she needed a l. operation** elle devait se faire opérer, c'était une question de vie ou de mort

life-size(d) ['laɪfsaɪz(d)] *adj* grandeur nature *inv*

lifestyle ['laɪfstaɪl] *n* style *m* *ou* mode *m* de vie

life-support ['laɪfsəpɔːt] *adj* **l. system** *or* **machine** respirateur *m* artificiel

life-threatening ['laɪfθretnɪŋ] *adj (disease)* potentiellement mortel(elle); **to be in a l. situation** être en danger de mort

lifetime ['laɪftaɪm] *n (of person)* vie *f*; **in my l.** de mon vivant; **it's the chance of a l.** une telle chance ne se présente qu'une fois dans la vie; **the holiday of a l.** des vacances exceptionnelles

lift [lɪft] **1** *n* **(a)** *(elevator)* ascenseur *m*; *(goods)* l. monte-charge *m inv*; **l. attendant** garçon *m* d'ascenseur; **l. shaft** cage *f* d'ascenseur

(b) *(car ride)* **to give sb a l.** prendre *ou* emmener qn en voiture; **could you give me a l. to the station?** est-ce que tu peux m'emmener à la gare?

(c) *Fam* **to give sb a l.** *(cheer up)* remonter le moral à qn

2 *vt* **(a)** *(one's head, eyes, arm)* lever; **he won't l. a finger**

to help il ne lèvera pas le petit doigt; **to l. sb (up)** *(after fall)* aider qn à se relever; **to l. a child up** prendre un enfant dans ses bras

(b) *Fam (take, steal)* piquer; *(arrest)* choper

(c) *(restrictions, siege)* lever

3 *vi (of mist, fog)* se lever, se dissiper

▶**lift off** *vi (of rocket)* décoller

liftoff ['lɪftɒf] *n (of rocket)* décollage *m*

ligament ['lɪgəmənt] *n* ligament *m*

light¹ [laɪt] **1** *n* **(a)** *(illumination)* lumière *f*; **by the l. of the moon** à la clarté de la lune; **things will look different in the cold l. of day** demain vous verrez les choses sous un autre jour; **to be in sb's l.** faire de l'ombre à qn; *Comptr* **l. pen** crayon *m* lumineux; **l. year** année-lumière *f*

(b) *(lamp)* lumière *f*; *Fam* **to go out like a l.** s'endormir aussitôt couché(e); **(traffic) lights** feux *mpl* de circulation; **l. bulb** ampoule *f*

(c) *(fire)* **to set l.** to sth mettre le feu à qch; **have you got a l.?** vous avez du feu?

(d) *(idioms)* **the l. at the end of the tunnel** le bout du tunnel; **to throw** *or* **cast l. on sth** faire la lumière sur qch; **to bring sth to l.** mettre qch en lumière; **to come to l.** être découvert(e); **to see sb/sth in a new/different l.** voir qn/qch sous un jour nouveau/différent; **in (the) l. of...** *(considering)* à la lumière de...

2 *adj (not dark)* clair(e); **it will soon be l.** il fera bientôt jour

3 *vt (pt & pp lit* [lɪt]*)* **(a)** *(fire, cigarette)* allumer **(b)** *(room, street)* éclairer, illuminer

light² **1** *adj* **(a)** *(not heavy)* léger(ère); **to be l. on one's feet** avoir le pas léger; **to be a l. sleeper** avoir le sommeil léger; **to have a l. touch** avoir la main légère; **l. aircraft** avion *m* petit porteur; **l. artillery** artillerie *f* légère; **l. infantry** infanterie *f* légère

(b) *(not severe) (job, exercise)* facile, peu fatigant(e); *(rain)* fin(e); *(prison sentence)* léger(ère)

(c) *(not serious)* léger(ère); **to make l. of sth** prendre qch à la légère; **l. entertainment** variétés *fpl*; **l. reading** lectures *fpl* récréatives; **l. verse** poésie *f* facile

2 *adv* **to travel l.** voyager léger

▶**light on** *(pt & pp lighted)* *vt insep* tomber sur

▶**light up** **1** *vt sep (house, room)* éclairer; *(cigarette)* allumer **2** *vi* s'éclairer; *Fam (of smoker)* allumer une cigarette

lighten¹ ['laɪtən] **1** *vt (make less dark)* éclaircir

2 *vi (of sky)* s'éclaircir

lighten² *vt (make less heavy)* alléger; *Fig* **to l. sb's load** soulager qn

▶**lighten up** *vi Fam* se détendre

lighter ['laɪtə(r)] *n* briquet *m*; **l. fluid** *or* **fuel** essence *f* à briquet

light-fingered [laɪt'fɪŋgəd] *adj Fam* **to be l.** être chapardeur(euse)

light-headed [laɪt'hedɪd] *adj* étourdi(e)

light-hearted [laɪt'hɑːtɪd] *adj (person, discussion)* enjoué(e); *(remark)* badin(e); **to take a l. look at sth** poser un regard amusé sur qch

lighthouse ['laɪthaʊs] *n* phare *m*; **l. keeper** gardien *m* de phare

lighting ['laɪtɪŋ] *n (act, system)* éclairage *m*

lighting-up time [laɪtɪŋ'ʌptaɪm] *n* = heure à laquelle les automobilistes sont tenus d'allumer leurs phares

lightly ['laɪtlɪ] *adv* légèrement; **to sleep l.** avoir le sommeil léger; **to get off l.** s'en tirer à bon compte; **to**

speak l. of sth parler de qch à la légère; **to speak l. of sb** parler de qn sur un ton léger; **to take a decision l.** prendre une décision à la légère

lightness ['laɪtnɪs] n (a) (brightness) clarté f (b) (in weight) légèreté f

lightning ['laɪtnɪŋ] n (a) (bolt) éclairs mpl, foudre f; **l. conductor** paratonnerre m (b) (idioms) **as quick as l., with l. speed** rapide comme l'éclair; **l. attack** attaque f éclair; **l. strike** grève f surprise; **l. visit** visite f éclair

lightweight ['laɪtweɪt] 1 n (in boxing) poids m léger; Fig & Pej (in character, intellect) personne f qui manque d'envergure
2 adj (garment, fabric) léger(ère)

lignite ['lɪgnaɪt] n lignite m

like¹ [laɪk] 1 n he and his l. lui et ses semblables; **it's not for the likes of me** ce n'est pas pour des gens comme moi; **music, painting and the l.** la musique, la peinture et autres choses du même genre; **I've never seen the l. of it** je n'ai jamais vu une chose pareille
2 adj semblable, pareil(eille); **they are as l. as two peas (in a pod)** ils se ressemblent comme deux gouttes d'eau
3 prep/a (similar to) to be l. sb/sth être semblable à qn/qch, ressembler à qn/qch; **to taste l. sth** avoir le même goût que qch; **to look l. sb/sth** ressembler à qn/qch; **what's the weather l.?** comment est le temps?; **people l. you** des gens comme vous; **you know what she's l.** tu sais comment elle est; **it costs something l. £10** cela coûte dans les 10 livres; **that's more l.** voilà qui est mieux; **we don't have anything l. as many as that** on est loin d'en avoir autant; **there's nothing l. it!** il n'y a rien de tel; **she is nothing l. as intelligent as you** elle est loin d'être aussi intelligente que vous; **that's not l. her** cela ne lui ressemble pas; **that's just l. him!** c'est bien de lui!; Prov **l. father, l. son** tel père, tel fils
(b) (in the manner of) comme; **just l. anybody else** comme tout le monde; Fam **don't be l. that!** ne fais pas l'idiot!
(c) (such as) tel (telle) que; **take more exercise, l. jogging** fais plus d'exercice, du jogging par exemple
4 adv Fam **as l. as not** à coup sûr
5 conj Fam **do it l. I said** fais comme je t'ai dit; **he looked l. he'd seen a ghost** on aurait dit qu'il avait vu un fantôme; **it's not l. he's ill or anything** ce n'est pas comme s'il était malade ou quoi que ce soit

like² 1 n likes goûts mpl, préférences fpl; **likes and dislikes** sympathies fpl et antipathies fpl
2 vt (a) (person) bien aimer; **she is well liked** elle est très appréciée
(b) (enjoy) aimer; **whether she likes it or not,...** que ça lui plaise ou non,...; **I l. to think my father would have agreed** j'aime à penser que mon père aurait approuvé; Fam Ironic **well, I l. that!** elle est bien bonne, celle-là!
(c) (want) **would you l. a cigarette?** aimerais-tu une cigarette?; **I would very much l. to go** j'aimerais beaucoup y aller; **I would l. nothing better than...** rien ne me ferait plus plaisir que...; **he doesn't l. people to talk about it** il n'aime pas que l'on en parle; **he thinks he can do anything he likes** il se croit tout permis; **if/when you l.** si/quand vous voulez; **as much as you l.** tant que vous voulez; **as often as you l.** aussi souvent que vous voulez; **I didn't l. to mention it** j'ai préféré ne pas le mentionner

likeable ['laɪkəbəl] adj sympathique

likelihood ['laɪklɪhʊd] n probabilité f; **in all l.** selon toute vraisemblance ou probabilité; **there is little l. of**

finding it il y a peu de chance pour qu'on le trouve; **the l. is that...** il est probable que... + subjunctive

likely ['laɪklɪ] 1 adj (a) (probable) probable; **it's more than l.** c'est plus que probable; **it's l. to rain** il est probable qu'il pleuve, il pleuvra probablement; Ironic **a l. story!** à d'autres! (b) (suitable) approprié(e)
2 adv very l. très probablement; **as l. as not** sûrement; Fam **not l.!** tu plaisantes?

like-minded [laɪk'maɪndɪd] adj du même avis; (having same tastes) qui ont les mêmes goûts

liken ['laɪkən] vt comparer (**to** à)

likeness ['laɪknɪs] n (a) (similarity) ressemblance f; **family l.** air m de famille (b) (portrait) portrait m

likewise ['laɪkwaɪz] adv (similarly) de même, aussi; **to do l.** en faire autant

liking ['laɪkɪŋ] n goût m, penchant m; **is it to your l.?** cela est-il à votre goût?; **to have a l. for sth** avoir du goût pour qch, aimer qch; **to take a l. to sth** prendre goût à qch; **to take a l. to sb** se prendre d'amitié pour qn

lilac ['laɪlək] 1 n lilas m
2 adj lilas inv

Lilo® ['laɪləʊ] n matelas m pneumatique

lilt [lɪlt] n (of voice) inflexions fpl

lilting ['lɪltɪŋ] adj chantant(e)

lily ['lɪlɪ] n (pl lilies) n lis m; **l. of the valley** muguet m

lily-livered ['lɪlɪlɪvəd] adj Fam froussard(e)

lima bean ['liːmə'biːn] n haricot m de Lima

limb [lɪm] n (a) (of body) membre m; **to tear sb l. from l.** déchiqueter qn, mettre qn en pièces (b) (of tree) grosse branche f; Fig **to be out on a l.** être dans une situation délicate

limber ['lɪmbə(r)] adj souple
►**limber up** vi s'échauffer

limbo ['lɪmbəʊ] n (pl limbos) (a) Rel les limbes mpl; Fig **to be in l.** être dans les limbes (b) (dance) limbo m

lime¹ [laɪm] n (a) (fruit) citron m vert; (citrus tree) limettier m; (linden tree) tilleul m; **l. green** vert m anis; **l. juice** jus m de citron vert

lime² n Chem chaux f

limelight ['laɪmlaɪt] n **to be in the l.** être sous les projecteurs

limerick ['lɪmərɪk] n = poème burlesque en cinq vers

limestone ['laɪmstəʊn] n calcaire m

limey ['laɪmɪ] n (pl limeys) n Am Fam (British person) Rosbif m

limit ['lɪmɪt] 1 n limite f; **within limits** jusqu'à un certain point; **off limits (to)** inaccessible (à); (forbidden) interdit(e) (à); **to know no limits** être sans limites; **that's the l.!** ce n'est plus possible!; **he's the l.!** il est impossible!
2 vt limiter; **to l. oneself to sth/to doing sth** se limiter à qch/à faire qch

limitation [lɪmɪ'teɪʃən] n limitation f; **to know one's limitations** connaître ses limites

limited ['lɪmɪtɪd] adj limité(e); **l. company** société f à responsabilité limitée; **l. edition** édition f à tirage limité; Law **l. liability** responsabilité f limitée

limitless ['lɪmɪtlɪs] adj (wealth, amount, supply) illimité(e); (generosity) sans bornes

limo ['lɪməʊ] n (pl limos) n Fam limousine f

limousine [lɪmə'ziːn] n limousine f

limp¹ [lɪmp] **1** *n* boitement *m*; **to have a l.** boiter
  2 *vi* boiter

limp² *adj* mou (molle); **to go l.** s'affaisser

limpet ['lɪmpɪt] *n* bernique *f*, patelle *f*; *Fig* **to stick to sb like a l.** ne pas lâcher qn; *Mil* **l. mine** *f* magnétique

limpid ['lɪmpɪd] *adj* limpide

limply ['lɪmplɪ] *adv* mollement

linchpin ['lɪntʃpɪn] *n* *Fig* (*person*) cheville *f* ouvrière; (*thing*) clé *f* de voûte

linctus ['lɪŋktəs] *n* sirop *m*

linden ['lɪndən] *n* **l.** (**tree**) tilleul *m*

line¹ [laɪn] **1** *n* (**a**) (*mark*) ligne *f*; (*drawn*) trait *m*; (*on face*) ride *f*; *Fig* **to draw the l. at doing sth** se refuser à faire qch; **l. drawing** dessin *m* au trait
  (**b**) (*row*) ligne *f*, rangée *f*; (*one behind the other*) file *f*; *Am* (*queue*) queue *f*; **to stand in a l.** être en rang; (*one behind the other*) être en file; *Am* **to stand in l.** (*queue*) faire la queue; *Fig* **to be out of l.** dépasser les bornes; **to be in l. with sth** être conforme à qch; *Fig* **to be in l. for promotion** être sur la liste des promotions; *Fig* **to be on the l.** (*of one's job, reputation*) être en jeu; *Com & Ind* **l. manager** chef *m* d'équipe
  (**c**) (*rope*) ligne *f*; (*for clothes*) fil *m* à linge
  (**d**) (*railway track*) voie *f*; (*railway route*) ligne *f*
  (**e**) (*direction*) **l. of argument** raisonnement *m*; **l. of attack** plan *m* d'attaque; **to be in the l. of fire** être dans la ligne de tir; **to be right** or **wrong about sth** être aux critiques; **to be on the right/wrong lines** être sur la bonne/mauvaise voie; **something along the lines of...** quelque chose dans le genre de...
  (**f**) (*policy*) ligne *f*; **the party l.** la ligne du parti; **to take a firm l. with sb** se montrer ferme avec qn
  (**g**) (*of text*) ligne *f*; (*of poem*) vers *m*; **to drop sb a l.** écrire un mot à qn; **to learn one's lines** apprendre son rôle; *Fig* **to read between the lines** lire entre les lignes
  (**h**) (*family*) lignée *f*; **in a direct l.** en ligne directe
  (**i**) (*telephone connection*) ligne *f*
  (**j**) *Fam* (*job*) **what l. (of business) are you in?** vous travaillez dans quelle branche?
  (**k**) *Com* (*of goods*) ligne *f*
  2 *vt* (*road, river*) border; **the crowd lined the street** la foule s'alignait le long du trottoir

▶**line up** **1** *vt sep* (**a**) (*form into a line*) mettre en ligne, aligner (**b**) (*prepare*) **to have sb lined up for sth** avoir qn en vue pour qch; **have you got anything lined up for this evening?** avez-vous quelque chose de prévu pour ce soir?
  2 *vi* (*form a line*) se mettre en rang

line² *vt* (*coat, curtain*) doubler (**with** de); (*box, drawer*) tapisser (**with** de); *Fig* **to l. one's pockets** se remplir les poches

lineage ['lɪnɪɪdʒ] *n* lignée *f*

linear ['lɪnɪə(r)] *adj* linéaire; *Math* **l. equation** équation *f* linéaire; *Comptr* **l. programming** programmation *f* linéaire

lined¹ [laɪnd] *adj* (*paper*) réglé(e); (*face*) ridé(e)

lined² *adj* (*coat, curtain*) doublé(e) (**with** de)

linen ['lɪnɪn] *n* (**a**) (*fabric*) lin *m*; **a l. dress** une robe en lin (**b**) (*clothes*) linge *m*; *Fig* **don't wash your dirty l. in public** il faut laver son linge sale en famille; **l. basket** panier *m* à linge

liner ['laɪnə(r)] *n* (*ship*) (paquebot *m*) transatlantique *m*

linesman ['laɪnzmən] *n* (*in tennis*) juge *m* de ligne; (*in football*) juge de touche

line-up ['laɪnʌp] *n* (**a**) (*of team*) composition *f*; (*on TV show*) plateau *m* (**b**) *Am* (*identity parade*) séance *f* d'identification

linger ['lɪŋgə(r)] *vi* (*of person*) s'attarder; (*of smell, custom*) subsister, persister; **to l. behind** rester en arrière; **to l. over doing sth** prendre son temps pour faire qch

lingerie ['lɒnʒəri] *n* lingerie *f*

lingo ['lɪŋgəʊ] (*pl* **lingoes**) *n* *Fam* (*language*) langue *f*; (*jargon*) charabia *m*

lingua franca ['lɪŋgwə'fræŋkə] *n* langue *f* véhiculaire

linguist ['lɪŋgwɪst] *n* (**a**) (*specialist in linguistics*) linguiste *mf* (**b**) (*polyglot*) **to be a l.** être doué(e) pour les langues

linguistic [lɪŋ'gwɪstɪk] *adj* linguistique

linguistics [lɪŋ'gwɪstɪks] *n* linguistique *f*

lining ['laɪnɪŋ] *n* (*of coat, curtain*) doublure *f*; (*of brakes*) garniture *f*; (*of stomach*) paroi *f*

link [lɪŋk] **1** *n* (**a**) (*of chain*) chaînon *m*, maillon *m*; *Fig* **the weak l.** (*in argument*) le point faible; (*in team*) l'élément *m* faible (**b**) (*connection*) lien *m* (**between** entre)
  2 *vt* (*physically*) relier; (*by association*) lier; **to l. hands** se donner la main

▶**link up** **1** *vt* relier
  2 *vi* (*of roads, travellers*) se rejoindre

lino ['laɪnəʊ] *n* *Fam* lino *m*

linoleum [lɪ'nəʊlɪəm] *n* linoléum *m*

linseed ['lɪnsiːd] *n* graine *f* de lin; **l. oil** huile *f* de lin

lintel ['lɪntəl] *n* linteau *m*

lion ['laɪən] *n* lion *m*; *Fig* **the l.'s share** la part du lion; **l. cub** lionceau *m*; **l. tamer** dresseur *m* de lions

lioness ['laɪənes] *n* lionne *f*

lion-hearted ['laɪən'hɑːtɪd] *adj* courageux(euse) comme un lion

lip [lɪp] *n* (**a**) (*of person*) lèvre *f*; (*of animal*) babine *f*; **to read sb's lips** lire sur les lèvres de qn; **to pay l. service to sth** faire semblant de s'intéresser à qch (**b**) (*of jug*) bec *m* (**c**) *Fam* (*impudence*) insolence *f*; **less of your l.!** sois un peu moins insolent(e)!

lip-read ['lɪpriːd] (*pt & pp* **lip-read** ['lɪpred]) **1** *vt* lire les lèvres de
  2 *vi* lire sur les lèvres

lipstick ['lɪpstɪk] *n* rouge *m* à lèvres

liquefy ['lɪkwɪfaɪ] (*pt & pp* **liquefied**) **1** *vt* liquéfier
  2 *vi* se liquéfier

liqueur [lɪ'kjʊə(r)] *n* liqueur *f*

liquid ['lɪkwɪd] **1** *n* liquide *m*
  2 *adj* liquide; *Fin* **l. assets** liquidités *fpl*; **l. crystal display** affichage *m* à cristaux liquides

liquidate ['lɪkwɪdeɪt] *vt* (**a**) *Fin* (*company, debt*) liquider; (*capital*) mobiliser (**b**) *Fam* (*kill*) liquider

liquidation [lɪkwɪ'deɪʃən] *n* *Fin* (*of company, debt*) liquidation *f*; (*of capital*) mobilisation *f*; **to go into l.** entrer en liquidation

liquidity [lɪ'kwɪdɪtɪ] *n* *Fin* liquidité *f*; **l. ratio** ratio *m* de liquidité

liquidize ['lɪkwɪdaɪz] *vt* (**a**) (*gas, solid*) liquéfier (**b**) (*food*) passer au mixeur

liquidizer ['lɪkwɪdaɪzə(r)] *n* mixeur *m*

liquor ['lɪkə(r)] *n* *Am* alcool *m*; **l. store** magasin *m* de vins et spiritueux

liquorice ['lɪkərɪs] *n* réglisse *f*

lira ['lɪərə] (*pl* **lire** ['lɪərə]) *n* lire *f*

Lisbon ['lızbən] *n* Lisbonne

lisp [lısp] **1** *n* zézaiement *m*; **to have a l.** avoir un cheveu sur la langue
  2 *vi* avoir un cheveu sur la langue

list¹ [lıst] **1** *n* liste *f*
  2 *vt* (*enter in list*) faire une liste de; **her phone number isn't listed in the directory** son numéro de téléphone ne figure pas dans l'annuaire; **to be listed on the Stock Exchange** être coté(e) en Bourse; **listed building** immeuble *m* classé

list² **1** *n* (*of ship*) bande *f*, gîte *f*
  2 *vi* (*of ship*) donner de la bande *ou* de la gîte

listen ['lısən] *vi* écouter; **to l. to sb/sth** écouter qn/qch; **to l. for sth** tendre l'oreille afin d'entendre qch; **to l. (out) for the phone** guetter la sonnerie du téléphone; **to l. to reason** entendre raison; **he wouldn't l.** il n'a rien voulu savoir
  ▸**listen in** *vi* to l. in (on sth) écouter (qch)

listener ['lısnə(r)] *n* **(a) to be a good l.** savoir écouter **(b)** (*to radio programme*) auditeur(trice) *m,f*

listing ['lıstıŋ] *n* (*list*) liste *f*; **listings** (*in newspaper*) rubrique *f* des spectacles; **listings magazine** programme *m* de spectacles

listless ['lıstlıs] *adj* apathique

lit [lıt] *pt & pp of* **light**

litany ['lıtənı] (*pl* **litanies**) *n* litanie *f*

liter *Am* = **litre**

literacy ['lıtərəsı] *n* alphabétisation *f*; **l. rate** taux *m* d'alphabétisation

literal ['lıtərəl] *adj* littéral(e)

literally ['lıtərəlı] *adv* littéralement; **to take sth l.** prendre qch au pied de la lettre

literary ['lıtərərı] *adj* littéraire

literate ['lıtərıt] *adj* to be l. (*able to read and write*) savoir lire et écrire; (*educated*) être cultivé(e)

literature ['lıtərıtʃə(r)] *n* **(a)** (*fiction, poetry*) littérature *f* **(b)** (*information*) documentation *f*

lithe [laıð] *adj* agile

lithium ['lıθıəm] *n* lithium *m*

lithograph ['lıθəgræf] *n* lithographie *f*

Lithuania [lıθjʊ'eınə] *n* la Lituanie

Lithuanian [lıθjʊ'eınən] **1** *n* **(a)** (*person*) Lituanien(enne) *m,f* **(b)** (*language*) lituanien *m*
  2 *adj* lituanien(enne)

litigant ['lıtıgənt] *n Law* partie *f*

litigate ['lıtıgeıt] *vi Law* intenter une action en justice

litigation [lıtı'geıʃən] *n Law* action *f* en justice

litmus ['lıtməs] *n* **l. paper** papier *m* (de) tournesol; *Fig* **l. test** test *m* décisif

litre, *Am* **liter** ['li:tə(r)] *n* litre *m*

litter ['lıtə(r)] **1** *n* **(a)** (*rubbish*) détritus *mpl*, ordures *fpl*; **l. bin** poubelle *f*; **l. lout** = personne qui jette des détritus n'importe où **(b)** (*of animal*) portée *f* **(c)** (*for cat*) litière *f*
  2 *vt* to be littered with être couvert(e) *ou* jonché(e) de

litterbug ['lıtəbʌg] *n Fam* = personne qui jette des détritus n'importe où

little ['lıtəl] **1** *pron* peu *m*; **to eat l. or nothing** manger peu ou pas du tout; **he knows very l.** il ne sait pas grand-chose; **a l. more** un peu plus; **a l. hot/slow** un peu chaud(e)/lent(e); **every l. helps** les petits ruisseaux font les grandes rivières
  2 *adj* **(a)** (*small*) petit(e); **a l. while** un petit moment; **l.**

finger petit doigt *m* **(b)** (*comparative* **less,** *superlative* **least**) (*not much*) peu de; **l. money** peu d'argent; **a l. money** un peu d'argent; **it makes l. sense** ça n'a pas beaucoup de sens

3 *adv* (*comparative* **less,** *superlative* **least**) peu; **l. by l.** peu à peu; **l. more than an hour ago** il y a à peine une heure; **that's l. short of bribery** ça frise la corruption; **l. did l think that...** j'étais loin de penser que...

littoral ['lıtərəl] **1** *n* littoral *m*
  2 *adj* littoral(e)

liturgy ['lıtədʒı] (*pl* **liturgies**) *n* liturgie *f*

live¹ [laıv] **1** *adj* **(a)** (*person, animal*) vivant(e), en vie; *Fam* **a real l. film star** une vedette de cinéma en chair et en os; **a l. issue** un sujet brûlant **(b)** (*performance, broadcast*) en direct **(c)** (*bomb*) non explosé(e); **l. ammunition** balles *fpl* réelles; **l. wire** fil *m* sous tension; *Fig* **to be a l. wire** déborder de vie
  2 *adv* (*broadcast*) en direct; **to perform l.** (*of comedian, dancer*) être sur scène; (*of band*) jouer en concert

live² [lıv] **1** *vt* vivre; **to l. a long life** vivre longtemps; **to l. a happy life** mener une vie heureuse; **to l. a lie** vivre dans le mensonge; **it makes life worth living** cela donne un sens à la vie
  2 *vi* vivre; (*reside*) habiter, vivre; **to l. with sb** vivre avec qn; **as long as I l.** tant que je vivrai; **to l. a little** profiter un peu de la vie; **l. and let l.!** un peu de tolérance!; **you l. and learn** on apprend tous les jours
  ▸**live down** *vt sep* (*mistake, one's past*) faire oublier; **I'll never l. it down!** je n'ai pas fini d'en entendre parler!
  ▸**live off** *vt insep* to l. off sth vivre de qch; **to l. off sb** vivre aux crochets de qn
  ▸**live on 1** *vt insep* (*food*) se nourrir de; (*capital*) vivre sur; **it's not enough to l. on** ce n'est pas suffisant pour vivre
    2 *vi* (*of person*) continuer à vivre; (*of memory*) survivre
  ▸**live out** *vt sep* to l. out one's life *or* days passer ses jours; **to l. out a fantasy** réaliser un fantasme
  ▸**live through** *vt insep* connaître, vivre
  ▸**live together** *vi* vivre ensemble
  ▸**live up** *vt sep Fam* to l. it up faire la fête
  ▸**live up to** *vt insep* to l. up to sb's expectations répondre aux attentes de qn; **to fail to l. up to expectations** ne pas tenir ses promesses; **to l. up to one's reputation** être à la hauteur de sa réputation

live-in ['lıvın] *adj* (*chauffeur, nanny*) logé(e) et nourri(e); *Fam* **l. lover** compagnon (compagne) qui

livelihood ['laıvlıhʊd] *n* gagne-pain *m inv*; **to earn one's l.** gagner sa vie

liveliness ['laıvlınıs] *n* vivacité *f*

lively ['laıvlı] *adj* (*person*) plein(e) de vie; (*place, party, conversation*) animé(e); (*music*) entraînant(e); (*imagination*) fertile; **to take a l. interest in sth** s'intéresser vivement à qch; *Fam* **look l.!** grouillez-vous!

▸**liven up** ['laıvən] **1** *vt sep* (*person*) égayer; (*place, party, conversation*) animer; (*proceedings*) activer
  2 *vi* (*of person*) s'égayer; (*of place, party, conversation*) s'animer

liver ['lıvə(r)] *n* foie *m*

Liverpool ['lıvəpu:l] *n* Liverpool

Liverpudlian [lıvə'pʌdlıən] **1** *n* = personne née ou habitant à Liverpool
  2 *adj* de Liverpool

livery ['lıvərı] *n* livrée *f*

lives [laıvz] *pl of* **life**

livestock ['laɪvstɒk] n bétail m

livid ['lɪvɪd] adj (a) (angry) furieux(euse) (b) (bluish-grey) livide, blême

living ['lɪvɪŋ] 1 n vie f; **to earn one's l.** gagner sa vie; **what does she do for a l.?** qu'est-ce qu'elle fait dans la vie?; l. **conditions** conditions fpl de vie; l. **expenses** faux frais mpl; l. **room** (salle f de) séjour m, salon m
2 adj vivant(e); **there is not a l. soul to be seen** il n'y a pas âme qui vive; **within l. memory** de mémoire d'homme

lizard ['lɪzəd] n lézard m

llama ['lɑːmə] n lama m

lo [ləʊ] exclam Lit or Hum **lo and behold...** ô surprise...

load [ləʊd] 1 n (a) (burden) fardeau m, charge f; **to share or spread the l.** répartir le travail; **that's a l. off my mind!** cela m'enlève un poids! (b) Fam (lot) **a l. of, loads of** plein de; **it's just a l. of rubbish!** c'est n'importe quoi; **we've got loads of time** on a largement le temps
2 vt (lorry, gun, camera) charger; (software) installer; (washing machine) remplir
3 vi (of lorry) prendre un chargement

▸**load up** 1 vt sep charger
2 vi prendre un chargement

loaded ['ləʊdɪd] adj (a) (lorry, gun, camera) chargé(e) (b) (dice) pipé(e); (question) insidieux(euse) (c) Fam (rich) plein(e) aux as

loading ['ləʊdɪŋ] n chargement m; l. **bay** aire f de chargement

loaf [ləʊf] (pl loaves [ləʊvz]) n **a l. (of bread)** un pain; Fig **to use one's l.** faire marcher son ciboulot

▸**loaf about, loaf around** vi traîner

loafer ['ləʊfə(r)] n (a) (person) fainéant(e) m,f (b) (shoe) mocassin m

loam [ləʊm] n terreau m

loan [ləʊn] 1 n (from lender's point of view) prêt m; (from borrower's point of view) emprunt m; **to give sb a l. of sth** prêter qch à qn; **to take out a l.** faire un emprunt; Fam l. **shark** usurier(ère) m,f
2 vt (money) prêter

loath [ləʊθ] adj **to be l. to do sth** répugner à faire qch

loathe [ləʊð] vt détester; **to l. doing sth** détester faire qch

loathing ['ləʊðɪŋ] n dégoût m, répugnance f

loathsome ['ləʊðsəm] adj répugnant(e)

loaves [ləʊvz] pl of loaf

lob [lɒb] 1 n (in tennis) lob m
2 vt (pt & pp lobbed) (a) (in tennis) lober (b) Fam (throw) balancer

lobby ['lɒbɪ] 1 n (pl lobbies) (a) (of hotel) hall m; (of theatre) foyer m (b) (pressure group) groupe m de pression, lobby m
2 vt (pt & pp lobbied) faire pression sur
3 vi **to l. for/against sth** faire pression en faveur de/contre qch

lobbyist ['lɒbɪɪst] n membre m d'un groupe de pression

lobe [ləʊb] n lobe m

lobotomy [lə'bɒtəmɪ] (pl lobotomies) n lobotomie f

lobster ['lɒbstə(r)] n homard m; **as red as a l.** (sunburnt) rouge comme une écrevisse; l. **pot** casier m à homards

local ['ləʊkəl] 1 n (a) (person) **the locals** les gens mpl du coin (b) Fam (pub) = pub du voisinage
2 adj local(e); l. **anaesthetic** anesthésie f locale; l. **government** ≃ administration f communale

locale [ləʊ'kɑːl] n (of events) lieu m; (for a film) lieu de tournage

locality [ləʊ'kælɪtɪ] (pl localities) n voisinage m, environs mpl

locally ['ləʊkəlɪ] adv dans le quartier

locate [ləʊ'keɪt] 1 vt (find) localiser; (situate) situer
2 vi (of company) s'installer

location [ləʊ'keɪʃən] n (a) (place) emplacement m; Cin **on l.** en extérieur; Cin l. **shot** plan m en extérieur (b) (act of finding) localisation f

loch [lɒx] n Scot (lake) loch m, lac m

lock¹ [lɒk] 1 n (a) (on door) serrure f; **under l. and key** (object) sous clef; (person) sous les verrous; Fig l., **stock and barrel** en entier (b) (in wrestling) clef f (c) (on canal) écluse f
2 vt (door, padlock) fermer à clef; **to be locked in each other's arms** être étroitement enlacés(ées); Fig **to l. horns with sb** livrer bataille à qn
3 vi (of door) se fermer; (of car wheels) se bloquer

▸**lock in** vt sep enfermer à clef

▸**lock out** vt sep enfermer dehors; **I locked myself out of my flat** je me suis enfermé dehors

▸**lock up** 1 vt sep (person, valuables) enfermer; (house) fermer à clef
2 vi fermer

lock² [lɒk] n (of hair) mèche f

locker ['lɒkə(r)] n casier m; Am l. **room** vestiaire m

locket ['lɒkɪt] n médaillon m

lockjaw ['lɒkdʒɔː] n Old-fashioned tétanos m

lock-out ['lɒkaʊt] n lock-out m inv

locksmith ['lɒksmɪθ] n serrurier m

lockup ['lɒkʌp] n (a) Br (for storage) garage m (b) Fam (police cells) violon m, bloc m

locomotion [ləʊkə'məʊʃən] n locomotion f

locomotive [ləʊkə'məʊtɪv] 1 n (train) locomotive f
2 adj locomotif(ive)

locum ['ləʊkəm] n Br remplaçant(e) m,f

locust ['ləʊkəst] n sauterelle f

locution [ləʊ'kjuːʃən] n locution f

lodge [lɒdʒ] 1 n (of porter, caretaker, masons) loge f; (small house) pavillon m
2 vt (a) (accommodate) loger, héberger (b) Law **to l. an appeal** faire appel; **to l. a complaint** porter plainte
3 vi (a) (live) loger (b) (become fixed) se loger; **to be lodged in sb's memory** être gravé(e) dans la mémoire de qn

lodger ['lɒdʒə(r)] n locataire mf (en meublé); (who has meals provided) pensionnaire mf

lodging ['lɒdʒɪŋ] n logement m; **lodgings** chambre f meublée; l. **house** (hôtel m) garni m

loft [lɒft] n grenier m

lofty ['lɒftɪ] adj (a) (aim, desire) noble (b) Lit (high) haut(e)

log [lɒg] 1 n (a) (of wood) bûche f; **to sleep like a l.** dormir comme une souche; l. **cabin** hutte f en rondins; l. **fire** feu m de bois (b) (record) registre m; (of ship, traveller) journal m de bord; (of plane) carnet m de vol
2 vt (pt & pp logged) (record) enregistrer; (in ship's, traveller's log) noter dans le journal de bord; (in plane's log) noter dans le carnet de vol

▸**log in** vi Comptr entrer

▸**log off** vi Comptr sortir

▸**log on** vi Comptr entrer

▸**log out** vi Comptr sortir

logarithm [ˈlɒɡərɪθəm] n logarithme m

logbook [ˈlɒɡbʊk] n (a) (of ship, traveller) journal m de bord; (of plane) carnet m de vol (b) Br (for car) ≃ carte f grise

loggerheads [ˈlɒɡəhedz] n Fam **to be at l. with sb** être en conflit avec qn

logic [ˈlɒdʒɪk] n logique f

logical [ˈlɒdʒɪkəl] adj logique

logically [ˈlɒdʒɪklɪ] adv logiquement

logistic(al) [ləˈdʒɪstɪk(əl)] adj logistique

logistics [ləˈdʒɪstɪks] npl logistique f

logjam [ˈlɒɡdʒæm] n impasse f

logo [ˈləʊɡəʊ] n sigle m, logo m

loin [lɔɪn] n (a) (of beef) aloyau m; (of mutton, pork) filet m; (of veal) longe f; **l. chop** côtes fpl premières (b) **loins** (of person) reins mpl

loincloth [ˈlɔɪnklɒθ] n pagne m

loiter [ˈlɔɪtə(r)] vi traîner; (suspiciously) rôder; Law **to l. with intent** = rôder d'une manière suspecte

lollipop [ˈlɒlɪpɒp] n sucette f; Br Fam **l. man/lady** = contractuel qui aide les écoliers à traverser la rue

lollop [ˈlɒləp] vi Fam **l. along** courir lourdement

lolly [ˈlɒlɪ] (pl **lollies**) n Fam (a) (ice) glace f à l'eau (b) (lollipop) sucette f (c) Br (money) fric m, flouze m

London [ˈlʌndən] n Londres

Londoner [ˈlʌndənə(r)] n Londonien(enne) m,f

lone [ləʊn] adj (single, solitary) solitaire; Fig **a l. wolf** un(e) solitaire

loneliness [ˈləʊnlɪnɪs] n (feeling) solitude f; (of place) isolement m

lonely [ˈləʊnlɪ] adj (person) seul(e); (life, job) solitaire; (place) isolé(e); **to feel l.** se sentir seul; **l. hearts club** club m de rencontres; **l. hearts column** rubrique f rencontres

loner [ˈləʊnə(r)] n solitaire mf

lonesome [ˈləʊnsəm] 1 n Fam **to be on one's l.** être abandonné(e) à son triste sort
2 adj Am solitaire, seul(e)

long[1] [lɒŋ] 1 n **the l. and the short of it is that...** bref,...
2 adj (a) (in size) long (longue); **how l. is the table?** quelle est la longueur de la table?; **to be 4 metres l.** faire 4 mètres de long; **to go the l. way (round)** prendre le chemin le plus long; Fig **the best by a l. way** de loin le meilleur (la meilleure); Fig **she'll go a l. way** elle ira loin; Fig **to go a l. way towards doing sth** beaucoup contribuer à faire qch; Fam **to be l. on charm/good ideas** être plein(e) de charme/de bonnes idées; **the l. arm of the law** (le bras de) la justice; Fig **to have a l. face** faire une tête de six pieds de long; **it's a l. shot** ça n'a pas beaucoup de chances de réussir; **not by a l. shot** or **chalk** loin s'en faut; **l. johns** caleçon m long; **l. jump** saut m en longueur
(b) (in time) long (longue); **a l. time ago** il y a longtemps; **it's been a l. day** ça a été une longue journée; **the days are getting longer** les jours rallongent; **to take a l. look at sth** regarder longuement qch; **in the l. term** or **run** à long terme, à longue échéance; **to have a l. memory** avoir bonne mémoire; **l. weekend** long week-end m, week-end prolongé
3 adv (a) (for a long period) longtemps; **l. live the King/Queen!** vive le roi/la reine!; **as l. as** (providing) du moment que, tant que; (while) tant que; **to think l. and**

hard (about sth) réfléchir longuement (à qch); **she won't be l.** elle ne tardera pas; (will soon have finished) elle n'en a pas pour longtemps; **I have l. been convinced of it** j'en suis convaincu depuis longtemps; **how l. have you known her?** depuis combien de temps la connais-tu?; Fam **so l.!** au revoir!, à bientôt!; **l. before/after** longtemps avant/après; **l. ago** il y a longtemps
(b) (for the duration of) **all day l.** toute la journée
(c) **I could no longer hear him** je ne l'entendais plus; **I couldn't wait any longer** je ne pouvais plus attendre; **five minutes longer** cinq minutes de plus

long[2] vi **to l. to do sth** rêver de faire qch; **to l. for sth** rêver de qch; (look forward to) attendre qch avec impatience; **we're longing for them to leave** il nous tarde qu'ils partent; **a longed-for holiday** des vacances fpl très attendues

long[3] (abbr **longitude**) long

longboat [ˈlɒŋbəʊt] n chaloupe f

longbow [ˈlɒŋbəʊ] n arc m

long-distance [lɒŋˈdɪstəns] 1 adj (runner, race) de fond; (telephone call) longue distance; Br **l. lorry driver** conducteur(trice) m,f de poids lourd
2 adv **to telephone l.** faire un appel longue distance

longevity [lɒnˈdʒevɪtɪ] n longévité f

long-forgotten [lɒŋfəˈɡɒtən] adj depuis longtemps oublié(e)

longhaired [ˈlɒŋheəd] adj (cat, dog) à poil(s) long(s); (person) aux cheveux longs

long-haul [ˈlɒŋhɔːl] adj long-courrier

longing [ˈlɒŋɪŋ] n profond désir m, grande envie f (**for** de)

longingly [ˈlɒŋɪŋlɪ] adv avec envie

longitude [ˈlɒndʒɪtjuːd] n longitude f

longitudinal [lɒndʒɪˈtjuːdɪnəl] adj longitudinal(e)

long-life [lɒŋˈlaɪf] adj (tyre, milk) longue conservation inv; (battery) longue durée inv

long-lost [ˈlɒŋlɒst] adj perdu(e) depuis longtemps; (relative) perdu de vue depuis longtemps

long-range [lɒŋˈreɪndʒ] adj (missile) longue portée; (forecast) à long terme; (plane) à long rayon d'action

longshoreman [ˈlɒŋʃɔːmən] n Am docker m

long-sighted [lɒŋˈsaɪtɪd] adj (from birth) hyper-métrope; (from adulthood) presbyte

long-sleeved [lɒŋˈsliːvd] adj à manches longues

long-standing [lɒŋˈstændɪŋ] adj (arrangement, friendship) de longue date

long-suffering [lɒŋˈsʌfərɪŋ] adj patient(e)

long-term [ˈlɒŋtɜːm] adj (prisoner) condamné(e) à une longue peine; (loan, planning) à long terme; **the l. unemployed** les chômeurs mpl de longue durée

long-winded [lɒŋˈwɪndɪd] adj verbeux(euse)

loo [luː] (pl **loos**) n Br Fam cabinets mpl, Br **l. paper** papier m toilette

loofah [ˈluːfə] n loofa m, luffa m

look [lʊk] 1 n (a) (act of looking) **to have** or **take a l. at sth** regarder qch; (quickly) jeter un coup d'œil à qch; **to have a l. for sth** chercher qch; **let me have a l.** fais-(moi) voir; **to have a l. round the town** faire un tour dans la ville; **to have a l. through some magazines** jeter un coup d'œil à des magazines
(b) (glance) regard m; **to give sb. a dirty l.** jeter un regard noir à qn; **if looks could kill** il y a des regards qui tuent
(c) (appearance) air m; **I don't like the l. of this** cela ne

me dit rien qu'vaille; **I don't like the l. of him** sa tête ne me revient pas; **by the l. of it,...** on dirait bien que...
(d) (good) looks beauté *f*; **to have lost one's looks** être moins beau (belle); **looks don't matter to him** le physique n'a pas d'importance

2 *vt* **to l. sb in the face** regarder qn en face *ou* dans les yeux; **to l. sb up and down** toiser qn; **l. what you've done!** regarde ce que tu as fait!; **l. where you're going!** vous ne pouvez pas faire attention, non?

3 *vi* **(a)** *(in general)* regarder; **to l. at sb/sth** regarder qn/qch; **he's not much to l. at** il n'est pas très beau; *Fig* **to l. the other way** fermer les yeux; **I'm just looking, thank you** je ne fais que regarder, merci; **to l. on the bright side** voir les choses du bon côté; **l. here!** dites donc!; **don't l. at it that way** je ne vois pas les choses comme ça; *Prov* **l. before you leap** il faut réfléchir avant d'agir

(b) *(search)* **to l. for sb/sth** chercher qn/qch; **we've looked everywhere** nous avons cherché partout

(c) *(seem, appear)* avoir l'air, paraître; **to l. old** avoir l'air vieux (vieille); **things are looking bad** les choses prennent une mauvaise tournure; **things are looking good** ça a l'air de bien se passer; **to l. one's age** faire son âge; **to l. the part** avoir l'allure qui convient; **what does she l. like?** comment est-elle?; **to l. like sb** ressembler à qn; **it looks like** *ou* **as if...** on dirait que...; **it looks like rain** on dirait qu'il va pleuvoir; **you l. as if you've slept badly** vous avez l'air d'avoir mal dormi

▸**look after** *vt insep (take care of)* s'occuper de; **to l. after oneself** se débrouiller tout(e) seul(e); **to l. after sb's house/bag** surveiller la maison/le sac de qn; **can you l. after the children tomorrow?** tu peux garder les enfants demain?

▸**look around 1** *vt insep (town, shops)* faire un tour dans
2 *vi (in town)* faire un tour; *(in shop)* jeter un coup d'œil; **to l. around for sth** essayer de trouver qch

▸**look back** *vi (in space)* regarder en arrière *ou* derrière soi **(b)** *(in time)* **to l. back on sth** revenir sur qch; **she has never looked back since that day** depuis ce jour sa situation n'a cessé de s'améliorer

▸**look down** *vi (from above)* regarder en bas *ou* vers le bas; *(lower one's eyes)* baisser les yeux; *Fig* **to l. down on sb** regarder qn de haut

▸**look forward to** *vt insep* **to l. forward to sth** attendre qch avec impatience; **I'm looking forward to seeing her again** il me tarde de la revoir; **I l. forward to hearing from you** *(in letter)* dans l'attente de vous lire

▸**look in** *vi* **to l. in (on sb)** passer (voir qn)

▸**look into** *vt insep* examiner

▸**look on 1** *vt insep (consider)* **to l. on sb/sth as** considérer qn/qch comme
2 *vi (watch)* regarder

▸**look out 1** *vt sep (find)* trouver, dénicher
2 *vi* **(a)** *(from indoors)* regarder dehors; **to l. out of the window** regarder par la fenêtre **(b)** *(be careful)* faire attention; **l. out!** attention!

▸**look out for** *vt insep* **(a)** *(look for) (person)* guetter; *(thing)* chercher **(b)** *(be on guard for)* faire attention à

▸**look over** *vt insep* jeter un coup d'œil sur

▸**look round** = **look around**

▸**look through** *vt insep* **(a)** *(inspect) (written material)* parcourir; *(clothes, CDs)* passer en revue **(b)** *(not see)* **to l. straight through sb** regarder qn sans le voir; *(deliberately)* ignorer qn

▸**look to** *vt insep* **(a)** *(rely on)* **to l. to sb (for sth)** compter sur qn (pour qch) **(b)** **to l. to the future** se tourner vers l'avenir

▸**look up 1** *vt sep (word, address)* chercher; *(person)* passer voir
2 *vi (from below)* regarder vers le haut; *(raise one's eyes)* lever les yeux; *Fig* **things are looking up** la situation s'améliore

▸**look upon** *vt insep (consider)* **to l. upon sb/sth as** considérer qn/qch comme

▸**look up to** *vt insep* respecter, estimer

lookalike ['lʊkəlaɪk] *n* sosie *m*

look-in ['lʊkɪn] *n Fam (chance)* **he won't have** *or* **get a l.** il n'a pas la moindre chance; *(in conversation)* il ne pourra pas en placer une

looking-glass ['lʊkɪŋglɑːs] *n Old-fashioned* miroir *m*

lookout ['lʊkaʊt] *n (person)* guetteur *m*; *(on ship)* vigie *f*; **to keep a l. for sb/sth** guetter qn/qch; **to be on the l. for sb/sth** être à la recherche de qn/qch; *Fam* **that's your l.!** ça c'est ton affaire!; **l. post/tower** poste *m*/tour *f* de guet

loom¹ [luːm] *n (for making cloth)* métier *m* à tisser

loom² [luːm] *vi* **1** *n* **to be on the l.** *(of danger, event)* être imminent(e); **to l. large** être très présent(e)

loony ['luːnɪ] *Fam* **1** *n (pl* **loonies)** dingue *mf*; **l. bin** maison *f* de fous
2 *adj* dingue

loop [luːp] **1** *n* boucle *f*
2 *vt* faire une boucle/des boucles à; **to l. sth around sth** enrouler qch autour de qch; **to l. the loop** *(in plane)* faire un looping

loophole ['luːphəʊl] *n (in law)* vide *m* juridique

loopy ['luːpɪ] *adj Fam* barjo(t)

loose [luːs] **1** *n* **to be on the l.** *(of prisoner)* être en cavale; *(of animal)* être en liberté
2 *adj (animal)* qui s'est échappé(e); *(tooth, plank)* qui bouge; *(piece of clothing)* large, ample; *(skin)* flasque; *(alliance, network)* peu structuré(e); *(translation)* approximatif(ive); *(morals, lifestyle)* dissolu(e); **to come l.** *(of knot)* se défaire; *(of screw)* se desserrer; **to let sb l.** relâcher qn; **to let sb l. in the kitchen!** ne le laisse pas faire la cuisine tout seul!; **to let l. a torrent of abuse** lâcher des torrents d'injures; **to buy sth l.** acheter qch en vrac; **l. change** petite *ou* menue monnaie *f*; **l. connection** *(in appliance)* faux contact *m*; **to be at a l. end** ne pas savoir quoi faire; *Fig* **to tie up the l. ends** régler les derniers détails; **l. talk** propos *mpl* irréfléchis; **a l. woman** une femme de mauvaise vie
3 *vt Lit (arrow)* décocher; *(bullet)* tirer

▸**loose off** *vt sep (arrow)* décocher; *(bullet)* tirer

loose-fitting ['luːsfɪtɪŋ] *adj* ample, large

loose-leaf ['luːsliːf] *adj* à feuilles mobiles; **l. binder** classeur *m*

loose-limbed ['luːs'lɪmd] *adj* souple

loosely ['luːslɪ] *adv* **(a)** *(attached)* de façon lâche; **l. packed** *(snow)* poudreux(euse) **(b)** *(roughly)* de façon approximative; **to be l. connected** avoir un lointain rapport; **l. speaking** en gros

loosen ['luːsən] **1** *vt (screw, knot, belt)* desserrer; *(restrictions)* assouplir; **to l. one's grip** relâcher son étreinte; **to l. sb's tongue** délier la langue à qn
2 *vi* se desserrer

▶**loosen up** *vi* (*relax*) se détendre

loot [luːt] **1** *n* (*booty*) butin *m*; *Fam* (*money*) oseille *f*
  2 *vt* piller

looter ['luːtə(r)] *n* pillard(e) *m,f*

looting ['luːtɪŋ] *n* pillage *m*

lopsided [lɒp'saɪdɪd] *adj* (*face*) asymétrique; (*picture*) de guingois, de travers; (*grin*) en coin

loquacious [ləˈkweɪʃəs] *adj* loquace

lord [lɔːd] **1** *n* (*a*) (*aristocrat*) noble *m*; (*feudal*) seigneur *m*; **L. Browne** lord Browne (*titre de noblesse masculin*); *Br* **the (House of) Lords** la Chambre des Lords; **the L. Mayor** le lord-maire (*b*) *Rel* **the L.** le Seigneur; **the L.'s Prayer** le Notre Père; *Fam* **good L.!** mon Dieu!; *Fam* **L. knows** Dieu seul le sait
  2 *vt* **to l. it over sb** traiter qn de haut

lordly ['lɔːdlɪ] *adj* (*noble*) altier(ère); *Pej* (*arrogant*) hautain(e)

lordship ['lɔːdʃɪp] *n* autorité *f*; *also Ironic* **His/Your L.** monsieur; (*to judge*) son/votre Honneur

lore [lɔː(r)] *n* tradition *f* orale

lorry ['lɒrɪ] *n* (*pl* **lorries**) *Br* camion *m*; *Fam Euph* **it fell off the back of a l.** (*was stolen*) c'est de la marchandise volée; **l. driver** chauffeur *m* de poids lourd

Los Angeles [lɒsˈændʒəliːz] *n* Los Angeles

lose [luːz] (*pt & pp* **lost** [lɒst]) **1** *vt* perdre; **to have nothing to l.** n'avoir rien à perdre; **he had lost interest in his work** son travail ne l'intéressait plus; **it loses something in translation** ça perd à la traduction; **to be lost at sea** périr en mer; **the joke was lost on him** il n'a pas saisi la plaisanterie; **that clock loses five minutes a day** cette pendule retarde de cinq minutes par jour; **that mistake lost her the match** cette erreur lui a coûté le match; **to l. one's way, to get lost** se perdre; *Fam* **get lost!** va te faire voir!; **to l. one's balance** perdre l'équilibre; **to l. sight of sb/sth** perdre qn/qch de vue; *Fam Fig* **you've lost me!** je ne vous suis plus!; **to l. weight** perdre du poids; **we lost him in the crowd** nous avons été séparés dans la cohue; **to l. oneself in a book/one's work** se plonger dans un livre/son travail
  2 *vi* (*in contest*) perdre

▶**lose out** *vi* être perdant(e) (**to sb** par rapport à qn); **to l. out on sth** laisser échapper qch

loser ['luːzə(r)] *n* (*a*) (*in contest*) perdant(e) *m,f*; **to be a bad l.** être mauvais(e) perdant(e) (*b*) *Fam* (*unsuccessful person*) minable *mf*; **a born l.** un(e) perdant(e)

losing ['luːzɪŋ] *adj* **to fight a l. battle** être battu(e) d'avance; **the l. side** (*in war*) les vaincus *mpl*; (*in contest*) l'équipe *f* perdante

loss [lɒs] *n* (*in contest, war*) perte *f*; **there was a great l. of life** il y a eu de grosses pertes en vies humaines; **to suffer heavy losses** subir de grosses pertes; **it's no great l.** ce n'est pas une grosse perte; *Fam* **it's your l.!** tu ne sais pas ce que tu perds!; **without l. of face** sans perdre la face; **to be at a l. to do sth** être incapable de faire qch; **she's never at a l. for an answer** elle a toujours réponse à tout (*b*) (*financial*) **to make a l.** perdre de l'argent, être déficitaire; **to sell at a l.** vendre à perte; *Fig* **to cut one's losses** sauver les meubles; **l. leader** article *m* ou produit *m* d'appel

loss-making ['lɒsmeɪkɪŋ] *adj* déficitaire

lost [lɒst] **1** *adj* perdu(e); **to give sb/sth up for l.** abandonner tout espoir de retrouver qn/qch; **l. cause** cause *f* perdue; **l. property** (*office*) (bureau *m* des) objets

mpl trouvés; **l. soul** âme *f* en peine
  2 *pt & pp of* **lose**

lot [lɒt] **1** *n* (*a*) (*large quantity*) **a l., lots** beaucoup; **the l.** tout; **I bought the l.** j'ai tout acheté; **a l. of** or **lots of people** beaucoup de monde; **I see quite a l. of her** je la vois assez souvent; **we had a l. of** or **lots of fun** nous nous sommes bien amusés; *Fam* **listen, you l.!** écoutez, vous tous!; *Fam* **that l. next door** la bande d'à côté; *Fam* **he's a bad l.** c'est un bon à rien
  (*b*) (*destiny*) sort *m*, destin *m*; **to draw** or **cast lots for sth** tirer qch au sort; **to throw in one's l. with sb** partager le sort de qn
  (*c*) (*piece of land*) (lot m de) terrain *m*; (*at auction*) lot *m*
  2 *adv* **a l.** beaucoup; **a l. bigger** beaucoup ou bien plus grand(e); **thanks a l.** merci beaucoup

lotion ['ləʊʃən] *n* lotion *f*

lottery ['lɒtərɪ] *n* (*pl* **lotteries**) *n also Fig* loterie *f*

lotto ['lɒtəʊ] *n* loto *m*

lotus ['ləʊtəs] *n* lotus *m*; **l. position** (position *f* du) lotus

loud [laʊd] **1** *adj* (*a*) (*noise*) bruyant(e); (*voice, music*) fort(e); *Pej* (*person*) fort(e) en gueule; **to be l. in one's praise/condemnation of sth** louer/condamner qch avec force (*b*) (*colour, clothes*) voyant(e)
  2 *adv* fort; **to think out l.** penser tout haut; **l. and clear** parfaitement

loudhailer [laʊd'heɪlə(r)] *n* porte-voix *m inv*

loudly ['laʊdlɪ] *adv* fort; (*complain*) bruyamment

loudmouth ['laʊdmaʊθ] *n Fam* **to be a l.** être ou avoir une grande gueule

loudmouthed ['laʊdmaʊðd] *adj Fam* fort(e) en gueule

loudness ['laʊdnɪs] *n* (*of noise, voice*) volume *m*

loudspeaker [laʊd'spiːkə(r)] *n* haut-parleur *m*

Louisiana [luːiːzɪ'ænə] *n* la Louisiane

lounge [laʊndʒ] **1** *n* (*in house, hotel*) salon *m*; **l. bar** = dans un pub, salle plus confortable où les prix sont légèrement plus élevés; **l. suit** complet-veston *m*
  2 *vi* fainéanter

▶**lounge about, lounge around** *vi* traîner

louse [laʊs] *n* (*a*) (*pl* **lice** [laɪs]) (*insect*) pou *m* (*b*) *Fam* (*pl* **louses**) (*person*) salaud *m*

lousy ['laʊzɪ] *adj Fam* nul (nulle); (*weather*) dégueulasse; (*trick*) sale; **to feel l.** se sentir vraiment mal; **we had a l. time on holiday** nous avons passé des vacances nulles

lout [laʊt] *n* voyou *m*

loutish ['laʊtɪʃ] *adj* de voyou

louvre door ['luːvəˈdɔː(r)] *adj* porte f à persiennes

lovable ['lʌvəbəl] *adj* attachant(e)

love [lʌv] **1** *n* (*a*) (*for family, country*) amour *m* (**of** or **for** de ou pour); **give my l. to your parents** embrasse tes parents pour moi; **with l. from...** (*at end of letter*) affectueusement,...; **Bill sends his l.** Bill vous fait ses amitiés; **there's no l. lost between them** ils ne peuvent pas se sentir; **I wouldn't do it for l. or money** je ne le ferais pour rien au monde; **to do sth for the l. of it** faire qch pour le plaisir
  (*b*) (*between lovers*) amour *m*; **to be/fall in l. with sb** être/tomber amoureux(euse) de qn; **to make l. with** or **to sb** faire l'amour avec qn; **the l. of my life** l'homme (la femme) de ma vie; **it was l. at first sight** ce fut le coup de foudre; (**my**) **l.** (*term of endearment*) mon amour; **a l.-hate relationship** une relation faite à la fois d'amour et de haine; **l. affair** aventure *f*; *Euph* **l. child** enfant *mf* de l'amour; **l. letter** lettre *f* d'amour; **l. life** vie *f* amoureuse;

l. match mariage *m* d'amour; **l. nest** nid *m* d'amour **(c)** *(in tennis)* **15 l.**15 à rien; **l. game** jeu *m* blanc **2** *vt (person)* aimer; *(thing)* adorer; **I l. Chinese food** j'adore manger chinois; **to l. to do** *or* **doing sth** adorer faire qch; **I'd l. to come** j'aimerais beaucoup venir

lovebird ['lʌvbɜːd] *n Fam Fig* **a pair of lovebirds** un couple de tourtereaux

lovebite ['lʌvbaɪt] *n* suçon *m*

loveless ['lʌvlɪs] *adj* sans amour

lovely ['lʌvlɪ] *adj (idea, smell)* très bon (bonne); *(weather)* beau (belle); *(person)* charmant(e); **to have a l. time** passer un bon moment; *Fam* **it's l. and warm** il fait bon

lovemaking ['lʌvmeɪkɪŋ] *n (sexual intercourse)* ébats *mpl* amoureux

lover ['lʌvə(r)] *n (of person) (man)* amant *m*; *(woman)* maîtresse *f*; *(of nature, good food)* amoureux(euse) *m,f*

lovesick ['lʌvsɪk] *adj* qui languit d'amour

lovey-dovey ['lʌvɪ'dʌvɪ] *adj Fam (talk)* mièvre, à la guimauve; *(person)* roucoulant(e)

loving ['lʌvɪŋ] *adj* affectueux(euse), tendre

low¹ [ləʊ] **1** *n* **(a)** *(to reach a new* or *an all-time* **l.** atteindre un niveau le plus bas **(b)** *(weather front)* zone *f* de basse pression

2 *adj* **(a)** *(not high, not loud)* bas (basse); *(neckline)* profond(e); **fuel is getting l.** on n'a plus beaucoup d'essence; **to cook sth over a l. heat** cuire qch à feu doux; **of l. birth** de basse extraction; **the lower classes** les classes les moins aisées; **lower ranks** *(in army)* rangs *mpl* inférieurs; **to have a l. opinion of sb** avoir une mauvaise opinion de qn; *Fig* **a l. blow** un coup bas; **the L. Countries** les Pays-Bas *mpl*; **l. tide** marée *f* basse **(b)** *(depressed)* déprimé(e) **(c)** *(ignoble)* **the lowest of the l.** le dernier des derniers (la dernière des dernières); **that's a l. trick!** c'est vraiment un coup vache!

3 *adv* bas; **the l. paid** les petits salaires *mpl*; **turn the music/the lights down l.** baisse la musique/la lumière; **to be running l. on sth** être presque à court de qch

low² *vi (of cattle)* meugler

lowbrow ['ləʊbraʊ] *adj (tastes, interests)* peu intellectuel(elle)

low-budget [ləʊ'bʌdʒɪt] *adj (film)* à petit budget; *(holiday)* bon marché *inv*

low-calorie [ləʊ'kælərɪ] *adj* basses calories, hypocalorique

low-cost [ləʊ'kɒst] *adj* économique; *(housing)* à loyer modéré

low-cut [ləʊ'kʌt] *adj* décolleté(e)

low-down ['ləʊdaʊn] *n Fam* **to give sb the l. on sth** tuyauter qn sur qch; **what's the l. on Peter's resignation?** tu as des tuyaux sur la démission de Peter?

lower¹ ['ləʊə(r)] *vt* baisser; *(sail)* amener; *also Fig* **to l. one's guard** baisser sa garde; **to l. one's voice** baisser la voix; **to l. oneself into/onto sth** se laisser glisser dans/sur qch; **to l. oneself (to do sth)** s'abaisser (à faire qch)

lower² ['laʊə(r)] *vi (of sky)* se couvrir; **to l. at sb** *(of person)* lancer des regards noirs à qn

low-flying [ləʊ'flaɪɪŋ] *adj* volant à basse altitude

low-grade [ləʊ'greɪd] *adj* de qualité inférieure

low-key [ləʊ'kiː] *adj (approach, debate)* modéré(e); *(film, style)* sobre, dépouillé(e); *(person)* réservé(e)

lowlands ['ləʊləndz] *npl* basses terres *fpl*; **the L.** *(of Scotland)* les Basses Terres de l'Écosse

low-level ['ləʊ'levəl] *adj* **(a)** *(discussion)* à bas niveau **(b)** *(radiation)* de faible intensité

lowly ['ləʊlɪ] *adj* humble, modeste

low-lying ['ləʊ'laɪɪŋ] *adj* de basse altitude

low-spirited ['ləʊ'spɪrɪtɪd] *adj* abattu(e)

low-tech ['ləʊtek] *adj* rudimentaire

loyal ['lɔɪəl] *adj (friend)* loyal(e), dévoué(e); **to be l. to sb/sth** être fidèle à qn/qch

loyalist ['lɔɪəlɪst] *n & adj* loyaliste *mf*

loyally ['lɔɪəlɪ] *adv* loyalement

loyalty ['lɔɪəltɪ] *n (pl* **loyalties)** loyauté *f*; **you'll have to decide where your loyalties lie** il faudra que vous décidiez de quel côté vous êtes; **to have divided loyalties** être partagé(e)

lozenge ['lɒzɪndʒ] *n (shape)* losange *m*; *(cough sweet)* pastille *f*

LP [el'piː] *n (abbr* **long player)** 33 tours *m*

LSD [eles'diː] *n (abbr* **lysergic acid diethylamide)** LSD *m*

Lt *(abbr* **Lieutenant)** lt

Ltd *Br (abbr* **limited)** ≃ SARL

lubricant ['luːbrɪkənt] *n* lubrifiant *m*

lubricate ['luːbrɪkeɪt] *vt* lubrifier

lubrication [luːbrɪ'keɪʃən] *n* lubrification *f*

lucid ['luːsɪd] *adj* lucide; *(explanation)* clair(e)

luck [lʌk] *n* chance *f*; *(good)* **l.** bonheur *m*, chance; **good l.!** bonne chance!; **bad l.** malchance *f*; **bad l.!** pas de chance!; **to wish sb l.** souhaiter bonne chance à qn; **to be in l.** avoir de la chance; **to be out of l.** ne pas avoir de chance; **to be down on one's l.** être sur la paille; **to try one's l.** tenter sa chance; **don't push your l.!** ne pousse pas le bouchon trop loin!; **some people have all the l.** il y a vraiment des gens qui ont de la veine; **just my l.!** c'est bien ma chance!; **no such l.!** j'en ai pas (eu) cette chance!; **with any l.** avec un peu de chance

luckily ['lʌkɪlɪ] *adv* par bonheur, heureusement

lucky ['lʌkɪ] *adj (person)* **to be l.** avoir de la chance; **to make a l. guess** tomber juste; **to have a l. escape** l'échapper belle; *Fam* **l. devil**, **l. beggar** veinard(e) *m,f*; *Ironic* **you'll be l.!** tu peux toujours courir!; **it's l. you came when you did** c'est une chance que tu sois arrivé à ce moment-là; **she's l. to be alive** elle a de la chance d'être encore en vie; **my l. number** mon chiffre porte-bonheur; **it's not my l. day** ce n'est pas mon jour de chance; **that was l.** ça a été un coup de chance; **to strike it l.** décrocher le gros lot; **l. charm** porte-bonheur *m inv*; *Br* **l. dip** = baquet rempli de sciure etc où l'on plonge la main pour en retirer une surprise; **you can thank your l. stars she didn't see you!** tu peux t'estimer heureux qu'elle ne t'ait pas vu!

lucrative ['luːkrətɪv] *adj* lucratif(ive)

lucre ['luːkə(r)] *n Pej* or *Hum* lucre *m*

ludicrous ['luːdɪkrəs] *adj* risible, ridicule

lug [lʌg] *(pt & pp* **lugged)** *vt Fam* trimbaler

luggage ['lʌgɪdʒ] *n* bagages *mpl*; **l. label** étiquette *f* à bagages; **l. locker** consigne *f* automatique; **l. rack** *(in train)* porte-bagages *m inv*; *(on car)* galerie *f*; *Br* **l. van** *(on train)* fourgon *m*

lughole ['lʌghəʊl] *n Br Fam* esgourde *f*

lugubrious [luː'guːbrɪəs] *adj* lugubre

lukewarm ['luːkwɔːm] *adj also Fig* tiède; **she was rather l. about my suggestion** ma suggestion ne l'a pas enthousiasmée

lull [lʌl] **1** *n (in fighting)* accalmie *f; (in conversation)* pause *f; Fig* **the l. before the storm** le calme avant la tempête
2 *vt to* **l. sb to sleep** endormir qn en le berçant; **to l. sb into a false sense of security** endormir la méfiance de qn

lullaby ['lʌləbaɪ] *(pl* **lullabies)** *n* berceuse *f*

lumbago [lʌm'beɪgəʊ] *n* lumbago *m*

lumbar ['lʌmbə(r)] *adj Anat* lombaire

lumber ['lʌmbə(r)] **1** *n* (a) *Br (junk)* bric-à-brac *m;* **l. room** débarras *m* (b) *Am (wood)* bois *m* de charpente *ou* de construction
2 *vt* **to get lumbered with sth** se taper *ou* se coltiner qch; **I got lumbered with a huge bill** je me suis retrouvé avec une facture gratinée
3 *vi to* **l. about** *or* **around** avancer d'un pas lourd

lumbering ['lʌmbərɪŋ] *adj (walk)* lourd(e), pesant(e)

lumberjack ['lʌmbədʒæk] *n* bûcheron *m*

luminary ['luːmɪnərɪ] *(pl* **luminaries)** *n Lit* sommité *f*

luminescent [luːmɪ'nesənt] *adj* luminescent(e)

luminous ['luːmɪnəs] *adj (paint, road sign, colour)* fluorescent(e)

lump [lʌmp] **1** *n* (a) *(of earth)* motte *f; (of stone, coal)* morceau *m; (in sauce)* grumeau *m; (on body)* grosseur *f;* **a l. of sugar** un sucre; *Fig* **it brought a l. to my throat** *(made me sad)* ma gorge se serra; *Fin* **l. sum** somme *f* forfaitaire; **to pay in a l. sum** payer en une seule fois (b) *Fam (person)* empoté(e) *m,f*
2 *vt* (a) *(group)* **to l. (together)** regrouper; *Pej* mettre dans le même sac (b) *Fam (endure)* **you'll just have to (like it or) l. it!** il faudra que tu fasses avec!

lumpy ['lʌmpɪ] *adj (sauce)* grumeleux(euse); *(mattress)* bosselé(e)

lunacy ['luːnəsɪ] *n* folie *f*

lunar ['luːnə(r)] *adj* lunaire; **l. eclipse** éclipse *f* de lune; **l. landing** alunissage *m*

lunatic ['luːnətɪk] **1** *n* fou (folle) *m,f;* **l. asylum** asile *m* d'aliénés
2 *adj (idea, behaviour)* dément(e); **the l. fringe** la frange extrémiste

lunch [lʌntʃ] *n* déjeuner *m;* **to have l.** prendre son déjeuner, déjeuner; *Fam Fig* **to be out to l.** *(be crazy)* débloquer; **l. hour** heure *f* du déjeuner
2 *vi* déjeuner **(on** de)

luncheon ['lʌntʃən] *n* (a) *Formal* déjeuner *m* (b) **l. meat** = viande à base de porc présentée en tranches; **l. voucher** chèque-restaurant *m*

lunchtime ['lʌntʃtaɪm] *n* heure *f* du déjeuner

lung [lʌŋ] *n* poumon *m;* **l. cancer** cancer *m* des poumons

lunge [lʌndʒ] **1** *n* mouvement *m* brusque en avant; **to make a l.** for se ruer vers
2 *vi* se ruer **(at** vers)

lupin ['luːpɪn] *n* lupin *m*

lurch [lɜːtʃ] **1** *n (of ship, car)* embardée *f;* **a l. to the left/right** *(of politician, party)* un virage à gauche/droite; *Fam* **to leave sb in the l.** laisser qn dans le pétrin
2 *vi (of ship, car)* faire une embardée; *(of person)* tituber; **to l. to the left/right** *(of politician, party)* virer à gauche/droite

lure ['lʊə(r)] **1** *n (attraction)* attrait *m*
2 *vt (into trap, ambush)* attirer; **nothing could l. her away from her computer** rien ne pouvait l'éloigner de son ordinateur

lurid ['lʊərɪd] *adj* (a) *(story, description)* cru(e); **she described it in l. detail** elle en a fait une description qui ne laissait rien à l'imagination (b) *(gaudy)* criard(e)

lurk [lɜːk] *vi* être tapi(e); *(of doubt, fear)* subsister

luscious ['lʌʃəs] *adj (woman)* appétissant(e); *(fruit)* succulent(e)

lush [lʌʃ] *adj (plant, vegetation)* luxuriant(e); *Fig (surroundings)* luxueux(euse)

lust [lʌst] *n (sexual)* désir *m* (charnel); *Fig (for power, knowledge)* soif *f* **(for** de)
▸**lust after** *vt insep* convoiter

luster *Am* = **lustre**

lustful ['lʌstfʊl] *adj* lubrique

lustre, *Am* **luster** ['lʌstə(r)] *n* lustre *m,* éclat *m*

lustrous ['lʌstrəs] *adj* brillant(e)

lusty ['lʌstɪ] *adj (person)* vigoureux(euse); *(cry, blow)* puissant(e)

lute [luːt] *n* luth *m*

Luxemb(o)urg ['lʌksəmbɜːg] *n* le Luxembourg

Luxemburger ['lʌksəmbɜːgə(r)] *n* Luxembourgeois(e) *m,f*

luxuriant [lʌg'zjʊərɪənt] *adj* luxuriant(e)

luxuriate [lʌg'zjʊərɪeɪt] *vi* se prélasser **(in** dans)

luxurious [lʌg'zjʊərɪəs] *adj* somptueux(euse)

luxury ['lʌkʃərɪ] **1** *n (pl* **luxuries)** luxe *m;* **to lead a life of l.** vivre dans le luxe
2 *adj* de luxe

lychee [laɪ'tʃiː] *n* litchi *m*

lying ['laɪŋ] **1** *n* mensonges *mpl*
2 *adj (person)* menteur(euse)

lymph [lɪmf] *n Anat* lymphe *f;* **l. node** ganglion *m* lymphatique

lymphatic [lɪm'fætɪk] *adj* lymphatique

lynch [lɪntʃ] *vt* lyncher

lynching ['lɪntʃɪŋ] *n* lynchage *m*

lynx [lɪŋks] *n* lynx *m*

Lyons [liːɒn] *n* Lyon *m*

lyre ['laɪə(r)] *n* lyre *f*

lyric ['lɪrɪk] *adj* lyrique

lyrical ['lɪrɪkl] *adj* lyrique

lyricism ['lɪrɪsɪzəm] *n* lyrisme *m*

lyricist ['lɪrɪsɪst] *n* parolier(ère) *m,f*

lyrics ['lɪrɪks] *npl (of song)* paroles *fpl*

M

M¹, m [em] *n (letter)* M, m *m inv*

M² *Br Aut (abbr* **motorway)** autoroute *f*

m (a) *(abbr* **metre(s))** m (b) *(abbr* **mile(s))** mile(s)

MA [em'eɪ] *n Univ (abbr* **Master of Arts)** to have an MA in linguistics avoir une maîtrise de linguistique; **John Smith MA** John Smith, titulaire d'une maîtrise de lettres/droit/*etc*

ma [mɑː] *n Fam* maman *f*

ma'am [mɑːm] *n Old-fashioned* madame *f*

mac [mæk] *n Br Fam (raincoat)* imper *m*

macabre [mə'kɑːbə(r)] *adj* macabre

macaroni [mækə'rəʊnɪ] *n* macaronis *mpl;* **m. cheese** gratin *m* de macaronis

macaroon [mækə'ruːn] *n* macaron *m*

macaw [mə'kɔː] *n* ara *m*

Mace® [meɪs] *n (spray)* gaz *m* lacrymogène

mace¹ [meɪs] *n (weapon, symbol of office)* masse *f*

mace² [meɪs] *n (spice)* macis *m*

Macedonia [mæsə'dəʊnɪə] *n* la Macédoine

Macedonian [mæsə'dəʊnɪən] **1** *n* (a) *(person)* Macédonien(enne) *m,f* (b) *(language)* macédonien *m*
2 *adj* macédonien(enne)

Mach [mæk] *n Phys* M. **(number)** (nombre *m* de) Mach

machete [mə'ʃetɪ] *n* machette *f*

Machiavellian [mækɪə'velɪən] *adj* machiavélique

machinations [mæʃɪ'neɪʃənz] *npl* machinations *fpl,* manœuvres *fpl*

machine [mə'ʃiːn] **1** *n* machine *f; Fig (person)* robot *m;* **party/propaganda m.** appareil *m* du parti/de la propagande; *Comptr* **m. code** code *m* machine; **m. gun** mitrailleuse *f; Comptr* **m. language** langage *m* machine; **m. shop** atelier *m* d'usinage; **m. tool** machine-outil *f*
2 *vt* (a) *Ind* usiner (b) *(with sewing machine)* coudre ou piquer à la machine

machine-gun [mə'ʃiːngʌn] *vt* mitrailler

machine-readable [mə'ʃiːn'riːdəbəl] *adj Comptr* lisible par ordinateur

machinery [mə'ʃiːnərɪ] *n (machines)* machines *fpl,* machinerie *f; Fig (of organization)* rouages *mpl*

machinist [mə'ʃiːnɪst] *n (on sewing machine)* mécanicienne *f; (on machine tool)* ouvrier(ère) *m,f*

machismo [mæ'tʃɪzməʊ] *n* machisme *m*

macho ['mætʃəʊ] *adj* macho *inv*

macintosh ['mækɪntɒʃ] = **mackintosh**

mackerel ['mækrəl] *n* maquereau *m*

mackintosh ['mækɪntɒʃ] *n* imperméable *m*

macro ['mækrəʊ] *n (pl* **macros)** *n Comptr* macro *f,* macrocommande *f*

macrobiotics ['mækrəʊbaɪ'ɒtɪks] *n* macrobiotique *f*

macroeconomics ['mækrəʊiː'kə'nɒmɪks] *n* macro-économie *f*

mad [mæd] *adj* (a) *(insane) (person)* fou (folle); *(idea, plan)* insensé(e); *(dog)* enragé(e); to go m. devenir fou; **as m. as a hatter** fou à lier; **m. with fear** mort(e) de peur; **there was a m. rush for the door** les gens se ruèrent vers la porte; *Fam* to run/work like m. courir/travailler comme un(e) fou (folle); *Fam* **m. cow disease** maladie *f* de la vache folle (b) *Fam (enthusiastic)* to be m. about sth être fou (folle) de qch; **the crowd went m.** ce fut le délire parmi les spectateurs (c) *Fam (angry)* furieux(euse) **(with** or **at** contre); to go m. piquer une colère

Madagascan [mædə'gæskən] **1** *n* Malgache *mf*
2 *adj* malgache

Madagascar [mædə'gæskə(r)] *n* Madagascar

madam ['mædəm] *n (as form of address)* madame *f; Br Fam* **she's a proper little m.** *(of child)* c'est une vraie petite pimbêche

madcap ['mædkæp] *adj* insensé(e)

madden ['mædən] *vt* exaspérer

maddening ['mædənɪŋ] *adj* exaspérant(e)

made [meɪd] *pt & pp of* **make**

Madeira [mə'dɪərə] *n (island)* Madère *f; (wine)* madère *m*

made-up [meɪ'dʌp] *adj* (a) *(story, excuse)* inventé(e) de toutes pièces (b) *(wearing make-up)* maquillé(e)

madhouse ['mædhaʊs] *n Fam* maison *f* de fous

madly ['mædlɪ] *adv* (a) *(insanely, desperately)* comme un(e) fou (folle) (b) *Fam (exciting, interested, jealous)* follement; **m. in love** follement *ou* éperdument amoureux(euse)

madman ['mædmən] *n* fou *m,* dément *m*

madness ['mædnɪs] *n* folie *f,* démence *f;* **it's sheer m.!** c'est de la folie pure!

madonna [mə'dɒnə] *n* madone *f*

Madrid [mə'drɪd] *n* Madrid

madwoman ['mædwʊmən] *n* folle *f,* démente *f*

maelstrom ['meɪlstrəm] *n (confusion)* tourbillon *m*

maestro ['maɪstrəʊ] *(pl* **maestros)** *n* maestro *m*

Mafia ['mæfɪə] *n* the M. la Mafia

mag [mæg] *n Fam* magazine *m,* revue *f*

magazine [mægə'ziːn] *n* (a) *(publication)* magazine *m,* revue *f* (b) *(on radio, TV)* **m. (show)** magazine *m* (c) *(for gun)* magasin *m; (ammunition store)* dépôt *m* de munitions

magenta [mə'dʒentə] **1** *n* magenta *m*
2 *adj* magenta *inv*

maggot ['mægət] *n* asticot *m*

Maghreb [mæ'greb] *n* the M. le Maghreb

Maghrebi [mɑ:ˈgreɪbɪ] **1** n Maghrébin(e) m,f
2 adj maghrébin(e)

Magi [ˈmeɪdʒaɪ] npl the M. les Rois mpl mages

magic [ˈmædʒɪk] **1** n magie f; **as if by m.** comme par enchantement; **black/white m.** magie noire/blanche
2 adj (a) magique; **m. wand** baguette f magique (b) Fam (excellent) génial(e)

▶**magic away** (pt & pp **magicked**) vt sep faire disparaître comme par enchantement

magical [ˈmædʒɪkəl] adj magique

magician [məˈdʒɪʃən] n magicien(enne) m,f

magisterial [mædʒɪsˈtɪərɪəl] adj magistral(e); Law de magistrat

magistrate [ˈmædʒɪstreɪt] n Law magistrat m; **magistrates' court** ≃ tribunal m d'instance

magnanimity [mægnəˈnɪmɪtɪ] n magnanimité f

magnanimous [mægˈnænɪməs] adj magnanime

magnate [ˈmægneɪt] n magnat m

magnesium [mægˈniːzɪəm] n Chem magnésium m

magnet [ˈmægnɪt] n aimant m; Fig (for tourists, investors) pôle m d'attraction

magnetic [mægˈnetɪk] adj also Fig magnétique; **m. compass** boussole f; **m. tape** bande f magnétique

magnetism [ˈmægnɪtɪzəm] n also Fig magnétisme m

magnification [mægnɪfɪˈkeɪʃən] n grossissement m; (of sound) amplification f

magnificence [mægˈnɪfɪsəns] n magnificence f

magnificent [mægˈnɪfɪsənt] adj magnifique; (meal, wine) excellent(e)

magnify [ˈmægnɪfaɪ] (pt & pp **magnified**) vt (image) grossir, agrandir; (sound) amplifier; Fig (importance, problem) exagérer

magnifying glass [ˈmægnɪfaɪɪŋˈglɑ:s] n loupe f

magnitude [ˈmægnɪtju:d] n ampleur f; **a problem of the first m.** un problème majeur

magnolia [mægˈnəʊlɪə] n (tree) magnolia m; (colour) rose m pâle

magnum [ˈmægnəm] n (of champagne) magnum m

magpie [ˈmægpaɪ] n pie f; Fig **he's a bit of a m.** il a quelque chose du collectionneur fou

mahogany [məˈhɒgənɪ] n (wood, colour) acajou m
2 adj en acajou

maid [meɪd] n (servant) bonne f, domestique f; **m. of honour** (to queen) demoiselle f d'honneur; Am (at wedding) première demoiselle d'honneur

maiden [ˈmeɪdən] **1** n Lit (girl) jeune fille f
2 adj (flight) inaugural(e); **m. aunt** tante f célibataire; **m. name** nom m de jeune fille; Parl **m. speech** premier discours m

mail¹ [meɪl] **1** n (a) (letters, parcels) courrier m; **it came in the m.** c'est arrivé au courrier (b) (system) poste f; **by m.** par la poste; Comptr **m. merge** publipostage m; Com **m. order catalogue/company** catalogue m/entreprise f de vente par correspondance; **by m. order** par correspondance; **m. train** train m postal
2 vt poster

mail² [meɪl] n (armour) mailles fpl

mailbag [ˈmeɪlbæg] n sac m postal; **she gets a huge m.** (of celebrity, politician) elle reçoit énormément de courrier

mailbox [ˈmeɪlbɒks] n Am & Comptr boîte f aux lettres

mailing [ˈmeɪlɪŋ] n (mailshot) publipostage m, mailing m; **m. list** fichier m d'adresses

mailshot [ˈmeɪlʃɒt] n publipostage m, mailing m

maim [meɪm] vt mutiler, estropier

main [meɪn] **1** n (a) (pipe) conduite f (principale); **the mains** (electricity) le secteur; **to turn the water off at the mains** couper l'arrivée d'eau; **gas from the mains** gaz de ville (b) **in the m.** (generally) en général, en gros
2 adj principal(e); **the m. thing is to...** l'essentiel est de...; Gram **m. clause** proposition f principale; **m. course** plat m de résistance; **m. entrance** entrée f principale; Rail **m. line** grande ligne f; **m. road** grande route f; Fam **m. squeeze** petit(e) ami(e) m,f; **m. street** rue f principale

mainframe [ˈmeɪnfreɪm] n Comptr ordinateur m central

mainland [ˈmeɪnlænd] n continent m; **m. Europe** l'Europe continentale

mainline [ˈmeɪnlaɪn] vi Fam (inject drugs) se piquer

mainly [ˈmeɪnlɪ] adv principalement; **the passengers were m. Spanish** la plupart des passagers étaient espagnols

mainspring [ˈmeɪnsprɪŋ] n Fig (of change, revolution) moteur m

mainstay [ˈmeɪnsteɪ] n (of economy, philosophy) pilier m, base f

mainstream [ˈmeɪnstri:m] **1** n courant m principal
2 adj ordinaire

maintain [meɪnˈteɪn] vt (a) (preserve) (order, reputation) maintenir; (silence, attitude) garder; **to m. one's enthusiasm** rester enthousiaste (b) (building, machine, road) entretenir (c) (family) subvenir aux besoins de (d) (state) **to m. that...** soutenir que...

maintenance [ˈmeɪntɪnəns] n (a) (of car, building, roads) entretien m; **m. costs** frais mpl d'entretien (b) Law (alimony) pension f alimentaire

maisonette [meɪzəˈnet] n (appartement m) duplex m

maize [meɪz] n maïs m

Maj (a) Mil (abbr **Major**) Cdt (b) Mus (abbr **Major**) M

majestic [məˈdʒestɪk] adj majestueux(euse)

majesty [ˈmædʒəstɪ] n majesté f; **His/Her M.** Sa Majesté le Roi/la Reine

major [ˈmeɪdʒə(r)] **1** n (a) Mil commandant m; **m. general** général m de division (b) Am Univ (subject) matière f principale
2 adj (a) (important) majeur(e); (most important) principal(e); (accident, illness) très grave; **of m. importance** de la plus haute importance (c) Mus majeur(e)
3 vi Am Univ **to m. in sth** se spécialiser en qch

Majorca [məˈjɔ:kə] n Majorque f

Majorcan [məˈjɔ:kən] **1** n Majorquin(e) m,f
2 adj majorquin(e)

majority [məˈdʒɒrɪtɪ] (pl **majorities**) n (a) (in vote) majorité f; **to be in a** or **the m.** être majoritaire; **m. decision** décision f prise à la majorité; Pol **m. rule** système m majoritaire; Law **m. verdict** verdict m de la majorité; Pol **there was a m. vote in favour of...** on a voté à la majorité pour... (b) Law (age) majorité f

make [meɪk] **1** vt (pt & pp **made** [meɪd]) (a) (produce, perform) faire; (payment) effectuer; (decision) prendre; **made in Spain** fabriqué(e) en Espagne; **made from** or **of stone/wood** en pierre/bois; **I'll show them what I'm made of!** je vais leur montrer de quel bois je me chauffe!; **I'm not made of money!** je ne suis pas millionnaire!; **to m. something of oneself** faire quelque chose de sa vie; **two and two m. four** deux et deux font quatre; **to m. a choice** prendre une décision; **it doesn't m. any difference** cela ne change rien; **to m. a noise** faire du bruit

(b) *(earn)* gagner; **to m. a living** gagner sa vie; **to m. a name for oneself** se faire un nom

(c) *(make successful)* **this is the book that made her** ce livre l'a rendue célèbre; *Fam* **to m. it** *(be successful)* réussir; **you've got it made** tu as la belle vie; **it's m. or break** ça passe ou ça casse; **it made my day** il m'a fait très plaisir

(d) *(cause to be)* **to m. sb happy/sad** rendre qn heureux(euse)/triste; **to m. sb hungry** donner faim à qn; **to m. sb tired** fatiguer qn

(e) *(compel)* **to m. sb do sth** faire faire qch à qn; **don't m. me laugh!** tu me fais rire!

(f) *(estimate, calculate)* **what time do you m. it?** quelle heure avez-vous?; **I m. it £50 in total** j'arrive à 50 livres en tout

(g) *(reach)* **to m. it** *(arrive in time)* arriver à temps; *(finish in time)* finir à temps; **to m. the final** *(of team, competitor)* arriver en finale; **to m. the first team** être sélectionné(e) pour jouer dans la première équipe

(h) *(become, be)* **she'll m. a good doctor/singer** elle fera un bon médecin/une bonne chanteuse; **the report makes interesting reading** le rapport est intéressant à lire

(i) *(manage to attend)* *(show, meeting)* assister à; **I can m. two o'clock** je peux être là à deux heures

2 vi (a) to m. as if or **as though to do sth** *(get ready to)* s'apprêter à faire qch; *(pretend)* faire semblant de faire qch

(b) to m. do *(cope)* se débrouiller; **to m. do with** se contenter de; **to m. believe (that)**... imaginer que...

(c) to m. sure or **certain of** s'assurer de

3 n (a) *(brand)* marque *f*

(b) *Fam* **to be on the m.** *(financially)* chercher à s'en mettre plein les poches; *(sexually)* draguer

▶**make after** *vt insep* *(chase)* se lancer à la poursuite de

▶**make for** *vt insep* **(a)** *(head towards)* se diriger vers **(b)** *(contribute to)* contribuer à

▶**make of** *vt sep* **what do you m. of the new manager?** que pensez-vous du nouveau directeur?; **I don't know what to m. of that remark** je ne sais pas comment interpréter cette remarque

▶**make off** *vi* *Fam* *(leave)* filer, décamper

▶**make off with** *vt insep* *Fam* *(steal)* filer avec

▶**make out 1** *vt sep* **(a)** *(understand, decipher)* comprendre; *(see, hear)* distinguer; *(handwriting)* déchiffrer **(b)** *(write)* *(list, cheque)* faire **(c)** *Fam* *(claim)* **to m. out (that)**... prétendre que...

2 *vi Am Fam* *(sexually)* se peloter

▶**make over** *vt sep* *(transfer)* céder (**to** à)

▶**make up 1** *vt sep* **(a)** *(story, excuses)* inventer **(b)** *(deficit, loss)* combler; **I'll m. it up to you later, I promise** je te le revaudrai, je te le promets **(c)** *(complete)* *(team, amount)* compléter **(d)** *(form)* constituer, composer; **to m. up one's mind** se décider **(e)** *(put together)* *(list)* faire; *(parcel, bed)* faire; **to m. up a prescription** préparer les médicaments prescrits sur une ordonnance **(f)** *(apply make-up to)* maquiller; **to m. oneself up** se maquiller

2 *vi* *(end quarrel)* se réconcilier

▶**make up for** *vt insep* compenser; *(lost time)* rattraper

make-believe ['meɪkbɪliːv] **1** *n* fantaisie *f*; **to live in a land of m.** ne pas avoir le sens des réalités

2 *adj* imaginaire

makeover ['meɪkəʊvə(r)] *n (of appearance)* séance *f* de maquillage; *Fig* transformation *f*

maker ['meɪkə(r)] *n* **(a)** *(manufacturer)* fabricant *m*; *(of planes, cars)* constructeur *m* **(b) to meet one's M.** monter au ciel

makeshift ['meɪkʃɪft] *adj* de fortune

make-up ['meɪkʌp] *n* **(a)** *(cosmetics)* maquillage *m*; **m. artist** maquilleur(euse) *m,f*; **m. bag** trousse *f* à maquillage; **m. remover** démaquillant *m* **(b)** *(composition)* *(of team, group)* composition *f*; *(of person)* caractère *m*

making ['meɪkɪŋ] *n (of goods)* fabrication *f*; **the film was three years in the m.** le tournage du film a duré trois ans; **history in the m.** l'histoire en train de se faire; **a poet in the m.** un poète en herbe; **the problem is of her own m.** c'est un problème qu'elle s'est elle-même créé; **he has the makings of an actor** il a tout ce qu'il faut pour devenir acteur

maladjusted [mælə'dʒʌstɪd] *adj* inadapté(e)

maladroit [mælə'drɔɪt] *adj* maladroit(e)

malady ['mælədɪ] *(pl* maladies*)* *n* *Fig* mal *m*

Malagasy ['mæləgæsɪ] **1** *n (language)* malgache *m*

2 *adj* malgache

malaise [mæ'leɪz] *n* malaise *m*

malaria [mə'leərɪə] *n* malaria *f*, paludisme *m*

Malawi [mə'lɑːwɪ] *n* le Malawi

Malawian [mə'lɑːwɪən] **1** *n* Malawien(enne) *m,f*

2 *adj* malawien(enne)

Malay [mə'leɪ] **1** *n* **(a)** *(person)* Malais(e) *m,f* **(b)** *(language)* malais *m*

2 *adj* malais(e)

Malaysia [mə'leɪzɪə] *n* la Malaisie

Malaysian [mə'leɪən] **1** *n* Malais(e) *m,f*

2 *adj* malais(e)

Maldives ['mɔːldiːvz] *npl* **the M.** les (îles *fpl)* Maldives *fpl*

male [meɪl] **1** *n (person)* homme *m*; *(animal)* mâle *m*

2 *adj* mâle; *(sex, attitude, public)* masculin(e); **m. chauvinist pig** phallocrate *m*; **m. nurse** infirmier *m*

malefactor ['mælɪfæktə(r)] *n* *Lit* malfaiteur(trice) *m,f*

malevolence [mə'levələns] *n* malveillance *f*

malevolent [mə'levələnt] *adj* malveillant(e)

malformed [mæl'fɔːmd] *adj* difforme

malfunction [mæl'fʌŋkʃən] **1** *n* mauvais fonctionnement *m*

2 *vi* mal fonctionner

Mali ['mɑːlɪ] *n* le Mali

malice ['mælɪs] *n* méchanceté *f*; *Law* **with m. aforethought** de préméditation

malicious [mə'lɪʃəs] *adj* méchant(e), malveillant(e)

maliciously [mə'lɪʃəslɪ] *adv* méchamment, avec malveillance

malign [mə'laɪn] **1** *adj* pernicieux(euse)

2 *vt* calomnier, diffamer

malignant [mə'lɪgnənt] *adj* *(person)* malveillant(e), méchant(e); *(tumour)* malin(igne)

malinger [mə'lɪŋgə(r)] *vi* faire semblant d'être malade

malingerer [mə'lɪŋgərə(r)] *n* simulateur(trice) *m,f*

mall [mɔːl] *n* *Am* **(shopping)** **m.** centre *m* commercial

mallard ['mælɑːd] *n* colvert *m*

malleable ['mælɪəbəl] *adj* also *Fig* malléable

mallet ['mælɪt] *n* maillet *m*

malnutrition [mælnjuː'trɪʃən] *n* malnutrition *f*

malpractice [mæl'præktɪs] n faute f professionnelle

malt [mɔːlt] n malt m; m. **vinegar** vinaigre m de malt; m. **whisky** whisky m de malt

Malta ['mɔːltə] n Malte f

Maltese [mɔːl'tiːz] 1 n (a) (person) Maltais(e) m,f; the M. les Maltais mpl (b) (language) maltais m
2 adj maltais(e); the M. cross la croix de Malte

maltreat [mæl'triːt] vt maltraiter

maltreatment [mæl'triːtmənt] n mauvais traitements mpl

mammal ['mæməl] n mammifère m

mammary ['mæmərɪ] adj Anat mammaire; m. **glands** glandes fpl mammaires

mammography [mæ'mɒgrəfɪ] n Med mammographie f

mammoth ['mæməθ] 1 n (animal) mammouth m
2 adj (huge) gigantesque

mammy ['mæmɪ] (pl mammies) n Fam maman f

man [mæn] 1 n (pl men [men]) (a) (adult male) homme m; Fam hey, m.! eh toi!; Fam how are you doing, m.? comment ça va, vieux?; a m.'s jacket/bicycle une veste/ bicyclette d'homme; the army will make a m. of him l'armée en fera un homme; he took it like a m. il a pris ça courageusement; this will separate the men from the boys ceci distinguera les hommes des gamins; to be m. enough to do sth être assez courageux pour faire qch; to talk to sb m. to m. parler à qn d'homme à homme; he's just the m. for the job c'est l'homme qu'il nous faut; to be one's own m. être son (propre) maître; he's a m.'s m. c'est un homme à vrai; the m. in the street l'homme de la rue; a m. of God un homme d'église; a m. of the world un homme d'expérience
(b) (individual, person) homme m; any m. n'importe qui; few men peu d'hommes; to reply as one m. répondre d'une seule voix; they were patriots to a m. ils étaient tous patriotes
(c) (husband, partner) my m. mon homme
(d) (humanity) l'homme m
(e) (employee) (in factory) homme m, ouvrier m; (servant) valet m, domestique m; (soldier) homme, soldat m; our m. in Rome (diplomat) notre envoyé à Rome; (spy) notre agent à Rome; (reporter) notre correspondant à Rome
(f) (in chess) pièce f; (in draughts) pion m
2 vt (pt & pp manned) (machine) assurer le fonctionnement de; (plane, boat) être membre de l'équipage de; to m. the phone répondre au téléphone; a manned flight un vol habité

manacles ['mænəkəlz] npl menottes fpl

manage ['mænɪdʒ] 1 vt (a) (company, project) diriger; (shop, hotel) être le gérant de; (economy, resources, money, time) gérer (b) (deal with) (situation) gérer; to know how to m. sb savoir (comment) prendre qn; to m. to do sth (succeed) réussir ou arriver à faire qch; I can't m. three suitcases je ne peux pas porter trois valises; £100 is the most that I can m. (to pay) je ne peux pas aller au-delà de 100 livres; can you m. dinner on Thursday? est-ce que vous pouvez venir dîner jeudi?
2 vi (cope) se débrouiller (with avec); to m. without sb/ sth pouvoir se passer de qn/qch; he'll never m. on his own il n'y arrivera pas tout seul

manageable ['mænɪdʒəbəl] adj (object, size, vehicle) maniable; (hair) facile à coiffer

management ['mænɪdʒmənt] n (a) (activity) (of company, project) gestion f, direction f; (of economy, resources, shop, hotel) gestion; m. **consultant** conseiller(ère) m,f en

gestion; m. **studies** études fpl de gestion (b) (managers, employers) direction f; **under new m.** (sign) changement de propriétaire; m. **buyout** = rachat d'une société par la direction; m. **team** équipe f dirigeante

manager ['mænɪdʒə(r)] n (of bank, company) directeur(trice) m,f; (of shop, hotel, bar) gérant(e) m,f; (of boxer, singer, football team) manager m

manageress [mænɪdʒə'res] n (of bank, company) directrice f; (of shop, hotel, bar) gérante f

managerial [mænɪ'dʒɪərɪəl] adj directorial(e); m. **staff** cadres mpl; m. **skills** qualités fpl de gestionnaire

managing director [mænɪdʒɪŋdaɪ'rektə(r)] n directeur(trice) m,f général(e)

Manchester ['mæntʃestə(r)] n Manchester

Mancunian [mæŋ'kjuːnɪən] 1 n = personne née à ou habitant Manchester
2 adj de Manchester

Mandarin ['mændərɪn] n (language) mandarin m

mandarin ['mændərɪn] n (a) (fruit) mandarine f (b) (official) mandarin m

mandate ['mændeɪt] n mandat m

mandatory ['mændətərɪ] adj obligatoire

mandible ['mændɪbəl] n (of insect) mandibule f; (of vertebrate) mâchoire f inférieure

mandolin ['mændəlɪn] n mandoline f

mane [meɪn] n crinière f

man-eater ['mæniːtə(r)] n (a) (animal) mangeur m d'hommes (b) Hum (woman) mangeuse f d'hommes

man-eating ['mæniːtɪŋ] adj mangeur(euse) d'hommes

maneuver Am = manoeuvre

manfully ['mænfʊlɪ] adv courageusement, vaillamment

manganese [mæŋgə'niːz] n Chem manganèse m

mange [meɪndʒ] n gale f

manger ['meɪndʒə(r)] n mangeoire f

mangle ['mæŋgəl] 1 n (for clothes) essoreuse f (à rouleaux)
2 vt (body) mutiler; (car) broyer; (text) massacrer

mango ['mæŋgəʊ] (pl mangoes) n mangue f

mangrove ['mæŋgrəʊv] n palétuvier m; m. **swamp** mangrove f

mangy ['meɪndʒɪ] adj (animal) galeux(euse); (carpet, coat) minable, miteux(euse)

manhandle ['mænhændəl] vt (person) malmener; (large object) transporter à la force des bras

manhole ['mænhəʊl] n (in road) bouche f d'égout; m. **cover** plaque f d'égout

manhood ['mænhʊd] n (a) (maturity) âge m d'homme; to reach m. devenir un homme (b) (masculinity) virilité f (c) (men collectively) Scottish m. les hommes écossais

man-hour ['mænaʊə(r)] n Econ heure f de travail

manhunt ['mænhʌnt] n chasse f à l'homme

mania ['meɪnɪə] n (liking) passion f (for pour); (psychological) manie f; to have a m. for doing sth avoir la manie de faire qch

maniac ['meɪnɪæk] n fou (folle) m,f; to drive like a m. conduire comme un fou

manic ['mænɪk] adj Fig (person) stressé(e); (activity) frénétique

manic-depressive ['mænɪkdɪ'presɪv] n & adj Psy maniaco-dépressif(ive) m,f

manicure ['mænɪkjʊə(r)] 1 n manucure f; **to have a m.** se faire faire les ongles

  2 vt **to m. one's nails** se faire les ongles

manifest ['mænɪfest] 1 n (of ship, aircraft) manifeste m

  2 adj manifeste, évident(e)

  3 vt manifester

manifestation [mænɪfes'teɪʃən] n manifestation f

manifestly ['mænɪfestlɪ] adv manifestement

manifesto [mænɪ'festəʊ] (pl **manifestos**) n Pol manifeste m

manifold ['mænɪfəʊld] 1 n Aut collecteur m

  2 adj Lit (numerous) multiple, nombreux(euse)

Manila [mə'nɪlə] n Manille

mani(l)la envelope [mə'nɪlə'envələʊp] n enveloppe f en papier kraft

manipulate [mə'nɪpjʊleɪt] vt also Fig manipuler

manipulation [mənɪpjʊ'leɪʃən] n also Fig manipulation f

manipulative [mə'nɪpjʊlətɪv] adj Pej manipulateur(trice)

mankind [mæn'kaɪnd] n l'humanité f

manliness ['mænlɪnɪs] n virilité f

manly ['mænlɪ] adj viril(e)

man-made [mænmeɪd] adj (fabric, product) synthétique; (lake, beach) artificiel(elle); **a m. disaster** un désastre provoqué par l'homme

mannequin ['mænɪkɪn] n (person) mannequin m

manner ['mænə(r)] n **(a)** (way, method, style) manière f, façon f; **the m. in which...** la manière ou façon dont...; **in a m. of speaking** pour ainsi dire, en quelque sorte **(b)** manners (etiquette) manières fpl; **it's bad manners to stare** il est mal élevé de dévisager les gens; **he's got no manners** il ne sait pas se tenir **(c)** (type) **all m. of people/things** toutes sortes de gens/choses; **by no m. of means, not by any m. of means** absolument pas **(d)** (attitude, behaviour) **I don't like his m.** je n'aime pas sa façon d'être; **she's got a very abrasive m.** elle est très acerbe **(e)** manners (social usages) mœurs fpl

mannered ['mænəd] adj maniéré(e)

mannerism ['mænərɪzəm] n manie f, tic m

manoeuvrable, Am **maneuverable** [mə'nu:vrəbl] adj maniable

manoeuvre, Am **maneuver** [mə'nu:və(r)] 1 n also Fig manœuvre f; Fig **there wasn't much room for m.** la marge de manœuvre était assez limitée; **to be on manoeuvres** (of soldiers) être en manœuvre(s)

  2 vt manœuvrer; **she manoeuvred the car into the space** elle a garé la voiture dans l'emplacement

  3 vi manœuvrer

manor ['mænə(r)] n **m. (house)** manoir m

manpower ['mænpaʊə(r)] n main-d'œuvre f

mansion ['mænʃən] n (in country) château m; (in town) hôtel m particulier

manslaughter ['mænslɔːtə(r)] n Law homicide m involontaire

mantelpiece ['mæntəlpiːs] n dessus m de cheminée; **on the m.** sur la cheminée

mantis ['mæntɪs] n Am mante f religieuse

mantle ['mæntl] n **(a)** Lit (of snow) manteau m; Fig **to take on the m. of office** assumer les responsabilités qui incombent au poste **(b)** (of gas lamp) manchon m **(c)** Geol manteau m

man-to-man [mæntə'mæn] adj & adv d'homme à homme

manual ['mænjʊəl] 1 n (handbook) manuel m

  2 adj (work, worker) manuel(elle); **m. dexterity** dextérité f

manually ['mænjʊəlɪ] adv manuellement

manufacture [mænjʊ'fæktʃə(r)] 1 n fabrication f; (of vehicles) construction f

  2 vt fabriquer; (vehicles) construire; (clothes) confectionner; Fig (evidence) fabriquer (de toutes pièces)

manufacturer [mænjʊ'fæktʃərə(r)] n Ind fabricant m; (of vehicles) constructeur m

manufacturing [mænjʊ'fæktʃərɪŋ] 1 n Ind l'industrie f (manufacturière)

  2 adj (centre, sector) industriel(elle); **m. capacity** capacité f de production; **m. industries** industries fpl manufacturières

manure [mə'njʊə(r)] 1 n fumier m; **liquid m.** purin m

  2 vt engraisser

manuscript ['mænjʊskrɪpt] n manuscrit m

many ['menɪ] (comparative **more** [mɔː(r)], superlative **most** [məʊst]) 1 pron beaucoup; **m. of us/them** beaucoup d'entre nous/eux; **not m.** pas beaucoup; **too m.** trop; **as m. as you like** autant que vous voulez; **there were as m. as 100 people there** il y avait bien jusqu'à 100 personnes; Fam **to have had one too m.** avoir bu un coup de trop

  2 adj beaucoup de; **m. people** beaucoup de gens; **m. times** souvent, bien des fois; **not m.** pas beaucoup de; **in m. ways** de bien des façons; **not in so m. words** pas aussi explicitement; **there were so m. people that...** il y avait tant de gens que...; **a good m. people** un bon nombre de gens; **too m.** trop de; **as m....** autant de... que; **m.'s the time I've done that** j'ai fait ça bien des fois; Prov **m. hands make light work** à plusieurs, l'ouvrage avance vite

many-coloured ['menɪ'kʌləd] adj multicolore

Maori ['maʊrɪ] 1 n Maori(e) m,f

  2 adj maori(e)

map [mæp] 1 n carte f; (of underground, town) plan m; Fig **this will put Stonybridge on the m.** cela va faire parler de Stonybridge; **m. reference** coordonnées fpl

  2 vt (pt & pp **mapped**) (region) dresser une carte de

▶**map out** vt sep (route) tracer; (plan, programme) élaborer; **she had her career all mapped out** sa carrière était toute tracée

maple ['meɪpl] n érable m; **m. leaf** feuille f d'érable; **m. syrup** sirop m d'érable

mar [mɑː(r)] (pt & pp **marred**) vt gâcher

Mar (abbr **March**) mars

maracas [mə'rækəz] npl Mus maracas fpl

marathon ['mærəθən] n also Fig marathon m; **a m. speech** un discours-marathon; **m. runner** marathonien(enne) m,f

marauder [mə'rɔːdə(r)] n maraudeur(euse) m,f

marauding [mə'rɔːdɪŋ] adj en maraude

marble ['mɑːbl] n **(a)** (stone) marbre m **(b)** (glass ball) bille f; **to play marbles** jouer aux billes; Fam Fig **to lose one's marbles** (go mad) perdre la boule

marbled ['mɑːbld] adj marbré(e)

March [mɑːtʃ] n mars m; see also **May**

march [mɑːtʃ] 1 n marche f; Fig **the m. of time** la marche du temps; **on the m.** en marche; **m. past** défilé m

2 vt (soldiers) faire défiler; **he was marched off to prison** il a été emmené en prison
3 vi (of soldiers) marcher au pas; (of soldiers on parade, demonstrators) défiler; **to m. off** partir; **to m. by** or **past (sb/sth)** défiler (devant qn/qch)

marcher ['mɑːtʃə(r)] n (demonstrator) manifestant(e) m,f

marching orders ['mɑːtʃɪŋ'ɔːdəz] npl Fam **to give sb his m.** mettre qn à la porte

mare [meə(r)] n jument f

margarine [mɑːdʒə'riːn], Fam **marge** [mɑːdʒ] n margarine f

margin ['mɑːdʒɪn] n (a) (on page) marge f; **in the m.** dans la marge (b) (edge) (of forest) orée f; **on the margin(s) of society** en marge de la société (c) (gap) **to win by a narrow m.** gagner de justesse; **to win by an enormous m.** gagner haut la main; **a m. of error** une marge d'erreur (d) Com marge f bénéficiaire

marginal ['mɑːdʒɪnəl] **1** n Br Pol siège m à majorité précaire
2 adj (a) (improvement, increase) léger(ère) (b) (note) en marge (c) Br Pol (seat) à majorité précaire

marginalize ['mɑːdʒɪnəlaɪz] vt marginaliser

marginally ['mɑːdʒɪnəlɪ] adv légèrement

marigold ['mærɪɡəʊld] n souci m

marihuana, marijuana [mærɪ'wɑːnə] n marijuana f

marina [mə'riːnə] n port m de plaisance

marinade ['mærɪneɪd] Culin **1** n marinade f
2 vt (faire) mariner

marinate ['mærɪneɪt] vt Culin (faire) mariner

marine [mə'riːn] **1** n (soldier) fusilier m marin; Am Fam **(go) tell it to the marines!** (allez dire ça) à d'autres!
2 adj (life, biology) marin(e); **m. engineering** génie m maritime

mariner ['mærɪnə(r)] n Lit marin m

marionette [mærɪə'net] n marionnette f à fils

marital ['mærɪtəl] adj conjugal(e); **m. status** situation f de famille

maritime ['mærɪtaɪm] adj maritime

marjoram ['mɑːdʒərəm] n marjolaine f

mark[1] ['mɑːk] n (German currency) mark m

mark[2] **1** n (a) (scratch, stain) tache f, marque f
(b) (symbol) marque f
(c) (sign, proof) signe m; **as a m. of respect** en signe de respect; **years of imprisonment had left their m. on him** les années de captivité l'avaient marqué; **to make one's m.** (succeed) faire ses preuves
(d) (target) **his comments hit the m.** ses remarques ont touché en plein dans le mille; **unemployment has passed the three million m.** le nombre des chômeurs a dépassé la barre des trois millions; **her accusation was wide of the m.** son accusation était complètement à côté de la plaque; **he's not up to the m.** il n'est pas à la hauteur
(e) (in test, exam) note f; **full marks** la note maximale
(f) (in race) **on your marks! get set! go!** à vos marques! prêts! partez!; **to be quick off the m.** démarrer vite; Fig avoir l'esprit vif; **to be slow off the m.** prendre un mauvais départ; Fig être long à la détente
(g) (model, of machine) **m.** II/III série II/III
(h) (on cooker) (gas) **m.** 4 thermostat m 4
2 vt (a) (put mark on) marquer
(b) (homework, exam) noter; **to m. sth right/wrong** compter qch comme juste/faux

(c) (indicate) indiquer; (anniversary, end, occasion) marquer; **this decision marks a change in policy** cette décision est le signe d'un changement de politique; Fig **to m. time** (wait) piétiner
(d) (characterize) caractériser; **his comments were marked by their sarcasm** ses commentaires étaient empreints de sarcasme
(e) (in sport) (opponent) marquer
(f) (pay attention to) **m. my words** notez bien ce que je vais dire
▶**mark down** vt sep (a) (make note of) noter; **they had him marked down as a troublemaker** ils l'avaient étiqueté comme fauteur de troubles (b) Com (price) baisser; (goods) démarquer
▶**mark off** vt sep (a) (area) délimiter (b) (tick off) cocher
▶**mark out** vt sep **to m. sb out** distinguer
▶**mark up** vt sep (price) augmenter, majorer; **to be marked up** (of goods) avoir augmenté

marked [mɑːkt] adj (a) (difference, improvement) marqué(e), sensible (b) cards cartes truquées ou marquées; **to be a m. man** être surveillé

markedly ['mɑːkɪdlɪ] adv nettement

marker ['mɑːkə(r)] n (a) (of essay, exam) correcteur(trice) m,f; **he's a hard m.** il note sévèrement (b) **m. (pen)** marqueur m (c) (flag, post) balise f; **m. buoy** bouée f de balisage

market ['mɑːkɪt] **1** n (a) marché m; **to put sth on the m.** mettre qch en vente; Fin **m. analyst** analyste mf du marché; **m. day** jour m de marché; Econ **(free) m. economy** économie f de marché; Econ **m. forces** tendances fpl du marché; **m. garden** jardin m maraîcher; Com **m. leader** leader m du marché; Econ **m. price** prix m du marché; Com **m. research** étude f de marché; Com **m. share** part f de marché; Com **m. survey** étude f de marché; **m. town** ville f de marché
2 vt commercialiser

marketable ['mɑːkɪtəbəl] adj commercialisable

marketing ['mɑːkɪtɪŋ] n Com (study, theory) marketing m, mercatique f; (of product) commercialisation f; **m. campaign** campagne f de marketing; **m. department** service m de marketing; **m. manager** responsable mf ou directeur(trice) m,f du marketing; **m. strategy** stratégie f marketing

marketplace ['mɑːkɪtpleɪs] n (a) (in village, town) place f du marché (b) Econ marché m; **in the m.** sur le marché

marking ['mɑːkɪŋ] n (a) **markings** (on animal) (spots) taches fpl; (stripes) rayures fpl; (on plane) insignes mpl (b) (of essay, exam) correction f; **I've got a lot of m. to do** j'ai beaucoup de copies à corriger

markka ['mɑːkə] n mark m finlandais

marksman ['mɑːksmən] n tireur m d'élite

mark-up ['mɑːkʌp] n (on price) majoration f

marmalade ['mɑːməleɪd] n confiture f d'oranges

maroon[1] [mə'ruːn] n (a) (colour) bordeaux m (b) (firework) fusée f de détresse

maroon[2] vt abandonner; **we were marooned by the floods** nous étions isolés à cause des inondations

marquee [mɑː'kiː] n grande tente f; (at circus) chapiteau m

marquis ['mɑːkwɪs] n marquis m

Marrakesh ['mærəkeʃ] n Marrakech f

marriage ['mærɪdʒ] n also Fig (wedding) mariage m; **a happy m.** un ménage heureux; **she's my aunt by m.**

c'est ma tante par alliance; **m. of convenience** mariage de convenance; *Fig* **it was a m. of minds** c'était la rencontre de deux esprits; **m. certificate** certificat *m* de mariage; **m. guidance counsellor** conseiller(ère) *m,f* conjugal(e); **m. vows** vœux *mpl* du mariage

marriageable ['mærɪdʒəbəl] *adj* **a girl of m. age** une fille en âge de se marier

married ['mærɪd] *adj* marié(e); **to get m. (to)** se marier (avec); **m. life** la vie maritale; **m. name** nom *m* de femme mariée; *Mil* **m. quarters** logements *mpl* pour familles

marrow ['mærəʊ] *n* **(a)** *(of bone)* moelle *f* **(b)** *(vegetable)* courge *f*

marrowbone ['mærəʊbəʊn] *n* os *m* à moelle

marrowfat pea ['mærəʊfæt'piː] *n* pois *m* carré

marry ['mærɪ] **1** *vt* **(a)** *(get married to)* épouser, se marier avec; *(of priest, parent)* marier; **will you m. me?** veux-tu m'épouser?; *Fig* **he's married to his job** il n'y a que son travail qui compte **(b)** *(combine)* marier
2 *vi* se marier

▸**marry off** *vt sep* marier

Mars [mɑːz] *n (planet)* Mars *f*

Marseilles [mɑːˈseɪ] *n* Marseille

marsh [mɑːʃ] *n* marais *m*, marécage *m*

marshal ['mɑːʃəl] **1** *n* **(a)** *(army officer)* maréchal *m* **(b)** *(at race, demonstration)* membre *m* du service d'ordre
2 *vt (pt & pp* **marshalled**, *Am* **marshaled)** *(vehicles, troops)* rassembler; *(crowd)* canaliser; *(arguments, thoughts)* mettre en ordre

marshland ['mɑːʃlænd] *n* région *f* marécageuse

marshmallow [mɑːʃ'mæləʊ] *n* guimauve *f*

marshy ['mɑːʃɪ] *adj* marécageux(euse)

marsupial [mɑːˈsuːpɪəl] *n* marsupial *m*

martial ['mɑːʃəl] *adj* martial(e); **m. arts** arts *mpl* martiaux; **to declare m. law** proclamer la loi martiale

Martian ['mɑːʃən] *n* Martien(enne) *m,f*

martyr ['mɑːtə(r)] **1** *n* martyr(e) *m,f*; *Fig* **to be a m. to rheumatism** souffrir le martyre à cause de rhumatismes
2 *vt* martyriser

martyrdom ['mɑːtədəm] *n* martyre *m*

marvel ['mɑːvəl] **1** *n* merveille *f*; **to work marvels** faire des merveilles; **it's a m. they survived** c'est un miracle qu'ils soient encore vivants; *Fam* **you're a m.!** tu es un as!
2 *vi (pt & pp* **marvelled**, *Am* **marveled)** s'émerveiller (**at** de)

marvellous, *Am* **marvelous** ['mɑːvələs] *adj* merveilleux(euse); *Ironic* **isn't it m.!** ça, c'est le bouquet *ou* le comble!

Marxism ['mɑːksɪzəm] *n* marxisme *m*

Marxist ['mɑːksɪst] *n & adj* marxiste *mf*

marzipan ['mɑːzɪpæn] *n* pâte *f* d'amandes

mascara [mæsˈkɑːrə] *n* mascara *m*

mascot ['mæskət] *n* mascotte *f*

masculine ['mæskjʊlɪn] **1** *n Gram* masculin *m*; **in the m.** au masculin
2 *adj* masculin(e)

masculinity [mæskjʊ'lɪnɪtɪ] *n* masculinité *f*

mash [mæʃ] **1** *n* **(a)** *Fam (mashed potato)* purée *f* **(b)** *(for pigs, poultry)* pâtée *f*
2 *vt* **to m. (up)** broyer; *(vegetables)* écraser

mashed potato [mæʃtpə'teɪtəʊ] *n* purée *f* de pommes de terre

mask [mɑːsk] **1** *n* masque *m*; *(for eyes only)* loup *m*
2 *vt (conceal)* dissimuler

masked [mɑːskt] *adj* masqué(e)

masking tape ['mɑːskɪŋteɪp] *n* ruban *m* de papier adhésif

masochism ['mæsəkɪzəm] *n* masochisme *m*

masochist ['mæsəkɪst] *n* masochiste *mf*

masochistic [mæsəˈkɪstɪk] *adj* masochiste

mason ['meɪsən] *n (builder)* maçon *m*; *(freemason)* franc-maçon *m*

masonry ['meɪsənrɪ] *n (stonework)* maçonnerie *f*

masquerade [mæskə'reɪd] **1** *n* **(a)** *Fig (disguise)* mascarade *f* **(b)** *(dance)* bal *m* masqué
2 *vi* **to m. as sb** se faire passer pour qn

mass¹ [mæs] **1** *n* **(a)** *(large number)* foule *f*, multitude *f*; *Fam* **I've got masses (of things) to do** j'ai des tas de choses à faire; *Fam* **there's masses of room** il y a plein de place; **m. grave** charnier *m*; **m. hysteria** hystérie *f* collective; **m. media** *(mass)* médias *mpl*; **m. meeting** grand rassemblement *m*; **m. murderer** tueur *m* fou; **m. production** fabrication *f* en série; **m. protest** protestation *f* en masse **(b)** *(shapeless substance)* masse *f* **(c)** *Pol* **the masses** le peuple *m* **(d)** *Phys* masse *f*
2 *vi (of troops, people, clouds)* se masser

mass² *n Rel* messe *f*; **to go to m.** aller à la messe

massacre ['mæsəkə(r)] **1** *n* massacre *m*; *Fam Fig* **it was a m.** *(in sport, election)* ça a été le massacre
2 *vt also Fig* massacrer

massage ['mæsɑːʒ] **1** *n* massage *m*; **m. parlour** salon *m* de massage
2 *vt (body)* masser; *Fig* **to m. the figures** manipuler les chiffres

masseur [mæ'sɜː(r)] *n* masseur *m*

masseuse [mæ'sɜːz] *n* masseuse *f*

massive ['mæsɪv] *adj (increase, scale, dose)* massif(ive); *(amount, building, obstacle)* énorme; *(room)* immense; *(heart attack, stroke)* foudroyant(e)

mass-produce [mæsprə'djuːs] *vt* fabriquer en série

mast [mɑːst] *n (of ship)* mât *m*; *(for radio, TV transmitter)* pylône *m*

mastectomy [mæs'tektəmɪ] *n (pl* **mastectomies)** *n Med* mastectomie *f*

master ['mɑːstə(r)] **1** *n* **(a)** *(man in charge)* maître *m*; *(of ship)* capitaine *m*; **the m. of the house** le maître de maison; **to be one's own m.** être son propre maître; **to be m. of the situation** être maître de la situation; **m. of ceremonies** maître des cérémonies; *(for TV programme)* présentateur *m*; **m. bedroom** chambre *f* principale; **m. copy** original *m*; **m. key** passe-partout *m*; **m. plan** plan *m* d'ensemble; **m. race** race *f* supérieure
(b) *(skilled person)* maître *m*, expert(e) *m,f*; *Univ* **M. of Arts** *(qualification)* ≃ maîtrise *f* ès lettres; *(person)* ≃ maître ès lettres; *Univ* **M. of Science** *(qualification)* ≃ maîtrise *f* ès sciences; *(person)* ≃ maître ès sciences; **m. mason/builder** maître maçon/d'œuvre; *Mus* **m. class** cours *m* de maître; *Univ* **m.'s (degree)** maîtrise *f* (in de)
(c) *(teacher)* professeur *m*; **fencing/dancing m.** maître d'escrime/de ballet
(d) *(young boy)* **M. David Thomas** Monsieur David Thomas
(e) *Art* **an old m.** une œuvre de maître
2 *vt* maîtriser; *(situation)* dominer

masterful ['mɑːstəfʊl] *adj* autoritaire

masterly ['mɑ:stəlɪ] *adj* magistral(e)

mastermind ['mɑ:stəmaɪnd] **1** *n* cerveau *m*
2 *vt* (*project*) diriger, organiser; (*plot, crime*) échafauder

masterpiece ['mɑ:stəpi:s] *n* chef-d'œuvre *m*

masterstroke ['mɑ:stəstrəʊk] *n* coup *m* de maître

mastery ['mɑ:stərɪ] *n* maîtrise *f*

mastiff ['mæstɪf] *n* mastiff *m*

mastitis ['mæs'taɪtəs] *n Med* mastite *f*

masturbate ['mæstəbeɪt] *vi* se masturber

masturbation [mæstə'beɪʃən] *n* masturbation *f*

mat [mæt] *n* (*on floor*) tapis *m*; (*of straw*) natte *f*; (*at door*) paillasson *m*; (*table*) **m.** (*for plates*) set *m* de table; (*for dishes*) dessous-de-plat *m inv*

match¹ [mætʃ] *n* (*for lighting fire, cigarette*) allumette *f*

match² [mætʃ] **1** *n* (a) (*in sport*) match *m*; **m. point** (*in tennis*) balle *f* de match (b) **they're a good m.** (*of clothes*) ils vont bien ensemble; **to meet one's m.** trouver son maître; **to be no m. for sb** ne pas être à l'hauteur par rapport à qn
2 *vt* (a) (*equal*) égaler (b) (*of colours, clothes*) être assorti(e) à; (*of description, account*) concorder avec (c) (*marriage*) **to make a good m.** faire un bon mariage; **we can't m. their prices** nous ne pouvons pas rivaliser avec leurs prix; **to m. sb against sb** opposer qn à qn; **to be well matched** (*of teams, players*) être de même niveau; **a well-matched couple** un couple bien assorti
3 *vi* (*of colours, clothes*) être assortis(ties); (*of descriptions, accounts*) concorder

▸**match up 1** *vt sep* (*colours, clothes*) assortir
2 *vi* (*of clothes, colours*) être assortis(ties); (*of explanations*) concorder; **to m. up to sb's expectations** répondre à l'attente de qn

matchbox ['mætʃbɒks] *n* boîte *f* d'allumettes

matching ['mætʃɪŋ] *adj* assorti(e)

matchless ['mætʃlɪs] *adj* sans pareil

matchmaker ['mætʃmeɪkə(r)] *n* marieur(euse) *m,f*

matchstick ['mætʃstɪk] *n* allumette *f*; **m. man or figure** bonhomme *m* dessiné de simples traits

mate¹ [meɪt] **1** *n* (a) (*sexual partner*) (*male animal*) mâle *m*; (*female animal*) femelle *f*; (*person*) partenaire *mf* (b) *Br Fam* (*friend*) copain (copine) *m,f*; **thanks, m.** merci mon vieux (c) (*assistant*) assistant(e) *m,f*, (d) (*on ship*) officier *m*; (*first*) **m.** second *m*
2 *vt* (*animals*) accoupler
3 *vi* (*of animals*) s'accoupler

mate² (*in chess*) **1** *n* mat *m*
2 *vt* mettre mat

material [mə'tɪərɪəl] **1** *n* (a) (*substance*) matériau *m*, matière *f*; *Fig* **he isn't officer m.** il n'a pas l'étoffe d'un officier (b) (*for book, article*) matériaux *mpl*; **reading m.** de quoi lire; **she writes all her own m.** (*of singer*) elle écrit ses chansons elle-même (c) (*cloth*) tissu *m* (d) **materials** (*equipment*) matériel *m*
2 *adj* (*needs, possessions*) matériel(elle) (b) (*important, relevant*) essentiel(elle); (*fact*) pertinent(e); **the point is m. to my argument** c'est un point essentiel de mon argumentation

materialism [mə'tɪərɪəlɪzəm] *n* matérialisme *m*

materialistic [mətɪərɪə'lɪstɪk] *adj* matérialiste

materialize [mə'tɪərɪəlaɪz] *vi* (*of hope, threat*) se réaliser; (*of event*) avoir lieu; (*of spirit*) apparaître

materially [mə'tɪərɪəlɪ] *adv* (a) (*in money, goods*) matériellement (b) (*appreciably*) sensiblement

maternal [mə'tɜ:nəl] *adj* maternel(elle)

maternity [mə'tɜ:nɪtɪ] *n* maternité *f*; **m. dress** robe *f* de grossesse; **m. hospital** maternité; **m. leave** congé *m* de maternité; **m. ward** maternité

matey ['meɪtɪ] *Fam* **1** *n* listen, **m.** écoute, mon pote
2 *adj* pote (**with** avec)

math [mæθ] *n Am* maths *fpl*

mathematical [mæθə'mætɪkəl] *adj* mathématique

mathematician [mæθəmə'tɪʃən] *n* mathématicien(enne) *m,f*

mathematics [mæθə'mætɪks] *n* (*subject*) mathématiques *fpl*; (*calculations*) calculs *mpl*

maths [mæθs] *n Br* maths *fpl*

matinée ['mætɪneɪ] *n* (*of play, film*) matinée *f*

mating ['meɪtɪŋ] *n* accouplement *m*; **m. call** appel *m* du mâle; **m. season** saison *f* des amours

matriarch ['meɪtrɪɑ:k] *n* = femme ayant le statut de chef de famille

matriarchal ['meɪtrɪɑ:kəl] *adj* matriarcal(e)

matriculate [mə'trɪkjʊleɪt] *vi* s'inscrire

matriculation [mətrɪkjʊ'leɪʃən] *n* inscription *f*

matrimonial [mætrɪ'məʊnɪəl] *adj* matrimonial(e)

matrimony ['mætrɪmənɪ] *n* mariage *m*

matrix ['meɪtrɪks] (*pl* **matrixes** ['meɪtrɪksɪz] *or* **matrices** ['meɪtrɪsi:z]) *n Math & Tech* matrice *f*

matron ['meɪtrən] *n* (a) *Br* (*in hospital*) infirmière *f* en chef; (*in school*) = intendante et infirmière (b) (*older woman*) matrone *f* (c) **m. of honour** (*at wedding*) première demoiselle *f* d'honneur

matt [mæt] *adj* mat(e)

matted ['mætɪd] *adj* (*hair*) emmêlé(e)

matter¹ ['mætə(r)] **1** *n* (a) (*affair, issue*) question *f*, problème *m*; **that's a m. of opinion/taste** c'est une question d'opinion/de goût; **it's no easy m.** ce n'est pas simple; **that's quite another m.** ce n'est pas du tout la même chose; **within a m. of hours** en quelques heures; **for that m.** d'ailleurs; **as a m. of course** bien évidemment; **as a m. of fact** en fait; **as matters stand** au point où en sont les choses; **and to make matters worse...** et pour aggraver les choses...; **military matters** questions *fpl* militaires; **business matters** affaires *fpl*
(b) (*problem*) **what's the m.?** qu'est-ce qu'il y a?; **what's the m. with you?** qu'est-ce que tu as?; **there's something the m. with the car/my foot** j'ai un problème avec la voiture/mon pied
(c) (*substance*) matière *f*
(d) (*with no*) **no m.!** peu importe!; **no m. who/where** qui/où que ce soit; **no m. how hard I try...** j'ai beau essayer; **no m. what** I do quoi que je fasse
2 *vi* avoir de l'importance (**to** pour); **it doesn't m.** cela n'a pas d'importance, ça ne fait rien; **nothing else matters** le reste est sans importance; **it doesn't m. to me** ça m'est égal

Matterhorn ['mætəhɔ:n] *n* the M. le mont Cervin

matter-of-fact ['mætərə'fækt] *adj* (*person, statement*) terre à terre; (*tone, voice*) neutre; **he was very m. about it** il avait l'air très détaché

matting ['mætɪŋ] *n* tapis *m* de sol tressé

mattress ['mætrɪs] *n* matelas *m*

mature [mə'tjʊə(r)] **1** *adj* (*person, fruit*) mûr(e); (*hard cheese*) fort(e); *Br Univ* **m. student** = adulte qui reprend des études
2 *vt* (*wine*) faire vieillir

3 vi (of person, fruit) mûrir; (of wine) vieillir; Fin (of investment) arriver à échéance

maturity [mə'tʃʊərɪtɪ] n maturité f; Fin **on m.** à l'échéance

maudlin ['mɔːdlɪn] adj larmoyant(e)

maul [mɔːl] vt (of lion, tiger) mutiler; Fig (criticize) tailler en pièces

Mauritania [mɒrɪ'teɪnɪə] n la Mauritanie

Mauritanian [mɒrɪ'teɪnɪən] **1** n Mauritanien(enne) m,f
2 adj mauritanien(enne)

Mauritian [mə'rɪʃən] **1** n Mauricien(enne) m,f
2 adj mauricien(enne)

Mauritius [mə'rɪʃəs] n l'île f Maurice

mausoleum [mɔːsə'liːəm] n mausolée m

mauve [məʊv] **1** n mauve m
2 adj mauve

maverick ['mævərɪk] n franc-tireur m, non-conformiste mf

mawkish ['mɔːkɪʃ] adj Pej mièvre

max [mæks] (abbr **maximum**) max

maxim ['mæksɪm] n maxime f

maximize ['mæksɪmaɪz] vt maximaliser

maximum ['mæksɪməm] **1** n (pl maximums or maxima ['mæksɪmə]) maximum m; **to the m.** au maximum
2 adj maximum inv; maximal(e)

May [meɪ] n mai m; **in M.** en mai, au mois de mai; **at the beginning/end of M.** début/fin mai; **during M.** en mai; **each** or **every M.** chaque année en mai; **in the middle of M.** mi-mai; **last/next M.** en mai dernier/prochain; **on the sixteenth of M.** le seize mai; **she was born on 22 M. 1953** elle est née le 22 mai 1953; **M. Day** le Premier Mai

may [meɪ] v aux (3rd person singular **may**, pt **might** [maɪt])

> **May** and **might** peuvent s'utiliser indifféremment ou presque dans les expressions de la catégorie (a).

(a) (expressing possibility) **he m. return at any moment** il pourrait rentrer à tout moment; **he m. have lost it** il se peut ou se pourrait qu'il l'ait perdu; **it m. be that...** il se peut ou se pourrait que... + subjunctive; **you m. be wondering why...** vous vous demandez peut-être pourquoi...; **you m. well ask!** bonne question!; **we m. as well go** autant y aller; **you m. as well tell them the truth** autant que tu leur dises la vérité
(b) (asking for or giving permission) **m. I come in?** puis-je entrer?; **if I m. say so** si je peux me permettre; **m. I?** (when borrowing) vous permettez?
(c) Formal (expressing wish, purpose) **m. she rest in peace!** paix à son âme!; **m. the best man win!** que le meilleur gagne!
(d) (with concessions) **he m. be very rich but I still don't like him** il est peut-être très riche, mais il me déplaît quand même; **be that as it m., that's as m. be** quoi qu'il en soit

Mayan ['maɪən] **1** n Maya mf
2 adj maya

maybe ['meɪbiː] adv peut-être; **m. she won't accept** elle n'acceptera peut-être pas

Mayday ['meɪdeɪ] n (distress signal) signal m de détresse, SOS m; **M.!** mayday!

mayhem ['meɪhem] n **it was m.** c'était la pagaille

mayonnaise [meɪə'neɪz] n mayonnaise f

mayor ['meə(r)] n maire m

mayoress ['meəres] n mairesse f; (mayor's wife) femme f du maire

maypole ['meɪpəʊl] n = mât autour duquel les gens dansent pour célébrer le Premier Mai

maze [meɪz] n labyrinthe m; Fig dédale m

MBA [embiː'eɪ] n Univ (abbr **Master of Business Administration**) MBA m

MBE [embiː'iː] n Br (abbr **Member of the Order of the British Empire**) = titre honorifique britannique

MBO [embiː'əʊ] n Com (abbr **management buyout**) = rachat d'une entreprise par ses cadres

MC [em'siː] n (abbr **Master of Ceremonies**) maître m des cérémonies; (for TV programme) présentateur m

MD [em'diː] n **(a)** Med (abbr **Doctor of Medicine**) docteur m en médecine **(b)** Com (abbr **Managing Director**) directeur(trice) m,f général(e)

ME [e'miː] n Med (abbr **myalgic encephalomyelitis**) encéphalomyélite f myalgique

me[1] [unstressed mɪ, stressed miː] pron **(a)** (direct object) me; **she hates me** elle me déteste; **she loves me** elle m'aime; **she can understand my son but not ME** elle comprend mon fils, mais, moi, elle ne me comprend pas
(b) (indirect object) **she gave me the book** elle m'a donné le livre; **she gave it to me** elle me l'a donné
(c) (after preposition) moi; **she's thinking of me** elle pense à moi
(d) (as complement of verb to be) moi; **it's me!** c'est moi!; **it was me who did it** c'est moi qui l'ai fait
(e) (with interjections) **silly me!** que je suis bête!; **poor me!** pauvre de moi!

me[2] [miː] n Mus mi m

meadow ['medəʊ] n prairie f, pré m

meagre, Am **meager** ['miːgə(r)] adj maigre

meal[1] [miːl] n repas m; Fig **to make a m. of sth** faire tout un plat de qch

meal[2] n (flour) farine f

mealtime ['miːltaɪm] n heure f du repas

mealy ['miːlɪ] adj farineux(euse)

mealy-mouthed [miːlɪ'maʊðd] adj Pej mielleux(euse)

mean[1] [miːn] **1** n (average) moyenne f
2 adj (average) moyen(enne)

mean[2] adj **(a)** (miserly) avare **(b)** (nasty) méchant(e); **she has a m. streak** elle peut être méchante quand elle veut; **that was a m. thing to do/say** ce n'est pas chic d'avoir dit ça/fait ça **(c)** (poor) **she's no m. photographer** c'est une sacrée photographe; **it was no m. feat** ce n'est pas un mince exploit **(d)** Fam (good) **he plays a m. game of pool** c'est un as du billard

mean[3] (pt & pp **meant** [ment]) vt **(a)** (signify) (of word, event) signifier; (of person) vouloir dire; **what does the word "tacky" m.?** que signifie le mot "tacky"?; **this is Tim, I m. Tom** je vous présente Tim, je veux dire Tom; **I know what you m.** je comprends; **what do you m.?** qu'est-ce que tu veux dire?; **it doesn't m. anything** ça ne veut rien dire
(b) (be serious about) **do you think he meant what he said?** pensez-vous qu'il l'ait dit sérieusement?; **I didn't m. that** ce n'est pas ce que je voulais dire; **I m. it** je parle sérieusement; **you don't m. it!** tu plaisantes!
(c) (be of importance) **the price means nothing to him** le prix importe peu pour lui; **it means a lot to me** c'est très important pour moi

(d) *(intend)* to m. to do sth avoir l'intention de faire qch; **I didn't m.** to do it je ne l'ai pas fait exprès; **I m.** him no harm je ne lui veux pas de mal; **she means well** ses intentions sont bonnes; **I m.** to succeed je veux réussir; **she meant** you to have this ring elle voulait que tu aies cette bague; **it was meant** as a **joke/compliment** c'était une blague/un compliment; **this portrait is meant to** be of the duke ce portrait est censé représenter le duc; **you were meant** to be here at **eight** vous étiez censé arriver à huit heures; **it's meant to be a good film** il paraît que c'est un bon film; **they were meant for each other** ils sont faits l'un pour l'autre

meander [mɪˈændə(r)] 1 *n* méandre *m*
2 *vi (of river, road)* serpenter; *(of person)* flâner

meaning [ˈmiːnɪŋ] *n* sens *m*, signification *f*; *Fam* **if you get my m.** si tu vois ce que je veux dire; **what's the m. of this?** *(expressing indignation)* qu'est-ce que ça signifie?; **the m.** of life le sens de la vie

meaningful [ˈmiːnɪŋfʊl] *adj* significatif(ive), *(relationship)* sérieux(euse)

meaningless [ˈmiːnɪŋlɪs] *adj* vide de sens, sans signification

meanness [ˈmiːnnɪs] *n* **(a)** *(miserliness)* avarice *f* **(b)** *(nastiness)* mesquinerie *f*

means [miːnz] 1 *n (pl* **means)** *(method)* moyen *m*; **by m. of...** au moyen de..., à l'aide de...; **there is no m. of escape** il n'y a aucun moyen de s'échapper; **by some m. or other** d'une manière ou d'une autre; **a m. to an end** un moyen (d'arriver à ses fins); **by all m.** *(certainly)* je vous en prie; **by no m.** pas du tout, nullement; **she is by no m. stupid** elle est loin d'être bête; **m. of communication** moyen de communication; **m. of production** moyens de production; **m. of transport** moyen de transport
2 *npl (income, wealth)* moyens *mpl*, ressources *fpl*; **a man of m.** un homme fortuné; **to live beyond/within one's m.** vivre au-dessus de/selon ses moyens; **m. test** *(for state benefit)* enquête *f* sur les revenus

meant [ment] *pt & pp of* **mean**

meantime [ˈmiːntaɪm], **meanwhile** [ˈmiːnwaɪl] 1 *n* **in the m.** *(at the same time)* pendant ce temps; *(between two events)* entre-temps
2 *adv* **(at the same time)** pendant ce temps; *(between two events)* entre-temps

measles [ˈmiːzəlz] *n* rougeole *f*; **to have (the) m.** avoir la rougeole

measly [ˈmiːzlɪ] *adj Fam* minable

measurable [ˈmeʒərəbəl] *adj* mesurable; *Fig (difference, improvement)* notable, sensible

measure [ˈmeʒə(r)] 1 *n* **(a)** *(measurement, quantity)* mesure *f*; **this was a m. of how serious the situation was** cela montrait à quel point la situation était sérieuse; **they allowed her a m. of freedom** on lui accordait une certaine liberté; **to get the m. of sb** jauger qn; **he called me a liar for good m.** par-dessus le marché, il m'a traité de menteur **(b)** *(degree)* **in some m.** dans une certaine mesure **(c)** *(action, step)* mesure *f*; **to take measures to do sth** prendre des mesures pour faire qch
2 *vt & vi* mesurer

▶**measure up** *vi* être à la hauteur **(to** de)

measured [ˈmeʒəd] *adj* mesuré(e)

measurement [ˈmeʒəmənt] *n* mesure *f*

measuring [ˈmeʒərɪŋ] *n* **m. jug** verre *m* gradué; **m. spoon** cuillère-mesure *f*; **m. tape** mètre *m* ruban

meat [miːt] *n* **(a)** *(food)* viande *f*; *Fig* **to be m.** and **drink to sb** être une aubaine pour qn **(b)** *Fig (substantial content)* substance *f*

meatball [ˈmiːtbɔːl] *n* boulette *f* de viande

meaty [ˈmiːtɪ] *adj (taste, smell)* de viande; *Fig (book, film)* riche

Mecca [ˈmekə] *n* La Mecque; *Fig* paradis *m*

mechanic [mɪˈkænɪk] *n* mécanicien(enne) *m,f*

mechanical [mɪˈkænɪkəl] *adj also Fig* mécanique; **m. engineer** ingénieur *m* mécanicien; **m. engineering** construction *f* mécanique

mechanics [mɪˈkænɪks] 1 *n* **(a)** *(science)* mécanique *f* **(b)** *(working parts)* mécanisme *m*
2 *npl Fig (processes)* mécanisme *m*

mechanism [ˈmekənɪzəm] *n* mécanisme *m*

mechanize [ˈmekənaɪz] *vt* mécaniser

mechanized [ˈmekənaɪzd] *adj* **m. industry** industrie *f* mécanisée; **m. troops** troupes *fpl* motorisées

MEd [eˈmed] *n Univ (abbr* **Master of Education)** maîtrise *f* en sciences de l'éducation

medal [ˈmedəl] *n* médaille *f*

medalist *Am* = **medallist**

medallion [mɪˈdæljən] *n* médaillon *m*

medallist, *Am* **medalist** [ˈmedəlɪst] *n* médaillé(e) *m,f*

meddle [ˈmedəl] *vi (interfere)* se mêler **(in** de); *(tamper)* toucher **(with** à)

meddler [ˈmedlə(r)] *n* indiscret(ète) *m,f*

meddlesome [ˈmedəlsəm] *adj* indiscret(ète)

media [ˈmiːdɪə] *n* **(a)** *(TV, press)* médias *mpl*; **m. coverage** couverture *f* médiatique; **m. studies** études *fpl* de communication **(b)** *pl of* **medium**

mediaeval [medɪˈiːvəl] *adj* médiéval(e)

median [ˈmiːdɪən] *Math* 1 *n* médiane *f*
2 *adj* médian(e)

mediate [ˈmiːdɪeɪt] *vi* servir de médiateur **(for/ between** pour/entre)

mediation [miːdɪˈeɪʃən] *n* médiation *f*; **to go to m.** recourir à une médiation

mediator [ˈmiːdɪeɪtə(r)] *n* médiateur(trice) *m,f*

medic [ˈmedɪk] *n Fam (student)* étudiant(e) *m,f* en médecine; *(doctor)* médecin *m*

medical [ˈmedɪkəl] 1 *adj (record, treatment, profession)* médical(e); *(book)* de médecine; *(student)* en médecine; **to seek m. advice** consulter un médecin; **m. insurance** assurance *f* maladie; **m. practitioner** médecin *m*; **m. records** dossier *m* médical
2 *n (physical examination)* visite *f* médicale; **to pass/fail a m.** être déclaré(e) apte/inapte à la visite médicale

medicated [ˈmedɪkeɪtɪd] *adj (soap)* médical(e); *(shampoo)* traitant(e)

medication [medɪˈkeɪʃən] *n* médicaments *mpl*; **to be on m.** être sous traitement

medicinal [meˈdɪsɪnəl] *adj* médicinal(e)

medicine [ˈmedɪsɪn] *n* **(a)** *(science)* médecine *f*; **to practise m.** exercer la médecine; **to study m.** faire des études de médecine **(b)** *(drugs)* médicament *m*; *Fig* **to give sb a taste of his own m.** rendre à qn la monnaie de sa pièce; **m. chest** *or* **cabinet** (armoire *f* à) pharmacie *f*; **m. man** *(traditional healer)* sorcier *m*, guérisseur *m*

medieval [medɪˈiːvəl] *adj* médiéval(e)

mediocre [miːdr'əʊkə(r)] *adj* médiocre

mediocrity [miːdr'ɒkrɪtɪ] *n* médiocrité *f*

meditate ['medɪteɪt] *vi* méditer (**on** sur)

meditation [medɪ'teɪʃən] *n* méditation *f*

Mediterranean [medɪtə'reɪnɪən] **1** *n* the M. la (mer) Méditerranée

2 *adj* méditerranéen(enne); **the M. Sea** la mer Méditerranée

medium ['miːdɪəm] **1** *n* (**a**) (*pl* **media** ['miːdɪə] *or* **mediums**) (*means of communication*) moyen *m* de communication; (*means of expression*) moyen d'expression; **through the m. of the press** par voie de presse (**b**) (*in spiritualism*) médium *mf*

2 *adj* moyen(enne); **of m. height** de taille moyenne; **in the m. term** à moyen terme; **m. dry** demi-sec; **m. rare** à point; **m. wave** ondes *fpl* moyennes

medley ['medlɪ] (*pl* **medleys**) *n* (*mixture*) mélange *m*; (*in music*) pot-pourri *m*; **the 400 metres m.** (*in swimming*) le 400 mètres quatre nages

meek [miːk] *adj* docile; **m. and mild** doux (douce) comme un agneau

meekly [miːklɪ] *adv* docilement

meet [miːt] (*prt & pp* **met** [met]) **1** *vt* (**a**) (*encounter*) (*by accident*) rencontrer; (*by arrangement*) rejoindre, retrouver; (*collect*) attendre, aller chercher; **his eyes met mine** nos regards se sont croisés; **a remarkable sight met our eyes** un spectacle extraordinaire s'offrait à nos yeux; **there's more to this than meets the eye** on ne connaît pas les dessous de cette affaire; **there's more to her than meets the eye** elle cache bien son jeu (**b**) (*become acquainted with*) rencontrer, faire la connaissance de; **have you met my husband?** connaissez-vous mon mari?; **m. Mr Ford** je vous présente M. Ford (**c**) (*join with*) (*river*) se jeter dans; (*road*) rejoindre (**d**) (*satisfy*) (*demand, order*) satisfaire; (*condition, requirement*) satisfaire à; (*objection, criticism*) répondre à; (*cost, expense*) prendre en charge, payer (**e**) (*danger*) affronter; (*difficulties*) rencontrer; **to m. one's death** trouver la mort; **to m. one's match** trouver son maître

2 *vi* (**a**) (*encounter*) (*by accident*) se rencontrer; (*by arrangement*) se rejoindre; **our eyes met** nos regards se sont croisés (**b**) (*become acquainted*) se rencontrer (**c**) (*of society, assembly*) se réunir (**d**) (*join*) se rencontrer; (*of rivers, roads*) se rejoindre

▶**meet up** *vi* (*by accident*) se rencontrer; (*by arrangement*) se retrouver; **to m. up with sb** (*by accident*) rencontrer qn; (*by arrangement*) retrouver qn

▶**meet with** *vt insep* (*difficulty, refusal*) se heurter à; (*danger*) affronter; **to m. with disaster** se solder par un désastre; **to m. with failure** échouer; **to m. with an accident** avoir un accident; **to m. with sb's approval** recevoir l'accord de qn

meeting ['miːtɪŋ] *n* (**a**) (*encounter*) (*by accident*) rencontre *f*; (*by arrangement*) rendez-vous *m*; **m. place** (lieu *m* de) rendez-vous (**b**) (*for business, discussion*) réunion *f*; (*of shareholders*) assemblée *f*; **to be in a m.** être en réunion; **to hold a m.** se réunir

megabyte ['megabaɪt] *n Comptr* mégaoctet *m*

megahertz ['megahɜːts] (*pl* **megahertz**) *n Elec* mégahertz *m*

megalomania [megələʊ'meɪnɪə] *n* mégalomanie *f*

megalomaniac [megələʊ'meɪnɪæk] *n* mégalomane *mf*

megaphone ['megəfəʊn] *n* mégaphone *m*, porte-voix *m inv*

megaton ['megatʌn] *n* mégatonne *f*

megawatt ['megawɒt] *n Elec* mégawatt *m*

melancholy ['melənkɒlɪ] **1** *n* mélancolie *f*

2 *adj* (*person*) mélancolique; (*atmosphere, news*) triste

melee ['meleɪ] *n* mêlée *f*

mellifluous [mə'lɪfluəs] *adj* mélodieux(euse)

mellow ['meləʊ] **1** *adj* (*flavour*) suave; (*voice, colour*) chaud(e); (*wine*) moelleux(euse); (*light*) doux (douce); (*person*) détendu(e), serein(e)

2 *vi* s'adoucir

melodic [mɪ'lɒdɪk] *adj* mélodique

melodious [mɪ'ləʊdɪəs] *adj* mélodieux(euse)

melodrama ['melədrɑːmə] *n* mélodrame *m*

melodramatic [melədrə'mætɪk] *adj* mélodramatique

melody ['melədɪ] (*pl* **melodies**) *n* mélodie *f*

melon ['melən] *n* melon *m*

melt [melt] **1** *vt also Fig* faire fondre

2 *vi* fondre; **to m. into thin air** s'évaporer, disparaître; **to m. into the crowd** se fondre dans la foule

▶**melt away** *vi* (*of snow*) fondre; (*of clouds, vapour*) se dissiper; (*of crowd*) se disperser; (*of objections, opposition*) s'évanouir

▶**melt down** *vt sep* (*metal*) fondre

meltdown ['meltdaʊn] *n Phys* fusion *f*

melting ['meltɪŋ] *n* **m. point** point *m* de fusion; *Fig* **m. pot** melting-pot *m*

member ['membə(r)] **1** *n* = membre *m*; *Br Pol* **M. of Parliament** député *m*

2 *adj* **m. country/state** pays *m*/État *m* membre

membership ['membəʃɪp] *n* (**a**) (*state*) adhésion *f*; **m. card** carte *f* de membre *ou* d'adhérent; **m. fee** cotisation *f* (**b**) (*members*) membres *mpl*, adhérents *mpl*; **a large/small m.** une forte/faible adhésion

membrane ['membreɪn] *n* membrane *f*

memento [mɪ'mentəʊ] (*pl* **mementos** *or* **mementoes**) *n* souvenir *m*

memo ['meməʊ] (*pl* **memos**) *n* note *f* de service; **m. pad** bloc-notes *m*

memoir ['memwɑː(r)] *n* (*essay*) mémoire *m*; (*biography*) biographie *f*; **memoirs** (*autobiography*) mémoires

memorable ['memərəbəl] *adj* mémorable

memorandum [memə'rændəm] (*pl* **memoranda** [memə'rændə] *or* **memorandums**) *n* note *f* de service

memorial [mɪ'mɔːrɪəl] **1** *n* (*monument*) mémorial *m*

2 *adj* commémoratif(ive)

memorize ['meməraɪz] *vt* mémoriser

memory ['memərɪ] (*pl* **memories**) *n* (**a**) (*faculty*) & *Comptr* mémoire *f*; **to have a good/bad m.** avoir (une) bonne/mauvaise mémoire; **if my m. serves me right** si ma mémoire est bonne; **from m.** de mémoire; **to lose one's m.** perdre la mémoire; **to commit sth to m.** apprendre qch par cœur; **within living m.** de mémoire d'homme (**b**) (*thing remembered*) souvenir *m*; **in m. of...** en souvenir de..., à la mémoire de...; **to take a trip down m. lane** se remémorer le passé

men [men] *pl of* **man**

menace ['menɪs] **1** *n* (*threat*) menace *f*; (*danger*) danger *m*; *Fam Fig* (*pest*) plaie *f*

2 *vt* menacer

menacing ['menəsɪŋ] *adj* menaçant(e)

menagerie [mɪ'nædʒərɪ] *n* ménagerie *f*

mend [mend] **1** *vt (repair)* réparer; *(clothing)* raccommoder; **to m. one's ways** s'amender

2 *vi (of broken bone)* se ressouder

3 *n Fam* **to be on the m.** aller mieux

menfolk ['menfəʊk] *npl* **the m.** les hommes *mpl*

menial ['mi:nɪəl] **1** *n Pej* laquais *m*

2 *adj (job)* subalterne

meningitis [menɪn'dʒaɪtɪs] *n* méningite *f*; **to have m.** avoir la méningite

menopause ['menəpɔ:z] *n* ménopause *f*

menstrual ['menstrʊəl] *adj* menstruel(elle)

menstruate ['menstrʊeɪt] *vi* avoir ses règles

menstruation [menstrʊ'eɪʃən] *n* menstruation *f*

menswear ['menzweə(r)] *n* vêtements *mpl* pour hommes

mental ['mentəl] *adj (a) (state, age)* mental(e); **to make a m. note of sth/to do sth** essayer de se souvenir de qch/de faire qch; **to have a m. block about sth** faire un blocage sur qch; **m. arithmetic** calcul *m* mental; **m. breakdown** dépression *f* (nerveuse); **m. health** santé *f* mentale; **m. hospital** hôpital *m* psychiatrique; **m. illness** maladie *f* mentale *(b) very Fam (mad)* malade, dingue; **to go m.** *(lose one's temper)* devenir dingue

mentality [men'tælɪtɪ] *(pl* **mentalities)** *n* mentalité *f*

mentally ['mentəlɪ] *adv* mentalement; **to be m. handicapped** être handicapé(e) mental(e); **to be m. ill** avoir une maladie mentale

menthol ['menθɒl] *n* menthol *m*; **m. cigarettes** cigarettes *fpl* mentholées

mention ['menʃən] **1** *n* mention *f*; **he gets a brief m. in her autobiography** elle le mentionne brièvement dans son autobiographie; **to make no m. of sth** ne pas faire référence à qch

2 *vt parler de; (allude to)* mentionner; **to m. that...** dire que...; **to m. sb in one's will** coucher qn sur son testament; **to be mentioned in dispatches** être cité(e) à l'ordre du jour; **not to m....** sans parler de...; **now (that) you m. it** maintenant que tu le dis; **don't m. it!** il n'y a pas de quoi!

menu ['menju:] *n (a) (in restaurant) (set)* menu *m*; *(à la carte)* carte *f (b) Comptr* menu *m*

MEP [emi:'pi:] *n Br Pol (abbr* **Member of the European Parliament)** député *m* au Parlement européen

mercantile ['mɜ:kəntaɪl] *adj* commercial(e)

mercenary ['mɜ:sɪnərɪ] **1** *n (pl* **mercenaries)** mercenaire *m*

2 *adj Pej* intéressé(e)

merchandise ['mɜ:tʃəndaɪz] **1** *n* marchandises *fpl*

2 *vt* marchandiser

merchandising ['mɜ:tʃəndaɪzɪŋ] *n* merchandising *m*, marchandisage *m*

merchant ['mɜ:tʃənt] *n (retail)* marchand(e) *m,f*; *(wholesale)* négociant(e) *m,f*; **m. bank** banque *f* d'affaires; **m. navy** marine *f* marchande; **m. seaman** marin *m* de la marine marchande; **m. ship** navire *m* marchand

merchantman ['mɜ:tʃəntmən] *n (ship)* navire *m* marchand

merciful ['mɜ:sɪfʊl] *adj (person)* clément(e); *(act)* charitable

mercifully ['mɜ:sɪfʊlɪ] *adv (a) (showing mercy)* avec clémence *(b) (fortunately)* heureusement

merciless ['mɜ:sɪlɪs] *adj* sans pitié, impitoyable

mercurial [mɜ:'kjʊərɪəl] *adj (lively)* vif (vive); *(changeable)* changeant(e), lunatique

Mercury ['mɜ:kjʊrɪ] *n (planet)* Mercure *f*

mercury ['mɜ:kjʊrɪ] *n (metal)* mercure *m*

mercy ['mɜ:sɪ] *(pl* **mercies)** *n (a) (clemency)* pitié *f*, clémence *f*; **to have m. on sb** avoir pitié de qn; **to beg for m.** demander grâce; **at the m. of** à la merci de; **m. killing** acte *m* d'euthanasie *(b) (blessing)* bonheur *m*, chance *f*; **it's a m. that...** c'est une chance que...; **to be thankful** *or* **grateful for small mercies** apprécier ce dont on dispose

mere [mɪə(r)] *adj* simple; **he's a m. child** ce n'est qu'un enfant

merely ['mɪəlɪ] *adv* simplement, seulement

merge [mɜ:dʒ] **1** *vt (of companies)* & *Comptr* fusionner

2 *vi (of colours, sounds)* se fondre, se confondre; *(of companies)* fusionner; **to m. into the background** se fondre dans le décor

merger ['mɜ:dʒə(r)] *n* fusion *f*

meridian [mə'rɪdɪən] *n* méridien *m*

meringue [mə'ræŋ] *n* meringue *f*

merit ['merɪt] **1** *n (advantage, worth)* mérite *m*; **of little/great m.** de peu de/grande valeur; **to judge sth on its merits** juger qch pour ce qu'il vaut; **in order of m.** par ordre de mérite

2 *vt* mériter

meritocracy [merɪ'tɒkrəsɪ] *(pl* **meritocracies)** *n* méritocratie *f*

meritorious [merɪ'tɔ:rɪəs] *adj Formal* méritoire, louable

mermaid ['mɜ:meɪd] *n* sirène *f*

merrily ['merɪlɪ] *adv* joyeusement, gaiement

merriment ['merɪmənt] *n* gaieté *f*

merry ['merɪ] *adj (a) (happy)* joyeux(euse), gai(e); **to make m.** s'amuser; **M. Christmas!** Joyeux Noël!; **the more the merrier** plus on est de fous, plus on rit *(b) (slightly drunk)* gai(e)

merry-go-round ['merɪgəʊraʊnd] *n* manège *m*

mesh [meʃ] **1** *n (of net, sieve)* mailles *fpl*

2 *vi (of gears)* s'engrener

mesmerize ['mezməraɪz] *vt* hypnotiser

mess [mes] **1** *n (a) (disorder)* désordre *m*; **you look a m.!** tu es dans un triste état!; **to be (in) a m.** *(of room)* être en désordre; *Fig (of person)* être dans le pétrin; *(of one's life)* être un désastre; *Fig* **to make a m. of sth** *(essay, job)* saloper qch; **he's a m.** il est dans un triste état *(b) (dirt)* saletés *fpl*; **to make a m. of sth** salir qch; **the dog's done a m. on the carpet** le chien a fait ses besoins sur le tapis *(c) Mil (for officers)* mess *m*; *(for soldiers)* réfectoire *m*; **m. tin** gamelle *f*

2 *vi Fam (of dog, cat)* faire ses besoins

▸**mess about, mess around 1** *vt sep (treat badly)* se moquer de

2 *vi (a) (fool about)* faire l'imbécile; *(waste time)* traîner *(b) (tinker)* **to m. about** *or* **around with sth** tripoter qch

▸**mess up** *vt sep (hair, room, papers)* mettre en désordre; *(plans)* ficher en l'air

message ['mesɪdʒ] *n* message *m*; **to leave a m. for sb** laisser un message pour qn; *Fam Fig* **to get the m.** piger

messenger ['mesɪndʒə(r)] *n* messager(ère) *m,f*; **m. boy** garçon *m* de courses, coursier *m*

Messiah [mɪ'saɪə] n Rel Messie m

messianic [mesɪ'ænɪk] adj messianique

messily ['mesɪlɪ] adv salement; Fig **to end m.** (of relationship) mal terminer

Messrs ['mesəz] (abbr **Messieurs**) MM

messy ['mesɪ] adj (a) (dirty) sale; (job) salissant(e); **to be a m. eater** manger salement (b) (untidy) (room, hair) en désordre; (handwriting) peu soigné(e); (appearance) négligé(e) (c) (unpleasantly complex) (affair, situation) embrouillé(e); (private life) troublé(e)

met [met] pt & pp of **meet**

metabolic [metə'bɒlɪk] adj métabolique

metabolism [mɪ'tæbəlɪzəm] n métabolisme m

metal ['metəl] 1 n métal m; **m. detector** détecteur m de métaux
 2 adj en métal

metalled road [metəld'rəʊd] n route f empierrée

metallic [mɪ'tælɪk] adj (sound, voice) métallique; (paint) métallisé(e); (taste) de métal

metallurgy [me'tælədʒɪ] n métallurgie f

metalwork ['metəlwɜːk] n ferronnerie f

metamorphosis [metə'mɔːfəsɪs] (pl **metamorphoses** [metə'mɔːfəsiːz]) n métamorphose f

metaphor ['metəfə(r)] n métaphore f

metaphoric(al) [metə'fɒrɪk(əl)] adj métaphorique

metaphysical [metə'fɪzɪkəl] adj métaphysique

metaphysics [metə'fɪzɪks] n métaphysique f

▶**mete out** [miːt] vt sep (punishment) infliger (**to** à); (justice) rendre

meteor ['miːtɪə(r)] n météore m

meteoric [miːtɪ'ɒrɪk] adj météorique; Fig **a m. rise** une ascension fulgurante

meteorite ['miːtɪəraɪt] n météorite f

meteorological [miːtɪərə'lɒdʒɪkəl] adj météorologique

meteorology [miːtɪə'rɒlədʒɪ] n météorologie f

meter[1] ['miːtə(r)] n compteur m; **to read the m.** relever le compteur; **(parking) m.** parcmètre m

meter[2] Am = **metre**

methane ['miːθeɪn] n méthane m

method ['meθəd] n méthode f; **there's m. in his madness** il n'est pas aussi fou qu'il en a l'air; **m. acting** méthode de Stanislavski

methodical [mɪ'θɒdɪkəl] adj méthodique

Methodism ['meθədɪzəm] n Rel méthodisme m

Methodist ['meθədɪst] n Rel méthodiste mf

methodology [meθə'dɒlədʒɪ] n méthodologie f

meths [meθs] n Br Fam (methylated spirits) alcool m à brûler

methylated spirits ['meθɪleɪtɪd'spɪrɪts] n Br alcool m à brûler

meticulous [mɪ'tɪkjʊləs] adj méticuleux(euse)

metre[1], Am **meter** ['miːtə(r)] n (measurement) mètre m

metre[2], Am **meter** n (of poetry) mètre m

metric ['metrɪk] adj métrique

metronome ['metrənəʊm] n métronome m

metropolis [mɪ'trɒpəlɪs] n métropole f

metropolitan [metrə'pɒlɪtən] adj urbain(e); **M. France** la France métropolitaine; **the M. Police** la police de Londres

mettle ['metəl] n (courage) courage m; **to be on one's m.** être fin prêt(e); **to show one's m.** montrer de quoi on est capable

mew [mjuː] 1 n miaulement m
 2 vi miauler

mews [mjuːz] (pl **mews**) n Br ruelle f; **m. cottage** = maison luxueuse aménagée dans une ancienne écurie

Mexican ['meksɪkən] 1 n Mexicain(e) m,f
 2 adj mexicain(e); **M. wave** (at match) vague f

Mexico ['meksɪkəʊ] n le Mexique; **M. City** Mexico

mezzanine ['metsəniːn] n m. **(floor)** mezzanine f

mg [em'dʒiː] n (abbr **milligram(s)**) mg

Mgr (abbr **Monsignor**) Mgr

MHz (abbr **megahertz**) MHz

mi [miː] n Mus mi m

MI5 [emaɪ'faɪv] n Br (abbr **Military Intelligence Section 5**) ≃ DST f

MI6 [emaɪ'sɪks] n Br (abbr **Military Intelligence Section 6**) ≃ DGSE f

miaow [miːˈaʊ] 1 n miaulement m; **m.!** miaou!
 2 vi miauler

mica ['maɪkə] n mica m

mice [maɪs] pl of **mouse**

Michelangelo ['maɪkəl'ændʒələʊ] n Michel-Ange

mickey ['mɪkɪ] n Br Fam **to take the m. (out of sb)** se moquer (de qn)

Mickey Mouse ['mɪkɪ'maʊs] adj Fam Pej (job, qualification) à la noix

micro ['maɪkrəʊ] (pl **micros**) n micro m

microbe ['maɪkrəʊb] n microbe m

microbiology [maɪkrəʊbaɪ'ɒlədʒɪ] n microbiologie f

microchip ['maɪkrəʊtʃɪp] n microprocesseur m

microcomputer ['maɪkrəʊkəm'pjuːtə(r)] n micro-ordinateur m

microcosm ['maɪkrəʊkɒzəm] n microcosme m

microfiche ['maɪkrəʊfiːʃ] n microfiche f

microfilm ['maɪkrəʊfɪlm] 1 n microfilm m
 2 vt microfilmer

micrometer [maɪ'krɒmɪtə(r)] n micromètre m

microphone ['maɪkrəfəʊn] n microphone m

microprocessor ['maɪkrəʊ'prəʊsesə(r)] n microprocesseur m

microscope ['maɪkrəskəʊp] n microscope m

microscopic [maɪkrə'skɒpɪk] adj microscopique

microsurgery [maɪkrəʊ'sɜːdʒərɪ] n microchirurgie f

microwave ['maɪkrəʊweɪv] 1 n Phys micro-onde f; **m. (oven)** (four m à) micro-ondes m inv
 2 vt faire cuire au micro-ondes

mid [mɪd] adj **in m. ocean** au milieu de l'océan; **m. June** mi-juin; **he stopped in m. sentence** il s'est arrêté au milieu d'une phrase

midair [mɪd'eə(r)] 1 n **in m.** en plein ciel
 2 adj (collision) en plein ciel

mid-Atlantic accent [mɪdət'læntɪk'æksent] n accent m mi-américain mi-britannique

midday ['mɪd'deɪ] n midi m; **m. meal** déjeuner m

middle ['mɪdəl] 1 n (a) (centre) milieu m; **to be in the m. of doing sth** être en train de faire qch; **in the m. of the night** en pleine nuit; **in the m. of nowhere** dans un coin perdu; Fig **to split sth down the m.** partager qch en deux **(b)** *(waist)* taille *f*

2 *adj* du milieu; **m. age** l'âge *m* mûr; *Hist* **the M. Ages** le Moyen Âge; *Mus* **m. C** do *m* du milieu du clavier; **the m. class** la classe moyenne; *Fig* **to steer a m. course** adopter une solution intermédiaire; **in the m. distance** au second plan; **the M. East** le Moyen-Orient; **M. Eastern** du Moyen-Orient; *Pol* **the m. ground** le centre; **m. management** cadres *mpl* moyens; **m. name** deuxième prénom *m*; *Fam* **"generosity" isn't exactly his m. name!** on ne peut pas dire qu'il soit particulièrement généreux!

middle-aged [mɪdəl'eɪdʒd] *adj* d'âge mûr

middlebrow ['mɪdəlbraʊ] *adj* moyen(enne); **a m. novelist** un romancier sans prétentions

middle-class [mɪdəl'klɑːs] *adj* bourgeois(e)

middleman ['mɪdəlmæn] *n* intermédiaire *mf*

middle-of-the-road ['mɪdəlɑvðə'rəʊd] *adj (policy)* modéré(e); *(music)* grand public *inv*

middle-sized ['mɪdəl'saɪzd] *adj* de taille moyenne

middleweight ['mɪdəlweɪt] *n (in boxing)* poids *m* moyen

middling ['mɪdlɪŋ] *adj (fairly good)* moyen(enne); *(mediocre)* médiocre

midfield [mɪd'fiːld] *n (in football)* milieu *m* de terrain; **m. player** milieu de terrain

midfielder [mɪd'fiːldə(r)] *n (in football)* milieu *m* de terrain

midge [mɪdʒ] *n* moucheron *m*

midget ['mɪdʒɪt] **1** *n (small person)* nain(e) *m,f*

2 *adj (miniature)* miniature

midi system ['mɪdɪsɪstəm] *n (stereo)* chaîne *f* midi

Midlands ['mɪdləndz] *npl* **the M.** les Midlands *fpl*

midlife crisis ['mɪdlaɪf'kraɪsɪs] *n* crise *f* aux alentours de la cinquantaine

midmorning [mɪd'mɔːnɪŋ] *n* milieu *m* de matinée

midnight ['mɪdnaɪt] *n* minuit *m*; **to burn the m. oil** travailler tard dans la nuit

midriff ['mɪdrɪf] *n* ventre *m*

midshipman ['mɪdʃɪpmən] *n* aspirant *m* de marine

midst [mɪdst] *n* milieu *m*, cœur *m*; **in the m. of** au milieu de; **in our/their m.** parmi nous/eux

midstream [mɪd'striːm] *n* **in m.** au milieu du courant; *Fig (when speaking)* en plein milieu d'une phrase

midsummer ['mɪdsʌmə(r)] *n* milieu *m* de l'été; **M.'s Day** la Saint-Jean

midterm ['mɪd'tɜːm] *n* **(a)** *Pol Br* **m. by-election** = élection législative en milieu de mandat; *Am* **m. elections** = élections qui ont lieu au milieu du mandat présidentiel **(b)** *Sch & Univ* milieu *m* du trimestre; **m. break** vacances *fpl* de milieu de trimestre

midway ['mɪdweɪ] **1** *adj* **at the m. point** *(in space)* à la mi-chemin; *(in time)* à la moitié

2 *adv* à mi-chemin

midweek [mɪd'wiːk] *adv* en milieu de semaine

Mid-West ['mɪd'west] *n* Midwest *m*

Mid-Western [mɪd'westən] *adj* du Midwest

midwife ['mɪdwaɪf] *(pl* **midwives** [mɪdwaɪvz]*) n* sage-femme *f*

midwifery [mɪd'wɪfərɪ] *n* profession *f* de sage-femme

midwinter ['mɪd'wɪntə(r)] *n* milieu *m* de l'hiver

might^1 [maɪt] *n (strength)* force *f*; **with all one's m.** de toutes ses forces; *Prov* **m. is right** la raison du plus fort est toujours la meilleure

might^2 *v aux*

> La forme négative **mightn't** s'écrit **might not** dans un style plus soutenu. **Might** et **may** peuvent s'utiliser indifféremment ou presque dans les expressions de la catégorie **(a)**.

(a) *(expressing possibility)* **it m. be difficult** il se peut ou se pourrait que ce soit difficile; **it m. be better to phone first** il vaudrait peut-être mieux téléphoner d'abord; **it m. be that...** il se peut ou se pourrait que... + *subjunctive*; **you m. want to...** tu pourrais peut-être...; **we m. as well go home** autant rentrer; **you m. as well stay here** autant que vous restiez ici; **I m. as well be talking to myself!** autant parler à un mur!

(b) *(as past form of may)* **I knew he m. be angry** je me doutais qu'il pourrait se fâcher; **he said he m. be late** il a dit qu'il se pourrait qu'il soit en retard

(c) *Formal (asking for permission)* **m. I have a word with you?** pourrais-je vous parler un instant?

(d) *(with concessions)* **it might not be the fastest car in the world, but...** ce n'est peut-être pas la voiture la plus rapide du monde, mais...

mightily ['maɪtɪlɪ] *adv* **(a)** *(powerfully)* avec force, vigoureusement **(b)** *Am Fam (for emphasis)* drôlement

mightn't ['maɪtənt] = **might not**

might've ['maɪtəv] = **might have**

mighty ['maɪtɪ] **1** *adj* **(a)** *(powerful) (nation, army)* puissant(e); *(blow)* grand(e) **(b)** *(large, imposing)* majestueux(euse)

2 *adv* *Am Fam (for emphasis)* drôlement

migraine ['miːgreɪn] *n* migraine *f*; **to have a m.** avoir la migraine

migrant ['maɪgrənt] **1** *n (person)* migrant(e) *m,f*; *(bird)* (oiseau *m*) migrateur *m*

2 *adj (bird)* migrateur(trice); **m. worker** travailleur *m* immigré

migrate [maɪ'greɪt] *vi (of bird)* migrer; *(of person)* émigrer

migration [maɪ'greɪʃən] *n (of birds)* migration *f*; *(of people)* émigration *f*

migratory ['maɪgrətrɪ] *adj* migratoire; *(bird)* migrateur(trice)

mike [maɪk] *n Fam (microphone)* micro *m*

mild [maɪld] **1** *adj (person, climate, soap, cheese)* doux (douce); *(curry)* peu épicé(e); *(punishment, annoyance, amusement, criticism)* léger(ère); *(illness)* bénin(igne)

2 *n Br (beer)* bière brune à faible teneur en houblon

mildew ['mɪldjuː] *n* moisissure *f*

mildly ['maɪldlɪ] *adv* **(a)** *(say)* doucement; **... to put it m.** ... pour ne pas dire plus **(b)** *(moderately)* légèrement

mildness ['maɪldnəs] *n (of person, weather, punishment)* douceur *f*; *(of criticism)* modération *f*

mile [maɪl] *n (distance)* ≃ 1609 m, mile *m*; **a 200-m. journey** ≃ un voyage de 320 km; **to see for miles** voir à des kilomètres; **it's miles from anywhere** c'est loin de tout; **miles per hour** ≃ kilomètres à l'heure; **he lives miles away** il habite très loin d'ici; *Fam Fig* **to be miles away** être dans la lune; *Fam* **miles better** cent fois mieux; *Fam* **it sticks** *ou* **stands out a m.** ça crève les yeux

mileage ['maɪlɪdʒ] *n* **(a)** *(distance travelled)* ≃ kilométrage *m*; **m. allowance** ≃ indemnité *f* kilométrique **(b)** *(rate of fuel consumption)* consommation *f*; *Fig* **to get a lot of m. out of sth** tirer le maximum de qch

milestone ['maɪlstəʊn] *n (on road)* ≃ borne *f* kilométrique; *Fig (in career, history)* étape *f* importante

milieu ['miːljə] n milieu m

militant ['mɪlɪtənt] adj & n militant(e), m,f

militarism ['mɪlɪtərɪzəm] n militarisme m

military ['mɪlɪtərɪ] 1 adj militaire; **m. academy** école f militaire; **m. man** militaire m; **m. police** police f militaire; **m. service** service m militaire 2 npl **the m.** les militaires mpl, l'armée f

militate ['mɪlɪteɪt] vi **to m. against sth** compromettre qch

militia [mɪ'lɪʃə] n milice f

milk [mɪlk] 1 n (a) lait m; **m. of magnesia** lait m de magnésie; **m. bottle** bouteille f de lait; **m. chocolate** chocolat m au lait; **m. churn** bidon m à lait; **m. float** camionnette f de laitier; **m. jug** pot m à lait; **m. round** tournée f du laitier; **m. shake** milk-shake m; **m. tooth** dent f de lait 2 vt (cow) traire; Fam Fig **to m. sb dry** dépouiller qn; Fig **they milked the story for all it was worth** ils ont tiré tout ce qu'ils ont pu de l'histoire

milking ['mɪlkɪŋ] n traite f; **m. machine** trayeuse f

milkman ['mɪlkmən] n = homme qui livre le lait à domicile

milky ['mɪlkɪ] adj (drink) avec du lait; (taste) de lait; (colour) laiteux(euse); **the M. Way** la Voie lactée

mill [mɪl] 1 n (a) (grinder) moulin m; Fam **to put sb through the m.** en faire baver à qn (b) (textile factory) filature f 2 vt (grain) moudre

▸**mill about, mill around** vi (of crowd) grouiller; (of thoughts, ideas) se bousculer

millennium [mɪ'lenɪəm] n millénaire m

miller ['mɪlə(r)] n meunier(ère) m,f

millet ['mɪlɪt] n millet m

milligram(me) ['mɪlɪɡræm] n milligramme m

millilitre, Am **milliliter** ['mɪlɪliːtə(r)] n millilitre m

millimetre, Am **millimeter** ['mɪlɪmiːtə(r)] n millimètre m

milliner ['mɪlɪnə(r)] n modiste mf

million ['mɪljən] n million m; **two m. men** deux millions d'hommes; Fam **I've told him a m. times** je le lui ai dit mille fois; Fam **thanks a m.!** merci mille fois!; Fam **she's one in a m.** elle est unique

millionaire [mɪljə'neə(r)] n millionnaire m

millionairess [mɪljə'neərɪs] n millionnaire f

millionth ['mɪljənθ] 1 n (a) (fraction) millionième m (b) (in series) millionième mf 2 adj millionième; see also **eighth**

millipede ['mɪlɪpiːd] n mille-pattes m inv

millpond ['mɪlpɒnd] n **as calm as a m.** (of sea) d'huile

millstone ['mɪlstəʊn] n meule f; Fig **it's a m. round my neck** c'est un boulet que je traîne

milometer [maɪ'lɒmɪtə(r)] n (in car) ≃ compteur m (kilométrique)

mime [maɪm] 1 n mime m; **m. (artist)** mime mf 2 vt mimer 3 vi mimer; (of singer) chanter en play-back

mimic ['mɪmɪk] 1 n imitateur(trice) m,f 2 vt (pt & pp mimicked) imiter

mimicry ['mɪmɪkrɪ] n imitation f

Min Mus (abbr **Minor**) m

min (a) (abbr **minute(s)**) min (b) (abbr **minimum**) min

minaret [mɪnə'ret] n minaret m

mince [mɪns] 1 n Br viande f hachée; **m. pie** (containing meat) tourte f à la viande hachée; (containing fruit) = tartelette fourrée aux fruits secs et aux épices 2 vt (chop up) hacher; Fig **she doesn't m. her words** elle ne mâche pas ses mots 3 vi (walk) marcher à petits pas

mincemeat ['mɪnsmiːt] n = mélange de fruits secs et d'épices utilisé en pâtisserie; Fam Fig **to make m. of** faire de la chair à pâté de qn

mincer ['mɪnsə(r)] n hachoir m

mincing ['mɪnsɪŋ] adj (walk, voice) affecté(e)

mind [maɪnd] 1 n (a) (thoughts) esprit m; in one's m.'s **eye** in imagination; **to put** or **set sb's m. at rest** rassurer qn; **to bear** or **keep sth in m.** garder qch à l'esprit ou en tête; **it went completely** or **clean out of my m.** ça m'est complètement sorti de l'esprit ou de la tête; **to have sth on one's m.** être préoccupé(e) par qch; **to take sb's m. off sth** distraire qn de qch; **I couldn't get it off my m.** je ne pouvais pas m'empêcher d'y penser; **it puts me in m. of sb/sth** ça me rappelle qn/qch (b) (opinion) **to my m.** à mon avis; **to speak one's m.** dire ce qu'on pense; **to change one's m. (about sth)** changer d'avis (au sujet de qch); Fam **to give sb a piece of one's m.** dire à qn sa façon de penser; **to be of one m., to be of the same m.** être du même avis (c) (will) **to know one's own m.** savoir ce qu'on veut; **to have a m. of one's own** savoir penser par soi-même; **to make up one's m.** se décider; **to be in two minds (about sth/about doing sth)** hésiter (sur qch/à faire qch); **to have a good m./half a m. to do sth** avoir bien envie/presque envie de faire qch; **this shopping trolley has a m. of its own** ce caddie n'en fait qu'à sa tête; **to have sb in m.** avoir qn en vue; **to have sth in m.** avoir qch en tête (d) (attention) **to keep one's m. on sth** se concentrer sur qch; **my m. isn't on the job** je n'ai pas la tête à ce que je fais; **if you put your m. to it you could do it** si tu t'y mettais, tu pourrais le faire (e) (reason) raison f; **her m. is going** elle perd la raison; Fam **to be out of one's m.** avoir perdu la tête; **to be bored out of one's m.** s'ennuyer à mourir; **to be out of one's m. with worry** être fou (folle) d'inquiétude; **no one in his right m. would do that** aucune personne saine d'esprit ne ferait ça (f) (person) esprit m; Prov **great minds think alike** les grands esprits se rencontrent 2 vt (a) (pay attention to) faire attention à; **m. you don't fall** fais attention à ne pas tomber; **m. you're not late!** fais en sorte de ne pas être en retard!; **m. the step!** attention à la marche!; **to m. one's language/manners** surveiller son langage/ses manières (b) (concern oneself with) never **m. the car/money** ne t'inquiète pas pour la voiture/l'argent; **m. you,...** remarque,... (c) (object to) **what I m. is...** ce qui me gêne, c'est...; **I don't m. the cold** le froid ne me gêne pas; **I don't m. trying** je veux bien essayer; **if you don't m. my asking,...** si je peux me permettre,...; **would you m. not doing that?** pourrais-tu arrêter ça?; **I wouldn't m. a cup of tea** je prendrais bien une tasse de thé (d) (look after) s'occuper de, garder 3 vi (a) (object) **I don't m.** ça m'est égal; **do you m.!** dites donc!; **do you m. if I smoke?** ça vous dérange si je fume?; **I don't m. if I do!** (accepting offer) ce n'est pas de refus!

(b) *(concern oneself)* never m.! ça ne fait rien!; **never m. about that now** ne t'inquiète pas de ça maintenant; *Fam* **never you m.!** occupe-toi de tes oignons!

▶**mind out** *vi Br* **m. out!** attention!

mind-boggling ['maɪndbɒɡlɪŋ], **mind-blowing** ['maɪndbləʊɪŋ] *adj Fam* époustouflant(e)

minded ['maɪndɪd] *adj* **to be m. to do sth** vouloir faire qch; **to be mechanically m.** avoir le sens de la mécanique; **to be scientifically m.** avoir l'esprit scientifique

minder ['maɪndə(r)] *n Fam (bodyguard)* gorille *m*

mindful ['maɪndfʊl] *adj* **to be m. of sth** être soucieux(euse) de qch

mindless ['maɪndlɪs] *adj (destruction, violence)* gratuit(e); *(task, job)* abrutissant(e)

mind-reader ['maɪndriːdə(r)] *n Fam Hum* **I'm not a m.!** je ne suis pas devin!

mine¹ [maɪn] **1** *n* **(a)** *(for coal, tin, diamonds)* mine *f*; *Fig* **a m. of information** une mine d'informations; **m. shaft** puits *m* de mine **(b)** *(bomb)* **(land) m.** mine *f*; **m. detector** détecteur *m* de mines

2 *vt* **(a)** *(coal, gold)* extraire; *(seam)* exploiter **(b)** *(place mines in)* miner

3 *vi* **m. for coal/gold** extraire du charbon/de l'or

mine² *possessive pron* **(a)** *(singular)* le mien (la mienne), *m,f*; *(plural)* les miens (les miennes) *mpl, fpl*; **her house is big but m. is bigger** elle a une grande maison, mais la mienne est plus grande encore **(b)** *(used attributively)* **this book is m.** c'est livre est à moi; **a friend of m.** un de mes amis; **where's that brother of m.?** où mon frère a-t-il bien pu passer?

minefield ['maɪnfiːld] *n* champ *m* de mines; *Fig* terrain *m* miné

miner ['maɪnə(r)] *n* mineur *m*

mineral ['mɪnərəl] *n* minéral *m*; *(extracted)* minerai *m*; **m. water** eau *m* minérale

minesweeper ['maɪnswiːpə(r)] *n* dragueur *m* de mines

mingle ['mɪŋɡəl] **1** *vt* mélanger, mêler

2 *vi (of things)* se mélanger, se mêler; *(of person)* parler un peu à tout le monde; **to m. with the crowd** se mêler à la foule

mini ['mɪnɪ] *n (miniskirt)* minijupe *f*

miniature ['mɪnɪtʃə(r)] **1** *n* miniature *f*

2 *adj* miniature

miniaturize ['mɪnɪtʃəraɪz] *vt* miniaturiser

minibus ['mɪnɪbʌs] *n* minibus *m*

minicab ['mɪnɪkæb] *n* radio-taxi *m*

minim ['mɪnɪm] *n Mus* blanche *f*

minimal ['mɪnɪməl] *adj* minime

minimize ['mɪnɪmaɪz] *vt (importance)* minimiser; *(noise, risk)* réduire au minimum

minimum ['mɪnɪməm] **1** *n* minimum *m*; **to keep sth to a m.** réduire qch au minimum

2 *adj* minimum *inv*, minimal(e); *Fin* **m. lending rate** taux *m* de base; **m. wage** salaire *m* minimum

mining ['maɪnɪŋ] *n* exploitation *f* minière; **m. engineer** ingénieur *m* des mines; **m. industry** industrie *f* minière

minion ['mɪnjən] *n* esclave *mf*

miniskirt ['mɪnɪskɜːt] *n* minijupe *f*

minister ['mɪnɪstə(r)] **1** *n* **(a)** *Pol* ministre *m*; *Br* **M. of Defence/Health** ministre de la Défense/de la Santé **(b)** *Rel* pasteur *m*

2 *vi* **to m. to sb** s'occuper de qn; **to m. to sb's needs** pourvoir aux besoins de qn

ministerial [mɪnɪ'stɪərɪəl] *adj Pol* ministériel(elle)

ministry ['mɪnɪstrɪ] *(pl* ministries*)* *n* **(a)** *Pol* ministère *m*; *Br* **the M. of Defence/Transport** le ministère de la Défense/des Transports **(b)** *Rel* **the m.** le sacerdoce

mink [mɪŋk] *n* vison *m*; **m. (coat)** *(manteau m de)* vison

minnow ['mɪnəʊ] *n (fish)* vairon *m*; *Fig* second couteau *m*

minor ['maɪnə(r)] **1** *adj* **(a)** *(unimportant)* mineur(e); *(operation)* bénin(igne); *(road)* secondaire **(b)** *Mus* mineur(e)

2 *n Law* mineur(e) *m,f*

Minorca [mɪ'nɔːkə] *n* Minorque

Minorcan [mɪ'nɔːkən] **1** *n* Minorquin(e) *m,f*

2 *adj* minorquin(e)

minority [maɪ'nɒrɪtɪ] *(pl* minorities*)* *n* minorité *f*; **to be in a** *or* **the m.** être en minorité; **m. party/ government** parti *m*/gouvernement *m* minoritaire

minstrel ['mɪnstrəl] *n* ménestrel *m*

mint¹ [mɪnt] *n (plant)* menthe *f*; *(sweet)* bonbon *m* à la menthe; **m. sauce** sauce *f* à la menthe; **m. tea** infusion *f* de menthe

mint² [mɪnt] *n* **the (Royal) M.** ≃ (l'hôtel *m* de) la Monnaie; *Fam* **to make a m.** gagner une fortune; **in m. condition** à l'état neuf

2 *vt (coins)* frapper

minuet [mɪnjʊ'et] *n Mus* menuet *m*

minus ['maɪnəs] **1** *n (sign)* moins *m*; *(negative aspect)* inconvénient *m*

2 *adj (quantity, number)* négatif(ive); *B* **m.** *(grade)* B moins; **on the m. side** quant aux inconvénients; **m. sign** signe *m* moins

3 *prep* moins; **ten m. eight leaves two** dix moins huit égale deux; **it's m. 12 (degrees)** il fait moins 12; **he managed to escape, but m. his luggage** il a réussi à s'enfuir, mais sans ses bagages

minuscule ['mɪnəskjuːl] *adj* minuscule

minute¹ ['mɪnɪt] **1** *n* **(a)** *(of time)* minute *f*; **ten minutes past/to three** trois heures dix/moins dix; **wait a m.!** attendez une minute!; **go downstairs this m.!** descends immédiatement!; **just a m.** une minute; **the m. my back was turned** dès que j'ai eu le dos tourné; **any m.** d'une minute à l'autre; **in a m.** dans une minute; **at the last m.** à la dernière minute; **m. hand** *(of watch)* grande aiguille *f*; **m. steak** steak *m* minute **(b)** *(note)* note *f*; **minutes** *(of meeting)* compte rendu *m*

2 *vt (make note of)* inscrire au procès-verbal

minute² [maɪ'njuːt] *adj* **(a)** *(small)* infine, minuscule **(b)** *(detailed)* minutieux(euse)

minutely [maɪ'njuːtlɪ] *adv* minutieusement

mips *Comptr (abbr* **million instructions per second)** MIPS *m*

miracle ['mɪrəkəl] *n also Fig* miracle *m*; **to perform** *or* **work miracles** faire des miracles; **by a** *or* **some m.** par miracle; **m. worker** faiseur(euse) *m,f* de miracles

miraculous [mɪ'rækjʊləs] *adj also Fig* miraculeux(euse)

mirage ['mɪrɑːʒ] *n* mirage *m*

MIRAS ['maɪræs] *n (abbr* **Mortgage Interest Relief at Source)** = système par lequel les intérêts dus à une société de crédit immobilier sont déductibles des impôts

mire [maɪə(r)] *n (mud)* boue *f*; *Fig* bourbier *m*

mirror ['mɪrə(r)] **1** *n* miroir *m*, glace *f*; *Fig* **to hold a m. to sth** refléter qch; **m. image** *(reversed image)* image *f*

inversée; *(exac copy)* copie *f* conforme
 2 *vt also Fig* refléter

mirth [mɜ:θ] *n* gaieté *f*, joie *f*

misadventure [mɪsəd'ventʃə(r)] *n* mésaventure *f*; *Law* **death by m.** mort *f* accidentelle

misanthropic [mɪsən'θrɒpɪk] *adj* misanthrope

misanthropist [mɪ'sænθrəpɪst] *n* misanthrope *mf*

misapprehension [mɪsæprɪ'henʃən] *n* malentendu *m*; **to be (labouring) under a m.** se méprendre

misappropriation ['mɪsəprəʊprɪ'eɪʃən] *n* détournement *m*

misbehave [mɪsbɪ'heɪv] *vi* se conduire mal

misbehaviour, *Am* **misbehavior** [mɪsbɪ'heɪvjə(r)] *n* mauvaise conduite *f*

misc *(abbr* **miscellaneous)** divers

miscalculate [mɪs'kælkjʊleɪt] **1** *vt* mal calculer; *Fig* mal évaluer
 2 *vi* faire une erreur de calcul; *Fig* faire un mauvais calcul

miscalculation [mɪskælkjʊ'leɪʃən] *n* erreur *f* de calcul; *Fig* mauvais calcul *m*

miscarriage [mɪs'kærɪdʒ] *n* **(a)** *Med* fausse couche *f*; **to have a m.** faire une fausse couche **(b)** *Law* **m. of justice** erreur *f* judiciaire

miscarry [mɪs'kærɪ] *(pt & pp* **miscarried)** *vi* **(a)** *(of woman)* faire une fausse couche **(b)** *Fig (of plan)* avorter

miscast [mɪs'kɑ:st] *(pt & pp* **miscast)** *vt* **to m. an actor** = donner à un acteur un rôle qui ne lui convient pas

miscellaneous [mɪsə'leɪnɪəs] *adj* divers(es)

miscellany [mɪ'selənɪ] *(pl* **miscellanies)** *n* mélange *m*

mischief ['mɪstʃɪf] *n* **(a)** *(naughtiness)* espièglerie *f*; **to get up to m.** faire des bêtises; *Hum* **to keep sb out of m.** occuper qn **(b)** *(trouble)* problèmes *mpl*; **to make m. (for sb)** créer des problèmes (à qn) **(c)** *Fam (injury)* **to do oneself a m.** se faire mal

mischievous ['mɪstʃɪvəs] *adj (naughty)* espiègle; *(malicious)* malveillant(e)

misconception [mɪskən'sepʃən] *n* idée *f* fausse

misconduct [mɪs'kɒndʌkt] *n* inconduite *f*

misconstrue [mɪskən'stru:] *vt* mal interpréter

misdemeanour, *Am* **misdemeanor** [mɪsdɪ-'mi:nə(r)] *n Law* délit *m*

misdiagnose [mɪsdaɪəg'nəʊz] *vt* mal diagnostiquer

misdirect [mɪsdɪ'rekt] *vt* **(a)** *(person)* mal orienter **(b)** *(letter)* mal adresser

miser ['maɪzə(r)] *n* avare *mf*

miserable ['mɪzərəbl] *adj* **(a)** *(unhappy)* malheureux(euse), triste; **to make sb's life m.** faire de la vie de qn un enfer **(b)** *(unpleasant)* déplorable; *(weather)* épouvantable **(c)** *(wretched)* misérable; **I only got a m. £70** je n'ai eu que 70 malheureuses livres

miserably ['mɪzərəblɪ] *adv* **(a)** *(unhappily)* tristement **(b)** *(wretchedly)* misérablement **(c)** *(very badly)* lamentablement

miserly ['maɪzəlɪ] *adj* avare

misery ['mɪzərɪ] *(pl* **miseries)** *n* **(a)** *(unhappiness)* détresse *f*; *(suffering)* malheur *m*; **to make sb's life a m.** faire de la vie de qn un enfer; **to put an animal out of its m.** achever un animal; *Hum* **to put sb out of his m.** *(tell secret)* mettre fin au supplice de qn **(b)** *Br Fam (person)* grincheux(euse) *m,f*

misery-guts ['mɪzərɪgʌts] *n Fam* grincheux(euse) *m,f*

misfire [mɪs'faɪə(r)] *vi (of gun)* faire long feu; *Fig (of plan)* rater

misfit ['mɪsfɪt] *n* inadapté(e) *m,f*

misfortune [mɪs'fɔ:tʃən] *n* malheur *m*, malchance *f*

misgiving [mɪs'gɪvɪŋ] *n* doute *m*; **to have misgivings (about sth)** avoir des doutes (sur qch)

misgovern [mɪs'gʌvən] *vt* mal gouverner

misguided [mɪs'gaɪdɪd] *adj (person, decision)* mal inspiré(e); *(attempt)* malencontreux(euse); *(energy, idealism)* mal placé(e)

mishandle [mɪs'hændəl] *vt (device)* mal utiliser; *(situation)* mal gérer; *(person)* malmener

mishap ['mɪshæp] *n* incident *m*; **without m.** sans encombre

mishear [mɪs'hɪə(r)] *(pt & pp* **misheard** [mɪs'hɜ:d]) *vt & vi* mal comprendre

mishmash ['mɪʃmæʃ] *n Fam* méli-mélo *m*

misinterpret [mɪsɪn'tɜ:prɪt] *vt (words)* mal interpréter; *(person)* mal interpréter les paroles de

misjudge [mɪs'dʒʌdʒ] *vt (person)* mal juger; *(distance, situation)* mal évaluer

misjudg(e)ment [mɪs'dʒʌdʒmənt] *n* erreur *f* de jugement

mislay [mɪs'leɪ] *(pt & pp* **mislaid** [mɪs'leɪd]) *vt* égarer

mislead [mɪs'li:d] *(pt & pp* **misled** [mɪs'led]) *vt* induire en erreur, tromper

misleading [mɪs'li:dɪŋ] *adj* trompeur(euse)

mismanage [mɪs'mænɪdʒ] *vt* mal gérer

mismanagement [mɪs'mænɪdʒmənt] *n* mauvaise gestion *f*

misnomer [mɪs'nəʊmə(r)] *n* terme *m* mal approprié

misogynist [mɪ'sɒdʒɪnɪst] *n* misogyne *mf*

misplace [mɪs'pleɪs] *vt* **(a)** *(mislay)* égarer **(b)** *(trust, confidence)* mal placer

misprint ['mɪsprɪnt] *n* faute *f* d'impression, coquille *f*

mispronounce [mɪsprə'naʊns] *vt* mal prononcer

mispronunciation [mɪsprənʌnsɪ'eɪʃən] *n* mauvaise prononciation *f*

misquote [mɪs'kwəʊt] *vt* citer incorrectement

misread [mɪs'ri:d] *(pt & pp* **misread** [mɪs'red]) *vt* **(a)** *(notice, timetable)* mal lire **(b)** *(misinterpret)* mal interpréter

misrepresent [mɪsreprɪ'zent] *vt (facts, theory)* dénaturer, déformer; *(person)* présenter sous un faux jour

misrepresentation [mɪsreprɪzen'teɪʃən] *n* déformation *f*

misrule [mɪs'ru:l] *n* mauvais gouvernement *m*

Miss [mɪs] *n* Mademoiselle *f*; **M. World** Miss Monde

miss [mɪs] **1** *n* coup *m* manqué; *Fam* **to give sth a m.** *(event)* s'abstenir d'aller à
 2 *vt* **(a)** *(target, bus, chance)* manquer, rater; *Fig* **to m. the boat** louper le coche; **you're missing the point** ce n'est pas le problème; **you've just missed him** tu l'as loupé de peu **(b)** *(not hear)* ne pas entendre; **she doesn't m. a thing** rien ne lui échappe **(c)** *(feel lack of)* **I m. you** tu me manques; **do you m. me?** est-ce que je te manque? **(d)** *(avoid)* **the car just missed me** la voiture m'a évité de peu; **she just missed being killed** elle a failli *ou* manqué être tuée **(e)** *(word, line)* sauter **(f)** *(lack)* **the table is missing one of its legs** il manque un pied à la table
 3 *vi (miss target)* rater *ou* manquer son coup

▸**miss out 1** *vt sep (accidentally)* oublier; *(intentionally)* omettre

2 vi (not benefit) to m. out on sth rater qch; you missed out there tu as raté quelque chose

missal ['mɪsəl] n Rel missel m

misshapen [mɪs'ʃeɪpən] adj difforme

missile ['mɪsaɪl, Am 'mɪsəl] n (rocket) missile m; (object thrown) projectile m; **m. launcher** lance-missiles m inv

missing ['mɪsɪŋ] adj (person) (lost) disparu(e); (absent) absent(e); (object) manquant(e); **nothing is m.** il ne manque rien; **m. link** chaînon m manquant; **m. person** personne f disparue

mission ['mɪʃən] n mission f

missionary ['mɪʃənərɪ] (pl **missionaries**) n Rel missionnaire mf; **the m. position** la position du missionnaire

missive ['mɪsɪv] n Formal missive f

misspell ['mɪs'spel] (pt & pp **misspelt** ['mɪs'spelt]) vt mal écrire

misspent ['mɪs'spent] adj (time, money) gaspillé(e); **m. youth** jeunesse f dissipée

missus ['mɪsɪz] n Fam (wife) **the m.** la patronne

mist [mɪst] n (fog) brume f; (condensation) buée f

▸**mist over, mist up** vi (of mirror, glasses) s'embuer

mistakable [mɪs'teɪkəbəl] adj facile à confondre (**for** avec)

mistake [mɪs'teɪk] **1** n erreur f; (in grammar, spelling) faute f; **to make a m.** faire ou commettre une erreur; **by m.** par erreur; Fam **this is hard work and no m.!** pas de doute, c'est vraiment très dur!

2 vt (pt **mistook** [mɪs'tʊk], pp **mistaken** [mɪs'teɪkən]) (a) (misunderstand) se tromper sur (b) (confuse) **to m. sb for** prendre qn pour; **there's no mistaking a voice like that!** avec une voix pareille, on ne peut pas se tromper!

mistakeable [mɪs'teɪkəbəl] = **mistakable**

mistaken [mɪs'teɪkən] adj (belief, impression) erroné(e), faux (fausse); **to be m.** se tromper

Mister ['mɪstə(r)] n Monsieur m

mistime [mɪs'taɪm] vt mal calculer

mistletoe ['mɪsəltəʊ] n gui m

mistranslation [mɪstrænz'leɪʃən] n erreur f de traduction

mistreat [mɪs'triːt] vt maltraiter

mistress ['mɪstrɪs] n maîtresse f; (in secondary school) professeur m

mistrial [mɪs'traɪəl] n Law Br jugement m entaché d'un vice de procédure; Am = procès dans lequel le jury ne parvient pas à prendre de décision

mistrust [mɪs'trʌst] **1** n méfiance f (**of** à l'égard de)
2 vt se méfier de, ne pas avoir confiance en

mistrustful [mɪs'trʌstfʊl] adj méfiant(e); **to be m. of** se méfier de

misty ['mɪstɪ] adj (place, weather) brumeux(euse); (outline, shape) flou(e)

misunderstand [mɪsʌndə'stænd] (pt & pp **misunderstood** [mɪsʌndə'stʊd]) vt & vi mal comprendre

misunderstanding [mɪsʌndə'stændɪŋ] n (a) (misconception) malentendu m (**about** sur) (b) (disagreement) mésentente f

misuse 1 n [mɪs'juːs] (of equipment, resources) mauvais emploi m; (of authority) abus m; (of funds) détournement m
2 vt [mɪs'juːz] (equipment, resources) mal employer; (authority) abuser de; (funds) détourner

mite [maɪt] n (a) (bug) acarien m (b) Fam (child) **poor little m.!** pauvre petit! (c) Fam (little bit) **a m. expensive/tired** un tantinet cher (chère)/fatigué(e)

miter Am = **mitre**

mitigate ['mɪtɪgeɪt] vt atténuer; Law **mitigating circumstances** circonstances fpl atténuantes

mitigation [mɪtɪ'geɪʃən] n atténuation f; Law **to say sth in m.** dire qch pour sa défense

mitre, Am miter ['maɪtə(r)] n Rel mitre f

mitt [mɪt] n (a) (mitten) moufle f; Am **baseball m.** gant m de baseball (b) Fam (hand) patte f

mitten ['mɪtən] n (glove) moufle f

mix [mɪks] **1** vt mélanger; (drink) préparer; **to m. business with pleasure** mélanger les affaires et le plaisir
2 vi (a) (blend) se mélanger (**with** avec) (b) (socially) **to m. with** fréquenter
3 n mélange m; (in music) remix m

▸**mix up** vt sep (a) (ingredients, papers) mélanger (b) (people, dates) confondre (c) Fam **to be mixed up in sth** (involved) être mêlé(e) à qch, être impliqué(e) dans qch; **to get mixed up with sb** se mettre à fréquenter qn

mixed ['mɪkst] adj mélangé(e); Fam **it was a m. bag** il y avait de tout; **to have m. feelings (about sth)** avoir des sentiments mitigés (envers qch); **m. doubles** (in tennis) double m mixte; **m. grill** assortiment m de grillades; **m. marriage** mariage m mixte; **m. school** école f mixte

mixed-up [mɪks'tʌp] adj Fam (person) déboussolé(e)

mixer ['mɪksə(r)] n (a) (for cooking) mixe(u)r m; Br **m. tap** (robinet m) mélangeur m (b) (socially) **to be a good m.** être très sociable (c) (drink) = boisson servant à allonger un alcool

mixing bowl ['mɪksɪŋ'bəʊl] n saladier m

mixture ['mɪkstʃə(r)] n mélange m

mix-up ['mɪksʌp] n confusion f (**over** ou **with** dans)

mktg Com (abbr **marketing**) marketing

ml (abbr **millilitre(s)**) ml

MLR [emel'ɑː(r)] n Fin (abbr **minimum lending rate**) taux m de base

mm (abbr **millimetre(s)**) mm

mnemonic [nɪ'mɒnɪk] n moyen m mnémotechnique

moan [məʊn] **1** n (a) (sound) gémissement m (b) (complaint) plainte f
2 vi (a) (make sound) gémir (b) (complain) ronchonner; **to m. about sth** se plaindre de qch

moat [məʊt] n douve f

mob [mɒb] **1** n (crowd) foule f; Fam **the M.** la Mafia; **m. rule** loi f de la rue
2 vt (pt & pp **mobbed**) prendre d'assaut

mobile ['məʊbaɪl] **1** adj mobile; **m. home** mobile home m; **m. phone** téléphone m mobile
2 n (hanging ornament) mobile m (b) Fam (mobile phone) (téléphone m) mobile m

mobility [məʊ'bɪlɪtɪ] n mobilité f

mobilize ['məʊbɪlaɪz] vt mobiliser

mobster ['mɒbstə(r)] n Am Fam gangster m

moccasin ['mɒkəsɪn] n mocassin m

mock [mɒk] **1** adj faux (fausse), factice; Br Sch **m. exam** examen m blanc
2 vt (ridicule) se moquer de

mockery ['mɒkərɪ] n (a) (ridicule) moqueries fpl (b) (travesty) parodie f; **to make a m. of sb** ridiculiser qn; **to make a m. of sth** faire perdre toute crédibilité à qch

mockingbird ['mɒkɪŋbɜːd] n moqueur m

mock-up ['mɒkʌp] n maquette f

MOD [eməʊ'diː] n Br (abbr **Ministry of Defence**) ministère m de la Défense

mod cons ['mɒd'kɒnz] npl Fam **with all m.** (house) tout confort; (car) avec toutes les options

mode [məʊd] n mode m

model ['mɒdəl] **1** n (a) (small version) maquette f, modèle m réduit; **m. aircraft** maquette d'avion (b) (example, paragon) modèle m; **m. pupil** élève mf modèle (c) (fashion model) mannequin m; (for artist) modèle m

2 vt (pt & pp **modelled**, Am **modeled**) (a) **to m. oneself on sb** prendre exemple sur qn (b) **to m. clothes** être mannequin (c) Comptr modéliser

3 vi (on catwalk, for photographer) travailler comme mannequin; (for artist) poser

modem ['məʊdem] n Comptr modem m

moderate 1 n ['mɒdərət] Pol modéré(e) m,f
2 adj modéré(e)
3 vt ['mɒdəreɪt] modérer
4 vi Formal présider

moderately ['mɒdərətlɪ] adv (a) (in moderation) modérément (b) (quite) assez

moderation [mɒdə'reɪʃən] n modération f; **in m.** avec modération

modern ['mɒdən] adj moderne; **m. languages** langues fpl vivantes

modernism ['mɒdənɪzəm] n modernisme m

modernization [mɒdənaɪ'zeɪʃən] n modernisation f

modernize ['mɒdənaɪz] **1** vt moderniser
2 vi se moderniser

modest ['mɒdɪst] adj (a) (unassuming, moderate) modeste (b) (chaste) pudique

modestly ['mɒdɪstlɪ] adv (a) (unassumingly) modestement (b) (moderately) assez, moyennement

modesty ['mɒdɪstɪ] n modestie f

modicum ['mɒdɪkəm] n **a m. of** un minimum de

modification [mɒdɪfɪ'keɪʃən] n modification f; **to make modifications to sth** apporter des modifications à qch

modify ['mɒdɪfaɪ] (pt & pp **modified**) vt modifier

modular ['mɒdjʊlə(r)] adj modulaire

modulate ['mɒdjʊleɪt] vt moduler

modulation [mɒdjʊ'leɪʃən] n modulation f

module ['mɒdjuːl] n module m

mogul ['məʊɡəl] n Fig magnat m

mohair ['məʊheə(r)] n mohair m; **m. sweater** pull m en mohair

Mohammed [məʊ'hæmɪd] n Mahomet m

moist [mɔɪst] adj humide; (skin, hand) moite; (cake) moelleux(euse)

moisten ['mɔɪsən] vt humecter

moisture ['mɔɪstʃə(r)] n humidité f

moisturize ['mɔɪstʃəraɪz] vt hydrater

moisturizer ['mɔɪstʃəraɪzə(r)] n crème f hydratante

molar ['məʊlə(r)] n molaire f

molasses [mə'læsɪz] n mélasse f

mold, molder etc Am = **mould, moulder** etc

Moldavia [mɒl'deɪvɪə], **Moldova** [mɒl'dəʊvə] n la Moldavie

Moldavian [mɒl'deɪvɪən], **Moldovan** [mɒl'dəʊvən] **1** n Moldave mf
2 adj moldave

mole[1] [məʊl] n (birthmark) grain m de beauté

mole[2] n (animal, spy) taupe f

molecular [mə'lekjʊlə(r)] adj moléculaire

molecule ['mɒlɪkjuːl] n molécule f

molehill ['məʊlhɪl] n taupinière f

molest [mə'lest] vt (pester) importuner; (sexually) agresser (sexuellement)

mollify ['mɒlɪfaɪ] (pt & pp **mollified**) vt calmer, apaiser

mollusc, Am mollusk ['mɒləsk] n mollusque m

mollycoddle ['mɒlɪkɒdəl] vt Fam dorloter

molten ['məʊltən] adj en fusion

mom [mɒm] n Am Fam maman f

moment ['məʊmənt] n moment m, instant m; **at the m.** en ce moment; **at the last m.** au dernier moment; **for the m.** pour le moment ou l'instant; **in a m.** dans un instant; **any m.** d'un instant à l'autre; **wait a m.!, one m.!** un moment!, un instant!; **the m. he arrives** dès qu'il arrive; **without a m.'s hesitation** sans une seconde d'hésitation; **to live for the m.** profiter du moment présent; **the man of the m.** l'homme du moment; **the m. of truth** le moment de vérité; **he's not a genius, but he has his moments** ce n'est pas un génie, mais il a parfois des moments d'inspiration

momentary ['məʊməntərɪ] adj momentané(e)

momentous [məʊ'mentəs] adj capital(e)

momentum [məʊ'mentəm] n Phys moment m; **to gather m.** (of campaign) prendre de l'ampleur; **to lose m.** (of campaign) s'essouffler

Mon (abbr **Monday**) lundi

Monaco ['mɒnəkəʊ] n Monaco

monarch ['mɒnək] n monarque m

monarchist ['mɒnəkɪst] n monarchiste mf

monarchy ['mɒnəkɪ] (pl **monarchies**) n monarchie f

monastery ['mɒnəstrɪ] (pl **monasteries**) n monastère m

monastic [mə'næstɪk] adj monastique, monacal(e)

Monday ['mʌndɪ] n lundi m; see also **Saturday**

monetarism ['mʌnɪtərɪzm] n monétarisme m

monetarist ['mʌnɪtərɪst] n & adj monétariste mf

monetary ['mʌnɪtərɪ] adj monétaire

money ['mʌnɪ] n argent m; **to do sth for the m.** faire qch pour l'argent; **to make m.** (of person) gagner de l'argent; (of business) rapporter de l'argent; **to be worth a lot of m.** (of thing) valoir cher; (of person) être très riche; **there's no m. in it** ça ne paie pas; Fam **to be in the m.** être plein(e) aux as; **to get one's m.'s worth** en avoir pour son argent; Fam **it was m. for old rope** c'était de l'argent facilement gagné; **to put one's m. where one's mouth is** joindre le geste à la parole; Fam **to spend m. like water** dépenser sans compter; Fam **m. doesn't grow on trees!** l'argent ne se trouve pas sous le sabot d'un cheval!; **for my m.,...** à mon avis,...; Fin **m. market** marché m monétaire; Econ **m. supply** masse f monétaire

moneybags ['mʌnɪbægz] n Fam (person) richard(e) m,f

moneybox ['mʌnɪbɒks] n tirelire f

moneyed ['mʌnɪd] adj fortuné(e)

moneylender ['mʌnɪlendə(r)] n prêteur(euse) m,f

moneymaker ['mʌnɪmeɪkə(r)] *n* to be a m. *(of shop, business, product)* rapporter

moneymaking ['mʌnɪmeɪkɪŋ] *adj* qui rapporte

Mongol ['mɒŋɡəl] *Hist* 1 *n* Mongol(e) *m,f*
2 *adj* mongol(e)

mongol ['mɒŋɡəl] *n Old-fashioned* mongolien(enne) *m,f*, = terme injurieux désignant un trisomique

Mongolia [mɒŋ'ɡəʊlɪə] *n* la Mongolie

Mongolian [mɒŋ'ɡəʊlɪən] 1 *n* Mongol(e) *m,f*
2 *adj* mongol(e)

mongoose [mɒŋ'ɡuːs] *n* mangouste *f*

mongrel ['mʌŋɡrəl] *n* bâtard *m*

monitor ['mɒnɪtə(r)] 1 *n* (a) *(supervisor)* superviseur *m* (b) *TV & Comptr (screen)* moniteur *m*
2 *vt (broadcast, conversation)* écouter; *(patient's condition, operation, results)* surveiller; *(performance)* suivre

monk [mʌŋk] *n* moine *m*

monkey ['mʌŋkɪ] *(pl* **monkeys)** *n (animal)* singe *m*; *Fam Fig (naughty child)* petit(e) diable(esse) *m,f*; *Fam* to make a m. out of sb se payer la tête de qn; *very Fam* I don't give a m.'s je m'en fous complètement; *Fam* m. **business** *(dishonest behaviour)* magouilles *fpl*; *(mischief)* bêtises *fpl*; m. **nut** cacah(o)uète *f*; m. **puzzle (tree)** désespoir *m* des singes; m. **wrench** clef *f* anglaise ou à molette
►**monkey about, monkey around** *vi Fam (fool around)* faire l'imbécile

monkfish ['mʌŋkfɪʃ] *n* lotte *f*

mono ['mɒnəʊ] *n* mono *f*

monochrome ['mɒnəkrəʊm] *adj* monochrome; *(photo)* en noir et blanc

monocle ['mɒnəkəl] *n* monocle *m*

monogamous [mɒ'nɒɡəməs] *adj* monogame

monogamy [mɒ'nɒɡəmɪ] *n* monogamie *f*

monogram ['mɒnəɡræm] *n* monogramme *m*

monograph ['mɒnəɡræf] *n* monographie *f*

monolingual [mɒnəʊ'lɪŋɡwəl] *adj* monolingue

monolithic [mɒnə'lɪθɪk] *adj* monolithique

monologue ['mɒnəlɒɡ] *n* monologue *m*

monopolize [mə'nɒpəlaɪz] *vt also Fig* monopoliser

monopoly [mə'nɒpəlɪ] *(pl* **monopolies)** *n also Fig* monopole *m*; to have a m. on sth avoir le monopole de qch

monorail ['mɒnəʊreɪl] *n* monorail *m*

monosyllabic [mɒnəʊsɪ'læbɪk] *adj (word)* monosyllabique; *(reply)* laconique

monosyllable [mɒnəʊ'sɪləb(ə)l] *n* monosyllabe *m*

monotone ['mɒnətəʊn] *n* ton *m* monotone; to speak in a m. parler d'une voix monotone

monotonous [mə'nɒtənəs] *adj* monotone

monotony [mə'nɒtənɪ] *n* monotonie *f*

Monsignor [mɒn'siːnjə(r)] *n* Monseigneur *m*

monsoon [mɒn'suːn] *n* mousson *f*

monster ['mɒnstə(r)] 1 *n* monstre *m*
2 *adj Fam (enormous)* monstre, colossal(e)

monstrosity [mɒn'strɒsɪtɪ] *(pl* **monstrosities)** *n* monstruosité *f*

monstrous ['mɒnstrəs] *adj* monstrueux(euse)

montage ['mɒntɑːʒ] *n* montage *m*

month [mʌnθ] *n* mois *m*; in the m. of August au mois d'août; *Fam* never in a m. of Sundays jamais de la vie

monthly ['mʌnθlɪ] 1 *n (pl* **monthlies)** *(magazine)* mensuel *m*
2 *adj* mensuel(elle); m. **payment** *or* **instalment** mensualité *f*
3 *adv* tous les mois

monument ['mɒnjʊmənt] *n also Fig* monument *m* (to à)

monumental [mɒnjʊ'mentəl] *adj* monumental(e); *(importance)* capital(e)

moo [muː] 1 *n (pl* **moos)** meuglement *m*, beuglement *m*; m.! meuh!
2 *vi (pt & pp* **mooed)** meugler, beugler

►**mooch about, mooch around** [muːtʃ] *vi Fam* traîner

mood [muːd] *n* (a) *(state of mind)* humeur *f*; to be in a good/bad m. être de bonne/mauvaise humeur; she's in one of her moods elle est de mauvaise humeur; to be in the m. for sth avoir envie de qch; to be in the m. for doing sth être d'humeur à faire qch (b) *Gram* mode *m*

moodily ['muːdɪlɪ] *adv (answer, speak)* d'un ton maussade

moody ['muːdɪ] *adj* (a) *(sulky)* maussade (b) *(changeable)* lunatique

moon [muːn] 1 *n* lune *f*; the M. la Lune; *Fam* to ask for the m. demander la lune; *Fam* to promise sb the m. promettre la lune à qn; *Fam* to be over the m. être aux anges; m. **landing** alunissage *m*
2 *vi Fam (expose one's buttocks)* montrer ses fesses

►**moon about, moon around** *vi* musarder, flâner

moonbeam ['muːnbiːm] *n* rayon *m* de lune

moonlight ['muːnlaɪt] 1 *n* clair *m* de lune; in the m., by m. au clair de lune; *Fam* to do a m. flit partir à la cloche de bois
2 *vi Fam (work illegally)* travailler au noir

moonlighting ['muːnlaɪtɪŋ] *n Fam* travail *m* au noir

moonlit ['muːnlɪt] *adj* éclairé(e) par la lune

moonshine ['muːnʃaɪn] *n Fam* (a) *(nonsense)* balivernes *fpl*, bêtises *fpl* (b) *Am (illegal alcohol)* alcool *m* de contrebande

Moor [mʊə(r)] *n* Maure *mf*

moor[1] [mʊə(r)] *n (heath)* lande *f*

moor[2] *vt (ship)* amarrer

mooring ['mʊərɪŋ] *n* (a) *(place)* mouillage *m* (b) **moorings** *(chains, ropes)* amarres *fpl*

Moorish ['mʊərɪʃ] *adj* maure, mauresque

moorland ['mʊələnd] *n* lande *f*

moose [muːs] *(pl* **moose)** *n* orignal *m*

moot [muːt] 1 *adj* it's a m. point c'est difficile à dire
2 *vt (suggest)* suggérer

mop [mɒp] 1 *n (for floor)* balai *m* à franges; *(with sponge)* balai-éponge *m*; *Fam* m. **(of hair)** tignasse *f*
2 *vt (pt & pp* **mopped)** to m. the floor laver par terre; to m. one's brow s'éponger le front

►**mop up** *vt sep (liquid)* éponger; *Fig (enemy forces)* liquider

►**mope about, mope around** [məʊp] *vi* broyer du noir

moped ['məʊped] *n (motorbike)* Mobylette® *f*

moral ['mɒrəl] 1 *n* (a) *(of story)* morale *f* (b) **morals** *(principles)* moralité *f*
2 *adj* moral(e); m. **fibre** force *f* de caractère; m. **support** soutien *m* moral; m. **victory** victoire *f* morale

morale [mɒ'rɑːl] *n* moral *m*; to be good/bad for m. être bon (bonne)/mauvais(e) pour le moral

moralistic [mɒrə'lɪstɪk] *adj* moraliste

morality [məˈralɪtɪ] n moralité f

moralize [ˈmɒrəlaɪz] vi faire la morale, moraliser

morally [ˈmɒrəlɪ] adv moralement; **m. right** moralement correct(e); **m. wrong** contraire à la morale

morass [məˈræs] n (marsh) marais m; Fig (of detail, despair) bourbier m

moratorium [mɒrəˈtɔːrɪəm] (pl **moratoria** [mɒrəˈtɔːrɪə] or **moratoriums**) n moratoire m (**on** sur)

morbid [ˈmɔːbɪd] adj morbide

morbidly [ˈmɔːbɪdlɪ] adv de façon morbide

mordant [ˈmɔːdənt] adj Formal (sarcasm, wit) mordant(e)

more [mɔː(r)] (comparative of **many**, **much**) 1 pron plus; **there are m. of us** nous sommes plus nombreux; **have (some) m.** reprenez-en; **there's no m.** il n'y en a plus; **let's say no m. about it** n'en parlons plus; **she knows m. than you** elle en sait plus long que toi; **we should see m. of each other** nous devrions nous voir plus souvent; **it's just m. of the same** c'est encore et toujours la même chose; **the m. I see her, the m. I like her** plus je la vois, plus elle me plaît; **what's m.,**... qui plus est,...; **what m. can I say?** que puis-je dire de plus?

2 adj **(a)** (larger quantity or number of) plus de; **m. water/children** plus d'eau/d'enfants; **m. than a hundred people were there** il y avait plus de cent personnes; **he has m. patience than I have** il a plus de patience que moi; **there are m. and m. accidents every year** chaque année, il y a de plus en plus d'accidents

(b) (additional quantity or number of) **one m. month** un mois de plus; **is there any m. bread?** est-ce qu'il y a encore du pain?; **I've no m. money** je n'ai plus d'argent; **I need m. time** il me faut plus de temps

3 adv **(a)** (to form comparative of adjectives and adverbs) plus (**than** que); **m. interesting** plus intéressant(e); **m. easily** plus facilement; **things are getting m. and m. difficult** les choses deviennent de plus en plus difficiles

(b) (to a greater extent) plus; **you should eat m.** tu devrais manger plus; **I'm m. than satisfied** je suis plus que satisfait; **he was m. surprised than annoyed** il était plus surpris que fâché; **I like her m. than I used to** je l'aime plus qu'avant; **that's m. like it!** voilà qui est mieux!; **m. or less** plus ou moins

(c) (with time) **once/twice m.** une/deux fois de plus; **he doesn't drink any m.** il ne boit plus; **I can't see you any m.** nous ne pouvons plus nous voir

moreover [mɔːˈrəʊvə(r)] adv de plus

mores [ˈmɔːreɪz] npl Formal mœurs fpl

morgue [mɔːg] n morgue f; Fig **this place is like a m.** c'est complètement mort ici

moribund [ˈmɒrɪbʌnd] adj moribond(e)

Mormon [ˈmɔːmən] n Rel mormon(e) m,f

morning [ˈmɔːnɪŋ] n matin m; (referring to duration) matinée f; **tomorrow m.** demain matin; **yesterday m.** hier matin; **the next m., the m. after** le lendemain matin; **the m. before** la veille au matin; Fam **it's the m. after (the night before)** c'est un lendemain de cuite; **m., noon and night** du matin au soir; **in the m.** le matin; **on Wednesday m.** mercredi matin; **good m.!,** Fam **m.!** bonjour!; **m. dress** habit m; **m. sickness** nausées fpl matinales; **m. star** étoile f du matin

morning-after pill [ˈmɔːnɪŋˈɑːftəpɪl] n pilule f du lendemain

Moroccan [məˈrɒkən] 1 n Marocain(e) m,f
2 adj marocain(e)

Morocco [məˈrɒkəʊ] n le Maroc

moron [ˈmɔːrɒn] n crétin(e) m,f

moronic [məˈrɒnɪk] adj débile

morose [məˈrəʊs] adj morose

Morse [mɔːs] n M. (code) morse m

morsel [ˈmɔːsəl] n morceau m

mortal [ˈmɔːtəl] 1 n mortel(elle) m,f; Fig & Ironic **mere mortals** de simples mortels
2 adj mortel(elle); **m. enemy** ennemi m mortel; **m. remains** dépouille f mortelle; **m. sin** péché m mortel; **m. wound** blessure f mortelle

mortality [mɔːˈtælɪtɪ] n mortalité f

mortally [ˈmɔːtəlɪ] adv mortellement

mortar [ˈmɔːtə(r)] n mortier m

mortgage [ˈmɔːgɪdʒ] 1 n (from lender's point of view) prêt m immobilier; (from borrower's point of view) emprunt m immobilier; **m. (re)payments** remboursements mpl d'emprunt; **m. rate** taux m de crédit immobilier
2 vt (property, one's future) hypothéquer

mortician [mɔːˈtɪʃən] n Am (undertaker) entrepreneur m de pompes funèbres

mortification [mɔːtɪfɪˈkeɪʃən] n Rel mortification f; Fig (embarrassment) honte f

mortify [ˈmɔːtɪfaɪ] (pt & pp **mortified**) vt Rel mortifier; Fig **to be mortified** être mort(e) de honte

mortise [ˈmɔːtɪs] n mortaise f; **m. lock** serrure f encastrée

mortuary [ˈmɔːtjʊərɪ] (pl **mortuaries**) n morgue f

mosaic [məʊˈzeɪk] n also Fig mosaïque f

Moscow [ˈmɒskəʊ] n Moscou

Moses [ˈməʊzɪz] n Moïse

Moslem [ˈmɒzləm] n & adj musulman(e) m,f

mosque [mɒsk] n mosquée f

mosquito [mɒsˈkiːtəʊ] (pl **mosquitos** or **mosquitoes**) n moustique m; **m. bite** piqûre f de moustique; **m. net** moustiquaire f

moss [mɒs] n mousse f

most [məʊst] (superlative of **many**, **much**) 1 pron **(a)** (the majority) la plupart; **m. of the people/time** la plupart des gens/du temps; **m. of us/them** la plupart d'entre nous/eux; **he is more interesting than m.** il est plus intéressant que la plupart des gens

(b) (greatest amount) **the m.** le plus; **he earns the m.** c'est lui qui gagne le plus; **at the (very) m.** au maximum; **to make the m. of sth** (situation, talents) tirer le meilleur parti de qch; (time, holiday) profiter au maximum de qch

2 adj **(a)** (the majority of) la plupart de; **m. women** la plupart des femmes

(b) (greatest amount of) **the m.** le plus de; **he has the m. money** c'est lui qui a le plus d'argent; **for the m. part** dans l'ensemble

3 adv **(a)** (to form superlative of adjectives and adverbs) plus; **the m. interesting book** le livre le plus intéressant; **the m. beautiful woman** la plus belle femme; **these are the m. expensive** ce sont les plus chers; **those who answered m. honestly** ceux qui ont répondu le plus franchement

(b) (to the greatest extent) le plus; **the one who works (the) m. is...** celui qui travaille le plus est...; **that's what worries me (the) m.** c'est ce qui m'inquiète le plus; **who do you like m.?** qui préfères-tu?; **what I want m.** ce que je veux par-dessus tout

(c) (very) extrêmement; **m. unhappy** extrêmement malheureux(euse)

mostly ['məʊstlɪ] *adv* (a) *(in the main)* principalement, surtout (b) *(most often)* le plus souvent, la plupart du temps

MOT [eməʊ'tiː] *n Br* ≃ contrôle *m* technique des véhicules

motel [məʊ'tel] *n* motel *m*

moth [mɒθ] *n* papillon *m* de nuit; *(in clothes)* mite *f*

mothball ['mɒθbɔːl] *n* boule *f* de naphtaline; *Fig* **to put a project in mothballs** mettre un projet au placard

moth-eaten ['mɒθiːtən] *adj* mité(e); *Fam (in poor condition)* miteux(euse)

mother ['mʌðə(r)] **1** *n* mère *f*; **M.'s Day** la fête des Mères; **m. country** patrie *f*; **M. Nature** Dame Nature *f*; *Rel* **M. Superior** Mère supérieure; **m. tongue** langue *f* maternelle
2 *vt* materner

motherboard ['mʌðəbɔːd] *n Comptr* carte *f* mère

motherhood ['mʌðəhʊd] *n* maternité *f*

mother-in-law ['mʌðərɪnlɔː] *(pl* **mothers-in-law)** *n* belle-mère *f*

motherland ['mʌðəlænd] *n* patrie *f*

mother-of-pearl ['mʌðərəv'pɜːl] *n* nacre *f*

mother-to-be ['mʌðətəˈbiː] *(pl* **mothers-to-be)** *n* future mère *f*

motif [məʊˈtiːf] *n* motif *m*

motion ['məʊʃən] **1** *n* (a) *(movement)* mouvement *m*; **to set sth in m.** *(machine)* mettre qch en marche; *(process)* déclencher qch; *Fig* **to go through the motions** agir machinalement; *Am* **m. picture** film *m* (b) *(in meeting, debate)* motion *f*; **to propose/second a m.** présenter/appuyer une motion (c) *(faeces)* selles *fpl*
2 *vt* **to m. sb to do sth** faire signe à qn de faire qch
3 *vi* **to m. to sb to do sth** faire signe à qn de faire qch

motionless ['məʊʃənlɪs] *adj* immobile

motivate ['məʊtɪveɪt] *vt* motiver

motivation [məʊtɪˈveɪʃən] *n* motivation *f*

motive ['məʊtɪv] **1** *n (reason)* motif *m*; *Law (for crime)* mobile *m*
2 *adj* **m. force** *or* **power** force *f* motrice

motley ['mɒtlɪ] *adj* hétéroclite; **m. crew** groupe *m* hétéroclite

motor ['məʊtə(r)] **1** *n (engine)* moteur *m*; *Fam (car)* bagnole *f*; **m. industry** industrie *f* automobile; **m. insurance** assurance *f* automobile; **m. racing** courses *fpl* automobiles; **m. show** salon *m* de l'automobile; **m. vehicle** véhicule *m* automobile
2 *vi* voyager en voiture

motorbike ['məʊtəbaɪk] *n* moto *f*

motorboat ['məʊtəbəʊt] *n* canot *m* à moteur

motorcade ['məʊtəkeɪd] *n* cortège *m* de voitures

motorcar ['məʊtəkɑː(r)] *n Br* voiture *f*

motorcycle ['məʊtəsaɪkəl] *n* moto *f*, motocyclette *f*

motorcyclist ['məʊtəsaɪklɪst] *n* motocycliste *mf*

motoring ['məʊtərɪŋ] *n* conduite *f*; **school of m.** auto-école *f*; **m. offence** infraction *f* au Code de la route

motorist ['məʊtərɪst] *n* automobiliste *mf*

motorize ['məʊtəraɪz] *vt* motoriser

motorized ['məʊtəraɪzd] *adj* motorisé(e)

motorway ['məʊtəweɪ] *n Br* autoroute *f*; **m. services** services *mpl* autoroutiers

mottled ['mɒtəld] *adj (skin)* marbré(e); *(coat, surface)* tacheté(e), moucheté(e)

motto ['mɒtəʊ] *(pl* **mottoes)** *n* devise *f*

mould¹, *Am* **mold** [məʊld] *n (fungus)* moisissure *f*

mould², *Am* **mold 1** *n (in art, cooking)* moule *m*; *Fig* **cast in the same m.** fait(e) dans le même moule; *Fig* **a star in the John Wayne m.** une star dans le style John Wayne; *Fig* **to break the m.** rompre avec la tradition
2 *vt (plastic, person's character)* modeler, façonner

moulder, *Am* **molder** ['məʊldə(r)] *vi (of food)* moisir; *(of building)* se délabrer

moulding, *Am* **molding** ['məʊldɪŋ] *n Archit* moulure *f*

mouldy, *Am* **moldy** ['məʊldɪ] *adj* moisi(e)

moult [məʊlt] *vi (of bird)* muer; *(of cat, dog)* perdre ses poils

mound [maʊnd] *n (hill)* butte *f*; *(of earth, sand)* tas *m*

mount¹ [maʊnt] *n (mountain)* mont *m*; **M. Vesuvius** le Vésuve

mount² 1 *n* (a) *(for painting)* carton *m* de montage; *(for slide)* cadre *m* (b) *(horse)* monture *f*
2 *vt* (a) *(bicycle, horse)* monter sur, enfourcher; *(stairs)* monter; *(ladder)* monter à (b) *(photograph, exhibition)* monter; *(machine gun)* installer; *(offensive)* lancer; **to m. guard** monter la garde
3 *vi* (a) *(get onto horse)* se mettre en selle (b) *(increase)* monter, augmenter

▶ **mount up** *vi (of cost, debts)* monter, augmenter

mountain ['maʊntɪn] *n also Fig* montagne *f*; **to make a m. out of a molehill** faire une montagne d'un rien; **m. bike** vélo *m* tout terrain; **m. climbing** alpinisme *m*; **m. lion** puma *m*; **m. range** chaîne *f* de montagnes; *Am* **m. rescue team** équipe *f* de secours en montagne; *Am* **M. Standard Time** heure *f* des montagnes Rocheuses

mountaineer [maʊntɪˈnɪə(r)] *n* alpiniste *mf*

mountaineering [maʊntɪˈnɪərɪŋ] *n* alpinisme *m*

mountainous ['maʊntɪnəs] *adj* montagneux(euse)

mounted ['maʊntɪd] *adj* monté(e), à cheval; **the m. police** la police montée

mounting ['maʊntɪŋ] **1** *n (for engine, gun)* support *m*
2 *adj (increasing)* croissant(e)

mourn [mɔːn] **1** *vt* pleurer
2 *vi* **to m. for sb/sth** pleurer qn/qch

mourner ['mɔːnə(r)] *n* ≃ personne assistant aux obsèques

mournful ['mɔːnfʊl] *adj* triste

mourning ['mɔːnɪŋ] *n* deuil *m*; **to be in m. (for sb)** être en deuil (de qn); **to go into m.** prendre le deuil

mouse [maʊs] *(pl* **mice** [maɪs]) *n also Comptr* souris *f*

mousetrap ['maʊstræp] *n* tapette *f*, souricière *f*

mousse [muːs] *n* mousse *f*; **chocolate m.** mousse au chocolat

moustache [məˈstɑːʃ], *Am* **mustache** ['mʌstæʃ] *n* moustache *f*

mousy ['maʊsɪ] *adj* (a) *(hair)* châtain terne *inv* (b) *(person, manner)* timide, effacé(e)

mouth 1 [maʊθ] *(of person, horse)* bouche *f*; *(of other animal)* gueule *f*; *(of tunnel)* entrée *f*; *(of river)* embouchure *f*; **we have seven mouths to feed** nous avons sept bouches à nourrir; *Fam* **keep your m. shut** about this garde ça pour toi; *Fam Fig* **to have a big m.** avoir une grande gueule; *Fam* **he's all m.** c'est une grande gueule; **don't put words into my m.** ne me fais pas dire ce que je n'ai pas dit; **m. organ** harmonica *m*
2 *vt* [maʊð] *(insincerely)* débiter; *(silently)* articuler silencieusement

mouthful ['maʊθfʊl] n (of food) bouchée f; (of drink) gorgée f; Fam Fig (long word) = mot long et difficile à prononcer; (long name) nom m à coucher dehors; Fam **to give sb a m.** enguirlander qn

mouthpiece ['maʊθpiːs] n (a) (of musical instrument) embouchure f; (of telephone) microphone m (b) (of government, political party) porte-parole m inv

mouth-to-mouth resuscitation ['maʊθtə'maʊθrɪsʌsɪ'teɪʃən] n bouche-à-bouche m inv

mouthwash ['maʊθwɒʃ] n bain m de bouche

mouthwatering ['maʊθwɔːtərɪŋ] adj (smell) appétissant(e); (prospect) alléchant(e)

movable ['muːvəbəl] adj mobile; Rel m. feast fête f mobile

move [muːv] 1 n (a) (motion) mouvement m; **to make a m.** (leave) partir; **to make a m. towards sb/sth** se diriger vers qn/qch; **on the m.** en mouvement; Fam **to get a m. on** se grouiller, se magner
(b) (action, step) pas m, démarche f; **to make the first m.** faire le premier pas
(c) (from home) déménagement m; (from job) changement m de poste
(d) (in games) coup m; **(it's) your m.** (c'est) à toi de jouer
2 vt (a) (change position of) déplacer; (set in motion) remuer; (employee) muter; **to m. house/premises** déménager; **to m. jobs** (within company, sector) changer de poste; Fam **to m. oneself** se remuer
(b) Fig (sway) faire changer d'avis; **to feel moved to do sth** se sentir obligé(e) de faire qch
(c) (affect emotionally) émouvoir; **to m. sb to anger** provoquer la colère de qn; **to m. sb to tears** émouvoir qn jusqu'aux larmes
(d) (in debate) proposer
3 vi (a) (change position) se déplacer; (stir) bouger; (progress, advance) avancer; (leave) partir; **to get things moving** faire avancer les choses; **could you m., please?** pourriez-vous vous pousser, s'il vous plaît?; Fam **come on, m.!** allez, remue-toi!
(b) (act) agir
(c) (to new home, office) emménager; **to m. to another job** changer de travail; **to m. to the country** s'installer à la campagne
(d) Fig (be swayed) céder
(e) (in games) (of player) jouer; (of piece) avancer

▶**move about, move around 1** vt sep (furniture) déplacer; (employee) muter, transférer
2 vi (change position) se déplacer; (stir) bouger; **he moves around a lot** (in job) il est souvent en déplacement

▶**move along = move on**

▶**move away 1** vt sep (object) éloigner, écarter (**from** de)
2 vi (from window, person) s'éloigner, s'écarter (**from** de); (move house) déménager

▶**move back 1** vt sep (further away) reculer; (to former position) remettre en place
2 vi (retreat) s'écarter, (se) reculer; (to former position) retourner (**to** à)

▶**move forward 1** vt sep (object, date, meeting) avancer; (troops) faire avancer
2 vi (of person, car) (s')avancer

▶**move in** vi (take up residence) emménager

▶**move off** vi (go away) partir, s'éloigner; (start journey) se mettre en marche; (of car) démarrer

▶**move on 1** vt sep (crowd) faire circuler
2 vi (a) **time's moving on** il se fait tard; **it's time we were moving on** il est temps de partir (b) (change subject)

passer à autre chose; **to m. on to sth** passer à qch (c) (progress, develop) changer

▶**move out** vi (leave home) déménager

▶**move over** vi (make room) se pousser

▶**move up** vi (a) (make room) sé pousser (b) (be promoted) avoir de l'avancement

moveable ['muːvəbəl] = **movable**

movement ['muːvmənt] n mouvement m; **to watch sb's movements** surveiller les faits et gestes de qn; (bowel) m. selles fpl

mover ['muːvə(r)] n (in debate) auteur m d'une motion; **the movers and shakers** les grands pontes mpl

movie ['muːvi] n Am film m; **to go to the movies** aller au cinéma; **to be in the movies** faire du cinéma; **m. actor/actress** acteur m/actrice f de cinéma; **m. camera** caméra f; **m. industry** industrie f cinématographique; **m. star** vedette f de cinéma; **m. theater** cinéma m

moviegoer ['muːviɡəʊə(r)] n Am spectateur(trice) m,f de cinéma

moving ['muːvɪŋ] adj (a) (in motion) en mouvement; (train, vehicle) en marche; (parts) mobile; **m. staircase** escalier m mécanique (b) (touching) émouvant(e)

mow [məʊ] (pp **mown** [məʊn]) vt (lawn) tondre; (hay) faucher

▶**mow down** vt sep (slaughter) faucher

Mozambican [məʊzæm'biːkən] 1 n Mozambicain(e) m,f
2 adj mozambicain(e)

Mozambique [məʊzæm'biːk] n le Mozambique

MP [em'piː] n (a) Br Pol (abbr **Member of Parliament**) député m (b) Mil (abbr **Military Police**) police f militaire

mpg [empiː'dʒiː] n (abbr **miles per gallon**) ≃ litre m aux cent (kilomètres)

mph [empiː'eɪtʃ] n (abbr **miles per hour**) ≃ km/h

Mr ['mɪstə(r)] (abbr **Mister**) Mr McLean M. McLean; **Mr Right** (ideal husband) l'homme m idéal

Mrs ['mɪsɪz] (abbr **Mistress**) Mrs Sole Mme Sole

Ms [mɪz] ≃ Mme (ne donne pas d'indications sur le statut de famille)

MS n (a) (abbr **multiple sclerosis**) sclérose f en plaques (b) (abbr **manuscript**) manuscrit m

ms (abbr **millisecond**) millième m de seconde

MSc [emes'siː] n Univ (abbr **Master of Science**) **to have an M. in chemistry** avoir une maîtrise de chimie; **John Smith M.** John Smith, titulaire d'une maîtrise de sciences

MSG [emes'dʒiː] n Culin (abbr **monosodium glutamate**) glutamate m de sodium

MST [emes'tiː] n Am (abbr **Mountain Standard Time**) heure f d'hiver des montagnes Rocheuses

Mt (abbr **Mount**) Mt.

much [mʌtʃ] (comparative **more** [mɔː(r)], superlative **most** [məʊst]) 1 pron beaucoup; **there isn't m. left** il n'en reste pas beaucoup; **it's not worth m.** ça ne vaut pas grand-chose; Formal **m. has happened since you left** il s'est passé beaucoup de choses depuis ton départ; **I'll say this m. for him, he's very polite** je dois reconnaître une chose, c'est qu'il est très poli; **I don't think m. of him** il n'ai pas grande estime pour lui; **it didn't come as m. of a surprise** ça n'a pas été une grande surprise; **she isn't m. of a singer** comme chanteuse, elle n'est pas très bonne; **twice as m.** deux fois plus; **I thought as m.** c'est ce que je pensais; **as m. as possible** autant que possible, **it was**

as m. as we could do to stay upright nous avions déjà assez de mal à rester debout; he left without so m. as saying goodbye il est parti sans même dire au revoir; he has drunk so m. that... il a tellement bu que...; so m. the better tant mieux; so m. so that... à tel point que...; so m. for her promises of help! c'était bien la peine de promettre qu'elle m'/nous/etc aiderait!; Fam that's a bit m.! c'est un peu fort!

2 adj

Hormis dans la langue soutenue et dans certaines expressions, ne s'utilise que dans des structures négatives ou interrogatives.

how m. money? combien d'argent?; there isn't m. traffic il n'y a pas beaucoup de circulation; too m. work trop de travail; so m. time tant de temps; as m. food as autant de nourriture que; Formal m. work still needs to be done il reste encore beaucoup de travail à faire

3 adv beaucoup; I don't like it m. ça ne me plaît pas beaucoup; m. better bien meilleur(e); m. more difficult beaucoup plus difficile; m. the best de loin le meilleur (la meilleure); m. the most interesting de loin le (la) plus intéressant(e); thank you very m. merci beaucoup; m. the same presque pareil(eille); m. to my astonishment à mon grand étonnement; m. as I like him, I don't really trust him j'ai beau l'apprécier, je ne lui fais pas vraiment confiance; the result was m. as I expected le résultat correspondait assez à mes attentes; so m. autant; I love him so m. je l'aime tellement; too m. trop; £10 too m. 10 livres de trop; this is (really) too m.! trop c'est trop!

muchness ['mʌtʃnɪs] n Fam they're much of a m. ils se valent

muck [mʌk] n Fam (dirt) saleté f; (manure) fumier m; (bad food) cochonneries fpl; (bad quality book, TV programme) idioties fpl

▸muck about, muck around Br Fam = mess about, mess around

▸muck in vi Br Fam (help) s'y mettre

▸muck out vt sep (stables) nettoyer

▸muck up vt sep Fam (a) (make dirty) cochonner (b) (task) bâcler; (plans) chambouler; (interview, exam) rater

muckraking ['mʌkreɪkɪŋ] n Fam (in journalism) = pratique consistant à révéler et exploiter à fond des scandales

mucky ['mʌkɪ] adj Br Fam sale

mucous ['mjuːkəs] adj muqueux(euse)

mucus ['mjuːkəs] n mucus m, mucosités fpl

mud [mʌd] n boue f; Fig to throw m. at sb couvrir qn de boue; Fam his name is m. il n'a pas la cote; m. hut hutte f en terre

mudbank ['mʌdbæŋk] n banc m de vase

mudflat ['mʌdflæt] n banc m de boue

muddle ['mʌdəl] 1 n confusion f; to be in a m. (of things) être en désordre; (of person) ne plus s'y retrouver; to get into a m. (of things) se mélanger; (of person) s'embrouiller

2 vt (a) (put in disorder) mélanger (b) (bewilder) embrouiller; to get muddled s'embrouiller

▸muddle along vi se débrouiller tant bien que mal

▸muddle through vi se débrouiller

▸muddle up vt sep (a) (put in disorder) mélanger (b) (confuse) embrouiller; to get muddled up s'embrouiller

muddleheaded [mʌdəl'hedɪd] adj (person) brouillon(onne); (thinking) confus(e)

muddy ['mʌdɪ] 1 adj (path, water) boueux(euse); (clothing, hands) couvert(e) de boue; (complexion) terreux(euse); (colour) sale

2 vt (pt & pp muddied) salir; Fig to m. the waters brouiller les pistes

mudguard ['mʌdɡɑːd] n garde-boue m inv

mudpack ['mʌdpæk] n masque m à l'argile

mudslinging ['mʌdslɪŋɪŋ] n Fam = fait de dénigrer systématiquement ses adversaires

muesli ['mjuːzlɪ] n muesli m

muff¹ [mʌf] vt Br Fam (bungle) rater, louper

muff² n (for hands) manchon m

muffin ['mʌfɪn] n Br (teacake) muffin m; Am (cake) = sorte de madeleine

muffle ['mʌfəl] vt (a) (sound) assourdir, étouffer (b) to m. oneself up s'emmitoufler

muffled ['mʌfəld] adj (sound, footstep) assourdi(e), étouffé(e)

muffler ['mʌflə(r)] n (a) (scarf) cache-nez m inv (b) Am (of car) silencieux m

mufti ['mʌftɪ] n Fam in m. (soldier) en civil

mug [mʌɡ] 1 n (a) (cup) grande tasse f (b) Fam (face) gueule f; m. shot photo f d'identité judiciaire (c) Br Fam (gullible person) poire f; it's a m.'s game on est toujours perdant à ce jeu-là

2 vt (pt & pp mugged) (attack) agresser

▸mug up vi Br Fam (study) bûcher; to m. up on sth potasser qch

mugger ['mʌɡə(r)] n agresseur m

mugging ['mʌɡɪŋ] n agression f

muggins ['mʌɡɪnz] n Br Fam mézigue

muggy ['mʌɡɪ] adj lourd(e), étouffant(e)

mulatto [mjuː'lætəʊ] (pl mulattos or mulattoes) n mulâtre mf

mulberry ['mʌlbərɪ] (pt mulberries) n (fruit) mûre f; (tree) mûrier m

mule [mjuːl] n mulet m; (female) mule f

▸mull over [mʌl] vt sep (consider) to m. sth over retourner qch dans sa tête

mulled wine [mʌld'waɪn] n vin m chaud épicé

mullet ['mʌlɪt] n grey m. mulet m gris; red m. rouget m

multi-access ['mʌltɪ'æksez] adj Comptr à accès multiple

multicoloured ['mʌltɪkʌləd] adj multicolore

multicultural [mʌltɪ'kʌltʃərəl] adj multiculturel(elle)

multifarious [mʌltɪ'feərɪəs] adj varié(e), divers(e)

multi-functional [mʌltɪ'fʌŋkʃənəl] adj multifonctions inv

multilateral [mʌltɪ'lætərəl] adj multilatéral(e)

multimedia [mʌltɪ'miːdɪə] adj multimédia

multimillionaire [mʌltɪmɪljə'neə(r)] n multimillionnaire mf

multinational [mʌltɪ'næʃənəl] 1 n multinationale f

2 adj multinational(e)

multiparty [mʌltɪ'pɑːtɪ] adj m. system pluripartisme m

multiple ['mʌltɪpəl] 1 n (a) Math multiple m (b) Com (chain store) chaîne f de magasins

2 adj multiple; m. sclerosis sclérose f en plaques

multiple-choice ['mʌltɪpl'tʃɔɪs] adj à choix multiple

multiplication [mʌltɪplɪ'keɪʃən] n multiplication f; **m. table** table f de multiplication

multiplicity [mʌltɪ'plɪsɪtɪ] n multiplicité f

multiply ['mʌltɪplaɪ] (pt & pp **multiplied**) 1 vt multiplier (**by** par)
  2 vi (reproduce) se multiplier

multipurpose [mʌltɪ'pɜːpəs] adj polyvalent(e)

multiracial [mʌltɪ'reɪʃəl] adj multiracial(e)

multistorey, Am **multistory** [mʌltɪ'stɔːrɪ] adj à étages; **m. (car park)** parking m à plusieurs niveaux

multitude ['mʌltɪtjuːd] n multitude f

mum [mʌm] Fam 1 n Br (mother) maman f; **m.'s the word!** motus et bouche cousue!
  2 adv **to keep m. (about sth)** ne pas souffler mot (de qch)

mumble ['mʌmbəl] 1 n marmonnement m
  2 vt & vi marmonner

mumbo jumbo ['mʌmbəʊ'dʒʌmbəʊ] n (nonsense) âneries fpl; (jargon) charabia m

mummify ['mʌmɪfaɪ] (pt & pp **mummified**) vt momifier

mummy[1] ['mʌmɪ] (pl **mummies**) n (embalmed body) momie f

mummy[2] n Br Fam (mother) maman f; **a m.'s boy** un petit garçon à sa maman

mumps [mʌmps] n (illness) oreillons mpl; **to have m.** avoir les oreillons

munch [mʌntʃ] vt mâcher

munchies ['mʌntʃɪz] npl Fam (a) (snacks) amuse-gueule mpl (b) (desire to eat) **to have the m.** avoir la fringale

mundane [mʌn'deɪn] adj banal(e), ordinaire

municipal [mjuː'nɪsɪpəl] adj municipal(e)

municipality [mjuːnɪsɪ'pælɪtɪ] (pl **municipalities**) n municipalité f

munitions [mjuː'nɪʃənz] npl munitions fpl

mural ['mjʊərəl] n peinture f murale

murder ['mɜːdə(r)] 1 n (a) (killing) meurtre m; Fig **she gets away with m.** elle peut tout se permettre; **m. case** affaire f de meurtre; **m. inquiry** enquête f sur une affaire de meurtre (b) Fam Fig (difficult task) cauchemar m, enfer m; **finding a parking place on a Saturday is m.** c'est l'enfer pour trouver à se garer le samedi
  2 vt (a) (kill) assassiner; Fam Fig **I'll m. you!** je vais te tuer!; Fam **I could m. a beer/pizza** je me taperais bien une bière/une pizza (b) Fig (song, tune) massacrer

murderer ['mɜːdərə(r)] n meurtrier(ère) m,f, assassin m

murky ['mɜːkɪ] adj (weather, sky) sombre; (details, past) trouble

murmur ['mɜːmə(r)] 1 n murmure m; **to do sth without a m.** faire qch sans broncher
  2 vt also Fig murmurer

muscle ['mʌsəl] n muscle m; Fig (power) poids m; **not to move a m.** rester immobile

▸**muscle in** vi intervenir (**on** dans)

muscleman ['mʌsəlmæn] n Monsieur m muscle

Muscovite ['mʌskəvaɪt] 1 n Moscovite mf
  2 adj moscovite

muscular ['mʌskjʊlə(r)] adj (tissue, pain) musculaire; (person) musclé(e); **m. dystrophy** myopathie f

Muse [mjuːz] n (in mythology) Muse f; (of poet) muse f

muse [mjuːz] vi rêvasser, songer (**on** or **about** à)

museum [mjuː'zɪəm] n musée m

mush [mʌʃ] n (a) (pulp) bouillie f (b) Fig (sentimentality) mièvrerie f

mushroom ['mʌʃrʊm] 1 n champignon m; **m. cloud** champignon atomique
  2 vi (of costs, prices) grimper (en flèche); (of town) se développer; (of houses, factories) pousser comme des champignons

mushy ['mʌʃɪ] adj (a) (food) en bouillie; (ground) détrempé(e) (b) Fam Fig (sentimental) à l'eau de rose, mièvre

music ['mjuːzɪk] n musique f; Fig **those words were m. to her ears** elle était ravie d'entendre ces mots; **m. box** boîte f à musique; **m. hall** music-hall m; **m. stand** pupitre m à musique; **m. teacher** professeur m de musique

musical ['mjuːzɪkəl] 1 n (show, film) comédie f musicale
  2 adj (tuneful) musical(e); (musically gifted) musicien(enne); **m. box** boîte f à musique; **m. chairs** (jeu m des) chaises fpl musicales; also Fig **to play m. chairs** jouer aux chaises musicales; **m. instrument** instrument m de musique

musician [mjuː'zɪʃən] n musicien(enne) m,f

musicologist [mjuːzɪ'kɒlədʒɪst] n musicologue mf

musings ['mjuːzɪŋz] npl rêverie(s) f(pl)

musk [mʌsk] n musc m

musket ['mʌskɪt] n mousquet m

musketeer [mʌskə'tɪə(r)] n mousquetaire m

muskrat ['mʌskræt] n rat m musqué

Muslim ['mʊzlɪm] n & adj musulman(e) m,f

muslin ['mʌzlɪn] n mousseline f

mussel ['mʌsəl] n moule f; **m. bed** parc m à moules

must [mʌst] 1 modal aux v (a) (expressing obligation) devoir; **you m. do it** tu dois le faire, il faut que tu le fasses; **they mustn't find out** il ne faut pas qu'ils l'apprennent; **you mustn't tell anyone** surtout, n'en parle à personne; **this plant m. be watered daily** cette plante doit être arrosée chaque jour; **I m. say** I thought it was rather good je dois avouer que j'ai trouvé ça plutôt bon; **will you come with me?** – **if I m.** tu viens avec moi? – s'il le faut; **take it if you m.** prends-le, si tu le veux vraiment; **you m. be silly** tu as le sens obligé d'être aussi bête? (b) (suggesting, inviting) **you m. come and visit us** il faut vraiment que vous nous rendiez visite; **we m. go out for a drink sometime** il faudrait que nous allions prendre un verre, un de ces jours (c) (expressing probability) devoir; **you m. be hungry** vous devez avoir faim; **I m. have made a mistake** j'ai dû faire une erreur; **you m. be joking!** tu veux rire!
  2 n Fam (a) (necessity) **to be a m.** être une nécessité; **sunglasses/hiking boots are a m.** il faut absolument emporter des lunettes de soleil/des chaussures de marche (b) (thing not to be missed) **this film's a m.** ce film est un must

mustache ['mʌstæʃ] Am = **moustache**

mustard ['mʌstəd] n moutarde f; Am Fam Fig **he couldn't cut the m.** il n'a pas été à la hauteur; **m. gas** gaz m moutarde

muster ['mʌstə(r)] 1 n Fig **to pass m.** être acceptable
  2 vt (gather) rassembler; **to m. one's strength/courage** rassembler ses forces/son courage

musty ['mʌstɪ] adj (smell) de moisi; **to have a m. smell** (of room) sentir le renfermé

mutant ['mjuːtənt] n & adj mutant(e) m,f

mutate [mjuːˈteɪt] vi muter

mutation [mjuːˈteɪʃən] n mutation f

mute [mjuːt] 1 n (a) (dumb person) muet(ette) m,f (b) Mus sourdine f
2 adj muet(ette)

muted ['mjuːtɪd] adj (sound) assourdi(e); (applause) faible; (protest, criticism) voilé(e); (colour) sourd(e)

mutilate ['mjuːtɪleɪt] vt also Fig mutiler

mutilation [mjuːtɪˈleɪʃən] n mutilation f

mutineer [mjuːtɪˈnɪə(r)] n mutiné(e) m,f

mutinous ['mjuːtɪnəs] adj rebelle

mutiny ['mjuːtɪnɪ] 1 n (pl mutinies) (on ship) mutinerie f; (of workers) révolte f
2 vi (pt & pp mutinied) (of crew, soldiers) se mutiner; (of workers) se révolter

mutt [mʌt] n Fam (dog) clébard m

mutter ['mʌtə(r)] 1 n murmure m
2 vt & vi marmonner

mutton ['mʌtən] n mouton m; Fam to look like m. dressed as lamb être habillé(e) trop jeune pour son âge

mutual ['mjuːtʃʊəl] adj (reciprocal) mutuel(elle), réciproque; (shared) commun(e); the feeling is m. c'est réciproque

mutually ['mjuːtʃʊəlɪ] adv mutuellement, réciproquement; to be m. exclusive s'exclure mutuellement

muzzle ['mʌzəl] 1 n (a) (dog's nose) museau m; (guard) muselière f (b) (of gun) canon m
2 vt also Fig museler

MW (a) (abbr **Medium Wave**) OM (b) Elec (abbr **Megawatts**) MW

my [maɪ] 1 possessive adj (a) (singular) mon (ma); (plural) mes; **my job** mon travail; **my wife** ma femme; **my parents** mes parents; **it wasn't MY idea!** ce n'est pas moi qui en ai eu l'idée! (b) (with parts of body) **I hit my head** je

me suis cogné la tête
2 exclam oh là là!

Myanmar [maɪənˈmɑː(r)] n le Myanmar

mynah ['maɪnə] n **m. (bird)** mainate m

myopia [maɪˈəʊpɪə] n myopie f; Fig manque m de perspicacité

myopic [maɪˈɒpɪk] adj myope; Fig à courte vue

myriad ['mɪrɪəd] adj Lit innombrable

myrrh [mɜː(r)] n myrrhe f

myrtle ['mɜːtəl] n myrte m

myself [maɪˈself] pron (a) (reflexive) **I hurt m.** je me suis blessé (b) (emphatic) moi-même; **I m. have never...** moi-même n'ai jamais...; **I told her m.** je le lui ai dit moi-même; **I'm not m. today** je ne suis pas dans mon état normal aujourd'hui (c) (after preposition) moi; **I live by m.** je vis seul; **I bought it for m.** je me le suis acheté; **I talk to m.** je parle tout seul

mysterious [mɪsˈtɪərɪəs] adj mystérieux(euse)

mysteriously [mɪsˈtɪərɪəslɪ] adv mystérieusement

mystery ['mɪstərɪ] 1 n (pl mysteries) mystère m; **m. tour** voyage m surprise
2 adj (guest, prize) surprise inv; (benefactor, witness) mystérieux(euse)

mystic ['mɪstɪk] n & adj mystique mf

mystical ['mɪstɪkəl] adj (person) mystique; (power, ceremony) occulte

mysticism ['mɪstɪsɪzəm] n mysticisme m

mystify ['mɪstɪfaɪ] (pt & pp mystified) vt déconcerter

mystique [mɪsˈtiːk] n mystère m

myth [mɪθ] n mythe m

mythical ['mɪθɪkəl] adj mythique

mythological [mɪθəˈlɒdʒɪkəl] adj mythologique

mythology [mɪˈθɒlədʒɪ] (pl mystologies) n mythologie f

myxomatosis [mɪksəmməˈtəʊsɪs] n myxomatose f

N

N, n [en] *n* (a) *(letter)* N, n *m inv* (b) *(abbr* **north)** N

NAACP [eneɪeɪsiːpiː] *n Am Pol (abbr* **National Association for the Advancement of Colored People)** = association pour la défense des droits des personnes de couleur

naan [nɑːn] *n* n. *(bread)* = sorte de pain indien servi comme accompagnement

nab [næb] *(pt & pp* **nabbed)** *vt Fam* (a) *(catch, arrest)* choper (b) *(steal)* piquer, faucher

nadir [ˈneɪdɪə(r)] *n Astron* nadir *m; Fig* to reach a n. atteindre son niveau le plus bas

naff [næf] *adj Br Fam (of poor quality)* nul (nulle); *(of poor taste)* ringard(e)

▸**naff off** *vi Br Fam* n. off! dégage!

nag¹ [næg] *n Fam (horse)* carne *f*

nag² **1** *n (person)* enquiquineur(euse) *m,f*
2 *(pt & pp* **nagged)** *vt (of person)* être sur le dos de; *(of doubt, conscience)* tourmenter; **to n. sb into doing sth** harceler qn pour qu'il fasse qch
3 *vi* **he's always nagging** il est tout le temps sur mon dos

nagging [ˈnægɪŋ] **1** *n* harcèlement *m;* **I've had enough of your n.** arrête de me harceler
2 *adj (pain, doubt, worry)* tenace

nail [neɪl] **1** *n* (a) *(in carpentry)* clou *m; Fig* **it was another n. in his coffin** c'était un pas de plus vers la fin; *Fig* **the final n. in the coffin** la goutte d'eau qui fait déborder le vase; *Fig* **to hit the n. on the head** mettre le doigt dessus (b) *(of person)* ongle *m;* **n. file** lime *f* à ongles; **n. scissors** ciseaux *mpl* à ongles; **n. varnish or polish** vernis *m* à ongles; **n. varnish or polish remover** dissolvant *m*
2 *vt* (a) *(clouer;* **to n. sth shut** clouer qch; *Fig* **to stand nailed to the spot** rester cloué(e) sur place (b) *(idioms) Fam* **to n. sb** *(for crime)* coincer qn; *Fam* **to n. a lie** dénoncer un mensonge

▸**nail down** *vt sep (fasten)* clouer, fixer avec des clous; *Fam Fig* **to n. sb down to a date/price** obtenir de qn qu'il fixe une date/un prix

nail-biting [ˈneɪlbaɪtɪŋ] *adj Fam (contest, finish)* palpitant(e); *(wait)* angoissant(e)

nailbrush [ˈneɪlbrʌʃ] *n* brosse *f* à ongles

naive [naɪˈiːv] *adj* naïf naïve(ive)

naively [naɪˈiːvli] *adv* naïvement

naivety [naɪˈiːvəti] *n* naïveté *f*

naked [ˈneɪkɪd] *adj (body, flame)* nu(e); *Fig (aggression, exploitation)* délibéré(e); **visible to the n. eye** visible à l'œil nu

namby-pamby [ˈnæmbɪˈpæmbi] **1** *n (pl* **namby-pambies)** mollasson(onne) *m,f*
2 *adj* gnangnan *inv*

name [neɪm] **1** *n* (a) *(in general)* nom *m;* **my n. is...** je m'appelle...; **what's your n.?** comment t'appelles-tu?; **to mention sb by n.** désigner nommément qn; **a big n. in the theatre** un grand nom du théâtre; **to put one's n. down (for sth)** s'inscrire (pour qch); **to go by or under the n. of...** être connu(e) sous le nom de...; **in the n. of...** au nom de...; **in the n. of God or Heaven!** au nom du Ciel!; **he was President in all but n.** c'était lui le président, même s'il n'en avait pas le titre; **to call sb names** insulter qn; **he hasn't got a penny to his n.** il n'a pas un sou (b) *(reputation)* réputation *f;* **to have a good/bad n.** avoir (une) bonne/mauvaise réputation; **to have a n. for** être réputé(e) pour; **to make a n. for oneself** se faire un nom
2 *vt* (a) *(give name to, appoint)* nommer; **to n. sb** *Br* **after** *or Am* **for sb** donner à qn le nom de qn (b) *(designate, identify)* citer; **to n. names** donner des noms; **n. your price** dites votre prix

name-calling [ˈneɪmkɔːlɪŋ] *n* insultes *fpl*

name-dropper [ˈneɪmdrɒpə(r)] *n Fam* = personne qui se vante de connaître des gens célèbres

name-dropping [ˈneɪmdrɒpɪŋ] *n Fam* = fait de se vanter de connaître des gens célèbres

nameless [ˈneɪmlɪs] *adj (person)* anonyme; **someone who shall remain n.** quelqu'un que je ne nommerai pas

namely [ˈneɪmli] *adv* c'est-à-dire, à savoir

nameplate [ˈneɪmpleɪt] *n* plaque *f*

namesake [ˈneɪmseɪk] *n* homonyme *mf*

Namibia [nəˈmɪbɪə] *n* la Namibie

Namibian [nəˈmɪbɪən] **1** *n* Namibien(enne) *m,f*
2 *adj* namibien(enne)

nancy [ˈnænsi] *n (pl* **nancies)** *n very Fam* **n. (boy)** *(homosexual)* tapette *f*, pédale *f; (effeminate man)* chochotte *f*

nanny [ˈnæni] *n (pl* **nannies)** *n* (a) *(for children)* jeune fille *f* au pair (b) **n. goat** chèvre *f*

nanosecond [ˈnænəʊsekənd] *n Phys* nanoseconde *f*

nap¹ [næp] **1** *n (sleep)* (petit) somme *m;* **to take or have a n.** faire un (petit) somme
2 *vi (pt & pp* **napped)** faire un (petit) somme; *Fig* **to be caught napping** être pris(e) au dépourvu

nap² *n (of cloth)* poil *m*

napalm [ˈneɪpɑːm] *n* napalm *m*

nape [neɪp] *n* n. **(of the neck)** nuque *f*

naphthalene [ˈnæfθəliːn] *n* naphtaline *f*

napkin [ˈnæpkɪn] *n* (a) *(table)* **n.** serviette *f* (de table); **n. ring** rond *m* de serviette (b) *Am (sanitary towel)* serviette *f* hygiénique

Naples [ˈneɪpəlz] *n* Naples

Napoleonic [nəpəʊlɪˈɒnɪk] *adj* napoléonien(enne)

nappy ['næpɪ] (*pl* **nappies**) *n Br* couche *f*; **n. rash** érythème *m* fessier

narc [nɑːk] *n Am Fam* agent *m* de la brigade des stups

narcissus [nɑːˈsɪsəs] (*pl* **narcissi** [nɑːˈsɪsaɪ]) *n* narcisse *m*

narcosis [nɑːˈkəʊsɪs] *n* narcose *f*

narcotic [nɑːˈkɒtɪk] 1 *n* (*medicine*) narcotique *m*; (*illegal drug*) stupéfiant *m*; *Am* **narcotics agent** agent *m* de la brigade des stupéfiants
2 *adj* narcotique

nark [nɑːk] *n Br Fam* (a) (*informer*) indic *m* (b) (*irritable person*) râleur(euse) *m,f*

narky ['nɑːkɪ] *adj Br Fam* grognon

narrate [nəˈreɪt] *vt* raconter

narrative ['nærətɪv] 1 *n* récit *m*
2 *adj* narratif(ive)

narrator [nəˈreɪtə(r)] *n* narrateur(trice) *m,f*

narrow ['nærəʊ] 1 *adj* étroit(e); (*majority*) faible; **to grow** *or* **become n.** se rétrécir; **to have a n. mind** avoir l'esprit étroit; **to have a n. escape** l'échapper belle; **to win/lose by a n. margin** gagner/perdre de justesse; **to take a n. view of sth** adopter un point de vue étroit sur qch
2 *vt* **to n. one's eyes** (*in suspicion, anger*) froncer les sourcils
3 *vi* (*of road*) se rétrécir, se resserrer

▸**narrow down** *vt sep* limiter, réduire

narrowly ['nærəʊlɪ] *adv* (*only just*) de peu; **she n. missed being run over** elle a failli se faire écraser

narrow-minded [nærəʊˈmaɪndɪd] *adj* étroit(e) d'esprit, borné(e)

NASA ['næsə] *n* (*abbr* **National Aeronautics and Space Administration**) NASA *f*

nasal ['neɪzəl] *adj* nasal(e); **to have a n. voice** parler du nez

nastily ['nɑːstɪlɪ] *adv* méchamment

nastiness ['nɑːstɪnɪs] *n* (*of person, remark*) méchanceté *f*

nasturtium [nəˈstɜːʃəm] *n* capucine *f*

nasty ['nɑːstɪ] *adj* mauvais(e); (*crime*) ignoble; (*shock, business*) sale; (*accident*) grave; **to be n. to sb** être méchant(e) avec qn; **to have a n. mind** penser toujours à mal; **to turn n.** (*of situation, weather*) se dégrader, se gâter; **that was a really n. thing to do** c'était vraiment ignoble de sa/ta/etc part; *Fig* **it left a n. taste in my mouth** ça m'a laissé un arrière-goût désagréable; **a n. piece of work** (*man*) un sale type; (*woman*) une vraie peste

nation ['neɪʃən] *n* nation *f*

national ['næʃənəl] 1 *n* (a) (*person*) ressortissant(e) *m,f* (b) (*newspaper*) journal *m* national
2 *adj* national(e); **n. anthem** hymne *m* national; **n. curriculum** programme *m* scolaire; **n. debt** dette *f* publique; **N. Front** = parti britannique d'extrême droite; **n. grid** réseau *m* national (d'électricité); *Br* **N. Health Service** = système *m* de santé britannique; *Br* **N. Insurance** contributions *fpl* sociales; **n. park** parc *m* national; **n. service** service *m* militaire; **N. Trust** = organisme britannique de conservation du patrimoine historique et naturel

nationalism ['næʃənəlɪzəm] *n* nationalisme *m*

nationalist ['næʃənəlɪst] *n & adj* nationaliste *mf*

nationalistic [næʃənəˈlɪstɪk] *adj* nationaliste

nationality [næʃəˈnælɪtɪ] (*pl* **nationalities**) *n* nationalité *f*

nationalization [næʃənəlaɪˈzeɪʃən] *n* nationalisation *f*

nationalize ['næʃənəlaɪz] *vt* nationaliser

nationally ['næʃənəlɪ] *adv* nationalement

nationwide ['neɪʃənwaɪd] 1 *adj* national(e)
2 *adv* dans tout le pays

native ['neɪtɪv] 1 *n* (*person*) natif(ive) *m,f*; (*plant*) plante *f* indigène; (*animal*) animal *m* indigène; **to be a n. of** être originaire de; **she speaks English like a n.** elle parle anglais comme si c'était sa langue maternelle
2 *adj* natal(e); **he returned to his n. London** il est retourné à Londres, sa ville natale; **n. American** Indien(enne) *m,f* d'Amérique; **n. land** pays *m* natal; **n. language** langue *f* maternelle; **I'm not a n. speaker of Spanish** ma langue maternelle n'est pas l'espagnol

Nativity [nəˈtɪvɪtɪ] *n Rel* **the N.** la Nativité *f*; **N. play** mystère *m* de la Nativité

NATO ['neɪtəʊ] *n Mil* (*abbr* **North Atlantic Treaty Organization**) l'OTAN *f*

natter ['nætə(r)] *Br Fam* 1 *n* **to have a n.** bavarder, papoter (**about** sur)
2 *vi* bavarder, papoter (**about** sur)

natty ['nætɪ] *adj Fam* chic *inv*

natural ['nætʃərəl] 1 *adj* (a) (*colour, taste*) naturel(elle); (*gift, talent*) inné(e); **to die from n. causes** mourir de mort naturelle; **n. childbirth** accouchement *m* naturel; **n. disaster** catastrophe *f* naturelle; **n. gas** gaz *m* naturel; **n. history** histoire *f* naturelle; **n. mother** mère *f* naturelle; **n. resources** ressources *fpl* naturelles; **n. sciences** sciences *fpl* naturelles; **n. yoghurt** yaourt *m* nature (b) (*normal*) naturel(elle); **it's only n.** c'est tout à fait naturel; *Ind* **n. wastage** = réduction des effectifs due aux départs d'employés non remplacés (c) (*unaffected*) naturel(elle)
2 *n* **he's a n. as an actor** c'est un acteur né

naturalism ['nætʃərəlɪzəm] *n* naturalisme *m*

naturalist ['nætʃərəlɪst] *n* naturaliste *mf*

naturalistic ['nætʃərəlɪstɪk] *adj* naturaliste

naturalization [nætʃərəlaɪˈzeɪʃən] *n* naturalisation *f*

naturalize ['nætʃərəlaɪz] *vt* naturaliser

naturally ['nætʃərəlɪ] *adv* (a) (*unaffectedly*) naturellement; (*by nature*) de nature; **to come n. to sb** être un don chez qn (b) (*of course*) naturellement

nature ['neɪtʃə(r)] *n* (a) (*the natural world*) nature *f*; **to let its course** laisser faire la nature; **n. reserve** réserve *f* naturelle; **n. trail** = sentier aménagé doté d'explications concernant la faune et la flore (b) (*character*) nature *f*; **to have a jealous n.** être d'une nature jalouse; **it's not in her n.** ça n'est pas dans sa nature; **to be shy by n.** être timide de nature (c) (*sort*) nature *f*, genre *m*; **problems of this n.** des problèmes de cette nature; *Formal* **what is the n. of your complaint?** quelle est la nature de votre réclamation?

naught [nɔːt] *n* (a) *Lit* (*nothing*) néant *m*; **to come to n.** se réduire à néant (b) *Am* = **nought**

naughtily ['nɔːtɪlɪ] *adv* **to behave n.** être vilain(e)

naughty ['nɔːtɪ] *adj* (*child*) méchant(e), vilain(e); (*book, picture*) coquin(e)

nausea ['nɔːzɪə] *n* nausée *f*

nauseate ['nɔːzɪeɪt] *vt* donner la nausée à; *Fig* écœurer

nauseating ['nɔːzɪeɪtɪŋ] *adj also Fig* écœurant(e)

nauseous ['nɔːzɪəs] *adj (disgusting)* écœurant(e); **to feel n.** avoir envie de vomir

nautical ['nɔːtɪkəl] *adj* nautique; **n. mile** mille *m* marin *ou* nautique

naval ['neɪvəl] *adj* naval(e); **n. battle** bataille *f* navale; **the N. College** ≃ l'École *f* navale; **n. officer** officier *m* de marine

nave [neɪv] *n (of church)* nef *f*

navel ['neɪvəl] *n* nombril *m*

navigable ['nævɪgəbəl] *adj* navigable

navigate ['nævɪgeɪt] **1** *vt (seas)* naviguer sur; *(ship, plane)* piloter
  2 *vi (in ship, plane)* naviguer; *(in car)* faire le pilote

navigation [nævɪ'geɪʃən] *n* navigation *f*

navigational [nævɪ'geɪʃənəl] *adj* de navigation

navigator ['nævɪgeɪtə(r)] *n (in ship, plane)* navigateur(trice) *m,f*; *(in car)* copilote *m*

navvy ['nævɪ] *(pl* navvies*)* *n Br* terrassier *m*

navy ['neɪvɪ] *(pl* navies*)* *n* marine *f*; **n. (blue)** bleu marine *m inv*

Nazi ['nɑːtsɪ] **1** *n* Nazi(e) *m,f*
  2 *adj* nazi(e)

Nazism ['nɑːtsɪzəm] *n* nazisme *m*

NB [en'biː] *(abbr* nota bene*)* NB

NBA [enbiː'eɪ] *n Am (abbr* **National Basketball Association**) = fédération américaine de basket-ball

NCO [ensiː'əʊ] *n Mil (abbr* **non-commissioned officer**) sous-officier *m*

NE *(abbr* **northeast**) N-E

Neanderthal [nɪ'ændətɑːl] **1** *n (a) (during Stone Age)* homme *m* de Neanderthal **(b)** *Fig (uncivilized man)* homme *m* des cavernes
  2 *adj (a) (during Stone Age)* **N. man** homme *m* de Neanderthal **(b)** *Fig (attitude, behaviour)* d'homme des cavernes

Neapolitan [nɪə'pɒlɪtən] **1** *n* Napolitain(e) *m,f*
  2 *adj* napolitain(e)

near [nɪə(r)] **1** *adj* proche; **to the nearest metre** au mètre près; **in the n. future** dans un avenir proche; **it was a n. thing** il s'en est fallu de peu; **the N. East** le Proche-Orient
  2 *adv* près; **to be n. to sth** *(in space)* être près de qch; *(in time)* être proche de qch; **n. at hand** *(of thing)* tout près; *(of event)* tout proche; **to be n. to doing sth** être sur le point de faire qch; **n. to tears/despair** au bord des larmes/du désespoir; **she's nowhere n. finished** elle est loin d'avoir fini; **a n. total failure** un échec presque total
  3 *prep* près de; **he came n. to being run over** il a failli se faire écraser; **nobody comes anywhere n. her** *(in skill, performance)* il n'y a personne à son niveau
  4 *n Fam* **my nearest and dearest** mes plus proches parents
  5 *vt (s')* approcher de; **to be nearing completion** être presque terminé(e)

nearby 1 *adj* ['nɪəbaɪ] proche
  2 *adv* [nɪə'baɪ] tout près

nearly ['nɪəlɪ] *adv* presque; **we're n. there** *(finished)* nous y sommes presque; *(at destination)* nous sommes presque arrivés; **he n. died** il a failli mourir; **not n. enough money/time** vraiment pas assez d'argent/de temps; **not n. so beautiful** bien moins beau (belle)

nearly-new ['nɪəlɪ'njuː] *adj* = d'occasion mais en parfait état

nearside ['nɪəsaɪd] **1** *n (on right)* côté *m* droit; *(on left)* côté *m* gauche
  2 *adj (on right)* droit(e); *(on left)* gauche

near-sighted [nɪə'saɪtɪd] *adj Am* myope

neat [niːt] *adj (a) (in habits)* ordonné(e); *(in appearance)* soigné(e); *(work, handwriting)* soigné; *(room, house)* bien rangé(e); **to make a n. job of doing sth** faire qch très bien **(b)** *(undiluted)* pur(e) **(c)** *Am Fam (good)* super *inv*

▶**neaten up** ['niːtən] *vt sep (hair, garden)* arranger; *(piece of work)* peaufiner

neatly ['niːtlɪ] *adv (a) (carefully)* soigneusement **(b)** *(skilfully)* habilement, adroitement

neatness ['niːtnɪs] *n (of appearance)* aspect *m* soigné; *(of work)* soin *m*; *(of handwriting)* netteté *f*; *(of room, house)* ordre *m*

nebula ['nebjʊlə] *(pl* nebulas *or* nebulae ['nebjʊlaɪ]) *n Astron* nébuleuse *f*

nebulous ['nebjʊləs] *adj (vague)* nébuleux(euse)

necessarily [nesɪ'serəlɪ] *adv* nécessairement, forcément

necessary ['nesɪsərɪ] **1** *adj* nécessaire; **it is n. to remind them** il faut le leur rappeler; **to do what is n.** faire le nécessaire; **when(ever) n.** si nécessaire, si besoin est; **a n. evil** un mal nécessaire
  2 *n Fam* **the n.** *(thing, action)* le nécessaire; *(money)* l'argent

necessitate [nɪ'sesɪteɪt] *vt* nécessiter, rendre nécessaire

necessity [nɪ'sesɪtɪ] *(pl* necessities*)* *n* nécessité *f*; **out of n.** par nécessité; **the necessities** *(things needed)* le nécessaire; **n. is the mother of invention** en cas de besoin, on trouve toujours une solution; *Prov*

neck [nek] **1** *n (a) (of person, animal)* cou *m*; *(of dress)* encolure *f*, col *m*; *(of bottle)* goulot *m*; *(of guitar, violin)* manche *f*; *(of land)* langue *f*; *(of lamb, beef)* collier *m* **(b)** *(idioms) Fam* **to risk one's n.** risquer sa peau; *Fam* **he got it in the n.** il s'est pris un savon; *Fam* **he's in it up to his n.** il est impliqué là-dedans jusqu'au cou; *Fam* **to finish n. and n.** finir au coude à coude; *Fam* **to stick one's n. out** se lancer; *Fam* **in this n. of the woods** dans le coin
  2 *vi Fam (of couple)* se peloter

necklace ['neklɪs] *n* collier *m*

neckline ['neklaɪn] *n* encolure *f*

necromancy ['nekrəʊmænsɪ] *n Formal* nécromancie *f*

nectar ['nektə(r)] *n* nectar *m*

nectarine ['nektəriːn] *n* nectarine *f*, brugnon *m*

née [neɪ] *adj* née; **Mrs Richardson, n. Johnston** Mme Richardson, née Johnston

need [niːd] **1** *n* besoin *m* (for de); **there is no n. to shout/worry** inutile de crier/de t'inquiéter; **if n. be** en cas de besoin; **to be in n.** *(poor)* être dans le besoin; **to be in n. of sth** avoir besoin de qch; **in time of n.** dans les moments difficiles; **their n. is greater than mine** ils en ont plus besoin que moi
  2 *vt* **to n. sth/to do sth** avoir besoin de qch/de faire qch; **I n. more time** il me faut plus de temps; **you'll n. to take more money** il te faudra prendre plus d'argent, il faudra que tu prennes plus d'argent; **I didn't n. to be reminded of it** je n'avais pas besoin qu'on me le rappelle, il était inutile de me le rappeler; **his hair needs cutting** il a besoin d'une coupe de cheveux; **the torch needs a new battery** la lampe a besoin d'une nouvelle pile; **this work needs a lot of patience** ce travail demande beaucoup de patience; *Ironic* **that's all I n.!** il ne (me) manquait plus que ça!

3 *modal aux v*

> La forme modale de **need** est la même à toutes les personnes, et s'utilise sans **do/does** (**he need only worry about himself; need she go?; it needn't matter**).

you needn't worry inutile de t'inquiéter; **you needn't wait** tu n'as pas besoin d'attendre; **n. I say more?** ai-je besoin d'en dire plus?

needful ['ni:dfʊl] *n Fam* **to do the n.** faire le nécessaire

needle ['ni:dəl] **1** *n* aiguille *f*; **it's like looking for a n. in a haystack** c'est comme chercher une aiguille dans une botte de foin; *Fam Fig* **to give sb the n.** taper sur les nerfs de qn; *Fam* **n. match** *(in football)* match *m* acharné

2 *vt Fam* asticoter

needlecraft ['ni:dəlkrɑ:ft] *n* travaux *mpl* d'aiguille

needless ['ni:dlɪs] *adj (waste, suffering, worry)* inutile; *(remark)* déplacé(e); **n. to say...** il va de soi que...

needlessly ['ni:dlɪslɪ] *adv* inutilement

needlework ['ni:dəlwɜ:k] *n (sewing)* couture *f*; *(embroidery)* broderie *f*

need-to-know [ni:dtə'nəʊ] *adj* **information is given on a n. basis** les renseignements ne sont donnés qu'aux personnes concernées

needy ['ni:dɪ] **1** *npl* **the n.** les nécessiteux *mpl*

2 *adj (person)* nécessiteux(euse), dans le besoin

nefarious [nɪ'feərɪəs] *adj* infâme, ignoble

negate [nɪ'geɪt] *vt (effect)* annuler; *(work, efforts)* anéantir

negation [nɪ'geɪʃən] *n (of work, efforts)* anéantissement *m*

negative ['negətɪv] **1** *n* (**a**) *Gram* **the n.** la forme négative; **to answer in the n.** répondre par la négative (**b**) *(of photo)* négatif *m*

2 *adj* négatif(ive); **don't be so n.** ne sois pas si négatif; *Fin* **n. equity** plus-value *f* immobilière négative; **n. feedback** réaction *f* négative

negatively ['negətɪvlɪ] *adv* négativement

negativity [negə'tɪvɪtɪ] *n* négativité *f*

neglect [nɪ'glekt] **1** *n (of person)* négligence *f*; *(of machine, garden)* manque *m* d'entretien; *(of duties, responsibilities)* manquement *m*; **from** *or* **through n.** par négligence

2 *vt* (**a**) *(not care for)* négliger; **to n. oneself** se négliger (**b**) *(ignore)* *(duties, responsibilities)* manquer à; *(post)* abandonner; **to n. to do sth** négliger de faire qch

neglectful [nɪ'glektfʊl] *adj* négligent(e); **to be n. of sb/sth** négliger qn/qch

negligée ['neglɪʒeɪ] *n* négligé *m*, déshabillé *m*

negligence ['neglɪdʒəns] *n* négligence *f*; *(of duties, responsibilities)* manquement *m* (**of** à)

negligent ['neglɪdʒənt] *adj* négligent(e)

negligently ['neglɪdʒəntlɪ] *adv* négligemment

negligible ['neglɪdʒɪbəl] *adj* négligeable

negotiable [nɪ'gəʊʃəbəl] *adj (demand, salary)* négociable; *(price)* à débattre; *(obstacle)* franchissable; *(road)* praticable

negotiate [nɪ'gəʊʃɪeɪt] **1** *vt* (**a**) *(price, treaty, salary, contract)* négocier (**b**) *(obstacle)* franchir; *(difficulty)* surmonter; *(bend)* négocier

2 *vi* négocier

negotiation [nɪgəʊʃɪ'eɪʃən] *n* négociation *f*; **under n.** en négociation

negotiator [nɪ'gəʊʃɪeɪtə(r)] *n* négociateur(trice) *m,f*

Negress ['ni:grɪs] *n Old-fashioned* négresse *f*

Negro ['ni:grəʊ] *Old-fashioned* **1** *n (pl* **Negroes**) nègre *m*

2 *adj* nègre; **N. spiritual** *(song)* Negro spiritual *m*

neigh [neɪ] **1** *n* hennissement *m*

2 *vi* hennir

neighbor, neighborhood *etc Am* = **neighbour, neighbourhood** *etc*

neighbour, *Am* **neighbor** ['neɪbə(r)] *n* voisin(e) *m,f*; **to be a good n.** être bon voisin

neighbourhood, *Am* **neighborhood** ['neɪbəhʊd] *n* (**a**) *(district)* quartier *m*; *(people)* voisinage *m*; **N. watch** = système de surveillance mis en œuvre par les habitants d'un quartier (**b**) *(vicinity)* voisinage *m*, environs *mpl*; **in the n.** dans les environs; **a figure in the n. of £2,000** un chiffre avoisinant les 2000 livres

neighbouring, *Am* **neighboring** ['neɪbərɪŋ] *adj* voisin(e)

neighbourliness, *Am* **neighborliness** ['neɪbəlɪnɪs] *n* (relations *fpl* de) bon voisinage *m*

neighbourly, *Am* **neighborly** ['neɪbəlɪ] *adj* **they're very n.** ce sont de très bons voisins

neither ['naɪðə(r), 'ni:ðə(r)] **1** *conj* **n.... nor...** ni... ni...; **n. you nor your brother** ni toi ni ton frère; **he n. drinks nor smokes** il ne boit pas et ne fume pas non plus; *Fig* **that's n. here nor there** là n'est pas la question

2 *adv* **n. do I** moi non plus; **if you don't go n. shall I** si tu n'y vas pas, moi non plus; **the workers aren't happy and n. is the management** les ouvriers ne sont pas contents et la direction non plus

3 *adj* **n. driver was injured** aucun des deux conducteurs n'a été blessé

4 *pron* **n. (of them) will do** aucun (des deux) ne fera l'affaire; **n. of my two brothers can come** aucun de mes deux frères ne peut venir

neo- ['ni:əʊ] *pref* néo-

neoclassical [ni:əʊ'klæsɪkəl] *adj* néoclassique

neofascist [ni:əʊ'fæʃɪst] *n & adj* néofasciste *mf*

neolithic [ni:əʊ'lɪθɪk] *adj* néolithique

neon ['ni:ɒn] *n* néon *m*; **n. light** lumière *f* au néon; **n. sign** enseigne *f* au néon

Nepal [nɪ'pɔ:l] *n* le Népal

Nepalese [nepə'li:z], **Nepali** [ne'pɔ:lɪ] **1** *n (pl* **Nepalese** *or* **Nepalis**) (**a**) *(person)* Népalais(e) *m,f* (**b**) *(language)* népalais *m*

2 *adj* népalais(e)

nephew ['nefju:] *n* neveu *m*

nepotism ['nepətɪzəm] *n* népotisme *m*

Neptune ['neptju:n] *n (planet)* Neptune *f*

nerd [nɜ:d] *n Fam* crétin(e) *m,f*

nerve [nɜ:v] **1** *n* (**a**) *(in body)* nerf *m*; *Fam* **to get on sb's nerves** taper sur les nerfs à qn; **her nerves were in a terrible state** elle était à bout de nerfs; *Anat* **n. cell** cellule *f* nerveuse; *Fig* **n. centre** *(of organization)* centre *m* nerveux; **n. gas** gaz *m* neurotoxique (**b**) *(courage)* courage *m*; **to have nerves of steel** avoir des nerfs d'acier; **to keep/lose one's n.** garder/perdre son sang-froid (**c**) *Fam (cheek)* culot *m*; **to have the n. to do sth** avoir le culot de faire qch

2 *vt* **to n. oneself to do sth** s'armer de courage pour faire qch

nerve-(w)racking ['nɜ:vrækɪŋ] *adj* éprouvant(e)

nervous ['nɜ:vəs] *adj* (**a**) *(apprehensive)* nerveux(euse), anxieux(euse); **to be n. about sth/doing sth** être nerveux *ou* anxieux à l'idée de qch/de faire qch (**b**) *(energy, exhaustion)* nerveux(euse); **n. breakdown** dépression *f* nerveuse; **n. system** système *m* nerveux

nervously ['nɜːvəslɪ] adv nerveusement

nervousness ['nɜːvəsnɪs] n nervosité f

nervy ['nɜːvɪ] adj Fam (tense) nerveux(euse)

nest [nest] 1 n (of bird, insects) nid m; Fig (of criminals) repaire m; Fig to fly the n. quitter le nid; n. of tables tables fpl gigognes; Fig n. egg pécule m

2 vi (of bird) faire son nid

nestle ['nesəl] vi se pelotonner, se blottir; to n. up to sb se blottir contre qn

nestling ['neslɪŋ] n oisillon m

Net [net] n Fam Comptr the N. le Net

net¹ [net] 1 n filet m; Fig to slip through the n. passer à travers les mailles du filet; n. curtain voilage m

2 vt (pt & pp netted) (animals, fish) prendre au filet; Fig (drugs, criminals) mettre la main sur; (donations, contracts) récolter

net² 1 adj (weight, price, profit) net (nette)

2 vt (earn) to n. £2,000 gagner 2000 livres net

netball ['netbɔːl] n = sport féminin proche du basket-ball

Netherlands ['neðələndz] npl the N. les Pays-Bas mpl

netting ['netɪŋ] n filet m

nettle ['netəl] 1 n (plant) ortie f

2 vt (irritate) irriter, énerver

network ['netwɜːk] 1 n réseau m

2 vi (make contacts) établir un réseau de contacts

networking ['netwɜːkɪŋ] n (making contacts) établissement m d'un réseau de contacts

neural ['njʊərəl] adj Anat neural(e)

neuralgia [njʊˈrældʒə] n névralgie f

neurologist [njʊəˈrɒlədʒɪst] n neurologue mf

neurology [njʊəˈrɒlədʒɪ] n neurologie f

neuron ['njʊərɒn] n Anat neurone m

neurosis [njʊəˈrəʊsɪs] n (pl neuroses [njʊəˈrəʊsiːz]) n névrose f

neurosurgery ['njʊərəʊsɜːdʒərɪ] n neurochirurgie f

neurotic [njʊˈrɒtɪk] 1 n névrosé(e) m,f

2 adj névrosé(e); to be n. about sth être obsédé(e) par qch

neuter ['njuːtə(r)] 1 n Gram neutre m

2 adj Gram neutre

3 vt (animal) castrer, châtrer

neutral ['njuːtrəl] 1 n (a) (country) pays m neutre; (person) personne f neutre (b) (of car) point m mort; in n. au point mort

2 adj (country, colour) neutre

neutrality [njuːˈtrælɪtɪ] n neutralité f

neutralize ['njuːtrəlaɪz] vt neutraliser

neutrino [njuːˈtriːnəʊ] n (pl neutrinos) n Phys neutrino m

neutron ['njuːtrɒn] n Phys neutron m; n. bomb bombe f à neutrons

never ['nevə(r)] adv (a) (not once) jamais; I've n. met him je ne l'ai jamais rencontré; n. again! plus jamais!; he's n. yet been beaten il n'a encore jamais été battu; I've n. yet understood why je n'ai jamais compris pourquoi (b) (emphatic negative) she n. said a word elle n'a pas dit un mot; I n. expected this je ne m'attendais vraiment pas à ça; he n. even congratulated me il ne m'a même pas félicité; Fam well I n.! ça alors!

never-ending [nevərˈendɪŋ] adj interminable

never-never ['nevə'nevə(r)] n Br Fam to buy sth on the n. acheter qch à crédit

nevertheless [nevəðəˈles] adv néanmoins, cependant

new [njuː] adj nouveau(elle); (not used) neuf (neuve); what's n.? quoi de neuf?; that's nothing n.! ça n'est pas nouveau!; she's n. to this work elle débute dans ce travail; to be n. to a town être nouveau dans une ville; N. Age (music, thinking) new age inv; N. Brunswick le Nouveau-Brunswick; N. Caledonia la Nouvelle-Calédonie; N. Delhi New Delhi; N. England la Nouvelle-Angleterre; N. Guinea la Nouvelle-Guinée; N. Man homme m de la nouvelle génération; N. Mexico le Nouveau-Mexique; n. moon nouvelle lune f; N. Orleans la Nouvelle-Orléans; N. South Wales la Nouvelle-Galles du Sud; the N. Testament le Nouveau Testament; n. town ville f nouvelle; n. wave (trend) Nouvelle Vague f; the N. World le Nouveau Monde; N. Year Nouvel An m; N. Year's Day le jour de l'an; N. Year's Eve la Saint-Sylvestre; N. Year's resolution résolution f du jour de l'an; N. York New York; N. Yorker New-Yorkais(e) m,f

newborn ['njuːbɔːn] adj nouveau-né(e); n. baby nouveau-né(e) m,f

newcomer ['njuːkʌmə(r)] n nouveau(elle) venu(e) m,f (to dans)

newfangled [njuːˈfæŋgəld] adj Pej (idea) nouveau(elle); (gadget) dernier cri inv

Newfoundland ['njuːfəndlænd] n Terre-Neuve

newly ['njuːlɪ] adv nouvellement, récemment

newlyweds ['njuːlɪwedz] npl jeunes mariés mpl

newness ['njuːnɪs] n (of design) nouveauté f; (of clothing) état m neuf

news [njuːz] n nouvelles fpl; (on TV, radio) informations fpl; a piece of n. une nouvelle; in the n. sous les feux de l'actualité; Fam he's bad n. il n'est pas fréquentable; Fam that's n. to me! première nouvelle!; Prov no n. is good n. pas de nouvelles, bonnes nouvelles; n. agency agence f de presse; n. bulletin bulletin m d'informations; n. conference conférence f de presse; n. item information f, nouvelle f; n. summary rappel m des titres

newsagent ['njuːzeɪdʒənt] n Br marchand(e) m,f de journaux; n.'s (shop) marchand m de journaux

newscaster ['njuːzkɑːstə(r)] n présentateur(trice) m,f du journal

newsdealer ['njuːzdiːlə(r)] n Am marchand(e) m,f de journaux

newsflash ['njuːzflæʃ] n flash m d'informations

newsgroup ['njuːzgruːp] n Comptr newsgroup m

newsletter ['njuːzletə(r)] n bulletin m

newspaper ['njuːzpeɪpə(r)] n journal m; n. report reportage m

newspaperman ['njuːzpeɪpəmæn] n (reporter) journaliste m; (proprietor) propriétaire m d'un journal

newsprint ['njuːzprɪnt] n papier m journal

newsreader ['njuːzriːdə(r)] n présentateur(trice) m,f du journal

newsreel ['njuːzriːl] n actualités fpl

newsroom ['njuːzruːm] n (salle f de) rédaction f

newsstand ['njuːzstænd] n kiosque m à journaux

newsworthy ['njuːzwɜːðɪ] adj d'un intérêt médiatique

newt [njuːt] n triton m

New Zealand [njuːˈziːlənd] n la Nouvelle-Zélande

New Zealander [njuːˈziːləndə(r)] n Néo-Zélandais(e) m,f

next [nekst] **1** adj (a) (in space) d'à côté; **n. door** à côté (b) (in time, order) prochain(e); (subsequent) suivant(e), d'après; **n. week** la semaine prochaine; **the n. week** la semaine suivante ou d'après; **the year after n.** pas l'année prochaine, celle d'après; **the n. time** la prochaine fois; **your name is n. on the list** votre nom est le suivant sur la liste; **the n. but one** pas le prochain, mais celui d'après; **(the) n. to arrive was Carmen** Carmen est arrivée ensuite; **who's n.?** c'est à qui?; **n. please!** au suivant!; **the n. size up/down** la taille au-dessus/au-dessous

2 adv (a) (in space) **n. to** à côté de (b) (in time, order) ensuite, après; Fam **what will they think of n.?** qu'est-ce qu'ils vont encore inventer?; **n. to Paris I like Madrid best** après Paris, la ville que je préfère, c'est Madrid; **when shall we meet n.?** quand nous reverrons-nous?; **the n. best thing would be to...** à défaut, le mieux serait de...; **the n. fastest after the Ferrari was...** la voiture la plus rapide après la Ferrari était...; **who is the n. oldest/youngest after Mark?** qui est le plus âgé/le plus jeune après Mark?; **n. to nothing** quasiment rien; **there is n. to no evidence** il n'y a pratiquement aucune preuve; **in n. to no time** en un rien de temps

next-door ['neks'dɔ:(r)] adj d'à côté; **n. neighbour** voisin(e) m,f d'à côté

next-of-kin [nekstəv'kın] n plus proche parent m

NFL [enef'el] n Am (abbr **National Football League**) = fédération nationale de football américain

NGO [endʒi:'əʊ] n (abbr **non-governmental organization**) ONG f

NHS [enetʃ'es] n Br (abbr **National Health Service**) = système de santé britannique

NI [en'aı] n Br (abbr **National Insurance**) contributions fpl sociales

nib [nıb] n plume f

nibble ['nıbəl] **1** n **to have a n. at sth** grignoter qch; **nibbles** (snacks) amuse-gueule mpl
2 vt grignoter

Nicaragua [nıkə'rægjʊə] n le Nicaragua

Nicaraguan [nıkə'rægjʊən] **1** n Nicaraguayen(enne) m,f
2 adj nicaraguayen(enne)

nice [naıs] adj (a) (pleasant) agréable; (physically attractive) beau (belle); (tasty) bon (bonne); **a n. idea** une bonne idée; **to be n. to sb** se montrer aimable avec qn; **to have a n. time** bien s'amuser; **have a n. day!** bonne journée!; **it was n. of her to...** c'était gentil de sa part de...; Ironic **that's a n. way to behave!** en voilà des manières! (b) (intensive) **n. and easy** très facile; **n. and handy** bien commode; **a n. warm bath** un bain bien chaud

nice-looking ['naıslʊkıŋ] adj beau (belle)

nicely ['naıslı] adv (ask) gentiment; (behave, sit) bien; **to be doing n.** aller bien; **to do n. for oneself** bien se débrouiller

niceties ['naısıtız] npl subtilités fpl

niche [ni:ʃ] n (in wall) niche f; (in market) créneau m; **to find one's n.** (in life) trouver sa voie

nick [nık] **1** n (a) (in wood, on face) entaille f (b) **in the n. of time** juste à temps (c) Fam (condition) **in good/bad n.** en bon/mauvais état (d) Br Fam (prison) taule f; (police station) poste m
2 vt (a) (cut) entailler (b) Br Fam (arrest) pincer, épingler (c) Br Fam (steal) piquer, faucher

nickel ['nıkəl] n (a) (metal) nickel m (b) Am (coin) pièce f de cinq cents

nickname ['nıkneım] **1** n surnom m
2 vt surnommer

nicotine ['nıkəti:n] n nicotine f

niece [ni:s] n nièce f

niff [nıf] Br Fam **1** n (bad smell) puanteur f
2 vi (smell bad) puer

nifty ['nıftı] adj Fam (a) (idea, device) génial(e) (b) (agile) vif (vive)

Niger ['naıdʒə] n le Niger

Nigeria [naı'dʒıərıə] n le Nigéria

Nigerian [naı'dʒıərıən] **1** n Nigérian(e) m,f
2 adj nigérian(e)

niggardly ['nıgədlı] adj (person) avare, pingre; (sum, portion) maigre

nigger ['nıgə(r)] n nègre (négresse) m,f, = terme raciste désignant un Noir

niggle ['nıg(ə)l] **1** vt (worry) tracasser
2 vi (be overfussy) couper les cheveux en quatre; **to n. (away) at sb** (worry) tracasser qn; (hassle) enquiquiner qn

niggling ['nıgəlıŋ] adj (detail) insignifiant(e); (pain, doubt) persistant(e); **I have a n. feeling that...** je ne peux pas m'empêcher de penser que...

nigh [naı] adv Lit (near) près, proche; **the end is n.!** la fin est proche! (b) **well n.** (almost) presque

night [naıt] n nuit f; (evening) soir m; **at n.** la nuit; (in the evening) le soir; **late at n.** tard dans la nuit; **all n.** toute la nuit; **last n.** la nuit dernière; (evening) hier soir; **tomorrow n.** demain soir; **on Thursday n.** jeudi soir; **good n.!** (when going to bed) bonne nuit!, bonsoir!; (when leaving) bonsoir!; **to work nights** travailler la nuit; **to have a n. out** sortir; **let's make a n. of it** et si on continuait la soirée?; **n. flight** vol m de nuit; **n. owl** oiseau m de nuit; **n. school** cours m du soir; **n. watchman** veilleur m de nuit

nightcap ['naıtkæp] n (a) (hat) bonnet m de nuit (b) (drink) petit verre m (avant d'aller se coucher)

nightclub ['naıtklʌb] n boîte f de nuit

nightdress ['naıtdres] n chemise f de nuit

nightfall ['naıtfɔ:l] n tombée f de la nuit; **at n.** à la nuit tombante

nightgown ['naıtgaʊn] n chemise f de nuit

nightie ['naıtı] n Fam chemise f de nuit

nightingale ['naıtıŋgeıl] n rossignol m

nightjar ['naıtdʒɑ:(r)] n engoulevent m (d'Europe)

nightlife ['naıtlaıf] n vie f nocturne; **there's not much n.** il n'y a pas grand-chose à faire le soir

nightlong ['naıtlɒŋ] adj qui dure toute la nuit

nightly ['naıtlı] **1** adj de toutes les nuits; (in the evening) du soir
2 adv toutes les nuits; (in the evening) tous les soirs

nightmare ['naıtmeə(r)] n also Fig cauchemar m

nightmarish ['naıtmeərıʃ] adj cauchemardesque

nightshirt ['naıtʃɜ:t] n chemise f de nuit

night-time ['naıttaım] **1** n nuit f; **at n.** la nuit
2 adj nocturne

nihilistic [naı(h)ı'lıstık] adj nihiliste

nil [nıl] n néant m; (in sport) zéro m; **two n.** deux à zéro

Nile [naıl] n **the N.** le Nil

nimble ['nımbəl] adj (person) souple; (leap, movement) leste; (fingers) preste; (mind) vif (vive)

nimbly ['nımblı] adv avec souplesse

nincompoop ['nɪŋkəmpuːp] n Fam nigaud(e) m,f

nine [naɪn] 1 n neuf m X inv; Fam **dressed up to the nines** sur son trente et un
2 adj neuf; n. **times out of ten** neuf fois sur dix; **a n.-to-five job** un travail de bureau; **to have n. lives** (of person) avoir l'âme chevillée au corps; see also **eight**

nineteen [naɪn'tiːn] 1 n dix-neuf m X inv; Br Fam **to talk n. to the dozen** bavarder comme une pie
2 adj dix-neuf; see also **eight**

nineteenth [naɪn'tiːnθ] 1 n (a) (fraction) dix-neuvième m (b) (in series) dix-neuvième mf (c) (of month) dix-neuf m inv
2 adj dix-neuvième; Fam Hum **the n. hole** (of golf course) le bar du golf; see also **eighth**

ninetieth ['naɪntɪθ] 1 n (a) (fraction) quatre-vingt-dixième m (b) (in series) quatre-vingt-dixième mf
2 adj quatre-vingt-dixième; see also **eighth**

ninety ['naɪntɪ] 1 n quatre-vingt-dix m inv
2 adj quatre-vingt-dix; n. **nine times out of a hundred** quatre-vingt-dix-neuf fois sur cent; see also **eighty**

ninth [naɪnθ] 1 n (a) (fraction) neuvième m (b) (in series) neuvième m (c) (of month) neuf m inv
2 adj neuvième; see also **eighth**

nip [nɪp] 1 n (a) (pinch) pincement m; (bite) morsure f légère (b) (of cold, frost) **there's a n. in the air** il fait frisquet (c) Fam (of drink) petit verre m
2 (pt & pp nipped) vt (a) (pinch) pincer; (bite) mordre légèrement; Fam Fig **to n. sth in the bud** étouffer qch dans l'œuf (b) (of cold, frost) pincer, piquer
3 vi (sting) piquer

▶**nip out** vi Br Fam sortir quelques instants; **to n. out to the supermarket/pub** faire un saut au supermarché/au pub

nipper ['nɪpə(r)] n Br Fam (child) gamin(e) m,f

nipple ['nɪp(ə)l] n mamelon m; (on baby's bottle) tétine f

nippy ['nɪpɪ] adj Fam (a) (person, car) rapide (b) (cold) vif (vive); **it's a bit n. today** il fait plutôt frisquet aujourd'hui

nit [nɪt] n (a) (in hair) lente f; **to have nits** avoir des poux (b) Br Fam (person) nigaud(e) m,f

nit-picker ['nɪtpɪkə(r)] n Fam chipoteur(euse) m,f

nit-picking ['nɪtpɪkɪŋ] Fam 1 n chipotage m
2 adj chipoteur(euse)

nitrate ['naɪtreɪt] n nitrate m

nitric ['naɪtrɪk] adj nitrique

nitrogen ['naɪtrədʒən] n azote m

nitroglycerine ['naɪtrəʊ'glɪsəriːn] n nitroglycérine f

nitrous ['naɪtrəs] adj nitreux(euse)

nitty-gritty ['nɪtɪ'grɪtɪ] n Fam **to get down to the n.** entrer dans le vif du sujet

nitwit ['nɪtwɪt] n Fam crétin(e) m,f

NNE (abbr north-northeast) NNE

NNW (abbr north-northwest) NNO

No, no (abbr number) no

no [nəʊ] 1 n (pl noes or nos) non m; **she won't take no for an answer** elle n'accepte pas qu'on lui dise non
2 adj (a) (not any) pas de; **there's no bread** il n'y a pas de pain; **of no importance** sans importance; **I am in no way surprised** je ne suis pas du tout surpris; **he's no friend of mine** je ne le compte certainement pas au nombre de mes amis; Fam **no way!** pas question!
(b) (with gerund) **there's no denying it** on ne peut pas le nier; **there's no pleasing him** il n'est jamais satisfait; **no smoking** (sign) interdiction de fumer
3 adv (a) (interjection) non

(b) (not any) **no richer/poorer** pas plus riche/pauvre; **no more/less than £100** pas plus/moins de 100 livres; **he no longer lives there** il n'habite plus là

Noah ['nəʊə] n Noé; N.'s ark l'arche f de Noé

nobble ['nɒbəl] vt Br Fam (a) (bribe) payer (b) (waylay) coincer

Nobel Prize [nəʊ'bel'praɪz] n prix m Nobel

nobility [nəʊ'bɪlɪtɪ] n noblesse f

noble ['nəʊbəl] 1 n noble mf
2 adj noble; Fig (building) majestueux(euse)

nobleman ['nəʊbəlmən] n noble m

nobleminded [nəʊbəl'maɪndɪd] adj (person) au cœur noble, magnanime; (sentiment, action) noble

noblewoman ['nəʊbəlwʊmən] n noble f

nobly ['nəʊbəlɪ] adv avec noblesse

nobody ['nəʊbədɪ] 1 pron personne m; **n. spoke to me** personne ne m'a parlé; **n. else** personne d'autre; **she's n.'s fool** elle n'est pas née de la dernière pluie; **if you don't have money, you're n.** si on n'a pas d'argent on est un moins que rien
2 n (pl nobodies) **a n.** un(e) moins que rien

no-claims bonus ['nəʊ'kleɪmz'bəʊnəs] n bonus m

nocturnal [nɒk'tɜːnəl] adj nocturne

nod [nɒd] 1 n (in greeting, as signal) signe m de tête; (in agreement) signe de tête affirmatif; Fig **to give sb/sth the n.** donner le feu vert à qn/qch
2 vt (pt & pp nodded) **to n. one's head** (in greeting, as signal) faire un signe de tête; (in agreement) faire oui de la tête; **to n. one's agreement/approval** consentir/ approuver d'un signe de tête
3 vi **to n. in agreement/approval** consentir/approuver d'un signe de tête

▶**nod off** vi Fam s'assoupir

node [nəʊd] n (of curve, plant) nœud m; Med ganglion m; Comptr noyau m

nodule ['nɒdjuːl] n nodule m

no-frills [nəʊ'frɪlz] adj tout(e) simple

no-go area ['nəʊ'gəʊ] adj zone f interdite

no-good ['nəʊgʊd] adj Fam **a n. idiot** un imbécile propre à rien; **that n. husband of hers** son bon à rien de mari

no-hoper [nəʊ'həʊpə(r)] n tocard(e) m,f

noise [nɔɪz] n bruit m; Fig **to make noises about doing sth** parler de faire qch; Fig **a big n.** une huile

noiselessly ['nɔɪzlɪslɪ] adv sans bruit, silencieusement

noisily ['nɔɪzɪlɪ] adv bruyamment

noisy ['nɔɪzɪ] adj bruyant(e)

nomad ['nəʊmæd] n & adj nomade mf

nomadic [nəʊ'mædɪk] adj nomade

no man's land ['nəʊmænz'lænd] n Fig no man's land m

nomenclature [nəʊ'menklətʃə(r)] n nomenclature f

nominal ['nɒmɪnəl] adj nominal(e); (damages) symbolique; (rent) insignifiant(e)

nominally ['nɒmɪnəlɪ] adv nominalement

nominate ['nɒmɪneɪt] vt (propose) proposer (for/as pour/comme); (appoint) nommer (to/as à/comme)

nomination [nɒmɪ'neɪʃən] n (a) (proposal) candidature f; (for film, TV awards) nomination f (b) (appointment) nomination f

nominee [nɒmɪ'niː] n (proposed) candidat(e) m,f; (appointed) personne f nommée

non- [nɒn] *pref* non(-)

non-aggression pact [nɒnə'greʃən'pækt] *n Pol* pacte *m* de non-agression

nonalcoholic [nɒnælkə'hɒlɪk] *adj* sans alcool

nonaligned [nɒnə'laɪnd] *adj Pol* non-aligné(e)

nonattendance [nɒnə'tendəns] *n* absence *f*

nonchalance ['nɒnʃələns] *n* désinvolture *f*

nonchalant ['nɒnʃələnt] *adj* désinvolte

nonchalantly [nɒnʃə'lɑntlɪ] *adv* avec désinvolture

noncombatant [nɒn'kɒmbətənt] *n & adj Mil* non-combattant(e) *m,f*

noncommissioned officer ['nɒnkə'mɪʃənd-'ɒfɪsə(r)] *n Mil* sous-officier *m*

noncommittal [nɒnkə'mɪtəl] *adj* (*answer*) de Normand; **to be n.** ne pas s'engager

nonconformist [nɒnkən'fɔːmɪst] *n & adj* non-conformiste *mf*

nondescript ['nɒndɪskrɪpt] *adj* banal(e); (*colour*) fade

none [nʌn] **1** *pron* aucun(e) *m,f*; **n. of you/us** aucun d'entre vous/nous; **n. of my friends** aucun de mes amis; **n. of this concerns me** rien de tout cela ne me concerne; **it was n. other than the President** c'était le Président, rien de moins; **there was/were n. left** il n'en restait plus; *Fam* **we'll have n. of that!** pas de ça!

2 *adv* **his answer left me n. the wiser** sa réponse ne m'a pas avancé; **n. too happy** pas très satisfait(e); **n. too soon** pas trop tôt

nonentity [nɒ'nentɪtɪ] (*pl* **nonentities**) *n* personne *f* sans intérêt

nonessential [nɒnɪ'senʃəl] *adj* qui n'est pas essentiel(elle)

nonetheless [nʌnðə'les] *adv* néanmoins, cependant

nonevent [nɒnɪ'vent] *n* **to be a n.** être décevant(e)

nonexecutive director [nɒnɪg'zekjʊtɪvdaɪ'rektə(r)] *n* = administrateur à titre consultatif

nonexistent [nɒnɪg'zɪstənt] *adj* inexistant(e)

non-fiction [nɒn'fɪkʃən] *n* ouvrages *mpl* généraux

nonflammable [nɒn'flæməbəl] *adj* ininflammable

non-linear [nɒn'lɪnɪə(r)] *adj Comptr* non linéaire

non-negotiable [nɒn'gəʊʃəbəl] *adj* non négociable

non-nuclear [nɒn'njuːklɪə(r)] *adj* (*country*) non nucléarisé(e); (*war, defence*) non nucléaire

no-no ['nəʊnəʊ] (*pl* **no-nos** *or* **no-noes**) *n Fam* **that's a n.** c'est à ne pas faire

no-nonsense [nəʊ'nɒnsəns] *adj* direct(e)

non-partisan [nɒn'pɑːtɪzæn] *adj* impartial(e)

non-payment [nɒn'peɪmənt] *n* non-paiement *m*

non-person ['nɒn'pɜːsən] *n* proscrit(e) *m,f*

nonplussed [nɒn'plʌst] *adj* interloqué(e)

non-profit-making [nɒn'prɒfɪtmeɪkɪŋ] *adj* à but non lucratif

non-racist [nɒn'reɪsɪst] *adj* non raciste

nonresident [nɒn'rezɪdənt] *n* (*of country*) non-résident(e) *m,f*; (*of hotel*) client(e) *m,f*

nonreturnable [nɒnrɪ'tɜːnəbəl] *adj* (*bottle*) non consigné(e); (*deposit*) non remboursable

nonsense ['nɒnsəns] *n* bêtises *fpl*, idioties *fpl*, **n.!** n'importe quoi!; **to talk (a lot of) n.** dire des bêtises; **to make a n. of sth** ôter tout sens à qch

nonsensical [nɒn'sensɪkəl] *adj* absurde, qui n'a pas de sens

non sequitur [nɒn'sekwɪtə(r)] *n* absurdité *f*

non-sexist [nɒn'seksɪst] *adj* non sexiste

non-smoker [nɒn'sməʊkə(r)] *n* non-fumeur(euse) *m,f*; (*train compartment*) compartiment *m* non-fumeurs

non-specialist [nɒn'speʃəlɪst] **1** *n* non-spécialiste *mf*

2 *adj* non spécialisé(e)

nonstarter [nɒn'stɑːtə(r)] *n* **to be a n.** (*of plan*) être fichu(e) d'avance

nonstick ['nɒn'stɪk] *adj* (*surface*) anti-adhésif(ive); (*frying pan*) qui n'attache pas

non-stop ['nɒn'stɒp] **1** *adj* (*journey*) sans arrêt; (*flight*) sans escale

2 *adv* sans arrêt; (*fly*) sans escale

non-tariff barrier ['nɒn'tærɪf'bærɪə(r)] *n Econ* barrière *f* non tarifaire

nontransferable ['nɒntræns'fɜːrəbəl] *adj* (*ticket, membership*) nominatif(ive); (*property, right*) incessible

nonverbal [nɒn'vɜːbəl] *adj* non-verbal(e)

nonviolent [nɒn'vaɪələnt] *adj* non-violent(e)

noodles ['nuːdəlz] *npl* nouilles *fpl*

nook [nʊk] *n* (*corner*) recoin *m*; (*retreat*) coin *m*; **every n. and cranny** le moindre recoin

nookie, nooky ['nʊkɪ] *n very Fam* crac-crac *m*

noon [nuːn] *n* midi *m*; **at n.** à midi

noonday ['nuːndeɪ] *n Lit* midi *m*; **the n. sun** le soleil de midi

no-one ['nəʊwʌn] = **nobody**

noose [nuːs] *n* nœud *m* coulant; *Fig* **to put one's head in a n.** signer son arrêt de mort

nope [nəʊp] *adv Fam* non

nor [nɔː(r)] **1** *conj* **neither you n. your brother** ni toi ni ton frère; **neither... n.** ni... ni; **he neither drinks n. smokes** il ne boit pas et ne fume pas non plus

2 *adv* **n. do I** moi non plus; **if you don't go n. shall I** si tu n'y vas pas, moi non plus

Nordic ['nɔːdɪk] *adj* nordique

norm [nɔːm] *n* norme *f*

normal ['nɔːməl] **1** *n* **above/below n.** (*temperature, rate*) au-dessus/au-dessous de la normale; **to get back to n.** redevenir normal(e)

2 *adj* normal(e)

normality [nɔː'mælɪtɪ, *Am* **normalcy** ['nɔːməlsɪ] *n* normalité *f*; **a return to n.** un retour à la normale

normalization [nɔːməlaɪ'zeɪʃən] *n* normalisation *f*

normalize ['nɔːməlaɪz] **1** *vt* normaliser

2 *vi* redevenir normal(e)

normally ['nɔːməlɪ] *adv* normalement

Norman ['nɔːmən] **1** *n* Normand(e) *m,f*

2 *adj* normand(e)

Normandy ['nɔːməndɪ] *n* la Normandie

north [nɔːθ] **1** *n* nord *m*; **to the n. (of)** au nord (de)

2 *adj* (*coast, side*) nord; (*wind*) du nord; **N. Africa** Afrique *f* du Nord; **N. African** nord-africain(e); (*person*) Nord-Africain(e) *m,f*; **N. America** Amérique *f* du Nord; **N. American** nord-américain(e); (*person*) Nord-Américain(e) *m,f*; **N. Carolina** la Caroline du Nord; **N. Dakota** le Dakota du Nord; **N. Korea** Corée *f* du Nord; **N. Korean** nord-coréen(enne); (*person*) Nord-Coréen(enne) *m,f*; **the N. Pole** le Pôle Nord; **the N. Sea** la mer du Nord

3 *adv* au nord; (*travel*) vers le nord; **to face n.** (*of house*) être exposé(e) au nord

northbound ['nɔ:θbaʊnd] *adj (train, traffic)* en direction du nord; n. **carriageway** voie *f* nord

northeast [nɔ:θ'i:st] **1** *n* nord-est *m*
  2 *adj (side) (wind)* du nord-est
  3 *adv* au nord-est; *(travel)* vers le nord-est

northeasterly [nɔ:θ'i:stəlɪ] **1** *n (wind)* vent *m* du nord-est
  2 *adj (direction)* vers le nord-est; *(wind)* du nord-est

northeastern [nɔ:θ'i:stən] *adj (region)* (du) nord-est

northerly ['nɔ:ðəlɪ] **1** *n (pl **northerlies**) (wind)* vent *m* du nord
  2 *adj (direction)* vers le nord; *(wind)* du nord; **the most n. point** le point le plus au nord

northern ['nɔ:ðən] *adj (region, accent)* du nord; **n. France** le nord de la France; **n. hemisphere** hémisphère *m* nord; **N. Ireland** l'Irlande *f* du Nord; **N. Irish** de l'Irlande du Nord; **the N. Irish** les Irlandais *mpl* du Nord; **N. Lights** aurore *f* boréale

northerner ['nɔ:ðərə(r)] *n* habitant(e) *m,f* du Nord *(de l'Angleterre)*

north-facing [nɔ:θ'feɪsɪŋ] *adj* exposé(e) au nord

north-northeast [nɔ:θnɔ:θ'i:st] *adv* au nord-nord-est; *(travel)* vers le nord-nord-est

north-northwest [nɔ:θnɔ:θ'west] *adv* au nord-nord-ouest; *(travel)* vers le nord-nord-ouest

northward ['nɔ:θwəd] **1** *adj* au nord
  2 *adv* vers le nord

northwards ['nɔ:θwədz] *adv* vers le nord

northwest [nɔ:θ'west] **1** *n* nord-ouest *m*
  2 *adj (side) (wind)* du nord-ouest
  3 *adv* au nord-ouest; *(travel)* vers le nord-ouest

northwesterly [nɔ:θ'westəlɪ] **1** *n (pl **northwesterlies**) (wind)* vent *m* du nord-ouest
  2 *adj (direction)* vers le nord-ouest; *(wind)* du nord-ouest

northwestern [nɔ:θ'westən] *adj (region)* (du) nord-ouest

North-West Territories ['nɔ:θ'west'terɪtri:z] *npl* les Territoires *mpl* du Nord-Ouest

Norway ['nɔ:weɪ] *n* la Norvège

Norwegian [nɔ:'wi:dʒən] **1** *n* (a) *(person)* Norvégien(enne) *m,f* (b) *(language)* norvégien *m*
  2 *adj* norvégien(enne)

nose [nəʊz] *n* (a) *(of person, animal, aeroplane)* nez *m*; her **n. is bleeding** elle saigne du nez; **to blow one's n.** se moucher (le nez); **to hold one's n.** se boucher le nez; *Fam* **to have a n. job** se faire refaire le nez; **the traffic was n. to tail** les voitures se suivaient pare-chocs contre pare-chocs (b) *(idioms)* **it's under your n.** vous l'avez sous le nez; **to turn one's n. up at sth** dédaigner qch; **she walked by with her n. in the air** elle passa, l'air dédaigneux; **to look down one's n. at sb** prendre qn de haut; **to pay through the n. for sth** payer qch une fortune; **to get up sb's n.** taper sur les nerfs à qn; **to lead sb by the n.** mener qn par le bout du nez; **to keep one's n. clean** se tenir à carreau; **to have a n. for sth** savoir flairer qch; **to poke one's n. into other people's business** fourrer son nez dans les affaires des autres

▶**nose about, nose around** *vi Fam* fouiner

nosebleed ['nəʊzbli:d] *n* **to have a n.** saigner du nez

nose-dive ['nəʊzdaɪv] **1** *n (of plane)* (vol *m* en) piqué *m*; *Fig (of prices)* chute *f* rapide
  2 *vi (of plane)* piquer du nez; *Fig (of prices)* chuter fortement

nosey ['nəʊzɪ] *adj Fam* fouineur(euse); *(questions)* indiscret(ète); *Br* **n. parker** fouineur(euse) *m,f*

nosh [nɒʃ] *Fam* **1** *n (food)* bouffe *f*
  2 *vi (eat)* bouffer

no-show [nəʊ'ʃəʊ] *n* défection *f*

nosiness ['nəʊzɪnəs] *n* curiosité *f*

no-smoking [nəʊ'sməʊkɪŋ] *adj (carriage, area)* non-fumeurs; *(seat)* non-fumeur

nostalgia [nɒs'tældʒə] *n* nostalgie *f*

nostalgic [nɒs'tældʒɪk] *adj* nostalgique

nostalgically [nɒs'tældʒɪklɪ] *adv* avec nostalgie

nostril ['nɒstrɪl] *n* narine *f*

nosy ['nəʊzɪ] = **nosey**

not [nɒt] *adv*

> À l'oral, et à l'écrit dans un style familier, on utilise généralement **not** à la forme contractée lorsqu'il suit un modal ou un auxiliaire (**don't go!**; **she wasn't there**; **he couldn't see me**).

n. me/him pas moi/lui; **I don't know** je ne sais pas; **don't move!** ne bouge pas!; **whether she likes it or n.** que ça lui plaise ou non; **I think/hope n.** je pense/ j'espère que non; **she asked me n.** to tell him elle m'a demandé de ne pas le lui dire; **n. wishing to cause an argument,** he said nothing ne voulant pas provoquer de dispute, il s'est tu; **you understand, don't you?** tu comprends, n'est-ce pas?; **n. at all** pas du tout; *(you're welcome)* je vous en prie; **n. any more** plus maintenant; **n. even** pas même, même pas; **n. only..., but also...** non seulement..., mais encore...; **n. yet** pas encore; **n. that I minded** non pas que ça me dérangeait; **n. that it matters** non pas que ça ait de l'importance; **n. that I know of** pas que je sache

notable ['nəʊtəbəl] *adj (person, thing)* notable; *(achievement, success)* remarquable; **with a few n. exceptions** à quelques exceptions près, et non des moindres

notably ['nəʊtəblɪ] *adv* notamment

notary ['nəʊtərɪ] *(pl **notaries**) n Law* **n. (public)** notaire *m*

notation [nəʊ'teɪʃən] *n* notation *f*

notch [nɒtʃ] **1** *n* (a) *(in stick)* encoche *f*; *(in belt)* cran *m* (b) *(grade, level)* cran *m*
  2 *vt* encocher

▶**notch up** *vt sep (victory, sale)* remporter; *(points)* marquer

note [nəʊt] **1** *n* (a) *(information, reminder)* note *f*; *(short letter)* mot *m*; *(lecture)* **notes** notes (de cours); **to take or make a n. of sth** prendre note de qch; **to take n. of sb/ sth** remarquer qn/qch (b) *(musical)* note *f*; *Fig (of impatience, anger)* pointe *f*; **on a lighter/more serious n.** pour en venir à un sujet moins/plus sérieux (c) *(banknote)* billet *m* (d) *(significance)* **of n.** remarquable
  2 *vt* noter, remarquer; *(error)* relever; *(fact)* constater

▶**note down** *vt sep* prendre note de, noter

notebook ['nəʊtbʊk] *n* carnet *m*; *(larger)* cahier *m*; *Comptr* agenda *m*

noted ['nəʊtɪd] *adj* éminent(e); **to be n. for sth** être réputé(e) pour qch

notepad ['nəʊtpæd] *n* bloc-notes *m*

notepaper ['nəʊtpeɪpə(r)] *n* papier *m* à lettres

noteworthy ['nəʊtwɜ:ðɪ] *adj* remarquable

nothing ['nʌθɪŋ] 1 *pron* rien; n. happened il ne s'est rien passé; **I have n. to do** je n'ai rien à faire; **to have n. to do with sb/sth** *(be unconnected to)* n'avoir rien à voir avec qn/qch; *(not get involved with)* n'avoir rien à faire avec qn/qch; **to say n. of...** sans parler de...; **she was n. if not discreet** elle a été très discrète; **n. new/ remarkable** rien de nouveau/d'exceptionnel; **n. but** rien que; **n. else** rien d'autre; **n. much** pas grand-chose; **there is n. more to be said** il n'y a plus rien à dire; **there's n. like a nice steak!** rien de tel qu'un bon steak!; **as a pianist, he has n. on his brother** en tant que pianiste, son frère n'a rien à lui envier; **there's n. in it** *(it's untrue)* il n'y a rien de vrai dans tout ça; **to think n. of doing sth** trouver normal de faire qch; *Fam* **there's n. to it** ce n'est pas sorcier; **£1,000 is n. to her** 1000 livres, ce n'est rien pour elle; **to get angry/worried for or about n.** se fâcher/s'inquiéter pour un rien; **to do sth for n.** *(in vain, free of charge)* faire qch pour rien

2 *n* **to come to n.** être anéanti(e); **a hundred pounds? - a mere n.!** cent livres? - une bagatelle!

3 *adv* **she looks n. like her sister** elle ne ressemble pas du tout à sa sœur; **it was n. like as difficult as they said** c'était loin d'être aussi difficile qu'on le disait

notice ['nəʊtɪs] 1 *n* **(a)** *(warning)* avertissement *m*; *(of resignation, redundancy)* préavis *m*; **to give sb n.** *(of sth)* avertir qn (de qch); *(of resignation, redundancy)* donner un préavis à qn (pour qch); **until further n.** jusqu'à nouvel ordre; **at short n.** au pied levé; **at a moment's n.** sur-le-champ; **to give in one's n.** *(resign)* donner sa démission, démissionner; **to give sb n.** *(of employer)* licencier qn **(b)** *(attention)* **to take n. of sb/sth** faire *ou* prêter attention à qn/qch; **to take no n. of sb/sth** ne pas prêter la moindre attention à qn/qch; **the fact escaped everyone's n.** ce fait a échappé à tout le monde; **it has come to my n. that...** *(I was told)* on m'a signalé que...; *(I read it)* je me suis rendu compte que... **(c)** *(sign)* écriteau *m*, pancarte *f*; *(poster)* affiche *f* **(d)** *(criticism of play, film)* critique *f*

2 *vt* remarquer, s'apercevoir de; **to be noticed, to get oneself noticed** se faire remarquer

3 *vi* remarquer

noticeable ['nəʊtɪsəbəl] *adj (change, difference)* sensible, perceptible; **it was n. that...** il était évident que...

noticeably ['nəʊtɪsəbli] *adv* sensiblement

noticeboard ['nəʊtɪsbɔːd] *n* panneau *m* d'affichage

notification [nəʊtɪfɪ'keɪʃən] *n* avis *m*, notification *f*; **to give sb n. of sth** notifier qch à qn

notify ['nəʊtɪfaɪ] *(pt & pp* **notified**) *vt* annoncer, notifier; **to n. sb of sth** avertir qn de qch

notion ['nəʊʃən] *n* notion *f*; **to have a n. that...** avoir dans l'idée que...; **to have a n. to do sth** avoir envie de faire qch

notoriety [nəʊtə'raɪətɪ] *n* notoriété *f*; **to achieve** *or* **gain n.** se rendre célèbre

notorious [nəʊ'tɔːrɪəs] *adj* tristement célèbre; *(criminal)* notoire; *(place)* mal famé(e); *(liar)* fieffé(e)

notoriously [nəʊ'tɔːrɪəslɪ] *adv* **to be n. tactless/rude** être bien connu(e) pour son manque de tact/son impolitesse; **Scottish weather is n. unpredictable** il est bien connu qu'en Écosse, le temps est très changeant

notwithstanding [nɒtwɪθ'stændɪŋ] *Formal* **1** *prep* en dépit de, malgré

2 *adv* néanmoins; **difficulties n.,...** ces difficultés mises à part,...

nougat ['nuːgɑː] *n* nougat *m*

nought [nɔːt] *n* zéro *m*; **noughts and crosses** ≃ morpion *m (jeu)*

noun [naʊn] *n* nom *m*

nourish ['nʌrɪʃ] *vt* nourrir

nourishing ['nʌrɪʃɪŋ] *adj* nourrissant(e)

nourishment ['nʌrɪʃmənt] *n* nourriture *f*; *(nourishing quality)* richesse *f* nutritive

nous [naʊs] *n Br Fam (common sense)* sens *m* commun, bon sens

Nov *(abbr* **November**) novembre

Nova Scotia ['nəʊvə'skəʊʃə] *n* la Nouvelle-Écosse

novel ['nɒvəl] **1** *n* roman *m*

2 *adj (original)* nouveau(elle), original(e)

novelist ['nɒvəlɪst] *n* romancier(ère) *m,f*

novelty ['nɒvəltɪ] *(pl* **novelties**) *n (newness)* nouveauté *f*; *(cheap object)* bricole *f*; **the n. will soon wear off** l'attrait de la nouveauté ne tardera pas à s'estomper; **n. value** attrait *m* de la nouveauté

November [nəʊ'vembə(r)] *n* novembre *m*; *see also* **May**

novice ['nɒvɪs] *n (beginner)* débutant(e) *m,f* **(at** en); *Rel* novice *mf*

now [naʊ] **1** *adv* **(a)** *(at this moment, these days)* maintenant; **it's n. or never** c'est maintenant ou jamais; **that'll do for n.** ça suffit pour le moment; **it's two years n. since his mother died** ça fait maintenant deux ans que sa mère est morte; **she won't be long n.** elle ne va plus tarder; **any minute/day n.** d'une minute/d'un jour à l'autre; **n. is the time to...** c'est le moment de...; **right n.** *(immediately)* tout de suite; *(at the moment)* pour le moment; **(every) n. and then, (every) n. and again** de temps en temps, de temps à autre; **up to** *or* **until n.** jusqu'à présent *ou* maintenant; **from n. on** dorénavant; **in three days from n.** dans trois jours; **she ought to be here by n.** elle devrait déjà être ici; **and n. for some music** et maintenant, un peu de musique **(b)** *(before statement, argument)* bon; **n., there are two ways of interpreting this** bon, il y a deux interprétations possibles; **come n.!** allons!; **n., n.!** stop quarrelling! allons, allons! arrêtez de vous disputer!

2 *conj* **n. (that)...** maintenant que...; **n. (that) you mention it,...** maintenant que tu le dis,...

nowadays ['naʊədeɪz] *adv* de nos jours

nowhere ['nəʊweə(r)] **1** *adv* nulle part; **n. else** nulle part ailleurs; **she was n. to be found** elle était introuvable; **qualifications alone will get you n.** les diplômes seuls ne servent à rien; **to be n. near as nice/stupid (as)** être loin d'être aussi agréable/stupide (que); **it's n. near the shopping centre** c'est à des kilomètres du centre commercial; **to finish n.** *(in contest)* finir loin derrière les autres; *Fam* **we're getting n. fast** on perd notre temps

2 *n* **in the middle of n.** dans un coin paumé; **he came from n. to win the race** il a gagné la course après une remontée spectaculaire

noxious ['nɒkʃəs] *adj* nocif(ive)

nozzle ['nɒzəl] *n (of petrol pump)* pistolet *m*; *(of vacuum cleaner)* suceur *m*; *(of pipe)* jet *m*; *(for icing)* douille *f*

nr *(abbr* **near**) près de

NRA [enɑː'reɪ] *n Am (abbr* **National Rifle Association**) = association américaine favorable à la généralisation des armes à feu

NSPCC [enespiːsiː'siː] *n Br (abbr* **National Society for the Prevention of Cruelty to Children**) = comité britannique pour la protection des enfants maltraités

nth [enθ] *adj Fam* énième

nuance ['nju:ɒns] *n* nuance *f*

nub [nʌb] *n* (*of question, argument*) cœur *m*

nubile ['nju:baɪl] *adj* désirable

nuclear ['nju:klɪə(r)] *adj* nucléaire; **n. disarmament** désarmement *m* nucléaire; **n. energy** énergie *f* nucléaire *ou* atomique; **n. family** famille *f* nucléaire; **n. physics** physique *f* nucléaire; **n. power** énergie *f* nucléaire; **n. power station** centrale *f* atomique *ou* nucléaire; **n. war** guerre *f* atomique *ou* nucléaire; **n. waste** déchets *mpl* nucléaires; **n. weapon** arme *f* atomique *ou* nucléaire; **n. winter** hiver *m* nucléaire

nuclear-free zone ['nju:klɪə'fri:'zəʊn] *n* zone *f* dénucléarisée

nucleus ['nju:klɪəs] (*pl* **nuclei** ['nju:klɪaɪ]) *n also Fig* noyau *m*

nude [nju:d] **1** *n* nu *m*; **in the n.** tout(e) nu(e)
2 *adj* nu(e)

nudge [nʌdʒ] **1** *n* coup *m* de coude
2 *vt* donner un coup de coude à

nudist ['nju:dɪst] *n* nudiste *mf*; **n. camp** *or* **colony** camp *m* de nudistes

nudity ['nju:dɪtɪ] *n* nudité *f*

nugatory ['nju:gətərɪ] *adj* sans valeur

nugget ['nʌgɪt] *n* (*of gold*) pépite *f*; *Fig* **a n. of information** un renseignement précieux

nuisance ['nju:səns] *n* **to be a n.** (*of person, situation*) être embêtant(e); **to make a n. of oneself** embêter le monde; **n. call** (*on telephone*) appel *m* anonyme

nuke [nju:k] *vt Fam* lâcher la bombe sur

null [nʌl] *adj* nul (nulle); **n. and void** nul et non avenu

nullify ['nʌlɪfaɪ] (*pt & pp* **nullified**) *vt* annuler; (*decree*) invalider

NUM [enju:'em] *n Br* (*abbr* **National Union of Mineworkers**) = syndicat britannique de mineurs

numb [nʌm] **1** *adj* engourdi(e); **to go n.** s'engourdir; **n. with cold** engourdi par le froid; **n. with fear** paralysé(e) par la peur
2 *vt* (*of cold*) engourdir; (*of fear*) paralyser

number ['nʌmbə(r)] **1** *n* **(a)** (*numeral*) nombre *m*; (*when written*) chiffre *m*; *Comptr* **n. crunching** calculs *mpl* (rapides)
(b) (*of house, page, telephone*) numéro *m*; **I live at n. 40** j'habite au (numéro) 40; (*telephone*) un numéro de téléphone; *Fam* **to look after n. one** s'occuper de sa petite personne; *Br* **N. Ten** le dix Downing Street (*résidence du premier ministre britannique*)
(c) (*quantity*) nombre *m*; **a large n. of** un grand nombre de; **in small/great numbers** en petit/grand nombre
(d) (*song*) chanson *f*
(e) (*idioms*) **he's my n. two** (*subordinate*) c'est mon adjoint; *Fam* **I've got your n.!** je sais ce que tu as en tête!; *Fam* **his n.'s up** son compte est bon; *Fam* **that car/dress is a nice little n.** c'est une jolie petite voiture/robe; *Fam* **she's got a nice little n. there** (*situation*) elle s'est dégoté un bon filon
2 *vt* **(a)** (*assign number to*) numéroter
(b) (*count*) compter; **his days are numbered** ses jours sont comptés; **to n. sb among one's friends** compter qn parmi *ou* au nombre de ses amis

numberplate ['nʌmbəpleɪt] *n Br* plaque *f* d'immatriculation *ou* minéralogique

numbly ['nʌmlɪ] *adv* (*say, react*) mollement; (*stare*) d'un air hébété

numbness ['nʌmnɪs] *n* (*in body*) engourdissement *m*; (*of emotions*) torpeur *f*

numbskull ['nʌmskʌl] *n Fam* bêta(asse) *m,f*

numeracy ['nju:mərəsɪ] *n* degré *m* d'aptitude en calcul

numeral ['nju:mərəl] *n* chiffre *m*

numerate ['nju:mərət] *adj* **to be n.** savoir compter

numerator ['nju:məreɪtə(r)] *n Math* numérateur *m*

numerical [nju:'merɪkəl] *adj* numérique

numerically [nju:'merɪklɪ] *adv* numériquement

numerous ['nju:mərəs] *adj* nombreux(euse); **on n. occasions** en de nombreuses occasions

nun [nʌn] *n* religieuse *f*, nonne *f*; **to become a n.** prendre la voile

nunnery ['nʌnərɪ] (*pl* **nunneries**) *n* couvent *m*

nuptial ['nʌpʃəl] **1** *npl Hum or Lit* **nuptials** noces *fpl*
2 *adj Lit* nuptial(e)

nurse [nɜːs] **1** *n* **(a)** (*medical*) infirmière *f*; (*male*) n. infirmier *m* **(b)** (*looking after children*) nurse *f*
2 *vt* **(a)** (*look after*) soigner; (*suckle*) allaiter; *Fig* (*feeling, hope*) nourrir; (*grievance*) entretenir; **to n. sb back to health** faire recouvrer la santé à qn

nursery ['nɜːsərɪ] (*pl* **nurseries**) *n* **(a)** (*for children*) (*establishment*) garderie *f*; (*room in house*) chambre *f* d'enfants; **n. education** enseignement *m* en maternelle; **n. rhyme** comptine *f*; **n. (school)** maternelle *f*; **n. slopes** (*in skiing*) pistes *fpl* pour débutants **(b)** (*for plants*) pépinière *f*

nursing ['nɜːsɪŋ] *n* (*profession*) profession *f* d'infirmière; (*care*) soins *mpl*; **n. home** (*for old people*) maison *f* de retraite; **n. staff** personnel *m* soignant

nurture ['nɜːtʃə(r)] *vt* **(a)** (*feed*) (*children, plants*) nourrir; (*plan, idea*) élaborer **(b)** (*bring up*) faire l'éducation de

NUS [enju:'es] *n Br* (*abbr* **National Union of Students**) = syndicat britannique d'étudiants

NUT [enju:'ti:] *n Br* (*abbr* **National Union of Teachers**) = syndicat britannique d'enseignants

nut [nʌt] *n* **(a)** (*food*) = noix, noisette, cacahuète, pistache ou autre fruit sec de cette nature; *Fig* **he's a hard** *or* **tough n.** c'est un dur; *Fig* **a tough** *or* **hard n. to crack** (*problem*) un problème difficile à résoudre **(b)** *Fam* (*head*) caboche *f*; **to do one's n.** piquer une crise **(c)** *Fam* (*mad person*) dingue *mf*; **a tennis n.** un dingue de tennis **(d)** (*for fastening bolt*) écrou *m*; *Fig* **the nuts and bolts** les notions de base **(e)** *very Fam* **nuts** (*testicles*) couilles *fpl*

nutcase ['nʌtkeɪs] *n Fam* cinglé(e) *m,f*

nutcrackers ['nʌtkrækəz] *npl* **(pair of) n.** casse-noisettes *m inv*, casse-noix *m inv*

nuthouse ['nʌthaʊs] *n Fam* maison *f* de fous

nutmeg ['nʌtmeg] *n* (*noix f de*) muscade *f*

nutrient ['nju:trɪənt] **1** *n* élément *m* nutritif
2 *adj* nutritif(ive)

nutrition [nju:'trɪʃən] *n* nutrition *f*

nutritional [nju:'trɪʃənəl] *adj* nutritionnel(elle); (*value*) nutritif(ive)

nutritious [nju:'trɪʃəs] *adj* nutritif(ive)

nuts [nʌts] *adj Fam* (*mad*) dingue; **to be n. about sb/sth** être dingue de qn/qch

nutshell ['nʌtʃel] *n* coquille *f* de noix/noisette/*etc*; *Fig* **in a n.,...** bref,...

nutter ['nʌtə(r)] *n Br Fam* (*mad person*) dingue *mf*

nutty ['nʌtɪ] *adj* (a) *(in taste)* au goût de noisette/noix/*etc*; *(containing nuts)* aux noisettes/noix/*etc* (b) *Fam (mad)* dingue

nuzzle ['nʌzəl] **1** *vt* renifler
2 *vi* **to n. against sb** renifler qn

NVQ [envi:'kju:] *n Br (abbr* **National Vocational Qualification**) = diplôme professionnel destiné notamment aux personnes travaillant déjà

NW *(abbr* **northwest**) N-O

NY [en'waɪ] *n Am (abbr* **New York**) New York

nylon ['naɪlɒn] *n* Nylon® *m*; **nylons** *(stockings)* bas *mpl* Nylon®

nymph [nɪmf] *n* nymphe *f*

nymphomania [nɪmfəʊ'meɪnɪə] *n* nymphomanie *f*

nymphomaniac [nɪmfəʊ'meɪnɪæk] *n* nymphomane *f*

NZ *(abbr* **New Zealand**) la Nouvelle-Zélande

O

O, o [əʊ] *n* **(a)** *(letter)* O, o *m inv; Br Sch Formerly* **O-level** = diplôme de fin de premier cycle de l'enseignement secondaire, sanctionnant une matière déterminée; *Br Sch* **O-levels** ≃ brevet *m* des collèges **(b)** *(zero)* zéro *m*

oaf [əʊf] *n* lourdaud *m*

oak [əʊk] *n* chêne *m*; **o. apple** noix *f* de galle

OAP [əʊeɪ'piː] *n Br (abbr* **old age pensioner)** retraité(e) *m,f*

oar [ɔː(r)] *n* aviron *m*, rame *f*; *Fig* **to put** *or* **stick one's o. in** mettre son grain de sel

oarsman ['ɔːzmən] *n* rameur *m*

oarswoman ['ɔːzwʊmən] *n* rameuse *f*

OAS [əʊeɪ'es] *n (abbr* **Organization of American States)** OEA *f*

oasis [əʊ'eɪsɪs] *(pl* **oases** [əʊ'eɪsiːz]) *n also Fig* oasis *f*

oatcake ['əʊtkeɪk] *n* galette *f* d'avoine

oath [əʊθ] *n* **(a)** *(pledge)* serment *m*; **o. of allegiance** serment d'allégeance; **to take** *or* **swear an o.** prêter serment; **on** *or* **under o.** sous serment **(b)** *(swear word)* juron *m*

oatmeal ['əʊtmiːl] *n* farine *f* d'avoine; *(colour)* beige *m*

oats [əʊts] *npl (plant)* avoine *f*; **(porridge) o.** *(food)* flocons *mpl* d'avoine; *Br very Fam* **to get one's o.** s'envoyer en l'air

OAU [əʊeɪ'juː] *n (abbr* **Organization of African Unity)** OUA *f*

obdurate ['ɒbdjʊrət] *adj* obstiné(e)

OBE [əʊbiː'iː] *n Br (abbr* **Officer of the Order of the British Empire)** = titre honorifique britannique

obedience [ə'biːdɪəns] *n* obéissance *f*

obedient [ə'biːdɪənt] *adj* obéissant(e)

obelisk ['ɒbəlɪsk] *n* obélisque *m*

obese [əʊ'biːs] *adj* obèse

obesity [əʊ'biːsɪtɪ] *n* obésité *f*

obey [ə'beɪ] **1** *vt* obéir à **2** *vi* obéir

obfuscation [ɒbfʌ'skeɪʃən] *n* obscurcissement *m*

obituary [ə'bɪtjʊərɪ] *(pl* **obituaries)** *n* nécrologie *f*; **o. column** rubrique *f* nécrologique; **o. notice** nécrologie

object 1 *n* ['ɒbdʒɪkt] **(a)** *(thing, recipient)* objet *m*; **an o. of contempt/desire** un objet de mépris/de désir; **an o. lesson in** un parfait exemple de **(b)** *(aim)* objet *m*, but *m*; **the o. of the exercise is to...** cet exercice a pour objet *ou* but de... **(c)** *(obstacle)* **money/distance is no o.** le prix/la distance importe peu **(d)** *Gram* complément *m* d'objet **2** *vi* [əb'dʒekt] émettre une objection; **to o. to sth/to doing sth** ne pas être d'accord avec qch/pour faire qch

objection [əb'dʒekʃən] *n* **(a)** *(protest)* objection *f*; **to have no o. to sth** ne voir aucune objection à qch; **I have**

no o. to going ça ne me dérange pas d'y aller **(b)** *(reason for objecting)* inconvénient *m* (to de)

objectionable [əb'dʒekʃənəbəl] *adj (unpleasant)* déplaisant(e)

objective [əb'dʒektɪv] **1** *n (aim, goal)* objectif *m* **2** *adj (impartial)* objectif(ive)

objectively [əb'dʒektɪvlɪ] *adv* objectivement

objectivity [ɒbdʒek'tɪvɪtɪ] *n* objectivité *f*

obligation [ɒblɪ'geɪʃən] *n* obligation *f*; **to be under an o. to** avoir une dette envers qn; **to be under an o. to do sth** être dans l'obligation de faire qch

obligatory [ə'blɪgətərɪ] *adj* obligatoire

oblige [ə'blaɪdʒ] *vt* **(a)** *(compel)* obliger; **to be obliged to do sth** être obligé(e) de faire qch **(b)** *(do a favour for)* rendre service à **(c)** *(be grateful)* **to be obliged to sb** être reconnaissant(e) à qn; **I'd be obliged if you'd...** ça me rendrait service si vous pouviez...; **much obliged** merci infiniment

obliging [ə'blaɪdʒɪŋ] *adj* serviable; **it was very o. of her** c'était très aimable de sa part

oblique [ə'bliːk] *adj (line, angle)* oblique; *(reference, hint)* indirect(e)

obliterate [ə'blɪtəreɪt] *vt* **(a)** *also Fig (erase)* effacer **(b)** *(destroy)* détruire; *(town)* rayer de la carte

oblivion [ə'blɪvɪən] *n* oubli *m*; **to sink into o.** sombrer dans l'oubli

oblivious [ə'blɪvɪəs] *adj* **to be o. to sth** ne pas avoir conscience de qch

oblong ['ɒblɒŋ] **1** *n* rectangle *m* **2** *adj* rectangulaire

obnoxious [əb'nɒkʃəs] *adj (person, action)* odieux(euse); *(smell)* repoussant(e)

oboe ['əʊbəʊ] *n* hautbois *m*

oboist ['əʊbəʊɪst] *n* hautboïste *mf*

obscene [əb'siːn] *adj* obscène; *Fig (profits, prices)* scandaleux(euse)

obscenely [əb'siːnlɪ] *adv* d'une manière obscène; *Fig (rich)* scandaleusement

obscenity [əb'senɪtɪ] *(pl* **obscenities)** *n* obscénité *f*

obscure [əb'skjʊə(r)] **1** *adj* obscur(e) **2** *vt* **(a)** *(hide from view)* cacher **(b)** *(make unclear)* obscurcir

obscurity [əb'skjʊərɪtɪ] *n* obscurité *f*; **to fall into o.** tomber dans l'oubli

obsequious [əb'siːkwɪəs] *adj* obséquieux(euse)

observable [əb'zɜːvəbəl] *adj* observable; *(change, difference)* perceptible

observance [əb'zɜːvəns] *n (of law, custom)* observation *f*

observant [əb'zɜːvənt] *adj* observateur(trice)

observation [ɒbzə'veɪʃən] *n* observation *f; (by police)* surveillance *f;* **to keep sb under o.** surveiller qn; *(in hospital)* garder qn en observation; **to escape o.** passer inaperçu(e); **to make an o.** faire une observation; *Mil* **o. post** poste *m* d'observation

observatory [əb'zɜ:vətəri] *(pl* observatories) *n* observatoire *m*

observe [əb'zɜ:v] *vt* observer

observer [əb'zɜ:və(r)] *n* observateur(trice) *m,f*

obsess [əb'ses] *vt* obséder; **to be obsessed with** *or* **by sb** faire une fixation sur qn; **to be obsessed with** *or* **by sth** être obsédé(e) par qch

obsession [əb'seʃən] *n* obsession *f;* **to become an o.** tourner à l'obsession

obsessive [əb'sesɪv] *adj (person)* à tendances obsessionnelles; *(fear, hatred, behaviour)* obsessionnel(elle)

obsolescence [ɒbsə'lesəns] *n* obsolescence *f*

obsolete ['ɒbsəli:t] *adj* obsolète; *(design, model)* dépassé(e), démodé(e)

obstacle ['ɒbstəkəl] *n* obstacle *m;* **to put obstacles in sb's way** mettre des bâtons dans les roues à qn; *also Fig* **o. course** course *f* d'obstacles

obstetrician [ɒbste'trɪʃən] *n* obstétricien(enne) *m,f*

obstetrics [ɒb'stetrɪks] *n* obstétrique *f*

obstinacy ['ɒbstɪnəsɪ] *n* obstination *f*

obstinate ['ɒbstɪnɪt] *adj* obstiné(e); **to be o. about doing sth** s'obstiner à vouloir faire qch

obstreperous [əb'strepərəs] *adj* tapageur(euse); **to get o. (about sth)** faire un scandale (à propos de qch)

obstruct [əb'strʌkt] *vt* **(a)** *(block) (road, pipe)* obstruer; *(view)* boucher, gêner **(b)** *(hinder)* gêner; *(in sport)* faire obstruction à; *Pol* **to o. a bill** faire de l'obstruction; *Law* **to o. the course of justice** entraver le cours de la justice

obstruction [əb'strʌkʃən] *n* **(a)** *(action) (of street, in sport)* obstruction *f* **(b)** *(blockage) (in road)* encombrement *m; (in pipe)* engorgement *m;* **to cause an o.** *(on road)* entraver la circulation

obstructive [əb'strʌktɪv] *adj* **to be o.** faire de l'obstruction

obtain [əb'teɪn] **1** *vt* obtenir
2 *vi Formal (of practice)* avoir cours; *(of rule)* être en vigueur

obtainable [əb'teɪnəbəl] *adj* que l'on peut se procurer; **easily o.** facile à obtenir

obtrusive [əb'tru:sɪv] *adj (person, behaviour)* importun(e); *(smell)* pénétrant(e)

obtuse [əb'tju:s] *adj* obtus(e)

obverse ['ɒbvɜ:s] **1** *n* **(a)** *(of medal)* avers *m* **(b)** *(opposite)* contraire *m*
2 *adj* **o. side** *(of medal)* avers *m*

obviate ['ɒbvɪeɪt] *vt Formal (difficulty, danger)* parer à

obvious ['ɒbvɪəs] **1** *n* **to state the o.** enfoncer une porte ouverte
2 *adj* évident(e)

obviously ['ɒbvɪəslɪ] *adv* **(a)** *(in an obvious way)* manifestement **(b)** *(of course)* évidemment; **o. not** certainement pas

occasion [ə'keɪʒən] **1** *n* **(a)** *(time)* occasion *f;* **on one o.** une fois; **on several occasions** plusieurs fois, à plusieurs reprises; **on o.** parfois, de temps en temps **(b)** *(event)* occasion *f*, événement *m;* **on the o. of...** à l'occasion de; **a sense of o.** une atmosphère de fête **(c)** *(opportunity)* occasion *f;* **I'd like to take this o. to...** j'aimerais profiter de cette occasion pour... **(d)** *Formal (cause)* sujet *m*, cause *f;*

to have o. for complaint avoir des raisons de se plaindre; **to have o. to do sth** avoir lieu de faire qch
2 *vt Formal (cause)* occasionner, causer

occasional [ə'keɪʒənəl] *adj* occasionnel(elle); *(showers)* intermittent(e); **I have the o.** cigar il m'arrive de fumer un cigare de temps en temps; **o. table** table *f* d'appoint

occasionally [ə'keɪʒənəlɪ] *adv* occasionnellement, de temps en temps

occidental [ɒksɪ'dentəl] *adj* occidental(e)

occult [ɒ'kʌlt] **1** *n* **the o.** l'occulte *m*
2 *adj* occulte

occupant ['ɒkjʊpənt] *n (of house, car)* occupant(e) *m,f; (of bus, plane)* passager(ère) *m,f*

occupation [ɒkjʊ'peɪʃən] *n* **(a)** *(profession)* métier *m*, profession *f;* *(pastime)* occupation *f* **(b)** *(of house, land)* occupation *f*

occupational [ɒkjʊ'peɪʃənəl] *adj* **o. disease** maladie *f* professionnelle; **o. hazard** risque *m* du métier; **o. therapist** ergothérapeute *mf;* **o. therapy** ergothérapie *f*

occupied ['ɒkjʊpaɪd] *adj* occupé(e); **to be o. with sth** être occupé à qch; **to keep sb o.** occuper qn

occupier ['ɒkjʊpaɪə(r)] *n (of house)* occupant(e) *m,f*

occupy ['ɒkjʊpaɪ] *(pt & pp* occupied) *vt (house, attention)* occuper; **to o. one's time (in doing sth)** occuper son temps (à faire qch)

occur [ə'kɜ:(r)] *(pt & pp* occurred) *vi* **(a)** *(happen) (of event)* avoir lieu; *(of opportunity)* se présenter; *(of problem)* surgir **(b)** *(be present)* apparaître **(c)** *(of idea)* **to o. to sb** venir à l'esprit de qn

occurrence [ə'kʌrəns] *n* **(a)** *(event)* événement *m* **(b)** *(of disease)* incidence *f;* **to be a regular o.** se produire régulièrement

ocean ['əʊʃən] *n* océan *m; Am* **the o.** *(the sea)* la mer; *Fam* **oceans of** plein de

ocean-going ['əʊʃəngəʊɪŋ] *adj* de haute mer

Oceania [əʊʃɪ'eɪnɪə] *n* l'Océanie *f*

oceanic [əʊʃɪ'ænɪk] *adj* océanique

ocelot ['ɒsəlɒt] *n* ocelot *m*

ochre, *Am* **ocher** ['əʊkə(r)] **1** *n* ocre *m*
2 *adj* ocre *inv*

o'clock [ə'klɒk] *adv* **(it's) one o.** (il est) une heure; **two o.** deux heures

OCR [əʊsɪ'ɑ:(r)] *n Comptr* **(a)** *(abbr* **optical character reader)** lecteur *m* optique **(b)** *(abbr* **optical character recognition)** ROC *f*

Oct *(abbr* **October)** octobre

octagon ['ɒktəgən] *n* octogone *m*

octagonal [ɒk'tægənəl] *adj* octogonal(e)

octane ['ɒkteɪn] *n Chem* octane *m;* **o. number** indice *m* d'octane

octave ['ɒktɪv] *n* octave *f*

October [ɒk'təʊbə(r)] *n* octobre *m; see also* **May**

octogenarian [ɒktədʒɪ'neərɪən] *n & adj* octogénaire *mf*

octopus ['ɒktəpəs] *n* pieuvre *f*, poulpe *m*

OD [əʊ'di:] *(pt & pp* OD'd, OD'ed) *vi Fam (abbr* **overdose)** faire une overdose (**on** de); *Fig* **I think I've rather OD'd on pizzas** je crois que j'y suis allé un peu fort sur les pizzas

odd [ɒd] **1** *adj* **(a)** *(strange)* bizarre, curieux(euse) **(b)** *(number)* impair(e); **to be the o. man out** être à part **(c)** *(one of a pair)* dépareillé(e) **(d)** *(occasional)* **I smoke the o. cigarette** il m'arrive de fumer une cigarette de temps en temps; **you've made the o. mistake** tu as fait deux ou trois fautes; **o. jobs** petits travaux *mpl*

2 *adv* **a hundred o. sheep** cent et quelques moutons; **she must be thirty o.** elle doit avoir trente ans ou plus

oddball ['ɒdbɔ:l] *n & adj Fam* excentrique *mf*

oddity ['ɒdɪtɪ] (*pl* **oddities**) *n* (**a**) (*strangeness*) bizarrerie *f* (**b**) (*person*) (*strange*) excentrique *mf*; (*exceptional*) cas *m* à part; (*thing*) curiosité *f*

oddly ['ɒdlɪ] *adv* bizarrement, curieusement; **o. enough,…** chose curieuse,…

oddness ['ɒdnɪs] *n* bizarrerie *f*

odds [ɒdz] *npl* (**a**) (*probability*) chances *fpl*; (*in betting*) cote *f*; **the o. are that…** il y a de grandes chances pour que… + *subjunctive*; **the o. are against her/in her favour** il y a peu de chance(s)/de grosses chances qu'elle réussisse; **against the o.** contre toute attente; **to pay over the o.** (**for sth**) payer (qch) plus cher que le tarif normal; *Fam* **it makes no o.** ça n'a pas d'importance **to be at o.** (**with sb**) (*of person*) être en désaccord (avec qn); **to be at o. with sth** (*of thing*) contredire qch (**c**) *Fam* **o. and ends, o. and sods** bricoles *fpl*

odds-on ['ɒd'zɒn] *adj* (*horse*) **o. favourite** grand favori *m*; *Fam* **it's o. that…** il y a gros à parier que…

ode [əʊd] *n* ode *f*

odious ['əʊdɪəs] *adj* odieux(euse)

odour, *Am* **odor** ['əʊdə(r)] *n* odeur *f*

odourless, *Am* **odorless** ['əʊdəlɪs] *adj* inodore

odyssey ['ɒdɪsɪ] (*pl* **odysseys**) *n* odyssée *f*

OECD [əʊi:si:'di:] *n* (*abbr* **Organization for Economic Co-operation and Development**) OCDE *f*

Oedipal ['i:dɪpəl] *adj* oedipien(enne)

oesophagus, *Am* **esophagus** [i:'sɒfəgəs] (*pl* **oesophagi** *or* **esophagi**) *n* oesophage *m*

oestrogen, *Am* **estrogen** ['i:strədʒən] *n* oestrogène *m*

of [ɒv, *unstressed* əv] *prep* (**a**) (*belonging to*) de; **a friend of mine** un de mes amis; **a car of her own** une voiture à elle; **the University of Manchester** l'université de Manchester

(**b**) (*with amount, quantity*) **a litre of milk** un litre de lait; **a bottle of wine** une bouteille de vin; **a year of her life** un an de sa vie; **many of us** beaucoup d'entre nous; **there are six of us** nous sommes six; **hundreds of people** des centaines de gens; **a girl of ten** une fille de dix ans; **you of all people should know that** si quelqu'un doit le savoir, c'est bien toi

(**c**) (*indicating agency*) **it was nice/clever of you to…** c'était gentil/intelligent de ta part de…

(**d**) (*with material*) **made of wood/glass** en bois/verre

(**e**) (*with dates, time*) **the 4th of October** le 4 octobre; *Am* **a quarter of one** une heure moins le quart

off [ɒf] **1** *adj* (**a**) (*not functioning*) (*light, TV*) éteint(e); (*water, electricity*) coupé(e); **the rain is o.** il ne pleut plus; **o. on, on and o.** (*intermittently*) par intermittence

(**b**) (*cancelled*) annulé(e); **the deal is o.** l'affaire ne se fera pas

(**c**) (*absent from work, school*) absent(e)

(**d**) (*food*) abîmé(e); (*milk*) tourné(e)

(**e**) (*unsuccessful*) **I'm having an o. day** c'est un jour sans; **the o. season** (*in tourism*) la morte-saison

(**f**) **to be well/badly o.** être aisé(e)/pauvre; **you'd be better o. staying where you are** tu ferais mieux de rester où tu es

2 *adv* (**a**) (*away*) **two weeks o.** dans deux semaines; **5**

---

miles o. ≃ à 8 kilomètres; **to be o.** (*leave*) s'en aller; **I'm o. to London** je pars pour Londres; **o. you go!** allez, file maintenant!

(**b**) (*indicating removal*) **to take o. one's coat** enlever son manteau; **the handle has come o.** la poignée est partie

(**c**) (*with prices*) **20 percent/£5 o.** 20 pour cent/5 livres de réduction

(**d**) (*away from work, school*) **to have a day/week o.** avoir un jour/une semaine de congé; **to take some time o.** prendre des vacances

3 *prep* (**a**) (*away from*) **o. the coast** au large de la côte; **o. the main road** qui donne dans la rue principale; **o. the record** officieusement

(**b**) (*indicating removal from*) **to fall/jump o. sth** tomber/sauter de qch; **the handle has come o. the saucepan** la poignée s'est détachée de la casserole

(**c**) (*with prices*) **20 percent/£5 o. the price** 20 pour cent/5 livres de réduction sur le prix

(**d**) (*absent from*) **to be o. work/school** être absent(e) de son travail/de l'école

(**e**) (*not liking*) **to be o. one's food** ne pas avoir d'appétit; **to go o. sb/sth** ne plus aimer qn/qch

(**f**) *Fam* (*from*) **to buy/borrow sth o. sb** acheter/emprunter qch à qn; **to get a cold o. sb** attraper le rhume de qn

offal ['ɒfəl] *n* abats *mpl*

offbeat ['ɒfbi:t] *adj Fam* original(e)

off-chance ['ɒftʃɑ:ns] *n* **on the o.** à tout hasard; **on the o. that…** en espérant que…

off-colour, *Am* **off-color** [ɒf'kʌlə(r)] *adj* (**a**) *Br* (*unwell*) **to be o.** ne pas se sentir dans son assiette (**b**) (*joke*) d'un goût douteux

offcut ['ɒfkʌt] *n* chute *f*

off-duty ['ɒf'dju:tɪ] *adj* qui n'est pas de service

offence, *Am* **offense** [ə'fens] *n* (**a**) *Law* infraction *f*; (*more serious*) délit *m* (**b**) (*displeasure*) **to cause sb o.** (*of person, remark*) vexer qn; (*of film, book*) choquer qn; **to take o. at sth** mal prendre qch; **no o., but…** ne le prends pas mal, mais…

offend [ə'fend] **1** *vt* (*of person, remark*) vexer; (*of book, film*) choquer; **to be offended at** *or* **by sth** mal prendre qch

2 *vi Law* commettre une infraction; (*more serious*) commettre un délit; **to o. against good taste** être une insulte au bon goût

offended [ə'fendɪd] *adj* vexé(e)

offender [ə'fendə(r)] *n Law* délinquant(e) *m,f*

offending [ə'fendɪŋ] *adj* fautif(ive)

offense *Am* = **offence**

offensive [ə'fensɪv] **1** *n also Fig* offensive *f*; **to be on/take the o.** être passé(e)/passer à l'attaque

2 *adj* choquant(e); (*smell*) repoussant(e); **to be o. to sb** se montrer blessant(e) envers qn; **o. weapon** arme *f* offensive

offer ['ɒfə(r)] **1** *n* offre *f*, proposition *f*; **to make sb an o.** faire une offre *ou* une proposition à qn; **on special o.** en promotion; **o. of marriage** demande *f* en mariage

2 *vt* offrir; (*explanation*) donner; (*apologies*) présenter; **to o. sb sth, to o. sth to sb** offrir qch à qn; **to o. to do sth** offrir *ou* proposer de faire qch

▶**offer up** *vt sep* offrir

offering ['ɒfərɪŋ] *n* offre *f*; (*in church*) offrande *f*

offhand ['ɒf'hænd] **1** *adj* désinvolte

2 *adv* (*immediately*) au pied levé; (*at a rough guess*) à première vue

office ['ɒfɪs] n (a) (place) bureau m; **o. boy** garçon m de bureau; **o. building** immeuble m de bureaux; **o. hours** heures fpl de bureau; **o. junior** = employé de bureau chargé de tâches mineures; **o. worker** employé(e) m,f de bureau (b) (position) charge f, fonctions fpl; **to hold o.** être au pouvoir; **to be out of o.** ne plus être au pouvoir

officeholder ['ɒfɪshəʊldə(r)] n responsable mf

officer ['ɒfɪsə(r)] n (in army) officier m; (in police) agent m de police; (in local government) fonctionnaire mf municipal(e)

official [ə'fɪʃəl] **1** n (in public sector) fonctionnaire mf; (of political party) responsable mf
2 adj officiel(elle); Br **O. Secrets Act** = document relatif au secret-défense, signé par tous les fonctionnaires

officialdom [ə'fɪʃəldəm] n Pej bureaucratie f

officialese [əfɪʃə'liːz] n Pej jargon m administratif

officially [ə'fɪʃəlɪ] adv officiellement

officiate [ə'fɪʃɪeɪt] vi Rel officier

officious [ə'fɪʃəs] adj trop zélé(e)

officiously [ə'fɪʃəslɪ] adv avec trop de zèle

offing ['ɒfɪŋ] n **in the o.** en perspective, en vue

off-key ['ɒf'kiː] **1** adj faux (fausse); Fig (remark) déplacé(e)
2 adv faux

off-licence ['ɒflaɪsəns] n Br ≃ magasin m de vins et spiritueux

off-line ['ɒflaɪn] adj Comptr (processing) en différé; (printer) déconnecté(e)

off-load ['ɒfləʊd] vt (surplus goods) écouler; **to o. sth onto sb** (task) se décharger de qch sur qn; (blame, responsibility) rejeter qch sur qn; **to o. sb on sb** refiler qn à qn

off-peak ['ɒf'piːk] adj (electricity) consommé(e) pendant les heures creuses; (holidays) en basse saison; (telephone call, travel) en dehors des heures de pointe

offprint ['ɒfprɪnt] n Typ tirage m à part

off-putting ['ɒfpʊtɪŋ] adj peu engageant(e)

off-sales ['ɒfseɪlz] n Br = vente de boissons alcoolisées à emporter

off-season ['ɒfsiːzən] adj hors saison, en basse saison

offset ['ɒfset] **1** n Typ offset m
2 vt (pt & pp offset) compenser

offshoot ['ɒfʃuːt] n (of tree) rejeton m; (of family) branche f; (of political party, artistic movement) ramification f

offshore **1** adj ['ɒfʃɔː(r)] (island) proche de la côte; (oil rig) off shore inv; Fin **o. investment** placement m off-shore
2 adv [ɒf'ʃɔː(r)] au large, en mer

offside **1** ['ɒfsaɪd] n **1** côté m du conducteur
2 adj (a) (of car) côté conducteur (b) [ɒf'saɪd] (in sport) hors jeu

offspring ['ɒfsprɪŋ] n progéniture f

offstage [ɒf'steɪdʒ] adj & adv dans les coulisses

off-the-cuff [ɒfðə'kʌf] **1** adj impromptu(e)
2 adv au pied levé

off-the-record [ɒfðə'rekɔːd] adj officieux(euse)

off-the-wall [ɒfðə'wɔːl] adj Fam loufoque

off-white ['ɒf'waɪt] **1** n blanc m cassé
2 adj blanc cassé inv

OFGAS ['ɒfɡæs] n Br (abbr **Office of Gas Supply**) = organisme chargé de contrôler les activités des sociétés de distribution de gaz en Grande-Bretagne

OFLOT ['ɒflɒt] n Br (abbr **Office of the National Lottery**) = organisme chargé de contrôler la gestion de la loterie nationale britannique

OFSTED ['ɒfsted] n Br (abbr **Office for Standards in Education**) = organisme chargé de veiller au maintien du niveau des élèves dans l'enseignement public en Grande-Bretagne

OFTEL ['ɒftel] n Br (abbr **Office of Telecommunications**) = organisme chargé de contrôler les activités des sociétés de télécommunications en Grande-Bretagne

often ['ɒfən, 'ɒftən] adv souvent; **how o.?** (how many times?) combien de fois?; (how frequently?) tous les combien?; **as o. as not** très souvent; **more o. than not** le plus souvent; **every so o.** de temps en temps, de temps à autre

OFWAT ['ɒfwɒt] n Br (abbr **Office of Water Services**) = organisme chargé de contrôler les activités des sociétés de distribution d'eau en Grande-Bretagne

ogle ['əʊɡəl] vt lorgner, reluquer

ogre ['əʊɡə(r)] n ogre m

ogress ['əʊɡrɪs] n ogresse f

oh [əʊ] exclam oh!

ohm [əʊm] n ohm m

OHMS [əʊeɪtʃem'es] Br (abbr **On Her/His Majesty's Service**) = formule apposée sur le courrier émis par les services gouvernementaux

oho [əʊ'həʊ] exclam ah ah!

oil [ɔɪl] **1** n (for cooking, lubricating) huile f; (petroleum) pétrole m; (for heating) mazout m; Fig **to pour o. on troubled waters** apaiser les esprits; **o. company** compagnie f pétrolière; **o. drum** bidon m à pétrole; **o. lamp** lampe f à pétrole; **o. painting** peinture f à l'huile; Fig Hum **she's no o. painting** ce n'est pas une beauté; **o. refinery** raffinerie f de pétrole; **o. rig** (on land) derrick m; (offshore) plate-forme f pétrolière ou de forage; **o. slick** nappe f de pétrole; **o. tanker** pétrolier m; **o. well** puits m de pétrole
2 vt huiler, lubrifier; Fig **to o. the wheels** faciliter les choses

oilcan ['ɔɪlkæn] n (for applying oil) burette f; (large container) bidon m à huile

oilfield ['ɔɪlfiːld] n gisement m de pétrole

oil-fired ['ɔɪlfaɪəd] adj (heating) au mazout

oilskin ['ɔɪlskɪn] n (fabric) toile f cirée; **oilskins** (garment) ciré m

oily ['ɔɪlɪ] adj (hands, rag) graisseux(euse); (skin, hair) gras (grasse); (food) huileux(euse) (b) Pej (manner) onctueux(euse)

oink [ɔɪŋk] vi grogner

ointment ['ɔɪntmənt] n pommade f

OK, okay ['əʊ'keɪ] Fam **1** adj (in order) correct(e), exact(e); (acceptable) pas mal; **that's OK by or with me** ça me va; **is it OK to wear jeans?** ça va si on vient en jean?; **no, it is NOT OK** (il n'en est) pas question; **she was OK about it** elle n'a pas fait d'histoires; **he's an OK sort of guy** c'est un type plutôt bien; **are we OK for time?** est-ce qu'on a assez de temps?
2 exclam OK!; **OK, OK! I'll do it now** OK, ça va, je vais le faire
3 n **to give (sb) the OK** donner le feu vert (à qn)
4 vt (pt & pp OK'd or okayed) donner le feu vert à

okra ['ɒkrə] n gombo m, okra m

old [əʊld] **1** adj **(a)** (aged) (person) vieux (vieille), âgé(e); (car) vieux; **to grow** ou **get older** vieillir; **o. age** vieillesse f; **o. age pension** (pension f de) retraite f; **o. age pensioner** retraité(e) m,f; **to go over** ou **do ground** revenir sur des choses qui ont déjà été dites; **to be an o. hand at sth** être rompu(e) à qch; **to be o. hat** être démodé(e); **Fig to be one of the o. school** être de la vieille école; **the O. Testament** l'Ancien Testament m; **o. wives' tale** conte m de bonne femme
(b) (with specific age) **how o. are you?** quel âge avez-vous?; **to be five years o.** avoir cinq ans; **when you're older** (to child) quand tu seras plus grand; **at six years o.** à l'âge de) six ans; **a two-year-o.** (child) un enfant (âgé de deux ans); **you're o. enough to do that yourself** tu es assez grand pour le faire toi-même
(c) (former) ancien(enne); **in the o. days** autrefois; **o. boy/girl** (of school) ancien(enne) élève mf; **the o. boy network** = la franc-maçonnerie des écoles privées et des universités; **an o. flame** un(e) ancien(enne) amoureux(euse)
(d) (longstanding) **an o. friend** un(e) vieil (vieille) ami(e); **o. habits die hard** il n'est pas facile de se défaire de ses habitudes
(e) Fam (intensifier) **any o. how** n'importe comment; **any o. thing** n'importe quoi
(f) Fam (affectionate) **o. Fred** ce vieux Fred; **the poor o. thing** le (la) pauvre vieux (vieille); **my** or **the o. man** (father) le pater; (husband) mon homme; **my** or **the o. woman** (mother) la mater; (wife) la bourgeoise
2 npl **the o.** les personnes fpl âgées

old-fashioned [əʊldˈfæʃənd] adj **(a)** (outdated) démodé(e); (person) vieux jeu inv **(b)** (traditional) à l'ancienne

old-timer [əʊldˈtaɪmə(r)] n Fam **(a)** (experienced person) ancien(enne) m,f **(b)** Am (form of address) vieux m

old-world [əʊldˈwɜːld] adj (atmosphere, elegance) suranné(e); (furnishings) à l'ancienne

oleander [əʊlɪˈændə(r)] n laurier-rose m

olfactory [ɒlˈfæktərɪ] adj olfactif(ive)

oligarchy [ˈɒlɪgɑːkɪ] (pl **oligarchies**) n oligarchie f

olive [ˈɒlɪv] **1** n olive f; Fig **to hold out the o. branch** proposer la paix; **o. grove** oliveraie f; **o. oil** huile f d'olive; **o. tree** olivier m
2 adj (skin) olivâtre; **o. (green)** (vert) olive inv

Olympic [əˈlɪmpɪk] **1** n **the Olympics** les Jeux mpl olympiques
2 adj olympique; **the O. Games** les Jeux mpl olympiques

Oman [əʊˈmæn] n Oman

Omani [əʊˈmænɪ] **1** n Omanais(e) m,f
2 adj omanais(e)

ombudsman [ˈɒmbʊdzmən] n ≃ médiateur m de la République

omelette, Am **omelet** [ˈɒmlɪt] n omelette f; **ham o.** omelette au jambon

omen [ˈəʊmən] n présage m, augure m

ominous [ˈɒmɪnəs] adj inquiétant(e); (event) de mauvais augure; **an o.-looking sky** un ciel menaçant; **an emergency meeting? – that sounds o.** une réunion d'urgence? – ça ne présage rien de bon

ominously [ˈɒmɪnəslɪ] adv **she spoke o.** ce qu'elle a dit ne présage rien de bon; **it was o. quiet** il régnait un silence inquiétant

omission [əʊˈmɪʃən] n omission f

omit [əʊˈmɪt] (pt & pp **omitted**) vt omettre; **to o. to do sth** omettre de faire qch

omnibus [ˈɒmnɪbəs] **1** n (a) (book) recueil m (b) Old-fashioned (bus) omnibus m
2 adj **o. edition** (of stories, poems) recueil m; (on TV, radio) rediffusion f de plusieurs épisodes en continu

omnipotence [ɒmˈnɪpətəns] n omnipotence f, toute-puissance f

omnipotent [ɒmˈnɪpətənt] adj omnipotent(e), tout-puissant (toute-puissante)

omnipresent [ɒmnɪˈprezənt] adj omniprésent(e)

omniscient [ɒmˈnɪsɪənt] adj omniscient(e)

omnivorous [ɒmˈnɪvərəs] adj omnivore; Fig (reader) qui lit de tout

on [ɒn] **1** adv **(a)** (in operation) (light, television) allumé(e); (engine) en marche; **the "on" position** la position marche
(b) (taking place) **what's on?** (on TV) qu'est-ce qu'il y a à la télé?; (at cinema) qu'est-ce qui passe au cinéma?; **is the meeting still on?** la réunion doit-elle toujours avoir lieu?; **I've got a lot on** j'ai beaucoup de choses à faire; **on and off, off and on** (intermittently) par intermittence
(c) (on duty) (in hospital, surgery) de garde; (in shop) de service
(d) (with clothing) **to have sth on** porter qch; **to put sth on** mettre qch; **to have nothing on** être nu(e)
(e) (in time) **earlier on** plus tôt; **later on** plus tard; **from that day on** à dater ou à partir de ce jour
(f) (expressing continuation) **to read/talk/work on** continuer à lire/bavarder/travailler; **he went on and on about it** il n'en finissait pas
(g) (in phrases) Fam **it's not on** c'est inadmissible
2 prep **(a)** (expressing position) **on;** on the table sur la table; **on the second floor** au deuxième étage; **on the wall** sur le mur; (hanging) au mur; **on page 4** à la page 4; **on the right/left** à droite/gauche; **on foot** à pied; **on horseback** à cheval; **on (the) television** à la télévision; **to be on a committee** faire partie d'un comité; **I haven't got any money on me** je n'ai pas d'argent sur moi
(b) (with time) **on the 15th** le 15; **on Sunday** dimanche; **on the hour** à l'heure pile; **on that occasion** à cette occasion
(c) (about) sur; **a book on France** un livre sur la France
(d) (introducing a gerund) **on completing the test, you should...** une fois l'examen terminé, les candidats devront...; **on discovering the corpse, she screamed** elle hurla lorsqu'elle découvrit le corps
(e) (expressing use, support) **to live on £200 a week** vivre avec 200 livres par semaine; **the drinks are on me** c'est ma tournée; **to be on antibiotics** prendre des antibiotiques; **to be on drugs** se droguer

once [wʌns] **1** adv **(a)** (on one occasion) une fois; **not o.** jamais; **o. a week** une fois par semaine; **o. or twice** une ou deux fois, une fois ou deux; **o. in a while** une fois de temps en temps; **o. more, o. again** encore une fois; **o. too often** une fois de trop; **o. and for all** une fois pour toutes; **a o.-in-a-lifetime opportunity** une occasion qui ne se présente qu'une fois **(b)** (formerly) autrefois; **o. upon a time there was a princess** il était une fois une princesse **(c) at o.** (immediately) immédiatement, tout de suite; (at the same time) à la fois, en même temps
2 conj **o.** une fois; **o. he reached home, he collapsed** une fois arrivé chez lui, il s'effondra; **o. he finishes, we can leave** une fois qu'il aura terminé, nous pourrons partir

once-over [ˈwʌnsəʊvə(r)] n Fam **to give sb/sth the o.** jeter un coup d'œil à qn/qch

oncoming ['ɒnkʌmɪŋ] *adj (traffic)* venant en sens inverse

one [wʌn] **1** *n (number)* un (une) *m,f;* **in ones and twos** par petits groupes; *Fam* **to get o. up on sb** prendre l'avantage sur qn

2 *pron* (a) *(identifying)* **this o.** celui-ci (celle-ci); **that o.** celui-là (celle-là); **these ones** ceux-ci (celles-ci); **those ones** ceux-là (celles-là); **which o. do you want?** lequel veux-tu?; **the o. I told you about** celui dont je t'ai parlé; **the big o.** le (la) grand(e); **the ones with the long sleeves** ceux aux manches longues; **that's a difficult o.!** *(question)* c'est une question difficile!

(b) *(indefinite)* un (une); **have you got o.?** tu en as un?; **any o. of us** n'importe lequel d'entre nous; **o. of my friends** un de mes amis; **she's o. of the family** elle fait partie de la famille; **o. of these days** un de ces jours; **it was just o. of those things** on n'y peut rien; **o. after the other** l'un après l'autre; **o. at a time** un à la fois; **o. by o.** un par un; **to have had o. too many** *(drinks)* avoir bu un coup de trop

(c) *(particular person)* **to act like o. possessed** se conduire comme un (une) possédé(e); **I, for o., do not believe it** quant à moi, je n'y crois pas; **I'm not o. to complain** je ne suis pas du genre à me plaindre; **she's not a great o.** for parties les soirées, ce n'est pas son fort

(d) *(people in general) (subject)* on; *(object)* vous; **never knows** on ne sait jamais; **it can make o. unhappy** cela peut vous rendre malheureux; **to do o.'s best** faire de son mieux

3 *adj* (a) *(number)* un (une); **page/number o.** page/ numéro un; **o. o'clock** une heure; **to be o.** *(year old)* avoir un an; **o. day/evening** un jour/soir; **o. or two people** une ou deux personnes; **for o. thing...** d'abord...

(b) *(single)* un (une) seul(e); **I have just o. thing to say** je n'ai qu'une seule chose à dire; **my o. regret** mon seul regret; **the o. person who...** la seule personne qui...; **my o. and only suit** mon seul et unique costume

(c) *(same)* **the same** (la même); **they all live in the o. house** ils habitent dans la même maison; **they are o. and the same thing/person** ils ne font qu'un; *Fam* **it's all o.** to me ça m'est égal

one-armed ['wʌnɑːmd] *adj (person)* manchot(e); *Br Fam* **o. bandit** machine *f* à sous

one-eyed ['wʌnaɪd] *adj* borgne

one-horse town ['wʌnhɔːs'taʊn] *n Fam* trou *m* perdu

one-legged [wʌn'legɪd] *adj* unijambiste

one-liner ['wʌn'laɪnə(r)] *n Fam* bon mot *m*

one-man ['wʌnmæn] *adj (job)* pour un seul homme; **o. band** homme-orchestre *m*; **o. show** one-man-show *m inv*; *Fig (company, team)* entreprise *f* individuelle

one-night stand ['wʌn'naɪt'stænd] *n Fam (sexual encounter)* rencontre *f* sans lendemain *ou* d'un soir; *(of performer)* représentation *f* unique; *(of musician)* concert *m* unique

one-off ['wʌnɒf] *Br Fam* **1** *n (object)* objet *m* unique; *(event)* événement *m* unique; **it was a o.** *(mistake, success)* ça ne se reproduira pas

2 *adj* unique

one-parent family ['wʌnpeərənt'fæmɪlɪ] *n* famille *f* monoparentale

one-party ['wʌn'pɑːtɪ] *adj* à parti unique

one-piece swimsuit ['wʌn'piːs'swɪmsuːt] *n* maillot *m* de bain une pièce

onerous ['əʊnərəs] *adj* lourd(e)

oneself [wʌn'self] *pron* (a) *(reflexive)* se; **to look after o.** *(when ill)* se soigner; *(generally)* s'occuper de soi; **to feel o. again** se sentir complètement rétabli(e) (b) *(emphatic)* soi-même; **to do sth all by o.** faire qch tout(e) seul(e); **to see for o.** regarder soi-même

one-sided [wʌn'saɪdɪd] *adj* (a) *(unequal) (contest)* inégal(e); *(relationship)* à sens unique (b) *(biased)* partial(e)

one-time ['wʌntaɪm] *adj* ancien(enne)

one-to-one ['wʌntə'wʌn] *adj (talk, meeting)* seul à seul, en tête-à-tête; **o. tuition** cours *mpl* particuliers

one-track ['wʌntræk] *adj* **to have a o. mind** *(be obsessed with one thing)* avoir une idée fixe; *(be obsessed with sex)* être obsédé(e), ne penser qu'à ça

one-upmanship [wʌn'ʌpmənʃɪp] *n Fam* = tendance à s'affirmer supérieur aux autres

one-way ['wʌnweɪ] *adj (street, traffic)* à sens unique; **o. ticket** aller *m* (simple)

ongoing ['ɒngəʊɪŋ] *adj* en cours; *(situation, problem)* qui dure

onion ['ʌnjən] *n* oignon *m*; *Br Fam* **to know one's onions** connaître son affaire

on-line [ɒn'laɪn] *adj & adv* Comptr en ligne

onlooker ['ɒnlʊkə(r)] *n* spectateur(trice) *m,f*; *(at accident)* badaud *m*

only ['əʊnlɪ] **1** *adj* seul(e), unique; **o. child** *(boy)* fils *m* unique; *(girl)* fille *f* unique; **you're not the o. one** tu n'es pas le seul

2 *adv* seulement, ne... que; **I was o. joking** c'était (uniquement) pour rire; **permit holders o.** *(sign)* stationnement réservé; **o. an expert could advise us** seul un expert pourrait nous conseiller; **I o. touched it** je n'ai fait que le toucher; **I shall be o. too pleased to come** je serais ravi de venir; **if o. they knew!**, **if they o. knew!** s'ils savaient!; **not o..., but also...** non seulement..., mais encore...; **I saw her o. yesterday** je l'ai vue pas plus tard qu'hier; **o. just** de justesse; **it's o. me** ce n'est que moi

3 *conj* mais

ono [əʊn'əʊ] *adv Com (abbr or nearest offer)* à débattre

on-off switch ['ɒn'ɒf'swɪtʃ] *n* interrupteur *m* marche-arrêt

onomatopoeic [ɒnəmætə'piːɪk] *adj* onomatopéique

onrush ['ɒnrʌʃ] *n (of emotions)* vague *f*; *(of people)* ruée *f*

onset ['ɒnset] *n* début *m*, commencement *m*

on-site [ɒn'saɪt] *adj & adv* sur place

onslaught ['ɒnslɔːt] *n* assaut *m*, attaque *f* (on contre)

onto ['ɒntʊ, *unstressed* 'ɒntə] *prep* (a) *(with direction)* sur (b) *(idioms)* **to be o. sb** être sur la piste de qn; **to get o. sb** contacter qn; **to be o. a good thing** avoir tiré le gros lot

onus ['əʊnəs] *n* responsabilité *f*, obligation *f*; **the o. is on the government to resolve the problem** il incombe au gouvernement de résoudre ce problème; *Law* **o. of proof** charge *f* de la preuve

onward ['ɒnwəd] **1** *adj* en avant

2 *adv* = **onwards**

onwards ['ɒnwədz] *adv* **from tomorrow o.** à partir de demain; **from now o.** désormais, dorénavant; **from then o.** à partir de ce moment-là

onyx ['ɒnɪks] *n* onyx *m*

oodles ['uːdəlz] *npl Fam* **o. of** des tonnes de; **to have o. of time** avoir largement le temps

oomph [umf] *n Fam (energy)* punch *m*; **to have plenty of o.** avoir du punch

oops [u:ps] *exclam* houp là!

ooze [u:z] **1** *n* (a) *(mud)* vase *f* (b) *(flow)* suintement *m*
2 *vt (liquid)* laisser suinter; *Fig (confidence)* déborder de; **to o. charm** avoir un charme fou
3 *vi (of liquid)* suinter (**from** de); *Fig* **to o. with confidence** déborder d'assurance

op [op] *n Fam (medical operation)* opération *f*

opal ['əʊpəl] *n* opale *f*

opaque [əʊ'peɪk] *adj* opaque; *Fig (difficult to understand)* obscur(e)

op cit [op'sɪt] *n (abbr opere citato)* op. cit.

OPEC ['əʊpek] *n (abbr* **Organization of Petroleum-Exporting Countries)** OPEP *f*

open ['əʊpən] **1** *n* **in the o.** *(outside)* dehors; *(not hidden)* sur la place publique; **to bring sth out into the o.** étaler qch au grand jour; **to come out into the o.** *(of person)* se découvrir; **to be o. about sth** révéler qch (b) *(sporting competition)* open *m*
2 *adj* (a) *(not shut)* ouvert(e); **o. to the public** ouvert au public; **o. late** ouvert en nocturne; **to be o. to sb/sth** *(accessible to)* être ouvert à qn/qch; **to be o. to doubt** être sujet(ette) à caution; **to be o. to ridicule** s'exposer à être ridiculisé(e); **to be o. to suggestions** être ouvert à toute suggestion; **in the o. air** au grand air; **to welcome sb with o. arms** accueillir qn à bras ouverts; **o. country** rase campagne *f*; *Law* **in o. court** en audience publique; *Br* **o. day,** *Am* **o. house** journée *f* portes ouvertes; **o. invitation** invitation *f* permanente; *Fig (to thieves)* invitation; *Econ* **o. market** marché *m* libre; **to keep an o. mind** *(on sth)* réserver son jugement (sur qch); **o. prison** prison *f* ouverte; **o. sandwich** canapé *m*; **the o. sea** le large, la haute mer; **o. season** *(for hunting)* saison *f* de la chasse; *Fig* **to declare o. season on sb/sth** partir en guerre contre qn/qch; **o. spaces** *(parks)* espaces *mpl* verts; **o. ticket** billet *m* open; *Br* **O. University** = organisme d'enseignement universitaire par correspondance doublé d'émissions de télévision et de radio; *Law* **o. verdict** verdict *m* de décès sans cause déterminée; **o. wound** plaie *f* béante (b) *(person, manner)* ouvert(e), franc (franche); *(conflict)* ouvert; **to be o. with sb** être franc avec qn; **to be o. about sth** être franc sur qch; **o. letter** *(in newspaper)* lettre *f* ouverte; **o. secret** secret *m* de Polichinelle
3 *adv* **to cut/break sth o.** couper/casser qch; **the door flew o.** la porte s'ouvrit brusquement
4 *vt* ouvrir; *(legs, arms)* écarter; *(negotiations, conversation)* entamer; **to o. fire (on sb)** ouvrir le feu (sur qn); **to o. one's heart to sb** ouvrir son cœur à qn, s'ouvrir à qn
5 *vi (of door, window, flower)* s'ouvrir; *(of shop, bank)* ouvrir; *(of film)* sortir; *(of meeting, negotiations)* commencer; **to o. late** *(of shop)* ouvrir en nocturne; **to o. onto sth** donner sur qch; **the play opens with a death scene** la pièce s'ouvre sur une scène de mort

▸**open out 1** *vt sep (paper, map)* ouvrir, déplier
2 *vi (of flower)* s'ouvrir; *(of wings)* se déployer; *(of view)* s'étendre; *(of road, valley)* s'élargir

▸**open up 1** *vt sep (shop, business, area)* ouvrir (**to** à); *(possibility, opportunity)* offrir
2 *vi (of shopkeeper, new shop)* ouvrir; *(of flower)* s'ouvrir; *Fig (of person)* s'ouvrir, s'épancher

open-air [əʊpə'neə(r)] *adj (restaurant, market)* en plein air; *(swimming pool)* découvert(e)

open-and-shut case [əʊpən'ən'ʃʌt'keɪs] *n* **to be an o.** ne pas faire l'ombre d'un doute

opencast ['əʊpənka:st] *adj* à ciel ouvert

open-door policy ['əʊpən'dɔ:polɪsɪ] *n (for immigrants)* politique *f* d'ouverture des frontières; *(for university)* politique non sélective

open-ended [əʊpən'endɪd] *adj (contract)* à durée indéterminée; *(question)* ouvert(e); *(discussion)* sans cadre strict

open-heart surgery ['əʊpən'hɑ:t'ss:dʒən] *n* opération *f* à cœur ouvert

opening ['əʊpənɪŋ] **1** *n* (a) *(of play, new era)* commencement *m*; *(of negotiations, Parliament)* ouverture *f* (b) *(gap)* ouverture *f*, trou *m* (c) *(of cave, tunnel)* entrée *f* (d) *(opportunity)* occasion *f* favorable; *(job)* débouché *m*
2 *adj* **o. address** *or* **speech** *(in court case)* déclaration *f* préliminaire; **o. batsman** *(in cricket)* premier batteur *m*; **o. ceremony** cérémonie *f* d'ouverture, inauguration *f*; **o. gambit** *(in chess)* gambit *m*; *(in conversation, negotiation)* manœuvre *f* d'approche; **o. hours** heures *fpl* d'ouverture; *Br* **o. time** *(of pub)* heure d'ouverture

openly ['əʊpənlɪ] *adv* ouvertement

open-minded [əʊpən'maɪndɪd] *adj* **to be o.** avoir l'esprit ouvert

open-mouthed [əʊpən'maʊðd] *adj & adv* bouche bée *inv*

openness ['əʊpənnɪs] *n* franchise *f*

open-plan ['əʊpənplæn] *adj (office)* paysager(ère); *(house)* sans cloisons; **o. kitchen** coin-cuisine *m*

opera ['ɒpərə] *n* opéra *m*; **o. glasses** jumelles *fpl* de théâtre; **o. house** opéra; **o. singer** chanteur(euse) *m,f* d'opéra

operable ['ɒpərəbəl] *adj* opérable

operate ['ɒpəreɪt] **1** *vt (machine)* faire fonctionner; *(bus service)* assurer; **to be operated by electricity** fonctionner à l'électricité
2 *vi* (a) *(of machine)* fonctionner; *(of company)* opérer, travailler (b) *(of surgeon)* opérer; **to o. on sb (for)** opérer qn (de); **to be operated on** se faire opérer

operatic [ɒpə'rætɪk] *adj* d'opéra

operating ['ɒpəreɪtɪŋ] *adj* **o. costs** coûts *mpl* ou frais *mpl* d'exploitation; *Comptr* **o. system** système *m* d'exploitation; **o. table** table *f* d'opération; *Br* **o. theatre,** *Am* **o. room** salle *f* d'opération

operation [ɒpə'reɪʃən] *n* (a) *(of machine)* fonctionnement *m*; **to be in o.** *(of machine)* être en service; *(of law)* être en vigueur; **to come into o.** *(of law)* entrer en vigueur (b) *(process)* opération *f* (c) *(of company)* activité *f* (d) *(military, surgical)* opération *f*; **to have an o. (for sth)** se faire opérer (de qch); *Mil* **operations room** salle *f* d'opérations *(d'un état-major)*

operational [ɒpə'reɪʃənəl] *adj (system, factory)* opérationnel(elle)

operative ['ɒpərətɪv] **1** *n (manual worker)* ouvrier(ère) *m,f*; *(of machine)* opérateur(trice) *m,f*; *Am (spy)* agent *m*
2 *adj (law, rule)* en vigueur; **to become o.** entrer en vigueur; **the o. word** le mot-clé

operator ['ɒpəreɪtə(r)] *n* (a) *(of machine)* opérateur(trice) *m,f* (b) *Tel (switchboard)* opérateur(trice) *m,f*; *(switchboard)* standardiste *mf* (c) *Fam* **a smooth o.** un petit finaud

operetta [ɒpə'retə] *n* opérette *f*

ophthalmology [ɒfθæl'mɒlədʒɪ] *n* ophtalmologie *f*

opinion [ə'pɪnjən] *n* opinion *f*; **in my o.** à mon avis; **to be of the o. that...** être d'avis *ou* estimer que...; **to ask sb's o.** demander l'avis *ou* l'opinion de qn; **to form an o.**

of sb/sth se faire une opinion sur qn/qch; **to have a high/low o. of sb** avoir une haute/mauvaise opinion de qn; **o. poll** sondage *m* (d'opinion)

opinionated [ə'pɪnjəneɪtɪd] *adj* dogmatique

opium ['əʊpɪəm] *n* opium *m*; **o. addict** opiomane *mf*; **o. den** fumerie *f* d'opium

opossum [ɒ'pɒsəm] *n* opossum *m*

opp (*abbr* **opposite**) ci-contre

opponent [ə'pəʊnənt] *n* adversaire *mf*; *(of government)* opposant(e) *m,f* (**of** à)

opportune [ˈɒpətjuːn] *adj* opportun(e)

opportunism [ɒpə'tjuːnɪzəm] *n* opportunisme *m*

opportunist [ɒpə'tjuːnɪst] *n & adj* opportuniste *mf*

opportunity [ɒpə'tjuːnɪtɪ] (*pl* **opportunities**) *n* occasion *f*; **to have the o. of doing** *or* **to do sth** avoir l'occasion de faire qch; **at every o.** à la moindre occasion; **at the first** *or* **earliest o.** à la première occasion; **if you get an o.** si tu en as l'occasion; **the o. of a lifetime** la chance de sa/ta/*etc* vie; **a job with opportunities** un emploi qui offre des perspectives

oppose [ə'pəʊz] *vt* s'opposer à; **to be opposed to sth** être opposé(e) à qch; **as opposed to...** par opposition à...

opposing [ə'pəʊzɪŋ] *adj* (*characters, viewpoints*) opposé(e); *(armies)* ennemi(e); *(team)* adverse

opposite ['ɒpəzɪt] **1** *n* **the o.** le contraire
2 *adj* (a) *(side, shore)* opposé(e); *(page)* d'en face; **on the o. side of the street** de l'autre côté de la rue (b) *(opinion)* contraire; **in the o. direction** en sens inverse, dans le sens opposé; **the o. sex** l'autre sexe
3 *adv* en face; **the house o.** la maison d'en face
4 *prep* en face de

opposition [ɒpə'zɪʃən] *n* (a) *(resistance)* opposition *f* (**to** à); **to meet with o.** *(of idea, plan)* être contesté(e) (b) *(contrast)* in **o.** to contre (c) *(opponents)* **the o.** le camp adverse; *Br Pol* **the O.** l'opposition *f*; *Br Pol* **to be in o.** être dans l'opposition

oppress [ə'pres] *vt* opprimer

oppressed [ə'prest] **1** *npl* **the o.** les opprimés *mpl*
2 *adj* opprimé(e)

oppression [ə'preʃən] *n* oppression *f*

oppressive [ə'presɪv] *adj* (a) *(law, regime)* oppressif(ive) (b) *(atmosphere, heat)* oppressant(e), étouffant(e)

opt [ɒpt] **1** *vt* **to o. to do sth** choisir de faire qch
2 *vi* **to o. for sth** opter pour qch

▸**opt out** *vi (of local authority control)* devenir autonome; *(of project, responsibilities)* se désengager

optic ['ɒptɪk] *adj* optique; **o. nerve** nerf *m* optique

optical ['ɒptɪkəl] *adj* optique; *(instrument)* d'optique; *Comptr* **o. character reader** lecteur *m* optique de caractères; *Comptr* **o. character recognition** reconnaissance *f* optique de caractères; *Comptr* **o. disk** disque *m* optique; **o. fibre** fibre *f* optique; **o. illusion** illusion *f* d'optique

optician [ɒp'tɪʃən] *n (prescribing)* ophtalmologue *mf*; *(dispensing)* opticien(enne) *m,f*

optics ['ɒptɪks] *n* optique *f*

optimism ['ɒptɪmɪzəm] *n* optimisme *m*

optimist ['ɒptɪmɪst] *n* optimiste *mf*

optimistic [ɒptɪ'mɪstɪk] *adj* optimiste (**about** quant à)

optimize ['ɒptɪmaɪz] *vt* optimiser

optimum ['ɒptɪməm] **1** *n* optimum *m*
2 *adj* optimum *inv*, optimal(e)

option ['ɒpʃən] *n* (a) *(choice)* option *f*, choix *m*; **to have the o. of doing sth** avoir la possibilité de faire qch; **to have no o. (but to do sth)** ne pas pouvoir faire autrement (que de faire qch); **a soft** *or* **easy o.** une solution de facilité; **to leave** *or* **keep one's options open** ne pas prendre de décision tout de suite (b) *Fin* option *f* (c) *(school or university subject)* option *f*

optional ['ɒpʃənəl] *adj* facultatif(ive); **o. extra** (accessoire *m* en) option *f*; **o. subject** *(at school, university)* matière *f* à option

opt-out ['ɒptaʊt] **1** *n* désengagement *m*
2 *adj* de désengagement

opulent ['ɒpjʊlənt] *adj* opulent(e)

OR [əʊ'ɑː(r)] *n Am (abbr* **operating room**) salle *f* d'opération

or [ɔː(r), *unstressed* ə(r)] *conj* (a) *(in general)* ou; **an hour or so** une heure environ; **in a day or two** dans un jour ou deux; **did she do it or not?** est-ce qu'elle l'a fait ou pas?; **snow or no snow, I'm going!** qu'il neige ou pas, j'y vais! (b) *(otherwise)* sinon; **stop it or I'll tell mum!** arrête, sinon je vais le dire à maman! (c) *(with negative)* ni; **she didn't write or phone** elle n'a ni écrit ni téléphoné

oracle ['ɒrəkəl] *n* oracle *m*

oral ['ɔːrəl] **1** *n (exam)* oral *m*
2 *adj* *(tradition, contraception)* oral(e); *(medication)* par voie orale; *(hygiene)* buccal(e); **o. examination** (examen *m*) oral *m*; **o. sex** rapports *mpl* bucco-génitaux

orally ['ɔːrəlɪ] *adv* oralement, de vive voix; *(take medicine)* par voie orale

orange ['ɒrɪndʒ] **1** *n (fruit)* orange *f*; *(colour)* orange *m*; **o. blossom** fleurs *fpl* d'oranger; **o. grove** orangeraie *f*; **o. juice** jus *m* d'orange; **o. peel** peau *f* ou écorce *f* d'orange; **o. squash** ≃ orangeade *f*; **o. tree** oranger *m*
2 *adj (colour)* orange *inv*

orang-outan(g) [ɔː'ræŋuːtæŋ] *n* orang-outan(g) *m*

oration [ɔː'reɪʃən] *n* allocution *f*

orator ['ɒrətə(r)] *n* orateur(trice) *m,f*

oratory ['ɒrətərɪ] *(pl* **oratories**) *n* (a) *(art of speaking)* art *m* oratoire, éloquence *f* (b) *Rel (chapel)* oratoire *m*

orb [ɔːb] *n (of regalia)* globe *m*; *Lit (sphere)* orbe *m*

orbit ['ɔːbɪt] **1** *n* (a) *(of planet)* orbite *f*; **in o.** en orbite; **to go into o.** se mettre en orbite (b) *(scope)* domaine *m*
2 *vt* être en orbite *ou* décrire une orbite autour de
3 *vi* être en orbite, décrire une orbite

orchard ['ɔːtʃəd] *n* verger *m*

orchestra ['ɔːkɪstrə] *n* orchestre *m*; **o. pit** fosse *f* d'orchestre

orchestral [ɔː'kestrəl] *adj* orchestral(e)

orchestrate ['ɔːkɪstreɪt] *vt also Fig* orchestrer

orchid ['ɔːkɪd] *n* orchidée *f*

ordain [ɔː'deɪn] *vt* (a) *Formal (decree)* ordonner; *(measure)* décréter; *Fig* **fate ordained that we should meet** il était écrit que nous devions nous rencontrer (b) *(priest)* ordonner

ordeal [ɔː'diːl] *n* épreuve *f*; **it was a bit of an o.** ça a été éprouvant

order ['ɔːdə(r)] **1** *n* (a) *(instruction)* ordre *m*; **to give sb an o.** donner un ordre à qn; **to be under orders (to do sth)** avoir reçu des ordres (pour faire qch); **to take orders from sb** recevoir des ordres de qn; *Fin* **pay to the o. of S. Fraser** payer à l'ordre de S. Fraser
(b) *Com* commande *f*; **to place an o. (with sb)** passer (une) commande (à qn); **to make sth to o.** faire qch sur

commande; **o. book** carnet *m* de commandes; **o. form** bon *m* de commande

(c) *(peace, tidiness)* ordre *m*; *Fig* **to put one's own house in o.** faire le ménage chez soi

(d) *(condition)* **out of o.** *(lift, toilets, machine)* hors service; *(telephone)* en dérangement; **in (good) working** or **running o.** en (bon) état de fonctionnement

(e) *(in meeting)* **o. of the day** ordre *m* du jour; **to call sb to o.** rappeler qn à l'ordre; *Fig* **I think a celebration is in o.** je pense que ça mérite d'être fêté; *Fam* **that's out of o.!** ça ne se fait vraiment pas!; *Rel* **o. of service** office *m*; *Pol* **o. paper** *(copie f de l')*ordre du jour

(f) *(system)* ordre *m*; **the new world o.** le nouvel ordre mondial

(g) *(sequence)* ordre *m*; **in the right/wrong o.** dans le bon ordre/le désordre; **in o.** en ordre; **out of o.** en désordre; **in o. of age/size** par ordre d'âge/de taille

(h) *(degree)* ordre *m*; **of the highest o.** de premier ordre; **the higher/lower orders** *(social classes)* les classes *fpl* supérieures/inférieures

(i) *Rel* ordre *m*; **to take holy orders** entrer dans les ordres

(j) **in o. to do sth** afin de *ou* pour faire qch; **in o. that...** afin *ou* pour que... + *subjunctive*

2 *vt* **(a)** *(instruct)* **to o. sb to do sth** ordonner à qn de faire qch; **to be ordered to do sth** recevoir l'ordre de faire qch; *Law* **to be ordered to pay costs** être condamné(e) aux dépens

(b) *Com & (in restaurant)* commander

(c) *(arrange) (papers, books)* classer, ranger; *(one's thoughts)* mettre de l'ordre dans; **to o. sth according to size** classer *ou* ranger qch par taille

3 *vi (in restaurant)* commander; **are you ready to o.?** vous avez choisi?

▶**order about, order around** *vt sep (person)* commander

▶**order in** *vt sep (supplies)* commander; *(troops)* faire venir

ordered ['ɔːdəd] *adj (organized)* ordonné(e); *(life)* régulier(ère)

orderly ['ɔːdəlɪ] **1** *n (pl* orderlies*) (in army)* planton *m*; *(in hospital)* aide-soignant(e) *m,f*

2 *adj* **(a)** *(tidy)* méthodique; *(life, room)* rangé(e) **(b)** *(well-behaved)* discipliné(e); **in an o. fashion** avec calme

ordinal ['ɔːdɪnəl] **1** *n (nombre m)* ordinal *m*

2 *adj* ordinal(e)

ordinance ['ɔːdɪnəns] *n Formal (decree)* ordonnance *f*

ordinarily ['ɔːdɪnərɪlɪ] *adv* normalement

ordinary ['ɔːdɪnrɪ] **1** *n* **out of the o.** qui sort de l'ordinaire, exceptionnel(elle)

2 *adj* ordinaire; **she was just an o. tourist** c'était une touriste comme une autre; *Br Naut* **o. seaman** ≃ matelot *m*; *Br Fin* **o. share** action *f* ordinaire

ordination [ɔːdɪ'neɪʃən] *n Rel* ordination *f*

ordnance ['ɔːdnəns] *n Mil (supplies)* matériel *m*; *(guns)* artillerie *f*; **o. factory** manufacture *f* d'artillerie; *Br* **O. Survey** ≃ Institut *m* Géographique National

ore [ɔː(r)] *n* minerai *m*

oregano [ɒrɪ'gɑːnəʊ] *n* origan *m*

organ ['ɔːgən] *n* **(a)** *(part of body, newspaper)* organe *m*; **o. donor** donneur(euse) *m,f* d'organe; **o. transplant** greffe *f* d'organe **(b)** *(musical instrument)* orgue *m*

organ-grinder ['ɔːgəngraɪndə(r)] *n* joueur(euse) *m,f* d'orgue de Barbarie

organic [ɔː'gænɪk] *adj (disease, chemistry)* organique; *(food, farming)* biologique; **an o. whole** un tout

organism ['ɔːgənɪzəm] *n* organisme *m*

organist ['ɔːgənɪst] *n* organiste *mf*

organization [ɔːgənaɪ'zeɪʃən] *n* organisation *f*

organize ['ɔːgənaɪz] **1** *vt* **(a)** *(put into order)* organiser; **to o. one's time** s'organiser **(b)** *(take care of)* s'occuper de

2 *vi (of workers)* se syndiquer

organizer ['ɔːgənaɪzə(r)] *n (person)* organisateur(trice) *m,f*; *(diary)* agenda *m*

orgasm ['ɔːgæzəm] *n* orgasme *m*; **to have an o.** avoir un orgasme

orgy ['ɔːdʒɪ] *n (pl* orgies*)* orgie *f*; *Fig* **an o. of violence** un déchaînement de violence

orient ['ɔːrɪənt] **1** *n* **the O.** l'Orient *m*

2 *vt* = **orientate**

oriental [ɔːrɪ'entəl] *n Old-fashioned* O. Oriental(e) *m,f*

2 *adj* oriental(e)

orientate ['ɔːrɪənteɪt] *vt* orienter **(to** or **towards** vers); **to o. oneself** s'orienter; **to be orientated towards sb/ sth** *(aimed at)* être destiné(e) à qn/qch

orientation [ɔːrɪən'teɪʃən] *n* orientation *f*; **o. course** stage *m* d'initiation

orienteering [ɔːrɪən'tɪərɪŋ] *n* course *f* d'orientation

orifice ['ɒrɪfɪs] *n* orifice *m*

origin ['ɒrɪdʒɪn] *n* origine *f*; **country of o.** pays *m* d'origine; **of Greek o.** d'origine grecque

original [ə'rɪdʒɪnəl] **1** *n (painting, document)* original *m*

2 *adj* **(a)** *(not copied, innovative)* original(e) **(b)** *(first)* d'origine; *Rel* **o. sin** péché *m* originel

originality [ərɪdʒɪ'nælɪtɪ] *n* originalité *f*

originally [ə'rɪdʒɪnəlɪ] *adv* **(a)** *(initially)* à l'origine, au départ; **where do you come from o.?** d'où êtes-vous originaire? **(b)** *(in an innovative way)* d'une façon originale

originate [ə'rɪdʒɪneɪt] **1** *vt* être à l'origine de

2 *vi (of fire)* prendre naissance; **to o. from** *(of person)* être originaire de; **to o. in** *(of custom)* être originaire de

Orkney ['ɔːknɪ] *n* **the O. Islands, the Orkneys** les Orcades *fpl*

ornament ['ɔːnəmənt] **1** *n* ornement *m*

2 *vt* ['ɔːnəment] orner

ornamental [ɔːnə'mentəl] *adj* ornemental(e), décoratif(ive); **o. lake** pièce *f* d'eau

ornate [ɔː'neɪt] *adj (building, surroundings)* orné(e), ornementé(e); *(style)* fleuri(e)

ornithology [ɔːnɪ'θɒlədʒɪ] *n* ornithologie *f*

orphan ['ɔːfən] **1** *n* orphelin(e) *m,f*; **to be left an o.** devenir orphelin

2 *adj* **an o. child** un (une) orphelin(e)

3 *vt* **to be orphaned** devenir orphelin(e)

orphanage ['ɔːfənɪdʒ] *n* orphelinat *m*

orthodontist [ɔːθəʊ'dɒntɪst] *n* orthodontiste *mf*

orthodox ['ɔːθədɒks] *adj* orthodoxe

orthodoxy ['ɔːθədɒksɪ] *n* orthodoxie *f*

orthopaedic, *Am* orthopedic [ɔːθə'piːdɪk] *adj* orthopédique; **o. surgeon** (chirurgien *m*) orthopédiste *mf*

orthopaedics, *Am* orthopedics [ɔːθə'piːdɪks] *n* orthopédie *f*

oscillate ['ɒsɪleɪt] *vi* osciller

osmosis [ɒz'məʊsɪs] *n also Fig* osmose *f*

osprey ['ɒspreɪ] *n (pl* ospreys*)* n balbuzard *m*

ossify ['ɒsɪfaɪ] *(pt & pp* ossified*) vi Anat* s'ossifier; *Fig (of person)* se fossiliser; *(of system, organization)* se scléroser

ostensible [ɒs'tensibəl] *adj* soi-disant *inv*

ostensibly [ɒs'tensibli] *adv* soi-disant

ostentation [ɒsten'teiʃən] *n* ostentation *f*

ostentatious [ɒsten'teiʃəs] *adj* (person) m'as-tu-vu *inv*; (thing) prétentieux(euse)

osteoarthritis [ɒstiəʊɑ:'θraitis] *n* ostéoarthrite *f*

osteopath ['ɒstiəpæθ] *n* ostéopathe *mf*

ostracism ['ɒstrəsizəm] *n* ostracisme *m*

ostracize ['ɒstrəsaiz] *vt* mettre en quarantaine

ostrich ['ɒstritʃ] *n* autruche *f*

OTC [əʊti:'si:] *n Br Mil* (abbr **Officers' Training Corps**) = centre de formation pour ceux qui envisagent de devenir officier dans l'armée

other ['ʌðə(r)] 1 *adj* autre; the o. one l'autre; every o. day/week un jour/une semaine sur deux; the o. day/week l'autre jour/semaine; the o. four les quatre autres; o. people seem to like it d'autres ont l'air de bien aimer ça; any o. book n'importe quel autre livre; somebody o. than me quelqu'un d'autre que moi

2 *pron* autre; others d'autres; the others les autres; one after the o. l'un(e) après l'autre; one or o. of us l'un d'entre nous; somewhere or o. quelque part; somebody or o. quelqu'un; some woman or o. une femme

3 *adv* the colour's odd, but o. than that, it's perfect la couleur est bizarre mais à part cela, il est très bien; she never speaks of him o. than admiringly elle ne parle jamais de lui autrement qu'avec admiration

otherwise ['ʌðəwaiz] 1 *adv* autrement; to be o. engaged avoir d'autres engagements; except where o. stated sauf indication contraire

2 *conj* autrement, sinon

other-worldly [ʌðə'wɜːldli] *adj* (person) détaché(e) de ce monde

OTT [əʊti:'ti:] *adj Br Fam* (abbr **over the top**) trop *inv*

Ottawa ['ɒtəwə] *n* Ottawa

otter ['ɒtə(r)] *n* loutre *f*

Ottoman ['ɒtəmən] *Hist* 1 *n* Ottoman(e) *m,f*

2 *adj* ottoman(e)

ottoman ['ɒtəmən] *n* (furniture) ottomane *f*

OU [əʊ'ju:] *n Br* (abbr **Open University**) = organisme d'enseignement universitaire par correspondance doublé d'émissions de télévision et de radio

ouch [aʊtʃ] *exclam* (expressing pain) aïe!, ouïe!

ought [ɔːt] *v aux*

> La forme négative **ought not** s'écrit **oughtn't** en forme contractée.

(a) (expressing obligation, desirability) I o. to be going je devrais m'en aller; you oughtn't to worry so much vous ne devriez pas vous inquiéter autant; he had drunk more than he o. to il n'aurait pas dû boire autant; this o. to have been done before on aurait dû le faire avant; they o. not to have waited ils n'auraient pas dû attendre (b) (expressing probability) they o. to be in Paris by now ils ont dû arriver à Paris maintenant; you o. to be able to get £150 for the painting vous devriez pouvoir tirer 150 livres de ce tableau

oughtn't ['ɔːtənt] = **ought not**

ounce [aʊns] *n* (unit of weight) = 28,35 g, once *f*; Fig an o. of une once de

our ['aʊə(r)] *possessive adj* (a) (singular) notre; (plural) nos; o. job notre travail; o. wives nos femmes; it wasn't OUR

idea! ce n'est pas nous qui en avons eu l'idée! (b) (for parts of body) we hit o. heads nous nous sommes cogné la tête

ours ['aʊəz] *possessive pron* (a) (singular) le nôtre *m,f*; (plural) les nôtres; their house is big but o. is bigger leur maison est grande, mais la nôtre est plus grande encore (b) (used attributively) this book is o. ce livre est à nous; a friend of o. un de nos amis; where's that brother of o.? où notre frère a-t-il bien pu passer?

ourselves [aʊə'selvz] *pron* (a) (reflexive) we hurt o. nous nous sommes blessés (b) (emphatic) nous-mêmes; we o. have never... nous-mêmes n'avons jamais...; we told you o. nous vous l'avons dit nous-mêmes; we're not o. today nous ne sommes pas dans notre état normal aujourd'hui (c) (after preposition) we live by o. nous vivons seuls; we bought it for o. nous nous la sommes acheté; we talk to o. nous parlons tous seuls

oust [aʊst] *vt* évincer (from de)

out [aʊt] 1 *adv* (a) (outside) dehors; to go o. sortir; o. here ici; o. there dehors; o.! (in tennis) faute!

(b) (not at home, not in) to be o. être sorti(e); to stay o. late rentrer tard

(c) (not concealed) the secret is o. on a révélé le secret; he's o. (openly gay) il a révélé son homosexualité; the sun is o. il y a du soleil; the moon is o. la lune est levée

(d) (published) sorti(e)

(e) (not in fashion) passé(e) de mode

(f) (indicating intent) to be o. to do sth chercher à faire qch; to be o. for money vouloir à tout prix de l'argent; Fam to be o. to get sb chercher la perte de qn

(g) (unconscious, asleep) to be o. cold or for the count être K-O; Fam to go o. like a light s'endormir comme une masse

(h) (extinguished) éteint(e)

(i) to be o. (on strike) faire grève

(j) (inaccurate) faux (fausse); I was £25 o. (over) j'avais 25 livres de trop; (under) il me manquait 25 livres

(k) (indicating completion) before the week is o. avant la fin de la semaine

(l) (in phrases with of) o. of (outside) hors de; to go o. of the office sortir du bureau; to look o. of the window regarder par la fenêtre; to be o. of the country être en voyage à l'étranger; o. of reach/danger hors de portée/danger; to be o. of cash/ideas ne plus avoir de liquide/d'idées; to do sth o. of friendship/curiosity faire qch par amitié/curiosité; she paid for it o. of her own money elle l'a payé de ses propres deniers; 20 o. of 20 20 sur 20; three days o. of four trois jours sur quatre; Fam to feel o. of it ne pas se sentir dans le coup

2 *prep* (through) to look o. the window regarder par la fenêtre

out-and-out [aʊtə'naʊt] *adj* (villain, liar) fieffé(e); (failure) total(e); (disgrace, scandal) véritable

outback ['aʊtbæk] *n* the o. l'intérieur *m*

outbid [aʊt'bid] (*pt & pp* outbid) *vt* enchérir avec succès sur

outboard ['aʊtbɔːd] 1 *n* (motor) moteur *m* hors-bord

2 *adj* o. motor moteur *m* hors-bord

outbreak ['aʊtbreik] *n* (of hostilities, war) déclenchement *m*; (of rioting, violence) flambée *f*; (of disease) épidémie *f*

outbuilding ['aʊtbildiŋ] *n* dépendance *f*

outburst ['aʊtbɜːst] *n* éclat *m*; (of activity, temper) accès *m*; (of hatred, violence) explosion *f*; (of enthusiasm) élan *m*

outcast ['aʊtkɑːst] *n* paria *m*

outclass [aʊt'klɑːs] *vt* surclasser

outcome ['aʊtkʌm] *n* résultat *m*, issue *f*

outcrop ['aʊtkrɒp] *n* affleurement *m*

outcry ['aʊtkraɪ] *(pl* outcries) *n (protest)* tollé *m*; **public o.** tollé général

outdated [aʊt'deɪtɪd] *adj* démodé(e)

outdid [aʊt'dɪd] *pt of* outdo

outdistance [aʊt'dɪstəns] *vt* distancer, dépasser

outdo [aʊt'du:] *(pt* outdid [aʊt'dɪd], *pp* outdone [aʊt'dʌn]) *vt* surpasser; **not to be outdone,…** pour ne pas être en reste,…

outdoor ['aʊtdɔ:(r)] *adj (life)* au grand air; *(activities, games)* de plein air; *(swimming pool)* découvert(e); **she's an o. person** elle aime le grand air

outdoors [aʊt'dɔ:z] **1** *n* **the great o.** les grands espaces *mpl*
2 *adv* dehors

outer ['aʊtə(r)] *adj* extérieur(e); **O. London** la grande banlieue de Londres; **o. space** espace *m* intersidéral

outermost ['aʊtəməʊst] *adj (nearest the outside)* le (la) plus à l'extérieur; *(most remote)* le (la) plus reculé(e)

outfit ['aʊtfɪt] *n* **(a)** *(clothes)* ensemble *m* **(b)** *Fam (organization)* boîte *f*

outflank [aʊt'flæŋk] *vt Mil* déborder; *Fig* prendre par surprise

outflow ['aʊtfləʊ] *n (of liquid)* écoulement *m*; *(of capital)* fuite *f*

outgoing ['aʊtɡəʊɪŋ] *adj* **(a)** *(departing)* sortant(e) **(b)** *(sociable)* communicatif(ive)

outgoings ['aʊtɡəʊɪŋz] *npl* dépenses *fpl*

outgrow [aʊt'ɡrəʊ] *(pt* outgrew [aʊt'ɡru:], *pp* outgrown [aʊt'ɡrəʊn]) *vt (habit, behaviour, toys)* passer l'âge de; **she's outgrown her jacket** son blouson est devenu trop petit pour elle

outhouse ['aʊthaʊs] *n* dépendance *f*

outing ['aʊtɪŋ] *n* **(a)** *(excursion)* excursion, sortie *f* **(b)** *(of homosexual)* = fait, principalement pour une organisation militante, de rendre publique l'homosexualité d'une personne connue

outlandish [aʊt'lændɪʃ] *adj* incongru(e), bizarre

outlast [aʊt'lɑ:st] *vt (object)* durer plus longtemps que; *(person)* survivre à

outlaw ['aʊtlɔ:] **1** *n* hors-la-loi *m inv*
2 *vt (practice)* rendre illégal(e); *(person)* mettre hors la loi

outlay ['aʊtleɪ] *n (expense)* frais *mpl*, dépenses *fpl*

outlet ['aʊtlet] *n* **(a)** *(for water, steam)* orifice *m* de sortie; *(for emotions, energy)* exutoire *m* **(b)** *(shop)* point *m* de vente

outline ['aʊtlaɪn] **1** *n* **(a)** *(shape)* silhouette *f*; *(drawing)* tracé *m* **(b)** *(summary) (of play, novel)* résumé *m*; *(of plan, policy)* grandes lignes *fpl*; **in o.** en gros, dans les grandes lignes
2 *vt* **(a)** *(shape)* repasser les contours de; **her figure was outlined against the sky** sa silhouette se découpait sur le ciel **(b)** *(plot of novel)* résumer; *(plan, policy)* donner les grandes lignes de

outlive [aʊt'lɪv] *vt* survivre à; **she will o. us all** elle nous enterrera tous; **to have outlived its usefulness** *(of machine, theory)* ne plus servir (à rien)

outlook ['aʊtlʊk] *n* **(a)** *(prospect)* perspectives *fpl*; *(of weather)* prévisions *fpl* **(b)** *(attitude)* façon *f* de voir les choses; **o. on life** conception *f* de la vie **(c)** *(view)* vue *f* *(over* sur)

outlying ['aʊtlaɪɪŋ] *adj* éloigné(e), isolé(e)

outmanoeuvre, *Am* **outmaneuver** [aʊtmə-'nu:və(r)] *vt Mil* l'emporter tactiquement sur; *(in politics, sport)* déjouer les tactiques de

outmoded [aʊt'məʊdɪd] *adj* démodé(e)

outnumber [aʊt'nʌmbə(r)] *vt* l'emporter en nombre sur; **we were outnumbered** ils étaient plus nombreux (que nous)

out-of-doors [aʊtəv'dɔ:z] *adv* = outdoors

out-of-pocket expenses [aʊtəv'pɒkɪt'ɪk'spensɪz] *npl* menues dépenses *fpl*

out-of-the-way [aʊtəvðə'weɪ] *adj (remote)* écarté(e), loin de tout; *(unusual)* insolite, qui sort de l'ordinaire

outpatient ['aʊtpeɪʃənt] *n* malade *mf* en consultation externe; **outpatients' (department)** service *m* des consultations externes

outplacement ['aʊtpleɪsmənt] *n* = aide à la recherche d'un nouvel emploi, fournie par l'employeur lors d'un licenciement

outpost ['aʊtpəʊst] *n Mil* poste *m* avancé; *Fig* bastion *m*

output ['aʊtpʊt] **1** *n (of goods)* production *f*; *(of data, information)* sortie *f*; *(of generator, machine)* débit *m*
2 *vt (pt & pp* output) produire; *(data, information)* sortir

outrage ['aʊtreɪdʒ] **1** *n* **(a)** *(act)* atrocité *f*; **it's an o.!** c'est un scandale! **(b)** *(indignation)* indignation *f* (**at** face à)
2 *vt (make indignant)* scandaliser, outrer

outrageous [aʊt'reɪdʒəs] *adj (shocking)* scandaleux(euse); *(clothes, haircut)* extravagant(e)

outrageously [aʊt'reɪdʒəslɪ] *adv (expensive)* scandaleusement; *(behave)* de façon scandaleuse; *(dressed)* de façon extravagante

outreach worker ['aʊtri:tʃwɜːkə(r)] *n* = employé d'une association travaillant sur le terrain

outright 1 *adv* **(a)** *(completely)* **to buy sth o.** acheter qch au comptant; **he was killed o.** il fut tué sur le coup **(b)** *(ask, tell)* franchement; *(refuse)* catégoriquement
2 *adj* ['aʊtraɪt] *(refusal)* catégorique; *(failure)* total(e); *(winner)* incontesté(e)

outrun [aʊt'rʌn] *(pt* outran [aʊt'ræn], *pp* outrun) *vt* courir plus vite que

outsell [aʊt'sel] *(pt & pp* outsold [aʊt'səʊld]) *vt* se vendre mieux que

outset ['aʊtset] *n* **at the o.** au départ; **from the o.** dès le départ

outshine [aʊt'ʃaɪn] *(pt & pp* outshone [aʊt'ʃɒn]) *vt (surpass)* éclipser

outside 1 [aʊtsaɪd, aʊt'saɪd] *n* extérieur *m*, dehors *m*; **on the o.** à l'extérieur; *Fig* extérieurement; **from the o.** du dehors, de l'extérieur; **at the o.** *(of estimate)* tout au plus
2 *adj (influence)* extérieur(e); *Rad & TV* **o. broadcast** reportage *m*; **o. lane** *(when driving on left)* file *f* de droite; *(when driving on right)* file de gauche; **the o. world** le monde extérieur; **an o. chance** une petite chance
3 *adv* dehors, à l'extérieur; **to go o.** sortir
4 *prep* **(a)** *(physically)* en dehors de, à l'extérieur de; *(in front of)* devant; **o. office hours** en dehors des heures de bureau **(b)** *(apart from)* en dehors de; **o. (of) a few friends** en dehors de quelques amis

outsider [aʊt'saɪdə(r)] *n* **(a)** *(socially)* étranger(ère) *m,f* **(b)** *(in race, election)* outsider *m*

outsize ['aʊtsaɪz] *adj (clothes)* très grande taille; *(appetite, ego)* démesuré(e)

outskirts ['aʊtskɜːts] *npl* **the o.** la banlieue

outsmart [aʊt'smɑːt] *vt* se montrer plus fin(e) que

outsourcing [ˈaʊtsɔːsɪŋ] n Com sous-traitance f

outspoken [aʊtˈspəʊkən] adj franc (franche)

outstanding [aʊtˈstændɪŋ] adj **(a)** (remarkable) exceptionnel(elle) **(b)** (unresolved) (business) en suspens **(c)** (unpaid) (amount, debt) impayé(e); (payment) en retard; (interest) échu(e)

outstay [aʊtˈsteɪ] vt **I hope I haven't outstayed my welcome** j'espère ne pas avoir abusé de votre hospitalité

outstretched [ˈaʊtstretʃt] adj (leg, arm) tendu(e)

outstrip [aʊtˈstrɪp] (pt & pp **outstripped**) vt dépasser

out-tray [ˈaʊttreɪ] n courrier m à expédier

outward [ˈaʊtwəd] 1 adj **(a)** (external) extérieur(e) **(b)** o. voyage or journey voyage m aller
2 adv = **outwards**

outwardly [ˈaʊtwədlɪ] adv en apparence

outwards [ˈaʊtwədz] adv vers l'extérieur

outweigh [aʊtˈweɪ] vt (be more important than) l'emporter sur

outwit [aʊtˈwɪt] (pt & pp **outwitted**) vt se montrer plus malin(igne) que

outworker [ˈaʊtwɜːkə(r)] n travailleur(euse) m,f à domicile

outworn [aʊtˈwɔːn] adj (theory, idea) périmé(e)

ova [ˈəʊvə] pl of **ovum**

oval [ˈəʊvəl] 1 n ovale m
2 adj ovale

ovarian [əʊˈveərɪən] adj Anat ovarien(enne)

ovary [ˈəʊvərɪ] (pl **ovaries**) n Anat ovaire m

ovation [əʊˈveɪʃən] n ovation f; **to give sb a standing o.** se lever pour applaudir qn

oven [ˈʌvən] n four m; **o. gloves** gants mpl isolants

oven-proof [ˈʌvənpruːf] adj qui va au four

oven-ready [ˈʌvənredɪ] adj prêt(e) à rôtir

ovenware [ˈʌvənweə(r)] n vaisselle f allant au four

over [ˈəʊvə(r)] 1 prep **(a)** (above) au-dessus de; **the plane flew o. our heads** l'avion est passé au-dessus de nos têtes; **I couldn't hear her o. the noise** impossible de l'entendre avec tout ce bruit; **Fig her talk was way o. my head** son exposé m'est passé complètement au-dessus de la tête
(b) (on top of) sur; **to put a blanket o. sb** mettre une couverture sur qn
(c) (from one side to the other of) par-dessus; **to throw sth o. the wall** jeter qch par-dessus le mur; **to read o. sb's shoulder** lire par-dessus l'épaule de qn
(d) (across) **to go o. the road** traverser la rue; **to live o. the road** habiter en face; **o. the border** de l'autre côté de la frontière; **the bridge o. the river** le pont qui traverse la rivière
(e) (about) **to laugh o. sth** rire de qch; **to fight o. sth** se battre pour qch
(f) (more than) plus de; **he's o. fifty** il a plus de cinquante ans; **children o. five** les enfants de plus de cinq ans; **o. and above** en plus de
(g) (during) pendant; **o. the last three years** les trois dernières années; **o. lunch** en déjeunant
(h) (recovered from) **to be o. sth** (illness, disappointment) s'être remis(e) de qch
(i) Fam Fig **o. the top** (excessive) excessif(ive)
2 adv **(a)** (across) **o. here** ici; **o. there** là-bas; **to cross o.** (the street) traverser; **to ask** or **invite sb o.** (to one's house) inviter qn (chez soi)
(b) (down) **to fall o.** tomber; **to bend o.** se pencher; **to**

push sb/sth o. faire tomber qn/qch
(c) (everywhere) **famous the world o.** célèbre dans le monde entier
(d) (expressing repetition) **three times o.** trois fois de suite; **o. and o. again** encore et encore; **to do sth all o. again** refaire qch
(e) (in excess) **children of five and o.** les enfants de cinq ans et plus; **there was £5 left o.** il restait 5 livres
(f) (on radio) **o.!** à vous!; **o. and out!** terminé!
3 adj **to be (all) o.** être fini(e); **to get sth o. (and done) with** en finir avec qch
4 n (in cricket) = série de six balles

overabundant [əʊvərəˈbʌndənt] adj surabondant(e)

overactive [əʊvərˈæktɪv] adj (imagination) débridé(e)

overall 1 [ˈəʊvərɔːl] adj global(e); (size, area) total(e); **she has o. responsibility for sales** elle est responsable de l'ensemble du service des ventes
2 adv dans l'ensemble; **£10 o.** 10 livres en tout; **third o.** troisième au classement général

overalls [ˈəʊvərɔːlz] npl **(a)** (work garment) bleu m de travail **(b)** Am (dungarees) salopette f

overanxious [əʊvərˈæŋkʃəs] adj trop inquiet(ète)

overawe [əʊvərˈɔː] vt **to be overawed by sb/sth** se laisser impressionner par qn/qch

overbalance [əʊvəˈbæləns] vi (of person) perdre l'équilibre; (of pile, load) se renverser

overbearing [əʊvəˈbeərɪŋ] adj autoritaire

overblown [əʊvəˈbləʊn] adj (style) ampoulé(e)

overboard [ˈəʊvəbɔːd] adv par-dessus bord; **man o.!** un homme à la mer!; Fig **to go o.** s'emballer (pour)

overbook [ˈəʊvəbʊk] vt faire du surbooking sur

overcapacity [ˈəʊvəkəˈpæsɪtɪ] n Ind surcapacité f

overcast [ˈəʊvəkɑːst] adj (sky, day) nuageux(euse)

overcautious [əʊvəˈkɔːʃəs] adj trop prudent(e)

overcharge [əʊvəˈtʃɑːdʒ] vt **to o. sb for sth** faire payer qch trop cher à qn; **he overcharged me by a pound** il m'a fait payer une livre en trop

overcoat [ˈəʊvəkəʊt] n pardessus m

overcome [əʊvəˈkʌm] (pt **overcame** [əʊvəˈkeɪm], pp **overcome**) vt (opponent, one's fears) vaincre; (problem, obstacle) surmonter; **to be overcome with** or **by grief** être accablé(e) de chagrin; **I was quite overcome** j'ai été bouleversé

overcompensate [əʊvəˈkɒmpenseɪt] vi **to o. for sth** surcompenser qch

overconfident [əʊvəˈkɒnfɪdənt] adj trop confiant(e)

overcook [əʊvəˈkʊk] vt (faire) trop cuire

overcrowded [əʊvəˈkraʊdəd] adj bondé(e)

overcrowding [əʊvəˈkraʊdɪŋ] n surpeuplement m

overdeveloped [əʊvədɪˈveləpt] adj trop développé(e)

overdo [əʊvəˈduː] (pt **overdid** [əʊvəˈdɪd], pp **overdone** [əʊvəˈdʌn]) vt exagérer; **to o. it** (work too hard) se surmener; **to o. the salt/make-up** forcer sur le sel/le maquillage

overdone [ˈəʊvədʌn] adj (food) trop cuit(e)

overdose [ˈəʊvədəʊs] 1 n overdose f
2 vi faire une overdose (on de); Fig **o. on chocolate** exagérer avec le chocolat

overdraft [ˈəʊvədrɑːft] n Fin découvert m

overdrawn [əʊvəˈdrɔːn] adj à découvert

overdressed [əʊvəˈdrest] adj trop habillé(e)

overdrive [ˈəʊvədraɪv] n Fig **to go into o.** passer à la vitesse supérieure

overdue [əʊvə'dju:] *adj (person, train)* en retard; *(bill)* impayé(e); *(library book)* qui n'a pas été rendu(e); **this measure is long o.** cette mesure aurait dû être prise il y a longtemps

overeat [əʊvə'ri:t] *(pt overate* [əʊvə'ret], *pp overeaten* [əʊvə'ri:tən]) *vi* trop manger

overemphasize [əʊvər'emfəsaɪz] *vt* trop mettre l'accent sur

overenthusiastic ['əʊvərɪnθju:zɪ'æstɪk] *adj* trop enthousiaste

overestimate [əʊvə'restɪmeɪt] *vt* surestimer; *(danger)* exagérer

overexcited [əʊvərɪk'saɪtɪd] *adj* surexcité(e)

overexpose [əʊvərɪks'pəʊz] *vt Phot* surexposer

overextended [əʊvərɪk'stendɪd] *adj Fin* incapable de faire face à ses engagements

overflow 1 n ['əʊvəfləʊ] *(liquid)* trop-plein *m*; **o. (pipe)** trop-plein

2 *vi* [əʊvə'fləʊ] déborder; **his desk was overflowing with papers** son bureau disparaissait sous la paperasse

overgrown [əʊvə'grəʊn] *adj (garden)* envahi(e) par les mauvaises herbes; **he's like an o. schoolboy** il se conduit comme un collégien

overhang 1 n ['əʊvəhæŋ] *(of roof, cliff)* surplomb *m*

2 *vt* [əʊvə'hæŋ] *(pt & pp overhung* [əʊvə'hʌŋ]) surplomber

overhaul 1 ['əʊvəhɔ:l] *n also Fig* révision *f*

2 *vt* [əʊvə'hɔ:l] **(a)** *(machine, policy)* réviser **(b)** *(overtake)* dépasser

overhead 1 n ['əʊvəhed] *Am Com* = **overheads**

2 *adj (cable)* aérien(enne); **o. projector** rétroprojecteur *m*

3 *adv* [əʊvə'hed] au-dessus; **a plane flew o.** un avion passa au-dessus de nos têtes

overheads ['əʊvəhedz] *npl Br Com* frais *mpl* généraux

overhear [əʊvə'hɪə(r)] *(pt & pp overheard* [əʊvə'hɜ:d]) *vt (person)* entendre (par hasard); *(words)* surprendre

overheat [əʊvə'hi:t] *vi (of engine)* chauffer; *(of economy)* être en surchauffe

overindulge [əʊvərɪn'dʌldʒ] **1** *vt (child)* trop gâter; **to o. oneself** *(drink, eat to excess)* faire des excès

2 *vi* faire des excès

overjoyed [əʊvə'dʒɔɪd] *adj* absolument ravi(e) *(at de)*

overkill ['əʊvəkɪl] *n* **it's o.** c'est exagéré, c'est trop; **media o.** matraquage *m*

overland ['əʊvəlænd] *adv & adj* par voie de terre

overlap 1 n ['əʊvəlæp] *(between planks, tiles)* chevauchement *m*

2 *vi* [əʊvə'læp] *(pt & pp overlapped) (of planks, tiles, periods)* se chevaucher; *(of theories)* avoir des points communs *(with avec)*; **to o. with** *(in time)* empiéter sur

overleaf [əʊvə'li:f] *adv* au verso; **see o.** voir au verso

overload 1 n ['əʊvələʊd] *Elec* surcharge *f*

2 *vt* [əʊvə'ləʊd] *also Fig* surcharger *(with de)*

overlong [əʊvə'lɒŋ] *adj* trop long (longue)

overlook [əʊvə'lʊk] *vt* **(a)** *(of building, window)* donner sur; **the town is overlooked by the castle** le château surplombe la ville **(b)** *(fail to notice)* oublier **(c)** *(disregard)* fermer les yeux sur

overly ['əʊvəlɪ] *adv* excessivement, trop

overmanning [əʊvə'mænɪŋ] *n* sureffectifs *mpl*

overmuch [əʊvə'mʌtʃ] *adv* outre mesure, trop

overnight 1 *adv* [əʊvə'naɪt] **(a)** *(during the night)* (pendant) la nuit; **to stay o.** passer la nuit; **leave to soak o.** laisser tremper toute la nuit **(b)** *(suddenly)* du jour au lendemain

2 *adj* ['əʊvənaɪt] **(a)** *(for one night)* **o. train/flight** train *m*/vol *m* de nuit; **o. bag** petit sac *m* de voyage; **o. stay** séjour *m* d'une nuit; *(in hotel)* nuit *f* **(b)** *(sudden)* soudain(e)

overoptimistic [əʊvərɒptɪ'mɪstɪk] *adj* trop optimiste *(about* quant à)

overpaid [əʊvə'peɪd] *adj* trop payé(e)

overpass ['əʊvəpɑ:s] *n (road)* pont *m*; *(for pedestrians)* passerelle *f*

overpayment [əʊvə'peɪmənt] *n* *(of taxes)* trop-perçu *m*; *(of employee)* rémunération *f* excessive

overpopulation [əʊvəpɒpjʊ'leɪʃən] *n* surpopulation *f*, surpeuplement *m*

overpower [əʊvə'paʊə(r)] *vt* maîtriser

overpowering [əʊvə'paʊərɪŋ] *adj (heat, smell)* suffocant(e); *(taste)* qui prend à la gorge; *(desire)* irrépressible

overpriced [əʊvə'praɪst] *adj* trop cher(ère)

overproduction [əʊvəprə'dʌkʃən] *n Econ* surproduction *f*

overrated [əʊvə'reɪtɪd] *adj* surfait(e)

overreach [əʊvə'ri:tʃ] *vt* **to o. oneself** trop présumer de ses forces

overreact [əʊvərɪ'ækt] *vi* réagir de façon excessive

override [əʊvə'raɪd] *vt (pt overrode* [əʊvə'rəʊd], *pp overridden* [əʊvə'rɪdən]) **(a)** *(objections, wishes, regulations)* passer outre à; *(decision)* annuler **(b)** *(take precedence over)* avoir la priorité sur; *Tech (device)* annuler

overriding [əʊvə'raɪdɪŋ] *adj (importance)* capital(e); *(factor)* prépondérant(e)

overrule [əʊvə'ru:l] *vt (opinion)* rejeter; *(decision)* annuler; **she was overruled by her boss** son patron a rejeté sa proposition

overrun 1 *vt* [əʊvə'rʌn] *(pt overran* [əʊvə'ræn], *pp overrun)* **(a)** *(country)* envahir; **the house was overrun with mice** la maison était infestée de souris **(b)** *(allotted time)* dépasser

2 *vi (of TV, radio programme)* déborder sur l'horaire

3 *n* ['əʊvərʌn] *Com (cost)* **o.** dépassement *m* du budget

overseas 1 *adj* ['əʊvəsi:z] d'outre-mer; *(trade, debt)* extérieur(e)

2 *adv* [əʊvə'si:z] à l'étranger

oversee [əʊvə'si:] *(pt oversaw* [əʊvə'sɔ:], *pp overseen* [əʊvə'si:n]) *vt* superviser

overseer ['əʊvəsɪə(r)] *n Old-fashioned* contremaître *m*

oversensitive [əʊvə'sensɪtɪv] *adj* hypersensible

oversexed [əʊvə'sekst] *adj* qui a une libido démesurée

overshadow [əʊvə'ʃædəʊ] *vt Fig (of atmosphere, threat)* planer sur; *(of person)* éclipser

overshoe ['əʊvəʃu:] *n Am* caoutchouc *m*

overshoot [əʊvə'ʃu:t] *(pt & pp overshot* [əʊvə'ʃɒt]) *vt* dépasser

oversight ['əʊvəsaɪt] *n* oubli *m*, omission *f*

oversimplify [əʊvə'sɪmplɪfaɪ] *(pt & pp over-simplified)* *vt* simplifier à outrance

oversized ['əʊvəsaɪzd] *adj (very big)* énorme; *(clothes)* trop grand(e)

oversleep [əʊvə'sli:p] *(pt & pp overslept* [əʊvə'slept]) *vi* ne pas se réveiller à temps

overspend [əʊvə'spend] (*pt & pp* **overspent** [əʊvə-'spent]) **1** *vt* to o. one's budget dépasser son budget
   2 *vi* trop dépenser

overspill ['əʊvəspɪl] *n* (*of population*) excédent *m*; (*from meeting, party*) trop-plein *m*

overstaffing [əʊvə'stɑːfɪŋ] *n* sureffectifs *mpl*

overstate [əʊvə'steɪt] *vt* exagérer

overstay [əʊvə'steɪ] = **outstay**

overstep [əʊvə'step] (*pt & pp* **overstepped**) *vt* outrepasser; *Fig* to o. the mark dépasser les bornes

oversubscribed [əʊvəsəb'skraɪbd] *adj Fin* sursouscrit(e)

overt [əʊ'vɜːt] *adj* manifeste

overtake [əʊvə'teɪk] (*pt* **overtook** [əʊvə'tʊk], *pp* **overtaken** [əʊvə'teɪkən]) **1** *vt & vi* (*vehicle*) doubler; to be overtaken by events être dépassé(e) par les événements

overthrow 1 *n* ['əʊvəθrəʊ] renversement *m*
   2 *vt* [əʊvə'θrəʊ] (*pt* **overthrew** [əʊvə'θruː], *pp* **overthrown** [əʊvə'θrəʊn]) renverser

overtime ['əʊvətaɪm] **1** *n* heures *fpl* supplémentaires
   2 *adv* to work o. faire des heures supplémentaires; *Fig (of imagination)* s'emballer

overtly [əʊ'vɜːtlɪ] *adv* ouvertement

overtone ['əʊvətəʊn] *n* (*of sadness, bitterness*) pointe *f*; (*of violence, racism*) relent *m*

overture ['əʊvətjʊə(r)] *n Mus* ouverture *f*; *Fig* to make overtures to sb faire des avances à qn

overturn [əʊvə'tɜːn] **1** *vt* (*table, government*) renverser; (*boat*) faire chavirer; (*decision*) annuler
   2 *vi* se renverser; (*of boat*) chavirer

overuse 1 *n* [əʊvə'juːs] emploi *m* excessif
   2 *vt* [əʊvə'juːz] abuser de

overvalue [əʊvə'væljuː] *vt* (*currency*) surévaluer; (*ability*) surestimer

overview ['əʊvəvjuː] *n* vue *f* d'ensemble

overweight [əʊvə'weɪt] *adj* trop gros (grosse); to be 10 kilos o. avoir 10 kilos de trop

overwhelm [əʊvə'welm] *vt* (*enemy, opponent*) écraser; **overwhelmed with joy** au comble de la joie; **overwhelmed by grief/with work** accablé(e) de chagrin/de travail

overwhelming [əʊvə'welmɪŋ] *adj* (*need, desire*) irrépressible; (*pressure, defeat, majority*) écrasant(e)

overwhelmingly [əʊvə'welmɪŋlɪ] *adv* massivement

overwork [əʊvə'wɜːk] **1** *n* surmenage *m*
   2 *vt* (*person*) surcharger de travail
   3 *vi* se surmener

overwrite [əʊvə'raɪt] (*pt* **overwrote** [əʊvə'rəʊt], *pp* **overwritten** [əʊvə'rɪtən]) *vt Comptr* (*file*) écraser

overwrought [əʊvə'rɔːt] *adj* à bout; **to get o.** beaucoup s'énerver

ovulate ['ɒvjʊleɪt] *vi Biol* ovuler

ovulation [ɒvjʊ'leɪʃən] *n Biol* ovulation *f*

ovum ['əʊvəm] (*pl* **ova** ['əʊvə]) *n Biol* ovule *m*

ow [aʊ] *exclam* aïe!, ouïe!

owe [əʊ] *vt also Fig* devoir; **to o. sb sth, to o. sth to sb** devoir qch à qn; **to o. sb an apology** devoir des excuses à qn; **to o. it to oneself to do sth** se devoir de faire qch

owing ['əʊɪŋ] *adj* (a) **the money o. to me** l'argent qui m'est dû (b) **o.** (*because of*) en raison de, à cause de

owl [aʊl] *n* hibou *m*, chouette *f*

own [əʊn] **1** *adj* propre; **her o. money** son propre argent; **I saw it with my o. eyes** je l'ai vu de mes propres yeux; **I do my o. accounts** je fais mes comptes moi-même; **she's famous in her o. right** elle est célèbre elle aussi; **o. goal** (*in football*) = but marqué contre son propre camp; *Fig* **to score an o. goal** apporter de l'eau au moulin de l'adversaire
   2 *pron* (a) **my o.** le mien (la mienne); **the house is my o.** la maison est à moi; **I have money of my o.** j'ai de l'argent à moi; **to make sth one's o.** s'approprier qch; **for reasons of her o.** pour des raisons qui ne regardent qu'elle (b) **to do sth on one's o.** (*without company*) faire qch tout(e) seul(e); **I am (all) on my o.** je suis seul; **you're on your o.!** (*I won't support you*) débrouille-toi tout seul! (c) (*idioms*) **to come into one's o.** montrer ce dont on est capable; **to get one's o. back (on sb)** se venger (de qn); **to hold one's o.** se maintenir
   3 *vt* (a) (*property*) posséder, être propriétaire de; **who owns this jumper?** à qui est ce pull?; **he behaves as if he owns the place** il se conduit comme en pays conquis (b) *Old-fashioned* (*admit*) avouer
   ▸**own up** *vi* (*confess*) avouer; **to o. up to sth** avouer qch

own-brand ['əʊnbrænd] *adj Com* vendu(e) sous la marque du distributeur

owner ['əʊnə(r)] *n* propriétaire *mf*

owner-occupier ['əʊnər'ɒkjʊpaɪə(r)] *n* propriétaire *mf* occupant(e)

ownership ['əʊnəʃɪp] *n* propriété *f*; **under new o.** (*sign*) changement de propriétaire; **to be in private/public o.** appartenir au secteur privé/public

ox [ɒks] (*pl* **oxen** ['ɒksən]) *n* bœuf *m*

Oxbridge ['ɒksbrɪdʒ] *n* les universités *fpl* d'Oxford et de Cambridge

oxide ['ɒksaɪd] *n Chem* oxyde *m*

oxidize ['ɒksɪdaɪz] *Chem* **1** *vt* oxyder
   2 *vi* s'oxyder

oxtail ['ɒksteɪl] *n* queue *f* de bœuf

oxyacetylene [ɒksɪə'setɪliːn] *n Chem* **o. torch** chalumeau *m* oxyacétylénique

oxygen ['ɒksɪdʒən] *n* oxygène *m*; **o. bottle** *or* **cylinder** bouteille *f* d'oxygène; **o. mask** masque *m* à oxygène

oyster ['ɔɪstə(r)] *n* huître *f*; *Fig* **the world's your o.** le monde t'appartient; **o. bed** parc *m* à huîtres

oystercatcher ['ɔɪstəkætʃə(r)] *n* huîtrier *m*

Oz [ɒz] *n Fam* l'Australie *f*

oz (*abbr* **ounce(s)**) once *f*

ozone ['əʊzəʊn] *n Chem* ozone *m*; **the o. layer** la couche d'ozone

ozone-friendly ['əʊzəʊn'frendlɪ] *adj* qui préserve la couche d'ozone

P

P, p [pi:] *n* (*letter*) P, p *m inv*; *Fam* to mind one's P's and Q's bien se tenir

p [pi:] *Br* (*abbr* **penny**) penny *m*; (*abbr* **pence**) pence *mpl*

PA ['pi:'eɪ] *n* (a) (*abbr* **public address**) PA (system) (système *m* de) sonorisation *f* (b) *Com* (*abbr* **personal assistant**) secrétaire *mf* de direction

pa [pɑ:] *n Am Fam* (*dad*) papa *m*

p.a. (*abbr* **per annum**) par an

pace [peɪs] **1** *n* (a) (*step*) pas *m*; *Fig* to put sb through his paces mettre qn à l'épreuve (b) (*speed*) vitesse *f*, allure *f*; at a slow/fast p. à petite/vive allure; to set the p. donner l'allure; *Fig* montrer la voie; to keep p. with sb suivre qn; *Fig (in activity)* suivre le rythme de qn

2 *vt* (*room, street*) arpenter; to p. oneself (*in race, work*) trouver son rythme

3 *vi* to p. up and down faire les cent pas

pacemaker ['peɪsmeɪkə(r)] *n* (a) (*in race*) meneur(euse) *m,f* de train (b) (*for heart*) stimulateur *m* cardiaque

Pacific [pə'sɪfɪk] *adj* the P. (Ocean) le Pacifique, l'océan *m* Pacifique; the P. Rim les pays *mpl* de l'Asie-Pacifique; *Am* P. Standard Time heure *f* de la côte ouest de l'Amérique du Nord

pacifier ['pæsɪfaɪə(r)] *n Am* tétine *f*

pacifism ['pæsɪfɪzəm] *n* pacifisme *m*

pacifist ['pæsɪfɪst] *n & adj* pacifiste *mf*

pacify ['pæsɪfaɪ] (*pt & pp* **pacified**) *vt* (*country*) pacifier; (*person*) apaiser, calmer

pack [pæk] **1** *n* (a) (*rucksack*) sac *m* à dos (b) (*of cigarettes, washing powder*) paquet *m*; (*of beer*) pack *m*; (*of playing cards*) jeu *m* (c) (*of thieves, photographers*) bande *f*; (*of runners, cyclists*) peloton *m*; (*in rugby*) pack *m*; (*of wolves*) meute *f*; a p. of lies un tissu de mensonges; p. animal animal *m* de bât; p. ice banquise *f*

2 *vt* (a) (*in box, suitcase*) mettre (b) (*cram*) (*earth into hole*) tasser; (*passengers into bus, train*) entasser (c) (*fill*) (*hole, box*) bourrer (with de); *also Fig* to p. one's bags faire ses valises (d) to p. a punch (*of fighter*) cogner dur; (*of drink*) être costaud

3 *vi* (a) (*prepare luggage*) faire ses valises *ou* bagages; *Fam Fig* to send sb packing envoyer promener qn (b) (*cram*) to p. into a room/bus s'entasser dans une pièce/un bus

▸**pack in Fam 1** *vt* (*job, course*) laisser tomber; p. it in! arrête!, ça suffit!

2 *vi* (*of car, machine*) tomber en rade

▸**pack off** *vt sep Fam* (*send away*) expédier

▸**pack up 1** *vt* (*tidy away*) ranger

2 *vi Fam* (a) (*of car, machine*) tomber en rade (b) (*finish work*) arrêter

package ['pækɪdʒ] **1** *n* (*parcel*) paquet *m*, colis *m*; (*of measures, laws*) ensemble *m*; (*contract*) contrat *m* global; p. deal *or* holiday forfait *m* (comprenant au moins transport et logement)

2 *vt* emballer, conditionner; *Fig* to p. sb (*pop star, politician*) créer l'image de marque de qn

packaging ['pækɪdʒɪŋ] *n* emballage *m*

packed [pækt] *adj* (*crowded*) bondé(e) (b) p. lunch = déjeuner qu'on emporte à l'école ou au bureau

packer ['pækə(r)] *n* (*person*) emballeur(euse) *m,f*

packet ['pækɪt] *n* (a) (*of food, washing powder, cigarettes*) paquet *m*; p. soup soupe *f* en sachet (b) *Fam (lot of money)* to make *or* earn a p. se faire un fric fou; that'll cost a p. ça va coûter bonbon

packhorse ['pækhɔ:s] *n* cheval *m* de bât

packing ['pækɪŋ] *n* (a) (*packing material*) emballage *m*; p. case caisse *f* d'emballage (b) (*for trip*) to do one's p. faire ses valises *ou* bagages

pact [pækt] *n* pacte *m*

pad [pæd] **1** *n* (a) (*for protection*) protection *f*; (*of dog's, cat's paw*) coussinet *m*; (*of cotton wool*) tampon *m*; (*for helicopters*) aire *f* d'atterrissage; (*writing*) p. bloc *m*; *Fam (home)* piaule *f*

2 *vt* (*pt & pp* **padded**) (*furniture*) capitonner (with avec)

3 *vi* to p. about aller et venir à pas feutrés

▸**pad out** *vt sep* (*speech, essay*) étoffer

padded ['pædɪd] *adj* (*furniture, wall, cell*) capitonné(e); (*jacket*) matelassé(e)

padding ['pædɪŋ] *n* (*for clothes*) ouate *f*; *Fig (in speech, essay*) remplissage *m*

paddle ['pædəl] **1** *n* (a) (*for canoe*) pagaie *f*; (*of paddle boat*) aube *f*; p. boat bateau *m* à aubes (b) (*walk in water*) to have a p. patauger

2 *vt* to p. a canoe pagayer

3 *vi* (a) (*in canoe*) pagayer; (*of duck*) nager (b) (*walk in water*) patauger

paddling pool ['pædlɪŋ'pu:l] *n* (a) (*inflatable*) piscine *f* gonflable (b) (*in park*) pataugeoire *f*

paddock ['pædək] *n* paddock *m*

Paddy ['pædɪ] (*pl* **Paddies**) *n Fam (Irish man)* Irlandais *m*

paddy ['pædɪ] (*pl* **paddies**) *n* p. (field) rizière *f*

padlock ['pædlɒk] **1** *n* cadenas *m*

2 *vt* cadenasser

padre ['pɑ:dreɪ] *n* aumônier *m* (militaire)

paediatric, *Am* **pediatric** [pi:dɪ'ætrɪk] *adj Med* (*ward*) de pédiatrie; (*specialist, nurse*) en pédiatrie

paediatrician, *Am* **pediatrician** [pi:dɪə'trɪʃən] *n Med* pédiatre *mf*

paediatrics, *Am* **pediatrics** [pi:dɪ'ætrɪks] *n Med* pédiatrie *f*

paedophile, *Am* **pedophile** ['pi:dəʊfaɪl] *n* pédophile *mf*

pagan ['peɪɡən] n & adj païen(enne) m,f

paganism ['peɪɡənɪzəm] n paganisme m

page¹ [peɪdʒ] n (of book) page f; **on p. 6** (à la) page 6

page² 1 n (servant, at wedding) page m

2 vt (call) (by loudspeaker) appeler par haut-parleur; (by electronic device) biper

pageant ['pædʒənt] n (procession) spectacle m grandiose; (historical) spectacle m historique

pageantry ['pædʒəntrɪ] n pompe f

pageboy ['peɪdʒbɔɪ] n page m; **p. (haircut)** coiffure f à la Jeanne d'Arc

pager ['peɪdʒə(r)] n récepteur m d'appel

pagination [pædʒɪ'neɪʃən] n Typ pagination f

pagoda [pə'ɡəʊdə] n pagode f

paid [peɪd] 1 adj (a) (person, work) rémunéré(e), payé(e) (b) **to put p. to sb's chances/hopes** réduire les chances/espoirs de qn à néant

2 pt & pp of **pay**

paid-up ['peɪdʌp] adj (member) qui a payé sa cotisation

pail [peɪl] n seau m

pain [peɪn] 1 n (a) (physical) douleur f; (emotional) peine f; **to cause sb p.** (physical) faire souffrir qn; (emotional) faire de la peine à qn; **to be in p.** souffrir; **I have a p. in my leg** j'ai une douleur à la jambe (b) (trouble) **to take pains** or **be at great pains to do sth** se donner du mal pour faire qch; **for my pains** pour ma peine (c) Formal **under p. of death** sous peine de mort (d) (idioms) Fam **he's a p. (in the neck)** il est casse-pieds; Vulg **it's a p. in the arse** c'est chiant; Fam **cooking is such a p.!** c'est tellement casse-pieds de faire la cuisine!

2 vt peiner

pained [peɪnd] adj (look, expression) peiné(e), affligé(e)

painful ['peɪnfʊl] adj (physically) douloureux(euse); (emotionally) pénible; **it's p. to watch** c'est un spectacle pénible

painfully ['peɪnfʊlɪ] adv (walk) avec difficulté; **she fell p. elle s'est fait mal en tombant;** Fig **p. shy** d'une timidité maladive

painkiller ['peɪnkɪlə(r)] n analgésique m

painless ['peɪnlɪs] adj (not painful) indolore; Fig (easy) facile

painstaking ['peɪnzteɪkɪŋ] adj minutieux(euse)

paint [peɪnt] 1 n peinture f; **wet p.** (sign) peinture fraîche; **p. gun** pistolet m à peinture; **p. remover** décapant m

2 vt peindre; Fam **to p. one's face** (put on make-up) se maquiller; **to p. one's nails** se faire les ongles; Fig **to p. a favourable picture of a situation** brosser un tableau favorable d'une situation; Fig **to p. the town red** faire la noce

3 vi peindre

paintbox ['peɪntbɒks] n boîte f de couleurs

paintbrush ['peɪntbrʌʃ] n pinceau m

painter ['peɪntə(r)] n peintre m; **p. and decorator** peintre-tapissier m

painting ['peɪntɪŋ] n (picture) tableau m, peinture f; (activity) la peinture

paintwork ['peɪntwɜːk] n peinture f

pair [peə(r)] 1 n paire f; **in pairs** deux par deux; **a p. of glasses** une paire de lunettes; **a p. of scissors** une paire de ciseaux; **a p. of trousers** un pantalon

2 vt **to p. sb with sb** mettre qn avec qn

▸**pair off** 1 vt sep (people) mettre deux par deux

2 vi (of people) se mettre deux par deux

▸**pair up** vi se mettre ensemble

pajamas Am = **pyjamas**

Pakistan [pɑːkɪ'stɑːn] n le Pakistan

Pakistani [pɑːkɪ'stɑːnɪ] 1 n Pakistanais(e) m,f

2 adj pakistanais(e)

PAL [pæl] n TV (abbr **phase alternation line**) PAL

pal [pæl] n Fam copain (copine) m,f; **listen, p.!** fais gaffe, mon vieux!

palace ['pælɪs] n palais m

palatable ['pælətəbəl] adj (food) agréable au palais; Fig (suggestion) acceptable

palate ['pælɪt] n (in mouth) palais m

palatial [pə'leɪʃəl] adj (impressive) grandiose; (luxurious) luxueux(euse)

palaver [pə'lɑːvə(r)] n Fam (fuss) histoire f

pale¹ ['peɪl] 1 adj pâle; **to turn p. (with fright)** pâlir; Br **p. ale** = bière brune de couleur claire

2 vi (of person) pâlir; **to p. into insignificance** être insignifiant(e)

pale² n beyond the p. (behaviour) inacceptable; (person) infréquentable

paleness ['peɪlnɪs] n pâleur f

Palestine ['pælɪstaɪn] n la Palestine

Palestinian [pælɪ'stɪnɪən] 1 n Palestinien(enne) m,f

2 adj palestinien(enne)

palette ['pælɪt] n Art palette f; **p. knife** couteau m à palette

palings ['peɪlɪŋz] npl (fence) palissade f

palisade [pælɪ'seɪd] n palissade f

pall¹ [pɔːl] n (of smoke) voile m

pall² vi (become uninteresting) perdre son attrait

pallbearer ['pɔːlbeərə(r)] n porteur m (du cercueil)

pallet ['pælɪt] n palette f

palliative ['pælɪətɪv] n palliatif m

pallid ['pælɪd] adj blême, blafard(e)

pally ['pælɪ] adj Fam **to be p. with sb** être copain (copine) avec qn

palm¹ [pɑːm] n **p. (tree)** palmier m; **p. (leaf)** palme f; **P. Sunday** Dimanche m des Rameaux

palm² n (of hand) paume f; Fig **to have sb in the p. of one's hand** avoir qn dans sa poche

▸**palm off** vt sep **to p. sth off on sb** refiler qch à qn

palmistry ['pɑːmɪstrɪ] n chiromancie f

palomino [pælə'miːnəʊ] (pl **palominos**) n (horse) palomino m

palpable ['pælpəbəl] adj (atmosphere) palpable; (lie) manifeste; (difference) sensible

palpate ['pælpeɪt] vt Med palper

palpitate ['pælpɪteɪt] vi also Fig palpiter

palpitations [pælpɪ'teɪʃəz] npl palpitations fpl

paltry ['pɔːltrɪ] adj (amount, sum) dérisoire; (excuse) piètre

pamper ['pæmpə(r)] vt (person) dorloter; **to p. oneself** se faire plaisir

pamphlet ['pæmflɪt] n (informative) brochure f; (political) pamphlet m

pan¹ [pæn] 1 n (saucepan) casserole f; (frying pan) poêle f; (of scales) plateau m; (of lavatory) cuvette f; Fam Fig **to go**

down the p. s'en aller en fumée

2 vi (pt & pp **panned**) **to p. for gold** faire de l'orpaillage

pan² [pæn] (pt & pp **panned**) vt Fam (criticize) descendre en flammes

▸**pan out** vi Fam (turn out) marcher; **it depends how things p. out** ça dépend de comment les choses vont s'arranger

panacea [pænə'sɪə] n panacée f

panache [pə'næʃ] n panache m

Pan-African [pæn'æfrɪkən] adj panafricain(e)

Panama ['pænəmɑː] n le Panama; **the P. Canal** le canal de Panama; **P. (hat)** panama m

Panamanian [pænə'meɪnɪən] **1** n Panaméen(enne) m,f

2 adj panaméen(enne)

Pan-American [pænə'merɪkən] adj panaméricain(e)

pancake ['pænkeɪk] n crêpe f; **P. Day** or **Tuesday** mardi m gras

pancreas ['pæŋkrɪəs] n Anat pancréas m

panda ['pændə] n panda m; Br **p. car** voiture f de police

pandemonium [pændɪ'məʊnɪəm] n (confusion) chaos m; (uproar) vacarme m assourdissant

pander ['pændə(r)] vi **to p. to sb/sth** flatter qn/qch

p & p [piːən'piː] n Br (abbr **postage and packing**) frais mpl de port et d'emballage

pane [peɪn] n **p. (of glass)** vitre f

panel ['pænəl] n (a) (of wood, metal) panneau m (b) (of switches, lights) tableau m de bord; **p. beater** carrossier m (c) (of experts) comité m; **p. discussion** table f ronde; (on radio, TV programme) invités mpl

panelling, Am **paneling** ['pænəlɪŋ] n lambris m

panellist, Am **panelist** ['pænəlɪst] n (on radio, TV programme) invité(e) m,f

pang [pæŋ] n (of guilt, jealousy) accès m; **pangs of hunger** tiraillements mpl d'estomac

panic ['pænɪk] **1** n panique f, affolement m; **in a p.** paniqué(e), affolé(e); **to get into a p.** paniquer, s'affoler; **p. attack** crise f d'angoisse; **p. button** bouton m déclencheur du signal d'alarme; Fin **p. buying/selling** achat m/vente f sous le coup de la panique; Fam **it was p. stations** c'était l'affolement général

2 vt (pt & pp **panicked**) affoler

3 vi paniquer, s'affoler

panicky ['pænɪkɪ] adj Fam **to be/get p.** paniquer, s'affoler

panic-stricken ['pænɪkstrɪkən] adj pris(e) de panique, affolé(e)

pannier ['pænɪə(r)] n (on bicycle) sacoche f; (on animal) panier m de bât

panoply ['pænəplɪ] n panoplie f

panorama [pænə'rɑːmə] n panorama m

panoramic [pænə'ræmɪk] adj panoramique

panpipes ['pænpaɪps] npl Mus flûte f de Pan

pansy ['pænzɪ] (pl **pansies**) n (a) (flower) pensée f (b) Fam (effeminate man) tante f

pant [pænt] vi haleter; **to p. for breath** chercher son souffle

panther ['pænθə(r)] n panthère f

panties ['pæntɪz] npl (petite) culotte f, slip m

pantomime ['pæntəmaɪm] n (a) Br (show) = spectacle de Noël inspiré d'un conte de fée (b) (mime) mime m

pantry ['pæntrɪ] (pl **pantries**) n garde-manger m inv

pants [pænts] npl (a) Br (underwear) slip m (b) Am (trousers) pantalon m; Fam **to scare the p. off sb** flanquer la trouille à qn

pantyhose, pantihose ['pæntɪhəʊz] n Am collant m

pap [pæp] n Fam Pej (nonsense) idioties fpl

papa [pə'pɑː] n Old-fashioned papa m

papacy ['peɪpəsɪ] n papauté f

papal ['peɪpəl] adj papal(e)

paper ['peɪpə(r)] **1** n (a) (material) papier m; **a piece of p.** un bout ou un morceau de papier; Fig **on p.** (in theory) sur le papier; **p. aeroplane** avion m en papier; **p. bag** sac m en papier; **p. cup** gobelet m en carton; Comptr **p. feed** alimentation f en papier; **p. mill** papeterie f; **p. money** papier-monnaie m; **p. towel** essuie-tout m inv; Comptr **p. tray** chariot m d'alimentation en papier (b) **papers** (documents) papiers mpl (c) (examination) épreuve f écrite (d) (scholarly study, report) article m; **to read** or **give a p.** faire un exposé (e) (newspaper) journal m; **p. boy/girl** livreur m/livreuse f de journaux; **p. round** tournée f de distribution des journaux; **p. shop** marchand m de journaux

2 vt (wall, room) tapisser

▸**paper over** vt sep Fig **to p. over the cracks** masquer les problèmes

paperback ['peɪpəbæk] n livre m de poche

paperclip ['peɪpəklɪp] n trombone m

paperknife ['peɪpənaɪf] (pl **paperknives**) n coupe-papier m

paperweight ['peɪpəweɪt] n presse-papiers m inv

paperwork ['peɪpəwɜːk] n travail m administratif, paperasserie f; (documentation) documents mpl

papery ['peɪpərɪ] adj (skin) parcheminé(e)

papier-mâché ['pæpjeɪ'mæʃeɪ] n papier m mâché

paprika ['pæprɪkə] n paprika m

Papuan ['pæpjʊən] **1** n Papou(e) m,f

2 adj papou(e)

Papua New Guinea ['pæpjʊənjuː'gɪnɪ] n Papouasie-Nouvelle-Guinée f

papyrus [pə'paɪrəs] n papyrus m

par [pɑː(r)] n (a) (equality) égalité f, pair m; **to be on a p. with sb/sth** être au même niveau que qn/qch (b) (in golf) par m; **a p.-three (hole)** un par trois; Fig **to be p. for the course** n'avoir rien de surprenant (c) Fin (of bills, shares) pair m; **above/below p.** au-dessus/au-dessous du pair; Fig **to feel below p.** ne pas être dans son assiette

parable ['pærəbəl] n parabole f

parabolic [pærə'bolɪk] adj parabolique

paracetamol [pærə'siːtəmɒl] n paracétamol m

parachute ['pærəʃuːt] **1** n parachute m; **p. jump** saut m en parachute; **to make a p. jump** sauter en parachute

2 vt parachuter

3 vi sauter en parachute

parachuting ['pærəʃuːtɪŋ] n parachutisme m; **to go p.** faire du parachutisme

parachutist ['pærəʃuːtɪst] n parachutiste mf

parade [pə'reɪd] **1** n (procession) défilé m; **on p.** (troops) à l'exercice; **a p. of shops** une rangée de magasins; **p. ground** terrain m de manœuvres

2 vt (troops) faire défiler; Fig (wealth, knowledge) faire étalage de

3 vi (of troops) défiler; **to p. about** or **around** (of person) se pavaner

paradigm ['pærədaɪm] n paradigme m

paradise ['pærədaɪs] n paradis m; **bird of p.** oiseau m de paradis

paradox ['pærədɒks] n paradoxe m

paradoxical [pærə'dɒksɪkəl] adj paradoxal(e)

paraffin ['pærəfɪn] n paraffine f; **p. heater** chauffage m à pétrole; **p. lamp** lampe f à pétrole; **p. wax** paraffine

paragliding ['pærəglaɪdɪŋ] n parapente m; **to go p.** faire du parapente

paragon ['pærəgən] n modèle m; **a p. of virtue** un modèle de vertu

paragraph ['pærəgrɑːf] n paragraphe m

Paraguay ['pærəgwaɪ] n Paraguay m

Paraguayan [pærə'gwaɪən] **1** n Paraguayen(enne) m,f
2 adj paraguayen(enne)

parakeet ['pærəkiːt] n perruche f

parallel ['pærəlel] **1** n Math parallèle f; Fig (analogy) parallèle m; **to draw a p. between two things** établir un parallèle entre deux choses; **without p.** sans égal, sans pareil
2 adj Math parallèle; Fig (analogous) pareil(eille), semblable; **to be** or **run p. to sth** être parallèle à qch; **p. bars** barres fpl parallèles; **p. lines** lignes fpl parallèles; Comptr **p. processing** traitement m en simultanéité
3 vt (be similar to) être analogue à; (be equal to) égaler

parallelogram [pærə'leləgræm] n parallélogramme m

paralyse, Am **paralyze** ['pærəlaɪz] vt also Fig paralyser

paralysis [pə'ræləsɪs] (pl **paralyses**) n paralysie f

paralytic [pærə'lɪtɪk] **1** n paralytique mf
2 adj paralytique; Fam (very drunk) complètement bourré(e)

paralyze Am = **paralyse**

paramedic [pærə'medɪk] n auxiliaire mf médical(e)

parameter [pə'ræmɪtə(r)] n paramètre m

paramilitary [pærə'mɪlɪtrɪ] adj paramilitaire

paramount ['pærəmaʊnt] adj primordial(e); **of p. importance** d'une importance capitale

paranoia [pærə'nɔɪə] n paranoïa f

paranoid ['pærənɔɪd] adj paranoïaque; **to be p. about sth** être obsédé(e) par qch

paranormal [pærə'nɔːməl] **1** n **the p.** le paranormal
2 adj paranormal(e)

parapet ['pærəpet] n parapet m

paraphernalia [pærəfə'neɪlɪə] n (equipment) attirail m; (things) affaires fpl; (clutter) bazar m

paraphrase ['pærəfreɪz] **1** n paraphrase f
2 vt paraphraser

paraplegic [pærə'pliːdʒɪk] n & adj paraplégique mf

parascending ['pærəsendɪŋ] n parachute m ascensionnel

parasite ['pærəsaɪt] n also Fig parasite m

parasitic [pærə'sɪtɪk] adj also Fig parasite; (existence) de parasite

parasol ['pærəsɒl] n ombrelle f

paratrooper ['pærətruːpə(r)] n parachutiste m

parboil ['pɑːbɔɪl] vt faire cuire à demi

parcel ['pɑːsəl] n (a) (package) colis m, paquet m; **p. bomb** colis piégé; **p. post** service m de colis postaux (b) (of land) parcelle f

▶**parcel out** (pt & pp **parcelled**, Am **parceled**) vt sep répartir

▶**parcel up** vt sep empaqueter, emballer

parchment ['pɑːtʃmənt] n parchemin m; **p. paper** papier m parchemin

pardon ['pɑːdən] **1** n (forgiveness) pardon m; Law grâce f; **(I beg your) p.?** (what did you say?) pardon?, comment?; **I beg your p.!** (in apology) je vous demande pardon!
2 vt (action, person) pardonner; Law gracier; **to p. sb for sth** pardonner qch à qn; **p. me?** (what did you say?) (je vous demande) pardon?; **p. me!** (in apology) pardonnez-moi!

pardonable ['pɑːdənəbəl] adj pardonnable, excusable

pare [peə(r)] vt (vegetable) éplucher; (apple) peler; (nails) rogner; (expenses) réduire

▶**pare down** vt sep (expenses) réduire

parent ['peərənt] n (father) père m; (mother) mère f; **parents** parents mpl; **p. company** société f ou maison f mère; **p.-teacher association** = association des parents d'élèves et des professeurs

parentage ['peərəntɪdʒ] n origine f

parental [pə'rentəl] adj parental(e)

parenthesis [pə'renθəsɪs] (pl **parentheses** [pə'renθəsiːz]) n parenthèse f; **in parentheses** entre parenthèses

parenthood ['peərənθʊd] n (fatherhood) paternité f; (motherhood) maternité f; **the joys of p.** le bonheur d'être parent

parenting ['peərəntɪŋ] n art m d'être parent; **p. skills** capacité f à élever des enfants

pariah [pə'raɪə] n paria m

Paris ['pærɪs] n Paris

parish ['pærɪʃ] n paroisse f; **p. church** église f paroissiale; **p. council** conseil m municipal

parishioner [pə'rɪʃənə(r)] n paroissien(enne) m,f

Parisian [pə'rɪzɪən] **1** n Parisien(enne) m,f
2 adj parisien(enne)

parity ['pærɪtɪ] n égalité f; **to achieve p.** (of pay) obtenir l'égalité

park [pɑːk] **1** n jardin m public, parc m; **p. keeper** gardien(enne) m,f de parc
2 vt (car) garer; Fam **to p. oneself in a chair/in front of the TV** s'installer dans un fauteuil/devant la télé

parka ['pɑːkə] n parka f

parking ['pɑːkɪŋ] n stationnement m; **no p.** (sign) défense de stationner; **p. attendant** gardien(enne) m,f de parking; **p. bay** place f de stationnement; **p. lights** (on car) feux mpl de position; Am **p. lot** parking m; **p. meter** parcmètre m; **p. space** place f (de parking); **p. ticket** contravention f

Parkinson's disease ['pɑːkɪnsənzdɪ'ziːz] n la maladie de Parkinson

parkland ['pɑːklænd] n espace m vert

parkway ['pɑːkweɪ] n Am route f bordée d'arbres et de verdure

parlance ['pɑːləns] n langage m; **in legal/political p.** en termes juridiques/politiques; **in common p.** en langage ordinaire

parley ['pɑːlɪ] vi parlementer (**with** avec); (more officially) être en pourparlers (**with** avec)

parliament ['pɑːləmənt] n parlement m

parliamentarian [pɑːləmen'teərɪən] n parlementaire mf

parliamentary [pɑːlə'mentərɪ] adj parlementaire; **p. privilege** immunité f parlementaire

parlour, *Am* **parlor** ['pɑːlə(r)] *n* salon *m*

Parmesan [pɑːmɪ'zæn] *n* **P.** (cheese) parmesan *m*

parochial [pə'rəʊkɪəl] *adj Rel* paroissial(e); *Fig & Pej* de clocher; **to be p.** (of person) avoir l'esprit de clocher

parody ['pærədɪ] **1** *n* (*pl* **parodies**) parodie *f* (of de)
  2 *vt* (*pt & pp* **parodied**) parodier

parole [pə'rəʊl] **1** *n* liberté *f* conditionnelle; **to be (out) on p.** être en liberté conditionnelle; **p. officer** contrôleur *m* judiciaire
  2 *vt* mettre en liberté conditionnelle

paroxysm ['pærəksɪzəm] *n* (of anger, guilt, jealousy) crise *f*; **to be in paroxysms of laughter** avoir le fou rire

parquet ['pɑːkeɪ] *n* **p.** (floor) parquet *m*

parrot ['pærət] **1** *n also Fig* perroquet *m*
  2 *vt* répéter comme un perroquet

parrot-fashion ['pærətfæʃən] *adv* comme un perroquet

parry ['pærɪ] (*pt & pp* **parried**) *vt* (blow) parer; (question) éluder

parsimonious [pɑːsɪ'məʊnɪəs] *adj* parcimonieux(euse)

parsley ['pɑːslɪ] *n* persil *m*

parsnip ['pɑːsnɪp] *n* panais *m*

parson ['pɑːsən] *n* pasteur *m*

parsonage ['pɑːsənɪdʒ] *n* presbytère *m*

part [pɑːt] **1** *n* (a) (portion, component) partie *f*; **p. of the body** partie du corps; **p. of speech** partie du discours; **(spare) parts** pièces *fpl* détachées; **p. two** (of TV series, story) deuxième partie; **in that p. of the world** dans cette région du monde; **in these parts** dans ces régions; **good in parts** bon (bonne) en partie; **the best/worst p. was when...** le meilleur/le pire ça a été quand...; **the difficult p. is remembering** ce qui est difficile, c'est de se souvenir; **for the best** *or* **greater p. of five years** pendant presque cinq ans; **the greater p. of the population** la plus grande partie de la population; **to be p. of sth** faire partie de qch; **it's all p. of growing up** c'est ce qui arrive quand on grandit; **it is p. and parcel of...** c'est partie intégrante de...; **in p.** en partie; **for the most p.** pour la plupart; **p. exchange** reprise *f* (en compte); **p. owner** copropriétaire *mf*
  (b) (role) rôle *m*; **to take p. (in sth)** prendre part (à qch); **to have** *or* **play a p. in sth** jouer un rôle dans qch; **I want no p. in it** je ne veux rien avoir à faire là-dedans
  (c) (side) **to take sb's p.** prendre le parti de qn; **on the p. of...** de la part de...; **for my p.** pour ma part
  (d) *Am* (in hair) raie *f*
  2 *adv* **she's p. French** elle est en partie française; **p. silk p. cotton** soie et coton
  3 *vt* (fighters, lovers) séparer; **to p. one's hair** se faire une raie; **to p. company** se séparer
  4 *vi* (separate) se rompre; **to p. (as) friends** se séparer (en) bons amis; **to p. with sth** se défaire de qch

partake [pɑː'teɪk] (*pt* **partook** [pɑː'tʊk], *pp* **partaken** [pɑː'teɪkən]) *vi Formal* (a) **to p. of** (eat, drink) prendre (b) (have quality) **to p.** relever de

partial ['pɑːʃəl] *adj* (a) (incomplete) partiel(elle) (b) (biased) partial(e) (c) (fond) **to be p. to sb/sth** avoir un faible pour qn/qch

partially ['pɑːʃəlɪ] *adv* (a) (in part) en partie, partiellement (b) (with bias) avec partialité

participant [pɑː'tɪsɪpənt] *n* participant(e) *m,f*

participate [pɑː'tɪsɪpeɪt] *vi* participer (in à)

participation [pɑːtɪsɪ'peɪʃən] *n* participation (in à)

participle ['pɑːtɪsɪpəl] *n Gram* participe *m*

particle ['pɑːtɪkəl] *n* (of matter) particule *f*; (of dust, sand) grain *m*; *Fig* (of truth) once *f*

particular [pə'tɪkjʊlə(r)] **1** *n* détail *m*; **in p.** en particulier; **I didn't see anything in p.** je n'ai rien vu de particulier; **to go into particulars** entrer dans les détails; **to take down sb's particulars** noter les coordonnées de qn
  2 *adj* (a) (specific) particulier(ère); (reason, case, example) précis(e); **which p. thing/person did you have in mind?** à quoi/à qui pensiez-vous en particulier?; **on that p. day** ce jour-là (b) (special) particulier(ère); **a p. favourite of mine** un (une) de mes favoris (favorites); **she is a p. friend of mine** c'est une de mes meilleures amies; **to take p. care over sth** mettre un soin particulier à qch (c) (exacting) méticuleux(euse); **to be p. about sth** être exigeant(e) pour qch; **I'm not p.** ça m'est égal

particularly [pə'tɪkjʊlələ] *adv* (especially) particulièrement, spécialement

parting ['pɑːtɪŋ] *n* (a) (separation) séparation *f*; **the p. of the ways** la croisée des chemins; **p. shot** pique *f* (lancée en partant); **p. words** mots *mpl* d'adieu (b) *Br* (in hair) raie *f*

partisan [pɑːtɪ'zæn] *n & adj* partisan(e) *m,f*

partition [pɑː'tɪʃən] **1** *n* (in room) cloison *f*
  2 *vt* (country) partager
▸**partition off** *vt sep* (room) cloisonner

partly ['pɑːtlɪ] *adv* partiellement, en partie

partner ['pɑːtnə(r)] **1** *n* (in games) partenaire *mf*; (in business) associé(e) *m,f*; (in dancing) cavalier(ère) *m,f*; (in relationship) compagnon (compagne) *m,f*; **p. in crime** complice *mf*
  2 *vt* (in games) faire équipe avec; (in dancing) être le (la) cavalier(ère) de

partnership ['pɑːtnəʃɪp] *n* association *f*; **to enter** *or* **go into p. (with sb)** s'associer (avec qn)

partridge ['pɑːtrɪdʒ] *n* perdrix *f*

part-time [pɑːt'taɪm] *adj & adv* à temps partiel

part-timer [pɑːt'taɪmə(r)] *n* travailleur(euse) *m,f* à temps partiel

partway ['pɑːtweɪ] *adv* **to be p. through sth** ne pas avoir complètement terminé qch; **this will go p. towards covering the costs** cela couvrira en partie les dépenses

party ['pɑːtɪ] **1** *n* (*pl* **parties**) (a) (political) parti *m*; **to follow** *or* **toe the p. line** suivre la ligne du parti; **p. member** membre *m* du parti; **p. political broadcast** émission *f* réservée à un parti politique (b) (celebration) fête *f*; **to have** *or* **give** *or* **throw a p.** organiser *ou* faire une fête; *Fig* **the p.'s over** la fête est finie; *Fam* **p. animal** fêtard(e) *m,f*; *Hum* **p. piece** numéro *m* favori (c) (group) groupe *m*; (of workers) équipe *f*; *Tel* **p. line** ligne *f* commune (à plusieurs abonnés); **p. wall** mur *m* mitoyen (d) *Law* (participant) partie *f*; **to be p. to sth** se faire complice de qch
  2 *vi* (*pt & pp* **partied**) *Fam* (celebrate) faire la fête

pass¹ [pɑːs] *n* (over mountains) col *m*

pass² **1** *n* (a) (permit) laissez-passer *m inv*; *Mil* sauf-conduit *m*; (for travel) carte *f* d'abonnement (b) (in examination) **to get a p.** avoir la moyenne; **p. mark** moyenne *f* (c) (in sport) passe *f* (d) *Fam* **to make a p. at sb** faire des avances à qn
  2 *vt* (a) (go past) (person) croiser; (destination) dépasser;

(frontier) traverser; *(car, runner)* dépasser, doubler

(b) *(exam, test)* réussir

(c) *(bill, resolution)* voter

(d) *(give)* passer; **p. (me) the salt, please** passe-moi le sel, s'il te plaît

(e) to p. the time *(of person)* passer le temps; **it passes the time** ça fait passer le temps

(f) *Law* **to p. sentence** prononcer le verdict; **to p. judgement on sb** porter un jugement sur qn

(g) to p. water uriner; **to p. wind** avoir des vents

3 *vi* **(a)** *(go past)* passer; *(overtake)* dépasser, doubler; **to p. unobserved** passer inaperçu(e); **to let sth p.** laisser tomber qch; *also Fig* **p.!** je passe!; **I think I'll p. on the onions** je crois que je ne prendrai pas d'oignons

(b) *(of time)* s'écouler

(c) *(go away)* passer

(d) *(in exam)* avoir la moyenne

(e) *Lit (take place)* **it came to p. that...** c'est alors qu'il arriva que...

▸**pass away** *vi Euph* décéder

▸**pass down** *vt sep (knowledge, tradition)* transmettre

▸**pass for** *vt insep* passer pour; **she'd p. for 25** on pourrait lui donner 25 ans

▸**pass off 1** *vt sep* **to p. oneself off as sb** se faire passer pour qn; **to p. sth off as sth** faire passer qch pour qch; **she passed it off as a joke** elle a prétendu que c'était une plaisanterie

2 *vi (take place)* se passer

▸**pass on 1** *vt sep (object)* faire passer; *(news, information)* faire circuler; *(disease)* passer

2 *vi Euph* décéder

▸**pass out** *vi* **(a)** *(faint)* perdre connaissance **(b)** *(of military cadet)* sortir avec ses diplômes

▸**pass over** *vt sep* **to p. sb over (for promotion)** ignorer qn au moment d'une promotion

▸**pass through 1** *vt insep* traverser

2 *vi* passer

▸**pass up** *vt sep (opportunity)* laisser passer

passable ['pɑ:səbəl] *adj* **(a)** *(of acceptable quality)* passable **(b)** *(road, bridge)* praticable; *(river)* franchissable

passage ['pæsɪdʒ] *n* **(a)** *(journey)* passage *m*; **with the p. of time** avec le temps; **to work one's p.** *(on ship)* travailler pour payer sa traversée **(b)** *(corridor)* couloir *m*, corridor *m*; *(alley)* passage *m* **(c)** *(extract)* passage *m*

passageway ['pæsɪdʒweɪ] *n (corridor)* couloir *m*, corridor *m*; *(alley)* passage *m*

passé [pæ'seɪ] *adj* dépassé(e)

passenger ['pæsɪndʒə(r)] *n* passager(ère) *m,f*; **p. seat** place *f* du passager

passer-by ['pɑ:sə'baɪ] *(pl* **passers-by)** *n* passant(e) *m,f*

passing ['pɑ:sɪŋ] **1** *n* **(a)** *(going past)* passage *m*; **to say sth in p.** dire qch en passant; **p. place** *(on road)* aire *f* de croisement **(b)** *(of time)* écoulement *m* **(c)** *(death)* décès *m*

2 *adj (car, motorist)* qui passe; *(remark)* en passant; *(whim, attraction)* passager(ère)

passion ['pæʃən] *n (desire)* passion *f*; *(anger, vehemence)* emportement *m*, colère *f*; **to have a p. for sth** adorer qch; **in a fit of p.** sous le coup de la passion; **she hates him with a p.** elle le hait de toute son âme; **crime of p.** crime *m* passionnel; *Rel* **the P. (of Christ)** la Passion (du Christ); **p. fruit** fruit *m* de la passion

passionate ['pæʃənɪt] *adj (lover, embrace)* passionné(e); *(plea, speech)* véhément(e); *(believer, defender)* fervent(e); **to make p. love** faire l'amour avec passion

passive ['pæsɪv] **1** *n Gram* **the p.** le passif; **in the p.** au passif

2 *adj* passif(ive); **p. resistance** résistance *f* passive; **p. smoking** tabagisme *m* passif

passively ['pæsɪvlɪ] *adv* passivement, avec passivité

passkey ['pɑ:ski:] *(pl* **passkeys)** *n* passe-partout *m*

Passover ['pɑ:səʊvə(r)] *n Rel* la Pâque (Juive)

passport ['pɑ:spɔ:t] *n* passeport *m*; **p. photo** photo *f* d'identité

password ['pɑ:swɜ:d] *n* mot *m* de passe

past [pɑ:st] **1** *n* passé *m*; **in the p.** autrefois; **a thing of the p.** une chose qui appartient au passé; **to live in the p.** vivre dans le passé

2 *adj* passé(e); **those days are p.** ces jours sont révolus; **in times p.** autrefois; **to be a p. master at sth** être passé(e) maître dans l'art de qch; **the p. week** la semaine dernière; **the p. few days** ces derniers jours; *Gram* **participle** participe *m* passé; **in the p. tense** au passé

3 *prep (beyond)* au-delà de; **to walk p. the house** passer devant la maison; **it's p. four (o'clock)** il est quatre heures passées; **ten p. four** quatre heures dix; **I'm p. caring** je n'en ai plus rien à faire; *Fam* **to be p. it** avoir fait son temps; *Fam* **I wouldn't put it p. her** elle en est bien capable

4 *adv* **to walk** *or* **go p.** passer; **to run p.** passer en courant

pasta ['pæstə] *n* pâtes *fpl*

paste [peɪst] **1** *n* **(a)** *(substance)* pâte *f* **(b)** *(pâté)* mousse *f* **(c)** *(glue)* colle *f*

2 *vt (glue)* coller

pastel ['pæstəl] **1** *n* pastel *m*

2 *adj* pastel *inv*; **p. shades** tons *mpl* pastel

pasteurize ['pæstjʊraɪz] *vt* pasteuriser; **pasteurized milk** lait *m* pasteurisé

pastiche [pæ'sti:ʃ] *n* pastiche *m*

pastille ['pæstɪl] *n* pastille *f*

pastime ['pɑ:staɪm] *n* passe-temps *m inv*

pasting ['peɪstɪŋ] *n Fam (beating)* raclée *f*; **to give sb a p.** flanquer une raclée à qn

pastor ['pɑ:stə(r)] *n Rel* pasteur *m*

pastoral ['pɑ:stərəl] *adj* **(a)** *(rural)* pastoral(e) **(b)** *(work, activities)* de conseiller/ère

pastry ['peɪstrɪ] *(pl* **pastries)** *n (dough)* pâte *f*; *(cake)* pâtisserie *f*; **p. chef** pâtissier(ère) *m,f*

pasture ['pɑ:stʃə(r)] *n* pâture *f*, pré *m*; **to be put out to p.** *(of animals)* être mis(e) au pré; *Fig (of person)* être mis au vert; *Fig* **to move on to pastures new** aller vers de nouveaux horizons

pasty¹ ['pæstɪ] *(pl* **pasties)** *n (savoury)* ≃ feuilleté *m*

pasty² ['peɪstɪ] *adj (face, complexion)* terreux(euse); **p.-faced** au teint terreux

pat [pæt] **1** *n* **(a)** *(tap)* petite tape *f*; *(on animal)* caresse *f*; *Fig* **to give sb a p. on the back** féliciter qn **(b)** *(of butter)* médaillon *m*

2 *adj (answer, explanation)* tout(e) prêt(e)

3 *adv* **to know** *or* **have sth off p.** savoir qch par cœur

4 *vt (pt & pp* **patted)** *(tap)* tapoter; **to p. sb on the head/shoulder** donner une tape sur la tête/l'épaule de qn; *Fig* **to p. sb on the back** féliciter qn

Patagonia [pætə'gəʊnɪə] *n* la Patagonie

patch [pætʃ] **1** *n* **(a)** *(of cloth)* pièce *f*; *(eye)* **p.** bandeau *m*; *Fam* **his last novel isn't a p. on the others** son dernier roman est loin de valoir les autres **(b)** *(of colour, light)* tache f; *(of fog, mist)* nappe f; *(of ice)* plaque f; **a p. of blue sky** un coin de ciel bleu; *Fam Fig* **to be going through a bad p.** traverser une mauvaise passe **(c)** *(of land)* lopin m; *(of prostitute, salesperson)* secteur m; *Fam* **keep off my p.!** hors de mon territoire!

2 vt *(hole, garment)* rapiécer

▶**patch up** vt sep *Fam (wounded person)* donner les premiers soins à; *(marriage, friendship)* raccommoder; **to p. things up** *(after argument)* se raccommoder

patchwork ['pætʃwɜːk] n *also Fig* patchwork m; **p. quilt** couvre-lit m en patchwork

patchy ['pætʃi] adj inégal(e)

pâté ['pæteɪ] n pâté m

patent ['peɪtənt] **1** n *(licence)* brevet m d'invention; **to take out a p. on sth** faire breveter qch; *Com* **p. applied for, p. pending** demande de brevet déposée

2 adj **(a)** *(patented)* breveté(e); **p. medicine** spécialité f pharmaceutique **(b)** *(evident)* manifeste **(c) p. leather** cuir m verni

3 vt *(of inventor)* faire breveter

patently ['peɪtəntlɪ] adv manifestement

paternal [pə'tɜːnəl] adj *(feelings)* paternel(elle); *(duty, responsibilities)* de père

paternally [pə'tɜːnəlɪ] adv paternellement

paternity [pə'tɜːnɪtɪ] n paternité f; *Law* **p. suit** action f en recherche de paternité

path [pɑːθ] n **(a)** *(track)* chemin m; *(narrow)* sentier m; *(in garden)* allée f; **their paths had crossed before** leurs chemins s'étaient croisés auparavant **(b)** *(of rocket, planet)* trajectoire f; *(of inquiry, to success)* voie f; **the storm destroyed everything in its p.** la tempête a tout détruit sur son passage **(c)** *Comptr* chemin m

pathetic [pə'θetɪk] adj *(useless)* lamentable; *(touching)* attendrissant(e)

pathetically [pə'θetɪklɪ] adv *(uselessly)* lamentablement; *(touchingly)* de manière attendrissante

pathological [pæθə'lɒdʒɪkəl] adj pathologique

pathologist [pə'θɒlədʒɪst] n pathologiste mf

pathology [pə'θɒlədʒɪ] n pathologie f

pathos ['peɪθɒs] n pathétique m

pathway ['pɑːθweɪ] n sentier m

patience ['peɪʃəns] n **(a)** *(quality)* patience f; **to try or tax sb's p.** mettre la patience de qn à l'épreuve; **to exhaust sb's p.** abuser de la patience de qn; **to lose one's p. (with sb)** perdre patience (avec qn); **I've no p. with him** il m'énerve **(b)** *(card game)* réussite f; **to play p.** faire une réussite

patient ['peɪʃənt] **1** n patient(e) m,f

2 adj patient(e)

patiently ['peɪʃəntlɪ] adv patiemment

patio ['pætɪəʊ] n *(pl patios)* patio m

patriarch ['peɪtrɪɑːk] n patriarche m

patriarchal [peɪtrɪ'ɑːkəl] adj patriarcal(e)

patriarchy ['peɪtrɪɑːkɪ] n *(pl patriarchies)* n patriarcat m

patrimony ['pætrɪmənɪ] n patrimoine m, héritage m

patriot ['pætrɪət, 'peɪtrɪət] n patriote mf

patriotic [pætrɪ'ɒtɪk, peɪtrɪ'ɒtɪk] adj patriotique

patriotism ['pætrɪətɪzəm, 'peɪtrɪətɪzəm] n patriotisme m

patrol [pə'trəʊl] **1** n patrouille f; **to be on p.** être de patrouille; **p. car** voiture f de police

2 vt *(pt & pp patrolled)* patrouiller dans

3 vi patrouiller; **to p. up and down** faire les cent pas

patrolman [pə'trəʊlmæn] n *Am* agent m de police

patron ['peɪtrən] n **(a)** *(of arts)* protecteur(trice) m,f, mécène m; *(of charity)* patron(onne) m,f; **p. saint** (saint(e)) patron(onne) m,f **(b)** *(of shop)* client(e) m,f

patronage ['peɪtrənɪdʒ] n **(a)** *(of arts, charity)* patronage m; **under the p. of** sous le patronage de **(b)** *Pej (in politics)* copinage m

patronize ['pætrənaɪz] vt **(a)** *(arts)* protéger; *(shop, restaurant)* fréquenter **(b)** *(treat condescendingly)* traiter avec condescendance

patronizing ['pætrənaɪzɪŋ] adj condescendant(e)

patter¹ ['pætə(r)] n **(a)** *(of footsteps)* petit bruit m; *(of rain)* crépitement m

2 vi *(of rain)* crépiter; **she pattered along the corridor** elle trottinait le long du couloir

patter² n *Fam (talk)* boniment m, baratin m

pattern ['pætən] **1** n **(a)** *(design)* dessin m, motif m; **p. book** catalogue m d'échantillons **(b)** *(of behaviour)* comportement m type; **a normal p. of events** une suite typique d'événements; **the evening followed the usual p.** la soirée s'est déroulée comme d'habitude **(c)** *(in sewing)* patron m; *(in knitting)* modèle m **(d)** *(norm)* modèle m; **to set a p.** créer un modèle

2 vt *(model)* **to p. sth on sth** modeler qch sur qch

patterned ['pætənd] adj à motifs

paunch [pɔːntʃ] n ventre m; **to have a p.** avoir du ventre

pauper ['pɔːpə(r)] n indigent(e) m,f; **p.'s grave** fosse f commune

pause [pɔːz] **1** n *(in conversation)* silence m; *(rest)* pause f; *(in music)* point m d'orgue

2 vi faire une pause; **to p. for breath** reprendre son souffle

pave [peɪv] vt *(road)* paver *(with de)*; *Fig* **to p. the way for sth** ouvrir la voie à qch

pavement ['peɪvmənt] n *Br (beside road)* trottoir m; *Am (roadway)* chaussée f; **p. artist** artiste mf qui dessine sur les trottoirs; **p. café** café m avec terrasse

pavilion [pə'vɪlɪən] n pavillon m

paving ['peɪvɪŋ] n *(with tiles)* carrelage m; *(with slabs)* dallage m; **p. stone** pavé m

paw [pɔː] **1** n patte f; *Fam* **paws off!** bas les pattes!

2 vt *(of animal)* donner un coup/des coups de patte à; **to p. the ground** frapper le sol du sabot

pawn¹ [pɔːn] vt mettre au mont-de-piété *ou* en gage

pawn² n *also Fig* pion m

pawnbroker ['pɔːnbrəʊkə(r)] n prêteur(euse) m,f sur gage

pawnshop ['pɔːnʃɒp] n mont-de-piété m, bureau m de prêt sur gage

pay [peɪ] **1** n paie f, salaire m; **the p.'s good/bad** ça paie bien/mal; **to be in sb's p.** être à la solde de qn; **p. cheque** chèque m de paie; **p. packet** enveloppe f de paie; **p. rise** augmentation f de salaire; **p. slip** bulletin m de salaire; **p. talks** négociations fpl salariales

2 vt *(pt & pp paid* [peɪd]*)* **(a)** *(person, money, bill)* payer; **I paid £5 for it** je l'ai payé 5 livres; **to be well/badly paid** être bien/mal payé(e); **I wouldn't do it if you paid me** je ne le ferais pas même si on me payait; **to p. one's way** payer son écot; **to p. cash** payer (argent) comptant; **to p. money into sb's account** verser de l'argent sur le compte de qn **(b)** *(give)* **to p. sb a compliment** faire un compliment à qn; **to p. sb a visit** rendre visite à qn; **to p. tribute to sb** rendre hommage à qn; **to p. one's respects to sb** présenter ses respects à qn **(c)** *(profit)* **it will p. you to do it** c'est dans votre intérêt de le faire

3 *vi* **(a)** *(give payment)* payer; **to p. through the nose** payer le prix fort; **to p. by cheque** payer par chèque **(b)** *(be profitable)* être rentable; **crime doesn't p.** le crime ne paie pas; **it pays to be honest** l'honnêteté est toujours récompensée

▸**pay back** *vt sep* *(loan, person)* rembourser; *Fig* **I'll p. you back for this!** tu me le paieras!

▸**pay in** *vt* *(cheque, money)* verser sur un compte

▸**pay off 1** *vt sep* **(a)** *(debt)* régler; *(mortgage)* purger; *Fam* **to p. sb off** *(bribe)* soudoyer qn **(b)** *(make redundant)* licencier
2 *vi* *(of work, efforts)* porter ses fruits

▸**pay out 1** *vt sep* **(a)** *(money)* débourser, dépenser **(b)** *(pt* **payed)** *(rope)* laisser filer
2 *vi* payer

▸**pay up** *vi* payer

payable ['peɪəbəl] *adj* payable; **to make a cheque p. to sb** libeller un chèque à l'ordre de qn

pay-as-you-earn [peɪæzjuː'ɜːn] *n Br* prélèvement *m* de l'impôt à la source

payday ['peɪdeɪ] *n* jour *m* de paie

PAYE [piːeɪwaɪ'iː] *n Br* *(abbr* **pay-as-you-earn)** prélèvement *m* de l'impôt à la source

payee [peɪ'iː] *n* bénéficiaire *mf*

paying ['peɪɪŋ] *adj* payant(e); **p. guest** hôte *m* payant

payload ['peɪləʊd] *n* charge *f* utile

paymaster ['peɪmɑːstə(r)] *n* caissier *m*

payment ['peɪmənt] *n* paiement *m*; **to make a p.** effectuer un versement; **to stop p. (on a cheque)** faire opposition sur un chèque; **on p. of £100** contre paiement de 100 livres; **p. by instalments** paiement par acomptes; **p. in full** paiement intégral

payoff ['peɪɒf] *n Fam* **(a)** *(bribe)* pot-de-vin *m* **(b)** *(reward)* récompense *f*

payphone ['peɪfəʊn] *n* téléphone *m* public

payroll ['peɪrəʊl] *n Com* liste *f* du personnel; **to be on the p.** faire partie du personnel

PC ['piː'siː] **1** *n* **(a)** *Br (abbr* **Police Constable)** = agent de police **(b)** *(abbr* **personal computer)** OI *m*
2 *adj (abbr* **politically correct)** politiquement correct(e)

pc *(abbr* **postcard)** carte *f* postale

PDQ *adv Fam (abbr* **pretty damn quick)** illico

PE ['piː'iː] *n (abbr* **physical education)** EPS *f*

pea [piː] *n* pois *m*; **like two peas in a pod** comme deux gouttes d'eau

peace [piːs] *n* paix *f*; **at p.** en paix; **to make (one's) p. with sb** faire la paix avec qn; **p. of mind** tranquillité *f* d'esprit; *Law* **to disturb the p.** troubler l'ordre public; **campaigner** militant(e) *m,f* pour la paix; **P. Corps** = organisation américaine d'aide aux pays du tiers-monde, composée de bénévoles intervenant sur le terrain; **p. movement** mouvement *m* pour la paix; **p. offering** cadeau *m* de réconciliation; **p. talks** pourparlers *mpl* de paix; **p. treaty** traité *m* de paix

peaceable ['piːsəbəl] *adj* pacifique

peaceful ['piːsfʊl] *adj (calm)* paisible; *(non-violent)* pacifique

peacekeeping ['piːskiːpɪŋ] *n* maintien *m* de la paix; **p. force** force *f* de maintien de la paix

peace-loving ['piːslʌvɪŋ] *adj* pacifique

peacetime ['piːstaɪm] *n* temps *m* de paix

peach [piːtʃ] *n (fruit)* pêche *f*; *Fam* **she's a p.** elle est canon; *Fam* **a p. of a goal** un but de toute beauté; **p. Melba** pêche Melba; **p. tree** pêcher *m*

peacock ['piːkɒk] *n* paon *m*

peak [piːk] **1** *n* **(a)** *(summit of mountain)* sommet *m*; *(mountain)* pic *m*; *Fig (of success, career)* apogée *m* **(b)** *(of price, inflation, fitness)* maximum *m*; **in p. condition** dans une forme excellente; **p. period** *(for traffic)* heures *fpl* de pointe; *(in shop)* heures d'affluence; **p. season** haute saison *f* **(c)** *(of cap)* visière *f*
2 *vi* culminer (**at** à)

peaky ['piːkɪ] *adj Fam* patraque

peal [piːl] *n (of bells)* sonnerie *f*; *(of thunder)* coup *m*; **peals of laughter** éclats *mpl* de rire

▸**peal out** *vi (of bells)* sonner à toute volée

peanut ['piːnʌt] *n* cacah(o)uète *f*; *Fam Fig* **peanuts** *(small sum of money)* clopinettes *fpl*; **p. butter** beurre *m* de cacah(o)uètes; **p. oil** huile *f* d'arachide

pear [peə(r)] *n* poire *f*; **p. tree** poirier *m*

pearl [pɜːl] *n* **(a)** *(jewel)* perle *f*; **p. diver** pêcheur(euse) *m,f* de perles; **p. necklace** collier *m* de perles **(b)** *(idiom)* **pearls of wisdom** paroles *fpl* pleines de sagesse; **to cast pearls before swine** jeter des perles aux cochons

pearly ['pɜːlɪ] *adj* nacré(e); **the P. Gates** les portes *fpl* du paradis

peasant ['pezənt] *n* paysan(anne) *m,f*; *Pej (ignorant person)* péquenaud(e) *m,f*

peashooter ['piːʃuːtə(r)] *n* petite sarbacane *f*

peat [piːt] *n* tourbe *f*; **p. bog** tourbière *f*

pebble ['pebəl] *n* caillou *m*; *(on beach)* galet *m*; **p. beach** plage *f* de galets

pebbledash ['pebəldæʃ] *n* crépi *m*

pebbly ['peblɪ] *adj* caillouteux(euse); *(beach)* de galets

pecan ['piːkən] *n* **p. (nut)** noix *f* de pecan

peccary ['pekərɪ] *(pl* **peccaries)** *n* pécari *m*

peck [pek] **1** *n* **(a)** *(of bird)* coup *m* de bec **(b)** *(kiss)* bise *f*; **to give sb a p. on the cheek** faire une bise à qn
2 *vt* **(a)** *(of bird) (grain)* picorer; *(person)* donner un coup/ des coups de bec à **(b)** *(kiss)* **to p. sb on the cheek** faire une bise à qn

peckish ['pekɪʃ] *adj Fam* **to be p.** avoir un creux

pecs [peks] *npl Fam (pectoral muscles)* pectoraux *mpl*

pectin ['pektɪn] *n Chem* pectine *f*

pectoral ['pektərəl] **1** *n* **pectorals** pectoraux *mpl*
2 *adj* pectoral(e)

peculiar [pɪ'kjuːlɪə(r)] *adj* **(a)** *(strange)* curieux(euse), bizarre **(b)** *(particular)* **p. to** particulier(ère) à, propre à; **this species is p. to France** cette espèce n'existe qu'en France

peculiarity [pɪkjuːlɪ'ærɪtɪ] *(pl* **peculiarities)** *n* **(a)** *(strangeness)* singularité *f*, bizarrerie *f*; *(unusual characteristic)* particularité *f*

peculiarly [pɪ'kjuːlɪəlɪ] *adv* **(a)** *(strangely)* singulièrement **(b)** *(especially)* particulièrement

pecuniary [pɪ'kjuːnɪərɪ] *adj Formal* pécuniaire

pedagogic(al) [pedə'gɒdʒɪk(əl)] *adj* pédagogique

pedagogy ['pedəgɒgɪ] *n* pédagogie *f*

pedal ['pedəl] **1** *n* pédale *f*; **p. bin** poubelle *f* à pédale
2 *vt (pt & pp* **pedalled,** *Am* **pedaled) to p. a bicycle**

être à bicyclette

3 vi pédaler

pedalo ['pedələʊ] (pl **pedaloes** or **pedalos**) n Pédalo® m

pedant ['pedənt] n pédant(e) m,f

pedantic [pɪ'dæntɪk] adj pédant(e)

pedantry ['pedəntrɪ] n pédantisme m, pédanterie f

peddle ['pedəl] vt (goods, ideas, theories) colporter; (drugs) faire du trafic de

peddler ['pedlə(r)] n (of goods, ideas, theories) colporteur (euse) m,f; (of drugs) trafiquant(e) m,f

pederast ['pedəræst] n Formal pédéraste m

pedestal ['pedɪstəl] n piédestal m; Fig **to put sb on a p.** mettre qn sur un piédestal; **p. lamp** lampe f sur piédestal

pedestrian [pɪ'destrɪən] **1** n piéton(onne) m,f; **p. crossing** passage m pour piétons, passage clouté; **p. precinct** zone f piétonnière

2 adj (unimaginative) banal(e)

pedestrianize [pɪ'destrɪənaɪz] vt transformer en zone piétonnière

pediatric, pediatrician Am = paediatric, paediatrician

pedicure ['pedɪkjʊə(r)] n **to have a p.** se faire soigner les pieds

pedigree ['pedɪɡriː] **1** n (a) (of animal) pedigree m (b) (of person) ascendance f, généalogie f; Fig (background) passé m, antécédents mpl

2 adj (animal) de race

pedlar ['pedlə(r)] n colporteur(euse) m,f

pedophile Am = paedophile

pee [piː] Fam **1** n pipi m; **to have a p.** faire pipi

2 vi faire pipi

peek [piːk] **1** n coup m d'œil furtif; **to take** or **have a p. (at)** jeter un coup d'œil furtif (à)

2 vi jeter un coup d'œil furtif (at à)

peel [piːl] **1** n (of apple, vegetable) peau f; (of orange, lemon) écorce f

2 vt (fruit) peler; (vegetable) éplucher; Fam **to keep one's eyes peeled** ouvrir l'œil

3 vi (of paint) s'écailler; (of skin, person) peler

▸**peel off** vt sep enlever

2 vi (of paint) s'écailler; (of skin) peler; (of label) s'enlever

peelings ['piːlɪŋz] npl (of potato, carrot) épluchures fpl

peep¹ [piːp] **1** n (furtive glance) coup m d'œil furtif; **to have** or **take a p. (at)** jeter un coup d'œil furtif (à)

2 vi **to p. at sb/sth** jeter un coup d'œil furtif à qn/qch; **to p. through the keyhole** regarder par le trou de la serrure

peep² n (sound) (of bird) pépiement m; (of mouse) cri m; Fam **I don't want to hear another p. out of you** je ne veux plus entendre un mot

peephole ['piːphəʊl] n judas m

Peeping Tom ['piːpɪŋ'tɒm] n Fam voyeur m

peer¹ [pɪə(r)] n (**a**) (equal) pair m; **p. group** pairs mpl; **p. pressure** influence f du groupe (**b**) Br (nobleman) pair m

peer² vi **to p. at sb/sth** scruter qn/qch du regard; **to p. over sth** jeter un coup d'œil par-dessus qch

peerage ['pɪərɪdʒ] n Br (rank) pairie f; **the p.** les pairs mpl

peeress [pɪə'res] n Br pairesse f

peerless ['pɪəlɪs] adj sans pareil(eille), hors pair

peeve [piːv] vt Fam mettre en rogne; **to be peeved (at)** être en rogne (à cause de)

peevish ['piːvɪʃ] adj irritable, maussade

peewit ['piːwɪt] n vanneau m (huppé)

peg [peɡ] **1** n (wooden) cheville f; (metal) fiche f; (for coat, hat) patère f; (clothes) p. pince f à linge; (tent) p. piquet m de tente; **to buy clothes off the p.** acheter du prêt-à-porter; Fig **to take sb down a p. (or two)** remettre qn à sa place

2 vt (pt & pp **pegged**) (**a**) **to p. sth in place** fixer qch avec des piquets; **to p. the washing on the line** étendre le linge (en utilisant des pinces à linge) (**b**) (prices) stabiliser

▸**peg out** vi Fam (die) casser sa pipe

pejorative [pɪ'dʒɒrətɪv] adj péjoratif(ive)

Pekinese [piːkɪ'niːz] n (dog) pékinois m

Peking [piː'kɪŋ] n Pékin

pelican ['pelɪkən] n pélican m; Br **p. crossing** feux mpl (à commande manuelle)

pellet ['pelɪt] n (of paper, bread, clay) boulette f; (for gun) plomb m

pell-mell ['pel'mel] adv (run) de façon désordonnée

pelmet ['pelmɪt] n cantonnière f

pelt¹ [pelt] n (animal skin) peau f, fourrure f

pelt² **1** vt bombarder (**with** de)

2 vi Fam (**a**) (rain) **it was pelting down** il pleuvait à verse (**b**) (go fast) aller à toute allure; **to p. upstairs** grimper l'escalier quatre à quatre; **she came pelting along the corridor** elle a déboulé de fond du couloir

pelvic ['pelvɪk] adj pelvien(enne)

pelvis ['pelvɪs] n pelvis m

pen¹ [pen] **1** n (for writing) stylo m; **to put to p. to paper** prendre la plume; **p. friend** or **pal** correspondant(e) m,f; **p. name** nom m de plume

2 vt (pt & pp **penned**) écrire, rédiger

pen² n (for sheep, cattle) enclos m

pen³ n Am Fam (prison) taule f

▸**pen in** vt sep (animals, people) parquer

penal ['piːnəl] adj pénal(e); **p. code** code m pénal; **p. colony** colonie f pénitentiaire; **p. servitude** travaux mpl forcés

penalize ['piːnəlaɪz] vt pénaliser

penalty ['penəltɪ] (pl **penalties**) n (**a**) (punishment) peine f; **to impose a p. (on sb)** prendre une sanction (contre qn); **on** or **under p. of death** sous peine de mort; Fig **to pay the p. for sth** subir les conséquences de qch; Com **p. clause** clause f pénale (**b**) (in football) penalty m; (in rugby) pénalité f; **p. area** surface f de réparation; **p. kick** penalty

penance ['penəns] n also Fig pénitence f; **to do p. (for sth)** faire pénitence (pour qch)

pence [pens] pl of **penny**

pencil ['pensəl] **1** n crayon m; **p. case** trousse f; **p. drawing** dessin m au crayon; **p. sharpener** taille-crayon m

2 vt (pt & pp **pencilled**, Am **penciled**) (draw) dessiner au crayon; (write) écrire au crayon

▸**pencil in** vt sep (date) fixer provisoirement; **to p. sb in** fixer provisoirement un rendez-vous à qn

pendant ['pendənt] n pendentif m

pending ['pendɪŋ] **1** adj (trial) en instance; (negotiations) en cours; (documents) en souffrance, en attente

2 prep en attendant

pendulum ['pendjʊləm] n pendule m

penetrate ['penɪtreɪt] vt & vi pénétrer

penetrating ['penɪtreɪtɪŋ] adj (sound, wind, cold) pénétrant(e); (voice, scream, stare) perçant(e)

penetration [penɪ'treɪʃən] n pénétration f

penguin ['peŋgwɪn] n manchot m

penicillin [penɪ'sɪlɪn] n pénicilline f

peninsula [pɪ'nɪnsjʊlə] n péninsule f; (smaller) presqu'île f

peninsular [pɪ'nɪnsjʊlə(r)] adj péninsulaire

penis ['piːnɪs] n pénis m

penitence ['penɪtəns] n pénitence f, repentir m

penitent ['penɪtənt] n & adj pénitent(e) m,f

penitentiary [penɪ'tenʃərɪ] n (pl **penitentiaries**) n Am pénitencier m

penknife ['pennaɪf] n (pl **penknives** ['pennaɪvz]) n canif m

pennant ['penənt] n flamme f

penniless ['penɪlɪs] adj sans le sou

Pennsylvania [pensɪl'veɪnɪə] n la Pennsylvanie

penny ['penɪ] n (a) Br (coin) (pl pence [pens]) penny m; a 10/50 pence piece une pièce de 10/50 pence; **it was worth every p.** ça a valait le coup; **it didn't cost them a p.** cela ne leur a pas coûté un sou; **p. farthing** vélocipède m; **p. pinching** économies fpl de bouts de chandelle; **p. whistle** flûtiau m (b) Am (cent) cent m (c) (idioms) **they haven't a p. to their name** il n'ont pas un sou vaillant; **the p.'s dropped** ça a fait tilt; **they're ten a p.** il y en a à la pelle; **a p. for your thoughts** à quoi penses-tu?; **a bad p.** un(e) bon (bonne) à rien

penny-pinching ['penɪpɪntʃɪŋ] adj (person) pingre; (ways, habits) de radin

pension ['penʃən] n pension f; (after retirement) (pension de) retraite f; **to be on a p.** recevoir une pension; (after retirement) recevoir une retraite; **p. fund** caisse f de retraite; **p. scheme** plan m de retraite

▸**pension off** vt sep mettre à la retraite

pensionable ['penʃənəbəl] adj **p. age** âge m de départ en retraite

pensioner ['penʃənə(r)] n (old-age) **p.** retraité(e) m,f

pensive ['pensɪv] adj pensif(ive), songeur(euse)

pensively ['pensɪvlɪ] adv pensivement

pentagon ['pentəgən] n pentagone m; **the P.** (building) le Pentagone

pentathlon [pen'tæθlən] n pentathlon m

Pentecost ['pentɪkɒst] n la Pentecôte

penthouse ['penthaʊs] n = appartement de standing au dernier étage d'un immeuble

pent-up [pen'tʌp] adj (desire) refoulé(e); (rage, energy) contenu(e)

penultimate [pe'nʌltɪmɪt] adj pénultième, avant-dernier(ère)

penury ['penjʊrɪ] n indigence f

peony ['piːənɪ] n (pl **peonies**) n pivoine f

people ['piːpəl] **1** npl (a) (as group) gens mpl; (as individuals) personnes fpl; **most p.** la plupart des gens; **old p.** les personnes âgées; **he's one of those p. who think (that)...** c'est le genre de type qui pense que...; **p. say (that)...** les gens disent que... (b) (citizens) peuple m; **the common p.** le peuple; **a man of the p.** un homme du peuple; **p. power** pouvoir m populaire; **P.'s Republic** République f populaire (c) Fam (family) **my/his p.** ma/sa famille

2 n (nation) peuple m; **the Scottish p.** les Écossais mpl

3 vt peupler

PEP [pep] n Fin (abbr **personal equity plan**) ≃ PEA m

pep [pep] n Fam entrain m, allant m; **p. pill** excitant m; **p. talk** petit discours m d'encouragement

▸**pep up** (pt & pp pepped) vt sep Fam (person) ragaillardir, revigorer; (event) animer; (dish) relever

pepper ['pepə(r)] **1** n (spice) poivre m; (vegetable) poivron m; **p. mill** moulin m à poivre; **p. pot** poivrière f

2 vt (a) (in cooking) poivrer (b) Fig (speech, essay) parsemer (with de); **to p. sb with bullets** cribler qn de balles

peppercorn ['pepəkɔːn] n grain m de poivre

peppermint ['pepəmɪnt] n (plant) menthe f poivrée; (sweet) bonbon m à la menthe; **p. tea** thé m à la menthe

peppery ['pepərɪ] adj (a) (dish) poivré(e) (b) (irritable) irascible, colérique

peptic ulcer ['peptɪk'ʌlsə(r)] n ulcère m gastro-duodénal

per [pɜː(r)] prep par; **p. day** par jour; **100 km p. hour** 100 km à l'heure; Formal **as p. your instructions** conformément à vos instructions; **as p. usual** comme d'habitude; **p. annum** par an; **p. capita** par habitant; **p. se** en soi

perceive [pə'siːv] vt percevoir

percent [pə'sent] **1** n pourcentage m

2 adv pour cent

percentage [pə'sentɪdʒ] n pourcentage m

perceptible [pə'septɪbəl] adj perceptible

perceptibly [pə'septɪblɪ] adv sensiblement

perception [pə'sepʃən] n perception f

perceptive [pə'septɪv] adj (person, remark) perspicace; (analysis, article) pertinent(e)

perch[1] [pɜːtʃ] **1** n (for bird) & Fig perchoir m; Fam Fig **to knock sb off his p.** détrôner qn

2 vi se percher

perch[2] n (fish) perche f

percolate ['pɜːkəleɪt] **1** vt (coffee) passer; **percolated coffee** = café préparé dans une cafetière à pression

2 vi (of liquid) passer; Fig (of information) filtrer

percolator ['pɜːkəleɪtə(r)] n cafetière f à pression

percussion [pə'kʌʃən] n percussion f; **p. instrument** instrument m à percussion

percussionist [pə'kʌʃənɪst] n percussionniste mf

peregrine falcon ['perɪgrɪn'fɔːlkən] n faucon m pèlerin

peremptory [pə'remptərɪ] adj péremptoire; (refusal) absolu(e)

perennial [pə'renɪəl] **1** n (plant) plante f vivace

2 adj (plant) vivace; (problem, beauty) éternel(elle); (worry) perpétuel(elle)

perfect 1 adj ['pɜːfɪkt] (a) (ideal) parfait(e); **nobody's p.** personne n'est parfait; **Tuesday would be p.** mardi me conviendrait parfaitement; **to have p. pitch** avoir l'oreille absolue (b) (complete) **it makes p. sense** c'est parfaitement logique; **she's a p. stranger** je ne la connais pas du tout; **he's a p. gentleman/fool** c'est un parfait homme du monde/imbécile (c) Gram **the p. (tense)** le passé composé

2 vt [pə'fekt] parfaire

perfection [pə'fekʃən] n perfection f

perfectionist [pə'fekʃənɪst] n perfectionniste mf

perfectly ['pɜːfɪktlɪ] adv (faultlessly) à la perfection; (completely) parfaitement

perfidious [pə'fɪdɪəs] adj Lit perfide

perforate ['pɜːfəreɪt] vt perforer

perforated ['pɜːfəreɪtɪd] adj perforé(e); **p. ulcer** perforation f ulcéreuse

perforation [pɜːfəˈreɪʃən] *n (hole)* perforation *f*; *(on stamp)* dentelure *f*

perform [pəˈfɔːm] **1** *vt (play, role, piece of music)* jouer; *(miracle)* faire; *(one's duty)* remplir; **to p. an operation on sb** opérer qn
2 *vi (of machine, car)* marcher; *(of actor)* jouer; *(of singer)* chanter

performance [pəˈfɔːməns] *n* **(a)** *(of task, duty)* accomplissement *m*; **p. appraisal** appréciation *f*, évaluation *f* **(b)** *(of sportsperson)* performance *f*; *(of actor)* interprétation *f*; *(of pupil, economy)* résultats *mpl*, performance; *(of machine, car)* performances *fpl* **(c)** *(of play)* représentation *f*; *Fig* **to make a p.** faire toute une histoire

performer [pəˈfɔːmə(r)] *n* artiste *mf (des arts du spectacle)*

performing [pəˈfɔːmɪŋ] *adj (dog, seal)* savant(e); **p. arts** arts *mpl* du spectacle

perfume 1 [ˈpɜːfjuːm] parfum *m*; **p. counter** rayon *m* parfumerie
2 [pəˈfjuːm] parfumer

perfumed [ˈpɜːfjuːmd] *adj* parfumé(e)

perfunctory [pəˈfʌŋktəri] *adj (examination, glance)* rapide; *(smile)* mécanique; *(letter, instructions)* sommaire

perhaps [pəˈhæps] *adv* peut-être; **p. so/not** peut-être que oui/non; **p. she'll come** elle viendra peut-être, peut-être qu'elle viendra

peril [ˈperəl] *n* péril *m*, danger *m*; **at one's p.** à ses risques et périls

perilous [ˈperɪləs] *adj* dangereux(euse)

perilously [ˈperɪləslɪ] *adv* dangereusement

perimeter [pəˈrɪmɪtə(r)] *n* périmètre *m*; **p. fence** clôture *f*

period [ˈpɪərɪəd] *n* **(a)** *(stretch of time)* période *f*; **within the agreed p.** dans les délais convenus; **sunny periods** intervalles *mpl* ensoleillés **(b)** *(in school)* heure *f* de cours; **a French/maths p.** un cours de français/maths **(c)** *(menstruation)* règles *fpl*; **to have one's p.** avoir ses règles; **p. pains** règles douloureuses **(d)** *(historical age)* époque *f*; **p. drama** *(on TV)* drame *m* historique; **p. dress** costume(s) *m(pl)* d'époque; **p. furniture** meubles *mpl* d'époque **(e)** *Am (full stop)* point *m*

periodic [pɪərˈɒdɪk] *adj* périodique; *Chem* **p. table** classification *f* périodique

periodical [pɪərˈɒdɪkəl] *n* périodique *m*

periodically [pɪərˈɒdɪklɪ] *adv* périodiquement

peripheral [pəˈrɪfərəl] **1** *n Comptr* périphérique *m*
2 *adj (area, vision)* périphérique; *(issue, importance)* accessoire

periphery [pəˈrɪfərɪ] *(pl* **peripheries**) *n* périphérie *f*

periscope [ˈperɪskəʊp] *n* périscope *m*

perish [ˈperɪʃ] *vi* **(a)** *(of person)* périr; **p. the thought!** loin de moi cette pensée! **(b)** *(of rubber, leather)* se détériorer; *(of food)* s'avarier

perishable [ˈperɪʃəbəl] **1** *n* **perishables** denrées *fpl* périssables
2 *adj* périssable

perishing [ˈperɪʃɪŋ] *adj Fam (very cold)* **it's p.** il fait un froid de canard

peritonitis [perɪtəˈnaɪtɪs] *n* péritonite *f*

perjure [ˈpɜːdʒə(r)] *vt Law* **to p. oneself** faire un faux témoignage

perjury [ˈpɜːdʒərɪ] *n Law* faux témoignage *m*; **to commit p.** faire un faux témoignage

perk [pɜːk] *n Br Fam* avantage *m*, à-côté *m*
▶**perk up** *Fam* **1** *vt sep (revive)* requinquer, ragaillardir; *(cheer up)* remonter le moral à
2 *vi (revive)* se requinquer, se ragaillardir; *(cheer up)* retrouver sa bonne humeur

perky [ˈpɜːkɪ] *adj Fam (lively)* plein(e) d'entrain; *(cheerful)* guilleret(ette)

perm [pɜːm] **1** *n* permanente *f*; **to have a p.** se faire faire une permanente
2 *vt* **to have one's hair permed** se faire faire une permanente

permanence [ˈpɜːmənəns] *n* permanence *f*

permanent [ˈpɜːmənənt] *adj* permanent(e); *(ink, stain)* indélébile; *(residence, address)* fixe; **p. wave** permanente *f*

permeate [ˈpɜːmɪeɪt] **1** *vt* **to be permeated with sth** *(liquid)* être saturé(e) de qch; *(smell)* être rempli(e) de qch; *Fig (feeling)* être imprégné(e) de qch
2 *vi* **to p. through sth** *(of liquid)* passer à travers qch; *(of smell)* se répandre dans qch; *Fig (of feeling)* imprégner qch

permissible [pəˈmɪsɪbəl] *adj* admissible, acceptable

permission [pəˈmɪʃən] *n* permission *f*, autorisation *f*; **to ask for p. to do sth** demander la permission de faire qch; **to give sb p. to do sth** donner à qn la permission de faire qch, autoriser qn à faire qch

permissive [pəˈmɪsɪv] *adj* permissif(ive)

permit 1 [ˈpɜːmɪt] *n* permis *m*; **p. holders only** *(sign)* réservé aux personnes autorisées
2 *vt* [pəˈmɪt] *(pt & pp* **permitted**) permettre; **to p. sb to do sth** permettre à qn de faire qch, autoriser qn à faire qch
3 *vi* **weather permitting** si le temps le permet

permutation [pɜːmjʊˈteɪʃən] *n* permutation *f*

pernicious [pəˈnɪʃəs] *adj* pernicieux(euse)

pernickety [pəˈnɪkɪtɪ] *adj Fam (person)* tatillon(onne), pointilleux(euse); *(task)* délicat(e), minutieux(euse)

peroxide [pəˈrɒksaɪd] *n Chem* peroxyde *m*; **p. blonde** blonde *f* décolorée

perpendicular [pɜːpənˈdɪkjʊlə(r)] **1** *n* perpendiculaire *f*
2 *adj* perpendiculaire

perpetrate [ˈpɜːpɪtreɪt] *vt (crime)* perpétrer; *(fraud, error)* commettre

perpetrator [ˈpɜːpɪtreɪtə(r)] *n* auteur *m*

perpetual [pəˈpetjʊəl] *adj (eternal)* perpétuel(elle), éternel(elle); *(constant)* incessant(e), continuel(elle); *Phys* **p. motion** mouvement *m* perpétuel

perpetually [pəˈpetjʊəlɪ] *adv* perpétuellement

perpetuate [pəˈpetjʊeɪt] *vt* perpétuer

perpetuity [pɜːpɪˈtjuːɪtɪ] *n Formal* perpétuité *f*; **in p.** à perpétuité

perplex [pəˈpleks] *vt* rendre *ou* laisser perplexe

perplexing [pəˈpleksɪŋ] *adj* difficile; *(person)* déconcertant(e)

perplexity [pəˈpleksɪtɪ] *n* perplexité *f*

persecute [ˈpɜːsɪkjuːt] *vt* persécuter

persecution [pɜːsɪˈkjuːʃən] *n* persécution *f*; *Psy* **p. complex** délire *m* de persécution

persecutor [ˈpɜːsɪkjuːtə(r)] *n* persécuteur(trice) *m,f*

perseverance [pɜːsɪˈvɪərəns] *n* persévérance *f*

persevere [pɜːsɪˈvɪə(r)] *vi* persévérer **(with** dans); **to p. in doing sth** persister à faire qch

Persia [ˈpɜːʒə] *n Hist* la Perse

Persian [ˈpɜːʒən] **1** *n* **(a)** *(person) Hist* Perse *mf*; *(after 7th century)* Persan(e) *m,f* **(b)** *(language)* persan *m*

2 *adj Hist* perse; *(after 7th century)* persan(e); **the P. Gulf** le golfe Persique

persimmon [pə'sɪmən] *n (arbre)* plaqueminier *m*; *(fruit)* kaki *m*

persist [pə'sɪst] *vi* persister; **to p. in doing sth** s'obstiner à faire qch; **to p. in one's belief that...** persister à croire que...

persistence [pə'sɪstəns] *n (of person)* ténacité *f*, obstination *f*; *(of fog, belief)* persistance *f*

persistent [pə'sɪstənt] *adj (person)* tenace; *(problems, pain)* incessant(e), continuel(elle); *(rumours)* persistant(e); **p. offender** récidiviste *mf*

persistently [pə'sɪstəntlɪ] *adv* continuellement

person ['pɜːsən] *(pl* **people** ['piːpəl], *Formal* **persons**) *n* personne *f*; **in p.** en personne; **on one's** p. sur soi; *Gram* **in the first/second/third p.** à la première/deuxième/troisième personne; *Law* **by a p. or persons unknown** par un ou plusieurs inconnus

personable ['pɜːsənəbəl] *adj* charmant(e)

personage ['pɜːsənɪdʒ] *n* personnage *m*

personal ['pɜːsənəl] *adj* personnel(elle); **to make a p. appearance** venir *ou* apparaître en personne; **for p. reasons** pour des raisons personnelles; **don't be p.** ne parle pas des choses aussi personnelles; **it's nothing p., but...** ça n'a rien de personnel, mais...; **p. friend** ami(e) *m,f* personnel(elle); **p. ad** petite annonce *f*; **p. assistant** secrétaire *mf* particulier(ère); **p. best** *(in sport)* record *m* personnel; **p. column** petites annonces; **p. computer** ordinateur *m* individuel; **p. effects** effets *mpl* personnels; **p. growth** développement *m* personnel; **p. hygiene** hygiène *f*; **p. loan** prêt *m* personnel; **p. organizer** *(book)* agenda *m*; *(electronic)* agenda électronique; *Gram* **p. pronoun** pronom *m* personnel; **p. stereo** baladeur *m*

personality [pɜːsə'nælɪtɪ] *(pl* **personalities**) *n* personnalité *f*; **p. cult** culte *m* de la personnalité; *Psy* **p. disorder** trouble *m* de la personnalité

personally [pɜːsənəlɪ] *adv* personnellement; **don't take it p.** n'en faites pas une affaire personnelle

personification [pɜːsɒnɪfɪ'keɪʃən] *n* incarnation *f*; **to be the p. of meanness** être l'avarice incarnée

personify [pɜː'sɒnɪfaɪ] *(pt & pp* **personified**) *vt* personnifier

personnel [pɜːsə'nel] *n* personnel *m*; **p. department** service *m* du personnel; **p. manager** directeur *m* du personnel

perspective [pə'spektɪv] *n* perspective *f*; **to see things in p.** relativiser les choses; **to put sth in(to) p.** relativiser qch

perspicacious [pɜːspɪ'keɪʃəs] *adj Formal* perspicace

perspiration [pɜːspə'reɪʃən] *n* transpiration *f*

perspire [pə'spaɪə(r)] *vi* transpirer

persuade [pə'sweɪd] *vt* persuader, convaincre; **to p. sb to do sth** persuader *ou* convaincre qn de faire qch; **to p. sb not to do sth** dissuader qn de faire qch

persuasion [pə'sweɪʒən] *n (a) (act, ability)* persuasion *f*; **powers of p.** pouvoir *m* de persuasion **(b)** *(beliefs)* **political p.** opinions *fpl* politiques; **religious p.** religion *f*, confession *f*

persuasive [pə'sweɪzɪv] *adj (person)* persuasif(ive); *(argument)* convaincant(e)

persuasively [pə'sweɪzɪvlɪ] *adv (say)* d'un ton persuasif; *(argue)* de façon convaincante

pert [pɜːt] *adj* **(a)** *(cheeky)* espiègle; *(reply)* direct(e) **(b)** *(nose, breasts)* pointu(e); *(bottom)* petit(e) et ferme

pertain [pə'teɪn] *vi Formal* **to p. to** *(belong to)* appartenir à; *(be relevant to)* se rapporter à

pertinent ['pɜːtɪnənt] *adj* pertinent(e); **to be p. to** avoir rapport à

perturb [pə'tɜːb] *vt* inquiéter, troubler

Peru [pə'ruː] *n* le Pérou

perusal [pə'ruːzəl] *n Formal* lecture *f*

peruse [pə'ruːz] *vt Formal (read carefully)* lire attentivement; *(read quickly)* feuilleter; *(article)* survoler

Peruvian [pə'ruːvɪən] **1** *n* Péruvien(enne) *m,f*
2 *adj* péruvien(enne)

pervade [pə'veɪd] *vt* imprégner

pervasive [pə'veɪsɪv] *adj (feeling)* général(e); *(smell)* envahissant(e)

perverse [pə'vɜːs] *adj* **(a)** *(contrary)* contrariant(e); **he's just being p.** il fait ça pour contrarier; **to take a p. pleasure in doing sth** prendre un malin plaisir à faire qch **(b)** *(sexually deviant)* pervers(e)

perversely [pə'vɜːslɪ] *adv (contrarily)* par pur esprit de contradiction

perversion [pə'vɜːʃən] *n (sexual)* perversion *f*; *(of truth, justice)* travestissement *m*

pervert 1 ['pɜːvɜːt] *(sexual deviant)* pervers(e) *m,f*
2 *vt* [pə'vɜːt] *(corrupt)* pervertir; *(distort)* altérer, dénaturer; *Law* **to p. the course of justice** entraver le bon fonctionnement de la justice

peseta [pə'seɪtə] *n* peseta *f*

pesky ['peskɪ] *adj Am Fam* embêtant(e), empoisonnant(e)

peso ['peɪsəʊ] *(pl* **pesos**) *n* peso *m*

pessary ['pesərɪ] *(pl* **pessaries**) *n* ovule *m*

pessimism ['pesɪmɪzəm] *n* pessimisme *m*

pessimist ['pesɪmɪst] *n* pessimiste *mf*

pessimistic [pesɪ'mɪstɪk] *adj* pessimiste

pest [pest] *n* **(a)** *(animal)* animal *m* nuisible; *(insect)* insecte *m* nuisible **(b)** *Fam (nuisance)* poison *m*, plaie *f*

pester ['pestə(r)] *vt* tourmenter, importuner; **to p. sb to do sth** harceler qn pour qu'il fasse qch; **to p. sb into doing sth** harceler qn jusqu'à ce qu'il fasse qch

pesticide ['pestɪsaɪd] *n* pesticide *m*

pestilence ['pestɪləns] *n Lit* peste *f*

pestle ['pesəl] *n* pilon *m*; **p. and mortar** pilon et mortier

pet [pet] **1** *n* **(a)** *(animal)* animal *m* familier *ou* domestique; **p. food** nourriture *f* pour animaux familiers; **p. shop** animalerie *f* **(b)** *(favourite)* **the teacher's p.** le chouchou du professeur; **p. hate** bête *f* noire; **p. name** surnom *m*; **p. subject** dada *m* **(c)** *(term of address)* mon petit chou
2 *vt (pt & pp* **petted**) *(person, dog)* caresser, câliner
3 *vi Fam (sexually)* se peloter

petal ['petəl] *n* pétale *m*

▶**peter out** ['piːtə(r)] *vi (of conversation, enthusiasm)* tarir; *(of scheme)* n'aboutir à rien; *(of path, stream)* disparaître

petite [pə'tiːt] *adj* menu(e)

petition [pɪ'tɪʃən] **1** *n* pétition *f*
2 *vt (court, sovereign)* adresser *ou* présenter une pétition à
3 *vi* **to p. for sth** faire une pétition pour qch; *Law* **to p. for divorce** faire une demande de divorce

petitioner [pɪ'tɪʃənə(r)] *n Law (for divorce)* pétitionnaire *mf*; requérant(e) *m,f*

petrify ['petrɪfaɪ] (*pt & pp* **petrified**) *vt* pétrifier

petrochemical [petrəʊ'kemɪkəl] **1** *n* produit *m* pétrochimique
2 *adj* pétrochimique

petrol ['petrəl] *n Br* essence *f*; **p. bomb** cocktail *m* Molotov; **p. can** bidon *m* d'essence; **p. pump** pompe *f* à essence; **p. station** station *f* d'essence, station-service *f*; **p. tank** réservoir *m* d'essence

petroleum [pə'trəʊlɪəm] *n* pétrole *m*; **p. jelly** vaseline *f*

petticoat ['petɪkəʊt] *n (from waist)* jupon *m*; *(full-length)* combinaison *f*

petty ['petɪ] *adj* **(a)** *(insignificant)* insignifiant(e); **p. cash** petite caisse *f*; **p. crime** petite délinquance *f*; *Naut* **p. officer** second maître *m* **(b)** *(small-minded)* mesquin(e)

petulance ['petjʊləns] *n* irascibilité *f*

petulant ['petjʊlənt] *adj* irascible

petunia [pɪ'tjuːnɪə] *n* pétunia *m*

pew [pjuː] *n* banc *m* d'église; *Fam* **take a p.!** assieds-toi!

pewter ['pjuːtə(r)] *n* étain *m*

PG [piː'dʒiː] *adj Br Cin (abbr* **Parental Guidance***)* = qui exige une autorisation parentale

pH [piː'eɪtʃ] *n Chem* pH *m*

phalanx ['fælæŋks] *n Mil Hist* phalange *f*; *Fig (of officials, journalists)* armée *f*

phallic ['fælɪk] *adj* phallique; **p. symbol** symbole *m* phallique

phallus ['fæləs] *n* phallus *m*

phantom ['fæntəm] *n* fantôme *m*, spectre *m*; **p. pregnancy** grossesse *f* nerveuse

Pharaoh ['feərəʊ] *n* pharaon *m*

pharmaceutical [fɑːmə'sjuːtɪkəl] **1** *n* **pharma-ceuticals** produits *mpl* pharmaceutiques
2 *adj* pharmaceutique

pharmacist ['fɑːməsɪst] *n* pharmacien(enne) *m,f*

pharmacology [fɑːmə'kɒlədʒɪ] *n* pharmacologie *f*

pharmacy ['fɑːməsɪ] (*pl* **pharmacies**) *n* pharmacie *f*

phase [feɪz] *n* phase *f*; **it's just a p. (he's going through)** ça lui passera; *Fig* **out of p.** déphasé(e)

►**phase in** *vt sep* mettre en place progressivement

►**phase out** *vt sep* éliminer progressivement

phased [feɪzd] *adj* progressif(ive)

PhD [piːeɪtʃ'diː] *n Univ (abbr* **Doctor of Philosophy***) (person)* docteur *m*; *(degree)* doctorat *m* **(in** de)

pheasant ['fezənt] *n* faisan *m*

phenomenal [fɪ'nɒmɪnəl] *adj* phénoménal(e)

phenomenally [fɪ'nɒmɪnəlɪ] *adv* prodigieusement

phenomenon [fɪ'nɒmɪnən] (*pl* **phenomena** [fɪ-'nɒmɪnə]) *n* phénomène *m*

phew [fjuː] *exclam (when hot)* pfff!; *(in relief)* ouf!

phial ['faɪəl] *n* fiole *f*

Philadelphia [fɪlə'delfɪə] *n* Philadelphie

philanderer [fɪ'lændərə(r)] *n Pej* coureur *m* de jupons

philanthropic [fɪlən'θrɒpɪk] *adj* philanthropique; *(person)* philanthrope

philanthropist [fɪ'lænθrəpɪst] *n* philanthrope *mf*

philanthropy [fɪ'lænθrəpɪ] *n* philanthropie *f*

philately [fɪ'lætəlɪ] *n* philatélie *f*

philharmonic [fɪlə'mɒnɪk] *Mus* **1** *n* (orchestre *m*) philharmonique *m*
2 *adj* philharmonique

Philippines ['fɪlɪpiːnz] *npl* **the P.** les Philippines *fpl*

philology [fɪ'lɒlədʒɪ] *n* philologie *f*

philosopher [fɪ'lɒsəfə(r)] *n* philosophe *mf*

philosophic(al) [fɪlə'sɒfɪk(əl)] *adj* philosophique; *(person, attitude)* philosophe

philosophize [fɪ'lɒsəfaɪz] *vi* philosopher

philosophy [fɪ'lɒsəfɪ] (*pl* **philosophies**) *n* philosophie *f*

phlegm [flem] *n* flegme *m*

phlegmatic [fleg'mætɪk] *adj* flegmatique

phobia ['fəʊbɪə] *n* phobie *f*; **to have a p. about sth** avoir la phobie de qch

phoenix ['fiːnɪks] *n* phénix *m*; **to rise like a p.** renaître tel un phénix

phone [fəʊn] **1** *n* téléphone *m*; **to be on the p.** *(talking)* être au téléphone; *(have a telephone)* avoir le téléphone; **to give sb a p.** donner un coup de téléphone à qn; **p. bill** facture *f* de téléphone; **p. book** annuaire *m* (du téléphone); **p. box/booth** cabine *f* téléphonique; **p. call** coup *m* de téléphone; **p. number** numéro *m* de téléphone
2 *vt* téléphoner à
3 *vi* téléphoner

phonecard ['fəʊnkɑːd] *n* carte *f* de téléphone

phone-in ['fəʊnɪn] *n* **p. (programme)** = émission au cours de laquelle les téléspectateurs ou les auditeurs peuvent intervenir par téléphone

phoneme ['fəʊniːm] *n* phonème *m*

phonetic [fə'netɪk] *adj* phonétique

phonetics [fə'netɪks] **1** *n (science)* phonétique *f*
2 *npl (symbols)* symboles *mpl* phonétiques

phoney, *Am* **phony** ['fəʊnɪ] (*pl* **phonies**) *Fam* **1** *n (impostor)* imposteur *m*; *(insincere person)* faux jeton *m*; *(thing)* faux *m*
2 *adj* bidon

phosphate ['fɒsfeɪt] *n* phosphate *m*

phosphorescent [fɒsfə'resənt] *adj* phosphorescent(e)

phosphorus ['fɒsfərəs] *n* phosphore *m*

photo ['fəʊtəʊ] (*pl* **photos**) *n* photo *f*; **to take sb's p.** prendre qn en photo; **p. album** album *m* (de) photos; **p. finish** photo-finish *f*; **it's just another p. opportunity** ce n'est qu'un nouveau prétexte pour se faire photographier

photocopier ['fəʊtəʊkɒpɪə(r)] *n* photocopieuse *f*

photocopy ['fəʊtəʊkɒpɪ] **1** *n* (*pl* **photocopies**) photocopie *f*
2 *vt* (*pt & pp* **photocopied**) photocopier

photoelectric [fəʊtəʊɪ'lektrɪk] *adj* photoélectrique; **p. cell** cellule *f* photoélectrique

photogenic [fəʊtə'dʒenɪk] *adj* photogénique

photograph ['fəʊtəgræf] **1** *n* photographie *f*; **to take sb's p.** prendre qn en photo; **p. album** album *m* de photographies
2 *vt* photographier, prendre en photo

photographer [fə'tɒgrəfə(r)] *n* photographe *mf*

photographic [fəʊtə'græfɪk] *adj* photographique; **to have a p. memory** avoir une mémoire photographique

photography [fə'tɒgrəfɪ] *n* photographie *f*

photosensitive [fəʊtəʊ'sensɪtɪv] *adj* photosensible

Photostat® ['fəʊtəʊstæt] *n* photostat *m*

photosynthesis [fəʊtəʊ'sɪnθɪsɪs] *n Bot* photosynthèse *f*

photosynthesize [fəʊtəʊ'sɪnθɪsaɪz] *vt Bot* fabriquer par photosynthèse

phrasal verb ['freɪzl'vɜːb] *n Gram* verbe *m* à particule

phrase [freɪz] **1** *n* phrase *f*; **p. book** manuel *m* ou guide *m* de conversation

2 *vt* **(a)** *(verbally)* exprimer; *(in writing)* tourner **(b)** *Mus* phraser

phraseology [freɪzɪ'ɒlədʒɪ] *n* phraséologie *f*

physical ['fɪzɪkl] **1** *n (examination)* visite *f* médicale

2 *adj* physique; **p. education** éducation *f* physique; **p. exercise** *or* **training** *(exercices mpl de)* gymnastique *f*; **p. fitness** forme *f* physique; **p. geography** géographie *f* physique; **p. impossibility** impossibilité *f* physique *ou* matérielle; **p. sciences** sciences *fpl* physiques

physically ['fɪzɪklɪ] *adv* physiquement; **p. fit** en bonne forme physique; **p. handicapped** handicapé(e) physique

physician [fɪ'zɪʃən] *n* médecin *m*

physicist ['fɪzɪsɪst] *n* physicien(enne) *m,f*

physics ['fɪzɪks] *n* physique *f*

physiognomy [fɪzɪ'ɒnəmɪ] *n Formal* physionomie *f*

physiological [fɪzɪə'lɒdʒɪkl] *adj* physiologique

physiology [fɪzɪ'ɒlədʒɪ] *n* physiologie *f*

physiotherapist [fɪzɪəʊ'θerəpɪst] *n* kinésithérapeute *mf*

physiotherapy [fɪzɪəʊ'θerəpɪ] *n* kinésithérapie *f*

physique [fɪ'ziːk] *n* physique *m*

pianist ['pɪənɪst] *n* pianiste *mf*

piano [pɪ'ænəʊ] *(pl* **pianos)** *n* piano *m*; **p. concerto** concerto *m* pour piano; **p. stool** tabouret *m* de piano; **p. tuner** accordeur *m* de pianos

piccolo ['pɪkələʊ] *(pl* **piccolos)** *n* piccolo *m*

pick [pɪk] **1** *n (tool)* pic *m*, pioche *f* **(b)** *(choice)* **to take one's p.** choisir; **the p. of the bunch** le (la) meilleur(e) du lot

2 *vt (choose)* choisir; **to p. a fight (with sb)** chercher la bagarre (avec qn) **(b)** *(flowers, fruit)* cueillir **(c)** *(other uses)* **to p. a lock** crocheter une serrure; **to p. a guitar** pincer la guitare; **to p. one's nose** mettre les doigts dans le nez; **to p. one's teeth** se curer les dents; **to p. a spot** tripoter un bouton; **to p. sb's pocket** voler dans les poches de qn; **to p. a hole in sth** faire un trou à qch en tirant dessus; *Fig* **to p. holes in sth** trouver des failles dans qch; **to p. sb's brains** soumettre quelque chose à la sagacité de qn

3 *vi* **to p. and choose** se permettre de choisir

▸**pick off** *vt sep (remove)* enlever, ôter; *(of gunman, sniper)* éliminer

▸**pick on** *vt insep* utiliser comme souffre-douleur

▸**pick out** *vt sep* **(a)** *(remove)* retirer **(b)** *(select)* choisir **(c)** *(recognize)* repérer

▸**pick up** **1** *vt sep* **(a)** *(lift up)* ramasser; *(to upright position)* relever; **to p. up the phone** décrocher (le téléphone); *Fig* **to p. oneself up** se remettre, se reprendre; *Fig* **to p. up the pieces** ramasser les morceaux; *Fig* **to p. up the bill** payer l'addition **(b)** *(collect)* prendre; *(arrest)* arrêter; **to p. up survivors** recueillir des survivants **(c)** *Fam (sexually)* ramasser **(d)** *(learn)* apprendre; *(acquire)* acquérir; **to p. up speed** prendre de la vitesse **(e)** *(radio station, message)* capter **(f)** *(notice)* relever **(g)** *(discussion)* reprendre **(h)** *(make better)* remonter

2 *vi (improve)* s'améliorer; *(after illness)* se remettre; *(of match, party)* s'animer; **business is picking up** les

affaires reprennent **(b)** *(continue)* **let's p. up where we left off** reprenons (là où nous en étions restés)

pickaxe ['pɪkæks] *n* pioche *f*, pic *m*

picket ['pɪkɪt] **1** *n* **(a)** *(in strike)* piquet *m* de grève; **p. line** piquet de grève **(b)** *(stake)* piquet *m*, pieu *m*; **p. fence** palissade *f*

2 *vt (during strike)* former un piquet de grève aux portes de

pickings ['pɪkɪŋz] *npl* bénéfices *mpl*; **rich p.** gros bénéfices

pickle ['pɪkl] **1** *n* = condiment à base de légumes conservés dans du vinaigre; **pickles** conserves *fpl* au vinaigre; *Fam Fig* **to be in a p.** être dans le pétrin

2 *vt* conserver dans du vinaigre; **pickled cabbage/onions** chou *m* rouge/oignons *mpl* au vinaigre

pick-me-up ['pɪkmɪʌp] *n Fam* remontant *m*

pickpocket ['pɪkpɒkɪt] *n* pickpocket *m*, voleur(euse) *m,f*, à la tire

pick-up ['pɪkʌp] *n* **(a)** **p. (arm)** *(on record player)* lecteur *m* (phonographique); **p. (truck)** pick-up *m inv (petite camionnette à plateau)*; **p. point** *for goods, passengers)* point *m* de ramassage **(b)** *Fam (improvement)* amélioration *f*; *(of business)* reprise *f*

picky ['pɪkɪ] *adj Fam* difficile **(about** sur)

picnic ['pɪknɪk] **1** *n* pique-nique *m*; **to go on a p.** aller faire un pique-nique, aller pique-niquer; *Fam Fig* **it was no p.** ça n'a pas été une partie de plaisir; **p. basket** *or* **hamper** panier *m* à pique-nique

2 *vi (pt & pp* **picnicked)** pique-niquer, faire un pique-nique

picnicker ['pɪknɪkə(r)] *n* pique-niqueur(euse) *m,f*

Pict [pɪkt] *n Hist* Picte *mf*

pictorial [pɪk'tɔːrɪəl] *adj (magazine)* illustré(e); *(representation)* en images

picture ['pɪktʃə(r)] **1** *n* **(a)** *(painting)* tableau *m*; *(drawing)* dessin *m*; *(in book, on TV)* image *f*; *(photograph)* photo *f*; *Fig (situation)* situation *f*; **to be the p. of health** respirer la santé; **her face was a p.** elle a fait une de ces têtes; *Fig* **to put sb in the p.** mettre qn au courant; *Fam Fig* **I get the p.** je pige; **p. book** livre *m* d'images; **p. frame** cadre *m*; **p. gallery** galerie *f* de peintures; **p. postcard** carte *f* postale illustrée; **p. window** baie *f* vitrée **(b)** *Br Fam (film)* film *m*; **the pictures** le cinéma

2 *vt (imagine)* **to p. sth (to oneself)** s'imaginer qch; **to p. sb/sth as sth** s'imaginer qn/qch en qch; **to p. sb doing sth** s'imaginer qn en train de faire qch **(b)** *(in photo, painting)* représenter; *Fig (in words)* dépeindre, décrire

picturesque [pɪktʃə'resk] *adj* pittoresque

pidgin ['pɪdʒɪn] *n* pidgin *m*; **p. English/French** ≃ petit nègre *m*

pie [paɪ] *n* tourte *f*; *Fam* **p. in the sky** des châteaux en Espagne; **p. chart** camembert *m*

piece [piːs] *n* **(a)** *(in general)* morceau *m*; *(smaller)* bout *m*; *(of cake)* part *f*; *(newspaper article)* article *m*; **p. of land** *(parcelle f de)* terrain *m,f*; **a p. of furniture** un meuble; **a p. of luggage** *(suitcase)* une valise; *(bag)* un sac; **a p. of advice** un conseil; **a p. of luck** un coup de chance; **a p. of news** une nouvelle; **p. rate** *(pay)* salaire *m* à la pièce **(b)** *(in chess, of jigsaw puzzle)* pièce *f*; *(in dominoes)* domino *m*; *(in draughts)* pion *m* **(c)** *(coin)* pièce *f* **(d)** *(of music)* morceau *m* **(e)** *(of artillery)* pièce *f*; *(firearm)* arme *f* **(f)** *(idioms)* **to be still in one p.** être encore entier(ère); **to give sb a p. of one's mind** dire ses quatre vérités à qn; **to say one's p.** dire ce qu'on a à dire; **p. by p.** par morceaux; *Fig* **to go to pieces** s'effondrer (complètement); **to fall to pieces** tomber en morceaux; *(of house)* se délabrer, crouler; *(of garment)* partir en morceaux; **to take sth to pieces** démonter qch; **to be a p. of cake** être facile comme tout; *Fam* **he's a nasty p. of work** c'est un sale type

▶**piece together** *vt sep (parts)* assembler les morceaux de; *(something broken)* recoller les morceaux de; *(facts)* reconstituer

piecemeal ['pi:smi:l] **1** *adj* fragmentaire, parcellaire; *(work)* fait(e) petit à petit
2 *adv* petit à petit

piecework ['pi:swɜ:k] *n* travail *m* à la tâche *ou* à la pièce

Piedmont ['pi:dmɒnt] *n* le Piémont

pier [pɪə(r)] *n (landing stage)* embarcadère *m*; *(at seaside resort)* jetée *f*; *(of bridge)* pilier *m*

pierce [pɪəs] *vt* percer, transpercer; **to have pierced ears** avoir les oreilles percées

piercing ['pɪəsɪŋ] *adj (cry, look)* perçant(e); *(cold)* vif (vive)

piety ['paɪətɪ] *n* piété *f*

pig [pɪg] **1** *n* **(a)** *(animal)* cochon *m*, porc *m* **(b)** *Fam (greedy person)* goinfre *m*, glouton(onne) *m,f*; *(unpleasant man)* salaud *m*; *(unpleasant woman)* salope *f* **(c)** *Fam (policeman)* poulet *m* **(d)** *Fam (idioms)* **to buy a p. in a poke** acheter chat en poche; **pigs might fly!** on peut toujours rêver!; **to make a p.'s ear of sth** bousiller qch, saloper qch; **to make a p. of oneself** s'en mettre plein la lampe
2 *vt (pt & pp pigged) Fam* **to p. oneself** s'en mettre plein la lampe

pig out *vi Fam* s'en mettre plein la lampe

pigeon ['pɪdʒɪn] *n* pigeon *m*

pigeonhole ['pɪdʒɪnhəʊl] **1** *n* casier *m*
2 *vt (person)* étiqueter, mettre une étiquette à

piggy ['pɪgɪ] *Fam* **1** *n (pl* **piggies)** petit cochon *m*; **p. bank** tirelire *f*
2 *adj (eyes)* de cochon

piggyback ['pɪgɪbæk] *n* **to give sb a p.** porter qn sur son dos

pig-headed [pɪg'hedɪd] *adj* entêté(e), têtu(e)

piglet ['pɪglɪt] *n* porcelet *m*

pigment ['pɪgmənt] *n* pigment *m*

pigmentation [pɪgmən'teɪʃən] *n* pigmentation *f*

pigmy ['pɪgmɪ] *(pl* **pigmies)** *n* Pigmée *mf*

pigsty ['pɪgstaɪ] *(pl* **pigsties)** *n also Fig* porcherie *f*

pigtail ['pɪgteɪl] *n* natte *f*

pike¹ [paɪk] *n (weapon)* pique *f*

pike² *n (fish)* brochet *m*

pilchard ['pɪltʃəd] *n* pilchard *m*

pile [paɪl] **1** *n* **(a)** *(heap)* tas *m*; *(stack)* pile *f*; **to put things in(to) a p.** *(heap)* mettre des choses en tas; *(stack)* empiler des choses; *Fam* **to make one's p.** faire fortune; *Fam* **to have piles of** *or* **a p. of things/work to do** avoir un tas de choses/des tonnes de travail à faire; *Fam Fig* **to be at the top/bottom of the p.** être favorisé(e)/défavorisé(e) **(b)** *(of carpet)* poils *mpl* **(c)** *Phys* **(atomic) p.** pile *f* atomique **(d)** *(building)* édifice *m*; *(column, pillar)* pilier *m*
2 *vt* entasser; *(stack)* empiler; **to p. food onto one's plate** bien remplir son assiette
3 *vi Fam* **to p. into a car** s'entasser dans une voiture

▶**pile in** *vi* s'entasser

▶**pile on** *vt sep* **to p. on the pressure** faire monter la pression; **to p. on the agony** dramatiser; *Fam* **to p. it on** en rajouter

▶**pile out** *vi* sortir en masse

▶**pile up** *vi* s'accumuler

pile-driver ['paɪldraɪvə(r)] *n* sonnette *f*

piles [paɪlz] *npl (haemorrhoids)* hémorroïdes *fpl*; **to have p.** avoir des hémorroïdes

pile-up ['paɪlʌp] *n Fam* carambolage *m*

pilfer ['pɪlfə(r)] *vt & vi* chaparder

pilgrim ['pɪlgrɪm] *n* pèlerin(e) *m,f*

pilgrimage ['pɪlgrɪmɪdʒ] *n* pèlerinage *m*; **to go on** *or* **make a p.** aller en pèlerinage, faire un pèlerinage

pill [pɪl] *n* pilule *f*; **the p.** *(contraceptive)* la pilule; **to be on the p.** prendre la pilule

pillage ['pɪlɪdʒ] **1** *n* pillage *m*
2 *vt & vi* piller

pillar ['pɪlə(r)] *n also Fig* pilier *m*; **to go from p. to post** courir à droite à gauche; **to be a p. of strength** être d'un grand soutien; **p. box** boîte *f* aux lettres

pillion ['pɪljən] **1** *n* **p. (seat)** siège *m* arrière
2 *adv* **to ride p.** monter derrière

pillory ['pɪlərɪ] **1** *n (pl* **pillories)** pilori *m*
2 *vt (pt & pp* **pilloried)** mettre au pilori

pillow ['pɪləʊ] *n* oreiller *m*

pillowcase ['pɪləʊkeɪs], **pillowslip** ['pɪləʊslɪp] *n* taie *f* d'oreiller

pilot ['paɪlət] **1** *n (of plane, ship)* pilote *m*; **p. (programme)** *(on TV)* émission *f* pilote; **p. light** veilleuse *f*; **p. scheme** projet-pilote *m*; **p. study** étude-pilote *f*
2 *vt (plane, ship)* piloter

pimp [pɪmp] *n* souteneur *m*, proxénète *m*

pimple ['pɪmpəl] *n* bouton *m*

pimply ['pɪmplɪ] *adj* boutonneux(euse)

PIN [pɪn] *n (abbr* **personal identification number)** code *m* confidentiel

pin [pɪn] **1** *n (for sewing)* épingle *f*; *(for surgery)* broche *f*; *(in grenade)* goupille *f*; **three-p. plug** prise *f* à trois broches; *(firing)* **p.** percuteur *m*; *(safety)* **p.** épingle à nourrice; *Fam* **to have pins and needles** avoir des fourmis; **you could hear a p. drop** on aurait entendu une mouche voler; **p. money** argent *m* de poche
2 *vt (pt & pp* **pinned)** *(fasten with pin)* épingler; *(with drawing pin, safety pin)* attacher; **to p. sb against** *or* **to a wall** plaquer qn contre un mur; **to p. the blame on sb** rejeter la responsabilité sur qn; **to p. one's hopes on sb/ sth** mettre tous ses espoirs en qn/qch

▶**pin down** *vt sep* **(a)** *(trap)* coincer **(b)** *(identify)* mettre le doigt sur **(c)** *(force to be definite)* **to p. sb down** obliger qn à s'engager; **to p. sb down to a date** obliger qn à donner une date

▶**pin up** *vt sep (notice)* fixer *ou* accrocher au mur; *(hair)* relever; *(hem)* rabattre avec des épingles

pinafore ['pɪnəfɔ:(r)] *n (apron)* tablier *m*; **p. (dress)** robe chasuble *f*

pinball ['pɪnbɔ:l] *n* flipper *m*

pincer ['pɪnsə(r)] *n (of crab, insect)* pince *f*; *Mil* **p. movement** mouvement *m* en tenailles

pincers ['pɪnsəz] *npl (tool)* tenailles *fpl*, pince *f*

pinch [pɪntʃ] **1** *n* **(a)** *(action)* pincement *m*; **to give sb a p.** pincer qn; *Fam Fig* **to feel the p.** être gêné(e); **at a p.** à la

rigueur (b) *(of salt, herbs)* pincée f; *Fig* **to take sth with a p. of salt** ne pas prendre qch pour argent comptant
2 vt (a) *(nip)* pincer; **these shoes p. my feet** ces chaussures me serrent (b) *Fam (steal)* piquer, faucher
3 vi *(of shoes)* serrer

pincushion [ˈpɪnkʊʃən] n pelote f à épingles

pine¹ [paɪn] n *(tree, wood)* pin m; **p. cone** pomme f de pin; **p. forest** pinède f; **p. needle** aiguille f de pin; **p. nut** pignon m

pine² vi **to p. for sb/sth** se languir de qn/qch
▶**pine away** vi languir

pineapple [ˈpaɪnæpəl] n ananas m

ping [pɪŋ] **1** n tintement m
2 vi tinter

ping-pong [ˈpɪŋpɒŋ] n ping-pong m

pinion [ˈpɪnjən] **1** n pignon m
2 vt *(restrain)* **to p. sb (to/against)** clouer *ou* plaquer qn (à/contre)

pink [pɪŋk] **1** n (a) *(colour)* rose m; *Fam* **to be in the p.** être en parfaite santé (b) *(flower)* œillet m
2 adj rose; **to turn p.** rosir; **p. gin** = cocktail à base de gin et d'angusture

pinkeye [ˈpɪŋkaɪ] n *Am* conjonctivite f infectieuse

pinkie [ˈpɪŋkɪ] n *Am & Scot* petit doigt m

pinnacle [ˈpɪnəkəl] n sommet m; *Fig (of fame, career)* apogée m

pinpoint [ˈpɪnpɔɪnt] vt déterminer, identifier; *(place)* localiser exactement

pinprick [ˈpɪnprɪk] n piqûre f d'aiguille

pinstripe [ˈpɪnstraɪp] n rayures fpl fines; **p. suit** costume m rayé

pint [paɪnt] n *(unit of measurement)* Br = 0,568 l, pinte f; Am = 0,473 l, pinte; *Br* **a p.** *(of beer)* ≃ un demi-litre de bière; **I'm going for a p.** je vais prendre une bière

pinto bean [ˈpɪntəʊˈbiːn] n haricot m pinto

pint-size(d) [ˈpaɪntsaɪz(d)] adj *Fam* minuscule

pin-up [ˈpɪnʌp] n *Fam* pin-up f inv

pioneer [paɪəˈnɪə(r)] **1** n *also Fig* pionnier(ère) m,f
2 vt **to p. sth** être le (la) premier(ère) à mettre au point qch

pioneering [paɪəˈnɪərɪŋ] adj *(work)* innovateur(trice); *(person)* qui fait œuvre de pionnier

pious [ˈpaɪəs] adj pieux(euse)

piously [ˈpaɪəslɪ] adv pieusement, avec piété

pip [pɪp] **1** n (a) *(of fruit)* pépin m (b) *(on card, die)* point m (c) *(sound)* **the pips** *(on radio)* les bips mpl sonores; *(on public telephone)* = la tonalité indiquant que le crédit est épuisé
2 vt *(pt & pp pipped) Fam* **to be pipped at the post** être coiffé(e) sur le poteau

pipe [paɪp] **1** n (a) *(tube)* tuyau m, canalisation f; *(musical instrument)* chalumeau m; **the pipes** la cornemuse; **p. band** orchestre m de cornemuses (b) *(for smoking)* pipe f; **to smoke a p.** fumer la pipe; *Fam Fig* **put that in your p. and smoke it!** mettez ça dans votre poche et votre mouchoir par-dessus!; **p. cleaner** cure-pipe m; **p. dream** chimère f
2 vt *(water, oil)* canaliser; *Fam* **piped music** musiquette f
▶**pipe down** vi *Fam (make less noise)* faire moins de bruit; *(not talk so much)* se taire
▶**pipe up** vi *(of person)* risquer un commentaire; *(of voice)* se faire entendre

pipeline [ˈpaɪplaɪn] n *(for oil)* pipeline m, oléoduc m; *(for gas)* gazoduc m; *Fig* **to be in the p.** être en préparation

piper [ˈpaɪpə(r)] n *(bagpipe player)* joueur(euse) m,f de cornemuse; *Prov* **he who pays the p. calls the tune** il est normal que celui qui paie ait le droit de choisir

pipette [pɪˈpet] n pipette f

piping [ˈpaɪpɪŋ] **1** n (a) *(pipes)* tuyauterie f, canalisations fpl (b) *(sound of bagpipes)* son m de la cornemuse (c) *(on uniform)* passepoil m
2 adj *(sound, voice)* flûté(e)
3 adv **p. hot** tout(e) chaud(e)

pipsqueak [ˈpɪpskwiːk] n *Fam* minus m

piquant [ˈpiːkənt] adj piquant(e)

pique [piːk] **1** n dépit m; **in a fit of p.** dans un accès de dépit
2 vt piquer

piracy [ˈpaɪrəsɪ] n (a) *(of ships)* piraterie f (b) *(of videos, software)* piratage m

piranha [pɪˈrɑːnə] n piranha m

pirate [ˈpaɪrət] n pirate m; **p. edition** édition f pirate; **p. radio** radio f pirate

pirouette [pɪrʊˈet] **1** n pirouette f
2 vi pirouetter

Pisa [ˈpiːzə] n Pise

Pisces [ˈpaɪsiːz] n les Poissons mpl; **to be (a) P.** être Poissons

piss [pɪs] *very Fam* **1** n *(urine)* pisse f; **to have a p.** pisser; *Fig* **to take the p. out of sb/sth** se foutre de qn/qch; **p. artist** soûlard(e) m,f
2 vt **to p. oneself, to p. one's pants** pisser dans son froc
3 vi pisser
▶**piss about, piss around** vi *very Fam (behave foolishly)* déconner; *(waste time)* glandouiller
▶**piss off** *very Fam* **1** vt sep *(annoy)* faire chier; **to be pissed off** en avoir plein le cul
2 vi *(go away)* foutre le camp

pissed [pɪst] adj *very Fam* (a) *Br (drunk)* bourré(e); **to get p.** se soûler la gueule (b) *Am (angry)* en rogne

piss-up [ˈpɪsʌp] n *very Fam* beuverie f

pistachio [pɪˈstɑːʃɪəʊ] *(pl pistachios)* n *(nut)* pistache f; *(tree)* pistachier m

pistol [ˈpɪstəl] n pistolet m; **p. shot** coup m de pistolet

piston [ˈpɪstən] n piston m

pit¹ [pɪt] n (a) *(hole in ground)* fosse f; *(coal mine)* mine f; **in the p. of one's stomach** au creux de l'estomac; *Fam* **to be the pits** être nul (nulle) le nul (nulle); **the pits** *(in motor racing)* les stands mpl de ravitaillement (c) *(on metal, glass)* piqûre f; *(on skin)* marque f, cicatrice f

pit² n *(of cherry, olive)* noyau m

pit³ *(pt & pp pitted)* vt **to p. sb against sb** mettre qn aux prises avec qn, opposer qn à qn; **to p. oneself against sb** se mesurer à qn; **to p. one's wits against sb** se mesurer intellectuellement à qn

pit-a-pat [ˈpɪtəpæt] **1** n *(of rain)* crépitement m; *(of feet)* trottinement m; *(of heart)* battement m
2 adv **to go p.** *(of rain)* crépiter; *(of feet)* trottiner; *(of heart)* palpiter

pitch¹ [pɪtʃ] **1** n (a) *Br (for market stall)* place f, emplacement m (b) *(for sport)* terrain m (c) *(in music)* hauteur f; *Fig* **to reach such a p. that...** atteindre un tel point que... (d) *(talk) (sales)* **p.** baratin m publicitaire (e) *(slope)* inclinaison f

2 vt (a) (throw) lancer (b) (aim) adapter (at à) (c) (tent) monter, dresser
3 vi (of ship, plane) tanguer
▶**pitch in** vi mettre du sien

pitch² [pɪtʃ] n (tar) poix f
pitch-black [pɪtʃ'blæk] adj noir(e) comme dans un four; **it's p. outside** il fait nuit noire
pitched [pɪtʃt] adj (a) (sloping) en pente (b) **p. battle** bataille f rangée
pitcher¹ [pɪtʃə(r)] n Am (jug) cruche f, pichet m
pitcher² n Am (in baseball) lanceur m
pitchfork [pɪtʃfɔːk] n fourche f
piteous [pɪtɪəs] adj pitoyable
pitfall [pɪtfɔːl] n piège m
pith [pɪθ] n (of orange) peau f blanche; (of argument, idea) essence f; **p. helmet** casque m colonial (en sola)
pithy [pɪθɪ] adj concis(e)
pitiable [pɪtɪəbəl] adj pitoyable
pitiful [pɪtɪfʊl] adj pitoyable
pitifully [pɪtɪfʊlɪ] adv pitoyablement
pitiless [pɪtɪlɪs] adj impitoyable
pitta bread [pɪtəbred] n pita m
pittance [pɪtəns] n salaire m de misère
pituitary gland [pɪˈtjuːɪtərɪˈglænd] n hypophyse f
pity [pɪtɪ] 1 n (a) (compassion) pitié f; **to take or have p. on sb** prendre qn en pitié; **for p.'s sake!** par pitié! (b) (misfortune) **it's a p. (that...)** c'est dommage (que... + subjunctive); **what a p.!** quel dommage!; **more's the p.** c'est bien dommage
2 vt (pt & pp pitied) plaindre, avoir pitié de
pitying [pɪtɪɪŋ] adj compatissant(e)
pivot [pɪvət] 1 n also Fig pivot m
2 vi pivoter (**on** sur); Fig (of plan) reposer (**on** or **around** sur)
pivotal [pɪvətəl] adj (position) clef; (importance) capital(e)
pixel [pɪksəl] n Comptr pixel m
pixie [pɪksɪ] n lutin m
pizza [piːtsə] n pizza f; **p. parlour** pizzeria f
Pk abbr **Park**
pkt (abbr **packet**) paquet
Pl abbr **Place**
placard [plækɑːd] n pancarte f
placate [pləˈkeɪt] vt apaiser, calmer
place [pleɪs] 1 n (a) (location) endroit m, lieu m; (in street names) rue f; **a p. to live/eat** un logement/un restaurant; **I can't be in two places at once** je ne peux pas être à deux endroits à la fois; Fam **all over the p.** (everywhere) un peu partout; **my hair was all over the p.** j'étais coiffé n'importe comment; **at the interview he was all over the p.** à l'entretien, il a raconté n'importe quoi; Fam Fig **to go places** réussir (dans la vie); **p. of birth/death/business** lieu de naissance/décès/travail; **p. of residence** domicile m; **p. of worship** lieu m de culte; **p. name** nom m de lieu
(b) (assigned to person, thing) place f; **to find a p. for sb** (job) trouver une place pour qn; **to get a p. at university** être admis(e) à l'université; **there's a time and a p. for everything** il y a un temps pour tout; **to hold sth in p.** tenir qch en place; **to lose one's p.** (in a book) perdre sa page; **to take p.** avoir lieu; **to take sb's p.** remplacer qn; (oust) prendre la place de qn; Fig **out of p.** (remark) déplacé(e); **to feel out of p.** ne pas se sentir à sa place

(c) Fam (residence) chez soi; **my parents' p.** chez mes parents; **your p. or mine?** on va chez toi ou chez moi?
(d) (seat, position in queue) place f; **to set** or **lay an extra p. at the table** mettre un couvert de plus; **to change places with sb** changer de place avec qn; Fig **être à la place de qn**; Fig **put yourself in my p.** mettez-vous à ma place; **p. mat** set m de table
(e) (in competition, society) place f, rang m; **in first/second p.** à la première/seconde place; **in the first p...., in the second p....** (parts of an argument) en premier lieu..., en second lieu...; **you shouldn't have said it in the first p.** d'abord, tu n'aurais pas dû le dire; **to know one's p.** savoir où est sa place; **to put sb in his p.** remettre qn à sa place
(f) Math **to three decimal places** à trois décimales
2 vt (a) (put) placer, mettre; **the house is well placed** la maison est bien située; **to be well placed to do sth** être bien placé(e) pour faire qch; **I know her face but I can't p. her** je l'ai déjà vue mais je ne sais pas où
(b) (Com & Fin (order) passer (**with** à); (contract) adjuger (**with** à); **to p. a bet (on sth)** parier (sur qch)
(c) (find a job for) placer
(d) (classify) classer; **to be placed third** se classer troisième

placebo [pləˈsiːbəʊ] (pl **placebos**) n Med also Fig placebo m
placement [pleɪsmənt] n stage m
placenta [pləˈsentə] n placenta m
placid [plæsɪd] adj placide, calme
plagiarism [pleɪdʒərɪzəm] n plagiat m
plagiarize [pleɪdʒəraɪz] vt plagier
plague [pleɪg] 1 n (disease) peste f; (of insects, frogs) invasion f; **to avoid sb/sth like the p.** éviter qn/qch comme la peste
2 vt (of person) harceler; (of problem) tourmenter; **to p. sb with questions** harceler qn de questions
plaice [pleɪs] n carrelet m
plaid [plæd] n (fabric) tissu m écossais; (garment) plaid m
plain [pleɪn] 1 n plaine f
2 adj (a) (clear, unambiguous) clair(e), évident(e); **to make sth p. to sb** faire comprendre qch à qn; **I'll be quite p. with you** je vais être franc avec vous; Fam **it's as p. as the nose on your face** ça se voit comme le nez au milieu de la figure; **in p. English** clairement; Fig **to be p. sailing** aller tout seul; **p. speaking** franc-parler m (b) (simple) simple; Fam **that's just p. foolishness/ignorance** c'est de la pure bêtise/ignorance; **one p., one purl** (in knitting) une maille à l'endroit, une maille à l'envers; **p. chocolate** chocolat m noir; **p. clothes policeman** un agent en civil; **p. flour** farine f (sans levure) (c) (not beautiful) quelconque; **a p. Jane** une jeune fille plutôt quelconque
plainly [pleɪnlɪ] adv (a) (clearly) clairement, nettement; **to speak p.** parler franchement ou sans détours (b) (simply) simplement
plain-spoken [pleɪnˈspəʊkən] adj franc (franche)
plaintiff [pleɪntɪf] n Law plaignant(e) m,f
plaintive [pleɪntɪv] adj plaintif(ive)
plaintively [pleɪntɪvlɪ] adv d'un ton plaintif
plait [plæt] 1 n natte f, tresse f
2 vt natter, tresser
plan [plæn] 1 n (a) (proposal, intention) projet m; **to go according to p.** marcher comme prévu; **the best p. would be to...** le mieux serait de... (b) (of building, town, essay) plan m

2 vt (pt & pp **planned**) **(a)** (arrange) projeter; (crime) comploter, tramer; **to p. to do sth** projeter de faire qch; **to go as planned** marcher comme prévu **(b)** (building, town) faire le plan de; (economy) planifier
3 vi faire des projets; **to p. for the future** faire des projets d'avenir

▶**plan out** vt sep prévoir (en détail)

plane¹ [plein] n (surface) plan m

plane² n (aeroplane) avion m; **by p.** en avion; **p. ticket** billet m d'avion

plane³ 1 n (tool) rabot m
2 vt raboter, aplanir

plane⁴ n **p.** (tree) platane m

planet ['plænɪt] n planète f

planetarium [plænɪ'teərɪəm] (pl **planetariums** or **planetaria** [plænɪ'teərɪə]) n planétarium m

planetary ['plænɪtərɪ] adj planétaire

plank [plæŋk] n (of wood) planche f; Fig (policy) point m

plankton ['plæŋktən] n plancton m

planner ['plænə(r)] n planificateur(trice) m,f; (for towns) urbaniste mf

planning ['plænɪŋ] n conception f, élaboration f; **it's still at the p. stage** c'est encore à l'état de projet; **p. permission** permis m de construire

plant [plɑːnt] **1** n **(a)** (living thing) plante f; **p. life** flore f **(b)** Ind (equipment) matériel m; (factory) usine f; **p. hire** location f de matériel industriel; **p. maintenance** entretien m du matériel
2 vt (tree, flower) planter; (crops, field) semer; (bomb) poser; **to p. an idea in sb's mind** mettre une idée dans l'esprit de qn; Fam **to p. sth on sb** cacher qch dans les affaires de qn (pour le/la compromettre en cas de découverte)

plantain ['plæntɪn] n (cereal) millet) plantain m **(b)** (fruit) banane f des Antilles; (tree) bananier m du paradis

plantation [plæn'teɪʃən] n plantation f

planter ['plɑːntə(r)] n (person) planteur(euse) m,f; (machine) planteuse

plaque [plɑːk] n **(a)** (sign) plaque f (commémorative) **(b)** (on teeth) plaque f dentaire

plasma ['plæzmə] n plasma m

plaster ['plɑːstə(r)] **1** n **(a)** (on wall) plâtre m; **p. of Paris** plâtre de Paris; **to put sb's leg in p.** mettre la jambe de qn dans le plâtre; **p. cast** (for broken bone) plâtre; (in art) moulage m en plâtre **(b)** Br **(sticking) p.** pansement m adhésif
2 vt **(a)** (wall) plâtrer **(b)** (cover) tapisser (**with** de); **plastered with mud** couvert(e) de boue; **her name was plastered over the front pages** son nom s'étalait en première page

plasterboard ['plɑːstəbɔːd] n placoplâtre® m

plastered ['plɑːstəd] adj Fam (drunk) beurré(e)

plasterer ['plɑːstərə(r)] n plâtrier m

plastic ['plæstɪk] **1** n **(a)** (material) plastique m **(b)** Fam (credit cards) cartes fpl de crédit; **do they take p.?** est-ce qu'ils acceptent les cartes de crédit?
2 adj (cup, bag) en plastique; (bullet) de plastique; **explosive plastic** m; **p. surgeon** chirurgien(enne) m,f esthétique; **p. surgery** (cosmetic) chirurgie f esthétique; (after accident) chirurgie réparatrice

plate [pleɪt] n **(a)** (for food) assiette f; (for church offering) plateau m de quête; Fam Fig **to have a lot on one's p.** avoir du pain sur la planche; Fam Fig **to hand sth to sb on a p.** apporter qch à qn sur un plateau; **p. rack** égouttoir m (sheet of glass, plastic) lamelle f; (sheet of metal) plaque f; **p. glass** vitrage m très épais
2 vt (with gold) plaquer en or; (with silver) plaquer en argent

plateau ['plætəʊ] (pl **plateaux** ['plætəʊz] or **plateaus**) n Geog plateau m; Fig **to reach a p.** (of career, economy) atteindre un palier

platform ['plætfɔːm] n **(a)** (raised flat surface) plate-forme f; (in train station) (where passengers stand) quai m; (where train stops) voie f; Rail **p. 4** quai n° 4; **p. shoes** chaussures fpl à semelles compensées (à la façon des années 70) **(b)** (at meeting) estrade f, tribune f; (political programme) programme m

platform-independent ['plætfɔːmɪndɪ'pendənt] adj Comptr indépendant(e) de la plate-forme

platinum ['plætɪnəm] n Chem platine m; **p. blond hair** cheveux blond platine

platitude ['plætɪtjuːd] n platitude f

platonic [plə'tɒnɪk] adj platonique

platoon [plə'tuːn] n Mil section f, peloton m

platter ['plætə(r)] n (serving plate) plat m

platypus ['plætɪpəs] n ornithorynque m

plausible ['plɔːzəbl] adj (excuse, argument) plausible; (person) convaincant(e)

play [pleɪ] **1** n **(a)** (drama) pièce f (de théâtre) **(b)** (of children) **at p.** en train de jouer; **to make great p. of sth** beaucoup insister sur qch; **p. on words** jeu m de mots
(c) (in sport) jeu m; **in p.** en jeu; **out of p.** hors jeu; Fig **to come into p.** entrer en jeu; Fig **to make a p. for sth** tenter sa chance à qch
(d) Tech jeu m
2 vt **(a)** (game, sport) jouer à; (opponent) affronter; (shot, card, position) jouer; **to p. football/chess** jouer au football/aux échecs; Fig **stop playing games!** arrête de te moquer de moi!; Fig **to p. ball** (co-operate) coopérer; Fig **to p. the Stock Exchange** jouer à la Bourse; **to p. a joke** or **a trick on sb** jouer un tour à qn
(b) (in play, film) jouer; **to p. Macbeth** jouer le rôle de Macbeth; Fig **to p. an important part in sth** jouer un rôle important dans qch; Fig **to p. no part in sth** ne pas intervenir dans qch; Fig **to p. the fool** faire l'idiot
(c) (musical instrument) jouer de; (piece, tune) jouer; (CD, tape, record) mettre; **to p. the piano/the flute** jouer du piano/de la flûte
3 vi **(a)** (of children) jouer; (of animals) folâtrer; **to p. with sth** (pen, hair) tripoter qch; Fig **to p. with fire** jouer avec le feu; Fam Fig **what's she playing at?** à quoi elle joue?
(b) (in sport/person) jouer; **to p. fair/dirty** jouer franc jeu/en traître; Fig **to p. for time** essayer de gagner du temps; Fig **to p. into sb's hands** faire le jeu de qn; Fig **to p. safe** ne pas prendre de risques

▶**play about, play around** vi jouer, s'amuser

▶**play along** vi coopérer

▶**play back** vt sep (tape, recording) (for first time) écouter; (replay) réécouter

▶**play down** vt sep minimiser

▶**play off** vt sep **to p. sb off against sb** monter qn contre qn

▶**play on 1** vt insep (feelings, fears) jouer sur
2 vi (of musician, sportsperson) continuer à jouer

▶**play out** vt sep **the drama being played out before them** le drame qui se déroule sous leurs yeux

▶**play up** vi Br Fam (of car, child, injury) faire des siennes

play-acting ['pleɪˌæktɪŋ] n comédie f

playboy ['pleɪbɔɪ] n play-boy m

player ['pleɪə(r)] n (of game, instrument) joueur(euse) m,f; (actor) acteur(trice) m,f

playful ['pleɪfʊl] adj (person, animal) joueur(euse); (mood, tone) enjoué(e); (remark) espiègle

playground ['pleɪgraʊnd] n (at school) cour f de récréation; (in park) aire f de jeu

playgroup ['pleɪgruːp] n garderie f

playhouse ['pleɪhaʊs] n (theatre) théâtre m

playing ['pleɪɪŋ] n p. card carte f à jouer; p. field terrain m de jeu

playmate ['pleɪmeɪt] n camarade mf de jeu

play-off ['pleɪɒf] n Sp match m de barrage

playpen ['pleɪpen] n parc m (pour bébé)

playroom ['pleɪruːm] n salle f de jeu

playschool ['pleɪskuːl] n garderie f

plaything ['pleɪθɪŋ] n jouet m

playtime ['pleɪtaɪm] n (at school) récréation f

playwright ['pleɪraɪt] n auteur m dramatique

plaza ['plɑːzə] n Am (shopping centre) centre m commercial

PLC, plc [piːel'siː] n Br Com (abbr **public limited company**) ≃ SARL f

plea [pliː] n (a) (appeal) appel m (for à) (b) (excuse) excuse f (c) Law to enter a p. of guilty/not guilty plaider coupable/non coupable; Am p. bargaining = possibilité donnée à l'accusé de voir ses charges réduites s'il plaide coupable

plead [pliːd] 1 vt Law to p. sb's case (of lawyer) plaider la cause de qn; Law to p. insanity plaider la démence; to p. ignorance faire l'ignorant(e)
2 vi to p. with sb (to do sth) supplier qn (de faire qch); Law to p. guilty/not guilty plaider coupable/non coupable

pleasant ['plezənt] adj agréable

pleasantly ['plezəntlɪ] adv (smile, behave) aimablement; (surprised) agréablement

pleasantry ['plezəntrɪ] (pl pleasantries) n (joke) plaisanterie f; to exchange pleasantries (polite remarks) échanger des politesses

please [pliːz] 1 adv s'il vous/te plaît; come in, p. entrez, je vous prie; p. don't cry s'il te plaît, ne pleure pas; p. tell me... dis-moi...; may I? – p. do puis-je? – je vous en prie; p. sit down asseyez-vous, je vous en prie; yes, p. oui, s'il te plaît
2 vt faire plaisir à; you can't p. everybody on ne peut pas contenter tout le monde; p. yourself! fais comme tu voudras!; to be easy/hard to p. être facile/difficile à contenter; p. God! plaise à Dieu!
3 vi (a) (like) to do as one pleases faire ce que l'on veut; this way, if you p. par ici, s'il vous plaît; and then, if you p., he blamed me for it! et le comble, c'est qu'il a dit que c'était de ma faute! (b) (give pleasure) to be eager to p. vouloir plaire

pleased [pliːzd] adj content(e) (with de); to be p. to do sth faire qch avec plaisir; to be p. for sb être content pour qn; to be as p. as Punch être content comme tout; he's very p. with himself il est très content de lui; p. to meet you! enchanté; I'm p. to say that... je suis heureux de vous dire que...

pleasurable ['pleʒərəbəl] adj agréable

pleasure ['pleʒə(r)] n (a) (contentment, enjoyment) plaisir m; to take p. in doing sth prendre plaisir à faire qch;

with p. avec plaisir; my p.! je t'en prie!; Formal I have p. in informing you that... j'ai le plaisir de vous informer que...; p. boat bateau m de plaisance; p. trip excursion f
(b) (will) at your p. à votre gré; Law to be detained at or during Her Majesty's p. être emprisonné(e)

pleat [pliːt] n pli m

pleated ['pliːtɪd] adj plissé(e)

plebeian [plə'biːən] n & adj plébéien(enne) m,f

plebiscite ['plebɪsɪt] n plébiscite m

plectrum ['plektrəm] n Mus médiator m

pledge [pledʒ] 1 n (a) (promise) promesse f (b) (object) gage m
2 vt (promise) to p. to do sth s'engager à faire qch; to p. one's loyalty/support accorder sa loyauté/son soutien; to p. money (in radio, television appeal) faire une promesse de don

plenary ['pliːnərɪ] adj plénier(ère); p. session séance f plénière

plentiful ['plentɪfʊl] adj abondant(e)

plenty ['plentɪ] 1 n abondance f; a land of p. un pays d'abondance
2 pron p. of beaucoup de; you've got p. of time tu as largement le temps; that's p. (of food) merci, j'en ai assez
3 adv Fam it's p. big enough c'est bien assez grand

plethora ['pleθərə] n pléthore f

pleurisy ['plʊərɪsɪ] n pleurésie f

pliable ['plaɪəbəl] adj (wood, plastic) souple; (person) malléable

pliers ['plaɪəz] npl pince f, tenaille f; a pair of p. une pince, une tenaille

plight [plaɪt] n situation f critique; (of refugees) détresse f

plimsolls ['plɪmsəlz] npl tennis mpl

plinth [plɪnθ] n socle m

PLO [piːel'əʊ] n (abbr **Palestine Liberation Organization**) OLP f

plod [plɒd] (pt & pp plodded) vi (a) (walk) marcher péniblement (b) (work) to p. (away) trimer

plonk¹ [plɒŋk] 1 n (sound) bruit m sourd
2 vt Fam just p. it down there tu n'as qu'à le poser là; p. oneself down in an armchair s'affaler dans un fauteuil

plonk² [plɒŋk] n Br Fam (wine) vin m ordinaire

plop [plɒp] 1 n plouf m
2 vi (pt & pp plopped) faire plouf

plot [plɒt] 1 n (a) (conspiracy) complot m (b) (of play, novel) intrigue f; Fig the p. thickens l'affaire se corse (c) (land) parcelle f; (vegetable) p. potager m
2 vt (pt & pp plotted) (a) (plan) comploter; to p. to do sth comploter de faire qch (b) (position, course) déterminer; (progress, development) suivre de près (c) Math tracer

plotter ['plɒtə(r)] n (conspirator) conspirateur(trice) m,f

plough, Am **plow** [plaʊ] 1 n charrue f; the P. (constellation) le Grand Chariot
2 vt (field) labourer; Fig (profits) réinvestir
3 vi labourer; Fig to p. through sth (work, reading) avancer péniblement dans qch; Fig to p. into sth (of vehicle) rentrer dans qch

▶**plough on with** vt insep poursuivre laborieusement

▶**plough up** vt sep (field) labourer

ploughman ['plaʊmən] n laboureur m; p.'s lunch = assiette de fromage ou jambon avec de la salade et des condiments

plover ['plʌvə(r)] n pluvier m

plow Am = **plough**

ploy [plɔɪ] n stratagème m, ruse f

pluck [plʌk] 1 n (courage) courage m
2 vt (hair, feathers) arracher; (flower) cueillir; (chicken, turkey) plumer; (string of guitar) pincer; **to p. one's eyebrows** s'épiler les sourcils; **they were plucked from danger by a helicopter** un hélicoptère les a sauvés du danger
3 vi **to p. at sb's sleeve** tirer qn par la manche

▸**pluck up** vt sep **to p. up the courage to do sth** trouver le courage de faire qch

plucky ['plʌkɪ] adj courageux(euse)

plug [plʌg] 1 n (a) (for sink) bonde f (b) (electrical) (on device) fiche f; (socket) prise f (de courant); Fam Fig **to pull the p. on sth** arrêter de financer qch (c) Aut (spark) p. bougie f (d) Fam (publicity) pub f
2 vt (pt & pp plugged) (a) (gap, hole) boucher; (leak) colmater (b) Fam (promote) faire de la pub pour

▸**plug away** vi Fam s'acharner (at sur)

▸**plug in** vt sep brancher

plughole ['plʌghəʊl] n trou m d'écoulement; Fam Fig **that's £300 down the p.!** c'est 300 livres foutues en l'air!

plug-in ['plʌgɪn] n Comptr module m externe

plum [plʌm] 1 n (fruit) prune f; **p. pudding** plum-pudding m; **p. tree** prunier m
2 adj (a) (colour) prune inv (b) Fam (very good) **a p. job** un boulot en or

plumage ['plu:mɪdʒ] n plumage m

plumb [plʌm] 1 n **p. (line)** fil m à plomb; **to be out of p.** ne pas être d'aplomb
2 adv (exactly) **p. in the centre** en plein centre
3 vt Fig **to p. the depths** toucher le fond; **that's really plumbing the depths!** c'est vraiment le comble du mauvais goût!

▸**plumb in** vt sep (washing machine) brancher

plumber ['plʌmə(r)] n plombier m

plumbing ['plʌmɪŋ] n (job, system) plomberie f

plume [plu:m] n (on hat) aigrette f; (of smoke) volute f

plummet ['plʌmɪt] vi (of morale, standards) chuter; (of prices) s'effondrer; **the plane plummeted to the ground** l'avion a piqué et s'est écrasé au sol

plummy ['plʌmɪ] adj Fam (voice, accent) snob inv

plump [plʌmp] adj dodu(e); (cheeks, face) rond(e)

▸**plump down** vt sep Fam laisser tomber lourdement

▸**plump for** vt insep Fam (choose) se décider pour

plunder ['plʌndə(r)] 1 n (action) pillage m; (loot) butin m
2 vt piller

plunge [plʌndʒ] 1 n (dive) plongeon m; Fig (decrease) chute f; Fam Fig **to take the p.** se jeter à l'eau
2 vt plonger (into dans)
3 vi (fall) plonger; Fig (decrease) chuter; **she plunged to her death** elle a fait une chute mortelle

plunger ['plʌndʒə(r)] n (of cafetière, syringe) piston m; (for clearing sink) ventouse f

plunging ['plʌndʒɪŋ] adj (prices) en chute libre; **p. neckline** décolleté m plongeant

pluperfect ['plu:'pɜ:fɪkt] n Gram **the p.** le plus-que-parfait

plural ['plʊərəl] Gram 1 adj pluriel(elle)
2 n pluriel m

pluralism ['plʊərəlɪzəm] n pluralisme m

plurality [plʊəˈrælɪtɪ] n pluralité f

plus [plʌs] 1 n (pl **plusses** ['plʌsɪz]) (a) **p. (sign)** (signe m) plus m (b) (advantage) plus m
2 adj **on the p. side...** mais d'un autre côté...; **fifteen p.** plus de quinze
3 prep plus; **seven p. nine** sept plus neuf

plush [plʌʃ] 1 n Tex peluche f
2 adj Fam luxueux(euse)

Pluto ['plu:təʊ] n (planet) Pluton f

plutonium [plu:ˈtəʊnɪəm] n Chem plutonium m

ply[1] [plaɪ] n **three-p.** (wood, paper handkerchief) triple épaisseur; (wool) à trois fils

ply[2] (pt & pp **plied**) 1 vt (trade) exercer; **to p. sb with questions** assaillir qn de questions; **to p. sb with drink** ne pas arrêter de verser à boire à qn
2 vi (of ship, bus) **to p. between** faire la navette entre

plywood ['plaɪwʊd] n contreplaqué m

PM [pi:'em] n (abbr **Prime Minister**) Premier ministre m

p.m. ['pi:em] adv (abbr **post meridiem**) 6 p.m. 18 h

PMT [pi:em'ti:] n (abbr **premenstrual tension**) syndrome m prémenstruel

pneumatic [nju:ˈmætɪk] adj pneumatique; **p. drill** marteau m piqueur

pneumonia [nju:ˈməʊnɪə] n pneumonie f

PO [pi:'əʊ] n (a) (abbr **Post Office**) poste f; **PO Box** BP (b) (abbr **postal order**) mandat m postal

poach[1] [pəʊtʃ] vt Culin (eggs, fish) pocher

poach[2] vt (a) (catch illegally) (fish) pêcher sans permis; (game) chasser sans permis (b) (employee) débaucher

poacher ['pəʊtʃə(r)] n (of fish, game) braconnier m

pocket ['pɒkɪt] 1 n (of clothes, bag) poche f; **to go through sb's pockets** faire les poches à qn; **prices to suit every p.** des prix pour toutes les bourses; **to be out of p.** en être de sa poche; **how much are you out of p.?** tu en as eu pour combien?; **to pay for sth out of one's own p.** payer qch de sa poche; Fig **to line one's pockets** se remplir les poches; Fig **to have sb in one's p.** avoir qn dans sa poche; **p. calculator** calculette f; **p. money** argent m de poche (b) (in snooker, pool) poche f; blouse f (c) (of gas, air, resistance) poche f
2 vt (put in pocket) empocher; Fam (steal) rafler

pocketbook ['pɒkɪtbʊk] n Am (wallet) portefeuille m; (handbag) sac m à main

pocketknife ['pɒkɪtnaɪf] n (pl **pocketknives** ['pɒkɪtnaɪvz]) n couteau m de poche

pockmarked ['pɒkmɑ:kt] adj grêlé(e)

pod [pɒd] n (of plant) gousse f

podgy ['pɒdʒɪ] adj grassouillet(ette)

podiatrist [pəˈdaɪətrɪst] n Am pédicure mf

podium ['pəʊdɪəm] n (for speaker, conductor) estrade f; (for winner) podium m

poem ['pəʊɪm] n poème m

poet ['pəʊɪt] n poète m

poetic [pəʊˈetɪk] adj poétique; **it's p. justice that...** ça n'est que justice que...; **p. licence** licence f poétique

poetical [pəʊˈetɪkəl] adj poétique

poetry ['pəʊɪtrɪ] n poésie f; **p. in motion** un véritable plaisir; **p. reading** lecture f de textes poétiques

poignancy ['pɔɪnjənsɪ] n caractère m poignant

poignant ['pɔɪnjənt] *adj* poignant(e)

point [pɔɪnt] **1** *n* (a) (*location*) endroit *m*; **the highest p.** le point le plus haut; **p. of sale** point *m* de vente; **p. of view** point *m* de vue

(b) (*in time*) moment *m*; **at this p. in time** actuellement; **at this p. the phone rang** à ce moment le téléphone a sonné; **to be on the p. of doing sth** être sur le point de faire qch; **to reach the p. of no return** arriver au point de non-retour; **to be at the p. of rudeness to sb** être d'une franchise qui frise l'impolitesse

(c) (*of argument, discussion*) point *m*; **the p. is,...** c'est que...; **I take your p.** je vois ce que tu veux dire; **she has a p.** elle a raison; **to make a p.** faire une remarque; **to get to the p.** en arriver au fait; **that's beside the p.** ça n'a rien à voir; **that's not the p.** il ne s'agit pas de cela; **what's the p.?** à quoi bon?; **to make a p. of doing sth** mettre un point d'honneur à faire qch; **there is no p. in waiting any longer** cela ne sert à rien d'attendre plus longtemps; **in p. of fact** en fait; **to the p.** (*relevant*) pertinent(e); **it has its good points** ça a ses avantages; **up to a p.** jusqu'à un certain point; **not to put too fine a p. on it...** pour parler franchement...; **p. of grammar/of law** question *f* de grammaire/de droit; **p. of order** question *f* de procédure

(d) (*punctuation mark*) point *m*; **Math (decimal) p.** virgule *f* (décimale); **three p. five** trois virgule cinq

(e) (*in game, exam, on scale*) point *m*; **to win on points** gagner aux points

(f) (*on compass*) point *m*

(g) (*of needle, pencil, sword*) pointe *f*; **to end in a p.** avoir un bout pointu

(h) (*plug socket*) prise *f* (de courant)

(i) (*of land*) pointe *f*

(j) *Rail* **points** aiguillage *m*

2 *vt* (*camera, gun*) braquer (**at** sur); *Fig* **to p. the finger at sb** montrer qn du doigt; **can you p. me in the right direction?** pouvez-vous me dire quelle direction je dois prendre?; **to p. the way (to)** montrer le chemin (à); *Fig* montrer la voie (à)

3 *vi* **to p. at** *or* **to sb/sth** (*with finger*) montrer qn/qch du doigt; **to p. north** (*of arrow, compass needle*) indiquer le nord; **to be pointing towards sth** (*of car, chair*) être face à qch; **this points to the fact that...** ceci montre *ou* indique que...; **all the evidence points to suicide** tout laisse penser à un suicide

▶**point out** *vt sep* (*with finger*) montrer; (*error, fact*) signaler

▶**point up** *vt sep* (*highlight*) mettre en évidence

point-blank ['pɔɪnt'blæŋk] **1** *adj* (*refusal, denial*) catégorique; **at p. range** à bout portant

2 *adv* (*fire*) à bout portant; (*ask*) de but en blanc; (*refuse, deny*) catégoriquement

pointed ['pɔɪntɪd] *adj* (a) (*sharp*) pointu(e) (b) (*remark*) mordant(e)

pointedly ['pɔɪntɪdlɪ] *adv* ostensiblement

pointer ['pɔɪntə(r)] *n* (a) (*indicator*) aiguille *f*; (*stick*) baguette *f* (b) *Fam* (*advice*) tuyau *m* (c) (*dog*) pointer *m*

pointless ['pɔɪntlɪs] *adj* inutile; (*life*) absurde; **it would be p.** ça ne servirait à rien

poise [pɔɪz] *n* (*composure*) assurance *f*; (*balance*) équilibre *m*

poised [pɔɪzd] *adj* (a) (*composed*) posé(e) (b) (*ready*) **to be p. to do sth** être prêt(e) à faire qch (c) (*suspended*) suspendu(e)

poison ['pɔɪzən] **1** *n* poison *m*; *Fam* **what's your p.?** qu'est-ce que tu veux boire?; **p. gas** gaz *m* toxique; **p. ivy** sumac *m* vénéneux; **p. pen letter** lettre *f* anonyme

2 *vt* (a) (*person, food*) empoisonner; **to p. sb's mind against sb** monter qn contre qn (b) (*pollute*) contaminer

poisoning ['pɔɪzənɪŋ] *n* (a) (*of person, food*) empoisonnement *m*; **to die of p.** mourir empoisonné(e) (b) (*pollution*) contamination *f*

poisonous ['pɔɪzənəs] *adj* (*snake, remark*) venimeux(euse); (*chemical, fumes*) toxique; (*plant, mushroom*) vénéneux(euse); *Fig* (*rumour, doctrine*) pernicieux(euse)

poke [pəʊk] **1** *n* coup *m* léger

2 *vt* (*person*) donner un coup à; (*object*) tâter; (*fire*) attiser; **to p. sb in the eye** mettre le doigt dans l'œil à qn; **to p. sb in the ribs** (*with elbow*) donner un coup de coude à qn; **to p. a hole in sth** faire un trou dans qch; **to p. one's nose into other people's business** mettre son nez dans les affaires des autres; **to p. one's head out of the window** passer la tête par la fenêtre; **to p. fun at se** moquer de

3 *vi* **to p. at sth** (*with one's finger/a stick*) tâter qch (du doigt/avec le bout d'un bâton)

▶**poke about, poke around** *vi* (*search*) (*of person*) fouiller; (*be nosy*) fourrer son nez partout

▶**poke out 1** *vt sep* **you nearly poked my eye out!** un peu plus et tu me crevais l'œil!

2 *vi* (*protrude*) sortir, dépasser

poker[1] ['pəʊkə(r)] *n* (*for fire*) tisonnier *m*

poker[2] *n* (*card game*) poker *m*

poker-faced ['pəʊkəfeɪst] *adj* au visage impassible

poky ['pəʊkɪ] *adj* **a p. little flat** un appartement riquiqui

Poland ['pəʊlənd] *n* la Pologne

polar ['pəʊlə(r)] *adj* polaire; **p. bear** ours *m* polaire *ou* blanc

polarity [pəʊ'lærɪtɪ] *n* polarité *f*

polarization [pəʊləraɪ'zeɪʃən] *n* (*of opinion, country*) division *f*

polarize ['pəʊləraɪz] *vt* (*opinion, country*) diviser

Polaroid® ['pəʊlərɔɪd] *n* (*camera, photo*) polaroïd® *m*

Pole [pəʊl] *n* Polonais(e) *m,f*

pole[1] [pəʊl] *n* (*post, stick*) perche *f*; (*for flag*) hampe *f*; **the p. vault** le saut à la perche

pole[2] *n* *Elec & Geog* pôle *m*; *Fig* **to be poles apart** être diamétralement opposés; **the P. Star** l'étoile *f* polaire

poleaxe ['pəʊlæks] *vt* (*physically*) assommer; (*emotionally*) abasourdir

polecat ['pəʊlkæt] *n* putois *m*

polemic [pə'lemɪk] *n* polémique *f*

polemical [pə'lemɪkəl] *adj* polémique

police [pə'liːs] **1** *npl* **the p.** la police; **two hundred p.** deux cents policiers; **p. car** voiture *f* de police; **p. constable** agent *m* de police; *Am* **p. department** service *m* de police; **p. dog** chien *m* policier; **p. force** police; **p. officer** policier *m*; **p. record** casier *m* judiciaire; **p. state** État *m* policier; **p. station** poste *m* de police

2 *vt* (*area, city*) maintenir l'ordre dans; *Fig* réglementer

policeman [pə'liːsmən] *n* agent *m* de police

policewoman [pə'liːswʊmən] *n* femme *f* agent de police

policy ['pɒlɪsɪ] (*pl* **policies**) *n* (a) (*of government, personal*) politique *f*; **it's a matter of p.** c'est une question de principe; **a good/bad p.** une bonne/mauvaise idée

(b) *Fin* **(insurance)** p. police *f* (d'assurance); *Fin* p. **holder** assuré(e) *m,f*

polio [ˈpəʊliəʊ] *n* polio *f*

Polish [ˈpəʊlɪʃ] **1** *n* (*language*) polonais *m*
2 *adj* polonais(e)

polish [ˈpɒlɪʃ] **1** *n* **(a)** *(for shoes)* cirage *m*; *(for furniture, floors)* cire *f*; *(for metal)* pâte *f* à polir; *(for nails)* vernis *m* à ongles **(b)** *(finish, shine)* éclat *m*, brillant *m*; **to give sth a p.** faire briller qch **(c)** *(refinement)* raffinement *m*
2 *vt* (*silver, brass*) astiquer; (*shoes, furniture, floor*) cirer; (*stone, metal*) polir

▶**polish off** *vt sep Fam (food)* avaler; *(drink)* descendre; *(work)* expédier; *(opponent)* liquider

▶**polish up** *vt sep (improve)* perfectionner

polished [ˈpɒlɪʃt] *adj (shoes, furniture, floor)* ciré(e); *(metal, stone, glass)* poli(e); *Fig (manners, style)* raffiné(e)

polite [pəˈlaɪt] *adj* poli(e) (**to** avec); **in p. society** chez les gens bien

politely [pəˈlaɪtlɪ] *adv* poliment

politeness [pəˈlaɪtnɪs] *n* politesse *f*

politic [ˈpɒlɪtɪk] *adj Formal* sage

political [pəˈlɪtɪkəl] *adj* politique; **she isn't very p.** elle ne s'intéresse pas beaucoup à la politique; **p. asylum** asile *m* politique; **p. prisoner** prisonnier(ère) *m,f* politique; **p. science** sciences *fpl* politiques

politically [pəˈlɪtɪklɪ] *adv* politiquement; **p. correct** politiquement correct(e)

politician [pɒlɪˈtɪʃən] *n* homme *m*/femme *f* politique

politicize [pəˈlɪtɪsaɪz] *vt* politiser

politics [ˈpɒlɪtɪks] **1** *n* politique *f*
2 *npl* **(a)** *(views)* opinions *fpl* politiques **(b)** **office p.** intrigues *fpl* de bureau

polka [ˈpɒlkə] *n* polka *f*; **a p. dot tie** une cravate à pois

poll [pəʊl] **1** *n (votes cast)* scrutin *m*; **(opinion) p.** *(survey)* sondage *m*; **to go to the polls** aller aux urnes; *Formerly* **the p. tax** = en Grande-Bretagne, anciens impôts locaux à payer à titre individuel
2 *vt (votes)* obtenir; *(people)* sonder

pollen [ˈpɒlən] *n* pollen *m*; **p. count** taux *m* de pollen dans l'atmosphère

pollinate [ˈpɒlɪneɪt] *vt* polliniser

polling [ˈpəʊlɪŋ] *n* élections *fpl*, scrutin *m*; **p. booth** isoloir *m*; **p. day** jour *m* du scrutin; **p. station** bureau *m* de vote

pollutant [pəˈluːtənt] *n* polluant *m*

pollute [pəˈluːt] *vt* polluer

polluter [pəˈluːtə(r)] *n* pollueur(euse) *m,f*

pollution [pəˈluːʃən] *n* pollution *f*

polo [ˈpəʊləʊ] *n (sport)* polo *m*; **p. neck (sweater)** *(pull m* à) col *m* roulé

poltergeist [ˈpɒltəɡaɪst] *n* esprit *m* frappeur

poly [ˈpɒlɪ] *(pl* **polys)** *n Br Fam (polytechnic)* établissement *m* d'enseignement supérieur

poly bag [ˈpɒlɪˈbæɡ] *n Fam* sac *m* en plastique

polyester [pɒlɪˈestə(r)] *n* polyester *m*

polygamy [pəˈlɪɡəmɪ] *n* polygamie *f*

polyglot [ˈpɒlɪɡlɒt] *n & adj* polyglotte *mf*

polygon [ˈpɒlɪɡən] *n* polygone *m*

polymer [ˈpɒlɪmə(r)] *n Chem* polymère *m*

Polynesia [pɒlɪˈniːziə] *n* la Polynésie

Polynesian [pɒlɪˈniːziən] **1** *n* Polynésien(enne) *m,f*
2 *adj* polynésien(enne)

polyp [ˈpɒlɪp] *n Med* polype *m*

polyphonic [pɒlɪˈfɒnɪk] *adj Mus* polyphonique

polystyrene [pɒlɪˈstaɪriːn] *n* polystyrène *m*

polytechnic [pɒlɪˈteknɪk] *n Br* établissement *m* d'enseignement supérieur

polythene [ˈpɒlɪθiːn] *n* polyéthylène *m*; **p. bag** sac *m* en plastique

polyunsaturated [pɒlɪʌnˈsætjʊəreɪtɪd] *adj* polyinsaturé(e)

polyurethane [pɒlɪˈjʊərɪθeɪn] *n* polyuréthane *m*

pom [pɒm] = **pommie**

pomegranate [ˈpɒmɪɡrænɪt] *n (fruit)* grenade *f*; *(tree)* grenadier *m*

pommie, pommy [ˈpɒmɪ] *(pl* **pommies)** *n Fam* Anglais(e) *m,f*

pomp [pɒmp] *n* pompe *f*; **p. and circumstance** grand apparat *m*

pompom [ˈpɒmpɒm] *n* pompon *m*

pomposity [pɒmˈpɒsɪtɪ] *n* suffisance *f*

pompous [ˈpɒmpəs] *adj* pompeux(euse)

ponce [pɒns] *n very Fam* **(a)** *(effeminate man)* tapette *f* **(b)** *(pimp)* maquereau *m*

▶**ponce about, ponce around** *vi Fam* **(a)** *(waste time)* traîner **(b)** *(of effeminate man)* se pavaner

poncho [ˈpɒntʃəʊ] *(pl* **ponchos)** *n* poncho *m*

pond [pɒnd] *n* étang *m*; *(smaller)* mare *f*

ponder [ˈpɒndə(r)] **1** *vt* réfléchir à, considérer
2 *vi* réfléchir (**on** *or* **over** à)

ponderous [ˈpɒndərəs] *adj (movement, person)* lourd(e); *(progress, piece of writing)* laborieux(euse)

pong [pɒŋ] *Fam* **1** *n (smell)* puanteur *f*
2 *vi* puer

pontiff [ˈpɒntɪf] *n* pontife *m*

pontificate [pɒnˈtɪfɪkeɪt] *vi* pontifier (**about** sur)

pontoon¹ [pɒnˈtuːn] *n (float)* ponton *m*; **p. bridge** pont *m* flottant

pontoon² *n (card game)* vingt-et-un *m*

pony [ˈpəʊnɪ] *(pl* **ponies)** *n* poney *m*; **p. trekking** randonnée *f* à dos de poney

ponytail [ˈpəʊnɪteɪl] *n* queue *f* de cheval

poo [puː] *n Fam* caca *m*; **to do** *or* **have a p.** faire caca

poodle [ˈpuːdəl] *n* caniche *m*

poof [pʊf], **poofter** [ˈpʊftə(r)] *n very Fam* pédé *m*, = terme injurieux désignant un homosexuel

pooh¹ [puː] *exclam* bah!

pooh² = **poo**

pooh-pooh [ˈpuːˈpuː] *vt* rejeter

pool¹ [puːl] *n (pond, of blood)* mare *f*; *(puddle)* flaque *f*; **(swimming) p.** piscine *f*

pool² **1** *n* **(a)** *(of money, helpers)* réserve *f*; *(of knowledge)* mine *f*; **car p.** parc *m* de voitures **(b)** **the (football) pools** = concours de pronostics des matchs de football
2 *vt (ideas, resources)* mettre en commun, grouper

pool³ *n (game)* billard *m* américain; **p. table** (table *f* de) billard

pooped [puːpt] *adj Fam* vanné(e)

poor [pʊə(r)] **1** *adj* **(a)** *(not rich)* pauvre; **the p. man's champagne** le champagne du pauvre **(b)** *(bad)* mauvais(e); *(chances)* faible; *(harvest, reward)* maigre; **to be in p. health** ne pas bien se porter; **to have a p. memory** ne pas avoir une bonne mémoire; **to be p. at maths** être faible en maths; **p. loser** mauvais(e) perdant(e) *m,f*; **in p. taste** de mauvais goût (c) *(expressing sympathy)* **you p. thing!** pauvre petit(e)!; **p. (old) Simon** le pauvre Simon

2 *npl* **the p.** les pauvres *mpl*

poorly ['pʊəlɪ] 1 *adv* mal; *(dressed)* pauvrement; **to be p. off** être pauvre

2 *adj* **Fam** patraque

pop[1] [pɒp] 1 *n (music)* pop *f*

2 *adj* **p. art** pop art *m*; **p. group** groupe *m* de pop; **p. music** musique *f* pop; **p. singer** chanteur(euse) *m,f* pop; **p. song** chanson *f* pop

pop[2] *n* **Am** *(father)* papa *m*

pop[3] 1 *n* (a) *(sound)* bruit *m* sec (b) **Fam** *(fizzy drink)* soda *m*

2 *vt (pt & pp popped)* (a) *(burst)* faire éclater (b) **Fam** *(put quickly)* mettre; **to p. one's head out of the window** passer la tête par la fenêtre; **Fam to p. the question** faire sa demande en mariage; **to p. pills** se bourrer de comprimés

3 *vi* (a) *(burst)* éclater; *(of cork)* sauter; *(of ears)* se déboucher (b) **Fam** *(go quickly)* **I'm just popping next door** je fais juste un saut chez les voisins; **we popped over to France for the weekend** nous avons fait un saut en France pour le week-end

▶**pop in** *vi* **Fam** passer

▶**pop off** *vi* **very Fam** *(die)* claquer

▶**pop out** *vi* **Fam** *(go out)* sortir

pop. *(abbr* **population)** population *f*

popcorn ['pɒpkɔːn] *n* pop-corn *m*

pope [pəʊp] *n* pape *m*

popgun ['pɒpgʌn] *n* pistolet *m* à bouchon

poplar ['pɒplə(r)] *n* peuplier *m*

poplin ['pɒplɪn] *n* popeline *f*

popper ['pɒpə(r)] *n* **Br Fam** *(fastener)* bouton-pression *m*

poppet ['pɒpɪt] *n* **Fam** *Old-fashioned* **she's a p.** elle est charmante; **my p.!** ma puce!

poppy ['pɒpɪ] *n (pl poppies)* coquelicot *m*; **p. seed** graine *f* de pavot

poppycock ['pɒpɪkɒk] *n* **Fam** *(nonsense)* bêtises *fpl*

populace ['pɒpjʊləs] *n* **Formal the p.** la population

popular ['pɒpjʊlə(r)] *adj* populaire; *(fashionable)* à la mode; *(restaurant, film)* qui a beaucoup de succès; **to make oneself p.** se faire valoir; **she is p. with her colleagues** elle est appréciée par ses collègues; **by p. demand** à la demande générale; **contrary to p. belief** contrairement à ce que les gens croient

popularity [pɒpjʊ'lærɪt] *n* popularité *f*; **p. rating** cote *f* de popularité

popularize ['pɒpjʊləraɪz] *vt* populariser

popularly ['pɒpjʊləlɪ] *adv* communément; **it is p. believed that...** les gens croient généralement que...

populate ['pɒpjʊleɪt] *vt* peupler

population [pɒpjʊ'leɪʃən] *n* population *f*; **p. explosion** explosion *f* démographique

populous ['pɒpjʊləs] *adj* populeux(euse)

porcelain ['pɔːslɪn] *n* porcelaine *f*; **p. ware** porcelaine

porch [pɔːtʃ] *n* **Br** *(entrance)* porche *m*; **Am** *(veranda)* véranda *f*

porcupine ['pɔːkjʊpaɪn] *n* porc-épic *m*

pore [pɔːr] *n* pore *m*

▶**pore over** *vt insep (examine closely)* étudier soigneusement

pork [pɔːk] *n* porc *m*; **p. chop** côte *f* de porc; **p. pie** ≃ pâté *m* en croûte

porn [pɔːn] *n* **Fam** porno *m*

pornographic [pɔːnə'græfɪk] *adj* pornographique

pornography [pɔː'nɒgrəfɪ] *n* pornographie *f*

porous ['pɔːrəs] *adj* poreux(euse)

porpoise ['pɔːpəs] *n* marsouin *m*

porridge ['pɒrɪdʒ] *n* porridge *m*; **p. oats** flocons *mpl* d'avoine

port[1] [pɔːt] *n (harbour, town)* port *m*; **in p.** au port; *also Fig* **p. of call** escale *f*; **Prov any p. in a storm** nécessité fait loi

port[2] *n* **Naut** *(left-hand side)* bâbord *m*

port[3] *n (drink)* porto *m*

portable ['pɔːtəbl] *adj* portable

Port-au-Prince [pɔːtəʊ'prɪs] *n* Port-au-Prince

portcullis [pɔːt'kʌlɪs] *n* sarrasine *f*

portend [pɔː'tend] *vt* **Formal** présager

portent [pɔː'tent] *n* **Formal** présage *m*

portentous [pɔː'tentəs] *adj* **Formal** majeur(e)

porter ['pɔːtə(r)] *n* *(for carrying luggage)* porteur *m*; *(door attendant)* chasseur *m*; *(in hospital)* brancardier *m*

portfolio [pɔːt'fəʊlɪəʊ] *n (pl portfolios) n (for documents)* porte-documents *m*; *(for drawings)* carton *m*; *(of shares, government minister)* portefeuille *m*; *(of model, artist)* portfolio *m*

porthole ['pɔːthəʊl] *n* hublot *m*

portion ['pɔːʃən] *n* part *f*, partie *f*; *(of food)* portion *f*

▶**portion out** *vt sep* partager

portly ['pɔːtlɪ] *adj* corpulent(e)

portrait ['pɔːtreɪt] *n also Fig* portrait *m*; **to have one's p. painted** faire faire son portrait; **p. gallery** galerie *f* de portraits; **Comptr p.** *(orientation)* orientation *f*) portrait; **p. painter** portraitiste *mf*

portray [pɔː'treɪ] *vt (describe)* dépeindre; *(of actor)* interpréter

portrayal [pɔː'treɪəl] *n (description)* tableau *m*; *(by actor)* interprétation *f*

Portugal ['pɔːtjʊgəl] *n* le Portugal

Portuguese [pɔːtjʊ'giːz] 1 *npl* **the P.** *(people)* les Portugais *mpl*

2 *n* (a) *(person)* Portugais(e) *m,f* (b) *(language)* portugais *m*

3 *adj* portugais(e)

POS [piːəʊˈes] *n* **Com** *(abbr* **point of sale)** PDV *m*

pose [pəʊz] 1 *n* (a) *(position)* pose *f* (b) **Pej** *(affectation)* **it's just a p.** c'est pour épater la galerie

2 *vt (problem, question)* poser; *(danger, threat)* représenter

3 *vi also Pej* poser; **to p. as** *(pretend to be)* se faire passer pour

poser ['pəʊzə(r)] *n* **Fam** (a) **Pej** *(affected person)* poseur(euse) *m,f* (b) *(difficult question)* colle *f*

posh [pɒʃ] **Br** 1 *adj (person)* huppé(e); *(accent)* snob *inv*; *(restaurant, area, clothes)* chic *inv*

2 *adv* **to talk p.** parler d'une manière snob

position [pə'zɪʃən] 1 *n* (a) *(of person)* *(posture, opinion)* position *f* (b) *(of object)* emplacement *m*; *(of enemy, plane, in team sport)* position *f*; **in the on/off p.** *(of switch, lever)* en position marche/arrêt; **in p.** en place; **out of p.** déplacé(e) (c) *(situation)* situation *f*; **to be in a strong p.**

être dans une position forte; **put yourself in my p.** mets-toi à ma place; **to be in a p. to do sth** être en mesure de faire qch; **to be in no p. to do sth** être mal placé(e) pour faire qch (d) *(job)* poste *m*; **a p. of responsibility** un poste à responsabilité

2 *vt (object)* placer; *(town)* situer; *(troops)* poster; **to p. oneself** se placer; **to be well/poorly positioned to do sth** être bien/mal placé(e) pour faire qch

positioning [pəˈzɪʃənɪŋ] *n Com* positionnement *m*

positive [ˈpɒzɪtɪv] *adj* (a) *(person, answer, test)* positif(ive); *(evidence, proof)* formel(elle); **to be p. about sth** être optimiste à propos de qch; **on the p. side,...** le bon côté des choses, c'est que...; **p. discrimination** = mesures antidiscriminatoires favorisant les groupes minoritaires (b) *(certain)* certain(e), sûr(e) *(about* de) (c) *Fam (for emphasis)* véritable (d) *Math & Elec* positif(ive)

positively [ˈpɒzɪtɪvlɪ] *adv* (a) *(identify)* formellement (b) *(think, react)* de façon positive (c) *(for emphasis)* absolument

posse [ˈpɒsɪ] *n (to catch criminal)* = dans le Far West, groupe d'hommes commandé par un shérif, lancé à la poursuite d'un criminel; *(of reporters)* troupe *f*; *Fam (of friends)* bande *f*

possess [pəˈzes] *vt* (a) *(property)* posséder; *(quality, faculty)* avoir (b) *(of evil spirit)* posséder; **possessed by fear** pris(e) de terreur; **what possessed you to do that?** qu'est-ce qui t'a pris de faire ça?

possession [pəˈzeʃən] *n (ownership)* possession *f*; *(thing possessed)* bien *m*; **to be in p. of sth** être en possession de qch; **in full p. of one's faculties** en pleine possession de ses facultés

possessive [pəˈzesɪv] **1** *n Gram* le possessif

2 *adj* possessif(ive); **she's very p. about** *or* **of her children** c'est une mère possessive

possessor [pəˈzesə(r)] *n* possesseur *m*

possibility [pɒsɪˈbɪlɪtɪ] *n (pl* **possibilities)** *n* possibilité *f*; **to be within/outside the bounds of p.** être dans la limite du possible/au delà des limites du possible; **it's a distinct p.** c'est bien possible

possible [ˈpɒsɪbəl] **1** *adj* possible; **it's p. that...** il est possible que... + *subjunctive*; **as soon as p.** dès que possible; **as much as p.** autant que possible; **anything's p.** tout est possible

2 *n (person)* candidat(e) possible *m,f*; *(thing)* option *f*

possibly [ˈpɒsɪblɪ] *adv* (a) *(perhaps)* peut-être; **p. not** peut-être pas (b) *(for emphasis)* **I can't accept it** je ne peux vraiment pas l'accepter; **I'll do all I p. can** je ferai tout mon possible

post¹ [pəʊst] **1** *n* (a) *(wooden stake)* piquet *m*; *(of goal)* poteau *m* (b) *(job, military position)* poste *m*

2 *vt (assign)* affecter

post² *vt (affix)* afficher; **p. no bills** *(sign)* défense d'afficher

post³ *Br* **1** *n (mail)* courrier *m*; **the first p.** la première distribution; **to miss the p.** manquer la levée; **it's in the p.** c'est parti au courrier; **p. office** poste *f*; **the P. Office** *(government department)* ≃ la Poste

2 *vt (letter)* poster; *Fam Fig* **to keep sb posted** tenir qn au courant

postage [ˈpəʊstɪdʒ] *n* affranchissement *m*; **p. and packing** frais *mpl* de port et d'emballage; **p. paid** port *m* payé; **p. stamp** timbre-poste *m*

postal [ˈpəʊstəl] *adj* postal(e); **p. order** mandat *m*; **p. vote** vote *m* par correspondance

postbag [ˈpəʊstbæg] *n Br* sac *m* postal

postbox [ˈpəʊstbɒks] *n Br* boîte *f* aux lettres

postcard [ˈpəʊstkɑːd] *n* carte *f* postale

postcode [ˈpəʊstkəʊd] *n Br* code *m* postal

postdate [pəʊstˈdeɪt] *vt* postdater

poster [ˈpəʊstə(r)] *n (for advertising)* affiche *f*; *(for decoration)* poster *m*; **p. paint** gouache *f*

posterior [pɒsˈtɪərɪə(r)] *n Hum (buttocks)* postérieur *m*

posterity [pɒsˈterɪtɪ] *n* postérité *f*

postgraduate [pəʊstˈgrædjʊət] **1** *n* étudiant(e) *m,f* de troisième cycle

2 *adj* de troisième cycle

posthaste [pəʊstˈheɪst] *adv* en toute hâte

posthumous [ˈpɒstjʊməs] *adj* posthume

posthumously [ˈpɒstjʊməslɪ] *adv* à titre posthume

posting [ˈpəʊstɪŋ] *n (assignment)* affectation *f*

postman [ˈpəʊstmən] *n Br* facteur *m*

postmark [ˈpəʊstmɑːk] *n* cachet *m* de la poste

postmaster [ˈpəʊstmɑːstə(r)] *n* receveur *m* des postes

postmistress [ˈpəʊstmɪstrɪs] *n* receveuse *f* des postes

postmortem [pəʊstˈmɔːtəm] *n* autopsie *f*

postnatal [pəʊstˈneɪtəl] *adj* postnatal(e)

postoperative [pəʊstˈɒpərətɪv] *adj* postopératoire

postpone [pəʊstˈpəʊn] *vt* reporter

postponement [pəʊstˈpəʊnmənt] *n* report *m*

postscript [ˈpəʊskrɪpt] *n* post-scriptum *m*

postulate [ˈpɒstjʊleɪt] *vt* poser comme hypothèse

posture [ˈpɒstʃə(r)] **1** *n* (a) *(physical)* posture *f*; **to have good/bad p.** se tenir bien/mal (b) *Fig (attitude)* position *f*

2 *vi* prendre des poses

postwar [ˈpəʊstwɔː(r)] *adj* d'après-guerre; **the p. period** l'après-guerre *m*

posy [ˈpəʊzɪ] *n (pl* **posies)** *n* petit bouquet *m*

pot [pɒt] **1** *n* (a) *(container)* pot *m*; *(saucepan)* casserole *f*; *(for tea)* théière *f*; *(for coffee)* cafetière *f*; **pots and pans** casseroles *fpl*; **a p. of tea** un thé; *Fam* **to have pots of money** avoir plein de fric; *Fam* **to go to p.** aller à la ruine; **to take a p. shot at sth** tirer à vue sur qch; **p. plant** plante *f* en pot (b) *Fam (marijuana)* hasch *m*

2 *vt (pt & pp* **potted)** (a) *(butter, meat)* mettre en pot; *(plant)* empoter (b) *(in snooker, pool)* blouser

potash [ˈpɒtæʃ] *n* potasse *f*

potassium [pəˈtæsɪəm] *n* potassium *m*

potato [pəˈteɪtəʊ] *n (pl* **potatoes)** *n* pomme *f* de terre; *Br* **p. crisps,** *Am* **p. chips** chips *mpl*; **p. peeler** épluche-légumes *m*; **p. salad** salade *f* de pommes de terre

potbellied [pɒtˈbelɪd] *adj (from overeating)* bedonnant(e); *(from malnourishment)* au ventre ballonné

potency [ˈpəʊtənsɪ] *n* puissance *f*; *(virility)* virilité *f*

potent [ˈpəʊtənt] *adj* puissant(e); *(drink)* fort(e)

potentate [ˈpəʊtənteɪt] *n* potentat *m*

potential [pəˈtenʃəl] **1** *n* potentiel *m*; **to have p.** avoir du potentiel; **to fulfil one's p.** aller au maximum de ses capacités

2 *adj* potentiel(elle)

potentially [pəˈtenʃəlɪ] *adv* potentiellement

pothole [ˈpɒthəʊl] *n (cave)* marmite *f* torrentielle; *(in road)* nid *m* de poule

potholer [ˈpɒthəʊlə(r)] *n* spéléologue *mf*

potholing [ˈpɒthəʊlɪŋ] *n* spéléologie *f*; **to go p.** faire de la spéléologie

potion ['pəʊʃən] n potion f

potluck ['pɒt'lʌk] n Fam **to take p.** prendre ce que l'on trouve

potpourri [pəʊ'pʊəri] n (of flowers, music) pot-pourri m

potted ['pɒtɪd] adj (a) (food) en terrine (b) (description, history) condensé(e)

potter ['pɒtə(r)] n potier(ère) m,f; **p.'s wheel** tour m de potier

▶**potter about, potter around** vi Br (do odd jobs) bricoler; (spend time leisurely) traîner

pottery ['pɒtəri] (pl **potteries**) n poterie f

potty[1] ['pɒtɪ] (pl **potties**) n pot m; **p. training** apprentissage m de la propreté

potty[2] adj Br Fam (crazy) dingue (**about** de)

potty-trained ['pɒtɪtreɪnd] adj propre

pouch [paʊtʃ] n (a) (for money) bourse f; (for tobacco) blague f; (for ammunition) étui m (b) (of marsupial) poche f

pouf(fe) [puːf] n pouf m

poulterer ['pəʊltərə(r)] n volailler(ère) m,f

poultice ['pəʊltɪs] n cataplasme m

poultry ['pəʊltri] n volaille f; **p. farm** élevage m de volaille; **p. farmer** éleveur(euse) m,f de volaille

pounce [paʊns] vi **to p. on** (of animal) bondir sur; (of person) se précipiter sur

pound[1] [paʊnd] n (a) (unit of weight) = 453,6 g, livre f (b) (British currency) livre f; **p. sign** symbole m de la livre sterling; **p. sterling** livre sterling

pound[2] n (for dogs, cars) fourrière f

pound[3] 1 vt (crush) (spices, garlic) piler; (meat) attendrir; (with artillery) pilonner; **to p. sth to pieces** réduire qch en miettes
2 vi (of heart) battre à tout rompre; **to p. on the door** cogner à la porte; **my head is pounding** j'ai des élancements dans la tête

pour [pɔː(r)] 1 vt verser (**into/down** dans); **to p. sb a drink** verser à boire à qn; **to p. money into sth** investir beaucoup d'argent dans qch
2 vi (of water) **it's pouring (with rain)** il pleut à verse; **sweat was pouring off him** il ruisselait de sueur; **tourists were pouring into the palace** les touristes entraient en masse dans le palais

▶**pour in** vt sep (liquid) verser
2 vi (of liquid) couler; (of people, letters) affluer

▶**pour out** 1 vt sep (tea, coffee) verser; Fig (anger, grief) déverser; (emotions) déballer
2 vi (of liquid) se déverser; Fig (of people) sortir en masse

pouring ['pɔːrɪŋ] adj (rain) torrentiel(elle)

pout [paʊt] 1 n moue f
2 vi faire la moue

poverty ['pɒvəti] n pauvreté f; Fig (of ideas, resources) pénurie f; **to live in p.** vivre dans la misère; **p. line** seuil m de pauvreté

poverty-stricken ['pɒvətistrɪkən] adj très pauvre

POW [piːəʊ'dʌbəljuː] n (abbr **prisoner of war**) prisonnier(ère) m,f de guerre

powder ['paʊdə(r)] 1 n poudre f; Fig **p. keg** poudrière f; **p. puff** houppe f; **p. room** toilettes fpl pour dames
2 vt saupoudrer (**with** de); **to p. one's face** se poudrer le visage; Euph **to p. one's nose** aller se laver les mains

powdered ['paʊdəd] adj (milk, eggs) en poudre

powdery ['paʊdəri] adj poudreux(euse)

power ['paʊə(r)] 1 n (a) (authority, capacity) pouvoir m; **to come to/be in p.** arriver/être au pouvoir; **to have sb in one's p.** tenir qn à sa merci; **to have the p. to do sth** avoir le pouvoir de faire qch; **to do everything in one's p. (to do sth)** faire tout ce qui est en son pouvoir (pour faire qch); **to be at the height or peak of one's powers** être au sommet de ses capacités; **it is beyond my p. to help you** je ne peux pas t'aider, cela dépasse mes capacités; Fam **to do sb a p. of good** faire énormément de bien à qn; **powers of concentration/persuasion** force f de concentration/persuasion; **p. of speech** usage m de la parole; **p. base** base f politique; **p. struggle** lutte f de pouvoir
(b) (physical strength) force f, puissance f; **p. steering** (in car) direction f assistée
(c) (powerful person, group, nation) puissance f; Fig **the p. behind the throne** l'éminence f grise; **the powers that be** les autorités fpl
(d) Law pouvoir m; **p. of attorney** procuration f
(e) (electricity) courant m; **p. cut** coupure f de courant; **p. pack** bloc m d'alimentation; **p. plant** centrale f électrique; **p. point** prise f de courant; **p. station** centrale f électrique
(f) Math puissance f; **three to the p. of ten** trois (à la) puissance dix
2 vt (provide with power) actionner; **powered by two engines** propulsé(e) par deux moteurs

power-assisted steering ['paʊərəsɪstɪd'stɪərɪŋ] n Aut direction f assistée

powerful ['paʊəfʊl] adj (muscles, engine, voice, country) puissant(e); (politician) influent(e); (drug, smell) fort(e); (speech, image) impressionnant(e)

powerhouse ['paʊəhaʊs] n Fam (person) moteur m

powerless ['paʊələs] adj impuissant(e); **to be p. to do sth** être impuissant(e) à faire qch

PR [piː'ɑː(r)] n (a) (abbr **public relations**) RP (b) Pol (abbr **proportional representation**) représentation f proportionnelle

practicable ['præktɪkəbəl] adj réalisable

practical ['præktɪkəl] 1 n (lesson) travaux mpl pratiques; (exam) épreuve f pratique
2 adj (a) (mind, solution) pratique; **she's very p.** elle a l'esprit pratique; **for all p. purposes** dans la pratique; **p. joke** farce f (b) (virtual) **it's a p. certainty** c'est pratiquement certain

practicality [præktɪ'kælɪtɪ] (pl **practicalities**) n (of suggestion, plan) aspect m pratique; **practicalities** détails mpl pratiques

practically ['præktɪklɪ] adv (a) (in a practical manner) de façon pratique (b) (almost) pratiquement, presque

practice ['præktɪs] 1 n (a) (action, exercise) pratique f; (in sport) entraînement m; **in p.** dans la ou en pratique; **to put sth into p.** mettre qch en pratique; **to be out of p.** avoir perdu l'habitude; Prov **p. makes perfect** c'est en forgeant qu'on devient forgeron; **p. match** (in football, rugby) match m d'entraînement (b) (of medicine, law) exercice m (c) (surgery) centre m médical; (lawyer's office) cabinet m d'avocat (d) (custom) pratique f; **to make a p. of doing sth** se faire une règle de faire qch; **to be good/bad p.** être conseillé(e)/déconseillé(e)
2 vt & vi Am = **practise**

practiced, practicing Am = **practised, practising**

practise, Am **practice** ['præktɪs] 1 vt (a) (musical instrument) travailler; (language, sport) pratiquer;

(b) (medicine, law) exercer **(c)** (religion, custom) pratiquer; **to p. what one preaches** mettre en pratique ce que l'on prêche

2 vi **(a)** (of musician) s'exercer; (of sportsperson) s'entraîner **(b)** (of doctor, lawyer) exercer

practised, Am **practiced** ['præktɪst] adj (teacher, nurse, speaker) expérimenté(e); (liar) professionnel(elle); (eye, ear) exercé(e); (charm) étudié(e)

practising, Am **practicing** ['præktɪsɪŋ] adj (doctor, lawyer) en exercice; (Christian) pratiquant(e)

pragmatic [præg'mætɪk] adj pragmatique

pragmatism ['prægmətɪzəm] n pragmatisme m

pragmatist ['prægmətɪst] n pragmatiste mf

Prague [pra:g] n Prague

prairie ['preərɪ] n prairie f; **p. dog** chien m de prairie; Am **p. schooner** chariot m bâché

praise [preɪz] **1** n éloges mpl; **to sing the praises of** faire l'éloge de

2 vt faire l'éloge de; (God) louer; **to p. sb to the skies** porter qn aux nues

praiseworthy ['preɪzwɜːðɪ] adj digne d'éloges

pram [præm] n Br landau m

prance [prɑːns] vi (of horse) caracoler; (of person) sautiller; **to p. in/out** entrer/sortir en sautillant

prank [præŋk] n farce f; **to play a p. on sb** faire une farce à qn

prat [præt] n Br Fam andouille f

prattle ['prætəl] **1** n papotage m

2 vi papoter (about de)

prawn [prɔːn] n crevette f rose; **p. cocktail** crevettes à la mayonnaise; **p. cracker** beignet m de crevette

pray [preɪ] vi prier (for pour); **to p. to God** prier Dieu; Fig **to p. for good weather/rain** prier pour qu'il fasse beau/qu'il pleuve

prayer [preə(r)] n prière f; **to say one's prayers** dire ses prières; Fam Fig **he doesn't have a p.** il n'a aucune chance; **p. beads** chapelet m; **p. book** livre m de prières; **p. mat** tapis m de prière; **p. meeting** réunion f de prière

preach [priːtʃ] **1** vt prêcher

2 vi prêcher; Fig (moralize) faire la morale; Fig **that's preaching to the converted** c'est essayer de prêcher un converti

preacher ['priːtʃə(r)] n prédicateur(trice) m,f

preamble ['priːæmbəl] n Formal préambule m

prearranged [priːə'reɪndʒd] adj convenu(e)

precarious [prɪ'keərɪəs] adj précaire

precariously [prɪ'keərɪəslɪ] adv de façon précaire; **p. balanced** en équilibre précaire

precaution [prɪ'kɔːʃən] n précaution f; **to take precautions** prendre des précautions; **as a p.** par précaution

precautionary [prɪ'kɔːʃənərɪ] adj préventif(ive)

precede [prɪ'siːd] vt précéder

precedence ['presɪdəns] n priorité f; **in order of p.** par ordre de préséance; **to take p. over sb** avoir la préséance sur qn; **to take p. over sth** passer avant qch

precedent ['presɪdənt] n précédent m

preceding [prɪ'siːdɪŋ] adj précédent(e)

precept ['priːsept] n précepte m

precinct ['priːsɪŋkt] n **(a)** Br (area) **(shopping) p.** quartier m commerçant piétonnier; **within the**

precincts of dans l'enceinte de **(b)** Am (administrative district) circonscription f; (police division) quartier m

precious ['preʃəs] **1** n (term of endearment) **my p.** mon trésor

2 adj also Pej précieux(euse); **that photo is very p. to me** cette photo m'est très chère; Ironic **you and your p. books!** toi et tes sacrés bouquins!

3 adv Fam (for emphasis) **p. little** très peu; **p. little money** très peu d'argent

precipice ['presɪpɪs] n précipice m

precipitate1 n [prɪ'sɪpɪtɪt] Chem précipité m

2 adj Formal précipité(e)

3 vt [prɪ'sɪpɪteɪt] Formal précipiter

precipitately [prɪ'sɪpɪtɪtlɪ] adv précipitamment

precipitation [prɪsɪpɪ'teɪʃən] n précipitation f; **annual p.** précipitations annuelles

precipitous [prɪ'sɪpɪtəs] adj (descent) à pic; (steps) raide

précis ['preɪsiː] (pl **précis** ['preɪsiːz]) n résumé m

precise [prɪ'saɪs] adj **(a)** (exact) précis(e); **..., to be p. ...,** pour être précis **(b)** (meticulous) méticuleux(euse)

precisely [prɪ'saɪslɪ] adv exactement, précisément; **at six (o'clock) p.** à six heures précises; **p.!** exactement!

precision [prɪ'sɪʒən] n précision f; Mil **p. bombing** bombardement m de précision; **p. instrument** instrument m de précision

preclude [prɪ'kluːd] vt empêcher; **to p. sb from doing sth** empêcher qn de faire qch

precocious [prɪ'kəʊʃəs] adj précoce

precociousness [prɪ'kəʊʃəsnɪs], **precocity** [prɪ'kɒsɪtɪ] n précocité f

preconceived [priːkən'siːvd] adj préconçu(e)

preconception [priːkən'sepʃən] n idée f préconçue; (prejudice) préjugé m

precondition [priːkən'dɪʃən] n condition f préalable

precooked [priː'kʊkt] adj précuit(e)

precursor [priː'kɜːsə(r)] n précurseur m

predate [priː'deɪt] vt **(a)** (precede) précéder **(b)** (put earlier date on) antidater

predator ['predətə(r)] n prédateur m

predatory ['predətərɪ] adj prédateur(trice); Fig avide

predecessor ['priːdɪsesə(r)] n (person) prédécesseur m; (object) précédent(e) m,f

predestination [priːdestɪ'neɪʃən] n prédestination f

predestine [priː'destɪn] vt **to be predestined to do sth** être prédestiné(e) à faire qch

predetermine [priːdɪ'tɜːmɪn] vt prédéterminer

predicament [prɪ'dɪkəmənt] n situation f difficile; **to be in a p.** être dans le pétrin

predicate1 n ['predɪkət] Gram prédicat m

2 vt ['predɪkeɪt] **to be predicated on sth** être fondé(e) sur qch

predict [prɪ'dɪkt] vt (from instinct) prédire; (from information) prévoir

predictable [prɪ'dɪktəbəl] adj prévisible; Fam **you're so p.!** j'aurais pu le deviner!

predictably [prɪ'dɪktəblɪ] adv de manière prévisible; **p., he arrived an hour late** comme on pouvait s'y attendre, il est arrivé une heure en retard

prediction [prɪ'dɪkʃən] n (from instinct) prédiction f; (from information) prévision f

predispose [pri:dɪsˈpəʊz] *vt* prédisposer; **to be predisposed to do sth** être prédisposé(e) à faire qch

predisposition [pri:dɪspəˈzɪʃən] *n* prédisposition *f* (**to** *or* **towards** envers)

predominance [prɪˈdɒmɪnəns] *n* prédominance *f*

predominant [prɪˈdɒmɪnənt] *adj* prédominant(e)

predominantly [prɪˈdɒmɪnəntlɪ] *adv* en majorité, principalement

predominate [prɪˈdɒmɪneɪt] *vi* prédominer

pre-eminence [prɪˈemɪnəns] *n* prééminence *f*

pre-eminent [prɪˈemɪnənt] *adj* prééminent(e)

pre-empt [prɪˈempt] *vt* devancer

pre-emptive [prɪˈemptɪv] *adj* préventif(ive)

preen [pri:n] *vt* (*of bird*) se lisser les plumes; **to p. oneself** (*of person*) se faire beau (belle)

pre-established [pri:ɪsˈtæblɪʃt] *adj* préétabli(e)

prefab [ˈpriːfæb] *n Fam* (*house*) préfabriqué *m*

prefabricated [priːˈfæbrɪkeɪtɪd] *adj* préfabriqué(e)

preface [ˈprefɪs] **1** *n* (*of book*) préface *f*; (*to speech*) préambule *m*
2 *vt* commencer (**with** par)

prefect [ˈpriːfekt] *n Sch* = élève des grandes classes chargé de la surveillance

prefer [prɪˈfɜː(r)] (*pt & pp* **preferred**) *vt* (a) (*favour*) préférer (**to** à); **to p. to do sth** préférer faire qch (b) *Law* **to p. charges** porter plainte

preferable [ˈprefərəbəl] *adj* préférable

preferably [ˈprefərəblɪ] *adv* de préférence

preference [ˈprefərəns] *n* préférence *f*; **to give sth p.**, **to give p. to sth** donner la préférence à qch; **in p. to** plutôt que; **in order of p.** par ordre de préférence

preferential [prefəˈrenʃəl] *adj* (*treatment*) de faveur; (*tariff*) préférentiel(elle)

preferred [prɪˈfɜːd] *adj* préféré(e)

prefigure [priːˈfɪɡə(r)] *vt* préfigurer

prefix [ˈpriːfɪks] *n* préfixe *m*

pregnancy [ˈpreɡnənsɪ] (*pl* **pregnancies**) *n* grossesse *f*; **p. test** test *m* de grossesse

pregnant [ˈpreɡnənt] *adj* (a) (*woman*) enceinte; (*animal*) pleine; **to be three months p.** être enceinte de trois mois (b) *Fig* (*pause, silence*) éloquent(e)

preheat [priːˈhiːt] *vt* préchauffer

prehensile [prɪˈhensaɪl] *adj* préhensile

prehistoric [priːhɪsˈtɒrɪk] *adj* préhistorique

prehistory [priːˈhɪstərɪ] *n* préhistoire *f*

prejudge [priːˈdʒʌdʒ] *vt* (*actions, motives*) préjuger de; (*person*) juger sans connaître

prejudice [ˈpredʒʊdɪs] **1** *n* (a) (*bias*) préjugé *m* (**against/in favour of** contre/en faveur de) (b) *Law* **without p. to** sans préjudice de
2 *vt* (a) (*bias*) prévenir (**against/in favour of** contre/en faveur de) (b) (*harm*) nuire à, faire du tort à

prejudiced [ˈpredʒʊdɪst] *adj* **to be p.** avoir des préjugés (**against/in favour of** contre/en faveur de)

prejudicial [predʒʊˈdɪʃəl] *adj* préjudiciable (**to** à)

preliminary [prɪˈlɪmɪnərɪ] **1** (*pl* **preliminaries**) *n* préliminaire *m*; **preliminaries** (*to investigation, meeting*) préliminaires
2 *adj* préliminaire

prelude [ˈpreljuːd] *n* prélude *m*

premarital [priːˈmærɪtəl] *adj* avant le mariage

premature [ˈpremətjʊə(r)] *adj* (*baby, action, comment*) prématuré(e); (*baldness, senility, ejaculation*) précoce; *Fam* **you're being a bit p.!** tu vas un peu vite!

prematurely [ˈpremətjʊəlɪ] *adv* prématurément

premeditated [priːˈmedɪteɪtɪd] *adj* prémédité(e)

premenstrual [priːˈmenstrʊəl] *adj* prémenstruel(elle); **p. syndrome** *or* **tension** syndrome *m* prémenstruel

premier [ˈpremɪə(r)] **1** *n* (*prime minister*) Premier ministre *m*
2 *adj* premier(ère)

premiere [ˈpremɪeə(r)] *n* (*of play, film*) première *f*

premise [ˈpremɪs] **1** *n* (*of argument, theory*) prémisse *f*
2 *vt* **to be premised on sth** être fondé(e) sur qch

premises [ˈpremɪsɪz] *npl* locaux *mpl*; **business p.** locaux commerciaux; **on the p.** sur place; **off the p.** en dehors de l'établissement; **to see sb off the p.** accompagner qn jusqu'au dehors

premium [ˈpriːmɪəm] *n* (a) *Fin* (*for insurance*) prime *f*; (*additional sum*) supplément *m*; **at a p.** au prix fort; *Br* **p. bonds** ≃ obligations *fpl* à lots (b) (*idioms*) **to be at a p.** être très recherché(e); **to put a p. on sth** accorder de l'importance à qch

premonition [priːməˈnɪʃən] *n* prémonition *f*; **to have a p. that...** avoir le pressentiment que...

prenatal [priːˈneɪtəl] *adj* prénatal(e)

preoccupation [priːɒkjʊˈpeɪʃən] *n* préoccupation *f* (**with** pour); **to have a p. with sth** être préoccupé(e) par qch

preoccupied [priːˈɒkjʊpaɪd] *adj* préoccupé(e) (**with** par)

preoccupy [priːˈɒkjʊpaɪ] (*pt & pp* **preoccupied**) *vt* préoccuper au plus haut point

prep [prep] *n Br Fam* (*homework*) devoirs *mpl*; **p. school** école *f* primaire privée

prepaid [priːˈpeɪd] *adj* prépayé(e)

preparation [prepəˈreɪʃən] *n* préparation *f*; **preparations** (*for ceremony, party*) préparatifs *mpl*

preparatory [prɪˈpærətərɪ] *adj* préparatoire; **p. school** *Br* école *f* primaire privée; *Am* école préparatoire

prepare [prɪˈpeə(r)] **1** *vt* préparer
2 *vi* se préparer (**for** à); **to p. to do sth** se préparer à faire qch

prepared [prɪˈpeəd] *adj* (a) (*willing*) **to be p. to do sth** être prêt(e) à faire qch (b) (*ready*) **to be p. for sth** s'attendre à qch (c) (*made in advance*) préparé(e) à l'avance; (*excuse, explanation*) tout(e) prêt(e)

prepayment [priːˈpeɪmənt] *n* paiement *m* d'avance

preponderance [prɪˈpɒndərəns] *n* prépondérance *f*

preposition [prepəˈzɪʃən] *n* préposition *f*

prepositional [prepəˈzɪʃənəl] *adj* prépositif(ive)

prepossessing [priːpəˈzesɪŋ] *adj* avenant(e), engageant(e)

preposterous [prɪˈpɒstərəs] *adj* ridicule

preppy [ˈprepɪ] *adj Am Fam* ≃ BCBG *inv*

preprogrammed [priːˈprəʊɡræmd] *adj Comptr* préprogrammé(e)

prerecorded [priːrɪˈkɔːdɪd] *adj* préenregistré(e)

prerequisite [priːˈrekwɪzɪt] *n* condition *f*

prerogative [prɪˈrɒɡətɪv] *n* prérogative *f*

presage [ˈpresɪdʒ] *Lit* **1** *n* présage *m*
2 *vt* présager

Presbyterian [prezbɪ'tɪərɪən] n & adj presbytérien(enne) m,f

preschool [pri:'sku:l] adj préscolaire

prescribe [prɪ'skraɪb] vt (medicine, punishment) prescrire; (solution) préconiser; (task, rule) exiger

prescription [prɪ'skrɪpʃən] n ordonnance f; **available only on p.** délivré(e) seulement sur ordonnance; **p. charge** = prix fixe payé sur chaque médicament prescrit sur ordonnance

presence ['prezəns] n présence f; **in the p. of** en présence de; **to have p.** avoir de la présence; **to make one's p. felt** ne pas passer inaperçu(e); **p. of mind** présence d'esprit

present¹ ['prezənt] **1** n **the p.** le présent; **at p.** en ce moment; **for the p.** pour l'instant
2 adj (a) (in attendance) présent(e) (**at** à) (b) (current) actuel(elle); **at the p. time** or **moment** actuellement; Gram **the p. tense** le présent; **p. participle** participe m présent

present² **1** n ['prezənt] (gift) cadeau m; **to give sb a p.** offrir un cadeau à qn
2 vt [prɪ'zent] (a) (introduce, put forward) présenter; **if the opportunity presents itself** si l'occasion se présente (b) (give) (gift) donner; (award, certificate) remettre; **to p. sth to sb, to p. sb with sth** (gift) donner qch à qn; (award, certificate) remettre qch à qn (c) Mil **p. arms!** présentez armes!

presentable [prɪ'zentəbəl] adj présentable; **to make oneself p.** s'arranger

presentation [prezən'teɪʃən] n (a) (of person) présentation f (b) (of gift, award) remise f; **to make a p. to sb** (give present) offrir un cadeau à qn; (give award) remettre un prix à qn (c) (formal talk) présentation f; (by student) exposé m (d) **on p. of** (passport, coupon) sur présentation de

present-day [prezənt'deɪ] adj actuel(elle)

presenter [prɪ'zentə(r)] n (on radio, TV) présentateur(trice) m,f

presentiment [prɪ'zentɪmənt] n pressentiment m

presently ['prezntlɪ] adv (a) (soon) bientôt; (soon afterwards) peu de temps après (b) Am (now) actuellement

preservation [prezə'veɪʃən] n (a) (maintenance) maintien m (b) (protection) (of species) protection f; (of building) conservation f; **to put a p. order on a building** classer un bâtiment monument historique

preservative [prɪ'zə:vətɪv] n conservateur m

preserve [prɪ'zə:v] **1** n (a) (jam) confiture f (b) (in hunting) réserve f; (area of dominance) domaine m; **engineering is no longer a male p.** le métier d'ingénieur n'est plus réservé aux hommes
2 vt (a) (custom, belief) préserver; (calm, sense of humour) garder; (dignity, self-respect) conserver (b) (leather, wood) entretenir (c) (fruit) mettre en conserve (d) (protect) préserver (**from** de); **saints p. us!** le ciel nous préserve!

preshrunk [pri:'ʃrʌŋk] adj lavé(e)

preside [prɪ'zaɪd] vi présider; **to p. over a meeting** présider une réunion

presidency ['prezɪdənsɪ] n (pl **presidencies**) n présidence f

president ['prezɪdənt] n (of country) président m; Am (of company) P-DG m

presidential [prezɪ'denʃəl] adj présidentiel(elle)

press [pres] **1** n (a) (act of pushing) pression f; **at the p. of a button** en appuyant sur le bouton; **p. stud** bouton-pression m
(b) (newspapers) **the p.** la presse; **to get a good/bad p.** avoir bonne/mauvaise presse; **p. agency** agence f de presse; **p. box** tribune f de la presse; **p. conference** conférence f de presse; **p. cutting** coupure f de presse; **p. photographer** photographe mf de presse; **p. release** communiqué m de presse
(c) (machine) (printing) **p.** presse f (typographique); **to go to p.** (of newspaper) partir à l'impression
2 vt (a) (button, switch) appuyer sur; (into clay, cement) enfoncer; **she pressed the note into my hand** elle m'a glissé le billet dans la main
(b) (squeeze) serrer
(c) (grapes, olives, flowers) presser
(d) (iron) repasser
(e) (pressurize) faire pression sur; **to p. sb to do sth** presser qn de faire qch; **to be pressed for time/money** être pressé(e) par le temps/l'argent
(f) (force) **to p. sth on sb** forcer qn à accepter qch; **to p. home one's advantage** profiter de son avantage; **to p. one's attentions on sb** faire des avances à qn
(g) (insist on) Law **to p. charges (against sb)** porter plainte (contre qn); **I didn't p. the point** je n'ai pas insisté
3 vi (push) appuyer; (of crowd) se presser

▸**press ahead** = **press on**

▸**press for** vt insep (demand) exiger

▸**press on** vi continuer; **to p. on with one's work** continuer de travailler

press-gang ['presgæŋ] vt **to p. sb into doing sth** forcer qn à faire qch

pressing ['presɪŋ] adj (urgent) pressant(e)

pressman ['presmæn] n Br journaliste m

press-up ['presʌp] n (exercise) pompe f

pressure ['preʃə(r)] **1** n pression f; **to put p. on sb (to do sth)** faire pression sur qn (pour qu'il/elle fasse qch); **to be under p.** être stressé(e); **p. of work** stress m lié au travail; **p. cooker** Cocotte-Minute® f, autocuiseur m; **p. gauge** manomètre m; **p. group** groupe m de pression; Med **p. point** point m de compression
2 vt **to p. sb to do sth** or **into doing sth** faire pression sur qn pour qu'il/elle fasse qch

pressurize ['preʃəraɪz] vt (a) Tech (container) pressuriser (b) (person) **to p. sb (into doing sth)** faire pression sur qn (pour qu'il/elle fasse qch)

prestige [pres'ti:ʒ] n prestige m

prestigious [pres'tɪdʒəs] adj prestigieux(euse)

presumably [prɪ'zju:məblɪ] adv sans doute; **p. she'll come** je suppose qu'elle viendra

presume [prɪ'zju:m] **1** vt présumer, supposer; **to p. to do sth** se permettre de faire qch; **I p. so** je suppose que oui
2 vi abuser; **I don't want to p. on you** je ne voudrais pas abuser

presumption [prɪ'zʌmpʃən] n présomption f

presumptuous [prɪ'zʌmptjʊəs] adj présomptueux(euse)

presuppose [pri:sə'pəʊz] vt présupposer, supposer

presupposition [pri:sʌpə'zɪʃən] n présupposition f

pretence [prɪ'tens] n simulation f; **he says... but it's all a p.** il dit... mais il fait semblant; **to make a p. of doing sth** faire semblant de faire qch

pretend [prɪ'tend] **1** *vt* **(a)** *(feign)* feindre, simuler; **to p. to do sth** faire semblant de faire qch; **they pretended that nothing had happened** ils ont fait comme si de rien n'était *(b)* *(claim)* prétendre

2 *vi* *(put on an act)* faire semblant

3 *adj* *Fam* **p. money** de l'argent pour faire semblant; **a. p. slap** une gifle pour rire

pretension [prɪ'tenʃən] *n* prétention *f*

pretentious [prɪ'tenʃəs] *adj* prétentieux(euse)

pretentiousness [prɪ'tenʃəsnəs] *n* prétention *f*

preterite ['pretərɪt] *n Gram* **the p.** le prétérit

pretext ['priːtekst] *n* prétexte *m*; **under** *or* **on the p. of doing sth** sous prétexte de faire qch

Pretoria [prɪ'tɔːrɪə] *n* Prétoria

pretty ['prɪtɪ] **1** *adj* joli(e); **it's not a p. sight** ce n'est pas beau à voir; **to cost a p. penny** coûter la peau des fesses

2 *adv* **(a)** *(fairly)* plutôt; **p. certain** pratiquement sûr(e); **they're p. much the same** ils sont pratiquement pareils **(b)** *Fam* **to be sitting p.** ne pas avoir à s'en faire

pretzel ['pretzəl] *n* bretzel *m*

prevail [prɪ'veɪl] *vi* **(a)** *(be successful)* l'emporter **(over** *sur***)** **(b)** *(persuade)* **to p. (up)on sb to do sth** amener qn à faire qch **(c)** *(predominate)* prédominer

prevailing [prɪ'veɪlɪŋ] *adj* prédominant(e); *(wind)* dominant(e)

prevalent ['prevələnt] *adj* très répandu(e)

prevaricate [prɪ'værɪkeɪt] *vi* tergiverser

prevarication [prɪværɪ'keɪʃən] *n* tergiversation *f*

prevent [prɪ'vent] *vt* empêcher, éviter; **to p. sb from doing sth** empêcher qn de faire qch; **to p. sth from happening** empêcher que qch n'arrive

preventable [prɪ'ventəbəl] *adj* évitable

preventative [prɪ'ventətɪv] = **preventive**

prevention [prɪ'venʃən] *n* prévention *f*; *Prov* **p. is better than cure** mieux vaut prévenir que guérir

preventive [prɪ'ventɪv] *adj* préventif(ive)

preview ['priːvjuː] **1** *n* *(of play, film)* avant-première *f*; *(of new product)* aperçu *m*

2 *vt* **to be previewed** *(of film)* sortir en avant-première

previous ['priːvɪəs] **1** *adj* précédent(e); **to have a p. engagement** être déjà pris(e); *Law* **p. conviction** condamnation *f* antérieure

2 *adv* **p. to** avant

previously ['priːvɪəslɪ] *adv* auparavant

prewar ['priːˈwɔː(r)] *adj* d'avant-guerre

prey [preɪ] *n* proie *f*; *Fig* **to be a p. to** être la proie de; **to fall p. to** devenir la proie de

▶**prey on, prey upon** *vt insep* *(person)* prendre pour cible; *(fears, doubts)* exploiter; **to p. on sb's mind** tourmenter qn

price [praɪs] **1** *n* prix *m*; **to rise** *or* **increase in p.** augmenter; **at any p.** à tout prix; **not at any p.** à aucun prix; *Fig* **to pay the p. (for sth)** faire les frais (de qch); *Fig* **it's too high a p. (to pay)** c'est trop cher payé; **to put** *or* **set a p. on sb's head** mettre la tête de qn à prix; *Fig* **everyone has his p.** il n'y a pas d'homme qu'on ne puisse acheter; *Fam* **what p. patriotism now?** que vaut le patriotisme maintenant?; **p. cut** baisse *f* des prix; **p. freeze** gel *m* des prix; **p. increase** hausse *f* des prix; **p. index** indice *m* des prix; **p. list** liste *f* de prix; **p. range** gamme *f* de prix; *(budget)* budget *m*; **p. tag** étiquette *f* de prix; **p. war** guerre *f* des prix

2 *vt* *(decide cost of)* fixer le prix de; *(indicate cost of)* mettre le prix sur; **the toy is priced at £10** le prix du jouet est 10 livres; **to p. oneself out of the market** perdre ses clients en pratiquant des prix trop élevés

price-cutting ['praɪsˌkʌtɪŋ] *n Com* baisse *f* des prix

price-fixing ['praɪsˌfɪksɪŋ] *n Com* alignement *m* des prix

priceless ['praɪsləs] *adj* **(a)** *(invaluable)* qui n'a pas de prix **(b)** *Fam* *(funny)* impayable

pricey ['praɪsɪ] *adj Fam* cher(ère)

prick [prɪk] **1** *n* **(a)** *(of needle)* piqûre *f*; *Fig* *(of conscience)* remords *m* **(b)** *Vulg* *(penis)* bite *f*; *(person)* con (conne) *m,f*

2 *vt* *(sausage, potato)* piquer; *(balloon)* percer; **to p. one's finger** se piquer le doigt; **to p. a hole in sth** percer qch

▶**prick up** *vt sep* **to p. up one's ears** *(of animal)* dresser les oreilles; *(of person)* tendre l'oreille

prickle ['prɪkəl] **1** *n* **(a)** *(of hedgehog)* piquant *m*; *(of plant)* épine *f* **(b)** *(sensation)* picotement *m*

2 *vi* *(of skin)* picoter

prickly ['prɪklɪ] *adj* **(a)** *(animal)* couvert(e) de piquants; *(plant)* à épines; *Fig* *(person)* susceptible; **p. pear** *(tree)* figuier *m* de Barbarie; *(fruit)* figue *f* de Barbarie **(b)** *(sensation)* de picotement; **p. heat** miliaire *f*

pride [praɪd] **1** *n* **(a)** *(satisfaction)* fierté *f*; *(self-esteem)* amour-propre *m*; *Pej* *(vanity)* orgueil *m*; **to take p. in sth** mettre sa fierté dans qch **(b)** *(person, thing)* **she is the p. of the family** elle fait la fierté de la famille; **the p. of my collection** le clou de ma collection; **she's his p. and joy** elle fait son bonheur; **to have p. of place** trôner **(c)** *(of lions)* troupe *f*

2 *vt* **to p. oneself on sth** être fier(ère) de qch

priest [priːst] *n* prêtre *m*

priestess ['priːstɪs] *n* prêtresse *f*

priesthood ['priːsthʊd] *n* prêtrise *f*; **to enter the p.** entrer dans les ordres

prig [prɪg] *n* prêcheur(euse) *m,f*

priggish ['prɪgɪʃ] *adj* prêcheur(euse)

prim [prɪm] *adj* **p. (and proper)** *(person, expression)* collet monté *inv*; *(manner)* guindé(e)

primacy ['praɪməsɪ] *n* primauté *f*

prima facie ['praɪmə'feɪʃɪ] **1** *adj Law* **p. case** = affaire qui, au premier abord, paraît légitime

2 *adv* de prime abord

primarily ['praɪmərɪlɪ] *adv* principalement

primary ['praɪmərɪ] **1** *n* *(pl* **primaries)** *(election)* primaire *f*

2 *adj* **(a)** *(main)* principal(e); **p. colours** couleurs *fpl* fondamentales **(b)** *(initial)* primaire; **p. education** enseignement *m* primaire; **p. school** école *f* primaire

primate ['praɪmeɪt] *n* **(a)** *(animal)* primate *m* **(b)** *Rel* primat *m*

prime [praɪm] **1** *n* *(best time)* **the p. of life** la fleur de l'âge; **to be in one's p.** être à la fleur de l'âge; **to be past one's p.** ne plus être de première jeunesse

2 *adj* **(a)** *(principal)* principal(e); *(importance)* capital(e); **p. minister** premier ministre *m*; *Math* **p. number** nombre *m* premier; **p. time** *(on TV)* prime time *m* **(b)** *(excellent)* excellent(e); **a p. example (of)** un exemple typique (de); **p. quality** de premier choix

3 *vt* **(a)** *(engine, pump)* amorcer; *(surface)* apprêter **(b)** *(provide with information)* **to p. sb for an interview/an exam** préparer qn à un entretien/un examen

primer[1] ['praɪmə(r)] *n* *(paint)* apprêt *m*

primer[2] *n* *(textbook)* manuel *m* élémentaire

primeval [praɪ'miːvəl] *adj* primitif(ive)

primitive ['prɪmɪtɪv] *adj (original)* primitif(ive); *(basic)* de base

primly ['prɪmlɪ] *adv* d'une manière guindée

primordial [praɪ'mɔːdɪəl] *adj* primordial(e); **p. soup** soupe *f* primordiale

primrose ['prɪmrəʊz] *n (plant)* primevère *f*; **p. yellow** jaune pâle *inv*

primula ['prɪmjʊlə] *n* primula *f*

primus (stove)® ['praɪməs('stəʊv)] *n* réchaud *m* portatif

prince [prɪns] *n* prince *m*; **the P. of Wales** le prince de Galles; **P. Charming** le prince charmant

princely ['prɪnslɪ] *adj also Fig* princier(ère)

princess [prɪn'ses] *n* princesse *f*; **the P. Royal** la princesse royale *(fille aînée du souverain)*

principal ['prɪnsɪpəl] **1** *(of school)* proviseur *m*; *(of university)* ≃ président *m*
  2 *adj* principal(e)

principality [prɪnsɪ'pælɪtɪ] *(pl* **principalities)** *n* principauté *f*

principle ['prɪnsɪpəl] *n* principe *m*; **in p.** en principe; **on p.** par principe

principled ['prɪnsɪpəld] *adj (person)* de principes; *(behaviour)* dicté(e) par des principes; **to be p.** avoir des principes

print [prɪnt] **1** *n* **(a)** *(of fingers)* empreinte *f* **(b)** *(printed matter)* texte *m*; **in p.** disponible en librairie; **out of p.** épuisé(e); **to appear in p.** être publié(e) **(c)** *(characters)* caractères *mpl*; *Fig* **to read the small p.** *(in contract)* lire ce qu'il y a d'écrit en petits caractères **(d)** *(engraving)* estampe *f*; *(photograph)* épreuve *f*; *(textile)* imprimé *m*
  2 *vt* **(a)** *(book, newspaper)* imprimer **(b)** *(write clearly)* écrire en script **(c)** *(in photography)* **to p. a negative** tirer une épreuve d'un négatif
  3 *vi (write clearly)* écrire en script

▶**print out** *vt sep Comptr* imprimer

printed ['prɪntɪd] *adj* imprimé(e); **p. circuit** circuit *m* imprimé; **p. matter** imprimés *mpl*

printer ['prɪntə(r)] *n (person)* imprimeur *m*; *(machine)* imprimante *f*

printing ['prɪntɪŋ] *n (process, industry)* imprimerie *f*; *(action)* tirage *m*; **p. error** faute *f* d'impression; **p. press** presse *f*

printout ['prɪntaʊt] *n Comptr* sortie *f* papier

prior¹ ['praɪə(r)] **1** *adj* antérieur(e); **to have p. knowledge (of sth)** avoir une connaissance préalable (de qch)
  2 *adv* **p. to** avant

prior² *n Rel* prieur *m*

prioritize [praɪ'ɒrɪtaɪz] **1** *vt* donner la priorité à
  2 *vi* établir ses priorités

priority [praɪ'ɒrɪtɪ] *(pl* **priorities)** *n* priorité *f*; **to have** or **take p. over sb/sth** avoir la priorité sur qn/qch; **to get one's priorities right/wrong** savoir/ne pas savoir ce qui est important

priory ['praɪərɪ] *(pl* **priories)** *n Rel* prieuré *m*

prise [praɪz] *vt* **to p. sth off/open** retirer/ouvrir qch en forçant; *Fig* **to p. sth out of sb** *(secret, truth)* soutirer qch à qn

prism ['prɪzəm] *n* prisme *m*

prison ['prɪzən] *n* prison *f*; **p. camp** camp *m* de prisonniers; **p. officer** gardien(enne) *m,f* de prison

prisoner ['prɪzənə(r)] *n* prisonnier(ère) *m,f*; **to take/ hold sb p.** faire/retenir qn prisonnier; *Fig* **to take no prisoners** être impitoyable; **p. of war** prisonnier de guerre

prissy ['prɪsɪ] *adj Fam* collet monté *inv*

pristine ['prɪstiːn] *adj* impeccable

privacy ['prɪvəsɪ, 'praɪvəsɪ] *n* intimité *f*; **in the p. of one's own home** dans l'intimité de son foyer

private ['praɪvɪt] **1** *adj* **(a)** *(personal)* personnel(elle); **can we go somewhere p.?** est-ce qu'on peut se voir en privé?; **p. life** vie *f* privée; *Parl* **p. member** simple député *m*; *Fam* **p. parts** parties *fpl* **(b)** *(secret)* confidentiel(elle); **p. and confidential** *(on letter)* confidentiel **(c)** *(for personal use)* privé(e); **p. house** maison *f* particulière; **p. lessons** leçons *fpl* particulières; **p. line** ligne *f* privée; **p. office** bureau *m* personnel; **p. secretary** secrétaire *mf* particulier(ère) **(d)** *(not state-run)* privé(e); **p. detective** or **investigator** détective *m* privé; **p. education** enseignement *m* privé; **p. enterprise** entreprise *f* privée; **p. school** école *f* privée **(e)** *(not for the public)* privé(e); **p. party** soirée *f* privée; **p. property** propriété *f* privée; **p. road** route *f* privée
  2 *n* **(a)** **in p.** en privé **(b)** *(soldier)* simple soldat *m*

privately ['praɪvɪtlɪ] *adv (in private)* en privé; **to be p. educated** faire sa scolarité dans le privé; **p. owned** *(company)* privé(e); *(hotel)* familial(e)

privation [praɪ'veɪʃən] *n* privation *f*

privatization [praɪvɪtaɪ'zeɪʃən] *n* privatisation *f*

privatize ['praɪvɪtaɪz] *vt* privatiser

privet ['prɪvɪt] *n* troène *m*

privilege ['prɪvɪlɪdʒ] **1** *n* privilège *m*; **to have the p. of doing sth** avoir le privilège de faire qch
  2 *vt* **to be privileged to do sth** avoir le privilège de faire qch

privy ['prɪvɪ] **1** *n (pl* **privies)** *Old-fashioned (toilet)* cabinets *mpl*
  2 *adj* **(a)** *Formal* **to be p. to sth** avoir connaissance de qch **(b)** *Br Pol* **the P. Council** le Conseil privé du souverain

prize¹ [praɪz] **1** *n (award)* prix *m*; **to win a p.** remporter un prix; *Fig* **no prizes for guessing** ce n'est pas difficile de deviner; **p. day** jour *m* de distribution des prix; **p. draw** tombola *f*; **p. money** argent *m* du prix
  2 *vt (value)* attacher de la valeur à

prize² = **prise**

prizefight ['praɪzfaɪt] *n* combat *m* professionnel

prizefighter ['praɪzfaɪtə(r)] *n* boxeur *m* professionnel

prizegiving ['praɪzgɪvɪŋ] *n* distribution *f* des prix

prizewinner ['praɪzwɪnə(r)] *n* gagnant(e) *m,f*

pro¹ [prəʊ] *(pl* **pros)** *n Fam (professional)* pro *mf*

pro² **1** *n (advantage)* **the pros and cons** le pour et le contre
  2 *prep (in favour of)* pour

proactive [prəʊ'æktɪv] *adj* qui fait preuve d'initiative

pro-am ['prəʊ'æm] *n Sp* tournoi *m* professionnel-amateur

probability [prɒbə'bɪlɪtɪ] *(pl* **probabilities)** *n* probabilité *f*; **in all p....** il y a de fortes chances que...

probable ['prɒbəbəl] *adj* probable

probably ['prɒbəblɪ] *adv* probablement

probation [prə'beɪʃən] *n (in job)* période *f* d'essai; *Law* mise *f* en liberté surveillée; **on p.** *(in job)* à l'essai; *Law* en liberté surveillée; **p. officer** agent *m* de probation

probationary [prə'beɪʃənərɪ] adj d'essai

probationer [prə'beɪʃənə(r)] n (in job) personne f à l'essai

probe [prəʊb] 1 n (a) (instrument) sonde f; (space) p. sonde spatiale (b) Fam (enquiry) enquête f
2 vt (a) (prod) sonder (b) (enquire into) enquêter sur
3 vi to p. into sth (past, private life) fouiller dans qch

probity ['prəʊbɪtɪ] n Formal probité f

problem ['prɒbləm] n problème m; Fam no p.! pas de problème!; p. area (in town) quartier m à problèmes (in project) source f de problèmes; p. child enfant mf à problèmes; p. page courrier m du cœur

problematic(al) [prɒblɪ'mætɪk(əl)] adj problématique

procedure [prə'siːdʒə(r)] n procédure f

proceed [prə'siːd] 1 vi to p. to do sth se mettre à faire qch
2 vi (a) (go on) se poursuivre; to p. to sth passer à qch; to p. with sth poursuivre qch; how shall we p.? comment allons-nous procéder? (b) (result) to p. from provenir de

proceedings [prə'siːdɪŋz] npl (a) (events) opérations fpl (b) Law poursuites fpl; to take p. (against sb) engager des poursuites (contre qn)

proceeds ['prəʊsiːdz] npl recette f

process¹ ['prəʊses] 1 n processus m; by a p. of elimination en procédant par élimination; she fell down the stairs, breaking her leg in the p. elle est tombée dans les escaliers, et s'est cassé la jambe; to be in the p. of doing sth être en train de faire qch
2 vt (raw material, information, application) traiter; (film) développer; processed food aliments mpl conditionnés

process² [prə'ses] vi (walk in procession) défiler

processing ['prəʊsesɪŋ] n (of raw material, information) traitement m; (of photographs) développement m; Comptr p. language langage m de traitement; Comptr p. speed vitesse f de traitement

procession [prə'seʃən] n défilé m; in p. en cortège

processor ['prəʊsesə(r)] n Comptr processeur m

pro-choice ['prəʊtʃɔɪs] adj partisan(e) de l'avortement

proclaim [prə'kleɪm] vt proclamer

proclamation [prɒklə'meɪʃən] n proclamation f

proclivity [prə'klɪvɪtɪ] (pl proclivities) n Formal tendance f (for à)

procrastinate [prəʊ'kræstɪneɪt] vi atermoyer

procrastination [prəʊkræstɪ'neɪʃən] n atermoiements mpl

procreate ['prəʊkrɪeɪt] vi procréer

procreation [prəʊkrɪ'eɪʃən] n procréation f

procure [prə'kjʊə(r)] vt procurer (for sb à qn); to p. sth (for oneself) se procurer qch

procurement [prə'kjʊəmənt] n acquisition f

prod [prɒd] 1 n to give sb a p. donner un petit coup à qn; Fig pousser qn; to give sth a p. donner un petit coup à qch
2 vt (pt & pp prodded) (poke) donner un petit coup dans; Fig to p. sb (into doing sth) pousser qn (à faire qch)

prodigal ['prɒdɪgəl] adj prodigue

prodigious [prə'dɪdʒəs] adj prodigieux(euse)

prodigy ['prɒdɪdʒɪ] (pl prodigies) n prodige m

produce 1 n ['prɒdjuːs] (products) produits mpl
2 vt [prə'djuːs] (a) (create) produire; (machine, car) fabriquer; (reaction, feeling) entraîner (b) (present) (ticket, passport) présenter; (documents, alibi) fournir; (from pocket, bag) sortir (c) (film, play, radio, TV programme) produire

producer [prə'djuːsə(r)] n (a) (of crops, goods) producteur(trice) m,f (b) (of film, play, radio, TV programme) producteur(trice) m,f

product ['prɒdʌkt] n produit m; Com p. development mise f au point de produit

production [prə'dʌkʃən] n (a) (manufacture) production f, fabrication f; to go into/out of p. être/ne plus être fabriqué(e); p. costs coûts mpl de production; p. line chaîne f de fabrication; p. manager directeur(trice) m,f de production; p. process procédé m de fabrication; p. target cible f de production (b) (of document, ticket) présentation f; on p. of sur présentation de (c) (play) mise f en scène; (film, radio, TV programme) production f

productive [prə'dʌktɪv] adj productif(ive)

productivity [prɒdʌk'tɪvɪtɪ] n Ind productivité f; p. agreement accord m de productivité; p. bonus prime f de rendement

Prof (abbr **Professor**) (a) (title) Professeur (b) Fam prof mf

profane [prə'feɪn] 1 adj (a) (language) grossier(ère) (b) Rel (secular) profane
2 vt profaner

profanity [prə'fænɪtɪ] (pl profanities) n grossièreté f

profess [prə'fes] vt (a) (declare) professer (b) (claim) prétendre

professed [prə'fest] adj (a) (self-declared) avoué(e) (b) (pretended) prétendu(e)

profession [prə'feʃən] n (a) (occupation) profession f; the medical/teaching p. le corps médical/enseignant; by p. de profession (b) (declaration) déclaration f

professional [prə'feʃənəl] 1 n professionnel(elle) m,f
2 adj (paid, competent) professionnel(elle); (soldier, army) de carrière; he made a very p. job of it il a fait du bon travail; to turn or go p. (of sportsperson) passer en catégorie professionnelle; to take p. advice on sth demander l'avis d'un professionnel sur qch; p. misconduct faute f professionnelle; p. training formation f professionnelle

professionalism [prə'feʃənəlɪzəm] n professionnalisme m

professor [prə'fesə(r)] n Univ Br ≃ professeur m; Am enseignant(e) m,f d'université

proficiency [prə'fɪʃənsɪ] n compétence f (in or at en ou dans); (in language) maîtrise f (in en)

proficient [prə'fɪʃənt] adj compétent(e) (in or at en ou dans)

profile ['prəʊfaɪl] 1 n (a) (side view, outline) profil m; to keep a low p. garder un profil bas (b) (description) portrait m
2 vt (describe) faire le portrait de

profit ['prɒfɪt] 1 n (a) (of company, on deal) bénéfice m, profit m; at a p. à profit; to make a p. réaliser un bénéfice; p. and loss account compte m de pertes et profits; p. margin marge f bénéficiaire (b) (advantage) avantage m
2 vi to p. by or from tirer profit de

profitability [prɒfɪtə'bɪlɪtɪ] n rentabilité f

profitable ['prɒfɪtəbəl] adj (company, deal) rentable; (experience) profitable

profitably ['prɒfɪtəblɪ] adv (trade, operate) à profit; (use one's time) profitablement

profiteer [profɪ'tɪə(r)] *Pej* **1** *n* profiteur(euse) *m,f*
2 *vi* profiter d'une situation pour faire des bénéfices

profit-making ['profitmeɪkɪŋ] *adj* rentable

profit-sharing ['profit'ʃeəriŋ] *n Com* intéressement *m*

profligate ['profligət] *adj Formal* prodigue

profound [prə'faʊnd] *adj* profond(e)

profundity [prə'fʌndɪtɪ] (*pl* **profundities**) *n* profondeur *f*

profuse [prə'fju:s] *adj* abondant(e)

profusely [prə'fju:slɪ] *adv* (*sweat, bleed*) abondamment; **to apologize p.** se confondre en excuses; **to thank sb p.** remercier qn avec effusion

profusion [prə'fju:ʒən] *n* profusion *f*

progeny ['prodʒɪnɪ] (*pl* **progenies**) *n Formal* progéniture *f*

prognosis [prog'nəʊsɪs] (*pl* **prognoses** [prog'nəʊsi:z]) *n Med* pronostic *m; Fig* pronostics

program¹ ['prəʊgræm] *Comptr* **1** *n* programme *m*
2 *vt & vi* programmer

program² *Am* = **programme**

programmable [prəʊ'græməbəl] *adj* programmable

programme, *Am* **program** ['prəʊgræm] **1** *n* (*for play, of political party*) programme *m*; (*on TV, radio*) émission *f*; **p. seller** vendeur(euse) *m,f* de programmes
2 *vt* (*machine*) programmer; **to p. sth to do sth** programmer qch pour faire qch

programmed ['prəʊgræmd] *adj Educ* **p. instruction** *or* **learning** enseignement *m* programmé

programmer ['prəʊgræmə(r)] *n Comptr* programmeur(euse) *m,f*

progress 1 *n* ['prəʊgres] (a) (*improvement*) progrès *m*; **to make p.** faire des progrès (b) (*movement*) marche *f*; **in p.** en cours; **to make p. (in sth)** progresser (dans qch); **p. report** rapport *m*
2 *vi* [prə'gres] (a) (*improve*) progresser (b) (*advance*) avancer; (*of meeting*) progresser

progression [prə'greʃən] *n* progression *f*

progressive [prə'gresɪv] **1** *adj* (a) (*increasing*) progressif(ive); **p. disease** maladie *f* évolutive (b) (*radical*) progressiste
2 *n* (*radical*) progressiste *mf*

progressively [prə'gresɪvlɪ] *adv* progressivement

prohibit [prə'hɪbɪt] *vt* interdire; **to p. sb from doing sth** interdire à qn de faire qch

prohibition [prəʊɪ'bɪʃən] *n* interdiction *f; Am Hist* la Prohibition

prohibitive [prə'hɪbɪtɪv] *adj* prohibitif(ive)

prohibitively [prə'hɪbɪtɪvlɪ] *adv* **p. expensive** à un prix prohibitif

project 1 *n* ['prodʒekt] (*undertaking, plan*) projet *m*; (*at school*) dossier *m*; (*at university*) mémoire *m*; *Com* **p. manager** directeur(trice) *m,f* de projet
2 *vt* [prə'dʒekt] (a) (*plan*) prévoir (b) (*propel*) projeter; **to p. one's voice** projeter sa voix
3 *vi* (*protrude*) dépasser

projectile [prə'dʒektaɪl] *n* projectile *m*

projection [prə'dʒekʃən] *n* (a) (*in general*) projection *f*; **p. room** (*in cinema*) salle *f* de projection (b) (*protruding part*) saillie *f*

projectionist [prə'dʒekʃənɪst] *n* projectionniste *mf*

projector [prə'dʒektə(r)] *n* projecteur *m*

prolapse ['prəʊlæps] *n Med* prolapsus *m*

proletarian [prəʊlɪ'teərɪən] **1** *n* prolétaire *mf*
2 *adj* prolétarien(enne)

proletariat [prəʊlɪ'teərɪət] *n* prolétariat *m*

pro-life ['prəʊlaɪf] *adj* contre l'avortement

proliferate [prə'lɪfəreɪt] *vi* proliférer

proliferation [prəlɪfə'reɪʃən] *n* prolifération *f*

prolific [prə'lɪfɪk] *adj* prolifique

prolix ['prəʊlɪks] *adj Formal* prolixe

prologue ['prəʊlog] *n* prologue *m*

prolong [prə'lɒŋ] *vt* prolonger

prom [prom] *n* (a) *Br Fam* (*at seaside*) front *m* de mer (b) *Br Fam* (*concert*) concert *m* (c) *Am* (*school dance*) soirée *f* dansante

promenade ['promənɑːd] **1** *n* (a) *Br* (*at seaside*) front *m* de mer; **p. deck** (*on ship*) pont *m* promenade
2 *vi* se promener

prominence ['promɪnəns] *n* (a) (*of land*) saillie *f*; (*of physical feature*) proéminence *f* (b) (*importance*) importance *f*; **to give sth p.** donner de l'importance à qch; **to come to p.** devenir célèbre

prominent ['promɪnənt] *adj* (a) (*peak, landscape*) en saillie; (*physical feature*) proéminent(e); **to be in a p. position** être en évidence (b) (*important*) important(e)

prominently ['promɪnəntlɪ] *adv* en bien en vue; **to figure p. in sth** figurer en bonne place dans qch

promiscuity [promɪs'kju:ɪtɪ] *n* promiscuité *f*

promiscuous [prə'mɪskjʊəs] *adj* qui a des partenaires multiples

promise ['promɪs] **1** *n* (a) (*pledge*) promesse *f*; **to make a p.** faire une promesse; **to keep/break one's p.** tenir/ne pas tenir sa promesse (b) (*potential*) **to show p.** promettre; **she never fulfilled her early p.** (*as a writer, musician*) elle n'a jamais eu le succès qu'elle promettait d'avoir
2 *vt* promettre (**to do** de faire); **to p. sth to sb, to p. sb sth** promettre qch à qn; **it promises to be hot** le temps promet d'être chaud

promising ['promɪsɪŋ] *adj* prometteur(euse)

promontory ['proməntərɪ] (*pl* **promontories**) *n* promontoire *m*

promote [prə'məʊt] *vt* (a) (*raise in rank, encourage*) promouvoir; **to be promoted** (*of officer, employee*) être promu(e); (*of football team*) passer dans la division supérieure; **to p. sb's interests** servir les intérêts de qn (b) *Com* faire la publicité de

promoter [prə'məʊtə(r)] *n* (*of theory, cause*) défenseur(euse) *m,f*; (*of boxing match*) organisateur(trice) *m,f*; (*of show*) imprésario *m*

promotion [prə'məʊʃən] *n* promotion *f*

promotional [prə'məʊʃənəl] *adj* promotionnel(elle)

prompt [prompt] **1** *adj* (a) (*swift*) rapide; **p. payment** paiement *m* dans les plus brefs délais (b) (*punctual*) ponctuel(elle)
2 *adv* **at three o'clock p.** à trois heures précises
3 *vt* (a) (*cause*) provoquer; **to p. sb to do sth** pousser qn à faire qch **to p. sb** (*encourage to speak*) aider qn à répondre en lui suggérant quelque chose; **"was he tall?" the policeman prompted** "est-ce qu'il était grand?" suggéra le policier (c) (*in theatre*) souffler à
4 *n* (a) **to give an actor a p.** souffler sa réplique à un acteur (b) *Comptr* invite *f*

prompter ['promptə(r)] *n Th* souffleur(euse) *m,f*

promptly ['promptlɪ] *adv (rapidly, punctually)* rapidement; *(immediately)* immédiatement

prone [prəʊn] *adj* (a) *(inclined)* to be p. to sth être sujet(ette) à qch; to be p. to do sth avoir tendance à faire qch (b) *Formal (lying face down)* couché(e) sur le ventre

prong [prɒŋ] *n (of fork)* dent *f*

pronoun ['prəʊnaʊn] *n Gram* pronom *m*

pronounce [prə'naʊns] 1 *vt* (a) *(word)* prononcer (b) *(declare) (opinion)* émettre; to p. that... déclarer que...; to p. oneself for/against sth se prononcer en faveur de/contre qch; he was pronounced dead/innocent il a été déclaré mort/innocent; *Law* to p. sentence rendre le verdict
2 *vi* to p. on se prononcer sur

pronounced [prə'naʊnst] *adj* prononcé(e)

pronouncement [prə'naʊnsmənt] *n Formal* déclaration *f*

pronto ['prɒntəʊ] *adv Fam* illico

pronunciation [prənʌnsɪ'eɪʃən] *n* prononciation *f*

proof [pruːf] 1 *n* (a) *(evidence)* preuve *f*; to give p. of sth prouver qch; p. of identity pièce *f* d'identité; p. of purchase preuve *f* d'achat; to put sth to the p. mettre qch à l'épreuve; *Prov* the p. of the pudding is in the eating il faut juger les choses à l'usage (b) *Typ* épreuve *f* (c) *(of alcohol)* teneur *f* en alcool; to be 40% p. faire 40 degrés
2 *adj (resistant)* to be p. against sth être résistant(e) à qch

proofread ['pruːfriːd] *(pt & pp proofread* ['pruːfred]*) vt Typ* relire, corriger

proofreader ['pruːfriːdə(r)] *n Typ* correcteur(trice) *m,f*

pro rata ['prəʊ'rɑːtə] *adj & adv* au prorata

prop [prɒp] 1 *n* (a) *(physical support)* support *m*; *(emotional support)* soutien *m* (b) *(in theatre)* accessoire *m*
2 *vt (pt & pp propped)* to p. sth against sth appuyer qch contre qch
▸**prop up** *vt sep (building, tunnel)* étayer; *Fig (economy, regime)* soutenir; to p. sth up against sth appuyer qch contre qch

propaganda [prɒpə'gændə] *n* propagande *f*

propagate ['prɒpəgeɪt] 1 *vt* propager
2 *vi* se propager

propagation [prɒpə'geɪʃən] *n* propagation *f*

propane ['prəʊpeɪn] *n Chem* propane *m*

propel [prə'pel] *(pt & pp propelled) vt* propulser; *Fig* pousser

propellant, propellent [prə'pelənt] *n (for rocket)* propergol *m*; *(for aerosol)* gaz *m* propulseur

propeller [prə'pelə(r)] *n* hélice *f*

propelling pencil [prə'pelɪŋ'pensəl] *n* porte-mine *m inv*

propensity [prə'pensɪtɪ] *(pl* propensities*) n* propension *f* (for à)

proper ['prɒpə(r)] *adj* (a) *(correct, real)* vrai(e); *(word)* correct(e); *Gram* p. noun nom *m* propre (b) *(appropriate)* bon (bonne); *(equipment, clothing)* adéquat(e); *(behaviour)* convenable (c) *(characteristic)* p. to propre à (d) *Br Fam (for emphasis)* it was a p. disaster c'était une véritable catastrophe; we're in a p. mess nous voilà propres; he's a p. fool c'est vraiment un imbécile

properly ['prɒpəlɪ] *adv* (a) *(correctly)* correctement (b) *(suitably)* convenablement

property ['prɒpətɪ] *(pl* properties*) n* (a) *(possessions)* biens *mpl*; *(land, house)* propriété *f*; p. developer promoteur(trice) *m,f* (immobilier(ère)); p. market marché *m* immobilier; p. tax impôt *m* foncier (b) *(quality)* propriété *f*

prophecy ['prɒfɪsɪ] *(pl* prophecies*) n* prophétie *f*

prophesy ['prɒfɪsaɪ] *(pt & pp* prophesied*) vt* prédire

prophet ['prɒfɪt] *n* prophète *m*

prophetic [prə'fetɪk] *adj* prophétique

prophylactic [prɒfɪ'læktɪk] *Med* 1 *n* prophylactique *m*; *(condom)* préservatif *m*
2 *adj* prophylactique

propitiate [prə'pɪʃɪeɪt] *vt Formal* gagner les faveurs de

propitious [prə'pɪʃəs] *adj Formal* favorable

proportion [prə'pɔːʃən] 1 *n* (a) *(relationship)* proportion *f*; in p. proportionné(e); out of p. disproportionné(e); the payment is out of all p. to the work involved la rétribution n'est pas du tout proportionnelle au travail requis (b) *(part, amount)* proportion *f*; to get sth out of p. exagérer qch; try to keep things in p. essaie de ne pas dramatiser (c) proportions *(dimensions)* proportions *fpl*
2 *vt* proportionner

proportional [prə'pɔːʃənəl] *adj* proportionnel(elle) (to à); *Pol* p. representation (représentation *f*) proportionnelle *f*

proportionate [prə'pɔːʃənɪt] *adj* proportionnel(elle) (to à)

proposal [prə'pəʊzəl] *n (offer)* proposition *f*; *(plan)* projet *m*; p. (of marriage) demande *f* en mariage

propose [prə'pəʊz] 1 *vt* proposer; to p. a toast porter un toast; to p. to do sth, to p. doing sth *(suggest)* suggérer de faire qch; *(intend)* avoir l'intention de faire qch
2 *vi* to p. to sb demander qn en mariage

proposition [prɒpə'zɪʃən] 1 *n* proposition *f*
2 *vt* faire des avances à

propound [prə'paʊnd] *vt Formal* exposer

proprietary [prə'praɪətərɪ] *adj (air, attitude)* possessif(ive); *Com* p. brand marque *f* déposée

proprietor [prə'praɪətə(r)] *n* propriétaire *mf*

propriety [prə'praɪətɪ] *n* bienséance *f*

propulsion [prə'pʌlʃən] *n* propulsion *f*

prosaic [prəʊ'zeɪɪk] *adj* prosaïque

proscribe [prəʊ'skraɪb] *vt* proscrire

prose [prəʊz] *n* prose *f*; *(translation in exam)* thème *m*

prosecute ['prɒsɪkjuːt] *Law* 1 *vt* poursuivre en justice
2 *vi (of lawyer)* représenter le ministère public

prosecution [prɒsɪ'kjuːʃən] *n Law (proceedings)* poursuites *fpl* judiciaires; the p. *(in trial)* les plaignants *mpl*; *(in crown case)* ≃ le ministère public

prosecutor ['prɒsɪkjuːtə(r)] *n Law* procureur *m*

prospect 1 *n* ['prɒspekt] (a) *(expectation, thought)* perspective *f* (b) *(chance, likelihood)* perspectives *fpl*; there is no p. of success il n'y a aucune chance de réussite; future prospects perspectives *fpl* d'avenir; a job with prospects un travail qui offre des perspectives d'avenir (c) *(view)* vue *f*
2 *vi* [prə'spekt] to p. for gold chercher de l'or

prospective [prə'spektɪv] *adj (future)* futur(e); *(potential)* potentiel(elle)

prospector [prə'spektə(r)] *n* prospecteur(trice) *m,f*; *(for gold)* chercheur(euse) *m,f*

prospectus [prə'spektəs] *n* prospectus *m*

prosper ['prɒspə(r)] *vi* prospérer

prosperity [prɒs'perɪtɪ] *n* prospérité *f*

prosperous ['prɒspərəs] *adj* prospère

prostate ['prɒsteɪt] *n Anat* p. **(gland)** prostate *f*

prosthesis [prɒs'θiːsɪs] (*pl* **prostheses** [prɒs'θiːsiːz]) *n* prothèse *f*

prostitute ['prɒstɪtjuːt] **1** *n* prostituée *f*; **male p.** prostitué *m*
  2 *vt also Fig* **to p. oneself** se prostituer

prostitution [prɒstɪ'tjuːʃən] *n* prostitution *f*

prostrate 1 *adj* ['prɒstreɪt] *(lying down)* couché(e); *Fig* p. **with grief** terrassé(e) par le chagrin
  2 *vt* [prɒ'streɪt] **to p. oneself** se prosterner

protagonist [prə'tægənɪst] *n* protagoniste *mf*; *(of idea, theory)* partisan(e) *m,f*

protect [prə'tekt] *vt* protéger **(from** *or* **against** de)

protection [prə'tekʃən] *n* protection *f*; p. **money =** argent versé à un racketteur; **p. racket** racket *m*

protectionism [prə'tekʃənɪzəm] *n Econ* protectionnisme *m*

protective [prə'tektɪv] *adj* protecteur(trice); **to put sb in p. custody** mettre qn en lieu sûr

protector [prə'tektə(r)] *n (device)* protecteur *m*; *(person)* protecteur(trice) *m,f*

protégé ['prɒtəʒeɪ] *n* protégé(e) *m,f*

protein ['prəutiːn] *n* protéine *f*

protest 1 *n* ['prəutest] protestation *f*; **to do sth under p.** faire qch contre son gré; **to do sth in p.** faire qch en signe de protestation; **p. song** chanson *f* engagée; **p. vote** vote *m* de protestation
  2 *vt* [prə'test] **(a)** *(protest against)* protester contre **(b)** *(one's innocence, love)* protester de; **to p. that...** protester en disant que...
  3 *vi* protester **(about/against** à propos de/contre)

Protestant ['prɒtɪstənt] *n & adj* protestant(e) *m,f*

Protestantism ['prɒtɪstəntɪzəm] *n* protestantisme *m*

protestation [prɒtes'teɪʃən] *n* protestation *f*

protester [prə'testə(r)] *n* protestataire *mf*

protocol ['prəutəkɒl] *n* protocole *m*

proton ['prəutɒn] *n Phys* proton *m*

prototype ['prəutətaɪp] *n* prototype *m*

protracted [prə'træktɪd] *adj* prolongé(e)

protractor [prə'træktə(r)] *n* rapporteur *m*

protrude [prə'truːd] *vi* dépasser **(from** de); *(of jaw, teeth)* avancer

protruding [prə'truːdɪŋ] *adj* en saillie; *(jaw, teeth)* qui avance

protuberance [prə'tjuːbərəns] *n* protubérance *f*

proud [praud] **1** *adj (person)* fier(ère) **(of** de); *(moment)* grand(e); **as p. as a peacock** fier comme un paon
  2 *adv* **to do sb p.** faire honneur à qn; **to do oneself p.** se distinguer

proudly ['praudlɪ] *adv* fièrement

prove [pruːv] (*pp* **proven** ['pruːvən, 'prəuvən] *or* **proved**) **1** *vt (demonstrate)* prouver; **to p. sb wrong/guilty** prouver que qn a tort/est coupable; **to p. oneself** se prouver quelque chose
  2 *vi* **to p. (to be) correct** se révéler correct(e)

proverb ['prɒvɜːb] *n* proverbe *m*

proverbial [prə'vɜːbɪəl] *adj* proverbial(e)

provide [prə'vaɪd] *vt* **(a)** *(supply)* fournir; *(service, support)* offrir; **to p. sb with sth** fournir qch à qn **(b)** *(stipulate)* stipuler

▶**provide against** *vt insep (danger, possibility)* parer à

▶**provide for** *vt insep* **(a)** *(support)* pourvoir aux besoins de; **he left his family well provided for** il a laissé sa famille à l'abri du besoin **(b)** *Formal (allow for)* parer à

provided [prə'vaɪdɪd] *conj* p. **(that)** à condition que + *subjunctive*

providence ['prɒvɪdəns] *n* providence *f*

providential [prɒvɪ'denʃəl] *adj* providentiel(elle)

provider [prə'vaɪdə(r)] *n* pourvoyeur(euse) *m,f*

providing [prə'vaɪdɪŋ] *conj* p. **(that)** à condition que + *subjunctive*

province ['prɒvɪns] *n* **(a)** *(of country)* province *f*; **in the provinces** en province **(b)** *Fig (domain)* domaine *m*

provincial [prə'vɪnʃəl] *adj* de province; *Pej (parochial)* provincial(e)

provision [prə'vɪʒən] *n* **(a)** **provisions** *(supplies)* provisions *fpl* **(b)** *(supplying)* approvisionnement *m* **(of** en); *(of services)* prestation *f* **(of** de) **(c)** *(allowance)* **to make p. for sth** prévoir qch **(d)** *(in treaty)* disposition *f*; *(in contract)* clause *f*

provisional [prə'vɪʒənəl] *adj* provisoire

provisionally [prə'vɪʒənəlɪ] *adv* provisoirement

proviso [prə'vaɪzəu] (*pl* **provisos** *or* **provisoes**) *n* condition *f*; **with the p. that** à condition que + *subjunctive*

provocation [prɒvə'keɪʃən] *n* provocation *f*; **at the slightest p.** pour un rien

provocative [prə'vɒkətɪv] *adj* provocateur(trice)

provoke [prə'vəuk] *vt* provoquer; **to p. sb into doing sth** pousser qn à faire qch

provoking [prə'vəukɪŋ] *adj (irritating)* agaçant(e)

provost ['prɒvəst] *n* **(a)** *Br Univ (head of college)* doyen *m* **(b)** *Scot (mayor)* maire *m*

prow [prau] *n (of ship)* proue *f*

prowess ['prauɪs] *n (skill)* prouesses *fpl*

prowl [praul] **1** *n* **to be on the p.** *(of person, animal)* être en chasse; **to be on the p. for sth** être à l'affût de qch
  2 *vt (streets, area)* rôder dans
  3 *vi* rôder

prowler ['praulə(r)] *n* rôdeur(euse) *m,f*

proxie ['prɒksɪ] *n Comptr* proxie *m*

proximity [prɒk'sɪmɪtɪ] *n* proximité *f*; **in p. to** à proximité de

proxy ['prɒksɪ] (*pl* **proxies**) *n (power)* procuration *f*; *(person)* mandataire *mf*; **by p.** par procuration

prude [pruːd] *n* prude *f*

prudence ['pruːdəns] *n* prudence *f*

prudent ['pruːdənt] *adj* prudent(e)

prudish ['pruːdɪʃ] *adj* pudibond(e)

prune¹ [pruːn] *n (fruit)* pruneau *m*

prune² *vt (bush, tree)* tailler; *Fig (article)* élaguer

prurient ['pruərɪənt] *adj* malsain(e)

Prussia ['prʌʃə] *n* la Prusse

Prussian ['prʌʃən] **1** *n* Prussien(enne) *m,f*
  2 *adj* prussien(enne)

pry [praɪ] (*pt & pp* **pried**) *vi* être indiscret(ète); **to p. into sth** mettre son nez dans qch

prying ['praɪɪŋ] *adj* indiscret(ète)

PS ['piː'es] *n (abbr* **postscript)** PS *m*

psalm [sɑːm] *n* psaume *m*

pseud [sju:d] *n Fam* prétentieux(euse) *m,f*

pseudo- ['sju:dəʊ] *pref Fam* pseudo-

pseudonym ['sju:dənɪm] *n* pseudonyme *m*

PST [pi:es'ti:] *n Am (abbr* **Pacific Standard Time)** PST *m*

psyche ['saɪkɪ] *n* psychisme *m*

▶**psyche out** [saɪk] *vt sep Fam (unnerve)* déstabiliser

▶**psyche up** [saɪk] *vt sep Fam* **to p. sb up (for sth)** préparer qn psychologiquement (à qch); **to p. oneself up (for sth)** se préparer psychologiquement (à qch)

psychedelic [saɪkə'delɪk] *adj* psychédélique

psychiatric [saɪkɪ'ætrɪk] *adj* psychiatrique

psychiatrist [saɪ'kaɪətrɪst] *n* psychiatre *mf*

psychiatry [saɪ'kaɪətrɪ] *n* psychiatrie *f*

psychic ['saɪkɪk] **1** *n* médium *m*
2 *adj* **(a)** *(paranormal)* paranormal(e) **(b)** *(clairvoyant)* **to be p., to have p. powers** être médium; *Fam* **I'm not p.!** je ne suis pas médium!

psycho ['saɪkəʊ] *(pl* **psychos)** *n Fam* dingue *mf*

psychoanalysis [saɪkəʊə'nælɪsɪs] *n* psychanalyse *f*

psychoanalyst [saɪkəʊ'ænəlɪst] *n* psychanalyste *mf*

psychoanalyze [saɪkəʊ'ænəlaɪz] *vt* psychanalyser

psychological [saɪkə'lɒdʒɪkəl] *adj* psychologique; **p. warfare** guerre *f* psychologique

psychologist [saɪ'kɒlədʒɪst] *n* psychologue *mf*

psychology [saɪ'kɒlədʒɪ] *n* psychologie *f*

psychometric [saɪkə'metrɪk] *adj* psychométrique

psychopath ['saɪkəʊpæθ] *n* psychopathe *mf*

psychosis [saɪ'kəʊsɪs] *(pl* **psychoses** [saɪ'kəʊsi:z]) *n* psychose *f*

psychosomatic [saɪkəʊsə'mætɪk] *adj* psychosomatique

psychotherapist [saɪkəʊ'θerəpɪst] *n* psychothérapeute *mf*

psychotherapy [saɪkəʊ'θerəpɪ] *n* psychothérapie *f*

psychotic [saɪ'kɒtɪk] *n & adj* psychotique *mf*

PT [pi:'ti:] *n (abbr* **physical training)** EPS *f*

PTA [pi:ti:'eɪ] *n Sch (abbr* **Parent-Teacher Association)** ≃ APE *f*

ptarmigan ['tɑːmɪgən] *n* lagopède *m*

Pte *Mil (abbr* **private)** p. Robbie McLean = Soldat Robbie McLean

PTO [pi:ti:'əʊ] *(abbr* **please turn over)** TSVP

pub [pʌb] *n Br* pub *m*

pub-crawl [pʌbkrɔːl] *n Br Fam* **to go on a p.** faire la tournée des bars

puberty ['pjuːbətɪ] *n* puberté *f*

pubic ['pjuːbɪk] *adj* pubien(enne), du pubis

public ['pʌblɪk] **1** *n* **the (general) p.** le grand public; **in p.** en public
2 *adj* public(ique); *(library, swimming pool)* municipal(e); **to go p. with sth** *(reveal information)* révéler qch *(à la presse)*; **the company's going p.** la compagnie va être cotée en Bourse; **to make sth p.** rendre qch public; **to make a p. appearance** faire une apparition en public; **to be in the p. domain** être dans le domaine public; **at p. expense** aux frais du contribuable; **to be in the p. eye** être très en vue; **a p. figure** une personnalité en vue; **in the p. interest** dans l'intérêt du public; **p. address system** sonorisation *f*; **p. call box** cabine *f* téléphonique; **p. convenience** toilettes *fpl* publiques;

Com **p. enterprise** entreprise *f* publique; **p. holiday** jour *m* férié; **p. house** pub *m*; **p. limited company** ≃ société *f* anonyme; **p. opinion** l'opinion *f* publique; *Law* **p. prosecutor** procureur *m*; **p. relations** relations *fpl* publiques; **p. school** *Br* école *f* privée, *Am* école publique; **p. sector** secteur *m* public; **p. spending** dépenses *fpl* publiques; **p. transport** transports *mpl* en commun; *Com* **p. utility** service *m* public

publican ['pʌblɪkən] *n* patron(onne) *m,f* d'un pub

publication [pʌblɪ'keɪʃən] *n* publication *f*

publicity [pʌb'lɪsɪtɪ] *n* publicité *f*; **p. campaign** campagne *f* publicitaire; **p. stunt** coup *m* de pub

publicize ['pʌblɪsaɪz] *vt* faire connaître au public

publicly ['pʌblɪklɪ] *adv* publiquement; **p. owned** à capitaux publics

public-spirited ['pʌblɪkspɪrɪtɪd] *adj (person)* qui a le sens civique; *(gesture, response)* dicté(e) par le sens civique

publish ['pʌblɪʃ] *vt* publier

publisher ['pʌblɪʃə(r)] *n (person)* éditeur(trice) *m,f*; *(company)* maison *f* d'édition

publishing ['pʌblɪʃɪŋ] *n* édition *f*; **p. house** maison *f* d'édition

pucker ['pʌkə(r)] **1** *vt (brow)* froncer; *(lips)* pincer
2 *vi (of face)* se rider; *(lips)* se plisser

pudding ['pʊdɪŋ] *n* **(a)** *(dessert)* dessert *m* **(b)** *(dish)* pudding *m*; **p. basin** *or* **bowl** jatte *f*

puddle ['pʌdəl] *n* flaque *f*

pudgy ['pʌdʒɪ] *adj* rondelet(ette)

puerile ['pjʊəraɪl] *adj Pej* puéril(e)

Puerto Rican [pweətəʊ'riːkən] **1** *n* Portoricain(e) *m,f*
2 *adj* portoricain(e)

Puerto Rico [pweətəʊ'riːkəʊ] *n* Porto Rico

puff [pʌf] **1** *n (of breath, air)* souffle *m*; *(of smoke, cigarette)* bouffée *f*; *Fam* **to be out of p.** être essoufflé(e); **p. pastry** pâte *f* feuilletée
2 *vt* **to p. smoke into sb's face** envoyer de la fumée à la figure de qn
3 *vi (of person)* souffler; *(of steam engine)* lancer des bouffées de vapeur; **to p. on a cigarette** fumer une cigarette

▶**puff out** *vt sep (cheeks, chest)* gonfler

▶**puff up** *vt sep (cheeks)* gonfler; **to be puffed up with pride** être gonflé(e) d'orgueil

puffin ['pʌfɪn] *n* macareux *m*

puffy ['pʌfɪ] *adj* gonflé(e)

pug [pʌg] *n (dog)* carlin *m*; **p.-nosed** au nez camus

pugnacious [pʌg'neɪʃəs] *adj* pugnace

puke [pjuːk] *Fam* **1** *n* dégueulis *m*
2 *vt & vi* dégueuler

pull [pʊl] **1** *n* **(a)** *(act of pulling)* traction *f*; *(of water current)* force *f*; **to give sth a p.** tirer qch; **to take a p. at a bottle** boire une gorgée d'une bouteille
(b) *Fam (influence)* influence *f*; **to have a lot of p.** avoir le bras long
2 *vt* **(a)** *(tug)* tirer; **to p. sth open/shut** ouvrir/fermer qch; **to p. a muscle** se froisser un muscle; **to p. a pint** servir une bière; **to p. the trigger** appuyer sur la gâchette; *Fig* **to p. sth to pieces** démolir qch; *Fam Fig* **to p. sb's leg** faire marcher qn; *Fam Fig* **p. the other one! (it's got bells on)** à d'autres!
(b) *(attract)* attirer
(c) *(extract)* *(cork)* retirer, enlever; *(tooth)* arracher; **to p. a gun on sb** braquer un pistolet sur qn; *Fam Fig* **it's like pulling teeth** il faut t'/lui/*etc* arracher les vers du nez

(d) *(sexually)* to p. sb se faire qn

(e) *(idioms)* to p. a face faire la grimace; *Fam* to p. a bank job se faire une banque; *Fam* to p. a fast one on sb rouler qn

3 *vi* tirer (on sur); to p. clear of sth s'éloigner de qch

▶pull about *vt sep (handle roughly)* malmener

▶pull ahead *vi (in race, election)* prendre la tête (of de)

▶pull apart *vt sep (break up)* séparer; *Fig (criticize)* massacrer

▶pull away *vi (of car, train)* partir; *(from embrace)* s'écarter

▶pull back 1 *vt sep (curtains)* ouvrir
   2 *vi (of person)* se retirer

▶pull down *vt sep (demolish)* démolir

▶pull in 1 *vt sep* (a) *(rope, fishing line)* ramener (b) *(money)* gagner; *(of deal)* rapporter; to p. sb in for questioning arrêter qn pour l'interroger (c) *(attract)* attirer
   2 *vi (of car)* s'arrêter; *(of train, bus)* arriver

▶pull off *vt sep (clothes)* retirer (b) *(task, deal)* réaliser; *(bank raid, burglary)* réussir; to p. it off réussir

▶pull on *vt sep (clothes)* mettre

▶pull out 1 *vt sep (tooth)* arracher; *Fam Fig* to p. out all the stops faire tout son possible
   2 *vi* (a) *(of car)* déboîter; *(of train)* partir (b) *(from race, agreement, deal)* se retirer (de)

▶pull over *vi (of driver)* s'arrêter

▶pull through *vi (recover)* s'en sortir

▶pull together 1 *vt sep* to p. oneself together se ressaisir
   2 *vi* s'entendre

▶pull up 1 *vt sep Fig* to p. one's socks up se ressaisir; to p. sb up *(short)* couper qn dans son élan
   2 *vi (of car)* s'arrêter

pull-down menu ['puldaun'menju:] *n Comptr* menu *m* déroulant

pullet ['pulɪt] *n* poulette *f*

pulley ['pulɪ] *(pl* pulleys) *n* poulie *f*

pull-out ['pulaut] *n (in newspaper, magazine)* supplément *m* détachable

pullover ['puləuvə(r)] *n* pull-over *m*

pulmonary ['pʌlmənəri] *adj* pulmonaire

pulp [pʌlp] 1 *n (of fruit)* pulpe *f*; to reduce sth to (a) p. écraser qch; *Fam* to beat sb to a p. mettre qn en bouillie; p. fiction romans *mpl* de gare
   2 *vt* écraser

pulpit ['pulpɪt] *n* chaire *f*

pulsate [pʌl'seɪt] *vi (of vein)* palpiter; *(of room, music)* vibrer; *(of heart)* battre

pulse¹ [pʌls] *n (of blood)* pouls *m*; *(of light, sound)* vibration *f*; to feel *or* take sb's p. prendre le pouls de qn

pulse² *n (seed)* légumineuse *f*

pulverize ['pʌlvəraɪz] *vt* pulvériser; *Fam Fig (beat up)* démolir; *(defeat heavily)* pulvériser

puma ['pju:mə] *n* puma *m*

pumice ['pʌmɪs] *n* p. (stone) pierre *f* ponce

pummel ['pʌml] *(pt & pp* pummelled, *Am* pummeled) *vt* marteler

pump¹ [pʌmp] *n (flat shoe)* escarpin *m*; *(ballet shoe)* ballerine *f*; *(plimsoll)* tennis *m* ou *f*

pump² *n (machine)* pompe *f*
   2 *vt* pomper; to p. sb's stomach faire un lavage d'estomac à qn; *Fig* to p. money into sth injecter des capitaux dans qch; *Fam* to p. sb for information tirer les vers du nez à qn; to p. sb's hand *(shake vigorously)* donner une poignée de main vigoureuse à qn; *Fam* to p. iron *(do weightlifting)* faire de la gonflette
   3 *vi (of heart)* battre; *(of machine)* pomper

▶pump out *vt sep* pomper

▶pump up *vt sep* gonfler

pumpkin ['pʌmpkɪn] *n* potiron *m*, citrouille *f*

pun [pʌn] *n* jeu *m* de mots

punch¹ [pʌntʃ] 1 *n (tool)* poinçon *m*; *(for tickets)* poinçonneuse *f*
   2 *vt (metal)* percer; *(ticket)* poinçonner

punch² 1 *n* (a) *(blow)* coup *m* (de poing); *Fig* she didn't pull her punches elle n'y est pas allée de main morte (b) *(energy)* punch *m*; p. line *(of joke, story)* chute *f*
   2 *vt (hit)* donner un coup de poing à; to p. sb in the face/on the nose donner un coup de poing à qn dans la figure/dans le nez

punch³ *n (drink)* punch *m*

Punch and Judy show ['pʌntʃən'dʒu:dɪ'ʃəu] *n* ≃ spectacle *m* de Guignol

punchbag ['pʌntʃbæg] *n* sac *m* de sable

punchball ['pʌntʃbɔ:l] *n* punching-ball *m*

punch-drunk ['pʌntʃdrʌŋk] *adj* assommé(e)

punch-up ['pʌntʃʌp] *n Fam* bagarre *f*

punchy ['pʌntʃɪ] *adj Fam* plein(e) de punch

punctilious [pʌŋk'tɪlɪəs] *adj* pointilleux(euse)

punctual ['pʌŋktjuəl] *adj* ponctuel(elle)

punctuality [pʌŋktjʊ'ælɪtɪ] *n* ponctualité *f*

punctually ['pʌŋktjuəlɪ] *adv* à l'heure

punctuate ['pʌŋktjueɪt] *vt* ponctuer (with de)

punctuation [pʌŋktjʊ'eɪʃən] *n* ponctuation *f*; p. mark signe *m* de ponctuation

puncture ['pʌŋktʃə(r)] 1 *n (in tyre)* crevaison *f*; *(in skin, metal)* perforation *f*; to have a p. *(of cyclist, driver)* crever; *(of bicycle, car)* avoir un pneu crevé
   2 *vt (tyre)* crever; *(metal, lung)* perforer; *(blister, abscess)* percer

pundit ['pʌndɪt] *n* expert(e) *m,f*

pungent ['pʌndʒənt] *adj (smell, taste)* âcre; *(style, wit)* mordant(e)

punish ['pʌnɪʃ] *vt* punir; to p. sb for doing sth punir qn pour avoir fait qch

punishment ['pʌnɪʃmənt] *n* punition *f*; *Law* peine *f*; to make the p. fit the crime adapter la punition à la faute; to take a lot of p. être mis(e) à rude épreuve

punitive ['pju:nɪtɪv] *adj* punitif(ive)

punk [pʌŋk] *n* punk *mf*; p. (rock) punk *m*

punnet ['pʌnɪt] *n* barquette *f*

punt¹ [pʌnt] 1 *n (boat)* barque *f* à fond plat
   2 *vi* to go punting faire de la barque

punt² [pɒnt] *n (Irish currency)* livre *f* irlandaise

punter ['pʌntə(r)] *n (gambler)* parieur(euse) *m,f*; *Fam (customer)* client(e) *m,f*

puny ['pju:nɪ] *adj* chétif(ive)

pup [pʌp] *n (of dog)* chiot *m*; *(of seal)* bébé-phoque *m*

pupil¹ ['pju:pəl] *n (student)* élève *mf*

pupil² *n (of eye)* pupille *f*

puppet ['pʌpɪt] *n also Fig* marionnette *f*; *Fig* p. government gouvernement *m* fantoche; p. show *(spectacle m de)* marionnettes *fpl*

puppy ['pʌpɪ] (*pl* **puppies**) *n* chiot *m*; p. fat rondeur *fpl* préadolescentes; **p. love** amour *m* d'adolescence

purchase ['pɜːtʃɪs] **1** *n* (a) (*action, thing bought*) achat *m*; **p. price** prix *m* d'achat (b) (*grip*) prise *f*; **to get a p. on sth** trouver une prise sur qch
2 *vt* acheter

purchaser ['pɜːtʃəsə(r)] *n* acheteur(euse) *m,f*

purchasing ['pɜːtʃəsɪŋ] *n* **p. manager** directeur(trice) *m,f* des achats; **p. power** pouvoir *m* d'achat

pure [pjʊə(r)] *adj* pur(e); **by p. chance** par pur hasard; **p. mathematics** mathématiques *fpl* pures

purebred ['pjʊəbred] *adj* (*dog*) de race pure; (*horse*) pur-sang *inv*

purée ['pjʊəreɪ] **1** *n* purée *f*
2 *vt* réduire en purée

purely ['pjʊəlɪ] *adv* purement; **p. and simply** purement et simplement

purgatory ['pɜːgətərɪ] *n* Rel purgatoire *m*; Fig enfer *m*

purge [pɜːdʒ] **1** *n* purge *f*
2 *vt* purger

purification [pjʊərɪfɪ'keɪʃən] *n* purification *f*

purify ['pjʊərɪfaɪ] (*pt & pp* **purified**) *vt* purifier

purist ['pjʊərɪst] *n* puriste *mf*

puritan ['pjʊərɪtən] *n* puritain(e) *m,f*

puritanical [pjʊərɪ'tænɪkəl] *adj* puritain(e)

purity ['pjʊərɪtɪ] *n* pureté *f*

purl [pɜːl] **1** *n* maille *f* à l'envers
2 *vt* tricoter à l'envers

purloin [pɜː'lɔɪn] *vt* dérober

purple ['pɜːpəl] **1** *n* violet *m*
2 *adj* violet(ette); **to turn** *or* **go p.** (*of person*) devenir cramoisi(e); **pages of p. prose** des pages d'un style ampoulé

purport Formal **1** *n* ['pɜːpɔːt] teneur *f*
2 *vt* [pɜː'pɔːt] **to p. to be sth** prétendre être qch

purpose ['pɜːpəs] *n* (a) (*object, aim*) but *m*, objectif *m*; **on p.** exprès; **what is the p. of your visit?** quel est l'objet de votre visite?; **to have a sense of p.** savoir ce que l'on veut; **to be to no p.** ne servir à rien (b) (*use*) utilité *f*; **to serve a p.** servir à quelque chose; **to serve no p.** ne servir à rien; **to serve sb's purpose(s)** faire l'affaire de qn; **for all practical purposes** à toutes fins utiles; **for the purposes of** pour les besoins de

purpose-built ['pɜːpəs'bɪlt] *adj* spécialement construit(e)

purposeful ['pɜːpəsfʊl] *adj* résolu(e)

purposely ['pɜːpəslɪ] *adv* délibérément; **to be p. rude** faire exprès d'être grossier(ère)

purr [pɜː(r)] **1** *n* ronron *m*, ronronnement *m*
2 *vi* ronronner

purse [pɜːs] **1** *n* Br (*wallet*) porte-monnaie *m inv*; Am (*handbag*) sac *m* à main; **the public p.** le Trésor public; Fig **to hold the p. strings** tenir les cordons de la bourse
2 *vt* **to p. one's lips** pincer les lèvres

pursue [pə'sjuː] *vt* poursuivre; (*pleasure, happiness*) rechercher; (*profession*) exercer

pursuer [pə'sjuːə(r)] *n* poursuivant(e) *m,f*

pursuit [pə'sjuːt] *n* (a) (*of person, animal*) poursuite *f*; (*of pleasure, knowledge, happiness*) quête *f*; **to be in p.** of être à la poursuite de; **in hot p.** à ses trousses (b) (*activity*) activité *f*

purveyor [pə'veɪə(r)] *n* Formal fournisseur(euse) *m,f*

pus [pʌs] *n* pus *m*

push [pʊʃ] **1** *n* (a) (*act of pushing*) poussée *f*; **to give sb/ sth a p.** pousser qn/qch; Fam **to give sb the p.** (*of employer*) virer qn; (*of lover*) plaquer qn; **at a p.** à la rigueur; **when p. comes to shove, if it comes to the p.** dans le pire des cas (b) Mil (*attack*) poussée *f*; **sales p.** campagne *f* de vente; **to make a p. for sth** lutter pour qch
2 *vt* (a) (*in general*) pousser; (*button*) appuyer sur; **to p. the door shut/open** fermer/ouvrir la porte; (*sign*) poussez; **to p. sb out of the way** écarter qn; **to p. one's way through the crowd** se frayer un chemin à travers la foule; Fig **don't p. yourself too hard** ne force pas trop; Fig **to p. sb into doing sth** pousser qn à faire qch; **to p. one's luck** y aller un peu fort; **to be pushed for time** être très pressé(e) (b) (*promote*) faire la promotion de; (*theory*) promouvoir (c) Fam (*drugs*) vendre (d) Fam **to be pushing sixty** approcher de la soixantaine
3 *vi* (*in general*) pousser; (*move forward*) avancer; **to p. past sb** passer devant qn en le bousculant; **to p. forward** pousser en avant

▶**push about, push around** *vt sep* Fam Fig (*bully*) **to p. sb about** faire de qn ce que l'on veut

▶**push ahead** *vi* continuer; **to p. ahead with sth** continuer qch

▶**push aside** *vt sep* also Fig écarter

▶**push in** *vi* (*in queue*) resquiller

▶**push off** *vi* Fam ficher le camp

▶**push on** *vi* (*continue*) continuer; **to p. on with sth** continuer qch

▶**push over** *vt sep* faire tomber

▶**push through** *vt sep* (*reform, law*) faire passer

push-bike ['pʊʃbaɪk] *n* Fam vélo *m*

push-button ['pʊʃ'bʌtən] *adj* à touches

pushchair ['pʊʃtʃeə(r)] *n* (*for baby*) poussette *f*

pusher ['pʊʃə(r)] *n* Fam (*drug*) p. dealer *m*

pushover ['pʊʃəʊvə(r)] *n* Fam **it's a p.** c'est un jeu d'enfant; **she's no p.** ce n'est pas facile de la faire changer d'avis

push-up ['pʊʃʌp] *n* pompe *f*

pushy ['pʊʃɪ] *adj* Fam batailleur(euse)

puss [pʊs] *n* Fam (*cat*) minou *m*

pussy ['pʊsɪ] (*pl* **pussies**) *n* Fam **p. (cat)** minou *m*; **p. willow** saule *m* blanc

pussyfoot ['pʊsɪfʊt] *vi* Fam **to p. (around** *or* **about)** (*when speaking*) tourner autour du pot; (*in one's actions*) toujours remettre les choses à plus tard

pustule ['pʌstjuːl] *n* pustule *f*

put [pʊt] (*pt & pp* **put**) **1** *vt* (a) (*place*) mettre; (*on flat surface*) poser; **to p. one's arms around sb** prendre qn dans ses bras; **to p. a man on the moon** envoyer un homme sur la lune; **to p. a limit on sth** mettre une limite à qch; Fam **p. it there!** (*shake hands*) tope là!; Fig **to p. oneself in sb's hands** s'en remettre à qn; Fig **to p. sb in his place** remettre qn à sa place; **p. yourself in my position** mets-toi à ma place; **to p. a matter right** mettre les choses au point; **to p. money on a horse** parier sur un cheval; **to p. a lot of work into sth** beaucoup travailler à qch; **to p. a stop to sth** mettre fin à qch; **to p. a child to bed** mettre un enfant au lit; **to p. sb to the test** mettre qn à l'épreuve; Fam Fig **I didn't know where to p. myself** je ne savais pas où me mettre
(b) (*present*) **to p. a question to sb** poser une question à

qn; **to p. a proposal to sb** soumettre une proposition à qn; **I p. it to you that...** *(in court)* n'est-il pas vrai que...? **(c)** *(express)* **to p. sth well** bien tourner qch; **I couldn't have put it better myself** je n'aurais pas mieux dit; **to p. it bluntly** pour parler franchement; **how shall I p. it...?** comment dire...?
(d) *(estimate)* estimer (at à); **I would p. her age at forty** je dirais qu'elle a quarante ans
2 *vi* **to p. to sea** prendre la mer

▶**put about** *vt sep (rumour)* faire courir; **to p. it about that...** faire courir le bruit que...

▶**put across** *vt sep (message, idea)* faire comprendre (**to** à); **to p. oneself across well/badly** *(at interview)* se mettre/ne pas se mettre en valeur

▶**put aside** *vt sep* **(a)** *(goods, money)* mettre de côté **(b)** *(problem, fact)* laisser de côté

▶**put away** *vt sep* **(a)** *(tidy away)* ranger **(b)** *Fam (prisoner)* enfermer **(c)** *Fam (eat, drink)* s'enfiler, ingurgiter

▶**put back** *vt sep* **(a)** *(replace)* remettre **(b)** *(postpone)* reporter; *(clock, schedule)* retarder; *Fig* **that puts the clock back ten years** cela nous ramène dix ans en arrière

▶**put by** *vt sep (save)* mettre de côté

▶**put down** *vt sep* **(a)** *(set down)* poser; **I couldn't put it down** *(book)* je ne pouvais pas m'arrêter de (le) lire **(b)** *(revolt, opposition)* réprimer **(c)** *(write)* écrire, mettre par écrit; **to p. sth down in writing** mettre qch par écrit; **to p. one's name down for sth** s'inscrire à qch *(d)* *(attribute)* **to p. sth down to sb/sth** attribuer qch à qn/qch **(e)** *(animal)* piquer; **to have a cat/dog put down** faire piquer un chat/un chien **(f)** *(criticize)* rabaisser; **to p. oneself down** se rabaisser

▶**put forward** *vt sep* **(a)** *(plan, theory, candidate)* proposer; *(proposal)* faire **(b)** *(clock, time of meeting)* avancer

▶**put in 1** *vt sep* **(a)** *(install)* installer **(b)** *(claim, application)* soumettre; **to p. in a (good) word for sb** dire un mot en faveur de qn **(c)** *(time)* passer; **they've p. in a lot of work** ils ont énormément travaillé
2 *vi (of ship)* faire escale

▶**put off** *vt sep* **(a)** *(postpone)* remettre à plus tard; **to p. off doing sth** retarder le moment de faire qch **(b)** *(cause to dislike)* **to p. sb off sth** dégoûter qn de qch **(c)** *(disturb)* gêner **(d)** *(discourage)* **to p. sb off doing sth** enlever à qn l'envie de faire qch **(e)** *(make wait)* faire patienter

▶**put on** *vt sep* **(a)** *(clothes)* mettre; **to p. on one's make-up** se maquiller; **to p. on an act** jouer la comédie; **to p. on an accent** prendre un accent; *Fam* **she's just putting it on!** elle fait semblant!; **to p. on weight** grossir, prendre du poids **(b)** *(light, TV, heating)* allumer; *(music, video)* mettre; **to p. the kettle on** mettre l'eau à chauffer **(c)** *(play, show)* monter

▶**put out** *vt sep* **(a)** *(fire, light)* éteindre **(b)** *(place outside)* mettre dehors **(c)** *(extend)* **to p. out one's hand** tendre la main **(d)** *(annoy)* **to be put out** être contrarié(e) **(g)** *(inconvenience)* déranger; **to p. oneself out (for sb)** se donner du mal (pour qn) **(h)** *(dislocate)* **to p. out one's shoulder/knee** se démettre l'épaule/le genou

▶**put through** *vt sep* **(a)** *(on phone)* **to p. sb through to sb** passer qn à qn **(b)** *(subject to)* **to p. sb through sth** faire subir qch à qn; **to p. sb through hell** faire souffrir le martyre à qn

▶**put together** *vt sep (assemble)* assembler; *(file, report)* préparer; *(meal, team)* composer; **she's more intelligent than the rest of them put together** elle est cent fois plus intelligente qu'eux; *Fig* **to p. two and two together** tirer ses conclusions

▶**put up** *vt sep* **(a)** *(tent, fence)* monter; *(ladder)* dresser; *(building)* construire; *(statue)* ériger; *(notice)* afficher; *(painting)* accrocher; *(umbrella)* ouvrir; **to p. up one's hand** lever la main; **to p. one's hair up** relever ses cheveux **(b)** *(increase)* augmenter **(c)** *(provide accommodation for)* loger, héberger **(d)** *(provide)* *(money)* verser, fournir; *(candidate)* présenter; **to p. sth up for sale** mettre qch en vente; **to p. up a fight** *or* **a struggle** se défendre

▶**put upon** *vt insep* **to feel put upon** se sentir exploité(e)

▶**put up to** *vt sep* **to p. sb up to doing sth** pousser qn à faire qch; **he put me up to it** c'est lui qui m'a poussé à le faire

▶**put up with** *vt insep* supporter

putative ['pju:tətɪv] *adj Formal* putatif(ive)

put-down ['pʊtdaʊn] *n Fam* remarque *f* humiliante

putrefy ['pju:trɪfaɪ] *(pt & pp* **putrefied***)* *vi* se putréfier

putrid ['pju:trɪd] *adj* putride

putsch [pʊtʃ] *n* putsch *m*

putt [pʌt] **1** *n (in golf)* putt *m*
2 *vi (in golf)* putter

putter ['pʌtə(r)] *n (golf club)* putter *m*

putty ['pʌtɪ] *n* mastic *m*; *Fig* **he's p. in her hands** elle en fait ce qu'elle veut

put-up job ['pʊtʌp'dʒɒb] *n Fam* coup *m* monté

puzzle ['pʌzl] **1** *n* **(a)** *(game)* casse-tête *m*; *(mental)* devinette *f*; *(jigsaw)* puzzle *m*; **p. book** livre *m* de devinettes et de jeux **(b)** *(mystery)* énigme *f*
2 *vt (person)* rendre perplexe

▶**puzzle out** *vt insep (solution, meaning)* trouver; *(action, motive)* essayer de comprendre

▶**puzzle over** *vt insep* essayer de comprendre

puzzled ['pʌzld] *adj* perplexe

puzzling ['pʌzlɪŋ] *adj* bizarre

PVC [pi:vi:'si:] *n (abbr* **polyvinyl chloride)** PVC *m*

pygmy ['pɪgmɪ] *(pl* **pygmies)** *n* pygmée *m*

pyjamas, *Am* **pajamas** [pə'dʒɑ:məz] *npl* pyjama *m*; **a pair of p.** un pyjama

pylon ['paɪlən] *n* pylône *m*

pyramid ['pɪrəmɪd] *n* pyramide *f*

pyre ['paɪə(r)] *n* bûcher *m* (funéraire)

Pyrenean [pɪrə'nɪən] *adj* pyrénéen(enne)

Pyrenees [pɪrə'ni:z] *npl* **the P.** les Pyrénées *fpl*

Pyrex® ['paɪreks] *n* pyrex® *m*; **P. dish** plat *m* en pyrex®

pyromaniac [paɪrəʊ'meɪnɪæk] *n* pyromane *mf*

pyrotechnics [paɪrəʊ'teknɪks] **1** *n (science)* pyrotechnie *f*
2 *npl (fireworks display)* feu *m* d'artifice; *Fig (in speech, writing)* prouesses *fpl*

python ['paɪθən] *n* python *m*

Q

Q, q [kjuː] n (letter) Q, q m inv

Qatar [kæˈtɑː(r)] n le Qatar

Qatari [kæˈtɑːrɪ] **1** n habitant(e) m,f du Qatar
2 adj du Qatar

QC [kjuːˈsiː] n Br Law (abbr **Queen's Counsel**) = membre haut placé du barreau

QED [kjuːiːˈdiː] (abbr **quod erat demonstrandum**) CQFD

qty Com (abbr **quantity**) qté

quack¹ [kwæk] **1** n (of duck) coin-coin m
2 vi (of duck) faire coin-coin

quack² n (doctor) Pej charlatan m; Hum toubib m

quad [kwɒd] n Fam (of school, college) cour f

quadrangle [ˈkwɒdræŋgəl] n (a) (shape) quadrilatère m (b) (of school, college) cour f

quadrant [ˈkwɒdrənt] n quart m de cercle

quadraphonic [kwɒdrəˈfɒnɪk] adj quadriphonique

quadratic equation [kwɒˈdrætɪkˈkweɪʒən] n Math équation f du second degré

quadrilateral [kwɒdrɪˈlætərəl] **1** n quadrilatère m
2 adj quadrilatéral(e)

quadriplegic [kwɒdrɪˈpliːdʒɪk] n & adj tétraplégique mf

quadruped [ˈkwɒdruped] n quadrupède m

quadruple [kwɒˈdruːpəl] **1** adj quadruple
2 vt & vi quadrupler

quadruplet [ˈkwɒdruplet] n quadruplé(e) m,f

quaff [kwɒf] vt Lit boire

quagmire [ˈkwægmaɪə(r)] n also Fig bourbier m

quail¹ [kweɪl] (pl **quail**) n (bird) caille f

quail² vi (of person) avoir un mouvement de recul

quaint [kweɪnt] adj (picturesque) pittoresque; (old-fashioned) vieillot(otte)

quake [kweɪk] **1** n Fam (earthquake) tremblement m de terre
2 vi trembler; **to q. in one's boots** trembler de peur

Quaker [ˈkweɪkə(r)] n Rel quaker(eresse) m,f

qualification [kwɒlɪfɪˈkeɪʃən] n (a) (diploma) diplôme m; (skill) compétence f (b) (completion of studies) **on/after q.** une fois le diplôme obtenu (c) (modification) précision f (d) (for competition) qualification f

qualified [ˈkwɒlɪfaɪd] adj (a) (having diploma) diplômé(e); (competent) compétent(e); **to be q. to do sth** (have diploma) avoir les diplômes requis pour faire qch; (be competent) avoir les compétences requises pour faire qch (b) (modified) mitigé(e); **a q. success** un demi-succès

qualifier [ˈkwɒlɪfaɪə(r)] n (a) (person, team) qualifié(e) m,f; (match) match m de qualification (b) Gram qualificatif m

qualify [ˈkwɒlɪfaɪ] (pt & pp **qualified**) **1** vt (a) (make competent) **to q. sb to do sth** donner les compétences nécessaires à qn pour faire qch (b) (modify) nuancer
2 vi (a) (in competition) se qualifier; **to q. as a doctor/teacher** obtenir son diplôme de médecin/professeur (b) (be eligible) **to q. for sth** avoir droit à qch

qualifying [ˈkwɒlɪfaɪɪŋ] adj (a) (round, match) éliminatoire (b) (exam) d'entrée

qualitative [ˈkwɒlɪtətɪv] adj qualitatif(ive)

quality [ˈkwɒlɪtɪ] (pl **qualities**) n qualité f; **of good/poor q.** de bonne/mauvaise qualité; **q. of life** qualité de la vie; **q. circle** cercle m de qualité; **q. control** contrôle m (de) qualité; **q. goods** marchandises fpl de qualité; Br **q. newspaper** journal m sérieux

qualm [kwɑːm] n doute m; **to have no qualms about doing sth** (doubts) ne pas hésiter une seconde avant de faire qch; (scruples) n'avoir aucun scrupule à faire qch

quandary [ˈkwɒndərɪ] (pl **quandaries**) n dilemme m; **to be in a q. (about sth)** être face à un dilemme (à propos de qch)

quango [ˈkwæŋgəʊ] (pl **quangoes**) n Br Pol (abbr **quasi-autonomous non-governmental organization**) = organisme créé par le gouvernement et doté de pouvoirs quasi autonomes

quantifier [ˈkwɒntɪfaɪə(r)] n Math quantificateur m

quantify [ˈkwɒntɪfaɪ] (pt & pp **quantified**) vt évaluer

quantitative [ˈkwɒntɪtətɪv] adj quantitatif(ive)

quantity [ˈkwɒntɪtɪ] (pl **quantities**) n quantité f; **q. surveyor** métreur vérificateur m

quantum [ˈkwɒntəm] n Phys quantum m; Fig **q. leap** bond m en avant; **q. mechanics** mécanique f quantique; **q. theory** théorie f des quanta

quarantine [ˈkwɒrəntiːn] **1** n quarantaine f; **to be in q.** être en quarantaine
2 vt mettre en quarantaine

quark [kwɑːk] n Phys quark m

quarrel [ˈkwɒrəl] **1** n (a) (argument) dispute f, querelle f; **to have a q.** se disputer; **to pick a q. with sb** chercher querelle à qn (b) (disagreement) désaccord m; **to have no q. with sth** n'avoir rien à reprocher à qch
2 vi (pt & pp **quarrelled**, Am **quarreled**) (a) (argue) se disputer (with avec) (b) (disagree) **to q. with sth** ne pas être d'accord avec qch

quarrelling, Am **quarreling** [ˈkwɒrəlɪŋ] n disputes fpl

quarrelsome [ˈkwɒrəlsəm] adj querelleur(euse)

quarry¹ [ˈkwɒrɪ] (pl **quarries**) n (prey) & Fig proie f

quarry² **1** (pl **quarries**) n (for stone) carrière f
2 vt (pt & pp **quarried**) (hill) exploiter; (stone) extraire

quart [kwɔːt] n (liquid measurement) Br = 1,136 l; Am = 0,946 l

quarter ['kwɔːtə(r)] **1** n (a) (fraction) quart m; (of orange, moon) quartier m; **a q. of a century** un quart de siècle; **a q. of an hour** un quart d'heure; **a q. (of a pound)** = 113,4 g, un quart de livre; **three quarters** trois quarts; **three and a q.** trois un quart; **three and a q. litres** trois litres un quart; **a q. full** au quart plein(e) (b) (in telling time) Br **a q. to six**, Am **a q. of six** six heures moins le quart; **it's a q. to six** il est moins le quart; Br **a q. past six**, Am **a q. after six** six heures un ou et quart; **it's a q. past** il est le quart (c) (three-month period) trimestre m (d) (area) quartier m (e) (group) milieu m; **help came from an unexpected q.** nous avons reçu une aide inespérée (f) Mil **quarters** (lodgings) quartiers mpl (g) Am (coin) pièce f de 25 cents

2 vt (a) (divide into four) partager en quatre (b) Mil (troops) loger

quarterback ['kwɔːtəbæk] n Am arrière m

quarterdeck ['kwɔːtədek] n (of ship) plage f arrière

quarterfinal [kwɔːtə'faɪnəl] n quart m de finale

quarterly ['kwɔːtəlɪ] **1** n (pl **quarterlies**) publication f trimestrielle

2 adj trimestriel(elle)

3 adv tous les trimestres

quartermaster ['kwɔːtəmɑːstə(r)] n Mil intendant m

quartet [kwɔː'tet] n quatuor m

quarto ['kwɔːtəʊ] n (pl **quartos**) n in-quarto m

quartz [kwɔːts] n quartz m; **q. watch** montre f à quartz

quasar ['kweɪzɑː(r)] n Astron quasar m

quash [kwɒʃ] vt (objection, plan) rejeter; (revolt, feeling) réprimer; Law (sentence) annuler

quaver ['kweɪvə(r)] **1** n (a) Mus croche f (b) (in voice) tremblement m

2 vi (of voice) trembler

quay [kiː] n quai m

quayside [kiːsaɪd] n quai m

queasy ['kwiːzɪ] adj **to feel q.** avoir mal au cœur

Quebec [kwɪ'bek] n le Québec; **Q. City** Québec

queen [kwiːn] n (a) (of country, in cards, chess) reine f; Br **Q.'s Counsel** = membre haut placé du barreau; **the Q.'s English** l'anglais m correct; **the Q. Mother** la reine mère (b) very Fam (homosexual) tante f, folle f, = terme injurieux désignant un homosexuel

queer ['kwɪə(r)] **1** adj (a) (strange) bizarre (b) very Fam (homosexual) homo, pédé

2 n very Fam (male homosexual) homo m, pédé m, = terme injurieux désignant un homosexuel

3 vt Fam **to q. the pitch for sb**, **to q. sb's pitch** bouleverser les plans de qn

quell [kwel] vt (revolt) réprimer; (doubt, worry) dissiper

quench [kwentʃ] vt (thirst) étancher

querulous ['kwerʊləs] adj (person) grincheux(euse); (tone) maussade, plaintif(ive)

query ['kwɪərɪ] **1** n (pl **queries**) question f

2 vt (pt & pp **queried**) mettre en question; **to q. if or whether...** mettre en question le fait que...

quest [kwest] Lit **1** n quête f, poursuite f (for de); **to go or be in q. of sth** être en quête ou à la poursuite de qch

2 vi **to q. after or for sth** être en quête ou à la poursuite de qch

question ['kwestʃən] **1** n (a) (query) question f; **to ask (sb) a q.** poser une question (à qn); **q. mark** point m d'interrogation; Fig **a q. mark hangs over the future of the project** l'avenir du projet reste en suspens; Br Pol **q. time** ≃ session f des questions orales (à l'Assemblée nationale) (b) (doubt) doute m; **to call sth into q.** mettre qch en doute; **beyond q.** indiscutable; **it's open to q. whether...** reste à savoir si...; **without q.** indiscutablement (c) (matter) question f, problème m; **it is a q. of...** il s'agit de...; **there is no q. of our agreeing to that** il n'est pas question que nous acceptions cela; **to be out of the q.** être hors de question; **it's only a q. of time** ce n'est qu'une question de temps; **the matter/person in q.** l'affaire/la personne en question

2 vt (a) (put questions to) interroger (**on** sur) (b) (cast doubt on) mettre en doute

questionable ['kwestʃənəbəl] adj discutable

questioning ['kwestʃənɪŋ] **1** n (interrogation) interrogation f; **to be held for q.** (by police) être interrogé(e)

2 adj (look) interrogateur(trice); (mind) curieux(euse)

questionnaire [kwestʃə'neə(r)] n questionnaire m

queue [kjuː] **1** n queue f, file f (d'attente); **to jump the q.** resquiller

2 vi faire la queue

queue-jump ['kjuːdʒʌmp] vi resquiller

quibble ['kwɪbəl] **1** n petite question f

2 vi chipoter (**about** or **over** à propos de)

quiche [kiːʃ] n quiche f

quick [kwɪk] **1** adj (a) (rapid) rapide; **to have a q. bath/drink** prendre un bain/un verre en vitesse; **to be q.** (hurry) faire vite; **that was q.!** tu as fait vite!; **as q. as a flash** rapide comme l'éclair; **to be q. to do sth** faire qch vite ou rapidement; **to be q. off the mark** (to act) réagir vite; (to understand) avoir l'esprit vif; **to have a q. temper** s'emporter facilement (b) (clever) vif (vive)

2 adv Fam (run, take, think) vite

3 n **to bite one's nails to the q.** se ronger les ongles jusqu'au sang; Fig **to cut sb to the q.** piquer qn au vif

quicken ['kwɪkən] **1** vt (a) (make faster) accélérer; **to q. one's pace** presser le pas (b) (imagination) stimuler; (interest) éveiller, exciter

2 vi (of pace, pulse) s'accélérer

quickfire ['kwɪkfaɪə(r)] adj rapide

quickie ['kwɪkɪ] Fam **1** n **to have a q.** (drink) prendre un verre en vitesse; (sex) faire l'amour en vitesse

2 adj **q. divorce** divorce m rapide

quicklime ['kwɪklaɪm] n chaux f vive

quickly ['kwɪklɪ] adv vite, rapidement

quickness ['kwɪknɪs] n (speed) rapidité f; (of mind) vivacité f

quicksand ['kwɪksænd] n sables mpl mouvants

quicksilver ['kwɪksɪlvə(r)] n Old-fashioned (mercury) vif-argent m

quick-tempered ['kwɪk'tempəd] adj emporté(e)

quick-witted ['kwɪk'wɪtɪd] adj vif (vive)

quid [kwɪd] (pl **quid**) n Br Fam (pound) livre f

quiescent [kwaɪ'esənt] adj Formal passif(ive)

quiet ['kwaɪət] **1** n silence m; Fam **to do sth on the q.** faire qch en cachette

2 adj (a) (not loud) silencieux(euse); (voice) petit(e); (music) doux (douce); **to keep sb q.** faire tenir qn tranquille; **to keep q.** (make no noise) ne pas faire de bruit; (say nothing) se taire; **to keep q. about sth** ne rien dire au sujet de qch; **to keep sth q.** cacher qch; **be q.!** tais-toi!; **as q. as a mouse** (person) silencieux (b) (discreet) discret(ète); **to have a q. laugh at sb/sth** se moquer discrètement de qn/qch **(c)** *(peaceful)* tranquille; **a q. wedding** un mariage célébré dans l'intimité **(d)** *(business, market)* calme

▶**quiet down = quieten down**

quieten ['kwaɪətən] *vt* calmer

▶**quieten down 1** *vt sep* calmer
  2 *vi* se calmer

quietly ['kwaɪətlɪ] *adv* **(a)** *(silently)* tranquillement, silencieusement **(b)** *(discreetly)* discrètement; **to be q. confident** être optimiste sans excès

quietness ['kwaɪətnɪs] *n (of person, place)* tranquillité *f*; *(of manner)* douceur *f*

quiff [kwɪf] *n (of hair)* toupet *m*

quill [kwɪl] *n (feather)* penne *f*; *(pen)* plume *f* d'oie; *(of porcupine)* piquant *m*

quilt [kwɪlt] **1** *n* édredon *m*; *(duvet)* couette *f*
  2 *vt (garment)* matelasser; **quilted jacket** veste *f* matelassée

quince [kwɪns] *n* coing *m*; **q. jelly** gelée *f* de coing

quinine [kwɪ'niːn] *n* quinine *f*

quintessential [kwɪntɪ'senʃəl] *adj Formal* quintessentiel(elle)

quintessentially [kwɪntɪ'senʃəlɪ] *adv Formal* fondamentalement

quintet [kwɪn'tet] *n* quintette *m*

quintuplet [kwɪn'tuplɪt] *n* quintuplé(e) *m,f*

quip [kwɪp] **1** *n* boutade *f*
  2 *vi (pt & pp quipped)* plaisanter

quirk [kwɜːk] *n* **(a)** *(of character)* particularité *f* **(b)** *(of fate, nature)* caprice *m*; **by a q. of fate** par un caprice du destin

quirky ['kwɜːkɪ] *adj* bizarre, insolite

quisling ['kwɪzlɪŋ] *n* collaborateur(trice) *m,f*

quit [kwɪt] **1** *vt (pt & pp quit) (person, place)* quitter; *Comptr (programme)* sortir de; **to q. one's job** démissionner; **to q. doing sth** arrêter de faire qch
  2 *vi (give up)* abandonner; *(resign)* démissionner; *Comptr* sortir
  3 *adj* **to be q. of** être débarrassé(e) de

quite [kwaɪt] *adv* **(a)** *(entirely)* tout à fait; **q. enough** bien assez; **that's q. enough of that!** ça suffit comme ça!; **q. apart from the fact that...** mis à part le fait que...; **q.!** tout à fait!; **that's q. all right** *(it doesn't matter)* ça n'a pas d'importance du tout; *(you're welcome)* mais pas du tout!; **you know q. well what I mean!** vous savez parfaitement ce que je veux dire!; **I q. understand** je comprends parfaitement
  (b) *(fairly)* assez, plutôt; **I q. like him** il me plaît bien; **q. a lot of people** pas mal de monde
  (c) *(for emphasis)* **it was q. a surprise** ça a été une véritable surprise; **it's been q. a day!** quelle journée!; **that film is q. something** ce film, c'est vraiment quelque chose!

quits [kwɪts] *adj* **to be q. (with sb)** être quitte (envers qn); **let's call it q.** restons-en là

quiver¹ ['kwɪvə(r)] *n (for arrows)* carquois *m*

quiver² **1** *n (tremble)* tremblement *m*
  2 *vi (tremble)* trembler **(with de)**; *(of flame)* vaciller

quivering ['kwɪvərɪŋ] *adj* tremblant(e)

quixotic [kwɪk'sɒtɪk] *adj* chimérique

quiz [kwɪz] **1** *n (pl quizzes) (on radio)* jeu *m* radiophonique; *(on TV)* jeu télévisé; *(in magazine)* questionnaire *m*
  2 *vt (pt & pp quizzed)* interroger

quizzical ['kwɪzɪkəl] *adj (look, air)* interrogateur(trice)

quorum ['kwɔːrəm] *n* quorum *m*

quota ['kwəʊtə] *n (share)* quota *m*

quotation [kwəʊ'teɪʃən] *n* **(a)** *(from author)* citation *f*; **q. marks** guillemets *mpl* **(b)** *Com (for work)* devis *m*

quote [kwəʊt] **1** *n Fam* **(a)** *(from author)* citation *f*; **in quotes** *(in quotation marks)* entre guillemets **(b)** *Com (for work)* devis *m*
  2 *vt* **(a)** *(author, passage)* citer; **she was quoted as saying that...** elle aurait dit que... **(b)** *Com (price)* indiquer; *Fin* **quoted company** société *f* cotée en Bourse

quotient ['kwəʊʃənt] *n Math* quotient *m*

R

R, r [ɑː(r)] *n (letter)* R, r *m inv*; *Fam* **the three R's** = la lecture, l'écriture et l'arithmétique, fondements de l'enseignement primaire

R *Am Pol (abbr* **Republican)** républicain(e)

RA [ɑːˈreɪ] *n Br (abbr* **Royal Academy)** = académie royale des beaux-arts

rabbi [ˈræbaɪ] *n* rabbin *m*

rabbit [ˈræbɪt] *n* lapin *m*; **r. hole** terrier *m*; **r. hutch** clapier *m*

▸**rabbit on** *vi Fam* ne pas cesser de parler

rabble [ˈræbəl] *n* foule *f* bruyante; **r. rouser** agitateur(trice) *m,f*

rabid [ˈræbɪd] *adj (animal)* & *Fig (person)* enragé(e); *(prejudice)* profondément enraciné(e)

rabies [ˈreɪbiːz] *n* rage *f*

RAC [ɑːreiˈsiː] *n Aut (abbr* **Royal Automobile Club)** = club automobile britannique offrant notamment des services de dépannage

raccoon [rəˈkuːn] *n* raton *m* laveur

race[1] [reɪs] *n (contest)* course *f*; *Fig* **a r. against time** une course contre la montre; **the races** *(horseraces)* les courses; **a r. meeting** *(for horseraces)* des courses de chevaux
2 *vt (a) (person)* faire la course avec; **I'll r. you home!** on fait la course jusqu'à la maison! **(b)** *(horse)* faire courir
3 *vi (a) (of athlete, horse)* courir **(b)** *(move quickly)* aller à toute vitesse; **to r. in/out** entrer/sortir à toute vitesse; **to r. down the street** dévaler la rue à toute vitesse; **to r. by** *(of time)* passer vite, filer **(c)** *(of engine)* s'emballer; *(of pulse, heart)* battre la chamade

race[2] *n (of people, animals)* race *f*; **the human r.** la race humaine; **r. relations** relations *fpl* interraciales

racecourse [ˈreɪskɔːs] *n* champ *m* de courses

racehorse [ˈreɪshɔːs] *n* cheval *m* de course

racer [ˈreɪsə(r)] *n (person)* coureur(euse) *m,f*; *(bicycle)* vélo *m* de course

racetrack [ˈreɪstræk] *n (for athletes, cars)* piste *f*; *Am (for horses)* champ *m* de courses

racial [ˈreɪʃəl] *adj* racial(e); **r. discrimination** discrimination *f* raciale

racing [ˈreɪsɪŋ] 1 *n* les courses *fpl*
2 *adj* **r. bicycle/car** vélo *m*/voiture *f* de course

racism [ˈreɪsɪzəm] *n* racisme *m*

racist [ˈreɪsɪst] *n* & *adj* raciste *mf*

rack [ræk] 1 *n (a) (for bottles)* casier *m*; *(for plates)* égouttoir *m*; *(for goods in shop)* présentoir *m*; *(for luggage)* porte-bagages *m inv*; *(for drying)* égouttoir *m*; **r. and pinion** crémaillère *f (b) (for torture)* chevalet *m*; *Fig* **to be on the r.** avoir des ennuis **(c)** *(idioms)* **to go to r. and ruin** aller de mal en pis
2 *vt (torment)* tourmenter; **to be racked with guilt** être

rongé(e) par le remords; **to be racked with pain** être tenaillé(e) par la douleur; **to r. one's brains** se creuser la tête

racket[1] [ˈrækɪt] *n (for tennis)* raquette *f*

racket[2] *n Fam (a) (noise)* vacarme *m*, tapage *m*; **to make a r.** faire du vacarme *ou* tapage **(b)** *(criminal activity)* racket *m*

racketeer [rækɪˈtɪə(r)] *n* racketteur *m*

racketeering [rækɪˈtɪərɪŋ] *n* racket *m*

racquet [ˈrækɪt] *n (for tennis)* raquette *f*

racy [ˈreɪsɪ] *adj (risqué)* osé(e); *(lively)* savoureux(euse), piquant(e)

RADA [ˈrɑːdə] *n Br (abbr* **Royal Academy of Dramatic Art)** ≃ le Conservatoire national d'art dramatique

radar [ˈreɪdɑː(r)] *n* radar *m*; **r. operator** radariste *mf*; **r. screen** écran *m* radar

radial [ˈreɪdɪəl] 1 *n (tyre)* pneu *m* radial
2 *adj* radial(e)

radiance [ˈreɪdɪəns] *n* éclat *m*, rayonnement *m*

radiant [ˈreɪdɪənt] *adj (light)* éclatant(e); *(person)* resplendissant(e)

radiate [ˈreɪdɪeɪt] 1 *vt (heat, light)* émettre; *Fig (happiness, health)* être rayonnant(e) de; *Fig (optimism, enthusiasm)* être débordant(e) de
2 *vi* rayonner **(from à partir de)**

radiation [reɪdɪˈeɪʃən] *n* radiation *f*

radiator [ˈreɪdɪeɪtə(r)] *n (heater)* radiateur *m*

radical [ˈrædɪkəl] *n* & *adj* radical(e) *m,f*

radicalism [ˈrædɪkəlɪzəm] *n* radicalisme *m*

radio [ˈreɪdɪəʊ] 1 *n (pl* **radios)** radio *f*; **r. cassette (recorder** *or* **player)** radiocassette *m*; **r. station** station *f* de radio
2 *vt (pt* & *pp* **radioed)** *(information)* communiquer par radio; *(person)* contacter par radio
3 *vi* **to r. for help** demander de l'aide par radio

radioactive [reɪdɪəʊˈæktɪv] *adj* radioactif(ive); **r. waste** déchets *mpl* radioactifs

radioactivity [reɪdɪəʊækˈtɪvɪtɪ] *n* radioactivité *f*

radio-controlled [reɪdɪəʊkənˈtrəʊld] *adj* télécommandé(e)

radiographer [reɪdɪˈɒɡrəfə(r)] *n* radiologue *mf*

radiography [reɪdɪˈɒɡrəfɪ] *n* radiographie *f*

radiologist [reɪdɪˈɒlədʒɪst] *n* radiologue *mf*

radiology [reɪdɪˈɒlədʒɪ] *n* radiologie *f*

radiotherapy [reɪdɪəʊˈθerəpɪ] *n* radiothérapie *f*

radish [ˈrædɪʃ] *n* radis *m*

radium [ˈreɪdɪəm] *n Chem* radium *m*

radius ['reɪdɪəs] (pl **radii** ['reɪdɪaɪ]) n rayon m; **within a r. of** dans un rayon de

radon ['reɪdɒn] n Chem radon m

RAF [ɑ:reɪ'ef] n Mil (abbr **Royal Air Force**) = armée de l'air britannique

raffia ['ræfɪə] n raphia m

raffish ['ræfɪʃ] adj canaille

raffle ['ræfəl] **1** n tombola f; **r. ticket** billet m de tombola
2 vt donner comme lot à une tombola

raft [rɑːft] n radeau m

rafter ['rɑːftə(r)] n chevron m

rag[1] [ræg] n (**a**) (piece of cloth) chiffon m; **rags** (clothes) haillons mpl, guenilles fpl; **hers is a rags to riches story** elle est partie de rien; **r. doll** poupée f de chiffon; **r. trade** la confection (**b**) Fam Pej (newspaper) torchon m

rag[2] **1** n Old-fashioned (prank) farce f, canular m; Univ **r. week** = semaine de divertissements organisés par les étudiants au profit d'œuvres de charité
2 vt (pt & pp **ragged**) Old-fashioned (tease) taquiner

ragamuffin ['rægəmʌfɪn] n polisson(onne) m,f

rag-and-bone man [rægən'bəʊnmæn] n chiffonnier m

ragbag ['rægbæg] n ramassis m

rage [reɪdʒ] **1** n (**a**) (fury) rage f, fureur f; **to be in a r.** être furieux(euse) (**b**) Fam (fashion) **to be all the r.** faire fureur
2 vi (**a**) (of person) être furieux(euse) (**against** or **at** contre) (**b**) (of sea) être démonté(e); (of epidemic, war) faire rage

ragged ['rægɪd] adj (clothes) en haillons, en lambeaux; (edge) irrégulier(ère); (person) en haillons; Fam **to run oneself r.** s'épuiser

raging ['reɪdʒɪŋ] adj (**a**) (person) furieux(euse); **to be in a r. temper** être furieux (**b**) (sea) démonté(e); (fever, headache) violent(e); (thirst) terrible

ragwort ['rægwɔːt] n séneçon m

raid [reɪd] **1** n (on bank) hold-up m inv; (by army) raid m; (by police) descente f
2 vt (of robbers) attaquer; (of army) faire un raid sur; (of police) faire une descente dans; Fig & Hum **to r. the fridge** faire la razzia dans le frigo

raider ['reɪdə(r)] n (criminal) voleur(euse) m,f

rail[1] [reɪl] n (**a**) (of stairway) rampe f; (of balcony) balustrade f (**b**) (train system) chemin m de fer; (track) rail m; **by r.** par le ou en chemin de fer; **to go off the rails** (of person) s'écarter du droit chemin; **r. network** réseau m ferroviaire; **r. strike** grève f des chemins de fer ou des cheminots

rail[2] vi **to r. at** or **against sth** s'insurger contre qch

railcar ['reɪlkɑː(r)] n Am wagon m

railcard ['reɪlkɑːd] n carte f d'abonnement de train; Br **young person's r.** ≃ carte Jeunes

railings ['reɪlɪŋz] npl grille f

railroad ['reɪlrəʊd] **1** n Am (system) chemin m de fer; (track) voie f ferrée
2 vt Fam **to r. sb into doing sth** forcer qn à faire qch

railway ['reɪlweɪ] n Br (system) chemin m de fer; (track) voie f ferrée; **r. carriage** voiture f; **r. line** ligne f de chemin de fer; **r. station** gare f

railwayman ['reɪlweɪmən] n cheminot m

rain [reɪn] **1** n pluie f; **in the r.** sous la pluie; **it looks like r.** on dirait qu'il va pleuvoir; **the rains** la saison des pluies; **come r. or shine** (whatever the weather) qu'il pleuve ou qu'il vente; (whatever the circumstances) quoi qu'il arrive; **r.**

cloud nuage m de pluie; **r. dance** danse f de la pluie
2 vt **to r. gifts on sb** couvrir qn de cadeaux; **to r. blows on sb** rouer qn de coups
3 vi pleuvoir; **it's raining** il pleut; Br Fam **it's raining cats and dogs** il pleut des cordes; Prov **it never rains but it pours** un malheur n'arrive jamais seul

rainbow ['reɪnbəʊ] n arc-en-ciel m; **r. coalition** coalition f des minorités; **r. trout** truite f arc-en-ciel

raincoat ['reɪnkəʊt] n imperméable m

raindrop ['reɪndrɒp] n goutte f de pluie

rainfall ['reɪnfɔːl] n précipitations fpl

rainforest ['reɪnfɒrɪst] n forêt f tropicale humide

rainproof ['reɪnpruːf] adj imperméable

rainstorm ['reɪnstɔːm] n pluie f torrentielle

rainwater ['reɪnwɔːtə(r)] n eau f de pluie

rainy ['reɪnɪ] adj pluvieux(euse); (day) de pluie; Fig **to save sth for a r. day** mettre qch de côté; **the r. season** la saison des pluies

raise [reɪz] **1** vt (**a**) (lift) lever; **to r. one's voice** élever la voix; **to r. one's glass to sb** porter son verre à ses lèvres; Fig **to r. one's hat to sb** tirer son chapeau à qn; Fam Fig **to r. the roof** faire du raffut (**b**) (price, salary) augmenter; (standard) élever; Fig **to r. the stakes** faire monter la mise (**c**) (problem, subject) soulever (**d**) (fears, doubts) faire naître; **to r. a smile/laugh** faire sourire/rire; **to r. sb's hopes** donner trop d'espoir à qn; **to r. the alarm** donner l'alarme; Fam **to r. hell** or **Cain** faire un foin d'enfer (**e**) (money) rassembler; (for charity) collecter (**f**) (children, cattle) élever; (crops) cultiver (**g**) (statue) dresser
2 n Am (pay increase) augmentation f (de salaire)

raisin ['reɪzən] n raisin m sec

rake [reɪk] **1** n (**a**) (garden tool) râteau m; **to be as thin as a r.** être maigre comme un clou (**b**) (dissolute man) libertin m
2 vt (leaves, soil) ratisser; **to r. one's memory** fouiller dans sa mémoire

▶**rake about, rake around** vi (search) fouiller (**for** pour trouver)

▶**rake in** vt sep Fam (money) rapporter; **she's raking it in!** elle s'en met plein les poches!

▶**rake off** vt sep Fam (money) empocher

▶**rake over** vt sep (subject, the past) ressasser

rakish ['reɪkɪʃ] adj (dissolute) libertin(e); (jaunty) désinvolte

rally ['rælɪ] **1** n (pl **rallies**) (**a**) (protest gathering) manifestation f (**b**) (in tennis) échange m (**c**) (car race) rallye m; **r. driver** pilote mf de rallye
2 vt (pt & pp **rallied**) (troops) rallier; **to r. support for sb/sth** gagner des appuis à la cause de qn/qch; **to r. sb's spirits** redonner courage à qn; **rallying cry** cri m de ralliement
3 vi (of prices) se redresser; (of patient) aller mieux; **to r. to sb's defence** se porter au secours de qn

▶**rally round 1** vt insep soutenir
2 vi apporter son soutien

RAM [ræm] n Comptr (abbr **random access memory**) mémoire f vive

ram [ræm] **1** n (**a**) (animal) bélier m (**b**) (implement) (battering) **r.** bélier m
2 vt (pt & pp **rammed**) (**a**) (crash into) percuter; (of ship) aborder (**b**) (force into place) tasser; Fam **to r. one's views down sb's throat** bassiner qn avec ses opinions

Ramadan [ræmə'dɑːn] n Rel le ramadan

ramble ['ræmbəl] 1 *n (walk)* randonnée *f* (pédestre)
2 *vi* (a) *(walk)* faire une randonnée (b) *(digress)* divaguer

▶**ramble on** *vi* divaguer; **to r. on about sth** radoter à propos de qch

rambler ['ræmblə(r)] *n (walker)* randonneur(euse) *m,f*

rambling ['ræmblɪŋ] 1 *n* (a) *(walking)* **to go r.** aller en randonnée (b) **ramblings** *(words)* divagations *fpl*
2 *adj* (a) *(letter, speech)* décousu(e) (b) *(house)* plein(e) de coins et de recoins; r. **rose** rosier *m* grimpant

ramification [ræmɪfɪ'keɪʃən] *n (consequence)* conséquence *f*

ramp [ræmp] *n* rampe *f*; *(to plane)* passerelle *f*; *(on road)* petit dos *m* d'âne

rampage 1 *n* ['ræmpeɪdʒ] **to go on the r.** *(lose control)* se déchaîner; *(cause damage)* tout saccager
2 *vi* [ræm'peɪdʒ] **to r. about** se déchaîner

rampant ['ræmpənt] *adj* endémique

rampart ['ræmpɑːt] *n* rempart *m*

ramrod ['ræmrɒd] *n (for rifle)* écouvillon *m*; *Fig* r. **straight** raide comme un piquet

ramshackle ['ræmʃækəl] *adj (building)* délabré(e); *(economy, organization)* qui s'effondre

ran [ræn] *pt of* **run**

ranch [rɑːntʃ] *n* ranch *m*

rancher ['rɑːntʃə(r)] *n* propriétaire *mf* de ranch

rancid ['rænsɪd] *adj* rance; **to go r.** rancir

rancour ['ræŋkə(r)] *n* rancœur *f*

rand [rænd] *n* rand *m*

random ['rændəm] 1 *n* **at r.** au hasard
2 *adj (choice, sample)* (fait(e)) au hasard; *Comptr* r. **access memory** mémoire *f* vive; r. **sampling** prélèvement *m* d'échantillons au hasard

randy ['rændɪ] *adj Br Fam* excité(e)

rang [ræŋ] *pt of* **ring**[2]

range [reɪndʒ] 1 *n* (a) *(of weapon, telescope)* portée *f*; **within r.** *(of fire)* à portée de tir; *(of hearing)* à portée de la voix; **out of r.** hors de portée (b) *(of prices, colours, products)* gamme *f*; *(of instrument, voice)* registre *m*; *(of knowledge, research)* étendue *f* (c) *(of hills, mountains)* chaîne *f* (d) *(practice area)* **(shooting) r.** champ *m* de tir (e) *(cooker)* fourneau *m*
2 *vt* (a) *(arrange in row)* ranger; **to r. oneself with sb** se ranger du côté de qn; **to r. oneself against sb** s'opposer à qn (b) *(travel)* parcourir
3 *vi* (a) *(extend)* **to r. from... to** aller de... à (b) **to r. over** *(include)* porter sur

rangefinder ['reɪndʒfaɪndə(r)] *n* télémètre *m*

ranger ['reɪndʒə(r)] *n (in forest)* garde *m* forestier; *Am Mil* commando *m*

rangy ['reɪndʒɪ] *adj* élancé(e)

rank[1] [ræŋk] 1 *n* (a) *(status)* grade *m*; *Fig* **to pull r.** abuser de son rang (b) *(row)* rangée *f*; *Mil* **the ranks** les hommes *mpl* du rang; *Fig* **to rise from the ranks** sortir du rang; *Fig* **the ranks of the unemployed** les rangs des chômeurs; *Fig* **to break ranks (with)** se désolidariser (de); *Fig* **to close ranks** se montrer solidaire; **(taxi) r. station** *f* de taxis
2 *vt* placer **(among** parmi); **to r. sb/sth as** considérer qn/qch comme
3 *vi* compter **(among** parmi); **to r. as** être considéré(e) comme; **to r. above/below sb** être supérieur(e)/inférieur(e) à qn; **this ranks as a major disaster** on peut qualifier ceci de catastrophe majeure

rank[2] *adj* (a) *(foul-smelling)* fétide (b) *(absolute)* total(e); **she's a r. outsider** elle n'est vraiment pas dans la course

rank-and-file [ræŋkən'faɪl] *n* **the r.** *(in army)* les hommes *mpl* du rang; *(of political party)* la base

ranking ['ræŋkɪŋ] *n (classification)* classement *m*

rankle ['ræŋkəl] *vi* **it still rankles with me** cela m'est resté sur l'estomac

ransack ['rænsæk] *vt (house, desk)* mettre sens dessus dessous; *(shop, town)* piller

ransom ['rænsəm] 1 *n* rançon *f*; **to hold sb to r.** rançonner qn; *Fig* retenir qn en otage
2 *vt* rançonner

rant [rænt] *vi Fam* déblatérer **(about/at** au sujet de/contre); **to r. and rave** tempêter **(about/at** au sujet de/contre)

rap [ræp] 1 *n* (a) *(sharp blow)* coup *m* sec; *Fig* **to take the r. for sth** écoper *ou* trinquer pour qch (b) *(music)* rap *m*
2 *vt (pt & pp* **rapped)** *(window, door)* frapper à; *(table)* frapper sur; *Fig* **to r. sb's knuckles, to r. sb over the knuckles** taper sur les doigts de qn
3 *vi* (a) *(hit)* frapper **(on** à) (b) *(sing)* rapper

rapacious [rə'peɪʃəs] *adj* rapace

rape[1] [reɪp] 1 *n* (a) *(crime)* viol *m*; *Fig (of countryside, environment)* destruction *f*
2 *vt* violer

rape[2] *n (crop)* colza *m*

rapid ['ræpɪd] *adj* rapide; r. **reaction force** force *f* d'intervention rapide

rapidity [rə'pɪdɪt] *n* rapidité *f*

rapidly ['ræpɪdlɪ] *adv* rapidement

rapids ['ræpɪdz] *npl (in river)* rapides *mpl*

rapier ['reɪpɪə(r)] *n* rapière *f*

rapist ['reɪpɪst] *n* violeur *m*

rapper ['ræpə(r)] *n (singer)* rappeur(euse) *m,f*

rapport [ræ'pɔː(r)] *n* **to have a good r. (with sb)** avoir de bons rapports (avec qn)

rapt [ræpt] *adj (attention)* profond(e); *(look)* absorbé(e); *(smile)* d'extase

rapture ['ræptʃə(r)] *n* extase *f*; **to be in raptures** être ravi(e); **to go into raptures over sb/sth** s'extasier devant qn/sur qch

rapturous ['ræptʃərəs] *adj (cries)* d'extase; *(applause)* frénétique; *(reception, welcome)* enthousiaste

rare [reə(r)] *adj* (a) *(animal, stamp)* rare; **to have a r. gift (for sth)** être exceptionnellement doué(e) (pour qch) (b) *(steak)* saignant(e)

rarefied ['reərɪfaɪd] *adj (air, gas)* raréfié(e); *Fig (atmosphere, ideas)* fermé(e)

rarely ['reəlɪ] *adv* rarement

raring ['reərɪŋ] *adj* **to be r. to do sth** être impatient(e) de faire qch; **to be r. to go** piaffer d'impatience

rarity ['reərɪtɪ] *(pl* **rarities)** *n* rareté *f*; **to be/become a r.** être/devenir rare; r. **value** rareté *f*

rascal ['rɑːskəl] *n (child)* coquin(e) *m,f*; *Old-fashioned or Hum (scoundrel)* vaurien(enne) *m,f*

rash[1] [ræʃ] *n* (a) *(on skin) (spots)* éruption *f*; *(red area)* rougeurs *fpl* (b) *(series)* série *f*

rash[2] *adj (imprudent)* irréfléchi(e)

rasher ['ræʃə(r)] *n Br (of bacon)* tranche *f*

rashly ['ræʃlɪ] *adv* sans réfléchir

rasp [rɑːsp] **1** n (a) *(tool)* râpe f (b) *(sound)* grincement m
2 vt *(say hoarsely)* grogner

raspberry ['rɑːzbərɪ] *(pl* **raspberries)** n *(fruit)* framboise f; *(plant)* framboisier m; *Fam Fig* **to blow a r.** souffler en signe de dérision; **r. jam** confiture f de framboises

rat [ræt] **1** n (a) *(animal)* rat m; **r. poison** mort-aux-rats f inv; **r. trap** piège m à rats, ratière f (b) *Fam (scoundrel)* dégueulasse mf (c) *(idioms)* **to smell a r.** flairer quelque chose de louche; **r. race** foire f d'empoigne
2 vi *(pt & pp* **ratted)** *Fam (inform)* **to r. on sb** dénoncer qn

ratchet ['rætʃɪt] n rochet m; **r. (wheel)** roue f à rochet

rate [reɪt] **1** n (a) *(of inflation, interest)* taux m; *Fin* **r. of return** taux de rendement (b) *(speed)* rythme m; **at this r.** à ce rythme (c) **at any r.** en tout cas (d) *(price, charge)* tarif m (e) *Br Formerly* **rates** *(local tax)* impôts mpl locaux
2 vt (a) *(classify)* placer *(among* parmi); **to r. sb/sth as** considérer qn/qch comme; **to r. sb/sth highly** tenir qn/qch en haute estime (b) *(deserve)* mériter; **to r. a mention** mériter d'être mentionné(e)
3 vi **to r. as** être considéré(e) comme

rateable value ['reɪtəbəl'væljuː] n *Br Formerly* valeur f locative nette

ratepayer ['reɪtpeɪə(r)] n *Br Formerly* contribuable mf *(pour les impôts locaux)*

rather ['rɑːðə(r)] adv (a) *(preferably)* **I'd r. stay** j'aimerais mieux rester; **I'd r. not go** j'aimerais mieux ne pas y aller; **I'd r. not** je n'y tiens pas; **r. you than me!** je n'aimerais pas être à ta place (b) *(more exactly)* plutôt; **he sounded surprised or, r., annoyed** il semblait surpris, ou plutôt, fâché (c) *(fairly)* assez; **I r. liked it** j'ai bien aimé (d) **r. than him** plutôt que lui; **r. than staying** plutôt que de rester

ratification [rætɪfɪkeɪʃən] n ratification f

ratify ['rætɪfaɪ] *(pt & pp* **ratified)** vt ratifier

rating ['reɪtɪŋ] n *(of popularity)* classement m; **the ratings** *(for TV, radio)* l'indice m d'écoute, l'audimat® m

ratio ['reɪʃɪəʊ] *(pl* **ratios)** n rapport m

ration ['ræʃən, Am 'reɪʃən] **1** n (a) ration f; *Fig (dose)* dose f; **rations** *(supplies)* provisions fpl; **r. book** carte f de rationnement
2 vt rationner

rational ['ræʃənəl] adj *(sensible)* raisonnable, sensé(e); *(sane)* rationnel(elle)

rationalism ['ræʃənəlɪzəm] n rationalisme m

rationalist ['ræʃənəlɪst] n rationaliste mf

rationalization [ræʃənəlaɪ'zeɪʃən] n *(of company)* rationalisation f

rationalize ['ræʃənəlaɪz] vt (a) *(action, dislike)* justifier (b) *(company)* rationaliser

rationally ['ræʃənəlɪ] adv *(sensibly)* raisonnablement; *(sanely)* rationnellement

rationing ['ræʃənɪŋ] n rationnement m

rattle ['rætəl] **1** n (a) *(for baby)* hochet m (b) *(noise)* (of train, chains, keys) cliquetis m; (of gunfire) crépitement m; (of door, window) frottement m
2 vt (a) *(chains, keys)* faire cliqueter; *(door, window)* faire vibrer (b) *Fam (make nervous)* démonter
3 vi *(of chains, keys)* cliqueter; *(of door, window)* vibrer
▸**rattle off** vt sep *Fam (list, facts)* débiter
▸**rattle on** vi *Fam* parler sans cesse
▸**rattle through** vt insep *Fam (work, book)* expédier

rattlesnake ['rætəlsneɪk] n serpent m à sonnette

ratty ['rætɪ] adj *Br Fam (annoyed)* irrité(e); *(irritable)* irritable

raucous ['rɔːkəs] adj *(hoarse)* rauque; *(rowdy)* bruyant(e)

raunchy ['rɔːntʃɪ] adj *Fam (film, scene, lyrics)* osé(e); *(dress)* provocant(e)

ravage [rævɪdʒ] **1** npl **ravages** ravages mpl
2 vt ravager

rave [reɪv] **1** n rave f
2 adj *(review)* dithyrambique
3 vi *(deliriously)* délirer; **to r. about sb/sth** *(enthusiastically)* être dithyrambique à propos de qn/qch

raven ['reɪvən] **1** n *(bird)* grand corbeau m
2 adj *(colour)* noir de jais inv

ravenous ['rævənəs] adj *(animal)* vorace; *(person)* affamé(e)

raver ['reɪvə(r)] n *Br Fam (socially active person)* noceur(euse) m,f; *(who goes to raves)* ravet mf

rave-up ['reɪvʌp] n *Br Fam* fiesta f, nouba f

ravine [rə'viːn] n ravin m

raving ['reɪvɪŋ] adj (a) *(delirious)* **r. mad** complètement fou (folle); **a r. lunatic** un fou furieux (une folle furieuse) (b) *(success)* éclatant(e)

ravish ['rævɪʃ] vt (a) *Lit (delight)* enchanter, ravir (b) *Old-fashioned (rape)* violenter

ravishing ['rævɪʃɪŋ] adj magnifique

raw [rɔː] adj (a) *(food)* cru(e); *(silk, sugar, statistics)* brut(e); **r. materials** matières fpl premières; **r. recruit** bleu m (b) *(skin)* écorché(e); *Fig* **to get a r. deal** être mal traité(e); *Fig* **to touch a r. nerve** toucher un point sensible (c) *(weather, wind)* glacial(e)

ray¹ [reɪ] n *(of light, sun)* rayon m; *Fig (of hope)* lueur f

ray² n *(fish)* raie f

rayon ['reɪɒn] n *(fabric)* rayonne f

raze [reɪz] vt **to r. sth to the ground** raser qch

razor ['reɪzə(r)] n rasoir m; **r. blade** lame f de rasoir

razor-sharp ['reɪzəʃɑːp] adj *(knife)* effilé(e); *Fig (intelligence, wit)* vif (vive)

razor-shell ['reɪzəʃel] n couteau m

razzmatazz ['ræzmətæz] n *Fam* tape-à-l'œil m inv

RC [ɑː'siː] n & adj *(abbr* **Roman Catholic)** catholique mf

R & D [ɑːrən'diː] n *Com (abbr* **research and development)** recherche et développement

Rd *(abbr* **Road)** rue

RDA [ɑːdiː'eɪ] n *(abbr* **recommended daily allowance)** recommandation f quotidienne officielle *(en vitamines, sels minéraux etc)*

RE [ɑː'iː] n *(abbr* **Religious Education)** instruction f religieuse

re¹ [riː] prep concernant; **re your letter** suite à votre lettre; **re: 1997 sales figures** Réf: les ventes de 1997

re² [reɪ] n *Mus* ré m

reach [riːtʃ] **1** n (a) *(accessibility)* portée f; **within r.** *(thing)* à portée de main; *(location)* tout(e) proche; **out of r.** hors de portée (b) *(of river)* **the upper reaches** l'amont m
2 vt (a) *(destination, conclusion)* atteindre, arriver à; *(agreement)* aboutir à; *(decision)* prendre; **the news didn't r. her** les nouvelles ne lui sont pas parvenues (b) *(contact)* joindre; **to r. a wider audience** toucher un public plus important (c) *(stretch as far as)* (one's shoulder, waist) atteindre, arriver jusqu'à
3 vi *(extend)* (of forest, property) s'étendre *(to* jusqu'à); *(of*

noise, voice) porter (**to** jusqu'à); **to r. for sth** tendre le bras pour prendre qch; *Fig* **to r. for the sky** *or* **the stars** viser très haut

▶**reach out** *vi* tendre le bras

reachable ['ri:tʃəbəl] *adj* accessible

react [rɪ'ækt] *vi* réagir (**against/to** contre/à)

reaction [rɪ'ækʃən] *n* réaction *f*

reactionary [rɪ'ækʃənərɪ] (*pl* **reactionaries**) *n & adj* réactionnaire *mf*

reactivate [rɪ'æktɪveɪt] *vt* réactiver

reactor [rɪ'æktə(r)] *n* réacteur *m*

read [ri:d] **1** *vt* **to have a r.** lire; **to be a good r.** être agréable à lire

2 *vt* (*pt & pp* **read** [red]) (**a**) (*book, newspaper, letter*) lire; **do you r. me?** (*on radio*) est-ce que vous me recevez?; *Fig* **to take it as read that…** considérer comme acquis que… (**b**) (*interpret*) interpréter; **to r. sb's mind** lire dans les pensées de qn; **to r. the future** prédire l'avenir (**c**) *Br Univ* (*study*) étudier (**d**) (*of dial, thermometer*) indiquer; (*of inscription*) être; **the sign read…** sur l'écriteau, on pouvait lire…

3 *vi* (**a**) (*of person*) lire; **to r. aloud** lire à haute voix; *Fig* **to r. between the lines** lire entre les lignes (**b**) (*of text*) **to r. well/badly** se lire facilement/difficilement

▶**read out** *vt sep* lire (à haute voix)

▶**read up on** *vt sep* étudier

readable ['ri:dəbəl] *adj* (*book*) facile à lire; (*handwriting*) lisible

reader ['ri:də(r)] *n* (**a**) (*person*) lecteur(trice) *m,f* (**b**) (*reading book*) livre *m* de lecture (**c**) (*device*) lecteur *m*

readily ['redɪlɪ] *adv* (*willingly*) volontiers; (*easily*) facilement

reading ['ri:dɪŋ] *n* (**a**) (*action, interpretation, pastime*) lecture *f*; **r. glasses** lunettes *fpl* de lecture (**b**) (*measurement*) relevé *m*

readjust [ri:ə'dʒʌst] **1** *vt* (*figures, salaries*) réajuster; (*instrument*) remettre au point; (*clothing*) rajuster

2 *vi* se réadapter (**to** à)

readjustment [ri:ə'dʒʌstmənt] *n* (*of figures, salaries*) réajustement *m*; (*of person*) réadaptation *f*

readmit [ri:əd'mɪt] (*pt & pp* **readmitted**) *vt* (*to club, party*) réintégrer (**to** à); **to r. sb** (*to hospital*) réhospitaliser qn

read-only memory ['ri:d'əʊnlɪ'memərɪ] *n Comptr* mémoire *f* morte

readvertise [ri:'ædvətaɪz] *vt* repasser une annonce pour

ready ['redɪ] **1** *adj* (**a**) (*prepared*) prêt(e) (**for** pour); **to be r. to do sth** être prêt à faire qch; **to get r.** se préparer; **to get sth r.** préparer qch; **to be r. for bed** être prêt à se coucher; **r.!, steady!, go!** à vos marques, prêts, partez!; **r. cash** argent *m* liquide (**b**) (*willing*) **to be r. to do sth** être prêt(e) *ou* disposé(e) à faire qch (**c**) (*quick*) **to have a r. wit** avoir l'esprit vif

2 *vt* (*pt & pp* **readied**) (*prepare*) préparer

3 *n* (**a**) **at the r.** prêt(e) (**b**) *Fam* **readies** (*cash*) ronds *mpl*

ready-made [redɪ'meɪd] *adj* (*food*) tout(e) préparé(e); (*excuse, phrase*) tout(e) fait(e)

reaffirm [ri:ə'fɜ:m] *vt* réaffirmer

reafforestation [ri:əfɒrɪ'steɪʃən] *n* reboisement *m*

real [rɪəl] **1** *adj* (**a**) (*authentic*) vrai(e); (*gold, leather*) véritable; (*danger, fear, effort*) réel(elle); **r. ale** = bière brune de fabrication traditionnelle (**b**) (*actual*) réel(elle); **the r. world** la réalité; **what does that mean in r. terms?**

qu'est-ce que cela signifie en clair?; *Com* **r. estate** (*property*) biens *mpl* immobiliers; (*profession*) l'immobilier *m* (**c**) (*for emphasis*) **a r. idiot** un véritable idiot

2 *adv Am Fam* (*very*) très

realism ['rɪəlɪzəm] *n* réalisme *m*

realist ['rɪəlɪst] *n* réaliste *mf*

realistic [rɪə'lɪstɪk] *adj* réaliste

reality [rɪ'ælɪtɪ] (*pl* **realities**) *n* réalité *f*; **in r.** en réalité

realize ['rɪəlaɪz] *vt* (**a**) (*become aware of*) se rendre compte de; **I r. he's busy, but…** j'ai bien conscience qu'il est occupé mais… (**b**) (*ambition, dream*) réaliser

really ['rɪəlɪ] *adv* vraiment; (*in actual fact*) en réalité

realm [relm] *n* (**a**) (*kingdom*) royaume *m* (**b**) (*field*) domaine *m*

realtor ['rɪəltə(r)] *n Am* agent *m* immobilier

ream [ri:m] *n* (*of paper*) rame *f*; *Fig* **reams of** des quantités de

reanimate [ri:'ænɪmeɪt] *vt* r(é)animer

reap [ri:p] *vt* moissonner; **to r. the benefits (of)** récolter les bénéfices (de)

reaper ['ri:pə(r)] *n* (*machine*) moissonneuse *f*

reappear [ri:ə'pɪə(r)] *vi* réapparaître

reappearance [ri:ə'pɪərəns] *n* réapparition *f*

reapply [ri:ə'plaɪ] (*pt & pp* **reapplied**) *vi* (*for job*) poser à nouveau sa candidature (**for** à)

reappraise [ri:ə'preɪz] *vt* réévaluer; (*policy*) réexaminer

rear[1] [rɪə(r)] *n* (**a**) (*back part*) arrière *m*; **at the r. of** (*inside*) à l'arrière de; (*behind*) derrière *m*; **in the r.** à l'arrière; **to bring up the r.** être en queue; **r. admiral** contre-amiral *m*; **r. entrance** entrée *f* de derrière; **r. legs** pattes *fpl* de derrière; **r. lights** feux *mpl* arrière; **r. window** vitre *f* arrière (**b**) *Fam* (*buttocks*) derrière *m*

rear[2] *vt* (**a**) (*child, livestock*) élever (**b**) (*one's head*) relever; *Fig* **to r. its ugly head** faire son apparition

▶**rear up** *vi* (*of horse*) se cabrer

rearguard ['rɪəgɑ:d] *n Mil* arrière-garde *f*; *also Fig* **r. action** combat *m* d'arrière-garde

rearm [ri:'ɑ:m] *vt & vi* réarmer

rearmament [ri:'ɑ:məmənt] *n* réarmement *m*

rearrange [ri:ə'reɪndʒ] *vt* (*books, furniture*) changer la disposition de; (*appointment*) changer

reason ['ri:zən] **1** *n* (**a**) (*cause, motive*) raison *f* (**for** de); **for no particular r.** sans raison précise; **I don't know the r. why** je ne sais pas pourquoi; *Ironic* **for reasons best known to himself** pour une raison connue de lui seul; **give me one good r. why I should!** donne-moi une raison valable de le faire! (**b**) (*sanity, common sense*) raison *f*; **to listen to** *or* **see r.** entendre raison; **it stands to r.** il va de soi *ou* sans dire; **within r.** dans des limites raisonnables

2 *vt* **to r. that** estimer que

3 *vi* raisonner (**about/with** sur/avec)

reasonable ['ri:zənəbəl] *adj* (**a**) (*fair*) raisonnable; (*excuse*) valable (**b**) (*quite good*) passable

reasonably ['ri:zənəblɪ] *adv* (**a**) (*behave, act*) raisonnablement (**b**) (*quite*) plutôt

reasoning ['ri:zənɪŋ] *n* (*thinking*) raisonnement *m*

reassemble [ri:ə'sembəl] **1** *vt* (*people*) rassembler; (*machine*) remonter

2 *vi* (*of people*) se rassembler

reassess [ri:ə'ses] *vt* (**a**) (*policy, situation*) reconsidérer (**b**) *Fin* (*tax, property*) réévaluer

reassurance [riːəˈʃʊərəns] n (comfort) réconfort m; (guarantee) assurance f

reassure [riːəˈʃʊə(r)] vt rassurer

reassuring [riːəˈʃʊərɪŋ] adj rassurant(e)

reawaken [riːəˈweɪkən] 1 vt (interest, feeling) faire renaître 2 vi (of person) se réveiller à nouveau

rebate ['riːbeɪt] n (refund) remboursement m; (discount) rabais m

rebel 1 n ['rebəl] rebelle mf
2 vi [rɪˈbel] (pt & pp rebelled) se rebeller (against contre)

rebellion [rɪˈbeljən] n rébellion f

rebellious [rɪˈbeljəs] adj rebelle

rebirth [riːˈbɜːθ] n renaissance f

reborn [riːˈbɔːn] adj to be r. renaître

rebound 1 n ['riːbaʊnd] (of ball) rebond m; Fig she married him on the r. elle l'a épousé à la suite d'une déception sentimentale
2 vi [rɪˈbaʊnd] (of ball) rebondir; Fig (of joke, lie) se retourner (on contre)

rebuff [rɪˈbʌf] 1 n (of person) rebuffade f; (of suggestion) refus m; to meet with a r. (of person) essuyer une rebuffade; (of suggestion) être repoussé(e)
2 vt repousser

rebuild [riːˈbɪld] (pt & pp rebuilt [riːˈbɪlt]) vt reconstruire

rebuke [rɪˈbjuːk] 1 n réprimande f
2 vt réprimander

rebut [rɪˈbʌt] (pt & pp rebutted) vt réfuter

rebuttal [rɪˈbʌtəl] n réfutation f

recalcitrant [rɪˈkælsɪtrənt] adj récalcitrant(e)

recall 1 n [rɪˈkɔːl] (memory) mémoire f; lost beyond r. irrévocablement perdu(e)
2 vt [rɪˈkɔːl] (a) (remember) se souvenir de, se rappeler; to r. doing sth se souvenir d'avoir fait qch, se rappeler avoir fait qch (b) (defective goods) rappeler; (library book) demander le retour de; Br Pol to r. Parliament rappeler le Parlement en session extraordinaire

recant [rɪˈkænt] 1 vt (opinion) rétracter
2 vi se rétracter

recap ['riːkæp] 1 n (summary) récapitulation f
2 vti (pt & pp recapped) récapituler

recapitulate [riːkəˈpɪtjʊleɪt] vt & vi récapituler

recapture [riːˈkæptʃə(r)] 1 n (of criminal) capture f; (of town, territory) reprise f
2 vt (a) (criminal) capturer; (town, territory) reprendre (b) Fig (memory, atmosphere) faire revivre; (one's youth) retrouver

recede [rɪˈsiːd] vi (of tide) se retirer; (of coastline) reculer; to have a receding chin avoir le menton fuyant; to have a receding hairline avoir le front qui se dégarnit

receipt [rɪˈsiːt] n (a) (act of receiving) réception f; to be in r. of sth avoir reçu qch (b) (proof of payment) reçu m; receipts (at box office) recette f, entrées fpl

receive [rɪˈsiːv] vt recevoir; (stolen goods) receler; to be well/badly received (of film, proposal) être bien/mal reçu(e); to r. sb into the Church admettre qn au sein de l'Église

received [rɪˈsiːvd] adj (idea) reçu(e); (opinion) admis(e); r. pronunciation la prononciation standard de l'anglais (celle du sud-est de l'Angleterre)

receiver [rɪˈsiːvə(r)] n (a) (of stolen goods) receleur(euse) m/f; (of telephone, radio set) récepteur m; to pick up the r. décrocher; to replace the r. raccrocher (c) Fin administrateur m judiciaire

receivership [rɪˈsiːvəʃɪp] n Fin to go into r. être placé(e) sous règlement judiciaire

receiving [rɪˈsiːvɪŋ] 1 n (of stolen goods) recel m
2 adj Fam to be on the r. end (of sth) faire les frais (de qch)

recent ['riːsənt] adj récent(e); (acquaintance) nouveau(elle); (development) dernier(ère); in r. months au cours des derniers mois; in r. times récemment

recently ['riːsəntlɪ] adv récemment; as r. as yesterday pas plus tard qu'hier; until quite r. jusqu'à ces derniers temps

receptacle [rɪˈseptəkəl] n récipient m

reception [rɪˈsepʃən] n (a) (of guests, announcement, book) accueil m; to get a warm r. être accueilli(e) chaleureusement; r. centre (for refugees) centre m d'accueil (b) (party) réception f; (wedding) r. réception (c) (in hotel) r. (desk) réception f (d) (of radio, TV programme) réception f

receptionist [rɪˈsepʃənɪst] n réceptionniste mf

receptive [rɪˈseptɪv] adj réceptif(ive)

recess [rɪˈses] n (a) (of law courts, Parliament) vacances fpl (b) (in wall) renfoncement m; (smaller) niche f; (of mind, past) recoins mpl (c) Am Sch (between classes) récréation f

recession [rɪˈseʃən] n récession f

recharge [riːˈtʃɑːdʒ] vt (battery) recharger; Fig to r. one's batteries recharger ses batteries

rechargeable [riːˈtʃɑːdʒəbəl] adj rechargeable

recidivism [rɪˈsɪdɪvɪzəm] n Law récidivisme m

recipe ['resɪpɪ] n also Fig recette f; a r. for success le secret de la réussite; to be a r. for disaster mener à la catastrophe; r. book livre m de recettes

recipient [rɪˈsɪpɪənt] n (of gift, letter) destinataire mf; (of cheque, money) bénéficiaire mf; (of award, honour) lauréat(e) m,f

reciprocal [rɪˈsɪprəkəl] adj réciproque

reciprocate [rɪˈsɪprəkeɪt] vt 1 retourner
2 vi rendre la pareille

recital [rɪˈsaɪtəl] n (of poetry, music) récital m

recitation [resɪˈteɪʃən] n (of poem) récitation f

recite [rɪˈsaɪt] 1 vt (poem) réciter; (complaints, details) énumérer
2 vi réciter

reckless ['reklɪs] adj imprudent(e); r. driver chauffard m

reckon ['rekən] 1 vt (a) (consider) considérer; she is reckoned to be... on la considère comme... (b) (calculate) calculer (c) Fam (think) penser
2 vi compter, calculer

▶**reckon on** vt insep compter sur

▶**reckon up** vt sep calculer

▶**reckon with** vt insep compter avec

reckoning ['rekənɪŋ] n estimation f; by my r. d'après mes calculs; day of r. moment m de vérité

reclaim [rɪˈkleɪm] vt (lost property, waste materials) récupérer; (expenses) se faire rembourser; to r. land from the sea/the desert gagner du terrain sur la mer/le désert

reclamation [rekləˈmeɪʃən] n (of waste materials) récupération f

recline [rɪˈklaɪn] vi s'allonger

reclining [rɪˈklaɪnɪŋ] adj in a r. position (person) en position allongée; r. seat siège m à dossier inclinable

recluse [rɪ'kluːs] *n* reclus(e) *m,f*

recognition [rekəg'nɪʃən] *n* reconnaissance *f*; **to have changed beyond** *or* **out of all r.** être devenu(e) méconnaissable; **in r.** en reconnaissance de

recognizable [rekəg'naɪzəbəl] *adj* reconnaissable

recognize ['rekəgnaɪz] *vt* reconnaître

recognized ['rekəgnaɪzd] *adj* reconnu(e); **to be a r. authority (on sth)** faire autorité (en matière de qch)

recoil 1 [rɪ'kɔɪl] (*of gun*) recul *m*
2 *vi* [rɪ'kɔɪl] (*of gun*) reculer; (*of person*) avoir un mouvement de recul

recollect [rekə'lekt] *vt* se souvenir de

recollection [rekə'lekʃən] *n* souvenir *m*; **to the best of my r.** autant que je m'en souvienne

recommend [rekə'mend] *vt* (a) (*praise*) recommander; **to r. sth to sb** recommander qch à qn; **the proposal has a lot to r. it** cette proposition présente de nombreux avantages (b) (*advise*) recommander, conseiller; **to r. sb to do sth** conseiller à qn de faire qch; *Com* **recommended retail price** prix *m* conseillé

recommendation [rekəmen'deɪʃən] *n* recommandation *f*

recompense ['rekəmpens] **1** *n* dédommagement *m*; **in r. for** en dédommagement de
2 *vt* dédommager

reconcile ['rekənsaɪl] *vt* (a) (*person*) réconcilier; **to be reconciled with sb** s'être réconcilié(e) avec qn; **to be reconciled to sth** se résigner à qch (b) (*facts, differences, opinions*) concilier

reconciliation [rekənsɪlɪ'eɪʃən] *n* réconciliation *f*

reconditioned [riːkən'dɪʃənd] *adj* (*TV, washing machine*) remis(e) à neuf

reconnaissance [rɪ'kɒnɪsəns] *n Mil* reconnaissance *f*; **r. flight/mission** vol *m*/mission *f* de reconnaissance

reconquer [riː'kɒŋkə(r)] *vt* reconquérir

reconquest [riː'kɒŋkwest] *n* reconquête *f*

reconsider [riːkən'sɪdə(r)] **1** *vt* réexaminer
2 *vi* réfléchir

reconstitute [riː'kɒnstɪtjuːt] *vt* reconstituer

reconstruct [riːkən'strʌkt] *vt* reconstruire; (*crime, event*) reconstituer

reconstruction [riːkən'strʌkʃən] *n* reconstruction *f*; (*of crime, event*) reconstitution *f*

record 1 *n* ['rekɔːd] (a) (*account*) rapport *m*; (*file*) dossier *m*; **we have no r. of this** nous n'en avons aucune trace; **to keep a r. of sth** garder une trace écrite de qch; **the coldest winter on r.** l'hiver le plus froid qu'on ait jamais enregistré; **she's on r. as saying that...** elle a déclaré officiellement que...; (**just) for the r.** au passage; **to put** *or* **set the r. straight** mettre les choses au point; **r. office** archives *fpl*
(b) (*personal history*) passé *m*; (*achievements*) résultats *mpl*; (*of criminal*) casier *m* judiciaire; **to have a good/bad safety r.** avoir bonne/mauvaise réputation en matière de sécurité
(c) (*musical*) disque *m*; **r. company** maison *f* de disques; **r. player** tourne-disques *m inv*
(d) (*best performance*) record *m*
(e) *Comptr* enregistrement *m*
2 *adj* record *inv*; **in r. time** en un temps record; **unemployment is at a r. high/low** le chômage a atteint son taux le plus haut/bas
3 *vt* [rɪ'kɔːd] (a) (*on video, cassette*) enregistrer

(b) (*write down*) noter; **to send sth recorded delivery** envoyer qch en recommandé

record-breaking ['rekɔːdbreɪkɪŋ] *adj* record *inv*

recorder [rɪ'kɔːdə(r)] *n* (*musical instrument*) flûte *f* à bec

record-holder ['rekɔːdhəʊldə(r)] *n* détenteur(trice) *m,f* du record

recording [rɪ'kɔːdɪŋ] *n* (*on tape*) enregistrement *m*; **r. studio** studio *m* d'enregistrement

recount [rɪ'kaʊnt] *vt* (*relate*) raconter

re-count ['riːkaʊnt] *n* (*in election*) deuxième décompte *m*

recoup [rɪ'kuːp] *vt* récupérer

recourse [rɪ'kɔːs] *n* recours *m*; **to have r. to** avoir recours à

recover [rɪ'kʌvə(r)] **1** *vt* (*territory, customers*) & *Comptr* récupérer; (*one's appetite, balance*) retrouver
2 *vi* (*from illness, setback*) se remettre; (*after running, travelling*) récupérer; *Fig* (*of economy*) se redresser; (*of sales*) reprendre

recoverable [rɪ'kʌvərəbəl] *adj* (*money*) recouvrable

recovery [rɪ'kʌvərɪ] *n* (*pl* **recoveries**) *n* (a) (*of lost or stolen item*) récupération *f*; **r. vehicle** dépanneuse *f* (b) (*from illness*) rétablissement *m*; *Fig* (*of economy*) redressement *m*; (*of sales*) reprise *f*; **to make a r.** se rétablir

re-create [riːkrɪ'eɪt] *vt* recréer

recreation [rekrɪ'eɪʃən] *n* (*leisure*) divertissement *m*; *Sch* (*break*) récréation *f*; **r. ground** terrain *m* de jeux; **r. room** salle *f* de jeux

recreational [rekrɪ'eɪʃənəl] *adj* de loisirs; **r. drug** = drogue prise occasionnellement, dans un but récréatif

recrimination [rɪkrɪmɪ'neɪʃən] *n* récrimination *f*

recruit [rɪ'kruːt] *also Mil* **1** *n* recrue *f*
2 *vt* recruter

recruitment [rɪ'kruːtmənt] *n also Mil* recrutement *m*

rectangle ['rektæŋgəl] *n* rectangle *m*

rectangular [rek'tæŋgjʊlə(r)] *adj* rectangulaire

rectify ['rektɪfaɪ] (*pt & pp* **rectified**) *vt* rectifier

rectitude ['rektɪtjuːd] *n Formal* rectitude *f*

rector ['rektə(r)] *n* (a) *Rel* pasteur *m* anglican (b) *Scot Univ* = personnalité élue par les étudiants pour les représenter; *Scot Sch* ≃ proviseur *m*

rectory ['rektərɪ] *n* (*pl* **rectories**) *n Rel* presbytère *m*

rectum ['rektəm] *n* rectum *m*

recumbent [rɪ'kʌmbənt] *adj Formal* allongé(e)

recuperate [rɪ'kuːpəreɪt] *vi* (*from illness*) se rétablir

recuperation [rɪkuːpə'reɪʃən] *n* (*from illness*) rétablissement *m*

recur [rɪ'kɜː(r)] (*pt & pp* **recurred**) *vi* (*of event, problem*) se reproduire; (*of theme, illness*) revenir, réapparaître

recurrence [rɪ'kʌrəns] *n* récurrence *f*

recurring [rɪ'kɜːrɪŋ] *adj* (*problem*) récurrent(e); (*nightmare*) qui revient souvent; **six point six r.** six virgule six à l'infini

recycle [riː'saɪkəl] *vt* recycler

recycling [riː'saɪklɪŋ] *n* recyclage *m*; **r. plant** usine *f* de recyclage

red [red] **1** *n* (*colour*) rouge *m*; *Fam Fig* **to see r.** (*get angry*) voir rouge; **to be in the r.** (*in debt*) être à découvert *ou* dans le rouge
2 *adj* (*redder, reddest*) (*hair*) roux (rousse); **to turn** *or* **go r.** rougir; **to be as r. as a beetroot** être rouge comme une pivoine; **r. alert** alerte *f* rouge; **the R. Army** l'Armée *f* rouge; **r.**

card (in football) carton m rouge; Fig **to roll out the r. carpet** dérouler le tapis rouge; **the R. Cross** la Croix-Rouge; Fig **r. herring** diversion f; (in film, book) fausse piste f; Old-fashioned **R. Indian** Peau-Rouge mf; **r. light** feu m rouge; **r. light district** quartier m chaud; **r. meat** viande f rouge; **r. pepper** poivron m rouge; **mentioning her name to him is like a r. rag to a bull** le simple fait d'entendre son nom le met dans une colère noire; (Little) **R. Riding Hood** le Petit Chaperon rouge; **the R. Sea** la mer Rouge; **r. tape** paperasserie f; **r. wine** vin m rouge

red-blooded [red'blʌdɪd] adj **a r. male** un homme viril

redbrick ['redbrɪk] adj (building) en brique rouge; **r. university** = université construite à la fin du XIXᵉ siècle

redcurrant [riːd'kʌrənt] n groseille f

redden ['redən] **1** vt rougir
2 vi (of sky) rougeoyer; (of person) rougir

reddish ['redɪʃ] adj (light, colour) rougeâtre; (hair) légèrement roux (rousse)

redecorate [riː'dekəreɪt] vt (repaint) refaire la peinture de; (re-wallpaper) retapisser

redeem [rɪ'diːm] vt (a) (pawned item) racheter; (promise) tenir; (gift token, coupon) échanger; (mortgage, loan) rembourser (b) (rescue) racheter; **to r. oneself** se racheter

Redeemer [rɪ'diːmə(r)] n Rel **the R.** le Rédempteur

redeeming [rɪ'diːmɪŋ] adj **he has no r. features** il n'a rien pour le racheter; **his one r. feature is...** la seule chose qui le rachète, c'est...

redemption [rɪ'dem(p)ʃən] n Rel rédemption f; also Fig **to be beyond** or **past r.** être irrécupérable

redeploy [riːdɪ'plɔɪ] vt (troops) redéployer; (staff) réaffecter

redeployment [riːdɪ'plɔɪmənt] n (of troops) redéploiement m; (of staff) réaffectation f

redevelop [riːdɪ'veləp] vt réaménager

red-faced [red'feɪst] adj (naturally) rougeaud(e); (with anger, embarrassment) rouge

red-handed ['red'hændɪd] adj **to be caught r.** être pris(e) la main dans le sac

redhead [redhed] n roux (rousse) m,f

red-hot [red'hɒt] adj (a) (very hot) brûlant(e) (b) Fam (very good) super bon (bonne); **r. news** des nouvelles de dernière minute

redial [riː'daɪəl] **1** n **r. button** (on phone) touche f bis
2 vt (pt & pp redialled, Am redialed) (phone number) recomposer

redirect [riːdɪ'rekt, riːdaɪ'rekt] vt (letter) faire suivre; (plane, traffic) dévier; (energy) canaliser

rediscover [riːdɪs'kʌvə(r)] vt redécouvrir

redistribute [riːdɪs'trɪbjuːt] vt redistribuer

red-letter day ['red'letə(r)deɪ] n journée f mémorable

redo [riː'duː] (pt redid [riː'dɪd], pp redone [riː'dʌn]) vt refaire

redolent ['redələnt] adj **to be r. of** (smell of) sentir; (suggest) avoir un parfum de

redraft [riː'drɑːft] vt rédiger de nouveau

redress [rɪ'dres] **1** n (of injustice, grievance) réparation f
2 vt (injustice, grievance) réparer; **to r. the balance** rétablir l'équilibre

redskin ['redskɪn] n Old-fashioned Peau-Rouge mf

reduce [rɪ'djuːs] vt (a) (cost, amount, tax) réduire; (importance) minimiser; (price) baisser; (number of people) faire baisser; (sauce) faire réduire; **to r. speed** ralentir (b)

(bring to a certain state) **to r. sth to ashes/dust** réduire qch en cendres/poussière; **to r. sb to silence** réduire qn au silence; **to r. sb to tears** faire fondre qn en larmes; **to be reduced to doing sth** être réduit(e) à faire qch

reduced [rɪ'djuːst] adj réduit(e); **to live in r. circumstances** vivre dans la gêne

reduction [rɪ'dʌkʃən] n (of price, temperature) baisse f (in de); (of spending, on item) réduction f (in/on de/sur)

redundancy [rɪ'dʌndənsɪ] (pl redundancies) n (dismissal) licenciement m; **r. notice** avis m de licenciement; **r. pay** prime f de licenciement

redundant [rɪ'dʌndənt] adj (a) (worker) **to make sb r.** licencier qn; **to be made r.** être licencié(e) (b) (superfluous) inutile

reed [riːd] n (a) (plant) roseau m (b) (of musical instrument) anche f

reef [riːf] n récif m

reek [riːk] **1** n relent m
2 vi also Fig **to r. (of sth)** puer (qch)

reel [riːl] **1** n (a) Br (for film, thread) bobine f; (for fishing line) moulinet m (b) (dance, music) quadrille m
2 vi (sway) chanceler; Fig **my head is reeling** la tête me tourne

►**reel off** vt sep (names, statistics) débiter

re-elect [riːɪ'lekt] vt réélire

re-election [riːɪ'lekʃən] n réélection f

re-enact [riːɪ'nækt] vt reconstituer

re-enter [riː'entə(r)] **1** vt entrer à nouveau dans
2 vi rentrer

re-establish [riːɪ'stæblɪʃ] vt rétablir

re-examine [riːɪg'zæmɪn] vt réexaminer

ref [ref] n (a) (abbr **reference**) réf (b) Fam (abbr **referee**) arbitre m

refectory [rɪ'fektərɪ] (pl refectories) n réfectoire m

refer [rɪ'fɜː(r)] (pt & pp referred) vt soumettre (**to** à); **to r. a patient to a specialist** envoyer un patient chez un spécialiste

►**refer to** vt insep (a) (mention) parler de; **she never refers to it** elle n'en parle jamais (b) (allude to) faire allusion à; **referred to as...** appelé(e)... (c) (consult) consulter (d) (apply to) s'appliquer à

referee [refə'riː] **1** n (a) (in sport) arbitre m (b) (for job) **please give the names of two referees** veuillez fournir deux références
2 vt & vi arbitrer

reference ['refərəns] n (a) (consultation, source) référence f; **for future r.** à titre d'information; **I can't do it without r. to Head Office** je ne peux pas le faire sans en référer au bureau central; **r. book** ouvrage m de référence; **r. number** (numéro m de) référence; **r. point, point of r.** point m de repère (b) (allusion) allusion f; **with r. to** (in letter) suite à (c) (from employer) lettre f de référence

referendum [refə'rendəm] n référendum m

refill 1 n ['riːfɪl] (for notebook) feuillets fpl de rechange; (for pen) cartouche f; (for lighter) recharge f; **would you like a r.?** (of drink) je te ressers?
2 vt [riː'fɪl] (glass) remplir à nouveau; (lighter, pen) recharger

refine [rɪ'faɪn] vt (a) (sugar, petroleum) raffiner (b) (improve) perfectionner

refined [rɪ'faɪnd] adj also Fig raffiné(e)

refinement [rɪ'faɪnmənt] n (a) (of manners, taste, person) raffinement m (b) (improvement) perfectionnement m; to make refinements to sth perfectionner qch

refinery [rɪ'faɪnərɪ] (pl **refineries**) n raffinerie f

refit 1 n ['riːfɪt] (of ship) remise f en état
2 vt [riː'fɪt] (pt & pp **refitted**) (ship) remettre en état

reflate [riː'fleɪt] vt Econ relancer

reflation [riː'fleɪʃən] n Econ relance f

reflect [rɪ'flekt] **1** vt (a) (image, light) réfléchir, refléter; to be reflected (in) se réfléchir ou se refléter (dans) (b) Fig (portray) refléter (c) (think) to r. that... se dire que...
2 vi (a) (think) réfléchir (on à) (b) to r. well/badly on sb/sth faire honneur/du tort à qn/qch

reflection [rɪ'flekʃən] n (a) (image, indication) reflet m; Fig it is no r. on your own capabilities cela ne remet pas en cause vos compétences (b) (thought) réflexion f; on r. après réflexion

reflective [rɪ'flektɪv] adj (a) (surface) réfléchissant(e) (b) (person) réfléchi(e)

reflector [rɪ'flektə(r)] n (on bicycle, vehicle) catadioptre m

reflex ['riːfleks] **1** n réflexe m
2 adj réflexe; r. action réflexe m; r. camera réflex m

reflexive [rɪ'fleksɪv] adj Gram r. pronoun pronom m réfléchi; r. verb verbe m pronominal réfléchi

reflexology [riːflek'sɒlədʒɪ] n réflexologie f

reforestation [riːfɒrɪ'steɪʃən] n reboisement m

reform [rɪ'fɔːm] **1** n réforme f
2 vt réformer
3 vi se réformer

re-form ['riː'fɔːm] vi (of organization, pop group) se reformer

re-format ['riː'fɔːmæt] (pt & pp **re-formatted**) vt Comptr (disk) reformater

reformation [refə'meɪʃən] n réforme f; Hist the R. la Réforme

reformatory [rɪ'fɔːmətərɪ] (pl **reformatories**) n Am centre m d'éducation surveillée

reformed [rɪ'fɔːmd] adj (alcoholic, drug addict) ancien(enne); he's a r. character il s'est assagi

reformer [rɪ'fɔːmə(r)] n réformateur(trice) m,f

reformist [rɪ'fɔːmɪst] n & adj réformiste mf

refract [rɪ'frækt] vt réfracter

refrain [rɪ'freɪn] **1** n also Fig refrain m
2 vi to r. from sth/doing sth s'abstenir de qch/de faire qch

re-freeze [riː'friːz] (pt **re-froze** [riː'frəʊz], pp **re-frozen** [riː'frəʊzən]) vt

refresh [rɪ'freʃ] vt (of drink) rafraîchir; (of nap, holiday) reposer; (bath) revigorer; Comptr actualiser; to r. one's memory se rafraîchir la mémoire; to r. sb's glass (top up) resservir à boire à qn

refreshing [rɪ'freʃɪŋ] adj (breeze, drink) rafraîchissant(e); (nap, holiday) reposant(e); (bath) revigorant(e); Fig (honesty) qui fait l'effet d'une bouffée d'air frais

refreshments [rɪ'freʃmənts] npl rafraîchissements mpl

refrigerate [rɪ'frɪdʒəreɪt] vt réfrigérer; r. after opening (on packet) à conserver au frais après ouverture

refrigeration [rɪfrɪdʒə'reɪʃən] n réfrigération f

refrigerator [rɪ'frɪdʒəreɪtə(r)] n (domestic) réfrigérateur m, frigidaire® m; (industrial) chambre f froide

refuel [riː'fjʊəl] (pt & pp **refuelled**, Am **refueled**) **1** vt (ship, aircraft) ravitailler en carburant
2 vi (of ship, aircraft) se ravitailler en carburant

refuge ['refjuːdʒ] n (from danger, weather) refuge m; (for battered women) foyer m; to seek r. chercher refuge; to take r. se réfugier

refugee [refjʊ'dʒiː] n réfugié(e) m,f; r. camp camp m de réfugiés; r. status statut m de réfugié

refund 1 n ['riːfʌnd] remboursement m
2 vt [riː'fʌnd] rembourser

refurbish [riː'fɜːbɪʃ] vt rénover

refusal [rɪ'fjuːzəl] n refus m; to give a flat r. refuser catégoriquement; to have first r. (on sth) avoir la priorité (pour qch)

refuse¹ ['refjuːs] n (rubbish) ordures fpl; r. collection ramassage m des ordures (ménagères); r. disposal traitement m des ordures; r. dump dépôt m d'ordures

refuse² [rɪ'fjuːz] **1** vt (invitation, offer) refuser; (request) rejeter; to r. to do sth refuser de faire qch; to r. sb sth refuser qch à qn
2 vi (of person) refuser; (of horse) refuser l'obstacle

refute [rɪ'fjuːt] vt (argument, theory) réfuter; (allegation) nier

regain [rɪ'geɪn] vt (a) (get back) retrouver; (power, political seat) reconquérir; to r. possession of sth rentrer en possession de qch; to r. consciousness revenir à soi; to r. the lead (in contest) reprendre l'avantage (b) (reach again) regagner

regal ['riːgəl] adj royal(e)

regale [rɪ'geɪl] vt to r. sb with sth gratifier qn de qch

regalia [rɪ'geɪlɪə] npl insignes mpl

regard [rɪ'gɑːd] **1** n (a) (admiration) respect m, estime f; to hold sb in high r. tenir qn en haute estime (b) (consideration) égard m; out of r. for par égard pour; without r. to sans tenir compte de (c) (connection) in this r. à cet égard; in all regards à tous égards; with r. to en ce qui concerne (d) regards (good wishes) amitiés fpl; give her my regards transmets-lui mes amitiés
2 vt (a) (admire, respect) estimer (b) (consider) to r. sb/sth as considérer qn/qch comme; to r. sb/sth with suspicion être soupçonneux(euse) à l'égard de qn/qch (c) (concern) concerner; as regards... en ce qui concerne..., concernant...

regarding [rɪ'gɑːdɪŋ] prep en ce qui concerne, concernant

regardless [rɪ'gɑːdlɪs] adv (a) (despite everything) quand même (b) r. of (without considering) sans tenir compte de; r. of the expense sans regarder à la dépense

regatta [rɪ'gætə] n régate f

regency ['riːdʒənsɪ] (pl **regencies**) n régence f

regenerate [rɪ'dʒenəreɪt] **1** vt (sector, city) régénérer; (interest, enthusiasm) raviver
2 vi se régénérer

regeneration [rɪdʒenə'reɪʃən] n régénération f

regent ['riːdʒənt] adj & n régent(e) m,f

reggae ['regeɪ] n reggae m

regime [reɪ'ʒiːm] n régime m

regiment ['redʒɪmənt] **1** n régiment m
2 vt enrégimenter

regimental [redʒɪ'mentəl] adj du régiment

regimentation [redʒɪmen'teɪʃən] n discipline f draconienne

regimented ['redʒɪmentɪd] adj très strict(e)

region ['ri:dʒən] n région f; *Fig* **in the r. of** environ

regional ['ri:dʒənəl] adj régional(e)

regionalism ['ri:dʒənəlɪzəm] n régionalisme m

register ['redʒɪstə(r)] **1** n registre m; *(at school)* cahier m d'appel; *(of voters)* liste f électorale; **to take the r.** *(at school)* faire l'appel; **r. of births, marriages and deaths** registre m de l'état civil; **(cash)** n caisse f (enregistreuse); *Br* **r. office** bureau m de l'état civil
2 vt **(a)** *(member, student)* inscrire; *(birth, marriage, death)* déclarer; *(complaint)* déposer; **to r. a protest** protester **(b)** *(temperature, speed)* enregistrer; *(astonishment, displeasure)* manifester **(c)** *(realize)* se rendre compte de **(d)** *(achieve)* *(victory, progress)* enregistrer
3 vi **(a)** *(for course)* s'inscrire; *(at hotel)* signer le registre; *(of voter)* s'inscrire sur les listes électorales **(b)** *Fam (of fact)* **I told him but it didn't r.** je lui ai dit mais il n'a pas enregistré

registered ['redʒɪstəd] adj *(charity)* reconnu(e) par l'État; *(childminder)* agréé(e); *(letter)* recommandé(e); **r. trademark** marque f déposée

registrar ['redʒɪstrɑ:(r)] n **(a)** *(record keeper)* officier m de l'état civil **(b)** *(in university)* responsable mf des inscriptions **(c)** *(in hospital)* chef m de clinique

registration [redʒɪ'streɪʃən] n *(of student)* inscription f; *(of voter)* inscription sur les listes électorales; *(of birth, death, marriage)* déclaration f; **r. number** *(of car)* numéro m d'immatriculation

registry office ['redʒɪstrɪ'ɒfɪs] n bureau m de l'état civil

regress [rɪ'gres] vi régresser

regression [rɪ'greʃən] n régression f

regressive [rɪ'gresɪv] adj régressif(ive)

regret [rɪ'gret] **1** n regret m; **to send one's regrets** *(apologies)* envoyer ses excuses; *(condolences)* envoyer ses condoléances
2 vt *(pt & pp* regretted) regretter; **to r. doing** or **having done sth** regretter d'avoir fait qch; **I r. to (have to) inform you that...** j'ai le regret de vous annoncer que...

regretful [rɪ'gretfʊl] adj *(voice, smile)* plein(e) de regret; *(person)* qui a des regrets

regrettable [rɪ'gretəbəl] adj regrettable

regroup [ri:'gru:p] **1** vt regrouper
2 vi se regrouper

regular ['regjʊlə(r)] **1** n *(in bar, restaurant)* habitué(e) m,f
2 adj **(a)** *(features, pulse, verb)* régulier(ère); **on a r. basis** régulièrement; **he comes twice a week, as r. as clockwork** il vient deux fois par semaine, c'est réglé comme du papier à musique **(b)** *(normal, habitual)* habituel(elle); *(in size)* moyen(enne); *(listener, viewer)* fidèle; *(customer)* régulier(ère); **she was a r. visitor to the house** elle venait régulièrement à la maison **(c)** *(army, soldier)* régulier(ère) **(d)** *Fam (for emphasis)* vrai(e)

regularity [regjʊ'lærɪtɪ] n régularité f

regulate ['regjʊleɪt] vt **(a)** *(adjust)* régler **(b)** *(control)* réglementer

regulation [regjʊ'leɪʃən] **1** n **(a)** *(action)* réglementation f **(b)** *(rule)* règlement m
2 adj *(statutory)* réglementaire

regulator ['regjʊleɪtə(r)] n régulateur m

regulatory [regjʊ'leɪtərɪ] adj de contrôle

regurgitate [rɪ'gɜ:dʒɪteɪt] vt régurgiter; *Fig* recracher

rehabilitate [ri:hə'bɪlɪteɪt] vt réhabiliter

rehabilitation [ri:həbɪlɪ'teɪʃən] n réhabilitation f

rehash *Fam* **1** n ['ri:hæʃ] resucée f
2 vt [ri:'hæʃ] *(ideas, proposal)* reprendre; *(film, book)* remanier

rehearsal [rɪ'hɜ:səl] n répétition f

rehearse [rɪ'hɜ:s] vt & vi répéter

rehouse [ri:'haʊz] vt reloger

reign [reɪn] **1** n règne m
2 vi *also Fig* régner

reigning ['reɪnɪŋ] adj *(monarch)* régnant(e); *(champion)* en titre

reimburse [ri:ɪm'bɜ:s] vt rembourser

rein [reɪn] n *also Fig* rêne f; *Fig* **to give sb free r. to do sth** donner carte blanche à qn pour qu'il/elle fasse qch; *Fig* **to give free r. to one's imagination** donner libre cours à son imagination; *Fig* **to keep a tight r. on sb** tenir la bride haute à qn

reincarnate [ri:ɪn'kɑ:neɪt] vt **to be reincarnated** être réincarné(e)

reincarnation [ri:ɪnkɑ:'neɪʃən] n réincarnation f

reindeer ['reɪndɪə(r)] n renne m

reinforce [ri:ɪn'fɔ:s] vt *also Fig* renforcer; **reinforced concrete** béton m armé

reinforcement [ri:ɪn'fɔ:smənt] n renforcement m; *also Fig* **reinforcements** renforts mpl

reinsert [ri:ɪn'sɜ:t] vt réinsérer

reinstate [ri:ɪn'steɪt] vt réintégrer

reinsurance [ri:ɪn'ʃʊərəns] n réassurance f

reinsure [ri:ɪn'ʃʊə(r)] vt réassurer

reinvent [ri:ɪn'vent] vt *Fig* **to r. the wheel** refaire ce qui a déjà été fait

reinvest [ri:ɪn'vest] vt réinvestir

reissue [ri:'ɪʃu:] **1** n *(of book, record)* réédition f
2 vt *(book, record)* rééditer

reiterate [ri:'ɪtəreɪt] vt réitérer

reiteration [ri:ɪtə'reɪʃən] n réitération f

reject 1 n ['ri:dʒekt] *(object)* rebut m; *Fam (person)* inadapté(e) m,f
2 vt [rɪ'dʒekt] rejeter; *(offer, goods)* refuser

rejection [rɪ'dʒekʃən] n rejet m; *(of offer, goods)* refus m; **to meet with r.** être rejeté(e)

rejoice [rɪ'dʒɔɪs] vi se réjouir

rejoicing [rɪ'dʒɔɪsɪŋ] n réjouissance f

rejoin¹ [rɪ'dʒɔɪn] vt **(a)** *(group, motorway)* rejoindre; *(race)* reprendre **(b)** *(join again)* réintégrer

rejoin² [rɪ'dʒɔɪn] vt & vi *(retort)* répliquer, rétorquer

rejoinder [rɪ'dʒɔɪndə(r)] n réplique f

rejuvenate [rɪ'dʒu:vɪneɪt] vt rajeunir

rekindle [ri:'kɪndəl] vt raviver

relapse 1 n [rɪ'læps] rechute f
2 vi [rɪ'læps] rechuter; **to r. into** retomber dans

relate [rɪ'leɪt] **1** vt **(a)** *(narrate)* raconter **(b)** *(connect)* mettre en rapport **(to avec)**
2 vi **(a)** *(be relevant)* **to r. to** avoir rapport à **(b)** **to r. to** *(understand)* *(person)* avoir des affinités avec; *(music)* apprécier; *(idea)* comprendre

related [rɪ'leɪtɪd] adj *(people, animals, languages)* apparenté(e); *(ideas, events, activities)* lié(e)

relation [rɪ'leɪʃən] n **(a)** *(relative)* parent(e) m,f **(b)** *(connection)* rapport m; **to bear no r. to** n'avoir aucun rapport avec

relationship [rɪ'leɪʃənʃɪp] n (a) (between people) relation f; (romantic, sexual) relation amoureuse; (between countries) relations fpl; (within family) lien m de parenté; **to have a good/bad r. with sb** s'entendre/ne pas bien s'entendre avec qn (b) (connection) rapport m

relative [relətɪv] 1 n (person) parent(e) m,f
2 adj (comparative) relatif(ive); **r. to** en rapport avec; Gram **r. clause** proposition f relative

relatively [relətɪvlɪ] adv relativement

relativity [relə'tɪvɪtɪ] n Phys relativité f

relax [rɪ'læks] 1 vt (person) détendre; (muscles, discipline) relâcher; (law, control) assouplir; **to r. one's grip (on)** relâcher son étreinte (sur); Fig relâcher son emprise (sur)
2 vi (of person) se détendre; (of muscles) se relâcher; **r.!** (calm down) du calme!

relaxation [riːlæk'seɪʃən] n (a) (of person) détente f; (of discipline) relâchement m; (of control) assouplissement m (b) (as therapy) relaxation f; **r. exercises/classes** exercices mpl/cours mpl de relaxation

relaxed [rɪ'lækst] adj détendu(e)

relaxing [rɪ'læksɪŋ] adj relaxant(e)

relay 1 n [riːleɪ] (of workers) équipe f de relais; **to work in relays** se relayer; **r. (race)** (course f de) relais m; Rad & TV **r. station** relais m
2 vt [rɪ'leɪ] retransmettre; (information) transmettre

release [rɪ'liːs] 1 n (a) (of prisoner) libération f; (of gas) émission f; (emotional) soulagement m (b) (of record, film) sortie f; **to be on general r.** (of film) être sorti(e) dans toutes les grandes salles de cinéma
2 vt (a) (prisoner) libérer; (gas, fumes) émettre; (balloon, bomb) lâcher; (funds) dégager; (brake) desserrer; **to r. sb from an obligation** dégager qn d'une obligation; **to r. sb's hand** lâcher la main de qn (b) (record, film) sortir; (news, information) communiquer

relegate ['relɪgeɪt] vt reléguer (**to** à); **to be relegated** (of team) descendre en division inférieure

relegation [relɪ'geɪʃən] n (of person) relégation f (**to** à); (of team) descente f en division inférieure

relent [rɪ'lent] vi (of storm, wind) se calmer; (of person) céder

relentless [rɪ'lentlɪs] adj (person, attitude) implacable; (rain, criticism) incessant(e)

relevance ['reləvəns] n pertinence f; **to have r. to sth** avoir un rapport avec qch

relevant ['reləvənt] adj (a) (apt) pertinent(e); **to be r. (to sth)** avoir un rapport (avec qch) (b) (appropriate) (chapter) correspondant(e); (authorities) compétent(e); (experience, qualifications) requis(e) (c) (topical) d'actualité

reliability [rɪlaɪə'bɪlɪtɪ] n (of person, information) sérieux m; (of machine) sûreté f, fiabilité f

reliable [rɪ'laɪəbəl] adj (person, machine) fiable; (information) sûr(e); **from a r. source** de source sûre

reliably [rɪ'laɪəblɪ] adv **to be r. informed that...** savoir de source sûre que...

reliance [rɪ'laɪəns] n (a) (dependence) dépendance f (**on** vis-à-vis de) (b) (trust) confiance f; **to place r. on sb/sth** faire confiance à qn/qch

reliant [rɪ'laɪənt] adj **to be r. on** être dépendant(e) de

relic ['relɪk] n Rel relique f; Fig vestige m

relief [rɪ'liːf] n (a) (comfort) soulagement m; **to bring r. to sb** soulager qn (b) (help) secours m, aide f; **r. fund** fonds m d'aide (c) (replacement) remplaçant(e) m,f, (d) (of besieged city, troops) libération f (e) (in art) relief m; **in r.** en relief; Fig

to throw sth into r. mettre qch en relief; **r. map** carte f en relief

relieve [rɪ'liːv] vt (a) (alleviate) soulager; (boredom) tromper; (pressure) réduire; Euph **to r. oneself** se soulager (b) (replace) remplacer (c) (liberate) libérer; **to r. sb of his duties** relever qn de ses fonctions; Hum **to r. sb of his wallet** soulager qn de son portefeuille

religion [rɪ'lɪdʒən] n religion f

religious [rɪ'lɪdʒəs] adj also Fig religieux(euse)

religiously [rɪ'lɪdʒəslɪ] adv also Fig religieusement

relinquish [rɪ'lɪŋkwɪʃ] vt (hope, habit, thought) abandonner; **to r. one's hold on sb/sth** relâcher son emprise sur qn/qch

relish ['relɪʃ] 1 n (a) (pleasure) goût m (**for** pour); **to do sth with r.** faire qch avec délectation (b) (pickle) condiments mpl
2 vt savourer; **I didn't r. the idea** l'idée ne m'enthousiasmait guère

relive [riː'lɪv] vt revivre

relocate [riːləʊ'keɪt] 1 vt (company) transférer; (person) muter
2 vi (of company) être transféré(e); (of person) se déplacer

relocation [riːləʊ'keɪʃən] n déménagement m

reluctance [rɪ'lʌktəns] n réticence f; **to do sth with r.** faire qch à contrecœur

reluctant [rɪ'lʌktənt] adj (smile, promise) accordé(e) à contrecœur; **to be r. to do sth** être réticent(e) à faire qch

▶**rely on, rely upon** [rɪ'laɪ] (pt & pp relied) vt insep (a) **to r. on sb (to do sth)** compter sur qn (pour faire qch) (b) (be dependent on) dépendre de

REM [ɑːrɪ'em] n (abbr rapid eye movement) mouvements mpl oculaires rapides

remain [rɪ'meɪn] vi (a) (stay behind, continue to be) rester (b) (be left) subsister; **it remains to be seen** cela reste à voir

remainder [rɪ'meɪndə(r)] n reste m

remaindered [rɪ'meɪndəd] adj (book) soldé(e)

remaining [rɪ'meɪnɪŋ] adj restant(e)

remains [rɪ'meɪnz] npl (of meal, fortune) restes mpl; (of civilization, building) vestiges mpl; (human) r. restes humains

remake 1 n ['riːmeɪk] (of film) remake m
2 vt [riː'meɪk] (pt & pp remade [riː'meɪd]) (film) faire un remake de

remand [rɪ'mɑːnd] Law 1 n **on r.** en détention préventive; **r. home** maison f de détention préventive
2 vt **to r. sb (in custody)** placer qn en détention préventive

remark [rɪ'mɑːk] 1 n remarque f; **to make** or **pass a r.** faire une remarque
2 vt faire remarquer

remarkable [rɪ'mɑːkəbəl] adj remarquable

remarkably [rɪ'mɑːkəblɪ] adv remarquablement

remarry [riː'mærɪ] (pt & pp remarried) vi se remarier

remedial [rɪ'miːdɪəl] adj (a) (class) de rattrapage; **r. education** rattrapage m scolaire (b) (corrective) **to take r. measures** prendre des mesures

remedy ['remɪdɪ] 1 n (pl remedies) also Fig remède m
2 vt (pt & pp remedied) remédier à

remember [rɪ'membə(r)] 1 vt (a) (recall) se souvenir de, se rappeler; **to r. doing sth** se souvenir d'avoir fait qch; **to r. to do sth** penser à faire qch; **a night to r.** une nuit mémorable (b) (commemorate) commémorer; **to r. the**

dead rendre hommage aux disparus **(c)** *(speak of)* **to r. sb to sb** rappeler qn au bon souvenir de qn

2 *vi* se souvenir, se rappeler; **as far as I r.** pour autant que je me souvienne

remembrance [rɪ'membrəns] *n Formal (memory)* souvenir *m*; **in r. of** en souvenir de; **R. Day** *or* **Sunday** = commémoration de la fin des deux guerres mondiales, ≃ le 11 novembre

remind [rɪ'maɪnd] *vt* **to r. sb of sth** rappeler qch à qn; **to r. sb to do sth** rappeler à qn de faire qch; **that reminds me...** à propos...

reminder [rɪ'maɪndə(r)] *n* rappel *m*

reminisce [remɪ'nɪs] *vi* évoquer des souvenirs; **to r. about sth** évoquer qch

reminiscence [remɪ'nɪsəns] *n* souvenir *m*

reminiscent [remɪ'nɪsənt] *adj* **to be r. of** rappeler

remiss [rɪ'mɪs] *adj* négligent(e); **it was very r. of him not to phone** c'était très négligent de sa part de ne pas téléphoner

remission [rɪ'mɪʃən] *n* **(a)** *Law* remise *f* de peine **(b)** *(of disease)* to be in r. être en phase de rémission

remit1 *n* ['riːmɪt] *(area of authority)* attributions *fpl*

2 *vt* [rɪ'mɪt] *(pt & pp* **remitted)** *(payment)* remettre

remittance [rɪ'mɪtəns] *n* versement *m*

remnant ['remnənt] *n* reste *m*; *(of civilization, building)* vestige *m*; *(of cloth)* coupon *m*

remonstrate ['remənstreɪt] *vi* protester; **to r. with sb** faire des remontrances à qn

remorse [rɪ'mɔːs] *n* remords *m*; **to feel r.** avoir du *ou* des remords

remorseful [rɪ'mɔːsfʊl] *adj* plein(e) de remords

remorseless [rɪ'mɔːslɪs] *adj* impitoyable

remote [rɪ'məʊt] *adj* **(a)** *(far-off)* *(in space)* éloigné(e) *(from* de); *(in time)* lointain(e) *(from* de); **r. control** télécommande *f* **(b)** *(aloof)* distant(e) **(c)** *(chance, possibility)* vague; **the remotest chance/idea** la moindre chance/idée

remote-controlled [rɪ'məʊtkən'trəʊld] *adj* télécommandé(e)

remotely [rɪ'məʊtlɪ] *adv* **(a)** *(distantly)* **r. situated** isolé(e) **(b)** *(slightly)* vaguement; **not r.** pas du tout

remould ['riːməʊld] *n (tyre)* pneu *m* rechapé

removal [rɪ'muːvəl] *n* **(a)** *(of politician, official)* renvoi *m*; *(of control, doubt, threat)* suppression *f*; *(of stain)* nettoyage *m* **(b)** *(moving house)* déménagement *m*; **r. man** déménageur *m*; **r. van** camion *m* de déménagement

remove [rɪ'muːv] *vt* **(a)** *(take away)* *(thing)* enlever; *(doubt)* dissiper; *(fear)* faire partir; *(politician, official)* renvoyer; **to r. one's child from a school** retirer son enfant d'une école **(b)** *(take off)* *(coat, hat)* enlever, retirer; *(tyre)* démonter

remover [rɪ'muːvə(r)] *n* **(a)** *(for paint)* décapant *m*; *(for nail varnish)* dissolvant *m* **(b)** *(furniture)* **removers** déménageurs *mpl*

remunerate [rɪ'mjuːnəreɪt] *vt Formal* rémunérer

remuneration [rɪmjuːnə'reɪʃən] *n Formal* rémunération *f*

remunerative [rɪ'mjuːnərətɪv] *adj Formal* rémunérateur(trice)

renaissance [rɪ'neɪsəns] *n* renouveau *m*; **the R.** la Renaissance

renal ['riːnəl] *adj* rénal(e)

rename [riː'neɪm] *vt* rebaptiser

rend [rend] *(pt & pp* **rent** [rent]) *vt Lit (tear)* déchirer

render ['rendə(r)] *vt Formal* rendre; **to r. homage to sb** rendre hommage à qn; **to r. sth into French** rendre qch en français; **for services rendered** pour services rendus; **the news rendered her speechless** la nouvelle l'a laissée sans voix

rendezvous ['rɒndɪvuː] **1** *n (pl* **rendezvous** ['rɒndɪvuːz]) rendez-vous *m inv*

2 *vi* *(pt & pp* **rendezvoused** ['rɒndɪvuːd]) se retrouver

rendition [ren'dɪʃən] *n* interprétation *f*

renegade ['renɪgeɪd] *n* renégat(e) *m,f*

renege [rɪ'neɪg] *vi* **to r. on sth** revenir sur qch

renew [rɪ'njuː] *vt (passport, membership)* renouveler; *(activity, negotiations, library book)* reprendre; *(optimism, strength, interest)* raviver; *(speculation)* relancer

renewable [rɪ'njuːəbəl] *adj* renouvelable

renewal [rɪ'njuːəl] *n (of passport, membership)* renouvellement *m*; *(of activity, negotiations)* reprise *f*; *(of library book)* renouvellement de prêt; *(of optimism, interest)* regain *m*

rennet ['renɪt] *n* présure *f*

renounce [rɪ'naʊns] *vt* renoncer à; *(treaty)* dénoncer; *(friends, faith, principles)* renier

renovate ['renəveɪt] *vt* rénover

renovation [renə'veɪʃən] *n* rénovation *f*

renown [rɪ'naʊn] *n* renommée *f*

renowned [rɪ'naʊnd] *adj* renommé(e) *(for* pour)

rent1 [rent] **1** *n (on flat, house)* loyer *m*; **for r.** à louer; *Br Fam* **r. boy** jeune prostitué *m*

2 *vt* louer

rent2 *pt & pp of* **rend**

rental ['rentəl] *n* **(a)** *(hire)* location *f* **(b)** *(money)* *(for house)* loyer *m*; *(for car, equipment, TV)* location *f*; *(for telephone)* abonnement *m*

rent-free [rent'friː] **1** *adj* exempt(e) de loyer

2 *adv* sans payer de loyer

reopen [riː'əʊpən] **1** *vt* rouvrir; *(talks)* reprendre; *Fig* **to r. old wounds** rouvrir une plaie

2 *vi (of talks)* reprendre; *(of shop, theatre)* rouvrir; **school reopens on the 21st of August** la rentrée des classes aura lieu le 21 août

reorder [riː'ɔːdə(r)] *vt* passer une nouvelle commande de

reorganization [riːɔːgənaɪ'zeɪʃən] *n* réorganisation *f*

reorganize [riː'ɔːgənaɪz] *vt* réorganiser

rep [rep] *n Fam (abbr* **representative)** VRP *m*

repaint [riː'peɪnt] *vt* repeindre

repair [rɪ'peə(r)] **1** *n* réparation *f*; **to be beyond r.** être irréparable; **to be in good/bad r.** être en bon/mauvais état; **to be under r.** être en réparation; **r. shop** atelier *m* de réparations

2 *vt* réparer

repairman [rɪ'peəmæn] *n* réparateur *m*

reparation [repə'reɪʃən] *n* **(a)** *Formal (compensation)* réparation *f*; **to make r. for sth** réparer qch **(b)** *(after war)* **reparations** réparations *fpl*

repartee [repɑː'tiː] *n* repartie *f*

repast [rɪ'pɑːst] *n Lit* repas *m*

repatriate [riː'pætrɪeɪt] *vt* rapatrier *(to* vers)

repatriation [riːpætrɪ'eɪʃən] *n* rapatriement *m*

repay [rɪ'peɪ] (*pt & pp* **repaid** [rɪ'peɪd]) *vt* (**a**) *(reimburse)* *(person, money)* rembourser (**b**) *(reward)* *(person)* remercier (**for** de); *(kindness)* payer de retour; *(loyalty)* récompenser

repayable [rɪ'peɪəbl] *adj* remboursable

repayment [rɪ'peɪmənt] *n* remboursement *m*; **r. plan** calendrier *m* des paiements

repeal [rɪ'piːl] *vt* abroger

repeat [rɪ'piːt] **1** *n* (*of event*) répétition *f*; (*of TV or radio programme*) rediffusion *f*; **r. prescription** ≃ ordonnance *f* renouvelable
2 *vt* répéter; *(attempt)* renouveler; *(TV programme)* rediffuser; **to r. oneself** se répéter

repeated [rɪ'piːtɪd] *adj* répété(e)

repeatedly [rɪ'piːtɪdlɪ] *adv* à maintes reprises

repel [rɪ'pel] (*pt & pp* **repelled**) *vt also Fig* repousser

repellent [rɪ'pelənt] **1** *n* (*for insects*) anti-moustiques *m inv*
2 *adj* (*disgusting*) repoussant(e)

repent [rɪ'pent] **1** *vt* se repentir de
2 *vi* se repentir (**of** de)

repentance [rɪ'pentəns] *n* repentir *m*

repentant [rɪ'pentənt] *adj* repentant(e) (**of** de)

repercussion [riːpə'kʌʃən] *n* répercussion *f*

repertoire ['repətwɑː(r)] *n* répertoire *m*

repertory ['repətərɪ] (*pl* **repertories**) *n Th* répertoire *m*; **r. company** troupe *f* de répertoire

repetition [repɪ'tɪʃən] *n* répétition *f*; (*of attempt*) renouvellement *m*

repetitive [rɪ'petɪtɪv] *adj* répétitif(ive); **r. strain injury** = douleurs dans les bras et les mains dues à la répétition de certains mouvements

rephrase [riː'freɪz] *vt* reformuler

replace [rɪ'pleɪs] *vt* (**a**) *(put back)* remettre qch à sa place; **to r. the receiver** (*on telephone*) raccrocher (**b**) *(substitute for)* remplacer

replacement [rɪ'pleɪsmənt] *n* (**a**) *(putting back)* remise *f* en place; *(substituting)* remplacement *m*; *Fin* **r. cost** coût *m* de remplacement; **r. parts** pièces *fpl* de remplacement; **r. value** valeur *f* de remplacement (**b**) *(person)* remplaçant(e) *m,f*

replay 1 *n* ['riːpleɪ] (*of match*) nouvelle rencontre *f*; (*action*) **r.** *(on TV)* = répétition d'une séquence précédente; (*at slow speed*) ralenti *m*
2 *vt* [riː'pleɪ] *(match)* rejouer

replenish [rɪ'plenɪʃ] *vt* (*cup, tank*) remplir à nouveau (**with** de); **to r. one's supplies** se réapprovisionner

replete [rɪ'pliːt] *adj Formal* rassasié(e) (**with** de)

replica ['replɪkə] *n* réplique *f*; *Fig* (*of person*) portrait *m*

replicate ['replɪkeɪt] *vt* reproduire

reply [rɪ'plaɪ] **1** *n* (*pl* **replies**) réponse *f*; **in r. to your letter** en réponse à votre lettre; **to say sth in r. (to sth)** répondre qch (à qch); **there was no r.** (*on telephone*) ça ne répondait pas
2 *vti* (*pt & pp* **replied**) répondre (**to** à)

report [rɪ'pɔːt] **1** *n* (**a**) *(account)* compte rendu *m*; *(analysis)* rapport *m*; *(in newspaper, on radio, television)* reportage *m*; **there are reports that...** il paraîtrait que...; **r. card** (*for primary school*) carnet *m* de notes; (*for secondary school*) bulletin *m* scolaire (**b**) *(sound)* détonation *f*
2 *vt* (*information*) rapporter; *(accident, theft)* signaler; **to r. sb missing** signaler la disparition de qn; **to r. sb to the police/the authorities** dénoncer qn à la police/aux autorités; **to r. one's findings (to sb)** faire un rapport (à qn)

3 *vi* (**a**) *(present oneself)* se présenter (**to** à); **to r. for duty** prendre son service (**b**) *(give account)* faire un rapport (**to** à); *(of journalist)* faire un reportage (**on** sur) (**c**) *(be accountable)* **to r. to sb** rendre compte à qn

reportedly [rɪ'pɔːtɪdlɪ] *adv* **he r. said that...** il aurait dit que...; **he is r. resident in Paris** il résiderait à Paris

reporter [rɪ'pɔːtə(r)] *n* (*for newspaper*) journaliste *mf*; (*on television, radio*) reporter *m*

repose [rɪ'pəʊz] *Formal* **1** *n* repos *m*
2 *vi* reposer

repository [rɪ'pɒzɪtərɪ] (*pl* **repositories**) *n* (*for books, furniture*) dépôt *m*

repossess [riːpə'zes] *vt* saisir

reprehensible [reprɪ'hensɪbl] *adj* répréhensible

represent [reprɪ'zent] *vt* représenter; *(describe)* présenter

representation [reprɪzen'teɪʃən] *n* (*in Parliament*) représentation *f*; *(of facts)* exposé *m*; *Formal* **to make representations (to sb)** faire des démarches (auprès de qn)

representative [reprɪ'zentətɪv] **1** *n* représentant(e) *m,f*
2 *adj* représentatif(ive)

repress [rɪ'pres] *vt* réprimer; *(memories, feelings)* refouler; **to be repressed** (*of person*) être un(e) refoulé(e)

repression [rɪ'preʃən] *n* répression *f*; (*of memories, feelings*) refoulement *m*

repressive [rɪ'presɪv] *adj* répressif(ive)

reprieve [rɪ'priːv] **1** *n Law* (*cancellation*) commutation *f* de la peine capitale; *(postponement)* sursis *m*; *Fig* **to win a r.** *(of project, company)* bénéficier d'un sursis
2 *vt Law* **to r. sb** *(cancel punishment of)* commuer la peine capitale de qn en réclusion à perpétuité; *(postpone punishment of)* accorder un sursis à qn

reprimand ['reprɪmɑːnd] **1** *n* (*to child*) réprimande *f*; (*to employee*) avertissement *m*
2 *vt* (*child*) réprimander; *(employee)* avertir

reprint 1 *n* ['riːprɪnt] réimpression *f*
2 *vt* [riː'prɪnt] réimprimer

reprisal [rɪ'praɪzəl] *n* représailles *fpl*; **to take reprisals** exercer des représailles; **in r. for** en représailles à

reproach [rɪ'prəʊtʃ] **1** *n* reproche *m*; **a look of r.** un regard plein de reproche; **beyond or above r.** irréprochable
2 *vt* faire des reproches à; **to r. sb for or with sth** reprocher qch à qn; **to r. oneself for sth** se reprocher qch

reproachful [rɪ'prəʊtʃfʊl] *adj* (*tone*) de reproche; (*look*) plein(e) de reproche

reprobate ['reprəbeɪt] *n* réprouvé(e) *m,f*; *Hum* dépravé(e) *m,f*

reproduce [riːprə'djuːs] **1** *vt* reproduire
2 *vi* se reproduire

reproduction [riːprə'dʌkʃən] *n* reproduction *f*; **r. furniture** copies *fpl* (de meubles anciens)

reproductive [riːprə'dʌktɪv] *adj* reproducteur(trice); **r. organs** organes *mpl* reproducteurs

reproof [rɪ'pruːf] *n Formal* réprobation *f*

reprove [rɪ'pruːv] *vt Formal* (*person*) réprimander; *(action)* condamner

reproving [rɪ'pruːvɪŋ] *adj Formal* réprobateur(trice)

reptile ['reptaɪl] *n* reptile *m*

reptilian [rep'tɪlɪən] *adj* reptilien(enne); *Fig* (*manner, looks*) de reptile

republic [rɪ'pʌblɪk] *n* république *f*

Republican [rə'pʌblɪkən] *n & adj (in US, Ireland)* républicain(e) *m,f*

republican [rə'pʌblɪkən] *n & adj* républicain(e) *m,f*

repudiate [rɪ'pju:dɪeɪt] *vt Formal (offer)* rejeter; *(person, belief)* renier; *(wife)* répudier; *(rumour)* démentir

repudiation [rɪpju:dɪ'eɪʃən] *n Formal (of offer)* rejet *m;* (of *person, belief)* reniement *m;* (of *wife)* répudiation *f;* (of *rumour)* démenti *m*

repugnant [rɪ'pʌgnənt] *adj* répugnant(e)

repulse [rɪ'pʌls] *vt* repousser

repulsive [rɪ'pʌlsɪv] *adj* repoussant(e)

reputable ['repjʊtəbəl] *adj* de bonne réputation

reputation [repju:'teɪʃən] *n* réputation *f;* **to have a good/bad r.** avoir (une) bonne/mauvaise réputation; **to have a r. for doing sth** avoir la réputation de faire qch; **to have a r. for frankness** avoir la réputation d'être franc (franche); **to live up to one's r.** être à la hauteur de sa réputation

repute [rɪ'pju:t] **1** *n Formal* réputation *f;* **to be held in high r.** être estimé(e); **of r.** réputé(e)
2 *vt* **she is reputed to be wealthy/a genius** on la dit riche/géniale

reputedly [rɪ'pju:tɪdlɪ] *adv* à ce qu'on dit

request [rɪ'kwest] **1** *n* demande *f* **(for** de**); available on r.** qui peut être obtenu(e) sur simple demande; **to make a r. (for)** faire une demande **(de); at sb's r.** à la demande de qn; **by popular r.** à la demande générale; **r. stop** *(for bus)* arrêt *m* facultatif
2 *vt* demander; **to r. sb to do sth** prier à qn de faire qch

requiem ['rekwɪəm] *n* requiem *m;* **r. (mass)** messe *f* de requiem

require [rɪ'kwaɪə(r)] *vt (of task, problem, situation)* requérir; *(of person)* avoir besoin de; **to be required to do sth** être tenu(e) de faire qch; **if required** si besoin est/était; **when required** quand il le faut/fallait/faudra

requirement [rɪ'kwaɪəmənt] *n (need)* exigence *f;* *(condition)* condition *f* (requise); **to meet** *or* **satisfy sb's requirements** *(needs)* correspondre aux besoins de qn; *(demands)* satisfaire aux exigences de qn

requisite ['rekwɪzɪt] **1** *n* élément *m* essentiel
2 *adj* requis(e)

requisition [rekwɪ'zɪʃən] *vt* réquisitionner

rerun 1 *n* ['ri:rʌn] *(on TV)* rediffusion *f; Fig (of situation, conflict)* répétition *f*
2 *vt* [ri:'rʌn] *(pt* **reran** [ri:'ræn], *pp* **rerun)** **(a)** *(TV programme)* rediffuser **(b)** *(race)* courir de nouveau

resale [ri:'seɪl] *n* revente *f*

reschedule [ri:'ʃedju:l] *vt* **(a)** *(meeting, flight)* change time of) changer l'heure de; *(change date of)* changer la date de **(b)** *(debt)* rééchelonner

rescind [rɪ'sɪnd] *vt (law)* abroger; *(contract)* résilier

rescue ['reskju:] **1** *n* secours *m;* (from drowning) sauvetage *m;* **to come to sb's r.** venir au secours de qn; **r. services** secours *mpl*
2 *vt (from death)* sauver; *(from difficulty)* secourir

rescuer ['reskju:ə(r)] *n* sauveteur *m*

research [rɪ'sɜ:tʃ] **1** *n* recherche *f;* **to do r.** faire de la recherche; **to do r. into sth** faire des recherches sur qch; **r. and development** recherche et développement *m;* **r. assistant/laboratory** assistant(e) *m,f*/laboratoire *m* de recherche
2 *vt* faire des recherches sur
3 *vi* faire des recherches **(into** sur**)**

researcher [rɪ'sɜ:tʃə(r)] *n* chercheur(euse) *m,f*

resemblance [rɪ'zembləns] *n* ressemblance *f* **(to** avec**); to bear a r. to** ressembler à

resemble [rɪ'zembəl] *vt* ressembler à

resent [rɪ'zent] *vt* ne pas apprécier du tout

resentful [rɪ'zentful] *adj* plein(e) de ressentiment; **to be** *or* **feel r.** éprouver du ressentiment

resentment [rɪ'zentmənt] *n* ressentiment *m;* **to feel r. towards sb** éprouver du ressentiment à l'égard de qn

reservation [rezə'veɪʃən] *n* **(a)** *(booking)* réservation *f;* **to make a r.** faire une réservation; **r. desk** bureau *m* des réservations **(b)** *(doubt)* réserve *f;* **to have reservations about** avoir des doutes sur **(c)** *(for Native Americans)* réserve *f* (indienne)

reserve [rɪ'zɜ:v] **1** *n* **(a)** *(supply)* réserve *f;* **to draw on one's reserves** puiser dans ses réserves; **to keep sth in r.** garder qch en réserve **(b)** *(in sport)* remplaçant(e) *m,f; Mil* **the reserves** les réservistes *mpl* **(c)** *(for birds, game)* réserve *f* **(d)** *(reticence)* réserve *f*
2 *vt (book, keep)* réserver; **to r. the right to do sth** se réserver le droit de faire qch; **to r. one's strength** ménager ses forces; **to r. judgement (on sth)** réserver son jugement (sur qch)

reserved [rɪ'zɜ:vd] *adj* réservé(e)

reservist [rɪ'zɜ:vɪst] *n Mil* réserviste *m*

reservoir ['rezəvwɑ:(r)] *n (lake)* réservoir *m; Fig (of strength, courage)* réserve *f*

reset [ri:'set] *(pt & pp* **reset)** *vt (a)* *(clock, watch)* mettre à l'heure; *(counter)* remettre à zéro; **r. button** bouton *m* de remise à zéro **(b)** *(fracture)* réduire

reshape [ri:'ʃeɪp] *vt* réorganiser

reshuffle ['ri:ʃʌfəl] *n* réorganisation *f; Br Pol* **(Cabinet) r.** remaniement *m* (ministériel)

reside [rɪ'zaɪd] *vi* résider **(at/in** à/dans/en**)**

residence ['rezɪdəns] *n* **(a)** *(stay)* séjour *m;* **to take up r.** s'installer; **place of r.** lieu *m* de résidence; **r. permit** permis *m* de séjour **(b)** *Formal (home)* demeure *f* **(c)** *Br Univ* **(hall of) r.** résidence *f* universitaire

resident ['rezɪdənt] **1** *n (of country, street)* habitant(e) *m,f;* *(of hotel)* pensionnaire *mf;* **residents' association** = association de propriétaires ou de locataires d'un immeuble ou d'un quartier
2 *adj* **to be r. in Manchester** résider à Manchester

residential [rezɪ'denʃəl] *adj* **(a)** *(neighbourhood)* résidentiel(elle) **(b)** *(staff)* à demeure; **r. course** = stage qui nécessite un déplacement de plusieurs jours

residual [rɪ'zɪdjuəl] *adj* résiduel(elle); *Fig (doubt, worry)* qui persiste; *(income)* net (nette)

residue ['rezɪdju:] *n* **(a)** *(remainder)* reste *m* **(b)** *Chem* résidu *m*

resign [rɪ'zaɪn] **1** *vt (a)* *(job, position)* démissionner de **(b) to r. oneself to sth/to doing sth** se résigner à qch/à faire qch
2 *vi* démissionner

resignation [rezɪg'neɪʃən] *n* **(a)** *(from job)* démission *f;* **to hand in one's r.** donner sa démission **(b)** *(attitude)* résignation *f*

resilience [rɪ'zɪlɪəns] *n (of material, metal)* élasticité *f;* (of *person, economy)* résistance *f*

resilient [rɪ'zɪlɪənt] *adj (material, metal)* élastique; *(person)* résistant(e)

resin ['rezɪn] *n* résine *f*

resist [rɪ'zɪst] **1** vt résister à; *Law* **to r. arrest** refuser d'obtempérer *(lors d'une arrestation)*; **to r. doing sth** s'empêcher de faire qch
2 vi résister

resistance [rɪ'zɪstəns] n résistance f *(to à)*; **to put up** or **offer r.** offrir une résistance; **to meet with r.** rencontrer une résistance; **to take the line of least r.** adopter la solution de facilité; **r. fighter** résistant(e) m,f

resistant [rɪ'zɪstənt] adj **to be r. to sth** résister à qch

resistor [rɪ'zɪstə(r)] n *Elec* résistance f

resit [ri:'sɪt] (pt & pp **resat** [ri:'sæt]) vt *(exam, driving test)* repasser

resolute ['rezəlu:t] adj résolu(e); *(refusal, opposition)* clair(e)

resolution [rezə'lu:ʃən] n **(a)** *(decision, solution)* résolution f; **to pass** or **carry a r.** adopter une résolution **(b)** *(firmness)* fermeté f

resolve [rɪ'zɒlv] **1** n résolution f
2 vt **(a)** *(decide)* **to r. to do sth** *(of individual)* se résoudre à faire qch; *(of committee)* décider de faire qch **(b)** *(solve)* résoudre
3 vi **to r. on/against doing sth** se résoudre à faire/ne pas faire qch

resonance ['rezənəns] n résonance f

resonant ['rezənənt] adj qui résonne

resonate ['rezəneɪt] vi résonner

resort [rɪ'zɔ:t] **1** n **(a)** *(recourse)* recours m; **without r. to** sans avoir recours à; **as a last r.** en dernier recours **(b)** *(holiday place)* lieu m de villégiature
2 vi **to r. to sth** recourir à qch; **to r. to doing sth** finir par faire qch

resound [rɪ'zaʊnd] vi résonner *(with de)*

resounding [rɪ'zaʊndɪŋ] adj *(crash, applause, failure)* retentissant(e); *(success)* éclatant(e)

resource [rɪ'zɔ:s] n **1** ressource f; **to be left to one's own resources** être livré(e) à soi-même; **r. management** gestion f des ressources
2 vt financer

resourceful [rɪ'zɔ:sfʊl] adj ingénieux(euse)

respect [rɪ'spekt] **1** n **(a)** *(admiration, consideration)* respect m; **to have r. for** avoir du respect pour; **treat mountains with r.** soyez prudent en montagne; **with all due r.** sauf le respect que je vous dois; **to pay one's last respects to sb** rendre les derniers hommages à qn **(b)** *(aspect)* égard m; **in many respects** à bien des égards; **in some** or **certain respects** à certains égards; **in all respects** or **every r.** à tous les égards; **with r. to, in r. of** concernant
2 vt respecter

respectability [rɪspektə'bɪlɪtɪ] n respectabilité f

respectable [rɪ'spektəbəl] adj *(decent, fairly large)* respectable; *(fairly good)* honorable

respectably [rɪ'spektəblɪ] adv **(a)** *(honourably, decently)* de manière respectable; *(dressed)* convenablement **(b)** *(fairly well)* honorablement

respecter [rɪ'spektə(r)] n **to be no r. of** n'avoir aucun respect pour

respectful [rɪ'spektfʊl] adj respectueux(euse)

respective [rɪ'spektɪv] adj respectif(ive)

respectively [rɪ'spektɪvlɪ] adv respectivement

respiration [respɪ'reɪʃən] n respiration f

respirator ['respɪreɪtə(r)] n respirateur m; **to be on a r.** être branché(e) sur un respirateur

respiratory [rɪ'spɪrətərɪ] adj respiratoire

respite ['respaɪt] n *(rest)* répit m; *(delay)* sursis m

resplendent [rɪ'splendənt] adj resplendissant(e)

respond [rɪ'spɒnd] vi *(answer)* répondre *(to à)*; *(react)* réagir *(to à)*; **to r.** *(to treatment)* *(of patient)* bien réagir (au traitement)

respondent [rɪ'spɒndənt] n **(a)** *Law* défendeur(eresse) m,f **(b)** *(to questionnaire)* sondé(e) m,f

response [rɪ'spɒns] n *(answer)* réponse f; *(reaction)* réaction f; **in r. to** en réponse à; **the appeal met with a** generous **r.** le public a répondu généreusement à l'appel; **r. time** temps m de réponse

responsibility [rɪspɒnsɪ'bɪlɪtɪ] (pl **responsibilities**) n responsabilité f *(for de)*; **to take** or **accept r. for sth** accepter la responsabilité de qch

responsible [rɪ'spɒnsəbəl] adj responsable *(for de)*; *(job)* à responsabilité; **to hold sb r.** tenir qn pour responsable

responsive [rɪ'spɒnsɪv] adj *(to kindness, praise)* sensible *(to à)*; *(to idea, suggestion)* réceptif(ive) *(to à)*

rest¹ [rest] **1** n **(a)** *(repose)* repos m; **to have** or **take a r.** se reposer; *Euph* **to be at r.** reposer en paix; **to put** or **set sb's mind at r.** rassurer qn; *Fam* **give it a r.!** tu veux bien arrêter cinq minutes!; **to come to r.** *(of ball, car)* s'arrêter **(b)** *(support)* support m **(c)** *Mus (pause)* silence m
2 vt **(a)** *(cause to repose)* **to r. one's eyes/legs** se reposer les yeux/les jambes; **God r. his soul!** que Dieu ait son âme! **(b)** *(lean)* poser *(on sur)* **(c)** *(argument, hopes, confidence)* fonder *(on sur)*; *Fig* **I r. my case!** sans commentaire!
3 vi **(a)** *(repose)* se reposer, prendre du repos; **I won't r. until she has been caught** je n'aurai de cesse qu'elle ne soit prise; **r. in peace** *(on gravestone)* qu'il/elle repose en paix **(b)** *(lean)* être posé(e) *(on sur)* **(c)** *(remain)* **to r. with sb** *(of decision, responsibility)* incomber à qn; **there the matter rests** l'affaire en est là; **I won't let it r. at that** je n'en resterai pas là; **r. assured…** soyez assuré que… **(d)** *(of argument, theory)* **to r. on** reposer sur

rest² [rest] n **the r.** *(remainder)* le reste; *(others)* les autres mpl; **the r. of the time/the men** le reste du temps/des hommes; **the r. of them will stay here** les autres resteront ici

restaurant ['restrɒnt] n restaurant m; **r. car** *(in train)* wagon-restaurant m

restful ['restfʊl] adj reposant(e)

restive ['restɪv] adj agité(e)

restless ['restlɪs] adj agité(e); **to have a r. night** passer une nuit agitée

restoration [restə'reɪʃən] n *(of furniture, monarchy)* restauration f; *(of communications, law and order)* rétablissement m; *(of property)* restitution f

restore [rɪ'stɔ:(r)] vt *(furniture, monarchy, faith, calm)* restaurer; *(communications, law and order, confidence)* rétablir; *(property)* restituer *(to à)*; **to r. sb to health/strength** redonner la santé/des forces à qn

restrain [rɪ'streɪn] vt *(person, dog)* maîtriser; *(passions)* refréner; *(anger, crowd)* contenir; **to r. sb from doing sth** retenir qn pour qu'il/elle ne fasse pas qch; **to r. oneself** *(from doing sth)* se retenir *(de faire qch)*

restrained [rɪ'streɪnd] adj *(person, manner)* réservé(e); *(tone, terms)* mesuré(e); *(style)* sobre

restraint [rɪ'streɪnt] n **(a)** *(moderation)* mesure f, modération f; **to show** or **exercise great r.** faire preuve d'une grande modération **(b)** *(restriction)* restriction f; **without r.** sans retenue

restrict [rɪ'strɪkt] vt (person, freedom) restreindre; **to r. oneself to sth/to doing sth** se limiter à qch/à faire qch

restricted [rɪ'strɪktɪd] adj restreint(e), limité(e); (document) secret(ète); **r. area** Mil zone f interdite; (for parking) zone bleue

restriction [rɪ'strɪkʃən] n restriction f; (of speed) limitation f; **to place restrictions on sth** apporter des restrictions à qch

restrictive [rɪ'strɪktɪv] adj restrictif(ive); Ind **r. practices** pratiques fpl restrictives

restroom ['restruːm] n Am toilettes fpl

restructure [riː'strʌktʃə(r)] vt restructurer

restructuring [riː'strʌktʃərɪŋ] n restructuration f

result [rɪ'zʌlt] 1 n résultat m; **as a r.** en conséquence; **as a r. of** à la suite de; **the r. is that...** il en résulte que...; **to yield** or **show results** donner des résultats
2 vi **to r. from** résulter de; **to r. in** entraîner

resultant [rɪ'zʌltənt] adj résultant(e)

resume [rɪ'zjuːm] 1 vt reprendre; (relations) renouer; (attempt) renouveler; (interest) retrouver
2 vi reprendre

résumé ['rezjʊmeɪ] n (summary) résumé m; Am (curriculum vitae) curriculum vitae m inv

resumption [rɪ'zʌmpʃən] n reprise f

resurface [riː'sɜːfɪs] 1 vt (road) refaire le revêtement de
2 vi also Fig refaire surface

resurgent [rɪ'sɜːdʒənt] adj renaissant(e); (economy) qui connaît une reprise

resurrect [rezə'rekt] vt Rel ressusciter; Fig (fashion) remettre au goût du jour; (argument) ressortir; (tradition) faire renaître

resurrection [rezə'rekʃən] n Fig réapparition f; Rel **the R.** la Résurrection (du Christ)

resuscitate [rɪ'sʌsɪteɪt] vt (person) ranimer; Fig (career) redonner un nouvel élan à; (scheme) ressortir

retail ['riːteɪl] 1 n Com (vente f au) détail m; **r. outlet** magasin m de détail; **r. price** prix m de détail; Econ **r. price index** indice m des prix de détail; **r. trade** commerce m de détail
2 vt (goods) vendre au détail
3 vi se vendre (**at** à)

retailer ['riːteɪlə(r)] n détaillant(e) m,f

retain [rɪ'teɪn] vt (a) (keep) conserver, garder (b) (hold in place) maintenir; **retaining wall** mur m de soutènement (c) (remember) retenir

retainer [rɪ'teɪnə(r)] n (a) (fee) appointements mpl (b) Old-fashioned (servant) serviteur m, servante f

retaliate [rɪ'tælɪeɪt] vi riposter

retaliation [rɪtælɪ'eɪʃən] n représailles fpl; **in r.** (**for sth**) en représailles (à qch)

retard [rɪ'tɑːd] vt retarder

retarded [rɪ'tɑːdɪd] adj (mentally) **r.** arriéré(e)

retch [retʃ] vi avoir des haut-le-cœur

retention [rɪ'tenʃən] n (of custom, practice) maintien m; (of fact, impression) mémorisation f

retentive [rɪ'tentɪv] adj (memory) fidèle; (person) qui a (une) bonne mémoire

rethink 1 ['riːθɪŋk] **to have a r.** (**about sth**) réfléchir à nouveau (à qch)
2 vt [riː'θɪŋk] (pt & pp **rethought** [riː'θɔːt]) repenser

reticent ['retɪsənt] adj peu communicatif(ive); **to be r. about sth** parler peu de qch

retina ['retɪnə] n rétine f

retinue ['retɪnjuː] n suite f, cortège m

retire [rɪ'taɪə(r)] 1 vt mettre à la retraite
2 vi (a) (of employee) prendre sa retraite (b) (withdraw) se retirer; (go to bed) (aller) se coucher

retired [rɪ'taɪəd] adj retraité(e), à la retraite

retirement [rɪ'taɪəmənt] n (from work, army) retraite f; **to take early r.** partir en retraite anticipée; **to come out of r.** reprendre sa carrière; **r. age** l'âge m de la retraite; **r. pension** (pension f de) retraite

retiring [rɪ'taɪərɪŋ] adj (a) (reserved) réservé(e) (b) (chairman, MP) sortant(e); (employee) qui prend sa retraite; **r. age** l'âge m de la retraite

retort [rɪ'tɔːt] 1 n (answer) réplique f
2 vt & vi répliquer

retrace [rɪ'treɪs] vt **to r. one's steps** revenir sur ses pas

retract [rɪ'trækt] 1 vt (a) (statement, offer) revenir sur (b) (claws, aircraft undercarriage) rentrer
2 vi (a) (of person) se rétracter (b) (of claws, aircraft undercarriage) rentrer

retractable [rɪ'træktəbəl] adj rétractable; (antenna, aircraft undercarriage) escamotable

retrain [riː'treɪn] 1 vt recycler
2 vi se recycler

retraining [riː'treɪnɪŋ] n recyclage m

retread ['riːtred] n pneu m rechapé

retreat [rɪ'triːt] 1 n (a) (withdrawal) retraite f; also Fig **to beat a (hasty) r.** battre en retraite (b) (place) retraite f
2 vi battre en retraite; Fig se réfugier

retrial [riː'traɪəl] n Law nouveau procès m

retribution [retrɪ'bjuːʃən] n châtiment m

retrieve [rɪ'triːv] vt récupérer; Comptr (file) ouvrir

retriever [rɪ'triːvə(r)] n (dog) retriever m

retroactive [retrəʊ'æktɪv] adj Formal rétroactif(ive)

retrograde ['retrəgreɪd] adj rétrograde

retrospect ['retrəspekt] n **in r.** après coup, rétrospectivement

retrospective [retrə'spektɪv] 1 n (exhibition) rétrospective f
2 adj rétrospectif(ive); (measure, decision) à effet rétroactif

return [rɪ'tɜːn] 1 n (a) (of person, peace, season, tennis service) retour m; (of goods) renvoi m; **on my r.** à mon retour; **by r. of post** par retour du courrier; **in r.** (**for**) en échange (de); **to do sth in r.** faire qch en retour; **many happy returns (of the day)!** bon anniversaire!; **r. journey** (voyage m de) retour; **r. match** match m retour; **r. ticket** (billet m) aller et retour m (b) Fin (profit) rapport m; **to bring a good r.** rapporter un bon bénéfice; **r. on investment** retour m sur investissement
2 vt (a) (give or send back) rendre; **to r. a favour** rendre la pareille; **r. to sender** (on letter) retour à l'envoyeur; **to r. service** (in tennis) renvoyer le service; **to r. sb's call** (on phone) rappeler qn; Law **to r. a verdict of guilty/not guilty** déclarer l'accusé(e) coupable/non coupable (b) Fin (profit) rapporter
3 vi (come back) revenir; (go back) retourner; **to r. to work** reprendre son travail

returnable [rɪ'tɜːnəbəl] adj (bottle) consigné(e)

reunification [riːjuːnɪfɪ'keɪʃən] n réunification f

reunify [riː'juːnɪfaɪ] (pt & pp **reunified**) vt réunifier

reunion [riː'juːnɪən] n réunion f

reunite [riːjuːˈnaɪt] vt réconcilier; **to be reunited with sb** retrouver qn

reusable [riːˈjuːzəbəl] adj réutilisable

reuse [riːˈjuːz] vt réutiliser

Rev Rel (abbr **Reverend**) R. Gray le révérend Gray

rev [rev] Fam **1** n (abbr **revolution**) tour m; **r. counter** compte-tours m inv
2 vt (pt & pp **revved**) **to r. the engine** faire monter le régime (du moteur)

revalue [riːˈvæljuː] vt Fin réévaluer

revamp [riːˈvæmp] vt Fam (image) rajeunir; (company) restructurer; (house) retaper

reveal [rɪˈviːl] vt révéler

revealing [rɪˈviːlɪŋ] adj (sign, comment) révélateur(trice); (clothing) qui ne cache pas grand-chose

revel [ˈrevəl] (pt & pp **revelled**, Am **reveled**) vi faire la fête; **to r. in sth** savourer qch

revelation [revəˈleɪʃən] n révélation f; **(the Book of) Revelations** l'Apocalypse f

reveller, Am **reveler** [ˈrevələ(r)] n fêtard(e) m,f

revenge [rɪˈvendʒ] **1** n (punishment) vengeance f; (getting one's own back) revanche f; **to take r. (on sb)** se venger (de qn); Prov **it's sweet** ça fait du bien de se venger!
2 vt venger

revenue [ˈrevənjuː] n revenu m; (from sales) recettes fpl

reverberate [rɪˈvɜːbəreɪt] vi (a) (of sound) résonner (b) (of news, rumour) se propager

reverberation [rɪvɜːbəˈreɪʃən] n (a) (sound) réverbération f (b) (of news, rumour) répercussion f

revere [rɪˈvɪə(r)] vt vénérer

reverence [ˈrevərəns] n révérence f

Reverend [ˈrevərənd] adj Rel révérend; **Right R.** très révérend

reverential [revəˈrenʃəl] adj révérencieux(euse)

reverie [ˈrevərɪ] n rêverie f

reversal [rɪˈvɜːsəl] n (of opinion, policy) revirement m; (of roles) renversement m; (of fortune) revers m; Law (of decision) annulation f

reverse [rɪˈvɜːs] **1** n (a) (opposite) contraire m; **quite the r.!** bien au contraire! (b) (of coin) revers m; (of fabric) envers m (c) (defeat) échec m; (misfortune) revers m; **to suffer a r.** (defeat) subir un échec; (misfortune) subir un revers (d) (gear) marche f arrière; **to put the car into r.** passer la marche arrière
2 adj inverse; **in r. order** en ordre inverse; **the r. side** of coin) le revers; (of fabric) l'envers m; Br **r.-charge call** communication f en PCV; **r. gear** marche f arrière
3 vt (a) (order, policy, roles) inverser; (decision) revenir sur; (situation, trend) renverser; Br **to r. the charges** appeler en PCV (b) (vehicle) faire reculer; **to r. the car** faire marche arrière

reversible [rɪˈvɜːsəbəl] adj (a) (jacket) réversible (b) (decree) révocable; (surgery) réversible; **not r.** (decision) irrévocable; (surgery) irréversible

▶revert to [rɪˈvɜːt] vt insep revenir à; **to r. to type** reprendre ses vieilles habitudes

review [rɪˈvjuː] **1** n (a) (of policy, salary) révision f; (of situation) examen m; **to be under r.** faire l'objet d'une révision (b) (of book, play, film) critique f (c) Mil revue f
2 vt (a) (policy, salary) réviser; (situation) faire le point sur (b) (book, play, film) faire la critique de (c) Mil (troops) passer en revue

reviewer [rɪˈvjuːə(r)] n (of book, play, film) critique mf

revile [rɪˈvaɪl] vt Formal vilipender

revise [rɪˈvaɪz] **1** vt (a) (text, law) réviser; (decision) réexaminer; **to r. one's opinion (of)** changer d'opinion (à l'égard de) (b) Br (for exam) (subject, notes) réviser
2 vi Br (for exam) réviser, faire des révisions

revision [rɪˈvɪʒən] n (a) (of text, law) révision f (b) Br (for exam) révisions fpl

revisionism [rɪˈvɪʒənɪzəm] n Pol révisionnisme m

revisit [riːˈvɪzɪt] vt (place) revisiter; (person) retourner voir

revitalize [riːˈvaɪtəlaɪz] vt (person) revigorer; (arts, industry) donner un nouvel essor à

revival [rɪˈvaɪvəl] n (of person) réanimation f; (of hopes) renaissance f; (of industry, custom, fashion) renouveau m; (of play) reprise f

revive [rɪˈvaɪv] **1** vt (person) ranimer; (industry, hopes, custom) faire renaître; (fashion) relancer
2 vi (of person) reprendre connaissance; (of industry) connaître un renouveau; (of hopes) renaître

revoke [rɪˈvəʊk] vt (law) abroger; (decision) revenir sur; (privilege) abolir; **to r. sb's licence** retirer son permis à qn

revolt [rɪˈvəʊlt] **1** n révolte f; **to be in r.** être en révolte
2 vt (disgust) dégoûter
3 vi (rebel) se révolter (**against** contre)

revolting [rɪˈvəʊltɪŋ] adj (disgusting) dégoûtant(e)

revolution [revəˈluːʃən] n (a) (radical change) révolution f (b) (turn) tour m, révolution f

revolutionary [revəˈluːʃənərɪ] (pl **revolutionaries**) n & adj révolutionnaire mf

revolutionize [revəˈluːʃənaɪz] vt révolutionner

revolve [rɪˈvɒlv] vi tourner (**around** autour de); Fig **to r. around sth** s'articuler autour de qch

revolver [rɪˈvɒlvə(r)] n revolver m

revolving [rɪˈvɒlvɪŋ] adj (chair) pivotant(e); (platform) tournant(e); Fin (credit) revolving inv; **r. door** porte f à tambour

revue [rɪˈvjuː] n Th revue f

revulsion [rɪˈvʌlʃən] n dégoût m

reward [rɪˈwɔːd] **1** n récompense f; **as a r. for** en récompense de
2 vt récompenser (**for** de ou pour)

rewarding [rɪˈwɔːdɪŋ] adj enrichissant(e), intéressant(e)

rewind [riːˈwaɪnd] (pt & pp **rewound** [riːˈwaʊnd]) vt (tape, film) rembobiner

rewire [riːˈwaɪə(r)] vt refaire l'installation électrique de

reword [riːˈwɜːd] vt reformuler

rework [riːˈwɜːk] vt retravailler

rewrite [riːˈraɪt] (pt **rewrote** [riːˈrəʊt], pp **rewritten** [riːˈrɪtən]) vt réécrire

Reykjavik [ˈrekjəvɪk] n Reykjavik

RFU [ɑːrefˈjuː] n Br Sp (abbr **Rugby Football Union**) = fédération britannique de rugby

rhapsodic(al) [ræpˈsɒdɪk(əl)] adj (prose, description) dithyrambique; (person) enthousiaste

rhapsodize [ˈræpsədaɪz] vi s'extasier (**over** or **about** sur)

rhapsody [ˈræpsədɪ] (pl **rhapsodies**) n Mus rhapsodie f; **to go into rhapsodies over sth** s'extasier sur qch

rhesus [ˈriːsəs] n **r. factor** facteur m rhésus; **r. positive/negative** rhésus m positif/négatif; **r. monkey** rhésus m

rhetoric [ˈretərɪk] n rhétorique f; **the speech was nothing but empty r.** le discours ne consistait qu'en de belles phrases creuses

rhetorical [rɪ'tɒrɪkəl] *adj (style, question)* rhétorique; *(term)* de rhétorique

rheumatic [ru:'mætɪk] *adj (pain)* rhumatismal(e); *(joint)* atteint(e) de rhumatisme; **r. fever** rhumatisme *m* articulaire aigu

rheumatoid arthritis ['ru:mətɔɪdɑ:'θ'raɪtɪs] *n* polyarthrite *f* rhumatoïde

Rhine [raɪn] *n* **the R.** le Rhin

rhinestone ['raɪnstəʊn] *n* faux diamant *m*

rhino ['raɪnəʊ] *(pl* **rhinos)** *n Fam* rhinocéros *m*

rhinoceros [raɪ'nɒsərəs] *n* rhinocéros *m*

Rhodes [rəʊdz] *n* Rhodes

rhododendron [rəʊdə'dendrən] *n* rhododendron *m*

rhomboid ['rɒmbɔɪd] *n* rhomboïde *m*

rhombus ['rɒmbəs] *(pl* **rhombuses** or **rhombi** ['rɒmbaɪ]) *n* losange *m*

Rhone [rəʊn] *n* **the R.** le Rhône

rhubarb ['ru:bɑ:b] *n* rhubarbe *f*; **r. jam/tart** confiture *f*/ tarte *f* à la rhubarbe

rhyme [raɪm] **1** *n (sound)* rime *f*; *(poem)* vers *mpl*; **without r. or reason** sans rime ni raison
2 *vi* rimer (**with** avec); **rhyming slang =** argot cockney où les mots sont remplacés par des locutions choisies pour la rime

rhythm ['rɪðəm] *n* rythme *m*; **r. method** *(of contraception)* méthode *f* du calendrier

rhythmic(al) ['rɪðmɪk(əl)] *adj* rythmé(e), cadencé(e)

rib [rɪb] **1** *n* **(a)** *(of person, animal)* côte *f* **(b)** *(of umbrella)* baleine *f*
2 *(pt & pp* **ribbed)** *Fam (tease)* taquiner (**about** à propos de)

ribald ['rɪbəld, 'raɪbɔld] *adj* grivois(e), paillard(e)

ribbed [rɪbd] *adj (fabric, jumper)* à côtes

ribbon ['rɪbən] *n (for hair, typewriter)* ruban *m*; *(of land)* bande *f* étroite; **to tear sth to ribbons** déchiqueter qch; *Fig (criticize)* éreinter qch

ribcage ['rɪbkeɪdʒ] *n* cage *f* thoracique

riboflavin(e) [raɪbəʊ'fleɪvɪn] *n Chem* riboflavine *f*

rice [raɪs] *n* riz *m*; **r. field** or **paddy** rizière *f*; **r. pudding** riz au lait

rich [rɪtʃ] **1** *npl* **the r.** les riches *mpl*; **riches** *(wealth)* richesses *fpl*
2 *adj* riche; *(harvest, supply)* abondant(e); *(colour)* intense; *(voice)* chaud(e); **to be r. in sth** être riche en qch; *Fam* **that's r.!** c'est un peu fort!

richly ['rɪtʃlɪ] *adv* richement; **r. deserved** bien mérité(e)

Richter Scale ['rɪktə'skeɪl] *n* échelle *f* de Richter

rick¹ [rɪk] *n (of hay, straw)* meule *f*

rick² *vt* **to r. one's neck** attraper un torticolis; **to r. one's back** se donner un tour de reins

rickets ['rɪkɪts] *npl* rachitisme *m*; **to have r.** être rachitique

rickety ['rɪkɪtɪ] *adj Fam (furniture, staircase)* branlant(e); *(alliance, alibi)* boiteux(euse)

ricochet ['rɪkəʃeɪ] **1** *n* ricochet *m*
2 *vi (pt & pp* **ricochetted)** ricocher (**off** sur)

rid [rɪd] *(pt* **rid**, *pp* **rid** or **ridden** ['rɪdən]) *vt* **to r. sb of sth** débarrasser qn de qch; **to get r. of sth** se débarrasser de qch

riddance ['rɪdəns] *n Fam* **good r.!** bon débarras!

ridden ['rɪdən] *pp of* **rid, ride**

riddle ['rɪdəl] **1** *n (puzzle)* devinette *f*; *(mystery)* énigme *f*
2 *vt* **to r. sb/sth with bullets** cribler qn/qch de balles; **riddled with mistakes** truffé(e) de fautes

ride [raɪd] **1** *n* **(a)** *(on bicycle, in car)* tour *m*; *(on horse)* promenade *f*; **to go for a r.** aller faire un tour; **to give sb a r.** *(in car)* conduire qn en voiture; **it's only a short r. away** ce n'est pas très loin; *Fig* **she was given a rough r.** on lui en a fait voir de toutes les couleurs; *Fig* **to take sb for a r.** mener qn en bateau **(b)** *(at funfair)* attraction *f*
2 *vi (pt* **rode** [rəʊd], *pp* **ridden** ['rɪdən]) *(horse, bicycle)* monter à; *(bus, train)* prendre
3 *vi (on horse)* faire du cheval; *(on bicycle)* faire de la bicyclette; *Fig* **to be riding high** connaître une période de succès; *Fam Fig* **to let it r.** laisser courir

▶**ride out** *vt sep (problem, crisis)* survivre à; *Fig* **to r. out the storm** surmonter la crise

rider ['raɪdə(r)] *n* **(a)** *(on horse)* cavalier(ère) *m,f*; *(on bicycle)* cycliste *mf*; *(on motorbike)* motocycliste *mf* **(b)** *Law (to document, treaty)* annexe *f*; *(to bill)* clause *f* additionnelle

ridge [rɪdʒ] *n (of mountain)* crête *f*; *(of roof)* faîte *m*; *(on surface)* strie *f*; *Met* **r. of high pressure** dorsale *f* barométrique

ridicule ['rɪdɪkju:l] **1** *n* ridicule *m*; **to hold sb/sth up to r.** tourner qn/qch en ridicule
2 *vt* ridiculiser, tourner en ridicule

ridiculous [rɪ'dɪkjʊləs] *adj* ridicule; **to make sb/sth look r.** rendre qn/qch ridicule; **to make oneself look r.** se rendre ridicule, se ridiculiser

riding ['raɪdɪŋ] *n* équitation *f*; **to go r.** faire du cheval; **r. boots** bottes *fpl* de cheval; **r. crop** or **whip** cravache *f*; **r. school** école *f* d'équitation

rife [raɪf] *adj* **to be r.** être très répandu(e); *(of rumours)* aller bon train

riffraff ['rɪfræf] *n* racaille *f*

rifle¹ ['raɪfəl] *n* fusil *m*; **r. range** champ *m* de tir; *(at funfair)* stand *m* de tir; **r. shot** coup *m* de fusil

rifle² *vt (house, office)* mettre sens dessus dessous; *(pockets, drawer)* fouiller dans

rifleman ['raɪfəlmən] *n Mil* fusilier *m*

rift [rɪft] *n (in earth, rock)* fissure *f*; *(in relationship)* rupture *f*; *(difference of opinion)* désaccord *m*

rig [rɪg] **1** *n* **(a)** *(of ship)* gréement *m* **(b)** *(oil)* **r.** derrick *m*; *(at sea)* plate-forme *f* pétrolière
2 *vt (pt & pp* **rigged)** **(a)** *(ship)* gréer **(b)** *Fam (election, contest)* truquer

▶**rig out** *vt sep Fam* **to be rigged out in** être attifé(e) de

▶**rig up** *vt sep* monter, installer

Riga ['ri:gə] *n* Riga

rigging ['rɪgɪŋ] *n (of ship)* gréement *m*

right¹ [raɪt] *n* **(a)** *(morality)* bien *m*; **to be in the r.** avoir raison; **to set things to rights** arranger les choses
(b) *(entitlement)* droit *m*; **to have the r. to do sth** avoir le droit de faire qch; **to be within one's rights** être dans son droit; **by rights** en principe; **by r. of** de droit; **to be famous in one's own r.** être soi-même une célébrité; **the r. to vote** le droit de vote; **r. of way** *(on land)* droit de passage; *(on road)* priorité *f*
(c) *(right-hand side)* droite *f*, côté *m* droit; **on** or **to the r.** à droite; **on my r.** à ou sur ma droite; **the r.** *(in politics)* la droite
2 *adj* **(a)** *(correct)* exact(e), bon (bonne); *(word)* juste; **to be r.** *(of person)* avoir raison; **to keep on the r. side of sb** veiller à ne pas se mettre qn à dos; **to be on the r. lines** être sur la bonne voie

(b) *(morally good)* bien *inv*; **to do the r. thing** faire ce qu'il faut

(c) *(appropriate)* bon (bonne); **the r. thing to do la** meilleure chose à faire; **to know the r. people** connaître les gens qu'il faut; **to be in the r. place at the r. time** se trouver là au bon moment

(d) *(mentally, physically well)* **I'm not feeling quite r.** je ne me sens pas très bien; **to be as r. as rain** être en parfaite santé; **no one in his r. mind would do that** aucune personne sensée ne ferait cela; **he's not quite r. in the head** il n'a pas toute sa tête

(e) *Fam (for emphasis)* véritable; **I felt a r. fool** je me suis vraiment senti stupide; **my hair was in a r. mess** mes cheveux étaient complètement en bataille

(f) *(right-hand)* droit(e); **on the r. side** à *ou* sur la droite; *Pol* **the r. wing** l'aile *f* droite

(g) *Math* **r. angle** angle *m* droit

3 *adv* **(a)** *(straight)* (tout) droit; **to put things r.** arranger les choses; **to put sb r.** détromper qn

(b) r. away *(immediately)* sur-le-champ, immédiatement; **I'll be r. back** je reviens tout de suite; **r. now** *(immediately)* tout de suite; *(at the moment)* en ce moment

(c) *(completely)* **to go r. through sth** traverser qch de part en part; **to go r. up to sb** se diriger (tout) droit vers qn; **to turn r. round** se retourner; **r. at the top/back** tout en haut/à l'arrière

(d) *(exactly)* **r. here/there** juste ici/là; **r. in the middle** en plein milieu; **r. behind** juste derrière; *Fig* **to be r. behind sb** soutenir qn à fond

(e) *(answer)* correctement; *(guess)* juste; **to understand/ remember r.** bien comprendre/se souvenir

(f) *(well)* **I'm sure it'll all come r.** je suis sûr que tout s'arrangera pour vous; *Fam* **to see sb r.** veiller à ce que qn ne soit pas à court d'argent; **it was a mistake, r. enough** c'était bien une erreur

(g) *(look, turn)* à droite; *Fig* **r., left and centre** de tous les côtés

4 *vt* **(a)** *(put upright)* redresser

(b) *(redress)* **to r. a wrong** réparer un tort

right-angled ['raɪtæŋgəld] *adj* à angle droit; *(triangle)* rectangle

righteous ['raɪtʃəs] *adj (person)* droit(e), vertueux(euse); *(indignation)* vertueux(euse)

rightful ['raɪtfəl] *adj (heir, owner)* légitime; *(share)* auquel (à laquelle) on a droit

right-hand ['raɪthænd] *adj* de droite, *(corner, side)* droit(e); **r. bend** virage *m* à droite; **r. drive** conduite *f* à droite; **on the r. side** à droite; **to be sb's r. man** être le bras droit de qn

right-handed [raɪt'hændɪd] **1** *adj* droitier(ère)
2 *adv* de la main droite

right-hander [raɪt'hændə(r)] *n (person)* droitier(ère) *m,f*

rightly ['raɪtlɪ] *adv (correctly)* bien; *(justifiably)* à juste titre; **I don't r. know why...** je ne sais pas exactement pourquoi...; **r. or wrongly** à tort ou à raison; **... and r. so ...** et non sans raison

right-minded [raɪt'maɪndɪd], **right-thinking** [raɪt'θɪŋkɪŋ] *adj* sensé(e)

right-wing [raɪt'wɪŋ] *adj Pol* de droite

right-winger [raɪt'wɪŋə(r)] *n Pol (man)* homme *m* de droite; *(woman)* femme *f* de droite

rigid ['rɪdʒɪd] *adj* rigide; *Fig (person, ideas)* inflexible; *Br Fam* **to be bored r.** s'ennuyer ferme

rigidity [rɪ'dʒɪdɪtɪ] *n* rigidité *f*

rigmarole ['rɪgmərəʊl] *n Fam (process)* procédure *f* compliquée; *(speech)* long discours *m*

rigor mortis ['rɪgə(r)'mɔːtɪs] *n* rigidité *f* cadavérique

rigorous ['rɪgərəs] *adj* rigoureux(euse)

rigour ['rɪgə(r)] *n* rigueur *f*

rigout ['rɪgaʊt] *n Fam (outfit)* tenue *f*

rile [raɪl] *vt Fam* agacer

rim [rɪm] *n (of cup, bowl)* bord *m*; *(of wheel)* jante *f*; *(of spectacles)* monture *f*

rind [raɪnd] *n (of fruit)* écorce *f*; *(of cheese)* croûte *f*; *(of bacon)* couenne *f*

ring¹ [rɪŋ] **1** *n* **(a)** *(for finger)* (with stone) bague *f*; *(without stone)* anneau *m*; *(for keys)* porte-clés *m inv*; **the rings** *(in gymnastics)* les anneaux; **r. binder** classeur *m* à anneaux; **r. finger** annulaire *m* **(b)** *(of people, chairs)* cercle *m*; *(on stove)* brûleur *m*; *(stain)* marque *f*; **to have rings under one's eyes** avoir des cernes sous les yeux; *Fig* **to run rings round sb** surpasser qn; **r. road** périphérique *m* **(c)** *(for boxing, wrestling)* ring *m* **(d)** *(of criminals)* bande *f*; *(of spies)* réseau *m*

2 *vt (surround)* encercler

ring² [rɪŋ] **1** *n (sound)* (of doorbell, telephone) sonnerie *f*; *(of small bell, coins)* tintement *m*; **there was a r. at the door** on sonna à la porte; *Fam* **to give sb a r.** passer un coup de fil à qn; **to have a r. of truth** avoir l'air vrai(e); **the name has a familiar r. to it** ce nom me dit quelque chose

2 *vt (pt* **rang** [ræŋ], *pp* **rung** [rʌŋ]) *(bell)* sonner; *(alarm)* déclencher; *(on phone)* appeler; **to r. the doorbell** sonner à la porte; *Fig* **that rings a bell** cela me dit quelque chose; *Fig* **to r. the changes** introduire des changements

3 *vi* **(a)** *(of bell, telephone)* sonner; **to r. at the door** sonner à la porte; *Fig* **to r. true** avoir l'air vrai(e); **to r. false** sonner faux **(b)** *(resonate)* *(of ears)* bourdonner; **to r. with** *(of street, room)* retentir de **(c)** *(make a phone call)* appeler

▸**ring back** *vt sep* (on phone) rappeler

▸**ring off** *vi (on phone)* raccrocher

▸**ring out** *vi (of voice, shout)* retentir

▸**ring up** *vt sep* **(a)** *(on phone)* téléphoner à, appeler **(b)** *(on cash register)* enregistrer; **to r. up a profit** enregistrer un bénéfice

ringleader ['rɪŋliːdə(r)] *n (of strike)* meneur(euse) *m,f*; *(of gang)* chef *m* de bande

ringlet ['rɪŋlɪt] *n* anglaise *f*

ringmaster ['rɪŋmɑːstə(r)] *n* ≃ Monsieur *m* Loyal

ring-pull ['rɪŋpʊl] *n* bague *f* (d'ouverture)

ringside ['rɪŋsaɪd] *n* **at the r.** près du ring; **to have a r. seat** avoir une place au premier rang; *Fig* être aux premières loges

ringworm ['rɪŋwɜːm] *n Med* teigne *f*

rink [rɪŋk] *n (for roller skating)* piste *f*; *(for ice skating)* patinoire *f*

rinse [rɪns] **1** *n* **to give sth a r.** rincer qch
2 *vt (clothes, dishes)* rincer; **to r. one's hands/hair** se rincer les mains/les cheveux

▸**rinse out** *vt sep* rincer

Rio (de Janeiro) ['riːəʊ(dɪdʒə'neərəʊ)] *n* Rio (de Janeiro)

riot ['raɪət] **1** *n (uprising)* émeute *f*; *Fig* **a r. of colour** une explosion de couleurs; **to run r.** se déchaîner; **her imagination was running r.** elle s'imaginait toutes sortes de choses; **to read sb the r. act** passer un savon à qn; **r. police** police *f* anti-émeute, ≃ CRS *mpl*

2 *vi* faire une émeute; *(of prisoners)* se mutiner

rioter ['raɪətə(r)] n émeutier(ère) m,f

rioting ['raɪətɪŋ] n émeutes fpl

riotous ['raɪətəs] adj (party, behaviour, event) tapageur(euse); **r. living** vie f déréglée

RIP [ɑːraɪˈpiː] (abbr **Rest In Peace**) qu'il/elle repose en paix

rip [rɪp] 1 n déchirure f

2 vt (pt & pp **ripped**) déchirer; **to r. sth to pieces** (cloth) mettre qch en lambeaux; (paper) déchirer qch en mille morceaux; Fig (criticize) mettre qch en pièces

3 vi (a) (of cloth, paper) se déchirer (b) Fam **to let r.** (in performance) se déchaîner; **to let r. at sb** s'en prendre violemment à qn

▸**rip off** vt sep (a) (tear) arracher (b) Fam (swindle) arnaquer; (steal) piquer

▸**rip open** vt sep **to r. open a letter** ouvrir une lettre en déchirant l'enveloppe; **to r. open a parcel** ouvrir un paquet en le déchirant

▸**rip up** vt sep (a) (letter) déchirer (b) (floorboards) arracher; (pavement) creuser des trous dans

ripe [raɪp] adj (fruit) mûr(e); (cheese) fait(e) à point; **to live to a r. old age** vivre jusqu'à un âge avancé; **the time is r.** (to do sth) le temps est venu (de faire qch)

ripen ['raɪpən] vti mûrir; (of cheese) se faire

rip-off ['rɪpɒf] n Fam arnaque f

riposte [rɪˈpɒst] n riposte f, réplique f

ripple ['rɪpəl] 1 n (on water) ride f; (of applause) vague f; (of excitement) frémissement m

2 vi (of water) se rider; **laughter rippled through the audience** des vagues de rires ont parcouru le public

rise [raɪz] 1 n (a) (in price, temperature, pressure) hausse f; (pay) r. augmentation f (de salaire); **to be on the r.** (of prices) être en hausse; (of crime, inflation) être en augmentation; **the r. and fall of** la grandeur et la décadence de

(b) (of leader, party) ascension f; **r. to power** accession f au pouvoir

(c) (in road, ground) éminence f

(d) (idioms) **to give r. to sth** donner lieu à qch; Fam **to take a r. out of sb** faire enrager qn

2 vi (pt **rose** [rəʊz], pp **risen** ['rɪzən]) (a) (get up) se lever; (after falling) se relever; Fam **r. and shine!** debout là-dedans!

(b) (of smoke, balloon, ground) monter; (of sun, moon) se lever; (in career) monter; **a murmur rose from the crowd** un murmure s'éleva de la foule; **to r. to the occasion** se montrer à la hauteur de la situation; **to r. to the position of managing director** accéder au poste de P-DG; **to r. to power** accéder au pouvoir; **to r. in sb's esteem** monter dans l'estime de qn

(c) (of temperature) s'élever, monter; (of price) augmenter; (of hope) grandir; (of dough) lever; **my spirits rose** je repris courage; **her voice rose in anger** elle a élevé la voix sous l'effet de la colère

(d) (revolt) se soulever; **to r. in arms** prendre les armes; **to r. in protest (against sth)** se soulever (contre qch)

▸**rise above** vt insep (problem, criticism) surmonter

▸**rise up** vi (revolt) se soulever; **to r. up in arms** prendre les armes; **to r. up in protest (against sth)** se soulever (contre qch)

risible ['rɪzɪbəl] adj risible

rising ['raɪzɪŋ] 1 n (revolt) soulèvement m

2 adj (sun) levant; (temperature) en hausse; (prices, inflation)

en augmentation; (artist, politician) qui monte; Fig **r. star** étoile f montante

risk [rɪsk] 1 n risque m; **to take a r.** prendre un risque; **at r.** (life, person) en danger; (job) menacé(e); **to put one's health at r.** risquer de s'abîmer la santé; **at the r. of doing sth** au risque de faire qch; **to run the r. of doing sth** courir le risque de faire qch; **at one's own r.** à ses risques et périls; **r. assessment** évaluation f des risques; **r. capital** capital m à risque; **r. management** gestion f des risques

2 vt (a) (life, reputation) risquer; **to r. one's neck** risquer sa peau (b) (take the chance of) **to r. failure** risquer d'échouer; **to r. death** risquer sa vie; **I can't r. going** je ne peux pas prendre le risque d'y aller; **they r. losing all their money** ils risquent de perdre tout leur argent; **we can't r. it** nous ne pouvons pas courir ce risque

risky ['rɪskɪ] adj risqué(e)

risotto [rɪˈzɒtəʊ] (pl **risottos**) n risotto m

risqué ['rɪskeɪ] adj osé(e)

rissole ['rɪsəʊl] n croquette f

rite [raɪt] n rite m

ritual ['rɪtjʊəl] 1 n rituel m

2 adj rituel(elle)

ritzy ['rɪtsɪ] adj Fam chic inv

rival ['raɪvəl] 1 n & adj rival(e) m,f

2 vt (pt & pp **rivalled**, Am **rivaled**) (compete with) rivaliser avec; (equal) égaler

rivalry ['raɪvəlrɪ] n rivalité f

river ['rɪvə(r)] n rivière f; (flowing into sea) fleuve m; Fig (of blood) flot m

riverbed ['rɪvəbed] n lit m de la rivière

riverside ['rɪvəsaɪd] n bord m de l'eau; **r. villa** villa f au bord de l'eau

rivet ['rɪvɪt] 1 n rivet m

2 vt river; **to be riveted (by)** être fasciné(e) (par); Fig **to be riveted to the spot** (with fear, surprise) être cloué(e) sur place

riveting ['rɪvɪtɪŋ] adj Fig fascinant(e)

Riviera [rɪvɪˈeərə] n **the (French) R.** la Côte d'Azur

RN [ɑːˈren] Br (abbr **Royal Navy**) ≃ Marine f Nationale

RNA [ɑːreˈnˈeɪ] n (abbr **ribonucleic acid**) ARN m

RNLI [ɑːrenelˈaɪ] n Br (abbr **Royal National Lifeboat Institution**) ≃ Société f nationale de sauvetage en mer

roach [rəʊtʃ] n (a) (fish) gardon m (b) Am Fam (cockroach) cafard m

road [rəʊd] n route f; (in town) rue f; **they live across** or **over the r.** ils habitent en face; **by r.** par la route; **to be off the r.** (of car) être en panne; **down/up the r.** un peu plus loin dans la rue; Fam **one for the r.** (final drink) un petit dernier pour la route; **to be on the r.** (of salesman) être sur la route; (of pop group) être en tournée; **after three hours on the r.** après trois heures de route; **to be on the r. to recovery** être en voie de guérison; Fig **to be on the right r.** être sur la bonne voie; Fam **let's get this show on the r.!** allez, c'est parti, on y va!; **a few years down the r.** dans quelques années; Fig **to come to the end of the r.** (of relationship) toucher à sa fin; **r. accident** accident m de la route; **r. conditions** états mpl des routes; Fam **r. hog** chauffard m; **r. map** carte f routière; **r. rage** violence f au volant; **r. sign** panneau m de signalisation; **r. tax** ≃ vignette f (automobile); **r. works** or **repairs** travaux mpl de voirie

roadblock ['rəʊdblɒk] n barrage m routier

roadside ['rəʊdsaɪd] *n* bord *m* de la route; **r. bar/hotel** bar *m*/hôtel *m* situé en bord de route

road-test ['rəʊdtest] *vt (car)* essayer sur route

roadway ['rəʊdweɪ] *n* chaussée *f*

roadworthy ['rəʊdwɜːðɪ] *adj* en état de rouler

roam [rəʊm] **1** *vt (streets, world)* parcourir; *(seas)* sillonner
2 *vi* to r. (about) errer; **to r. about the streets** traîner dans les rues

roar [rɔː(r)] **1** *n (of person, crowd)* hurlement *m*; *(of animal, engine)* rugissement *m*; *(of sea, wind)* mugissement *m*; *(of cars)* vacarme *m*
2 *vi (of person, crowd)* hurler; *(of animal, engine)* rugir; *(of sea, wind)* mugir; *(of cars)* vrombir; **to r. with laughter** hurler de rire

roaring ['rɔːrɪŋ] *adj* **r. drunk** ivre mort(e); **a r. fire** une belle flambée; **a r. success** un succès fou; **to do a r. trade** faire des affaires en or

roast [rəʊst] **1** *n (piece of meat)* rôti *m*
2 *adj* rôti(e)
3 *vt* **(a)** *(meat, potatoes)* faire rôtir; *(nuts, coffee)* faire griller **(b)** *Fam (criticize)* éreinter

roasting ['rəʊstɪŋ] *Fam* **1** *n* **to give sb a r.** *(reprimand)* passer un savon à qn; *(criticize)* descendre qn en flammes
2 *adj* **r. (-hot)** brûlant(e); **it's r. in here** il fait une chaleur à crever ici

rob [rɒb] *(pt & pp robbed) vt (bank)* dévaliser; *(person)* voler; *(house)* cambrioler; **to r. sb of sth** *(money, possession)* voler qch à qn; *Fig (youth, opportunity)* priver qn de qch

robber ['rɒbə(r)] *n* voleur(euse) *m,f*

robbery ['rɒbərɪ] *(pl robberies) n* vol *m*

robe [rəʊb] *n (of priest, judge)* robe *f*; *Am (dressing gown)* robe de chambre

robin ['rɒbɪn] *n* rouge-gorge *m*

robot ['rəʊbɒt] *n* robot *m*

robotics [rəʊ'bɒtɪks] *n* robotique *f*

robust [rəʊ'bʌst] *adj (person)* robuste; *(material, suitcase)* solide; *(defence, speech)* musclé(e)

rock [rɒk] **1** *n* **(a)** *(substance)* roche *f*; *(large stone)* rocher *m*; *Fig* **to be on the rocks** *(of marriage, company)* être en pleine débâcle; **on the rocks** *(drink)* avec des glaçons; **the R. of Gibraltar** le Rocher de Gibraltar; **to reach** *or* **hit r. bottom** toucher le fond; **r. climbing** varappe *f*; **r. face** paroi *f* rocheuse; **r. garden** rocaille *f*; **r. pool** = flaque d'eau dans les rochers à marée basse; **r. salt** sel *m* gemme; **r. solid** solide comme le roc **(b)** *Br (sweet)* = sucrerie en forme de bâton parfumée à la menthe **(c)** *(rocking motion)* **to give the cradle a r.** balancer un peu le berceau **(d)** *(music)* rock *m*; **r. and roll** rock-and-roll *m*; **r. concert** concert *m* de rock; **r. group** groupe *m* de rock; **r. singer** chanteur(euse) *m,f* de rock
2 *vt (boat, chair)* balancer; *(building)* secouer; **to r. a baby to sleep** bercer un enfant pour qu'il s'endorme; *Fig* **to r. the boat** faire des histoires; *Fig* **the country has been rocked by these revelations** le pays a été secoué par ces révélations
3 *vi (sway)* se balancer; *(of building)* trembler; **to r. with laughter** être secoué(e) par un fou rire

rock-bottom ['rɒkbɒtəm] *adj* **r. prices** prix *mpl* incroyables

rocker ['rɒkə(r)] *n* **(a)** *(chair)* fauteuil *m* à bascule; *Fam* **to be off one's r.** être givré(e) **(b)** *(musician, fan)* rocker(euse) *m,f*

rockery ['rɒkərɪ] *(pl rockeries) n* rocaille *f*

rocket ['rɒkɪt] **1** *n* fusée *f*; *Fig* **to give sb a r.** engueuler qn; **r. launcher** lance-fusées *m inv*
2 *vi (of prices, inflation, unemployment)* monter en flèche

rockfall ['rɒkfɔːl] *n* éboulement *m*

rock-hard [rɒk'hɑːd] *adj* dur(e) comme (de la) pierre

Rockies ['rɒkɪz] *npl* **the R.** les Rocheuses *fpl*

rocky ['rɒkɪ] *adj* **(a)** *(path, soil)* rocailleux(euse); **the R. Mountains** les Montagnes *fpl* Rocheuses **(b)** *Fig (economy, relationship)* instable

rod [rɒd] *n (wooden)* baguette *f*; *(metal)* tige *f*; *(for curtain)* tringle *f*; *(for fishing)* canne *f* à pêche; *Fig* **to rule with a r. of iron** gouverner d'une main de fer; *Fig* **to make a r. for one's own back** se préparer des ennuis

rode [rəʊd] *pt of* **ride**

rodent ['rəʊdənt] *n* rongeur *m*

rodeo ['rəʊdɪəʊ] *(pl rodeos) n* rodéo *m*

roe[1] [rəʊ] *n* **r. (deer)** chevreuil *m*

roe[2] *n (of fish)* œufs *mpl* de poisson

roger[1] ['rɒdʒə(r)] *exclam (in radio message)* bien reçu!

roger[2] *vt very Fam (have sex with)* baiser

rogue [rəʊg] *n (dishonest)* filou *m*; *(mischievous)* coquin(e) *m,f*; **r. elephant** éléphant *m* solitaire

roguish ['rəʊgɪʃ] *adj* canaille

role [rəʊl] *n* rôle *m*; *Fig* **to play an important/a leading r. (in sth)** jouer un rôle important/prépondérant (dans qch); **r. model** modèle *m*

role-playing ['rəʊlpleɪŋ] *n* jeu *m* de rôle

roll [rəʊl] **1** *n* **(a)** *(of paper)* rouleau *m*; *(of fat)* bourrelet *m*; *(of banknotes)* liasse *f*; **a r. of film** une pellicule (photo) **(b)** *(bread)* petit pain *m*; **cheese r.** ≃ sandwich *m* au fromage **(c)** *(of drum, thunder)* roulement *m* **(d)** *(movement)* roulis *m*; *Fam* **to be on a r.** avoir la chance de son côté **(e)** *(list)* liste *f*; **r. call** appel *m*; *Mil* **r. of honour** liste de ceux qui sont morts pour la patrie
2 *vt* **(a)** *(ball)* faire rouler; **to r. sth along the ground** faire rouler qch sur le sol; **to r. one's eyes** lever les yeux au ciel; **to r. one's r's** rouler les r; **the animal rolled itself into a ball** l'animal se mit en boule **(b)** *(lawn)* passer au rouleau; *(road)* cylindrer; *(metal)* laminer **(c)** *(cigarette)* rouler
3 *vi (of ball, ship)* rouler; *(of camera)* tourner; *Fig* **heads will r.** il y a des têtes qui vont tomber; *Fam* **to be rolling in money, to be rolling in it** rouler sur l'or; *Fig* **to start the ball rolling** mettre les choses en route **(b)** *(of thunder)* gronder

▶**roll down 1** *vt sep (sleeves)* redescendre; *(blind, car window)* descendre
2 *vi (of tears, sweat)* couler

▶**roll on** *vi Fam* **r. on Friday/Christmas!** vivement vendredi/Noël!

▶**roll over** *vi (of person) (once)* se retourner; *(several times)* se rouler; *(of car) (once)* capoter; *(several times)* faire des tonneaux

▶**roll up 1** *vt sep (newspaper)* rouler; *(sleeves)* retrousser; *(blind, car window)* remonter; **to r. sth up in paper** envelopper qch dans du papier
2 *vi Fam (arrive)* rappliquer; **r. up!, r. up!** venez nombreux!

rolled-up [rəʊl'dʌp] *adj (sleeves, trousers)* retroussé(e); *(umbrella)* replié(e); *(newspaper)* roulé(e)

roller ['rəʊlə(r)] n (for paint, garden) rouleau m; (for hair) bigoudi m; **r. blind** store m (à cylindre); **r. coaster** montagnes fpl russes; **r. skates** patins mpl à roulettes

rollerblades ['rəʊləbleɪdz] npl patins mpl en ligne

rollerblading ['rəʊləbleɪdɪŋ] n **to go r.** faire du patin à roulettes (avec des patins en ligne)

roller-skate ['rəʊləskeɪt] vi faire du patin à roulettes

roller-skating ['rəʊləskeɪtɪŋ] n **to go r.** faire du patin à roulettes

rolling ['rəʊlɪŋ] adj (hills, fields) ondulant(e); (sea, waves) gros (grosse); (thunder) qui gronde; **r. mill** (for steel) laminoir m; **r. pin** rouleau m à pâtisserie; Rail **r. stock** matériel m roulant

rollneck ['rəʊlnek] adj (sweater) à col roulé

roll-on ['rəʊlɒn] adj (a) **r.** (deodorant) déodorant m à bille (b) Naut **r.-roll-off ferry** ferry m de type roll-on-roll-off

rollover ['rəʊləʊvə(r)] n (in lottery) = à la loterie nationale, situation où, personne n'ayant gagné le gros lot, celui-ci est ajouté à l'enjeu du tirage suivant

roll-top desk ['rəʊltɒp'desk] n bureau m à cylindre

roll-up ['rəʊlʌp] n Fam (cigarette) cigarette f roulée

roly-poly ['rəʊlɪ'pəʊlɪ] adj Fam (plump) grassouillet(ette)

ROM [rɒm] n Comptr (abbr **read only memory**) mémoire f morte

Roman ['rəʊmən] 1 n Romain(e) m,f
2 adj romain(e); **R. Catholic** catholique; **R. nose** nez m aquilin; **R. numerals** chiffres mpl romains

roman ['rəʊmən] Typ 1 n romain m
2 adj romain(e)

romance ['rəʊmæns, rə'mæns] n (a) (book) roman m d'amour; (film) histoire f d'amour (b) (love affair) aventure f (c) (charm) charme m

Romania [rə'meɪnɪə] n la Roumanie

Romanian [rə'meɪnɪən] 1 n (a) (person) Roumain(e) m,f (b) (language) roumain m
2 adj roumain(e)

romantic [rəʊ'mæntɪk, rə'mæntɪk] 1 n romantique mf
2 adj romantique; (scheme, notion) romanesque

romanticism [rəʊ'mæntɪsɪzəm] n romantisme m

romanticize [rə'mæntɪsaɪz] vt (incident) romancer; (idea, war) présenter sous un jour romantique

Romany ['rəʊmənɪ] 1 n (pl **Romanies**) (a) (person) Tzigane mf (b) (language) tzigane m
2 adj tzigane

Rome [rəʊm] n Rome; **R. wasn't built in a day** Paris ne s'est pas fait en un jour; **when in R., do as the Romans do** (b) il faut adopter les usages de l'endroit où l'on se trouve

romp [rɒmp] 1 n **to have a r.** chahuter
2 vi **to r.** (about or around) s'ébattre; **to r. through an exam** réussir un examen les doigts dans le nez

romper ['rɒmpə(r)] n **r. suit, rompers** barboteuse f

roof [ruːf] 1 n (of building, car) toit m; (of tunnel, cave) plafond m; **to have a r. over one's head** avoir un endroit où vivre; **to live under one or the same roof** vivre sous le même toit; Fam **to hit the r.** sortir de ses gonds; Fam **to go through the r.** connaître une flambée; **r. of the mouth** voûte f du palais; **r. garden** jardin m aménagé sur le toit; **r. rack** galerie f
2 vt couvrir

roofing ['ruːfɪŋ] n toiture f; **r. material** matériaux mpl de couverture

rooftop ['ruːftɒp] n toit m; Fig **to shout sth from the rooftops** crier qch sur les toits

rook [rʊk] n (bird) freux m; (in chess) tour f

rookery ['rʊkərɪ] (pl **rookeries**) n colonie f de freux

rookie ['rʊkɪ] n Am Fam bleu m

room [ruːm] 1 n (a) (in house) pièce f; (bedroom, in hotel) chambre f; (large, public) salle f; **r. and board** chambre et pension; **r. service** service m dans les chambres; **r. temperature** température f ambiante (b) (space) place f; **there's no r. to move** il n'y a pas de place; **to make r. (for sb)** faire de la place (pour qn); **there's no r. for doubt** cela ne fait aucun doute; **there is r. for improvement** ça pourrait être mieux
2 vi Am **to r. with sb** partager une chambre avec qn

roomy ['ruːmɪ] adj spacieux(euse); (clothes) ample

roost [ruːst] 1 n perchoir m; **to rule the r.** faire la loi
2 vi se percher; Fig **her actions have come home to r.** ses actions se sont retournées contre elle

rooster ['ruːstə(r)] n coq m

root [ruːt] 1 n (a) (of plant, tooth, word, hair) racine f; **to pull up by the roots** (plant) déraciner; also Fig **to take r.** prendre racine; **they destroyed the party r. and branch** ils ont entièrement détruit le parti; Fig **to put down roots** s'intégrer; Fig **to get back to one's roots** retrouver ses racines; Am **r. beer** = boisson gazeuse aux extraits de plantes; **r. crops** racines comestibles; **r. vegetables** légumes mpl à racine comestible (b) (origin) origine f; Prov **money is the r. of all evil** l'argent est la source de tous les maux
2 vt **to be rooted to the spot** être figé(e) sur place
3 vi (a) **to r. about or around** (for sth) fouiller (pour trouver qch) (b) Am **to r. for sb** appuyer qn

▸**root for** vt insep (support) être pour

▸**root out** vt sep supprimer

rope [rəʊp] 1 n (a) corde f; (of pearls) sautoir m; (of onions) chapelet m; **r. ladder** échelle f de corde (b) (idioms) **to be on the ropes** (of company) battre de l'aile; **to learn the ropes** apprendre les ficelles; **to show sb the ropes** former qn; **to give sb plenty of r.** donner du mou à qn
2 vt (fasten) lier (avec une corde) (to à); **they roped themselves together** (for climbing) ils se sont encordés

▸**rope in** vt sep Fam (recruit) recruter; **to get roped in to do sth** se laisser convaincre de faire qch

▸**rope off** vt sep **to r. sth off** interdire l'accès de qch avec une corde

rop(e)y ['rəʊpɪ] adj Fam (unreliable) pas terrible; (ill) patraque

rosary ['rəʊzərɪ] (pl **rosaries**) n Rel chapelet m; **to say one's r.** dire son chapelet

rose¹ [rəʊz] 1 n (a) (flower) rose f; (on watering can) pomme f; **r. bed** parterre m de rosiers; **r. bush** rosier m; **r. garden** roseraie f; **r. grower** rosiériste mf; **r. window** rosace f (b) (idioms) **life isn't a bed of roses** tout n'est pas rose dans la vie; **to come up roses** se passer à merveille
2 adj (colour) rose

rose² pt of **rise**

rosé ['rəʊzeɪ] n rosé m

rosebud ['rəʊzbʌd] n bouton m de rose

rose-coloured ['rəʊzkʌləd], **rose-tinted** ['rəʊz-tɪntɪd] adj **to see things through r. glasses** or **spectacles** voir la vie en rose

rosehip ['rəʊzhɪp] n gratte-cul m

rosemary ['rəʊzmərɪ] n romarin m

rosette [rəʊ'zet] *n* rosette *f*

rosewater ['rəʊzwɔːtə(r)] *n* eau *f* de rose

rosewood ['rəʊzwʊd] *n* bois *m* de rose

roster ['rɒstə(r)] *n* liste *f* de service

rostrum ['rɒstrəm] (*pl* **rostrums** *or* **rostra** ['rɒstrə]) *n* (*for speaker*) estrade *f*; (*for prizewinner*) podium *m*

rosy ['rəʊzɪ] *adj* (*pink*) rose; (*complexion*) de rose; *Fig* (*future*) prometteur(euse)

rot [rɒt] **1** *n* (a) (*in house, wood*) pourriture *f*; *Fig* **the r. has set in** ça se gâte; *Fig* **to stop the r.** empêcher la situation de se dégrader (b) *Fam* (*nonsense*) bêtises *fpl*
2 *vt* (*pt & pp* **rotted**) (faire) pourrir
3 *vi* pourrir; **to r. in prison** moisir en prison

rota ['rəʊtə] *n* roulement *m*

rotary ['rəʊtərɪ] **1** *n* (*pl* **rotaries**) *Am* (*roundabout*) rond-point *m*
2 *adj* rotatif(ive)

rotate [rəʊ'teɪt] *vt* (a) (*turn*) faire tourner (b) (*alternate*) (*duties*) remplir à tour de rôle; (*crops*) alterner
2 *vi* (a) (*turn*) tourner (b) (*in job*) remplir des fonctions à tour de rôle

rotation [rəʊ'teɪʃən] *n* (a) (*of planet*) rotation *f* (b) (*in job*) roulement *m*; (*of crops*) alternance *f*; **by** *or* **in r.** à tour de rôle

rote [rəʊt] *n* **by r.** par cœur; **r. learning** apprentissage *m* par cœur

rotor ['rəʊtə(r)] *n* rotor *m*

rotten ['rɒtən] *adj* (a) (*wood, egg, fruit*) pourri(e) (b) *Fam* (*bad*) nul (nulle); (*weather*) pourri(e); **to feel r.** (*ill*) ne pas se sentir dans son assiette; (*guilty*) ne pas être fier(ère) (**about** de); **to have r. luck** avoir la guigne (c) (*unpleasant*) dégueulasse; **a r. trick** un tour de cochon

rotter ['rɒtə(r)] *n* *Fam Old-fashioned* peau *f* de vache

rottweiler ['rɒtvaɪlə(r)] *n* rottweiler *m*

rotund [rəʊ'tʌnd] *adj* rond(e)

rouble ['ruːbəl] *n* rouble *m*

rouge [ruːʒ] *n* rouge *m* (à joues)

rough [rʌf] **1** *n* (a) (*in golf*) rough *m*
(b) *Fam Old-fashioned* (*hooligan*) voyou *m*
(c) (*difficulty*) **you have to take the r. with the smooth** on ne peut pas tout avoir dans la vie
2 *adj* (a) (*surface, skin*) rugueux(euse); (*terrain*) accidenté(e)
(b) (*unrefined*) (*manners*) fruste; *Fig* **a r. diamond** un cœur d'or sous des dehors frustes; **r. draft** brouillon *m*; **r. sketch** ébauche *f*
(c) *Fam* (*to feel/look*) **r.** se sentir/avoir l'air patraque
(d) (*violent*) brutal(e); (*crossing, sea*) agité(e)
(e) (*harsh*) (*voice*) rude; (*wine, spirits*) âpre; *Fam* **it was r. on her** c'était dur pour elle; **r. justice** justice *f* sommaire
(f) (*approximate*) approximatif(ive); **at a r. guess** à vue de nez; **I've got a r. idea of what he wants** j'ai une petite idée de ce qu'il veut
3 *adv* **to play r.** jouer avec brutalité; *Fig* ne pas faire de cadeaux; *Fam* **to sleep r.** coucher à la dure
4 *vt Fam* **to r. it** vivre à la dure

▸**rough up** *vt sep Fam* (*beat up*) tabasser

roughage ['rʌfɪdʒ] *n* fibres *fpl* (alimentaires)

rough-and-ready [rʌfən'redɪ] *adj* (*meal, accommodation*) sommaire; (*person*) rustre

rough-and-tumble [rʌfən'tʌmbəl] *n* bousculade *f*; *Fig* **the r. of politics** le monde sans pitié de la politique

roughly ['rʌflɪ] *adv* (a) (*violently*) brutalement; **to treat sb r.** rudoyer qn (b) (*crudely*) grossièrement (c) (*approximately*) à peu près; **r. (speaking)** en gros

roughness ['rʌfnɪs] *n* (a) (*of surface, skin*) rugosité *f* (b) (*of behaviour*) rudesse *f*

roughshod ['rʌfʃɒd] *adv* **to ride r. over sth** ne faire aucun cas de qch

rough-spoken [rʌf'spəʊkən] *adj* au langage grossier

roulette [ruː'let] *n* roulette *f*; **r. table** table *f* de roulette; **r. wheel** roulette

round [raʊnd] **1** *n* (a) (*slice*) (*of bread*) tranche *f*; **a r. of sandwiches** = un sandwich au pain de mie coupé en deux ou en quatre
(b) (*stage of match*) manche *f*; (*stage of tournament*) tour *m*; (*in boxing*) round *m*; (*of golf*) partie *f*; **to get/be through to the next r.** se qualifier/s'être qualifié(e) pour le tour suivant
(c) (*of talks, visits*) série *f*; (*of drinks*) tournée *f*; **r. of applause** applaudissements *mpl*; **to give sb a r. of applause** applaudir qn
(d) **to do one's rounds** (*of doctor*) faire ses visites; **to do the rounds** (*of rumour, illness*) circuler; **the daily r.** (*of tasks*) le train-train quotidien
(e) *Mil* (*bullet*) balle *f*
(f) *Mus* canon *m*
2 *adj* rond(e); **to have r. shoulders** avoir le dos rond; **a r. dozen** une douzaine exactement; **in r. figures** en arrondissant; **r. table (conference)** table *f* ronde; **r. trip** aller (et) retour *m*
3 *adv* autour; **all (the) year r.** toute l'année; **all r.** (*on the whole*) dans l'ensemble; **the wrong way r.** à l'envers; **the right way r.** (*not back to front*) à l'endroit; (*in the correct order*) dans le bon ordre; **the other way r.** (*in the other direction*) dans l'autre sens; **do it the other way r.** fais l'inverse; **to go r.** (*to sb's house*) passer (chez qn); **to invite sb r.** inviter qn
4 *prep* (a) (*position*) autour de; **r. here** dans le coin
(b) (*motion*) **to look r. a room** parcourir une pièce du regard; **to travel r. the world** parcourir le monde; **to go r. an obstacle** contourner un obstacle; **to go r. the corner** (*of person*) tourner le coin; (*of vehicle*) prendre le virage; **it's just r. the corner** c'est juste au coin (de la rue); *Fig* **to drive** *or* **send sb r. the bend** rendre qn maboul(e)
(c) (*approximately*) **r. about** environ; **r. about midday** vers midi
5 *vt* (a) (*make round*) arrondir
(b) (*obstacle*) contourner; (*corner*) tourner

▸**round down** *vt sep* (*figure*) arrondir au chiffre inférieur

▸**round off** *vt sep* (*conclude*) conclure

▸**round up** *vt sep* (a) (*cattle*) rassembler; (*criminals, suspects*) ramasser (b) (*figure*) arrondir au chiffre supérieur

roundabout ['raʊndəbaʊt] **1** *n* (a) (*at fairground*) manège *m* (b) (*for cars*) rond-point *m*
2 *adj* (*approach, route*) détourné(e); **to lead up to a question in a r. way** aborder une question de biais

rounders ['raʊndəz] *n* = jeu similaire au base-ball

roundly ['raʊndlɪ] *adv* (*praise, condemn*) vivement; (*beat*) sévèrement

round-trip ['raʊndtrɪp] *adj Am* (*ticket*) aller (et) retour

roundup ['raʊndʌp] *n* (*of criminals*) rafle *f*; (*of events, news*) résumé *m*

rouse [raʊz] *vt* réveiller; **to r. oneself (to do sth)** se secouer (et faire qch); **to r. sb to action** pousser qn à agir; **to r. sb to anger** susciter la colère de qn

rousing ['raʊzɪŋ] *adj* (*music, speech*) exaltant(e); (*welcome, cheers*) enthousiaste

rout [raʊt] **1** *n* déroute *f*
2 *vt* mettre en déroute

▶**rout out** *vt sep* (*get rid of*) se débarrasser de

route [ru:t] **1** *n* (*of traveller*) itinéraire *m*; (*of plane, ship*) route *f*; (*of bus, parade*) parcours *m*; *Fig* (*to success*) voie *f* (**to** de)
2 *vt* (*parcel, goods*) acheminer; (*bus, train, flight*) faire passer

routine [ru:'ti:n] **1** *n* (**a**) (*habit*) routine *f*; **the daily r.** le train-train quotidien (**b**) (*of performer, comedian*) numéro *m*; *Fam* **Fig don't give me that r.** arrête ton numéro (**c**) *Comptr* sous-programme *m*
2 *adj* (**a**) (*normal*) de routine (**b**) (*dull*) routinier(ère)

routinely [ru:'ti:nlɪ] *adv* systématiquement

rove [raʊv] **1** *vt* parcourir
2 *vi* rôder, vagabonder; **her eyes roved around the room** son regard parcourait la pièce

row[1] [raʊ] *n* (*line*) rangée *f*; **in a r.** en rang; **two Sundays in a r.** deux dimanches d'affilée; **in the front r.** (*of seats*) au premier rang

row[2] [raʊ] *n* (*in boat*) promenade *f* en canot; **to go for a r.** canoter
2 *vt* (*boat*) faire aller à la rame; (*person*) transporter en canot
3 *vi* (*in boat*) ramer

row[3] [raʊ] **1** *n* (**a**) (*noise*) vacarme *m*; (*protest*) tollé *m* (**b**) (*quarrel*) dispute *f*; **to have a r. (with sb)** se disputer (avec qn)
2 *vi* (*quarrel*) se disputer (**about** à propos de)

rowan ['raʊən] *n* sorbier *m*

rowboat ['raʊbəʊt] *n Am* bateau *m* à rames

rowdy ['raʊdɪ] **1** *n* (*pl* **rowdies**) chahuteur(euse) *m,f*
2 *adj* (*person*) chahuteur(euse); (*event, party*) bruyant(e); **to be r.** chahuter

rower ['raʊə(r)] *n* rameur(euse) *m,f*

rowing ['raʊɪŋ] *n* canotage *m*; (*as sport*) aviron *m*; **r. boat** bateau *m* à rames; **r. machine** rameur *m*

royal ['rɔɪəl] **1** *adj* royal(e); *Fig* (*splendid*) princier(ère); **His/Her R. Highness** Son Altesse Royale; **r. blue** bleu roi *m inv*; **the R. Family** la famille royale; **r. flush** (*in cards*) quinte *f* royale; **r. jelly** gelée *f* royale; **R. Mail** = la Poste britannique; **the R. Navy** = la marine nationale britannique
2 *n Fam* membre *m* de la famille royale; **the Royals** la famille royale

royalist ['rɔɪəlɪst] *n & adj* royaliste *mf*

royally ['rɔɪəlɪ] *adv* (*entertain, welcome*) royalement

royalty ['rɔɪəltɪ] *n* (**a**) (*rank, position*) royauté *f*; **to be r.** faire partie de la famille royale; **to be treated like r.** être traité(e) royalement (**b**) **royalties** (*for author, singer*) droits *mpl* d'auteur

RP [ɑː'piː] *n Ling* (*abbr* **received pronunciation**) = prononciation de l'anglais considérée comme la norme

RPI [ɑːpiː'aɪ] *n Econ* (*abbr* **retail price index**) indice *m* des prix de détail

rpm [ɑːpiː'em] *n Aut* (*abbr* **revolutions per minute**) tr/min

R & R [ɑːrən'ɑː(r)] *n Mil* (*abbr* **rest and recreation**) permission *f*

RRP [ɑːrɑː'piː] *n Com* (*abbr* **recommended retail price**) prix *m* conseillé

RS [ɑː'res] *n Br* (*abbr* **Royal Society**) ≃ Académie *f* des Sciences

RSA [ɑːres'eɪ] *n* (*abbr* **Republic of South Africa**) Afrique *f* du Sud

RSI [ɑːres'aɪ] *n* (*abbr* **repetitive strain injury**) = douleurs dans les bras et les mains dues à la répétition de certains mouvements

RSPB [ɑːrespiː'biː] *n Br* (*abbr* **Royal Society for the Protection of Birds**) = ligue pour la protection des oiseaux

RSPCA [ɑːrespiːsiː'eɪ] *n Br* (*abbr* **Royal Society for the Prevention of Cruelty to Animals**) ≃ SPA *f*

RSVP [ɑːresviː'piː] (*abbr* **répondez s'il vous plaît**) (*on invitation*) RSVP

Rt Hon *Br Parl* (*abbr* **Right Honourable**) = formule accolée au nom des ministres et anciens ministres

rub [rʌb] **1** *n* **to give sth a r.** frotter qch; *Fig* **there's the r.** voilà le hic!
2 *vt* (*pt & pp* **rubbed**) frotter; **to r. one's hands together** se frotter les mains; *Fig* **to r. shoulders with sb** côtoyer qn; *Fam* **to r. sb up the wrong way** prendre qn à rebrousse-poil
3 *vi* (*of straps, shoes*) frotter (**against** contre)

▶**rub along** *vi Fam* (**a**) (*manage*) se débrouiller (**b**) (*get on*) s'entendre (**with** avec)

▶**rub in** *vt sep* (*lotion, ointment*) faire pénétrer; *Fam* **to r. it in** retourner le couteau dans la plaie

▶**rub off 1** *vt sep* (*dirt, stain*) enlever en frottant; (*writing*) effacer
2 *vi* partir, s'enlever; *Fig* **to r. off on sb** (*of manners, enthusiasm*) déteindre sur qn

▶**rub out** *vt sep* (**a**) (*erase*) effacer (**b**) *Fam* (*murder*) descendre

rubber ['rʌbə(r)] *n* (**a**) (*substance*) caoutchouc *m*; **r. ball/gloves** balle *f*/gants *mpl* en caoutchouc; **r. band** élastique *m*; **r. dinghy** canot *m* pneumatique; **r. plant** caoutchouc; **r. ring** bouée *f*; **r. stamp** tampon *m* (**b**) (*eraser*) gomme *f*; (*for blackboards*) brosse *f* (**c**) *Am Fam* (*condom*) capote *f*

rubber-stamp [rʌbə'stæmp] *vt Fig* (*approve*) approuver sans discussion

rubbery ['rʌbərɪ] *adj* caoutchouteux(euse)

rubbish ['rʌbɪʃ] *Br* **1** *n* (**a**) (*refuse*) détritus *mpl*; (*from house*) ordures *fpl*; (*junk*) cochonneries *fpl*; **r. bag** sac *m* poubelle; **r. bin** poubelle *f*; **r. collection** ramassage *m* des ordures; **r. dump** dépotoir *m*; *Fig* **to throw sb/sth on the r. heap** mettre qn/qch au rancart (**b**) *Fam* (*nonsense*) idioties *fpl*; **that book/film is a load of r.** ce livre/film est nul; **r.!** n'importe quoi!
2 *vt Fam* (*book, plan*) descendre en flammes

rubble ['rʌbəl] *n* décombres *mpl*

rubella [ru:'belə] *n* rubéole *f*

rubric ['ru:brɪk] *n* instructions *fpl*

ruby ['ru:bɪ] **1** *n* (*pl* **rubies**) rubis *m*
2 *adj* (*colour*) rubis

RUC [ɑːrjuː'siː] *n* (*abbr* **Royal Ulster Constabulary**) = forces de l'ordre d'Irlande du Nord

ruck[1] [rʌk] *n* (**a**) (*in rugby*) mêlée *f* ouverte (**b**) (*fight*) bagarre *f*

ruck[2] **1** *n* (*in cloth*) faux pli *m*
2 *vi* **to r. up** (*of sheet*) se froisser

rucksack ['rʌksæk] *n* sac *m* à dos

ructions ['rʌkʃənz] *npl Fam* grabuge *m*

rudder ['rʌdə(r)] *n* gouvernail *m*

ruddy ['rʌdɪ] *adj* (a) *(complexion)* rose (b) *Br Fam (euphemism for bloody)* fichu(e); **the r. fool!** quel espèce d'imbécile!

rude [ru:d] *adj* (a) *(impolite)* impoli(e) (b) *(vulgar)* grossier(ère); *(gesture)* obscène (c) *(primitive)* rudimentaire (d) *(shock, surprise)* **to receive a r. awakening** être brutalement rappelé(e) à la réalité (e) *(vigorous)* **to be in r. health** jouir d'une santé robuste

rudeness ['ru:dnɪs] *n* (a) *(impoliteness)* impolitesse *f* (b) *(vulgarity)* grossièreté *f*

rudimentary [ru:dɪ'mentərɪ] *adj* rudimentaire

rudiments ['ru:dɪmənts] *npl* rudiments *mpl*

rue [ru:] *vt Lit* regretter amèrement; **I r. the day I met her** je maudis le jour où je l'ai rencontrée

rueful ['ru:fʊl] *adj (voice, smile)* de regret; *(person)* qui a des regrets

ruff [rʌf] *n (on costume)* fraise *f*

ruffian ['rʌfɪən] *n Old-fashioned* voyou *m*

ruffle ['rʌfəl] *vt (water)* troubler; *(hair)* ébouriffer; **to r. sb's feathers** froisser qn; **to r. sb's composure** faire perdre contenance à qn

rug [rʌg] *n* (a) *(carpet)* tapis *m*, *Fig* **to pull the r. from under sb's feet** couper l'herbe sous le pied à qn (b) *(blanket)* couverture *f*

rugby ['rʌgbɪ] *n* rugby *m*; **r. ball** ballon *m* de rugby; **r. league** rugby à treize; **r. player** rugbyman *m*; **r. tackle** plaquage *f*; **r. union** rugby à quinze

rugby-tackle ['rʌgbɪtækəl] *vt* **to r. sb** plaquer qn au sol

rugged ['rʌgɪd] *adj (ground, country)* accidenté(e); *(features, manner)* rude; **r. good looks** beauté *f* un peu rude

rugger ['rʌgə(r)] *n Fam (rugby)* rugby *m*

ruin ['ru:ɪn] **1** *n* ruine *f*; **to fall into ruin(s)** tomber en ruine(s); **it will be the r. of him** ça le perdra

2 *vt (suit, shoes)* abîmer; *(person)* ruiner; *(meal, evening, holiday)* gâcher; **to r. one's health** se ruiner la santé; **to r. one's eyesight** s'user la vue; **tourism has ruined the town** le tourisme a défiguré la ville; **a ruined castle** un château en ruine(s)

ruinous ['ru:ɪnəs] *adj (expensive)* ruineux(euse)

rule [ru:l] **1** *n* (a) *(principle)* règle *f*; *(regulation)* règlement *m*; **rules** *(of club, school)* règlement *m*; **as a r.** en règle générale; **to make it a r. to do sth** se faire un principe de faire qch; **rules and regulations** règles; *Ind* **to work to r.** faire la grève du zèle; **it's against the rules** c'est contraire au règlement; **as a r. of thumb** pour avoir une idée approximative; **r. book** règlement (b) *(government)* autorité *f* (c) *(for measuring)* règle *f*

2 *vt* (a) *(country, people)* gouverner; **to let sth r. one's life** laisser qch dominer toute sa vie; *Fig* **to r. the roost** commander (b) *(decide, decree)* décider; **to be ruled illegal** être décrété(e) illégal(e) (c) *(paper)* régler

3 *vi* (a) *(of monarch)* régner (b) *(of judge)* statuer (on sur); **to r. in favour of/against sb** décider en faveur de/contre qn

▸**rule out** *vt sep* exclure

ruler ['ru:lə(r)] *n* (a) *(of country)* dirigeant(e) *m,f* (b) *(for measuring)* règle *f*

ruling ['ru:lɪŋ] *n (of judge, umpire)* décision *f*

2 *adj* (a) *(party)* au pouvoir; *(class)* dirigeant(e) (b) *(passion)* dominant(e); *(consideration)* premier(ère)

rum¹ [rʌm] *n (drink)* rhum *m*

rum² *adj Fam (strange)* bizarre; *(suspect)* louche

Rumania [ru:'meɪnɪə] = **Romania**

Rumanian [ru:'meɪnɪən] = **Romanian**

rumble ['rʌmbəl] **1** *n (of thunder, gunfire, traffic)* grondement *m*; *(of voices)* bourdonnement *m*; *(of stomach)* gargouillement *m*; **rumbles of discontent** murmures *mpl* de protestation

2 *vt Fam (find out) (person)* deviner le jeu de; *(plot)* découvrir

3 *vi (of thunder, traffic)* gronder; *(of stomach)* gargouiller

rumbustious [rʌm'bʌstɪəs] *adj* exubérant(e)

ruminant ['ru:mɪnənt] *n Zool* ruminant *m*

ruminate ['ru:mɪneɪt] *vi Formal* **to r. (about** *or* **on sth)** ruminer (qch)

rummage ['rʌmɪdʒ] **1** *vi* **to r. about** *or* **around (for sth)** farfouiller (à la recherche de qch); **to r. through sth** fouiller qch

2 *n Am* **r. sale** vente *f* de charité

rumour ['ru:mə(r)] **1** *n* rumeur *f*, bruit *m*; **r. has it...** on raconte que...; **there's a r. going round that...** le bruit court que...

2 *vt* **it is rumoured that...** le bruit court que...; **he is rumoured to be very rich/in hiding** le bruit court qu'il est très riche/qu'il se cache

rump [rʌmp] *n* (a) *(of animal)* croupe *f*; *Fam (of person)* postérieur *m*; **r. steak** romsteck *m* (b) *(of political party, assembly)* restant *m*

rumple ['rʌmpəl] *vt (clothes, sheets)* friper, froisser; *(hair)* ébouriffer

rumpus ['rʌmpəs] *n Fam (noise)* chahut *m*; **to kick up** *or* **cause a r. (about sth)** faire un scandale (à propos de qch)

run [rʌn] **1** *n* (a) *(act of running)* course *f*; **at a r.** en courant; **to go for a r.** aller courir; **to be on the r.** être en fuite; *Fig* **we've got them on the r.** nous les avons mis en déroute; **to give sb the r. of the house** mettre sa maison à la disposition de qn; *Fam* **to make a r. for it** *(escape)* se tirer; *(to catch train)* se grouiller; *Fam* **to give sb a r. for his money** donner du fil à retordre à qn; *Fam* **to have the runs** avoir la courante

(b) *(trip)* trajet *m*; *(for pleasure)* balade *f*; **to go for a r.** *(in car)* aller se balader en voiture

(c) *Com (of book)* tirage *m*; *(of product)* série *f*

(d) *(sequence, series)* série *f*; *(in cards)* suite *f*; **a r. of good luck** une période faste; **a r. of bad luck** une série de malheurs; **in the short/long r.** à court/long terme

(e) *Fin (on currency, stock exchange)* ruée *f* (on sur); *(on bank)* retrait *m* massif

(f) *(in stocking)* échelle *f*

(g) *(in cricket, baseball)* point *m*

(h) *(for skier)* piste *f*

(i) *(for chickens, rabbits)* enclos *m*

(j) *Mus* roulade *f*

2 *vt (pt ran* [ræn], *pp run)* (a) *(distance, race)* courir; **to r. an errand** faire une course; **to allow things to r. their course** laisser les choses se faire; **to r. sb close** talonner qn; *Fam* **to be run off one's feet** être débordé(e)

(b) *(drive)* **to r. sb to the airport** conduire qn à l'aéroport

(c) *(drugs, arms)* faire le trafic de

(d) *(machine)* faire fonctionner; *(tests)* effectuer; *Comptr (program)* exécuter

(e) *(business)* diriger; *(hotel)* tenir; *(car)* avoir; **to r. sb's life for him** dire à qn comment vivre sa vie

(f) *(cables, pipes)* faire passer; **to r. one's fingers over/ through sth** passer la main sur/dans qch; **to r. one's**

eye over sth parcourir qch du regard
(g) (water, bath) faire couler
(h) to r. a temperature avoir de la température
(i) to r. a deficit enregistrer un déficit
(j) to r. an article publier un article
3 vi (a) (of person) courir; **to r. up/down the street** monter/descendre la rue en courant; **to r. about** courir çà et là; **I'll just r. across/round to the shop** je fais un saut à l'épicerie; **to r. after sb** courir après qn; **to r. for help** courir chercher de l'aide; **to r. in/out** entrer/sortir en courant
(b) (flee) s'enfuir, se sauver; **r. for it!** sauve qui peut!
(c) (compete in race) courir; **to r. for Parliament** se présenter aux législatives
(d) (flow) couler; **the river runs into a lake** la rivière se jette dans un lac; **my nose is running** j'ai le nez qui coule; **my blood ran cold** mon sang se glaça
(e) **to r. aground** (of ship) s'échouer; Fig (of project, economy) échouer
(f) (of contract, lease) courir; (of play) être à l'affiche; **it runs in the family** c'est de famille; **the total ran to £2,000** le montant total s'élevait à 2000 livres
(g) (of bus, train) circuler; **to be running late** (of bus, train) avoir du retard; (of person) être en retard
(h) (operate) (of machine) marcher, fonctionner; (of engine) tourner; **to r. on gas/electricity** marcher ou fonctionner au gaz/à l'électricité; **to r. off the mains** marcher ou fonctionner sur secteur; **the car runs on unleaded petrol** la voiture roule à l'essence sans plomb; **things are running smoothly** tout marche comme sur des roulettes
(i) (of road, railway) passer; **the line runs along the coast** la ligne suit ou longe la côte
(j) feelings or tempers are running high les esprits sont échauffés; **to be running low** (of funds, supplies) s'épuiser; **to r. dry** (of river) s'assécher
(k) (of colour, dye) déteindre

▶**run away** vi (of person) s'enfuir, se sauver (from de); **to r. away from home** faire une fugue; Fig **to r. away from the facts** refuser l'évidence; Fig **don't r. away with the idea that...** ne va pas t'imaginer que...

▶**run down 1** vt sep (a) (in car) renverser (b) (find) dénicher (c) (criticize) dénigrer (d) (reduce) (production, stocks) diminuer, réduire; (industry, factory) fermer progressivement
2 vi (of battery) se décharger

▶**run in** vt sep (a) Fam (arrest) pincer (b) (engine) roder

▶**run into** vt insep (a) (collide with) rentrer dans; Fig (difficulties) rencontrer; **to r. into trouble** s'attirer des ennuis (b) (meet by chance) tomber sur

▶**run off 1** vt sep (a) (print) imprimer; (photocopy) photocopier; **to r. off a copy of sth** faire une copie de qch
2 vi (of person) s'enfuir, se sauver (with avec)

▶**run on** vi (a) (of meeting) durer (b) Fam (talk a lot) parler sans arrêt

▶**run out** vi (of lease, contract) expirer; (of money, supplies) s'épuiser; **to have run out of sth** ne plus avoir de qch; **time is running out** il ne reste plus beaucoup de temps; Fig **to r. out of steam** (of person, project) s'essouffler

▶**run over 1** vt sep (in car) renverser, écraser
2 vt insep (speech, lines) revoir
3 vi (of speech, TV programme) déborder

▶**run to** vt insep (amount to) s'élever à; **we can't r. to a new car** (afford) nous ne pouvons pas nous permettre d'acheter une nouvelle voiture

▶**run up** vt sep (a) (debts) accumuler (b) (flag) hisser (c) (clothes) confectionner à la hâte

run-around ['rʌnəraʊnd] n Fam **to give sb the r.** faire tourner qn en bourrique

runaway ['rʌnəwei] **1** n fugitif(ive) m,f; (child) fugueur(euse) m,f
2 adj (prisoner, slave) en fuite; (train, lorry) fou (folle); (inflation) galopant(e); (victory) remporté(e) haut la main; (success) fou (folle)

rundown ['rʌndaʊn] n (summary) résumé m; **to give sb a r. (on sth)** mettre qn au courant (de qch)

run-down [rʌn'daʊn] adj (building) délabré(e); (person) fatigué(e)

rung[1] [rʌŋ] n (of ladder) échelon m; Fig **on the bottom/ top r.** tout en bas/en haut de l'échelle

rung[2] pp of **ring**[2]

run-in ['rʌnɪn] n Fam **to have a r. with sb** avoir un accrochage avec qn

runner ['rʌnə(r)] n (a) (athlete) coureur(euse) m,f; (messenger) coursier(ère) m,f; (for drugs, guns) passeur(euse) m,f (b) **r. bean** haricot m d'Espagne (c) (on sleigh) patin m; (on drawer) glissière f (d) Fam **to do a r.** se tirer

runner-up [rʌnə'rʌp] (pl **runners-up**) n suivant(e) m,f; (in second place) second(e) m,f

running ['rʌnɪŋ] **1** n (a) (activity) course f; **to go r.** courir; Fig **to be out of the r.** (in competition, race) n'avoir aucune chance; **to be in the r.** avoir des chances; **to make all the r.** (in relationship) prendre toutes les initiatives; Am Pol **r. mate** = candidat à la vice-présidence accompagnant dans sa campagne le candidat à la présidence des Etats-Unis; **r. shoe** chaussure f de course; **r. track** piste f (b) (of machine, car) **r. costs** frais mpl d'entretien (c) (management) gestion f
2 adj (battle, feud) incessant(e); Fam **go take a r. jump!** va voir ailleurs si j'y suis!; **r. board** (on car) marchepied m; **r. commentary** commentaire m en direct; **r. repairs** petites réparations fpl; **r. sore** plaie f qui suppure; **to keep a r. total (of sth)** comptabiliser (qch) au fur et à mesure; **r. water** eau f courante

runny ['rʌnɪ] adj (liquid) liquide; **to have a r. nose** avoir le nez qui coule

run-off ['rʌnɒf] n (a) (election) deuxième tour m; (contest) manche f pour départager deux candidats (b) (from fields) eaux fpl de ruissellement

run-of-the-mill [rʌnəvðə'mɪl] adj ordinaire

runt [rʌnt] n (a) (of litter) **the r.** le (la) plus faible de la portée (b) (weak person) avorton m

run-up ['rʌnʌp] n (before jump) course f d'élan; **the r. to the wedding/the election** la période précédant le mariage/les élections

runway ['rʌnwei] n piste f

rupee [ru:'pi:] n roupie f

rupture ['rʌptʃə(r)] **1** n rupture f
2 vt (relations) rompre; (container) faire éclater
3 vi also Med éclater

rural ['rʊərəl] adj rural(e)

ruse [ru:z] n ruse f

rush[1] [rʌʃ] n (plant) jonc m; **r. matting** natte f (de jonc)

rush[2] **1** n (a) (hurry) **what's the r.?** pourquoi tant de hâte?; **to be in a r.** être pressé(e); **to do sth in a r.** faire qch à toute vitesse; **there's no r.** il n'y a rien qui presse; **to make a r. for sth** se précipiter vers qch; **r. hour** heures *fpl* de pointe; **a r. job** *(urgent)* un travail urgent; *(hurried)* un travail bâclé **(b)** *(surge)* *(of air)* bouffée *f*; *(of water)* flot *m* soudain; *(of requests)* flot **(c)** *(demand)* ruée *f*; **there's been a r. on tickets** les gens se sont rués sur les billets **(d)** *Cin* **rushes** rush(e)s *mpl*

2 *vt* **(a)** *(hurry)* *(task)* faire à la hâte; *(person)* bousculer; **to r. sb into doing sth** bousculer qn pour qu'elle fasse qch; **to be rushed off one's feet** être débordé(e) **(b)** *(transport quickly)* transporter d'urgence **(c)** *(attack)* prendre d'assaut

3 *vi* *(move quickly)* se ruer **(at/towards** sur/vers); *(act quickly)* se dépêcher; **the blood rushed to her cheeks** le sang afflua à ses joues; **to r. to do sth** s'empresser de faire qch; **to r. into doing sth** faire qch sans réfléchir; **to r. into marriage** se marier sans réfléchir

▶**rush about, rush around** *vi* courir à droite et à gauche

▶**rush in** *vi* *(enter)* entrer précipitamment

▶**rush off** *vi* partir précipitamment

▶**rush out 1** *vt sep* *(book)* publier à la hâte

   2 *vi* *(exit)* sortir précipitamment

▶**rush through 1** *vt sep* *(bill)* faire passer à la hâte; *(decision)* prendre à la hâte

   2 *vt insep* *(book)* lire à toute vitesse; *(meal, work)* expédier

rusk [rʌsk] *n* gros biscuit *m* *(pour bébés)*

russet [ˈrʌsɪt] **1** *n* *(colour)* brun *m* roux

   2 *adj* brun roux *inv*

Russia [ˈrʌʃə] *n* la Russie

Russian [ˈrʌʃən] **1** *n* **(a)** *(person)* Russe *mf* **(b)** *(language)* russe *m*

   2 *adj* russe; **R. roulette** roulette *f* russe

rust [rʌst] **1** *n* rouille *f*

   2 *adj* *(colour)* rouille *inv*

   3 *vi* rouiller

rustic [ˈrʌstɪk] *adj* rustique

rustle¹ [ˈrʌsəl] **1** *n* *(of leaves, paper)* bruissement *m*

   2 *vt* *(leaves, paper)* faire bruire

   3 *vi* *(of leaves, paper)* bruire

rustle² *vt* *(cattle)* voler

▶**rustle up** *vt sep* *Fam* *(meal, snack)* improviser; **to r. up support** rassembler des partisans

rustler [ˈrʌslə(r)] *n* *(cattle thief)* voleur(euse) *m,f* de bétail

rustproof [ˈrʌstpruːf] *adj* *(paint)* antirouille *inv*; *(metal)* inoxydable

rusty [ˈrʌstɪ] *adj also Fig* rouillé(e); *(colour)* rouille *inv*

rut¹ [rʌt] *n* *(groove)* ornière *f*; *Fig* **to be in a r.** être prisonnier(ère) de la routine

rut² **1** *n* *(of stag)* rut *m*

   2 *vi* *(pt & pp* **rutted)***(of stag)* être en rut

rutabaga [ruːtəˈbeɪgə] *n Am* rutabaga *m*

ruthless [ˈruːθlɪs] *adj* impitoyable

RV [ɑːˈviː] *n Am* *(abbr* **recreational vehicle)** mobile home *m*

Rwanda [rəˈwændə] *n* le Rwanda

Rwandan [rəˈwændən] **1** *n* Rwandais(e) *m,f*

   2 *adj* rwandais(e)

rye [raɪ] *n* seigle *m*; **r. bread** pain *m* de seigle

S

S, s [es] n (a) (letter) S, s m inv (b) (abbr **south**) S

Sabbath ['sæbəθ] n (Jewish) (jour m du) sabbat m; (Christian) jour du seigneur

sabbatical [sə'bætɪkəl] Univ **1** n congé m sabbatique; **to be on s.** être en congé sabbatique
2 adj (term, year) sabbatique

sable ['seɪbəl] **1** n (animal) zibeline f; **s. coat** manteau m de ou en zibeline
2 adj Lit (black) noir(e)

sabotage ['sæbətɑːʒ] **1** n sabotage m
2 vt saboter

saboteur [sæbə'tɜː(r)] n saboteur(euse) m,f

sabre ['seɪbə(r)] n sabre m

sac [sæk] n Biol sac m

saccharin ['sækərɪn] n saccharine f

saccharine ['sækərɪn] adj Pej (smile, words) mielleux(euse); (film) à l'eau de rose

sachet ['sæʃeɪ] n sachet m

sack[1] [sæk] **1** n (a) (bag) sac m; Fam **to hit the s.** se pieuter (b) Fam (dismissal) renvoi m; **to give sb the s.** virer qn; **to get the s.** se faire virer
2 vt Fam (dismiss) virer

sack[2] **1** n (plundering) sac m
2 vt (plunder) mettre à sac

sacking ['sækɪŋ] n (a) (textile) grosse toile f (b) Fam (dismissal) renvoi m

sacrament ['sækrəmənt] n Rel sacrement m; **to take or receive the sacraments** communier

sacred ['seɪkrɪd] adj sacré(e); Fig **s. cow** (belief, institution) véritable institution f

sacrifice ['sækrɪfaɪs] **1** n sacrifice m; **to make sacrifices** faire des sacrifices
2 vt sacrifier (to à); **to s. oneself** se sacrifier

sacrificial [sækrɪ'fɪʃəl] adj sacrificiel(elle); Fig **s. lamb or victim** bouc m émissaire

sacrilege ['sækrɪlɪdʒ] n also Fig sacrilège m

sacrilegious [sækrɪ'lɪdʒəs] adj also Fig sacrilège

sacristan ['sækrɪstən] n Rel sacristain m

sacrosanct ['sækrəʊsæŋkt] adj sacro-saint(e)

SAD [sæd] n Med (abbr **Seasonal Affective Disorder**) = dépression due au manque de soleil en hiver

sad [sæd] adj (a) (unhappy, depressing) triste; **to make sb s.** attrister qn (b) Fam (pathetic) pitoyable

sadden ['sædən] vt attrister

saddle ['sædəl] **1** n (on horse, bicycle) selle f; **to be in the s.** être en selle; Fig être aux commandes
2 vt (horse) seller; Fam Fig **to s. sb with sth** refiler qn/qch à qn; **to get saddled with sb/sth** se retrouver avec qn/qch sur les bras

saddlebag ['sædəlbæg] n sacoche f

sadism ['seɪdɪzəm] n sadisme m

sadist ['seɪdɪst] n sadique mf

sadistic [sə'dɪstɪk] adj sadique

sadly ['sædlɪ] adv (a) (unhappily) tristement (b) (unfortunately) malheureusement (c) (greatly) **to be s. mistaken** se tromper lourdement; **he is s. missed** il nous/leur/etc manque beaucoup

sadness ['sædnɪs] n tristesse f

sadomasochism [seɪdəʊ'mæsəkɪzəm] n sadomasochisme m

sadomasochist [seɪdəʊ'mæsəkɪst] n sadomasochiste mf

SAE [eser'iː] n (abbr **stamped addressed envelope**) enveloppe f timbrée

safari [sə'fɑːrɪ] n safari m; **to go on s.** faire un safari; **s. jacket** saharienne f; **s. park** réserve f d'animaux sauvages

safe [seɪf] **1** adj (a) (not in danger) en sécurité; (house, activity) sûr(e); (topic of conversation) sans danger; **s. from sth** à l'abri de qch; **s. and sound** sain et sauf (saine et sauve); **as s. as houses** qui ne présente aucun risque; Prov **better s. than sorry** deux précautions valent mieux qu'une; **s. seat** (in parliament) = siège parlementaire en principe acquis à un parti donné (b) (not dangerous) **it is s. to say that...** on peut dire sans risque de se tromper que...; **it's a s. bet that...** il y a fort à parier que...; **at a s. distance** à distance respectueuse; **in s. hands** entre de bonnes mains; **to wish sb a s. journey** souhaiter bon voyage à qn; **...to be on the s. side** ...pour plus de sûreté; **s. house** (for spies) cachette f sûre; **s. sex** rapports mpl sexuels protégés
2 n (for money) coffre-fort m
3 adv **to play it) s.** ne pas prendre de risques

safe-conduct [seɪf'kɒndʌkt] n sauf-conduit m

safeguard ['seɪfgɑːd] **1** n garantie f
2 vt sauvegarder
3 vi **to s. against sth** se protéger contre qch

safe-keeping [seɪf'kiːpɪŋ] n **in s.** en lieu sûr; **to give sth to sb for s.** confier qch à la garde de qn

safely ['seɪflɪ] adv (a) (without risk) en toute sécurité; (drive) prudemment; **to arrive s.** (of person) bien arriver; (of goods) arriver sans dommage (b) (with certainty) avec certitude

safety ['seɪftɪ] n sûreté f; **for s.'s sake** pour plus de sûreté; **to be s. conscious** se préoccuper beaucoup de la sécurité; Prov **(there's) s. in numbers** plus on est nombreux, moins on court de risques; **s. belt** ceinture f de sécurité; **s. catch** cran m de sûreté; **s. glass** verre m de sécurité; **s. matches** allumettes *fpl* de sûreté; **s. measures** mesures *fpl* de sûreté; **s. net** filet *m*; *Fig* mesure *f* de sécurité; **s. pin** épingle *f* de sûreté; *also Fig* **s. valve** soupape *f* de sûreté

saffron ['sæfrən] **1** *n* safran *m*
 2 *adj* safran *inv*

sag [sæg] *(pt & pp* **sagged)** *vi (of roof, bridge)* s'affaisser; *(of flesh)* être flasque; *(of rope)* pendre; *(of breasts)* être tombant(e); *(of prices, support)* baisser

saga ['sɑ:gə] *n also Fig (story)* saga *f*

sagacious [sə'geɪʃəs] *adj Formal* sagace

sagacity [sə'gæsɪtɪ] *n Formal* sagacité *f*

sage¹ [seɪdʒ] **1** *n (wise man)* sage *m*
 2 *adj (person, conduct)* sage

sage² *n (herb)* sauge *f*

Sagittarius [sædʒɪ'teərɪəs] *n (sign of zodiac)* le Sagittaire; **to be (a) S.** être (du) Sagittaire

Sahara [sə'hɑ:rə] *n* **the S. (Desert)** le Sahara

said [sed] *pt & pp of* **say**

sail [seɪl] **1** *n (on boat)* voile *f*; *(of windmill)* aile *f*; **to set s.** prendre la mer; **to go for a s.** faire un tour en voilier
 2 *vi (of ship, person)* naviguer; *(start voyage)* prendre la mer; *Fig* **the clouds sailed by** les nuages passaient dans le ciel; *Fig* **his book sailed out of the window** son livre vola par la fenêtre; *Fig* **to s. close to the wind** jouer avec le feu; *Fam* **to s. through an examination** réussir un examen les doigts dans le nez

sailing ['seɪlɪŋ] *n (activity)* voile *f*; *(departure)* appareillage *m*; **to go s.** faire de la voile; *Br* **s. boat/ship** voilier *m*

sailor ['seɪlə(r)] *n* marin *m*; **to be a good/bad s.** avoir/ ne pas avoir le pied marin; **s. suit** costume *m* marin *(d'enfant)*

saint [seɪnt] *n* saint(e) *m,f*; **All Saints' (Day)** la Toussaint; **S. Bernard** *(dog)* saint-bernard *m inv*

saintly ['seɪntlɪ] *adj (life, behaviour)* de saint; *(smile)* d'ange

sake [seɪk] *n* **for the s. of sb, for sb's s.** *(for the good of)* pour le bien de qn; *(out of respect for)* par égard de qn; **for God's** *or* **heaven's s.!** mais pour bon sang!; **for the s. of peace** pour avoir la paix; **for old times' s.** en souvenir du passé; **this is just talking for talking's s.** c'est parler pour parler; **let's say, for the s. of argument...** admettons que...

salacious [sə'leɪʃəs] *adj* salace

salad ['sæləd] *n* salade *f*; **s. bowl** saladier *m*; *Br* **s. cream** = sorte de mayonnaise liquide; *Fig* **s. days** années *fpl* de jeunesse; **s. dressing** = vinaigrette ou sauce pour salade

salamander ['sæləmændə(r)] *n* salamandre *f*

salami [sə'lɑ:mɪ] *n* salami *m*

salaried ['sælərɪd] *adj* salarié(e)

salary ['sælərɪ] *(pl* **salaries)** *n* salaire *m*; **s. earner** salarié(e) *m,f*; **s. grade** échelon *m* de salaire; **s. scale** échelle *f* des salaires

sale [seɪl] *n* **(a)** *(action, event)* vente *f*; **for s.** à vendre; **to put sth up for s.** mettre qch en vente; **on s.** en vente; *Br* **sales assistant** vendeur(euse) *m,f*; **sales department** service *m* commercial; **sales drive** campagne *f* de vente; **sales force** force *f* de vente; **sales forecast** prévision *f* des ventes; **sales manager** directeur(trice) *m,f* commercial(e); **sales pitch** arguments *mpl* de vente; **sales target** objectif *m* de vente; **s. price** prix *m* de vente **(b)** *(at reduced prices)* soldes *mpl*; **the sales** les soldes; **in the sales** en solde

saleable ['seɪləbəl] *adj* vendable

saleroom ['seɪlru:m] *n* salle *f* des ventes

salesclerk ['seɪlzklɑ:k] *n Am* vendeur(euse) *m,f*

salesgirl ['seɪlzgɜ:l] *n* vendeuse *f*

salesman ['seɪlzmən] *n (for company)* représentant *m*; *(in shop)* vendeur *m*

salesmanship ['seɪlzmənʃɪp] *n* technique *f* de vente

salesperson ['seɪlzpɜ:sən] *(pl* **salespeople)** *n (for company)* représentant(e) *m,f*; *(in shop)* vendeur(euse) *m,f*

saleswoman ['seɪlzwʊmən] *n (for company)* représentante *f*; *(in shop)* vendeuse *f*

salient ['seɪlɪənt] *adj (feature)* marquant(e); *(point)* essentiel(elle)

saline ['seɪlaɪn] *adj* salin(e); **s. drip** perfusion *f* de solution saline; **s. solution** solution *f* saline

saliva [sə'laɪvə] *n* salive *f*

salivate ['sælɪveɪt] *vi also Fig* saliver

sallow ['sæləʊ] *adj* jaunâtre

▶**sally forth** ['sælɪ] *(pt & pp* **sallied)** *vi Lit* partir

salmon ['sæmən] *(pl* **salmon)** *n* saumon *m*; **s. (pink)** (rose *m*) saumon; **s. trout** truite *f* saumonée

salmonella [sælmə'nelə] *n* salmonelle *f*

salon ['sælɒn] *n (beauty)* **s.** institut *m* de beauté; *(hairdressing)* **s.** salon *m* de coiffure

saloon [sə'lu:n] *n* **(a)** *(room)* salle *f*; *Am (bar)* bar *m* **(b)** **s. (car)** berline *f*

SALT [sɔ:lt] *n (abbr* **Strategic Arms Limitation Talks)** SALT *m*

salt [sɔ:lt] **1** *n* **(a)** sel *m*; **s. flat** marais *m* salant; **s. mine** mine *f* de sel **(b)** *(idioms)* **to be worth one's s.** être à la hauteur; **to rub s. in sb's wounds** remuer le couteau dans la plaie; **the s. of the earth** le sel de la terre **(c)** *Fam* **an old s.** *(sailor)* un vieux loup de mer
 2 *adj* **s. beef** bœuf *m* salé; **s. cod** morue *f* salée; **s. water** eau *f* salée
 3 *vt (food)* saler; *(roads)* sabler

▶**salt away** *vt sep (money)* mettre de côté

saltcellar ['sɔ:ltselə(r)] *n* salière *f*

salt-free ['sɔ:ltfri:] *adj* sans sel

saltpetre [sɔ:lt'pi:tə(r)] *n* salpêtre *m*

saltwater ['sɔ:ltwɔ:tə(r)] *adj (lake)* salé(e); *(fish)* de mer

salty ['sɔ:ltɪ] *adj* salé(e)

salubrious [sə'lu:brɪəs] *adj Formal* salubre

salutary ['sæljʊtərɪ] *adj* salutaire

salute [sə'lu:t] **1** *n* salut *m*; **to take the s.** passer les troupes en revue
 2 *vt also Fig* saluer
 3 *vi* faire un salut

salvage ['sælvɪdʒ] **1** *n (of ship)* sauvetage *m*; *(of waste material)* récupération *f*; **s. vessel** bateau *m* de sauvetage
 2 *vt also Fig* sauver

salvation [sæl'veɪʃən] *n* salut *m*; **S. Army** Armée *f* du Salut

salve [sælv] *vt* **to s. one's conscience** se donner bonne conscience

salver ['sælvə(r)] *n (tray)* plateau *m* (de présentation)

salvo ['sælvəʊ] *(pl* **salvos** *or* **salvoes)** *n also Fig* salve *f*; *(of questions)* flot *m*; *(of insults)* torrent *m*

Samaritan [sə'mærɪtən] *n also Fig* **the Good S.** le bon Samaritain; **the Samaritans** ≃ S.O.S. Amitié

same [seɪm] **1** *adj* the s. man le même homme; the s. woman la même femme; the s. children les mêmes enfants; in the s. way de la même façon; Fig to go the s. way prendre le même chemin; the s. day le même jour; the *or* that (very) s. day (for emphasis) le jour même; it all comes to the s. thing cela revient au même; at the s. time (regularly) au même moment; (simultaneously) en même temps, à la fois

2 *pron* s. le même, la même; (plural) les mêmes; I would have done the s. j'aurais fait la même chose *ou* pareil; if it's all the s. to you si cela vous est égal; Fam (the) s. again? (in pub) la même chose?; Fam s. here! (me do I) moi aussi; (neither do I) moi non plus!; (I did the same thing) pareil!; the house isn't the s. without her la maison n'est plus la même sans elle

3 *adv* to think/feel the s. penser/ressentir la même chose; to look the s. (of two things) sembler pareils; to taste the s. avoir le même goût; all the s. (nevertheless) tout de même

sameness ['seɪmnɪs] *n* monotonie *f*

Samoa [sə'məʊə] *n* Samoa *m*

Samoan [sə'məʊən] **1** *n* (a) (person) Samoan(e) *m,f* (b) (language) samoan *m*
2 *adj* samoan(e)

samosa [səm'əʊsə] *n* samosa *m*

sample ['saːmpəl] **1** *n* échantillon *m*; (of blood, urine) prélèvement *m*
2 *vt* (a) (food, experience) goûter (b) (public opinion) sonder (c) (piece of music) sampler

sanatorium [sænə'tɔːrɪəm] (*pl* **sanatoria** [sænə'tɔːrɪə]) *n* sanatorium *m*

sanctify ['sæŋ(k)tɪfaɪ] *vt* sanctifier; Fig consacrer

sanctimonious [sæŋ(k)tɪ'məʊnɪəs] *adj* moralisateur(trice)

sanction ['sæŋ(k)ʃən] **1** *n* (a) (penalty) sanction *f*; to impose sanctions on a country imposer des sanctions à un pays (b) Formal (consent) consentement *m*, accord *m*
2 *vt* Formal (consent to) sanctionner

sanctity ['sæŋ(k)tɪtɪ] *n* sainteté *f*; Fig of (life, marriage) caractère *m* sacré

sanctuary ['sæŋ(k)t(ʊ)ərɪ] *n* Rel sanctuaire *m*; (for fugitive, refugee) refuge *m*, asile *m*; (for birds, wildlife) réserve *f*; to seek/find s. chercher/trouver refuge

sand [sænd] **1** *n* sable *m*; s. castle château *m* de sable; s. dune dune *f*
2 *vt* (a) (smooth with sandpaper) poncer (b) (cover with sand) sabler

sandal ['sændəl] *n* sandale *f*

sandbag ['sændbæg] *n* sac *m* de sable

sandbank ['sændbæŋk] *n* banc *m* de sable

sandblast ['sændblaːst] *vt* décaper à la sableuse

sandpaper ['sændpeɪpə(r)] **1** *n* papier *m* de verre
2 *vt* poncer, passer au papier de verre

sandpit ['sændpɪt] *n* bac *m* à sable

sandstone ['sændstəʊn] *n* grès *m*

sandstorm ['sændstɔːm] *n* tempête *f* de sable

sandwich ['sændwɪtʃ] **1** *n* sandwich *m*; ham s. sandwich au jambon; Br s. course stage *m* de formation (professionnelle) en alternance
2 *vt* to be sandwiched between (of layer) être intercalé(e) entre; (of person, building) être coincé(e) entre

sandy ['sændɪ] *adj* (a) (earth) sablonneux(euse); (beach) de sable (b) (hair) blond roux *inv*

sane [seɪn] *adj* (person) sain(e) d'esprit; (action, remark) sensé(e)

San Franciscan ['sænfrən'sɪskən] **1** *n* habitant(e) *m,f* de San Francisco
2 *adj* de San Francisco

San Francisco ['sænfrən'sɪskəʊ] *n* San Francisco

sang [sæŋ] *pt of* **sing**

sanguine ['sæŋgwɪn] *adj* optimiste

sanitary ['sænɪtərɪ] *adj* (a) (clean) hygiénique (b) (relating to hygiene) sanitaire; Br s. towel serviette *f* hygiénique

sanitation [sænɪ'teɪʃən] *n* installations *fpl* sanitaires

sanitize ['sænɪtaɪz] *vt* expurger

sanity ['sænɪtɪ] *n* santé *f* mentale

sank [sæŋk] *pt of* **sink²**

San Marino [sænmə'riːnəʊ] *n* Saint-Marin

Santa (Claus) ['sæntə('klɔːz)] *n* le père Noël

sap¹ [sæp] *n* (of plant) sève *f*

sap² *n* Fam (gullible person) andouille *f*

sap³ (*pt & pp* **sapped**) *vt* (weaken) saper

sapling ['sæplɪŋ] *n* jeune arbre *m*

sapper ['sæpə(r)] *n* Mil soldat *m* du génie

sapphire ['sæfaɪə(r)] *n* saphir *m*

Sarajevo [særə'jeɪvəʊ] *n* Sarajevo

sarcasm ['saːkæzəm] *n* sarcasme *m*

sarcastic [saː'kæstɪk] *adj* sarcastique

sarcastically [saː'kæstɪklɪ] *adv* de manière sarcastique; (speak) d'un ton sarcastique

sarcophagus [saː'kɒfəgəs] (*pl* **sarcophagi** [saː-'kɒfəgaɪ]) *n* sarcophage *m*

sardine [saː'diːn] *n* sardine *f*; Fam Fig to be packed like sardines être serrés(es) comme des sardines

Sardinia [saː'dɪnɪə] *n* la Sardaigne

Sardinian [saː'dɪnɪən] **1** *n* Sarde *mf*
2 *adj* sarde

sardonic [saː'dɒnɪk] *adj* sardonique

sari ['saːrɪ] *n* sari *m*

sarong [sə'rɒŋ] *n* paréo *m*

sartorial [saː'tɔːrɪəl] *adj* Formal vestimentaire

SAS [eseɪ'es] *n* Br (abbr **Special Air Service**) = service d'intervention spécial de l'Armée britannique

sash [sæʃ] *n* (around waist) large ceinture *f* de tissu; (around shoulder) écharpe *f*; s. cord corde *f* (actionnant une fenêtre à guillotine); s. window fenêtre *f* à guillotine

Sassenach ['sæsənæx] *n* Scot Pej Anglais(e) *m,f*

Sat (abbr **Saturday**) samedi

sat [sæt] *pt & pp of* **sit**

Satan ['seɪtən] *n* Satan *m*

satanic [sə'tænɪk] *adj* satanique, diabolique

satchel ['sætʃəl] *n* cartable *m*

sate [seɪt] *vt* Formal assouvir

satellite ['sætəlaɪt] *n* satellite *m*; s. dish antenne *f* parabolique; s. (state) (État *m*) satellite; s. television télévision *f* par satellite; s. town ville *f* satellite

satiate ['seɪʃɪeɪt] *vt* Formal assouvir

satin ['sætɪn] *n* satin *m*

satire ['sætaɪə(r)] *n* satire *f*

satirical [sə'tɪrɪkəl] *adj* satirique

satirist ['sætɪrɪst] *n* écrivain *m* satirique

satirize ['sætɪraɪz] vt faire la satire de
satisfaction [sætɪs'fækʃən] n satisfaction f; **to have the s. of doing sth** avoir la satisfaction de faire qch
satisfactory [sætɪs'fæktərɪ] adj satisfaisant(e)
satisfied ['sætɪsfaɪd] adj satisfait(e)
satisfy ['sætɪsfaɪ] (pt & pp **satisfied**) vt (a) (meet needs of) (person, curiosity) satisfaire; (condition) remplir (b) (convince) convaincre, persuader
saturate ['sætʃəreɪt] vt saturer; **to s. the market** saturer le marché; **saturated fats** graisses fpl saturées
saturation [sætʃə'reɪʃən] n saturation f; **to reach s. point** arriver à saturation; Mil **s. bombing** bombardement m intensif
Saturday ['sætədɪ] n samedi m; **this S.** samedi prochain ou qui vient; **on S.** samedi; **on S. morning/ afternoon/evening** samedi matin/après-midi/soir; **on Saturdays** le samedi; **every S.** tous les samedis; **every other S.** un samedi sur deux; **last S.** samedi dernier; **the S. before last** pas samedi dernier mais celui d'avant; **next S.** samedi prochain; **the S. after next, a week on S., S. week** le samedi d'après, samedi en huit; **the following S.** le samedi suivant; **S.'s paper** le journal de samedi; **S. job** petit boulot m (du samedi)
Saturn ['sætɜːn] n (planet) Saturne f
sauce [sɔːs] n (a) (for food) sauce f; **tomato/cheese s.** sauce tomate/au fromage; **s. boat** saucière f (b) Fam (impudence) culot m
saucepan ['sɔːspən] n casserole f
saucer ['sɔːsə(r)] n soucoupe f
saucy ['sɔːsɪ] adj Fam (impertinent) insolent(e); (risqué) coquin(e)
Saudi ['saʊdɪ] 1 n (person) Saoudien(enne) m,f; Fam (country) l'Arabie f Saoudite
2 adj saoudien(enne)
Saudi Arabia ['saʊdɪə'reɪbɪə] n l'Arabie f Saoudite
Saudi Arabian ['saʊdɪə'reɪbɪən] 1 n Saoudien(enne) m,f
2 adj saoudien(enne)
sauna ['sɔːnə] n sauna m; **to have a s.** aller au sauna
saunter ['sɔːntə(r)] 1 n balade f; **to go for a s.** partir en balade
2 vi **to s.** (along) flâner
sausage ['sɒsɪdʒ] n saucisse f; Fam **not a s.** (nothing) que dalle; Hum **you silly s.!** patate, val; Fam **s. dog** saucisson m à pattes; **s. meat** chair f à saucisse; Br **s. roll** feuilleté m à la viande
sauté ['səʊteɪ] 1 adj sauté(e)
2 vt (pt & pp **sautéed**) faire sauter
savage ['sævɪdʒ] 1 n Old-fashioned sauvage mf
2 adj (animal, person) féroce, brutal(e); (attack, criticism) violent(e)
3 vt (attack physically) attaquer; Fig (criticize) descendre en flammes
savagely ['sævɪdʒlɪ] adv (beat, attack) sauvagement; Fig (criticize) violemment, avec virulence
savanna(h) [sə'vænə] n savane f
save¹ [seɪv] prep Formal (except) hormis
save² [seɪv] 1 vt (rescue) sauver; **to s. sb's life** sauver la vie à qn; Fam **she can't sing to s. her life** elle chante comme un pied; Fam **to s. one's (own) neck** or **skin** sauver sa peau; **to s. sb from falling** empêcher qn de tomber; **to s. a goal** arrêter un but; **God s. the King/ the Queen!** vive le Roi/la Reine! (b) (keep for future)

garder, conserver; (money) mettre de côté; Comptr sauvegarder; **to s. oneself for sth** se réserver pour qch (c) (not waste) (money, space) économiser; (time) gagner; **s. your breath** économise ton souffle (d) (spare) **to s. sb sth** éviter qch à qn; **to s. sb (from) doing sth** éviter à qn de faire qch
2 vi faire des économies (for/on pour/sur)
3 n (of goalkeeper) arrêt m; **to make a s.** arrêter un but
▸**save up** vi mettre de l'argent de côté (for pour)
saver ['seɪvə(r)] n épargnant(e) m,f
saving ['seɪvɪŋ] 1 n (a) (economy) économie f (b) savings (money saved) économies fpl; **to live off one's savings** vivre sur ses économies; **savings account** compte m d'épargne; **savings bank** caisse f d'épargne
2 adj **her/its s. grace** ce qui la/le sauve
saviour ['seɪvjə(r)] n sauveur m; **the S.** le Sauveur
savour ['seɪvə(r)] 1 n saveur f
2 vt also Fig savourer
3 vi Formal **to s. of** sentir
savoury ['seɪvərɪ] adj (a) (food) salé(e) (b) (conduct) honorable
saw¹ [sɔː] pt of **see²**
saw² 1 n (tool) scie f
2 vt (pp **sawn** [sɔːn] or **sawed**) scier
▸**saw off** vt sep scier
▸**saw up** vt sep découper à la scie
sawdust ['sɔːdʌst] n sciure f
sawmill ['sɔːmɪl] n scierie f
sawn [sɔːn] pp of **saw²**
sawn-off shotgun ['sɔːnɒf'ʃɒtgʌn] n fusil m à canon scié
sax [sæks] n Fam (saxophone) sax m
Saxon ['sæks(ə)n] 1 n (a) (person) Saxon(onne) m,f (b) (language) saxon m
2 adj saxon(onne)
Saxony ['sæksənɪ] n Saxe f
saxophone ['sæksəfəʊn] n saxophone m
saxophonist [sæk'sɒfənɪst] n saxophoniste mf
say [seɪ] 1 vt (pt & pp **said** [sed]) dire; (of clock, watch) indiquer; **to s. sth to sb** dire qch à qn; (of text, sign) il y a écrit que...; **I wouldn't s. no to a cup of tea** je prendrais volontiers une tasse de thé; **I didn't s. a word** je n'ai pas dit un mot; **it's not for me to s.** ce n'est pas à moi de le dire; **there's no saying what might happen if...** inutile de vous dire ce qui se passerait si...; **what have you got to s. for yourself?** as-tu une excuse valable?; **there's a lot to be said for living in the country** il y a bien des avantages à vivre à la campagne; **you're honest, I'll s. that for you** tu es honnête, je te l'accorde; **it says a lot about her** ça en dit long sur sa personne; **don't s. you've forgotten already!** ne me dis pas que tu as déjà oublié!; **you can s. that again!** c'est le cas de le dire!, tu l'as dit!; **need I s. more?** ai-je besoin d'en dire plus?; **they s. that..., it is said that...** on dit que...; **s. we won first prize** supposons que nous gagnions le premier prix; **if I had, s., £100,000** si j'avais, mettons, 100 000 livres
2 vi **I need hardly s. that...** je ne dirai rien; **as they s.** comme on dit; **I s.!** dis-donc!; **I'll s.!** absolument!, tout à fait!; Fam **you don't s.!** sans blagues!
3 n **to have one's s.** avoir son mot à dire; **to have a s./ no s. in sth** avoir/ne pas avoir voix au chapitre concernant qch

saying ['seɪɪŋ] n maxime f; **as the s. goes** comme dit la maxime

say-so ['seɪsəʊ] n Fam (permission) permission f

scab [skæb] n (a) (on skin) croûte f (b) Fam (strikebreaker) jaune mf

scabbard ['skæbəd] n fourreau m, gaine f

scabies ['skeɪbiːz] n gale f

scaffold ['skæfəld] n (outside building) échafaudage m; (for execution) échafaud m

scaffolding ['skæfəldɪŋ] n échafaudage m

scald [skɔːld] **1** n brûlure f

2 vt ébouillanter; **to s. one's hand** s'ébouillanter la main

scalding ['skɔːldɪŋ] adj brûlant(e)

scale¹ [skeɪl] **1** n (on fish, reptile) écaille f; (in pipes, kettle) dépôt m calcaire

2 vt (fish) écailler

scale² n (a) (of instrument) gamme f; (of salaries) barème m; on a s. of one to ten sur une échelle allant de un à dix (b) (of map, drawing) échelle f; Fig (of problem, changes) étendue f; **to s. à la bonne échelle; s. model** modèle m réduit (c) (of ruler, thermometer) graduation f

scale³ vt (climb) escalader

▸**scale down** vt sep (reduce) revoir à la baisse

▸**scale up** vt sep (increase) augmenter

scales [skeɪlz] npl (set of) **s.** (for kitchen) balance f; (for bathroom) pèse-personne m

scallop ['skæləp, 'skɒləp] **1** n (a) (shellfish) coquille f Saint-Jacques (b) (in sewing) feston m

2 vt (in sewing) festonner

scallywag ['skælɪwæg] n Fam coquin(e) m,f

scalp [skælp] **1** n cuir m chevelu; (as war trophy) scalp m

2 vt (in war) scalper

scalpel ['skælpəl] n scalpel m

scaly ['skeɪlɪ] adj (fish) écailleux(euse); (skin) squameux(euse)

scam [skæm] n Fam arnaque f, magouille f

scamp [skæmp] n (rascal) coquin(e) m,f

scamper ['skæmpə(r)] vi gambader, galoper

▸**scamper away, scamper off** vi détaler, partir en courant

scampi ['skæmpɪ] n scampi mpl

scan [skæn] **1** vt (pt & pp scanned) (a) (examine closely) scruter; Comptr balayer; Med faire une scanographie de; (with ultrasound) faire une échographie de (b) (glance at) parcourir

2 n Med scanographie f; (with ultrasound) échographie f

scandal ['skændəl] n (a) (outrage) scandale m; **to create or cause a s.** créer ou provoquer un scandale (b) (gossip) ragots mpl

scandalize ['skændəlaɪz] vt scandaliser, choquer

scandalous ['skændələs] adj scandaleux(euse)

Scandinavia [skændɪ'neɪvɪə] n la Scandinavie

Scandinavian [skændɪ'neɪvɪən] **1** n Scandinave mf

2 adj scandinave

scanner ['skænə(r)] n Med & Comptr scanner m

scant [skænt] adj insuffisant(e)

scantily ['skæntɪlɪ] adv insuffisamment, sommairement; **s. dressed or clad** légèrement vêtu(e)

scanty ['skæntɪ] adj (dress) léger(ère); (amount, information) maigre, limité(e)

scapegoat ['skeɪpgəʊt] n bouc m émissaire

scar [skɑː(r)] **1** n also Fig cicatrice f; **s. tissue** tissu m cicatriciel

2 vt (pt & pp scarred) marquer de cicatrices; Fig marquer; **to be scarred for life** garder des cicatrices toute sa vie; Fig être marqué(e) à vie

3 vi (of wound) laisser une cicatrice

scarce [skeəs] adj rare; Fam **to make oneself s.** filer

scarcely ['skeəslɪ] adv à peine; **she could s. speak** elle pouvait à peine parler; **s. ever/anyone** presque jamais/personne; **it is s. likely that...** il est peu probable que...

scarcity ['skeəsɪtɪ], **scarceness** ['skeəsnɪs] n manque m, pénurie f

scare [skeə(r)] **1** n frayeur f; **pollution s.** alerte f à la pollution; **you gave me an awful s.** tu m'as fait une belle frayeur

2 vt effrayer; Fam **to s. the life out of sb, to s. the living daylights out of sb** faire une de ces trouilles à qn

3 vi s'effrayer

▸**scare away, scare off** vt sep faire fuir

scarecrow ['skeəkrəʊ] n épouvantail m

scared [skeəd] adj effrayé(e); **to be s. of sb/sth** avoir peur de qn/qch; **to be s. stiff, to be s. to death** être mort(e) de peur

scaremongering ['skeəmʌŋgərɪŋ] n alarmisme m

scarf [skɑːf] (pl **scarves** [skɑːvz]) n (long) écharpe f; (square) foulard m

scarlet ['skɑːlɪt] **1** n écarlate f

2 adj écarlate; Fig **to go or turn s.** (with anger, embarrassment) devenir rouge; **s. fever** scarlatine f

scarper ['skɑːpə(r)] vi Br Fam ficher le camp, se tailler

scary ['skeərɪ] adj Fam effrayant(e)

scat [skæt] exclam Fam fiche le camp!, dégage!

scathing ['skeɪðɪŋ] adj (remark, sarcasm) acerbe; **to be s. about sb/sth** faire des remarques acerbes sur qn/qch

scatological [skætə'lɒdʒɪkəl] adj scatologique

scatter ['skætə(r)] **1** vt (clouds, demonstrators) disperser, éparpiller; (corn, seed) jeter ou semer à la volée; (crumbs, papers) laisser traîner

2 vi (of crowd) se disperser

scatterbrain ['skætəbreɪn] n Fam tête f de linotte

scatty ['skætɪ] adj Br Fam farfelu(e)

scavenge ['skævɪndʒ] **1** vt récupérer

2 vi **to s. for sth** fouiller pour trouver qch; **to s. in the dustbins** fouiller dans ou parmi les poubelles

scavenger ['skævɪndʒə(r)] n (animal) charognard m; Fig (person) fouilleur(euse) m,f de poubelles

scenario [sɪ'nɑːrɪəʊ] (pl **scenarios**) n (a) (of film) scénario m (b) (situation) hypothèse f

scene [siːn] n (a) (in book, film, play) scène f; also Fig a touching/terrifying s. une scène touchante/terrifiante; also Fig **behind the scenes** dans les coulisses; Th **s. shifter** machiniste mf (b) (of event) lieu m, endroit m; **a change of s.** un changement de décor; **to arrive or come on the s.** faire son apparition; **the s. of the crime/accident** le lieu du crime/de l'accident; **a s. of devastation** un spectacle de dévastation; **I can picture the s.** j'imagine la scène; Fam **it's not my s.** ce n'est pas mon truc (c) (fuss) scandale m; **to make a s.** faire un scandale

scenery ['siːnərɪ] n (a) (in play) décor(s) m(pl) (b) (landscape) paysage m; Fam **to need a change of s.** avoir besoin de changer d'air

scenic ['si:nɪk] *adj* pittoresque; **s. railway** petit train *m* (touristique); **s. route** route *f* touristique

scent [sent] **1** *n* (a) *(smell)* odeur *f* (b) *(perfume)* parfum *m* (c) *(in hunting)* fumet *m*; **to pick up the s.** trouver la piste; **to be on the s. of sth** être sur la trace de qch; **to lose the s.** perdre la trace; **she threw her pursuers off the s.** elle sema ses poursuivants
2 *vt* (a) *(smell)* flairer; *Fig* **to s. danger** flairer le danger (b) *(perfume)* parfumer

sceptic ['skeptɪk] *n* sceptique *mf*

sceptical ['skeptɪkəl] *adj* sceptique

sceptically ['skeptɪklɪ] *adv* avec scepticisme

scepticism ['skeptɪsɪzəm] *n* scepticisme *m*

sceptre ['septə(r)] *n* sceptre *m*

schedule ['ʃedju:l, *Am* 'skedju:l] **1** *n* (a) *(plan)* programme *m*, calendrier *m*; *Am (for trains, buses)* horaire *m*; **on s.** *(train, bus)* à l'heure; *(person)* dans les temps; **to be behind/ahead of s.** être en retard/en avance sur le programme; **to go according to s.** se dérouler comme prévu; **to work to a tight s.** avoir un emploi du temps serré (b) *Com (list of prices)* barème *m*
2 *vt* prévoir; **we're scheduled to arrive at 21.45** notre arrivée est prévue à 21h45; **the museum is scheduled to open in August** l'ouverture du musée est prévue pour le mois d'août

scheduled ['ʃedju:ld, *Am* 'skedju:ld] *adj* prévu(e); **s. flight** vol *m* régulier

schematic [skɪ'mætɪk] *adj* schématique

scheme [ski:m] **1** *n (arrangement, system)* arrangement *m*; *(plan)* plan *m*; *(plot)* machination *f*, complot *m*; **in the (great) s. of things** dans le fond; **(housing) s.** lotissement *m*
2 *vi Pej* comploter, intriguer

schilling ['ʃɪlɪŋ] *n* schilling *m*

schism ['s(k)ɪzəm] *n* schisme *m*

schizoid ['skɪtsɔɪd] *n & adj* schizoïde *mf*

schizophrenia [skɪtsəʊ'fri:nɪə] *n* schizophrénie *f*

schizophrenic [skɪtsəʊ'frenɪk] *n & adj* schizophrène *mf*

schmaltzy ['ʃmɔ:ltsɪ] *adj Fam* à l'eau de rose, cucul *inv*

scholar ['skɒlə(r)] *n (learned person)* érudit(e) *m,f*

scholarly ['skɒlərlɪ] *adj* érudit(e)

scholarship ['skɒləʃɪp] *n* (a) *(learning)* érudition *f*, savoir *m* (b) *(grant)* bourse *f* (d'études)

scholastic [skə'læstɪk] *adj Formal* scolaire

school¹ [sku:l] **1** *n* (a) *(for children)* école *f*; **to go to s.** aller à l'école; **s. of art, art s.** école d'art; **of s. age** d'âge scolaire; **s. bag** cartable *m*; *Br* **s. board** conseil *m* d'administration de l'établissement; **s. book** manuel *m* ou livre *m* scolaire; **s. day** journée *f* d'école ou scolaire; **s. friend** camarade *mf* d'école; **s. leaver** = jeune qui vient de terminer ses études secondaires; **s. report** *(for primary school)* carnet *m* de notes; *(for secondary school)* bulletin *m* scolaire; **s. uniforme** uniforme *m* scolaire; **s. year** année *f* scolaire (b) *Am (college, university)* faculté *f*, université *f* (c) *(of artists, thinkers)* école *f*; **s. of thought** école de pensée; *Fig* **he's one of the old s.** il est de la vieille école
2 *vt (educate)* scolariser; *(train)* former, entraîner; **to s. sb in sth** former qn à qch

school² *n (of fish)* banc *m*

schoolboy ['sku:lbɔɪ] *n* écolier *m*, élève *m*

schoolchild ['sku:ltʃaɪld] *n* écolier(ère) *m,f*, élève *mf*

schoolfellow ['sku:lfeləʊ] *n* camarade *mf* de classe

schoolgirl ['sku:lgɜ:l] *n* écolière *f*, élève *f*

schooling ['sku:lɪŋ] *n* scolarité *f*, éducation *f*

schoolmaster ['sku:lmɑ:stə(r)] *n Formal (primary)* instituteur *m*, maître *m* d'école; *(secondary)* professeur *m*

schoolmate ['sku:lmeɪt] *n* camarade *mf* de classe

schoolmistress ['sku:lmɪstrɪs] *n Formal (primary)* institutrice *f*, maîtresse *f* d'école; *(secondary)* professeur *m*

schoolroom ['sku:lru:m] *n* salle *f* de classe

schoolteacher ['sku:lti:tʃə(r)] *n (primary)* instituteur(trice) *m,f*; *(secondary)* professeur *m*

schooner ['sku:nə(r)] *n* (a) *(ship)* schooner *m* (b) *(glass)* grand verre *m* (à xérès)

sciatica [saɪ'ætɪkə] *n* sciatique *f*

science ['saɪəns] *n* science *f*; **she's good at s.** elle est bonne en sciences; **s. fiction** science-fiction *f*; **s. teacher** professeur *m* de sciences

scientific [saɪən'tɪfɪk] *adj* scientifique

scientist ['saɪəntɪst] *n* scientifique *mf*

sci-fi ['saɪfaɪ] *Fam* **1** *n* SF *f*
2 *adj* SF

Scilly ['sɪlɪ] *n* **the S. Isles, the Scillies** les Sorlingues *fpl*

scimitar ['sɪmɪtə(r)] *n* cimeterre *m*

scintillating ['sɪntɪleɪtɪŋ] *adj* brillant(e)

scissors ['sɪzəz] *npl* ciseaux *mpl*; **a pair of s.** une paire de ciseaux

sclerosis [sklə'rəʊsɪs] *n Med* sclérose *f*

scoff [skɒf] **1** *vt Br Fam (eat)* bouffer
2 *vi (mock)* se moquer (**at** de)

scold [skəʊld] *vt* gronder

scone [skɒn] *n* scone *m*

scoop [sku:p] **1** *n* (a) *(device)* (for ice cream) cuillère *f* à glace; (for flour, sugar) pelle *f*; (for mashed potato) cuillère *f* (b) *(portion)* (of ice cream) boule *f*; (of mashed potato) portion *f* (c) *Fam (in journalism)* scoop *m*
2 *vt* (a) *(with hands, spoon)* ramasser (b) *(story)* publier en exclusivité

▸**scoop up** *vt sep* ramasser

scoot [sku:t] *vi Fam* **to s. (off or away)** filer

scooter ['sku:tə(r)] *n (for child)* trottinette *f*; *(small motorbike)* scooter *m*

scope [skəʊp] *n (of action)* possibilité *f*; *(of enquiry)* étendue *f*, portée *f*; **to give s. for...** *(interpretation, explanation)* laisser le champ libre à...

scorch [skɔ:tʃ] **1** *vt* roussir; **scorched earth policy** politique *f* de la terre brûlée
2 *n* **s. mark** brûlure *f*

scorcher ['skɔ:tʃə(r)] *n Fam (hot day)* **it's been a s.** ça a été la canicule

scorching ['skɔ:tʃɪŋ] *adj (day, weather)* torride; *(sun)* brûlant(e)

score [skɔ:(r)] **1** *n* (a) *(in sport, quiz)* score *m*; **there was still no s.** personne n'avait encore marqué; **to keep the s.** compter les points; *Fam Fig* **to know the s.** connaître le topo
(b) *(line)* rayure *f*, entaille *f*
(c) *(quarrel)* **to have a s. to settle with sb** avoir un compte à régler avec qn
(d) *(reason, grounds)* **on that s.** à ce sujet, sur ce point
(e) *(in music)* partition *f*
(f) *Old-fashioned (twenty)* **a s.** vingt; *Fam* **scores of** *(a lot)* des tas de

2 *vt* **(a)** *(in sport)* marquer; **to s. a hit** *(hit target)* atteindre la cible; *Fig (of person, film)* remporter un grand succès; *Fig* **to s. points off sb** avoir le dessus

(b) *(cut line in)* entailler

(c) *Fam (buy)* **to s. drugs** se procurer de la drogue

3 *vi* **(a)** *(score a goal)* marquer un but

(b) *Fam (sexually)* faire une touche; *(buy drugs)* se procurer de la drogue

▸**score off** *vt sep (delete)* biffer, barrer

▸**score out** *vt sep (delete)* biffer, barrer

scoreboard ['skɔːbɔːd] *n* tableau *m* d'affichage (des scores)

scorecard ['skɔːkɑːd] *n* carte *f* de score

scorer ['skɔːrə(r)] *n* marqueur(euse) *m,f*

scorn [skɔːn] **1** *n* mépris *m*; **to pour s. on sb/sth** n'avoir que du mépris pour qn/qch

2 *vt* mépriser

scornful ['skɔːnfʊl] *adj* méprisant(e); **to be s. of sb/ sth** considérer qn/qch avec mépris

Scorpio ['skɔːpɪəʊ] *n (sign of zodiac)* Scorpion *m*; **to be (a) S.** être (du) Scorpion

scorpion ['skɔːpɪən] *n* scorpion *m*

Scot [skɒt] *n* Écossais(e) *m,f*

Scotch [skɒtʃ] **1** *n (whisky)* scotch *m*

2 *adj* **S. broth** = potage écossais à base de légumes et d'orge perlé; **S. egg** = œuf dur enrobé de chair à saucisse et pané; *Am* **S. tape**® scotch®*m*; **S. terrier** scotch-terrier *m*; **S. whisky** scotch *m*

scotch [skɒtʃ] *vt (rumour)* étouffer

scot-free ['skɒt'friː] *adj Fam* **to get off s.** s'en tirer sans la moindre punition

Scotland ['skɒtlənd] *n* l'Écosse *f*

Scots [skɒts] **1** *n (dialect)* écossais *m*

2 *adj* écossais(e)

Scotsman ['skɒtsmən] *n* Écossais *m*

Scotswoman ['skɒtswʊmən] *n* Écossaise *f*

Scottie dog ['skɒtɪ'dɒg] *n Fam* scotch-terrier *m*

Scottish ['skɒtɪʃ] *adj* écossais(e); **S. terrier** scotch-terrier *m*

scoundrel ['skaʊndr(ə)l] *n* crapule *f*; *Fam (child)* coquin(e) *m,f*

scour ['skaʊə(r)] *vt* **(a)** *(pot, surface)* récurer, frotter **(b)** *(area, house)* ratisser, fouiller

scourer ['skaʊərə(r)] *n* tampon *m* à récurer

scourge [skɜːdʒ] *n* fléau *m*

scout [skaʊt] **1** *n* **(a)** *(boy)* **s.** (boy-)scout *m*, éclaireur *m*; *(girl)* **s.** éclaireuse *f*; *(talent)* **s.** dénicheur(euse) *m,f* de talents **(b)** *(action)* **to have a s. around (for sth)** chercher (qch)

2 *vi* **to s. for talent** dénicher des talents

scoutmaster ['skaʊtmɑːstə(r)] *n* chef *m* scout

scowl [skaʊl] **1** *n* regard *m* noir

2 *vi* lancer des regards noirs **(at à)**

scrabble ['skræbəl] *vi* **to s. about** *or* **around for sth** chercher qch à tâtons

scraggy ['skrægɪ] *adj* maigre, décharné(e)

scram [skræm] *(pt & pp* **scrammed)** *vi Fam* se tirer

scramble ['skræmbəl] **1** *n* **(a)** *(rush)* ruée *f*; *(struggle)* bousculade *f* **(for** pour)

2 *vt Tel (signal)* brouiller

3 *vi* **to s. for sth** se précipiter pour qch; **to s. up a hill** gravir une colline avec les mains

scrambled eggs ['skræmbəld'egz] *npl* œufs *mpl* brouillés

scrap¹ [skræp] **1** *n* **(a)** *(of material, paper)* bout *m*; *(of information)* bribe *f*; *(of evidence)* semblant *m*; **scraps** *(of food)* restes *mpl*; **a s. of truth** une once de vérité; **s. paper** *(papier m)* brouillon *m* **(b)** *(metal)* ferraille *f*; **s. merchant** *or* **dealer** ferrailleur *m*; **to sell sth for s.** vendre qch à la casse

2 *vt (pt & pp* **scrapped)** *(car)* envoyer à la casse; *(submarine, missile)* mettre au rebut; *(project)* abandonner

scrap² [skræp] *Fam* **1** *n (fight)* bagarre *f*; **to have a s., to get into a s.** se bagarrer

2 *vi (fight)* se bagarrer

scrapbook ['skræpbʊk] *n* album *m (de coupures de presse etc)*

scrape [skreɪp] **1** *n* **(a)** *(action)* coup *m* de grattoir; *(mark)* éraflure *f*; *(sound)* raclement *m*; **to give sb a s.** donner un coup de grattoir à qch **(b)** *Fam* **to get into a s.** se mettre dans le pétrin

2 *vt* **(a)** *(skin, side of car)* érafler; *(dirt, wallpaper, vegetables)* gratter; **to s. one's plate clean** nettoyer son assiette; *Fig* **to s. the bottom of the barrel** être tombé(e) bien bas **(b)** *(barely obtain)* **to s. a living** arriver tout juste à vivre; **to s. a pass** *(in exam)* passer de justesse

3 *vi* **(a)** *(make sound)* gratter, grincer **(b)** *(barely manage)* **to s. home** *(in contest)* réussir de justesse; **to s. into college** passer de justesse à l'université

▸**scrape through** *vt insep* passer de justesse

▸**scrape together** *vt sep (money, resources)* parvenir à rassembler

scraper ['skreɪpə(r)] *n (tool)* grattoir *m*

scrapheap ['skræphiːp] *n* tas *m* de ferraille; *Fig* **to be on the s.** être au rebut

scrappy ['skræpɪ] *adj (performance)* décousu(e); *(knowledge)* limité(e)

scratch [skrætʃ] **1** *n* **(a)** *(on skin)* égratignure *f*; *(on record, furniture)* rayure *f*; *(by claw)* griffure *f* **(b)** *(action)* **to give one's arm a s.** se gratter le bras **(c)** *Fam (idioms)* **to start from s.** recommencer à zéro; **to come up** *or* **be up to s.** être à la hauteur; **to bring sth/sb up to s.** mettre qch/ qn à niveau

2 *adj (meal, team)* improvisé(e)

3 *vt* **(a)** *(skin)* *(by accident)* égratigner; *(to relieve itching)* gratter; *(with claw, nail)* griffer; *(glass, record)* rayer; **to s. oneself** se gratter; **to s. one's arm** se gratter le bras; *Fig* **you s. my back and I'll s. yours** un service en vaut un autre; *Fig* **we've only scratched the surface of the problem** nous n'avons fait que survoler le problème **(b)** *(write, draw)* griffonner **(c)** *(in sport)* retirer

4 *vi (of person)* se gratter; *(of pen, new clothes)* gratter; *(of thorns)* piquer; **the dog was scratching at the door** le chien grattait à la porte

▸**scratch out** *vt sep (number, name)* rayer; *Fig* **to s. sb's eyes out** arracher les yeux à qn

scratchcard ['skrætʃkɑːd] *n* = carte de loterie à gratter

scratchy ['skrætʃɪ] *adj (garment, towel)* qui gratte; *(record)* rayé(e)

scrawl [skrɔːl] **1** *n (writing)* gribouillage *m*

2 *vt & vi* gribouiller

scrawny ['skrɔːnɪ] *adj* maigrelet(ette)

scream [skriːm] **1** *n* **(a)** *(of person)* hurlement *m*; **screams of laughter** éclats *mpl* de rire **(b)** *Fam (good fun)* **it/he was a s.** c'était/il était tordant

2 *vt* hurler; **the headlines screamed "guilty"** le mot "coupable" s'étalait en gros à la une des journaux

3 vi hurler; **the car screamed past** la voiture est passée en rugissant; **to s. with pain** hurler de douleur; **to s. with laughter** se tordre de rire

screamingly ['skri:mɪŋlɪ] adv Fam **s. funny** tordant(e)

scree [skri:] n éboulis m

screech [skri:tʃ] **1** n (of bird, person) cri m strident; (of brakes) crissement m; (of laughter) éclat m

2 vt hurler

3 vi (of bird) pousser des cris stridents; (of person) hurler; (of brakes) crisser; **the car screeched to a halt** la voiture s'est arrêtée dans un crissement de pneus

screen [skri:n] **1** n (a) (barrier) écran m; (folding) paravent m; **s. door** moustiquaire f (b) (of TV, computer, in cinema) écran m; **the big/small s.** le grand/petit écran; **s. actor/actress** acteur m/actrice f de cinéma; Comptr **s. saver** économiseur m d'écran; Cin **s. test** bout m d'essai; Aut **s. wash** liquide m lave-glace

2 vt (a) (protect) protéger; **to s. sth from view** cacher qch aux regards (b) (film) projeter; (TV programme) diffuser (c) (test) (for security) effectuer une enquête sur; (for disease) tester

screening ['skri:nɪŋ] n (a) Cin projection f (b) (for security) enquête f; (for disease) dépistage m

screenplay ['skri:npleɪ] n Cin scénario m

screenwriter ['skri:nraɪtə(r)] n Cin scénariste mf

screw [skru:] **1** n (a) (for fixing) vis f; Fam Fig **she's got a s. loose** elle a une case en moins; Fam Fig **to put the screws on sb** faire pression sur qn; **s. top** (of bottle, jar) couvercle m qui se visse (b) (propeller) hélice f (c) very Fam (prison officer) maton(onne) m,f (d) Vulg (sex) **to have a s.** s'envoyer en l'air

2 vt (a) (fix) visser (to à); **to s. one's face into a smile** se forcer à sourire; Fam **to s. money out of sb** extorquer de l'argent à qn (b) Vulg (have sex with) baiser; **go and s. yourself!** va te faire foutre!

3 vi Vulg (have sex) baiser

▸**screw around** vi Vulg baiser à droite et à gauche

▸**screw on** vt sep (attach) visser; Fam **she's got her head screwed on** elle a la tête sur les épaules

2 vi (of lid) se visser

▸**screw up** vt sep (a) (paper) froisser; **to s. up one's face** faire la grimace; Fig **to s. up one's courage** prendre son courage à deux mains (b) very Fam (spoil) foutre en l'air

2 vi very Fam (fail) cafouiller

screwdriver ['skru:draɪvə(r)] n tournevis m

scribble ['skrɪbəl] **1** n gribouillage m

2 vt & vi griffonner

scribe [skraɪb] n scribe m

scrimmage ['skrɪmɪdʒ] n (a) (pushing) bousculade f (b) Am (in football) mêlée f

scrimp [skrɪmp] vi **to s. (and save)** se serrer la ceinture

script [skrɪpt] n (a) (for play) texte m; (for film, TV programme) script m; (in exam) copie f d'examen (b) (handwriting) script m

Scripture ['skrɪptʃə(r)] n **(Holy) S., the Scriptures** les saintes Écritures fpl

scriptwriter ['skrɪptraɪtə(r)] n Cin & TV scénariste mf

scroll [skrəʊl] **1** n (a) (of paper, parchment) rouleau m (b) Archit volute f

2 vi Comptr défiler

▸**scroll down** vi Comptr défiler vers le bas

▸**scroll up** vi Comptr défiler vers le haut

scrooge [skru:dʒ] n avare mf

scrotum ['skrəʊtəm] n scrotum m

scrounge [skraʊndʒ] Fam **1** n **to be on the s.** venir quémander

2 vt **to s. sth from** or off **sb** taper qch à qn

3 vi **to s. off sb** vivre aux crochets de qn

scrounger ['skraʊndʒə(r)] n Fam parasite m

scrub [skrʌb] **1** n (a) (bushes) broussailles fpl (b) (wash) **to give sth a (good) s.** (bien) frotter qch (c) (for skin, face) gommage m

2 vt (pt & pp **scrubbed**) (a) (floor) frotter; (pots) récurer; **to s. one's hands** bien se frotter les mains (b) Fam (cancel) annuler

▸**scrub up** vi Med se brosser les mains

scrubber ['skrʌbə(r)] n (for dishes) tampon m à récurer

scrubbing brush ['skrʌbɪŋ'brʌʃ] n brosse f en chiendent

scrubland ['skrʌblænd] n brousse f

scruff [skrʌf] n (a) **by the s. of the neck** par la peau du cou (b) Fam (unkempt person) **he's a bit of a s.** il n'est pas très soigné

scruffily ['skrʌfɪlɪ] adv **to be s. dressed** être dépenaillé(e)

scruffy ['skrʌfɪ] adj (person) peu soigné(e); (clothes) miteux(euse)

scrum [skrʌm] n (in rugby) mêlée f; Fig bousculade f; **s. half** demi m de mêlée

scrumptious ['skrʌm(p)ʃəs] adj Fam fameux(euse)

scrunch [skrʌntʃ] **1** vt (paper) froisser en boule; (can, cigarette) écraser

2 vi crisser

scrunchie ['skrʌntʃɪ] n (for hair) chouchou m

scruple ['skru:pəl] n scrupule m; **to have no scruples** n'avoir aucun scrupule

scrupulous ['skru:pjʊləs] adj scrupuleux(euse)

scrupulously ['skru:pjʊləslɪ] adv scrupuleusement

scrutineer [skru:tɪ'nɪə(r)] n scrutateur(trice) m,f

scrutinize ['skru:tɪnaɪz] vt (document, contract) éplucher; (votes) vérifier

scrutiny ['skru:tɪnɪ] n (of document, votes) examen m minutieux; **to come under s.** être examiné(e)

scuba ['sku:bə] n **s. diver** plongeur(euse) m,f sous-marin(e); **s. diving** plongée f sous-marine

scuff [skʌf] **1** n **s. mark** éraflure f

2 vt (shoe) érafler

scuffle ['skʌfəl] **1** n échauffourée f

2 vi se bagarrer

scull [skʌl] **1** n (oar) aviron m

2 vi ramer

scullery ['skʌlərɪ] n Br arrière-cuisine f

sculpt [skʌlpt] vt sculpter

sculptor ['skʌlptə(r)] n sculpteur m

sculpture ['skʌlptʃə(r)] **1** n sculpture f

2 vt sculpter

scum [skʌm] n (a) (layer of dirt) crasse f; (froth) écume f (b) very Fam Pej (person) ordure f; (people) racaille f; **the s. of the earth** le rebut de la société

scupper ['skʌpə(r)] vt (ship, project) couler

scurrilous ['skʌrɪləs] adj calomnieux(euse)

scurry ['skʌrɪ] vi (dash) courir

▸**scurry away, scurry off** vi se sauver

scurvy ['skɜːvɪ] n Med scorbut m

scuttle¹ ['skʌtəl] 1 n (coal) s. seau m à charbon
2 vt (ship, plan) saborder

scuttle² vi (run) courir

►**scuttle away, scuttle off** vi déguerpir

scythe [saɪð] 1 n faux f
2 vt faucher

SDLP [esdiːelˈpiː] n Br (abbr **Social Democratic Labour Party**) = parti démocrate d'Irlande du Nord en faveur de la réunification de l'Irlande

SDP [esdiːˈpiː] n Br Formerly (abbr **Social Democratic Party**) parti social-démocrate

SE [esˈiː] n (abbr **southeast**) SE

sea [siː] n mer f; by the s. au bord de la mer; to go to s. (become a sailor) devenir marin; Fig a s. of people une marée humaine; heavy seas mer démontée; on the high seas, out at s. en haute mer; to find or get one's s. legs s'habituer au roulis; Fig to be all at s. être complètement perdu(e); s. air air m marin; s. anemone anémone f de mer; s. battle bataille f navale; s. breeze brise f de mer; s. change changement m radical; Fam (old) s. dog (vieux) loup m de mer; s. horse hippocampe m; Naut s. lane couloir m maritime; s. level niveau m de la mer; s. lion otarie f; s. salt sel m de mer; s. urchin oursin m; s. voyage voyage m en mer

seaboard ['siːbɔːd] n côte f

seaborne ['siːbɔːn] adj (trade) maritime; (invasion) naval(e)

seafarer ['siːfeərə(r)] n marin m

seafaring ['siːfeərɪŋ] adj (people) de navigateurs

seafood ['siːfuːd] n fruits mpl de mer

seafront ['siːfrʌnt] n front m de mer

seagoing ['siːgəʊɪŋ] adj (boat) de mer

seagull ['siːgʌl] n mouette f

seal¹ [siːl] n (animal) phoque m

seal² 1 n (a) (stamp) sceau m; to give one's s. of approval to sth donner son approbation à qch; to set the s. on sth (on alliance, friendship) sceller qch; (on victory, defeat) confirmer qch (b) (device) joint m (d'étanchéité); (on food container) = fermeture garantissant la fraîcheur d'un produit
2 vt (document, envelope) cacheter; (with official seal) sceller; (jar) fermer hermétiquement; (joint) assurer l'étanchéité de; to s. sb's fate décider du sort de qn; my lips are sealed je ne dirai rien

►**seal in** vt sep enfermer

►**seal off** vt sep (area) boucler; (people) isoler

sealing wax ['siːlɪŋwæks] n cire f à cacheter

sealskin ['siːlskɪn] n peau f de phoque

seam [siːm] n (a) (of garment) couture f; (in metalwork) soudure f; to be coming apart at the seams (of clothing) craquer de partout; Fig (of plan, organization) s'effondrer (b) (of coal) veine f

seaman ['siːmən] n Naut marin m

seamanship ['siːmənʃɪp] n Naut qualités fpl de navigateur

seamstress ['semstrɪs] n couturière f

seamy ['siːmɪ] adj sordide

seance ['seɪɒns] n séance f de spiritisme

seaplane ['siːpleɪn] n hydravion m

seaport ['siːpɔːt] n port m maritime

sear [sɪə(r)] vt (skin) brûler; Fig the image was seared on her memory l'image était gravée dans sa mémoire

search [sɜːtʃ] 1 n recherches fpl; (of building, room) fouille f; to have a s. for sth chercher qch; in s. of à la recherche de; to make a s. faire des recherches; Comptr to do a s. faire une recherche; s. party équipe f de secours; Law s. warrant mandat m de perquisition
2 vt (person, place) fouiller; Comptr (file, directory) rechercher dans; Fam s. me! je n'en ai pas la moindre idée!
3 vi chercher; to s. for sth chercher qch; Comptr s. and replace rechercher et remplacer

searching ['sɜːtʃɪŋ] adj (examination) minutieux(euse); (look) pénétrant(e)

searchlight ['sɜːtʃlaɪt] n projecteur m

searing ['sɪərɪŋ] adj (pain, heat) fulgurant(e); (criticism, indictment) virulent(e)

seascape ['siːskeɪp] n Art marine f

seashell ['siːʃel] n coquillage m

seashore ['siːʃɔː(r)] n rivage m

seasick ['siːsɪk] adj to be s. avoir le mal de mer

seasickness ['siːsɪknɪs] n mal m de mer

seaside ['siːsaɪd] n the s. le bord de la mer; at the s. au bord de la mer; s. resort station f balnéaire

season¹ ['siːzən] n saison f; (of films) cycle m; S.'s Greetings meilleurs vœux de fin d'année; the high s. (for tourism) la haute saison; cherries are out of s. ce n'est pas la saison des cerises; s. ticket abonnement m

season² vt (a) (with salt, pepper) assaisonner; (with spice) épicer (b) (wood) faire sécher

seasonable ['siːzənəbəl] adj s. weather un temps de saison

seasonal ['siːzənəl] adj (work, fluctuations) saisonnier(ère)

seasoned ['siːzənd] adj (a) (food) assaisonné(e); a highly s. dish un plat très relevé (b) (wood) sec (sèche) (c) (person) expérimenté(e); (soldier) aguerri(e)

seasoning ['siːzənɪŋ] n Culin assaisonnement m

seat [siːt] 1 n (a) (chair) chaise f; (on bus, train, in theatre, cinema) place f, siège m; (in Parliament) siège m; to take a s. s'asseoir; s. belt ceinture f de sécurité (b) (part of chair, toilet) siège m; (of trousers) fond m (c) (centre) of government siège m; a s. of learning un haut lieu du savoir; country s. (of aristocrat) demeure f familiale
2 vt (a) (cause to sit) (child) asseoir; (guests) faire asseoir; to be/remain seated être/rester assis(e); Formal please be seated veuillez vous asseoir (b) (accommodate) the bus seats thirty il y a trente places assises dans le bus; this table seats twelve on tient douze à cette table; the hall seats two hundred la salle compte deux cents places

seating ['siːtɪŋ] n (seats) sièges mpl; (positioning) placement m; s. capacity nombre m de places assises; s. plan plan m de table

SEATO ['siːtəʊ] n (abbr **Southeast Asia Treaty Organization**) OTASE f

seaway ['siːweɪ] n route f (maritime)

seaweed ['siːwiːd] n algues fpl

seaworthy ['siːwɜːðɪ] adj en état de naviguer

sebaceous [sɪˈbeɪʃəs] adj sébacé(e)

sec¹ (abbr **second(s)**) s.

sec² [sek] n Fam (second) I'll be there in a s. j'arrive tout de suite; wait a s.! attends une seconde!

secateurs [sekəˈtɜːz] npl sécateur m

secede [sɪ'siːd] *vi* faire sécession (**from** de)

secession [sɪ'seʃən] *n* sécession *f*

secluded [sɪ'kluːdɪd] *adj (place)* reculé(e); *(life)* de reclus(e)

seclusion [sɪ'kluːʒən] *n* isolement *m*

second[1] ['sekənd] *n (of time)* seconde *f*; **I won't be a s.** j'en ai pour deux secondes; **s. hand** *(of clock)* trotteuse *f*

second[2] 1 *n* (a) *(in series)* deuxième *mf*, second(e) *m,f*; **Edward the S.** Edward II; **I was s. in the race** je suis arrivé deuxième à la course
(b) *(of month)* deux *m*; **the s. of May** le deux mai
(c) *Com* **seconds** articles *mpl* défectueux
(d) *(in duel)* témoin *m*; *(in boxing)* soigneur *m*
(e) *Br Univ* **to get a s.** *(in degree)* ≃ avoir sa licence avec mention assez bien
(f) **s. (gear)** seconde *f*
(g) *Fam* **anyone for seconds?** *(at meal)* quelqu'un veut du rab?

2 *adj* deuxième, second(e); **twenty-s.** vingt-deuxième; **ninety-s.** quatre-vingt-douzième; **to be s.** to none être sans égal(e); **s. in command** *Mil* commandant *m* en second; *(in organization)* adjoint(e) *m,f*; **the s. largest city in England** la deuxième ville d'Angleterre; **a s. Picasso/Churchill** un nouveau Picasso/Churchill; **on s. thoughts** tout bien réfléchi; **to have s. thoughts (about sth)** ne plus être très sûr(e) (de qch); *Fig* **to play s. fiddle to sb** être dans l'ombre de qn; **it's s. nature to her** elle le fait automatiquement; **to get one's s. wind** trouver un second souffle; **s. chance** deuxième chance *f*; **to be in one's s. childhood** être retombé(e) en enfance; **s. class** *(on train)* deuxième classe *f*; *Rel* **the S. Coming** le second avènement; **s. cousin** petit(e) cousin(e) *m,f*; **s. floor** *Br* deuxième étage *m*, *Am* premier étage *m*; **s. language** seconde langue *f*; **s. name** nom *m* de famille; *Law* **s. offence** récidive *f*; **s. opinion** deuxième avis *m*; *Gram* **s. person** deuxième personne *f*; **s. sight** don *m* de double vue; **s. violin** second violon *m*; **the S. World War** la Seconde Guerre mondiale

second[3] *vt (motion)* appuyer

second[4] [sɪ'kɒnd] *vt (officer, employee)* détacher (**from**/**to** de/à)

secondary ['sekəndərɪ] *adj* secondaire; **s. school** établissement *m* secondaire

second-best ['sekənd'best] 1 *n* pis-aller *m*; **to be content with s.** se contenter d'un pis-aller
2 *adv* **to come off s.** être battu(e)

second-class ['sekənd'klɑːs] 1 *adj (ticket, carriage)* de deuxième classe; **s. citizen** citoyen(enne) *m,f* de second rang; *Br Univ* **s. degree** licence *f* avec mention assez bien; **s. mail** courrier *m* au tarif lent
2 *adv* **to travel s.** voyager en seconde classe

seconder ['sekəndə(r)] *n* = personne qui appuie une motion

second-guess ['sekənd'ges] *vt* **to s. sb** anticiper ce que qn va faire

second-hand ['sekənd'hænd] 1 *adj (car, clothes)* d'occasion
2 *adv (buy)* d'occasion; **to hear news s.** avoir des nouvelles de seconde main

secondly ['sekəndlɪ] *adv* deuxièmement

secondment [sɪ'kɒndmənt] *n* **to be on s.** être en détachement

second-rate ['sekəndreɪt] *adj* médiocre

secrecy ['siːkrɪsɪ] *n* secret *m*; **in s.** en secret; **to swear sb to s.** faire jurer le silence à qn

secret ['siːkrɪt] 1 *n* secret *m*; **to do sth in s.** faire qch secrètement; **I make no s. of it** je ne m'en cache pas; **it's no s.** tout le monde le sait
2 *adj* secret(ète); **to keep sth s. from sb** cacher qch à qn; **s. agent** agent *m* secret; **s. police** police *f* secrète; **s. service** services *mpl* secrets; **the S. Service** = service de sécurité du président américain; *also Fig* **s. weapon** arme *f* secrète

secretarial [sekrə'teərɪəl] *adj (work)* administratif(ive); *(job, college, course)* de secrétariat

secretariat [sekrə'teərɪət] *n* secrétariat *m*

secretary ['sekrətərɪ] *n* (a) *(in office)* secrétaire *mf* (b) *Br Pol* ministre *m*

secretary-general ['sekrətərɪ'dʒenərəl] *n* *Pol* secrétaire *m* général

secrete [sɪ'kriːt] *vt* (a) *(discharge)* sécréter (b) *(hide)* cacher

secretion [sɪ'kriːʃən] *n* sécrétion *f*

secretive ['siːkrɪtɪv] *adj* secret(ète); **to be s. about sth** faire des cachotteries à propos de qch

secretly ['siːkrɪtlɪ] *adv* secrètement

sect [sekt] *n* secte *f*

sectarian [sek'teərɪən] *adj* sectaire

sectarianism [sek'teərɪənɪzəm] *n* sectarisme *m*

section ['sekʃən] 1 *n* (a) *(in general)* partie *f*; *(of road, railway)* tronçon *m*; *(of machine)* élément *m*; *(of organization)* département *m*; *(in orchestra)* section *f*; *(of law, treaty)* article *m*; **all sections of society** toutes les catégories sociales (b) *(of soldiers)* section *f* (c) *(cross-section)* coupe *f*
2 *vt (cut)* sectionner

sector ['sektə(r)] *n* secteur *m*

secular ['sekjʊlə(r)] *adj (history, art)* laïque; *(music)* profane

secure [sɪ'kjʊə(r)] 1 *adj* (a) *(free from anxiety)* en sécurité; **s. in the knowledge that...** ayant l'assurance que... (b) *(investment, place)* sûr(e); *(foothold)* ferme; *(nomination, future)* assuré(e); *(load, rope)* bien attaché(e); *(foundations, lock)* solide
2 *vt* (a) *(make safe)* *(position, future)* assurer (b) *(fasten)* *(load)* bien amarrer; *(door, window)* bien fermer (c) *(obtain)* *(support, promise, loan)* obtenir

securely [sɪ'kjʊəlɪ] *adv* (a) *(stored, hidden)* en toute sécurité; *(protected)* bien (b) *(firmly)* solidement; **the door was s. fastened** la porte était bien fermée

security [sɪ'kjʊərɪtɪ] *n* (a) *(stability, safety)* sécurité *f*; **s. of tenure** sécurité de l'emploi; **the S. Council** le Conseil de sécurité; **s. forces** forces *fpl* de sécurité; **s. guard** garde *m*; **s. officer** agent *m* de sécurité; **to be a s. risk** être un danger pour la sécurité (b) *Fin (for loan)* garantie *f* (c) *Fin* **securities** titres *mpl*

sedan [sɪ'dæn] *n* (a) *Am (car)* berline *f* (b) **s. chair** chaise *f* à porteurs

sedate [sɪ'deɪt] 1 *adj* tranquille
2 *vt* donner des calmants à

sedately [sɪ'deɪtlɪ] *adv* tranquillement

sedation [sɪ'deɪʃən] *n* **under s.** sous calmants

sedative ['sedətɪv] *n* sédatif *m*, calmant *m*

sedentary ['sedəntrɪ] *adj* sédentaire

sediment ['sedɪmənt] *n* sédiment *m*

sedition [sɪ'dɪʃən] *n* sédition *f*

seditious [sɪˈdɪʃəs] *adj* séditieux(euse)

seduce [sɪˈdjuːs] *vt* (*sexually*) séduire; *Fig* **to s. sb into doing sth** persuader qn de faire qch

seducer [sɪˈdjuːsə(r)] *n* séducteur(trice) *m,f*

seduction [sɪˈdʌkʃən] *n* séduction *f*

seductive [sɪˈdʌktɪv] *adj* (*look*) séducteur(trice); (*argument, offer*) séduisant(e)

see¹ [siː] *n* Rel évêché *m*

see² (*pt* **saw** [sɔː], *pp* **seen** [siːn]) **1** *vt* (a) (*with eyes, perceive*) voir; **now s. what you've done!** regarde ce que tu as fait!; **s. page 50** voir page 50; **to be seeing things** (*hallucinate*) avoir des visions; **it has to be seen to be believed** il faut le voir pour le croire; **to s. sb do** *or* **doing sth** voir qn faire qch; **I can't s. a way out of this problem** je ne vois pas comment on peut s'en sortir; **could you s. your way to lending me your car?** cela te serait-il possible de me prêter ta voiture?; **to s. sense** *or* **reason** entendre raison; **the city has seen many changes** la ville a connu de grands changements; **I don't know what you s. in her** je ne vois pas ce que tu lui trouves; **it remains to be seen whether...** reste à savoir si...; **I'll s. what I can do** je vais voir ce que je peux faire

(b) (*understand*) voir; **I s. what you mean** je vois ce que tu veux dire; **I don't s. the point** je n'en vois pas l'intérêt

(c) (*envisage, imagine*) imaginer, voir; **what do you s. happening next?** à ton avis, qu'est-ce qui va se passer maintenant?; **I can't s. them arriving before six** ça m'étonnerait qu'ils arrivent avant six heures; **I can't s. you as a boxer** je ne t'imagine pas boxeur

(d) (*make sure*) **I shall s. that he comes** je ferai en sorte qu'il vienne; **s. that this doesn't happen again!** fais en sorte que ça ne se reproduise pas!

(e) (*meet*) (*person, doctor, solicitor*) voir; **I'm seeing Bill tomorrow** je vois Bill demain; **s. you (soon)!** à bientôt!

(f) (*accompany*) **to s. sb home** accompagner qn chez lui; **to s. sb to the door** accompagner qn jusqu'à la porte

2 *vi* (a) (*with eyes*) voir; **s. for yourself** à toi de juger; **we shall s.** nous verrons bien

(b) (*understand*) comprendre; **ah, I s.!** ah, je vois!

(c) (*consider*) **let me s.!, let's s.!** voyons!; **have you got a free room? – let me s.** avez-vous une chambre libre? – voyons voir

(d) (*find out*) **I'll go and s.** je vais voir

▸**see about** *vt insep* (a) (*deal with*) s'occuper de (b) (*consider*) voir; *Fam* **we'll (soon) s. about that!** c'est ce qu'on va voir!

▸**see in** *vt sep* **to s. the New Year in** fêter le Nouvel An

▸**see off** *vt sep* (a) (*say goodbye to*) dire au revoir à (b) (*attacker*) faire fuir

▸**see out** *vt sep* accompagner jusqu'à la porte; **I'll s. myself out** inutile de me raccompagner

▸**see through** **1** *vt sep* (*project, policy*) mener à bien

2 *vt insep* (*person, lie, plan*) percer à jour

▸**see to** *vt insep* (*deal with*) s'occuper de; **to get sth seen to** (*machine, roof*) faire réparer qch; (*wound, injury*) faire examiner qch; **I'll s. to it that you're not disturbed** je ferai en sorte que tu ne sois pas dérangé

seed [siːd] *n* **1** (a) (*for sowing*) graine *f*, (*of fruit*) pépin *m*; **to go** *or* **run to s.** (*of plant*) monter en graine; **s. corn** blé *m* de semence; *Fig* capital *m* initial; **s. merchant** grainetier(ère) *m,f*; **s. potatoes** pommes *fpl* de terre de semence (b) *Sp* (*in tournament*) tête *f* de série (c) *Lit* (*semen*) semence *f*

2 *vt* (a) (*remove seeds from*) épépiner (b) (*lawn*)

ensemencer (c) (*in tournament*) **seeded players** joueurs *mpl* classés tête de série

3 *vi* (*of plant*) monter en graine

seedless [ˈsiːdlɪs] *adj* sans pépins

seedling [ˈsiːdlɪŋ] *n* plant *m*

seedy [ˈsiːdɪ] *adj* (a) (*shabby*) (*person, hotel, area*) miteux(euse) (b) *Fam* (*unwell*) mal fichu(e)

seeing [ˈsiːɪŋ] **1** *conj* **s. (that** *or* **how)...** étant donné que...

2 *n* **s. is believing** voir c'est croire

seek [siːk] (*pt & pp* **sought** [sɔːt]) *vt* (a) (*look for*) (*thing lost, job*) chercher; (*sb's friendship, promotion*) essayer d'obtenir; (*request*) **to s. sth from sb** demander qch à qn; **to s. sb's advice** demander conseil à qn (c) (*try*) **to s. to do sth** essayer de faire qch

▸**seek after** *vt insep* **to be much sought after** être très recherché(e)

▸**seek out** *vt sep* (*person*) dénicher

seem [siːm] *vi* sembler; **to s. tired** avoir l'air fatigué(e); **do what seems best** fais au mieux; **it seemed like a dream** j'avais l'impression de rêver; **I s. to have heard her name somewhere** il me semble avoir entendu son nom quelque part; **I can't s. to get it right** je n'y arrive pas; **it seems (that)..., it would s. that...** il semble que...+ *subjunctive*; **it seems to me that...** il me semble que...; **it seems** *or* **would s. so** il paraît; **it seems** *or* **would s. not** il paraît que non

seeming [ˈsiːmɪŋ] *adj* apparent(e)

seemingly [ˈsiːmɪŋlɪ] *adv* apparemment

seemly [ˈsiːmlɪ] *adj* Formal bienséant(e)

seen [siːn] *pp of* **see²**

seep [siːp] *vi* suinter; **s. into sth** s'infiltrer dans qch

seepage [ˈsiːpɪdʒ] *n* (*oozing*) suintement *m*; (*into surface*) infiltration *f*

seer [sɪə(r)] *n* Lit voyant(e) *m,f*

seesaw [ˈsiːsɔː] *n* **1** tapecul *m*

2 *vi* Fig (*of prices*) être en dents de scie

seethe [siːð] *vi* (*of liquid*) bouillonner; (*of street*) grouiller (**with** de); **to be seething (with anger)** bouillir (de rage)

see-through [ˈsiːθruː] *adj* transparent(e)

segment 1 *n* [ˈsegmənt] segment *m*; (*of orange*) quartier *m*

2 *vt* [segˈment] (*orange*) couper en quartiers; (*line*) segmenter

segmentation [segmenˈteɪʃən] *n* Econ segmentation *f*

segregate [ˈsegrɪgeɪt] *vt* séparer (**from** de); (*prisoner*) isoler (**from** de)

segregation [segrɪˈgeɪʃən] *n* ségrégation *f*; (*of prisoner*) isolement *m*

Seine [sem] *n* **the S.** la Seine

seismic [ˈsaɪzmɪk] *adj* sismique

seismograph [ˈsaɪzməɡrɑːf] *n* sismographe *m*

seismology [saɪzˈmɒlədʒɪ] *n* sismologie *f*

seize [siːz] *vt* (a) (*grab*) *& Fig* (*opportunity*) saisir; **to s. hold of sth** saisir (b) (*city, territory*) s'emparer de; (*drugs, stolen goods*) saisir

▸**seize on, seize upon** *vt insep* sauter sur

▸**seize up** *vi* (*of engine, back*) se bloquer

seizure [ˈsiːʒə(r)] *n* (a) (*of land, city*) prise *f*; *Law* (*of property, drugs*) saisie *f* (b) *Med* crise *f*

seldom ['seldəm] *adv* rarement; **s. have I seen such courage** j'ai rarement vu un tel courage

select [sɪ'lekt] **1** *adj (exclusive)* sélect(e); **a s. few** quelques privilégiés(ées); *Br Parl* **s. committee** commission *f* d'enquête
2 *vt* sélectionner

selected [sɪ'lektɪd] *adj* choisi(e)

selection [sɪ'lekʃən] *n* sélection *f*, choix *m*; **to make a s.** faire un choix; **a wide s.** un grand choix

selective [sɪ'lektɪv] *adj* sélectif(ive)

selector [sɪ'lektə(r)] *n (of team)* sélectionneur(euse) *m,f*

self [self] *(pl* **selves** [selvz]*) n* **(a)** **he's quite his old s. again** il est redevenu comme avant; **she was her usual cheerful s.** comme à son habitude, elle était gaie **(b)** *Psy* **the s.** le moi

self-addressed envelope ['selfə'drest'envələup] *n* enveloppe *f* libellée à ses nom et adresse

self-appointed ['selfə'pɔɪntɪd] *adj* **he's the s. spokesman** il s'est proclamé porte-parole

self-assured ['selfə'ʃʊəd] *adj* plein(e) d'assurance

self-catering ['self'keɪtərɪŋ] *adj (holiday)* en appartement meublé; *(accommodation)* meublé(e)

self-centred ['self'sentəd] *adj* égocentrique

self-confessed ['selfkən'fest] *adj* **he's a s. liar/cheat** il est menteur/tricheur de son propre aveu

self-confidence ['self'kɒnfɪdəns] *n* confiance *f* en soi

self-confident ['self'kɒnfɪdənt] *adj* plein(e) d'assurance

self-conscious ['self'kɒnʃəs] *adj* timide, gêné(e)

self-contained ['selfkən'teɪnd] *adj (person)* réservé(e); *(apartment)* indépendant(e)

self-contradictory ['selfkɒntrə'dɪktərɪ] *adj* qui contient des contradictions

self-control ['selfkən'trəʊl] *n* maîtrise *f* de soi

self-deception ['selfdɪ'sepʃən] *n* aveuglement *m*

self-defeating ['selfdɪ'fiːtɪŋ] *adj* qui va à l'encontre du but recherché

self-defence, *Am* **self-defense** ['selfdɪ'fens] *n* autodéfense *f*; *Law* légitime défense *f*; **in s.** en état de légitime défense

self-denial ['selfdɪ'naɪəl] *n* abnégation *f*

self-destruct ['selfdɪ'strʌkt] *vi* s'autodétruire

self-determination ['selfdɪtɜːmɪ'neɪʃən] *n* autodétermination *f*

self-discipline ['self'dɪsɪplɪn] *n* autodiscipline *f*

self-doubt ['self'daʊt] *n* manque *m* de confiance en soi

self-effacing ['selfɪ'feɪsɪŋ] *adj* effacé(e)

self-employed ['selfɪm'plɔɪd] *adj* indépendant(e)

self-esteem [selfə'stiːm] *n* confiance *f* en soi

self-evident ['self'evɪdənt] *adj* évident(e)

self-explanatory ['selfɪk'splænətərɪ] *adj* **to be s.** se passer d'explications

self-expression ['selfɪk'spreʃən] *n* expression *f* individuelle

self-government ['self'gʌvənmənt] *n* autonomie *f*

self-help ['self'help] *n* **s. group** groupe *m* d'entraide

self-important ['selfɪm'pɔːtənt] *adj* suffisant(e)

self-indulgent [selfɪn'dʌldʒənt] *adj* complaisant(e)

self-inflicted ['selfɪn'flɪktɪd] *adj* que l'on s'inflige à soi-même

self-interest ['self'ɪntərest] *n* intérêt *m* personnel

selfish ['selfɪʃ] *adj* égoïste

selfishness ['selfɪʃnɪs] *n* égoïsme *m*

self-knowledge ['self'nɒlɪdʒ] *n* connaissance *f* de soi

selfless ['selfləs] *adj* désintéressé(e)

self-made man ['selfmeɪd'mæn] *n* self-made-man *m*

self-pity ['self'pɪtɪ] *n* apitoiement *m* sur son propre sort; **to be full of s.** s'apitoyer sur son sort

self-portrait ['self'pɔːtreɪt] *n* autoportrait *m*

self-possessed ['selfpə'zest] *adj* qui a une grande maîtrise de soi

self-preservation ['selfprezə'veɪʃən] *n* **instinct for s.** instinct *m* de conservation

self-raising flour ['selfreɪzɪŋ'flaʊə(r)], *Am* **self-rising flour** ['selfraɪzɪŋ'flaʊə(r)] *n* = farine contenant de la levure chimique

self-reliant ['selfrɪ'laɪənt] *adj* indépendant(e)

self-respect ['selfrɪ'spekt] *n* amour-propre *m*

self-respecting ['selfrɪ'spektɪŋ] *adj* qui se respecte

self-restraint ['selfrɪs'treɪnt] *n* retenue *f*, maîtrise *f* de soi

self-righteous ['self'raɪtʃəs] *adj* suffisant(e)

self-rising flour ['selfraɪzɪŋ'flaʊə(r)] *n Am* = **self-raising flour**

selfsame ['selfseɪm] *adj* **the s. day** le même jour exactement; **the s. thing** la même chose exactement

self-satisfied ['self'sætɪsfaɪd] *adj* suffisant(e), content(e) de soi

self-service ['self'sɜːvɪs] **1** *n* self-service *m*
2 *adj* self-service

self-starter ['self'stɑːtə(r)] *n (person)* personne *f* très motivée

self-styled ['self'staɪld] *adj* prétendu(e), soi-disant *inv*

self-sufficient ['selfsə'fɪʃənt] *adj (person)* indépendant(e); *(country)* auto-suffisant(e)

self-taught ['self'tɔːt] *adj* autodidacte

sell [sel] *(pt & pp* **sold** [səʊld]*) **1** *vt* vendre; **to s. sb sth**, **to s. sth to sb** vendre qch à qn; **scandal sells newspapers** le scandale fait vendre les journaux; *Fig* **to s. oneself** *(present oneself)* se vendre; *Fig* **to s. sb an idea** faire accepter une idée à qn; *Fig* **to s. sb down the river** trahir qn
2 *vi (of product)* se vendre; *(of person)* vendre; **to s. like hot cakes** se vendre comme des petits pains

▶**sell off** *vt sep* liquider

▶**sell out 1** *vt sep* **(a) to be sold out** *(of book, item)* être épuisé(e); *(of show, concert)* afficher complet; **the tickets are sold out** il n'y a plus de billets **(b)** *(betray)* trahir, vendre
2 *vi* **(a) to s. out of sth** ne plus avoir de qch **(b)** *(betray beliefs)* se vendre

▶**sell up** *vi (sell home, business)* tout vendre

sell-by date ['selbaɪdeɪt] *n* date *f* limite de vente

seller ['selə(r)] *n* vendeur(euse) *m,f*; *Econ* **s.'s market** marché *m* favorable au vendeur

selling ['selɪŋ] *n* vente *f*; **s. point** atout *m*; **s. price** prix *m* de vente

sell-off ['selɒf] *n (of state-owned company)* vente *f*

Sellotape® ['seləteɪp] *n* Scotch® *m*

sellotape ['seləteɪp] *vt* scotcher

sellout ['selaʊt] n (a) **the play was a s.** il n'y avait plus de places pour cette pièce, la pièce a joué à guichets fermés (b) (betrayal) trahison f

semantic [sɪ'mæntɪk] adj sémantique

semantics [sɪ'mæntɪks] n sémantique f

semaphore ['seməfɔ:(r)] n signaux mpl à bras

semblance ['sembləns] n semblant m

semen ['si:men] n sperme m

semester [sɪ'mestə(r)] n semestre m

semi ['semɪ] n Br Fam (semi-detached house) maison f jumelée

semiautomatic ['semɪɔ:tə'mætɪk] adj semi-automatique

semicircle ['semɪsɜ:kəl] n demi-cercle m

semicircular ['semɪ'sɜ:kjʊlə(r)] adj semi-circulaire, en demi-cercle

semicolon ['semɪ'kəʊlən] n point-virgule m

semiconductor ['semɪkən'dʌktə(r)] n Elec semi-conducteur m

semiconscious ['semɪ'kɒnʃəs] adj à demi conscient(e)

semidetached ['semɪdɪ'tætʃt] 1 n maison f jumelée
2 adj jumelé(e)

semifinal ['semɪ'faɪnəl] n demi-finale f

semifinalist ['semɪ'faɪnəlɪst] n demi-finaliste mf

seminal ['semɪnəl] adj majeur(e), de première importance

seminar ['semɪnɑ:(r)] n séminaire m

semi-precious ['semɪ'preʃəs] adj semi-précieux(euse)

semiquaver ['semɪkweɪvə(r)] n Mus double croche f

semi-skimmed [semɪ'skɪmd] adj (milk) demi-écrémé(e)

Semite ['si:maɪt] n Sémite mf

Semitic [sɪ'mɪtɪk] adj (language) sémitique; (people) sémite

semitone ['semɪtəʊn] n Mus demi-ton m

semitropical ['semɪ'trɒpɪkəl] adj semi-tropical(e)

semolina [semə'li:nə] n semoule f

Senate ['senɪt] n the S. le Sénat

senator ['senətə(r)] n sénateur m

send [send] (pt & pp **sent** [sent]) vt (letter, message, person) envoyer; **to s. sb sth, to s. sth to sb** envoyer qch à qn; **to s. sb home** renvoyer qn chez soi; **to s. sb to prison** envoyer qn en prison; **to s. sb on an errand** envoyer qn faire une course; Fig **to s. sb/sth flying** envoyer qn/qch valser; **to s. sb into fits of laughter** faire rire qn aux larmes

▸ **send away** 1 vt sep (person) renvoyer
2 vi **to s. away for sth** se faire envoyer qch

▸ **send back** vt sep renvoyer

▸ **send down** vt sep Br (a) (expel from university) renvoyer (b) Fam (send to prison) mettre en taule (for pour)

▸ **send for** vt insep (help, supplies) envoyer chercher; (doctor) faire venir

▸ **send in** vt sep envoyer

▸ **send off** 1 vt sep (a) (letter, order) expédier, envoyer (b) (player) expulser
2 vi **to s. off for sth** se faire envoyer qch

▸ **send on** vt sep (ahead) expédier; (later) faire suivre

▸ **send out** 1 vt sep envoyer
2 vi **to s. out for sth** envoyer chercher qch

▸ **send up** vt sep Br Fam (parody) se moquer de

sender ['sendə(r)] n expéditeur(trice) m,f

send-off ['sendɒf] n Fam **to give sb a good s.** faire des adieux en règle à qn

send-up ['sendʌp] n Br Fam parodie f, pastiche m

Senegal ['senɪ'gɔ:l] n le Sénégal

Senegalese [senɪgə'li:z] 1 n (person) Sénégalais(e) m,f
2 adj sénégalais(e)

senile ['si:naɪl] adj sénile; **s. dementia** démence f sénile

senility [sɪ'nɪlɪtɪ] n sénilité f

senior ['si:nɪə(r)] 1 n (a) (in age) **to be sb's s.** être l'aîné(e) de qn; **she's three years his s.** elle est son aînée de trois ans (b) (in rank) supérieur(e) m,f
2 adj (a) (in age) aîné(e); Thomas Smith, S. Thomas Smith père; **he's two years s. to me** il a deux ans de plus que moi; **s. citizen** personne f du troisième âge (b) (in rank, position) supérieur(e); **s. officer** officier m supérieur; **s. partner** (in company) associé(e) m,f principal(e)

seniority [si:nɪ'ɒrɪtɪ] n (in age, length of service) ancienneté f; (in rank) supériorité f

sensation [sen'seɪʃən] n (a) (feeling) sensation f; **a tingling/burning s.** une sensation de picotement/brûlure (b) (excitement) **to cause a s.** faire sensation

sensational [sen'seɪʃənəl] adj sensationnel(elle)

sensationalism [sen'seɪʃənəlɪzəm] n sensationnalisme m

sense [sens] 1 n (a) (faculty) sens m; **to come to one's senses** (recover consciousness) revenir à soi; (see reason) revenir à la raison; **s. of direction** sens de l'orientation; **s. of duty** sens du devoir; **s. of hearing** ouïe f; **s. of humour** sens de l'humour (b) (rationality) bon sens m, intelligence f; **there's no s. in staying/leaving** ça ne sert à rien de rester/partir (c) (feeling) sentiment m; **to lose all s. of time/reality** perdre toute notion du temps/de la réalité; **a s. of achievement** un sentiment de satisfaction (d) (meaning) sens, signification f; **to make s.** être logique; **to make no s.** n'avoir aucun sens; **to make s. of sth** comprendre qch; **in a s.** dans un sens
2 vt (perceive) sentir, deviner; **to s. that** sentir que

senseless ['senslɪs] adj (a) (unconscious) sans connaissance (b) (pointless) absurde

sensibilities [sensɪ'bɪlɪtɪz] npl susceptibilité f

sensible ['sensɪbəl] adj (a) (rational) sensé(e) (b) (practical) pratique (c) Formal (aware) **to be s. of sth** être sensible à qch

sensibly ['sensɪblɪ] adv (rationally) raisonnablement

sensitive ['sensɪtɪv] adj (a) (person) sensible (**to** à) (b) (subject, issue) délicat(e); (document, information) confidentiel(elle)

sensor ['sensə(r)] n détecteur m

sensory ['sensərɪ] adj sensoriel(elle); **s. organs** organes mpl sensoriels

sensual ['sensjʊəl] adj sensuel(elle)

sensuality [sensjʊ'ælɪtɪ] n sensualité f

sensuous ['sensjʊəs] adj sensuel(elle)

sent [sent] pt & pp of **send**

sentence ['sentəns] 1 n (a) (phrase) phrase f (b) (in prison) peine f; **to pass s.** prononcer la sentence
2 vt (criminal) condamner (**to** à)

sententious [sen'tenʃəs] *adj Formal* sentencieux(euse)

sentient ['sentɪənt] *adj* sensible

sentiment ['sentɪmənt] *n* (a) *(opinion)* sentiment *m*; my sentiments exactly je suis tout à fait du même avis (b) *(sentimentality)* sentimentalité *f*

sentimental [sentɪ'mentəl] *adj* sentimental(e)

sentimentality [sentɪmen'tælɪtɪ] *n* sentimentalité *f*, sensiblerie *f*

sentry ['sentrɪ] *n* sentinelle *f*; to be on s. duty être de garde; s. box guérite *f*

Seoul [səʊl] *n* Séoul

Sep *(abbr* **September**) septembre

separable ['sepərəbəl] *adj* séparable

separate 1 *adj* ['sepərət] *(parts)* séparé(e), distinct(e); *(box, room, document)* à part; *(occasion, attempt, entrance)* différent(e); *(organization)* indépendant(e); fish and meat should be kept s. le poisson et la viande doivent être gardés séparément; to lead s. lives avoir chacun sa vie; *also Fig* they went their s. ways ils sont partis chacun de leur côté

2 *vt* ['sepərett] séparer **(from** de)

3 *vi* se séparer **(from** de)

separation [sepə'reɪʃən] *n* séparation *f*

separatist ['sepərətɪst] *n Pol* séparatiste *mf*

sepia ['siːpɪə] *n* sépia *f*

sepsis ['sepsɪs] *n* infection *f*

Sept *(abbr* **September**) septembre

September [sep'tembə(r)] *n* septembre *m*; *see also* **May**

septet [sep'tet] *n* septuor *m*

septic ['septɪk] *adj* septique; to go s. s'infecter; s. tank fosse *f* septique

septicaemia, *Am* **septicemia** [septɪ'siːmɪə] *n* septicémie *f*

sepulchre, *Am* **sepulcher** ['sepəlkə(r)] *n Formal* sépulcre *m*

sequel ['siːkwəl] *n* (a) *(book, film)* suite *f* **(to** de) (b) *(result)* conséquence *f* **(to** de)

sequence ['siːkwəns] *n* (a) *(order)* ordre *m*, suite *f*; in s. par ordre; out of s. dans le désordre (b) *(of numbers, events)* suite *f*, série *f*; *(in film)* séquence *f*

sequential [sɪ'kwenʃəl] *adj* séquentiel(elle)

sequestrate [sɪ'kwestreɪt] *vt Law* séquestrer

sequestration [siːkwe'streɪʃən] *n Law* mise *f* sous séquestre

sequin ['siːkwɪn] *n* paillette *f*

sequoia [se'kwɔɪə] *n* séquoia *m*

Serbia ['sɜːbɪə] *n* la Serbie

Serb(ian) ['sɜːb(ɪən)] **1** *n* Serbe *mf*
2 *adj* serbe

Serbo-Croat ['sɜːbəʊ'krəʊæt] **1** *n* serbo-croate *m*
2 *adj* serbo-croate

serenade [serə'neɪd] **1** *n* sérénade *f*
2 *vt* chanter une sérénade à

serene [sɪ'riːn] *adj* serein(e)

serenity [sɪ'renɪtɪ] *n* sérénité *f*

serf [sɜːf] *n Hist* serf (serve) *m,f*

serfdom ['sɜːfdəm] *n Hist* servage *m*

serge [sɜːdʒ] *n* serge *f*

sergeant ['sɑːdʒənt] *n (in police)* brigadier *m*; *Mil* sergent *m*

sergeant-major [sɑːdʒənt'meɪdʒə(r)] *n* sergent-major *m*

serial ['sɪərɪəl] **1** *n (in magazine)* roman-feuilleton *m*; *(on TV)* feuilleton *m*
2 *adj* d'une série, en série; s. killer tueur(euse) *m,f* en série; s. number numéro *m* de série

serialize ['sɪərɪəlaɪz] *vt (in magazine)* publier en feuilleton; *(on TV)* adapter en feuilleton

series ['sɪəriːz] *(pl* series) *n* série *f*

serious ['sɪərɪəs] *adj (person)* sérieux(euse); *(situation, problem, injury)* grave; to be s. about doing sth envisager sérieusement de faire qch; are you s.? tu parles sérieusement?; *Fam* s. money un bon paquet d'argent

seriously ['sɪərɪəslɪ] *adv* (a) *(in earnest)* sérieusement; to take sb/sth s. prendre qn/qch au sérieux; to take oneself too s. se prendre trop au sérieux; you can't s. expect... sérieusement, vous ne pensez pas que... (b) *(gravely, critically)* gravement

sermon ['sɜːmən] *n also Fig* sermon *m*

serpent ['sɜːpənt] *n Lit* serpent *m*

serpentine ['sɜːpəntaɪn] *adj Lit* qui serpente, sinueux(euse)

SERPS [sɜːps] *n Br Fin (abbr* **State Earnings Related Pension Scheme**) = retraite versée par l'État, calculée sur le salaire

serrated [se'reɪtɪd] *adj* en dents de scie

serum ['sɪərəm] *n* sérum *m*

servant ['sɜːvənt] *n* domestique *mf*

serve [sɜːv] **1** *vt* (a) *(country, cause)* servir; to s. one's own interests servir ses propres intérêts
(b) *(be useful to)* servir à, être utile à; to s. a purpose avoir une utilité; it doesn't s. my purpose cela ne me sert à rien; it has served me well ça m'a fait de l'usage; if my memory serves me right si ma mémoire est bonne
(c) *(prison sentence)* purger; *(apprenticeship)* faire
(d) *(meal, customer, drink)* servir; s. chilled *(on wine)* servir frais; serves four *(on packet, in recipe)* pour quatre personnes
(e) *Law* to s. sb with a summons remettre une assignation à qn
(f) *(it)* serves her right! bien fait pour elle!
2 *vi* servir; to s. as *(be used as)* servir de
3 *n (in tennis)* service *m*; *(it's)* your s.! à toi de servir!

▶**serve up** *vt sep* servir

server ['sɜːvə(r)] *n* (a) *(in tennis)* serveur(euse) *m,f* (b) *Comptr* serveur *m*

service ['sɜːvɪs] **1** *n* (a) *(with army, firm)* service *m*; *Mil* the services les forces *fpl* armées; to do sb a s. rendre un service à qn; to be at sb's s. être au service de qn; to be of s. to sb être utile à qn; to offer one's services offrir ses services
(b) *(in shop, restaurant)* service *m*; s. included/not included service compris/non compris; s. charge service; s. industry industrie *f* de services; *Br* s. lift ascenseur *m* de service
(c) *(system)* postal/air/train s. service *m* postal/aérien/des trains
(d) *(maintenance) (of machine)* entretien *m*; *(of car)* révision *f*; s. area *(on motorway)* aire *f* de service; s. station *(on motorway)* station-service *f*
(e) *(in church)* service *m*, office *m*
(f) *(in tennis)* service *m*; s. line ligne *f* de service

(g) *Old-fashioned* **to be in/go into s.** *(of servant)* être/
devenir domestique

2 *vt (machine)* entretenir; *(car)* réviser

serviceable ['sɜːvɪsəbəl] *adj* **(a)** *(in working order)* en état
de marche **(b)** *(durable)* résistant(e)

serviceman ['sɜːvɪsmən] *n* militaire *m*

servicewoman ['sɜːvɪswʊmən] *n* femme *f* soldat

serviette [sɜːvɪˈet] *n Br* serviette *f* (de table)

servile ['sɜːvaɪl] *adj* servile, obséquieux(euse)

serving ['sɜːvɪŋ] *n (portion)* portion *f*; **s. hatch** passe-
plat *m*

servitude ['sɜːvɪtjuːd] *n* servitude *f*, asservissement *m*

servo ['sɜːvəʊ] **1** *n (pl servos) Fam (servomechanism)*
servomécanisme *m*

2 *adj* **s. brake** servofrein *m*

sesame ['sesəmɪ] *n* **(a)** **s. oil** huile *f* de sésame; **s. seeds**
graines *fpl* de sésame **(b)** **open s.!** sésame, ouvre-toi!

session ['seʃən] *n* **(a)** *(period of activity)* séance *f*, session *f*
(b) *(meeting)* séance *f*; **to be in s.** siéger **(c)** *(university,
school term)* trimestre *m*; *(university year)* année *f*
universitaire; *(school year)* année scolaire

set [set] **1** *n* **(a)** *(of keys)* jeu *m*; *(of saucepans)* série *f*,
assortiment *m*; *(of books)* collection *f*; *(of tyres)* train *m*; *(of
problems, rules, symptoms)* ensemble *m*; **s. of teeth**
dentition *f*
(b) *(of people)* cercle *m*
(c) *(TV, radio)* poste *m*
(d) *(in theatre)* décor *m*; *(in cinema)* plateau *m*
(e) *(in tennis)* set *m*; **s. point** balle *f* de set

2 *adj* **(a)** *(fixed) (look)* figé(e); *(ideas)* déterminé(e); *(price)*
fixe; **to be s. in one's ways** tenir à ses habitudes; **s.
menu** menu *m*; **s. phrase** expression *f* figée; **s. piece** *(in
play, film)* morceau *m* de bravoure; *(in sport)* tactique *f*
(b) *(ready)* **to be (all) s. for sth/to do sth** être *(b)*
prêt(e) pour qch/à faire qch
(c) *(determined)* **to be (dead) s. on sth** avoir fixé son
choix sur qch; **to be (dead) s. on doing sth** être
fermement décidé(e) à faire qch; **to be dead s. against**
être formellement opposé(e) à

3 *vt (pt & pp set)* **(a)** *(place)* placer, mettre; *(jewel)* sertir;
to s. the table mettre la table; **to s. a trap (for sb)**
tendre un piège (à qn); **the novel/film is set in
Edinburgh** le roman/film se passe à Édimbourg
(b) *(fix) (date, day, limit, price)* fixer, déterminer; *(watch)*
régler; *(alarm clock)* mettre; *(record)* établir; **to s. a value
on sth** estimer la valeur de qch; **to s. the scene** planter
le décor
(c) *(cause to start)* **to s. sb thinking** faire réfléchir qn; **to
s. sb free** libérer qn; **to s. sth on fire** mettre le feu à qch
(d) *(task)* fixer; *(essay, homework)* donner
(e) *(bone, fracture)* réduire

4 *vi* **(a)** *(of sun, moon)* se coucher
(b) *(become firm) (of jelly, concrete)* prendre; *(of broken bone)*
se ressouder

▶**set about** *vt insep* **(a)** *(task, job)* se mettre à; **to s.
about doing sth** se mettre à faire qch **(b)** *(attack)*
attaquer

▶**set against** *vt sep* **(a)** *(cause to oppose)* **to s. sb
against sb** monter qn contre qn **(b)** *(compare)* **to s. sth
against sth** comparer qch à qch **(c)** *(deduct)* **to s.
expenses against tax** déduire les dépenses des impôts

▶**set apart** *vt sep* distinguer **(from** de)

▶**set aside** *vt sep* **(a)** *(put down, disregard)* laisser de côté
(b) *(save) (money)* mettre de côté; *(time)* réserver

▶**set back** *vt sep* **(a)** *(delay)* retarder **(b)** *Fam (cost)* coûter

▶**set down** *vt sep (put down)* poser, laisser; **to s. sth
down in writing** coucher qch par écrit

▶**set forth** *vi Lit (depart)* partir, se mettre en route

▶**set in** *vi (of winter, mood)* s'installer; *(of fog, night)* tomber;
(of infection) se déclarer

▶**set off 1** *vt sep* **(a)** *(bomb, explosion, alarm)* déclencher;
(argument, chain of events) provoquer; **to s. sb off
(laughing)** faire éclater qn de rire; **to s. sb off (crying)**
faire éclater qn en sanglots **(b)** *(enhance)* mettre en valeur,
rehausser
2 *vi (depart)* partir, se mettre en route

▶**set out 1** *vt sep (arrange)* disposer
2 *vi* **(a)** *(depart)* partir, se mettre en route; *(in job, task)*
démarrer **(b)** *(intend)* **to s. out to do sth** avoir
l'intention de faire qch

▶**set to** *vi* **(a)** *(start working)* s'y mettre **(b)** *Fam (start
arguing)* recommencer à se disputer

▶**set up 1** *vt sep* **(a)** *(statue)* ériger; *(tent, barrier)* monter;
(roadblock) mettre en place **(b)** *(meeting)* arranger;
(company) créer, fonder; *(system)* mettre en place; **to s. up
house** *or* **home** s'installer; **to s. sb up in business (as)**
installer qn (comme) **(c)** *(trick, frame)* monter un coup
contre; **to be set up** être victime d'un coup monté
2 *vi (establish oneself)* s'installer **(as** comme); **to s. up in
business (as)** s'installer (comme)

▶**set upon** *vt insep (attack)* attaquer

setback ['setbæk] *n* revers *m*, échec *m*

set-square ['setskweə(r)] *n* équerre *f* (à dessin)

settee [se'tiː] *n* canapé *m*

setter ['setə(r)] *n (dog)* setter *m*

setting ['setɪŋ] **1** *n* **(a)** *(of story, film)* cadre *m* **(b)** *(of sun)*
coucher *m* **(c)** *(on machine)* réglage *m* **(d)** **s. lotion** lotion *f*
pour mise en plis
2 *adj (sun)* couchant(e)

settle ['setəl] **1** *vt* **(a)** *(put in place)* installer; **to s. oneself**
s'installer **(b)** *(nerves)* calmer; **to s. one's stomach**
calmer ses douleurs d'estomac **(c)** *(day, venue)* décider,
régler **(d)** *(problem, dispute, bill)* régler; **to s. one's affairs**
régler ses affaires; *Fam* **that settles it!** c'est décidé!; *Law*
to s. a matter out of court régler une affaire à l'amiable
(e) *(colonize)* coloniser

2 *vi* **(a)** *(of bird, insect)* se poser; *(of dust, liquid, beer)* se
déposer **(b)** *(of person, family)* s'installer, s'établir; *(of crowd)*
se calmer, s'apaiser; **to s. into an armchair** s'installer
confortablement dans un fauteuil **(c)** *Law* **to s. out of
court** régler l'affaire à l'amiable

▶**settle down 1** *vt sep* **(a)** *(make comfortable)* installer **(b)**
(make calm) calmer
2 *vi* **(a)** *(make oneself comfortable)* s'installer confortablement; **to s. down to work** se mettre au travail
(b) *(become quieter, more disciplined)* s'assagir; **to s. down
with sb** mener une vie stable avec qn **(c)** *(of situation,
excitement)* se calmer

▶**settle for** *vt insep* accepter, se contenter de

▶**settle in** *vi (in new home)* s'installer; *(in new school, job)*
s'adapter

▶**settle on** *vt insep* se décider pour, choisir

▶**settle up** *vi (pay bill)* régler

settled ['setəld] *adj (person, life)* rangé(e), établi(e);
(weather) stable

settlement ['setəlmənt] *n* **(a)** *(of problem, dispute, bill)* règlement *m*; **to reach a s.** parvenir à un accord **(b)** *(village)* village *m*

settler ['setlə(r)] *n* colon *m*

set-to ['set'tu:] *n Fam* bagarre *f*

setup ['setʌp] *n Fam (arrangement)* système *m*

seven ['sevən] **1** *n* sept *m inv*
2 *adj* sept *m*; **the s. deadly sins** les sept péchés capitaux; *Lit* **to sail the s. seas** parcourir les mers; *see also* **eight**

seventeen [sevən'ti:n] **1** *n* dix-sept *m inv*
2 *adj* dix-sept; *see also* **eight**

seventeenth [sevən'ti:nθ] **1** *n* **(a)** *(fraction)* dix-septième *m* **(b)** *(in series)* dix-septième *mf* **(c)** *(of month)* dix-sept *m inv*
2 *adj* dix-septième; *see also* **eighth**

seventh ['sevənθ] **1** *n* **(a)** *(fraction)* septième *m* **(b)** *(in series)* septième *mf* **(c)** *(of month)* sept *m inv*
2 *adj* septième; **to be in s. heaven** être au septième ciel; *see also* **eighth**

seventieth ['sevəntnθ] **1** *n* **(a)** *(fraction)* soixante-dixième *m* **(b)** *(in series)* soixante-dixième *mf*
2 *adj* soixante-dixième

seventy ['sevəntɪ] **1** *n* soixante-dix *m inv*
2 *adj* soixante-dix; *see also* **eighty**

sever ['sevə(r)] *vt (arm, finger)* couper, trancher; *Fig (link, relationship)* rompre

several ['sevərəl] **1** *adj* plusieurs
2 *pron* plusieurs; **s. of us/them** plusieurs d'entre nous/eux

severance ['sevərəns] *n* rupture *f*; **s. pay** indemnité *f* de licenciement

severe [sɪ'vɪə(r)] *adj (person, punishment, criticism)* sévère; *(pain)* vif (vive); *(illness, injury)* grave; *(winter)* rude; *(weather)* très mauvais(e); *(style)* austère, sévère

severity [sɪ'verɪtɪ] *n (of person, punishment, criticism)* sévérité *f*; *(of pain)* intensité *f*; *(of injury, illness)* gravité *f*; *(of winter)* rigueur *f*; *(of style)* austérité *f*, sévérité *f*

sew [səʊ] *vt & vi* coudre
▶**sew up** *vt sep* **(a)** *(stitch)* coudre **(b)** *Fam* **it's all sewn up** *(decided, settled)* l'affaire est dans le sac

sewage ['su:ɪdʒ] *n* eaux *fpl* usées *ou* d'égout; **s. disposal** évacuation *f* des eaux usées; **s. works** champ *m* d'épandage

sewer ['su:ə(r)] *n* égout *m*; *Fam* **to have a mind like a s.** avoir l'esprit mal tourné

sewing ['səʊɪŋ] *n (activity)* couture *f*; *(work)* ouvrage *m*; **s. machine** machine *f* à coudre

sewn [səʊn] *pp of* **sew**

sex [seks] *n* sexe *m*; **to have s. with sb** faire l'amour avec qn; **s. appeal** sex-appeal *m*; **s. education** éducation *f* sexuelle; **s. life** vie *f* sexuelle; **s. maniac** obsédé(e) *m,f* sexuel(elle); **s. shop** sex-shop *m*; **s. symbol** sex-symbol *m*

sexagenarian [seksədʒə'neərɪən] *n* sexagénaire *mf*

sexism ['seksɪzəm] *n* sexisme *m*

sexist ['seksɪst] *n & adj* sexiste *mf*

sexologist [sek'sɒladʒɪst] *n* sexologue *mf*

sextant ['sekstənt] *n* sextant *m*

sextet [seks'tet] *n* sextuor *m*

sexton ['sekstən] *n* sacristain *m*, bedeau *m*

sexual ['seksjʊəl] *adj* sexuel(elle); **s. assault** agression *f* sexuelle; **s. discrimination** discrimination *f* sexuelle; **s.**

harassment harcèlement *m* sexuel; **s. intercourse** rapports *mpl* sexuels; **s. reproduction** reproduction *f* sexuée

sexuality [seksjʊ'ælɪtɪ] *n* sexualité *f*

sexually ['seksjʊəlɪ] *adv* sexuellement; **s. transmitted disease** maladie *f* sexuellement transmissible

sexy ['seksɪ] *adj Fam* sexy *inv*; *Fig (car, hi-fi)* branché(e)

Seychelles [seɪ'ʃelz] *npl* **the S.** les Seychelles *fpl*

Sgt *(abbr* **Sergeant)** Sgt

sh [ʃ] *exclam* chut!

shabbily ['ʃæbɪlɪ] *adv* **(a)** *(furnished, dressed)* pauvrement **(b)** *(treat, behave)* avec mesquinerie

shabbiness ['ʃæbɪnɪs] *n* **(a)** *(of person, clothes, area)* apparence *f* miteuse **(b)** *(of treatment, behaviour)* mesquinerie *f*

shabby ['ʃæbɪ] *adj* **(a)** *(dingy, worn out)* miteux(euse) **(b)** *(behaviour, treatment)* minable, mesqui(e)

shack [ʃæk] *n* cabane *f*, hutte *f*
▶**shack up** *vi Fam* **to s. up with sb** être *ou* vivre à la colle avec qn

shackle ['ʃækəl] **1** *n* **shackles** chaînes *fpl*, fers *mpl*
2 *vt (prisoner)* enchaîner

shade [ʃeɪd] **1** *n* **(a)** *(shadow)* ombre *f*; **in the s.** à l'ombre; *Fig* **to put sb in the s.** éclipser qn **(b)** *(of reminders, suggestions)* réminiscences *fpl* de **(b)** *(of colour, meaning, opinion)* nuance *f*, ton *m*; **a s. better/longer** un tout petit mieux/plus long **(c)** *Fam* **shades** *(sunglasses)* lunettes *fpl* de soleil
2 *vt (from sun)* **to s. one's eyes** se protéger les yeux

shaded ['ʃeɪdɪd] *adj* **(a)** *(garden, path)* à l'ombre, ombragé(e) **(b)** *(area on diagram, map)* hachuré(e)

shading ['ʃeɪdɪŋ] *n (on drawing)* ombres *fpl*; *(on diagram, map)* hachure *f*

shadow ['ʃædəʊ] **1** *n* ombre *f*; **to cast a s.** projeter une ombre; *Fig* **to cast a s. over sth** jeter une ombre sur qch; **to be a s. of one's former self** n'être plus que l'ombre de soi-même; **without a s. of doubt** sans l'ombre d'un doute; **the s. of death/war** le spectre de la mort/de la guerre; **to have shadows under one's eyes** avoir des cernes, avoir les yeux cernés
2 *adj Br Pol* **S. Cabinet** cabinet *m* fantôme; **S. Minister** = député de l'opposition chargé d'un dossier administratif tel que l'Intérieur, les Affaires étrangères *etc*
3 *vt (follow)* filer, prendre en filature

shadowy ['ʃædəʊɪ] *adj (dark)* ombragé(e); *(form, outline)* vague

shady ['ʃeɪdɪ] *adj* **(a)** *(garden, lane)* ombragé(e) **(b)** *Fam (suspicious)* louche

shaft [ʃɑ:ft] **1** *n* **(a)** *(of golf club, tool)* manche *m*; *(of light)* rayon *m* **(b)** *(of mine)* puits *m*; *(for lift)* cage *f*
2 *vt very Fam (cheat)* entuber

shag[1] [ʃæg] *n (tobacco)* tabac *m*

shag[2] *Br Vulg* **1** *n (sexual intercourse)* **to have a s.** baiser
2 *vt & vi (pt & pp* **shagged)** baiser

shagged [ʃægd] *adj very Fam (exhausted)* crevé(e)

shaggy ['ʃægɪ] *adj (hairy)* hirsute; *Fam* **s. dog story** histoire *f* sans queue ni tête

shah [ʃɑː] *n* schah *m*

shake [ʃeɪk] **1** *n* **(a)** *(action)* secousse *f*; **to give sb/sth a s.** secouer qn/qch; *Fig* **to give oneself a s.** se secouer; *Fam* **to have the shakes** avoir la tremblote; *Fam* **in two shakes (of a lamb's tail)** en un rien de temps; *Fam* **to be no great shakes** ne pas casser trois pattes à un canard (b) **(milk)** s. (milk-)shake *m*

2 *vt* (*pt* **shook** [ʃʊk], *pp* **shaken** [ˈʃeɪkən]) (*person, box, bottle*) secouer; (*building*) faire trembler, ébranler; Fig **to s. sb's faith/trust** ébranler la foi/la confiance de qn; **to s. one's head** faire non de la tête; **to s. one's fist at sb** menacer qn du poing; **to s. hands with sb** serrer la main à qn; **to s. hands on a deal** conclure un accord par une poignée de mains

3 *vi* (a) (*of person, building, voice*) trembler; **to s. like a leaf** trembler comme une feuille (b) Fam **to s. on it** (*shake hands*) toper; **s. on it!** tope là!

▸**shake off** *vt sep* (*illness, depression*) sortir de; (*pursuer*) semer

▸**shake up** *vt sep* (a) (*upset*) secouer (b) (*reorganize*) réorganiser de fond en comble

shaken [ˈʃeɪkən] *pp of* **shake**

Shakespearean [ʃeɪksˈpɪərɪən] *adj* shakespearien(enne)

shake-up [ˈʃeɪkʌp] *n* Fam (*reorganization*) chambardement *m*

shakily [ˈʃeɪkɪlɪ] *adv* (*walk*) d'un pas vacillant; (*write*) d'une main tremblante; (*speak*) d'une voix tremblante

shaky [ˈʃeɪkɪ] *adj* (*table, ladder*) branlant(e); (*handwriting*) tremblé(e); (*voice*) tremblant(e); (*health, position*) précaire

shale [ʃeɪl] *n* schiste *m* argileux

shall [stressed ʃæl, unstressed ʃəl]

> On trouve généralement **I/you/he/etc shall** sous leurs formes contractées **I'll/you'll/he'll/***etc.* La forme négative correspondante est **shan't**, que l'on écrira **shall not** dans des contextes formels.

modal aux **v** (a) (*with first person*) (*expressing future tense*) **I s. be there** j'y serai; **where s. I sit?** où veux-tu que je m'asseye?; **I shan't say this more than once** je ne te dirai pas plus d'une fois; **as we s. see** comme nous le verrons

(b) (*making suggestions, offers*) **s. I make some coffee?** veux-tu que je fasse du café?; **let's go in, s. we?** entrons, tu veux bien?

(c) Formal (*with 2nd and 3rd person*) (*expressing determination*) **you s. pay for this!** tu me le paieras!

(d) (*indicating general truth*) **all members s. be entitled to vote** tous les membres auront le droit de vote

shallot [ʃəˈlɒt] *n* échalote *f*

shallow [ˈʃæləʊ] *adj* (a) (*water, dish*) peu profond(e); **s. end** (*of swimming pool*) petit bain *m* (b) Fig (*person, mind*) superficiel(elle)

sham [ʃæm] 1 *n* (*trial, election*) comédie *f*, farce *f*; (*person*) imposteur *m*

2 *adj* feint(e)

3 *vt* (*pt & pp* **shammed**) feindre, simuler

4 *vi* faire semblant

shamble [ˈʃæmbəl] *vi* **to s. along** marcher en traînant les pieds

shambles [ˈʃæmbəlz] *n* désordre *m*, pagaille *f*; **this place is a s.!** quel désordre!, quelle pagaille!

shambolic [ʃæmˈbɒlɪk] *adj* Fam bordélique

shame [ʃeɪm] 1 *n* (a) (*disgrace, guilt*) honte *f*; **to my s.** à ma grande honte; **s. on you!** tu devrais avoir honte!; **to put sb to s.** faire honte à qn (b) (*pity*) dommage *m*; **it's a s. (that...)** c'est dommage (que... + *subjunctive*); **what a s.!** quel dommage!

2 *vt* (a) (*cause to feel ashamed*) faire honte à; **to s. sb into doing sth** obliger qn à faire qch en lui faisant honte (b) (*bring shame on*) couvrir de honte

shamefaced [ˈʃeɪmfeɪst] *adj* honteux(euse), penaud(e)

shameful [ˈʃeɪmfʊl] *adj* honteux(euse), scandaleux(euse)

shamefully [ˈʃeɪmfʊlɪ] *adv* honteusement

shameless [ˈʃeɪmlɪs] *adj* impudique; **to be s. about doing sth** n'avoir aucun scrupule à faire qch

shammy [ˈʃæmɪ] *n* **s. (leather)** peau *f* de chamois

shampoo [ʃæmˈpuː] 1 *n* shampoing *m*

2 *vt* **to s. one's hair** se faire un shampoing

shamrock [ˈʃæmrɒk] *n* trèfle *m*

shandy [ˈʃændɪ] *n* panaché *m*

shank [ʃæŋk] *n* (*of lamb, beef*) jarret *m*

shan't [ʃɑːnt] = **shall not**

shanty¹ [ˈʃæntɪ] *n* (*hut*) baraque *f*, cabane *f*; **s. town** bidonville *m*

shanty² *n* (*song*) chanson *f* de marins

shape [ʃeɪp] 1 *n* (a) (*form*) forme *f*; **what s. is it?** quelle forme cela a-t-il?; **to be the same s. as...** avoir la même forme que...; **to take s.** (*of plan*) prendre forme; Fig **in any s. or form** quel (quelle) qu'il (elle) soit; Fig **in the s. of** sous la forme de; (*person*) en la personne de (b) (*condition*) **to be in good/bad s.** (*of person*) être en bonne/mauvaise forme; (*of company, economy*) bien/mal marcher; **to get into/keep in s.** (*of person*) retrouver/garder la forme

2 *vt* (a) (*clay*) modeler; (*wood*) façonner (b) Fig (*perception, events, future*) influencer; (*character*) former

▸**shape up** *vi* (*of person*) progresser; (*of team, plans*) prendre forme

shapeless [ˈʃeɪplɪs] *adj* informe

shapely [ˈʃeɪplɪ] *adj* bien fait(e)

shard [ʃɑːd] *n* (*of glass*) éclat *m*; (*of pottery*) tesson *m*

share [ʃeə(r)] 1 *n* (a) (*portion*) part *f*; **in equal shares** à parts égales; **to have a s. in sth** avoir une part dans qch; **to do one's s.** mettre la main à la pâte; *also* Fig **to get one's fair s. of sth** avoir sa part de qch (b) Fin action *f*; **s. capital** capital *m* social; **s. certificate** certificat *m* ou titre *m* d'actions

2 *vt* partager

3 *vi* partager; **to s. in sth** partager qch; **s. and s. alike!** chacun sa part!

▸**share out** *vt sep* partager, répartir

shareholder [ˈʃeəhəʊldə(r)] *n* Fin actionnaire *mf*

shareholding [ˈʃeəhəʊldɪŋ] *n* Fin actionnariat *m*

shark [ʃɑːk] *n also* Fig requin *m*

sharp [ʃɑːp] 1 *adj* (a) (*knife*) bien aiguisé(e); (*pencil*) bien taillé(e); (*scissors, razor*) qui coupe bien; (*point*) aigu(uë); (*claws*) acéré(e)

(b) (*features*) anguleux(euse); (*turning, rise, fall*) brusque; (*photo, outline, focus*) net (nette); (*contrast*) marqué(e); (*hearing*) fin(e); (*eyesight*) perçant(e); Fig **to be at the s. end** être en première ligne

(c) (*intelligent*) vif (vive)

(d) (*harsh*) (*voice, words*) cinglant(e); (*person*) mordant(e); **to have a s. tongue** être mordant

(e) (*taste, sauce*) acide; (*sound*) perçant(e); (*pain, wind*) vif (vive)

(f) (*in music*) **C s.** do dièse

2 *adv* (a) (*punctually*) pile; **at four o'clock s.** à quatre heures pile précises

(b) (*immediately*) **to turn s. left/right** tourner tout de suite à gauche/à droite

(c) *(idioms) Fam* **look s.!** grouille-toi!
3 *n (in music)* dièse *m*

sharpen ['ʃɑːpən] *vt* **(a)** *(knife, tool)* aiguiser; *(pencil)* tailler **(b)** *(pain)* accentuer; *(passion, desire)* exacerber; **to s. one's wits** faire travailler sa matière grise

sharpener ['ʃɑːpənə(r)] *n (for knife)* aiguisoir *m* (à couteaux); *(for pencil)* taille-crayon *m*

sharp-eyed ['ʃɑːpaɪd] *adj* observateur(trice)

sharply ['ʃɑːplɪ] *adv* **(a)** *(contrast)* nettement **(b)** *(rise, fall, brake)* brusquement

sharpness ['ʃɑːpnɪs] *n* **(a)** *(of knife)* tranchant *m* **(b)** *(of outline, photo)* netteté *f* **(c)** *(of mind, hearing, sight)* acuité *f* **(d)** *(of voice, words)* brusquerie *f* **(e)** *(of pain)* acuité *f*; *(of wind)* âpreté *f*

sharpshooter ['ʃɑːpʃuːtə(r)] *n* tireur *m* d'élite

sharp-sighted [ʃɑːp'saɪtɪd] *adj* observateur(trice)

sharp-tongued [ʃɑːp'tʌŋd] *adj* mordant(e)

shat [ʃæt] *pt of* **shit**

shatter ['ʃætə(r)] **1** *vt* **(a)** *(glass, bone)* briser en mille morceaux; *Fig (hopes, silence, nerves)* briser; *(health)* ruiner **(b)** *Fam* **to be shattered** *(stunned)* être accablé(e); *(exhausted)* être crevé(e)
2 *vi* se briser en mille morceaux

shattering ['ʃætərɪŋ] *adj* **(a)** *(defeat)* accablant(e); **it was a s. blow** ça a été un coup terrible **(b)** *Fam (stunning)* accablant(e); *(exhausting)* crevant(e)

shatterproof ['ʃætəpruːf] *adj (glass)* Sécurit®; *(windscreen, door)* en verre Sécurit®

shave [ʃeɪv] **1** *n* **to have a s.** se raser; *Fig* **that was a close s.** il était moins une
2 *vt* **(a)** *(face, legs)* raser; **to s. one's legs** se raser les jambes **(b)** *(wood)* raboter
3 *vi* se raser

▸**shave off** *vt sep* se raser

shaven ['ʃeɪvən] *adj* rasé(e)

shaver ['ʃeɪvə(r)] *n* rasoir *m* électrique

shaving ['ʃeɪvɪŋ] *n* **(a)** *(action)* rasage *m*; **s. brush** blaireau *m*; **s. foam** mousse *f* à raser **(b)** *(piece of wood)* copeau *m*; *(piece of metal)* rognure *f*

shawl [ʃɔːl] *n* châle *m*

she [ʃiː] **1** *pron* elle; **she's Scottish** elle est écossaise; **SHE hasn't got it!** ce n'est pas elle qui l'a!
2 *n* **it's a s.** *(of animal)* c'est une femelle

sheaf [ʃiːf] *(pl* **sheaves** [ʃiːvz]) *n (of corn)* gerbe *f*; *(of papers)* liasse *f*

shear [ʃɪə(r)] *(pp* **shorn** [ʃɔːn] *or* **sheared**) **1** *vt (sheep)* tondre; *Fig* **to be shorn of sth** être dépouillé(e) de qch
2 *vi (cut)* **to s. through sth** couper qch

shears [ʃɪəz] *npl* cisailles *fpl*

sheath [ʃiːθ] *n* **(a)** *(for sword, knife)* fourreau *m*; *(for electric cable)* gaine *f*; **s. knife** couteau *m* à gaine **(b)** *(contraceptive)* préservatif *m*

shed¹ [ʃed] *n (in garden)* abri *m*, remise *f*; *(in factory)* atelier *m*

shed² [ʃed] *(pt & pp* **shed**) *vt (leaves)* perdre; *(tears)* verser; **to s. its skin** *(of snake)* muer; **to s. light on sth** jeter de la lumière sur qch; **to s. weight** perdre du poids; **to s. its load** *(of lorry)* perdre son chargement

she'd [ʃiːd] = **she had, she would**

sheen [ʃiːn] *n (on metal, silk)* lustre *m*; *(on hair)* brillant *m*

sheep [ʃiːp] *(pl* **sheep**) *n* mouton *m*

sheepdog ['ʃiːpdɒg] *n* chien *m* de berger

sheepfold ['ʃiːpfəʊld] *n* parc *m* à moutons

sheepish ['ʃiːpɪʃ] *adj* penaud(e)

sheepskin ['ʃiːpskɪn] *n* peau *f* de mouton; **s. jacket** veste *f* en peau de mouton

sheer [ʃɪə(r)] *adj* **(a)** *(pure)* pur(e); **it's s. madness** c'est de la folie pure; **by s. chance** tout à fait par hasard **(b)** *(steep)* à pic *inv* **(c)** *(stockings, fabric)* très fin(e)

sheet [ʃiːt] *n* **(a)** *(on bed)* drap *m*; *(of paper)* feuille *f*; *(of glass, ice, metal)* plaque *f*; *(of flame)* rideau *m*; **s. lightning** éclair *m* en nappe(s); **s. metal** tôle *f*; **s. music** partitions *fpl*

sheetfeed ['ʃiːtfiːd] *n Comptr* avancement *m* du papier

sheik(h) [ʃeɪk] *n* cheikh *m*

shekel ['ʃekəl] *n* shekel *m*

shelf [ʃelf] *(pl* **shelves** [ʃelvz]) *n* **(a)** *(in cupboard, bookcase)* étagère *f*; **(set of) shelves** étagère *f*; *Fig* **to be left on the s.** rester vieille fille; *Com* **s. life** *(of goods)* durée *f* de conservation avant vente **(b)** *(of cliff, rock face)* rebord *m*

shell [ʃel] **1** *n* **(a)** *(of snail, oyster, egg, nut)* coquille *f*; *(of lobster, tortoise)* carapace *f*; *(on beach)* coquillage *m*; *Fig* **to come out of one's s.** sortir de sa coquille; **s. suit** = survêtement en synthétique brillant **(b)** *(of building)* carcasse *f* **(c)** *(bomb)* obus *m*; **s. shock** psychose *f* traumatique *(à la suite d'une explosion)*
2 *vt (nuts)* décortiquer; *(peas)* écosser; *(eggs)* écaler **(b)** *(bombard)* bombarder

▸**shell out** *Fam* **1** *vt sep (money)* casquer
2 *vi* **to s. out (for sth)** casquer (pour qch)

she'll [ʃiːl] = **she will, she shall**

shellfire ['ʃelfaɪə(r)] *n* tirs *mpl* d'obus

shellfish ['ʃelfɪʃ] *n (crustacean)* crustacé *m*; *(mollusc)* coquillage *m*; *(as food)* fruits *mpl* de mer

shelling ['ʃelɪŋ] *n* bombardement *m*

shellshocked ['ʃelʃɒkt] *adj (soldier)* commotionné(e) *(à la suite d'une explosion)*; *Fig* sous le choc

shelter ['ʃeltə(r)] **1** *n (place, protection)* abri *m*; **to take s.** se mettre à l'abri, s'abriter
2 *vt* abriter **(from** de); *(criminal, refugee)* accueillir
3 *vi* s'abriter, se mettre à l'abri **(from** de)

sheltered ['ʃeltəd] *adj (place)* abrité(e); *(life, childhood)* protégé(e); **s. housing** = logements spécialement conçus pour les personnes âgées

shelve [ʃelv] *vt (postpone)* mettre au placard

shelving ['ʃelvɪŋ] *n* étagères *fpl*

shepherd ['ʃepəd] **1** *n* berger *m*; **s.'s pie** ≃ hachis *m* Parmentier
2 *vt (sheep)* garder; *Fig (people)* guider, conduire

shepherdess [ʃepə'des] *n* bergère *f*

sherbet ['ʃɜːbət] *n Br (powder)* poudre *f* acidulée; *Am (sorbet)* sorbet *m*

sheriff ['ʃerɪf] *n Br* = plus haut fonctionnaire du comté, dont le rôle est essentiellement protocolaire; *Scot* ≃ juge *m* au tribunal de grande instance; *Am* shérif *m*

sherry ['ʃerɪ] *n* sherry *m*, xérès *m*

she's [ʃiːz] = **she has, she is**

Shetland ['ʃetlənd] *n* **the S. Islands, the Shetlands** les (îles *fpl*) Shetland *fpl*; **S. pony** poney *m* des Shetland

shield [ʃiːld] **1** *n (of knight) & Fig (protection)* bouclier *m*; *(police badge)* badge *m*; *(trophy)* trophée *m* en forme d'écusson
2 *vt (protect)* protéger **(from** de); **to s. one's eyes** se protéger les yeux

shift [ʃɪft] **1** n (a) (change of position) changement m; a s. in meaning un glissement de sens; a s. to the right/left (in politics) un revirement à droite/gauche; s. key (on typewriter, computer) touche f des majuscules (b) (period) poste m; (workers) équipe f; to work (in) shifts avoir un travail posté (c) s. (dress) robe f chasuble

2 vt (a) (move) déplacer; (stain) enlever, faire partir; to s. the blame onto sb rejeter la responsabilité sur qn (b) Fam (sell) écouler

3 vi (move) bouger; (of stain) partir; Fam (move quickly) foncer

shiftless [ˈʃɪftlɪs] adj fainéant(e)

shiftwork [ˈʃɪftwɜːk] n travail m posté

shifty [ˈʃɪftɪ] adj (person) louche; (look) fuyant(e)

shilling [ˈʃɪlɪŋ] n shilling m

shimmer [ˈʃɪmə(r)] **1** n (of light) scintillement m; (of water) miroitement m; (of silk) chatoiement m

2 vi (of light) scintiller; (of water) miroiter; (of silk) chatoyer

shimmering [ˈʃɪmərɪŋ] adj (light) scintillant(e); (water) miroitant(e); (silk) chatoyant(e)

shin [ʃɪn] n tibia m; s. guard or pad (in sport) jambière f

▶**shin up** [ʃɪn] (pt & pp shinned) vt insep (climb) grimper à

shinbone [ˈʃɪnbəʊn] n tibia m

shindy [ˈʃɪndɪ] n Fam (din) boucan m; to kick up a s. faire du boucan

shine [ʃaɪn] **1** n (a) brillant m, éclat m (b) (idioms) to take the s. off sth faire perdre son éclat à qch, ternir qch; Fam to take a s. to sb prendre qn en affection

2 vt (pt & pp shone [ʃɒn]) (a) (light, torch) braquer (on sur) (b) (pt & pp shined) (polish) faire briller

3 vi shine; Fig to s. at sth briller en qch; her face shone with joy son visage rayonna de joie

shiner [ˈʃaɪnə(r)] n Fam (black eye) œil m au beurre noir

shingle [ˈʃɪŋgəl] n (a) (wooden tile) bardeau m (b) (pebbles) galets mpl

shingles [ˈʃɪŋgəlz] n (disease) zona m; to have s. avoir un zona

shining [ˈʃaɪnɪŋ] adj brillant(e); Fig a s. example (of) un parfait exemple (de)

shiny [ˈʃaɪnɪ] adj brillant(e)

ship [ʃɪp] **1** n navire m; Fig when my s. comes in quand je serai riche

2 vt (pt & pp shipped) (transport) transporter; (send) expédier; (take on board) embarquer

▶**ship off** vt sep Fam expédier

shipboard [ˈʃɪpbɔːd] n Naut on s. à bord

shipbuilder [ˈʃɪpbɪldə(r)] n constructeur m naval

shipbuilding [ˈʃɪpbɪldɪŋ] n construction f navale; the s. industry (l'industrie f de) la construction navale

shipload [ˈʃɪpləʊd] n cargaison f; Fig by the s. en masse

shipmate [ˈʃɪpmeɪt] n Naut camarade m de bord

shipment [ˈʃɪpmənt] n cargaison f

shipowner [ˈʃɪpəʊnə(r)] n armateur m

shipping [ˈʃɪpɪŋ] n (ships) navires mpl; s. agent (person) agent m maritime; (company) agence f maritime; s. lane voie f de navigation

shipshape [ˈʃɪpʃeɪp] adj rangé(e), en ordre

shipwreck [ˈʃɪprek] **1** n (disaster) naufrage m; (ship) épave f

2 vt to be shipwrecked faire naufrage

shipwrecked [ˈʃɪprekt] adj naufragé(e)

shipwright [ˈʃɪpraɪt] n Naut (company) constructeur m naval; (worker) ouvrier(ère) m,f de chantier naval

shipyard [ˈʃɪpjɑːd] n chantier m naval

shire [ˈʃaɪə(r)] n comté m; s. horse shire m

shirk [ʃɜːk] **1** vt (task) éviter de faire; (obligation, responsibility) se dérober à

2 vi (avoid work) tirer au flanc

shirker [ˈʃɜːkə(r)] n tire-au-flanc mf inv

shirt [ʃɜːt] n chemise f; Fam keep your s. on! on se calme!

shirtmaker [ˈʃɜːtmeɪkə(r)] n fabricant(e) m,f de chemises

shirtsleeves [ˈʃɜːtsliːvz] npl to be in s. être en bras de chemise

shirt-tail [ˈʃɜːtteɪl] n pan m de chemise

shirty [ˈʃɜːtɪ] adj Br Fam en rogne; to get s. (with sb) se mettre en rogne (contre qn)

shit [ʃɪt] Vulg **1** n (a) (excrement) merde f; (mess) bordel m; (nonsense) conneries fpl; to have a s. chier (b) (nasty man) salaud m; (nasty woman) salope f (c) (idioms) to talk s. dire des conneries; to be in the s. être dans la merde; he doesn't give a s. il n'en a rien à foutre; to beat the s. out of sb casser la gueule à qn; to scare the s. out of sb foutre une de ces trouilles à qn

2 vt (pt & pp shitted or shat [ʃæt]) to s. oneself chier dans son froc

3 vi chier

4 exclam merde!

shitty [ˈʃɪtɪ] adj Vulg (a) (nappies, trousers) dégueulasse (b) (weather, job) merdique; (behaviour, remark) dégueulasse; to feel s. (ill) avoir la tête dans le cul; (guilty) se sentir merdeux(euse)

shiver [ˈʃɪvə(r)] **1** n (of cold, fear) frisson m; to send shivers down sb's spine donner le frisson à qn

2 vi frissonner, trembler (with de)

shoal [ʃəʊl] n (of fish) banc m; Fig (of people) foule f

shock¹ [ʃɒk] n (of hair) crinière f

shock² [ʃɒk] **1** n (a) (impact) choc m; (of earthquake) secousse f; s. absorber amortisseur m; s. tactics tactique f de choc; Mil s. troops troupes fpl de choc; also Fig s. wave onde f de choc (b) (emotional blow) choc m, coup m; I got a real s. when... cela m'a vraiment fait un choc quand...; to be in s. être en état de choc (c) (electric) décharge f (électrique); s. therapy (traitement m par) électrochocs mpl

2 vt (surprise, startle) stupéfier; (scandalize) choquer; to s. sb into doing sth pousser qn à faire qch en lui faisant peur

shocked [ʃɒkt] adj (startled) stupéfié(e); (scandalized) choqué(e)

shocking [ˈʃɒkɪŋ] adj (a) (scandalous) choquant(e); s. pink rose m bonbon (b) (very bad) atroce

shockproof [ˈʃɒkpruːf] adj (watch) antichoc inv

shoddy [ˈʃɒdɪ] adj (goods) de mauvaise qualité; (workmanship) mal fait(e); (conduct) méprisable

shoe [ʃuː] **1** n chaussure f; (horseshoe) fer m (à cheval); Fig I wouldn't like to be in her shoes je n'aimerais pas être à sa place; Fig put yourself in my shoes mets-toi à ma place; s. polish cirage m; s. shop magasin m de chaussures

2 vt (pt & pp shod [ʃɒd] or shoed) (horse) ferrer

shoebrush [ˈʃuːbrʌʃ] n brosse f à chaussures

shoehorn [ˈʃuːhɔːn] n chausse-pied m

shoelace [ʃuːleɪs] n lacet m (de chaussure)

shoemaker [ʃuːmeɪkə(r)] n (manufacturer) bottier m; (seller) chausseur m

shoeshine [ʃuːʃaɪn] n Am (person) cireur m de chaussures

shoestring [ʃuːstrɪŋ] n (a) Fam on a s. avec trois fois rien (b) Am lacet m (de chaussure)

shone [ʃɒn] pt & pp of shine

shoo [ʃuː] exclam ouste!

▸**shoo away, shoo off** vt sep chasser

shook [ʃʊk] pt of shake

shoot [ʃuːt] 1 n (pt & pp shot [ʃɒt]) (a) (fire) (bullet) tirer; (arrow) & Fig (glance) lancer
(b) to s. sb (wound) blesser qn par balle; (kill) tuer qn par balle; (execute) fusiller qn; to be shot in the arm recevoir une balle dans le bras; to s. rabbits/grouse chasser le lapin/la grouse; Fig to s. oneself in the foot compromettre ses chances
(c) (film, TV programme) tourner
(d) (pass rapidly) to s. the rapids franchir les rapides; to s. the lights (in car) brûler ou griller le feu rouge
(e) to s. dice/pool jouer aux dés/au billard
2 vi (a) (with gun) tirer (at sur); (in football) tirer, shooter
(b) (move rapidly) filer; he shot into/out of the house il se précipita dans/hors de la maison; the pain shot up her left side elle ressentit soudain une vive douleur au côté gauche
3 n (a) (of plant) pousse f
(b) (hunting party) chasse f

▸**shoot down** vt sep (person) descendre; (plane) abattre

▸**shoot off** vi (leave quickly) filer

▸**shoot out** vi (emerge quickly) jaillir

▸**shoot up** vi (a) (of plant) pousser vite; (of child) monter en graine; (of buildings) pousser comme des champignons (b) (of rocket) s'élever; (of prices) monter ou grimper en flèche (c) Fam (with drugs) se shooter

shooting [ʃuːtɪŋ] 1 n (a) (gunfire) coups mpl de feu; (incident) fusillade f; s. stick canne-siège f (b) (of film, TV programme) tournage m
2 adj s. star étoile f filante

shoot-out [ʃuːtaʊt] n fusillade f

shop [ʃɒp] 1 n (a) (for goods) magasin m; s. assistant vendeur(euse) m,f; s. window vitrine f (b) Fam to do a s. (go shopping) faire ses courses (c) (workshop) atelier m; Fig the s. floor les ouvriers mpl (d) (idioms) Fam to talk s. parler boutique; Fam Fig all over the s. (everywhere) un peu partout; Fig his explanation was all over the s. son explication ne tenait pas debout; my hair was all over the s. j'étais coiffé n'importe comment; at the interview he was all over the s. à l'entretien, il a raconté n'importe quoi
2 vt (pt & pp shopped) Br Fam (betray) balancer
3 vi faire ses courses; to go shopping faire les courses; (for food) faire ses courses; to s. around comparer les prix

shopgirl [ʃɒpgɜːl] n vendeuse f

shopkeeper [ʃɒpkiːpə(r)] n commerçant(e) m,f

shoplifter [ʃɒplɪftə(r)] n voleur(euse) m,f à l'étalage

shoplifting [ʃɒplɪftɪŋ] n vol m à l'étalage

shopper [ʃɒpə(r)] n client(e) m,f

shopping [ʃɒpɪŋ] n courses fpl; to do the s. faire les courses; to do one's s. faire ses courses; s. bag sac m à provisions, cabas m; s. basket panier m (à provisions); s.

centre or precinct centre m commercial; s. list liste f des courses; s. trolley chariot m

shore [ʃɔː(r)] n (of sea) rivage m; (of lake) bord m; on s. à terre; to go on s. (from ship) débarquer

▸**shore up** vt sep (house, wall) étayer; Fig (reputation) consolider

shoreline [ʃɔːlaɪn] n littoral m

shorn [ʃɔːn] pp of shear

short [ʃɔːt] 1 adj (a) (physically) court(e); (person) petit(e); Bill is s. for William Bill est le diminutif de William; the s. answer is "no" c'est tout simplement "non"; to have a s. temper or fuse être coléreux(euse); s. story nouvelle f
(b) (in time) court(e), bref (brève); in s. en bref; to make s. work of sb/sth expédier qn/qch; s. and sweet clair(e) et net (nette)
(c) (abrupt) brusque, sec (sèche) (with avec)
(d) (insufficient, lacking) insuffisant(e); to be in s. supply manquer; to be s. of sth être à court ou manquer de qch; I'm 50 pence s. il me manque 50 pence; little or not far s. of (almost) pas loin de; he's not far s. of forty il n'est pas loin de la quarantaine; it was nothing s. of miraculous that she survived c'est vraiment un miracle qu'elle ait survécu
2 adv (a) (suddenly) to stop s. s'arrêter net; to bring sb up s. arrêter net qn
(b) (in length, duration) to stop s. of doing sth se retenir tout juste de faire qch; to cut sb s. couper la parole à qn, interrompre qn; to cut sth s. abréger qch
(c) (without) to go s. (of sth) se priver (de qch)
(d) (insufficiency) to be running s. of sth n'avoir presque plus de qch; to fall s. of sth (target) ne pas atteindre qch; (expectations) ne pas répondre à qch; Fig to sell sb s. rouler qn; to be taken or caught s. être pris(e) d'un besoin pressant
3 n Fam (a) (short film) court-métrage m
(b) (drink) alcool m fort
(c) (short circuit) court-circuit m

shortage [ʃɔːtɪdʒ] n pénurie f; petrol/food s. pénurie d'essence/de nourriture; housing s. crise f du logement; to have no s. of sth ne pas manquer de qch

shortbread [ʃɔːtbred], **shortcake** [ʃɔːtkeɪk] n sablés mpl au beurre

short-change [ʃɔːt'(t)ʃeɪndʒ] vt (in shop) ne pas rendre assez de monnaie à; Fig (cheat) escroquer

short-circuit [ʃɔːt'sɜːkɪt] 1 n court-circuit m
2 vt also Fig court-circuiter
3 vi se mettre en court-circuit

shortcomings [ʃɔːtkʌmɪŋz] npl défauts mpl

shorten [ʃɔːtən] vt (skirt, text) raccourcir; (visit, task) abréger

shortfall [ʃɔːtfɔːl] n manque m, insuffisance f

shorthaired [ʃɔːtheəd] adj (cat, dog) à poil(s) court(s); (person) aux cheveux courts

shorthand [ʃɔːthænd] n sténographie f, sténo f; s. typist sténodactylo mf

short-haul [ʃɔːthɔːl] adj moyen-courrier m

shortlist [ʃɔːtlɪst] 1 n = liste de candidats après une première selection
2 vt to be shortlisted (for sth) être parmi les candidats retenus (à qch)

short-lived [ʃɔːt'lɪvd] adj de courte durée

shortly [ʃɔːtlɪ] adv (a) (soon) bientôt; s. after(wards) peu (de temps) après (b) (abruptly) sèchement

short-range ['ʃɔ:treɪndʒ] *adj (missile)* de courte portée

shorts [ʃɔ:ts] *npl (short trousers)* short *m*

short-sighted [ʃɔ:t'saɪtɪd] *adj* myope; *Fig* peu clairvoyant(e)

short-sleeved [ʃɔ:t'sli:vd] *adj* à manches courtes

shortstop ['ʃɔ:tstɒp] *n Am Sp* bloqueur *m*

short-tempered [ʃɔ:t'tempəd] *adj* coléreux(euse)

shot [ʃɒt] 1 *n* (a) *(act of firing, sound)* coup *m* (de feu); **to fire a s.** tirer; *Fig* **like a s.** sans hésiter; *Fig* **to take a s. in the dark** tenter le coup; *Fig* **to call the shots** faire la loi; **s. put** lancer *m* du poids (b) *(marksman)* tireur *m* (c) *(in football, rugby)* coup *m* de pied; *(in basketball)* lancer *m*; **good s.!** bien joué! (d) *(photograph)* photo *f*; *(of film, TV programme)* prise *f* de vue, plan *m* (e) *Fam (injection)* piqûre *f* (f) *(attempt)* tentative *f*, essai *m*; **to have a s. at sth/at doing sth** essayer qch/de faire qch (g) *(drink)* petit verre *m*

2 *pt & pp of* **shoot**

shotgun ['ʃɒtgʌn] *n* fusil *m* de chasse; *Fam* **s. wedding** mariage *m* en catastrophe

should [ʃʊd]

> La forme négative **should not** s'écrit **shouldn't** en forme contractée.

modal aux v (a) *(expressing obligation, desirability)* **you s. do it at once** vous devriez le faire tout de suite; **you s. have come earlier** vous auriez dû venir plus tôt; **she shouldn't have told them** elle n'aurait pas dû leur dire

(b) *(expressing probability)* **the weather s. improve from now on** le temps devrait s'améliorer à partir de maintenant; **she s. have arrived by this time** elle devrait être arrivée à l'heure qu'il est

(c) *(in exclamations, rhetorical questions)* **why s. you suspect me?** pourquoi me soupçonnez-vous?; **who s. I meet but Martin!** et qui a-t-il fallu que je rencontre! Martin!, je n'ai rencontré que Martin!; **I s. think so, too!** il s'est excusé – j'espère bien!

(d) *(in subordinate clauses)* **he ordered that they s. be released** il a ordonné leur libération; **she insisted that he s. meet her parents** elle a insisté pour qu'il rencontre ses parents

(e) *(in conditional clauses)* **if he s. come** *or Formal* **s. he come, let me know** s'il vient, fais-le-moi savoir

(f) *(expressing opinions, preferences)* **I s. like a drink** je prendrais bien un verre; **I s. imagine he was rather angry** j'imagine qu'il était plutôt en colère; **I shouldn't be surprised if...** cela ne m'étonnerait pas si...

shoulder ['ʃəʊldə(r)] 1 *n* (a) *(of person, meat)* épaule *f*; **to stand s. to s.** *(of two people)* se tenir l'une(e) contre l'autre; *Fig* **to rub shoulders with sb** côtoyer qn; *Fig* **to be looking over one's s.** être constamment sur ses gardes; *Fig* **to cry on sb's s.** pleurer sur l'épaule de qn; **s. bag** (sac *m*) besace *f*; **s. blade** omoplate *f*; **s. pad** épaulette *f*; **s. strap** *(of bag)* bandoulière *f*; *(of garment)* bretelle *f*

2 *vt* (a) *(push)* **to s. one's way through a crowd** se frayer un passage à travers la foule à coups d'épaule; **to s. sb aside** écarter qn d'un coup d'épaule (b) *(put on shoulder)* mettre sur son épaule; *Fig* **to s. the responsibility** endosser la responsabilité

shouldn't ['ʃʊdnt] = **should not**

shout [ʃaʊt] 1 *n* cri *m*; **shouts of laughter** des éclats *mpl* de rire; **give me a s. when you're ready** appelle-moi quand tu seras prêt

2 *vt* crier; **to s. sth at sb** crier qch à qn

3 *vi* crier; **to s. at sb** crier après qn; **to s. for help** crier

au secours; *Fig* **to have something to s. about** pouvoir être fier(ère) de qch

▸**shout down** *vt sep* **to s. sb down** huer qn

shouting ['ʃaʊtɪŋ] *n* cris *mpl*

shove [ʃʌv] 1 *n* poussée *f*; **to give sb/sth a s.** pousser qn/qch

2 *vt & vi* pousser

▸**shove around** *vt sep Fam (bully)* chahuter

▸**shove off** *vi Fam (leave)* dégager

shovel ['ʃʌvəl] 1 *n* pelle *f*

2 *vt (pt & pp* **shovelled)** pelleter; *Fam* **to s. food into one's mouth** enfourner de la nourriture

shovelful ['ʃʌvəlfʊl] *n* pelletée *f*

show [ʃəʊ] 1 *n* (a) *(exhibition)* exposition *f*; **to be on s.** être exposé(e); **to put sth on s.** exposer qch; **s. house** maison *f* témoin; **s. jumper** = cavalier(ère) spécialisé(e) dans le jumping; **s. jumping** jumping *m*; *Pej* **s. trial** procès *m* à grand spectacle

(b) *(concert, play)* spectacle *m*; *(on TV, radio)* émission *f*; *Fig* **to run the s.** commander; **s. business** show-business *m*, monde *m* du spectacle; **s. girl** girl *f*; *Fam* **to be a s. stopper** être le clou du spectacle

(c) *(act of showing)* démonstration *f*, manifestation *f*; **s. of hands** vote *m* à main levée; **it's all s.** tout ça, c'est de la comédie; **to do sth for s.** faire qch pour épater la galerie; *Fam* **good s.!** *(well done)* bravo!

2 *vt (pp* **shown** [ʃəʊn]) (a) *(display)* montrer; *(picture)* exposer; *(courage, talent)* faire preuve de; **to s. sb sth, to s. sth to sb** montrer qch à qn; *Fig* **to s. one's cards** *or* **one's hand** abattre ses cartes; **they had nothing to s. for all that work** ils avaient fait tout ce travail pour rien; **he won't s. his face round here again** on ne le reverra pas de sitôt; **to s. oneself** se montrer; **to s. a profit/a loss** enregistrer un bénéfice/une perte; **you're showing your age** ça ne te rajeunit pas!; **to s. oneself to be...** se révéler...

(b) *(indicate)* montrer, indiquer

(c) *(prove, demonstrate)* démontrer, prouver; **it goes to s. that...** cela montre bien que...

(d) *(teach)* montrer; **to s. sb how to do sth** montrer à qn comment faire qch

(e) *(film)* passer; *(TV programme)* diffuser

(f) *(escort, lead)* **to s. sb the way** montrer le chemin à qn; **to s. sb to his/her room** conduire qn à sa chambre; **to s. sb round the town** faire visiter la ville à qn

3 *vi* (a) *(be visible)* se voir

(b) *(of film)* passer

show in *vt sep (escort in)* faire entrer

▸**show off** 1 *vt sep* exhiber

2 *vi* frimer

▸**show out** *vt sep (escort out)* reconduire, raccompagner

▸**show up** 1 *vt sep* (a) *(reveal)* révéler (b) *(embarrass)* faire honte à

2 *vi* (a) *(stand out)* ressortir, se voir (b) *Fam (arrive)* se pointer

showbiz ['ʃəʊbɪz] *n Fam* show-biz *m*, monde *m* du spectacle

showcase ['ʃəʊkeɪs] *n* vitrine *f*

showdown ['ʃəʊdaʊn] *n* confrontation *f*

shower ['ʃaʊə(r)] 1 *n* (a) *(of rain)* averse *f*; *(of stones, insults)* pluie *f* (b) *(for washing)* douche *f*; **to have** *or* **take a s.** prendre une douche; **s. cap** bonnet *m* de douche; **s. curtain** rideau *m* de douche; **s. gel** gel *m* douche; **s. head** pomme *f* de douche (c) *Br Fam (group)* **what a s.!**

quelle bande de crétins!

2 *vt* **to s. sb with sth, to s. sth on sb** couvrir qn de qch

3 *vi* *(take a shower)* se doucher

showery ['ʃaʊərɪ] *adj* pluvieux(euse)

showing ['ʃəʊɪŋ] *n (exhibition)* exposition *f; (of film)* séance *f*

showman ['ʃəʊmən] *n (at circus)* forain *m; Fig* cabotin *m*

showmanship ['ʃəʊmənʃɪp] *n* sens *m* du spectacle

shown [ʃəʊn] *pp of* **show**

show-off ['ʃəʊɒf] *n Fam* frimeur(euse) *m,f*

showpiece ['ʃəʊpiːs] *n* joyau *m*

showroom ['ʃəʊruːm] *n* magasin *m*

showy ['ʃəʊɪ] *adj* voyant(e)

shrank [ʃræŋk] *pt of* **shrink**

shrapnel ['ʃræpnəl] *n* éclats *mpl* d'obus

shred [ʃred] 1 *n* lambeau *m;* **in shreds** en lambeaux; **to tear sth to shreds** mettre qch en lambeaux; *Fig* **there isn't a s. of evidence** il n'y a pas l'ombre d'une preuve

2 *vt (pt & pp* **shredded***) (documents)* déchiqueter; *(food)* couper grossièrement

shredder ['ʃredə(r)] *n (for paper)* déchiqueteuse *f*

shrew [ʃruː] *n* **(a)** *(animal)* musaraigne *f* **(b)** *(nagging woman)* mégère *f*

shrewd [ʃruːd] *adj (person)* perspicace; *(decision)* judicieux(euse)

shrewdly ['ʃruːdlɪ] *adv* judicieusement

shriek [ʃriːk] 1 *n* cri *m* strident; **shrieks of laughter** hurlements *mpl* de rire; **to give a s.** pousser un cri strident

2 *vt* hurler

3 *vi* pousser un cri strident; **to s. with laughter** hurler de rire

shrift [ʃrɪft] *n* **to give sb short s.** envoyer qn promener

shrill [ʃrɪl] *adj* perçant(e), aigu(uë)

shrimp [ʃrɪmp] *n* crevette *f*

shrine [ʃraɪn] *n (tomb)* tombeau *m; (place)* lieu *m* de pèlerinage; *Fig* mausolée *m*

shrink [ʃrɪŋk] 1 *vt (pt* **shrank** [ʃræŋk]*, pp* **shrunk** [ʃrʌŋk]*)* faire rétrécir

2 *vi* **(a)** *(of material)* rétrécir; *(of income, budget)* diminuer, se réduire **(b)** *(move back)* **to s. from sth** se dérober devant qch; **to s. from doing sth** répugner à faire qch

3 *n Fam (psychiatrist)* psy *mf*

shrinkage ['ʃrɪŋkɪdʒ] *n (of material)* rétrécissement *m; Fig (in sales, profit)* diminution *f*

shrink-wrapped ['ʃrɪŋkræpt] *adj* emballé(e) sous film plastique

shrivel ['ʃrɪvəl] *(pt & pp* **shrivelled***, Am* **shriveled***)* 1 *vt* dessécher

2 *vi* se dessécher

▶**shrivel up** *vi* se dessécher

shroud [ʃraʊd] 1 *n* linceul *m; Fig (of mystery, darkness)* voile *m*

2 *vt Fig* **to be shrouded in sth** être enveloppé(e) de qch

Shrove Tuesday ['ʃrəʊv'tjuːzdɪ] *n* Mardi *m* gras

shrub [ʃrʌb] *n* arbuste *m*

shrug [ʃrʌg] 1 *n* haussement *m* d'épaules

2 *vt (pt & pp* **shrugged***)* **to s. one's shoulders** hausser les épaules

3 *vi* hausser les épaules

▶**shrug off** *vt sep* ignorer

shrunk [ʃrʌŋk] *pp of* **shrink**

shrunken ['ʃrʌŋkən] *adj* rétréci(e)

shudder ['ʃʌdə(r)] 1 *n (of person)* frisson *m*

2 *vi (of person)* frissonner; *(of vehicle)* vibrer; **I s. to think!** j'ai des frissons quand j'y pense!

shuffle ['ʃʌfəl] 1 *n* **(a)** *(in walk)* **to walk with a s.** marcher en traînant les pieds **(b)** **to give the cards a s.** battre les cartes

2 *vt (papers)* brasser; *(cards)* battre

3 *vi (when walking)* traîner les pieds

shun [ʃʌn] *(pt & pp* **shunned***) vt* fuir, éviter

shunt [ʃʌnt] *vt (train, carriages)* aiguiller; *Fam Fig (people)* transbahuter

shush [ʃʊʃ] 1 *vt* faire taire

2 *exclam* chut!

shut [ʃʌt] 1 *adj* fermé(e); *Fam* **to keep one's mouth s.** se taire

2 *vt (pt & pp* **shut***)* fermer; **to s. the door on sb** fermer la porte au nez de qn; **to s. one's finger in the door** se coincer le doigt dans la porte; *Fam* **s. your mouth!** ferme-la!

3 *vi (of door)* se fermer; *(of shop)* fermer

▶**shut down** 1 *vt sep* fermer; *(production)* arrêter

2 *vi* fermer

▶**shut in** *vt sep (confine)* enfermer

▶**shut off** *vt sep* **(a)** *(electricity, water, funds)* couper **(b)** *(road, exit)* fermer **(c)** *(isolate)* isoler *(from de)*

▶**shut out** *vt sep* **(a)** *(exclude)* exclure; *(light, view)* bloquer **(b)** *(keep outside)* empêcher d'entrer; **to s. oneself out** s'enfermer dehors

▶**shut up** 1 *vt sep* **(a)** *(confine)* enfermer **(b)** *(close)* fermer **(c)** *Fam (silence)* faire taire

2 *vi Fam (be quiet)* se taire

shutdown ['ʃʌtdaʊn] *n (of factory)* fermeture *f*

shut-eye ['ʃʌtaɪ] *n Fam* roupillon *m;* **to get some s.** roupiller

shutter ['ʃʌtə(r)] *n (a) (on window)* volet *m; (of shop)* store *m;* **to put up the shutters** *(of shop)* fermer le magasin **(b)** *(in camera)* obturateur *m*

shuttle ['ʃʌtəl] 1 *n (a) (in sewing, train, bus, plane)* navette *f;* **s. service** service *m* de navettes **(b)** *(in badminton)* volant *m*

2 *vt* véhiculer

3 *vi* faire la navette **(between** entre*)*

shuttlecock ['ʃʌtəlkɒk] *n* volant *m*

shy [ʃaɪ] 1 *adj* timide; **to be s. of sb** être intimidé(e) par qn; **to be s. of doing sth** éviter de faire qch à tout prix

2 *vi (pt & pp* **shied***) (of horse)* s'effaroucher **(at** devant*)*

▶**shy away** *vi* **to s. away from sth/from doing sth** éviter qch/de faire qch

shyly ['ʃaɪlɪ] *adv* timidement

Siamese [saɪə'miːz] 1 *n (pl* **Siamese***) (cat)* siamois *m*

2 *adj* siamois(e); **S. cat** chat *m* siamois; **S. twins** *(boys)* frères *mpl* siamois; *(girls)* sœurs *fpl* siamoises

Siberia [saɪ'bɪərɪə] *n* la Sibérie

Siberian [saɪ'bɪərɪən] 1 *n* Sibérien(enne) *m,f*

2 *adj* sibérien(enne)

sibling ['sɪblɪŋ] *n (brother)* frère *m; (sister)* sœur *f;* **s. rivalry** rivalité *f* entre frères et sœurs

sic [sɪk] *adv* sic

Sicilian [sɪ'sɪljən] 1 *n* Sicilien(enne) *m,f*

2 *adj* sicilien(enne)

Sicily ['sɪsɪlɪ] *n* la Sicile

sick [sɪk] **1** *adj* **(a)** *(ill)* malade; **to be s.** *(be ill)* être malade; *(vomit)* vomir; **to feel s.** avoir envie de vomir; *Fig* **it makes me s.!** ça me dégoûte!; *Fig* **to be worried s.** se faire un sang d'encre; **s. bay** infirmerie *f*; **s. leave** congé *m* de maladie; **s. note** *(from parents)* mot *m* d'absence; *(from doctor)* certificat *m* médical; **s. pay** indemnité *f* de maladie **(b)** *(fed up)* **to be s. of sb/sth** en avoir assez de qn/qch; **to be s. and tired of** en avoir ras le bol de qn/qch **(c)** *(humour, joke)* de mauvais goût; *(person)* malsain(e); **to have a s. mind** avoir l'esprit dérangé

2 *n Fam (vomit)* vomi *m*

3 *npl* **the s.** les malades *mpl*

▸**sick up** *vt sep Br Fam (vomit)* vomir

sicken ['sɪkən] **1** *vt (make ill)* rendre malade; *Fig (disgust)* écœurer

2 *vi* **to be sickening for something** couver quelque chose

sickening ['sɪkənɪŋ] *adj* écœurant(e)

sickle ['sɪkəl] *n* faucille *f*

sickly ['sɪklɪ] *adj* **(a)** *(person, complexion)* maladif(ive); *(plant)* rabougri(e); *(colour, light, smile)* faible **(b)** *(taste, sentiment)* écœurant(e); **s. sweet** douceâtre

sickness ['sɪknɪs] *n (illness)* maladie *f*; *(nausea)* écœurement *m*; **s. benefit** indemnité *f* journalière

sickroom ['sɪkruːm] *n* chambre *f* de malade

side [saɪd] **1** *n* **(a)** *(of person, animal, object)* côté *m*; *(of mountain)* flanc *m*, versant *m*; **by sb's s.** aux côtés de qn; **s. by s.** côte à côte; *Fam* **to split one's sides (laughing)** se tordre de rire; **s. door/entrance** porte *f*/entrée *f* latérale

(b) *(of record)* face *f*; *(paper)* côté *m*

(c) *(adjacent area)* côté *m*; **on this/that s. (of)** de ce côté (de); **on the other s. (of)** de l'autre côté (de); **from all sides, from every s.** de toutes parts; **to move from s. to s.** osciller; **the left-/right-hand s.** le côté gauche/droit; **to lean to one s.** se pencher sur le côté; **to stand to one s.** se tenir à l'écart; **s. dish** plat *m* d'accompagnement; **s. salad** salade *f*; **s. view** vue *f* latérale

(d) *(aspect)* côté *m*; **to look on the bright/gloomy s.** *(of things)* voir le bon/mauvais côté (des choses)

(e) *(in game)* camp *m*; *(in dispute)* côté *m*; **to be on sb's s.** être du côté de qn; **to take sides** prendre parti; **to change sides** changer de camp; **he had let the s. down** il nous/les/*etc* avait laissés tomber

(f) *(secondary)* **s. effects** effets *mpl* secondaires; **s. issue** question *f* d'intérêt secondaire; **s. road** petite route *f*; **s. street** ruelle *f*

(g) *(idioms)* **on his mother's s.** *(of family)* du côté de sa mère; **to put sth to one s.** mettre qch de côté; **to take sb to one s.** prendre qn à part; **to be on the wrong s. of forty** avoir plus de quarante ans; **to get on the right s. of sb** se faire bien voir de qn; **to get on the wrong s. of sb** prendre qn à rebrousse-poil; **it's a bit on the expensive/long s.** c'est un peu cher/long; **to do sth on the s.** *(as extra job)* faire qch pour arrondir ses fins de mois; *Fam* **to have a bit on the s.** *(of man)* avoir une maîtresse; *(of woman)* avoir un amant

2 *vi* **to s. with** prendre le parti de; **to s. against** prendre parti contre

sideboard ['saɪdbɔːd] *n* buffet *m*

sideboards ['saɪdbɔːdz] *npl (facial hair)* pattes *fpl*

sidecar ['saɪdkɑː(r)] *n* side-car *m*

sidekick ['saɪdkɪk] *n Fam* acolyte *m*

sidelight ['saɪdlaɪt] *n* feu *m* de position

sideline ['saɪdlaɪn] *n* **(a)** *(of football, rugby pitch)* ligne *f* de touche; *Fig* **to sit on the sidelines** rester sur la touche **(b)** *(business, job)* à-côté *m*; **we sell guide books as a s.** nous vendons également des guides

side-saddle ['saɪdsædəl] *adv* **to ride s.** monter en amazone

sideshow ['saɪdʃəʊ] *n (at fair)* attraction *f*; *Fig* événement *m* mineur

side-splitting ['saɪdsplɪtɪŋ] *adj Fam* tordant(e)

sidestep ['saɪdstep] *(pt & pp* **sidestepped)** **1** *vt (tackle, player)* éviter; *Fig (question)* éluder

2 *vi (in boxing)* esquiver

sideswipe ['saɪdswaɪp] *n* remarque *f* désobligeante

sidetrack ['saɪdtræk] *vt* distraire

sidewalk ['saɪdwɔːk] *n Am* trottoir *m*

sideways ['saɪdweɪz] **1** *adj (look, movement)* de côté

2 *adv (move, walk)* latéralement; *(turn, fall, lean)* sur le côté

siding ['saɪdɪŋ] *n (on railway)* voie *f* de garage

sidle ['saɪdəl] *vi* **to s. up to sb** se glisser vers qn

siege [siːdʒ] *n* siège *m*; **to lay s. to a town** assiéger une ville; **under s.** assiégé(e); **to have a s. mentality** se sentir persécuté(e)

Sierra Leone [sɪˈerəlɪˈəʊn] *n* la Sierra Leone

sieve [sɪv] **1** *n* crible *m*; *(in kitchen)* passoire *f*; *Fam* **to have a memory like a s.** avoir la tête comme une passoire

2 *vt* tamiser

sift [sɪft] **1** *vt (flour, sugar)* tamiser

2 *vi Fig* **to s. through sth** passer qch au crible

sigh [saɪ] **1** *n* soupir *m*

2 *vi* soupirer; *(of wind)* gémir

sight [saɪt] *n* **(a)** *(faculty)* vue *f*; **to lose one's s.** perdre la vue

(b) *(act of seeing)* **to catch s. of sb/sth** apercevoir qn/qch; **to lose s. of sb/sth** perdre qn/qch de vue; **I hate the s. of him** je ne peux pas le voir; **I can't stand the s. of blood** je ne supporte pas la vue du sang; **to shoot on s.** tirer à vue; **at first s.** à première vue; **it was love at first s.** ça a été le coup de foudre; **to know sb by s.** connaître qn de vue; **to buy sth s. unseen** acheter qch sans l'avoir vu

(c) *(range of vision)* **to come into s.** apparaître; **in s.** en vue; **to keep sb in s.** garder un œil sur qn; **out of s.** caché(e); **to put sth out of s.** cacher qch; **to keep out of s.** se cacher; *Prov* **out of s., out of mind** loin des yeux, loin du cœur

(d) *(of instrument, gun)* viseur *m*; *Fig* **to have sb/sth in one's sights** avoir qn/qch en vue; *Fig* **to have or set one's sights on sb/sth** avoir des vues sur qn/qch

(e) *(spectacle)* spectacle *m*; **you're/it's a s. for sore eyes** c'est un plaisir de te voir/de voir ça; *Fam* **to look a s.** ne pas être beau (belle) à voir; **sights** *(of city)* attractions *fpl* touristiques

(f) *Fam (for emphasis)* **a damn s.** easier/longer bien plus facile/long (longue)

2 *vt (see)* apercevoir

sighted ['saɪtɪd] **1** *npl* **the s.** les voyants *mpl*

2 *adj (person)* voyant(e)

sighting ['saɪtɪŋ] *n* **several sightings of the fugitive have been reported** on a aperçu le fugitif à plusieurs reprises; **there have been several UFO sightings in the area** on a aperçu plusieurs ovnis dans les parages

sightless ['saɪtləs] *adj* aveugle

sight-read ['saɪtriːd] (*pt & pp* **sight-read** ['saɪtred]) *vt & vi* déchiffrer

sightseeing ['saɪtsiːɪŋ] *n* tourisme *m*; **to go s.** faire du tourisme

sightseer ['saɪtsiːə(r)] *n* touriste *mf*

sign [saɪn] **1** *n* (a) *(gesture, symbol, indication)* signe *m*; **to make a s.** to sb faire un signe à qn; **it's a sure s. that...** on peut être sûr que...; **a s. of the times** un signe des temps; **there's no s. of an improvement** il n'y a rien qui annonce une quelconque amélioration; **there's no s. of it/him** je ne le vois nulle part; **she gave no s. of having heard** elle n'a pas semblé avoir entendu; **all the signs are that...** tout laisse à penser que...; **the equipment showed signs of having been used** on voyait que l'équipement avait déjà été utilisé; **s. language** langage *m* des sourds-muets (b) *(notice)* panneau *m*; *(of pub, shop)* enseigne *f*; *(on road)* panneau de signalisation routière; **follow the signs for Manchester** suivre la direction de Manchester

2 *vt* (a) *(write signature on)* signer (b) *(in sign language)* dire en langage des sourds-muets (c) *(in sport)* engager

3 *vi* (a) *(write signature)* signer (b) *(in sport)* signer (**for** avec)

▶**sign away** *vt sep (rights)* renoncer à

▶**sign for** *vt insep (delivery, parcel)* signer un reçu pour

▶**sign in** *vi (in factory)* pointer; *(in hotel)* signer le registre en arrivant

▶**sign off** *vi* (a) *(of radio, TV presenter)* terminer l'émission (b) *(close letter)* finir la lettre

▶**sign on** *vi Fam (for unemployment benefit)* (initially) s'inscrire au chômage; *(regularly)* pointer

▶**sign out 1** *vt sep* **to s. sth out** *(book, equipment)* signer un registre pour emprunter qch

2 *vi (from hotel)* signer le registre à son départ

▶**sign up 1** *vi* (a) *(register)* s'inscrire (**for** à) (b) *(of soldier)* s'engager

signal ['sɪgnəl] **1** *n* signal *m*; *Fig* **to send the wrong signals** ne pas être clair(e); **s. box** poste *m* d'aiguillage; **s. flare** fusée *f* éclairante; **s. rocket** fusée *f* de signalisation

2 *vt (pt & pp* **signalled**, *Am* **signaled**) (a) *(make gesture to)* faire signe à; **to s. sb to do sth** faire signe à qn de faire qch (b) *(be sign of)* être le signe de

3 *vi* (a) *(make gesture)* faire signe (**to** à) (b) *(in car)* clignoter

signalman ['sɪgnəlmən] (*pl* **signalmen**) *n* aiguilleur *m*

signatory ['sɪgnətərɪ] (*pl* **signatories**) *n* signataire *mf*

signature ['sɪgnətʃə(r)] *n* signature *f*; **s. tune** *(of radio, TV programme)* indicatif *m*

signboard ['saɪnbɔːd] *n* enseigne *f*

signet ring ['sɪgnɪt'rɪŋ] *n* chevalière *f*

significance [sɪg'nɪfɪkəns] *n* (a) *(importance)* importance *f*; **of great s.** d'une grande importance; **of no s.** sans importance (b) *(meaning)* signification *f*

significant [sɪg'nɪfɪkənt] *adj (important)* important(e), considérable; *(meaningful)* significatif(ive); **s. other** ami(e) *m,f*

significantly [sɪg'nɪfɪkəntlɪ] *adv* (a) *(appreciably)* nettement; **to vary/change s.** varier/changer considérablement (b) *(meaningfully)* d'une manière significative; **s., no one mentioned it** fait révélateur, personne n'en a parlé

signify ['sɪgnɪfaɪ] (*pt & pp* **signified**) *vt* signifier

signpost ['saɪnpəʊst] **1** *n* poteau *m* indicateur; *Fig* indice *m*

2 *vt* signaliser

Sikh [siːk] *n & adj* sikh *mf*

silage ['saɪlɪdʒ] *n* ensilage *m*

silence ['saɪləns] **1** *n* silence *m*; **to listen/watch in s.** écouter/regarder en silence; *Prov* **s. is golden** le silence est d'or

2 *vt* faire taire

silencer ['saɪlənsə(r)] *n (on car, gun)* silencieux *m*

silent ['saɪlənt] *adj (person, place)* silencieux(euse); *(letter)* muet(ette); **to fall s.** se taire; **to remain** *or* **keep s.** garder le silence; **s. film** film *m* muet; **s. majority** majorité *f* silencieuse; **s. protest** manifestation *f* silencieuse

silently ['saɪləntlɪ] *adv* silencieusement

silhouette [sɪluː'et] **1** *n* silhouette *f*

2 *vt* **she was silhouetted against the light** sa silhouette se détachait à contre-jour

silica ['sɪlɪkə] *n* silice *f*

silicon ['sɪlɪkən] *n* silicium *m*; **s. chip** puce *f* électronique

silk [sɪlk] *n* soie *f*; **s. screen printing** sérigraphie *f*

silkworm ['sɪlkwɜːm] *n* ver *m* à soie

silky ['sɪlkɪ] *adj* soyeux(euse); *(voice)* suave

sill [sɪl] *n (of window)* rebord *m*

silliness ['sɪlɪnɪs] *n* stupidité *f*

silly ['sɪlɪ] **1** *adj* idiot(e), stupide; **the s. thing is that...** ce qui est idiot, c'est que...; **to look s.** avoir l'air ridicule; **to say/do something s.** dire/faire une bêtise; **to laugh/worry oneself s.** mourir de rire/d'inquiétude; **to knock sb s.** assommer qn

2 *n Fam* bêta(asse) *mf*

silo ['saɪləʊ] (*pl* **silos**) *n* silo *m*

silt [sɪlt] *n* vase *f*

▶**silt up** *vi* s'envaser

silver ['sɪlvə(r)] **1** *n* (a) *(metal)* argent *m*; *Prov* **every cloud has a s. lining** à quelque chose malheur est bon; **s. haired** aux cheveux argentés; **s. medal** médaille *f* d'argent; **s. paper** papier *m* d'argent; **s. plate** *(coating)* plaqué *m* argent; *(articles)* argenterie *f*; **the s. screen** le grand écran; **s. wedding** noces *fpl* d'argent (b) *Br (coins)* pièces *fpl* en argent (c) *(silverware)* argenterie *f*

2 *adj (made of silver)* en argent (b) **s.(-coloured)** argenté(e)

silver-plated [sɪlvə'pleɪtɪd] *adj* plaqué(e) argent

silversmith ['sɪlvəsmɪθ] *n* orfèvre *mf*

silverware ['sɪlvəweə(r)] *n* argenterie *f*

silverwork ['sɪlvəwɜːk] *n* orfèvrerie *f*

silvery ['sɪlvərɪ] *adj (colour)* argenté(e); *(sound)* argentin(e)

simian ['sɪmɪən] *adj* simien(enne)

similar ['sɪmɪlə(r)] *adj* semblable, similaire (**to** à); **s. in appearance/size** d'apparence/de taille semblable; **they are very s.** ils se ressemblent beaucoup

similarity [sɪmɪ'lærɪtɪ] (*pl* **similarities**) *n* ressemblance *f*

similarly ['sɪmɪləlɪ] *adv* de la même façon

simile ['sɪmɪlɪ] *n* comparaison *f*

simmer ['sɪmə(r)] **1** *n* **at a s.** à feu doux

2 *vt* mijoter

3 *vi* mijoter; *Fig (of revolt, discontent)* couver; **to s. with rage** bouillonner de rage

▶**simmer down** *vi Fam* se calmer

simper ['sɪmpə(r)] *vi* minauder

simple ['sɪmpəl] *adj* (a) *(easy)* simple; **in s. terms** dit simplement; **the s. truth** la vérité pure et simple (b) *(unintelligent)* simplet(ette)

simple-minded [sɪmpəl'maɪndɪd] *adj (person)* simple d'esprit; *(ideas, belief)* naïf(ive)

simpleton ['sɪmpəltən] *n* simple *mf* d'esprit

simplicity [sɪm'plɪsɪtɪ] *n* simplicité *f*

simplification [sɪmplɪfɪ'keɪʃən] *n* simplification *f*

simplify ['sɪmplɪfaɪ] *(pt & pp* **simplified)** *vt* simplifier

simplistic [sɪm'plɪstɪk] *adj* simpliste

simply ['sɪmplɪ] *adv* (a) *(in simple manner)* simplement (b) *(absolutely)* absolument (c) *(just)* simplement; **it's s. a question of time** c'est une simple question de temps; **she s. had to snap her fingers and...** elle n'avait qu'à claquer des doigts et...

simulate ['sɪmjʊleɪt] *vt* simuler

simulated ['sɪmjʊleɪtɪd] *adj (leather, marble)* faux (fausse); *(surprise, anger)* simulé(e)

simulation [sɪmjʊ'leɪʃən] *n* simulation *f*

simultaneous [sɪməl'teɪnɪəs, *Am* saɪməl'teɪnɪəs] *adj* simultané(e); **s. broadcast** retransmission *f* simultanée; **s. translation** traduction *f* simultanée

simultaneously [sɪməl'teɪnɪəslɪ, *Am* saɪməl'teɪnɪəslɪ] *adv* simultanément

sin [sɪn] **1** *n* péché *m*; *Old-fashioned or Hum* **to be living in s.** *(of unmarried couple)* vivre dans le péché; *Fam* **it would be a s. to...** ce serait un crime de...
2 *vi (pt & pp* **sinned)** pécher

since [sɪns] **1** *adv* depuis; **long s.** depuis longtemps
2 *prep* depuis; **s. June/1984** depuis le mois de juin/1984; **s. then** depuis
3 *conj* (a) *(in time)* depuis que; **it's a long time s. I saw her** cela fait longtemps que je ne l'ai pas vue (b) *(because)* puisque

sincere [sɪn'sɪə(r)] *adj* sincère

sincerely [sɪn'sɪəlɪ] *adv* sincèrement; **Yours s.** *(ending letter)* Veuillez agréer, Monsieur/Madame, l'expression de mes salutations distinguées

sincerity [sɪn'serɪtɪ] *n* sincérité *f*; **in all s.** en toute sincérité

sinecure ['saɪnɪkjʊə(r)] *n* sinécure *f*

sinew ['sɪnjuː] *n* tendon *m*

sinewy ['sɪnjuːɪ] *adj* musclé(e)

sinful ['sɪnfʊl] *adj (act, life)* coupable; *(waste)* scandaleux(euse); **s. person** pécheur(eresse) *m,f*

sing [sɪŋ] *(pt* **sang** [sæŋ]*, pp* **sung** [sʌŋ]) **1** *vt (song)* chanter
2 *vi (of person, bird, kettle)* chanter

▶**sing out** *vi (sing loudly)* chanter fort

Singapore [sɪŋə'pɔː(r)] *n* Singapour

Singaporean [sɪŋə'pɔːrɪən] **1** *n* Singapourien(enne) *m,f*
2 *adj* singapourien(enne)

singe [sɪndʒ] *vt* roussir

singer ['sɪŋə(r)] *n* chanteur(euse) *m,f*; **s. songwriter** auteur-compositeur-interprète *m*

singing ['sɪŋɪŋ] *n* chant *m*; **his s. is awful** il chante atrocement; **s. lessons** cours *mpl* de chant; **to have a fine s. voice** chanter admirablement

single ['sɪŋɡəl] **1** *adj* (a) *(just one)* seul(e); **every s. day** tous les jours; **not a s. one** pas un(e); **don't say a s. word** ne dis pas un mot; **s. cream** ≃ crème *f* fraîche liquide; *Fin* **s. currency** monnaie *f* unique; *Econ* **s. European market** marché *m* unique européen (b) *(not double)* **in s. figures** inférieur à dix; **in s. file** en file indienne; **s. bed** lit *m* à une place; **s. room** chambre *f* pour une personne (c) *(not married)* célibataire; **s. mother** mère *f* célibataire; **s. parent** parent *m* isolé; **s. parent family** famille *f* monoparentale
2 *n* (a) *(record)* single *m* (b) *(ticket)* aller *m* simple (c) *(hotel room)* chambre *f* pour une personne (d) **singles** *(in tennis)* simple *m*

▶**single out** *vt sep* distinguer; **she was singled out for praise** on a choisi de faire des compliments qu'à elle

single-breasted ['sɪŋɡəl'brestɪd] *adj (jacket, suit)* droit(e)

single-decker ['sɪŋɡəl'dekə(r)] *n* autobus *m* sans impériale

single-handedly ['sɪŋɡəl'hændɪdlɪ] *adv* tout(e) seul(e)

single-minded ['sɪŋɡəl'maɪndɪd] *adj (person)* résolu(e); *(determination, conviction)* farouche

single-sex school ['sɪŋɡəl'seks'skuːl] *n* école *f* non mixte

singlet ['sɪŋɡlɪt] *n* maillot *m* de corps

single-track railway ['sɪŋɡəl'træk'reɪlweɪ] *n* chemin *m* de fer à une seule voie

singsong ['sɪŋsɒŋ] **1** *n* (a) *(voice, tone)* voix *f* chantante (b) *Fam (singing session)* **to have a s.** chanter en chœur
2 *adj (voice, tone)* chantant(e)

singular ['sɪŋɡjʊlə(r)] **1** *n Gram* singulier *m*; **in the s.** au singulier
2 *adj* (a) *Gram* singulier(ère) (b) *(remarkable)* remarquable

singularly ['sɪŋɡjʊləlɪ] *adv* remarquablement

Sinhalese [sɪnə'liːz] **1** *n (pl* **Sinhalese)** (a) *(person)* Cinghalais(e) *m,f* (b) *(language)* cinghalais *m*
2 *adj* cinghalais(e)

sinister ['sɪnɪstə(r)] *adj* sinistre

sink¹ [sɪŋk] *n (in kitchen)* évier *m*; *(in bathroom)* lavabo *m*

sink² [sɪŋk] *(pt* **sank** [sæŋk]*, pp* **sunk** [sʌŋk]) **1** *vt* (a) *(ship)* couler; **to be sunk in thought** être perdu(e) dans ses pensées; *Fam Fig* **to be sunk** être fichu(e) (b) *(well)* creuser; **s. one's teeth into sth** mordre à pleines dents dans qch; **to s. money into sth** investir des capitaux dans qch; *Fam* **to s. a pint** s'envoyer une pinte de bière
2 *vi (in water, mud)* couler; **her heart sank** son cœur s'est serré; **his spirits sank** il a perdu tout son courage; **to s. into sb's memory** *(of information)* se graver dans la mémoire de qn; **to s. into oblivion** tomber dans l'oubli; **to s. into a deep sleep** sombrer dans un profond sommeil; **to s. into an armchair** s'affaler dans un fauteuil; **to s. to the ground** s'effondrer par terre; **to s. in sb's estimation** baisser dans l'estime de qn; **how could you s. so low?** comment peux-tu tomber aussi bas?

▶**sink in** *vi (of liquid)* pénétrer; *(of information)* être assimilé(e); *Fig* **it hasn't sunk in yet** je n'ai/il n'a/*etc* pas encore digéré la nouvelle

sinking ['sɪŋkɪŋ] **1** n (a) (of ship) naufrage m (b) Fin s. fund fonds m d'amortissement

2 adj (feeling) d'angoisse; **with a s. heart** avec un serrement de cœur

sinner ['sɪnə(r)] n pécheur(eresse) m,f

sinuous ['sɪnjʊəs] adj (river, curves) sinueux(euse); (snake, dancer) qui ondule; (movement) ondulant(e)

sinus ['saɪnəs] n sinus m

sinusitis [saɪnə'saɪtɪs] n sinusite f

sip [sɪp] **1** n petite gorgée f; **to take a s. (of sth)** boire une petite gorgée (de qch)

2 vt (pt & pp **sipped**) siroter

3 vi **to s. at sth** siroter qch

siphon ['saɪfən] **1** n siphon m

2 vt siphonner

▶**siphon off** vt sep (liquid) siphonner; Fig (money, supplies) détourner

sir [sɜː(r)] n (a) (form of address) monsieur m; **Dear S./ Sirs** (in letter) Monsieur/Messieurs (b) (title) **S. Clyde** sir Clyde (titre de noblesse masculin)

sire ['saɪə(r)] **1** n (a) (father of animal) père m (b) Old-fashioned (address to sovereign) sire m

2 vt engendrer

siren ['saɪərən] n sirène f

sirloin ['sɜːlɔɪn] n s. (steak) steak m d'aloyau

sissy ['sɪsɪ] n Fam (weak male) poule f mouillée; (effeminate male) garçon m efféminé

sister ['sɪstə(r)] n (a) (sibling, nun) sœur f; **s. company** société f sœur; **s. ship** sister-ship m (b) (nurse) infirmière-chef f

sisterhood ['sɪstəhʊd] n (a) (community of nuns) communauté f religieuse (b) (solidarity) solidarité f féminine

sister-in-law ['sɪstərɪnlɔː] (pl **sisters-in-law**) n belle-sœur f

sisterly ['sɪstəlɪ] adj fraternel(elle)

sit [sɪt] (pt & pp sat [sæt]) **1** vt (a) **to s. a child on one's knee** asseoir un enfant sur ses genoux (b) Br (exam) passer

2 vi (a) (of person) s'asseoir; **to be sitting** être assis(e); **to be sitting reading** être assis en train de lire; **s.!** (to dog) assis!; Fam **to s. tight** (not move) ne pas bouger de sa place; (not take action) ne rien faire (b) (of assembly, court) siéger; **to s. on a jury** faire partie d'un jury (c) (of object) **to be sitting on the radiator/outside** être sur le radiateur/dehors

▶**sit about, sit around** vi rester assis(e) à ne rien faire

▶**sit back** vi (a) (lean back) to **s. back in one's chair** s'installer confortablement sur sa chaise (b) Fam (relax) se détendre; (not intervene) ne rien faire

▶**sit down 1** vt sep asseoir; Fam **s. yourself down!** assieds-toi donc!

2 vi s'asseoir; **to be sitting down** être assis(e)

▶**sit in** vi (at meeting) assister (**on** à)

▶**sit on** vt insep Fam (a) (not deal with) laisser traîner (b) (repress) rembarrer

▶**sit out 1** vt sep (not participate in) ne pas participer à

2 vi (in garden) s'asseoir dehors

▶**sit through** vt insep rester jusqu'au bout de

▶**sit up** vi (a) (straighten one's back) se redresser; (from lying position) s'asseoir; Fig **to make sb s. up (and take notice)** secouer qn (b) (not go to bed) veiller

sitar ['sɪtɑː(r)] n sitar m

sitcom ['sɪtkɒm] n sitcom m

site [saɪt] **1** n (a) (of building) emplacement m; (archaeological) site m (b) (building) s. chantier m (de construction)

2 vt situer

sit-in ['sɪtɪn] n occupation f des locaux

sitting ['sɪtɪŋ] **1** n (of committee, for portrait) séance f; (for meal) service m; **at one s.** d'un trait; **s. room** (in house) salon m

2 adj (a) (seated) assis(e); Fam Fig **s. duck** or target cible f facile (b) (current) Pol **s. member** député m en exercice; **s. tenant** locataire mf dans les lieux

situate ['sɪtjʊeɪt] vt situer

situated ['sɪtjʊeɪtɪd] adj situé(e)

situation [sɪtjʊ'eɪʃən] n (a) (circumstances) situation f; s. comedy (on TV) sitcom m (b) (job) **situations vacant/ wanted** (in advertisements) offres fpl/demandes fpl d'emploi (c) (location) emplacement m

sit-up ['sɪtʌp] n **to do sit-ups** faire des abdominaux

six [sɪks] **1** n six m inv; Fam **it's s. of one and half a dozen of the other** c'est kif-kif; **at sixes and sevens** sens dessus dessous; Fam **to knock sb for s.** étendre qn

2 adj six; see also **eight**

six-figure ['sɪks'fɪgə(r)] adj **a s. sum** une somme à six chiffres

sixpence ['sɪkspəns] n Br Formerly = ancienne pièce de 6 pence

six-shooter ['sɪks'ʃuːtə(r)] n six-coups m inv

sixteen [sɪks'tiːn] **1** n seize m inv

2 adj seize; see also **eight**

sixteenth [sɪks'tiːnθ] **1** n (a) (fraction) seizième m (b) (in series) seizième mf (c) (of month) seize m inv

2 adj seizième; see also **eighth**

sixth [sɪksθ] **1** n (a) (fraction) sixième m (b) (in series) sixième mf (c) (of month) six m inv

2 adj sixième; Br Sch **the s. form** ≃ les classes fpl de première et de terminale; Br Sch **s. former** ≃ élève mf de première ou de terminale; **s. sense** sixième sens m; see also **eighth**

sixtieth ['sɪkstɪɪθ] **1** n (a) (fraction) soixantième m (b) (in series) soixantième mf

2 adj soixantième

sixty ['sɪkstɪ] **1** n soixante m inv

2 adj soixante; see also **eighty**

size [saɪz] n (of person, clothes) taille f; (of shoe) pointure f; (of place, object) dimensions fpl; (of country) superficie f; (of problem, undertaking) ampleur f; Fam **that's about the s. of it** c'est à peu près ça; **s. 10 shoes** ≃ des chaussures du 44; **to try sth (on) for s.** essayer qch pour voir si la taille convient

▶**size up** vt sep (person) jauger; (situation) évaluer

sizeable ['saɪzəbəl] adj non négligeable; (improvement) net(nette)

sizzle ['sɪzəl] **1** n grésillement m

2 vi grésiller

skate¹ [skeɪt] n (fish) raie f

skate² **1** n patin m; Fam Fig **to get one's skates on** se dépêcher

2 vi (on ice skates) faire du patin à glace; (on roller skates) faire du roller; Fig **to s. round sth** tourner autour de qch

▶**skate over** vt insep (deal with superficially) survoler

skateboard ['skeɪtbɔːd] n planche f à roulettes

skater ['skeɪtə(r)] n patineur(euse) m,f

skating ['skeɪtɪŋ] *n* patinage *m*; **s. rink** *(for ice skating)* patinoire *f*; *(for roller skating)* piste *f*

skeletal ['skelɪtəl] *adj* squelettique

skeleton ['skelɪtən] *n* *(of person)* squelette *m*; *(of building)* charpente *f*; *Fig* **to have a s. in the cupboard** *or* **closet** avoir un secret honteux; **s. staff/crew** personnel *m*/ équipage *m* réduit; **s. key** passe-partout *m inv*

sketch [sketʃ] **1** *n* (a) *(drawing, description)* croquis *m*; **s. pad** bloc *m* à dessin (b) *(on stage, TV)* sketch *m*
2 *vt also Fig* esquisser

▶**sketch in** *vt sep also Fig* esquisser

▶**sketch out** *vt sep* ébaucher

sketchbook ['sketʃbʊk] *n* carnet *m* de croquis

sketchily ['sketʃɪlɪ] *adv* vaguement

sketchy ['sketʃɪ] *adj* vague (**about** à propos de)

skew [skju:] **1** *n* **on the s.** de travers
2 *vt (distort)* fausser

skewer ['skju:ə(r)] **1** *n* brochette *f*
2 *vt* embrocher

ski [ski:] **1** *n* ski *m*; **s. boots** chaussures *fpl* de ski; **s. instructor** moniteur(trice) *m,f* de ski; **s. jump** saut *m* à skis; **s. jumper** sauteur(euse) *m,f* à ski; **s. lift** remontée *f* mécanique; **s. pants** fuseau *m*; **s. resort** station *f* de ski; **s. run** *or* **slope** piste *f* de ski; **s. stick** bâton *m* de ski
2 *vi (pt & pp skied)* skier, faire du ski

skid [skɪd] **1** *n* (a) *(of car)* dérapage *m*; **to go into a s.** faire un dérapage (b) *(idioms) Fam* **to put the skids under sb/sth** faire accélérer qn/qch; *Fam* **to be on the skids** battre de l'aile; *Am Fam* **to be on s. row** être à la rue
2 *vi (pt & pp skidded)* déraper

skier ['ski:ə(r)] *n* skieur(euse) *m,f*

skiing ['ski:ɪŋ] *n* ski *m*; **to go s.** aller faire du ski; **s. instructor** moniteur(trice) *m,f* de ski

skilful, *Am* **skillful** ['skɪlfʊl] *adj* habile

skilfully, *Am* **skillfully** ['skɪlfʊlɪ] *adv* habilement

skill [skɪl] *n (ability)* qualités *fpl*; *(technique)* compétence *f*, connaissances *fpl*

skilled [skɪld] *adj (person, work)* qualifié(e); **to be s. in doing sth** être habile à faire qch; **s. worker** ouvrier(ère) *m,f* qualifié(e)

skillful, skillfully *Am* = **skilful, skilfully**

skim [skɪm] *(pt & pp skimmed)* **1** *vt* (a) *(milk)* écrémer; *(soup)* écumer (b) *(surface)* effleurer; **to s. stones on water** faire des ricochets
2 *vi* **to s. along** *or* **over the ground** voler au ras du sol; **to s. over the water** raser la surface de l'eau;

▶**skim off** *vt sep (fat, cream)* enlever; *Fig (money)* ponctionner

▶**skim through** *vt insep (novel, document)* lire en diagonale

skimmed milk ['skɪmd'mɪlk], *Am* **skim milk** ['skɪm'mɪlk] *n* lait *m* écrémé

skimp [skɪmp] **1** *vt* lésiner sur; *(work)* bâcler
2 *vi* **to s. on sth** lésiner sur qch

skimpy ['skɪmpɪ] *adj (meal)* maigre; *(clothes)* étriqué(e)

skin [skɪn] *n* (a) *(of person, animal, fruit, on milk, sauce)* peau *f*; **to be all s. and bone** n'avoir que la peau et les os; *Fam* **to jump out of one's s.** sauter au plafond; *Fig* **by the s. of one's teeth** de justesse; **to save one's (own) s.** sauver sa peau; *Fam* **to get under sb's s.** taper sur les nerfs de qn; *Fam* **it's no s. off my nose** je m'en balance; **s. cancer** cancer *m* de la peau; **s. complaint** problème *m*

de peau; **s. cream** crème *f* pour la peau; **s. disease** maladie *f* de peau; **s. diving** plongée *f* sous-marine; *Am Fam* **s. flick** *(porn film)* film *m* porno; *Med* **s. graft** greffe *f* de peau (b) *Fam (skinhead)* skin *mf*
2 *vt (pt & pp skinned) (animal)* écorcher; *(tomato)* peler; **to s. one's knees** s'écorcher les genoux

▶**skin up** *vi very Fam* rouler un pétard

skinflint ['skɪnflɪnt] *n Fam* radin(e) *m,f*

skinhead ['skɪnhed] *n* skinhead *mf*

skinny ['skɪnɪ] *adj* maigre

skint [skɪnt] *adj Br Fam* fauché(e)

skintight ['skɪntaɪt] *adj* moulant(e)

skip[1] [skɪp] **1** *n (jump)* saut *m*
2 *vt (pt & pp skipped) (meal, page, stage)* sauter
3 *vi (of lambs, children)* gambader; *(with rope)* sauter à la corde

skip[2] *n (for rubbish)* benne *f*

skipper ['skɪpə(r)] **1** *n (of ship, team)* capitaine *m*
2 *vt Fam* commander

skipping ['skɪpɪŋ] *n* saut *m* à la corde; **s. rope** corde *f* à sauter

skirmish ['skɜ:mɪʃ] **1** *n Mil* escarmouche *f*; *Fig* accrochage *m*
2 *vi* s'engager dans une escarmouche

skirt [skɜ:t] **1** *n* jupe *f*
2 *vt (village, hill)* contourner; **to s. (a)round a problem** contourner un problème

skirting board ['skɜ:tɪŋbɔ:d] *n Br* plinthe *f*

skit [skɪt] *n* satire *f*

skittish ['skɪtɪʃ] *adj* espiègle

skittle ['skɪtəl] *n* quille *f*

skive [skaɪv] *vi Br Fam* tirer au flanc

▶**skive off** *vi Br Fam* s'esquiver

skiver ['skaɪvə(r)] *n Br Fam* tire-au-flanc *m inv*

skivvy ['skɪvɪ] *(pl skivvies) n Br Pej* bonne *f* à tout faire

skulduggery [skʌl'dʌgərɪ] *n* magouille *f*

skulk [skʌlk] *vi* rôder

skull [skʌl] *n* crâne *m*; **s. and crossbones** tête *f* de mort

skullcap ['skʌlkæp] *n* calotte *f*

skunk [skʌŋk] *n (animal)* mouffette *f*; *Fam Pej (person)* mufle *m*

sky [skaɪ] *n* ciel *m*; *Fam* **the s.'s the limit** tout est possible; *Fam* **to praise sb to the skies** porter qn aux nues; **s. high** *(price, costs)* astronomique

sky-blue [skaɪ'blu:] *adj* bleu ciel *inv*

skydiver ['skaɪdaɪvə(r)] *n* parachutiste *mf* qui pratique la chute libre

skydiving ['skaɪdaɪvɪŋ] *n* parachutisme *m* en chute libre

skylark ['skaɪlɑ:k] *n* alouette *f* des champs

skylight ['skaɪlaɪt] *n* lucarne *f* faîtière *f*

skyline ['skaɪlaɪn] *n (horizon)* horizon *m*; *(of city)* silhouette *f*

skyscraper ['skaɪskreɪpə(r)] *n* gratte-ciel *m inv*

slab [slæb] *n (of stone, concrete)* dalle *f*; *(of cake)* tranche *f*; *(of meat)* pavé *m*; *(of chocolate)* plaque *f*; *(in mortuary)* table *f* d'autopsie

slack [slæk] **1** *adj* (a) *(not tight)* mou (molle); **trade is s.** le commerce marche mal; **in s. periods** en période creuse (b) *(careless)* négligent(e)
2 *n* **to take up the s.** *(in rope)* tendre la corde; *Fig*

prendre le relais

3 *vi Fam* se relâcher

▶**slack off** *vi (of rain)* se calmer; *(of trade, demand)* se ralentir

slacken ['slækən] 1 *vt (pace)* ralentir; *(rope)* détendre

2 *vi (of person, rope)* se relâcher; *(of speed)* se ralentir; *(of storm, wind)* se calmer; *(of energy, enthusiasm)* retomber

▶**slacken off** *vi (of rain)* se calmer; *(of trade, demand)* se ralentir

slacker ['slækə(r)] *n Fam* flemmard(e) *m,f*

slackness ['slæknɪs] *n* (a) *(negligence)* négligence *f*; *(laziness)* fainéantise *f* (b) *(of rope)* mou *m* (c) *(of business)* stagnation *f*

slacks [slæks] *npl (trousers)* pantalon *m*

slag [slæg] *n* (a) *(from coalmine)* scories *fpl*; **s. heap** terril *m* (b) *very Fam Pej (woman)* salope *f*

▶**slag off** *(pt & pp slagged) vt sep very Fam (criticize)* débiner

slain [sleɪn] 1 *npl* **the s.** les morts *mpl*

2 *pp of* **slay**

slake [sleɪk] *vt Lit* **to s. one's thirst** étancher sa soif

slalom ['slɑːləm] *n* slalom *m*

slam [slæm] 1 *vt (pt & pp slammed)* (a) *(door)* claquer; *(lid, drawer)* fermer violemment; **to s. the door in sb's face** claquer la porte au nez de qn; **to s. sth down** flanquer qch (b) *Fam (criticize)* éreinter

2 *vi (of door)* claquer; **to s. on the brakes** freiner à fond

3 *n (of door)* claquement *m*

slander ['slɑːndə(r)] 1 *n* calomnie *f*

2 *vt* calomnier

slanderous ['slɑːndərəs] *adj* calomnieux(euse)

slang [slæŋ] 1 *n* argot *m*

2 *vt Fam (insult)* injurier; **slanging match** échange *m* d'insultes

slant [slɑːnt] 1 *n* (a) *(slope)* pente *f* (b) *(point of view)* perspective *f*; *(bias)* parti *m* pris; **to put a s. on sth** présenter qch d'une manière partiale

2 *vt* (a) *(set at angle)* incliner (b) *(bias)* présenter avec parti pris

3 *vi (slope)* être incliné(e)

slanting ['slɑːntɪŋ] *adj (roof)* en pente; *(writing)* penché(e)

slap [slæp] 1 *n (with hand)* claque *f*; *also Fig* **a s. in the face** une gifle; **to get a s. on the wrist** *(reprimand)* se faire taper sur les doigts

2 *adv Fam* **s. (bang) in the middle** en plein milieu

3 *vt (pt & pp slapped)* donner une claque à; **to s. sb's face**, **to s. sb in the face** gifler qn; **to s. sb on the back** donner une tape dans le dos à qn; *Fig* **to s. sb down** remettre qn à sa place; **to s. some paint on sth** passer un coup de peinture sur qch

slapdash ['slæpdæʃ] *adj* brouillon(onne)

slapstick ['slæpstɪk] *n* **s. (comedy)** comique *m* tarte à la crème

slap-up ['slæpʌp] *adj Br Fam* **s. meal** gueuleton *m*

slash [slæʃ] 1 *n* (a) *(cut)* coupure *f*, balafre *f* (b) *Typ* barre *f* oblique (c) *Br very Fam* **to have/go for a s.** pisser/aller pisser un coup

2 *vt (cut)* taillader, balafrer; *(reduce)* réduire considérablement; **prices slashed** *(sign)* prix sacrifiés

slat [slæt] *n* latte *f*

slate [sleɪt] 1 *n* (a) *(stone)* ardoise *f*; **s. grey** ardoise *m inv*; **s. quarry** ardoisière *f* (b) *(idioms) Fam* **put it on the s.**

mettez-le-moi sur mon ardoise; **to wipe the s. clean** faire table rase

2 *vt Fam (criticize)* éreinter

slaughter ['slɔːtə(r)] 1 *n (of animals)* abattage *m*; *(of people)* massacre *m*

2 *vt (animals)* abattre; *(people)* massacrer; *Fam (defeat heavily)* massacrer

slaughterhouse ['slɔːtəhaʊs] *n* abattoir *m*

Slav [slɑːv] *n* Slave *mf*

slave [sleɪv] 1 *n* esclave *mf*; *Fam* Fig **s. driver** négrier *m*; **s. labour** travail *m* de forçat; **s. trade** commerce *m* des esclaves

2 *vi* trimer (**over** sur); **I've been slaving over a hot stove all day** j'ai passé ma journée aux fourneaux

slaver ['slævə(r)] *vi* baver

slavery ['sleɪvərɪ] *n* esclavage *m*

Slavic ['slɑːvɪk] *adj* slave

slavish ['sleɪvɪʃ] *adj* servile

Slavonic [slə'vɒnɪk] *adj* slave

slay [sleɪ] *(pt slew* [sluː], *pp slain* [sleɪn]) *vt Lit (kill)* tuer

sleaze [sliːz] *n Fam* (a) *(immorality)* côté *m* scabreux (b) *(in politics)* scandales *mpl*

sleazy ['sliːzɪ] *adj Fam* sordide

sledge [sledʒ], *Am* **sled** [sled] 1 *n* luge *f*, *(for transporting)* traîneau *m*

2 *vi (Am pt & pp sledded)* faire de la luge

sledgehammer ['sledʒhæmə(r)] *n* masse *f*; *Fig* **to use a s. to crack a nut** avoir recours à des moyens démesurés

sleek [sliːk] *adj (hair)* lisse et brillant(e); *(manner)* mielleux(euse)

▶**sleek down** *vt sep* **to s. down one's hair** se lisser les cheveux

sleep [sliːp] 1 *n* (a) *(rest)* sommeil *m*; **to go to s.** s'endormir; **to put sb to s.** *(anaesthetize)* endormir qn; **to put an animal to s.** *(kill)* faire piquer un animal; *Fig* **to send sb to s.** *(bore)* endormir qn; **I won't lose any s. over it** cela ne va pas m'empêcher de dormir; **to walk in one's s.** être somnambule; **to talk in one's s.** parler en dormant; **my foot has gone to s.** je ne sens plus mon pied (b) *(in eye)* **to have s. in one's eyes** avoir les yeux chassieux

2 *vi (pt & pp slept* [slept]) dormir; *Euph* **to s. with sb** coucher avec qn; **I slept through the alarm** je n'ai pas entendu le réveil; **I'll s. on it** la nuit porte conseil; **to s. rough** dormir à la dure

3 *vt* **the flat sleeps four** on peut dormir à quatre dans l'appartement; **I haven't slept a wink all night** je n'ai pas fermé l'œil de la nuit

▶**sleep around** *vi Fam* coucher à droite et à gauche

▶**sleep in** *vi* ne pas se réveiller à l'heure

▶**sleep off** *vt sep* **to s. off a hangover** cuver son vin

▶**sleep together** *vi* coucher ensemble

sleeper ['sliːpə(r)] *n* (a) *(person)* dormeur(euse) *m,f*; **to be a light/heavy s.** avoir le sommeil léger/lourd (b) *Rail (train)* train-couchettes *m*; *Br (on track)* traverse *f*

sleepily ['sliːpɪlɪ] *adv* d'un air endormi

sleeping ['sliːpɪŋ] 1 *n* **s. arrangements** couchage *m*; **s. bag** sac *m* de couchage; **s. car** *(on train)* wagon-lit *m*; **s. pill** somnifère *m*

2 *vt* endormi(e); *Prov* **let s. dogs lie** ne réveillez pas le chat qui dort; **s. partner** *(in company)* commanditaire *m*; *Br* **s. policeman** *(in road)* ralentisseur *m*

sleepless ['sli:pləs] *adj* **to have a s. night** ne pas fermer l'œil de la nuit

sleepwalk ['sli:pwɔ:k] *vi* être somnambule

sleepwalker ['sli:pwɔ:kə(r)] *n* somnambule *mf*

sleepy ['sli:pɪ] *adj* somnolent(e); **to be** *or* **feel s.** avoir sommeil

sleet [sli:t] **1** *n* neige *f* fondue
2 *vi* **it's sleeting** il tombe de la neige fondue

sleeve [sli:v] *n* **(a)** *(of shirt, jacket)* manche *f*; *Fig* **he's still got something up his s.** il n'a pas encore dit son dernier mot **(b)** *(of record)* pochette *f*

sleeveless ['sli:vlɪs] *adj* sans manches

sleigh [sleɪ] *n* traîneau *m*

sleight [slaɪt] *n* **s. of hand** tour *m* de passe-passe

slender ['slendə(r)] *adj* **(a)** *(person, figure)* svelte; *(waist)* fin(e) **(b)** *(hope)* mince; *(income)* maigre; *(majority)* faible; **of s. means** qui a peu de moyens

slept [slept] *pt & pp of* **sleep**

sleuth [slu:θ] *n Fam* limier *m*

slew [slu:] *pt of* **slay**

slice [slaɪs] **1** *n* **(a)** *(of bread, meat, cake)* tranche *f*; *(of pizza)* part *f*; *(of cheese)* lamelle *f*; *(of salami)* rondelle *f*; *Fig* **a s. of the profits** une part des bénéfices
2 *vt* **(a)** *(bread, meat, cake)* couper en tranches; *(cheese)* couper en lamelles; *(salami)* couper en rondelles; **to s. sth in two** *or* **in half** couper qch en deux **(b)** *(in sport)* slicer

▸**slice off** *vt sep* couper

▸**slice through** *vt insep* trancher

▸**slice up** *vt sep* couper en tranches

sliced bread ['slaɪst'bred] *n* pain *m* en tranches; *Fam* **it's the best thing since s.** on n'a rien fait de mieux depuis l'invention du fil à couper le beurre

slick [slɪk] **1** *adj* **(a)** *(campaign, event)* bien mené(e) **(b)** *Pej (reply, person, manner)* habile **(c)** *(surface, tyre)* lisse
2 *n* **(oil) s.** marée *f* noire

▸**slick back** *vt sep* **to s. one's hair back** se lisser les cheveux

slide [slaɪd] **1** *n* **(a)** *(fall)* *(in prices, popularity)* chute *f*; *Math* **s. rule** règle *f* à calcul **(b)** *(in playground)* toboggan *m* **(c)** *(for microscope)* lame *f*; *(photographic)* diapositive *f*; **s. projector** projecteur *m* de diapositives **(d)** *Br (for hair)* barrette *f*
2 *vt (pt & pp* **slid** [slɪd]*)* glisser; **s. the lid off** faites glisser le couvercle
3 *vi* **(a)** *(slip)* *(of person)* glisser; *(of door, hatch)* coulisser; **the door slid open** la porte coulissante s'est ouverte; *Fig* **to let things s.** laisser les choses se dégrader; **to s. down a rope** glisser le long d'une corde **(b)** *(move quietly)* se glisser

sliding ['slaɪdɪŋ] *adj* coulissant(e); **s. door** porte *f* coulissante; **s. scale** échelle *f* mobile

slight [slaɪt] **1** *adj* **(a)** *(small, unimportant)* léger(ère); **not the slightest danger/interest** pas le moindre danger/intérêt; **not in the slightest** pas du tout **(b)** *(person)* menu(e)
2 *n (affront)* affront *m*
3 *vt* blesser

slightly ['slaɪtlɪ] *adv* **(a)** *(to a small degree)* légèrement **(b)** **s. built** menu(e)

slim [slɪm] **1** *adj* *(person)* mince, svelte; *(book, chance, hope)* mince; *(majority)* faible
2 *vi (pt & pp* **slimmed***)* faire un régime

▸**slim down 1** *vt sep Fig (budget, company)* réduire
2 *vi (of person)* perdre du poids; *Fig (of company)* réduire ses effectifs

slime [slaɪm] *n (mud)* vase *f*; *(of snail, slug)* bave *f*

slimmer ['slɪmə(r)] *n* personne *f* qui fait un régime amaigrissant

slimming ['slɪmɪŋ] *n* **s. can be bad for you** les régimes amaigrissants peuvent être dangereux pour la santé; **s. diet** régime *m* amaigrissant; **s. product** produit *m* amaigrissant

slimy ['slaɪmɪ] *adj* *(frog, snail)* visqueux(euse); *(person)* mielleux(euse)

sling [slɪŋ] **1** *n* **(a)** *(for injured arm)* écharpe *f* **(b)** *(weapon)* fronde *f*
2 *vt (pt & pp* **slung** [slʌŋ]*) (throw)* lancer; **to s. sth over one's shoulder** mettre qch sur son épaule; *Fam Fig* **s. your hook!** dégage!

▸**sling out** *vt sep Fam (throw away)* balancer; *(person)* vider

slingshot ['slɪŋʃɒt] *n Am* lance-pierres *m inv*

slink [slɪŋk] *(pt & pp* **slunk** [slʌŋk]*) vi* **to s. off** *or* **away** s'éclipser

slinky ['slɪŋkɪ] *adj (dress)* long (longue) et sexy

slip [slɪp] **1** *n* **(a)** *(fall)* chute *f*; *(of land)* glissement *m*; *(in prices, standards)* chute
(b) *(error)* erreur *f*; **a s. of the pen/tongue** un lapsus
(c) **to give sb the s.** semer qn
(d) *(of paper)* bout *m* de papier; *(printed)* bordereau *m*
(e) a s. of a girl un petit bout de femme; **a s. of a lad** un gamin
(f) *Br Aut* **s. road** bretelle *f*
(g) *(garment)* combinaison *f*; *(pillow)* **s.** taie *f* d'oreiller
2 *vt (pt & pp* **slipped***)* **(a)** *(escape)* **her name has slipped my mind** son nom m'échappe; **the ship slipped its moorings** le bateau a quitté son mouillage
(b) *(put)* glisser; **to s. sth into the conversation** glisser qch dans la conversation; **to s. a coat on/off** enfiler/ quitter un manteau softreturn;
(c) **to s. a disc** se faire une hernie discale
3 *vi* **(a)** *(slide)* *(of person, foot)* glisser; *(of prices, popularity)* chuter; **to s. from sb's hands** *or* **grasp** glisser des mains de qn; *Fig* **to s. through sb's fingers** glisser entre les doigts de qn; **to let one's guard/concentration s.** relâcher sa vigilance/concentration
(b) *(move quickly)* **to s. into sth** *(bed, room, shoes)* se glisser dans qch; *(clothes)* enfiler qch; **to s. out of sth** *(clothes)* quitter qch
(c) *(make mistake)* faire une erreur; **you're slipping!** tu baisses!
(d) **to let sth s.** *(words, information)* lâcher qch

▸**slip away** *vi (leave)* s'éclipser

▸**slip by** *vi (of time, years)* passer vite

▸**slip out** *vi (escape)* s'échapper; **to s. out to the shop** faire un saut au magasin

▸**slip through** *vi (of mistake)* échapper à l'attention

▸**slip up** *vi (make mistake)* se planter

slip-on ['slɪpɒn] **1** *n Fam* **slip-ons** chaussures *fpl* sans lacets
2 *adj (shoes)* sans lacets

slipper ['slɪpə(r)] *n* pantoufle *f*

slippery ['slɪpərɪ] *adj* glissant(e); *(person)* fuyant(e); *Fig* **to be on a s. slope** être sur une pente savonneuse

slippy ['slɪpɪ] *adj* glissant(e)

slipshod ['slɪpʃɒd] *adj (work)* bâclé(e)

slipstream ['slɪpstriːm] n sillage m

slip-up ['slɪpʌp] n bourde f

slipway ['slɪpweɪ] n Naut (for repairs) cale f de construction; (for launching) cale de lancement

slit [slɪt] 1 n fente f
2 vt (pt & pp slit) fendre; to s. sth open ouvrir qch; to s. sb's throat couper la gorge à qn

slither ['slɪðə(r)] vi glisser

sliver ['slɪvə(r)] n (of ham, cheese) mince tranche f; (of wood, glass) éclat m

slob [slɒb] n Fam (untidy person) dégueulasse mf; (lazy person) flemmard(e) m,f

slobber ['slɒbə(r)] vi baver

sloe [sləʊ] n (fruit) prunelle f; s. gin alcool m de prunelles

slog [slɒɡ] Fam 1 vi (pt & pp slogged) (work hard) trimer (at sur)
2 n it was a bit of a s. ça a été dur; it's a long s. (walk) ça fait une trotte

slogan ['sləʊɡən] n slogan m

sloop [sluːp] n (ship) sloop m

slop [slɒp] 1 n (pig food) pâtée f (b) Fam (sentimentality) sensiblerie f
2 vt (pt & pp slopped) renverser
3 vi se renverser

slope [sləʊp] 1 n pente f
2 vi être en pente
▶**slope off** vi Fam se tailler

sloping ['sləʊpɪŋ] adj (roof, ground) en pente; (handwriting) penché(e); s. shoulders épaules fpl tombantes

sloppy ['slɒpɪ] adj (a) (careless) (person) sans soin; (attitude) négligé(e); (work) bâclé(e) (b) Fam (sentimental) sentimental(e)

slosh [slɒʃ] vi (of liquid) clapoter; (spill) se renverser

sloshed [slɒʃt] adj Fam (drunk) bourré(e)

slot [slɒt] 1 n (in box, machine) fente f; (in schedule, list) créneau m; s. machine (for vending) distributeur m automatique; (for gambling) machine f à sous
2 vt (pt & pp slotted) (part) insérer
▶**slot in** 1 vt sep (into schedule) caser
2 vi (of part) rentrer; (into team) s'intégrer

sloth [sləʊθ] n (a) (laziness) paresse f (b) (animal) paresseux m

slothful ['sləʊθfʊl] adj paresseux(euse)

slouch [slaʊtʃ] 1 n Fam he's no s. il n'est pas empoté
2 vi (on chair) être avachi(e); she slouched out of the room elle est sortie de la pièce en traînant les pieds; don't s.! tiens-toi droit!

slough [slʌf] vt to s. its skin (of reptile) muer

Slovak ['sləʊvæk] 1 n (a) (person) Slovaque mf (b) (language) slovaque m
2 adj slovaque

Slovakia [sləʊ'vækɪə] n la Slovaquie

Slovakian [sləʊ'vækɪən] 1 n Slovaque mf
2 adj slovaque

Slovene ['sləʊviːn] 1 n (a) (person) Slovène mf (b) (language) slovène m
2 adj slovène

Slovenia [sləʊ'viːnɪə] n la Slovénie

Slovenian [sləʊ'viːnɪən] 1 n Slovène mf
2 adj slovène

slovenly ['slʌvənlɪ] adj (untidy) négligé(e); (careless) négligent(e)

slow [sləʊ] 1 adj (not fast, stupid) lent(e); business is s. les affaires tournent au ralenti; my watch is s. ma montre a du retard; to be s. to do sth être lent à faire qch; to be s. off the mark (in race) être lent à démarrer; (to understand) être lent à la détente; Culin in a s. oven à four doux; we're making s. progress nous avançons lentement; she's a s. worker elle travaille lentement; Aut s. lane voie f lente; Cin & TV (in) s. motion (au) ralenti m; s. train (train m) omnibus m
2 adv lentement
3 vi ralentir
▶**slow down, slow up** vt sep & vi ralentir

slowcoach ['sləʊkəʊtʃ] n Br Fam lambin(e) m,f

slowly ['sləʊlɪ] adv lentement; s. but surely lentement mais sûrement

slowness ['sləʊnɪs] n lenteur f

slowpoke ['sləʊpəʊk] n Am Fam lambin(e) m,f

slow-witted ['sləʊ'wɪtɪd] adj à l'esprit lent

slow-worm ['sləʊwɜːm] n orvet m

SLR [esel'ɑː(r)] n Phot (abbr single-lens reflex) reflex m monoculaire

sludge [slʌdʒ] n vase f, boue f

slug [slʌɡ] n (a) (mollusc) limace f (b) Fam (bullet) balle f (c) Fam (of drink) goutte f
2 vt (pt & pp slugged) Fam (hit) cogner

sluggish ['slʌɡɪʃ] adj (person) paresseux(euse); (business, market) au ralenti

sluice [sluːs] 1 n (a) (channel) canal m (b) (sluicegate) écluse f
2 vt to s. sth down/out laver qch à grande eau

sluicegate ['sluːsɡeɪt] n écluse f

slum [slʌm] 1 n (district) quartier m délabré; (shantytown) bidonville m; (house) taudis m
2 vt (pt & pp slummed) to s. it s'encanailler

slumber ['slʌmbə(r)] 1 n (a) Lit sommeil m (b) Am s. party = soirée entre fillettes, où les invitées restent dormir chez leur hôte
2 vi dormir

slump [slʌmp] 1 n (in prices, sales) effondrement m; (economic depression) crise f (économique)
2 vi (of person, economy, prices) s'effondrer

slung [slʌŋ] pt & pp of **sling**

slunk [slʌŋk] pt & pp of **slink**

slur [slɜː(r)] 1 n (a) (insult) insulte f; to cast a s. on sb's reputation entacher la réputation de qn (b) (in speech) there was a s. in her voice elle avait du mal à articuler
2 vt (pt & pp slurred) mal articuler

slurp [slɜːp] vt & vi (drink) boire bruyamment; (eat) manger bruyamment

slush [slʌʃ] n (a) (snow) neige f fondue (b) Pol s. fund caisse f noire (c) Fam (sentimentality) sensiblerie f

slut [slʌt] n (promiscuous woman) salope f

sluttish ['slʌtɪʃ] adj (slovenly) négligé(e)

sly [slaɪ] 1 adj (a) (cunning) rusé(e) (b) (dishonest) sournois(e) (c) (mischievous) espiègle
2 n on the s. en douce

smack [smæk] 1 n (a) (blow) claque f; (on bottom) fessée f; (sound) claquement m; a s. in the face une gifle (b) Fam (heroin) héro f
2 adv Fam to bump s. into a tree rentrer en plein dans un arbre

3 vt (hit) donner une claque à; (on bottom) donner une fessée à; **to s. one's lips** faire claquer ses lèvres

▶**smack of** vt insep (suggest) avoir des relents de

smacker ['smækə(r)] n Fam (**a**) (kiss) grosse bise (**b**) 50 **smackers** (pounds) 50 livres; (dollars) 50 dollars

small [smɔːl] **1** adj (**a**) (not large) petit(e); **to make sth smaller** rapetisser qch; Fig **it made me feel s.** (inconsequential) je me suis senti tout petit; **the s. hours** le petit matin; Journ **s. ads** petites annonces fpl; **s. arms** armes fpl portatives; **s. business** petite entreprise f; **s. businessman** petit entrepreneur m; **s. letters** (not capitals) minuscules fpl; **s. talk** banalités fpl (**b**) (not important) peu important(e); **it's s. wonder that...** ce n'est pas très étonnant que...; **in a s. way** à sa façon; Fam **to be s. beer** (of money) être que dalle; **s. change** petite monnaie f; **s. fry** menu fretin m

2 adv (chop) menu; (write) petit; **to think s.** voir petit

3 n **s. of the back** la chute des reins (**b**) Fam **smalls** (underwear) sous-vêtements mpl

smallholder ['smɔːlhəʊldə(r)] n petit(e) exploitant(e) m,f

smallholding ['smɔːlhəʊldɪŋ] n petite exploitation f

small-minded [smɔːl'maɪndɪd] adj étroit(e) d'esprit

smallness ['smɔːlnɪs] n petitesse f

smallpox ['smɔːlpɒks] n variole f

small-scale ['smɔːlskeɪl] adj (model) réduit(e); (research, project) à petite échelle

small-time ['smɔːltaɪm] adj Fam (criminal, businessman) petit(e)

smarmy ['smɑːmɪ] adj Pej mielleux(euse)

smart [smɑːt] **1** adj (**a**) (clever, sharp) (person) futé(e); (decision, move) habile; **don't get s. with me** n'essaie pas de faire le malin avec moi; Fam **s. aleck** petit malin m; **s. bomb** bombe f intelligente; **s. card** carte f à puce (**b**) (elegant) (clothes) élégant(e); (hotel, area) chic inv; **the s. set** le beau monde; **to be a s. dresser** bien s'habiller (**c**) (quick) (pace, work) rapide; **look s. (about it)!** et que ça saute! (**d**) Fam (excellent) génial(e); (pretty) canon inv

2 vi (sting) (of wound, graze) brûler; (of eyes) piquer; Fig (of person) être piqué(e) au vif

▶**smarten up** ['smɑːtən] **1** vt sep égayer; **to s. oneself up** se faire beau

2 vi (improve) se reprendre

smarty-pants ['smɑːtɪpænts] n (pl smarty-pants) n Fam petit(e) malin(igne) m,f

smash [smæʃ] **1** n (blow) coup m; (noise) fracas m; (collision) collision f; (in tennis) smash m; **s.** (hit) (record, film) gros succès m

2 vt (**a**) **to s. sth (to pieces)** fracasser qch; **to s. sth open** défoncer qch; **to s. down a door** défoncer une porte (**b**) (ruin) néantir; **to s. a drugs ring** démanteler un réseau de trafiquants de drogue; **she smashed the world record** elle a pulvérisé le record du monde

3 vi (**a**) (strike) **to s. into sth** s'écraser contre qch (**b**) **to s. (into pieces)** éclater (en morceaux)

▶**smash up** vt sep (room, car, furniture) saccager

smash-and-grab raid [smæʃən'græbreɪd] n pillage m de vitrines

smashed [smæʃt] adj Fam (drunk) pété(e)

smasher ['smæʃə(r)] n **what a s.!** (person) il/elle est génial(e)!

smashing ['smæʃɪŋ] adj (**a**) (blow) violent(e) (**b**) Fam (excellent) génial(e); **we had a s. time!** on s'est éclatés!

smattering ['smætərɪŋ] n notions fpl

smear [smɪə(r)] **1** n (**a**) (stain) tache f; Med **s. test** frottis m (**b**) (slander) propos m diffamatoire; **s. campaign** campagne f de diffamation

2 vt (**a**) (stain) tacher; (spread) enduire, barbouiller; (smudge) (paint) salir (**b**) (slander) calomnier

smell [smel] **1** n (**a**) (sense) odorat m (**b**) (odour) odeur f; **there's a bad s.** ça sent mauvais; **to have a s. of sth** sentir qch

2 vt (pt & pp smelled or smelt [smelt]) also Fig sentir; Fig **I s. a rat** ça sent l'embrouille

3 vi sentir; (stink) sentir mauvais; **to s. of sth** sentir qch; **his breath smells** il a mauvaise haleine

smelly ['smelɪ] adj qui sent mauvais

smelt [smelt] **1** vt (ore) fondre

2 pt & pp of **smell**

smile [smaɪl] **1** n sourire m; **to give sb a s.** sourire à qn; **she was all smiles** elle était tout sourire; **to take** or **wipe the s. off sb's face** passer l'envie de sourire à qn

2 vi sourire (**at** à); **fortune smiled on them** la fortune leur sourit; **s.!** (for photograph) un petit sourire!

smiling ['smaɪlɪŋ] adj souriant(e)

smirk [smɜːk] **1** n sourire m en coin

2 vi sourire en coin

smite [smaɪt] (pt smote [sməʊt], pp smitten ['smɪtən]) vt (**a**) Lit (strike) frapper (**b**) **smitten with terror** terrorisé(e); **smitten with remorse** envahi(e) par les remords

smith [smɪθ] n forgeron m

smithereens [smɪðə'riːnz] npl **to smash/blow sth to s.** réduire qch en miettes

smithy ['smɪðɪ] (pl smithies) n forge f

smitten ['smɪtən] **1** adj (in love) très épris(e) (**with** de)

2 pp of **smite**

smock [smɒk] n blouse f

smog [smɒg] n smog m

smoke [sməʊk] **1** n fumée f; **to have a s.** fumer une cigarette; Fig **to go up in s.** partir en fumée; Prov **there's no s. without fire** il n'y a pas de fumée sans feu; **s. bomb** bombe f fumigène; **s. detector** détecteur m de fumée; also Fig **s. screen** rideau m de fumée; **s. signals** signaux mpl de fumée

2 vt (**a**) (cigarette) fumer; **to s. a pipe** fumer la pipe (**b**) (meat, fish) fumer

3 vi (**a**) (of person) fumer (**b**) (of chimney, oil) fumer

▶**smoke out** vt sep (insects) enfumer; Fig (rebels) débusquer

smoked [sməʊkt] adj fumé(e); **s. glass** verre m fumé; **s. salmon** saumon m fumé

smokeless ['sməʊklɪs] adj **s. fuel** combustible m non polluant; **s. zone** = zone où l'usage de combustible polluant n'est pas autorisé

smoker ['sməʊkə(r)] n fumeur(euse) m,f; **to be a cigarette/pipe s.** fumer des cigarettes/la pipe; **to be a heavy s.** être un grand fumeur; **s.'s cough** toux f de fumeur

smoking ['sməʊkɪŋ] n **s. can damage your health** fumer ou le tabac nuit à la santé; **no s.** (sign) défense de fumer; **s. compartment** compartiment m fumeurs; **s. jacket** veste f d'intérieur; **s. room** salle f fumeurs

smoky ['sməʊkɪ] adj (atmosphere, room) enfumé(e); (fire) qui dégage de la fumée; (surface) noirci(e) par la fumée; (taste) de fumée

smolder Am = smoulder

smooch [smuːtʃ] vi Fam se bécoter

smooth [smuːð] 1 adj **a** (not rough) lisse; (sea) calme; (sauce) homogène; (skin, wine, whisky) doux (douce); (style) coulant(e); (flight, crossing) calme; **a s. shave** un rasage de près (**b**) (person, manner) onctueux(euse); **he's a s. talker** c'est un beau parleur; **to be a s. operator** savoir y faire (**c**) (without problems) sans problèmes; **to get off to a s. start** commencer sans problèmes

2 vt (feathers, hair) lisser; (pillow, sheet, clothing) défroisser; (surface) égaliser; **to s. the way for sb** faciliter les choses à qn; **to s. the way for sth** faciliter qch

▸**smooth back** vt sep **to s. back one's hair** lisser ses cheveux en arrière

▸**smooth down** vt sep lisser

▸**smooth out** vt sep (map, sheets) défroisser; (crease) faire disparaître; Fig (difficulty) aplanir

▸**smooth over** vt sep (difficulties) aplanir; (differences) atténuer; **to s. things over** arranger les choses

smoothly [smuːðlɪ] adv sans problèmes; **to go s.** se passer sans problèmes

smoothness [smuːðnɪs] n (of skin, wine, whisky) douceur f; (of surface) aspect m lisse; (of flight, crossing) calme m; (of sauce) homogénéité f

smooth-talking [smuːðˈtɔːkɪŋ] adj mielleux(euse)

smote [sməʊt] pt of **smite**

smother [ˈsmʌðə(r)] vt **a** (person, fire, yawn) étouffer; **to s. sb with kisses** couvrir qn de baisers (**b**) (cover) **to s. sth in sth** recouvrir qch de qch

smoulder, Am **smolder** [ˈsməʊldə(r)] vi (of fire) couver; Fig **to s. with anger/passion** se consumer de colère/passion

smudge [smʌdʒ] 1 n tache f
2 vt (ink, lipstick) étaler; (drawing) maculer
3 vi (of ink, lipstick) s'étaler

smug [smʌg] adj suffisant(e)

smuggle [ˈsmʌgəl] vt (arms, drugs) faire de la contrebande de; **to s. sth in/out** faire entrer/sortir qch en contrebande; **to s. sb in/out** faire entrer/sortir qn clandestinement; **to s. sth through customs** passer qch en fraude à la douane

smuggler [ˈsmʌglə(r)] n contrebandier(ère) m,f; (of drugs) trafiquant(e) m,f

smuggling [ˈsmʌglɪŋ] n contrebande f; (of drugs) trafic m

smut [smʌt] n (**a**) (soot) tache f de suie (**b**) (obscenity) cochonneries fpl

smutty [ˈsmʌtɪ] adj (**a**) (dirty) sale, noirci(e) (**b**) (obscene) cochon(onne)

snack [snæk] 1 n casse-croûte m inv; **to have a s.** grignoter quelque chose; **s. bar** snack-bar m
2 vi **to s. on sth** grignoter qch

snag [snæg] 1 n (problem) problème m
2 vt (pt & pp snagged) (clothing) faire un accroc à

snail [sneɪl] n escargot m; **at a s.'s pace** (move) comme un escargot; (change, learn, progress) très lentement; Fam **s. mail** = terme humoristique désignant les services postaux par opposition aux messageries électroniques

snake [sneɪk] 1 n serpent m; Fig **s. in the grass** traître(esse) m,f; **snakes and ladders** ≃ jeu m de l'oie; **s. charmer** charmeur(euse) m,f de serpent
2 vi (of road, river) serpenter

snakebite [ˈsneɪkbaɪt] n (**a**) (of snake) morsure f de serpent (**b**) (drink) = boisson composée d'une mesure de bière et d'une mesure de cidre

snakeskin [ˈsneɪkskɪn] n peau f de serpent

snap [snæp] 1 n (**a**) (bite) coup m de dents (**b**) (sound) craquement m; **a s. of the fingers** un claquement de doigts (**c**) (of weather) **a cold s.** une brusque vague de froid (**d**) Fam (photograph) photo f (**e**) (card game) = jeu de cartes dont le but est de crier "snap" lorsque l'on pose sur la table une carte similaire à celle qui vient d'être posée; Fam **I'm going to Paris – s.!** je vais à Paris – tiens, moi aussi

2 adj (judgement, decision) hâtif(ive); **to call a s. election** procéder à une élection surprise

3 vt (pt & pp snapped) (**a**) (break) casser net; **to s. sth in two** casser qch en deux (**b**) **to s. one's fingers** faire claquer ses doigts (**c**) (say sharply) dire sèchement (**d**) Fam (take photograph of) prendre en photo

4 vi (**a**) (break cleanly) casser net; (break noisily) casser avec un bruit sec (**b**) (bite) **to s. (at)** essayer de mordre; **to s. shut** (of jaws, lid) se refermer avec un bruit sec (**c**) (speak abruptly) parler sèchement (at à) (**d**) (idioms) **to s. out of it** (of depression, apathy) se secouer; (of sulk) arrêter de faire la tête

▸**snap off** 1 vt sep (**a**) (break) casser net (**b**) Fam **to s. sb's head off** rembarrer qn
2 vi casser net

▸**snap up** vt sep (**a**) (seize in jaws) attraper (**b**) (buy, take quickly) rafler

snapdragon [ˈsnæpdrægən] n gueule-de-loup f

snappy [ˈsnæpɪ] adj Fam (style, prose) vif (vive); (slogan) accrocheur(euse); **to be a s. dresser** s'habiller toujours à la mode; **make it s.!** (be quick) au trot!

snapshot [ˈsnæpʃɒt] n Fam (photograph) photo f

snare [sneə(r)] 1 n collet m; Fig piège m; **s. drum** caisse f claire
2 vt prendre au collet; Fig prendre au piège

snarl [snɑːl] 1 n grognement m
2 vi grogner (at après)

▸**snarl up** vi être paralysé(e)

snarl-up [ˈsnɑːlʌp] n (of traffic) bouchon m; (in system) paralysie f

snatch [snætʃ] 1 n (of conversation) bribe f; **to sleep in snatches** avoir un sommeil fragmenté; **a s. of music** quelques notes de musique
2 vt (**a**) (grab) saisir; **to s. something to eat** avaler quelque chose à la hâte; **to s. some sleep** dormir un peu (**b**) (steal, abduct) (wallet, handbag) arracher; (person) enlever
3 vi **to s. at sth** essayer de saisir qch

▸**snatch away** vt sep arracher

snazzy [ˈsnæzɪ] adj Fam sympa inv

sneak [sniːk] 1 n (**a**) Fam (telltale) mouchard(e) m,f (**b**) **to get a s. preview of sth** voir qch en avant-première
2 vt (pt & pp sneaked, Am snuck [snʌk]) **to s. sth past sb** passer qch subrepticement devant qn; **to s. sb in/out** faire entrer/sortir qn subrepticement; **to s. a glance at sb** jeter un coup d'œil furtif à qn
3 vi (**a**) (tell tales) rapporter (**b**) (move furtively) se déplacer furtivement; **to s. past sb** passer furtivement devant qn; **to s. in/out** entrer/sortir furtivement

▸**sneak away, sneak off** vi s'esquiver

sneaker [ˈsniːkə(r)] n Am (running shoe) chaussure f de sport

sneaky ['sni:kɪ] *adj* sournois(e)

sneer [snɪə(r)] 1 *n (expression)* sourire *m* méprisant
2 *vt* "you couldn't do that," he sneered "vous n'en seriez pas capable", dit-il d'un air méprisant
3 *vi* ricaner; **to s. at sb/sth** se moquer de qn/qch

sneering ['snɪərɪŋ] 1 *n (laughter)* ricanement *m; (remarks)* sarcasmes *mpl*
2 *adj* méprisant(e)

sneeze [sni:z] 1 *n* éternuement *m*
2 *vi* éternuer; *Fam* it's not to be sneezed at il ne faut pas cracher dessus

snicker ['snɪkə(r)] *Am* 1 *n* ricanement *m*
2 *vi* ricaner

snide [snaɪd] *adj* méprisant(e)

sniff [snɪf] 1 *vt* (a) *(smell)* sentir; *(detect)* flairer (b) *(inhale) (air)* respirer; *(cocaine, glue)* sniffer
2 *vi* renifler; *(disdainfully)* avoir une moue de dédain; *Fam* it's not to be sniffed at il ne faut pas cracher dessus
3 *n* to take a s. at sth sentir qch; **with a s. of disgust** avec une moue de dégoût

▸**sniff out** *vt sep (of dog)* découvrir à l'odeur; *Fig (of investigator)* découvrir

sniffer dog ['snɪfədɒg] *n* chien *m* renifleur

sniffle ['snɪfəl] 1 *n (slight cold)* petit rhume *m;* **to have the sniffles** avoir un petit rhume
2 *vi* (a) *(sniff repeatedly)* renifler (b) *(cry quietly)* pleurer *(doucement)*

sniffy ['snɪfɪ] *adj Fam (disdainful)* dédaigneux(euse); **to be s. about sth** éprouver du dédain pour qch

snifter ['snɪftə(r)] *n Fam Old-fashioned (drink)* petit verre *m*

snigger ['snɪgə(r)] 1 *n* ricanement *m* étouffé
2 *vi* ricaner

snip [snɪp] 1 *n* (a) *(cut)* petite entaille *f* (b) *(piece cut off)* bout *m* (c) *Br Fam (bargain)* (bonne) affaire *f*
2 *vt (pt & pp snipped)* couper

▸**snip off** *vt sep* couper

snipe¹ [snaɪp] *n (pl snipe) (bird)* bécassine *f*

snipe² *vi (shoot)* tirer (d'une position cachée); **to s. at sb** tirer sur qn (d'une position cachée); *Fig (criticize)* critiquer qn de façon malveillante

sniper ['snaɪpə(r)] *n* tireur(euse) *m,f* embusqué(e)

snippet ['snɪpɪt] *n (of information, conversation)* bribe *f;* **a s. of news** une nouvelle brève

snitch [snɪtʃ] *Fam* 1 *n* (a) *(informer)* mouchard(e) *m,f* (b) *(nose)* pif *m*
2 *vi* moucharder; **to s. on sb** moucharder qn

snivel ['snɪvəl] *(pt & pp snivelled, Am sniveled) vi* pleurnicher

snivelling, *Am* **sniveling** ['snɪvəlɪŋ] *adj* pleurnicheur(euse)

snob [snɒb] *n* snob *mf*

snobbery ['snɒbərɪ] *n* snobisme *m*

snobbish ['snɒbɪʃ] *adj* snob *inv*

snog [snɒg] *Br Fam* 1 *n* **to have a s.** se bécoter
2 *vi (pt & pp snogged)* se bécoter

snooker ['snu:kə(r)] 1 *n (game)* = billard qui se joue avec vingt-deux billes
2 *vt* **to s.** *(in game)* laisser qn dans une position difficile; *Fig* mettre qn dans l'embarras

snoop [snu:p] *Fam* 1 *n* (a) *(person)* fouineur(euse) *m,f* (b) *(look)* **to have a s. (around)** jeter un coup d'œil
2 *vi* fouiner, fureter

snooper ['snu:pə(r)] *n Fam* fouineur(euse) *m,f*

snooty ['snu:tɪ] *adj Fam* prétentieux(euse)

snooze [snu:z] *Fam* 1 *n* petit somme *m;* **to have a s.** faire un petit somme
2 *vi* faire un petit somme

snore [snɔ:(r)] 1 *n* ronflement *m*
2 *vi* ronfler

snoring ['snɔ:rɪŋ] *n* ronflements *mpl*

snorkel ['snɔ:kəl] 1 *n* tuba *m*
2 *vi (pt & pp snorkelled, Am snorkeled)* nager sous l'eau avec un tuba

snort [snɔ:t] 1 *n (of person)* grognement *m; (of horse)* ébrouement *m*
2 *vt Fam (drugs)* sniffer
3 *vi (of person)* grogner; *(of horse)* s'ébrouer

snot [snɒt] *n Fam* morve *f*

snotty ['snɒtɪ] *adj Fam* (a) *(nose)* qui coule (b) *(arrogant)* arrogant(e)

snout [snaʊt] *n (of pig)* groin *m; (of other animal)* museau *m; Fam (of person)* pif *m*

snow [snəʊ] 1 *n* neige *f;* **s. blindness** cécité *f* des neiges; **s. line** limite *f* des neiges éternelles
2 *vi* neiger; **it's snowing** il neige

▸**snow in** *vt sep* **to be snowed in** être bloqué(e) par la neige

▸**snow under** *vt sep* **to be snowed under (with)** *(work)* être débordé(e) (de); *(invitations, offers)* être submergé(e) (de)

snowball ['snəʊbɔ:l] 1 *n* boule *f* de neige; **s. fight** bataille *f* de boules de neige; *Fam* she hasn't a s.'s chance (in hell) elle n'a pas la moindre chance
2 *vi Fig* faire boule de neige

snowboarding ['snəʊbɔ:dɪŋ] *n* snowboard *m;* **to go s.** faire du snowboard

snowbound ['snəʊbaʊnd] *adj* bloqué(e) par la neige

snowcapped ['snəʊkæpt] *adj* couronné(e) de neige

snowdrift ['snəʊdrɪft] *n* congère *f*

snowdrop ['snəʊdrɒp] *n (flower)* perce-neige *m ou f inv*

snowfall ['snəʊfɔ:l] *n* chute *f* de neige

snowflake ['snəʊfleɪk] *n* flocon *m* de neige

snowman ['snəʊmæn] *n* bonhomme *m* de neige

snowmobile ['snəʊməʊbi:l] *n (enclosed)* autoneige *f; (open)* motoneige *f*

snowplough, *Am* **snowplow** ['snəʊplaʊ] *n* chasse-neige *m inv*

snowshoe ['snəʊʃu:] *n* raquette *f*

snowstorm ['snəʊstɔ:m] *n* tempête *f* de neige

snowsuit ['snəʊsu:t] *n* combinaison *f* de ski *(pour enfants)*

Snow White ['snəʊ'waɪt] *n* **S. and the Seven Dwarfs** Blanche-Neige et les sept nains

snowy ['snəʊɪ] *adj (landscape, field)* enneigé(e); *(weather)* neigeux(euse); *(day)* de neige

SNP [esen'pi:] *n Br Pol (abbr* **Scottish National Party**) = parti politique écossais indépendantiste

Snr *(abbr* **Senior**) **Jonathan Pye-Finch** S. Jonathan Pye-Finch père

snub [snʌb] **1** n (refusal) rebuffade f; (insult) affront m
2 vt (pt & pp **snubbed**) snober

snub nose ['snʌb'nəʊz] n nez m retroussé

snuck [snʌk] Am pt & pp of **sneak**

snuff [snʌf] **1** n tabac m à priser
2 vt (candle) moucher; Br Fam **to s. it** (die) casser sa pipe

▶**snuff out** vt sep (candle) moucher; (life, opposition) mettre fin à

snuffbox ['snʌfbɒks] n tabatière f

snuffle ['snʌfəl] **1** n (sniff) reniflement m
2 vi (sniff) renifler

snug [snʌɡ] adj (a) (place) douillet(ette); (person) bien au chaud (b) (tight-fitting) bien ajusté(e)

▶**snuggle up** ['snʌɡəl] vi **to s. up to sb** se blottir contre qn

snugly ['snʌɡlɪ] adv (comfortably) confortablement; **to fit s.** être bien ajusté(e)

so [səʊ] **1** adv (a) (to such an extent) tellement, si (that que); **I was so angry (that) I almost hit him** j'étais tellement en colère que j'ai failli le frapper; **he's not so clever as she is** il n'est pas aussi intelligent qu'elle; **it isn't so very old** il n'est pas si vieux; **I'm not so sure of that** je n'en suis pas si sûr; **so much money/many people** tant ou autant d'argent/de gens; **so difficult, so much so that...** c'était difficile, à tel point que...

(b) (for emphasis) tellement; **I was so disappointed!** j'étais tellement déçu; **we enjoyed ourselves so much!** nous nous sommes tellement amusés!

(c) (expressing agreement) **you're late – so I am!** tu es en retard – ah oui, tu as raison!; **that's Mrs Thatcher! – so it is!** c'est Madame Thatcher! – ah oui, tu as raison!

(d) (referring to statement already mentioned) **I hope so** je l'espère bien; **I think so** je crois; **I suppose so** je le suppose; **so I believe** c'est ce que je crois; **I told you so!** je vous l'avais bien dit!; **I'm not very organized – so I see!** je ne suis pas très bien organisé – c'est ce que je vois!; **so be it!** soit!

(e) (also) **so am I** moi aussi; **so do we** nous aussi; **so can they** eux aussi; **so is my brother** mon frère aussi

(f) (in this way) ainsi; **do it (like) so** fais-le comme ça; **and so on, and so forth** et ainsi de suite

2 conj (a) (because of this) donc; **she has a bad temper, so be careful** elle a un mauvais caractère, donc fais attention

(b) (introducing remark) alors; **so you're not coming?** alors, tu ne viens pas?; **so that's why!** alors, c'est pour ça!; **so (what)?** et alors?, et après?

(c) **so as to** afin de; **we hurried so as not to be late** nous nous sommes dépêchés afin de ne pas être en retard

(d) **so that** pour que + subjunctive; **she sat down so that I could see better** elle s'est assise pour que je puisse mieux voir; **we hurried so that we wouldn't be late** nous nous sommes dépêchés pour ne pas arriver en retard

soak [səʊk] **1** vt (leave in water) faire ou laisser tremper; (make very wet) tremper (**with** de)
2 vi (of food, clothes) tremper; **to leave sth to s.** faire ou laisser tremper qch

▶**soak in** vt (liquid) pénétrer

▶**soak up** vt sep (liquid) absorber; Fig **to s. up the sun** prendre un bain de soleil

soaked [səʊkt] adj trempé(e); **s. to the skin** trempé(e) jusqu'aux os

so-and-so ['səʊənsəʊ] n Fam (a) (unspecified person) untel (unetelle) m,f; **Mr S. M. Untel**; **Mrs S.** Mme Unetelle (b) (unpleasant person) peau de vache

soap [səʊp] **1** n savon m; **a bar of s.** un morceau de savon; **s.** (opera) feuilleton m populaire; **s. powder** lessive f (en poudre)
2 vt savonner

soapbox ['səʊpbɒks] n tribune f improvisée à l'extérieur

soapdish ['səʊpdɪʃ] n porte-savon m

soapflakes ['səʊpfleɪks] npl savon m en paillettes

soapsuds ['səʊpsʌdz] npl mousse f de savon

soapy ['səʊpɪ] adj (water) savonneux(euse); (body) couvert(e) de savon; (taste, smell) de savon

soar [sɔ:(r)] vi (of bird, plane) & Fig (of prices) monter en flèche; Fig (of building) se dresser

soaring ['sɔ:rɪŋ] adj Fig (prices) en forte hausse; (building) élancé(e)

sob [sɒb] **1** n sanglot m; Fam **s. story** histoire f larmoyante
2 vi (pt & pp **sobbed**) sangloter

s.o.b. [esəʊ'bi:] n Am very Fam (abbr **son of a bitch**) salaud m

sobbing ['sɒbɪŋ] n sanglots mpl

sober ['səʊbə(r)] adj (a) (not drunk) qui n'a pas bu (b) (sensible) sobre

▶**sober up** vt sep & vi dessoûler

sobering ['səʊbərɪŋ] adj (news, thought) qui donne à réfléchir

sobriety [səʊ'braɪətɪ] n sobriété f

Soc n (abbr **society**) club m, société f

so-called [səʊ'kɔ:ld] adj soi-disant inv; **s. digital multiplexes** ce que l'on appelle des bouquets numériques

soccer ['sɒkə(r)] n football m; **s. match** match m de football

sociable ['səʊʃəbəl] adj sociable

social ['səʊʃəl] **1** adj social(e); **s. class** classe f sociale; **s. climber** arriviste mf; Pol **s. democrat** social(e)-démocrate m,f; **s. intercourse** relations fpl avec les gens; **s. life** vie f sociale; **s. outcast** paria m; **s. sciences** sciences fpl humaines; **s. security** prestations fpl sociales; **the s. services** les services mpl sociaux; **s. work** assistance f sociale; **s. worker** assistant(e) social(e),m,f
2 n (party) fête f

socialism ['səʊʃəlɪzəm] n socialisme m

socialist ['səʊʃəlɪst] n & adj socialiste mf

socialite ['səʊʃəlaɪt] n mondain(e) m,f

socialize ['səʊʃəlaɪz] vi fréquenter des gens; **to s. with sb** fréquenter qn

socially ['səʊʃəlɪ] adv socialement; **to see sb s.** fréquenter qn

society [sə'saɪətɪ] (pl **societies**) n (a) (community) société f; (high) **s.** haute société, (beau) monde m (b) (club) club m, société f

socioeconomic [səʊsɪəʊɪkə'nɒmɪk] adj socioéconomique

sociological [səʊsɪə'lɒdʒɪkəl] adj sociologique

sociologist [səʊsɪ'ɒlədʒɪst] n sociologue mf

sociology [səʊsɪ'ɒlədʒɪ] n sociologie f

sock [sɒk] **1** *n* (a) *(garment)* chaussette *f*; Br Fam Fig to **pull one's socks up** se secouer (b) *Fam (blow)* coup *m* de poing

2 *vt Fam (hit)* donner un coup de poing à; Fig to **s. it to sb** montrer à qn de quoi on est capable

socket [ˈsɒkɪt] *n (of eye)* orbite *f*; *(for plug)* prise *f* de courant

sod[1] [sɒd] *n (of earth)* motte *f*

sod[2] **1** *n very Fam (man)* salaud *m*; *(woman)* salope *f*; **poor s.!** pauvre bougre!; **s. all** que dalle; **S.'s law** la loi de l'emmerdement maximum

2 *vt Vulg* **s. it!** merde!; **s. you!** va te faire voir!; **s. the party, I'm tired** tant pis pour la soirée, je suis fatigué

▶**sod off** *(pt & pp sodded)* *vi Br Vulg (go away)* aller se faire voir

soda [ˈsəʊdə] *n* (a) **s. (water)** eau *f* de Seltz; **s. fountain** cafétéria *f* (b) *Am (fizzy drink)* boisson *f* gazeuse (c) *Chem* soude *f*

sodden [ˈsɒdən] *adj* trempé(e)

sodium [ˈsəʊdɪəm] *n Chem* sodium *m*; **s. bicarbonate** bicarbonate *m* de soude; **s. chloride** chlorure *m* de sodium

sodomize [ˈsɒdəmaɪz] *vt* sodomiser

sodomy [ˈsɒdəmɪ] *n* sodomie *f*

sofa [ˈsəʊfə] *n* canapé *m*; **s. bed** canapé-lit *m*

Sofia [ˈsəʊfɪə] *n* Sofia

soft [sɒft] *adj* (a) *(in texture)* mou (molle); *(ground)* meuble; *(pillow, carpet)* moelleux(euse); *(fabric, skin)* doux (douce); **s. cheese** fromage *m* frais; Comptr **s. copy** visualisation *f* sur écran; **s. furnishings** tissus *mpl* d'ameublement; Comptr **s. return** retour *m* de chariot conditionnel, changement *m* de ligne facultatif; Anat **s. tissue** parties *fpl* charnues; **s. toy** peluche *f*

(b) *(voice)* doux (douce); *(rain)* léger(ère); *(colour)* doux, tendre; **s. currency** devise *f* faible; **s. drinks** boissons *fpl* non alcoolisées; **s. drugs** drogues *fpl* douces; Phot **in s. focus** dans le flou artistique; Fin **s. loan** prêt *m* offrant des conditions avantageuses; Com **s. sell** méthode *f* de vente non agressive

(c) *(not strict)* indulgent(e), faible; **to have a s. spot for sb** avoir un faible pour qn; **to have a s. heart** avoir le cœur tendre

(d) *Fam (stupid)* idiot(e)

(e) *(easy) (job, life)* facile; Fam **to be a s. touch** être bonne pâte; **s. option** solution *f* de facilité

softback [ˈsɒftbæk] *n* livre *m* broché

softball [ˈsɒftbɔːl] *n Am* = sorte de base-ball joué sur un plus petit terrain avec une balle moins dure

soft-boiled [ˈsɒftbɔɪld] *adj (egg)* à la coque

soften [ˈsɒfən] **1** *vt (wax, butter)* ramollir; *(leather, fabric)* assouplir; *(skin, light)* adoucir; Fig to **s. the blow** amortir le choc

2 *vi (of wax, butter)* ramollir; Fig *(of person)* se radoucir; *(of opinions, resolve, stance)* devenir plus modéré(e)

▶**soften up** *vt sep Fam (before attack)* affaiblir; *(before request)* amadouer

softener [ˈsɒfənə(r)] *n* adoucissant *m*

softhearted [sɒftˈhɑːtɪd] *adj* qui se laisse facilement attendrir

softie [ˈsɒftɪ] *n Fam* = **softy**

softly [ˈsɒftlɪ] *adv (quietly, gently)* doucement; **to be s. lit** être légèrement éclairé(e)

softly-softly [ˈsɒftlɪˈsɒftlɪ] *adj Fam (approach, attitude)* en douceur

softness [ˈsɒftnɪs] *n (of ground)* consistance *f* meuble; *(of fabric, skin, voice)* douceur *f*

soft-pedal [sɒftˈpedəl] *(pt & pp soft-pedalled, Am soft-pedaled)* *vi also Fig* mettre la pédale douce

soft-soap [sɒftˈsəʊp] *vt Fam* amadouer

soft-spoken [sɒftˈspəʊkən] *adj* qui a une voix douce

software [ˈsɒftweə(r)] *n Comptr* logiciel *m*; **s. package** progiciel *m*

softy [ˈsɒftɪ] *(pl softies)* *n Fam (gentle person)* bonne pâte *f*; *(coward)* troussard(e) *m,f*

soggy [ˈsɒgɪ] *adj* trempé(e)

soh [səʊ] *n Mus* sol *m*

soil [sɔɪl] **1** *n (earth)* terre *f*; **on British s.** sur le sol britannique

2 *vt (clothes, sheet)* salir; Fig to **s. one's hands** se salir les mains

solace [ˈsɒləs] *n Lit* réconfort *m*

solar [ˈsəʊlə(r)] *adj* solaire; **s. eclipse** éclipse *f* solaire; **s. plexus** plexus *m* solaire; **s. system** système *m* solaire

sold [səʊld] *pt & pp of* **sell**

solder [ˈsəʊldə(r)] **1** *n* soudure *f*

2 *vt* souder

soldering iron [ˈsəʊldərɪŋˈaɪən] *n* fer *m* à souder

soldier [ˈsəʊldʒə(r)] **1** *n* soldat *m*

2 *vi* être soldat

▶**soldier on** *vi* persévérer

sole[1] [səʊl] **1** *n (of foot)* plante *f*; *(of shoe)* semelle *f*

2 *vt (shoe)* ressemeler

sole[2] *n (fish)* sole *f*

sole[3] *adj (only)* unique; Com **s. agent** agent *m* exclusif

solely [ˈsəʊllɪ] *adv* uniquement

solemn [ˈsɒləm] *adj* solennel(elle)

solemnity [səˈlemnɪtɪ] *n* solennité *f*

sol-fa [sɒlˈfɑː] *n Mus* solfège *m*

solicit [səˈlɪsɪt] **1** *vt (request)* solliciter, demander

2 *vi (of prostitute)* racoler

solicitor [səˈlɪsɪtə(r)] *n Br (for property, wills)* notaire *m*; *(in court cases)* avocat(e) *m,f*; **S. General** conseiller *m* juridique de la Couronne

solicitous [səˈlɪsɪtəs] *adj Formal* empressé(e); *(caring)* plein(e) de sollicitude; *(concerned)* soucieux(euse) **(for de)**

solid [ˈsɒlɪd] **1** *n* solide *m*; **solids** *(food)* aliments *mpl* solides

2 *adj* (a) *(not liquid)* solide; **s. food** aliments *mpl* solides; **s. fuel** combustible *m* solide (b) *(not hollow)* plein(e); *(gold, silver)* massif(ive); **made of s. brick** construit(e) entièrement en brique (c) *(worker)* sérieux(euse)

3 *adv* **ten hours s.** dix heures d'affilée

solidarity [sɒlɪˈdærɪtɪ] *n* solidarité *f*

solidify [səˈlɪdɪfaɪ] *(pt & pp solidified)* *vi* se solidifier

solidity [səˈlɪdɪtɪ] *n* solidité *f*

solidly [ˈsɒlɪdlɪ] *adv (firmly)* solidement; *(without interruption)* sans arrêt

solid-state [sɒlɪdˈsteɪt] *adj Elec* transistorisé(e)

soliloquy [səˈlɪləkwɪ] *(pl soliloquies)* *n* soliloque *m*

solitaire [sɒlɪˈteə(r)] *n (card game)* réussite *f*; *(board game, jewellery)* solitaire *m*

solitary ['sɒlɪtərɪ] *adj* (a) *(single)* seul(e) (b) *(alone)* solitaire; **s. confinement** isolement *m* cellulaire

solitude ['sɒlɪtjuːd] *n* solitude *f*

solo ['səʊləʊ] **1** *n* *(pl* **solos**) *(musical)* solo *m*
2 *adj (flight, crossing)* en solitaire; *(performance)* solo
3 *adv* en solitaire; **to go s.** *(of musician)* faire une carrière solo; *(of business partner)* s'établir à son compte

soloist ['səʊləʊɪst] *n* soliste *mf*

Solomon Islands ['sɒləmən'aɪləndz] *npl* **the S.** les îles *fpl* Salomon

solstice ['sɒlstɪs] *n* solstice *m*

soluble ['sɒljʊbəl] *adj* soluble

solution [sə'luːʃən] *n* solution *f*

solve [sɒlv] *vt* résoudre

solvency ['sɒlvənsɪ] *n* solvabilité *f*

solvent ['sɒlvənt] **1** *n* solvant *m*, dissolvant *m*; **s. abuse** = utilisation de solvants comme stupéfiants
2 *adj (financially)* solvable

Somali [sə'mɑːlɪ] **1** *n* (a) *(person)* Somalien(enne) *m,f* (b) *(language)* somali *m*
2 *adj* somalien(enne)

Somalia [sə'mɑːlɪə] *n* la Somalie

sombre, *Am* **somber** ['sɒmbə(r)] *adj* sombre

some [sʌm] **1** *pron* (a) *(certain quantity or number)* **there is/are s.** over there il y en a là-bas; *(a few)* il y en a quelques-uns là-bas; **give me s. (of them)** donne-m'en; *(a few)* donne-m'en quelques-uns; **do you want s.?** en veux-tu?; *(a few)* en veux-tu quelques-uns?; **s. of my wine** un peu de mon vin; **s. of my sweets** quelques-uns de mes bonbons; **s. of the time** une partie du temps
(b) *(as opposed to others)* certains *mpl*, certaines *fpl*; **s. say...** certains disent que..., il y en a qui disent que...; **s. of the guests** certains invités; **they went off, s. one way, s. another** ils sont partis, certains par là, d'autres par là-bas
2 *adj* (a) *(certain quantity or number of)* **s. wine** du vin; **s. ice cream** de la glace; **s. water** de l'eau; **s. books** des livres; *(a few)* quelques livres; **in s. ways** par certains côtés; **to s. extent** jusqu'à un certain point
(b) *(as opposed to other)* certain(e); **s. people say...** certains disent que..., il y a des gens qui disent que...
(c) *(considerable quantity or number of)* **I've been waiting for s. time/hours** ça fait un moment/plusieurs heures que j'attends; **s. distance away** assez loin; **s. miles away** à plusieurs kilomètres
(d) *(unspecified)* **for s. reason or other** pour une raison ou pour une autre; **she'll come s. day** elle viendra un jour (ou l'autre); **at s. time in the future** plus tard; **in s. book or other** dans un livre quelconque; **s. fool left the door open** un imbécile a laissé la porte ouverte
(e) *Fam (for emphasis)* **that was s. storm/meal!** quel orage/repas!; *Ironic* **s. hope!** je peux/il peut/*etc* toujours y compter!; *Ironic* **s. friend you are!** quel ami tu fais!
3 *adv (approximately)* environ; **s. fifteen minutes** environ quinze minutes

somebody ['sʌmbɒdɪ] **1** *pron* quelqu'un; **she's s. you can trust** c'est quelqu'un en qui vous pouvez avoir confiance; **s.'s coming** on vient; **s. important/taller** quelqu'un d'important/de plus grand; **s. else** quelqu'un d'autre
2 *n* **she thinks she's s.** elle se croit importante; **I want to be s.** je veux devenir quelqu'un

somehow ['sʌmhaʊ] *adv* (a) *(in some way or other)* d'une façon ou d'une autre (b) *(for some reason or other)* pour une raison ou pour une autre

someone ['sʌmwʌn] *pron* = **somebody**

somersault ['sʌməsɔːlt] **1** *n* *(on the ground)* roulade *f*; *(in the air)* saut *m* périlleux
2 *vi* *(of person)* *(on the ground)* faire une roulade; *(in the air)* faire un saut périlleux; *(of car)* faire un tonneau

something ['sʌmθɪŋ] **1** *pron* quelque chose; **there's s. about him I don't like** il y a quelque chose chez lui que je n'aime pas; **s. tells me she'll be there** quelque chose me dit qu'elle sera là; **s. to drink/to eat/to read** quelque chose à boire/à manger/à lire; **s. red/different/special** quelque chose de rouge/de différent/de spécial; **he's s. in publishing** il a un poste important dans l'édition; **in nineteen-fifty s.** dans les années cinquante; **she's eighty s.** elle a quatre-vingts ans et quelques; **what's his name? – Simon s.** comment s'appelle-t-il? – Simon quelque chose; **at least he apologized, that's s.!** au moins, il s'est excusé, c'est déjà ça!; **there's s. in what you say** il y a quelque chose d'intéressant dans ce que vous dites; **she has s. to do with what happened** elle a quelque chose à voir avec ce qui s'est passé; **that was quite s.!** ce n'était pas mal du tout!; **he's a mechanic or s.** il est mécanicien ou un truc comme ça; **she's got a cold or s.** *(like that)* elle a un rhume, je crois
2 *adv* (a) *(expressing degree)* **there's been s. of an improvement** il y a eu une certaine amélioration; **she's s. of a miser** elle est plutôt avare; **it's s. like a guinea pig** ça ressemble à un cobaye (b) *(for emphasis)* **it hurt s. awful!** ça faisait mal, quelque chose de bien!
3 *n* **a little s.** un petit quelque chose

sometime ['sʌmtaɪm] *adv* **see you s.** à un de ces jours; **s. last week** la semaine dernière; **s. before Christmas** avant Noël; **you'll have to make up your mind s.** il faudra bien que tu te décides un jour; **s. soon** d'ici peu, bientôt; **s. or other** un jour ou l'autre

sometimes ['sʌmtaɪmz] *adv* quelquefois

somewhat ['sʌmwɒt] *adv* quelque peu, un peu

somewhere ['sʌmweə(r)] *adv* (a) *(some place)* quelque part; **s. else** ailleurs; **do you have s. to stay?** est-ce que tu as trouvé à te loger?; *Fig* **now we're getting s.!** nous voilà enfin sur la bonne route ou voie! (b) *(approximately)* environ; **she's s. around fifty** elle a environ cinquante ans; **it costs s. in the region of £500** cela coûte environ 500 livres

somnolent ['sɒmnələnt] *adj Formal* somnolent(e)

son [sʌn] *n* fils *m*; *Am very Fam* **s. of a bitch** salaud *m*

sonar ['səʊnɑː(r)] *n* sonar *m*

sonata [sə'nɑːtə] *n* sonate *f*

song [sɒŋ] *n* (a) chanson *f*; **to burst** *or* **break into s.** se mettre à chanter; **s. book** livre *m* de chansons (b) *(idioms)* **to buy sth for a s.** acheter qch pour une bouchée de pain; **to make a s. and dance (about sth)** faire toute une histoire (de qch)

songbird ['sɒŋbɜːd] *n* oiseau *m* chanteur

songwriter ['sɒŋraɪtə(r)] *n* auteur-compositeur *m*

sonic ['sɒnɪk] *adj* sonique; **s. boom** bang *m*

son-in-law ['sʌnɪnlɔː] *n* *(pl* **sons-in-law**) *n* gendre *m*

sonnet ['sɒnɪt] *n* sonnet *m*

sonny ['sʌnɪ] *n Fam* fiston *m*

sonorous ['sɒnərəs] *adj (deep)* sonore; *(impressive)* imposant(e)

soon [su:n] *adv* (a) *(within a short time)* bientôt; *(in past)* vite; **it will s. be Friday** c'est bientôt vendredi; **she s. changed her mind** elle a vite changé d'avis; **s. after(wards)** peu après; **s. after four** peu après quatre heures; **no sooner had she left than...** elle n'était pas plus tôt partie que... (b) *(early)* tôt; **none too s.** pas trop tôt; **how s. can you get here?** quand pouvez-vous être ici au plus tôt?; **sooner or later** tôt ou tard; **the sooner the better** le plus tôt sera le mieux; **as s. as** aussitôt que, dès que; **as s. as possible** aussitôt que possible, dès que possible (c) *(expressing preference)* **I would just as s. stay** j'aimerais autant rester; **I would sooner do it alone** je préférerais le faire seul

soot [sʊt] *n* suie *f*

soothe [su:ð] *vt* apaiser

soothing ['su:ðɪŋ] *adj* apaisant(e)

soothsayer [su:θseɪə(r)] *n* devin *(devineresse)* *m,f*

sooty ['sʊtɪ] *adj (covered in soot)* couvert(e) de suie; *(black)* noir(e) comme de la suie

sop [sɒp] *n (concession)* concession *f* (**to** à)

sophist ['sɒfɪst] *n* sophiste *mf*

sophisticated [sə'fɪstɪkeɪtɪd] *adj (person, taste)* raffiné(e); *(style, humour)* recherché(e); *(machinery, technique)* sophistiqué(e)

sophistication [səfɪstɪ'keɪʃən] *n (of person, taste)* raffinement *m*; *(of style, humour)* recherche *f*; *(of machinery, technique)* sophistication *f*

sophistry ['sɒfɪstrɪ] *n (reasoning)* sophistique *f*; *(argument)* sophisme *m*

sophomore ['sɒfəmɔ:(r)] *n Am* étudiant(e) *m,f* de deuxième année

soporific [sɒpə'rɪfɪk] *adj Formal* soporifique

sopping ['sɒpɪŋ] *adj* **s. (wet)** trempé(e)

soppy ['sɒpɪ] *adj Fam* sentimental(e)

soprano [sə'prɑ:nəʊ] *(pl* **sopranos** *or* **soprani** [sə'prɑ:ni:]*)* *n (singer)* soprano *mf*; **s. voice** voix *f* de soprano

sorbet ['sɔ:beɪ] *n* sorbet *m*

sorcerer ['sɔ:sərə(r)] *n* sorcier *m*

sorceress ['sɔ:sərɪs] *n* sorcière *f*

sorcery ['sɔ:sərɪ] *n* sorcellerie *f*

sordid ['sɔ:dɪd] *adj* sordide

sore [sɔ:(r)] **1** *adj* (a) *(painful)* douloureux(euse); **to have a s. throat/back** avoir mal à la gorge/au dos; **my feet are s.** mes pieds me font mal (b) *Fam (annoyed)* en colère (**about** à propos de); **it's a s. point (with him)** c'est un sujet douloureux (pour lui)
2 *n (wound)* plaie *f*

sorely ['sɔ:lɪ] *adv (greatly)* sérieusement; **she will be s. missed** elle nous/leur manquera beaucoup; **to be s. in need of sth** avoir vraiment besoin de qch; **s. tempted** sérieusement tenté(e)

sorrow ['sɒrəʊ] *n* chagrin *m*; **to my great s.** à mon grand regret

sorrowful ['sɒrəfʊl] *adj* triste

sorry ['sɒrɪ] *adj* (a) *(regretful, disappointed)* désolé(e); **to be s. about sth** être désolé de qch; **to be s. one did sth** regretter d'avoir fait qch; **to say s. (to sb)** s'excuser (auprès de qn); **I'm s. you didn't like it** je suis désolé que tu n'aies pas aimé; **to keep you waiting** je suis désolé de vous faire attendre; **I'm s. to hear (that)...** je suis désolé d'apprendre que...; *Fam* **you'll be s.!** tu vas le

regretter!; **s.?** *(pardon?)* pardon?
(b) *(sympathetic)* **to feel s. for sb** plaindre qn; **to feel s. for oneself** s'apitoyer sur son propre sort; **I'm just feeling a bit s. for myself** je suis juste un peu déprimé
(c) *(pathetic)* triste; **to be a s. sight** être dans un triste état; **to be in a s. state** être dans un triste état

sort [sɔ:t] **1** *n* (a) *(kind)* sorte *f*; **all sorts of** toutes sortes de; **what s. of tree is it?** qu'est-ce que c'est comme arbre?; **that s. of thing** ce genre de chose; **she's that s. of person** elle est comme ça; **something of the s.** quelque chose de ce genre; **I did nothing of the s.** je n'ai jamais fait ça; **he's so arrogant – he's nothing of the s.!** il est vraiment arrogant – pas du tout!; **it takes all sorts** il faut de tout pour faire un monde; *Fam* **she's a good s.** c'est une brave fille; **she's not the s. to give in easily** elle n'est pas du genre à abandonner facilement; **we don't want your s. here** nous ne voulons pas de personnes de votre genre ici; **to be out of sorts** *(unwell)* être mal fichu(e); *(in a bad mood)* être de mauvaise humeur; **coffee of a s.** une espèce de café; **an artist of sorts** espèce d'artiste
(b) *Fam* **this is s. of embarrassing** c'est plutôt gênant; **I s. of expected it** je m'y attendais un peu; **do you like it?** – **s. of** ça te plaît? – oui, plus ou moins
(c) *(in order to organize)* **to have a s. through sth** faire du tri dans qch
2 *vt also Comptr* trier

▸**sort out** *vt sep* (a) *(organize)* ranger; **to s. oneself out** se reprendre (b) *(problem)* régler; *Fam* **to s. sb out** régler son compte à qn

sortie ['sɔ:ti:] *n Mil* sortie *f*; *Fig* escapade *f*

sorting ['sɔ:tɪŋ] *n* **s. office** bureau *m* de tri

SOS [esəʊ'es] *n* S.O.S. *m*; **to send out an S.** lancer un S.O.S.

soufflé ['su:fleɪ] *n* soufflé *m*; **cheese s.** soufflé au fromage

sought [sɔ:t] *pt & pp of* **seek**

sought-after ['sɔ:tɑ:ftə(r)] *adj* recherché(e)

soul [səʊl] *n* (a) *(spirit)* âme *f*; **to sell one's s.** vendre son âme au diable; *Fig* **she's the s. of discretion** c'est la discrétion même; *Fig* **it lacks s.** cela n'a pas d'âme; **All Souls' Day** le jour des Morts (b) *(person)* personne *f*; **he's a good s.** c'est une bonne personne; **there wasn't a s. in the street** il n'y avait pas âme qui vive dans la rue; **poor s.!** le/la pauvre! (c) *(music)* soul *f*

soul-destroying ['səʊldɪstrɔɪɪŋ] *adj* démoralisant(e)

soulful ['səʊlfʊl] *adj* émouvant(e)

soulless ['səʊllɪs] *adj (person)* insensible; *(place)* sans âme

soulmate ['səʊlmeɪt] *n* âme f sœur

soul-searching ['səʊlsɑ:tʃɪŋ] *n* examen *m* de conscience

sound[1] [saʊnd] **1** *n* son *m*; *(noise)* bruit *m*; **not a s. could be heard** on n'entendait pas un bruit; **she likes the s. of his own voice** elle aime s'écouter parler; **to turn the s. up/down** *(on TV, radio)* monter/baisser le son; *Fig* **I don't like the s. of it** cela ne me dit rien qui vaille; **she's angry, by the s. of it** elle est en colère, on dirait; **s. barrier** mur *m* du son; **s. bite** petite phrase *f*; **s. effects** bruitage *m*; **s. engineer** ingénieur *m* du son; **s. wave** onde *f* sonore
2 *vi* (a) *(bell)* sonner; *also Fig (alarm)* donner; **to s. one's horn** klaxonner (b) *(pronounce)* prononcer; **the "h" is not sounded** le "h" ne se prononce pas
3 *vi* (a) *(make sound)* (of trumpet, bell) sonner (b) *(seem)*

avoir l'air, sembler; **she sounds French** on dirait qu'elle est française; **that sounds like a good idea** ça me semble une bonne idée; **he sounds like a nice guy** ça a l'air d'être un type bien; **it sounds like Mozart** on dirait du Mozart; **that sounds like trouble!** c'est signe de problèmes!; **how does that s. to you?** *(referring to suggestion)* qu'en pensez-vous?

▸**sound off** *vi Fam* se plaindre **(about** de)

▸**sound out** *vt sep* sonder **(about** à propos de)

sound² **1** *adj* **(a)** *(healthy)* sain(e); *(in good condition)* en bon état; **to be of s. mind** être sain d'esprit **(b)** *(sensible, logical)* *(argument)* valable; *(basis)* solide; *(advice)* bon (bonne) **(c)** *(reliable)* *(investment)* sûr(e); *(business)* sain(e); *(person)* compétent(e)

2 *adv* **to be s. asleep** être profondément endormi(e)

sounding board ['saʊndɪŋbɔːd] *n* (*on pulpit, stage*) abat-voix *m*; *Fig* **I use John as a s.** j'utilise John pour tester mes idées

soundings ['saʊndɪŋz] *npl* **to take s.** faire des sondages

soundly ['saʊndlɪ] *adv* **(a)** *(solidly)* solidement **(b)** *(logically)* judicieusement **(c)** *(thoroughly)* **to sleep s.** dormir profondément; **to thrash sb s.** donner une bonne correction à qn

soundproof ['saʊndpruːf] **1** *adj* insonorisé(e)

2 *vt* insonoriser

soundtrack ['saʊndtræk] *n* bande *f* sonore

soup [suːp] *n* soupe *f*; *Fig* **to be in the s.** être dans le pétrin; **s. kitchen** soupe populaire; **s. ladle** louche *f*; **s. plate** assiette *f* creuse; **s. spoon** cuillère *f* à soupe

▸**soup up** *vt sep Fam* *(engine)* gonfler; *(car)* gonfler le moteur de

sour ['saʊə(r)] **1** *adj* *(fruit, milk, taste)* aigre; *Fig* *(person)* aigri(e); **to turn s.** *(of milk)* tourner; *Fig* *(of situation, relationship)* tourner à l'aigre, mal tourner; **s. cream** crème *f* aigre; *Fig* **it was just s. grapes** c'était par dépit

2 *vt* *(milk)* faire tourner; *Fig* *(atmosphere, relationship)* empoisonner

3 *vi* *(of milk)* tourner; *Fig* *(atmosphere, relationship)* détériorer

source [sɔːs] *n* source *f*; *(of unrest, discontent)* origine *f*; *(of infection)* foyer *m*

sourly ['saʊəlɪ] *adv* avec aigreur

souse [saʊs] *vt* tremper

south [saʊθ] **1** *n* sud *m*; **to the s. of** au sud de

2 *adj* *(coast, side)* sud; *(wind)* du sud; **S. Africa** Afrique *f* du Sud; **S. African** sud-africain(e); *(person)* Sud-Africain(e) *m,f*; **S. America** Amérique *f* du Sud; **S. American** sud-américain(e); *(person)* Sud-Américain(e) *m,f*; **S. Carolina** la Caroline du Sud; **S. China Sea** mer *f* de Chine du Sud; **S. Dakota** le Dakota du Sud; **S. Korea** Corée *f* du Sud; **S. Korean** sud-coréen(enne); *(person)* Sud-Coréen(enne) *m,f*; **S. Pole** pôle *m* sud

3 *adv* au sud; *(travel)* vers le sud; **to face s.** *(of house)* être exposé(e) au sud

southbound ['saʊθbaʊnd] *adj* *(train, traffic)* en direction du sud; **s. carriageway** voie *f* sud

southeast [saʊθ'iːst] **1** *n* sud-est *m*

2 *adj* *(side)* sud-est; *(wind)* du sud-est

3 *adv* au sud-est; *(travel)* vers le sud-est

southeasterly [saʊθ'iːstəlɪ] **1** *n* *(wind)* vent *m* du sud-est

2 *adj* *(direction)* vers le sud-est; *(wind)* du sud-est

southeastern [saʊθ'iːstən] *adj* *(region)* (du) sud-est

southerly ['sʌðəlɪ] **1** *n* *(wind)* vent *m* du sud

2 *adj* *(direction)* vers le sud; *(wind)* du sud; **the most s. point** le point le plus au sud

southern ['sʌðən] *adj* *(region, accent)* du sud; **s. France** le sud de la France; **s. hemisphere** hémisphère *m* sud

southerner ['sʌðənə(r)] *n* habitant(e) *m,f* du Sud *(de l'Angleterre)*

south-facing ['saʊθfeɪsɪŋ] *adj* exposé(e) au sud

south-southeast ['saʊθsaʊθ'iːst] *adv* au sud-sud-est; *(travel)* vers le sud-sud-est

south-southwest ['saʊθsaʊθ'west] *adv* au sud-sud-ouest; *(travel)* vers le sud-sud-ouest

southward ['saʊθwəd] **1** *adj* au sud

2 *adv* vers le sud

southwards ['saʊθwədz] *adv* vers le sud

southwest [saʊθ'west] **1** *n* sud-ouest *m*

2 *adj* *(side)* sud-ouest; *(wind)* du sud-ouest

3 *adv* au sud-ouest; *(travel)* vers le sud-ouest

southwesterly [saʊθ'westəlɪ] **1** *n* *(wind)* vent *m* du sud-ouest

2 *adj* *(direction)* vers le sud-ouest; *(wind)* du sud-ouest

southwestern [saʊθ'westən] *adj* *(region)* (du) sud-ouest

souvenir [suːvə'nɪə(r)] *n* souvenir *m*

sovereign ['sɒvrɪn] *n & adj* souverain(e) *m,f*

sovereignty ['sɒvrəntɪ] *n* souveraineté *f*

Soviet ['saʊvɪət] **1** *n* *(person)* Soviétique *mf*

2 *adj* soviétique; *Formerly* **the S. Union** l'Union *f* soviétique

sow¹ [saʊ] *(pt* sowed [saʊd], *pp* sown [saʊn] *or* sowed*)* *vt* *(seeds)* & *Fig* *(discord, doubt)* semer; *(field)* ensemencer **(with** en)

sow² [saʊ] *n* *(female pig)* truie *f*

sown [saʊn] *pp of* **sow¹**

soya ['sɔɪə] *n* soja *m*

soy sauce [sɔɪ'sɔːs] *n* sauce *f* de soja

sozzled ['sɒzəld] *adj Fam* *(drunk)* bourré(e); **to get s.** se cuiter

spa [spɑː] *n* *(place)* ville *f* d'eau; *(spring)* source *f* thermale

space [speɪs] **1** *n* **(a)** *(room)* espace *m*; **to stare into s.** regarder dans le vide **(b)** *(individual place)* place *f*; *(on printed form)* espace *m*; **wide open spaces** grands espaces; **s. bar** *(on keyboard)* barre *f* d'espacement **(c)** *(period of time)* espace *m*; **in the s. of a year** en l'espace d'une année **(d)** *(outer space)* espace *m*; **the s. age** l'ère *f* spatiale; *Fam* **s. cadet** planer; **s. rocket** fusée *f* spatiale; **s. shuttle** navette *f* spatiale; **s. suit** combinaison *f* spatiale; **s. travel** voyages *mpl* dans l'espace **(e)** *(gap)* espace *m*, vide *m*; *(in timetable)* trou *m*

2 *vt* espacer

▸**space out** *vt sep* espacer

space-age ['speɪseɪdʒ] *adj* futuriste

spacecraft ['speɪskrɑːft] *n* vaisseau *m* spatial

spaceman ['speɪsmæn] *n* astronaute *m*

spaceship ['speɪsʃɪp] *n* vaisseau *m* spatial

spacing ['speɪsɪŋ] *n* espacement *m*; *Typ* **single/double s.** simple/double interligne *m*

spacious ['speɪʃəs] *adj* spacieux(euse)

spade [speɪd] *n* **(a)** *(tool)* bêche *f*; **to call a s. a s.** appeler un chat un chat **(b)** *(in cards)* pique *m*

spaghetti [spə'getɪ] *n* spaghetti *mpl*

Spain [speɪn] *n* l'Espagne *f*

span [spæn] **1** *n* (a) (of hand) empan *m*; (of wing) envergure *f* (b) (of arch) portée *f*; (of bridge) travée *f* (c) (period of time) période *f* (d) (of knowledge, interests) étendue *f*
2 *vt* (pt & pp **spanned**) (of bridge) franchir; *Fig* (of life, knowledge) couvrir

Spaniard ['spænjəd] *n* Espagnol(e) *m,f*

spaniel ['spænjəl] *n* épagneul *m*

Spanish ['spænɪʃ] **1** *npl* (people) **the S.** les Espagnols *mpl*
2 *n* (language) espagnol *m*
3 *adj* espagnol(e); **the S. Inquisition** l'Inquisition *f* espagnole

spank [spæŋk] **1** *n* **to give sb a s.** donner une claque sur les fesses à qn
2 *vt* donner une claque sur les fesses à

spanking ['spæŋkɪŋ] **1** *n* fessée *f*; **to give sb a s.** donner une fessée à qn
2 *adv Fam* **s. new** flambant neuf (neuve); **they had a s. good time** ils se sont rudement bien amusés

spanner ['spænə(r)] *n Br* clef *f*; *Fig* **to throw a s. in the works** compliquer les choses

spar¹ [spɑː(r)] *n* (on ship) espar *m*

spar² (pt & pp **sparred**) *vi* **to s. with sb** (in boxing) s'entraîner avec qn; (argue) se chamailler avec qn

spare ['speə(r)] **1** *n* (spare part) pièce *f* de rechange; (tyre) pneu *m* de rechange
2 *adj* (available) disponible; (surplus) en trop, qui reste; (reserve) de rechange; **do you have a s. pen?** tu as un stylo à me prêter?; **to be going s.** être en trop; **a s. moment** un moment de libre; **s. part** pièce *f* de rechange; **s. ribs** travers *mpl* de porc; **s. room** chambre *f* d'amis; **s. time** temps *m* (de) libre; **s. tyre** pneu *m* de rechange; *Br Fam Fig* (around waist) bourrelet *m*; **s. wheel** roue *f* de secours
(b) (frugal) (meal) frugal(e); (style) dépouillé(e); (room) austère
(c) *Br Fam* (angry) **to go s.** sortir de ses gonds
3 *vt* (a) (give away, go without) (person) se passer de; **to have no time to s.** ne pas avoir le temps; **can you s. the time?** avez-vous le temps?; **with five minutes to s.** avec cinq minutes d'avance; **to have a few moments to s.** disposer de quelques minutes; **can you s. me a few moments?** pouvez-vous m'accorder quelques minutes?; **could you s. me some milk?** est-ce que tu peux me donner un peu de lait?; **to s. a thought for sb** penser à qn
(b) (avoid) **to s. no expense** ne pas regarder à la dépense
(c) (save from) **to s. sb sth** épargner qch à qn; **s. me the details!** épargnez-moi les détails! (d) (show mercy towards) épargner; **to s. sb's life** épargner la vie de qn; **to s. sb's feelings** ménager les sentiments de qn

sparing ['speərɪŋ] *adj* économe (**with** avec); **to be s. with one's compliments** être avare de compliments

sparingly ['speərɪŋlɪ] *adv* en petite quantité

spark [spɑːk] **1** *n* (electrical, from fire) étincelle *f*; *Fig* (of intelligence, interest) lueur *f*; *Fig* **sparks will fly** cela va faire des étincelles; *Fig* **s. plug** bougie *f*
2 *vi* jeter ou faire des étincelles

▶**spark off** *vt sep* déclencher

sparkle ['spɑːkəl] **1** *n also Fig* éclat *m*
2 *vi* (of light, eyes) & *Fig* (of person, conversation) briller; (of diamond) scintiller

sparkler ['spɑːklə(r)] *n* (a) (firework) cierge *m* magique (b) *Fam* (diamond) diam *m*

sparkling ['spɑːklɪŋ] *adj* (light, eyes) & *Fig* (person, conversation) brillant(e); (diamond) scintillant(e); (wine) pétillant(e)

sparring partner ['spɑːrɪŋ'pɑːtnə(r)] *n* (in boxing) partenaire *mf* d'entraînement; *Fig* adversaire *mf*

sparrow ['spærəʊ] *n* moineau *m*

sparse [spɑːs] *adj* clairsemé(e)

sparsely ['spɑːslɪ] *adv* (populated, furnished) peu; **s. covered with trees** aux arbres clairsemés

spartan ['spɑːtən] *adj also Fig* spartiate

spasm ['spæzəm] *n* spasme *m*; *Fig* (of coughing) quinte *f*; (of jealousy) crise *f*

spasmodic [spæz'mɒdɪk] *adj* (irregular) irrégulier(ère)

spasmodically [spæz'mɒdɪklɪ] *adv* (irregularly) irrégulièrement

spastic ['spæstɪk] *n* (a) *Med* handicapé(e) *m,f* moteur (b) *very Fam Pej* (clumsy, useless person) empoté(e) *m,f*

spat¹ [spæt] *n* (quarrel) querelle *f*

spat² *pt & pp of* **spit²**

spate [speɪt] *n* (of letters, calls) avalanche *f*; (of crimes) vague *f*

spatial ['speɪʃəl] *adj* spatial(e)

spatter ['spætə(r)] *vt* éclabousser (**with** avec)

spatula ['spætjʊlə] *n* spatule *f*

spawn [spɔːn] **1** *n* (of frog, fish) œufs *mpl*
2 *vt* (give rise to) engendrer
3 *vi* (of frog, fish) frayer

speak [spiːk] (pt **spoke** [spəʊk], pp **spoken** ['spəʊkən]) **1** *vt* (a) (utter) dire (b) (language) parler
2 *vi* (talk, give a speech) parler (**to/about** à/de); **they're not speaking** (to each other) ils ne se parlent pas; **I know her to s.** on se parle quelquefois; **legally/morally speaking** légalement/moralement parlant; (on phone) **who's speaking?** (on phone) qui est à l'appareil?; **Mr Curry?** — yes, **speaking** Mr Curry? — lui-même

▶**speak for** *vt insep* **to s. for sb** (on behalf of) parler pour qn; **s. for yourself!** parle pour toi!; **the facts s. for themselves** les faits parlent d'eux-mêmes

▶**speak out** *vi* parler franchement; **to s. out against sth** s'élever contre qch

▶**speak up** *vi* (a) (speak more loudly) parler plus fort (b) (speak in favour of) **to s. up for sb/sth** parler en faveur de qn/qch; **to s. up for oneself** se défendre

speaker ['spiːkə(r)] *n* (a) (at meeting) intervenant(e) *m,f*; (at conference) conférencier(ère) *m,f*; **an Italian s.** une personne qui parle italien; **to be a slow/fast s.** parler lentement/vite; *Pol* **the S.** *Br* le Président de la Chambre des Communes; *Am* le Président du Congrès (b) (loudspeaker) enceinte *f*

speaking ['spiːkɪŋ] *adj* (doll, robot) parlant(e); **s. clock** horloge *f* parlante; **s. part** (in play, film) rôle *m* parlant

spear ['spɪə(r)] **1** *n* lance *f*
2 *vt* transpercer d'un coup de lance

spearhead ['spɪəhed] **1** *n* also Fig fer *m* de lance
2 *vt* (attack, campaign) être le fer de lance de

spearmint ['spɪəmɪnt] *n* menthe *f* verte

spec [spek] *n Fam* **on s.** à tout hasard

special ['speʃəl] **1** *adj* spécial(e); (friend) proche; (reason, effort, attention) particulier(ère); **what's so s. about the**

19th of November? qu'est-ce que le 19 novembre a de si spécial?; **s. agent** agent *m* secret; *Br* **S. Branch** = service de renseignements britannique; **s. delivery** envoi *m* en exprès; **s. effects** effets *mpl* spéciaux; **s. needs** difficultés *fpl* d'apprentissage; **s. offer** offre *f* spéciale; *Pol* **s. powers** pouvoirs *mpl* exceptionnels
   2 (*on menu*) plat *m* du jour

specialist ['speʃəlɪst] **1** *n* spécialiste *mf*; *Med* **heart s.** cardiologue *mf*; **lung s.** pneumologue *mf*
   2 *adj* (*skills, equipment*) d'un spécialiste; (*shop*) spécialisé(e)

speciality [speʃɪˈælɪtɪ] (*pl* **specialities**) *n* spécialité *f*

specialization [speʃəlaɪˈzeɪʃən] *n* spécialisation *f*

specialize ['speʃəlaɪz] *vi* se spécialiser (**in** en)

specially ['speʃəlɪ] *adv* (*expressly*) spécialement

specialty ['speʃəltɪ] (*pl* **specialties**) *n Am* spécialité *f*

species ['spiːʃiːz] (*pl* **species**) *n* espèce *f*

specific [spəˈsɪfɪk] **1** *adj* précis(e) (**about** au sujet de); **to be s.,...** pour être précis,...; *Phys* **s. gravity** densité *f*
   2 *npl* **specifics** détails *mpl*

specifically [spəˈsɪfɪkəlɪ] *adv* (**a**) (*explicitly*) expressément (**b**) (*specially*) spécialement (**c**) (*precisely*) précisément

specification [spesɪfɪˈkeɪʃən] *n* spécification *f*

specify ['spesɪfaɪ] (*pt & pp* **specified**) *vt* (**a**) (*state exactly*) préciser (**b**) (*stipulate*) stipuler

specimen ['spesɪmɪn] *n* (**a**) (*sample amount*) (*of handwriting, blood*) échantillon *m*; **s. copy** spécimen *m* (**b**) (*individual example*) spécimen *m*; *Fam* **he's an odd s.** c'est un drôle de spécimen

specious ['spiːʃəs] *adj* spécieux(euse)

speck [spek] *n* (*of dust*) grain *m*; (*of paint, ink*) petite tache *f*; **s. of dirt** une poussière

speckled ['spekəld] *adj* tacheté(e) (**with** de)

specs [speks] *npl Fam* (*spectacles*) lunettes *fpl*

spectacle ['spektəkəl] *n* (**a**) (*show, sight*) spectacle *m*; **to make a s. of oneself** se donner en spectacle (**b**) **spectacles** (*glasses*) lunettes *fpl*

spectacular [spekˈtækjʊlə(r)] **1** *n* production *f* à grand spectacle
   2 *adj* spectaculaire

spectator [spekˈteɪtə(r)] *n* spectateur(trice) *m,f*; **sport** sport *m* à grand public

spectre, *Am* **specter** ['spektə(r)] *n* spectre *m*

spectrum ['spektrəm] (*pl* **spectra** ['spektrə]) *n* spectre *m*; *Fig* éventail *m*

speculate ['spekjʊleɪt] *vi* (**a**) (*hypothesize*) faire des suppositions (**about** au sujet de) (**b**) *Fin* **to s.** (**on the Stock Market**) spéculer (à la Bourse)

speculation [spekjʊˈleɪʃən] *n* suppositions *fpl*

speculative ['spekjʊlətɪv] *adj* spéculatif(ive)

speculator ['spekjʊleɪtə(r)] *n Fin* spéculateur(trice) *m,f*

sped [sped] *pt & pp* of **speed**

speech [spiːtʃ] *n* (**a**) (*faculty*) parole *f*; **s. defect** *or* **impediment** défaut *m* d'élocution; **s. therapist** orthophoniste *mf*; **s. therapy** orthophonie *f* (**b**) (*address*) discours *m*; **to give** *or* **make a s.** faire un discours; *Br Sch* **s. day** remise *f* des prix (**c**) (*way of speaking*) langue *f* (**d**) *Gram* **part of s.** partie *f* du discours

speechless ['spiːtʃləs] *adj* muet(ette) (**with** de); **to be left s.** rester sans voix

speechwriter ['spiːtʃraɪtə(r)] *n* personne *f* qui écrit des discours

speed [spiːd] **1** *n* (**a**) (*rapidity*) vitesse *f*; **the s. of light/ sound** la vitesse de la lumière/du son; **at s.** à toute vitesse; **to gather** *or* **pick up/lose s.** prendre/perdre de la vitesse; *Fam* **s. cop** motard *m*; **s. limit** limitation *f* de vitesse; **s. trap** contrôle *m* de vitesse (**b**) (*gear*) vitesse *f*; **five-s. gearbox** boîte *f* à cinq vitesses (**c**) *Fam* (*amphetamine*) amphés *fpl*, speed *m*
   2 *vi* (**a**) (*pt & pp* **sped** [sped] *or* **speeded**) (*move quickly*) **to s. along** foncer; **to s. away/out** partir/sortir à toute vitesse (**b**) (*exceed speed limit*) faire un excès de vitesse; **to be caught speeding** être arrêté pour excès de vitesse (**c**) *Fam* **to be speeding** (*under effect of amphetamines*) être sous amphés

▸**speed off** *vi* partir à toute vitesse

▸**speed up 1** *vt sep* (*person*) faire aller plus vite; (*work, project, process*) accélérer
   2 *vi* aller plus vite

speedboat ['spiːdbəʊt] *n* vedette *f*; (*with outboard motor*) hors-bord *m inv*

speedily ['spiːdɪlɪ] *adv* vite, rapidement

speeding ['spiːdɪŋ] *n* excès *m* de vitesse

speedometer [spiːˈdɒmɪtə(r)] *n* compteur *m* de vitesse

speedway ['spiːdweɪ] *n* speedway *m*

speedy ['spiːdɪ] *adj* rapide

spell[1] [spel] *n* (*magic words*) formule *f* magique; **to cast a s. on sb** jeter un sort à qn; **to break the s.** rompre le charme; **to be under a s.** être envoûté(e); **to be under sb's s.** être sous le charme de qn

spell[2] [spel] (*pt & pp* **spelt** [spelt] *or* **spelled**) **1** *vt* (**a**) (*in writing*) écrire, orthographier; (*aloud*) épeler; **how do you s. it?** comment ça s'écrit? (**b**) (*signify*) signifier; **to s. disaster** être un désastre; **to s. trouble** être mauvais signe
   2 *vi* **he can s. well** il a une bonne orthographe; **he can't s.** il a une mauvaise orthographe

▸**spell out** *vt sep* (*address, name*) épeler; *Fig* (*explain explicitly*) expliquer clairement; **do I have to s. it out for you?** est-ce qu'il faut que je te fasse un dessin?

spell[3] [spel] *n* (**a**) (*period*) période *f*; **after a s. as a teacher, he...** après avoir été professeur pendant un temps, il...; **a cold s.** une période de froid; **a good/bad s.** une bonne/ mauvaise période

spellbound ['spelbaʊnd] *adj* fasciné(e)

spell-checker ['speltʃekə(r)] *n Comptr* correcteur *m* d'orthographe

speller ['spelə(r)] *n Am* manuel *m* d'orthographe

spelling ['spelɪŋ] *n* orthographe *f*; **to be good/bad at s.** être bon (bonne) /mauvais(e) en orthographe; **s. mistake** faute *f* d'orthographe

spelt [spelt] *pt & pp* of **spell**[2]

spend [spend] (*pt & pp* **spent** [spent]) *vt* (**a**) (*money*) dépenser; **to s. money on sb** dépenser de l'argent pour qn; **to s. money on sth** (*object*) dépenser de l'argent en qch; (*holidays, education*) dépenser de l'argent pour qch (**b**) (*time*) passer; **to s. time on sth/doing sth** passer du temps sur qch/à faire qch

spender ['spendə(r)] *n* **to be a big s.** être dépensier(ère)

spending ['spendɪŋ] *n* dépenses *fpl*; **s. money** argent *m* de poche; **s. power** pouvoir *m* d'achat; **to go on a s. spree** faire des folies

spendthrift ['spendθrɪft] *n* dépensier(ère) *m,f*

spent [spent] **1** *adj (bullet, match)* utilisé(e); **to be a s. force** ne plus avoir d'influence

2 *pt & pp of* **spend**

sperm [spa:m] *n (semen)* sperme *m*; **s. bank** banque *f* de sperme; **s. donor** donneur *m* de sperme; **s. whale** cachalot *m*

spermicide ['spa:mɪsaɪd] *n* spermicide *m*

spew [spju:] *vt & vi Fam (vomit)* dégobiller

sphere [sfɪə(r)] *n also Fig* sphère *f*; **that's outside my s.** ce n'est pas dans mes compétences; **s. of influence** sphère d'influence

spherical ['sferɪkəl] *adj* sphérique

sphincter ['sfɪŋktə(r)] *n Anat* sphincter *m*

sphinx [sfɪŋks] *n* sphinx *m*

spice [spaɪs] **1** *n (seasoning)* épice *f*; *Fig (excitement)* sel *m*, piquant *m*; **s. rack** présentoir *m* à épices

2 *vt (food)* épicer; *Fig* **to s. sth (up)** *(make more exciting)* ajouter du piquant à qch

spick [spɪk] *n Am very Fam* = terme injurieux désignant une personne originaire d'Amérique latine

spick-and-span [spɪkən'spæn] *adj* impeccable

spicy [spaɪsɪ] *adj (food)* épicé(e); *Fig (story, gossip)* croustillant(e)

spider ['spaɪdə(r)] *n* araignée *f*; **s.'s web** toile *f* d'araignée; **s. plant** chlorophytum *m*

spiel [ʃpi:l] *n Fam* baratin *m*

spike [spaɪk] **1** *n* pointe *f*; **spikes** *(running shoes)* pointes *fpl*

2 *vt* **to s. sb's guns** mettre des bâtons dans les roues de qn; **to s. sb's drink** ajouter de l'alcool dans la boisson de qn

spiky ['spaɪkɪ] *adj (plant)* couvert(e) de piquants; *(hair)* en épis

spill [spɪl] **1** *n* **to take a s.** *(fall)* faire une chute

2 *vt (pt & pp* **spilt** [spɪlt] *or* **spilled***)* renverser; *Fig* **to s. the beans** vendre la mèche

3 *vi (of liquid)* se répandre

▸**spill over** *vi (of liquid)* déborder; *Fig (of conflict)* s'étendre

spillage ['spɪlɪdʒ] *n* déversement *m*

spilt [spɪlt] *pt & pp of* **spill**

spin [spɪn] **1** *n* **(a)** *(turning movement)* tournoiement *m*; **to go into a s.** *(of car)* faire un tête-à-queue; **s. doctor** = spécialiste en communication chargé de présenter l'information de façon à mettre en valeur un parti politique **(b)** *Fam (in car)* **to go for a s.** aller faire un tour **(c)** *(on ball)* effet *m*; **to put s. on a ball** donner de l'effet à une balle

2 *vt (pt & pp* **spun** [spʌn]*)* **(a)** *(wool, cotton)* filer **(b)** *(wheel, top)* faire tourner, faire tournoyer; **to s. a coin** jouer à pile ou face **(c)** *(spin-dry)* essorer

3 *vi* tourner, tournoyer; **my head's spinning** j'ai la tête qui tourne; **the room's spinning** la pièce tourne *(autour de moi)*

▸**spin out** *vt sep (speech, debate)* faire traîner (en longueur); *(money)* faire durer

spinach ['spɪnɪtʃ] *n* épinards *mpl*

spinal ['spaɪnəl] *adj* vertébral(e); **s. column** colonne *f* vertébrale; **s. cord** moelle *f* épinière; **s. injury** lésion *f* de la colonne vertébrale

spindly ['spɪndlɪ] *adj (person)* chétif(ive); *(arms, legs)* maigre

spin-dry ['spɪn'draɪ] *(pt & pp* **spin-dried***) vt* essorer

spin-dryer ['spɪn'draɪə(r)] *n* essoreuse *f*

spine [spaɪn] *n* **(a)** *(backbone)* colonne *f* vertébrale **(b)** *(of book)* dos *m* **(c)** *(of plant, hedgehog)* piquant *m*

spine-chilling ['spaɪntʃɪlɪŋ] *adj* à vous glacer le sang

spineless ['spaɪnlɪs] *adj (weak)* mou (molle)

spinney ['spɪnɪ] *(pl* spinneys*) n* bosquet *m*

spinning top ['spɪnɪŋ'tɒp] *n* toupie *f*

spinning wheel ['spɪnɪŋ'wi:l] *n* rouet *m*

spin-off ['spɪnɒf] *n* **(a)** *(result)* retombée *f* **(b)** *(TV programme)* feuilleton tiré d'un film ou d'un autre feuilleton

spinster ['spɪnstə(r)] *n* vieille fille *f*

spiny ['spaɪnɪ] *adj* couvert(e) de piquants; **s. lobster** langouste *f*

spiral ['spaɪərəl] **1** *n* spirale *f*; **s. staircase** escalier *m* en colimaçon

2 *vi (pt & pp* **spiralled***) (of smoke)* s'élever *ou* monter en spirale; *(of prices)* s'envoler

spire ['spaɪə(r)] *n (of church)* flèche *f*

spirit ['spɪrɪt] *n* **(a)** *(soul, being)* esprit *m*; **the Holy S.** le Saint-Esprit **(b)** *(mood, attitude)* esprit *m*; **to enter into the s. of sth** participer de bon cœur à qch; **to take sth in the right/wrong s.** bien/mal prendre qch; **to be in good/poor spirits** être de bonne humeur/déprimé(e); *Fam* **that's the s.!** à la bonne heure! **(c)** *(determination)* courage *m*; **to break sb's s.** entamer le courage de qn **(d) spirits** *(drinks)* spiritueux *mpl*; **s. lamp** lampe *f* à alcool; **s. level** niveau *m* (à bulle)

▸**spirit away, spirit off** *vt sep* faire disparaître (comme par enchantement)

spirited ['spɪrɪtɪd] *adj (person, defence)* courageux(euse); *(reply)* énergique; *(performance)* plein de brio

spiritual ['spɪrɪtjʊəl] **1** *adj* spirituel(elle); **France is my s. home** c'est en France que je me sens vraiment chez moi

2 *n (Negro)* **s.** Negro spiritual *m*

spiritualism ['spɪrɪtjʊəlɪzəm] *n* spiritisme *m*

spirituality [spɪrɪtjʊ'ælɪtɪ] *n* spiritualité *f*

spit¹ [spɪt] *n* **(a)** *(for cooking)* broche *f* **(b)** *(of land)* pointe *f*

spit² *n (saliva)* salive *f*; *(spittle)* crachat *m*; *Fam* **s. and polish** astiquage *m*

2 *vt (pt & pp* **spat** [spæt]*)* cracher

3 *vi (of person, cat)* cracher; *(of hot fat)* sauter; *Fig* **to be within spitting distance (of)** être à deux pas (de); **it's spitting** *(with rain)* il pleuvote

▸**spit out** *vt sep* cracher; *Fam* **s. it out!** *(say what you want to)* allez, accouche!

spite [spaɪt] **1** *n* **(a)** *(malice)* dépit *m*; **out of s.** par dépit **(b)** **in s. of** malgré; **to do sth in s. of oneself** faire qch malgré soi

2 *vt* vexer

spiteful ['spaɪtfʊl] *adj* vexant(e)

spitting image ['spɪtɪŋ'ɪmɪdʒ] *n Fam* **he's the s. of his father** c'est son père tout craché

spittle ['spɪtəl] *n* crachat *m*

spiv [spɪv] *n Br very Fam* aigrefin *m*

splash [splæʃ] **1** *n* **(a)** *(of liquid)* éclaboussure *f*; *(sound)* plouf *m*; *Fam Fig* **to make a s.** faire sensation **(b)** *(of colour, light)* tache *f*

2 *vt* éclabousser **(with de)**; **to s. one's face with water** se passer de l'eau sur le visage; **the photo was splashed across the front page** la photo était étalée à la une

3 *vi (of liquid, waves)* faire des éclaboussures

▸**splash about, splash around** *vi* patauger

▶**splash down** *vi (of spacecraft)* amerrir

▶**splash out** *vt sep Fam* claquer des ronds (**on** en achetant)

splatter ['splætə(r)] **1** *n* éclaboussure *f; (sound)* crépitement *m*
2 *vt* éclabousser (**with** de)

splay [spleɪ] *vt* écarter

spleen [spliːn] *n (a) (part of body)* rate *f (b) Formal (anger)* mauvaise humeur *f;* **to vent one's s. (on sb)** passer sa mauvaise humeur (sur qn)

splendid ['splendɪd] *adj* magnifique

splendour, *Am* **splendor** ['splendə(r)] *n* splendeur *f*

splice [splaɪs] *vt (film)* coller; *(rope)* épisser; *Fam* **to get spliced** *(marry)* se caser

splint [splɪnt] *n* attelle *f*

splinter ['splɪntə(r)] **1** *n (of wood, glass)* éclat *m; (in finger)* écharde *f; (of bone)* esquille *f; Pol* **s. group** groupe *m* dissident
2 *vt* briser
3 *vi* se briser; *Fig (of political party)* se scinder

split [splɪt] **1** *n (in wood)* fente *f; (in group)* division *f; (in garment) (tear)* déchirure *f; (by design)* fente; **to do the splits** faire le grand écart
2 *adj* brisé(e); **s. ends** *(in hair)* fourches *fpl;* **s. peas** pois *mpl* cassés; **s. personality** dédoublement *m* de la personnalité; **s. screen** écran *m* divisé; **in a s. second** en quelques dixièmes de seconde
3 *vt (pt & pp* **split***) (a) (wood)* fendre; *(cloth)* déchirer; *(seam)* faire craquer; *(group)* diviser; *(political party)* scinder; **to s. one's head open** se fendre le crâne; **to s. the vote** éparpiller les voix; *Fam* **to s. one's sides (laughing)** se tordre de rire; **to s. hairs** couper les cheveux en quatre *(share)* partager; **to s. the difference** partager la différence
4 *vi (a) (of wood)* se fendre; *(of cloth)* se déchirer; *(of seam)* craquer; *(of group)* se diviser; *(of political party)* se scinder; *Fam* **my head's splitting** j'ai un mal de tête atroce **(b)** *very Fam (leave)* se casser

▶**split up** *vt sep (share out)* diviser, partager
2 *vi (of couple, group)* se séparer; **to s. up with sb** rompre avec qn

split-second ['splɪtsekənd] *adj (decision)* pris(e) en un rien de temps; *(timing)* au quart de seconde

splitting ['splɪtɪŋ] *adj* **to have a s. headache** avoir un mal de tête atroce

splodge [splɒdʒ] *n Fam* tache *f*

splutter ['splʌtə(r)] *vi (of person)* bredouiller; *(of engine)* tousser; *(of flame, candle)* crépiter

spoil [spɔɪl] *(pt & pp* **spoilt** [spɔɪlt] *or* **spoiled***)* **1** *vt (a) (ruin)* gâcher; **to s. sb's fun** gâcher le plaisir de qn; **to s. sb's appetite** couper l'appétit à qn; *Pol* **spoilt ballot** vote *m* nul **(b)** *(indulge)* gâter; **to be spoilt for choice** avoir l'embarras du choix
2 *vi (a) (of food)* s'abîmer **(b) to be spoiling for a fight** chercher la bagarre

spoils [spɔɪlz] *npl (of war, crime)* butin *m*

spoilsport ['spɔɪlspɔːt] *n Fam* rabat-joie *mf inv*

spoilt [spɔɪlt] *pt & pp of* **spoil**

spoke[1] [spəʊk] *n (of wheel)* rayon *m; Fig* **to put a s. in sb's wheel** mettre des bâtons dans les roues à qn

spoke[2] *pt of* **speak**

spoken ['spəʊkən] *pp of* **speak**

spokesman ['spəʊksmən] *n* porte-parole *m*

spokesperson ['spəʊkspɜːsən] *n* porte-parole *m*

spokeswoman ['spəʊkswʊmən] *n* porte-parole *m*

sponge [spʌndʒ] **1** *n* éponge *f; Fig* **to throw in the s.** jeter l'éponge; **s. bag** trousse *f* de toilette; **s. cake** génoise *f;* **s. pudding** = sorte de génoise, cuite à la vapeur et servie avec une sauce au chocolat, de la confiture etc
2 *vt (a) (wash)* nettoyer avec une éponge **(b)** *Fam (scrounge)* taper (**off** *or* **from** à)
3 *vi Fam (scrounge)* taper les autres

▶**sponge down** *vt sep (wash)* nettoyer avec une éponge

▶**sponge off 1** *vt sep (stain)* faire partir d'un coup d'éponge
2 *vt insep Fam (scrounge from)* taper

sponger ['spʌndʒə(r)] *n Fam* tapeur(euse) *m,f*

spongy ['spʌndʒɪ] *adj* spongieux(euse)

sponsor ['spɒnsə(r)] **1** *n* sponsor *m; (of student, club member)* parrain *m*
2 *vt* sponsoriser; *(student)* financer les études de; *(club member)* parrainer; **sponsored walk** marche *f* parrainée

sponsorship ['spɒnsəʃɪp] *n* sponsoring *m; (of student, club member)* parrainage *m;* **s. deal** *(for athlete, team)* contrat *m* de sponsoring

spontaneity [spɒntə'neɪtɪ] *n* spontanéité *f*

spontaneous [spɒn'teɪnɪəs] *adj* spontané(e)

spoof [spuːf] *n Fam (a) (parody)* parodie *f* (**on** de) **(b)** *(hoax)* canular *m*

spook [spuːk] *n Fam* fantôme *m*

spooky ['spuːkɪ] *adj Fam* qui fait froid dans le dos

spool [spuːl] *n* bobine *f*

spoon [spuːn] **1** *n* cuillère *f*
2 *vt* **to s. sth onto sth** mettre qch sur qch avec une cuillère

spoon-feed ['spuːnfiːd] *(pt & pp* **spoon-fed** ['spuːnfed]*) vt* faire manger à la cuillère; *Fig* mâcher le travail de

spoonful ['spuːnfʊl] *n* cuillerée *f*

sporadic [spə'rædɪk] *adj* sporadique

spore [spɔː(r)] *n* spore *f*

sporran ['spɒrən] *n Scot* = bourse portée sur le devant du kilt

sport [spɔːt] **1** *n (a) (activity)* sport *m* **(b)** *Fam (person)* **to be a (good) s.** *(man)* être un chic type; *(woman)* être une chic fille; **to be a bad s.** être mauvais(e) joueur(euse)
2 *vt (wear)* arborer

sporting ['spɔːtɪŋ] *adj (a) (related to sport)* sportif(ive) **(b)** *(fair)* chic *inv;* **to give sb a s. chance** donner sa chance à qn

sports [spɔːts] *adj* **s. car** voiture *f* de sport; **s. centre** complexe *m* sportif; **s. day** = compétition sportive annuelle organisée dans l'école; **s. ground** terrain *m* de sport; *Br* **s. jacket** veste *f* sport; **s. page** page *f* des sports; **s. shop** magasin *m* de sports

sportsman ['spɔːtsmən] *n* sportif *m*

sportsmanship ['spɔːtsmənʃɪp] *n* esprit *m* sportif

sportsperson ['spɔːtspɜːsən] *n* sportif(ive) *m,f*

sportswoman ['spɔːtswʊmən] *n* sportive *f*

sporty ['spɔːtɪ] *adj (person)* sportif(ive); *(car, clothing)* de sport

spot [spɒt] **1** *n (a) (place)* endroit *m;* **on the s.** sur place; *Fam* **to put sb on the s.** prendre qn au dépourvu; *Fam* **to be in a (tight) s.** être dans le pétrin; **s. check** contrôle *m* surprise **(b)** *(stain)* tache *f* **(c)** *(pimple)* bouton *m* **(d)**

(forming pattern on cloth) pois *m*; *(on leopard)* tache *f* **(e)** Br Fam *(small amount)* goutte *f*; **to have a s. of lunch** manger un morceau; **a s. of bother** de petits problèmes *mpl* **(f)** *(spotlight)* projecteur *m*; *(smaller)* spot *m* **(g)** *(on TV, radio, in show)* numéro *m*

2 *vt (pt & pp spotted)* **(a)** *(stain, mark)* tacher **(b)** *(notice)* remarquer; *(opportunity, opening)* repérer; **to s. sb doing sth** apercevoir qn en train de faire qch; **well spotted!** bien vu!

spotless ['spotlɪs] *adj* impeccable; Fig *(reputation)* irréprochable

spotlight ['spotlaɪt] *n* projecteur *m*; *(smaller)* spot *m*; Fig **to be in the s.** être sous le feu des projecteurs

spot-on ['spot'ɒn] *adj Fam* tout à fait exact(e)

spotter plane ['spotə'pleɪn] *n* avion-espion *m*

spotty ['spotɪ] *adj (pimply)* boutonneux(euse)

spouse [spauz] *n* époux (épouse) *m,f*

spout [spaut] **1** *n (of teapot, kettle)* bec *m*; *Fam Fig* **to be up the s.** être fichu(e); *(of economy, business)* s'être cassé la figure; *(pregnant)* être enceinte

2 *vt (water)* faire jaillir; *Fam Fig (speech, nonsense)* débiter

3 *vi (of liquid)* jaillir; *Fam Fig (of person)* faire des discours

sprain [spreɪn] **1** *n (injury)* entorse *f*

2 *vt* **to s. one's ankle/wrist** se fouler la cheville/le poignet

sprang [spræŋ] *pt of* **spring**

sprat [spræt] *n* sprat *m*

sprawl [sprɔːl] *vi (of person)* s'affaler; *(of town)* s'étendre

sprawling ['sprɔːlɪŋ] *adj (person)* affalé(e); *(town)* tentaculaire

spray¹ [spreɪ] *n (of flowers)* bouquet *m*

spray² **1** *n* **(a)** *(of liquid)* fines gouttelettes *fpl*; *(from sea)* embruns *mpl* **(b)** *(act of spraying)* **to give sth a s.** *(flowers, crops)* pulvériser; *(room)* vaporiser **(c)** *(device)* bombe *f*; *(for perfume)* atomiseur *m*; **s. can** bombe aérosol; **s. gun** *(for paint)* pistolet *m* (à peinture)

2 *vt (flowers, crops)* pulvériser; *(room)* vaporiser; **to s. oneself with sth** *(perfume, deodorant)* se vaporiser qch; **to s. sb with sth** asperger qn de qch

spray-paint ['spreɪ'peɪnt] **1** *n* peinture *f* en bombe

2 *vt (with spray can)* peindre à la bombe; *(with spray gun)* peindre au pistolet

spread [spred] **1** *n* **(a)** *(of idea, religion, language)* diffusion *f*; *(of disease)* propagation *f* **(b)** *(of products, ages)* éventail *m* **(c)** *(in newspaper)* **full-page s.** pleine page *f*; **two-page s.** double page *f* **(d)** *(paste)* **cheese/ chocolate s.** fromage *m*/chocolat *m* à tartiner **(e)** *(of wings, sails)* envergure *f* **(f)** *Fam (big meal)* festin *m*

2 *vt (pt & pp spread)* **(a)** *(arms, legs)* écarter; Fig **to s. one's wings** acquérir de l'indépendance **(b)** *(sand, sawdust, terror)* répandre; *(rumour, disease, germs)* propager; *(payments)* étaler **(c)** *(butter, ointment)* étaler; **to s. a surface with sth** étaler qch sur une surface

3 *vi* se répandre; *(of rumour, disease, fire)* se propager

▶**spread out 1** *vt sep* **(a)** *(map, newspaper)* étaler **(b)** **to be spread out** *(of fields, city)* s'étendre

2 *vi (of person)* s'étendre; *(of search party)* se disperser

spreadsheet ['spredʃiːt] *n Comptr* tableur *m*

spree [spriː] *n Fam* **to go on a s.** *(go drinking)* prendre une cuite; **to go on a shopping** *or* **spending s.** faire des folies dans les magasins

sprig [sprɪg] *n (of parsley)* brin *m*; *(of holly, mistletoe)* branche *f*

sprightly ['spraɪtlɪ] *adj* alerte

spring [sprɪŋ] **1** *n* **(a)** *(of water)* source *f* **(b)** *(season)* printemps *m*; **in (the) s.** au printemps; **s. onion** ciboule *f*; **s. roll** rouleau *m* de printemps; **s. tide** grande marée *f* **(c)** *(leap)* bond *m* **(d)** *(elasticity)* élasticité *f*; **to walk with a s. in one's step** marcher d'un pas souple **(e)** *(device)* ressort *m*

2 *vt (pt sprang* [spræŋ]*, pp sprung* [sprʌŋ]*)* **(a)** *(reveal unexpectedly)* **to s. sth on sb** annoncer qch à qn de but en blanc; **to s. a surprise on sb** faire une surprise à qn **(b)** *(develop)* **to s. a leak** commencer à fuir; *(of boat)* commencer à prendre l'eau **(c)** *Fam (prisoner)* faire évader

3 *vi* **(a)** *(jump)* bondir, sauter; **to s. to one's feet** se lever d'un bond; **to s. into action** passer rapidement à l'action; **to s. to life** *(of person, town)* s'animer; *(of machine)* se mettre en marche; **to s. to sb's defence** prendre vivement la défense de qn; **to s. open/shut** s'ouvrir/se fermer brusquement; **to s. to mind** venir à l'esprit **(b)** *(originate)* **to s. from** venir de; **to s. into existence** voir le jour; *Fam* **where did you s. from?** d'où sortez-vous?

▶**spring up** *vi* **(a)** *(jump to one's feet)* se lever d'un bond **(b)** *(appear suddenly)* surgir; *(of wind)* se lever; *(of feeling)* prendre naissance

springboard ['sprɪŋbɔːd] *n also Fig* tremplin *m*

spring-clean ['sprɪŋ'kliːn] **1** *n* grand nettoyage *m*

2 *vt* nettoyer à fond

spring-cleaning ['sprɪŋ'kliːnɪŋ] *n* grand nettoyage *m*; **to do the s.** faire le grand nettoyage

springtime ['sprɪŋtaɪm] *n* printemps *m*

springy ['sprɪŋɪ] *adj* souple

sprinkle ['sprɪŋkəl] **1** *n (of salt, flour)* pincée *f*

2 *vt (with liquid)* arroser, asperger **(with de)**; *(with salt, flour)* saupoudrer **(with de)**; **to s. liquid on sth** arroser *ou* asperger qch de liquide; **to s. salt/flour on sth** saupoudrer qch de sel/farine

sprinkler ['sprɪŋklə(r)] *n (for lawns)* arroseur *m*; *(as fire prevention)* sprinkler *m*

sprinkling ['sprɪŋklɪŋ] *n* **a s. of** *(liquid)* quelques gouttes de; *(salt, flour)* un peu de; Fig *(people)* quelques

sprint [sprɪnt] **1** *n (fast run)* sprint *m*; *(running race)* course *f* (de vitesse); **to put on a s.** piquer un sprint

2 *vi (run fast)* piquer un sprint; **to s. off** partir en courant

sprinter ['sprɪntə(r)] *n* sprinter(euse) *m,f*

sprocket ['sprɒkɪt] *n* **s. (wheel)** pignon *m*

sprout [spraut] **1** *n (of plant)* pousse *f*; **(Brussels) s.** chou *m* de Bruxelles

2 *vt (leaves, shoots)* faire; *Fam (moustache, beard)* se laisser pousser

3 *vi (of leaves, hair)* pousser

▶**sprout up** *vi (of plant, child)* pousser; *(of new buildings, towns)* surgir

spruce¹ [spruːs] *n (tree)* épicéa *m*

spruce² *adj* impeccable

▶**spruce up** *vt sep (room)* bien nettoyer; **to s. oneself up** se faire beau (belle)

sprung [sprʌŋ] **1** *adj* **s. mattress** à ressorts

2 *pp of* **spring**

spry [spraɪ] *adj* alerte

spud [spʌd] *n Fam (potato)* patate *f*

spun [spʌn] **1** *adj* **s. silk** schappe *f*

2 *pt & pp of* **spin**

spunk [spʌŋk] n (a) Fam (courage) cran m (b) Vulg (semen) sperme m

spur [spɜ:(r)] 1 n (a) (for riding) éperon m; Fig (stimulus) motivation f; Fig **to win one's spurs** faire ses preuves; **on the s. of the moment** sur un coup de tête (b) (of land, rock) éperon m

2 vt (pt & pp **spurred**) (horse) éperonner; Fig **to s. sb on** stimuler qn; **to s. sb on to do sth** inciter qn à faire qch; Fig **to s. sb into action** inciter qn à agir

spurious ['spjʊərɪəs] adj (argument, reasoning) spécieux(euse); (claim, story, charge) sans fondement

spurn [spɜ:n] vt repousser, rejeter

spurt [spɜ:t] 1 n (of liquid) giclée f; (of activity, energy) regain m; (increase in speed) accélération f; **to do sth in spurts** faire qch par à-coups; **to put on a s.** accélérer

2 vt **the wound was spurting blood** le sang giclait de la blessure; **the pen spurted ink** l'encre giclait du stylo

3 vi (a) (of liquid) gicler (b) (move quickly) **to s. off** s'élancer brusquement

sputter ['spʌtə(r)] vi (of engine) toussoter; (of flame, candle) crépiter

spy [spaɪ] 1 n espion(onne) m,f; **s. plane** avion m espion; **s. ring** réseau m d'espionnage; **s. satellite** satellite m espion

2 vt (notice) repérer

3 vi espionner, faire de l'espionnage; **to s. on sb** espionner qn

▶**spy out** vt sep Fig **to s. out the land** tâter le terrain

Sq (abbr **Square**) pl

sq (abbr **square**) carré; **sq. ft.** (abbr **square foot** or **feet**) ≃ mètres mpl carrés

squabble ['skwɒbəl] 1 n querelle f

2 vi se quereller (**about** or **over** à propos de)

squabbling ['skwɒblɪŋ] n querelles fpl

squad [skwɒd] n (of workmen) équipe f; (of athletes, footballers) délégation f; (of soldiers) section f; (of police) brigade f; **s. car** voiture f de patrouille

squadron ['skwɒdrən] n Mil (of planes) escadron m; (of ships) escadrille f

squalid ['skwɒlɪd] adj (dirty) crasseux(euse); (sordid) sordide

squall [skwɔ:l] 1 n (of wind) bourrasque f

2 vi (cry) pousser des hurlements

squalor ['skwɒlə(r)] n (dirtiness) crasse f; (poverty) misère f noire

squander ['skwɒndə(r)] vt (money, resources, talents) gaspiller; (time) perdre; (fortune, inheritance) dilapider; (opportunity) laisser passer

square [skweə(r)] 1 n (a) (shape) carré m; (on chessboard, map) case f; Fig **to be back at s. one** être de retour à la case départ (b) Math carré m (c) (of town, village) place f (d) Fam (unfashionable person) **to be a s.** être ringard(e)

2 adj (a) (in shape) carré(e) (b) (right-angled) **s. corner** angle m droit; Math carré(e); **s. root** racine f carrée (d) Fam (unfashionable) vieux jeu inv (in idioms) **to be s. with sb** être honnête avec qn; **that's us s.** nous sommes quittes; **to feel like a s. peg in a round hole** ne pas se sentir à sa place; **s. deal** arrangement m équitable; **s. meal** bon repas m

3 adv **to hit sb s. on the jaw** frapper qn en pleine mâchoire; **to look sb s. in the eye** regarder qn bien en face

4 vt (a) (make square) mettre en forme de carré; Math (number) élever au carré; **squared paper** papier m

quadrillé (b) (settle) (account, debt) régler (c) (arrange) **to s. sth with sb** arranger qch avec qn

5 vi (agree) coller; **to s. with** correspondre à

▶**square up** vi (a) (settle debts) régler ses comptes (b) (of fighters) se mettre en garde; Fig **to s. up to a problem/an opponent** faire face à un problème/un adversaire

squarely ['skweəlɪ] adv (a) (directly) **to hit sb s. in the chest/face** frapper qn en pleine poitrine/figure (b) (honestly) honnêtement

squash¹ [skwɒʃ] 1 n (a) (crush) cohue f; **it was a s. on** était serrés comme des sardines (b) (drink) **orange/lemon s.** ≃ sirop m d'orange/de citron (c) (sport) squash m; **s. court** court m de squash

2 vt écraser

3 vi **to s. into a room/car** s'entasser dans une pièce/voiture

squash² n Am (vegetable) courge f

▶**squash up** vi se serrer

squat [skwɒt] 1 n (illegally occupied dwelling) squat m

2 adj (person, object, building) trapu(e)

3 vi (pt & pp **squatted**) (a) (crouch down) (of person) s'accroupir; (of animal) se tapir (b) (occupy illegally) squatter

squatter ['skwɒtə(r)] n squatter m

squaw [skwɔ:] n squaw f

squawk [skwɔ:k] 1 n (of bird) cri m rauque; Fam (of person) braillement m

2 vi (of bird) pousser un cri rauque; Fam (of person) brailler

squeak [skwi:k] 1 n (of animal, person) cri m aigu; (of door, hinges) grincement m; Fam **I don't want to hear another s. out of you** je ne veux plus vous entendre

2 vi (of animal, person) pousser un cri aigu; (of door, hinges) grincer; (of shoes) craquer

squeaky ['skwi:kɪ] adj (voice) aigu(uë); (door, hinges) qui grince; (shoes) qui craque; **s. clean** impeccable

squeal [skwi:l] 1 n (of person, animal) cri m perçant; (of brakes) crissement m

2 vi crier

3 vi (a) (of person, animal) pousser un cri perçant; (of brakes) crisser; Fam **to s. about sth** (complain) se lamenter au sujet de qch (b) very Fam (inform) moucharder; **to s. on sb** balancer qn

squeamish ['skwi:mɪʃ] adj de nature délicate; **to be s. about sth** ne pas supporter qch

squeeze [skwi:z] 1 n pression f; **to give sb a s.** presser qch; **to give sb a s.** (hug) serrer qn dans ses bras; **a s. of lemon** quelques gouttes de citron; Fam **it was a tight s.** nous étions serrés comme des sardines; Fam **to put the s. on sb** (pressurize) faire pression sur qn

2 vt (a) (press) presser; **to s. sb's hand** serrer la main à qn; Fig **to s. sb** (pressurize) faire pression sur qn (b) (squash) **to s. sth into sth** faire rentrer qch dans qch; **I think we can just s. you in** je pense qu'on peut vous trouver une place

3 vi **to s. into sth** s'entasser dans qch; **to s. past sb** se glisser devant qn; **s. up a bit!** serrez-vous un peu!

▶**squeeze out** vt sep (juice) exprimer

squelch [skwelt∫] vi patauger; **to s. through the mud** avancer en pataugeant dans la boue

squib [skwɪb] n (firework) pétard m; Fig **to be a damp s.** être bidon inv

squid [skwɪd] n (pl **squid**) n calmar m

squiggle ['skwɪgəl] n gribouillis m

squint [skwɪnt] **1** n (a) (eye defect) strabisme m; to have a s. loucher (b) (quick look) coup d'œil m; to have a s. at jeter un coup d'œil à

2 vi (have eye defect) loucher (b) (narrow one's eyes) plisser les yeux; to s. at plisser les yeux pour voir

squire ['skwaɪə(r)] n (landowner) châtelain m; Hist écuyer m

squirm [skwɜːm] vi (wriggle) se tortiller; Fig to s. (with embarrassment) être mal à l'aise

squirrel ['skwɪrəl] n écureuil m

squirt [skwɜːt] **1** n (a) (of liquid) giclée f (b) Fam (insignificant person) petit(e) morveux(euse) m,f

2 vt (liquid) faire gicler; to s. sth on sb/sth, to s. sb/sth with sth asperger qn/qch de qch

3 vi (of liquid) to s. out gicler

Sr (abbr **Senior**) Thomas Smith, Sr Thomas Smith père

Sri Lanka [sriːˈlæŋkə] n le Sri Lanka

Sri Lankan [sriːˈlæŋkən] **1** n Sri Lankais(e) m,f

2 adj sri lankais(e)

SSE (abbr **south-southeast**) sud-sud-est

SSW (abbr **south-southwest**) sud-sud-ouest

St (a) (abbr **Street**) rue f (b) (abbr **Saint**) st(e); **St Kitts and Nevis** Saint-Kitts-et-Nevis; **St Lucia** Sainte-Lucie; **St Petersburg** Saint-Petersbourg; **St Vincent and the Grenadines** Saint-Vincent-et-Grenadines

stab [stæb] **1** n (a) (with knife) coup m de couteau; Fig a s. of pain un élancement; a s. of envy un pincement de jalousie; a s. of guilt un accès de culpabilité (b) Fam (attempt) to have a s. at sth/at doing sth essayer qch/de faire qch

2 vt (pt & pp stabbed) (with knife) poignarder; (with other weapon) transpercer; to s. sb to death tuer qn d'un coup de couteau; Fig to s. sb in the back poignarder qn dans le dos

stabbing ['stæbɪŋ] **1** n (attack) agression f au couteau

2 adj (pain) lancinant(e)

stability [stəˈbɪlɪti] n stabilité f

stabilize ['steɪbɪlaɪz] **1** vt stabiliser

2 vi se stabiliser

stabilizer ['steɪbɪlaɪzə(r)] n (on bicycle) stabilisateur m

stable¹ ['steɪbl] **1** n écurie f; Fig to lock the s. door after the horse has bolted prendre des mesures trop tard

2 vt mettre à l'écurie

stable² adj stable

stack [stæk] **1** n (a) (pile) pile f; Fam stacks of des tas de (b) (chimney) cheminée f

2 vt empiler; to be stacked with sth (full of) être plein(e) de qch; the odds were stacked against them ils n'avaient aucune chance

stadium ['steɪdɪəm] n (pl stadiums or stadia ['steɪdɪə]) n stade m

staff [stɑːf] **1** n (a) (stick) bâton m (b) (personnel) personnel m; teaching/nursing s. personnel m enseignant/infirmier; s. nurse infirmier(ère) m,f; s. room (in school) salle f des professeurs (c) Mus (pl staves [steɪvz]) portée f

2 vt the office is staffed by volunteers le personnel du bureau est composé de volontaires; the desk is staffed at all times il y a toujours quelqu'un au bureau

stag [stæg] n (animal) cerf m; s. beetle cerf-volant m; s. night or party (before wedding) enterrement m de la vie de garçon

stage [steɪdʒ] **1** n (a) (platform) plate-forme f; (in theatre) scène f; to go on the s. faire du théâtre; Fig to set the s. for sth préparer le terrain à qch; s. directions indications fpl scéniques; s. door entrée f des artistes; s. fright trac m; s. manager régisseur m; s. name nom m de scène; s. whisper aparté m (b) (phase) stade m; at this s. in... à ce stade de...; to do sth in stages faire qch par étapes (c) s. (coach) diligence f

2 vt (play) monter, mettre en scène; Fig (demonstration, invasion) organiser

stagehand ['steɪdʒhænd] n machiniste m

stage-manage ['steɪdʒˌmænɪdʒ] vt (play) s'occuper de la régie de; Fig (event, demonstration) mettre en scène

stage-struck ['steɪdʒstrʌk] adj fou (folle) de théâtre

stagflation [stægˈfleɪʃən] n Econ stagflation f

stagger ['stægə(r)] **1** vt (a) (astound) stupéfier (b) (tea-breaks, holidays) échelonner

2 vi (stumble) tituber; to s. along/in/out marcher/entrer/sortir en titubant; to s. to one's feet se relever péniblement

stagnant ['stægnənt] adj stagnant(e)

stagnate [stægˈneɪt] vi stagner

stagnation [stægˈneɪʃən] n stagnation f

staid [steɪd] adj collet monté inv

stain [steɪn] **1** n (a) (mark) tache f; (dye) teinture f; s. remover détachant m

2 vt (mark) tacher; (dye) teindre; Fig (reputation) salir

stained-glass ['steɪndɡlɑːs] n vitrail m; s. window vitrail

stainless steel ['steɪnlɪsˈstiːl] n acier m inoxydable, inox® m

stair [steə(r)] n (single step) marche f; stairs (staircase) escalier m

staircase ['steəkeɪs] n escalier m

stairway ['steəweɪ] n escalier m

stairwell ['steəwel] n cage f d'escalier

stake [steɪk] **1** n (a) (piece of wood) pieu m; (piece of metal) piquet m; (for plant) tuteur m; to be burnt at the s. périr sur le bûcher (b) (bet) enjeu m; to be at s. être en jeu (c) (share) to have a s. in sth avoir des intérêts dans qch; Fig être concerné(e) par qch

2 vt (a) (money) miser (on sur); Fig (one's reputation, job) risquer (on sur); I'd s. my life on it j'en mettrais ma tête à couper (b) to s. a claim (to sth) revendiquer un droit (à qch)

stakeout ['steɪkaʊt] n surveillance f

stalactite ['stæləktaɪt] n stalactite f

stalagmite ['stæləɡmaɪt] n stalagmite f

stale [steɪl] adj (a) (bread, cake) rassis(e); (air) confiné(e); (smell) âcre (b) Fig (social life, politics) sans intérêt; (excuse, joke) éculé(e); (person) blasé(e)

stalemate ['steɪlmeɪt] n (in chess) pat m; (in negotiations) impasse f; to reach a s. être dans l'impasse

stalk¹ [stɔːk] **1** vt (suspect, wild animal) traquer; (obsessively) harceler

2 vi (walk angrily) to s. in/out entrer/sortir d'un air furieux mais digne

stalk² n (of plant, flower) tige f; (of fruit) queue f

stalker ['stɔːkə(r)] n = admirateur obsessionnel qui harcèle une célébrité ou une de ses connaissances

stall [stɔːl] 1 *n* (a) *(in stable)* stalle *f; (for shower, toilet)* cabine *f* (b) *(in market)* étal *m; (at exhibition)* stand *m* (c) *the* **stalls** *(in theatre)* l'orchestre *m*
2 *vt (hold off)* faire patienter
3 *vi (of car)* caler; *Fig (of campaign)* être interrompu(e)
(b) *(delay)* **to s.** *(for time)* essayer de gagner du temps

stallion [ˈstæljən] *n* étalon *m*

stalwart [ˈstɔːlwət] 1 *n* fidèle *mf*
2 *adj* résolu(e)

stamen [ˈsteɪmən] *n* étamine *f*

stamina [ˈstæmɪnə] *n* résistance *f* physique

stammer [ˈstæmə(r)] 1 *n* bégaiement *m;* **to have a s.** bégayer
2 *vi* bégayer
3 *vt* balbutier

▸**stammer out** *vt insep* balbutier

stamp [stæmp] 1 *n* (a) *(for letter)* timbre *m; (mark)* cachet *m; (device)* tampon *m; Fig* **to bear the s. of sth** porter l'empreinte de qch; *Fig* **s. of approval** aval *m*, approbation *f;* **s. album** album *m* de timbres; **s. collector** philatéliste *mf; Fin* **s. duty** droit *m* de timbre; **s. machine** distributeur *m* de timbres-poste
2 *vt (document)* tamponner; **to s. the date on sth** tamponner la date sur qch; **stamped addressed envelope** enveloppe *f* timbrée libellée à ses noms et adresse (b) **to s. one's foot** taper du pied
3 *vi* **to s. on sth** *(on purpose)* écraser qch avec le pied; *(accidentally)* écraser qch du pied; **to s. off/out** partir/ sortir en tapant des pieds

▸**stamp out** *vt sep* (a) *(resistance, dissent)* anéantir; *(poverty)* éradiquer (b) *(fire)* éteindre en piétinant

stampede [stæmˈpiːd] 1 *n* débandade *f;* **there was a s. for the door** il y a eu une ruée vers la porte
2 *vi* se ruer

stance [stɑːns] *n also Fig* position *f*

stand [stænd] 1 *n* (a) *(opinion)* position *f;* **to take a s.** *(on sth)* prendre position *(sur qch)*
(b) *(of lamp, microphone)* pied *m; (for books, postcards)* présentoir *m*
(c) *(stall) (outside)* étalage *m; (at exhibition)* stand *m*
(d) *(at sports ground)* tribune *f*
(e) *(taxi rank)* station *f*
2 *vt (pt & pp* **stood** [stʊd]) (a) *(place)* poser; **to s. sth against sth** mettre qch contre qch
(b) *(endure)* supporter; **to s. comparison with sb/sth** soutenir la comparaison avec qn/qch; **to s. one's ground** tenir bon
(c) *(pay for)* **to s. sb a drink/meal** payer à boire/ manger à qn
(d) *(have)* **to s. a chance (of doing sth)** avoir des chances (de faire qch); **she doesn't s. a chance** elle n'a aucune chance
(e) *Law* **to s. trial** passer en jugement
3 *vi* (a) *(of person) (get up)* se mettre debout; *(be upright)* être debout; *(remain upright)* rester debout; **to s. on one's head** faire le poirier; **I could hardly s.** je tenais à peine debout; **don't just s. there!** ne reste pas planté là les bras ballants!; **to s. fast or firm** tenir bon; **to s. still** *(of person)* se tenir immobile; **time seemed to s. still** le temps semblait s'être arrêté
(b) *(of building)* se dresser; *(of object)* être, se trouver
(c) *(be in situation)* **inflation/unemployment stands at...** le taux d'inflation/de chômage s'élève à...; **to s. in need of sth** avoir besoin de qch; **to s. to do sth** risquer de faire qch; **it stands to reason that...** il est clair que...

(d) *(idioms)* **to be standing right behind sb** être avec qn; **to s. on one's own two feet** se débrouiller tout(e) seul(e); **I don't know where I s.** je ne sais pas à quoi m'en tenir; **to know how things** savoir où j'en suis les choses; **I s. corrected** autant pour moi; **to s. for Parliament** se présenter aux élections législatives; **the offer still stands** l'offre tient toujours

▸**stand aside** *vi* s'écarter

▸**stand back** *vi (move away)* reculer **(from** de); *Fig* prendre de la distance **(from** par rapport à)

▸**stand by** 1 *vt insep* (a) *(person, cause)* défendre, soutenir (b) *(promise, decision)* maintenir
2 *vi* (a) *(be ready)* **to s. by (for sth/to do sth)** *(of person)* se tenir prêt(e) (pour qch/à faire qch); *(of vehicle)* être prêt (pour qch/à faire qch) (b) *(not get involved)* rester sans rien faire

▸**stand down** *vi (retire)* se retirer

▸**stand for** *vt insep* (a) *(mean, represent)* vouloir dire (b) *(tolerate)* supporter

▸**stand out** *vi* (a) *(be prominent)* ressortir; **to s. out in a crowd** se détacher dans la foule; *Fam* **it stands out a mile** ça se voit comme le nez au milieu de la figure (b) *(oppose)* **to s. out against sth** résister à qch

▸**stand up** 1 *vt sep* (a) *(put in upright position)* mettre à la verticale (b) *Fam* **to s. sb up** *(on date)* poser un lapin à qn
2 *vi* (a) *(get up)* se mettre debout; *(be standing)* être debout; *Fig* **to s. up for sb/sth** défendre qn/qch; *Fig* **to s. up to sb** tenir tête à qn (b) *(of argument, theory)* faire le poids; **to s. up to sth** résister à qch; **it'll never s. up in court** ça ne sera pas valable au tribunal

stand-alone word processor [ˈstændələʊn-ˈwɜːdprəʊsesə(r)] *n Comptr* machine *f* à traitement de texte autonome

standard [ˈstændəd] 1 *n* (a) *(point of reference)* référence *f; (set requirement)* norme *f; (for weight, measurement)* étalon *m* (b) *(required level)* niveau *m;* **to be up to/below s.** être du/en dessous du niveau requis; **s. of living** niveau de vie; **s. of accommodation** qualité *f* du logement (c) **standards** *(morals)* principes *mpl* moraux; **to have high/low standards** être/ne pas être exigeant(e) (d) *(flag)* étendard *m; also Fig* **s. bearer** porte-drapeau *m*
2 *adj* (a) *(design, size)* standard *inv; Math* **s. deviation** écart *m* type; **s. lamp** lampadaire *m;* **s. measure** mesure *f* étalon (b) *(usual)* habituel(elle); **s. English** anglais *m* standard; **s. practice** pratique *f* courante

standardization [stændədaɪˈzeɪʃən] *n* normalisation *f*

standardize [ˈstændədaɪz] *vt* normaliser

stand-by [ˈstændbaɪ] *n* (a) *(fuel, food)* réserve *f;* **to have sth as a s.** avoir qch en réserve; **to be on s.** *(of troops, emergency services)* être en état d'alerte; *(for air travel)* **to be on s.** être en stand-by; **s. passenger** passager(ère) *m,f;* **en stand-by; s. ticket** billet *m* en stand-by

stand-in [ˈstændɪn] *n* remplaçant(e) *m,f; (for actor)* doublure *f*

standing [ˈstændɪŋ] 1 *n* (a) *(status)* réputation *f* (b) *(duration)* **of long s.** de longue date
2 *adj* (a) *(upright)* debout; **to give sb a s. ovation** se lever pour applaudir qn (b) *(permanent)* permanent(e); **I have a s. invitation** je peux y aller quand je veux; **s. army** armée *f* de métier; **s. charges** *(on bill)* frais *mpl* d'abonnement; **s. joke** plaisanterie *f* classique; *Fin* **s. order** virement *m* automatique

stand-offish [stændˈɒfɪʃ] *adj* distant(e)

standpoint [ˈstændpɔɪnt] *n* point *m* de vue

standstill ['stændstɪl] *n* **to be at a s.** (*of traffic*) être immobilisé(e); (*of production, economy*) être paralysé(e); **to come to a s.** (*of traffic*) s'immobiliser; (*of production*) s'arrêter; (*of economy*) être paralysé(e)

stand-up ['stændʌp] *adj* (**a**) **s. comedian** comique *mf* de scène; **s. comedy** spectacle *m* comique (**b**) (*fight, argument*) en règle

stank [stæŋk] *pt of* **stink**

stanza ['stænzə] *n* strophe *f*

staple¹ ['steɪpəl] **1** *n* (*for fastening paper*) agrafe *f*; **s. gun** agrafeuse *f*
2 *vt* agrafer

staple² *n* (*basic food*) aliment *m* de base; (*basic product*) principale production *f*; *Fig* **such stories are a s. of the tabloid press** la presse à sensation se nourrit de telles histoires

stapler ['steɪplə(r)] *n* agrafeuse *f*

star [stɑː(r)] **1** *n* (**a**) (*heavenly body*) étoile *f*; **the Stars and Stripes** (*US flag*) la bannière étoilée; *Fig* **to reach for the stars** essayer d'atteindre les sommets; *Fig* **to see stars** (*after blow to head*) voir trente-six chandelles; **s. fruit** carambole *f*; **s. sign** signe *m* du zodiaque (**b**) (*famous person*) star *f*, vedette *f*; **s. player** vedette *f* (**c**) *Fam* **stars** (*horoscope*) horoscope *m*
2 *vt* (*pt & pp* **starred**) (*of film, play*) avoir pour vedette
3 *vi* **to s. in a film/play** jouer dans un film/une pièce

starboard ['stɑːbəd] *n Naut* tribord *m*

starch [stɑːtʃ] **1** *n* (*for shirts, in food*) amidon *m*
2 *vt* (*shirt*) amidonner

starchy ['stɑːtʃɪ] *adj* (**a**) (*food*) riche en féculents (**b**) *Fam* (*person, manner*) guindé(e)

stardom ['stɑːdəm] *n* célébrité *f*

stare [steə(r)] **1** *n* regard *m* fixe
2 *vi* **to be staring sb in the face** (*be obvious*) crever les yeux à qn
3 *vt* **to s. at sb** dévisager qn; **to s. at sth** regarder qch fixement; **to s. into space** regarder dans le vague; **it's rude to s.** ce n'est pas poli de dévisager les gens

starfish ['stɑːfɪʃ] *n* étoile *f* de mer

stark [stɑːk] **1** *adj* (*contrast*) net (nette); (*light, colours*) cru(e); (*truth, facts*) brut(e); (*landscape*) nu(e)
2 *adv* **s. naked** tout(e) nu(e); *Fam* **s. staring mad** complètement dingue

starkers ['stɑːkəz] *adj Fam* à poil

starlet ['stɑːlɪt] *n* (*young actress*) starlette *f*

starlight ['stɑːlaɪt] *n* lumière *f* des étoiles

starling ['stɑːlɪŋ] *n* étourneau *m*

starlit ['stɑːlɪt] *adj* étoilé(e)

starry ['stɑːrɪ] *adj* étoilé(e)

starry-eyed [stɑːrɪ'aɪd] *adj* naïf(ïve)

start [stɑːt] **1** *n* (**a**) (*beginning*) début *m*; (*starting place, of journey, race*) départ *m*; **for a s.** pour commencer; **at the s.** au début; **from the s.** dès le départ; **from s. to finish** du début à la fin; **to make a s. on sth** commencer qch; **he lent her £50 to give her a s.** il lui a prêté 50 livres pour l'aider à démarrer; **to give sb a 60 metre s.** (*in race*) laisser 60 mètres d'avance à qn (**b**) (*sudden movement*) sursaut *m*; **to wake with a s.** se réveiller en sursaut; **to give sb a s.** faire sursauter qn
2 *vt* (**a**) (*begin*) commencer; (*conversation, talks*) entamer; (*fire*) déclencher; (*fashion, rumour*) lancer; (*business*) monter; **to s. doing sth, to s. to do sth** commencer de faire qch; **to s. crying/laughing/sneezing** se

mettre à pleurer/rire/éternuer; **to get started** démarrer (**b**) (*machine, engine*) mettre en marche; (*car*) démarrer
3 *vi* (**a**) (*begin*) commencer; **to s. at the beginning** commencer par le commencement; **to s. by doing sth** commencer par faire qch; **to s. on sth** commencer qch; **she had started as a doctor** elle avait commencé sa carrière comme médecin; **to s. with** au début; d'abord; **now don't YOU s.!** tu ne vas pas t'y mettre aussi! (**b**) (*make sudden movement*) sursauter (**c**) (*begin journey*) se mettre en route (**d**) (*of car, engine*) démarrer

▸**start off 1** *vt sep* (*argument, debate*) commencer; **to s. sb off** (*in business*) aider qn à démarrer; (*on a subject*) lancer qn
2 *vi* (*begin*) commencer; (*on journey*) se mettre en route

▸**start out** *vi* (*begin*) débuter; (*on journey*) se mettre en route

▸**start up 1** *vt sep* (*car*) démarrer; (*machine*) mettre en marche; (*business*) monter
2 *vi* (*of engine*) démarrer; **to s. up in business** monter son entreprise

starter ['stɑːtə(r)] *n* (**a**) (*competitor*) partant(e) *m,f*; (*official*) starter *m* (**b**) **to be a late s.** (*of child*) ne pas être très précoce; **to be a slow s.** (*of person*) être lent(e) à démarrer (**c**) (*device*) starter *m* (**d**) (*in meal*) hors-d'œuvre *m inv*; *Fig* **for starters** pour commencer

starting ['stɑːtɪŋ] *n* (**a**) (*in sport*) **s. block** starting-block *m*; **s. line** ligne *f* de départ; **s. pistol** pistolet *m* de starter (**b**) (*initial*) **s. point** or **place** point *m* de départ; **s. price** (*in betting*) cote *f* au départ; **s. salary** salaire *m* de départ

startle ['stɑːtəl] *vt* faire sursauter

startling ['stɑːtlɪŋ] *adj* (*noise*) effrayant(e); (*news, event*) incroyable

start-up ['stɑːtʌp] *n Com* démarrage *m*; **s. costs** coûts *mpl* d'installation

starvation [stɑː'veɪʃən] *n* privation *f* totale de nourriture; **to die of s.** mourir de faim; **to be on a s. diet** (*not have enough to eat*) n'avoir presque rien à manger; **s. wages** salaires *mpl* de misère

starve [stɑːv] **1** *vt* (*deprive of nourriture*); **to s. sb to death** faire mourir de faim; *Fig* **to be starved of sth** être privé(e) de qch
2 *vi* (*lack food*) souffrir de la faim; **to s. (to death)** mourir de faim; *Fam* **I'm starving** je meurs de faim

starving ['stɑːvɪŋ] *adj* famélique

stash [stæʃ] *Fam* **1** *n* réserve *f*
2 *vt* planquer

state [steɪt] **1** *n* (**a**) (*condition*) état *m*; (*situation*) situation *f*; **I'm not in a fit s. to travel** je ne suis pas en état de voyager; **s. of war/emergency** état de guerre/d'urgence; **s. of affairs** situation *f*; **s. of health** état de santé; **s. of mind** état d'esprit; **in a s. of terror** terrifié(e); **in a s. of shock** en état de choc; **to be in a terrible s.** être dans un état lamentable; **to lie in s.** (*of dead person*) être exposé(e) au public (**b**) (*country, administrative region*) État *m*; *Fam* **the States** (*the USA*) les États-Unis; **s. control** étatisme *m*; *Am* **S. Department** ≃ ministère *m* des Affaires étrangères; **s. occasions** cérémonie *f* officielle; **s. school** école *f* publique; **s. secret** secret *m* d'État; **s. sector** secteur *m* public; **s. visit** visite *f* officielle
2 *vt* (*declare*) déclarer; (*address, age*) indiquer, préciser; **to s. the obvious** enfoncer une porte ouverte; **as stated earlier/above** comme mentionné précédemment/ci-dessus; **at the stated times** aux heures prévues

stateless ['steɪtlɪs] *adj* apatride

stately ['steɪtlɪ] *adj* imposant(e); **s. home** ≃ château *m*

statement ['steɪtmənt] *n* (**a**) *(of opinion)* déclaration *f*; *(of facts)* exposé *m*; **to make a s.** *(of spokesperson)* faire une déclaration; *(of witness)* faire une déposition; *Fig (of lifestyle, behaviour)* faire passer un message (**b**) *(from bank)* relevé *m* de compte

state-of-the-art [steɪtəvɒr'ɑ:t] *adj* ultramoderne

state-owned ['steɪt'əʊnd] *adj (company)* d'État; *(property)* de l'État

statesman ['steɪtsmən] *n* homme *m* d'État

statesmanlike ['steɪtsmənlaɪk] *adj* digne d'un homme d'État

static ['stætɪk] **1** *adj* statique; **s. electricity** électricité *f* statique

2 *n* électricité *f* statique

station ['steɪʃən] **1** *n* (**a**) *(for trains)* gare *f*; **s. master** chef *m* de gare; *Am* **s. wagon** *(car)* break *m* (**b**) *(post)* poste *m*; *(police)* poste *m* de police; *(radio/television)* station *f* de radio/télévision (**c**) *(social condition)* condition *f*; **to have ideas above one's s.** ne pas avoir les moyens de ses ambitions

2 *vt (person)* placer; *(soldier, troops)* poster

stationary ['steɪʃənərɪ] *adj* immobile

stationer ['steɪʃənə(r)] *n* **s.'s (shop)** papeterie *f*

stationery ['steɪʃənərɪ] *n (writing materials)* papeterie *f*; *(writing paper)* papier *m* à lettres

statistic [stə'tɪstɪk] *n* chiffre *m* statistique; **statistics** statistiques *fpl*

statistical [stə'tɪstɪkəl] *adj* statistique

statistician [stætɪs'tɪʃən] *n* statisticien(enne) *m,f*

statue ['stætju:] *n* statue *f*

statuesque [stætjʊ'esk] *adj* sculptural(e)

statuette [stætjʊ'et] *n* statuette *f*

stature ['stætʃə(r)] *n (physical build)* stature *f*; *(reputation)* envergure *f*, réputation *f*

status ['steɪtəs] *n (position, prestige)* statut *m*; *Comptr* **s. line** ligne *f* d'état; **s. report** rapport *m* de situation; **s. symbol** marque *f* de prestige

status quo ['steɪtəs'kwəʊ] *n* statu quo *m inv*

statute ['stætju:t] *n* texte *m* de loi; **by s.** par la loi; **s. book** recueil *m* de lois

statutory ['stætjʊtərɪ] *adj* légal(e); **s. duty** obligation *f* légale; **s. holiday** jour *m* férié

staunch[1] [stɔ:ntʃ] *adj (resolute)* convaincu(e); *(supporter)* ardent(e)

staunch[2] *vt (blood)* étancher

staunchly ['stɔ:ntʃlɪ] *adv* résolument

stave [steɪv] *n* (**a**) *(of barrel)* douve *f* (**b**) *Mus* portée *f*

▸**stave in** *(pt & pp* staved *or* stove [stəʊv]) *vt sep* défoncer; *(ribs)* enfoncer

▸**stave off** *vt sep (problem, disaster)* éviter; *(hunger)* tromper

stay [steɪ] **1** *vi* (**a**) *(endure)* **to s. the course** *or* **distance** tenir la distance

2 *vi* (**a**) *(not move, remain)* rester; *Fam* **to s. put** rester tranquille; **to s. still** rester tranquille; **computers are here to s.** l'informatique est entrée dans les mœurs (**b**) *(reside temporarily)* **I stayed 5 years in the States** j'ai passé cinq ans aux États-Unis; **to s. with sb** loger chez qn (**c**) *Scot (live)* habiter

3 *n* (**a**) *(visit)* séjour *m* (**b**) *Law & Fig* **s. of execution** sursis *m*

▸**stay away** *vi* **to s. away from sb/sth** ne pas s'approcher de qn/qch; **to s. away from school** ne pas aller à l'école

▸**stay in** *vi (not go out)* rester chez soi

▸**stay on** *vi* rester

▸**stay out** *vi* (**a**) *(not go home)* ne pas rentrer; **to s. out all night** ne pas rentrer de la nuit; **to s. out late** rentrer tard (**b**) *(of strikers)* continuer la grève (**c**) *(not interfere)* **to s. out of sth** ne pas se mêler de qch

▸**stay up** *vi* ne pas aller se coucher

staying power ['steɪɪŋ'paʊə(r)] *n* endurance *f*

STD [esti:'di:] *n* (**a**) *(abbr* **subscriber trunk dialling)** indicatif *m* (**b**) *(abbr* **sexually transmitted disease)** MST *f*

stead [sted] *n* **to stand sb in good s.** être fort utile à qn; **in sb's s.** à la place de qn

steadfast ['stedfɑ:st] *adj* dévoué(e); *(opponent, resistance)* constant(e)

steadily ['stedɪlɪ] *adv (change, grow)* progressivement; *(work)* assidûment; *(walk)* d'un pas régulier; *(look)* fixement; *(breathe, increase)* régulièrement

steady ['stedɪ] **1** *adj* (**a**) *(stable)* stable; **in a s. voice** d'une voix assurée (**b**) *(regular)* régulier(ère); *(progress)* constant(e); *(relationship)* durable; **to have a s. girlfriend** avoir une copine (attitrée); **to drive at a s. 50 mph** ≃ rouler à une vitesse régulière de 80 km/h

2 *adv* **to be going s.** sortir ensemble sérieusement; *Fam* **s. (on)!** du calme!

3 *vt* faire tenir; **to s. oneself** trouver son équilibre; **to s. one's nerves** se calmer; **to s. one's voice** contrôler sa voix

steak [steɪk] *n (beef)* steak *m*; *(of fish)* darne *f*; **s. and kidney pie** = tourte à la viande de bœuf et aux rognons

steal [sti:l] *(pt* stole [stəʊl], *pp* stolen ['stəʊlən]) **1** *vt* (**a**) *(thieve)* voler; **to s. sth from sb** voler qch à qn (**b**) *(idioms)* **to s. a glance at sb** jeter un coup d'œil à qn; **to s. the show** ravir la vedette

2 *vi* (**a**) *(thieve)* voler (**b**) *(move quietly)* **to s. away/in/out** s'en aller/rentrer/sortir sans faire de bruit; **to s. up on sb** s'approcher de qn sans faire de bruit; *Fig* prendre qn par surprise

stealth [stelθ] *n* ruse *f*

stealthily ['stelθɪlɪ] *adv* furtivement

stealthy ['stelθɪ] *adj* furtif(ive)

steam [sti:m] **1** *n* (**a**) *vapeur f; (on glass)* buée *f*; **s. bath** bain *m* de vapeur; **s. engine** locomotive *f* à vapeur; **s. iron** fer *m* à vapeur; **s. shovel** pelleteuse *f* (**b**) *(idioms)* **to get up s.** prendre de l'élan; **to run out of s.** s'essouffler; **to let off s.** se défouler; **to do sth under one's own s.** faire qch tout(e) seul(e)

2 *vt (food)* faire cuire à la vapeur

3 *vi (give off steam)* fumer

▸**steam open** *vt sep (envelope)* décacheter à la vapeur

▸**steam up 1** *vi* **to get all steamed up (about sth)** *(of person)* se mettre dans tous ses états (à propos de qch)

2 *vi (of window, glasses)* s'embuer

steamer ['sti:mə(r)] *n* (**a**) *(ship)* bateau *m* à vapeur *m* (**b**) *(for food)* panier *m* de cuisson à la vapeur

steamroller ['sti:mrəʊlə(r)] **1** *n* rouleau *m* compresseur

2 *vt* **to s. sb into doing sth** forcer qn à faire qch

steamship ['sti:mʃɪp] *n* bateau *m* à vapeur

steamy ['sti:mɪ] adj (a) (room) plein(e) de vapeur; (mirror) embué(e) (b) Fam (novel, film) torride

steel [sti:l] 1 n acier m; **nerves of s.** nerfs mpl d'acier; **the s. industry** la sidérurgie; **s. band** steel band m; **s. mill** aciérie f; **s. wool** paille f de fer
2 vt **to s. oneself to do sth** s'armer de courage pour faire qch; **to s. oneself against sth** se blinder contre qch

steelworker ['sti:lwɜːkə(r)] n employé(e) m,f de la sidérurgie

steep¹ [sti:p] adj (a) (path, hill) pentu(e), escarpé(e); (climb) raide; Fig (increase) considérable (b) Fam (expensive) salé(e); (unreasonable) raide

steep² vt (soak) faire tremper; Fig **steeped in history/tradition** imprégné(e) d'histoire/de tradition

steeple ['sti:pəl] n clocher m

steeplechase ['sti:pəltʃeɪs] n steeple-chase m

steeplejack ['sti:pəldʒæk] n réparateur m de clochers et de cheminées d'usines

steer¹ [stɪə(r)] 1 vt (car) conduire; (ship) barrer; **to s. sb out of trouble** sortir qn du pétrin
2 vi (of person) conduire; (of ship) se diriger (**for** vers); **to s. clear of sb/sth** éviter qn/qch

steer² n (bull) bouvillon m

steering ['stɪərɪŋ] n (mechanism) direction f; **s. column** colonne f de direction; Pol **s. committee** comité m d'organisation; **s. wheel** volant m

stem [stem] 1 n (of plant) tige f; (of glass) pied m; (of pipe) tuyau m; (of word) radical m
2 vt (pt & pp stemmed) (halt) stopper; **to s. the tide of sth** enrayer le flot de qch
3 vi **to s. from** provenir de

stench [stentʃ] n puanteur f

stencil ['stensəl] 1 n pochoir m
2 vt (pt & pp stencilled, Am stenciled) dessiner au pochoir

stenographer [stə'nɒɡrəfə(r)] n sténographe mf

step [step] 1 n (a) (movement, sound) pas m; **to take a s.** faire un pas; **s. by s.** pas à pas; Fig petit à petit; also Fig **to watch one's s.** faire attention où l'on met les pieds; **to keep in s.** (in dance) danser en mesure; Fig **to be out of s.** (**with sb**) être en décalage (par rapport à qn)
(b) (action, measure) mesure f; **to take steps** (to do sth) prendre des mesures (pour faire qch); **the next s. is to...** la prochaine chose à faire, c'est de...; **a s. in the right direction** un pas dans la bonne direction
(c) (stage) étape f; **at every s.** à chaque étape; **every s. of the way** sur toute la ligne
(d) (of staircase) marche f; (of stepladder) échelon m; (flight of) **steps** escalier m; (on outside of building) perron m
(e) (exercise) step m; **s. class** cours m de step
2 vi (pt & pp stepped) (take a step) faire un pas; (walk) marcher; **to s. on sth** marcher sur qch; **s. this way** venez par ici; Fam Fig **to s. on it** se grouiller

▶**step back** vi reculer (**from** de); Fig prendre du recul (**from** par rapport à)

▶**step down** vi (resign) démissionner

▶**step forward** vi (volunteer) se porter volontaire

▶**step in** vi (intervene) intervenir

▶**step up** vt sep (increase) accélérer; (pressure) augmenter

stepbrother ['stepbrʌðə(r)] n = fils du conjoint m des parents

stepchild ['steptʃaɪld] n (boy) beau-fils m; (girl) belle-fille f

stepdaughter ['stepdɔːtə(r)] n belle-fille f

stepfather ['stepfɑːðə(r)] n beau-père m

stepladder ['steplædə(r)] n escabeau m

stepmother ['stepmʌðə(r)] n belle-mère f

stepparent ['steppeərənt] n (father) beau-père m; (mother) belle-mère f

steppe [step] n steppe f

stepsister ['stepsɪstə(r)] n = fille du conjoint d'un des parents

stepson ['stepsʌn] n beau-fils m

stereo ['steriəu] 1 n (pl stereos) (equipment) chaîne f stéréo; (sound) stéréo f; **in s.** en stéréo
2 adj stéréo inv

stereophonic [steriə'fɒnɪk] adj stéréophonique

stereoscopic [steriəu'skɒpɪk] adj stéréoscopique

stereotype ['steriətaɪp] n stéréotype m

stereotyped ['steriətaɪpt] adj stéréotypé(e)

sterile ['steraɪl] adj stérile

sterility [ste'rɪlɪtɪ] n stérilité f

sterilization [sterɪlaɪ'zeɪʃən] n stérilisation f

sterilize ['sterɪlaɪz] vt stériliser

sterling ['stɜːlɪŋ] 1 n (British currency) livre f sterling
2 adj (a) (silver) fin(e) (b) (effort, quality) remarquable

stern¹ [stɜːn] adj (person, look) sévère

stern² n (of boat) poupe f

sternum ['stɜːnəm] n (pl sternums or sterna ['stɜːnə]) sternum m

steroid ['steroid] n stéroïde m

stethoscope ['steθəskəup] n stéthoscope m

stevedore ['sti:vədɔː(r)] n docker m

stew [stju:] 1 n ragoût m; Fam Fig **to be in a s.** (of person) être dans le pétrin
2 vt (meat) faire cuire en ragoût; (fruit) faire de la compote de
3 vi (of meat) mijoter; Fam **to let sb s.** (in his/her own juice) laisser qn mariner

steward ['stjuːəd] n (on estate) régisseur m; (on ship, plane) steward m; (at sporting event) organisateur m; (at demonstration) membre m du service d'ordre

stewardess [stjuː'des] n (on ship, plane) hôtesse f

stewed [stjuːd] adj **s. beef** bœuf m en ragoût; **s. fruit** compote f de fruits; **this tea is s.** ce thé a trop infusé

stick¹ [stɪk] n (a) (of wood, glue, chewing gum) bâton m; (for walking) canne f; (of celery, rhubarb) tige f; Fam Fig **to get hold of the wrong end of the s.** comprendre de travers; Fam **she lives out in the sticks** elle habite dans un trou perdu; **s. insect** phasme m (b) Fam (criticism) **to give sb s.** (for sth) taper sur les doigts de qn (à cause de qch); **to take a lot of s.** se faire beaucoup critiquer

stick² [stɪk] (pt & pp stuck [stʌk]) 1 vt (a) (insert) **to s. sth in(to)** sth planter qch dans qch (b) Fam (put) mettre, poser (c) (attach with glue) coller (**on**/**in** sur/dans) (d) Fam (endure) supporter
2 vi (a) (adhere) coller; Fig **the name stuck** ce nom lui/leur/etc est resté; Fig **to s. to one's guns** ne pas en démordre; **to s. to the facts** s'en tenir aux faits; **to s. to one's principles** rester fidèle à ses principes (b) (become jammed) se coincer; Fig **it sticks in my throat** c'est dur à avaler

▶**stick around** vi Fam attendre

▶**stick at** vt insep (persevere with) persévérer dans; **to s. at nothing** ne reculer devant rien

▶**stick by** vt insep (friend) soutenir; (promise, statement) maintenir

▶**stick out 1** vt sep (a) (cause to protrude) faire sortir; **to s. one's tongue out** (at sb) tirer la langue (à qn); Fam **to s. one's neck out** (for sb) prendre des risques (pour qn) (b) Fam (endure) **to s. it out** tenir bon
2 vi (a) (protrude) ressortir; (of ears) être décollé(es); (of teeth) avancer (b) Fam (be noticeable) se voir; **it sticks out a mile** or **like a sore thumb** ça se voit comme le nez au milieu de la figure

▶**stick together 1** vt sep coller
2 vi (a) (with glue) être collé(e) (b) (of friends) rester ensemble

▶**stick up 1** vt sep (sign, poster) mettre; Fam **s. 'em up!** haut les mains!
2 vi (of building, hair) se dresser

▶**stick up for** vt insep (person, rights) prendre la défense de

▶**stick with** vt insep (not give up) rester avec

sticker ['stɪkə(r)] n autocollant m

stick-in-the-mud ['stɪknðəmʌd] n Fam rabat-joie m inv

stickleback ['stɪklbæk] n épinoche f

stickler ['stɪklə(r)] n **to be a s. for sth** être à cheval sur qch

stick-on ['stɪkɒn] adj autocollant(e)

stick-up ['stɪkʌp] n Fam (robbery) braquage m

sticky ['stɪkɪ] adj (a) (substance) collant(e); (climate) humide, moite; (label) adhésif(ive); Fig **to have s. fingers** avoir une tendance pickpocket; **s. tape** ruban m adhésif (b) Fig (awkward) délicat(e); **to come to a s. end** mal finir; Fam **to be on a s. wicket** être dans une situation délicate

stiff [stɪf] adj (a) (rigid) rigide; (paste) ferme; **as s. as a board** tout(e) raide; **to be bored s.** s'ennuyer à mourir; **to be scared s.** avoir une trouille bleue; **to be frozen s.** être frigorifié(e) (b) (joint) ankylosé(e); **to be s.** (of person) avoir des courbatures; **to have a s. neck** avoir un torticolis; **my leg is s.** j'ai la jambe ankylosée (c) (handle, hinge, drawer) dur(e) (d) (severe) (punishment, fine) sévère; (resistance) opiniâtre; (competition) rude; (exam) dur(e); (breeze) fort(e); **a s. drink** une boisson forte (e) (formal) rigide; (smile) forcé(e)

stiffen ['stɪfən] **1** vt renforcer; (paste) épaissir
2 vi se raidir

stiffly ['stɪflɪ] adv (bow) avec raideur; (answer, greet) avec froideur

stifle ['staɪfəl] vt also Fig étouffer

stifling ['staɪflɪŋ] adj étouffant(e)

stigma ['stɪgmə] (pl stigmas) n honte f

stigmata [stɪg'mɑːtə] npl (of saint) stigmates mpl

stigmatize ['stɪgmətaɪz] vt stigmatiser

stile [staɪl] n échalier m

stiletto [stɪ'letəʊ] (pl stilettos) n (dagger) stylet m; (shoe) talon m aiguille; **s. heels** talons aiguille

still¹ [stɪl] **1** adj (motionless) immobile; (calm) calme; (silent) silencieux(euse); (drink) non gazeux(euse); **to stand s.** ne pas bouger; Art **s. life** nature f morte; Prov **s. waters run deep** il faut se méfier de l'eau qui dort
2 vt calmer, apaiser

3 n (a) **in the s. of the night** dans le silence de la nuit (b) (photograph) photo f de plateau

still² adv (a) (up to given point in time) toujours, encore; **she's s. alive** elle vit toujours; **I s. think/say that...** je continue de penser/dire que...; **I s. have 500 francs** il me reste encore 500 francs (b) (nonetheless) tout de même; **s., it could have been worse** enfin, ç'aurait pu être pire (c) (even) encore; **s. more/better** encore plus/mieux

still³ n (distilling equipment) alambic m

stillbirth ['stɪlbɜːθ] n enfant m mort-né

stillborn ['stɪlbɔːn] adj mort-né(e)

stillness ['stɪlnɪs] n tranquillité f

stilt [stɪlt] n (for walking) échasse f; (for building) pilotis m

stilted ['stɪltɪd] adj qui manque de naturel

stimulant ['stɪmjʊlənt] n stimulant m

stimulate ['stɪmjʊleɪt] vt stimuler

stimulating ['stɪmjʊleɪtɪŋ] adj stimulant(e)

stimulation [stɪmjʊ'leɪʃən] n stimulation f

stimulus ['stɪmjʊləs] (pl stimuli ['stɪmjʊlaɪ]) n encouragement m; (physiological) stimulus m inv

sting [stɪŋ] **1** n (a) (of bee) dard m; (of scorpion) aiguillon m; (wound) piqûre f (b) (sensation) brûlure f (c) (idioms) **to have a s. in the tail** (of story, proposal) avoir une fin inattendue; **to take the s. out of sth** atténuer les effets de qch
2 vt (pt & pp stung [stʌŋ]) (of bee, nettle) piquer; Fig (of remark) blesser, piquer au vif; Fig **to s. sb into action** inciter qn à agir; Fam Fig **they stung him for £10** ils l'ont arnaqué de 10 livres
3 vi (of eyes, skin) piquer

stinging ['stɪŋɪŋ] adj (pain) cuisant(e); (remark, criticism) cinglant(e); **s. nettle** ortie f

stingray ['stɪŋreɪ] n pastenague f

stingy ['stɪndʒɪ] adj (person) pingre; (portion) minuscule; **to be s. with one's praise** être avare de compliments

stink [stɪŋk] **1** n (smell) puanteur f; Fam Fig **to kick up a s.** (about sth) faire tout un scandale (à propos de qch)
2 vi (pt stank [stæŋk] or stunk [stʌŋk], pp stunk) (a) (smell) puer; **to s. of sth** puer qch; Fam Fig **to s. of corruption** sentir la corruption à plein nez (b) Fam Fig (be of bad quality) craindre

stinkbomb ['stɪŋkbɒm] n boule f puante

stinker ['stɪŋkə(r)] n Fam (person) peau f de vache; (difficult task) casse-tête m; **a s. of a cold** un rhume carabiné

stinking ['stɪŋkɪŋ] **1** adj puant(e); **a s. cold** un rhume carabiné
2 adv Fam **to be s. rich** être bourré(e) de fric

stint [stɪnt] **1** n (period) période f; (share of work) part f de travail; **to take a s. at the wheel** prendre le volant; **he had a two-year s. in the army** il a fait deux ans d'armée
2 vt épargner; **to s. oneself** se sacrifier
3 vi **to s. on sth** lésiner sur qch

stipend ['staɪpend] n traitement m

stipulate ['stɪpjʊleɪt] vt stipuler

stipulation [stɪpjʊ'leɪʃən] n stipulation f

stir [stɜː(r)] **1** vt (pt & pp stirred) (a) (liquid, mixture) remuer; (leaves) agiter (b) Fig (person) émouvoir, remuer; (emotion) réveiller; (curiosity) exciter; **to s. sb to do sth** inciter qn à faire qch; Fam **to s. oneself** se remuer; Fam **to s. it** (make trouble) envenimer les choses
2 vi (move) bouger, remuer

3 n (a) to give sth a s. remuer qch (b) *Fig* to cause a s. faire du bruit

▸**stir up** vt sep (a) (dust, leaves) remuer (b) *Fig* (rebellion, anger, resentment) attiser; (workers, crowd) inciter à la révolte; to s. up trouble semer la zizanie; to s. things up envenimer les choses

stir-fry ['stɜ:fraɪ] (pt & pp stir-fried) vt Culin faire sauter

stirrer ['stɜ:rə(r)] n Fam (trouble-maker) semeur(euse) m,f de zizanie

stirring ['stɜ:rɪŋ] **1** n the first stirrings of les premiers signes de
   2 adj (speech, film) poignant(e)

stirrup ['stɪrəp] n étrier m

stitch [stɪtʃ] **1** n (a) (in sewing) point m; (in knitting) maille f; Med point (de suture); Fam she didn't have a s. on elle était nue comme un ver; Prov a s. in time saves nine un point à temps en vaut cent (b) (sharp pain) point m (de côté); to get a s. prendre un point (c) Fam we were in stitches (laughing) on était pliés
   2 vt (clothing) coudre; Med recoudre

▸**stitch up** vt sep Fam (falsely incriminate) faire porter le chapeau à

stoat [stəʊt] n hermine f

stock [stɒk] **1** n (a) (supply) provisions fpl; Com stock m; Com while stocks last jusqu'à épuisement des stocks; to have sth in s. avoir qch en stock; to be out of s. être épuisé(e); to take s. faire le point; Com s. control gestion f des stocks; Com s. list inventaire m des stocks (b) (livestock) bétail m (c) Fin valeurs fpl, actions fpl; Fig her s. is going up/down sa cote est en hausse/baisse; stocks and shares valeurs mobilières; s. exchange Bourse f (des valeurs); s. market marché m des valeurs (d) (descent) of German s. de souche allemande (e) (of rifle) fût m (f) stocks (for punishment) pilori m (g) (in cooking) bouillon m; s. cube bouillon cube m
   2 adj (argument, excuse) classique
   3 vt (a) (goods) vendre (b) (supply) (shop) approvisionner (with en)

▸**stock up** vi faire des provisions (with de)

stockade [stɒ'keɪd] n palissade f

stockbroker ['stɒkbrəʊkə(r)] n Fin agent de change

stockholder ['stɒkhəʊldə(r)] n Fin actionnaire mf

Stockholm ['stɒkhəʊm] n Stockholm

stocking ['stɒkɪŋ] n (garment) bas m

stockist ['stɒkɪst] n Com stockiste mf

stockpile ['stɒkpaɪl] **1** n réserves fpl
   2 vt faire des réserves de

stockroom ['stɒkru:m] n réserve f, magasin m

stock-still ['stɒk'stɪl] adv to stand s. se tenir complètement immobile

stocktaking ['stɒkteɪkɪŋ] n Com inventaire m des stocks; Fig a s. exercise un examen de situation

stocky ['stɒkɪ] adj trapu(e)

stodge [stɒdʒ] n Fam (food) aliments mpl bourratifs

stodgy ['stɒdʒɪ] adj (food) bourratif(ive); (book) indigeste

stoic ['stəʊɪk] n & adj stoïque mf

stoical ['stəʊɪkəl] adj stoïque

stoicism ['stəʊɪsɪzəm] n stoïcisme m

stoke [stəʊk] vt (fire, boiler) alimenter; Fig entretenir

STOL [stɒl] n Av (abbr short take-off and landing) ADAC m

stole[1] [stəʊl] n (garment) étole f

stole[2] pt of steal

stolen ['stəʊlən] **1** adj volé(e)
   2 pp of steal

stolid ['stɒlɪd] adj impassible

stomach ['stʌmək] **1** n ventre m; (organ) estomac m; on an empty s. à jeun; Fig it turns my s. ça m'écœure; Fig to have no s. for sth ne pas avoir envie de qch; to have (a) s. ache avoir mal au ventre; (in organ) avoir mal à l'estomac; Med s. pump pompe f stomacale
   2 vt Fig (tolerate) supporter

stomp [stɒmp] vi marcher en tapant des pieds; to s. in/out entrer/sortir en tapant des pieds

stone [stəʊn] **1** n (a) (material, piece of rock) pierre f; (smaller) caillou m; Fig to leave no s. unturned remuer ciel et terre; Fig a s.'s throw from here à deux pas d'ici; the S. Age l'âge m de pierre (b) (of fruit) noyau m (c) (unit of weight) = 6,35kg
   2 adj en pierre; (jug) en grès
   3 vt (a) (fruit) dénoyauter (b) (person) lapider

stone-cold ['stəʊn'kəʊld] adj glacé(e)

stoned [stəʊnd] adj very Fam (on drugs) défoncé(e)

stone-dead ['stəʊn'ded] adj raide mort(e)

stone-deaf ['stəʊn'def] adj sourd(e) comme un pot

stonemason ['stəʊnmeɪsən] n maçon m

stonewall [stəʊn'wɔ:l] vi (in game) pratiquer un jeu défensif; (in inquiry) refuser de répondre

stoneware ['stəʊnweə(r)] n poterie f en grès

stonework ['stəʊnwɜ:k] n maçonnerie f

stonily ['stəʊnɪlɪ] adv froidement

stony ['stəʊnɪ] adj (ground, beach) caillouteux(euse); Fig (look, silence) glacial(e); Fam Fig to be s. broke n'avoir pas un rond

stood [stʊd] pt & pp of stand

stooge [stu:dʒ] n (comedian's fall-guy) faire-valoir m; (minion) larbin m

stool [stu:l] n (a) (seat) tabouret m; Fig to fall between two stools être assis(e) entre deux chaises; Fam s. pigeon balance f, indic m (b) Med (faeces) selles fpl

stoop[1] [stu:p] **1** n to have a s. être voûté(e); to walk with a s. marcher le dos courbé
   2 vi (bend down) se pencher; Fig to s. to (doing) sth s'abaisser à (faire) qch

stoop[2] n Am (of house) (with roof) véranda f; (without roof) perron m

stop [stɒp] **1** n (a) (halt) arrêt m; to put a s. to sth mettre fin à qch; to come to a s. s'arrêter; put a s. stop m (b) (pause) (in work) pause f; (in journey) halte f; (of plane) escale f; (of train) arrêt m (c) (for bus, train) arrêt m (d) (full stop) point m; (in telegram) stop m (e) Mus (on organ) jeu m; Fig to pull out all the stops tout mettre en œuvre
   2 vt (pt & pp stopped) (a) (halt) (person, vehicle) arrêter; (conversation, speaker) interrompre; (corruption, abuse) mettre fin à; Fin to a cheque faire opposition à un chèque; s., thief! au voleur! (b) (cease) arrêter; to s. doing sth arrêter de faire qch (c) (prevent) empêcher; to s. sb from doing sth empêcher qn de faire qch; I couldn't s. myself je n'ai pas pu m'en empêcher (d) (fill in) (hole, gap) boucher
   3 vi (a) (halt) (of moving person, vehicle) s'arrêter (b) (cease) (of speaker, worker) s'arrêter; (of pain, bleeding) cesser; (of rain) s'arrêter, cesser; she'll s. at nothing rien ne l'arrêtera; to s. short s'arrêter net (c) (stay) rester

▶**stop by** *vi (visit)* passer; **I'll s. by your place tomorrow** je passerai chez toi demain

▶**stop off** *vi* faire une halte

▶**stop over** *vi Av* faire escale

▶**stop up** *vt sep (hole, sink, pipe)* boucher

stopcock ['stɒpkɒk] *n* robinet *m* d'arrêt

stopgap ['stɒpgæp] *n (thing, person)* bouche-trou *m*; **s. measure** mesure *f* transitoire

stoplight ['stɒplaɪt] *n Am Aut* feux *mpl* (tricolores *ou* de signalisation)

stopover ['stɒpəʊvə(r)] *n Av* escale *f*

stoppage ['stɒpɪdʒ] *n (a) (of flow, traffic)* arrêt *m*; *(strike)* débrayage *m* **(b)** *Fin (deduction)* retenue *f*

stopper ['stɒpə(r)] *n* bouchon *m*

stop-press ['stɒppres] *adj Journ* de dernière minute

stopwatch ['stɒpwɒtʃ] *n* chronomètre *m*

storage ['stɔːrɪdʒ] *n (a) (action)* emmagasinage *m*; *(space available)* (espace *m* de) rangement *m*; **s. into s.** entreposer qch; **s. heater** radiateur *m* à accumulation; **s. space** espace *m* de rangement; **s. tank** citerne *f* **(b)** *Comptr* mémoire *f*

store [stɔː(r)] **1** *n (a) (supply) (of goods, food)* provision *f*; *Fig (of knowledge)* fonds *m*; **stores** réserves *fpl* **(b)** *(warehouse)* entrepôt *m* **(c)** *Am (shop)* magasin *m*; *also Br* **s. detective** vigile *m* **(d)** *(idioms)* **to hold** *or* **keep sth in s.** tenir *ou* garder qch en réserve; **I have a surprise in s. for her** je lui réserve une surprise; **to set great s. by sth** faire grand cas de qch

2 *vt (put in storage)* entreposer; *(food)* ranger; *(electricity, heat)* emmagasiner; **in a cool place** conserver au frais

▶**store up** *vt sep* accumuler

storehouse ['stɔːhaʊs] *n* entrepôt *m*

storeroom ['stɔːruːm] *n (in office, factory)* réserve *f*; *(at home)* débarras *m*

storey, Am story ['stɔːrɪ] *n* étage *m*; **a four-s. building** un immeuble de quatre étages

stork [stɔːk] *n* cigogne *f*

storm [stɔːm] **1** *n (a) (bad weather)* tempête *f*; *(thunderstorm)* orage *m*; *Fig* **a s. in a teacup** une tempête dans un verre d'eau; **s. cloud** nuée *f* d'orage; **s. door** double porte *f* **(b)** *Fig (scandal, of protest)* tempête *f*; *(of abuse)* bordée *f* **(c)** *Mil* **to take sth by s.** prendre qch d'assaut; *Fig* **she took London by s.** elle a eu un succès foudroyant à Londres; **s. troops** troupes *fpl* d'assaut

2 *vt (town, fortress)* prendre d'assaut

3 *vi (of person)* tempêter (**at sb** contre qn); **to s. in/out** entrer/sortir comme un ouragan

stormy ['stɔːmɪ] *adj also Fig* orageux(euse)

story[1] ['stɔːrɪ] *(pl* **stories)** *n (a) (account)* histoire *f*; *Fig* **to tell stories** *(lie)* raconter des histoires **(b)** *(plot) (of novel, play)* intrigue *f*, histoire *f* **(c)** *(in newspaper)* article *m* **(d)** *(idioms)* **that's quite another s.** ça c'est une autre histoire; **it's the same old s.** c'est toujours la même histoire; *Fam* **it's the s. of my life** je suis le/la spécialiste de ce genre de choses; **it's a long s.** c'est une longue histoire; **to cut a long s. short,...** bref, pour résumer...

story[2] *Am (of building) =* **storey**

storybook ['stɔːrɪbʊk] *n* livre *m* d'histoires

storyteller ['stɔːrɪtelə(r)] *n* conteur(euse) *m,f*

stout [staʊt] **1** *n (beer)* stout *f*, bière *f* brune forte
2 *adj (a) (fat)* corpulent(e) **(b)** *(solid) (door, shoes)* solide **(c)** *(brave) (person, resistance)* acharné(e)

stouthearted [staʊt'hɑːtɪd] *adj Lit* vaillant(e)

stoutly ['staʊtlɪ] *adv (resist, maintain)* avec fermeté

stove [stəʊv] *n (for cooking)* cuisinière *f*; *(for heating)* poêle *m*

stow [stəʊ] *vt (put away)* ranger; *Naut* arrimer

▶**stow away** *vi (on ship)* s'embarquer clandestinement

stowaway ['stəʊəweɪ] *n* passager(ère) *m,f* clandestin(e)

straddle ['strædəl] *vt (horse)* enfourcher; *(chair)* se mettre à califourchon sur; *Fig (period of time, subject)* couvrir

strafe [streɪf] *vt Mil* mitrailler en rase-mottes

straggle ['strægəl] *vi (a) (lag behind)* être à la traîne **(b)** *(of hair)* pendouiller

straggler ['stræglə(r)] *n* retardataire *mf*

straggly ['stræglɪ] *adj (hair)* épars(e)

straight [streɪt] **1** *adj (a) (level, not curved) (line, tie, skirt, picture, back)* droit(e); *(hair)* raide; **to keep a s. face** garder son sérieux; **to put things** *or* **matters s.** arranger les choses; **to put sb s. about sth** éclairer qn sur qch **(b)** *(consecutive)* consécutif(ive); **s. flush** *(in cards)* quinte *f* flush

(c) *(honest) (person) (answer)* clair(e); **to be s. with sb** jouer franc jeu avec qn **(d)** *(conventional)* conformiste; *Th* **s. man** faire-valoir *m* **(e)** *Fam (heterosexual)* hétéro **(f)** *(undiluted)* pur(e)

2 *adv (a) (in straight line)* droit; **sit up s.!** tiens-toi droit sur ton siège!; **to see s.** voir bien; **I can't think s.** je n'ai pas les idées claires; **to look s. ahead** regarder droit devant soi; **go s. on** allez tout droit; *Fig* **to go s.** *(of criminal)* se ranger

(b) *(immediately)* immédiatement; **I'll be s. back** je reviens tout de suite; **s. away** *or* **off** tout de suite

(c) *(directly)* directement; **to come** *or* **get s. to the point** allez droit au fait; **to come s. out with sth** dire qch tout net

3 *n (a)* **to keep to the s. and narrow** rester sur le droit chemin

(b) *(on running track, racecourse)* ligne *f* droite

straightaway ['streɪtəweɪ] *adv* tout de suite

straighten ['streɪtən] *vt (bent road, rod)* redresser; *(picture)* remettre droit; *(tie, hat)* ajuster; **to s. one's back** se redresser

▶**straighten out** *vt sep (problem)* régler; *(one's affairs)* mettre de l'ordre dans

straight-faced ['streɪt'feɪst] *adj* à l'air sérieux

straightforward [streɪt'fɔːwəd] *adj (a) (honest)* direct(e), franc (franche) **(b)** *(simple)* simple

strain[1] [streɪn] **1** *n (a) (on rope, beam, economy, friendship)* tension *f*; *(on muscle, ankle)* foulure *f*; **to put a s. on** *(economy)* grever; *(friendship)* éprouver **(b)** *(mental stress)* stress *m*; **to be under a lot of s.** être très stressé(e)

2 *vt (muscle, ankle)* se fouler; *(economy)* grever; *(friendship)* éprouver; **to s. one's back** se faire mal au dos; **to s. one's ears** tendre l'oreille **(b)** *Culin (liquid)* filtrer, passer; *(vegetables)* égoutter

3 *vi* **to s. at a rope** tirer sur une corde; *Fig* **to s. at the leash** ne plus tenir en place

strain[2] *n (variety) (of virus)* souche *f*; *(of plant)* variété *f*

strained [streɪnd] *adj (muscle)* froissé(e); *Fig (atmosphere, relationship)* tendu(e)

strainer ['streɪnə(r)] *n* passoire *f*

strait [streɪt] *n* détroit *m*; **the Straits of Gibraltar** le détroit de Gibraltar

straitlaced ['streɪt'leɪst] *adj* collet monté *inv*

strand¹ [strænd] vt (ship) échouer; **to be stranded** (of person) être bloqué(e)

strand² n (of rope, cotton) brin m; (of hair) mèche f; Fig (of plot) fil m

strange [streɪndʒ] adj (a) (odd) (person, behaviour) bizarre (b) (unfamiliar) inconnu(e)

strangely ['streɪndʒlɪ] adv (behave, dress) bizarrement; **s. enough,...** chose bizarre,...

strangeness ['streɪndʒnɪs] n (a) (oddness) bizarrerie f (b) (unfamiliarity) étrangeté f

stranger ['streɪndʒə(r)] n (unknown person) inconnu(e) m,f; (from somewhere else) étranger(ère) m,f; **I'm a s. here myself** je ne suis pas d'ici

strangle ['stræŋgəl] vt also Fig étrangler

stranglehold ['stræŋgəlhəʊld] n Fig **to have a s. on sth** avoir la mainmise sur qch

strangulation [stræŋgjʊ'leɪʃən] n strangulation f

strap [stræp] **1** n (of leather, canvas) sangle f, lanière f; (on dress, bra) bretelle f; (for watch) bracelet m; (for shoe) bride f
2 vt (pt & pp strapped) **to s. sth to sth** sangler qch à qch; Fam **to be strapped (for cash)** être un peu juste
▶**strap in** vt sep attacher; **to s. oneself in** attacher sa ceinture de sécurité

strapless ['stræplɪs] adj (dress, bra) sans bretelles

strapping ['stræpɪŋ] adj costaud(e)

Strasbourg ['stræzbɜːg] n Strasbourg

strategic [strə'tiːdʒɪk] adj stratégique

strategist ['strætədʒɪst] n stratège m

strategy ['strætədʒɪ] n (pl strategies) n stratégie f

stratification [strætɪfɪ'keɪʃən] n stratification f

stratosphere ['strætəsfɪə(r)] n stratosphère f

stratum ['strɑːtəm] n (pl strata ['strɑːtə]) n strate f; Fig couche f

straw [strɔː] n (a) (from wheat, for drinking) paille f; **s. hat** chapeau m de paille; Fig **s. man** homme m de paille; **s. poll** sondage m d'opinion (b) (idioms) **to clutch** or **grasp at straws** se raccrocher à de faux espoirs; **that's the last s.!** ça c'est le comble!

strawberry ['strɔːbərɪ] n (pl strawberries) n fraise f; **s. jam** confiture f de fraises

straw-coloured ['strɔːkʌləd] adj jaune paille inv

stray [streɪ] **1** n (dog) chien m errant; (cat) chat m égaré
2 adj (animal) égaré(e); (dog) errant(e); (bullet) perdu(e)
3 vi (of person, animal) s'égarer; **to s. from the point** s'écarter du sujet

streak [striːk] **1** n (stripe) (of paint, dirt) traînée f; (of light) rai m; (in hair) mèche f; **a s. of lightning** un éclair; **a s. of luck** une période de chance; **to be on a winning/losing s.** être dans une période de chance/poisse; **to have a mean/cruel s.** avoir tendance à être radin(e)/cruel(elle)
2 vt **streaked with dirt** plein(e) de traînées sales; **streaked with tears** strié(e) de larmes; **his hair is streaked with silver** ses cheveux sont parsemés de cheveux gris; **to have one's hair streaked** se faire faire des mèches
3 vi (move quickly) **to s. off** partir à toute vitesse; **to s. past** passer en trombe (b) Fam (run naked) courir nu(e) (en public)

streaker ['striːkə(r)] n Fam = personne qui court nue en public

streaky ['striːkɪ] adj (surface, pattern) strié(e); **s. bacon** bacon m entrelardé

stream [striːm] **1** n (a) (brook) ruisseau m (b) (of light, blood, water) jet m; (of tears, insults) torrent m; (of people) flot m; **to come on s.** (of industrial plant) entrer en production
2 vi (a) (spurt) **to s. blood** ruisseler de sang (b) Br Sch **to s. pupils** répartir des élèves par niveau
3 vi (a) (of liquid) ruisseler; (of people) affluer; (of traffic) s'écouler; **her eyes were streaming** ses yeux étaient ruisselants de larmes (b) (of hair, banner) flotter

streamer ['striːmə(r)] n banderole f

streamline ['striːmlaɪn] vt (vehicle) caréner; Fig (system) rationaliser; (department) dégraisser

streamlined ['striːmlaɪnd] adj (vehicle) caréné(e); Fig (system) rationalisé(e); (department) dégraissé(e)

street [striːt] n (a) rue f; **on the s.** dans la rue; **s. fighting** combats mpl de rue; **s. lamp** lampadaire m; **s. map** plan m (de la ville); **s. market** marché m de plein air; **s. sweeper** balayeur(euse) m,f; **s. theatre** théâtre m de rue; **s. value** (of drugs) valeur f à la revente (b) (idioms) **to walk the streets** (of prostitute) faire le tapin ou le trottoir; **the man in the s.** Monsieur Tout-le-Monde; Fam **to be streets ahead** dépasser tout le monde; **that's right up my s.** c'est tout à fait mon rayon; Fam **to have s. cred** être très branché(e)

streetcar ['striːtkɑː(r)] n Am tramway m

streetwalker ['striːtwɔːkə(r)] n racoleuse f

streetwise ['striːtwaɪz] adj débrouillard(e)

strength [streŋθ] n (a) (of person, wind, emotion, currency) force f; (of rope, fabric) solidité f; (of light, alcohol, army) puissance f; **to be at full s.** (of department, regiment) avoir des effectifs complets; **to be under s.** (of department, regiment) ne pas avoir des effectifs complets; **in s.** en force; **to go from s. to s.** aller de mieux en mieux; **on the s. of** sur la base de; **on the s. of her qualifications** grâce à ses diplômes (b) (strong point) point m fort

strengthen ['streŋθən] **1** vt (wall, building) renforcer, consolider; (muscle) affermir; (friendship) consolider; (determination, position) renforcer
2 vi (of friendship) se consolider; (of determination) se renforcer; (of currency) se raffermir; (of wind) souffler plus fort

strenuous ['strenjʊəs] adj (activity, lifestyle) fatigant(e); (effort, opposition) vigoureux(euse); (denial) énergique

strenuously ['strenjʊəslɪ] adv (campaign, deny) énergiquement; (resist) vigoureusement

stress [stres] **1** n (a) (tension) (physical) tension f; (mental) stress m; **to be under a lot of s.** être très stressé(e); **s. factor** facteur m de stress (b) (emphasis) insistance f; Ling accentuation f; **to put s. on sth** insister sur qch
2 vt (emphasize) insister sur; Ling accentuer

stressful ['stresfʊl] adj stressant(e)

stretch [stretʃ] **1** n (a) (of body) **to have a s.** s'étirer; Fig **by no s. of the imagination** même avec beaucoup d'imagination; **s. marks** vergetures fpl (b) (of water, land) étendue f; (of road) tronçon m; (of time, silence) période f; **at one s.** d'une traite (c) **at full s.** (factory) au maximum de ses capacités
2 vt (a) (elastic) étirer; (belt, arm, hand) tendre; **to s. the truth** exagérer; **to s. one's legs** se dégourdir les jambes (b) (put demands on) (person) pousser à son maximum; (resources) utiliser au maximum; **to s. sb's patience** abuser de; **we're fully stretched at the moment** nous sommes au maximum de notre rendement en ce moment (c) (make last) (income, supplies) faire durer
3 vi (a) (of elastic) s'étendre; (of person, fabric) s'étirer (b) (of road, land, years) s'étendre, s'étaler (c) (of resources, budget)

my budget won't s. to a new car je n'ai pas les moyens de m'acheter une nouvelle voiture

▶**stretch out 1** vt sep (arm, hand) tendre

2 vi (**a**) (of person) s'étirer (**b**) (of road, land, time) s'étaler, s'étendre

stretcher ['stretʃə(r)] n brancard m; **s. bearer** brancardier m

stretchy ['stretʃɪ] adj extensible

strew [stru:] (pp strewed or strewn [stru:n]) vt (objects) éparpiller; **to be strewn with sth** (of surface) être jonché/e de qch

stricken ['strɪkən] adj (with grief, guilt) accablé(e) (**with** de); (with illness, by disaster) frappé(e) (**with** par)

strict [strɪkt] adj (**a**) (person, instruction, discipline) strict(e); **s. morals** morale f sévère; **a s. Moslem** un musulman de stricte obéissance (**b**) (meaning, minimum) strict(e); **in strictest confidence** en toute confiance

strictly ['strɪktlɪ] adv (**a**) (severely, only) strictement (**b**) (exactly) **s. speaking** à proprement parler; **not s. true** pas tout à fait vrai(e)

strictness ['strɪktnɪs] n (of discipline, rules) sévérité f

stride [straɪd] **1** n (**a**) pas m; (when running) foulée f (**b**) (idioms) **to make great strides** faire des pas de géant; **to take sth in one's s.** prendre qch calmement; **to get into one's s.** trouver son rythme

2 vi (pt strode [strəʊd], pp stridden ['strɪdən]) **to s. in/out** entrer/sortir à grands pas

strident ['straɪdənt] adj strident(e)

strife [straɪf] n conflits mpl

strike [straɪk] **1** n (**a**) (refusal to work) grève f; **to be on s.** être en grève; **s. fund** = caisse de prévoyance permettant d'aider les grévistes; **s. pay** indemnité f de grève

(**b**) (discovery) (of ore, oil) découverte f

(**c**) (blow) coup m; Mil attaque f, raid m

2 vt (pt & pp **struck** [strʌk]) (**a**) (hit) frapper; (collide with) heurter, taper contre; **to be struck by lightning** être frappé(e) par la foudre; **to s. sb in the face** frapper qn à la figure; **to s. a blow** donner un coup; Fig **to s. a blow for freedom** se battre pour défendre sa liberté; Fig **the clock struck ten** l'horloge a sonné dix heures; Fig **to s. the right/wrong note** (of speech, remark) sonner juste/faux; **to s. terror into sb** frapper qn de terreur; **to be struck dumb/blind** être frappé(e) de mutisme/cécité; **he was struck dead by a heart attack** il a été emporté par une crise cardiaque

(**b**) (match) craquer

(**c**) (coin, medal) frapper

(**d**) (impress) frapper; **she strikes me as a reasonable person** elle me paraît raisonnable; **it struck me that...** il m'a semblé que...

(**e**) (discover) (gold, oil) découvrir; Fam **to s. it rich** faire fortune; Fam **to s. it lucky** avoir un coup de chance

(**f**) (reach) (bargain, deal) conclure; **to s. a balance** trouver un équilibre

3 vi (**a**) (attack) (of enemy) attaquer; (of criminal) frapper; (of disaster, earthquake) se produire; (of clock) sonner; **to s. home** (of criticism) faire mouche; **s. while the iron is hot** il faut battre le fer pendant qu'il est chaud

(**b**) (of workers) faire grève

▶**strike back** vi (retaliate) riposter

▶**strike down** vt sep (of disease) terrasser; (of bullet) abattre

▶**strike off** vt sep (doctor, lawyer) radier

▶**strike out 1** vt sep (delete) rayer

2 vi (**a**) (hit out) **to s. out at sb** essayer de frapper qn (**b**) (leave) s'élancer (**for** vers)

▶**strike up** vt sep (song) entonner; (conversation) entamer; **to s. up a friendship (with sb)** se lier d'amitié (avec qn)

strikebreaker ['straɪkbreɪkə(r)] n briseur(euse) m,f de grève

striker ['straɪkə(r)] n (**a**) (striking worker) gréviste mf (**b**) (in football) buteur m

striking ['straɪkɪŋ] adj (**a**) (similarity, appearance) frappant(e), saisissant(e) (**b**) (worker) en grève

string [strɪŋ] **1** n (**a**) (for tying) ficelle f; (of violin, tennis racket, bow) corde f; (of puppet) fil m; Mus **the strings** (in orchestra) les cordes; Fig **to have more than one s. to one's bow** avoir plus d'une corde à son arc; Fig **with no strings attached** sans conditions; Fig **to pull strings** faire jouer ses relations; Mus **s. quartet** quatuor m à cordes; Br **s. vest** maillot m de corps à grosses mailles (**b**) (of onions, islands) chapelet m; (of words, shops, defeats) série f; Comptr **série**

2 vt (pp & pt **strung** [strʌŋ]) (**a**) (violin) monter; (tennis racket) corder; (bow) bander (**b**) (pearls, beads) enfiler

▶**string along** vi sep Fam mener en bateau

▶**string up** vt sep Fam (hang) (criminal) pendre

stringed [strɪŋd] adj (instrument) à cordes

stringent ['strɪndʒənt] adj rigoureux(euse)

strip¹ [strɪp] n (**a**) (of cloth, paper) bande f; (of metal) lame f; Fam **to tear sb off a s.** passer un savon à qn; **s. cartoon** bande f dessinée; **s. lighting** éclairage m au néon (**b**) (of sports team) tenue f

strip² [strɪp] n **to do a s.** (undress) se déshabiller; (for show) faire un strip-tease; **s. club** boîte f de strip-tease; **s. poker** strip-poker m; **s. show** strip-tease m

2 vt (pt & pp **stripped**) (person) déshabiller; (bed) défaire; (paint) gratter; (wallpaper) décoller; **to s. sb of sth** dépouiller qn de qch

3 vi (undress) se déshabiller

▶**strip off 1** vt sep (paint) gratter; (wallpaper) décoller

2 vi (undress) se déshabiller

stripe [straɪp] n (**a**) (on cloth, animal's coat) rayure f, raie f (**b**) (indicating rank) galon m

striped [straɪpt] adj à rayures, rayé(e)

stripling ['strɪplɪŋ] n tout jeune homme m

stripper ['strɪpə(r)] n (**a**) strip-teaseuse f; (male) **s.** = homme qui se livre à un striptease

strip-search ['strɪpsɜːtʃ] **1** n fouille f corporelle

2 vt **to s. sb** faire subir une fouille corporelle à qn

striptease ['strɪptiːz] n strip-tease m

strive [straɪv] (pt **strove** [strəʊv], pp **striven** ['strɪvən]) vi **to s. to do sth** s'efforcer de faire qch; **to s. for** after **sth** se battre pour obtenir qch

strobe [strəʊb] n Phys stroboscope m; **s. lighting** lumières fpl stroboscopiques

strode [strəʊd] pt of **stride**

stroke [strəʊk] **1** n (**a**) (blow, tennis shot) coup m; (in rowing, swimming) (style) nage f; (single movement) mouvement m; **a brush s.** un coup de pinceau (**b**) (of clock, bell) **on the s. of nine** à neuf heures sonnantes (**c**) (caress) caresse f; **to give sb/sth a s.** caresser qn/qch (**d**) Med attaque f (**e**) (idioms) **she hasn't done a s.** of work elle n'a rien fichu; **a s. of luck** un coup de chance; **a s. of genius** un trait de génie; **at a s.** d'un seul coup

2 vt (caress) caresser

stroll [strəʊl] **1** *n* promenade *f*, tour *m*; **to go for a s.** aller se promener *ou* faire un tour

2 *vi* se promener, flâner

strong [strɒŋ] **1** *adj* **(a)** *(physically, mentally)* fort(e); *(candidate, team)* bon (bonne); *(friendship, argument)* solide; **the pound is s. against the dollar** la livre est solide face au dollar **(b)** *(in degree)* *(colour, light, protest)* vif (vive); *(smell, drink, accent, possibility)* fort(e); *(resemblance)* grand(e); *(measures)* énergique; **s. language** grossièretés *fpl*; **s. point** point *m* fort **(c)** *(sturdy)* *(rope, chair, shoes)* solide

2 *adv* **to be still going s.** bien se maintenir

3 *npl* **the s.** les forts *mpl*

strong-arm tactics [strɒŋɑːmˈtæktɪks] *npl* manière *f* forte

strong-box [ˈstrɒŋbɒks] *n* coffre-fort *m*

stronghold [ˈstrɒŋhəʊld] *n* *(fortress)* forteresse *f*; Fig *(of political party, religion)* bastion *m*

strongly [ˈstrɒŋlɪ] *adv* *(oppose, endorse)* vigoureusement; *(believe)* fermement; **s. built** solide; **a s. worded letter** une lettre bien sentie; **to feel s. about sth** être convaincu(e) de qch

strongman [ˈstrɒŋmæn] *n* *(in circus)* hercule *m* (de foire); Fig *(dictator)* homme *m* fort

strong-minded [strɒŋˈmaɪndɪd] *adj* résolu(e)

strongroom [ˈstrɒŋruːm] *n* chambre *f* forte

strong-willed [strɒŋˈwɪld] *adj* résolu(e)

strontium [ˈstrɒntɪəm] *n* Chem strontium *m*

stroppy [ˈstrɒpɪ] *adj* Br Fam hargneux(euse); **to get s.** monter sur ses grands chevaux

strove [strəʊv] *pt of* **strive**

struck [strʌk] *pt & pp of* **strike**

structural [ˈstrʌktʃərəl] *adj* structurel(elle); **s. damage** dégâts *mpl* de structure; **s. survey** = inspection pour vérifier la solidité d'un bâtiment

structurally [ˈstrʌktʃərəlɪ] *adv* structurellement

structure [ˈstrʌktʃə(r)] *n* **1 (a)** *(of society, language, story)* structure *f* **(b)** *(building, monument)* édifice *m*, construction *f*

2 *vt* structurer

struggle [ˈstrʌɡəl] *n* **1** lutte *f* (for pour); **without a s.** sans résistance; **life is a s.** la vie est un combat

2 *vi* lutter (for pour); **to s. to do sth** lutter pour faire qch; **to be struggling** *(of person, company)* avoir des difficultés *ou* du mal

strum [strʌm] *(pt & pp strummed)* *vt* *(guitar)* gratter

strung [strʌŋ] *pt & pp of* **string**

strut [strʌt] *n* *(for frame)* étai *m*; Av pilier *m*

strut [strʌt] *(pt & pp strutted)* *vi* se pavaner

strychnine [ˈstrɪkniːn] *n* strychnine *f*

stub [stʌb] **1** *n* *(of pencil)* bout *m*; *(of cigarette)* mégot *m*; *(of cheque)* talon *m*

2 *vt* *(pt & pp stubbed)* **to s. one's toe** (on *or* against) se cogner l'orteil (contre)

▸**stub out** *vt sep* *(cigarette)* écraser

stubble [ˈstʌbəl] *n* **(a)** *(in field)* chaume *m* **(b)** *(on face)* barbe *f* de plusieurs jours

stubborn [ˈstʌbən] *adj* *(person)* têtu(e); *(determination, resistance)* farouche; *(stain, infection)* rebelle

stubbornness [ˈstʌbənnɪs] *n* *(of person)* entêtement *m*, obstination *f*; *(of determination, resistance)* inflexibilité *f*

stubby [ˈstʌbɪ] *adj* court(e) et boudiné(e)

stucco [ˈstʌkəʊ] *n* stuc *m*

stuck [stʌk] **1** *adj* bloqué(e), coincé(e); **to get s.** être coincé; *(in mud, sand, with problem)* s'enliser; **to be s. for sth** être à court de qch; Fam **to be s. with sb/sth** ne pas pouvoir se débarrasser de qn/qch

2 *pt & pp of* **stick**[2]

stuck-up [stʌkˈʌp] *adj* Fam snob *inv*

stud[1] [stʌd] *n* *(fastener)* bouton-pression *m*; *(on football, rugby boots)* crampon *m*; *(earring)* clou *m* d'oreille

stud[2] *n* **(a)** *(farm)* haras *m*; *(stallion)* étalon *m* **(b)** Fam *(man)* étalon *m*

student [ˈstjuːdənt] *n* **(a)** *(at university)* étudiant(e) *m,f*; *(at school)* élève *mf*; **law s.** étudiant(e) *m,f* en droit; **s. card** carte *f* d'étudiant; **s. life** vie *f* étudiante; **s. nurse** élève infirmier(ère); **s. teacher** enseignant(e) *m,f* stagiaire; **students' union** *(association)* = association d'aide et de services aux étudiants; *(place)* foyer *m* des étudiants

studied [ˈstʌdɪd] *adj* *(manner, attitude)* calculé(e)

studio [ˈstjuːdɪəʊ] *(pl* **studios)** *n* studio *m*; *(of artist)* atelier *m*; TV **s. audience** public *m* présent lors de l'enregistrement; Br **s. flat** studio *m*

studious [ˈstjuːdɪəs] *adj* studieux(euse)

study [ˈstʌdɪ] **1** *n* **(a)** *(investigation, by artist)* étude *f*; **to make a s. of sth** faire une étude sur qch; **s. group** groupe *m* d'étude; **s. trip** voyage *m* d'études **(b)** *(room)* bureau *m*, cabinet *m* de travail

2 *vt* *(pt & pp studied)* *(facts, evidence)* examiner; *(behaviour, school subject)* étudier; *(university subject)* faire des études de

3 *vi* *(revise)* travailler; *(be at university)* faire des études

stuff [stʌf] **1** *n* **(a)** *(objects, possessions)* affaires *fpl*; **some s.** *(substance)* un truc; Fam **he reads all that intellectual s.** il lit tous ces trucs intellectuels; Fam **she writes good s.** c'est bien, ce qu'elle écrit; Fam **he knows his s.** il s'y connaît; Fam **that's the s.!** c'est bien! **(b)** *(cloth)* étoffe *f*

2 *vt* *(fill)* *(cushion)* rembourrer; *(chicken, tomatoes)* farcir; *(pocket)* remplir; **to s. sth into sth** fourrer qch dans qch; Fam **to s. oneself** s'empiffrer; Br very Fam **get stuffed!** va te faire foutre!

stuffing [ˈstʌfɪŋ] *n* *(for furniture)* rembourrage *m*; *(for chicken)* farce *f*; Fam **to knock the s. out of sb** ficher un coup à qn

stuffy [ˈstʌfɪ] *adj* **(a)** *(room)* qui sent le renfermé **(b)** *(person)* vieux jeu *inv*

stultifying [ˈstʌltɪfaɪɪŋ] *adj* abrutissant(e)

stumble [ˈstʌmbəl] **1** *n* faux-pas *m*

2 *vi* *(when walking, speaking)* trébucher

▸**stumble across** *vt insep* *(find)* tomber par hasard sur

stump [stʌmp] **1** *n* **(a)** *(of tree)* souche *f*; *(of arm, leg)* moignon *m* **(b)** *(in cricket)* piquet *m* **(c)** Am Fam *(of politician)* **to be on the s.** être en campagne électorale

2 *vt* *(baffle)* laisser perplexe; **to be stumped for an answer** ne pas savoir quoi répondre

▸**stump up** *vt insep* Br Fam *(pay)* cracher

stumpy [ˈstʌmpɪ] *adj* court(e) et boudiné(e)

stun [stʌn] *(pt & pp stunned)* *vt* *(make unconscious)* assommer; Fig *(shock)* abasourdir

stung [stʌŋ] *pt & pp of* **sting**

stunk [stʌŋk] *pt & pp of* **stink**

stunning [ˈstʌnɪŋ] *adj* *(shocking)* étourdissant(e); *(excellent)* excellent(e); *(beautiful)* superbe

stunt[1] [stʌnt] *vt* *(person)* ralentir la croissance de; *(growth)* ralentir

stunt² *n* (*in film*) cascade *f*; (*for publicity*) coup *m* de pub; **s. man** cascadeur *m*

stupefy ['stju:pɪfaɪ] (*pt & pp* **stupified**) *vt* (*of alcohol, drugs*) abrutir; (*of news, behaviour*) stupéfier

stupefying ['stju:pɪfaɪɪŋ] *adj* stupéfiant(e)

stupendous [stju:'pendəs] *adj* fantastique

stupid ['stju:pɪd] *adj* bête, stupide; **the s. TV keeps breaking down** cette saleté de télé est sans arrêt en panne; **what a s. thing to do!** c'est vraiment idiot d'avoir fait ça!

stupidity [stju:'pɪdɪtɪ] *n* bêtise *f*, stupidité *f*

stupidly ['stju:pɪdlɪ] *adv* bêtement

stupor ['stju:pə(r)] *n* état *m* d'abrutissement

sturdy ['stɜ:dɪ] *adj* (*person, object*) robuste; (*opposition, resistance*) résolu(e)

sturgeon ['stɜ:dʒən] *n* esturgeon *m*

stutter ['stʌtə(r)] 1 *n* bégaiement *m*
 2 *vi* bégayer

sty¹ [staɪ] *n* (*for pigs*) & *Fig* porcherie *f*

sty², stye [staɪ] *n* (*in eye*) orgelet *m*

style [staɪl] 1 *n* (a) (*manner, design*) style *m* (b) (*sophistication*) classe *f*; **to live in s.** mener grand train
 2 *vt* (*design*) créer; (*hair*) coiffer

stylish ['staɪlɪʃ] *adj* élégant(e), chic *inv*

stylist ['staɪlɪst] *n* (*hairdresser*) coiffeur(euse) *m,f*

stylistic [staɪ'lɪstɪk] *adj* stylistique

stylized ['staɪlaɪzd] *adj* stylisé(e)

stylus ['staɪləs] (*pl* **styluses** *or* **styli** ['staɪlaɪ]) *n* (*for engraving*) style *m*; (*on record player*) pointe *f* de lecture

stymie ['staɪmɪ] *vt Fam* coincer

suave [swɑ:v] *adj* affable; *Pej* mielleux(euse)

sub [sʌb] *Fam* 1 *n* (a) (*abbr* **subscription**) cotisation *f* (b) (*abbr* **substitute**) remplaçant(e) *m,f* (c) (*abbr* **submarine**) sous-marin *m* (d) *Journ* (*abbr* **subeditor**) secrétaire *mf* de rédaction
 2 *vt* (*pt & pp* **subbed**) *Journ* mettre au point
 3 *vi* (*abbr* **substitute**) **to s. for sb** remplacer qn

subaltern ['sʌbəltən] *n Mil* officier *m* subalterne

subcommittee ['sʌbkəmɪtɪ] *n* sous-comité *m*

subconscious [sʌb'kɒnʃəs] 1 *n* **the s.** l'inconscient *m*
 2 *adj* inconscient(e)

subcontinent [sʌb'kɒntɪnənt] *n* sous-continent *m*

subcontract 1 [sʌb'kɒntrækt] sous-traitance *f*
 2 *vt* [sʌbkən'trækt] sous-traiter

subcontractor ['sʌbkəntræktə(r)] *n* sous-traitant *m*

subculture ['sʌbkʌltʃə(r)] *n* phénomène *m* de groupe

subdivision [sʌbdɪ'vɪʒən] *n* subdivision *f*

subdue [səb'dju:] *vt* (*enemy, rioter*) soumettre; (*emotions*) maîtriser

subdued [səb'dju:d] *adj* (*person, event*) inhabituellement calme; (*light*) tamisé(e); (*sound, voice*) bas (basse)

subedit [sʌb'edɪt] *vt Journ* mettre au point

subeditor [sʌb'edɪtə(r)] *n Journ* secrétaire *mf* de rédaction

subhuman [sʌb'hju:mən] 1 *n* sous-homme *m*
 2 *adj* inférieur(e) (aux humains)

subject 1 ['sʌbdʒɪkt] (a) (*of conversation, book, painting, photograph*) sujet *m*; (*at school, university*) matière *f*; **while we're on the s.** à ce propos; **to change the s.** parler d'autre chose; **s. matter** (*of letter*) contenu *m*; (*of book*)

sujet (b) *Gram* sujet *m* (c) (*of monarch*) sujet(ette) *m,f*
 2 *adj* (a) (*prone*) **to be s. to** (*illness*) être sujet(ette) à; (*fine, taxation*) être passible de; **to be s. to jealousy/depression** avoir tendance à être jaloux(ouse)/dépressif(ive) (b) **s. to** (*dependent on*) sous réserve de
 3 *vt* [səb'dʒekt] (*control*) soumettre, assujettir; **to s. sb to sth** (*force to undergo*) soumettre qn à qch

subjective [səb'dʒektɪv] *adj* subjectif(ive)

subjectivity [sʌbdʒek'tɪvɪtɪ] *n* subjectivité *f*

sub judice ['sʌb'dʒu:dɪsɪ] *adj Law* en instance

subjugate ['sʌbdʒʊgeɪt] *vt* assujettir

subjunctive [səb'dʒʌŋktɪv] *Gram* 1 *n* subjonctif *m*
 2 *adj* subjonctif(ive)

sublet [sʌb'let] (*pt & pp* **sublet**) *vt* sous-louer

sublimate ['sʌblɪmeɪt] *vt* sublimer

sublime [sə'blaɪm] 1 *adj* sublime; (*utter*) suprême
 2 *n* **from the s. to the ridiculous** du sublime au ridicule

subliminal [sʌb'lɪmɪnəl] *adj* subliminal(e)

sub-machine gun [sʌbmə'ʃi:ngʌn] *n* mitraillette *f*

submarine [sʌbmə'ri:n] *n* sous-marin *m*

submerge [səb'mɜ:dʒ] 1 *vt* (*immerse*) immerger; (*cover*) submerger; *Fig* **to be submerged in sth** être submergé(e) par qch
 2 *vi* plonger

submersion [səb'mɜ:ʃən] *n* submersion *f*

submission [səb'mɪʃən] *n* (a) (*to will, authority*) soumission *f*; **to starve sb into s.** réduire qn à la soumission en le/la privant de nourriture; **to beat sb into s.** battre qn jusqu'à ce qu'il/elle se soumette (b) (*of document*) présentation *f* (c) (*report*) soumission *f*

submissive [səb'mɪsɪv] *adj* soumis(e)

submit [səb'mɪt] (*pt & pp* **submitted**) 1 *vt* soumettre (*for* à)
 2 *vi* (*to person, authority*) se soumettre (*to* à)

subnormal [sʌb'nɔ:məl] *adj* arriéré(e)

subordinate 1 *n* [sə'bɔ:dɪnət] subordonné(e) *m,f*
 2 *adj* (*rank*) subalterne; (*role*) secondaire; **to be s. to sb** être subordonné(e) à qn; *Gram* **s. clause** proposition *f* subordonnée
 3 *vt* [sə'bɔ:dɪnet] subordonner

subordination [səbɔ:dɪ'neɪʃən] *n* subordination *f*

subplot ['sʌbplɒt] *n* intrigue *f* secondaire

subpoena [sə'pi:nə] *Law* 1 *n* citation *f* ou assignation *f* à comparaître
 2 *vt* citer *ou* assigner à comparaître

subscribe [səb'skraɪb] *vi* (a) (*to newspaper, magazine*) s'abonner (*to* à); (*to charity, organization*) être membre (*to* de) (b) **to s. to** (*opinion, theory*) souscrire à

subscriber [səb'skraɪbə(r)] *n* (*to newspaper, magazine, telephone*) abonné(e) *m,f*; (*to charity, organization*) membre *m*

subscript ['sʌbskrɪpt] *n Typ* indice *m*

subscription [səb'skrɪpʃən] *n* (*to newspaper, magazine*) abonnement *m*; (*to charity, organization, club*) cotisation *f*

subsection ['sʌbsekʃən] *n* subdivision *f*

subsequent ['sʌbsɪkwənt] *adj* ultérieur(e)

subservient [səb'sɜ:vɪənt] *adj* servile

subside [səb'saɪd] *vi* (*of ground, building*) s'affaisser; (*of water*) baisser; (*of bump*) dégonfler; (*of storm, excitement, fever*) s'apaiser; (*of noise, pain*) s'affaiblir

subsidence [səb'saɪdəns] *n* (*of ground, building*) affaissement *m*; (*of water*) baisse *f*

subsidiarity [səbsɪdɪ'ærɪtɪ] *n* subsidiarité *f*

subsidiary [sʌb'sɪdɪərɪ] **1** *n* (*pl* **subsidiaries**) (*company*) filiale *f*
2 *adj* subsidiaire

subsidize ['sʌbsɪdaɪz] *vt* subventionner

subsidy ['sʌbsɪdɪ] (*pl* **subsidies**) *n* subvention *f*

subsist [səb'sɪst] *vi* to s. on vivre de

subsistence [səb'sɪstəns] *n* subsistance *f*; **s. allowance** faux frais *mpl*; **s. wage** salaire *m* à peine suffisant pour vivre

substance ['sʌbstəns] *n* (a) (*matter*) substance *f*; **s. abuse** usage *m* de stupéfiants (b) (*essential element*) fond *m* (c) (*solidity, worth*) fondement *m*

substandard [sʌb'stændəd] *adj* de qualité inférieure

substantial [səb'stænʃəl] *adj* (a) (*significant*) important(e); (*meal*) substantiel(elle); **a. number of** un nombre important de (b) (*solid, robust*) solide

substantially [səb'stænʃəlɪ] *adv* (a) (*considerably*) considérablement (b) (*for the most part*) pour l'essentiel; **they are the same** ils sont pareils dans l'ensemble (c) (*solidly*) solidement

substantiate [səb'stænʃɪeɪt] *vt* (*statement*) corroborer; (*claim*) justifier

substantive ['sʌbstəntɪv] **1** *n Gram* substantif *m*
2 *adj* important(e)

substitute ['sʌbstɪtjuːt] **1** *n* (*person*) remplaçant(e) *m,f*; (*foodstuff, drug*) succédané *m*; **to be a s./no s. for** remplacer/ne pas remplacer
2 *vt* to **A for B** remplacer B par A
3 *vi* to **s. for sb** remplacer qn

substitution [sʌbstɪ'tjuːʃən] *n* substitution *f*; (*of person, player*) remplacement *m*

subsume [səb'sjuːm] *vt Formal* subsumer

subterfuge ['sʌbtəfjuːdʒ] *n* subterfuge *m*

subterranean [sʌbtə'reɪnɪən] *adj* souterrain(e)

subtitle ['sʌbtaɪtəl] **1** *n* sous-titre *m*
2 *vt* sous-titrer

subtle ['sʌtəl] *adj* subtil(e)

subtlety ['sʌtəltɪ] (*pl* **subtleties**) *n* subtilité *f*

subtly ['sʌtəlɪ] *adv* subtilement

subtotal ['sʌbtəʊtəl] *n* sous-total *m*

subtract [səb'trækt] *vt* soustraire (**from** de)

subtraction [səb'trækʃən] *n* soustraction *f*

subtropical [sʌb'trɒpɪkəl] *adj* subtropical(e)

suburb ['sʌbɜːb] *n* banlieue *f*; **the suburbs** la banlieue

suburban [sə'bɜːbən] *adj* (a) (*of suburb*) de banlieue; (*population, development*) suburbain(e) (b) *Pej* (*narrow-minded*) étriqué(e)

suburbia [sə'bɜːbɪə] *n* la banlieue

subversion [səb'vɜːʃən] *n* subversion *f*

subversive [səb'vɜːsɪv] *n & adj* subversif(ive) *m,f*

subvert [səb'vɜːt] *vt* renverser, subvertir

subway ['sʌbweɪ] *n* (a) *Br* (*underpass*) passage *m* souterrain (b) *Am* (*underground railway*) métro *m*

sub-zero [sʌb'zɪərəʊ] *adj* au-dessous de zéro

succeed [sək'siːd] **1** *vt* (*follow*) succéder à
2 *vi* (a) (*be successful*) réussir; **to s. in doing sth** réussir à faire qch (b) **to s. to the throne** monter sur le trône

succeeding [sək'siːdɪŋ] *adj* (*following*) suivant(e)

success [sək'ses] *n* réussite *f*, succès *m*; **to be a s.** avoir du succès; **s. story** réussite *f*

successful [sək'sesfʊl] *adj* (*person*) brillant(e); (*project, application*) couronné(e) de succès; **to be s.** réussir; **to be s. in doing sth** réussir à faire qch

successfully [sək'sesfʊlɪ] *adv* avec succès

succession [sək'seʃən] *n* succession *f*, série *f*; **two years in s.** deux années de suite

successive [sək'sesɪv] *adj* successif(ive); **on five s. Sundays** cinq dimanches consécutifs

successor [sək'sesə(r)] *n* successeur *m*

succinct [sʌk'sɪŋ(k)t] *adj* succinct(e)

succulent ['sʌkjʊlənt] **1** *adj* (*delicious*) succulent(e)
2 *n* (*plant*) plante *f* grasse

succumb [sə'kʌm] *vi* succomber (**to** à)

such [sʌtʃ] **1** *pron* tel (telle) *m,f*; **if s. were the case** si tel était le cas; **and s. et des choses comme ça**; **as s.** en tant que tel; **s. is life!** c'est la vie!
2 *adj* tel (telle), pareil(eille); **s. a question** une telle question, une question pareille; **animals s. as the lion or the tiger** des animaux tels que le lion ou le tigre; **books as these, books s. as these** de tels livres, des livres pareils; **here's my bedroom, s. as it is** voici ce qui me sert de chambre; **as? par exemple?**; **do you have s. a thing as a screwdriver?** est-ce que tu aurais un tournevis, par hasard?; **there's no s. thing as aliens** les extraterrestres n'existent pas; **I said/did no s. thing** je n'ai rien dit/fait de tel; **in s. a way that** d'une façon telle que; **on s. and s. a day** tel jour
3 *adv* (a) (*in comparisons*) **s. a big house** une si ou aussi grande maison; **I had never heard s. good music** je n'avais jamais entendu de si bonne musique
(b) (*for emphasis*) **we had s. a good time** nous nous sommes tellement bien amusés; **it was s. a long time ago** ça fait tellement longtemps; **s. a lot of people** tant de gens

suchlike ['sʌtʃlaɪk] *pron* **...and s.** ...et autres

suck [sʌk] **1** *vt* (*lollipop, thumb*) sucer; (*liquid, air*) aspirer; (*mother's milk*) téter
2 *vi Am very Fam* (*be of bad quality*) être nul (nulle)

▸**suck in** *vt sep* aspirer; *Fig* **to get sucked into sth** se laisser entraîner dans qch

▸**suck up 1** *vt sep* (*liquid, dust*) aspirer
2 *vi very Fam* **to s. up to sb** lécher les bottes a qn

sucker ['sʌkə(r)] *n* (a) (*of octopus*) suçoir *m*; (*of plant*) rejeton *m* (b) *Fam* (*gullible person*) niais(e) *m,f*; **to be a s. for sth** craquer pour qch

suckle ['sʌkəl] **1** *vt* allaiter
2 *vi* téter

sucrose ['suːkrəʊs] *n* saccharose *m*

suction ['sʌkʃən] *n* succion *f*

Sudan [suː'dæn] *n* le Soudan

Sudanese [suːdə'niːz] **1** *npl* (*people*) **the S.** les Soudanais
2 *n* Soudanais(e) *m,f*
3 *adj* soudanais(e)

sudden ['sʌdən] *adj* soudain(e), subit(e); **all of a s.** tout à coup; *Fig* **s. death** (*in match, contest*) la mort subite

suddenly ['sʌdənlɪ] *adv* soudain, tout à coup; (*die, happen*) subitement

suddenness ['sʌdənnɪs] *n* soudaineté *f*

suds [sʌdz] *npl* (*of soap*) mousse *f*

sue [su:] **1** *vt* intenter un procès à (**for** en)
2 *vi* **to s. for divorce** entamer une procédure de divorce; **to s. for damages** demander des dommages-intérêts

suede [sweɪd] *n* daim *m*

suet ['su:ɪt] *n* graisse *f* de rognon

Suez ['su:ɪz] *n* **the S. Canal** le canal de Suez

suffer ['sʌfə(r)] **1** *vt* (a) (*loss, defeat, consequence*) subir; (*pain*) avoir (b) (*tolerate*) supporter; **she doesn't s. fools gladly** elle ne supporte pas les imbéciles
2 *vi* (*of person*) souffrir (**from** de); (*of health, work*) en pâtir

sufferance ['sʌf(ə)rəns] *n* **I'm just here on s.** on me tolère tout juste ici

sufferer ['sʌfərə(r)] *n* victime *f*

suffering ['sʌfərɪŋ] *n* souffrance *f*

suffice [sə'faɪs] *vi Formal* suffire

sufficient [sə'fɪʃənt] *adj* suffisant(e); **to be s.** suffire, être suffisant

sufficiently [sə'fɪʃəntlɪ] *adv* suffisamment

suffix ['sʌfɪks] *n Gram* suffixe *m*

suffocate ['sʌfəkeɪt] **1** *vt also Fig* étouffer
2 *vi* suffoquer

suffocating ['sʌfəkeɪtɪŋ] *adj* suffocant(e)

suffocation [sʌfə'keɪʃən] *n* suffocation *f*

suffrage ['sʌfrɪdʒ] *n* droit *m* de vote

suffragette [sʌfrə'dʒet] *n* suffragette *f*

suffuse [sə'fju:z] *vt Lit* (*of light, liquid, colour*) inonder; (*of heat*) envahir

sugar ['ʃʊɡə(r)] **1** *n* (a) (*food*) sucre *m*; **two sugars, please** deux sucres, s'il te plaît; **s. almond** dragée *f*; **s. beet** betterave *f* sucrière; **s. bowl** sucrier *m*; **s. cane** canne *f* à sucre; **s. daddy** vieux *m* plein de fric (*qui entretient une jeune femme*); **s. lump** morceau *m* de sucre; **s. plantation** plantation *f* de canne à sucre; **s. refinery** raffinerie *f* de sucre (b) *Fam* (*term of address*) mon trésor
2 *vt* (*coffee, tea*) sucrer; *Fig* **to s. the pill** dorer la pilule

sugar-coated ['ʃʊɡə'kəʊtɪd] *adj* recouvert(e) de sucre

sugar-free ['ʃʊɡə'fri:] *adj* sans sucre

sugary ['ʃʊɡərɪ] *adj* (a) (*containing sugar*) sucré(e) (b) *Fig* (*smile, tone*) mielleux(euse), doucereux(euse)

suggest [sə'dʒest] *vt* (a) (*propose*) suggérer (b) (*imply*) indiquer

suggestible [sə'dʒestɪbəl] *adj* influençable

suggestion [sə'dʒestʃən] *n* (a) (*proposal*) suggestion *f*; **suggestions box** boîte *f* à idées (b) (*insinuation, hint*) indication *f*; **there is no s. that...** rien ne dit que...; **a s. of** une pointe de

suggestive [sə'dʒestɪv] *adj* suggestif(ive); **to be s. of** évoquer

suicidal [suɪ'saɪdəl] *adj* suicidaire

suicide ['suɪsaɪd] *n* suicide *m*; **to commit s.** se suicider; **s. attempt** tentative *f* de suicide; **s. mission** mission *f* suicide; **s. note** lettre *f* (*laissée par un suicidé*)

suit [su:t] **1** *n* (a) (*clothing*) (*man's*) complet *m*; (*woman's*) tailleur *m*; **s. of armour** armure *f* complète (b) (*in cards*) couleur *f*; *Fig* **to follow s.** faire de même; *Fig* **politeness is not her strong s.** la politesse n'est pas son fort (c) *Law* procès *m*
2 *vt* (a) (*of clothes, colours*) aller à (b) (*of arrangement, time, job*) convenir à; **to be suited to or for sth** (*purpose, job*) être fait(e) pour qch; **to s. sb down to the ground** convenir parfaitement à qn; **they are well suited** ils

sont vraiment faits l'un pour l'autre; *Fam* **s. yourself** fais comme tu voudras (c) (*adapt*) **to s. sth to sth** adapter qch à qch

suitability [su:tə'bɪlɪt] *n* convenance *f*; (*of person*) aptitude *f*

suitable ['su:təbəl] *adj* (*clothes, subject*) convenable; (*candidate, date, title*) adéquat(e); **the film is not s. for children** ce n'est pas un film pour les enfants

suitably ['su:təblɪ] *adv* (*behave, dress*) convenablement; **s. impressed/embarrassed** vraiment impressionné(e)/gêné(e)

suitcase ['su:tkeɪs] *n* valise *f*

suite [swi:t] *n* (a) (*of rooms*) suite *f* (b) (*of furniture*) (**three-piece**) **s.** canapé *m* avec deux fauteuils assortis (c) *Mus* suite *f*

suitor ['su:tə(r)] *n Old-fashioned* (*admirer*) soupirant *m*

sulfate, sulfide *etc Am* = **sulphate, sulphide** *etc*

sulk [sʌlk] **1** *n* **to be in a s.** bouder
2 *vi* bouder

sulky ['sʌlkɪ] *adj* boudeur(euse)

sullen ['sʌlən] *adj* renfrogné(e)

sully ['sʌlɪ] *vt Lit* (*reputation*) ternir; *Fig* **to s. one's hands** (**with sth**) se salir les mains (en faisant qch)

sulphate, *Am* **sulfate** ['sʌlfeɪt] *n Chem* sulfate *m*

sulphide, *Am* **sulfide** ['sʌlfaɪd] *n Chem* sulfure *m*

sulphur, *Am* **sulfur** ['sʌlfə(r)] *n Chem* soufre *m*; **s. dioxide** anhydride *m* sulfureux

sulphuric, *Am* **sulfuric** [sʌl'fjʊərɪk] *adj Chem* sulfurique; **s. acid** acide *m* sulfurique

sultan ['sʌltən] *n* sultan *m*

sultana [sʌl'tɑ:nə] *n* raisin *m* de Smyrne

sultry ['sʌltrɪ] *adj* (*heat*) étouffant(e); (*weather*) lourd(e); (*look, smile*) sensuel(elle)

sum [sʌm] *n* (*amount of money*) somme *f*; (*mathematical problem*) problème *m*; **the s. of** la somme de; **s. total** somme totale

▶**sum up** (*pt & pp* **summed**) **1** *vt sep* (a) (*summarize*) résumer (b) (*assess quickly*) jauger, évaluer
2 *vi* (*summarize*) résumer

summarily ['sʌmərɪlɪ] *adv* sommairement

summarize ['sʌməraɪz] *vt* résumer

summary ['sʌmərɪ] **1** *n* (*pl* **summaries**) résumé *m*
2 *adj* (*brief*) sommaire

summer ['sʌmə(r)] **1** *n* été *m*; **in (the) s.** en été; **s. holidays** vacances *fpl* d'été; **s. school** cours *mpl* d'été
2 *vi* passer l'été

summerhouse ['sʌməhaʊs] *n* (*in garden*) pavillon *m*

summertime ['sʌmətaɪm] *n* été *m*

summery ['sʌmərɪ] *adj* d'été

summing-up [sʌmɪŋ'ʌp] *n Law* résumé *m* des débats

summit ['sʌmɪt] *n* sommet *m*; **to hold a s.** tenir un sommet

summon ['sʌmən] *vt* (*person, meeting*) convoquer; (*police, doctor, help*) appeler, faire venir; *Law* (*witness*) assigner ou citer à comparaître

▶**summon up** *vt sep* rassembler

summons ['sʌmənz] *Law* **1** *n* (*pl* **summonses** ['sʌmənzɪz]) assignation *f* ou citation *f* à comparaître
2 *vt* assigner ou citer à comparaître

sump [sʌmp] *n* (a) (*in engine*) carter *m* à huile (b) (*cesspool*) fosse *f* d'aisance

sumptuous ['sʌm(p)tjʊəs] *adj* somptueux(euse)

Sun (*abbr* **Sunday**) dimanche

sun [sʌn] **1** *n* soleil *m*; **in the s.** au soleil; **to catch the s.** prendre le soleil; **everything under the s.** tout ce qu'il est possible d'imaginer; **s. lamp** lampe *f* à bronzer; **s. lotion** lotion *f* solaire; **s. shield** *or* **visor** (*in car*) pare-soleil *m*

2 *vt* (*pt & pp* **sunned**) **to s. oneself** prendre le soleil

sunbathe ['sʌnbeɪð] *vi* se faire bronzer

sunbeam ['sʌnbiːm] *n* rayon *m* de soleil

sunbed ['sʌnbed] *n* lit *m* à ultraviolets

sunburn ['sʌnbɜːn] *n* coup *m* de soleil; **to have s.** avoir un coup de soleil

sunburnt ['sʌnbɜːnt], **sunburned** ['sʌnbɜːnd] *adj* **to be s.** avoir un coup de soleil

sundae ['sʌndeɪ] *n* coupe *f* glacée

Sunday ['sʌndeɪ] *n* dimanche *m*; **S. best** habits *mpl* du dimanche; **S. paper** journal *m* du dimanche; **S. school** ≃ catéchisme *m*; *see also* **Saturday**

sundial ['sʌndaɪəl] *n* cadran *m* solaire

sundown ['sʌndaʊn] *n* coucher *m* du soleil

sun-drenched ['sʌndren(t)ʃt] *adj* inondé(e) de soleil

sun-dried ['sʌndraɪd] *adj* séché(e) au soleil

sundry ['sʌndrɪ] **1** *n* (a) **all and s.** tout le monde (b) **sundries** (*items*) articles *mpl* divers; (*costs*) frais *mpl* divers

2 *adj* divers(e)

sunflower ['sʌnflaʊə(r)] *n* tournesol *m*; **s. oil** huile *f* de tournesol; **s. seeds** (*as snack*) graines *fpl* de tournesol

sung [sʌŋ] *pp of* **sing**

sunglasses ['sʌnglɑːsɪz] *npl* lunettes *fpl* de soleil

sunhat ['sʌnhæt] *n* chapeau *m* de soleil

sunk [sʌŋk] *pp of* **sink²**

sunken ['sʌŋkən] *adj* (*ship*) englouti(e); (*eyes*) enfoncé(e); (*rock*) immergé(e)

sunlight ['sʌnlaɪt] *n* lumière *f* du soleil; **in the s.** au soleil

sunlit ['sʌnlɪt] *adj* éclairé(e) par le soleil

sunny ['sʌnɪ] *adj* (a) (*day, place*) ensoleillé(e); **it's s.** il fait du soleil (b) *Fig* (*face*) radieux(euse); **to have a s. personality** être toujours content(e)

sunray lamp ['sʌnreɪlæmp] *n* lampe *f* à bronzer

sunrise ['sʌnraɪz] *n* lever *m* de soleil; **at s.** au lever du soleil, au soleil levant; *Econ* **s. industry** industrie *f* d'avenir

sunroof ['sʌnruːf] *n* toit *m* ouvrant

sunset ['sʌnset] *n* coucher *m* de soleil; **at s.** au coucher du soleil, au soleil couchant

sunshade ['sʌnʃeɪd] *n* parasol *m*

sunshine ['sʌnʃaɪn] *n* soleil *m*

sunspot ['sʌnspɒt] *n* (a) (*on sun*) tache *f* solaire (b) *Fam* (*holiday resort*) destination *f* ensoleillée

sunstroke ['sʌnstrəʊk] *n* insolation *f*; **to have s.** avoir une insolation

suntan ['sʌntæn] *n* bronzage *m*; **to have a s.** être bronzé(e); **s. lotion** lotion *f* solaire

suntrap ['sʌntræp] *n* coin *m* très ensoleillé

sup [sʌp] (*pt & pp* **supped**) *vt* boire à petites gorgées

super ['suːpə(r)] **1** *adj Fam* (*excellent*) super *inv*

2 *n* (*petrol*) super *m*

superannuation [suːpərænjʊ'eɪʃən] *n Fin* retraite *f*

superb [suː'pɜːb] *adj* excellent(e)

supercharger ['suːpətʃɑːdʒə(r)] *n Aut & Av* compresseur *m*

supercilious [suːpə'sɪlɪəs] *adj* hautain(e)

superconductor [suːpəkən'dʌktə(r)] *n Phys* supraconducteur *m*

super-duper ['suːpə'duːpə(r)] *adj Fam* super, génial(e)

superego ['suːpərɪgəʊ] *n Psy* surmoi *m*

superficial [suːpə'fɪʃəl] *adj* superficiel(elle)

superficiality [suːpəfɪʃɪ'ælɪtɪ] *n* superficialité *f*

superficially [suːpə'fɪʃəlɪ] *adv* superficiellement

superfluous [suː'pɜːflʊəs] *adj* superflu(e)

superhuman [suːpə'hjuːmən] *adj* surhumain(e)

superimpose [suːpərɪm'pəʊz] *vt* superposer

superintend [suːpərɪn'tend] *vt* (*run*) diriger; (*supervise*) surveiller

superintendent [suːpərɪn'tendənt] *n* (*supervisor*) directeur(trice) *m,f*; (*police officer*) ≃ commissaire *m* de police

superior [suː'pɪərɪə(r)] **1** *adj* (a) (*better, more senior*) supérieur(e) (b) (*arrogant*) (*person*) qui se croit supérieur(e); (*tone, air, smile*) de supériorité

2 *n* (*senior*) supérieur(e) *m,f*

superiority [suːpɪərɪ'ɒrɪtɪ] *n* supériorité *f*

superlative [suː'pɜːlətɪv] **1** *n Gram* superlatif *m*

2 *adj* (a) (*excellent*) excellent(e) (b) *Gram* superlatif(ive)

superman ['suːpəmæn] *n* surhomme *m*

supermarket ['suːpəmɑːkɪt] *n* supermarché *m*

supermodel ['suːpəmɒdl] *n* top model *m*

supernatural [suːpə'nætʃərəl] **1** *n* **the s.** le surnaturel

2 *adj* surnaturel(elle)

superpower ['suːpəpaʊə(r)] *n* superpuissance *f*

supersede [suːpə'siːd] *vt* supplanter, détrôner

supersonic [suːpə'sɒnɪk] *adj* supersonique

superstar ['suːpəstɑː(r)] *n* superstar *f*

superstition [suːpə'stɪʃən] *n* superstition *f*

superstitious [suːpə'stɪʃəs] *adj* superstitieux(euse)

superstore ['suːpəstɔː(r)] *n* hypermarché *m*

superstructure ['suːpəstrʌktʃə(r)] *n* superstructure *f*

supertanker ['suːpətæŋkə(r)] *n* supertanker *m*

supervise ['suːpəvaɪz] *vt* (*children*) surveiller; (*staff*) superviser

supervision [suːpə'vɪʒən] *n* (*of children*) surveillance *f*; (*of staff*) supervision *f*

supervisor ['suːpəvaɪzə(r)] *n* (a) (*in office*) chef *m* de service; (*in factory*) chef *m* d'équipe (b) (*for thesis*) directeur *m* de thèse

supervisory [suːpə'vaɪzərɪ] *adj* de supervision

supine ['suːpaɪn] **1** *adj* couché(e) sur le dos; *Fig* (*inactive*) mou (molle)

2 *adv* **to lie s.** être couché(e) sur le dos

supper ['sʌpə(r)] *n* (*evening meal*) dîner *m*; (*snack before going to bed*) ≃ casse-croûte pris avant d'aller se coucher

supplant [sə'plɑːnt] *vt* supplanter

supple ['sʌpəl] *adj* souple

supplement ['sʌplɪmənt] **1** *n* supplément *m*

2 *vt* compléter

supplementary [sʌplɪ'mentərɪ] *adj* supplémentaire

supplication [sʌplɪ'keɪʃən] *n* supplication *f*

supplier [sə'plaɪə(r)] *n* fournisseur(euse) *m,f*

supply [sə'plaɪ] **1** n (pl **supplies**) (stock) provision f; (act of supplying) approvisionnement m, fourniture f; a week's/month's s. of sth une provision de qch pour une semaine/un mois; **petrol is in short s.** on manque d'essence; **Econ s. and demand** l'offre f et la demande; **s. lines** lignes fpl de ravitaillement; **s. ship** ravitailleur m; **s. teacher** remplaçant(e) m,f, suppléant(e) m,f
2 vt (pt & pp **supplied**) (provide) fournir; **to s. sb with sth** fournir qch à qn

support [sə'pɔːt] **1** n (a) (backing) soutien m; **to give sb/sth s.** appuyer qn/qch; **in s. of** (theory, claim) à l'appui de; (cause) en faveur de; **s. band** (at concert) première partie f **(b)** (person supporting) soutien m; (thing supporting) support m
2 vt (hold up) supporter, soutenir; **I supported her with my arm** je lui ai donné le bras pour qu'elle s'appuie dessus **(b)** (encourage, aid) soutenir, apporter son soutien à; (team in sport) supporter **(c)** (sustain) pourvoir aux besoins de; **to s. oneself** subvenir à ses propres besoins

supporter [sə'pɔːtə(r)] n (of opinion, party, policy) défenseur m, sympathisant(e) m,f; (of team) supporter m

supporting [sə'pɔːtɪŋ] adj (film) qui passe en première partie; **s. cast** seconds rôles mpl

supportive [sə'pɔːtɪv] adj d'un grand soutien

suppose [sə'pəʊz] vt supposer; **I s. so/not** je suppose que oui/non; **s. or supposing** he came back supposons qu'il revienne; **I don't s. you'd consider sharing it?** je suppose que tu ne veux pas partager?; **s. we change the subject?** et si nous changions de sujet?

supposed [sə'pəʊzd] adj (a) (meant) **to be s. to do sth** être censé(e) faire qch; **there's s. to be a meeting today** il est censé y avoir une réunion aujourd'hui **(b)** (reputed) **the film's s. to be very good** il paraît que c'est un très bon film

supposition [sʌpə'zɪʃən] n supposition f; **on the s. that...** en supposant que...

suppository [sə'pɒzɪtrɪ] n (pl **suppositories**) n Med suppositoire m

suppress [sə'pres] vt (revolt) réprimer; (fact, evidence) faire disparaître; (emotions) refouler; (cough, smile) réprimer

suppressed [sə'prest] adj (emotion) refoulé(e)

suppression [sə'preʃən] n (of revolt) répression f; (of fact, evidence) dissimulation f; (of emotions) refoulement m

suppurate [ˈsʌpjʊəreɪt] vi suppurer

supranational [suːprə'næʃənəl] adj supranational(e)

supremacy [suː'preməsɪ] n suprématie f

supreme [suː'priːm] adj suprême; **to make the s. sacrifice** se sacrifier; **Fig to reign s.** régner; **Mil S. Commander** commandant m en chef; **Am Law S. Court** Cour f suprême

supremely [suː'priːmlɪ] adv suprêmement

supremo [suː'priːməʊ] n (pl **supremos**) n Fam grand chef m

surcharge [ˈsɜːtʃɑːdʒ] **1** n supplément m
2 vt faire payer un supplément à

sure [ʃʊə(r)] **1** adj sûr(e); **to be s. of or about sth** être sûr de qch; **to be s. to do sth** ne pas oublier de faire qch; **to be s. of oneself** être sûr de soi; **to make s. of sth** s'assurer de qch; **to make s. that...** s'assurer que...; **I don't know for s.** je ne suis pas absolument certain(e); **that's for s.** ça, c'est sûr; Fam **s. thing!** bien sûr!
2 adv (a) Am Fam (really) **it s. is cold** il fait vachement froid; **are you tired? – I s. am** tu es fatigué? – ça oui **(b)** (yes) bien sûr **(c)** **s. enough he was there** il était bien là

surefooted [ʃʊə'fʊtɪd] adj **to be s.** avoir le pied sûr

surely [ˈʃʊəlɪ] adv (a) (certainly) sûrement; **s. you don't believe that!** tu ne crois quand même pas ça!; **s. not!** c'est pas vrai! **(b)** (in a sure manner) **slowly but s.** lentement mais sûrement

surety [ˈʃʊərətɪ] n Law caution f; **to stand s. (for sb)** se porter caution (pour qn)

surf [sɜːf] **1** n surf m
2 vi (go surfing) faire du surf
3 vt Comptr **to s. the Net** naviguer sur l'Internet

surface [ˈsɜːfɪs] **1** n surface f; **Fig on the s.** en apparence; **Fig beneath the s.** au fond; **s. mail** courrier m par voie de terre; **s. tension** tension f de surface; **s. water** eaux fpl de surface
2 vt (road) revêtir
3 vi (from water) & Fam Hum (from bed) faire surface; Fig (of person, emotion) réapparaître

surface-to-air missile [ˈsɜːfɪstə'eə'mɪsaɪl] n Mil missile m sol-air

surface-to-surface missile [ˈsɜːfɪstə'sɜːfɪs'mɪsaɪl] n Mil missile m sol-sol

surfboard [ˈsɜːfbɔːd] n (planche f de) surf m

surfeit [ˈsɜːfɪt] n surabondance f

surfer [ˈsɜːfə(r)] n surfer m

surfing [ˈsɜːfɪŋ] n surf m; **to go s.** aller faire du surf

surge [sɜːdʒ] **1** n (of electricity) surtension f; (of enthusiasm, support, demand) sursaut m; (of profits) hausse f soudaine; (of crowd) ruée f
2 vi (of water, crowd) déferler; (of feeling) monter

surgeon [ˈsɜːdʒən] n chirurgien m

surgery [ˈsɜːdʒərɪ] n (a) (technique) chirurgie f; (operation) intervention f chirurgicale; **to perform s. on sb** opérer qn **(b)** Br (doctor's office) cabinet m (de consultation); (period) heures fpl de consultation **(c)** Br (of MP) permanence f

surgical [ˈsɜːdʒɪkəl] adj chirurgical(e); Fig **with s. precision** avec une précision mathématique; **s. instruments** instruments mpl de chirurgie; **s. spirit** alcool m à 90°; Mil **s. strike** offensive f chirurgicale

Surinam [ˈsʊərɪnæm] n le Surinam

surly [ˈsɜːlɪ] adj revêche

surmise [sə'maɪz] vt conjecturer

surmount [sə'maʊnt] vt surmonter

surname [ˈsɜːneɪm] n nom m de famille

surpass [sə'pɑːs] vt (person) surpasser; (record) battre; (expectation) dépasser; **to s. oneself** se surpasser

surplice [ˈsɜːplɪs] n Rel surplis m

surplus [ˈsɜːpləs] **1** n surplus m; Econ (of trade) excédent m
2 adj (items) en trop, en surplus; **to be s. to requirements** être en trop

surprise [sə'praɪz] **1** n surprise f; **to take sb by s.** prendre qn par surprise; **to give sb a s.** faire une surprise à qn; **it was no s.** cela n'a étonné personne
2 adj (attack, defeat) surprise inv; **s. party** soirée f surprise
3 vt surprendre, étonner; **I'm not surprised** ça ne m'étonne pas

surprising [sə'praɪzɪŋ] adj surprenant(e), étonnant(e)

surprisingly [sə'praɪzɪŋlɪ] adv étonnamment; **not s.** comme il fallait s'y attendre; **s. enough,...** chose surprenante...

surreal [sə'rɪəl] adj (surrealist) surréaliste; (strange) délirant(e)

surrealism [sə'rɪəlɪzəm] *n Art* surréalisme *m*

surrealist [sə'rɪəlɪst] *n & adj Art* surréaliste *mf*

surrender [sə'rendə(r)] **1** *n* (a) *(of army, weapons)* reddition *f*; **no s.!** nous ne nous rendrons pas! (b) *Fin* **s. value** valeur *f* de rachat
2 *vt (town)* livrer; *(right, possessions)* abandonner; *(advantage)* perdre; **to s. control of sth** abandonner la direction de qch
3 *vi* se rendre

surreptitious [sʌrəp'tɪʃəs] *adj* furtif(ive)

surrogate ['sʌrəgət] *n* substitut *m*; **s. mother** mère *f* porteuse

surround [sə'raʊnd] **1** *vt* entourer; *(of police)* cerner
2 *n* encadrement *m*

surrounding [sə'raʊndɪŋ] *adj* environnant(e)

surroundings [sə'raʊndɪŋz] *npl* environnement *m*

surtax ['sɜːtæks] **1** *n* surtaxe *f*
2 *vt* surtaxer

surveillance [sə'veɪləns] *n* surveillance *f*; **under s.** sous surveillance

survey 1 *n* [sɜː'veɪ] (a) *(look at)* contempler (b) *(of subject, situation)* étude *f*; *(of opinions)* sondage *m* (b) *(of house)* expertise *f*; *(of land)* relevé *m*
2 *vt* [sɜː'veɪ] (a) *(look at)* contempler (b) *(subject, situation)* étudier, examiner (c) *(house)* faire l'expertise de; *(land)* faire un relevé de

surveying [sɜː'veɪɪŋ] *n (of house)* expertise *f*; *(of land)* relevé *m*

surveyor [sə'veɪə(r)] *n (of building)* expert *m*; *(of land)* géomètre *mf*

survival [sə'vaɪvəl] *n* (a) *(continued existence)* survie *f*; *also Fig* **the s. of the fittest** la survie du plus apte; **s. kit** équipement *m* de survie (b) *(relic)* vestige *m*

survive [sə'vaɪv] **1** *vt (of person)* survivre à; *(of object)* résister à; **he is survived by a wife and son** il laisse une épouse et un fils
2 *vi* survivre

surviving [sə'vaɪvɪŋ] *adj (person)* survivant(e); *(remains, copy)* restant(e)

survivor [sə'vaɪvə(r)] *n* survivant(e) *m,f*

susceptible [sə'septɪbəl] *adj* sensible (**to** à)

suspect 1 *n* ['sʌspekt] suspect(e) *m,f*
2 *adj* suspect(e)
3 *vt* [sə'spekt] (a) *(person)* soupçonner (b) *(have intuition of)* se douter de; **to s. the truth** soupçonner la vérité (c) *(consider likely)* croire

suspend [sə'spend] *vt* (a) *(hang)* suspendre (**from** à) (b) *(service, employee, player)* suspendre; *(pupil)* renvoyer temporairement

suspended [sə'spendɪd] *adj* suspendu(e); **in s. animation** en hibernation; *Law* **s. sentence** condamnation *f* avec sursis

suspender [sə'spendə(r)] *n* (a) *Br (for stocking)* jarretelle *f*; *(for sock)* fixe-chaussette *m*; **s. belt** porte-jarretelles *m inv* (b) *Am* **suspenders** *(braces)* bretelles *fpl*

suspense [sə'spens] *n (uncertainty)* incertitude *f*; *(in film)* suspense *m*; **to keep sb in s.** tenir qn en haleine

suspension [sə'spenʃən] *n* (a) *(of car)* suspension *f*; **s. bridge** pont *m* suspendu (b) *(of service, employee)* suspension *f*; *(of pupil)* renvoi *m*

suspicion [sə'spɪʃən] *n* (a) *(belief of guilt)* soupçon *m*; **to be under s.** être soupçonné(e); **to be above s.** être au-dessus de tout soupçon; **to have one's suspicions**

about sb/sth avoir des doutes sur qn/qch; **to arouse s.** éveiller les soupçons (b) *(small amount)* soupçon *m*

suspicious [sə'spɪʃəs] *adj (arousing suspicions)* suspect(e); *(having suspicions)* méfiant(e) (**of** *or* **about** à l'égard de); **to make sb s.** éveiller les soupçons de qn

suspiciously [sə'spɪʃəslɪ] *adv (behave)* d'une manière suspecte; *(ask)* avec méfiance; *Fam* **it looks s. like...** ça ressemble étrangement à...

▸**suss out** [sʌs] *vt sep Br Fam* piger; *(person)* cerner

sustain [sə'steɪn] *vt* (a) *(maintain)* soutenir; *(life)* maintenir; **a proper breakfast will s. you until lunchtime** un bon petit déjeuner vous permettra de tenir jusqu'à midi; *Law* **objection sustained** objection accordée (b) *(loss, attack, damage)* subir; **to s. an injury** être blessé(e)

sustainable [sə'steɪnəbl] *adj (growth, development)* durable

sustained [sə'steɪnd] *adj* soutenu(e); **s. applause** applaudissements *mpl* prolongés

sustenance ['sʌstɪnəns] *n* subsistance *f*

suture ['suːtʃə(r)] *n* suture *f*

svelte [svelt] *adj* svelte

SW *n* (a) *(abbr* **southwest**) SO (b) *Rad (abbr* **Short Wave**) OC

swab [swɒb] **1** *n (cotton wool)* tampon *m*
2 *vt (pt & pp* **swabbed**) *(wound)* nettoyer; *(floor)* laver

swag [swæg] *n very Fam (of thief)* butin *m*

swagger ['swægə(r)] **1** *n* démarche *f* balancée et crâneuse
2 *vi (strut)* se pavaner

swallow¹ ['swɒləʊ] **1** *n (of drink)* gorgée *f*; *(of food)* bouchée *f*
2 *vt* (a) *(food, drink)* avaler; *Fig (pride, anger)* ravaler; **to s. sth whole** avaler qch tout rond (b) *Fam (believe)* gober, avaler
3 *vi* avaler; **to s. hard** *(when nervous, afraid)* avaler sa salive

swallow² *n (bird)* hirondelle *f*; *Prov* **one s. doesn't make a summer** une hirondelle ne fait pas le printemps

▸**swallow up** *vt sep Fig (company, country)* engloutir

swam [swæm] *pt of* **swim**

swamp [swɒmp] **1** *n* marais *m*
2 *vt (flood)* inonder; *Fig* **to be swamped with sth** être submergé(e) de qch

swan [swɒn] **1** *n* cygne *m*; *Fig* **s. song** chant *m* du cygne
2 *vi (pt & pp* **swanned**) *Fam* **to s. in/out/off** arriver/sortir/partir tranquillement

▸**swan about, swan around** *vi Fam* musarder

swank [swæŋk] *Fam* **1** *n (ostentation)* épate *f*; *(ostentatious person)* frimeur(euse) *m,f*
2 *vi* frimer

swanky ['swæŋkɪ] *adj Fam* chic *inv*

swap [swɒp] **1** *n* échange *m*; **to do a s.** faire un échange
2 *vt (pt & pp* **swapped**) **to s. sth for sth** échanger qch contre qch; **to s. places with sb** changer de place avec qn; **to s. insults/ideas** échanger des insultes/idées
3 *vi* échanger

swarm [swɔːm] **1** *n (of bees)* essaim *m*; *(of people)* nuée *f*
2 *vi (of bees)* essaimer; *(of people)* accourir en masse; **to be swarming with** *(of place)* grouiller de

swarthy ['swɔːðɪ] *adj* basané(e)

swashbuckling ['swɒʃbʌklɪŋ] *adj* de cape et d'épée

swastika ['swɒstɪkə] *n* svastika *m*

SWAT [swɒt] *n Am* (*abbr* **Special Weapons and Tactics**) S. team = groupe d'intervention d'élite de la police américaine

swat [swɒt] (*pt & pp* **swatted**) *vt* écraser

swatch [swɒtʃ] *n* échantillon *m*

swathe [sweɪð] **1** *n* (*of grass*) andain *m*; (*of material, land*) bande *f*; *Fig* **to cut a s. through sth** (*of fire, storm*) détruire qch sur son passage
2 *vt* envelopper (**in** de)

sway [sweɪ] **1** *n* (**a**) (*movement*) balancement *m* (**b**) (*influence*) influence *f*; **to be under sb's s.** être sous l'influence de qn; **to hold s. over sb/sth** tenir qn/qch sous sa domination
2 *vt* (*influence*) influencer
3 *vi* se balancer; **to s. from side to side** se balancer d'un côté à l'autre

Swazi ['swɑːzɪ] **1** *n* (**a**) (*person*) Swazi(e) *m,f* (**b**) (*language*) swazi *m*
2 *adj* swazi(e)

Swaziland ['swɑːzɪlænd] *n* le Swaziland

swear [sweə(r)] (*pt* **swore** [swɔː(r)], *pp* **sworn** [swɔːn]) **1** *vt* (*vow*) jurer; **to s. to do sth** jurer de faire qch; *Law* **to s. an oath** prêter serment
2 *vi* (*use swearwords*) jurer; **to s. at sb** injurier qn

▸**swear by** *vt insep* (*have confidence in*) se fier à

▸**swear in** *vt insep Law* (*jury, witness*) faire prêter serment à

swearing ['sweərɪŋ] *n* grossièretés *fpl*

swearword ['sweəwɜːd] *n* juron *m*, mot *m* grossier

sweat [swet] **1** *n* transpiration *f*, sueur *f*; *Fig* **to be in a s. about sth** avoir des sueurs froides à propos de qch; *very Fam* **no s.!** pas de problèmes!; **s. gland** glande *f* sudoripare
2 *vt Fam* **to s. buckets** être en nage; *Fig* **to s. blood** suer sang et eau
3 *vi* (**a**) (*perspire*) transpirer, suer; *Fam* **to s. like a pig** suer comme un bœuf (**b**) *Fam Fig* (*worry*) se faire de la bile; **to make sb s.** laisser mariner qn

sweatband ['swetbænd] *n* (*on head*) bandeau *m*; (*on wrist*) poignet *m*

sweater ['swetə(r)] *n* pullover *m*, pull *m*

sweatshirt ['swetʃɜːt] *n* sweatshirt *m*

sweatshop ['swetʃɒp] *n* = atelier de confection où l'on exploite le personnel

sweaty ['swetɪ] *adj* (*person*) en sueur; (*hands*) moite; (*clothes*) imprégné(e) de sueur; (*work*) qui fait transpirer

Swede [swiːd] *n* (*person*) Suédois(e) *m,f*

swede [swiːd] *n Br* (*vegetable*) rutabaga *m*

Sweden ['swiːdən] *n* la Suède

Swedish ['swiːdɪʃ] **1** *npl* (*people*) **the S.** les Suédois *mpl*
2 *n* (*language*) suédois *m*
3 *adj* suédois(e)

sweep [swiːp] **1** *n* (**a**) (*action*) coup *m* de balai; **to give sth a s.** donner un coup de balai à qch; *Fig* **at one s.** d'un seul coup; *Fig* **to make a clean s.** (*win everything*) tout gagner (**b**) (*movement*) **with a s. of the arm** d'un geste large (**c**) (*of land, hills*) étendue *f*; (*of road, river*) courbe *f*
2 *vt* (*pt & pp* **swept** [swept]) (**a**) (*floor, street*) balayer; (*chimney*) ramoner; **to be swept overboard** être emporté(e) par une vague (**b**) (*idioms*) **to s. sth under the carpet** tirer le rideau sur qch; **to s. the board** (*in competition*) tout gagner; **the latest craze to s. the country** la dernière folie qui a envahi le pays; *Fig* **to s.**
sb off their feet faire perdre la tête à qn
3 *vi* (**a**) (*with broom*) balayer (**b**) (*move rapidly*) **to s. in/out** faire une entrée/une sortie majestueuse; **to s. to power** être propulsé(e) au pouvoir

▸**sweep aside** *vt sep* (*opposition, criticism*) écarter

▸**sweep away** *vt sep* (*building*) emporter; *Fig* (*obstacle, difficulty*) balayer; *Fig* **to be swept away by sth** (*enthusiasm, passion*) être emporté(e) par qch

▸**sweep up** *vt sep & vi* balayer

sweeper ['swiːpə(r)] *n* (**a**) (*carpet*) **s.** balai *m* mécanique (**b**) (*footballer*) arrière *mf* volant(e)

sweeping ['swiːpɪŋ] *adj* (*gesture*) large; (*statement*) généralisateur(trice); (*change, proposal*) radical(e)

sweepstake ['swiːpsteɪk] *n* sweepstake *m*

sweet [swiːt] **1** *adj* (**a**) (*sugary*) doux (douce); (*wine*) doux (douce); **to taste s.** avoir un goût sucré; **as s. as honey** doux comme le miel; **to have a s. tooth** aimer les sucreries; **s. pea** pois *m* de senteur; **s. potato** patate *f* douce; **s. william** œillet *m* de poète (**b**) (*smell*) agréable; (*sound*) doux (douce) (**c**) (*pretty, kind*) adorable; **to whisper s. nothings to sb** dire des mots doux à qn
2 *n Br* (*piece of confectionery*) bonbon *m*; (*dessert*) dessert *m*; **s. shop** confiserie *f*

sweetbreads ['swiːtbredz] *npl* ris *m* (*de veau, d'agneau*)

sweet-and-sour ['swiːtən'saʊə(r)] *adj* aigre-doux (aigre-douce)

sweetcorn ['swiːtkɔːn] *n* maïs *m*

sweeten ['swiːtən] *vt* (*food*) sucrer; *Fig* **to s. sb up** amadouer qn

sweetener ['swiːtənə(r)] *n* (**a**) (*in food*) édulcorant *m* (**b**) *Fam* (*bribe*) pot-de-vin *m*

sweetheart ['swiːthɑːt] *n* (*term of address*) (*to woman*) chérie *f*; (*to man*) chéri *m*

sweetie ['swiːtɪ] *n Fam* (**a**) *Br* (*piece of confectionery*) bonbon *m* (**b**) (*darling*) chou *m*; **he's such a s.** il est adorable

sweetly ['swiːtlɪ] *adv* (*sing*) d'une voix douce; (*smile, answer*) gentiment

sweetness ['swiːtnɪs] *n* douceur *f*; **to be all s. and light** être tout sucre tout miel

sweet-talk ['swiːttɔːk] *vt Fam* **to s. sb into doing sth** baratiner qn pour qu'il fasse qch

sweet-tempered [swiːt'tempəd] *adj* doux (douce)

swell [swel] **1** *vt* (*pp* **swollen** ['swəʊlən] *or* **swelled**) (*numbers, crowd*) gonfler
2 *vi* (*of part of body*) enfler; (*of number, crowd*) grossir; (*of sea*) se soulever; **to s. with pride** se gonfler d'orgueil
3 *n* (*of sea*) houle *f*
4 *adj Am Fam* (*excellent*) super *inv*

▸**swell up** *vi* (*part of body*) enfler

swelling ['swelɪŋ] *n* gonflement *m*, enflure *f*; **the s. had gone down** ça avait désenflé

sweltering ['sweltərɪŋ] *adj* étouffant(e)

swept [swept] *pt & pp* of **sweep**

swerve [swɜːv] **1** *n* (*of car*) embardée *f*; (*of player*) écart *m*
2 *vi* (*of car, driver*) faire une embardée; (*of player*) faire un écart; (*of ball*) décrire une courbe

swift [swɪft] **1** *n* (*bird*) martinet *m*
2 *adj* rapide

swift-footed ['swɪftfʊtɪd] *adj* rapide à la course

swiftly ['swɪftlɪ] *adv* rapidement, vite

swiftness ['swɪftnɪs] *n* rapidité *f*

swig [swɪg] *Fam* **1** *n* lampée *f*; **to take a s. from a bottle** boire un coup à une bouteille

2 *vt* (*pt & pp* **swigged**) boire à grands traits

swill [swɪl] **1** *n* (*food*) (*for pigs*) pâtée *f*; *Pej* (*for people*) nourriture *f* infâme

2 *vt Fam* (*drink*) écluser

▶**swill about, swill around** *vi* (*of liquid*) se répandre

▶**swill out** *vt sep* (*rinse*) rincer à grande eau

swim [swɪm] **1** *n* **to go for** *or* **have a s.** aller nager

2 *vi* (*pt* **swam** [swæm], *pp* **swum** [swʌm]) nager; **to s. the breast stroke** nager la brasse; **to s. the Channel** traverser la Manche à la nage

3 *vi* (a) nager; **to go swimming** aller nager; **to s. across** traverser qch à la nage; *Fig* **to s. with the tide** suivre le courant (b) (*be dizzy*) **my head is swimming** j'ai la tête qui tourne

swimmer ['swɪmə(r)] *n* nageur(euse) *m,f*

swimming ['swɪmɪŋ] *n* natation *f*; **s. cap** bonnet *m* de bain; **s. costume** maillot *m* de bain; **s. lesson** cours *m* de natation; **s. pool** piscine *f*; **s. trunks** slip *m* de bain

swimmingly ['swɪmɪŋlɪ] *adv Fam* au mieux; **things are going s.** ça baigne

swimsuit ['swɪmsuːt] *n* maillot *m* de bain

swindle ['swɪndəl] **1** *n* escroquerie *f*

2 *vt* escroquer; **to s. sb out of sth** soutirer qch à qn

swindler ['swɪndlə(r)] *n* escroc *m*

swine [swaɪn] *n* (*pl* **swine**) *n* (a) *Lit* (*pig*) porc *m*; **s. fever** peste *f* porcine (b) *Fam* (*man*) salaud *m*; (*woman*) garce *f*

swing [swɪŋ] **1** *n* (a) (*movement*) (*of rope, chain*) balancement *m*; (*in golf*) swing *m*; *Fam* **to take a s. at sb/sth** balancer un coup de poing à qn/qch; **to be in full s.** battre son plein; *Fam* **to go with a s.** marcher comme sur des roulettes; *Fam* **to get into the s. of things** se mettre dans le bain; **s. door** porte *f* battante (b) (*change*) (*in opinion*) revirement *m* (**in** de); (*in economy*) fluctuation *f* (**in** de); (*in mood*) saute *f* (**in** de) (c) (*in playground*) balançoire *f*; *Fam* **it's swings and roundabouts** ce qu'on gagne d'un côté on le perd de l'autre

2 *vt* (*pt & pp* **swung** [swʌŋ]) (*arms, racquet, axe*) balancer; **to s. one's hips** balancer les hanches; **to s. sb/sth onto one's shoulder** hisser qn/qch sur ses épaules; *Fam* **to s. it so that...** arranger les choses de manière à ce que... + *subjunctive*

3 *vi* (a) (*move to and fro*) se balancer; **to s. open** (*of door*) s'ouvrir; **to s. into action** passer à l'action; *Fam* **he should s. for this** (*be hanged*) il mérite d'être pendu; *Fam* **the party was really swinging** la fête battait son plein (b) (*change direction*) virer; **to s. round** se retourner

swingeing ['swɪndʒɪŋ] *adj* énorme

swipe [swaɪp] **1** *vt* (a) (*through electronic reader*) passer dans un lecteur de cartes (b) *Fam* (*steal*) faucher

2 *vi* (*hit*) **to s. at** essayer de frapper

3 *n* **to take a s. at** (*aim blow at*) essayer de frapper; *Fig* (*criticize*) s'en prendre à

swirl [swɜːl] **1** *n* (*of cream*) spirale *f*; (*of smoke, leaves, dust*) tourbillon *m*

2 *vt* remuer

3 *vi* tourbillonner, tournoyer

swish [swɪʃ] **1** *n* (*of cane, whip*) sifflement *m*; (*of dress, silk*) froufrou *m*

2 *adj Fam* (*elegant*) chic *inv*

3 *vt* (*cane*) faire siffler; **to s. its tail** (*of animal*) remuer la

queue

4 *vi* (*of cane, whip*) siffler; (*of dress, silk*) froufrouter

Swiss [swɪs] **1** *npl* **the S.** (*people*) les Suisses *mpl*

2 *adj* suisse; **S. army knife** couteau *m* suisse; **S. chard** bette *f*; **S. cheese plant** philodendron *m*; **s. roll** roulé *m*

Switch® [swɪtʃ] *n* **to pay by S.** ≃ payer par carte bleue®; **S. card** ≃ carte *f* bleue®

switch [swɪtʃ] **1** *n* (a) (*electrical*) interrupteur *m* (b) (*change*) revirement *m*; **to make a s.** effectuer un changement (c) (*stick*) baguette *f*

2 *vt* (a) (*change*) **to s. channels/jobs** changer de chaîne/d'emploi; **they switched their attention to...** leur attention s'est portée sur...; **he's been switched to another department** il a été muté dans un autre service (b) (*exchange*) échanger

3 *vi* (*change*) **to s. to** passer à; *Comptr* basculer vers

▶**switch off 1** *vt sep* (*appliance, heating*) éteindre

2 *vi* (a) (*of appliance, heating*) s'éteindre (b) *Fam* (*of person*) décrocher

▶**switch on 1** *vt sep* (*appliance, heating*) allumer

2 *vi* (*of appliance, heating*) s'allumer

▶**switch over** *vi* (*change TV channel*) passer sur une autre chaîne; **to s. over to sth** passer à qch

switchback ['swɪtʃbæk] *n* route *f* en lacets

switchboard ['swɪtʃbɔːd] *n* standard *m*; **s. operator** standardiste *mf*

Switzerland ['swɪtsələnd] *n* la Suisse

swivel ['swɪvəl] **1** *n* pivot *m*; **s. chair** chaise *f* pivotante

2 *vi* (*pt & pp* **swivelled**) pivoter

swizz [swɪz] *n Fam* arnaque *f*

swollen ['swəʊlən]

1 *pp of* **swell**

2 *adj* enflé(e)

swoon [swuːn] **1** *n* évanouissement *m*

2 *vi* s'évanouir

swoop [swuːp] **1** *n* (*of bird, plane*) descente *f* en piqué; (*of police*) descente *f*

2 *vi* (*of bird, plane*) descendre en piqué; (*of police*) faire une descente

swop [swɒp] = **swap**

sword [sɔːd] *n* épée *f*; **s. dance** danse *f* du sabre

swordfish ['sɔːdfɪʃ] *n* espadon *m*

swore [swɔː(r)] *pt of* **swear**

sworn [swɔːn] **1** *adj* **s. enemy** ennemi(e) *m,f* juré(e)

2 *pp of* **swear**

swot [swɒt] *Br Fam* **1** *n* (*studious pupil*) bûcheur(euse) *m,f*

2 *vi* (*pt & pp* **swotted**) (*study hard*) bûcher

▶**swot up on** *vt insep Br Fam* (*subject*) potasser

swum [swʌm] *pp of* **swim**

swung [swʌŋ] *pt & pp of* **swing**

sycamore ['sɪkəmɔː(r)] *n* sycomore *m*

sycophant ['sɪkəfənt] *n* flagorneur(euse) *m,f*

sycophantic [sɪkə'fæntɪk] *adj* flagorneur(euse)

Sydney ['sɪdnɪ] *n* Sydney

syllable ['sɪləbəl] *n* syllabe *f*

syllabus ['sɪləbəs] *n* programme *m*

sylph-like ['sɪlflaɪk] *adj Hum* **a s. woman** une sylphide

symbiotic [sɪmb(a)ɪ'ɒtɪk] *adj* symbiotique

symbol ['sɪmbəl] *n* symbole *m*

symbolic [sɪm'bɒlɪk] *adj* symbolique

symbolism ['sɪmbəlɪzəm] *n Art* symbolisme *m*
symbolist ['sɪmbəlɪst] *n & adj Art* symboliste *mf*
symbolize ['sɪmbəlaɪz] *vt* symboliser
symmetrical [sɪ'metrɪkəl] *adj* symétrique
symmetry ['sɪmɪtrɪ] *n* symétrie *f*
sympathetic [sɪmpə'θetɪk] *adj (understanding)* com-péhensif(ive); *(compassionate)* compatissant(e); **to be s. to a proposal/cause** être favorable à une proposition/cause
sympathize ['sɪmpəθaɪz] *vi* **(a)** *(show compassion)* compatir **(with** avec) **(b)** *(show understanding)* **to s. (with sb)** comprendre (qn)
sympathizer ['sɪmpəθaɪzə(r)] *n* sympathisant(e) *m,f*
sympathy ['sɪmpəθɪ] *n* **(a)** *(pity, compassion)* compassion *f*; **to feel s. for sb** éprouver de la compassion pour qn **(b)** *(understanding, support)* sympathie *f*; **to feel s. for sb** éprouver de la sympathie pour qn; **s. strike** grève *f* de solidarité
symphony ['sɪmfənɪ] *n* symphonie *f*; **s. orchestra** orchestre *m* symphonique
symposium [sɪm'pəʊzɪəm] *(pl* **symposia** [sɪm'pəʊzɪə]) *n* symposium *m*
symptom ['sɪm(p)təm] *n also Fig* symptôme *m*
symptomatic [sɪm(p)tə'mætɪk] *adj* symptomatique
synagogue ['sɪnəgɒg] *n* synagogue *f*
sync [sɪŋk] *n Fam* synchronisation *f*; **in/out of s.** **(with)** synchrone/pas synchrone (avec)
synchronization [sɪŋkrənaɪ'zeɪʃən] *n* synchro-nisation *f*
synchronize ['sɪŋkrənaɪz] *vt* synchroniser
syncopation [sɪŋkə'peɪʃən] *n Mus* syncope *f*
syndicalism ['sɪndɪkəlɪzəm] *n Pol* syndicalisme *m*
syndicalist ['sɪndɪkəlɪst] *n & adj Pol* syndicaliste *mf*
syndicate 1 *n* ['sɪndɪkət] syndicat *m*
2 *vt* ['sɪndɪkeɪt] *Journ* publier simultanément dans plusieurs journaux; **syndicated columnist** journaliste *mf* d'agence
syndrome ['sɪndrəʊm] *n Fig* syndrôme *m*
synergy ['sɪnədʒɪ] *n* synergie *f*
synod ['sɪnəd] *n Rel* synode *m*
synonym ['sɪnənɪm] *n* synonyme *m*
synonymous [sɪ'nɒnɪməs] *adj* synonyme **(with** de)
synopsis [sɪ'nɒpsɪs] *(pl* **synopses** [sɪ'nɒpsi:z]) *n* résumé *m*; *(of film)* synopsis *m*
syntax ['sɪntæks] *n Ling* syntaxe *f*; *Comptr* **s. error** erreur *f* de syntaxe
synthesis ['sɪnθɪsɪs] *(pl* **syntheses** ['sɪnθɪsi:z]) *n* synthèse *f*
synthesize ['sɪnθəsaɪz] *vt* synthétiser
synthesizer ['sɪnθəsaɪzə(r)] *n* synthétiseur *m*
synthetic [sɪn'θetɪk] **1** *adj* synthétique
2 *n* **synthetics** synthétique *m*
syphilis ['sɪfɪlɪs] *n* syphilis *f*
syphon [saɪfən] = **siphon**
Syria ['sɪrɪə] *n* la Syrie
Syrian ['sɪrɪən] **1** *n* Syrien(enne) *m,f*
2 *adj* syrien(enne)
syringe [sɪ'rɪndʒ] **1** *n* seringue *f*
2 *vt (ears)* déboucher
syrup ['sɪrəp] *n* sirop *m*
syrupy ['sɪrəpɪ] *adj (smile, music)* sirupeux(euse)
system ['sɪstəm] *n* **(a)** *(structure)* système *m*; **the S.** *(established order)* le système; *Fam* **it was a shock to the s.** ça a été un choc; *Fam* **to get sb/sth out of one's s.** se sortir qn/qch de la tête **(b)** *Comptr* système *m*; **systems analyst** analyste *m* programmeur **(c)** *(method)* méthode *f*
systematic [sɪstə'mætɪk] *adj* systématique
systematize ['sɪstəmətaɪz] *vt* systématiser

T

T, t [tiː] n (a) (letter) T, m inv (b) (idioms) that's you to a T c'est tout à fait toi; to suit sb to a T convenir parfaitement à qn

t (abbr **ton(s)**) t

TA [tiːˈeɪ] n Br (abbr **territorial army**) = armée de réserve, constituée de volontaires

ta [tɑː] exclam Br Fam merci!

tab [tæb] n (a) (on garment) étiquette f; Fam to keep tabs on sb/sth avoir qn/qch à l'œil (b) (on typewriter, word processor) tabulation f; t. (key) tabulateur m (c) Am Fam (for meal, drinks) addition f (d) (of LSD, ecstasy) pilule f

tabby [ˈtæbɪ] n t. (cat) chat m tigré

tabernacle [ˈtæbənækəl] n (church) temple m; (on altar) tabernacle m

table [ˈteɪbəl] 1 n (a) (furniture) table f; to lay or set the t. mettre ou dresser la table; to clear the t. débarrasser la table; t. lamp petite lampe f; t. linen linge m de table; to have good/bad t. manners bien/mal se tenir à table; t. mat set m de table; t. salt sel m de table; t. tennis tennis m de table; t. wine vin m de table (b) (of facts, figures) tableau m, table f; t. of contents table des matières; twelve times t. table de douze (c) (idioms) the offer is still on the t. l'offre tient toujours; to turn the tables on sb renverser les rôles

2 vt to t. a motion/proposal Br (present) présenter une motion/une proposition; Am (postpone) ajourner une motion/une proposition

tablecloth [ˈteɪbəlklɒθ] n nappe f

tablespoon [ˈteɪbəlspuːn] n cuillère f à soupe

tablet [ˈtæblɪt] n (a) (pill) cachet m (b) (inscribed stone) tablette f (c) (of soap) pain m

tableware [ˈteɪbəlweə(r)] n vaisselle f

tabloid [ˈtæblɔɪd] n (newspaper) tabloïd m; the t. press la presse populaire

taboo [təˈbuː] 1 n (pl taboos) tabou m
2 adj tabou(e)

tabular [ˈtæbjʊlə(r)] adj in t. form sous forme de tableau

tabulate [ˈtæbjʊleɪt] vt présenter sous forme de tableau

tachometer [tækˈɒmɪtə(r)] n compte-tours m

tacit [ˈtæsɪt] adj tacite

tacitly [ˈtæsɪtlɪ] adv tacitement

taciturn [ˈtæsɪtɜːn] adj taciturne

tack [tæk] 1 n (a) (small nail) clou m; Am (drawing pin) punaise f (b) Naut (course) bordée f; Fig to change t. changer de tactique
2 vt (a) (fasten) clouer; Am (with drawing pin) punaiser; Fig to t. sth on (add) rajouter qch (b) (in sewing) faufiler
3 vi Naut louvoyer

tackle [ˈtækəl] 1 n (a) (equipment) matériel m, équipement m (b) (in football) tacle m; (in rugby) placage m
2 vt (a) (deal with) (problem) s'attaquer à; (subject) aborder; to t. sb about sth (confront) confronter qn à propos de qch (b) (in football) tacler; (in rugby) plaquer

tacky [ˈtækɪ] adj (a) (sticky) collant(e) (b) Fam (tasteless) de mauvais goût; (person) vulgaire

tact [tækt] n tact m

tactful [ˈtæktfʊl] adj (person) qui a du tact; (answer, remark) diplomatique

tactic [ˈtæktɪk] n tactique f

tactical [ˈtæktɪkəl] adj tactique; Pol t. voting vote m utile

tactician [tækˈtɪʃən] n tacticien(enne) m,f

tactile [ˈtæktaɪl] adj tactile

tactless [ˈtæktlɪs] adj dépourvu(e) de tact

tactlessly [ˈtæktlɪslɪ] adv sans tact

tad [tæd] n Fam a t. un peu

tadpole [ˈtædpəʊl] n têtard m

Tadzhikistan [tædʒɪkɪˈstɑːn] n le Tadjikistan

taffeta [ˈtæfɪtə] n taffetas m

tag [tæg] 1 n (a) (label) étiquette f; Gram t. question tag m (b) (game) to play t. jouer à chat
2 vt (pt & pp tagged) (label) étiqueter

▶**tag along** vi she always tags along elle me/le/etc suit partout; to t. along with sb venir avec qn

▶**tag on** vt sep to t. sth on rajouter qch

Tagus [ˈteɪgəs] n the T. le Tage

Tahiti [təˈhiːtɪ] n Tahiti f

Tahitian [təˈhiːʃən] 1 n Tahitien(enne) m,f
2 adj tahitien(enne)

tail [teɪl] 1 n (a) (of animal, plane) queue f; (of shirt) pan m; heads or tails? (when tossing coin) pile ou face?; tails, t. coat queue-de-pie f; t. end (last part) fin f (b) (idioms) with one's t. between one's legs la queue entre les jambes; Fam to put a t. on sb prendre qn en filature; Fam to turn t. tourner les talons
2 vt Fam (follow) filer

▶**tail away** vi décliner; (of voice) baisser

tailback [ˈteɪlbæk] n (traffic jam) bouchon m

tailboard [ˈteɪlbɔːd], Am **tailgate** [ˈteɪlgeɪt] n hayon m

taillight [ˈteɪllaɪt] n Am feu m arrière

tailor [ˈteɪlə(r)] 1 n tailleur m; t.'s dummy mannequin m; t.'s shop atelier m de tailleur
2 vt (suit) faire; Fig (speech, policy) adapter (to à)

tailored [ˈteɪləd] adj ajusté(e)

tailor-made [ˈteɪləmeɪd] adj also Fig fait(e) sur mesure

tailplane [ˈteɪlpleɪn] n Av stabilisateur m

tailspin ['teɪlspɪn] *n Av* descente *f* en vrille; **to go into a t.** descendre en vrille; *Fig* paniquer

tailwind ['teɪlwɪnd] *n* vent *m* arrière

taint [teɪnt] **1** *n* contamination *f*; *Fig* tare *f*
2 *vt (contaminate)* contaminer; *Fig* souiller

Taiwan [taɪ'wɑːn] *n* Taiwan

Taiwanese [taɪwə'niːz] **1** *n* Taiwanais(e) *m,f*
2 *adj* taiwanais(e)

Tajikistan [tædʒɪkɪ'stɑːn] = **Tadzhikistan**

take [teɪk] **1** *vt (pt* took [tʊk], *pp* taken ['teɪkən]) **(a)** *(grasp)* prendre; **to t. hold of** prendre *ou* saisir; **to t. sb by the arm** prendre qn par le bras; **to t. sb in one's arms** prendre qn dans ses bras; **to t. the opportunity to do sth** profiter de l'occasion pour faire qch
(b) *(remove)* prendre; **to t. sth away from sb** prendre qch à qn; **to t. sth out of sth** prendre qch dans qch
(c) *(tolerate)* supporter; **he can't t. a joke** il prend mal la plaisanterie; **I can't t. (it) any more** je n'en peux plus
(d) *(lead, carry)* amener; **to t. sb home/to the station** conduire qn chez lui/à la gare; **to t. sb to court** faire un procès à qn; **to t. the dog for a walk** aller promener le chien; **her job takes her all over the world** son travail l'amène à voyager dans le monde entier; **if you can get the money we'll t. it from there** quand tu auras l'argent on verra comment on procède
(e) *(go by) (bus, road, turning)* prendre
(f) *(require)* prendre; **it takes courage (to do)** il faut du courage (pour faire); **how long does it t.?** combien de temps cela prend-il?; **it took me an hour to get here** il m'a fallu une heure pour venir; **that will t. a lot of explaining** ça ne va pas être facile de se faire pardonner
(g) *(adopt) (precautions, measures)* prendre; **to t. legal advice** consulter un avocat; **to t. sth as an example** prendre qch comme exemple
(h) *(record) (temperature, notes)* prendre
(i) *(capture) (power, town, chess piece)* prendre; **to t. first prize** remporter le premier prix
(j) *(assume)* **I t. it (that)...** je suppose que...
(k) *(accept) (cheque, credit card)* accepter; **my car only takes unleaded** ma voiture ne marche qu'à l'essence sans plomb; **t. it or leave it!** c'est à prendre ou à laisser!; **to t. sth well/badly** prendre bien/mal qch; **to t. sth the wrong way** mal comprendre qch; **how much or what will you t. for it?** combien est-ce que tu en veux?; **you can t. it from me that...** je peux te garantir que...
(l) *(contain)* avoir une capacité de
(m) *(subject) (class, course)* suivre; *(exam)* passer; **he takes them for English** il leur enseigne l'anglais
(n) *(in phrases)* **to t. a bath** prendre un bain; **to t. drugs** se droguer; **to t. fright** prendre peur; **to be taken ill** tomber malade; **to t. a look at sth** jeter un coup d'œil à qch; **to t. a photograph of sb/sth** prendre qn/qch en photo; **to t. a seat** s'asseoir; **to t. a walk** se promener
2 *vi (be successful) (of fire, plant cutting, dye)* prendre
3 *n* **(a)** *(of film, music)* prise *f*
(b) *(money)* recette *f*; *Fam* **to be on the t.** toucher des pots-de-vin

▶**take after** *vt insep* ressembler à

▶**take apart** *vt (machine, engine)* démonter; *(argument)* démolir

▶**take away 1** *vt sep (remove)* enlever, retirer; *(deduct)* ôter; **to t. sth away from sb** enlever qch à qn; *Br* **sandwiches to t. away** sandwichs à emporter
2 *vi* **to t. away from the pleasure/value of sth** diminuer le plaisir/la valeur de qch

▶**take back** *vt sep* **(a)** *(return)* ramener, rapporter; **that takes me back to my childhood** cela me rappelle mon enfance **(b)** *(accept)* reprendre **(c)** *(withdraw)* retirer; **t. that back!** retire ce que tu viens de dire!

▶**take down** *vt sep* **(a)** *(remove) (from shelf)* prendre; *(downstairs)* descendre; *(poster, decorations)* enlever **(b)** *(lower)* baisser; *Fam* **to t. sb down a peg or two** remettre qn à sa place **(c)** *(dismantle) (tent, scaffolding)* démonter; *(wall, barricade)* démolir **(d)** *(record)* noter; *(notes)* prendre

▶**take for** *vt sep* **to t. sb for somebody else** prendre qn pour quelqu'un d'autre; **what do you t. me for?** pour qui est-ce que tu me prends?

▶**take in** *vt sep* **(a)** *(lead, carry) (person)* faire entrer; *(harvest)* rentrer **(b)** *(orphan)* recueillir; *(lodger)* prendre **(c)** *(garment)* reprendre **(d)** *(include)* inclure, comprendre **(e)** *(understand)* saisir **(f)** *(deceive)* tromper, rouler

▶**take off 1** *vt sep (remove)* enlever; **to t. sth off sb's hands** retirer qch des mains de qn; **to t. years off sb** *(of clothes, diet)* rajeunir qn; **he took £10 off (the price)** il a baissé (le prix) de 10 livres; **he never took his eyes off us** il ne nous a pas quittés des yeux **(b)** *(lead) (person)* emmener; **to t. oneself off** s'en aller **(c)** *(mimic)* imiter
2 *vi* **(a)** *(of plane)* décoller **(b)** *Fam (of person)* se casser **(c)** *Fam (succeed)* prendre

▶**take on** *vt sep* **(a)** *(task, responsibility)* assumer; *(problem)* s'occuper de; *(opponent)* défier; *(fuel, supplies)* prendre **(b)** *(employ)* embaucher **(c)** *(acquire)* prendre

▶**take out** *vt sep* **(a)** *(remove)* sortir; *Fam* **to t. it or a lot out of sb** épuiser qn; **to t. it out on sb** passer sa colère sur qn **(b)** *(person)* inviter (à sortir) **(c)** *(obtain) (licence)* obtenir; *(insurance policy)* souscrire; *(subscription)* prendre

▶**take over 1** *vt sep* **(a)** *(become responsible for) (job, business)* reprendre **(b)** *(take control of) (place)* envahir; *(company)* racheter
2 *vi* **(a)** *(assume power)* prendre le pouvoir **(b)** *(relieve)* prendre la relève **(from** de)

▶**take to** *vt insep* **(a)** *(go to)* **to t. to one's heels** prendre ses jambes à son cou; **to t. to one's bed** s'aliter; **to t. to the hills** se réfugier dans les collines **(b)** *(adopt habit)* **to t. to doing sth** se mettre à faire qch **(c)** *(like)* **to t. to sb** se prendre d'affection pour qn

▶**take up 1** *vt sep* **(a)** *(carry)* monter **(b)** *(lead) (person)* faire monter **(c)** *(lift)* enlever **(d)** *(shorten) (skirt, hem)* raccourcir **(e)** *(challenge)* relever; *(offer, suggestion)* accepter; **to t. sb up on an offer** accepter l'offre de qn **(f)** *(subject, problem)* parler de **(with** sb avec qn) **(g)** *(assume) (position, post)* prendre **(h)** *(hobby, studies)* se mettre à; **we t. up the story just after...** nous reprenons l'histoire juste après... **(i)** *(space, time)* prendre
2 *vi* **to t. up with sb** se lier avec qn

▶**take upon** *vt sep* **to t. it upon oneself to do sth** prendre sur soi de faire qch

takeaway ['teɪkəweɪ] *Br* **1** *n (food)* plat *m* à emporter; *(restaurant)* restaurant *m* qui fait des plats à emporter
2 *adj (food)* à emporter

take-home pay ['teɪkhəʊmpeɪ] *n* salaire *m* net

taken ['teɪkən] **1** *adj* **(a)** *(occupied)* pris(e) **(b)** *(impressed)* **I was very t. with him** il m'a fait très bonne impression
2 *pp* of **take**

takeoff ['teɪkɒf] *n* **(a)** *(imitation)* imitation *f*; **to do a t.** of faire une imitation de **(b)** *(of plane)* décollage *m*

takeover ['teɪkəʊvə(r)] *n* **(a)** *Com (of company)* rachat *m*; **t. bid** offre *f* publique d'achat **(b)** *(of government, country)* prise *f* de pouvoir

taker ['teɪkə(r)] *n* any takers? y a-t-il des amateurs?; there were no takers il n'y a pas eu d'amateurs

taking ['teɪkɪŋ] *n* (a) it's yours for the t. tu n'as plus qu'à accepter (b) *Com* takings recette *f*

talc [tælk] *n* talc *m*

talcum powder ['tælkəmpaʊdə(r)] *n* talc *m*

tale [teɪl] *n* (a) *(story)* histoire *f*, *(legend)* conte *m*; to live to tell the t. survivre (b) *(lie)* histoire *f*, salades *fpl* (c) to tell tales (on sb) moucharder (qn)

talent ['tælənt] *n* (a) *(person, ability)* talent *m*; t. scout or spotter dénicheur(euse) *m,f* de talents (b) *Br Fam (attractive women)* belles nanas *fpl*; *(attractive men)* beaux mecs *mpl*

talented ['tæləntɪd] *adj* talentueux(euse)

talisman ['tælɪzmən] *n* talisman *m*

talk [tɔːk] 1 *n* (a) *(conversation)* conversation *f*; to have a t. with sb parler *ou* s'entretenir avec qn; *Fam* to be all t. (and no action) parler beaucoup (et ne pas faire grand-chose); t. show *(on TV, radio)* talk-show *m*
(b) talks *(negotiations)* pourparlers *mpl*
(c) *(gossip)* there is some t. of him resigning le bruit court qu'il va démissionner; it's the t. of the town on ne parle que de cela
(d) *(lecture)* intervention *f*
2 *vt (speak)* to t. nonsense dire des bêtises; to t. business/politics parler business/politique; to t. sense tenir des propos sensés; to t. (some) sense into sb faire entendre raison à qn; she can t. her way out of anything avec son bagou elle arrive toujours à se tirer d'affaire; to t. sb into/out of doing sth convaincre/dissuader qn de faire qch
3 *vi* (a) *(speak)* parler (to/about à/de); to t. to oneself parler tout(e) seul(e); talking of embarrassing situations,... à propos de situations embarrassantes,...; *Fam* now you're talking! voilà qui est mieux!; *Fam* you can t.!, look who's talking! tu peux parler!
(b) *(gossip)* cancaner, jaser
(c) *(give lecture)* faire une intervention (on sur)

▶**talk back** *vi* répondre avec insolence

▶**talk down** *vt insep* to t. down to sb parler à qn sur un ton de supériorité

▶**talk over** *vt sep* discuter

talkative ['tɔːkətɪv] *adj* bavard(e)

talker ['tɔːkə(r)] *n* he was never much of a t. il n'a jamais été très bavard

talking ['tɔːkɪŋ] *adj* t. book livre *m* enregistré; t. point sujet *m* de conversation; *Fam* t. shop = organisation où l'on parle beaucoup mais où l'on agit peu

talking-to ['tɔːkɪŋtuː] *n Fam* savon *m*; to give sb a t. passer un savon à qn

tall [tɔːl] *adj (person)* grand(e); *(building)* haut(e); how t. are you? combien est-ce que tu mesures?; to be 2 metres t. *(of person)* mesurer 2 mètres; *(of object)* faire 2 mètres de haut; *Fig* that's a t. order ça va être dur; *Fig* a t. story une histoire invraisemblable
2 *adv* to walk or stand t. marcher la tête haute

tallboy ['tɔːlbɔɪ] *n* commode *f* haute

Tallin(n) ['tælɪn] *n* Tallinn

tallow ['tæləʊ] *n* suif *m*

tally ['tælɪ] 1 *n* compte *m*; to keep a t. of sth tenir le compte de qch
2 *vi (of figure, report)* concorder

talon ['tælən] *n* serre *f*

tamarind ['tæmərɪnd] *n (fruit)* tamarin *m*; *(tree)* tamarinier *m*

tambourine [tæmbə'riːn] *n* tambourin *m*

tame [teɪm] 1 *adj* (a) *(not timid or vicious)* familier(ère); *(domesticated)* apprivoisé(e) (b) *(unadventurous)* timide; *(speech, attempt)* mou (molle); *(party, evening)* morne
2 *vt (animal)* apprivoiser; *Fig (emotion)* dominer

tamely ['teɪmlɪ] *adv (say, ask)* timidement; *(accept)* docilement

Tamil ['tæmɪl] 1 *n* (a) *(person)* Tamoul(e) *m,f* (b) *(language)* tamoul *m*
2 *adj* tamoul(e)

▶**tamper with** ['tæmpə(r)] *vt insep* toucher à; *(lock)* tripoter; *(documents, records)* trafiquer

tampon ['tæmpon] *n* tampon *m* (hygiénique)

tan¹ [tæn] *n Math (abbr* tangent) tan *f*, tg *f*

tan² [tæn] 1 *n* (a) *(colour)* marron *m* clair (b) *(from sun)* bronzage *m*
2 *adj (colour)* marron clair *inv*
3 *vt (pt & pp* tanned) (a) *(of sun) (skin)* hâler (b) *(leather)* tanner; *Fam* to t. sb, to t. sb's hide tanner le cuir à qn
4 *vi (of person, skin)* bronzer

tandem ['tændəm] *n* (a) *(bicycle)* tandem *m* (b) to do sth in t. faire qch à deux

tang [tæŋ] *n (taste)* saveur *f* acidulée; *(smell)* odeur *f* acidulée

tangent ['tændʒənt] *n Math* tangente *f*; *Fig* to go off at a t. changer de sujet

tangerine [tændʒə'riːn] 1 *n (fruit, colour)* mandarine *f*
2 *adj (colour)* mandarine *inv*

tangible ['tændʒɪbəl] *adj* tangible; *Fig (real)* évident(e); *Fin* t. assets biens *mpl* corporels

tangibly ['tændʒɪblɪ] *adv* manifestement

Tangier(s) [tæn'dʒɪə(r)(z)] *n* Tanger

tangle ['tæŋgəl] 1 *n* enchevêtrement *m*; to be in a t. être emmêlé(e); *Fig (of person, figures, accounts)* être embrouillé(e); to get into a t. s'emmêler; *Fig (of person, figures, accounts)* s'embrouiller
2 *vt* to get tangled up in sth se prendre dans qch; *Fig* se retrouver mêlé(e) à qch

▶**tangle with** *vt insep Fam* s'en prendre à

tangled ['tæŋgəld] *adj* emmêlé(e); *Fig* embrouillé(e)

tango ['tæŋgəʊ] 1 *n (pl* tangos) *(dance)* tango *m*
2 *vi* danser le tango; *Fam* it takes two to t. chacun a sa part de responsabilité

tangy ['tæŋɪ] *adj* acidulé(e)

tank [tæŋk] *n* (a) *(container)* réservoir *m* (b) *Mil* tank *m*
(c) t. top *(garment)* débardeur *m* en laine

▶**tank along** *vi Fam* foncer

▶**tank up** *vt sep Br very Fam* to be tanked up être bourré(e); to get tanked up se prendre une biture

tankard ['tæŋkəd] *n* chope *f*

tanker ['tæŋkə(r)] *n (ship)* navire-citerne *m*; *(lorry)* camion-citerne *m*

tanned [tænd] *adj* bronzé(e)

tanner ['tænə(r)] *n* tanneur(euse) *m,f*

tannery ['tænərɪ] *n* tannerie *f*

tannin ['tænɪn] *n* tan(n)in *m*

tannoy® ['tænɔɪ] *n* système *m* de haut-parleurs; over the t. au haut-parleur

tantalize ['tæntəlaɪz] *vt* allécher (with avec)

tantalizing ['tæntəlaızıŋ] *adj* alléchant(e)

tantamount ['tæntəmaʊnt] *adj* t. to équivalent(e) à

tantrum ['tæntrəm] *n* caprice *m*; **to throw a t.** faire un caprice

Tanzania [tænzə'nıə] *n* la Tanzanie

Tanzanian [tænzə'nıən] 1 *n* Tanzanien(enne) *m,f*
2 *adj* tanzanien(enne)

tap¹ [tæp] 1 *n* (**a**) *Br (for water, gas)* robinet *m*; **to be on t.** *(of beer)* être à la pression; *Fig (of person, information)* être toujours disponible; **t. water** eau *f* du robinet (**b**) **to put a t. on a phone** mettre un téléphone sur écoute
2 *vt (pt & pp tapped)* (**a**) *(tree)* inciser; *(resources)* puiser dans; *Fam* **to t. sb for money** taper de l'argent à qn (**b**) *(phone)* mettre sur écoute

tap² 1 *n* (**a**) *(light blow)* petit coup *m*; *(with hand)* tape *f* (**b**) **t. dancer** danseur(euse) *m,f* de claquettes; **t. dancing** claquettes *fpl*
2 *vt (pt & pp tapped)* donner un petit coup à; *(with hand)* donner une tape à
3 *vi* **to t.** (**at** *or* **on**) frapper doucement (à)

tape [teıp] 1 *n* (**a**) *(ribbon)* ruban *m*; *(of paper)* bande *f*; (**adhesive** *or Fam* **sticky**) **t.** ruban *m* adhésif, Scotch® *m*; *Sp* *(finishing)* **t.** ligne *f* d'arrivée; **t.** *(measure)* mètre *m* (**b**) *(for recording)* bande *f*; *(cassette)* cassette *f*; **t. deck** platine *f* cassette; **t. recorder** magnétophone *m*; **t. recording** enregistrement *m*
2 *vt* (**a**) *(stick with tape)* scotcher; *Fig* **to have sb taped** connaître qn comme sa poche; **to have sth taped** avoir compris qch (**b**) *(record)* enregistrer

taper ['teıpə(r)] 1 *n* *(candle)* bougie *f* filée
2 *vi* s'effiler; *tip* **t. to a point** se terminer en pointe
▶**taper off** *vi* *(of object)* s'effiler; *Fig (decrease)* s'amenuiser

tape-record ['teıprıkɔːd] *vt* enregistrer

tapestry ['tæpıstrı] *n* tapisserie *f*

tapeworm ['teıpwɜːm] *n* ver *m* solitaire

tapioca [tæpı'əʊkə] *n* tapioca *m*

tapping ['tæpıŋ] *n* *(sound)* petits coups *mpl*

tar [tɑː(r)] 1 *n* (**a**) *(substance)* goudron *m* (**b**) *Fam Old-fashioned (sailor)* matelot *m*
2 *vt (pt & pp tarred)* goudronner; **to t. and feather sb** rouler qn dans le goudron et les plumes; *Fig* **we've been tarred with the same brush** on nous a mis dans le même sac

tarantula [tə'ræntjʊlə] *n* tarentule *f*

tardily ['tɑːdılı] *adv (late)* tardivement; *(slowly)* lentement

tardy ['tɑːdı] *adj (late)* tardif(ive); *(slow)* lent(e)

target ['tɑːgıt] 1 *n* (**a**) *(of bullet, missile, joke)* cible *f*; **t. language** *(in translating)* langue *f* d'arrivée; **t. practice** exercices *mpl* de tir (**b**) *Fig (goal)* objectif *m*; **to set oneself a t.** se fixer un objectif; **to be on t.** *(to do sth)* être dans les temps (pour faire qch); **t. audience** type *m* d'écoute ciblé; **t. market** marché *m* ciblé
2 *vt* (**a**) *(aim)* **to t. sth at sth** *(missile)* diriger qch sur qch; *Fig (campaign, TV programme, benefits)* destiner qch à qch (**b**) *also Fig (aim at)* viser

tariff ['tærıf] *n* *(tax)* tarif *m*, droit *m* de douane; *(price list)* tarif; **t. barrier** barrière *f* douanière

tarmac® ['tɑːmæk] 1 *n* macadam *m*; **the t.** *(runway)* le tarmac
2 *vt (pt & pp tarmacked)* goudronner

tarnish ['tɑːnıʃ] 1 *vt also Fig* ternir
2 *vi* se ternir

tarot ['tærəʊ] *n* tarot *m*; **t. card** carte *f* de tarot

tarpaulin [tɑː'pɔːlın] *n* bâche *f*

tarragon ['tærəgən] *n* estragon *m*

tart [tɑːt] 1 *n* (**a**) *(cake) (large)* tarte *f*; *(small)* tartelette *f* (**b**) *Fam Pej (promiscuous woman, prostitute)* pute *f*
2 *adj* (**a**) *(in taste)* âpre (**b**) *(tone, remark)* aigrelet(ette)
▶**tart up** *vt sep Fam (room, pub)* retaper; **to t. oneself up** se faire une beauté

tartan ['tɑːtən] *n* tartan *m*, écossais *m*; **t. tie/jacket** cravate *f*/veste *f* écossaise

Tartar ['tɑːtə(r)] *n* Tatar(e) *m,f*

tartar ['tɑːtə(r)] *n* *(on teeth)* tartre *m*

tartar(e) sauce ['tɑːtə'sɔːs] *n* sauce *f* tartare

tartly ['tɑːtlı] *adv* avec aigreur

task [tɑːsk] *n* tâche *f*; **to take sb to t. for sth/for doing sth** reprocher qch à qn/à qn d'avoir fait qch

taskforce ['tɑːskfɔːs] *n Mil* corps *m* expéditionnaire; *Fig* commission *f*

taskmaster ['tɑːskmɑːstə(r)] *n* **to be a hard t.** être très exigeant(e)

Tasmania [tæz'meınıə] *n* la Tasmanie

Tasmanian [tæz'meınıən] 1 *n* Tasmanien(enne) *m,f*
2 *adj* tasmanien(enne)

Tasman Sea ['tæzmən'siː] *n* **the T.** la mer de Tasman

tassel ['tæsəl] *n* gland *m*

taste [teıst] 1 *n* (**a**) *(flavour, sense)* goût *m*; **t. bud** papille *f* gustative (**b**) *(sample) also Fig* **to have a t. of sth** goûter à qch; **a t. of things to come** un avant-goût des choses à venir; **to give sb a t. of his own medicine** rendre la pareille à qn (**c**) *(liking)* goût *m* (**for** pour); **to acquire** *or* **develop a t. for sth** prendre goût à qch; **add sugar to t.** ajouter du sucre à volonté; **violent films are not to my t.** les films violents ne me plaisent pas (**d**) *(judgement)* goût *m*; **in good/bad** *or* **poor t.** de bon/mauvais goût
2 *vt* (**a**) *(detect flavour of)* sentir (le goût de) (**b**) *(sample)* goûter; *Fig (happiness, success)* goûter à
3 *vi* **to t. of** *or* **like sth** avoir un goût de qch; **to t. good/bad** être bon (bonne)/mauvais(e)

tasteful ['teıstfʊl] *adj* de bon goût

tastefully ['teıstfəlı] *adv* avec goût

tasteless ['teıstlıs] *adj* (**a**) *(food)* insipide (**b**) *(remark, clothes)* de mauvais goût

taster ['teıstə(r)] *n* (**a**) *(person)* goûteur(euse) *m,f* (**b**) *(foretaste)* avant-goût *m*

tasty ['teıstı] *adj* (**a**) *(food)* savoureux(euse) (**b**) *Fam (good-looking)* bien foutu(e)

tat [tæt] *n Fam* camelote *f*

ta-ta [tæ'tɑː] *exclam Br Fam* au revoir!

tatters ['tætəz] *npl also Fig* **in t.** en lambeaux

tattered ['tætəd] *adj* déguenillé(e)

tattle ['tætəl] 1 *n* potins *mpl*, commérages *mpl*
2 *vi* commérer

tattoo¹ [tə'tuː] *n* (**a**) *(on drum)* retraite *f* du soir (**b**) *(military show)* parade *f* militaire

tattoo² 1 *n* *(design)* tatouage *m*
2 *vt* tatouer

tatty ['tætı] *adj Fam* minable

taught [tɔːt] *pt & pp of* **teach**

taunt [tɔːnt] 1 *n* *(words)* raillerie *f*
2 *vt* railler

Taurus ['tɔːrəs] *n* le Taureau; **to be (a) T.** être Taureau

taut [tɔːt] *adj* tendu(e)

tauten ['tɔːtən] **1** *vt* tendre
2 *vi* se tendre

tautness ['tɔːtnɪs] *n* tension *f*

tautological [tɔːtə'lɒdʒɪkəl] *adj* tautologique

tautology [tɔː'tɒlədʒɪ] *n* tautologie *f*

tavern ['tævən] *n* taverne *f*

tawdry ['tɔːdrɪ] *adj* (a) *(conduct, motive)* lâche (b) *(decor, jewellery)* tape-à-l'œil *inv*

tawny ['tɔːnɪ] *adj* fauve; **t. owl** chouette *f* hulotte

tax [tæks] **1** *n* impôt *m*, taxe *f*; **t. allowance** abattement *m* fiscal; **t. avoidance** évasion *f* fiscale; **t. bracket** tranche *f* d'imposition; **t. collector** percepteur(trice) *m,f*; **t. cut** réduction *f* d'impôt; *Br* **t. disc** ≃ vignette *f* automobile; **t. evasion** évasion *f* fiscale; **t. exile** = personne vivant à l'étranger pour échapper au fisc; **t. haven** paradis *m* fiscal; **t. incentive** incitation *f* fiscale; **t. inspector** inspecteur(trice) *m,f* des impôts; **t. relief** dégrèvement *m* fiscal; **t. return** déclaration *f* d'impôt
2 *vt* (a) *(subject to tax)* imposer, frapper d'un impôt (b) *(put under strain)* mettre à l'épreuve (c) *Formal (accuse)* **to t. sb with sth** taxer qn de qch

taxable ['tæksəbl] *adj* imposable

taxation [tæk'seɪʃən] *n* imposition *f*; **an increase in t.** une augmentation des impôts

tax-deductible [tæksdɪ'dʌktɪbl] *adj* déductible des impôts

tax-free [tæks'friː] *adj* exempt(e) d'impôt

taxi ['tæksɪ] **1** *n* taxi *m*; **t. driver** chauffeur *m* de taxi; **t. rank** station *f* de taxi
2 *vi (of aircraft)* rouler

taxidermist ['tæksɪdɜːmɪst] *n* taxidermiste *mf*

taxing ['tæksɪŋ] *adj* ardu(e)

taxonomy [tæk'sɒnəmɪ] *n* taxonomie *f*

taxpayer ['tækspeɪə(r)] *n* contribuable *mf*

TB [tiː'biː] *n (abbr* **tuberculosis)** tuberculose *f*

T-bone steak [tiːbəʊn'steɪk] *n* côte *f* de bœuf à l'os

te [tiː] *n Mus* si *m*

tea [tiː] *n* (a) *(plant, drink)* thé *m*; *(herbal infusion)* tisane *f*; **t. break** ≃ pause-café *f*; **t. caddy** boîte *f* à thé; **t. cosy** couvre-théière *m*; **t. leaves** feuilles *fpl* de thé; **t. party** goûter *m*; **t. set** service *m* à thé; **t. strainer** passoire *f* à thé; **t. towel** torchon *m* (pour la vaisselle); **t. tray** plateau *m* (b) *Br (evening meal)* dîner *m*; *(afternoon)* **t.** thé *m*

teabag ['tiːbæg] *n* sachet *m* de thé

teach [tiːtʃ] *(pt & pp* **taught** [tɔːt]*)* **1** *vt* enseigner; **to t. sb sth, to t. sth to sb** enseigner qch à qn; **to t. sb (how) to do sth** apprendre à qn à faire qch; **to t. oneself sth** apprendre qch tout seul; *Am* **to t. school** enseigner; *Fig* **to t. sb a lesson** donner une leçon à qn; *Fam* **that'll t. him!** ça lui apprendra!
2 *vi* enseigner

teacher ['tiːtʃə(r)] *n* (at primary school) instituteur(trice) *m,f*; *(at secondary school)* professeur *m*, enseignant(e) *m,f*; **t.'s pet** chouchou(te) *m,f* du professeur; **t. training** formation *f* pédagogique; **t. training college** ≃ IUFM *m*

teaching ['tiːtʃɪŋ] *n* (a) *(profession, action)* enseignement *m*; **t. hospital** CHU *m*; **t. practice** stage *m* pratique d'enseignement; **t. staff** personnel *m* enseignant (b) *(doctrine)* doctrine *f*

teacup ['tiːkʌp] *n* tasse *f* à thé

teak [tiːk] *n* teck *m*

team [tiːm] *n* équipe *f*; **a t. effort** un travail d'équipe; **t. games** jeux *mpl* d'équipe; **t. player** joueur(euse) *m,f* qui a l'esprit d'équipe; **t. spirit** esprit *m* d'équipe

▶**team up** *vi* s'associer (**with** avec)

team-mate ['tiːmmeɪt] *n* coéquipier(ère) *m,f*

teamwork ['tiːmwɜːk] *n* travail *m* d'équipe

teamster ['tiːmstə(r)] *n Am (lorry driver)* routier *m*

teapot ['tiːpɒt] *n* théière *f*

tear¹ [tɪə(r)] *n* larme *f*; **in tears** en larmes; **t. duct** canal *m* lacrymal; **t. gas** gaz *m* lacrymogène

tear² [teə(r)] **1** *vt (pt* **tore** [tɔː(r)], *pp* **torn** [tɔːn]*) (rip)* déchirer; *(snatch)* arracher (**from** à); **to t. sth in two** or **in half** déchirer qch en deux; **to t. sth to pieces** déchirer qch en mille morceaux; *Fig* démolir qch; *Fig* **to t. sb to pieces** mettre qn en pièces; **to be torn between two things** se sentir tiraillé(e) entre deux choses; *Fam* **that's torn it!** il ne manquait plus que ça!
2 *vi* (a) *(rip)* se déchirer (b) **to t. at sth** déchirer qch (c) *(move quickly)* **to t. along/past/away** aller/passer/partir à toute vitesse
3 *n* déchirure *f*

▶**tear apart** *vt sep Fig* déchirer

▶**tear away** *vt sep Fig* **to t. oneself away from sth** s'arracher de qch

▶**tear down** *vt sep (building)* démolir; *(statue)* renverser; *(poster)* arracher

▶**tear into** *vt insep* **to t. into sb** *(physically)* se jeter sur qn; *(verbally)* passer un savon à qn

▶**tear off 1** *vt sep (remove)* arracher
2 *vi (run away)* se sauver à toute vitesse

▶**tear out** *vt sep* arracher; *Fig* **to t. one's hair out** s'arracher les cheveux

▶**tear up** *vt sep (document, photo)* déchirer; *(plant)* déraciner; *(floorboards)* enlever

tearaway ['teərəweɪ] *n* casse-cou *m inv*

teardrop ['tɪədrɒp] *n* larme *f*

tearful ['tɪəfəl] *adj* en pleurant; **in a t. voice** avec des larmes dans la voix

tearfully ['tɪəfəlɪ] *adv* en pleurant

tearjerker ['tɪədʒɜːkə(r)] *n Fam (film, book)* it's a real t. c'est complètement mélo

tearoom ['tiːruːm] *n* salon *m* de thé

tearstained ['tɪəsteɪnd] *adj* barbouillé(e) de larmes

tease [tiːz] **1** *vt* taquiner (**about** sur ou à propos de)
2 *vi* plaisanter
3 *n (person)* taquin(e) *m,f*

▶**tease out** *vt sep* clarifier

teaser ['tiːzə(r)] *n Fam (problem)* colle *f*

teashop ['tiːʃɒp] *n* salon *m* de thé

teaspoon ['tiːspuːn] *n* cuillère *f* à café

teat [tiːt] *n (of animal)* trayon *m*; *(of feeding bottle)* tétine *f*

teatime ['tiːtaɪm] *n (in the afternoon)* l'heure *f* du thé; *(in the evening)* l'heure du dîner

technical ['teknɪkəl] *adj* technique; *Br* **t. college** ≃ institut *m* universitaire; **t. drawing** *(school subject)* dessin *m* industriel; **t. hitch** incident *m* technique

technicality [teknɪ'kælɪtɪ] *n* détail *m* technique

technically ['teknɪklɪ] *adv* techniquement

technician [tek'nɪʃən] *n* technicien(enne) *m,f*

technique [tek'niːk] n technique f

technological [teknə'lɒdʒɪkəl] adj technologique

technology [tek'nɒlədʒɪ] n technologie f

teddy [ˈtedɪ] n t. (bear) ours m en peluche

tedious [ˈtiːdɪəs] adj ennuyeux(euse); (task) fastidieux(euse)

tedium [ˈtiːdɪəm] n ennui m

tee [tiː] n (in golf) tee m

▸**tee off** vi (in golf) jouer le départ

teem [tiːm] vi (a) (rain) to t. (down) pleuvoir à verse (b) to be teeming with sth (insects, ideas) grouiller de qch

teeming [ˈtiːmɪŋ] adj grouillant(e)

teenage [ˈtiːneɪdʒ] adj adolescent(e)

teenager [ˈtiːneɪdʒə(r)] n adolescent(e) m,f

teen [ˈtiːn] adj adolescent(e); t. idol idole f des jeunes

teens [tiːnz] npl adolescence f; to be in one's t. être adolescent(e)

teensy(-weensy) [ˈtiːnzɪ(ˈwiːnzɪ)] adj Fam tout(e) petit(e)

teeny-bopper [ˈtiːnɪbɒpə(r)] n Fam petite minette f

teeny(-weeny) [ˈtiːnɪ(ˈwiːnɪ)] adj Fam tout(e) petit(e)

teeshirt [ˈtiːʃɜːt] n tee-shirt m

teeter [ˈtiːtə(r)] vi chanceler; Fig to t. on the brink of sth être au bord de qch

teeth [tiːθ] pl of tooth

teethe [tiːð] vi to be teething faire ses dents

teething [ˈtiːðɪŋ] n poussée f dentaire; Fig t. troubles (of project) difficultés fpl initiales

teetotal [tiː'təʊtəl] adj qui ne boit jamais d'alcool

teetotaller, Am **teetotaler** [tiː'təʊtələ(r)] n = personne qui ne boit jamais d'alcool

TEFL [ˈtefəl] n (abbr Teaching of English as a Foreign Language) enseignement m de l'anglais langue étrangère

Teh(e)ran [teə'rɑːn] n Téhéran

tel (abbr telephone) tél

telecommunications [telɪkəmjuːnɪˈkeɪʃənz] npl télécommunications fpl

telecommuting [telɪkə'mjuːtɪŋ] n télétravail m

teleconference [telɪ'kɒnfərəns] n téléconférence f

telegenic [telɪ'dʒenɪk] adj télégénique

telegram [ˈtelɪɡræm] n télégramme m

telegraph [ˈtelɪɡrɑːf] 1 n télégraphe m; t. pole/wire poteau m/fil m télégraphique

2 vt télégraphier

telegraphic [telɪ'ɡræfɪk] adj télégraphique

telemarketing [telɪ'mɑːkɪtɪŋ] n télémarketing m

telepathic [telɪ'pæθɪk] adj télépathique

telepathy [tɪ'lepəθɪ] n télépathie f

telephone [ˈtelɪfəʊn] 1 n téléphone m; to be on the t. (talking) être au téléphone; (have a telephone) avoir le téléphone; Com t. banking transactions fpl bancaires télématiques; t. bill facture f de téléphone; t. box cabine f téléphonique; t. call appel m téléphonique, coup m de téléphone; t. directory or book annuaire m (téléphonique); t. exchange central m téléphonique; t. number numéro m de téléphone

2 vt téléphoner à

3 vi téléphoner

telephonist [tɪ'lefənɪst] n Br téléphoniste mf

telephoto lens [ˈtelɪfəʊtəʊlenz] n téléobjectif m

teleprinter [ˈtelɪprɪntə(r)] n téléimprimeur m

telesales [ˈtelɪseɪlz] npl Com téléventes fpl

telescope [ˈtelɪskəʊp] n télescope m

telescopic [telɪs'kɒpɪk] adj télescopique; t. sight (of rifle) lunette f

teleshopping [ˈtelɪʃɒpɪŋ] n téléachat m

teletext [ˈtelɪtekst] n Télétexte® m

televise [ˈtelɪvaɪz] vt téléviser

television [telɪ'vɪʒən] n télévision f; on t. à la télévision; t. camera caméra f de télévision; t. licence redevance f télévision; t. programme émission f de télévision; t. screen écran m de télévision; t. set téléviseur m, poste m de télévision

telex [ˈteleks] 1 n télex m

2 vt (message) télexer

tell [tel] (pt & pp told [təʊld]) 1 vt (a) (say) dire; (story, joke) raconter; to t. sb sth, to t. sth to sb dire qch à qn; to t. the truth/a lie dire la vérité/un mensonge; to t. you the truth, I don't know je t'avouerai que je ne sais pas; can you t. me the way to the station? est-ce que vous pouvez m'indiquer le chemin de la gare?; I told you so! je te l'avais bien dit!; you're telling me! à qui le dis-tu!; let me t. you, I was frightened laisse-moi te dire que j'ai eu peur!; to t. the time (of clock) donner l'heure; to t. sb the time (of person) donner l'heure à qn; he can't t. the time il ne sait pas lire l'heure

(b) (discern) I could t. he was lying je savais qu'il mentait; you can t. she's lived abroad ça se voit qu'elle a vécu à l'étranger; there's no telling what she'll do next qui sait ce qu'elle va inventer maintenant

(c) (distinguish) to t. sth from sth distinguer qch de qch; to t. two people/things apart distinguer deux personnes/choses; to t. right from wrong discerner le bien du mal; I can't t. the difference je ne vois pas la différence

(d) (order) to t. sb to do sth dire à qn de faire qch; do as you're told! fais ce qu'on te dit!; I'm not asking you, I'm telling you! ce n'est pas une question, c'est un ordre!; he wouldn't be told il refusait d'écouter ce qu'on lui disait

(e) (Pol) (votes) compter; all told au total

2 vi (a) (say) dire; that would be telling! je ne veux pas cafarder!

(b) (discern) dire; it's difficult or hard to t. c'est difficile à dire; it's too early to t. il est trop tôt pour se prononcer; you never can t. on ne sait jamais

(c) (have effect) se faire sentir

▸**tell off** vt sep (scold) to t. sb off disputer qn

▸**tell on** vt insep Fam (inform on) dénoncer, balancer

teller [ˈtelə(r)] n (a) (of votes) scrutateur(trice) m,f (b) (in bank) guichetier(ère) m,f

telling [ˈtelɪŋ] 1 n (of story) narration f

2 adj (a) (revealing) révélateur(trice) (b) (decisive) qui porte

telling-off n réprimande f; to give sb a t. disputer qn

telltale [ˈtelteɪl] 1 n (person) rapporteur(euse) m,f

2 adj (revealing) révélateur(trice)

telly [ˈtelɪ] n Br Fam télé f; on t. à la télé; t. addict accro mf de la télé

temerity [tɪ'merɪtɪ] n témérité f, audace f; to have the t. to do sth avoir l'audace de faire qch

temp [temp] *Fam* **1** *n* intérimaire *mf*; **to be a t.** faire de l'intérim

2 *vi* faire de l'intérim

temper ['tempə(r)] **1** *n* (*character*) caractère *m*, tempérament *m*; (*mood*) humeur *f*; (*bad mood*) mauvaise humeur *f*; **to be in a good/bad t.** être de bonne/mauvaise humeur; **to have a short t.** être coléreux(euse); **to lose one's t.** se mettre en colère; **to fly into a t.** piquer une colère; *Fam* **t.!** on se calme!; **t. tantrum** caprice *m*

2 *vt* (a) (*steel*) tremper (b) (*action*) tempérer

temperament ['tempərəmənt] *n* tempérament *m*, caractère *m*

temperamental [tempərə'mentəl] *adj* capricieux(euse)

temperance ['tempərəns] *n* (a) (*moderation*) modération *f* (b) (*abstinence from alcohol*) tempérance *f*; *Hist* **t. movement** mouvement *m* antialcoolique

temperate ['tempərət] *adj* (a) *Geog* (*climate, zone*) tempéré(e) (b) *Formal* (*language, criticism*) mesuré(e)

temperature ['tempərətʃə(r)] *n* température *f*; **to take sb's t.** prendre la température de qn; **to have a t.** avoir de la température

tempered ['tempəd] *adj* (*steel*) trempé(e)

tempest ['tempɪst] *n Lit* tempête *f*

tempestuous [tem'pestjʊəs] *adj* tempétueux(euse)

template ['templeɪt] *n* gabarit *m*; *Comptr* modèle *m*

temple¹ ['tempəl] *n* (*place of worship*) temple *m*

temple² ['tempəl] *n* (*side of head*) tempe *f*

tempo ['tempəʊ] (*pl* **tempos** *or* **tempi** ['tempiː]) *n Mus* tempo *m*

temporal ['tempərəl] *adj* temporel(elle)

temporarily [tempə'reərɪlɪ] *adv* temporairement

temporary ['tempərərɪ] *adj* temporaire

tempt [tem(p)t] *vt* tenter; **to t. sb to do sth** inciter qn à faire qch; **to be tempted to do sth** être tenté(e) de faire qch; **to t. fate** tenter le diable

temptation [tem(p)'teɪʃən] *n* tentation *f*

tempting ['tem(p)tɪŋ] *adj* tentant(e)

temptress ['tem(p)trɪs] *n Lit* tentatrice *f*

ten [ten] **1** *n* (a) dix *m inv* (b) (*idioms*) **they're a penny** on en trouve à la pelle; **t. to one he'll find out** je te parie qu'il finira par le savoir

2 *adj* dix; **the T. Commandments** les dix commandements; *see also* **eight**

tenable ['tenəbəl] *adj* défendable

tenacious [te'neɪʃəs] *adj* tenace

tenacity [te'næsɪtɪ] *n* ténacité *f*

tenancy ['tenənsɪ] *n* location *f*; **t. agreement** bail *m* (de location)

tenant ['tenənt] *n* locataire *mf*

tend¹ [tend] *vt* (*look after*) s'occuper de

tend² [tend] *vi* pencher (*towards* vers); **to t. to do sth** avoir tendance à faire qch

▸**tend to** *vt insep* (*look after*) s'occuper de

tendency ['tendənsɪ] *n* tendance *f* (*towards* à); **to have a t. to do sth** avoir tendance à faire qch

tendentious [ten'denʃəs] *adj Formal* tendancieux(euse)

tender¹ ['tendə(r)] *n Naut* navette *f*; *Rail* tender *m*

tender² *adj* (a) (*affectionate*) tendre (b) (*sore*) sensible (c) (*meat*) tendre (d) (*young*) **at the t. age of...** dès l'âge de...

tender³ **1** *n Com* (*bid*) offre *f*, soumission *f*; **to make** *or* **put in a t.** soumissionner

2 *vt* (*services, money*) offrir; (*resignation*) donner; (*apology*) présenter

3 *vi Com* **to t. for a contract** soumissionner à un appel d'offres

tenderhearted [tendə'hɑːtɪd] *adj* au cœur tendre

tenderly ['tendəlɪ] *adv* tendrement

tenderness ['tendənɪs] *n* (a) (*affection*) tendresse *f* (b) (*soreness*) sensibilité *f* (c) (*of meat*) tendreté *f*

tendon ['tendən] *n* tendon *m*

tendril ['tendrɪl] *n* vrille *f*

tenement ['tenɪmənt] *n* immeuble *m*

tenet ['tenɪt] *n* (*principle*) dogme *m*; (*belief*) croyance *f*

tenfold ['tenfəʊld] **1** *adj* décuple

2 *adv* dix fois plus; **to increase t.** être multiplié(e) par dix

tenner ['tenə(r)] *n Br Fam* (*sum*) dix livres *fpl*; (*note*) billet *m* de dix livres

tennis ['tenɪs] *n* tennis *m*; **t. ball** balle *f* de tennis; **t. club** club *m* de tennis; **t. court** court *m* de tennis; **t. elbow** tennis-elbow *m*; **t. player** joueur(euse) *m,f* de tennis; **t. racquet** *or* **racket** raquette *f* de tennis; **t. shoe** (chaussure *f* de) tennis *m ou f*

tenor ['tenə(r)] *n* (a) (*singer*) ténor *m*; **t. saxophone** saxophone *m* ténor (b) *Formal* (*content, sense*) teneur *f*

tenpin bowling ['tenpɪn'bəʊlɪŋ] *n* bowling *m* (*jeu*)

tense¹ [tens] *n Gram* temps *m*

tense² **1** *adj* (*cord, person, situation*) tendu(e); (*voice*) étranglé(e); (*muscle*) contracté(e)

2 *vt* (*cord*) tendre; (*muscle*) contracter; **to t. oneself** se raidir

3 *vi* se tendre, se raidir

▸**tense up** *vi* se crisper

tensely ['tenslɪ] *adv* nerveusement

tension ['tenʃən] *n* tension *f*

tent [tent] *n* tente *f*; **t. peg** piquet *m* de tente; **t. pole** mât *m* de tente

tentacle ['tentəkəl] *n* tentacule *m*

tentative ['tentətɪv] *adj* (*hesitant*) hésitant(e), timide; (*provisional*) provisoire

tentatively ['tentətɪvlɪ] *adv* (*hesitantly*) timidement; (*provisionally*) provisoirement

tenterhooks ['tentəhʊks] *npl* **to be on t.** être sur des charbons ardents; **to keep sb on t.** mettre qn au supplice

tenth [tenθ] **1** *n* (a) (*fraction*) dixième *m* (b) (*in series*) dixième *mf* (c) (*of month*) dix *m inv*

2 *adj* dixième; *see also* **eighth**

tenuous ['tenjʊəs] *adj* (*connection*) ténu(e); (*comparison*) subtil(e); (*argument*) faible

tenure ['tenjə(r)] *n* (*of land*) fermage *m*; (*of office*) occupation *f*; (*of university teaching job*) titularisation *f*

tepid ['tepɪd] *adj also Fig* tiède

tequila [tɪ'kiːlə] *n* tequila *f*

term [tɜːm] *n* (a) (*word, expression*) terme *m*; **I told her in no uncertain terms** je le lui ai dit carrément; **in terms of salary/pollution** en ce qui concerne le salaire/la pollution

(b) **to be on good/bad terms (with sb)** (*relations*) être en bons/mauvais termes (avec qn); **to be on friendly terms with sb** avoir des relations amicales avec qn; **to be on speaking terms** (*of two people*) se parler; **to come** to terms with sth accepter qch; **in terms of** du point de vue de; **we should think in terms of leaving** il faudrait songer à partir

(c) Com **terms** *(conditions)* conditions *fpl*; *(of contract)* termes *mpl*; **terms of reference** *(of commission)* attributions *fpl*; **terms of payment** conditions de paiement

(d) *(at school, university)* trimestre *m*; **t. of office** *(of politician)* mandat *m*; **t. of imprisonment** peine *f* de prison; **in the long/short t.** à long/court terme; **to have reached (full) t.** *(of pregnancy)* arriver à terme

2 *vt* appeler

terminal ['tɜːmɪnəl] **1** *n* **(a)** *(of battery)* pôle *m*, borne *f* **(b)** *(rail, bus)* terminus *m*; *(at airport)* terminal *m* **(c)** Comptr terminal *m*

2 *adj* terminal(e); *(illness)* en phase terminale

terminally ['tɜːmɪnəlɪ] *adv* **to be t. ill** être en phase terminale

terminate ['tɜːmɪneɪt] **1** *vt* **(a)** *(employment, project)* mettre fin à; *(contract)* résilier **(b)** *(pregnancy)* interrompre

2 *vi* **(a)** *(of contract)* prendre fin **(b)** *(of bus, train)* aller jusqu'à

termination [tɜːmɪ'neɪʃən] *n* **(a)** *(of employment, project)* fin *f*; *(of contract)* résiliation *f* **(b)** **t. (of pregnancy)** interruption *f* de grossesse

terminology [tɜːmɪ'nɒlədʒɪ] *n* terminologie *f*

terminus ['tɜːmɪnəs] *(pl* **terminuses** *or* **termini** ['tɜːmɪnaɪ]*)* *n* terminus *m*

termite ['tɜːmaɪt] *n* termite *m*

tern [tɜːn] *n* sterne *f*

Terr *abbr* **Terrace**

terrace ['terɪs] *n* **(a)** *(beside house, on hillside)* terrasse *f* **(b)** Br **the terraces** *(in football ground)* les gradins *mpl* **(c)** Br *(of houses)* = rangée de maisons attenantes

terraced ['terɪst] *adj* **(a)** *(hillside)* en terrasses **(b)** Br **t. house** = maison située dans une rangée d'habitations attenantes

terracotta ['terə'kɒtə] *n* terre *f* cuite

terrain [tə'reɪn] *n* terrain *m*

terrapin ['terəpɪn] *n* tortue *f* d'eau douce

terrestrial [tɪ'restrɪəl] *adj* terrestre

terrible ['terɪbəl] *adj* *(shocking)* terrible; *(of poor quality)* épouvantable

terribly ['terɪblɪ] *adv* **(a)** *(badly)* affreusement mal; *(injured)* très gravement **(b)** Fam *(very)* extrêmement

terrier ['terɪə(r)] *n* *(dog)* terrier *m*; Fig **he's a real t.** il n'abandonne jamais

terrific [tə'rɪfɪk] *adj* Fam **(a)** *(excellent)* super *inv* **(b)** *(enormous)* incroyable

terrifically [tə'rɪfɪklɪ] *adv* Fam *(very)* extrêmement

terrified ['terɪfaɪd] *adj* terrifié(e); **to be t.** avoir une peur bleue de

terrify ['terɪfaɪ] *vt* terrifier

terrifying ['terɪfaɪɪŋ] *adj* terrifiant(e)

territorial [terɪ'tɔːrɪəl] *adj* territorial(e); *(animal)* qui défend son territoire; Br **the T. Army** = armée de réserve, constituée de volontaires; **t. waters** eaux *fpl* territoriales

territory ['terɪtərɪ] *(pl* **territories***)* *n* territoire *m*; Fig *(area of activity)* domaine *m*

terror ['terə(r)] *n* terreur *f*; **reign of t.** régime *m* de terreur; Fam **that child is a t.** cet enfant est une vraie terreur

terrorism ['terərɪzəm] *n* terrorisme *m*

terrorist ['terərɪst] *n & adj* terroriste *mf*

terrorize ['terəraɪz] *vt* terroriser

terror-stricken ['terəstrɪkən] *adj* terrorisé(e)

terse [tɜːs] *adj* *(person, reply)* sec *(sèche)*; *(style, prose)* concis(e)

terseness ['tɜːsnɪs] *n* *(of person, reply)* brusquerie *f*; *(of style, prose)* concision *f*

tertiary ['tɜːʃərɪ] *adj* tertiaire; **t. education** enseignement *m* supérieur

TESL ['tesəl] *n* *(abbr* **Teaching of English as a Second Language)** enseignement *m* de l'anglais deuxième langue

TESOL ['tiːsɒl] *n* *(abbr* **Teaching of English to Speakers of Other Languages)** enseignement *m* de l'anglais langue étrangère

TESSA ['tesə] *n* Br Fin *(abbr* **tax-exempt special savings account)** = plan d'épargne exonéré d'impôts

test [test] **1** *n* **(a)** *(trial, check)* test *m*; **to put sb/sth to the t.** mettre qn/qch à l'épreuve; **to pass the t.** se montrer à la hauteur; **to stand the t. of time** résister à l'épreuve du temps; **t. ban** interdiction *f* des essais nucléaires; Law **t. case** précédent *m*; **t. drive** essai *m* sur route; **t. flight** vol *m* d'essai; **t. pilot** pilote *m* d'essai; **t. tube** tube *m* à essai, éprouvette *f*; **t. tube baby** bébé-éprouvette *m* **(b)** *(examination)* examen *m*; *(driving)* **t.** examen du permis de conduire; **French/maths t.** examen de français/maths **(c)** *(in cricket, rugby)* **(match)** match *m* international

2 *vt* **(a)** *(examine)* *(pupil)* interroger *(on* sur*)*; *(sight, hearing)* examiner; **to t. sb's knowledge** tester les connaissances de qn; **to t. sb for Aids** faire subir à qn le test de dépistage du sida **(b)** *(try out)* tester, mettre à l'épreuve

3 *vi* **to t. for Aids** faire un test de dépistage du sida; **to t. positive/negative** *(for drugs)* être positif/négatif; *(for Aids)* être séropositif(ive)/séronégatif(ive)

▶**test out** *vt sep* tester

testament ['testəmənt] *n* **(a)** Law *(will)* testament *m* **(b)** *(tribute)* preuve *f* (to de)

test-bed ['testbed] *n* banc *m* d'essai

test-drive ['testdraɪv] *vt* essayer

testicle ['testɪkəl] *n* testicule *m*

testify ['testɪfaɪ] Law **1** *vt* **to t. that...** attester que...

2 *vi* témoigner *(for/against* en faveur de/contre*)*; Fig **to t. to sth** *(be proof of)* témoigner de qch

testily ['testɪlɪ] *adv* d'un ton irrité

testimonial [testɪ'məʊnɪəl] *n* **(a)** *(character reference)* références *fpl* **(b)** *(in football)* **t. (match)** = match en l'honneur d'un footballeur

testimony ['testɪmənɪ] *n* Law témoignage *m*, déposition *f*; Fig **to be a t. to sth** *(proof of)* témoigner de qch

testing ['testɪŋ] **1** *n* essai *m*; **t. ground** terrain *m* d'essai

2 *adj* éprouvant(e)

testis ['testɪs] *(pl* **testes** ['testiːz]*)* *n* testicule *m*

testosterone [tes'tɒstərəʊn] *n* testostérone *f*

testy ['testɪ] *adj* *(person, mood)* irritable; *(tone, manner)* irrité(e)

tetanus ['tetənəs] *n* tétanos *m*

tetchy ['tetʃɪ] *adj* Fam irritable

tether ['teðə(r)] **1** *n* *(for tying animal)* longe *f*; Fig **to be at the end of one's t.** être à bout

2 *vt* *(animal)* attacher

Texan ['teksən] **1** n Texan(e) m,f

2 adj texan(e)

Texas ['teksəs] n le Texas

Tex-Mex [teks'meks] adj tex-mex inv

text [tekst] n texte f; Comptr t. editor éditeur m de texte

textbook ['tekstbʊk] n manuel m; Fig a t. example (of) un parfait exemple (de)

textile ['tekstaɪl] **1** n textile m

2 adj textile

textual ['tekstjʊəl] adj de texte

texture ['tekstʃə(r)] n texture f

Thai [taɪ] **1** n (a) (person) Thaïlandais(e) m,f (b) (language) thaï m

2 adj thaïlandais(e)

Thailand ['taɪlænd] n la Thaïlande

Thames [temz] n the T. la Tamise

than [ðæn, unstressed ðən] conj que; he's taller t. me il est plus grand que moi; he was taller t. I had expected il était plus grand que je (ne) l'imaginais; more/less t. ten plus/moins de dix; more t. once plus d'une fois

thank [θæŋk] vt remercier; to t. sb for sth/for doing sth remercier qn pour qch/d'avoir fait qch; t. God! Dieu merci!; t. you merci; t. you very much merci beaucoup; no, t. you non merci; t. you for coming merci d'être venu; Ironic I'll t. you to mind your own business! je te prierai de te mêler de tes affaires!; also Ironic we have Mike to t. for this c'est à Mike que nous devons cela

thankful ['θæŋkfʊl] adj reconnaissant(e) (for de); to be t. that... être heureux/euse que...

thankfully ['θæŋkfəlɪ] adv (a) (gratefully) avec gratitude (b) (fortunately) heureusement

thankless ['θæŋklɪs] adj ingrat(e)

thanks [θæŋks] **1** npl remerciements mpl; t. to (because of) grâce à; no t. to you/them! ce n'est pas grâce à toi/eux!

2 exclam Fam t.! merci!; Fam no t. non merci; t. for coming/your letter merci d'être venu/pour ta lettre; Fam Ironic t. for nothing! je te remercie!

thanksgiving [θæŋks'gɪvɪŋ] n action f de grâces; Am T. (Day) = 4ème jeudi de novembre, fête commémorant la première action de grâce des colons anglais

thank you ['θæŋkju] n merci m, remerciement m; to say t. to sb dire merci à qn, remercier qn; t. letter lettre f de remerciement

that [ðæt] **1** demonstrative pron (pl those [ðəʊz]) (a) (subject) ce, cela, ça (in more informal contexts); (object) cela, ça (in more informal contexts); who's t.? qui est-ce?; what's t.? qu'est-ce que c'est?; t.'s strange c'est bizarre; t.'s what she told me c'est ce qu'elle m'a dit; is t. all the luggage you're taking? c'est tout ce que vous prenez comme bagages?; t.'s where he lives c'est là qu'il habite; can you run as fast as t.? tu peux courir aussi vite que ça?; t.'s it! c'est ça!; t.'s t.! un point, c'est tout!

(b) (as opposed to this) celui-là (celle-là) m,f; in a case like t. dans un cas comme celui-là

2 demonstrative adj (pl those) (a) (indicating person, thing) ce (cette); t. book ce livre; t. question cette question; t. man cet homme

(b) (as opposed to this) ce...-là (cette...-là); I prefer t. film je préfère ce film-là; take t. cup prends cette tasse-là; t. one celui-là (celle-là)

3 adv t. high/big haut(e)/grand(e) comme ça; I tasted it but it wasn't t. good j'y ai goûté mais ce n'était pas si bon que ça; I've never seen one t. good je n'en ai jamais vu d'aussi bon que ça; he's t. stupid he... il est tellement stupide qu'il...

4 [unstressed ðət] relative pron

> On peut omettre le pronom relatif that sauf s'il est en position sujet.

(a) (subject) qui; (object) que; the letter t. came yesterday la lettre qui est arrivée hier; the woman t. I saw la femme que j'ai vue

(b) (with preposition) the person t. I gave it to la personne à qui je l'ai donné; the woman t. we're talking about la femme dont nous parlons; the room t. he's sleeping in la chambre où il dort

(c) (when) où; the day t. you arrived le jour où tu es arrivé

5 [unstressed ðət] conj

> Sauf dans la langue soutenue, la conjonction that est souvent omise.

que; she said t. she would come elle a dit qu'elle viendra

thatch [θætʃ] **1** n (on roof) chaume m; Fam (of hair) tignasse f

2 vt (roof) couvrir de chaume; thatched cottage chaumière f; thatched roof toit m de chaume

thaw [θɔː] **1** n also Fig dégel m

2 vt (snow, ice) faire fondre; (food) décongeler

3 vi (of snow, ice) fondre; (of food) se décongeler; Fig (of person) se dérider

▸**thaw out** vi (of lake) dégeler; (of food) se décongeler; Fig (of person) se dérider

the [before consonant sounds ðə, before vowel sounds ðɪ, stressed ðiː] definite art (a) (singular) le (la); (plural) les; t. pen le stylo; t. house la maison; t. airport l'aéroport; in t. summer (this summer) cet été; (every summer) l'été; to have t. measles/flu avoir la rougeole/la grippe; at t. time à ce moment-là; t. Europe of today l'Europe d'aujourd'hui; Fam how's t. knee? et ce genou?

(b) (denoting concept, group) t. poor/blind les pauvres/aveugles; t. Wilsons les Wilson; t. supernatural le surnaturel

(c) (with titles) Edward t. Eighth Édouard VIII; Catherine t. Great la Grande Catherine

(d) (with proportions, rates) to be paid by t. hour être payé(e) à l'heure; 15 kilometres to t. litre 15 kilomètres au litre

(e) (in exclamations) t. arrogance/stupidity of it! quelle arrogance/stupidité!

(f) [stressed ðiː] not THE Professor Branestorm? pas le célèbre professeur Branestorm?; it's THE car for the nineties c'est LA voiture des années 90

(g) (in comparisons) t. more... t. more... plus... plus...; t. sooner t. better le plus tôt sera le mieux; t. more I see him, t. less I like him plus je le vois, moins je l'apprécie

(h) (with dates) t. sixties les années soixante; t. eighteen hundreds le dix-neuvième siècle

theatre, Am **theater** ['θɪətə(r)] n (a) (drama, building) théâtre m; t. company compagnie f théâtrale, troupe f de théâtre (b) Br (operating) t. salle f d'opération (c) (area) t. of war théâtre m des hostilités

theatre-goer, Am **theater-goer** ['θɪətəɡəʊə(r)] n amateur(trice) m,f de théâtre

theatrical [θɪ'ætrɪkəl] adj also Fig théâtral(e); t. company compagnie f théâtrale, troupe f de théâtre

thee [ði:] *pron Lit or Rel* te; *(after preposition)* toi

theft [θeft] *n* vol *m*

theftproof ['θeftpru:f] *adj (lock)* antivol *inv*; *(vehicle)* muni(e) d'un dispositif antivol

their [ðeə(r)] *possessive adj* (a) *(singular)* leur; *(plural)* leurs; **t. job** leur travail; **t. wives** leurs femmes; **it wasn't THEIR idea!** ce n'est pas eux qui en ont eu l'idée! (b) *(for parts of body)* **they hit t. heads** ils se sont cogné la tête (c) *(indefinite use)* **someone's left t. umbrella** quelqu'un a oublié son parapluie

theirs [ðeəz] *possessive pron* (a) *(singular)* le leur (la leur) *m,f*; *(plural)* les leurs; **our house is big, but t. is bigger** notre maison est grande, mais la leur est plus grande encore
(b) *(used attributively)* **this book is t.** ce livre est à eux/à elles; **a friend of t.** un de leurs amis; **where's that brother of t.?** où leur frère a-t-il bien pu passer?
(c) *(indefinite use)* **if anyone hasn't got t. they can use mine** si quelqu'un n'a pas le sien, il pourra utiliser le mien

theism ['θi:ɪzəm] *n Rel* théisme *m*

them [ðem, *unstressed* ðəm] *pron* (a) *(direct object)* les; **I hate t.** je les déteste; **I can understand their son but not THEM** je comprends leur fils, mais eux, je ne les comprends pas
(b) *(indirect object)* leur; **I gave t. the book** je leur ai donné le livre; **I gave it to t.** je le leur ai donné
(c) *(after preposition)* eux (elles) *mpl,fpl*; **I'm thinking of t.** je pense à eux/elles
(d) *(as complement of verb to be)* eux (elles) *mpl,fpl*; **it's t.!** ce sont eux/elles!; **it was t. who did it** c'est eux/elles qui l'ont fait
(e) *(indefinite use)* **if anyone comes, tell t....** si quelqu'un vient, dis-lui...

thematic [θi:'mætɪk] *adj* thématique

theme [θi:m] *n* thème *m*; **t. park** parc *m* à thème; **t. restaurant** restaurant *m* à thème; **t. song or tune** chanson *f* du générique

themselves [ðəm'selvz, *stressed* ðem'selvz] *pron* (a) *(reflexive)* **they hurt t.** ils se sont blessés
(b) *(emphatic)* eux-mêmes (elles-mêmes) *mpl,fpl*; **they t. have never...** eux-mêmes/elles-mêmes n'ont jamais...; **they told me t.** ils me l'ont dit eux-mêmes; **they're not t. today** ils ne sont pas dans leur état normal aujourd'hui
(c) *(after preposition)* **they live by t.** ils vivent seuls; **they bought it for t.** ils se le sont acheté; **they talk to t.** ils parlent tout seuls

then [ðen] **1** *adv* (a) *(at that time)* alors, à ce moment-là; **since t.** depuis (ce moment-là), depuis (lors); **until t.** *(in future)* jusque-là; *(in past)* jusqu'à ce moment-là; **by t.** d'ici là; **there and t., there and t.** there sur-le-champ
(b) *(next)* ensuite, puis; **what t.?** et alors, qu'est-ce qui va se passer?
(c) *(in that case)* alors; **if it rains, t. we get wet** s'il pleut, alors on va se mouiller
(d) *(therefore)* donc; **you already knew, t.?** donc, tu le savais déjà?
2 *adj* **the t. President** le Président de l'époque

thence [ðens] *adv Formal* de là

theologian [θi:ə'ləʊdʒ(ɪ)ən] *n* théologien(enne) *m,f*

theological [θi:ə'lɒdʒɪkəl] *adj* théologique

theology [θi:'ɒlədʒɪ] *n* théologie *f*

theorem ['θɪərəm] *n* théorème *m*

theoretical [θi:ə'retɪkəl] *adj* théorique

theoretically [θi:ə'retɪklɪ] *adv* théoriquement

theoretician [θi:ərɪ'tɪʃən] *n* théoricien(enne) *m,f*

theorist ['θɪərɪst] *n* théoricien(enne) *m,f*

theorize ['θɪəraɪz] *vi* théoriser **(about** sur)

theory ['θɪərɪ] *n* théorie *f*; **in t.** en théorie

therapeutic [θerə'pju:tɪk] *adj also Fig* thérapeutique

therapist ['θerəpɪst] *n* thérapeute *mf*

therapy ['θerəpɪ] *n* thérapie *f*

there [ðeə(r), *unstressed* ðə(r)] **1** *pron* **t. is/are** il y a; **t. was/were** il y avait; **t.'s somebody at the door** il y a quelqu'un à la porte; **t. isn't/aren't any** il n'y en a pas; **t. are** *or Fam* **t.'s two left** il (en) reste deux; **t.'s a page missing** il manque une page; **t. comes a time when...** il arrive un moment où...
2 *adv* (a) *(in that place)* là; *(over there)* là-bas; **he isn't t.** il n'est pas là; **the weather's nice t.** il fait beau là-bas; **I'm going t. tomorrow** j'y vais demain; **give me that book t.** donne-moi ce livre-là; **do we have time to get t. and back?** avons-nous le temps d'y aller et de revenir?; **t. it is!** le voilà!; **t. you are!** *(I was looking for you)* te voilà!; *(when handing over something)* voilà!; *(expressing triumph, satisfaction)* tu vois!; **t. and then, then and t.** sur-le-champ; *Fam* **he's not all t.** il n'a pas toute sa tête
(b) *(at that point)* là; **t.'s the difficulty** voilà la difficulté; **we'll stop t.** for today nous nous arrêterons là pour aujourd'hui; *Fam* **you've got me t.!** alors là, vous me posez une colle!
3 *exclam* voilà!; **t., t.!** allons, allons!; **t., I told you so!** et voilà, je te l'avais bien dit!; **t. now, that wasn't so bad!** voilà, ce n'était pas si terrible!

thereabouts ['ðeərə'baʊts] *adv* (a) *(with place)* dans les environs; **he's from Stirling or t.** il est de Stirling, ou quelque part par là (b) *(with number, quantity, distance)* environ, à peu près; **it costs £500 or t.** ça coûte environ *ou* à peu près 500 livres

thereafter [ðeər'ɑ:ftə(r)] *adv Formal* après cela, par la suite

thereby ['ðeəbaɪ] *adv Formal* ainsi; **t. hangs a tale!** c'est une longue histoire!

therefore ['ðeəfɔ:(r)] *adv Formal* donc

thereupon [ðeərə'pɒn] *adv Formal* sur ce

thermal ['θɜ:məl] **1** *n Met* ascendance *f* thermique
2 *adj* thermique; **t. energy** énergie *f* thermique; *Comptr* **t. paper** papier *m* thermique; **t. springs** sources *fpl* thermales; **t. underwear** sous-vêtements *mpl* en Thermolactyl®

thermodynamics [θɜ:məʊdaɪ'næmɪks] *n* thermodynamique *f*

thermoelectric [θɜ:məʊɪ'lektrɪk] *adj* thermoélectrique

thermometer [θə'mɒmɪtə(r)] *n* thermomètre *m*

Thermos® ['θɜ:məs] *n* **T. (flask)** (bouteille *f*) Thermos® *f ou m*

thermostat ['θɜ:məstæt] *n* thermostat *m*

thesaurus [θɪ'sɔ:rəs] *(pl* **thesauruses** *or* **thesauri** [θɪ'sɔ:raɪ]*) n* dictionnaire *m* de synonymes

these [ði:z] **1** *demonstrative pron* ceux-ci (celles-ci) *mpl,fpl*; **in cases like t.** dans des cas comme ceux-ci; **t. are the ones I want** voici ceux que je veux; **t. are my parents** je te présente mes parents
2 *demonstrative adj* (a) *(indicating people or things)* ces; **t. children** ces enfants (b) *(as opposed to those)* ces...-ci; **I**

like t. shoes j'aime bien ces chaussures-ci; **t. ones** ceux-ci (celles-ci) *mpl,fpl*

thesis ['θiːsɪs] (*pl* **theses** ['θiːsiːz]) *n* thèse *f*

thespian ['θespɪən] *n Lit ou Hum* comédien(enne) *m,f*

they [ðeɪ] *pron* (a) (*subject*) ils (elles) *mpl,fpl*; **they're** Scottish (*masculine*) ils sont écossais; (*feminine*) elles sont écossaises; **THEY haven't got it!** ce ne sont pas eux/elles qui l'ont! (b) (*indefinite use*) **somebody called – what did t. want?** quelqu'un a appelé – qu'est-ce qu'il voulait?; **t. say that… on dit que…**

they'd [ðeɪd] = **they had, they would**

they'll [ðeɪl] = **they will, they shall**

they're [ðeə(r)] = **they are**

they've [ðeɪv] = **they have**

thick [θɪk] 1 *adj* (a) (*in general*) épais(aisse); **to be a metre t.** faire un mètre d'épaisseur; **the air was t. with smoke** l'air était empli d'une épaisse fumée; **the snow was t. on the ground** il y avait une épaisse couche de neige sur le sol; *Fig* **to be t. on the ground** (*plentiful*) être légion
(b) (*voice*) pâteux(euse); (*accent*) fort(e)
(c) *Fam* (*stupid*) bouché(e); **to be as t. as two short planks or as a brick** être bête comme ses pieds
(d) (*idioms*) **to have a t. skin** ne pas être susceptible; **to give sb a t. ear** donner une gifle à qn; *Fam* **to be as t. as thieves** s'entendre comme larrons en foire; *Fam* **that's a bit t.!** ça, c'est un peu fort!
2 *adv* (a) (*cut*) en tranches épaisses; (*spread*) en couche épaisse
(b) (*idioms*) **to come t. and fast** (*of questions, orders*) pleuvoir; *Fam* **to lay it on a bit t.** exagérer
3 *n* **in the t. of the forest** au beau milieu de la forêt; **to be in the t. of it or things** être au cœur de l'action; **through t. and thin** quoi qu'il arrive

thicken ['θɪkən] 1 *vt* épaissir
2 *vi* s'épaissir; *Hum* **the plot thickens…** les choses se compliquent…

thicket ['θɪkɪt] *n* fourré *m*

thickly ['θɪklɪ] *adv* (a) (*cut*) en tranches épaisses; (*spread*) en couche épaisse (b) (*populated*) fortement (c) (*speak*) d'une voix pâteuse

thickness ['θɪknɪs] *n* épaisseur *f*

thickset ['θɪk'set] *adj* trapu(e)

thick-skinned [θɪk'skɪnd] *adj Fig* peu susceptible

thief [θiːf] (*pl* **thieves** [θiːvz]) *n* voleur(euse) *m,f*

thieve [θiːv] *vt & vi* voler

thieving ['θiːvɪŋ] 1 *n* vol *m*
2 *adj* voleur(euse)

thigh [θaɪ] *n* cuisse *f*

thighbone ['θaɪbəʊn] *n* fémur *m*

thimble ['θɪmbəl] *n* dé *m* à coudre

thin [θɪn] 1 *adj* (a) (*person, wall*) mince; (*paper, slice, layer*) fin(e), mince; (*blanket, clothing*) léger(ère); (*book*) peu épais(aisse); **to get thinner** (*of person*) maigrir
(b) (*sparse*) (*hair, crowd, vegetation*) clairsemé(e)
(c) (*soup, sauce*) liquide; (*paint*) dilué(e); (*blood*) appauvri(e)
(d) (*idioms*) grêle
(e) (*idioms*) **to vanish into t. air** se volatiliser; **to have a t. time (of it)** avoir la vie dure; **to be t. on the ground** être rare; **it's just the t. end of the wedge** ce n'est qu'un début

2 *adv* (*cut*) en tranches fines *ou* minces; *Fig* **our forces/resources are spread very t.** nos forces/ressources sont très éparpillées

3 *vt* (*pt & pp* **thinned**) (*paint*) diluer; (*sauce*) éclaircir

4 *vi* (*of crowd*) s'éclaircir; (*of fog, mist*) se lever; **his hair is thinning** il perd ses cheveux

thing [θɪŋ] *n* (a) (*action, remark, fact*) chose *f*; **the important t. is that…** l'important, c'est que…; **it's the only t. we can do** c'est tout ce que nous pouvons faire; **that's another t. altogether** c'est une autre affaire; **the t. is,…** le problème, c'est que…; **that was a silly t. to do/say** c'était stupide de faire/dire ça; **for one t.** d'abord; **what with one t. and another** avec tout ce qui s'est passé; **I don't know a t. about algebra** je n'y connais rien en algèbre; **to know a t. or two (about sth)** s'y connaître (en qch); **to take things too seriously** prendre les choses trop au sérieux; **it's just one of those things** ce sont des choses qui arrivent; **things are going well/badly** les choses vont bien/mal; *Fam* **how are things?, how's things?** comment ça va?
(b) (*object*) chose *f*; *Fam* **what's that t.?** qu'est-ce que c'est que ce truc?; *Fam* **where's that spanner t. I was using?** où est cette espèce de clé dont je me suis servi tout à l'heure?; **things** (*belongings*) affaires *fpl*
(c) *Fam* (*person*) **you poor t.!** pauvre de toi!; **you lucky t.!** sacré veinard!; **you silly t.!** espèce d'idiot!
(d) (*idioms*) **to have a t. about sb/sth** (*like*) avoir un faible pour qn/qch; (*dislike*) avoir quelque chose contre qn/qch; **to have a t. about tidiness/punctuality** être très à cheval sur la propreté/la ponctualité; **it's not the done t.** ça ne se fait pas; **the latest t. in shoes** la dernière mode en matière de chaussures

thingummy ['θɪŋəmɪ], **thingamajig** ['θɪŋəmɪdʒɪg], **thingumabob** ['θɪŋəmɪbɒb] *n Fam* (*object*) truc *m*; (*person*) machin(e) *m,f*

think [θɪŋk] 1 *vt* (*pt & pp* **thought** [θɔːt]) (a) (*have in mind*) **to t. that…** penser que…; **what are you thinking?** à quoi penses-tu?; **to t. evil thoughts** avoir de mauvaises pensées; **to t. to do sth** penser à faire qch
(b) (*believe, have as opinion*) croire, penser; **he thinks he knows everything** il croit tout savoir; **anyone would t. she was asleep** on jurerait qu'elle dort; **who'd have thought it!** qui l'eût cru!; **what do you t.?** qu'en penses-tu?; **I t. so** je pense (que oui); **I don't t. so, I t. not** je ne pense pas, je pense que non; **I thought so, I thought as much** c'est ce que je pensais; **I should t. so, too!** j'espère bien!; **that's what you t.!** c'est ce que tu crois!; **what do you t. about that idea?** qu'est-ce que tu penses de cette idée?
(c) (*imagine*) imaginer; **I can't t. why/what/where…** je me demande bien pourquoi/ce que/où…; **t. what we could do with all that money!** imagine ce qu'on pourrait faire avec tout cet argent!; **to t. that he's only twenty!** et dire qu'il n'a que vingt ans

2 *vi* réfléchir, penser; **to t. ahead** voir loin; **to t. aloud** penser tout haut; **to t. long and hard before doing sth** bien réfléchir avant de faire qch; **to t. on one's feet** réagir vite; **it makes you t.** ça fait réfléchir; **you can t. again!** tu te fourres le doigt dans l'œil!

3 *n* **to have a t.** réfléchir; *Fam* **you've got another t. coming!** tu te fourres le doigt dans l'œil!

▶**think about** *vt insep* (*have in mind, take into account*) penser à; (*consider*) réfléchir à; **to t. about doing sth** songer à faire qch; **it's quite cheap when you t. about it** ça n'est pas très cher quand on y pense; **that will give them something to t. about** voilà qui va leur donner matière à réflexion

▶**think back to** vt insep repenser à

▶**think of** vt insep (a) (have in mind, take into account) penser à; **to t. of doing sth** songer à faire qch; **come to t. of it, I did see her that night** maintenant que j'y pense, je l'ai effectivement vue ce soir-là; **what were you thinking of walking home alone?** qu'est-ce qui t'a pris de rentrer à pied tout seul? (b) (have opinion about) **what do you t. of this?** qu'est-ce que tu penses de cela?; **to t. well/badly of sb** avoir une bonne/mauvaise opinion de qn; **I don't t. much of the idea** cette idée ne me dit pas grand-chose (c) (recall) se rappeler; **I can't t. of the right word** le mot m'échappe

▶**think out** vt sep réfléchir à

▶**think over** vt sep réfléchir à

▶**think through** vt sep **to t. sth through** bien réfléchir à qch

▶**think up** vt sep imaginer, inventer

thinker ['θɪŋkə(r)] n penseur m

thinking ['θɪŋkɪŋ] 1 n (a) (process of thought) réflexion f; **to do some t.** réfléchir (b) (opinion) avis m, opinion f; **to my (way of) t.** à mon avis

2 adj Br Hum **the t. man's crumpet** une jolie fille avec quelque chose dans la tête

think-tank ['θɪŋktæŋk] n comité m d'experts

thinly ['θɪnlɪ] adv (a) (cut) en tranches fines ou minces; (spread) en couche fine ou mince (b) (populated) faiblement

thinner ['θɪnə(r)] n diluant m

thinness ['θɪnnɪs] n (of person, wall) minceur f; (of paper, slice, layer) finesse f; (of liquid) fluidité f; (of blanket, clothing) légèreté f

third [θɜːd] 1 n (a) (fraction) tiers m inv (b) (in series) troisième mf (c) (of month) trois m inv (d) Mus tierce f (e) Br Univ **to get a t.** (in degree) ≃ avoir sa licence avec mention passable

2 adj troisième; **t. degree burns** brûlures fpl au troisième degré; Fam **to give sb the t. degree** cuisiner qn; Law **t. party** tiers m, tierce personne f; **t. party cover** (in insurance) assurance f au tiers; **t. rate** (mediocre) très mauvais(e); **the T. World** le tiers-monde; see also **eighth**

thirdly ['θɜːdlɪ] adv troisièmement

thirst [θɜːst] 1 n soif f; Fig **the t. for sth** la soif de qch

2 vi Fig **être assoiffé(e) (for** de)

thirsty ['θɜːstɪ] adj also Fig assoiffé(e); **to be** or **feel t.** avoir soif; Fam **all this talking is t. work** ça donne soif de parler autant

thirteen [θɜː'tiːn] 1 n treize m inv

2 adj treize; see also **eight**

thirteenth [θɜː'tiːnθ] 1 n (a) (fraction) treizième m (b) (in series) treizième mf (c) (of month) treize m inv

2 adj treizième; see also **eighth**

thirtieth ['θɜːtɪɪθ] 1 n (a) (fraction) trentième m (b) (in series) trentième mf (c) (of month) trente m inv

2 adj trentième; see also **eighth**

thirty ['θɜːtɪ] 1 n trente m inv

2 adj trente; see also **eighty**

this [ðɪs] 1 demonstrative pron (pl **these** [ðiːz]) (a) (subject) ce, ceci; (object) ceci; **who's t.?** qui est-ce?; **what's t.?** qu'est-ce que c'est?; **t. is ridiculous!** c'est ridicule!; **t. leads me to believe that...** ceci me mène à croire que...; **I do it like t.** je le fais comme ceci; **t. is what she told me** voici ce qu'elle m'a dit; **listen to t.** écoute ça; **t. is Sarah Jervis** (on telephone) c'est Sarah Jervis à l'appareil;

(introducing another person) je te présente Sarah Jervis; Fam **to talk about t. and that** parler de choses et d'autres (b) (as opposed to that) celui-ci (celle-ci) m,f; **in a case like t.** dans un cas comme celui-ci

2 demonstrative adj (pl **these**) (a) (indicating person, thing) ce (cette); **t. book** ce livre; **t. question** cette question; **t. man** cet homme

(b) (as opposed to that) ce...-ci (cette...-ci); **I prefer t. film** je préfère ce film-ci; **take t. cup** prends cette tasse-ci; **t. one** celui-ci (celle-ci)

3 adv **t. high/big** haut(e)/grand(e) comme ça; **I didn't think it would be t. good** je ne pensais pas que ce serait aussi bon; **I've never seen one t. good** je n'en ai jamais vu d'aussi bon que ça; **t. much is certain,...** une chose est sûre,...

thistle ['θɪsəl] n chardon m

thither ['ðɪðə(r)] adv Lit hither and t. çà et là

thong [θɒŋ] n lanière f

thorax ['θɔːræks] n Anat thorax m

thorn [θɔːn] n épine f; Fig **to be a t. in sb's flesh** or **side** être un sujet d'irritation pour qn

thorny ['θɔːnɪ] adj also Fig épineux(euse)

thorough ['θʌrə] adj (a) (search, cleaning, preparation) minutieux(euse), (knowledge, examination, revision) approfondi(e); **to do** or **make a t. job of sth** faire qch très consciencieusement (b) (work, worker) conscien-cieux(euse) (c) (complete) intégral(e)

thoroughbred ['θʌrəbred] 1 n pur-sang m inv

2 adj (horse) pur-sang inv

thoroughfare ['θʌrəfeə(r)] n voie f de communication

thoroughgoing ['θʌrəgəʊɪŋ] adj (search) minu-tieux(euse); (knowledge, revision) approfondi(e)

thoroughly ['θʌrəlɪ] adv (a) (with thoroughness) à fond (b) (completely) tout à fait

thoroughness ['θʌrənɪs] n minutie f

those [ðəʊz] (plural of **that**) 1 demonstrative pron ceux-là (celles-là) mpl,fpl; **t. are cases like t.** dans des cas comme ceux-là; **t. are the ones I want** voilà ceux que je veux; **t. of us who...** ceux d'entre nous qui...

2 demonstrative adj ces; **t. ones** ceux-là (celles-là) mpl, fpl

though [ðəʊ] 1 conj bien que + subjunctive; **t. I say so myself** sans fausse modestie; **strange t. it may seem** aussi étrange que cela puisse paraître; **even t.** même si; **as t.** comme si

2 adv pourtant

thought [θɔːt] 1 n (a) (thinking, idea) pensée f; **it's quite a t.!** (pleasant) le rêve!; (unpleasant) quelle horreur!; **what a kind t.!** quelle délicate attention!; **the very t. of it...** le simple fait d'y penser...; **I didn't give it another t.** je n'y ai plus pensé; **her thoughts were elsewhere** son esprit était ailleurs; **what are your thoughts on the matter?** quelle est votre opinion sur le sujet? (b) (reflection) réflexion f; **after much t.** après mûre réflexion; **to give some/no t. to sth** réfléchir/ne pas réfléchir à qch; **to be deep** or **lost in t.** être perdu(e) ou plongé(e) dans ses pensées (c) (intention) intention f; **to have no t. of doing sth** ne pas avoir l'intention de faire qch; **you must give up all thought(s) of seeing him** tu dois renoncer à le voir

2 pt & pp of **think**

thoughtful ['θɔːtfʊl] adj (a) (pensive) (person) pen-sif(ive); (book, writer) sérieux(euse) (b) (considerate) (person) attentionné(e); (gesture, remark) gentil(ille)

thoughtfully ['θɔ:tfəlɪ] adv (a) (pensively) pensivement (b) (considerately) gentiment

thoughtless ['θɔ:tlɪs] adj irréfléchi(e)

thought-out ['θɔ:t'aʊt] adj well/poorly t. (plan, scheme) bien/mal étudié(e)

thought-provoking ['θɔ:tprəvəʊkɪŋ] adj qui donne à réfléchir

thousand ['θaʊzənd] 1 n a mille m inv; one or a t. mille; **thousands of people** des milliers de gens; **she's one in a t.** elle est unique
  2 adj mille inv; a t. years mille ans; two t. men deux mille hommes; Fam **to have a t. and one things to do** avoir mille choses à faire

thousandth ['θaʊzənθ] 1 n (a) (fraction) millième m (b) (in series) millième mf
  2 adj millième

thrash [θræʃ] vt (beat) battre; Fam Fig (defeat heavily) écraser, battre à plate(s) couture(s)
▸**thrash about, thrash around** 1 vt sep to t. one's arms and legs about se débattre
  2 vi (move wildly) se débattre
▸**thrash out** vt sep discuter ou débattre de

thread [θred] 1 n (a) (for sewing) fil m; Fig **his life hung by a t.** sa vie ne tenait qu'à un fil; **to lose the t. (of sth)** perdre le fil (de qch) (b) (of screw, bolt) filetage m
  2 vt (a) (needle, beads) enfiler (b) (move) to t. one's way between the cars se faufiler entre les voitures; to t. one's way through the crowd se frayer un chemin à travers la foule

threadbare ['θredbeə(r)] adj (clothes) élimé(e); Fig (argument, joke) éculé(e)

threat [θret] n menace f

threaten ['θretən] 1 vt menacer; to t. to do sth menacer de faire qch; to t. sb with sth menacer qn de qch
  2 vi menacer

threatening ['θretənɪŋ] adj (look, gesture) menaçant(e); (letter) de menaces

three [θri:] 1 n trois m inv; come with us – no, (two's company,) t.'s a crowd viens avec nous – non, je me sentirais de trop
  2 adj trois inv; see also **eight**

three-cornered [θri:'kɔ:nəd] adj triangulaire

three-course meal ['θri:kɔ:s'mi:l] n repas m à trois plats (entrée, plat principal, dessert)

three-dimensional [θri:daɪ'menʃənəl] adj (object) tridimensionnel(elle), en trois dimensions; (character) qui semble réel; (film, picture) en relief

threefold ['θri:fəʊld] 1 adj triple
  2 adv to increase t. être multiplié(e) par trois

three-legged [θri:'legd] adj (stool) à trois pieds; t. race = course dont les participants sont attachés deux à deux par une jambe

three-piece [θri:'pi:s] adj t. suit (costume m) trois-pièce m inv; t. suite canapé m avec deux fauteuils assortis

three-point turn [θri:'pɔɪnt'tɜ:n] n demi-tour m en trois manœuvres

threescore ['θri:skɔ:(r)] adj Lit soixante inv; t. (years) and ten soixante-dix inv

threesome ['θri:səm] n groupe m de trois personnes

three-wheeler [θri:'wi:lə(r)] n (car) voiture f à trois roues; (tricycle) tricycle m

thresh [θreʃ] vt battre

threshold ['θreʃəʊld] n also Fig seuil m; to cross the t. franchir le seuil; Fig to be on the t. of sth être au seuil de qch

threw [θru:] pt of **throw**

thrice [θraɪs] adv Lit trois fois

thrift [θrɪft] n économie f, épargne f

thriftless ['θrɪftlɪs] adj dépensier(ère)

thrifty ['θrɪftɪ] adj économe

thrill [θrɪl] 1 n (excitement) sensation f; (trembling) frisson m; to get a t. out of doing sth adorer faire qch
  2 vt exalter, donner des frissons à; to be thrilled for sb/with sth être ravi(e) pour qn/de qch
  3 vi Lit tressaillir, frissonner

thriller ['θrɪlə(r)] n thriller m

thrilling ['θrɪlɪŋ] adj (story, film, match) palpitant(e); (idea, proposal, situation) exaltant(e)

thrive [θraɪv] (pt & pp thrived [θraɪvd], pt also throve [θrəʊv]) vi (of child, plant) se développer; (of adult) s'épanouir; (of business) prospérer; to t. on sth (stress, danger) avoir besoin de qch pour s'épanouir

thriving ['θraɪvɪŋ] adj (plant, person, animal) vigoureux(euse); (business) prospère, florissant(e)

throat [θrəʊt] n (a) gorge f; to clear one's t. se racler la gorge, s'éclaircir la voix (b) (idioms) to ram or shove sth down sb's t. rebattre les oreilles à qn de qch; to jump down sb's t. sauter sur qn; to be at each other's throats se battre

throaty ['θrəʊtɪ] adj rauque

throb [θrɒb] 1 n (of heart) battement m; (of pain) élancement m; (of engine) vibration f
  2 vi (pt & pp throbbed) (of heart) battre; (of engine) vibrer; my head is throbbing j'ai une douleur lancinante dans la tête

throes [θrəʊz] npl t. of death, death t. affres fpl de la mort, l'agonie f; to be in the t. of sth/of doing sth être en plein qch/en train de faire qch

thrombosis [θrɒm'bəʊsɪs] (pl thromboses) n thrombose f

throne [θrəʊn] n trône m

throng [θrɒŋ] 1 n foule f
  2 vt se presser dans; the streets were thronged with people les rues étaient noires de monde
  3 vi affluer, se presser; to t. round sb se presser autour de qn

throttle ['θrɒtəl] 1 n (valve) papillon m des gaz; (accelerator) manette f des gaz; at full t. à pleins gaz
  2 vt also Fig étrangler

through [θru:] 1 prep (a) (with place) par, à travers; to go t. a tunnel passer par un tunnel; to look t. a hole regarder par un trou; to come in t. the window entrer par la fenêtre; we went t. Belgium nous sommes passés par la Belgique
  (b) (in the course of) all t. his life toute sa vie durant; halfway t. a book/film à la moitié d'un livre/film; to get t. sth (finish) venir à bout de qch; Fam he's been t. a lot il en a bavé
  (c) (by means of) par; to send sth t. the post envoyer qch par la poste; (accelerator) I found out t. my brother/the newspaper je l'ai appris par mon frère/le journal
  (d) (because of) à cause de; t. ignorance/carelessness par ignorance/négligence
  (e) Am (up to) Tuesday t. Thursday de mardi à jeudi
  2 adv (a) (from side to side) to go t. (of bullet, nail) traverser; to let sb t. laisser passer qn; to get t. to the final être en

finale

(b) *(from start to finish)* **to sleep all night t.** dormir toute la nuit; **to read a book right t.** lire un livre tout entier; **he's bad t. and t.** il est vraiment méchant

(c) *(in contact)* **to get t. to sb** *(on phone)* joindre qn; **to put sb t. to sb** *(on phone)* passer qn à qn; *Fam* **I just can't get t. to him** *(make myself understood)* je n'arrive pas à le lui faire comprendre

3 *adj* **(a)** *(finished)* fini(e); **to be t. with sb/sth** en avoir fini avec qn/qch

(b) *(direct)* **t. train** train *m* direct

throughout [θruːˈaʊt] **1** *prep (in every part of)* partout dans; *(during)* tout au long de; **t. the country** dans tout le pays; **t. her life** tout au long de sa vie, pendant toute sa vie

2 *adv (everywhere)* partout; *(the whole time)* tout le temps

throughput [ˈθruːpʊt] *n Com* débit *m*

throve [θrəʊv] *pt of* **thrive**

throw [θrəʊ] **1** *vt (pt* **threw** [θruː]*, pp* **thrown** [θrəʊn]*)* **(a)** *(in general)* jeter, lancer; *(javelin, discus)* lancer; **to t. sth at sb/sth** lancer qch à/contre qn/qch; **to t. sth in sb's face** lancer qch à la figure de qn; *Fig* jeter qch à la figure de qn; **to t. sb forwards/backwards** projeter qn en avant/en arrière; *Fig* **to t. oneself into sth** *(after traumatic event)* se jeter dans qch; *(enthusiastically)* se lancer dans qch; **to t. oneself at sb** se jeter sur qn; **to t. sb into confusion** plonger qn dans l'embarras; **to t. a switch** appuyer sur un interrupteur; **to t. open the door** ouvrir la porte en grand; *Fam* **to t. one's weight about** *or* **around** la ramener

(b) *(image, shadow)* projeter (**on** sur); *Fig* **to t. light on sth** éclairer qch

(c) *(have)* **to t. a fit** piquer une crise; *Fam* **to t. a party** organiser une fête

(d) *(in wrestling)* renverser

(e) *(of horse)* désarçonner

(f) *Fam (disconcert)* désarçonner, déconcerter

2 *n* **(a)** *(in general)* jet *m*; *(of javelin, discus)* lancer *m*; *(in wrestling)* mise *f* à terre

(b) *(for furniture, bed)* jeté *m*

(c) *Fam* **£50 a t.** *(each)* 50 livres chaque

▸**throw away** *vt sep* **(a)** *(discard)* jeter **(b)** *(chance, life)* gâcher; *(money)* gaspiller

▸**throw in** *vt sep* **(a)** *(in general)* jeter; *Fig* **to t. in the sponge** *or* **the towel** jeter l'éponge; *Fig* **to t. in one's lot with sb** s'associer avec qn **(b)** *(add)* placer; *(give as extra)* ajouter, donner en plus

▸**throw out** *vt sep* **(a)** *(eject)* *(person)* exclure, mettre à la porte; *(thing)* jeter; *(proposal)* rejeter **(b)** *(emit)* *(light, heat)* émettre

▸**throw together** *vt sep (assemble or gather hurriedly)* assembler à la hâte; *(make hurriedly)* faire à la hâte; **chance had thrown us together** le hasard nous avait réunis

▸**throw up 1** *vt sep* **(a)** *(raise)* **to t. up one's hands** *(in horror, dismay)* lever les bras au ciel **(b)** *(reveal)* *(facts, information)* révéler **(c)** *(abandon)* *(career)* abandonner

2 *vi Fam (vomit)* vomir

throwaway [ˈθrəʊəweɪ] *adj* **(a)** *(disposable)* jetable **(b)** *(line, remark)* fait(e) sans y penser

throwback [ˈθrəʊbæk] *n Biol* régression *f* (**to** à); *Fig* retour *m* (**to** à)

throw-in [ˈθrəʊɪn] *n (in football)* remise *f* en jeu

thrown [θrəʊn] *pp of* **throw**

thru [θruː] = **through**

thrush[1] [θrʌʃ] *n (bird)* grive *f*

thrush[2] *n (disease)* muguet *m*

thrust [θrʌst] **1** *n* **(a)** *(forward movement)* mouvement *m* en avant; *(of army)* attaque *f* **(b)** *(of argument)* idée *f* principale **(c)** *(force of engine)* poussée *f*

2 *vt (pt & pp* **thrust***)* **to t. sth into sth** enfoncer qch dans qch; **to t. one's way through the crowd** se frayer un chemin à travers la foule

▸**thrust aside** *vt sep* repousser, écarter

▸**thrust forward** *vt sep* pousser en avant; *Fig* **to t. oneself forward** se mettre en avant

▸**thrust on** *vt sep* **to t. sth on sb** imposer qch à qn; **he thrust himself on them** il s'est imposé

▸**thrust out** *vt sep (arm, leg)* allonger; *(chest)* bomber; *(chin)* avancer

▸**thrust upon** = **thrust on**

thrusting [ˈθrʌstɪŋ] *adj* entreprenant(e), dynamique

thruway [ˈθruːweɪ] *n Am* autoroute *f*

thud [θʌd] **1** *n* bruit *m* sourd

2 *vi* faire un bruit sourd; **to t. against sth** frapper qch avec un bruit sourd

thug [θʌɡ] *n* voyou *m*

thumb [θʌm] **1** *n* **(a)** pouce *m*; *Fig* **she's got him under her t.** il est sous sa coupe; *Fam* **to be all thumbs** être maladroit(e); *Fam* **to give sth the thumbs up/down** accepter/rejeter qch

2 *vt* **to t. one's nose at sb** faire un pied de nez à qn; *Fam* **to t. a lift** *or* **ride** faire de l'auto-stop; **a well thumbed book/magazine** un livre/magazine qui a beaucoup servi

3 *vi* **to t. through a book/magazine** feuilleter un livre/magazine

thumbnail [ˈθʌmneɪl] *n* ongle *m* du pouce; **t. sketch** description *f* rapide

thumbprint [ˈθʌmprɪnt] *n* empreinte *f* du pouce

thumbtack [ˈθʌmtæk] *n Am* punaise *f*

thump [θʌmp] **1** *n (blow)* coup *m*; *(sound)* bruit *m* sourd

2 *vt (hit)* cogner, frapper; *(put down heavily)* poser lourdement

3 *vi* **(a)** **to t. on sth** *(table, door)* cogner, frapper qch **(b)** *(walk heavily)* **to t. around** *or* **about** marcher à pas lourds **(c)** *(of heart)* battre la chamade

thumping [ˈθʌmpɪŋ] *Fam* **1** *adj* **(a)** *(very large)* énorme **(b)** *(headache)* lancinant(e)

2 *adv* **a t. great book/salary** un livre/un salaire énorme

thunder [ˈθʌndə(r)] **1** *n* tonnerre *m*; **with a face like t.** le visage déformé par la colère

2 *vi Fig* tonner; **to t. along** *(of train, lorry)* passer dans un bruit de tonnerre

thunderbolt [ˈθʌndəbəʊlt] *n* éclair *m* suivi d'un coup de tonnerre

thunderclap [ˈθʌndəklæp] *n* coup *m* de tonnerre

thundercloud [ˈθʌndəklaʊd] *n* nuage *m* orageux

thunderous [ˈθʌndərəs] *adj (voice)* tonitruant(e); **t. applause** un tonnerre d'applaudissements

thunderstorm [ˈθʌndəstɔːm] *n* orage *m*

thunderstruck [ˈθʌndəstrʌk] *adj* abasourdi(e)

Thur *(abbr* **Thursday***)* jeudi

Thursday [ˈθɜːzdɪ] *n* jeudi *m; see also* **Saturday**

thus [ðʌs] *adv Formal* **(a)** *(in this way, therefore)* ainsi **(b)** **t. far** *(in present)* jusqu'ici; *(in past)* jusque-là

thwart [θwɔːt] *vt* contrecarrer

thyme [taɪm] n thym m

thyroid ['θaɪrɔɪd] **1** n thyroïde f
2 adj thyroïde; **t. gland** thyroïde f

tiara [tɪ'ɑːrə] n (jewellery) diadème m

Tibet [tɪ'bet] n le Tibet

Tibetan [tɪ'betən] **1** n (**a**) (person) Tibétain(e) m,f (**b**) (language) tibétain m
2 adj tibétain(e)

tibia ['tɪbɪə] n Anat tibia m

tic [tɪk] n tic m

tick¹ [tɪk] n (parasite) tique f

tick² n Br Fam (credit) **to buy sth on t.** acheter qch à crédit

tick³ [tɪk] **1** n (**a**) (of clock) tic-tac m inv; Fam (moment) instant m (**b**) (mark) coche f; **to put a t. beside sth** cocher qch
2 vt (mark) cocher
3 vi (of clock) faire tic-tac; **the minutes were ticking by** or **away** les minutes passaient; Fam **I don't know what makes him t.** je ne sais pas ce qui se passe dans sa tête
▸**tick off** vt sep (**a**) (on list) cocher (**b**) Br Fam (reprimand) passer un savon à (**c**) Am Fam (irritate) énerver
▸**tick over** vi (of engine) tourner au ralenti; (of business) tourner

ticket ['tɪkɪt] **1** n (**a**) (for train, plane, cinema, lottery) billet m; (for underground, bus) ticket m; (parking) **t.** P-V m; **t. inspector** contrôleur(euse) m,f; **t. office** guichet m, billetterie f; **t. tout** revendeur(euse) m,f de billets (**b**) (label) (price) **t.** étiquette f (**c**) Am Pol (list of candidates) liste f électorale; **she ran on an anti-corruption t.** elle a fondé son programme électoral sur la lutte contre la corruption (**d**) Fam **it was just the t.!** c'était juste ce qu'il fallait!
2 vt (goods) étiqueter

ticking ['tɪkɪŋ] n (**a**) (of clock) tic-tac m inv (**b**) (fabric) toile f à matelas

ticking off n Br Fam (reprimand) savon m; **to give sb a t.** passer un savon à qn

tickle ['tɪkəl] **1** n chatouillement m; **to have a t. in one's throat** avoir des picotements dans la gorge
2 vt chatouiller; Fig (amuse) amuser; **to t. sb's fancy** plaire à qn; **to be tickled pink** être ravi(e)
3 vi chatouiller

ticklish ['tɪklɪʃ] adj (**a**) (person) chatouilleux(euse) (**b**) Fam (situation, problem) délicat(e)

tidal ['taɪdəl] adj régi(e) par les marées; **t. energy** énergie f marémotrice; **t. wave** raz de marée m inv

tiddler ['tɪdlə(r)] n Br Fam (small fish) petit poisson m; (child) mioche m

tiddly ['tɪdlɪ] adj Br Fam (**a**) (small) minuscule (**b**) (drunk) paf inv

tiddlywinks ['tɪdlɪwɪŋks] n jeu m de puce

tide [taɪd] **1** n (of sea) marée f; (of events) cours m; **high/low t.** marée haute/basse; Fig **to go against the t.** aller à contre-courant; Fig **the t. has turned** le vent a tourné
▸**tide over** vt sep **to t. sb over** dépanner qn

tidemark ['taɪdmɑːk] n (mark left by tide) laisse f de haute mer; Br Fam (in bath, around neck) ligne f de crasse

tidings ['taɪdɪŋz] npl Lit nouvelles fpl

tidy ['taɪdɪ] **1** adj (**a**) (room, house) rangé(e), en ordre; (hair) bien coiffé(e); (appearance, handwriting) soigné(e); (person) (in habits) ordonné(e); (in appearance) soigné (**b**) Fam (considerable) joli(e)

2 vt ranger; (garden) nettoyer; **to t. one's hair** se recoiffer
▸**tidy up** vt sep & vi ranger

tie [taɪ] **1** n (**a**) (link) lien m (**b**) (garment) cravate f (**c**) (draw) (in match) match m nul; **there was a t. for second place** (in race, competition) il y a eu égalité pour la deuxième place (**d**) (peg) match m
2 vt (shoelace, string) attacher, nouer; **to t. a knot** faire un nœud; **to t. sth to sth** attacher qch à qch; Fig **to have one's hands tied** avoir les mains liées; Fig **to be tied to one's desk** être cloué(e) à son bureau
3 vi (in race, contest) être à égalité; **to t. for first/second place** être premiers(ères)/deuxièmes ex aequo
▸**tie back** vt sep (hair, curtains) relever
▸**tie down** vt sep (immobilize) attacher; Fig **children t. you down** les enfants sont une contrainte; **she didn't want to feel tied down** elle voulait garder sa liberté
▸**tie in** vi (of facts, story) concorder, cadrer
▸**tie on** vt attacher
▸**tie up** vt sep (**a**) (person, animal) attacher; (parcel) ficeler; (boat) amarrer (**b**) (deal) conclure; (money) immobiliser (**c**) **to be tied up** (busy) être occupé(e)

tie-break(er) ['taɪbreɪk(ər)] n (in tennis) tie-break m; (in quiz, competition) question f subsidiaire

tie-in ['taɪɪn] n (link) lien m, rapport m (**with** avec); **a film/TV t.** = livre, jouet etc commercialisé à la suite d'un film ou d'une série télévisée

tier [tɪə(r)] n (of theatre, stadium) gradin m; (of wedding cake) étage m; (administrative) échelon m

tiff [tɪf] n Fam querelle f

tiger ['taɪgə(r)] n tigre m

tight [taɪt] **1** adj (**a**) (clothes, knot, screw) serré(e); **to be a t. fit** (of clothes) être un peu juste; **to keep a t. hold** or **grip on sth** s'agripper à qch; **it was a t. squeeze** il a fallu se serrer un peu; Fig **to be in a t. spot** or **corner** être dans une mauvaise passe; Fig **to run a t. ship** bien mener sa barque (**b**) (competition, race, bend, schedule) serré(e); (restrictions) strict(e); **a t. finish** (in race) une arrivée disputée; Fam **money's a bit t. at the moment** je suis un peu à court d'argent en ce moment (**c**) Fam (mean) radin(e) (**d**) Fam (drunk) bourré(e)
2 adv (hold, squeeze) fortement; (seal, shut) bien; **hold t.!** tiens bon!; **sleep t.!** dors bien!

tighten ['taɪtən] **1** vt (screw, knot) serrer; (rope) tendre; (restrictions, security) renforcer; (conditions, rules) durcir; **to t. one's grip on sth** (rope, handle) resserrer sa prise sur qch; Fig (power, control) renforcer son emprise sur qch; Fig **to t. one's belt** se serrer la ceinture
2 vi (of knot, grip) se resserrer; (of rope) se tendre
▸**tighten up** vt sep (screw) resserrer; (restrictions, security) renforcer

tightfisted [taɪt'fɪstɪd] adj Fam radin(e)

tightknit ['taɪt'nɪt] adj (community) uni(e)

tight-lipped ['taɪtlɪpt] adj (silent) peu bavard(e); (angry) renfrogné(e)

tightly ['taɪtlɪ] adv (hold, squeeze) fortement; (seal, shut) bien

tightness ['taɪtnɪs] n (of link, clothing) étroitesse f; (of regulations, security) rigueur f

tightrope ['taɪtrəʊp] n corde f raide; Fig **to walk a t.** être sur la corde raide; **t. walker** funambule mf

tights [taɪts] npl Br (garment) collant m

tigress ['taɪgrɪs] n tigresse f

'til [tɪl] = **until**

tile [taɪl] **1** *n* (*on roof*) tuile *f*; (*on floor, wall*) carreau *m*
2 *vt* (*roof*) couvrir de tuiles; (*floor, wall*) carreler

tiled [taɪld] *adj* (*roof*) de tuiles; (*floor, wall*) carrelé(e)

till[1] [tɪl] *vt* (*field*) labourer

till[2] *n* (*cash register*) caisse *f*; *Fig* **to be caught with one's hand** *or* **fingers in the t.** être pris(e) la main dans le sac

till[3] = **until**

tiller ['tɪlə(r)] *n* (*on boat*) barre *f*

tilt [tɪlt] **1** *n* (**a**) (*angle*) inclinaison *f* (**b**) **at full t.** à toute vitesse
2 *vt* (*head, chair*) incliner, pencher; **to t. the balance of opinion in favour of** faire pencher l'opinion en faveur de
3 *vi* (**a**) (*incline*) pencher; **to t. backwards/forwards** pencher vers l'arrière/vers l'avant (**b**) *Fig* **to t. at windmills** se battre contre des moulins à vent
▸**tilt over** *vi* basculer

timber ['tɪmbə(r)] *n* (*wood*) bois *m*; **t. merchant** marchand *m* de bois

time [taɪm] **1** *n* (**a**) (*in general*) temps *m*; *Fig* **to have no t. for sb/sth** ne pas avoir de temps à perdre avec qn/qch; **to take t.** prendre du temps; **to take one's t. (doing sth)** prendre son temps (pour faire qch); **you took your t.!** tu as pris ton temps!; **in one's own t.** (*out of working hours*) pendant son temps libre; (*at one's own pace*) à son rythme; **in t.** (*eventually*) avec le temps; **in t. for sth/to do sth** à temps pour qch/pour faire qch; **in good t.** (*early*) à temps; (*in due course*) en temps voulu; **all in good t.** chaque chose en son temps; **she'll do it in her own good t.** elle le fera quand elle le pourra; **now my t. is my own** maintenant, je suis libre de mon temps; **in no t. at all, in next to no t.** en un rien de temps; **t.'s getting on** l'heure avance; **t.'s up!** c'est l'heure!; **t. will tell** l'avenir le dira; *Prov* **t. is money** le temps, c'est de l'argent; *Fam* **to do t.** (*go to prison*) faire de la taule; *also Fig* **t. bomb** bombe *f* à retardement; **to be in a t. warp** être hors du temps

(**b**) (*period*) temps *m*; **in a short/long t.** dans peu de temps/longtemps; **for some t.** pendant quelque temps; **in three weeks' t.** dans trois semaines; **to take a long t. over sth/to do sth** passer beaucoup de temps sur qch/à faire qch; **for the t. being** pour le moment; **to have a good t.** bien s'amuser; **to give sb a hard t.** faire passer un mauvais moment à qn

(**c**) (*age*) époque *f*; **before my t.** avant ma naissance; **to be ahead of one's t.** être en avance sur son temps; **to move with the times** vivre avec son temps; **she was a good singer in her t.** c'était une bonne chanteuse à son époque; **she's seen a few things in her t.** elle a vu pas mal de choses dans sa vie; **t. capsule** = conteneur rempli d'objets que l'on enterre pour permettre aux générations futures de comprendre comment on vivait à une époque donnée

(**d**) (*moment*) moment *m*; **at the t.** à ce moment-là; **at the present t.** en ce moment; **at one t.** à une époque; **at no t.** jamais, à aucun moment; **at the same t.** en même temps; **at times** parfois, par moments; **this t. next year** l'année prochaine à la même époque; **from t. to t.** de temps en temps; **at this t. of (the) year** à cette époque de l'année; **the t. has come to...** le moment est venu de...; *Fam* **it's high t. (that)...** il est grand temps que.... + *subjunctive*

(**e**) (*on clock*) heure *f*; **what's the t.?** quelle heure est-il?; **to pass the t. of day with sb** parler de la pluie et du beau temps avec qn; *Fam* **he wouldn't give you the t.**

of day il n'est vraiment pas aimable; **this t. tomorrow** demain à la même heure; **on t.** à l'heure; **it's t. we left** il est temps de partir; **t. difference** décalage *m* horaire; **t. lag** décalage; *Ind* **t. sheet** fiche *f* horaire; **t. switch** minuterie *f*

(**f**) (*occasion*) fois *f*; **five times** cinq fois; **t. and t. again**, **t. after t.** encore et encore

(**g**) (*in multiplication*) **four times two is eight** quatre fois deux égalent huit; **three times as big/expensive as** trois fois plus grand(e)/cher (chère) que

(**h**) (*in music*) mesure *f*; **to keep t.** rester en mesure

2 *vt* (**a**) (*meeting, visit*) prévoir
(**b**) (*remark, action*) **well timed** opportun(e); **badly timed** mal venu(e)
(**c**) (*athlete, race*) chronométrer

time-consuming ['taɪmkənsju:mɪŋ] *adj* qui prend du temps

time-honoured ['taɪmɒnəd] *adj* consacré(e) (par l'usage)

timekeeper ['taɪmkiːpə(r)] *n* (*in competition*) chronométreur *m*

timekeeping ['taɪmkiːpɪŋ] *n* (**a**) (*in factory*) contrôle *m* de présence (**b**) (*punctuality*) ponctualité *f*

timeless ['taɪmlɪs] *adj* intemporel(elle)

timely ['taɪmlɪ] *adj* opportun(e)

time-out ['taɪmaʊt] *n* (*in sport*) temps *m* mort; *Fig* pause *f*; **to take t.** faire une pause

timepiece ['taɪmpiːs] *n* (*clock*) pendule *f*; (*watch*) montre *f*

timer ['taɪmə(r)] *n* minuteur *m*

time-saving ['taɪmseɪvɪŋ] *adj* qui permet de gagner du temps

timescale ['taɪmskeɪl] *n* période *f*

time-share ['taɪmʃeə(r)] *n* (*flat*) appartement *m* en multipropriété; (*house*) maison *f* en multipropriété

timespan ['taɪmspæn] *n* laps *m* de temps

timetable ['taɪmteɪbl] **1** *n* (*at school, university*) emploi *m* du temps; (*for event, project*) calendrier *m*; (*for trains, buses*) horaire *m*; **to work to a t.** suivre un emploi du temps
2 *vt* (*talks, meeting*) fixer une date pour; (*classes*) établir un emploi du temps pour

time-wasting ['taɪmweɪstɪŋ] *n* perte *f* de temps

timid ['tɪmɪd] *adj* timide

timidity [tɪ'mɪdɪtɪ] *n* timidité *f*

timidly ['tɪmɪdlɪ] *adv* timidement

timing ['taɪmɪŋ] *n* (**a**) (*of announcement, election*) moment *m* choisi (de pour) (**b**) (*of remark, action*) **good t.** à-propos *m*; **bad t.** manque *m* d'à-propos; **perfect t.!** ça tombe bien! (**c**) (*of musician*) sens *m* du rythme

timorous ['tɪmərəs] *adj* timoré(e)

tin [tɪn] *n* (**a**) (*metal*) étain *m*; **t. mine** mine *f* d'étain; **t. plate** fer-blanc *m*; **t. soldier** soldat *m* de plomb (**b**) (*mould*) moule *m* (**c**) (*container*) boîte *f*; (*for biscuits, cakes*) boîte en fer; **t. opener** ouvre-boîte *m*

tinder ['tɪndə(r)] *n* petit bois *m*

tinderbox ['tɪndəbɒks] *n Fig* poudrière *f*

tinfoil ['tɪn'fɔɪl] *n* papier *m* aluminium

ting-a-ling ['tɪŋəlɪŋ] *n* dring-dring *m inv*

tinge [tɪn(d)ʒ] **1** *n* (*of colour, emotion*) pointe *f*
2 *vt* **tinged with** teinté(e) de

tingle ['tɪŋgl] **1** *n* (*physical sensation*) picotement *m*; (*of fear*) frisson *m*; (*of excitement*) frémissement *m*

2 *vi* picoter; **to t. with fear** frissonner de peur; **to t. with excitement** frémir d'excitation

tingling ['tɪŋglɪŋ] *n* picotement *m*

tinker ['tɪŋkə(r)] **1** *n* (*travelling person*) rétameur *m*
2 *vi* **to t. with sth** bricoler qch

tinkle ['tɪŋkəl] **1** *n* (*of bell*) tintement *m*; *Br Fam* (*phone call*) **to give sb a t.** passer un coup de fil à qn
2 *vi* tinter

tinned [tɪnd] *adj Br* (*food*) en boîte

tinnitus ['tɪnɪtəs] *n* acouphène *m*

tinny ['tɪnɪ] *adj* (*sound*) métallique

tinsel ['tɪnsəl] *n* guirlandes *fpl* de Noël

tint [tɪnt] **1** *n* teinte *f*, nuance *f*; (*in hair*) rinçage *m*
2 *vt* teinter

tiny ['taɪnɪ] *adj* minuscule; **a t. bit** un tout petit peu

tip¹ [tɪp] **1** *n* (*end*) bout *m*; **on the tips of one's toes** sur la pointe des pieds; **it's on the t. of my tongue** je l'ai sur le bout de la langue; *Fig* **that's just the t. of the iceberg** ce n'est que la partie visible de l'iceberg
2 *vt* (*pt & pp* **tipped**) **to be tipped with sth** avoir le bout recouvert de qch

tip² [tɪp] **1** *n* (a) (*payment*) pourboire *m* (b) (*piece of advice*) truc *m*
2 *vt* (*pt & pp* **tipped**) (a) (*give money to*) donner un pourboire à (b) (*predict*) **to t. a winner** (*in horse race*) pronostiquer un cheval gagnant; **to t. sb for success/promotion** prédire à qn le succès/une promotion; **the film is tipped to win an Oscar** on pressent que ce film va gagner un Oscar

tip³ [tɪp] *n* (*for rubbish*) & *Fig* dépotoir *m*
2 *vt* (*pt & pp* **tipped**) (a) (*pour*) (*rubbish*) déverser; (*liquid*) verser; **to t. sth over sb/sth** renverser qch sur qn/qch (b) **to t. the scales at 95 kg** peser 95 kg; *Fig* **to t. the scales** *or* **balance (in sb's favour)** faire pencher la balance (en faveur de qn)

▸**tip off** *vt sep* (*warn*) avertir

▸**tip out** *vt sep* (*empty*) vider; (*discard*) jeter

▸**tip over 1** *vt sep* renverser
2 *vi* se renverser

▸**tip up 1** *vt sep* renverser
2 *vi* basculer

tip-off ['tɪpɒf] *n Fam* tuyau *m*

Tipp-Ex® ['tɪpeks] **1** *n* Tipp-Ex® *m inv*
2 *vt* **to t. sth out** effacer qch avec du Tipp-Ex®

tipple ['tɪpəl] *n Fam* **what's your t.?** qu'est-ce que vous buvez habituellement?; **sherry's her favourite t.** ce qu'elle préfère, c'est le sherry

tipsy ['tɪpsɪ] *adj* pompette

tiptoe ['tɪptəʊ] **1** *n* **on t.** sur la pointe des pieds
2 *vi* marcher sur la pointe des pieds; **to t. in/out** entrer/sortir sur la pointe des pieds

tiptop ['tɪptɒp] *adj* excellent(e)

tirade [taɪ'reɪd] *n* diatribe *f*

tire¹ ['taɪə(r)] **1** *vt* fatiguer
2 *vi* se fatiguer; **to t. of sth/of doing sth** se lasser de qch/de faire qch

▸**tire out** *vt sep* (*exhaust*) épuiser

tire² *Am* = **tyre**

tired ['taɪəd] *adj* fatigué(e); **to be t. of sth/of doing sth** en avoir assez de qch/de faire qch

tireless ['taɪələs] *adj* infatigable

tiresome ['taɪəsəm] *adj* ennuyeux(euse)

tiring ['taɪərɪŋ] *adj* fatigant(e)

tissue ['tɪʃuː] *n* (a) *Biol* tissu *m* (b) (*paper handkerchief*) mouchoir *m* en papier; *Fig* **a t. of lies** un tissu de mensonges; **t. paper** papier *m* de soie

tit¹ [tɪt] *n* (*bird*) mésange *f*

tit² *n* **t. for tat** un prêté pour un rendu; **to give sb t. for tat** rendre à qn la monnaie de sa pièce

tit³ *n very Fam* (a) (*breast*) nichon *m*; **to get on sb's tits** courir sur le haricot à qn (b) (*idiot*) con (conne) *m,f*

titanic [taɪ'tænɪk] *adj* (*conflict, struggle*) titanesque

titanium [taɪ'teɪnɪəm] *n Chem* titane *m*

titbit ['tɪtbɪt] *n* (*snack*) morceau *m* de choix; *Fig* **t. of gossip** potin *m*; **t. of information** nouvelle *f*

titch [tɪtʃ] *n Br Fam* (*small person*) microbe *m*

titchy ['tɪtʃɪ] *adj Br Fam* minuscule

tit-for-tat [tɪtfə'tæt] *adj* (*murder*) en représailles; **it's just t.** c'est un prêté pour un rendu

titillate ['tɪtɪleɪt] *vt* titiller

titillation [tɪtɪ'leɪʃən] *n* titillation *f*

title ['taɪtəl] **1** *n* titre *m*; **the titles** le générique; **t. deeds** titres de propriété; **t. fight** combat *m* comptant pour le titre; **t. page** page *f* de titre; **t. role** (*in play, film*) rôle-titre *m*; **t. track** (*of album*) morceau *m* qui donne son titre à l'album
2 *vt* intituler

titled ['taɪtəld] *adj* (*person*) titré(e)

titleholder ['taɪtəlhəʊldə(r)] *n* (*in sport*) tenant(e) *m* du titre

titter ['tɪtə(r)] **1** *n* petit rire *m*
2 *vi* rire bêtement

tittle-tattle ['tɪtəltætəl] *Fam* **1** *n* potins *mpl*, cancans *mpl*
2 *vi* cancaner

titular ['tɪtjʊlə(r)] *adj* en titre

tizzy ['tɪzɪ] *n Fam* **to be in/get into a t.** être/se mettre dans tous ses états

T-junction ['tiːdʒʌŋkʃən] *n* carrefour *m* en T

TNT [tiːen'tiː] *n Chem* (*abbr* **trinitrotoluene**) TNT *m*

to [tuː, *unstressed* tə] **1** *prep* **a** (*towards*) à; **to go to church/school** aller à l'église/à l'école; **to go to France/Japan/the USA** aller en France/au Japon/aux États-Unis; **to go to sb's house** aller chez qn; **to the left/right** à gauche/droite
(b) (*until*) jusqu'à; **it's ten to (six)** il est (six heures) moins dix; **to count to ten** compter jusqu'à dix; **a year to the day** un an pour jour
(c) (*expressing indirect object*) **to give sth to sb** donner qch à qn; **to speak to sb** parler à qn
(d) (*with result*) **to my surprise/joy** à ma grande surprise/joie; **to my horror, I discovered that...** et, horreur!, je découvris que...
(e) (*expressing proportion*) **six votes to four** six voix contre quatre; **there are 8 francs to the pound** une livre vaut 8 francs
2 *particle* (a) (*with infinitive*) **to go** aller; **to have things to do** avoir des choses à faire; **it's too hot to go out** il fait trop chaud pour sortir; **he came to help me** il est venu m'aider; **I want him to know** je veux qu'il sache; **she told me to stay** elle m'a dit de rester
(b) (*representing verb*) **I want/ought to** je veux/devrais le faire; **I was told to** on m'a dit de le faire

toad [təʊd] *n* (*animal*) crapaud *m*; *Fam Pej* (*man*) type *m* répugnant; *Br* **t. in the hole** = saucisses cuites au four dans de la pâte à crêpes

toadstool ['təudstu:l] n champignon m non comestible

toady ['təudɪ] Fam 1 n lèche-bottes mf inv
2 vi to t. to sb lécher les bottes de qn

toast [təust] 1 n (a) (toasted bread) pain m grillé; **a slice or piece of t.** un toast; **t. rack** porte-toasts m inv (b) (tribute) toast m; **to drink a t. to sb/sth** porter un toast à qn/qch
2 vt (a) (bread) (faire) griller; **toasted cheese** fromage m fondu; **toasted sandwich** sandwich m grillé (b) (tribute) porter un toast à

toaster ['təustə(r)] n grille-pain m inv

toastie ['təustɪ] n Fam (toasted sandwich) sandwich m grillé

tobacco [tə'bækəu] (pl tobaccos) n tabac m; **t. pouch** blague f à tabac

tobacconist [tə'bækənɪst] n marchand(e) m,f de tabac; Br **t.'s (shop)** (bureau m de) tabac m

toboggan [tə'bɒgən] 1 n luge f
2 vi faire de la luge

today [tə'deɪ] adv aujourd'hui; **a week ago t.** il y a juste une semaine aujourd'hui; **t.'s date** la date d'aujourd'hui; **t.'s paper** le journal du jour

toddle ['tɒdəl] vi (of infant) commencer à marcher; Fam **to t. off** ficher le camp

toddler ['tɒdlə(r)] n enfant mf qui commence à marcher

to-do [tə'du:] n Fam remue-ménage m inv; **what a t.!** quelle histoire!

toe [təu] 1 n (a) (of foot) orteil m, doigt m de pied; (of sock, shoe) bout m; **big/little t.** gros/petit orteil (b) (idioms) **to be on one's toes** être en alerte; **to keep sb on his toes** ne pas laisser de répit à qn; **to tread on sb's toes** marcher sur les pieds de qn
2 vt **to t. the line** bien se tenir

toehold ['təuhəuld] n (in climbing) prise f de pied; Fig **to gain a t. in the market** mettre un pied sur le marché

toenail ['təuneɪl] n ongle m de pied

toff [tɒf] n Br Fam Old-fashioned aristo mf

toffee ['tɒfɪ] n caramel m (au beurre); Fam **he can't sing for t.** il chante comme un pied; **t. apple** pomme f d'amour

tofu ['təufu:] n tofu m

together [tə'geðə(r)] 1 adv ensemble; **t. with** ainsi que, en même temps que
2 adj Fam (person) équilibré(e)

togetherness [tə'geðənɪs] n unité f, harmonie f

toggle ['tɒgəl] 1 n (on coat) olive f; Comptr & Elec **t. switch** commande f à bascule
2 vi Comptr basculer

Togo ['təugəu] n le Togo

Togolese [təugəu'li:z] 1 n Togolais(e) m,f
2 adj togolais(e)

togs [tɒgz] npl Fam (clothes) fringues fpl

toil [tɔɪl] 1 n Lit labeur m
2 vi (work hard) travailler dur; **to t. away at sth** peiner sur qch; **to t. up a hill** gravir péniblement une colline

toilet ['tɔɪlɪt] n (a) (lavatory) toilettes fpl; **to go to the t.** aller aux toilettes; **t. paper** papier m hygiénique; **t. roll** rouleau m de papier hygiénique; **t. seat** siège m des toilettes (b) Old-fashioned (washing and dressing) toilette f; **t. bag** trousse f de toilette; **t. soap** savon m de toilette

toiletries ['tɔɪlɪtrɪz] npl articles mpl de toilette

toilet-trained ['tɔɪlɪttreɪnd] adj propre

toilet-training ['tɔɪlɪttreɪnɪŋ] n apprentissage m de la propreté

token ['təukən] 1 n (a) (symbol) signe m, marque f; **as a t. of respect** en signe de respect; **by the same t.** de même, pareillement (b) (for vending machine) jeton m
2 adj (resistance, effort) symbolique; **I was the t. woman on the committee** j'étais la seule femme de la commission, parce qu'il en fallait une

Tokyo ['təukɪəu] n Tokyo

told [təuld] pt & pp of **tell**

tolerable ['tɒlərəbəl] adj (a) (bearable) tolérable, supportable (b) (reasonably good) acceptable

tolerance ['tɒlərəns] n tolérance f; **to have a high/low t. for sth** bien/mal tolérer qch

tolerant ['tɒlərənt] adj tolérant(e); **to be t. of sb/sth** tolérer qn/qch

tolerate ['tɒləreɪt] vt tolérer

toleration [tɒlə'reɪʃən] n tolérance f

toll[1] [təul] n (a) (charge) péage m; **t. bridge** pont m à péage; **t. road** route f à péage (b) (of dead, injured) nombre m de victimes; Fig **to take its t.** faire des dégâts

toll[2] vt (bell) sonner
2 vi (of bell) sonner

toll-free ['təul'fri:] Am 1 adj **t. number** ≃ numéro m vert
2 adv (call) gratuitement

Tom [tɒm] n Fam **any T., Dick or Harry** le premier venu

tom [tɒm] n Fam matou m

tomahawk ['tɒməhɔ:k] n tomahawk m

tomato [tə'mɑ:təu, Am tə'meɪtəu] (pl tomatoes) n tomate f; **t. juice** jus m de tomate; **t. ketchup** ketchup m; **t. purée** concentré m de tomates; **t. sauce** (for pasta) sauce f tomate; (ketchup) ketchup m; **t. soup** soupe f à la tomate

tomb [tu:m] n tombe f

tomboy ['tɒmbɔɪ] n garçon m manqué

tombstone ['tu:mstəun] n pierre f tombale

tomcat ['tɒmkæt] n matou m

tome [təum] n Formal gros volume m

tomfoolery [tɒm'fu:lərɪ] n Fam bêtises fpl

tomorrow [tə'mɒrəu] n demain m; Fam **to do sth like there's no t.** faire qch frénétiquement
2 adv demain; **t. morning/evening** demain matin/soir

tom-tom ['tɒmtɒm] n tam-tam m

ton [tʌn] n (a) (weight) tonne f (b) (idioms) Fam **to weigh a t.** peser une tonne; Fam **tons of** des tonnes de; Fam **to come down on sb like a t. of bricks** tomber dessus à qn

tone [təun] n (a) (of voice) ton m; (quality of sound) sonorité f; **don't speak to me in that t. of voice** ne me parle pas sur ce ton; **leave your name and number after the t.** (on answering machine) laissez votre nom et votre numéro de téléphone après le signal sonore; Fig **it set the t. for the evening** et le ton a été donné pour le reste de la soirée; Fig **to raise/lower the t. of the neighbourhood** améliorer/faire baisser le standing du quartier (b) (colour) ton m

▶**tone down** vt sep (colour) adoucir; Fig (remarks) modérer

▶**tone up** vt sep (muscles) raffermir, tonifier

tone-deaf [təun'def] adj **to be t.** ne pas avoir d'oreille

Tonga ['tɒŋgə] *n* les îles *fpl* Tonga

Tongan ['tɒŋgən] **1** *n* **(a)** *(person)* Tonguien(enne) *m,f* **(b)** *(language)* tongan *m*
2 *adj* tonguien(enne)

tongs [tɒŋz] *npl* **(pair of)** t. pince *f*; **(curling)** t. *(for hair)* fer *m* à friser

tongue [tʌŋ] *n* **(a)** *(in mouth, of land, flame)* langue *f*; *(of shoe)* languette *f*; *(language)* langue *f*; **to stick one's** t. out tirer la langue; **t. twister** = mot ou phrase difficile à prononcer **(b)** *(idioms)* **hold your** t.! tiens ta langue!, tais-toil; **have you lost your** t.? tu as perdu ta langue?; **to say sth t. in cheek** dire qch en plaisantant

tongue-tied ['tʌŋtaɪd] *adj* muet(ette)

tonic ['tɒnɪk] *n also Fig* tonique *m*, remontant *m*; **(water)** Schweppes® *m*

tonight [tə'naɪt] **1** *n* (*evening*) ce soir *m*; *(night)* cette nuit *f*
2 *adv* (*evening*) ce soir; *(night)* cette nuit

tonnage ['tʌnɪdʒ] *n Naut (of ship)* tonnage *m*

tonne [tʌn] *n* tonne *f*

tonsil ['tɒnsəl] *n* amygdale *f*; **to have one's tonsils out** se faire opérer des amygdales

tonsillitis [tɒnsɪ'laɪtɪs] *n* angine *f*; **to have** t. avoir une angine

too [tu:] *adv* **(a)** *(excessively)* trop; t. **many people** trop de gens; **I know her all** *or* **only t. well** je ne la connais que trop; **you're t. kind** vous êtes trop aimable; **he's not t. well today** il ne va pas trop bien aujourd'hui; t. **bad** tant pis; *Fam* t. **right!** et comment! **(b)** *(also)* aussi **(c)** *(moreover)* en plus

took [tʊk] *pt of* **take**

tool [tu:l] *n* *(implement)* outil *m*; *(set of)* **tools** outillage *m*; t. **bag** trousse *f* à outils; *also Comptr* t. **box** boîte *f* à outils; t. **kit** trousse *f* à outils; t. **shed** remise *f* **(b)** *(means, instrument)* instrument *m*

toot [tu:t] **1** *n* t. coup *m* de Klaxon®
2 *vt* to t. **the horn** klaxonner; **to t. sb** klaxonner qn
3 *vi* klaxonner

tooth [tu:θ] *(pl* **teeth** [ti:θ]) *n* **(a)** *(of person, saw, comb)* dent *f*; **to cut a** t. percer une dent; t. **decay** carie *f* **(b)** *(idioms)* **to fight t. and nail** se défendre bec et ongles; **to lie through one's teeth** mentir effrontément; **in the teeth of opposition** malgré l'opposition; **armed to the teeth** armé(e) jusqu'aux dents; *Fam* **to get one's teeth into sth** se mettre à fond dans qch; *Fam* **to be fed up to the back teeth with sb/sth** en avoir ras le bol de qn/qch; *Fam* **to be long in the** t. n'être plus tout jeune

toothache ['tu:θeɪk] *n* mal *m* de dents; **to have** t. avoir mal aux dents

toothbrush ['tu:θbrʌʃ] *n* brosse *f* à dents

toothless ['tu:θlɪs] *adj* édenté(e), sans dents; *Fig (powerless)* sans pouvoir

toothpaste ['tu:θpeɪst] *n* dentifrice *m*

toothpick ['tu:θpɪk] *n* cure-dents *m inv*

toothy ['tu:θɪ] *adj* t. **grin** large sourire *m*

top[1] [tɒp] *n* (*toy*) toupie *f*

top[2] **1** *n* **(a)** *(highest part)* (*of tree, mountain, tower, head*) sommet *m*; *(of page, map)* haut *m*; **at the** t. **of the stairs/street** en haut des escaliers/de la rue; **to be (at the) t. of the class** être premier(ère) de la classe; **from t. to bottom** de haut en bas; *Fig* de fond en comble; **at the** t. **of one's voice** à tue-tête; **to go over the** t. *Mil* partir à l'assaut; *Fig* aller trop loin; *Fig* **over the** t. *(excessive)* exagéré(e); **to make it to the** t. parvenir au sommet

(b) *(lid)* (*of box*) couvercle *m*; *(of bottle)* bouchon *m*; *(of pen)* capuchon *m*
(c) *(surface)* dessus *m*
(d) *(garment)* haut *m*
(e) on t. dessus; **on t. of** sur; *Fig* **to be on t. of sth** maîtriser qch; **you mustn't let things get on t. of you** il ne faut pas te laisser dépasser par les événements; *Fig* **to come out on t.** prendre le dessus; **to feel on t. of the world** se sentir en pleine forme
2 *adj* **(a)** *(highest)* (*shelf, drawer*) du haut; *(floor)* dernier(ère); **the** t. **people** *(in society)* les gens *mpl* en vue; *(in an organization)* la direction *f*; *Fam* **the** t. **brass** les gros bonnets *mpl*; t. **coat** *(of paint)* dernière couche *f*; t. **deck** *(of bus)* impériale *f*; *Fam Fig* t. **dog** chef *m*; **to feel on** t. **form** se sentir en pleine forme; *Aut* t. **gear** *(fourth)* quatrième *f* (*vitesse f*); *(fifth)* cinquième *f* (*vitesse f*); t. **hat** haut-de-forme *m*; t. **security** haute sécurité *f*; t. **speed** vitesse *f* de pointe; *Fig* **at** t. **speed** à toute vitesse
(b) *(best, major)* premier(ère); **the** t. **ten** les dix premiers; **to come t. in sth** arriver premier en qch
3 *vt* **(a)** *(place on top of)* couvrir (**with** de); **and to t. it all** et pour couronner le tout
(b) *(exceed)* dépasser
(c) *(be at the top of)* être en tête de; **to t. the bill** être la tête d'affiche
(d) *very Fam* **to t. oneself** *(commit suicide)* se foutre en l'air

▶**top up** *vt sep* (*glass, tank*) remplir; *(sum of money)* compléter

top-heavy [tɒp'hevɪ] *adj* *(structure)* trop lourd(e) du haut, déséquilibré(e); *Fig (organization)* aux dirigeants trop nombreux

topic ['tɒpɪk] *n* sujet *m*, thème *m*

topical ['tɒpɪk(ə)l] *adj* d'actualité

topless ['tɒplɪs] *adj* (*woman*) aux seins nus; **to go** t. faire du monokini

top-level [tɒplevəl] *adj* au plus haut niveau

topmost ['tɒpməʊst] *adj* le (la) plus haut(e)

top-notch ['tɒpnɒtʃ] *adj Fam* de première classe

topography [tə'pɒgrəfɪ] *n* topographie *f*

topping ['tɒpɪŋ] *n* (*for pizza*) garniture *f*; (*for cake, ice cream*) nappage *m*

topple ['tɒpəl] **1** *vt* faire tomber, renverser
2 *vi* tomber

top-secret ['tɒpsi:krɪt] *adj* top secret(ète)

topsoil ['tɒpsɔɪl] *n* couche *f* arable

topsy-turvy [tɒpsɪ'tɜ:vɪ] *Fam* **1** *adj* (*untidy*) sens dessus dessous; *(confused)* tordu(e)
2 *adv* (*untidily*) sens dessus dessous

torch [tɔ:tʃ] **1** *n* **(a)** *(burning)* torche *f*; *Fig* **to carry a** t. **for sb** aimer qn secrètement **(b)** *Br (electric)* lampe *f* de poche
2 *vt* incendier, mettre le feu à

torchlight ['tɔ:tʃlaɪt] *n* **by** t. à la lumière d'une lampe de poche; t. **procession** retraite *f* aux flambeaux

tore [tɔ:] *pt of* **tear**[2]

torment 1 [tɔ:ment] supplice *m*; **to be in** t. être au supplice
2 *vt* [tɔ:'ment] tourmenter

tormentor [tɔ:'mentə(r)] *n* bourreau *m*

torn [tɔ:n] *pp of* **tear**[2]

tornado [tɔ:'neɪdəʊ] *n* tornade *f*

Toronto [tə'rɒntəʊ] *n* Toronto

torpedo [tɔ:ˈpiːdəʊ] **1** n torpille f; **t. boat** torpilleur m, vedette f lance-torpilles
2 vt also Fig torpiller

torpid [ˈtɔ:pɪd] adj engourdi(e), léthargique

torpor [ˈtɔ:pə(r)] n torpeur f

torrent [ˈtɒrənt] n torrent m; Fig (of abuse, insults) flot m; **it's raining in torrents** il pleut à torrents

torrential [təˈrenʃəl] adj torrentiel(elle)

torrid [ˈtɒrɪd] adj also Fig torride

torso [ˈtɔ:səʊ] n torse m

tortoise [ˈtɔ:təs] n tortue f

tortoiseshell [ˈtɔ:təʃel] n écaille f (de tortue); **t. (cat)** chat m noir, blanc et roux

tortuous [ˈtɔ:tjʊəs] adj tortueux(euse)

torture [ˈtɔ:tʃə(r)] **1** n torture f; Fig **it was sheer t.!** c'était un vrai supplice!; **t. chamber** chambre f de torture
2 vt also Fig torturer

Tory [ˈtɔ:rɪ] n & adj Tory m, conservateur(trice) m,f

tosh [tɒʃ] n Br Fam bêtises fpl

toss [tɒs] **1** n (a) (of ball) lancer m; (of head) mouvement m brusque; **to decide sth on the t. of a coin** décider qch à pile ou face; **to argue the t.** discuter inutilement
(b) Br very Fam **not to give a t.** s'en ficher
2 vt (throw) lancer; (pancake) faire sauter; (salad) remuer; **to t. sth to sb** lancer qch à qn; **to t. a coin** jouer à pile ou face; **to t. one's head** rejeter la tête en arrière; **the ship was tossed by the sea** le bateau était ballotté par la mer
3 vi **to t. (up) for sth** jouer à pile ou face; **to t. and turn** (in bed) se tourner et se retourner (pour trouver le sommeil)

▶**toss about, toss around** vt sep (ship) ballotter; Fig (idea) lancer

▶**toss off** vt sep (a) (write) expédier (b) Vulg (masturbate) **to t. oneself off** se branler; **to t. sb off** branler qn

▶**toss out** vt sep jeter

tosser [ˈtɒsə(r)] n Br very Fam con (conne) m,f

toss-up [ˈtɒsʌp] n **to have a t.** jouer à pile ou face; Fam **it was a t. between the pub and the cinema** nous n'arrivions pas à nous décider entre le pub et le cinéma; **it's a t. whether or not she'll say yes** je ne sais vraiment pas si elle va dire oui

tot [tɒt] n (a) (child) tout-petit m (b) (of drink) (petite) goutte f

▶**tot up** vt sep additionner

total [ˈtəʊtəl] **1** n total m; **in t.** au total
2 adj total(e); **t. eclipse** éclipse f totale
3 vt (a) (sum) se monter à (b) Am Fam (wreck) bousiller

totalitarian [təʊtælɪˈteərɪən] adj totalitaire

totality [təʊˈtælɪtɪ] n totalité f

totally [ˈtəʊtəlɪ] adv totalement

tote[1] [təʊt] n (in betting) totalisateur m, totaliseur m

tote[2] vt Fam (carry) trimbal(l)er

totem pole [ˈtəʊtəmˈpəʊl] n totem m

totter [ˈtɒtə(r)] vi also Fig chanceler; **to t. in/out** entrer/sortir d'un pas chancelant

toucan [ˈtuːkæn] n toucan m

touch [tʌtʃ] **1** n (a) (act of touching) toucher m, contact m; **I felt a t. on my arm** j'ai senti qu'on me touchait le bras; **it was t. and go whether...** il n'était pas certain que... + subjunctive
(b) (sense) toucher m; (feel) contact m; **hard/soft to the t.** dur/doux au toucher; **he's lost his t.** il a perdu la main

(c) (detail) **there were some nice touches in the film** il y avait quelques bons passages dans le film
(d) (small amount) pointe f; **a t. (too) strong/short** un peu trop fort(e)/court(e); **to have a t. of flu** être un peu grippé(e)
(e) (communication) **to be/get in t. with sb** être/se mettre en contact avec qn; **to stay in/lose t. with sb** rester en/perdre contact avec qn
(f) (in football, rugby) **in t.** en touche; **t. judge** juge m de touche
2 vt (physically, emotionally) toucher; (interfere with) toucher à; **to t. bottom** (of ship, economy) toucher le fond; Fam **t. wood!** je touche du bois!; **I never t. alcohol** je ne touche jamais à l'alcool; **you haven't touched your meal** tu n'as pas touché à ton repas; **the law can't t. her** la loi ne peut rien contre elle; Fig **there's nothing to t. it** c'est sans égal; **there's nothing to t. her** elle est imbattable

▶**touch down** vi (of plane) atterrir

▶**touch on** vt insep aborder

▶**touch up** vt sep (a) (picture) retoucher (b) Br Fam (molest) peloter

touchdown [ˈtʌtʃdaʊn] n (a) (of plane) atterrissage m (b) (in American football) but m

touched [tʌtʃt] adj (a) (moved) touché(e), ému(e) (b) Fam (mad) toqué(e)

touching [ˈtʌtʃɪŋ] adj (moving) touchant(e), émouvant(e)

touchline [ˈtʌtʃlaɪn] n ligne f de touche

touch-sensitive screen [ˈtʌtʃˈsensɪtɪvˈskriːn] n Comptr écran m tactile

touchstone [ˈtʌtʃstəʊn] n pierre f de touche

touch-type [ˈtʌtʃtaɪp] vi taper au toucher

touchy [ˈtʌtʃɪ] adj (subject) délicat(e); (person) susceptible (about à propos de)

tough [tʌf] **1** adj (a) (strict, severe) dur(e); (resistant) résistant(e), solide; Fam **a t. guy** un dur à cuire; **to get t. (with sb)** se montrer plus sévère (avec qn) (b) (difficult) dur(e), difficile; (unfair) dur(e); Fam **t. luck!** pas de chance!; Ironic **tant pis!**
2 adv **to act t.** jouer au dur
3 n dur(e) m,f

toughen [ˈtʌfən] vt (person, skin) endurcir; (penalties, conditions) durcir; **toughened glass** verre m trempé

toughness [ˈtʌfnɪs] n (of meat, skin, conditions) dureté f; (of task) difficulté f; (of person) (strength) force f; (hardness) dureté f

toupee [ˈtuːpeɪ] n postiche m

tour [tʊə(r)] **1** n (by tourist) voyage m; (of building, town) visite f; (by pop group, theatre company) tournée f; **to go on a t.** (of tourist) faire un voyage organisé; **to go on t.** (of pop group, theatre company) partir en tournée; Mil **t. of duty** service m; **t. of inspection** tournée f d'inspection; **t. guide** (person) guide mf; **t. operator** voyagiste m
2 vt (country, hospital) visiter; (of pop group, theatre company) être en tournée à/en
3 vi (of tourist) faire du tourisme, voyager; (of pop group, theatre company) être en tournée

tour de force [ˈtʊədəˈfɔːs] n tour m de force

tourism [ˈtʊərɪzəm] n tourisme m

tourist [ˈtʊərɪst] n touriste mf; **t. attraction** site m touristique; **t. class** classe f touriste; **t. (information) office** syndicat m d'initiative, office m du tourisme; Fam **t. trap** piège m à touristes

tournament ['tʊənəmənt] *n* tournoi *m*

tourniquet ['tʊənɪkeɪ] *n Med* garrot *m*

tousle ['taʊzəl] *vt* ébouriffer

tout [taʊt] **1** *n* (*ticket*) **t.** revendeur(euse) *m,f* de billets (*au marché noir*)

2 *vt* (*tickets, goods*) revendre

3 *vi* **to t. for trade** racoler des clients

tow [taʊ] **1** *n* **to give sb a t.** remorquer qn; **on t.** en remorque; *Fam* **to have someone in t.** avoir qn dans son sillage; **t. truck** dépanneuse *f*

2 *vt* remorquer; **to t. a car away** enlever une voiture

toward [tə'wɔːd] = **towards**

towards [tə'wɔːdz] *prep* (**a**) (*in space, time*) vers (**b**) (*directed at*) (*of feelings, behaviour*) envers (**c**) (*contributing to*) **to contribute t.** the cost of sth participer au coût de qch; **15% of the budget will go t. improving safety** 15% du budget sera destiné à l'amélioration de la sécurité

towbar ['taʊbɑː(r)] *n* barre *f* de remorquage

towel ['taʊəl] **1** *n* serviette *f* (de toilette); **t. rail** porte-serviette *m*

2 *vt* **to t. oneself (dry)** se sécher, s'essuyer

towelling ['taʊəlɪŋ] *n* tissu-éponge *m*

tower ['taʊə(r)] **1** *n* tour *f*; *Fig* **a t. of strength** un roc; *Br* **t. block** tour; *Comptr* **t. system** tour

2 *vi* **to t. over sb/sth** dominer qn/qch

towering ['taʊərɪŋ] *adj* immense

town [taʊn] *n* ville *f*; **to go into t.** aller en ville; **to go out on the t.** faire la fête en ville; *Fam Fig* **to go to t. (on sth)** mettre le paquet (sur qch); **t. centre** centre-ville *m*; **t. clerk** secrétaire *mf* de mairie; **t. council** conseil *m* municipal; **t. hall** mairie *f*; **t. planner** urbaniste *mf*; **t. planning** urbanisme *m*

townsfolk ['taʊnzfəʊk] *npl* citadins *mpl*

township ['taʊnʃɪp] *n* (*in North America*) municipalité *f*; (*in South Africa*) township *f*

townspeople ['taʊnzpiːpəl] *npl* citadins *mpl*

towpath ['taʊpɑːθ] *n* chemin *m* de halage

towrope ['taʊrəʊp] *n* câble *m* de remorque

toxic ['tɒksɪk] *adj* toxique

toxin ['tɒksɪn] *n* toxine *f*

toy [tɔɪ] **1** *n* jouet *m*; **t. soldier** petit soldat *m*; **t. shop** magasin *m* de jouets

2 *vi* **to t. with sb** jouer avec qn; **to t. with an idea** caresser une idée; **to t. with sb's affections** jouer avec les sentiments de qn

toyboy ['tɔɪbɔɪ] *n Fam* jeune amant *m* (*d'une femme plus âgée*)

trace [treɪs] **1** *n* trace *f*; **without t.** sans laisser de traces; *Chem* **t. element** oligo-élément *m*

2 *vt* (**a**) (*diagram, picture*) tracer (**b**) (*person*) retrouver (la trace de); (*development, history*) retracer

trachea [trə'kiːə] (*pl* **tracheae** [trə'kiːiː]) *n Anat* trachée *f*

track [træk] **1** *n* (**a**) (*mark*) trace *f*; (*trail*) piste *f* (**b**) (*path*) piste *f*, chemin *m*; (*in athletics*) piste *f*; *Sp* **t. and field events** épreuves *fpl* d'athlétisme; *Fig* **t. record** passé *m*; **t. shoes** chaussures *fpl* d'athlétisme (**c**) (*on record, CD*) morceau *m* (**d**) (*of tank, tractor*) chenille *f* (**e**) (*railway line*) voie *f* (**f**) (*idioms*) **to be on the right t.** être sur la bonne voie; **to keep t. of sth** surveiller qch; **to lose t. of sb** perdre qn de vue; **I've lost t. of how much money I've spent** je ne sais plus combien d'argent j'ai dépensé; **to stop sb in his tracks** stopper qn net; *Fam* **to make tracks** filer, mettre les voiles

2 *vt* (*animal*) suivre à la trace; (*missile*) suivre la trajectoire de; (*person*) traquer

▶**track down** *vt sep* (*locate*) trouver

tracked [trækt] *adj* (*vehicle*) chenillé(e)

tracker dog ['trækə'dɒg] *n* chien *m* policier

tracksuit ['træksjuːt] *n* survêtement *m*; **t. top** veste *f* de survêtement; **t. trousers** *or* **bottoms** pantalon *m* de survêtement

tract¹ [trækt] *n* (**a**) (*of land*) étendue *f* (**b**) *Anat* (*respiratory, digestive*) appareil *m*

tract² *n* (*pamphlet*) tract *m*

tractable ['træktəbəl] *adj* (*person, animal*) docile

traction ['trækʃən] *n* (*force*) traction *f*; *Med* **to be in t.** être en extension; **t. engine** locomobile *f*

tractor ['træktə(r)] *n* (*vehicle*) tracteur *m*; *Comptr* **t. feed** alimentation *f* par entraînement

trade [treɪd] **1** *n* (**a**) *Com* (*commerce*) commerce *m*; **t. association** association *f* professionnelle; **t. deficit** déficit *m* commercial; **t. discount** remise *f* professionnelle; **t. embargo** embargo *m* commercial; **t. fair** foire *f* ou exposition *f* commerciale; **t. gap** déficit commercial; **t. name** (*of product*) nom *m* de marque; (*of firm*) raison *f* commerciale; *also Fig* **t. secret** secret *m* de fabrication; *Geog* **t. winds** alizés *mpl* (**b**) (*swap*) échange *m*; **to do a t.** faire un échange (**c**) (*profession*) métier *m*; **he's a plumber by t.** il est plombier (de son métier); **t. union** syndicat *m*; **t. unionist** syndicaliste *mf*

2 *vt* **to t. sth (for sth)** échanger qch (contre qch); **to t. places with sb** changer de place avec qn; **to t. insults/blows** échanger des insultes/coups

3 *vi* commercer, faire du commerce

▶**trade in** *vt sep* faire reprendre

▶**trade on** *vt insep* (*exploit*) profiter de

trade-in ['treɪdɪn] *n* reprise *f*

trademark ['treɪdmɑːk] *n* marque *f* (de fabrique); *Fig* signe *m* distinctif

trade-off ['treɪdɒf] *n* compromis *m*

trader ['treɪdə(r)] *n* commerçant(e) *m,f*, marchand(e) *m,f*; (*on stock exchange*) opérateur(trice) *m,f*

tradesman ['treɪdzmən] *n* commerçant(e) *m,f*

trading ['treɪdɪŋ] *n* **t. partner** partenaire *m* commercial; **t. post** comptoir *m* commercial; **t. stamp** timbre-prime *m*

tradition [trə'dɪʃən] *n* tradition *f*

traditional [trə'dɪʃənəl] *adj* traditionnel(elle)

traditionalist [trə'dɪʃənəlɪst] *n & adj* traditionaliste *mf*

traffic ['træfɪk] **1** *n* (**a**) (*vehicles*) circulation *f*, trafic *m*; **t. cone** cône *m* de signalisation; *Fam* **t. cop** agent *m* de la circulation; **t. island** refuge *m*; **t. jam** embouteillage *m*; *Br* **t. lights** feux *mpl* (tricolores *ou* de signalisation); **t. police** police *f* de la route; *Br* **t. warden** contractuel(elle) *m,f* (**b**) (*trade*) trafic *m*

2 *vi* faire le trafic de

3 *vi* faire du trafic (**in** de)

trafficker ['træfɪkə(r)] *n* trafiquant(e) *m,f*

tragedy ['trædʒɪdɪ] *n* tragédie *f*

tragic ['trædʒɪk] *adj* tragique

tragically ['trædʒɪklɪ] *adv* tragiquement

trail [treɪl] **1** *n* (**a**) (*of smoke, blood*) traînée *f*; **to be on the t. of sb/sth** être sur les traces *ou* la piste de qn/qch (**b**) (*path*) sentier *m*, piste *f*; **t. bike** moto *f* de cross

2 *vt* (*drag*) traîner

3 *vi* (a) *(drag)* traîner (b) *(move slowly)* se traîner (c) *(in sport, contest)* to be trailing (behind) être mené(e)

►**trail away, trail off** *vi (of voice)* se taire; *(of sound)* s'arrêter

trailblazer ['treɪlbleɪzə(r)] *n* pionnier(ère), *m,f*

trailer ['treɪlə(r)] *n* (a) *(vehicle)* remorque *f; Am (caravan)* camping-car *m* (b) *(for film, TV programme)* bande-annonce *f*

train [treɪn] **1** *n* (a) *(means of transport)* train *m* (b) *(series)* suite *f*, enchaînement *m*; **t. of thought** enchaînement d'idées (c) *(retinue)* suite *f* (d) *(of dress)* traîne *f*

2 *vt* (a) *(person)* former; *(animal)* dresser; **to t. sb for sth/to do sth** former qn à qch/à faire qch (b) *(gun, telescope)* braquer (on sur)

3 *vi (of athlete, soldier)* s'entraîner; **to t. as a nurse/teacher** suivre une formation d'infirmière/de professeur

trained [treɪnd] *adj (animal)* dressé(e) (b) *(teacher, nurse)* diplômé(e) (c) *(eye, ear)* exercé(e)

trainee [treɪ'niː] *n* stagiaire *mf*

trainer ['treɪnə(r)] *n* (a) *(of athlete, team, racehorse)* entraîneur *m; (of animals)* dresseur(euse) *m,f* (b) *(shoe)* chaussure *f* de sport (c) **t. (aircraft)** avion-école *m*

training ['treɪnɪŋ] *n* (a) *(in sport)* entraînement *m*; *(for job)* formation *f*; **to be in t. (for)** *(of athlete, team)* s'entraîner (pour); **to be out of t.** manquer d'entraînement; **t. course** stage *m* (de formation); **t. officer** officier *m* instructeur

trainload ['treɪnləʊd] *n* **a t.** of un train plein de

trainspotter ['treɪnspɒtə(r)] *n Br* = personne dont le passe-temps est de noter les numéros des trains; *Fam Pej* **he's a bit of a t.** il est vraiment ringard

traipse [treɪps] *vi Fam* traîner

trait [treɪt] *n* trait *m* (de caractère)

traitor ['treɪtə(r)] *n* traître(esse) *m,f*

trajectory [trə'dʒektəri] *n* trajectoire *f*

tram [træm] *n Br* tramway *m*

tramline ['træmlaɪn] *n* ligne *f* de tramway; **tramlines** *(in tennis)* lignes *fpl* de côté

tramp [træmp] **1** *n* (a) *(vagabond)* clochard(e) *m,f* (b) *Am very Fam (immoral woman)* traînée *f* (c) **t. (steamer)** tramp *m* (d) *(walk)* promenade *f*

2 *vt (country)* arpenter, parcourir; **to t. the streets** battre le pavé

3 *vi* marcher (d'un pas lourd)

trample ['træmpəl] **1** *vt* piétiner; **to t. sth underfoot** fouler qch aux pieds

2 *vi* **to t. on sb/sth** piétiner qn/qch

trampoline ['træmpə'liːn] *n* trampoline *m*

trance [trɑːns] *n* transe *f*; **to go into a t.** entrer *ou* se mettre en transe

tranquil ['træŋkwɪl] *adj* tranquille, calme

tranquillity, *Am* **tranquility** [træŋ'kwɪltɪ] *n* tranquillité *f*, calme *m*

tranquillizer, *Am* **tranquilizer** ['træŋkwɪlaɪzə(r)] *n* tranquillisant *m*, calmant *m*

transaction [træn'zækʃən] *n* transaction *f*, opération *f*

transatlantic [trænzət'læntɪk] *adj* transatlantique

transcend [træn'send] *vt (go beyond)* transcender; *(be superior to)* surpasser

transcendental [trænsen'dentəl] *adj* transcendantal(e); **t. meditation** méditation *f* transcendantale

transcontinental [trænzkɒntɪ'nentəl] *adj* transcontinental(e)

transcribe [træn'skraɪb] *vt* transcrire

transcript ['trænskrɪpt] *n* transcription *f*

transcription [træns'krɪpʃən] *n* transcription *f*

transfer 1 *n* ['trænsfɜː(r)] (a) *(move)* transfert *m*; *(of employee)* mutation *f*; *(of power)* passation *f*; **t. fee** *(for footballer)* prime *f* de transfert; **t. lounge** *(in airport)* salle *f* de transit; **t. passenger** passager *m* en transit; *Comptr* **t. speed** vitesse *f* de transfert (b) *(sticker)* transfert *m*

2 *vt* [træns'fɜː(r)] transférer; *(employee)* muter; *(attention, affection)* déplacer

3 *vi* être transféré(e) (to dans); *(between planes, trains)* changer

transferable [træns'fɜːrəbəl] *adj* transmissible; **not t.** *(on ticket)* titre de transport nominal

transfigure [træns'fɪgə(r)] *vt* transfigurer

transfix [træns'fɪks] *vt* transpercer; *Fig* **to be transfixed with fear** être pétrifié(e) par la peur

transform [træns'fɔːm] *vt* transformer (into en)

transformation [trænsfə'meɪʃən] *n* transformation *f*

transformer [træns'fɔːmə(r)] *n Elec* transformateur *m*

transfusion [træns'fjuːʒən] *n* **(blood) t.** transfusion *f* (sanguine)

transgress [trænz'gres] *Formal* **1** *vt (law)* transgresser, enfreindre

2 *vi (violate law)* transgresser la loi; *(sin)* pécher

transient ['trænzɪənt] *adj* éphémère

transistor [træn'zɪstə(r)] *n Elec* transistor *m*; **t. (radio)** transistor

transit ['trænzɪt] *n* transit *m*; **in t.** en transit; **t. camp** camp *m* de transit; **t. visa** visa *m* de transit

transition [træn'zɪʃən] *n* transition *f*; **the t. from sth to sth** le passage de qch à qch

transitional [træn'zɪʃənəl] *adj* transitoire, de transition

transitive [trænz'ɪtɪv] *adj Gram* transitif(ive)

transitory ['trænzɪtəri] *adj* transitoire

translate [trænz'leɪt] **1** *vt* traduire (from/into de/en); *Fig* **to t. one's ideas into action** mettre ses idées en pratique

2 *vi (of person)* faire de la traduction; *(of word, expression)* se traduire (as par)

translation [trænz'leɪʃən] *n (of language)* traduction *f*

translator [trænz'leɪtə(r)] *n* traducteur(trice) *m,f*

transliterate [trænz'lɪtəreɪt] *vt* transcrire

translucent [trænz'luːsənt] *adj* translucide

transmission [trænz'mɪʃən] *n (action)* transmission *f*; *(TV, radio programme)* émission *f*; **t. shaft** *(in vehicle)* arbre *m* de transmission

transmit [trænz'mɪt] *vt* transmettre; *(TV, radio programme)* diffuser

transmitter [trænz'mɪtə(r)] *n (emitter)* émetteur *m*; *(relay station)* réémetteur *m*

transparent [træns'pærənt] *adj* (a) *(see-through)* transparent(e) (b) *(obvious)* évident(e)

transpire [træns'paɪə(r)] **1** *vt (become apparent)* **it transpired that...** il s'est avéré que...; **she transpired to be...** elle s'est avérée être...

2 *vi (happen)* arriver, se passer

transplant 1 *n* ['trænsplɑːnt] *(of organ)* transplantation *f*, greffe *f*

2 vt [træns'plɑ:nt] *n* (a) (organ) transplanter, greffer (b) (population) transplanter

transport 1 *n* ['trænspɔ:t] transport *m*; *Br* t. café routier *m* (restaurant); t. costs frais *mpl* de transport
2 vt [træns'pɔ:t] transporter

transportation [trænspɔ:'teɪʃən] *n* transport *m*; *Hist* (as punishment) transportation *f*

transporter [træns'pɔ:tə(r)] *n* (vehicle) camion *m* pour transport d'automobiles

transpose [træns'pəʊz] vt transposer

transsexual [træn(z)'seksjuəl] *n* transsexuel(elle) *m,f*

Transvaal ['trɑ:nzvɑ:l] *n* the T. le Transvaal

transverse ['trænzvɜ:s] *adj* transversal(e)

transvestite [trænz'vestaɪt] *n* travesti *m*

trap [træp] **1** *n* (a) (in hunting) & Fig piège *m*; to set a t. tendre un piège; Fig to **walk** or **fall straight into the t.** tomber en plein dans le piège (b) very Fam (mouth) gueule *f*
2 vt piéger, prendre au piège; to **t. sb into saying/ doing sth** faire dire/faire qch à qn en usant de ruse

trapdoor ['træp'dɔ:(r)] *n* trappe *f*

trapeze [trə'pi:z] *n* trapèze *m*; t. **artist** trapéziste *mf*

trapper ['træpə(r)] *n* trappeur *m*

trappings ['træpɪŋz] *npl* signes *mpl* extérieurs

trash [træʃ] **1** *n* (worthless objects) camelote *f*; *Am* (refuse) ordures *fpl*; Fam **that book/film is a load of t.** ce livre/ film est nul; *Am* t. **can** poubelle *f*
2 vt Fam (a) (vandalize) saccager (b) (criticize) descendre en flammes

trashy ['træʃɪ] *adj* Fam à la noix

trauma ['trɔ:mə] *n* traumatisme *m*

traumatic [trɔ:'mætɪk] *adj* traumatisant(e)

traumatize ['trɔ:mətaɪz] vt traumatiser

travail ['træveɪl] *n* Lit labeur *m*

travel ['trævəl] **1** *n* voyage *m*; **on my travels** au cours de mes voyages; **I spend half my money on t.** (to and from work) la moitié de mon argent part dans les transports; t. **agency** agence *f* de voyages; t. **agent** agent *m* de voyages; t. **documents** titre *m* de transport; t. **writer** auteur *m* de récits de voyage
2 vt (road, country) parcourir
3 vi (a) (of person) voyager; (vehicle, of light, sound, electricity) se déplacer; **wine doesn't t. well** le vin supporte mal d'être transporté; Fam **(good) news travels fast** les nouvelles vont vite

traveller, *Am* **traveler** ['trævələ(r)] *n* voyageur(euse) *m,f*; *Br* **(new age)** t. voyageur new age; t.'s **cheque** chèque *m* de voyage

travelling, *Am* **traveling** ['trævəlɪŋ] **1** *n* déplacement *m*; t. **bag** sac *m* de voyage; t. **companion** compagnon *m* de voyage; t. **expenses** frais *mpl* de déplacement
2 *adj* (performer, circus) itinérant(e); t. **salesman** voyageur *m* de commerce

traverse [trə'vɜ:s] vt Lit traverser

travesty ['trævəstɪ] *n* travestissement *m*; t. **of justice** simulacre *m* de justice

trawl [trɔ:l] **1** *n* (a) (net) chalut *m* (b) Fig (search) to **carry out** or **make a t. through sth** passer qch au crible
2 vt (a) (sea) aller à la pêche au chalut en (b) Fig (search through) passer au crible
3 vi (a) (fish) pêcher au chalut (b) Fig to **t. through sth** passer qch au crible

trawler ['trɔ:lə(r)] *n* (ship) chalutier *m*

tray [treɪ] *n* plateau *m*; (in office) corbeille *f*

treacherous ['tretʃərəs] *adj* traître

treachery ['tretʃərɪ] *n* traîtrise *f*

treacle ['tri:kəl] *n* mélasse *f*

tread [tred] **1** (vt pt **trod** [trod], pp **trodden** ['trodən]) marcher sur; to **t. sth underfoot** fouler qch aux pieds; to **t. sth into the carpet** mettre qch sur le tapis (avec ses chaussures); to **t. the boards** (appear on stage) monter sur les planches; to **t. grapes** fouler le raisin; to **t. water** faire du surplace; Fig (of company) se maintenir à flot
2 vi marcher (on sur); also Fig to **t. on sb's toes** marcher sur les pieds de qn; Fig to **t. carefully** or **warily** y aller doucement
3 *n* (a) (sound of footstep) pas *m* (b) (of tyre) chape *f*

treadmill ['tredmɪl] *n* (in gym) tapis *m* roulant de jogging; (in prison) = roue ou manège auxquels étaient attachés les prisonniers; Fig (routine) routine *f*

treason ['tri:zən] *n* trahison *f*

treasonable ['tri:zənəbəl] *adj* qui constitue un acte de trahison

treasure ['treʒə(r)] **1** *n* also Fig trésor *m*; t. **hunt** chasse *f* au trésor
2 vt (person, possession) tenir beaucoup à; (memory) chérir

treasurer ['treʒərə(r)] *n* trésorier(ère) *m,f*

treasure-trove ['treʒərəʊv] *n* Law & Fig trésor *m*

treasury ['treʒərɪ] *n* trésorerie *f*; **the T.** (government department) ≃ le ministère des Finances; Fin t. **bond** ≃ bon *m* du Trésor

treat [tri:t] **1** *n* (pleasure) plaisir *m*; (gift) cadeau *m*; to **give sb a t.** faire plaisir à qn; **it's my t.** (I'm paying) c'est moi qui régale; also Ironic **you've got a real t. in store** attends-toi à une belle surprise; Fam **to work a t.** marcher à merveille
2 vt (a) (person, illness, metal) traiter; to **t. sth as a joke** prendre qch à la rigolade (b) (give present to) to **t. sb to sth** offrir qch à qn; to **t. oneself to sth** s'offrir qch; **I'll t. you** (pay for you) je t'invite; Ironic **she treated us to one of her tantrums** nous avons eu droit à une de ses colères
3 vi Formal (negotiate) to **t. with sb/sth** traiter avec qn/ qch

treatise ['tri:tɪs] *n* traité *m*

treatment ['tri:tmənt] *n* traitement *m*; Fam **to give sb the t.** rosser qn

treaty ['tri:tɪ] *n* (international) traité *m*; (between individuals) accord *m*, contrat *m*

treble ['trebəl] **1** *n* Mus (person, voice) soprano *m*
2 *adj* (triple) triple; Mus t. **clef** clef *f* de sol
3 vt & vi tripler

tree [tri:] *n* arbre *m*; Fig **at the top of the t.** en haut de l'échelle; *Am* Fam **to be out of one's t.** débloquer; t. **trunk** tronc *m* d'arbre

treetop ['tri:top] *n* cime *f* d'un arbre

trek [trek] **1** *n* (long walk) randonnée *f* (pédestre); Fig **it's quite a t. to the shops** ça fait loin à pied jusqu'aux magasins
2 vi faire de la randonnée; Fig to **t. to the shops/home** se taper le chemin à pied jusqu'aux magasins/jusqu'à chez soi

trellis ['trelɪs] *n* treillis *m*, treillage *m*

tremble ['trembəl] **1** *n* tremblement *m*
2 vi trembler (with de)

tremendous [trɪ'mendəs] *adj* (a) (enormous) énorme (b) Fam (excellent) formidable

tremendously [trɪ'mendəslɪ] *adv (very)* extrêmement

tremor ['tremə(r)] *n* tremblement *m*

tremulous ['tremjʊləs] *adj (voice, hand)* tremblant(e); *(person, smile)* timide

trench [trentʃ] *n (ditch)* fossé *m; Mil* tranchée *f;* **t. coat** trench-coat *m;* **t. warfare** guerre *f* de tranchées

trenchant ['tren(t)ʃənt] *adj* tranchant(e)

trend [trend] *n (tendency)* tendance *f; (fashion)* mode *f;* **to set** *or* **start a t.** lancer une mode

trendsetter ['trendsetə(r)] *n* lanceur(euse) *m,f* de mode

trendy ['trendɪ] *Br Fam n & adj* branché(e) *m,f*

trepidation [trepɪ'deɪʃən] *n Formal* inquiétude *f*

trespass ['trespəs] *vi Law* s'introduire illégalement dans une propriété privée

trespasser ['trespəsə(r)] *n Law* intrus(e) *m,f;* **trespassers will be prosecuted** *(sign)* défense d'entrer sous peine de poursuites

tresses ['tresɪz] *npl Lit (hair)* chevelure *f*

trestle ['tresəl] *n* tréteau *m;* **t. table** table *f* à tréteaux

trial ['traɪəl] *n* **(a)** *Law* procès *m;* **to bring sb to t.** traduire qn en justice; **to be on t. (for)** passer en jugement (pour) **(b)** *(test)* essai *m;* **on t.** à l'essai; **by t. and error** par tâtonnements; **t. period** période *f* d'essai; **t. run** essai; **t. separation** *(of couple)* séparation *f* à l'essai **(c)** *(ordeal)* épreuve *f*

triangle ['traɪæŋgəl] *n* triangle *m*

triangular [traɪ'æŋgjʊlə(r)] *adj* triangulaire

triathlon [traɪ'æθlɒn] *n* triathlon *m*

tribal ['traɪbəl] *adj* tribal(e)

tribalism ['traɪbəlɪzəm] *n* tribalisme *m*

tribe [traɪb] *n* tribu *f*

tribesman ['traɪbzmən] *n* membre *m* d'une tribu

tribulation [trɪbjʊ'leɪʃən] *n Formal* malheur *m*

tribunal [traɪ'bjuːnəl] *n Law* tribunal *m*

tributary ['trɪbjʊtərɪ] *n (of river)* affluent *m*

tribute ['trɪbjuːt] *n* **(a)** *(homage)* hommage *m;* **to pay t.** **to** rendre hommage à **(b)** *(testimony)* **our success is a t.** **to all your hard work** c'est grâce à vos efforts soutenus que nous avons réussi

trice [traɪs] *n* **in a t.** en un clin d'œil

triceps ['traɪseps] *n Anat* triceps *m*

trick [trɪk] *n* **1** *n* **(a)** *(ruse)* tour *m; (practical joke)* farce *f;* **to** **play a t. on sb** jouer un tour à qn; *(practical joke)* faire une farce à qn; **t. photography** truquage *m;* **t. question** question *f* piège **(b)** *(by magician)* tour *m* **(c)** *(in card game)* pli *m* **(d)** *(idiom)* **to do the t.** marcher; **to know all the** **tricks** connaître toutes les astuces; **the tricks of the** **trade** les ficelles du métier; **she doesn't miss a t.** rien ne lui échappe; **he's been up to his old tricks again** il a encore fait des siennes; *Fam* **how's tricks?** comment vas-tu?

2 *vt (person)* duper; **to t. sb into doing sth** amener qn à faire qch par la ruse

trickery ['trɪkərɪ] *n* duperie *f*, ruse *f*

trickle ['trɪkəl] **1** *vi (liquid)* faire couler goutte à goutte

2 *vi (of liquid)* couler goutte à goutte; **to t. in/out** *(of* *people)* entrer/sortir au compte-gouttes

3 *n (of liquid)* filet *m; (of complaints, letters)* petit nombre *m;* **t.-down theory** = théorie selon laquelle la richesse de quelques-uns finira par profiter à toute la société

tricky ['trɪkɪ] *adj* délicat(e)

tricycle ['traɪsɪkəl] *n* tricycle *m*

trident ['traɪdənt] *n* trident *m*

tried-and-tested ['traɪdən'testɪd] *adj* qui a fait ses preuves

trier ['traɪə(r)] *n Fam* **to be a t.** être persévérant(e)

trifle ['traɪfəl] *n* **(a)** *(insignificant thing)* brouille *f* **(b)** **a t.** **wide/short** un tantinet trop large/court(e) **(c)** *Br* *(dessert)* = dessert où alternent une couche de génoise imbibée d'alcool et de fruits en gelée et une couche de crème anglaise, et recouvert de chantilly

▸**trifle with** *vt insep* plaisanter avec

trifling ['traɪflɪŋ] *adj* insignifiant(e)

trigger ['trɪgə(r)] **1** *n (of gun)* détente *f; Fig (of change,* *decision)* élément *m* déclencheur; *Fam* **to be t. happy** avoir la gâchette facile

2 *vt* déclencher

▸**trigger off** *vt sep* déclencher

trigonometry [trɪgə'nɒmɪtrɪ] *n* trigonométrie *f*

trilby ['trɪlbɪ] *n Br (chapeau m en)* feutre *m*

trill [trɪl] **1** *n* trille *m*

2 *vi* triller

trillion ['trɪljən] *n* trillion *m; Fam* **trillions of** *(lots of)* un milliard de

trilogy ['trɪlədʒɪ] *n (pl* **trilogies)** *n* trilogie *f*

trim [trɪm] **1** *adj* **(a)** *(neat)* soigné(e) **(b)** *(slim)* svelte

2 *vt (pt & pp* **trimmed)** **(a)** *(cut)* *(hair)* rafraîchir; *(hedge)* tailler, élaguer; *(meat)* parer; *(budget)* réduire **(b)** *(decorate)* orner, décorer **(with de)**

3 *n* **(a)** **to give sb's hair a t.** faire une coupe d'entretien à qn; **to give the hedge a t.** tailler la haie **(b)** **to be/** **keep in t.** *(keep fit)* être en/garder la forme

▸**trim down** *vt sep (text)* élaguer; *(company, expenditure)* réduire

trimaran ['traɪməræn] *n* trimaran *m*

trimester [trɪ'mestə(r)] *n* trimestre *m*

trimming ['trɪmɪŋ] *n* **(a)** *(on clothes)* garniture *f* **(b)** **trimmings** *(of meal)* accompagnements *mpl* traditionnels

Trinidad and Tobago ['trɪnɪdædəntə'beɪgəʊ] *n* Trinité-et-Tobago

Trinity ['trɪnɪtɪ] *n Rel* **the T.** la Trinité

trinket ['trɪŋkɪt] *n* babiole *f*

trio ['triːəʊ] *n (pl* **trios)** *n* trio *m*

trip [trɪp] **1** *n* **(a)** *(journey)* voyage *m; (for one day)* excursion *f* **(b)** *Fam (on drugs)* trip *m* **(c)** *(stumble)* faux pas *m;* **t. wire** fil *m* de détente

2 *vt (pt & pp* **tripped)** **(a)** *(make stumble)* faire un croche-pied à **(b)** **to a switch** déclencher un interrupteur

3 *vi* **(a)** *(stumble)* trébucher **(b)** *(step lightly)* marcher d'un pas léger; **to t. off the tongue** *(of name)* bien couler **(c)** *Fam (on drugs)* **to be tripping** être en plein trip

▸**trip over 1** *vt insep* trébucher sur

2 *vi* trébucher

▸**trip up 1** *vt sep (cause to stumble)* faire un croche-pied à; *Fig (cause to make mistake)* désarçonner

2 *vi (stumble)* trébucher

tripe [traɪp] *n (food)* tripes *fpl; Fam (nonsense)* foutaises *fpl*

triple ['trɪpəl] **1** *adj* triple; **t. jump** triple saut *m*

2 *adv* **t. the number/amount** trois fois le nombre/la quantité

3 *vt & vi* tripler

triplet ['trɪplɪt] *n* **(a)** *(person)* triplé(e) *m,f* **(b)** *Mus* triolet *m*

triplicate ['trɪplɪkət] *n* **in t.** en trois exemplaires

tripod ['traipɒd] n trépied m

Tripoli ['trɪpəlɪ] n Tripoli

trite [trait] adj banal(e)

triumph ['traɪəmf] 1 n triomphe m; **in t.** triomphant(e) 2 vi triompher (**over** de)

triumphant [traɪ'ʌmfənt] adj triomphant(e)

triumvirate [traɪ'ʌmvɪrɪt] n triumvirat m

trivet ['trɪvɪt] n (on open fire) trépied m; (stand) = support métallique surélevé pour plats chauds

trivia ['trɪvɪə] npl (unimportant details) détails mpl; (useless information) futilités fpl

trivial ['trɪvɪəl] adj (detail, matter) sans importance, insignifiant(e); (person) superficiel(elle)

trivialize ['trɪvɪəlaɪz] vt banaliser

trod [trɒd] pt of **tread**

trodden ['trɒdən] pp of **tread**

Trojan ['trəʊdʒən] Hist 1 n Troyen(enne) m,f 2 adj de Troie, troyen(enne); **T. Horse** cheval m de Troie; **the T. War** la guerre de Troie

troll [trəʊl] n troll m

trolley ['trɒlɪ] (pl trolleys) n Br chariot m; Fam **to be off one's t.** débloquer

trolley car ['trɒlɪ'kɑː(r)] n Am tramway m

trollop ['trɒləp] n Old-fashioned or Hum gourgandine f, catin f

trombone [trɒm'bəʊn] n trombone m

trombonist [trɒm'bəʊnɪst] n trombone m

troop [truːp] 1 n (a) troops (soldiers) troupes fpl (b) (of people) groupe m 2 vi **to t. in/out** entrer/sortir en groupe

trooper ['truːpə(r)] n (soldier) cavalier m; Am (mounted policeman) membre m de la police montée; Fam **to swear like a t.** jurer comme un charretier

trophy ['trəʊfɪ] n trophée m

tropic ['trɒpɪk] n tropique m; **the tropics** les tropiques

tropical ['trɒpɪkəl] adj tropical(e)

trot [trɒt] 1 n trot m; **at a t.** au trot; Fam **on the t.** (consecutively) de suite; Fam **to have the trots** avoir la courante 2 vi (pt & pp trotted) (of horse) aller au trot; (of person) trotter

▶**trot out** vt sep Fam débiter

Trotskyism ['trɒtskɪɪzəm] n trotskisme m

Trotskyist ['trɒtskɪɪst], **Trotskyite** ['trɒtskɪaɪt] n & adj trotskiste mf

trotter ['trɒtə(r)] n (of pig) pied m

trouble ['trʌbəl] 1 n (a) (problem) ennui m; **to have t. with sb/sth** avoir des problèmes avec qn/qch; **to have t. doing sth** avoir du mal à faire qch; **to be in/get into t.** avoir/s'attirer des ennuis; **to get sb into t.** attirer des ennuis à qn; **to get sb out of t.** tirer qn d'affaire; **to make t. (for sb)** créer des ennuis (à qn); **it's more t. than it's worth** le jeu n'en vaut pas la chandelle; Fam **man/woman t.** ennuis mpl de cœur (b) (inconvenience) problème m; **to go to the t. of doing sth** se donner la peine de faire qch; **it's not worth the t.** ça n'en vaut pas la peine; (it's) no t. (ça ne pose) aucun problème (c) (disorder, unrest) troubles mpl; **t. spot** point m chaud 2 vt (worry) inquiéter; (inconvenience) déranger 3 vi **to t. to do sth** se donner la peine de faire qch

troubled ['trʌbəld] adj (person) inquiet(ète); (region) agité(e) de troubles; (period) troublé(e)

trouble-free ['trʌbəlfriː] adj sans souci

troublemaker ['trʌbəlmeɪkə(r)] n semeur(euse) m,f de troubles

troubleshooter ['trʌbəlʃuːtə(r)] n (for organizational problems) expert m; (for industrial disputes) conciliateur(trice) m,f; (for machines) dépanneur(euse) m,f

troublesome ['trʌbəlsəm] adj pénible

trough [trɒf] n (for food) mangeoire f; (for drink) abreuvoir m; (of wave, on graph) creux m; (in weather front) dépression f

trounce [traʊns] vt battre à plates coutures

troupe [truːp] n troupe f

trouser press ['traʊzə'pres] n presse-pantalon m

trousers ['traʊzəz] npl (a) Br pantalon m (b) (idioms) Fam **to wear the t.** porter la culotte; Fam **to be caught with one's t. down** être pris(e) en flagrant délit

trouser suit ['traʊzə'suːt] n tailleur-pantalon m

trousseau ['truːsəʊ] n trousseau m

trout [traʊt] (pl trout) n truite f

trowel ['traʊəl] n truelle f

truancy ['truːənsɪ] n absentéisme m scolaire

truant ['truːənt] n (pupil) élève m qui fait l'école buissonnière; **to play t.** faire l'école buissonnière

truce [truːs] n also Fig trêve f; **to call a t.** demander une trêve

truck [trʌk] 1 n (a) (lorry) camion m; **t. driver** conducteur(trice) m,f de camion, camionneur m; Am **t. farm** exploitation f maraîchère; **t. stop** relais m routier (b) (rail wagon) wagon m (c) Fam **to have no t. with sb/ sth** ne rien avoir à faire avec qn/qch 2 vt (goods) acheminer par camion 3 vi Am (drive a truck) être conducteur(trice) m,f de camion

trucker ['trʌkə(r)] n Am (truck driver) camionneur m

truculent ['trʌkjʊlənt] adj agressif(ive)

trudge [trʌdʒ] 1 n trajet m pénible 2 vi marcher péniblement, se traîner

true [truː] 1 adj (a) (not fictional) vrai(e); **to come t.** se réaliser; **to hold t. (for)** être vrai (de) (b) (genuine) véritable; **t. love** grand amour m; **t. north** le nord géographique (c) (faithful) fidèle; **to be t. to sb** être loyal(e) envers qn; **to be t. to sth** être fidèle à qch; **t. to life** fidèle à la réalité; **t. to form** ou **type** fidèle à soi-même (d) (accurate) exact(e) 2 n **out of t.** hors d'aplomb

truffle ['trʌfəl] n truffe f

truism ['truːɪzəm] n truisme m

truly ['truːlɪ] adv vraiment; **yours t.** (at end of letter) = je vous prie d'agréer, Madame/Monsieur, l'expression de mes sentiments distingués; Fam (myself) mézigue

trump [trʌmp] 1 n atout m; **spades are trumps** c'est atout pique; Fig **to play one's t. card** jouer son atout; Fam Fig **to turn up trumps** sauver la mise 2 vt couper à l'atout

trumped up ['trʌmptʌp] adj fabriqué(e)

trumpet ['trʌmpɪt] n trompette f; Fig **to blow one's own t.** vanter ses propres mérites 2 vt (proclaim) claironner 3 vi (of elephant) barrir

trumpeter ['trʌmpɪtə(r)] n trompettiste mf

truncate [trʌŋ'keɪt] vt tronquer

truncheon ['trʌn(t)ʃən] n Br matraque f

trundle ['trʌndəl] 1 *vt* pousser péniblement
2 *vi* rouler péniblement

trunk [trʌŋk] *n* (a) *(of tree, body)* tronc *m*; *Br* **t. call** appel *m* interurbain; *Br* **t. road** route *f* nationale (b) *(case)* malle *f* (c) *Am (of car)* coffre *m* (d) *(of elephant)* trompe *f* (e) **trunks** *(swimming costume)* slip *m* de bain

truss [trʌs] 1 *n* (a) *Med (for hernia)* bandage *m* herniaire (b) *(for roof, bridge)* ferme *f*
2 *vt (tie up)* ligoter

▶**truss up** *vt sep (person)* ligoter; *(chicken, turkey)* trousser

trust [trʌst] 1 *n* (a) *(faith)* confiance *f* (**in** en); **to put one's t. in sb/sth** se fier à qn/qch; **to take sth on t.** croire qch sur parole (b) *Law* **in t.** par fidéicommis; *Fin* **t. fund** fonds *m* en fidéicommis (c) *Com (group of companies)* trust *m*
2 *vt* (a) *(believe in)* faire confiance à; **to t. sb with sth** confier qch à qn; **to t. sb to do sth** laisser à qn le soin de faire qch; *Fam* **t. him to say that!** c'est bien de lui! (b) *Formal (hope)* **to t. (that)…** espérer que…
3 *vi* **to t. in sb/sth** faire confiance à qn/qch; **to t. to luck** s'en remettre au hasard

trusted ['trʌstɪd] *adj* de confiance

trustee [trʌs'tiː] *n* (a) *Law (of fund, property)* fidéicommissaire *m*; *(of charity)* administrateur(trice) *m,f*

trusting ['trʌstɪŋ] *adj* qui fait confiance aux gens

trustworthy ['trʌstwɜːðɪ] *adj (person)* digne de confiance; *(thing)* fiable

trusty ['trʌstɪ] *adj* fidèle

truth [truːθ] *n* vérité *f*; **to tell the t.** dire la vérité

truthful ['truːθfʊl] *adj (person)* sincère; *(story)* véridique

try [traɪ] 1 *vt (sample, attempt)* essayer; *(food, drink)* goûter (à); **to t. to do sth** essayer de faire qch; **I'll t. anything once** il faut tout essayer dans la vie (b) *Law (case, person)* juger (c) *(test)* tester; *(person)* mettre à l'épreuve; **to t. sb's patience** mettre la patience de qn à l'épreuve
2 *vi* essayer; **to t. harder** faire plus d'efforts; **just you t.!** essaie un peu pour voir!
3 *n* (a) *(attempt)* essai *m*; **to give sth a t.** essayer qch; **to have a t. at sth/at doing sth** essayer qch/de faire qch; **it's worth a t.** ça vaut le coup d'essayer (b) *(in rugby)* essai *m*

▶**try on** *vt sep* (a) *(clothes)* essayer (b) *Fam* **to t. it on (with sb)** tenter le coup (avec qn); *(sexually)* draguer (qn)

▶**try out** *vt sep* essayer; **to t. sth out on sb** expérimenter qch sur qn

trying ['traɪɪŋ] *adj* difficile

tsar [zɑː(r)] *n* tsar *m*

tsarist ['zɑːrɪst] *n & adj* tsariste *mf*

tsetse ['t(s)etsɪ] *n* **t. (fly)** (mouche *f*) tsé-tsé *f inv*

T-shirt ['tiːʃɜːt] *n* tee-shirt *m*

tub [tʌb] *n* (a) *(for washing clothes)* baquet *m*; *(bath)* baignoire *f* (b) *(for food, plants)* pot *m*

tuba ['tjuːbə] *n* tuba *m*

tubby ['tʌbɪ] *adj Fam* boulot(otte)

tube [tjuːb] *n* (a) *(cylindrical container)* tube *m*; *(pipe)* tuyau *m*; *Fam* **to go down the tubes** *(of money)* être foutu en l'air; *(of work, plan)* tomber à l'eau (b) *Br Fam* **the t.** *(underground railway)* le métro; **t. station** station *f* de métro (c) *Am Fam (TV)* télé *f*

tuber ['tjuːbə(r)] *n* tubercule *m*

tuberculosis [tjɔbɜːkjʊ'ləʊsɪs] *n* tuberculose *f*

tubing ['tjuːbɪŋ] *n* tuyaux *mpl*

tubular ['tjuːbjʊlə(r)] *adj* tubulaire; **t. bells** carillon *m*

TUC [tiːjuː'siː] *n Br (abbr* **Trades Union Congress)** = confédération des syndicats britanniques

tuck [tʌk] 1 *n* (a) *(in sewing)* pli *m* (b) *Br Fam (food)* sucreries *fpl*; **t. shop** *(in school)* boutique *f* de friandises (c) *(in cosmetic surgery) (for face)* lifting *m*
2 *vt* **to t. one's shirt into one's trousers** rentrer sa chemise dans son pantalon; **to t. sth under one's arm** mettre qch sous son bras; **to t. sb up in bed** border qn; **to t. sth into a drawer** glisser qch dans un tiroir

▶**tuck in** 1 *vt sep (sheets, child)* border; *(clothes)* rentrer
2 *vi Fam (start to eat)* attaquer

▶**tuck into** *vt insep Fam (meal)* attaquer

Tudor ['tjuːdə(r)] 1 *n Hist* **the Tudors** les Tudor
2 *adj* des Tudor

Tue(s) *(abbr* **Tuesday)** mardi

Tuesday ['tjuːzdɪ] *n* mardi *m*; *see also* **Saturday**

tuft [tʌft] *n* touffe *f*

tug [tʌg] 1 *vt (pt & pp* **tugged)** (a) *(pull)* tirer sur (b) *(tow)* remorquer
2 *vi* **to t. at sth** tirer sur qch
3 *n* (a) *(pull)* **to give sth a t.** tirer sur qch (b) *(boat)* remorqueur *m*

tug-of-love [tʌgəv'lʌv] *n Br* = conflit de parents séparés à propos de la garde d'un enfant

tug-of-war [tʌgəv'wɔː(r)] *n (game)* lutte *f* de (traction) à la corde; *Fig* lutte acharnée

tuition [tjʊ'ɪʃən] *n* cours *mpl*, leçons *fpl*

tulip ['tjuːlɪp] *n* tulipe *f*

tum [tʌm] *n (in children's language)* ventre *m*

tumble ['tʌmbəl] 1 *vi (of person)* faire une chute; *Fig (of prices)* chuter
2 *n (fall)* chute *f*; **to take a t.** *(of person)* faire une chute; *Fig (of prices)* chuter

▶**tumble down** *vi* s'écrouler

tumbledown ['tʌmbəldaʊn] *adj* qui tombe en ruines

tumble-drier [tʌmbəl'draɪə(r)] *n* sèche-linge *m inv*

tumble-dry ['tʌmbəldraɪ] *vt* faire sécher au sèche-linge

tumbler ['tʌmblə(r)] *n* verre *m* droit

tummy ['tʌmɪ] *n Fam* ventre *m*; **to have (a) t. ache** avoir mal au ventre

tumour, *Am* **tumor** ['tjuːmə(r)] *n* tumeur *f*

tumult ['tjuːmʌlt] *n* tumulte *m*

tumultuous [tjʊ'mʌltjʊəs] *adj* tumultueux(euse)

tuna ['tjuːnə] *n* thon *m*

tundra ['tʌndrə] *n* toundra *f*

tune [tjuːn] 1 *n* (a) *(air)* air *m*, mélodie *f*; **to be in/out of t.** *(of person)* chanter juste/faux; *(of instrument)* être accordé(e)/désaccordé(e); *Fig (idioms)* **to be in t. with sb/sth** être en harmonie avec qn/qch; **to call the t.** commander; **to change one's t.** changer de discours; **to be in debt to the t. of £200** avoir 200 livres de dettes
2 *vt (musical instrument)* accorder; *(engine, TV, radio)* régler

▶**tune in** *vi* brancher son poste

tuneful ['tjuːnfʊl] *adj* mélodieux(euse)

tuneless ['tjuːnlɪs] *adj* discordant(e)

tuner ['tjuːnə(r)] *n* (a) *(person)* accordeur(euse) *m,f* (b) *(on TV, radio)* tuner *m*

tungsten ['tʌŋstən] *n* tungstène *m*; **t. steel** acier *m* au tungstène

tunic ['tjuːnɪk] *n* tunique *f*

tuning fork ['tju:nɪŋ'fɔːk] n diapason m

Tunis ['tju:nɪs] n Tunis

Tunisia [tju:'nɪzɪə] n la Tunisie

Tunisian [tju:'nɪzɪən] 1 n Tunisien(enne) m,f
2 adj tunisien(enne)

tunnel ['tʌnəl] 1 n tunnel m; **to have t. vision** souffrir d'un rétrécissement du champ visuel; Fig avoir des œillères
2 vt (pt & pp tunnelled) **to t. one's way out of prison** s'échapper de prison en creusant un tunnel
3 vi creuser un tunnel

turban ['tɜːbən] n turban m

turbine ['tɜːbaɪn] n turbine f

turbo-charged ['tɜːbəʊtʃɑːdʒd] adj turbo-compressé(e)

turbo-charger ['tɜːbəʊtʃɑːdʒə(r)] n turbocompresseur m

turbojet ['tɜːbəʊdʒet] n (engine) turboréacteur m; (plane) avion m à turboréacteur

turboprop ['tɜːbəʊprɒp] n (engine) turbopropulseur m; (plane) avion m à turbopropulseur

turbot ['tɜːbət] n turbot m

turbulence ['tɜːbjʊləns] n turbulence f

turbulent ['tɜːbjʊlənt] adj agité(e)

turd [tɜːd] n very Fam (a) (excrement) étron m (b) (person) connard (connasse) m,f

tureen [tjʊə'riːn] n soupière f

turf [tɜːf] 1 n (a) (grass-covered earth) gazon m; Fam (territory) territoire m; **t. accountant** bookmaker m
2 vt gazonner
▶**turf out** vt sep Br Fam (person) vider; (thing) balancer

Turk [tɜːk] n Turc (Turque) m,f

Turkey ['tɜːkɪ] n la Turquie

turkey ['tɜːkɪ] n (pl turkeys) n (a) (bird) dinde f (b) Fam (bad play, film) navet m

Turkish ['tɜːkɪʃ] 1 n (language) turc m
2 adj turc (turque); **T. bath** bain m turc; **T. delight** loukoum m

Turkmenistan [tɜːkmenɪ'stɑːn] n le Turkménistan

turmeric ['tɜːmərɪk] n curcuma m

turmoil ['tɜːmɔɪl] n (of person) émoi m; (of country) agitation f; **to be in a t.** (of person) être dans tous ses états; (of country) être en ébullition; **his mind was in t.** il était très troublé

turn [tɜːn] 1 n (a) (of wheel, screw) tour m; **the meat is done to a t.** la viande est cuite à point
(b) (change of direction) demi-tour m; (in road) virage m; **no right/left t.** (on sign) défense de tourner à droite/gauche; Fig **at every t.** à tout bout de champ; **to take a t. for the better** s'améliorer; **to take a t. for the worse** se détériorer; **events took an unexpected t.** les événements ont pris une tournure inattendue; **the t. of the century** le tournant du siècle; **the t. of the tide** le changement de marée; Fig **le renversement de tendances**
(c) (in game, queue) tour m; **to take (it in) turns (to do sth)** se relayer (pour faire qch); **in t.** à tour de rôle
(d) Fam (fit) crise f
(e) Th (performance) numéro m
(f) (service) **to do sb a good t.** rendre un service à qn; **one good t. deserves another** un service en vaut un autre
(g) **t. of phrase** tournure f de phrase
2 vt (a) (cause to move) tourner; Fam Fig **without turning**

a hair sans broncher; Fam Fig **success has turned her head** le succès lui a tourné la tête; **to t. sb's stomach** soulever le cœur à qn
(b) (direct) **to t. the conversation to sb/sth** orienter la conversation sur qn/qch
(c) (go round) **to t. the corner** tourner au coin de la rue; Fig passer le moment critique; **she's just turned forty** elle vient d'avoir quarante ans
(d) (change) **to t. sth into sth** transformer qch en qch; **to t. sth green/black** verdir/noircir qch; **to t. sb against sb** monter qn contre qn
(e) (on lathe) tourner
3 vi (a) (rotate) (of wheel) tourner; (of person) se retourner; **she turned to me** elle s'est tournée vers moi; **to t. to sb (for help/advice)** se tourner vers qn (pour obtenir de l'aide/des conseils); **to t. (to the) right/left** tourner à droite/gauche
(b) (change) **to t. against sb** se retourner contre qn; **to t. nasty** (of person) devenir méchant(e); (of situation) mal tourner; **to t. red** devenir rouge; (of milk) **to t. sour** (of milk) tourner; Fig (of relationship) tourner au vinaigre
▶**turn away** 1 vt sep (refuse entry, help to) refuser
2 vi se détourner
▶**turn back** 1 vt sep (person) refouler; (sheets) rabattre; **to t. the clocks back** retarder les pendules; Fig faire machine arrière
2 vi faire demi-tour; **t. back to page 20** revenez à la page 20
▶**turn down** vt sep (a) (volume, heat) baisser (b) (request, application) rejeter, refuser
▶**turn in** 1 vt sep (lost property) rapporter à la police; (person) livrer à la police
2 vi Fam (go to bed) aller se pieuter
▶**turn into** vt insep (become) devenir
▶**turn off** 1 vt sep (a) (water, gas) fermer; (light, TV, engine) éteindre (b) Fam **to t. sb off** dégoûter qn; (sexually) couper l'envie à qn
2 vt insep **to t. off the road** quitter la route
3 vi (leave road) sortir
▶**turn on** 1 vt sep (a) (water, gas) ouvrir; (light, TV, engine) allumer (b) Fam **to t. sb on** (excite) brancher; (sexually) exciter
2 vt insep (a) (attack) **to t. on sb** attaquer qn. n (b) (depend on) dépendre de
▶**turn out** 1 vt sep (a) (light) éteindre; (gas) fermer (b) (eject) mettre à la porte (c) (pocket, container) vider (d) (produce) produire, fabriquer; **to be well turned out** (of person) être élégant(e)
2 vi (a) (appear, attend) se déplacer (b) (result) se terminer; **to t. out to be** s'avérer (être); **it turns out that...** il se trouve que...
▶**turn over** 1 vt sep (a) (change position of) retourner; **to t. sth over in one's mind** retourner qch dans sa tête; Fig **to t. over a new leaf** tourner la page (b) (hand in) **to t. sth over to sb** remettre qn/qch entre les mains de qn
2 vi (a) (of person) se retourner; (of car) faire un tonneau, capoter (b) (change TV channels) changer de chaîne
▶**turn round** 1 vt sep (object) retourner; (situation) renverser; (company, economy) remettre sur pied
2 vi (of person) se retourner
▶**turn up** 1 vt sep (a) (collar) relever; (trousers) retrousser (b) (volume, heat) mettre plus fort
2 vi (a) (of person) arriver; (of lost object) réapparaître; **something is sure to t. up** quelque chose finira bien par se présenter

turnabout ['tɜːnəbaʊt] *n (in situation, opinion)* revirement *m*

turnaround ['tɜːnəraʊnd] *n* (a) *(in situation, opinion)* revirement *m* (b) *Com* t. time délai *m* d'exécution

turncoat ['tɜːnkəʊt] *n* renégat(e) *m,f*

turning ['tɜːnɪŋ] *n* (a) *(off road) (in country)* route *f* transversale; *(in town)* rue *f* transversale; **the second t. on the left** la deuxième rue à gauche (b) **t. circle** *(of car)* rayon *m* de braquage; *Fig* **t. point** tournant *m*

turnip ['tɜːnɪp] *n* navet *m*

turn-off ['tɜːnɒf] *n* (a) *(on road)* sortie *f* (b) *Fam* to be a t. être rébarbatif(ive); *(sexually)* couper l'envie

turn-on ['tɜːnɒn] *n Fam* **to be a t.** *(sexually)* être excitant(e)

turnout ['tɜːnaʊt] *n (attendance)* assistance *f; (at election)* taux *m* de participation

turnover ['tɜːnəʊvə(r)] *n* (a) *(of company)* chiffre *m* d'affaires (b) *(cake)* chausson *m;* **apple t.** chausson *m* aux pommes

turnpike ['tɜːnpaɪk] *n Am (road)* autoroute *f*

turnstile ['tɜːnstaɪl] *n* tourniquet *m*

turntable ['tɜːnteɪbəl] *n* platine *f*

turn-up ['tɜːnʌp] *n Br (on trousers)* revers *m* (b) *Fam* **what a t. for the books!** quel événement!

turpentine ['tɜːpəntaɪn] *n* essence *f* de térébenthine

turquoise ['tɜːkwɔɪz] **1** *n* (a) *(stone)* turquoise *f* (b) *(colour)* turquoise *m* 2 *adj* turquoise *inv*

turret ['tʌrɪt] *n* tourelle *f; (gun)* t. *(on ship, tank)* tourelle *f*

turtle ['tɜːtəl] *n Br* tortue *f* de mer; *Am* tortue *f;* **to turn t.** *(of ship)* chavirer; **t. dove** tourterelle *f;* **t. soup** potage *m* à la tortue

turtleneck ['tɜːtəlnek] *n* col *m* montant; **t. sweater** pull *m* à col montant

Tuscan ['tʌskən] *adj* toscan(e)

Tuscany ['tʌskənɪ] *n* la Toscane

tusk [tʌsk] *n* défense *f*

tussle ['tʌsəl] **1** *n* empoignade *f;* **to have a t. (with sb)** *(physically)* se battre (avec qn); *(verbally)* se disputer (avec qn) 2 *vi (physically)* se battre; *(verbally)* se disputer

tutor ['tjuːtə(r)] **1** *n (at university)* directeur(trice) *m,f* d'études; *(for private lessons)* professeur *m* particulier 2 *vt* **to t. sb (in sth)** donner des leçons particulières (de qch) à qn

tutorial [tjʊ'tɔːrɪəl] *n Br Univ* travaux *mpl* dirigés

tux [tʌks] *n Fam* smoking *m*

tuxedo [tʌk'siːdəʊ] *n* smoking *m*

TV [tiː'viː] *n (television)* télé *f,* TV *f;* **TV dinner** plateau *m* télé; **TV movie** téléfilm *m*

TVP [tiːviː'piː] *n (abbr* **textured vegetable protein)** protéine *f* végétale texturée

twaddle ['twɒdəl] *n Fam* fadaises *fpl*

twang [twæŋ] **1** *n (sound)* vibration *f; (nasal voice)* ton *m* nasillard 2 *vi (of string)* vibrer

tweak [twiːk] **1** *n* **to give sth a t.** *(nose)* pincer qch; *(ear)* tirer qch; *Fam Fig (statistics, mechanism)* ajuster légèrement 2 *vt (nose)* pincer; *(ear)* tirer; *Fam Fig (statistics, mechanism)* ajuster légèrement

twee [twiː] *adj Br Fam Pej* cucul (la praline) *inv*

tweed [twiːd] *n* tweed *m;* **tweeds** *(suit)* costume *m* de tweed

tweet [twiːt] **1** *n* pépiement *m* 2 *vi* pépier

tweezers ['twiːzəz] *npl* pince *f* à épiler

twelfth [twelfθ] **1** *n* (a) *(fraction)* douzième *m* (b) *(in series)* douzième *mf* (c) *(of month)* douze *m inv* 2 *adj* douzième; **T. Night** ≃ la fête des Rois; *see also* **eighth**

twelve [twelv] **1** *n* douze *m inv;* **half past t.** *(in the afternoon)* douze heure trente, midi et demi; *(at night)* zéro heures trente, minuit et demi 2 *adj* douze; *see also* **eight**

twentieth ['twentɪəθ] **1** *n* (a) *(fraction)* vingtième *m* (b) *(in series)* vingtième *mf* (c) *(of month)* vingt *m inv* 2 *adj* vingtième; *see also* **eighth**

twenty ['twentɪ] **1** *n* vingt *m inv* 2 *adj* vingt; **to have t.-t. vision** avoir dix sur dix à chaque œil; *see also* **eighty**

twenty-first ['twentɪ'fɜːst] **1** *n* (a) *(in series)* vingt et unième *mf* (b) *(of month)* vingt et un *m inv* 2 *adj* vingt et unième

twenty one ['twentɪ'wʌn] **1** *n* vingt et un *m inv* 2 *adj* vingt et un

twerp [twɜːp] *n Fam* crétin(e) *m,f*

twice [twaɪs] *adv* deux fois; **t. a week** deux fois par semaine; **t. as big (as)** deux fois plus grand (que); **it would cost t. as much elsewhere** ça coûterait le double ailleurs; **t. over** à deux reprises; **to think t. before doing sth** réfléchir à deux fois avant de faire qch; **he didn't have to be asked t.** il ne s'est pas fait prier

twiddle ['twɪdəl] **1** *vt* tripoter; **to t. one's thumbs** se tourner les pouces 2 *vi* **to t. with sth** tripoter qch

twig[1] [twɪg] *n (small branch)* brindille *f*

twig[2] *(pt & pp* **twigged)** *vt & vi Br Fam* piger

twilight ['twaɪlaɪt] *n* crépuscule *m*

twin [twɪn] **1** *n* jumeau(elle) *m,f;* **t. brother** frère *m* jumeau; **t. sister** sœur *f* jumelle 2 *adj (paired)* jumeau(elle), jumelé(e); **t. beds** lits *mpl* jumeaux; **t.-engine(d) aircraft** avion *m* bimoteur 3 *vt (pt & pp* **twinned)** *(town)* jumeler

twine [twaɪn] **1** *n (string)* ficelle *f* 2 *vt* **to t. sth around sb/sth** enrouler qch autour de qn/qch

twinge [twɪn(d)ʒ] *n (of pain)* élancement *m;* **a t. of conscience** un léger remords

twinkle ['twɪŋkəl] **1** *vi (of star, light)* scintiller; *(of eyes)* pétiller 2 *n (of star, light)* scintillement *m; (of eyes)* pétillement *m*

twirl [twɜːl] **1** *n (movement)* tournoiement *m* 2 *vt* faire tournoyer 3 *vi (of person)* tournoyer

twist [twɪst] **1** *n* (a) *(action)* tour *m;* **to give sth a t.** *(to open)* dévisser qch; *(to close)* visser qch (b) *(bend)* tortillement *m;* **twists and turns** *(in road)* tours *mpl* et détours; *Fig (of events)* rebondissements *mpl;* *Br Fam* **to be round the t.** être cinglé(e) (c) *(in story, plot)* tour *m* inattendu (d) **a t. of lemon** une rondelle de citron (e) *(dance)* **the t.** le twist 2 *vt (hair, rope, thread)* tordre, tortiller; *Fig (words, meaning)* déformer; **to t. one's ankle** se fouler la cheville; **to t. sb's arm** tordre le bras à qn; *Fig* forcer la main à qn; *Fig* **to t. the knife in the wound** retourner *ou* remuer le couteau dans la plaie

  3 *vi (of smoke)* faire des volutes; *(of road)* faire des lacets; **to t. and turn** *(of road)* être en lacets

▶**twist off 1** *vt sep (lid)* dévisser

  2 *vi* se dévisser

twisted ['twɪstɪd] *adj also Fig* tordu(e)

twister ['twɪstə(r)] *n* **(a)** *Br Fam (dishonest person)* escroc *m* **(b)** *Am (tornado)* tornade *f*

twit [twɪt] *n Fam* andouille *f*

twitch [twɪtʃ] **1** *n (pull)* coup *m* sec; **to have a nervous t.** avoir un tic (nerveux)

  2 *vt (pull)* tirer d'un coup sec

  3 *vi (of muscle, limb, face)* se contracter nerveusement

twitter ['twɪtə(r)] **1** *vi (of bird)* gazouiller; *Fig (of person)* jacasser

  2 *n (of bird)* gazouillis *m*

two [tu:] **1** *n (pl twos)* deux *m*; **to break/fold sth in t.** casser/plier qch en deux; **to walk in twos** *or* **t. by t.** marcher deux par deux; *Fig* **to put t. and t. together** faire le rapprochement; *Fam* **that makes t. of us** comme ça, on est deux

  2 *adj* deux; *see also* **eight**

two-bit ['tu:bɪt] *adj Am Fam (cheap)* de quatre sous

two-dimensional [tu:daɪ'menʃənəl] *adj* à deux dimensions; *Fig (character, film)* simpliste

two-faced ['tu:feɪst] *adj* hypocrite

twofold ['tu:fəʊld] *adj* double

two-legged [tu:'legɪd] *adj* bipède

twopence ['tʌpəns] *n Br* deux pence *mpl*; *Fam* **it isn't worth t.** ça ne vaut pas tripette

two-piece ['tu:pi:s] *adj (suit, swimsuit)* deux pièces

two-pin ['tu:pɪn] *adj (plug, socket)* à deux fiches

twosome ['tu:səm] *n* couple *m*

two-time ['tu:taɪm] *vt Fam (boyfriend, girlfriend)* tromper

two-way ['tu:weɪ] *adj* **t. mirror** miroir *m* sans tain; **t. radio** poste *m* émetteur-récepteur

tycoon [taɪ'ku:n] *n* magnat *m*

type [taɪp] **1** *n* **(a)** *(kind)* type *m*, genre *m*; *Fam* **he's not my t.** ce n'est pas mon genre de mec **(b)** *Typ* caractères *mpl*; **in bold t.** en caractères gras

  2 *vt & vi* taper (à la machine)

▶**type up** *vt sep* taper (à la machine)

typecast ['taɪpkɑ:st] *(pt & pp* **typecast***)* *vt* **to be typecast** être cantonné(e) dans un rôle

typeface ['taɪpfeɪs] *n* police *f* de caractères

typescript ['taɪpskrɪpt] *n* tapuscrit *m*

typesetter ['taɪpsetə(r)] *n* typographe *mf*

typewriter ['taɪpraɪtə(r)] *n* machine *f* à écrire

typhoid ['taɪfɔɪd] *n* **t. (fever)** *(fièvre f)* typhoïde *f*; **to have t.** avoir la typhoïde

typhoon [taɪ'fu:n] *n* typhon *m*

typhus ['taɪfəs] *n* typhus *m*

typical ['tɪpɪkəl] *adj* typique; **that's t. (of him/her)!** ça ne m'étonne pas (de lui/d'elle)!

typify ['tɪpɪfaɪ] *(pt & pp* **typified***)* *vt* caractériser

typing ['taɪpɪŋ] *n* dactylographie *f*, frappe *f*; **t. error** faute *f* de frappe; **t. paper** papier *m* à machine; **t. pool** équipe *f* de dactylos; **t. speed** vitesse *f* de frappe

typist ['taɪpɪst] *n* dactylo *mf*

typographic(al) [taɪpə'græfɪk(əl)] *adj* typographique

typography [taɪ'pɒgrəfɪ] *n* typographie *f*

tyrannical [tɪ'rænɪkəl] *adj* tyrannique

tyrannize ['tɪrənaɪz] *vt* tyranniser

tyranny ['tɪrənɪ] *n* tyrannie *f*

tyrant ['taɪrənt] *n* tyran *m*

tyre, *Am* **tire** ['taɪə(r)] *n* pneu *m*; **t. marks** traces *fpl* de pneu; **t. pressure** pression *f* des pneus

tzar [zɑ:(r)], **tzarist** ['zɑ:rɪst] = **tsar**, **tsarist**

U

U, u [juː] *n (letter)* U, u *m inv;* **U bend** tuyau *m* U; **U boat** sous-marin *m* allemand; **U turn** *(in car)* demi-tour *m;* *Fig* virage *m* à 180 degrés

UAE [juːeɪˈiː] *n (abbr* **United Arab Emirates)** EAU *mpl*

UB40 [juːbiːˈfɔːtɪ] *n Br* = carte de pointage de demandeur d'emploi

ubiquitous [juːˈbɪkwɪtəs] *adj* omniprésent(e)

UCAS [ˈjuːkæs] *n Br (abbr* **Universities and Colleges Admissions Service)** = centre national d'inscriptions à l'université

UDA [juːdiːˈeɪ] *n Br Pol (abbr* **Ulster Defence Association)** = groupement paramilitaire protestant d'Irlande du Nord

udder [ˈʌdə(r)] *n* pis *m,* mamelle *f*

UDI [juːdiːˈaɪ] *n Pol (abbr* **Unilateral Declaration of Independence)** déclaration *f* unilatérale d'indépendance

UEFA [juːˈeɪfə] *n (abbr* **Union of European Football Associations)** UEFA *f*

UFO [juːefˈəʊ] *n (abbr* **unidentified flying object)** OVNI *m*

Uganda [juːˈgændə] *n* l'Ouganda *m*

Ugandan [juːˈgændən] **1** *n* Ougandais(e) *m,f*
2 *adj* ougandais(e)

ugh [ʌx] *exclam* berk!

ugly [ˈʌglɪ] *adj (a) (in appearance)* laid(e); *Fig* **u. duckling** vilain petit canard *m* **(b)** *(unpleasant)* désagréable, déplaisant(e)

UHF [juːeɪtʃˈef] *n (abbr* **ultra-high frequency)** UHF

UHT [juːeɪtʃˈtiː] *adj (abbr* **ultra-heat-treated)** UHT

UK [juːˈkeɪ] *n (abbr* **United Kingdom)** *(written)* RU; *(spoken)* Royaume-Uni *m*

Ukraine [juːˈkreɪn] *n* the U. l'Ukraine *f*

Ukrainian [juːˈkreɪnɪən] **1** *n (a) (person)* Ukrainien(enne) *m,f* **(b)** *(language)* ukrainien *m*
2 *adj* ukrainien(enne)

ukulele [juːkəˈleɪlɪ] *n* ukulélé *m*

ulcer [ˈʌlsə(r)] *n* ulcère *m; (in mouth)* aphte *m*

ulcerate [ˈʌlsəreɪt] **1** *vt* ulcérer
2 *vi* s'ulcérer

ulna [ˈʌlnə] *n* cubitus *m*

Ulster [ˈʌlstə(r)] *n* l'Ulster *m*

ulterior [ʌlˈtɪərɪə(r)] *adj* ultérieur(e); **u. motive** arrière-pensée *f*

ultimate [ˈʌltɪmət] **1** *adj (a) (last)* final(e) **(b)** *(supreme, best)* absolu(e); **the u. holiday** les vacances idéales
2 *n Fam* **the u. (in)** le summum (de)

ultimately [ˈʌltɪmətlɪ] *adv* **(a)** *(finally)* finalement **(b)** *(basically)* en fin de compte

ultimatum [ʌltɪˈmeɪtəm] *n* ultimatum *m*

ultra- [ˈʌltrə] *pref* ultra-

ultramarine [ʌltrəməˈriːn] *n* bleu *m* outremer

ultramodern [ʌltrəˈmɒdən] *adj* ultramoderne

ultrasound [ˈʌltrəsaʊnd] *n* ultrasons *mpl*

ultraviolet [ʌltrəˈvaɪələt] *adj* ultraviolet(ette)

Ulysses [ˈjuːlɪsiːz] *n* Ulysse

umbilical cord [ʌmˈbɪlɪkəlkɔːd] *n* cordon *m* ombilical

umbrage [ˈʌmbrɪdʒ] *n* **to take u. (at sth)** prendre ombrage (de qch)

umbrella [ʌmˈbrelə] *n* parapluie *m; Fig* **under the u. of** sous les auspices de; **u. organization** organisme *m* de tutelle; **u. stand** porte-parapluie *m*

umpire [ˈʌmpaɪə(r)] **1** *n* arbitre *mf*
2 *vt* arbitrer

umpteen [ʌmpˈtiːn] *adj Fam* je ne sais combien de

umpteenth [ʌmpˈtiːnθ] *adj Fam* énième

UN [juːˈen] *n (abbr* **United Nations)** ONU *f*

unabashed [ʌnəˈbæʃt] *adj* imperturbable

unable [ʌnˈeɪbəl] *adj* **to be u. to do sth** être incapable de faire qch

unabridged [ʌnəˈbrɪdʒd] *adj* intégral(e)

unacceptable [ʌnəkˈseptəbəl] *adj* inacceptable

unaccompanied [ʌnəˈkʌmpənɪd] **1** *adj (person)* non accompagné(e); *(violin, singer)* sans accompagnement
2 *adv (travel)* seul(e); *(play, sing)* sans accompagnement

unaccomplished [ʌnəˈkʌmplɪʃt] *adj* médiocre

unaccountable [ʌnəˈkaʊntəbəl] *adj* **(a)** *(not answerable)* **to be u. (to sb)** ne pas avoir de comptes à rendre (à qn) **(b)** *(puzzling)* inexplicable

unaccounted [ʌnəˈkaʊntɪd] *adj* **to be u. for** *(of person)* ne pas être retrouvé(e)

unaccustomed [ʌnəˈkʌstəmd] *adj (a) (not used)* **to be u. to sth/to doing sth** ne pas être habitué(e) à qch/à faire qch **(b)** *(not usual)* inhabituel(elle)

unacknowledged [ʌnəkˈnɒlɪdʒd] **1** *adj* non reconnu(e)
2 *adv* **to go u.** *(of talent, achievement)* ne pas être reconnu(e)

unacquainted [ʌnəˈkweɪntɪd] *adj* **to be u. with sb/sth** ne pas connaître qn/qch

unadulterated [ʌnəˈdʌltəreɪtɪd] *adj* **(a)** *(food)* naturel(elle) **(b)** *(total, sheer)* pur(e)

unadventurous [ʌnədˈventʃərəs] *adj* peu audacieux(euse)

unaffected [ʌnə'fektɪd] *adj* (a) *(sincere)* simple (b) *(not touched)* **to be u. (by sth)** ne pas être affecté(e) (par qch)

unaffiliated [ʌnə'fɪlɪeɪtɪd] *adj* non affilié(e)

unafraid [ʌnə'freɪd] *adj* **to be u.** ne pas avoir peur

unaided [ʌn'eɪdɪd] *adv* sans aide

unaltered [ʌn'ɔːltəd] *adj* inchangé(e)

unambiguous [ʌnæm'bɪgjʊəs] *adj* sans équivoque

unambitious [ʌnæm'bɪʃəs] *adj* sans ambition

unanimity [juːnə'nɪmɪtɪ] *n* unanimité *f*

unanimous [juː'nænɪməs] *adj* unanime

unanimously [juː'nænɪməslɪ] *adv* à l'unanimité

unannounced [ʌnə'naʊnst] **1** *adj* non annoncé(e) **2** *adv* sans prévenir

unanswerable [ʌn'ɑːnsərəbəl] *adj* irréfutable

unanswered [ʌn'ɑːnsəd] **1** *adj* sans réponse **2** *adv* **to go u.** (of question, letter) rester sans réponse

unappealing [ʌnə'piːlɪŋ] *adj* peu attrayant(e)

unappetizing [ʌn'æpɪtaɪzɪŋ] *adj* peu appétissant(e)

unappreciated [ʌnə'priːʃɪeɪtɪd] *adj* non reconnu(e)

unapproachable [ʌnə'prəʊtʃəbəl] *adj* inaccessible

unarmed [ʌn'ɑːmd] *adj* non armé(e); **u. combat** combat *m* à mains nues

unashamed [ʌnə'ʃeɪmd] *adj* (joy, greed) non dissimulé(e); **he's u. about his background** il n'a absolument pas honte de ses origines

unassailable [ʌnə'seɪləbəl] *adj* (castle, position) imprenable; (argument, theory) inattaquable

unassuming [ʌnə'sjuːmɪŋ] *adj* sans prétention

unattached [ʌnə'tætʃt] *adj* (a) (not connected) détaché(e) (b) (without partner) sans attaches

unattainable [ʌnə'teɪnəbəl] *adj* inaccessible

unattractive [ʌnə'træktɪv] *adj* peu attrayant(e)

unauthorized [ʌn'ɔːθəraɪzd] *adj* non autorisé(e)

unavailable [ʌnə'veɪləbəl] *adj* non disponible; **to be u.** ne pas être disponible

unavailing [ʌnə'veɪlɪŋ] *adj* vain(e)

unavoidable [ʌnə'vɔɪdəbəl] *adj* inévitable

unaware [ʌnə'weə(r)] *adj* ignorant(e); **to be u. of sth** ignorer qch

unawares [ʌnə'weəz] *adv* **to catch sb u.** prendre qn au dépourvu

unbalanced [ʌn'bælənst] *adj* (a) (person) instable (b) (biased) partial(e)

unbearable [ʌn'beərəbəl] *adj* insupportable

unbeatable [ʌn'biːtəbəl] *adj* imbattable

unbecoming [ʌnbɪ'kʌmɪŋ] *adj* (behaviour) inconvenant(e); (dress) peu seyant(e)

unbeknown(st) [ʌnbɪ'nəʊn(st)] *adv* **u. to me/him** à mon/son insu

unbelievable [ʌnbɪ'liːvəbəl] *adj* incroyable

unbending [ʌn'bendɪŋ] *adj* inflexible

unbias(s)ed [ʌn'baɪəst] *adj* impartial(e)

unblock [ʌn'blɒk] *vt* (sink, pipe) déboucher; (road) dégager

unborn [ʌn'bɔːn] *adj* (child) à naître

unbounded [ʌn'baʊndɪd] *adj* sans bornes

unbreakable [ʌn'breɪkəbəl] *adj* (a) (glass, toy) incassable (b) (promise, rule) sacré(e)

unbridled [ʌn'braɪdəld] *adj* débridé(e)

unbroken [ʌn'brəʊkən] *adj* (a) (intact) intact(e) (b) (uninterrupted) ininterrompu(e)

unburden [ʌn'bɜːdən] *vt* **to u. oneself to sb** se confier à qn

unbusinesslike [ʌn'bɪznɪslaɪk] *adj* peu professionnel(elle)

unbutton [ʌn'bʌtən] *vt* déboutonner

uncalled-for [ʌn'kɔːldfɔː(r)] *adj* (of behaviour, remark) déplacé(e); (insult) gratuit(e)

uncanny [ʌn'kænɪ] *adj* étrange, troublant(e)

uncaring [ʌn'keərɪŋ] *adj* indifférent(e)

unceasing [ʌn'siːsɪŋ] *adj* incessant(e)

uncertain [ʌn'sɜːtən] *adj* incertain(e); **to be u. about sth** ne pas être certain(e) de qch; **it is u. if...** on ne sait pas si...; **in no u. terms** en termes on ne peut plus clairs

uncertainty [ʌn'sɜːtəntɪ] *n* (pl **uncertainties**) *n* incertitude *f*

unchallenged [ʌn'tʃælɪndʒd] *adj* incontesté(e)

unchanged [ʌn'tʃeɪndʒd] *adj* inchangé(e)

unchanging [ʌn'tʃeɪndʒɪŋ] *adj* immuable

uncharacteristic [ʌnkærəktə'rɪstɪk] *adj* inhabituel(elle)

uncharitable [ʌn'tʃærɪtəbəl] *adj* peu charitable

uncharted [ʌn'tʃɑːtɪd] *adj* inexploré(e)

unchecked [ʌn'tʃekt] **1** *adj* (a) (not restrained) incontrôlé(e) (b) (not verified) non vérifié(e) **2** *adv* **to go u.** rester incontrôlé(e)

uncivil [ʌn'sɪvɪl] *adj* impoli(e)

uncivilized [ʌn'sɪvɪlaɪzd] *adj* non civilisé(e)

unclaimed [ʌn'kleɪmd] *adj* non réclamé(e); **to go u.** ne pas être réclamé(e)

uncle ['ʌŋkəl] *n* oncle *m*; *Am* **U. Sam** l'oncle Sam

unclean [ʌn'kliːn] *adj* sale, souillé(e)

unclear [ʌn'klɪə(r)] *adj* vague

unclothed [ʌn'kləʊðd] *adj* nu(e)

uncoil [ʌn'kɔɪl] *vt* dérouler

uncombed [ʌn'kəʊmd] *adj* pas peigné(e)

uncomfortable [ʌn'kʌmfətəbəl] *adj* inconfortable; (silence) gêné(e); **to feel u.** (physically) ne pas être à l'aise; (ill at ease) être mal à l'aise

uncommitted [ʌnkə'mɪtɪd] *adj* indécis(e)

uncommon [ʌn'kɒmən] *adj* peu commun(e)

uncommunicative [ʌnkə'mjuːnɪkətɪv] *adj* peu communicatif(ive)

uncomplicated [ʌn'kɒmplɪkeɪtɪd] *adj* simple, non compliqué(e)

uncomplimentary [ʌnkɒmplɪ'mentərɪ] *adj* peu flatteur(euse)

uncomprehending [ʌnkɒmprɪ'hendɪŋ] *adj* **to be u. of sth** ne pas comprendre qch; **with an u. look** l'air perplexe

uncompromising [ʌn'kɒmprəmaɪzɪŋ] *adj* (person, opposition) intransigeant(e)

unconcealed [ʌnkən'siːld] *adj* non dissimulé(e)

unconcerned [ʌnkən'sɜːnd] **1** *adj* indifférent(e); **to be u. about sth** ne pas s'inquiéter de qch **2** *adv* avec indifférence

unconditional [ʌnkən'dɪʃənəl] *adj* sans condition

unconfirmed [ʌnkən'fɜːmd] *adj* non confirmé(e)

unconnected [ʌnkə'nektɪd] *adj* sans lien

unconscious [ʌnˈkɒnʃəs] **1** adj (a) (having fainted) sans connaissance; (asleep) profondément endormi(e) (b) (unaware) inconscient(e); **to be u. of sth** ne pas avoir conscience de qch **2** n **the u.** l'inconscient m

unconsciously [ʌnˈkɒnʃəslɪ] adv inconsciemment

unconstitutional [ʌnkɒnstɪˈtjuːʃənəl] adj inconstitutionnel(elle)

uncontaminated [ʌnkənˈtæmɪneɪtɪd] adj non contaminé(e)

uncontested [ʌnkənˈtestɪd] adj incontesté(e)

uncontrollable [ʌnkənˈtrəʊləbəl] adj incontrôlable

uncontroversial [ʌnkɒntrəˈvɜːʃəl] adj anodin(e)

unconventional [ʌnkənˈvenʃənəl] adj non-conformiste

unconvinced [ʌnkənˈvɪnst] adj sceptique

unconvincing [ʌnkənˈvɪnsɪŋ] adj peu convaincant(e)

uncooked [ʌnˈkʊkt] adj cru(e)

uncool [ʌnˈkuːl] adj Fam ringard(e)

uncooperative [ʌnkəʊˈɒpərətɪv] adj peu coopératif(ive)

uncoordinated [ʌnkəʊˈɔːdɪneɪtɪd] adj qui manque de coordination

uncork [ʌnˈkɔːk] vt déboucher

uncorroborated [ʌnkəˈrɒbəreɪtɪd] adj non corroboré(e)

uncountable [ʌnˈkaʊntəbəl] adj indénombrable

uncouth [ʌnˈkuːθ] adj fruste

uncover [ʌnˈkʌvə(r)] vt also Fig découvrir

uncritical [ʌnˈkrɪtɪkəl] adj peu critique; **to be u. of sb/sth** ne pas être critique envers qn/qch

UNCTAD [ˈʌŋktæd] n Econ (abbr United Nations Conference on Trade and Development) CNUCED f

unction [ˈʌŋkʃən] n Rel onction f

unctuous [ˈʌŋktjʊəs] adj Pej onctueux(euse)

uncultivated [ʌnˈkʌltɪveɪtɪd] adj inculte

uncultured [ʌnˈkʌltʃəd] adj inculte

uncut [ʌnˈkʌt] adj (gem) brut(e); (text, film) intégral(e)

undamaged [ʌnˈdæmɪdʒd] adj intact(e)

undated [ʌnˈdeɪtɪd] adj non daté(e)

undaunted [ʌnˈdɔːntɪd] adj qui n'est pas impressionné(e); **to be u. by sth** ne pas se laisser impressionner par qch

undecided [ʌndɪˈsaɪdɪd] adj (a) (question, problem) sans réponse; **that's still u.** aucune décision n'a encore été prise (b) (person) indécis(e) (about à propos de)

undefeated [ʌndɪˈfiːtɪd] adj invaincu(e)

undefended [ʌndɪˈfendɪd] adj sans défense

undemanding [ʌndɪˈmɑːndɪŋ] adj (job) peu prenant(e); (person) peu exigeant(e)

undemocratic [ʌndeməˈkrætɪk] adj antidémocratique

undemonstrative [ʌndɪˈmɒnstrətɪv] adj peu démonstratif(ive)

undeniable [ʌndɪˈnaɪəbəl] adj indéniable

undeniably [ʌndɪˈnaɪəblɪ] adv indéniablement

under [ˈʌndə(r)] **1** prep (a) (beneath) sous; **u. the table/the stairs** sous la table/l'escalier; Fam **to be u. the weather** ne pas être dans son assiette (b) (less than) moins de; **he's u. thirty** il a moins de trente ans; **children u. five** les enfants de moins de cinq ans (c) (under the control of) sous; **he had a hundred men u. him** il avait cent hommes sous ses ordres; **Spain u. Franco** l'Espagne de Franco (d) (subject to) **to be u. orders to do sth** avoir pour ordre de faire qch; **u. the terms of the agreement** d'après les termes de l'accord; **u. these conditions** dans ces conditions; **u. the circumstances** dans ces circonstances (e) (in the process of) **u. repair/observation** en réparation/observation; **to be u. investigation** faire l'objet d'une enquête; **to get u. way** (of meeting, campaign) commencer **2** adv (a) (underneath) dessous; (underwater) sous l'eau; **to go u.** (of company) faire faillite (b) (less) au-dessous; **children of five and u.** les enfants de cinq ans et au-dessous

underachiever [ʌndərəˈtʃiːvə(r)] n = personne qui ne tire pas profit de ses capacités intellectuelles

under-age [ʌndərˈeɪdʒ] adj mineur(e); **u. drinking** consommation f d'alcool par les mineurs; **u. sex** relations fpl sexuelles entre personnes mineures

undercarriage [ˈʌndəkærɪdʒ] n train m d'atterrissage

undercharge [ʌndəˈtʃɑːdʒ] vt se tromper dans l'addition de (à l'avantage du client); **he undercharged me by £5** il aurait dû me faire payer 5 livres de plus

underclass [ˈʌndəklɑːs] n sous-prolétariat m

underclothes [ˈʌndəkləʊðz] npl sous-vêtements mpl

underclothing [ˈʌndəkləʊðɪŋ] n sous-vêtements mpl

undercoat [ˈʌndəkəʊt] n sous-couche f

undercook [ʌndəˈkʊk] vt ne pas faire cuire assez longtemps

undercover [ˈʌndəkʌvə(r)] **1** adj secret(ète) **2** adv clandestinement

undercurrent [ˈʌndəkʌrənt] n (in sea) courant m sous-marin; Fig (of emotion, unrest) courant sous-jacent

undercut [ʌndəˈkʌt] (pt & pp **undercut**) vt vendre moins cher que

underdeveloped [ʌndədɪˈveləpt] adj sous-développé(e)

underdog [ˈʌndədɒg] n (a) (in contest) outsider m (b) (in society) **the u.** les opprimés mpl

underestimate 1 n [ʌndərˈestɪmɪt] sous-estimation f **2** vt [ʌndərˈestɪmeɪt] sous-estimer

underexposed [ˈʌndərɪksˈpəʊzd] adj sous-exposé(e)

underfed [ʌndəˈfed] adj sous-alimenté(e)

underfoot [ʌndəˈfʊt] adv sous les pieds; **it's wet u.** le sol est mouillé; **to trample sth u.** piétiner qch

underfunding [ʌndəˈfʌndɪŋ] n insuffisance f de financement

undergarment [ˈʌndəgɑːmənt] n sous-vêtement m

undergo [ʌndəˈgəʊ] (pt **underwent** [ʌndəˈwent], pp **undergone** [ʌndəˈgɒn]) vt (change) connaître; (test) subir; **to u. surgery** être opéré(e); **to u. treatment** (of patient) suivre un traitement

undergraduate [ʌndəˈgrædjʊət] n étudiant(e) m, f qui prépare une licence

underground 1 adj [ˈʌndəgraʊnd] (a) (below ground) souterrain(e) (b) (clandestine) clandestin(e) **2** adv [ʌndəˈgraʊnd] (a) (below ground) sous terre (b) **to go u.** (into hiding) passer dans la clandestinité

3 _n_ (a) _Br (railway system)_ métro _m_ (b) _(resistance movement)_ mouvement _m_ de résistance

undergrowth ['ʌndəgrəʊθ] _n_ broussailles _fpl_

underhand ['ʌndəhænd] _adj_ sournois(e)

underlain [ʌndə'leɪn] _pp of_ **underlie**

underlay ['ʌndəleɪ] _n (for carpet)_ thibaude _f_

underlie [ʌndə'laɪ] (_pt_ **underlay** [ʌndə'leɪ], _pp_ **underlain** [ʌndə'leɪn]) _vt_ sous-tendre

underline [ʌndə'laɪn] _vt also Fig_ souligner

underlying [ʌndə'laɪɪŋ] _adj_ sous-jacent(e)

undermanning [ʌndə'mænɪŋ] _n_ manque _m_ de main-d'œuvre

undermentioned ['ʌndəmenʃənd] _adj Formal_ ci-dessous

undermine [ʌndə'maɪn] _vt (weaken)_ saper

underneath [ʌndə'ni:θ] **1** _prep_ sous
2 _adv_ dessous
3 _n_ **the u.** le dessous

undernourished [ʌndə'nʌrɪʃt] _adj_ sous-alimenté(e)

underpaid [ʌndə'peɪd] _adj_ sous-payé(e)

underpants ['ʌndəpænts] _npl_ slip _m_

underpass ['ʌndəpɑ:s] _n_ passage _m_ souterrain

underperform [ʌndəpə'fɔ:m] _vi Fin (of shares, investment)_ ne pas être performant(e)

underpin [ʌndə'pɪn] (_pt & pp_ **underpinned**) _vt_ étayer

underpopulated [ʌndə'pɒpjʊleɪtɪd] _adj_ sous-peuplé(e)

underprivileged [ʌndə'prɪvɪlɪdʒd] _adj_ défavorisé(e)

underqualified [ʌndə'kwɒlɪfaɪd] _adj_ sous-qualifié(e)

underrate [ʌndə'reɪt] _vt_ sous-estimer

underside ['ʌndəsaɪd] _n_ dessous _m_

undersized [ʌndə'saɪzd] _adj_ trop petit(e)

underskirt ['ʌndəskɜ:t] _n_ jupon _m_; _(full-length)_ combinaison _f_

understaffed [ʌndə'stɑ:ft] _adj_ **to be u.** manquer de personnel

understand [ʌndə'stænd] (_pt & pp_ **understood** [ʌndə'stʊd]) **1** _vt_ (a) _(comprehend)_ comprendre; **to make oneself understood** se faire comprendre; **they u. each other** ils se comprennent (b) _(believe, assume)_ to u. that croire que; **I u. that you're coming to work here** j'ai appris que vous venez travailler ici; **to give sb to u.** that laisser entendre à qn que; **are we to u. that...?** devons-nous en conclure que...?
2 _vi_ comprendre

understandable [ʌndə'stændəbəl] _adj_ compréhensible

understandably [ʌndə'stændəblɪ] _adv_ naturellement

understanding [ʌndə'stændɪŋ] **1** _n_ (a) _(comprehension, sympathy)_ compréhension _f_ (b) _(agreement)_ accord _m_; **to come to** _or_ **to reach an u.** parvenir à un accord; **on the u. that** à condition que + _subjunctive_
2 _adj_ compréhensif(ive)

understatement [ʌndə'steɪtmənt] _n_ **that's an u.!** c'est peu dire!

understood [ʌndə'stʊd] _pt & pp of_ **understand**

understudy ['ʌndəstʌdɪ] _n_ doublure _f_

undertake [ʌndə'teɪk] (_pt_ **undertook** [ʌndə'tʊk], _pp_ **undertaken** [ʌndə'teɪkən]) _vt_ entreprendre; **to u. to do sth** entreprendre de faire qch

undertaker ['ʌndəteɪkə(r)] _n_ entrepreneur _m_ de pompes funèbres

undertaking [ʌndə'teɪkɪŋ] _n_ (a) _(enterprise)_ entreprise _f_ (b) _(promise)_ engagement _m_, promesse _f_

undertone ['ʌndətəʊn] _n (low voice)_ voix _f_ basse; _Fig (hint, suggestion)_ fond _m_

undertook [ʌndə'tʊk] _pt of_ **undertake**

undertow ['ʌndətəʊ] _n_ ressac _m_

undervalue [ʌndə'vælju:] _vt (property)_ sous-évaluer; _Fig (person, ability)_ sous-estimer

underwater 1 _adj_ ['ʌndəwɔ:tə(r)] de plongée
2 _adv_ [ʌndə'wɔ:tə(r)] sous l'eau

underwear ['ʌndəweə(r)] _n_ sous-vêtements _mpl_

underweight [ʌndə'weɪt] _adj_ trop maigre

underwent [ʌndə'went] _pt of_ **undergo**

underworld ['ʌndəwɜ:ld] _n_ (a) _(in mythology)_ **the U.** les Enfers _mpl_ (b) _(of criminals)_ pègre _f_

underwrite ['ʌndəraɪt] (_pt_ **underwrote** [ʌndə'rəʊt], _pp_ **underwritten** [ʌndə'rɪtən]) _vt_ souscrire

underwriter ['ʌndəraɪtə(r)] _n (in insurance)_ souscripteur _m_

underwritten [ʌndə'rɪtən] _pp of_ **underwrite**

underwrote [ʌndə'rəʊt] _pt of_ **underwrite**

undeserved [ʌndɪ'zɜ:vd] _adj_ immérité(e)

undeserving [ʌndɪ'zɜ:vɪŋ] _adj_ peu méritant(e); **to be u. of sth** ne pas mériter qch

undesirable [ʌndɪ'zaɪərəbəl] _n & adj_ indésirable _mf_

undetected [ʌndɪ'tektɪd] **1** _adj_ non détecté(e)
2 _adv_ **to go u.** passer inaperçu(e)

undetermined [ʌndɪ'tɜ:mɪnd] _adj_ indéterminé(e)

undeterred [ʌndɪ'tɜ:d] **1** _adj_ **to be u. (by sth)** ne pas se laisser décourager (par qch)
2 _adv_ sans se laisser décourager

undeveloped [ʌndɪ'veləpt] _adj_ non développé(e); _(land)_ inexploité(e)

undid [ʌn'dɪd] _pt of_ **undo**

undies ['ʌndɪz] _npl Fam_ sous-vêtements _mpl_

undigested [ʌndaɪ'dʒestɪd] _adj also Fig_ non digéré(e)

undignified [ʌn'dɪgnɪfaɪd] _adj_ indigne

undiluted [ʌndaɪ'lu:tɪd] _adj (liquid)_ non dilué(e); _Fig (emotion)_ pur(e)

undiminished [ʌndɪ'mɪnɪʃt] _adj_ intact(e)

undiplomatic [ʌndɪplə'mætɪk] _adj_ peu diplomate

undisciplined [ʌn'dɪsɪplɪnd] _adj_ indiscipliné(e)

undisclosed [ʌndɪs'kləʊzd] _adj_ non révélé(e)

undiscovered [ʌndɪs'kʌvəd] **1** _adj_ inconnu(e)
2 _adv_ **to go/continue u.** rester ignoré(e)

undiscriminating [ʌndɪs'krɪmɪneɪtɪŋ] _adj_ **to be u.** manquer de discernement

undisputed [ʌndɪs'pju:tɪd] _adj_ incontesté(e)

undistinguished [ʌndɪs'tɪŋgwɪʃt] _adj_ médiocre

undisturbed [ʌndɪs'tɜ:bd] _adj (sleep)_ paisible; **to leave sth u.** ne pas toucher à qch

undo [ʌn'du:] (_pt_ **undid** [ʌn'dɪd], _pp_ **undone** [ʌn'dʌn]) _vt_ (a) _(mistake, damage)_ réparer; _Comptr (command)_ annuler (b) _(knot, button, shoelaces)_ défaire; _(parcel, zip)_ ouvrir; _(bra, dress)_ dégrafer

undoing [ʌn'du:ɪŋ] _n_ ruine _f_; **her pride was her u.** c'est sa fierté qui l'a perdue

undone [ʌn'dʌn] _pp of_ **undo**

undoubted [ʌn'dautɪd] *adj* indubitable

undoubtedly [ʌn'dautɪdlɪ] *adv* indubitablement

undreamed-of [ʌn'dri:mdɒv], **undreamt-of** [ʌn'dremtɒv] *adj* inimaginable

undress [ʌn'dres] **1** *vt* déshabiller; **to get undressed** se déshabiller
2 *vi* se déshabiller
3 *n* **in a state of u.** *(naked)* nu(e); *(nearly naked)* en petite tenue

undue [ʌn'dju:] *adj* excessif(ive)

undulate ['ʌndjʊleɪt] *vi* onduler

undulation [ʌndjʊ'leɪʃən] *n* ondulation *f*

unduly [ʌn'dju:lɪ] *adv* trop

unearned [ʌn'ɜ:nd] *adj (reward, punishment)* immérité(e); *Fin* **u. income** rentes *fpl*

unearth [ʌn'ɜ:θ] *vt (buried object)* déterrer; *Fig (information, secret)* mettre à jour

unearthly [ʌn'ɜ:θlɪ] *adj* **(a)** *(supernatural)* mystérieux(euse) **(b)** *Fam* **at an u. hour** à une heure impossible; **an u. din** *or* **racket** un vacarme de tous les diables; **for some u. reason** pour une raison étrange

unease [ʌn'i:z] *n* malaise *m*

uneasily [ʌn'i:zɪlɪ] *adv* d'un air gêné

uneasy [ʌn'i:zɪ] *adj (person)* mal à l'aise; *(sleep)* agité(e); *(silence)* gêné(e)

uneconomical [ʌni:kə'nɒmɪkəl] *adj* peu économique

uneducated [ʌn'edjʊkeɪtɪd] *adj* sans instruction; **to be u.** ne pas avoir d'instruction

unemotional [ʌnɪ'məʊʃənəl] *adj* impassible

unemployable [ʌnɪm'plɔɪəbəl] *adj* inemployable

unemployed [ʌnɪm'plɔɪd] **1** *npl* **the u.** les sans-emploi *mpl*, les chômeurs *mpl*
2 *adj* sans emploi, au chômage

unemployment [ʌnɪm'plɔɪmənt] *n* chômage *m*; *Br* **u. benefit** allocation *f* chômage

unending [ʌn'endɪŋ] *adj* interminable

unendurable [ʌnɪn'djʊərəbəl] *adj* insupportable

unenlightened [ʌnɪn'laɪtənd] *adj (person)* peu éclairé(e)

unenlightening [ʌnɪn'laɪtnɪŋ] *adj* obscur(e)

unenterprising [ʌn'entəpraɪzɪŋ] *adj* qui manque d'initiative

unenthusiastic [ʌnɪnθju:zɪ'æstɪk] *adj* peu enthousiaste

unenviable [ʌn'envɪəbəl] *adj* peu enviable

unequal [ʌn'i:kwəl] *adj* inégal(e)

unequivocal [ʌnɪ'kwɪvəkəl] *adj* sans équivoque

unerring [ʌn'ɜ:rɪŋ] *adj* infaillible

UNESCO [ju:'neskəʊ] *n (abbr* **United Nations Educational, Scientific and Cultural Organization)** UNESCO *f*

unethical [ʌn'eθɪkəl] *adj* contraire à l'éthique

uneven [ʌn'i:vən] *adj* inégal(e)

uneventful [ʌnɪ'ventfʊl] *adj* sans histoires

unexceptionable [ʌnɪk'sepʃənəbəl] *adj* tout à fait convenable

unexceptional [ʌnɪk'sepʃənəl] *adj* qui n'a rien d'exceptionnel

unexciting [ʌnɪk'saɪtɪŋ] *adj* peu intéressant(e)

unexpected [ʌnɪks'pektɪd] *adj* inattendu(e), imprévu(e)

unexplained [ʌnɪks'pleɪnd] *adj* inexpliqué(e)

unexplored [ʌnɪks'plɔ:d] *adj* inexploré(e)

unfailing [ʌn'feɪlɪŋ] *adj* à toute épreuve

unfair [ʌn'feə(r)] *adj* injuste; **to be u. to sb** être injuste envers qn; **to have an u. advantage (over sb)** être injustement favorisé(e) (par rapport à qn); *Com* **u. competition** concurrence *f* déloyale; *Law* **u. dismissal** licenciement *m* abusif

unfairly [ʌn'feəlɪ] *adv (act, treat)* injustement; *(share, distribute)* inéquitablement; *(dismiss)* abusivement

unfairness [ʌn'feənɪs] *n* injustice *f*

unfaithful [ʌn'feɪθfʊl] *adj* infidèle

unfamiliar [ʌnfə'mɪlɪə(r)] *adj* **(a)** *(unknown)* inconnu(e) **(b)** *(unacquainted)* **to be u. with** ne pas connaître

unfashionable [ʌn'fæʃənəbəl] *adj* démodé(e)

unfasten [ʌn'fɑ:sən] **1** *vt* défaire
2 *vi* se défaire

unfathomable [ʌn'fæðəməbəl] *adj* insondable

unfavourable, *Am* **unfavorable** [ʌn'feɪvərəbəl] *adj* défavorable; *(moment)* peu propice

unfeeling [ʌn'fi:lɪŋ] *adj* insensible

unfinished [ʌn'fɪnɪʃt] *adj* inachevé(e); **to have (some) u. business (with sb)** avoir des affaires à régler (avec qn)

unfit [ʌn'fɪt] *adj* **(a)** *(unsuitable)* inapte; **to be u. to do sth** être incapable de faire qch; **he's u. for the job** il est incapable d'assumer ce travail; **u. for human consumption** impropre à la consommation; **u. mother** mère *f* indigne **(b)** *(physically)* qui n'est pas en forme; **to be u.** ne pas être en forme

unflagging [ʌn'flægɪŋ] *adj (optimism, courage, enthusiasm)* inépuisable; *(attention, interest)* sans faille

unflappable [ʌn'flæpəbəl] *adj* imperturbable

unflattering [ʌn'flætərɪŋ] *adj* peu flatteur(euse)

unflinching [ʌn'flɪntʃɪŋ] *adj (courage)* inépuisable; *(resolve, loyalty, support)* à toute épreuve

unfold [ʌn'fəʊld] **1** *vt* **(a)** *(newspaper, map)* déplier **(b)** *(intentions, proposal)* dévoiler
2 *vi (of story, events)* se développer, se dérouler

unforced [ʌn'fɔ:st] *adj* naturel(elle)

unforeseeable [ʌnfɔ:'si:əbəl] *adj* imprévisible

unforeseen [ʌnfɔ:'si:n] *adj* imprévu(e)

unforgettable [ʌnfə'getəbəl] *adj* inoubliable

unforgivable [ʌnfə'gɪvəbəl] *adj* impardonnable

unforgiving [ʌnfə'gɪvɪŋ] *adj* implacable, impitoyable

unforthcoming [ʌnfɔ:θ'kʌmɪŋ] *adj* réticent(e)

unfortunate [ʌn'fɔ:tjənɪt] *adj (person)* malchanceux(euse); *(accident, event)* fâcheux(euse), regrettable; **it is u. that...** il est fâcheux *ou* regrettable que... + *subjunctive*

unfortunately [ʌn'fɔ:tjənɪtlɪ] *adv* malheureusement

unfounded [ʌn'faʊndɪd] *adj* infondé(e), sans fondement

unfriendly [ʌn'frendlɪ] *adj (person)* peu sympathique; *(reception, tone, look)* froid(e)

unfulfilled [ʌnfʊl'fɪld] *adj (promise)* non tenu(e); *(desire, ambition)* insatisfait(e); *(potential)* non réalisé(e); **to feel u.** se sentir insatisfait

unfunny [ʌn'fʌnɪ] *adj* qui n'a rien de drôle

unfurl [ʌnˈfɜːl] **1** *vt* déployer
2 *vi* se déployer

unfurnished [ʌnˈfɜːnɪʃt] *adj* non meublé(e)

ungainly [ʌnˈgeɪnlɪ] *adj* disgracieux(euse)

ungenerous [ʌnˈdʒenərəs] *adj* (person) qui manque de générosité; (remark) pas gentil(ille)

ungodly [ʌnˈɡɒdlɪ] *adj* impie; Fam **at an u. hour** à une heure impossible

ungovernable [ʌnˈɡʌvənəbəl] *adj* (people, country) ingouvernable; (feelings) irrépressible

ungracious [ʌnˈɡreɪʃəs] *adj* peu aimable

ungrateful [ʌnˈɡreɪtfʊl] *adj* ingrat(e)

ungrudging [ʌnˈɡrʌdʒɪŋ] *adj* accordé(e) de bon cœur; **to be u. in one's praise** être généreux(euse) avec ses compliments

unguarded [ʌnˈɡɑːdɪd] *adj* (place) sans surveillance (b) (remark) irréfléchi(e); **in an u. moment** dans un moment d'inattention

unhampered [ʌnˈhæmpəd] *adj* non entravé(e) (by par)

unhappily [ʌnˈhæpɪlɪ] *adv* (a) (unfortunately) malheureusement (b) (sadly) sans joie, sans bonheur

unhappiness [ʌnˈhæpɪnɪs] *n* tristesse *f*

unhappy [ʌnˈhæpɪ] *adj* (a) (sad) triste, malheureux(euse) (b) (worried) **to be u. about doing sth** ne pas vouloir faire qch (c) (not pleased) mécontent(e) (with de) (d) (unfortunate) malheureux(euse), regrettable

unharmed [ʌnˈhɑːmd] *adj* indemne

UNHCR [juːˈenetʃsiːˈɑː(r)] *n* (abbr **United Nations High Commission for Refugees**) HCR *m*

unhealthy [ʌnˈhelθɪ] *adj* (a) (person) maladif(ive); (environment, climate) malsain(e) (b) (unwholesome) malsain(e)

unheard-of [ʌnˈhɜːdɒv] *adj* (a) (unknown) inconnu(e) (b) (unprecedented) inouï(e); **it was u. in my youth!** c'était inconcevable dans ma jeunesse!

unheeded [ʌnˈhiːdɪd] *adj* ignoré(e); **to go u.** rester ignoré

unhelpful [ʌnˈhelpfʊl] *adj* (person) peu serviable; (criticism, advice) de peu d'utilité

unhesitating [ʌnˈhezɪteɪtɪŋ] *adj* (support) résolu(e), ferme; (reply, reaction) immédiat(e)

unhindered [ʌnˈhɪndəd] **1** *adj* (progress) sans encombre; **to be u. by sth** (doubts, worry) ne pas être gêné(e) par qch
2 *adv* sans encombres

unhinged [ʌnˈhɪndʒd] *adj* (mad) déséquilibré(e)

unhip [ʌnˈhɪp] *adj* Fam (untrendy) ringard(e)

unholy [ʌnˈhəʊlɪ] *adj* impie; Fam **an u. mess/noise** une pagaille/un bruit invraisemblable; **u. alliance** alliance *f* contre nature

unhurt [ʌnˈhɜːt] *adj* indemne

unhygienic [ʌnhaɪˈdʒiːnɪk] *adj* contraire à l'hygiène; (person) qui manque d'hygiène

UNICEF [ˈjuːnɪsef] *n* (abbr **United Nations International Children's Emergency Fund**) UNICEF *m*

unicorn [ˈjuːnɪkɔːn] *n* licorne *f*

unidentified [ʌnaɪˈdentɪfaɪd] *adj* non identifié(e); **u. flying object** objet *m* volant non identifié

unification [juːnɪfɪˈkeɪʃən] *n* unification *f*

uniform [ˈjuːnɪfɔːm] **1** *n* uniforme *m*
2 *adj* (colour, size) uniforme; (temperature) constant(e)

uniformity [juːnɪˈfɔːmɪtɪ] *n* uniformité *f*

uniformly [ˈjuːnɪfɔːmlɪ] *adv* uniformément

unify [ˈjuːnɪfaɪ] (pt & pp **unified**) **1** *vt* unifier
2 *vi* s'unifier

unilateral [juːnɪˈlætərəl] *adj* unilatéral(e)

unimaginable [ʌnɪˈmædʒɪnəbəl] *adj* inimaginable

unimaginative [ʌnɪˈmædʒɪnətɪv] *adj* qui manque d'imagination, peu imaginatif(ive)

unimpaired [ʌnɪmˈpeəd] *adj* intact(e)

unimportant [ʌnɪmˈpɔːtənt] *adj* sans importance

unimpressed [ʌnɪmˈprest] *adj* qui n'est pas impressionné(e); (unconvinced) qui n'est pas convaincu(e)

uninformed [ʌnɪnˈfɔːmd] *adj* mal informé(e) (about sur)

uninhabitable [ʌnɪnˈhæbɪtəbəl] *adj* inhabitable

uninhabited [ʌnɪnˈhæbɪtɪd] *adj* inhabité(e)

uninhibited [ʌnɪnˈhɪbɪtɪd] *adj* (person) sans complexes; (feeling) non refréné(e)

uninitiated [ʌnɪˈnɪʃɪeɪtɪd] *adj* non initié(e)

uninspiring [ʌnɪnˈspaɪrɪŋ] *adj* peu stimulant(e)

unintelligible [ʌnɪnˈtelɪdʒɪbəl] *adj* inintelligible

unintended [ʌnɪnˈtendɪd] *adj* involontaire

unintentional [ʌnɪnˈtenʃənəl] *adj* involontaire

uninterested [ʌnˈɪntərestɪd] *adj* indifférent(e)

uninteresting [ʌnˈɪntərestɪŋ] *adj* inintéressant(e)

uninterrupted [ʌnɪntəˈrʌptɪd] *adj* ininterrompu(e)

uninvited [ʌnɪnˈvaɪtɪd] **1** *adj* (comment, advice) non désiré(e); **u. guest** invité(e)-surprise *m,f*
2 *adv* sans invitation

uninviting [ʌnɪnˈvaɪtɪŋ] *adj* peu attrayant(e); (food) peu appétissant(e)

union [ˈjuːnjən] *n* (a) (between countries, people) union *f*; **the U. Jack** l'Union Jack *m* (drapeau du Royaume-Uni) (b) (trade union) syndicat *m*

unionist [ˈjuːnjənɪst] *n* (a) (supporter of trade union) syndicaliste *mf* (b) (in Northern Ireland) unioniste *mf*

unionize [ˈjuːnjənaɪz] *vt* syndiquer

unique [juːˈniːk] *adj* unique; **to be u. to** être propre à

unisex [ˈjuːnɪseks] *adj* unisexe

UNISON [ˈjuːnɪsən] *n* Br = principal syndicat de la fonction publique

unison [ˈjuːnɪsən] *n* **in u.** (sing, play) à l'unisson; (speak, reply) en même temps

unit [ˈjuːnɪt] *n* (a) (in general) unité *f*; **u. of measurement** unité de mesure; Com **u. price** prix *m* à l'unité; Fin **u. trust** fonds *m* commun de placement, SICAV *f* (b) (part of system, machine) bloc *m*, élément *m* (c) (in hospital) service *m*, département *m*; (in army) unité *f* (d) (of furniture) élément *m*

unitary [ˈjuːnɪtərɪ] *adj* unitaire

unite [juːˈnaɪt] **1** *vt* unir, rassembler
2 *vi* s'unir; **to u. in doing sth** s'unir pour faire qch

united [juːˈnaɪtɪd] *adj* uni(e); **the U. Arab Emirates** les Émirats *mpl* arabes unis; **the U. Kingdom** le Royaume-Uni; **the U. Nations** les Nations *fpl* unies; **the U. States (of America)** les États-Unis *mpl* (d'Amérique)

unity [ˈjuːnɪtɪ] *n* unité *f*

univ (abbr **university**) univ

universal [juːnɪˈvɜːsəl] *adj* universel(elle); **u. suffrage** suffrage *m* universel

universally [juːnɪˈvɜːsəlɪ] adv universellement

universe [ˈjuːnɪvɜːs] n univers m

university [juːnɪˈvɜːsɪtɪ] n université f

UNIX [ˈjuːnɪks] n Comptr (abbr **Uniplexed Information and Computing System**) UNIX m

unjust [ʌnˈdʒʌst] adj injuste

unjustifiable [ʌndʒʌstɪˈfaɪəbəl] adj injustifiable

unjustified [ʌnˈdʒʌstɪfaɪd] adj injustifié(e)

unkempt [ʌnˈkem(p)t] adj négligé(e)

unkind [ʌnˈkaɪnd] adj pas gentil(ille); **to be u. to sb** ne pas être gentil avec qn

unkindly [ʌnˈkaɪndlɪ] adv méchamment; **to take u. to sth** mal accepter qch

unknowingly [ʌnˈnəʊɪŋlɪ] adv inconsciemment

unknown [ʌnˈnəʊn] **1** adj inconnu(e); Fig **to be an u. quantity** rester une inconnue; **the U. Soldier** le Soldat inconnu

2 adv **u. to me/us** à mon/notre insu

3 n (person) inconnu(e) m,f; **the u.** l'inconnu m

unlace [ʌnˈleɪs] vt délacer, défaire

unladylike [ʌnˈleɪdɪlaɪk] adj (person) qui se conduit pas comme une jeune fille; (behaviour) qui n'est pas digne d'une jeune fille

unlawful [ʌnˈlɔːfʊl] adj illégal(e), illicite

unleaded [ʌnˈledɪd] **1** adj sans plomb

2 n sans plomb m

unleash [ʌnˈliːʃ] vt (dog) détacher, lâcher; Fig (emotion, criticism) susciter

unleavened [ʌnˈlevənd] adj sans levain

unless [ʌnˈles] conj à moins que + subjunctive; **u. I hear to the contrary** sauf avis contraire

unlike [ʌnˈlaɪk] prep **to be u. sb/sth** ne pas être comme qn/qch; **he's not u. his sister** il ressemble assez à sa sœur; **he, u. his father,...** lui, à la différence de son père...; **it's u. her to do such a thing** cela ne lui ressemble pas de faire une chose pareille

unlikely [ʌnˈlaɪklɪ] adj improbable; (story, explanation) invraisemblable; **it's u. to happen** il est peu probable que cela se produise; **she's u. to do it** il est peu probable qu'elle le fasse; **in the u. event of an accident** dans le cas fort peu probable d'un accident

unlimited [ʌnˈlɪmɪtɪd] adj illimité(e), sans limites; **u. mileage** (of hired car) ≃ kilométrage m illimité

unlisted [ʌnˈlɪstɪd] adj **(a)** Fin non inscrit(e) à la cote **(b)** Am Tel (phone number) qui est sur liste rouge

unlit [ʌnˈlɪt] adj (fire, cigarette) non allumé(e); (place) non éclairé(e)

unload [ʌnˈləʊd] **1** vt (boat, gun, goods) décharger; Fig **to u. one's problems onto sb** se soulager de ses problèmes en en parlant à qn

2 vi (of lorry, ship) décharger

unlock [ʌnˈlɒk] vt (door) ouvrir; Fig (mystery) dévoiler, révéler

unlovable [ʌnˈlʌvəbəl] adj peu attachant(e)

unloved [ʌnˈlʌvd] adj mal aimé(e)

unlovely [ʌnˈlʌvlɪ] adj déplaisant(e)

unluckily [ʌnˈlʌkɪlɪ] adv malheureusement

unlucky [ʌnˈlʌkɪ] adj (coincidence, decision) malheureux(euse); (day) de malchance; **to be u.** (of person) être malchanceux(euse); (of thing) porter malheur

unmanageable [ʌnˈmænɪdʒəbəl] adj (person, situation) difficile; (hair) impossible à coiffer

unmanly [ʌnˈmænlɪ] adj (effeminate) effeminé(e), peu viril(e); (cowardly) lâche

unmanned [ʌnˈmænd] adj (spaceship) inhabité(e)

unmarked [ʌnˈmɑːkt] adj **(a)** (grave) sans inscription; **u.** (police) car voiture f (de police) banalisée **(b)** (uncorrected) non corrigé(e)

unmarried [ʌnˈmærɪd] adj non marié(e)

unmask [ʌnˈmɑːsk] vt démasquer

unmentionable [ʌnˈmenʃənəbəl] adj à ne pas mentionner

unmistakable [ʌnmɪsˈteɪkəbəl] adj caractéristique

unmitigated [ʌnˈmɪtɪɡeɪtɪd] adj total(e), absolu(e)

unmoved [ʌnˈmuːvd] **1** adj **to be u. by sth** rester insensible à qch; **he was u. by her** elle le laissait complètement indifférent

2 adv sans broncher

unnamed [ʌnˈneɪmd] adj (person) anonyme; (thing) sans nom

unnatural [ʌnˈnætʃərəl] adj **(a)** (abnormal) anormal(e) **(b)** (affected) affecté(e)

unnecessary [ʌnˈnesɪsərɪ] adj inutile, superflu(e)

unnerve [ʌnˈnɜːv] vt troubler

unnerving [ʌnˈnɜːvɪŋ] adj troublant(e)

unnoticed [ʌnˈnəʊtɪst] **1** adj inaperçu(e)

2 adv **to pass** or **go u.** passer inaperçu(e)

UNO [juːenˈəʊ] n (abbr **United Nations Organization**) ONU f

unobservant [ʌnəbˈzɜːvənt] adj peu observateur(trice)

unobserved [ʌnəbˈzɜːvd] **1** adj inaperçu(e)

2 adv **to do sth u.** faire qch sans être vu(e)

unobstructed [ʌnəbˈstrʌktɪd] adj dégagé(e); (pipe) non obstrué(e)

unobtainable [ʌnəbˈteɪnəbəl] adj impossible à obtenir

unobtrusive [ʌnəbˈtruːsɪv] adj discret(ète)

unoccupied [ʌnˈɒkjʊpaɪd] adj (person) qui n'est pas occupé(e); (seat) libre; (house) inhabité(e), inoccupé(e)

unofficial [ʌnəˈfɪʃəl] adj **(a)** officieux(euse), non officiel(elle); Ind **u. strike** grève f sauvage

unopened [ʌnˈəʊpənd] adj non ouvert(e)

unopposed [ʌnəˈpəʊzd] **1** adj sans opposition; **to be u.** ne pas rencontrer d'opposition

2 adv **to go u.** ne pas rencontrer d'opposition

unorthodox [ʌnˈɔːθədɒks] adj peu orthodoxe

unpack [ʌnˈpæk] **1** vt (suitcase) défaire; (contents) déballer; (box) ouvrir

2 vi défaire ses bagages

unpaid [ʌnˈpeɪd] adj **(a)** (work, volunteer) non rémunéré(e) **(b)** (bill, debt) impayé(e)

unpalatable [ʌnˈpælətəbəl] adj (food) qui n'est pas très bon (bonne); Fig (truth) désagréable à entendre

unparalleled [ʌnˈpærəleld] adj incomparable, sans pareil(eille)

unpardonable [ʌnˈpɑːdənəbəl] adj impardonnable

unpatriotic [ʌnpætrɪˈɒtɪk, ʌnpeɪtrɪˈɒtɪk] adj (person) peu patriote; (song, remark) antipatriotique

unperturbed [ʌnpəˈtɜːbd] **1** adj **to be u. by sth** ne pas se laisser perturber par qch

2 adv imperturbablement

unplanned [ʌnˈplænd] adj imprévu(e); (pregnancy) accidentel(elle)

unpleasant [ʌnˈplezənt] adj désagréable, déplaisant(e)

unpleasantness [ʌn'plezəntnɪs] n (a) (unpleasant nature) côté m désagréable (b) (ill-feeling) désagréments mpl

unplug [ʌn'plʌg] (pt & pp **unplugged**) vt débrancher

unpolished [ʌn'polɪʃt] adj (shoes, surface) non ciré(e); Fig (performance, style) imparfait(e)

unpolluted [ʌnpə'luːtɪd] adj non pollué(e)

unpopular [ʌn'pɒpjʊlə(r)] adj impopulaire; **she's very u. with the boss at the moment** elle n'est pas dans les bonnes grâces du patron en ce moment

unpopularity [ʌnpɒpjʊ'lærɪt] n impopularité f

unpredictable [ʌnprɪ'dɪktəbəl] adj imprévisible

unprejudiced [ʌn'predʒʊdɪst] adj (view, person) impartial(e)

unprepared [ʌnprɪ'peəd] adj (speech) improvisé(e); **to be u. for sth** être mal préparé(e) à qch; (not expect) ne pas s'attendre à qch

unprepossessing [ʌnpriːpə'zesɪŋ] adj peu avenant(e)

unpresentable [ʌnprɪ'zentəbəl] adj qui n'est pas présentable

unpretentious [ʌnprɪ'tenʃəs] adj sans prétention(s)

unprincipled [ʌn'prɪnsɪpəld] adj sans scrupules

unprintable [ʌn'prɪntəbəl] adj inédit(e)

unproductive [ʌnprə'dʌktɪv] adj improductif(ive)

unprofessional [ʌnprə'feʃənəl] adj qui n'est pas professionnel(elle)

unprofitable [ʌn'profɪtəbəl] adj peu rentable

unpromising [ʌn'promɪsɪŋ] adj peu prometteur(euse)

unpronounceable [ʌnprə'naʊnsəbəl] adj imprononçable

unprotected [ʌnprə'tektɪd] adj sans protection; (sex) non protégé(e)

unprovoked [ʌnprə'vəʊkt] adj gratuit(e)

unpublished [ʌn'pʌblɪʃt] adj inédit(e)

unpunished [ʌn'pʌnɪʃt] 1 adj impuni(e)
2 adv **to go u.** rester impuni(e)

unqualified [ʌn'kwolɪfaɪd] adj (a) (doctor, teacher) non qualifié(e); **to be u. to do sth** ne pas être qualifié pour faire qch (b) (support) inconditionnel(elle), sans réserve; (disaster, success) total(e), complet(ète)

unquestionable [ʌn'kwestʃənəbəl] adj indubitable, incontestable

unquestioning [ʌn'kwestʃənɪŋ] adj (trust, obedience) absolu(e), aveugle

unravel [ʌn'rævəl] (pt & pp **unravelled**) 1 vt (wool, knitting) défaire; (threads) démêler; Fig (plot) dénouer; (mystery) éclaircir
2 vi (of wool, knitting) se défaire; Fig (of plan) péricliter; (of mystery) s'éclaircir

unreadable [ʌn'riːdəbəl] adj illisible

unreal [ʌn'rɪəl] adj irréel(elle)

unrealistic [ʌnrɪə'lɪstɪk] adj irréaliste

unreasonable [ʌn'riːzənəbəl] adj déraisonnable

unrecognizable [ʌnrekəg'naɪzəbəl] adj méconnaissable

unrecognized [ʌn'rekəgnaɪzd] 1 adj méconnu(e)
2 adv **to go u.** rester méconnu(e)

unrecorded [ʌn'kɔːdɪd] adj non enregistré(e)

unrefined [ʌnrɪ'faɪnd] adj (a) (sugar, petrol) non raffiné(e) (b) (person, taste) qui manque de raffinement

unregistered [ʌn'redʒɪstəd] adj (birth) non déclaré(e)

unrelated [ʌnrɪ'leɪtɪd] adj **to be u.** (of events) ne pas avoir de rapport; (of people) n'avoir aucun lien de parenté

unrelenting [ʌnrɪ'lentɪŋ] adj incessant(e); (person) tenace

unreliable [ʌnrɪ'laɪəbəl] adj peu fiable

unrelieved [ʌnrɪ'liːvd] adj (pain) constant(e)

unremarkable [ʌnrɪ'mɑːkəbəl] adj quelconque

unremitting [ʌnrɪ'mɪtɪŋ] adj inlassable, infatigable

unrepentant [ʌnrɪ'pentənt] adj impénitent(e)

unreported [ʌnrɪ'pɔːtɪd] 1 adj non signalé(e)
2 adv **to go u.** ne pas être signalé(e)

unrepresentative [ʌnreprɪ'zentətɪv] adj non représentatif(ive)

unrepresented [ʌnreprɪ'zentɪd] adj non représenté(e)

unrequited love ['ʌnrɪkwaɪtɪd'lʌv] n amour m non partagé

unreserved [ʌnrɪ'zɜːvd] adj (a) (praise, support) sans réserve (b) (seat, table) non réservé(e)

unresponsive [ʌnrɪ'spɒnsɪv] adj sans réaction; **to be u. to sth** être insensible à qch

unrest [ʌn'rest] n agitation f, troubles mpl

unrestricted [ʌnrɪ'strɪktɪd] adj illimité(e); (access) libre

unrewarding [ʌn'wɔːdɪŋ] adj (financially) qui ne rapporte pas; (intellectually) ingrat(e)

unripe [ʌn'raɪp] adj qui n'est pas mûr(e)

unrivalled [ʌn'raɪvəld] adj sans pareil(eille), incomparable

unromantic [ʌnrə'mæntɪk] adj peu romantique

unruffled [ʌn'rʌfəld] adj imperturbable

unruly [ʌn'ruːlɪ] adj (child, hair) indiscipliné(e); (crowd) incontrôlé(e)

unsaddle [ʌn'sædəl] vt (horse) desseller

unsafe [ʌn'seɪf] adj (a) (in danger) en danger (b) (dangerous) dangereux(euse)

unsaid [ʌn'sed] adj **to leave sth u.** passer qch sous silence; **it's better left u.** il vaut mieux garder le silence là-dessus

unsalted [ʌn'sɔːltɪd] adj sans sel; **u. butter** beurre m doux

unsatisfactory [ʌnsætɪs'fæktərɪ] adj peu satisfaisant(e)

unsatisfying [ʌn'sætɪsfaɪɪŋ] adj peu satisfaisant(e)

unsavoury [ʌn'seɪvərɪ] adj (person, place) peu recommandable; (reputation) sale

unscathed [ʌn'skeɪðd] adj indemne

unscheduled [ʌn'ʃedjuːld] adj imprévu(e)

unscientific [ʌnsaɪən'tɪfɪk] adj non scientifique

unscramble [ʌn'skræmbəl] vt décoder

unscrew [ʌn'skruː] 1 vt dévisser
2 vi se dévisser

unscrupulous [ʌn'skruːpjʊləs] adj (person) sans scrupules; (action) malhonnête

unseat [ʌn'siːt] vt (rider) désarçonner; Fig (MP) faire perdre son siège à; (leader) faire tomber

unseemly [ʌn'siːmlɪ] adj inconvenant(e), indécent(e)

unseen [ʌn'siːn] 1 adj invisible; **u. translation** traduction f à vue
2 adv **to do sth u.** faire qch sans qu'on vous voie

unselfconscious [ʌnself'kɒnʃəs] adj naturel(elle)

unselfish [ʌn'selfɪʃ] adj généreux(euse)

unsentimental [ʌnsentɪ'mentəl] *adj (person)* peu sentimental(e); *(book, film)* dénué(e) de tout sentimentalisme

unsettle [ʌn'setəl] *vt* perturber

unshakeable [ʌn'ʃeɪkəbəl] *adj* inébranlable

unshaven [ʌn'ʃeɪvən] *adj* pas rasé(e)

unsightly [ʌn'saɪtlɪ] *adj* laid(e)

unsigned [ʌn'saɪnd] *adj* non signé(e)

unskilful [ʌn'skɪlf(ʊ)l] *adj* maladroit(e), malhabile

unskilled [ʌn'skɪld] *adj* non qualifié(e)

unsociable [ʌn'səʊʃəbəl] *adj (by nature)* sauvage; **she's feeling rather u. at the moment** elle n'a pas envie de voir du monde en ce moment

unsold [ʌn'səʊld] *adj* invendu(e)

unsolicited [ʌnsə'lɪsɪtɪd] *adj* non sollicité(e)

unsolved [ʌn'sɒlvd] *adj* non résolu(e)

unsophisticated [ʌnsə'fɪstɪkeɪtɪd] *adj* simple

unsound [ʌn'saʊnd] *adj* **(a)** *(health)* précaire; *Law* **to be of u. mind** ne pas jouir de toutes ses facultés mentales **(b)** *(decision, advice)* peu judicieux(euse); *(investment)* hasardeux(euse)

unsparing [ʌn'speərɪŋ] *adj* **to be u. of one's time/with one's advice** ne pas être avare de son temps/de ses conseils

unspeakable [ʌn'spi:kəbəl] *adj* indescriptible

unspecified [ʌn'spesɪfaɪd] *adj* non spécifié(e)

unspoilt [ʌn'spɔɪlt] *adj (beach, landscape)* préservé(e)

unspoken [ʌn'spəʊkən] *adj (fear, threat)* inexprimé(e); *(agreement)* tacite

unsporting [ʌn'spɔ:tɪŋ], **unsportsmanlike** [ʌn'spɔ:tsmənlaɪk] *adj* qui n'est pas fair-play

unstable [ʌn'steɪbəl] *adj* instable

unsteady [ʌn'stedɪ] *adj (table, chair)* bancal(e); *(hand, voice)* mal assuré(e); **to be u. on one's feet** ne pas être très solide sur ses jambes

unstinting [ʌn'stɪntɪŋ] *adj (praise, effort)* sans réserve

unstressed [ʌn'strest] *adj Ling* inaccentué(e)

unstuck [ʌn'stʌk] *adj Fam* **to come u.** *(of person, plan)* se casser la figure

unsubstantiated [ʌnsəb'stænʃɪeɪtɪd] *adj (accusation)* sans fondement

unsuccessful [ʌnsək'sesfʊl] *adj* **to be u.** *(of person, project)* ne pas réussir

unsuccessfully [ʌnsək'sesfəlɪ] *adv* en vain, sans succès

unsuitable [ʌn'su:təbəl] *adj (candidate)* inadéquat(e); *(friend)* pas convenable; *(time)* inopportun(e); *(choice)* inapproprié(e); **to be u. for sth** ne pas convenir à qch; **this film is u. for children** ce n'est pas un film pour les enfants

unsuited [ʌn'su:tɪd] *adj* **to be u. to sth** ne pas être fait(e) pour qch; **to be u.** *(of couple)* être mal assorti(e)

unsupported [ʌnsə'pɔ:tɪd] *adj* **(a)** *(statement, charges)* sans fondement **(b)** *(structure)* non soutenu(e)

unsure [ʌn'ʃʊə(r)] *adj* incertain(e), peu sûr(e); **to be u. of or about sth** ne pas être sûr de qch

unsurpassed [ʌnsə'pɑ:st] *adj* inégalé(e)

unsuspected [ʌnsəs'pektɪd] *adj* insoupçonné(e)

unsuspecting [ʌnsəs'pektɪŋ] *adj* qui ne se doute de rien

unsweetened [ʌn'swi:tənd] *adj* non sucré(e), sans sucre ajouté

unswerving [ʌn'swɜ:vɪŋ] *adj* à toute épreuve

unsympathetic [ʌnsɪmpə'θetɪk] *adj* peu compatissant(e) (**to** à); *(to cause, request)* insensible (**to** à)

unsystematic [ʌnsɪstə'mætɪk] *adj* non systématique

untainted [ʌn'teɪntɪd] *adj (food)* qui n'a pas été contaminé(e); *(reputation)* qui n'a pas été entaché(e)

untalented [ʌn'tæləntɪd] *adj* peu doué(e)

untamed [ʌn'teɪmd] *adj (animal)* sauvage

untangle [ʌn'tæŋgəl] *vt* démêler; *Fig (plot)* dénouer

untapped [ʌn'tæpt] *adj* inexploité(e)

untenable [ʌn'tenəbəl] *adj (position)* intenable; *(theory)* indéfendable

untested [ʌn'testɪd] *adj (drug, product)* non testé(e); *(method, system)* qui n'a pas été mis(e) à l'épreuve

unthinkable [ʌn'θɪŋkəbəl] *adj* impensable, inconcevable

untidiness [ʌn'taɪdɪnɪs] *n* désordre *m*

untidy [ʌn'taɪdɪ] *adj (person)* désordonné(e); *(place)* en désordre

untie [ʌn'taɪ] *vt (knot, shoelaces)* défaire; *(string)* dénouer; *(person, animal)* détacher

until [ʌn'tɪl] **1** *prep* jusqu'à; **u. April** jusqu'en avril; **u. now** jusqu'à présent; **not u. tomorrow** pas avant demain; **I didn't see her u. Sunday** c'est seulement dimanche que je l'ai vue

2 *conj* jusqu'à ce que + *subjunctive*; **u. she gets back** jusqu'à ce qu'elle revienne; **don't move u. I tell you** ne bouge pas avant que je (ne) te le dise

untimely [ʌn'taɪmlɪ] *adj (death)* prématuré(e); *(remark)* inopportun(e); *(moment)* mauvais(e)

untiring [ʌn'taɪərɪŋ] *adj* infatigable, inlassable

untold [ʌn'təʊld] *adj (wealth, beauty)* immense

untouchable [ʌn'tʌtʃəbəl] **1** *n* intouchable *mf*; *Fig* paria *m*

2 *adj* intouchable

untouched [ʌn'tʌtʃt] *adj* qui n'a pas été touché(e); **to leave sth u.** ne pas toucher à qch

untoward [ʌntə'wɔ:d] *adj* fâcheux(euse), malencontreux(euse)

untrained [ʌn'treɪnd] *adj (animal)* non dressé(e); *(person)* sans formation

untranslatable [ʌntræns'leɪtəbəl] *adj* intraduisible

untried [ʌn'traɪd] *adj* **(a)** *(person, system)* qui n'a pas encore fait ses preuves **(b)** *Law (person, case)* non jugé(e)

untroubled [ʌn'trʌbəld] *adj* tranquille, calme; **to be u. by sth** ne pas être perturbé(e) par qch

untrue [ʌn'tru:] *adj* **(a)** *(false)* faux (fausse) **(b)** *(unfaithful)* infidèle (**to** à)

untrustworthy [ʌn'trʌstwɜ:ðɪ] *adj (person)* qui n'est pas digne de confiance; *(information)* qui n'est pas fiable

untruth [ʌn'tru:θ] *n* mensonge *m*

untruthful [ʌn'tru:θfʊl] *adj (person)* menteur(euse); *(story, reply)* mensonger(ère)

unusable [ʌn'ju:zəbəl] *adj* inutilisable

unused *adj* **(a)** [ʌn'ju:zd] *(not in use)* inutilisé(e) **(b)** *(never yet used)* neuf (neuve) **(c)** [ʌn'ju:st] *(unaccustomed)* **to be u. to sth/to doing sth** ne pas avoir l'habitude de qch/de faire qch

unusual [ʌnˈjuːʒʊəl] *adj (not common)* inhabituel(elle); *(strange)* bizarre, étrange; **it's u. of her not to notice** c'est rare qu'elle ne s'en rende pas compte

unusually [ʌnˈjuːʒʊəlɪ] *adv* exceptionnellement

unvaried [ʌnˈveərɪd] *adj* monotone

unvarnished [ʌnˈvɑːnɪʃt] *adj* non verni(e); *Fig* **the u. truth** la vérité pure et simple

unveil [ʌnˈveɪl] *vt also Fig* dévoiler

unverifiable [ʌnˈverɪfaɪəbəl] *adj* invérifiable

unvoiced [ʌnˈvɔɪst] *adj* **(a)** *Ling* non voisé(e) **(b)** *(unspoken)* inexprimé(e)

unwaged [ʌnˈweɪdʒd] **1** *npl* **the u.** ceux qui n'ont pas d'activité rémunérée
2 *adj* qui n'a pas d'activité rémunérée

unwanted [ʌnˈwɒntɪd] *adj* non désiré(e); **to feel u.** se sentir de trop

unwarranted [ʌnˈwɒrəntɪd] *adj* injustifié(e)

unwary [ʌnˈweərɪ] *adj* sans méfiance

unwavering [ʌnˈweɪvərɪŋ] *adj (devotion)* inébranlable; *(loyalty, support)* à toute épreuve; *(gaze)* fixe

unwelcome [ʌnˈwelkəm] *adj (visit, visitor)* importun(e); *(news)* fâcheux(euse); **to make sb feel u.** faire sentir à qn qu'il n'est pas le bienvenu

unwell [ʌnˈwel] *adj* souffrant(e)

unwholesome [ʌnˈhəʊlsəm] *adj* malsain(e)

unwieldy [ʌnˈwiːldɪ] *adj (object)* difficile à manier; *Fig (system, method)* lourd(e)

unwilling [ʌnˈwɪlɪŋ] *adj* réticent(e); **to be u. to do sth** être réticent à faire qch

unwillingness [ʌnˈwɪlɪŋnɪs] *n* réticence *f*

unwind [ʌnˈwaɪnd] *(pt & pp* **unwound** [ʌnˈwaʊnd]*)* **1** *vt (string, wool)* dérouler
2 *vi* **(a)** *(of string, wool)* se dérouler **(b)** *Fam (relax)* se détendre, se relaxer

unwise [ʌnˈwaɪz] *adj (person)* imprudent(e); *(decision, action)* peu judicieux(euse)

unwitting [ʌnˈwɪtɪŋ] *adj* involontaire

unworkable [ʌnˈwɜːkəbəl] *adj* infaisable

unworthy [ʌnˈwɜːðɪ] *adj* indigne *(of* de)

unwrap [ʌnˈræp] *(pt & pp* **unwrapped**) *vt* déballer

unwritten [ʌnˈrɪtən] *adj (language)* non écrit(e); *(agreement)* verbal(e); **it's an u. rule that...** il est entendu que...

unyielding [ʌnˈjiːldɪŋ] *adj* inflexible

unzip [ʌnˈzɪp] *(pt & pp* **unzipped**) *vt* ouvrir (la fermeture Éclair® de)

up [ʌp] **1** *adv* **(a)** *(with motion)* **to come/go up** monter; **to go up to sb** s'approcher de qn; **to go up north** aller au nord; **to put one's hand up** lever la main; **to put a poster up** accrocher un poster; **petrol has gone up in price** l'essence a augmenté
(b) *(with position)* en haut; **up here** ici; **up there** là-haut; **up above** au-dessus; **further up** plus haut; **petrol is up in price** l'essence a augmenté
(c) *(ahead)* **to be one goal/five points up** avoir un but/cinq points d'avance
(d) *(in phrases with to)* **up to now/the age of seven** jusqu'à maintenant/l'âge de sept ans; **what are the children up to?** que fabriquent les enfants?; **she's up to something** elle prépare quelque chose; **what have you been up to?** qu'est-ce que tu deviens?; **it's up to you to do it** c'est à vous de le faire; **it's up to you** *(you*

decide) c'est à vous de décider; **he's not up to the job** il n'est pas à la hauteur de la tâche; **I don't feel up to it** je ne m'en sens pas capable; **it's not up to much** *(not very good)* ce n'est pas extraordinaire
2 *prep* **(a)** *(with motion)* **to go up the stairs/the street** monter les escaliers/la rue; **to run up the stairs/the street** monter les escaliers/la rue en courant; **to climb up a hill** monter à une colline; *Vulg* **up yours!** va te faire foutre!
(b) *(with position)* **to be up a tree/ladder** être dans un arbre/sur une échelle; **to live up the street (from sb)** habiter plus haut dans la rue (que qn); *Fig* **to be up against sth** avoir affaire à qch
3 *adj* **(a)** *(out of bed)* levé(e); **I was up at seven** j'étais levé à sept heures; **we were up all night** nous sommes restés debout toute la nuit; **to be up and about** être debout; *(after illness)* être sur pied
(b) *(finished)* **the two weeks were up** les deux semaines étaient terminées; **(your) time's up** c'est terminé
(c) *Fam (wrong)* **something's up** quelque chose ne va pas; **what's up?** qu'est-ce qu'il y a?; **what's up with her?** qu'est-ce qu'elle a?
(d) *(idiom)* **to be up and running** *(of machine, system)* être opérationnel(elle)
4 *n* **ups and downs** des hauts et des bas
5 *vt Fam (price, offer)* augmenter
6 *vi Fam* **to up and go** *or* **leave** filer

up-and-coming [ˈʌpəndˈkʌmɪŋ] *adj* qui monte

upbeat [ˈʌpbiːt] *adj* optimiste

upbraid [ʌpˈbreɪd] *vt* réprimander; **to u. sb for sth** reprocher qch à qn; **to u. sb for doing sth** reprocher à qn d'avoir fait qch

upbringing [ˈʌpbrɪŋɪŋ] *n* éducation *f*

update 1 *n* [ˈʌpdeɪt] mise *f* à jour, actualisation *f*
2 *vt* [ʌpˈdeɪt] mettre à jour, actualiser; **to u. sb on sth** mettre qn au courant de qch

upend [ʌpˈend] *vt* renverser

upfront [ʌpˈfrʌnt] **1** *adj Fam (frank)* franc (franche), direct(e)
2 *adv (in advance)* d'avance

upgrade 1 *n* [ˈʌpgreɪd] *Comptr (of hardware)* augmentation *f* de puissance; *(of software)* nouvelle version *f*
2 *vt* [ʌpˈgreɪd] **(a)** *(improve)* améliorer; *(promote)* promouvoir **(b)** *Comptr (hardware)* augmenter la puissance de; *(software)* acquérir la dernière version de

upheaval [ʌpˈhiːvəl] *n* bouleversement *m*

uphill [ˈʌphɪl] **1** *adj* qui monte; *Fig (struggle)* ardu(e), pénible
2 *adv* **to go u.** monter

uphold [ʌpˈhəʊld] *(pt & pp* **upheld** [ʌpˈheld]*)* *vt (opinion, principle)* soutenir; *(decision)* maintenir; **to u. the law** faire respecter la loi

upholstered [ʌpˈhəʊlstəd] *adj* tapissé(e)

upholstery [ʌpˈhəʊlstərɪ] *n* tapisserie *f*; *(in car)* sièges *mpl*

upkeep [ˈʌpkiːp] *n* entretien *m*

uplift 1 *n* [ˈʌplɪft] élévation *f* morale *ou* spirituelle
2 *vt* [ʌpˈlɪft] élever

uplifting [ʌpˈlɪftɪŋ] *adj* édifiant(e)

up-market [ˈʌpmɑːkɪt] *adj (product)* haut de gamme *inv*; *(area, place)* chic *inv*

upon [əˈpɒn] *prep* sur; **u. my word!** ma parole!

upper ['ʌpə(r)] **1** *adj* supérieur(e); **u. class** aristocratie *f*; **to get/have the u. hand** prendre/avoir le dessus; *Br Pol* **the U. House** la Chambre des Lords

2 *n* (*of shoe*) empeigne *f*; *Fam* **to be on one's uppers** manger de la vache enragée

upper-class ['ʌpəklɑ:s] *adj* aristocratique

upper-crust ['ʌpəkrʌst] *adj Fam* aristo

uppermost ['ʌpəməʊst] *adj* le (la) plus haut(e); *Fig* **it was u. in my mind** c'était la première de mes préoccupations

uppity ['ʌpɪtɪ] *adj Fam* crâneur(euse); **to get u.** crâner

upright ['ʌpraɪt] **1** *adj* **(a)** (*vertical*) droit(e); **u. piano** piano *m* droit; **u. vacuum cleaner** aspirateur *m* balai **(b)** (*honest*) droit(e)

2 *adv* droit

3 *n* (*beam*) montant *m*

uprising ['ʌpraɪzɪŋ] *n* soulèvement *m*, révolte *f*

uproar ['ʌprɔ:(r)] *n* (*noise, protest*) tumulte *m*; **the house was in an u.** ce fut le tumulte dans la maison

uproarious [ʌp'rɔ:rɪəs] *adj* (*noisy*) tonitruant(e); (*funny*) hilarant(e)

uproot [ʌp'ru:t] *vt* déraciner

upset [ʌp'set] **1** *vt* (*pt & pp* upset) **(a)** (*liquid, container*) renverser **(b)** (*person, plans, schedule*) bouleverser

2 *n* ['ʌpset] (*disturbance*) bouleversement *m*; (*surprise*) défaite *f*; **to have a stomach u.** avoir l'estomac dérangé

3 *adj* (*unhappy*) bouleversé(e) (**about** par); **to have an u. stomach** avoir l'estomac dérangé

upsetting [ʌp'setɪŋ] *adj* bouleversant(e)

upshot ['ʌpʃɒt] *n* conséquence *f*, résultat *m*

upside down ['ʌpsaɪd'daʊn] **1** *adj* à l'envers

2 *adv* à l'envers; **to turn sth u.** retourner qch; *Fig* mettre qch sens dessus dessous

upstage [ʌp'steɪdʒ] **1** *adv Th* (*move*) vers le fond de la scène; **u. of sb/sth** à l'arrière-plan par rapport à qn/qch

2 *vt Th & Fig* éclipser, voler la vedette à

upstairs 1 *n* [ʌp'steəz] étage *m*

2 *adj* ['ʌpsteəz] de l'étage du dessus; **u. neighbours** les voisins du dessus; **the u. bathroom** la salle de bains du haut

3 *adv* [ʌp'steəz] en haut; **to come/go u.** monter; **he lives u.** il habite à l'étage au-dessus

upstanding [ʌp'stændɪŋ] *adj* droit(e)

upstart ['ʌpstɑ:t] *n* parvenu(e) *m,f*

upstream [ʌp'stri:m] *adv* en amont; (*with movement*) vers l'amont

upsurge ['ʌpsɜ:dʒ] *n* vague *f*

upswing ['ʌpswɪŋ] *n* amélioration *f* (**in** de); (*in economy*) redressement *m* (**in** de)

uptake ['ʌpteɪk] *n Fam* **to be quick on the u.** piger vite; **to be slow on the u.** être lent(e) à la détente

uptight [ʌp'taɪt] *adj Fam* (*nervous*) tendu(e), crispé(e); (*inhibited*) coincé(e)

up-to-date [ʌptə'deɪt] *adj* **(a)** (*most recent*) à jour; (*news*) récent(e); **to bring sb u.** (**on sth**) mettre qn au courant (de qch) **(b)** (*modern*) à la mode

up-to-the-minute [ʌptəðə'mɪnɪt] *adj* (*news, information*) de dernière minute; (*style, fashion*) dernier cri *inv*

upturn ['ʌptɜ:n] *n* amélioration *f* (**in** de); (*in economy*) redressement *m* (**in** de)

upturned ['ʌptɜ:nd] *adj* (*bucket, box*) retourné(e); (*nose*) retroussé(e)

upward ['ʌpwəd] **1** *adj* vers le haut; **u. mobility** ascension *f* sociale; **an u. trend** une tendance à la hausse

2 *adv* = **upwards**

upwardly mobile ['ʌpwədlɪ'məʊbaɪl] *adj* qui connaît une ascension sociale rapide

upwards ['ʌpwədz] *adv* vers le haut; **from £100 u.** à partir de 100 livres; **u. of** plus de

Urals ['jʊərəlz] *npl* **the U.** l'Oural *m*

uranium [jʊ'reɪnɪəm] *n* uranium *m*

Uranus [jʊ'reɪnəs] *n* (*planet*) Uranus *f*

urban ['ɜ:bən] *adj* urbain(e); **u. legend** *or* **myth** = anecdote souvent inventée mais qui passe pour vraie; **u. renewal** rénovations *fpl* urbaines; **u. sprawl** étalement *m* urbain

urbane [ɜ:'beɪm] *adj* urbain(e), courtois(e)

urbanization [ɜ:bənaɪ'zeɪʃən] *n* (*process*) urbanisation *f*

urchin ['ɜ:tʃɪn] *n* galopin(e) *m,f*

Urdu ['ʊədu:] *n* ourdou *m*

urethra [jʊ'ri:θrə] *n* urètre *m*

urge [ɜ:dʒ] **1** *n* terrible envie *f*; **to have an u. to do sth** avoir très envie de faire qch

2 *vt* **(a)** (*encourage*) **to u. sb to do sth** presser qn de faire qch **(b)** (*recommend*) conseiller; **to u. that sth be done** insister pour que qch soit fait

▸**urge on** *vt sep* encourager; **to u. sb on to do sth** encourager qn à faire qch

urgency ['ɜ:dʒənsɪ] *n* urgence *f*; **it's a matter of u.** il y a urgence

urgent ['ɜ:dʒənt] *adj* urgent(e); **to be in u. need of sth** avoir un besoin urgent de qch

urgently ['ɜ:dʒəntlɪ] *adv* d'urgence

urinal [jə'raɪnəl] *n* urinoir *m*

urinary ['jʊərɪnərɪ] *adj* urinaire

urinate ['jʊərɪneɪt] *vi* uriner

urine ['jʊərɪn] *n* urine *f*

urn [ɜ:n] *n* urne *f*; (**tea**) **u.** fontaine *f* (à thé)

urology [jʊ'rɒlədʒɪ] *n Med* urologie *f*

Uruguay ['jʊərəgwaɪ] *n* l'Uruguay *m*

Uruguayan [jʊərə'gwaɪən] **1** *n* Uruguayen(enne) *m,f*

2 *adj* uruguayen(enne)

us [stressed ʌs, unstressed əs] *pron* **(a)** (*direct object*) nous; **she hates us** elle nous déteste; **she can understand our son but not us** elle comprend notre fils, mais nous, elle ne nous comprend pas **(b)** (*indirect object*) nous; **she gave us the book** elle nous a donné le livre; **she gave it to us** elle nous l'a donné **(c)** (*after preposition*) nous; **she's thinking of us** elle pense à nous **(d)** (*as complement of verb to be*) nous; **it's us!** c'est nous!; **it was us who did it** c'est nous qui l'avons fait

US [ju:'es] **1** *n* (*abbr* **United States**) **the US** les USA *mpl*

2 *adj* (*forces, officials*) américain(e), des États-Unis

USA [ju:es'eɪ] *n* **(a)** (*abbr* **United States of America**) **the U.** les USA *mpl* **(b)** *Am* (*abbr* **United States Army**) armée *f* de terre des États-Unis

usable ['ju:zəbəl] *adj* utilisable

USAF [ju:eseɪ'ef] *n Am* (*abbr* **United States Air Force**) armée *f* de l'air des États-Unis

usage ['ju:sɪdʒ] *n* usage *m*

use 1 *n* [ju:s] **(a)** (*utilization*) utilisation *f*, emploi *m*; **to make (good) u. of sth** faire (bon) usage de qch; **to be in u.** être utilisé(e); **not in u., out of u.** hors d'usage **(b)**

(ability, permission to use) usage *m*; **to have the u. of sth** pouvoir utiliser qch; **she has full u. of her faculties** elle jouit de toutes ses facultés **(c)** *(usefulness)* **to be of u.** être utile; **can I be of any u. to you?** puis-je vous être d'une quelconque utilité?; **it's not much u.** cela ne sert pas à grand-chose; **to have no u. for sth** ne pas avoir l'usage de qch; *Fam* **he's no u.** il n'est bon à rien; **it's no u.** cela ne sert à rien; **it's no u. crying** cela ne sert à rien de pleurer; **what's the u. of worrying?** à quoi bon s'inquiéter?

2 *vt* [ju:z] **(a)** *(utilize)* utiliser, se servir de; *(force, diplomacy)* avoir recours à; *Fam* **u. your head!** réfléchis un peu!; *Fam* **I could u. some sleep** un peu de sommeil ne me ferait pas de mal **(b)** *(exploit)* utiliser, se servir de **(c)** *(consume) (petrol, electricity)* consommer; **who's used all the milk?** qui a pris tout le lait?

3 *v aux* **used to** *(translated by imperfect of main verb)* **we used to live abroad** (autrefois,) nous vivions à l'étranger; **I didn't u. to like him** avant, je ne l'aimais pas; **do you travel much? – I used to** tu voyages beaucoup? – autrefois, oui

▸**use up** *vt sep (food, fuel)* finir; *(ideas)* épuiser; *(money)* dépenser

use-by date ['ju:zbaideit] *n* date *f* limite de consommation

used *adj* **(a)** [ju:zd] *(second-hand)* d'occasion **(b)** [ju:st] *(accustomed)* **to be u.** to sth/to doing sth être habitué(e) à qch/à faire qch; **to get u. to sb/sth** s'habituer à qn/qch

useful ['ju:sfəl] *adj* utile; **to make oneself u.** se rendre utile

usefully ['ju:sfəli] *adv* utilement

usefulness ['ju:sfʊlnis] *n* utilité *f*

useless ['ju:slis] *adj* **(a)** *(not useful)* inutile; **to be worse than u.** ne servir strictement à rien **(b)** *(incompetent)* nul (nulle) **(at en)**

user ['ju:zə(r)] *n (of road, dictionary)* utilisateur(trice) *m,f*; *(of telephone)* usager *m*; *(of drugs)* consommateur(trice) *m,f*

user-friendly [ju:zə'frendli] *adj* convivial(e)

usher ['ʌʃə(r)] **1** *n (in court)* huissier *m*; *(in theatre, cinema)* ouvreur *m*; *(at wedding)* placeur *m*

2 *vt* **to u. sb in/out** faire entrer/sortir qn

usherette [ʌʃə'ret] *n* ouvreuse *f*

USIA [ju:esar'er] *n Am (abbr* **United States Information Agency)** renseignements *mpl* généraux américains

USN [ju:es'en] *n Am (abbr* **United States Navy)** marine *f* de guerre des États-Unis

USP [ju:es'pi:] *n Com (abbr* **unique selling point** *or* **proposition)** avantage *m* unique

USS [ju:es'es] *n Am (abbr* **United States Ship)** U. Lexington le Lexington *(bâtiment de la marine américaine)*

USSR [ju:eses'ɑ:(r)] *n Formerly (abbr* **Union of Soviet Socialist Republics)** URSS *f*

usual ['ju:ʒʊəl] **1** *adj* habituel(elle); **you're not your u. cheery self today** tu n'es pas aussi gai que d'habitude aujourd'hui; **earlier/later than u.** plus tôt/tard que d'habitude; **as u.** comme d'habitude

2 *n Fam (drink)* the u., sir? comme d'habitude, monsieur?

usually ['ju:ʒʊəli] *adv* habituellement, d'habitude; **he was more than u. polite** il était plus poli que d'habitude

usurer ['ju:ʒərə(r)] *n* usurier(ère) *m,f*

usurp [ju:'zɜ:p] *vt* usurper

usurper [ju:'zɜ:pə(r)] *n* usurpateur(trice) *m,f*

usury ['ju:ʒʊri] *n* usure *f*

utensil [ju:'tensəl] *n* ustensile *m*

uterus ['ju:tərəs] *(pl* **uteri** ['ju:tərai]*) n* utérus *m*

utilitarian [ju:tili'teəriən] **1** *adj (approach, design)* utilitaire; *(in philosophy)* utilitariste

2 *n (in philosophy)* utilitariste *mf*

utility [ju:'tiliti] *n* **(a)** *(usefulness)* utilité *f*; *Comptr* **u. program** *(programme m)* utilitaire *m*; **u. room** pièce *f* de rangement **(b)** *(public)* **utilities** services *mpl* (publics) **(c)** *Am* **utilities** *(service charges)* charges *fpl*

utilize ['ju:tilaiz] *vt* utiliser, se servir de

utmost ['ʌtməʊst] **1** *n* **to the u.** au plus haut point; **to do one's u. (to do sth)** faire de son mieux (pour faire qch)

2 *adj* **(a)** *(greatest)* **the u.** le (la) plus grand(e); **it is of the u. importance that...** il est de la plus haute importance que... + *subjunctive* **(b)** *(furthest)* **to the u. ends of the earth** au bout du monde

utopia [ju:'təʊpiə] *n* utopie *f*

utopian [ju:'təʊpiən] **1** *n* utopiste *mf*

2 *adj* utopique

utter¹ ['ʌtə(r)] *adj* total(e); **it's u. madness** c'est de la folie pure; **it's u. rubbish** c'est complètement absurde

utter² *vt (cry)* pousser; *(word)* prononcer

utterance ['ʌtərəns] *n (act)* énonciation *f*; *(words spoken)* paroles *fpl*, déclaration *f*

utterly ['ʌtəli] *adv* complètement, tout à fait

uttermost ['ʌtəməʊst] *adj* = **utmost**

UV [ju:'vi:] *adj Phys (abbr* **ultra-violet)** UV *inv*; **UV rays** UV *mpl*

uvula ['ju:vjələ] *n* luette *f*

Uzbekistan [ʊzbekɪ'stɑ:n] *n* l'Ouzbékistan *m*

V

V, v [viː] n (a) (letter) V, v m inv; **V. sign** (for victory) signe m de la victoire; (as insult) cornes fpl (b) (abbr **very**) t (c) (abbr **versus**) contre (d) (abbr **verse**) (pl vv) V

V (abbr **volt**) V

VA [viːˈeɪ] n Am (abbr **Veterans Administration**) ≃ ministère m des Anciens Combattants

vacancy ['veɪkənsɪ] n (a) (position, job) poste m vacant (b) (at hotel) chambre f libre ou à louer; **no vacancies** (sign) complet

vacant ['veɪkənt] adj (a) (seat, space) libre, inoccupé(e) (b) (expression, look) absent(e)

vacantly ['veɪkəntlɪ] adv d'un air absent

vacate [vəˈkeɪt] vt (seat, flat) libérer, quitter; (one's post) démissionner de

vacation [vəˈkeɪʃən] n Br Univ & Am vacances fpl; Am **to take a v.** prendre des vacances

vaccinate ['væksɪneɪt] vt vacciner

vaccination [væksɪˈneɪʃən] n vaccination f

vaccine ['væksiːn] n vaccin m

vacillate ['væsɪleɪt] vi hésiter (**between** entre)

vacuous ['vækjʊəs] adj (person, look) vide, sans expression; (book, remark) dénué(e) de sens

vacuum ['vækjʊm] 1 n Phys vacuum m; Fig vide m; **v. cleaner** aspirateur m; **v. flask** thermos® m
2 vt (room) passer l'aspirateur dans
3 vi passer l'aspirateur

vacuum-packed [vækjʊmˈpækt] adj (emballé(e)) sous vide

vagabond ['væɡəbɒnd] n vagabond(e) m,f

vagary ['veɪɡərɪ] n caprice m

vagina [vəˈdʒaɪnə] n vagin m

vagrancy ['veɪɡrənsɪ] n vagabondage m

vagrant ['veɪɡrənt] n vagabond(e) m,f

vague [veɪɡ] adj (idea, feeling) vague; (shape, outline) flou(e), indistinct(e); **I haven't the vaguest idea** je n'en ai pas la moindre idée

vaguely ['veɪɡlɪ] adv vaguement

vagueness ['veɪɡnɪs] n imprécision f, flou m

vain [veɪn] 1 adj (a) (conceited) vaniteux(euse) (b) (hopeless) vain(e)
2 **in v.** en vain

vale [veɪl] n Lit val m, vallée f; Fig **v. of tears** vallée de larmes

valency ['veɪlənsɪ] n Chem valence f

valentine ['væləntaɪn] n **v. (card)** carte f de la Saint-Valentin; **V.'s Day** la Saint-Valentin

valet ['væleɪ] n valet m de chambre

valiant ['væljənt] adj Lit vaillant(e)

valiantly ['væljəntlɪ] adv vaillamment

valid ['vælɪd] adj valable; **v. for six months** valable six mois; **no longer v.** périmé(e)

validate ['vælɪdeɪt] vt (document) valider; (theory) confirmer

validation [vælɪˈdeɪʃən] n (of document) validation f; (of theory) confirmation f

validity [vəˈlɪdɪtɪ] n validité f

valise [vəˈliːz] n Am mallette f

valley ['vælɪ] n vallée f

valour, Am **valor** ['vælə(r)] n bravoure f

valuable ['væljʊəbəl] 1 adj (object) de valeur; (advice, time, contribution) précieux(euse) (**to** à)
2 n **valuables** objets mpl de valeur

valuation [væljʊˈeɪʃən] n (a) (act) estimation f (b) (price) évaluation f

value ['væljuː] 1 n (a) (worth) valeur f; **to be of v.** avoir de la valeur; **to be good/poor v. (for money)** être d'un bon/mauvais rapport qualité-prix; **to set a v. upon sth** estimer la valeur de qch; **to the v. of** pour une valeur de; **to make a v. judgment** faire un jugement de valeur (b) **values** (principles) valeurs fpl
2 vt (a) (evaluate) estimer (b) (appreciate) apprécier

value-added tax ['væljuːædɪd'tæks] n taxe f sur la valeur ajoutée

valued ['væljuːd] adj précieux(euse)

valueless ['væljʊlɪs] adj sans valeur

valve [vælv] n (in body) valve f; Tech soupape f

vampire ['væmpaɪə(r)] n vampire m; **v. bat** vampire m

van[1] [væn] n (a) (vehicle) camionnette f, fourgonnette f; **v. driver** chauffeur m de camionnette (b) Br Rail fourgon m

van[2] = **vanguard**

Vancouver [væŋˈkuːvə(r)] n Vancouver

vandal ['vændəl] n vandale mf

vandalism ['vændəlɪzəm] n vandalisme m

vandalize ['vændəlaɪz] vt saccager

vane [veɪn] n girouette f

vanguard ['vænɡɑːd] n avant-garde f; **to be in the v. of** être à l'avant-garde de

vanilla [vəˈnɪlə] n vanille f; **v. essence** extrait m de vanille; **v. ice cream** glace f à la vanille

vanish ['vænɪʃ] vi disparaître

vanishing ['vænɪʃɪŋ] adj **to do a v. act** disparaître dans la nature; **v. point** point m de fuite

vanity ['vænɪtɪ] n vanité f; **v. case** vanity-case m, mallette f de toilette

vanquish ['væŋkwɪʃ] vt Lit vaincre

vantage point ['vɑːntɪdʒˌpɔɪnt] *n* point *m* de vue; *Fig* position *f* objective

Vanuatu [vænuˈɑːtuː] *n* Vanuatu *m*

vapid ['væpɪd] *adj* insipide

vapor ['veɪpə(r)] *Am* = **vapour**

vaporize ['veɪpəraɪz] 1 *vt* vaporiser
2 *vi* se vaporiser

vapour, *Am* **vapor** ['veɪpə(r)] *n* vapeur *f*; **v. trail** traînée *f* de condensation

variable ['veərɪəbəl] 1 *n* variable *f*
2 *adj* variable

variance ['veərɪəns] *n* désaccord *m*; **to be at v. with sb/sth** être en désaccord avec qn/qch

variant ['veərɪənt] 1 *n* variante *f*
2 *adj* différent(e)

variation [veərɪˈeɪʃən] *n* variation *f*

varicose vein ['værɪkəʊsˈveɪn] *n* varice *f*

varied ['veərɪd] *adj* varié(e)

variegated ['veərɪgeɪtɪd] *adj* panaché(e)

variety [vəˈraɪətɪ] *n* (a) (*diversity*) variété *f*; **a v. of toutes sortes de;** *Prov* **v. is the spice of life** la diversité est le sel de la vie (b) (*of plant*) variété *f* (c) (*in theatre, on TV*) variétés *fpl*; **v. show** spectacle *m* de variétés

various ['veərɪəs] *adj* (*different*) divers(e); (*several*) plusieurs

variously ['veərɪəslɪ] *adv* **v. described as a hero or a rogue** parfois décrit comme un héros, d'autres fois comme un escroc

varnish ['vɑːnɪʃ] 1 *n* vernis *m*
2 *vt* vernir

▶**varnish over** *vt sep Fig* maquiller, dissimuler

vary ['veərɪ] 1 *vt* varier
2 *vi* varier (**in/with** en/selon)

varying ['veərɪɪŋ] *adj* qui varie, variable

vase [*Br* vɑːz, *Am* veɪz] *n* vase *m*

vasectomy [vəˈsektəmɪ] *n* vasectomie *f*; **to have a v.** subir une vasectomie

Vaseline® ['væsɪliːn] *n* vaseline *f*

vast [vɑːst] *adj* immense

vastly ['vɑːstlɪ] *adv* à l'extrême; (*superior*) infiniment

VAT [viːeɪˈtiː] *n* (*abbr* **value added tax**) TVA *f*

vat [væt] *n* (*container*) cuve *f*, bac *m*

Vatican ['vætɪkən] *n* **the V.** le Vatican; **V. City** la cité du Vatican, le Vatican

vaudeville ['vɔːdəvɪl] *n* music-hall *m*

vault¹ [vɔːlt] *n* (a) (*roof*) voûte *f* (b) (*cellar*) cave *f*; (*for burial*) caveau *m*; (*of bank*) chambre *f* forte, salle *f* des coffres

vault² *vt & vi* sauter

vaulted ['vɔːltɪd] *adj* (*ceiling*) voûté(e)

vaulting horse ['vɔːltɪŋˌhɔːs] *n* cheval *m* d'arçons

vaunt [vɔːnt] *vt* vanter; **his much vaunted reputation as...** sa réputation tant vantée de...

VC [viːˈsiː] *n* (a) (*abbr* **Vice-Chairman**) vice-président *m* (b) (*abbr* **Victoria Cross**) = la plus haute distinction militaire britannique

VCR [viːsiːˈɑː(r)] *n* (*abbr* **video cassette recorder**) magnétoscope *m*

VD [viːˈdiː] *n* (*abbr* **venereal disease**) maladie *f* vénérienne

VDU [viːdiːˈjuː] *n* *Comptr* (*abbr* **visual display unit**) moniteur *m*

veal [viːl] *n* veau *m*

vector ['vektə(r)] *n* vecteur *m*

veer ['vɪə(r)] *vi* virer; **to v. to the left/right** virer à gauche/droit

▶**veer round** *vi* tourner, changer de direction; *Fig* **she has veered round to our point of view** elle s'est ralliée à notre point de vue

veg [vedʒ] *npl Br Fam* (*abbr* **vegetables**) légumes *mpl*

vegan ['viːgən] *n* végétalien(enne) *m,f*

vegetable ['vedʒtəbəl] *n* (a) légume *m*; **v. garden** potager *m* (b) (*brain-damaged person*) légume *m*

vegetarian [vedʒɪˈteərɪən] *n & adj* végétarien(enne) *m,f*

vegetate ['vedʒɪteɪt] *vi* végéter

vegetation [vedʒɪˈteɪʃən] *n* végétation *f*

veggie ['vedʒɪ] *n & adj Br Fam* (*abbr* **vegetarian**) végétarien(enne) *m,f*

vehemence ['viːməns] *n* véhémence *f*

vehement ['viːmənt] *adj* véhément(e)

vehicle ['viːɪkəl] *n* véhicule *m*

vehicular [vɪˈhɪkjʊlə(r)] *adj* de véhicules; **v. traffic** circulation *f* automobile

veil [veɪl] *n also Fig* voile *m*; *Fig* **to draw a v. over sth** jeter un voile sur qch; *Fig* **under a v. of secrecy** sous le voile du secret
2 *vt* voiler; *Fig* **veiled in secrecy** secret(ète)

veiled [veɪld] *adj also Fig* voilé(e)

vein [veɪn] *n* (a) (*in body, wood, marble*) veine *f*; (*in leaf*) nervure *f*; (*in rock*) filon *m* (b) (*idioms*) **and now, in a lighter v.**... et maintenant, dans un registre plus léger...; **in similar v.** de la même veine

Velcro® ['velkrəʊ] *n* (bande *f*) Velcro® *m*

vellum ['veləm] *n* vélin *m*; **v. (paper)** papier *m* vélin

velocity [vɪˈlɒsɪtɪ] *n* vélocité *f*

velvet ['velvɪt] *n* velours *m*; **v. jacket** veste *f* en velours

velveteen [velvɪˈtiːn] *n* velvantine *f*

velvety ['velvɪtɪ] *adj* velouté(e)

venal ['viːnəl] *adj* vénal(e)

vendetta [venˈdetə] *n* vendetta *f*; **to carry on a v. against sb** mener une vendetta contre qn

vending machine ['vendɪŋməˈʃiːn] *n* distributeur *m* automatique

vendor ['vendɔː(r)] *n* vendeur(euse) *m,f*

veneer [vəˈnɪə(r)] *n* placage *m*; *Fig* vernis *m*, apparence *f*

venerable ['venərəbəl] *adj* vénérable

venerate ['venəreɪt] *vt* vénérer

veneration [venəˈreɪʃən] *n* vénération *f*

venereal [vɪˈnɪərɪəl] *adj* vénérien(enne); **v. disease** maladie *f* vénérienne

Venetian [vɪˈniːʃən] 1 *n* Vénitien(enne) *m,f*
2 *adj* vénitien(enne); **V. blind** store *m* vénitien

Venezuela [veneˈzweɪlə] *n* le Venezuela

Venezuelan [veneˈzweɪlən] 1 *n* Vénézuélien(enne) *m,f*
2 *adj* vénézuélien(enne)

vengeance ['vendʒəns] *n* vengeance *f*; **to take v. on sb** se venger de qn; *Fig* **with a v.** de plus belle; **the problem has returned with a v.** le problème s'est reposé avec d'autant plus d'acuité

vengeful ['vendʒfʊl] *adj* vengeur(eresse)

venial ['vi:nɪəl] *adj* véniel(elle)

Venice ['venɪs] *n* Venise

venison ['venɪsən] *n* venaison *f*

venom ['venəm] *n also Fig* venin *m*

venomous ['venəməs] *adj also Fig* venimeux(euse)

vent [vent] **1** *n* conduit *m*; *Fig* **to give v. to sth** donner *ou* laisser libre cours à qch
2 *vt* **to v. one's anger (on)** décharger sa colère (sur)

ventilate ['ventɪleɪt] *vt* ventiler, aérer

ventilation [ventɪ'leɪʃən] *n* ventilation *f*, aération *f*

ventilator ['ventɪleɪtə(r)] *n* **(a)** *Tech* ventilateur *m* **(b)** *Med* respirateur *m*; **to be on a v.** être branché(e) sur respirateur

ventriloquism [ven'trɪləkwɪzəm] *n* ventriloquie *f*

ventriloquist [ven'trɪləkwɪst] *n* ventriloque *mf*; **v.'s dummy** poupée *f* de ventriloque

venture ['ventʃə(r)] **1** *n* entreprise *f* hasardeuse; *(in business)* entreprise; *Fin* **v. capital** capital-risque *m*
2 *vt* risquer; **to v. to do sth** se risquer à faire qch; *Prov* **nothing ventured, nothing gained** qui ne risque rien n'a rien
3 *vi* s'aventurer

▶**venture on, venture upon** *vt insep* s'aventurer dans

venue ['venju:] *n* *(for meeting, concert)* salle *f*; *(for football match)* stade *m*

Venus ['vi:nəs] *n* *(planet)* Vénus *f*

veracity [və'ræsɪtɪ] *n* *Formal* véracité *f*

veranda(h) [və'rændə] *n* véranda *f*

verb [vɜ:b] *n* verbe *m*

verbal [vɜ:bəl] *adj* verbal(e); **v. abuse** insultes *fpl* verbales

verbalize ['vɜ:bəlaɪz] *vt* verbaliser

verbally ['vɜ:bəlɪ] *adv* verbalement

verbatim [vɜ:'beɪtɪm] **1** *adj* textuel(elle)
2 *adv* mot pour mot

verbiage ['vɜ:bɪɪdʒ] *n* verbiage *m*

verbose [vɜ:'bəʊs] *adj* verbeux(euse)

verbosity [vɜ:'bɒsɪtɪ] *n* verbosité *f*

verdict ['vɜ:dɪkt] *n also Fig* verdict *m*; **to return a v. of guilty/not guilty** rendre un verdict de culpabilité/non-culpabilité

verge [vɜ:dʒ] *n* *(of road)* bord *m*; *Fig* **on the v. of sth** au bord de qch; *(victory, defeat)* à deux doigts de qch; *Fig* **to be on the v. of doing sth** être sur le point de faire qch

▶**verge on** *vt insep* friser

verger ['vɜ:dʒə(r)] *n* *(in Church of England)* bedeau *m*

verifiable ['verɪfaɪəbəl] *adj* vérifiable

verification [verɪfɪ'keɪʃən] *n* vérification *f*

verify ['verɪfaɪ] *(pt & pp* **verified)** *vt* vérifier

verisimilitude [verɪsɪ'mɪlɪtju:d] *n* *Formal* vraisemblance *f*

veritable ['verɪtəbəl] *adj* *Formal* véritable

vermilion [və'mɪljən] **1** *n* vermillon *m*
2 *adj* vermillon *inv*

vermin ['vɜ:mɪn] *npl also Fig* vermine *f*

vermouth ['vɜ:məθ] *n* vermouth *m*

vernacular [və'nækjʊlə(r)] **1** *n* langue *f* vernaculaire
2 *adj* vernaculaire

verruca [ve'ru:kə] *n* verrue *f* plantaire

versatile ['vɜ:sətaɪl] *adj* polyvalent(e)

versatility [vɜ:sə'tɪlɪtɪ] *n* polyvalence *f*

verse [vɜ:s] *n* **(a)** *(poetry)* vers *mpl* **(b)** *(stanza)* strophe *f* **(c)** *(of Bible)* verset *m*

versed [vɜ:st] *adj* **to be (well) v. in sth** être versé(e) dans qch

version ['vɜ:ʃən] *n* version *f*

versus ['vɜ:səs] *prep* **(a)** *(in law, sport)* contre **(b)** *(compared to)* comparé(e) à

vertebra ['vɜ:tɪbrə] *(pl* **vertebrae** ['vɜ:tɪbri:]) *n* vertèbre *f*

vertebral column ['vɜ:tɪbrəl'kɒləm] *n* colonne *f* vertébrale

vertebrate ['vɜ:tɪbrɪt] **1** *n* vertébré *m*
2 *adj* vertébré(e)

vertex ['vɜ:teks] *(pl* **vertices** ['vɜ:tɪsi:z]) *n* sommet *m*

vertical ['vɜ:tɪkəl] **1** *n* verticale *f*
2 *adj* vertical(e)

vertically ['vɜ:tɪklɪ] *adv* à la verticale

vertigo ['vɜ:tɪgəʊ] *n* vertige *m*

verve [vɜ:v] *n* verve *f*

very ['verɪ] **1** *adv* **(a)** *(extremely)* très; **v. little** très peu; **v. much** beaucoup; **are you hungry? – yes, v.** as-tu faim? – oui, très; *Rad* **v. high frequency** hyperfréquences *fpl* **(b)** *(emphatic use)* **the v. first/last** le (la) tout(e) premier(ère)/dernier(ère); **the v. best** tout ce qu'il y a de mieux; **at the v. most/least** tout au plus/moins; **at the v. earliest/latest** au plus tôt/tard; **the v. same** exactement le même; **I v. nearly died** j'ai bien failli mourir; **the v. next day** le lendemain même
2 *adj* *(emphatic use)* **this v. house** cette maison même; **this v. day** aujourd'hui même; **those were her v. words** c'est ce qu'elle a dit mot pour mot; **at the v. beginning** au tout début; **the v. thought of it!** rien que d'y penser!

vessel ['vesəl] *n* **(a)** *(ship)* vaisseau *m* **(b)** *(container)* récipient *m*

vest [vest] *n* *Br (undershirt)* maillot *m* de corps; *Am (waistcoat)* gilet *m*

vested ['vestɪd] *adj* **to have a v. interest in sth/in doing sth** avoir un intérêt personnel dans qch/à faire qch

vestibule ['vestɪbju:l] *n* hall *m*

vestige ['vestɪdʒ] *n* vestige *m*

vestments ['vestmənts] *npl Rel* habits *mpl* sacerdotaux

vestry ['vestrɪ] *n Rel* sacristie *f*

vet¹ [vet] *n* *(veterinary surgeon)* vétérinaire *mf*

vet² *(pt & pp* **vetted)** *vt* effectuer une enquête sur

vet³ *n Am Fam Mil (veteran)* ancien combattant *m*

veteran ['vetərən] **1** *n Mil* ancien combattant *m*; *Fig* vétéran *m*
2 *adj* de longue date

veterinarian [vetərɪ'neərɪən] *n Am* vétérinaire *mf*

veterinary ['vetərɪnərɪ] *adj* vétérinaire; **v. medicine** médecine *f* vétérinaire; *Formal* **v. surgeon** vétérinaire *mf*

veto ['vi:təʊ] **1** *n* *(pl* **vetoes)** veto *m*; **right** *or* **power of v.** droit *m* de veto; **to impose a v. on sth** mettre son veto à qch
2 *vt* mettre son veto à

vetting ['vetɪŋ] *n* enquête *f* personnelle

vex [veks] *vt* contrarier

vexation [vek'seɪʃən] *n* *(annoyance)* contrariété *f*

vexed [vekst] *adj* (a) *(annoyed)* très contrarié(e) (b) v. question question *f* controversée

VHF [viːeɪtʃ'ef] *n (abbr* **very high frequency)** VHF *f*

VHS [viːeɪtʃ'es] *n (abbr* **video home system)**VHS *m*

via ['vaɪə] *prep* par, via

viability [vaɪə'bɪlɪtɪ] *n* viabilité *f*

viable ['vaɪəbəl] *adj* viable

viaduct ['vaɪədʌkt] *n* viaduc *m*

vibes [vaɪbz] *npl Fam* ambiance *f*; **I got good/bad v. from her** je la sentais/je ne la sentais pas bien

vibrant ['vaɪbrənt] *adj* très actif(ive)

vibrate [var'breɪt] *vi* vibrer

vibration [var'breɪʃən] *n* vibration *f*

vibrator [var'breɪtə(r)] *n* vibromasseur *m*

vicar ['vɪkə(r)] *n (in Church of England)* pasteur *m*

vicarage ['vɪkərɪdʒ] *n* presbytère *m*

vicarious [var'keərɪəs, vɪ-] *adj* indirect(e)

vice¹ [vaɪs] *n (immorality, immoral activity)* vice *m*; **the V. Squad** ≃ **la brigade des mœurs**

vice² *n (tool)* étau *m*

vice-chairman [vaɪs'tʃeəmən] *n* vice-président(e) *m,f*

vice-president [vaɪs'prezɪdənt] *n* vice-président(e) *m,f*

viceroy ['vaɪsrɔɪ] *n* vice-roi *m*

vice versa [vaɪs'vɜːsə] *adv* vice versa

vicinity [vɪ'sɪnɪtɪ] *n* **in the v. (of)** dans les alentours (de); **a sum in the v. of £25,000** un chiffre aux alentours de 25 000 livres

vicious ['vɪʃəs] *adj (violent)* violent(e); *(malicious, cruel)* malveillant(e); **v. circle** cercle *m* vicieux

vicissitudes [vɪ'sɪsɪtjuːdz] *npl Formal* vicissitudes *fpl*

victim ['vɪktɪm] *n* victime *f*; **to be the v. of sth** être victime de qch

victimization [vɪktɪmaɪ'zeɪʃən] *n* brimades *fpl*

victimize ['vɪktɪmaɪz] *vt (bully)* prendre comme tête de Turc; *(penalize)* pénaliser

victor ['vɪktə(r)] *n* vainqueur *m*

Victorian [vɪk'tɔːrɪən] **1** *n* Victorien(enne) *m,f*
2 *adj* victorien(enne)

victorious [vɪk'tɔːrɪəs] *adj* victorieux(euse); **to be v. over sb** vaincre qn

victory ['vɪktərɪ] *n* victoire *f*; **v. celebrations** = fêtes pour célébrer une victoire

victuals ['vɪtəlz] *npl Old-fashioned (food)* victuailles *fpl*

video ['vɪdɪəʊ] **1** *n (pl* **videos)** *(medium)* vidéo *f*; *(cassette)* (cassette *f*) vidéo; *(recorder)* magnétoscope *m*; **v. camera** caméra *f* vidéo; **v. cassette** *or* **tape** cassette *f* vidéo; **v. (cassette) recorder** magnétoscope; **v. game** jeu *m* vidéo; **v. nasty** = film vidéo à contenu très violent ou pornographique
2 *vt (on video recorder)* enregistrer (b) *(on camcorder)* filmer en vidéo

vie [vaɪ] *(pt & pp* **vied** [vaɪd]) *vi* **to v. with sb (for sth/to do sth)** rivaliser avec qn (pour qch/pour faire qch)

Vienna [vɪ'enə] *n* Vienne

Viennese [vɪə'niːz] **1** *n* Viennois(e) *m,f*
2 *adj* viennois(e)

Vietnam [vɪet'næm] *n* le Viêt Nam; **the V. War** la guerre du Viêt Nam

Vietnamese [vɪetnə'miːz] **1** *npl (people)* **the V. les** Vietnamiens *mpl*

2 *n* (a) *(person)* Vietnamien(enne) *m,f* (b) *(language)* vietnamien *m*
3 *adj* vietnamien(enne)

view [vjuː] **1** *n* (a) *(sight, scene, prospect)* vue *f*; **a room with a v.** une chambre avec vue; **to have a good v. of sth** avoir une belle vue de qch; **in full v. of** sous les yeux de; *Fig* **in v. of** *(considering)* compte tenu de, étant donné (b) *(opinion)* opinion *f*; **in my v.** à mon avis (c) *(intention)* intention *f*; **with this in v.** *(prospective property, exhibition)* dans cette intention; **with a v. to doing sth** dans l'intention de faire qch
2 *vt* (a) *(look at)* voir; *(prospective property, exhibition)* visiter (b) *(consider)* voir, considérer; **to v. sth with horror/delight** envisager qch avec horreur/ravissement

viewer ['vjuːə(r)] *n* (a) *(of TV)* téléspectateur(trice) *m,f* (b) *(for slides)* visionneuse *f*

viewfinder ['vjuːfaɪndə(r)] *n* viseur *m*

viewpoint ['vjuːpɔɪnt] *n* point *m* de vue

vigil ['vɪdʒɪl] *n* veillée *f*; **to keep v.** veiller

vigilance ['vɪdʒɪləns] *n* vigilance *f*

vigilant ['vɪdʒɪlənt] *adj* vigilant(e)

vigilante [vɪdʒɪ'læntɪ] *n* = membre d'une milice privée

vignette [vɪn'jet] *n (photo, picture)* buste *m* sur un fond dégradé; *(short essay)* court portrait *m*

vigor ['vɪgə(r)] *Am* = **vigour**

vigorous ['vɪgərəs] *adj* vigoureux(euse)

vigour, *Am* **vigor** ['vɪgə(r)] *n* vigueur *f*

Viking ['vaɪkɪŋ] **1** *n* Viking *mf*
2 *adj* viking *inv*

vile [vaɪl] *adj (weather, person, thought)* abominable; *(food, drink)* infecte; *(temper)* exécrable

vilification [vɪlɪfɪ'keɪʃən] *n* calomnie *f*

vilify ['vɪlɪfaɪ] *(pt & pp* **vilified)** *vt* calomnier

villa ['vɪlə] *n* villa *f*

village ['vɪlɪdʒ] *n* village *m*; **v. idiot** idiot *m* du village

villager ['vɪlɪdʒə(r)] *n* villageois(e) *m,f*

villain ['vɪlən] *n (scoundrel)* scélérat *m*; *Hum* **the v. of the piece** le/la coupable

villainous ['vɪlənəs] *adj* diabolique

villainy ['vɪlənɪ] *n* infamie *f*

Vilnius ['vɪlnɪəs] *n* Vilnius

vindicate ['vɪndɪkeɪt] *vt (decision, action)* donner raison à; *(right, claim)* justifier

vindication [vɪndɪ'keɪʃən] *n (of decision, action)* bien-fondé *m*; *(of right, claim)* justification *f*

vindictive [vɪn'dɪktɪv] *adj* vindicatif(ive)

vine [vaɪn] *n* vigne *f*; **v. leaf** feuille *f* de vigne

vinegar ['vɪnɪgə(r)] *n* vinaigre *m*

vineyard ['vɪnjəd] *n* vigne *f*

vintage ['vɪntɪdʒ] *n (year)* année *f*; *(wine)* cru *m*; *Fig* **a v. year (for)** une grande année (pour); **v. car** = voiture construite entre 1919 et 1930; **v. wine** vin *m* de cru

vinyl ['vaɪnɪl] *n* vinyle *m*

viola [vɪ'əʊlə] *n* alto *m*

violate ['vaɪəleɪt] *vt (agreement)* violer; *(rule, law)* enfreindre

violation [vaɪə'leɪʃən] *n* violation *f*

violence ['vaɪələns] *n* violence *f*

violent ['vaɪələnt] *adj* violent(e); **to take a v. dislike to sb/sth** se prendre d'une aversion violente pour qn/qch

violently ['vaɪələntlɪ] *adv* violemment; *(die)* de mort violente; **to be v. sick** être pris(e) de violents vomissements

violet ['vaɪələt] **1** *n* (a) *(flower)* violette f (b) *(colour)* violet *m*
2 *adj* v.(-coloured) violet(ette)

violin [vaɪə'lɪn] *n* violon *m*

violinist [vaɪə'lɪnɪst] *n* violoniste *mf*

VIP [viːaɪ'piː] *n (abbr* **very important person)** VIP *mf;* **V. lounge** salon *m* de luxe; **to get V. treatment** recevoir un accueil princier

viper ['vaɪpə(r)] *n* vipère f

viral ['vaɪrəl] *adj* viral(e)

virgin ['vɜːdʒɪn] **1** *n* vierge *mf;* **the (Blessed) V.** la Sainte Vierge; **the V. Islands** les îles *fpl* Vierges
2 *adj* vierge

Virginia [və'dʒɪnjə] *n* la Virginie

virginity [və'dʒɪnɪtɪ] *n* virginité f

Virgo ['vɜːgəʊ] *n (sign of zodiac)* la Vierge; **to be (a) V.** être Vierge

virile ['vɪraɪl] *adj* viril(e)

virility [vɪ'rɪlɪtɪ] *n* virilité f

virology [vaɪ'rɒlədʒɪ] *n* virologie f

virtual ['vɜːtjʊəl] *adj* (a) quasi; **it's a v. impossibility** c'est quasiment impossible (b) *Comptr* virtuel(elle); **v. reality** réalité f virtuelle

virtually ['vɜːtjʊəlɪ] *adv* quasiment, pratiquement

virtue ['vɜːtjuː] *n* (a) *(goodness)* vertu f; **by v. of** en vertu de; **to make a v. of necessity** faire de nécessité vertu (b) *(advantage)* avantage *m*

virtuoso [vɜːtjʊ'əʊzəʊ] *(pl* **virtuosos** *or* **virtuosi** [vɜːtjʊ'əʊziː]) *n* virtuose *mf*

virtuous ['vɜːtjʊəs] *adj* vertueux(euse)

virulent ['vɪr(j)ʊlənt] *adj* virulent(e)

virus ['vaɪrəs] *n Med & Comptr* virus *m*

visa ['viːzə] *n* visa *m*

vis-à-vis ['viːzɑːviː] *prep* par rapport à, vis-à-vis de

visceral ['vɪsərəl] *adj* viscéral(e)

viscount ['vaɪkaʊnt] *n* vicomte *m*

viscous ['vɪskəs] *adj* visqueux(euse)

visibility [vɪzɪ'bɪlɪtɪ] *n* visibilité f

visible ['vɪzɪbəl] *adj* visible

visibly ['vɪzɪblɪ] *adv* visiblement

vision ['vɪʒən] *n* (a) *(eyesight)* vue f; **to have good/poor v.** avoir une bonne/mauvaise vue (b) *(foresight, imagination)* clairvoyance f (c) *(apparition)* vision f; **I had visions of being left homeless** je me suis vu devenir sans-abri

visionary ['vɪʒənərɪ] *(pl* **visionaries)** *n & adj* visionnaire *mf*

visit ['vɪzɪt] **1** *n* visite f; **to pay sb a v.** rendre visite à qn; **to be on a v.** être en visite
2 *vt (person)* rendre visite à; *(museum, monument)* visiter
3 *vi to* **be visiting** être de passage

visiting ['vɪzɪtɪŋ] **1** *n* **v. card** carte f de visite; **v. hours** heures *fpl* de visite; **v. rights** *(of divorced parent)* droits *mpl* de visite
2 *adj* **v. professor** professeur *m* invité

visitor ['vɪzɪtə(r)] *n* visiteur(euse) *m,f;* **visitors' book** livre *m* d'or

visor ['vaɪzə(r)] *n* visière f

vista ['vɪstə] *n* vue f; *Fig* perspective f

visual ['vɪʒʊəl] *adj* visuel(elle); **v. aid** support *m* visuel; **v. arts** arts *mpl* plastiques; *Comptr* **v. display unit** console f de visualisation

visualize ['vɪʒʊəlaɪz] *vt (imagine)* visualiser, se représenter; *(foresee)* envisager

visually ['vɪʒʊəlɪ] *adv* visuellement; **v. handicapped** malvoyant(e)

vital ['vaɪtəl] *adj* (a) *(essential)* vital(e); **v. organ** organe *m* vital; *Hum* **v. statistics** *(of woman)* mensurations *fpl* (b) *(vigorous)* vigoureux(euse)

vitality [vaɪ'tælɪtɪ] *n* vitalité f

vitally ['vaɪtəlɪ] *adv* **supplies are v. needed** on a un besoin vital de vivres; **v. important** d'une importance vitale

vitamin [*Br* 'vɪtəmɪn, *Am* 'vaɪtəmɪn] *n* vitamine f; **with added vitamins** vitaminé(e)

vitreous ['vɪtrɪəs] *adj* **v. enamel** émail *m* vitrifié; **v. humour** humeur f vitrée

vitriol ['vɪtrɪəl] *n also Fig* vitriol *m*

vitriolic [vɪtrɪ'ɒlɪk] *adj* au vitriol

vituperative [vɪ'tjuːpərətɪv] *adj Formal* injurieux(euse)

viva ['vaɪvə] *n v.* **(voce)** oral *m*

vivacious [vɪ'veɪʃəs] *adj* enjoué(e)

vivacity [vɪ'væsɪtɪ] *n* vivacité f

vivid ['vɪvɪd] *adj* vif (vive); *(memory)* clair(e)

vividly ['vɪvɪdlɪ] *adv* vivement; *(remember)* clairement; *(describe)* de manière vivante

vivisection [vɪvɪ'sekʃən] *n* vivisection f

vixen ['vɪksən] *n* renarde f

viz [vɪz] *adv (abbr* **videlicet)** à savoir

VOA [viːəʊ'eɪ] *n Am (abbr* **Voice of America)** = station de radio américaine de diffusion mondiale

vocabulary [və'kæbjʊlərɪ] *n* vocabulaire *m*

vocal ['vəʊkəl] **1** *adj* (a) *(relating to the voice)* vocal(e); **v. cords** cordes *fpl* vocales (b) *(outspoken)* franc (franche); **to be v. about sth** se faire entendre à propos de qch
2 *npl* **vocals** chant *m;* **on vocals** au chant

vocalist ['vəʊkəlɪst] *n* chanteur(euse) *m,f*

vocation [vəʊ'keɪʃən] *n* vocation f; **to have a v. (for sth)** avoir une vocation (pour qch)

vocational [vəʊ'keɪʃənəl] *adj* professionnel(elle)

vocative ['vɒkətɪv] *n* vocatif *m*

vociferous [və'sɪfərəs] *adj* bruyant(e)

vociferously [və'sɪfərəslɪ] *adv* bruyamment

vodka ['vɒdkə] *n* vodka f

vogue [vəʊg] *n* vogue f; **to be in v.** être en vogue

voice [vɔɪs] **1** *n* (a) *(of person)* voix f; **to raise/lower one's v.** élever/baisser la voix; **at the top of one's v.** à tue-tête; **I've lost my v.** je n'ai plus de voix; **v. box** larynx *m* (b) *Gram* **active/passive** voix f active/passive (c) *(idioms)* **the v. of reason** la voix de la raison; **with one v.** d'une seule voix; **to make one's v. heard** se faire entendre; **these reforms would give small parties a v.** ces réformes donneraient voix au chapitre aux petits partis
2 *vt* (a) *(opinion, feelings)* exprimer (b) *(consonant)* sonoriser

voiced [vɔɪst] *adj (consonant)* sonore

voiceless ['vɔɪslɪs] *adj (consonant)* sans voix

voice-over ['vɔɪsəʊvə(r)] *n* voix f off

void [vɔɪd] **1** *n* vide *m*; **to fill the v.** combler le vide
2 *adj* (**a**) *(devoid)* **v. of** dépourvu(e) de (**b**) *Law (deed, contract)* **(null and) v.** nul (nulle) et non avenu(e)

volatile ['vɔlətaɪl] *adj* (**a**) *(person)* inconstant(e); *(situation)* explosif(ive); *(economy, market)* instable (**b**) *Chem* volatil(e)

volcanic [vɔl'kænɪk] *adj* volcanique

volcano [vɔl'keɪnəʊ] *(pl* **volcanoes***) n* volcan *m*

vole [vəʊl] *n* campagnol *m*

volition [və'lɪʃən] *n Formal* **of one's own v.** de son propre gré

volley ['vɔlɪ] *n* (**a**) *(of gunfire, blows, stones)* volée *f*; *Fig (of insults)* bordée *f* (**b**) *(in tennis)* volée *f*

volleyball ['vɔlɪbɔːl] *n* volley(-ball *m*) *m*

volt [vəʊlt] *n* volt *m*

voltage ['vəʊltɪdʒ] *n* voltage *m*

volte-face ['vɔltfɑːs] *n* volte-face *f inv*

voluble ['vɔljʊbəl] *adj* volubile

volubly ['vɔljʊblɪ] *adv* avec volubilité

volume ['vɔljuːm] *n* (**a**) *(book)* volume *m*, tome *m*; *Fig* **to speak volumes (about)** *(of action, expression)* en dire long (sur) (**b**) *(amount, space occupied)* volume *m*; *(of work)* quantité *f* (**c**) *(loudness)* volume *m*; **to turn the v. up/down** *(on TV, radio)* monter/baisser le volume; **v. control** bouton *m* de réglage du volume

voluminous [və'ljuːmɪnəs] *adj (garment)* ample; *(container)* volumineux(euse)

voluntarily [vɔlən'teərɪlɪ] *adv* de plein gré

voluntary ['vɔləntərɪ] *adj* volontaire; **v. redundancy** départ *m* volontaire; **v. work** travail *m* bénévole

volunteer [vɔlən'tɪə(r)] **1** *n* volontaire *mf*; *(for charity)* bénévole *mf*
2 *vt (information)* donner spontanément; *(advice)* offrir; **to v. to do sth** se porter volontaire pour faire qch
3 *vi* (**a**) *(for military service)* s'engager (**b**) *(to help, for charity)* se porter volontaire (**for** pour)

voluptuous [və'lʌptjʊəs] *adj* voluptueux(euse)

vomit ['vɔmɪt] **1** *n* vomi *m*
2 *vti* vomir

voodoo ['vuːduː] *n* vaudou *m*

voracious [və'reɪʃəs] *adj* vorace

vortex ['vɔːteks] *(pl* **vortices** ['vɔːtɪsiːz]*) n* vortex *m*; *Fig* tourbillon *m*

vote [vəʊt] **1** *n (choice)* vote *m*; *(election)* scrutin *m*; *(paper)* voix *f*; **to put sth to the v.** soumettre qch au vote; **to**

take a **v. on sth** voter sur qch; **to have the v.** avoir le droit de vote; **they got 52% of the v.** ils ont remporté 52% des voix; **the party has increased its share of the v.** le parti a amélioré ses résultats aux élections; **v. of confidence** vote de confiance; **v. of no confidence** motion *f* de censure; **to propose a v. of thanks** faire un discours de remerciement
2 *vt* **to v. Communist** voter communiste; **to v. to do sth** voter pour faire qch; **to v. sth down** voter contre qch; **to v. sb in** élire qn; **to v. sb out** ne pas réélire qn; **I v. (that) we go** je propose qu'on y aille
3 *vi* voter (**for/against** pour/contre); **to v. on sth** voter sur qch

voter ['vəʊtə(r)] *n* électeur(trice) *m,f*

voting ['vəʊtɪŋ] **1** *n* scrutin *m*; **v. booth** isoloir *m*
2 *adj (member)* votant(e)

votive ['vəʊtɪv] *adj Rel* votif(ive)

▶**vouch for** [vaʊtʃ] *vt insep (person)* se porter garant(e) de; *(quality, truth)* attester de

voucher ['vaʊtʃə(r)] *n* coupon *m*, bon *m*; *(gift)* **v.** chèque-cadeau *m*

vow [vaʊ] **1** *n* vœu *m*; **to make a v.** faire un vœu; **to take a v. of poverty/silence** faire vœu de pauvreté/silence
2 *vt* jurer; **to v. to do sth** jurer de faire qch; **to v. that** jurer que

vowel ['vaʊəl] *n* voyelle *f*; **v. sound** son *m* vocalique

voyage ['vɔɪdʒ] *n* voyage *m*

voyager ['vɔɪdʒə(r)] *n* voyageur(euse) *m,f*

vs *(abbr* **versus***)* contre

VSO [viːes'əʊ] *n Br (abbr* **Voluntary Service Overseas***)* ≃ service *m* de la coopération

VTOL [viːtiːəʊ'el] *n (abbr* **vertical take-off and landing***)* ADAV *m*

VTR [viːtiːɑː(r)] *n (abbr* **video tape recorder***)* magnétoscope *m*

vulgar ['vʌlgə(r)] *adj* vulgaire; *Math* **v. fraction** fraction *f* ordinaire

vulgarity [vʌl'gærɪtɪ] *n* vulgarité *f*

vulnerability [vʌlnərə'bɪlɪtɪ] *n* vulnérabilité *f*

vulnerable ['vʌlnərəbəl] *adj* vulnérable

vulture ['vʌltʃə(r)] *n also Fig* vautour *m*

vulva ['vʌlvə] *(pl* **vulvas** or **vulvae** ['vʌlviː]*) n* vulve *f*

W

W, w [ˈdʌbəlju:] *n* (**a**) (*letter*) W, w *m inv* (**b**) (*abbr* **west**) O

W *n* (*abbr* **watt(s)**) W

WAAF [wæf] *n* (*abbr* **Women's Auxiliary Air Force**) = groupe de femmes, auxiliaires de l'armée de l'air britannique durant la Seconde Guerre mondiale

wacky [ˈwækɪ] *adj Fam* farfelu(e)

wad [wɒd] *n* (*of cotton wool*) morceau *m*; (*of paper, bank notes*) liasse *f*

wadding [ˈwɒdɪŋ] *n* ouate *f*

waddle [ˈwɒdəl] *vi* se dandiner

wade [weɪd] *vi* (*in water*) marcher dans l'eau; **to w. across a stream** traverser une rivière à gué; *Fam Fig* **to w. in** intervenir

▶**wade into** *vt insep Fam Fig* (*task*) s'attaquer à; (*person*) tomber sur

wader [ˈweɪdə(r)] *n* (**a**) (*bird*) échassier *m* (**b**) **waders** (*boots*) bottes *fpl* de pêcheur

wafer [ˈweɪfə(r)] *n* (**a**) (*biscuit*) gaufrette *f* (**b**) *Rel* (*for communion*) hostie *f*

wafer-thin [weɪfəˈθɪn] *adj* ultramince

waffle[1] [ˈwɒfəl] *n* (*food*) gaufre *f*

waffle[2] *Fam* **1** *n Br* remplissage *m*
2 *vi Br* faire du remplissage

waft [wɒft] **1** *vt* (*smell, sound*) porter
2 *vi* (*of smell, sound*) parvenir

wag[1] [wæg] **1** *vt* (*pt & pp* **wagged**) agiter, remuer; **to w. one's finger at sb** menacer qn du doigt; **to w. its tail** (*of dog*) remuer la queue
2 *vi* frétiller, remuer; **its tail was wagging** (*of dog*) il remuait la queue; *Fam* **tongues will w.** les langues vont aller bon train
3 *n* (*action*) frétillement *m*; **with a w. of its tail** la queue frétillante

wag[2] *n Fam* (*joker*) farceur(euse) *m,f*

wage [weɪdʒ] **1** *n* (*pay*) **wage(s)** salaire *m*, paie *f*; **w. claim** revendication *f* salariale; **w. cut** diminution *f* de salaire; **w. differential** écart *m* salarial; **w. earner** salarié(e) *m,f*; **w. freeze** gel *m* des salaires; **w. packet** (*envelope*) enveloppe *f* de paie; (*money*) paie
2 *vt* **to w. war (on)** faire la guerre (à); **to w. a campaign against smoking** mener une campagne anti-tabac

wager [ˈweɪdʒə(r)] **1** *n* pari *m*
2 *vt* parier

waggle [ˈwægəl] *vt & vi* remuer

wag(g)on [ˈwægən] *n* (*horse-drawn*) charrette *f*; *Br* (*for railway freight*) wagon *m* (découvert); *Fam Fig* **to be on the w.** être au régime sec

waif [weɪf] *n* (*abandoned child*) enfant *mf* abandonné(e); (*very thin girl*) fille *f* excessivement maigre; **waifs and strays** (*children*) enfants *mpl* abandonnés; (*animals*) animaux *mpl* abandonnés

wail [weɪl] **1** *n* (*of person*) gémissement *m*; (*of siren*) hurlement *m*
2 *vi* (*of person*) gémir, pousser des gémissements; (*of siren*) hurler

waist [weɪst] *n* taille *f*

waistband [ˈweɪstbænd] *n* ceinture *f*

waistcoat [ˈweɪskəʊt] *n Br* gilet *m*

waistline [ˈweɪstlaɪn] *n* taille *f*; **to watch one's w.** surveiller sa ligne

wait [weɪt] **1** *n* attente *f*; **to have a long w.** attendre longtemps; **to lie in w. for sb** guetter qn
2 *vi* attendre; **to w. one's turn** attendre son tour
3 *vi* (**a**) attendre; **to w. for sb/sth** attendre qn/qch; **to keep sb waiting** faire attendre qn; **I can't w. to see her** j'ai vraiment hâte de la voir; **repairs while you w.** (*sign*) réparations minute; **we must w. and see** on verra bien (**b**) **to w. at table** (*serve*) faire le service

▶**wait about, wait around** *vi* attendre

▶**wait on** *vt insep* (*serve*) servir; **to w. on sb hand and foot** être aux petits soins pour qn

▶**wait up** *vi* **to w. up for sb** attendre qn pour aller se coucher

waiter [ˈweɪtə(r)] *n* serveur *m*

waiting [ˈweɪtɪŋ] *n* attente *f*; **to play the w. game** faire de l'attentisme; **w. list** liste *f* d'attente; **w. room** salle *f* d'attente

waitress [ˈweɪtrɪs] *n* serveuse *f*

waive [weɪv] *vt* (*rights, claim*) renoncer à; (*rule*) ignorer

wake[1] [weɪk] *n* (*of ship*) sillage *m*; *Fig* **in the w. of sth** à la suite de qch; *Fig* **to follow in sb's w.** suivre l'exemple de qn

wake[2] *n* (*on night before funeral*) veillée *f* de corps

wake[3] (*pt* **woke** [wəʊk] *or* **waked**, *pp* **woken** [ˈwəʊkən] *or* **waked**) **1** *vt* réveiller
2 *vi* se réveiller

▶**wake up** *vt sep* réveiller
2 *vi* se réveiller; *Fig* **to w. up to sth** prendre conscience de qch

wakeful [ˈweɪkfʊl] *adj* (**a**) (*sleepless*) éveillé(e); **to have a w. night** ne pas fermer l'œil de la nuit (**b**) (*vigilant*) vigilant(e)

waken [ˈweɪkən] *vt* réveiller

wakey [ˈweɪkɪ] *exclam Fam* **w., w.!** réveille-toi!

Wales [weɪlz] *n* le pays de Galles

walk [wɔːk] **1** *n* (**a**) (*short*) promenade *f*; (*long*) marche *f*; **its a long w.** c'est loin à pied; **its a ten-minute w.** c'est à dix minutes à pied; **to go for a w.** aller se promener **(b)** *(gait)* démarche *f*; **I know her by her w.** je la reconnais à sa démarche **(c)** *(speed)* **at a w.** au pas **(d)** *(path)* avenue *f* **(e)** *(profession, situation)* **people from all walks of life** des gens de tous les milieux

2 *vt* **to w. the dog** promener le chien; **to w. sb home** raccompagner qn; **to w. the streets** battre le pavé; *Euph (of prostitute)* faire le trottoir

3 *vi (move on foot)* marcher; *(as opposed to riding, driving)* aller à pied; *(for exercise, pleasure)* se promener (à pied); **to w. home** rentrer à pied

▶**walk away** *vi* s'en aller; *Fig* **to w. away from trouble** éviter les ennuis; *Fig* **to w. away with a prize** remporter un prix

▶**walk in** *vi* entrer

▶**walk into** *vt insep* **(a)** *(enter)* entrer dans **(b)** *(collide with)* rentrer dans

▶**walk off** *vi* s'en aller; **to w. off with sth** *(steal)* partir avec qch; *(win easily)* remporter qch

▶**walk out** *vi* **(a)** *(leave)* sortir; **to w. out on sb** quitter qn **(b)** *(go on strike)* se mettre en grève

▶**walk over** *vt insep Fam* **to w. all over sb** marcher sur les pieds de qn

walkabout ['wɔːkəbaut] *n (of politician)* bain *m* de foule

walker ['wɔːkə(r)] *n* marcheur(euse) *m, f*

walkie-talkie [wɔːkɪ'tɔːkɪ] *n* talkie-walkie *m*

walk-in cupboard ['wɔːkɪn'kʌbəd] *n (for clothes)* débarras *m*; *(for food)* cellier *m*

walking ['wɔːkɪŋ] **1** *n* marche *f*; **w. frame** déambulateur *m*; **w. shoes** chaussures *fpl* de marche; **w. stick** canne *f*

2 *adj* **at a w. pace** au pas; *Fam* **she's a w. encyclopedia** c'est une encyclopédie ambulante; **the w. wounded** les blessés *mpl* en état de marcher

Walkman® ['wɔːkmən] *n* baladeur *m*

walk-on part ['wɔːkɒn'pɑːt] *n (in film, play)* rôle *m* de figurant(e)

walkout ['wɔːkaut] *n (strike)* débrayage *m*; *(from meeting)* départ *m* en signe de protestation

walkover ['wɔːkəuvə(r)] *n Fam* **it was a w.!** c'était du gâteau!

walkway ['wɔːkweɪ] *n* passage *m* (couvert)

wall [wɔːl] **1** *n* **(a)** *(of building, room)* mur *m*; **the Great W. of China** la grande muraille de Chine; **w. cupboard** placard *m* mural; **w. hanging** tenture *f* murale **(b)** *(idioms)* **a w. of silence** un mur de silence; **to go to the w.** faire faillite; *Fam* **to drive sb up the w.** rendre qn dingue; *Fam* **I might as well talk to the w.!** c'est comme parler à un mur

▶**wall in** *vt sep* entourer

▶**wall off** *vt sep* séparer

▶**wall up** *vt sep* murer

wallaby ['wɒləbɪ] *n* wallaby *m*

wallet ['wɒlɪt] *n* portefeuille *m*

wallflower ['wɔːlflauə(r)] *n (plant)* giroflée *f*; *Fig* **to be a w.** *(of person)* faire tapisserie

Walloon [wɒ'luːn] **1** *n* **(a)** *(person)* Wallon(onne) *m, f* **(b)** *(language)* wallon *m*

2 *adj* wallon(onne)

wallop ['wɒləp] *Fam* **1** *n* beigne *f*, grand coup *m*

2 *vt* filer un grand coup à

walloping ['wɒləpɪŋ] *Fam* **1** *n* raclée *f*

2 *adv (for emphasis)* super; **a w. great lie** un mensonge gros comme ça

wallow ['wɒləu] *vi* se vautrer; **to w. in self-pity** s'apitoyer sur son propre sort

wallpaper ['wɔːlpeɪpə(r)] **1** *n* papier *m* peint

2 *vt* tapisser

wall-to-wall ['wɔːltəwɔːl] *adj* **w. carpeting** moquette *f*; *Fig* **w. coverage** couverture *f* complète

wally ['wɒlɪ] *n Br Fam (idiot)* andouille *f*

walnut ['wɔːlnʌt] *n (fruit)* noix *f*; *(tree, wood)* noyer *m*

walrus ['wɔːlrəs] *(pl* **walruses)** *n* morse *m*

waltz [wɔːls] **1** *n* valse *f*

2 *vi* **(a)** *(dance)* valser **(b)** *Fam (move confidently)* **to w. in/out** entrer/sortir avec désinvolture; *Fam* **to w. off with sth** partir avec qch

WAN ['dʌbəljuːeɪ'en] *n Comptr (abbr* **wide area network)** grand réseau *m*

wan [wɒn] *adj* blême

wand [wɒnd] *n* baguette *f*

wander ['wɒndə(r)] **1** *vt (streets)* traîner dans; *(world)* courir

2 *vi* **(a)** *(roam)* errer; **to w. around the town** se promener dans la ville; **she had wandered from the path** elle s'était éloignée du chemin **(b)** *(verbally)* radoter; *(mentally)* dérailler; **to w. from the subject** s'écarter du sujet

3 *n* balade *f*; **to go for a w.** aller faire un tour

wanderer ['wɒndərə(r)] *n* vagabond(e) *m, f*

wandering ['wɒndərɪŋ] *adj (person, life)* errant(e); *(tribe)* nomade

wanderlust ['wɒndəlʌst] *n* soif *f* de voyages

wane [weɪn] **1** *vi (of moon)* décroître; *(of popularity, enthusiasm, power)* décliner

2 *n* **to be on the w.** *(of moon)* décroître; *(of popularity, enthusiasm, power)* être en déclin

wangle ['wæŋgl] *vt Fam* se débrouiller pour avoir; **to w. sth, to w. sth for sb** se débrouiller pour avoir qch à qn; **to w. it so that** se débrouiller pour que + *subjunctive*

wank [wæŋk] *Br Vulg* **1** *vi* se branler

2 *n* branlette *f*; **to have a w.** se branler

wanker ['wæŋkə(r)] *n Br Vulg* connard *m*

want [wɒnt] **1** *vt* **(a)** *(wish, desire)* vouloir; **to w. to do sth** vouloir faire qch; **to w. sb to do sth** vouloir que qn fasse qch; **that's the last thing we w.** nous ne voulons surtout pas cela; **I know when I'm not wanted** je sais quand je suis de trop; **what does she w. with me?** qu'est-ce qu'elle me veut? **(b)** *Fam (need)* avoir besoin de; **the lawn wants cutting** la pelouse a besoin d'être tondue; **you w. to be careful with him** il faut que tu fasses attention avec lui **(c)** *(seek)* **to be wanted by the police** être recherché(e) par la police; **you're wanted on the phone** on te demande au téléphone

2 *vi* **to w. for nothing** ne manquer de rien

3 *n* **(a)** *(lack)* besoin *m* **(b)** *(lack)* manque *m* (**of** de); **for w. of sth/of doing sth** faute de qch/de faire qch; **for w. of anything better** faute de mieux

wanting ['wɒntɪŋ] *adj* **to be w. in sth** manquer de qch; **to be found w.** *(of person)* se révéler incapable; *(of thing)* laisser à désirer

wanton ['wɒntən] *adj* **(a)** *(unjustified)* gratuit(e) **(b)** *(unrestrained)* dévergondé(e); *(sexually)* licencieux(euse)

war [wɔː(r)] n guerre f; **to be at w. (with)** être en guerre (avec); **to go to w. (with/over)** entrer en guerre (contre/à propos de); Fig **w. of words** altercation f; Fam Fig **you look as if you've been through the wars** tu es dans un bel état!; **w. correspondent** correspondant(e) mf de guerre; **w. criminal** criminel m de guerre; **w. cry** cri m de guerre; **w. games** Mil manœuvres fpl; (with model soldiers) wargame m; **w. memorial** monument m aux morts

warble ['wɔːbəl] 1 n gazouillement m

2 vi gazouiller

warbler ['wɔːblə(r)] n fauvette f

ward [wɔːd] n (a) (in hospital) salle f (b) (electoral division) circonscription f (c) Law **w. of court** pupille mf sous tutelle judiciaire

▶**ward off** vt sep (blow) éviter; (danger) chasser

warden ['wɔːdən] n (of institution, hostel) directeur(trice) m,f; (of park) gardien(enne) mf

warder ['wɔːdə(r)] n Br (of prison) gardien(enne) m,f

wardrobe ['wɔːdrəʊb] n (a) (cupboard) armoire f (b) (clothes) garde-robe f; **to have a large w.** avoir une garde-robe importante (c) (theatrical costumes) costumes mpl; **w. mistress** habilleuse f

warehouse ['weəhaʊs] n entrepôt m

wares [weə(r)z] npl articles mpl

warfare ['wɔːfeə(r)] n guerre f

warhead ['wɔːhed] n ogive f

warhorse ['wɔːhɔːs] n Fig **an old w.** un vétéran

warily ['weərɪlɪ] adv avec une prudence circonspecte

wariness ['weərɪnɪs] n prudence f circonspecte

warlike ['wɔːlaɪk] adj guerrier(ère)

warm [wɔːm] 1 adj (a) (in temperature) chaud(e); **to be w.** (of person) avoir chaud; (of object, water, clothing) être chaud; **it's w.** (of weather) il fait chaud; **you're getting warmer** (in guessing game) tu chauffes (b) (kind, friendly) chaleureux(euse)

2 vt chauffer; **to w. oneself by the fire** se chauffer près du feu

3 vi **to w. to sb** se prendre de sympathie pour qn; **to w. to sth** se laisser séduire par qch

▶**warm up 1** vt sep (food) réchauffer

2 vi (a) (of person, room) se réchauffer (b) (of dancer, athlete) s'échauffer (c) (of engine) chauffer

warm-blooded [wɔːm'blʌdɪd] adj à sang chaud

warm-hearted [wɔːm'hɑːtɪd] adj chaleureux(euse)

warmly ['wɔːmlɪ] adv (a) (dress) chaudement (b) (applaud, thank) chaleureusement

warmonger ['wɔːmʌŋɡə(r)] n belliciste mf

warmth [wɔːmθ] n chaleur f

warm-up ['wɔːmʌp] n (of dancer, athlete) échauffement m

warn [wɔːn] vt avertir, prévenir; **to w. sb about sb/sth** mettre qn en garde contre qn/qch; **to w. sb about doing sth** dire à qn de ne pas faire qch; **to w. sb not to do sth** déconseiller à qn de faire qch; **you have been warned!** te voilà prévenu!

warning ['wɔːnɪŋ] n (a) (caution) avertissement m; (against danger) mise f en garde; **to give sb a w.** donner un avertissement à qn; (against danger) mettre qn en garde; Fig **w. sign** signe m (b) (advance notice) avis m; **without w.** sans prévenir

warp [wɔːp] 1 vt (a) (wood, metal) gauchir (b) (person, mind) pervertir

2 vi (of wood, metal) gauchir

warpath ['wɔːpɑːθ] n Fam **to be on the w.** en vouloir à tout le monde

warped [wɔːpt] adj (a) (wood, metal) gauchi(e) (b) (person, mind) perverti(e)

warrant ['wɒrənt] 1 n Law mandat m; Mil **w. officer** adjudant m

2 vt (a) (justify) justifier (b) (guarantee) garantir

warranty ['wɒrəntɪ] (pl warranties) n garantie f; **under w.** sous garantie

warren ['wɒrən] n (of rabbit) garenne f; Fig (of streets) labyrinthe m

warring ['wɔːrɪŋ] adj en guerre

warrior ['wɒrɪə(r)] n guerrier(ère) m,f

Warsaw ['wɔːsɔː] n Varsovie; Formerly **the W. Pact** le pacte de Varsovie

warship ['wɔːʃɪp] n navire m de guerre

wart [wɔːt] n verrue f; **warts and all** (biography, portrait) sans complaisance

warthog ['wɔːthɒɡ] n phacochère m

wartime ['wɔːtaɪm] n temps m de guerre; **in w.** en temps de guerre

wary ['weərɪ] adj méfiant(e); **to be w. of sth/sb** se méfier de qch/qn

was [wɒz] pt of **be**

wash [wɒʃ] 1 n (a) (action) lavage m; **to have a w.** se laver; **to give sth a w.** laver qch; **your jeans are in the w.** ton jean est au lavage; Fig **it will all come out in the w.** tout va s'arranger (b) (of ship) remous m

2 vt (a) (clean) laver; **to w. oneself** se laver; **to w. one's face/one's hands** se laver la figure/les mains; Fig **to w. one's hands of sth** se laver les mains de qch (b) (carry) **to w. sb/sth ashore** rejeter qn/qch sur le rivage; **he was washed overboard** une vague l'a emporté par-dessus bord

3 vi (wash oneself) se laver; Fam **that won't w.!** ça ne marche pas!

▶**wash away** vt sep emporter

▶**wash down** vt sep (a) (walls, car) laver à grande eau (b) (pill) faire descendre (with avec); **to w. down one's dinner with a bottle of wine** arroser son dîner d'une bouteille de vin

▶**wash off 1** vt sep enlever

2 vi partir

▶**wash out 1** vt sep (a) (cup, bottle) rincer (b) (stain, dirt) faire partir; **to be completely washed out** (exhausted) être complètement lessivé(e)

2 vi (of stain, dirt) partir

▶**wash up 1** vt sep (a) Br (clean) laver (b) (carry ashore) rejeter sur le rivage

2 vi (a) Br (do dishes) faire la vaisselle (b) Am (have a wash) se débarbouiller

washbasin ['wɒʃbeɪsən] n (cuvette f de) lavabo m

washboard ['wɒʃbɔːd] n planche f à laver

washbowl ['wɒʃbəʊl] n (small) cuvette f; (large) bassine f

washcloth ['wɒʃklɒθ] n Am (face cloth) lingette f

washer ['wɒʃə(r)] n (a) Fam (for clothes) machine f à laver (b) (for screw) rondelle f; (made of rubber) joint m

washer-dryer [ˈwɒʃəˈdraɪə(r)] *n* machine *f* à laver qui fait sèche-linge

wash(-)hand basin [ˈwɒʃhændˈbeɪsən] *n* lavabo *m*

washing [ˈwɒʃɪŋ] *n* (a) *(action)* lavage *m*; **to do the w.** faire la lessive; **w. machine** machine *f* à laver; **w. powder** poudre *f* à laver, lessive *f* (en poudre) (b) *(dirty clothes)* linge *m* sale; *(clean clothes)* linge (propre)

Washington [ˈwɒʃɪŋtən] *n* Washington; **W. (State)** l'État *m* de Washington; **W. DC** Washington

washing-up [ˈwɒʃɪŋˈʌp] *n Br* vaisselle *f*; **to do the w.** faire la vaisselle; **w. bowl** cuvette *f*; **w. liquid** liquide *f* vaisselle

washout [ˈwɒʃaʊt] *n Fam* bide *m*

washroom [ˈwɒʃruːm] *n Am* toilettes *fpl*

wasn't [ˈwɒznt] = **was not**

wasp [wɒsp] *n* guêpe *f*

waspish [ˈwɒspɪʃ] *adj* **to be w.** avoir une langue de vipère

wastage [ˈweɪstɪdʒ] *n* gaspillage *m*

waste [weɪst] **1** *n* (a) *(of food, effort)* gaspillage *m*; *(of time, money)* perte *f*; **to go to w.** être gaspillé(e) (b) *(rubbish)* déchets *mpl*; **w. disposal unit** broyeur *m* d'ordures (c) **wastes** *(desert)* étendues *fpl* désertiques

2 *adj (heat, fuel)* gaspillé(e); *(water)* usé(e)

3 *vt (money)* gaspiller; *(time)* perdre; *(opportunity)* gâcher; **to w. no time doing sth** ne pas perdre de temps pour faire qch; *Prov* **w. not, want not** il ne faut pas gaspiller

▶**waste away** *vi* dépérir

wasted [ˈweɪstɪd] *adj (effort)* gaspillé(e); *(opportunity)* gâché(e)

wasteful [ˈweɪstfʊl] *adj* **to be w.** *(of process, practice)* ne pas être rentable; *(of person)* être gaspilleur(euse)

wasteland [ˈweɪstlænd] *n* désert *m*

wastepaper [weɪstˈpeɪpə(r)] *n* vieux papiers *mpl*; **w. basket/bin** corbeille *f* à papier

waster [ˈweɪstə(r)] *n Fam (idle person)* bon (bonne) *m,f* à rien

wasting disease [ˈweɪstɪŋdɪˈziːz] *n* maladie *f* dégénérative

watch [wɒtʃ] **1** *n* (a) *(timepiece)* montre *f* (b) *(period of guard duty)* garde *f*; *(guard)* sentinelle *f*; **to be on w.** monter la garde; **to keep a close w. on sb/sth** surveiller qn/qch de près

2 *vt (a) (observe)* regarder; **to w. television** regarder la télévision; **to w. sb doing sth** regarder qn faire qch (b) *(keep an eye on)* surveiller (c) *(be careful of)* faire attention à; **w. your language!** surveille ton langage!; *Fam* **w. it!** attention!

3 *vi* regarder

▶**watch out** *vi* faire attention; **w. out!** attention!

▶**watch out for** *vt insep* (a) *(look for)* (person) guetter; *(thing)* chercher (b) *(be on guard for)* faire attention à

▶**watch over** *vt insep* veiller sur

watchdog [ˈwɒtʃdɒg] *n* chien *m* de garde; *Fig (organization)* organisme *m* de contrôle

watchful [ˈwɒtʃfʊl] *adj* vigilant(e)

watchmaker [ˈwɒtʃmeɪkə(r)] *n* horloger(ère) *m,f*

watchman [ˈwɒtʃmən] *n* gardien *m*

watchstrap [ˈwɒtʃstræp] *n* bracelet *m* de montre

watchtower [ˈwɒtʃtaʊə(r)] *n* tour *f* de guet

watchword [ˈwɒtʃwɜːd] *n* mot *m* d'ordre

water [ˈwɔːtə(r)] **1** *n* (a) eau *f*; **to pass w.** *(urinate)* uriner; **w. bed** matelas *m* d'eau; **w. biscuit** = biscuit sec non salé; **w. bottle** gourde *f*; **w. chestnut** macre *f*; *Old-fashioned* **w. closet** waters *mpl*; **w. heater** chauffe-eau *m*; **w. level** niveau *m* d'eau; **w. lily** nénuphar *m*; **w. meter** compteur *m* d'eau; **w. pistol** pistolet *m* à eau; **w. polo** water-polo *m*; **w. rat** rat *m* d'eau; **w. skiing** ski *m* nautique; **w. wings** brassards *mpl* de natation (b) *(idioms)* **to spend money like w.** jeter l'argent par les fenêtres; **the argument doesn't hold w.** cet argument ne tient pas debout; **to keep one's head above w.** garder la tête hors de l'eau; **that's all w. under the bridge now** c'est de l'histoire ancienne

2 *vt (a) (fields, plants)* arroser (b) *(horse)* donner à boire à

3 *vi (of eyes)* pleurer; **it makes my mouth w.** ça me met l'eau à la bouche; **my mouth is watering** j'en ai l'eau à la bouche

▶**water down** *vt sep (liquid, chemical)* diluer; *Fig (criticism, legislation)* atténuer

waterborne [ˈwɔːtəbɔːn] *adj (goods)* transporté(e) par voie d'eau; *(disease)* d'origine hydrique

watercourse [ˈwɔːtəkɔːs] *n* cours *m* d'eau

watercolour [ˈwɔːtəkʌlə(r)] *n* aquarelle *f*

watercress [ˈwɔːtəkres] *n* cresson *m* (de fontaine)

waterfall [ˈwɔːtəfɔːl] *n* cascade *f*

waterfowl [ˈwɔːtəfaʊl] *(pl* **waterfowl**) *n* gibier *m* d'eau

waterfront [ˈwɔːtəfrʌnt] *n (by river)* bord *m* de l'eau; *(by sea)* front *m* de mer

watering can [ˈwɔːtərɪŋˈkæn] *n* arrosoir *m*

watering hole [ˈwɔːtərɪŋˈhəʊl] *n (for animals)* point *m* d'eau; *Fam (bar)* bar *m*

waterlogged [ˈwɔːtəlɒgd] *adj (shoes, clothes)* trempé(e); *(land)* détrempé(e)

watermark [ˈwɔːtəmɑːk] *n* filigrane *m*

watermelon [ˈwɔːtəmelən] *n* pastèque *f*

waterproof [ˈwɔːtəpruːf] **1** *adj* imperméable; *(watch, joint, seal)* étanche; *(make-up)* waterproof *inv*; *(sun lotion)* résistant(e) à l'eau

2 *n (raincoat)* imperméable *m*

3 *vt* imperméabiliser

water-resistant [ˈwɔːtərɪzɪstənt] *adj (watch)* étanche; *(fabric)* qui résiste à l'eau

watershed [ˈwɔːtəʃed] *n Geog* ligne *f* de partage des eaux; *Fig (turning point)* tournant *m*; *Br* **the (nine o'clock) w.** *(on television)* = heure après laquelle sont diffusées des programmes ne convenant pas aux enfants

waterside [ˈwɔːtəsaɪd] *n* bord *m* de l'eau

water-ski [ˈwɔːtəskiː] *vi* faire du ski nautique

watertight [ˈwɔːtətaɪt] *adj (seal)* hermétique; *(compartment)* étanche; *Fig (argument, alibi)* inattaquable

waterway [ˈwɔːtəweɪ] *n* voie *f* navigable

waterworks [ˈwɔːtəwɜːks] *n* station *f* hydraulique; *Br Euph (urinary system)* voies *fpl* urinaires; *Fam* **to turn on the w.** *(cry)* se mettre à pleurer comme une madeleine

watery [ˈwɔːtərɪ] *adj (soup)* trop liquide; *(beer, tea, coffee)* insipide, fade; *(eyes)* qui pleure; *(colour)* délavé(e)

watt [wɒt] *n* watt *m*

wattage [ˈwɒtɪdʒ] *n* puissance *f* en watts

wave [weɪv] **1** *n* (a) *(of water, dislike, crime)* vague *f*; *Fig* **to make waves** faire des vagues (b) *(gesture)* signe *m* (de la main); **to give sb a w.** faire signe à qn (c) *(in hair)* ondulation *f* (d) *(in physics)* onde *f*

2 vt (arm, flag) agiter; (stick) brandir; **to w. one's arms about** agiter les bras; **to w. goodbye to sb** faire au revoir de la main à qn

3 vi (a) (of person) faire signe; **to w. to sb** faire signe à qn (b) (of flag) flotter au vent

▸**wave aside** vt insep Fig (objection, criticism) écarter

waveband ['weivbænd] n bande f de fréquences

wavelength ['weivleŋθ] n longueur f d'ondes; Fig **to be on the same w.** être sur la même longueur d'ondes

waver ['weivə(r)] vi (of person) vaciller; (of voice) trembler; (of courage) faiblir

waverer ['weivərə(r)] n indécis(e) m,f

wavy ['weivi] adj ondulé(e)

wax[1] [wæks] **1** n (for candles, polishing) cire f; (in ear) cérumen m
2 vt (polish) cirer

wax[2] vi (a) (of moon) croître (b) (become) **to w. lyrical (about sth)** devenir lyrique (à propos de qch)

waxed [wækst] adj ciré(e)

waxen ['wæksən] adj (complexion) de cire

waxwork ['wækswɜːk] n w. (dummy) mannequin m de cire; **waxworks** musée m de cire

way [wei] **1** n (a) (route) & Fig chemin m; **the w. in** l'entrée f; **the w. out** la sortie; **the w. to the station** le chemin pour aller à la gare; **to ask sb the w.** demander son chemin à qn; **to show sb the w.** montrer le chemin à qn; **to lose one's w.** se perdre; **to know one's w. about** savoir se débrouiller; **on the w.** en chemin, en route; Fam **they've got a baby on the w.** ils ont un bébé en route; **I must be on my w.** je dois partir; **out of the w.** isolé(e); **to go out of one's w. to help sb** se mettre en quatre pour aider qn; Fig **to find a w. out of a problem** trouver une issue à un problème; Fig **she is well on the w. to success** elle est bien partie pour réussir; **to make one's w. to a place** se diriger vers un endroit; **to make one's w. through the crowd** se frayer un chemin à travers la foule; Fig **to make w. for sb** laisser la place à qn; Fig **to make one's w. in the world** réussir dans la vie; also Fig **to stand in sb's w.** barrer le passage à qn; also Fig **to be/get in the w.** gêner; also Fig **to get out of the w.** s'écarter; also Fig **to keep out of the w.** se tenir à l'écart

(b) (manner) manière f, façon f; **in this w.** de cette manière; **to do things in one's own w.** faire les choses à sa manière; **I don't like the w. things are going** je n'aime pas la façon dont les choses tournent; **one w. or another** d'une manière ou d'une autre; **to find a w. of doing sth** trouver un moyen de faire qch; **to get into the w. of doing sth** s'habituer à faire qch; **to have a w. with children/animals** savoir s'y prendre avec les enfants/animaux; **to get one's (own) w.** arriver à ses fins; **to get used to sb's ways** se faire aux habitudes de qn

(c) (distance) **to go a part of the w.** faire un bout de chemin; **to go all the w.** aller jusqu'au bout; Fig **I'm with you all the w.** je suis tout à fait d'accord avec toi; **San Francisco is a long w. from New York** San Francisco est loin de New York; **we've still got a long w. to go** nous avons encore du chemin à faire; **to be a little/long w. off** être proche/loin

(d) (direction) direction f, sens m; **which w. ...?** dans quel sens...?; **this/that w.** par ici/là; **to look the other w.** se boucher les yeux; Fam **down our w.** chez nous; Fig **it works both ways** cela marche dans les deux sens; **to split sth three ways** partager qch en trois

(e) (street) rue f

(f) (respect) égard m; **in a w.** d'une certaine manière; **in every w.** en tous points; **in no w.** en aucune façon

(g) (state, condition) **to be in a good w.** bien aller; **to be in a bad w.** être mal en point

2 adv Fam **w. back in the 1920s** dans les années vingt; **Lucy and I go w. back** Lucy et moi sommes des amis de longue date; **w. ahead** devant tout le monde; **w. down south** tout au sud; **your guess was w. out** tu étais loin de la vérité

wayfarer ['weifeərə(r)] n voyageur(euse) m,f

waylay [wei'lei] (pt & pp **waylaid** [wei'leid]) vt (attack) agresser; Fig (stop) arrêter au passage

way-out [wei'aut] adj Fam (person) excentrique; (ideas, beliefs) curieux(euse)

wayside ['weisaid] n bord m de la route; Fig **to fall by the w.** se retrouver à la traîne

wayward ['weiwəd] adj difficile

WBA [dʌbəljuːbiː'ei] n (abbr **World Boxing Association**) WBA, = association mondiale de boxe

WC [dʌbəljuː'siː] n (abbr **water closet**) WC mpl

we [wiː] pron nous; **we're Scottish** nous sommes écossais; **we haven't got it!** ce n'est pas nous qui l'avons!; **as we say in England** comme on dit en Angleterre; **we French are...** nous autres Français, nous sommes...

WEA [dʌbəljuːiː'ei] n Br (abbr **Workers' Educational Association**) = association d'enseignement des travailleurs

weak [wiːk] adj (person, currency, character) faible; (heart) fragile; (argument, excuse) peu convaincant(e); (tea, coffee) peu fort(e); **to grow w.** s'affaiblir; **to be w. at sth** (school subject) être faible en qch; Fig **to go w. at the knees** avoir les jambes en coton; Fig **w. spot** point m faible

weaken ['wiːkən] **1** vt affaiblir
2 vi s'affaiblir

weak-kneed [wiːk'niːd] adj Fig Fam mou (molle)

weakling ['wiːklıŋ] n mauviette f, faible mf

weakly ['wiːklı] adv faiblement

weakness ['wiːknıs] n faiblesse f; **to have a w. for sb/sth** avoir un faible pour qn/qch

weak-willed [wiːk'wıld] adj sans volonté

weal [wiːl] n trace f de coup

wealth [welθ] n richesse f; Fig **a w. of sth** une abondance de qch

wealthy ['welθı] **1** npl **the w.** les riches
2 adj riche

wean [wiːn] vt (baby) sevrer; Fig **to w. sb off sth** (bad habit) faire passer qch à qn; (alcohol, drugs) sevrer qn de qch

weapon ['wepən] n arme f

wear [weə(r)] **1** vt (pt **wore** [wɔː(r)], pp **worn** [wɔːn]) (a) (garment, glasses) porter; **to w. black** porter du noir; **to w. one's hair up** avoir les cheveux relevés (b) (erode) user; **to w. a hole in sth** faire un trou dans qch (c) Fam (believe, accept) avaler

2 vi (of clothing) s'user; **to w. thin** s'user; Fig **that excuse is wearing thin** cette excuse ne prend plus; **my patience is wearing thin** je suis à bout de patience; **to w. smooth** devenir lisse; **to w. well** (of clothing, person, film) bien vieillir

3 n (a) (clothing) vêtements mpl; **evening w.** habits mpl de soirée; **children's w.** vêtements pour enfants (b) (use) usure f; **to get a lot of w. out of sth** porter qch longtemps; *Fam* **to be the worse for w.** être bien éméché(e); **w. and tear** usure f naturelle

▶**wear away 1** vt sep user
2 vi s'user

▶**wear down 1** vt sep user; *Fig* **to w. sb down** avoir qn à l'usure
2 vi s'user

▶**wear off** vi *(of pain)* disparaître; *(of effect)* cesser; *(of anaesthetic)* cesser de faire effet; **the novelty soon wore off** l'attrait de la nouveauté n'a pas duré

▶**wear on** vi *(of time)* s'écouler

▶**wear out** vt sep user; **to w. oneself out** s'épuiser

wearily ['wɪərɪlɪ] adv avec lassitude

weariness ['wɪərɪnɪs] n lassitude f

wearing ['weərɪŋ] adj fatigant(e)

wearisome ['wɪərɪsəm] adj fatigant(e)

weary ['wɪərɪ] **1** adj las (lasse); **to be w. of sth/of doing sth** être las de qch/de faire qch; **to grow w. of sth** se lasser de qch
2 vt fatiguer, lasser
3 vi se lasser **(of** de)

weasel ['wi:zəl] n belette f

weather ['weðə(r)] **1** n *(atmospheric conditions)* temps m; **what's the w. like?** quel temps fait-il?; **the w. is good/bad** il fait beau/mauvais; **in this w.** par un temps pareil; **w. permitting** si le temps le permet; **w. forecast** prévisions fpl météorologiques; **w. map** carte f météorologique **(b)** *(idioms)* **to make heavy of sth** faire tout un plat de qch; **to be under the w.** se sentir patraque
2 vt **(a)** *(rock)* éroder **(b)** *(problem, situation)* surmonter; *Fig* **to w. the storm** tenir le coup
3 vi *(of rock)* s'éroder

weatherbeaten ['weðəbi:tən] adj *(person, face)* hâlé(e); *(cliff, rock)* battu(e) par les vents

weathercock ['weðəkɒk] n girouette f

weathergirl ['weðəgɜːl] n présentatrice f de la météo

weatherman ['weðəmæn] n présentateur m de la météo

weatherproof ['weðəpru:f] adj résistant(e) aux intempéries

weave [wi:v] **1** vt *(pt* **wove** [wəʊv] *or* **weaved**, *pp* **woven** ['wəʊvən]) tisser; *Fig* **a skilfully woven plot** une intrigue bien ficelée
2 vi tisser; *Fig* **to w. through the traffic** se faufiler parmi les voitures
3 n *(pattern)* tissage m

weaver ['wiːvə(r)] n tisserand(e) m,f

weaving ['wiːvɪŋ] n tissage m

web [web] n **(a)** *(of spider)* toile f; *Fig (of lies)* tissu m; *(of intrigue)* nid m **(b)** *(of duck, frog)* palmure f **(c)** *Comptr* **the W.** le Web; **w. site** site m Web

webbed [webd] adj *(foot)* palmé(e)

webbing ['webɪŋ] n *(on chair, bed)* sangles fpl

web-footed ['web'fʊtɪd] adj palmipède

we'd [wi:d] = **we had, we would**

Wed *(abbr* **Wednesday)** mercredi

wed [wed] *(pt & pp* **wedded) 1** vt épouser; *Fig* **to be wedded to sth** être totalement dévoué(e) à qch
2 vi se marier

wedding ['wedɪŋ] n mariage m; **w. anniversary** anniversaire m de mariage; **w. breakfast** repas m de noces; **w. cake** gâteau m de mariage; **w. day** jour m du mariage; **w. dress** robe f de mariée; **w. night** nuit f de noces; **w. ring** alliance f

wedge [wedʒ] **1** n *(for door, wheel)* cale f; *(of cake)* part f; *(of cheese)* morceau m; *Fig* **it has driven a w. between them** ça les a éloignés l'un de l'autre
2 vt coincer; **to w. a door open** maintenir une porte ouverte avec une cale

wedlock ['wedlɒk] n *Law* mariage m; **to be born out of w.** naître de parents non mariés

Wednesday ['wenzdɪ] n mercredi m; *see also* **Saturday**

wee[1] [wiː] adj *Scot (small)* petit(e); **a w. bit** un petit peu

wee[2] *Br Fam* **1** n pipi m; **to do a w.** faire pipi
2 vi faire pipi

weed [wiːd] n **(a)** *(plant)* mauvaise herbe f **(b)** *Pej (weak person)* mauviette f
2 vt désherber

▶**weed out** vt sep *Fig* éliminer

weedkiller ['wiːdkɪlə(r)] n désherbant m

weedy ['wiːdɪ] adj *Pej (person)* malingre

week [wiːk] n semaine f; **next/last w.** la semaine prochaine/dernière; **once/twice a w.** une fois/deux fois par semaine; **within a w.** sous huitaine; **w. in w. out** chaque semaine; **tomorrow/Tuesday w.** demain/mardi en huit

weekday ['wiːkdeɪ] n jour m de semaine

weekend [wiːk'end] n week-end m; *Br at or Am* **on the w.** ce week-end; *(every weekend)* le week-end; **w. break** week-end

weekly ['wiːklɪ] **1** n *(magazine)* hebdomadaire m
2 adj hebdomadaire
3 adv chaque semaine; **twice w.** deux fois par semaine

weeknight ['wiːknaɪt] n soir m de semaine

weep [wiːp] **1** n **to have a w.** pleurer un coup
2 vt & vi *(pt & pp* **wept** [wept]) pleurer

weeping ['wiːpɪŋ] n pleurs mpl
2 adj qui pleure; **w. willow** saule m pleureur

weepy ['wiːpɪ] adj *Fam (book, film)* mélo; **to be w.** *(of person)* avoir envie de pleurer

wee(-)wee ['wiː'wiː] n *Fam* pipi m; **to do a w.** faire pipi

weft [weft] n trame f

weigh [weɪ] **1** vt **(a)** *(measure)* peser **(b)** *(consider)* mesurer; **to w. sth against sth** mettre qch en balance avec qch **(c)** *Naut* **to w. anchor** lever l'ancre
2 vi *(of person, parcel)* peser; **how much do you w.?** combien tu pèses?; **it's weighing on my conscience** ça me pèse sur la conscience; **her experience weighed in her favour** son expérience a fait pencher la balance en sa faveur

▶**weigh down** vt sep lester; *Fig* **to be weighed down with sth** *(grief, responsibilities)* être accablé(e) de qch

▶**weigh in** vi *(of boxer, jockey)* être pesé(e); **to w. in at 75 kilos** peser 75 kilos

▶**weigh out** vt sep peser

▶**weigh up** vt sep *(consider)* mesurer

weighbridge ['weɪbrɪdʒ] n pont-bascule f

weight [weɪt] **1** n **(a)** *(measure)* poids m; **they're the same w.** ils font le même poids; **to lose/put on w.** perdre/prendre du poids; **to have a w. problem** avoir un problème de poids; **weights and measures** poids et mesures; **w. training** entraînement m aux haltères **(b)** *(idioms)* **to throw one's w. about** affirmer son autorité; **to pull**

one's w. faire sa part de travail; **that's a w. off my mind** ça m'ôte un poids; **to carry w.** avoir du poids

2 *vt Fig* **to be weighted in favour of sb/sth** peser en faveur de qn/qch

▶**weight down** *vt sep (to keep in place)* maintenir avec un poids; *(to make sink)* lester

weighting ['weɪtɪŋ] *n Fin* pondération *f*; **London w.** *(in salary)* indemnité *f* de résidence à Londres

weightless ['weɪtlɪs] *adj (astronaut)* en apesanteur; *(conditions)* d'apesanteur

weightlifter ['weɪtlɪftə(r)] *n* haltérophile *mf*

weightlifting ['weɪtlɪftɪŋ] *n* haltérophilie *f*

weighty ['weɪtɪ] *adj (heavy)* lourd(e); *Fig (serious, important)* grave

weir [wɪə(r)] *n* barrage *m*

weird [wɪəd] *adj* bizarre

weirdo ['wɪədəʊ] *(pl* **weirdos)** *n Fam* type *m* bizarre

welcome ['welkəm] 1 *adj (person, news, change)* bienvenu(e); **to make sb w.** faire un bon accueil à qn; **to feel w.** se sentir le (la) bienvenu(e); **she's always w.** elle est toujours la bienvenue; **w. home!** ça fait plaisir de te revoir!; **w. to Scotland!** bienvenue en Écosse!; **you're w. to borrow it** n'hésite pas à l'emprunter si tu veux

2 *vt (person)* souhaiter la bienvenue à; *(news, change)* accueillir favorablement; *(opportunity)* profiter de

3 *n* accueil *m*; **to give sb a warm w.** faire un accueil chaleureux à qn

welcoming ['welkəmɪŋ] *adj* accueillant(e)

weld [weld] 1 *n* soudure *f*

2 *vt* souder

welder ['weldə(r)] *n* soudeur(euse) *m,f*

welding ['weldɪŋ] *n* soudure *f*

welfare ['welfeə(r)] *n* (a) *(wellbeing)* bien-être *m*; *Br* **the W. State** *m* providence; **w. work** assistance *f* sociale (b) *Am (social security)* **to be on w.** recevoir l'aide sociale

we'll [wiːl] = **we will, we shall**

well¹ [wel] *n (for water, oil)* puits *m*; *(for lift, stairwell)* cage *f*

▶**well up** *vi (of tears)* monter

well² *(comparative* **better** ['betə(r)], *superlative* **best** [best]) 1 *adj* bien; **to be w.** aller bien; **to get w.** se remettre; **it's just as w....** heureusement que...; **that's all very w., but...** tout ça, c'est très bien, mais...; **it's all very w. for you to say that** c'est facile pour toi de dire ça

2 *adv* (a) *(satisfactorily)* bien; **to speak w. of sb** dire du bien de qn; **I did as w. as I could** j'ai fait de mon mieux; **w. done!** bravo!; **you would do w. to keep quiet about it** tu ferais bien de vous taire à ce sujet; **he apologized, as w. he might** il s'est excusé, et c'était bien la moindre des choses; **very w.!** *(OK)* très bien!

(b) *(for emphasis)* **to be w. able to do sth** être parfaitement capable de faire qch; **to be w. aware of sth** avoir parfaitement conscience de qch; **to leave w. alone** ne pas s'en mêler; *Fam* **to be w. in with sb** être dans les petits papiers de qn; **it is w. known that...** il est bien connu que...; **it's worth the effort** ça vaut vraiment la peine; **I can w. believe it** je n'ai aucun mal à le croire; **w. before/after** bien avant/après

(c) **as w.** *(also)* aussi, également; **she has a flat in town as w. as a house in the country** elle a un appartement en ville ainsi qu'une maison à la campagne

3 *exclam (expressing surprise, enquiry)* eh bien!; *(expressing resignation, qualifying previous remark)* enfin; **w., who would have believed it!** eh bien, qui l'eût cru!; **w., who was it?** eh bien, qui était-ce?; **w., if you must!** enfin, si tu es vraiment obligé!; **he's nice, w.** sometimes il est gentil, enfin quelquefois

well-adjusted [welə'dʒʌstɪd] *adj* équilibré(e)

well-advised [weləd'vaɪzd] *adj* sage; **you'd be w. to stay indoors today** tu ferais bien de ne pas sortir aujourd'hui

well-appointed [welə'pɔɪntɪd] *adj* bien équipé(e)

well-argued [wel'ɑːgjuːd] *adj* bien argumenté(e)

well-balanced [wel'bælənst] *adj* équilibré(e)

well-behaved [welbɪ'heɪvd] *adj* sage

wellbeing ['welbiːɪŋ] *n* bien-être *m*

well-built [wel'bɪlt] *adj (building)* solide; *(person)* bien bâti(e)

well-chosen [wel'tʃəʊzən] *adj* bien choisi(e)

well-disposed [weldɪs'pəʊzd] *adj* **to be w. towards sb** être bien disposé(e) envers qn; **to be w. towards sth** être favorable à qch

well-dressed [wel'drest] *adj* bien habillé(e)

well-earned [wel'ɜːnd] *adj* bien mérité(e)

well-fed [wel'fed] *adj* bien nourri(e)

well-founded [wel'faʊndɪd] *adj* fondé(e)

well-heeled [wel'hiːld] *adj Fam* cossu(e)

well-informed [welɪn'fɔːmd] *adj* bien informé(e)

wellington ['welɪŋtən] *n Br* **wellingtons, w. boots** bottes *fpl* en caoutchouc

well-intentioned [welɪn'tenʃənd] *adj* bien intentionné(e)

well-kept [wel'kept] *adj (garden)* bien entretenu(e); *(secret)* bien gardé(e)

well-known [wel'nəʊn] *adj* connu(e)

well-loved [wel'lʌvd] *adj* très aimé(e)

well-made [wel'meɪd] *adj* bien fait(e)

well-meaning [wel'miːnɪŋ] *adj* bien intentionné(e)

well-nigh [wel'naɪ] *adv* pratiquement

well-off [wel'ɒf] *adj Br (wealthy)* riche; *Fig* **you don't know when you're w.** tu ne connais pas ton bonheur

well-paid [wel'peɪd] *adj* bien payé(e)

well-read [wel'red] *adj* cultivé(e)

well-spoken [wel'spəʊkən] *adj* qui s'exprime bien

well-timed [wel'taɪmd] *adj* opportun(e)

well-to-do [weltə'duː] *adj* aisé(e)

wellwisher ['welwɪʃə(r)] *n* sympathisant(e) *m,f*

well-worn [wel'wɔːn] *adj (garment)* très usé(e); *(argument)* éculé(e)

well-written [wel'rɪtən] *adj* bien écrit(e)

Welsh [welʃ] 1 *npl (people)* **the W.** les Gallois *mpl*

2 *n (language)* gallois *m*

3 *adj* gallois(e); **W. dresser** vaisselier *m*

Welshman ['welʃmən] *n* Gallois *m*

Welshwoman ['welʃwʊmən] *n* Galloise *f*

welt [welt] *n* trace *f* de coup

welter ['weltə(r)] *n (of forms, details)* masse *f*; *(of ideas, activities)* multitude *f*

welterweight ['weltəweɪt] *n Sp* poids *m* welter

wench [wentʃ] *n Old-fashioned or Hum* jeune fille *f*, jeune femme *f*

wend [wend] *vt Lit* **to w. one's way homewards** prendre le chemin du retour

went [went] *pt of* **go**

wept [wept] *pt & pp of* **weep**

we're [wɪə(r)] = **we are**

were [wɜ:(r)] *pt of* **be**

weren't [wɜ:nt] = **were not**

werewolf ['wɪəwʊlf] (*pl* **werewolves** ['wɪəwʊlvz]) *n* loup-garou *m*

west [west] **1** *n* ouest *m*; **to the w. (of)** à l'ouest (de); **the W.** l'Occident *m*, l'Ouest *m*

2 *adj* (*coast, side*) ouest *inv*; (*wind*) d'ouest; **W. Africa** l'Afrique *f* de l'Ouest; **the W. Bank** la Cisjordanie; **the W. Country** le sud-ouest de l'Angleterre; **the W. End** = quartier chic de Londres et Glasgow où l'on trouve théâtres et restaurants; *Formerly* **W. Germany** l'Allemagne *f* de l'Ouest; **W. Indian** antillais(e); (*person*) Antillais(e) *m,f*; **the W. Indies** les Antilles *fpl*; **the W. Side** = les quartiers ouest de New York; **W. Virginia** la Virginie occidentale

3 *adv* à l'ouest; (*travel*) vers l'ouest; *Fam Fig* **to go w.** (*of TV, car*) rendre l'âme

westbound ['westbaʊnd] *adj* (*train, traffic*) en direction de l'ouest

westerly ['westəlɪ] **1** *n* (*wind*) vent *m* d'ouest

2 *adj* (*point*) à l'ouest; (*wind*) d'ouest, qui vient de l'ouest; **in a w. direction** vers l'ouest

western ['westən] **1** *n* (*film*) western *m*; (*novel*) roman-western *m*

2 *adj* (*region*) de l'ouest; (*in politics, sociology*) occidental(e); **w. France** l'ouest *m* de la France; **W. Europe** l'Europe *f* de l'Ouest; **the W. Isles** (*of Scotland*) les Hébrides *fpl*; **W. Samoa** les Samoa *fpl*; **W. Samoan** samoan(e); (*person*) Samoan(e) *m,f*

westernized ['westənaɪzd] *adj* occidentalisé(e)

westward ['westwəd] **1** *adj* (*in the west*) à l'ouest, dans l'ouest

2 *adv* = **westwards**

westwards ['westwədz] *adv* (*face, point*) à l'ouest; (*go, travel*) vers l'ouest

wet [wet] **1** *adj* **(a)** (*not dry*) mouillé(e); (*weather*) pluvieux(euse); **to get w.** se mouiller; **the ink/paint was still w.** l'encre/la peinture n'était pas sèche; *Fig* **w. blanket** rabat-joie *mf*; **w. paint** (*sign*) peinture fraîche; **w. suit** combinaison *f* de plongée **(b)** *Br Fam* (*feeble*) minable

2 *vt* (*pt & pp* **wet** *or* **wetted**) mouiller; **to w. the bed** faire pipi au lit; **to w. oneself** mouiller sa culotte

3 *n* **(a)** (*dampness*) humidité *f*; (*rain*) pluie *f* **(b)** *Br Pol* modéré(e) *m,f*

WEU [dʌbəlju:iː'u:] *n* (*abbr* **Western European Union**) UEO *f*

we've [wiːv] = **we have**

whack [wæk] *Fam* **1** *n* **(a)** (*blow*) grand coup *m*; **to give sb/sth a w.** donner un grand coup à qn/qch **(b)** (*share*) part *f*

2 *vt* **(a)** (*hit*) donner un grand coup à; **to w. sb on** *or* **over the head** donner un grand coup sur la tête de qn **(b)** *Am very Fam* (*murder*) liquider

whacked [wækt] *adj Fam* (*exhausted*) nase, vanné(e)

whacking ['wækɪŋ] *adv Fam* **a w. great increase/fine** une vache d'augmentation/d'amende

whale [weɪl] *n* baleine *f*; *Fam* **to have a w. of a time** s'éclater

whaler ['weɪlə(r)] *n* baleinier *m*

whaling ['weɪlɪŋ] *n* pêche *f ou* chasse *f* à la baleine

wharf [wɔ:f] (*pl* **wharves** [wɔ:vz]) *n* quai *m*

what [wɒt] **1** *pron* **(a)** (*in questions*) (*subject*) qu'est-ce qui; (*object*) qu'est-ce que, que; (*after preposition*) quoi; **w.'s happening?** qu'est-ce qui se passe?; **w. do you want?** qu'est-ce que tu veux?, que veux-tu?; **w. are you thinking about?** à quoi penses-tu?; **w.'s that?** qu'est-ce que c'est?; **w.'s that to you?** qu'est-ce que ça peut vous faire?; **w. for?** (*for what purpose?*) pour quoi faire?; (*why*) pourquoi?; **w.'s a modem for?** à quoi ça sert, un modem?; **w. did he do that for?** pourquoi est-ce qu'il a fait ça?; **w.'s French for "dog"?** comment dit-on "dog" en français?; **w.'s he like?** comment est-il?; **w. about the money I lent you?** et l'argent que je vous ai prêté?; **w. about a game of tennis?** et si on faisait une partie de tennis?; **w. about me?** et moi?; **if that doesn't work, w. then?** si ça ne marche pas, qu'est-ce qui reste?; *Fam* **w. of it?** et alors?; *Fam* **are you coming or w.?** tu viens ou quoi?

(b) (*in relative constructions*) (*subject*) ce qui; (*object*) ce que; **I don't know w. has happened** je ne sais pas ce qui s'est passé; **I can't remember w. she said** je ne me souviens plus de ce que tu m'as dit; **w. is surprising is that…** ce qu'il y a de surprenant, c'est que…; **w. I like is…** ce que j'aime, c'est…; *Fam* **he knows w.'s w.** il sait ce qu'il en est; *Fam* **to give sb w. for** frotter les oreilles à qn

2 *adj* **(a)** (*in questions*) quel (quelle); (*plural*) quels (quelles); **w. time is it?** quelle heure est-il?; **tell me w. time it is** dis-moi l'heure qu'il est; **show me w. books you want** montre-moi quels livres tu veux

(b) (*in relative constructions*) **I'll give you w. money I have** je vais vous donner l'argent que j'ai; **he took w. little food was left** il a pris le peu de nourriture qui restait

(c) (*in exclamations*) **w. an idea!** quelle idée!; **w. a fool he is!** qu'il est bête!; **w. a lot of people!** quel monde!

3 *exclam* quoi?; **w. next!** et quoi encore!

what-d'ye-call-her ['wɒtjəkɔːlə(r)] *n Fam* (*person*) Machine *f*

what-d'ye-call-him ['wɒtjəkɔːlɪm] *n Fam* (*person*) Machin *m*

what-d'ye-call-it ['wɒtjəkɔːlɪt] *n Fam* (*thing*) machin *m*, truc *m*

whatever [wɒt'evə(r)] **1** *pron* **(a)** (*no matter what*) quoi que + *subjunctive*; **w. it is, w. it may be** quoi que ce soit; **w. happens** quoi qu'il arrive **(b)** (*anything*) ce que; **do w. you like** fais ce que tu veux; **give him w. he wants** donne-lui tout ce qu'il veut; **w. you say** comme tu voudras (*c*) (*what on earth*) **w. does that mean?** qu'est-ce que ça peut bien vouloir dire?

2 *adj* **(a)** (*no matter what*) **take w. food you want** prends toute la nourriture que tu veux; **pay w. price they ask** donne-leur le prix qu'ils en demandent, quel qu'il soit **(b)** (*emphatic*) **for no reason w.** sans aucune raison; **nothing w.** absolument rien

what's-her-name ['wɒtsəneɪm], **what's-his-name** ['wɒtsɪzneɪm], **what's-its-name** ['wɒtsɪts-neɪm] = **what-d'ye-call-her/him/it**

whatsit ['wɒtsɪt] *n Fam* machin *m*, truc *m*

whatsoever [wɒtsəʊ'evə(r)] *adj* **for no reason w.** sans aucune raison; **none w.** aucun(e); **nothing w.** absolument rien

wheat [wiːt] *n* blé *m*; **w. germ** germe *m* de blé

wheaten ['wiːtən] *adj* (*loaf, roll*) de blé *ou* froment

wheatfield ['wi:tfi:ld] *n* champ *m* de blé

wheedle ['wi:dəl] *vt* **to w. sth out of sb** soutirer qch à qn par des cajoleries; **to w. sb into doing sth** amadouer qn pour qu'il/elle fasse qch

wheel [wi:l] **1** *n* (a) *(on car, bike, pram)* roue *f*; *(on trolley, suitcase)* roulette *f* (b) *(steering wheel)* volant *m*; **to be at the w.** être au volant

2 *vt (push)* pousser

3 *vi (turn)* **to w. (about or around)** *(of person)* se retourner brusquement; *(of plane)* tourner

wheelbarrow ['wi:lbærəʊ] *n* brouette *f*

wheelbase ['wi:lbeɪs] *n* empattement *m*

wheelchair ['wi:ltʃeə(r)] *n* fauteuil *m* roulant

-wheeled [wi:ld] *suff* **two/three/four-w.** à deux/trois/quatre roues

wheeling and dealing ['wi:lɪŋəndi:lɪŋ] *n* tractations *fpl*

wheeze [wi:z] **1** *n* (a) *(noise)* respiration *f* sifflante (b) *Fam (trick)* astuce *f*, combine *f*

2 *vi (breathe heavily)* respirer péniblement

whelk [welk] *n* bulot *m*

whelp [welp] *n* petit *m*

when [wen] **1** *adv (in questions)* quand; **w. will you come?** quand viendras-tu?; **tell me w. it happened** dis-moi quand cela s'est produit; *Fam* **say w.!** *(when pouring drink)* tu me dis stop!

2 *conj* (a) *(with time)* quand, lorsque; **w. I came into the room** quand *ou* lorsque je suis entré dans la pièce; **tell me w. you've finished** dis-moi quand tu auras terminé; **what's the good of talking w. you never listen?** à quoi sert de parler puisque tu n'écoutes jamais? (b) *(whereas)* alors que

whence [wens] *adv Lit* d'où

whenever [wen'evə(r)] **1** *conj* (a) *(every time that)* chaque fois que; **I go w. I can** j'y vais aussi souvent que je peux (b) *(no matter when)* n'importe quand; **come w. you like** viens quand tu veux

2 *adv* (a) *(referring to unspecified time)* n'importe quand; **Sunday, Monday or w.** dimanche, lundi ou n'importe quel autre jour (b) *(in questions)* **w. did you do that?** quand est-ce que tu as fait ça?

where [weə(r)] **1** *adv (in questions)* où; **w. are you going?** où vas-tu?; **w. does he come from?** d'où vient-il?; **tell me w. she is** dis-moi où elle est; **w. would we be if...?** que serions-nous devenus si...?

2 *conj* (a) **I'll stay w. I am** je reste (là) où je suis; **that's w. he lives** c'est là qu'il habite; **that is w. you are mistaken** c'est là que vous vous trompez; **they went to Paris, w. they stayed a week** ils sont allés à Paris, où ils ont séjourné une semaine

whereabouts 1 *npl* ['weərəbaʊts] **nobody knows her w., her w. are unknown** personne ne sait où elle est

2 *adv* [weərə'baʊts] *(where)* où

whereas [weər'ræz] *conj* alors que, tandis que

whereby [weə'baɪ] *adv Formal* par lequel (par laquelle)

whereupon [weərə'pɒn] *conj Lit* sur quoi

wherever [weər'evə(r)] **1** *conj* (a) *(everywhere that)* où que; **I see him w. I go** où que j'aille, je le vois; **w. possible** partout où cela est possible (b) *(no matter where)* n'importe où; **we'll go w. you want** nous irons où tu voudras

2 *adv* (a) *(referring to unknown or unspecified place)* **at home, in the office or w.** chez soi, au bureau ou n'importe où; **it's in Coatbridge, w. that is** c'est à Coatbridge, mais je ne sais pas où se trouve Coatbridge (b) *(in questions)* **w. can he be?** où peut-elle bien être?

wherewithal ['weəwɪðɔ:l] *n* **to have the w. (to do sth)** avoir les moyens (de faire qch)

whet [wet] *(vt & pp* **whetted)** *vt (tool, blade, appetite)* aiguiser

whether ['weðə(r)] *conj* (a) *(with indirect questions)* si; **I don't know w. it's true** je ne sais pas si c'est vrai (b) *(conditional)* **w. she comes or not we shall leave** qu'elle vienne ou non, nous partirons

whew [hju:] *exclam (of relief)* ouf!; *(of fatigue)* pff!; *(of astonishment)* dis donc!

whey [weɪ] *n* petit-lait *m*

which [wɪtʃ] **1** *pron* (a) *(in questions)* lequel (laquelle) *m,f*; *(plural)* lesquels (lesquelles) *mpl,fpl*; **w. (one) is better?** lequel est le meilleur?; **w. of you is going?** qui d'entre vous y va?; **I can never remember w. is w.** je ne me rappelle jamais la différence

(b) *(relative) (subject)* qui; *(object)* que; **the house w. is for sale** la maison qui est à vendre; **the film w. I saw last week** le film que j'ai vu la semaine dernière

(c) *(referring back to whole clause) (subject)* ce qui; *(object)* ce que; **he's getting married, w. surprises me** il va se marier, ce qui m'étonne; **she was back in London, w. I didn't know** elle était de retour à Londres, ce que je ne savais pas

(d) *(with prepositions)* **behind/in front of w.** derrière/devant lequel (laquelle); **beside/above w.** à côté/au-dessus duquel (de laquelle); **the countries w. we are going to** les pays où nous allons; **the town w. we live in** la ville où nous habitons; **after w. he went out** après quoi, il est sorti

2 *adj* (a) *(in questions)* quel (quelle); *(plural)* quels (quelles); **w. colour do you like best?** quelle couleur préférez-vous?; **w. way do we go?** de quel côté allons-nous?; **w. one?** lequel (laquelle)?; **w. ones?** lesquels (lesquelles)?

(b) *(in relative constructions)* **I was there for a week, during w. time...** j'y suis resté une semaine, période pendant laquelle...; **she came at noon, by w. time I had left** elle est arrivée à midi, heure à laquelle j'étais déjà parti

whichever [wɪtʃ'evə(r)] **1** *pron* (a) *(no matter which)* quel (quelle) que soit celui (celle) qui; **w. you choose, I'm sure she'll like it** quel que soit celui que tu choisisses, je suis sûr que ça lui plaira (b) *(any)* **take w. you want** prends celui (celle) que tu voudras (c) *(according to which)* **come on Saturday or Sunday, w. suits you** viens samedi ou dimanche, suivant ce qui t'arrange

2 *adj (no matter which)* **take w. book you like best** choisis le livre que tu préfères

whiff [wɪf] *n* odeur *f*; **to catch a w. of sth** sentir qch; *Fig* **a w. of scandal** un parfum de scandale

while [waɪl] **1** *n* (a) *(time)* **a w.** un moment; **after/in a w.** après/dans un moment; **a short or little w. ago** il y a un petit moment; **a good w., quite a w.** un bon moment; **a long w.** longtemps; **once in a w.** de temps en temps

(b) **it's not worth my w.** ça n'en vaut pas la peine; **it's not worth my w. going** ça ne vaut pas la peine que j'y aille; **I'll make it worth your w.** vous serez récompensé de votre peine

2 *conj* (a) *(during the time that)* pendant que; **w. reading I fell asleep** je me suis endormi en lisant

(b) *(as long as)* tant que; **it won't happen w. I'm in**

charge! ça ne se produira pas tant que ce sera moi le responsable!

(c) *(although)* bien que + *subjunctive*; **w. I admit it's difficult,...** bien que j'admette que ce soit difficile...

(d) *(whereas)* alors que; **one wore white, w. the other was in black** l'un portait du blanc, alors que l'autre était en noir

▶**while away** *vt sep* **to w. away the time** passer le temps

whilst [waɪlst] *conj Br* = **while²**

whim [wɪm] *n* lubie *f*, fantaisie *f*; **to do sth on a w.** faire qch sur un coup de tête

whimper ['wɪmpə(r)] **1** *n* gémissement *m*, geignement *m*; *Fig* **without a w.** sans broncher
2 *vi* gémir, geindre

whimsical ['wɪmzɪkəl] *adj (person, behaviour)* fantasque; *(remark, story)* saugrenu(e)

whine [waɪn] **1** *n (of person, animal)* gémissement *m*; *(of machine)* grincement *m*
2 *vi also Fig* gémir *(about* à propos de)

whinge [wɪndʒ] *vi* pleurnicher

whinny ['wɪnɪ] **1** *n* hennissement *m*
2 *vi* hennir

whip [wɪp] **1** *n* **(a)** *(for punishment)* fouet *m* **(b)** *Pol* chef *m* de file
2 *vt (pt & pp* **whipped)** **(a)** *(beat with whip)* fouetter; **whipped cream** crème *f* fouettée; *Fig* **he whipped the crowd into a frenzy** son discours rendit la foule frénétique **(b)** *Fam (defeat)* battre à plates coutures **(c)** *Fam (steal)* faucher

▶**whip off** *vt sep Fam (clothes)* ôter rapidement

▶**whip out** *vt sep Fam* sortir soudainement

▶**whip round** *vi Fam (turn quickly)* se retourner brusquement

▶**whip up** *vt sep* **(a)** *(support, enthusiasm)* susciter; *(audience)* galvaniser **(b)** *(prepare quickly) (dish, meal)* préparer vite fait

whiplash ['wɪplæʃ] *n* lésion *f* des cervicales

whippersnapper ['wɪpəsnæpə(r)] *n Fam* garnement *m*

whippet ['wɪpɪt] *n* whippet *m*

whipround ['wɪpraʊnd] *n Fam* **to have a w. (for sb)** organiser une collecte (pour qn)

whirl [wɜːl] **1** *n also Fig* tourbillon *m*; **the social w.** le tourbillon de la vie mondaine; **my head's in a w.** j'ai la tête qui tourne; *Fam* **let's give it a w.** on va tenter le coup
2 *vt* **to w. sb/sth around** faire tournoyer qn/qch
3 *vi* tourbillonner; **my head's whirling** j'ai la tête qui tourne

▶**whirl along** *vi (of car, train)* filer à toute vitesse

▶**whirl round** *vi* se retourner brusquement

whirlpool ['wɜːlpuːl] *n* tourbillon *m*; **w. bath** bain *m* à remous

whirlwind ['wɜːlwɪnd] *n* tourbillon *m*; **w. romance** passion *f* enivrante; **w. tour** visite *f* éclair

whirr [wɜː(r)] **1** *n* ronflement *m*
2 *vi* ronfler

whisk [wɪsk] **1** *n* batteur *m*, fouet *m*
2 *vt* **(a)** *(eggs)* battre **(b)** *(move quickly)* **to w. sb into hospital** transporter qn d'urgence à l'hôpital
3 *vi (move quickly)* **she whisked past me** elle est passée devant moi comme un éclair

▶**whisk away, whisk off** *vt sep (person)* emmener rapidement; *(object)* enlever rapidement

whisker ['wɪskə(r)] *n* **whiskers** *(of cat, mouse)* moustaches *fpl*; *(of man)* favoris *mpl*; *Fam* **to win by a w.** gagner de justesse

whisky, *Am* **whiskey** ['wɪskɪ] *n* whisky *m*

whisper ['wɪspə(r)] **1** *n* chuchotement *m*; **to speak in a w.** chuchoter
2 *vt* chuchoter; **to w. sth to sb** chuchoter qch à qn; **it's being whispered that...** le bruit court que...
3 *vi* chuchoter; **to w. to sb** chuchoter à l'oreille de qn

whist [wɪst] *n* whist *m*

whistle ['wɪsəl] **1** *n* **(a)** *(noise)* sifflement *m* **(b)** *(musical instrument)* flageolet *m*; *(of referee, policeman)* sifflet *m*
2 *vt (tune)* siffler
3 *vi* siffler; *Fam* **he can w. for his money** s'il compte récupérer son argent, il peut toujours courir

whistle-stop tour ['wɪsəlstɒp'tʊə(r)] *n* tournée *f* rapide

Whit [wɪt] *n* Pentecôte *f*; **W. Sunday** la Pentecôte

whit [wɪt] *n* **it doesn't matter a w.** ça n'a aucune importance; **it won't make a w. of difference** ça ne changera absolument rien

white [waɪt] **1** *n* **(a)** *(colour, of egg, eye)* blanc *m*; **w. doesn't suit her** le blanc ne lui va pas **(b)** *(person)* Blanc (Blanche) *m,f*
2 *adj* blanc (blanche); **a w. man** un Blanc; **a w. woman** une Blanche; **to turn** *or* **go w.** *(person)* devenir blême; *(object, hair)* blanchir; **w. with fear** vert(e) de peur; **w. as a ghost/sheet** pâle comme la mort/un linge; **w. chocolate** chocolat *m* blanc; **w. coffee** café *m* au lait; *Fig* **w. elephant** = chose coûteuse et peu rentable; **w. fish** poisson *m* à chair blanche; **w. flag** drapeau *m* blanc; **w. flour** farine *f* blanche; **the W. House** la Maison-Blanche; **w. lie** pieux mensonge *m*; **w. meat** viande *f* blanche; *Pol* **w. paper** livre *m* blanc; **w. sauce** sauce *f* blanche; **w. spirit** white-spirit *m*; **w. stick** canne *f* blanche; **w. tie** *(formal dress)* tenue *f* de soirée; **w. wedding** mariage *m* en blanc

whitebait ['waɪtbeɪt] *n* friture *f*

white-collar worker ['waɪt'kɒlə'wɜːkə(r)] *n* col *m* blanc

white-haired ['waɪt'heəd] *adj* aux cheveux blancs

Whitehall ['waɪthɔːl] *n* = rue de Londres où se trouvent les ministères

white-hot ['waɪt'hɒt] *adj* chauffé(e) à blanc

whiteness ['waɪtnɪs] *n* blancheur *f*

whitewash ['waɪtwɒʃ] **1** *n (paint)* badigeon *m* à la chaux; *Fig (cover-up)* blanchiment *m*
2 *vt (paint)* badigeonner à la chaux; *Fig (cover up)* blanchir

whither ['wɪðə(r)] *adv Lit* **w. Britain/education?** où va la Grande-Bretagne/l'enseignement?

whiting ['waɪtɪŋ] *n (fish)* merlan *m*

whitish ['waɪtɪʃ] *adj* blanchâtre

Whitsun ['wɪtsən] *n* Pentecôte *f*

whittle ['wɪtəl] *vt* tailler (au couteau); *Fig* **to w. sth down** réduire qch

▶**whittle away** *vt sep Fig* **to w. sth away** réduire qch à presque rien

whizz [wɪz] **1** *n Fam (expert)* crack *m*; **w. kid** jeune prodige *m*
2 *vi (of bullet)* siffler; *(of person, car)* passer à toute vitesse;

to w. **through** a book/meal lire un livre/manger à toute vitesse

WHO [dʌbəlju:eɪtʃˈəu] n (abbr **World Health Organization**) OMS f

who [hu:] pron (a) (in questions) qui; **w. is it?** qui est-ce?; **w. with?** avec qui?; **do you know w. she is?** sais-tu qui elle est?; **w.'s speaking?** (on phone) qui est à l'appareil?; **w. did you say was there?** qui était là, déjà?; **w. does he think he is?** pour qui se prend-il? (b) (relative) qui; **the people w. came yesterday** les gens qui sont venus hier; **those w. have already paid can leave** ceux qui ont déjà payé peuvent s'en aller; **Louise's father, w. is a doctor, was there** le père de Louise, qui est médecin, était la

whodun(n)it [hu:ˈdʌnɪt] n Fam polar m

whoever [hu:ˈevə(r)] pron (a) (no matter who) qui que + subjunctive; **w. you are** qui que vous soyez; **w. wrote that letter** la personne qui a écrit cette lettre; **Fam ask Simon or Cris or w.** demande à Simon ou à Cris ou à n'importe qui d'autre (b) (anyone that) celui (celle) qui; **w. finds it may keep it** celui qui le trouvera pourra le garder (c) (in questions) **w. can that be?** qui cela peut-il être?

whole [həul] 1 adj (a) (entire, intact) entier(ère); **the w. truth** toute la vérité; **the w. world** le monde entier; **a w. week** toute une semaine, une semaine entière; **to swallow sth w.** avaler qch sans le mâcher; Fig avaler qch; **w. milk** lait m entier (b) Fam (for emphasis) **a w. lot** of tout un tas de; **the w. lot of you** vous tous

2 n totalité f, ensemble m; **the w. of the village/the money** tout le village/l'argent; **as a w.** dans sa totalité; **on the w.** dans l'ensemble

wholefood ['həulfu:d] n aliments mpl complets; **w. restaurant** restaurant m bio

wholehearted [həul'hɑ:tɪd] adj sans réserve, total(e)

wholemeal ['həulmi:l] adj **w. bread** pain m complet; **w. flour** farine f complète

wholesale ['həulseɪl] 1 adj de gros; Fig (large-scale) à grande échelle

2 adv en gros; Fig (on a large scale) à grande échelle

3 n (vente f en) gros m

wholesaler ['həulseɪlə(r)] n grossiste mf

wholesome ['həulsəm] adj (food, entertainment) sain(e); (person) comme il faut

wholly ['həulli] adv entièrement

whom [hu:m] pron Formal (a) (in questions) qui; **w. did you see?** qui avez-vous vu?; **for/to/of w.?** pour/à/de qui? (b) (relative) que; **the woman w. you saw** la femme que vous avez vue; **the man w. you gave the money to** l'homme à qui vous avez donné l'argent; **the person of w. we were speaking** la personne dont nous parlions; **the men, both of w. were quite young,...** les hommes, tous deux assez jeunes...

whoop [wu:p] 1 n cri m de joie

2 vi crier de joie

whoopee 1 n ['wʊpi] Fam **to make w.** (have fun) faire la bombe; (have sex) faire crac-crac

2 exclam [wʊˈpi:] youpi!

whooping cough ['hu:pɪŋˈkɒf] n coqueluche f

whoops [wʊps] exclam houp-là!

whopper ['wɒpə(r)] n Fam (a) (huge thing) truc m énorme (b) (lie) gros bobard m

whopping ['wɒpɪŋ] adj Fam **w. (great)** énorme

whore [hɔ:(r)] n very Fam putain f

whorehouse ['hɔ:haʊs] n bordel m

whose [hu:z] 1 possessive pron (in questions) à qui; **w. are these gloves?** à qui sont ces gants?; **w. is this?** à qui est-ce?; **tell me w. they are** dis-moi à qui ils sont

2 possessive adj (in questions) à qui; **w. gloves are these?** à qui sont ces gants?; **w. daughter are you?** de qui es-tu la fille? (b) (relative) dont; **the pupil w. work I showed you** l'élève dont je t'ai montré le travail; **the man to w. wife I gave the money** l'homme à la femme de qui j'ai donné l'argent

why [waɪ] 1 adv (a) (in questions) pourquoi; **w. didn't you say so?** pourquoi ne l'as-tu pas dit?; **w. get angry?** pourquoi se mettre en colère?; **w. not?** pourquoi pas? (b) (in suggestions) **w. don't you phone him?** pourquoi ne lui téléphones-tu pas?; **w. don't I come with you?** pourquoi est-ce que je ne viendrais pas avec toi?; **w. not sell the car?** pourquoi ne pas vendre la voiture?

2 conj pourquoi; **I'll tell you w. I don't like her** je vais vous dire pourquoi je ne l'aime pas; **that's w....** voilà pourquoi...; **the reason w....** la raison pour laquelle...

3 n **the whys and wherefores (of sth)** le pourquoi et le comment (de qch)

4 exclam **w., it's David!** mais voilà David!

WI [dʌbəlju:ˈaɪ] n Br (abbr **Women's Institute**) = association de femmes en milieu rural qui organise diverses activités

wick [wɪk] n (a) (of lamp, candle) mèche f (b) Fam **to get on sb's w.** taper sur les nerfs à qn

wicked ['wɪkɪd] adj (a) (evil) méchant(e); Fig (dreadful) affreux(euse) (b) Fam (excellent) génial(e)

wickedness ['wɪkɪdnɪs] n méchanceté f

wicker ['wɪkə(r)] n osier m

wickerwork ['wɪkəwɜ:k] n vannerie f

wicket ['wɪkɪt] n (in cricket) guichet m

wicketkeeper ['wɪkɪtki:pə(r)] n (in cricket) gardien m de guichet

wide [waɪd] 1 adj (a) (broad) large; **to be 100 metres w.** faire 100 mètres de large; **in the whole w. world** dans le monde entier (b) (extensive) vaste

2 adv **w. open** (eyes, mouth, door) grand ouvert(e); **to be w. open to criticism** prêter le flanc à la critique; **w. apart** très espacé(e); (legs) très écarté(e); **w. awake** complètement réveillé(e); **the shot went w.** la balle est passée à côté; **w. of the mark** loin de la vérité

wide-angle ['waɪdæŋgl] adj grand angle inv

wide-eyed ['waɪdaɪd] adj aux yeux écarquillés

widely ['waɪdlɪ] adv (a) (extensively) largement; **it is w. believed that...** beaucoup de gens pensent que...; **w. known** connu(e) de tout le monde (b) (at a distance) **w. spaced** très espacé(e)

widen ['waɪdən] 1 vt agrandir; (garment) élargir; Fig (influence, scope) étendre; **to w. one's horizons** élargir son horizon

2 vi s'élargir; (of gap, eyes) s'agrandir

▸**widen out** vi s'élargir

widespread ['waɪdspred] adj répandu(e)

widow ['wɪdəu] 1 n veuve f; **w.'s pension** allocation f veuvage

2 vt **to be widowed** devenir veuf (veuve)

widowed ['wɪdəud] adj veuf (veuve)

widower ['wɪdəuə(r)] n veuf m

width [wɪdθ] n largeur f

wield [wiːld] vt (a) (sword, pen) manier (b) (power, influence) exercer

wife [waɪf] (pl **wives** [waɪvz]) n femme f, épouse f

wifely ['waɪflɪ] adj de bonne épouse

wig [wɪg] n perruque f

wiggle ['wɪgəl] 1 n trémoussement m
2 vt remuer
3 vi se trémousser

wiggly ['wɪglɪ] adj Fam (line) ondulé(e)

wigwam ['wɪgwæm] n wigwam m

wild [waɪld] 1 adj (a) (not domesticated) (animal, flower, countryside) sauvage; Fig **it was a w. goose chase** ça n'a rien donné; Fam **w. horses wouldn't drag it out of me** rien au monde ne me le ferait dire; Fig **to sow one's w. oats** jeter sa gourme; **the W. West** le Far West
(b) (unrestrained) (wind) violent(e); (weather) très mauvais(e); (hair) en bataille; (child) turbulent(e); (enthusiasm) délirant(e); (promise, rumour) insensé(e); **w. eyes** regard m fou; **to be w.** (person) mener une vie agitée; **to drive sb w.** rendre qn fou (folle)
(c) (random) **it was just a w. guess** j'ai dit ça au hasard; Comptr & Typ **w. card** joker m
(d) Fam (enthusiastic) **to be w. about sb/sth** être dingue de qn/qch
(e) Fam (excellent) génial(e)
2 adv **to grow w.** (of plant) pousser à l'état sauvage; **to run w.** être livré(e) à soi-même; **the audience went w.** le public s'est déchaîné
3 n **in the w.** à l'état sauvage; **in the wilds** en pleine brousse

wildcat ['waɪldkæt] n chat m sauvage; Ind **w. strike** grève f sauvage

wilderness ['wɪldənɪs] n région f sauvage; Fig (overgrown garden) jungle f; Fig **to be in the w.** être en pleine traversée du désert

wildfire ['waɪldfaɪə(r)] n **to spread like w.** se répandre comme une traînée de poudre

wildfowl ['waɪldfaʊl] (pl **wildfowl**) n gibier m d'eau

wildlife ['waɪldlaɪf] n nature f; **w. programme** (on TV) émission f sur les animaux

wildly ['waɪldlɪ] adv (a) (cheer, applaud) frénétiquement; **to rush about w.** courir dans tous les sens (b) (guess) au hasard (c) (for emphasis) extrêmement; (inaccurate, exaggerated) complètement

wildness ['waɪldnɪs] n (of countryside, animal) état m sauvage; (of wind, waves) fureur f; (of applause) frénésie f; (of ideas, words) extravagance f

wilful ['wɪlfʊl] adj (a) (stubborn) têtu(e) (b) (deliberate) délibéré(e); Law **w. murder** homicide m volontaire

wilfully ['wɪlfʊlɪ] adv (a) (stubbornly) avec entêtement (b) (deliberately) délibérément

will[1] [wɪl] 1 n (a) (resolve, determination) volonté f (**to do** de faire); **at w.** à volonté; (cry) à la demande; (fire) au hasard; Mil **fire at w.!** feu à volonté; **to show good w.** faire preuve de bonne volonté; **with the best w. in the world** avec la meilleure volonté du monde; Prov **where there's a w. there's a way** quand on veut, on peut (b) (document) testament m; **the last w. and testament of...** les dernières volontés de...; **to make one's w.** faire son testament
2 vt (a) **to w. sb to do sth** souhaiter ardemment que qn fasse qch; **to w. oneself to do sth** faire un effort de volonté pour faire qch (b) (leave in one's will) **to w. sth to sb** léguer qch à qn par testament

will[2]

On trouve généralement **I/you/he/**etc **will** sous leurs formes contractées **I'll/you'll/he'll/**etc. La forme négative correspondante est **won't**, que l'on écrira **will not** dans des contextes formels.

modal aux v (a) (expressing future tense) **I'll do it tomorrow** je le ferai demain; **it won't take long** ça ne prendra pas longtemps; **when w. he be coming?** quand viendra-t-il?; **I'll have finished by five** j'aurai fini avant cinq heures; **w. you be there? – yes I w./no I won't** tu seras là? – oui/non; **you'll write to me, won't you?** tu m'écriras, n'est-ce pas?
(b) (expressing wish, determination) **I won't allow it!** je ne le permettrai pas!; **w. you help me?** tu veux bien m'aider?; **she won't let me see him** elle refuse que je le voie; **won't you sit down?** vous ne voulez pas vous asseoir?; **be quiet, w. you!** tais-toi, s'il te plaît!; **if she will insist on doing everything herself...** si elle continue à tout vouloir faire elle-même...; **will you go away!** va-t-en, je te dis!; **it won't open** ça ne s'ouvre pas
(c) (expressing general truth) **these things w. happen** ça arrive parfois; **the restaurant w. seat a hundred people** le restaurant peut accueillir cent personnes
(d) (expressing conjecture) **you'll be tired** vous devez être fatigué; **they'll be home by now** ils ont dû arriver chez eux maintenant

William ['wɪljəm] n **W. the Conqueror** Guillaume le Conquérant

willie ['wɪlɪ] n Fam (penis) zizi m

willies ['wɪlɪz] npl Fam **to have the w.** avoir la trouille; **to give sb the w.** flanquer la trouille à qn

willing ['wɪlɪŋ] adj (assistant, participant) plein(e) de bonne volonté; **he was a w. accomplice** c'est de son plein gré qu'il est devenu complice; **to be w. to do sth** bien vouloir faire qch; **to show w.** faire preuve de bonne volonté

willingly ['wɪlɪŋlɪ] adv (voluntarily) de son plein gré; (with pleasure) volontiers

willingness ['wɪlɪŋnɪs] n bonne volonté f

will-o'-the-wisp [wɪləðə'wɪsp] n also Fig feu m follet

willow ['wɪləʊ] n **w.** (tree) saule m

willpower ['wɪlpaʊə(r)] n volonté f

willy ['wɪlɪ] n Fam (penis) zizi m

willy-nilly ['wɪlɪ'nɪlɪ] adv bon gré, mal gré

wilt [wɪlt] vi (of plant) se flétrir; Fig (of person) fatiguer

wily ['waɪlɪ] adj rusé(e)

wimp [wɪmp] n Fam mauviette f

wimpish ['wɪmpɪʃ] adj Fam mauviette

win [wɪn] 1 n victoire f
2 vt (pt & pp **won** [wʌn]) (a) (battle, race, prize) gagner; **to w. an argument** avoir le dernier mot; Fam **you can't w. them all, you w. some you lose some** on ne peut pas toujours être gagnant (b) (popularity, recognition) acquérir; (confidence, love) gagner (parliamentary seat, election) remporter
3 vi gagner; Fam **you can't w.** j'aurai/tu auras/etc toujours tort; **OK, you w.!** bon, d'accord!

▸**win back** vt sep reconquérir

▸**win out** vi réussir

▸**win over, win round** vt sep persuader

▸**win through** vi réussir

wince [wɪns] **1** *n* grimace *f*

2 *vi* to w. (with pain/embarrassment) grimacer de douleur/d'embarras

winch [wɪntʃ] **1** *n* treuil *m*

2 *vt* hisser

wind¹ [wɪnd] **1** *n* (a) (air current) vent *m*; to sail into or against the w. naviguer vent debout; *Fig* to sail close to the w. (take risks) jouer avec le feu; (be risqué) friser l'indécence; w. energy or power énergie *f* éolienne; w. instrument instrument *m* à vent; w. tunnel soufflerie *f* (b) (breath) souffle *m*; let me get my w. back laisse-moi reprendre mon souffle (c) (abdominal) gaz *m*, vent *m*; to have w. avoir des gaz; to break w. lâcher un vent (d) (idioms) Fam to put the w. up sb faire une peur bleue à qn; to take the w. out of sb's sails couper l'herbe sous le pied à qn; to get w. of sth avoir vent de qch

2 *vt* to w. sb (with punch) couper la respiration à qn

wind² [waɪnd] (pt & pp wound [waʊnd]) **1** *vt* (a) (thread, string) enrouler (round autour de) (b) (handle) tourner; (clock, watch) remonter; to w. a cassette on/back faire avancer/rembobiner une cassette

2 *vi* (of path, river) serpenter

▸**wind down 1** *vt sep* (a) (car window) baisser (b) (reduce) (production) réduire progressivement; (company) fermer progressivement

2 *vi* (of party) se calmer; (of meeting) tirer à sa fin; *Fam* (of person) se détendre, décompresser

▸**wind up 1** *vt sep* (a) (car window) remonter (b) (finish) (speech, meeting) terminer (c) *Fam* (tease) faire marcher; (annoy) mettre en boîte

2 *vi* (end speech, meeting) terminer (b) *Fam* (end up) finir; to w. up doing sth finir par faire qch; she'll w. up in prison elle va finir en prison

windbag [ˈwɪndbæg] *n Fam* moulin *m* à paroles

windbreak [ˈwɪndbreɪk] *n* brise-vent *m inv*

windcheater [ˈwɪndtʃiːtə(r)] *n* (jacket) coupe-vent *m inv*

windchill factor [ˈwɪndtʃɪlfæktə(r)] *n* = abaissement de la température dû au vent

winder [ˈwaɪndə(r)] *n* (on watch) remontoir *m*; (on car door) lève-glace *m inv*

windfall [ˈwɪndfɔːl] *n* (fruit) fruit *m* abattu par le vent; *Fig* (money) aubaine *f*; *Fin* w. profits (of company) bénéfices *mpl* inattendus

winding [ˈwaɪndɪŋ] *adj* (path, stream) sinueux(euse); (staircase) en colimaçon

windmill [ˈwɪndmɪl] *n* moulin *m* à vent

window [ˈwɪndəʊ] *n* (a) (of house) & Comptr fenêtre *f*; (of vehicle) vitre *f*, glace *f*; (of shop) vitrine *f*; w. box jardinière *f*; w. cleaner laveur(euse) *m,f* de carreaux; w. frame châssis *m*; w. ledge rebord *m* de fenêtre; w. seat (in vehicle, plane) place *f* côté fenêtre (b) (idioms) to provide a w. on sth procurer une ouverture sur qch; w. of opportunity ouverture *f*; *Fam* that's my holiday out of the w. voilà mes vacances fichues en l'air

window-dressing [ˈwɪndəʊdresɪŋ] *n* (in shop) vitrine *f*; *Fig* façade *f*

windowpane [ˈwɪndəʊpeɪn] *n* vitre *f*, carreau *m*

window-shopping [ˈwɪndəʊʃɒpɪŋ] *n* to go w. faire du lèche-vitrines

windowsill [ˈwɪndəʊsɪl] *n* rebord *m* de fenêtre

windpipe [ˈwɪndpaɪp] *n* trachée *f*

windscreen [ˈwɪndskriːn], *Am* **windshield** [ˈwɪndʃiːld] *n* pare-brise *m inv*; w. wiper essuie-glace *m inv*

windsock [ˈwɪndsɒk] *n Av* manche *f* à air

windsurf [ˈwɪndsɜːf] *vi* faire de la planche à voile

windsurfing [ˈwɪndsɜːfɪŋ] *n* planche *f* à voile; to go w. faire de la planche à voile

windswept [ˈwɪndswept] *adj* (hillside, scene) balayé(e) par le vent; (hair) décoiffé(e) par le vent; (person) échevelé(e)

wind-up [ˈwaɪndʌp] *n Fam* plaisanterie *f*

windward [ˈwɪndwəd] *adj* au vent; the W. Islands les îles *fpl* du Vent

windy¹ [ˈwɪndɪ] *adj* (day) venteux(euse); (place) venté(e); I hate w. weather je déteste le vent

windy² [ˈwɪndɪ] *adj* (road) sinueux(euse)

wine [waɪn] **1** *n* vin *m*; w. bar bar *m* à vin; w. bottle bouteille *f* de vin; w. box cubitainer *m* de vin; w. cellar cave *f* à vin; w. gum bonbon *m* à la gomme; w. list carte *f* des vins; w. tasting dégustation *f*; w. vinegar vinaigre *m* de vin

2 *vt* to w. and dine sb inviter qn dans de bons restaurants

wineglass [ˈwaɪnglɑːs] *n* verre *m* à vin

wing [wɪŋ] *n* (a) (of bird, plane) aile *f*; *Fig* to take sb under one's w. prendre qn sous son aile; *Fig* to spread or stretch one's wings élargir son horizon; w. nut papillon *m* (b) (of car) aile *f*; w. mirror rétroviseur *m* extérieur (c) (of building, hospital) aile *f* (d) (in football, rugby) (player) ailier *m*; (area) aile *f* (e) the wings (in theatre) les coulisses *fpl*; *Fig* to be waiting in the wings attendre son heure (f) *Pol* the left/right w. l'aile *f* gauche/droite

2 *vt* (a) (injure) (bird) blesser à l'aile; (person) blesser au bras (b) *Fam* (improvise) to w. it improviser (c) (fly) to w. its way towards sth (of bird) voler vers qch; *Fig* my report should be winging its way towards you j'ai posté mon rapport, tu devrais l'avoir bientôt

winger [ˈwɪŋə(r)] *n* (in football, rugby) ailier *m*

wingspan [ˈwɪŋspæn] *n* envergure *f*

wink [wɪŋk] **1** *n* clin *m* d'œil; to give sb a w. faire un clin d'œil à qn; *Fam* to tip sb the w. refiler un tuyau à qn; *Fam* I didn't sleep a w. je n'ai pas fermé l'œil

2 *vi* cligner de l'œil; (of star, light) clignoter

▸**wink at** *vt insep* (person) faire un clin d'œil à; *Fig* (offence, illegal practice) fermer les yeux sur

winkle [ˈwɪŋkəl] *n* (mollusc) bigorneau *m*

▸**winkle out** *vt sep Fam* to w. sth out of sb soutirer qch à qn

winner [ˈwɪnə(r)] *n* gagnant(e) *m,f*; this book will be a w. ce livre est assuré d'avoir du succès

winning [ˈwɪnɪŋ] **1** *npl* winnings gains *mpl*

2 *adj* (a) (victorious) gagnant(e); w. post poteau *m* d'arrivée (b) (attractive) charmant(e)

winnow [ˈwɪnəʊ] *vt* vanner

wino [ˈwaɪnəʊ] (pl winos) *n Fam* (alcoholic) soûlot(ote) *m,f*

winsome [ˈwɪnsəm] *adj* charmant(e)

winter [ˈwɪntə(r)] **1** *n* hiver *m*; in (the) w. en hiver; w. break vacances *fpl* d'hiver; w. clothing vêtements *mpl* d'hiver

2 *vi* passer l'hiver

wintertime [ˈwɪntətaɪm] *n* hiver *m*

wint(e)ry [ˈwɪnt(ə)rɪ] *adj* (weather) d'hiver; *Fig* (hostile) glacial(e)

wipe [waɪp] **1** n (a) (action) to give sth a w. essuyer qch (b) (moist tissue) lingette f

2 vt (a) (table, plate) essuyer; **to w. one's nose** s'essuyer le nez; **to w. one's hands (on)** s'essuyer les mains (avec); **to w. one's shoes (on)** s'essuyer les pieds (sur); Fam Fig **to w. the floor with sb** ne faire qu'une bouchée de qn (b) (recording, tape) effacer

▶**wipe away** vt sep (tears) essuyer; (mark) enlever

▶**wipe off** vt sep Fam **that'll w. the smile off his face!** ça lui fera passer l'envie de rire!
  2 vi (of stain) partir

▶**wipe out** vt sep (a) (erase) effacer; (debt) liquider (b) (destroy) décimer

▶**wipe up** vt sep essuyer

wiper ['waɪpə(r)] n essuie-glace m inv

wire ['waɪə(r)] **1** n (a) (of metal) fil m de fer; (electrical) fil (électrique); **w. brush** brosse f métallique; **w. fence** clôture f en fil de fer; **w. mesh** toile f métallique; **w. wool** paille f de fer (b) Am (telegram) télégramme m (c) (idioms) Fam **to get one's wires crossed** s'emmêler les pinceaux; **the tournament went right down to the w.** l'issue du tournoi a été incertaine jusqu'au bout

2 vt (a) (house) faire l'installation électrique de; **to w. sth to sth** (connect electrically) relier qch à qch; (attach with wire) attacher qch à qch avec du fil de fer (b) (send telegram to) télégraphier à

wirecutters ['waɪəkʌtəz] npl **(pair of) w.** pince f coupante

wireless ['waɪəlɪs] n Old-fashioned **w. (set)** (poste m de) TSF f

wiretapping ['waɪətæpɪŋ] n mise f sur écoute d'une ligne téléphonique

wiring ['waɪərɪŋ] n installation f électrique

wiry ['waɪərɪ] adj (hair) crépu(e); (person) petit(e) et musclé(e)

wisdom ['wɪzdəm] n sagesse f; **w. tooth** dent f de sagesse

wise [waɪz] adj (knowledgeable) sage; (advisable) prudent(e); Fam Pej **a w. guy** un gros malin; **the Three W. Men** les Rois mpl mages; **it's easy to be w. after the event** c'est facile de savoir ce qui est bien ou pas bien après coup; **to be none the wiser** ne pas être plus avancé(e); Fam **to get w. to sth** se rendre compte de qch; Fam **to get w. to sb** percer qn à jour

▶**wise up** vi Fam **to w. up to sb** voir qn sous son vrai jour; **to w. up to sth** se rendre compte de qch; **w. up!** ouvre les yeux!

-wise [waɪz] suff Fam (with reference to) **health-/salary-/etc w.** du point de vue de la santé/du salaire

wisecrack ['waɪzkræk] Fam **1** n vanne f, blague f
  2 vi sortir des vannes

wisely ['waɪzlɪ] adv sagement

wish [wɪʃ] **1** n (a) (desire) désir m; (thing desired) vœu m; **to make a w.** faire un vœu; **to do sth against sb's wishes** faire qch contre le souhait de qn (b) (greeting) **best wishes** meilleurs vœux; (in letter) amicalement

2 vt (a) (want) désirer; **to w. to do sth** désirer faire qch; **to w. sb well** souhaiter à qn que tout se passe bien; **to w. sb luck/a pleasant journey** souhaiter bonne chance/bon voyage à qn; **to w. sth on sb** souhaiter qch à qn (b) (want something impossible, unlikely) **I w. she could come** j'aurais bien aimé qu'elle vienne; **I w. I had seen it!** j'aurais bien voulu voir ça!; **I w. I hadn't left so early** je regrette d'être parti aussi tôt; **I w. she wouldn't**

say things like that je préférerais qu'elle s'abstienne de dire des choses pareilles; **w. you were here!** (on postcard) je pense bien à toi

3 vi **to w. for sth** souhaiter qch; **what more could you w. for?** que souhaiter de plus?; **as you w.** comme tu voudras

wishbone ['wɪʃbəʊn] n bréchet m

wishful ['wɪʃfʊl] adj **that's w. thinking** tu te fais/il se fait/etc des illusions

wishy-washy ['wɪʃɪwɒʃɪ] adj Fam mou (molle); (couleur) délavé(e)

wisp [wɪsp] n (of straw, wool) brin m; (of hair) mèche f; (of smoke, cloud) traînée f

wistful ['wɪstfʊl] adj nostalgique

wit [wɪt] n (a) (intelligence, presence of mind) esprit m; **to have the w. to do sth** être assez intelligent(e) pour faire qch; **to have quick wits** avoir l'esprit vif; **to have lost one's wits** avoir perdu l'esprit; **to keep/keep one's wits about one** être/rester très vigilant(e); **to be at one's wits' end** ne plus savoir que faire; **to live by one's wits** vivre d'expédients; **to scare sb out of their wits** faire une peur bleue à qn (b) (humour) esprit m (c) (witty person) (man) homme m d'esprit; (woman) femme f d'esprit

witch [wɪtʃ] n sorcière f; **w. doctor** sorcier m

witchcraft ['wɪtʃkrɑːft] n sorcellerie f

witch-hunt ['wɪtʃhʌnt] n Pol chasse f aux sorcières

with [wɪð] prep (a) (expressing accompaniment) avec; **w. me/him** avec moi/lui; **to live w. one's parents** vivre chez ses parents; **I was left w. nobody to talk to** je me suis retrouvé sans personne à qui parler

(b) (having) **the girl w. glasses/blue eyes** la fille aux lunettes/aux yeux bleus; **w. one's hands in one's pockets** les mains dans les poches

(c) (expressing association) **to be pleased w. sb** être content(e) de qn; **to be angry w. sb** être en colère contre qn; **to fight/compete w. sb** se battre/être en concurrence avec qn; **to be in love w. sb** être amoureux(euse) de qn; **covered w. mud** couvert(e) de boue

(d) (expressing manner) **w. pleasure/difficulty** avec plaisir/difficulté; **to say sth w. a smile** dire qch avec un sourire

(e) (expressing instrument, agent) **to hit sb w. sth** frapper qn avec qch; **to cut sth w. a knife** couper qch avec un couteau; **it's pouring w. rain** il pleut à verse

(f) (because of) **to tremble w. rage** trembler de rage; **to cry w. laughter** pleurer de rire; **w. her money, she can surely afford it** avec l'argent qu'elle a, elle peut bien se permettre ça

(g) (expressing simultaneity) **to improve w. age** s'améliorer avec l'âge; **w. those words, he left** sur ces mots, il partit; **w. Christmas coming,…** puisque c'est bientôt Noël,…

(h) (idioms) **to be w. it** être dans le vent; **get w. it!** (wake up) réveille-toi!; (face reality) ouvre les yeux!; **I'm w. you** (I support you) je suis avec vous; **I'm not w. you** (I don't understand) je ne vous suis pas

withdraw [wɪð'drɔː] (pt **withdrew** [wɪð'druː], pp **withdrawn** [wɪð'drɔːn]) **1** vt retirer (from de)

2 vi se retirer (from de); **to w. in favour of sb** se désister en faveur de qn; **to w. into oneself** se replier sur soi-même

withdrawal [wɪð'drɔːəl] n retrait m; **to make a w.** (from bank) faire un retrait; **w. symptoms** symptômes *mpl* de manque; **to have w. symptoms** être en (état de) manque

withdrawn [wɪð'drɔːn] *adj* replié(e) sur soi-même

wither ['wɪðə(r)] *vi (of plant)* se flétrir; *(of limb)* s'atrophier

withered ['wɪðəd] *adj (plant)* flétri(e); *(limb)* atrophié(e)

withering ['wɪðərɪŋ] *adj (look)* foudroyant(e); *(tone)* cinglant(e)

withhold [wɪð'həʊld] *(pt & pp **withheld** [wɪð'held])* *vt (consent, help)* refuser; *(money)* retenir; *(truth)* cacher; *(information)* faire de la rétention de

within [wɪð'ɪn] **1** *prep* **(a)** *(inside)* à l'intérieur de; **problems w. the company** des problèmes au sein de l'entreprise **(b)** *(not beyond)* **w. 10 miles of the town** ≃ à moins de 16 km de la ville; **w. a radius of** dans un rayon de; **w. limits** jusqu'à un certain point; **w. reason** dans des limites raisonnables; **to stay w. budget** rester dans les limites du budget; **to come w. an inch of doing sth** bien faillir faire qch **(c)** *(with expressions of time)* **w. an hour/a week** en moins d'une heure/d'une semaine; **w. minutes** en quelques minutes; **w. the next five years** *(in the space of)* *(in future)* au cours des cinq années à venir; *(in past)* au cours des cinq années suivantes; *(before the end of)* *(in future)* avant cinq ans; *(in past)* en moins de cinq ans; **they died w. a few days of each other** ils sont morts à quelques jours d'intervalle

2 *adv* à l'intérieur; **from w.** de l'intérieur

without [wɪð'aʊt] **1** *prep* sans; **w. any money/difficulty** sans argent/difficulté; **w. doing sth** sans faire qch; **do it w. him knowing** fais-le sans qu'il le sache; **it goes w. saying that...** il va sans dire que...; **to do** *or* **go w. sth** se passer de qch

2 *adv* **to do** *or* **go w.** se priver

withstand [wɪð'stænd] *(pt & pp **withstood** [wɪð'stʊd])* *vt* supporter

witless ['wɪtlɪs] *adj (person, remark)* stupide; **to scare sb w.** faire une peur bleue à qn

witness ['wɪtnɪs] **1** *n* **(a)** *(person)* témoin *m*; **to call sb as w.** citer qn comme témoin; **w. for the defence/prosecution** témoin à décharge/charge; **w. box** barre *f* des témoins **(b)** *(testimony)* **to bear w. (to sth)** témoigner (de qch)

2 *vt* être témoin de; *Fig* **this town has witnessed many battles** cette ville a été le théâtre de nombreuses batailles

3 *vi Law* **to w. to sth** témoigner de qch

witter ['wɪtə(r)] *vi Fam* **to w. (on)** bavasser

witticism ['wɪtɪsɪzəm] *n* mot *m* d'esprit

wittily ['wɪtɪlɪ] *adv* avec esprit

wittingly ['wɪtɪŋlɪ] *adv* sciemment

witty ['wɪtɪ] *adj* spirituel(elle), plein(e) d'esprit

wives [waɪvz] *pl of* **wife**

wizard ['wɪzəd] *n* magicien *m*; *Fig* as *m*

wizened ['wɪzənd] *adj* ratatiné(e)

wk *(abbr* **week)** semaine

wobble ['wɒbəl] *vi (of chair, table)* branler; *(of building, jelly)* trembler; *(of person)* être chancelant(e)

wobbly ['wɒblɪ] **1** *n Fam* **to throw a w.** piquer une crise

2 *adj (chair, table)* bancal(e); *(shelf, ladder)* branlant(e); *(person)* chancelant(e)

woe [wəʊ] *n Lit* malheur *m*; *Hum* **w. betide you if you're late** malheur à toi si tu es en retard

woebegone ['wəʊbɪgɒn] *adj* abattu(e)

woeful ['wəʊfʊl] *adj* **(a)** *(sad)* affligé(e) **(b)** *(very bad)* déplorable

wog [wɒg] *n very Fam* = terme injurieux désignant une personne qui n'est pas blanche

wok [wɒk] *n* poêle *f* chinoise

woke [wəʊk] *pt of* **wake³**

woken ['wəʊkən] *pp of* **wake³**

wolf [wʊlf] *(pl* **wolves** [wʊlvz]) *n* **(a)** loup *m*; **w. cub** louveteau *m*; **w. whistle** = sifflement admiratif au passage de quelqu'un **(b)** *(idioms)* **I don't earn much but it keeps the w. from the door** je ne gagne pas beaucoup mais je ne manque de rien; **to throw sb to the wolves** abandonner qn à son sort; **a w. in sheep's clothing** un loup déguisé en brebis; **to cry w.** crier au loup

▶**wolf down** *vt sep* engloutir

woman ['wʊmən] *(pl* **women** ['wɪmɪn]) *n* femme *f*; **women's magazine** magazine *m* féminin; **women's movement** mouvement *m* de libération de la femme; **women's page** page *f* des lectrices; *Euph* **women's problems** des trucs *mpl* de femme; **w. doctor** femme médecin *f*; **w. driver** conductrice *f*

womanizer ['wʊmənaɪzə(r)] *n* coureur *m* (de jupons)

womanly ['wʊmənlɪ] *adj* féminin(e)

womb [wuːm] *n* utérus *m*

women ['wɪmɪn] *pl of* **woman**

womenfolk ['wɪmɪnfəʊk] *n* femmes *fpl*

won [wʌn] *pt & pp of* **win**

wonder ['wʌndə(r)] **1** *n* **(a)** *(miracle)* miracle *m*, merveille *f*; **to work** *or* **do wonders** faire des miracles; **it's a w. (that)...** c'est un miracle que... + *subjunctive*; **(it's) no w....** ce n'est pas étonnant que... + *subjunctive*; **w. drug** remède *m* miracle **(b)** *(astonishment)* émerveillement *m*; **in w.** avec émerveillement

2 *vi* se demander; **one wonders whether...** c'est à se demander si...; **I was wondering if you were free tonight** je voulais savoir si tu étais libre ce soir

3 *vi* **(a)** *(be curious)* se demander; *Fam* **I w. about her sometimes!** je me pose parfois des questions à son sujet! **(b)** *Lit (be amazed)* s'étonner **(at** de)

wonderful ['wʌndəfʊl] *adj* merveilleux(euse), formidable

wonky ['wɒŋkɪ] *adj Fam* déglingué(e)

won't [wəʊnt] = **will not**

wont [wəʊnt] *Formal* **1** *n* habitude *f*; **as is her w.** comme à son habitude

2 *adj* **to be w. to do sth** avoir l'habitude de faire qch

woo [wuː] *(pt & pp* **wooed)** *vt* **(a)** *Lit (woman)* courtiser **(b)** *Fig (supporters, investors)* attirer

wood [wʊd] *n* **(a)** *(forest, material)* bois *m*; **w. carving** sculpture *f* sur bois **(b)** *(idioms)* **she can't see the w. for the trees** elle se perd dans les détails; **we're not out of the woods yet** nous ne sommes pas encore tirés d'affaire; **touch w.!** je touche du bois!

woodbine ['wʊdbaɪn] *n (plant)* vigne *f* vierge

woodcock ['wʊdkɒk] *n* bécasse *f*

woodcut ['wʊdkʌt] *n* gravure *f* sur bois

woodcutter ['wʊdkʌtə(r)] *n* bûcheron *m*

wooded ['wʊdɪd] *adj* boisé(e)

wooden ['wʊdən] *adj (made of wood)* en bois; *Fig (unexpressive)* impassible; **w. spoon** cuillère *f* de bois; *Fig* **to get the w. spoon** *(in contest)* arriver dernier au classement

woodland ['wʊdlənd] *n* bois *mpl*

woodlouse ['wʊdlaʊs] (*pl* **woodlice** ['wʊdlaɪs]) *n* cloporte *m*

woodpecker ['wʊdpekə(r)] *n* pic *m*

woodpile ['wʊdpaɪl] *n* tas *m* de bois

woodshed ['wʊdʃed] *n* remise *f* à bois

woodwind ['wʊdwɪnd] *n Mus* the w. (*instruments*) les bois *mpl*; **w. instrument** bois *m*

woodwork ['wʊdwɜːk] *n* (*craft*) travail *m* du bois; (*in house*) boiserie *f*, *Fig* **to come** *or* **crawl out of the w.** faire soudain surface

woodworm ['wʊdwɜːm] *n* ver *m* à bois

woof [wʊf] **1** *n* aboiement *m*
2 *exclam* ouah!

wool [wʊl] *n* laine *f*; *Fam* **to pull the w. over sb's eyes** embobiner qn

woollen ['wʊlən] **1** *n* **woollens** lainages *mpl*
2 *adj* (*garment*) en laine

woolly ['wʊlɪ] **1** *n Fam* (*garment*) **woollies** lainages *mpl*
2 *adj* (*garment*) en laine; *Fig* (*idea, theory*) nébuleux(euse)

woozy ['wuːzɪ] *adj Fam* dans les vapes

wop [wɒp] *n very Fam* rital(e) *m,f*, = terme raciste désignant un Italien

word [wɜːd] **1** *n* (a) (*in general*) mot *m*; **w. for w.** mot pour mot; **in a w.** en un mot; **in other words** autrement dit; **not in so many words** pas en ces termes-là; **not a w.** pas un mot; **in one's own words** à sa façon; **I can't put it into words** je n'arrive pas à trouver les mots; **he's a man of few words** c'est un homme qui parle peu; **I couldn't get a w. in (edgeways)** je n'ai pas pu placer un mot; **the w. of God** la parole de Dieu; **I'll take your w. for it** je te crois sur parole; **to take sb at his/her w.** prendre qn au mot; **it was too ridiculous for words** c'était d'un ridicule sans nom; **my w.!** ma parole!
(b) (*remarks, conversation*) **to have a w. with sb** parler à qn; **to have words with sb** avoir des mots avec qn; **just say the w.** tu n'as qu'à me faire signe; **you're putting words into my mouth** tu me fais dire des choses que je n'ai pas voulu dire; **you took the words right out of my mouth** c'est justement ce que j'allais dire; **to put in a good w. for sb** glisser un mot en faveur de qn; **he never has a good w. for anyone** il ne peut pas s'empêcher de dire du mal des gens; **a w. of warning** une mise en garde; **a w. of advice** un petit conseil
(c) (*news*) **to receive w. from sb** avoir des nouvelles de qn; **to send sb w. of sth** faire part à qn de qch; **the w. is that...** on raconte que...; **by w. of mouth** de bouche à oreille
(d) (*promise*) parole *f*; **w. of honour** parole d'honneur; **to give sb one's w.** donner sa parole à qn; **to keep one's w.** tenir sa promesse; **to go back on one's w.** manquer à sa parole
(e) **words** (*lyrics*) paroles *fpl*
2 *vt* (*express in words*) formuler

wording ['wɜːdɪŋ] *n* formulation *f*

word-processing [wɜːd'prəʊsesɪŋ] *n Comptr* traitement *m* de texte

word processor ['wɜːdprəʊsesə(r)] *n Comptr* machine *f* à traitement de texte

wordy ['wɜːdɪ] *adj* prolixe

wore [wɔː(r)] *pt of* **wear**

work [wɜːk] **1** *n* (a) (*labour*) travail *m*; **to be at w. on sth** travailler à *ou* sur qch; **to get to w.** se mettre au travail;

w. in progress (*sign*) travaux *m*; *Comptr* **w. station** poste *m* de travail
(b) (*task*) travail *m*; **to put a lot of w. into sth** beaucoup travailler à qch; **to have one's w. cut out (to do sth)** avoir du mal (à faire qch); **to make quick** *or* **short w. of sth** venir rapidement à bout de qch; **good w.!** c'est du bon travail!
(c) (*literary, artistic*) œuvre *f*; **a w. of art** une œuvre d'art
(d) (*employment*) travail *m*; **to be out of w.** être sans travail; **w. permit** permis *m* de travail
(e) *Ind* **works council** comité *m* d'entreprise; **works outing** sortie *f* organisée par le comité d'entreprise
(f) **works** (*construction*) travaux *mpl*; **road works ahead** (*sign*) attention travaux
(g) **works** (*mechanism*) mécanisme *m*
(h) *Fam* **the works** (*everything*) le grand jeu; **to give sb the works** (*beating*) passer qn à tabac; (*luxury treatment*) jouer le grand jeu à qn

2 *vt* (a) (*person*) **to w. sb hard** exiger beaucoup de qn; **to w. oneself to death** se tuer au travail
(b) (*operate*) (*machine*) faire fonctionner
(c) (*bring about*) (*miracle, cure, change*) opérer; **to w. it** *or* **things so that** parvenir en sorte que
(d) (*move*) **to w. one's hands free** se libérer les mains; **to w. one's way through a book/list** avancer progressivement dans la lecture d'un livre/dans une liste
(e) (*exploit*) (*mine, quarry*) exploiter; (*land*) travailler

3 *vi* (a) (*of person*) travailler; **to w. against sb/in sb's favour** jouer en la défaveur/la faveur de qn
(b) (*function*) (*of machine, system*) marcher, fonctionner
(c) (*have effect*) (*of medicine*) faire effet; (*of plan, method*) marcher

▸**work in** *vt sep* (*include*) introduire, glisser

▸**work off** *vt sep* (*anger*) évacuer; **he worked off 5 kilos** il a perdu 5 kilos en faisant de l'exercice

▸**work on 1** *vt insep* **to w. on sth** travailler à *ou* sur qch
2 *vi* (*continue to work*) continuer à travailler

▸**work out 1** *vt sep* (*cost, total*) calculer; (*answer*) trouver; **to w. out how to do sth** trouver comment faire qch; **I'm sure we can w. this thing out** je suis sûr qu'on peut arranger ça
2 *vi* (a) (*turn out*) **to w. out well/badly (for sb)** bien/mal se passer (pour qn); **it all worked out in the end** finalement, tout s'est arrangé (b) (*total*) **to w. out at** revenir à (c) (*exercise*) s'entraîner

▸**work up** *vt sep* (a) (*develop*) **to w. up enthusiasm/interest for sth** s'enthousiasmer pour/s'intéresser à qch; **I worked up an appetite** ça m'a ouvert l'appétit (b) (*excite*) **to get worked up (about sth)** se mettre dans tous ses états (à propos de qch)

▸**work up to** *vt insep* se préparer à

workable ['wɜːkəbəl] *adj* possible

workaday ['wɜːkədeɪ] *adj* de tous les jours

workaholic [wɜːkə'hɒlɪk] *n Fam* bourreau *m* de travail

workbench ['wɜːkbentʃ] *n* établi *m*

workday ['wɜːkdeɪ] *n Am* jour *m* ouvrable

worker ['wɜːkə(r)] *n* travailleur(euse) *m,f*; (*in industry*) ouvrier(ère) *m,f*; **to be a fast/slow w.** travailler vite/lentement; **w. bee** ouvrière *f*; **w. participation** participation *f* des travailleurs à la gestion

workforce ['wɜːkfɔːs] *n* main-d'œuvre *f*

workhouse ['wɜːkhaʊs] *n Hist* asile *m* des pauvres

working ['wɜːkɪŋ] **1** *n* (a) (*operation*) (*of machine*) fonctionnement *m* (b) **workings** (*mechanism*) mécanisme *m*

2 *adj (person)* qui travaille; **to have a w. knowledge of sth** avoir de bonnes bases en qch; **in w. order** en état de marche; **the w. class** la classe ouvrière; **w. clothes** vêtements *mpl* de travail; **w. hours** heures *fpl* de travail; **w. lunch** déjeuner *m* d'affaires; **w. majority** majorité *f* suffisante; **w. model** maquette *f* animée; **w. party** groupe *m* de travail

working-class ['wɜːkɪŋˈklɑːs] *adj* ouvrier(ère); *(accent)* prolétaire

workload ['wɜːkləʊd] *n* charge *f* de travail

workman ['wɜːkmən] *n* ouvrier *m*

workmanlike ['wɜːkmənlaɪk] *adj* de professionnel

workmanship ['wɜːkmənʃɪp] *n* travail *m*; **a fine piece of w.** du beau travail

workout ['wɜːkaʊt] *n* séance *f* d'entraînement

workplace ['wɜːkpleɪs] *n* lieu *m* de travail

workshop ['wɜːkʃɒp] *n* atelier *m*

workshy ['wɜːkʃaɪ] *adj* fainéant(e)

worktop ['wɜːktɒp] *n (in kitchen)* plan *m* de travail

work-to-rule [wɜːktəˈruːl] *n Ind* grève *f* du zèle

world [wɜːld] *n* **(a)** *(the earth)* monde *m*; **the best/biggest in the w.** le (la) meilleur(e)/plus grand(e) du monde; **the w. over, all over the w.** dans le monde entier; **the W. Bank** la Banque mondiale; **w. champion** champion(onne) *m,f* du monde; **the W. Cup** la Coupe du monde; **w. map** mappemonde *f*; **w. music** world music *f*; **w. record** record *m* du monde; **W. Series** = championnat national américain de base-ball; **W. War One/Two** la Première/Seconde ou Deuxième Guerre mondiale

(b) *(sphere of activity)* **the literary/political/business w.** le monde littéraire/politique/des affaires

(c) *(society)* **man of the w.** homme *m* d'expérience; **to go up in the w.** faire du chemin; **to come down in the w.** déchoir; **to have the w. at one's feet** avoir le monde à ses pieds

(d) *(for emphasis)* **to do sb the w. of good** faire le plus grand bien à qn; **a w. of difference** une différence énorme; **to think the w. of sb** admirer énormément qn; **they carried on for all the w. as if nothing had happened** ils ont continué comme si de rien n'était

(e) *(idioms)* **she's not long for this w.** elle n'en a plus pour longtemps; **to bring a child into the w.** mettre un enfant au monde; **to have the best of both worlds** avoir tous les avantages et aucun des inconvénients; **she lives in a w. of her own** elle vit dans un monde à elle; *Fam* **it's out of this w.** c'est extraordinaire; **not for (anything in) the w.** pour rien au monde; **it's a small w.!** le monde est petit!; **what is the w. coming to?** où va-t-on?

world-beater ['wɜːldbiːtə(r)] *n* leader *m* mondial

world-famous ['wɜːldˈfeɪməs] *adj* célèbre dans le monde entier

worldly ['wɜːldlɪ] *adj (pleasure, goods)* matériel(elle)

worldly-wise ['wɜːldlɪˈwaɪz] *adj* qui a de l'expérience

world-weary ['wɜːldwɪərɪ] *adj* désabusé(e)

worldwide ['wɜːldwaɪd] **1** *adj* mondial(e); *Comptr* **the W. Web** le Worldwide Web
2 *adv* dans le monde entier

worm [wɜːm] **1** *n* ver *m*; *(maggot)* asticot *m*; **to have worms** *(of person, animal)* avoir des vers; *Fig* **the w. has turned** il/elle/*etc* a fini par se rebiffer
2 *vt* **(a)** *(animal)* traiter contre les vers **(b) to w. one's way out of a situation** réussir à se tirer d'une situation; **to w. oneself into sb's favour/confidence** s'insinuer

dans les bonnes grâces/la confiance de qn; **to w. a secret out of sb** arracher un secret à qn

wormeaten ['wɜːmiːtən] *adj (wood)* vermoulu(e); *(fruit)* véreux(euse)

worn [wɔːn] *pp of* **wear**

worried ['wʌrɪd] *adj* inquiet(ète); **to be w. about sb** être inquiet pour qn; **I'm w. about his safety** je m'inquiète pour sa sécurité; **he's w. about losing his job** il a peur de perdre son emploi

worrier ['wʌrɪə(r)] *n* anxieux(euse) *m,f*

worry ['wʌrɪ] **1** *n* souci *m*; **that's the least of my worries** c'est le cadet de mes soucis
2 *vt (pt & pp* **worried)** *(cause anxiety to)* inquiéter; **to w. oneself sick (about sth)** se faire un sang d'encre (à propos de qch)
3 *vi* s'inquiéter, se faire du souci; **to w. about sb** s'inquiéter pour qn; **to w. about the future** s'inquiéter pour l'avenir; **to w. about doing sth** avoir peur de faire qch; **not to w.!** ce n'est pas grave!; **there's/it's nothing to w. about** il n'y a pas de quoi s'inquiéter

worrying ['wʌrɪɪŋ] *adj* inquiétant(e)

worse [wɜːs] **1** *adj (comparative of* **bad)** pire (que); **there's nothing w. than...** il n'y a rien de pire que...; **to get w.** aller en empirant; **things could be w.** les choses pourraient aller plus mal; **and to make matters w.** et, pour tout arranger...; **to go from bad to w.,...** aller de mal en pis; **I'm none the w. for it** je n'en porte pas plus mal; **to be the w. for drink** être éméché(e); *Fam* **to be the w. for wear** *(of car, book)* être en mauvais état; *(of drunk person)* être dans un sale état; **w. luck!** quelle poisse!
2 *adv (comparative of* **badly)** plus mal; **you could do w.** tu aurais pu tomber plus mal; **I don't think any w. of her for it** elle n'a pas pour autant baissé dans mon estime; **he is w. off than before** sa situation a empiré
3 *n* **there was w. to come** le pire restait à venir; **I've seen w.** j'ai vu pire; **a change for the w.** une détérioration

worsen ['wɜːsən] **1** *vt* aggraver
2 *vi* empirer

Worship ['wɜːʃɪp] *n (title)* **His/Her W.** *(referring to mayor)* monsieur/madame le maire; *(referring to magistrate)* monsieur/madame le juge

worship ['wɜːʃɪp] **1** *n (of deity)* vénération *f*, culte *m*; *(of person)* adoration *f*; **place of w.** lieu *m* de culte
2 *vt (pt & pp* **worshipped)** *(deity)* vénérer; *(person)* adorer

worst [wɜːst] **1** *adj (superlative of* **bad)** **the w.** le (la) pire; **the book I've ever read** le plus mauvais livre que j'aie jamais lu; **her w. mistake** sa plus grave erreur; **the w. thing was...** le pire, c'était que...
2 *adv (superlative of* **badly)** **le plus mal; the elderly are the w. off** ce sont les personnes âgées qui sont le plus mal loties
3 *n* **at the w.** le pire; **the w. that could happen** le pire qui puisse arriver; **the w. of it is that...** le pire dans tout ça, c'est que...; **if the w. comes to the w.** au pire; *Fam* **do your w.!** essaie un peu pour voir!; **the w. is over** on a passé le plus dur

worst-case scenario ['wɜːstkeɪsɪˈnɑːrɪəʊ] *(pl* **worst-case scenarios)** *n* le pire qui puisse se produire

worsted ['wʊstɪd] *n* peigné *m*

worth [wɜːθ] **1** *prep* **(a)** *(having a value of)* **to be w. sth** valoir qch; **how much is it w.?** combien est-ce que cela vaut?; **that's my opinion, for what it's w.** c'est mon opinion, elle vaut ce qu'elle vaut; **he's w. millions** il est millionnaire; **he was pulling for all he was w.** il tirait de toutes ses forces **(b)** *(meriting)* **the museum is w. a visit** le musée vaut le détour; **this book is not w. buying** ce livre ne vaut pas la peine d'être acheté; **it's w./it isn't w.** it ça en vaut/ça n'en vaut pas la peine; **it's w. thinking about** ça vaut le coup d'y réfléchir

2 *n* valeur *f*; **give me £20 w. of petrol** donnez-moi pour 20 livres d'essence; **to get one's money's w.** en avoir pour son argent

worthless ['wɜːθlɪs] *adj* **to be w.** *(of object)* ne rien valoir; *(of person)* être un(e) bon (bonne) à rien

worthwhile [wɜːθ'waɪl] *adj* **to be w.** valoir la peine *ou* le coup

worthy ['wɜːðɪ] **1** *adj* *(person, life)* digne; **to be w. of sth** être digne de qch
2 *n* notable *m*

would [wʊd]

> On trouve généralement **I/you/he/etc would** sous leurs formes contractées **I'd/you'd/he'd**/*etc*. La forme négative correspondante est **wouldn't**, que l'on écrira **would not** dans des contextes formels.

modal aux v **(a)** *(expressing conditional tense)* **she w. come if you invited her** elle viendrait si vous l'invitiez; **if he had let go, he w. have fallen** s'il avait lâché prise, il serait tombé; **if she had asked me, I w. have refused** si elle m'avait demandé, j'aurais refusé; **w. you do it?** – yes **I w./no I wouldn't** tu le ferais? – oui/non; **you wouldn't do it, w. you?** tu ne le ferais pas, dis? **(b)** *(expressing wish, determination)* **w. you pass the salt, please?** pourrais-tu passer le sel, s'il te plaît?; **w. you like a drink?** tu veux boire quelque chose?; **she wouldn't let me speak to him** elle m'empêchait de lui parler; **be quiet, w. you!** tais-toi, s'il te plaît!; **the car wouldn't start** la voiture ne démarrait pas
(c) *(for emphasis)* **you would insist on going!** il fallait que tu insistes pour y aller!; **I forgot – you w.!** j'ai oublié – c'est bien (de) toi!
(d) *(expressing past habit)* **she w. often return home exhausted** il lui arrivait souvent de rentrer épuisée; **there w. always be some left over** il en restait toujours
(e) *(in reported speech)* **she told me she w. be there** elle m'a dit qu'elle serait là; **I said I w. do it** j'ai dit que je le ferais
(f) *(expressing conjecture)* **w. that be my pen you're using?** est-ce que, par hasard, ce serait mon stylo que vous utilisez?; **they w. have been tired after their journey** ils devaient être fatigués après leur voyage; **I wouldn't know** je n'en ai aucune idée

would-be ['wʊdbɪ] *adj* *(actor, artist)* en puissance

wouldn't ['wʊdnt] = **would not**

wound¹ [wuːnd] **1** *n* blessure *f*
2 *vt also Fig* blesser; **to w. sb's feelings** blesser qn, heurter la sensibilité de qn

wound² [waʊnd] *pt & pp of* **wind²**

wounded ['wuːndɪd] **1** *adj* blessé(e)
2 *npl* **the w.** les blessés *mpl*

wounding ['wuːndɪŋ] *adj* blessant(e)

wove [wəʊv] *pt of* **weave**

woven ['wəʊvən] *pp of* **weave**

wow [waʊ] *Fam* **1** *vt* séduire, emballer
2 *exclam* la vache!

WP [dʌbəljuː'piː] *n* Comptr **(a)** *(abbr* **word processor)** *(machine)* machine *f* à traitement de texte; *(software)*

logiciel *m* de traitement de texte **(b)** *(abbr* **word-processing)** *(skill)* traitement *m* de texte

WPC [dʌbəljuːpiː'siː] *n* *(abbr* **woman police constable)** = femme agent de police

wpm [dʌbəljuːpiː'em] *(abbr* **words per minute)** mots par minute

WRAC [ræk] *n Br Mil* *(abbr* **Women's Royal Army Corps)** = section féminine de l'armée britannique

wrangle ['ræŋgəl] **1** *n* dispute *f*
2 *vi* se disputer **(about** *or* **over** à propos de)

wrap [ræp] **1** *n* *(shawl)* châle *m*; *Fig* **to keep sth under wraps** garder qch secret
2 *vt* *(pt & pp* **wrapped)** envelopper, emballer **(in** dans); **to w. sth around sth** enrouler qch autour de qch; *Fig* **wrapped in mystery** enveloppé(e) de mystère

▸ **wrap up 1** *vt sep* **(a)** *(parcel, present)* envelopper; *Fig* **to be wrapped up in sth** être absorbé(e) par qch **(b)** *Fam (bring to an end)* conclure
2 *vi* *(dress warmly)* s'emmitoufler

wrapper ['ræpə(r)] *n* *(of sweet)* papier *m*

wrapping ['ræpɪŋ] *n* emballage *m*; **w. paper** papier *m* d'emballage

wrath [rɒθ] *n Lit* courroux *m*

wreak [riːk] *vt* **to w.** havoc faire des ravages; **to w. vengeance on sb** assouvir sa vengeance sur qn

wreath [riːθ] *n* couronne *f*

wreathe [riːð] *vt Lit* couronner

wreck [rek] **1** *n* *(ship, car, train, plane)* épave *f*; *Fig* **to be a physical/nervous w.** être physiquement/nerveusement au bout du rouleau
2 *vt* *(ship)* faire faire naufrage à; *(car)* démolir; *(room, house)* saccager; *Fig (plans, hopes, happiness)* ruiner, anéantir; *(marriage, career)* ruiner; **to w. one's health** se ruiner la santé

wreckage ['rekɪdʒ] *n* épave *f*

wrecker ['rekə(r)] *n Am (salvage vehicle)* dépanneuse *f*

wren [ren] *n* troglodyte *m*

wrench [rentʃ] **1** *n* **(a)** *(pull) (to ankle, shoulder)* faux mouvement *m*; *Fig (emotional)* déchirement *m* **(b)** *(tool)* clef *f*
2 *vt* **to w. one's ankle/shoulder** se fouler la cheville/l'épaule; **to w. sth out of sb's hands** arracher qch des mains de qn

wrest [rest] *vt* **to w. sth from sb** arracher qch à qn

wrestle ['resəl] *vi (with person)* lutter **(with** contre); *Fig* **to w. with sth** se débattre avec qch

wrestler ['reslə(r)] *n* lutteur(euse) *m,f*

wrestling ['reslɪŋ] *n* lutte *f*, catch *m*; **w. match** match *m* de catch

wretch [retʃ] *n* malheureux(euse) *m,f*

wretched ['retʃɪd] *adj* **(a)** *(very bad)* atroce **(b)** *(unhappy)* démoralisé(e) **(c)** *Fam (for emphasis)* **I can't find the w. umbrella!** je ne trouve pas ce maudit parapluie!

wriggle ['rɪgəl] **1** *vt* **to w. one's way out of a situation** se sortir d'une situation
2 *vi* **w. (about)** gigoter, se tortiller; **to w. out of sth** couper à qch; **he managed to w. out of paying me back** il s'est débrouillé pour ne pas me rembourser

wring [rɪŋ] *vt* *(pt & pp* **wrung** [rʌŋ]) *(clothes)* essorer; **to w. one's hands** se tordre les mains; **to w. sb's neck** tordre le cou à qn; *Fam* **I'd like to w. his neck!** j'ai envie de lui tordre le cou; *Fig* **to w. sth from sb** réussir à arracher qch à qn

▶**wring out** *vt sep* (*clothes*) essorer

wringer ['rɪŋə(r)] *n* essoreuse *f*; *Fam Fig* **to put sb through the w.** faire passer un mauvais quart d'heure à qn

wringing ['rɪŋɪŋ] *adj* **w. (wet)** trempé(e)

wrinkle ['rɪŋkəl] **1** *n* (*on skin, paper*) ride *f*; (*in cloth*) faux pli *m*
2 *vi* se froisser

wrinkled ['rɪŋkəld] *adj* (*skin*) ridé(e); (*clothes, fabric*) froissé(e)

wrinkly ['rɪŋklɪ] *adj* fripé(e)

wrist [rɪst] *n* poignet *m*

wristwatch ['rɪstwɒtʃ] *n* montre-bracelet *f*

writ [rɪt] *n Law* ordre *m*, assignation *f*; **to serve a w. on sb** assigner qn en justice

write [raɪt] (*pt* **wrote** [rəʊt], *pp* **written** ['rɪtən]) **1** *vt* (*answer, name*) écrire; (*cheque*) faire; *Am* **to w. sb** écrire à qn; **she had guilt written all over her face** la culpabilité se lisait sur son visage
2 *vi* écrire; *Br* **to w. to sb** écrire à qn; *Fam* **it's nothing to w. home about** ça n'a rien d'extraordinaire

▶**write away for** *vt insep* **to w. away for sth** écrire pour recevoir qch

▶**write back** *vi* répondre

▶**write down** *vt sep* noter

▶**write in 1** *vt sep* (*insert*) inscrire
2 *vi* (*send letter*) écrire

▶**write off 1** *vt sep* (a) (*debt*) annuler (b) *Fam* (*car*) bousiller (c) *Fam* (*person*) enterrer; **to w. sb off as a has-been** considérer qn comme un(e) ringard(e)
2 *vi* **to w. off for sth** écrire pour recevoir qch

▶**write out** *vt sep* (*instructions, recipe*) noter; (*cheque*) faire

▶**write up** *vt sep* (*notes, thesis*) rédiger; (*diary, journal*) tenir

write-off ['raɪtɒf] *n* (a) *Fam* (*car*) **to be a w.** être bon (bonne) pour la casse (b) (*of debt*) annulation *f*

write-protected ['raɪtprə'tektɪd] *adj Comptr* protégé(e) en écriture

writer ['raɪtə(r)] *n* (*by profession*) écrivain *m*, auteur *m*; (*of article, book*) auteur *m*

write-up ['raɪtʌp] *n* (*of play*) critique *f*

writhe [raɪð] *vi* se tordre (**in de**)

writing ['raɪtɪŋ] *n* (a) (*action, profession*) écriture *f*; **w. desk** bureau *m*, secrétaire *m*; **w. paper** papier *m* à lettres (b) (*handwriting*) écriture *f*; **in w.** par écrit (c) (*thing written*) écrit *m*; *Fig* **the w. is on the wall** la fin est proche

written ['rɪtən] **1** *adj* écrit(e); **w. consent** consentement *m* par écrit; **w. examination** écrit *m*,

épreuve *f* écrite
2 *pp* of **write**

WRNS [renz] *n Br Mil* (*abbr* **Women's Royal Naval Service**) = section féminine de la marine britannique

wrong [rɒŋ] **1** *n* (*immoral action*) mal *m*; **to know right from w.** distinguer le bien du mal; *Ironic* **he can do no w.** il est parfait; **to do sb w.** faire du tort à qn; *Prov* **two wrongs don't make a right** on ne répare pas le mal par le mal; **to be in the w.** être dans son tort
2 *adj* (a) (*morally bad*) mauvais(e); **stealing is w.** c'est mal de voler; **it was w. of you not to tell me** ce n'est pas bien de ta part de ne pas me l'avoir dit
(b) (*incorrect, mistaken*) mauvais(e); **to be w.** (*of person*) avoir tort; **my watch is w.** ma montre n'est pas à l'heure; **don't get the w. idea** ne te fais pas de fausses idées; **I did/said the w. thing** j'ai fait/dit ce qu'il ne fallait pas; *Fig* **to go the w. way about doing sth** mal s'y prendre pour faire qch; *Fig* **to get on the w. side of sb** se faire mal voir de qn; **you've got the w. number** (*on phone*) vous vous êtes trompé de numéro
(c) (*amiss*) **what's w.?** qu'est-ce qui ne va pas?; **what's w. with you?** qu'est-ce que tu as?; **is anything w.?** quelque chose ne va pas?; **there's something w. with the car** il y a quelque chose qui ne va pas dans cette voiture; *Fam* **he's w. in the head** il ne tourne pas rond
3 *adv* (a) (*morally*) mal; **to do w.** mal agir
(b) (*incorrectly*) mal; **to go w.** se gâter; **where did I go w.?** qu'est-ce que j'ai fait qui n'allait pas?; **don't get me w., I like her** je n'ai pas dit que je ne l'aimais pas
4 *vt* faire du tort à, léser

wrongdoer ['rɒŋduːə(r)] *n* auteur *m* d'un tort

wrongdoing ['rɒŋduːɪŋ] *n* (*immoral action*) méfait *m*; (*crime*) infraction *f*

wrongful ['rɒŋfʊl] *adj* arbitraire; **w. dismissal** licenciement *m* abusif

wrong-headed [rɒŋ'hedɪd] *adj* buté(e), borné(e)

wrongly ['rɒŋlɪ] *adv* (a) (*unjustly*) à tort (b) (*incorrectly*) incorrectement

wrote [rəʊt] *pt* of **write**

wrought-iron ['rɔːt'aɪən] *adj* en fer forgé

wrought-up ['rɔːt'ʌp] *adj* **to be w.** être dans tous ses états

wrung [rʌŋ] *pt & pp* of **wring**

wry [raɪ] *adj* ironique

wt (*abbr* **weight**) p.

WW (*abbr* **World War**) **WWI/II** la Première/Deuxième *ou* Seconde Guerre mondiale

WWF [dʌbəljuːdʌbəljuː'ef] *n* (*abbr* **World Wildlife Fund, Worldwide Fund for Nature**) WWF *m*

WYSIWYG ['wɪzɪwɪg] *n Comptr* (*abbr* **what you see is what you get**) WYSIWYG *m*

X

X, x [eks] *n (letter)* X, x *m inv;* **for x number of years** pendant x années; *Formerly* **X (certificate)** film film *m* X

xenon ['zenɒn] *n Chem* xénon *m*

xenophobia [zenə'fəʊbɪə] *n* xénophobie *f*

xenophobic [zenə'fəʊbɪk] *adj* xénophobe

Xerox® ['zɪərɒks] **1** *n (machine)* photocopieur *m;* *(copy)* photocopie *f*

2 *vt* photocopier

XL ['eks'el] *(abbr* **extra large)** XL

Xmas ['eksməs] *n (abbr* **Christmas)** Noël *m*

X-ray ['eksreɪ] **1** *n (radiation)* rayon *m* X; *(picture)* radio *f;* **to have an X.** passer une radio

2 *vt* radiographier

xylophone ['zaɪləfəʊn] *n* xylophone *m*

Y

Y, y [waɪ] *n (letter)* Y, y *m inv;* **Y-fronts** slip *m* ouvert

yacht [jɒt] *n (sailing boat)* voilier *m; (large private boat)* yacht *m;* **y. club** club *m* de voile; **y. race** régate *f*

yachting ['jɒtɪŋ] *n* voile *f;* **to go y.** faire de la voile

yachtsman ['jɒtsmən] *n* navigateur *m*

yachtswoman ['jɒtswʊmən] *n* navigatrice *f*

yak [jæk] *n* yack *m*

yam [jæm] *n Br* igname *f; Am* patate *f* douce

Yank [jæŋk], **Yankee** ['jæŋkɪ] *n Br Fam (person from the USA)* Ricain(e) *m,f; Am Fam (person from north-eastern states of the USA)* habitant(e) *m,f* des États du Nord

yank [jæŋk] *Fam* **1** *n* **to give sth a y.** tirer qch d'un coup sec

2 *vt* tirer d'un coup sec; **to y. sth open/out** ouvrir/arracher qch d'un coup sec

yap [jæp] *(pt & pp yapped)* *vi (of dog)* japper; *Fam (of person)* jacasser

yard¹ [jɑːd] *n (unit of measurement)* = 0,914 m, yard *m*

yard² *n* **(a)** *(of house, school, farm)* cour *f; Am (garden)* jardin *m* **(b)** *(for working)* chantier *m; (builder's)* **y.** chantier de construction **(c)** *(for storage)* dépôt *m* de marchandises

yardstick ['jɑːdstɪk] *n (standard)* point *m* de référence

yarn [jɑːn] *n* **(a)** *(thread, wool)* fil *m* (à tricoter) **(b)** *Fam (story)* histoire *f* à dormir debout; **to spin a y.** raconter une histoire

yawn [jɔːn] **1** *n* bâillement *m; Fam (boring thing)* plaie *f*

2 *vi* **(a)** *(of person)* bâiller **(b)** *(of chasm)* béer

yd *(abbr* **yard(s))** yard *m*

ye [jiː] **1** *pron Lit =* **you**

2 *definite art Lit or Hum =* **the**

yea [jeɪ] **1** *n* **yeas and nays** voix *fpl* pour et voix contre

2 *adv Lit =* **yes**

yeah [jeə] *adv Fam* ouais

year [jɪə(r)] *n (twelve-month period)* an *m; (referring to duration)* année *f;* **in the y. 1931** en 1931; **this y.** cette année; **last/next y.** l'année dernière/prochaine; **every y.** chaque année, tous les ans; **twice a y.** deux fois par an; **to earn £10,000 a y.** gagner 10 000 livres par an; **to be ten years old** avoir dix ans; **he got five years** *(prison sentence)* il en a pris pour cinq ans; **for many years** pendant des années; **y. in, y. out** chaque année; **over the years** au fil des ans, avec les années; **years ago** il y a des années; **it's years since I saw him, I haven't seen him for** *or* **in years** ça fait des années que je ne l'ai pas vu; **from her earliest years** dès son plus jeune âge; **to be getting on in years** prendre de l'âge

yearbook ['jɪəbʊk] *n* almanach *m*

yearlong ['jɪəlɒŋ] *adj* d'un an

yearly ['jɪəlɪ] **1** *adj* annuel(elle)

2 *adv* annuellement; **twice y.** deux fois par an

yearn [jɜːn] *vi* **to y. for sth** désirer qch ardemment; **to y. to do sth** brûler de faire qch

yearning ['jɜːnɪŋ] *n* désir *m* ardent

yeast [jiːst] *n* levure *f*

yell [jel] **1** *n* hurlement *m;* **to give a y.** pousser un hurlement

2 *vt & vi* hurler

yellow ['jeləʊ] **1** n jaune m

2 adj (a) (in colour) jaune; **to turn** or **go y.** jaunir; **y. card** (in football) carton m jaune; **y. fever** fièvre f jaune; **the Y. Pages®** les Pages fpl Jaunes; **the Y. River** le fleuve Jaune (b) Fam (cowardly) trouillard(e)

3 vi jaunir

yelp [jelp] **1** n jappement m

2 vi japper

Yemen ['jemən] n le Yémen

Yemeni ['jemənɪ] **1** n Yéménite mf

2 adj yéménite

yen¹ [jen] n (Japanese currency) yen m

yen² n to have a y. for sth/to do sth avoir envie de qch/de faire qch

Yerevan [jerə'væn] n Erevan

yes [jes] **1** adv oui; (after negative question) si; **haven't you seen the film? – y.(, I have)** tu n'as pas vu ce film? – mais si

2 n oui m inv

yes-man ['jesmæn] n Fam béni-oui-oui m inv

yesterday ['jestədeɪ] **1** n hier m

2 adv hier; **y. morning/evening** hier matin/soir

yet [jet] **1** adv (a) (still) encore; **I haven't finished y.** je n'ai pas encore fini; **don't go y.** ne pars pas tout de suite; **I'll catch her y.!** je finirai bien par l'attraper!; **as y.** jusqu'à présent; **not y.** pas encore; **y. again** encore une fois; **y. more** encore plus; **y. another mistake** encore une erreur (b) (in questions) **have they decided y.?** est-ce qu'ils ont décidé?

2 conj cependant; **small y. strong** petit(e) mais fort(e); **and y. I like her** et pourtant, elle me plaît

yeti ['jetɪ] n yéti m

yew [juː] n if m

YHA [waɪeɪtʃ'eɪ] n (abbr **Youth Hostels Association**) = association des auberges de jeunesse

Yiddish ['jɪdɪʃ] **1** n yiddish m

2 adj yiddish inv

yield [jiːld] **1** n (of field, shares) rendement m; (of mine) production f

2 vt (a) (interest) rapporter; (results) donner; **to y. a profit** rapporter (b) (territory, right) céder

3 vi (surrender) se rendre; **to y. to force** céder devant la force; **to y. to reason** se rendre à la raison; **to y. to temptation** céder à la tentation

yippee [jɪ'piː] exclam youpi!

YMCA [waɪemsiː'eɪ] n (abbr **Young Men's Christian Association**) = association chrétienne proposant hébergement et activités sportives

yob [jɒb], **yobbo** ['jɒbəʊ] (pl yobbos or yobboes) n Fam loubard m

yodel ['jəʊdəl] (pt & pp yodelled) vi iodler

yoga ['jəʊgə] n yoga m

yoghurt, yogurt ['jɒgət] n yaourt m

yoke [jəʊk] **1** n (a) (for oxen) & Fig joug m (b) (for carrying) palanche f

2 vt (oxen) atteler; Fig **to be yoked to sth** être lié(e) à qch

yokel ['jəʊkəl] n Pej or Hum péquenaud(e) m,f

yolk [jəʊk] n jaune m (d'œuf)

yonder ['jɒndə(r)] adv (over) y. là-bas

yonks [jɒŋks] npl Fam une éternité; **it was y. ago** ça fait une paye

Yorkshire pudding ['jɔːkʃə'pʊdɪŋ] n = croquette de pâte à frire servie avec le rosbif

you [juː] pron (a) (subject) (familiar) tu; (formal, familiar plural) vous; **you're late** tu es/vous êtes en retard; **have you got it?** c'est toi qui l'as/vous qui l'avez?

(b) (direct object) (familiar) te; (formal, familiar plural) vous; **I hate y.** je te/vous déteste; **I love y.** je t'aime/je vous aime; **I can understand your son but not you** je comprends ton fils, mais toi, je ne te comprends pas

(c) (indirect object) (familiar) te; (formal, familiar plural) vous; **I gave y. the book** je t'ai/vous ai donné le livre; **I gave it to y.** je te/vous l'ai donné

(d) (after preposition) (familiar) toi; (formal, familiar plural) vous; **I'm thinking of y.** je pense à toi/vous

(e) (as complement of verb to be) (familiar) toi; (formal, familiar plural) vous; **it's y.** c'est toi/vous; **it was y. who did it** c'est toi qui l'as fait/vous qui l'avez fait

(f) (impersonal) on; **y. never know** on ne sait jamais; **y. have to be careful with her** il faut faire attention avec elle; **smoking is bad for y.** fumer est mauvais pour la santé

(g) (in apposition) **y. men/French** vous les hommes/les Français; **y. idiot!** espèce d'idiot!

(h) (with imperative) **y. sit down here** toi, tu t'assois ici; **don't y. dare!** je t'interdis de le faire!

(i) (with interjections) **silly y.!** que tu es bête!; **poor y.!** pauvre de toi!

you'd [juːd] = **you had, you would**

you-know-who [juːnəʊ'huː] n qui-tu-sais

you'll [juːl] = **you will, you shall**

young [jʌŋ] **1** adj jeune; **she's younger than me** elle est plus jeune que moi; **she's two years younger than me** elle a deux ans de moins que moi; **you're only y.** once on n'a pas tous les jours vingt ans; **when I was a y. man/woman** quand j'étais jeune; **in his younger days** dans sa jeunesse; **the night is y.!** la soirée ne fait que commencer!; **y. people** les jeunes mpl; **she's y. for her age** elle fait plus jeune que son âge; **y. in spirit** or **at heart** jeune d'esprit

2 npl (a) (people) **the y.** les jeunes mpl (b) (animals) petits mpl

youngster ['jʌŋstə(r)] n jeune mf

your [jɔː(r)] possessive adj (a) (with singular possession) (familiar) ton (ta); (formal, familiar plural) votre; (with plural possession) (familiar) tes; (formal, familiar plural) vos; **y. job** ton/votre travail; **y. wife** ta/votre femme; **y. parents** tes/vos parents; **it wasn't YOUR idea!** ce n'est pas toi qui en as eu l'idée!

(b) (for parts of body) **did you hit y. head?** vous vous êtes cogné la tête?

(c) (impersonal) **you should buy y. ticket first** on doit acheter son billet d'abord; **smoking is bad for y. health** fumer est mauvais pour la santé; Fam **y. average Frenchman** le Français moyen

you're [jɔː(r)] = **you are**

yours [jɔːz] possessive pron (a) (replacing singular possession) (familiar) le tien (la tienne) m,f; (formal, familiar plural) le vôtre (la vôtre) m,f; (replacing plural possession) (familiar) les tiens (les tiennes) mpl,fpl; (formal, familiar plural) les vôtres mpl,fpl; **my house is big, but y. is bigger** ma maison est grande, mais la tienne est plus grande encore

(b) (used attributively) **this book is y.** ce livre est à toi/à vous; **a friend of y.** un de tes/vos amis; **where's that brother of y.?** où ton frère a-t-il bien pu passer?

yourself [jɔːˈself] *pron* (a) *(reflexive)* did you hurt y.? *(familiar)* tu t'es blessé?; *(formal)* vous vous êtes blessé?

(b) *(emphatic)* *(familiar)* toi-même; *(formal)* vous-même; **you y. have never...** vous-même n'avez jamais...; **you told me y.** vous me l'avez dit vous-même; **you're not y. today** tu n'es pas dans ton état normal aujourd'hui

(c) *(after preposition)* **do you live by y.?** vous vivez seul(e)?; **did you buy it for y.?** vous l'avez acheté pour vous-même?; **do you talk to y.?** tu parles tout(e) seul(e)?

yourselves [jɔːˈselvz] *pron* (a) *(reflexive)* **have you hurt y.?** vous vous êtes blessés(ées)?

(b) *(emphatic)* vous-mêmes; **you y. have never...** vous-mêmes n'avez jamais...; **you told me y.** vous me l'avez dit vous-mêmes; **you're not y. today** vous n'êtes pas dans votre état normal aujourd'hui

(c) *(after preposition)* **do you live by y.?** vous vivez seuls(es)?; **did you buy it for y.?** vous l'avez acheté pour vous-mêmes?; **do you talk to y.?** vous parlez tout(es) seuls(es)?

youth [juːθ] *n* (a) *(period)* jeunesse *f* (b) *(young man)* adolescent *m*, jeune *m* (c) *(young people)* jeunes *mpl*; **y. club** centre *m* de loisir pour les jeunes; **y. hostel** auberge *f* de jeunesse

youthful [ˈjuːθfʊl] *adj (person, looks)* jeune; *(enthusiasm)* juvénile

you've [juːv] = **you have**

yowl [jaʊl] 1 *n* hurlement *m*
  2 *vi* hurler

yo-yo® [ˈjəʊjəʊ] *n (pl* **yo-yos)** *n* yo-yo® *m*

yr *(abbr* **year)** année *f*

yuan [juːˈæn] *n* yuan *m*

yucca [ˈjʌkə] *n* yucca *m*

yuck [jʌk] *exclam Fam* berk!

yucky [ˈjʌkɪ] *adj Fam* berk *inv*

Yugoslav [ˈjuːɡəʊslɑːv] 1 *n* Yougoslave *mf*
  2 *adj* yougoslave

Yugoslavia [juːɡəʊˈslɑːvɪə] *n* la Yougoslavie

Yugoslavian [juːɡəʊˈslɑːvɪən] *adj* yougoslave

yuletide [ˈjuːltaɪd] *n* Noël *m*

yummy [ˈjʌmɪ] *adj Fam* délicieux(euse)

yuppie [ˈjʌpɪ] *n* yuppie *mf*; **y. area** quartier *m* riche et branché; *Fam* **y. flu** syndrome *m* de la fatigue chronique

YWCA [waɪdʌbəljuːsiːˈeɪ] *n (abbr* **Young Women's Christian Association)** = association chrétienne proposant hébergement et activités sportives

Z

Z, z [zed, *Am* ziː] *n (letter)* Z, z *m inv*

Zaire [zɑːˈɪə(r)] *n* le Zaïre

Zairean [zɑːˈɪərɪən] 1 *n* Zaïrois(oise) *m,f*
  2 *adj* zaïrois(oise)

Zambia [ˈzæmbɪə] *n* la Zambie

Zambian [ˈzæmbɪən] 1 *n* Zambien(enne) *m,f*
  2 *adj* zambien(enne)

zany [ˈzeɪnɪ] *adj* loufoque

zap [zæp] *(pt & pp* **zapped)** *Fam* 1 *vt* (a) *(destroy, disable)* éliminer (b) *Comptr (delete)* effacer
  2 *vi* (a) *(change TV channel)* zapper (b) *(move quickly)* **to z. in/out/off** entrer/sortir/partir à toute pompe

zapper [ˈzæpə(r)] *n Fam (TV remote control)* télécommande *f*

zeal [ziːl] *n* zèle *m*

zealot [ˈzelət] *n* fanatique *mf*

zealous [ˈzeləs] *adj* zélé(e); *(campaigner, supporter)* fervent(e)

zebra [ˈziːbrə, ˈzebrə] *n* zèbre *m*; *Br* **z. crossing** passage *m* pour piétons

zeds [zedz] *npl Fam (sleep)* **to catch some z.** piquer un roupillon

zenith [ˈzenɪθ] *n also Fig* zénith *m*; **at the z. of her powers/influence** au sommet de son pouvoir/influence

zephyr [ˈzefə(r)] *n* zéphyr *m*

zero [ˈzɪərəʊ] 1 *n (pl* **zeros)** zéro *m*; **22 degrees below z.** 22 degrés en dessous de zéro
  2 *adj Fam* aucun(e); **to have z. charm** n'avoir aucun charme
  3 *vi* **to z. in on sb** foncer sur qn; **to z. in on sth** se concentrer sur qch

zero-rated [ˈzɪərəʊreɪtɪd] *adj Fin (for VAT)* exonéré(e) de TVA

zest [zest] *n* (a) *(enjoyment)* enthousiasme *m* (b) *(of orange, lemon)* zeste *m*

zigzag [ˈzɪɡzæɡ] 1 *n* zigzag *m*
  2 *vi (pt & pp* **zigzagged)** zigzaguer

zilch [zɪltʃ] *n Fam* que dalle

Zimbabwe [zɪmˈbɑːbweɪ] *n* le Zimbabwe

Zimbabwean [zɪmˈbɑːbweɪən] 1 *n* Zimbabwéen(enne) *m,f*
  2 *adj* zimbabwéen(enne)

zinc [zɪŋk] *n* zinc *m*

Zionism [ˈzaɪənɪzəm] *n* sionisme *m*

Zionist [ˈzaɪənɪst] *n & adj* sioniste *mf*

zip [zɪp] 1 *n* (a) *Br* **z. (fastener)** fermeture *f* Éclair® (b) *Fam (vigour)* punch *m* (c) *Am* **z. code** code *m* postal
  2 *vi (pt & pp* **zipped) to z. past** *(of car)* passer en trombe; *(of bullet)* passer en sifflant

▸**zip through** *vt insep Fam* I zipped through the book j'ai lu le livre à toute vitesse; we zipped through the work nous avons fait le travail à toute vitesse

▶**zip up 1** *vt sep (clothes)* remonter la fermeture Éclair® de
  2 *vi* se fermer par une fermeture Éclair®

zipper ['zɪpə(r)] *n Am* fermeture *f* Éclair®

zippy ['zɪpɪ] *adj Fam* plein(e) de punch

zit [zɪt] *n Fam* bouton *m*

zither ['zɪðə(r)] *n* cithare *f*

zodiac ['zəʊdɪæk] *n* zodiaque *m*

zombie ['zɒmbɪ] *n* zombi *m*

zone [zəʊn] **1** *n* zone *f*
  2 *vt* diviser en zones

zonked (out) [zɒŋkt('aʊt)] *adj Fam (exhausted)*
cassé(e); *(drugged)* défoncé(e); *(drunk)* pété(e)

zoo [zuː] *n* zoo *m*

zoological [zəʊə'lɒdʒɪkəl] *adj* zoologique; **z.
garden(s)** jardin *m* zoologique

zoologist [zəʊ'ɒlədʒɪst] *n* zoologiste *mf*

zoology [zəʊ'ɒlədʒɪ] *n* zoologie *f*

zoom [zuːm] **1** *n* **(a)** *(noise)* vrombissement *m* **(b) z. lens**
zoom *m*
  2 *vi Fam* **(a)** *(move quickly)* **to z. in/out/past** entrer/
sortir/passer comme une flèche **(b)** *(increase quickly)*
monter en flèche

▶**zoom in** *vi (of camera)* faire un zoom avant **(on** sur)

zucchini [zuː'kiːnɪ] *(pl* **zucchini** *or* **zucchinis)** *n Am*
courgette *f*

Zulu ['zuːluː] **1** *n* Zoulou *mf*
  2 *adj* zoulou(e)

English Irregular Verbs

Verbes Anglais Irréguliers

Infinitif	Prétérit	Participe passé
arise	arose	arisen
awake	awoke	awoken
awaken	awoke, awakened	awakened, awoken
be	were/was	been
bear	bore	borne
beat	beat	beaten
become	became	become
begin	began	begun
bend	bent	bent
beseech	besought, beseeched	besought, beseeched
bet	bet, betted	bet, betted
bid	bade, bid	bidden, bid
bind	bound	bound
bite	bit	bitten
bleed	bled	bled
blow	blew	blown
break	broke	broken
breed	bred	bred
bring	brought	brought
build	built	built
burn	burnt, burned	burnt, burned
burst	burst	burst
bust	bust, busted	bust, busted
buy	bought	bought
cast	cast	cast
catch	caught	caught
chide	chided, chid	chided, chidden
choose	chose	chosen
cleave	cleaved, cleft, clove	cleaved, cleft, cloven
cling	clung	clung
clothe	clad, clothed	clad, clothed
come	came	come
cost	cost	cost
creep	crept	crept
crow	crowed, crew	crowed
cut	cut	cut
deal	dealt	dealt
dig	dug	dug
dive	dived, *Am* dove	dived
do	did	done
draw	drew	drawn
dream	dreamt, dreamed	dreamt, dreamed
drink	drank	drunk
drive	drove	driven
dwell	dwelt	dwelt
eat	ate	eaten
fall	fell	fallen
feed	fed	fed

(1)

Infinitif	Prétérit	Participe passé
feel	felt	felt
fight	fought	fought
find	found	found
flee	fled	fled
fling	flung	flung
fly	flew	flown
forget	forgot	forgotten
forgive	forgave	forgiven
forsake	forsook	forsaken
freeze	froze	frozen
get	got	got, *Am* gotten
gild	gilded, gilt	gilded, gilt
gird	girded, girt	girded, girt
give	gave	given
go	went	gone
grind	ground	ground
grow	grew	grown
hang	hung/hanged	hung/hanged
have	had	had
hear	heard	heard
hew	hewed	hewn, hewed
hide	hid	hidden
hit	hit	hit
hold	held	held
hurt	hurt	hurt
keep	kept	kept
kneel	knelt	knelt
knit	knitted, knit	knitted, knit
know	knew	known
lay	laid	laid
lead	led	led
lean	leant, leaned	leant, leaned
leap	leapt, leaped	leapt, leaped
learn	learnt, learned	learnt, learned
leave	left	left
lend	lent	lent
let	let	let
lie	lay	lain
light	lit	lit
lose	lost	lost
make	made	made
mean	meant	meant
meet	met	met
mow	mowed	mown
pay	paid	paid
plead	pleaded, *Am* pled	pleaded, *Am* pled
prove	proved	proved, proven
put	put	put
quit	quit	quit
read	read	read
rend	rent	rent

Infinitif	Prétérit	Participe passé
rid	rid	rid
ride	rode	ridden
ring	rang	rung
rise	rose	risen
run	ran	run
saw	sawed	sawn, sawed
say	said	said
see	saw	seen
seek	sought	sought
sell	sold	sold
send	sent	sent
set	set	set
sew	sewed	sewn
shake	shook	shaken
shear	sheared	shorn, sheared
shed	shed	shed
shine	shone	shone
shit	shitted, shat	shitted, shat
shoe	shod	shod
shoot	shot	shot
show	showed	shown
shrink	shrank	shrunk
shut	shut	shut
sing	sang	sung
sink	sank	sunk
sit	sat	sat
slay	slew	slain
sleep	slept	slept
slide	slid	slid
sling	slung	slung
slink	slunk	slunk
slit	slit	slit
smell	smelled, smelt	smelled, smelt
smite	smote	smitten
sow	sowed	sown, sowed
speak	spoke	spoken
speed	sped	sped
spell	spelt, spelled	spelt, spelled
spend	spent	spent
spill	spilt, spilled	spilt, spilled
spin	span	spun
spit	spat, *Am* spit	spat, *Am* spit
split	split	split
spoil	spoilt, spoiled	spoilt, spoiled
spread	spread	spread
spring	sprang	sprung
stand	stood	stood
stave in	staved in, stove in	staved in, stove in
steal	stole	stolen
stick	stuck	stuck
sting	stung	stung

Infinitif	Prétérit	Participe passé
stink	stank, stunk	stunk
strew	strewed	strewed, strewn
stride	strode	stridden
strike	struck	struck
string	strung	strung
strive	strove	striven
swear	swore	sworn
sweep	swept	swept
swell	swelled	swollen, swelled
swim	swam	swum
swing	swung	swung
take	took	taken
teach	taught	taught
tear	tore	torn
tell	told	told
think	thought	thought
thrive	thrived, throve	thrived
throw	threw	thrown
thrust	thrust	thrust
tread	trod	trodden
wake	woke	woken
wear	wore	worn
weave	wove, weaved	woven, weaved
weep	wept	wept
wet	wet, wetted	wet, wetted
win	won	won
wind	wound	wound
wring	wrung	wrung
write	wrote	written

French Conjugation
Tables

Full listings of the conjugations of French regular -er, -ir and -re verbs
are given on pages (8) and (9). On the following pages you will find a
list of model irregular verbs. Numbers after verbs in the French-
English side of the dictionary, eg [20], refer you to these tables where
you will find their irregular forms.

The more common verbs such as **aller**, **avoir**, **être** and **faire** are shown
in full for all persons and all tenses. In other cases, where complete
forms have not been shown they follow the pattern indicated by the
first person singular and/or plural.

As the perfect tense is always formed simply by **avoir** or **être** plus the
past participle, this has not been shown apart from the verbs
mentioned above. Similarly, the conditional tense can always be
formed in the same way as the future tense but with the endings **-ais, -
ais, -ait, -ions, -iez** and **-aient**. When not shown, the imperative has the
same form as the present tense ("tu", "nous" and "vous" forms).

Toutes les formes des verbes réguliers en **-er**, **-ir** et **-re** sont données
pages (8) et (9), suivies d'une liste de conjugaisons irrégulières types.
Les nombres apparaissant après les verbes dans la partie français-
anglais du dictionnaire, par exemple [20], renvoient à cette liste.

Toutes les personnes et tous les temps sont donnés systématiquement
pour les verbes d'usage fréquent tels qu'**aller**, **avoir**, **être** et **faire**. Dans
tous les autres cas, seules les formes particulières, c'est-à-dire celles qui
ne suivent pas le modèle déterminé par la première personne du
singulier et/ou du pluriel, sont indiquées.

Le passé composé étant toujours formé sur le modèle avoir/être +
participe passé, il n'a pas été inclus dans nos listes, sauf pour les verbes
mentionnés ci-dessus. De même, le conditionnel se construira à partir
du futur.

	INDICATIVE Present	Imperfect	Perfect	Past Historic	Future

1 avoir

j'ai	j'avais	j'ai eu	j'eus	j'aurai
tu as	tu avais	tu as eu	tu eus	tu auras
il a	il avait	il a eu	il eut	il aura
nous avons	nous avions	nous avons eu	nous eûmes	nous aurons
vous avez	vous aviez	vous avez eu	vous eûtes	vous aurez
ils ont	ils avaient	ils ont eu	ils eurent	ils auront

2 être

je suis	j'étais	j'ai été	je fus	je serai
tu es	tu étais	tu as été	tu fus	tu seras
il est	il était	il a été	il eut	il sera
nous sommes	nous étions	nous avons été	nous fûmes	nous serons
vous êtes	vous étiez	vous avez été	vous fûtes	vous serez
ils sont	ils étaient	ils ont été	ils furent	ils seront

3a absoudre

j'absous	j'absolvais		j'absolus	j'absoudrai
il absout				
nous absolvons				

3b résoudre *follows the above pattern except for the following*

			je résolus	

4a accroître

j'accrois	j'accroissais		j'accrus	j'accroîtrai
il accroît				
nous accroissons				

4b croître *follows the above pattern except for the following*

je croîs			je crûs	

5 accueillir

j'accueille	j'accueillais		j'accueillis	j'accueillerai
nous accueillons				

6 acheter

j'achète	j'achetais		j'achetai	j'achèterai
nous achetons				
ils achètent				

7 acquérir

j'acquiers	j'acquérais		j'acquis	j'acquerrai
il acquiert				
nous acquérons				
ils acquièrent				

8 aller

je vais	j'allais	je suis allé	j'allai	j'irai
tu vas	tu allais	tu es allé	tu allas	tu iras
il va	il allait	il est allé	il alla	il ira
nous allons	nous allions	nous sommes allés	nous allâmes	nous irons
vous allez	vous alliez	vous êtes allés	vous allâtes	vous irez
ils vont	ils allaient	ils sont allés	ils allèrent	ils iront

CONDITIONAL Present	SUBJUNCTIVE Present	Imperfect	IMPERATIVE	PARTICIPLE Present	Past
j'aurais	j'aie	j'eusse		ayant	eu
tu aurais	tu aies	tu eusses	aie		
il aurait	il ait	il eût			
nous aurions	nous ayons	nous eussions	ayons		
vous auriez	vous ayez	vous eussiez	ayez		
ils auraient	ils aient	ils eussent			
je serais	je sois	je fusse		étant	été
tu serais	tu sois	tu fusses	sois		
il serait	il soit	il fût			
nous serions	nous soyons	nous fussions	soyons		
vous seriez	vous soyez	vous fussiez	soyez		
ils seraient	ils soient	ils fussent			
	j'absolve	*not used*		absolvant	absous(oute)
	nous absolvions				
					résolu
	j'accroisse	j'accrusse		accroissant	accru
	nous accroissions	nous accrussions			
		je crûsse			crû
	j'accueille	j'accueillisse	accueille	accueillant	accueilli
	nous accueillions	nous accueillissions	accueillons		
		accueillez			
	j'achète	j'achetasse		achetant	acheté
	nous achetions	nous achetassions			
	j'acquière	j'acquisse		acquérant	acquis
	nous acquérions	nous acquissions			
j'irais	j'aille	j'allasse		allant	allé
tu irais	tu ailles	tu allasses	va		
il irait	il aille	il allât			
nous irions	nous allions	nous allassions	allons		
vous iriez	vous alliez	vous allassiez	allez		
ils iraient	ils aillent	ils allassent			

(7)

INDICATIVE Present	Imperfect	Perfect	Past Historic	Future
9 appeler				
j'appelle	j'appelais		j'appelai	j'appellerai
nous appelons				
ils appellent				
10a s'asseoir				
je m'assieds/	je m'asseyais/		je m'assis	je m'assiérai/assoirai
assois	assoyais			
il s'assied/assoit				
nous nous				
asseyons/				
assoyons				
10b surseoir *follows pattern of oi forms of* **s'asseoir**				
				je surseoirai
11 battre				
je bats	je battais		je battis	je battrai
il bat				
nous battons				
12 boire				
je bois	je buvais		je bus	je boirai
il boit				
nous buvons				
ils boivent				
13 bouillir				
je bous	je bouillais		je bouillis	je bouillirai
il bout				
nous bouillons				
14 choir				
je chois			il chut	
il chut				
ils choient				
15 clore				
je clos				je clorai
il clôt				
ils closent				
16 commencer				
je commence	je commençais		je commençai	je commencerai
nous commençons				
vous commencez				
ils commencent				
17 conclure				
je conclus	je concluais		je conclus	je conclurai
il conclut				
nous concluons				

CONDITIONAL Present	SUBJUNCTIVE Present	Imperfect	IMPERATIVE	PARTICIPLE Present	Past
	j'appelle nous appelions	j'appelasse nous appelassions		appelant	appelé
	je m'asseye/ assoie nous nous asseyions/ assoyions	je m'assisse nous nous assissions		asseyant/ assoyant	assis
je surseoirais					
	je batte nous battions	je battisse nous battissions		battant	battu
	je boive nous buvions	je busse nous bussions		buvant	bu
	je bouille nous bouillions	je bouillisse nous bouillissions		bouillant	bouilli
					chu
	je close nous closions				clos
	je commence nous commencions	je commençasse nous commençassions		commençant	commencé
	je conclue nous concluions	je conclusse nous conclussions		concluant	conclu

INDICATIVE Present	Imperfect	Perfect	Past Historic	Future
18 conduire				
je conduis	je conduisais		je conduisis	je conduirai
il conduit				
nous conduisons				
19a confire				
je confis	je confisais		je confis	je confirai
il confit				
nous confisons				
19b suffire PAST PARTICIPLE suffi (invariable)				
20 connaître				
je connais	je connaissais		je connus	je connaîtrai
il connaît				
nous connaissons				
21 coudre				
je couds	je cousais		je cousis	je coudrai
il coud				
nous cousons				
22 courir				
je cours	je courais		je courus	je courrai
il court				
nous courons				
23 craindre				
je crains	je craignais		je craignis	je craindrai
il craint				
nous craignons				
24 créer				
je crée	je créais		je créai	je créerai
nous créons				
25 croire				
je crois	je croyais		je crus	je croirai
il croit				
nous croyons				
ils croient				
26 devoir				
je dois	je devais		je dus	je devrai
il doit				
nous devons				
ils doivent				
27a dire				
je dis	je disais		je dis	je dirai
il dit				
nous disons				
vous dites				

	je conduise	je conduisisse		conduisant	conduit
	nous conduisions	nous conduisissions			
	je confise	je confisse		confisant	confit
	nous confisions	nous confissions			
	je connaisse	je connusse		connaissant	connu
	nous connaissions	nous connussions			
	je couse	je cousisse		cousant	cousu
	nous cousions	nous cousissions			
	je coure	je courusse		courant	couru
	nous courions	nous courussions			
	je craigne	je craignisse		craignant	craint
	nous craignions	nous craignissions			
	je crée nous créions	je créasse nous créassions		créant	créé
	je croie	je crusse		croyant	cru
	nous croyions	nous crussions			
	je doive	je dusse		devant	dû (due), dus (dues)
	nous devions	nous dussions			
	je dise	je disse		disant	dit
	nous disions	nous dissions			

27b contredire, interdire etc PRESENT vous contredisez, interdisez

28 distraire

je distrais	je distrayais			je distrairai
il distrait				
nous distrayons				
ils distraient				

29 dormir

je dors	je dormais		je dormis	je dormirai
il dort				
nous dormons				

30 écrire

j'écris	j'écrivais		j'écrivis	j'écrirai
il écrit				
nous écrivons				

31a émouvoir

j'émeus	j'émouvais		j'émus	j'émouvrai
il émeut				
nous émouvons				
ils émeuvent				

31b mouvoir PAST PARTICIPLE mû (mue), mus (mues)

32 employer

j'emploie	j'employais		j'employai	j'emploierai
nous employons				
ils emploient				

33 envoyer

j'envoie	j'envoyais		j'envoyai	j'enverrai
nous envoyons				
ils envoient				

34 espérer

j'espère	j'espérais		j'espérai	j'espérerai
nous espérons				
ils espèrent				

35 faillir

je faillis				je faillirai

36 faire

je fais	je faisais	j'ai fait	je fis	je ferai
tu fais	tu faisais	tu as fait	tu fis	tu feras
il fait	il faisait	il a fait	il fit	il fera
nous faisons	nous faisions	nous avons fait	nous fîmes	nous ferons
vous faites	vous faisiez	vous avez fait	vous fîtes	vous ferez
ils font	ils faisaient	ils ont fait	ils firent	ils feront

37 falloir

il faut	il fallait		il fallut	il faudra

| CONDITIONAL | SUBJUNCTIVE | | IMPERATIVE | PARTICIPLE | |
Present	Present	Imperfect		Present	Past
	je meure	je mourusse		mourant	mort
	nous mourions	nous mourussions			
	je naisse	je naquisse		naissant	né
	nous naissions	nous naquissions			
	j'oie	j'ouïsse		oyant	ouï
	nous oyions				
	j'ouvre		ouvre	ouvrant	ouvert
	nous ouvrions		ouvrons		
			ouvrez		
	je paie/paye	je payasse		payant	payé
	nous payions	nous payassions			
	je peigne	je peignisse		peignant	peint
	nous peignions	nous peignissions			
	je plaise	je plusse		plaisant	plu
	nous plaisions	nous plussions			
	il pleuve	il plût		pleuvant	plu
	je puisse	je pusse		pouvant	pu
	nous puissions	nous pussions			
	je prenne	je prisse		prenant	pris
	nous prenions	nous prissions			

59 protéger

| je protège
nous protégeons

ils protègent | je protégeais | | je protégeai | je protégerai |

60 recevoir

| je reçois
il reçoit
nous recevons
ils reçoivent | je recevais | | je reçus | je recevrai |

61 rire

| je ris
il rit
nous rions | je riais | | je ris | je rirai |

62 savoir

| je sais

il sait
nous savons | je savais | | je sus | je saurai |

63 servir

| je sers
il sert
nous servons | je servais | | je servis | je servirai |

64a sortir

| je sors
il sort
nous sortons | je sortais | | je sortis | je sortirai |

64b mentir PAST PARTICIPLE is invariable

65 suivre

| je suis
il suit
nous suivons | je suivais | | je suivis | je suivrai |

66 supplier

| je supplie
nous supplions | je suppliais | | je suppliai | je supplierai |

67 tressaillir

| je tressaille
nous tressaillons | je tressaillais | | je tressaillis | je tressaillirai |

68 vaincre

| je vaincs
il vainc
nous vainquons | je vainquais | | je vainquis | je vaincrai |

69 valoir

| je vaux
il vaut
nous valons | je valais | | je valus | je vaudrai |

CONDITIONAL Present	SUBJUNCTIVE Present	Imperfect	IMPERATIVE	PARTICIPLE Present	Past
	je protège	je protégeasse		protégeant	protégé
	nous protégions	nous protégeassions			
	je reçoive	je reçusse		recevant	reçu
	nous recevions	nous reçussions			
	je rie	je risse		riant	ri
	nous riions	nous rissions			
	je sache	je susse	sache	sachant	su
	nous sachions	nous sussions	sachons sachez		
	je serve	je servisse		servant	servi
	nous servions	nous servissions			
	je sorte	je sortisse		sortant	sorti
	nous sortions	nous sortissions			
	je suive	je suivisse		suivant	suivi
	nous suivions	nous suivissions			
	je supplie	je suppliasse		suppliant	supplié
	nous suppliions	nous suppliassions			
	je tressaille	je tressaillisse		tressaillant	tressailli
	nous tressaillions	nous tressaillissions			
	je vainque	je vainquisse		vainquant	vaincu
	nous vainquions	nous vainquissions			
	je vaille	je valusse		valant	valu
	nous valions	nous valussions			

INDICATIVE Present	Imperfect	Perfect	Past Historic	Future
70 venir				
je viens il vient nous venons ils viennent	je venais		je vins	je viendrai
71 vêtir				
je vêts il vêt nous vêtons	je vêtais		je vêtis	je vêtirai
72 vivre				
je vis il vit nous vivons	je vivais		je vécus	je vivrai
73a voir				
je vois il voit nous voyons ils voient	je voyais		je vis	je verrai

73b pourvoir *follows the above pattern except for the following*

			Past Historic	Future
			je pourvus	je pourvoirai

73c prévoir *follows the above pattern except for the following*

			Past Historic	Future
			je prévus	je prévoirai

INDICATIVE Present	Imperfect	Perfect	Past Historic	Future
74 vouloir				
je veux	je voulais		je voulus	je voudrai
il veut nous voulons				
ils veulent				

CONDITIONAL Present	SUBJUNCTIVE Present	Imperfect	IMPERATIVE	PARTICIPLE Present	Past
	je vienne	je vinsse		venant	venu
	nous venions	nous vinssions			
	je vête	je vêtisse		vêtant	vêtu
	nous vêtions	nous vêtissions			
	je vive	je vécusse		vivant	vécu
	nous vivions	nous vécussions			
	je voie	je visse		voyant	vu
	nous voyions	nous vissions			
je pourvoirais					
je prévoirais					
	je veuille	je voulusse	veuille	voulant	voulu
	nous voulions	nous voulussions	veuillons veuillez		

Français-Anglais
French-English

A

A, a [ɑ] *nm inv* A, a; **connaître un sujet de A à Z** to know a subject inside out; **prouver qch par A plus B** to prove sth in a logical or scientific fashion

A [ɑ] *nf (abrév* **autoroute)** A1 *Br* ≃ M1, *Am* ≃ I1

a *voir* **avoir**

à [a] *prép*

> **à + le** contracts to form **au** [o], **à + les** contracts to form **aux** [o].

(a) *(indique la direction)* to; **aller/venir à Paris** to go/come to Paris; **aller à la pêche** to go fishing; **partir au Venezuela** to leave for Venezuela; **rentrer à la maison** to go/come home; **au lit!** off to bed!

(b) *(indique la position)* at; **être à la maison/à la campagne/à Marseille** to be at home/in the countryside/in Marseilles; **j'habite au 3, place des Cardeurs** I live at number 3, place des Cardeurs; **à la page deux** on page two; **à 2 kilomètres/dix minutes d'ici** 2 kilometres/ten minutes from here; **à la télévision** on (the) television; **un livre à la main** a book in his/her hand

(c) *(dans l'expression du temps)* **à huit heures** at eight (o'clock); **au vingtième siècle** in the twentieth century; **à la tombée de la nuit** at nightfall; **au printemps** in the spring; **à mon arrivée** when I arrive/arrived; **le 2 au soir** on the evening of the 2nd; **à lundi!/ce soir!** see you Monday/tonight!

(d) *(avec de)* to; **de Paris à Lyon** from Paris to Lyons; **du lundi au vendredi** from Monday to Friday, *Am* Monday to *or* thru Friday; **de 2 à 4** *(heure)* from 2 till *or* to 4; **de 10 à 15%** *(environ)* between 10 and 15%

(e) *(introduit le complément d'objet indirect)* to; **donner/prêter qch à qn** to give/lend sth to sb, to give/lend sb sth; **penser à qn /qch** to think of *or* about sb/sth

(f) *(indique l'appartenance)* **c'est à lui/à Paul** it's his/Paul's; *Fam* **un ami à moi** a friend of mine; **c'est à vous de...** *(il vous incombe de)* it's up to you to...; *(c'est votre tour de)* it's your turn to...; **à toi!** your turn!

(g) *(indique le moyen, la manière)* **à bicyclette** by bicycle; **à pied/cheval** on foot/horseback; **au crayon** in pencil; **à la française** in the French style; **fonctionner à l'électricité** to run on electricity; **jouer un air au violon** to play a tune on the violin

(h) *(distributif)* **faire qch à deux/trois** to do sth in twos/threes; **se mettre à plusieurs pour faire qch** to team up to do sth; **100 km à l'heure** 100 km an *or* per hour; **être payé à l'heure** to be paid by the hour

(i) *(indique la caractéristique)* **l'homme à la barbe/aux lunettes noires** the man with a beard/with the dark glasses; **un timbre à 3 F** a 3-franc stamp

(j) *(indique le but)* **maison à vendre** house for sale; **à louer** *(sur panneau)* Br to let, *Am* to rent; **j'ai une lettre à écrire/des courses à faire** I've got a letter to write/some errands to run

(k) *(indique la conséquence)* **c'était à mourir de rire** it was hilarious; **laid à faire peur** hideously ugly; **c'est à se demander si...** you begin to wonder if...

abaisser [abese] **1** *vt* **(a)** *(levier, manette, pont-levis)* to lower; *(store)* to pull down **(b)** *(prix, coût, pression)* to reduce **(c)** *Litt (humilier)* to humble, to abase **(d)** *Culin (pâte)* to roll out

2 s'abaisser *vpr* **(a)** *(descendre)* to slope down **(b)** **s'a. à faire qch** to lower oneself to do sth

abandon [abɑ̃dɔ̃] *nm* **(a)** *(d'un enfant, d'un projet)* abandonment; **exiger l'a. des hostilités** to call for an end to hostilities; *Jur* **a. du domicile conjugal** desertion; *Mil* **a. de poste** desertion of one's post **(b)** *(en sport)* **gagner par a.** to win by default; **être contraint à l'a.** to be forced to withdraw **(c)** *(d'un lieu)* neglect; **à l'a.** neglected; **laisser qch à l'a.** to neglect sth **(d)** *(nonchalance)* abandon **(e)** *Ordinat* abort

abandonner [abɑ̃dɔne] **1** *vt* **(a)** *(personne, village)* to desert, to abandon; *(voiture)* to abandon; **a. le navire** to abandon ship; **a. le domicile conjugal** to desert the marital home; **mes forces m'abandonnent** my strength is failing me **(b)** *(privilège, pouvoir, combat)* to give up; *(projet)* to abandon; *(course)* to withdraw from; **a. ses études** to drop out (of school/university); **a. ses études de médecine** to give up medicine; *aussi Fig* **a. la partie** to throw in one's hand **(c)** *(céder)* to give (à to) **(d)** *Ordinat* abort

2 *vi* **(a)** *(renoncer)* to give up **(b)** *(en sport)* to withdraw

3 s'abandonner *vpr (se laisser aller)* to let oneself go; **s'a. au sommeil** to drift off to sleep

abasourdi, -e [abazurdi] *adj* stunned

abat-jour [abaʒur] *nm inv* lampshade

abats [aba] *nmpl Br* offal, *Am* variety meat; *(de volaille)* giblets

abattage [abataʒ] *nm* **(a)** *(d'animal)* slaughter, slaughtering **(b)** **avoir de l'a.** *(acteur, politicien)* to be full of go

abattant [abatɑ̃] *nm (d'une table)* flap; *(des toilettes)* lid

abattement [abatmɑ̃] *nm* **(a)** *(physique)* exhaustion **(b)** *(moral)* dejection, depression **(c)** *Fin* **a. (fiscal)** tax allowance

abattis [abati] *nmpl* **(a)** *(de volaille)* giblets **(b)** *très Fam* **numéroter ses a.** to start saying one's prayers

abattoir [abatwar] *nm* slaughterhouse, abattoir; *Fig* **envoyer qn à l'a.** to send sb to the slaughter

abattre [11] [abatr] **1** *vt* **(a)** *(faire tomber)* (mur, cloison) to knock down, to pull down; *(arbre)* to fell, to cut down; **a.** *(sujet: vent)* (arbre) to blow down; *(avion)* to bring down; **a. de la besogne** to get through a lot of work **(b)** *(tuer)* (personne) to kill; *(animal de boucherie)* to slaughter; *(animal malade ou dangereux)* to destroy; *Fig* **c'est l'homme à a.** he needs to be removed **(c)** *Fig (fatiguer)* (sujet: maladie) to lay low; **la chaleur nous a complètement abattus** the heat drained us of all energy (**d**) *Fig (démoraliser)* to dishearten, to depress; **ne vous laissez pas a.!** keep your chin up! (**e**) *aussi Fig* **a. ses cartes** *ou* **son jeu** to lay one's cards on the table

2 s'abattre *vpr (arbre, mur)* to crash down (**sur** on); *(pluie)* to pour down (**sur** on); *(oiseau)* to swoop down (**sur** on)

abattu, -e [abaty] *adj* dejected, depressed

abbaye [abei] *nf* abbey

abbé [abe] *nm* (**a**) *(d'une abbaye)* abbot (**b**) *(prêtre)* priest; **j'en parlerai à Monsieur l'a.** I'll mention it to the priest; **l'a. Martin** Father Martin

abc [abese] *nm inv (rudiments)* basics

abcès [apsɛ] *nm* abscess; *Fig* **crever** *ou* **vider l'a.** to resolve the situation

abdiquer [abdike] *vt (trône)* to abdicate; *(droits)* to renounce, to surrender; **être contraint d'a.** to be forced to abdicate

abdomen [abdɔmɛn] *nm* abdomen

abdominal, -e, -aux, -ales [abdɔminal, -o] **1** *adj* abdominal

2 *nmpl* **abdominaux** stomach muscles; **faire des abdominaux** to do exercises for the stomach muscles

abdos [abdo] *nmpl Fam* stomach muscles; **faire des a.** to do exercises for the stomach muscles

abécédaire [abesedɛr] *nm* ABC, alphabet book

abeille [abɛj] *nf* bee

aberrant, -e [aberɑ̃, -ɑ̃t] *adj* absurd

aberration [aberasjɔ̃] *nf* aberration; **c'est une a.!** it's absurd!

abêtir [abetir] **1** *vt* **a. qn** to dull sb's mind

2 s'abêtir *vpr* to become stupid

abêtissant, -e [abetisɑ̃, -ɑ̃t] *adj* mind-numbing

abhorrer [abɔre] *vt Litt* to abhor

Abidjan [abidʒɑ̃] *n* Abidjan

abîme [abim] *nm (de l'océan)* abyss, depths; *Fig (entre deux personnes)* gulf; *Fig* **être au bord de l'a.** to be on the brink of disaster

abîmer [abime] **1** *vt (objet)* to spoil, to damage; *(vêtement, chaussures)* to ruin

2 s'abîmer *vpr* (**a**) *(fruit)* to go bad; *(objet)* to get damaged; *(vêtement, chaussures)* to get ruined (**b**) **s'a. les yeux** to ruin one's eyesight (**c**) *Litt* **s'a. en mer** to be engulfed by the sea

abject, -e [abʒɛkt] *adj Péj* contemptible, despicable

abjurer [abʒyre] *vt (religion)* to abjure

ablation [ablasjɔ̃] *nf* removal

ablette [ablɛt] *nf* bleak

ablutions [ablysjɔ̃] *nfpl Litt ou Hum* **faire ses a.** to perform one's ablutions

abnégation [abnegasjɔ̃] *nf* abnegation, self-sacrifice

aboiement [abwamɑ̃] *nm* bark; **des aboiements** barking

abois [abwa] *nmpl* **être aux a.** *(cerf)* to be at bay; *Fig* **il est aux a.** *(personne)* the net's closing in on him

abolir [abɔlir] *vt* to abolish

abolition [abɔlisjɔ̃] *nf* abolition

abominable [abɔminabl] *adj* appalling, abominable; *(crime)* heinous; *(odeur)* foul; **l'a. homme des neiges** abominable snowman

abominablement [abɔminabləmɑ̃] *adv* abominably; *(laid)* hideously

abomination [abɔminasjɔ̃] *nf* abomination; *Litt* **avoir qn/qch en a.** to loathe sb/sth

abondamment [abɔ̃damɑ̃] *adv (parler, critiquer)* at length; **se servir a.** to help oneself to large amounts of food

abondance [abɔ̃dɑ̃s] *nf* abundance; *(d'informations, détails)* wealth; **il y avait des fruits en a.** there was plenty of fruit; **vivre dans l'a.** to live a life of ease

abondant, -e [abɔ̃dɑ̃, -ɑ̃t] *adj* abundant, plentiful; *(repas)* hearty; *(pluie)* heavy; *(saignement)* profuse; **une chevelure abondante** a thick head of hair; **peu a.** *(récolte, chevelure)* poor; *(pluie)* light; *(repas)* frugal

abonder [abɔ̃de] *vi* (**a**) *(foisonner)* to be plentiful; **a. en qch** to abound in sth (**b**) **a. dans le sens de qn** to agree entirely with sb

abonné, -e [abɔne] *nm,f (d'une revue)* subscriber; *(du gaz, de l'électricité)* consumer; *(de la SNCF, d'un théâtre)* season-ticket holder; **il n'y a pas d'a. au numéro que vous avez demandé** ≃ the number you have dialled has not been recognized

2 *adj* **être a. à qch** *(revue)* to have a subscription to sth; *(SNCF, théâtre)* to have a season ticket to sth; *Fam (être habitué à)* to be prone to sth

abonnement [abɔnmɑ̃] *nm (à une revue)* subscription (**à** to); *(de train, de théâtre)* season ticket; *(au téléphone)* line rental; **prendre un a.** *(à une revue)* to take out a subscription; *(pour le train, pour le théâtre)* to buy a season ticket

abonner [abɔne] **1** *vt* **a. qn à une revue** to take out a subscription to a magazine for sb

2 s'abonner *vpr (à une revue)* to take out a subscription (**à** to); *(au théâtre)* to buy a season ticket (**à** for)

abord [abɔr] *nm* (**a**) *(d'un lieu)* **l'île est d'un a. difficile** the island is not easily accessible (**b**) **abords** *(d'un bâtiment)* surroundings; *(d'une ville)* outskirts (**c**) *(d'une personne)* **être d'un a. facile/difficile** to be approachable/unapproachable; **au premier a.**, **de prime a.** at first sight (**d**) **d'a., tout d'a.** *(pour commencer)* at first, to begin with; *(premièrement)* first (and foremost), in the first place; *Fam* **toi, d'a., je ne te parle plus!** I'm not talking to you, so there!

abordable [abɔrdabl] *adj* (**a**) *(lieu)* accessible (**b**) *(prix)* affordable (**c**) *(personne)* approachable

abordage [abɔrdaʒ] *nm (pour attaquer)* boarding; *(pour s'amarrer)* coming alongside; **monter à l'a.** to board a ship

aborder [abɔrde] **1** *vt* (**a**) *(personne)* to approach; **se faire a.** to be approached (**b**) *(question)* to deal with; *(virage)* to approach (**c**) *(navire)* *(attaquer)* to board; *(se mettre le long de)* to come alongside

2 *vi* to land

aborigène [abɔriʒɛn] **1** *nmf (d'un pays)* native; **les aborigènes d'Australie** the (Australian) Aborigines

2 *adj* native, indigenous (**de** to); *(des peuplades australiennes)* Aboriginal

abortif, -ive [abɔrtif, -iv] *adj voir* **pilule**

abouler [abule] *très Fam* **1** *vt* to hand over

2 s'abouler *vpr* to turn up, to show up; **alors, tu t'aboules?** well, are you coming or not?

aboutir [abutir] *vi* (a) *(réussir)* to be successful; **ne pas a.** to fall through (b) *(dans l'espace)* **a. à/dans** *(sujet: personne)* to end up at/in; **a. à** *(sujet: chemin, escalier)* to lead to; *Fig (sujet: efforts, recherches)* to result in; **n'a. à rien** *(personne)* to get nowhere; *(efforts, recherches)* to come to nothing

aboutissants [abutisã] *nmpl voir* **tenant**

aboutissement [abutismã] *nm* result, outcome

aboyer [32] [abwaje] *vi* to bark

abracadabrant, -e [abrakadabrã, -ãt] *adj Fam (histoire)* cock-and-bull

abrasif, -ive [abrazif, -iv] *adj & nm* abrasive

abrégé [abreʒe] *nm* (a) *(livre)* **un a. d'histoire de France** a short history of France; **un a. de philosophie** a short guide to philosophy (b) **écrire en a.** to write in abbreviated form

abréger [59] [abreʒe] *vt (article, exposé)* to shorten, to cut down; *(visite)* to cut short; *(mot)* to abbreviate; *Fam* **allez, abrège!** come on, get to the point!

abreuver [abrœve] **1** *vt (chevaux, bétail)* to water; *Fig* **a. qn d'injures** to shower sb with insults
  2 s'abreuver *vpr (cheval, bétail)* to drink

abreuvoir [abrœvwar] *nm (dans une rivière)* watering place; *(baquet)* drinking trough

abréviation [abrevjasjõ] *nf* abbreviation

abri [abri] *nm* shelter; **mettre qn/qch à l'a.** to shelter sb/sth; **se mettre à l'a.** to (take) shelter; **être à l'a. (de qch)** to be sheltered (from sth); **être à l'a. du besoin** to have no financial worries; **personne n'est à l'a. d'une erreur** anybody can make a mistake; **a. antiatomique** fallout shelter; **a. à vélos** bike shed

abribus® [abribys] *nm* bus shelter

abricot [abriko] *nm* apricot
  2 *adj inv* apricot-coloured

abricotier [abrikɔtje] *nm* apricot tree

abrier [abrije] *Can* **1** *vt* to wrap up (well)
  2 s'abrier *vpr* to wrap oneself up (well)

abriter [abrite] **1** *vt (protéger)* to shelter (**de** from)
  2 s'abriter *vpr* **s'a. (de la pluie)** to (take) shelter (from the rain); **s'a. (du soleil)** to shade oneself (from the sun)

abrogation [abrɔgasjõ] *nf (d'une loi)* repeal

abroger [45] [abrɔʒe] *vt (loi)* to repeal

abrupt, -e [abrypt] *adj (rocher, pente)* steep; *Fig (manière)* abrupt, blunt; **d'un ton a.** abruptly

abruti, -e [abryti] **1** *nm,f Fam* idiot, fool
  2 *adj* (a) *(hébété)* stupefied, dazed; **a. par l'alcool** stupefied with drink (b) *Fam (bête)* stupid, idiotic

abrutir [abrytir] **1** *vt (hébéter)* to daze; **a. qn de travail** to work sb to the point of exhaustion
  2 s'abrutir *vpr* **s'a. de travail** to work oneself to the point of exhaustion; **on s'abrutit à trop regarder la télévision** too much television numbs the brain

abrutissant, -e [abrytisã, -ãt] *adj* mind-numbing; *(bruit)* wearing

ABS [abeɛs] *nm Aut (système)* A. ABS

abscisse [apsis] *nf Math* x-axis

abscons, -e [apskõ, -ɔ̃s] *adj Litt* abstruse

absence [apsãs] *nf* (a) *(d'une personne)* absence; **en ou pendant mon a.** in or during my absence, while I am/was/etc away (b) *(manque)* lack (c) **avoir des absences** to be prone to absent-mindedness; **dans un moment d'a.** in a moment of absent-mindedness

absent, -e [apsã, -ãt] **1** *adj* (a) *(qui n'est pas présent)* absent (**de** from) (b) *(inexistant)* missing (c) *(distrait)* **avoir un air a.** to be miles away
  2 *nm,f* absentee; **les absents ont toujours tort** it's always those who aren't there who get the blame

absentéisme [apsãteism] *nm* absenteeism

absenter [apsãte] **s'absenter** *vpr (sortir)* to go away (**de** from); **elle a dû s'a. quelques minutes** she had to go out for a few minutes

absinthe [apsɛ̃t] *nf* absinthe

absolu, -e [apsɔly] **1** *nm* **l'a.** the absolute; **dans l'a.,...** in principle,...
  2 *adj* absolute; *(règle)* hard-and-fast; **être dans l'impossibilité absolue de faire qch** to be quite unable to do sth

absolument [apsɔlymã] *adv* (a) *(complètement)* absolutely; **a. pas!** absolutely not! (b) *(sans faute)* **vous devez a. y aller!** you simply MUST go!

absolution [apsɔlysjõ] *nf Rel* absolution

absolvais *etc voir* **absoudre**

absorbant, -e [apsɔrbã, -ãt] *adj* (a) *(matériau)* absorbent (b) *(livre, tâche)* absorbing

absorber [apsɔrbe] *vt* (a) *(liquide)* to absorb, to soak up (b) *(nourriture)* to eat; *(boisson)* to drink; *(médicament)* to take (c) *(entreprise)* to take over (d) *(sujet: lecture)* to absorb, to engross; **son travail l'absorbe** she is absorbed or engrossed in her work; **être absorbé dans ses pensées** to be lost in thought

absorption [apsɔrpsjõ] *nf* (a) *(de liquide)* absorption (b) *(de nourriture)* eating; *(d'une boisson)* drinking; *(d'un médicament)* taking (c) *(d'une entreprise)* takeover

absoudre [3a] [apsudr] *vt Litt ou Rel* **a. qn de qch** to forgive sb sth

abstenir [70] [apstənir] **s'abstenir** *vpr (ne pas voter)* to abstain (from voting); **s'a. de faire qch** to refrain from doing sth; **dans le doute, abstiens-toi** when in doubt, don't; **pas sérieux s'a.** *(dans une petite annonce)* no timewasters

abstention [apstãsjõ] *nf* abstention

abstentionniste [apstãsjonist] *nmf* abstainer

abstinence [apstinãs] *nf* abstinence

abstraction [apstraksjõ] *nf* (a) **faire a. de qch** to disregard sth; **a. faite de cette dépense** leaving aside this expense (b) *(idée abstraite)* abstract idea, abstraction

abstrait, -e [apstrɛ, -ɛt] **1** *adj* abstract
  2 *nm* **dans l'a.** in the abstract

absurde [apsyrd] **1** *adj* absurd
  2 *nm* **l'a.** *(d'une situation, d'une remarque)* absurdity; **démonstration par l'a.** reductio ad absurdum

absurdité [apsyrdite] *nf* (a) *(caractère absurde)* absurdity (b) *(chose absurde)* absurdity, piece of nonsense; **dire des absurdités** to talk nonsense

abus [aby] *nm* (a) *(excès)* overindulgence (**de** in); **l'a. d'alcool** alcohol abuse; **l'a. de médicaments est dangereux** taking too much medication is dangerous (b) *(pratique)* abuse; *Fam* **il y a de l'a.!** that's going too far! (c) *Jur* **a. de biens sociaux** misappropriation of funds; **a. de confiance** breach of trust; **a. de pouvoir** abuse of power

abuser [abyze] **1** vt Litt to deceive
2 abuser de vt ind (exploiter, violer) to take advantage of; **a. du tabac** to smoke too much; **a. de ses forces** to overexert oneself; **il ne faut pas a. des bonnes choses** good things should be enjoyed in moderation; **je voudrais pas a.** I don't want to cause you any inconvenience; **alors là, vous abusez!** this is a bit much!
3 s'abuser vpr **si je ne m'abuse** if I'm not mistaken

abusif, -ive [abyzif, -iv] adj (a) (emploi d'un mot) incorrect (b) (excessif) excessive; (mère) possessive

abysse [abis] nm abyssal zone

acabit [akabi] nm Péj **du même a.** of that type

acacia [akasja] nm acacia

académicien, -enne [akademisjɛ̃, -ɛn] nm,f = member of the "Académie française"

académie [akademi] nf (a) (des lettres, des sciences, d'art) academy; **l'A. française** = learned society responsible for promoting the French language and imposing standards (b) (école) school, academy; **a. de musique/dessin** music/art school (c) (dans l'Éducation nationale) Br ≃ local education authority, Am ≃ school district

académique [akademik] adj (a) Scol = relating to a local education authority (b) Péj (style) conventional

acajou [akaʒu] **1** nm mahogany
2 adj inv reddish-brown

a cap(p)ella [akapela] adv a cappella

acariâtre [akarjɑtr] adj cantankerous

acarien [akarjɛ̃] nm dust mite

accablant, -e [akablɑ̃, -ɑ̃t] adj (a) (responsabilités) overwhelming; (chaleur) oppressive (b) (témoignage) damning

accablement [akabləmɑ̃] nm dejection, depression

accabler [akable] vt (a) (sujet: chaleur, malheur) to overwhelm; **a. qn de travail** to overload sb with work; **a. qn de reproches** to heap criticism on sb (b) (sujet: témoignage) to damn

accalmie [akalmi] nf lull

accaparer [akapare] vt (personne, conversation) to monopolize; (places, morceaux de choix) to grab

accéder [34] [aksede] **accéder à** vt ind (a) (atteindre) to reach, to get to (b) Fig (responsabilités, rang) to gain; **a. au trône** to accede to the throne (c) (requête) to comply with (d) Ordinat (programme) to access

accélérateur [akseleratœr] nm (de voiture, d'ordinateur) accelerator; **appuyer sur l'a.** to step on the accelerator; Ordinat **a. graphique** graphic(s) accelerator

accélération [akselerasjɔ̃] nf acceleration

accéléré, -e [akselere] **1** nm Cin **en a.** in accelerated motion
2 adj quick, fast; (mouvement) accelerated; **cours a.** crash course

accélérer [34] [akselere] **1** vt to speed up; Fig **a. le mouvement** to get a move on
2 vi (en voiture) to accelerate
3 s'accélérer vpr to accelerate, to speed up

accent [aksɑ̃] nm (a) (sur une lettre) accent; **a. aigu/grave/circonflexe** acute/grave/circumflex (accent); **e a. circonflexe** e circumflex (b) (en phonétique) stress; **a. tonique** (primary) stress (c) (prononciation) accent (d) Fig (inflexion) **avoir des accents de vérité** to have a ring of truth; **mettre l'a. sur qch** to stress or emphasize sth

accentuation [aksɑ̃tɥasjɔ̃] nf (a) (en phonétique) stress (b) (à l'écrit) accentuation (c) (d'un phénomène) intensification

accentué, -e [aksɑ̃tɥe] adj (a) (syllabe) stressed (b) (lettre) accented (c) Fig (net) pronounced, marked

accentuer [aksɑ̃tɥe] **1** vt (a) (syllabe) to stress (b) (lettre) to put an accent on (c) Fig (renforcer) to emphasize; (avance) to increase
2 s'accentuer vpr to become more pronounced or marked

acceptable [akseptabl] adj (a) (recevable) acceptable (b) (passable) satisfactory

acceptation [akseptasjɔ̃] nf acceptance

accepter [aksepte] vt to accept; **a. de faire qch** to agree to do sth; **il est hors de question que j'accepte** I can't possibly accept

acception [aksepsjɔ̃] nf Formel (a) (d'un mot) meaning, sense (b) **sans a. de race/de sexe** irrespective of race/sex

accès [aksɛ] nm (a) (approche) access, approach (à to); **être facile/difficile d'a.** to be easy/hard to reach; **avoir a. à qch** to have access to sth; **donner a. à qch** (sujet: porte, chemin) to lead to sth; (sujet: ticket) to allow entry to sth; **a. aux quais** (sur panneau) to the trains (b) (d'une personne) **être d'un a. facile/difficile** to be approachable/unapproachable (c) (poussée) fit, attack; **a. de colère** fit of anger; **a. de fièvre** bout of fever; **a. de toux** coughing fit (d) Ordinat access; **avoir a. à** to be able to access

accessible [aksesibl] adj (a) (lieu, livre) accessible; (prix) affordable (b) (personne) approachable

accession [aksesjɔ̃] nf **a. au pouvoir/au trône** accession (to power)/to the throne; **l'a. à la propriété** home ownership

accessoire [akseswar] **1** nm (d'appareil ménager, de mode) accessory; Th **accessoires** props
2 adj minor; **c'est a.** it's a minor detail

accessoirement [akseswarmɑ̃] adv if necessary, if need be; (en plus) also

accessoiriste [akseswarist] nmf Th prop man, f prop woman

accident [aksidɑ̃] nm (a) (collision, malheur) accident; **a. d'avion** plane or air crash; **a. de chemin de fer** train crash; **a. de la circulation** traffic accident; **a. de la route** road accident; **a. du travail** industrial accident; **a. de voiture** car accident or crash (b) (événement inattendu) mishap; **par a.** by accident, by chance; **a. de parcours** hitch (c) **a. de terrain** (bosse) bump; (trou) hole

accidenté, -e [aksidɑ̃te] **1** nm,f accident victim; **accidentés de la route** road accident victims
2 adj (a) (terrain) uneven (b) (voiture) damaged

accidentel, -elle [aksidɑ̃tɛl] adj accidental

accidentellement [aksidɑ̃tɛlmɑ̃] adv (par hasard) accidentally, by chance; (mourir) in an accident

acclamation [aklamasjɔ̃] nf cheer; **sous les acclamations de la foule** to the cheers of the crowd

acclamer [aklame] vt to cheer

acclimatation [aklimatasjɔ̃] nf acclimatization, Am acclimation (à to)

acclimater [aklimate] **1** vt to acclimatize, Am to acclimate (à to)
2 s'acclimater vpr to become or get acclimatized or Am acclimated (à to)

accointances [akwɛ̃tɑ̃s] *nfpl* contacts

accolade [akɔlad] *nf* (a) *(embrassade)* (formal) embrace; **donner l'a. à qn** to embrace sb (b) *(signe typographique)* curly bracket, brace

accoler [akɔle] *vt (mettre côte à côte)* to put side by side

accommodant, -e [akɔmɔdɑ̃, -ɑ̃t] *adj* accommodating

accommoder [akɔmɔde] **1** *vt (nourriture)* to prepare; *(restes)* to use up
2 *vi (œil)* to focus
3 s'accommoder *vpr* **s'a. de qch** to put up with sth

accompagnateur, -trice [akɔ̃paɲatœr, -tris] *nm,f* (a) *(pianiste)* accompanist (b) *(d'un voyage organisé)* courier, tour guide; *(d'une sortie scolaire)* accompanying adult

accompagnement [akɔ̃paɲmɑ̃] *nm* (a) *(de morceau de musique)* accompaniment; **chanter sans a.** to sing unaccompanied (b) *(légumes)* accompaniment

accompagner [akɔ̃paɲe] **1** *vt* (a) *(venir avec)* to come with, to accompany; *(aller avec)* to go with, to accompany; **il est venu accompagné d'une amie** he came with a friend (b) *(conduire)* **a. qn à la gare** to take sb to the station (c) *(chanteur)* to accompany (à on) (d) *(ajouter à)* **il a accompagné ses mots d'un sourire** he said it with a smile; **elle a accompagné son exposé de diapositives** she complemented her talk with a slide show
2 s'accompagner *vpr* (a) **s'a. au piano** to accompany oneself on the piano (b) *(se produire simultanément)* **s'a. de qch** to be accompanied by sth

accompli, -e [akɔ̃pli] *adj (excellent)* accomplished

accomplir [akɔ̃plir] **1** *vt* (a) *(tâche)* to carry out; *(bonne action)* to do; *(exploit)* to accomplish; *(souhait, promesse)* to fulfil (b) *(terminer)* to complete, to finish
2 s'accomplir *vpr (souhait)* to come true

accord [akɔr] *nm* (a) *(traité)* agreement; *(non formel)* understanding; *(pour résoudre un conflit)* settlement; **arriver ou parvenir à un a.** to come to *or* reach an agreement *(entente)* agreement (sur on); **être d'a. avec qn** to agree with sb; **se mettre d'a.** *ou* **tomber d'a. avec qn** to come to an agreement with sb; **(c'est) d'a.!** all right!, OK!; **d'un commun a.** by common consent, by mutual agreement; **faire qch en a. avec qn** to do sth in agreement with sb (c) *(autorisation)* consent (d) *Gram* agreement (avec with) (e) *(en musique)* chord; **a. parfait** common chord

accordéon [akɔrdeɔ̃] *nm* accordion; *Fig* **en a.** *(chaussettes)* at half-mast

accordéoniste [akɔrdeɔnist] *nmf* accordionist, accordion player

accorder [akɔrde] **1** *vt* (a) **a. qch à qn** *(faveur)* to grant sb sth; *(augmentation, dommages-intérêts)* to award sb sth; *(prêt, découvert bancaire)* to authorize sth to sb; **a. son pardon à qn** to pardon sb; **a. la plus grande importance à qch** to attach the utmost importance to sth; **pouvez-vous m'a. quelques minutes?** can you spare me a few minutes? *Formel* **je ne l'aime pas, je vous l'accorde** I don't like him, I must admit (b) *Gram* **a. qch avec qch** to make sth agree with sth (c) *(instrument de musique)* to tune; *Fig* **il faudrait a. nos violons** we'd better get our story straight (d) *(harmoniser)* *(couleurs)* to co-ordinate
2 s'accorder *vpr* (a) *(se mettre d'accord)* to agree, to come to an agreement (avec/sur with/on); **s'a. à penser que...** there is a general belief *or* it is generally believed that... (b) *(couleurs)* to go together (c) *Gram* to agree (avec with) (d) *(à soi-même)* **s'a. qch** to allow *or* give oneself sth

accordeur [akɔrdœr] *nm* (piano) tuner

accoster [akɔste] **1** *vt (personne)* to approach
2 *vi Naut* to dock

accotement [akɔtmɑ̃] *nm* (a) *(d'une route)* verge; **accotements non stabilisés** *(sur panneau)* soft verges (b) *(de voie ferrée)* shoulder

accouchement [akuʃmɑ̃] *nm* childbirth, delivery; **avoir un a. difficile** to have a difficult birth; **a. sans douleur =** childbirth made less painful by the use of relaxation techniques

accoucher [akuʃe] **1** *vi* **a. qn** to deliver sb's baby
2 accoucher de *vt ind* (a) *(enfant)* to give birth to; **elle doit a. dans un mois** her baby's due in a month (b) *Fam* **accouche!** come on, spit it out!

accoucheur [akuʃœr] *nm* **(médecin) a.** obstetrician

accoucheuse [akuʃøz] *nf* midwife

accouder [akude] **s'accouder** *vpr* **s'a. à** *ou* **sur qch** to lean one's elbow(s) on sth

accoudoir [akudwar] *nm* armrest

accouplement [akuplɑ̃mɑ̃] *nm (d'animaux)* pairing, mating

accoupler [akuple] **s'accoupler** *vpr (animaux)* to mate

accourir [22] [akurir] *vi* to run up, to rush up

accoutrement [akutrəmɑ̃] *nm* rig-out, get-up

accoutrer [akutre] **1** *vt* to rig out (de in)
2 s'accoutrer *vpr* to rig oneself out (de in)

accoutumance [akutymɑ̃s] *nf (adaptation)* familiarization (à with); *(à l'alcool, à la drogue)* addiction; **créer une a.** to be addictive

accoutumé, -e [akutyme] *adj* usual; **comme à l'accoutumée** as usual

accoutumer [akutyme] **1** *vt* **a. qn à qch** to accustom sb to sth, to get sb used to sth
2 s'accoutumer *vpr* **s'a. à** to get used *or* accustomed to

accréditer [akredite] *vt* (a) *(ambassadeur, journaliste)* to accredit (b) *(rendre plausible)* to substantiate

accro [akro] *adj Fam (drogué) & Fig* addicted (à to), hooked (à on)

accroc [akro] *nm* (a) *(à un tissu)* tear, catch (b) *Fig* hitch, snag; **sans a.** without a hitch

accrochage [akrɔʃaʒ] *nm* (a) *(accident)* minor accident (b) *(dispute)* row; *Mil* skirmish

accroche [akrɔʃ] *nf* slogan

accroche-cœur [akrɔʃkœr] *nm* (*pl* **accroche-cœurs**) kiss curl

accrocher [akrɔʃe] **1** *vt* (a) *(suspendre)* to hang up (à on); *(wagon)* to hitch on, to couple; *Fig* **une robe qui accroche le regard** an eye-catching dress; **avoir le cœur bien accroché** to have strong nerves *or* a strong stomach (b) *(abîmer)* *(vêtement)* to catch (à on); *(pare-chocs)* to clip
2 *vi* (a) *(achopper)* to hit a stumbling block; **un titre qui accroche** an eye-catching title; *Fam* **ça n'a pas du tout accroché entre eux** they didn't hit it off at all; *Fam* **je n'accroche pas du tout en maths** I just can't get into maths at all
3 s'accrocher *vpr* (a) *aussi Fig (s'agripper)* **s'a. à qn/qch** to cling to sb/sth; *Fam* **accroche-toi, tu n'as pas tout entendu!** brace yourself, you haven't heard everything yet! (b) *Fam (persévérer)* to stick at it (c) *(voitures)* to crash

into each other **(d)** *Fam (se disputer)* to have a row **(avec** with**) (e)** *(se fixer)* to fasten

accrocheur, -euse [akrɔʃœr, -øz] *adj* **(a)** *(tenace)* tenacious, stubborn **(b)** *(titre, slogan)* catchy

accroissement [akrwasmã] *nm* increase **(de in)**

accroître [akrwatr] **1** *vt* to increase, to enlarge

2 s'accroître *vpr* to increase, to grow

accroupir [akrupir] **s'accroupir** *vpr* to squat (down), to crouch (down); **être accroupi** to be squatting *or* crouching

accu [aky] *nm* battery

accueil [akœj] *nm (façon d'accueillir)* reception, welcome; *(lieu)* reception; **faire bon a. à qn** to welcome sb; **faire mauvais a. à qn** to give sb a cool reception

accueillant, -e [akœjã, -ãt] *adj* welcoming

accueillir [5] [akœjir] *vt* **(a)** *(personne, proposition)* to greet; **bien a. qn** to give sb a warm welcome; **nous avons été mal accueillis** we weren't given a very warm welcome; **le film a été mal accueilli par le public** the film was badly received by the public **(b)** *(loger; sujet: ami)* to put up; *(sujet: hôtel)* to accommodate

acculer [akyle] *vt* to drive back **(contre** against**)**; *Fig* **a. qn à faire qch** to give sb no choice but to do sth; *Fig* **être acculé à la faillite** to be forced into bankruptcy

accumulateur [akymylatœr] *nm Él* battery

accumulation [akymylasjõ] *nf* accumulation; *(d'énergie)* storage; **chauffage par a.** storage heating

accumuler [akymyle] **1** *vt* to accumulate, to amass; *(énergie)* to store; **a. les erreurs** to make a series of mistakes

2 s'accumuler *vpr* to accumulate; *(nuages)* to gather, to build up; *Fin (intérêts)* to accrue; **les preuves s'accumulent contre elle** the evidence against her is growing

accusateur, -trice [akyzatœr, -tris] **1** *adj (regard, doigt)* accusing

2 *nm,f* accuser

accusation [akyzasjõ] *nf* accusation; **lancer** *ou* **porter une a. contre qn** to make an accusation against sb; *Jur* **mettre qn en a.** to commit sb for trial

accusé, -e [akyze] **1** *adj (trait)* prominent, pronounced

2 *nm,f (d'un crime)* accused; *(au tribunal)* defendant

3 *nm* **a. de réception** *(pour une lettre)* acknowledgement (of receipt); *Ordinat* acknowledge, acknowledgement

accuser [akyze] **1** *vt* **(a)** *(incriminer)* to accuse; **a. qn de qch/de faire qch** to accuse sb of sth/of doing sth **(b)** *(tendance, baisse)* to show; **a. le coup** to be obviously shaken **(c)** **a. réception de qch** to acknowledge (receipt of) sth

2 s'accuser *vpr* **(a)** *(se déclarer coupable)* to confess **(de** to**) (b)** *(se renforcer)* to become more pronounced *or* marked

acerbe [asɛrb] *adj* acerbic; **d'un ton a.** sharply

acéré, -e [asere] *adj (lame)* sharp; *Fig (remarque)* cutting

acériculteur [aserikyltœr] *nm Can* maple syrup and sugar producer

acériculture [aserikyltyr] *nf Can* production of maple syrup and sugar

acétone [aseton] *nf* acetone

ACF [aseɛf] *nm (abrév* **Automobile Club de France)** = French motoring organization

achalandé, -e [aʃalãde] *adj* **magasin bien/mal a.** well/poorly stocked shop

achaler [aʃale] *vt Can* to annoy, to bother

acharné, -e [aʃarne] *adj (lutte, concurrence)* fierce; *(travail)* relentless; *(joueur)* inveterate

acharnement [aʃarnəmã] *nm* relentlessness; **avec a.** relentlessly; **se battre avec a.** to fight tooth and nail

acharner [aʃarne] **s'acharner** *vpr* **s'a. après** *ou* **contre** *ou* **sur qn** *(persécuter)* to be always after sb; **s'a. sur qn** *(sujet: meurtrier)* to savage sb; *(sujet: examinateur)* to give sb a hard time; **s'a. à faire qch** to try very hard to do sth

achat [aʃa] *nm* **(a)** *(action)* purchase, buying; **faire un a.** to make a purchase, to buy something; **faire l'a. de qch** to buy sth **(b)** *(ce qu'on a acheté)* purchase; **achats** *(provisions, paquets)* shopping; **aller faire ses achats** to go shopping

acheminement [aʃminmã] *nm (de troupes)* transportation **(sur** *ou* **vers** to**)**; *(de marchandises)* shipping **(sur** *ou* **vers** to**)**; **a. du courrier** mail handling

acheminer [aʃmine] **1** *vt (troupes)* to transport **(sur** *ou* **vers** to**)**; *(marchandises)* to ship **(sur** *ou* **vers** to**)**; *(courrier)* to handle

2 s'acheminer *vpr* **s'a. vers** to make one's way towards

acheter [6] [aʃte] **1** *vt* **(a)** *(acquérir)* to buy, to purchase; **a. qch à qn** *(faire une transaction)* to buy sth from sb; *(en cadeau)* to buy sth sb; **je vais lui a. un livre** I'm going to buy him/her a book; **j'ai acheté ce livre 50 francs** I bought this book for 50 francs **(b)** *Fam (corrompre)* to buy off

2 s'acheter *vpr* **(a)** *(pour soi-même)* **je vais m'a. une glace** I'm going to buy (myself) an ice cream **(b)** *(être acheté)* **ça s'achète en pharmacie** you can buy it/them in any pharmacy; **l'amour, ça ne s'achète pas** love can't be bought and sold

acheteur, -euse [aʃtœr, -øz] *nm,f* buyer, purchaser; **je suis a.!** I'm interested!

achevé, -e [aʃve] *adj (artiste, style)* accomplished; *(travail)* perfect; **c'est d'un ridicule a.!** it's utterly ridiculous!

achèvement [aʃɛvmã] *nm* completion

achever [46] [aʃve] **1** *vt* **(a)** *(finir) (discours)* to end, to conclude; *(travail)* to complete **(b)** *(tuer) (personne, proie)* to finish off; *(animal malade ou blessé)* to put out of its misery; *Fam* **ça m'a achevé!** that really finished me (off)!

2 s'achever *vpr (finir)* to end

achigan [aʃigã] *nm Can* (black) bass

achoppement [aʃɔpmã] *nm voir* **pierre**

acide [asid] **1** *adj* acid(ic); *(au goût)* sour

2 *nm* acid

acidité [asidite] *nf* acidity; *(au goût)* sourness

acidulé, -e [asidyle] *adj* slightly acid; **bonbons acidulés** acid drops

acier [asje] *nm* steel; **a. inoxydable** stainless steel

aciérie [asjeri] *nf* steelworks *(singulier)*

acné [akne] *nf* acne; **a. juvénile** acne

acolyte [akɔlit] *nm Péj* accomplice

acompte [akõt] *nm* deposit, down payment; **recevoir un a.** to receive something on account; **verser un a.** to make a down payment

acoquiner [akɔkine] **s'acoquiner** *vpr* to team up **(avec** with**)**

Açores [asɔr] *nfpl* **les A.** the Azores

à-côté *(pl* **à-côtés)** [akote] *nm* **(a)** *(élément secondaire)* side issue **(b)** *(financier)* extra

à-coup (*pl* **à-coups**) [aku] *nm* jolt; **travailler par à-coups** to work in fits and starts; **le moteur a des à-coups** the engine judders

acoustique [akustik] **1** *adj* acoustic
2 *nf* (*discipline*) acoustics (*singulier*); (*qualité*) acoustics (*pluriel*)

acquéreur [akerœr] *nm* purchaser, buyer; **notre voiture n'a pas trouvé a.** we couldn't find a buyer for our car

acquérir [7] [akerir] *vt* **a** (*obtenir, prendre*) to acquire; **nous avons acquis la certitude de son innocence** we have established beyond doubt that he/she is innocent; **a. de la valeur** to increase in value **(b)** (*acheter*) to purchase, to buy

acquière, acquiers *etc voir* **acquérir**

acquiescer [16] [akjese] *vi* to acquiesce (**à** to); **a. d'un signe de tête** to nod in agreement

acquis, -e [aki, -iz] **1** *pp voir* **acquérir**
2 *adj* (*savoir, caractères*) acquired; **tenir qch pour a.** to take sth for granted; **son aide nous est acquise** we can take it for granted that he will help us; **cela est a.** that's been established
3 *nm* (*connaissances*) knowledge; **il ne fonctionne que sur ses acquis** he gets by on what he knows already; **les a. sociaux** social benefits

acquisition [akizisjɔ̃] *nf* (*a*) (*action*) acquisition; **faire l'a. de qch** (*acheter*) to purchase sth **(b)** (*bien acheté*) purchase

acquit [aki] *nm Com* receipt; **pour a.** received (with thanks), paid; **par a. de conscience** to ease one's conscience

acquittement [akitmɑ̃] *nm* **(a)** *Jur* acquittal **(b)** (*d'une dette*) payment

acquitter [akite] **1** *vt* **a** (*accusé*) to acquit **(b)** (*dette, facture*) to pay
2 **s'acquitter** *vpr* **s'a. d'une obligation/d'un devoir** to fulfil an obligation/a duty; **s'a. envers qn** to repay sb

acre [akr] *nm ou nf Can* acre

âcre [ɑkr] *adj* (*goût*) bitter; (*odeur*) acrid

acrobate [akrɔbat] *nmf* acrobat

acrobatie [akrɔbasi] *nf* (*art*) acrobatics (*singulier*); **faire des acrobaties** to perform acrobatics; **a. aérienne** aerobatics (*singulier*)

acrobatique [akrɔbatik] *adj* acrobatic

acronyme [akrɔnim] *nm* acronym

Acropole [akrɔpɔl] *nf* **l'A.** the Acropolis

acrylique [akrilik] *adj & nm* acrylic

acte [akt] *nm* **(a)** (*action*) act; **faire a. d'autorité** to exercise one's authority; **faire a. de candidature à un emploi** to apply for a job; **faire a. de présence** to put in an appearance; **passer aux actes** to take action; **a. de terrorisme** terrorist act
(b) *Jur* deed, title; **dont a.** duly noted *or* acknowledged; **prendre a. de qch** to take note of sth; *Formel* **nous prenons a. de votre candidature** we acknowledge your application; **a. d'accusation** bill of indictment, charges; **a. de propriété** title deed; **a. unique européen** Single European Act; **a. de vente** bill of sale **(c)** (*certificat*) record; **a. de décès** death certificate; **a. d'état civil** = certificate of birth, marriage or death; **a. de mariage** marriage certificate; **a. de naissance** birth certificate
(d) **actes** (*d'un procès, d'un colloque*) proceedings; (*d'un*

organisme scientifique) transactions
(e) *Th* act

acteur [aktœr] *nm* **(a)** (*artiste*) actor; **a. de cinéma/de théâtre** film/stage actor **(b)** (*d'un événement*) **les différents acteurs de la négociation** the different participants in *or* parties involved in the negotiations

actif, -ive [aktif, -iv] **1** *adj* **a** (*défenseur, participation, substance*) active; **femme active** working woman **(b)** (*énergique*) (*personne*) active **(c)** *Gram* active
2 *nm* **a** *Com* assets; *Fig* **avoir qch à son a.** to have sth to one's name; **il faut mettre sa patience à son a.** you have to give him credit for patience **(b)** *Gram* **verbe à l'a.** verb in the active voice

action [aksjɔ̃] *nf* **a** (*acte*) action, act; **bonne/mauvaise a.** good/bad deed **(b)** (*influence, effet*) (*d'une substance*) action, effect (**sur** on) **(c)** (*activité*) **entrer en a.** (*loi*) to come into force; **mettre qch en a.** to put sth into operation; **passer à l'a.** to take action, to act; **homme d'a.** man of action **(d)** (*histoire*) action; *TV & Cin* **a.!** action! **(e)** *Fin* share **(f)** *Jur* action; **intenter une a. judiciaire** *ou* **en justice contre** to take legal action against **(g)** *Mil* action

actionnaire [aksjɔnɛr] *nmf Fin* shareholder

actionner [aksjɔne] *vt* (*mettre en marche*) to start up, to turn on; (*faire fonctionner*) to operate, to drive

activement [aktivmɑ̃] *adv* actively

activer [aktive] **1** *vt* **a** (*accélérer*) to speed up; (*feu*) to stoke **(b)** *Ordinat* to activate; **a. une option** to select an option
2 *vi Fam* to get a move on
3 **s'activer** *vpr* to be busy

activiste [aktivist] *adj & nmf* activist

activité [aktivite] *nf* activity; **en a.** (*volcan*) active; (*usine*) in production; (*personne*) working

actrice [aktris] *nf* actress

actualisation [aktɥalizasjɔ̃] *nf* (*d'un texte, d'une méthode de travail*) updating

actualiser [aktɥalize] *vt* (*texte, méthode de travail*) to update

actualité [aktɥalite] *nf* **l'a.** the news, current affairs; **l'a. politique française** the current French political scene; **cette question est toujours d'a.** this is still a topical question; **les actualités** (*à la télé, à la radio*) the news; **les actualités télévisées** the television news

actuel, -elle [aktɥɛl] *adj* present, current; **dans la situation actuelle** as things are *or* stand at the moment

actuellement [aktɥɛlmɑ̃] *adv* at present, at the present time

acuité [akɥite] *nf* (*de la douleur*) acuteness; (*d'un argument*) pointedness; (*d'un son*) shrillness; **a. visuelle/auditive** keenness of vision/hearing

acupuncture, acuponcture [akypɔ̃ktyr] *nf* acupuncture

adage [adaʒ] *nm* adage, (common) saying; **selon l'a.** as the saying goes

adaptateur, -trice [adaptatœr, -tris] **1** *nm* (*dispositif*) adapter
2 *nm,f* (*d'une œuvre*) adapter

adaptation [adaptasjɔ̃] *nf* **a** (*à une situation*) adaptation (**à** to); **faire un effort d'a.** to try to adapt; **faculté d'a.** adaptability **(b)** (*d'une œuvre*) adaptation; **a. théâtrale** stage adaptation

adapter [adapte] 1 *vt* (a) *(ajuster)* to adapt (à to); est-ce vraiment adapté à la situation? is it really suitable for the situation? (b) *(œuvre)* to adapt
2 s'adapter *vpr* (a) *(s'acclimater)* to adapt (à to); savoir s'a. to be very adaptable *or* flexible (b) *(être compatible)* la prise s'adapte à toutes les télévisions the plug fits all types of television

Addis-Abeba [adisabeba] *n* Addis Ababa

additif [aditif] *nm* (a) *(ajout)* addition (b) *(substance)* additive; sans additifs additive free

addition [adisjɔ̃] *nf* (a) *(fait d'ajouter)* addition, adding (à to); *(pour faire un total)* adding up; faire une a. to do a sum (b) *(extension)* addition, extension (c) *(au restaurant)* Br bill, Am check

additionnel, -elle [adisjɔnel] *adj* additional, extra; *Ordinat* add-on

additionner [adisjɔne] 1 *vt* to add (up); lait additionné d'eau watered-down milk; café additionné d'eau-de-vie coffee laced with brandy
2 s'additionner *vpr* to add up; aux longues heures de travail s'additionnent celles passées dans le métro along with the long working hours, there are those spent on the underground

adduction [adyksjɔ̃] *nf Tech* admission, intake; *Constr* a. d'eau canalization

adepte [adept] *nmf* *(d'une doctrine, d'une personnalité)* follower; *(d'une activité)* enthusiast; faire des adeptes to attract a following

adéquat, -e [adekwa, -at] *adj (personne, lieu, expression, méthode)* appropriate, suitable; *(montant, quantité)* adequate

adéquation [adekwasjɔ̃] *nf* appropriateness, suitability

adhérence [aderɑ̃s] *nf* adhesion, adherence; *(de pneus)* grip

adhérent, -e [aderɑ̃, -ɑ̃t] 1 *adj (substance, propriétés)* adhesive
2 *nm,f* member

adhérer [34] [adere] *vi* (a) *(coller)* to adhere, to stick (à to); à la route *(pneus)* to grip the road (b) a. à *(opinion, doctrine)* to subscribe to (c) *(s'inscrire)* a. à un parti to join a party

adhésif, -ive [adezif, -iv] *adj* adhesive, sticky

adhésion [adezjɔ̃] *nf* (a) *(accord)* support (à for) (b) *(inscription)* joining (à of)

ad hoc [adɔk] *adj & adv* ad hoc

adieu, -x [adjø] 1 *exclam* goodbye!, farewell!; dire a. à qn to say goodbye to sb; *Fam Fig* dire a. à qch to kiss *or* say goodbye to sth
2 *nm* farewell; faire ses adieux to say one's goodbyes; faire ses adieux à qn to say goodbye to sb

adipeux, -euse [adipø, -øz] *adj (tissu)* adipose; *(visage)* fat

adjacent, -e [adʒasɑ̃, ɑ̃t] *adj* adjacent (à to)

adjectif [adʒɛktif] *nm* adjective

adjoint, -e [adʒwɛ̃, -ɛ̃t] 1 *adj* assistant, deputy
2 *nm,f* assistant; a. au maire deputy mayor

adjonction [adʒɔ̃ksjɔ̃] *nf* addition; produit sans a. de sucre product with no added sugar

adjudant [adʒydɑ̃] *nm Br* warrant officer class II, *Am* warrant officer (junior grade); a.-chef *Br* warrant officer class I, *Am* chief warrant officer

adjudication [adʒydikasjɔ̃] *nf* sale by auction

adjuger [45] [adʒyʒe] 1 *vt* a. qch à qn *(prix, contrat)* to award sth to sb; *(aux enchères)* to knock sth down to sb; une fois, deux fois, trois fois, adjugé, vendu! going, going, gone!
2 s'adjuger *vpr* s'a. qch to appropriate sth

admettre [47] [admetr] *vt* (a) *(accueillir)* a. qn to admit sb, to let sb in; les chiens ne sont pas admis *(sur la porte d'un magasin)* no dogs allowed; être admis à l'université to win a place at university; être admis à un concours to pass an examination (b) *(accepter)* to allow; je n'admets pas qu'on me mente I won't tolerate being lied to; cette règle n'admet aucune exception there can be no exceptions to this rule (c) *(reconnaître)* to admit, to accept; admettons que ce soit possible assuming it's possible; admettons que j'ai tort *(pour clore une discussion)* I stand corrected

administrateur, -trice [administratœr, -tris] *nm,f* (a) *(d'une société, d'une banque)* director (b) *(de fondation)* trustee

administratif, -ive [administratif, -iv] *adj* administrative

administration [administrasjɔ̃] *nf* (a) *(d'affaires)* administration, management; *(d'un pays)* governing (b) *(ensemble des directeurs)* board of directors; *(d'une institution)* governing body (c) l'A. *(service public)* ≃ the Civil Service; *(fonctionnaires)* civil servants

administré, -e [administre] *nm,f* citizen

administrer [administre] *vt* (a) *(propriété)* to administer, to manage; *(pays)* to govern (b) *(justice)* to dispense; *Rel (sacrements)* to administer; *(remède)* to administer; je vais lui a. une bonne correction I'm going to give him/her a good hiding

admirable [admirabl] *adj* admirable; *(très compétent)* wonderful; elle a été a. de courage she showed admirable courage

admirablement [admirabləmɑ̃] *adv* admirably; *(très bien)* wonderfully; a. bien wonderfully

admirateur, -trice [admiratœr, -tris] *nm,f* admirer

admiratif, -ive [admiratif, -iv] *adj* admiring

admiration [admirasjɔ̃] *nf* admiration; avoir de l'a. pour qn to admire sb; être en a. devant qch to be filled with admiration for sth; tomber en a. devant qch to be stopped in one's tracks by the beauty of sth; faire l'a. de tous to be universally admired

admirer [admire] *vt* to admire

admis, -e [admi, -iz] 1 *adj* (a) *(autorisé à entrer)* admitted, allowed (in) (b) *(accepté)* allowed, accepted
2 *nm,f (à un examen)* successful candidate

admissible [admisibl] *adj (excuse, preuve, conduite)* admissible, allowable; (candidats) admissibles candidates who have qualified for the oral examination

admission [admisjɔ̃] *nf* (a) *(entrée)* admission (à/dans to) (b) *Tech* intake; *Aut* induction

ADN [adeɛn] *nm (abrév* acide désoxyribonucléique) DNA

ado [ado] *nmf Fam* teenager

adolescence [adolesɑ̃s] *nf* adolescence; pendant mon a. when I was a teenager

adolescent, -e [adolesɑ̃, -ɑ̃t] 1 *nm,f* adolescent, teenager
2 *adj* adolescent, teenage

adon [adɔ̃] *nm Can Fam* coincidence

adonner [adɔne] s'adonner *vpr* s'a. à qch to devote oneself to sth; s'a. à la boisson to be an alcoholic

adopter [adɔpte] vt (a) (enfant) to adopt (b) (accepter) to accept (c) (choisir) to adopt (d) (projet de loi, résolution) to adopt, to pass

adoptif, -ive [adɔptif, -iv] adj (enfant) adopted; (parent) adoptive

adoption [adɔpsjɔ̃] nf (a) (d'un enfant) adoption (b) (d'une idée, d'une mode) adoption; **mon pays d'a.** my adopted country (c) (d'un projet de loi) adoption, passing

adorable [adɔrabl] adj adorable, charming

adoration [adɔrasjɔ̃] nf aussi Fig adoration; **être en a. devant qn** to worship sb

adorer [adɔre] 1 vt aussi Fig to adore; **j'adore monter à cheval** I adore riding
 2 **s'adorer** vpr to adore each other

adosser [adose] 1 vt **a. qch à** ou **contre qch** to lean sth (with its back) against sth
 2 **s'adosser** vpr **s'a. à** ou **contre qch** to lean (back) against sth; **le village est adossé à la colline** the village stands at the foot of the hill

adoucir [adusir] 1 vt (a) (voix, eau, linge, peau) to soften; (contraste, couleur) to tone down; **sa nouvelle coiffure adoucit son visage** her new haircut softens her face (b) (douleur, chagrin) to ease; Prov **la musique adoucit les mœurs** music hath charms to soothe the savage breast
 2 **s'adoucir** vpr (a) (voix, ton) to soften (b) (personne, caractère) to mellow

adoucissant, -e [adusisɑ̃, -ɑ̃t] 1 adj softening
 2 nm (pour le linge) fabric softener

adoucisseur [adusisœr] nm (water) softener

adr. (abrév **adresse**) address

adrénaline [adrenalin] nf adrenalin(e)

adresse [adrɛs] nf (a) (coordonnées) address; **changer d'a.** to change one's address; Fig **tu te trompes d'a.** you've come to the wrong person; **il connaît de bonnes adresses** (de restaurants, de magasins) he knows all the good places to go to; **je l'ai dit à l'a. de ceux qui…** I said it for the benefit of those who…; **a. électronique** e-mail address (b) (habileté) skill; (savoir-faire) diplomacy; **avec a.** skilfully (c) Ordinat address; **a. virtuelle** virtual address

adresser [adrese] 1 vt (a) (lettre) to address; **a. qch à qn** to send sth to sb (b) (personne) **on m'a adressé à vous** I have been referred to you (c) **a. qch à qn** (compliments, remerciements) to present sth to sb; **cette remarque était adressée à Martin** that remark was aimed at or meant for Martin; **a. un sourire à qn** to smile at sb; **a. la parole à qn** to speak to sb
 2 **s'adresser** vpr **s'a. à qn** (sujet: personne) to speak to sb; (pour un renseignement) to ask sb; (sujet: remarque, recommandation) to apply to sb; **s'a. ici** (sur écriteau) enquire within

Adriatique [adrijatik] nf **l'A.** the Adriatic

adroit, -e [adrwa, -at] adj (a) (habile) skilful (b) (réponse, diplomate) shrewd, clever

adroitement [adrwatmɑ̃] adv skilfully

aduler [adyle] vt to worship

adulte [adylt] 1 adj (personne) adult, grown-up; (plante, animal) fully-grown
 2 nmf adult, grown-up

adultère [adylter] nm adultery

advenir [70] [advənir] v impersonnel (aux **être**) to happen; **or, il advint que…** it so happened that…; **quoi qu'il advienne** no matter what happens; **advienne que pourra** come what may

adverbe [adverb] nm adverb

adverbial, -e, -aux, -ales [adverbjal, -o] adj adverbial

adversaire [adverser] nmf opponent; (dans un conflit, dans une guerre) enemy

adverse [advers] adj (équipe) opposing; Jur **la partie a.** the other side

AELE [aɛlə] nf (abrév **Association européenne de libre-échange**) **l'A.** EFTA

aérateur [aeratœr] nm ventilator

aération [aerasjɔ̃] nf (d'une pièce) ventilation

aérer [34] [aere] 1 vt (a) (pièce, linge) to air (b) (texte, exposé) to lighten
 2 **s'aérer** vpr to get some fresh air

aérien, -enne [aerjɛ̃, -ɛn] adj (a) (défense, attaque, transport) air (b) (texture) (light and) airy; (grâce, allure) ethereal (c) (câble) overhead; (voie ferrée) elevated

aérobic [aerobik] nm aerobics (singulier)

aérodrome [aerodrom] nm aerodrome, airfield

aérodynamique [aerodinamik] adj (forme, voiture) streamlined

aérogare [aerogar] nf (air) terminal

aéroglisseur [aeroglisœr] nm hovercraft

aérogramme [aerogram] nm aerogramme, airmail letter

aéromodélisme [aeromodelism] nm making model aircraft

aéronautique [aeronotik] 1 adj aeronautic(al)
 2 nf aeronautics (singulier)

aéronaval, -e, -als, -ales [aeronaval] 1 adj (forces) air and sea
 2 nf **l'Aéronavale** Br ≃ the Fleet Air Arm, Am ≃ the Naval Air Service

aéronef [aeronef] nm aircraft

aérophagie [aerofaʒi] nf flatulence; **avoir** ou **faire de l'a.** to suffer from flatulence

aéroport [aeropor] nm airport

aéroporté, -e [aeroporte] adj airborne

aérosol [aerosol] nm aerosol; **vendu en a.** sold in spray form

aérospatial, -e, -aux, -ales [aerospasjal, -o] adj aerospace

aérostat [aerosta] nm (montgolfière) hot-air balloon; (dirigeable) airship

affabilité [afabilite] nf affability

affable [afabl] adj affable

affabulation [afabylasjɔ̃] nf fabrication

affabuler [afabyle] vi to make things up

affaiblir [afeblir] 1 vt (a) (sujet: maladie) to weaken (b) (réduire) to lessen, to reduce
 2 **s'affaiblir** vpr (personne) to get weaker; (vue, ouïe) to get worse, to deteriorate; (sentiment) to wane; (son) to grow fainter; **le sens du mot s'est affaibli** the word has lost much of its meaning

affaiblissement [afeblismɑ̃] nm (d'une personne, d'un gouvernement, de l'économie) weakening; (d'un sentiment) waning; (d'une lumière, d'un son) fading

affaire [afɛr] nf (a) (occupation) business, concern; **ce n'est pas votre a.** it's none of your business; **j'en fais mon a.** I'll handle it; **c'est une a. de goût** it's a matter or question of taste; **c'est l'a. d'une minute** it won't take a minute; **ça, c'est une autre a.** that's another matter; **avoir a. à qn** to be dealt with by sb; **s'il continue à mentir, il aura a. à moi!** if he carries on lying, he'll have me to deal with!

(b) (usage) **cela fera parfaitement l'a.** that will do nicely; **Fam faire son a. à qn** to do sb in

(c) (histoire, problème) affair, business; **une a. de pots-de-vin** a bribery scandal; **a. de cœur** love affair; **ça n'a pas été une mince a.** it wasn't easy; **c'est toute une a.** it's quite a business; **la belle a.!** big deal; **ça ne change rien à l'a.** that doesn't change anything; **tirer qn d'a.** to get sb out of trouble; **ce n'est pas une a. d'État!** it's no big deal!

(d) (transaction) deal; (achat à bon marché) bargain; **il a fait une a. en achetant cette voiture** he got a bargain when he bought that car; **faire a. avec qn** to make a deal with sb; **une a. en or** the bargain of the century

(e) (entreprise) firm, business

(f) **affaires** (effets personnels) things, belongings

(g) **les affaires** (activités commerciales) business (singulier); **comment vont les affaires?** how's business?; **il est dur en affaires** he's a hard-headed businessman; **les affaires sont les affaires** business is business

(h) **les Affaires étrangères** Br ≃ the Foreign (and Commonwealth) Office, Am ≃ the State Department

affairé, -e [afere] adj busy

affairer [afere] **s'affairer** vpr to busy oneself; **s'a. autour de qn** to fuss (a)round sb

affairiste [aferist] nmf wheeler-dealer

affaissement [afɛsmɑ̃] nm (de terrain) subsidence; (du plancher, d'une poutre) sagging

affaisser [afɛse] **s'affaisser** vpr (a) (s'enfoncer) (terrain) to subside; (poutre, fauteuil) to sag (b) (tomber, s'écrouler) to collapse

affalé, -e [afale] adj **être a. dans un fauteuil** to be slumped in an armchair

affaler [afale] **s'affaler** vpr to collapse

affamé, -e [afame] adj starving

affectation [afɛktasjɔ̃] nf (a) Péj (pose) affectation, affectedness; (simulacre) pretence, affectation; **avec a.** affectedly; **sans a.** unaffectedly (b) (de fonds, de crédits, de locaux) assignment, allocation (à) (à un poste) appointment (à to); (d'un soldat) posting (à to) (d) Ordinat (de touche) assignment; **a. de mémoire** memory allocation

affecté, -e [afɛkte] adj Péj (personne, manière) affected

affecter [afɛkte] vt (a) (fonds, crédits, locaux) to assign (à to), to allocate (à to) (b) (employé) to appoint (à to); (soldat) to post (à to) (c) (feindre) to affect; **a. de faire qch** to pretend to do sth (d) (émouvoir) to affect, to move (e) (frapper) (carrière, santé) to affect, to have an effect on; **la grève a affecté plusieurs usines** the strike has affected or hit several factories

affectif, -ive [afɛktif, -iv] adj emotional, Spéc affective

affection [afɛksjɔ̃] nf (a) (attachement) affection (pour for); **prendre qn en a.** to become fond of sb; **avoir de l'a. pour qn** to be fond of sb (b) Litt (maladie) ailment

affectionner [afɛksjɔne] vt to be fond of; **votre cousin affectionné** (dans une lettre) your affectionate cousin

affectivité [afɛktivite] nf feelings

affectueusement [afɛktyøzmɑ̃] adv affectionately; (dans une lettre) love (from)

affectueux, -euse [afɛktyø, -øz] adj affectionate

afférent, -e [aferɑ̃, -ɑ̃t] adj **a. à** (concernant) relating to

affermir [afɛrmir] **1** vt (a) (muscles, chairs) to tone (up) (b) (pouvoir, position, autorité) to strengthen, to consolidate **2 s'affermir** vpr (chairs, muscles) to tone up; (pouvoir, position, autorité) to be strengthened

affichage [afiʃaʒ] nm (a) (pose d'affiches) billsticking, billposting; **a. interdit** (sur panneau) stick no bills (b) Ordinat display; **montre à a. digital ou numérique** digital watch; **a. à cristaux liquides** liquid crystal display

affiche [afiʃ] nf notice; (de publicité) poster; **être à l'a.** (spectacle) to be on; **être en tête de l'a.** to be top of the bill; **a. électorale** election poster

afficher [afiʃe] **1** vt (a) (annonce, poster) to put up; (prix, honaires, résultats) to display; **défense d'a.** (sur panneau) stick no bills; **a. complet** (spectacle) to be sold out (b) (mépris, indifférence) to show, to display; (savoir) to flaunt; (déficit, excédent) to show (c) Ordinat (message) to display **2 s'afficher** vpr (a) (personne) to flaunt oneself (b) (sur écran) to be displayed

affichette [afiʃɛt] nf small notice; (publicitaire) poster

afficheur [afiʃœr] nm (personne) billsticker, billposter; (société) publicity company

affilée [afile] **d'affilée** adv in a row; **cinq heures d'a.** five hours solid or at a stretch

affiler [afile] vt to sharpen

affiliation [afiljasjɔ̃] nf joining (à of)

affilier [66] [afilje] **s'affilier** vpr to join; **s'a. à un parti** to join a party

affiner [afine] **1** vt (a) (métal) to refine; (fromage) to mature (b) (esprit) to sharpen; (goût) to refine **2 s'affiner** vpr (goût) to become more refined; (visage) to get thinner; (traits) to become better defined; (esprit) to become sharper

affinité [afinite] nf affinity (entre between)

affirmatif, -ive [afirmatif, -iv] **1** adj (a) (réponse) affirmative, positive; **faire un signe a. de la tête** to nod in agreement (b) (personne) positive **2** nf **dans l'affirmative** if so, if the answer is yes; **répondre par l'affirmative** to answer yes **3** exclam affirmative!

affirmation [afirmasjɔ̃] nf assertion

affirmer [afirme] **1** vt (a) (soutenir) to maintain; **il affirme vous connaître** he maintains that he knows you (b) (manifester) to assert; **a. sa volonté de faire qch** to declare one's willingness to do sth **2 s'affirmer** vpr (personnalité) to assert itself; (tendance, talent) to be confirmed

affleurer [aflœre] vi (récif) to be near the surface; Fig (mépris, racisme) to come to the surface; Géol (filon) to outcrop

affliction [afliksjɔ̃] nf affliction

affligé, -e [afliʒe] adj **a) être a. de** (atteint) to be afflicted with (b) (peiné) distressed

affligeant, -e [afliʒɑ̃, -ɑ̃t] adj (nouvelle, vision) distressing; (bêtise, ignorance, résultats) appalling

affliger [45] [aflige] 1 *vt* (a) (*atteindre*) to afflict; **région affligée par le choléra** area afflicted with cholera; **la nature l'a affligé d'un grand nez** nature has cursed him with a big nose (b) (*peiner*) (*sujet: nouvelle, événement*) to distress

2 **s'affliger** *vpr* to be distressed (**de** about)

affluence [aflyās] *nf* (*de personnes*) crowd; (*de marchandises*) abundance

affluent [aflyā] *nm* tributary

affluer [aflye] *vi* (*liquide*) to flow (**vers/dans** to/into); (*sang*) to rush (**à** to); (*foule*) to flock (**vers** to)

afflux [afly] *nm* (*de sang*) rush; (*de visiteurs*) flood; (*de capitaux*) influx

affolant, -e [afɔlā, -āt] *adj* (*spectacle, nouvelle*) distressing; *Fam* **c'est a.!** it's incredible!

affolé, -e [afɔle] *adj* (*personne*) panic-stricken

affolement [afɔlmā] *nm* panic; **pas d'a.!** don't panic!

affoler [afɔle] 1 *vt* to throw into a panic

2 **s'affoler** *vpr* (a) (*paniquer*) to panic (b) (*aiguille de boussole*) to spin (c) (*machine*) to race

affranchir [afrāʃir] 1 *vt* (a) (*lettre, colis*) to put a stamp/stamps on; (*avec une machine*) to frank (b) (*esclave*) to free

2 **s'affranchir** *vpr* (*peuple, personne*) to free oneself (**de** from)

affranchissement [afrāʃismā] *nm* (a) (*montant payé*) (*de lettre, paquet*) postage (b) (*d'un esclave*) freeing

affres [afr] *nfpl Litt* (*du doute, de la jalousie, de la faim*) pangs; **les a. de la mort** death throes

affréter [34] [afrete] *vt* to charter

affreusement [afrøzmā] *adv* horribly; **il parle a. mal l'anglais** his English is awful

affreux, -euse [afrø, -øz] *adj* (a) (*laid*) hideous (b) (*atroce*) (*nouvelle, pauvreté, crime*) dreadful (c) *Fam* (*épouvantable*) (*temps, migraine*) awful, dreadful; **qu'est-ce que ça a augmenté, c'est a.!** it's dreadful or shocking how the price has gone up!; **un a. jojo** a little horror

affriolant, -e [afrijɔlā, -āt] *adj* alluring

affront [afrō] *nm* affront, insult; **faire un a. à qn** to affront *or* insult sb

affrontement [afrōtmā] *nm* clash, confrontation

affronter [afrōte] 1 *vt* (*adversaire, danger, mort*) to face, to confront; **a. la colère de qn** to brave the wrath of sb

2 **s'affronter** *vpr* (*ennemis*) to clash; (*équipes, joueurs*) to clash; **deux thèses s'affrontent** there are two conflicting theories

affubler [afyble] 1 *vt* **a. qn de qch** to set sb up in sth

2 **s'affubler** *vpr* **s'a. de qch** to get oneself up in sth

affût [afy] *nm* (a) (*à la chasse*) **être à l'a.** to lie in wait; *Fig* **être à l'a. de qch** to be on the lookout for sth

affûter [afyte] *vt* to sharpen

afghan, -e [afgā, -an] 1 *adj* Afghan

2 *nm,f* A. Afghan

3 *nm* (*langue*) Afghan

Afghanistan [afganistā] *nm* **l'A.** Afghanistan

afin [afē] *adv* **a. de faire qch** (in order) to do sth, so as to do sth; **a. que** + *subjunctive* so that; **a. que les autres puissent le voir** so that the others may see it

AFNOR [afnɔr] *nf* (*abrév* **Association française de normalisation**) = French industrial standards authority, *Br* ≃ BSI, *Am* ≃ ANSI

a fortiori [aforsjɔri] *adv* all the more so

AF-P [aefpe] *nf* (*abrév* **Agence France-Presse**) = French international news agency

africain, -e [afrikē, -en] 1 *adj* African

2 *nm,f* A. African

Afrique [afrik] *nf* **l'A.** Africa; **l'A. du Nord** North Africa; **l'A. du Sud** South Africa

afro-américain, -e [afroamerikē, -en] (*mpl* afro-américains, *fpl* afro-américaines) 1 *adj* Afro-American, African American

2 *nm,f* A. Afro-American, African American

after-shave [aftɔrʃev] 1 *nm inv* aftershave

2 *adj* **lotion a.** aftershave (lotion)

A.G. [aʒe] *nf* (*abrév* **assemblée générale**) AGM

agaçant, -e [agasā, -āt] *adj* annoying, irritating

agacer [16] [agase] *vt* (a) (*énerver*) to annoy, to irritate; **il m'agace avec ses questions** he's getting on my nerves, asking all those questions (b) (*dents, nerfs*) to set on edge

agapes [agap] *nfpl Litt* feast; *Hum* **nous allons faire des a. chez Jeannot** we're going to have a real slap-up meal at Jeannot's

agate [agat] *nf* (*pierre*) agate; (*bille*) marble

âge [ɑʒ] *nm* (a) (*d'une personne*) age; **quel â. avez-vous?** how old are you?; **à ton â., je travaillais** when I was your age, I was working; **à l'â. de six ans** at the age of six; **on ne lui donne pas son â.** he doesn't look his age; **faire son â.** to look one's age; **un homme d'un grand â.** a very old man; **entre deux âges** middle-aged; **être en â. de faire qch**, **être d'â. à faire qch** to be old enough to do sth; **ce n'est plus de mon â.** I'm too old for that type of thing; **un whisky de quinze ans d'â.** a fifteen-year-old whisky; **l'â. adulte** adulthood; **l'â. bête** *ou* **ingrat** the awkward *or* difficult age; **l'â. mental** mental age; **une femme d'â. mûr** a mature woman; **avoir l'â. de raison** to have reached the age of reason (b) (*époque*) age; **l'â. de (la) pierre** the Stone Age; **l'â. d'or du cinéma muet** the golden age of silent movies

âgé, -e [ɑʒe] *adj* (a) (*qui a tel âge*) **être â. de dix ans** to be ten years old; **un enfant â. de deux ans** a two-year-old child (b) (*vieux*) old; **être plus/moins â. que qn** to be older/younger than sb

agence [aʒās] *nf* agency; (*de banque*) branch; **a. immobilière** *Br* estate agent's *or* agency, *Am* real estate agency; **a. matrimoniale** marriage bureau; **A. nationale pour l'emploi** = French national employment bureau, *Br* ≃ job centre; **a. de presse** press *or* news agency; **a. de voyages** travel agent's *or* agency

agencement [aʒāsmā] *nm* (*d'éléments*) arrangement; (*d'une maison, d'une pièce*) layout

agencer [16] [aʒāse] 1 *vt* (*éléments*) to arrange; (*maison, pièce*) to lay out, to design

2 **s'agencer** *vpr* **les parties du discours s'agencent bien/mal** the different parts of the speech hang/don't hang together well

agenda [aʒēda] *nm* diary; **a. électronique** personal organizer

agenouiller [aʒnuje] **s'agenouiller** *vpr* to kneel (down) (**devant** in front of)

agent [aʒā] *nm* (a) (*employé, espion*) agent; **a. (de police)** police officer; **pardon, Monsieur l'a.** excuse me, officer; **a. d'assurance(s)** insurance broker; **a. de change** stockbroker; **a. de la circulation** traffic policeman; **a. immobilier** *Br* estate agent, *Am* realtor; **a. secret** secret agent (b) (*facteur*) factor (c) *Gram* agent

agglomération [aglɔmerasjɔ̃] *nf (ville)* town, built-up area; **l'a. lyonnaise/parisienne** Lyons/Paris and its suburbs

aggloméré [aglɔmere] *nm* chipboard

agglomérer [34] [aglɔmere] 1 *vt* to bind together
2 **s'agglomérer** *vpr* to bind together

agglutiner [aglytine] **s'agglutiner** *vpr (personnes)* to congregate, to gather

aggravant, -e [agravɑ̃, -ɑ̃t] *adj* aggravating

aggravation [agravasjɔ̃] *nf (d'une maladie)* aggravation; *(du temps, d'un conflit)* worsening

aggraver [agrave] 1 *vt (situation, état de santé)* to make worse; *(difficultés)* to increase; **pour a. les choses** to make matters worse
2 **s'aggraver** *vpr (situation)* to get worse; *(état de santé)* to deteriorate; *(difficultés)* to increase

agile [aʒil] *adj* agile, nimble

agilement [aʒilmɑ̃] *adv* agilely, nimbly

agilité [aʒilite] *nf* agility

agios [aʒjo] *nmpl* bank charges

agir [aʒir] 1 *vi* (a) *(faire quelque chose)* to act; **bien/mal a. envers qn** to behave well/badly towards sb; **je n'aime pas sa façon *ou* manière d'a.** I don't like his behaviour (b) *(produire un effet) (médicament, substance)* to act (**sur** on); **a. sur le moral** to have a demoralizing effect (c) *Jur* **a. au nom de qn** to act on behalf of sb
2 **s'agir de** *v impersonnel* (a) *(être question de)* **de quoi s'agit-il?** what's it about?; **l'affaire dont il s'agit** the matter in hand; **il ne s'agit pas d'argent** it's not a question of money; **quand il s'agit d'aider, il est toujours occupé!** when it comes to helping, he always seems to be busy! (b) *(falloir)* **il s'agit de prendre une décision** we have to take a decision; **il s'agirait de savoir si...** the question is whether...; **il s'agirait de se dépêcher** we've got to hurry

agissements [aʒismɑ̃] *nmpl* dealings

agitateur, -trice [aʒitatœr, -tris] *nm,f Pol* agitator

agitation [aʒitasjɔ̃] *nf (inquiétude)* agitation; *(bougeotte)* restlessness; *(troubles)* unrest

agité, -e [aʒite] *adj (mer)* rough; *(patient, nuit)* restless; *(sommeil)* troubled; *(enfant)* fidgety; *(époque)* unsettled; *(vie)* hectic

agiter [aʒite] 1 *vt* (a) *(mouchoir, drapeau, bras)* to wave; *(bouteille)* to shake; *(sujet: vent) (arbre, branches)* to sway; **a. la queue** *(chien)* to wag its tail; *(cheval)* to flick its tail (b) *(inquiéter)* to trouble; *(malade)* to excite
2 **s'agiter** *vpr* (a) *(bouger)* to fidget; *(s'affairer)* to bustle around; **s'a. dans son sommeil** to toss and turn in one's sleep (b) *(s'énerver)* to get excited

agneau, -x [aɲo] *nm* lamb; **(peau d')a.** lambskin

agnelle [aɲɛl] *nf* ewe lamb

agnostique [agnɔstik] *adj & nmf* agnostic

agonie [agɔni] *nf aussi Fig* death throes; **être à l'a.** to be at death's door; *Fig (régime)* to be in its death throes

agonisant, -e [agɔnizɑ̃, -ɑ̃t] 1 *adj* dying
2 *nm,f* dying person

agoniser [agɔnize] *vi* to be dying; *Fig (régime)* to be in its death throes

agoraphobie [agɔrafɔbi] *nf Méd* agoraphobia; **souffrir d'a.** to be agoraphobic

agrafe [agraf] *nf* (a) *(de bureau)* staple; *(de robe)* hook; *Méd* clip (b) *Constr* cramp (iron)

agrafer [agrafe] *vt* (a) *(avec une agrafeuse)* to staple; *(robe)* to fasten (b) *Fam (arrêter)* to nick; **se faire a.** to get nicked

agrafeuse [agraføz] *nf* stapler

agraire [agrɛr] *adj (économie, société)* agrarian

agrandir [agrɑ̃dir] 1 *vt* (a) *(rendre plus grand)* to enlarge; *(maison, influence)* to extend; *(cercle de relations)* to widen (b) *(sujet: loupe, microscope)* to magnify; **ce papier peint agrandit la pièce** this wallpaper makes the room look bigger
2 **s'agrandir** *vpr (ville)* to grow, to get bigger; *(nombre, influence)* to increase; *(entreprise)* to expand

agrandissement [agrɑ̃dismɑ̃] *nm* (a) *(d'une maison)* extension; *(d'une ville)* growth; *(d'une entreprise)* expansion (b) *(cliché)* enlargement

agréable [agreabl] *adj (personne, endroit, journée)* nice, pleasant; *(apparence)* pleasing; **a. au goût** tasty; **a. à regarder** nice to look at

agréablement [agreablɑ̃mɑ̃] *adv* pleasantly

agréer [24] [agree] *vt (fournisseur, équipement)* to approve; **veuillez a. l'expression de mes sentiments distingués** *(à une personne dont on connaît le nom)* yours sincerely; *(à une personne dont on ne connaît pas le nom)* yours faithfully

agrégation [agregasjɔ̃] *nf* **(le concours de) l'a.** = competitive examination for posts on the teaching staff of lycées and universities

agrégé, -e [agreʒe] 1 *adj* = who has passed the agrégation examination
2 *nm,f* = graduate who has passed the agrégation examination

agrément [agremɑ̃] *nm* (a) *(plaisir)* **voyage d'a.** pleasure trip (b) *(charme)* **une ville sans a.** an unattractive town (c) *(accord)* approval, consent

agrémenter [agremɑ̃te] *vt* **a. qch de** *(décorer)* to adorn sth with; **texte agrémenté de citations** text spiced with quotations

agrès [agrɛ] *nmpl* (a) *Sp (gymnastics)* apparatus; **faire des a.** to do apparatus work (b) *Naut* tackle

agresser [agrese] *vt* to attack, to assault; *(en paroles)* attack; *(tympans)* to assault; *(yeux)* to hurt; *(peau)* to damage; **se faire a.** to be attacked; *(pour son argent)* to be mugged

agresseur [agresœr] *nm* attacker

agressif, -ive [agresif, -iv] *adj* aggressive

agression [agresjɔ̃] *nf (d'une personne)* attack, assault; *(pour son argent)* mugging; *(d'un pays)* act of aggression; **être victime d'une a.** to be attacked; *(pour son argent)* to be mugged; **les agressions de la vie moderne** the stresses of modern life

agressivement [agresivmɑ̃] *adv* aggressively

agressivité [agresivite] *nf* aggressiveness

agricole [agrikɔl] *adj* agricultural; *(population)* farming; *(produits)* farm

agriculteur, -trice [agrikyltœr, -tris] *nm,f* farmer

agriculture [agrikyltyr] *nf* farming, agriculture

agripper [agripe] 1 *vt* to clutch
2 **s'agripper** *vpr* to cling on (**à** to)

agroalimentaire [agroalimɑ̃tɛr] 1 *adj (industrie, secteur)* food
2 *nm* **l'a.** the food-processing industry

agronome [agrɔnɔm] *nmf* agronomist

agronomie [agrɔnɔmi] *nf* agronomy

agrume [agrym] *nm* citrus fruit

aguets [agɛ] **aux aguets** adv on the lookout; **être** ou **se tenir aux a.** to be on the lookout

aguichant, -e [agiʃɑ̃, -ɑ̃t] adj seductive

aguicher [agiʃe] vt to seduce

ahuri, -e [ayri] 1 adj astounded 2 nm,f numbskull

ahurissant, -e [ayrisɑ̃, -ɑ̃t] adj astounding

aide [ɛd] 1 nf help, assistance; **demander de l'a. à qn** to ask sb for help; **venir en a. à qn** to help sb; **appeler à l'a.** to call for help; **à l'a.! help!; à l'a. de qch** with the aid of sth; Ordinat **a. à la césure** hyphenation help; **a. de l'État** government aid; **a. humanitaire** aid; **a. judiciaire** legal aid; Ordinat **a. en ligne** on-line help; **a. sociale** Br social security, Am welfare
2 nmf assistant; **un a. de camp** aide-de-camp; **une a. familiale** a home help; **une a. ménagère** a home help

aide-mémoire [ɛdmemwar] nm inv aide-mémoire

aider [ede] 1 vt to help; (sujet: gouvernement) to aid; **que puis-je faire pour vous a.?** how may I help you?; **je me suis fait a. par un ami** I got a friend to help me; **a. qn à faire qch** to help sb to do sth; **a. qn à monter/sortir** to help sb up/out; Ironique **tu veux que je t'aide?** stop that!; **elle n'aide jamais** she never helps (out)
2 **aider à** vt ind to contribute towards; **a. à faire qch** to help to do sth
3 **s'aider** vpr (a) (soi-même) **s'a. de qch** to use sth; **marcher en s'aidant d'une canne/de béquilles** to walk with the aid of a stick/crutches; Prov **aide-toi et le ciel t'aidera** God helps those who help themselves (b) (l'un l'autre) to help each other

aide-soignant, -e (mpl aides-soignants, fpl aides-soignantes) [edswaɲɑ̃, -ɑ̃t] nm,f nursing auxiliary

aïe [aj] exclam (cri de douleur) ow!, ouch!; Fig **a., j'ai fait une gaffe!** oh no, I've put my foot in it!

aïeul [ajœl] nm,f, Vieilli grandfather, f grandmother, **aïeuls** grandparents

aïeux [ajø] nmpl Litt ancestors

aigle [ɛgl] nm eagle; Fig **ce n'est pas un a.** he's no genius; **avoir un œil d'a.** to be eagle-eyed

aiglefin [ɛgləfɛ̃] nm haddock

aigre [ɛgr] adj (goût, lait) sour; Fig (propos) cutting; **d'un ton a.** sharply

aigre-doux, -douce (mpl aigres-doux, fpl aigres-douces) [ɛgrədu, -dus] adj (sauce) sweet-and-sour; Fig (remarque) snide

aigrelet, -ette [ɛgrəlɛ, -ɛt] adj (vin, goût) (rather) sour; (son, voix) shrill

aigrette [ɛgrɛt] nf (a) (d'un oiseau) crest (b) (panache) plume

aigreur [ɛgrœr] nf (a) (d'un goût) sourness; (d'une remarque) sharpness, bitterness (b) Méd **aigreurs (d'estomac)** heartburn

aigri, -e [egri] adj embittered

aigu, -uë [egy] adj (a) (douleur) acute, sharp; (regard) penetrating; (esprit) keen; **avoir un sens a. de qch** to have a keen sense of sth (b) (instrument) sharp; (angle) acute (c) (son) high-pitched (d) Méd acute

aigue-marine (pl aigues-marines) [ɛgmarin] nf aquamarine

aiguillage [egɥijaʒ] nm (a) (manœuvre) Br shunting, Am switching; (appareil) Br points, Am switches (b) Fig **faire une erreur d'a.** to take the wrong course

aiguille [egɥij] nf (a) (instrument, objet pointu) needle; Fig **chercher une a. dans une botte de foin** to look for a needle in a haystack; **a. à coudre/repriser/tricoter** sewing/darning/knitting needle; Méd **a. hypodermique** hypodermic needle; **a. de pin** pine needle (b) (de boussole, de compteur de vitesse) needle; (de montre, d'horloge) hand; **petite a.** hour hand; **grande a.** minute hand (c) (d'une église) spire (d) (sommet) sharp peak

aiguiller [egɥije] vt (train) Br to shunt, Am to switch; Fig **a. qn vers** (profession) to steer sb towards; **a. ses recherches vers** to direct one's investigations towards; **a. la police sur une fausse piste** to put the police off the scent; **il a été mal aiguillé dans ses études** he was badly advised about his studies

aiguilleur [egɥijœr] nm (de trains) signalman; **a. du ciel** air-traffic controller

aiguillon [egɥijɔ̃] nm (a) (pique-bœuf) goad; Fig spur (b) (d'une guêpe) sting

aiguiser [egize] vt (a) (outil, couteau) to sharpen (b) Fig (curiosité, jalousie) to arouse; (appétit) to whet

aïkido [ajkido] nm aikido; **faire de l'a.** to do aikido

ail (pl ails [aj], Vieilli aulx [o]) nm garlic; Can **a. des bois** wild garlic

aile [ɛl] nf (a) (d'oiseau, de papillon) wing; Fig **battre de l'a.** to be struggling; **la peur nous donnait des ailes** fear lent us wings; Fam **avoir un coup dans l'a.** to have had a bit too much to drink (b) (d'une voiture) Br wing, Am fender; (d'un bâtiment) wing; (d'une armée) flank (c) (d'un avion) wing; (d'un moulin) sail; (d'une hélice, d'une turbine) blade (d) (au football, au rugby) wing

ailé, -e [ele] adj winged

aileron [ɛlrɔ̃] nm (a) (d'oiseau) pinion; (de requin) fin (b) Av aileron

ailette [ɛlɛt] nf (d'une turbine, d'un ventilateur) blade; (d'une bombe, d'un missile) wing, fin

ailier [elje] nm (au football) winger; (au rugby, au basket) wing

aille etc voir **aller**

ailler [aje] vt to put garlic in

ailleurs [ajœr] adv (a) (à un autre endroit) elsewhere, somewhere else; Fig **être a., avoir l'esprit a.** to be miles away; **partout a.** everywhere else; (n'importe où) anywhere else; **nulle part a.** nowhere else; **vous mangerez ici comme nulle part a.** you'll eat better here than anywhere else; Fam **va voir a. si j'y suis!** take a hike! (b) **d'a.** (de plus) besides, anyway; (au fait) by the way (c) **par a.** (par d'autres côtés) in other respects; (d'autre part) moreover

ailloli [ajoli] nm = **aïoli**

aimable [ɛmabl] adj (gentil) kind, nice; **vous êtes bien a., c'est très a. de votre part** it's very kind of you; **peu a.** (personne) not very nice; (propos) unkind

aimablement [ɛmabləmɑ̃] adv kindly

aimant¹ [ɛmɑ̃] nm magnet

aimant², -e [ɛmɑ̃, -ɑ̃t] adj (personne) loving

aimanter [ɛmɑ̃te] vt to magnetize

aimer [eme] 1 vt (a) (d'amour) to love (apprécier, avoir de l'affection pour) to like; **a. beaucoup qn/qch** to like sb/sth a lot, to be fond of sb/sth; **a. bien qn/qch** to like sb/sth; **a. faire qch** to like doing sth; **j'aurais aimé le voir** I would like to have seen him; **je n'aime pas que tu fréquentes ces gens** I don't like you mixing with those people; **j'aime(rais) autant ou mieux rester ici** I would rather stay here; **j'aime autant qu'il ne m'attende pas** I would rather he didn't wait for me; **a. mieux** to prefer; **ah, j'aime mieux ça!** now that's more like it!; *Fam* **j'aime mieux pas** I'd rather not; **je vais prendre un pot – qui m'aime me suive!** I'm going for a drink – anyone want to join me?

2 aimer à *vt ind Litt* **a. à faire qch** to take pleasure in doing sth; **j'aime à croire que...** I like to think (that)...

3 s'aimer *vpr* (*a*) (*l'un l'autre*) to love each other (*b*) (*être fier de soi*) to be in love with oneself; **je ne m'aime pas dans cette veste** I don't like myself in this jacket

aine [ɛn] *nf* groin

aîné, -e [ene] **1** *adj* (*de deux enfants*) elder; (*de plus de deux enfants*) eldest

2 *nmf* (*de deux enfants*) elder (child); (*de plus de deux enfants*) eldest (child); **nos aînés** our elders; **il est mon a.** he is older than me; **il est mon a. de deux ans** he is two years older than me

aînesse [ɛnɛs] *nf voir* **droit**

ainsi [ɛsi] *adv* (**a**) (*de cette façon*) like this, in this way; **c'est a. qu'il est devenu soldat** that's how he became a soldier; **et a. de suite** and so on, and so forth; **pour a. dire** so to speak, as it were; *Rel* **a. soit-il** amen (**b**) **a.** (*donc*) (*alors*) so; **a. vous ne venez pas?** so you're not coming? (**c**) (*par exemple*) for example, for instance (**d**) **a. que** (*et*) as well as, and

aïoli [ajɔli] *nm Culin* garlic mayonnaise

air [ɛr] *nm* (**a**) (*gaz*) air; **cela manque d'a. ici** it's stuffy in here; **faire de l'a.** to let some air in; **sortir prendre l'a.** to go out for some fresh air; **laisser qch à l'a.** to leave sth uncovered; **au grand a.** in the fresh air; **en plein a., à l'a. libre** outside; **concert en plein a.** open-air concert; **activités de plein a.** outdoor pursuits; *Fam* **allez, de l'a.!** go on, clear off!; **a. comprimé** compressed air; **avoir l'a. conditionné** to have air-conditioning (**b**) (*ciel*) **l'a.** the air; **s'élever dans les airs** to rise into the air; **regarder en l'a.** to look up (**c**) *Fig* (*atmosphère*) **changer d'a.** to have a change of scene; **il y a de la dispute/de l'orage dans l'a.** there's an argument/a storm brewing (**d**) (*vent*) **il y a** *ou* **il fait de l'a.** there's a breeze (**e**) (*allure*) look; (*mine*) expression; **avoir un drôle d'a.** to look odd or funny; **avoir l'a. fatigué/de s'ennuyer** to look tired/bored; *Fam* **avoir l'a. fin** to look daft; **tu as l'a. de ne pas comprendre** you look as if you don't understand; **n'avoir l'a. de rien** (*travail*) to look (deceptively) easy; **il n'a l'a. de rien, mais...** he doesn't look much, but...; **se donner** *ou* **prendre des airs** to give oneself airs; **ne prends pas tes grands airs!** don't get on your high horse!; **a. de famille** family likeness (**f**) (*musique*) tune; **un a. d'opéra** an (operatic) aria (**g**) (*locutions*) *Fam* **ficher qch en l'a.** to mess sth up; **mettre qch en l'a.** (*en désordre*) to make an awful mess of sth; **c'est dans l'a. du temps** it's the in-thing

air-air [ɛrɛr] *adj inv Mil* air-to-air

aire [ɛr] *nf* (**a**) (*surface plane*) area; **a.** (*de battage*) threshing floor; **a. d'atterrissage** (*pour avions*) landing strip; (*pour hélicoptères*) helipad; **a. de jeux** play area; **a. de lancement** (*de fusée*) launch pad; **a. de repos** (*sur l'autoroute*) rest area; **a. de stationnement** lay-by (**b**) (*d'un champ, d'un triangle, d'un bâtiment*) area; *Fig* **a. d'influence** sphere of influence (**c**) (*d'un aigle*) eyrie

airelle [ɛrɛl] *nf* (*rouge*) cranberry

air-sol [ɛrsɔl] *adj inv Mil* air-to-ground

aisance [ɛzɑ̃s] *nf* (**a**) (*facilité, grâce*) ease (**b**) (*financière*) **vivre dans l'a.** to live comfortably

aise [ɛz] **1** *nf* **être à l'a.** (*bien installé*) to be comfortable; (*avoir beaucoup de place*) to have plenty of room; (*financièrement*) to be comfortably off; (*dans une situation*) to feel comfortable *or* at ease; **on tient à l'a. à six dans cette voiture** this car holds six comfortably; *Fam* **à l'a.!** (*c'est facile*) easy!; **ne pas être à son a., sentir mal à l'a.** to feel uncomfortable; **mettre qn à l'a.** to put sb at his ease; **se mettre à l'a.** to make oneself comfortable; *Ironique* **elle peut en parler à son a.!** it's easy (enough) for her to say that!; **à ton a.!** suit yourself!; **prendre ses aises** to make oneself at home

2 *adj Litt* **être bien** *ou* **tout a.** to be delighted to do sth

aisé, -e [ɛze] *adj* (**a**) (*financièrement*) comfortably off (**b**) (*tâche, mouvements*) easy

aisément [ɛzemɑ̃] *adv* easily

aisselle [ɛsɛl] *nf* armpit

Aix-la-Chapelle [ɛkslaʃapɛl] *n* Aachen, Aix-la-Chapelle

AJ [aʒi] *nf* (*abrév* **auberge de jeunesse**) youth hostel

ajonc [aʒɔ̃] *nm* gorse

ajouré, -e [aʒure] *adj* (*pull*) loose-knit; (*broderie, en architecture*) openwork

ajourner [aʒurne] *vt* (*réunion, décision, voyage*) to postpone, to put off; (*après le début de la séance*) to adjourn; *Scol* (*candidat*) to refer

ajout [aʒu] *nm* addition (**à** to)

ajouter [aʒute] **1** *vt* to add (**à** to); *Ordinat* (*à une base de données*) to append

2 ajouter à *vt ind* to add to

3 s'ajouter *vpr* **s'a. à** to be added to; **à ceci viennent s'a. les frais de déplacement** on top of this there are travel expenses to be added

ajustable [aʒystabl] *adj* adjustable

ajustage [aʒystaʒ] *nm* fitting

ajuster [aʒyste] **1** *vt* (*a*) (*régler*) (*appareil, outil*) to adjust; (*chapeau, coiffure*) to adjust; **a. le tir** to aim (*b*) (*adapter*) to fit (**à** to); (*vêtement*) to alter; **veste ajustée** fitted jacket

2 s'ajuster *vpr* (*a*) (*personne*) to straighten one's clothes (*b*) (*s'adapter*) **s'a. à** to fit; **s'a. sur** to fit onto

ajusteur [aʒystœr] *nm* fitter

alaise [alɛz] *nf* undersheet

alambic [alɑ̃bik] *nm* still

alambiqué, -e [alɑ̃bike] *adj* convoluted

alangui, -e [alɑ̃gi] *adj* languid

alarmant, -e [alarmɑ̃, -ɑ̃t] *adj* alarming; **son état est a.** his condition is giving serious cause for concern

alarme [alarm] *nf* alarm; **donner/sonner l'a.** to give/sound the alarm; **une fausse a.** a false alarm; **a. antivol** car alarm; **a. incendie** fire alarm

alarmer [alarme] **1** *vt* to alarm

2 s'alarmer *vpr* to get alarmed; **il n'y a pas lieu de s'a.** there is no cause for alarm

albanais, -e [albanɛ, -ɛz] **1** *adj* Albanian

2 *nmf*, **A.** Albanian

3 *nm* (*langue*) Albanian

Albanie [albani] *nf* **l'A.** Albania

albâtre [albɑtr] *nm* alabaster

albatros [albatros] *nm* albatross

albinos [albinos] *adj & nmf* albino

album [albɔm] *nm* album; **a. de timbres/de photos** stamp/photo album

albumen [albymɛn] *nm Biol* albumen

albumine [albymin] *nf Chim* albumin

alcalin, -e [alkalɛ̃, -in] *adj Chim* alkaline

alchimie [alʃimi] *nf* alchemy

alchimiste [alʃimist] *nm* alchemist

alcool [alkɔl] *nm* (a) *Chim* alcohol; **à 90°** *Br* surgical spirit, *Am* rubbing alcohol; **a. à brûler** methylated spirits (b) *(digestif)* liqueur; **l'a.** *(boissons alcoolisées)* alcohol; **il ne tient pas l'a.** he can't hold his drink; **l'a. au volant** drink-driving; **a. de poire** pear brandy

alcoolémie [alkɔlemi] *nf* **taux d'a.** blood alcohol level

alcoolique [alkɔlik] *adj & nmf* alcoholic; **être a.** to be an alcoholic

alcoolisé, -e [alkɔlize] *adj* alcoholic

alcoolisme [alkɔlism] *nm* alcoholism

alcolo [alkɔlo] *adj & nmf Fam* drunk, alky; **être a.** to be a drunk

Alcotest® [alkɔtɛst] *nm* breath test; **faire passer un A. à qn** to breathalyze sb

alcôve [alkov] *nf* recess *(for bed)*

aléa [alea] *nm* hazard

aléatoire [aleatwar] *adj* random; *(résultat)* uncertain

alémanique [alemanik] *adj* **la Suisse a.** German-speaking Switzerland

ALENA [alena] *nm (abrév* **Accord de libre-échange nord-américain)** l'A. NAFTA

alentour [alɑ̃tur] **1** *adv* around, round about; **les villages a.** the surrounding villages
2 alentours *nmpl (voisinage)* surroundings; **aux alentours** in the vicinity; **aux alentours de la ville/300 francs** in the vicinity of the town/300 francs; **aux alentours de midi** (some time) around midday

Aléoutiennes [aleusjɛn] *adj & nfpl* **les (îles) A.** the Aleutian Islands

alerte [alɛrt] **1** *nf* (a) *(avertissement)* alarm; **donner/sonner l'a.** to give/sound the alarm; **a. à la bombe** bomb scare (b) *(menace)* threat; *(problème de santé)* scare; **à la première a.** at the first sign of danger; **fausse a.** false alarm
2 *adj (personne) (physiquement)* sprightly; *(mentalement)* alert; *(esprit, style)* lively; **d'un pas a.** at a brisk pace
3 *(exclam)* look out!

alerter [alɛrte] *vt* to alert **(sur** to)

alèse [alɛz] = **alaise**

alevin [alvɛ̃] *nm* young fish

Alexandre [alɛksɑ̃dr] *npr* **A. le Grand** Alexander the Great

Alexandrie [alɛksɑ̃dri] *n* Alexandria

alexandrin [alɛksɑ̃drɛ̃] *nm* alexandrine

alezan, -e [alzɑ̃, -an] **1** *adj (cheval)* chestnut
2 *nm* chestnut *(horse)*

algèbre [alʒɛbr] *nf* algebra

algébrique [alʒebrik] *adj* algebraic

Alger [alʒe] *n* Algiers

Algérie [alʒeri] *nf* **l'A.** Algeria

algérien, -enne [alʒerjɛ̃, -ɛn] **1** *adj* Algerian
2 *nm,f* **A.** Algerian

algérois, -e [alʒerwa, -az] **1** *adj* of Algiers
2 *nm,f* **A.** person from Algiers

algorithme [algɔritm] *nm Math & Ordinat* algorithm; *Ordinat* **a. de tri** sorting algorithm

algue [alg] *nf* piece of seaweed; **algues** seaweed

alias [aljɑs] *adv* alias

alibi [alibi] *nm* alibi

aliénation [aljenasjɔ̃] *nf* (a) *(de l'esprit)* alienation; *Psy* **a. mentale** insanity (b) *(de liberté)* loss; *Jur (des droits, de biens)* alienation

aliéné, -e [aljene] **1** *adj* insane
2 *nm,f* insane person

aliéner [34] [aljene] **1** *vt* (a) *(personne)* to alienate; **ce commentaire vous a aliéné la sympathie de l'auditoire** you lost the audience's sympathy when you made that comment (b) *Jur (biens, droits)* to alienate
2 s'aliéner *vpr* **s'a. la sympathie de l'électorat** to lose the goodwill of the electorate; **s'a. un ami** to alienate a friend

alignement [aliɲmɑ̃] *nm* (a) *(opération)* alignment, aligning; *Pol (sur un pays, une politique)* alignment **(sur** with); (b) *(ligne)* line; **être dans l'a. de qch** to be in line with sth (c) *(de monolithes)* = line of standing stones

aligner [aliɲe] **1** *vt* (a) *(mettre en ligne)* to align, to line up; *(politique, monnaie)* to align **(sur** with); (b) *(mettre à la suite) (arguments)* to reel off; **je passe ma journée à a. des chiffres** I spend my day producing lists of figures
2 s'aligner *vpr (se mettre en rang)* to line up; *Pol (sur un pays, une politique)* to align oneself **(sur** with); *Fam* **tu peux toujours t'a.!** not a chance!

aliment [alimɑ̃] *nm* (a) *(nourriture)* food (b) *Jur* **aliments** alimony

alimentaire [alimɑ̃tɛr] *adj* (a) *(plante)* edible; **habitudes alimentaires** eating habits; **l'industrie a.** the food industry *Fig* **ce n'est qu'un travail a.** I just do this job to keep body and soul together

alimentation [alimɑ̃tasjɔ̃] *nf* (a) *(régime alimentaire)* diet; **avoir une a. équilibrée** to have a balanced diet; **(magasin d')a.** grocer's; **(rayon) a.** grocery department (b) *(action) (de personne, de plante, d'animal)* feeding; *(d'une ville, d'un marché)* supply; **l'a. d'une ville en eau** the water supply to a town (c) *Tech (d'une chaudière)* feeding; *(en électricité)* power supply; **a. papier** *(d'une imprimante)* sheetfeed, paper feed

alimenter [alimɑ̃te] **1** *vt (personne, plante, animal, chaudière)* to feed; *(cours d'eau)* to flow into; *Fin (compte)* to pay money into; *Fig (conversation)* to keep going; *(sentiment)* to fuel; **a. une usine en courant** to supply a factory with power
2 s'alimenter *vpr* to eat

alinéa [alinea] *nm* (a) *(renfoncement)* indent (b) *(texte)* paragraph

aliter [alite] **s'aliter** *vpr* to take to one's bed; **être alité** *(temporairement)* to be confined to one's bed; *(grabataire)* to be bedridden

alizé [alize] *adj & nm* **les (vents) alizés** the trade winds

Allah [ala] *npr* Allah

allaitement [alɛtmɑ̃] *nm* feeding; *(d'un animal)* suckling; **a. au biberon** bottle-feeding; **a. maternel** breast-feeding

allaiter [alɛte] *vt (enfant)* to breast-feed; *(sujet: animal)* to suckle; **est-ce que vous allaitez?** are you breast-feeding?

allant [alɑ̃] *nm* **avoir de l'a., être plein d'a.** to be full of energy

alléchant, -e [aleʃɑ̃, -ɑ̃t] *adj (offre)* tempting; *(odeur, plat)* appetizing

allécher [34] [aleʃe] *vt* to tempt

allée [ale] *nf* (a) *(dans un jardin)* path; *(devant une résidence)* driveway; *(dans une ville)* avenue; *(dans un supermarché, un cinéma)* aisle (b) **allées et venues** coming(s) and going(s); **faire des allées et venues** to go back and forth

allégation [alegasjɔ̃] *nf* allegation

allégé, -e [aleʒe] *adj (en matières grasses)* low-fat; *(en sucre)* low-sugar

allègement [alɛʒmɑ̃] *nm* (a) *(d'impôts, de charges)* reduction; *(des emplois de temps scolaires)* streamlining; **a. fiscal** tax relief (b) *(d'un véhicule, d'un fardeau)* lightening

alléger [59] [aleʒe] *vt* (a) *(impôts, charges)* to reduce; *(douleur, chagrin)* to soothe (b) *(véhicule, fardeau)* to lighten; *(emploi du temps scolaire)* to streamline

allégorie [alegɔri] *nf* allegory

allégorique [alegɔrik] *adj* allegorical

allègre [alɛgr] *adj* lively, cheerful; **d'un ton a.** cheerfully, light-heartedly; **d'un pas a.** with a spring in one's step

allègrement [alɛgrəmɑ̃] *adv* cheerfully; *(marcher)* with a spring in one's step; **il m'a a. refilé ses enfants pour le week-end** he cheerfully palmed his children off on me for the weekend

allégresse [alegrɛs] *nf* joy; **a. générale** general rejoicing

alléluia [aleluja] *nm & exclam Rel* hallelujah

Allemagne [alman] *nf* l'A. Germany; *Anciennement* l'A. de l'Ouest/de l'Est West/East Germany

allemand, -e [almɑ̃, -ɑ̃d] 1 *adj* German
2 *nm,f* A. German; *Anciennement* A. de l'Est/de l'Ouest East/West German
3 *nm (langue)* German

aller¹ [8] [ale] *(aux être)* 1 *vi* (a) *(se déplacer)* to go; **a. à Toulon** to go to Toulon; **ce train va à Lille** this train goes to Lille; **a. à la pêche** to go fishing; **a. et venir** to come and go
(b) *(sujet: chemin, route)* **a.** à to go to
(c) *(arriver)* **a. jusqu'à** *(dans l'espace)* to go as far as; *(dans le temps)* to last until; **jusqu'où ira-t-il?** *(pour atteindre son but)* to what lengths will he go?; **a. jusqu'à faire qch** to go so far as to do sth
(d) *(fonctionner)* to go; *(bien fonctionner)* to go well; **si tu touches à mes affaires, ça va a. mal!** touch my things and there'll be trouble!; **ça va** *(comme ça)*, **merci** *(à table)* that's enough, thanks; **je vous en offre 100 francs, ça va?** I'll give you 100 francs for it, OK?; *Fam* **non mais ça va pas(, la tête)!** are you crazy?
(e) *(se porter)* **a. bien/mal** to be well/ill; **comment allez-vous?** how are you?; **ça va? - ça va!** how's things? - OK!
(f) *(indique le but)* **a. faire qch** to go and do sth; **a. se coucher** to go to bed; **a. se promener** to go for a walk; **va voir!** go and see!; **n'allez pas vous imaginer que...** don't you go thinking that...
(g) *(convenir)* **a. à qn** to suit sb; **a. bien à qn** *(vêtement, couleur)* to look good on sb; **a. (bien) avec qch** *(vêtement, couleur)* to go (well) with sth, to match sth; *Fam* **ça lui va mal de donner des conseils** he's a fine one to be giving advice
(h) *(se ranger, s'adapter)* **où vont les couteaux?** where do the knives go *or* belong?; **un plat qui va au four** an ovenproof dish
(i) *(agir)* **il est allé un peu vite dans cette affaire** he was a bit hasty; *Fam* **vas-y doucement** take it easy; *Fam* **comme tu y vas!** that's a bit much!
(j) *(locutions)* **y a.** *(partir)* to go; *(commencer)* to get on with it; **allez!** *(pour encourager)* come on!; *(pour consoler)* come now!; **allons!** *(pour encourager, réprimander)* come on!; **ça passera, va** don't worry, you'll get over it; **va pour 1000 francs/mardi prochain** 1,000 francs/next Tuesday, that's fine; **a. de soi** to be obvious; **a. sur ses quarante ans** to be nearing forty
2 *v aux* (a) *(indique le futur proche)* **a. faire qch** to be going to do sth; **il va s'en occuper** he's going to deal with it; **j'allais m'endormir quand...** I was about to fall asleep when... (b) *(indique la progression)* **a. en empirant** to be getting worse and worse
3 *v impersonnel* **il en va de même pour moi/lui** it's the same for me/him
4 **s'en aller** *vpr* (a) *(personne)* to go (away) (b) *(tache)* to come out; *(couleur)* to fade; *(peinture)* to flake off

aller² *nm (trajet)* outward journey; **à l'a.** on the way there (b) *(billet)* **a. (simple)** *Br* single (ticket), *Am* round-trip (ticket); *Fam Fig* **un a. et retour** *(gifle)* a slap on the face

allergie [alerʒi] *nf* allergy; **avoir** *ou* **faire une a. à qch** to be allergic to sth

allergique [alerʒik] *adj aussi Fig* allergic (à to)

allergologiste [alergɔloʒist], **allergologue** [alergɔlɔg] *nmf Méd* allergist

alliage [aljaʒ] *nm (métallique)* alloy

alliance [aljɑ̃s] *nf* (a) *(entente)* alliance; *(d'un couple)* marriage; **parent par a.** relative by marriage (b) *(bague)* wedding ring (c) *(combinaison)* *(de parfums, de couleurs)* combination

allié, -e [alje] 1 *nm,f (partisan)* ally; **parents et alliés** extended family; *Hist* **les Alliés** the Allies
2 *adj* (a) *(nation)* allied (b) *Hist* Allied

allier [66] [alje] 1 *vt* (a) *(pays)* to ally; *(familles)* to unite by marriage (b) *(métaux)* to alloy; *(couleurs)* to combine; **a. l'intelligence à la beauté** to combine intelligence and beauty
2 **s'allier** *vpr* (a) *(s'unir)* to become allies (avec with); **s'a. contre qn/qch** to unite against sb/sth (b) *(goûts, parfums, couleurs)* to combine

alligator [aligatɔr] *nm* alligator

allitération [aliterasjɔ̃] *nf* alliteration; **a. en s** alliteration of the letter s

allô, allo [alo] *exclam* hello!

allocation [alɔkasjɔ̃] *nf* (a) *(d'argent, de terres)* allocation; *(de titres financiers)* allotment (b) *(prestation financière)* allowance; **les allocations (familiales)** child benefit; **a. (de) chômage** unemployment benefit; **a. (de) logement** housing benefit

allocs [alɔk] *nfpl Fam* child benefit

allocution [alɔkysjɔ̃] *nf* address

allongé, -e [alɔ̃ʒe] *adj (forme, silhouette)* elongated; **avoir le visage a.** to have a long face (b) *(couché)* **être a.** to be lying down

allongement [alɔ̃ʒmɑ̃] *nm* (a) *(agrandissement)* lengthening (b) *(dans le temps)* extension; **a. de l'espérance de vie** increase in life expectancy

allonger [45] [alɔ̃ʒe] **1** *vt* (a) *(rendre plus long)* to lengthen; *(vêtement)* to let down; *(sauce)* to thin (down); **cette robe allonge la silhouette** this dress makes you look taller (b) *(bras)* to stretch out; *(cou)* to crane; **a. le pas** to quicken one's pace; *Sp* **a. l'allure** to increase the pace (c) *(personne)* to lie down (d) *(vacances, délai)* to extend (e) *Fam* **a. une gifle à qn** to give sb a slap; **a. le fric/1000 balles** to hand over the money/1,000 francs
2 *vi (jours)* to get longer
3 s'allonger *vpr* (a) *(ombres, jours)* to get longer; *Fig (enfant)* to grow (b) *(se coucher)* to lie down; *Fam* **s'a. (par terre)** *(tomber)* to fall flat on the ground

allopathie [alɔpati] *nf Méd* allopathy

allouer [alwe] *vt* **a. qch à qn** *(salaire, indemnité, délai)* to grant sb sth; *(actions, ration)* to allocate sb sth

allumage [alymaʒ] *nm (d'un feu)* lighting; *(d'une lampe)* switching on; *(d'un moteur)* ignition

allume-cigare (*pl* **allume-cigares**) [alymsigar] *nm* cigar lighter

allume-gaz [alymgaz] *nm inv* gas lighter

allumer [alyme] **1** *vt* (a) *(cigarette, briquet, feu)* to light; *(lampe, télévision, électricité)* to switch on, to turn on; *(incendie)* to start; **a. (la lumière)** to switch *or* turn the light on; **a. le salon** to switch *or* turn the light on in the lounge; **laisser la cuisinière allumée** to leave the cooker on (b) *Fig (passions)* to arouse; *Fam (séduire)* to tease
2 s'allumer *vpr (lumière, lampe, téléviseur)* to come on; **où est-ce que ça s'allume?** where does it switch *or* turn on?

allumette [alymɛt] *nf* match

allumeuse [alymøz] *nf Fam* prick-teaser

allure [alyr] *nf* (a) *(vitesse)* speed; **à toute a.** at top speed (b) *(démarche)* walk, gait; *(manière de se tenir)* bearing; **avoir de l'a.** to be stylish; **avoir fière a.** to cut a fine figure; **avoir une drôle d'a.** to look funny; **avoir des allures de malfrat** to look like a crook

allusion [alyzjɔ̃] *nf* allusion (à to); **faire a.** à to refer to, to allude to

alluvial, -e, -aux, -ales [alyvjal, -o] *adj* alluvial

alluvions [alyvjɔ̃] *nfpl* alluvium

almanach [almana] *nm* almanac

aloès [alɔɛs] *nm* aloe

aloi [alwa] *nm* **de bon a.** *(succès)* deserved; *(plaisanterie)* in good taste; **de mauvais a.** *(succès)* undeserved; *(plaisanterie)* in bad taste

alors [alɔr] *adv* (a) *(à ce moment-là)* then; *(dans ce cas)* then, in that case; **jusqu'a.** (up) until then; **le ministre d'a.** the minister at the time; **a. a.?** so what?; **a., qu'est-ce qu'il a répondu?** so what did he say?; *Fam* **a., tu viens?** so are you coming?; *Fam* **non mais a., pour qui il se prend, celui-là?** really, just who does he think he is?; *Fam* **ça a.!** blimey! (b) *(donc)* so; **il n'était pas là, a. je suis revenu** he wasn't there, so I came back (c) **a. que** *(au moment où)* when; *(bien que)* even though; **il a une maison, a. que moi j'habite dans un appartement** he's got a house, whereas I live in a flat

alouette [alwɛt] *nf* lark

alourdir [alurdir] **1** *vt (chose)* to make heavier; *Fig (phrase)* to make cumbersome; *(charges sociales)* to increase
2 s'alourdir *vpr* to get heavy; *(taille)* to get bigger

aloyau, -x [alwajo] *nm* sirloin

alpaga [alpaga] *nm* alpaca

alpage [alpaʒ] *nm* mountain pasture

alpaguer [alpage] *vt très Fam* to collar; **se faire a. par qn** to get collared by sb

Alpes [alp] *nfpl* **les A.** the Alps; **les A. suisses** the Swiss Alps

alphabet [alfabɛ] *nm* alphabet

alphabétique [alfabetik] *adj* alphabetical

alphabétiquement [alfabetikmɑ̃] *adv* alphabetically

alphabétisation [alfabetizasjɔ̃] *nf* teaching of literacy

alphanumérique [alfanymerik] *adj* alphanumeric

alpinage [alfapaʒ] *nm* bleeper

alpin, -e [alpɛ̃, -in] *adj* alpine

alpinisme [alpinism] *nm* mountaineering, climbing; **faire de l'a.** to go mountaineering *or* climbing

alpiniste [alpinist] *nmf* mountaineer, climber

Alsace [alzas] *nf* **l'A.** Alsace

alsacien, -enne [alzasjɛ̃, -ɛn] **1** *adj* of Alsace, Alsatian
2 *nm, f* **A.** Alsatian

altercation [alterkasjɔ̃] *nf* altercation

alter ego [alterego] *nm inv* alter ego

altérer [34] [altere] *vt* (a) *(détériorer) (viande, vin)* to spoil; *(santé)* to damage (b) *(changer)* to affect

alternance [alternɑ̃s] *nf* alternation; *Pol* change of government; **en a.** alternately

alternateur [alternatœr] *nm Él* alternator

alternatif, -ive [alternatif, -iv] **1** *adj* (a) *(successif)* & *Él* alternating (b) *(de remplacement)* alternative
2 *nf* **alternative** alternative

alternativement [alternativmɑ̃] *adv* alternately, in turn

alterner [alterne] **1** *vt (cultures)* to rotate
2 *vi (se succéder)* to alternate (**avec** with); *(personnes)* to take turns (**avec** with)

altesse [altɛs] *nf* **son A. royale** His/Her Royal Highness

altier, -ère [altje, -ɛr] *adj* haughty

altimètre [altimɛtr] *nm* altimeter

altitude [altityd] *nf* altitude; **à basse/haute a.** at low/ high altitude; **à 100 mètres d'a.** at an altitude of 100 metres; **en a.** at altitude; **prendre de l'a.** to climb

alto [alto] *Mus* **1** *nm (instrument)* viola
2 *nf (chanteuse)* alto

altruisme [altrɥism] *nm* altruism

altruiste [altrɥist] *adj* altruistic

aluminium [alyminjɔm] *nm* aluminium

alunir [alynir] *vi* to land on the moon

alunissage [alynisaʒ] *nm* moon landing

alvéole [alveɔl] *nf (de ruche)* cell; *(pulmonaire)* alveolus; *(de dent)* socket

amabilité [amabilite] *nf* kindness; **auriez-vous l'a. de me le faire savoir?** would you be so kind as to let me know?

amadouer [amadwe] *vt* to coax

amaigrir [amegrir] **1** *vt* to make thin; **la maladie l'a beaucoup amaigri** he's much thinner following his illness
2 s'amaigrir *vpr* to get thinner

amaigrissant, -e [amegrisɑ̃, -ɑ̃t] *adj (régime)* slimming

amaigrissement [amegrismɑ̃] *nm (involontaire)* weight loss; *(volontaire)* slimming

amalgame [amalgam] *nm* combination

amalgamer [amalgame] *vt (confondre)* to lump together

amanché, -e [amɑ̃ʃe] *adj Can* **mal a.** badly dressed

amande [amɑ̃d] *nf (fruit)* almond; *(dans un noyau)* kernel; **des yeux en a.** almond(-shaped) eyes

amandier [amɑ̃dje] *nm* almond tree

amanite [amanit] *nf* **a. phalloïde** death cap; **a. tue-mouches** fly agaric

amant [amɑ̃] *nm* lover

amarrage [amaraʒ] *nm Naut* mooring

amarre [amar] *nf Naut* (mooring) rope; **rompre ses amarres** to break its moorings

amarrer [amare] *vt Naut* to moor

amaryllis [amarilis] *nf* amaryllis

amas [ama] *nm* heap, pile

amasser [amase] **1** *vt* to amass
2 s'amasser *vpr (preuves, foule)* to build up; *(neige)* to pile up; *(troupes)* to mass

amateur [amatœr] **1** *nm* **(a)** *(passionné)* **a. de tennis/de jardinage** tennis/gardening enthusiast; **a. d'art** art lover; **a. de bons vins** connoisseur of fine wines; *Fig* **est-ce qu'il y a des amateurs?** any takers?; **avis aux amateurs!** anyone interested? **(b)** *(non professionnel)* amateur; **faire de la photo en a.** to be an amateur photographer; *Péj* **c'est du travail d'a.** it's amateurish work
2 *adj* **photographe a.** amateur photographer

amateurisme [amatœrism] *nm* amateurism

Amazone [amazon] *nf* **l'A.** the Amazon

amazone [amazon] *nf* **(a)** *(dans la mythologie)* **les Amazones** the Amazons **(b)** *(cavalière)* horsewoman; **monter en a.** to ride side-saddle

Amazonie [amazoni] *nf* **l'A.** the Amazon (Basin)

amazonien, -enne [amazonjɛ̃, -ɛn] *adj* Amazonian; *(forêt)* Amazon

ambages [ɑ̃baʒ] **sans ambages** *adv* without beating about the bush

ambassade [ɑ̃basad] *nf* embassy; **l'a. de France au Japon** the French embassy in Japan

ambassadeur, -drice [ɑ̃basadœr, -dris] **1** *nm,f* ambassador; **l'a. de France au Japon** the French ambassador to Japan; *Fig* **être l'a. de son pays** to be an ambassador for one's country
2 *nf* **ambassadrice** *(épouse)* ambassador's wife

ambiance [ɑ̃bjɑ̃s] *nf* atmosphere, ambience; *Fam* **mettre de l'a.** to liven things up; *Fam* **il y a de l'a. ici** there's a good atmosphere here

ambiant, -e [ɑ̃bjɑ̃, -ɑ̃t] *adj (gaieté, enthousiasme)* pervading; **température ambiante** room temperature

ambidextre [ɑ̃bidɛkstr] *adj* ambidextrous

ambigu, -uë [ɑ̃bigy] *adj* ambiguous

ambiguïté [ɑ̃biguite] *nf* ambiguity; **répondre sans a.** to give an unambiguous answer

ambitieux, -euse [ɑ̃bisjø, -øz] **1** *adj* ambitious
2 *nm,f* ambitious person

ambition [ɑ̃bisjɔ̃] *nf* ambition; **avoir de l'a.** to be ambitious; **j'ai l'a. de devenir médecin** my ambition is to be a doctor

ambitionner [ɑ̃bisjone] *vt* to aspire to; **il ambitionne de gagner le Tour de France** his ambition is to win the Tour de France

ambivalent, -e [ɑ̃bivalɑ̃, -ɑ̃t] *adj* ambivalent

ambre [ɑ̃br] *nm (résine)* amber

ambulance [ɑ̃bylɑ̃s] *nf* ambulance

ambulancier, -ère [ɑ̃bylɑ̃sje, -ɛr] *nm,f* ambulance-man, *f* ambulancewoman

ambulant, -e [ɑ̃bylɑ̃, -ɑ̃t] *adj* itinerant, travelling; *Fam* **c'est un dictionnaire a.** he's a walking dictionary

âme [ɑm] *nf* **(a)** *Rel & Phil* soul; *Fig (animateur)* moving spirit; **être artiste dans l'â.** to have an artistic temperament; **rendre l'â.** to give up the ghost; **aller comme une â. en peine** to wander around like a lost soul; **trouver l'â. sœur** to find one's soul mate; **de toute mon â.** with all my heart; **ils ne rencontrèrent â. qui vive** they didn't meet a (living) soul; **un hameau de cinquante âmes** a hamlet of fifty inhabitants; **â. damnée** devoted servant; *Hum* partner in crime **(c)** *(d'un câble)* core

amélioration [ameljorasjɔ̃] *nf* improvement; **apporter des améliorations à qch** to make improvements to sth

améliorer [ameljore] **1** *vt* to improve
2 s'améliorer *vpr* to improve; **ça ne s'améliore pas** it's not getting any better

amen [amen] *inv* **am** *inv*; *Fig* **dire â. à qch** to go along with sth

aménagement [amenaʒmɑ̃] *nm (changement)* adjustment; *(d'une pièce)* conversion **(en** into); *(d'une ville, d'une région)* development; **a. du temps de travail** flexibility of working hours; **a. du territoire** regional development, physical planning

aménager [45] [amenaʒe] *vt (changer)* to adjust; *(pièce, maison)* to convert **(en** into)

amende [amɑ̃d] *nf* **(a)** *(contravention)* fine; **avoir 200 francs d'a.** to get a 200 franc fine **(b)** **faire a. honorable** to apologize

amendement [amɑ̃dmɑ̃] *nm Pol* amendment

amender [amɑ̃de] **1** *vt (loi, texte)* to amend
2 s'amender *vpr* to turn over a new leaf

amener [46] [amne] **1** *vt* **(a)** *(apporter)* to bring; **a. l'eau à ébullition** to bring the water to the boil; **a. qn à faire qch** to get sb to do sth; *(sujet: circonstances)* to lead sb to do sth; **... ce qui nous amène à parler du chômage ...** which brings us to the issue of unemployment **(b)** *(occasionner)* to bring about **(c)** *(tirer à soi)* to pull in; *(voile)* to lower
2 s'amener *vpr Fam* to turn up; **amène-toi!** come here!

amenuiser [amənɥize] **1** *vt* to wear down
2 s'amenuiser *vpr* to dwindle; *(écart)* to get smaller

amer, -ère [amer] *adj* bitter

amèrement [amermɑ̃] *adv* bitterly

américain, -e [amerikɛ̃, -ɛn] **1** *adj* American
2 *nm,f* **A.** American
3 *nm (langue)* American (English)
4 *nf* **américaine** *Culin* **homard à l'américaine** = lobster cooked in a tomato, white wine and brandy sauce

américaniser [amerikanize] **1** *vt* to Americanize
2 s'américaniser *vpr* to become Americanized

américanisme [amerikanism] *nm Ling* Americanism

amérindien, -enne [ameredjɛ̃, -ɛn] **1** *adj* Amerindian, American Indian **2** *nm,f* **A.** Amerindian, American Indian

Amérique [amerik] *nf* l'A. America; l'A. **centrale** Central America; l'A. **latine** Latin America; l'A. **du Nord/du Sud** North/South America

Amerloque [amerlɔk] *nmf très Fam* American

amerrir [amerir] *vi* to make a landing at sea; *(vaisseau spatial)* to splash down

amerrissage [amerisaʒ] *nm* landing at sea; *(d'un vaisseau spatial)* splashdown

amertume [amertym] *nf* bitterness

améthyste [ametist] *nf* amethyst

ameublement [amœblǝmɑ̃] *nm* (a) *(action de meubler)* furnishing (b) *(meubles)* furniture

ameuter [amøte] *vt (gens)* to bring out; **elle va a. tout le voisinage si elle continue à hurler comme ça!** she'll have the whole neighbourhood out if she carries on shouting like that!

ami, -e [ami] **1** *nm,f* friend; **(petit) a.** *(amant)* boyfriend; **(petite) amie** *(maîtresse)* girlfriend; **a. d'enfance** childhood friend; **a. intime** close friend
2 *adj* friendly; **être a. avec qn** to be friends with sb

amiable [amjabl] *Jur* **1** *adj* amicable
2 à l'amiable *adv* out of court

amiante [amjɑ̃t] *nm* asbestos

amical, -e, -aux, -ales [amikal, -o] **1** *adj* friendly; **peu a.** unfriendly
2 *nf* **amicale** association

amicalement [amikalmɑ̃] *adv* in a friendly way

amidon [amidɔ̃] *nm* starch

amidonner [amidone] *vt* to starch

amincir [amɛ̃sir] **1** *vt* to make thinner; **cette robe t'amincit** that dress makes you look thinner
2 s'amincir *vpr* to get thinner

amincissant, -e [amɛ̃sisɑ̃, -ɑ̃t] *adj (produit, crème)* slimming

amincissement [amɛ̃sismɑ̃] *nm (d'une personne)* slimming

aminé, -e [amine] *adj Chim* **acide a.** amino acid

amiral, -aux [amiral, -o] *nm* admiral

amitié [amitje] *nf* (a) *(sentiment)* friendship; **avoir de l'a. pour qn** to like sb; **se lier d'a. avec qn** to make friends with sb; **prendre qn en a.** to befriend sb (b) *(amabilité)* **faites-moi l'a. de le lui dire** would you be so kind as to tell him?; **mes amitiés à votre sœur** my best wishes to your sister

ammoniaque [amɔnjak] *nf* ammonia

amnésie [amnezi] *nf* amnesia; **souffrir d'a.** to have amnesia

amnésique [amnezik] **1** *adj* amnesic; **être a.** to have amnesia
2 *nmf* amnesiac

amniocentèse [amnjosɛ̃tɛz] *nf Méd* amniocentesis

amniotique [amnjɔtik] *adj* amniotic

amnistie [amnisti] *nf* amnesty

amnistier [66] [amnistje] *vt* to grant an amnesty to

amocher [amɔʃe] *Fam* **1** *vt (personne)* to beat up; *(objet)* to ruin; **se faire (sérieusement) a.** to get (badly) beaten up
2 s'amocher *vpr* to smash oneself up

amoindrir [amwɛ̃drir] **1** *vt* to diminish
2 s'amoindrir *vpr* to diminish

amollir [amɔlir] **1** *vt* to soften
2 s'amollir *vpr* to soften

amonceler [11] [amɔ̃sle] **1** *vt* to pile up; *(preuves)* to accumulate
2 s'amonceler *vpr* to pile up; *(preuves)* to accumulate

amoncellement [amɔ̃sɛlmɑ̃] *nm (pile)* heap, pile

amont [amɔ̃] *nm* upstream section; *aussi Ind* **en a. (de)** upstream (from); **la Seine en a. de Paris** the Seine above Paris

amoral, -e, -aux, -ales [amɔral, -o] *adj* amoral

amorçage [amɔrsaʒ] *nm* (a) *Ordinat* booting; **système d'a.** *(d'une bombe)* detonating system (b) *(pour pêcher)* baiting

amorce [amɔrs] *nf* (a) *(commencement)* beginning (b) *(détonateur)* detonator; *(d'une petite arme)* cap; **pistolet à amorces** cap gun (c) *(appât)* bait

amorcer [16] [amɔrse] **1** *vt* (a) *(commencer)* to begin (b) *Ordinat* to boot (up); **a. de nouveau** to reboot (c) *(bombe)* to arm (d) *(hameçon)* to bait
2 s'amorcer *vpr* (a) *(commencer)* to begin; *(tendance)* to develop (b) *Ordinat* to boot (up)

amorphe [amɔrf] *adj* lifeless, apathetic

amortir [amɔrtir] **1** *vt* (a) *(bruit)* to deaden; *(choc)* to break; *(choc)* to absorb; *(au football)* to trap; *(au tennis)* to kill (b) *Fin (dette)* to pay off (c) *(rentabiliser)* **il a amorti sa nouvelle voiture en six mois** he recouped the cost of his new car in six months; **le matériel a été amorti dès la première année** the equipment started to pay for itself after the first year

amortissement [amɔrtismɑ̃] *nm* (a) *(de matériel)* depreciation (b) *(d'un bruit)* deadening; *(d'une chute)* breaking; *(d'un choc)* absorption (c) *Fin (d'une dette)* paying off

amortisseur [amɔrtisœr] *nm (d'une voiture)* shock absorber

amour [amur] **1** *nm* (a) *(sentiment)* love; **avec a.** lovingly; **être fou d'a. pour qn** to be madly in love with sb; **faire qch par a. pour qn** to do sth out of love for sb; **faire l'a. (avec)** to make love (with); **pour l'a. du Ciel!** for heaven's sake!; **l'a. maternel/filial** a mother's/child's love; **l'a. du prochain** love of one's neighbour; **le grand a.** true love (b) *(personne)* **mon a.** my love, my darling; **tu es un a.!** you're an angel!; **quel a. d'enfant!** what an adorable child!
2 *nfpl* **amours** *(vie amoureuse)* love life; **à tes amours!** *(en buvant)* your health!, cheers!; *(quand on éternue)* bless you!

amouracher [amuraʃe] **s'amouracher** *vpr* **s'a. de qn** to become infatuated with sb

amourette [amuret] *nf* fling

amoureusement [amurøzmɑ̃] *adv* lovingly

amoureux, -euse [amurø, -øz] **1** *nm,f (amateur)* **un a. de** a lover of
2 *nm (petit ami)* boyfriend; **un couple d'a.** a pair of lovers
3 *adj (soin, regard)* loving; **vie amoureuse** love life; **tomber a. (de)** to fall in love (with); **être a. de qn** to be in love with sb

amour-propre [amurpropr] *nm* self-respect, pride; **elle est blessée dans son a.** her pride is hurt

amovible [amɔvibl] *adj* detachable, removable; *Ordinat (disque dur)* removable

ampère [ɑ̃per] *nm Él* ampere

amphés [ɑ̃fe] *nfpl Fam* speed

amphétamine [ɑ̃fetamin] *nf* amphetamine

amphi [ɑ̃fi] *nm Fam* lecture hall

amphibie [ãfibi] *adj* amphibious

amphibien [ãfibjɛ̃] *nm Zool* amphibian

amphithéâtre [ãfiteatr] *nm* (a) *(d'université)* lecture hall (b) *Archit* amphitheatre; **en a.** in a semicircle

amphore [ãfɔr] *nf* urn

ample [ãpl] *adj (robe, jupe)* full; *(geste)* sweeping; *Fig* de **plus amples renseignements** more detailed information; **jusqu'à plus a. informé** until further information is available

amplement [ãpləmã] *adv* amply, fully; **nous avons a. le temps** we have plenty of time; **c'est a. suffisant** it's more than enough

ampleur [ãplœr] *nf* (a) *(d'un vêtement)* fullness (b) *(importance)* scale, extent; **prendre de l'a.** to grow in size

ampli [ãpli] *nm Fam* amp

amplificateur [ãplifikatœr] *nm* amplifier

amplification [ãplifikasjɔ̃] *nf (d'un son)* amplification; *(d'une tendance, d'un phénomène)* intensification

amplifier [66] [ãplifje] **1** *vt (son)* to amplify; *(tendance, phénomène)* to intensify
2 s'amplifier *vpr (son)* to increase; *(tendance, phénomène)* to intensify

amplitude [ãplityd] *nf* (a) *(d'un désastre)* magnitude, scale (b) *(d'un geste)* fullness (c) *(variation)* range; **a. thermique** temperature range (d) *(d'une oscillation)* amplitude

ampoule [ãpul] *nf* (a) *(d'une lampe)* (light) bulb; **a. à baïonnette/vis** bayonet/screw-in light bulb (b) *(sur la peau)* blister (c) *(fiole)* phial

ampoulé, -e [ãpule] *adj* bombastic

amputation [ãpytasjɔ̃] *nf* amputation

amputer [ãpyte] *vt* to amputate; *Fig* to slash; **il fut amputé du bras gauche** his left arm was amputated

Amsterdam [amsterdam] *n* Amsterdam

amulette [amylɛt] *nf* amulet

amusant, -e [amyzã, -ãt] **1** *adj* amusing, funny; *(divertissant)* entertaining; *(bizarre)* weird
2 le plus a., c'est que... the funniest thing is that...

amuse-gueule [amyzgœl] *nm inv* appetizer

amusement [amyzmã] *nm* amusement

amuser [amyze] **1** *vt* to amuse; **cette histoire m'a beaucoup amusé** I found the story very amusing; **si tu crois que ça m'amuse!** do you think I enjoy this?
2 s'amuser *vpr (se distraire)* to amuse oneself; **bien s'a.** to have a good time; **s'a. avec qn** to play with sb; **s'a. à faire qch** to amuse oneself doing sth; **faire qch pour s'a.** to do sth for the fun of it

amuseur, -euse [amyzœr, -øz] *nm,f* entertainer

amygdales [amidal] *nfpl* tonsils; **se faire opérer des a.** to have one's tonsils out

an [ã] *nm* year; **l'an passé** *ou* **dernier** last year; **l'an prochain** next year; **tous les ans** every year; **tous les trois ans** every three years; **en l'an 2000** in the year 2000; **en l'a. de grâce 1172** in the year of Our Lord 1172; **dans trois ans** in three years' time, three years from now; **par an** per year; *Fin* per annum; **avoir dix ans** to be ten (years old); **bon an, mal an** on average over the years

anabolisant [anaboliza] *nm* anabolic steroid

anachronique [anakrɔnik] *adj* anachronistic

anachronisme [anakrɔnism] *nm* anachronism

anagramme [anagram] *nf* anagram

anal, -e, -aux, -ales [anal, -o] *adj* anal

analgésique [analʒezik] *nm* analgesic

anallergique [analɛrʒik] *adj* hypoallergenic

analogie [analɔʒi] *nf* analogy; **par a. avec** by analogy with

analogique [analɔʒik] *adj* (a) *(dictionnaire)* analogical (b) *Él* analogue

analogue [analɔg] *adj* similar (à to)

analphabète [analfabɛt] **1** *adj* illiterate
2 *nmf* illiterate person

analyse [analiz] *nf* (a) *(étude)* analysis; **en dernière a.** in the final analysis; **faire l'a. de qch** to analyse sth (b) *Méd* test; **a. de sang/d'urine** blood/urine test; **faire une a. de sang** to have a blood test (c) *Psy* (psycho)analysis

analyser [analize] *vt* to analyse; *Méd (sang, urine)* to test

analyseur [analizœr] *nm Ordinat* **a. logique** logic analyzer; *Ordinat* **a. syntaxique** parser

analyste [analist] *nmf Ordinat* analyst; *Psy* (psycho)analyst

analyste-programmeur *(pl* **analystes-programmeurs)** [analistprɔgramœr] *nm Ordinat* systems analyst

analytique [analitik] *adj* analytical

ananas [anana(s)] *nm* pineapple

anarchie [anarʃi] *nf aussi Fig* anarchy

anarchique [anarʃik] *adj aussi Fig* anarchic

anarchisant, -e [anarʃizã, -ãt] *adj (discours)* advocating anarchy

anarchisme [anarʃism] *nm* anarchism

anarchiste [anarʃist] *adj & nmf* anarchist

anatomie [anatɔmi] *nf* anatomy

anatomique [anatɔmik] *adj* anatomical

ancestral, -e, -aux, -ales [ãsestral, -o] *adj* ancestral

ancêtre [ãsetr] *nmf* ancestor; *Fam (vieillard)* granddad, *f* grandma

anche [ãʃ] *nf Mus* reed

anchois [ãʃwa] *nm* anchovy

ancien, -enne [ãsjɛ̃, -ɛn] **1** *adj* (a) *(vieux)* old; **livre a.** antiquarian book; **meubles anciens** antique furniture; **dans l'a. temps** in the old days; **je suis plus a. que vous dans la profession** I've been in the profession longer than you (b) *(d'autrefois) (professeur, voisin)* former, old; *(voiture, maison)* old; **c'est un a. boxeur** he used to be a boxer; **a. combattant** *Br* ex-serviceman, *Am* veteran; **a. élève** former student; *Hist* **l'A. Régime** the Ancien Régime
2 *nm* (a) *Rel & Pol* elder (b) **l'a.** *(meubles)* antiques
3 *nm,f (par l'expérience)* **c'est un a. de la maison** he's been with the firm a long time

anciennement [ãsjɛnmã] *adv* formerly

ancienneté [ãsjɛnte] *nf* (a) *(âge)* age (b) *(expérience)* seniority; **avoir quinze ans d'a.** to have fifteen years' service

ancrage [ãkraʒ] *nm Naut* anchoring

ancre [ãkr] *nf* anchor; **lever l'a.** to weigh anchor; **jeter l'a.** to anchor

ancrer [ãkre] **1** *vt (navire)* to anchor; **cette idée est profondément ancrée en lui** this idea is firmly rooted in his mind
2 s'ancrer *vpr Fig (idée, concept)* to become rooted

andalou, -se [ɑ̃dalu, -uz] 1 *adj* Andalusian 2 *nm,f* A. Andalusian

Andalousie [ɑ̃daluzi] *nf* l'A. Andalusia

Andes [ɑ̃d] *nfpl* les A. the Andes

andorran, -e [ɑ̃dɔrɑ̃, -an] 1 *adj* Andorran 2 *nm,f* A. Andorran

Andorre [ɑ̃dɔr] *nf* Andorra; **la principauté d'A.** the Principality of Andorra

Andorre-la-Vieille [ɑ̃dɔrlavjɛj] *n* Andorra la Vella

andouille [ɑ̃duj] *nf* (a) *Culin* = sausage made from pigs' intestines (b) *Fam* (*imbécile*) fool, twit; **faire l'a.** to play the fool

andouillette [ɑ̃dujɛt] *nf Culin* = small sausage made from pigs' intestines

androgyne [ɑ̃drɔʒin] *adj* androgynous

âne [ɑn] *nm* (a) (*animal*) donkey; **à dos d'â.** by donkey (b) *Fam* (*idiot*) ass; (*ignare*) dunce

anéantir [aneɑ̃tir] *vt* (*ville*) to destroy; (*armée*) to crush; (*espoirs*) to shatter; **la nouvelle l'a anéantie** she was staggered by the news

anéantissement [aneɑ̃tismɑ̃] *nm* (a) (*d'une ville, d'un empire*) destruction; (*d'un espoir*) shattering (b) (*abattement*) **dans un état d'a.** total completely crushed

anecdote [anɛkdɔt] *nf* anecdote

anecdotique [anɛkdɔtik] *adj* anecdotal

anémie [anemi] *nf* anaemia; **faire de l'a.** to have anaemia

anémique [anemik] *adj* anaemic; *Fig* feeble, weak

anémone [anemɔn] *nf* anemone; **a. de mer** sea anemone

ânerie [ɑnri] *nf* (*paroles*) stupid remark; (*acte*) stupid act; **dire des âneries** to talk rubbish; **faire des âneries** to behave stupidly

ânesse [ɑnɛs] *nf* she-ass

anesthésie [anɛstezi] *nf* anaesthesia; **être sous a.** to be under anaesthetic; **a. générale/locale** general/local anaesthetic

anesthésier [66] [anɛstezje] *vt* to anaesthetize

anesthésiste [anɛstezist] *nmf Br* anaesthetist, *Am* anesthesiologist

aneth [anɛt] *nm* dill

ange [ɑ̃ʒ] *nm Fig* angel; **un visage d'a.** an angelic face; **être aux anges** to be in seventh heaven; **un a. passe** someone must have walked over my grave; **a. gardien** guardian angel

angélique [ɑ̃ʒelik] 1 *adj* angelic 2 *nf Culin* angelica

angine [ɑ̃ʒin] *nf* sore throat; **a. de poitrine** angina (pectoris)

angiome [ɑ̃ʒjom] *nm Méd* angioma

anglais, -e [ɑ̃glɛ, -ɛz] 1 *adj* English; (*britannique*) British 2 *nm,f* A. Englishman, *f* Englishwoman; (*Britannique*) British man, *f* British woman; **les A.** the English; (*Britanniques*) the British 3 *nm* (*langue*) English

anglaise (*boucles*) ringlets

angle [ɑ̃gl] *nm* (a) (*d'une pièce, d'une rue, d'une table*) corner; **faire l'a. avec la rue du Bac** to intersect the rue du Bac; **la maison qui fait l'a.** the house on the corner (b) (*point de vue*) angle (c) (*en géométrie*) angle; **a. droit** right angle; **se couper à angles droits** to cross at right angles; *Aut* **a. mort** blind spot

Angleterre [ɑ̃glətɛr] *nf* l'A. England; (*Grande-Bretagne*) Britain

anglican, -e [ɑ̃glikɑ̃, -an] *adj & nm,f* Anglican

anglicisme [ɑ̃glisism] *nm* Anglicism

anglo-américain, -e (*mpl* anglo-américains, *fpl* anglo-américaines) [ɑ̃gloamerikɛ̃, -ɛn] *adj* Anglo-American

anglo-irlandais, -e (*mpl* anglo-irlandais, *fpl* anglo-irlandaises) [ɑ̃gloirlɑ̃dɛ, -ɛz] *adj* Anglo-Irish

anglo-normand, -e (*mpl* anglo-normands, *fpl* anglo-normandes) [ɑ̃glonɔrmɑ̃, -ɑ̃d] *adj voir* **île**

anglophone [ɑ̃glɔfɔn] 1 *adj* English-speaking 2 *nmf* English speaker

anglo-saxon, -onne (*mpl* anglo-saxons, *fpl* anglo-saxonnes) [ɑ̃glosaksɔ̃, -ɔn] 1 *adj* Anglo-Saxon 2 *nm,f* A. Anglo-Saxon

angoissant, -e [ɑ̃gwasɑ̃, -ɑ̃t] *adj* (*nouvelle*) distressing; (*attente*) agonizing; (*film, livre*) frightening; (*situation*) alarming

angoisse [ɑ̃gwas] *nf* anguish, distress; *Méd* **une crise d'a.** an anxiety attack; *Fam* **c'est l'a.!** what a drag!

angoissé, -e [ɑ̃gwase] 1 *adj* anxious 2 *nm,f* anxious person

angoisser [ɑ̃gwase] 1 *vt* **a. qn** to make sb anxious 2 *vi Fam* to worry, to get worked up 3 **s'angoisser** *vpr* to get anxious; **s'a. pour un rien** to get worked up over nothing

Angola [ɑ̃gɔla] *nm* l'A. Angola

angolais, -e [ɑ̃gɔlɛ, -ɛz] 1 *adj* Angolan 2 *nm,f* A. Angolan

angora [ɑ̃gɔra] 1 *nm* (a) (*lapin*) angora rabbit; (*chat*) Persian cat (b) (*laine*) angora (wool) 2 *adj* angora

anguille [ɑ̃gij] *nf* eel; *Fig* **il y a a. sous roche** there's something going on

angulaire [ɑ̃gylɛr] *adj* angular

anguleux, -euse [ɑ̃gylø, -øz] *adj* (*visage*) angular; (*contours*) rugged

anicroche [anikrɔʃ] *nf* hitch, snag; **sans a.** without a hitch

animal, -e, -aux, -ales [animal, -o] 1 *nm aussi Fig* animal; **animaux de boucherie** animals raised for slaughter; **a. domestique** pet 2 *adj* animal

animalerie [animalri] *nf Can* pet shop

animalier, -ère [animalje, -ɛr] *adj* **parc a.** safari park; **peintre a.** wildlife painter

animateur, -trice [animatœr, -tris] *nm,f* (a) (*de télé, de radio*) presenter (b) (*dans un club*) leader

animation [animasjɔ̃] *nf* (a) (*vie*) life; **une ville pleine d'a.** a lively town; **parler avec a.** to speak animatedly; **mettre de l'a. dans une soirée** to liven up a party (b) (*divertissement*) event; **faire de l'a.** (*de centre aéré*) to be an entertainment officer; (*de télé, de radio*) to be a presenter (c) *Cin* animation (d) *Météo* **a. satellite** satellite picture

animé, -e [anime] *adj* (*personne, discussion*) lively, animated; (*rue, quartier*) busy, bustling

animer [anime] **1** vt (a) *(sujet: désir, ambition)* to drive (b) *(conversation, soirée, quartier)* to liven up (c) *(débat)* to conduct; *(jeu télévisé)* to present
 2 s'animer vpr *(personne)* to come to life; *(conversation, soirée)* to get more lively; *(visage)* to light up

animisme [animism] nm animism

animosité [animozite] nf animosity **(contre** towards), hostility **(contre** towards); **dire qch sans a.** to say sth calmly

anis [ani(s)] nm *(plante)* anise; **(sirop d')a.** aniseed cordial; **(graine d')a.** *(en cuisine)* aniseed; **à l'a.** aniseed-flavoured

anisette [anizet] nf anisette

Ankara [ākara] n Ankara

ankylose [ākiloz] nf stiffness, *Spéc* ankylosis

ankyloser [ākiloze] **1** vt **être ankylosé** to be stiff
 2 s'ankyloser vpr to get stiff; *Fig (dans un métier, des habitudes)* to get into a rut

annales [anal] nfpl annals; **les a. du bac** = past baccalauréat examination papers (with sample answers); **a. de géographie/littéraires** geographical/literary review; *Fig* **ça restera dans les a.** it will go down in history

anneau, -x [ano] nm (a) *(cercle, bague)* ring; *(de chaîne)* link; **a. nuptial** ou **de mariage** wedding ring; **a. de rideau** curtain ring; **les anneaux** *(en gymnastique)* the rings (b) *(d'un serpent)* coil (c) *Astron* ring

année [ane] nf year; **Bonne A.!** Happy New Year!; **une a. de vacances** a year's holiday; **d'a. en a.** year by year; **les années 80** the 80s; **en quelle a ....?** in what year...?; **l'a. prochaine/dernière** next/last year; **elle entre dans sa trentième a.** she's just turned twenty-nine; **entrer en troisième a. de médecine** to start the third year of one's medical course; **a. civile** calendar year; **a. comptable** *Br* accounting ou financial year, *Am* fiscal year

année-lumière *(pl* **années-lumière)** [anelymjɛr] nf light year; **à des années-lumière** *(étoile, planète)* light years away; *Fig* **nous sommes à des années-lumière l'un de l'autre** we're light years apart

annexe [anɛks] **1** nf (a) *(bâtiment)* annexe (b) *(de lettre)* enclosure; *(de livre, de rapport)* appendix; *(de projet de loi)* rider; *(de loi)* schedule; **en a. veuillez trouver... please find enclosed...
 2 adj (a) *(complémentaire)* *(pièces)* enclosed; *(revenus)* supplementary; *(industries)* subsidiary (b) *(mineur)* secondary

annexer [anɛkse] **1** vt (a) *(territoire)* to annex (b) *(document)* to append (à to); **pièces annexées** *(à une lettre)* enclosures
 2 s'annexer vpr **s'a. qch** to get hold of sth for oneself

annexion [anɛksjɔ̃] nf annexation

annihilation [aniilasjɔ̃] nf *(d'une ville, d'une armée)* annihilation; *(d'efforts, d'espoirs)* destruction

annihiler [aniile] vt *(ville, armée)* to annihilate; *(efforts, espoirs)* to destroy

anniversaire [aniverser] **1** nm *(d'une naissance)* birthday; *(d'une victoire, d'une mort)* anniversary; **bon** ou **joyeux a.!** happy birthday!; **gâteau/carte d'a.** birthday cake/card; **a. de mariage** wedding anniversary
 2 adj anniversary; **date a.** anniversary

annonce [anɔ̃s] nf (a) *(déclaration)* announcement; *(par écrit)* notice; *(aux cartes)* declaration, bid; *Fig* sign, indication **(de** of) (b) *(publicitaire, de vente)* advert, advertisement; **passer une (petite) a. dans un journal** to put an advert in a newspaper; **petites annonces** *Br* small ads, *Am* want ads; **annonces classées** classified ads

annoncer [16] [anɔ̃se] **1** vt (a) *(déclarer)* to announce; **a. la nouvelle à qn** to tell sb the news (b) *(dans la presse)* *(soldes, exposition)* to advertise (c) *(indiquer)* to herald; **cela n'annonce rien de bon** things aren't looking too good (d) **a. qn** *(visiteur)* to show sb in; *(lors d'une occasion officielle)* to announce sb; **se faire a.** to give one's name
 2 s'annoncer vpr (a) *(prévenir de sa visite)* to announce one's arrival (b) *(situation)* **cela s'annonce bien/mal** things aren't looking too bad/good; **l'avènement de la démocratie s'annonce dans plusieurs pays** there are signs in several countries that democracy is on the way

annonceur [anɔ̃sœr] nm *(de publicité)* advertiser

annonciateur, -trice [anɔ̃sjatœr, -tris] adj **signes annonciateurs de crise** signs that a crisis is on the way

Annonciation [anɔ̃sjasjɔ̃] nf **l'A.** the Annunciation

annotation [anɔtasjɔ̃] nf annotation; **faire des annotations dans un texte** to annotate a text

annoter [anɔte] vt to annotate

annuaire [anɥɛr] nm *(d'un organisme)* yearbook; *(liste d'adresses)* directory; **l'a. du téléphone** ou **téléphonique** the telephone directory; **je suis dans l'a.** I'm in the (phone) book; **a. électronique** electronic telephone directory; **a. des marées** tide table

annuel, -elle [anɥɛl] adj annual, yearly

annuellement [anɥɛlmɑ̃] adv annually, yearly

annuité [anɥite] nf *(sur un emprunt)* annual repayment

annulaire [anɥlɛr] **1** nm ring finger
 2 adj annular, ring-shaped

annulation [anɥlasjɔ̃] nf (a) *(d'une commande, d'un rendez-vous, de vacances)* cancellation; *(d'une dette)* writing off; *(d'un mariage, d'un contrat)* annulment; *(d'un jugement)* quashing (b) *Ordinat* deletion; **a. d'entrée** *(commande)* cancel entry

annuler [anɥle] **1** vt (a) *(commande, rendez-vous, vacances)* to cancel; *(dette)* to write off; *(mariage, contrat)* to annul; *(jugement)* to quash (b) *(remplacer)* to supersede (c) *Sp* *(but, essai)* to disallow
 2 s'annuler vpr to cancel each other out

anoblir [anɔblir] vt to ennoble

anode [anɔd] nf *Él* anode

anodin, -e [anɔdɛ̃, -in] adj *(remarque)* harmless; *(personne)* insignificant; *(blessure, changement)* slight, minor; *(infection)* mild

anomalie [anɔmali] nf anomaly; *Méd* abnormality

ânon [anɔ̃] nm little donkey

ânonner [anɔne] vt to stumble through

anonymat [anɔnima] nm anonymity; **garder l'a.** to remain anonymous

anonyme [anɔnim] adj anonymous; *Fig (décor, intérieur)* impersonal

anorak [anɔrak] nm anorak

anorexie [anɔrɛksi] nf anorexia; **faire de l'a.** to suffer from anorexia; **a. mentale** anorexia nervosa

anorexique [anɔrɛksik] adj & nmf anorexic

anormal, -e, -aux, -ales [anɔrmal, -o] **1** *adj* **(a)** *(non conforme)* abnormal; *(mentalement)* educationally subnormal **(b)** il fait une chaleur anormale it's abnormally hot **(b)** *(injuste)* unfair; **il est a. que tu sois si peu payé** it's unfair that you're paid so little
2 *nm,f (mentalement)* educationally subnormal person

anormalement [anɔrmalmɑ̃] *adv* abnormally

ANPE [aɛnpeø] *nf (abrév* **Agence nationale pour l'emploi)** = French state employment agency

anse [ɑ̃s] *nf* **(a)** *(d'une cruche, d'un panier)* handle **(b)** *(crique)* cove

antagonisme [ɑ̃tagɔnism] *nm* antagonism

antagoniste [ɑ̃tagɔnist] **1** *nmf* antagonist
2 *adj (opinions, parties)* antagonistic

antalgique [ɑ̃talʒik] *adj & nm Méd* analgesic

antan [ɑ̃tɑ̃] **d'antan** *adj Litt* of yesteryear

antarctique [ɑ̃tarktik] **1** *nm* **l'A.** the Antarctic, Antarctica
2 *adj* Antarctic

antécédent [ɑ̃tesedɑ̃] *nm* **(a)** **antécédents** *(d'une personne)* previous history, past record; **il y a des antécédents cancéreux dans ma famille** my family has a history of cancer; **avoir de bons/mauvais antécédents** to have a good/bad record; **antécédents médicaux** medical history **(b)** *Ling* antecedent

Antéchrist [ɑ̃tekrist] *nm* Antichrist

antédiluvien, -enne [ɑ̃tedilyvjɛ̃, -ɛn] *adj Hum* **ma télévision est antédiluvienne** my television is an antique

anténatal, -e, -als, -ales [ɑ̃tenatal] *adj Méd* antenatal

antenne [ɑ̃tɛn] *nf* **(a)** *(de radio)* aerial, antenna; *(d'un satellite, d'un robot)* antenna; **être à l'a.** to be on the air; **passer à l'a.** *(émission)* to be broadcast; *(personne)* to be on the television/radio; **rendre l'a.** to hand over; **à vous l'a.** over to you; **hors a.** off the air; **a. parabolique** (satellite) dish **(b)** *(d'un insecte)* antenna, feeler; *Fig* **avoir des antennes** *(de l'intuition)* to have a sixth sense **(c)** *Mil* **a. chirurgicale** field hospital **(d)** *(de société)* branch

antépénultième [ɑ̃tepenyltjɛm] *adj* antepenultimate

antérieur, -e [ɑ̃terjœr] *adj* **(a)** *(période)* former; *(date)* earlier; *(année)* previous; *(engagement)* prior; **tous ces événements sont antérieurs à la révolution** all these events took place before the revolution; **dans une vie antérieure** in a previous life **(b)** *(muscle)* anterior; *(membre)* fore

anthologie [ɑ̃tɔlɔʒi] *nf* anthology

anthracite [ɑ̃trasit] **1** *nm* **(a)** *(minerai)* anthracite **(b)** *(couleur)* charcoal grey
2 *adj inv* charcoal grey

anthropologie [ɑ̃trɔpɔlɔʒi] *nf* anthropology

anthropologiste [ɑ̃trɔpɔlɔʒist], **anthropologue** [ɑ̃trɔpɔlɔg] *nmf* anthropologist

anthropophage [ɑ̃trɔpɔfaʒ] **1** *nmf* cannibal
2 *adj* cannibalistic

anti [ɑ̃ti] *préf (contre)* anti-

antiadhésif, -ive [ɑ̃tiadezif, -iv] **1** *adj (revêtement, poêle)* nonstick **2** *nm* antiadhesive

antiaérien, -enne [ɑ̃tiaerjɛ̃, -ɛn] *adj* anti-aircraft

anti-âge [ɑ̃tiɑʒ] *adj inv* anti-aging

antialcoolique [ɑ̃tialkɔlik] *adj (ligue)* temperance

antiatomique [ɑ̃tiatɔmik] *adj* antinuclear

antibactérien, -enne [ɑ̃tibakterjɛ̃, -ɛn] *adj* antibacterial

antibiotique [ɑ̃tibjɔtik] **1** *nm* antibiotic; **être sous antibiotiques** to be on antibiotics
2 *adj* antibiotic

antiblocage [ɑ̃tiblɔkaʒ] *adj inv* Aut **système a. (des roues)** anti-lock brakes

antibrouillard [ɑ̃tibrujar] *adj inv & nm Aut* **(phare) a.** fog lamp

antibruit [ɑ̃tibrɥi] *adj inv (mur)* soundproof; **lutte a.** noise abatement campaign

antibuée [ɑ̃tibɥe] *adj inv & nm Aut (dispositif)* a. demister

anticalcaire [ɑ̃tikalker] *adj inv* **produit a.** *(pour machine à laver)* water softener

anticancéreux, -euse [ɑ̃tikɑ̃serø, -øz] *adj* **centre/ sérum a.** cancer hospital/serum

anticasseurs [ɑ̃tikasœr] *adj inv* **loi a.** = law banning violent behaviour during demonstrations

antichambre [ɑ̃tiʃɑ̃br] *nf* waiting room, antechamber

antichar [ɑ̃tiʃar] *adj Mil* anti-tank

antichoc [ɑ̃tiʃɔk] *adj inv* shock-proof

anticipation [ɑ̃tisipasjɔ̃] *nf* anticipation; **payer par a.** to pay in advance; **littérature d'a.** science fiction; **film d'a.** science-fiction film

anticipé, -e [ɑ̃tisipe] *adj (paiement)* advance; *(départ, retour)* early; **avec mes remerciements anticipés** thanking you in advance

anticiper [ɑ̃tisipe] **1** *vt (réaction, réponse)* to anticipate; *(action)* to forestall; *(tendance, résultat d'élections)* to forecast; **j'anticipais déjà le pire** I was expecting the worst
2 *vi* **a.** to anticipate, to look or think ahead; *(aux échecs)* to anticipate what one's opponent will do next; **n'anticipons pas** let's not look too far ahead; **a. sur qch** to anticipate sth

anticlérical, -e, -aux, -ales [ɑ̃tiklerikal, -o] *adj & nm,f* anticlerical

anticoagulant, -e [ɑ̃tikɔagylɑ̃, -ɑ̃t] *adj & nm* anticoagulant

anticolonialiste [ɑ̃tikɔlɔnjalist] *adj* anti-colonialist

anticommunisme [ɑ̃tikɔmynism] *nm* anti-communism

anticommuniste [ɑ̃tikɔmynist] *adj & nmf* anti-communist

anticonceptionnel, -elle [ɑ̃tikɔ̃sepsjɔnel] *adj (pilule)* contraceptive

anticonformiste [ɑ̃tikɔ̃fɔrmist] *adj & nmf* non-conformist

anticonstitutionnel, -elle [ɑ̃tikɔ̃stitysjɔnel] *adj* unconstitutional

anticorps [ɑ̃tikɔr] *nm* antibody

anticyclone [ɑ̃tisiklon] *nm Météo* anticyclone

antidater [ɑ̃tidate] *vt* to backdate, to antedate

antidémocratique [ɑ̃tidemɔkratik] *adj* undemocratic

antidépresseur [ɑ̃tidepresœr] *adj m & nm* antidepressant

antidérapant, -e [ɑ̃tiderapɑ̃, -ɑ̃t] *adj (pneu, route)* non-skid; *(semelle, tapis)* non-slip

antidopage [ɑ̃tidɔpaʒ], **antidoping** [ɑ̃tidɔpiŋ] *adj inv Sp* **contrôle a.** drug(s) test

antidote [ɑ̃tidɔt] *nm aussi Fig* antidote (**contre** for)

antiesclavagiste [ɑ̃tiesklavaʒist] *adj* anti-slavery

antifasciste [ātifaʃist] *adj* anti-fascist

antifongique [ātifɔ̃ʒik] **1** *adj* fungicidal
2 *nm* fungicide

antigel [ātiʒɛl] *nm* antifreeze

antigrippal, -e, -aux, -ales [ātigripal, -o] *adj* anti-flu

antihéros [ātiero] *nm* antihero

antihistaminique [ātiistaminik] *adj & nm Méd* antihistamine

anti-inflammatoire [ātiɛ̃flamatwar] *adj & nm Méd* anti-inflammatory

anti-inflationniste [ātiɛ̃flasjɔnist] *adj* anti-inflationary

antillais, -e [ātije, -ɛz] **1** *adj* West Indian
2 *nm,f* A. West Indian

Antilles [ātij] *nfpl* les A. the West Indies

antilope [ātilɔp] *nf* antelope

antimatière [ātimatjɛr] *nf Phys* antimatter

antimilitariste [ātimilitarist] *adj & nmf* antimilitarist

antimite [ātimit] **1** *adj inv* (*produit*) moth-repellent; **bombe a.** moth spray
2 *nm* mothkiller

antinazi, -e [ātinazi] *adj* anti-Nazi

antinomie [ātinɔmi] *nf* antinomy

antinucléaire [ātinykleər] *adj* anti-nuclear

Antiope [ātjɔp] *n* = French teletext system, providing subtitles for the deaf

antioxydant, -e [ātiɔksidā, -āt] *adj & nm* antioxidant

antipathie [ātipati] *nf* antipathy; **avoir** *ou* **éprouver de l'a. pour qn** to dislike sb

antipathique [ātipatik] *adj* unpleasant; **il m'est très a.** I don't like him at all

antipelliculaire [ātipelikylɛr] *adj* **shampooing a.** dandruff shampoo

antiphrase [ātifraz] *nf Ling* antiphrasis

antipodes [ātipɔd] *nmpl Géog* antipodes; **être aux a. de** to be on the other side of the world from; *Fig* to be the exact opposite of

antipoison [ātipwazɔ̃] *adj inv Méd* **centre a.** poisons unit

antiquaire [ātikɛr] *nmf* antique dealer

antique [ātik] *adj* (*de l'Antiquité*) ancient; (*mobilier*) antique; *Hum* (*voiture, télévision*) antiquated; **la Grèce/la Rome a.** ancient Greece/Rome

antiquité [ātikite] *nf* (a) *Hist* l'a. **grecque/romaine** ancient Greek/Rome (b) **antiquités** (*meubles et objets anciens*) antiques; **magasin d'antiquités** antique shop (c) **antiquités** (*dans un musée*) antiquities

antirabique [ātirabik] *adj Méd* anti-rabies

antiracisme [ātirasism] *nm* anti-racism

antiraciste [ātirasist] *adj* anti-racist

antiradar [ātiradar] *nm* anti-radar device

antireflet [ātirəflɛ] *adj inv* non-reflecting; *Ordinat* non-reflecting, antiglare

antirides [ātirid] *adj inv* anti-wrinkle

antirouille [ātiruj] **1** *adj inv* rustproofing
2 *nm* rustproofing agent

antiroulis [ātiruli] *adj Aut* **barre a.** anti-roll bar

anti-scintillements [ātisɛ̃tijmā] *adj inv Ordinat* flicker-free

antisèche [ātisɛʃ] *nf Fam* crib sheet

antisémite [ātisemit] **1** *adj* anti-Semitic
2 *nmf* anti-Semite

antisémitisme [ātisemitism] *nm* anti-Semitism

antiseptique [ātiseptik] *adj & nm* antiseptic

antisocial, -e, -aux, -ales [ātisɔsjal, -o] *adj* antisocial

antispasmodique [ātispasmɔdik] *adj & nm Méd* antispasmodic

antitabac [ātitaba] *adj inv* **lutte** *ou* **campagne a.** anti-smoking campaign

antiterroriste [ātiterɔrist] *adj* anti-terrorist

antithèse [ātitɛz] *nf* antithesis; *Fig* **être l'a. de** to be the opposite of

antitrust [ātitrœst] *adj inv Br* anti-monopoly, *Am* anti-trust

antivariolique [ātivarjɔlik] *adj Méd* **vaccin a.** smallpox vaccine

antivenimeux, -euse [ātivənimø, -øz] *adj Méd* antivenin

antivol [ātivɔl] **1** *adj inv* (*dispositif*) anti-theft
2 *nm* anti-theft device

antre [ātr] *nm* (*caverne*) cave, cavern; (*d'animaux, de brigands*) den, lair; *Fig* (*d'une personne*) den

anus [anys] *nm* anus

Anvers [āvɛr(s)] *n* Antwerp

anxiété [āksjete] *nf* anxiety; **éprouver de l'a.** to feel anxious; **avec a.** anxiously

anxieux, -euse [āksjø, -øz] **1** *adj* anxious, worried; **a. de faire qch** anxious to do sth
2 *nm,f* worrier

anxiolytique [āksjɔlitik] *Méd* **1** *adj* anxiety-reducing
2 *nm* tranquillizer

AOC [aɔse] *nf* (*abrév* **appellation d'origine contrôlée**) = (guarantee of) high-quality wine from an identified vineyard

aorte [aɔrt] *nf* aorta

août [u(t)] *nm* August; **le quinze a.** (*fête*) Assumption Day; *voir aussi* **janvier**

aoûtat [auta] *nm Br* harvest mite, *Am* chigger

aoûtien, -enne [ausjɛ̃, -ɛn] *nm,f* August *Br* holidaymaker *ou Am* vacationer

apache [apaʃ] **1** *nm* A. Apache
2 *adj* Apache

apaisant, -e [apezā, -āt] *adj* soothing, calming

apaisement [apezmā] *nm* (*de la douleur*) alleviation; (*calme*) calm

apaiser [apeze] **1** *vt* (*personne*) to calm (down); (*douleur*) to soothe; (*faim*) to satisfy; (*soif*) to quench; (*craintes*) to allay
2 **s'apaiser** *vpr* (*personne*) to calm down; (*vent, douleur, craintes*) to subside

apanage [apanaʒ] *nm* prerogative; **elle croit avoir l'a. de la sagesse** she thinks she has a monopoly on wisdom

aparté [aparte] *nm* (a) *Th* aside; **en a. in** an aside (b) (*entre deux personnes*) private conversation; **en a.** in private

apartheid [aparted] *nm* apartheid

apathie [apati] *nf* apathy, listlessness

apathique [apatik] *adj* apathetic, listless

apatride [apatrid] *nmf* stateless person

APEC [apɛk] *nf* (*abrév* **Association pour l'emploi des cadres**) = employment agency for executives and graduates

apercevoir [60] [apɛrsəvwar] **1** *vt* to see; (*soudain, rapidement*) to catch sight of; **laisser a. qch** to let sth show

2 s'apercevoir *vpr* **s'a. de qch** (*comprendre, réaliser*) to realize *or* notice sth; **s'a. que...** to realize *or* notice that...

aperçu [apɛrsy] *nm* (*idée générale*) general idea; *Ordinat* **a. avant impression** print preview

apéritif [aperitif] *nm* aperitif; **prendre l'a.** to have a drink before the meal

apéro [apero] *Fam* = **apéritif**

apesanteur [apəzɑ̃tœr] *nf* weightlessness; **en (état d')a.** in weightless conditions

à-peu-près [apøprɛ] *nm inv* vague approximation; **il y a trop d'à. dans votre exposé** there is too much vagueness in your report

apeuré, -e [apœre] *adj* frightened, scared

apeurer [apœre] *vt* to frighten, to scare

aphasie [afazi] *nf Méd* aphasia

aphasique [afazik] *adj & nmf Méd* aphasic

aphone [afon] *adj Méd* voiceless; **elle était a. d'avoir trop crié** she'd lost her voice because she'd been shouting too much

aphorisme [aforism] *nm* aphorism; *Péj* platitude

aphrodisiaque [afrodizjak] *adj & nm* aphrodisiac

aphte [aft] *nm* mouth ulcer

aphteux, -euse [aftø, -øz] *adj* **fièvre aphteuse** foot-and-mouth disease

à-pic [apik] *nm inv* sheer face

apiculteur, -trice [apikyltœr, -tris] *nm,f* beekeeper

apiculture [apikyltyr] *nf* beekeeping

apitoiement [apitwamɑ̃] *nm* pity; **pas d'a.!** don't let pity get the better of you!

apitoyer [32] [apitwaje] **1** *vt* **a. qn** to move sb to pity

2 s'apitoyer *vpr* **s'a. sur (le sort de) qn** to feel sorry for sb; **s'a. sur soi-même** *ou* **sur son sort** to feel sorry for oneself

APL [apeɛl] *nf* (*abrév* **Aide personnalisée au logement**) housing benefit

aplanir [aplanir] **1** *vt* (*bois*) to plane; (*route*) to level; *Fig* (*difficultés*) to iron out

2 s'aplanir *vpr* (*sol*) to level out

aplati, -e [aplati] *adj* (*ballon, nez*) flat; (*figure géométrique*) oblate

aplatir [aplatir] **1** *vt* (*objet*) to flatten; **a. qch à coups de marteau** to hammer sth flat

2 s'aplatir *vpr* (*coiffure*) to go flat; (*chapeau*) to get flattened; **s'a. contre un mur** to flatten oneself against a wall; *Fig* **s'a. devant qn** to grovel to sb

aplomb [aplɔ̃] *nm* (a) (*ligne droite*) perpendicularity; **mettre qch d'a.** to stand sth up straight; **les étagères ne sont pas d'a.** the shelves aren't level; **je ne me sens pas d'a. aujourd'hui** I'm feeling out of sorts today; **remettre qn d'a.** to perk sb up (b) (*assurance*) (self-)confidence; *Péj* nerve, cheek; *Péj* **il ne manque pas d'a.** he's got a nerve *or* a cheek

apnée [apne] *nf* **plonger en a.** to dive without breathing apparatus

apocalypse [apokalips] *nf* apocalypse; **l'A.** (*dans la Bible*) the Book of Revelation; *Fig* **d'a.** apocalyptic

apocalyptique [apokaliptik] *adj* apocalyptic

apogée [apoʒe] *nm Astron* apogee; *Fig* **être à l'a. de sa carrière** to be at the height of one's career

apolitique [apolitik] *adj* apolitical

apollon [apolɔ̃] *nm* (*bel homme*) Adonis

apologie [apoloʒi] *nf* (*défense*) apologia (**de** for); (*éloge*) eulogy; **faire l'a. de** (*louer*) to eulogize

apoplectique [apoplɛktik] *adj & nmf Méd* apoplectic

apoplexie [apoplɛksi] *nf Méd* apoplexy

a posteriori [aposterjɔri] *adv* with hindsight

apostolat [apostɔla] *nm* (*métier*) vocation

apostrophe [apostrɔf] *nf* (a) (*signe, figure de style*) apostrophe (b) (*interpellation*) rude remark

apostropher [apostrɔfe] **1** *vt* (*pour attirer l'attention*) to shout to; (*être impoli envers*) to shout at

2 s'apostropher *vpr* to shout at one another

apothéose [apoteoz] *nf* (*consécration*) crowning glory; **finir en a.** to end spectacularly

apothicaire [apotikɛr] *nm Vieilli* apothecary; *Fig* **tenir des comptes d'a.** to know where every penny goes

apôtre [apotr] *nm* apostle; *Fig* **se faire l'a. de qch** to become an advocate of sth

Appalaches [apalaʃ] *nmpl* **les (monts) A.** the Appalachians

apparaître [20] [aparɛtr] (*aux être*) **1** *vi* (a) (*devenir visible*) to appear; **il lui est apparu en rêve** he came *or* appeared to her in a dream (b) (*phénomène, espèce*) to appear (c) (*vérité, solution*) to become apparent (d) (*sembler*) **il m'apparaît comme le seul capable d'y parvenir** he seems to me to be the only person capable of doing it

2 *v impersonnel* **il apparaît que...** it appears (that)...

apparat [apara] *nm* pomp, show; **tenue d'a.** ceremonial dress; **en grand a.** with great pomp and ceremony

appareil [aparɛj] *nm* (a) (*instrument*) apparatus; **a. (dentaire)** (*correctif*) brace; (*dentier*) dentures; **appareils ménagers** household appliances; **a. (photographique)**, **a. photo** camera (b) (*téléphone*) telephone; **Paul à l'a.** Paul speaking *or* here; **qui est à l'a.?** who's speaking? (c) (*avion*) aircraft, plane (d) (*structure, système*) apparatus; **l'a. de la justice** the legal system; **a. de production** (*industriel*) production facilities (e) *Anat* system; **a. digestif** digestive system; **a. génital** genital system; **a. respiratoire** respiratory system (f) *Litt ou Hum* **dans le plus simple a.** in one's birthday suit

appareillage [aparɛjaʒ] *nm* (a) *Naut* getting under way (b) (*matériel*) equipment; *Ind* plant

appareiller [aparɛje] *vi Naut* to get under way

apparemment [aparamɑ̃] *adv* apparently

apparence [aparɑ̃s] *nf* (a) (*aspect extérieur*) appearance, look; **un homme à l'a. négligée/soignée** an untidy-looking/a tidy-looking man; **en dépit des apparences** in spite of appearances (b) (*aspect trompeur*) **il ne faut pas se fier aux apparences** appearances can be deceptive; **il a l'air gentil, mais ce n'est qu'une a.** he seems nice, but it's only a façade; **en a.** outwardly; **pour sauver les apparences** to keep up appearances

apparent, -e [aparã, -ãt] *adj* (**a**) *(visible)* visible, apparent; **peu a.** hardly noticeable; **sans raison apparente** for no apparent reason (**b**) *(prétendu)* apparent; **sous cette apparente bonté se cache un grand égoïsme** beneath that kind exterior there lies great selfishness

apparenté, -e [aparãte] *adj* (**a**) *(par le mariage)* related; *(en rapport)* related, connected (**b**) *Pol* **candidat a. à un parti** = candidate who, though not a member of a party, can count on its support in an election

apparenter [aparãte] **s'apparenter** *vpr (ressembler)* to have something in common (**à** with)

appariteur [aparitœr] *nm (d'université)* porter

apparition [aparisjɔ̃] *nf* (**a**) *(manifestation)* appearance; **faire son a.** *(personne)* to make one's appearance (**b**) *(fantôme)* apparition; **avoir des apparitions** to see things

appartement [apartəmã] *nm Br* flat, *Am* apartment; *(dans un hôtel)* suite; **vivre en a.** to live in a flat; **les grands appartements** *(d'un château)* the state apartments

appartenance [apartənãs] *nf* belonging (**à** to); *(à un parti)* membership (**à** of)

appartenir [70] [apartənir] **appartenir à 1** *vt ind* (**a**) *(être possédé par)* to belong to (**b**) *(faire partie de)* club, parti, espèce) to belong to, to be a member of; **elle appartient à une famille très riche** she comes from a very wealthy family
  2 *v impersonnel* **il appartient au comité de prendre la décision** it is up to the committee to decide

appât [apɑ] *nm (de pêche)* bait; *Fig (du succès)* lure; **l'a. du gain** the lure of money

appâter *vt* (**a**) *(animaux)* to lure; *Fig (personne)* to entice (**b**) *(hameçon)* to bait

appauvrir [apovrir] **1** *vt* to impoverish
  2 s'appauvrir *vpr* to get poorer; *(sol, langue)* to become impoverished

appeau, -x [apo] *nm* birdcall *(instrument)*

appel [apɛl] *nm* (**a**) *(invitation, sollicitation)* appeal; **faire a. à qn** to appeal to sb; *(plombier, médecin)* to send for sb; **faire a. à la générosité de qn** to appeal to sb's generosity; **cette formation fait a. à des connaissances commerciales** this training course calls for some knowledge of business; **faire a. à ses souvenirs** to search one's memory; **un a. à la révolte** a call to revolt; *Com* **lancer un a. d'offres** to invite bids (**b**) *(cri)* call; **a. au secours** call for help; **faire un a. de phares à qn** to flash one's headlights at sb; *Fig* **a. du pied** veiled hint (**c**) *(attirance)* call; **l'a. du large/de la nature** the call of the sea/of the wild; **a. d'air** *(courant d'air)* draught (**d**) **a. (téléphonique)** (tele)phone call; **a. gratuit** *Br* freefone call, *Am* toll-free call (**e**) *(pour vérifier)* **faire l'a.** to have a roll call; *Scol* to take the register; **manquer/répondre à l'a.** to be absent/present (**f**) *Jur* appeal; **faire a. d'une décision** to appeal against a decision; *Fig* **faire sans a.** *(décision)* to be final (**g**) *Typ* **a. de note** reference figure (**h**) *(pour sauter)* take-off (**i**) *Ordinat* call; *(de commande)* selection

appelé [aple] *nm* (**a**) *Mil* conscript (**b**) *Fig* **il y a beaucoup d'appelés, mais peu d'élus** many are called, but few are chosen

appeler [aple] **1** *vt* (**a**) *(personne, chien)* to call (to); *(taxi)* to hail; **a. (qn) au secours** to call to sb for help; **il arrive qu'il appelle la nuit** he sometimes calls out in the night
  (**b**) **a. qn (au téléphone)** to call sb, to ring sb (up); **a. un taxi/un médecin** to call or ring for a taxi/a doctor; **laisse-la a. la première** wait for her to call you
  (**c**) *(faire venir)* to send for; *(ascenseur)* to call; **faire a. un médecin** to send for a doctor; **a. qn à faire qch** *(inviter)* to call on sb to do sth; *aussi Hum* **le devoir t'appelle** duty calls
  (**d**) *(désigner)* to call
  (**e**) **être appelé à faire qch** *(être destiné à)* to be destined to do sth; *(avoir l'obligation de)* to be called upon to do sth
  (**f**) *(demander, réclamer)* (solution, mesures) to call for; *(critique)* to invite
  2 en appeler à *vt ind* to appeal to
  3 s'appeler *vpr* (**a**) *(avoir pour nom)* to be called; **comment vous appelez-vous?** what's your name?; **je m'appelle David** my name's David (**b**) *(se téléphoner)* **alors, on s'appelle, hein?** talk to you on the phone, okay?

appellation [apɛlasjɔ̃] *nf* name; *(de produit)* designation; **a. contrôlée** *(de vin)* guaranteed vintage; **a. d'origine** = guarantee of wine quality

appendice [apɛ̃dis] *nm* (**a**) *Anat* appendix; *Zool & Bot* appendage (**b**) *(d'un livre)* appendix

appendicite [apɛ̃disit] *nf* appendicitis; **une crise d'a.** appendicitis; **se faire opérer de l'a.** to have one's appendix out

appesantir [apəzɑ̃tir] **1** *vt (démarche)* to slow down; **les paupières appesanties par le sommeil** eyes heavy with sleep
  2 s'appesantir *vpr (démarche)* to slow down; *Fig* **s'a. sur qch** *(sujet)* to dwell at length on sth

appétissant, -e [apetisɑ̃, -ɑ̃t] *adj (nourriture)* appetizing, tempting

appétit [apeti] *nm* (**a**) *(de nourriture)* appetite; **couper l'a. à qn** to spoil sb's appetite; **donner de l'a. à qn, mettre qn en a.** to give sb an appetite; **manger de bon a.** to tuck in; **avoir un a. d'oiseau** to have a poor appetite; **avoir bon ou un gros a.** to have a good appetite; **bon a.!** enjoy your meal!; *Prov* **l'a. vient en mangeant** it's only when you start eating that you realize you're hungry (**b**) *(désir)* (de culture, de connaissances) appetite (**de** for)

applaudimètre [aplodimɛtr] *nm* clapometer

applaudir [aplodir] **1** *vt* to applaud
  2 *vi* to applaud, to clap
  3 applaudir à *vt ind (décision, changement)* to applaud

applaudissements [aplodismɑ̃] *nmpl* applause, clapping; **un tonnerre ou une tempête d'a.** thunderous applause

applicable [aplikabl] *adj* applicable (**à** to)

applicateur [aplikatœr] *nm (dispositif)* applicator

application [aplikasjɔ̃] *nf* (**a**) *(de peinture, de pommade)* application (**b**) *(d'un règlement)* application; *(de la loi, d'une peine)* enforcement; **mettre une théorie en a.** to put a theory into practice; **mettre une loi en a.** to enforce a law; **entrer en a.** to come into force (**c**) *(emploi)* application (**d**) *(assiduité)* application; **travailler avec a.** to apply oneself to one's work (**e**) *Ordinat* application

applique [aplik] *nf (lampe)* wall light

appliqué, -e [aplike] *adj* (**a**) *(personne)* hard-working, diligent; *(écriture)* careful (**b**) *(sciences)* applied

appliquer [aplike] **1** vt (a) (mettre) to apply (sur to) (b) (utiliser) to apply (à to); (loi, peine) to enforce

2 s'appliquer vpr (a) (se concentrer) to apply oneself (à to); s'a. à faire qch to take pains to do sth (b) s'a. à (concerner) to apply to (c) (se placer) to be applied

appoint [apwɛ̃] nm (a) (monnaie) exact money or change; faire l'a. to give the exact money (b) (revenu supplémentaire) extra income; d'a. (chauffage, éclairage) additional

appointements [apwɛ̃tmã] nmpl salary

apport [apɔr] nm (contribution) contribution (à to); Fin a. en capital/numéraire capital/cash contribution

apporter [apɔrte] vt (a) (porter) to bring (à to); (capitaux) to bring in; je t'ai apporté la cassette vidéo I've brought you the video (b) (mettre) a. du soin à faire qch to exercise care in doing sth (c) (bonheur, soulagement) to bring (d) (preuve) to provide; (changements) to bring about; ce travail ne m'apporte pas grand-chose I don't very much out of this work

apposer [apoze] vt (affiche) to put up; (signature, scellés, sceau) to affix (à to)

apposition [apozisjɔ̃] nf (a) (d'un sceau, de scellés, de signature) affixing (à to) (b) Gram apposition; en a. in apposition

appréciable [apresjabl] adj (a) (visible) appreciable, noticeable (b) (non négligeable) considerable, appreciable (c) (agréable) (qualités) praiseworthy; (changement) welcome

appréciation [apresjasjɔ̃] nf (a) (évaluation) valuation (b) (opinion) judgement, opinion; (sur devoir scolaire) comment; laisser qch à l'a. de qn to leave sth to sb's discretion (c) (augmentation de valeur) appreciation

apprécier [66] [apresje] **1** vt (a) (température, distance, son) to estimate; (différences, nuances) to appreciate; tu ne l'apprécies pas à sa juste valeur you don't appreciate her true worth (b) (aimer) to like; Fam elle n'a pas apprécié she wasn't too pleased

2 s'apprécier vpr (a) (personnes) to like each other (b) (monnaie) to appreciate

appréhender [apreɑ̃de] vt (a) Jur (arrêter) to arrest, to apprehend (b) (craindre) to dread; a. de faire qch to dread doing sth (c) (comprendre) to grasp

appréhensif, -ive [apreɑ̃sif, -iv] adj apprehensive

appréhension [apreɑ̃sjɔ̃] nf (crainte) apprehension (de about); avoir une a. to be apprehensive

apprendre [58] [aprɑ̃dr] **1** vt (a) (leçon, langue, instrument de musique) to learn; a. à faire qch to learn how to do sth; a. vite/lentement to be a fast/slow learner (b) (nouvelle) to hear; (mort, mariage) to hear of; a. que... to hear that... (c) (enseigner) a. qch à qn to teach sb sth; a. à qn à faire qch to teach sb how to do sth; Fam je t'apprendrai à me parler sur ce ton! I'll teach you to speak to me like that!; Fam ça vous apprendra! that'll teach you! (d) (informer de) a. qch à qn to tell sb sth; vous ne m'apprenez rien! you're telling me!

2 s'apprendre vpr ça s'apprend vite it can be learned quickly; ça s'apprend facilement it's easy to learn

apprenti, -e [aprɑ̃ti] nm,f apprentice; a. menuisier carpenter's apprentice; Fig jouer les apprentis sorciers to bite off more than one can chew

apprentissage [aprɑ̃tisaʒ] nm (a) (professionnel) training; (chez un artisan) apprenticeship; être en a. chez qn to be apprenticed to sb (b) (d'une matière, d'une langue) l'a. de qch learning sth; Fig faire l'a. de qch to learn about sth

apprêté, -e [aprete] adj (style, attitude) affected

apprêter [aprete] **1** vt (a) (repas) to prepare (b) (tissu, cuir) to finish

2 s'apprêter vpr (se préparer) to get ready; s'a. à faire qch to get ready to do sth

apprivoisé, -e [aprivwaze] adj tame

apprivoiser [aprivwaze] **1** vt (animal) to tame; Fig (personne) to win over

2 s'apprivoiser vpr (animal) to become tame; Fig (personne) to become more sociable

approbateur, -trice [aprobatœr, -tris] adj approving

approbation [aprobasjɔ̃] nf approval (de of); le film a reçu l'a. du public the film was well received by the public; pour a. (sur document) for approval

approchant [aprɔʃɑ̃] adj je n'ai jamais rien vu d'a. I've never seen anything like it; voilà ce qu'il a dit ou quelque chose d'a. that's what he said, or something similar

approche [aprɔʃ] nf (a) (dans le temps) approach; à l'a. de la vieillesse as old age draws/drew near; aux approches de la trentaine elle a voulu avoir des enfants as she approached thirty she wanted children (b) (dans l'espace) à son a. as she approached; Fig d'une a. difficile (personne) unapproachable; (livre) hard to understand (c) (d'une question) approach (d) approches (d'une ville, d'un village) outskirts (e) Av approach

approcher [aprɔʃe] **1** vt (a) (mettre plus près) to bring up; a. qch de qn/qch to bring sth near (to) sb/sth (b) (venir près de) to approach, to get closer to; (aborder) to go up to

2 vi (a) (dans l'espace, dans le temps) to approach, to get closer; l'heure ou le moment approche it will soon be time; la nuit approchait it was beginning to get dark; approche, je vais te montrer quelque chose come (over) here, I've got something to show you; a. de qn/qch to approach sb/sth; a. du but to be nearing one's goal; il approche de la trentaine he's getting on for thirty (b) Fig a. de qch (être semblable à) to be close to sth

3 s'approcher vpr to approach, to get closer; s'a. de qn/qch to approach sb/sth; Fig s'a. de qch (être semblable à) to be close to sth

approfondi, -e [aprofɔ̃di] adj (recherche) detailed, extensive; (connaissances, enquête) thorough, in-depth

approfondir [aprofɔ̃dir] vt (examiner) to go thoroughly into

approprié, -e [aproprije] adj appropriate (à for)

approprier [66] [aproprije] **1** vt Belg (nettoyer) to clean; (ranger) to tidy

2 s'approprier vpr s'a. qch to appropriate sth

approuver [apruve] vt (a) (décision, choix) to approve of; a. qn (d'avoir fait qch) to think sb is right (to have done sth) (b) (facture, contrat, projet de loi) to approve

approvisionnement [aprovizjɔnmã] nm (a) (ravitaillement) (d'une ville, d'une armée) supplying (en with); (d'un magasin) stocking (en with) (b) approvisionnements (stocks) supplies

approvisionner [aprovizjɔne] **1** vt (a) (ville, armée, personne) to supply (en with); (magasin) to stock (en with) (b) (compte bancaire) to pay money into; son compte en banque n'est plus approvisionné his bank account is no longer in credit

2 s'approvisionner vpr to get in supplies (en of); s'a. chez qn to get one's supplies from sb; (faire ses courses) to shop at sb's

approximatif, -ive [apɔksimatif, -iv] *adj (calcul, estimation)* approximate; **dans un anglais a.** in broken English

approximation [apɔksimasjɔ̃] *nf* approximation

approximativement [apɔksimativmɑ̃] *adv* approximately

appt *(abrév* **appartement)** *Br* flat, *Am* apartment

appui [apɥi] *nm* (a) *(support)* support; **prendre a. sur qch** *(personne)* to lean on sth; **prendre a. sur le pied gauche** *(pour sauter)* to take off from the left foot; **a. de fenêtre** window ledge *or* sill (b) *(moral)* support, backing; **à l'a. de qch** in support of sth; **preuves à l'a.** with supporting evidence

appui-tête *(pl* **appuis-tête)** [apɥitɛt] *nm* headrest

appuyé, -e [apɥije] *adj (plaisanterie, ironie)* laboured; **il lui lançait des regards appuyés** he stared at him intently

appuyer [32] [apɥije] **1** *vt* **a** *(poser)* to lean, to rest *(contre* against) (b) *(appliquer)* **a. qch sur qch** to press sth on sth; **a. le pied sur la pédale de frein** to put one's foot on the brake; *Fig (demande, pétition, candidat)* to support, to back; *(proposition)* to second

2 *vi (presser)* to press; **a. sur un bouton** to press a button **3** **s'appuyer** *vpr* (a) *(reposer)* **s'a. sur/contre** to lean on/against; *Fig* **s'a. sur qch** *(être basé sur)* to be based on sth; *(se servir de)* to draw on sth (b) *Fam* **s'a. qch** *(corvée)* to get lumbered with sth

âpre [apr] *adj* (a) *(aigre)* bitter; *(vin)* rough (b) *(vent)* raw (c) *(concurrence)* fierce; **être â. au gain** to be money-grabbing

âprement [aprəmɑ̃] *adv* fiercely

après [apɛ] **1** *prép* (a) *(dans le temps, dans l'espace)* after; **jour a. jour** day after day; **a. s'être rasé** after shaving; **a. vous, Monsieur/Madame!** after you!; *Fam* **courir a. qn** to run after sb; *Fig (faire la cour à)* to chase sb; **il est toujours a. moi** he's always nagging me; *Fam* **en avoir a. qn** to have it in for sb; **a. coup** after the event; **a. tout** after all (b) **d'a.** *(selon)* according to; **d'a. l'article 12** under article 12

2 *adv* afterwards; **six semaines a.** six weeks later; **a. que** after, when; **avec lui, la famille, ça passe a.** his family takes second place; **le jour d'a.** the next *or* following day; **et a.?** what happened next?; *Fam* **et puis a.?** so what?

après- [apɛ] *préf* post-; **l'a.-68** the post-1968 period; **l'a.-Gorbatchev** the post-Gorbachev era

après-demain [apɛdəmɛ̃] *adv* the day after tomorrow

après-guerre *(pl* **après-guerres)** [apɛgɛʁ] *nm* post-war period

après-midi [apɛmidi] *nm inv ou nf inv* afternoon; **trois heures de l'a.** three (o'clock) in the afternoon

après-rasage *(pl* **après-rasages)** [apɛʁazaʒ] *nm & adj inv* aftershave

après-ski *(pl* **après-skis)** [apɛski] *nm* snowboot

après-soleil [apɛsɔlɛj] *adj inv voir* **lait**

après-vente [apɛvɑ̃t] *adj inv Com* **service a.** aftersales service

âpreté [apʁəte] *nf* (a) *(aigreur)* bitterness; *(du vin)* roughness (b) *(du vent)* rawness (c) *(de la concurrence)* fierceness

a priori [apʁijɔʁi] **1** *adv* in principle

2 *nm inv* preconception; **avoir des a.** (contre/en faveur de qch) to be prejudiced (against/in favour of sth); **être sans a.** to be impartial

apr. J.-C. *(abrév* **après Jésus-Christ)** AD

à-propos [apʁopo] *nm (d'une remarque, d'une réaction)* appropriateness; **avoir l'esprit d'à.** to have presence of mind; **répondre avec à.** to give an appropriate reply

apte [apt] *adj* **a. à qch/à faire qch** fit for sth/for doing sth; *Mil* **a. au service** fit for military service

aptitude [aptityd] *nf (capacité)* aptitude, ability (à *ou* pour for)

aquaplanage [akwaplanaʒ], **aquaplaning** [akwaplaniŋ] *nm Aut* aquaplaning

aquarelle [akwaʁɛl] *nf* watercolour; **peindre à l'a.** to paint in watercolours

aquarium [akwaʁjɔm] *nm* aquarium

aquatique [akwatik] *adj* aquatic

aqueduc [akədyk] *nm* aqueduct

aqueux, -euse [akø, -øz] *adj Anat & Chim* aqueous; *(soupe)* watery

aquilin, -e [akilɛ̃, -in] *adj* aquiline

Aquitaine [akitɛn] *nf* l'A. Aquitaine

arabe [aʁab] **1** *adj (monde, littérature, pays)* Arab, Arabic; *(chiffres, langue)* Arabic; *(cheval)* Arab; *(coutumes, civilisation)* Arabian, Arabic

2 *nmf* A. Arab

3 *nm (langue)* Arabic

arabesque [aʁabɛsk] *nf* arabesque

arabica [aʁabika] *nm* arabica

Arabie [aʁabi] *nf* l'A. Arabia; **l'A. saoudite** Saudi Arabia

arable [aʁabl] *adj* arable

arachide [aʁaʃid] *nf (plante)* peanut, groundnut; **huile d'a.** peanut *or* groundnut oil

araignée [aʁeɲe] *nf* spider; *Fam* **avoir une a. au plafond** to have a screw loose; **a. de mer** spider crab

Aral [aʁal] *n voir* **mer**

arbalète [aʁbalɛt] *nf* crossbow

arbitrage [aʁbitʁaʒ] *nm* (a) *(au tennis)* umpiring; *(au football)* refereeing (b) *(dans un conflit)* arbitration

arbitraire [aʁbitʁɛʁ] *adj* arbitrary

arbitrairement [aʁbitʁɛʁmɑ̃] *adv* arbitrarily

arbitre [aʁbitʁ] *nm* (a) *(au tennis)* umpire; *(au football)* referee (b) *(dans un conflit)* arbitrator (c) *Phil* **libre a.** free will

arbitrer [aʁbitʁe] *vt* (a) *(match de tennis)* to umpire; *(match de football)* to referee (b) *(dans un conflit)* to arbitrate

arborer [aʁbɔʁe] *vt (porter, exhiber)* to wear, to sport

arborescence [aʁbɔʁesɑ̃s] *nf Ordinat* tree diagram

arborescent, -e [aʁbɔʁesɑ̃, -ɑ̃t] *adj* (a) *Bot* arborescent (b) *Math & Ordinat* **structure arborescente** tree diagram

arboriculteur, -trice [aʁbɔʁikyltœʁ, -tʁis] *nm,f* tree grower

arboriculture [aʁbɔʁikyltyʁ] *nf* tree growing

arbre [aʁbʁ] *nm* (a) *(végétal)* tree; *Fig* **les arbres cachent la forêt** you can't see the wood for the trees; **a. fruitier** fruit tree; **a. de Noël** Christmas tree (b) **a. généalogique** family tree; **faire son a. généalogique** to trace one's family tree (c) *Tech* shaft; **a. à cames** camshaft; **a. de transmission** transmission shaft

arbrisseau, -x [aʁbʁiso] *nm* shrub

arbuste [aʁbyst] *nm* shrub

arc [ark] *nm* (**a**) (*arme*) bow (**b**) *Archit & Anat* arch; **a. de triomphe** triumphal arch (**c**) (*de cercle*) arc; **assis en a. de cercle** sitting in a semicircle

arcade [arkad] *nf* (**a**) *Archit* archway; **arcades** (*d'une place*) arcade (**b**) *Anat* **a. sourcilière** arch of the eyebrows

arc-bouter [arkbute] **s'arc-bouter** *vpr* to brace oneself

arceau, -x [arso] *nm* (**a**) (*d'une voûte*) arch (**b**) (*au croquet*) hoop; **a. de sécurité** roll bar

arc-en-ciel (*pl* arcs-en-ciel) [arkãsjel] *nm* rainbow

archaïque [arkaik] *adj* archaic

archaïsme [arkaism] *nm* archaism

archange [arkãʒ] *nm* archangel

arche[1] [arʃ] *nf* **l'a. de Noé** Noah's ark

arche[2] *nf* (*d'un pont*) arch

archéologie [arkeɔlɔʒi] *nf* archaeology

archéologique [arkeɔlɔʒik] *adj* archaeological

archéologue [arkeɔlɔg] *nmf* archaeologist

archer [arʃe] *nm* archer

archet [arʃe] *nm* bow (*for violin*)

archétype [arketip] *nm* archetype; **c'est l'a. du père de famille** he is the archetypal father figure

archevêque [arʃəvek] *nm* archbishop

archiconnu, -e [arʃikɔny] *adj Fam* very well-known

archiduc [arʃidyk] *nm* archduke

archiduchesse [arʃidyʃes] *nf* archduchess

archifaux, -fausse [arʃifo, -fos] *adj Fam* dead wrong

Archimède [arʃimed] *npr* Archimedes

archipel [arʃipel] *nm* archipelago

architecte [arʃitekt] *nm* architect

architectural, -e, -aux, -ales [arʃitektyral, -o] *adj* architectural

architecture [arʃitektyr] *nf aussi Ordinat* architecture; *Fig* structure

architecturé, -e [arʃitektyre] *adj Ordinat* **a. autour de** with its architecture built around

archiver [arʃive] *vt* (*documents officiels*) to archive; (*factures*) to file

archives [arʃiv] *nfpl* archives, records; **les a. nationales** ≃ the (Public) Record Office

archiviste [arʃivist] *nmf* archivist; (*employé de bureau*) filing clerk

arçon [arsõ] *nm* saddle bow

arctique [arktik] **1** *adj* arctic
2 *nm* **l'A.** the Arctic

ardemment [ardamã] *adv* (*aimer*) passionately; **désirer qch a.** to long for sth

ardent, -e [ardã, -ãt] *adj* (**a**) (*braises, soleil*) scorching, blazing; (*soif, fièvre*) raging (**b**) (*tempérament, jeunesse*) fiery; (*désir*) burning; (*lutte*) fierce

ardeur [ardœr] *nf* (**a**) (*enthousiasme*) ardour, fervour; **travailler avec a.** to work enthusiastically (**b**) (*du soleil, du feu*) intense heat

ardoise [ardwaz] *nf* (**a**) (*matière, plaque, pour écrire*) slate; **toit d'ardoises** slate roof (**b**) *Fam* (*compte*) tab; **il a des ardoises dans tous les bars de la ville** he owes money in every bar in town

ardu, -e [ardy] *adj* arduous

are [ar] *nm* are, = 100 m²

aréna [arena] *nf Can* = sports centre including an ice rink

arène [aren] *nf* (*d'amphithéâtre*) arena; (*de tauromachie*) bullring; **arènes** (*antiques*) amphitheatre; *Fig* **descendre dans l'a.** to enter the fray; *Fig* **l'a. politique** the political arena

arête [aret] *nf* (**a**) (*de poisson*) bone; **sans arêtes** boneless; **enlever les arêtes d'un poisson** to fillet a fish (**b**) (*du nez*) bridge (**c**) (*d'un solide*) edge (**d**) *Géog* ridge

argent [arʒã] *nm* (**a**) (*métal*) silver; **bracelet d'a.** *ou* **en a.** silver bracelet (**b**) (*monnaie*) money; **en avoir pour son a.** to get one's money's worth; *Fig* **prendre qch pour a. comptant** to take sth at face value; *Prov* **l'a. ne fait pas le bonheur** money can't buy you happiness; **a. liquide** cash; **a. de poche** pocket money (**c**) (*couleur*) silver
2 *adj inv* silver

argenté, -e [arʒãte] *adj* (**a**) (*couleur*) silver (**b**) (*plaqué*) silver-plated

argenterie [arʒãtri] *nf* (silver) plate, silverware

argentin, -e [arʒãtẽ, -in] **1** *adj* Argentinian, Argentine
2 *nm,f* **A.** Argentinian, Argentine

Argentine [arʒãtin] *nf* **l'A.** Argentina

argile [arʒil] *nf* clay

argileux, -euse [arʒilø, -øz] *adj* clayey

argot [argo] *nm* slang

argotique [argotik] *adj* slang, slangy

arguer [arge, argɥe] **arguer de** *vt ind Litt* **a. de qch** to give sth as a reason

argument [argymã] *nm* argument; **a. de vente** selling point

argumentaire [argymãter] *nm* sales blurb

argumentation [argymãtasjõ] *nf* (*arguments*) argument

argumenter [argymãte] *vi* to argue (**contre/en faveur de** against/for)

argus [argys] *nm* = guide to used car prices

aria [arja] *nf Mus* aria

aride [arid] *adj* (*pays*) arid, barren; (*œuvre, sujet*) dry

aridité [aridite] *nf* aridity, barrenness

aristocrate [aristokrat] *nmf* aristocrat

aristocratie [aristokrasi] *nf* aristocracy

aristocratique [aristokratik] *adj* aristocratic

Aristote [aristot] *npr* Aristotle

arithmétique [aritmetik] **1** *adj* arithmetical
2 *nf* (*matière, calculs*) arithmetic

arlequin [arləkẽ] *nm Th* Harlequin

armagnac [armaɲak] *nm* Armagnac

armateur [armatœr] *nm* shipowner

armature [armatyr] *nf* framework; (*dans le béton*) reinforcement; (*de tente, d'abat-jour*) frame; (*de soutien-gorge*) underwiring

arme [arm] *nf* (**a**) (*de combat*) arm, weapon; **peuple/ville en armes** nation/town in arms; **prendre les armes** to take up arms (**contre** against); **aux armes!** to arms!; **le métier** *ou* **la carrière des armes** the military profession; **passer qn par les armes** to send sb to the firing squad; *Fam* **passer l'a. à gauche** to snuff it, to kick the bucket; **faire ses premières armes** to earn one's spurs; **à armes égales** on equal terms; **avec armes et bagages** with bag and baggage; **a. blanche** knife; **a. à feu** firearm (**b**) (*section de l'armée*) service (**c**) **armes** (*blason*) (coat of) arms

armé, -e [arme] *adj* (a) *(muni d'une arme)* armed; **a. jusqu'aux dents** armed to the teeth; *aussi Fig* **être a. de qch** to be armed with sth; *Fig* **être a. pour qch** *(préparé)* to be equipped for sth (b) *(renforcé)* fortified, strengthened

armée [arme] *nf aussi Fig* army; **être dans l'a.** to be in the army; **être à l'a.** to be doing one's military service; **l'a. de l'air** the air force; **a. de métier** professional army; **a. régulière** *ou* **active** regular army; **a. de réserve** reserves; **l'A. du salut** the Salvation Army; **l'a. de terre** the army

armement [armamɑ̃] *nm* (a) *(action) (d'un pays, d'une région)* armament; *(d'une armée)* arming (b) **armements** *(armes)* armaments, weaponry (c) *(d'une arme à feu)* cocking; *(d'un appareil photo)* setting (d) *(de navire)* commissioning, fitting out

Arménie [armeni] *nf* l'A. Armenia

arménien, -enne [armenjɛ̃, -ɛn] **1** *adj* Armenian **2** *nm,f* A. Armenian **3** *nm (langue)* Armenian

armer [arme] **1** *vt* (a) *(munir d'armes)* to arm **(de** with); **je sors toujours armé** I always carry a weapon when I go out (b) *(navire)* to commission, to fit out (c) *(arme à feu)* to cock; *(appareil photo)* to set **2** **s'armer** *vpr* to arm oneself; **s'a. de courage/de patience** to summon up (one's) courage/patience

armistice [armistis] *nm* armistice

armoire [armwar] *nf (placard)* Br cupboard, Am closet; *(pour les vêtements)* Br wardrobe, Am closet; **a. à glace** mirrored wardrobe; *Fam* **c'est une a. à glace** he's built like a tank; **a. de toilette** *ou* **de salle de bain** bathroom cabinet

armoiries [armwari] *nfpl* (coat of) arms

armure [armyr] *nf* armour

armurier [armyrje] *nm* (a) *(vendeur)* gun dealer (b) *(dans une caserne)* armourer

ARN [aɛrɛn] *nm (abrév* **acide ribonucléique)** RNA

arnaque [arnak] *nf Fam* rip-off; **c'est de l'a.!** what a rip-off!

arnaquer [arnake] *vt Fam* to rip off; **se faire a.** to get ripped off

arnaqueur, -euse [arnakœr, -øz] *nm,f Fam* rip-off merchant

arnica [arnika] *nm ou nf* arnica

aromate [arɔmat] *nm (herbe)* herb; *(épice)* spice

aromathérapie [arɔmaterapi] *nf* aromatherapy

aromatique [arɔmatik] *adj* aromatic

aromatisé, -e [arɔmatize] *adj* flavoured; **a. à la vanille** vanilla-flavoured

arôme [arom] *nm (parfum)* aroma; *(goût)* flavour; **crème glacée, a. vanille** vanilla ice cream

arpège [arpɛʒ] *nm Mus* arpeggio

arpent [arpɑ̃] *nm =* former land measurement approximately equivalent to one acre

arpenter [arpɑ̃te] *vt* (a) *(mesurer)* to survey, to measure (b) *(parcourir)* to pace up and down

arqué, -e [arke] *adj (sourcils)* arched; *(nez)* hooked; **jambes arquées** bow legs

arquer [arke] **s'arquer** *vpr* to bend, to curve

arrachage [araʃaʒ] *nm (de plantes)* uprooting; *(de pommes de terre)* lifting; *(d'une dent, d'un clou, de piquets)* pulling out

arraché [araʃe] *nm (en haltérophilie)* snatch; *Fig* **gagner à l'a.** to snatch victory; *Fig* **ils ont obtenu le contrat à l'a.** it was a struggle for them to get the contract

arrachement [araʃmɑ̃] *nm (peine)* wrench

arrache-pied [araʃpje] **d'arrache-pied** *adv* relentlessly

arracher [araʃe] **1** *vt* (a) *(arbre)* to uproot; *(légumes)* to lift; *(dent, mauvaises herbes, piquets)* to pull out; *(page)* to tear out; *(affiche)* to tear down; *(vêtement, membre, toit)* to tear off; **se faire a. une dent** to have a tooth out; **a. qch à qn/des mains de qn** to snatch sth from sb/from sb's hands; *Fig* **je vais lui a. les yeux!** I'll scratch his eyes out! (b) *(obtenir)* **a. qch à qn** *(argent)* to get sth off sb; *(secret)* to drag sth out of sb; *(promesse, sourire)* to force sth out of sb; *Fig* **nous sommes finalement parvenus à lui a. quelques mots** nevertheless, we did manage to get a few words out of him (c) *(séparer)* **a. un enfant à sa mère** to take a child away from its mother; **a. qn à la mort** to snatch sb from the jaws of death; **a. qn à son travail** to tear or drag sb away from his work (d) *Fam (sujet: alcool, piment)* **ça arrache!** it brings tears to your eyes!

2 **s'arracher** *vpr* (a) *(se disputer)* **s'a. qn/qch** to fight over sb/sth (b) *(se retirer)* **c'est à s'a. les cheveux!** it's enough to make you tear your hair out!; **s'a. à son travail** to tear oneself away from one's work (c) *très Fam (partir)* to hit the road

arracheur [araʃœr] *nm* **mentir comme un a. de dents** to lie through one's teeth

arraisonner [arɛzɔne] *vt* to stop and examine

arrangeant, -e [arɑ̃ʒɑ̃, -ɑ̃t] *adj* helpful

arrangement [arɑ̃ʒmɑ̃] *nm* (a) *(fait de disposer)* arranging; *(manière d'être disposé)* arrangement (b) *(accord)* agreement, settlement (c) *Mus* arrangement

arranger [45] [arɑ̃ʒe] **1** *vt* (a) *(meubles, fleurs)* to arrange; *(pièce, maison)* to put in order; *(cravate, col)* to straighten (b) *(réparer)* to repair (c) *(organiser)* to arrange, to organize; **j'ai tout arrangé** I've made all the arrangements (d) *(régler) (problème)* to settle; **cela n'arrangera rien** that won't help things; *Ironique* **pour tout a., il s'est mis à pleuvoir** just to help matters, it started to rain (e) *Fam* **a. qn** *(maltraiter)* to give sb a going over; *(critiquer)* to tear sb to pieces (f) *(convenir à)* to suit; **faire qch pour a. qn** to do sth to help sb out (g) *Mus* to arrange

2 **s'arranger** *vpr* (a) *(s'organiser)* to manage; **arrangez-vous pour être là/finir à temps** make sure you're there/you finish on time; *Fam* **je ne sais pas comment tu t'arranges, tu es toujours en retard** I don't know how you manage it, but you're always late (b) *(s'améliorer)* to work out; **ça ne s'arrange pas!** things aren't getting any better! (c) *(rectifier son apparence)* to tidy oneself up (d) *(se mettre d'accord)* to come to an agreement (avec with); **ça ne me regarde pas, arrange-toi avec elle** it's got nothing to do with me, sort it out with her (e) *(se contenter)* **s'a. de qch** to make do with sth

arrestation [arɛstasjɔ̃] *nf* arrest; **en état d'a.** under arrest

arrêt [arɛ] *nm* (a) *(interruption) (des combats, des hostilités, de la production)* stop; **Clermont-Ferrand, dix minutes d'a.** *(en train)* this is Clermont-Ferrand, there will be a ten-minute stop; **sans a.** continuously; **tomber en a. devant qn/qch** to stop and stare at sb/sth; **marquer un temps d'a.** to pause; **a. du cœur** heart failure; *Ordinat* **a. de défilement** scroll lock; *TV & Cin* **a. sur image** freeze frame; **a. de jeu** stoppage; **a. de travail** sick leave (b) *(de véhicule)* stop; **ne pas descendre avant**

l'a. complet du train *(sur la portière)* do not get off before the train has come to a complete stop; **le train est sans a. jusqu'à Hendaye** the train is non-stop to Hendaye; **a. de bus** bus stop; **a. facultatif** request stop (C) *Jur* judgement; *aussi Fig* **a. de mort** death sentence

arrêté -e [arete] **1** *adj (idées)* fixed

2 *nm (décret)* order, decree; **a. ministériel** ministerial order; **a. municipal** bylaw; **a. préfectoral** bylaw

arrêter [arete] **1** *vt* (a) *(personne, animal, véhicule)* to stop; *(machine, moteur, musique)* to turn off; *(fuite)* to stem; *(études)* to give up; **là je vous arrête, je ne suis pas d'accord!** hold it right there, I don't agree!; **arrête-moi au carrefour** drop me off at the crossroads; **rien ne l'arrête** nothing will stop him; **a. de faire qch** to stop doing sth; **elle n'arrête pas de me déranger** she keeps disturbing me; **ce détail retint mon attention** this detail caught my attention (b) *(criminel)* to arrest (C) *(déterminer)* to decide; *(date, prix)* to fix

2 *vi* to stop; **arrête!** stop it!

3 s'arrêter *vpr* (a) *(cesser, s'immobiliser)* to stop; **s'a. de faire qch** to stop doing sth; **s'a. chez qn** to call in at sb's house (b) **s'a. à qch** *(faire attention à)* to pay attention to sth

arrhes [ar] *nfpl* deposit

arrière [arjɛr] **1** *adj inv back;* **feu a.** rear light; **roue a.** rear *or* back wheel

2 *nm* (a) *(d'une maison, d'un avion)* back; *(d'un bateau)* stern; **à l'a. de la voiture** in the back of the car (b) *Mil* **l'a. the rear;** *Fig* **protéger ses arrières** to leave oneself a way out (C) *(au football, au rugby)* full back

3 *exclam* stand back!

4 en arrière *adv* (a) *(derrière)* behind; **rester en a.** to lag behind; **en a. de qn/qch** behind sb/sth (b) *(dans la direction inverse)* backwards; **pencher la tête en a.** to lean one's head back; **retourner en a.** to go *or* turn back

arriéré -e [arjere] **1** *adj* (a) *(paiement)* overdue (b) *(dans ses idées, son développement)* backward

2 *nm* arrears

arrière-boutique *(pl* arrière-boutiques*)* [arjɛr-butik] *nf Br* back shop, *Am* back store

arrière-cour *(pl* arrière-cours*)* [arjɛrkur] *nf* backyard

arrière-garde *(pl* arrière-gardes*)* [arjɛrgard] *nf* rearguard

arrière-goût *(pl* arrière-goûts*)* [arjɛrgu] *nm aussi Fig* aftertaste

arrière-grand-mère *(pl* arrière-grands-mères*)* [arjɛrgrɑ̃mɛr] *nf* great-grandmother

arrière-grand-père *(pl* arrière-grands-pères*)* [arjɛrgrɑ̃pɛr] *nm* great-grandfather

arrière-grands-parents [arjɛrgrɑ̃parɑ̃] *nmpl* great-grandparents

arrière-pays [arjɛrpei] *nm inv* hinterland

arrière-pensée *(pl* arrière-pensées*)* [arjɛrpɑ̃se] *nf* ulterior motive

arrière-petite-fille *(pl* arrière-petites-filles*)* [arjɛrpətitfij] *nf* great-granddaughter

arrière-petit-fils *(pl* arrière-petits-fils*)* [arjɛrpətifis] *nm* great-grandson

arrière-petits-enfants [arjɛrpətizɑ̃fɑ̃] *nmpl* great-grandchildren

arrière-plan *(pl* arrière-plans*)* [arjɛrplɑ̃] *nm aussi Fig* background; **à l'a.** in the background

arrière-saison *(pl* arrière-saisons*)* [arjɛrsɛzɔ̃] *nf Br* late autumn, *Am* late fall

arrière-train *(pl* arrière-trains*)* [arjɛrtrɛ̃] *nm (d'un animal)* (hind)quarters; *Fam (d'une personne)* rump, rear

arrimer [arime] *vt* (a) *Naut (cargaison)* to stow (b) *(fixer)* to secure *or* fasten (à to)

arrivage [ariva3] *nm* consignment

arrivant -e [arivɑ̃, -ɑ̃t] *nm,f* arrival; **les nouveaux arrivants** the new arrivals, the newcomers

arrivé -e [arive] **1** *adj* **être a.** *(socialement)* to have arrived, to have made it

2 *nm (personne)* **le premier/dernier a.** the first/last (person) to arrive

arrivée [arive] *nf* (a) *(venue)* arrival; **depuis son a. au pouvoir** since he came to power; **à mon a.** when I arrive/arrived; **arrivées** *(sur panneau)* arrivals (b) *Tech* inlet (C) *(d'une course)* winning post, finish

arriver [arive] *(aux être)* **1** *vi* (a) *(venir)* to arrive; **a. à Lyon/in France** to arrive in Lyons/in France; **a. le premier/dernier** *(à une soirée)* to arrive first/last; **a. premier/second** *(dans un concours, une course)* to come first/second; **j'arrive!** (I'm) coming!; **c'est à cette heure-là que tu arrives?** and what time do you call this?; **nous sommes presque arrivés** we're almost there

(b) *(atteindre)* **l'eau m'arrive aux chevilles** the water comes up to my ankles; **ses cheveux lui arrivent aux épaules** her hair comes down to her shoulders *or* is shoulder-length

(c) **en a. à faire qch** to get to the stage of doing sth; **c'est malheureux d'en a. là** it's a shame it's got to that stage; **j'en arrive à penser que.../me demander si...** I'm beginning to think.../wonder if...

(d) *(socialement)* to arrive, to make it

(e) *(parvenir)* **a. à un résultat** to achieve a result; **a. à faire qch** to manage to do sth; **je n'arrive pas à l'ouvrir** I can't get it open; **il n'arrivera jamais à rien** he'll never make anything of himself

(f) *(se produire)* to happen (à to)

2 *v impersonnel* **quoi qu'il arrive** whatever happens; **il lui est arrivé quelque chose** something's happened to him; **il m'arrive d'y penser** I sometimes think about it; **il arrive à tout le monde de se tromper** anyone can make a mistake; **qu'est-ce qu'il t'arrive?** what's wrong (with you)?

arrivisme [arivism] *nm* unscrupulous ambition

arriviste [arivist] *nmf* social climber, arriviste

arrogance [arɔgɑ̃s] *nf* arrogance; **avec a.** arrogantly

arrogant -e [arɔgɑ̃, -ɑ̃t] *adj* arrogant

arroger [45] [arɔʒe] **s'arroger** *vpr* **s'a. un droit/un privilège** to claim a right/a privilege

arrondi -e [arɔ̃di] **1** *adj (objet, visage)* round

2 *nm* (a) *(forme)* roundness, rounded form (b) *(d'une jupe)* hemline

arrondir [arɔ̃dir] **1** *vt* (a) *(forme)* **a. qch** to make sth round; **cette coiffure lui arrondit le visage** that haircut makes her face look round; *Fig* **a. les angles** to smooth things over (b) *(chiffre, somme)* *(vers le haut)* to round up; *(vers le bas)* to round down; *Fam* **a. ses fins de mois** to supplement one's income; **a. au franc supérieur/inférieur** to round up/down to the nearest franc

2 s'arrondir *vpr (corps, visage)* to fill out

arrondissement [arɔ̃dismɑ̃] *nm* = administrative subdivision of Paris, Lyons and Marseilles

arrosage [arozaʒ] *nm (des plantes, du sol)* watering; *(des rues)* spraying; *(d'une pelouse)* sprinkling

arroser [aroze] **1** *vt* **(a)** *(plantes, sol)* to water; *(pelouse)* to sprinkle; *(rues)* to spray; *(rôti)* to baste; **région très peu arrosée** area with little rainfall; **a. qch d'essence** to douse sth in petrol **(b)** *(fêter)* to drink to; **un repas bien arrosé** a meal washed down with plenty of alcohol **(c)** *(sujet: rivière)* to flow through

2 s'arroser *vpr (se fêter)* **ça s'arrose!** that calls for a drink!

arroseur [arozœr] *nm (appareil)* sprinkler

arrosoir [arozwar] *nm* watering can

arsenal, -aux [arsenal, -o] *nm* **(a)** *Mil* arsenal; **a. maritime** *ou* **de la marine** naval dockyard **(b)** *Fam (attirail)* gear

arsenic [arsenik] *nm* arsenic

art [ar] *nm* **(a)** *(esthétique)* art; **c'est du grand a.!** it's a work of art; **le septième a.** cinema; **a. dramatique** drama, dramatic art; **les arts graphiques** graphic arts; **l'a. lyrique** opera; **arts martiaux** martial arts; **arts plastiques** fine art **(b)** *(savoir-faire)* **l'a. de faire qch** the art of doing sth; **cultiver l'a. de vivre** to enjoy the finer things in life; **préparer le café, c'est tout un a.** there's quite an art to making coffee; *Fig* **avoir l'a. de faire qch** to have a knack for doing sth

Arte [arte] *n* = French-German TV channel showing cultural programmes

artère [arter] *nf* **(a)** *(vaisseau)* artery **(b)** *(route)* arterial road; *(en ville)* main thoroughfare

artériel, -elle [arterjɛl] *adj (système, maladie)* arterial

artériosclérose [arterjoskleroz] *nf* hardening of the arteries, *Spéc* arteriosclerosis

arthrite [artrit] *nf* arthritis

arthrose [artroz] *nf* osteoarthritis

Arthur [artyr] *npr Fam* **je vais me faire appeler A.!** I'm going to get a real telling-off!

artichaut [artiʃo] *nm* artichoke

article [artikl] *nm* **(a)** *Com* item; **articles de toilette** toiletries; **faire l'a.** to make a sales pitch **(b)** *Journ* article; *(de dictionnaire)* entry **(c)** *(d'un traité, d'un règlement)* article **(d)** *Gram* article; **a. défini/indéfini** definite/indefinite article **(e)** **être à l'a. de la mort** to be on the point of death **(f)** *Ordinat (dans base de données)* record; *(commande)* command

articulaire [artikylɛr] *adj Anat* articular, articulatory

articulation [artikylasjɔ̃] *nf* **(a)** *Anat & Tech* joint **(b)** *(prononciation)* articulation **(c)** *(organisation)* structure

articuler [artikyle] **1** *vt* **(a)** *(idées, arguments)* to link **(b)** *(mots)* to articulate; **articule!** speak clearly!

2 s'articuler *vpr (pièces, idées)* to be linked; **les différentes parties du texte s'articulent bien** the different parts of the text hang well together; **s'a. autour de qch** *(théorie)* to centre on sth

artifice [artifis] *nm* trick

artificiel, -elle [artifisjɛl] *adj* **(a)** *(non naturel)* artificial; *Fig (personne)* false; *(rire)* forced **(b)** *(arbitraire)* arbitrary

artificiellement [artifisjɛlmɑ̃] *adv* **(a)** *(de façon non naturelle)* artificially **(b)** *(arbitrairement)* arbitrarily

artificier [artifisje] *nm (fabricant)* firework manufacturer; *(dans un feu d'artifice)* master of ceremonies

artillerie [artijri] *nf* artillery; **a. légère/lourde** light/heavy artillery; **pièce d'a.** artillery cannon

artilleur [artijœr] *nm* artilleryman

artisan [artizɑ̃] *nm* craftsman, *f* craftswoman; *Fig* architect

artisanal, -e, -aux, -ales [artizanal, -o] *adj* traditionally-made; *(à la main)* hand-made; **métier a.** craft

artisanat [artizana] *nm* craft industry

artiste [artist] **1** *adj (tempérament, style)* artistic; **se donner un genre a.** to cultivate an arty image

2 *nmf* **(a)** *(personne créative)* artist **(b)** *(qui pratique un art)* artiste; *(musicien)* performer; *(acteur)* actor, *f* actress; *(chanteur)* singer; *(danseur)* dancer; **a. (peintre)** artist

artistique [artistik] *adj* artistic

as¹ *voir* **avoir**

as² [as] *nm* **(a)** *(aux cartes)* ace; *(aux dominos, aux dés)* one; *Fam* **être ficelé** *ou* **fichu comme l'as de pique** to be dressed like a tramp; **être plein aux as** to be rolling in it; *Fam* **passer à l'as** to go out of the window **(b)** *Fam (champion)* whizz; **as du volant** crack racing driver; **un as du bricolage** a DIY expert

ascendance [asɑ̃dɑ̃s] *nf (ancêtres)* ancestry

ascendant, -e [asɑ̃dɑ̃, -ɑ̃t] **1** *adj (échelle)* rising; *(mouvement, courant)* upward

2 *nm* **(a)** *(influence)* influence; **avoir de l'a. sur qn** to have influence over sb **(b)** **ascendants** *(ancêtres)* ancestry

ascenseur [asɑ̃sœr] *nm* **(a)** *(dans un bâtiment)* Br lift, Am elevator; *Fam* **je lui renverrai l'a.** I'll return the favour **(b)** *Ordinat* scroll box

ascension [asɑ̃sjɔ̃] *nf* **(a)** *(escalade)* ascent; **faire l'a. d'une montagne** to climb a mountain **(b)** *(progression)* **a. sociale** social climbing **(c)** *Rel* **(la fête** *ou* **le jeudi de) l'A.** Ascension Day

ascensionnel, -elle [asɑ̃sjɔnɛl] *adj (mouvement)* upward

ascète [asɛt] *nmf* ascetic

ascorbique [askɔrbik] *adj (acide)* ascorbic

aseptique [asɛptik] *adj* aseptic

aseptiser [asɛptize] *vt (blessure)* to sterilize; *(pièce)* to disinfect; *Fig & Péj* **un univers aseptisé** a sterile environment

asexué, -e [asɛksɥe], **asexuel, -elle** [asɛksɥɛl] *adj aussi Fig* asexual

ashkénaze [aʃkenaz] *adj & nmf* Ashkenazi

asiatique [azjatik] **1** *adj* oriental

2 *nmf* **A.** Oriental

Asie [azi] *nf* **l'A.** Asia; **l'A. centrale** Central Asia; **l'A. du Sud-Est** South-east Asia

asile [azil] *nm* **(a)** *(abri)* refuge; *Vieilli* **a. (d'aliénés)** mental hospital; **a. de nuit** night shelter; **a. de vieillards** old folk's home **(b)** *(statut)* **a. politique/diplomatique** political/diplomatic asylum; **demander l'a. politique** to ask for political asylum

asocial, -e, -aux, -ales [asɔsjal, -o] **1** *adj* asocial

2 *nm,f* asocial person

aspartam(e) [aspartam] *nm* aspartame

aspect [aspɛ] *nm* **(a)** *(air)* appearance, look **(b)** *(angle)* angle, point of view; **sous tous ses aspects** from every angle, from all points of view **(c)** *Gram* aspect

asperge [aspɛrʒ] *nf* **(a)** *(plante)* asparagus **(b)** *Fam (personne)* beanpole

asperger [45] [aspɛrʒe] **1** *vt (linge, plante)* to spray with water; **a. qn de qch** to splash sb with sth; **se faire a.** to get splashed

2 s'asperger *vpr* **s'a. de qch** to splash oneself with sth

aspérité [asperite] *nf* **(a)** *(d'une surface)* rough part **(b)** *(d'un caractère)* harshness

aspersion [aspɛrsjɔ̃] nf spraying

asphalte [asfalt] nm asphalt

asphyxiant, -e [asfiksjɑ̃, -ɑ̃t] adj asphyxiating, suffocating; **gaz a.** poison gas

asphyxie [asfiksi] nf asphyxiation

asphyxier [65] [asfiksje] 1 vt (a) (personne, animal) to asphyxiate (b) Fig (économie, industrie) to paralyse
2 **s'asphyxier** vpr (suffoquer) to choke; (se suicider) to gas oneself

aspirateur [aspiratœr] nm Hoover®, vacuum (cleaner); **passer l'a. dans la maison** to hoover or vacuum the house

aspiration [aspirasjɔ̃] nf (a) (inhalation) inhalation; Tech (d'eau dans une pompe) suction (b) (désir) yearning (à for); (ambition) aspiration (à for) (c) Ling aspiration

aspiré, -e [aspire] adj Ling aspirate(d)

aspirer [aspire] 1 vt (a) (air, parfum) to inhale, to breathe (in) (b) (liquide) to suck up (c) Ling to aspirate
2 **aspirer à** vt ind to aspire to; **a. à faire qch** to aspire to do sth

aspirine [aspirin] nf aspirin; **un cachet d'a.** an aspirin; **blanc comme un cachet d'a.** white as a ghost

assagir [asaʒir] 1 vt to quieten down
2 **s'assagir** vpr to settle down

assaillant, -e [asajɑ̃, -ɑ̃t] nm,f assailant, attacker

assaillir [67] [asajir] vt to assault, to attack; Fig (sujet: difficultés, remords, doute) to beset; **a. qn de questions** to bombard sb with questions; **il a été assailli par les journalistes** he was set upon by the journalists

assainir [asenir] vt (maison, rivière) to clean up; (atmosphère) to purify; (marais) to drain; (économie) to stabilize

assainissement [asenismɑ̃] nm (d'une maison, d'une rivière) cleaning up; (de l'atmosphère) purifying; (d'un marais) drainage; (de l'économie) stabilization

assaisonnement [asɛzɔnmɑ̃] nm (de plat) seasoning; (de salade) dressing

assaisonner [asɛzɔne] vt (plat) to season (de with); (salade) to dress; Fam Fig **se faire a.** to get a good telling-off

assassin [asasɛ̃, -in] 1 nm murderer; (d'une personnalité politique) assassin; **à l'a.!** murder!
2 adj (a) (méchant) (regard) murderous; (remarque) crushing (b) (provocant) (sourire, œillade) provocative

assassinat [asasina] nm murder; (d'une personnalité politique) assassination

assassiner [asasine] vt to murder; (personnalité politique) to assassinate; Fig (chanson, texte) to murder; (sujet: critique) to crucify

assaut [aso] nm (attaque) assault, attack; Mil charge; **donner l'a. à** to storm, to launch an attack on; **prendre qch d'a.** Mil to storm sth; Fig (buffet, guichets) to make a run for sth

assèchement [asɛʃmɑ̃] nm (d'un terrain, d'un marécage) drainage; (d'un cours d'eau) drying out

assécher [34] [aseʃe] 1 vt (terrain, marécage) to drain; (cours d'eau) to dry out
2 **s'assécher** vpr to dry up

ASSEDIC [asedik] nfpl (abrév **Association pour l'emploi dans l'industrie et le commerce**) = French unemployment benefits department, Br ≃ Unemployment Benefit Office; **toucher les A.** to get Br unemployment benefit or Am welfare

assemblage [asɑ̃blaʒ] nm (a) (de pièces détachées) assembly; (en menuiserie) joint; (en couture) making up; (de feuillets) collating (b) (structure) assembly

assemblée [asɑ̃ble] nf (a) (réunion) assembly; (plus petite) meeting; **a. générale** annual general meeting (b) Pol **l'A. nationale** the National Assembly, Br ≃ the House of Commons, Am ≃ the House of Representatives (c) (foule) crowd

assembler [asɑ̃ble] 1 vt (a) (machine, meuble en kit) to assemble, to put together; (feuillets) to collate (b) (timbres) to join (c) Ordinat (programme) to assemble; (modules) to link
2 **s'assembler** vpr to gather

assembleur [asɑ̃blœr] nm Ordinat assembler

asséner [34] [asene] vt **a. qch à qn** (coup) to deliver sth to sb; (remarque) to hurl sth at sb

assentiment [asɑ̃timɑ̃] nm assent

asseoir [10a] [aswar] 1 vt (a) (installer) (personne) to seat, to sit; **être assis** to be sitting (b) Fig (autorité, réputation) to establish
2 vi **faire a. qn** to ask sb to sit down or to take a seat
3 **s'asseoir** vpr to sit (down); (depuis la position allongée) to sit up; **s'a. sur une chaise/dans un fauteuil** to sit on a chair/in an armchair; Fam Fig **s'a. sur qch** not to give a damn about sth

assermenté [asɛrmɑ̃te] adj sworn (in); (témoin) under or on oath; **fonctionnaire a.** sworn official; Hist (prêtre) **non a.** non-juring (priest)

assertion [asɛrsjɔ̃] nf assertion

asservir [asɛrvir] vt to enslave

asservissement [asɛrvismɑ̃] nm enslavement; **a. à qn/qch** subjection to sb/sth

assesseur [asesœr] nm assessor

asseyais etc voir **asseoir**

assez [ase] adv (a) (suffisamment) enough; **a. grand/intelligent (pour faire qch)** big/clever enough (to do sth); **a. bien** well enough; (appréciation scolaire) fair; **tu as a. mangé** you've eaten enough; **a.!** that's enough!; **a. parlé!** that's enough talk!; **nous sommes a. de trois** three of us is enough (b) **a. de** enough; **il y a a. de pain/de pâtes** there's enough bread/pasta; **j'en ai a.** (suffisamment) I've got enough; (je suis agacé) I've had enough (c) (plutôt) quite, rather

assidu, -e [asidy] adj (a) (toujours présent) regular; **être a. aux cours** to attend classes regularly (b) (appliqué) diligent; **un soin a.** painstaking care (c) (attentionné) **être a. auprès de qn** to be attentive to sb; **faire une cour assidue à qn** to pay constant court to sb

assiduité [asiduite] nf (a) (présence régulière) regularity; **a. aux cours** regular attendance at classes (b) (zèle) diligence (c) **poursuivre qn de ses assiduités** to force one's attentions on sb

assidûment [asidymɑ̃] adv (a) (régulièrement) regularly (b) (avec application) diligently

assied etc voir **asseoir**

assiéger [59] [asjeʒe] vt aussi Fig to besiege

assiéra etc voir **asseoir**

assiette [asjɛt] nf (a) (vaisselle) plate; (contenu) plateful; Culin **a. anglaise** assorted cold meats; **a. creuse** soup plate; **a. à dessert** dessert plate; **a. plate** dinner plate (b) (d'un impôt, d'un taux) base (c) (d'un cavalier) seat (d) **ne pas être dans son a.** to be out of sorts

assiettée [asjete] nf plateful

assignation [asiɲasjɔ̃] nf (a) (d'une tâche) assignment (à to); (de fonds, d'une part) allotment (à to) (b) Jur summons; a. à résidence house arrest

assigner [asiɲe] vt (a) (tâche) to assign (à to); (fonds, part) to allot (à to) (b) Jur (témoin) to summon; a. qn à résidence to place sb under house arrest

assimilable [asimilabl] adj (comparable) comparable (à to)

assimilation [asimilasjɔ̃] nf (a) (absorption) & Fig assimilation (b) (comparaison) comparison (à with)

assimilé, -e [asimile] adj (de même nature) similar; cadres et assimilés executives and those in similar categories

assimiler [asimile] 1 vt (a) (aliment, connaissances, immigrés) to assimilate; un élève qui a du mal à a. a pupil who finds it hard to take things in (b) (comparer) to compare (à with)
  2 s'assimiler vpr (a) (immigré) to assimilate (b) (être comparable) to be comparable (à with)

assis, -e [asi, -iz] 1 pp voir asseoir
  2 adj sitting, seated; je travaille a. toute la journée I spend the whole day at work sitting down; Fig une situation bien assise a secure job

assise [asiz] nf (d'une théorie) basis, foundation

assises [asiz] nfpl (a) (congrès) conference (b) Jur les a. the assizes

assistanat [asistana] nm assistantship

assistance [asistɑ̃s] nf (a) (public) audience (b) (aide) assistance; prêter a. à qn to give sb assistance (c) être à l'A. (publique) to be in care

assistant, -e [asistɑ̃, -ɑ̃t] nm,f assistant; (de langue) language assistant; a. metteur en scène assistant director; assistante maternelle child minder; assistante sociale social worker

assisté, -e [asiste] 1 nm,f Péj person living on handouts
  2 adj a. par ordinateur computer-aided

assister [asiste] 1 vt (personne) to assist
  2 assister à vi ind to be (present) at, to attend; (accident) to witness; je ne peux pas vous répondre, je n'ai pas assisté à la scène I can't give you an answer, I wasn't there

associatif, -ive [asɔsjatif, -iv] adj mouvement a. association; vie associative community life

association [asɔsjasjɔ̃] nf (a) (groupe, société) association; Com partnership; a. à but non lucratif Br non-profit-making or Am not-for-profit organization; l'A. européenne de libre-échange European Free Trade Association; a. de parents d'élèves parent-teacher association; a. sportive sports club (b) (de mots, d'idées) association; (d'aliments, de substances, de couleurs) combination (c) Jur a. de malfaiteurs criminal conspiracy

associé, -e [asɔsje] 1 nm,f associate; Com partner
  2 adj membre a. associate member

associer [66] [asɔsje] 1 vt (a) (lier) to combine (à with) (b) (mentalement) to associate (à with)
  2 s'associer vpr (a) s'a. à un projet to join in a project; s'a. à ou avec qn (dans une lutte) to join forces with sb; Com to enter into partnership with sb (à with) (se mêler) to combine (à with)

assoiffé, -e [aswafe] adj thirsty; Fig a. de sang bloodthirsty; a. de savoir thirsty for knowledge

assolement [asɔlmɑ̃] nm crop rotation

assombrir [asɔ̃brir] 1 vt to darken; (avenir) to cast a shadow over
  2 s'assombrir vpr (ciel, visage) to darken, to cloud over; (personne) to become gloomy

assommant, -e [asɔmɑ̃, -ɑ̃t] adj very boring

assommer [asɔme] vt a. qn (étourdir) to knock sb senseless; (engourdir) to make sb lethargic; (ennuyer) to bore sb to death

Assomption [asɔ̃psjɔ̃] nf (la fête de) l'A. (the feast of) the Assumption

assonance [asɔnɑ̃s] nf assonance

assorti, -e [asɔrti] adj (a) (en harmonie) matching; bien a. well-matched; mal a. ill-matched; pull avec jupe assortie jumper with matching skirt; le pull n'était pas a. à la jupe the jumper didn't match the skirt (b) (bonbons) assorted, mixed (c) bien a. (magasin) well-stocked (d) (accompagné) a. de accompanied by

assortiment [asɔrtimɑ̃] nm (de produits) assortment

assortir [asɔrtir] vt (a) (couleurs) to match (à to) (b) Com to restock

assoupir [asupir] s'assoupir vpr to doze off

assouplir [asuplir] 1 vt (chaussures, cuir, corps) to make supple; Fig (réglementation) to relax
  2 s'assouplir vpr (chaussures, cuir, corps) to get supple

assouplissant [asuplisɑ̃] nm fabric softener

assouplissement [asuplismɑ̃] nm (du corps) making supple; Fig (de la réglementation) relaxing; exercices d'a., assouplissements limbering-up exercises

assourdir [asurdir] vt (a) (personne) to deafen (b) (son) to deaden

assourdissant, -e [asurdisɑ̃, -ɑ̃t] adj deafening

assouvir [asuvir] vt (faim, désir) to satisfy

assouvissement [asuvismɑ̃] nm (de la faim, du désir) satisfaction

assoyant voir asseoir

assujettir [asyʒetir] vt (a) (province) to subjugate (b) (soumettre) a. qn à qch to subject sb to sth; être assujetti à l'impôt to be liable for tax (c) (objet) to fix, to fasten (à to)

assujettissement [asyʒetismɑ̃] nm (a) (dépendance) subjection (à to) (b) (à l'impôt) liability (à for)

assumer [asyme] 1 vt (a) (responsabilité) to assume, to take on; (risque) to take (b) (accepter) (conséquences) to take
  2 vi Fam tu vas devoir a. you'll have to live with it
  3 s'assumer vpr to come to terms with oneself

assurance [asyrɑ̃s] nf (a) (confiance) (self-)assurance (b) (garantie) assurance; je vous donne l'a. que tout sera fini demain I assure you that everything will be finished tomorrow; demander/recevoir des assurances to ask for/to receive assurance (c) (contre le vol, les accidents) insurance; prendre une a. to take out insurance; Fam je vais écrire à mon a. I'm going to write to my insurance company; a. auto car insurance; a. maladie health insurance; a. au tiers third-party insurance; a. tous risques comprehensive insurance; a. sur la vie, a.-vie life insurance; a. vieillesse retirement pension

assuré, -e [asyre] 1 adj (pas, voix) firm; (air, personne) assured, confident; d'une voix mal assurée in an unsteady voice (b) (succès, victoire) guaranteed, certain
  2 nm,f l'a. the insured; les assurés sociaux ≃ people who pay Br national insurance or Am social security

assurément [asyremɑ̃] adv Vieilli certainly

assurer [asyre] **1** vt (a) (garantir) to ensure, to guarantee; **a. une rente à qn** to settle an annuity on sb; **ma retraite m'assure de quoi vivre** my pension gives me enough to live on; **a. ses arrières** to leave oneself a way out (b) (certifier) **a. qch à qn, a. qn de qch** to assure sb of sth; **a. qn que** to assure sb that; **c'est bien vrai, je t'assure** it's absolutely true, I assure you (c) (se charger de) to be in charge of; **a. les fonctions de directeur de la production** to be production manager; **un service régulier est assuré entre Paris et Londres** there is a regular service between Paris and London; **j'assure la permanence ce matin** I'm on duty this morning; **a. la défense de qn** (sujet: avocat) to defend sb (d) (immobiliser) to steady; (attacher) to secure (e) (par contrat d'assurance) to insure (**contre** against)

2 vi Fam **a. en maths** to be brilliant at maths; **à l'entretien, j'ai assuré un max** I did brilliantly at the interview

3 s'assurer vpr (a) **s'a. de qch** (vérifier) to make sure of sth; **je vais m'en a.** I'll check (b) (par contrat d'assurance) to insure oneself (**contre** against); **s'a. au tiers/sur la vie** to take out third-party/life insurance (c) (se procurer) **s'a. la collaboration de qn** to secure sb's collaboration; **les Allemands se sont assuré la victoire** the Germans are assured of victory

assureur [asyrœr] nm insurer

astérisque [asterisk] nm asterisk

astéroïde [asteroid] nm asteroid

asthmatique [asmatik] adj & nmf asthmatic

asthme [asm] nm asthma; **avoir de l'a.** to have asthma; **crise d'a.** asthma attack

asticot [astiko] nm maggot

asticoter [astikɔte] vt Fam to bug

astigmate [astigmat] adj & nmf astigmatic

astiquer [astike] vt (faire briller) to polish; (récurer) to scour; **a. sa maison** to get one's house spotlessly clean

astrakan [astrakã] nm astrakhan

astre [astr] nm star; **beau comme un a.** as pretty as a picture

astreignant, -e [astrɛɲã, -ãt] adj exacting, demanding

astreindre [54] [astrɛ̃dr] **1** vt **a. qn à faire qch** to compel or oblige sb to do sth

2 s'astreindre vpr **s'a. à un régime sévère** to strictly follow a diet; **s'a. à faire qch** to force oneself to do sth

astreinte [astrɛ̃t] nf constraint

astrologie [astrɔlɔʒi] nf astrology

astrologique [astrɔlɔʒik] adj astrological

astrologue [astrɔlɔg] nmf astrologer

astronaute [astrɔnot] nmf astronaut

astronautique [astrɔnotik] nf astronautics (singulier)

astronome [astrɔnɔm] nmf astronomer

astronomie [astrɔnɔmi] nf astronomy

astronomique [astrɔnɔmik] adj aussi Fig astronomical

astrophysique [astrofizik] nf astrophysics (singulier)

astuce [astys] nf (a) (finesse) shrewdness (b) (truc) trick; (conseil) tip; **il doit y avoir une a.** there must be a trick to it (c) (plaisanterie) witticism; (jeu de mots) pun; **je ne saisis pas l'a.** I don't get it

astucieusement [astysjøzmã] adv shrewdly

astucieux, -euse [astysjø, -øz] adj (personne) shrewd; (solution) clever

asymétrie [asimetri] nf asymmetry

asymétrique [asimetrik] adj asymmetrical

asynchrone [asɛ̃krɔn] adj Ordinat asynchronous

atavisme [atavism] nm atavism; **faire qch par a.** to do sth because it's in one's genes

atchoum [atʃum] exclam atishoo!

atelier [atəlje] nm (a) (lieu) workshop; (dans une maison) workroom; (d'artiste) studio; **a. de carrosserie** bodyshop; **a. de montage** assembly shop; TV & Cin **a. de production** production studio; **a. de réparations** repair shop (b) (personnel) workshop staff (c) (groupe de travail) work-group

atermoiements [atɛrmwamã] nmpl procrastination

athée [ate] **1** adj atheistic

2 nmf atheist

athéisme [ateism] nm atheism

Athènes [atɛn] n Athens

athénien, -enne [atenjɛ̃, -ɛn] **1** adj Athenian

2 nm, f A. Athenian

athlète [atlɛt] nmf athlete

athlétique [atletik] adj athletic

athlétisme [atletism] nm athletics (singulier); **épreuves d'a.** athletic events

atlantique [atlãtik] **1** adj Atlantic

2 nm **l'A.** the Atlantic (Ocean)

atlas [atlas] nm (livre) atlas

atmosphère [atmɔsfɛr] nf aussi Fig atmosphere

atmosphérique [atmɔsferik] adj atmospheric

atoca [atɔka] nm Can cranberry

atoll [atɔl] nm atoll

atome [atom] nm atom; Fig **avoir des atomes crochus avec qn** to hit it off with sb; **elle n'a pas un a. de bon sens** she doesn't have a bit of common sense

atomique [atɔmik] adj atomic

atomiser [atɔmize] vt (a) (pulvériser) to atomize (b) (ville, région) to destroy with nuclear weapons

atomiseur [atɔmizœr] nm atomizer, spray; **parfum en a.** perfume spray

atone [atɔn] adj (a) (inerte) lacklustre (b) (voyelle) unstressed

atours [atur] nmpl Litt ou Hum finery; **parée de ses plus beaux a.** in all her finery

atout [atu] nm (aux cartes) trump; Fig asset; **a. carreau** diamonds are trumps; aussi Fig **avoir tous les atouts dans son jeu** to hold all the winning cards

être [ɔtr] nm Litt hearth; **au coin de l'â.** by the fireplace

atriqué, -e [atrike] adj Can **mal a.** badly dressed

atroce [atrɔs] adj (crime) atrocious; (douleur) excruciating; (odeur, cauchemar, repas) dreadful, horrible; **j'avais une peur a. de le rencontrer** I dreaded meeting him

atrocement [atrɔsmã] adv (cruellement) atrociously; (très mal) dreadfully, horribly; **avoir a. mal** to be in dreadful pain; **sentir a. mauvais** to smell really horrible

atrocité [atrɔsite] nf atrocity

atrophie [atrɔfi] nf atrophy

atrophier [66] [atrɔfje] **1** vt to atrophy

2 s'atrophier vpr to atrophy

attabler [atable] **s'attabler** vpr to sit down at the/a table

attachant, -e [ataʃã, -ãt] adj engaging

attache [ataʃ] *nf* (a) *(lien)* fastener; *Fig* **attaches** *(amis)* links; *Fig* **sans attaches** unattached; **je n'avais plus aucune a. dans cette ville** there was nothing to keep me in the town (b) **avoir les attaches fines** *(chevilles et poignets)* to have delicate wrists and ankles

attaché, -e [ataʃe] **1** *adj* (a) *(fixé)* fastened; *(chien)* chained up (b) *(affectivement)* **a. à** attached to (c) *(dépendant)* **les avantages attachés à une fonction** the benefits attached to a post
  2 *nm,f* attaché; **a. d'ambassade** attaché; **a. culturel** cultural attaché; **a. militaire** military attaché; **a. de presse** press officer

attaché-case *(pl* **attachés-cases)** [ataʃekɛz] *nm* attaché case

attachement [ataʃmɑ̃] *nm* attachment (à to)

attacher [ataʃe] **1** *vt* (a) **a. qch à qch** *(fixer)* to fasten sth to sth; *(avec de la ficelle, avec une corde)* to tie sth to sth; *(avec une chaîne)* to chain sth to sth; **a. ses cheveux** to tie one's hair back; **a. ses lacets** *ou* **chaussures** to do one's shoelaces up (b) *(accorder)* **a. de l'importance/de la valeur à qch** to attach importance/great value to sth
  2 *vi (dans une poêle, une casserole)* to stick to the pan; **une casserole qui n'attache pas** a non-stick saucepan
  3 s'attacher *vpr* (a) *(se fixer)* to be fastened (à to); **cette jupe s'attache par derrière** this skirt does up at the back (b) *(affectivement)* **s'a. à qn** to get attached to sb; **je ne veux pas m'a.** I don't want to commit myself (c) *(se concentrer)* **s'a. aux faits** to stick to the facts; **s'a. à faire qch** to strive to do sth (d) *(s'assurer)* **s'a. les services de qn** to procure sb's services

attaquant, -e [atakɑ̃, -ɑ̃t] **1** *nm,f Sp* attacker
  2 *adj* attacking

attaque [atak] *nf* (a) *(agression, en sport)* attack; *aussi Fig* **passer à l'a.** to go on the offensive; **à l'a.!** attack!; **a. aérienne** air raid; **a. à main armée** armed robbery (b) *Fam* **être d'a.** to be on top form; **se sentir d'a. pour faire qch** to feel up to doing sth (c) *Méd (crise)* attack; **une a.** *(apoplexie)* a stroke; *(crise cardiaque)* a heart attack

attaquer [atake] **1** *vt* (a) *(physiquement, verbalement)* to attack; *(sujet: acide)* to attack; *Jur* **a. qn en justice** to bring an action against sb (b) *(repas, sujet, travail)* to tackle; *Fam* **on attaque?** *(à table)* shall we get stuck in? (c) *Mus (morceau)* to strike up; *(note)* to attack
  2 s'attaquer *vpr* **s'a. à** *(adversaire)* to attack; *(problème)* to tackle; **s'a. à plus fort que soi** to bite off more than one can chew

attardé, -e [atarde] **1** *nm,f* **a.** *(mental)* (mentally) retarded person
  2 *adj* (a) *(qui flâne)* **il ne restait plus que quelques passants attardés** there were only a few people still about (b) *(vieux)* old-fashioned (c) *(mentalement)* (mentally) retarded

attarder [atarde] **s'attarder** *vpr* to linger; **s'a. à des détails** to dwell over details; **ne nous attardons pas sur ce point** let's not dwell on this point

atteignais *etc voir* **atteindre**

atteindre [54] [atɛ̃dr] **1** *vt* to reach; *(cible)* to hit; **être atteint d'une maladie** to be suffering from a disease; **il a été atteint dans son amour-propre** his pride has been wounded; **le poumon est atteint** the lung is affected; *Fig* **rien ne l'atteint** nothing affects him; *Fam* **il est très atteint** *(fou)* he's completely cracked
  2 atteindre à *vt ind* **a. à la perfection** to be close to perfection

atteinte [atɛ̃t] *nf (attaque)* **a. à** attack on; **porter a. à** to undermine

attelage [atlaʒ] *nm (animaux)* team

atteler [42] [atle] **1** *vt (chevaux)* to harness; *(bœufs)* to yoke; **a. une voiture** to hitch up horses to a carriage
  2 s'atteler *vpr* **s'a. à une tâche** to buckle down to a task

attelle [atɛl] *nf* splint

attenant, -e [atnɑ̃, -ɑ̃t] *adj* adjoining; **a. à** adjoining

attendre [atɑ̃dr] **1** *vt* to wait for; **a. son tour** to wait one's turn; **a. un bébé** to be expecting (a baby); **se faire a.** *(personne)* to keep people waiting; **la réponse ne s'est pas fait a.** the reply wasn't long in coming; **je l'attends d'une minute à l'autre** I'm expecting him any minute now; **a. qch de qn/qch** to expect sth from sb/sth; **qu'est-ce que tu attends pour le lui dire?** what are you waiting for? go and tell him; **a. que qn fasse qch** to wait for sb to do sth; *Fig* **a. qn au tournant** to be waiting to catch sb out
  2 *vi* to wait; **a. une heure** to wait (for) an hour; **sans plus a.** without further ado; **faire a. qn** to keep sb waiting; *Fam* **on ne va pas a. cent sept ans** we're not going to wait forever; **en attendant** meanwhile; *(néanmoins)* all the same; **en attendant son arrivée** until he arrives/arrived
  3 s'attendre *vpr* **s'a. à qch** to expect sth; **je m'attends à tout** I'm ready for anything; **je m'y attendais** I expected as much; **il fallait s'y a.** it was only to be expected; **je m'attendais à ce que tu le lui dises** I was expecting you to tell him

attendrir [atɑ̃drir] **1** *vt* (a) *(émouvoir)* to move; *(rendre indulgent)* to soften (b) *(viande)* to tenderize
  2 s'attendrir *vpr* to be moved *(sur* by)

attendrissant, -e [atɑ̃drisɑ̃, -ɑ̃t] *adj* moving

attendu, -e [atɑ̃dy] **1** *adj* expected; **le jour tant a. est arrivé** the long-awaited day arrived
  2 *prép Formel* **a. les circonstances** considering the circumstances
  3 attendu que *conj Formel* considering that; *Jur* whereas

attentat [atɑ̃ta] *nm* attack; **a. à la bombe** bombing; **a. à la pudeur** indecent assault; **a. à la sûreté de l'État** high treason; **a. à la voiture piégée** car-bomb attack

attente [atɑ̃t] *nf* (a) *(fait d'attendre)* waiting; *(période)* wait; **être dans l'a. de qch** to be waiting for sth; **en a.** *(au téléphone)* on hold; *Ordinat* **liste de fichiers à imprimer en a.** print queue (b) *(espoir)* expectations; **contre toute a.** against all expectations; **répondre à l'a.** *ou* **aux attentes de qn** to live up to sb's expectations; **dans l'a. de votre réponse/de vous rencontrer** *(dans une lettre)* I look forward to receiving your reply/to meeting you

attenter [atɑ̃te] **attenter à** *vt ind* to make an attempt on; **a. à ses jours** to attempt suicide

attentif, -ive [atɑ̃tif, -iv] *adj* attentive; **être a. aux autres** to be attentive to others; **être a. à qch** to pay attention to sth; *(ses intérêts, sa santé)* to look after sth; **écouter d'une oreille attentive** to listen attentively

attention [atɑ̃sjɔ̃] *nf* (a) *(soin)* attention; **écouter avec a.** to listen attentively; **faire a. à qch** to pay attention to sth; *(sa santé, ses intérêts)* to look after sth; **il a fait a. de ne pas la blesser** he took care not to hurt her; **ne pas prêter la moindre a. à** to take no notice of; **(faites) a.!** look out!; **a. si je t'attrape!** if I catch you there'll be trouble!; **a., peinture fraîche** *(sur écriteau)* wet paint; **a. à la fermeture des portières, a. au départ!** stand clear of the doors, the train is about to depart!; **à l'a. de qn** *(sur une lettre)* for the attention of sb **(b)** *(amabilité)* attention; **être plein d'attentions envers qn** to be very attentive towards sb

attentionné, -e [atɑ̃sjɔne] *adj* attentive **(auprès de** towards)

attentisme [atɑ̃tism] *nm* wait-and-see policy

attentivement [atɑ̃tivmɑ̃] *adv* attentively

atténuation [atenɥasjɔ̃] *nf (d'un effet, de la douleur)* reduction; *(d'une lumière)* dimming; *(d'une couleur)* toning down; *(d'une chute)* breaking

atténuer [atenɥe] **1** *vt (effet, douleur)* to reduce; *(lumière)* to dim; *(couleur)* to tone down; *(chute)* to break
  2 s'atténuer *vpr (douleur)* to ease; *(lumière, couleurs, bruit)* to fade

atterrant, -e [aterɑ̃, -ɑ̃t] *adj* appalling

atterrer [atere] *vt* to appal

atterrir [aterir] *vi* to land; **a. en catastrophe** to make an emergency landing; *Fam* **a. dans un bar/en prison** to land up in a bar/in prison

atterrissage [aterisaʒ] *nm* landing; **a. en douceur** soft landing; **a. forcé** forced landing

attestation [atɛstasjɔ̃] *nf* certificate

attester [atɛste] *vt (témoigner)* to testify to; **a. que** to testify that; **aucun dictionnaire n'atteste l'existence de ce mot** this word is not attested in any dictionary

attifer [atife] *Fam* **1** *vt* to dress **(de** in)
  2 s'attifer *vpr* to dress; **s'a. de qch** to put sth on

attirail [atiraj] *nm* paraphernalia

attirance [atirɑ̃s] *nf* attraction; **éprouver de l'a. pour ou envers qn** to be attracted to sb

attirant, -e [atirɑ̃, -ɑ̃t] *adj* attractive

attirer [atire] **1** *vt (a) (sujet: aimant, planète)* to attract; *Fig* **a. qn dans un piège** to lure sb into a trap; **a. qn dans un coin** to take sb into a corner; **a. l'attention de qn** *(sujet: chose)* to catch sb's attention; **a. l'attention de qn sur qch** to draw sb's attention to sth; **a. les regards** to catch the eye **(b)** *(séduire)* to attract; *(sujet: matière, pays)* to appeal to
  2 s'attirer *vpr (a) (mutuellement)* to be attracted to each other **(b)** *(sur soi)* **s'a. des critiques** to come in for criticism; **s'a. des ennuis** to get oneself into trouble; **s'a. la colère de qn** to incur sb's anger

attiser [atize] *vt (a) (feu)* to poke **(b)** *Fig (désir, colère, racisme)* to stir up

attitré, -e [atitre] *adj (a) (habituel)* usual **(b)** *(chargé d'une fonction)* appointed

attitude [atityd] *nf (a) (conduite, position)* attitude **(envers** *ou* **à l'égard de** towards); **tu as eu une a. déplorable** your behaviour was appalling **(b)** *(affectation)* pose

attouchement [atuʃmɑ̃] *nm* fondling; **se livrer à des attouchements sur qn** to fondle sb

attraction [atraksjɔ̃] *nf (a) (d'un aimant)* attraction; **l'a. terrestre** the earth's gravitational pull **(b)** *aussi Fig (spectacle)* attraction

attrait [atrɛ] *nm* attraction

attrape [atrap] *nf (farce)* trick

attrape-nigaud *(pl* **attrape-nigauds)** [atrapnigo] *nm* trick

attraper [atrape] **1** *vt (a) (capturer, saisir)* to catch; **se faire a.** to be caught; *Fam* **a. qn à faire qch** to catch sb doing sth **(b)** *(maladie)* to catch; **a. froid** to catch cold; **a. mal** to catch a chill **(c)** *(tromper)* **a. qn** to take sb in; **là, tu es bien attrapé** you fell for it good and proper **(d)** *Fam (gronder)* **se faire a.** to get a good talking to
  2 s'attraper *vpr (maladie)* to be caught; *(habitude)* to be picked up

attrayant, -e [atrejɑ̃, -ɑ̃t] *adj* attractive; **peu a.** unattractive

attribuable [atribɥabl] *adj* attributable **(à** to)

attribuer [atribɥe] **1** *vt (a) (allouer)* to assign, to allot **(à** to); *(prix, récompense, bourse)* to award **(à** to) **(b)** *(œuvre, crime, erreur)* to attribute **(à** to); **a. de l'importance à qch** to attach importance to sth
  2 s'attribuer *vpr* **s'a. qch** to claim sth; **il s'en est attribué tout le mérite** he claimed all the credit for it

attribut [atriby] **1** *nm* attribute
  2 *adj* attributive

attribution [atribysjɔ̃] *nf (a) (allocation)* assigning, allocation **(à** to); *(d'un prix, d'une récompense, d'une bourse)* awarding **(à** to); **attributions** *(fonctions)* duties; **entrer dans les attributions de qn** to be part of sb's duties **(b)** *(d'une œuvre, d'un crime, d'une erreur)* attribution **(à** to)

attristant, -e [atristɑ̃, -ɑ̃t] *adj* depressing

attrister [atriste] **1** *vt* to sadden; **cela m'attriste** it makes me sad
  2 s'attrister *vpr* to be saddened **(de** by)

attroupement [atrupmɑ̃] *nm* crowd; **provoquer un a.** to draw a crowd

attrouper [atrupe] **s'attrouper** *vpr* to gather

atypique [atipik] *adj* atypical

au [o] *voir* **à**

aubaine [oben] *nf* godsend; **profiter de l'a.** to take advantage of one's good luck

aube [ob] *nf (a) (matin)* dawn; **à l'a.** at dawn; *Fig* **l'a. de la civilisation** the dawn of civilization **(b)** *Rel* alb

aubépine [obepin] *nf* hawthorn; **fleurs d'a.** may blossom

auberge [oberʒ] *nf* inn; *Fig* **ici, c'est l'a. espagnole** you have to bring everything yourself here; *Fam* **on n'est pas sorti de l'a.** we're not out of the wood yet; **a. de jeunesse** youth hostel

aubergine [oberʒin] *nf (a) (plante)* *Br* aubergine, *Am* eggplant **(b)** *Fam (contractuelle)* (female) traffic warden

aubergiste [oberʒist] *nmf* innkeeper

auburn [obœrn] *adj inv* auburn

aucun, -e [okœ̃, -yn] **1** *pron indéfini (a) (personne, rien)* none; **a. des deux** neither (of them); **a. d'entre eux** none of them; **je ne me fie à a. d'entre eux** I don't trust any of them **(b)** *Litt* **d'aucuns** some people
  2 *adj indéfini (a) (négatif)* no, not any; **je n'en ai aucune idée** I've (got) no idea; **sans aucune exception** without any exception; **sans a. doute** without a doubt **(b)** *(positif)* any; **plus rapide qu'a. autre coureur** faster than any other runner

aucunement [okynmɑ̃] *adv* not at all, not in the slightest

audace [odas] *nf (a) (courage)* boldness, daring **(b)** *(culot)* audacity, impudence **(c)** *(originalité)* boldness **(d)** *(action audacieuse)* **avoir toutes les audaces** to do the most daring things

audacieusement [odasjøzmɑ̃] adv (a) (avec courage) boldly, daringly (b) (avec culot) impudently

audacieux, -euse [odasjø, -øz] adj (a) (courageux) bold, daring (b) (culotté) impudent (c) (original) bold

au-dedans [odədɑ̃] adv inside; a. de inside

au-dehors [odəɔr] adv outside; a. de outside

au-delà [odəla] 1 nm l'a. the next world
2 prép a. de beyond
3 adv beyond; jusqu'à une certaine somme mais pas a. up to a certain sum but no more

au-dessous [odəsu] adv below, underneath; on en trouve à 50 francs et même a. you can get them for 50 francs or even less; a. de (dans l'espace) below, under; (nombre, somme) under; (dans une hiérarchie) below; 15 degrés a. de zéro 15 degrees below zero; Fig être a. de tout to be beneath contempt

au-dessus [odəsy] adv above; (à l'étage supérieur) upstairs; une terrasse avec une marquise a. a terrace with an awning over it; 1000 francs et a. 1,000 francs and upwards; a. de (dans l'espace, dans une hiérarchie) above; (nombre, somme) over; a. de nos têtes (dans le ciel) overhead; c'est a. de mes forces it's beyond me; vivre a. de ses moyens to live beyond one's means; Fig je suis a. de ça I'm above all that

au-devant [odəvɑ̃] au-devant de prép aller/courir a. de qn to go/run to meet sb; aller a. des désirs de qn to anticipate sb's wishes; aller a. du danger to court danger

audible [odibl] adj audible

audience [odjɑ̃s] nf (a) (entrevue) audience; Jur hearing; l'a. est suspendue the case is adjourned (b) (intérêt) trouver a. auprès des jeunes to find a following among young people (c) (public) audience

Audimat® [odimat] nm (appareil) = device for calculating television audience ratings; (résultats) audience ratings; faire de l'A. to increase audience ratings

audioconférence [odjokɔ̃ferɑ̃s] nf audioconference

audionumérique [odjonymerik] adj digital audio; disque a. compact disc

audiovisuel, -elle [odjovizɥɛl] 1 adj (a) (méthodes) audiovisual (b) TV & Rad television and radio
2 nm TV & Rad l'a. television and radio

auditeur, -trice [oditœr, -tris] nm,f (a) (d'un programme de radio) listener (b) Univ suivre un cours en a. libre = to follow a course without being officially registered as a student, Am to audit a course

auditif, -ive [oditif, -iv] adj (nerf) auditory; (troubles) hearing

audition [odisjɔ̃] nf (a) (faculté) hearing (b) (de chanteur, d'acteur) audition; passer une a. to have an audition (c) Jur a. des témoins examination of the witnesses

auditionner [odisjone] vt & vi to audition

auditoire [oditwar] nm (a) (public) audience (b) Belg & Suisse auditorium

auditorium [oditɔrjom] nm auditorium; Rad & TV recording studio

auge [oʒ] nf (mangeoire) trough

augmentation [ɔgmɑ̃tasjɔ̃] nf (a) (accroissement) increase (de in); a. (de salaire) Br (pay-)rise, Am raise; demander une a. to ask for a (pay-)rise; être en a. to be on the increase (b) Ordinat a. de puissance upgrade

augmenter [ɔgmɑ̃te] 1 vt to increase; édition augmentée enlarged edition; a. qn to raise sb's salary
2 vi to increase (de by)

augure [ogyr] nm (a) (devin) augur (b) (présage) omen; de bon a. auspicious; de mauvais a. ominous

augurer [ogyre] vt a. bien/mal de qch to augur well/ill for sth

auguste [ogyst] adj august

aujourd'hui [oʒurdɥi] adv (a) (ce jour) today; le journal d'a. today's paper; Fam c'est pour a. ou pour demain? I/we haven't got all day! (b) (à l'heure actuelle) nowadays, today; les jeunes gens d'a. young people today; l'Europe d'a. present-day Europe

aulne [on] nm alder

aumône [omon] nf alms; demander l'a. to ask for charity; faire l'a. à qn to give alms to sb

aumônier [omonje] nm chaplain

aune [on] nm alder

auparavant [oparavɑ̃] adv (avant) before(hand); (d'abord) first

auprès [oprɛ] auprès de prép (a) (près de) by, next to; ambassadeur a. des Nations unies ambassador to the United Nations (b) (en comparaison de) compared with (c) (en s'adressant à) se renseigner a. de qn to ask sb

auquel [okɛl] voir lequel

aura¹ etc voir avoir

aura² [ora] nf aura

auréole [oreol] nf (a) (de saint, d'un astre) halo; Fig parer qn d'une a. to idolize sb (b) (trace) ring

auréoler [oreole] vt tout auréolé de gloire crowned with glory

auriculaire [orikyler] nm little finger

aurifère [orifer] adj gold-bearing; gisement a. goldfield

Aurigny [oriɲi] n Alderney

aurore [oror] nf dawn, daybreak; à l'a. at dawn; Fam aux aurores at the crack of dawn; a. boréale aurora borealis, northern lights

auscultation [oskyltasjɔ̃] nf auscultation

ausculter [oskylte] vt (malade, cœur) to listen to

auspices [ospis] nmpl sous les a. de (sous l'égide de) under the auspices of; sous d'heureux a. auspiciously; sous de fâcheux a. inauspiciously

aussi [osi] 1 adv (a) (également) too, as well; lui a. il sait le faire he, too, knows how to do it, he knows how to do it as well (b) (tellement) so; une a. belle journée such a nice day (c) (dans les phrases comparatives) as; a. grand que moi as tall as me; pas a. gros que not as big as, not so big as; a. bien que moi as well as me (d) (quelque) however; a. bizarre que cela soit however odd it may be
2 conj therefore, so

aussitôt [osito] 1 adv immediately, straight away; a. avant/après immediately before/after; a. après son retour je suis parti as soon as he returned I left; a. l'argent reçu je vous paierai as soon as I get the money I'll pay you; a. dit, a. fait no sooner said than done
2 conj a. que as soon as

austère [oster] adj (vie, style) austere; (vêtement) severe; (expression) stern

austérité [osterite] nf (de la vie, d'un style) austerity; (d'un vêtement) severity; (d'une expression) sternness; mesures d'a. austerity measures

austral, -e, -als *ou* **-aux** [ostral, -o] *adj* southern

Australasie [ostralazi] *nf* l'A. Australasia

Australie [ostrali] *nf* l'A. Australia

australien, -enne [ostraljɛ̃, -ɛn] **1** *adj* Australian **2** *nm,f* A. Australian

autant [otɑ̃] *adv* **(a)** *(tellement)* so much; **a. de** *(quantité)* so much; *(nombre)* so many; **je n'avais jamais vu a. de neige/de bateaux** I had never seen so much snow/so many boats

(b) *(la même quantité, le même nombre)* **remettez-m'en encore a.** give me the same again; **il m'en veut, mais je lui en veux tout a.** he's angry with me, but I'm just as angry with him; **le coût de la vie a augmenté de 5% mais les salaires n'ont pas augmenté d'a.** the cost of living has increased by 5% but salaries have not risen by the same amount; **a. que** *(quantité)* as much as; *(nombre)* as many as; **a. que possible** as far as possible; **a. de... que** *(quantité)* as much... as; *(nombre)* as many... as; **ils ont a. de terrain/d'amis que vous** they have as much land/as many friends as you

(c) *(de même)* **on ne peut pas en dire a. de tout le monde** you can't say the same for everybody; **essaie un peu d'en faire a.** try to do the same

(d) *(locutions)* **a. elle est expansive, a. il est réservé** she's as extroverted as he is shy; **a. pour moi!** I stand corrected!; **(pour) a. que je sache** as far as I know, to the best of my knowledge; **ce sera a. de moins à payer** it will be that much less to pay; **a. rester ici** we may as well stay here; **a. dire que...** which amounts to saying that...; **j'aimerais a. aller au cinéma** I'd rather go to the cinema; **j'aime a. te dire que je n'étais pas contente!** I wasn't too happy, I can tell you!; **... d'a. (plus) que...,** especially since...; **d'a. plus/moins que** all the more/less because; **cela vous sera d'a. plus facile que vous êtes jeune** it will be that much easier for you since you are young; **pour a.** *(malgré cela)* for all that

autarcie [otarsi] *nf Pol* autarky; **vivre en a.** to be self-sufficient

autel [otɛl] *nm aussi Fig* altar; **conduire sa fille à l'a.** to give one's daughter away

auteur [otœr] *nm* **(a)** *(de livre)* author, writer; *(de chanson)* composer; *(de tableau)* painter **(b)** *(responsable)* author; *(d'un crime)* perpetrator; *(d'un projet)* instigator

authenticité [otɑ̃tisite] *nf* authenticity

authentification [otɑ̃tifikasjõ] *nf* authentication

authentifier [66] [otɑ̃tifje] *vt* to authenticate

authentique [otɑ̃tik] *adj* authentic, genuine; *(fait, histoire)* true

authentiquement [otɑ̃tikmɑ̃] *adv* authentically, genuinely

autisme [otism] *nm* autism

autiste [otist] **1** *adj* autistic **2** *nmf* person with autism

auto [oto] *nf* car; **autos tamponneuses** bumper cars, *Br* Dodgems®; **petite a.** *(jouet)* toy car

auto- *préf* auto-, self-

autoaccusation [otoakyzasjõ] *nf* self-accusation

autobiographie [otobjografi] *nf* autobiography

autobiographique [otobjografik] *adj* autobiographical

autobronzant, -e [otobrɑ̃zɑ̃, -ɑ̃t] **1** *adj* self-tanning **2** *nm* self-tanning cream

autobus [otobys] *nm* bus; **a. à impériale** double-decker (bus)

autocar [otokar] *nm* bus, *Br* coach; **a. de luxe** luxury coach

autocassable [otokasabl] *adj* **ampoule a.** break-open phial

autocensurer [otosɑ̃syre] **s'autocensurer** *vpr* to practise self-censorship

autochtone [otɔkton] **1** *nmf aussi Hum* native **2** *adj* native

autocollant, -e [otokɔlɑ̃, -ɑ̃t] **1** *adj* self-adhesive; *(enveloppe)* self-seal **2** *nm* sticker

autocorrecteur, -trice [otokɔrɛktœr, -tris] *adj Ordinat* self-correcting

autocouchette(s) [otokuʃɛt] *adj inv voir* **train**

autocrate [otokrat] *nmf* autocrat

autocratie [otokrasi] *nf* autocracy

autocratique [otokratik] *adj* autocratic

autocritique [otokritik] *nf* self-criticism; **faire son a.** to criticize oneself

autocuiseur [otokɥizœr] *nm* pressure cooker

autodafé [otodafe] *nm Hist* auto-da-fé

autodéfense [otodefɑ̃s] *nf* self-defence

autodestructeur, -trice [otodestryktœr, -tris] *adj* self-destructive

autodestruction [otodestryksjõ] *nf* self-destruction

autodétermination [otodeterminasjõ] *nf Pol* self-determination

autodidacte [otodidakt] **1** *adj* self-taught **2** *nmf* self-taught person

autodrome [otodrom] *nm* motor-racing track; *(pour les essais)* car-testing track

auto-école *(pl* **auto-écoles)** [otoekɔl] *nf* driving school

autofinancement [otofinɑ̃smɑ̃] *nm* self-financing

autofinancer [45] [otofinɑ̃se] **s'autofinancer** *vpr* to be self-financing

autofocus [otofɔkys] *adj & nm Phot* autofocus

autogéré, -e [otoʒere] *adj* self-managed

autogestion [otoʒestjõ] *nf* self-management

autographe [otograf] *nm & adj* autograph

automate [otomat] *nm aussi Fig* automaton

automation [otomasjõ] *nf* automation

automatique [otomatik] **1** *adj* automatic; **il est absent tous les lundis, c'est a.** he's off every Monday without fail
2 *nm* **(a)** *Tél* direct dialling **(b)** *(pistolet)* automatic

automatiquement [otomatikmɑ̃] *adv* automatically

automatisation [otomatizasjõ] *nf* automation

automatiser [otomatize] *vt* to automate

automatisme [otomatism] *nm* **(a)** *(réflexe)* automatism; **agir par a.** to act automatically; **fermer la porte à double tour est devenu un a.** double-locking the door has become automatic **(b)** *(dispositif)* automatic device

automédication [otomedikasjõ] *nf* self-medication

automitrailleuse [otomitrajøz] *nf* armoured car

automnal, -e, -aux, -ales [otɔnal, -o] *adj* autumnal

automne [otɔn] *nm* autumn, *Am* fall; **en a., à l'a.** in autumn; **une soirée d'a.** an autumn evening; *Fig* **à l'a. de sa vie** in the autumn of his/her life

automobile [otɔmɔbil] **1** *nf* (*a*) (*voiture*) car, *Am* automobile (**b**) (*industrie*) **l'a.** the car industry

2 *adj* (**a**) (*véhicule*) self-propelling (**b**) (*industrie, accessoires*) car, *Am* automobile

automobiliste [otɔmɔbilist] *nmf* motorist

autonettoyant, -e [otɔnetwajã, -ãt] *adj* **four a.** self-cleaning oven

autonome [otɔnɔm] *adj* (*état, région*) autonomous, self-governing; (*appareil*) self-contained; (*personne*) self-sufficient; *Ordinat* **calculateur a.** stand-alone (computer)

autonomie [otɔnɔmi] *nf* (**a**) *Pol* autonomy, self-government (**b**) (*de personne*) self-sufficiency (**c**) (*de voiture*) range; (*de batterie*) life; *Av* **a.** (**de vol**) range

autonomiste [otɔnɔmist] *nmf Pol* separatist

autoportrait [otɔpɔrtrɛ] *nm* self-portrait

autopsie [otɔpsi] *nf* autopsy, post-mortem; *Fig* **faire l'a. d'une œuvre** to dissect a work

autopsier [66] [otɔpsje] *vt* to perform an autopsy or a post-mortem on

autopunition [otɔpynisjɔ̃] *nf* self-punishment

autoradio [otɔradjo] *nm* car radio

autorail [otɔraj] *nm* railcar

autorégulation [otɔregylasjɔ̃] *nf* self-regulation

autoreverse [otɔrivœrs] *adj* **appareil a.** auto-reverse

autorisation [otɔrizasjɔ̃] *nf* (**a**) (*permission*) authorization, permission; **donner à qn l'a. de faire qch** to give sb permission to do sth; **demander à qn l'a. de faire qch** to ask (sb) permission to do sth; *Ordinat* **a. d'accès** access authorization; **a. de sortie du territoire** = parental authorization for a minor to travel abroad; *Av* **a. de vol** flight clearance (**b**) (*document*) authorization

autorisé, -e [otɔrize] *adj* (**a**) (*qualifié*) **tenir qch de source autorisée** to have sth from an authoritative source; **les milieux autorisés** official circles (**b**) (*permis*) permitted, allowed

autoriser [otɔrize] *vt* (**a**) (*permettre à*) **a. qn à faire qch** to authorize *or* permit sb to do sth (**b**) (*permettre*) **ces découvertes (nous) autorisent à penser que...** these discoveries entitle us to believe that...

autoritaire [otɔritɛr] *adj* authoritarian

autoritairement [otɔritɛrmã] *adv* in an authoritarian manner

autoritarisme [otɔritarism] *nm* authoritarianism

autorité [otɔrite] *nf* (**a**) (*domination, fermeté*) authority; **avoir de l'a. sur qn** to have authority over sb; **faire qch d'a.** to do sth on one's own authority (**b**) (*poids*) **faire a. en qch** (*personne*) to be an authority on sth; **ce livre fait a.** this book is the authoritative work (**c**) (*gouvernement*) **les représentants de l'a.** the representatives of authority; **les autorités** the authorities (**d**) (*personne respectée*) authority

autoroute [otɔrut] *nf* (**a**) *Aut Br* motorway, *Am* freeway; **a. à péage** *Br* toll motorway, *Am* turnpike (road) (**b**) *Ordinat* **a. de l'information** information superhighway

autoroutier, -ère [otɔrutje, -ɛr] *adj* **réseau a.** *Br* motorway *or Am* freeway system

autosatisfaction [otosatisfaksjɔ̃] *nf* self-satisfaction

auto-stop [otɔstɔp] *nm* hitch-hiking, hitching; **faire de l'a.** to hitch-hike, to hitch; **prendre qn en a.** to give sb a lift; **faire le tour de l'Europe en a.** to hitch-hike around Europe

auto-stoppeur, -euse (*mpl* **auto-stoppeurs**, *fpl* **auto-stoppeuses**) [otɔstɔpœr, -øz] *nm,f* hitch-hiker, hitcher

autosuggestion [otosygʒɛstjɔ̃] *nf* auto-suggestion

autour [otur] *adv* around; **une ville avec des murs tout a.** a town with walls all around it; **a. de** (*dans l'espace*) around, round; (*environ*) about; *Fig* **discuter qch a. d'un verre** to discuss sth over a drink

autre [otr] **1** *adj indéfini* (**a**) (*différent*) other; **l'a. côté** the other side; **un a. jour** another day; **as-tu d'autres questions?** do you have any other questions?; **les choux et autres légumes** cabbages and other vegetables; **je l'ai vu l'a. jour/soir** I saw him the other day/evening

(**b**) (*avec un pronom personnel*) **nous autres Français** we French (people); *Fam* **eh, vous autres, venez par ici!** hey, you lot, come over here!

(**c**) (*locutions*) **a. chose** something else; **avez-vous a. chose à faire?** have you got anything else to do?; *Fig* **il est assez bon musicien, mais sa femme c'est autre c.!** he's not a bad musician, but his wife's in another league!; **a. part** somewhere else

2 *pron indéfini* (**a**) **l'a.** (*personne, chose*) the other (one); *Fam* **et l'a. qui se plaint tout le temps!** and then there's him and his constant complaining!; *Fam* **comme dit l'a.** as the saying goes, as they say; **un a.** (*personne, chose*) another (one); **il n'est pas plus bête qu'un a.** he is no more stupid than anyone else; **c'était un touriste comme un a.** he was just an ordinary tourist; **c'est une raison comme une a.** it's as good a reason as any; **les autres** (*personnes, choses*) the others, the other ones; **tu devrais penser un peu aux autres** you should think of others; *Fam* **à d'autres!** who do you think you're kidding?; *Fam* **j'en ai vu d'autres** I've seen worse than that

(**b**) (*avec l'un, les uns*) **l'un et l'a.** both; **l'un dit ceci, l'a. dit cela** one says this and the other says that; **les uns disent ceci, les autres disent cela** some say this and others say that; **les uns et les autres** (*deux groupes*) both parties; **l'un ou l'a.** either; **c'est l'un ou l'autre** (*il faut choisir*) it's one or the other; **ni l'un ni l'a.** neither; **je ne les connais ni l'un ni l'a.** I don't know either of them; **ni les uns ni les autres** none of them; **je n'ai vu ni les uns ni les autres** I didn't see any of them; **l'un l'a.** each other, one another; **les uns les autres** one another; **ils dépendent l'un de l'a.** they depend on each other; *Fig* **l'un dans l'a.** on the whole

(**c**) (*avec de*) **quelque chose d'a.** something else; (*dans les questions*) anything else; **rien d'autre** nothing else; **il n'y en a pas d'a.** there aren't any others; **personne d'a.** nobody else; **quelqu'un d'a.** somebody else; (*dans les questions*) anyone else; **que pouvait-il faire d'a.?** what else could he do?; **qui d'a. sera là?** who else will be there?

autrefois [otrəfwa] *adv* in the past, once; **d'a.** of long ago

autrement [otrəmã] *adv* (**a**) (*différemment*) differently; **il ne put faire a. que d'obéir** he had no alternative but to obey; **a. dit** in other words (**b**) (*sinon*) otherwise (**c**) (*bien plus*) far more; **a. plus dangereux (que)** far more dangerous (than) (**d**) **pas a.** not particularly; **cela ne me surprend pas a.** that doesn't particularly surprise me

Autriche [otriʃ] *nf* l'A. Austria

autrichien, -enne [otriʃjɛ̃, -ɛn] **1** *adj* Austrian

  2 *nm,f* A. Austrian

autruche [otryʃ] *nf* ostrich; **sac en a.** ostrich-skin handbag; *Fig* **avoir un estomac d'a.** to have a cast-iron stomach; **pratiquer la politique de l'a., faire l'a.** to bury one's head in the sand

autrui [otrɥi] *pron indéfini* others, other people; **ne fais pas à a. ce que tu ne voudrais pas qu'on te fît** do as you would be done by

auvent [ovɑ̃] *nm (toit)* porch roof; *(de tente)* canopy, awning

auvergnat, -e [ovɛrɲa, -at] **1** *adj* of the Auvergne

  2 *nm,f* A. person from the Auvergne

aux [o] *voir* à

auxiliaire [oksiljɛr] **1** *adj* auxiliary

  2 *nmf (aide)* assistant; *(dans les hôpitaux)* auxiliary; *(dans l'administration)* temporary worker; **a. familiale** mother's help

  3 *nm Gram* auxiliary verb

auxquels, auxquelles [okɛl] *voir* **lequel**

av. *abrév* **avenue**

avachi, -e [avaʃi] *adj* **(a)** *(vêtement, bottes, canapé)* misshapen **(b)** *(personne, muscles)* flabby; **être à dans un fauteuil** to be slumped in an armchair

avachir [avaʃir] **s'avachir** *vpr* **(a)** *(vêtement, bottes, canapé)* to lose its shape **(b)** *(personne) (physiquement)* to get flabby; *(moralement)* to let oneself go; **s'a. dans un fauteuil** to flop into an armchair

avais *etc voir* **avoir**

aval¹, -als [aval] *nm Fin (d'un effet de commerce)* endorsement; **a. bancaire** bank guarantee; *Fig* **donner son a. à un projet** to give a project one's backing or support

aval² *nm (d'un cours d'eau)* downstream section; *aussi Ind* **en a.(de)** downstream (from); **la Seine en a. de Paris** the Seine below Paris

avalanche [avalɑ̃ʃ] *nf* avalanche; *Fig (d'injures)* shower; *(de lettres, de compliments)* flood

avaler [avale] *vt* to swallow; *(goulûment) (nourriture)* to bolt; *(boisson)* to gulp down; *Fig (livre)* to devour; *(colère)* to swallow; **j'ai avalé de travers** it went down the wrong way; **je meurs de faim, je n'ai rien avalé depuis hier** I'm starving, I haven't had a thing to eat since yesterday; **a. la fumée** to inhale; *Fig* **a. ses mots** to mumble; **a. une carte de crédit** *(distributeur automatique)* to eat up a credit card; **a. les kilomètres** to eat up the miles; **tu as avalé ta langue?** have you lost your tongue?

avaleur [avalœr] *nm* **a. de sabres** sword-swallower

avance [avɑ̃s] *nf* **(a)** *(progression)* advance; **a. rapide** *(sur magnétophone)* fast-forwarding **(b)** *(avantage)* lead; **avoir de l'a. sur qn** to be ahead of sb; **prendre de l'a. sur qn** to take the lead over sb; **avoir 2 minutes/2 km d'a. sur qn** to have a 2-minute/2-km lead over sb; **avoir un but/point d'a.** *(sur qn)* to be one goal/point ahead (of sb); *Scol* **avoir un an d'a.** to be a year ahead; **arriver avec cinq minutes d'a.** to arrive five minutes early; **d'a., à l'a., par a.** in advance; **en a.** early; **être en a.** to be **d'une demi-heure** to be half an hour early; **être en a. pour son âge** to be advanced for one's age; **être en a. sur son temps** to be ahead of one's time **(c)** *(d'argent)* advance; **faire une a. à qn** to give sb an advance **(d)** **faire des avances à qn** *(chercher à séduire)* to make advances to sb

avancé, -e [avɑ̃se] *adj* **(a)** *(dans l'espace)* advanced **(b)** *(précoce)* **être a. pour son âge** to be advanced for one's age **(c)** *(idées, technologie)* advanced **(d)** *(tardif)* **à une heure avancée de la nuit** late in the night; **à un âge a.** at an advanced age **(e)** *(presque à terme)* **à un stade a.** at an advanced stage; **mon travail est bien a.** I'm making good progress with my work; *Fig* **vous voilà bien a.!** a lot of good that's done you!

avancée [avɑ̃se] *nf* **(a)** *(saillie)* projection; *Constr* **a. du toit** eaves **(b)** *(de troupes, de la recherche)* advance

avancement [avɑ̃smɑ̃] *nm* **(a)** *(d'un projet)* progress; **état d'a. des travaux** progress report **(b)** *(promotion)* promotion; **avoir ou obtenir de l'a.** to be promoted **(c)** *Ordinat* **a. automatique** automatic feed; **a. ligne par ligne** line feed; **a. du papier** paper feed; **a. par friction** friction feed

avancer [16] [avɑ̃se] **1** *vt* **(a)** *(mettre en avant)* to move forward; *(pion)* to advance; *(présenter) (main, verre, assiette)* to hold out; *Formel ou Hum* **l'automobile de Monsieur est avancée** Sir's carriage awaits

  (b) *Fig (thèse)* to advance, to put forward

  (c) *(dans le temps)* to bring forward; **a. sa montre d'une heure** to put one's watch forward one hour

  (d) *(argent)* **a. qch à qn** to advance sb sth; *(prêter)* to lend sb sth

  (e) *(faire progresser)* **à quoi cela vous avancera-t-il?** what good will that do you?; **ça ne t'avancera à rien de te mettre en colère** losing your temper won't get you anywhere; **ses réponses ne m'ont pas beaucoup avancé** his answers didn't leave me much the wiser

  2 *vi* **(a)** *(aller de l'avant)* to move forward; *(armée)* to advance; **a. d'un pas** to take a step forward; **faire a. qn** to move sb along; **allez, avance! on va être en retard** come on, move! we're going to be late

  (b) *(faire des progrès)* to progress; **alors, ça avance?** so how's it coming along?; **faire a. les choses** to get things moving

  (c) *(montre)* to be fast; **ma montre avance d'une minute par jour** my watch gains a minute a day; **vous avancez de dix minutes** your watch is ten minutes fast

  (d) *(promontoire, toit)* to jut out

  3 **s'avancer** *vpr* **(a)** *(aller devant)* to move forward; **s'a. vers qch** to head towards sth; **s'a. d'un pas** to take a step forward

  (b) *(faire son travail à l'avance)* to get ahead

  (c) *Fig (s'engager hâtivement)* to commit oneself

avant [avɑ̃] **1** *prép* **a. (a)** *(dans le temps, dans l'espace)* before; **a. une heure** by one o'clock; *(dans moins d'une heure)* within an hour; **800 a. Jésus-Christ** 800 BC; **a. impôt** before tax; **je vous reverrai a. de partir** I'll see you before I leave; **je ne fais rien a. d'être tout à fait sûr** don't do anything until you're absolutely sure; **je vous reverrai a. que vous (ne) partiez** I'll see you before you leave; **je serai parti a. que vous ayez fini** I'll have left by the time you've finished; **ne partez pas a. qu'on vous le dise** don't go until you are told; *Fam* **celle-là, a. qu'elle se décide!** she takes forever to make her mind up!

  (b) *(par ordre de priorité)* before; **faire passer qch a. le reste** to put sth before everything else; **pour lui, la famille passe a. tout** for him, (the) family comes first; **a. tout** *(surtout)* above all; **a. toute chose** before anything else

  2 *adv* **(a)** *(auparavant)* before; *(d'abord)* beforehand; **j'avais les cheveux longs** I used to have long hair; **tu ferais mieux de téléphoner a.** you'd better phone first; **le jour d'a.** the day before

(b) *(dans l'espace)* **vous voyez l'église? sa maison est juste a.** you see the church? his house is just before you get to it

(c) *Litt (loin)* far; *(tard)* late; *Fig* **poussons plus a. notre enquête** let's take our investigation(s) further

(d) **en a.** *(devant les autres)* in front, ahead; *(se pencher, tomber)* forwards; *Mil* **en a., marche!** forward march!; **partir en a.** to go on ahead; **faire deux pas en a.** to take two steps forward; *Fig* **se mettre en a.** to push oneself forward; **en a. de** in front of

3 *adj inv* front

4 *nm* **(a)** *(d'un véhicule, d'une salle)* front; **à l'a.** *(d'un véhicule)* in the front; **aller de l'a.** to get on with it **(b)** *(en sport)* forward; **jouer a.** to be a forward

avantage [avɑ̃taʒ] *nm* **(a)** *(intérêt)* advantage; **cette solution a ou présente l'a. d'être rapide** this solution has the advantage of being quick **(b)** *(supériorité)* advantage **(sur** over**)**; **être à son a.** *(physiquement)* to look one's best **(c)** *(profit)* advantage; **tu aurais a. à être poli** you'd do well to be polite; **être/tourner à l'a. de qn** to be/to turn to sb's advantage; **tirer a. de qch** to turn sth to one's advantage; **a. fiscal** tax benefit; **a. en nature** benefit in kind; **avantages sociaux** social security benefits **(d)** *Sp* advantage; **prendre/conserver l'a.** to gain/retain the advantage

avantager [45] [avɑ̃taʒe] *vt* **(a)** *(favoriser)* **a. qn (par rapport à)** to give sb an advantage (over) **(b)** *(physiquement)* **a. qn** to show sb off to advantage

avantageux, -euse [avɑ̃taʒø, -øz] *adj* **(a)** *(offre)* attractive; *(conditions)* favourable; *(prix)* reasonable; *(produit)* good value **(b)** *(vaniteux)* **(ton)** superior

avant-bras [avɑ̃bra] *nm inv* forearm

avant-centre *(pl* **avants-centres)** [avɑ̃sɑ̃tr] *nm (au football)* centre forward

avant-coureur *(pl* **avant-coureurs)** [avɑ̃kurœr] *adj m voir* **signe**

avant-dernier, -ère [mpl **avant-derniers,** fpl **avant-dernières)** [avɑ̃dɛrnje, -ɛr] **1** *adj* last but one, second to last; **l'avant-dernière fois** the time before last **2** *nm,f* last but one, second to last

avant-garde *(pl* **avant-gardes)** [avɑ̃gard] *nf* **(a)** *Mil* advance guard **(b) l'a.** *(modernité)* the avant-garde; **d'a.** *(œuvre, théâtre)* avant-garde; **être à l'a. de la mode** to be at the cutting edge of fashion

avant-goût *(pl* **avant-goûts)** [avɑ̃gu] *nm* foretaste **(de** of**)**

avant-guerre *(pl* **avant-guerres)** [avɑ̃gɛr] *nm ou nf* pre-war period

avant-hier [avɑ̃tjɛr] *adv* the day before yesterday; **a. au soir** the evening before last

avant-poste *(pl* **avant-postes)** [avɑ̃post] *nm Mil* outpost

avant-première *(pl* **avant-premières)** [avɑ̃prəmjɛr] *nf* preview; **(présenté) en a.** *(film, pièce)* previewed

avant-propos [avɑ̃propo] *nm inv* foreword, preface

avant-scène *(pl* **avant-scènes)** [avɑ̃sɛn] *nf Th* apron

avant-toit *(pl* **avant-toits)** [avɑ̃twa] *nm* eaves

avant-veille *(pl* **avant-veilles)** [avɑ̃vɛj] *nf* **l'a. (de qch)** two days before (sth)

avare [avar] **1** *adj* mean, miserly; *Fig* **il n'est pas a. de compliments** he's generous with his compliments **2** *nmf* miser

avarice [avaris] *nf* miserliness, avarice

avarie [avari] *nf* damage; **subir une a.** to be damaged

avarié, -e [avarje] *adj (nourriture)* rotten

avarier [66] [avarje] **s'avarier** *vpr (nourriture)* to go off, to go bad

avatar [avatar] *nm* **(a)** *(incarnation)* incarnation **(b)** *(mésaventure)* mishap, misadventure

avec [avɛk] **1** *prép* **(a)** *(en compagnie de)* with; **être gentil/méchant a. qn** to be nice/nasty to sb; **être bien/mal a. qn** *(s'entendre bien/mal)* to get on well/badly with sb; **je suis a. vous** *(je vous soutiens)* I'm right behind you; *Fam* **et a. ça?** *(chez le marchand)* anything else?
(b) *(indique la manière)* **a. enthousiasme** enthusiastically, with enthusiasm; **a. beaucoup de gentillesse** very kindly, with great kindness; **c'est a. émotion que j'accepte** I'm thrilled to accept
(c) *(indique la simultanéité)* **diminuer a. l'âge** to decrease with age; **cela viendra a. le temps** it will come in time
(d) *(indique le moyen)* with; **ouvrir qch a. une clef** to open sth with a key; **j'ai eu un accident a. cette voiture** I had an accident in this car
(e) *(à cause de)* **a. tous les ennuis que j'ai en ce moment...** with all the problems I have at the moment...; **impossible de sortir a. cette pluie** it's impossible to go out in this rain
(f) *(en ce qui concerne)* **a. elle, on ne sait jamais** you never can tell with her
(g) **divorcer d'a. qn** to divorce sb
2 *adv Fam* **je suis venu a.** *(mon parapluie, mes gants)* I came with it/them; **il faut bien faire a.** I'll/we'll just have to put up with it

avenant, -e [avnɑ̃, -ɑ̃t] **1** *adj (personne, manières)* pleasant
2 *nm* **(a)** *(de police d'assurance)* endorsement **(b) le bâtiment est beau et le jardin est à l'a.** the building is beautiful and the garden is in keeping with it

avènement [avɛnmɑ̃] *nm (du Christ, d'une ère)* advent; *(d'un roi)* accession

avenir [avnir] *nm* future; **assurer l'a. de qn** to make provision for sb; **dans un très proche a.** in the very near future; **avoir de l'a.** *(personne, technique)* to have a future; **un métier d'a.** a career with good prospects; **un avocat d'a.** a lawyer with a great future; **à l'a.** in future

Avent [avɑ̃] *nm* **l'A.** Advent

aventure [avɑ̃tyr] *nf* **(a)** *(histoire)* adventure; **pour trouver des fruits en hiver, c'est tout une a.** it's quite a job finding fruit in winter **(b)** *(liaison)* (love) affair **(c)** *(le risque)* adventure; **tenter l'a.** to seek adventure; **partir à l'a.** to set off in search of adventure; *(sans préparation)* to set out without making plans **(d)** **dire la bonne a.** to tell sb's fortune

aventurer [avɑ̃tyre] **s'aventurer** *vpr* to venture **(dans** into**)**; **je ne m'aventurerai pas à dire que...** I wouldn't go so far as to say (that)...

aventureux, -euse [avɑ̃tyrø, -øz] *adj (vie, personne)* adventurous; *(projet)* risky

aventurier, -ère [avɑ̃tyrje, -ɛr] *nm,f* adventurer, *f* adventuress

avenue [avny] *nf* avenue

avérer [34] [avere] **s'avérer** *vpr (se révéler)* to prove to be; **il s'est avéré que...** it turned out that...

averse [avɛrs] *nf* shower; *Can* **a. de neige** snow flurry

aversion [avɛrsjɔ̃] *nf* aversion **(pour** to**)**, dislike **(pour** of**)**; **prendre qn en a.** to take a dislike to sb

averti, -e [averti] *adj (bien informé)* (well-)informed; **vous voilà a.!** don't say I didn't warn you!; *Prov* **un homme a. en vaut deux** forewarned is forearmed

avertir [avertir] *vt* **a. qn de qch** *(informer)* to inform sb of sth; *(d'un danger)* to warn sb of sth; **je vais me mettre en colère, je t'avertis!** I'm going to get angry, I'm warning you!

avertissement [avertismã] *nm* **(a)** *(avis préalable)* warning; **a. (au lecteur)** foreword **(b)** *(réprimande)* warning; *Sp (de l'arbitre)* warning, caution **(c)** *(signal)* warning sign

avertisseur [avertisœr] *nm (dispositif)* alarm; *(Klaxon®)* horn; **a. d'incendie** fire alarm

aveu, -x [avø] *nm* confession; **passer aux aveux** to make a confession; **je dois vous faire un a...** I must confess...; **de l'a. de tout le monde...** it is commonly acknowledged that...

aveuglant, -e [avœglã, -ãt] *adj* blinding, dazzling; *Fig (preuve)* blindingly obvious

aveugle [avœgl] **1** *adj aussi Fig* blind; **a. d'un œil** blind in one eye; **avoir une confiance a. en qn** to trust sb implicitly

2 *nmf* blind man, *f* blind woman; **les aveugles** the blind

aveuglement [avœgləmã] *nm (moral, mental)* blindness

aveuglément [avœgləmã] *adv* blindly

aveugle-né, -e *(mpl* **aveugles-nés,** *fpl* **aveugles-nées)** [avœglane] **1** *adj* blind from birth

2 *nm,f* person blind from birth

aveugler [avœgle] *vt aussi Fig* to blind; **aveuglé par la colère** blind with rage

aveuglette [avœglɛt] **à l'aveuglette** *adv* blindly; **aller à l'a.** to grope one's way

aviateur, -trice [avjatœr, -tris] *nm,f* aviator

aviation [avjasjɔ̃] *nf* **(a)** *(activité)* flying; **faire de l'a.** to go flying **(b)** *(secteur)* aviation; **a. civile/commerciale** civil/commercial aviation; **a. de tourisme** civil aviation **(c)** *Mil* air force

aviculteur, -trice [avikyltœr, -tris] *nm,f (de volailles)* poultry farmer

aviculture [avikyltyr] *nf (de volailles)* poultry farming

avide [avid] *adj* **(a)** *(passionné)* eager **(de** for); **a. de sang** bloodthirsty **(b)** *Péj (cupide)* greedy

avidement [avidmã] *adv (voracement)* greedily; *(avec passion)* eagerly

avidité [avidite] *nf (voracité, cupidité)* greed; *(passion)* eagerness; **avec a.** *(manger)* greedily; *(écouter, regarder)* eagerly

aviez *voir* **avoir**

avilir [avilir] **1** *vt (dégrader)* to degrade, to demean

2 s'avilir *vpr (personne)* to demean oneself

avilissant, -e [avilisã, -ãt] *adj* degrading

avilissement [avilismã] *nm (dégradation)* degradation

aviné, -e [avine] *adj (personne)* inebriated; *(haleine)* reeking of wine

avion [avjɔ̃] *nm* plane, *Br* aeroplane, *Am* airplane; **par a.** *(sur lettre)* airmail; **voyager en a.** to travel by plane or by air; **a. charter** charter plane; **a. de chasse** fighter (plane); **a. gros-porteur** jumbo jet; **a. de ligne** airliner; **a. à réaction** jet (plane); **a. supersonique** supersonic plane; **a. de tourisme** private plane

avion-cargo *(pl* **avions-cargos)** [avjɔ̃kargo] *nm* freight plane, cargo plane

avions *voir* **avoir**

aviron [avirɔ̃] *nm* **(a)** *(rame)* oar; *Can* paddle **(b)** *(sport)* **l'a.** rowing; **faire de l'a.** to row

avironner [avirone] *vi Can* to paddle

avis [avi] *nm* **(a)** *(opinion)* opinion; **changer d'a.** to change one's mind; **les a. sont partagés** opinion is divided; **à mon a.** in my opinion; **être de l'a. de qn** to be of the same opinion as sb; **de l'a. de tous...** the general opinion is that...; **être d'a. de faire qch** to be of a mind to do sth; *Prov* **deux a. valent mieux qu'un** two heads are better than one **(b)** *(conseils)* advice **(c)** *(avertissement)* notice; **jusqu'à nouvel a.** until further notice; **sauf a. contraire** unless I/you/*etc* hear to the contrary; **a. de livraison** delivery note; **a. de prélèvement** direct debit advice; **a. de réception** acknowledgement of receipt

avisé, -e [avize] *adj (sage)* sensible, wise; *(acheteur, consommateur)* shrewd; **tu serais bien/mal a. de...** you'd be well-/ill-advised to...

aviser [avize] **1** *vt* **(a)** *(informer)* **a. qn de qch** to inform sb of sth; **a. qn que...** to inform sb that... **(b)** *Fam (entrevoir)* to spot

2 *vi (prendre une décision)* to make up one's mind

3 s'aviser *vpr* **(a)** *(se rendre compte)* **s'a. que** to notice that **(b)** *(oser)* **s'a. de faire qch** to get it into one's head to do sth; **et ne t'avise pas de recommencer!** don't you dare start again!

aviver [avive] *vt (couleurs)* to brighten up; *(passion, querelle, feu)* to stir up; *(appétit)* to sharpen

av. J.-C. *(abrév* **avant Jésus-Christ)** BC

avocat¹, -e [avɔka, -at] *nm,f* **(a)** *Jur* lawyer; **a. d'affaires** business lawyer; **a. général** assistant public prosecutor *(in a Court of Appeal)* **(b)** *Fig* advocate; **se faire l'a. du diable** to play devil's advocate

avocat² *nm (fruit)* avocado (pear)

avocette [avɔsɛt] *nf* avocet

avoine [avwan] *nf* **(a)** *(céréale)* oats **(b)** *Fam (argent)* dough

avoir¹ [avwar] **[1]** *v aux* to have; **je n'ai pas encore fini** I haven't finished it yet; **je te l'ai dit hier** I told you yesterday; **j'avais déjà vu ce film** I had already seen the film before; **il faut que je l'aie fini pour demain** I have to finish it by tomorrow

2 *vt* **(a)** *(posséder)* to have; **il a une fille** he has or he's got a daughter; **a. les yeux bleus** to have blue eyes; **a. une drôle de forme** to have a funny shape; **a. un rhume** to have a cold; **a. du diabète** to be diabetic; **a. mal au cœur** to feel sick; **j'ai le nez qui pique** I've got an itchy nose; **a. de l'ambition** to be ambitious; **a. de l'humour** to have a sense of humour; **a. 20 ans** to be 20 (years old); **a. de quoi manger** to have something to eat; **elle a Guy pour voisin** Guy is her neighbour; **qui as-tu comme prof de math?** who's your maths teacher?

(b) *(obtenir)* to get; **a. qn au téléphone** to speak to sb on the telephone; **a. son train** to catch one's train; **je l'ai eu pour 50 francs** I bought it for 50 francs; **j'ai eu mon bac en 1995** I passed my "bac" in 1995

(c) *(porter) (vêtement)* to wear; *(objet)* to carry

(d) *(faire)* **il a eu un sourire étrange** he smiled strangely

(e) *(atteindre) (cible)* to hit

(f) *Fam (duper) (personne)* to take for a ride, to con; **tu nous a bien eus!** you really had us going!; **se faire a.** to be conned; **se faire a. de 100 francs** to be conned out of 100 francs

(g) *(locutions)* **a. faim/froid** to be hungry/cold; **a. quelque chose à faire** to have something to do; **j'ai à**

faire I've got things to do; **j'ai à lui parler** I've got to talk to him; **tu n'as qu'à le lui dire** just tell her; **tu en as pour combien de temps?** how long will you be?; **j'en ai pour 10 minutes** I'll be 10 minutes; **je n'en ai pas pour longtemps** I won't be long; **qu'est-ce que tu as?** what's wrong?; **j'ai que je suis fatigué** I'm tired, that's all; **qu'est-ce qu'il a à se plaindre sans arrêt?** why is he complaining all the time?; **on les aura!** we'll have them!

3 il y a *v impersonnel* there is/are; **il y a un problème** there's a problem; **il y a des problèmes** there are some problems; **il y a six ans** six years ago; **il y a un mois que je suis arrivé** I've been here for a month; **il n'y a qu'à le faire** we'll just have to do it; **il n'y a pas que ça dans la vie** there's more to life than that; **il n'y a pas de quoi!** don't mention it!; **qu'y a-t-il?, qu'est-ce qu'il y a?** what is it?, what's wrong?

avoir² *nm (d'une compagnie)* assets; *(d'un compte)* credit; *(dans un magasin)* voucher

avoisinant, -e [avwazinã, -ãt] *adj* neighbouring, nearby

avoisiner [avwazine] *vt* **une somme avoisinant les 500 francs** a sum in the region of 500 francs

avons *voir* **avoir**

avortement [avɔrtəmã] *nm* **(a)** *(chez une femme)* a. **(provoqué)** abortion; **a. spontané** miscarriage; **a. thérapeutique** termination for medical reasons **(b)** *(chez un animal)* casting **(c)** *Fig (d'un projet)* failure

avorter [avɔrte] **1** *vi* **(a)** *(subir une IVG)* to have an abortion; *(faire une fausse couche)* to miscarry **(b)** *(animal)* to cast **(c)** *Fig (projet)* to fall through
2 *vt (sujet: médecin)* to abort; **se faire a.** to have an abortion

avorteur, -euse [avɔrtœr, -øz] *nm,f* abortionist

avorton [avɔrtɔ̃] *nm Péj* runt

avoué¹ [avwe] *nm Jur Br* ≃ solicitor, *Am* ≃ attorney

avoué, -e *adj* **(a)** *(auteur, partisan)* confessed **(b)** *(but)* declared

avouer [avwe] **1** *vt (faute, crime)* to confess to, to own up to; **il a fini par a.** he finally confessed; **a. que** to admit that; **ceci me surprend, je l'avoue** this surprises me, I must confess; **il faut bien a. que...** it must be admitted that...
2 s'avouer *vpr* **s'a. coupable** to admit one's guilt; **s'a. vaincu** to acknowledge defeat

avril [avril] *nm* April; **le premier a.** *(jour des farces)* April Fools' Day; *Prov* **en a., ne te découvre pas d'un fil** ne'er cast a clout till May is out; *voir aussi* **janvier**

axe [aks] *nm* **(a)** *(géométrique)* axis; **a. des abscisses/des ordonnées** x-/y-axis; **être dans l'a. de qch** to be in line with sth; **(grand) a.** *(routier)* main road; *Fig* **les grands axes de sa politique** the main thrust of his policy **(b)** *(de machine, de roue de vélo)* axle **(c)** *Hist* **l'A. (Rome-Berlin)** the (Rome-Berlin) Axis

axer [akse] *vt* to centre; **être axé sur** *ou* **autour de** to centre on

axiome [aksjom] *nm* axiom

ayant *etc voir* **avoir**

ayant droit *(pl* **ayants droit)** [ɛjãdrwa] *nm Jur* beneficiary

ayatollah [ajatola] *nm* ayatollah

azalée [azale] *nf* azalea

Azerbaïdjan [azɛrbajdʒã] *nm* **l'A.** Azerbaijan

azerbaïdjanais, -e [azɛrbajdʒanɛ, -ez] **1** *adj* Azerbaijani
2 *nm,f* **A.** Azerbaijani

azéri, -e [azeri] **1** *adj* Azeri
2 *nm,f* **A.** Azeri

azimuts [azimyt] *nmpl Fam* **une campagne électorale tous a.** an all-out electoral campaign

azote [azɔt] *nm* nitrogen

AZT® [azedte] *nm Méd (abrév* **azidothymidine)** AZT

aztèque [aztɛk] **1** *adj* Aztec
2 *nmf* **A.** Aztec

azur [azyr] *nm Litt* **(a)** *(couleur)* azure **(b)** **l'a.** *(ciel)* the sky

azyme [azim] *adj m voir* **pain**

B

B, b [be] *nm inv* B, b

baba¹ [baba] *nm* b. au rhum rum baba; *Fam* elle l'a dans le b. she's had it

baba² *adj inv Fam* flabbergasted

baba cool (*pl* babas cool) [babakul] *nmf* hippie

Babel [babɛl] *n* la tour de B. the Tower of Babel

babil [babil] *nm (d'un enfant)* prattling; *(des oiseaux)* twittering; *(d'un ruisseau)* babbling

babiller [babije] *vi (enfant)* to prattle; *(oiseau)* to twitter; *(ruisseau)* to babble

babines [babin] *nfpl aussi Hum* chops; d'avance, je m'en lèche les b. my mouth's watering in anticipation

babiole [babjɔl] *nf* (a) *(bibelot)* knick-knack, trinket (b) *(broutille)* trifle

bâbord [babɔr] *nm* port (side); à b. to port

babouche [babuʃ] *nf* Turkish slipper

babouin [babwɛ̃] *nm* baboon

baboune [babun] *nf Can Fam* faire la b. to sulk

baby-boom (*pl* baby-booms) [bebibum] *nm* baby boom

baby-foot [babifut] *nm inv* table football

baby-sitter (*pl* baby-sitters) [bebisitœr] *nmf* baby-sitter

baby-sitting [bebisitiŋ] *nm* baby-sitting; faire du b. to baby-sit

bac¹ [bak] *nm* (a) *(bateau)* ferry(-boat) (b) *(récipient)* tank; *(d'imprimeur, de photographe)* tray; *Ordinat* b. d'alimentation sheet feed; b. à glace ice tray; b. à légumes salad drawer; *Belg* b. à ordures *Br* dustbin, *Am* garbage can; b. de ou à papier *(d'imprimante)* paper tray; b. à sable sandpit

bac² *Fam* = **baccalauréat**

baccalauréat [bakalɔrea] *nm* = secondary school examination qualifying for entry to university, *Br* ≃ A levels, *Am* ≃ high school diploma; b. L ou littéraire = arts-based "baccalauréat"; b. S ou scientifique = science-based "baccalauréat"

bacchantes [bakɑ̃t] *nfpl Hum* moustache

bâche [baʃ] *nf (toile)* tarpaulin

bachelier, -ère [baʃalje, -ɛr] *nm,f* = student who has passed the "baccalauréat"

bâcher [baʃe] *vt* b. qch to cover sth with a tarpaulin

bachot [baʃo] *nm Fam Vieilli* = **baccalauréat**

bachotage [baʃɔtaʒ] *nm Fam Vieilli* cramming, *Br* swotting

bachoter [baʃɔte] *vi Fam Vieilli* to cram, *Br* to swot

bacille [basil] *nm Biol* bacillus

bâcler [bakle] *vt Fam* to botch

bacon [bekɔn] *nm* bacon

bactérie [bakteri] *nf* bacterium

bactériologique [bakterjɔlɔʒik] *adj* bacteriological; guerre b. germ warfare

badaboum [badabum] *exclam Fam* et b., il est tombé! he fell down, crash, bang, wallop!

badaud [bado] *nm (promeneur)* stroller; *(curieux) Br* gawper, *Am* rubberneck

badge [badʒ] *nm Br* badge, *Am* button

badigeonner [badiʒɔne] *vt* (a) *(surface)* to daub (de with); *(mur)* to whitewash; *Culin* to brush (de with) (b) *(gorge, plaie)* to paint (de with)

badin, -e [badɛ̃, -in] *adj* playful

badinage [badinaʒ] *nm* banter

badine [badin] *nf* switch

badiner [badine] *vi* to jest, to joke; il ne badine pas avec la ponctualité he's very strict about punctuality

badinerie [badinri] *nf* jest

badminton [badminton] *nm* badminton

bâdrant, -e [badrɑ̃, -ɑ̃t] *adj Can* bothersome

bâdrer [badre] *vt Can* to bother

baffe [baf] *nf Fam* clout

baffle [bafl] *nm* baffle

bafouer [bafwe] *vt (personne)* to jeer at; *(règlement, autorité)* to flout

bafouiller [bafuje] *vt & vi* to stammer

bâfrer [bafre] *vi très Fam* to stuff oneself

bagage [bagaʒ] *nm* (a) *(sac, valise)* bagages luggage, baggage; faire ses bagages to pack one's bags; b. à main piece of hand luggage (b) *Fig (connaissances)* knowledge (en of)

bagagiste [bagaʒist] *nm* baggage handler

bagarre [bagar] *nf* fight, brawl; chercher la b. to look for a fight

bagarrer [bagare] se bagarrer *vpr Fam* to fight

bagarreur, -euse [bagarœr, -øz] *Fam* 1 *adj (personne, caractère)* aggressive
2 *nm,f* brawler

bagatelle [bagatɛl] *nf (chose sans importance)* trifle; pour la b. de 2000 francs for a mere 2,000 francs

Bagdad [bagdad] *n* Baghdad

bagnard [baɲar] *nm* convict

bagne [baɲ] *nm Hist (prison)* convict prison; *(peine)* penal servitude

bagnole [baɲɔl] *nf Fam* car

bagou(t) [bagu] *nm* glibness; avoir du b. to have the gift of the gab

bague [bag] *nf* (a) *(bijou)* ring; *Fig* **passer à qn la b. au doigt** to marry sb; **b. de fiançailles** engagement ring (b) *(d'une boîte de conserve)* ring-pull; *(de cigare)* band (c) *(d'oiseau)* ring (d) *Tech* bush, ring; **b. de serrage** jubilee clip

baguenauder [bagnode] **1** *vi* to saunter around
2 se baguenauder *vpr* to saunter around

baguer [bage] *vt (oiseau, arbre)* to ring

baguette [baget] *nf (tige)* stick; *(de chef d'orchestre)* baton; *(pain)* French stick; **baguettes** *(pour manger)* chopsticks; **mener** *ou* **faire marcher qn à la b.** to rule sb with a rod of iron; **b. magique** magic wand; **d'un coup de b. magique** with a wave of my/his/*etc* magic wand; **baguettes de tambour** drumsticks

bah [ba] *exclam* bah!

Bahamas [baamas] *nfpl* **les B., l'archipel des B.** the Bahamas

Bahreïn [barajn], **Bahrayn** [barɛ̃] *n* Bahrain

bahut [bay] *nm* (a) *(coffre)* chest; *(buffet)* sideboard (b) *Fam (collège, lycée)* school

bai, -e [bɛ] *adj (cheval)* bay

baie¹ [bɛ] *nf Géog* bay; **la b. d'Hudson** Hudson Bay

baie² *nf* **b. vitrée** picture window

baie³ *nf (fruit)* berry

baignade [bɛɲad] *nf* (a) *(activité)* swimming; *Br* bathing; **b. interdite** *(sur panneau)* no swimming (b) *(endroit)* swimming *or Br* bathing place

baigner [bɛɲe] **1** *vt (pieds, œil, blessure)* to bathe; *(bébé, chien) Br* to bath, *Am* to bathe; *(sujet: mer)* to wash; *(sujet: rivière)* to water; **être baigné de sueur** to be bathed in sweat; **visage baigné de larmes** face streaming with tears; **baigné de lumière** bathed in light
2 *vi (tremper)* to soak, to steep *(dans* in); **les légumes baignent dans la sauce** the vegetables are swimming in sauce; **il baignait dans son sang** he was lying in a pool of his own blood; *Fam* **ça baigne (dans l'huile)!** everything's hunky dory!
3 se baigner *vpr* (a) *(se laver)* to have *or* take a bath (b) *(nager)* to have a swim

baigneur, -euse [bɛɲœʀ, -øz] **1** *nm,f* swimmer, *Br* bather
2 *nm (poupée)* doll

baignoire [bɛɲwaʀ] *nf* (a) *(dans la salle de bains)* bath (b) *Th* ground-floor box

Baïkal [bajkal] *n voir* **lac**

bail [baj] *(pl* **baux** [bo]) *nm* lease; *Fam* **ça fait un b. que je ne l'ai pas vu** I haven't seen him for ages

bâillement [bajmɑ̃] *nm* yawn

bâiller [baje] *vi* (a) *(personne)* to yawn; *Fam* **b. à s'en** *ou* **se décrocher la mâchoire** to yawn one's head off (b) *(couture, col)* to gape; *(porte)* to be ajar

bâillon [bajɔ̃] *nm* gag; **mettre un b. à qn** to gag sb

bâillonner [bajone] *vt aussi Fig* to gag

bain [bɛ̃] *nm* (a) *(pour se laver)* bath; **prendre un b.** to have *or* take a bath; *Fam Fig* **être/se mettre dans le b.** to be in/get into the swing of things; **b. de bouche** mouthwash; **faire un b. de bouche** to use mouthwash; **b. de boue** mud bath; **prendre un b. de foule** *(personnalité)* to go on a walkabout; **b. moussant** bubble bath; **prendre un b. de pieds** to soak one's feet; **prendre un b. de soleil** to sunbathe; **b. turc** Turkish bath; **b. de vapeur** steam bath; *(à la piscine)* **petit/grand b.** small/large pool (b) *(à la mer, en rivière)* swim, *Br*

bathe; *Vieilli* **bains de mer** swimming in the sea (d) *Phot* bath (e) *Tex* dye

bain-marie *(pl* **bains-marie)** [bɛ̃maʀi] *nm* bain-marie *(cooking pan set over second pan of boiling water)*; **faire cuire qch au b.** to cook sth in a bain-marie

baïonnette [bajonet] *nf* bayonet

baisemain [bɛzmɛ̃] *nm* **faire le b. à qn** to kiss sb's hand

baiser¹ [beze] **1** *vt* (a) *Litt (embrasser)* to kiss (b) *Vulg (coucher avec)* to fuck (c) *Vulg (tromper)* to screw; **se faire baiser** to get screwed
2 *vi Vulg* to fuck

baiser² *nm* kiss; **gros baisers** *(dans une lettre)* love and kisses

baisse [bɛs] *nf* fall, drop *(de* in); **être en b.** *(température, actions)* to be falling; *(popularité)* to be on the decline

baisser [bese] **1** *vt* (a) *(rideau, store, vitre de voiture)* to lower; **b. la tête** to lower one's head; *(de honte, de découragement)* to hang one's head; **b. les yeux** to look down; *Fig* **b. les bras** to give in (b) *(lumière, son, chauffage)* to turn down; *(prix)* to lower; **b. la voix** to lower one's voice; **je vous prie de b. le ton!** please keep your voice down!
2 *vi* (a) *(diminuer)* (température, niveau de l'eau, prix) to fall; *(marée)* to ebb; **elle a baissé dans mon estime** she's gone down in my estimation (b) *(s'affaiblir)* (malade) to get weaker; *(enthousiasme)* to fall off; *(feu)* to burn low; *(vue, mémoire)* to fail; **le jour baisse** night is falling
3 se baisser *vpr* to bend down; *(pour éviter un coup)* to duck; *Fig* **il n'y a qu'à se b. pour les ramasser** there are loads of them around

baissier [besje] *adj m voir* **marché**

bajoues [baʒu] *nfpl (d'animal)* chops; *Péj (d'une personne)* flabby cheeks

Bakou [baku] *n* Bakı

bal [bal] *(pl* **bals)** *nm (populaire)* dance; *(élégant)* ball; **b. costumé** *ou* **masqué** fancy dress ball; **b. musette** = dance to accordion music; **b. populaire** = dance, usually outdoors, open to the public

balade [balad] *nf Fam (à pied)* walk; *(en voiture)* drive; *(à bicyclette, à moto)* ride; **faire une b.** *(à pied)* to go for a walk; *(en voiture)* to go for a drive; *(à bicyclette, à moto)* to go for a ride

balader [balade] *Fam* **1** *vt (personne, chien)* to take for a walk; *(avoir avec soi) (objet)* to drag around
2 envoyer b. qn to send sb packing
3 se balader *vpr (à pied)* to go for a walk; *(en voiture)* to go for a drive; *(à bicyclette, à moto)* to go for a ride

baladeur, -euse [baladœr, -øz] **1** *adj Fam* **avoir les mains baladeuses** to have wandering hands
2 *nm* personal stereo, Walkman®
3 *nf* **baladeuse** *(lampe)* inspection lamp

baladin [baladɛ̃] *nm* strolling player

balafre [balafr] *nf* (a) *(coupure)* gash (b) *(cicatrice)* scar

balafré [balafre] *nm* scarface

balafrer [balafre] *vt* to gash; **visage balafré** scarred face

balai [balɛ] *nm* (a) *(de ménage)* broom; **passer le b.** to give the floor a sweep; **donner un coup de b.** *(balayer)* to give the floor a sweep; *Fig (dans une entreprise)* to have a shake-out; **du b.!** clear off!; **b. mécanique** carpet sweeper (b) *Aut (d'essuie-glace)* blade (c) *(percussion)* brush (d) *Fam (an)* **avoir quarante/cinquante balais** to be forty/fifty

balai-brosse (*pl* **balais-brosses**) [balɛbrɔs] *nm* long-handled scrubbing brush

balaise [balɛz] = **balèze**

balalaïka [balalaika] *nf* balalaika

balance [balɑ̃s] *nf* (a) (*appareil*) (pair of) scales; (*publique*) weighing machine; *Fig* **ce facteur pèse dans la b.** this factor carries some weight; **faire pencher la b.** to tip the scales (b) *Astron & Astrol* **la B.** Libra; **être B.** to be a Libran (c) *Écon* balance; **b. commerciale** balance of trade; **b. des paiements** balance of payments (d) *Fam* (*mouchard*) squealer

balancé, -e [balɑ̃se] *adj Fam* **être bien b.** (*personne*) to have a good figure

balancelle [balɑ̃sɛl] *nf* (*de jardin*) *Br* swing hammock, *Am* glider

balancement [balɑ̃smɑ̃] *nm* swaying

balancer [16] [balɑ̃se] **1** *vt* a (*bras, jambes, trompe, pendule*) to swing; (*hanches*) to sway (b) *Fam* (*projectile, objet*) to chuck, to throw; **b. des vannes/remarques** to make snide/unpleasant remarks (c) *Com* (*compte*) to balance (d) *Fam* (*se débarrasser de*) (*objet*) to chuck or throw out; **qn** to give sb the push; **elle a tout balancé** (*tout abandonné*) she's given it all up (e) *Fam* (*dénoncer*) to squeal on

2 *vi Litt* (*hésiter*) to waver

3 se balancer *vpr* (a) (*arbres, blés*) to sway; **se b. sur sa chaise** to rock backwards and forwards on one's chair; **se b. d'un pied sur l'autre** to rock from one foot to the other (b) (*sur une balançoire*) to swing (c) *très Fam* **je m'en balance!** I don't give a toss! (d) *Fam* **il s'est balancé du haut de la tour Eiffel** he chucked himself off the top of the Eiffel Tower

balancier [balɑ̃sje] *nm* (a) (*d'un funambule*) balancing pole (b) (*d'horloge*) pendulum

balançoire [balɑ̃swar] *nf* (*suspendue*) swing; (*bascule*) seesaw

balayage [balɛjaʒ] *nm* (a) (*pour nettoyer*) sweeping (b) *Rad, Él & TV* scanning

balayer [53] [balɛje] *vt* a (*nettoyer*) to sweep; (*saletés*) to sweep up; *Fig* (*objections, obstacles*) to brush aside; **le vent a balayé les nuages** the wind has swept the clouds away; *Fig* **b. devant sa porte** to put one's own house in order (b) *Rad, Él & TV* to scan; (*sujet: projecteurs*) to sweep

balayette [balɛjɛt] *nf* small brush

balayeur, -euse [balɛjœr, -øz] *nm,f* road-sweeper **2** *nf* **balayeuse** *Can* (*aspirateur*) vacuum cleaner

balbutiement [balbysimɑ̃] *nm* (a) (*en parlant*) stammering (b) **balbutiements** (*d'une science, d'une discipline*) early stages

balbutier [66] [balbysje] **1** *vi* to stammer **2** *vt* to stammer (out)

balcon [balkɔ̃] *nm* (a) (*d'édifice*) balcony (b) (*dans un théâtre*) circle; **premier/deuxième b.** dress/upper circle

baldaquin [baldakɛ̃] *nm* canopy

Bâle [bal] *n* Basel

Baléares [balear] *nfpl* **les (îles) B.** the Balearic Islands

baleine [balɛn] *nf* (a) (*animal*) whale; **b. blanche/bleue** white/blue whale (b) (*d'un parapluie*) rib; (*d'un corset*) (whale)bone

baleineau, -x [balɛno] *nm* whale calf

baleinière [balɛnjɛr] *nf* whaleboat

balèze [balɛz] *adj Fam* (*grand & fort*) hefty; (*intelligent*) brainy; **b. en maths** brilliant at maths

balisage [balizaʒ] *nm* (a) (*signaux*) *Naut & Rad* beacons; *Av* lights (b) (*action*) *Naut & Rad* beaconing; *Av* lighting

balise [baliz] *nf Naut & Rad* beacon; *Av* light; (*de piste de ski, d'épave*) marker; *Ordinat* tag; *Naut* **b. flottante** buoy; *Rad* **b. radar** radar beacon

baliser [balize] *vt* (*chenal*) to beacon; (*aéroport*) to equip with lights; (*route*) to mark out with beacons; (*piste de ski*) to mark out

balistique [balistik] **1** *adj* (*missile*) ballistic **2** *nf* ballistics (*singulier*)

balivernes [balivern] *nfpl* twaddle

balkanisation [balkanizasjɔ̃] *nf aussi Fig* Balkanization

Balkans [balkɑ̃] *nmpl* **les B.** the Balkans

ballade [balad] *nf* ballad

ballant, -e [balɑ̃, -ɑ̃t] *adj* (*bras, jambes*) dangling

ballast [balast] *nm* (a) *Constr* (*d'une route, d'une voie ferrée*) ballast (b) *Naut* ballast tank

balle¹ [bal] *nf* (a) (*pour jouer*) ball; **jouer à la b.** to play ball; *Fig* **prendre** *ou* **saisir la b. au bond** to seize the opportunity; *Fig* **se renvoyer la b.** to pass the buck; *Fig* **la b. est dans votre camp** the ball's in your court; **b. de golf/de tennis** golf/tennis ball; **b. de break/de match** break/match point (b) (*d'arme*) bullet; **b. à blanc** blank; **b. perdue** stray bullet (c) *Fam* **balles** (*francs*) francs

balle² *nf* (*de coton, de laine*) bale

balle³ *nf* (*de blé*) husk

ballerine [balrin] *nf* (a) (*danseuse*) ballerina (b) (*chaussure*) pump

ballet [balɛ] *nm* ballet

ballon [balɔ̃] *nm* (a) (*aéronef*) balloon; **b. d'essai** pilot balloon (b) (*balle*) ball; **jouer au b.** to play with a ball; **b. de football** football; **le b. ovale** rugby; **le b. rond** football (c) (*pour boire*) (*verre*) **b.** round wine glass (d) **b.** (*de baudruche*) balloon; **souffler dans le b.** (*d'alcotest*) to blow into the bag; **b. d'oxygène** oxygen bottle

ballonné, -e [balɔne] *adj* (*ventre, personne*) bloated

ballon-sonde (*pl* **ballons-sondes**) [balɔ̃sɔ̃d] *nm Météo* sounding balloon

ballot [balo] *nm* (a) (*paquet*) bundle (b) *Fam* (*imbécile*) twit

ballottage [balɔtaʒ] *nm Pol* **il y a b.** there will be a second ballot

ballottement [balɔtmɑ̃] *nm* (*de train*) rocking; (*des passagers*) shaking; (*de navire*) tossing

ballotter [balɔte] **1** *vt* (*bateau*) to toss about; (*passagers*) to shake about; *Fig* **un enfant ballotté entre son père et sa mère** a child passed backwards and forwards between its father and mother

2 *vi* (*bagages, bateau*) to be tossed about; (*poitrine*) to bounce up and down

ball-trap [baltrap] *nm* (*sport*) clay-pigeon shooting

balluchon [balyʃɔ̃] *nm Fam* (*de vêtements*) bundle; **faire son b.** to pack one's bags

balnéaire [balneɛr] *adj voir* **station**

balourd, -e [balur, -urd] **1** *adj* (*personne*) oafish **2** *nm,f* clumsy oaf

balsa [balza] *nm* balsawood

balte [balt] **1** *adj* Baltic; **les pays Baltes** the Baltic states **2** *nmf* Balt

Baltique [baltik] *nf* **la (mer) B.** the Baltic (Sea)

baluchon [balyʃɔ̃] = **balluchon**

balustrade [balystrad] *nf* (a) *Archit* balustrade (b) (*clôture*) railing

bambin [bãbɛ̃] *nm Fam* toddler

bambou [bãbu] *nm (plante)* bamboo; *Fam* c'est le coup de b.! it's a rip-off!

bamboula [bãbula] *nf Fam* spree; faire la b. to live it up

ban [bã] *nm (a) (applaudissements)* round of applause (b) bans *(de mariage)* banns (c) être au b. de la société to be an outcast from society; le b. et l'arrière-b. *(tout le monde)* the world and his wife

banal, -e, -als, -ales [banal] *adj (objet, gens, occupation)* ordinary; *(idée, remarque, style)* trite, banal; *(accident, exemple)* common; pas b. unusual

banalisation [banalizasjõ] *nf* la b. de qch the way sth is becoming more common

banaliser [banalize] 1 *vt (rendre commun)* to trivialize; véhicule banalisé unmarked police car
2 se banaliser *vpr* to become more common

banalité [banalite] *nf (a) (d'un objet, de gens, d'une occupation)* ordinariness; *(d'une idée, d'une remarque, d'un style)* triteness, banality; *(d'un accident, d'un exemple)* commonness (b) banalités platitudes

banane [banan] *nf (a) (fruit)* banana (b) *(coiffure)* quiff (c) *(petit sac) Br* bum bag, *Am* fanny pack

bananier, -ère [banaɲe, -ɛr] 1 *adj (plantation, production)* banana
2 *nm (arbre)* banana tree

banc [bã] *nm (a) (siège)* bench; ils se sont connus sur les bancs de l'école they got to know each other at school; b. des accusés dock; b. d'église pew; b. des témoins *Br* witness box, *Am* witness stand (b) *(de roche)* layer; *Can* b. de neige snowbank; b. de sable sandbank (c) *(de poissons)* shoal; b. d'huîtres oyster bed (d) *(établi)* (work)bench; b. d'essai *Ind* test bed; *Ordinat* benchtest; *Fig* testing ground; *Ordinat* b. de mémoire memory bank

bancaire [bãker] *adj (opération)* banking; *(chèque, compte)* bank

bancal, -e, -als, -ales [bãkal] *adj (meuble)* wobbly; *Fig (raisonnement, projet)* unsound

bandage [bãdaʒ] *nm (pansement)* bandage; *(action)* bandaging

bandana [bãdana] *nm* bandana

bande¹ [bãd] *nf (a) (de tissu, de papier, de terre)* strip; *(motif)* stripe; b. dessinée comic strip (b) *(pansement)* bandage; b. Velpeau® crêpe bandage (c) *(magnétique)* tape; *(pellicule)* film; *Ordinat* b. en cassettes cassette tape; *Ordinat* b. de défilement scroll bar; *Ordinat* b. de données data tape; b. originale *(d'un film)* original soundtrack; b. sonore soundtrack (d) *Aut* b. d'arrêt d'urgence *Br* hard shoulder, *Am* shoulder; b. médiane *(sur la route)* central line; b. de roulement *(de pneu)* tread (e) *Rad* band (f) *(d'une mitrailleuse)* cartridge belt (g) *Naut* donner de la b. to list

bande² *nf (de personnes)* band, group; *(de voleurs)* gang, band; faire b. à part *(agir seul)* to do one's own thing; viens avec nous, ne fais pas b. à part come with us, don't stay all on your own; faire qch en b. to do sth in a group; une b. d'incapables/d'imbéciles a bunch of incompetents/idiots

bande-annonce *(pl* bandes-annonces*)* [bãdanõs] *nf* trailer *(de* for*)*

bandeau, -x [bãdo] *nm (a) (pour les cheveux)* headband (b) *(sur les yeux)* blindfold; mettre un b. à qn to blindfold sb

bandelette [bãdlɛt] *nf (de tissu)* strip; bandelettes *(de momie)* bandages

bander [bãde] 1 *vt (a) (blessure, main)* to bandage; b. les yeux à qn to blindfold sb (b) *(ressort)* to tighten; *(arc)* to bend; *(muscles)* to flex
2 *vi Vulg* to have a hard-on

banderille [bãdrij] *nf* banderilla

banderole [bãdrɔl] *nf* banner

bande-son *(pl* bandes-son*)* [bãdsõ] *nf* soundtrack

bandit [bãdi] *nm (escroc)* crook; *Vieilli (brigand)* bandit; b. de grand chemin highwayman

banditisme [bãditism] *nm* crime; le grand b. organized crime

bandoulière [bãduljɛr] *nf (d'un sac)* shoulder strap; en b. over one's shoulder

bang [bãg] *nm inv Av* sonic boom

Bangkok [bãgkɔk] *n* Bangkok

Bangladesh [bãgladɛʃ, bɛ̃gladɛʃ] *nm* le B. Bangladesh

banjo [bãdʒo] *nm* banjo

banlieue [bãljø] *nf* suburbs; la b. parisienne/marseillaise the suburbs of Paris/Marseilles; la grande/proche b. the outer/inner suburbs; vivre en b. to live in the suburbs; de b. suburban

banlieusard, -e [bãljøzar, -ard] *nm,f* suburbanite

bannière [banjɛr] *nf* banner; la b. étoilée the Star-spangled Banner

bannir [banir] *vt (personne, idée)* to banish *(de* from*)*; *(sujet de conversation)* to ban *(de* from*)*; vous devez b. le sucre de votre alimentation you must exclude sugar from your diet

bannissement [banismã] *nm* banishment

banque [bãk] *nf (a) (établissement)* bank; la b. *(activité)* banking; employé/directeur de b. bank clerk/manager; b. d'affaires *Br* merchant bank, *Am* investment bank; b. centrale central bank; la B. de France the Bank of France; la B. mondiale the World Bank (b) *(au jeu)* bank; faire sauter la b. to break the bank (c) *Ordinat* b. de données data bank; *Méd* b. d'organes/du sperme organ/sperm bank

banquer [bãke] *vi Fam* to cough up

banqueroute [bãkrut] *nf Jur* bankruptcy; faire b. to go bankrupt

banquet [bãke] *nm* banquet

banquette [bãket] *nf (siège)* seat; la b. arrière *(d'une voiture)* the back seat

banquier, -ère [bãkje, -ɛr] *nm,f* banker

banquise [bãkiz] *nf* ice floe

bantou, -e [bãtu] 1 *adj* Bantu
2 *nm,f* B. Bantu

baobab [baobab] *nm* baobab (tree)

baptême [batɛm] *nm (a) Rel* baptism, christening; donner le b. à qn to baptize or christen sb (b) *(d'un navire)* naming; *(d'une cloche)* blessing (c) b. de l'air first flight; b. du feu baptism of fire

baptiser [batize] *vt (a) Rel* to baptize, to christen (b) *(nommer)* to name; *(surnommer)* to christen (c) *(navire)* to name; *(cloche)* to bless

baptismal, -e, -aux, -ales [batismal, -o] *adj* baptismal

baptistère [batister] *nm Rel* baptistry

baquet [bake] *nm (cuve)* tub

bar¹ [bar] *nm (café, comptoir)* bar

bar² *nm (poisson)* bass

bar³ *nm Phys* bar

barachois [baraʃwa] *nm Can (dans une rivière)* sandbar

baragouiner [baragwine] *Fam* **1** *vt (langue étrangère)* to speak badly; **qu'est-ce qu'il baragouine?** what's he jabbering about?
2 *vi* to jabber

baraque [barak] *nf* **(a)** *(cabane)* hut, shack; *(de forain)* stall, stand **(b)** *Fam (maison)* place

baraqué, -e [barake] *adj Fam* hefty

baraquement [barakmɑ̃] *nm* shacks; *Mil* camp

baratin [baratɛ̃] *nm Fam* **(a)** *(d'un vendeur)* sales talk, patter; *(d'un séducteur)* smooth talk **(b)** *(verbiage)* waffle

baratiner [baratine] *Fam* **1** *vt (sujet: vendeur)* to give the sales talk to; *(sujet: séducteur) Br* to chat up, *Am* to hit on
2 *vi* to waffle

baratineur, -euse [baratinœr, -øz] *nm,f Fam* smooth talker

baratte [barat] *nf* churn

Barbade [barbad] *nf* **la B.** Barbados

barbant, -e [barbɑ̃, -ɑ̃t] *adj Fam* boring

barbare [barbar] **1** *adj (cruel, sauvage)* barbaric
2 *nmf* barbarian

barbarie [barbari] *nf* **(a)** *(cruauté)* barbarity **(b)** *(manque de civilisation)* barbarism

barbarisme [barbarism] *nm* barbarism

barbe [barb] *nf* **(a)** *(d'homme)* beard; **b. de trois jours** stubble; **Fig à la b. de qn** right under sb's nose; **parler dans sa b.** to mutter, to mumble; **rire dans sa b.** to laugh up one's sleeve; *Fam* **quelle b.!** what a drag!; **b. à papa** *Br* candy floss, *Am* cotton candy **(b)** *(de chèvre, d'épi)* beard; *(de plume, d'hameçon)* barb **(c)** *Tech (de métal)* burr; *(de papier)* ragged edge

barbecue [barbəkju] *nm* barbecue; **faire un b.** to have a barbecue

barbelé [barbəle] **1** *adj m voir* **fil**
2 *nmpl* **barbelés** barbed wire

barber [barbe] *Fam* **1** *vt* **b. qn** to bore sb stiff
2 se barber *vpr* to be bored stiff

barbiche [barbiʃ] *nf* goatee (beard)

barbichette [barbiʃet] *nf Fam* small goatee (beard)

barbier [barbje] *nm* **(a)** *Vieilli* barber **(b)** *Can (coiffeur pour hommes)* (men's) hairdresser

barbiturique [barbityrik] *nm* barbiturate

barboter [barbote] **1** *vi* to splash about
2 *vt Fam (voler)* to pinch

barboteuse [barbotøz] *nf* romper-suit

barbouiller [barbuje] *vt* **(a)** *(salir)* to smear **(de** with); *(peindre)* to daub **(b)** *Fam* **b. l'estomac** *ou* **le cœur à qn** to make sb feel queasy; **se sentir barbouillé** to feel queasy

barbouze [barbuz] *nf Fam (agent secret)* secret agent

barbu, -e [barby] **1** *adj* bearded
2 *nm* bearded man

Barcelone [barsələn] *n* Barcelona

barda [barda] *nm Fam* gear; *Mil* kit

barde¹ [bard] *nf Culin (sur un rôti)* bard

barde² [bard] *nm* bard

barder¹ [barde] *v impersonnel Fam* **ça va b.!** there's going to be trouble!

barder² *vt* **(a)** *Culin* to bard **(b)** **bardé de fer/cuir** steel-/leather-clad; **être bardé de décorations** to be covered with decorations; **être bardé de diplômes** to have a whole string of qualifications

barème [barem] *nm* **(a)** *(de notes, de salaires, de prix)* scale **(b)** *(pour calcul rapide)* ready reckoner

barge [barʒ] *nf (péniche)* barge

baril [baril] *nm (de vin, de pétrole)* barrel; *(de poudre)* keg; *(de lessive)* drum

barillet [barije] *nm (de revolver)* cylinder

bariolé, -e [barjole] *adj* multicoloured

barjo(t) [barʒo] *adj Fam* nutty

barman [barman] *(pl* **barmans** *ou* **barmen** [barmɛn]*) nm Br* barman, *Am* bartender

baromètre [barɔmetr] *nm aussi Fig* barometer

baron [barɔ̃] *nm (seigneur)* baron; *Fig* **les barons de la finance/de l'industrie** financial/industrial tycoons

baronne [barɔn] *nf* baroness

baroque [barɔk] **1** *adj (architecture, art, musique)* baroque; *(idées)* bizarre, odd
2 *nm* **le b.** the Baroque

baroud [barud] *nm* **b. d'honneur** last stand

barouder [barude] *vi Fam (voyager)* to knock about

baroudeur [barudœr] *nm Fam* **(a)** *(combattant)* fighter **(b)** *(voyageur)* keen traveller

barouf(le) [baruf(l)] *nm Fam* din, row

barque [bark] *nf* boat; *Fig* **bien mener** *ou* **bien conduire sa b.** to manage one's affairs well; *Fig* **c'est elle qui mène la b.** she's the boss

barquette [barket] *nf* **(a)** *(pour plat à emporter)* container; *(de fruits)* punnet **(b)** *(gâteau)* pastry boat

barrage [baraʒ] *nm (sur l'eau)* dam; **b. de police** police roadblock; **b. routier** roadblock

barre [bar] *nf* **(a)** *(de métal)* bar, rod; *(de bois)* rod; **b. d'appui** *(d'une fenêtre)* rail; **b. de chocolat** bar of chocolate; **b. à mine** = metal bar used for breaking stone surfaces
(b) *(pour la danse)* barre; *Sp* **barres asymétriques** asymmetric bars; **b. fixe** horizontal bar; **barres parallèles** parallel bars; **b. transversale** *(de but)* crossbar; *Fig* **placer la b. trop haut** to set too high a standard
(c) *(trait)* line, stroke; *(d'un t)* cross; **b. oblique** oblique, slash; *Mus* **b. de mesure** bar (line)
(d) *Naut (à l'arrière)* tiller; *(volant)* helm; *aussi Fig* **être à** *ou* **tenir la b.** to be at the helm
(e) *Jur (de tribunal)* bar; **b. des témoins** *Br* witness box, *Am* witness stand; **être appelé à la b.** to be called to the witness box
(f) *(de clavier)* **b. d'espacement** space bar
(g) *Ordinat* **b. d'outils** tool bar; **b. de sélection** menu bar; **b. de titre** title bar

barreau, -x [baro] *nm* **(a)** *(d'une fenêtre, d'une cage)* bar; *(d'une échelle, d'une chaise)* rung; *Fig* **b. de chaise** fat cigar; **être derrière les barreaux** to be behind bars **(b)** *Jur* **le b.** the bar

barrer [bare] 1 vt (a) (route, passage, chemin) to block off; (porte, fenêtre) to bar; Can (fermer à clef) to lock; **route barrée** (sur panneau) road closed; **b. le passage** ou **la route à qn** to bar sb's way (b) (chèque) to cross (c) (mot, paragraphe) to cross out (d) Naut (bateau) to steer; (à l'aviron) to cox (e) Fam **on est mal barrés** things don't look good

2 **se barrer** vpr Fam to clear off, to beat it

barrette [baret] nf (a) (pour les cheveux) Br (hair) slide, Am barrette (b) (broche) brooch (c) Ordinat **b. de mémoire vive** RAM module

barreur [barœr] nm Naut helmsman; (à l'aviron) cox

barricade [barikad] nf barricade

barricader [barikade] 1 vt (rue, porte) to barricade
2 **se barricader** vpr to barricade oneself in

barrière [barjer] nf (obstacle) barrier; (clôture) fence; (d'un passage à niveau) gate; Aut **b. de dégel** = ban on the use of a road by heavy traffic during a thaw; Com **barrières douanières** trade barriers; **la Grande B. de Corail** the Great Barrier Reef

barrique [barik] nf barrel; Fam Fig **plein** ou **rond comme une b.** blind drunk

barrir [barir] vi (éléphant) to trumpet

barrissements [barismã] nmpl (d'un éléphant) trumpeting

bar-tabac (pl **bars-tabacs**) [bartaba] nm = bar that also sells cigarettes and tobacco

baryton [baritõ] nm Mus baritone

baryum [barjɔm] nm Chim barium

bas¹ [ba], **basse** [bas] 1 adj (a) (dans l'espace, en quantité, en intensité) low; (marée) out, low; **à b. prix** cheaply; **avoir la vue basse** to be short-sighted

(b) (dans une hiérarchie) low; Péj ou Hum **le b. peuple** the hoi polloi; **les b. quartiers** the poor districts

(c) (note) low; (instrument de musique), bass

(d) (dans le temps) late; **le b. Moyen Âge** the late Middle Ages

(e) Péj (acte) mean, low; (besognes) menial

2 adv (a) (dans l'espace) low (down); **voir plus b.** (dans un article) see below; Fig **mettre qn plus b. que terre** to treat sb like dirt; **tomber b.** (température, prix d'une action) to plummet; Fam **b. les mains** ou **les pattes!** hands off!, keep your paws off!

(b) (dans une hiérarchie) low

(c) (parler) quietly; (chanter) (dans le registre) low; (doucement) softly; **rire tout b.** to chuckle to oneself

(d) **en b.** at the bottom; (à l'étage inférieur) downstairs; **les gens d'en b.** the people below ou downstairs; **la tête en b.** upside down; **en b. de** at the bottom of

(e) **à b. la dictature/la police!** down with dictatorship/the police!

3 nm (partie inférieure) bottom; **l'étagère du b.** the bottom shelf; **le b. du dos** the small of the back; **au b. de** at the bottom of; **de b. en haut** upwards

4 nf **basse** Mus (partie) bass part; (voix, chanteur) bass (b) (contrebasse) (double) bass; (guitare) bass (guitar)

bas² nm (vêtement) stocking; **b. de contention** elastic stocking; Fig **b. de laine** nest egg; **b. nylon** nylons; **b. résille** fishnet stocking; **b. à varices** support stocking

basalte [bazalt] nm basalt

basané, -e [bazane] adj (bronzé) tanned; (tanné) weatherbeaten; (naturellement) swarthy

bas-côté (pl **bas-côtés**) [bakote] nm (a) (d'une route) verge (b) (d'une église) (side) aisle

basculant, -e [baskylã, -ãt] adj **benne basculante** (de camion) tipping body; **pont b.** drawbridge

bascule [baskyl] nf (a) (balançoire) seesaw (b) (balance) weighing machine

basculer [baskyle] 1 vt (a) (brouette, charrette) to tip up; (chargement) to tip over (b) Ordinat to toggle
2 vi (a) (tomber) to topple over; **faire b.** (personne) to knock over; (chargement) to tip over; **le pays a basculé dans l'anarchie** the country tipped over into anarchy (b) Ordinat to toggle

base [baz] nf (a) (partie inférieure) base; Fig (d'un syndicat, d'un parti politique) rank and file; **b. de maquillage** foundation (b) Mil (d'opérations) base; **b. aérienne/navale** air/naval base; **b. de lancement** launch site (c) (principe) basis; **jeter** ou **poser les bases de qch** to lay the foundations for sth; **de b.** basic; **denrées de b.** staple commodities; **à b. d'amidon/de gin** starch/gin-based (d) Math & Chim base (e) Ordinat **b. de données** database

base-ball [bezbol] nm baseball

baser [baze] 1 vt to base; **être basé sur qch** to be based on sth
2 **se baser** vpr **se b. sur qch** (sujet: personne) to base one's argument on sth; **sur quoi te bases-tu pour dire que...?** what basis do you have for saying that...?

bas-fond [bafõ] nm (a) (dans la mer, la rivière) shallow; **les bas-fonds** (d'une ville) the rough areas

basic [bazik] nm Ordinat BASIC

basilic [bazilik] nm (plante) basil

basilique [bazilik] nf basilica

basket [basket] 1 nm ou nf (chaussure) baseball boot
2 nm (sport) basketball

basket-ball [basketbol] nm basketball

basketteur, -euse [basketœr, -øz] nm,f basketball player

basque¹ [bask] 1 adj Basque
2 nmf **B.** Basque
3 nm (langue) Basque

basque² [bask] nf (d'une veste) tail; Fig **être toujours pendu aux basques de qn** to be always at sb's heels

bas-relief (pl **bas-reliefs**) [baraljef] nm bas-relief

basse [bas] voir **bas¹**

basse-cour (pl **basses-cours**) [baskur] nf (a) (cour) farmyard (b) (volaille) poultry

bassement [basmã] adv **être b. intéressé** to have one's own interests at heart

bassesse [bases] nf (a) (d'une action, d'un caractère) lowness (b) (action) low act

basset [base] nm (chien) basset (hound)

bassin [basɛ̃] nm (a) (récipient) basin, bowl; **b. (hygiénique)** bedpan (b) (dans un jardin) ornamental lake; (de fontaine) basin; (réservoir) tank; **petit b.** (de la piscine) children's pool; **grand b.** (de la piscine) large pool (c) (d'un port) dock, basin (d) Géol basin; **b. houiller** coal basin; **b. minier** mining area; **le B. parisien** the Paris Basin (e) (partie du corps) pelvis

bassine [basin] nf (en plastique) basin, bowl; (contenu) basinful, bowlful (b) (en cuivre) pan; (contenu) panful

bassiner [basine] vt Fam (ennuyer) to bore stiff

bassiste [basist] nmf (contrebassiste) double bass player; (guitariste) bass guitarist

basson [basõ] nm (a) (instrument) bassoon (b) (joueur) bassoonist

basta [basta] *exclam Fam* that'll do!

bastide [bastid] *nf* (a) *(maison)* country house; *(ferme)* farm (b) *Hist (ville fortifiée)* fortified town

bastille [bastij] *nf* fortress; *Hist* **la B.** the Bastille; **la prise de la B.** the storming of the Bastille

bastingage [bastēgaʒ] *nm Naut (garde-corps)* rail

bastion [bastjɔ̃] *nm aussi Fig* bastion

baston [bastɔ̃] *nm ou nf Fam* punch-up

bastringue [bastrε̃g] *nm Fam* (a) *(dancing)* (seedy) dance hall (b) *(affaires)* gear, stuff; **et tout le b.** and the whole caboodle

bas-ventre *(pl bas-ventres)* [bavātr] *nm* lower abdomen

bât [ba] *nm* packsaddle; *Fig* **c'est là que le b. blesse** there's the rub

bataclan [bataklã] *nm Fam (affaires)* stuff, gear; **et tout le b.** and the whole caboodle

bataille [bataj] *nf* (a) *(lutte)* battle, fight; *(électorale)* contest; **b. terrestre/aérienne/navale** land/air/naval battle; *(cheveux* **en b.** dishevelled hair (b) *(jeu de cartes)* beggar-my-neighbour

batailler [bataje] *vi Fam* **b. pour faire qch** to battle to do sth

batailleur, -euse [batajœr, -øz] *adj* aggressive

bataillon [batajɔ̃] *nm Mil* battalion; *Fam* **un b. de** a troop of

bâtard, -e [batar, -ard] **1** *adj (enfant)* illegitimate; *Péj* bastard; *(style, solution)* hybrid
2 *nm,f (enfant)* illegitimate child; *Péj* bastard
3 *nm (chien)* mongrel; *(pain)* = small French stick

batavia [batavja] *nf* batavia lettuce

bateau, -x [bato] **1** *nm* (a) *(embarcation)* boat; **faire du b.** to go boating; **prendre le b.** to go/come by boat; **en** *ou* **par b.** by boat; *Fam Fig* **mener qn en b.**, **monter un b. à qn** to wind sb up; **b. à moteur** motorboat; **b. de pêche** fishing boat; **b. de plaisance** pleasure boat; **b. à vapeur** steamboat, steamer; **b. à voiles** *Br* sailing boat, *Am* sailboat (b) *(sur le trottoir)* driveway entrance (c) **encolure b.** boat neck
2 *adj inv Fam (banal)* hackneyed

bateau-mouche *(pl bateaux-mouches)* [batomuʃ] *nm* river boat *(on the Seine)*

bateleur, -euse [batlœr, -øz] *nm,f Vieilli (jongleur)* juggler; *(acrobate)* acrobat

batelier, -ère [batalje, -εr] *nm,f* boatman, *f* boatwoman; *(sur un bac)* ferryman, *f* ferrywoman

bat-flanc [baflã] *nm inv (dans un dortoir, une prison)* wooden partition

bâti, -e [bati] **1** *adj (personne)* **être bien b.** to be well-built; **être mal b.** to have an odd shape
2 *nm* (a) *Constr* frame, framework (b) *(en couture)* tacking, basting

batifoler [batifole] *vi Fam* to lark about

batik [batik] *nm* batik

bâtiment [batimã] *nm* (a) *(immeuble)* building; **b. d'habitation** residential building (b) *(secteur)* **le b.** building; **être dans le b.** to be in the building trade (c) *Naut* ship; **b. de guerre** warship, battleship

bâtir [batir] **1** *vt* (a) *(maison, ville)* to build; *Fig (fortune, hypothèse)* to build (up); **(se) faire b. une maison** to have a house built; **terrain bâti** developed *or* built-up site (b) *(en couture)* to tack, to baste
2 se bâtir *vpr* **se b. une réputation (de)** to build up a reputation (as)

bâtisse [batis] *nf* ugly building

batiste [batist] *nf* batiste

bâton [batɔ̃] *nm* (a) *(en bois, de colle, de craie)* stick; *(d'agent de police)* Br truncheon, *Am* nightstick; *(de majorette)* baton; **mener une vie de b. de chaise** to lead a wild life; **mettre des bâtons dans les roues à qn** to put a spoke in sb's wheel; **parler à bâtons rompus** to talk about this and that; **conversation à bâtons rompus** rambling conversation; **b. de rouge à lèvres** lipstick; **bâtons de ski** ski sticks or poles (b) *(trait vertical)* vertical line

bâtonnet [batɔnɛ] *nm* stick

batracien [batrasjε̃] *nm Zool* amphibian

battage [bataʒ] *nm* (a) *Fam (publicité)* hype; **faire du b. autour de qch** to hype sth up (b) *(du blé)* threshing

battant, -e [batã, -ãt] **1** *adj (pluie)* lashing; **le cœur b.** with a pounding heart
2 *nm,f (personne combative)* fighter
3 *nm* (a) *(d'une cloche)* clapper, tongue (b) *(d'une porte, d'un volet)* leaf; **porte à double b.** double door

batte [bat] *nf* bat; **b. de base-ball/de cricket** baseball/cricket bat

battement [batmã] *nm* (a) *(de tambour)* beat, beating; *(de mains)* clapping; *(d'ailes, de voiles)* flapping; *(de porte)* banging; **j'entendais les battements de son cœur** I could hear his heart beating (b) *(entre deux événements)* gap; **deux heures de b.** a two-hour gap

batterie [batri] *nf* (a) *(dans un orchestre)* drums; **être à la b.** to be on drums (b) *Mil* battery; *Fig* **dévoiler ses batteries** to show one's hand; **b. antiaérienne/antichars** anti-aircraft/antitank battery (c) *(ensemble, groupe)* battery; *(de tests, de questions)* series; **élevage en b.** battery farming; **poulet de b.** battery hen; **b. de cuisine** kitchen utensils (d) *Él* battery; **fonctionner sur b.** to be battery-operated *or* battery-powered; **b. de secours** emergency battery

batteur [batœr] *nm* (a) *(dans un groupe)* drummer (b) *(au cricket)* batsman; *(au base-ball)* batter, striker (c) *(de cuisine)* mixer

batteuse [batøz] *nf (machine agricole)* threshing machine, thresher

battoir [batwar] *nm* (a) *(pour les tapis)* (carpet) beater; *(pour le linge)* beetle (b) *Fam (grande main)* great paw or mitt

battre [11] [batr] **1** *vt* (a) *(frapper) (personne, chien, tapis)* to beat; *(blé)* to thresh; *(métal)* to hammer; **b. qn à coups de poings/avec une canne** to punch/cane sb; **b. le tambour** to beat the drum; **b. le rappel** *Mil* to call to arms; *Fig* to call everyone together; **b. la campagne** to scour or comb the countryside; *(esprit)* to wander; *Prov* **il faut b. le fer quand il** *ou* **pendant qu'il est chaud** strike while the iron is hot (b) *(cartes)* to shuffle; *(beurre)* to churn; *(œufs, préparation culinaire)* to beat, to whisk; **b. les blancs en neige** to beat the whites stiffly (c) *(adversaire)* to beat; *(record)* to break; **b. qn à plate(s) couture(s)** to beat sb hollow; *Fig* **b. tous les records** to take some beating (d) *Mus* **b. la mesure** to beat time (e) *Naut* **b. pavillon français/britannique** to fly the French/ British flag
2 *vi* (a) *(cœur)* to beat; *(porte, volet)* to bang; *(voile)* to flap; **il a le cœur qui bat** *(d'émotion)* his heart is pounding (b) **b.**

en retraite to beat a retreat
3 battre de vt ind **b. des mains** to clap one's hands; **b. des cils** to flutter one's eyelashes
4 se battre vpr aussi Fig to fight (**avec/contre** with/against); **se b. comme des chiffonniers** to fight like cat and dog; **se b. au couteau** to fight with knives; très Fam **je m'en bats l'œil** I don't give a toss

battu, -e [baty] adj (femme, enfant) battered; **un air ou regard de chien b.** a hangdog look; **avoir les yeux battus** to have dark circles under one's eyes

battue [baty] nf (à la chasse) beat; (pour retrouver quelqu'un) search

batture [batyr] nf Can sandbank

baud [bo] nm Tél & Ordinat baud

baudet [bode] nm ass, donkey; **chargé comme un b.** loaded down like a packhorse

baudrier [bodrije] nm shoulder strap; (pour épée) baldric; (d'escalade) harness

baudroie [bodrwa] nf monkfish

baudruche [bodryʃ] nf (ballon de) b. balloon

baume [bom] nm aussi Fig balm; **mettre du b. au cœur de qn** (événement) to be a consolation for sb

baux [bo] voir bail

bauxite [boksit] nf bauxite

bavard, -e [bavar, -ard] **1** adj (a) (qui parle beaucoup) chatty; (style, essai) wordy; **il est b. comme une pie** he'd talk the hind legs off a donkey **(b)** (indiscret) indiscreet
2 nm,f (a) (qui parle beaucoup) chatterbox **(b)** (indiscret) gossip

bavardage [bavardaʒ] nm **(a)** (action) chatting; (commérage) gossiping **(b) bavardages** (paroles) chat; (commérage) gossip

bavarder [bavarde] vi (parler) to chat; (commérer) to gossip

bavarois, -e [bavarwa, -az] **1** adj Bavarian
2 nm,f B. Bavarian
3 nm Culin bavarois, -e = dessert consisting of set custard and whipped cream mixed with fruit purée

bave [bav] nf (de personne) dribble; (de chien) slaver; (de cheval, de chien enragé) froth, foam; (d'escargot) slime; (de crapaud) spittle

baver [bave] vi (personne) to dribble; (chien) to slaver; (chien enragé) to foam at the mouth; (stylo) to leak, to run; (encre) to smudge; Fam **en b. (des ronds de chapeaux)** to have a hard time of it; Fam **en faire b. (des ronds de chapeaux) à qn** to give sb a hard time

bavette [bavet] nf **(a)** (d'un bébé, d'un tablier) bib **(b)** Culin skirt (of beef) **(c)** Fam **tailler une b.** to have a chat

baveux, -euse [bavø, -øz] **1** adj (bouche, enfant) dribbling; (omelette) runny
2 nm,f Can (morveux) pain, pest

Bavière [bavjer] nf la B. Bavaria

bavoir [bavwar] nm bib

bavure [bavyr] nf (a) (tache) smudge, smear **(b)** (erreur) slip-up; **sans bavure(s)** faultless; **b. policière** case of police misconduct

bayer [53] [baje] vi **b. aux corneilles** to stare into space

bazar [bazar] nm **(a)** (marché) bazaar **(b)** (magasin) general store **(c)** Fam (désordre) shambles (singulier); (bruit) racket; (affaires) stuff, gear; **et tout le b.** and the whole caboodle; **mettre du** ou **le b. dans qch** to make a shambles of sth

bazarder [bazarde] vt Fam (se débarrasser de) to get shot of; (jeter) to chuck out; (vendre) to flog

bazooka [bazuka] nm bazooka

BCBG [besebeʒe] adj inv (abrév **bon chic bon genre**) Br ≃ Sloany, Am ≃ preppy

BCG® [beseʒe] nm Méd BCG

BD [bede] nf (a) (abrév **bande dessinée**) comic strip, cartoon **(b)** Ordinat (abrév **base de données**) dbase

bd abrév **boulevard**

béant, -e [beã, -ãt] adj (bouche, porte) wide open; (blessure, gouffre) gaping

béat, -e [bea, -at] adj Rel blessed; (heureux) blissful; Péj (niais) inane; **être b. d'admiration** to be open-mouthed in admiration; **elle nous observait d'un air b.** she watched us open-mouthed

béatement [beatmã] adv (sourire) inanely

béatifier [66] [beatifje] vt Rel to beatify

béatitude [beatityd] nf **(a)** Rel beatitude **(b)** (bonheur parfait) bliss

beau, belle [bo, bel]
bel is used before masculine singular nouns beginning with a vowel or h mute.

1 adj **(a)** (d'apparence) (femme, enfant) beautiful, good-looking; (homme) handsome, good-looking; (objet, maison) lovely, beautiful; **b. comme un dieu** like a Greek god; **ce n'est pas b. à voir** it's not a pretty sight; **se faire b.** to smarten oneself up; Fam Fig **te voilà b.!** you're in a fine mess!
(b) (de qualité) (œuvre, spectacle, discours) fine; **avoir une belle situation** to have a good job
(c) (moralement) fine, noble; **un b. geste** a noble gesture; **ce n'est pas b. de mentir** it isn't nice to tell lies
(d) (bien) **c'est trop b. pour être vrai** it's too good to be true; **ce serait trop b.!** that would be too much (to hope for)!; **le plus b. jour de ma vie** the best day of my life
(e) Ironique **une belle grippe** a nasty dose of the flu; **une belle correction** a good thrashing; **te voilà dans un bel état!** look at the state of you!; **j'ai eu une belle peur** I had an awful fright; **vous avez fait du b. travail!** well done!; très Fam **un b. salaud** a real or right bastard; **j'en ai entendu de belles sur votre compte!** I've heard some unpleasant things about you!; **il en a fait de belles** he got up to some real tricks
(f) (intensif) **au b. milieu de la rue** right or bang in the middle of the road; **une belle somme** a tidy sum; **un b. poulet** a nice big chicken
(g) (locutions) **bel et bien** (complètement) well and truly; **il est bel et bien venu** he really did come; **il s'est bel et bien trompé** he has indeed made a mistake; **de plus belle** with a vengeance; **il reprit l'entraînement de plus belle** he resumed training with a vengeance or more enthusiastically than ever
2 adv **il fait b.** it's fine; **il ferait b. voir ça!** that'll be the day!; **j'ai b. le lui expliquer...** no matter how many times I explain it to him...; **j'ai b. pousser, la porte ne bouge pas** try as I might, I can't get the door to open
3 nm **le b.** (beauté) beauty; **mais le plus b., c'est que...** but the best bit or part is that ...; Fam Ironique **c'est du b.!** that's great!; **le temps est au b. (fixe)** the weather is set fair; Fig **avoir le moral au b. fixe** to be permanently in a good mood; **un vieux b.** an old roué; **faire le b.** (chien) to sit up and beg
4 nf **belle (a)** (partie) decider **(b)** Hum (amie) lady friend **(c)** Fam **se faire la b.** to run away; (de prison) to escape

beaucoup [boku] *adv* **(a)** *(intensément, en grande quantité)* a lot; **ça te plaît?** – **pas b.** do you like it? – not much or not a lot **(b)** *(une grande quantité, un grand nombre)* **il reste encore b. à faire** there's still a lot to do; **c'est déjà b. qu'il veuille bien vous parler** it's quite something that he condescended to speak to you; **il y est pour b.** he has had a lot or a great deal to do with it; **b. pensent que...** a lot of or many people think that...; **b. d'entre nous** a lot or many of us; **de b.** *(de loin)* by far; **il s'en faut de b. que je sois riche** I'm far from rich
(c) b. *(quantité)* a lot of, many; **b. de vin/chance** a lot of wine/luck; **b. de fautes** a lot of or many mistakes; **pas b. de** *(argent, courage)* not much; *(gens, problèmes)* not many; **avec b. de soin** with great care, very carefully; **j'en veux b.!** I want a lot!
(d) *(avec des comparatifs)* a lot, much; **b. moins/plus vite** a lot or much slower/faster; **il parle b. trop** he talks far too much; **b. moins d'enfants** a lot or many fewer children; **b. moins de temps** a lot or much less time

beauf [bof] *Fam* **1** *adj Péj* **il est un peu b.** he's a bit of a narrow-minded average Frenchman
2 *nm* **(a)** *(beau-frère)* brother-in-law **(b)** *Péj* = stereotypical narrow-minded, average Frenchman

beau-fils *(pl* **beaux-fils)** [bofis] *nm* **(a)** *(gendre)* son-in-law **(b)** *(après remariage)* stepson

beau-frère *(pl* **beaux-frères)** [bofʀɛʀ] *nm* brother-in-law

beaujolais [boʒɔlɛ] *nm* Beaujolais

beau-père *(pl* **beaux-pères)** [bopɛʀ] *nm* **(a)** *(père du conjoint)* father-in-law **(b)** *(après remariage)* stepfather

beaupré [bopʀe] *nm Naut* bowsprit

beauté [bote] *nf* beauty; **être en b.** to be looking magnificent; **de toute b.** magnificent; **finir en b.** to end on a high note; **faire qch pour la b. du geste** to do sth for the sake of it; **se refaire une b.** to put one's face on

beaux-arts [bozaʀ] *nmpl* fine art; **école des B.,** B. art school

beaux-parents [bopaʀɑ̃] *nmpl* parents-in-law

bébé [bebe] *nm* **(a)** *(nourrisson)* baby; **faire le b.** to behave like a baby; **être très b.** to be very babyish **(b)** *(animal)* **b. gazelle/lapin** baby gazelle/rabbit

bébé-éprouvette *(pl* **bébés-éprouvettes)** [bebe-epʀuvɛt] *nm* test-tube baby

bébelle [bebɛl] *nf Can (gadget)* gadget; *(bibelot)* ornament; *(jouet)* toy

bébête [bebɛt] *Fam* **1** *adj* silly
2 *nf* creepy-crawly

bec [bɛk] *nm* **(a)** *(d'oiseau, de tortue, de pieuvre)* beak **(b)** *Fam (bouche)* mouth; **il n'a pas ouvert le b. de la journée** he hasn't opened his mouth all day; **la clope au b.** with a fag in one's mouth; **rester le b. dans l'eau** to be left high and dry; **b. fin** gourmet **(c)** *(de pot)* lip; *(de cafetière)* spout; *(d'instrument à vent)* mouthpiece; **b. Bunsen** Bunsen burner; **b. de gaz** *(réverbère)* gas lamp; **b. verseur** spout **(d)** *Can (baiser)* **donner un b. à qn** to give sb a kiss

bécane [bekan] *nf Fam (vélo)* bike; *(machine, ordinateur)* machine

bécarre [bekaʀ] *adj & nm Mus* natural

bécasse [bekas] *nf* **(a)** *(oiseau)* woodcock **(b)** *Fam (idiote)* silly thing

bec-de-lièvre *(pl* **becs-de-lièvre)** [bɛkdəljɛvʀ] *nm* harelip

béchamel [beʃamɛl] *nf (sauce)* **b.** béchamel sauce

bêche [bɛʃ] *nf* spade

bêcher [beʃe] *vt* to dig, to turn over

bêcheur, -euse [beʃœʀ, -øz] *nm,f Fam (snob)* stuck-up person

bécosses [bekos] *nfpl Can Fam* privy, *Am* john

bécoter [bekote] *Fam* **1** *vt* to snog
2 se bécoter *vpr* to snog

becqueter [42] [bɛkte] **1** *vt (sujet: oiseau)* to peck at
2 *vi très Fam (personne)* to eat

becter [bɛkte] *vi* = **becqueter**

bedaine [bədɛn] *nf Fam* pot(-belly), paunch; **prendre de la b.** to get a pot(-belly) or a paunch

bédé [bede] *nf Fam* comic strip, cartoon

bedeau, -x [bədo] *nm* verger

bedon [bədɔ̃] *nm Fam* pot(-belly), paunch

bedonnant, -e [bədɔnɑ̃, -ɑ̃t] *adj Fam* pot-bellied, paunchy

bédouin, -e [bedwɛ̃, -in] **1** *adj* Bedouin
2 *nm,f* B. Bedouin

bée [be] *adj* **bouche b.** open-mouthed; **j'en suis restée bouche b.** I was speechless; **regarder qch bouche b.** to gape at sth

beffroi [befʀwa] *nm* belfry

bégaiement [begemɑ̃] *nm* stuttering, stammering

bégayer [53] [begeje] **1** *vi* to stutter, to stammer
2 *vt* to stammer (out)

bégonia [begɔnja] *nm* begonia

bègue [bɛg] **1** *adj* **être b.** to stutter, to stammer
2 *nmf* stutterer, stammerer

bégueule [begœl] *adj* prudish

béguin [begɛ̃] *nm Fam (personne)* crush; **avoir le b. pour qn** to have a crush on sb; **avoir le b. pour qch** to have taken a fancy to sth

BEI [beœi] *nf (abrév* **Banque européenne d'investissement)** EIB

beige [bɛʒ] *adj & nm* beige

beigne¹ [bɛɲ] *nf Fam* clout

beigne² *nm Can* doughnut

beignet [bɛɲɛ] *nm (salé)* fritter; *(au sucre, à la confiture)* doughnut, donut; **b. de** ou **aux pommes** apple fritter

bel [bɛl] *voir* **beau**

bêlement [bɛlmɑ̃] *nm aussi Fig* bleat; **des bêlements** bleating

bêler [bele] *vi aussi Fig* to bleat

belette [bəlɛt] *nf* weasel

Belfast [belfast] *n* Belfast

belge [bɛlʒ] **1** *adj* Belgian
2 *nmf* B. Belgian

belgicisme [bɛlʒisism] *nm (mot)* Belgian-French word; *(tournure)* Belgian-French expression

Belgique [bɛlʒik] *nf* la B. Belgium

Belgrade [bɛlgʀad] *n* Belgrade

bélier [belje] *nm* **(a)** *(animal)* ram **(b)** *Mil* battering ram **(c)** *Astron & Astrol* **le B.** Aries; **être** *(un)* **b.** to be (an) Aries

Belize [beliz] *nm* **le B.** Belize

belladone [beladɔn] *nf* belladonna, deadly nightshade

bellâtre [belɑtʀ] *nm Péj* smoothie

belle [bɛl] *voir* **beau**

belle-famille *(pl* **belles-familles)** [bɛlfamij] *nf* in-laws

belle-fille (*pl* **belles-filles**) [bɛlfij] *nf* (a) (*épouse du fils*) daughter-in-law (b) (*après remariage*) stepdaughter

belle-mère (*pl* **belles-mères**) [bɛlmɛr] *nf* (a) (*mère du conjoint*) mother-in-law (b) (*après remariage*) stepmother

belle-sœur (*pl* **belles-sœurs**) [bɛlsœr] *nf* sister-in-law

belligérant, -e [beliʒerɑ̃, -ɑ̃t] **1** *adj* belligerent
2 *nm* **les belligérants** the warring nations

belliqueux, -euse [belikø, -øz] *adj* (*pays, peuple*) warlike; (*personne, humeur*) aggressive

belote [bəlɔt] *nf* = card game

bélouga [beluga], **béluga** [belyga] *nm* beluga whale

belvédère [bɛlvedɛr] *nm* (a) (*construction*) belvedere, gazebo (b) (*sur un site naturel*) viewpoint

bémol [bemɔl] *Mus* **1** *nm* flat; *Fam Fig* **mettre un b.** to tone it down
2 *adj* flat

ben [bɛ̃] *adv Fam* **b. oui!** well, yes!; **b. voilà, euh...** yeah, well, er...

bénédictin, -e [benediktɛ̃, -in] *adj, nmf & af* Benedictine

bénédiction [benediksjɔ̃] *nf Rel* blessing, benediction; (*d'une église*) consecration; *Fig* blessing

bénéfice [benefis] *nm* (a) (*gain*) profit; **b. d'exploitation** operating profit (b) (*avantage*) benefit, advantage; **tirer un certain b. de qch** to derive some benefit *ou* advantage from sth; **avoir le b. de l'âge** to have the benefit of age; **accorder** *ou* **laisser le b. du doute à qn** to give sb the benefit of the doubt; **au b. de** (*œuvre charitable*) in aid of

bénéficiaire [benefisjɛr] **1** *adj Com* (*entreprise*) profit-making; (*compte*) in credit
2 *nmf* (*d'un chèque*) payee; *Jur* beneficiary

bénéficier [benefisje] **bénéficier de** *vt ind* (a) (*profiter de*) to benefit from; **faire b. qn de son expérience** to give sb the benefit of one's experience (b) (*avoir*) to have; **cette carte d'abonnement vous fait b. d'une remise** this season ticket entitles you to a 20 per cent reduction

bénéfique [benefik] *adj* beneficial (**à** to)

Benelux [benelyks] *nm* **le B.** Benelux

benêt [bənɛ] **1** *adj m* simple
2 *nm* simpleton

bénévolat [benevɔla] *nm* voluntary work

bénévole [benevɔl] **1** *adj* (*travail, infirmière*) voluntary
2 *nmf* volunteer, voluntary worker

Bengale [bɛ̃gal] *nm* **le B.** Bengal

Bénin [benɛ̃] *nm* **le B.** Benin

bénin, -igne [benɛ̃, -iɲ] *adj* (*accident, opération*) minor; (*tumeur*) benign

béninois, -e [beninwa, -az] **1** *adj* Beninese
2 *nm,f* **B.** Beninese

bénir [benir] *vt aussi Fig* to bless; (*église*) to consecrate; (*que*) **Dieu vous bénisse!** (may) God bless you!; **être béni des dieux** to have been touched by God

bénit, -e [beni, -it] *adj voir* **eau, pain**

bénitier [benitje] *nm Rel* holy-water stoup

benjamin, -e [bɛ̃ʒamɛ̃, -in] *nm,f* (a) (*le plus jeune*) youngest (b) *Sp* junior (*10 to 12 years old*)

benjoin [bɛ̃ʒwɛ̃] *nm* (gum) benzoin, benjamin

benne [bɛn] *nf* (*de camion*) tipping *ou* dump body; (*dans une mine*) tub, truck; (*de téléphérique*) (cable) car; **b. à ordures** bin lorry

benzine [bɛ̃zin] *nf* benzine

BEP [beape] *nm Scol* (*abrév* **brevet d'études professionnelles**) = vocational diploma taken at age eighteen

BEPC [beapese] *nm Anciennement Scol* (*abrév* **brevet d'études du premier cycle**) = school-leaving certificate taken at age fifteen

béquille [bekij] *nf* (a) (*pour marcher*) crutch; **marcher avec des béquilles** to be on crutches (b) (*d'un vélo, d'une moto*) stand

berbère [bɛrbɛr] **1** *adj* Berber
2 *nmf* **B.** Berber
3 *nm* (*langue*) Berber

bercail [bɛrkaj] *nm* (*de l'Église*) fold; *Hum* **rentrer au b.** to return to the fold

berçante [bɛrsɑ̃t] *adj f & nf Can* (**chaise**) **b.** rocking chair

berce [bɛrs] *nf Belg & Suisse* (*berceau*) cradle

berceau, -x [bɛrso] *nm* (*de bébé*) cradle; *Fig* (*d'une civilisation, d'un mouvement*) birthplace; **dès le b.** from the cradle, from birth; *Fam* **il les prend au b.** he's a cradle-snatcher

bercer [16] [bɛrse] **1** *vt* (a) (*bébé, passager*) to rock; *Fig* **mon enfance a été bercée par la musique de Debussy** I was brought up listening to Debussy (b) *Fig* **b. qn de promesses** to delude sb with promises
2 se bercer *vpr* **se b. d'illusions** to delude oneself

berceuse [bɛrsøz] *nf* (*chanson*) lullaby

BERD [bɛrd] *nf* (*abrév* **Banque européenne pour la reconstruction et le développement**) EBRD

béret [berɛ] *nm* beret

bergamote [bɛrgamɔt] *nf* bergamot

berge¹ [bɛrʒ] *nf* (*bord*) bank

berge² *nf Fam* **il a quarante berges** he's forty

berger, -ère [bɛrʒe, -ɛr] **1** *nm,f* shepherd, *f* shepherdess
2 *nm* (*chien*) **b. allemand** German shepherd, *Br* Alsatian; **b. des Pyrénées** Pyrenean mountain dog
3 *nf* **bergère** (*fauteuil*) wing chair

bergerie [bɛrʒəri] *nf* sheepfold

bergeronnette [bɛrʒərɔnɛt] *nf* wagtail

Béring [beriŋ] *n voir* **détroit**

berk [bɛrk] *exclam* yuk!

Berlin [bɛrlɛ̃] *n* Berlin; **B.-Ouest/-Est** West/East Berlin

berline [bɛrlin] *nf Aut Br* (four-door) saloon, *Am* (four-door) sedan

berlingot [bɛrlɛ̃go] *nm* (a) (*bonbon*) *Br* boiled sweet, *Am* hard candy (b) (*de lait*) carton; (*de produit d'entretien*) pack

berlinois, -e [bɛrlinwa, -az] **1** *adj* from Berlin
2 *nm,f* **B.** Berliner

berlue [bɛrly] *nf Fam* **avoir la b.** to be seeing things

bermuda [bɛrmyda] *nm* Bermuda shorts, Bermudas

Bermudes [bɛrmyd] *nfpl* **les (îles) B.** Bermuda

bernard-l'(h)ermite [bɛrnarlɛrmit] *nm inv* hermit crab

Berne [bɛrn] *n* Bern

berne [bɛrn] **en berne** *adj Naut* at *Br* half mast *ou Am* half staff; *Mil* furled

berner [bɛrne] *vt* to fool

bernois, -e [bɛrnwa, -az] **1** *adj* Bernese
2 *nm,f* **B.** Bernese

besace [bəzas] *nf (de mendiant)* bag; *(de pèlerin)* scrip; **sac b.** = large, soft handbag

bésef [bezef] = **bézef**

besogne [bəzɔɲ] *nf* job, task; **aller vite en b.** to get things done quickly; *Fig & Péj* to jump the gun

besoin [bəzwɛ̃] *nm* (a) *(nécessité)* need **(de qch** for sth); **avoir b. de qn/qch** to need sb/sth; **avoir b. de faire qch** to need to do sth; **j'ai b. que tu m'aides** I need you to help me; **éprouver le b. de faire qch** to feel the need to do sth; **pour les besoins de la cause** for the sake of the cause; **au b.** if necessary, if need be; **en cas de b.** if need be; **si b. est** if necessary, if need be **(b) faire ses besoins** *(personne)* to relieve oneself; *(animal)* to do its business **(c)** *(misère)* **être dans le b.** to be in need

bestial, -e, -aux, -ales [bestjal, -o] *adj* bestial

bestiaux [bestjo] *nmpl* livestock

bestiole [bestjɔl] *nf* small animal; *(insecte)* creepy-crawly

best-seller *(pl* **best-sellers)** [bestselœr] *nm* best-seller

bêta, -asse [beta, -as] *Fam* **1** *adj* silly
2 *nm,f* silly-billy

bêtabloquant [betablɔkɑ̃] *nm Méd* beta-blocker

bétail [betaj] *nm* livestock; **gros b.** cattle and horses

bétaillère [betajɛr] *nf* cattle truck

bêta-test *(pl* **bêta-tests)** [betatest] *nm Ordinat* beta test

bête [bɛt] **1** *adj* stupid, silly; **c'est b., on a loupé le film!** what a pity or a shame, we've missed the film!; **ce n'est pas b.** *(suggestion)* that's not a bad idea; **rester tout b.** *(décontenancé)* to be open-mouthed; *Fam* **être b. comme ses pieds** to be as thick as two short planks; **être b. à pleurer** to be pathetically stupid; **c'est b. comme chou, c'est tout b.** it's as easy as pie
2 *nf* (a) *(animal)* animal; **travailler comme une b.** to work flat out; **elle m'a regardé comme une b. curieuse** she looked at me as if I was from another planet; *Péj* **b. à concours** *Fr* swot, *Am* grind; **b. à cornes** horned animal; **b. fauve** big cat; **b. féroce** wild animal; **b. noire** *(personne)* bête noire; *(chose)* pet hate; **b. de somme** beast of burden **(b)** *(insecte)* insect; *Fig* **chercher la petite b.** to nit-pick; **b. à bon Dieu** *Br* ladybird, *Am* ladybug

bêtement [betmɑ̃] *adv (rire, regarder)* stupidly; **mourir b.** to die senselessly; **tout b.** quite simply, purely and simply

bêtifier [66] [betifje] *vi (avec un enfant)* to use baby-talk

bêtise [betiz] *nf* (a) *(manque d'intelligence)* stupidity, silliness; *(action idiote)* stupid thing (to do); *(parole idiote)* stupid thing to say; **dire/faire une b.** to say/do something stupid; **dire des bêtises** to talk nonsense **(c)** *(chose sans importance)* trivial thing; **se disputer pour des bêtises** to argue over nothing **(d)** *Can* **bêtises** *(injures)* insults **(e) bêtises de Cambrai** *Br* ≃ mint humbugs, *Am* ≃ hard mint candies

béton [betɔ̃] *nm* (a) *(matériau)* concrete; *Fig* **des muscles en b.** rock-hard muscles; **un alibi en b.** a cast-iron alibi; **b. armé** reinforced concrete **(b)** *Fam* **laisse b.!** drop it!

bétonner [betone] *vt* to concrete

bétonneuse [betonøz], **bétonnière** [betɔnjɛr] *nf* cement mixer, concrete mixer

bette [bɛt] *nf* (Swiss) chard

betterave [betrav] *nf* **b. (rouge)** *Br* beetroot, *Am* beet; **b. fourragère** mangel-wurzel; **b. sucrière** sugar beet

beuglement [bøgləmɑ̃] *nm (d'une vache)* moo; *(d'un taureau)* bellow; *(de la radio, de la télé)* blaring; **des beuglements** mooing/bellowing; **pousser des beuglements** *(personne)* to bellow

beugler [bøgle] **1** *vi (vache)* to moo; *(taureau, personne)* to bellow; *(radio, télé)* to blare
2 *vt (chanson)* to bawl out, to bellow out

beur [bœr] **1** *nmf* = North African born in France of immigrant parents
2 *adj inv* = of North Africans born in France of immigrant parents

beurre [bœr] *nm* butter; **au b.** *(pâtisserie)* made with butter; *Fam* **ça compte pour du b.** that doesn't count; *Fam* **faire son b.** to make a packet; **ça mettra du b. dans les épinards** that will make life a bit easier; **elle veut le b. et l'argent du b.** she wants to have her cake and eat it; **b. de cacahouètes** peanut butter; **b. de cacao** cocoa butter; **b. salé/demi-sel** salted/slightly salted butter

beurré, -e [bœre] *adj très Fam (ivre)* plastered, legless

beurrer [bœre] *vt* to butter

beurrier [bœrje] *nm* butter dish

beuverie [bøvri] *nf* binge, drinking session

bévue [bevy] *nf* slip-up

Beyrouth [berut] *n* Beirut

bézef [bezef] *adv Fam* **il n'y en a pas b.** *(pain, confiture)* there's not much or a lot (of it); *(légumes, livres)* there aren't many or a lot (of them)

Bhoutan [butɑ̃] *nm* **le B.** Bhutan

bi- [bi-] *préf* bi-

biais [bjɛ] *nm* (a) *(d'un mur)* slant; **regarder qn de b.** to look sideways at sb; **en b.** at an angle; **tailler un tissu dans le b.** to cut material on the bias **(b)** *(moyen)* way; **par le b. de** through **(c)** *(aspect)* angle; **par quel b. envisager la chose?** from what angle should we look at the issue?

biaiser [bjeze] *vi (ruser)* to dodge the issue

biathlon [biatlɔ̃] *nm* biathlon

bibelot [biblo] *nm* curio, knick-knack

biberon [bibrɔ̃] *nm (baby's or feeding)* bottle; **nourrir ou élever un enfant au b.** to bottle-feed a child; **c'est l'heure du b.** it's the baby's feeding time

bibi¹ [bibi] *nm (chapeau)* (woman's) hat

bibi² *pron Fam (moi)* yours truly

bibine [bibin] *nf Fam (boisson)* dishwater

bibite [bibit] *nf Can* bug, insect

bible [bibl] *nf aussi Fig* bible; **la B.** the Bible

bibliographie [bibliografi] *nf* bibliography

bibliographique [bibliografik] *adj* bibliographical

bibliophile [bibliofil] *nmf* book-lover

bibliothécaire [biblioteker] *nmf* librarian

bibliothèque [bibliɔtɛk] *nf* (a) *(bâtiment, salle)* library; **b. municipale** public library; **b. de prêt** lending library; **b. universitaire** university library **(b)** *(meuble)* bookcase

biblique [biblik] *adj* biblical

Bic® [bik] **1** *adj* **stylo B., pointe B.** ballpoint (pen), *Br* Biro®
2 *nm* ballpoint (pen), *Br* Biro®

bicarbonate [bikarbonat] *nm Chim* bicarbonate; **b. de soude** bicarbonate of soda

bicentenaire [bisɑ̃tner] *nm Br* bicentenary, *Am* bicentennial

biceps [biseps] nm biceps; Fam **avoir des b.** to have big biceps

biche [biʃ] nf (a) (animal) hind, doe (b) Fam **ma b.** darling

bicher [biʃe] vi Fam Vieilli (se réjouir) to be tickled pink

bichonner [biʃɔne] **1** vt (a) (préparer) to doll up (b) (soigner) to pamper
2 se bichonner vpr to doll oneself up

bicolore [bikɔlɔr] adj two-colour(ed)

bicoque [bikɔk] nf Fam (maison) house, place

bicorne [bikɔrn] nm cocked hat

bicyclette [bisiklɛt] nf bicycle; **aller en ville à ou en b.** to cycle into town, to go into town by bicycle; **faire de la b.** to go cycling; **il ne sait pas faire de la b.** he can't ride a bicycle

bidasse [bidas] nm très Fam Br squaddie, Am G.I.

bide [bid] nm Fam (a) (ventre) belly; **avoir/prendre du b.** to have/develop a belly (b) (échec) **faire un b.** Br to flop, Am to bomb

bidet [bidɛ] nm (a) (de toilette) bidet (b) Hum (cheval) nag

bidimensionnel, -elle [bidimãsjɔnɛl] adj bi-dimensional

bidoche [bidɔʃ] nf très Fam meat

bidon [bidõ] **1** adj inv Fam (excuse, argument) phoney, fake; (élections) rigged
2 nm (a) (d'huile, d'essence) can; (de lait) churn; (gourde) water bottle; **b. d'essence** petrol can, jerry can (b) Fam (ventre) belly (c) Fam (bluff) **c'est du b.** it's a load of tosh

bidonnant, -e [bidɔnã, -ãt] adj Fam hilarious

bidonner [bidɔne] **se bidonner** vpr Fam to laugh one's head off

bidonville [bidõvil] nm shantytown

bidouiller [biduje] vt Fam to patch up; Ordinat (programme) to modify

bidule [bidyl] nm Fam thingy, whatsit; **B.** (personne) what's-his-name, f what's-her-name

bielle [bjɛl] nf Aut connecting rod, con-rod

biélorusse [bjelɔrys] **1** adj Byelorussian
2 nmf **B.** Byelorussian

Biélorussie [bjelɔrysi] nf la **B.** Belarus

bien [bjɛ̃] **1** adv (a) (convenablement) well; **un livre b. écrit** a well-written book; **écoutez-moi b.** listen carefully; Ironique **ça commence b.!** that's a good start!
(b) (moralement) right; **se conduire ou se tenir b.** to behave (well); **vous avez b. fait** you did the right thing; **tu fais b. de me le dire** it's a good thing you've told me; **tu ferais b. de te méfier** you would be wise to beware
(c) (emphatique) **regarder qn b. en face** to look sb right in the face; **c'est b. cela** that's right; **c'est b. une erreur** that's definitely a mistake; **est-ce b. le train pour Paris?** is this the right train for Paris?; **j'ai b. dû lire dix de ses livres** I must have read at least ten of his books; **j'irais b. avec vous mais...** I'd love to go with you but...; **j'y suis b. obligé** I just have to; **je sais b.** I'm well aware of it; **je vous l'avais b. dit!** I told you so!; **c'est b. ce que je pensais** that's what I thought; **nous verrons b.!** we'll see!; **qu'est-ce que ça peut b. être/vouloir dire?** what on earth can it be/mean?; **est-ce b. raisonnable?** is that really reasonable?; **B. à vous** (dans une lettre) Yours
(d) (très) very; **vous arrivez b. tard** you're very late; **que ce soit b. clair, je...** let's get this clear, I...
(e) (beaucoup) (réfléchir, changer) a lot, a great deal; **b. plus** much or a lot more; **b. moins** much or a lot less; **des**

gens a lot of people; **b. d'autres** many others; **b. des fois** often; **avoir b. de la peine ou du mal à faire qch** to have a lot of difficulty doing sth; **tu as b. de la chance!** you're really lucky!
(f) (locutions) **b. que** although, though; **b. que je le sache** although I know it; **b. entendu, b. sûr, b. évidemment** of course; **b. sûr que je viendrai** of course I'll come; **b. sûr que non!** of course not!
2 exclam **eh b.!** well!; **b.! je vous appelle demain!** OK, I'll call you tomorrow!
3 adj inv (a) (satisfaisant) good; **c'est b.!** good!
(b) (à l'aise) comfortable; **être b. avec qn** (en bons termes) to be on good terms with sb; **se mettre b. avec qn** to get into sb's good books; Fam **nous voilà b.!** we're in a right mess!
(c) (en forme) well
(d) (moral) decent; **ce n'est pas b. de vous moquer de lui** it's not nice or kind of you to make fun of him
(e) (beau) (personne) good-looking, attractive; **elle est b. sur cette photo** she looks good in this photo
4 nm (a) Phil & Rel good; **le b. et le mal** good and evil, right and wrong; **faire le b.** to do good; **faire du b. à qn** to do sb good; **grand b. vous fasse!** much good may it do you!; **dire du b. de qn** to speak well of sb; **c'est pour ton b.** it's for your own good; **c'était en tout b. tout honneur** it was quite innocent
(b) (chose matérielle) possession; Jur assets; **biens** possessions, property; **avoir du b.** to have property; Prov **b. mal acquis ne profite jamais** ill-gotten gains never prosper; **biens de consommation** consumer goods; **biens immobiliers ou immeubles** real estate or property

bien-aimé, -e [bjɛ̃neme] (mpl bien-aimés, fpl bien-aimées) [bjɛ̃neme] adj beloved

bien-être [bjɛ̃nɛtr] nm well-being

bienfaisance [bjɛ̃fəzãs] nf œuvre de **b.** charity, charitable organization

bienfaisant, -e [bjɛ̃fəzã, -ãt] adj (a) (personne) charitable (b) (remède) beneficial; (vent, pluie) refreshing

bienfait [bjɛ̃fɛ] nm (a) (acte) kindness (b) (avantage) benefit

bienfaiteur, -trice [bjɛ̃fɛtœr, -tris] nm,f benefactor, f benefactress

bien-fondé [bjɛ̃fõde] nm validity; Jur cogency

bienheureux, -euse [bjɛ̃nœrø, -øz] adj blissful; Rel blessed

biennal, -e, -aux, -ales [bjenal, -o] adj biennial

bien-pensant, -e (mpl bien-pensants, fpl bien-pensantes) [bjɛ̃pãsã, -ãt] adj & nm,f conformist

bienséance [bjɛ̃seãs] nf propriety, decorum

bientôt [bjɛ̃to] adv soon; **il est b. deux heures** it's nearly two o'clock; **on est b. arrivés?** will we soon be there?; Fam **tu n'as pas b. fini?** have you quite finished?; **à b.!** see you soon!

bienveillance [bjɛ̃vɛjãs] nf kindness; **avec b.** kindly

bienveillant, -e [bjɛ̃vɛjã, -ãt] adj kind

bienvenu, -e [bjɛ̃vny] **1** adj (remarque) apposite; (repas, explication) welcome
2 nmf **soyez le b.!** welcome!; **vous serez toujours la bienvenue** you're always welcome

bienvenue [bjɛ̃vny] **1** nf welcome; **souhaiter la b. à qn** to welcome sb
2 exclam welcome! (à to); Can (de rien) you're welcome!

bière¹ [bjɛr] *nf (boisson)* beer; *Fam* **ce n'est pas de la petite b.** it's no small thing; **b. blonde** lager; **b. brune** *Br* brown ale, *Am* dark beer; **b. pression** *Br* draught beer, *Am* draft beer

bière² *nf (cercueil)* coffin; **assister à la mise en b.** to be present when the body is placed in the coffin

biffer [bife] *vt* to cross out; **b. un nom d'une liste to** cross a name off a list

biffure [bifyr] *nf* crossing out

bifidus [bifidys] *nm* live culture

bifocal, -e, -aux, -ales [bifɔkal, -o] *adj (lentille)* bifocal; **lunettes bifocales** bifocals

bifteck [biftɛk] *nm (beef)steak*; **b. haché** *Br* mince, *Am* mincemeat; *Fam* **gagner son b.** to earn one's bread and butter

bifurcation [bifyrkasjɔ̃] *nf* fork

bifurquer [bifyrke] *vi (route, chemin)* to fork; *(automobiliste)* to turn off; **bifurquez à droite** take the right fork

bigame [bigam] *adj* bigamous

bigamie [bigami] *nf* bigamy

bigarré, -e [bigare] *adj (tissu)* multicoloured; **une foule bigarrée** a motley crew

bigarreau, -x [bigaro] *nm* = type of cherry

bigler [bigle] *Fam* **1** *vi* (a) *(loucher)* to have a squint (b) **b. sur qch** to have a good look at sth
2 *vt (personne)* to eye up

bigleux, -euse [biglø, -øz] *adj Fam (qui louche)* cross-eyed; *(myope)* short-sighted

bigophone [bigɔfɔn] *nm Fam Br* blower, *Am* horn

bigorneau, -x [bigɔrno] *nm* winkle

bigot, -e [bigo, -ɔt] **1** *nm,f (religious)* bigot
2 *adj* sanctimonious

bigoterie [bigɔtri] *nf (religious)* bigotry

bigoudi [bigudi] *nm (hair)* curler *or* roller; **se mettre des bigoudis** to put one's hair in curlers

bigre [bigr] *exclam Fam* Vieilli gosh!

bigrement [bigrəmɑ̃] *adv Fam (très)* awfully; *(beaucoup)* a heck of a lot

bihebdomadaire [biɛbdɔmadɛr] *adj* twice-weekly

bijou, -x [biʒu] *nm* jewel; *Fig* gem; **des bijoux** jewellery, jewels; **b. de famille** family jewel; **un b. fantaisie** a piece of costume jewellery

bijouterie [biʒutri] *nf (boutique)* jeweller's (shop); *(commerce, fabrication)* jeweller's trade

bijoutier, -ère [biʒutje, -ɛr] *nm,f* jeweller

bikini® [bikini] *nm* bikini

bilan [bilɑ̃] *nm* (a) *Fin* balance sheet; **faire** *ou* **dresser un b.** to draw up a balance sheet; *Com* **déposer son b.** to file one's petition (in bankruptcy); *Com* **un dépôt de b.** a petition in bankruptcy; **b. comptable** balance sheet (b) *(appréciation)* *(d'une situation, de faits)* assessment, evaluation; *(résultats)* results; *(d'une catastrophe)* toll; **faire le b. de la situation** to take stock of the situation; **accident sur l'autoroute, b. quatre morts** *(titre)* motorway accident, four dead; **b. de santé** complete check-up

bilatéral, -e, -aux, -ales [bilateral, -o] *adj* bilateral

bilboquet [bilbɔkɛ] *nm* cup-and-ball

bile [bil] *nf* bile; **décharger sa b. sur qn** to vent one's spleen on sb; *Fam* **se faire de la b. (pour)** to fret (about)

biler [bile] **se biler** *vpr Fam* to fret

biliaire [biljɛr] *adj* biliary

bilingue [bilɛ̃g] *adj* bilingual

billard [bijar] *nm* (a) *(jeu)* billiards; **faire un b.** *ou* **une partie de b.** to have a game of billiards; **b. américain** pool; **b. électrique** pinball (b) *(table)* billiard table (c) *Fam* **passer sur le b.** to go under the knife

bille¹ [bij] *nf* (a) *(de verre)* marble; *Fig* **reprendre ses billes** to pull out; *Fam* **toucher sa b. en qch** to know a thing *or* two about sth (b) *(de billard)* (billiard) ball; *Fam* **aller b. en tête** not to beat about the bush (c) *Tech* ball (d) *très Fam (visage)* mug; **avoir une bonne b.** to look pleasant enough

bille² *nf (pièce de bois)* billet

billet [bijɛ] *nm* (a) *(argent)* **b. (de banque)** *Br* (bank)note, *Am* bill; **un b. de 100 francs** a 100-franc note; **un faux b.** a forged banknote; **le b. vert** the dollar; *Fam* **je me fiche mon b. qu'il ne viendra pas!** I bet my bottom dollar he won't come! (b) *(pour voyager, pour le cinéma)* ticket; **b. d'avion/de train** plane/train ticket; **b. de première/de seconde** first/second-class ticket; **b. simple** *Br* single *or Am* one-way ticket; **b. aller (et) retour** *Br* return *or Am* round-trip ticket (c) *Com & Fin (effet)* bill; **b. au porteur** bill payable to bearer (d) *Litt (lettre)* note; *Scol* **b. d'absence** absence slip; **b. doux** love letter; *Scol* **b. de retard** = note given to pupil who is late, specifying the time of arrival

billetterie [bijɛtri] *nf* (a) *(lieu)* ticket office (b) *(de billets de transport)* **b. automatique** ticket machine

billion [biljɔ̃] *nm* trillion

billot [bijo] *nm* block

bimensuel, -elle [bimɑ̃sɥɛl] **1** *adj Br* fortnightly, *Am* semimonthly
2 *nm Br* fortnightly *or Am* semimonthly magazine

bimestriel, -elle [bimɛstriel] *adj & nm* bimonthly

bimoteur [bimɔtœr] *adj & nm (avion)* **b.** twin-engine aircraft

binaire [binɛr] *adj Math* binary; **langage b.** binary notation

biner [bine] *vt* to hoe

binette¹ [binɛt] *nf (outil)* hoe

binette² *nf très Fam (visage)* mug

biniou [binju] *nm* Breton bagpipes

binoclard, -e [binɔklar, -ard] *nm,f Fam* specs wearer

binocle [binɔkl] *nm* pince-nez *inv*; *Fam* **binocles** *(lunettes)* specs

binôme [binom] *nm* (a) *Math* binomial (b) *Scol* **travailler en b.** to work in twos

bio [bjo] *adj inv Fam (produit, yaourt)* organic

biocarburant [bjokarbyrɑ̃] *nm* biofuel

biochimie [bjoʃimi] *nf* biochemistry

biodégradable [bjodegradabl] *adj* biodegradable

biographe [bjograf] *nmf* biographer

biographie [bjografi] *nf* biography

biographique [bjografik] *adj* biographical

bio-industrie [*pl* **bio-industries**] [bjoɛ̃dystri] *nf* biotechnology industry

biologie [bjɔlɔʒi] *nf* biology

biologique [bjɔlɔʒik] *adj* biological; *(sans engrais chimiques)* organic

biologiste [bjɔlɔʒist] *nmf* biologist

biomasse [bjomas] *nf* biomass

biophysique [bjɔfizik] *nf* biophysics *(singulier)*

biopsie [bjɔpsi] *nf* biopsy

biorythme [bjɔritm] *nm* biorhythm

biosphère [bjɔsfɛr] *nf* biosphere

biotechnique [bjɔtɛknik], **biotechnologie** [bjɔtɛknɔlɔʒi] *nf* biotechnology

bip [bip] **1** *exclam* beep!
2 *nm* (a) *(son)* beep; **faire b.** to beep (b) *(appareil)* beeper, pager

biparti, -e [biparti], **bipartite** [bipartit] *adj* bipartite

bipède [biped] *adj & nm* biped

biplace [biplas] *adj & nm Aut & Av* two-seater

biplan [biplɑ̃] *nm* biplane

bipolaire [bipɔlɛr] *adj Él & Phys* bipolar

bique [bik] *nf Fam* (a) *(chèvre)* nanny goat (b) *Péj (femme)* **vieille b.** old bag

biquet, -ette [bikɛ, -ɛt] *nm,f* (a) *(chevreau)* kid (b) *Fam* **mon b.** my pet

biréacteur [bireaktœr] *nm* twin-engine jet

birman, -e [birmɑ̃, -an] **1** *adj* Burmese
2 *nm,f* B. Burmese
3 *nm (langue)* Burmese

Birmanie [birmani] *nf* **la B.** Burma

bis¹, -e [bi, biz] *adj* greyish-brown

bis² [bis] *adv* (a) *Th* encore; *Mus* repeat (b) *(d'une adresse)* **10 b.** ≃ 10A

bisaïeul, -e [bizajœl] *nm,f Litt* great-grandfather, f great-grandmother

bisannuel, -elle [bizanɥɛl] *adj* biennial

bisbille [bisbij] *nf Fam* squabble; **être en b. avec qn** to be at odds with sb

biscornu, -e [biskɔrny] *adj* (a) *(chapeau)* misshapen; *(bâtiment, objet)* oddly shaped (b) *Fam (idées)* cranky; *(raisonnement, esprit)* tortuous

biscoteaux [biskɔto] *nmpl Fam* biceps; **avoir des b.** to have bulging biceps

biscotte [biskɔt] *nf* rusk

biscuit [biskɥi] *nm* (a) *(gâteau)* Br biscuit, Am cookie; **b. à la cuiller** Br sponge finger, Am lady finger; **biscuits salés** crackers (b) *(porcelaine)* biscuit

bise¹ [biz] *nf (vent)* north wind

bise² [biz] *nf (baiser)* kiss; **donner** ou **faire une b. à qn** to give sb a kiss; **se faire la b.** to give each other a kiss; **grosses bises** *(sur une lettre)* love and kisses

biseau, -x [bizo] *nm* (a) *(bord)* bevel; **taillé en b.** bevel-edged (b) *(outil)* bevel

biseauter [bizote] *vt* (a) *(tailler)* to bevel (b) *(cartes à jouer)* to mark

bisexualité [biseksɥalite] *nf* bisexuality

bisexuel, -elle [biseksɥɛl] *adj* bisexual

bismuth [bismyt] *nm* bismuth

bison [bizɔ̃] *nm* bison

Bison Futé [bizɔ̃fyte] *n* = organization which advises drivers of driving conditions on French motorways

bisou [bizu] *nm Fam* kiss

bisque [bisk] *nf Culin* **b. de homard** lobster bisque

bisquer [biske] *vi Fam* **faire b. qn** to wind sb up

bissectrice [bisektris] *nf* bisector

bisser [bise] *vt* (a) *(sujet: artiste) (chanson)* to give an encore of (b) *(sujet: spectateur) (chanson)* to call for an encore of; **b. un chanteur** to call on a singer to give an encore

bissextile [bisɛkstil] *adj* **année b.** leap year

bistouri [bisturi] *nm* lancet

bistro(t) [bistro] *nm Fam* bar

BIT [beite] *nm (abrév* **Bureau international du travail)** ILO

bit [bit] *nm Ordinat* bit; **b. d'arrêt** stop bit; **b. de contrôle** control bit; **b. de départ** start bit

bite¹ [bit] = **bitte**

bitoniau [bitɔnjo] *nm Fam* thingy

bitte¹ [bit] *nf Vulg* cock

bitte² *nf Naut* **b. d'amarrage** bollard

bitture [bityr] *nf très Fam* **prendre une b.** to get plastered

bitturer [bityre] **se bitturer** *vpr très Fam* to get plastered

bitume [bitym] *nm (revêtement)* asphalt

bitumer [bityme] *vt (route)* to asphalt

bitum(in)eux, -euse [bitym(in)ø, -øz] *adj* bituminous

biture [bityr] = **bitture**

biturer [bityre] = **bitturer**

bivouac [bivwak] *nm* bivouac

bivouaquer [bivwake] *vi* to bivouac

bizarre [bizar] *adj* strange, odd

bizarrement [bizarmɑ̃] *adv* strangely, oddly

bizarrerie [bizarri] *nf (d'une situation, d'une idée, d'une attitude)* strangeness, oddness; **bizarreries** oddities; *(d'une personne)* eccentricities

bizarroïde [bizarɔid] *adj Fam* weird

bizut [bizy] *nm Fam* = first-year student on whom practical jokes are played

bizutage [bizytaʒ] *nm Fam* = practical jokes played on first-year students

bizuter [bizyte] *vt Fam (étudiant)* to play practical jokes on

bizuth [bizy] = **bizut**

bla-bla [blabla] *nm Fam* claptrap

blackbouler [blakbule] *vt Fam (à un examen)* to fail; **se faire b.** to fail, Am to flunk

blafard, -e [blafar, -ard] *adj* pallid

blague [blag] *nf* (a) *(plaisanterie)* joke; **faire une b. à qn** to play a joke on sb; **b. à part** joking apart; **sans b.?** no kidding? (b) *(mensonge)* **raconter des blagues** to lie

blaguer [blage] *vi Fam* to joke; **aimer b.** to like a joke

blagueur, -euse [blagœr, -øz] *Fam* **1** *adj* **il est très b.** he really likes a joke
2 *nm,f* (qui dit des blagues) joker; *(qui fait des blagues)* practical joker

blair [blɛr] *nm très Fam Br* conk, Am schnozzle

blaireau, -x [blɛro] *nm* (a) *(animal)* badger (b) *(pinceau)* shaving brush

blairer [blere] *vt Fam* **je ne peux pas le b.** I can't stick him

blâme [blɑm] *nm* (a) *(reproche)* blame (b) *(sanction)* reprimand

blâmer [blɑme] *vt* (a) *(désapprouver)* to blame (b) *(sanctionner)* to reprimand

blanc, blanche [blɑ̃, blɑ̃ʃ] **1** *adj* (a) *(couleur)* white; **b. comme neige** as white as snow (b) *(peau)* pale; *(pas bronzé)* white; **b. comme un linge** as white as a sheet (c) *(page)* blank (d) *(sourd)* **d'une voix blanche** in a toneless voice

2 *nm* (a) *(couleur)* white; **le b. est à la mode** white is in; **b. cassé** off-white (b) *(partie blanche) (d'une cible)* bull's-eye; **le b. des yeux** the whites of the eyes; **regarder qn dans le b. des yeux** to look sb straight in the eye; **b. d'œuf** egg white; **b. de poulet** chicken breast (c) *(espace)* blank (d) *(aux dominos)* blank (e) **chauffé à b.** white-hot; **tirer à b.** to fire a blank/blanks (f) *(linge)* **(articles de) b.** linen; **je lave le b. séparément** I wash my whites separately (g) *(vin)* white wine

3 *nm, f* B. White (man), *f* White (woman); **les Blancs** the Whites

4 *nf* **blanche** *Mus Br* minim, *Am* half note

blanc-bec [blɑ̃bɛk] *(pl* blancs-becs) *nm* total novice

blanchâtre [blɑ̃ʃɑtr] *adj* whitish

blanche [blɑ̃ʃ] *voir* **blanc**

Blanche-Neige [blɑ̃ʃnɛʒ] *npr* Snow White

blancheur [blɑ̃ʃœr] *nf* whiteness

blanchiment [blɑ̃ʃimɑ̃] *nm (d'argent)* laundering

blanchir [blɑ̃ʃir] **1** *vt* (a) *(rendre blanc)* to whiten; *(linge)* to launder; **b. à la chaux** to whitewash (b) *(disculper)* to clear (c) *(argent)* to launder (d) *Culin* to blanch
2 *vi* (a) *(devenir blanc)* to turn or go white (b) *(pâlir)* to blanch

blanchissage [blɑ̃ʃisaʒ] *nm* (a) *(du linge)* laundering (b) *Can Sp* shutout

blanchissement [blɑ̃ʃismɑ̃] *nm* whitening

blanchisserie [blɑ̃ʃisri] *nf* laundry

blanchisseur, -euse [blɑ̃ʃisœr, -øz] *nm, f* laundryman, *f* laundrywoman

blanchon [blɑ̃ʃɔ̃] *nm Can* whitecoat *(seal pup)*

blanquette¹ [blɑ̃kɛt] *nf Culin* **b. (de veau)** = veal stew in a white sauce

blanquette² *nf* **b. de Limoux** = sparkling white wine from Limoux

blasé, -e [blɑze] *adj* blasé

blason [blazɔ̃] *nm* coat of arms

blasphème [blasfɛm] *nm* blasphemy

blasphémer [34] [blasfeme] *vi* to blaspheme

blatte [blat] *nf* cockroach

blazer [blazɛr, blazœr] *nm* blazer

bld *abrév* **boulevard**

blé [ble] *nm* (a) *(céréale)* wheat, *Br* corn; **b. dur** durum wheat; **b. en herbe** wheat in the blade; *Fig* **manger son b. en herbe** to eat one's seed corn; **Can b. d'Inde** *Br* maize, *Am* (Indian) corn (b) *Fam (argent)* bread

bled [blɛd] *nm Fam (lieu isolé)* dump, hole; **dans un b. perdu** in the middle of nowhere

blême [blɛm] *adj (personne, matin)* pale; **b. de colère** livid with anger; **devenir b.** to turn or go pale

blêmir [blemir] *vi* to turn or go pale; **b. de colère** to turn livid with anger

blennorragie [blenoraʒi] *nf* gonorrhoea

blessant, -e [blesɑ̃, -ɑ̃t] *adj* hurtful

blessé, -e [blese] **1** *adj (par arme)* wounded; *(dans un accident)* injured; *(moralement)* hurt; **être b. dans son amour-propre** to have had one's pride hurt; **êtes-vous b.?** are you hurt?
2 *nm, f (victime d'un accident)* injured person; *(victime d'une agression)* wounded person; **les blessés** the injured/wounded

blesser [blese] **1** *vt* (a) *(par arme)* to wound; *(dans un accident)* to injure, to hurt; *(sujet: chaussures)* to hurt; **il a été blessé au bras** *(par arme)* he was wounded in the arm; *(dans un accident)* his arm was injured (b) *(moralement)* to hurt
2 se blesser *vpr (avec une arme)* to wound oneself; *(accidentellement)* to hurt or injure oneself *(avec* with); **se b. à la tête** *(avec une arme)* to wound oneself in the head; *(accidentellement)* to hurt one's head

blessure [blesyr] *nf (par arme)* wound; *(dans un accident)* injury; *Fig (morale)* wound, hurt

blette [blɛt] = **bette**

bleu, -e [blø] **1** *adj* blue; *(bifteck)* very rare; **b. de froid** blue with cold
2 *nm* (a) *(couleur)* blue; **le b. est à la mode** blue is in; **b. canard** peacock blue; **b. ciel** sky blue; **b. électrique** electric blue; **b. marine** navy (blue); **b. nuit** midnight blue; **b. de Prusse** Prussian blue; **b. roi** royal blue (b) *(ecchymose)* bruise; **se faire un b.** to bruise oneself (c) *Fam (novice)* novice; *Mil* rookie (d) *(fromage)* blue cheese; **b. d'Auvergne/de Bresse** = blue cheese from Auvergne/Bresse (e) **b. (de chauffe ou de travail)** overalls; *(salopette)* dungarees

bleuâtre [bløɑtr] *adj* bluish

bleuet [bløɛ] *nm* (a) *(plante)* cornflower (b) *Can (baie)* blueberry

bleuetière [bløtjɛr] *nf Can* blueberry field

bleuté, -e [bløte] *adj* bluish; *(verres)* blue-tinted

blindage [blɛ̃daʒ] *nm Mil* armour-plating

blindé, -e [blɛ̃de] **1** *adj* (a) *(véhicule militaire)* armoured, armour-plated; *(voiture)* bulletproof; **porte blindée** steel security door (b) *Fam* **je suis b.** I'm hardened to it
2 *nm Mil* armoured vehicle

blinder [blɛ̃de] *vt* (a) *(véhicule)* to armour-plate; *(porte)* to reinforce with steel (b) *Fam (personne)* to harden (contre to)

blini [blini] *nm* blini

blizzard [blizar] *nm* blizzard

bloc [blɔk] *nm* (a) *(de bois, de pierre)* block (b) *(de maisons)* block (c) *Pol* bloc; **faire b. (avec/contre qn)** to join forces (with/against sb) (d) *(de papier)* pad; **b. de papier à lettres** writing pad (e) *(ensemble d'éléments)* unit; **b. opératoire** operating theatre (f) *très Fam (prison)* clink; **être au b.** to be in the clink (g) *Ordinat* block; **b. d'alimentation secteur** mains power unit; **b. de données** data block; **b. de touches** keypad (h) *(locutions)* **tout refuser en b.** to reject everything in its entirety; **serrer qch à b.** to screw sth as tightly as possible

blocage [blɔkaʒ] *nm* (a) *(d'un mécanisme)* jamming; *(des freins)* locking; *(des prix, des salaires)* freezing; *Psy (mental)* block; *Psy* **faire un b.** to get a (mental) block (b) *Ordinat (dans réseau)* lockout; **b. majuscule** caps lock

blockhaus [blɔkos] *nm* blockhouse

bloc-moteur *(pl* blocs-moteurs) [blɔkmɔtœr] *nm* engine block

bloc-notes *(pl* blocs-notes) [blɔknɔt] *nm* notepad

blocus [blɔkys] nm blockade; **lever/forcer le b.** to raise/run the blockade

blond, -e [blɔ̃, -ɔ̃d] **1** adj (cheveux) fair, blond; (personne) fair-haired, blond; (sable, blés) golden; **être b. comme les blés** (sujet: personne) to have golden-blond hair

2 nm,f (personne) **et** **a.** a fair-haired man; **une blonde a.** a blonde, a fair-haired woman; **une blonde décolorée** a peroxide blonde

3 nm (couleur) **b. cendré** ash blond; **b. platine** platinum blond; **b. vénitien** strawberry blond

4 nf **blonde (a)** (bière) lager **(b)** Can Fam (amie) girlfriend

blondinet, -ette [blɔ̃dine, -et] nm,f fair-haired child

blondir [blɔ̃dir] **1** vt (cheveux) to bleach

2 vi (cheveux, personne) to go or turn blond; **faire b. des oignons** to cook onions until they turn pale yellow

bloquer [blɔke] **1** vt (a) (mécanisme, porte) to jam; **il m'a bloqué contre un mur** he jammed me up against a wall; Fam **je suis bloqué à l'hôpital** I'm stuck in hospital (b) (réunir) to group together; (jours de congé) to lump together (c) (compte en banque) to block; (prix, salaires) to freeze (d) (route, ballon) to block; **b. le chemin ou le passage à qn** to block sb's way (e) Belg Fam (sujet:) to bone up on **(f)** Psy **ça me bloque de me sentir observé** I get a (mental) block if I feel I'm being watched; **être bloqué** to have a (mental) block

2 se bloquer vpr (a) (machine, ascenseur) to get stuck (b) Psy to get a (mental) block

blottir [blɔtir] **se blottir** vpr to snuggle up; **se b. contre qn/dans les bras de qn** to snuggle up to sb/in sb's arms; **blottis les uns contre les autres** huddled up together

blousant, -e [bluzɑ̃, -ɑ̃t] adj loose-fitting

blouse [bluz] nf (a) (tablier) overall; **b. de laboratoire/blanche** lab/white coat (b) (de femme) blouse

blouser [bluze] **1** vt Fam (personne) to con

2 vi (corsage) to be loose-fitting

blouson [bluzɔ̃] nm (lumber-)jacket; (plus léger) blouson; **b. en ou de cuir** leather jacket; **b. d'aviateur** bomber jacket; Fam Vieilli **b. noir** young hoodlum (wearing a black leather jacket)

blue-jean [bludʒin] (pl blue-jeans [bludʒins]) nm Vieilli jeans

blues [bluz] nm blues

bluff [blœf] nm bluff; **y aller au b.** to try and bluff

bluffer [blœfe] **1** vi (aux cartes) to bluff; Fam (personne) to take in

2 vt (aux cartes) & Fam to bluff

blush [blœʃ] nm blusher

BN [been] nf (abrév **Bibliothèque nationale**) = French national library, based in Paris

boa [bɔa] nm (a) (serpent) boa; **b. constricteur** boa constrictor (b) (en plumes) boa

boat people [botpipœl] nmpl boat people

bob [bɔb] nm Fam (chapeau) sun hat

bobard [bɔbar] nm Fam tall story

bobine [bɔbin] nf (a) (de ruban, de fil) reel; (de machine à coudre) bobbin; (de machine à écrire, d'appareil photo) spool; (de film, de papier) roll (b) Él coil (c) Fam (visage) mug

bobo [bɔbo] nm (langage enfantin) (coupure) cut; (piqûre) sting; **ça fait b.?** does it hurt?; **se faire b.** to hurt oneself

bobsleigh [bɔbslɛg] nm bobsleigh

bocage [bɔkaʒ] nm bocage (countryside with many hedges, trees and small fields)

bocal, -aux [bɔkal, -o] nm jar; (aquarium) (fish)bowl

Boche [bɔʃ] nmf Fam Péj Kraut, = offensive term referring to a German

bock [bɔk] nm beer glass

body [bɔdi] nm (vêtement) body

body-building [bɔdibildiŋ] nm body building; **faire du b.** to do body building

bœuf [bœf, pl bø] **1** nm (a) (animal) bullock; (de trait) ox; Fam **on n'est pas des bœufs** we're not superhuman (b) (viande) beef; **b. bourguignon** bœuf bourguignon; Culin **b. mode** stewed beef (c) Fam (improvisation) jam session; **faire un b.** to jam

2 adj inv Fam **avoir un succès b.** to be incredibly successful; **faire un effet b.** to make a really big impression

bof [bɔf] exclam Fam **ça te plaît? – b., pas tellement** do you like it? – not really, no; **il est chouette, hein, mon nouveau pull? – b.** my new sweater's great, isn't it? – I suppose so

Bogota [bɔgɔta] n Bogota

bogue [bɔg] nf (a) (de châtaigne) Br burr, Am shuck (b) Ordinat bug; **dépourvu/plein de bogues** bug-free/-ridden; **b. de logiciel** software bug

bohème [bɔɛm] **1** adj bohemian

2 nmf **mener une vie de b.** to lead a bohemian life

Bohême [bɔɛm] nf **la B.** Bohemia

bohémien, -enne [bɔemjɛ̃, -ɛn] nm,f gypsy

boire¹ [12] [bwar] **1** vt (a) (sujet: personne) to drink; Fig **b. les paroles de qn** to drink in sb's every word (b) (sujet: plante, matière poreuse) to soak up, to absorb

2 vi (personne) to drink; (plante) to soak up or absorb water; Can (bébé) to feed; **b. comme un trou** to drink like a fish; **b. à la bouteille** to drink from the bottle; **b. au succès de qn/qch** to drink to the success of sb/sth; **donner à b. à qn** to give sb a drink; **faire b. qn** to give sb something to drink; **faire b. les chevaux** to water the horses; Fig **il y a à b. et à manger là-dedans** it's a bit of a mixed bag; Prov **qui a bu boira** old habits die hard

3 se boire vpr to be drunk

boire² nm **le b. et le manger** food and drink

bois [bwa] nm (a) (forêt) wood (b) (matériau) wood; **des meubles en b.** wooden furniture; Fig **elle n'est pas de b.** she's only human; Fig **je vais leur faire voir de quel b. je me chauffe!** I'll show them (what I'm made of)!; **petit b.** kindling; **b. de charpente** ou **de construction** Br timber, Am lumber; **b. de chauffage** firewood; **b. mort** deadwood; **b. de rose** rosewood (c) (de chaise, de raquette) frame; **faire un b.** (au tennis) to hit the ball off the frame; **b. de lit** bed frame (d) Mus **les b.** the woodwind (e) **les b.** (d'un cerf) the antlers

boisé, -e [bwaze] adj (région) wooded

boisement [bwazmɑ̃] nm afforestation

boiseries [bwazri] nfpl panelling

boisson [bwasɔ̃] nf drink; Can (spiritueux) hard liquor, spirits; **b. alcoolisée/non alcoolisée** alcoholic/soft drink; **b. chaude** hot drink; **b. gazeuse** fizzy drink

boîte [bwat] nf (a) (récipient) box; **les haricots en b.** canned or Br tinned beans; **mettre qch en b.** (marchandises) to box sth; (aliments) to can sth, Br to tin sth; Fam **mettre qn en b.** to pull sb's leg; **b. d'allumettes** (pleine) box of matches; (vide) matchbox; **b. à bijoux** jewel box; **b. de conserve** can, Br tin; **b. à couture** ou **couture** ou **ouvrage** sewing box; **b. à gants** glove compartment; **b. à** ou **aux lettres** Br postbox, Am mailbox; (chez soi) Br letterbox, *Am* mailbox; **b. à lettres électronique** mailbox; **b. à musique** music box; *Av* **b. noire** black box; **b. à outils** toolbox; **b. postale** Post Office Box; *Aut* **b. de vitesses** gearbox **(b)** *Fam (entreprise)* firm; *(école)* school **(c) b. (de nuit)** nightclub; **aller** *ou* **sortir en b.** to go to a nightclub

boiter [bwate] *vi* to limp

boiteux, -euse [bwatø, -øz] *adj (personne, cheval, explication)* lame; *(raisonnement)* shaky; *(phrase)* badly constructed

boîtier [bwatje] *nm* case; *Phot* (camera) body; *Ordinat* **b. de commande** command box; *Ordinat* **b. commutateur** data switch

boîtiller [bwatije] *vi* to limp slightly

boive *etc voir* **boire**

bol [bɔl] *nm* **(a)** *(récipient)* bowl **(b)** *(contenu)* bowl(ful); **prendre un b. d'air frais** *ou* **pur** to get a good breath of fresh air **(c)** *Fam (chance)* luck; **avoir du b.** to be lucky; **ne pas avoir de b.** to be unlucky; **manque de b., il avait déjà demandé!** just my luck, he'd already asked! **(d) le B. d'or** = 24-hour motorcycle race

bolchevique [bɔlʃevik, bɔlʃevik] *adj & nmf* Bolshevik

bolduc [bɔldyk] *nm* gift-wrap ribbon

bolée [bɔle] *nf* bowl(ful)

boléro [bɔlero] *nm (vêtement, pièce musicale)* bolero

bolet [bɔle] *nm* boletus

bolide [bɔlid] *nm (voiture)* racing car; **comme un b.** like a rocket

Bolivie [bɔlivi] *nf* **la B.** Bolivia

bolivien, -enne [bɔlivjɛ̃, -ɛn] **1** *adj* Bolivian **2** *nm,f* **B.** Bolivian

bolognais, -e [bɔlɔɲe, -ez] *adj* Bolognese; *Culin* **spaghetti bolognaise** spaghetti bolognese

Bologne [bɔlɔɲ] *n* Bologna

bombage [bɔ̃baʒ] *nm Fam* (aerosol) graffiti; **faire des bombages sur un mur** to spray-paint a wall with graffiti

bombance [bɔ̃bɑ̃s] *nf Fam* **faire b.** to feast

bombardement [bɔ̃bardəmɑ̃] *nm (avec des obus)* shelling; *(avec des bombes)* bombing; **b. aérien** air raid

bombarder [bɔ̃barde] *vt* **(a)** *(avec des obus)* to shell; *(avec des bombes)* to bomb; **b. qn de questions/de lettres** to bombard sb with questions/letters **(b)** *Fam* **on l'a bombardé ministre** he's been pitchforked into the post of minister

bombardier [bɔ̃bardje] *nm (avion)* bomber; *(aviateur)* bombardier

bombe [bɔ̃b] *nf* **(a)** *(explosif)* bomb; *Fig* **faire l'effet d'une b.** to be a bombshell; **b. atomique** atom(ic) bomb; **b. à eau** water bomb; *Culin* **b. glacée** bombe glacée; **b. H** H bomb; **b. à hydrogène** hydrogen bomb; **b. lacrymogène** tear-gas grenade; **b. à retardement** time bomb **(b)** *(atomiseur)* spray, aerosol **(c)** *(chapeau)* riding hat **(d)** *Fam* **faire la b.** to live it up

bombé, -e [bɔ̃be] *adj* bulging

bomber [bɔ̃be] **1** *vt (gonfler)* **b. qch** to cause sth to bulge; **b. le torse** to throw out one's chest; *Fig* to swagger (around)
2 *vi (mur)* to bulge; *(planche)* to warp

bombonne [bɔ̃bɔn] = **bonbonne**

bôme [bom] *nf Naut* boom

bon¹, bonne [bɔ̃, bɔn] **1** *adj* **(a)** *(agréable)* good; **passer une bonne soirée** to spend a pleasant evening; **l'eau est bonne** *(en se baignant)* the water's great; **de bons petits plats** nice little meals; **souhaiter une** *ou* **la bonne année à qn** to wish sb a happy New Year; **bonnes vacances!** have a good holiday!
(b) *(satisfaisant) (travail, qualité)* good; **c'est b.** *(d'accord)* that's fine; **c'est b., j'ai compris** all right or OK, I understand
(c) *(correct)* right; **c'est la bonne réponse/le b. bus** that's the right answer/bus; **un intellectuel, au b. sens du terme** an intellectual in the true sense of the word
(d) *(compétent)* good (en at); **un b. médecin/père a** good doctor/father
(e) *(profitable) (investissement, conseil, idée)* good; **cet exercice est b. pour le dos** this exercise is good for the back; **c'est b. à savoir** it's worth knowing; **il serait b. que vous lui en parliez** it would be a good idea if you spoke to her about it; **à quoi b.?** what's the point *or* the use?; **à quoi b. se plaindre?** what's the point *or* the use of complaining?; **quand b. vous semble** whenever you like
(f) *(apte)* **b. à manger** fit *or* safe to eat; **b. pour le service** *Mil* fit for duty; **j'ai** serviceable; **elle n'est bonne à rien** she's useless; **tu es b. pour une contravention** you're in for a fine
(g) *(valable) (billet, abonnement)* valid; **la balle est bonne** *(au tennis)* the ball is in *or* good; **les yaourts sont-ils encore bons?** are the yoghurts still all right to eat?
(h) *(moralement)* good; *(généreux)* good, kind (**envers** *ou* **avec** to)
(i) *(en intensif)* good; **j'ai attendu deux bonnes heures** I waited for a good two hours; **il m'a fallu un b. moment pour comprendre** it took me a while to understand; **un b. rhume** a bad cold
(j) *(locutions)* **elle est bien bonne!** that's a good one!; **il en a de bonnes!** he must be joking *or* kidding!; **avoir qn à la bonne** to have a soft spot for sb; **pour de b.** *(partir, revenir)* for good
2 *exclam (d'accord)* right!, fine!; **b., on y va?** right, shall we go?; **allons b.!** what!; **ah b., je ne le savais pas** really? I didn't know
3 *adv (sentir)* good, nice; **il fait b.** it's lovely; **un pays où il fait b. vivre** a country that's good to live in
4 *nm,f* **les bons et les méchants** *(dans un film)* the goodies and the baddies; **un b. à rien** a good-for-nothing
5 *nm* **cela a du b.** it has some good points

bon² *nm* **(a)** *(papier)* voucher, coupon; **b. d'achat** gift voucher; **b. de commande** order form; **b. de garantie** guarantee; **b. de livraison** delivery note; **b. de réduction** money-off coupon **(b)** *Fin* bond; **b. du Trésor** treasury bond

bonard, -e [bɔnar, -ard] *adj Fam* **c'est b.!** that's pretty good!

bonasse [bɔnas] *adj* soft; **d'un ton b.** meekly

bonbon [bɔ̃bɔ̃] *nm* **(a)** *(sucrerie)* *Br* sweet, *Am* candy; **b. à la menthe** mint **(b)** *Belg* biscuit

bonbonne [bɔ̃bɔn] *nf* demijohn; *(de gaz)* cylinder

bonbonnière [bɔ̃bɔnjɛr] *nf Br* sweet *or Am* candy box

bond [bɔ̃] *nm* **(a)** *(saut)* leap, jump; **faire un b.** to leap up; *Fig* to shoot up; **faire un b. en avant/en arrière** to leap forwards/back; **franchir qch d'un b.** to clear sth at one leap; **se lever d'un b.** to jump to one's feet **(b)** *(d'une balle)* bounce; **faire faux b. à qn** to leave sb in the lurch

bonde [bɔ̃d] nf (a) (bouchon) (d'un évier, d'une baignoire) plug; (d'un tonneau) bung; (d'un bassin) sluice gate (b) (trou) (d'un évier, d'une baignoire) plughole; (d'un tonneau) bunghole; (d'un bassin) drainage hole

bondé, -e [bɔ̃de] adj packed, crammed

bondir [bɔ̃dir] vi to leap, to jump; **b. sur** to pounce on; Fig **cela me fait b.** it makes me hopping mad

bon enfant [bɔnɑ̃fɑ̃] adj inv easy-going

bonheur [bɔnœr] nm (a) (bien-être) happiness; **faire le b. de qn** to make sb happy (b) (chance) good fortune, (good) luck; **j'ai le b. de la connaître** I have the good fortune to know her; **porter b. à qn** to bring sb (good) luck; **il ne connaît pas son b.** he doesn't know how lucky he is; **par b.** luckily; **au petit b. (la chance)** at random (c) Litt (réussite) **avec b.** felicitously

bonhomie [bɔnɔmi] nf good-naturedness; **avec b.** good-naturedly

bonhomme [bɔnɔm] (pl **bonshommes** [bɔ̃zɔm]) nm Fam fellow, guy; **c'est un sacré b.** he's a hell of a guy; **on se retrouvera, mon b.!** I'll get even with you, my friend!; **aller son petit b. de chemin** to be jogging along nicely; **b. de neige** snowman

boniche [bɔniʃ] nf maid, Br skivvy

bonification [bɔnifikasjɔ̃] nf (a) (d'une terre, d'un vin) improvement (b) Com bonus (c) Sp advantage

bonifier [66] [bɔnifje] **1** vt (terre, caractère) to improve
2 se bonifier vpr to improve

boniment [bɔnimɑ̃] nm (a) (discours) sales talk, patter; Fam **faire du b. à qn** Br to chat sb up, Am to hit on sb (b) Fam (mensonges) tall story; **tout ça, c'est du b.** that's all claptrap

bonite [bɔnit] nf bonito

bonjour [bɔ̃ʒur] nm hello; (le matin) good morning; (l'après-midi) good afternoon; **dire b. à qn** to say hello/good morning/good afternoon to sb; **dis b. à ta mère de ma part** say hello to your mother for me; **facile ou simple comme b.** easy as pie; Fam **b. l'ambiance!** there was one hell of an atmosphere!; Fam **b. la soirée!** what an evening!; Fam **le périphérique à six heures du soir, b.!** the ring road at six o'clock at night, forget it!

bon marché [bɔ̃marʃe] adj inv cheap; **acheter/vendre qch (à) b.** to buy/sell sth cheap(ly)

bonne [bɔn] **1** voir **bon**[1]
2 nf (domestique) maid, Vieilli maidservant; Fam **dis-donc, je ne suis pas ta b.!** I'm not your maid, you know!; **b. à tout faire** maid, Vieilli maidservant; **b. d'enfants** nanny

Bonne-Espérance [bɔnespərɑ̃s] voir **cap**

bonnement [bɔnmɑ̃] adv tout b. simply

bonnet [bɔnɛ] nm (a) (coiffure) hat; **c'est b. blanc et blanc b.** it's six of one and half a dozen of the other; **b. d'âne** dunce's cap; **b. de bain** bathing cap; **b. de nuit** nightcap; **b. de ski** ski cap (b) (d'un soutien-gorge) cup; **quelle profondeur de b.?** what size cup?

bonneterie [bɔnɛtri] nf (a) (bas) hosiery (b) (commerce) hosiery trade; (magasin) hosier's (shop)

bonniche [bɔniʃ] = **boniche**

bonsaï [bɔnzaj, bɔ̃zaj] nm bonsai

bonsoir [bɔ̃swar] nm good evening; (quand on se quitte tard, quand on se couche) goodnight; **dire b. à qn** to say good evening/goodnight to sb

bonté [bɔ̃te] nf (a) (gentillesse) kindness, goodness; **une femme d'une grande b.** a very kind woman; **un sourire plein de b.** a kind smile; **avoir la b. de faire qch** to be so good as to do sth; **faire qch par b. d'âme** to do sth out of the goodness of one's heart; Vieilli **b. divine! good heavens!** (b) (acte) **remercier qn pour ses bontés** to thank sb for his/her kindness

bonus [bɔnys] nm (prime de salaire) bonus; (d'assurance) no-claims bonus

bon vivant [bɔ̃vivɑ̃] adj m **être b.** to enjoy life

bonze [bɔ̃z] nm Buddhist priest

bookmaker [bukmɛkœr] nm bookmaker

booléen, -enne [buleɛ̃, -ɛn] adj Math & Ordinat Boolean

boom [bum] nm boom

boomerang [bumrɑ̃g] nm boomerang

booter [bute] vi Ordinat **b. (sur le lecteur B)** to boot up (off the B drive)

boots [buts] nmpl ankle boots

borborygmes [bɔrbɔrigm] nmpl rumbling

bord [bɔr] nm (a) (limite) edge; (d'un chapeau) brim; (d'une tasse, d'un verre) rim; **un chapeau à larges bords** a wide-brimmed hat; **le b. du trottoir** Br the kerb, Am the curb; **sur le ou au b. de** (route) at the side of; (lac, rivière) beside; **aller au b. de la mer** to go to the seaside; **une maison en b. de mer** a house beside the sea; **au b. des larmes/de la catastrophe** on the verge of tears/of disaster; Fam **un peu voleur sur les bords** a bit light-fingered; **b. à b.** edge to edge; Ordinat **b. de reliure** inside margin (b) **à b. de** (bateau, avion) on board; **prendre qn à son b.** to take sb on board; **par-dessus b.** overboard; Fig **être du même b.** to be on the same side

bordages [bɔrdaʒ] nmpl Can (glace) inshore ice

bordeaux [bɔrdo] **1** nm Bordeaux (wine); **b. rouge** claret
2 adj inv maroon

bordée [bɔrde] nf (a) Naut (de coups de feu) broadside; Fig **b. de jurons** torrent of swearwords (b) Fam **être en b.** to be on a binge (c) Can **b. (de neige)** heavy snowfall

bordel [bɔrdɛl] nm très Fam (hôtel de passe) brothel; (désordre) mess; (vacarme) racket; **mettre ou foutre le b. dans qch** to make a mess of sth; **et tout le b.** the whole damn lot; Vulg **b.!** shit!

bordelais, -e [bɔrdəlɛ, -ɛz] **1** adj of Bordeaux
2 nm, f **B.** = person from Bordeaux
3 nm le **B.** (région) the Bordeaux region

bordélique [bɔrdelik] adj Fam (pièce, organisation) shambolic; **être b.** (personne) to be a slob

border [bɔrde] vt (a) (garnir) **b. qch de** to edge sth with (b) (sujet: arbres) (route) to line; (sujet: bateau) (côte) to skirt (c) (lit, draps) to tuck in; **b. qn (dans son lit)** to tuck sb in

bordereau, -x [bɔrdəro] nm (liste) schedule; **b. de livraison** delivery note

bordure [bɔrdyr] nf (a) (bord) edge; (d'un vêtement) border; **en b. de route/de mer** by the roadside/the sea (b) (d'un miroir, d'un tableau) frame

boréal, -e, -als ou **-aux, -ales** [bɔreal, -o] adj northern

borgne [bɔrɲ] **1** adj (a) (personne) one-eyed; (mur) blind; (fenêtre) obstructed (b) (louche) shady
2 nmf one-eyed man, f one-eyed woman

borne [bɔrn] *nf* (a) *(limite)* boundary marker; *(pierre)* boundary stone; *Fig* **sans bornes** boundless; **b. d'incendie** *Br* (fire) hydrant, *Am* fireplug; **b. kilométrique** kilometre marker, ≃ milestone (b) *Fam (kilomètre)* kilometre (c) *Él* terminal (d) *Ordinat* **b. (interactive)** terminal

borné, -e [bɔrne] *adj (esprit)* narrow; *(personne)* narrow-minded

borne-fontaine [bɔrnfɔ̃tɛn] *(pl* **bornes-fontaines)** *nf Can (bouche d'incendie) Br* (fire) hydrant, *Am* fireplug

borner [bɔrne] **1** *vt (terrain)* to mark out
2 se borner *vpr* (a) **se b. à qch/à faire qch** *(personne)* to restrict oneself to sth/to doing sth (b) **se b. à qch** *(choses)* to be limited to sth

borsalino [bɔrsalino] *nm* fedora

bosniaque [bɔsnjak] **1** *adj* Bosnian
2 *nmf* **B.** Bosnian

Bosnie [bɔsni] *nf* **la B.** Bosnia; **la B.-Herzégovine** Bosnia-Herzegovina

bosquet [bɔskɛ] *nm* copse, grove

bosse [bɔs] *nf* (a) *(d'un bossu, d'un chameau)* hump; *Fig* **avoir la b. du commerce/des maths** to have a good head for business/maths; *Fam* **il a roulé sa b.** he's knocked about a bit (b) *(sur la tête)* bump, lump; *(sur le sol)* bump; *(sur une piste de ski)* mogul; **se faire une b.** to get a bump

bosselé, -e [bɔsle] *adj (casserole, pare-chocs)* dented

bosser [bɔse] *Fam* **1** *vi* to work
2 *vt Scol* to bone up on, *Br* to swot up

bosseur, -euse [bɔsœr, -øz] *Fam* **1** *adj* hardworking
2 *nm,f* hard worker

bossu, -e [bɔsy] **1** *adj (personne)* hunchbacked; *(animal)* humped
2 *nm,f* hunchback

bot [bo] *adj m voir* **pied**

botanique [bɔtanik] **1** *adj* botanical
2 *nf* botany

botaniste [bɔtanist] *nmf* botanist

Botswana [bɔtswana] *nm* **le B.** Botswana

botte[1] [bɔt] *nf (de fleurs, de carottes, de radis)* bunch; *(de foin, de paille)* bale

botte[2] [bɔt] *nf (chaussure)* boot; *Fig* **sous la b.** de under the heel of; *Fam* **en avoir plein les bottes (de)** to be fed up to the back teeth (with); **bottes de** *ou* **en caoutchouc** rubber boots, *Br* wellingtons; **bottes de cavalier** *ou* **de cheval** riding boots

botte[3] *nf (en escrime)* thrust; **porter une b. à qn** to make a thrust at sb; *Fig* **b. secrète** secret weapon

botter [bɔte] *vt* (a) *(chausser)* **botté de cuir** wearing leather boots (b) *Fam* **b. les fesses** *ou* **le derrière à qn** to boot sb up the backside (c) *Fam (plaire à)* **ça me botte** I dig it

bottier [bɔtje] *nm* bootmaker

bottillon [bɔtijɔ̃] *nm* ankle boot

Bottin® [bɔtɛ̃] *nm (annuaire téléphonique)* phone book, telephone directory; **B. mondain** ≃ Who's Who

bottine [bɔtin] *nf* ankle boot

botulisme [bɔtylism] *nm Méd* botulism

boubou [bubu] *nm* = long traditional African robe

bouc [buk] *nm (animal)* (billy) goat; *(barbe)* goatee (beard); *Fam* **puer comme un b.**, **puer le b.** to stink to high heaven; **b. émissaire** scapegoat

boucan [bukɑ̃] *nm Fam* row, din; **faire du b.** to kick up a row

boucane [bukan] *nf Can* smoke

boucané, -e [bukane] *adj (teint)* weatherbeaten

boucanier [bukanje] *nm* buccaneer

bouche [buʃ] *nf* (a) *(de personne, d'animal)* mouth; **avoir/parler la b. pleine** to have/to talk with one's mouth full; **une pipe à la b.** with a pipe in his mouth; *Fig* **faire la fine b.** to be fussy; **c'est une fine b.** he's a gourmet; **b. cousue!** mum's the word!; **de b. à oreille** by word of mouth (b) *(d'une rivière, d'un cratère, d'un four)* mouth; *(d'un fusil, d'un canon)* muzzle; **b. d'égout** manhole; **b. d'incendie** *Br* (fire) hydrant, *Am* fireplug; **b. de métro** *Br* underground *or Am* subway entrance

bouché, -e [buʃe] *adj (conduite, rue)* blocked; *(temps)* cloudy, overcast; **j'ai le nez b.** my nose is stuffed up; **j'ai les oreilles bouchées** my ears are blocked up; *Fam* **être b.** *(personne)* to be dense; *Fam* **être b. à l'émeri** to be a complete moron

bouche-à-bouche [buʃabuʃ] *nm inv* mouth-to-mouth resuscitation, *Br* kiss of life; **faire du b. à qn** to give sb mouth-to-mouth resuscitation

bouchée [buʃe] *nf* (a) *(quantité)* mouthful; *Fig* **ne faire qu'une b. de qn/qch** to make short work of sb/sth; **acheter qch pour une b. de pain** to buy sth for a song; **mettre les bouchées doubles** to really get a move on (b) *Culin* **b. (au chocolat)** chocolate; **b. à la reine** chicken vol-au-vent

boucher[1] [buʃe] **1** *vt (fente, trou)* to fill in; *(conduite, fenêtre)* to block up; *(vue)* to block; *(bouteille)* to cork; **b. le passage à qn** to block sb's way; **b. elle/ça m'en a bouché un coin** she/that took the wind out of my sails
2 se boucher *vpr (conduite)* to get blocked up; **se b. le nez** to hold one's nose; **se b. les oreilles** to put one's fingers in one's ears

boucher[2], **-ère** [buʃe, -ɛr] *nm,f aussi Fig* butcher

boucherie [buʃri] *nf (boutique)* butcher's (shop); *(activité)* butchery; *Fig (massacre)* slaughter; **b. chevaline** horse butcher's (shop)

bouche-trou *(pl* **bouche-trous)** [buʃtru] *nm Fam* stopgap; **servir de b.** to act as a stopgap

bouchon [buʃɔ̃] *nm* (a) *(en liège)* cap, top; *(d'un tonneau)* stopper; **b. (de liège)** cork; **vin qui sent le b.** corked wine; *Aut* **b. de réservoir** *Br* petrol cap, *Am* fuel cap (b) *(embouteillage)* hold-up, traffic jam; **3 kilomètres de b.** a 3-kilometre tailback (c) *(d'une ligne de pêche)* float (d) *(de paille)* wisp (e) *Fam* **tu pousses le b. un peu loin!** you're going a bit too far!

bouchonné, -e [buʃɔne] *adj* corked

bouchonner [buʃɔne] **1** *vt (cheval)* to rub down
2 *vi Fam* **ça bouchonne** *(sur la route)* there's congestion

bouchot [buʃo] *nm* mussel bank

boucle [bukl] *nf* (a) *(de ceinture, de chaussure, de harnais)* buckle; **b. d'oreille** earring (b) *(nœud, méandre, looping)* loop; **faire une b.** *(en marchant, en voiture)* to loop back (c) *(de cheveux)* curl (d) *Sp* lap (e) *Ordinat* loop

bouclé, -e [bukle] *adj (cheveux)* curly; *(personne)* curly-haired; *Ordinat* **système b.** looped system

boucler [bukle] 1 vt (a) (ceinture, valise) to buckle; Fam (affaire) to finish off; b. sa valise (se préparer à partir) to pack one's bags; avoir du mal à b. ses fins de mois to find it hard to make ends meet at the end of the month; Fam boucle-la! belt up! (b) (quartier) to seal off; Fam (chambre, maison) to lock up; Fam (prisonnier) to bang up (c) b. la boucle Av to loop the loop; Fig to come full circle

2 vi (cheveux) to be curly; (personne) to have curly hair

bouclette [buklεt] nf (de cheveux) small curl; (de laine, de moquette) curl

bouclier [buklije] nm aussi Fig shield; b. atomique ou nucléaire nuclear shield; b. thermique (d'engin spatial) heat shield

Bouddha [buda] npr Buddha

bouddhisme [budism] nm Buddhism

bouddhiste [budist] adj & nmf Buddhist

bouder [bude] 1 vi to sulk

2 vt b. qn/qch to refuse to have anything to do with sb/ sth; en été, les Parisiens boudent les salles de cinéma Parisians stay away from the cinema in summer

bouderie [budεr, -øz] 1 adj sulky

2 nm,f sulky person

boudin [budε̃] nm (a) (charcuterie) b. (noir) Br black pudding, Am blood sausage; b. blanc white pudding (b) (de pâte à modeler, de terre) roll (c) (traversin) bolster (d) Fam Péj (femme) fat lump

boudiné, -e [budine] adj (a) je suis b. dans ce pantalon I'm bursting out of these trousers (b) (doigts) podgy

boudoir [budwar] nm (a) (salon) boudoir (b) (biscuit) Br sponge finger, Am lady finger

boue [bu] nf (a) (terre détrempée) mud; Fig traîner qn dans la b. to drag sb through the mud (b) (dans une rivière) silt; (dans l'océan) ooze

bouée [bwe] nf Naut buoy; (pour nager) rubber ring; b. de sauvetage lifebelt; Fig lifeline

boueux, -euse [bwø, -øz] 1 adj muddy

2 nm Fam Br dustman, Am garbage man

bouffant, -e [bufɑ̃, -ɑ̃t] 1 adj (manche) puff(ed); (jupe) full; (pantalon) baggy; cheveux bouffants bouffant hairdo

2 nm (des cheveux) body

bouffée [bufe] nf (a) (de fumée) puff; (de parfum) whiff; (d'air) breath; aussi Fig une b. d'air pur a breath of fresh air; Méd b. de chaleur Br hot flush, Am hot flash (b) (d'éloquence, de colère) outburst; (d'orgueil) fit

bouffer [bufe] 1 vt b. (manger) to eat; Fig je l'aurais bouffé I could have killed him; elle se laisse b. par ses enfants/son travail she has no time for anything but her children/her work; b. du curé to rant against the clergy; elle a bouffé du lion! she's full of beans! (b) (argent, économies) to blow; b. de l'essence (voiture) to be heavy on petrol

2 vi (a) Fam (manger) to eat (b) (manche, jupe) to puff out; (cheveux) to have body; faire b. ses cheveux to give body to one's hair

3 se bouffer vpr Fam elles se bouffent constamment le nez they're always having a go at each other

bouffi, -e [bufi] adj (yeux, visage) puffy, swollen; b. d'orgueil puffed up with pride

bouffon, -onne [bufɔ̃, -ɔn] 1 nm buffoon; Hist jester

2 adj farcical

bouge [buʒ] nm Péj (maison) hovel; (bar) dive

bougeoir [buʒwar] nm (plat) candleholder; (haut) candlestick

bougeotte [buʒɔt] nf Fam avoir la b. to be fidgety; (envie de voyager) to have itchy feet

bouger [45] [buʒe] 1 vt to move, to shift

2 vi (remuer, se déplacer) to move; rester sans b. to keep still; ne bougeons plus! (pour une photo) hold it there!; je n'ai pas bougé (de chez moi) pendant deux jours I haven't been out for two days; Fig ce chemisier ne bouge pas au lavage (ne déteint pas) this blouse doesn't run in the wash; (ne rétrécit pas) this blouse doesn't shrink in the wash; Fam ça bouge pas mal, dans cette ville there's a lot going on in this town

3 se bouger vpr Fam (se déplacer) to move; (s'activer) to get a move on; bouge-toi de là! shift yourself!

bougie [buʒi] nf (a) (en cire) candle; s'éclairer à la b. to use candles for lighting (b) Aut b. (d'allumage) spark plug

bougnat [buɲa] nm Fam Vieilli coal-merchant

bougnoul(e) [buɲul] nmf Br wog, = racist term referring to a North African person

bougon, -onne [buɡɔ̃, -ɔn] Fam 1 adj grumpy

2 nm,f grumbler

bougonner [buɡɔne] vi Fam to grumble

bougre [buɡr] nm Fam (a) Vieilli (individu) le pauvre b. the poor devil; un drôle de b. an odd sort; il n'est pas un mauvais b. he's not a bad sort (b) b. d'imbécile damn(ed) fool

bougrement [buɡrəmɑ̃] adv damn(ed)

boui-boui (pl bouis-bouis) [bwibwi] nm Fam dingy café

bouillabaisse [bujabεs] nf bouillabaisse (Provençal fish soup)

bouillant, -e [bujɑ̃, -ɑ̃t] adj (a) (qui bout) boiling; (très chaud, fiévreux) boiling hot (b) Fig (ardent) fiery

bouille [buj] nf Fam (visage) mug; il a une bonne b. he looks a good sort

bouilleur [bujœr] nm b. de cru home distiller

bouilli, -e [buji] 1 adj boiled

2 nm boiled meat; Can = beans, cabbage, potatoes, salt pork and ham cooked together for several hours; b. de bœuf boiled beef

bouillie [buji] nf (pour bébés) baby food; (à base de céréales) baby cereal; b. de légumes mashed vegetables; réduire qch en b. (légumes, fruits) to mash sth; (au mixer) to liquidize; (personne) to smash sth up; Fam mettre ou réduire qn en b. to beat sb to a pulp

bouillir [13] [bujir] vi to boil; faire b. qch to boil sth; b. de colère to seethe with anger; b. d'impatience to burst with impatience; cela me fait b. that makes my blood boil

bouilloire [bujwar] nf kettle

bouillon [bujɔ̃] nm (a) (d'un liquide en ébullition) bubble; bouillir à gros bouillons to boil hard; le sang sortait à gros bouillons the blood was gushing out (b) Culin (liquide) stock; Fam boire un b. (en nageant) to get a mouthful; (professionnellement) to come to grief; b. cube stock cube; b. de culture culture medium; b. de légumes vegetable stock

bouillonnant, -e [bujɔnɑ̃, -ɑ̃t] adj bubbling; (torrent) foaming; Fig b. de colère seething; Fig b. de vie/d'idées bubbling over with life/ideas

bouillonner [bujɔne] vi (eau, soupe, bain) to bubble; (torrent) to foam; **b. de colère** to seethe with anger; **b. d'idées** to bubble over with ideas

bouillotte [bujɔt] nf hot-water bottle

boul. abrév **boulevard**

boulanger, -ère [bulɑ̃ʒe, -ɛr] nmf baker

boulangerie [bulɑ̃ʒri] nf (magasin) baker's (shop); (industrie) bakery trade; **b.-pâtisserie** baker's and confectioner's (shop)

boule [bul] nf (a) (sphère) ball; Fam (tête) nut; **se rouler ou se mettre en b.** (animal) to roll up into a ball; Fig **se mettre en b.** (en colère) to fly off the handle; Fam **avoir la b. à zéro** to be a skinhead; Fam **avoir les boules** (être énervé) to be pissed off; (avoir peur) to be wetting oneself; Fam **perdre la b.** to go off one's head; **b. de neige** snowball; Fig **faire b. de neige** to snowball; **c'est une b. de nerfs** he's/she's a bundle of nerves; **b. puante** stink bomb; **b. Quiès®** earplug (b) (de pétanque, de bowling) bowl; (de billard) ball; **jouer aux boules** to play bowls (c) (de machine à écrire) golf ball

bouleau, -x [bulo] nm (silver) birch; (bois) birch(wood)

bouledogue [buldɔg] nm bulldog

bouler [bule] vi Fam **envoyer b. qn** to send sb packing

boulet [bulɛ] nm (a) (projectile) **b. (de canon)** cannonball; **passer comme un b. (de canon)** to hurtle past; **tirer à boulets rouges sur qn** to go for sb hammer and tongs (b) (de bagnard) ball and chain; Fig **c'est un b. qu'il traînera toute sa vie** it'll be a millstone round his neck all his life

boulette [bulɛt] nf (a) (de papier, de pâte) small ball (b) Culin meatball (c) Fam (gaffe) Br boob, Am boo-boo

boulevard [bulvar] nm boulevard; **les Grands Boulevards** (à Paris) the main boulevards; **b. périphérique** Br ring road, Am beltway

bouleversant, -e [bulvɛrsɑ̃, -ɑ̃t] adj (émouvant) deeply moving; (perturbant) distressing

bouleversement [bulvɛrsəmɑ̃] nm (a) (de projets, d'habitudes) disruption; **bouleversements politiques/ économiques** political/economic upheavals (b) (d'une personne) emotion

bouleverser [bulvɛrse] vt (a) (projets, habitudes) to disrupt; (vie) to turn upside down (b) (émouvoir) to move deeply; (perturber) to distress

boulier [bulje] nm abacus

boulimie [bulimi] nf Méd bulimia

boulimique [bulimik] adj & nmf Méd bulimic; **être b.** to be bulimic, to have bulimia

bouliste [bulist] nmf bowls player

boulocher [bulɔʃe] vi (vêtement) to pill

boulodrome [bulodrom] nm bowling alley

boulon [bulɔ̃] nm bolt

boulonner [bulɔne] **1** vt to bolt
2 vi Fam (travailler) to slog away

boulot¹, -otte [bulo, -ɔt] adj Fam tubby

boulot² [bulo] Fam **1** nm (travail, lieu de travail) work; (emploi) job; **allez, au b.!** come on, get to work!; **refaire les peintures dans une maison, c'est du b.** to repaint a whole house is quite a job; Fig **faire le sale b.** to do the dirty work
2 adj inv **être b. b.** to be a workaholic

boum [bum] **1** exclam bang!
2 nm Fam (a) (bruit) bang (b) (succès) **le b. du multimédia/de l'informatique** the multimedia/ computer boom; **en plein b.** in full swing
3 nf Fam (fête) party (for young people)

boumer [bume] vi Fam Vieilli **ça boume?** how's things?

bouquet¹ [bukɛ] nm (a) (fleurs) bunch of flowers; (imposant) bouquet; (petit) posy; (d'arbres) clump; **un b. de roses** a bunch/bouquet of roses; **le b. de la mariée** the bride's bouquet; Culin **b. garni** bouquet garni (bunch of mixed herbs) (b) (d'un vin) bouquet, nose (c) (d'un feu d'artifice) **b. (final)** grand finale; Fam Fig **ça, c'est le b.!** that takes the Br biscuit or Am cake! (d) TV **b. numérique** multiplex (bundle of digital TV channels)

bouquet² nm (crevette) prawn

bouquetin [buktɛ̃] nm ibex

bouquin [bukɛ̃] nm Fam book

bouquiner [bukine] vti Fam to read

bouquiniste [bukinist] nmf second-hand bookseller

bourbeux, -euse [burbø, -øz] adj muddy

bourbier [burbje] nm aussi Fig quagmire

bourbon [burbɔ̃] nm (whisky) bourbon

bourde [burd] nf Fam (a) (balivernes) fib (b) (gaffe) blunder; **faire une b.** to put one's foot in it

bourdon [burdɔ̃] nm (a) (insecte) bumblebee; Fam **avoir le b.** to be down (in the dumps) (b) (cloche) great bell (c) Mus (de cornemuse) drone; (d'orgue) bourdon stop

bourdonnement [burdɔnmɑ̃] nm (d'insectes) buzz(ing); (de machine, de moteur) hum(ming); **avoir des bourdonnements d'oreilles** to have a buzzing in one's ears

bourdonner [burdɔne] vi (insectes, oreilles) to buzz; (machine, moteur) to hum

bourg [bur] nm market town

bourgade [burgad] nf village

bourge [burʒ] Fam **1** adj (a) (de la bourgeoisie) upper-class (b) Péj snobby
2 nmf (a) (de la bourgeoisie) upper-class person (b) Péj snob

bourgeois, -e [burʒwa, -az] **1** adj (a) (personne) middle-class; **cuisine bourgeoise** home cooking (b) Péj (conventionnel) middle-class, bourgeois
2 nmf (a) (de la classe moyenne) middle-class person; **les grands/petits b.** the upper/lower middle class (b) Hist (roturier) commoner

bourgeoisie [burʒwazi] nf middle class, bourgeoisie; **la haute/petite b.** the upper/lower middle class

bourgeon [burʒɔ̃] nm bud; **en bourgeons** in bud

bourgeonner [burʒɔne] vi (a) (plante, arbre) to bud (b) Fam (avoir des boutons) to come out in spots

bourgmestre [burgmɛstr] nm burgomaster

Bourgogne [burgɔɲ] **1** nf **la B.** Burgundy
2 nm burgundy

bourguignon, -onne [burgiɲɔ̃, -ɔn] **1** adj Burgundian
2 nm, f **B.** Burgundian

bourlinguer [burlɛ̃ge] vi (personne) (naviguer) to sail the seven seas; Fam (voyager) to knock about

bourrade [burad] nf push, shove

bourrasque [burask] nf squall, gust (of wind); **b. de neige** snow flurry; **souffler en bourrasques** to gust

bourratif, -ive [buratif, -iv] adj Fam stodgy

bourre [bur] *nf* (a) *(pour rembourrer)* stuffing, padding; *(de coton, de soie)* waste (b) *(des bourgeons)* down (c) *(d'arme à feu)* wad (d) *Fam* **de première b.** first-rate; **à la b.** in a rush

bourré, -e [bure] *adj* (a) *(plein)* packed, crammed *(de with)*; **b. à craquer** full to bursting; *Fam* **être b. de complexes** to be a mass of complexes; *Fam* **être b. de fric** to have pots of money (b) *très Fam (ivre)* plastered

bourreau, -x [buro] *nm* (a) *(exécuteur)* executioner; *(qui pend)* hangman; *(tortionnaire)* torturer (b) *Fig* tormentor; **b. des cœurs** ladykiller; **b. d'enfants** child-beater; *Hum* child tormentor; **b. de travail** workaholic

bourrée [bure] *nf (danse)* bourrée

bourrelé, -e [burle] *adj* **b. de remords** stricken with remorse

bourrelet [burlɛ] *nm* (a) *Fam* **b. (de graisse)** *(au ventre)* spare tyre (b) *(contre les courants d'air)* weather strip, *Br* draught excluder

bourrer [bure] **1** *vt* (a) *(chaise, coussin)* to stuff, to pad (b) *(placard, sac)* to cram *(de with)*; *(pipe)* to fill; **ça bourre** *(aliment)* it's filling; **b. qn de qch** *(gaver)* to fill sb up with sth; **b. qn de coups** to beat sb up; *Fam* **b. le crâne à qn** *(élève)* to stuff sb's head with facts; *(politiquement)* to brainwash sb; *Fam* **b. le mou à qn** to pull the wool over sb's eyes

2 se bourrer *vpr* (a) **se b. de qch** *(se gaver)* to stuff oneself with sth (b) *très Fam* **se b. la gueule** to get plastered

bourriche [buriʃ] *nf (d'huîtres)* basket

bourrichon [buriʃɔ̃] *nm Fam* **se monter le b.** to get worked up

bourricot [buriko] *nm (small) donkey*

bourrin [burɛ̃] *nm Fam (cheval)* nag

bourrique [burik] *nf (ânesse)* she-ass; *Fam (personne têtue)* pigheaded individual; **faire tourner qn en b.** to drive sb crazy

bourru, -e [bury] *adj* surly

bourse [burs] *nf* (a) *(porte-monnaie)* purse; **la b. ou la vie!** your money or your life!; **sans b. délier** without spending a penny; **faire b. commune** to pool one's money (b) *Scol & Univ* **b. (d'études)** grant (c) *Fin* **la B. (des valeurs)** the Stock Exchange, the Stock Market; **jouer à la B.** to play the market; **b. de commerce** commodities exchange (d) *Anat* **bourses** scrotum

boursicoter [bursikɔte] *vi* to dabble on the Stock Market

boursier, -ère [bursje, -ɛr] **1** *adj* (a) *Fin* Stock Exchange, Stock Market (b) *Scol & Univ* **étudiant b.** grant holder

2 *nm,f* (a) *Scol & Univ* grant holder (b) *Fin* (Stock Exchange) operator

boursouflé, -e [bursufle] *adj (visage, yeux)* swollen, puffy; *(peinture)* blistered; *Fig (style, discours)* turgid

bous *voir* **bouillir**

bousculade [buskylad] *nf (agitation)* pushing and shoving; **être pris dans la b.** to be caught up in the rush

bousculer [buskyle] **1** *vt* (a) *(pousser)* to jostle; *Fig (habitudes)* to disrupt; *(préjugés)* to overturn (b) *(presser)* to rush

2 se bousculer *vpr (foule)* to push and shove; **les idées se bousculaient dans sa tête** his head was buzzing with ideas; *Fig* **les candidats ne se bousculent pas au portillon** applicants aren't exactly queuing up for the job

bouse [buz] *nf* **de la b. (de vache)** cow dung; **une b.** a cowpat

bouseux [buzø] *nm Fam Péj* yokel

bousiller [buzije] *Fam* **1** *vt (voiture, appareil photo)* to wreck; *(travail)* to botch (up), to bungle

2 se bousiller *vpr* **se b. la santé** to ruin one's health

boussole [busɔl] *nf* compass; **s'orienter à la b.** to use a compass to get one's bearings; *Fam Fig* **perdre la b.** to go off one's head

boustifaille [bustifaj] *nf très Fam* grub

bout¹ [bu] *voir* **bouillir**

bout² *nm* (a) *(extrémité)* end; **b. à b.** end to end; **de b. en b., d'un b. à l'autre** *(dans l'espace)* from one end to the other; *(reprendre un travail, lire)* from start to finish; **à l'autre b., au b. du fil** *(au téléphone)* on the other end; *Fig* **je n'en vois pas le b.** I'm nowhere near the end of it; *Fig* **voir le b. du tunnel** to see the light at the end of the tunnel; **au b. de la rue** at the end of the street; **aller au b. du monde** to go to the ends of the earth; *Fig* **ce n'est pas le b. du monde** it's not exactly difficult; **au b. d'une heure/de quelques jours** after an hour/a few days

(b) *(du doigt, du nez)* tip, end; *(d'une pipe)* mouthpiece; *(d'une chaussure)* toe; **b. filtre** *(d'une cigarette)* filter tip; **b. du sein** nipple

(c) *(morceau)* bit; **elle en connaît un b. sur la question** she knows a thing or two about it; **faire un b. de chemin** to go part of the way; **un b. de temps** a little while; *Fig* **b. de chou** little child; *Cin & TV* **b. d'essai** screen test

(d) *(locutions)* **être à b.** *(épuisé)* to be exhausted; *(exaspéré)* to be at the end of one's patience; **pousser qn à b.** to push sb too far; **être à b. d'arguments** to have run out of arguments; **venir à b. de qch** *(travail)* to get through sth; *(obstacle)* to overcome sth; **à b. de bras** at arm's length; *Fig* **porter une entreprise à b. de bras** to carry a firm; **à b. portant** point-blank; **on ne sait jamais par quel b. le prendre** it's hard to know how to handle him; **avoir un mot sur le b. de la langue** to have a word on the tip of one's tongue; **tenir le bon b.** to be well on the way to success

boutade [butad] *nf (trait d'esprit)* quip

boute-en-train [butɑ̃trɛ̃] *nm inv* live wire

bouteille [butɛj] *nf* bottle; *(de gaz, d'oxygène)* cylinder; *(contenu)* bottle(ful); **c'est une bonne b.** it's a good bottle of wine; **mettre du vin en bouteilles** to bottle wine; *Fam* **prendre de la b.** to be getting long in the tooth

boutique [butik] *nf Br* shop, *Am* store; **fermer b.** to shut up shop; **b. hors taxes** duty-free shop; **b. de mode** fashion shop, boutique

boutiquier, -ère [butikje, -ɛr] *nm,f Br* shopkeeper, *Am* storekeeper

bouton [butɔ̃] *nm* (a) *(de fleur)* bud; **b. de rose** rosebud; **en b.** in bud (b) *(sur un vêtement)* button; *(de col)* stud; **boutons de manchette** cufflinks (c) *(de porte, de radio)* knob; *(qu'on pousse)* & *Ordinat* button; *(interrupteur)* switch; *Ordinat* **b. de réinitialisation** reset button (d) *(sur le visage)* spot

bouton-d'or *(pl* **boutons-d'or)** [butɔ̃dɔr] *nm* buttercup

boutonnage [butɔnaʒ] *nm* buttoning (up); **veste à double b.** double-breasted jacket

boutonner [butɔne] **1** *vt (vêtement)* to button (up), to fasten (up)

2 se boutonner *vpr (vêtement)* to button (up)

boutonneux, -euse [butɔnø, -øz] *adj* spotty

boutonnière [butɔnjɛr] *nf (de vêtement)* buttonhole; **porter une fleur à la b.** to wear a *Br* buttonhole *or Am* boutonnière

bouton-pression (*pl* **boutons-pression**) [butɔ̃-presjɔ̃] *nm Br* press stud, *Am* snap fastener

bouture [butyr] *nf* cutting; **faire des boutures** to take cuttings

bouturer [butyre] *vt* to propagate by cuttings

bouvier, -ère [buvje, -ɛr] *nm,f* cowherd
2 *nm (chien)* sheepdog

bouvreuil [buvrœj] *nm* bullfinch

bovin, -e [bovɛ̃, -in] 1 *adj aussi Fig* bovine
2 *nm Zool* bovine

bowling [buliŋ] *nm* (a) *(jeu)* (tenpin) bowling (b) *(lieu)* (tenpin) bowling alley

box (*pl* **boxes**) [bɔks] *nm (dans un dortoir)* cubicle; *(dans une écurie)* stall; *(garage)* lock-up (garage); *Jur* **b. des accusés** dock

boxe [bɔks] *nf* boxing; **faire de la b.** to box; **b. anglaise** boxing; **b. française** kick boxing

boxer[1] [bɔkse] 1 *vi* to box
2 *vt Fam (frapper)* to punch up

boxer[2] [bɔksɛr] *nm (chien)* boxer

boxeur [bɔksœr] *nm* boxer

box-office (*pl* **box-offices**) [bɔksɔfis] *nm* box office; **être en tête du b.** to be a box-office hit

boyau, -x [bwajo] *nm* (a) *(d'animal)* gut; *(corde)* (cat)gut (b) *(de vélo)* tubular tyre (c) *(allée)* narrow alleyway; *(de mine)* narrow gallery; *Mil* communication trench

boycott(age) [bɔjkɔt(aʒ)] *nm* boycott(ing)

boycotter [bɔjkɔte] *vt* to boycott

boy-scout (*pl* **boy-scouts**) [bɔjskut] *nm Vieilli* boy scout; *Fig* **mentalité de b.** boy-scout mentality

BP [bepe] *nf (abrév* **boîte postale)** PO Box

BPF [bepeɛf] *Fin (abrév* **bon pour francs)** = letters printed on cheques before amount to be written in figures

bracelet [braslɛ] *nm* (a) *(bijou)* bracelet; *(rigide)* bangle; *(de montre)* strap (b) *(élastique)* rubber *or* elastic band

bracelet-montre (*pl* **bracelets-montres**) [braslɛmɔ̃tr] *nm* wristwatch

braconnage [brakɔnaʒ] *nm* poaching

braconner [brakɔne] *vi* to poach

braconnier [brakɔnje] *nm* poacher

brader [brade] *vt (solder)* to sell off

braderie [bradri] *nf (liquidation)* clearance sale; *(vente par des particuliers) Br* ≃ car boot sale, *Am* ≃ garage sale; *(magasin)* discount store

braguette [bragɛt] *nf* flies

braille [braj] *nm* Braille; **lire en b.** to read Braille

braillements [brajmɑ̃] *nmpl* yelling; *(d'enfant)* howling

brailler [braje] 1 *vi* to yell; *(enfant)* to howl
2 *vt (chanson)* to bawl out; *(slogan)* to chant

braire [28] [brɛr] *vi (âne)* to bray; *Fam Fig* to yell

braise [brɛz] *nf (charbons)* (glowing) embers; **des yeux de b.** glowing eyes

braiser [breze] *vt Culin* to braise

bramer [brame] *vi (cerf)* to bell; *Fig (hurler)* to howl

brancard [brɑ̃kar] *nm* (a) *(d'une civière, d'une charrette)* shaft; *Fig* **ruer dans les brancards** to kick over the traces (b) *(civière)* stretcher

brancardier, -ère [brɑ̃kardje, -ɛr] *nm,f* stretcher bearer

branchage [brɑ̃ʃaʒ] *nm (des arbres)* branches; **branchages** *(coupés)* cut branches

branche [brɑ̃ʃ] *nf* (a) *(d'un arbre)* branch; *(de céleri)* stick; *Fig (de l'industrie, de la science, d'une famille)* branch; *(professionnelle)* line of business; **la b. maternelle** the mother's side; *Fam* **vieille b.** old stick (b) *(d'un compas)* leg; *(de lunettes)* side piece; *(d'un chandelier)* branch

branché, -e [brɑ̃ʃe] *adj Fam (à la mode)* trendy, hip; **il est b. tennis/techno** he's really into tennis/techno music

branchement [brɑ̃ʃmɑ̃] *nm (sur un réseau)* connecting (up) (**sur** to); *(à une prise)* plugging in; *(assemblage de fils)* connection

brancher [brɑ̃ʃe] 1 *vt* (a) *(à un réseau)* to connect (up) (**sur** to); *(à une prise)* to plug in; *Fig* **b. qn sur un sujet** to get sb onto a subject (b) *Fam (plaire à)* **la peinture moderne, ça ne me branche pas tellement** I'm not really into modern art; **on se fait un resto ce soir, ça te branche?** fancy going to a restaurant tonight?
2 **se brancher** *vpr* (a) *(appareil électrique)* to plug in (b) **se b. sur** *(une station de radio)* to tune in to

branchie [brɑ̃ʃi] *nf* gill

brandade [brɑ̃dad] *nf Culin* **b. (de morue)** = salt cod puréed with garlic, oil and cream

brandebourg [brɑ̃dbur] *nm* frog

brandir [brɑ̃dir] *vt* to brandish

brandy [brɑ̃di] *nm* brandy

branlant, -e [brɑ̃lɑ̃, -ɑ̃t] *adj (dent)* loose; *(chaise, escalier)* rickety

branle [brɑ̃l] *nm* **mettre qch en b.** *(processus)* to set sth in motion; **se mettre en b.** *(partir)* to get moving; *(entrer en fonctionnement)* to get going

branle-bas [brɑ̃lba] *nm inv* **b. (de combat)** *(agitation)* commotion

branlée [brɑ̃le] *nf Fam* thrashing; **prendre** *ou* **recevoir une b.** to get a thrashing

branler [brɑ̃le] 1 *vt Vulg (masturber)* to jerk off, *Br* to wank off; *Fig* **mais qu'est-ce qu'il branle?** what the hell's he up to?
2 *vi (dent)* to be loose; *(chaise, escalier)* to be rickety
3 **se branler** *vpr Vulg (se masturber)* to jerk off, *Br* to wank; *Fig* **je m'en branle!** I don't give a shit!

branleur, -euse [brɑ̃lœr, -øz] *nm,f Vulg (bon à rien)* nerd, *Br* wanker

braquage [brakaʒ] *nm* (a) *Aut (des roues)* turning; **(angle de) b.** steering lock (b) *Fam (vol)* hold-up; **faire un b.** to do a hold-up

braque [brak] *nm (chien)* pointer

braquer [brake] 1 *vt* (a) *(diriger)* to point (**sur** at); *(regard)* to fix (**sur** on) (b) *(rendre hostile)* **b. qn contre qn/qch** to turn sb against sb/sth (c) *Fam (banque)* to hold up
2 *vi Aut* to turn (the steering) wheel; **b. à fond** to apply full lock; **voiture qui braque mal** car that has a poor lock
3 **se braquer** *vpr* to dig one's heels in; **se b. contre qn** to set one's face against sb

braquet [brakɛ] *nm* gear ratio; **changer de b.** to change gear

bras [bra] *nm* (a) *(membre)* arm; **donner le b. à qn** to give sb one's arm; **un panier au b.** with a basket on one's arm; **les b. croisés** with one's arms folded; *Fig* **rester les b. croisés** *(être passif)* to stand by with one's arms folded; **b. dessus, b. dessous** arm in arm; **être le b. droit de qn** to be sb's right-hand man; **accueillir qn à b. ouverts** to welcome sb with open arms; *Fam* **tomber sur qn à bras raccourcis** to get stuck into sb; *Fig* **avoir le b. long** to have a lot of influence; *Fig* **avoir qn/qch sur les b.** to have sb/sth on one's hands; **les b. m'en tombent!** I'm flabbergasted!; **en b. de chemise** in (one's) shirtsleeves; **une partie de b. de fer** an arm-wrestling match; **faire un b. d'honneur à qn** $\simeq$ to stick two fingers up at sb **(b)** *(d'un fauteuil, d'un levier, d'une ancre)* arm; *(d'une grue)* jib; *(d'une croix)* limb; **b. de lecture** pickup arm **(c)** *(de fleuve)* arm; **b. de mer** arm of the sea

brasero [brazero] *nm* brazier

brasier [brazje] *nm (incendie)* blaze, inferno

Brasilia [brazilja] *n* Brasilia

bras-le-corps [bralkɔr] **à bras-le-corps** *adv* **saisir qn à b.** to seize sb round the waist; **prendre un problème à b.** to get to grips with a problem

brassage [brasaʒ] *nm* (a) *(de la bière)* brewing **(b)** *(mélange)* mixing

brassard [brasar] *nm* armband; **b. de deuil** black armband

brasse [bras] *nf Sp (style)* breaststroke; *(mouvement)* stroke; **nager la b.** to swim breaststroke; **b. coulée** = breaststroke in which face is submerged; **b. papillon** butterfly (stroke)

brassée [brase] *nf* armful

brasser [brase] *vt* (a) *(bière)* to brew **(b)** *(mélanger)* to mix; *Fig* **b. de l'argent** to handle large amounts of money; **b. de l'air** *ou* **du vent** to work without getting anything done

brasserie [brasri] *nf* (a) *(fabrique)* brewery; *(industrie)* brewing **(b)** *(restaurant)* brasserie

brasseur, -euse [brascr, -øz] *nm,f* (a) *(fabricant de bière)* brewer *Fig* **b. d'affaires** big businessman

brassière [brasjɛr] *nf* (a) *(de bébé)* *Br* vest, *Am* undershirt **(b)** *Can (soutien-gorge)* bra

Bratislava [bratislava] *n* Bratislava

bravade [bravad] *nf* bravado; **par b.** out of bravado

brave [brav] **1** *adj* (a) *(courageux)* brave, courageous **(b)** *(bon)* good; **de braves gens** good people **(c)** *Péj* **il est bien b.** *(pas futé)* he means well
2 *nm* (a) *(héros)* brave man **(b)** *Vieilli* **mon b.** my good man

bravement [bravmã] *adv* (a) *(courageusement)* bravely, courageously **(b)** *(avec résolution)* boldly

braver [brave] *vt (mort, danger)* to brave; *(personne, lois, règlements)* to defy

bravo [bravo] **1** *exclam* bravo!; *(dans un débat)* hear, hear!; *Ironique* well done!
2 *nm* **un grand b. à toute l'équipe technique** a big hand for all the technical crew; **des bravos** cheers

bravoure [bravur] *nf* bravery, courage

Brazzaville [brazavil] *n* Brazzaville

break¹ [brek] *nm (voiture) Br* estate car, *Am* station wagon

break² *nm (pause) & Sp* break

brebis [brəbi] *nf* (a) *(animal)* ewe; *Fig* **b. galeuse** black sheep **(b)** *Rel* sheep

brèche [brɛʃ] *nf (dans un mur, une haie)* gap; *(dans la coque d'un bateau)* hole; *Mil* breach; *Fig* **être toujours sur la b.** to be always on the go; **battre qch en b.** to demolish sth

bréchet [breʃe] *nm* breastbone

bredouille [brəduj] *adj* empty-handed

bredouiller [brəduje] *vt & vi* to mumble, to mutter

bref, -ève [brɛf, brɛv] **1** *adj* brief, short; *Ling (voyelle)* short; **soyez b.!** be brief!
2 *adv* in short; **une cousine ou une tante, enfin b., quelqu'un de sa famille** a cousin or an aunt, well anyway, one of his relatives; **l'actualité en b.** the news in brief
3 *nf* **brève** *(nouvelle)* short news item

brelan [brəlã] *nm* three of a kind; **b. d'as** three aces

breloque [brəlɔk] *nf (sur un bracelet)* charm

brème [brɛm] *nf* bream

Brême [brɛm] *n* Bremen

Brésil [brezil] *nm* **le B.** Brazil

brésilien, -enne [breziljɛ̃, -ɛn] **1** *adj* Brazilian
2 *nm,f* **B.** Brazilian

Bretagne [brətaɲ] *nf* **la B.** Brittany

bretelle [brətɛl] *nf* (a) *(de soutien-gorge, de robe)* (shoulder) strap; **(paire de) bretelles** *(pour pantalon)* (pair of) *Br* braces *or Am* suspenders **(b)** *(lanière)* strap; *(de fusil)* sling **(c)** *(route)* **b. (d'accès)** access road; **b. (d'autoroute)** *Br* slip road

breton, -onne [brətɔ̃, -ɔn] **1** *adj* Breton
2 *nm,f* **B.** Breton
3 *nm (langue)* Breton

bretzel [brɛdzɛl] *nm* pretzel

breuvage [brœvaʒ] *nm (potion)* potion; *Hum (boisson)* concoction

brève [brɛv] *voir* **bref**

brevet [brəvɛ] *nm (certificat)* certificate; *(diplôme)* diploma; *Scol* **b. (des collèges)** = general exam taken at fifteen; **b. d'études professionnelles** = vocational diploma; **b. (d'invention)** patent; **b. de pilote** *Av* pilot's licence; *Mil* wings; **b. de technicien supérieur** = advanced vocational training certificate

breveter [42] [brəvte] *vt (invention)* to patent; **faire b. qch** to take out a patent on sth

bréviaire [brevjɛr] *nm Rel* breviary

briard [brijar] *nm (chien)* Briard

bribes [brib] *nfpl* **b. de conversation** snatches of conversation; **des b. de finlandais** a few scraps of Finnish

bric-à-brac [brikabrak] *nm inv (vieux objets)* odds and ends, bric-à-brac; *(mélange)* jumble **(de** of); **(boutique de) b.** second-hand shop

bric et de broc [brikedəbrɔk] **de bric et de broc** *adv* haphazardly

brick [brik] *nm (carton)* carton

bricolage [brikɔlaʒ] *nm* (a) *(travail)* DIY, do-it-yourself; **faire du b.** to do some DIY **(b)** *Péj (réparation)* botch-up

bricole [brikɔl] *nf (objet)* trinket; *(chose sans importance)* trifle; *Fam* **il va lui arriver des bricoles** he's/she's going to get into a pickle

bricoler [brikɔle] **1** *vt (construire)* to put together; *(réparer)* to tinker with
2 *vi* to do-it-yourself *or Br* DIY; **j'ai passé la matinée à b. dans la maison** I spent the morning doing odd jobs about the house

bricoleur, -euse [brikœlœr, -øz] **1** *adj* être **b.** to be good with one's hands

2 *nm,f* handyman, *f* handywoman

bride [brid] *nf* (a) (*de harnais*) bridle; *Fig* lâcher la **b.** à qn to give sb his/her head; *Fig* avoir la **b.** sur le cou to have a free rein; aller à **b.** abattue to ride full tilt (b) (*de boutonnière*) bar

bridé, -e [bride] *adj* (*yeux*) slanting

brider [bride] *vt* (*cheval*) to bridle; (*personne, passions, impulsion*) to curb, to restrain

bridge [bridʒ] *nm* (*jeu, prothèse*) bridge

brie [bri] *nm* Brie

brièvement [brievmɑ̃] *adv* briefly

brièveté [brievte] *nf* brevity, briefness

brigade [brigad] *nf* (a) *Mil* brigade; (*de police, de gendarmerie*) squad; **b. antigang** organized crime squad; *Hist* **Brigades internationales** International Brigades; **b. des stupéfiants** *ou Fam* **des stups** drug squad (b) (*d'ouvriers*) team

brigadier [brigadje] *nm* (a) *Mil* corporal; (*d'artillerie*) bombardier (b) **b. (de police)** (police) sergeant

brigand [brigɑ̃] *nm* (*bandit*) brigand; (*personne malhonnête*) crook

briguer [brige] *vt* (*honneur, poste*) to solicit

brillamment [brijamɑ̃] *adv* brilliantly

brillant, -e [brijɑ̃, -ɑ̃t] **1** *adj* (a) (*lumière, couleur*) bright, brilliant; (*pierre précieuse*) sparkling; (*cheveux, chaussures, cuir*) shiny; **b. de fièvre** bright with fever (b) (*carrière, élève, avenir*) brilliant; (*conversation*) sparkling

2 *nm* (a) (*d'un métal*) brilliance, brightness; (*d'une pierre précieuse*) sparkle; (*d'un papier, d'un tissu, de cheveux*) shininess (b) (*diamant*) brilliant (c) **b. à lèvres** lip gloss

brillantine [brijɑ̃tin] *nf* brilliantine

briller [brije] *vi* (a) (*soleil, étoiles, yeux*) to shine; (*bougie*) to glimmer; (*pierre précieuse*) to sparkle; (*eau, satin*) to shimmer; (*braises*) to glow; **faire b. ses chaussures** to shine *or* polish one's shoes; **des yeux qui brillent de colère/de joie** eyes shining with anger/happiness; **b. de mille feux** to sparkle brilliantly; *Prov* **tout ce qui brille n'est pas or** all that glitters is not gold (b) (*exceller*) to shine; **b. par son absence** to be conspicuous by one's absence; **elle ne brille pas par sa ponctualité** she's not noted for her punctuality

brimade [brimad] *nf* instance of bullying; **faire subir des brimades à qn** to bully sb

brimbaler [brɛ̃bale] = **bringuebaler**

brimer [brime] *vt* to bully; **se sentir brimé** to feel victimized

brin [brɛ̃] **1** *nm* (a) (*de persil, de romarin*) sprig; (*de mimosa, de muguet*) spray; (*de paille*) wisp; **un b. d'herbe** a blade of grass; **un b. de qch** a bit of sth (b) *Fam* (*petite quantité*) bit (de of); **un b. d'ironie/de jalousie** a touch of irony/jealousy; **faire un b. de toilette** to have a quick wash (and brush-up); **un beau b. de fille** a fine-looking girl (c) (*de laine, corde, fibre*) strand

2 *adv Fam* **un b.** a bit

brindille [brɛ̃dij] *nf* twig

bringue¹ [brɛ̃g] *nf Fam* **grande b.** (*fille*) beanpole

bringue² *nf Fam* (*fête*) binge; **faire la b.** to go on a binge

bringuebaler [brɛ̃gbale], **brinquebaler** [brɛ̃kbale] *vt & vi Fam* to shake about

brio [brijo] *nm* brilliance; **avec b.** brilliantly

brioche [brijɔʃ] *nf* brioche; *Fam Fig* **avoir/prendre de la b.** to have/develop a paunch

brioché, -e [brijɔʃe] *adj* **pain b.** = milk bread

brique [brik] **1** *nf* (a) (*de construction*) brick; **mur de** *ou* **en briques** brick wall (b) *très Fam* (*10 000 francs*) 10,000 francs

2 *adj inv* brick-red

briquer [brike] *vt* (*nettoyer*) to scrub down; (*pont de navire*) to holystone

briquet [brike] *nm* (*cigarette*) lighter

briqueterie [briketri] *nf* brickyard

briquette [briket] *nf* (a) (*petite brique*) small brick (b) (*de jus de fruit*) small carton (c) (*de charbon*) briquette

bris [bri] *nm* (*de verre, de scellés*) breaking; **b. de glaces** broken windows

brisant [brizɑ̃] *nm* (*écueil*) reef; **brisants** (*vagues*) breakers

brise [briz] *nf* breeze; *Naut* **forte b.** stiff breeze

brise-glace [brizglas] *nm inv* (a) (*navire*) ice breaker (b) (*d'une pile de pont*) ice breaker; (*d'un navire*) ice beam

brise-lames [brizlam] *nm inv* breakwater

briser [brize] **1** *vt* (*casser*) to break; (*opposition, résistance, espérances*) to crush; (*carrière*) to wreck; (*grève*) to break; **b. qn** (*sujet: effort, marche*) to shatter sb; **brisé par la douleur** crushed by grief; **la voix brisée par l'émotion** his/her voice choked with emotion; **cela me brise le cœur** it breaks my heart

2 se briser *vpr* (*vagues, porcelaine, verre*) to break; *Fig* (*espoirs*) to be shattered

brise-tout [briztu] *nmf inv* clumsy person (*who is always breaking things*)

briseur, -euse [brizœr, -øz] *nm,f* **b. de grève** strike breaker

brise-vent [brizvɑ̃] *nm inv* windbreak

bristol [bristɔl] *nm* Bristol board; (*carte de visite*) visiting card

britannique [britanik] **1** *adj* British; **les îles Britanniques** the British Isles

2 *nmf* **B.** Briton; **les Britanniques** the British

broc [bro] *nm* pitcher, jug

brocante [brokɑ̃t] *nf* (*commerce*) secondhand trade; (*magasin*) secondhand shop; (*marché aux puces*) secondhand market

brocanteur, -euse [brokɑ̃tœr, -øz] *nm,f* secondhand dealer

brocard [brokar] *nm* brocade

brocarder [brokarde] *vt Litt* to gibe at

brocha [broʃ] *nf* (a) (*pour rôtir*) spit; **faire cuire qch à la b.** to spit-roast sth (b) (*bijou*) brooch (c) *Tech, Él & Méd* pin

brocher [broʃe] *vt* (a) (*livre*) to stitch (b) (*tissu*) to brocade

brochet [broʃɛ] *nm* pike

brochette [broʃɛt] *nf* (*broche*) skewer; (*plat*) kebab

brochure [broʃyr] *nf* brochure, pamphlet

brocoli [brokoli] *nm* broccoli; **des brocolis** broccoli

brodequin [brodkɛ̃] *nm* laced boot

broder [brode] *vt & vi aussi Fig* to embroider

broderie [brodri] *nf* (a) (*ouvrage*) piece of embroidery; (*activité*) embroidery; **b. anglaise** broderie anglaise (b) (*activité*) embroidery

broie *voir* **broyer**

bromure [bromyr] *nm* bromide

bronche [brɔ̃ʃ] *nf* bronchial tube; **être fragile des bronches** to have a weak chest

broncher [brɔ̃ʃe] *vi* (a) *(réagir)* **sans b.** without batting an eyelid; **il n'a pas bronché** he didn't bat an eyelid (b) *(cheval)* to stumble

bronchite [brɔ̃ʃit] *nf* bronchitis; **avoir une b.** to have bronchitis

broncho-pneumonie (*pl* **broncho-pneumonies**) [brɔ̃kɔpnømɔni] *nf Méd* bronchopneumonia

bronzage [brɔ̃zaʒ] *nm (activité)* tanning; *(hâle)* (sun)tan; **b. intégral** all-over tan

bronze [brɔ̃z] *nm (métal, objet d'art)* bronze

bronzé, -e [brɔ̃ze] *adj (peau)* (sun)tanned; *Euph ou Péj (personne)* coloured

bronzer [brɔ̃ze] *vi (personne)* to go brown, to tan

bronzette [brɔ̃zɛt] *nf Fam* sunbathing; **faire b.** to do a bit of sunbathing

brosse [brɔs] *nf* (a) *(ustensile)* brush; **donner un coup de b. à qch** to give sth a brush; **donner un coup de b. à qn** to give sb's hair a brush; **avoir les cheveux en b.** to have a crew cut; *Fig* **manier la b. à reluire** to bow and scrape; **b. à cheveux** hairbrush; **b. à dents** toothbrush; **b. à habits** clothes brush; **b. à ongles** nailbrush (b) *(pinceau large)* (paint)brush

brosser [brɔse] **1** *vt* (a) *(tapis, manteau, cheveux)* to brush; *(sol)* to scrub; *(cheval)* to brush down; *Belg* **b. un cours** to skip a lecture (b) *(décrire)* **b. un tableau optimiste de la situation** to paint an optimistic picture of the situation
2 se brosser *vpr (se nettoyer)* to brush oneself down; **se b. les dents/les cheveux** to brush one's teeth/one's hair; *Fam* **tu peux toujours te b.!** not a chance!

brou [bru] *nm* (a) *(enveloppe)* husk, *Am* shuck (b) *(teinture)* **b. de noix** walnut stain

broue [bru] *nf Can* froth; *très Fam Fig* **faire ou péter de la b.** to talk big

brouette [bruɛt] *nf* wheelbarrow

brouhaha [bruaa] *nm* hubbub

brouillard [brujar] *nm* fog; **il y a du b.** it's foggy; *Fig* **être dans le b.** to be in a fog; **b. givrant** freezing fog

brouille [bruj] *nf* quarrel, disagreement

brouillé, -e [bruje] *adj* (a) *(teint)* blotchy (b) **être b. avec qn** to have fallen out with sb; **être b. avec les dates/la grammaire** to be hopeless at dates/grammar

brouiller [bruje] **1** *vt* (a) *(rendre trouble) (idées)* to muddle up; *(vue)* **yeux brouillés de larmes** eyes blurred with tears; *Fig* **b. les cartes** to confuse the issue; *Fig* **b. les pistes** to cover one's tracks (b) *(fâcher)* **b. qn avec qn** to set sb against sb (c) *Rad & Él (accidentellement)* to cause interference to; *(intentionnellement)* to jam
2 se brouiller *vpr* (a) *(idées, dates)* to get muddled up (b) *(vue)* to get blurred (c) *(se détériorer)* **le temps se brouille** it's clouding over (d) *(se disputer)* to fall out *(avec qn* with sb)

brouillon, -onne [brujɔ̃, -ɔn] **1** *adj (mal organisé)* disorganized, unmethodical; *(mal présenté)* untidy
2 *nm (ébauche)* (rough) draft; *(papier)* **b.** *Br* scrap or *Am* scratch paper; **faire un exercice au b.** to do an exercise in rough; *(cahier de)* **b.** rough book; *Ordinat* **version b.** draft version

broussaille [brusaj] *nf* **broussailles** scrub; **en b.** *(cheveux)* tousled; *(sourcils)* bushy

broussailleux, -euse [brusajø, -øz] *adj (terrain)* scrubby; *(cheveux)* tousled; *(sourcils)* bushy

brousse [brus] *nf* **la b.** the bush

brouter [brute] **1** *vt (herbe)* to graze
2 *vi* (a) *(animal)* to graze (b) *(embrayage)* to judder

broutille [brutij] *nf* trifle

broyer [32] [brwaje] *vt (pierre, aliments, couleurs)* to grind; *(membre, main, personne)* to crush; *Fig* **b. du noir** to be down in the dumps

broyeur, -euse [brwajœr, -øz] **1** *adj (appareil)* grinding
2 *nm (machine)* grinder; **b. à ordures** *Br* waste or *Am* garbage disposal unit

bru [bry] *nf* daughter-in-law

brugnon [brynɔ̃] *nm* nectarine

bruine [brɥin] *nf* drizzle

bruiner [brɥine] *v impersonnel* to drizzle

bruire [brɥir] *vi Litt (feuilles, étoffe)* to rustle; *(ruisseau, vent)* to murmur

bruissement [brɥismɑ̃] *nm (des feuilles, d'une étoffe)* rustle, rustling; *(d'un ruisseau, du vent)* murmur(ing)

bruit [brɥi] *nm* (a) *(son)* sound, noise; **b. de pas** (sound of) footsteps; **des bruits de voix** the sound of voices; **sans b.** without a sound (b) *(vacarme)* noise; **faire du b.** to make a noise; *Fig (affaire, histoire)* to cause a sensation; **b. de fond** background noise; **beaucoup de b. pour rien** a lot of fuss over nothing (c) *(rumeur)* rumour; **faire courir un b.** to spread a rumour; **le b. court que...** rumour has it that...

bruitage [brɥitaʒ] *nm* sound effects

bruiteur, -euse [brɥitœr, -øz] *nm,f* sound-effects man, *f* woman

brûlant, -e [bryla, -ɑ̃t] *adj (plat, casserole)* red-hot; *(café)* boiling (hot); *(soleil)* scorching; *Fig* **b. de désir** burning with desire; **question brûlante** burning question; **le sujet est d'une actualité brûlante** it's one of the burning issues of the day

brûlé, -e [bryle] **1** *nm,f (accidenté)* burns victim; *Méd* **les grands brûlés** people with third-degree burns
2 sentir le b. to smell burnt; **une odeur de b.** a burnt smell; **avoir un goût de b.** to taste burnt

brûle-parfum (*pl* **brûle-parfums**) [brylparfœ̃] *nm* perfume burner

brûle-pourpoint [brylpurpwɛ̃] **à brûle-pourpoint** *adv* point-blank

brûler [bryle] **1** *vt* (a) *(sujet: flamme, acide)* to burn; *(sujet: eau bouillante)* to scald; *(sujet: fer à repasser)* to scorch; *(café)* to roast; **gazon brûlé par le soleil** lawn scorched by the sun; **être brûlé vif** *(dans un accident)* to be burnt alive; *(être supplicié)* to be burnt at the stake; **l'argent lui brûle les doigts** money burns a hole in his pocket (b) *(consommer) (électricité, combustible)* to use; *(calories)* to burn (c) **b. un feu rouge** to go through a red light; **b. un stop** to go straight past a stop sign
2 *vi* (a) *(flamber, être carbonisé)* to burn; *(être très chaud)* to be red-hot; *(liquide)* to be boiling (hot); *(blessure)* to smart; **attention, ça brûle!** careful, it's hot!; **tu brûles** *(dans un jeu)* you're getting hot (b) *Fig* **b. de faire qch** to be burning to do sth; **b. d'impatience** to be bursting with impatience; **b. de désir** to be burning with desire
3 se brûler *vpr (par accident)* to burn oneself *(avec* on); **se b. la langue/la main** to burn one's tongue/hand

brûleur [brylœr] *nm* burner

brûlot [brylo] *nm Can (moustique)* gnat, midge

brûlure [brylyr] *nf (blessure)* burn; *(sensation)* burning; **b. de cigarette** cigarette burn; **brûlures d'estomac** heartburn

brume [brym] *nf* mist, haze; **b. de chaleur** heat haze

brumeux, -euse [brymø, -øz] *adj* misty, hazy; *Fig (idées, explication)* hazy

Brumisateur® [brymizatœr] *nm* atomizer, spray

brun, -e [brœ̃, bryn] **1** *adj (cheveux)* dark, brown; *(peau, personne) (naturellement)* dark; *(bronzé)* brown; **être b. de peau** to be dark-skinned
 2 *nm,f (personne)* dark-haired man, *f* dark-haired woman
 3 *nm (couleur)* brown
 4 *nf* **brune** *(bière)* brown ale

brunante [brynɑ̃t] *nf Can* dusk

brunâtre [brynɑtr] *adj* brownish

Brunei [brynei] *nm* **le B.** Brunei

brunir [brynir] *vi (peau, personne)* to tan; *(cheveux)* to darken

brushing® [brœʃiŋ] *nm* blow-dry

brusque [brysk] *adj* abrupt

brusquement [bryskəmɑ̃] *adv* abruptly

brusquer [bryske] *vt* **(a) b. qn** *(être impoli envers)* to be abrupt with sb; *(maltraiter)* to treat sb harshly **(b)** *(hâter) (décision)* to rush; **il ne faut rien b.** we mustn't rush things

brusquerie [bryskəri] *nf* abruptness; **avec b.** abruptly

brut, -e [bryt] **1** *adj (a) (pétrole, minerai)* crude; *(sucre)* unrefined; *(pierre précieuse)* uncut; *(champagne)* extra-dry; *(cidre)* dry; **à l'état b.** in its raw state **(b)** *(bénéfice, poids, salaire)* gross
 2 *nm (a) (pétrole)* crude (oil) **(b)** *(champagne)* extra-dry champagne
 3 *adv* gross

brutal, -e, -aux, -ales [brytal, -o] *adj (a) (personne, paroles, manières)* brutal; *(choc)* violent; **être b. avec qn** to be rough with sb **(b)** *(changement)* abrupt

brutalement [brytalmɑ̃] *adv (violemment)* brutally; *(avec brusquerie)* roughly; *(soudainement)* abruptly

brutaliser [brytalize] *vt* to ill-treat

brutalité [brytalite] *nf (violence, brusquerie)* brutality; *(soudaineté)* abruptness; **brutalités** brutality

brute [bryt] *nf (personne violente)* brute; *(personne grossière)* boor; **taper sur qch comme une b.** to bang at sth like a madman; **une b. épaisse** a great brute; **grosse b.!** you big brute!

Bruxelles [brysɛl] *n* Brussels

bruxellois, -e [bryksɛlwa, -az] **1** *adj* of Brussels
 2 *nm,f* **B.** = person from Brussels

bruyamment [brɥijamɑ̃] *adv (parler, rire)* loudly; *(manger)* noisily

bruyant, -e [brɥijɑ̃, -ɑ̃t] *adj (rue, voisin)* noisy; *(rire, applaudissements)* loud

bruyère [brɥjɛr] *nf (plante)* heather; *(terre)* heath; **pipe de b.** briar pipe; **terre de b.** peat

BTP [betepe] *nm (abrév* **bâtiment et travaux publics)** construction industry

BTS [betees] *nm (abrév* **brevet de technicien supérieur)** = advanced vocational training certificate

bu, -e *pp voir* **boire**

buanderie [bɥɑ̃dri] *nf* laundry (room)

bubonique [bybɔnik] *adj voir* **peste**

Bucarest [bykarɛst] *n* Bucharest

buccal, -e, -aux, -ales [bykal, -o] *adj* buccal; **par voie buccale** orally

bûche [byʃ] *nf (a) (morceau de bois)* log; **b. de Noël** Yule log **(b)** *Fam (chute)* fall; **prendre une b.** to come a cropper

bûcher¹ [byʃe] *nm (a) (pour le bois)* woodshed **(b)** *(de supplice)* stake **(c)** *(funéraire)* (funeral) pyre

bûcher² *Fam Scol* **1** *vt* to bone up on, *Br* to swot up
 2 *vi Br* to swot, *Am* to grind

bûcheron [byʃrɔ̃] *nm* woodcutter

bûcheur, -euse [byʃœr, -øz] *Fam Scol* **1** *adj* hardworking
 2 *nm,f Br* swot, *Am* grind

bucolique [bykɔlik] *adj* pastoral

Budapest [bydapɛst] *n* Budapest

budget [bydʒɛ] *nm* budget

budgétaire [bydʒetɛr] *adj (dépenses, contrôle)* budgetary; *(année)* financial; **déficit/excédent b.** budget deficit/surplus

buée [bɥe] *nf (sur les vitres)* condensation; *(sur un miroir)* mist

Buenos Aires [bɥenozɛr] *n* Buenos Aires

buffet [byfɛ] *nm (a) (meuble) (bas)* sideboard; *(haut)* dresser **(b)** *(repas)* buffet; **b. campagnard** = cold buffet made with country produce; **b. froid** cold buffet **(c)** *Fam (ventre)* belly

buffle [byfl] *nm* buffalo

building [bildiŋ] *nm* tower block

buis [bɥi] *nm (arbre)* box (tree); *(bois)* box(wood)

buisson [bɥisɔ̃] *nm* bush

buissonnière [bɥisɔnjɛr] *adj f voir* **école**

bulbe [bylb] *nm (a) Bot* bulb **(b)** *Anat* **b. pileux** hair bulb; **b. rachidien** medulla oblongata **(c)** *Archit* onion dome

bulgare [bylgar] **1** *adj* Bulgarian
 2 *nmf* **B.** Bulgarian
 3 *nm (langue)* Bulgarian

Bulgarie [bylgari] *nf* **la B.** Bulgaria

bulldozer [byldozœr] *nm* bulldozer

bulle [byl] *nf (d'air, de savon, stérile)* bubble; *(de bandes dessinées)* balloon; **faire des bulles** to blow bubbles; *Fam* **coincer la b.** to sleep, *Br* to kip; *Ordinat* **b. d'aide** help pop-up **(b)** *(lettre du pape)* (papal) bull

buller [byle] *vi Fam* to laze around

bulletin [byltɛ̃] *nm (communiqué)* bulletin; *(d'entreprise)* newsletter; *(formulaire)* form; *Scol* **b. (scolaire)** (school) report; **b. blanc** blank ballot paper; **b. d'informations** news bulletin; **b. météorologique** weather report; **b. de paie** *ou* **de salaire** pay slip; *Méd* **b. de santé** medical bulletin; **b. trimestriel** end-of-term report; **b. de vote** ballot paper; **b. (de vote) nul** spoiled ballot paper

bulletin-réponse *(pl* **bulletins-réponse)** [byltɛ̃repɔ̃s] *nm* reply form

bungalow [bœ̃galo] *nm* bungalow

bunker [bunkœr] *nm Mil* bunker; *(en golf) Br* bunker, *Am* sand trap

buraliste [byralist] *nmf (a) (de bureau de tabac)* tobacconist **(b)** *(dans un bureau)* clerk

bure [byr] *nf (étoffe)* frieze; *(habit religieux)* frock

bureau, -x [byro] *nm* (**a**) *(meuble)* desk
(**b**) *(lieu)* office; *(à la maison)* study
(**c**) *(comité)* committee
(**d**) *(agence)* office; **b. de change** bureau de change; **b. d'études** design office; *(de recherche)* R & D department; **B. international du travail** International Labour Office; **b. de poste** post office; **b. de tabac** tobacconist's (shop)
(**e**) *(organisme)* **b. d'aide sociale** welfare office

bureaucrate [byrokrat] *nmf* bureaucrat

bureaucratie [byrokrasi] *nf (système)* bureaucracy; *(ensemble des fonctionnaires)* bureaucrats

bureaucratique [byrokratik] *adj* bureaucratic

Bureautique® [byrotik] *nf* office automation

burette [byrɛt] *nf (pour l'huile)* oilcan; *(de chimiste)* burette

burin [byrɛ̃] *nm* (**a**) *(de graveur)* burin (**b**) *(pour découper)* (cold) chisel

buriné, -e [byrine] *adj (visage)* seamed

Burkina [byrkina] *nm* le B. Burkina Faso

burkinabé [byrkinabe] **1** *adj* of Burkina Faso
2 *nmf* **B.** = person from Burkina Faso

burlesque [byrlɛsk] **1** *adj* (**a**) *(ridicule)* ludicrous, ridiculous (**b**) *(film, genre)* burlesque
2 *nm (genre)* **le b.** the burlesque

Burundi [burundi] *nm* le B. Burundi

bus [bys] *nm (autobus)* & *Ordinat* bus

buse [byz] *nf* buzzard

busqué, -e [byske] *adj (nez)* hook(ed)

buste [byst] *nm (torse)* chest; *(seins, sculpture)* bust

bustier [bystje] *nm (corsage)* bustier; *(soutien-gorge)* long-line (strapless) bra

but [by, byt] *nm* (**a**) *(objectif)* aim, goal; *(intention)* purpose; *(d'un trajet)* destination, goal; **dans ce b.** with this aim in view; **c'est le b. de l'opération** that's the point of the operation; **errer sans b.** to wander about aimlessly (**b**) *Sp* goal; **marquer un b.** to score a goal; **gagner/perdre (par) 3 buts à 1** to win/lose by 3 goals to 1; **les buts** *(zone)* the goal (**c**) **demander/dire qch de b. en blanc** to ask/say sth straight out

butane [bytan] *nm* butane

buté, -e [byte] *adj* stubborn, obstinate

butée [byte] *nf* (**a**) *(pièce)* **b. (d'arrêt)** stop (**b**) *Archit* abutment

buter [byte] **1** *vt* (**a**) *(braquer)* **b. qn** to put sb's back up (**b**) *très Fam (tuer)* to bump off
2 *vi* **b. contre qch** *(cogner)* to bump into sth; *(trébucher)* to stumble over sth; **b. sur un problème/une difficulté** to come up against a problem/a difficulty
3 se buter *vpr (s'entêter)* to dig one's heels in

buteur [bytœr] *nm (au football)* goalscorer; *(au rugby)* kicker

butin [bytɛ̃] *nm (d'une armée)* booty; *(de pillards)* spoils; *(de voleur)* loot

butiner [bytine] **1** *vi (abeille)* to gather pollen
2 *vt (sujet: abeille)* to gather pollen from; *(renseignements)* to gather

butoir [bytwar] *nm Rail* buffer; *(de porte)* door stop

butte [byt] *nf (colline)* hillock; *Fig* **être en b. à qch** to be exposed to sth

buvable [byvabl] *adj* (**a**) *(potable)* drinkable (**b**) *(médicament)* to be taken orally

buvard [byvar] *nm (feuille)* sheet of blotting paper; *(sous-main)* blotter; **(papier) b.** blotting paper

buvette [byvɛt] *nf (dans une gare, à une fête)* refreshment bar

buveur, -euse [byvœr, -øz] *nm,f* drinker; **un gros b.** a heavy drinker

buviez *etc voir* **boire**

C

C, c [se] *nm inv* C, c; **c cédille** c cedilla

C (*abrév* **Celsius**) C

c' *voir* **ce**

CA [sea] *nm* **(a)** *Él* (*abrév* **courant alternatif**) AC **(b)** *Com* (*abrév* **chiffre d'affaires**) turnover

ça [sa] *pron démonstratif* **(a)** (*en désignant*) (*cela*) that; (*ceci*) this; **donne-moi ça** give that to me; **c'est bien vrai ça!** that's very true!; **écoute-moi ça!** just listen to this!; **ce n'est pas si facile que ça** it isn't as easy as that; **ça oui!** oh yes!; **à part ça** apart from that; **qui/quand/où ça?** who/when/where?; **c'est ça!** that's right!; *Ironique* if you say so!; **comment ça, elle est partie?** what do you mean she's gone?; **ça alors!, ça par exemple!** my goodness!; **ça y est, j'ai fini** that's it, I'm finished; **et insolent avec ça!** and you're/she's/*etc* rude! **(b)** (*sujet indéterminé*) it; **ça m'ennuie/me choque** it annoys/shocks me; **ça m'amuse** I find it funny; **ça me ferait plaisir** I'd enjoy it **(c)** *Fam* **ça criait dans tous les coins** there was shouting going on everywhere; *Hum* **ça travaille là-dedans!** you're not just a pretty face!

çà [sa] **çà et là** *adv* here and there

cabale [kabal] *nf* **(a)** (*complot, comploteurs*) cabal; **monter une c. contre qn** to plot against sb **(b)** *Rel* cabbala

cabalistique [kabalistik] *adj* cabbalistic

caban [kabɑ̃] *nm* reefer

cabane [kaban] *nf* **(a)** (*baraque*) hut; (*en rondins*) cabin; (*à outils*) shed; **c. à lapins** rabbit hutch; *Can* **c. à sucre** sugar shack **(b)** *très Fam* (*prison*) **en c.** in the clink; **faire de la c.** to do time

cabanon [kabanɔ̃] *nm* **(a)** (*petite cabane*) hut, shed **(b)** (*en Provence*) (*maison de campagne*) (country) cottage

cabaret [kabarɛ] *nm* cabaret

cabas [kaba] *nm* shopping bag

cabestan [kabɛstɑ̃] *nm* capstan

cabillaud [kabijo] *nm* (fresh) cod

cabine [kabin] *nf* **(a)** (*de bateau, de vaisseau spatial*) cabin; **c. de pilotage** (*de petit avion*) cockpit; (*de gros avion*) flight deck **(b)** **c. à lapins** rabbit hutch; **c. de douche** (*pièce*) shower room; (*installation*) shower cubicle; **c. de bain(s)** (*de plage*) beach hut; (*de piscine*) changing cubicle; **c. d'essayage** fitting room **(c)** (*de grue, de locomotive, de camion*) cab; (*d'ascenseur*) *Br* cage, *Am* car; **c. téléphonique** phone box

cabinet [kabinɛ] *nm* **(a)** (*petite pièce*) small room; *Fam* **les cabinets** *Br* the loo, *Am* the john; **c. noir** cubbyhole; **c. de toilette** (small) bathroom; **c. de travail** study **(b)** (*de pub*) agency; (*d'architectes, de notaire*) office; (*de médecin*) *Br* surgery, practice, *Am* office; **c. dentaire** dental surgery or practice **(c)** (*entreprise*) **c. conseil** consultancy; **c. juridique** law firm **(d)** *Pol* (*d'un ministre*) departmental staff

câble [kabl] *nm* **(a)** (*fil*) cable; **c. métallique** wire cable **(b)** *Vieilli* (*message*) cable

câbler [kable] *vt* **(a)** *TV* (*ville, quartier*) to install cable television in **(b)** *Vieilli* (*message*) to cable

câblo-opérateur (*pl* **câblo-opérateurs**) [kablooperatœr] *nm* cable company

cabochard, -e [kabɔʃar, -ard] *Fam* **1** *adj* pigheaded **2** *nm,f* pigheaded person

caboche [kabɔʃ] *nf Fam* (*tête*) nut; **mets-toi dans la c.!** get that into your thick skull!

cabosser [kabɔse] *vt* (*métal, voiture*) to bash up; (*chapeau*) to bash in; **un vieux chapeau cabossé** a battered old hat

cabot [kabo] *nm Fam* **(a)** (*chien*) pooch **(b)** (*acteur*) ham (actor)

cabotage [kabɔtaʒ] *nm Naut* coasting

caboteur [kabɔtœr] *nm Naut* coaster

cabotin, -e [kabɔtɛ̃, -in] **1** *adj* (*acteur*) ham **2** *nm,f* **(a)** (*acteur*) ham (actor, *f* actress) **(b)** (*vantard*) show-off

cabrer [kabre] **se cabrer** *vpr* (*cheval*) to rear (up); *Fig* (*personne*) to recoil

cabriole [kabrijɔl] *nf* (*saut, bond*) caper; (*en danse*) cabriole; (*en équitation*) capriole; (*de gymnaste*) somersault; **faire des cabrioles** to caper about

cabriolet [kabrijɔlɛ] *nm* **(a)** (*auto*) convertible **(b)** (*voiture à cheval*) cabriolet

CAC [kak] *n* (*abrév* **Compagnie des agents de change**) **le C.-40** = the Paris Stock Exchange index

caca [kaka] *nm* (*langage enfantin*) (*excrément*) poo; **faire c.** to do a poo; **c. d'oie** yellowish green

cacah(o)uète [kakawɛt] *nf* peanut

cacao [kakao] *nm* (*boisson, poudre*) cocoa; (*fève*) cocoa bean

cacaoui [kakawi] *nm Can* long-tailed duck

cacatoès [kakatɔɛs] *nm* cockatoo

cacatois [kakatwa] *nm Naut* (*voile*) royal sail; **(mât de) c.** royal mast

cachalot [kaʃalo] *nm* sperm whale

cache [kaʃ] **1** *nf* hiding place; **c. d'armes** arms cache **2** *nm* (*sur un texte*) masking card

caché, -e [kaʃe] *adj* hidden; (*sentiment*) secret

cache-cache [kaʃkaʃ] *nm* **jouer à c.** to play hide-and-seek

cache-col [kaʃkɔl] *nm inv Vieilli* scarf

Cachemire [kaʃmir] *nm* **le C.** Kashmir

cachemire [kaʃmir] *nm* (*laine*) cashmere; **à impression c.** paisley

cache-nez [kaʃne] *nm inv* scarf

cache-pot [kaʃpo] nm inv flowerpot holder

cacher [kaʃe] 1 vt to hide; **il ne cache pas que... he** makes no secret of the fact that...; **c. qch à qn** (omettre de lui dire) to hide sth from sb; **pour ne rien te c.** to be completely open with you; **je ne vous cache pas que j'ai été surpris** I won't pretend (that) I wasn't surprised; **le mur nous cache la vue** the wall hides our view

2 se cacher vpr (personne, soleil) to hide; **se c. de qn** to hide from sb; **sa timidité se cache derrière une certaine rudesse** his shyness is hidden behind a bluff exterior; **je ne m'en cache pas** I make no secret of it; **en se cachant** secretly; **sans se c.** openly

cache-sexe [kaʃsɛks] nm inv G-string; (d'indigène) apron

cachet [kaʃe] nm (a) (médicament) tablet, pill (b) (tampon) stamp; (sceau) seal; (de fabricant) (trade)mark; **c. de la poste** postmark (c) (style) (d'un endroit) character; (d'un vêtement) style (d) (salaire) fee

cacheter [42] [kaʃte] vt to seal

cachette [kaʃɛt] nf hiding place; **en c.** secretly; **boire en c.** (habituellement) to be a secret drinker; **faire qch en c. de qn** to do sth without sb's knowing

cachot [kaʃo] nm (a) (cellule) dungeon (b) (isolement) solitary confinement

cachotterie [kaʃɔtri] nf **faire des cachotteries** to be secretive

cachottier, -ère [kaʃɔtje, -ɛr] 1 adj secretive

2 nm,f secretive person; **petit c.!** you secretive little thing!

cachou [kaʃu] nm (bonbon) cachou (liquorice sweet)

cacophonie [kakɔfɔni] nf cacophony

cactus [kaktys] nm cactus

c.-à-d. (abrév **c'est-à-dire**) i.e.

cadastre [kadastr] nm (registre) cadastre; (administration) cadastral survey office

cadavérique [kadaverik] adj (teint) deathly pale; Méd cadaveric

cadavre [kadavr] nm (a) (de personne) corpse, (dead) body; (d'animal) carcass, body; Fam **c'est un c. ambulant** he's a walking skeleton (b) Fam (bouteille) empty

caddie [kadi] nm (a) Sp caddie (b) (chariot) Br trolley, Am cart

cadeau, -x [kado] nm present, gift; (avec un achat) free gift; **en c.** as a present; **en c. avec** (achat) free with; **faire un c. à qn** to give sb a present; **faire c. de qch à qn** (donner) to make sb a present of sth; Fam Fig **il ne lui a pas fait de cadeaux** he didn't spare him/her; Fam **ton frère, ce n'est pas un c.** your brother's a real pain; **c'est un c. empoisonné** it's more trouble than it's worth

cadenas [kadna] nm padlock

cadenasser [kadnase] 1 vt (porte, pièce) to padlock

2 se cadenasser vpr (personne) to lock oneself away

cadence [kadãs] nf (a) (rythme régulier) rhythm; (vitesse) rate; **en c.** in time; **c. de production** rate of production; **c. de tir** rate of fire

cadencé, -e [kadãse] adj (rythmé) rhythmic(al); **marcher au pas c.** to walk in time (b) Ordinat **c. à** running at

cadet, -ette [kadɛ, -ɛt] 1 adj (de deux) younger; (de plus de deux) youngest

2 nm,f (a) (de deux) younger (one); (de plus de deux) youngest (one); **il est mon c. de deux ans** he's two years younger than I am; **c'est le c. de mes soucis** that's the least of my worries (b) Sp junior (16 to 18 years old) (c) Hist & Mil cadet

cadrage [kadraʒ] nm Cin & Phot (de l'image) centring; (plan) frame; Ordinat positioning

cadran [kadrã] nm (d'horloge, de baromètre) face; (d'instrument, de téléphone) dial; Can (réveil) alarm-clock; Fig **faire le tour du c.** (dormir) to sleep round the clock; Aut **cadrans (de bord)** display panels; **c. solaire** sundial

cadre [kadr] nm (a) (de tableau, de porte, de vélo) frame (b) (domaine) limits; (structure) framework; **dans le c. de** within the framework of (c) (décor) setting; **c. (de vie)** environment (d) (dans un formulaire) box; Ordinat (pour graphique) box; **c. réservé à l'administration** (sur formulaire) for official use only (e) (dans une entreprise) executive, manager; **les cadres** the management; Mil the officers; **c. moyen** middle manager; **c. supérieur** senior executive; **jeune c. dynamique** dynamic young executive (f) **être rayé des cadres** to be dismissed

cadre-adresse (pl cadres-adresses) [kadradrɛs] nm address space

cadrer [kadre] 1 vt (photo) to centre; (plan) to frame; Ordinat to position

2 vi (correspondre) to tally (**avec** with)

cadreur [kadrœr] nm TV & Cin cameraman

caduc, caduque [kadyk] adj (a) (feuille) deciduous (b) Jur (accord) lapsed; (loi) null and void

caducée [kadyse] nm caduceus

CAF [seaɛf] (abrév **Caisse d'allocations familiales**) = child benefit office

cafard [kafar] nm (a) (insecte) cockroach (b) Fam **avoir le c.** ou **un coup de c.** to feel down or low (c) Fam (rapporteur) sneak

cafarder [kafarde] vi Fam (a) (rapporter) to sneak (b) (avoir le cafard) to feel down or low

cafardeur, -euse [kafardœr, -øz] nm,f Fam sneak

cafardeux, -euse [kafardø, -øz] adj Fam **se sentir** ou **être c.** to feel down or low

café [kafe] 1 nm (a) (produit, boisson) coffee; **glace au c.** coffee ice cream; **c. crème** white coffee; **c. décaféiné** decaffeinated coffee; **c. en grains** coffee beans; **c. au lait** white coffee; **c. liégeois** = coffee ice cream topped with whipped cream; **c. moulu** ground coffee; Suisse **c. nature** black coffee; **c. noir** black coffee; **c. en poudre** ou **instantané** instant coffee (b) (bar) café (also serving alcoholic drinks); **c. tabac** = café-cum-tobacconist's

2 adj inv (couleur) **c. (au lait)** coffee-coloured

caféine [kafein] nf caffeine

cafétéria [kafeterja] nf cafeteria

café-théâtre (pl cafés-théâtres) [kafeteatr] nm Br ≃ pub theatre

cafetier [kaftje] nm café owner

cafetière [kaftjɛr] nf (récipient) coffee pot; (électrique) coffee machine; **c. à pression** percolator

cafouillage [kafujaʒ] nm Fam (a) (confusion) muddle, shambles (b) (de moteur de voiture) misfiring

cafouiller [kafuje] vi Fam (a) (personne) to get into a muddle; (projet) to fall apart (b) (moteur de voiture) to misfire; (poste de télévision) to be on the blink

cage [kaʒ] *nf* (a) (*pour oiseaux, dans un zoo*) cage; (*pour poules*) coop; (*pour lapins*) hutch; **mettre un oiseau en c.** to put a bird in a cage; *Fam Fig* **c. à lapins** rabbit hutch (b) (*de foot*) goal (c) **c. d'ascenseur** lift *or Am* elevator shaft; **c. d'escalier** stairwell (d) *Anat* **c. thoracique** rib cage

cageot [kaʒo] *nm* (a) (*caisse*) crate (b) *Fam Péj* (*femme*) dog

cagibi [kaʒibi] *nm Fam* storage room

cagneux, -euse [kaɲø, -øz] *adj* **avoir les genoux c.** to have knock-knees

cagnotte [kaɲɔt] *nf* (*caisse commune*) kitty; (*de jeux*) pool; (*économies*) nest egg

cagoule [kagul] *nf* (*de moine*) cowl; (*de pénitent, de terroriste*) hood

cahier [kaje] *nm* (a) (*livre*) notebook; (*d'écolier*) exercise book; **c. de brouillon** rough book; **c. de textes** homework book (b) *Typ* signature (c) (*d'un journal*) section (d) **Cahiers de...** (*revue*) Journal of... (e) *Com* **c. des charges** (*d'un contrat*) terms and conditions; (*de fabrication*) specifications

cahin-caha [kaɛ̃kaa] *adv Fam* **aller c.** (*se déplacer*) to struggle along; **ça va, la santé? – ça va, c.** how are you keeping? – oh, so-so

cahot [kao] *nm* (*secousse*) jolt

cahoter [kaɔte] **1** *vt* **être cahoté** (*dans un véhicule*) to be jolted about
2 *vi* to jolt along

cahoteux, -euse [kaɔtø, -øz] *adj* bumpy

cahute [kayt] *nf* shack

caïd [kaid] *nm Fam* (*chef de bande*) gang leader; **un c. de la drogue** a drugs baron; **faire le c., jouer les caïds** to act high and mighty

caillasse [kajas] *nf Fam* loose stones

caille [kaj] *nf* quail; *Fam* **ma petite c.** my little dove

caillé [kaje] *nm* curds

caillebotis [kajbɔti] *nm* (a) *Naut* grating (b) (*plancher*) duckboard

caillebotte [kajbɔt] *nf* curds

cailler [kaje] **1** *vt* (*lait*) to curdle; (*sang*) to clot
2 *vi* (*lait*) to curdle; (*sang*) to clot; **faire c. du lait** to curdle milk (b) *Fam* **ça caille** it's freezing
3 **se cailler** *vpr Fam* **on (les) caille** it's freezing

caillot [kajo] *nm* (*de sang*) clot

caillou, -x [kaju] *nm* (a) (*petite pierre*) stone; (*sur la plage*) (b) *Fam* (*pierre précieuse*) stone (c) *Fam* (*tête*) nut, pebble; **il n'a plus un poil sur le c.** he's as bald as a coot

caillouteux, -euse [kajutø, -øz] *adj* (*route*) stony; (*plage*) pebbly

caïman [kaimɑ̃] *nm* cayman

Caire [kɛr] *voir* **Le Caire**

cairote [kerɔt] **1** *adj* of Cairo
2 *nmf* **C.** person from Cairo, Cairene

caisse [kɛs] *nf* (a) (*pour marchandises*) case; (*à outils*) box; (*de champagne, de vin*) case; (*pour plantes*) tub; (*de fruits*) crate (b) *Com & Fin* (*coffre*) cash box; (*d'une caisse enregistreuse*) till; (*où l'on paie*) (*dans un magasin*) cash desk; (*dans un supermarché*) checkout; **les caisses de l'État** the coffers of the State; **tenir la c.** (*dans un restaurant, dans un magasin*) to be the cashier; **passer à la c.** (*se faire licencier*) to be paid off; *Fam* (*payer*) to pay; *Fam* (*se faire payer*) to be paid; **c. (enregistreuse)** cash register; *Pol* **c. noire** slush fund (c) (*argent*) cash (in hand); **faire la ou sa c.** to do the till (d) (*organisme*) **c. d'allocations familiales** = child

benefit office; **c. d'épargne** savings bank; **Can c. populaire** credit union; **c. primaire d'assurance maladie** = French government department dealing with health insurance; **c. de retraite** pension fund (e) *Mus* **c. claire** snare drum; **c. de résonance** sound box (f) (*de piano, d'horloge*) case; (*de véhicule*) body (g) *très Fam* (*voiture*) car

caissette [kɛset] *nf* small box

caissier, -ère [kesje, -er] *nm,f* cashier; (*dans un supermarché*) checkout operator

caisson [kɛsɔ̃] *nm* (a) *Fam* **se faire sauter le c.** to blow one's brains out (b) *Archit* **plafond à caissons** coffered ceiling (c) (*de plongée*) caisson

cajoler [kaʒɔle] *vt* to cuddle

cajolerie [kaʒɔlri] *nf* cuddle

cajou [kaʒu] *nm* **noix c.** ou **noix c.**

cake [kek] *nm* fruit cake

cal (*pl* **cals**) [kal] *nm* (*durillon*) callus

calamar [kalamar] = **calmar**

calamine [kalamin] *nf* (*dépôt*) carbon deposits

calamité [kalamite] *nf* (*fléau*) calamity; (*malheur*) great misfortune; *Fam* **ce mec, c'est une vraie c.!** this guy is a real disaster!

calamiteux, -euse [kalamitø -øz] *adj* calamitous

calandre [kalɑ̃dr] *nf* (a) (*machine*) calender (b) *Aut* radiator grille

calanque [kalɑ̃k] *nf* deep narrow creek (*in the Mediterranean*)

calcaire [kalker] **1** *adj* (*sol, terrain*) chalky; (*roche*) calcareous; (*eau*) hard
2 *nm* (a) *Géol* limestone (b) (*dépôt*) fur

calcification [kalsifikasjɔ̃] *nf Méd* calcification

calciner [kalsine] **1** *vt* (*brûler*) to char; **calciné** (*trop cuit*) burnt to a cinder
2 **se calciner** *vpr* to burn

calcium [kalsjɔm] *nm* calcium

calcul¹ [kalkyl] *nm* (a) (*compte*) calculation; **faire un c.** to make a calculation (b) *Scol* **le c.** arithmetic; **c. mental** mental arithmetic (c) *Math* **c. différentiel/intégral** differential/integral calculus (d) (*prévision*) calculation; **agir par c.** to act from selfish motives; **faire un mauvais c.** to miscalculate

calcul² *nm Méd* stone, *Spéc* calculus; **c. biliaire/rénal** gall/kidney stone

calculateur, -trice [kalkylatœr, -tris] **1** *adj* (*personne, politique*) calculating
2 *nm Ordinat* (desktop) calculator; **c. (électronique)** (electronic) computer
3 *nf* **calculatrice (de poche)** (pocket) calculator

calculé, -e [kalkyle] *adj* (*insulte, risque*) calculated; (*méchanceté*) premeditated; (*insolence*) deliberate

calculer [kalkyle] **1** *vt* (*compter*) (*prix, superficie*) to work out, to calculate; (*comportement, propos*) to plan; (*conséquences, chances*) to weigh (up); **tout bien calculé** taking everything into account
2 *vi* to calculate; *Fig* (*économiser*) to count every penny

calculette [kalkylet] *nf* (pocket) calculator

Calcutta [kalkyta] *n* Calcutta

caldoche [kaldɔʃ] **1** *adj* White New Caledonian
2 *nmf* **C.** New Caledonian

cale¹ [kal] *nf Naut* (a) (*de navire*) hold; **à fond de c.** down in the hold (b) (*rampe*) **c. sèche** dry dock

cale² nf (pour meuble, pour porte) wedge; (pour bloquer une roue) chock

calé, -e [kale] adj Fam (a) (personne) être c. en qch to be well up in sth (b) (problème, question, devoir) tough

calebasse [kalbas] nf calabash

calèche [kalɛʃ] nf barouche

caleçif [kalsif] nm Fam Br pants, Am shorts

caleçon [kalsɔ̃] nm boxer shorts; (de femme) leggings; Vieilli c. de bain bathing trunks; Vieilli c. long long johns

calédonien, -enne [kaledɔnjɛ̃, -ɛn] 1 adj Caledonian
2 nm,f C. Caledonian

calembour [kalɑ̃bur] nm pun, play on words; faire des calembours to make puns

calendes [kalɑ̃d] nfpl renvoyer qch aux c. grecques to put sth off indefinitely

calendrier [kalɑ̃drije] nm (a) (système, tableau) calendar (b) (de voyage, de travail) timetable

cale-pied (pl cale-pieds) [kalpje] nm toe clip

calepin [kalpɛ̃] nm notebook

caler¹ [kale] 1 vt (a) (meuble, porte) to wedge; (roue) to chock; (chargement) to secure; c. un malade avec des coussins to prop up a patient with cushions (b) Fam (remplir) ça cale (l'estomac) it fills you up; je suis calé I'm full up
2 vi (moteur) to stall
3 se caler vpr (dans un fauteuil) to settle oneself comfortably

caler² vi (a) Fam (abandonner) to give up (b) Can (se dégarnir) to have a receding hairline

calfater [kalfate] vt Naut to caulk

calfeutrer [kalføtre] 1 vt (a) (brèches) to block up (b) (pièce, fenêtre) to draught-proof
2 se calfeutrer vpr (pour avoir chaud) to make oneself snug; (pour être seul) to shut oneself away

calibre [kalibr] nm (a) (d'arme à feu, de tuyau, de balle) calibre; (d'œufs, de fruits) grade; Fig sa sœur est d'un autre c. his sister is of quite a different calibre (b) (outil) gauge (c) très Fam (revolver) shooter

calibrer [kalibre] vt (pièce) to gauge; (instrument de mesure) to calibrate; Com (œufs, fruits) to grade

calice¹ [kalis] nm Rel chalice; Fig boire le c. jusqu'à la lie to drain the cup to the dregs

calice² nm Bot calyx

calife [kalif] nm caliph

Californie [kaliforni] nf la C. California

californien, -enne [kalifɔrnjɛ̃, -ɛn] 1 adj Californian
2 nm,f C. Californian

califourchon [kalifurʃɔ̃] à califourchon adv astride; se mettre à c. sur qch to sit astride sth

câlin, -e [kalɛ̃, -in] 1 adj affectionate
2 nm cuddle; faire un c. à qn to give sb a cuddle

câliner [kaline] vt to cuddle

calisson [kalisɔ̃] nm = lozenge-shaped sweet made of marzipan

calleux, -euse [kalø, -øz] adj callous

call-girl (pl call-girls) [kolgœrl] nf call girl

calligramme [kaligram] nm calligram

calligraphe [kaligraf] nmf calligrapher

calligraphie [kaligrafi] nf calligraphy

calmant, -e [kalmɑ̃, -ɑ̃t] Méd 1 adj (pour les nerfs) sedative; (pour la douleur) painkilling
2 nm (pour les nerfs) sedative; (pour la douleur) painkiller; sous calmants under sedation

calmar [kalmar] nm squid

calme [kalm] 1 adj (a) (personne) (qui garde son sang-froid) calm; (tranquille) quiet (b) (mer) calm; (ciel) clear; les affaires sont calmes en août business is quiet in August
2 nm (absence d'agitation) calm, calmness; (sang-froid) composure; (du paysage) peace and quiet; être au c. to have peace and quiet; du c.! (taisez-vous) keep quiet!; (ne vous affolez pas) keep calm!; garder/perdre son c. to keep/lose one's composure; Naut c. plat dead calm; c'est le c. plat dans ma vie sentimentale my love life is in the doldrums

calmement [kalməmɑ̃] adv calmly

calmer [kalme] 1 vt (personne) to calm (down); (craintes) to calm; (douleur) to soothe; (fièvre) to reduce; (soif) to quench; (faim) to appease; (ardeur, passion) to cool
2 se calmer vpr (personne) to calm down; (tempête, vent) to die down; (mer) to become calm; (pluie) to ease off; (douleur, fièvre) to subside

calomnie [kalɔmni] nf (en paroles) slander; (par écrit) libel

calomnier [66] [kalɔmnje] vt (en paroles) to slander; (par écrit) to libel

calomnieux, -euse [kalɔmnjø, -øz] adj (paroles) slanderous; (écrits) libellous

calorie [kalɔri] nf calorie; régime basses calories low-calorie diet

calorifère [kalɔrifɛr] 1 adj heat-conveying
2 nm Vieilli (slow-combustion) stove; Can radiator

calorifique [kalɔrifik] adj calorific

calorifuge [kalɔrifyʒ] 1 adj (heat-)insulating
2 nm heat insulation; (pour chaudière, tuyau) lagging

calorique [kalɔrik] adj calorific

calot [kalo] nm (coiffure militaire) Br forage cap, Am garrison cap

calotte [kalɔt] nf (a) (chapeau rond) skullcap; Rel calotte; (de chapeau) crown; très Fam Péj la c. (le clergé) the clergy (b) Fam (gifle) clout (c) Anat c. crânienne skullcap (d) Géol c. glaciaire ice cap

calque [kalk] nm (copie) tracing; Fig (de poème, de portrait) exact copy; (traduction) calque; prendre un c. de qch to make a tracing of sth; (papier) c. tracing paper

calquer [kalke] vt (reproduire) to trace; Fig to copy exactly; expression calquée sur l'anglais expression copied from the English; il calque sa conduite sur celle de son frère he models his behaviour on his brother's

calumet [kalymɛ] nm peace pipe; Fig fumer le c. de la paix to bury the hatchet

calvados [kalvados] nm Calvados

calvaire [kalvɛr] nm (a) (du Christ) calvary; Fig (épreuve pénible) ordeal (b) (croix) calvary

calviniste [kalvinist] adj & nmf Calvinist

calvitie [kalvisi] nf baldness; avoir un début de c. to be starting to go bald; c. précoce premature baldness

camaïeu, -x [kamajø] nm (peinture) monochrome; (gravure) tint drawing; un c. de bleu (papiers peints, vêtements) different shades of blue

camarade [kamarad] *nmf* friend; *Pol (terme d'adresse)* comrade; **c. de classe** classmate; **c. d'école** school friend

camaraderie [kamaradri] *nf* camaraderie

cambiste [kɑ̃bist] *nmf Fin* foreign exchange dealer

Cambodge [kɑ̃bɔdʒ] *nm* **le C.** Cambodia

cambodgien, -enne [kɑ̃bɔdʒjɛ̃, -ɛn] **1** *adj* Cambodian
2 *nm,f* **C.** Cambodian

cambouis [kɑ̃bwi] *nm* dirty oil

cambré, -e [kɑ̃bre] *adj (pied)* with a high instep; *(personne)* with an arched back

cambrer [kɑ̃bre] **1** *vt (dos, pied)* to arch; **c. la taille** *ou* **les reins** to arch one's back
2 se cambrer *vpr* to arch one's back

cambrien, -enne [kɑ̃brijɛ̃, -ɛn] *Géol* **1** *adj* Cambrian
2 le C. the Cambrian period

cambriolage [kɑ̃brijɔlaʒ] *nm* burglary, break-in

cambrioler [kɑ̃brijɔle] *vt (maison, personne)* Br to burgle, Am to burglarize

cambrioleur, -euse [kɑ̃brijɔlœr, -øz] *nm,f* burglar

cambrousse [kɑ̃brus], **cambrouse** [kɑ̃bruz] *nf Fam* country; **en pleine c.** in the middle of nowhere

cambrure [kɑ̃bryr] *nf (du pied, du dos)* arch; **c. des reins** small of the back

cambuse [kɑ̃byz] *nf* **(a)** *Naut* storeroom **(b)** *très Fam Vieilli (chambre)* hole

came¹ [kam] *nf Tech* cam

came² [kam] *nf très Fam (drogue)* dope

camé, -e [kame] *très Fam* **1** *adj* high
2 *nm,f* junkie

camée [kame] *nm* cameo

caméléon [kameleɔ̃] *nm aussi Fig* chameleon

camélia [kamelja] *nm* camellia

camelote [kamlɔt] *nf Fam* **(a)** *(pacotille)* junk **(b)** *(marchandise)* stuff

camembert [kamɑ̃bɛr] *nm* **(a)** *(fromage)* Camembert **(b)** *(diagramme)* pie-chart

camer [kame] **se camer** *vpr très Fam* to do drugs; **se c. à l'héroïne** to do heroin

caméra [kamera] *nf Cin & TV* camera; **c. cachée** *ou* **invisible** *(émission)* candid camera; **c. de télévision** television camera; **c. vidéo** video camera

cameraman [kameraman] *(pl* **cameramans** *ou* **cameramen** [kameramɛn]) *nm Cin & TV* cameraman

Cameroun [kamrun] *nm* **le C.** Cameroon

camerounais, -e [kamrunɛ, -ɛz] **1** *adj* Cameroonian
2 *nm,f* **C.** Cameroonian

Caméscope® [kameskɔp] *nm* camcorder

camion [kamjɔ̃] *nm Br* lorry, *Am* truck; **c. à benne** dump truck; **c. de déménagement** removal van; **c. de dépannage** breakdown truck; **c. frigorifique** *ou* **réfrigéré** refrigerated lorry

camion-benne *(pl* **camions-bennes** [kamjɔ̃bɛn]) *nm* dumper truck

camion-citerne *(pl* **camions-citernes** [kamjɔ̃sitɛrn]) *nm* tanker

camionnette [kamjɔnɛt] *nf* van; **c. de livraison** delivery van

camionneur [kamjɔnœr] *nm* **(a)** *(conducteur)* Br lorry driver, *Am* truck driver **(b)** *(transporteur)* Br haulier, *Am* trucker

camisole [kamizɔl] *nf* **(a)** *Can (tricot de corps)* Br vest, *Am* undershirt **(b)** *(chemise de nuit)* nightshirt **(c)** **c. de force** straitjacket

camomille [kamɔmij] *nf* camomile; *(tisane)* camomile tea

camouflage [kamuflaʒ] *nm Mil* camouflage; *(de la vérité, d'intentions)* disguising; *(de bénéfices)* concealment

camoufler [kamufle] **1** *vt Mil* to camouflage; *(vérité, intentions)* to disguise; *(bénéfices)* to conceal; **c. un meurtre en suicide** to make a murder look like suicide
2 se camoufler *vpr* to camouflage oneself

camp [kɑ̃] *nm* **(a)** *(campement)* camp; **établir un c.** to pitch camp; **lever le c.** to strike camp; *Fam Fig (partir)* to hit the road; **c. (de vacances)** *Br (children's)* holiday camp, *Am* summer camp; **c. de concentration** concentration camp; **c. de loisirs** holiday camp; **c. de prisonniers** prison camp **(b)** *(parti)* camp, side **(c)** *(de jeux)* side; **faire deux camps** to form two teams

campagnard, -e [kɑ̃paɲar, -ard] *adj* country

campagne [kɑ̃paɲ] *nf* **(a)** *(par opposition à la ville)* country; *(paysage)* countryside; **à la c.** in the country; **en pleine c.** deep in the countryside; **en rase c.** in the open country **(b)** *Mil, Pol & Com (campagne)* Pol **entrer en c.** to go on the campaign trail; **faire c. pour/contre** to campaign for/against; **partir en c. contre le tabac** to launch an anti-smoking campaign; **c. électorale** election campaign; **c. de presse** press campaign; **c. publicitaire** *ou* **de publicité** advertising campaign

campanile [kɑ̃panil] *nm Archit* bell tower

campanule [kɑ̃panyl] *nf* campanula

campement [kɑ̃pmɑ̃] *nm (installation)* camp; *(lieu)* camping place; **établir un c.** to pitch camp

camper [kɑ̃pe] **1** *vi* **(a)** *(faire du camping)* to camp **(b)** *Fig (chez quelqu'un)* to camp out
2 *vt* **(a)** *Vieilli* **c. son chapeau sur sa tête** to plant one's hat on one's head **(b)** *(décrire)* to put in context; **c. un personnage** *(sujet: acteur)* to play a part effectively
3 se camper *vpr* **se c. devant qn** to plant oneself in front of sb

campeur, -euse [kɑ̃pœr, -øz] *nm,f* camper

camphre [kɑ̃fr] *nm* camphor

camphré, -e [kɑ̃fre] *adj* camphorated

camping [kɑ̃piŋ] *nm* **(a)** *(activité)* camping; **faire du c.** to go camping; **c. à la ferme** farm camping; **c. sauvage** unauthorized camping **(b)** *(lieu)* camp site; **c. aménagé** camp site with facilities

camping-car *(pl* **camping-cars** [kɑ̃piŋkar]) *nm* camper

camping-caravaning [kɑ̃piŋkaravaniŋ] *nm* camping-caravanning

Camping-Gaz® [kɑ̃piŋgaz] *nm inv* camping stove

campus [kɑ̃pys] *nm* campus; **habiter sur le c.** to live on campus

camus [kamy] *adj m (nez)* flat

Canada [kanada] *nm* **le C.** Canada

Canadair® [kanader] *nm* fire-fighting plane

canadianisme [kanadjanism] *nm Ling* Canadianism

canadien, -enne [kanadjɛ̃, -ɛn] **1** *adj* Canadian
2 *nm,f* **C.** Canadian
3 *nf* **canadienne** *(veste)* sheepskin jacket; *(tente)* ridge tent

canaille [kanɑj] **1** *adj (chanson, paroles)* vulgar; *(air)* roguish
2 *nf (crapule)* scoundrel; **petite c.!** *(à un enfant)* you little devil!

canal, -aux [kanal, -o] *nm* **(a)** *(cours d'eau)* canal; **c. d'irrigation** irrigation canal; **le c. de Panama/de Suez** the Panama/Suez Canal **(b)** *(conduite)* conduit **(c)** *Anat & Bot* duct **(d)** *Rad & TV* channel; **TV C. +** = French pay television channel **(e)** *Fig (moyen)* channel; **par le c. de la poste** through the post **(f)** *Com* channel; **c. de distribution** distribution channel

canalisation [kanalizasjɔ̃] *nf* **(a)** *(conduite)* pipe; *(pour pétrole)* pipeline **(b)** *(de rivière)* canalization

canaliser [kanalize] *vt* **(a)** *(région, rivière)* to canalize **(b)** *(énergie)* to channel; *(trafic, foule)* to direct

canapé [kanape] *nm* **(a)** *(meuble)* sofa, couch; **c. convertible** sofa bed; **c. deux places** two-seater sofa **(b)** *(pour l'apéritif)* canapé

canapé-lit *(pl* **canapés-lits)** [kanapeli] *nm* sofa bed

canaque [kanak] **1** *adj* Kanak *(of New Caledonia)*
2 *nmf* **C.** Kanak *(from New Caledonia)*

canard [kanar] *nm* **(a)** *(oiseau)* duck; *(mâle)* drake; *Fam* **mon petit c.** my pet; **marcher en c.** to walk with one's feet turned out; **c. laqué** Peking duck; **c. à l'orange** duck à l'orange; **c. sauvage** wild duck **(b)** *Fam (journal)* rag **(c)** *(morceau de sucre)* = sugar lump dipped in coffee or alcoholic drink **(d)** *Mus* false note

canarder [kanarde] *vt Fam* to snipe at

canari [kanari] *nm* canary

Canaries [kanari] *nfpl* **les (îles) C.** the Canary Islands

canasson [kanasɔ̃] *nm Fam (cheval)* nag

cancan [kɑ̃kɑ̃] *nm* **(a)** *cancans (ragots)* gossip **(sur** about) **(b)** *(danse)* cancan

cancaner [kɑ̃kane] *vi* **(a)** *(médire)* to gossip **(sur** about) **(b)** *(canard)* to quack

cancanier, -ère [kɑ̃kanje, -ɛr] *Fam* **1** *adj* gossipy
2 *nm,f* gossip

cancer [kɑ̃ser] *nm* **(a)** *Méd & Fig* cancer; **c. du poumon/du sein** lung/breast cancer; **avoir un c.** to have cancer **(b)** *Astron & Astrol* **le C.** Cancer; **être C.** to be **(a)** Cancer

cancéreux, -euse [kɑ̃serø, -øz] **1** *adj (tumeur)* cancerous
2 *nm,f* cancer sufferer

cancérigène [kɑ̃seriʒɛn] *adj* carcinogenic; **produit c.** carcinogen

cancérologie [kɑ̃serɔlɔʒi] *nf* cancerology

cancérologue [kɑ̃serɔlɔg] *nmf* cancer specialist

cancre [kɑ̃kr] *nm Fam* dunce

cancrelat [kɑ̃krəla] *nm* cockroach

candélabre [kɑ̃delabr] *nm (chandelier)* candelabra

candeur [kɑ̃dœr] *nf* guilelessness; **un regard plein de c.** a guileless look

candi [kɑ̃di] *adj m voir* **sucre**

candidat, -e [kɑ̃dida, -at] *nm,f (à un poste)* applicant *(à* for); *(à un examen)* candidate *(à* for); **être c. aux élections** to stand *or* run for election

candidature [kɑ̃didatyr] *nf (aux élections)* candidature; *(à un poste)* application *(à* for); **poser sa c. à un poste** to apply for a post; **c. spontanée** unsolicited application

candide [kɑ̃did] *adj* guileless

candidement [kɑ̃didmɑ̃] *adv* guilelessly

candidose [kɑ̃didoz] *nf Méd* candidiasis

cane [kan] *nf (femelle)* duck

caneton [kantɔ̃] *nm (male)* duckling

canette¹ [kanet] *nf (petite cane)* (female) duckling

canette² = **cannette**

canevas [kanva] *nm* **(a)** *(trame)* canvas **(b)** *(de film, de roman)* outline

caniche [kaniʃ] *nm* poodle

canicule [kanikyl] *nf* heatwave

canif [kanif] *nm* penknife

canin, -e [kanɛ̃, -in] **1** *adj* canine; **exposition canine** dog show
2 *nf* **canine** (tooth)

caniveau, -x [kanivo] *nm* gutter

cannabis [kanabis] *nm* cannabis

cannage [kanaʒ] *nm (partie en rotin)* canework

canne [kan] *nf* **(a)** *(tige)* cane; **c. à pêche** fishing rod; **c. à sucre** sugar cane **(b)** *(pour s'appuyer)* (walking) stick; **c. blanche** white stick **(c)** *très Fam (jambe)* leg, pin

canné, -e [kane] *adj (chaise)* cane

canneberge [kanberʒ] *nf* cranberry

cannelé, -e [kanle] *adj (colonne)* fluted; *(pneu)* grooved

cannelle [kanɛl] *nf* cinnamon; **bâton de c.** cinnamon stick; **à la c.** cinnamon(-flavoured)

cannelloni [kaneloni] *nmpl* cannelloni

cannelure [kanlyr] *nf (rainure)* groove; *(de colonne)* fluting

cannette [kanet] *nf* **(a)** *(petite bouteille)* bottle; *(boîte)* can **(b)** *Tex* spool

cannibale [kanibal] **1** *nmf* cannibal
2 *adj (pratiques)* cannibalistic; **tribu c.** tribe of cannibals

cannibalisme [kanibalism] *nm* cannibalism

canoë [kanoe] *nm* canoe; **faire du c.** to go canoeing

canoë-kayak [kanoekajak] *nm* canoeing

canon¹ [kanɔ̃] *nm* **(a)** *(pièce d'artillerie)* gun; *Hist* cannon **(b)** *(de carabine)* barrel **(c)** *Anciennement (mesure)* = wine measure equivalent to 0.058 l; *Fam* **boire un c.** to have a glass of wine

canon² **1** *nm* **(a)** *Rel & Fig (règle)* canon **(b)** *Mus* canon; **c. à deux/trois voix** canon for two/three voices; **chanter qch en c.** to sing sth in canon **(c)** *Fam (personne)* stunner
2 *adj inv Fam (beau)* stunning

canonique [kanɔnik] *adj* canonical; *Fig* **être d'un âge c.** to be advanced in years

canoniser [kanɔnize] *vt Rel* to canonize

canonnade [kanɔnad] *nf* gunfire; **une c.** a burst of gunfire

canot [kano] *nm Naut* **(a)** *(petit bateau)* boat; **c. pneumatique** rubber dinghy; **c. de sauvetage** lifeboat **(b)** *Can (canoë)* canoe

canotage [kanɔtaʒ] *nm* boating; *Can (en canoë)* canoeing; **faire du c.** to go boating/canoeing

canoter [kanɔte] *vi Naut* to go boating; *Can (en canoë)* to go canoeing

canotier [kanɔtje] *nm* **(a)** *(rameur)* rower **(b)** *(chapeau)* boater

cantal, -als [kɑ̃tal] *nm* Cantal

cantate [kɑ̃tat] *nf* cantata

cantatrice [kɑ̃tatris] *nf (chanteuse d'opéra)* opera singer; *(de concert)* (concert) singer

cantine [kɑ̃tin] *nf* **(a)** *(réfectoire)* canteen; *(à l'école)* dining hall; **déjeuner à la c.** *(de l'école)* to have school meals **(b)** *(malle)* trunk

cantique [kɑ̃tik] *nm* Rel hymn; **le C. des cantiques** the Song of Solomon

canton [kɑ̃tɔ̃] *nm (en France)* canton *(administrative division of a department)*; *(en Suisse)* canton *(semi-autonomous administrative region of Switzerland)*; **Can les cantons de l'Est** the Eastern Townships

cantonade [kɑ̃tɔnad] **à la cantonade** *adv* to everybody present; *(au théâtre)* off

cantonais, -e [kɑ̃tɔnɛ, -ɛz] **1** *adj* Cantonese
2 *nm,f* C. Cantonese
3 *nm (langue)* Cantonese

cantonal, -e, -aux, -ales [kɑ̃tɔnal, -o] *adj* cantonal; **les (élections) cantonales** the cantonal elections

cantonnement [kɑ̃tɔnmɑ̃] *nm* Mil *(des troupes)* quartering; *(lieu)* quarters

cantonner [kɑ̃tɔne] **1** *vt (a) Mil (troupes)* to quarter **(b) c. qn dans/à** to confine sb to
2 se cantonner *vpr (se limiter)* **se c. dans/à** to confine oneself to

cantonnier [kɑ̃tɔnje] *nm* roadmender; *Rail* lineman

canular [kanylar] *nm* Fam hoax; **monter un c.** to play a hoax

canule [kanyl] *nf Méd* cannula

canyon [kanjɔ̃] *nm* canyon; **le Grand C.** the Grand Canyon

CAO [seao] *nf Ordinat (abrév* **conception assistée par ordinateur)** CAD

caoutchouc [kautʃu] *nm* **(a)** *(substance)* rubber; **C. Mousse®** foam rubber; **c. synthétique** synthetic rubber **(b)** *(plante)* rubber plant

caoutchouteux, -euse [kautʃutø, -øz] *adj* Péj rubbery

CAP [seɑpe] *nm (abrév* **certificat d'aptitude professionnelle)** = vocational training certificate

Cap [kap] *voir* **Le Cap**

cap [kap] *nm* **(a)** *Géog* cape, headland; **passer ou franchir ou doubler un c.** to round a cape; **quand on a franchi le c. de la quarantaine** when you've turned forty; **notre usine va passer le c. des mille employés** our factory will soon pass the thousand-employee mark; **le c. de Bonne-Espérance** the Cape of Good Hope; **le c. Horn** Cape Horn **(b)** *Naut & Av (direction)* course; **mettre le c. sur...** to set course for...

capable [kapabl] *adj* **(a)** *(susceptible)* **être c. de qch** to be capable of sth; **être c. de faire qch** to be capable of doing sth, to be able to do sth; **il est c. de tout** he's capable of anything; **c. du meilleur comme du pire** capable of the best as well as the worst; **elle est bien c. d'oublier les clefs!** she's quite capable of forgetting the keys! **(b)** *(compétent)* capable, able **(c)** *Jur* competent *(de faire* to do)

capacité [kapasite] *nf* **(a)** *(contenance)* capacity; **c. d'accueil** *(d'un hôtel)* accommodation capacity **(b)** *(aptitude)* ability, capability; **de grandes capacités (intellectuelles)** great intellectual abilities; *Ordinat* **c. d'adressage** address capability; **c. de concentration** attention span; *Ordinat* **c. de mémoire** memory capacity **(c)** *Jur* capacity; **avoir c. pour faire qch** to be (legally) entitled to do sth **(d)** *Univ* **c. en droit** = certificate entitling holder to practise in some branches of the legal profession

cape [kap] *nf (vêtement)* cape; *(plus longue)* cloak; **film/roman de c. et d'épée** swashbuckling film/novel; *Fig* **rire sous c.** to laugh up one's sleeve

capeline [kaplin] *nf (chapeau)* floppy hat

CAPES [kapɛs] *nm (abrév* **certificat d'aptitude au professorat de l'enseignement du second degré)** = postgraduate teaching certificate

CAPET [kapɛt] *nm (abrév* **certificat d'aptitude au professorat de l'enseignement technique)** = postgraduate technical teaching certificate

capétien, -enne [kapesjɛ̃, -ɛn] **1** *adj* Capetian
2 *nmpl* **les Capétiens** the Capetians

capharnaüm [kafarnaɔm] *nm* Fam *(pièce en désordre)* pigsty; *(désordre)* mess

capillaire [kapiler] **1** *adj* capillary
2 *nm* **(a)** *(plante)* maidenhair (fern) **(b)** *Anat* capillary

capillarité [kapilarite] *nf* Phys capillarity

capilotade [kapilɔtad] **en capilotade** *adv* **j'ai le dos en c.** my back's killing me

capitaine [kapiten] *nm* **(a)** Mil & Naut captain; *Av Br* flight lieutenant, *Am* captain; **c. de gendarmerie** police superintendent; **c. des pompiers** fire chief; **c. de port** harbour master **(b)** Sp captain

capitainerie [kapitenri] *nf* harbour master's office

capital, -e, -aux, -ales [kapital, -o] **1** *adj* **(a)** *(essentiel)* major; **il est c. qu'il soit présent à la réunion** it is essential for him to be at the meeting **(b)** *Typ* **lettre capitale** capital letter
2 *nm* Fin capital; *Fig (culturel, artistique)* wealth; **posséder un c.** to have some capital; **capitaux propres** equity; **c. social** (issued) share capital
3 *nf* **capitale (a)** *(ville)* capital (city) **(b)** *Typ* capital; **écrire en capitales d'imprimerie** to write in block letters

capitalisable [kapitalizabl] *adj (intérêts)* capitalizable

capitalisation [kapitalizasjɔ̃] *nf (d'intérêts)* capitalization

capitaliser [kapitalize] **1** *vt (intérêts)* to capitalize
2 *vi* to save

capitalisme [kapitalism] *nm* capitalism

capitaliste [kapitalist] *adj & nmf* capitalist

capiteux, -euse [kapitø, -øz] *adj (vin, parfum)* heady; *(charme)* sensuous; *(femme)* alluring

capitonnage [kapitɔnaʒ] *nm (action, matière)* padding, stuffing

capitonné, -e [kapitɔne] *adj (siège, cellule)* padded

capitulation [kapitylasjɔ̃] *nf* surrender; **c. sans conditions** unconditional surrender

capituler [kapityle] *vi* to surrender

caporal, -aux [kapɔral, -o] *nm* Mil Br lance corporal, Am private first class

capot¹ [kapo] *nm Aut Br* bonnet, *Am* hood; *Av (de moteur d'avion)* cowl; *Naut (bâche)* tarpaulin; *Ordinat* c. d'imprimante printer hood

capot² *adj inv* être c. *(aux cartes)* to have made no tricks at all

capote [kapɔt] *nf (a) Aut (de décapotable) Br* hood, *Am* top; **baisser la c.** to put the hood down **(b)** *Mil (manteau)* greatcoat **(c)** *Fam* c. **(anglaise)** rubber

capoté, -e [kapote] *adj Can Fam* annoyed

capoter [kapote] *vi Naut* to capsize; *Aut & Av* to overturn; *Fig (échouer) (projet)* to fall through

cappuccino [kaput∫ino] *nm* cappuccino

câpre [kɑpr] *nf* caper

caprice [kapris] *nm (a) (fantaisie)* whim, caprice; **on lui passe tous ses caprices** they indulge his/her every whim; **par un c. du destin** by a whim of fate **(b)** *(crise de colère)* tantrum; **faire un c.** to throw a tantrum

capricieux, -euse [kaprisjø, -øz] *adj (personne, courant, vent)* capricious; *(moteur)* temperamental; *(temps)* changeable

capricorne [kaprikɔrn] *nm (a) (insecte)* capricorn beetle **(b)** *Astron & Astrol* **le C.** Capricorn; **être C.** to be (a) Capricorn

caprin, -e [kaprɛ̃, -in] *adj Zool* goat, *Spéc* caprine

capsule [kapsyl] *nf (a) Anat, Bot & Méd* capsule **(b)** *(de bouteille)* cap, top **(c)** c. **(spatiale)** (space) capsule

capter [kapte] *vt (a) (l'attention de quelqu'un)* to gain, to capture **(b)** *(courant électrique)* to pick up; *(eaux)* to harness **(c)** *Rad & Tél (messages, station)* to pick up

capteur [kaptœr] *nm Phys* sensor; *Ordinat* c. **photosensible** photosensitive sensor; **c. solaire** solar panel

captif, -ive [kaptif, -iv] *adj & nm,f* captive

captivant, -e [kaptivɑ̃, -ɑ̃t] *adj* captivating

captiver [kaptive] *vt* to captivate

captivité [kaptivite] *nf* captivity; **en c.** in captivity

capture [kaptyr] *nf (a) (d'un ennemi, d'un animal)* capture **(b)** *(proie)* catch **(c)** *Ordinat* c. **vidéo** video capture

capturer [kaptyre] *vt* to capture

capuche [kapy∫] *nf* hood; *(de poche)* rainhood

capuchon [kapy∫ɔ̃] *nm (a) (de manteau)* hood; *(de moine)* cowl **(b)** *(de stylo, de tube de dentifrice)* cap, top; *(de cheminée)* cowl

capucine [kapysin] *nf* nasturtium

capverdien, -enne [kapvɛrdjɛ̃, -ɛn] **1** *adj* of Cape Verde

2 *nm,f* **C.** = person from Cape Verde

Cap-Vert [kapvɛr] *nm* **le C., les îles du C.** Cape Verde

caquelon [kaklɔ̃] *nm* fondue dish

caquet [kakɛ] *nm (a) (de poules)* cackle **(b)** *Fam (bavardage)* prattle; **quel c. elle a!** she doesn't half prattle on!; **rabattre** *ou* **rabaisser le c. à qn** to shut sb up

caqueter [42] [kakte] *vi (a) (poule)* to cackle **(b)** *Fam (bavarder)* to prattle

car¹ [kar] *conj* for, because

car² *nm (véhicule)* bus, *Br* coach; **c. de police** police van; **c. de ramassage scolaire** school bus

carabine [karabin] *nf* rifle; **c. à air comprimé** air gun

carabiné, -e [karabine] *adj Fam (vent)* stiff; *(orage, fièvre)* violent; *(rhume)* stinking

carabinier [karabinje] *nm (a) (en Espagne)* frontier guard **(b)** *(en Italie)* carabiniere **(c)** *Hist* carabineer

Caracas [karakas] *n* Caracas

caraco [karako] *nm* camisole

caracoler [karakɔle] *vi (cheval)* to caracole; *Fam (sautiller)* to prance about

caractère [karaktɛr] *nm (a) (nature)* character, nature; *(détermination, style)* character; **avoir bon c.** to be good-natured; **avoir mauvais** *ou* **sale c.** to be bad-tempered; *Fam* **avoir un c. de cochon** to have a foul temper; **ce n'est pas dans son c. de...** it's not in his nature to... **(b)** *(attribut)* characteristic, feature; *(aspect)* nature, character; **publication à c. officiel** publication of an official nature; *Biol* **c. héréditaire/acquis** hereditary/acquired characteristic **(c)** *(signe)* character, letter; *Typ* **caractères** *(en métal)* type; **en petits caractères** in small print; **écrivez en caractères d'imprimerie** *(sur formulaire)* write in block letters **(d)** *Ordinat* character; **c. de changement de ligne** line feed character; **c. de changement de page** page break character; **c. de contrôle** control character; **c. d'effacement** delete character; **c. imprimable** printable character; **c. d'interruption** break character; **c. en mode point** bitmap character; **c. de retour arrière** backspace character; **c. à sept bits** seven-bit character

caractériel, -elle [karakterjɛl] *Psy* **1** *adj (troubles)* emotional; **enfant c.** problem child

2 *nm,f* emotionally disturbed person; *(enfant)* problem child

caractérisé, -e [karakterize] *adj* **une rougeole caractérisée** a clear case of measles; **c'est de la méchanceté caractérisée** it's sheer spite

caractériser [karakterize] **1** *vt* to characterize; **la bonté qui la caractérise** her characteristic kindness

2 se caractériser *vpr* **se c. par** to be characterized by

caractéristique [karakteristik] **1** *adj* characteristic *(de* of*)*

2 *nf (particularité)* characteristic, feature; **caractéristiques** *(d'une voiture, d'un avion)* specifications

carafe [karaf] *nf (a) (pour le vin, l'eau)* carafe; *(pour le whisky)* decanter **(b)** *Fam* **rester en c.** to be (left) stranded

carafon [karafɔ̃] *nm (pour le vin)* small carafe; *(pour le whisky)* small decanter

Caraïbes [karaib] *nfpl* **les C.** the Caribbean

carambolage [karɑ̃bɔlaʒ] *nm (multiple)* pile-up

caramboler [karɑ̃bɔle] **se caramboler** *vpr Fam* to collide

caramel [karamɛl] *nm (sucre brûlé)* caramel; **des caramels** *(mous)* fudge; *(durs)* toffees

caraméliser [karamelize] *vt & vi* to caramelize

carapace [karapas] *nf aussi Fig* shell

carapater [karapate] **se carapater** *vpr Fam* to beat it

carat [kara] *nm* carat; **or (à) 18 carats** 18-carat gold; *Fam* **tu as jusqu'à trois heures, dernier c.** you've got until three o'clock at the latest

caravanage [karavanaʒ] **= caravaning**

caravane [karavan] *nf (a) (de tourisme)* caravan, *Am* trailer **(b)** *(du désert)* caravan

caravaning [karavaniŋ] *nm* caravanning; **faire du c.** to go caravanning

carbonate [karbɔnat] *nm Chim* carbonate; **c. de soude** sodium carbonate; *(dans le commerce)* washing soda

carbone [karbon] *nm Chim* carbon; **c. 14** carbon-14; **datation au c. 14** carbon dating; **(papier) c.** carbon (paper)

carbonique [karbonik] *adj* carbonic; **gaz c.** carbon dioxide; **neige c.** dry ice

carbonisé, -e [karbonize] *adj (nourriture)* burnt to a cinder; *(corps)* charred; **mourir c.** to burn to death

carburant [karbyrã] *nm* fuel

carburateur [karbyratœr] *nm Aut* carburettor

carbure [karbyr] *nm Chim* carbide; **c. d'hydrogène** hydrogen carbide

carburer [karbyre] *vi* **(a)** *(moteur)* **mal c.** to be badly tuned **(b)** *Fam* **ça carbure ici** everyone here's working like mad; **il carbure au café** coffee keeps him going

carcajou [karkaʒu] *nm* wolverine

carcan [karkã] *nm Fig* yoke; **le c. des horaires** scheduling constraints

carcasse [karkas] *nf* **(a)** *(d'animal mort)* carcass; *Fam (de personne)* body **(b)** *(de maison, de bateau)* shell; **à c. radiale** *(pneu)* radial-ply

carcéral, -e, -aux, -ales [karseral, -o] *adj* prison

carcinogène [karsinoʒɛn] *adj Méd* carcinogenic

cardan [kardã] *nm* universal joint

carder [karde] *vt* to card

cardiaque [kardjak] **1** *adj (arrêt, massage)* cardiac; **être c.** to have a heart condition
2 *nmf* person with a heart condition

cardigan [kardigã] *nm* cardigan

cardinal, -e, -aux, -ales [kardinal, -o] **1** *adj (point, nombre, vertu)* cardinal
2 *nm (religieux)* cardinal

cardiologie [kardjoloʒi] *nf* cardiology

cardiologue [kardjolog] *nmf* cardiologist

cardio-vasculaire [*pl* **cardio-vasculaires**) [kardjovaskyler] *adj* cardiovascular

carême [karɛm] *nm* **(a)** *(période)* **le c.** Lent **(b)** *(jeûne)* fast; **faire c.** to fast

carence [karãs] *nf (manque)* deficiency; **c. en vitamine E** vitamin E deficiency; **c. alimentaire** nutritional deficiency; **c. affective** emotional deprivation

carène [karɛn] *nf* hull

caréner [34] [karene] *vt* **(a)** *Naut* to careen **(b)** *Av & Aut* to streamline

caressant, -e [karesã, -ãt] *adj* affectionate; **d'une voix caressante** affectionately

caresse [kares] *nf* caress; **faire des caresses à** *(personne)* to caress; *(animal)* to stroke

caresser [karese] *vt (personne)* to caress; *(animal)* to stroke; *Fig (espoir, rêve)* to cherish

car-ferry (*pl* **car-ferrys**) [karferi] *nm* car ferry

cargaison [kargezõ] *nf* cargo; *Fam* **il est arrivé avec une c. de cadeaux** he arrived weighed down with presents

cargo [kargo] *nm Naut* freighter

cariatide [karjatid] *nf* caryatid

caribou [karibu] *nm* caribou

caricatural, -e, -aux, -ales [karikatyral, -o] *adj (récit, description)* caricatured

caricature [karikatyr] *nf* caricature

caricaturer [karikatyre] *vt* to caricature

caricaturiste [karikatyrist] *nmf* caricaturist

carie [kari] *nf* **c. (dentaire)** tooth decay; *Spéc* dental caries; **avoir une c.** to have a cavity

carié, -e [karje] *adj* decayed

carier [66] [karje] **se carier** *vpr* to rot, to decay

carillon [karijõ] *nm* **(a)** *(sonnerie)* chimes; **c. électrique** doorbell **(b)** *(ensemble de cloches)* bells **(c)** *(horloge)* chiming clock

carillonner [karijone] **1** *vi (cloches)* to chime; **c. à la porte** to ring the (door)bell loudly
2 *vt (air)* to chime; *(fête religieuse)* to announce with a peal of bells

carioca [karjoka] **1** *adj* of Rio de Janeiro
2 *nmf* C. person from Rio de Janeiro

caritatif, -ive [karitatif, -iv] *adj* charitable; **association caritative** charity

carlingue [karlɛ̃g] *nf* **(a)** *Av* cabin **(b)** *Naut* keelson

carmélite [karmelit] *nf* Carmelite (nun)

carmin [karmɛ̃] **1** *nm* carmine
2 *adj inv* carmine, crimson

carnage [karnaʒ] *nm* carnage

carnassier, -ère [karnasje, -ɛr] **1** *adj (animal)* flesh-eating; *Fig (sourire)* cruel
2 *nm* carnivore

carnaval, -als [karnaval] *nm* carnival; **un masque de c.** a carnival mask

carnet [karnɛ] *nm (cahier)* notebook; *(de tickets de métro)* = book of ten tickets; *Scol* **c. (de notes)** report card; **c. d'adresses** address book; **c. de chèques** cheque book; *Scol* **c. de correspondance** = book of forms to be completed by parents of schoolchildren in the event of absence; *Journ* **c. mondain** society column; **c. de santé** health record; **c. de timbres** book of stamps

carnivore [karnivor] **1** *adj (animal)* carnivorous
2 *nm* carnivore

Caroline [karolin] *nf* **la C. du Nord/du Sud** North/South Carolina

carolingien, -enne [karolɛ̃ʒjɛ̃, -ɛn] **1** *adj* Carolingian
2 *nmpl* **les Carolingiens** the Carolingians

carotène [karoten] *nm* carotene

carotide [karotid] *nf* carotid

carotte [karot] **1** *nf (a) (légume)* carrot; **la c. et** *ou* **le bâton** the carrot and the stick; *Fam* **les carottes sont cuites** you've/he's/*etc* had it **(b)** *(enseigne)* tobacconist's sign
2 *adj inv* **cheveux (roux) c.** carroty hair

carotter [karote] *vt Fam (objet, argent)* to pinch, *Br* to nick; **il m'a carotté 50 francs** he cheated me out of 50 francs

caroube [karub] *nf* carob (bean)

Carpates [karpat] *nfpl* **les C.** the Carpathians

carpe¹ [karp] *nm Anat* carpus

carpe² *nf* carp

carpette [karpet] *nf* rug; *Fam Péj* **c'est une vraie c.** he's a doormat

carquois [karkwa] *nm* quiver

carre [kar] *nf (de patin, de ski)* edge

carré, -e [kare] **1** *adj* (a) *(figure, jardin, visage)* square; *(épaules)* square, broad (b) *Math* **10 mètres carrés** 10 square metres (c) *(tranché) (personne)* straightforward; **être c. en affaires** to be straightforward in one's business dealings

2 *nm* (a) *(forme)* square; *Can (place)* (public) square; **c. de soie** silk scarf; *Naut* **c. des officiers** wardroom; **c. de valets** *(aux cartes)* four jacks; **avoir une coupe au c.** *ou* **un c.** to have one's hair in a bob; *Fam* **faire la tête au c. à qn** to punch sb's face in (b) *Math (d'un nombre)* square; **élever au c.** to square; **le c. de six, six au c.** six squared (c) *Culin* **c. d'agneau** rack of lamb (d) *Rail* **c. Jeunes** = reduced-rate railcard for young people within France

carreau, -x [karo] *nm* (a) *(motif)* square; *(sur du tissu)* check; **tissu à carreaux** check(ed) material (b) *(de céramique)* tile (c) *(vitre)* (window) pane; *Fam* **carreaux** *(lunettes)* specs, glasses (d) *(cartes)* diamond; *(couleur)* diamonds; *Fam* **se tenir à c.** to keep a low profile (e) *(locations)* **Fam rester sur le c.** *(être tué)* to be killed; *(être blessé)* to be badly injured; *(être éliminé)* to be given the boot

carreauté, -e [karote] *adj Can (chemise)* check(ed)

carrefour [karfur] *nm* (a) *(croisement)* crossroads *(singulier)*; *Fig* **être à un c.** to be at a crossroads (b) *(réunion)* forum

carrelage [karlaʒ] *nm (carreaux)* tiles; *(sol)* (tiled) floor

carreler [42] [karle] *vt* to tile

carrelet [karlɛ] *nm* plaice

carreleur [karlœr] *nm* tiler

carrément [karemɑ̃] *adv Fam* (a) *(franchement)* straight out; **vas-y c.** get on with it (b) *(très)* really; **c'était c. immangeable** it was absolutely inedible

carrière¹ [karjɛr] *nf (profession)* career; **faire c. (dans)** to make a career (in)

carrière² *nf (lieu)* quarry

carriériste [karjerist] *nmf Péj* careerist

carriole [karjol] *nf* (a) *(petite charrette)* light cart (b) *Can* sleigh, sled

carrossable [karosabl] *adj (chemin, route)* suitable for motor vehicles

carrosse [karos] *nm* (horse-drawn) coach

carrosser [karose] *vt* to fit the body to; **une voiture bien carrossée** a sturdily built car

carrosserie [karosri] *nf (de voiture)* bodywork

carrossier [karosje] *nm* coachbuilder

carrousel [karuzɛl] *nm (d'une aérogare)* carousel

carrure [karyr] *nf (de personne)* build; *(de vêtement)* width across the shoulders; **un homme à la forte c.** a broad-shouldered man; *Fig* **un homme d'une c. exceptionnelle** a man of exceptional qualities

cartable [kartabl] *nm* school bag

carte [kart] *nf* (a) *(géographique)* map; *Naut* chart; **faire la c. d'une région** to map (out) an area; *Astrol* **c. du ciel** astronomical chart; *Br* **c. d'état-major** ≃ Ordnance Survey map, *Am* ≃ Geological Survey map; **c. routière** road map

(b) *(carton)* card; **c. (à jouer)** (playing) card; **jouer aux cartes** to play cards; **donner les cartes** to deal (the cards); *Fig* **donner c. blanche à qn** to give sb carte-blanche; *Fig* **jouer cartes sur table** to put one's cards on the table; **c. d'anniversaire** birthday card; **c. maîtresse** trump card; **c. postale** postcard; **c. de visite** *Br* visiting *or Am* calling card; **c. de vœux** greetings card

(c) *(document officiel)* card; **c. d'abonnement** *(de bibliothèque)* library card; *(de transports, de théâtre)* season ticket; **c. d'adhérent** membership card; **c. d'électeur** voting card; **c. d'embarquement** boarding pass; **c. d'étudiant** student card; **c. de fidélité** loyalty card; *Aut* **c. grise** ≃ (vehicle) registration document; **c. d'identité** identity card; *Rail* **c. Jeunes** = reduced-rate railcard for young people, valid in certain European countries; **C. Orange** *(à Paris)* = combined monthly season ticket for the underground, bus and suburban train; **c. de presse** press card; **c. de Sécurité sociale** ≃ National Insurance Card; **c. de séjour** residence permit; *Rail* **C. Vermeil** = reduced-rate railcard for people over sixty within France; *Aut* **c. verte** green card

(d) *(document informatisé)* card; **c. bancaire** bank card; **c. Bleue®** debit card, *Br* ≃ Switch card; **c. de crédit** credit card; **c. de paiement** payment card; **c. à puce** smart card; **c. de téléphone** phonecard

(e) *(de restaurant)* menu; **manger à la c.** to eat à la carte; **c. des vins** wine list

(f) *Ordinat (carte)*; *(de clavier)* map; **c. accélératrice** accelerator card; **c. à circuit imprimé** *ou* **de circuits imprimés** printed circuit board, PCB; **c. à circuit(s) intégré(s)** integrated circuit card, IC card; **c. d'extension** expansion card *or* board; **c. mémoire** memory card; **c. mère** motherboard; **c. modem** modem card; **c. de polices de caractères** font card; **c. processeur** processor card; **c. réseau** network card; **c. SCSI** SCSI card; **c. son** *ou* **sonore** sound card; **c. unité centrale** CPU board; **c. vidéo** video card; **c. vocale** voice card

carte-adaptateur *(pl* cartes-adaptateurs*)* [kart-adaptatœr] *nf Ordinat* **c. réseau** network adaptor card

cartel [kartɛl] *nm Écon* cartel; **c. de l'acier/de la drogue** steel/drug cartel

carte-lettre *(pl* cartes-lettres*)* [kartəlɛtr] *nf* letter-card

carter [kartɛr] *nm (d'engrenages)* casing; *(de bicyclette)* chain guard; *Aut (de vilebrequin)* crankcase

carte-réponse *(pl* cartes-réponses*)* [kartrepɔ̃s] *nf* reply card

carterie [kartəri] *nf* card shop

cartésien, -enne [kartezjɛ̃, -ɛn] *adj* (a) *Math* Cartesian (b) *(logique)* logical

cartilage [kartilaʒ] *nm* cartilage

cartilagineux, -euse [kartilaʒinø, -øz] *adj* cartilaginous; *(viande)* gristly

cartographe [kartograf] *nmf* cartographer

cartographie [kartografi] *nf* cartography

cartomancien, -enne [kartomɑ̃sjɛ̃, -ɛn] *nm,f* fortune-teller *(who uses cards)*

carton [kartɔ̃] *nm* (a) *(matière)* cardboard; *(feuille)* piece of cardboard; **c. d'invitation** invitation (card); **c. jaune/rouge** *(au football)* yellow/red card (b) *(boîte)* (cardboard) box; **faire des cartons** to pack one's things up in cardboard boxes; **c. à chapeau(x)** hatbox (c) *Art (dessin)* cartoon, sketch; **c. à dessin** portfolio (d) *(locutions)* **faire un c.** *(au tir)* to have a shot; *Fam (sur quelqu'un)* to shoot somebody; *Fam (à un examen)* to pass with flying colours; *Fam Scol* **(se) prendre un c.** *(une mauvaise note)* to get a bad mark

cartonner [kartone] **1** *vt (livre)* to case; **livre cartonné** hardback (book)

2 *vi Fam (à l'école)* to get excellent marks (**en** in)

cartonneux, -euse [kartonø, -øz] *adj* like cardboard

carton-pâte [kartɔ̃pat] *nm* pasteboard

cartouche [kartuʃ] *nf (de fusil, de stylo, d'imprimante)* cartridge; *(de cigarettes)* carton

cartouchière [kartuʃjɛr] *nf* cartridge belt

caryatide [karjatid] = **cariatide**

cas [ka] *nm* (a) *(situation)* case, situation; *Jur & Méd* case; **c. particulier** exception; **envisager tous les c. possibles** to consider all the possibilities; **c'est le c. de le dire** you can say that again; **en pareil c.** in a similar situation; **si c'est votre c.** if that applies to you; **il parle trois langues mais ce n'est pas mon c.** he speaks three languages but I don't; *Fam* **c'est un c.!** he is a case!; **un c. social** a person with social problems (b) *Gram* case

(c) *(locutions)* **en aucun c.** under no circumstances, on no account; **en tout c., dans tous les c.** in any case, anyway; **dans ce c.** *(puisqu'il en est ainsi)* in that case; **dans tous les c. de figure** in all cases; **le c. échéant** if necessary, if need be; **selon le c.** as the case may be; **en c. d'urgence** in an emergency; **en c. de besoin** if need be; **j'ai pris un pull supplémentaire en c. de besoin** I took an extra sweater just in case; **au c. où il viendrait** in case he comes; *Fam* **je te le laisse au c. où** I'll leave it for you just in case; **faire grand c. de qn/qch** to have a high opinion of sb/sth; **faire peu de c. de qch** to have a low opinion of sth; **ne faire aucun c. de qch** to take no notice of sth

Casablanca [kazablɑ̃ka] *n* Casablanca

casanier, -ère [kazanje, -ɛr] *adj* home-loving; *Péj* stay-at-home

casaque [kazak] *nf (de jockey)* blouse; *Fig* **tourner c.** *(partir)* to turn tail; *(changer d'opinion)* to change sides

cascade [kaskad] *nf* (a) *(chute d'eau)* waterfall; *Fig* **des rires en c.** peals of laughter; *Ordinat* **ouvrir des fenêtres en c.** to cascade windows (b) *(au cinéma)* stunt

cascadeur, -euse [kaskadœr, -øz] *nm,f* stuntman, f stuntwoman

case [kaz] *nf* (a) *(de tiroir)* compartment; *(de formulaire)* box; *(de mots croisés, de damier)* square; *Fam* **il lui manque une c., il a une c. de vide** he's got a screw loose; *(de)* **départ** *(dans les jeux)* start; *Fig* **retour à la c. départ** back to square one (b) *(hutte)* hut (c) *Ordinat* button; *(en forme de boîte)* box

casemate [kazmat] *nf* blockhouse

caser [kaze] 1 *vt* (a) *(placer)* to fit in (b) *Fam* **c. qn** *(établir)* to fix sb up with a job; *(marier)* to marry sb off

2 se caser *vpr Fam (trouver un emploi)* to get oneself a job; *(se marier)* to get married and settle down

caserne [kazɛrn] *nf* barracks; **c. de pompiers** fire station

cash [kaʃ] *adv Fam* **payer c.** to pay cash (down)

cash-flow *(pl* **cash-flows)** [kaʃflo] *nm Com* cash flow

casier [kazje] *nm* (a) *(compartiment)* compartment; *(pour le courrier)* pigeonhole; *(à vêtements)* locker; **c. à bouteilles** bottle rack (b) *Jur* **c. judiciaire** police *or* criminal record; **avoir un c. (judiciaire)** to have a record (c) *(pour pêcher)* pot

casino [kazino] *nm* casino

Caspienne [kaspjɛn] *adj f voir* **mer**

casque [kask] *nm* (a) *(de soldat, de pompier)* helmet; *(de motocycliste)* (crash) helmet; **le port du c. est obligatoire** *(sur panneau)* safety helmets must be worn; **c. intégral** full-face crash helmet; **les Casques bleus** the Blue Berets (b) *(écouteurs)* headphones, headset (c) *(de salon de coiffure)* hairdryer

casqué, -e [kaske] *adj* helmeted

casquer [kaske] *vi Fam (payer)* to fork out

casquette [kaskɛt] *nf* cap

cassable [kasabl] *adj* breakable

cassant, -e [kasɑ̃, -ɑ̃t] *adj* brittle; *Fig (personne, ton)* brusque

cassation [kasasjɔ̃] *nf Jur* annulment

cassé[1] [kas] *nf Typ* case; **bas/haut de c.** lower/upper case

cassé[2] *nf* (a) *(action de casser)* **il va y avoir de la c.** something will get broken; *Fam (des ennuis)* there'll be trouble; **aller** *ou* **partir à la c.** *(voiture)* to go for scrap (b) *(objets cassés)* breakages

cassé[3] *nm très Fam (cambriolage)* break-in

cassé, -e [kase] *adj (objet, jambe)* broken; *(voix)* cracked; *très Fam (ivre)* smashed, plastered; *(drogué)* stoned

casse-cou [kasku] **1** *adj inv (personne)* reckless

2 *nmf inv (personne)* daredevil

casse-croûte [kaskrut] *nm inv* (a) *Fam (repas)* snack, bite (b) *Can (snack)* snack bar

casse-cul [kasky] *très Fam* **1** *adj inv* damned annoying

2 *nmf inv* pain in the arse

casse-gueule [kasgœl] *très Fam* **1** *adj inv (endroit)* dangerous; *(entreprise)* risky

2 *nm inv (endroit)* danger spot; *(entreprise)* risky business

casse-noisettes [kasnwazɛt] *nm inv* nutcrackers

casse-noix [kasnwa] *nm inv* nutcrackers

casse-pieds [kaspje] *Fam* **1** *adj inv* damned annoying; **ce qu'il peut être c.!** he can be a real pain (in the neck)!

2 *nmf inv* pain (in the neck)

casse-pipe [kaspip] *nm inv Fam* **aller au c.** to go to the front

casser [kase] **1** *vt* (a) *(briser)* to break; *(noix)* to crack; *(voix)* to strain; *(chaussures)* to break in; *Fam (personne)* to humiliate; **c. les prix** to slash prices; *aussi Fig* **c. le moral des troupes** to discourage the ranks; *Fig* **c. du sucre sur le dos de qn** to talk about sb behind his/her back; *Fam* **c. la croûte** *ou* **la graine** to have a bite to eat; *Fam* **ça ne casse pas trois pattes à un canard, Fam ça ne casse pas des briques** it's nothing to write home about; *Fam* **c. la baraque** *(pièce, acteur)* to bring the house down; *Fam* **à tout c.** *(au maximum)* at the very most

(b) *Fam (locutions avec parties du corps)* **c. les pieds à qn** *(ennuyer)* to bore the pants off sb; *(agacer)* to get on sb's nerves; **ça fait deux mois qu'elle me casse les pieds pour que j'y aille** she's been bugging me to go for two months now; **c. les oreilles à qn** to deafen sb; **c. la figure** *ou* très *Fam* **la gueule à qn** to smash sb's face in; *Fam* **c. sa pipe** to kick the bucket; *Vulg* **il nous casse les couilles, il nous les casse** he gets on our tits

(c) *Jur (verdict)* to quash; *(mariage)* to annul; *(fiançailles)* to break off

2 *vi* (a) *(se briser)* to break; **attention, ça casse!** be careful, it's fragile!

(b) *Fam (se séparer)* to split up

3 se casser *vpr* (a) *(se briser)* to break

(b) **se c. une** *ou* **la jambe** to break one's leg; *Fig* **se c. le nez** to fail; *Fig* **se c. la tête** to rack one's brains; *Fam* **se c.**

la figure *ou très Fam* la gueule *(tomber)* to fall flat on one's face; *(échouer)* to fail

(c) *Fam (se fatiguer)* il ne s'est pas cassé pour m'aider he didn't exactly strain himself helping me; *Vulg* se c. le cul à faire qch to bust a gut trying to do sth

(d) *Fam (partir)* to split, to clear off; tu viens? on se casse we're off, are you coming?; casse-toi! get lost!

casserole [kasʀɔl] *nf* **(a)** *(de cuisine)* (sauce)pan; *très Fam* passer à la c. *(sexuellement)* to be given a good seeing-to; *(être tué)* to get bumped off **(b)** *Fam* chanter comme une c. to be a rotten singer

casse-tête [kastɛt] *nm inv* **(a)** *(jeu)* puzzle **(b)** *(problème)* headache

cassette [kasɛt] *nf* **(a)** *(magnétique)* cassette, tape; enregistrer qch sur c. to tape sth; c. vidéo video (cassette) **(b)** *Ordinat* c. à bande magnétique mag tape cassette

casseur, -euse [kasœʀ, -øz] *nm,f* **(a)** *(manifestant)* rioter **(b)** *très Fam (cambrioleur)* burglar

cassis [kasis] *nm* **(a)** *(baie)* blackcurrant **(b)** *(arbuste)* blackcurrant bush **(c)** *(liqueur)* blackcurrant liqueur

cassonade [kasɔnad] *nf* brown sugar

cassoulet [kasulɛ] *nm* cassoulet *(stew of beans, pork, goose etc, a speciality of Languedoc)*

cassure [kasyʀ] *nf* break; *Géol* fault

castagnettes [kastaɲɛt] *nfpl* castanets

caste [kast] *nf* caste

castillan, -e [kastijɑ̃, -an] **1** *adj* Castilian
2 *nm,f* C. Castilian
3 *nm (langue)* Castilian

Castille [kastij] *nf* la C. Castile

casting [kastiŋ] *nm Cin & Th* casting

castor [kastɔʀ] *nm* beaver

castrat [kastʀa] *nm Mus* castrato

castrer [kastʀe] *vt* to castrate; *(chat, chien)* to neuter

cataclysme [kataklism] *nm* cataclysm

cataclysmique [kataklismik] *adj* cataclysmic

catacombes [katakɔ̃b] *nfpl* catacombs

catadioptre® [katadjɔptʀ] *nm (de véhicule)* reflector; *(sur la route)* cat's-eye®

catafalque [katafalk] *nm* catafalque

catalan, -e [katalɑ̃, -an] **1** *adj* Catalan
2 *nm,f* C. Catalan
3 *nm (langue)* Catalan

Catalogne [katalɔɲ] *nf* la C. Catalonia

catalogue [katalɔg] *nm* catalogue; faire le c. de to catalogue; acheter sur c. to buy things from a catalogue

cataloguer [katalɔge] *vt* to catalogue; *Fig & Péj* to label

catalyser [kataalize] *vt aussi Fig* to catalyse

catalyseur [katalizœʀ] *nm aussi Fig* catalyst

catalytique [katalitik] *adj Chim* catalytic

catamaran [katamaʀɑ̃] *nm Naut* catamaran

Cataphote® [katafɔt] = **catadioptre**

cataplasme [kataplasm] *nm* poultice

catapulte [katapylt] *nf* catapult

catapulter [katapylte] *vt* to catapult; *Fig* c. qn à un poste to catapult sb into a post

cataracte [kataʀakt] *nf (maladie, chute d'eau)* cataract

catastrophe [katastʀɔf] *nf* disaster, catastrophe; c. ferroviaire/aérienne rail/air disaster; c'est la c.! it's a disaster!; c.! il est déjà là! panic stations! he's here already!; en c. *(à toute vitesse)* in a mad rush *or* panic

catastrophé, -e [katastʀɔfe] *adj Fam* stunned

catastrophique [katastʀɔfik] *adj* disastrous, catastrophic

catch [katʃ] *nm* wrestling; faire du c. to wrestle

catcheur, -euse [katʃœʀ, -øz] *nm,f* wrestler

catéchisme [kateʃism] *nm* catechism

catégorie [kategɔʀi] *nf* category, type; *(d'hôtel, de personnel)* grade; *(de boxeur)* class; c. sociale social class; c. socioprofessionnelle socio-professional group

catégorique [kategɔʀik] *adj (réponse, refus)* categoric(al); je suis absolument c., c'est lui I'm absolutely positive it's him

catégoriquement [kategɔʀikmɑ̃] *adv* categorically

catégoriser [kategɔʀize] *vt* to categorize

Cathares [kataʀ] *nmpl Hist* les C. the Cathars

catharsis [kataʀsis] *nf* catharsis

cathédrale [katedʀal] *nf* cathedral

cathéter [katetɛʀ] *nm Méd* catheter

catho [kato] *adj Fam* Catholic

cathode [katod] *nf El* cathode

cathodique [katodik] *adj El* cathodic; tube c. cathode ray tube

catholicisme [katɔlisism] *nm* (Roman) Catholicism

catholique [katɔlik] **1** *adj* (Roman) Catholic; *Fam* ce n'est pas très c. it's a bit shady
2 *nmf* (Roman) Catholic

catimini [katimini] en catimini *adv* on the sly

catogan [katɔgɑ̃] *nm (nœud)* hair ribbon *(for ponytail)*; *(queue de cheval)* ponytail

Caucase [kokaz] *nm* le C. the Caucasus

caucasien, -enne [kokazjɛ̃, -ɛn] *adj* Caucasian

cauchemar [koʃmaʀ] *nm aussi Fig* nightmare; une vision de c. a nightmarish vision; faire un c. to have a nightmare

cauchemarder [koʃmaʀde] *vi* to have nightmares

cauchemardesque [koʃmaʀdɛsk] *adj* nightmarish

causal, -e, -als *ou* **-aux, -ales** [kozal, -o] *adj* causal

causant, -e [kozɑ̃, -ɑ̃t] *adj Fam* chatty

cause [koz] *nf* **(a)** *(origine)* cause; quelle est la c. de son départ? why is he leaving?; il s'est mis en colère, et pour c. he got angry, and with good reason; fermé pour c. d'inventaire/de décès *(sur panneau)* closed for stocktaking/due to bereavement; à c. de because of **(b)** *Jur* case; *Fig* la c. est entendue there's nothing more to be said; être en c. *(sujet à caution)* to be in question; mettre qch en c. to doubt sth, to question sth; mettre qn en c. *(impliquer)* to implicate sb; mettre qn hors de c. to clear sb; en tout état de c. in any case **(c)** *(parti)* cause; faire c. commune avec qn to join forces with sb

causer[1] [koze] *vt (provoquer)* to cause; c. des ennuis à qn to cause sb problems

causer[2] [koze] *vi* **(a)** *(parler)* to chat, to talk *(de* about); c. affaires to talk business; c. avec *ou* à qn to chat with sb; *Fam* je ne lui cause plus! I'm not talking to him!; *Ironique* cause toujours(, tu m'intéresses)! riveting! **(b)** *(cancaner)* to talk, to gossip; on en cause au village it's the talk of the village

causerie [kozri] *nf* (a) *(discussion)* chat, talk (b) *(conférence)* (informal) talk

causette [kozet] *nf Fam* little chat; **faire la c.** *ou* **un brin de c. avec qn** to have a little chat with sb

causse [kos] *nm* = limestone plateau in central and southern France

caustique [kostik] *adj aussi Fig* caustic

cautériser [koterize] *vt* to cauterize

caution [kosjɔ̃] *nf* (a) *(pour appartement)* deposit; *Jur* bail; *Fig (appui)* support, backing; *Jur* **sous c.** on bail; **sujet à c.** *(information)* unconfirmed (b) *(personne)* guarantor

cautionner [kosjone] *vt (personne)* to stand surety for; *Jur* to stand bail for; *Fig (approuver)* to support, to back

cavalcade [kavalkad] *nf Fam (bousculade)* stampede

cavale [kaval] *nf Fam (évasion)* escape; **être en c.** to be on the run

cavaler [kavale] *vi Fam (se démener)* to rush around; *(fuir)* to run off; **c. après qn** to chase after sb

cavalerie [kavalri] *nf Mil* cavalry

cavaleur, -euse [kavalœr, -øz] *Fam* **1** *adj (homme)* womanizing; *(femme)* man-chasing
2 *nm,f (homme)* skirt-chaser; *(femme)* man-chaser

cavalier, -ère [kavalje, -ɛr] **1** *adj (manière, personne)* cavalier
2 *nm,f* (a) *(à cheval)* rider, horseman, *f* horsewoman (b) *(de bal)* partner; *Fig* **faire c. seul** to go it alone
3 *nm* (a) *(aux échecs)* knight (b) *(accompagnateur)* escort (c) *Ordinat* jumper

cavalièrement [kavaljɛrmɔ̃] *adv* in a cavalier manner

cave¹ [kav] *adj (joues, yeux)* hollow, sunken

cave² *nf (cellier)* cellar; **c. à charbon/vin** coal/wine cellar; *Fig* **de la c. au grenier** from top to bottom

caveau, -x [kavo] *nm* (a) *(petite cave)* small cellar (b) *(funéraire)* burial vault

caverne [kavɛrn] *nf* cave, cavern; **homme des cavernes** caveman

caverneux, -euse [kavɛrnø, -øz] *adj (voix)* deep

caviar [kavjar] *nm* caviar

caviarder [kavjarde] *vt* to censor

caviste [kavist] *nm* cellarman

cavité [kavite] *nf* cavity, hollow; **c. buccale** oral cavity

Cayenne [kajɛn] *n* (a) *(ville)* Cayenne (b) **poivre de C.** cayenne pepper

CC [sese] *nm (abrév* **compte courant)** CA

CCI [sesei] *nf (abrév* **Chambre de commerce et d'industrie)** Chamber of Commerce and Industry

CCP [sesepe] *nm (abrév* **compte courant postal, compte chèque postal)** *Br* ≃ Giro account, *Am* ≃ Post Office checking account

CD [sede] *nm* (a) *(abrév* **Compact Disc)** CD (b) *(abrév* **corps diplomatique)** CD

CDD [sedede] *nm (abrév* **contrat à durée déterminée)** fixed-term contract

CDI [sedei] *nm inv* (a) *(abrév* **centre des impôts)** tax office (b) *(abrév* **contrat à durée indéterminée)** permanent contract (c) *(abrév* **centre de documentation et d'information)** school library *(with special resources on how to find information)*

CD-I [sedei] *(abrév* **Compact Disc interactif)** CDI

CD-Rom [sederom] *nm inv* CD-Rom; **C. interactif** interactive CD-Rom

CE [seə] **1** *nm* (a) *(abrév* **Conseil de l'Europe)** Council of Europe (b) *(abrév* **cours élémentaire)** CE1 = second year of primary school; CE2 = third year of primary school
2 *nf (abrév* **Communauté européenne)** EC

ce¹ [sə] *pron démonstratif*

> ce becomes c' before a vowel.

(a) *(pour désigner)* **c'est mon père** that's my father; *(au téléphone)* it's my father; **ce sont** *ou Fam* **c'est mes amis** those are my friends; *(qui arrivent)* there are my friends; **c'était mon idée** it was my idea; **c'est le plus beau jour de ma vie** this is the best day of my life; **c'est moi** it's me; **qui est-ce?**, *Fam* **qui c'est?** who is it?; **c'est lui qui l'a écrit** HE wrote it; **qui a fait ça? – c'est moi!** who did that? – I did!; **c'est un bon traducteur** he's a good translator; **c'est la première voiture que j'aie eue** that was my first car; **c'est ici que je suis né** this is where I was born, I was born here; **c'est jeudi aujourd'hui** today's Thursday, it's Thursday today; **c'était il y a longtemps** it was a long time ago

(b) *(pour qualifier ou pour expliquer)* **c'est facile/joli** it's easy/nice; **c'est exact!** that's right!; **c'est que maman est déjà partie** the thing is, Mum's already left; **s'il chante, (alors) c'est qu'il est de bonne humeur** if he's singing, it means he's in a good mood; *Fam* **c'est bizarre qu'il n'ait pas appelé!** it's strange that he hasn't called!; *Fam* **ce qu'il est pénible!** he's such a pain!

(c) *(avec des pronoms relatifs)* **ce qui...**, **ce que...** what...; **je sais ce qui s'est passé** I know what happened; **ce que je crois, c'est que...** what I think is...; **voici ce dont il s'agit** this is what it's all about; **voilà ce à quoi j'avais pensé** this is what I thought of; **ce qui compte, c'est que...** what counts is that...; **j'ai appris tout ce qui se trouve dans le chapitre 4** I've learned everything in chapter 4; **j'ai oublié tout ce qu'elle m'a dit** I've forgotten everything she told me; **pour ce qui est de la qualité** with regards to or as regards quality

(d) *(locutions)* **ce faisant** in so doing, whilst doing so; **il y est allé, et ce malgré mon interdiction** he went despite the fact that I had forbidden him; **sur ce, je m'en vais** on that note, I'm leaving; **... et, sur ce, il sortit son album de photos ...** whereupon he brought out his photo album

ce², cet, cette, ces [sə, sɛt, se] *adj démonstratif*

> cet is used before a masculine singular noun or adjective beginning with a vowel or mute h.

(a) *(par référence)* **ce garçon** this boy; **cet enfant** this child; **cette fille** this girl; **ces gens/animaux/couleurs** these people/animals/colours (b) *(en désignant)* **ce vin-ci** this wine; **ce vin-là** that wine; **ces voitures-ci** these cars; **ces voitures-là** those cars (c) *Fam (intensif)* **alors, cette lettre, tu me la montres?** so do I get to see this or that letter of yours?; **et ce café, il arrive?** is that coffee on its way or what?; **je lui ai envoyé une de ces lettres!** I wrote him such a letter!; **j'ai une de ces faims!** I'm so hungry!

ceci [səsi] *pron démonstratif* this; **c. (étant) dit** having said that; **c. n'explique pas cela** that's no explanation

cécité [sesite] *nf* blindness; **être atteint de c.** to be blind

CED [seəde] *nf (abrév* **Communauté européenne de défense)** EDC

céder [34] [sede] **1** vt (a) (donner) (objet, droit) to give up (à to); (dans un testament) to leave (à to); **c. sa place à qn** to give up one's seat to sb; **c. du terrain** to give ground; **cédez le passage** (sur panneau) Br give way, Am yield (b) (vendre) to sell; **à c.** (sur panneau) for sale

2 vi (a) (plancher, branche) to give way (b) (se soumettre) to give in (**devant** to)

3 **céder à** vt ind (personne, tentation, revendication) to give in to

Cedex [sedɛks] nm (abrév **Courrier d'entreprise à distribution exceptionnelle**) = postal code ensuring rapid delivery of business mail

cédille [sedij] nf cedilla

cédrat [sedra] nm (fruit) citron

cèdre [sedr] nm (arbre, bois) cedar; **c. du Liban** cedar of Lebanon

CEE [seɔə] nf (abrév **Communauté économique européenne**) EEC

CEEA [seɔɔa] nf (abrév **Communauté européenne de l'énergie atomique**) Euratom

cégep [seʒɛp] nm Can (abrév **collège d'enseignement général et professionnel**) = college of further education

CEI [seɔi] nf (abrév **Communauté d'États indépendants**) CIS

ceindre [54] [sɛ̃dr] vt Litt (a) (épée) to strap on (b) (sujet: couronne) to encircle

ceinture [sɛ̃tyr] nf (a) (accessoire) belt; **être c. noire de judo** to be a black belt in judo; Fam **se serrer la c., faire c.** to tighten one's belt; **c. de chasteté** chastity belt; **c. de sécurité** seat belt; **attacher sa c. (de sécurité)** to fasten one's seat belt (b) (taille) (de vêtement) waistband; (d'une personne) waist; **frapper au-dessous de la c.** to hit below the belt (c) **la petite C.** = circular bus route around centre of Paris

ceinturer [sɛ̃tyre] vt to grab around the waist

ceinturon [sɛ̃tyrɔ̃] nm belt

cela [səla, sla] pron démonstratif that; **c'est pour c. que je viens** that's what I've come for or why I've come; **il y a deux ans de c.** that was two years ago; **et pourquoi c.?** why is that?; **s'il n'y avait que c.** if that were the only problem; **et avec c.?** (dans un magasin) (will there be) anything else?

célébration [selebrasjɔ̃] nf celebration

célèbre [selebr] adj famous (**pour** for); **se rendre c. par qch** to become famous for sth; **tristement c.** notorious

célébrer [34] [selebre] vt (a) (fêter) (anniversaire, victoire, messe) to celebrate (b) (vanter) **c. les mérites/le talent de qn** to extol sb's merits/talent

célébrité [selebrite] nf (notoriété) fame; (personne) celebrity

céleri [sɛlri] nm celery; Culin **c. rémoulade** = grated celeriac in mayonnaise

céleri-rave (pl **céleris-raves**) [sɛlrirav] nm celeriac

céleste [selɛst] adj (a) (du firmament) (phénomènes, corps) celestial, heavenly (b) Rel heavenly

célibat [seliba] nm single life; (des prêtres) celibacy

célibataire [selibater] **1** adj (non marié) unmarried, single
2 nm bachelor; **un c. endurci** a confirmed bachelor
3 nf single woman

celle [sɛl] voir **celui**

cellier [selje] nm storeroom; (cave) cellar

Cellophane® [selɔfan] nf cellophane®; **sous C.** cellophane-wrapped

cellulaire [selyler] adj (a) Biol cell (b) Jur **régime c.** solitary confinement (c) Tél cellular

cellule [selyl] nf (a) (d'une prison, d'un couvent) cell (b) Biol cell; **c. nerveuse** nerve cell (c) Fig (élément) unit; (de parti politique) cell (d) Él **c. photoélectrique** photoelectric cell

cellulite [selylit] nf cellulite

Celluloïd® [selylɔid] nm celluloid®

cellulose [selyloz] nf cellulose

celte [sɛlt] **1** adj Celtic
2 nmf **C.** Celt

celtique [sɛltik] adj & nm Celtic

celui, celle [səlɥi, sɛl] (mpl **ceux** [sø], fpl **celles**) pron démonstratif the one; **mon livre et c. de Paul** my book and Paul's; **mes livres et ceux de Paul** my books and Paul's; **c. que je t'ai donné** the one I gave you; **celles dont je t'ai parlé** the ones I talked to you about; **c.-ci** this one; (ce dernier) the latter; **c.-là** that one; (le premier) the former; **ceux-ci** these ones; (ces derniers) the latter; **ceux-là** those ones; (les premiers) the former; **ah, c.-là, quel idiot!** he's such an idiot, that one!; **autre exemple, plus technique c.-là** another example, a more technical one this time; **elle est bien bonne, celle-là!** that's a good one!

cendre [sɑ̃dr] nf ash(es); **faire cuire des pommes de terre sous la c.** to roast potatoes in the ashes; **réduire qch en cendres** to reduce sth to ashes; **cendres** (après incinération) ashes; Rel **le mercredi des Cendres** Ash Wednesday

cendré, -e [sɑ̃dre] adj voir **blond**

cendrée [sɑ̃dre] nf Sp (piste) cinder track; (mâchefer) cinders

cendrier [sɑ̃drije] nm ashtray

Cendrillon [sɑ̃drijɔ̃] npr Cinderella

Cène [sɛn] nf **la C.** the Last Supper

censé, -e [sɑ̃se] adj **être c. faire qch** to be supposed to do sth

censeur [sɑ̃sœr] nm (a) Scol (d'un lycée) Br deputy head, Am assistant principal (b) (dans les médias) censor (c) Litt (juge) critic

censure [sɑ̃syr] nf (activité) censorship; (personnes) (board of) censors

censurer [sɑ̃syre] vt (a) (film, livre, scène) to censor (b) Litt (critiquer) to censure

cent¹ [sɑ̃] **1** adj a or one hundred; **deux cents hommes** two hundred men; **deux c. cinquante** two hundred and fifty; **je te l'ai dit c. fois** I've told you a hundred times; **vous avez c. fois raison** you're absolutely right; Fam **je ne vais pas t'attendre** (pendant) **c. sept ans** I'm not going to wait for you forever; **faire les c. pas** to pace up and down; Fam **être aux c. coups** to be frantic; Fam **faire les quatre cents coups** to get up to all sorts of tricks

2 nm a hundred; **pour c.** per cent; **c. pour c.** a hundred per cent; voir aussi **trois**

cent² [sɛnt] nm (monnaie) cent

centaine [sɑ̃tɛn] nf **une c. (de)** about a hundred, a hundred or so; **des centaines de livres** hundreds of books; **plusieurs centaines de personnes** several hundred people

centaure [sɑ̃tor] nm centaur

centenaire [sɑ̃tnɛr] **1** adj (personne, arbre) hundred-year-old; **être c.** (avoir cent ans) to be a hundred (years old); (avoir plus de cent ans) to be over a hundred (years old); **plusieurs fois c.** hundreds of years old
  2 nmf centenarian
  3 nm centenary

centième [sɑ̃tjɛm] **1** nmf, nm & adj hundredth; voir aussi **cinquième**
  2 nf Th hundredth performance

centigrade [sɑ̃tigrad] adj degré **c.** degree centigrade

centigramme [sɑ̃tigram] nm centigram

centilitre [sɑ̃tilitr] nm centilitre

centime [sɑ̃tim] nm centime; **je ne lui donnerai pas un c.!** I won't give him a penny!

centimètre [sɑ̃timɛtr] nm (a) (unité de mesure) centimetre (b) (ruban) tape measure

centrafricain, -e [sɑ̃trafrikɛ̃, -ɛn] **1** adj of the Central African Republic
  2 nm,f **C.** person from the Central African Republic

central, -e, -aux, -ales [sɑ̃tral, -o] **1** adj (a) (au centre) central (b) (principal) central, main (c) (l'École) **Centrale** = Grande École specializing in engineering
  2 nm **c. téléphonique** telephone exchange
  3 nf **centrale** (a) (usine) **centrale (électrique)** power station; **centrale thermique/nucléaire** thermal/nuclear power station (b) (prison) county jail (c) (groupement) **centrale (syndicale)** group of affiliated trade unions; Com **centrale d'achat** (central) purchasing group

centralisation [sɑ̃tralizasjɔ̃] nf centralization

centraliser [sɑ̃tralize] vt to centralize

centralisme [sɑ̃tralism] nm Pol centralism

centre [sɑ̃tr] nm (a) (milieu) centre; **il se prend pour le c. du monde** he thinks the world revolves round him; **cette question est au c. du débat** this question is at the heart of the debate; Phys **c. de gravité** centre of gravity; **c. d'intérêt** centre of interest (b) Pol centre; **le c. droit/gauche** the centre right/left (c) (au football) (passe) cross; **faire un c.** to make a cross (d) (organisme, lieu) centre; **c. aéré** outdoor activity centre; **c. commercial** shopping centre; **c. culturel** arts centre; **c. hospitalier** hospital complex; **c. des impôts** tax office; **c. de loisirs** leisure centre; **c. de tri** sorting office

centre-ville (pl **centres-villes**) [sɑ̃trəvil] nm town centre; (d'une grande ville) Br city centre, Am downtown area; **habiter au c.** to live in the town centre

centrifuge [sɑ̃trifyʒ] adj centrifugal

centrifuger [45] [sɑ̃trifyʒe] vt to centrifuge

centrifugeur [sɑ̃trifyʒœr] nm, **centrifugeuse** [sɑ̃trifyʒøz] nf (en chimie, en biologie) centrifuge; (pour jus de fruits) juice extractor

centripète [sɑ̃tripɛt] adj centripetal

centrisme [sɑ̃trism] nm Pol centrism

centriste [sɑ̃trist] adj & nmf Pol centrist

centuple [sɑ̃typl] nm **le c. de dix** a hundred times ten; **je te le rendrai au c.** I'll repay you a hundred times over

cep [sɛp] nm **c. (de vigne)** vine-stock

cépage [sepaʒ] nm variety of vine

cèpe [sɛp] nm cep

cependant [səpɑ̃dɑ̃] **1** conj however, nevertheless; **le directeur, c., n'est pas d'accord** the manager, however, does not agree; **c., vous ne m'avez pas averti** nevertheless, you didn't tell me
  2 adv Litt meanwhile; **c. que** while

céphalée [sefale] nf Méd headache, Spéc cephalalgia

céramique [seramik] nf (art) ceramics (singulier); (matière, objet) ceramic

cerceau, -x [sɛrso] nm hoop

cercle [sɛrkl] nm (a) (figure) circle; **en c.** in a circle; **c. vicieux** vicious circle; **décrire des cercles** (avion, oiseau) to circle (b) (groupe de personnes) circle (c) (association) club; **c. littéraire** literary society (d) (objet circulaire) hoop, ring (e) Géog **c. (polaire) arctique** Arctic Circle

cerclé, -e [sɛrkle] adj **lunettes cerclées d'écaille** horn-rimmed spectacles; **un tonneau c. de fer** a barrel with iron hoops

cercueil [sɛrkœj] nm coffin

céréale [sereal] nf cereal, grain; **céréales** (au petit déjeuner) cereal

céréalier, -ère [serealje, -ɛr] adj (production, culture) cereal; (région) cereal-growing

cérébral, -e, -aux, -ales [serebral, -o] adj cerebral; **hémorragie cérébrale** brain haemorrhage

cérémonial, -als [seremɔnjal] nm ceremonial

cérémonie [seremɔni] nf ceremony; **habit de c.** dress suit; **uniforme de c.** dress uniform; Fig **sans cérémonies** (réception, repas) informal; (recevoir quelqu'un) informally; (renvoyer quelqu'un) unceremoniously; **faire des cérémonies** to stand on ceremony; **sans plus de c.** without further ado

cérémonieux, -euse [seremɔnjø, -øz] adj ceremonious

cerf [sɛr] nm stag

cerfeuil [sɛrfœj] nm chervil

cerf-volant (pl **cerfs-volants**) [sɛrvɔlɑ̃] nm (a) (jeu) kite (b) (insecte) stag beetle

cerise [səriz] **1** nf cherry
  2 adj inv cherry(-red)

cerisier [sərizje] nm (arbre) cherry tree; (bois) cherrywood

CERN [sɛrn] nm (abrév **Conseil européen pour la recherche nucléaire**) CERN

cerne [sɛrn] nm ring

cerné, -e [sɛrne] adj **avoir les yeux cernés** to have rings under one's eyes

cerner [sɛrne] vt (a) (encercler) to surround (b) (définir) (problème) to identify; **une personne difficile à c.** a difficult person to figure out

certain, -e [sɛrtɛ̃, -ɛn] **1** adj (sûr) certain; **il viendra, c'est c.** he'll definitely come; **être c. de qch** to be certain of sth; **aller à une mort certaine** to be heading for certain death
  2 adj indéfini (avant le nom) certain; **il a un c. charme** he has a certain charm; **un c. temps** a while; **jusqu'à un c. point** up to a (certain) point; **d'une certaine façon** in a way; **dans une certaine mesure** to a certain extent; **d'un c. âge** elderly; **avoir un c. âge** to be getting on; **cela demande un c. culot/courage** it takes some nerve/courage; **une certaine Martine** someone called Martine
  3 pron indéfini **certains pensent que...** some (people)

think (that)...; **certaines d'entre nous/vous** some of us/you

certainement [sɛrtɛnmɑ̃] *adv* (*probablement*) most probably; **c.!** of course!; **c. pas!** certainly not!

certes [sɛrt] *adv* certainly; **il n'est pas sans défauts, c., mais...** he has his faults, certainly, but...; **c. oui!** yes indeed!; **c. non!** certainly not!

certificat [sɛrtifika] *nm* certificate; **c. d'assurance** insurance certificate; **c. de garantie** certificate of guarantee; **c. médical** medical certificate; **c. de scolarité** school attendance record; **c. de travail** certificate of employment

certifié, -e [sɛrtifje] *adj* **professeur c.** = qualified (graduate) teacher

certifier [66] [sɛrtifje] *vt* (**a**) (*authentifier*) to certify; (*signature*) to witness (**b**) (*assurer*) **c. qch à qn** to assure sb of sth

certitude [sɛrtityd] *nf* certainty; **j'en ai la c.** I'm certain of it

cérumen [serymɛn] *nm* earwax, *Spéc* cerumen

cerveau, -x [sɛrvo] *nm Anat & Fig* brain; (*esprit*) mind, brains; (*personne intelligente*) brainy person; (*d'un projet*) mastermind

cervelas [sɛrvəla] *nm* saveloy

cervelet [sɛrvəle] *nm Anat* cerebellum

cervelle [sɛrvɛl] *nf Anat* (*substance*) brain; **se brûler** *ou* **se faire sauter la c.** to blow one's brains out; **il n'a rien dans la c.** he's got nothing between his ears; **avoir une c. de moineau** to be bird-brained; *Culin* **c. d'agneau** lamb's brains

cervical, -e, -aux, -ales [sɛrvikal, -o] *adj Anat* cervical

CES [seɔɛs] *nm* (**a**) (*abrév* **contrat emploi-solidarité**) = short-term contract subsidised by the government (**b**) (*abrév* **collège d'enseignement secondaire**) = former secondary school for pupils aged 12 to 15

ces [se] *voir* **ce²**

César [sezar] **1** *npr* **Jules C.** Julius Caesar
2 *nm Cin* = French cinema award

césarienne [sezarjɛn] *nf* Caesarean (section)

cessant, -e [sesɑ̃, -ɑ̃t] *adj* **toutes affaires cessantes** forthwith

cessation [sesasjɔ̃] *nf* cessation; **c. des hostilités** cease-fire; **c. de paiements** suspension of payments

cesse [sɛs] *nf* (**a**) **sans c.** constantly, continually (**b**) *Litt* **il n'aura (pas) de c. qu'il ne réussisse** he won't rest until he has succeeded

cesser [sese] **1** *vi* to stop, to cease; (*vent*) to die down; **faire c. qch** to put a stop to sth; **il faudra que ça cesse** this has to stop
2 *vt* (*interrompre*) to stop; *Mil* **cessez le feu!** cease fire!; **c. de faire qch** to stop doing sth

cessez-le-feu [seselfø] *nm inv* cease-fire

cession [sesjɔ̃] *nf Jur* transfer

c'est-à-dire [sɛtadir] *conj* that is (to say); **vous l'avez prévenu?** – **eh bien, c. que non** did you let him know? – well, actually, no; **c. que je n'étais pas au courant** the thing is that no one told me; **il faut aller de l'avant!** – **c.?** we must forge ahead! – what do you mean by that?

césure [sezyr] *nf* (*en poésie*) caesura; *Ordinat* break, hyphenation

cet [sɛt] *voir* **ce²**

cétacé [setase] *nm* cetacean

cette [sɛt] *voir* **ce²**

ceux [sø] *voir* **celui**

Ceylan [selɑ̃] *n* Ceylon

cf (*abrév* **confer**) cf

CFA [seɛfa] (*abrév* **Communauté financière africaine**) **franc C.** CFA franc

CFAO [seɛfao] *nf* (*abrév* **conception et fabrication assistées par ordinateur**) CADCAM

CFC [seɛfse] *nm* (*abrév* **chlorofluorocarbone**) CFC

CFDT [seɛfdete] *nf* (*abrév* **Confédération française démocratique du travail**) = French trade union

CFTC [seɛftese] *nf* (*abrév* **Confédération française des travailleurs chrétiens**) = French trade union

CGC [seʒese] *nf* (*abrév* **Confédération générale des cadres**) = French trade union for managerial staff

CGT [seʒete] *nf* (*abrév* **Confédération générale du travail**) = French trade union

chacal, -als [ʃakal] *nm* jackal; *Fig* vulture

chacun, -e [ʃakœ̃, -yn] *pron indéfini* (**a**) (*chaque personne*) each (one), every one; **3 francs c.** 3 francs each; **nous avons pris c. notre chapeau** each of us took our hat (**b**) (*tout le monde*) everyone, everybody; **c. pour soi** every man for himself; **c. ses goûts** everyone to their own taste; **c. son tour** (*dans une file d'attente*) each in turn; (*son tour!*) wait your turn!; **tout un c.** everyone

chagrin, -e [ʃagrɛ̃, -in] **1** *nm* (*peine*) grief, sorrow; **avoir du c.** to be upset; **avoir un gros c.** (*langage enfantin*) to be very unhappy; **faire du c. à qn** to distress sb; **un c. d'amour** an unhappy love affair
2 *adj Litt* woeful; **esprits chagrins** malcontents

chagriner [ʃagrine] *vt* (*peiner*) to grieve; (*contrarier*) to bother

chahut [ʃay] *nm Fam* racket, din; **faire du c.** to make a racket

chahuter [ʃayte] *Fam* **1** *vi* (*faire du tapage*) to make a racket; (*jouer brutalement*) to be rowdy
2 *vt* (*professeur*) to bait; (*orateur*) to heckle; **se faire c.** (*professeur*) to get baited; (*orateur*) to get heckled

chai [ʃe] *nm* wine and spirits storehouse

chaîne [ʃɛn] *nf* (**a**) (*pour attacher, pour décorer*) chain; **faire la c.** to form a chain; **chaînes** *Aut* (snow) chains; *Fig* (*contraintes*) chains, shackles (**b**) (*de transmission*) chain; **c. de vélo** bicycle chain (**c**) (*série*) (*d'hôtels, de magasins*) chain; **c. alimentaire** food chain; **c. de montagnes** range *or* chain of mountains (**d**) (*TV*) television channel; **c. de télévision** television channel; **c.** (*dans l'industrie*) **c. (de montage)** assembly line, production line; **travail à la c.** assembly line work; **travailler à la c.** to work on the assembly line (**f**) *Tex* warp (**g**) *Ordinat* string; **c. de caractères** character string; **c. de recherche** search string (**h**) **c. (haute-fidélité)** hi-fi

chaînette [ʃɛnɛt] *nf* small chain

chaînon [ʃɛnɔ̃] *nm* link; *Fig* **le c. manquant** the missing link

chair [ʃɛr] **1** *nf* (*d'humain, d'animal, de fruit*) flesh; **en c. et en os** in the flesh; **être bien en c.** to be plump; **la c. est faible** the flesh is weak; **c. à canon** cannon fodder; **avoir la c. de poule** to have *Br* goose pimples *or Am* goose bumps; **donner la c. de poule à qn** to give sb goose pimples; **c. à saucisse** sausagemeat; *Fam Fig* **je vais en faire de la c. à saucisse** I'll make mincemeat of him
2 *adj inv* (*couleur*) **c.** flesh-coloured

chaire [ʃɛr] nf (a) (dans une église) pulpit (b) Univ (fonction, tribune) chair; **être titulaire d'une c.** to hold a chair

chaise [ʃɛz] nf chair; Fig **être assis** ou **très** Fam **avoir le cul entre deux chaises** to be in an awkward position; Can **c. berçante** rocking chair; **chaises musicales** musical chairs; **c. électrique** electric chair; **c. haute** high chair; **c. longue** deckchair; **c. à porteurs** sedan chair; **c. roulante** wheelchair

chaland [ʃalɑ̃] nm barge

châle [ʃɑl] nm shawl

chalet [ʃalɛ] nm (a) (de montagne) chalet (b) Can cottage

chaleur [ʃalœr] nf (a) (température) heat; **les grandes chaleurs** the hot season; **il fait une c. terrible** it's terribly hot; **coup de c.** heatstroke (b) (d'une personne, d'une couleur, d'une voix, d'un accueil) warmth; **c. humaine** human warmth; **avec c.** warmly (c) Zool **être en c.** to be Br on heat or Am in heat

chaleureusement [ʃalœrøzmɑ̃] adv warmly

chaleureux, -euse [ʃalœrø, -øz] adj (accueil, atmosphère) warm; (paroles) glowing

challenge [ʃalɑ̃ʒ] nm (a) Sp tournament (b) (défi) challenge

challenger [tʃalɑ̃ʒœr] nm challenger

chaloupe [ʃalup] nf launch; (à rames) Br rowing boat, Am rowboat; **c. à moteur** motor launch; **c. de sauvetage** lifeboat

chaloupé, -e [ʃalupe] adj swaying

chalumeau, -x [ʃalymo] nm (a) Tech Br blowlamp, Am blowtorch (b) Can spout (for collecting sap of maple tree)

chalut [ʃaly] nm trawl; **pêcher au c.** to trawl

chalutier [ʃalytje] nm trawler

chamade [ʃamad] nf **battre la c.** to beat wildly

chamailler [ʃamaje] **se chamailler** vpr to squabble

chamailleur, -euse [ʃamajœr, -øz] 1 adj quarrelsome
2 nmf squabbler

chamarré, -e [ʃamare] adj richly coloured

chambardement [ʃɑ̃bardəmɑ̃] nm Fam upheaval

chambarder [ʃɑ̃barde] vt Fam (projets, maison) to turn upside down

chambouler [ʃɑ̃bule] vt Fam (projets, maison) to turn upside down

chambranle [ʃɑ̃brɑ̃l] nm (d'une porte, d'une fenêtre) frame

chambre [ʃɑ̃br] nf (a) (pièce) bedroom; (d'un hôtel) room; **c. à un lit/deux lits** single/twin room; **vous auriez une c. (de) libre?** do you have any vacancies?; **faire c. à part** to sleep in separate rooms; **faire sa c.** to tidy (up) one's room; **garder la c.** to keep to one's room; **sportif/ politicien en c.** armchair sportsman/politician; **c. d'amis** spare room; **c. de bonne** maid's room; **c. à coucher** (pièce) bedroom; (mobilier) bedroom furniture; **c. forte** strongroom; **c. frigorifique** ou **froide** cold store; **c. à gaz** gas chamber; **c. d'hôte** ≃ guest house; **c. meublée** furnished room, Br bed-sit(ter) (b) Jur (d'un tribunal) division; **c. d'accusation** Court of Criminal Appeal; **C. de commerce** Chamber of Commerce (c) Pol **la C.** the House; **siéger à la C.** to sit in the House; **C. des députés** = lower chamber of Parliament (d) Tech (d'un fusil, d'un appareil photo) chamber; **c. à air** inner tube

chambrée [ʃɑ̃bre] nf (a) (occupants d'une chambre) room(ful) (b) Mil barrackroom

chambrer [ʃɑ̃bre] vt (a) **c. qch** (bouteille, vin) to bring sth to room temperature (b) Fam **c. qn** to pull sb's leg

chameau, -x [ʃamo] nm (a) (animal) camel (b) Fam (homme) bastard; (femme) cow

chamelier [ʃamɔlje] nm camel-driver

chamelle [ʃamɛl] nf she-camel

chamois [ʃamwa] nm (a) (animal) chamois (b) Sp **c. d'or/d'argent/de bronze** = gold/silver/bronze skiing proficiency medal

champ [ʃɑ̃] nm (a) (étendue) field; **c. de blé** field of wheat, wheatfield; **prendre** ou **couper à travers champs** to cut across country; **à tout bout de c.** at every possible opportunity; Fig **laisser le c. libre à qn** to leave the field free for sb; **c. de bataille** battlefield; **c. de courses** Br racecourse, Am racetrack; **c. de foire** fairground; **mort** ou **tombé au c. d'honneur** killed in action; **c. de mines** minefield; **c. de tir** rifle range; Mil practice ground; (d'un fusil) field of fire (b) Fig (portée) scope; **c. d'action** field of activity; **élargir le c. de ses activités** to extend the scope of one's activities (c) Phot shot, picture; (d'un instrument optique) field; **être dans le c.** to be in shot; **c. visuel** field of vision (d) Él & Rad field; **c. magnétique** magnetic field (e) Ordinat field; **c. numérique** numeric field; **c. de texte** text field

champagne [ʃɑ̃paɲ] nm champagne

champenois, -e [ʃɑ̃pənwa, -az] 1 adj (a) (de la région) of Champagne (b) **méthode champenoise** champagne method
2 nm,f C. person from Champagne

champêtre [ʃɑ̃pɛtr] adj rustic, rural

champignon [ʃɑ̃piɲɔ̃] nm (a) (plante) mushroom; Fig **pousser comme un c.** (enfant) to shoot up; (ville) to mushroom; **c. atomique** mushroom cloud; **c. hallucinogène** magic mushroom; **c. de Paris** button mushroom; **c. vénéneux** poisonous mushroom, toadstool (b) Méd fungus (c) Fam (accélérateur) **appuyer sur le c.** Br to put one's foot down, Am to step on the gas

champion, -onne [ʃɑ̃pjɔ̃, -ɔn] 1 nm,f (a) (dans une discipline) champion; **le c. du monde d'escrime** the world fencing champion; Fam **c'est un c. du bricolage** he's an ace handyman (b) (d'une cause) champion
2 adj (a) Sp **l'équipe championne du monde** the world champions (b) Fam great; **pour les gaffes, il est c.!** he's a great one for putting his foot in it!

championnat [ʃɑ̃pjona] nm championship

chance [ʃɑ̃s] nf (a) (sort favorable) (good) luck; **souhaiter bonne c. à qn** to wish sb luck; **bonne c.!** good luck!; **quelle c.!** what a stroke of luck!; **avec un peu de c....** with a bit of luck...; **avoir de la c.** to be lucky or fortunate; **ne pas avoir de c.** to be unlucky; **porter c. à qn** to bring sb luck; **c'est mon jour de c.** it's my lucky day; **c'est bien ma c.!** just my luck!; **pas de c.!** hard luck!; **par c.** luckily, fortunately (b) (possibilité) chance; **avoir des chances de faire qch** to stand a (good) chance of doing sth; **avoir peu de chances de faire qch** to have little chance of doing sth; **donner une** ou **sa c. à qn** to give sb a chance; **elle a une c. sur deux de gagner** she has a fifty-fifty chance of winning; Fam **il y a des chances** probably; **il y a de grandes** ou **fortes chances (pour) qu'on le lui propose** there's every chance that she will be offered it

chancelant, -e [ʃɑ̃slɑ̃, -ɑ̃t] adj (pas) unsteady; (mémoire) shaky; (santé) delicate; (pouvoir, gouvernement) tottering; (détermination) wavering

chanceler [42] [ʃɑ̃sle] vi (personne) to stagger, to totter; (objet) to wobble; (régime, gouvernement) to totter; **l'uppercut le fit c.** the uppercut sent him reeling

chancelier [ʃɑ̃səlje] *nm Pol* chancellor; *(d'ambassade)* chief secretary

chancellerie [ʃɑ̃sɛlri] *nf* (a) *(d'une ambassade)* chancery (b) *(ministère de la Justice)* ≃ *Br* Lord Chancellor's Department

chanceux, -euse [ʃɑ̃sø, -øz] *adj* lucky

chancre [ʃɑ̃kr] *nm Méd & Fig* canker

chandail [ʃɑ̃daj] *nm* sweater, jumper

Chandeleur [ʃɑ̃dlœr] *nf* **la C.** Candlemas

chandelier [ʃɑ̃dəlje] *nm (à une branche)* candlestick; *(à plusieurs branches)* candelabra

chandelle [ʃɑ̃dɛl] *nf* (a) *(bougie)* candle; **s'éclairer à la c.** to use candlelight; **un dîner aux chandelles** a candlelit dinner; **faire des économies de bouts de c.** to make cheeseparing economies; **brûler la c. par les deux bouts** to burn the candle at both ends; **le jeu n'en vaut pas la c.** the game is not worth the candle; **tenir la c.** *Br* to play gooseberry, *Am* to feel like a fifth wheel; **voir trente-six chandelles** to see stars; **devoir une fière c. à qn** to owe sb a great debt (b) *(en gymnastique)* **faire la c.** to do a shoulder stand (c) *Av* **(montée en) c.** vertical climb

chanfrein [ʃɑ̃frɛ̃] *nm (de cheval)* nose

change [ʃɑ̃ʒ] *nm* (a) *Fin* exchange; **le c. est avantageux** the exchange rate is good; *Fig* **gagner/ne pas perdre au c.** to gain on/not to lose on the exchange (b) *Fig* **donner le c. à qn** to put sb off the scent; *(couche-culotte)* **c. (complet)** disposable *Br* nappy *or Am* diaper

changeant, -e [ʃɑ̃ʒɑ̃, -ɑ̃t] *adj (temps)* unsettled; **d'humeur changeante** moody

changement [ʃɑ̃ʒmɑ̃] *nm (modification)* change; **ça va te faire un drôle de c.** it'll be quite a change for you; **c. de décor** *Th* scene change; *Fig* change of scenery; **c. de direction** *(sur un écriteau)* under new management (b) *(dans les transports)* change; **il y a un c. à Valence** you have to change at Valence (c) **c. de vitesse** *(action)* change of gear; *(levier) Br* gear lever, *Am* gear shift; *Ordinat* **c. de ligne** line feed

changer [45] [ʃɑ̃ʒe] 1 *vt* (a) *(remplacer) (draps, couche de bébé, roue)* to change; **qch contre qch** to change *or* exchange sth for sth
(b) *(enfant, bébé)* to change
(c) *(convertir) (argent)* to change (**en** into)
(d) *(transformer)* **c. qn/qch en** to change sb/sth into
(e) *(modifier)* to change, to alter; **ça va les c.!** that'll be a change for them!; **ça lui changera les idées** that'll take his mind off things; **ça nous change du café du coin!** that makes a change from the local!; **cela ne change rien à l'affaire** that makes no difference; **sa nouvelle coiffure la change** she looks different with her new hairstyle; **mais cela change tout!** that changes everything!; **c. qch de place** to move sth
2 *vi* (a) *(se modifier)* to change; **c. en bien** *ou* **en mieux** to change for the better; **c. en mal** *ou* **en pire** to change for the worse; *Ironique* **pour c.** for a change
(b) *(dans les transports)* to change
3 **changer de** *vt ind* to change; **c. de train/de travail** to change trains/jobs; **c. de place avec qn** to change places with sb; **c. de coiffure** to change one's hairstyle; **c. de vêtements** to change (one's clothes), to get changed; **c. de couleur** to change colour; *Aut* **c. de vitesse** to change gear; **je te prie de c. de ton!** don't talk to me in that tone of voice!; *Fam Fig* **change de disque!** put another record on!
4 **se changer** *vpr* (a) *(mettre d'autres vêtements)* to change

(b) **se c. les idées** to change one's ideas
(c) *(se transformer)* **se c. en** to change *or* turn into

chanoine [ʃanwan] *nm Rel* canon

chanson [ʃɑ̃sɔ̃] *nf* (a) *(air)* song; **la c. française** French songs; *Fam* **c'est toujours la même c.!** it's always the same old story!; *Fam* **on connaît la c.** I've heard that one before!; **c. d'amour** love song; **c. à boire** drinking song (b) *(genre littéraire)* song; **c. de geste** chanson de geste

chansonnette [ʃɑ̃sɔnɛt] *nf* ditty

chansonnier [ʃɑ̃sɔnje] *nm* satirical cabaret singer

chant [ʃɑ̃] *nm* (a) *(chanson)* song; *(d'un instrument de musique, de la mer, du vent)* sound; *(d'un oiseau)* singing; *(du grillon, de la cigale)* chirping; *(du coq)* crowing; **au c. du coq** at cockcrow; *Fig* **c. du cygne** swan song; **c. funèbre** dirge; **c. de Noël** Christmas carol; **c. sacré** hymn (b) *(art)* singing; **leçon/professeur de c.** singing lesson/teacher; **apprendre le c.** to take singing lessons; **c. choral** choral singing; **c. grégorien** Gregorian chant (c) *(d'un poème)* canto

chantage [ʃɑ̃taʒ] *nm* blackmail; **faire du c.** to use blackmail; **il lui fait du c. au suicide** he's blackmailing her with suicide threats

chantant, -e [ʃɑ̃tɑ̃, -ɑ̃t] *adj (musique, air)* tuneful; *(accent, voix)* lilting

chanter [ʃɑ̃te] 1 *vt (chanson)* to sing; *Fam* **qu'est-ce que vous me chantez là?** what are you on about?; *Fam* **elle le chante sur tous les tons** she's always going on about it
2 *vi* (a) *(personne, oiseau)* to sing; *(coq)* to crow; *(grillon, cigale)* to chirp; **c. juste/faux** to sing in tune/out of tune (b) **faire c. qn** *(exercer un chantage sur)* to blackmail sb (c) *(plaire)* **viens, si ça te chante** come along, if you fancy the idea; **il vient quand ça lui chante** he comes when he feels like it

chanterelle[1] [ʃɑ̃trɛl] *nf Mus (corde)* top string

chanterelle[2] *nf (champignon)* chanterelle

chanteur, -euse [ʃɑ̃tœr, -øz] *nm,f* singer; **c. de charme** crooner; **c. des rues** street singer

chantier [ʃɑ̃tje] *nm* (a) *(lieu de construction)* (building) site; *(sur la route)* roadworks; **c. interdit au public** *(sur panneau)* no admittance to the public; **mettre qch en c.** to get sth under way; **c. naval** shipyard (b) *Fam (désordre)* **quel c.!** what a shambles!; **ils ont tout laissé en c.** they left the place in a complete shambles

chantilly [ʃɑ̃tiji] *nf (crème)* **c.** whipped cream

chantonner [ʃɑ̃tɔne] *vt & vi* to sing softly; *(sans paroles)* to hum

chantre [ʃɑ̃tr] *nm (défenseur)* champion

chanvre [ʃɑ̃vr] *nm* hemp; **c. indien** Indian hemp

chaos [kao] *nm* chaos

chaotique [kaotik] *adj* chaotic

chaparder [ʃaparde] *vt Fam* to pinch

chapardeur, -euse [ʃapardœr, -øz] *nm,f Fam* thief

chape [ʃap] *nf (de béton)* screed; *(d'un pneu)* tread; **la chaleur pèse sur la ville comme une c. de plomb** the heat lies on the town like a lead weight

chapeau, -x [ʃapo] *nm* (a) *(coiffure)* hat; *Fig* **porter le c.** to carry the can; *Fig* **tirer son c. à qn** to take off one's hat to sb; **c.!** well done!; **c. melon** bowler hat; **c. mou** *Br* trilby, *Am* fedora; **c. de paille** straw hat (b) *(d'un champignon)* cap (c) *(partie supérieure) (de vol-au-vent, de bouchée à la reine)* lid; **prendre un virage sur les chapeaux de roues** to take a corner at top speed

démarrer sur les chapeaux de roues *(projet, soirée)* to get off to a cracking start **(d)** *Typ & Journ* lead-in

chapeauter [ʃapote] *vt (contrôler)* to head

chapelain [ʃaplɛ̃] *nm Rel* chaplain

chapelet [ʃaplɛ] *nm (de prière)* rosary; *Fig (d'invectives, d'insultes)* stream; *(d'objets)* string; **dire son c.** to say the rosary

chapelier, -ère [ʃapəlje, -ɛr] *nm,f* hatter

chapelle [ʃapɛl] *nf* chapel; **c. ardente** chapel of rest

chapelure [ʃaplyr] *nf* breadcrumbs

chaperon [ʃaprɔ̃] *nm* **(a)** *(personne)* chaperon **(b)** *le Petit C. rouge* Little Red Riding Hood

chaperonner [ʃaprɔne] *vt aussi Fig* to chaperon

chapiteau, -x [ʃapito] *nm* **(a)** *Archit (d'une colonne)* capital **(b)** *(d'un cirque)* big top; **sous c.** in a marquee

chapitre [ʃapitr] *nm* **(a)** *(d'un livre)* chapter; *(d'un budget)* item; **inscrire une somme au c. des recettes/ dépenses** to enter a sum under revenue/expenditure; **elle est sévère sur le c. de la discipline** she is strict in the matter of discipline; **en voilà assez sur ce c.** that's enough of that; **et maintenant, au c. des faits divers...** and now for the news in brief... **(b)** *Rel (assemblée)* chapter; *Fig* **avoir voix au c.** to have a say in the matter

chapitrer [ʃapitre] *vt* **c. qn** *(réprimander)* to tell sb off; *(faire la morale à)* to lecture sb

chapon [ʃapɔ̃] *nm (coq)* capon

chaptaliser [ʃaptalize] *vt* to chaptalize

chaque [ʃak] *adj indéfini* each, every; **c. femme doit pouvoir travailler et élever ses enfants** every woman should be able to work as well as bring up her children; **ces livres coûtent 100 francs c.** these books cost 100 francs each; **c. chose à sa place** everything in its place; **c. chose en son temps** all in good time; **c. fois qu'il vient** whenever he comes; **j'y pense à c. instant** I think about it all the time

char [ʃar] *nm* **(a)** *Mil* **c. (d'assaut ou de combat)** tank **(b)** *(romain)* chariot **(c)** *Can Fam (voiture)* car **(d)** *Sp* **c. à voile** sand yacht; **faire du c. à voile** to go sand yachting **(f)** *Fam* **arrête ton c.!** come off it!

charabia [ʃarabja] *nm Fam* gibberish

charade [ʃarad] *nf* = charade which is described rather than acted out

charançon [ʃarɑ̃sɔ̃] *nm* weevil

charbon [ʃarbɔ̃] *nm* **(a)** *(combustible)* coal; **c. (de bois)** charcoal; **chauffage au c.** coal-fired heating; *Fig* **être sur des charbons ardents** to be on tenterhooks **(b)** *Art* charcoal; **dessin au c.** charcoal drawing **(c)** *Méd (médicament)* charcoal

charbonnage [ʃarbɔnaʒ] *nm (exploitation)* coal mining **(b)** **charbonnages** *(houillères)* collieries

charbonneux, -euse [ʃarbɔnø, -øz] *adj (noir)* coal-black; *(yeux)* heavy with black make-up

charbonnier, -ère [ʃarbɔnje, -ɛr] **1** *adj (industrie)* coal **2** *nm,f(a) (marchand de charbon)* coal merchant; *Prov* **c. est maître dans sa maison ou chez soi** a man is master in his own home **(b)** *Naut* coaler **3** *nf* **charbonnière** *(mésange)* great tit

charcuter [ʃarkyte] *Fam* **1** *vt* **c. qn** to hack sb about **2 se charcuter** *vpr* to cut oneself to ribbons; **se c. le menton/le doigt** to cut one's chin/finger to ribbons

charcuterie [ʃarkytri] *nf* **(a)** *(magasin)* pork butcher's (shop) **(b)** *(activité)* cooked meats trade **(c)** *(produits)* cooked meats

charcutier, -ère [ʃarkytje, -ɛr] *nm,f (a) (commerçant, fabricant)* pork butcher **(b)** *Fam Péj (chirurgien)* butcher

chardon [ʃardɔ̃] *nm (plante)* thistle

chardonneret [ʃardɔnrɛ] *nm* goldfinch

charentais, -e [ʃarɑ̃tɛ, -ɛz] **1** *adj* of Charente **2** *nm,f* C. person from Charente **3** *nf* **charentaise** *(chausson)* slipper

charge [ʃarʒ] *nf* **(a)** *(poids)* load; *(sur bateau)* cargo; *Fig* **être une c. pour qn** to be a burden to sb; **c. utile** *(d'un véhicule)* capacity **(b)** *(responsabilité)* responsibility; **être en c. de qch** to be in charge of sth; **prendre qn/qch en c.** to take charge of sb/sth; **se prendre en c.** to be responsible for oneself **(c)** *(fonction)* office; *(d'avoué)* practice **(d)** *(obligation financière)* **être à la c. de qn** *(personne)* to be dependent on sb; *(appel, transport, réparations)* to be chargeable to sb; **avoir deux enfants à c.** to have two dependent children; **prendre un client en c.** *(taxi)* to pick up a fare; **prendre pris en c. à cent pour cent par la Sécurité sociale** to have one's medical expenses fully paid for by Social Security; **charges (locatives)** *(d'un appartement)* maintenance charges; **charges d'exploitation** operating costs; **charges sociales** *Br* national insurance contributions, *Am* social security charges *(paid by the employer)* **(e)** *(d'une arme, d'explosifs)* charge **(f)** *Constr (pression)* load **(g)** *Él (d'une batterie, d'une particule)* charge **(h)** *Mil* charge; *Fig* **revenir à la c.** to return to the attack **(i)** *Jur (preuve)* charge

chargé, -e [ʃarʒe] **1** *adj (a) (camion, navire)* loaded, laden (**de** with); *(revolver, appareil photo)* loaded; *Fig (style)* ornate; **la voiture est trop chargée** the car is overloaded; **être c. comme un bourricot ou un mulet** to be loaded down; **avoir la langue chargée** to have a furred tongue; **un regard c. de reconnaissance** a look full of gratitude **(b)** *(occupé) (journée, programme)* full **(c)** *(responsable)* **être c. de qch** *(mission)* to be entrusted with sth; *(tâche)* to be responsible for sth; **être c. de famille** to have family responsibilities; **être c. de faire qch** to be responsible for doing sth **(d)** *Phys* charged **2** *nm* **c. d'affaires** chargé-d'affaires; **c. de mission** official representative **3** *nm,f Univ* **c. de cours** = part-time lecturer; *Can* lecturer

chargement [ʃarʒəmɑ̃] *nm* **(a)** *(action)* loading; *Él (d'une batterie)* charging; **machine à laver à c. frontal** front-loading washing machine **(b)** *(marchandises)* load; *(sur bateau)* cargo

charger [45] [ʃarʒe] **1** *vt (a) (camion, navire, marchandises)* to load **(b)** *(remplir)* to fill (**de** with) **(c)** *(fusil, appareil photo)* to load; *Él (batterie)* to charge; *Ordinat* to load (up) **(d)** *(donner une responsabilité à)* **c. qn de qch** to entrust sb with sth; **c. qn de faire qch** to give sb the responsibility for doing sth **(e)** *(attaquer)* to charge (at) **2** *vi (a) Ordinat* to load up **(b)** *Mil* to charge **3 se charger** *vpr (a) (s'alourdir)* to weigh oneself down **(b) se c. de qn/qch** *(prendre la responsabilité de)* to take care of sb/sth; **se c. de faire qch** to undertake to do sth

chargeur [ʃarʒœr] *nm (d'arme)* magazine; *Phot* cartridge; *Él (battery)* charger; *Ordinat* loader; **c. automatique** self loader

chariot [ʃarjo] *nm* (*petite charrette*) wagon; (*de supermarché*) *Br* trolley, *Am* cart; (*pour diapositives*) cartridge; (*pour la manutention*) truck; (*d'hôpital*) *Br* trolley, *Am* gurney; *Cin* dolly; (*d'une machine à écrire*) carriage; **c. à bagages** luggage trolley

charismatique [karismatik] *adj* charismatic

charisme [karism] *nm* charisma

charitable [ʃaritabl] *adj* charitable (**envers** towards); (*conseil*) friendly

charité [ʃarite] *nf* (**a**) (*altruisme*) charity; **faites-moi ou ayez la c. de…** please be kind enough to…; *Prov* **c. bien ordonnée commence par soi-même** charity begins at home (**b**) (*don*) charity; **faire la c. à qn** to give money to sb; **demander la c.** to ask for charity; **la c., Messieurs Dames** (*dans la rue*) can you spare some change, please?

charlatan [ʃarlatã] *nm Péj* (*mauvais médecin*) quack; (*escroc*) charlatan

Charles [ʃarl] *npr* **C. Quint** Charles the Fifth

charlot [ʃarlo] *nm Fam* (*personne peu sérieuse*) clown

charlotte [ʃarlɔt] *nf Culin* charlotte; **c. aux poires/au chocolat** pear/chocolate charlotte

charmant, -e [ʃarmã, -ãt] *adj* (*personne, chose, soirée*) charming, delightful; *Ironique* **et voilà qu'il pleut, ah, c'est c.!** how charming, marvellous!

charme[1] [ʃarm] *nm* (**a**) (*attrait*) charm; **avoir du c.** to have charm; **c'est ce qui en fait le c.** that's what makes it so attractive; **faire du c. à qn** to turn on the charm with sb; **charmes** (*d'une femme*) charms; **vivre de ses charmes** to sell one's charms (**b**) (*magie*) spell; **être/tomber sous le c.** to be/fall under the spell; *Fig* **se porter comme un c.** to be as fit as a fiddle

charme[2] *nm* (*arbre*) hornbeam

charmer [ʃarme] *vt* (**a**) (*plaire à*) to charm; **j'ai été charmé de vous rencontrer** it's been a pleasure to meet you (**b**) (*envoûter*) to charm

charmeur, -euse [ʃarmœr, -øz] **1** *nm,f* charmer; **c. de serpents** snake charmer
2 *adj* (*regard, sourire*) charming

charnel, -elle [ʃarnɛl] *adj* carnal

charnier [ʃarnje] *nm* mass grave

charnière [ʃarnjɛr] *nf* (*de porte, de fenêtre*) hinge; *Fig* **à la c. de deux grandes périodes** at the junction of two great eras; **époque/œuvre c.** transitional period/work

charnu, -e [ʃarny] *adj* (*partie du corps, lèvres*) fleshy; (*fruit*) pulpy; *Hum* **la partie charnue de son anatomie** his posterior

charognard [ʃarɔɲar] *nm* (**a**) *Zool* carrion-eater (**b**) (*exploiteur*) vulture

charogne [ʃarɔɲ] *nf* (**a**) (*d'animal*) carrion (**b**) *Fam* (*homme*) bastard; (*femme*) bitch

charpente [ʃarpɑ̃t] *nf* (*d'un bâtiment, d'un roman*) framework; (*du corps*) frame; **avoir une solide c.** (*personne*) to be solidly built

charpenterie [ʃarpɑ̃tri] *nf* (*métier*) carpentry

charpentier [ʃarpɑ̃tje] *nm* carpenter

charpie [ʃarpi] *nf* **mettre qch en c.** to tear sth to shreds; *Fam* **mettre qn en c.** to make mincemeat out of sb

charretier [ʃartje] *nm* **jurer comme un c.** to swear like a trooper

charrette [ʃaret] *nf* (**a**) (*véhicule*) cart (**b**) (*de licenciements*) round of redundancies (**c**) *Suisse Fam* **c. de Paul!** blinking Paul!

charrier [66] [ʃarje] **1** *vt* (**a**) (*transporter*) to cart (**b**) (*entraîner*) to carry along (**c**) *Fam* (*se moquer de*) **c. qn** *Br* to have sb on, *Am* to put sb on; **se faire c.** to be had on
2 *vi Fam* (*exagérer*) to go too far; **faut pas c.!** (*n'exagère pas*) come off it!

charrue [ʃary] *nf* (**a**) (*pour labourer*) plough; *Fig* **mettre la c. avant les bœufs** to put the cart before the horse (**b**) *Can* snowplough

charte [ʃart] *nf* charter

charter [ʃartɛr] *nm* (**avion**) **c.** charter plane

chartreux, -euse [ʃartrø, -øz] **1** *nm,f Rel* Carthusian
2 *nf* **chartreuse** (**a**) (*couvent*) Carthusian monastery (**b**) (*alcool*) Chartreuse

chas [ʃa] *nm* eye

chasse[1] [ʃas] *nf* (**a**) (*activité*) hunting; (*au fusil*) shooting; **aller à la c.** to go hunting/shooting; **la c. est ouverte/fermée** the shooting season has begun/ended; *Prov* **qui va à la c. perd sa place** if you leave your place someone will take it; **c. à courre** hunting; **c. au lapin** rabbit shooting (**b**) (*événement*) hunt; (*au fusil*) shoot (**c**) (*réserve*) **c. gardée** private game preserve; *Fig* (*domaine*) preserve (**d**) (*poursuite*) chase; **donner la c. à qn/qch, prendre qn/qch en c.** to give chase to sb/sth; **c. à l'homme** manhunt; *Pol* **c. aux sorcières** witch hunt; **c. au trésor** treasure hunt (**e**) **c. (d'eau)** flush; **tirer la c. (d'eau)** to flush the toilet (**f**) **être en c.** (*chienne, chatte*) to be *Br* on heat *or Am* in heat

châsse[2] [ʃas] *nf Rel* shrine

chassé-croisé (*pl* **chassés-croisés**) [ʃasekrwaze] *nm* (*de personnes*) comings and goings; (*de conversations*) babble

chasse-neige [ʃasnɛʒ] *nm inv* (**a**) (*engin*) snowplough (**b**) (*en ski*) snowplough; **descendre une piste en c.** to snowplough down a ski slope

chasser [ʃase] **1** *vt* (**a**) (*animaux*) to hunt; **c. le renard/la perdrix** to go foxhunting/partridge shooting (**b**) (*expulser*) to chase *or* chase away (**de** from); (*employé*) to dismiss; (*mouches*) to brush away; (*sujet: vent; nuages*) to blow away; **je ne veux pas vous c. mais il est tard** I'm not trying to get rid of you but it's getting late; *Fig* **c. qn/qch de son esprit** to dismiss sb/sth from one's thoughts
2 *vi* (**a**) (*aller à la chasse*) to hunt, to go hunting; (*au fusil*) to shoot, to go shooting (**b**) *Aut* to skid

chasseur, -euse [ʃasœr, -øz] **1** *nm,f* hunter; **c. de primes** bounty hunter; *aussi Fig* **c. de têtes** headhunter
2 *nm* (**a**) (*dans un hôtel*) *Br* pageboy, *Am* bellboy (**b**) (*avion de chasse*) fighter (**c**) *Mil* **les chasseurs alpins** the mountain light infantry

châssis [ʃasi] *nm* (**a**) (*charpente*) frame (**b**) *Art* stretcher (**c**) (*de jardin*) (cold) frame (**d**) *Aut* chassis

chaste [ʃast] *adj* chaste

chastement [ʃastəmã] *adv* chastely

chasteté [ʃastəte] *nf* chastity

chasuble [ʃazybl] *nf* (**a**) (**robe**) *Br* pinafore dress, *Am* jumper (**b**) *Rel* chasuble

chat, chatte [ʃa, ʃat] **1** *nm,f* cat; **petit c.** kitten; *Fam* **mon petit c., ma petite chatte** my pet; *Fig* **il n'y avait pas un c.** there wasn't a soul there; **appeler un c. un c.** to call a spade a spade; **avoir un c. dans la gorge** to have a frog in one's throat; **jouer au c. et à la souris avec qn** to play cat-and-mouse with sb; *Prov* **c. échaudé craint l'eau froide** once bitten, twice shy; **quand le c. n'est pas là, les souris dansent** when the cat's away the mice will play; **c. de gouttière** alley cat; **c. persan** Persian (cat); **c. sauvage** wildcat; *Can* (*raton laveur*) raccoon; **c.**

siamois Siamese (cat)

2 *nf* **chatte** *Vulg (sexe féminin)* pussy

châtaigne [ʃɑtɛɲ] *nf* **(a)** *(fruit)* (sweet) chestnut **(b)** *très Fam (coup de poing)* clout; **flanquer une c. à qn** to clout sb; **se prendre une c.** *(décharge)* to get a shock

châtaignier [ʃɑtɛɲe] *nm (arbre, bois)* chestnut

châtain [ʃɑtɛ̃] **1** *adj (cheveux)* (chestnut-)brown; *(personne)* brown-haired

2 *nm* chestnut brown

château, -x [ʃɑto] *nm* **(a)** *(forteresse)* castle; *(manoir)* mansion; *(de famille aristocratique)* stately home; *(palais)* palace; **les châteaux de la Loire** the châteaux of the Loire; *Fig* **bâtir des châteaux en Espagne** to build castles in the air; **c. de cartes** house of cards; **c. d'eau** water tower; **c. fort** castle **(b)** *(exploitation vinicole)* château; **mis en bouteille au c.** *(sur bouteille)* = indicates that wine was bottled at source

châtelain [ʃɑtlɛ̃] *nm (au Moyen Âge)* lord of the manor; *(propriétaire d'un château)* château owner

châtelaine [ʃɑtlɛn] *nf (au Moyen Âge)* lady of the manor; *(propriétaire d'un château)* (woman) château owner; *(épouse du propriétaire)* wife of a château owner

chat-huant *(pl* **chats-huants)** [ʃayɑ̃] *nm* tawny owl

châtié, -e [ʃɑtje] *adj (style)* polished; *(langage)* refined

châtier [66] [ʃɑtje] *vt Litt (personne)* to chastise; *Prov* **qui aime bien châtie bien** spare the rod and spoil the child

chatière [ʃɑtjɛr] *nf* **(a)** *(pour chat)* cat flap **(b)** *(pour aénation)* ventilation hole

châtiment [ʃɑtimɑ̃] *nm* **(a)** *Litt* chastisement **(b)** **c. corporel** corporal punishment

chaton¹ [ʃatɔ̃] *nm* **(a)** *(petit chat)* kitten **(b)** *Bot* catkin

chaton² [ʃatɔ̃] *nm* **(a)** *(d'une bague)* bezel **(b)** *(pierre)* stone

chatouille [ʃatuj] *nf* **faire des chatouilles à qn** to tickle sb; **craindre les chatouilles** to be ticklish

chatouiller [ʃatuje] *vt* **(a)** *(pour rire)* to tickle **(b)** *Fig (curiosité)* to arouse; *(amour-propre)* to flatter; **ah, ça chatouille!** oh, that tickles!

chatouilleux, -euse [ʃatujø, -øz] *adj* ticklish; *Fig* sensitive *(sur* about)

chatoyant, -e [ʃatwajɑ̃, -ɑ̃t] *adj* shimmering; *(pierre, imagination)* sparkling

chatoyer [32] [ʃatwaje] *vi* to shimmer; *(pierre)* to sparkle

châtrer [ʃɑtre] *vt (homme, taureau)* to castrate; *(étalon)* to geld; *(chat)* to neuter

chatte [ʃat] *nf voir* **chat**

chatterton [ʃatɛrtɔn] *nm Br* insulating tape, *Am* friction tape

chaud, -e [ʃo, ʃod] **1** *adj* **(a)** *(modérément)* warm; *(intensément)* hot; *Fig (voix) (couleur)* warm; **la soupe est toute chaude** the soup is piping hot; **l'été va être c.** it'll be a hot summer; *Fig* there'll be a lot of unrest this summer; **l'alerte fut chaude** it was a close thing; **une nouvelle toute chaude** some hot news **(b)** *(passionné) (discussion)* heated; *(partisan)* keen; **elle n'est pas chaude pour le projet** she's not keen on the plan

2 *adv* **j'aime manger c.** I like my food hot

3 *nm (modéré)* warmth; *(intense)* heat; **garder** *ou* **tenir qch au c.** to keep sth warm; **chez soi, au c.** at home, in the warmth; **avoir c.** to be or feel hot; *Fam (échapper de justesse)* to have a narrow escape; **il fait c.** it's hot; *Fig* **cela ne me fait ni c. ni froid** it's all the same to me; **interroger les spectateurs à c.** to question the

audience on the spot; **attraper un c. et froid** to catch a chill

chaudement [ʃodmɑ̃] *adv (s'habiller, féliciter, recommander)* warmly

chaudière [ʃodjɛr] *nf (de chauffage)* boiler; **c. à mazout/à gaz** oil-fired/gas boiler

chaudron [ʃodrɔ̃] *nm* cauldron

chaudronnier, -ère [ʃodrɔnje, -ɛr] *nm,f* boiler maker

chauffage [ʃofaʒ] *nm (d'une pièce, d'un bâtiment)* heating; *(appareils)* heating (system); *(dans une voiture)* heater; **c. à l'électricité/au gaz/au mazout** electric/gas/oil-fired heating; **c. central** central heating

chauffagiste [ʃofaʒist] *nm* heating engineer

chauffant, -e [ʃofɑ̃, -ɑ̃t] *adj voir* **couverture, plaque**

chauffard [ʃofar] *nm* reckless driver

chauffe-biberon *(pl* **chauffe-biberons)** [ʃofbibrɔ̃] *nm* bottle-warmer

chauffe-eau [ʃofo] *nm inv* water heater; **c. électrique** immersion heater

chauffe-plat *(pl* **chauffe-plats)** [ʃofpla] *nm* hot plate

chauffer [ʃofe] **1** *vt (pièce, bâtiment)* to heat (up); *(moteur)* to warm up; **c. une maison au gaz** to heat a house with gas; **la chambre n'est pas chauffée** there's no heating in the bedroom; *Fig* **c. son public** to warm up one's audience

2 *vi* **(a)** *(devenir chaud)* to heat up; **ce radiateur chauffe bien/mal** this radiator gives out/doesn't give out a lot of heat; **faire c. qch, mettre qch à c.** to heat sth up **(b)** *(s'échauffer) (moteur)* to overheat **(c)** *Fam* **ça va c. s'il est en retard!** there'll be trouble if he's late!; **tu chauffes!** *(dans un jeu)* you're getting warmer!

3 **se chauffer** *vpr* to warm oneself; **se c. (les muscles)** to warm up; **se c. au mazout/à l'électricité** to have oil-fired/electric heating

chaufferette [ʃofrɛt] *nf (pour les pieds)* footwarmer

chaufferie [ʃofri] *nf* boiler room

chauffeur [ʃofœr] *nm (de voiture, de bus)* driver; *(employé)* chauffeur; **les chauffeurs du dimanche** Sunday drivers; **c. de camion** *Br* lorry driver, *Am* truck driver; **c. de taxi** taxi driver

chauffeuse [ʃoføz] *nf (fauteuil)* low armless chair

chauler [ʃole] *vt (murs)* to whitewash; *(terres)* to treat with lime

chaume [ʃom] *nm* **(a)** *(pour toits)* thatch **(b)** *(des céréales)* stubble

chaumière [ʃomjɛr] *nf (maison pauvre)* cottage; *(maison à toit de chaume)* thatched cottage

chaussée [ʃose] *nf (route)* roadway

chausse-pied *(pl* **chausse-pieds)** [ʃospje] *nm* shoehorn

chausser [ʃose] *vt* **1 (a)** *(chaussures, lunettes, skis)* to put on; *(enfant) (de pantoufles)* wearing slippers; **elle chausse du 37** she takes a size 37 **(b)** *(mettre des chaussures à)* to put shoes on **(c)** *(aller à)* to fit; **souliers qui chaussent bien** shoes that fit well

2 **se chausser** *vpr (mettre ses chaussures)* to put one's shoes on

chausses [ʃos] *nfpl (vêtement)* breeches

chaussette [ʃosɛt] *nf* sock; **en chaussettes** in one's socks; **laisser tomber qn comme une vieille c.** to cast sb aside like an old rag

chausseur [ʃosœr] nm (magasin) shoe shop; (fabricant) shoe manufacturer

chausson [ʃosɔ̃] nm (a) (pantoufle) slipper; (de danse) ballet shoe; (de bébé) bootee (b) Culin c. aux pommes apple turnover

chaussure [ʃosyr] nf shoe; (l'industrie de) la c. the shoe industry; **chaussures de ville/de sport/ habillées** town/sports/dress shoes; **chaussures à lacets** lace-up shoes; **chaussures de marche** ou **de montagne** walking boots; **chaussures montantes** ankle boots; **chaussures de ski** ski boots; **chaussures à talons** high-heeled shoes; Fig **trouver c. à son pied** to find the right woman/man

chauve [ʃov] **1** adj bald
2 nm bald(-headed) man

chauve-souris (pl **chauves-souris**) [ʃovsuri] nf bat

chauvin, -e [ʃovɛ̃, -in] **1** adj chauvinistic
2 nm,f chauvinist

chauvinisme [ʃovinism] nm chauvinism

chaux [ʃo] nf lime; **blanchir un mur à la c.** to whitewash a wall; **c. vive** quicklime

chavirer [ʃavire] **1** vi (a) (bateau) to capsize; **faire c. un bateau** to capsize a boat (b) (tourner) **tout chavire autour de moi** everything's spinning
2 vt (bouleverser) to overwhelm

check-up [tʃɛkœp] nm inv Méd check-up; **se faire faire un c.** to have a check-up

chef [ʃɛf] nm (a) (d'un parti politique, d'une bande) leader; (d'une tribu) chief; Fam (patron) boss; **ingénieur/ rédacteur en c.** chief engineer/editor; **se débrouiller comme un c.** to be getting on very well; **c. d'atelier** (shop) foreman; **c. d'entreprise** company head; **c. d'État** head of state; **c. de famille** head of the family; **c. de file** leader; **c. de gare** station manager; **le c. du gouvernement** the head of government; **c. d'orchestre** conductor; **c. de service** departmental head (b) (cuisinier) chef (c) Jur **c. d'accusation** charge (d) (tête) head; **faire qch de son propre c.** to do sth on one's own authority

chef-d'œuvre (pl **chefs-d'œuvre**) [ʃedœvr] nm masterpiece

chef-lieu (pl **chefs-lieux**) [ʃefljø] nm = administrative centre of a département

cheik(h) [ʃɛk] nm sheik(h)

chelem [ʃlɛm] nm Sp **grand c.** grand slam

chemin [ʃəmɛ̃] nm (a) (route étroite) path, track; **c. de grande randonnée** hiking trail; **c. de ronde** parapet walk; **c. de terre** track; **c. de traverse** path across the fields (b) (itinéraire) way (**de** to); Fig (de la gloire, du bonheur) road (**de** to); **en c.** on the way; **se mettre en c.** to set out or off; **nous ne pouvons pas nous arrêter en si bon c.** we can't give up now when we're doing so well; **ne pas y aller par quatre chemins** to get straight to the point; **prendre le c. des écoliers** to take the long way round; **suivre le droit c.** to stay on the straight and narrow (c) (distance) way; aussi Fig **avoir beaucoup de c. à faire** to have a long way to go; **nous avons fait la moitié du c. ensemble/à pied** we went half the way together/on foot; Fig **faire son c.** (idée) to gain ground (d) Ordinat path; **c. d'accès** path

chemin de fer (pl **chemins de fer**) [ʃəmɛ̃dfɛr] nm Br railway, Am railroad; Ordinat (affichage) thumbnail; **les chemins de fer** (société d'exploitation) the railway

cheminée [ʃəmine] nf (a) (dans une maison) fireplace; (dessus) mantelpiece (b) (conduit) (de maison, d'usine) chimney; (de bateau à vapeur) funnel (c) Géol chimney

cheminement [ʃəminmɑ̃] nm (de personnes) movement; Fig **le c. de la pensée** the development of thought

cheminer [ʃəmine] vi (personne) to make one's way; Fig (idée) to gain ground

cheminot [ʃəmino] nm Br railwayman, Am railroader

chemise [ʃəmiz] nf (a) (vêtement) shirt; **c. à manches longues/courtes** long-/short-sleeved shirt; Fig **changer de qch comme de c.** to change sth at the drop of a hat; **c. de nuit** (de femme) nightdress; (d'homme) nightshirt (b) (classeur) folder

chemisette [ʃəmizɛt] nf (d'homme) short-sleeved shirt

chemisier [ʃəmizje] nm (a) (corsage) blouse (b) (fabricant) shirt-maker; (marchand) men's outfitter

chenal, -aux [ʃənal, -o] nm (d'une rivière, d'un port) channel

chenapan [ʃənapɑ̃] nm Vieilli scoundrel

chêne [ʃɛn] nm oak; **table en c. massif** solid oak table; **c. vert** holm oak

chêne-liège (pl **chênes-lièges**) [ʃɛnljɛʒ] nm cork oak

chenet [ʃəne] nm firedog

chenil [ʃəni] nm (a) (abri, élevage) kennels (b) Suisse (désordre) shambles

chenille [ʃənij] nf (a) (insecte) caterpillar (b) (de char, d'autoneige) caterpillar track; **véhicule à chenilles** tracked vehicle (c) (tissu) chenille

chenu, -e [ʃəny] adj Litt (personne, tête) hoary; (arbre) leafless

cheptel [ʃɛptɛl] nm (d'un agriculteur) livestock

chèque [ʃɛk] nm **c.** (bancaire) Br cheque, Am check; **c. de 60 francs** cheque for 60 francs; **faire un c. à qn** to write sb a cheque; **payer qch par c.** to pay for sth by cheque; **c. barré** crossed cheque; **c. en blanc** blank cheque; Fam **c. en bois** rubber cheque; **c. sans provision** bad cheque; **j'ai fait un c. sans provision** my cheque bounced; **c. de voyage** traveller's cheque

chèque-cadeau (pl **chèques-cadeaux**) [ʃɛkkado] nm gift token

chèque-repas (pl **chèques-repas**) [ʃɛkrəpa], **chèque-restaurant** (pl **chèques-restaurant**) [ʃɛkrɛstɔrɑ̃] nm luncheon voucher

chéquier [ʃekje] nm Br cheque book, Am check book

cher, -ère [ʃɛr] **1** adj (a) (coûteux) dear, expensive; Fam **pas c.** cheap; **la vie est chère en ville** it's expensive to live in town; (aimé) dear; Litt **être c. à qn** to be dear to sb; **c'est mon vœu le plus c.** it's my dearest wish; **il a retrouvé sa chère maison/son c. bureau** he's back in his beloved house/office; **C. Monsieur** (dans une lettre) Dear Mr X; (officiel) Dear Sir
2 adv **payer qch c./trop c.** to pay a high price/too much for sth; Fam **je l'ai eu pour pas c.** I got it cheap; **coûter c.** to cost a lot; **je donnerais c. pour savoir ce qu'il leur a dit** I'd give anything to know what he said to them
3 nm,f **mon c., ma chère** my dear

chercher [ʃɛrʃe] **1** *vt* **(a)** *(objet, personne, emploi, solution)* to look for; *(dans un dictionnaire)* to look up; *(dans ses souvenirs)* to try to think of; **c. qn du regard** *ou* **des yeux** to look around for sb; **cherche!** *(à un chien)* fetch!; *Fig* **où va-t-il donc c. tout cela?** where on earth does he get that from?; **il l'a bien cherché** he was asking for it; **c. midi à quatorze heures** to look for problems where there are none **(b)** *(prendre)* **aller/venir c. qn/qch** to (go/come and) fetch sb/sth **(c)** *(essayer)* **c. à faire qch** to try to do sth **(d)** *Fam (atteindre)* **cela va c. dans les 10 000 francs** you're talking about something like 10,000 francs **(e)** *Fam (provoquer)* to get at; **tu me cherches?** are you looking for a fight?

2 se chercher *vpr (chercher son identité)* to try to find oneself

chercheur, -euse [ʃɛrʃœr, -øz] *nm,f* **(a)** *(scientifique)* researcher **(b) c. d'or** gold digger

chère [ʃɛr] *nf Litt* **aimer la bonne c.** to be a lover of good food

chèrement [ʃɛrmɑ̃] *adv* **vendre c. sa peau** to sell one's life dearly

chéri, -e [ʃeri] **1** *adj* dear
2 *nm,f* darling; **mon c., ma chérie** darling

chérir [ʃerir] *vt Litt* to cherish

cherra *etc voir* **choir**

cherry *(pl* **cherrys** *ou* **cherries)** [ʃeri] *nm* cherry brandy

cherté [ʃɛrte] *nf* high cost; **la c. de la vie** the high cost of living

chérubin [ʃerybɛ̃] *nm aussi Fig* cherub

chétif, -ive [ʃetif, -iv] *adj (personne)* puny, sickly; *(arbuste)* stunted

cheval, -aux [ʃəval, -o] *nm* **(a)** *(animal)* horse; *Péj (femme)* carthorse; **à c. on** horseback; **monter à c.** to ride; *aussi Fig* **être à c. sur qch** to straddle sth; **être à c. sur l'étiquette** to be a stickler for etiquette; *Fam* **ce n'est pas un mauvais c.** he's not such a bad sort; **monter sur ses grands chevaux** to get on one's high horse; **petits chevaux** = type of board game; **c. d'arçons** (vaulting) horse; **c. à bascule** rocking horse; **c'est son c. de bataille** that's her hobby-horse; **chevaux de bois** *Br* roundabout, *Am* carousel; **c. de course** racehorse; **c. de labour** workhorse; **c. de trait** carthorse **(b)** *Aut* horsepower; **une automobile de 20 chevaux** a 20-horsepower car

chevalerie [ʃəvalri] *nf* **(a)** *(dignité)* knighthood **(b)** *(institution)* chivalry

chevalet [ʃəvalɛ] *nm* **(a)** *(de peintre)* easel; *(de menuisier, de charpentier)* trestle **(b)** *Mus (de violon)* bridge

chevalier [ʃəvalje] *nm* **(a)** *(seigneur)* knight; **c. servant** faithful admirer **(b)** *(de la Légion d'honneur)* chevalier

chevalière [ʃəvaljɛr] *nf* signet ring

chevalin, -e [ʃəvalɛ̃, -in] *adj* equine; *Fig (traits)* horsey

cheval-vapeur [ʃəvalvapœr] *(pl* **chevaux-vapeur** [ʃəvovapœr]) *nm* horsepower

chevauchée [ʃəvoʃe] *nf (course)* ride

chevaucher [ʃəvoʃe] **1** *vt (mur, chaise)* to straddle; *Litt (cheval, âne)* to ride
2 *vi Litt* to ride
3 se chevaucher *vpr* to overlap

chevelu, -e [ʃəvly] *adj Péj* long-haired

chevelure [ʃəvlyr] *nf* (head of) hair; **femme à la c. rousse/blonde** red-haired/blonde woman

chevet [ʃəvɛ] *nm* **(a)** *(tête de lit)* bedhead; **rester au c. de qn** to stay at sb's bedside **(b)** *Archit (d'une église)* chevet

cheveu, -x [ʃəvø] *nm* **(a)** *(poil)* hair; **avoir le c. terne** to have dull hair; **un c. blanc** a grey hair; **arriver comme un c. sur la soupe** to come at an awkward moment; **il s'en est fallu d'un c. qu'il n'éclate de rire** he very nearly burst out laughing; **rater qch d'un c.** to miss sth by a whisker; **à un c. près, je ratais mon train** I caught my train by a hair's breadth **(b) cheveux** hair; **avoir les cheveux longs/courts** to have long/short hair; **un vieillard à cheveux blancs** a white-haired old man; **argument tiré par les cheveux** far-fetched argument; **cheveux d'ange** *(pâtes)* angel-hair pasta

cheville [ʃəvij] *nf* **(a)** *(partie du corps)* ankle; *Fig* **il ne vous arrive pas à la c.** he can't hold a candle to you; *Fam Péj* **tu as les chevilles qui enflent** you're getting too big for your *Br* boots or *Am* britches **(b)** *(pour accrocher)* peg; *(pour boucher un trou)* plug; *(de violon, de guitare)* peg; **être en c. avec qn** to be in cahoots with sb; *Fig* **c. ouvrière** mainspring

chèvre [ʃɛvr] **1** *nf* goat; *Fam* **devenir c.** to go round the bend; *Fam* **rendre qn c.** to drive sb round the bend
2 *nm* goat's cheese

chevreau, -x [ʃəvro] *nm* kid; **gants en c.** kid gloves

chèvrefeuille [ʃɛvrəfœj] *nm* honeysuckle

chevreuil [ʃəvrœj] *nm* roe deer; *Can* deer; *(gibier)* venison

chevron [ʃəvrɔ̃] *nm* **(a)** *Constr (d'un toit)* rafter **(b)** *Mil* stripe, chevron **(c)** *(motif)* **tissu à chevrons** herringbone-pattern material

chevronné, -e [ʃəvrɔne] *adj (qui a de l'expérience)* experienced

chevrotant, -e [ʃəvrɔtɑ̃, -ɑ̃t] *adj (voix)* quavering

chevroter [ʃəvrɔte] *vi (voix)* to quaver

chevrotine [ʃəvrɔtin] *nf* buckshot

chewing-gum *(pl* **chewing-gums)** [ʃwiŋgɔm] *nm* chewing-gum

chez [ʃe] *prép* **(a)** *(dans la maison de)* **il n'est pas c. lui** he's not at home, he's not in; **elle est rentrée c. elle** she's gone home; **faites comme c. vous** make yourself at home; **je vais c. ma sœur** I'm going to my sister's; **venez c. nous** come to our place; **il vit c. nous** he lives with us; **aller c. le dentiste** to go to the dentist; **chez...** *(sur une lettre)* c/o... **(b)** *(en, dans)* **c'est devenu une habitude c. moi** it's become a habit with me; **ce que j'admire c. cet homme, c'est...** what I admire about the man is...; **c. les Espagnols, on dîne tard** the Spaniards have dinner late **(c)** *(au temps de)* during the time of **(d)** *(parmi)* among; **cette expression est courante c. les jeunes** this expression is common among young people

chez-soi [ʃeswa] *nm inv* **son petit c.** one's own little home

chialer [ʃjale] *vi très Fam* to blubber

chiant, -e [ʃjɑ̃, -ɑ̃t] *adj très Fam* damned annoying

chianti [kjɑ̃ti] *nm* Chianti

chiasse [ʃjas] *nf Vulg* **avoir la c.** *(la diarrhée)* to have the shits; *(avoir peur)* to be shit-scared

chic [ʃik] **1** *adj inv* **(a)** *(élégant)* stylish, smart; **les gens c.** the smart set **(b)** *Fam Vieilli (aimable)* decent
2 *nm* **(a)** *(savoir-faire)* **avoir le c. pour faire qch** to have the knack of doing sth **(b)** *(élégance)* style; **bon c. bon genre** ≃ *Br* Sloany, *Am* preppy
3 *exclam Fam Vieilli* **c. (alors)!** great!

Chicago [ʃikago] n Chicago

chicaner [ʃikane] **1** vt (chercher querelle à) to quibble with (sur about)
2 chicaner sur vt ind to quibble over
3 se chicaner vpr to squabble

chicaneur, -euse [ʃikanœr, -øz], **chicanier, -ère** [ʃikanje, -er] nmf quibbler

chiche [ʃiʃ] adj (repas) scanty; (personne) mean; **être c. de louanges** to be sparing in one's praise; Fam **tu n'es pas c. d'y aller!** I bet you don't go!; Fam **c.! (pour défier)** I dare you!; (pour relever le défi) you're on!

chichement [ʃiʃmã] adv meanly

chichi [ʃiʃi] nm Fam **faire du c. ou des chichis** (se donner des airs) to put on airs; (compliquer les choses) to make a fuss; **repas sans c.** informal meal

chicorée [ʃikɔre] nf (a) (plante) c. (frisée) endive; c. **sauvage** chicory (b) (en poudre) chicory

chicot [ʃiko] nm (dent) stump

chiée [ʃje] nf très Fam (toute) **une c. de** a hell of a lot of

chien, chienne [ʃjɛ̃, ʃjɛn] nmf, f dog, f bitch; **jeune c.** puppy, pup; (attention) **c. méchant** (sur écriteau) beware of the dog; **traiter qn comme un c.** to treat sb like a dog; Fam **quel temps de c.!** what foul weather!; Fam **vie de c.** dog's life; **être comme c. et chat** to fight like cat and dog; **entre c. et loup** at dusk; **se regarder en chiens de faïence** to stare at one another; **c. d'arrêt** pointer; **c. d'aveugle** guide dog; **c. de berger** sheepdog; **c. de chasse** retriever; **c. de garde** guard dog; **c. policier** police dog; **c. de race** pedigree dog; **c. savant** (dans un cirque) performing dog; Fig performing monkey; **c. de traîneau** husky
2 nm (a) Fam (style) **avoir du c.** to have a certain something (b) (d'un fusil) hammer; **dormir en c. de fusil** to sleep curled up

chiendent [ʃjɛ̃dã] nm couch grass; **brosse en ou de c.** scrubbing brush; **pousser comme du c.** to sprout up

chien-loup [ʃjɛ̃lu] (pl chiens-loups) nm wolfhound

chienne [ʃjɛn] nf voir chien

chier [ʃje] vi Vulg to shit, to crap; **faire c. qn** (énerver) to piss sb off; (ennuyer) to bore sb shitless; **se faire c.** (s'ennuyer) to be bored shitless; **se faire c. (à faire qch)** (avoir du mal) to bust a gut (doing sth); **je me suis fait c. à l'attendre** I did myself in waiting for him

chiffe [ʃif] nf Fam **c'est une c. molle** he's a drip

chiffon [ʃifɔ̃] nm rag; **c. à poussière** duster; **passer un coup de c.** to have a dust; **passer un coup de c. sur qch** to give sth a dust; Fam **parler chiffons** to talk clothes

chiffonner [ʃifɔne] **1** vt (a) (robe, morceau de papier) to crumple (b) Fam (ennuyer) to bother
2 se chiffonner vpr to crumple

chiffonnier, -ère [ʃifɔnje, -er] **1** nm, f rag picker; **se disputer comme des chiffonniers** to go at it hammer and tongs
2 nm (meuble) chiffonier

chiffrable [ʃifrabl] adj **facilement/difficilement c.** easy/difficult to calculate; **ne pas être c.** to be impossible to calculate

chiffre [ʃifr] nm (a) (nombre) figure, number; **chiffres arabes/romains** Arabic/Roman numerals; **nombre à trois chiffres** three-figure number; Ordinat **c. binaire** binary digit; Ordinat **c. ASCII** ASCII number (b) (total) total; **c. d'affaires** (annuel) turnover; **faire un c. d'affaires de 4 millions de francs** to have a turnover of 4 million francs

chiffrement [ʃifrəmã] nm Ordinat **c. de données** data encryption

chiffrer [ʃifre] **1** vt (a) (montant, coût) to work out, to calculate; (réparations) to assess (b) **message chiffré** coded message
2 se chiffrer vpr **se c. à** to add up to, to amount to

chignole [ʃinɔl] nf hand drill; (électrique) electric drill

chignon [ʃinɔ̃] nm bun, chignon; **se faire un c.** to put one's hair in a bun

chihuahua [ʃiwawa] nm chihuahua

chiite [ʃiit] adj & nmf Rel Shiite

Chili [ʃili] nm **le C.** Chile

chili (con carne) [ʃili(kɔnkarne)] nm Culin chilli (con carne)

chilien, -enne [ʃiljɛ̃, -en] **1** adj Chilean
2 nm, f **C.** Chilean

chimère [ʃimer] nf (monstre) chimera; Fig (rêve) pipe dream

chimie [ʃimi] nf chemistry

chimiothérapie [ʃimjoterapi] nf Méd chemotherapy; **faire une c.** to have chemotherapy

chimique [ʃimik] adj chemical

chimiste [ʃimist] nmf chemist; **ingénieur c.** chemical engineer

chimpanzé [ʃɛ̃pãze] nm chimpanzee

chinchilla [ʃɛ̃ʃila] nm (animal, fourrure) chinchilla; **veste en c.** chinchilla jacket

Chine [ʃin] nf **la C.** China

chiné, -e [ʃine] adj (tissu) flecked

chiner [ʃine] **1** vt Fam (personne) to kid
2 vi to hunt for second-hand goods

chinetoque [ʃintɔk] nmf très Fam Chink, = racist term used to refer to a Chinese

chinois, -e [ʃinwa, -az] **1** adj Chinese
2 nm, f **C.** Chinese; **les C.** the Chinese
3 nm (a) (langue) Chinese; Fam **c'est du c.** it's all Greek to me (b) (ustensile) conical strainer

chinoiserie [ʃinwazri] nf (a) (objet) Chinese curio (b) Fam **chinoiseries** (complications) pointless complications

chintz [ʃints] nm chintz; **des rideaux en c.** chintz curtains

chiot [ʃjo] nm puppy, pup

chiottes [ʃjɔt] nfpl très Fam Br bog, Am john; Vulg **aux c., l'arbitre!** the referee's a wanker!

chiper [ʃipe] vt Fam to pinch, to swipe

chipie [ʃipi] nf Fam minx

chipolata [ʃipɔlata] nf chipolata (sausage)

chipoter [ʃipɔte] vi (a) (picorer) to pick at one's food (b) (contester) to quibble (sur about)

chips [ʃips] nf Br crisp, Am chip; **des (pommes) c.** Br crisps, Am chips

chique [ʃik] nf (a) (de tabac) quid (b) Belg sweet

chiqué [ʃike] nm Fam **faire du c.** to put on an act; **c'est du c.** it's all put on

chiquenaude [ʃiknod] nf flick; **d'une c., il l'envoya sur le bureau** he flicked it onto the desk

chiquer [ʃike] **1** vt to chew
2 vi to chew tobacco

chiromancien, -enne [kirɔmãsjɛ̃, -en] nm, f palmist

chirurgical, -e, -aux, -ales [ʃiryrʒikal, -o] adj surgical

chirurgie [ʃiryrʒi] *nf* surgery; **c. esthétique** plastic surgery

chirurgien [ʃiryrʒjɛ̃] *nm* surgeon

chirurgien-dentiste (*pl* **chirurgiens-dentistes**) [ʃiryrʒjɛ̃dɑ̃tist] *nm* dental surgeon

chiure [ʃjyr] *nf* c. **de mouche** fly-speck

ch-l. (*abrév* **chef-lieu**) = administrative centre of a *département*

chleuh, -e [ʃlø] *adj & nm,f très Fam* Kraut, = offensive term used to refer to a German

chlinguer [ʃlɛ̃ge] *vi très Fam* to stink

chlorate [klɔrat] *nm Chim* chlorate

chlore [klɔr] *nm* chlorine

chlorer [klɔre] *vt* to chlorinate

chlorhydrique [klɔridrik] *adj (acide)* hydrochloric

chlorofluorocarbure [klɔrɔflyɔrɔkarbyr] *nm Chim* chlorofluorocarbon

chloroforme [klɔrɔfɔrm] *nm* chloroform

chloroformer [klɔrɔfɔrme] *vt* to chloroform

chlorophylle [klɔrɔfil] *nf* chlorophyll

chlorure [klɔryr] *nm Chim* chloride; **c. de sodium** sodium chloride

chnoque [ʃnɔk] = **schnock**

choc [ʃɔk] *nm* (a) *(coup)* impact; *Fig (conflit)* clash; *(forte impression)* impact; *Écon* **c. pétrolier** oil crisis (b) *Méd* shock; **c. opératoire** post-operative shock (c) *(émotion brutale)* shock; **faire un c. à qn** to give sb a shock; **être en état de c.** to be in a state of shock; **être sous le c.** to be in shock (d) **équipe de c.** team of troubleshooters; **troupes de c.** shock troops

-choc [ʃɔk] *suff* **image-c.** shocking image; **prix-chocs** *(sur une vitrine)* drastic reductions

chochotte [ʃɔʃɔt] *nf Fam Péj* la-di-da type; *(homme)* namby-pamby; **faire sa c.** to put on airs

chocolat [ʃɔkɔla] **1** *nm* (a) *(produit)* chocolate; **gâteau au c.** chocolate cake; **blanc** white chocolate; **un c. (chaud)** a hot chocolate; **c. à cuire** cooking chocolate; **c. au lait** milk chocolate; **c. noir ou à croquer** plain *or* dark chocolate; **c. aux noisettes** hazelnut chocolate; **c. en poudre** drinking chocolate (b) *(bonbon)* chocolate

2 *adj inv* chocolate-coloured; *Fam* **être c.** to have lost out

chocolaté, -e [ʃɔkɔlate] *adj* chocolate

chocolatier, -ère [ʃɔkɔlatje, -ɛr] **1** *nm,f (fabricant)* chocolate-maker; *(vendeur)* chocolate-seller

2 *adj (industrie)* chocolate

chocottes [ʃɔkɔt] *nfpl Fam* **avoir les c.** to have the jitters

chœur [kœr] *nm* choir; *(d'opéra)* chorus; **les chœurs** the chorus; **chanter en c.** to sing in chorus; **répétez tous en c.** repeat all together now

choir [14] [ʃwar] *vi (aux être) Litt (tomber)* to fall; **se laisser c.** to sink down; *Fam* **laisser c. qn** to drop sb

choisi, -e [ʃwazi] *adj* (a) *(sélectionné)* **morceaux choisis de...** selected extracts from... (b) *(langage, termes)* careful

choisir [ʃwazir] *vt* to choose, to pick; **c. de faire qch** to choose to do sth; **il a bien choisi son moment!** he really picked his moment!; **à toi de c.,** **cette fois** it's your turn to choose now

choix [ʃwa] *nm* choice; **un grand c. de cravates** a wide choice *or* selection of ties; **avoir le c.** to have a choice; **faire son c.** to take one's pick; **faire le bon c.** to make the right choice; **mon c. est fait** I've made my choice; **laisser le c. à qn** to let sb choose; **viande ou poisson au c. (sur un menu)** choice of meat or fish; **de premier c.** top-grade; **de second c.** second-grade

choléra [kɔlera] *nm* cholera; **avoir le c.** to have cholera

cholestérol [kɔlesterɔl] *nm* cholesterol; **taux de c.** cholesterol level; *Fam* **avoir du c.** to have a high cholesterol level

cholestérolémie [kɔlesterɔlemi] *nf Méd* cholesterol level

chômage [ʃomaʒ] *nm* unemployment; **être au c.** to be unemployed, to be out of work; **toucher le c.** to claim unemployment benefit; **s'inscrire au c.** to sign on; **le c. des jeunes** youth unemployment; **être en c. technique** to have been laid off

chômé, -e [ʃome] *adj* **jour c.** public holiday, *Br* bank holiday

chômer [ʃome] *vi* **vous n'avez pas chômé!** you've not been idle!

chômeur, -euse [ʃomœr, -øz] *nm,f* unemployed person; **les chômeurs** the unemployed

chope [ʃɔp] *nf (récipient)* beer mug; *(contenu)* ≃ pint

choper [ʃɔpe] *vt Fam* (a) *(arrêter, prendre)* to nab; **se faire c.** to get nabbed (b) *(maladie)* to catch

chopine [ʃɔpin] *nf Fam (bouteille)* half-litre bottle; **tu viens boire une c.?** are you coming for a drink?

choquant, -e [ʃɔkɑ̃, -ɑ̃t] *adj* shocking

choquer [ʃɔke] *vt* (a) *(indigner)* to shock (b) *(traumatiser)* **c. qn** to shake sb badly

choral, -e, -aux *ou* **-als, -ales** [kɔral] **1** *adj* choral **2** *nf* **chorale** *(club)* choral society; *(chanteurs)* choir

chorégraphe [kɔregraf] *nmf* choreographer

chorégraphie [kɔregrafi] *nf* choreography; **faire la c. d'un spectacle** to choreograph a show

chorégraphique [kɔregrafik] *adj* choreographic

choriste [kɔrist] *nmf* choir member; *(d'église)* chorister; *(d'opéra)* chorus member; *(d'un chanteur)* backing singer

chorizo [tʃɔrizo] *nm* chorizo

chorus [kɔrys] *nm (de jazz)* chorus

chose [ʃoz] **1** *nf* (a) *(objet, parole, événement)* thing; **il s'est passé une c. incroyable** something unbelievable has happened; **je vais te dire une c.** I'm going to tell you something; **il a très bien pris la c.** he took it very well (b) *(locutions)* **avant toute c.** first of all; **les choses étant ce qu'elles sont** with things as they are; **aller au fond des choses** to get to the heart of the matter; **bien faire les choses** to do things in style; **il ne fait pas les choses à moitié** he doesn't do things by halves; **parler de choses et d'autres** to talk about this and that; **c'est c. faite** it's done; **de deux choses l'une, soit il parle, soit...** either he talks or...; **c. curieuse, personne n'en savait rien** curiously enough, nobody knew anything about it; **et, c. rare, il a demandé pardon** he apologized for once; **dites bien des choses de ma part à...** remember me to...

2 *nm (truc)* whatsit, thingummy; **Monsieur/Madame C.** Mr/Mrs thingummy

3 *adj inv Fam* **se sentir tout c.** to feel a bit funny

chou¹, -x [ʃu] *nm* (a) *(légume)* cabbage; **faire ses choux gras de qch** to have a field day with sth; **faire c. blanc** to draw a blank; **mon petit c.** darling; **c. de Bruxelles** Brussels sprout; **c. rouge** red cabbage (b) *(gâteau)* **c. à la crème** cream puff

chou² *adj inv Fam* cute

chouchou, -oute [ʃuʃu, -ut] **1** *nm,f Fam* c'est le c. (de la maîtresse) he's teacher's pet; **c'est le c. de sa maman** he's his mother's little blue-eyed boy **2** *nm (pour les cheveux)* scrunchie

chouchouter [ʃuʃute] *vt Fam* to pamper; **elle aime se faire c.** she enjoys being pampered

choucroute [ʃukrut] *nf (chou)* sauerkraut; **c. (garnie)** = sauerkraut served with different types of sausages and bacon

chouette¹ [ʃwɛt] *nf* owl; **c. hulotte** tawny owl; *Fam Péj* **une vieille c.** an old shrew

chouette² *Fam* **1** *adj* great, terrific; **il a été très c. avec elle** he's been really nice to her **2** *exclam* great!, terrific!

chou-fleur [ʃuflœr] *(pl* **choux-fleurs)** *nm* cauliflower; **oreille en c.** cauliflower ear

chouia [ʃuja] *nm Fam* **un c. (de qch)** a tiny bit (of sth)

chouraver [ʃurave], **chourer** [ʃure] *vt très Fam* to swipe; **se faire c. qch** to have sth swiped

choyer [32] [ʃwaje] *vt* to pamper

CHR [seaʃɛr] *nm (abrév* **centre hospitalier régional)** regional hospital

chrétien, -enne [kretjɛ̃, -ɛn] *adj & nm,f* Christian

chrétienté [kretjɛ̃te] *nf* Christendom

Christ [krist] *nm* (a) **le C.** Christ (b) *(crucifix)* **c.** crucifix

christianisme [kristjanism] *nm* Christianity

chromatique [kromatik] *adj* (a) *(des couleurs) & Mus* chromatic (b) *Biol* chromosomal

chrome [krom] *nm Chim* chromium; **chromes** *(d'une voiture)* chrome

chromé, -e [krome] *adj* chromium-plated; **acier c.** chrome steel

chromosome [kromozom] *nm* chromosome

chromosomique [kromozomik] *adj* chromosomal

chronique¹ [kronik] *adj* chronic

chronique² *nf* (a) *Journ* column; **tenir la c. sportive** to write the sports column (b) *(annale)* chronicle

chroniqueur, -euse [kronikœr, -øz] *nm,f Journ* columnist; **c. sportif** sports reporter

chrono [krono] *nm Fam* stopwatch; **faire du 220 km/h c.** to be timed at 220 kph

chronologie [kronolɔʒi] *nf* chronology

chronologique [kronolɔʒik] *adj* chronological

chronomètre [kronometr] *nm (montre de précision)* chronometer; *(pour le sport)* stopwatch

chronométrer [34] [kronometre] *vt Sp* to time

chrysalide [krizalid] *nf* chrysalis

chrysanthème [krizɑ̃tɛm] *nm* chrysanthemum

ch'timi [ʃtimi] **1** *nmf Fam* Northerner *(from Northern France)* **2** *nm (patois)* = dialect spoken in Northern France

CHU [seaʃy] *nm inv (abrév* **centre hospitalo-universitaire)** teaching hospital

chu *voir* **choir**

chuchotement [ʃyʃotmɑ̃] *nm* whisper; **des chuchotements** whispering

chuchoter [ʃyʃote] *vt & vi* to whisper

chuintement [ʃɥɛ̃tmɑ̃] *nm* hissing

chuinter [ʃɥɛ̃te] *vi (siffler)* to hiss

chut [ʃyt] *exclam* sh!, hush!

chute [ʃyt] *nf* (a) *(fait de tomber) & Fig Fam; (diminution)* drop, fall; **faire une c. (de cheval/moto)** to have a fall (from one's horse/motorbike); **prévenir la c. des cheveux** to prevent hair loss; **il m'a entraîné dans sa c.** he has dragged me down with him; **c. libre** free fall; **descendre en c. libre** to be in free fall; **c. de neige** snowfall (b) **c. d'eau** waterfall; **les chutes Victoria** the Victoria Falls (c) *(d'histoire drôle)* punchline (d) *(de tissu, de métal)* scrap; *(de bois)* off-cut

chuter [ʃyte] *vi (diminuer)* to fall, to drop; *Fam (tomber)* to fall (down)

Chypre [ʃipr] *n* Cyprus

chypriote [ʃiprijɔt] **1** *adj* Cypriot **2** *nmf* **C.** Cypriot

ci¹ [si] *adv* **c. livre-ci** this book; **ces jours-ci** these days; **de-ci de-là** here and there; **par-ci par-là** here and there

ci² *pron démonstratif Fam* **faire ci et ça** to do this and that

CIA [seia] *nf* **la C.** the CIA

ciao [tʃao] *exclam Fam* ciao!

ci-après [siaprɛ] *adv* below; *Jur* hereinafter

cibiste [sibist] *nmf* CB user

cible [sibl] *nf aussi Fig* target

ciblé, -e [sible] *adj* well-targeted

ciboire [sibwar] *nm Rel* ciborium

ciboulette [sibulet] *nf* chives

ciboulot [sibulo] *nm très Fam (tête)* nut; **se creuser le c.** to rack one's brains

cicatrice [sikatris] *nf aussi Fig* scar

cicatrisant, -e [sikatrizɑ̃, -ɑ̃t] *adj* healing

cicatrisation [sikatrizasjɔ̃] *nf* healing

cicatriser [sikatrize] **1** *vt & vi* to heal **2 se cicatriser** *vpr* to heal

ci-contre [sikɔ̃tr] *adv* opposite

ci-dessous [sidəsu] *adv* below

ci-dessus [sidəsy] *adv* above

ci-devant [sidəvɑ̃] *adv Vieilli* formerly

CIDJ [seideʒi] *nm (abrév* **centre d'information et de documentation de la jeunesse)** = library offering careers information and literature to young people

cidre [sidr] *nm* cider; **c. bouché** = traditionally-made cider, fermented twice; **c. doux/brut** sweet/dry cider

Cie *(abrév* **compagnie)** Co

ciel [sjɛl] *nm* (a) *(air)* sky; **les ciels de Turner** Turner's skies; **à c. ouvert** open-air; **sous d'autres cieux** in other climes; **lever les bras/les yeux au c.** to raise one's arms/one's eyes heavenwards; *Fam* **être au septième c.** to be in seventh heaven; *Fam* **tomber du c. (à qn)** *(héritage)* to be a godsend (to sb); *(solution)* to come (to sb) out of the blue (b) *(pl* **cieux** [sjø] *) (paradis)* heaven; **il est au c.** he's in heaven; **notre Père qui êtes aux cieux** our Father who art in Heaven (c) **c. de lit** canopy

cierge [sjɛrʒ] *nm Rel* candle; **brûler un c.** to light a candle

cigale [sigal] *nf* cicada

cigare [sigar] nm (a) (à fumer) cigar (b) très Fam (tête) ne rien avoir dans le c. to be completely brainless

cigarette [sigarɛt] nf cigarette

ci-gît [siʒi] voir gésir

cigogne [sigɔɲ] nf stork

ciguë [sigy] nf hemlock

ci-inclus, -e (mpl ci-inclus, fpl ci-incluses) [siẽkly, -yz] 1 adj la copie ci-incluse the enclosed copy
2 adv (vous trouverez) c. copie de votre lettre please find enclosed a copy of your letter

ci-joint, -e (mpl ci-joints, fpl ci-jointes) [siʒwẽ, -ẽt] 1 adj les pièces ci-jointes the enclosed documents
2 adv (vous trouverez) c. copie de votre lettre please find enclosed a copy of your letter

cil [sil] nm eyelash; **faux cils** false eyelashes

ciller [sije] vi to blink; Fig **il n'a pas cillé** he didn't bat an eyelid

cime [sim] nf (d'une montagne) summit; (pic) peak; (d'un arbre, d'un mât) top

ciment [simã] nm cement

cimenter [simãte] vt aussi Fig to cement

cimetière [simtjɛr] nm cemetery; (d'église) graveyard; c. de voitures scrapyard

ciné [sine] nm Fam Br pictures, Am movies

cinéaste [sineast] nmf film maker

ciné-club (pl ciné-clubs) [sineklœb] nm film club

cinéma [sinema] nm (a) (art, industrie) Br cinema, Am movies; **faire du c.** to be a film actor, to act in films; Fam **c'est du c.** it's all an act; Fam **arrête ton c.!** stop making such a fuss!; **c. d'art et d'essai** art films; **c. muet** silent films; **c. parlant** talking films (b) (salle) Br cinema, Am movie theater; **aller au c.** to go to the cinema

CinémaScope® [sinemaskɔp] nm CinemaScope®

cinémathèque [sinematɛk] nf film library

cinématographie [sinematografi] nf cinematography

cinématographique [sinematografik] adj cinema, film

ciné-parc (pl cinés-parcs) [sinepark] nm Can drive-in movie theater

cinéphile [sinefil] 1 adj **être c.** to be a film or Am movie buff
2 nmf Br film or Am movie enthusiast

cinéraire [sinerɛr] adj (urne) cinerary

cinétique [sinetik] adj (énergie) kinetic

cinglant, -e [sẽglã, -ãt] adj (pluie) lashing; (vent, remarque) cutting

cinglé, -e [sẽgle] Fam 1 adj crazy
2 nmf loony

cingler[1] [sẽgle] vi Naut **c. vers** to make for

cingler[2] vt (frapper) to lash; **la grêle lui cinglait le visage** the hail was stinging his face

cinoche [sinɔʃ] nm Fam Br cinema, Am movie theater

cinq [sẽk] 1 adj inv five
2 nm inv five; **recevoir qn c. sur c.** to receive sb loud and clear; Fam **c'était moins c.** it was a close shave; voir aussi **trois**

cinquantaine [sẽkãtɛn] nf **une c. de personnes** about fifty people, fifty or so people; **avoir la c.** to be about fifty

cinquante [sẽkãt] adj & nm inv fifty; voir aussi **trois**

cinquantenaire [sẽkãtnɛr] 1 nm (anniversaire) fiftieth anniversary
2 adj **être c.** to be fifty years old

cinquantième [sẽkãtjɛm] nmf, nm & adj fiftieth; voir aussi **cinquième**

cinquième [sẽkjɛm] 1 adj fifth; **le c. jour** the fifth day; **arriver c.** to finish fifth
2 nmf fifth; **le c. en partant de la droite** the fifth from the right; **arriver le c.** to finish fifth
3 nm (a) (fraction) fifth (b) (étage) fifth floor; **habiter au c.** to live on the Br fifth or Am sixth floor (c) (arrondissement) fifth arrondissement
4 nf (a) (classe) Br ≃ second year of secondary school, Am ≃ sixth grade (b) (vitesse) fifth (gear); **passer la c.** to go into fifth (gear)

cinquièmement [sẽkjɛmmã] adv fifthly

cintre [sẽtr] nm (coat)hanger

cintré, -e [sẽtre] adj (veste) fitted; (taille) nipped-in

CIO [seio] nm (abrév **Comité international olympique**) IOC

cirage [siraʒ] nm (shoe) polish; Fam **être dans le c.** to be feeling woozy

circoncire [sirkɔ̃sir] vt to circumcise

circoncision [sirkɔ̃sizjɔ̃] nf circumcision

circonférence [sirkɔ̃ferãs] nf circumference; **avoir 10 centimètres de c.** to have a circumference of 10 centimetres

circonflexe [sirkɔ̃flɛks] adj voir **accent**

circonlocution [sirkɔ̃lɔkysjɔ̃] nf circumlocution; **parler par circonlocutions** to speak in a roundabout way

circonscription [sirkɔ̃skripsjɔ̃] nf division, district; **c. électorale** (au niveau municipal) ward; (au niveau national) constituency

circonscrire [30] [sirkɔ̃skrir] vt Math to circumscribe; (encercler) to encircle; (incendie) to contain

circonspect, -e [sirkɔ̃spɛ, -ɛkt] adj circumspect, cautious

circonstance [sirkɔ̃stãs] nf circumstance; **dans les circonstances actuelles** in the present circumstances; **en pareille c.** under such circumstances; **être à la hauteur des circonstances** to be equal to the occasion; **des paroles de c.** appropriate words; **habillé pour la c.** appropriately dressed; **circonstances aggravantes** aggravating circumstances; Jur **circonstances atténuantes** extenuating circumstances

circonstancié, -e [sirkɔ̃stãsje] adj detailed

circonstanciel, -elle [sirkɔ̃stãsjɛl] adj voir **complément**

circonvolution [sirkɔ̃vɔlysjɔ̃] nf convolution

circuit [sirkɥi] nm (a) (chemin) way; (boucle) tour; Fig **ça fait longtemps que je ne suis plus dans le c.** I've been out of circulation for ages; **c. touristique** (organized) tour (b) (de course automobile, de cyclisme) circuit; **c. automobile** racing circuit (c) Él circuit (d) Tech **c. de refroidissement** cooling circuit; **c. de commande** command circuit; **c. imprimé** printed circuit; **c. intégré** integrated circuit; **c. de liaison** link circuit; **c. logique** logic circuit (f) Écon **c. de distribution** distribution network; **circuits de vente** commercial channels

circulaire [sirkylɛr] 1 nf circular
2 adj circular; **billet c.** round-trip ticket

circulation [sirkylasjɔ̃] nf (a) (d'autos, d'avions) traffic; **c. interdite** (sur panneau) no thoroughfare; **c. aérienne** air traffic; **c. routière** road traffic (b) (du sang, de l'information, des marchandises) circulation; **mettre qch en c.** to put sth into circulation; **retirer un produit de la c.** to take a product off the market (c) Fin (des billets, des capitaux) circulation (d) Pol & Écon **libre c. des personnes et des biens** free movement of persons and goods

circulatoire [sirkylatwar] adj circulatory

circuler [sirkyle] vi (a) (sang, air, rumeur) to circulate; **faire c. un plat** to pass or hand a dish round; **faire c. une pétition** to circulate a petition (b) (voyageur) to travel; (train, autobus) to run; **on circule très mal dans Paris** it's very difficult to drive about in Paris; **circulez, il n'y a rien à voir!** move along now, there's nothing to see!

cire [sir] nf wax; (pour le bois) polish; (dans l'oreille) (ear)wax; **c. d'abeille** beeswax; **c. à cacheter** sealing wax; **personnage en c.** waxwork (model)

ciré [sire] nm oilskin

cirer [sire] vt (chaussures, meubles) to polish; Fam **c. les pompes à qn** to lick sb's boots; très Fam **il en a rien à c. (de tes histoires)** he doesn't give a damn (about your stories)

cireur, -euse [sirœr, -øz] **1** nm,f (de chaussures) shoeblack
2 nf **cireuse** (machine) (floor) polisher

cireux, -euse [sirø, -øz] adj waxy

cirque [sirk] nm (a) (spectacle) circus; Fam **quel c. dans ce bureau!** it's like a zoo in this office!; Fam **faire tout un c.** to make a scene (b) Géol corrie

cirrhose [siroz] nf **c. (du foie)** cirrhosis (of the liver); **avoir une c.** to have cirrhosis

cisaille [sizaj] nf **c., cisailles** (de jardinier) shears

cisailler [sizaje] vt (branches, haie) to prune

ciseau, -x [sizo] nm (a) (de jardin) shears; **(une paire de) ciseaux** (pour papier, pour tissu) (a pair of) scissors; **des ciseaux à ongles** nail scissors (b) Sp **sauter en ciseaux** to do a scissors jump (c) Tech chisel

ciseler [39] [sizle] vt (or, argent) to chase; (marbre) to chisel; (bijou) to engrave a design on

Cisjordanie [sisʒɔrdani] nf **la C.** the West Bank

cisjordanien, -enne [sisʒɔrdanjɛ̃, -ɛn] **1** adj from the West Bank
2 nm,f **C.** person from the West Bank

cistercien, -enne [sistɛrsjɛ̃, -ɛn] adj & nm Rel Cistercian

citadelle [sitadɛl] nf citadel

citadin, -e [sitadɛ̃, -in] **1** nm,f city-dweller
2 adj city

citation [sitasjɔ̃] nf (a) (extrait) quotation; **fin de c.** unquote (b) Jur **c. à comparaître** (d'un accusé) summons; (d'un témoin) subpoena

cité [site] nf (a) (ville) city (b) (groupe d'immeubles) (housing) Br estate or Am development; **c. universitaire** Br halls of residence, Am dormitory complex

cité-dortoir (pl **cités-dortoirs**) [sitedɔrtwar] nf dormitory town

citer [site] vt (a) (rapporter) to quote (from); **c. qn en exemple** to quote sb as an example; **il a dit, je cite...** he said, and I quote,... (b) (énumérer) to name (c) Jur (personne en justice) to summons; (témoin) to subpoena (d) Mil **c. qn (à l'ordre du jour)** to mention sb in dispatches

citerne [sitɛrn] nf tank; **c. à mazout** oil tank

cithare [sitar] nf (instrument moderne) zither

citizen band [sitizɛnbɑ̃d] nf Citizens' Band, CB

citoyen, -enne [sitwajɛ̃, -ɛn] nm,f citizen; **c. d'honneur** freeman (of a city)

citoyenneté [sitwajente] nf citizenship; **la c. française** French citizenship

citrique [sitrik] adj (acide) citric

citron [sitrɔ̃] nm (a) (fruit) lemon; **un c. givré** = lemon sorbet served inside the skin of a whole lemon; **un c. pressé** = freshly squeezed lemon juice served with water and sugar; **c. vert lime** (b) Fam (tête) nut

citronnade [sitronad] nf Br lemon squash, Am lemonade

citronnelle [sitronɛl] nf (plante, huile) citronella

citronnier [sitronje] nm lemon tree

citrouille [sitruj] nf pumpkin

civelle [sivɛl] nf elver

civet [sive] nm Culin **c. de lapin** rabbit stew; **c. de lièvre** ≃ jugged hare

civière [sivjɛr] nf stretcher

civil, -e [sivil] **1** adj (a) (du citoyen, non ecclésiastique) civil (b) (non militaire) civilian; **dans la vie civile** in civilian life (c) Litt (courtois) civil
2 nm (a) (personne) (non ecclésiastique) layman, civilian (b) **dans le c.** in civilian life; **en c.** (policier) in plain clothes; (militaire) in civilian clothes (c) Jur **poursuivre qn au c.** to bring a civil action against sb

civilement [sivilmɑ̃] adv (a) **Jur se marier c.** to have a civil wedding (b) Litt (avec courtoisie) civilly

civilisation [sivilizasjɔ̃] nf civilization

civilisé, -e [sivilize] adj civilized

civilité [sivilite] nf Litt (a) (courtoisie) civility (b) **civilités** (politesses) courtesies

civique [sivik] adj civic; **avoir le sens c.** to have a sense of civic responsibility

civisme [sivism] nm sense of civic responsibility

clac [klak] exclam (d'un fouet) crack!; (d'un objet qui se casse) snap!; (d'une porte) slam!

clafoutis [klafuti] nm clafoutis (fruit, usually cherries, baked in a dish of batter)

claie [klɛ] nf (a) (treillis) rack (b) (clôture) fence

clair, -e [klɛr] **1** adj (a) (transparent) (eau, teint, voix) clear; **par temps c.** on a clear day (b) (pièce, couleur) light (sens, explication) clear; **il a été très c. là-dessus** he was very clear about it; **il est c. qu'il a tort** he's clearly wrong; **être c. comme de l'eau de roche** to be crystal clear; **avoir les idées claires** to have a clear head; **c'est c. et net** there are no two ways about it; Fam **un individu pas très c.** a bit of a shady character (d) (soupe) thin
2 adv clearly; **il fait c.** it's light; Fig **je commence à y voir c.** I'm beginning to understand
3 nm (a) (lumière) **c. de lune** moonlight; **au c. de lune** in the moonlight (b) **en c.** (autrement dit) in plain language; **émission en c.** non-crypted broadcast (c) Fig **tirer une affaire au c.** to clear a matter up; **passer le plus c. de**

son temps à faire qch to spend the better part of one's time doing sth

clairement [klɛrmɑ̃] *adv* clearly

claire-voie (*pl* **claires-voies**) [klɛrvwa] *nf* (a) *(treillage)* à c. open-work (b) *Archit* clerestory

clairière [klɛrjɛr] *nf* clearing, glade

clair-obscur (*pl* **clairs-obscurs**) [klɛrɔpskyr] *nm* (*en peinture*) chiaroscuro

clairon [klɛrɔ̃] *nm* (a) *(instrument)* bugle; **sonner le c.** to sound the bugle (b) *(joueur)* bugler

claironner [klɛrɔne] *vt (nouvelle)* to trumpet forth

clairsemé, -e [klɛrsəme] *adj (population, cheveux, gazon)* sparse; *(arbres)* scattered

clairvoyant, -e [klɛrvwajɑ̃, -ɑ̃t] *adj* perceptive

clamer [klame] *vt* to proclaim

clameur [klamœr] *nf* clamour; **une c. de joie** a shout of joy; **les clameurs de la foule** the clamour of the crowd

clamser [klamse] *vi très Fam (mourir)* to kick the bucket

clan [klɑ̃] *nm (tribu)* clan; *Péj (groupe)* clique

clandestin, -e [klɑ̃dɛstɛ̃, -in] **1** *adj (réunion, atelier)* clandestine; *(travailleur, immigré)* illegal; *(mouvement)* underground
2 *nm,f (voyageur)* stowaway; *(immigré)* illegal immigrant; *(travailleur)* illegal worker

clandestinement [klɑ̃dɛstinmɑ̃] *adv (secrètement)* clandestinely; *(illégalement)* illegally

clandestinité [klɑ̃dɛstinite] *nf* **dans la c.** *(secrètement)* clandestinely; *(illégalement)* illegally; **entrer dans/sortir de la c.** to go into/to come out of hiding

clap [klap] *nm Cin* clapperboard; **c. de fin** end board

clapet [klapɛ] *nm* (a) *Tech* valve (b) *Fam* **ferme ton c.!** shut your trap!

clapier [klapje] *nm (rabbit)* hutch

clapoter [klapɔte] *vi* to lap

clapotis [klapɔti] *nm* lapping

claquage [klakaʒ] *nm (blessure)* pulled muscle; **se faire un c.** to pull a muscle

claque [klak] *nf* (a) *(gifle)* slap; **donner une c. à qn** to give sb a slap; *Fam Fig* **il va se prendre une c.** it'll be a slap in the face for him; **une paire de claques** a slap (b) *Fam* **j'en ai ma c.** I've had it up to here (c) *Can* **claques** galoshes

claqué, -e [klake] *adj Fam (fatigué)* Br shattered, Am bushed

claquement [klakmɑ̃] *nm (de porte)* slam(ming); *(de dents)* chattering; *(d'un fouet)* crack(ing); *(d'un drapeau)* flap(ping); *(de doigts)* snap(ping); *(de talons, de la langue)* click(ing); *(de sabots)* clatter(ing)

claquer [klake] **1** *vt* (a) *(porte)* to slam; **c. la langue** to click one's tongue (b) *Fam (dépenser)* to blow; **il claque un fric monstre chez le coiffeur** he spends a fortune at the hairdresser's
2 *vi* (a) *(porte)* to slam; *(drapeau)* to flap; *(talons)* to click; *(sabots)* to clatter; **c. des mains** to clap; **c. des doigts** to snap one's fingers; **elle claque des dents** her teeth are chattering; **faire c. sa langue** to click one's tongue (b) *(ampoule électrique)* to go; *Fam (personne)* to kick the bucket
3 se claquer *vpr* **c. un muscle** to pull a muscle

claquettes [klakɛt] *nfpl* tap dancing; **faire des c.** to do tap dancing; **danseur de c.** tap dancer

clarification [klarifikasjɔ̃] *nf aussi Fig* clarification

clarifier [66] [klarifje] **1** *vt (liquide, situation)* to clarify
2 se clarifier *vpr (situation)* to become clear

clarinette [klarinɛt] *nf* clarinet

clarinettiste [klarinetist] *nmf* clarinettist

clarté [klarte] *nf* (a) *(lumière)* light (b) *(transparence)* clearness (c) *Fig (du style)* clarity; **avec c.** clearly; **manquer de c.** *(personne)* not to make oneself clear; *(texte, argument)* to be unclear

classe [klas] **1** *nf* (a) *(catégorie)* class; *(dans une hiérarchie)* grade; **c. affaires/économique** business/economy class; **c. d'âge** age group; **la c. dirigeante** the ruling class; **les classes moyennes** the middle class(es); **la c. ouvrière** the working class(es); **c. sociale** social class
(b) *(qualité)* class; **un sportif de c. internationale** a world-class sportsman; **avoir de la c.** *(personne)* to have class; *(objet, vêtement)* to be classy; *Fam* **ce type, c'est la c.!** he's got real class!
(c) *(à l'école)* *(niveau)* year; *(groupe d'élèves)* class; **les grandes classes, les classes supérieures** the senior school; **les petites classes** the junior school; **c. de mer/ de neige** school study trip to the seaside/to the mountains; **partir en c. de mer** to go on a school study trip to the seaside; **c. préparatoire (aux grandes écoles)** = preparatory class for the entrance examinations for the Grandes Écoles; **c. verte** school study trip to the countryside
(d) *(leçon)* class; **la c. de français** the French class; **aller en c.** to go to school; **être en c.** *(à l'école)* to be at school; *(en cours)* to be in class; **faire la c.** to teach
(e) *(pièce)* **(salle de) c.** classroom
(f) *Mil (de conscrits)* levy; **faire ses classes** to undergo basic training
2 *adj inv Fam* classy

classé, -e [klase] *adj (monument)* listed

classement [klasmɑ̃] *nm* (a) *(dans une classe ou une course)* position, place; *(liste d'équipes, de concurrents)* classification; *(au foot, au rugby)* table; *(des plantes)* classification; **être troisième au c.** to be in third place; **c. général** overall classification (b) *(rangement)* *(de documents)* filing; *(d'articles)* sorting out; **faire du c.** to do some filing; **c. (par ordre) alphabétique** alphabetical classification

classer [klase] **1** *vt* (a) *(classifier)* to classify; *(étudiants)* to grade; **être classés par pays** to be classed according to country (b) *(ranger)* *(documents)* to file; *(articles)* to sort out; **c. une affaire** to consider a matter closed; **c'est une affaire classée** the matter's closed
2 se classer *vpr* **se c. parmi les meilleurs** to rank among the best; *Sp* **se c. troisième** to be placed third

classeur [klasœr] *nm* (a) *(dossier)* ring binder (b) *(meuble)* filing cabinet (c) *Ordinat* filer

classicisme [klasisism] *nm* classicism

classification [klasifikasjɔ̃] *nf* classification; *Chim* **c. périodique des éléments** periodic table

classifier [66] [klasifje] *vt* to classify

classique [klasik] **1** *adj* (a) *(période)* classical; *(beauté)* classic (b) *(conventionnel)* *(vêtement, style, exemple, plaisanterie)* classic; *(arme, guerre)* conventional; *Fam* **c'est le coup c.** it's the same old story
2 *nm* (a) *(auteur)* classical author (b) *(œuvre, film, chanson)* classic; **c'est un c. du genre** it's a classic of its kind (c) *(style musical)* **le c.** classical music

claudication [klodikasjɔ̃] *nf* limp

clause [kloz] *nf Jur* clause; **c. d'exclusivité** exclusivity clause

claustrophobe [klostrofob] *adj* claustrophobic

claustrophobie [klostrofobi] *nf* claustrophobia

clavecin [klavsɛ̃] *nm* harpsichord

claveciniste [klavsinist] *nmf* harpsichordist

clavicule [klavikyl] *nf* collarbone, *Spéc* clavicle

clavier [klavje] *nm* keyboard; *Ordinat* **c. multifonction** multifunctional keyboard; **c. numérique** numerical *or* numeric keypad

claviste [klavist] *nmf Ordinat* keyboarder; *Typ* typesetter

clé [kle] = **clef**

clean [klin] *adj inv Fam* (a) *(BCBG)* clean-cut (b) *(qui ne se drogue pas)* clean

clébard [klebar], **clebs** [kleps] *nm Fam* pooch

clef [kle] 1 *nf* (a) *(d'une porte, d'un cadenas)* key; **fermer qch à c.** to lock sth; **tenir/mettre qch sous c.** to keep/put sth under lock and key; **usine clefs en main** turnkey factory; **prix clefs en main** *(d'une voiture)* on-the-road price; *(d'une maison)* all-inclusive price; *Fig* **mettre la c. sous la porte** to move away; *(commerçant)* to shut up shop; **prendre la c. des champs** *(prisonnier)* to make a bid for freedom; **c. de contact** ignition key; **c. passe-partout** passkey, master key (b) *(outil)* spanner; **c. anglaise** monkey wrench; **c. à molette** adjustable spanner; **c. plate** open-end *Br* spanner *or Am* wrench (c) *Mus (d'un instrument à cordes)* peg; *(d'un instrument à vent)* key; **c. de sol/de fa** treble/bass clef; **il y a une forte somme d'argent à la c.** there is a large sum of money at the end of it (d) *(moyen d'accès, solution)* **la c. du placard/mystère** the key to the cupboard/mystery (e) **c. de voûte** *(d'une arche)* keystone; *Fig* cornerstone (f) *Ordinat* key; *(du DOS)* switch; **c. de contrôle** control key; **c. gigogne** dongle; **c. à puce** computerized key

2 *adj (vital)* key; **un secteur(-)c. de la recherche** a key area of research

clématite [klematit] *nf* clematis

clémence [klemɑ̃s] *nf* (a) *(de la température)* mildness (b) *(d'un juge, d'un maître)* clemency (**envers** towards)

clément, -e [klemɑ̃, -ɑ̃t] *adj* (a) *(température)* mild (b) *(juge, maître)* clement (**envers** towards)

clémentine [klemɑ̃tin] *nf* clementine

Cléopâtre [kleopatr] *npr* Cleopatra

cleptomane [kleptoman] *adj & nmf* kleptomaniac

cleptomanie [kleptomani] *nf* kleptomania

clerc [klɛr] *nm* (a) *(dans un bureau)* **c. de notaire** ≃ solicitor's clerk (b) *Rel* cleric (c) *Litt* **il n'est pas besoin d'être grand c. pour...** you don't have to be a genius in order to...

clergé [klɛrʒe] *nm* clergy

clérical, -e, -aux, -ales [klerikal, -o] *adj* clerical

clic [klik] *nm* click; **faire c.** to click

clic-clac [klikklak] *nm inv* (a) *(d'un appareil photo)* click; *(des talons)* click-clack (b) *(canapé)* sofa bed

cliché [kliʃe] *nm* (a) *(photo)* photo; *(négatif)* negative (b) *(lieu commun)* cliché

client, -e [klijɑ̃, -ɑ̃t] *nm,f (d'un magasin, d'une entreprise)* customer; *(d'un médecin)* patient; *(d'un avocat)* client; *(d'un hôtel)* guest; *(d'un taxi)* fare; **ici, le c. est roi** the customer is always right

clientèle [klijɑ̃tɛl] *nf (d'un magasin, d'une entreprise)* customers; *(d'un médecin, d'un avocat)* practice; *(d'un hôtel)* clientèle; *(d'un taxi)* fares; **c. de passage** passing trade (b) *(fait d'acheter)* custom; **accorder sa c. à** to give one's custom to

cligner [kliɲe] *vi* **c. des yeux** to blink; **c. de l'œil** to wink

clignotant, -e [kliɲotɑ̃, -ɑ̃t] 1 *adj (étoile)* twinkling; *(lumière)* flashing

2 *nm (de voiture) Br* indicator, *Am* flasher; **mettre son c.** (**à gauche/droite**) to indicate (left/right)

clignoter [kliɲote] *vi (étoile)* to twinkle; *(lumière, voyant)* to flash; *Ordinat (d'un marqueur)* to flash, to blink

climat [klima] *nm aussi Fig* climate; **sous des climats plus ensoleillés** in sunnier climes; **c. de détente** relaxed climate

climatique [klimatik] *adj (conditions)* climatic

climatisation [klimatizasjɔ̃] *nf* air conditioning

climatisé, -e [klimatize] *adj* air-conditioned

climatiser [klimatize] *vt* to air-condition

climatiseur [klimatizœr] *nm* air-conditioner

clin d'œil *(pl* clins d'œil*)* [klɛ̃dœj] *nm* wink; **faire un c. à qn** to wink at sb; **en un c. in a flash**

clinique [klinik] 1 *nf* (a) *(hôpital privé)* clinic (b) *(médecine)* clinical medicine

2 *adj* clinical

clinquant, -e [klɛ̃kɑ̃, -ɑ̃t] 1 *adj* flashy

2 *nm (éclat trompeur)* flashiness

clip [klip] *nm* (a) *(vidéo)* (music) video (b) *(bijou)* clip

clique [klik] *nf* (a) *Fam (gang)* clique, gang; **et toute la c.** and the rest of the gang (b) *(d'une fanfare militaire)* drum-and-bugle band

cliquer [klike] *vi Ordinat* to click (**sur** on); **c. deux fois** to double-click

cliques [klik] *nfpl Fam* **prendre ses c. et ses claques** to pack one's bags and go

cliqueter [42] [klikte] *vi (chaînes)* to rattle; *(épées, aiguilles à tricoter)* to click; *(monnaie, clefs)* to jingle

cliquetis [klikti] *nm (de chaînes)* rattling; *(de pièces de monnaie, de clefs)* jingling; *(d'épées, d'aiguilles à tricoter)* clicking

clitoris [klitoris] *nm* clitoris

clivage [klivaʒ] *nm (dans la société)* divide; *(dans un parti politique)* split

cloaque [kloak] *nm aussi Fig* cesspool

clochard, -e [kloʃar, -ard] *nm,f* tramp, *Am* hobo

clochardiser [kloʃardize] 1 *vt* to turn into a tramp

2 **se clochardiser** *vpr* to turn into a tramp

cloche [kloʃ] 1 *nf* (a) *(d'église, de bétail)* bell; **déménager à la c. de bois** to do a moonlight flit; *Fig* **entendre plusieurs sons de c.** to hear several different versions of events (b) *(pour couvrir)* Chem bell jar; *(pour cultures)* cloche; *(pour garder au chaud)* dish cover; **c. à fromage(s)** covered cheese dish; **c. à plongeur** diving bell (c) *Fam (imbécile)* twit (d) *(chapeau)* **c.** cloche (hat) (e) *Fam* **être de la c.** *(être clochard)* to be a tramp *or Am* hobo

2 *adj Fam* stupid

cloche-pied [kloʃpje] **à cloche-pied** *adv* **sauter à c.** to hop

clocher¹ [kloʃe] *nm (d'une église)* bell tower, steeple

clocher² *vi Fam* **il y a quelque chose qui cloche** there's something wrong somewhere; **il y a quelque chose qui cloche dans son histoire** there's something not quite right about her story

clochette [kloʃɛt] *nf* (a) *(petite cloche)* small bell (b) *(fleur)* bell-flower; *(corolle)* bell-shaped flower

clodo [klodo] *nm Fam* tramp, *Am* bum

cloison [klwazɔ̃] nf (a) (entre des pièces) partition (b) Anat c. nasale nasal septum

cloisonner [klwazɔne] vt (pièce) to partition (off); Fig to compartmentalize

cloître [klwatr] nm (a) (partie d'un monastère) cloister (b) (bâtiment) (pour moines) monastery; (pour religieuses) convent

cloîtrer [klwatre] **1** vt Rel to cloister; Fig to shut up or away; **nonne cloîtrée** nun in an enclosed order
2 se cloîtrer vpr (moine) to enter a monastery; (religieuse) to enter a convent; Fig to shut oneself away

clonage [klɔnaʒ] nm Biol cloning

clone [klɔn] nm Biol clone

clope [klɔp] nf Fam Br fag, Am smoke

clopin-clopant [klɔpɛ̃klɔpɑ̃] adv **aller c.** to hobble along; Fig (commerce) to struggle along

clopiner [klɔpine] vi to hobble

clopinettes [klɔpinet] nfpl Fam **des c.** Br sweet FA, Am zilch; **travailler pour des c.** to work for peanuts

cloporte [klɔpɔrt] nm (insecte) woodlouse

cloque [klɔk] nf (a) (sur la peau, sur la peinture) blister; **faire des cloques** to blister (b) très Fam **être en c.** (enceinte) Br to be up the spout, to be knocked up

clore [15] [klɔr] **1** vt (réunion, discussion) to conclude, to end; (débat, compte) to close; Ordinat **c. une session** to log off, to log out
2 se clore vpr (réunion, film, livre) to end (**sur** with)

clos, -e [klo, kloz] **1** pp voir **clore**
2 adj (a) (fermé) (porte, volets) closed (b) (achevé) finished, concluded; **l'incident est c.** the matter is closed; **les inscriptions seront closes le 5 mars** the closing date for applications is 5 March (c) (clôturé) (jardin) enclosed
3 nm enclosure; **c. (de vigne)** vineyard

clôture [klotyr] nf (a) (barrière) fence (b) (d'une réunion, d'une discussion) conclusion, end; (d'un débat, d'un compte) closing; **c. des inscriptions le 3 mars** closing date for applications is 3 March; **c. de la chasse** close of the hunting season; **Fin c. de l'exercice** end of the financial year (c) (à la Bourse) close; **à la c.** at the close (d) Ordinat close; **c. de session** logging off

clôturer [klotyre] **1** vt (a) (champ, terrain) to enclose, to fence in (b) (session, débats) to close (c) Fin (comptes) to close
2 vi (valeur, indice) **c.** à to close at

clou [klu] nm (a) (pointe) nail; **être maigre comme un c.** to be as thin as a rake; Fam **ça ne vaut pas un c.** it's not worth a penny; Fam **des clous!** not a sausage!; Fam **travailler pour des clous** to work for peanuts (b) Culin **c. de girofle** clove (c) (d'un spectacle) main attraction; **ça a été le c. de la soirée** it was the highlight of the evening (d) **les clous** (passage piéton) Br the pedestrian crossing, Am the crosswalk (e) Fam (vieux) **c.** (voiture) old banger; (vélo) old boneshaker (f) Fam **mettre qn au c.** (en prison) to lock sb up; Vieilli **mettre qch au c.** (en gage) to pawn sth

clouer [klue] vt (a) (au mur) to nail up; (ensemble) to nail together; (caisse) to nail down; Fam **c. le bec à qn** to shut sb up (b) Fig (immobiliser) **c. qn au sol** to pin sb down; **rester cloué sur place** to be rooted to the spot; **être cloué au lit** to be stuck in bed

clouté, -e [klute] adj (chaussures) studded

clown [klun] nm aussi Fig clown; **faire le c.** to clown around

club [klœb] nm (a) (culturel, sportif, politique) club; **c. automobile** car club; **c. de foot** football club; **c. de vacances** Br holiday club, Am vacation center (b) (canne de golf) club

CM [seem] nm (abrév **cours moyen**) **CM1** = fourth year of primary school; **CM2** = fifth year of primary school

cm (abrév **centimètre(s)**) cm

CNPF [seenpeef] nm (abrév **Conseil national du patronat français**) = national employers' association

CNRS [seeneres] nm (abrév **Centre national de la recherche scientifique**) = national organization for scientific research

coach [kotʃ] nm (entraîneur) coach

coagulant, -e [kɔagylɑ̃, -ɑ̃t] **1** adj coagulating
2 nm coagulant

coagulation [kɔagylasjɔ̃] nf coagulation

coaguler [kɔagyle] **1** vt & vi (sang) to clot; (lait) to curdle
2 se coaguler vpr (sang) to clot; (lait) to curdle

coaliser [kɔalize] **se coaliser** vpr to unite; (partis, pays) to form a coalition

coalition [kɔalisjɔ̃] nf (a) (alliance) coalition (b) Fig & Péj conspiracy; **former une c. contre** to join forces against

coaltar [koltar] nm coaltar; Fam **être dans le c.** to be in a daze

coasser [kɔase] vi (grenouille) to croak

coassurance [kɔasyrɑ̃s] nf mutual assurance

coauteur [kootœr] nm (a) (d'un livre) co-author (b) Jur accomplice

COB [kɔb] nf Fin (abrév **Commission des opérations de Bourse**) = French Stock Exchange watchdog

cobalt [kɔbalt] nm cobalt

cobaye [kɔbaj] nm aussi Fig guinea pig

cobol [kɔbɔl] nm Ordinat COBOL

cobra [kɔbra] nm cobra

Coca® [kɔka] nm inv Fam (boisson) Coke®

coca [kɔka] **1** nm (plante) coca
2 nf (feuilles) coca

Coca-Cola® [kɔkakɔla] nm inv Coca-Cola®

cocagne [kɔkaɲ] nf voir **mât**

cocaïne [kɔkain] nf cocaine

cocaïnomane [kɔkainɔman] nmf cocaine addict

cocarde [kɔkard] nf (insigne) rosette; Hist (sur un chapeau) cockade

cocasse [kɔkas] adj Fam comical

coccinelle [kɔksinel] nf (a) (insecte) Br ladybird, Am ladybug (b) (voiture) beetle

coccyx [kɔksis] nm coccyx

coche [kɔʃ] nm Vieilli stagecoach; Fam **rater** ou **louper le c.** to miss the boat

cochenille [kɔʃnij] nf cochineal

cocher¹ [kɔʃe] nm coachman

cocher² vt Br to tick (off), Am to check

cochère [kɔʃer] adj f voir **porte**

cochon, -onne [kɔʃɔ̃, -ɔn] **1** *nm* (a) *(animal, personne sale)* pig; *(viande)* pork; **sale comme un c.** filthy; **gros ou gras comme un c.** as round as a barrel; **manger comme un c.** to eat like a pig; **tu écris comme un c.** your writing's an absolute mess; *Fig* **nous n'avons pas gardé les cochons ensemble!** but we hardly know each other!; *Fam* **Fig eh ben, mon c.!** you old devil!; **c. de lait** suck(l)ing pig (b) **c. d'Inde** guinea pig (c) *(personne malfaisante)* swine (d) *(personne grivoise)* dirty devil; **un vieux c.** a dirty old man **2** *adj (histoire, film)* dirty

cochonner [kɔʃɔne] *vt Fam (travail)* to bungle, to botch

cochonnerie [kɔʃɔnri] *nf* (a) *(chose sans valeur)* trash, rubbish (b) *(nourriture de mauvaise qualité)* muck (c) *(saleté)* mess; **faire des cochonneries** to make a mess (d) *(obscénité)* smutty remark; **dire des cochonneries** to say smutty things

cochonnet [kɔʃɔne] *nm* (a) *(aux boules)* jack (b) *(petit cochon)* piglet

cocker [kɔkɛr] *nm* cocker spaniel

cockpit [kɔkpit] *nm Naut & Av* cockpit

cocktail [kɔktɛl] *nm* (a) *(boisson) & Fig* cocktail; *(soirée)* cocktail party; **c. de fruits** fruit cocktail; **c. Molotov** Molotov cocktail

coco¹ [koko] *nm* (a) *(plante)* coconut (b) *Fam* **mets-toi ça dans le c.!** *(dans la tête)* get that into your thick skull!; *(dans l'estomac)* get that inside you!

coco² *nm* (a) *Fam (type)* **un drôle de c.** a strange character; **toi, mon c., je t'ai à l'œil** just watch it, mate (b) *(terme d'affection)* **mon petit c.** my pet

coco³ *adj & nmf Fam (communiste)* commie

cocon [kɔkɔ̃] *nm aussi Fig* cocoon; *Fig* **le c. familial** the family nest

cocorico [kɔkɔriko] **1** *exclam* cock-a-doodle-doo! **2** *nm (cri du coq)* cock-a-doodle-doo; *aussi Fig* **faire c.** to crow

cocoter [kɔkɔte] *vi Fam* to stink

cocotier [kɔkɔtje] *nm (arbre)* coconut palm

cocotte [kɔkɔt] *nf* (a) *(marmite)* large casserole dish (b) *(poule)* hen (c) *(pliage)* paper bird (d) *(terme d'affection)* **ma c.** darling (e) *Fam* **hue, c.!** gee up! (f) *Fam Vieilli* tart

Cocotte-Minute® *(pl Cocottes-Minute)* [kɔkɔtminyt] *nf* pressure cooker

cocu, -e [kɔky] *Fam* **1** *adj* **un mari c.** a cuckold; **je suis c./cocue** my wife's/husband's cheating on me **2** *nm* cuckold; **faire c. son mari** to cheat on one's husband

cocufier [66] [kɔkyfje] *vt* to be unfaithful to

coda [kɔda] *nf Mus* coda

codage [kɔdaʒ] *nm* coding

code [kɔd] *nm* (a) *(symboles)* code; **mettre qch en c.** to put sth into code; **c. confidentiel** security code; *(d'une carte bancaire)* PIN; **c. postal** *Br* postcode, *Am* zip code (b) *Ordinat.* code; **c. abrégé** shortcode; **c. d'accès** access code; **c. d'arrêt** stop code; **c. d'autorisation d'accès** access authorization code; **c. de caractère** character code; **c. de commande** command code; **c. de contrôle** control code; **c. de départ** start code; **c. d'erreur** error code; **c. d'imprimante** printer code; **c. natif** native code; **c. objet** object code; **c. source** source code (c) *(ensemble de lois, livre)* code; **passer le c.** *(du permis de conduire)* to sit the written part of one's driving test; **c. civil** civil code, ≃ common law; **c. de la nationalité** = laws governing French nationality; **c. pénal** penal code;

c. de la route Highway Code; **c. du travail** employment legislation (d) *(phare)* **codes** *Br* dipped headlights, *Am* low beams; **se mettre en codes** *Br* to dip one's headlights, *Am* to switch on one's low beams; **rouler en codes** to drive with *Br* dipped headlights *or Am* low beams (e) *Biol* **c. génétique** genetic code

code-barres *(pl* **codes-barres)** [kɔdbar] *nm* bar code

codéine [kɔdein] *nf* codeine

coder [kɔde] *vt* to code

codétenu, -e [kɔdetny] *nm,f* fellow prisoner

CODEVI [kɔdevi] *nm* = type of government savings account

codicille [kɔdisil] *nm Jur* codicil

codification [kɔdifikasjɔ̃] *nf Ordinat.* **c. binaire** binary code; **c. décimale** decimal coding

codifier [66] [kɔdifje] *vt* to codify

codirecteur, -trice [kɔdirɛktœr, -tris] *nm,f* joint manager, *f* joint manageress

coédition [kɔediʒjɔ̃] *nf* joint publication

coefficient [kɔefisjɑ̃] *nm* coefficient; *Aut* **c. aérodynamique ou de pénétration dans l'air** drag coefficient

coentreprise [kɔɑ̃trapriz] *nf* joint venture

coéquipier, -ère [kɔekipje, -ɛr] *nm,f* team-mate

coercitif, -ive [kɔɛrsitif, -iv] *adj* coercive

coercition [kɔɛrsiʒjɔ̃] *nf* coercion

cœur [kœr] *nm* (a) *(organe)* heart; **être malade du c.** to have a weak heart; **être opéré à c. ouvert** to have open-heart surgery; **recevoir une balle en plein c.** to get a bullet right in the heart; **en (forme de) c.** heart-shaped (b) *(poitrine)* **serrer ou presser qn contre son c.** to hold sb close (c) *(estomac)* **avoir mal au c.** to feel sick; **soulever le c. à qn** to turn sb's stomach; *Fig* **avoir le c. solide ou bien accroché** to have a strong stomach (d) *(symbole de la bonté)* **avoir bon c.** to be kind-hearted; **ne pas avoir de c.** to be heartless; **avoir un c. d'or/de pierre** to have a heart of gold/stone; **avoir le c. sur la main** to be very generous; **à votre bon c., M'sieurs Dames** can you spare a few coins? (e) *(siège des sentiments)* **donner son c. à qn** to lose one's heart to sb; **de tout (son) c.** with all one's heart; **aller droit au c. de qn** to go straight to sb's heart; **avoir le c. brisé** to be broken-hearted; *Fig* **ça (me) fait mal au c.** it's sickening; **faire qch le c. léger** to do sth with a light heart; **avoir le c. gros ou serré** to have a heavy heart; **si tu aimes les pâtes, tu vas t'en donner à c. joie** if you like pasta, you'll be able to eat it to your heart's content; **ne pas porter qn dans son c.** to be not very fond of sb; **du fond du c.** from the bottom of one's heart; **au fond de mon c.** in my heart of hearts; *Prov* **le c. a ses raisons que la raison ne connaît point** the heart has its reasons (f) *(pensées intimes)* **dire ce qu'on a sur le c.** to say what's on one's mind; **en avoir le c. net** to get to the bottom of it; **ouvrir son c. à qn** to open one's heart to sb (g) **par c.** by heart; *Fam* **connaître qn par c.** to know sb inside out (h) *(courage)* courage; **ne pas avoir le c. de faire qch** not to have the heart to do sth; *Fam* **avoir du c. au ventre** to have plenty of guts (i) *(envie, désir)* **ils n'ont pas le c. à l'ouvrage** their hearts aren't in it; **le c. n'y est pas** his/my/etc heart isn't in it; **elle n'a plus le c. à rien** she hasn't the heart for anything any more; **avoir le c. à rire** to be in the mood for laughing; **si le c. vous en dit** if you feel like it; **avoir à c. de faire qch** to have one's heart set on doing sth; **ce projet lui tient à c.** this project is close to his heart; **de bon c.** (*volontiers*) willingly; (*rire*) heartily; **y aller de bon c.** to get down to it

(j) (*personne*) **c'est un c.** she's got a heart of gold; **merci, mon c.** thank you, darling

(k) (*centre*) heart; (*d'un réacteur nucléaire*) core; **fromage fait à c.** ripe cheese; **au c. de l'hiver/l'été** in the depths of winter/height of summer; **au c. de la ville** in the heart of the town; **au c. du débat** at the heart of the debate; **c. d'artichaut** artichoke heart; *Fig* **avoir un c. d'artichaut** to fall in love with every girl/man one meets; **c. de palmier** palm heart

(l) (*objet en forme de cœur*) heart; (*carte*) heart; (*couleur*) hearts

coexistence [kɔɛgzistɑ̃s] *nf* coexistence (**avec** with); *Pol* **c. pacifique** peaceful coexistence

coexister [kɔɛgziste] *vi* to coexist (**avec** with)

coffrage [kɔfraʒ] *nm* (*pour ouvrages en béton*) formwork

coffre [kɔfr] *nm* **(a)** (*meuble*) chest; **c. à linge** linen chest **(b)** (*pour objets de valeur*) safe; (*à la banque*) safe deposit box; **les coffres de l'État** the coffers of the State **(c)** *Fam* **avoir du c.** (*avoir du souffle*) to have a lot of puff; (*avoir de la voix*) to have a powerful voice **(d)** (*d'une voiture*) *Br* boot, *Am* trunk; **c. à bagages** baggage compartment

coffre-fort (*pl* **coffres-forts**) [kɔfrəfɔr] *nm* safe

coffrer [kɔfre] *vt Fam* (*mettre en prison*) to put inside; **se faire c.** to get put inside

coffret [kɔfrɛ] *nm* **(a)** (*petit coffre*) box; **c. à bijoux** jewellery box **(b)** (*de livres, de disques*) box **(c)** *Ordinat* case

cogérant, -e [kɔʒerɑ̃, -ɑ̃t] *nm,f* joint manager, *f* joint manageress

cogestion [kɔʒɛstjɔ̃] *nf* joint management

cogitation [kɔʒitasjɔ̃] *nf Hum* cogitation

cogiter [kɔʒite] *vi Hum* to cogitate

cognac [kɔɲak] *nm* cognac

cognement [kɔɲəmɑ̃] *nm* (*bruit*) banging; (*d'un moteur*) knocking

cogner [kɔɲe] **1** *vt* **(a)** (*heurter*) to knock **(b)** *Fam* (*battre*) to knock about

2 *vi* **(a)** (*buter*) to bang (**sur/contre** on); **sa tête a cogné contre le mur** he banged his head on the wall; **c. du poing sur la table** to bang (one's fist) on the table; **c. à une porte** to bang on a door **(b)** *Fam* (*frapper*) **il cogne dur** he knows how to use his fists; **se faire c. dessus** to get knocked about **(c)** *Fam* **ça cogne** (*il fait chaud*) it's scorching **(d)** (*moteur*) to knock

3 se cogner *vpr* to bang oneself; **se c. à** *ou* **contre qch** to bang into sth; **se c. la tête contre qch** to bang one's head on sth; *Fig* **se c. la tête contre les murs** to bang one's head against a brick wall

cohabitation [kɔabitasjɔ̃] *nf* living together, cohabitation; *Pol* cohabitation

cohabiter [kɔabite] *vi* to live together; **c. avec qn** to live with sb

cohérence [kɔerɑ̃s] *nf* (*d'une argumentation, d'un discours*) coherence; (*d'une attitude*) consistency

cohérent, -e [kɔerɑ̃, -ɑ̃t] *adj* (*argumentation, discours*) coherent; (*attitude*) consistent

cohéritier, -ère [kɔeritje, -ɛr] *nm,f* joint heir, *f* joint heiress

cohésion [kɔezjɔ̃] *nf* cohesion

cohorte [kɔɔrt] *nf* (*de gens*) horde

cohue [kɔy] *nf* crowd

coi, coite [kwa, kwat] *adj* **se tenir c.** to keep quiet; **en rester c.** to be speechless

coiffe [kwaf] *nf* (*coiffure régionale, religieuse*) headdress

coiffé, -e [kwafe] *adj* **(a)** **je ne suis pas encore coiffée** I haven't done my hair yet; **elle est bien coiffée** her hair is lovely; **il est mal c.** his hair's a mess **(b)** **être c. de qch** to be wearing sth (*on one's head*)

coiffer [kwafe] **1** *vt* **(a)** (*peigner*) **c. qn** to do sb's hair; **il coiffe bien** he's a good hairdresser; **se faire c.** (**chez/par qn**) to have one's hair done (at sb's/by sb) **(b)** (*mettre un chapeau à*) **c. qn de qch** to put sth on sb's head; *Fig* **c. sainte Catherine** to be twenty-five and still unmarried **(c)** (*service*) to head **(d)** *Sp & Fig* **se faire c.** (**au poteau**) to be pipped at the post

2 se coiffer *vpr* **(a)** (*se peigner*) to do one's hair **(b)** (*mettre*) **se c. de qch** to put sth on

coiffeur, -euse [kwafœr, -øz] **1** *nm,f* hairdresser

2 *nf* **coiffeuse** (*meuble*) dressing-table

coiffure [kwafyr] *nf* **(a)** (*coupe de cheveux*) hairstyle **(b)** (*activité*) hairdressing **(c)** (*chapeau*) headgear; (*de costume régional*) headdress

coin [kwɛ̃] *nm* **(a)** (*angle*) corner; **faire le c.** to be on the corner; **à tous les coins de rue** on every street corner; **aux quatre coins du monde** in all corners of the earth; **mettre un enfant au c.** (*pour le punir*) to make a child stand in the corner; *Fig* **rester dans son c.** to keep to oneself; **les coins et les recoins de qch** the nooks and crannies of sth; **je ne voudrais pas le rencontrer au c. d'un bois** I wouldn't like to meet him on a dark night; *Av & Rail* **c. fenêtre/couloir** window/aisle seat; **au c. du feu** by the fire(side); **lancer un regard en c. à qn** to give sb a sidelong glance; **sourire en c.** half smile; **regarder qn du c. de l'œil** to look at sb out of the corner of one's eye **(b)** (*endroit quelconque*) spot, place; **un petit c. tranquille** a quiet little spot; *Euph* **le petit c.** the smallest room (in the house); **dans un c. de ma mémoire** in a corner of my mind; **j'ai dû le mettre dans un c.** I must have put it somewhere; **chercher qch dans tous les coins** to look high and low for sth **(c)** (*voisinage*) **du c.** local; **il habite dans le c.** he lives around here **(d)** (*parcelle*) patch; **c. de ciel bleu** patch of blue sky **(e)** (*cale*) wedge

coincé, -e [kwɛ̃se] *adj* **(a)** (*fermeture, porte, mécanisme*) jammed, stuck **(b)** *Fam* (*inhibé*) hung up **(c)** **il faut que je paie, je suis c.** I'll have to pay, I've no choice

coincer [16] [kwɛ̃se] **1** *vt* **(a)** (*accidentellement*) (*tiroir, clef*) to jam; **j'ai coincé mes cheveux dans ma fermeture Éclair®** I got my hair caught in my zip; **la voiture est coincée entre deux camions** (*en stationnement*) the car is boxed in by two lorries; **être coincé** (*personne*) (*dans un embouteillage, un endroit*) to be stuck; (*être occupé*) to be tied up **(b)** (*volontairement*) to wedge; **elle l'a coincé dans le couloir** she cornered him in the corridor; **il m'a coincé** (*je n'ai pas su répondre*) he had me cornered **(c)** *Fam* (*arrêter*) to nick; **se faire c.** to get nicked

2 *vi* (*tiroir, mécanisme*) to jam, to stick; *Fam* **ça coince** there's a hitch

3 se coincer *vpr* (*tiroir, mécanisme*) to jam, to stick; **se c. le doigt dans la porte** to catch one's finger in the door; **je me suis coincé le dos** my back's seized up

coïncidence [kɔɛ̃sidɑ̃s] *nf* coincidence

coïncider [kɔɛ̃side] *vi* (*événements, versions*) to coincide (avec with); **leurs intérêts coïncident** they have similar interests; **tous les témoignages coïncident** the witnesses all bear each other out

coin-coin [kwɛ̃kwɛ̃] **1** *nm inv* (*des canards*) quacking
2 *exclam* quack! quack!

coin-cuisine (*pl* **coins-cuisines**) [kwɛ̃kɥizin] *nm* kitchen area

coïnculpé, -e [kɔɛ̃kylpe] *nm,f* co-defendant

coing [kwɛ̃] *nm* quince

coin-repas (*pl* **coins-repas**) [kwɛ̃rəpa] *nm* dining area

coït [kɔit] *nm* coitus

coite [kwat] *voir* **coi**

coke [kɔk] **1** *nm* (*combustible*) coke
2 *nf Fam* (*cocaïne*) coke

col [kɔl] *nm* **a** (*d'une robe, d'une chemise*) collar; **c. de fourrure/de dentelle** fur/lace collar; **c. blanc** (*employé de bureau*) white-collar worker; **c. bleu** (*ouvrier*) blue-collar worker; **c. cheminée** *ou* **montant** *Br* turtleneck, *Am* mock turtleneck; **c. rond** round neck; **c. roulé** *Br* polo neck, *Am* turtleneck; **c. en V** V-neck; **faux c.** false collar **(b)** (*d'une bouteille*) neck **(c)** *Géog* col **(d)** *Anat* (*d'un os*) neck; **c. de l'utérus** cervix

colchique [kɔlʃik] *nm* autumn crocus

coléoptère [kɔleɔptɛr] *nm* beetle, *Spéc* coleopteran

colère [kɔlɛr] *nf* anger; **être en c.** (**contre qn**) to be angry (with sb); **mettre qn en c.** to make sb angry; **se mettre en c.** to get angry; **se mettre dans une c. bleue** *ou* **noire** to fly into a towering rage; **piquer une c.** to fly into a rage; **passer sa c. sur qn** to take one's anger out on sb; **avec c.** angrily; *Litté* **la c. de Dieu** the wrath of God; **c. froide** cold fury

coléreux, -euse [kɔlerø, -øz], **colérique** [kɔlerik] *adj* (*personne*) quick-tempered; (*disposition*) irritable

colibri [kɔlibri] *nm* humming-bird

colifichet [kɔlifiʃɛ] *nm* trinket, knick-knack

colimaçon [kɔlimasɔ̃] *nm voir* **escalier**

colin [kɔlɛ̃] *nm* (*merlu*) hake; (*lieu noir*) coley

colin-maillard [kɔlɛ̃majar] *nm* blindman's-buff; **jouer à c.** to play blindman's-buff

colique [kɔlik] *nf* (*diarrhée*) diarrhoea; **avoir la c.** to have diarrhoea; (*douleur*) **coliques** stomach pains, colic; **c. néphrétique** renal colic

colis [kɔli] *nm* parcel; **par c. postal** by parcel post

Colisée [kɔlize] *nm* **le C.** the Coliseum

colistier, -ère [kɔlistje, -ɛr] *nm,f Pol* fellow candidate

colite [kɔlit] *nf Méd* colitis

collabo [kɔlabo] *nmf Fam Hist* collaborator

collaborateur, -trice [kɔlabɔratœr, -tris] *nm,f* **(a)** (*aide*) assistant **(b)** *Journ* contributor (**de** to) **(c)** *Hist* collaborator

collaboration [kɔlabɔrasjɔ̃] *nf* **(a)** (*aide*) collaboration (**à** on); **travailler en étroite c.** (**avec qn**) to work closely (with sb) **(b)** *Journ* contribution **(c)** *Hist* collaboration

collaborer [kɔlabɔre] *vi* **(a)** (*travailler ensemble*) to collaborate (**avec** with); **c. à qch** (*projet*) to take part in sth; (*journal*) to contribute to sth **(b)** *Hist* to collaborate

collage [kɔlaʒ] *nm* **(a)** (*d'affiches*) sticking up; (*de bois*) gluing; (*de papier*) pasting **(b)** (*composition*) collage

collagène [kɔlaʒɛn] *nm* collagen

collant, -e [kɔlɑ̃, -ɑ̃t] **1** *adj* **a** (*adhésif*) sticky **(b)** (*poisseux*) sticky **(c)** (*moulant*) skin-tight **(d)** *Fam* (*personne*) **qu'est-ce qu'il est c.!** you just can't shake him off!
2 *nm Br* (pair of) tights, *Am* pantihose; **c. de danse** dance tights

collation [kɔlasjɔ̃] *nf* (*repas*) light meal

colle [kɔl] *nf* **(a)** (*transparente*) glue; (*blanche*) paste; **c. à bois** woodworking glue; **c. forte** strong glue; **de la c. en pot/stick/tube** a pot/stick/tube of glue **(b)** *Fam* (*question difficile*) poser; **là, tu me poses une c.** you've got me there **(c)** *Fam* (*punition*) detention **(d)** *Fam* (*examen oral*) oral test **(e)** *très Fam* **vivre** *ou* **être à la c.** to be shacked up together

collecte [kɔlɛkt] *nf* collection; **faire une c.** (**au profit de**) to make a collection (in aid of)

collecter [kɔlɛkte] *vt* to collect

collecteur, -trice [kɔlɛktœr, -tris] **1** *nm,f* collector; **c. d'impôts** tax collector
2 *nm* **(a)** (*d'eaux pluviales*) main sewer **(b)** *Aut* **c. d'échappement** exhaust manifold

collectif, -ive [kɔlɛktif, -iv] **1** *adj* (*action, travail, responsabilité*) collective; (*billet*) group; (*licenciements*) mass
2 *nm* **(a)** *Fin* **c. budgétaire** bill of supply **(b)** (*association*) collective

collection [kɔlɛksjɔ̃] *nf* **(a)** (*action*) collecting; **faire la c. de qch** to collect sth **(b)** (*série*) (*de timbres, de papillons, d'œuvres d'art*) collection; (*de périodiques*) series; (*d'échantillons*) line; **j'en ai toute une c.** I've got a whole collection of them **(c)** (*de haute couture, de prêt-à-porter*) collection

collectionner [kɔlɛksjɔne] *vt* to collect

collectionneur, -euse [kɔlɛksjɔnœr, -øz] *nm,f* collector

collectivisme [kɔlɛktivism] *nm Écon* collectivism

collectivité [kɔlɛktivite] *nf* **(a)** (*groupe*) community **(b)** **collectivités locales** local communities

collège [kɔlɛʒ] *nm* **(a)** (*école*) school; **c. d'enseignement secondaire** = former secondary school for pupils aged 12 to 15; **c. d'enseignement technique** technical school; **le C. de France** the Collège de France (*prestigious higher education institution*) **(b)** *Pol* **c. électoral** electoral college

collégial, -e, -aux, -ales [kɔleʒjal, -o] **1** *adj* collegiate
2 *nf* **collégiale** collegiate church

collégien, -enne [kɔleʒjɛ̃, -ɛn] *nm,f* schoolboy, *f* schoolgirl; **je me suis fait avoir comme un c.** I fell for it like a fool

collègue [kɔlɛg] *nmf* **c.** (**de travail**) colleague

coller [kɔle] **1** *vt* **a** (*faire adhérer*) to stick (**à/sur** to/on); **il avait les cheveux collés par la sueur/la peinture** his hair was matted with sweat/paint; **il est resté collé à la télé toute la soirée** he was glued to the TV all evening **(b)** (*appuyer*) **c. qch à** *ou* **contre qch** to press sth against sth **(c)** *Fam* (*mettre*) to stick; **ils ont collé le bébé à la grand-mère** they've dumped the baby on the grandmother; **on m'a collé à la comptabilité sans que j'aie dit oui** I got shoved into accounts without any say in the matter; **c. une gifle à qn** to slap sb in the face; **si tu continues, je t'en colle une!** if you don't stop, I'll slap you one!; **c. une contravention à qn** to slap a fine on sb **(d)** *Fam* (*retenir en punition*) to keep in; **se faire c.** to be kept in **(e)** (*refuser*) (*candidat*) to fail; **se faire c.** to fail **(f)** *Fam* (*suivre*) to follow closely; **il me colle!** he sticks to me like glue! **(g)** *Ordinat* to paste

2 *vi Fam* **(a)** *(coincider)* to tally **(avec** with) **(b)** *(aller bien)* **ça colle!** that's OK!; **ça ne va pas c. pour mercredi** it's no go for Wednesday; **ça ne colle pas entre eux** they don't hit it off

3 coller à *vt ind aussi Fig* to stick to; *Fam* **c. aux fesses à qn** to stick to sb's tail; **sa réputation lui colle à la peau** he can't shake off his reputation

4 se coller *vpr* **(a)** *(adhérer les uns aux autres)* to stick **(s')aplatir)** **se c. contre un mur** to flatten oneself against a wall; **se c. contre qn** to cling to sb; *Fam* **se c. devant la télé** to plonk oneself down in front of the TV; *Fam* **c'est encore toi qui t'y colles** you're landed with it again

collerette [kɔlʀɛt] *nf* **(a)** *(de vêtement)* collar; *Hist (fraise)* ruff **(b)** *Bot (de champignon)* annulus **(c)** *(de tuyau)* flange

collet [kɔlɛ] *nm* **(a)** *(de vêtement)* collar; **saisir** *ou* **prendre qn au c.** to grab sb by the scruff of the neck; **mettre la main au c. à qn** *(l'arrêter)* to get hold of sb; **être c. monté** to be strait-laced **(b)** *(piège)* snare

colleter [42] [kɔlte] **se colleter** *vpr Fam* to tussle **(avec qn** with sb); **se c. avec qch** to grapple with sth

collier [kɔlje] *nm* **(a)** *(bijou)* necklace; **c. de perles** pearl necklace; **c. de fleurs** garland of flowers **(b)** *(de chien)* collar; *Fig* **donner un coup de c.** to put one's back into it **(c)** *(barbe)* **c. de barbe** fringe of beard **(d)** *Culin (de bœuf, de mouton)* neck **(e)** *Tech* collar; **c. de serrage** clamp collar **(f)** *Zool (d'oiseau)* collar

collimateur [kɔlimatœʀ] *nm Fig* **avoir qn dans le c.** to keep one's eye on sb

colline [kɔlin] *nf* hill

collision [kɔlizjɔ̃] *nf (entre véhicules, entre objets)* collision; **entrer en c. avec qch** to collide with sth; *Aut* **c. frontale/latérale** head-on/side-on collision

colloque [kɔlɔk] *nm (conférence)* seminar

collusion [kɔlyzjɔ̃] *nf* collusion

collutoire [kɔlytwaʀ] *nm* throat spray

collyre [kɔliʀ] *nm* eyewash

colmater [kɔlmate] *vt* to fill in

colo [kɔlo] *nf Fam Br* (children's) holiday camp, *Am* summer camp

colocataire [kɔlokatɛʀ] *nmf Br* flatmate, *Am* roommate

Colomb [kɔlɔ̃] *npr* **Christophe C.** Christopher Columbus

colombage [kɔlɔ̃baʒ] *nm Constr* half-timbering; **maison à colombages** half-timbered house

colombe [kɔlɔ̃b] *nf* dove

Colombie [kɔlɔ̃bi] *nf* **la C.** Colombia

Colombie-Britannique [kɔlɔ̃bibʀitanik] *nf* **la C.** British Columbia

colombien, -enne [kɔlɔ̃bjɛ̃, -ɛn] **1** *adj* Colombian
2 *nmf* **C.** Colombian

colombier [kɔlɔ̃bje] *nm (pigeonnier)* dovecote

colon [kɔlɔ̃] *nm* **(a)** *(pionnier)* settler, colonist **(b)** *(dans une colonie de vacances)* child (at camp)

côlon [kɔlɔ̃] *nm* colon

colonel [kɔlɔnɛl] *nm (dans l'armée de terre)* colonel; *(dans l'armée de l'air)* *Br* group captain, *Am* colonel

colonial, -e, -aux, -ales [kɔlɔnjal, -o] **1** *adj* colonial
2 *nf Hist* **la coloniale** the Colonial Army

colonialisme [kɔlɔnjalism] *nm* colonialism

colonialiste [kɔlɔnjalist] *adj & nmf* colonialist

colonie [kɔlɔni] *nf* **(a)** *(territoire, immigrés)* colony **(b)** **c. (de vacances)** *Br* (children's) holiday camp, *Am* summer camp; **envoyer ses enfants en c.** to send one's children to camp

colonisation [kɔlɔnizasjɔ̃] *nf* colonization

coloniser [kɔlɔnize] *vt* to colonize

colonnade [kɔlɔnad] *nf* colonnade

colonne [kɔlɔn] *nf* **(a)** *(pilier)* column, pillar; **c. Morris** = pillar used to advertise forthcoming events **(b)** *(file)* column; **en c. par deux/trois** in columns of two/three **(c)** *(d'un dictionnaire, d'un journal)* column **(d)** *(de fumée, de mercure)* column **(e)** *Anat* **c. vertébrale** spine, spinal column **(f)** *Aut* **c. de direction** steering column

coloquinte [kɔlɔkɛ̃t] *nf (plante)* bitter apple

colorant, -e [kɔlɔʀɑ̃, -ɑ̃t] **1** *adj* colouring
2 *nm* **(a)** *(pour teindre)* colorant **(b)** *(alimentaire)* colouring; **sans colorants** *(sur étiquette)* no artificial colouring

coloration [kɔlɔʀasjɔ̃] *nf* **(a)** *(fait de colorer)* colouring; **se faire faire une c.** to have one's hair tinted **(b)** *(de la peau)* colouring **(c)** *Fig* **c. politique** political colour

coloré, -e [kɔlɔʀe] *adj* coloured; *(teint)* ruddy; *Fig (style)* colourful

colorer [kɔlɔʀe] **1** *vt* to colour; *Fig (récit)* to lend colour to; **c. qch en vert** to colour sth green
2 se colorer *vpr (visage)* to become flushed

coloriage [kɔlɔʀjaʒ] *nm (action)* colouring (in); *(dessin)* drawing; **album** *ou* **livre de c.** colouring (in) book

colorier [66] [kɔlɔʀje] *vt* to colour (in)

coloris [kɔlɔʀi] *nm* shade

coloriser [kɔlɔʀize] *vt Cin* to colourize

colossal, -e, -aux, -ales [kɔlɔsal, -o] *adj* colossal, huge

colosse [kɔlɔs] *nm (homme)* giant; *Fig* **un c. aux pieds d'argile** a giant with feet of clay

colostomie [kɔlɔstɔmi] *nf Méd* colostomy

colporter [kɔlpɔʀte] *vt (marchandises)* to hawk; *(nouvelle, rumeurs)* to spread

colporteur, -euse [kɔlpɔʀtœʀ, -øz] *nm,f* hawker

colt [kɔlt] *nm* Colt®

coltiner [kɔltine] **se coltiner** *vpr Fam* **se c. qn/qch** to get landed with sb/sth

colvert [kɔlvɛʀ] *nm* mallard

colza [kɔlza] *nm* rape

coma [kɔma] *nm* coma; **être/tomber dans le c.** to be in/go into a coma

comateux, -euse [kɔmatø, -øz] **1** *adj* comatose
2 *nm,f* patient in a coma

combat [kɔ̃ba] *nm* **(a)** *Mil (bataille)* fight; *(activité)* combat; **c. aérien** dog fight; *aussi Fig* **c. d'arrière-garde** rearguard action; **c. naval** naval engagement **(b)** *(dispute)* fight; **c. de boxe** boxing match; **c. de coqs** cockfight **(c)** *Fig (lutte)* fight **(contre** against)

combatif, -ive [kɔ̃batif, -iv] *adj* combative

combativité [kɔ̃bativite] *nf* combativeness

combattant, -e [kɔ̃batɑ̃, -ɑ̃t] **1** *nm,f* combatant; **anciens combattants** veterans
2 *adj (troupes, unité)* fighting

combattre [11] [kɔ̃batʀ] **1** *vt (ennemi)* to fight (against); *(maladie, inflation, racisme)* to fight
2 *vi* to fight **(pour/contre** for/against)

combien [kɔ̃bjɛ̃] **1** adv **(a)** (comme) how (much); **j'ai pu constater c. tu avais changé** I could see how much you'd changed **(b)** (en nombre) how many; **c. sont-ils?** how many (of them) are there?; **c. de** how many; **c. de gens furent tués dans cette guerre!** what a lot of people were killed in that war! **(c)** (en quantité, en poids) how much; **ça fait c.?** (d'argent) how much is that?; **c. y a-t-il d'ici à Londres?** how far is it to London?; **à c. sommes-nous de Paris?** how far are we from Paris?; **c. mesure-t-il?** how tall is he?; **elle est enceinte – de c.?** she's pregnant – how many months?; **c. de** how much; **c. de temps** how long
2 nm inv Fam **c. sommes-nous?** what's the date (today)?; **il y a un car tous les c.?** how often do the buses run?; **tu chausses du c.?** what size shoe do you take?

combientième [kɔ̃bjɛ̃tjɛm] Fam **1** nmf **c'est le c. sur la liste?** where is it on the list?
2 adj **tu as été reçu c. à l'examen?** where did you come in the exam?; **c'est la c. fois que tu viens?** how often have you been here now?

combinaison [kɔ̃binɛzɔ̃] nf **(a)** (assemblage) combination; **la c. gagnante** (au tiercé) the winning combination; Ordinat **c. de touches** key combination **(b)** (vêtement) (de travail) Br boiler suit, Am coveralls; Av flying suit; (de femme) catsuit; (sous-vêtement) slip; **c. de plongée** wet suit; **c. de ski** ski suit

combine [kɔ̃bin] nf Fam trick; **il a une c. pour entrer sans payer** he knows a way of getting in without paying; **mettre qn dans la c.** to let sb in on it

combiné, -e [kɔ̃bine] **1** adj (action, efforts) combined
2 nm **(a)** **c. (téléphonique)** receiver **(b)** (en ski) **c. alpin** alpine competition

combiner [kɔ̃bine] vt **(a)** (unir) to combine **(b)** Fam (plan) to concoct; **qu'est-ce que tu combines encore?** what are you cooking up now?
2 se combiner vpr to combine

comble [kɔ̃bl] **1** adj (jam-)packed; **faire salle c.** (au théâtre) to have a full house
2 nm **(a)** (maximum) **le c. de** the height of; (du désespoir) the depth of; **ça, c'est le ou un c.!** that's the last straw!; **être au c. de la joie** to be overjoyed **(b)** Archit (en bois) roof timbers; (en métal) roof structure; **les combles** (grenier) the attic; **loger sous les combles** to live in an attic

combler [kɔ̃ble] vt **(a)** (puits, fossé, trou) to fill in; (perte) to make good; (découvert) to pay off; (lacune) to fill; **c. son retard** to make up for lost time **(b)** (satisfaire) to satisfy; **c. qn de cadeaux** to shower sb with gifts; **un mari comblé** a happily married man

combustible [kɔ̃bystibl] **1** nm fuel
2 adj combustible

combustion [kɔ̃bystjɔ̃] nf combustion

comédie [kɔmedi] nf (pièce, film, genre) comedy; **jouer la c.** to act; Fig to put on an act; **allons, pas de c.!** (caprice) come on, stop your nonsense!; **c'est une vraie c. quand il faut aller à l'école** it's a real fuss when it's time to go to school; **c. de mœurs** comedy of manners; **c. musicale** musical

Comédie-Française [kɔmedifʀɑ̃sɛz] nf la C. = state-run theatre company presenting plays from the established repertoire

comédien, -enne [kɔmedjɛ̃, -ɛn] **1** nm,f (acteur) actor, f actress; Fig **c'est une comédienne** she's always putting on an act; **comédiens ambulants** strolling players
2 adj **elle est très comédienne** she's always putting on an act

comédon [kɔmedɔ̃] nm blackhead

comestible [kɔmɛstibl] adj edible; **denrées comestibles** foodstuffs

comète [kɔmɛt] nf comet; Fig **tirer ou faire des plans sur la c.** to build castles in the air

comice [kɔmis] nm **c. agricole** agricultural association; **comices agricoles** (foire) agricultural show

comique [kɔmik] **1** adj **(a)** (acteur, film, rôle) comedy; **le genre c.** comedy **(b)** (amusant) comical, funny
2 nm **(a)** (genre) comedy; **c. de situation** situation comedy **(b)** (acteur) comic actor; Péj (bouffon) comedian **(c)** **le c. de l'histoire, c'est que...** the funny part is that...

comité [kɔmite] nm committee; **faire partie d'un c.** to sit on a committee; Fig **nous serons en petit c.** we'll just have a small get-together; **c. d'entreprise** works council; **C. international olympique** International Olympic Committee

commandant [kɔmɑ̃dɑ̃] nm **(a)** (officier) (d'unité) commander; (de camp, de base) commandant; (de bateau) captain (whatever his rank); Av **c. de bord** captain; **c. en chef** commander-in-chief; Naut executive officer **(b)** (rang) (dans l'armée de terre) major; (dans l'armée de l'air) Br squadron leader, Am major

commande [kɔmɑ̃d] nf **(a)** Com order; **faire ou passer une c.** to put in or place an order; **sur c.** to order; Fig **at will; on ne peut pas tire sur c.** you can't laugh to order; **ouvrage de c.** commissioned work; (action, manette) control; (mécanisme) drive; **c. à distance** remote control; **commandes** (d'un avion) controls; **prendre les commandes** (d'un avion) to take over the controls; (d'une société) to take control **(c)** Ordinat command; **c. d'annulation/d'effacement** undo/delete command; **à c. vocale** voice-activated

commandement [kɔmɑ̃dmɑ̃] nm **(a)** (ordre) Mil command; **à mon c.** when I give the command; Rel **les dix commandements** the Ten Commandments **(b)** (pouvoir) command; **avoir/prendre le c.** to be in/to take command; **c. suprême, haut c.** high command

commander [kɔmɑ̃de] **1** vt **(a)** (diriger, ordonner) to command; Fam **sans vous c., est-ce que vous pourriez fermer la fenêtre?** I wonder if you'd mind closing the window **(b)** (marchandises, dîner) to order; (peinture, ouvrage) to commission; **c. qch à qn** to order/commission sth from sb **(c)** (mouvement, valve) to control; (machine) to drive **(d)** Ordinat to drive; **commandé par menu** menu-driven
2 vi **c. à qn de faire qch** to order sb to do sth; **qui est-ce qui commande ici?** who's in charge here?
3 se commander vpr **ces choses-là ne se commandent pas** (sont incontrôlables) these things are beyond our control

commanditaire [kɔmɑ̃ditɛʀ] adj & nm Com (associé) **c.** Br sleeping or Am silent partner; **les commanditaires de l'attentat** the people behind the attack

commandite [kɔmɑ̃dit] nf Com **(société en) c.** mixed liability company

commandité [kɔmɑ̃dite] adj & nm Com (associé) **c.** active partner

commanditer [kɔmɑ̃dite] vt Com to finance; (meurtre, attentat) to be behind

commando [kɔmɑ̃do] nm (groupe) commando (unit)

comme [kɔm] **1** adv (a) (devant un nom, un pronom) like; **il n'est pas c. les autres** he isn't like the others; **c. ça** like that; (du coup) that way; **c'est c. ça, un point c'est tout!** too bad, that's the way it is!; **alors c. ça, vous venez de Paris?** you come from Paris, don't you?; Fam **c. ça!** (formidable) great!, fab!; **quelque chose c. deux cents personnes** something like two hundred people

(b) (devant une proposition) as; **il écrit c. il parle** he writes as he speaks; **insolent c. il est...** insolent as he is...; **il leva la main c. pour me frapper** he lifted his hand as if or as though to strike me; **c. il faut** (se conduire) properly; **des gens très c. il faut** very respectable people; **c. si as**, as though; **c. si je ne le savais pas!** as if I didn't know!

(c) (dans des images) as; **doux c. un agneau** (as) gentle as a lamb

(d) (et) **les femmes c. les hommes** men and women alike; **tout le monde fera la vaisselle, toi c. les autres** everyone's going to do the washing-up, and you're no exception

(e) (tel que) such as, like; **les bois durs c. le chêne** hard woods like or such as oak; P **c. pomme** P as in pomme

(f) (en tant que) as; **je l'ai eue c. professeur** she was my teacher; **qu'est-ce que vous avez c. desserts?** what have you got in the way of desserts?; **ce n'est pas mal c. film** it's not a bad film

(g) (en quelque sorte) **elle a eu c. une hésitation** she seemed to hesitate; **j'étais c. hypnotisé** it was as if or as though I was hypnotized

(h) (comment) how; **tu sais bien c. il est** you know what he's like; Fam **elle a fait les carreaux, faut voir c.!** you should see the way she's done the windows!

(i) (exclamatif) how; **c. tu as grandi!** how you've grown!; **c. elle est bête!** she's so stupid!; **c. elle a de beaux cheveux!** what lovely hair she has!

(j) Fam (locutions) **c'est tout c.** it amounts to the same thing; **c. ci c. ça** so-so; **c. qui dirait** as it were; **c. quoi** (disant que) to the effect that; (ce qui prouve que) which goes to show that; **drôle c. tout** as funny as anything

2 conj (a) (puisque) as, since; **c. vous êtes mon ami, je vais tout vous dire** as you're my friend I'll tell you everything

(b) (alors que) **c. il allait frapper, la porte s'ouvrit** he was just about to knock when the door opened

commémoratif, -ive [kɔmemɔratif, -iv] adj (plaque, cérémonie) commemorative; (service) memorial; **monument c.** memorial

commémoration [kɔmemɔrasjɔ̃] nf commemoration; **en c. de** in commemoration of

commémorer [kɔmemɔre] vt to commemorate

commencement [kɔmɑ̃smɑ̃] nm beginning, start; **au c.** at the beginning or start; **il faut un c. à tout** you've got to start somewhere; Fam **c'est le c. de la fin** it's the beginning of the end

commencer [16] [kɔmɑ̃se] **1** vt (a) (entreprendre) to begin, to start; (traitement, régime) to go on, to start; **nous avons mal commencé l'année** we've made a bad start to the year (b) (être au début de) to begin, to start

2 vi to begin, to start; **pour c., je dois vous dire...** to begin with, I must tell you...; Ironique **ça commence bien!** that's a good start!; **c. par qch/par faire qch** to begin or start with sth/by doing sth; **par où c.?** where shall I begin?; **à c. par...** beginning with...

3 commencer à vt ind **c. à faire qch** to begin or start to

do sth, to begin or start doing sth; Fam **je commence à en avoir assez!** I've had just about enough!; Fam **ça commence à bien faire** it's getting a bit too much

comment [kɔmɑ̃] **1** adv how; **c. allez-vous?** how are you?; **c.?** (pour faire répéter) I beg your pardon?; **c. faire?** what can I/we/etc do?; **c. est-il, ce garçon?** what's this young man like?; **elle me dira c. faire** she'll tell me how to do it

2 exclam what!; **mais c. donc!** why, of course!; Fam **ça vous a plu? – et c.!** did you like it? – you bet I did!

commentaire [kɔmɑ̃tɛr] nm (a) (remarque) comment, remark; **faire des commentaires** to make comments; **cela se passe de c.** it speaks for itself; Fam **sans c.!** no comment!; Scol **c. de texte** textual commentary (b) (à la radio, à la télévision) commentary; **c. sportif** sports commentary

commentateur, -trice [kɔmɑ̃tatœr, -tris] nm,f (à la radio, à la télévision) commentator; **c. sportif** sports commentator

commenter [kɔmɑ̃te] vt (expliquer, donner son avis sur) to comment on; (à la radio, à la télévision) (compétition) to commentate on; **c. l'actualité** to comment on current affairs

commérage [kɔmeraʒ] nm (piece of) gossip; **commérages** gossip

commerçant, -e [kɔmɛrsɑ̃, -ɑ̃t] **1** nm,f trader; (qui tient un magasin) shopkeeper; **petits commerçants** small traders

2 adj **quartier c.** shopping area; **rue très commerçante** busy shopping street; **il n'est pas très c.** he doesn't look after his customers very well

commerce [kɔmɛrs] nm (a) **le c.** (activité, secteur) trade; (affaires) business; **ça se trouve dans le c.** you can buy it in the shops; **faire du c. avec** to do business with; **hors c.** not for (general) sale; **c. en gros/de gros/de détail** wholesale/retail trade; **c. intérieur/extérieur** home/ foreign trade; **c. international** world trade; **c. maritime** seaborne trade; **le petit c.** small traders (b) (magasin) business

commercer [16] [kɔmɛrse] vi to trade (avec with)

commercial, -e, -aux, -ales [kɔmɛrsjal, -o] **1** adj (rapports, pratiques) business, commercial; (embargo, tribunal) trade; (droit) commercial; Péj (film, chanson) commercial; **suivre une formation commerciale** to do a business studies course

2 nm,f salesman, f saleswoman

3 nf **commerciale** (voiture) Br estate car, Am station wagon

commercialisation [kɔmɛrsjalizasjɔ̃] nf marketing

commercialiser [kɔmɛrsjalize] vt (produit) to market

commère [kɔmɛr] nf gossip

commettre [47] [kɔmɛtr] **1** vt (a) (crime, péché, injustice) to commit; (erreur) to make; Hum **il a déjà commis deux pièces de théâtre** he's already to blame for two plays (b) Jur **avocat commis d'office** counsel appointed by the court

2 se commettre vpr Litt **se c. avec qn** to compromise oneself by associating with sb

commis¹, -e voir **commettre**

commis² [kɔmi] nm (a) (employé) clerk; (dans un magasin) (shop) assistant (b) Vieilli **c. voyageur** commercial traveller

commisération [kɔmizerasjɔ̃] nf commiseration; **témoigner de la c. à qn** to commiserate with sb

commissaire [kɔmisɛr] *nm* (a) c. (de police) *Br* ≃ (police) superintendent, *Am* ≃ (police) captain (b) *Fin* c. aux comptes government auditor (c) *(membre d'une commission)* commissioner (d) *Sp* steward

commissaire-priseur *(pl* **commissaires-priseurs**) [kɔmisɛrprizœr] *nm* auctioneer

commissariat [kɔmisarja] *nm* (a) c. (de police) police station (b) *(fonction)* commissionership (c) *(service)* commission; le C. à l'énergie atomique the Atomic Energy Commission

commission [kɔmisjɔ̃] *nf* (a) *(course)* faire les commissions to go shopping (b) *(service)* errand; *(message)* message; faire une c. à qn to run an errand; faire une c. à qn to give sb a message (c) *(comité)* commission, committee; c. d'enquête board of inquiry; C. européenne European Commission; C. des opérations de Bourse = French Stock Exchange watchdog (d) *(pourcentage)* Com commission; *Fin* brokerage; être payé à la c. to be paid on a commission basis; c. bancaire bank commission (e) *Fam* la petite/grosse c. number one/two

commissionnaire [kɔmisjɔnɛr] *nm* (a) *(messager)* messenger; *(à l'hôtel, au théâtre)* commissionaire (b) *Com* (commission) agent

commissionner [kɔmisjɔne] *vt* to commission

commissures [kɔmisyr] *nfpl* c. des lèvres *ou* de la bouche corners of the mouth

commode [kɔmɔd] 1 *adj* (a) *(heure, lieu)* convenient; *(outil, système)* handy (b) pas c. *(difficile)* tricky (c) pas c. *(peu aimable)* awkward
2 *nf* chest of drawers

commodément [kɔmɔdemɑ̃] *adv* *(assis, installé)* comfortably

commodité [kɔmɔdite] *nf* (a) *(facilité)* convenience; pour plus de c. for greater convenience; les commodités de la vie moderne the comforts of modern life (b) *Vieilli* commodités *(toilettes)* Br toilet, Am rest room

commotion [kɔmosjɔ̃] *nf* (a) *Méd* c. cérébrale concussion (b) *(émotion)* shock

commotionner [kɔmosjɔne] *vt* (a) *Méd* to concuss (b) *(choquer)* to shake (up)

commuer [kɔmɥe] *vt* *Jur* *(peine)* to commute (en to)

commun, -e [kɔmœ̃, -yn] 1 *adj* (a) *(non exclusif)* common (à to); *(travail)* joint; *(ami)* mutual; jardin c. à deux maisons garden shared by two houses; en c. *(travailler)* together; *(vivre)* communally; avoir qch en c. *(se ressembler)* to have sth in common; se mettre *ou* mettre de l'argent en c. pour acheter un cadeau to club together to buy a present (b) *(répandu)* common; il est d'une force peu commune he's unusually strong (c) *(vulgaire)* common
2 *nm* (a) *(majorité)* le c. des mortels the ordinary man; hors du c. out of the ordinary (b) communs *(dépendances)* outbuildings

communal, -e, -aux, -ales [kɔmynal, -o] *adj* *(de la commune)* *(terrain, salle)* Br ≃ council, Am ≃ district; école communale ≃ local Br primary or Am grade school

communautaire [kɔmynotɛr] *adj* *(en commun)* communal; *(de la Communauté européenne)* Community

communauté [kɔmynote] *nf* (a) *(collectivité)* & Rel community; *(de hippies)* commune; vivre en c. to live in a commune; la C. économique européenne the European Economic Community; la C. d'États indépendants the Commonwealth of Independent States (b) *(d'intérêts, d'idées)* similarity; *Jur* être mariés sous le régime de la c. to be married on the basis of a joint settlement of property

commune [kɔmyn] *nf* (a) *(municipalité)* commune *(smallest territorial division)* (b) *Hist* la C. the Commune *(in 1789 and 1874)*

communément [kɔmynemɑ̃] *adv* commonly

communiant, -e [kɔmynjɑ̃, -ɑ̃t] *nm,f* Rel communicant; premier c. person taking his first communion

communicatif, -ive [kɔmynikatif, -iv] *adj* (a) *(qui parle)* communicative; peu c. uncommunicative (b) *(rire, bonne humeur)* infectious

communication [kɔmynikasjɔ̃] *nf* (a) *(échange)* communication; entrer *ou* se mettre en c. avec qn to get in touch or in contact with sb; toutes les communications sont coupées all lines of communication are cut; c. de masse mass communication (b) c. (téléphonique) (telephone) call; je vous passe la c. I'll put you through; la c. est mauvaise the line is bad (c) *(exposé)* communication, message; faire une c. *(dans un colloque)* to read a paper

communier [66] [kɔmynje] *vi* Rel to receive Communion

communion [kɔmynjɔ̃] *nf* (a) *(communauté)* communion; être en c. avec la nature to commune with nature (b) Rel Communion; première c. first Communion; c. solennelle solemn Communion; faire sa c. to make one's first/solemn Communion

communiqué [kɔmynike] *nm* communiqué; c. de presse press release

communiquer [kɔmynike] 1 *vt* to communicate (à to); *(maladie)* to pass on (à to)
2 *vi* (a) *(être en relation)* to communicate (avec with) (b) *(pièce)* to communicate (avec with); porte qui communique avec le jardin door that leads into the garden
3 se communiquer *vpr* *(se transmettre)* to spread (à to)

communisme [kɔmynism] *nm* communism

communiste [kɔmynist] *adj* & *nmf* communist

commutateur [kɔmytatœr] *nm* Él *(bouton)* switch; Ordinat c. de données data switch

commutation [kɔmytasjɔ̃] *nf* (a) *Jur* *(de peine)* commutation (b) *(changement)* & Gram substitution; *(entre documents)* switching (c) Ordinat c. de message/ de paquets message/packet switching

Comores [kɔmɔr] *nfpl* les C., l'archipel des C. the Comoros

comorien, -enne [kɔmɔrjɛ̃, -ɛn] 1 *adj* Comoran
2 *nm,f* C. Comoran

compact, -e [kɔ̃pakt] 1 *adj* (a) *(de petit format)* compact (b) *(masse, terre)* compact; *(foule)* dense
2 *nm* (CD) compact disc

Compact Disc® *(pl* **Compact Discs**) [kɔ̃paktdisk] *nm* compact disc

compacter [kɔ̃pakte] *vt* Ordinat *(fichier, données)* to compress; *(base de données)* to pack

compacteur [kɔ̃paktœr] *nm Ordinat* c. de données data compressor; **c. d'exécutables** execute file compressor

compagne [kɔ̃paɲ] *nf* **(a)** *(camarade)* companion; **mes compagnes de captivité** my fellow captives **(b)** *(concubine)* partner

compagnie [kɔ̃paɲi] *nf* **(a)** *(présence)* company; **tenir c. à qn** to keep sb company **(b)** *(groupe)* **et toute la c.** and everybody **(c)** *Com & Th* company; *Com* **Thomas et C. Thomas and Company; c. aérienne** airline; **c. d'assurances** insurance company; **c. maritime** shipping line; **c. pétrolière** oil company; **c. de transports** carrier **(d)** *Mil* company **(e)** *(de perdrix)* covey

compagnon [kɔ̃paɲɔ̃] *nm* **(a)** *(camarade)* companion; **c. de voyage** travelling companion **(b)** *(ouvrier)* journeyman **(c)** *(concubin)* partner

comparable [kɔ̃parabl] *adj* comparable (**à** *ou* **avec** to or with); **ce n'est pas c.** there's no comparison

comparaison [kɔ̃parezɔ̃] *nf* **(a)** *(action de comparer)* comparison; **faire la c. entre** to make a comparison between; **c'est sans c. avec...** it can't be compared with...; **il est sans c. le plus grand** he is by far the tallest; **en c. de...** in comparison with...; **par c.** by comparison; **par c. avec** *ou* **à** compared with or to **(b)** *(figure de style)* simile

comparaître [kɔ̃parɛtr] *vi Jur* **c. (en justice)** to appear (in court); **être appelé à c.** to be summoned to appear

comparatif, -ive [kɔ̃paratif, -iv] **1** *adj* comparative **2** *nm Gram* comparative; **c. de supériorité/ d'infériorité** comparative of greater/lesser degree

comparativement [kɔ̃parativmɑ̃] *adv* comparatively

comparé, -e [kɔ̃pare] *adj (anatomie, histoire, littérature)* comparative; **c. à** compared with or to

comparer [kɔ̃pare] **1** *vt* to compare (**à** *ou* **avec** to or with)
2 se comparer *vpr* **(a)** *(soi-même)* **se c. à** *ou* **avec** to compare oneself to or with **(b)** *(être comparé)* **Händel ne peut pas se c. à Mozart** Handel can't be compared with Mozart

comparse [kɔ̃pars] *nmf Péj* associate

compartiment [kɔ̃partimɑ̃] *nm (de wagon, de boîte, de tiroir)* compartment; **c. fumeurs** smoking compartment, smoker; **c. non-fumeurs** no-smoking compartment, non-smoker; **c. à bagages** *(d'autocar)* luggage compartment

compartimenter [kɔ̃partimɑ̃te] *vt (diviser en espaces)* to partition; *Fig* **une société compartimentée** a compartmentalized society

comparution [kɔ̃parysjɔ̃] *nf Jur* appearance

compas [kɔ̃pa] *nm* **(a)** *Math* (pair of) compasses; *Fig* **avoir le c. dans l'œil** to have an accurate eye; **c. à pointes sèches** dividers **(b)** *Naut* compass

compassé, -e [kɔ̃pase] *adj* stiff, starchy

compassion [kɔ̃pasjɔ̃] *nf* compassion; **avec c.** compassionately

compatibilité [kɔ̃patibilite] *nf* compatibility

compatible [kɔ̃patibl] *adj aussi Ordinat* compatible (**avec** with)

compatir [kɔ̃patir] *vi* to sympathize; **c. au chagrin de qn** to sympathize with sb in his/her grief

compatissant, -e [kɔ̃patisɑ̃, -ɑ̃t] *adj* compassionate, sympathetic

compatriote [kɔ̃patriot] *nmf* compatriot

compensable [kɔ̃pɑ̃sabl] *adj (chèque)* clearable

compensation [kɔ̃pɑ̃sasjɔ̃] *nf* **(a)** *(d'une perte, d'un inconvénient)* compensation; **en c. de qch** as compensation for sth **(b)** *(de chèque)* clearing

compensé, -e [kɔ̃pɑ̃se] *adj* **chaussures à semelles compensées** platform shoes

compenser [kɔ̃pɑ̃se] **1** *vt* **(a)** *(perte, défaut)* to compensate for, to make up for **(b)** *(chèque)* to clear
2 se compenser *vpr* to make up for each other

compère [kɔ̃pɛr] *nm Vieilli (camarade)* friend

compétence [kɔ̃petɑ̃s] *nf* **(a)** *(capacité)* competence; **compétences** *(connaissances)* ability; **cela n'entre pas dans mes compétences** it's beyond my capabilities **(b)** *Jur (d'un tribunal, d'un maire)* competence; **cela n'est pas de sa c.** that doesn't come within her province

compétent, -e [kɔ̃petɑ̃, -ɑ̃t] *adj* **(a)** *(capable)* competent; **c. en qch** conversant with sth **(b)** *Jur (tribunal, autorité)* competent; **adressez-vous au service c.** apply to the relevant department

compétitif, -ive [kɔ̃petitif, -iv] *adj* competitive

compétition [kɔ̃petisjɔ̃] *nf* **(a)** *(rivalité)* competition; **être en c. avec qn** to compete with sb **(b)** *Sp (épreuve)* **c. (sportive)** *(sporting)* event; **faire de la c.** to go in for competitive sport

compétitivité [kɔ̃petitivite] *nf* competitiveness

compilateur [kɔ̃pilatœr] *nm Ordinat* compiler; **c. croisé** cross-compiler

compilation [kɔ̃pilasjɔ̃] *nf* compilation

compiler [kɔ̃pile] *vt aussi Ordinat* to compile

complaire [kɔ̃plɛr] **se complaire** *vpr* **se c. dans qch/à faire qch** to delight or revel in sth/in doing sth

complaisance [kɔ̃plezɑ̃s] *nf* **(a)** *(bienveillance)* kindness; **faire qch par c.** to do sth out of kindness **(b)** *Péj (indulgence)* indulgence; **certificat médical de c.** = medical certificate to which one is not entitled **(c)** *(autosatisfaction)* complacency, smugness

complaisant, -e [kɔ̃plezɑ̃, -ɑ̃t] *adj* **(a)** *(bienveillant)* obliging, kind *(envers* towards) **(b)** *Péj (indulgent)* indulgent **(c)** *(satisfait)* complacent, smug

complément [kɔ̃plemɑ̃] *nm* **(a)** *(reste)* rest, remainder; **demander un c. d'information** to ask for further information **(b)** *Gram* complement; **c. d'attribution** indirect object; **c. circonstanciel de temps/de manière** adverbial phrase of time/of manner; **c. de nom** possessive phrase; **c. d'objet direct/indirect** direct/indirect object

complémentaire [kɔ̃plemɑ̃tɛr] *adj (couleur)* complementary; **pour tout renseignement c., s'adresser à...** for further information, apply to...

complet, -ète [kɔ̃plɛ, -ɛt] **1** *adj (entier, intégral) (tenue, service)* complete, whole; **deux jours complets** two full or whole days; **formation très complète** thorough training; *Fam* **c'est c.!** that's the last straw! **(b)** *(détaillé)* full **(c)** *(absolu)* complete; **un c. abruti** a complete moron; **ce fut un échec c.** it was a complete failure **(d)** *(bus, salle de théâtre)* full; **c.** *(sur panneau) (parking)* full; *(pension, hôtel)* no vacancies **(e)** *(pain, pâtes)* wholemeal; *(riz)* brown
2 *nm* **(a)** *(.-veston)* suit **(b)** **est-ce que nous sommes au c.?** are we all here? **j'ai invité la famille au (grand) c. pour Noël** I've invited the whole family for Christmas

complètement [kɔ̃plɛtmɑ̃] *adv* (a) *(terminé, guéri)* completely, totally; **je n'ai pas c. fini** I haven't quite finished (b) *(vraiment) (perdu, idiot)* completely, totally

compléter [34] [kɔ̃plete] *vt* **1** *vt (collection, formation)* to complete; *(somme)* to make up; *(formulaire)* to complete, to fill in

2 se compléter *vpr* to complement one another

complexe [kɔ̃plɛks] **1** *adj (compliqué)* complex

2 *nm* (a) *(ensemble de bâtiments, d'industries)* complex; **c. hôtelier** hotel complex; **c. sportif** sports complex (b) *(gêne)* hang-up; *Psy* complex; **avoir des complexes (à cause de qch)** to have a hang-up (about sth); **être sans c.** to have no hang-ups; **c. d'infériorité** inferiority complex; **c. d'Œdipe** Oedipus complex

complexé, -e [kɔ̃plɛkse] *adj* hung up (**par** about)

complexer [kɔ̃plɛkse] *vt* **c. qn** to give sb a hang-up

complexité [kɔ̃plɛksite] *nf* complexity

complication [kɔ̃plikasjɔ̃] *nf* (a) *(ennui)* complication; **faire des complications** to create complications (b) *(complexité)* complexity (c) *Méd* **complications** complications

complice [kɔ̃plis] **1** *nmf* accomplice

2 *adj (regard, sourire)* knowing; **être c. de qch** to be party to sth

complicité [kɔ̃plisite] *nf* complicity; **agir en c. avec qn** to act in collusion with sb; **accusé de c. de meurtre** accused of being an accessory to murder

compliment [kɔ̃plimɑ̃] *nm* compliment; **faire des compliments à qn (sur qch)** to pay sb compliments (on sth); **(je vous fais) mes compliments!** I congratulate you!; *Ironique* **mes compliments!** congratulations!

complimenter [kɔ̃plimɑ̃te] *vt* **c. qn pour** *(courage, présence d'esprit)* to congratulate sb on; **c. qn sur** *(toilette, coiffure)* to compliment sb on

compliqué, -e [kɔ̃plike] *adj* complicated; **ce n'est pourtant pas c.!** it's quite simple!

compliquer [kɔ̃plike] **1** *vt* to complicate; **c. les choses** to complicate matters

2 se compliquer *vpr (situation, problème)* to get complicated; **se c. l'existence** to make life complicated for oneself

complot [kɔ̃plo] *nm* plot, conspiracy

comploter [kɔ̃plɔte] **1** *vt* to plot

2 *vi* to plot (**contre** against); **c. de faire qch** to plot to do sth

comportement [kɔ̃pɔrtəmɑ̃] *nm* behaviour; *Écon* **c. d'achat** buying behaviour

comporter [kɔ̃pɔrte] **1** *vt* (a) *(être constitué de)* to consist of, to be made up of (b) *(contenir)* to contain (c) *(difficultés, inconvénients)* to involve

2 se comporter *vpr (agir)* to behave (**vis-à-vis de** ou **envers** towards) (b) *(fonctionner) (voiture)* to handle

composant [kɔ̃pozɑ̃] *nm* component

composante [kɔ̃pozɑ̃t] *nf* component

composé, -e [kɔ̃poze] *adj & nm* compound

composer [kɔ̃poze] **1** *vt* (a) *(symphonie, poème)* to compose, to write; *(bouquet)* to make up (b) *(faire partie de)* to make up; **être composé de qch** to be made up or composed of sth (c) *(numéro de téléphone)* to dial (d) *Typ* to set (e) **c. son visage** to compose one's features

2 *vi* (a) *(s'entendre)* to compromise (**avec** with) (b) *Scol* to take a test

3 se composer *vpr* (a) **se c. de qch** to be made up or

composed of sth (b) **se c. un visage de circonstance** to put on a suitable expression

composite [kɔ̃pozit] *adj* composite

compositeur, -trice [kɔ̃pozitœr, -tris] *nm,f* (a) *Mus* composer (b) *Typ* typesetter

composition [kɔ̃pozisjɔ̃] *nf* (a) *(d'une symphonie, d'un poème)* composition, writing; **un poème de ma c.** a poem I wrote (myself) (b) *(éléments)* composition; *(d'un aliment)* ingredients; **la c. des équipes n'est pas encore connue** the teams haven't been announced yet (c) *(œuvre musicale, littéraire)* composition (d) *(rédaction)* essay; *(examen)* test (e) *(caractère)* **être de bonne c.** to be good-natured (f) *Typ* typesetting

compost [kɔ̃pɔst] *nm* compost

composter [kɔ̃pɔste] *vt (billet)* to cancel

compote [kɔ̃pɔt] *nf* compote, stewed fruit; **c. de pommes** apple compote, stewed apples; *Fam* **j'ai les jambes en c.** my legs feel like jelly

compotier [kɔ̃pɔtje] *nm* fruit dish

compréhensible [kɔ̃preɑ̃sibl] *adj* (a) *(clair)* comprehensible (**par** to) (b) *(justifié)* understandable

compréhensif, -ive [kɔ̃preɑ̃sif, -iv] *adj* understanding

compréhension [kɔ̃preɑ̃sjɔ̃] *nf* (a) *(fait de comprendre)* comprehension, understanding (b) *(bienveillance)* understanding

comprendre [58] [kɔ̃prɑ̃dr] **1** *vt* (a) *(par l'esprit)* to understand; **dois-je c. que...?** am I to understand that...?; **mal c. qn/qch** to misunderstand sb/sth; **je ne le comprends pas** *(il est étrange, il n'articule pas)* I can't understand him; **il faut la c.** you have to see things from her point of view; **je n'y comprends rien** I can't make head nor tail of it; **c'est à n'y rien c.** it's incomprehensible; **ne cherche pas, il n'y a rien à c.** don't even try to understand; **va y c. quelque chose!** YOU try to make head or tail of it!; **faire c. à qn que...** to give sb to understand that...; *(avec autorité)* to make it clear to sb that...; **se faire c.** to make oneself understood; **me suis-je bien fait c.?** have I made myself clear?; **elle comprend vite** she's quick on the uptake; **ça va, j'ai compris!** OK, I understand!; **tu comprends...** you see... (b) *(être composé de)* to consist of, to be made up of (c) *(inclure)* to include

2 se comprendre *vpr (l'un l'autre)* to understand each other; **ça se comprend** it's understandable; **je me comprends!** I know what I mean!

compresse [kɔ̃prɛs] *nf* compress

compresser [kɔ̃prese] *vt* to compress

compresseur [kɔ̃presœr] *nm* (a) *Tech (de gaz, de vapeur)* compressor; *(de moteur)* supercharger (b) *Ordinat* **c. de données** data compressor

compression [kɔ̃prɛsjɔ̃] *nf* (a) *(de gaz, de vapeur)* compression (b) *(réduction)* reduction; **c. des dépenses** spending cuts

comprimé, -e [kɔ̃prime] **1** *adj (gaz)* compressed

2 *nm (médicament)* tablet; **un c. d'aspirine** an aspirin

comprimer [kɔ̃prime] *vt (gaz, artère, fichier informatique)* to compress; **cette jupe me comprime la taille** this skirt is too tight round my waist (b) *Fig (dépenses)* to reduce

compris, -e [kɔ̃pri, -iz] **1** *pp voir* **comprendre**
2 *adj* (a) *(enregistré)* **bien c.** (fully) understood; **mal c.** misunderstood; **alors, c'est c.?** so, do you understand?; *Fam* **tu fais tes devoirs immédiatement, c.?** you'll do your homework right now, (is that) understood? (b) *(inclus)* included; **service non c.** service not included; **tout c.** all in; **y c.** including (c) *(situé)* **être c. entre** to be between

compromettant, -e [kɔ̃prɔmetɑ̃, -ɑ̃t] *adj* compromising

compromettre [47] [kɔ̃prɔmetr] **1** *vt* (a) *(personne, réputation)* to compromise; **être compromis dans qch** to be implicated in sth (b) *(sécurité, vacances, chances)* to jeopardize
2 se compromettre *vpr* to compromise oneself; **se c. dans qch** to be implicated in sth

compromis [kɔ̃prɔmi] *nm (arrangement)* compromise

compromission [kɔ̃prɔmisjɔ̃] *nf Péj* compromise

comptabiliser [kɔ̃tabilize] *vt (recettes, dépenses)* to enter in the accounts; *(points)* to count

comptabilité [kɔ̃tabilite] *nf* (a) *(livres)* accounts; *(technique)* book-keeping, accounting; **tenir la c.** to keep the accounts (b) *(service)* accounts department

comptable [kɔ̃tabl] **1** *adj (travail, technique)* book-keeping, accounting
2 *nmf* accountant; **c. agréé** *Br* chartered accountant, *Am* certified public accountant

comptage [kɔ̃taʒ] *nm* counting

comptant [kɔ̃tɑ̃] **1** *adv* **payer c.** to pay (in) cash
2 *nm* cash; **payer/acheter au c.** to pay (in)/buy for cash

compte [kɔ̃t] *nm* (a) *(dans une banque, chez un commerçant)* account; **comptes** *(comptabilité)* accounts; **tenir les comptes** to keep the accounts; **faire ses comptes** to do one's accounts; **verser une somme sur son c.** to pay a sum into one's account; **se mettre** *ou* **s'installer à son c.** to start one's own business; **faire qch pour le c. de qn** to do sth on sb's behalf; **c. en banque** *ou* **bancaire** bank account; **c. chèques** *Br* current account, *Am* checking account; **c. chèques postal** ≃ giro account; **c. courant** *Br* current account, *Am* checking account; **c. de dépôt** deposit account; **c. d'épargne** savings account; **c. joint** joint account
(b) *(calcul)* calculation; **faire le c. de** *(dépenses)* to add up; *(temps restant)* to calculate; *(objets, personnes)* to count; **le c. y est** *(somme)* it's the right amount; *(objets, personnes)* they're all here; **c. à rebours** countdown
(c) *(explication)* **demander des comptes à qn** to ask sb for an explanation; **rendre des comptes** to explain oneself; **je n'ai de comptes à rendre à personne** I'm not answerable to anyone; **rendre c. de qch** to account for sth
(d) *(locutions) Fam* **avoir son c.** to have had enough; **être loin du c.** *(se tromper)* to be wide of the mark; *Fam* **régler son c. à qn** to sort sb out; **on réglera nos comptes plus tard** we'll settle scores later; **apprendre qch sur le c. de qn** to learn sth about sb; *Fam* **son c. est bon** he's for it; **tenir c. de qch** to take sth into account; **c. tenu de** considering; **s'en tirer à bon c.** to get off lightly; **y trouver son c.** to get something out of it; **à ce c.-là** in that case; **au bout du c., en fin de c.** in the end; **tout c. fait** all things considered; *Prov* **les bons comptes font les bons amis** pay your debts and keep your friends

compte-gouttes [kɔ̃tgut] *nm inv* dropper; *Fig* **au c.** in dribs and drabs

compter [kɔ̃te] **1** *vt* (a) *(dénombrer)* to count; **on ne compte plus les mécontents** we've lost count of the malcontents; *Fig* **c. les points** to watch from the sidelines (b) *(donner avec parcimonie)* **il compte chaque sou** he begrudges every penny he spends; **ses jours sont comptés** his days are numbered (c) *(inclure)* to include; **sans c....** not counting...; **sans c. que...** besides the fact that...; **je le compte parmi mes meilleurs amis** I number him among my best friends (d) *(prévoir)* to allow; **j'ai compté 200 grammes par personne** I've allowed 200 grams per person; **c. faire qch** *(espérer)* to expect to do sth; *(avoir intention de)* to intend to do sth (e) *(facturer)* **c. qch à qn** to charge sb for sth
2 *vi* (a) *(calculer)* to count; **dépenser sans c.** *(dépenser trop)* to spend money like water; **à c. du 1ᵉʳ janvier** (with effect) from 1 January (b) *(être parcimonieux)* to count the pennies (c) *(être important)* to count, to matter; **il compte beaucoup pour elle** he means a lot to her; **c. double** to count double; **à table, il compte pour deux** he eats enough for two (d) *(figurer)* **c. parmi les meilleurs** to rank among the best (e) **c. avec qn/qch** to reckon with sb/sth (f) **c. sur qn/qch** to count or rely on sb/sth; **j'y compte bien!** I should hope so!; *Fam* **compte là-dessus et bois de l'eau!** you'll be lucky!
3 se compter *vpr* **les membres de cette secte se comptent par milliers** this sect has thousands of members

compte rendu *(pl* **comptes rendus***)* [kɔ̃trɑ̃dy] *nm* report; *(d'un roman, d'un film)* review; *(d'une réunion)* minutes

compte-tours [kɔ̃ttur] *nm inv* rev counter

compteur [kɔ̃tœr] *nm* meter; **c. d'eau/d'électricité/à gaz** water/electricity/gas meter; **c. (de) Geiger** Geiger counter; *Aut* **c. kilométrique** *Br* mileometer, *Am* odometer; *Aut* **c. de vitesse** speedometer

comptine [kɔ̃tin] *nf* nursery rhyme

comptoir [kɔ̃twar] *nm* (a) *(dans un magasin)* counter; *(dans un bar)* bar; **prendre une consommation au c.** to have a drink at the bar; **c. d'enregistrement** check-in desk; **c. d'information** information desk; **c. de réception** reception desk; **c. de vente** sales counter (b) *(dans un pays éloigné)* trading post

compulser [kɔ̃pylse] *vt (documents, livres)* to consult

comte [kɔ̃t] *nm* count; *(en Grande-Bretagne)* earl

comté [kɔ̃te] *nm* (a) *Hist* earldom (b) *(subdivision administrative)* county (c) *(fromage)* = type of hard cheese (d) *Can Pol* riding

comtesse [kɔ̃tes] *nf* countess

con, conne [kɔ̃, kɔn] **1** *adj très Fam (stupide)* bloody stupid; *Fam* **être c. comme la lune** *ou* **un balai** to be as daft as a brush; **c'est pas c.!** that's pretty smart! (b) *(facile)* **c'est tout c.!** it's dead easy!
2 *nm, f très Fam* stupid bastard; **faire le c.** to arse around; **pauvre c.!** stupid bastard!; **à la c.** *(ordinateur, voiture)* bloody useless; *(idée, histoire)* bloody stupid
3 *nm Vulg (sexe)* cunt

conard [kɔnar] *nm très Fam* jerk

conasse [kɔnas] *nf très Fam* silly bitch

concasser [kɔ̃kase] *vt (roche)* to crush; *(poivre)* to grind

concave [kɔ̃kav] *adj* concave

concéder [34] [kɔ̃sede] *vt* (a) *(privilège, droit, terrain, concession)* **c. qch à qn** to grant sb sth, to grant sth to sb (b) *(reconnaître)* **c. qu'on a tort** to admit that one is wrong; **il fait chaud, je vous le concède** it's warm, I grant you (c) *Sp (point, but, victoire)* to concede

concentration [kɔ̃sɑ̃trasjɔ̃] nf concentration

concentrationnaire [kɔ̃sɑ̃trasjɔner] adj of concentration camps; **la vie c.** life in a concentration camp

concentré, -e [kɔ̃sɑ̃tre] **1** adj (a) (solution) concentrated; (lait) condensed (b) (intellectuellement) il était très c. he was concentrating hard
2 nm Chim & Culin concentrate; **c. de tomate** tomato purée

concentrer [kɔ̃sɑ̃tre] **1** vt (troupes, forces, efforts) to concentrate; (rayons du soleil) to focus
2 se concentrer vpr (a) (être attentif) to concentrate (**sur** on) (b) (s'assembler) (foule) to gather; **la population se concentre dans les grandes villes** the population is concentrated in the big cities

concentrique [kɔ̃sɑ̃trik] adj concentric

concept [kɔ̃sɛpt] nm concept

conception [kɔ̃sɛpsjɔ̃] nf (a) (d'un enfant, d'une idée) conception (b) (idée) concept (c) (création) design; **c. assistée par ordinateur** computer-aided or -assisted design

concernant [kɔ̃sɛrnɑ̃] prép concerning

concerner [kɔ̃sɛrne] vt to concern; **en ce qui me concerne** as far as I am concerned; **cela ne vous concerne pas** (cela ne vous regarde pas) it's none of your business; (vous n'êtes pas visé) it doesn't concern you

concert [kɔ̃sɛr] nm (a) (de musique) concert (b) (accord) agir de c. avec qn to act jointly with sb

concertation [kɔ̃sɛrtasjɔ̃] nf consultation

concerté, -e [kɔ̃sɛrte] adj (action) concerted

concerter [kɔ̃sɛrte] **1** vt (projet) to devise together
2 se concerter vpr to consult together

concertiste [kɔ̃sɛrtist] nmf concert performer

concerto [kɔ̃sɛrto] nm concerto

concession [kɔ̃sesjɔ̃] nf (a) (compromis) concession; **faire des concessions** to make concessions; **sans concessions** uncompromising (b) (attribution) (de terrain) granting (c) (terrain) concession; (au cimetière) plot (d) (droit exclusif de vente) dealership

concessionnaire [kɔ̃sesjoner] nmf dealer

concevable [kɔ̃səvabl] adj conceivable

concevoir [60] [kɔ̃səvwar] **1** vt (a) (enfant, plan, idée) to conceive; (produit) to design (b) (comprendre) to understand (c) (éprouver) **c. de l'amitié pour qn** to take a liking to sb
2 se concevoir vpr ça se conçoit that's understandable

concierge [kɔ̃sjɛrʒ] nmf (d'immeuble, d'appartements) & Scol Br caretaker, Am janitor; (dans un hôtel) porter; Fam **c'est une vraie c.** she's a terrible gossip

concile [kɔ̃sil] nm Rel council

conciliabule [kɔ̃siljabyl] nm (conversation) confab

conciliant, -e [kɔ̃siljɑ̃, -ɑ̃t] adj conciliatory

conciliation [kɔ̃siljasjɔ̃] nf reconciliation

concilier [66] [kɔ̃silje] **1** vt (deux choses) to reconcile; **c. sa vie professionnelle et sa vie de famille** to combine one's professional life with one's family life
2 se concilier vpr (être compatible) **se c.** avec to go with (b) **se c. qn** ou **la faveur de qn** to win sb's goodwill

concis, -e [kɔ̃si, -iz] adj concise

concision [kɔ̃sizjɔ̃] nf conciseness; **avec c.** concisely

concitoyen, -enne [kɔ̃sitwajɛ̃, -ɛn] nm,f fellow citizen

concluant, -e [kɔ̃klyɑ̃, -ɑ̃t] adj conclusive; **peu c.** inconclusive

conclure [17] [kɔ̃klyr] **1** vt (a) (terminer) to conclude, to end (**par** with) (b) (accord, pacte) to finalize; (marché) to clinch; **marché conclu!**, **affaire conclue!** it's a deal! (c) (déduire) to conclude (**de** from); **dois-je en c. que...?** am I to conclude that...?
2 conclure à vt ind **ils ont conclu au suicide/meurtre** they concluded it was suicide/murder

conclusion [kɔ̃klyzjɔ̃] nf (a) (fin) (d'un discours, d'une réunion) conclusion, end (b) (déduction) conclusion; **tirer une c. de qch** to draw a conclusion from sth; Fam **c., l'échafaudage s'est écroulé** the result was that the scaffolding collapsed

concocter [kɔ̃kɔkte] vt Fam to concoct

concombre [kɔ̃kɔ̃br] nm cucumber

concordance [kɔ̃kɔrdɑ̃s] nf (a) (de preuves, de témoignages, de dates) tallying (b) Gram **c. des temps** sequence of tenses

concorder [kɔ̃kɔrde] vi (preuves, dates, témoignages) to tally (**avec** with)

concourir [22] [kɔ̃kurir] vi (a) Sp to compete (b) (lignes) to converge
2 concourir à vt ind **c. à qch/à faire qch** to contribute to sth/to doing sth

concours [kɔ̃kur] nm (a) (compétition) competition, contest; (examen) competitive examination; **c. agricole/hippique** agricultural/horse show; **c. de beauté** beauty contest; **c. d'entrée (à)** entrance examination (to) (b) (aide) aid, assistance (c) **c. de circonstances** combination of circumstances

concret, -ète [kɔ̃krɛ, -ɛt] adj concrete

concrètement [kɔ̃krɛtmɑ̃] adv in concrete terms

concrétiser [kɔ̃kretize] **1** vt (rêve) to realize; (projet, promesse) to carry out
2 se concrétiser vpr to materialize

conçu, -e voir **concevoir**

concubin, -e [kɔ̃kybɛ̃, -in] nm,f Jur cohabitant

concubinage [kɔ̃kybinaʒ] nm cohabitation; **vivre en c.** to cohabit

concupiscent, -e [kɔ̃kypisɑ̃, -ɑ̃t] adj concupiscent

concurrence [kɔ̃kyrɑ̃s] nf (rivalité, concurrents) competition; **faire c. à** to compete with; **faire jouer la c.** to shop around (b) **jusqu'à c. de...** up to...

concurrencer [16] [kɔ̃kyrɑ̃se] vt to compete with

concurrent, -e [kɔ̃kyrɑ̃, -ɑ̃t] **1** adj (industries, produits) competing, rival
2 nm,f (a) Com competitor (b) (dans une épreuve, un concours) competitor

concurrentiel, -elle [kɔ̃kyrɑ̃sjɛl] adj competitive

condamnation [kɔ̃danasjɔ̃] nf (a) Jur (jugement) conviction (**pour** for); (peine) sentence (**à** to); **c. à mort** death sentence (b) (critique) condemnation

condamné, -e [kɔ̃dane] **1** adj (malade) terminally ill
2 nm,f convicted person; **un c. à mort** a condemned man

condamner [kɔ̃dane] vt (a) Jur to sentence (**à** to); **c. qn à 1000 francs d'amende** to fine sb 1,000 francs (b) (obliger à) **c. qn à qch** to force sb into sth; **être condamné à la solitude** to be condemned to loneliness; **je suis condamnée à les attendre** I have to wait for them (c) (blâmer) to condemn (d) (porte) to block up; (pièce) to seal up (e) (interdire) to forbid

condensateur [kɔ̃dɑ̃satœr] *nm* *Él* condenser

condensation [kɔ̃dɑ̃sɑsjɔ̃] *nf* condensation

condensé, -e [kɔ̃dɑ̃se] **1** *adj* condensed
 2 *nm* digest

condenser [kɔ̃dɑ̃se] **1** *vt* (*article, récit*) to condense
 2 se condenser *vpr* to condense

condescendant, -e [kɔ̃desɑ̃dɑ̃, -ɑ̃t] *adj* condescending

condescendre [kɔ̃desɑ̃dr] *vi* **c. à faire qch** to condescend to do sth

condiment [kɔ̃dimɑ̃] *nm* condiment

condisciple [kɔ̃disipl] *nmf* *Univ* fellow student; *Scol* schoolmate

condition [kɔ̃disjɔ̃] *nf* (**a**) (*stipulation*) condition; **sans c.** unconditionally; **à une c.:...** on one condition...; **à c. que tu viennes avec moi** providing that *or* on condition that you come with me; **tu peux y aller à c. de rentrer pour minuit** you can go providing that *or* on condition that you're home by midnight (**b**) **conditions** (*circonstances*) conditions; (*d'une vente, d'un accord*) terms; **dans ces conditions, je n'y vais pas** if that's the way it is, I'm not going; **conditions atmosphériques** atmospheric conditions; **conditions de paiement** terms of payment; **conditions de vie/travail** living/ working conditions (**c**) (*état*) condition; **être en bonne/ mauvaise c. physique** to be in good/bad shape (**d**) (*sort*) condition; **la c. humaine** the human condition; **la c. des ouvriers/des paysans** the workers'/farmers' lot (**e**) (*classe sociale*) station, status

conditionnel, -elle [kɔ̃disjɔnɛl] **1** *adj* conditional
 2 *nm* *Gram* conditional

conditionnement [kɔ̃disjɔnmɑ̃] *nm* (**a**) (*fait d'emballer, emballage*) packaging (**b**) *Psy* conditioning

conditionner [kɔ̃disjɔne] *vt* (**a**) (*être la condition de*) to govern (**b**) (*emballer*) to package (**c**) *Psy* (*personne*) to condition

condoléances [kɔ̃dɔleɑ̃s] *nfpl* condolences; **présenter ses c. à qn** to offer one's condolences to sb; **toutes mes c.** (please accept) my condolences

condominium [kɔ̃dɔminjɔm] *nm* *Pol* condominium

condor [kɔ̃dɔr] *nm* condor

conducteur, -trice [kɔ̃dyktœr, -tris] **1** *nm,f* (*d'une voiture, d'un train*) driver; (*de machine*) operator; **c. de travaux** clerk of works
 2 *nm* *Él & Phys* conductor
 3 *adj* *Él & Phys* conductive

conduction [kɔ̃dyksjɔ̃] *nf* *Él* conduction

conductivité [kɔ̃dyktivite] *nf* *Él* conductivity

conduire [18] [kɔ̃dɥir] **1** *vt* (**a**) (*emmener*) to take; (*en voiture*) to drive, to take (**b**) (*mener*) (*troupeau, aveugle*) to lead (**c**) (*entraîner*) **c. qn à faire qch** to lead sb to do sth; **c. qn au désespoir/suicide** to drive sb to despair/suicide (**d**) (*voiture, camion*) to drive; (*moto*) to ride; (*bateau*) to steer (**e**) (*acheminer*) (*eau, gaz*) to carry (**f**) (*diriger*) (*opérations*) to manage, to run
 2 *vi* (**a**) (*en voiture*) to drive; (*en moto*) to ride; **elle conduit bien** she's a good driver (**b**) (*sujet: porte, couloir, études*) **c. à** to lead to
 3 se conduire *vpr* (*se comporter*) to behave; **se c. mal** (*d'un enfant*) to misbehave; **se c. bien/mal avec qn** to behave well/badly towards sb

conduit [kɔ̃dɥi] *nm* (**a**) (*tuyau*) conduit, pipe; **c. d'aération** air duct; **c. de ventilation** ventilation shaft (**b**) *Anat* **c. auditif** auditory canal

conduite [kɔ̃dɥit] *nf* (**a**) (*de voiture, de camion*) driving; (*de moto*) riding; **leçons de c.** driving lessons; **c. à gauche/ droite** (*position du volant*) left-/right-hand drive; (*sur la route*) driving on the left/right; **c. accompagnée** = learning to drive accompanied by someone holding a full driving licence; **c. intérieure** *Br* saloon (car), *Am* sedan; **c. sur route** driving on the open road (**b**) (*des affaires, des opérations*) management, running; (*d'une armée*) command; (*de travaux*) supervision (**c**) (*comportement*) behaviour, conduct; **faire une c.** to turn over a new leaf (**d**) (*tuyau*) pipe; **c. d'eau/de gaz** water/gas main

cône [kon] *nm* cone

confection [kɔ̃fɛksjɔ̃] *nf* (**a**) (*d'un vêtement, d'un repas*) making (**b**) (*industrie*) (ready-made) clothing industry; **vêtements de c.** ready-made clothes

confectionner [kɔ̃fɛksjɔne] *vt* to make

confédération [kɔ̃federasjɔ̃] *nf* confederation; **la C. helvétique** the Swiss Confederation

conférence [kɔ̃ferɑ̃s] *nf* (**a**) (*congrès, colloque*) conference; **c. de presse** press conference; **c. au sommet** summit (conference) (**b**) (*exposé*) lecture; **faire une c. sur...** to give a lecture on...

conférencier, -ère [kɔ̃ferɑ̃sje, -ɛr] *nm,f* lecturer

conférer [34] [kɔ̃fere] **1** *vt* (*titre*) to confer (**à** on); **l'âge confère certains privilèges** age brings with it certain privileges
 2 *vi* to confer (**avec** with)

confesser [kɔ̃fese] **1** *vt* (**a**) *Rel* to confess (**b**) (*reconnaître*) to confess, to admit
 2 se confesser *vpr* to confess; (*aller*) **se c.** to go to confession

confession [kɔ̃fesjɔ̃] *nf* (**a**) *Rel & Fig* confession; *Fam* **on lui donnerait le bon Dieu sans c.** he/she looks as though butter wouldn't melt in his/her mouth (**b**) (*croyance*) denomination

confessionnal, -aux [kɔ̃fesjɔnal, -o] *nm* confessional

confetti [kɔ̃feti] *nm* (piece of) confetti; **confettis** confetti

confiance [kɔ̃fjɑ̃s] *nf* (*foi*) trust, confidence; **avoir c. en qn/qch, faire c. à qn/qch** to trust sb/sth, to have confidence in sb/sth; **faites-moi c.** trust me; *Fam* (*croyez-moi*) believe me; **digne de c.** trustworthy; **de c.** (*mission*) of trust; (*personne*) trustworthy (**b**) (*assurance*) confidence; **c. en soi** self-confidence; **avoir c. en soi** to be self-confident

confiant, -e [kɔ̃fjɑ̃, -ɑ̃t] *adj* (**a**) (*qui fait confiance*) trusting (**b**) (*optimiste*) confident (**dans** in) (**c**) (*qui a confiance en soi*) self-confident

confidence [kɔ̃fidɑ̃s] *nf* confidence; **faire une c. à qn** to confide in sb; **mettre qn dans la c.** to let sb into the secret

confident, -e [kɔ̃fidɑ̃, -ɑ̃t] *nm,f* confidant, *f* confidante

confidentiel, -elle [kɔ̃fidɑ̃sjɛl] *adj* confidential

confidentiellement [kɔ̃fidɑ̃sjɛlmɑ̃] *adv* confidentially

confier [66] [kɔ̃fje] **1** *vt* (**a**) (*laisser*) **c. qch à qn** to entrust sth with sth; **je leur ai confié les enfants** I left the children with them (**b**) (*dire*) **c. qch à qn** to confide sth to sb; **c. un secret à qn** to share a secret with sb
 2 se confier *vpr* **se c. à qn** to confide in sb

configuration [kɔ̃figyrasjɔ̃] nf (a) (disposition) configuration; (de bâtiment) layout; **la c. du terrain** the lie of the land (b) Ordinat configuration; **c. matérielle** hardware configuration

configurer [kɔ̃figyre] vt Ordinat to configure

confiné, -e [kɔ̃fine] adj (a) (atmosphère) enclosed; (air) stale (b) (enfermé) shut up

confiner [kɔ̃fine] **1** vt (enfermer) to confine, to shut up
2 confiner à vt ind to border on
3 se confiner vpr **se c. chez soi** to shut oneself up indoors

confins [kɔ̃fɛ̃] nmpl (de région, d'État) confines, borders; **aux c. de** on the edge of

confirmation [kɔ̃firmasjɔ̃] nf confirmation

confirmer [kɔ̃firme] **1** vt (nouvelle, jugement) to confirm; **c. qn dans son opinion** to confirm sb in his/her opinion
2 se confirmer vpr (nouvelle, bruit) to be confirmed; (tendance) to continue

confiserie [kɔ̃fizri] nf (a) (magasin) Br sweetshop, Am candy store (b) (bonbon) **confiseries** Br sweets, Am candy (c) (secteur) confectionery

confiseur, -euse [kɔ̃fizœr, -øz] nm,f confectioner

confisquer [kɔ̃fiske] vt to confiscate

confit, -e [kɔ̃fi, -it] **1** adj (fruits) crystallized, candied
2 nm **c. d'oie/de canard** potted goose/duck

confiture [kɔ̃fityr] nf jam; **c. de fraises** strawberry jam; **c. d'oranges** (orange) marmalade; Fig **ce serait donner de la c. aux cochons** that would be throwing pearls before swine

conflictuel, -elle [kɔfliktɥel] adj (témoignages, intérêts) conflicting; **situation conflictuelle** situation of potential conflict; **ils ont des rapports conflictuels** they have a tempestuous relationship

conflit [kɔ̃fli] nm conflict; **c. armé** armed conflict; **conflits sociaux** industrial disputes

confluent [kɔ̃flyɑ̃] nm confluence; **au c. du Cher et de la Loire** where the Cher and the Loire meet

confondre [kɔ̃fɔ̃dr] **1** vt (a) (personnes, noms, dates) to confuse, to mix up; **je l'ai confondu avec son frère** I mistook him for his brother; **toutes catégories confondues** all categories taken together (b) (sidérer) to astound (c) (démasquer) to confound
2 se confondre vpr (a) (couleurs, formes) to merge, to blend (en into) (b) (être similaire) (intérêts) to merge (c) (se répandre) **se c. en excuses** to apologize profusely; **se c. en remerciements** to be profuse in one's thanks

conforme [kɔ̃fɔrm] adj (a) (identique) **copie c. à l'original** exact copy; **pour copie c.** (sur document) certified true copy; Fig **c'est la copie c. de sa mère** she's the image of her mother (b) (qui correspond) **être c. à** to be in accordance with

conformément [kɔ̃fɔrmemɑ̃] **conformément à** prép in accordance with

conformer [kɔ̃fɔrme] **1** vt to model (à on)
2 se conformer vpr **se c. à qch** to conform to sth

conformisme [kɔ̃fɔrmism] nm conformism

conformiste [kɔ̃fɔrmist] adj & nmf conformist

conformité [kɔ̃fɔrmite] nf (d'un produit aux normes) compliance (à with); **en c. avec** in accordance with

confort [kɔ̃fɔr] nm comfort; **maison/hôtel tout c.** house/hotel with every modern convenience; **c. d'emploi** (d'un ordinateur) user-friendliness

confortable [kɔ̃fɔrtabl] adj comfortable

confortablement [kɔ̃fɔrtabləmɑ̃] adv comfortably; **installe-toi c.** make yourself comfortable

conforter [kɔ̃fɔrte] vt (position, avance) to consolidate; **c. qn dans son opinion** to confirm sb's opinion

confrère [kɔ̃frɛr] nm (de profession) colleague; (de société) fellow member

confrérie [kɔ̃freri] nf Rel brotherhood

confrontation [kɔ̃frɔ̃tasjɔ̃] nf (a) (face-à-face) confrontation; Fig (d'opinions, d'idéaux) clash, conflict (b) (comparaison) comparison

confronter [kɔ̃frɔ̃te] vt (a) (personnes) to confront; **être confronté à** to be confronted with (b) (comparer) to compare

confucianisme [kɔ̃fysjanism] nm Confucianism

confus, -e [kɔ̃fy, -yz] adj (a) (indistinct) (masse, explication, idées) confused; (bruit) indistinct; (style, texte) obscure (b) (embarrassé) embarrassed

confusément [kɔ̃fyzemɑ̃] adv vaguely

confusion [kɔ̃fyzjɔ̃] nf (a) (désordre) confusion; **jeter la c. dans les esprits** to confuse people (b) (méprise) mix-up, confusion (c) (gêne) embarrassment

congé [kɔ̃ʒe] nm (a) (vacances) Br holiday, Am vacation; **en c.** on holiday; **un jour/une semaine de c.** a day/a week off; **congés payés** paid holiday (b) (arrêt de travail) leave; **c. de maladie** sick leave; **c. de maternité** maternity leave (c) (avis de renvoi) notice; **donner son c. à qn** to give sb his notice; **demander son c.** to hand in one's notice (d) **prendre c. de qn** to take one's leave of sb

congédier [66] [kɔ̃ʒedje] vt to dismiss

congélateur [kɔ̃ʒelatœr] nm freezer

congélation [kɔ̃ʒelasjɔ̃] nf freezing

congeler [39] [kɔ̃ʒle] **1** vt (aliments) to freeze
2 se congeler vpr to freeze

congénital, -e, -aux, -ales [kɔ̃ʒenital, -o] adj congenital

congère [kɔ̃ʒɛr] nf snowdrift

congestion [kɔ̃ʒɛstjɔ̃] nf congestion; **c. cérébrale** stroke; **c. pulmonaire** congestion of the lungs

congestionné, -e [kɔ̃ʒestjone] adj (visage) flushed; (routes) congested

conglomérat [kɔ̃glɔmera] nm conglomerate

Congo [kɔ̃go] nm **le C.** the Congo

congolais, -e [kɔ̃gɔlɛ, -ɛz] **1** adj Congolese
2 nm,f **C.** Congolese
3 nm (pâtisserie) coconut cake

congratuler [kɔ̃gratyle] vt to congratulate

congre [kɔ̃gr] nm conger (eel)

congrégation [kɔ̃gregasjɔ̃] nf Rel congregation

congrès [kɔ̃grɛ] nm conference; **le C.** (aux États-Unis) Congress

congru, -e [kɔ̃gry] adj voir **portion**

conifère [kɔnifɛr] nm conifer

conique [kɔnik] adj conical

conjecture [kɔ̃ʒɛktyr] nf conjecture

conjecturer [kɔ̃ʒɛktyre] vt to conjecture

conjoint, -e [kɔ̃ʒwɛ̃, -ɛt] **1** adj joint
2 nm spouse; **les conjoints** the husband and wife

conjointement [kɔ̃ʒwɛ̃tmɑ̃] adv jointly

conjonctif, -ive [kɔ̃ʒɔ̃ktif, -iv] adj (a) Gram conjunctive (b) Anat connective

conjonction [kɔ̃ʒɔ̃ksjɔ̃] nf (a) (union) union; **la c. de nos efforts** our combined efforts (b) Gram conjunction; **c. de coordination/subordination** coordinating/subordinating conjunction

conjonctivite [kɔ̃ʒɔ̃ktivit] nf conjunctivitis

conjoncture [kɔ̃ʒɔ̃ktyr] nf (situation) circumstances, situation; **dans la c. actuelle** in the present circumstances

conjugaison [kɔ̃ʒygɛzɔ̃] nf (a) (d'un verbe) conjugation (b) (union) combination

conjugal, -e, -aux, -ales [kɔ̃ʒygal, -o] adj (devoir) conjugal; **bonheur c.** wedded bliss; **le domicile c.** the matrimonial home; **le lit c.** the marital bed; **la vie conjugale** married life

conjuguer [kɔ̃ʒyge] vt (a) (verbe) to conjugate (b) (unir) to combine

conjurer [kɔ̃ʒyre] 1 vt (a) (implorer) **c. qn de faire qch** to beg or implore sb to do sth; **je t'en conjure** I beg you (b) (écarter) (danger, mauvais sort) to avert, to ward off
2 **se conjurer** vpr to conspire (together) (contre against)

connaissance [kɔnɛsɑ̃s] nf (a) (fait de connaître) knowledge; **avoir c. de qch** to be aware of sth; **prendre c. de qch** to acquaint oneself with sth; **à ma c.** to my knowledge; **en (toute) c. de cause** with full knowledge of the facts (b) (contact) **faire la c. de qn** to make sb's acquaintance; **faire c. avec qn** to get to know sb; **quelqu'un de ma c.** someone I know, an acquaintance of mine (c) (personne) acquaintance (d) (savoir) knowledge; **elle a de bonnes connaissances en astronomie** she has a good knowledge of astronomy (e) (conscience) consciousness; **sans c.** unconscious

connaisseur, -euse [kɔnɛsœr, -øz] 1 nm,f connoisseur, expert
2 adj expert

connaître [20] [kɔnɛtr] 1 vt (a) (personne, détails, endroit) to know; **c. qn de nom/de vue** to know sb by name/by sight; **il n'y connaît rien** he doesn't know anything about it; **c'est ce livre qui l'a fait c.** this is the book that made his/her name; **tu connais la nouvelle?** have you heard the news?; **c'est mal le c.** you/they/etc don't know him; Fam **je connais la musique ou la chanson** I've heard it all before; Fam **si tu fais ça, je ne te connais plus** if you do that, I'll have nothing more to do with you (b) (rencontrer) to meet (c) (éprouver) (famine, guerre civile) to experience; (amour, peur, faim) to know; **c. des moments difficiles** to go through some difficult times; **c. un destin tragique** to have a tragic fate; **c. un succès considérable** to enjoy considerable success (d) (avoir) **ne pas c. de limites** to know no bounds
2 **se connaître** vpr (a) **se c. (soi-même)** to know oneself (b) **s'y c. en qch** to know a lot about sth (c) (se rencontrer) to meet

connard [kɔnar] = **conard**

conne [kɔn] voir **con**

connecter [kɔnɛkte] vt Él to connect; Ordinat **connecté on line; connecté en anneau/bus/étoile** in a ring/bus/star configuration

connerie [kɔnri] nf très Fam (a) (acte stupide) **faire une c./des conneries** to do a bloody stupid thing/some bloody stupid things (b) (remarque stupide) bloody stupid thing; **dire ou raconter des conneries** to talk bullshit (c) (caractère stupide) stupidity

connexion [kɔnɛksjɔ̃] nf connection

connivence [kɔnivɑ̃s] nf connivance; **agir/être de c. avec qn** to act/be in connivance with sb; **des regards de c.** conniving looks

connotation [kɔnɔtasjɔ̃] nf connotation

connu, -e [kɔny] 1 adj (écrivain, chanteur) well-known; **c'est bien c.!** everyone knows that!
2 pp voir **connaître**

conquérant, -e [kɔ̃kerɑ̃, -ɑ̃t] 1 adj (air) triumphant
2 nm,f conqueror

conquérir [7] [kɔ̃kerir] vt (pays, territoire, sommet) to conquer; (marché) to capture; **ils ont été conquis par son charme** they were won over by his charm

conquête [kɔ̃kɛt] nf conquest; **faire la c. de** (pays) to conquer; (personne) to make a conquest of; **se lancer à la c. de** (pouvoir) to make a bid for; (sommet) to set out to conquer

conquis, -e voir **conquérir**

conquistador [kɔ̃kistadɔr] nm conquistador

consacré, -e [kɔ̃sakre] adj (coutume) established; **selon l'expression consacrée** as the saying goes; **c. par l'usage** sanctioned by usage

consacrer [kɔ̃sakre] 1 vt (a) Rel to consecrate (b) (temps, énergie) **c. qch à** to devote sth to; **combien de temps pouvez-vous me c.?** how much time can you spare me? (c) (entériner) to establish
2 **se consacrer** vpr **se c. à son travail/sa famille** to devote oneself to one's work/family

consanguin, -e [kɔ̃sɑ̃gɛ̃, -in] adj **frère c.** half-brother (on the father's side); **sœur consanguine** half-sister (on the father's side); **mariage c.** intermarriage

consciemment [kɔ̃sjamɑ̃] adv consciously

conscience [kɔ̃sjɑ̃s] nf (a) (esprit) consciousness; **perdre/reprendre c.** to lose/regain consciousness; **avoir/prendre c. de qch** to be/become aware or conscious of sth (b) (morale) conscience; **avoir bonne/mauvaise c.** to have a clear/bad conscience; **se donner bonne c.** to ease one's conscience; **avoir la c. tranquille, avoir sa c. pour soi** to have a clear conscience; **avoir qch sur la c.** to have sth on one's conscience (c) **c. professionnelle** professional integrity

consciencieusement [kɔ̃sjɑ̃sjøzmɑ̃] adv conscientiously

consciencieux, -euse [kɔ̃sjɑ̃sjø, -øz] adj conscientious

conscient, -e [kɔ̃sjɑ̃, -ɑ̃t] adj (a) (décision, choix) conscious; **être c. de qch** to be aware or conscious of sth (b) (lucide) conscious

consécration [kɔ̃sekrasjɔ̃] nf (a) (d'une église, d'un évêque) consecration; (d'un prêtre) ordination (b) (aboutissement) (des efforts, d'une œuvre) recognition; (d'une carrière) crowning moment

consécutif, -ive [kɔ̃sekytif, -iv] adj consecutive; **c. à** resulting from

consécutivement [kɔ̃sekytivmɑ̃] adv consecutively; **c. à** following

conseil [kɔ̃sɛj] nm (a) (recommandation) piece of advice; **des conseils** advice; **donner un c. à qn** to give sb a piece of advice; **être de bon c.** to give good advice (b) (assemblée) council, committee; (d'une entreprise) board; (réunion) meeting; **c. d'administration** board of directors; **c. de classe** = staff meeting with participation of class representatives to discuss school matters; **C. constitutionnel** = independent body which pronounces on the constitutionality of government decisions; **c. de discipline** disciplinary committee; **C. d'État** Council of State; **C. de l'Europe** Council of Europe; **C. général** regional council; **c. de guerre** *(réunion)* council of war; *(tribunal)* court martial; **le c. des ministres** ≃ the Cabinet; **c. municipal** local council; *Can* **C. national des autochtones du Canada** Native Council of Canada; **C. de sécurité** *de l'ONU)* Security Council **(c)** *(personne)* consultant **(en in)**

conseiller[1] [kɔ̃seje] *vt* **(a)** *(guider) (personne)* to advise **(b)** *(recommander)* **c. qch à qn** to recommend sth to sb; **c. à qn de faire qch** to advise sb to do sth; **il est conseillé de ne pas fumer** it is advisable not to smoke

conseiller[2], **-ère** [kɔ̃seje, -ɛr] *nm,f* **(a)** *(spécialiste)* adviser, consultant; **c. d'orientation** careers adviser; **c. technique** technical adviser **(b)** *Pol* **c. général** regional councillor; **c. municipal** local councillor

consensuel, -elle [kɔ̃sɑ̃sɥɛl] *adj* consensual

consensus [kɔ̃sɛ̃sys] *nm* consensus (of opinion)

consentant, -e [kɔ̃sɑ̃tɑ̃, -ɑ̃t] *adj* consenting; **être c.** to consent

consentement [kɔ̃sɑ̃tmɑ̃] *nm* consent; **donner son c. à qch** to give one's consent to sth; **divorce par c. mutuel** divorce by mutual consent

consentir [64a] [kɔ̃sɑ̃tir] **1** *vi* to consent, to agree (**à qch/à faire** to sth/to do sth); **je consens (à ce) qu'il vienne** I consent to his coming **2** *vt* **c. un prêt à qn** to grant sb a loan; **c. une remise à qn** to allow sb a discount

conséquence [kɔ̃sekɑ̃s] *nf* consequence; **une erreur sans c.** an inconsequential mistake; **tirer les conséquences de qch** to draw conclusions from sth; **la baisse des taxes a eu pour c. de créer des emplois** the tax reduction resulted in the creation of jobs; **agir en c.** to take appropriate action; **en c. (de quoi)** consequently

conséquent, -e [kɔ̃sekɑ̃, -ɑ̃t] *adj* **(a)** *(cohérent)* consistent **(b)** *Fam (somme)* tidy **(c)** **par c.** consequently

conservateur, -trice [kɔ̃sɛrvatœr, -tris] **1** *adj Pol* Conservative **2** *nm,f* **(a)** *(de musée)* curator; *(de bibliothèque)* librarian **(b)** *Pol* Conservative **3** *nm (alimentaire)* preservative; **sans c.** *(sur emballage)* free of preservatives

conservation [kɔ̃sɛrvasjɔ̃] *nf (de fruits, de viande)* preserving; *(de bâtiments)* preservation; *(d'archives)* keeping

conservatoire [kɔ̃sɛrvatwar] *nm (de musique, d'art dramatique)* school, academy; **le C. (de Paris)** the (Paris) Conservatoire; **le C. des arts et métiers** = museum and college of applied sciences

conserve [kɔ̃sɛrv] *nf (aliment)* canned or *Br* tinned food; *(en bocal)* preserve; *(boîte)* can, *Br* tin; **en c.** canned, *Br* tinned; *(en bocal)* preserved; **mettre qch en c.** to can sth, *Br* to tin sth; *(en bocal)* to preserve sth

conserver [kɔ̃sɛrve] **1** *vt* **(a)** *(aliment)* to keep; *(dans le sel, le vinaigre)* to preserve; **c. à l'abri de la lumière** *(sur emballage)* keep away from direct sunlight; **c. au froid** *(sur emballage)* keep in a cold place; **être bien conservé** *(personne)* to be well preserved **(b)** *(garder) (objet, emploi, sang-froid)* to keep; *(droits)* to retain; **c. un bon souvenir de qch** to have good memories of sth **2 se conserver** *vpr (aliment)* to keep

considérable [kɔ̃siderabl] *adj* considerable

considérablement [kɔ̃siderabləmɑ̃] *adv* considerably

considération [kɔ̃siderasjɔ̃] *nf* **(a)** *(examen)* **prendre qch en c.** to take sth into consideration; *(offre, demande d'emploi)* to consider sth **(b)** *(estime)* regard, esteem; **agir avec/sans c.** to act considerately/inconsiderately; **jouir d'une grande c.** to be highly regarded **(c)** *(observations)* **considérations (sur)** *(observations)* observations (on); **je ne peux pas entrer dans ces considérations** I can't go into that

considérer [34] [kɔ̃sidere] **1** *vt* **(a)** *(étudier, regarder)* to consider; **tout bien considéré** all things considered **(b)** *(estimer)* **c. que** to consider that; **c. qn/qch comme...** to regard sb/sth as...
2 se considérer *vpr* **se c. désavantagé** to consider oneself disadvantaged; **se c. comme un artiste/un révolutionnaire** to consider oneself an artist/a revolutionary

consigne [kɔ̃siɲ] *nf* **(a)** *(ordres)* orders; **avoir pour c. de...** to have orders to...; **passer la c.** to pass on the orders; **consignes en cas d'incendie** fire notice **(b)** *(punition) Mil* confinement to barracks; *Scol* detention **(c)** *(pour les bagages)* **c. (à bagages)** *Br* left-luggage office, *Am* checkroom; **c. automatique** lockers **(d)** *(de bouteille)* deposit

consigner [kɔ̃siɲe] *vt (bouteille, emballage)* to charge a deposit on **(b)** *(noter)* to record **(c)** *(punir) (soldat)* to confine to barracks; *(élève)* to keep in **(d)** *(laisser à la consigne)* *Br* to deposit in the left-luggage office, *Am* to check

consistance [kɔ̃sistɑ̃s] *nf (d'un corps)* consistency; **sans c.** *(pâte, fromage)* too soft; *Fig (personne)* bland; *(personnage de fiction)* insubstantial

consistant, -e [kɔ̃sistɑ̃, -ɑ̃t] *adj (substance)* firm; *(sauce, soupe)* thick; *(repas)* substantial; *(argument)* sound

consister [kɔ̃siste] *vi* **c. en qch** to consist of sth; **c. à faire qch** to consist in doing sth

consœur [kɔ̃sœr] *nf (female)* colleague

consolation [kɔ̃sɔlasjɔ̃] *nf* consolation, comfort

console [kɔ̃sɔl] *nf* console

consoler [kɔ̃sɔle] **1** *vt* to console, to comfort; **si ça peut te c.** if that's any consolation to you
2 se consoler *vpr* to console oneself; *(l'un l'autre)* to console each other; **se c. d'une perte/d'un échec** to get over a loss/a failure; **elles se sont consolées mutuellement** they consoled each other

consolidation [kɔ̃sɔlidasjɔ̃] *nf* **(a)** *aussi Fig (renforcement)* strengthening **(b)** *Méd (d'une fracture)* knitting

consolider [kɔ̃sɔlide] **1** *vt* **(a)** *aussi Fig (renforcer)* to strengthen **(b)** *(fracture)* to knit **(c)** *Fin (dette)* to fund; *(bilan)* to consolidate
2 se consolider *vpr* **(a)** *(régime)* to strengthen its position; *(amitié, liens)* to become stronger **(b)** *(fracture)* to knit

consommateur, -trice [kɔ̃sɔmatœr, -tris] *nm,f Écon* consumer; *(dans un restaurant, un café)* customer; **je suis un grand c. de café** I'm a great coffee drinker; *Écon* **c. final** end-user

consommation [kɔ̃sɔmasjɔ̃] *nf* **(a)** *(d'électricité, de pétrole, de nourriture)* consumption; *(d'une voiture)* (fuel) consumption; **faire une grande c. de qch** to consume great quantities of sth **(b)** *(dans un café)* drink **(c)** *(du mariage)* consummation

consommé, -e [kɔ̃sɔme] **1** *nm Culin* consommé
2 *adj* consummate

consommer [kɔ̃sɔme] **1** vt (a) (électricité, pétrole, nourriture) to consume; **à c. avant fin novembre** (sur emballage) best before end November; **cette voiture consomme trop (d'essence)** this car is heavy on fuel; **c. au bar** to drink at the bar (b) (mariage) to consummate
2 se consommer vpr **ce plat se consomme froid** this dish is eaten cold

consonance [kɔ̃sɔnɑ̃s] nf Mus & Ling consonance; **langue à c. germanique** German-sounding language

consonne [kɔ̃sɔn] nf consonant

consortium [kɔ̃sɔrsjɔm] nm Com & Fin consortium

conspirateur, -trice [kɔ̃spiratœr, -tris] **1** nm,f conspirator
2 adj conspiratorial

conspiration [kɔ̃spirasjɔ̃] nf conspiracy, plot

conspirer [kɔ̃spire] vi (a) (comploter) to conspire, to plot (**contre** against) (b) (contribuer) to conspire (**à faire qch** to do sth)

constamment [kɔ̃stamɑ̃] adv constantly

constance [kɔ̃stɑ̃s] nf (a) (dans une tâche) perseverance; (en amour) constancy; **travailler avec c.** to work steadily (b) (de la température, d'un phénomène) constancy

constant, -e [kɔ̃stɑ̃, -ɑ̃t] **1** adj (a) (souci, température, va-et-vient) constant; (effort) persistent; (amitié, intérêt) steady (b) (personne) être c. dans ses opinions to stick to one's opinions; **être c. dans ses amitiés** to be faithful to one's friends (c) Écon **en francs constants** in real terms
2 nf **constante** (en sciences) constant

constat [kɔ̃sta] nm (a) Jur official report; **dresser un c. d'accident** to write out an accident report; **c. amiable** = report of road accident agreed by parties involved (b) (bilan) assessment; **faire un c. d'échec** to acknowledge failure

constatation [kɔ̃statasjɔ̃] nf (a) (observation) observation; **c'est une simple c.** it's a simple statement of fact (b) **constatations** (d'une enquête) findings

constater [kɔ̃state] vt (a) (observer) to note (**que** that); **vous pouvez c. vous-même qu'elle est partie** you can see for yourself that she's gone (b) Jur (enregistrer) to record; (décès) to certify; (dégâts) to assess

constellation [kɔ̃stelasjɔ̃] nf constellation

constellé, -e [kɔ̃stele] adj **un ciel c. d'étoiles** a star-studded sky

consternant, -e [kɔ̃stɛrnɑ̃, -ɑ̃t] adj (nouvelle) dismaying; **d'une bêtise consternante** appallingly stupid

consternation [kɔ̃stɛrnasjɔ̃] nf dismay, consternation; **jeter la c. dans/parmi** to fill with dismay; **à la c. générale** to everyone's dismay

consterner [kɔ̃stɛrne] vt to dismay

constipation [kɔ̃stipasjɔ̃] nf constipation

constipé, -e [kɔ̃stipe] adj constipated; Fam (mal à l'aise) ill at ease

constituer [kɔ̃stitɥe] **1** vt (a) (composer) to make up; **être constitué de** to be made up of (b) (équivaloir à) to constitute (c) (comité, gouvernement, équipe) to form; (bibliothèque, fortune, stocks) to build up; **c. une rente/une dot à qn** to settle an annuity/a dowry on sb
2 se constituer vpr (a) (devenir) **se c. prisonnier** to give oneself up; Jur **se c. partie civile** to bring a civil suit for damages (b) (se réunir) **se c. en commission/en association** to form a committee/an association

constitution [kɔ̃stitysjɔ̃] nf (a) (physique, d'un pays) constitution; **avoir une bonne c.** to have a sound constitution (b) (de comité, de société, de gouvernement) formation; (de stocks, de bibliothèque) building up

constitutionnel, -elle [kɔ̃stitysjɔnɛl] adj constitutional

constructeur [kɔ̃stryktœr] nm (bâtisseur) builder; **c. automobile** car manufacturer; **c. naval** shipbuilder

constructif, -ive [kɔ̃stryktif, -iv] adj constructive

construction [kɔ̃stryksjɔ̃] nf (a) (d'une maison, d'une route, d'un voilier) building, construction; (d'une phrase) structure; **en c.** under construction; **c. navale** shipbuilding (b) (bâtiment) building

construire [18] [kɔ̃strɥir] **1** vt to build, to construct; (roman, phrase, théorie) to construct
2 se construire vpr Gram **"après que" se construit avec l'indicatif** 'après que' takes the indicative

consul [kɔ̃syl] nm consul; **le c. de France** the French consul; **c. général** consul general

consulaire [kɔ̃syler] adj consular

consulat [kɔ̃syla] nm (lieu) consulate; (charge) consulship

consultant, -e [kɔ̃syltɑ̃, -ɑ̃t] **1** nm,f consultant
2 adj consulting; **médecin c.** consultant

consultation [kɔ̃syltasjɔ̃] nf (a) (d'un expert, d'un médecin) consultation; **le médecin est en c.** the doctor is with a patient; **heures de c.** consulting or Br surgery hours (b) (de livre) consultation (c) Pol **c. populaire** consultation of the people

consulter [kɔ̃sylte] **1** vt to consult
2 vi (docteur) to see patients, Br to take surgery
3 se consulter vpr to consult each other

consumer [kɔ̃syme] **1** vt (brûler) to consume; Fig **consumé par le remords** consumed with remorse
2 se consumer vpr (brûler) to burn; Fig **se c. d'inquiétude/de chagrin** to be consumed with worry/with grief

contact [kɔ̃takt] nm (a) (relation, personne) contact; **garder/perdre le c. avec qn** to keep in touch/lose touch with sb; **prendre c.** ou **se mettre en c. avec qn** to get in touch or in contact with sb; **être/entrer en c. avec qn** to be in/come into contact with sb; **être d'un c. facile/difficile** to be approachable/unapproachable; **au c. de qn** through spending time with sb (b) (toucher) contact; **au c. agréable** pleasant to the touch; **être/entrer en c. avec qch** to be in/come into contact with sth; **au c. de qch** on contact with sth (c) Él contact (d) Aut contact; **mettre/couper le c.** to switch on/off

contacter [kɔ̃takte] vt to contact

contagieux, -euse [kɔ̃taʒjø, -øz] adj (maladie, virus, personne) contagious; (rire, enthousiasme) infectious

contagion [kɔ̃taʒjɔ̃] nf Méd contagion

container [kɔ̃tener] nm container

contamination [kɔ̃taminasjɔ̃] nf (pollution) contamination; Méd infection

contaminer [kɔ̃tamine] vt (polluer) to contaminate; Méd to infect

conte [kɔ̃t] nm story, tale; **c. de fées** fairy tale; Fig **elle vit un c. de fées** her life is a fairy tale

contemplatif, -ive [kɔ̃tɑ̃platif, -iv] adj & nm,f contemplative

contemplation [kɔ̃tɑ̃plasjɔ̃] nf contemplation; **être en c. devant qch** to gaze at sth

contempler [kɔ̃tɑ̃ple] **1** vt to contemplate, to gaze at **2 se contempler** vpr (soi-même) to gaze at oneself

contemporain, -e [kɔ̃tɑ̃pɔrɛ̃, -ɛn] **1** adj (a) (moderne) contemporary (b) (du même âge) contemporary (de with); **être c. de qn** to be a contemporary of sb; **ils sont contemporains** they are contemporaries **2** nm,f contemporary

contenance [kɔ̃tnɑ̃s] nf (a) (d'un récipient) capacity (b) (allure) attitude, bearing; **faire qch pour se donner une c.** to do sth to give an impression of composure; **faire bonne c.** to put on a bold front; **perdre c.** to lose one's composure

contenant [kɔ̃tnɑ̃] nm container

conteneur [kɔ̃tnœr] nm container

contenir [70] [kɔ̃tnir] **1** vt (a) (renfermer) to contain; **le théâtre contient mille places** the theatre holds or seats a thousand (b) (foule, ennemi) to contain, to keep in check; (colère) to curb; (larmes) to hold back **2 se contenir** vpr to contain oneself

content, -e [kɔ̃tɑ̃, -ɑ̃t] **1** adj (satisfait) happy, content (de with); (joyeux) glad (de faire to do); **je suis très c. de vous voir** I'm very pleased to see you; **être c. de faire qch** to be pleased with doing sth; **tu peux être c. de toi, tu as vu ce que tu as fait!** I hope you're happy, just look what you've done!; **non c. de mentir, il vole!** not content with lying, he steals as well!; **je suis vraiment c. que vous soyez venu** I'm so glad you've come; **j'am et si tu n'es pas c., c'est pareil** you can like it or lump it **2** nm **manger tout son c.** to eat one's fill; **avoir c. de qch** to have had one's fill of sth

contentement [kɔ̃tɑ̃tmɑ̃] nm (état) satisfaction, contentment; **un sourire de c.** a contented smile

contenter [kɔ̃tɑ̃te] **1** vt (personne) to satisfy, to please **2 se contenter** vpr **se c. de qch/de faire qch** to content oneself with sth/with doing sth; **se c. de peu** to be easily satisfied; **je me contenterai de faire remarquer que...** I will merely point out that...

contentieux [kɔ̃tɑ̃sjø] nm (querelle) dispute; Jur litigation; (service) legal department; **avoir un c. avec qn** to be in dispute with sb

contenu, -e [kɔ̃tny] **1** nm (d'un paquet, d'une bouteille, d'une boîte) contents; (d'une lettre, d'un livre) content **2** adj (émotion) restrained

conter [kɔ̃te] vt to tell; **elle ne s'en laisse pas c.** you can't fool her

contestataire [kɔ̃testater] **1** adj Pol anti-establishment; (mécontent) rebellious **2** nmf Pol protester; (mécontent) rebel

contestation [kɔ̃testasjɔ̃] nf (a) (protestation) protest; **il y a matière ou sujet à c.** there are grounds for dispute; **sans c. possible** beyond dispute (b) Pol protest

conteste [kɔ̃test] **sans conteste** adv indisputably

contester [kɔ̃teste] vt to dispute; **je lui conteste le droit de...** I dispute his right to...; **elle est très contestée** she is very controversial; **faire qch sans c.** to do sth without protest

conteur, -euse [kɔ̃tœr, -øz] nm,f storyteller

contexte [kɔ̃tɛkst] nm context; **dans le c. de** in the context of; **hors c.** out of context

contigu, -ë [kɔ̃tigy] adj (maisons, pièces) adjoining; **c. à qch** adjoining sth

continent [kɔ̃tinɑ̃] nm (a) (étendue) continent; **l'Ancien/le Nouveau C.** the Old/the New World (b) (par rapport à une île) mainland

continental, -e, -aux, -ales [kɔ̃tinɑtal, -o] **1** adj (climat, plateau) continental; (par rapport à une île) mainland **2** nm,f mainlander

contingent [kɔ̃tɛ̃ʒɑ̃] nm (a) Mil contingent; **les soldats du c.** the conscripted soldiers (b) (quota) quota

continu, -e [kɔ̃tiny] adj (ligne, effort) continuous; (soin, attention) constant; **en c.** continuously; Ordinat **papier en c.** continuous paper

continuation [kɔ̃tinɥasjɔ̃] nf continuation; **bonne c.!** all the best!

continuel, -elle [kɔ̃tinɥɛl] adj (ininterrompu) continuous; (qui se répète) continual

continuellement [kɔ̃tinɥɛlmɑ̃] adv (de façon ininterrompue) continuously; (de façon répétitive) continually

continuer [kɔ̃tinɥe] **1** vt (études, efforts, politique) to continue (with), to carry on with; (trait, route) to continue; **c. sa route** ou **son chemin** to continue on one's way; **continuez!** carry on!; **si tu continues comme ça,...** if you carry on like that,... **2** vi to continue **3 continuer à** ou **de** vt ind **c. à** ou **de faire qch** to continue doing sth, to carry on doing sth; **je continue à** ou **de me demander si...** I keep wondering if... **4 se continuer** vpr to continue

continuité [kɔ̃tinɥite] nf (d'une action) continuity; (d'une tradition, d'une politique) continuation

contondant, -e [kɔ̃tɔ̃dɑ̃, -ɑ̃t] adj blunt

contorsion [kɔ̃tɔrsjɔ̃] nf contortion

contorsionner [kɔ̃tɔrsjɔne] **se contorsionner** vpr to contort oneself

contorsionniste [kɔ̃tɔrsjɔnist] nmf contortionist

contour [kɔ̃tur] nm (silhouette) outline

contourner [kɔ̃turne] vt to go round; Fig (loi, difficulté) to get round

contraceptif, -ive [kɔ̃traseptif, -iv] Méd **1** adj contraceptive **2** nm contraceptive; **c. oral** oral contraceptive

contraception [kɔ̃trasepsjɔ̃] nf contraception

contractant, -e [kɔ̃traktɑ̃, -ɑ̃t] adj Jur (partie) contracting

contracté, -e [kɔ̃trakte] adj (a) (muscles, visage, personne) tense (b) Ling contracted

contracter[1] [kɔ̃trakte] vt (a) (alliance, dette) to contract; (assurance) to take out (b) (habitude, goût, manie) to acquire; (maladie) to contract

contracter[2] **1** vt (muscles, visage) to tense; **visage contracté par la douleur** face drawn with pain **2 se contracter** vpr (a) (cœur, muscle) to contract; (personne) to tense (up) (b) Ling to contract

contraction [kɔ̃traksjɔ̃] nf (a) (d'un muscle, d'un gaz, d'un mot) contraction; **contractions** (à l'accouchement) contractions (b) Scol **c. de texte** précis

contractuel, -elle [kɔ̃traktɥɛl] **1** adj (obligations) contractual; **agent c. =** contractor working for the local council **2** nm,f (auxiliaire de police) Br ≃ traffic warden, Am ≃ traffic policeman, f traffic policewoman

contracture [kɔ̃traktyr] nf Méd spasm

contradiction [kɔ̃tradiksjɔ̃] *nf* (a) *(opposition)* contradiction; **avoir l'esprit de c.** to be contrary; **il ne supporte pas la c.** he can't stand being contradicted (b) *(illogisme)* contradiction; **être en c. avec qch** to contradict sth; **être en c. avec soi-même** to contradict oneself

contradictoire [kɔ̃tradiktwar] *adj* contradictory (**avec** to); **débat c.** debate

contraignant, -e [kɔ̃trɛɲɑ̃, -ɑ̃t] *adj* restricting

contraindre [23] [kɔ̃trɛ̃dr] **1** *vt (obliger)* **c. qn à faire qch** to force *or* compel sb to do sth; **être contraint de faire qch** to be forced *or* compelled to do sth; **contraint et forcé** under duress
2 se contraindre *vpr* **se c. à faire qch** to force oneself to do sth

contrainte [kɔ̃trɛ̃t] *nf* (a) *(obligation, limitation, retenue)* constraint; **parler sans c.** to speak freely (b) *(force)* force; **obtenir qch par la c.** to get sth by force; **faire qch sous la c.** to do sth under duress (c) *Tech* stress

contraire [kɔ̃trɛr] **1** *adj* (a) *(opposé) (intérêts, avis)* conflicting; **vent c.** headwind; **c. à** contrary to; **en sens c.** in the opposite direction (b) *(défavorable)* **le sort nous/m'est c.** fate is against us/me
2 *nm* opposite; **le c. de** the opposite of; **sa sœur est tout le c. de lui** his sister is the exact opposite of him; **(bien) au c.** on the contrary

contrairement [kɔ̃trɛrmɑ̃] *contrairement à prép* contrary to; **c. à moi,...** unlike me,...

contralto [kɔ̃tralto] *nm Mus* contralto

contrariant, -e [kɔ̃trarjɑ̃, -ɑ̃t] *adj* (a) *(personne)* contrary; **elle n'est pas contrariante** she's easy-going; *Péj* she says yes to everything (b) *(situation)* annoying, irritating

contrarier [66] [kɔ̃trarje] *vt* (a) *(ennuyer)* to annoy, to irritate (b) *(contrecarrer) (projets, desseins)* to thwart, to frustrate

contrariété [kɔ̃trarjete] *nf* annoyance; **éprouver une vive c.** to feel extremely annoyed

contraste [kɔ̃trast] *nm* contrast; **faire c. (avec)** to contrast (with); **par c. avec** in contrast to; **effet de c.** contrasting effect

contrasté, -e [kɔ̃traste] *adj* (a) *(différencié)* contrasting; **photo bien/mal contrastée** photo with the right amount of/with not enough contrast (b) *Ordinat* highlighted

contraster [kɔ̃traste] *vi* to contrast (**avec** with)

contrat [kɔ̃tra] *nm* (a) *(accord)* contract, agreement; **passer un c. (avec qn)** to enter into an agreement (with sb); **c. d'assurance** contract of insurance; **c. collectif** collective agreement; **c. à durée déterminée/indéterminée** fixed-term/permanent contract; **c. emploi-solidarité** = short-term contract subsidized by the government; **c. de mariage** marriage contract; **c. de travail** *Br* contract of employment, *Am* labor contract (b) *(au bridge)* contract

contravention [kɔ̃travɔ̃sjɔ̃] *nf (envers un règlement)* contravention; *(amende)* fine; *(pour stationnement non autorisé) (amende)* parking fine; *(avis)* parking ticket

contre [kɔ̃tr] **1** *prép* (a) *(se battre, jouer)* against; **se fâcher c. qn** to get angry with sb; **la campagne c. l'avortement** the anti-abortion campaign; **je n'ai rien**

c., je ne suis pas c. I've got nothing against it; **par c.** on the other hand
(b) *(pour se protéger de)* **sirop c. la toux** cough mixture; **être assuré c. le vol** to be insured against theft
(c) *(en échange de)* (in exchange) for; **échanger une chose c. une autre** to exchange one thing for another
(d) *(en proportion de)* to; **parier à cinq c. un** to bet five to one; **10 voix c. 2** 10 votes to 2
(e) *(en contact avec)* against; **s'appuyer c. qch** to lean against sth; **leur maison est tout à c. la mienne** their house is right next to mine; **joue c. joue** cheek to cheek; **le radiateur est allumé, assieds-toi tout c.** the heater is on, sit right next to it
(f) *(en dépit de)* **toute logique** against all logic; **c. toute attente** against all expectations
(g) *(en comparaison de)* (compared to) **la livre est à 9 francs c. 8 francs le mois dernier** the pound stands at 9 francs compared to 8 francs last month
2 *nm* (a) **peser le pour et le c.** to weigh up the pros and cons
(b) *(au volley, au basket)* block

contre-allée (*pl* contre-allées) [kɔ̃trale] *nf* side road

contre-attaque (*pl* contre-attaques) [kɔ̃tratak] *nf* counter-attack

contre-attaquer [kɔ̃tratake] *vi* to counter-attack

contrebalancer [16] [kɔ̃trəbalɑ̃se] **1** *vt (poids)* to counterbalance; *(inconvénient)* to offset
2 se contrebalancer *vpr Fam* **se c. de qch** not to give a damn about sth

contrebande [kɔ̃trəbɑ̃d] *nf* (a) *(activité)* smuggling; **faire de la c.** to smuggle goods; **faire entrer des marchandises en c.** to smuggle in goods; **de c.** smuggled (b) *(marchandises)* contraband

contrebandier, -ère [kɔ̃trəbɑ̃dje, -ɛr] *nm,f* smuggler

contrebas [kɔ̃trəba] **en contrebas** *adv* (down) below; **en c. de** below

contrebasse [kɔ̃trəbas] *nf (instrument)* (double) bass; *(musicien)* (double) bass player

contrebassiste [kɔ̃trəbasist] *nmf* (double) bass player

contre-braquer [kɔ̃trəbrake] *vi Aut* to steer into the skid

contrecarrer [kɔ̃trəkare] *vt* to thwart

contrechamp [kɔ̃trəʃɑ̃] *nm Cin* reverse shot

contre-chant (*pl* contre-chants) [kɔ̃trəʃɑ̃] *nm Mus* counterpoint

contrecœur [kɔ̃trəkœr] **à contrecœur** *adv* reluctantly, unwillingly

contrecoup [kɔ̃trəku] *nm (conséquence)* repercussions

contre-courant [kɔ̃trəkurɑ̃] **à contre-courant** *adv (nager)* against the current; *(sur la route)* in the wrong direction; *Fig* **aller à c. de qch** to go against the current of sth

contredanse [kɔ̃trədɑ̃s] *nf Fam (amende)* parking fine; *(avis)* (parking) ticket; **flanquer une c. à qn** to give sb a (parking) ticket

contredire [27b] [kɔ̃trədir] **1** *vt* to contradict
2 se contredire *vpr (soi-même)* to contradict oneself; *(l'un l'autre)* to contradict each other

contrée [kɔ̃tre] *nf Litt (région)* region; *(pays)* land

contre-emploi (*pl* contre-emplois) [kɔ̃trɑ̃plwa] *nm Th & Cin* miscasting; **utiliser qn à c.** to miscast sb

contre-enquête (*pl* contre-enquêtes) [kɔ̃trɑ̃kɛt] *nf Jur* counter-inquiry

contre-espionnage [kɔ̃trɛspjɔnaʒ] *nm* counter-espionage

contre-exemple (*pl* contre-exemples) [kɔ̃trɛgzɑ̃pl] *nm* counter-example

contre-expertise (*pl* contre-expertises) [kɔ̃trɛkspɛrtiz] *nf* second valuation

contrefaçon [kɔ̃trafasɔ̃] *nf* (a) (*pratique*) counterfeiting; (*de signature*) forging (b) (*produit*) fake, imitation

contrefaire [36] [kɔ̃trafɛr] *vt* (a) (*voix, écriture*) to disguise (b) (*pièce, produit de marque*) to counterfeit; (*signature*) to forge

contreficher [kɔ̃trafiʃe] **se contreficher** *vpr très Fam* se c. de qch not to give a damn about sth

contre-filet (*pl* contre-filets) [kɔ̃trafile] *nm Culin* sirloin

contrefort [kɔ̃trafɔr] *nm* (a) *Archit* buttress (b) *Géog* contreforts foothills (c) (*de chaussure*) stiffener

contre-indication (*pl* contre-indications) [kɔ̃trɛ̃dikasjɔ̃] *nf* contraindication

contre-interrogatoire (*pl* contre-interrogatoires) [kɔ̃trɛ̃tɛrɔgatwar] *nm Jur* cross-examination

contre-jour (*pl* contre-jours) [kɔ̃traʒur] *nm* (a) (*éclairage défavorable*) light from behind; **à c.** against the light (b) *Art, Cin & Phot* backlighting

contre-la-montre [kɔ̃tralamɔ̃tr] *nm inv Sp* time-trial

contremaître, -esse [kɔ̃tramɛtr, -ɛs] *nm,f* foreman, f forewoman

contre-manifestation (*pl* contre-manifestations) [kɔ̃tramanifɛstasjɔ̃] *nf* counter-demonstration

contremarche [kɔ̃tramarʃ] *nf* (*d'un escalier*) riser

contremarque [kɔ̃tramark] *nf* (*au spectacle*) passout ticket

contre-mesure (*pl* contre-mesures) [kɔ̃tramazyr] *nf* countermeasure

contre-offensive (*pl* contre-offensives) [kɔ̃trɔfɑ̃siv] *nf* counter-offensive

contrepartie [kɔ̃traparti] *nf* (*compensation*) compensation; **en c. (de)** in return (for)

contre-performance (*pl* contre-performances) [kɔ̃trapɛrfɔrmɑ̃s] *nf* substandard performance

contrepèterie [kɔ̃trapɛtri] *nf* spoonerism

contre-pied [kɔ̃trapje] *nm* (a) **prendre le c. de qch** (*faire le contraire*) to do the opposite of sth; (*dire le contraire*) to take the opposite view to sth (b) *Sp* **prendre son adversaire à c.** to wrong-foot one's opponent; **prendre la balle à c.** to take the ball on the wrong foot

contreplaqué [kɔ̃traplake] *nm* plywood

contre-plongée (*pl* contre-plongées) [kɔ̃traplɔ̃ʒe] *nf Cin & TV* low-angle shot; **filmer qch en c.** to film sth from below

contrepoids [kɔ̃trapwɑ] *nm aussi Fig* counterbalance; *Fig* **faire c. à qch** to counterbalance sth

contre-poil [kɔ̃trapwal] **à contre-poil** *adv* the wrong way; *Fam* **prendre qn à c.** to rub sb up the wrong way

contrepoison [kɔ̃trapwazɔ̃] *nm* antidote

contre-pouvoir (*pl* contre-pouvoirs) [kɔ̃trapuvwar] *nm* anti-establishment force

contre-proposition (*pl* contre-propositions) [kɔ̃trapropozisjɔ̃] *nf* counter-proposal

contrer [kɔ̃tre] *vt* (a) (*attaque, argument, personne*) to counter (b) (*au volley, au basket*) to block (c) (*aux cartes*) to double

contre-révolution (*pl* contre-révolutions) [kɔ̃trarevɔlysjɔ̃] *nf* counter-revolution

contre-révolutionnaire (*pl* contre-révolutionnaires) [kɔ̃trarevɔlysjɔner] *adj & nmf* counter-revolutionary

contresens [kɔ̃trasɑ̃s] *nm* (a) (*mauvaise compréhension*) misinterpretation; (*mauvaise traduction*) mistranslation; **faire un c.** (*mal comprendre*) to make a mistake in interpretation; (*mal traduire*) to make a mistake in translation (b) *Aut* **à c.** the wrong way; **prendre une rue à c.** to go the wrong way down a street

contresigner [kɔ̃trasiɲe] *vt* to countersign

contretemps [kɔ̃tratɑ̃] *nm* (a) (*ennui*) hitch, mishap (b) *Mus* offbeat; **à c.** off the beat; *Fig* at the wrong moment

contre-ténor (*pl* contre-ténors) [kɔ̃tratenɔr] *nm* counter-tenor

contre-torpilleur (*pl* contre-torpilleurs) [kɔ̃tratorpijœr] *nm* destroyer

contrevenant, -e [kɔ̃travnɑ̃, -ɑ̃t] *nm,f* offender

contrevenir [70] [kɔ̃travnir] **contrevenir à** *vt ind* to contravene

contrevent [kɔ̃travɑ̃] *nm* (*volet*) (outside) shutter

contrevérité [kɔ̃traverite] *nf* untruth, falsehood

contribuable [kɔ̃tribɥabl] *nmf* taxpayer

contribuer [kɔ̃tribɥe] **contribuer à** *vt ind* to contribute to; **financièrement à qch** to contribute (money) to sth; **c. à faire qch** to help (to) do sth

contribution [kɔ̃tribysjɔ̃] *nf* (a) (*impôt*) tax; contributions (*à l'État*) taxes; (*à la collectivité locale*) *Br* rates, *Am* local taxes; (**bureau des**) **contributions** tax office, *Br* Inland Revenue, *Am* Internal Revenue; **contributions directes/indirectes** direct/indirect taxation; **c. sociale généralisée** = income-based tax deducted at source (b) (*collaboration, aide financière*) contribution (à to); **mettre qn à c.** to call on sb's services

contrit, -e [kɔ̃tri, -it] *adj* contrite

contrôle [kɔ̃trol] *nm* (a) (*vérification*) checking; *Scol* test; *Univ* **c. continu** continuous assessment; **c. douanier** customs control; **c. fiscal** tax inspection; **c. d'identité** identity check; **c. de police** police check; **c. radar** (*sur la route*) radar speed check; *Aut* **c. technique** *Br* ≃ MOT (test) (b) (*surveillance*) (*d'opérations*) monitoring; *Fin* **c. des changes** exchange control; **sous c. judiciaire** on probation; **sous c. médical** under medical supervision; **c. des prix** price control (c) (*maîtrise*) control; **avoir le c. de qch** to have control of sth, to be in control of sth; **perdre le c. de son véhicule** to lose control of one's vehicle; **c. de soi** self-control; **sous c. serbe** under Serb control; **c. des naissances** birth control (d) *Ordinat* **touche c.** control key; **c. d'accès** access control; **faire un c. croisé de** to cross-check

contrôler [kɔ̃trole] **1** *vt* (a) (*vérifier*) to check (b) (*surveiller*) (*opérations*) to monitor (c) (*maîtriser*) to control (d) *Ordinat* **contrôlé par le logiciel** software-controlled; **contrôlé par menu** menu-driven, menu-controlled

2 se contrôler *vpr* to control oneself

contrôleur, -euse [kɔ̃trolœr, -øz] **1** *nm,f* (*dans les trains, les bus*) ticket inspector; **c. aérien** air-traffic controller; **c. des impôts** tax inspector

2 *nm Ordinat* **c. d'affichage** display or screen controller

contrordre [kɔ̃trɔrdr] *nm* countermand; **il y a c. the** orders have been changed; **sauf c.** unless otherwise directed

controverse [kɔ̃trɔvɛrs] *nf* controversy; **prêter à c.** to be controversial

controversé, -e [kɔ̃trɔvɛrse] *adj* controversial

contumace [kɔ̃tymas] **par contumace** *adv Jur* in absentia

contusion [kɔ̃tyzjɔ̃] *nf* bruise, *Spéc* contusion

contusionné, -e [kɔ̃tyzjɔne] *adj* bruised

convaincant, -e [kɔ̃vɛ̃kɑ̃, -ɑ̃t] *adj* convincing

convaincre [68] [kɔ̃vɛ̃kr] *vt* (a) *(persuader)* to convince **(de/que** of/that); **c. qn de faire qch** to persuade sb to do sth; **se laisser c.** to let oneself be persuaded (b) *(prouver la culpabilité de)* **être convaincu de meurtre** to be convicted *or* found guilty of murder

convaincu, -e [kɔ̃vɛ̃ky] *adj* convinced; *(pacifiste, partisan)* committed; **être c. de/que** to be convinced of / that; **d'un ton c.** with conviction

convalescence [kɔ̃valesɑ̃s] *nf* convalescence; **être en c.** to be convalescing

convalescent, -e [kɔ̃valesɑ̃, -ɑ̃t] *adj & nm,f* convalescent

convecteur [kɔ̃vɛktœr] *nm* convector (heater)

convenable [kɔ̃vnabl] *adj* (a) *(décent)* decent, respectable; **il n'est pas c. de faire du bruit en mangeant** it is not polite to make a noise when eating (b) *(acceptable)* *(salaire, délai)* decent (c) *(approprié)* appropriate, suitable

convenablement [kɔ̃vnabləmɑ̃] *adv* decently

convenance [kɔ̃vnɑ̃s] *nf* (a) *(fait de convenir)* **pour (des raisons de) c. personnelle** for personal reasons; **trouver qch à sa c.** to find sth to one's liking; **il le fera à sa c.** he'll do it at his own convenience (b) **les convenances** the proprieties; **contraire aux convenances** improper

convenir [70] [kɔ̃vnir] **1 convenir à** *vt ind (aller à, plaire à)* to suit; **il est difficile de trouver le mot qui convient** it's hard to find the right word

2 convenir de *vt ind* (a) *(reconnaître)* to admit; **j'ai eu tort, j'en conviens** I was wrong, I admit it; **il convient qu'il a eu tort** he admits that he was wrong (b) *(décider de)* to agree on; **c. de faire qch** to agree to do sth

3 *v impersonnel* (a) **il convient de...** *(il est souhaitable de)* it is advisable to...; *(il est de bon ton de)* it is proper to... (b) *(être décidé)* **il fut convenu qu'ils le feraient venir** it was agreed that they would send for him

convention [kɔ̃vɑ̃sjɔ̃] *nf* (a) *(accord)* agreement; **c. collective** collective agreement (b) *(règle arbitraire)* convention; **les conventions (sociales)** the (social) conventions; *Péj* **amabilité/sourire de c.** superficial courtesy/smile (c) *Pol (assemblée)* assembly

conventionné, -e [kɔ̃vɑ̃sjɔne] *adj (médecin, clinique)* attached to the health system, *Br* ≃ NHS; **médecin non c.** private doctor

conventionnel, -elle [kɔ̃vɑ̃sjɔnɛl] *adj* (a) *(style, personne, armes)* conventional (b) *Jur (clause)* contractual

convenu, -e [kɔ̃vny] *adj* (a) *(décidé)* agreed; **comme c.** as agreed (b) *Péj (peu original)* conventional

convergence [kɔ̃vɛrʒɑ̃s] *nf* convergence

convergent, -e [kɔ̃vɛrʒɑ̃, -ɑ̃t] *adj* convergent

converger [45] [kɔ̃vɛrʒe] *vi (routes, lignes)* to converge **(vers** on); **c. vers** *(efforts)* to be focused on; **leurs opinions convergent** they are of like mind

conversation [kɔ̃vɛrsasjɔ̃] *nf* conversation; **être en grande c. (avec qn)** to be deep in conversation (with sb); **engager la c.** to start a conversation; **faire la c. (à qn)** to make conversation (with sb); **n'avoir aucune c.** to be a poor conversationalist; **c. téléphonique** telephone conversation

conversationnel, -elle [kɔ̃vɛrsasjɔnɛl] *adj Ordinat* **mode c.** conversational *or* interactive mode

converser [kɔ̃vɛrse] *vi Formel* to converse **(avec** with)

conversion [kɔ̃vɛrsjɔ̃] *nf* (a) *(changement)* conversion **(en** into); *Ordinat* **c. de fichier** file conversion (b) *(à une doctrine)* conversion **(à** to)

converti, -e [kɔ̃vɛrti] **1** *nm,f Rel* convert; *Fig* **prêcher un c.** to preach to the converted

2 *adj* converted

convertibilité [kɔ̃vɛrtibilite] *nf Fin* convertibility

convertible [kɔ̃vɛrtibl] **1** *adj* convertible **(en** into)

2 *nm (canapé)* sofa bed

convertir [kɔ̃vɛrtir] **1** *vt* (a) *(changer)* to convert **(en** into) (b) *(à une doctrine)* to convert **(à** to)

2 se convertir *vpr* (a) *(à une doctrine)* to be converted **(à** to) (b) **se c. en** *(se changer en)* to be converted into

convertisseur [kɔ̃vɛrtisœr] *nm Tech* converter; *Ordinat* **c. analogique numérique** digitizer

convexe [kɔ̃vɛks] *adj* convex

conviction [kɔ̃viksjɔ̃] *nf* (a) *(certitude)* conviction; **avoir la c. que...** to be convinced that... (b) **convictions** *(opinions)* convictions

convier [66] [kɔ̃vje] *vt Formel (inviter)* to invite **(à** to); **c. qn à faire qch** to invite sb to do sth

convive [kɔ̃viv] *nmf* guest

convivial, -e, -aux, -ales [kɔ̃vivjal, -o] *adj* convivial; *Ordinat* user-friendly

convivialité [kɔ̃vivjalite] *nf* conviviality; *Ordinat* user-friendliness

convocation [kɔ̃vɔkasjɔ̃] *nf* (a) *(lettre)* notice to attend; *Jur* summons; **c. à un examen** notification of an examination (b) *(d'une assemblée)* convening

convoi [kɔ̃vwa] *nm* (a) *(de véhicules, de troupes, de prisonniers)* convoy; **c. exceptionnel** *(sur un camion) (dangereux)* dangerous load; *(large)* wide load (b) *(train)* train; **c. de marchandises** goods *or* freight train; **c. postal** mail train (c) *(cortège)* **c. funèbre** funeral procession

convoiter [kɔ̃vwate] *vt (poste, richesse)* to covet; *(femme)* to lust after

convoitise [kɔ̃vwatiz] *nf* covetousness; **regarder qch avec c.** to look covetously at sth; **exciter les convoitises** to excite envy

convoler [kɔ̃vɔle] *vi Hum* **c. (en justes noces)** to marry

convoquer [kɔ̃vɔke] *vt* (a) *(assemblée)* to convene; **c. les actionnaires** to call the shareholders to a meeting (b) *(témoin)* to summon; *(employé)* to call in; **c. qn à un examen** to notify sb of an examination

convoyer [32] [kɔ̃vwaje] *vt (troupes)* to convoy; *(fonds)* to transport under armed guard

convoyeur [kɔ̃vwajœr] *nm* (a) *(personne)* **c. de fonds** security guard (b) *Ind* conveyer

convulser [kɔ̃vylse] **1** *vt* to convulse

2 se convulser *vpr* to be convulsed

convulsif, -ive [kɔ̃vylsif, -iv] *adj* convulsive

convulsion [kɔ̃vylsjɔ̃] *nf* convulsion; **être pris de convulsions** to go into convulsions

convulsivement [kɔ̃vylsivmɑ̃] *adv* convulsively

cool [kul] *adj inv Fam* cool

coopérant, -e [kɔɔperɑ̃, -ɑ̃t] **1** *nm,f (à l'étranger)* aid worker
2 *nm (pendant le service militaire)* = man doing voluntary work overseas instead of military service

coopératif, -ive [kɔɔperatif, -iv] **1** *adj (société, personne)* co-operative
2 *nf* **coopérative** *(association, magasin)* co-operative, co-op; **coopérative d'achat** wholesale co-operative

coopération [kɔɔperasjɔ̃] *nf* **(a)** *(appui)* co-operation; **en c. avec qn** in co-operation with sb **(b)** *Pol* overseas development; *(service militaire)* = voluntary work overseas instead of military service

coopérer [34] [kɔɔpere] *vi* to co-operate **(à** in)

cooptation [kɔɔptasjɔ̃] *nf* co-option; **par c.** by co-option

coordinateur, -trice [kɔɔrdinatœr, -tris] **=** **coordonnateur**

coordination [kɔɔrdinasjɔ̃] *nf (d'un projet, des mouvements)* co-ordination

coordonnateur, -trice [kɔɔrdɔnatœr, -tris] *nm,f* co-ordinator

coordonné, -e [kɔɔrdɔne] **1** *adj (mouvement, efforts)* co-ordinated; *(draps, vêtements)* matching
2 *nmpl* **coordonnés** *(vêtements)* co-ordinates
3 *nfpl* **coordonnées (a)** *Math, Géog & Astron* co-ordinates **(b)** *(d'une personne)* address and phone number

coordonner [kɔɔrdɔne] *vt* to co-ordinate **(à** *ou* **avec** with)

copain, copine [kɔpɛ̃, kɔpin] *Fam* **1** *nm,f* **(a)** *(camarade)* pal, mate; **salut les copains!** *(en arrivant)* hi guys!; *(en partant)* see you guys!; **c. de classe** classmate **(b)** *(fiancé)* **(petit) c.** boyfriend; **(petite) copine** girlfriend
2 *adj* **ils sont très copains** they're great pals; **être copains comme cochons** to be thick as thieves; **ils sont très c.-c.** they're very pally

copeau, -x [kɔpo] *nm (de bois, de chocolat)* shaving; *(de métal)* cutting

Copenhague [kɔpenag] *n* Copenhagen

copie [kɔpi] *nf* **(a)** *(double, manuscrit)* copy **(b)** *Scol (d'examen)* paper; **rendre c. blanche** to hand in a blank paper; **c. simple/double** single/double sheet of paper **(c)** *(d'une œuvre d'art)* copy, reproduction; *(d'un roman, d'un style)* imitation **(d)** *TV & Cin* copy **(e)** *Ordinat* **c. sur papier** hard copy, printout; **c. de sauvegarde** *ou* **de secours** backup (copy), security copy

copier [66] [kɔpje] *vt* **(a)** *(texte, musique, document informatique)* to copy; **c. qch au propre** *ou* **au net** to make a fair copy of sth, to copy sth out neatly **(b)** *(œuvre d'art)* to copy; *(personne, style)* to imitate **(c)** *(à un devoir sur table)* to copy **(sur** from)

copier-coller [kɔpjekɔle] *nm inv Ordinat* copy-and-paste

copieur, -euse [kɔpjœr, -øz] *nm,f (élève)* copier
2 *nm (photocopieuse)* (photo)copier

copieusement [kɔpjøzmɑ̃] *adv (manger, boire)* copiously; **il s'est servi c.** he took a generous helping; **un repas c. arrosé** a meal washed down with a lot of wine; **je me suis fait c. insulter** I got well and truly insulted

copieux, -euse [kɔpjø, -øz] *adj (repas)* copious; *(portion, part, pourboire)* generous

copilote [kɔpilɔt] *nmf (d'avion)* co-pilot; *(de rallye automobile)* navigator

copinage [kɔpinaʒ] *nm Fam* **obtenir un poste par c.** to get a job through one's connections

copiste [kɔpist] *nmf (scribe)* copyist

coprésentateur, -trice [koprezɑ̃tatœr, -tris] *nm,f* co-presenter

coprésidence [koprezidɑ̃s] *nf* co-chairmanship

coprésident, -e [koprezidɑ̃, -ɑ̃t] *nm,f* co-chairman, *f* co-chairwoman

coprocesseur [koprosesœr] *nm Ordinat* co-processor; **c. arithmétique** maths co-processor

coproduction [koprodyksjɔ̃] *nf* coproduction

coproduire [18] [koprodɥir] *vt* to coproduce

copropriétaire [koproprijeter] *nmf* co-owner, joint owner

copropriété [koproprijete] *nf* co-ownership, joint ownership; **acheter/posséder une maison en c.** to buy/own a house jointly

copte [kɔpt] **1** *adj* Coptic
2 *nmf* **C.** Copt

copulation [kɔpylasjɔ̃] *nf* copulation

copuler [kɔpyle] *vi* to copulate

copyright [kɔpirajt] *nm* copyright

coq¹ [kɔk] *nm* **(a)** *(oiseau)* cock, *Am* rooster; **jeune c.** cockerel; *Fig* young upstart; **le c. gaulois** the French cockerel; *Fig* **le c. du village** the local Casanova; *Fig* **passer** *ou* **sauter du c. à l'âne** to jump from one subject to another; **être comme un c. en pâte** to be in clover; **c. de bruyère** capercaillie; **c. de combat** fighting cock; *Culin* **c. au vin** coq au vin *(chicken cooked in red wine)*; *(girouette)* weathercock

coq² *nm Naut* (ship's) cook

coq-à-l'âne [kɔkalan] *nm inv* **faire un c.** to jump from one subject to another

coquard, coquart [kɔkar] *nm Fam* shiner

coque [kɔk] *nf* **(a)** *(d'une noix, d'un fruit)* shell; *Fig* **c. de noix** flimsy craft **(b)** *(d'un navire)* hull; *(d'un avion)* fuselage; *(d'une voiture)* body **(c)** *(mollusque)* cockle

coquelet [kɔkle] *nm* cockerel

coquelicot [kɔkliko] *nm* (red) poppy

coqueluche [kɔklyʃ] *nf (maladie)* whooping cough; **avoir la c.** to have whooping cough; **il est devenu la c. de ces dames** he's become a heart-throb

coquet, -ette [kɔke, -et] **1** *adj (ville, intérieur)* charming; **elle est coquette** she's very clothes-conscious; *Fam* **une coquette somme** a tidy sum
2 *nf* **coquette** *Vieilli* coquette

coquetier [kɔktje] *nm* egg-cup; *Fam* **gagner** *ou* **décrocher le c.** to hit the jackpot

coquetterie [kɔketri] *nf* **(a)** *(vestimentaire)* consciousness of one's appearance; *(désir de plaire)* coquetry; **avec c.** *(s'habiller)* stylishly **(b)** *Fam* **avoir une c. dans l'œil** to have a cast in one's eye

coquillage [kɔkijaʒ] *nm* (a) *(mollusque)* shellfish (b) *(coque vide)* shell

coquille [kɔkij] *nf* (a) *(de mollusque, d'œuf, de noix)* shell; *Fig* **rentrer dans/sortir de sa c.** to withdraw into/to come out of one's shell; *Fig* **c. de noix** flimsy craft; **c. d'œuf** *(couleur)* eggshell; **c. Saint-Jacques** *Culin* scallop; *(coquillage)* scallop shell (b) *Typ* misprint

coquillettes [kɔkijɛt] *nfpl* pasta shells

coquin, -e [kɔkɛ̃, -in] **1** *adj (sourire, air)* mischievous; *(sous-vêtement)* naughty; *(histoire)* risqué
2 *nmf (garnement)* rascal

cor [kɔr] *nm* (a) *(instrument)* horn; **c. de chasse** hunting horn; **sonner du c.** to sound *or* blow the horn; *Fig* **réclamer qch à c. et à cri** to clamour for sth (b) *(durillon)* corn

corail, -aux [kɔraj, -o] **1** *nm* coral
2 *adj inv* **(rouge)** c. coral-red

Coran [kɔrɑ̃] *nm* **le C.** the Koran

coranique [kɔranik] *adj* Koranic

corbeau, -x [kɔrbo] *nm* (a) *(oiseau)* crow (b) *(auteur de lettres anonymes)* poison-pen letter writer

corbeille [kɔrbɛj] *nf* (a) *(panier)* basket; **c. à linge** laundry basket; **c. de mariage** wedding presents; **c. à ouvrage** workbasket; **c. à pain** breadbasket; **c. à papier** wastepaper basket (b) *(à la Bourse de Paris)* trading floor (c) *Th* dress circle (d) *Ordinat* wastebasket, *Am* trash

corbillard [kɔrbijar] *nm* hearse

cordage [kɔrdaʒ] *nm* (*corde*) rope; *(d'une raquette)* stringing; *Naut* **cordages** rigging

corde [kɔrd] *nf* (a) *(lien)* rope; **échelle de c.** rope ladder; **c. à linge** clothes *or* washing line; **c. lisse** climbing rope; **c. à nœuds** knotted climbing rope; **c. raide** tightrope; *Fig* **être sur la c. raide** to be walking a tightrope; **c. à sauter** *Br* skipping rope, *Am* jump-rope (b) *(d'instrument, de raquette)* string; **les cordes** *(d'un orchestre)* the strings; *Fig* **avoir plus d'une c. à son arc** to have more than one string to one's bow; *Fig* **j'ai dû toucher la c. sensible** I must have touched a raw nerve (c) *Sp* **tenir la c.** *(coureur)* to be on the inside; *(cheval)* to hug the rails; **les cordes** *(d'un ring)* the ropes (d) *Anat* **cordes vocales** vocal cords; *Fig* **ce n'est pas dans mes cordes** it's not in my line

cordeau, -x [kɔrdo] *nm* (*corde*) string; *Fig* **tiré au c.** as straight as a die

cordée [kɔrde] *nf (d'alpinistes)* roped party; **premier de c.** leader

cordelette [kɔrdəlɛt] *nf* cord

cordelière [kɔrdəljɛr] *nf (ceinture)* cord

cordial, -e, -aux, -ales [kɔrdjal, -o] **1** *adj (accueil, personne)* cordial
2 *nm (médicament)* tonic

cordialement [kɔrdjalmɑ̃] *adv* cordially; **détester c. qn** to heartily dislike sb; **bien c.** *(dans une lettre)* best wishes

cordier [kɔrdje] *nm (de violon)* tailpiece

cordillère [kɔrdijɛr] *nf* mountain range; **la c. des Andes** the Andes

cordon [kɔrdɔ̃] *nm* (a) *(lien)* cord, string; *Fig* **tenir les cordons de la bourse** to hold the purse-strings; *Anat* **c. ombilical** umbilical cord; *aussi Fig* **couper le c. (ombilical)** to cut the umbilical cord (b) *(de policiers, de soldats)* cordon

cordon-bleu (*pl* **cordons-bleus**) [kɔrdɔ̃blø] *nm Fam* cordon bleu (cook)

cordonnerie [kɔrdɔnri] *nf* (a) *(métier)* shoe-repairing (b) *(boutique)* shoe repairer's (shop)

cordonnier, -ère [kɔrdɔnje, -ɛr] *nm,f* shoe repairer; *Prov* **les cordonniers sont toujours les plus mal chaussés** the shoemaker's wife is always the worst shod

Corée [kɔre] *nf* **la C. du Nord/du Sud** North/South Korea

coréen, -enne [kɔreɛ̃, -ɛn] **1** *adj* Korean
2 *nm,f* **C.** Korean

Corfou [kɔrfu] *nf* Corfu

coriace [kɔrjas] *adj* (a) *(viande)* tough (b) *(personne, adversaire)* tough

coriandre [kɔrjɑ̃dr] *nf* coriander

Corinthe [kɔrɛ̃t] *n voir* raisin

cormoran [kɔrmɔrɑ̃] *nm* cormorant

corne [kɔrn] *nf* (a) *(d'animal)* horn; **c. d'abondance** horn of plenty, cornucopia; **c. de brume** foghorn; **la C. de l'Afrique** the Horn of Africa (b) *(matériau)* horn; **peigne de c.** horn comb (c) *(d'un croissant)* end; **faire une c. à une page** to turn down the corner of a page (d) *(aux pieds, aux mains)* hard skin

corned-beef [kɔrnbif] *nm* corned beef

cornée [kɔrne] *nf* cornea

cornéen, -enne [kɔrneɛ̃, -ɛn] *adj* corneal

corneille [kɔrnɛj] *nf* crow

cornemuse [kɔrnəmyz] *nf* bagpipes

corner[1] [kɔrne] *vt* (a) *(page)* to turn down the corner of; *(abîmer)* to make dog-eared (b) *Fam* **c. qch aux oreilles de qn** to shout sth into sb's ear

corner[2] [kɔrnɛr] *nm (au football)* corner; **tirer un c.** to take a corner

cornet [kɔrne] *nm (de papier)* cone; *(de marrons, de frites)* cornet; **mettre les mains en c.** to cup one's hands together; **c. (à pistons)** cornet; **c. de glace** ice cream cone *or Br* cornet

cornette [kɔrnɛt] *nf (coiffe)* cornet

cornettiste [kɔrnetist] *nmf* cornetist

corn flakes [kɔrnflɛks] *nmpl* cornflakes

corniaud [kɔrnjo] *nm* (a) *(chien)* mongrel (b) *Fam (personne)* twit

corniche [kɔrniʃ] *nf* (a) *(de bâtiment)* cornice (b) *(de rochers)* ledge; *(de glace, de neige)* cornice; **(route de) c.** coast road

cornichon [kɔrniʃɔ̃] *nm* gherkin

Cornouailles [kɔrnwaj] *nf* **la C.** Cornwall

cornu, -e [kɔrny] *adj (animal, diable)* horned

corollaire [kɔrɔlɛr] *nm (suite)* consequence

corolle [kɔrɔl] *nf* corolla

coron [kɔrɔ̃] *nm* mining village

coronaire [kɔrɔnɛr] *adj* coronary

coronarien, -enne [kɔrɔnarjɛ̃, -ɛn] *adj* coronary

corporation [kɔrpɔrasjɔ̃] *nf* corporate body

corporatiste [kɔrpɔratist] *adj* corporatist

corporel, -elle [kɔrpɔrɛl] *adj (punition)* corporal; *(besoins)* bodily; *(hygiène)* personal

corps [kɔr] *nm* (a) *(organisme)* body; **trembler de tout son c.** to tremble all over; **lutter c. à c.** to fight hand to hand; *Fig* **faire qch à son c.** défendant to do sth reluctantly; *Fig* **se jeter à c. perdu dans qch** to throw oneself into sth; *Fig* **se donner c. et âme à qn/qch** to give oneself body and soul to sb/sth (b) *(cadavre)* body, corpse (c) *Chim & Phys* body; *Astron* **c. céleste** heavenly body; **c. composé** compound; **c. gras** fat; **c. simple** element (d) *(consistance)* body; **avoir du c.** *(vin)* to have body; *Fig* **prendre c.** *(projet, idée)* to take shape (e) *(partie principale)* main part; *(d'un texte)* body; *Naut* **perdu c. et biens** lost with all hands; **jur le c. du délit** the corpus delicti (f) *(groupe)* **c. d'armée** army corps; **c. de ballet** corps de ballet; **c. diplomatique** diplomatic corps; **c. électoral** electorate; **plaisanterie de c. de garde** barrackroom joke; **le c. médical** the medical profession; **c. de métier** trade; *Hist* corporation; **les grands c. de l'État** = the highest sections of the French administration *(Conseil d'État, Cour des comptes etc)*

corpulence [kɔrpylɑ̃s] *nf* stoutness, corpulence

corpulent, -e [kɔrpylɑ̃, -ɑ̃t] *adj* stout, corpulent

corpus [kɔrpys] *nm Jur & Ling* corpus

corpuscule [kɔrpyskyl] *nm* corpuscle

correct, -e [kɔrekt] *adj* (a) *(sans fautes)* correct (b) *(courtois)* *(personne)* correct; **cela n'est pas c. de sa part** that's not right of him; **elle a été correcte avec moi** she behaved properly towards me (c) *Fam (acceptable)* *(repas, travail, salaire)* reasonable

correctement [kɔrektəmɑ̃] *adv* (a) *(sans faire d'erreur, décemment)* correctly (b) *Fam (de façon acceptable)* reasonably; **gagner c. sa vie** to make a reasonable living

correcteur, -trice [kɔrektœr, -tris] 1 *nm,f* *(de copies d'examen)* examiner; *(en typographie)* proofreader; *(dans la presse)* copy reader
2 *nm Ordinat* checker; **c. liquide** correcting fluid; *Ordinat* **c. d'orthographe** *ou* **orthographique** spellchecker
3 *adj* (verres) correcting

correction [kɔreksjɔ̃] *nf* (a) *(d'une faute)* correction; *Scol (d'un exercice)* correcting, marking; *Typ (d'épreuves)* proofreading (b) *(punition)* beating (c) *(décence, courtoisie)* correctness

correctionnel, -elle [kɔreksjɔnɛl] *Jur* 1 *adj* **peine correctionnelle** = penalty of more than five days' (but less than five years') imprisonment; **tribunal c.** criminal court
2 *nf* **correctionnelle** criminal court; **passer en correctionnelle** to go before the criminal court

corrélation [kɔrelasjɔ̃] *nf* correlation

correspondance [kɔrespɔ̃dɑ̃s] *nf* (a) *(lettres, échange de lettres)* correspondence (b) *(entre trains, avions)* connection; **assurer la c. avec...** *(train, bateau)* to connect with... (c) *(entre deux choses)* correspondence; *(d'idées, de principes)* conformity

correspondant, -e [kɔrespɔ̃dɑ̃, -ɑ̃t] 1 *adj* corresponding (à to)
2 *nm,f* (a) *(journaliste)* correspondent; **c. de guerre** war correspondent; **c. permanent à Londres** London correspondent (b) *(au téléphone)* caller; *(par lettre)* pen-friend; **le numéro de votre c. a changé** *(au téléphone)* the number you have dialled has been changed

correspondre [kɔrespɔ̃dr] *vi* (a) *(être conforme, équivaloir)* **c. à qch** to correspond to sth; **les vis et les écrous qui correspondent** the screws and the nuts that go with them (b) *(par lettres)* **c. avec qn** to correspond with sb

corrida [kɔrida] *nf* bullfight; *Fam (problèmes)* hassle, *Br* carry-on

corridor [kɔridɔr] *nm* corridor

corrigé, -e [kɔriʒe] 1 *adj* corrected; **en données corrigées des variations saisonnières** seasonally adjusted
2 *nm Scol (d'un exercice)* correct answers (**de** to); *(à la fin d'un ouvrage)* key

corriger [45] [kɔriʒe] 1 *vt* (a) *(erreur, faute d'orthographe, myopie, défauts)* to correct; *(exercice, examen)* to correct, to mark; *(épreuves typographiques)* to read; *(article de journal)* to sub-edit; **c. qn de qch** to cure sb of sth (b) *(pour punir)* **c. qn** to give sb a beating
2 **se corriger** *vpr (personne)* to mend one's ways; **se c. de qch** to cure oneself of sth

corroborer [kɔrɔbɔre] *vt* to corroborate

corroder [kɔrɔde] *vt* to corrode

corrompre [kɔrɔ̃pr] *vt* (a) *(personne, goût)* to corrupt (b) *(soudoyer)* to bribe

corrompu, -e [kɔrɔ̃py] *adj* corrupt

corrosif, -ive [kɔrozif, -iv] *adj* corrosive; *Fig (propos, humour)* caustic

corrosion [kɔrozjɔ̃] *nf (d'un métal)* corrosion

corruption [kɔrypsjɔ̃] *nf (perversion)* corruption; *(fait de soudoyer)* bribery

corsage [kɔrsaʒ] *nm* blouse

corsaire [kɔrsɛr] 1 *nm* (a) *Hist (navire, homme)* corsair (b) *(pantalon)* breeches
2 *adj* **pantalon c.** breeches

Corse [kɔrs] *nf* **la C.** Corsica

corse [kɔrs] 1 *adj* Corsican
2 *nmf* **C.** Corsican
3 *nm (langue)* Corsican

corsé, -e [kɔrse] *adj (vin)* full-bodied; *(sauce, plat)* spicy; *(café)* full-flavoured; *Fig (histoire)* spicy

corser [kɔrse] 1 *vt (plat)* to spice up; *Fig (récit)* to liven up
2 **se corser** *vpr (intrigue)* to thicken; **ça se corse** things are getting complicated

corset [kɔrsɛ] *nm* corset; **c. orthopédique** surgical corset

cortège [kɔrtɛʒ] *nm* procession; *Fig* **la vie de famille et son c. de problèmes** family life and its attendant problems; **c. funèbre** funeral cortège

cortex [kɔrtɛks] *nm Anat & Bot* cortex

corticoïde [kɔrtikɔid] *nm* corticoid

cortisone [kɔrtizon] *nf* cortisone

corvée [kɔrve] *nf* (a) *(obligation pénible)* chore; **je suis de c. de vaisselle ce soir** I'm on washing-up duty tonight; **quelle c.!** what a drag! (b) *Mil* fatigue duty; **être de c.** to be on fatigue duty (c) *Hist* corvée

corvette [kɔrvɛt] *nf* corvette

coryza [kɔriza] *nm* head cold, *Spéc* coryza

cosaque [kɔzak] *nm* cossack

cosignataire [kɔsiɲatɛr] *adj & nmf* cosignatory

cosinus [kɔsinys] *nm* cosine

cosmétique [kɔsmetik] *adj & nm* cosmetic

cosmique [kɔsmik] *adj* cosmic

cosmologie [kɔsmɔlɔʒi] *nf* cosmology

cosmonaute [kɔsmɔnot] *nmf* cosmonaut

cosmopolite [kɔsmɔpɔlit] *adj* cosmopolitan

cosmos [kɔsmos] *nm (univers)* cosmos; *(espace)* outer space

cosse [kɔs] *nf (de petits pois)* pod

cossu, -e [kɔsy] *adj (maison, intérieur)* opulent; *(personne)* well-to-do

costard [kɔstar] *nm Fam* suit

Costa Rica [kɔstarika] *nm* le C. Costa Rica

costaud, -e [kɔsto, -od] **1** *adj (fort, solide)* sturdy **2** *nm,f* sturdy man, *f* woman

costume [kɔstym] *nm (habit)* costume; *(complet)* suit

costumé, -e [kɔstyme] *adj voir* **bal**

costumier, -ère [kɔstymje, -ɛr] *nm,f (de théâtre)* wardrobe master, *f* wardrobe mistress; *(de cinéma)* costume supervisor

cotation [kɔtasjɔ̃] *nf* c. **(en Bourse)** quotation (on the Stock Exchange)

cote [kɔt] *nf (a) (d'une action) (valeur)* quotation; *(liste)* share index; *(d'un cheval)* odds; **c. de popularité** popularity rating; *Fam* **avoir la c.** (avec ou auprès de) to be popular (with) **(b)** *(servant à classer)* classification mark **(c)** *(altitude)* altitude; **atteindre la c. d'alerte** *(fleuve)* to reach danger level; *Fig* to reach crisis point

coté, -e [kɔte] *adj (a) (estimé)* **bien/très/mal c.** highly/very highly/not highly thought of **(b)** **action cotée en Bourse** share quoted on the Stock Exchange; **être c. à 100 francs** to be trading at 100 francs; **être c. à l'argus** to be listed in the car buyer's guide

côte [kot] *nf (a) (os)* rib; **c. à c.** side by side; *Fam* **on lui voit les côtes** he's nothing but skin and bone; **c. d'agneau/de porc** lamb/pork chop; **c. de bœuf** rib of beef **(b)** *(de melon, de feuille)* rib; **tissu à côtes** ribbed material **(c)** *(d'une montagne)* slope; **monter/descendre une c.** to go up/down a hill **(d)** *(rivage)* coast; **la C. (d'Azur)** the (French) Riviera

côté [kote] *nm (a) (du corps humain)* side; **couché sur le c.** lying on one's side; *Fig* **être aux côtés de qn** to be at sb's side

(b) *(d'une route, d'un triangle, d'une feuille)* side; **de l'autre c. (de qch)** on the other side (of sth); **siège c. couloir/fenêtre** aisle/window seat; *Th* **c. jardin/cour** on stage left/right

(c) *(aspect)* side; **il a de bons côtés** he's got a good side to him; **prendre la vie du bon c.** to look on the bright side of life

(d) *(endroit)* **de tous côtés** on all sides; *(affluer)* from all directions; **du c. de** *(près de)* near; **ils s'en allèrent chacun de son c.** they went their separate ways; **de quel c.?** *(direction)* which way?; *(position)* which side?; *Fig* **être du c. de qn** to be on sb's side; **ma tante du c. maternel** my aunt on my mother's side; **d'un c...., d'un autre c....** on the one hand..., on the other hand...

(e) *Fam (en ce qui concerne)* **c. argent, ça va** things are OK moneywise; **de ce c., il n'y a rien à craindre** there's nothing to worry about on that score

(f) **à c.** *(près)* nearby; **à c. de** *(près de)* next to; *(comparé à)* compared with; **les voisins d'à c.** the next-door neighbours; **à c. l'un de l'autre** side by side; *Fig* **passer à c. de qch** to miss out on sth

(g) **faire un saut de c.** to leap to one side or aside; *Fig* **mettre qch de c.** to put sth aside; *Fig* **laisser qn/qch de c.** to leave sb/sth out

coteau, -x [kɔto] *nm (versant)* hillside; *(colline)* hill

Côte d'Ivoire [kotdivwar] *nf* la C. the Ivory Coast

côtelé, -e [kotle] *adj voir* **velours**

côtelette [kotlɛt, kɔtlɛt] *nf* chop; **c. d'agneau/de porc** lamb/pork chop

coter [kɔte] *vt (a) (prix, actions)* to quote **(b)** *(documents)* to classify

côtier, -ère [kotje, -ɛr] *adj (fleuve, navigation)* coastal; *(pêche)* inshore

cotillon [kɔtijɔ̃] *nm* **accessoires de c., cotillons** party novelties

cotisation [kɔtizasjɔ̃] *nf (a) (à une caisse)* contribution; **cotisations de Sécurité Sociale** ≃ National Insurance contributions **(b)** *(à un club)* subscription

cotiser [kɔtize] **1** *vi (à une caisse de retraite, à une mutuelle)* to contribute (à to) **2 se cotiser** *vpr* to club together

coton [kɔtɔ̃] **1** *nm (a) (plante, tissu)* cotton; **chemise 100% c.** 100% cotton shirt; *Fam* **filer un mauvais c.** *(financièrement, physiquement)* to be in a bad way **(b)** **c. (hydrophile)** *Br* cotton wool, *Am* absorbent cotton; **un c.** a piece of *Br* cotton wool *or Am* absorbent cotton; *Fig* **élever un enfant dans du c.** to wrap a child in cotton wool; *Fam* **j'ai les jambes en c.** my legs feel like jelly **2** *adj Fam* tough, tricky

cotonnade [kɔtɔnad] *nf* cotton fabric

cotonneux, -euse [kɔtɔnø, -øz] *adj (feuille)* downy; *(nuage)* fluffy; *(fruit)* mushy

Coton-Tige® *(pl* **Cotons-Tiges)** [kɔtɔ̃tiʒ] *nm* cotton bud

côtoyer [32] [kotwaje] *vt (a) (personnes)* to mix with **(b)** *(rivière, forêt)* to border on

cotte [kɔt] *nf* **c. de mailles** coat of mail

cou [ku] *nm* neck; **tendre le c.** to crane one's neck; **avoir un c. de taureau** to have a neck like a bull; **se jeter au c. de qn** to throw one's arms round sb's neck; *Fam* **endetté jusqu'au c.** up to one's eyes in debt

couac [kwak] *nm (fausse note)* false note; *Fig* discordant note; **faire un c.** to play a false note; *(chanteur)* to sing a false note

couchage [kuʃaʒ] *nm voir* **sac**

couchant, -e [kuʃɑ̃, -ɑ̃t] **1** *adj* **le soleil c.** the setting sun **2** *nm (ouest)* west; **dans la direction du c.** in a westerly direction

couche [kuʃ] *nf (a) (de peinture)* coat; *(de beurre, de crème, de poussière)* layer; *(classe sociale)* level; *Géol* layer, stratum; **la c. d'ozone** the ozone layer; *Fam* **il en tient une c.!** he's really stupid! **(b)** *(de bébé) Br* nappy, *Am* diaper **(c)** *Vieilli* **femme en couches** woman in labour; **mourir en couches** to die in childbirth **(d)** *Lit (lit)* bed

couché, -e [kuʃe] *adj (a) (allongé)* lying (down); *(au lit)* in bed **(b)** *(écriture)* slanting, sloping

couche-culotte *(pl* **couches-culottes)** [kuʃkylɔt] *nf* disposable *Br* nappy *or Am* diaper

coucher¹ [kuʃe] *nm (a) (fait d'aller au lit)* **l'heure du c.** bedtime **(b)** *(gîte)* accommodation **(c)** *(du soleil)* setting; **un superbe c. de soleil** a magnificent sunset; **au c. du soleil** at sunset

coucher² [kuʃe] *vt (a) (mettre au lit)* **c. qn** to put sb to bed **(b)** *(allonger, poser)* to lay down **(c)** *(écrire)* **c. qn sur testament** to mention sb in one's will

2 *vi (a) (passer la nuit)* to sleep; *Fig* **c. sous les ponts** to sleep rough **(b)** *Fam* **c. avec qn** to sleep with sb; **c. ensemble** to sleep together **(c)** *(à un chien)* **couché!** (lie) down!

3 se coucher *vpr (a) (au lit)* to go to bed; **aller se c.** to go to bed; *Fam* **se c. avec les poules** to go to bed early; *Prov* **comme on fait son lit, on se couche** as we make our bed, so we must lie in it (**b**) *(s'allonger)* to lie down; **se c. à plat ventre** to lie flat on one's stomach (**c**) **se c. sur le flanc** *(navire)* to keel over (**d**) *(soleil, lune)* to set, to go down

coucheries [kuʃri] *nf Fam* sleeping around

couchette [kuʃɛt] *nf (de navire)* bunk; *(de train)* couchette

coucheur [kuʃœr] *nm Fam* **c'est un mauvais c.** he's an awkward customer

couci-couça [kusikusa] *adv Fam* so-so

coucou [kuku] **1** *nm* (**a**) *(oiseau)* cuckoo (**b**) *(horloge)* cuckoo clock (**c**) *(plante)* cowslip (**d**) *Fam (avion)* old crate
2 *exclam (langage enfantin)* peekaboo!; *(bonjour)* cooee!

coude [kud] *nm* (**a**) *(articulation)* elbow; **être au c. à c.** to be neck and neck; **jouer des coudes** to push and shove; *Fig* to manœuvre; *Fig* **se serrer les coudes** to stick together; *Fig* **garder qch sous le c.** to hold on to sth; *Fam* **lever le c.** to booze (**b**) *(tournant)* sharp bend; *(de barre, de tuyau)* bend; *(d'arbre)* crank

coudé, -e [kude] *adj* bent

coudée [kude] *nf* **avoir les coudées franches** to have plenty of elbow room

cou-de-pied *(pl* **cous-de-pied)** [kudapje] *nm* instep

coudre [21] [kudr] *vt (ourlet)* to sew; *(bouton)* to sew on; *(deux morceaux d'étoffe)* to sew together; *(jupe, plaie)* to sew up; **c. un bouton à une robe** to sew a button on a dress; **je ne sais pas c.** I can't sew

coudrier [kudrije] *nm* hazel (tree)

couenne [kwan] *nf* rind

couette[1] [kwet] *nf (édredon)* duvet, continental quilt

couette[2] *nf (coiffure)* bunch; **se faire des couettes** to put one's hair in bunches

couille [kuj] *nf Vulg (testicule)* ball; *(problème)* balls-up

couillon, -onne [kujɔ̃, -ɔn] *nm, f très Fam* twat

couillonner [kujɔne] *vt très Fam (personne)* to con; **se faire c.** to be conned

couiner [kwine] *vi (animal)* to squeak; *(enfant)* to whine

coulant, -e [kulɑ̃, -ɑ̃t] *adj (fromage)* runny; *Fig (style)* flowing; *Fam (personne)* easy-going

coulée [kule] *nf* **c. de boue** mudslide; **c. de lave** lava flow

coulemelle [kulmɛl] *nf* parasol mushroom

couler [kule] **1** *vt* (**a**) *(liquide, cire, ciment)* to pour; *(métal, statue)* to cast (**b**) *(navire)* to sink; *Fig* **c. qn** to bring sb down (**c**) *(passer)* **c. des jours heureux** to lead a happy life; *Fam* **se la c. douce** to take things easy
2 *vi* (**a**) *(liquide, rivière)* to flow, to run; *(fromage, maquillage)* to run; **la sueur coule sur son front** sweat is trickling down his/her forehead; **cette affaire a fait c. beaucoup d'encre** a lot has been written about this affair; **faire c. un bain à qn** to run a bath for sb; *Fig* **c. de source** to be obvious (**b**) *(navire)* to sink, to go down; *(entreprise)* to go under (**c**) *(tonneau, stylo)* to leak; *(nez)* to run; **avoir le nez qui coule** to have a runny nose
3 se couler *vpr (se glisser)* to slip

couleur [kulœr] **1** *nf* (**a**) *(teinte, orientation politique)* colour; **de quelle c. est...?** what colour is...?; **de c.** coloured; **télévision/photographie en c.** *ou* **couleurs** colour television/photography; **les couleurs** *(linge)* coloureds; *Fig* **pour faire c. locale** to add a bit of local colour; *Fam* **elle nous en a fait voir de toutes les couleurs** she gave us a hard time; *Fam* **je n'en ai pas encore vu la c.** I've seen no sign of it yet (**b**) *(teint)*

prendre des couleurs to get some colour in one's cheeks (**c**) *Mil* **couleurs** *(drapeau)* colours (**d**) **couleurs** *(d'un club, d'une écurie)* colours; **défendre les couleurs de** to represent (**e**) *(peinture)* paint; **une boîte de couleurs** a paintbox (**f**) *(aux cartes)* suit; **annoncer la c.** to call (trumps); *Fam* to lay one's cards on the table (**g**) *(en coiffure)* dye; **se faire une c.** *(soi-même)* to dye one's hair; *(chez le coiffeur)* to have one's hair dyed
2 *adj inv (télévision, pellicule)* colour; **une chevelure c. de feu** flame-coloured hair

couleuvre [kulœvr] *nf* **c. (à collier)** grass snake; *Fig* **avaler des couleuvres** *(se faire humilier)* to eat humble pie; *(être naïf)* to swallow anything

coulis [kuli] *nm* **c. de tomates/framboises** tomato/raspberry coulis

coulissant, -e [kulisɑ̃, -ɑ̃t] *adj* sliding

coulisse [kulis] *nf* (**a**) *(glissière)* runner; **porte à c.** sliding door (**b**) *Th* **les coulisses** the wings; **en coulisses, dans les coulisses** in the wings; *Fig* behind the scenes

coulisser [kulise] *vi* to slide

couloir [kulwar] *nm* (**a**) *(de maison)* corridor, passage; *(de train)* corridor; *(en athlétisme, en natation)* lane; *(au tennis) Br* tramlines, *Am* alley; **c. aérien** air corridor; **c. d'autobus** bus lane (**b**) *Géog* gully

coulommiers [kulɔmje] *nm =* type of soft cheese

coulpe [kulp] *nf* **battre sa c.** to beat one's breast

coup [ku] *nm* (**a**) *(choc)* blow; **donner un c. à qn** to hit sb; **se donner un c. contre qch** to knock against sth; **donner un c. de bâton à qn** to hit sb with a stick; **donner un c. de couteau à qn** to knife sb; **donner un c. de coude à qn** to nudge sb; *Fam* **c. de pied** kick; **donner un c. de pied à qn/qch** to kick sb/sth; **c. de poing** punch; **donner un c. de poing à qn** to punch sb; **c. de poing américain** knuckle-duster; *Fig* **donner un c. de pouce à qn** to push sb; **c. de tête** header; *Fam* **faire qch sur un c. de tête** to do sth on the spur of the moment; **donner un c. de griffe à qn/qch** to claw at sb/sth; **rendre c. pour c.** to give as good as one gets; *Fig* **tous les coups sont permis** there are no holds barred; *Fig* **c'était un c. bas** that was below the belt; *Jur* **coups et blessures** grievous bodily harm

(**b**) *(choc émotionnel)* blow; **faire un c. à qn** to be a blow; **accuser le c.** to show that one has been affected; *Fam* **tenir le c.** to hold out; *Fam* **en prendre un c.** to be devastated; *Fam* **c. dur** a setback

(**c**) *(action soudaine, événement soudain)* **c. de vent** gust of wind; *Fam* **passer en c. de vent** to pay a flying visit; **donner un c. de frein** to brake; **donner un c. de volant** to turn the wheel sharply; **donner un c. d'arrêt à qch** to call a halt to sth; *Fam* **prendre un c. de vieux** to age; *Fam* **avoir un c. de barre** *ou* **de pompe** to have the munchies; **c. de chance** *ou* **c. de pot** stroke of luck; *Fam* **avoir un c. de cœur pour qch** to absolutely love sth; **c. d'État** coup (d'État); **ça a été le c. de foudre** it was love at first sight; **attraper un c. de froid** to catch a cold; *Fam* **pousser un c. de gueule** to yell; *Fam* **un c. de pub** a publicity stunt; **prendre un c. de soleil** to get sunburned; **c. de théâtre** coup de théâtre; *(dans la vie)* sudden turn of events

(**d**) *(bruit)* **c. de feu** shot; **c. de fusil** shot; **c. de sifflet** whistle; **c. de sonnette** ring; **c. de tonnerre** clap of thunder; **tirer deux coups** to fire twice; **l'horloge sonna trois coups** the clock struck three; *Fig* **sur le c. de midi** on the stroke of twelve; **les trois coups** *(au théâtre)* = the three knocks given just before the curtain rises

(e) *(influence)* sous le c. de la colère in a fit of anger; tomber sous le c. de la loi to be an offence

(f) *(essai)* attempt, go; Fig **réussir son** c. to be a great success; **d'un seul** c. in one go; **du premier** c. at the first attempt; Fam **à tous les coups, le patron va nous repérer** the boss is bound to see us; **il n'en est pas à son c. d'essai** it's not the first time he's done it; c. **de maître** masterstroke

(g) *(au golf)* stroke; *(aux échecs)* move; c. **droit** *(au tennis)* forehand; Fig **faire** c. **double** to kill two birds with one stone; c. **d'envoi** *(au football, au rugby)* kickoff; Fig **donner le** c. **d'envoi de qch** to launch sth; c. **franc** *(au football)* free kick; c. **de pied de réparation** penalty kick

(h) Fam *(tour, combine)* **réussir un bon** c. to do well for oneself; **faire un sale** c. **à qn** to play a dirty trick on sb; **être sur un** c. to be on to a good thing; **être dans le** c. *(impliqué)* to be involved; *(à la mode)* to be trendy; **fourré,** c. **de Jarnac** dirty trick; **c. monté** put-up job

(i) Vulg **tirer un** c. to have a screw

(j) *(locutions)* **tout à** c., **tout d'un** c. suddenly, all of a sudden; **à** c. **sûr** for certain, definitely; **au** c. **par** c. step by step; c. **sur** c. one after the other; **après** c. after the event; Fam **du** c. and so; **pleurer un bon** c. to have a good cry; **mourir sur le** c. to die on the spot; **sur le** c., **je n'ai pas compris** at the time I didn't understand; **faire les quatre cents coups** to sow one's wild oats; **donner le** c. **de grâce à qn** to finish sb off; **avoir le** c. **de main (pour faire qch)** to have the knack (of doing sth); **donner un** c. **de main à qn** to give sb a hand; Fam **boire un** c. to have a drink; Fam **avoir un** c. **dans le nez** to be smashed; Fam **valoir le** c. to be worth it; Fam **il va falloir en mettre un** c. we're going to have to pull out all the stops

coupable [kupabl] **1** *adj (personne)* guilty (**de** of); *(action, négligence)* culpable; *(faiblesse)* reprehensible; **se sentir** c. **(de faire qch)** to feel guilty (about doing sth)

2 *nmf* culprit

coupant, -e [kupɑ̃, -ɑ̃t] *adj* sharp

coupe¹ [kup] *nf* (a) *(récipient)* bowl; c. **à champagne** champagne glass; Fig **la** c. **est pleine** that's the limit; Prov **il y a loin de la** c. **aux lèvres** there's many a slip 'twixt cup and lip (b) *(trophée)* cup; **la C. du monde de football** the Football World Cup; **la C. Davis** the Davis Cup

coupe² *nf* (a) *(action) (du blé)* cutting; *(de tissu)* cutting out; *(d'arbres)* cutting down; c. **(de cheveux)** haircut; **acheter du fromage à la** c. to buy cheese from the fresh cheese counter; c. **sombre** *(dans une forêt)* slight thinning; *(du personnel, des dépenses)* drastic (b) *(d'un vêtement)* cut (c) *(plan)* section (d) *(aux cartes)* cut; Fig **être sous la** c. **de qn** to be under sb's thumb

coupé, -e [kupe] **1** *adj* (a) *(taillé)* cut; **un costume mal** c. a badly cut suit (b) *(au tennis)* **une balle coupée** a slice (c) *(castré) (chat)* neutered

2 *nm (voiture)* coupé; c. **sport** sports coupé

coupe-coupe [kupkup] *nm inv* machete

coupe-faim [kupfɛ̃] *nm inv* appetite suppressant

coupe-feu [kupfø] *nm inv* firebreak; **porte** c. fire-door

coupe-gorge [kupgɔrʒ] *nm inv* dangerous back alley

coupe-légumes [kuplegym] *nm inv* vegetable slicer

coupelle [kupɛl] *nf* (a) *(petite coupe)* small dish (b) *(de laboratoire)* cupel

coupe-ongles [kupɔ̃gl] *nm inv* nail clippers

coupe-papier [kuppapje] *nm inv* paper knife, letter opener

couper [kupe] **1** *vt* (a) *(trancher)* to cut; *(arbre)* to cut down; *(vêtement)* to cut out; c. **qch en morceaux** to cut sth up (into pieces); c. **qch en trois** to cut sth into three; c. **les cheveux à qn** to cut sb's hair; c. **la tête à qn** to cut off sb's head; c. **les cheveux en quatre** to split hairs; **un brouillard à** c. **au couteau** fog you could cut with a knife; **j'en donnerais ma main** *ou* **ma tête à** c. I'd stake my life on it

(b) *(supprimer, raccourcir)* to cut; c. **dans le vif** to take drastic measures

(c) *(traverser)* to cut across; c. **la route à qn** to cut in in front of sb; c. **à travers champs** to cut across country; c. **par le jardin** to cut through the garden

(d) *(séparer)* to divide; c. **en deux** (in two); **être coupé du monde** to be cut off from the outside world

(e) *(interrompre) (personne)* to cut in on; *(son)* to turn right down; c. **l'eau** *(pour réparation)* to turn off the water; *(pour non-paiement)* to cut off the water; c. **le courant** *ou* **l'électricité** *(pour réparation)* to switch off the current; *(pour non-paiement)* to cut off the power; c. **le téléphone à qn** to cut off sb's telephone; **nous avons été coupés, la communication a été coupée** we were cut off; c. **le contact** *(d'une voiture)* to switch off the ignition; c. **l'appétit à qn** to spoil sb's appetite; **ces bas me coupent la circulation** these stockings are cutting off my circulation; Fam **ça te la coupe!** that's taken the wind out of your sails!

(f) *(châtrer) (chat)* to neuter

(g) c. **du vin** *(en mélangeant)* to blend wine; *(avec de l'eau)* to water down wine

(h) *(paquet de cartes)* to cut; *(prendre avec l'atout)* to trump; **à toi de** c. it's your turn to cut; c. **à carreau** to trump with a diamond

(i) *(au tennis) (balle)* to slice

2 *vi (être tranchant)* to be sharp

3 couper *vt ind* (a) Fam c. **à qch** *(se dérober)* to get out of sth (b) c. **court à qch** to cut sth short

4 se couper *vpr* (a) *(se blesser)* to cut oneself; **se** c. **le** *ou* **au doigt** to cut one's finger; **se** c. **les veines** to slash one's wrists (b) **se** c. **les ongles/les cheveux** to cut one's nails/hair (c) *(routes)* to intersect, to cross (d) **se** c. **de qn** to cut oneself off from sb

couper-coller [kupekɔle] *nm inv Ordinat* cut and paste

couperet [kupʁɛ] *nm* (a) *(pour la viande)* cleaver (b) *(de la guillotine)* blade

couperose [kupʁoz] *nf* blotches

couperosé, -e [kupʁoze] *adj* blotchy

coupe-vent [kupvɑ̃] *nm inv* (a) *(dispositif)* windbreak (b) *(blouson)* Br windcheater, Am Windbreaker®

couple [kupl] *nm (de personnes)* couple; *(d'animaux)* pair; **vivre en** c. to live together; **un** c. **sans enfants** a childless couple

couplet [kuplɛ] *nm (de chanson)* verse; Fam tirade (**sur** about)

coupole [kupɔl] *nf* dome, cupola

coupon [kupɔ̃] *nm* (a) *(ticket)* c. **de réduction** money-off coupon (b) *(de tissu)* remnant (c) Fin c. **d'action** coupon

coupon-réponse *(pl* **coupons-réponse)** [kupɔ̃repɔ̃s] *nm* reply coupon

coupure [kupyr] *nf* (a) *(blessure)* cut (b) *(suppression)* cut (c) **c. (de courant)** power cut (d) *Fig (séparation)* break (e) **c. de journal** *ou* **de presse** newspaper *or* press cutting (f) *Fin* denomination; **50 000 francs en petites coupures** 50,000 francs in small notes *or* denominations

cour [kur] *nf* (a) *(de maison, de ferme)* yard; **c. d'honneur** main courtyard; **c. de récréation** *Br* playground, *Am* schoolyard (b) *(de souverain)* court; **vivre à la c.** to live at court (c) *(tribunal)* court; **Messieurs, la C.!** all rise!; **Haute C.** High Court *(for impeachment of president or ministers)*; **c. d'appel** court of appeal; **c. d'assises** court of assizes; **c. de cassation** ≃ Supreme Court of Appeal; **la C. des comptes** the Audit Office; **la C. internationale de justice** the International Court of Justice; **c. martiale** court martial; **passer en c. martiale (pour qch)** to be court-martialled (for sth); **Can la C. suprême** the Supreme Court (d) **faire la c. à qn** to court sb

courage [kuraʒ] *nm* courage, bravery; **avec c.** bravely, courageously; **perdre c.** to lose heart; **prendre son c. à deux mains** to pluck up courage; **avoir/se sentir le c. de ses opinions** to have the courage of one's convictions; **avoir/se sentir le c. de faire qch** to be/to feel up to doing sth; **bon c.!** good luck!

courageusement [kuraʒøzmɑ̃] *adv* *(bravement)* courageously, bravely; *(résolument)* with a will

courageux, -euse [kuraʒø, -øz] *adj* (a) *(brave)* courageous, brave (b) *(énergique)* energetic

courailler [kuraje] *vi Can Fam* to chase women

courailleur [kurajœr] *nm Can Fam* womanizer

couramment [kuramɑ̃] *adv* (a) *(parler)* fluently (b) *(généralement)* commonly; **ce mot s'emploie c.** this word is in common use

courant, -e [kurɑ̃, -ɑ̃t] **1** *adj* (a) *(commun)* common; **dans la vie courante** in everyday life (b) *(en cours)* current; **le 5 c.** the 5th inst.

2 *nm* (a) *(dans une rivière)* current; *Fig (tendance)* trend; **suivre/remonter le c.** to go with/against the current; **c. d'air** draught; **c. de pensée** way of thinking (b) *Él* **c. (électrique)** (electric) current; **c. continu/alternatif** direct/alternating current; *Fig* **le c. ne passe pas** we're/they're/you're not on the same wavelength (c) *(durée)* **dans le c. de** in the course of; **c. janvier** during the month of January (d) **être au c. (de qch)** to know (about sth); **mettre qn au c. (de qch)** to tell sb (about sth); **tenir qn au c. (de qch)** to keep sb up-to-date (on sth)

3 *nf courante Fam* **avoir la courante** to have the runs

courbatu, -e [kurbaty] *adj* aching (all over)

courbature [kurbatyr] *nf* ache; **avoir des courbatures** to be aching (all over)

courbaturé, -e [kurbatyre] *adj* aching (all over)

courbe [kurb] **1** *adj* curved

2 *nf* curve; *(graphe)* graph; **c. de niveau** contour (line); **c. des prix/des salaires** price/salary curve; **c. de température** temperature curve

courber [kurbe] **1** *vt* to bend; **c. la tête** to bow *or* bend one's head; *Fig* **c. l'échine** to submit

2 *vi* to bend

3 se courber *vpr (personne)* to bend down, to stoop; **c. en deux** to bend double

courbette [kurbɛt] *nf (salut)* bow; *Fig* **faire des courbettes (à qn)** to bow and scrape (to sb)

courbure [kurbyr] *nf (d'une surface, d'une ligne)* curvature; *(d'un morceau de bois, du dos)* curve

coureur, -euse [kurœr, -øz] **1** *nm,f (à pied)* runner; **c. (automobile)** (racing) driver; **c. (cycliste)** (racing) cyclist

2 *adj (homme)* womanizing; *(femme)* manhunting

3 *nm* **c. (de jupons)** womanizer

4 *nf* **coureuse** *(dévergondée)* manhunter

courge [kurʒ] *nf* (a) *(plante)* *Br* marrow, *Am* squash (b) *Fam (imbécile)* wally

courgette [kurʒɛt] *nf Br* courgette, *Am* zucchini

courir [22] [kurir] **1** *vi* (a) *(personne)* to run; **monter/descendre la colline en courant** to run up/down the hill; **arriver en courant** to come running (up); **je cours le prévenir** I'll run and warn him; **c. après qn/qch** to run after sb/sth; **c. après la gloire** to chase after glory; **c. à sa perte** to be heading for disaster; **l'assassin court toujours** the murderer is still at large; **ça ne court pas les rues** *(personnes)* they're not thick on the ground; *(objets)* you don't see that every day; *Fam* **tu peux toujours c.!** not a chance!; *Fam* **laisse c.!** forget it!; *Prov* **rien ne sert de c., il faut partir à point** slow and steady wins the race (b) *(se propager)* **le bruit court que...** rumour has it that...; **faire c. un bruit** to spread a rumour (c) *(eau, ruisseau)* to rush (d) *(participer à une course)* *(à pied)* to run; *(automobile)* to drive; *(cycliste)* to ride

2 *vt (tenter)* **c. un risque** to run a risk (b) *Sp* **c. le 100 mètres** to run the 100 metres (c) *(parcourir, fréquenter)* **c. le monde** to roam the world; **c. les théâtres** to go to the theatre all the time (d) *(chasser)* **c. les filles** to chase women; *Fig* **c. deux lièvres à la fois** to have two irons in the fire

3 *v impersonnel* **il court des bruits sur lui** there are rumours going round about him

courlis [kurli] *nm* curlew

couronne [kuron] *nf* (a) *(de fleurs, de lauriers)* wreath; **c. funéraire** *ou* **mortuaire** funeral wreath; *(de souverain)* crown; *(de noble)* coronet; **la C. de France** the French Crown (c) *(monnaie)* crown (d) *(pain)* ring-shaped loaf; *(de dent)* crown; **se faire poser une c.** to have a tooth crowned

couronnement [kuronmɑ̃] *nm (de souverain)* coronation; *Fig (réussite)* crowning achievement

couronner [kurone] *vt* (a) *(sacrer)* to crown; *Fig* **mes efforts furent couronnés de succès** my efforts were crowned with success; **et pour c. le tout...** and to crown it all... (b) *(dent)* to crown

courra *etc voir* **courir**

courre [kur] *voir* **chasse**

courrier [kurje] *nm* (a) *(lettres)* mail, *Br* post; **c. électronique** electronic mail, e-mail; **c. interne** internal mail (b) *Journ* **c. du cœur** problem page; **c. des lecteurs** letters to the Editor (c) *Vieilli (messager)* courier

courroie [kurwa] *nf (de cuir, de toile)* strap (b) *Méc* belt; **c. de transmission** driving belt; **c. de ventilateur** fanbelt

courroucé, -e [kuruse] *adj Litt* incensed

courroux [kuru] *nm Litt* ire, wrath

cours¹ [kur] *nm* (a) *(leçon)* *Univ* lecture; *Scol* lesson; *(ensemble des leçons)* course; **aller en c.** *Univ* to go to lectures; *Scol* to go to school; **prendre ou suivre un c.** to take or do a course; **donner des c.** *Univ* to give lectures; *Scol* to give classes; **c. par correspondance** correspondence course; **c. intensif** crash course; **c. magistral** lecture; **c. particulier** private lesson; **c. du soir** evening class (b) *(classe)* **c. élémentaire** = second and third years of primary school; **c. moyen** = fourth and fifth years of primary school; **c. préparatoire** = first year of primary school **(c)** *(de rivière, d'un astre)* course; **suivre la c. de ses pensées** to follow one's train of thought; **donner libre c. à qch** to give free rein to sth; **c. d'eau** waterway **(d)** *(évolution)* course; **suivre son c.** to run its course; **en c.** *(affaires)* in hand; *(travaux)* in progress, *(année)* current; **en c. de route** on the way; **au c. de qch** in the course of sth **(e)** *(d'une monnaie)* currency; **avoir c.** *(monnaie)* to be legal tender; *(pratique)* to be current **(f)** *Fin (d'une action)* price; *(de devises)* rate; **c. des changes** exchange rates

cours² *voir* **courir**

course [kurs] *nf* **(a)** *Sp (épreuve)* race; *(discipline)* racing; **les courses** *(de chevaux)* the races; *Fam* **ça va encore être la c.** it's going to be another mad rush; **la c. aux armements** the arms race; **c. automobile** motor race; *(discipline)* motor racing; **c. de chevaux** horse race; *Sp & Fig* **c. contre la montre** race against the clock; **c. cycliste** cycle race; **c. de haies** *(en athlétisme)* hurdles; *(course de chevaux)* steeplechase; **c. d'obstacles** steeplechase; **c. à pied** race; *(discipline)* running; **c. de taureaux** *(corrida)* bullfight **(b)** *(action de courir)* running **(c)** *(achat)* **faire une c.** to get something from the shops; **courses** shopping; **faire des courses** to go shopping **(d)** *(trajet en taxi)* journey; *(prix)* fare **(e)** *(de planète, de projectile)* course

courser [kurse] *vt Fam* to chase after

coursier, -ère [kursje, -er] *nm,f* messenger; *(en moto)* motorcycle courier

coursive [kursiv] *nf Naut* gangway

court¹, -e [kur, kurt] **1** *adj* short; *Fam* **100 francs, c'est un peu c.** 100 francs, it's not very much

2 *adv* short; **pour faire c.** to cut a long story short; **on l'appelle Charles tout c.** people just call him Charles; **prendre qn de c.** *(en lui laissant peu de temps)* to give sb short notice; *(sans le prévenir)* to catch sb unawares; **à c. de** short of

court² *nm* **c.** *(de tennis)* (tennis) court

court³ *voir* **courir**

court-bouillon *(pl* **courts-bouillons)** [kurbujõ] *nm* court-bouillon

court-circuit *(pl* **courts-circuits)** [kursirkųi] *nm* short circuit

court-circuiter [kursirkųite] *vt El & Fam Fig* to short-circuit

courtier, -ère [kurtje, -er] *nm,f* broker; **c. d'assurances** insurance broker

courtisan [kurtizã] *nm* **(a)** *Hist* courtier **(b)** *Péj (flatteur)* sycophant

courtisane [kurtizan] *nf Litt* courtesan

courtiser [kurtize] *vt* **(a)** *(femme)* to court **(b)** *(flatter)* to fawn on

courtois, -e [kurtwa, -az] *adj (poli)* courteous **(envers ou avec** towards)

courtoisement [kurtwazmã] *adv* courteously

courtoisie [kurtwazi] *nf* courtesy **(envers** towards)

court-vêtu, -e *(mpl* **court-vêtus,** *fpl* **court-vêtues)** [kurvety] *adj* in a short skirt; **être c.** to be wearing a short skirt

couru, -e [kury] *adj* **(a)** *(lieu, spectacle)* popular **(b)** *Fam* **c'est c.** *(d'avance)* it's a sure thing

cousais *etc voir* **coudre**

couscous [kuskus] *nm* couscous

cousin¹, -e [kuzɛ̃, -in] *nm,f* cousin; **c. germain** first cousin

cousin² *nm (insecte)* mosquito

coussin [kusɛ̃] *nm* **(a)** *(de siège)* cushion; *Belg (oreiller)* pillow **(b)** **c. d'air** air cushion

coussinet [kusine] *nm* **(a)** *(coussin)* small cushion **(b)** *(d'animal)* pad

cousu¹, -e [kuzy] *adj* sewn; **c.** *(à la)* **main** hand-sewn; *Fam Fig* **c'est du c.** main it's first-rate; **une histoire cousue de fil blanc** a blatant lie

cousu², -e *voir* **coudre**

coût [ku] *nm aussi Fig* cost; **le c. de la vie** the cost of living

coûtant [kutã] *adj m voir* **prix**

couteau, -x [kuto] *nm* **(a)** *(ustensile)* knife; **être à couteaux tirés (avec qn)** to be at daggers drawn (with sb); *Fig* **avoir le c. sous la gorge** to have a gun at one's head; **c. de cuisine** kitchen knife; **c. à fromage** cheese-knife; **c. à pain** breadknife **(b)** *(mollusque)* razor shell **(c)** *Fig* **deuxième** *ou* **second c.** *(en politique, dans la Mafia)* minion

couteau-scie *(pl* **couteaux-scies)** [kutosi] *nm* serrated knife

coutelas [kutla] *nm* large knife

coûter [kute] *vi* to cost; **combien ça coûte?** how much is it?, how much does it cost?; **ça coûte 100 francs** it costs 100 francs, it's 100 francs; **c. les yeux de la tête** to cost a fortune; **ça ne coûte rien d'essayer** there's no harm in trying; **c. cher** to cost a lot, to be expensive; **cela vous coûtera cher** it'll cost you a lot; *Fig* **you'll pay for that;** **c. la vie à qn** to cost sb his/her life; **ça m'a beaucoup coûté** it was very painful for me; **coûte que coûte** at all costs

coûteux, -euse [kutø, -øz] *adj* costly, expensive; **peu c.** inexpensive

coutume [kutym] *nf* **(a)** *(habitude)* custom; **avoir c. de faire qch** to be accustomed to doing sth; **plus aimable que de c.** nicer than usual; **comme de c.** as usual; **une fois n'est pas c.** it won't hurt for once **(b)** *(tradition)* custom

coutumier, -ère [kutymje, -er] *adj* **(a)** *(habituel)* customary, usual **(b)** *(personne)* **il est c. du fait** it's not the first time he's done that **(c)** *Jur* **droit c.** common law

couture [kutyr] *nf* **(a)** *(de vêtement)* seam; *Fig* **examiner qn/qch sous toutes les coutures** to examine sb/sth from every angle **(b)** *(activité)* sewing, needlework; **faire de la c.** to sew

couturier [kutyrje] *nm* fashion designer, couturier; **grand c.** big fashion designer

couturière [kutyrjɛr] *nf* dressmaker

couvaison [kuvɛzõ] *nf* incubation

couvée [kuve] *nf* **(a)** *(œufs)* clutch **(b)** *(d'oisillons, d'enfants)* brood

couvent [kuvã] *nm* **(a)** *(communauté religieuse)* *(de femmes)* convent; *(d'hommes)* monastery **(b)** *(pensionnat)* convent school

couver [kuve] **1** *vt* **(a)** *(œufs)* to sit on; *Fig (personne)* to mollycoddle; **c. qn des yeux** to look fondly at sb **(b)** *(maladie)* to be coming down with

2 *vi (poule)* to brood; *(feu, passion)* to smoulder; *(émeute)* to be brewing

couvercle [kuvɛrkl] *nm* lid; *(qui se visse)* cap, top

couvert¹, -e [kuver, -ert] **1** adj **(a)** (allée, marché) covered; (piscine) indoor; (ciel) overcast **(b)** (jonché, plein) **c. de** covered with or in **(c)** (habillé) covered up; **chaudement ou bien c.** warmly dressed **(d)** (ciel) overcast

2 pp voir **couvrir**

couvert² nm **(a)** (ustensiles) **un c. en argent** a silver knife, fork and spoon; **couverts** cutlery **(b)** (pour chaque convive) place setting; **mettre le c.** to set or Br lay the table; **mettre trois couverts** to set or Br lay the table for three **(c)** **sous le c. de** (sous l'apparence de) under the cover of

couverture [kuvertyr] nf **(a)** (de lit) blanket; Fig **tirer la c. à soi** to take all the credit; **c. chauffante** electric blanket **(b)** (d'un livre, d'un magazine, d'un cahier) cover; **en c.** on the cover **(c)** (protection) **c. sociale** social security cover **(d)** (d'un bâtiment) roofing **(e)** (d'un événement médiatique) coverage

couveuse [kuvøz] nf **(a)** (pour nouveau-nés) incubator **(b)** (poule) brooder

couvre-chef (pl couvre-chefs) [kuvrəʃef] nm Hum hat

couvre-feu (pl couvre-feux) [kuvrəfø] nm Mil curfew

couvre-lit (pl couvre-lits) [kuvrəli] nm bedspread

couvre-pied(s) (pl couvre-pieds) [kuvrəpje] nm quilt

couvreur [kuvrœr] nm roofer

couvrir [52] [kuvrir] **1** vt **(a)** (casserole, meuble, livre) to cover (**de** with) **(b)** **c. qn de** (cadeaux, honneurs, compliments) to shower sb with **(c)** (protéger, justifier) to cover; **être couvert par ses supérieurs** to be acting with the authority of one's superiors **(d)** (parcourir, englober) & Journ to cover **(e)** (bruit, voix) to drown (out) **(f)** (sujet: assurance) to cover **(g)** Zool (femelle) to cover

2 se couvrir vpr **(a)** (pour sortir) to wrap up; (pour cacher sa nudité) to cover oneself up; (mettre son chapeau) to put on one's hat **(b)** (ciel) to cloud over; **le temps** ou **ça se couvre** it's clouding over **(c)** **se c. de** (honte, ridicule) to cover oneself with; **se c. de feuilles** (arbre) to come into leaf

cow-boy (pl cow-boys) [kobɔj] nm cowboy

coyote [kɔjɔt] nm coyote

CP [sepe] nm (abrév **cours préparatoire**) = first year of primary school

CPAM [sepeaɛm] nf (abrév **caisse primaire d'assurance maladie**) = French government department dealing with health insurance

cpp Ordinat (abrév **caractères par pouce**) cpi

cps Ordinat (abrév **caractères par seconde**) cps

crabe [krab] nm crab

crac [krak] **1** exclam (bruit de cassure) crack!; Fam **et c., elle est tombée malade!** and what do you know, she fell ill!

2 nm crack

crachat [kraʃa] nm gob of spit; **crachats** spit

craché, -e [kraʃe] adj Fam **c'est sa mère tout c., c'est le portrait (tout)** ou **de sa mère** he's the spitting image of his mother; **c'est lui tout c.!** that's just like him!

cracher [kraʃe] **1** vi **(a)** (personne) to spit; Fam Fig **ne pas c. sur qch** not to say no to sth; Fam Fig **c. dans la soupe** to bite the hand that feeds **(b)** (stylo) to splutter **(c)** (haut-parleur, téléphone, radio) to crackle

2 vt **(a)** (chewing-gum, nourriture) to spit out; **c. du sang** to spit blood **(b)** (fumée) to belch out **(c)** très Fam (somme d'argent) to cough up

cracheur, -euse [kraʃœr, -øz] nm,f **c. de feu** fire-eater

crachin [kraʃɛ̃] nm (fine) drizzle

crachoir [kraʃwar] nm spittoon; Fam Fig **tenir le c.** to monopolize the conversation; Fam Fig **tenir le c. à qn** to listen to sb rambling on and on

crachoter [kraʃɔte] vi (feu) to splutter; (radio, téléphone) to crackle

crack [krak] nm **(a)** Fam (personne) ace (**en** at) **(b)** (drogue) crack

cracker [krakœr] nm cracker

Cracovie [krakɔvi] n Cracow

cracra [krakra] adj inv Fam filthy

crade [krad], **cradingue** [kradɛ̃g], **crado** [krado] adj Fam filthy

craie [krɛ] nf (matière) chalk; (bâtonnet) stick of chalk

craignais etc voir **craindre**

craignos [krɛɲos] adj Fam (laid) hideous; (louche) dodgy

craindre [23] [krɛ̃dr] **1** vt **(a)** (redouter) to fear, to be afraid of; **ne craignez rien!** (n'ayez pas peur) don't be frightened!; (ne vous inquiétez pas) don't worry!; **je crains qu'il (ne) soit parti** I'm afraid he's left; **c. de faire qch** to be afraid of doing sth **(b)** (ne pas supporter) **ces plantes craignent le gel** these plants don't like frost; **craint l'humidité/la chaleur** (sur emballage) keep dry/cool

2 vi Fam **ça craint!** (c'est ennuyeux) what a pain!; (c'est très laid) it's hideous!; (c'est louche) it's dodgy

craint, -e voir **craindre**

crainte [krɛ̃t] nf fear; **de c. de tomber** for fear of falling; **de c. qu'on ne l'entende** for fear of being overheard; **soyez sans c., n'ayez c.** have no fear

craintif, -ive [krɛ̃tif, -iv] adj timid

cramer [krame] Fam **1** vi & vt to burn

2 se cramer vpr to burn oneself; **se c. les doigts** to burn one's fingers

cramoisi, -e [kramwazi] adj crimson

crampe [krɑ̃p] nf cramp; **j'ai une c. au pied** I've got cramp in my foot; **crampes d'estomac** stomach cramps

crampon [krɑ̃pɔ̃] nm **(a)** (de chaussure de sport) stud; (pour alpinisme) crampon; **crampons** (chaussures) boots with studs **(b)** Constr cramp (iron) **(c)** Fam (personne) leech

cramponner [krɑ̃pɔne] **se cramponner** vpr to hold on; **se c. à** to hold on to; Fig (vie, espoir) to cling to; (fonction) to hang on to

cran [krɑ̃] nm **(a)** (entaille) notch; (de ceinture) hole; **serrer sa ceinture d'un c.** to take one's belt in a notch; **c. de sûreté** ou **d'arrêt** safety catch; (couteau à) **c. d'arrêt** Br flick knife, Am switchblade **(b)** Fig (degré) avancer/reculer d'un **c.** to go up/come down a notch **(c)** Fam **être à c.** to be wound up **(d)** Fam (courage) guts; **avoir du c.** to have guts **(e)** (dans les cheveux) crimp

crâne [krɑn] nm skull; Spéc cranium; Fam **avoir mal au c.** to have a headache; Fam **mets-toi ça dans le c.!** get that into your head!

crâner [krɑne] vi Fam to swagger, to show off

crâneur, -euse [krɑnœr, -øz] Fam **1** adj swaggering; **être c.** to be a show-off

2 nm,f show-off

crânien, -enne [krɑnjɛ̃, -ɛn] adj Anat cranial

crapahuter [krapayte] vi Fam **(a)** (marcher) to traipse about **(b)** Mil (soldat) to trudge along

crapaud [krapo] nm **(a)** (animal) toad **(b)** (défaut) flaw

crapule [krapyl] nf scoundrel, villain

crapuleux, -euse [krapylø, -øz] adj voir **crime**

craqueler [42] [krakle] **1** *vt* to crack
2 se craqueler *vpr* to crack

craquement [krakmã] *nm (de branche)* crack; *(d'escalier, de plancher)* creak; **des craquements** cracking/creaking

craquer [krake] **1** *vi* **(a)** *(branche)* to crack; *(escalier, plancher)* to creak; **faire c. ses doigts** to crack one's fingers **(b)** *(se déchirer)* to rip; *(se casser)* to snap **(c)** *(perdre le contrôle de soi)* to crack up **(d)** *Fam (succomber)* **c. pour qn** to fall for sb; **ce mec me fait c.** I really fancy that guy
2 *vt* **(a)** *(allumette)* to strike **(b)** *(déchirer)* to rip

crasse [kras] **1** *adj (ignorance)* crass
2 *nf* **(a)** *(saleté)* filth **(b)** *Fam (mauvais tour)* dirty trick; **faire une c. à qn** to play a dirty trick on sb

crasseux, -euse [krasø, -øz] *adj* filthy

cratère [krater] *nm* crater

cravache [kravaʃ] *nf (riding) crop; Fig* **mener qn à la c.** to rule sb with a rod of iron

cravacher [kravaʃe] **1** *vt (cheval)* to use the crop on
2 *vi Fam (travailler vite)* to work like mad

cravate [kravat] *nf* tie; *Fam* **s'en jeter un derrière la c.** to knock back a drink

crawl [krol] *nm* crawl; **nager le c.** to do the crawl

crayeux, -euse [krejø, -øz] *adj (matière, teint)* chalky

crayon [krejõ] *nm* **(a)** *(pour écrire)* pencil; **c. de couleur** coloured pencil, crayon; **c. gras** soft lead pencil; *Ordinat* **c. lumineux** *ou* **optique** light pen **(b)** *(bâton)* stick; **c. à lèvres** lip pencil

créance [kreãs] *nf* debt; **c. douteuse** bad debt

créancier, -ère [kreãsje, -ɛr] *nm,f* creditor

créateur, -trice [kreatœr, -tris] **1** *adj (génie)* creative; **industrie créatrice d'emplois** job-creating industry
2 *nm,f* creator; *Rel* **le C.** the Creator

créatif, -ive [kreatif, -iv] *adj* creative

création [kreasjõ] *nf* **(a)** *(fait de créer)* creation; **c. d'emplois** job creation **(b)** *(produit)* new product; *(d'un couturier)* creation **(c)** *(univers)* **la c.** creation **(d)** *(première représentation) (d'une pièce)* first production; *(d'un rôle)* creation; *(d'une œuvre musicale)* first performance

créativité [kreativite] *nf* creativity

créature [kreatyr] *nf* **(a)** *(être vivant)* creature; *Hum* **une c. de rêve** *(femme)* a magnificent woman **(b)** *Péj (protégé)* creature

crécelle [kresɛl] *nf* rattle; **une voix de c.** a rasping voice

crèche [krɛʃ] *nf* **(a)** *(garderie)* crèche, day nursery **(b)** *(de Noël)* crib

crécher [34] [kreʃe] *vi Fam* to live; *(temporairement)* to crash

crédibilité [kredibilite] *nf* credibility

crédible [kredibl] *adj* credible

crédit [kredi] *nm* **(a)** *(prêt)* credit; **à c.** on credit; **faire c. à qn** to give sb credit; **la maison ne fait pas c.** *(sur panneau)* we do not give credit; **c. à la consommation** consumer credit; **c. gratuit** interest-free credit; **c. immobilier** home loan, mortgage **(b)** *(en comptabilité)* credit side; **porter une somme au c. de qn** to credit sb with a sum **(c)** **crédits** *(somme d'argent)* funds **(d)** *Litt (influence)* credit

crédit-bail *(pl* **crédits-bails)** [kredibaj] *nm* leasing

créditer [kredite] *vt* **(a)** *Fin (compte)* to credit **(b)** *Fig* **c. qn de qch** to give sb credit for sth

créditeur, -trice [kreditœr, -tris] *adj (solde, compte)* credit; **être c.** to be in credit

crédit-relais *(pl* **crédits-relais)** [kredirəlɛ] *nm* bridging loan

credo [kredo] *nm inv* credo, creed

crédule [kredyl] *adj* credulous

crédulité [kredylite] *nf* credulity

créer [24] [kree] **1** *vt* **(a)** *(emplois, poste)* to create; *(entreprise)* to set up **(b)** *(œuvre, nouveau produit, vêtement)* to create **(c)** *(difficultés, problème)* to create (à for) **(d)** *(interpréter pour la première fois) (rôle)* to create; *(pièce de théâtre)* to produce for the first time; *(œuvre musicale)* to perform for the first time
2 se créer *vpr* **(a)** *(être créé)* to be created **(b)** *(pour soi-même)* **se c. une clientèle** to build up a clientèle; **se c. des problèmes** to create problems for oneself

crémaillère [kremajɛr] *nf (dans la cheminée)* trammel (hook); **pendre la c.** to have a housewarming (party)

crémant [kremã] *nm* slightly sparkling champagne

crémation [kremasjõ] *nf* cremation

crématoire [krematwar] *adj voir* **four**

crématorium [krematɔrjɔm] *nm* crematorium

crème [krɛm] **1** *nf* **(a)** *(du lait, dessert)* cream; *Fig* **c'est la c. des hommes** he's the best of men; **c. anglaise** custard; **c. au beurre** = butter, sugar, eggs and cream, baked together and used as a cake filling; **c. brûlée** crème brûlée; **c. (au) caramel** caramel custard, crème caramel; **c. Chantilly** whipped cream *(with sugar added)*; **c. fouettée** whipped cream; **c. fraîche** crème fraîche; **c. glacée** ice cream; **c. pâtissière** confectioner's custard; **c. renversée** crème caramel *(turned out of its mould)* **(b)** *(produit cosmétique)* cream; **c. antirides** anti-wrinkle cream; **c. hydratante** moisturizing cream; **c. à raser** shaving cream **(c)** *(liqueur)* **c. de menthe** crème de menthe; **c. de cassis** blackcurrant liqueur
2 *nm Fam* **un grand c.** a large white coffee
3 *adj inv* cream(-coloured)

crémerie [krɛmri] *nf (magasin)* dairy

crémeux, -euse [kremø, -øz] *adj* creamy

crémier, -ère [kremje, -ɛr] *nm,f* dairyman, *f* dairywoman

crémone [kremɔn] *nf* espagnolette

créneau, -x [kreno] *nm* **(a)** *(de rempart)* crenel **(b)** *(manœuvre)* **faire un c.** to reverse into a (parking) space **(c)** *Com* niche **(d)** *(dans un programme, un emploi du temps)* slot; **c. horaire** time slot

crénelé, -e [krenle] *adj* crenellated

créole [kreɔl] **1** *adj* Creole
2 *nmf* **C.** Creole
3 *nm (langue)* Creole
4 *nfpl* **créoles** *(boucles d'oreille)* hoop earrings

crêpe [krɛp] **1** *nf* pancake
2 *nm* **(a)** *(tissu)* crêpe **(b)** *(caoutchouc)* crêpe (rubber); **semelles (de) c.** crêpe soles

crêper [krepe] **1** *vt* **(a)** *(cheveux)* to backcomb **(b)** *(tissu)* to crimp
2 se crêper *vpr Fam Fig* **se c. le chignon** to have a dust-up

crêperie [krɛpri] *nf* pancake restaurant

crépi, -e [krepi] *adj & nm Constr* roughcast

crépir [krepir] *vt Constr* to roughcast

crépitement [krepitmã] *nm (du feu)* crackling

crépiter [krepite] *vi (feu)* to crackle

crépon [krepɔ̃] nm (papier) crêpe paper

crépu, -e [krepy] adj frizzy

crépuscule [krepyskyl] nm aussi Fig twilight

crescendo [kreʃɛndo] 1 adv crescendo; **aller c.** to get louder and louder; Fig (difficultés) to get worse and worse 2 nm crescendo

cresson [kresɔ̃, krəsɔ̃] nm watercress

crétacé, -e [kretase] Géol 1 adj Cretaceous 2 nm **le C.** the Cretaceous period

Crète [krɛt] nf **la C.** Crete

crête [krɛt] nf (a) (d'oiseau) crest; (de coq) comb (b) (de montagne, de vague, de toit) crest

crétin, -e [kretɛ̃, -in] nm,f Fam cretin

crétois, -e [kretwa, -az] 1 adj Cretan 2 nm,f C. Cretan

cretonne [krətɔn] nf cretonne

cretons [krətɔ̃] nmpl Can potted pork

creuser [krøze] 1 vt (a) (trou, tranchée, puits) to dig; Fig **c. l'écart entre** to widen the gap between; Fig **c. un abîme entre deux personnes** to create a gulf between two people (b) (évider) to hollow (out); **c. la terre** to dig (c) (problème, question) to look into (d) (donner faim à) **c. qn** to give sb an appetite; **le grand air, ça creuse** the fresh air gives you an appetite; (e) (cambrer) **c. les reins** to arch one's back (f) (amaigrir) **il avait le visage creusé par la fatigue/la maladie** his face was gaunt with exhaustion/illness
2 vi to dig
3 **se creuser** vpr (a) (s'agrandir) (écart) to widen (b) **se c. (la tête** ou **la cervelle) (pour faire qch)** to rack one's brains (to do sth) (c) (visage) to grow hollow

creuset [krøzɛ] nm (a) Chim crucible (b) Fig melting pot

creux, -euse [krø, krøz] 1 adj (a) (vide) (arbre, mur, dent) hollow; (chemin) sunken; Fig **avoir le ventre c.** to be hungry (b) (période, question) off-peak (c) (joues) hollow; (visage) gaunt (d) Péj (débat, discours, personne) hollow
2 adv **sonner c.** to sound hollow; Fig to sound empty
3 nm (a) (de la main, dans le sol, sur une route) hollow; **le c. des reins** the small of the back (b) (d'une vague, d'une courbe) trough; Fig **être au c. de la vague** to have hit rock bottom (c) Fam **avoir un (petit) c.** to be feeling (a bit) peckish

crevaison [krəvɛzɔ̃] nf (d'un pneu) puncture, flat

crevant, -e [krəvɑ̃, -ɑ̃t] adj Fam (a) (fatigant) exhausting (b) (drôle) priceless

crevasse [krəvas] nf (a) (sur la peau) crack; **avoir des crevasses aux mains** to have chapped hands (b) (dans un mur, le sol) crack; (dans un glacier) crevasse

crevé, -e [krəve] adj (a) (éclaté) (ballon, pneu) burst (b) Fam (fatigué) dead beat (c) très Fam (mort) dead

crève [krɛv] nf très Fam **avoir la c.** (gros rhume) to have a stinking cold; **attraper la c.** to catch one's death of cold

crève-cœur [krɛvkœr] nm inv heartbreak; **c'est un c. de partir** it's heartbreaking to leave

crève-la-faim [krɛvlafɛ̃] nm inv Fam down-and-out

crever [46] [krəve] 1 vt (a) (ballon, sac, pneu) to burst; **c. un œil à qn** to put sb's eye out; **ça me crève le cœur** I'm heartbroken about it; Fig **ça crève les yeux** it sticks out a mile; Fig **c. l'écran** to fill the screen with one's presence (b) (épuiser) to wear out (c) très Fam **c. la dalle** to be bloody starving
2 vi (a) (éclater) to burst; **mon pneu a** ou Fam **j'ai crevé** I've got a puncture; **c. de** (jalousie, orgueil) to be bursting

with (b) (mourir) (bête, plante) to die; très Fam (personne) to kick the bucket; Fam **il fait une chaleur à c.** it's boiling hot; Fam **c. d'envie de faire qch** to be dying to do sth; Fam **c. de faim** (mourir) to starve to death; (avoir faim) to be starving; Fam **c. de froid/de chaud** to be freezing/boiling; Fam **c. de rire** to split one's sides laughing; Fam **qu'il crève!** he can go to hell!; Fam **plutôt c.!** I'd rather die!
3 **se crever** vpr Fam to wear oneself out

crevette [krəvɛt] nf (a) (rose) prawn; **c. grise** shrimp

cri [kri] nm (a) (d'une personne) cry, shout; (perçant) scream; **j'ai entendu des cris** I heard shouting; Fig **pousser les hauts cris** to kick up a fuss; **c'est le c. du cœur** it's a cry from the heart; Mil **c. de guerre** war cry (b) (d'un animal, d'un oiseau) cry

criailler [kriaje] vi (a) (crier sans arrêt) to bawl (b) (faisan, pintade) to cry; (oie) to honk

criant, -e [krijɑ̃, -ɑ̃t] adj (erreur) glaring; (preuve, contraste) striking; (vérité) obvious; (abus, injustice) blatant; **c. de vérité** (témoignage, reportage) obviously true

criard, -e [krijar, -ard] adj (a) (aigu) (voix) shrill (b) (couleur) loud (c) (enfant) noisy

crible [kribl] nm sieve; Fig **passer qch au c.** to go through sth with a fine-tooth comb

criblé, -e [krible] adj **c. de** (trous, balles) riddled with; Fig **être c. de dettes** to be up to one's eyes in debt

cric [krik] nm jack

cricket [krikɛt] nm cricket

criée [krije] nf (vente) (sale by) auction; (salle) auction room; (dehors) auction area; **à la c.** by auction

crier [66] [krije] 1 vi (a) (personne) to shout, to cry (out); (fort) to scream; (parler très fort) to shout; **c. de douleur** to cry out or scream with pain; **c. contre** ou **après qn** to shout at sb; **c. au secours** to shout for help; **c. au scandale** to protest, to be up in arms; **c. qch sur les toits** to shout sth from the rooftops (b) (souris) to squeak; (oiseau) to call
2 vt (ordre, injures) to shout (à at); **c. à qn de faire qch** to shout to sb to do sth; **c. son innocence** to protest one's innocence

crime [krim] nm (a) Jur & Fig crime; **ce n'est pas un c.!** it's not a crime!; **c. crapuleux** crime committed for financial gain; **c. d'État** treason; **crimes de guerre** war crimes; **c. contre l'humanité** crime against humanity (b) (meurtre) murder; **c. passionnel** crime of passion

criminalité [kriminalite] nf crime

criminel, -elle [kriminɛl] 1 adj (acte) criminal; Fam **ce serait c. de la jeter** it would be criminal to throw it away
2 nm,f (a) (malfaiteur) criminal; **c. de guerre** war criminal (b) (assassin) murderer

criminologie [kriminɔlɔʒi] nf criminology

crin [krɛ̃] nm horsehair; Fig **à tout c., à tous crins** out-and-out

crinière [krinjer] nf aussi Fig mane

crinoline [krinɔlin] nf crinoline

crique [krik] nf creek

criquet [krikɛ] nm locust

crise [kriz] *nf* (a) *(marasme, période d'instabilité)* crisis; c. de l'énergie energy crisis; c. du logement housing crisis *or* shortage (b) *(d'une maladie)* attack; c. cardiaque heart attack; c. de foie bilious attack (C) *(accès)* c. de colère fit of anger; c. de conscience attack of conscience; c. de larmes crying fit; c. de nerfs attack of nerves, fit of hysterics; la c. (de rire)! what a hoot! (d) *Fam (colère)* fit of rage; piquer *ou* faire une c. to throw a fit

crispant, -e [krispɑ̃, -ɑ̃t] *adj Fam* irritating, annoying

crispé, -e [krispe] *adj (visage, personne)* tense; *(sourire, rire)* forced

crisper [krispe] **1** *vt* (a) *(poings, mains)* to clench; *(corps)* to tense (b) *(énerver)* to irritate, to annoy
2 se crisper *vpr (muscle, visage)* to tense; *(sourire)* to become strained; *(personne)* to get tense

crissement [krismɑ̃] *nm (de la craie sur le tableau)* squeak; *(des pneus, des freins)* squeal; *(du gravier, de la neige)* crunch

crisser [krise] *vi (pneus, freins)* to squeal; *(gravier, neige)* to crunch; *(craie)* to squeak

cristal, -aux [kristal, -o] *nm* crystal; c. de roche rock crystal; cristaux *(verre)* crystal(ware); *(de sel, de glace)* crystals; *Tech* cristaux liquides liquid crystal

cristallin, -e [kristalɛ̃, -in] **1** *adj* (a) *(roche)* crystalline (b) *Fig (eau, voix)* crystal-clear; *(son, note)* ringing
2 *nm (de l'œil)* crystalline lens

cristalliser [kristalize] **1** *vi* to crystallize
2 se cristalliser *vpr* to crystallize

critère [kriter] *nm* criterion; *Ordinat* c. de tri sort criterion

critérium [kriterjɔm] *nm Sp* criterium

critique¹ [kritik] *adj (décisif, crucial)* critical

critique² **1** *adj (esprit, personne, édition)* critical
2 *nmf* critic; c. d'art/de cinéma art/film critic; c. gastronomique restaurant critic
3 *nf* (a) *(condamnation)* criticism; si je peux me permettre de vous faire une c.,... if I could just make one criticism,...; il n'accepte pas la c. he can't take criticism (b) *(article)* critical article; *Th & Cin* review; faire la c. de qch to review sth (C) la c. *(l'ensemble des critiques)* the critics

critiquer [kritike] *vt (personne, attitude)* to criticize (pour for); ce n'est pas pour te c., mais... I don't mean to criticize, but...; c'est facile de c. it's easy to criticize

croassement [krɔasmɑ̃] *nm* caw; des croassements cawing

croasser [krɔase] *vi* to caw

croate [krɔat] **1** *adj* Croatian
2 *nmf* C. Croat, Croatian

Croatie [krɔasi] *nf* la C. Croatia

croc [kro] *nm* (a) *(de loup, de chien)* fang; *Fam* avoir les crocs to be famished (b) *(crochet)* hook

croc-en-jambe [krɔkɑ̃ʒɑ̃b] *(pl* crocs-en-jambe) *nm* trip; faire un c. à qn to trip sb up

croche [krɔʃ] *nf Mus Br* quaver, *Am* eighth note

croche-pied *(pl* croche-pieds) [krɔʃpje] = croc-en-jambe

crochet [krɔʃɛ] *nm* (a) *(pour accrocher)* hook; *Fig* vivre aux crochets de qn to live off sb (b) *(pour tricoter)* crochet hook; *(technique)* crochet; faire du c. to (do) crochet (C) *(détour)* faire un c. (par) *(personne)* to make a detour (through) (d) *Typ* square bracket; entre crochets in square brackets (e) *(coup de poing)* c. du gauche/du droit left/right hook (f) *(d'un serpent)* fang

crocheter [39] [krɔʃte] *vt (serrure)* to pick; *(porte)* to pick the lock on

crochu, -e [krɔʃy] *adj (nez, bec)* hooked; *(doigts)* claw-like

crocodile [krɔkɔdil] *nm* crocodile; en c. *(sac, chaussures)* crocodile(-skin)

crocus [krɔkys] *nm* crocus

croire [25] [krwar] **1** *vt* (a) *(accepter, faire confiance à)* to believe; *Fam Ironique* c'est ça, je te crois! is that so?; *Fam* faut pas c.! don't you believe it!; croyez-moi, ce n'était pas facile believe (you) me, it wasn't easy; à l'en c.,... to hear him, you'd think...; je n'en croyais pas mes yeux/mes oreilles I couldn't believe my eyes/my ears (b) *(penser)* to think; je crois que oui I think so; je crois que non I don't think so; vous croyez? do you really think so?; je vous croyais anglais/riche I thought you were English/rich; j'ai cru nécessaire de... I thought it necessary to...; j'ai cru bien faire I thought *or* believed I was doing the right thing; elle ne croyait pas si bien dire she didn't know how right she was; je n'aurais pas cru cela de lui I would never have thought it of him; on croirait qu'il dort you'd think he was asleep
2 *vi (avoir la foi)* to be a believer
3 croire à *vt ind* (a) *(envisager)* le médecin crut à une rougeole the doctor thought it was measles (b) *(accepter)* to believe; veuillez c. ou je vous prie de c. à l'expression de mes sentiments distingués yours sincerely (C) *(avoir confiance en, adhérer à)* to believe in
4 croire en *vt ind (personne, talent, Dieu)* to believe in
5 se croire *vpr* il se croit intelligent he thinks he's clever; il se croit tout permis he thinks he can get away with anything; on se serait cru en octobre it felt like October; *Fam* se c. sorti de la cuisse de Jupiter to think a lot of oneself; *Fam* il s'y croit he thinks a lot of himself

croisade [krwazad] *nf Hist & Fig* crusade; partir en c. to go on a crusade

croisé, -e [krwaze] **1** *adj (manteau, veste)* double-breasted
2 *nm Hist* crusader

croisement [krwazmɑ̃] *nm* (a) *(carrefour)* crossroads *(singulier),* intersection (b) *(d'animaux)* crossing; *(animal)* cross (entre between)

croiser [krwaze] **1** *vt* (a) *(couper) (ligne, route)* to cross; c. le regard de qn to meet sb's gaze (b) *(passer à côté de) (véhicule, personne)* to pass (C) *(mettre l'un sur l'autre)* c. les jambes to cross one's legs; c. les bras to fold one's arms; *Fig* c. les doigts to keep one's fingers crossed (d) *(animaux, espèces)* to cross (avec with); *(race)* to cross(breed)
2 *vi (navire)* to cruise
3 se croiser *vpr* (a) *(lignes, routes)* to cross, to intersect; *(regards)* to meet (b) *(personnes) (dans la rue)* to walk past each other; *(se voir rapidement)* to meet briefly; *(lettres)* to cross

croiseur [krwazœr] *nm Naut* cruiser

croisière [krwazjer] *nf* cruise; faire une c. to go on a cruise

croisillon [krwazijɔ̃] *nm* (a) *(de croix)* crosspiece (b) *croisillons* *(de fenêtre, de barrière)* latticework; *(sur une tarte)* lattice

croissais *etc voir* **croître**

croissance [krwasɑ̃s] *nf (d'un enfant) & Écon* growth; **en pleine c.** growing rapidly; **finir sa c.** *(enfant)* to stop growing

croissant¹, -e [krwasɑ̃, -ɑ̃t] *adj (plante, tendance, angoisse)* growing; *(ordre)* ascending; *(chaleur, température)* increasing

croissant² *nm* (a) *(arc de cercle)* crescent; **un c. de lune** a crescent moon; **en c.** crescent-shaped (b) *(pâtisserie)* croissant; **c. au beurre/ordinaire** croissant made with/without butter

croissant³ *voir* **croître**

croître [4b] [krwatr] *vi* (a) *(enfant, plantes)* to grow (b) *(vente, chiffre)* to grow, to increase **(de** by); *(jours)* to get longer; *(lune)* to wax; **aller croissant** *(succès)* to grow and grow; *(suspense)* to get worse and worse

croix [krwa] *nf* cross; **signer d'une c.** to make one's mark; *Fam Fig* **faire une c. sur qch** to say goodbye to sth; **en (forme de) c.** cross-shaped; **les bras en c.** with one's arms stretched out at the sides; **c. de bois c. de fer, si je mens je vais en enfer** cross my heart and hope to die; **c'est la c. et la bannière** it's the devil of a job; **c. gammée** swastika; **la C.-Rouge** the Red Cross

croquant, -e [krɔkɑ̃, -ɑ̃t] *adj* crisp, crunchy

croque-au-sel [krɔkosɛl] **à la croque-au-sel** *adv* = raw and seasoned only with salt

croque-madame [krɔkmadam] *nm inv* = toasted cheese and ham sandwich topped with fried egg

croque-monsieur [krɔkməsjø] *nm inv* = toasted cheese and ham sandwich

croque-mort *(pl* **croque-morts)** [krɔkmɔr] *nm Fam* undertaker

croquer [krɔke] **1** *vt* (a) *(pomme, bonbon)* to crunch; *Fig (fortune, héritage)* to squander; **à sucer ou à c.** *(sirop de médicaments)* may be sucked or chewed; *Fig* **c. la vie à belles dents** to make the most of life; **il est à c.** *(enfant)* he looks good enough to eat; **joli** *ou* **mignon à c.** as pretty as a picture (b) *(faire un croquis de)* to sketch **2** *vi* (a) *(pomme, salade)* to be crunchy (b) *(mordre)* **c. dans** to bite into

croquet [krɔke] *nm (jeu)* croquet

croquette [krɔkɛt] *nf (de pomme de terre, de viande, de poisson)* croquette; **croquettes** *(pour chien, chat)* biscuits

croquis [krɔki] *nm* sketch; **faire un c. de qch** to make a sketch of sth

cross [krɔs] *nm (sport)* cross-country running; *(événement)* cross-country run

crosse [krɔs] *nf* (a) *(de fusil)* butt; *(de pistolet)* grip; *(d'évêque)* crook (b) *(de hockey)* stick; *Fam Fig* **chercher des crosses à qn** to try to pick a fight with sb

crotte [krɔt] *nf* (a) *(de cheval, de mouton, de lapin)* dung, droppings; **une c. de chien** dog dirt; *Fam* **c.!** blast! (b) **une c. de chocolat** a chocolate (c) *Vieilli (boue)* mud

crotter [krɔte] **1** *vt (chaussures, manteau)* to cover in mud **2 se crotter** *vpr* to get covered in mud

crottin [krɔtɛ̃] *nm* (a) *(excrément) (de cheval)* dung *Fam* (b) *(fromage)* small goat's-milk cheese

croulant, -e [krulɑ̃, -ɑ̃t] **1** *adj (bâtiment)* crumbling **2** *nm, f très Fam (vieux)* **c.** (old) wrinkly

crouler [krule] *vi (bâtiment)* to crumble; **c. sous le poids de qch** to give way under the weight of sth; **c. sous le travail** to be snowed under with work; **la salle croulait sous les applaudissements** the audience brought the house down

croupe [krup] *nf* rump; **monter en c.** to ride behind

croupi, -e [krupi] *adj (eau)* stagnant

croupier [krupje] *nm* croupier

croupion [krupjɔ̃] *nm (d'oiseau)* rump; *(d'une volaille) Br* parson's *ou Am* pope's nose

croupir [krupir] *vi* (a) *(eau)* to stagnate (b) *(végéter)* **c. en prison** to rot in prison

croupissant, -e [krupisɑ̃, -ɑ̃t] *adj (eau, vie)* stagnant

CROUS [krus] *nm (abrév* **Centre régional des œuvres universitaires et scolaires)** = organization responsible for student accommodation and catering etc

croustillant, -e [krustijɑ̃, -ɑ̃t] *adj* (a) *(biscuit, pâte)* crisp; *(pain)* crusty (b) *Fig (histoire, détails)* spicy

croustiller [krustije] *vi (biscuit, pâte)* to be crisp; *(pain)* to be crusty

croûte [krut] *nf* (a) *(de pain, de tarte)* crust; *(de fromage)* rind; *(d'une plaie)* scab; **la c. terrestre** the earth's crust; *Fam* **gagner sa c.** to earn one's bread and butter (b) *Fam (mauvaise peinture)* daub

croûton [krutɔ̃] *nm* (a) *(de pain)* end (b) *(dans la soupe, les salades)* crouton (c) *Fam* **(vieux) c.** old fossil

croyable [krwajabl] *adj* believable, credible; **ce n'est pas c.!** it's unbelievable!, it's incredible!

croyais *etc voir* **croire**

croyance [krwajɑ̃s] *nf* belief **(en** in)

croyant, -e [krwajɑ̃, -ɑ̃t] **1** *adj* **être c.** to be a believer **2** *nm,f* believer

CRS [seɛrɛs] *nm (abrév* **compagnie républicaine de sécurité)** = French riot policeman; **les C.** = French riot police

cru¹, -e [kry] *adj* (a) *(viande, poisson, légumes)* raw; *(lait)* unpasteurized (b) *(couleur, lumière)* garish (c) *(licencieux) (langage)* crude (d) *(direct) (réponse, personne)* blunt (e) **monter à c.** to ride bareback

cru² *nm (terroir)* vineyard; *(vin)* wine; **un grand c.** a vintage wine; **du c.** local; *Fig* **une histoire de son (propre) c.** a story of his/her own invention

cru³, -e *voir* **croire**

cruauté [kryote] *nf* (a) *(dureté)* cruelty **(envers** to) (b) *(acte)* (act of) cruelty

cruche [kryʃ] *nf* (a) *(récipient, contenu) Br* jug, *Am* pitcher; *Prov* **tant va la c. à l'eau qu'à la fin elle se casse** the pitcher has gone to the well once too often (b) *Fam (imbécile)* ass

cruchon [kryʃɔ̃] *nm (récipient, contenu)* small *Br* jug *ou Am* pitcher

crucial, -e, -aux, -ales [krysjal, -o] *adj* crucial

crucifier [66] [krysifje] *vt* to crucify

crucifix [krysifi] *nm* crucifix

crucifixion [krysifiksjɔ̃] *nf* crucifixion

cruciforme [krysifɔrm] *adj* cruciform; **vis/tournevis c.** Phillips® screw/screwdriver

cruciverbiste [krysiverbist] *nmf* crossword enthusiast

crudité [krydite] *nf* (a) **crudités** *(légumes)* assorted raw vegetables (b) *(d'une couleur, d'une lumière)* garishness (c) *(d'une expression)* crudeness

crue [kry] nf (montée) swelling; (inondation) flood; **rivière en c.** river in spate

cruel, -elle [kryɛl] adj cruel (**envers** ou **avec** to)

cruellement [kryɛlmɑ̃] adv cruelly; **être c. éprouvé** to be deeply affected; **faire c. défaut** to be sadly lacking

crûment [krymɑ̃] adv (a) (parler) (sans détours) bluntly; (grossièrement) crudely (b) **éclairé c.** garishly lit

crustacé [krystase] nm Zool crustacean; **crustacés** crustaceans; Culin seafood

cruzado [kruzado] nm cruzado

cryogénie [krijɔʒeni] nf cryogenics (singulier)

cryptage [kriptaʒ] nm encoding

crypte [kript] nf crypt

crypté, -e [kripte] adj (message) & TV coded

crypter [kripte] vt to encode

CSA [seesa] nm (abrév **Conseil supérieur de l'audiovisuel**) = organization regulating French broadcasting, Br ≃ ITC

CSG [seesʒe] nf (abrév **Contribution sociale généralisée**) = income-based tax deducted at source

Cuba [kyba] n Cuba

cubain, -e [kybɛ̃, -ɛn] **1** adj Cuban
2 nm,f C. Cuban

cube [kyb] **1** nm cube; (de jeu) building block; **élever un nombre au c.** to cube a number
2 adj (mètre, centimètre) cubic

cubique [kybik] adj cubic

cubisme [kybism] nm cubism

cubitus [kybitys] nm ulna

cucul [kyky] adj inv Fam **c. (la praline)** (personne, décoration) twee; (film, livre) corny

cueillette [kœjɛt] nf (action) gathering, picking; (fruits, noisettes, baies) harvest

cueillir [5] [kœjir] vt (fleurs, fruits) to gather, to pick; Fig **la mort l'a cueilli en pleine jeunesse** he was cut down in his prime; Fam **c. qn** to pick sb up

cui-cui [kɥikɥi] **1** nm cheeping
2 exclam cheep!

cuiller, cuillère [kɥijɛr] nf (a) (couvert) spoon; (contenu) spoon(ful); Fam Fig **il n'y va pas avec le dos de la c.** he doesn't go in for half measures; Fam Fig **en deux** ou **trois coups de c. à pot** in two shakes (of a lamb's tail); **être à ramasser à la petite c.** (épuisé) to be all in; (déprimé) to be down in the dumps; **c. à café, petite c.** teaspoon; **c. à soupe** tablespoon (b) (pour la pêche) spoon (bait); **pêcher la truite à la c.** to troll for trout

cuillerée [kɥijere] nf spoonful; **une c. à café** a teaspoonful; **une c. à soupe** a tablespoonful

cuir [kɥir] nm (a) (matière) leather; (veste) leather jacket; **chaussures/pantalon en c.** leather shoes/trousers (b) (d'un éléphant, d'un rhinocéros) hide (c) **c. chevelu** scalp

cuirasse [kɥiras] nf (a) (protection) breastplate; Fig **trouver le défaut dans la c. de qn** to find the chink in sb's armour (b) (d'un navire de guerre, d'un blindé) armour (plating)

cuirassé [kɥirase] nm battleship

cuirassier [kɥirasje] nm cuirassier

cuire [18] [kɥir] **1** vt (a) (aliment) to cook; **c. qch à l'eau** to boil sth; **c. qch à la vapeur** to steam sth; **c. qch au four** to bake sth (b) (briques, poterie) to fire (c) (chauffer) (sujet: soleil) to bake
2 vi (a) (aliments, plat) to cook; **faire trop c. qch** to overcook sth; **faire c. qch à feu doux** to cook sth over a low heat (b) (brûler) **les joues me cuisent** my cheeks are burning; Fam (avoir très chaud) to be boiling
3 v impersonnel **il vous en cuira** you'll regret it

cuisais etc voir **cuire**

cuisant, -e [kɥizɑ̃, -ɑ̃t] adj (douleur) burning; (froid) biting; (déception, échec) bitter

cuisine [kɥizin] nf (a) (pièce) kitchen; (sur un navire) galley (b) (art) cooking, cookery; **faire la c.** to do the cooking; **bien faire la c.** to be a good cook; **c. au beurre/à l'huile** cooking with butter/oil; **la c. française/chinoise** French/Chinese cooking ou cuisine (c) Fam (magouilles) scheming

cuisiner [kɥizine] **1** vi to cook; **bien c.** to be a good cook
2 vt (a) (préparer) to cook; **plats cuisinés** ready-cooked meals (b) Fam (interroger) to grill

cuisinier, -ère [kɥizinje, -ɛr] **1** nm,f cook
2 nf cuisinière stove, Br cooker; **cuisinière électrique/à gaz** electric/gas stove ou Br cooker; **c. mixte** combined gas and electric stove ou Br cooker

cuissardes [kɥisard] nfpl (bottes de femme) thigh boots; (de pêche) waders

cuisse [kɥis] nf thigh; **cuisses de grenouilles** frogs' legs; **c. de poulet** chicken leg, drumstick

cuisson [kɥisɔ̃] nf (d'aliments) cooking; (de pain, de gâteau) baking; **temps de c.** cooking time; **c. à la vapeur** steaming (b) (des briques, de la porcelaine) firing

cuissot [kɥiso] nm (de venaison) haunch

cuistot [kɥisto] nm Fam cook

cuit, -e [kɥi, kɥit] adj (aliment) cooked; **bien c.** well done; **c. à point** done to a turn; **trop c.** overcooked; **pas assez c.** undercooked; **au four** baked (b) Fam Fig **être c.** to have had it; **c'est c.!** we've had it!; **c'est du tout c.** it's a cinch

cuite [kɥit] nf Fam **avoir/prendre une c.** to be/get plastered

cuivre [kɥivr] nm (a) (métal) **c. (rouge)** copper; **c. jaune** brass; **les cuivres** (objets) copper(ware); (en cuivre jaune) brasses (b) Mus **les cuivres** the brass (section)

cuivré, -e [kɥivre] adj (peau, teint) (naturellement) copper-coloured; (par le soleil) bronzed

cul [ky] nm **1** (a) Fam (d'une personne) backside, Br bum; **en rester** ou **tomber sur le c.** to be flabbergasted; **c'est à se taper le c. par terre** it's an absolute scream; **de c.** (magazine, film) porn; **être comme c. et chemise** to be as thick as thieves; Vulg **l'avoir dans le c.** to be screwed up; Vulg **en avoir plein le c.** to be pissed off; **avoir qn au c.** to have sb on one's tail (b) Fam (chance) **avoir du c.** to be jammy (c) (d'un sac, d'un tonneau, d'une bouteille) bottom; **boire c. sec** to down one's drink in one go; **c. sec!** bottoms up!
2 adj Fam (personne, décoration) twee; (livre) corny

culasse [kylas] nf (a) (de fusil, de pistolet) breech (b) (de moteur) cylinder head

culbute [kylbyt] nf (a) (cabriole) somersault; **faire la c.** to do a somersault (b) (chute) tumble; **faire la c.** to take a tumble

culbuter [kylbyte] **1** *vi* (*vase, statue*) to topple over; (*personne*) to take a tumble; (*voiture*) to overturn

2 *vt* (*objet*) to knock over

cul-de-jatte (*pl* culs-de-jatte) [kydʒat] *nmf* legless cripple

cul-de-poule [kydpul] *nm* **avoir la bouche en c.** to have pursed lips

cul-de-sac (*pl* culs-de-sac) [kydsak] *nm* dead end, cul-de-sac; *Fig* dead end

culinaire [kyliner] *adj* culinary

culminant, -e [kylminã, -ãt] *adj* **point c.** (*d'une chaîne de montagnes*) highest point; (*de la gloire, d'une carrière*) height, peak

culminer [kylmine] *vi* (a) **le mont Blanc culmine à 4807 mètres** Mont Blanc is 4,807 metres at its highest point (b) (*crise, tension*) to peak

culot [kylo] *nm* (a) *Fam* (*audace*) cheek, nerve; **il a un de ces culots!** he's got a nerve!; **y aller au c.** to brazen it out (b) (*de douille, de cartouche*) base

culotte [kylɔt] *nf* (a) (*sous-vêtement*) (*de femme*) panties, knickers; (*d'enfant*) pants (b) (*pantalon*) c. **courte** short trousers; **c. de cheval** jodhpurs; *Fam Fig* jodhpur thighs; **c. de golf** plus-fours; *Fam Fig* **c'est elle qui porte la c.** she's the one who wears the trousers; *Fam* **faire dans sa c.** to dirty one's pants; *Fig* to wet oneself (c) (*de bœuf*) rump

culotté, -e [kylɔte] *adj Fam* cheeky

culpabiliser [kylpabilize] **1** *vt* **c. qn** to make sb feel guilty

2 *vi* to feel guilty

culpabilité [kylpabilite] *nf* guilt

culte [kylt] *nm* (a) (*vénération*) worship; *Fig* cult; *Fig* **vouer un c. à qn** to (hero-)worship sb; **c. de la personnalité** personality cult (b) (*religion*) religion; **liberté du c.** freedom of worship

cul-terreux (*pl* culs-terreux) [kyterø] *nm Fam Péj* country bumpkin, yokel

cultivable [kyltivabl] *adj* suitable for cultivation

cultivateur, -trice [kyltivatœr, -tris] **1** *nm,f* farmer; **petits cultivateurs** small farmers, *Br* smallholders

2 *nm* (*machine*) cultivator

cultivé, -e [kyltive] *adj* (a) (*terre, champs*) cultivated (b) (*personne*) cultured, cultivated

cultiver [kyltive] **1** *vt* (*sol, champ*) to cultivate, to farm; (*plantes*) to grow (b) (*art, relations, amitié*) to cultivate

2 se cultiver *vpr* to improve one's mind

culture [kyltyr] *nf* (a) (*du sol*) cultivation; (*de plantes*) growing; **cultures** land under cultivation (b) (*espèce cultivée*) crop (c) (*connaissances*) culture; **un homme d'une grande c.** a highly cultured man; **c. générale** general knowledge (d) (*civilisation*) culture (e) *Biol* **c. microbienne/de tissus** bacteria/tissue culture (f) **c. physique** physical training

culturel, -elle [kyltyrel] *adj* cultural

culturisme [kyltyrism] *nm* body-building

culturiste [kyltyrist] *nmf* body-builder

cumin [kymɛ̃] *nm* cumin

cumul [kymyl] *nm* **c. des fonctions** plurality of offices; **c. des traitements** drawing of more than one salary

cumulable [kymylabl] *adj* (*fonctions*) which can be held concurrently; (*traitements*) which can be drawn concurrently

cumulatif, -ive [kymylatif, -iv] *adj* cumulative

cumuler [kymyle] *vt* **c. des fonctions** to hold more than one office; **c. plusieurs traitements** to draw several salaries; **c. plusieurs emplois** to have several jobs

cumulo-nimbus [kymylonɛ̃bys] *nm inv* cumulo-nimbus

cumulus [kymylys] *nm inv* cumulus

cupide [kypid] *adj* avaricious

cupidité [kypidite] *nf* cupidity

Cupidon [kypidɔ̃] *npr* Cupid

curable [kyrabl] *adj* (*maladie*) curable

curaçao [kyraso] *nm* curaçao (liqueur)

curage [kyraʒ] *nm* cleaning out

curare [kyrar] *nm* curare

cure [kyr] *nf* (a) (*traitement*) (course of) treatment; **c. d'amaigrissement** (course of) slimming treatment; **faire une c. de désintoxication** (*alcoolique*) to receive treatment for alcohol dependency; (*toxicomane*) to receive treatment for drug dependency; **faire une c. de vitamines** to go/be on a course of vitamins; **faire une c. de fruits** to eat a lot of fruit; **faire une c. de repos/de sommeil** to go/be on a rest cure/sleep cure (b) (*dans une ville d'eau*) c. (**thermale**) spa cure; **faire une c.** to take the waters (c) (*fonction de curé*) office of a parish priest

curé [kyre] *nm* parish priest; **aller à l'école chez les curés** to be educated by priests

cure-dents [kyrdɑ̃] *nm inv* toothpick

curée [kyre] *nf* (*lutte*) scramble; **ce fut la c. entre les héritiers** the heirs started to fight over the spoils

cure-pipe (*pl* cure-pipes) [kyrpip] *nm* pipe-cleaner

curer [kyre] **1** *vt* to clean out

2 se curer *vpr* **se c. les ongles/les oreilles** to clean one's nails/one's ears

curetage [kyrtaʒ] *nm* (*en chirurgie*) curettage

curieusement [kyrjøzmɑ̃] *adv* curiously (enough)

curieux, -euse [kyrjø, -øz] **1** *adj* (a) (*intéressé*) curious; **je serais c. de voir cela** I'd be curious to see that (b) (*indiscret*) inquisitive, inquisitive (c) (*étrange*) curious, strange; **chose curieuse,...** curiously enough,...

2 *nm,f* inquisitive person; (*badaud*) onlooker

curiosité [kyrjozite] *nf* (a) (*intellectuelle*) curiosity; **avec c.** curiously (b) (*indiscrétion*) curiosity, inquisitiveness; **par c.** out of curiosity; *Prov* **la c. est un vilain défaut** curiosity killed the cat (c) (*objet*) curio; **les curiosités d'une ville** the interesting sights of a town

curiste [kyrist] *nmf* = patient taking a spa cure

curriculum vitae [kyrikylɔmvite] *nm inv Br* curriculum vitae, *Am* résumé

curry [kyri] *nm* curry; **poulet au c., c. de poulet** chicken curry

curseur [kyrsœr] *nm aussi Ordinat* cursor

cursif, -ive [kyrsif, -iv] *adj* (*écriture*) cursive

cursus [kyrsys] *nm Univ* degree course

cutané, -e [kytane] *adj* skin, *Spéc* cutaneous

cuti [kyti] *nf* skin test; **virer sa c.** to have a positive skin test; *Fam Fig* to change radically

cuti-réaction (*pl* cuti-réactions) [kytireaksjɔ̃] *nf* skin test

cutter [kœtœr, kyter] *nm* Stanley knife®

cuve [kyv] *nf* (*réservoir*) (storage) tank; (*de machine à laver*) tub; (*pour la fermentation des alcools, du vin*) vat; (*en photographie*) tank

cuvée [kyve] *nf* **(a)** *(quantité)* vatful **(b)** *(produit)* vintage; *Fig* batch

cuver [kyve] *vt Fam* **c. (son vin)** to sleep it off

cuvette [kyvet] *nf* **(a)** *(récipient)* basin, bowl **(b)** *(de W.-C.)* bowl **(c)** *Géog* basin

CV¹ [seve] *Aut (abrév* **cheval-vapeur***)* hp

CV² *nm (abrév* **curriculum vitae***) Br* CV, *Am* résumé

cyanure [sjanyr] *nm* cyanide

cybercafé [siberkafe] *nm* cybercafé

cyberespace [siberespas] *nm* cyberspace

cybernétique [sibernetik] **1** *adj* cybernetic **2** *nf* cybernetics *(singulier)*

cyclable [siklabl] *adj voir* **piste**

cyclamen [siklamɛn] *nm* cyclamen

cycle [sikl] *nm* **(a)** *(suite, mouvement)* cycle; **c. menstruel** menstrual cycle **(b)** *(dans l'éducation)* **premier/second c.** *Scol* lower/upper classes *(in secondary school)*; *Univ* first/last two years *(of degree course)*; *Univ* **troisième c.** postgraduate studies; **c. I/II/III** = subdivisions of primary school (between the ages of 2 and 4, 5 and 7, and 8 and 10 respectively) **(c)** *(bicyclette)* cycle

cyclique [siklik] *adj* cyclical

cyclisme [siklism] *nm* cycling

cycliste [siklist] **1** *nmf* cyclist **2** *adj voir* **coureur, course**

cyclo-cross [siklokrɔs] *nm inv* cyclo-cross

cyclomoteur [siklomɔtœr] *nm* moped

cyclone [siklon] *nm* cyclone

cyclope [siklɔp] *nm* cyclops

cyclothymique [siklotimik] *adj Psy* manic-depressive

cyclotourisme [sikloturism] *nm* bicycle touring

cygne [siɲ] *nm* swan

cylindre [silɛ̃dr] *nm* **(a)** *aussi Aut* cylinder; **une quatre cylindres** a four-cylinder car **(b)** *(rouleau)* roller

cylindrée [silɛ̃dre] *nf* (cubic) capacity; **petite/grosse c.** *(moto)* motorbike with a small/large engine; *(voiture)* car with a small/large engine

cylindrique [silɛ̃drik] *adj* cylindrical

cymbale [sɛ̃bal] *nf* cymbal

cynique [sinik] **1** *adj* cynical **2** *nmf* cynic

cyniquement [sinikmɑ̃] *adv* cynically

cynisme [sinism] *nm* cynicism

cyprès [siprɛ] *nm* cypress (tree)

cypriote [siprijɔt] **1** *adj* Cypriot **2** *nmf* **C.** Cypriot

cyrillique [sirilik] *adj (alphabet, caractères)* Cyrillic

cystite [sistit] *nf* cystitis

cytoplasme [sitoplasm] *nm Biol* cytoplasm

D

D, d [de] *nm inv* D, d

D [de] *nf* (*abrév* **route départementale**) = designation of secondary road

DAB [deabe] *nm* (*abrév* **distributeur automatique de billets**) ATM

dactylo [daktilo] **1** *nmf* (*abrév* **dactylographe**) typist **2** *nf* (*abrév* **dactylographie**) typing

dactylographe [daktilograf] *nmf* typist

dactylographie [daktilografi] *nf* typing

dactylographier [66] [daktilografje] *vt* to type

dada [dada] *nm* (a) (*langage enfantin*) (*cheval*) gee-gee (b) *Fam* (*sujet favori*) hobby-horse

dadais [dade] *nm Fam* **un grand d.** a great gawk

dague [dag] *nf* (*épée*) dagger

dahlia [dalja] *nm* dahlia

daigner [dene] *vt* **d. faire qch** to deign to do sth

daim [dɛ̃] *nm* (a) (*animal*) (*fallow*) deer; (*mâle*) buck (b) (*peau*) suede; **gants/veste en d.** suede gloves/jacket

dais [dɛ] *nm* canopy

Dakar [dakar] *n* Dakar

dalaï-lama [dalailama] *nm* dalai lama

dallage [dalaʒ] *nm* (*action, revêtement*) paving

dalle [dal] *nf* (a) (*de pierre*) paving stone; (*de marbre*) slab; (*de moquette, de lino*) tile (b) *Fam* **que d.** (*rien*) damn all; **j'y vois que d.** I can't see a damn thing (c) *Fam* **avoir ou crever la d.** to be starving

daller [dale] *vt* to pave

dalmatien, -enne [dalmasjɛ̃, -ɛn] *nm,f* (*chien*) Dalmatian

daltonien, -enne [daltɔnjɛ̃, -ɛn] **1** *adj* colour-blind **2** *nm,f* colour-blind person

daltonisme [daltɔnism] *nm* colour blindness

dam [dã] *nm* **au grand d. de qn** to the great displeasure of sb

damage [damaʒ] *nm* (*de la terre, de la neige*) packing down

Damas [damas] *n* Damascus

damas [dama] *nm* damask

dame [dam] *nf* (a) (*femme*) lady; **d. de compagnie** lady's companion; **d. d'honneur** lady-in-waiting (b) (*aux cartes, aux échecs*) queen; (*au jeu de dames*) king (c) **dames** (*jeu*) *Br* draughts, *Am* checkers

damer [dame] *vt* (a) *Fam Fig* **d. le pion à qn** to put one over on sb (b) (*terre, neige*) to pack down

dameuse [daməz] *nf* piste basher

damier [damje] *nm Br* draughtboard, *Am* checkerboard; **tissu à damiers** checked material

damnation [danasjõ] *nf* damnation

damné, -e [dane] **1** *adj* damned **2** *nm,f* damned soul; *Fig* **souffrir comme un d.** to suffer sheer torture

damner [dane] **1** *vt* to damn **2 se damner** *vpr* to damn oneself; **il se damnerait pour...** he'd sell his soul to the devil for...

Damoclès [damokles] *n voir* **épée**

dancing [dãsiŋ] *nm Vieilli* dance hall

dandinement [dãdinmã] *nm* waddle

dandiner [dãdine] **se dandiner** *vpr* to waddle; **se d. d'un pied sur l'autre** to shift from foot to foot

dandy [dãdi] *nm* dandy

Danemark [danmark] *nm* **le D.** Denmark

danger [dãʒe] *nm* danger; **être en d.** to be in danger; **mettre en d. la vie de qn** to endanger sb's life; **d. de mort** (*sur panneau*) danger of death; **hors de d.** out of danger; **d. public** public menace

dangereusement [dãʒrøzmã] *adv* dangerously

dangereux, -euse [dãʒrø, -øz] *adj* dangerous

danois, -e [danwa, -az] **1** *adj* Danish **2** *nm,f* **D.** Dane **3** *nm* (a) (*langue*) Danish (b) (*chien*) Great Dane

dans [dã] *prép* (a) (*à l'intérieur de*) in; **d. une boîte** in(side) a box; **il est d. sa chambre** he's in his room; **lire qch d. un journal** to read sth in a newspaper; **tomber d. l'escalier** to fall down the stairs; **il pleut d. tout le pays** it's raining all over the country; **être d. le commerce/l'informatique** to be in business/computers; **travailler d. le bruit/la saleté** to work in noisy/dirty surroundings (b) (*avec mouvement*) into); **il est entré d. leur chambre** he went into their room (c) (*exprime la temporalité*) in; **d. vingt ans** in twenty years, in twenty years' time (d) (*indique une provenance*) out of; **boire d. un verre** to drink out of a glass; **découper un article d. le journal** to cut an article out of the paper (e) (*indique une approximation*) **d. les quarante ans/les 3000 francs** about forty (years old)/3,000 francs (f) (*pour indiquer un état*) in; **d. mon excitation/ma hâte** in my excitement/hurry

dansant, -e [dãsã, -ãt] *adj voir* **soirée, thé**

danse [dãs] *nf* (*ensemble de mouvements, musique*) dance; **la d.** (*art*) dancing; **d. classique** ballet; **d. folklorique** folk dance/dancing; **Méd d. de Saint-Guy** St Vitus's dance; **la d. du ventre** belly-dancing

danser [dãse] **1** *vi* to dance; **le bouchon/le bateau danse sur l'eau** the cork/the boat is bobbing up and down on the water; *Fig* **avec lui je ne sais jamais sur quel pied d.** I never know where I am with him **2** *vt* (*valse, tango*) to dance

danseur, -euse [dɑ̃sœr, -øz] *nm,f* dancer; **d. (classique** *ou* **de ballet)** ballet-dancer; **d. étoile** lead dancer; **danseuse étoile** prima ballerina; **être en danseuse** (*en cyclisme*) to stand on the pedals

Danube [danyb] *nm* **le D.** the Danube

dard [dar] *nm* (*d'insecte, de scorpion*) sting

darder [darde] *vt* **il a dardé sur moi un regard furieux** he shot a furious look at me; **le soleil darde ses rayons** the sun is beating down

dare-dare [dardar] *adv Fam* at the double

darne [darn] *nf* (*de poisson*) steak

dartre [dartr] *nf* dry patch of skin

darwinisme [darwinism] *nm* Darwinism

datation [datasjɔ̃] *nf* dating

date [dat] *nf* date; **prendre d. pour qch** to fix a date for sth; **faire d.** to be a landmark; **amitié de fraîche/ longue d.** recent/long-standing friendship; **je la connais de longue d.** I've known her (for) a long time; **d. limite** deadline; **d. limite de consommation/de vente/de fraîcheur** use-by/sell-by/best-before date; **d. de naissance** date of birth

dater [date] **1** *vt* (*lettre*) to date
2 *vi* **à du 15** as from the 15th; **ça date un peu** it's a bit dated; **ça ne date pas d'hier** that's nothing new

dateur [datœr] *adj m* **tampon** *ou* **timbre d.** date stamp

datte [dat] *nf* date

dattier [datje] *nm* date palm

dauphin [dofɛ̃] *nm* (**a**) (*animal*) dolphin (**b**) *Hist* D. Dauphin (**c**) *Fig* (*successeur*) heir apparent

daurade [dorad] *nf* sea bream

davantage [davɑ̃taʒ] *adv* more; **elle est jolie, mais tu l'es bien d.** she's pretty but you're even prettier; **nous ne resterons pas d.** we won't stay any longer

DCA [desea] *nf Mil* (*abrév* **Défense contre avions**) anti-aircraft defence

DD *Ordinat* (*abrév* **disque dur**) HD

DDASS [das] *nf* (*abrév* **Direction départementale de l'action sanitaire et sociale**) = local social work department, one of whose tasks is to deal with children who have been abandoned or ill-treated

DDT [dedete] *nm* (*abrév* **dichloro-diphényl-trichloréthane**) DDT

de [də]

de becomes **d'** before vowel and h mute; **de + le** contracts to form **du**, and **de + les** to form **des**.

1 *prép* (**a**) (*indique l'origine*) from; **venir/être de** to come/ be from; **sortir de chez soi** to leave the house; **l'idée est de vous** it's your idea; **de vous à moi...** between ourselves...
(**b**) (*indique une progression*) **de... à...** from... to...; **du matin au soir** from morning till night; **de vingt à trente personnes** between twenty and thirty people; **de... en...** from... to...; **errer de ville en ville** to go from town to town
(**c**) (*introduit l'agent, l'auteur*) by; (*introduit l'instrument*) with; **accompagné de ses amis** accompanied by his friends; **la statue est de Rodin** the statue is by Rodin; **armé de pierres** armed with stones; **couvert de puces** covered in fleas
(**d**) (*indique la manière*) **d'un air amusé** with an amused expression; **d'une voix douce** gently, in a gentle voice
(**e**) (*indique la cause*) **sauter de joie** to jump for joy; **resplendissant de santé** blooming with health
(**f**) (*introduit une mesure*) **un enfant de dix ans** a child of ten, a ten-year-old child; **il est plus grand que moi de 5 cm** he's 5 cm taller than I am; **une pièce de 20 centimes** a 20-centime coin; **la terrasse fait 20 mètres de long** the terrace is 20 metres long; **20 francs de l'heure** 20 francs an hour
(**g**) (*indique l'appartenance*) of; **le livre de Pierre** Pierre's book; **le toit de la maison** the roof of the house
(**h**) (*pour préciser la nature, la matière*) **un problème d'algèbre** an algebra problem; **un hôtel de la rive gauche** a hotel on the left bank; **le journal d'hier** yesterday's paper; **à quatre heures de l'après-midi** at four (o'clock) in the afternoon; **une robe de soie** a silk dress; **un verre de vin** a glass of wine
(**i**) (*dans, parmi*) of; **l'un d'eux** one of them; **le meilleur élève de la classe** the best pupil in the class; **la moitié de ses économies** half (of) her savings
(**j**) (*pendant*) **je ne l'ai pas vu de la soirée** I haven't seen him all evening; **de nuit** by night
(**k**) (*introduit un infinitif*) **il est honteux de mentir** it is shameful to lie; **j'aime mieux attendre que de me faire mouiller** I would rather wait than get wet
(**l**) (*pour insister*) **c'est d'un ridicule!** it's utterly ridiculous!
(**m**) (*dans un titre*) **de l'amour** (on) love
2 *art partitif* some; **je bois du café tous les matins** I drink coffee every morning; **donnez-moi du vin** give me some wine; **c'est du Bach** it's Bach; **avez-vous du pain?** have you any bread?
3 *art indéfini* **je n'ai plus d'amis/de problèmes** I haven't got any friends/problems any more

dé¹ [de] *nm* (*pour jouer*) dice; **jouer aux dés** to play dice; **couper qch en dés** (*légumes*) to dice sth

dé² *nm* **dé** (**à coudre**) thimble

DEA [deəa] *nm* (*abrév* **diplôme d'études approfondies**) = postgraduate qualification which is a prerequisite for PhD candidates

dealer [dilœr] *nm Fam* (*de drogue*) dealer

déambulateur [deãbylatœr] *nm* Zimmer® (frame)

déambuler [deãbyle] *vi* to stroll about

débâcle [debakl] *nf* (**a**) (*d'un cours d'eau gelé*) breaking up (**b**) *Mil* rout; *Fig* (*d'une affaire, d'une monnaie*) collapse

déballage [debalaʒ] *nm* (**a**) (*action*) unpacking (**b**) *Fam* (*aveu*) outpouring

déballer [debale] *vt* (**a**) (*affaires, produits, caisses*) to unpack (**b**) *Fam* (*sa vie privée, ses sentiments*) to pour out

débandade [debãdad] *nf* (*d'une armée, d'une équipe*) rout; **c'est la d. dans l'entreprise** the company's in disarray

débaptiser [debatize] *vt* (*personne, rue*) to rename

débarbouillage [debarbujaʒ] *nm* face wash

débarbouiller [debarbuje] **1** *vt* **d. qn** to wash sb's face
2 se débarbouiller *vpr* to wash one's face

débarbouillette [debarbujet] *nf Can* (face) flannel, face cloth, *Am* washrag

débarcadère [debarkadɛr] *nm* landing stage; (*pour les marchandises*) wharf

débardeur [debardœr] *nm* (**a**) (*vêtement*) vest (**b**) (*personne*) docker, stevedore

débarquement [debarkəmã] *nm* (**a**) (*de cargaison*) unloading; (*de passagers*) landing (**b**) (*de troupes*) landing; *Hist* **le D.** the Normandy landings

débarquer [debarke] **1** *vt* (*cargaison*) to unload; (*passagers*) to land
2 *vi* (**a**) (*d'un bateau, d'un avion*) to disembark (**b**) *Fam Fig* to turn up; **il a toujours l'air de d.** he never seems to know what's going on

débarras [debara] *nm* (**a**) (*endroit*) junk room (**b**) *Fam* **bon d.!** good riddance!

débarrasser [debarase] **1** *vt* (*table, bureau, pièce*) to clear; **d. qn de qch** to relieve sb of sth; *Fam Fig* **d. le plancher** to clear out
2 **se débarrasser** *vpr* **se d. de** to get rid of

débat [deba] *nm* debate; *Pol* **débats (parlementaires)** (parliamentary) proceedings

débattre [11] [debatr] **1** *vt* (*discuter*) to debate, to discuss; **prix à d.** price negotiable
2 débattre de *vt ind* to discuss
3 se débattre *vpr* to struggle; **se d. contre les difficultés** to be up against difficulties

débauche [deboʃ] *nf* debauchery; **lieu de d.** den of vice; *Fig* **une d. de couleurs** a riot of colour

débauché, -e [deboʃe] **1** *adj* debauched
2 *nm,f* debauchee

débaucher [deboʃe] *vt* (**a**) (*inciter à la débauche*) to corrupt (**b**) (*licencier*) to lay off

débecter [debekte] *vt très Fam* to sicken

débile [debil] **1** *adj* (**a**) (*qui manque de vigueur*) (*enfant*) sickly; (*corps*) weak; (*santé*) poor (**b**) *Fam* (*stupide*) stupid
2 *nmf* **d. mental** mental defective; *Fam Fig* complete idiot

débilitant, -e [debilitā, -āt] *adj* debilitating; *Fig* demoralizing

débilité [debilite] *nf* (**a**) (*faiblesse*) debility; **d. mentale** mental deficiency (**b**) *Fam* (*stupidité*) stupidity

débiliter [debilite] *vt* to debilitate

débiner [debine] *Fam* **1** *vt* to run down
2 se débiner *vpr* to clear off

débit [debi] *nm* (**a**) *Fin* debit (**b**) (*ventes*) turnover (**c**) (*commerce*) **d. de boissons** bar; **d. de tabac** tobacconist's (shop) (**d**) (*de bois*) cutting up (**e**) (*d'une rivière, de liquide*) flow; (*d'une machine*) output; *Ordinat* **d. de données** data throughput (**f**) (*d'un orateur*) delivery; *Fam* **il a un de ces débits** he's really got the gift of the gab!

débitant, -e [debitā, -āt] *nm,f* **d. de boissons** bar owner; **d. de tabac** tobacconist

débiter [debite] *vt* (**a**) (*sujet: usine*) to produce; (*sujet: cours d'eau*) to have a flow rate of (**b**) *Fin* (*somme, compte*) to debit (**c**) (*bois, viande*) to cut up (**d**) (*vendre*) to sell (**e**) *Péj* (*dire*) to spout

débiteur, -trice [debitœr, -tris] **1** *adj* (*compte*) debit
2 *nm,f* debtor

déblaiement [deblemā] *nm* clearing

déblatérer [34] [deblatere] *vi Fam* **d. contre** *ou* **sur qn/qch** to rail against sb/sth

déblayage [debleʒaʒ] *nm* clearing

déblayer [53] [debleje] *vt* (**a**) (*terre, gravats, neige*) to clear (**b**) (*terrain*) to clear; *Fig* **d. le terrain** (*faire des préparatifs*) to prepare the ground

déblocage [deblɔkaʒ] *nm* (*d'une porte, d'un tiroir, d'un mécanisme*) unjamming; (*des prix, des salaires*) unfreezing

débloquer [deblɔke] **1** *vt* (**a**) (*porte, tiroir, mécanisme*) unjam; (*prix, salaires*) to unfreeze; **d. des fonds** to release funds (**b**) *Psy* **d. qn** (*lui ôter ses complexes*) to rid sb of his/her complexes; (*le rendre moins timide*) to make sb less inhibited
2 *vi Fam* (*être fou*) to be off one's rocker; (*raconter n'importe quoi*) to talk drivel; (*être gâteux*) to go gaga

déboguer [deboge] *vt Ordinat* to debug

débogueur [debogœr] *nm Ordinat* debugger

déboires [debwar] *nmpl* (*déceptions*) disappointments; (*ennuis*) problems

déboisement [debwazmā] *nm* deforestation

déboiser [debwaze] *vt* to deforest

déboîtement [debwatmā] *nm* (**a**) (*d'un membre, d'une articulation*) dislocation (**b**) (*en voiture*) pulling out

déboîter [debwate] **1** *vt* (**a**) (*objets encastrés*) to disconnect (**b**) (*articulation, membre*) to dislocate
2 *vi* (*en voiture*) to pull out
3 se déboîter *vpr* (*articulation, membre*) to become dislocated; **se d. l'épaule/le genou** to dislocate one's shoulder/knee

débonnaire [debonɛr] *adj* (*personne*) good-natured, easy-going; **répondre d'un ton d.** to answer good-naturedly

débordant, -e [debordā, -āt] *adj* (*activité*) tireless; (*imagination*) boundless; **d. de santé/d'enthousiasme** bursting with health/with enthusiasm

débordé, -e [deborde] *adj* **d. (de travail)** snowed under (with work)

débordement [debordǝmā] *nm* (**a**) (*d'une rivière*) overflowing; *Fig* (*d'enthousiasme, de joie*) outburst (**b**) **débordements** excesses (**c**) *Mil* (*de l'ennemi*) outflanking

déborder [deborde] **1** *vi* (**a**) (*liquide, rivière*) to overflow; **l'eau déborde du vase** the vase is overflowing; **les papiers débordent de la corbeille** the wastepaper basket is overflowing with paper; **d. sur le temps prévu** to overrun (**b**) *Fig* **d. de vie** to be bursting with vitality; **d. d'imagination** to have boundless imagination
2 *vt* (*dépasser*) (*alignement*) to stick out from; (*limite*) to go beyond; *Mil* (*l'ennemi*) to outflank; *Sp* (*coureur*) to overtake; **cela déborde le cadre de...** that is beyond the scope of...

débouchage [debuʃaʒ] *nm* (**a**) (*d'un tuyau, d'un évier*) unblocking (**b**) (*d'une bouteille*) uncorking

débouché [debuʃe] *nm* (*professionnel*) opening, job opportunity; *Com* outlet

déboucher [debuʃe] **1** *vt* (**a**) (*tuyau, évier*) to unblock (**b**) (*bouteille*) to uncork
2 *vi* (**a**) (*dans l'espace*) (*personne, voiture*) to emerge (*de* from), to come out (*de* of); **d. dans/sur** to lead to (**b**) *Fig* **d. sur qch** (*avoir pour résultat*) to lead to sth
3 se déboucher *vpr* (*tuyau, évier, oreilles*) to clear; **la bouteille se débouche facilement** the bottle opens easily

débouler [debule] *Fam* **1** *vt* **d. l'escalier** to race down the stairs
2 *vi* (**a**) (*descendre*) to race down (**b**) (*arriver*) to turn up

déboulonner [debulɔne] *vt* (**a**) *Tech* to unbolt; (*statue*) to take down (**b**) *Fam Fig* (*critiquer*) to debunk; (*de son poste*) to kick out

débourser [deburse] *vt* (*argent*) to lay out; **sans rien d.** without spending a penny

déboussoler [debusole] *vt Fam* to throw

debout [dəbu] adv (a) (verticalement) (chose) upright; (personne) standing; **cent ans plus tard, la maison est encore d.** the house is still standing a hundred years later; **elle est d. toute la journée** she's on her feet all day; **mettre qch d.** to stand sth up; **se mettre d.** to stand up; **rester d.** to stand; **tenir d.** (objet) to stay upright; (personne) to stay on one's feet; Fig **un argument qui ne tient pas d.** an argument that won't stand up; **se tenir d.** to stand; **conte** ou **histoire à dormir d.** cock-and-bull story (b) (hors du lit) **être d.** to be up; **allons, d.!** come on, get up!

débouter [debute] vt Jur to nonsuit

déboutonner [debutɔne] **1** vt to unbutton
2 se déboutonner vpr (personne) to undo one's coat/jacket/etc; (vêtement) to unbutton; Fig (se confier) to open up

débraillé, -e [debraje] adj slovenly

débrancher [debrɑ̃ʃe] vt to unplug

débrayage [debrejaʒ] nm (a) Aut declutching (b) (grève) stoppage

débrayer [53] [debreje] vi (a) Aut to release the clutch (b) (se mettre en grève) to stop work

débridé, -e [debride] adj (passion) unbridled; (imagination) vivid

débris [debri] nmpl (d'un avion, d'une voiture) debris, wreckage; (de verre, de bois) fragments; **d. de métal** scrap (metal)
2 nm Fam **un vieux d.** an old wreck

débrouillard, -e [debrujar, -ard] Fam **1** adj resourceful
2 nm,f resourceful person

débrouillardise [debrujardiz] nf resourcefulness

débrouiller [debruje] **1** vt (fil, mystère) to unravel
2 se débrouiller vpr to manage, to cope; (dans une langue, un domaine) to get by; **débrouillez-vous!** you'll just have to manage!; **elle s'est débrouillée pour rencontrer le directeur** she worked it so that she got to meet the director

débroussailler [debrusaje] vt to clear of undergrowth; Fig (question) to clarify

débusquer [debyske] vt to flush out

début [deby] nm (a) (commencement) beginning, start; **au d. (de)** at the start or beginning (of); **au tout d., tout au d.** at the very start or beginning; **dès le d.** from the start; **je le savais depuis le d.** I knew all along; **du d. à la fin** from start to finish; **en d. de** at the start of; Hum **il faut** ou **il y a un d. à tout** there's a first time for everything (b) **débuts** (d'un acteur, d'un chanteur) debut, first appearance; **faire ses débuts** to make one's debut; **en être à ses débuts** (société, projet) to be in its early stages (c) Ordinat home; **aller au d.** (commande) go top

débutant, -e [debytɑ̃, -ɑ̃t] **1** adj novice
2 nm,f (dans une discipline) beginner; **grand d.** complete beginner

débuter [debyte] **1** vi (a) (commencer) to begin, to start (par with) (b) (dans le spectacle) to make one's debut; (dans la vie professionnelle) to start out; **mal/bien d. dans la vie** to get off to a bad/good start in life
2 vt Fam to start, to begin (par with)

deçà [dəsa] **en deçà de** prép (dans l'espace) (on) this side of; **rester (très) en d. de la vérité** to be (very) short of the truth

déca [deka] nm Fam (café) decaf

décacheter [42] [dekaʃte] vt to unseal, to open

décadenasser [dekadnase] vt to take the padlock off

décadence [dekadɑ̃s] nf (état) decadence; (processus) decline; **tomber en d.** to go into decline

décadent, -e [dekadɑ̃, -ɑ̃t] adj decadent

décaféiné [dekafeine] nm decaffeinated coffee

décagonal, -e, -aux, -ales [dekagonal, -o] adj decagonal

décagone [dekagon] nm Math decagon

décalage [dekalaʒ] nm (a) (désaccord) gap (b) (dans le temps) time lag; **d. horaire** time difference; **souffrir du d. horaire** to have jet lag

décalaminer [dekalamine] vt to decoke

décalcification [dekalsifikasjɔ̃] nf Méd decalcification

décalcifier [66] [dekalsifje] Méd **1** vt to decalcify
2 se décalcifier vpr to become decalcified

décalcomanie [dekalkomani] nf (procédé) Br transfer process, Am decal; (image) Br transfer, Am decal; **faire de la d.** to do Br transfers or Am decals

décaler [dekale] **1** vt (a) (dans l'espace) to move, to shift (de from) (b) (dans le temps) (avancer) to bring forward (de by); (reculer) to put back (de by)
2 se décaler vpr to move, to shift; **vous pourriez vous d. d'un rang/vers la gauche?** could you move up a row/move to the left?

décalitre [dekalitr] nm decalitre

décalquer [dekalke] vt to trace

décamètre [dekametr] nm decametre

décamper [dekɑ̃pe] vi Fam to clear off

décan [dekɑ̃] nm = one of three divisions of each sign of the zodiac

décaniller [dekanije] vi Fam to clear off

décanter [dekɑ̃te] **1** vt (vin) to decant
2 se décanter vpr (vin) to settle; Fig (situation) to become clearer

décapage [dekapaʒ] nm (avec un produit) stripping; (au papier de verre) sanding (down); (d'un four) cleaning

décapant, -e [dekapɑ̃, -ɑ̃t] **1** adj (a) **produit d.** (pour vernis, peinture) paint stripper; (pour four) oven cleaner (b) Fig (humour) caustic
2 nm (pour vernis, peinture) paint stripper; (pour four) oven cleaner

décaper [dekape] vt (a) (avec un produit) to strip; (au papier de verre) to sand (down); (four) to clean (b) Fam Fig **ça décape!** (alcool) it takes the roof of your mouth off!

décapeuse [dekapøz] nf scraper

décapitation [dekapitasjɔ̃] nf decapitation

décapiter [dekapite] vt (personne) to decapitate; (arbre) to pollard

décapotable [dekapotabl] **1** adj convertible; (coupé) drop-head
2 nf convertible

décapoter [dekapote] vt to lower the top of

décapsuler [dekapsyle] vt to take the top off

décapsuleur [dekapsylœr] nm bottle opener

décarcasser [dekarkase] **se décarcasser** vpr Fam to sweat blood (**pour faire** to do)

décasyllabe [dekasilab] **1** adj decasyllabic
2 nm decasyllable

décathlon [dekatlɔ̃] nm decathlon

décati, -e [dekati] adj (visage) age-worn; (personne) decrepit

décatir [dekatir] **se décatir** vpr to become decrepit

décédé, -e [desede] *adj* deceased

décéder [34] [desede] *vi* to die

décelable [deslabl] *adj* detectable

déceler [39] [desle] *vt* (a) *(découvrir)* to detect (b) *(indiquer)* to indicate

décélération [deselerasjɔ̃] *nf* deceleration

décélérer [34] [deselere] *vi* to decelerate

décembre [desɑ̃br] *nm* December; *voir aussi* **janvier**

décemment [desamɑ̃] *adv* (a) *(convenablement) (se comporter)* properly; *(s'habiller)* decently (b) *(raisonnablement)* reasonably well (c) *(raisonnablement)* reasonably; **je ne pouvais pas d. refuser** I couldn't reasonably refuse

décence [desɑ̃s] *nf* (a) *(bienséance) (de comportement)* propriety; *(d'habillement)* decency (b) *(tact)* decency; **avoir la d. de faire qch** to have the decency to do sth

décennal, -e, -aux, -ales [desenal, -o] *adj* ten-year

décennie [deseni] *nf* decade

décent, -e [desɑ̃, -ɑ̃t] *adj* (a) *(comportement)* proper; *(vêtements)* decent; **peu d.** improper/indecent (b) *(passable)* reasonable

décentralisation [desɑ̃tralizasjɔ̃] *nf* decentralization

décentraliser [desɑ̃tralize] *vt* to decentralize

décentrer [desɑ̃tre] **1** *vt* to move off centre
2 se décentrer *vpr* to move off centre

déception [desɛpsjɔ̃] *nf* disappointment; **d. sentimentale** disappointment in love

décerner [deserne] *vt* (prix, médaille) to award (à to)

décès [desɛ] *nm* death; **fermé pour cause de d.** *(sur la porte d'un magasin)* closed due to bereavement

décevant, -e [desəvɑ̃, -ɑ̃t] *adj* disappointing

décevoir [60] [desəvwar] *vt* to disappoint; **il/ce voyage m'a beaucoup déçu** I was very disappointed in him/with the trip

déchaîné, -e [deʃene] *adj (passion)* unbridled; *(mer, vent)* raging; *(personne)* wild

déchaînement [deʃɛnmɑ̃] *nm (des éléments)* fury; *(des passions)* outburst

déchaîner [deʃene] **1** *vt (passions, colère)* to unleash; **d. l'hilarité** to provoke laughter
2 se déchaîner *vpr (tempête, vent)* to rage; *(personne)* to fly into a rage (**contre** with)

déchanter [deʃɑ̃te] *vi Fam* to become disillusioned

décharge [deʃarʒ] *nf* (a) *(tirs)* discharge (b) *(électrique)* (electric) shock; **d. d'adrénaline** rush of adrenaline (c) *(d'ordures)* dump; *(publique) Br* rubbish *or Am* garbage dump; **d. interdite** *(sur panneau)* no dumping (d) *Jur (d'un accusé)* acquittal; *(d'un témoin)* discharge; *Fig* **dire qch à la d. de qn** to say sth in sb's defence

déchargement [deʃarʒəmɑ̃] *nm* unloading

décharger [45] [deʃarʒe] **1** *vt* (a) *(vider) (camion, bateau, cargaison)* to unload; *(sujet: camion) (sable, gravier)* to dump; *(arme à feu)* to fire, to discharge; *Fig* **d. sa conscience** to unburden one's conscience (**de** of) (b) *(soulager)* **d. qn de qch** *(tâche, responsabilité)* to relieve sb of sth; *Jur (d'une accusation)* to acquit sb of sth
2 se décharger *vpr* (a) *(personne)* **se d. d'une tâche/ d'une responsabilité sur qn** to offload a task/a responsibility onto sb (b) *(pile, batterie)* to go flat

décharné, -e [deʃarne] *adj (corps, membres, visage)* emaciated; *Fig (arbre)* bare

déchaussé, -e [deʃose] *adj* (a) *(sans chaussures)* barefoot (b) *(dent)* loose

déchausser [deʃose] **1** *vt (enlever ses chaussures à)* **d. qn** to take off sb's shoes; **d. ses skis** to take off one's skis
2 se déchausser *vpr* (a) *(enlever ses chaussures)* to take off one's shoes (b) *(dent)* to work loose

dèche [dɛʃ] *nf Fam* **être dans la d.** to be stony broke; **c'est la d.** I'm/we're/etc stony broke

déchéance [deʃeɑ̃s] *nf* (a) *(physique, morale)* decline (b) *Jur (de droits)* forfeiture; **d. de l'autorité parentale** loss of parental rights

déchet [deʃɛ] *nm* (a) **déchets** waste; **déchets radioactifs/industriels** radioactive/industrial waste (b) *(perte)* **il y a du d.** there's some wastage (c) *Péj (personne)* down-and-out; **un d. de la société** a social outcast

déchiffrable [deʃifrabl] *adj* decipherable

déchiffrage [deʃifraʒ] *nm Mus* sight-reading

déchiffrement [deʃifrəmɑ̃] *nm* deciphering; *Ordinat* decryption

déchiffrer [deʃifre] *vt* (a) *(inscription, écriture, message)* to decipher; *(signaux)* to interpret; *Fig (pensées, sentiments, mystère)* to fathom (b) *(musique)* to sight-read

déchiqueté, -e [deʃikte] *adj* (a) *(irrégulier)* jagged (b) *(vêtements, papiers)* torn to shreds; *(corps) (dans une explosion)* blown to pieces

déchiqueter [42] [deʃikte] *vt (vêtements, papiers)* to tear to shreds; *(sujet: explosion) (corps)* to blow to pieces

déchirant, -e [deʃirɑ̃, -ɑ̃t] *adj (spectacle, adieux)* heartrending

déchiré, -e [deʃire] *adj aussi Méd & Fig* torn; **être d. entre deux personnes** to be torn between two people

déchirement [deʃirmɑ̃] *nm (peine)* heartbreak

déchirer [deʃire] **1** *vt* (a) *(accidentellement)* to tear; *(volontairement)* to tear up; *(enveloppe)* to tear open (b) *Fig (famille, pays)* to tear apart; *(silence)* to pierce; **des sons qui déchirent le tympan** ear-splitting sounds
2 se déchirer *vpr (tissu, papier)* to tear (b) *Méd* **se d. un muscle** to tear a muscle (c) *Fig (couple)* to tear each other apart

déchirure [deʃiryr] *nf (dans un tissu) & Méd* tear; *Fig (peine)* heartbreak; **se faire une d. musculaire** to tear a muscle

déchoir [14] [deʃwar] *vi* **ce serait d. (que de...)** it would be demeaning (to...); **par ce mariage il déchoit de son rang** he is marrying beneath him

déchu, -e [deʃy] *adj (dépossédé) (roi)* deposed; **être d. de qch** *(droit, nationalité)* to be stripped of sth

décibel [desibɛl] *nm* decibel

décidé, -e [deside] *adj* (a) *(fixé)* settled (b) *(caractère, personne, manière)* determined; **d'un ton d.** in a decisive tone; **être d. à faire qch** to be determined to do sth

décidément [desidemɑ̃] *adv* really; **d. je n'ai pas de chance!, je n'ai d. pas de chance!** I really don't have any luck!

décider [deside] **1** *vt* (a) *(déterminer)* **d. que/quand/si** to decide that/when/if; **il fut décidé qu'on attendrait** it was decided that we/they/etc should wait; **c'est moi qui décide ici** I'm the one who makes the decisions here; **je déciderai pour toi** I'll decide for you (b) *(convaincre)* **d. qn à faire qch** to persuade sb to do sth
2 décider de *vt ind* (a) *(fixer)* **d.** to decide on sth; **un événement qui a décidé de sa carrière** an event that determined his career; **d. de faire qch** to decide to do sth
3 se décider *vpr (prendre une décision)* to make up one's mind, to come to a decision; **se d. à faire qch** to

make up one's mind to do sth; **je ne peux pas me d. à le faire** I can't bring myself to do it; *Fig* **il ne se décide pas à faire beau** the weather can't make up its mind whether to be fine or not; **se d. pour qn/qch** to decide on sb/sth (b) *(problème, question)* to be settled

décideur, -euse [desidœr, -øz] *nm,f* decision-maker

décigramme [desigram] *nm* decigram

décilitre [desilitr] *nm* decilitre

décimal, -e, -aux, -ales [desimal, -o] **1** *adj* decimal **2** *nf* **décimale** decimal

décimer [desime] *vt* to decimate

décimètre [desimetr] *nm* decimetre; **double d.** *(règle)* ruler *(20 cm long)*

décisif, -ive [desizif, -iv] *adj (bataille, argument)* decisive; *(preuve)* conclusive; *(moment)* critical

décision [desizjɔ̃] *nf* (a) *(choix)* decision; *Jur* ruling; **arriver à/prendre une d.** to come to/to make a decision; **prendre la d. de faire qch** to decide to do sth; **la d. ne m'appartient pas** it's not my decision (b) *(détermination)* determination; **avec d.** decisively; **esprit de d.** decisiveness

déclamation [deklamasjɔ̃] *nf (éloquence)* declamation

déclamatoire [deklamatwar] *adj Péj (style)* declamatory; *(discours)* bombastic

déclamer [deklame] *vt (discours, vers)* to declaim; *Péj* to spout

déclaration [deklarasjɔ̃] *nf* (a) *(annonce orale, écrite)* statement; **d. (d'amour)** declaration of love; **faire une ou sa d. à qn** to declare one's love to sb; **le chef de l'État a une importante d. à faire** the President has an important announcement to make; **faire une d. à la police** to make a statement to the police; **D. des droits de l'homme** Declaration of Human Rights; **d. de guerre** declaration of war; *Hist* **D. d'indépendance** Declaration of Independence; **d. de principe** statement of principle (b) *(acte officiel) (de naissance, de décès)* registration; *(à une compagnie d'assurances)* claim (**de** for); *(à la police)* report; **d. en douane** customs declaration; **d. d'impôts** tax return; **faire sa d. d'impôts** to fill in one's tax return; **d. de revenus** income tax return (c) *Ordinat* **d. de champ** field definition

déclaré, -e [deklare] *adj (ennemi, intention)* declared; *(partisan)* avowed

déclarer [deklare] **1** *vt (annoncer)* to declare; *(revenus, décès, naissance)* to register; *(à une compagnie d'assurances)* to make a claim for; *(à la police)* to report; **d. que** to declare (that); **d. forfait** *(en sport)* to scratch; **d. la guerre à qn** to declare war on sb; **rien à d.** *(en douane)* nothing to declare; **être déclaré coupable** to be found guilty
2 se déclarer *vpr (feu, maladie, guerre)* to break out (b) *(se prononcer)* **se d. pour/contre qch** to declare oneself in favour of/against sth (c) *(se dire)* **se d. satisfait/surpris** to declare oneself satisfied/surprised; **se d. coupable** to admit one's guilt (d) *(faire une déclaration d'amour)* to declare one's love

déclasser [deklase] *vt* (a) *(faire changer de classe) Sp* to relegate; *(hôtel)* to downgrade; *(passagers)* to transfer from one class to another (b) *(déranger)* to get out of order

déclenchement [deklɑ̃ʃmɑ̃] *nm (d'un appareil)* starting; *(d'un mécanisme)* activation; *(d'une sonnerie)* setting off; *(d'un événement)* triggering

déclencher [deklɑ̃ʃe] *vt (appareil)* to start; *(mécanisme)* to activate; *(sonnerie)* to set off; *(événement, critiques, questions)* to trigger; *Mil (attaque)* to launch

déclencheur [deklɑ̃ʃœr] *nm Phot* shutter release

déclic [deklik] *nm (bruit)* click; **la vue de cette photo a été pour elle un véritable d.** when she looked at the photo things fell into place

déclin [deklɛ̃] *nm (du talent, de la santé, d'une civilisation)* decline; *(de la beauté)* fading; *(du jour)* close; **être en d.** to be in decline; **le soleil est à son d.** the sun is setting; **au d. de sa vie** in her declining years

déclinaison [deklinɛzɔ̃] *nf Gram* declension

déclinant, -e [deklinɑ̃, -ɑ̃t] *adj (beauté, lumière)* fading; *(pouvoirs)* declining

décliner [dekline] **1** *vi (jour)* to draw to a close; *(talent, santé)* to decline; *(beauté)* to fade
2 *vt* (a) *Formel (refuser) (offre, invitation)* to decline; **d. toute responsabilité** to accept no liability (b) *Gram* to decline (c) *(réciter) (identité)* to state
3 se décliner *vpr Gram* to be declined

déclivité [deklivite] *nf* slope, incline

décloisonnement [deklwazɔnmɑ̃] *nm* decompartmentalization

décloisonner [deklwazɔne] *vt* to decompartmentalize

déco [deko] *nf Fam (d'une pièce)* décor; *(métier)* (interior) decorating; **j'aime beaucoup faire de la d.** I love decorating

décocher [dekɔʃe] *vt* (a) *(flèche)* to shoot; **d. un coup/une ruade à qn** to hit out at/to kick sb (b) *Fig (remarque)* to fire off (**à** at); *(sourire, œillade)* to flash (**à** at)

décoction [dekɔksjɔ̃] *nf* decoction

décodage [dekodaʒ] *nm* decoding

décoder [dekode] *vt* to decode

décodeur [dekodœr] *nm TV* decoder

décoiffer [dekwafe] **1** *vt (ébouriffer)* **d. qn** to mess up sb's hair; **tu es tout décoiffé** your hair's in a mess; *Fam Fig* **un film qui décoiffe** a mind-blowing film
2 se décoiffer *vpr* (a) *(se dépeigner)* to mess up one's hair (b) *(ôter son chapeau)* to remove one's hat

décoincer [16] [dekwɛ̃se] **1** *vt (tiroir, mécanisme)* to loosen; *Fam Fig (personne)* to loosen up
2 se décoincer *vpr (tiroir, mécanisme)* to loosen; *Fam Fig (personne)* to loosen up

déçois *etc voir* **décevoir**

décolérer [34] [dekolere] *vi* to calm down; **il ne décolérait pas** he was still angry; **il n'a pas décoléré depuis huit jours** he's been angry for a week

décollage [dekɔlaʒ] *nm* (a) *aussi Fig (démarrage)* takeoff (b) *(d'un timbre, de papier peint, d'une affiche)* peeling off

décollement [dekɔlmɑ̃] *nm* (a) *Méd* **d. de la rétine** detachment of the retina (b) *(d'un timbre, de papier peint, d'une affiche)* peeling off

décoller [dekɔle] **1** *vt (timbre, papier peint, affiche)* to peel off; **d. une enveloppe à la vapeur** to steam open an envelope; *Fam Fig* **d. qn de la télé/du bar** to tear sb away from the TV/the bar
2 *vi* (a) *(avion, fusée, économie)* to take off (b) *Fam (partir)* to leave; **bon, on décolle?** shall we get moving?; **je ne décollerai pas d'ici tant que…** I'm not budging until…; *Sp* **d. du peloton** to pull away from the pack
3 se décoller *vpr (se détacher)* to peel off; *Méd (rétine)* to become detached

décolleté, -e [dekɔlte] **1** *adj (vêtement)* low-cut; **une femme très décolletée** a woman in a very low-cut dress; **robe décolletée dans le dos** dress cut low at the back
2 *nm (de vêtement)* low neckline; *(haut des seins)* cleavage

décolonisation [dekɔlɔnizasjɔ̃] *nf* decolonization

décoloniser [dekɔlɔnize] *vt* to decolonize

décolorant, -e [dekɔlɔrɑ̃, -ɑ̃t] **1** *adj* bleaching
2 *nm* bleaching agent

décoloration [dekɔlɔrasjɔ̃] *nf (d'un tissu)* fading; *(des cheveux)* bleaching; **se faire faire une d.** to have one's hair bleached

décolorer [dekɔlɔre] **1** *vt (tissu)* to fade; *(cheveux)* to bleach
2 se décolorer *vpr (tissu)* to fade; **se d. les cheveux** to bleach one's hair

décombres [dekɔ̃br] *nmpl* ruins, debris

décommander [dekɔmɑ̃de] **1** *vt (réunion, dîner)* to cancel, to call off; *(invité)* to put off
2 se décommander *vpr* to cancel

décomplexer [dekɔ̃plekse] *vt Fam* **d. qn** to cure sb of his/her hang-ups

décomposer [dekɔ̃poze] **1** *vt* **(a)** *(élément chimique)* to decompose; *(problème, phrase, mouvement)* to break down **(en** into**) (b)** *(matière organique)* to decompose **(c)** *(traits, visage)* to distort; **il est arrivé complètement décomposé** *(par l'émotion)* he arrived quite distraught
2 se décomposer *vpr* **(a)** *(corps, viande, feuilles)* to decompose; *(fruit)* to rot **(b)** *(visage, traits)* to become distorted

décomposition [dekɔ̃pozisjɔ̃] *nf* **(a)** *(d'un élément chimique)* decomposition; *(d'un problème, d'une phrase, d'un mouvement)* breaking down **(en** into**) (b)** *(de viande, de feuilles, de corps)* decomposition; *Fig (décadence)* decay

décompresser [dekɔ̃prese] **1** *vt Tech* to decompress; *Ordinat* to decompress, to unbundle, to uncrunch
2 *vi Fam* to unwind

décompression [dekɔ̃presjɔ̃] *nf* decompression; *Ordinat* decompression, unbundling; **avoir un accident de d.** *(plongeur)* to get the bends

décompte [dekɔ̃t] *nm (sur une somme à payer)* deduction; *(calcul)* calculation

décompter [dekɔ̃te] *vt* to deduct **(de** from**)**

déconcentrer [dekɔ̃sɑ̃tre] **1** *vt* **(a)** *(pouvoirs, administration)* to devolve, to decentralize **(b)** *(distraire)* to distract
2 se déconcentrer *vpr* to lose concentration

déconcertant, -e [dekɔ̃sertɑ̃, -ɑ̃t] *adj* disconcerting

déconcerté, -e [dekɔ̃serte] *adj* disconcerted

déconcerter [dekɔ̃serte] *vt* to disconcert

déconfit, -e [dekɔ̃fi, -it] *adj (personne, mine)* crestfallen

déconfiture [dekɔ̃fityr] *nf (échec)* defeat

décongeler [39] [dekɔ̃ʒle] *vt* to defrost, to thaw

décongestionner [dekɔ̃ʒɛstjɔne] *vt aussi Fig* to relieve congestion in

déconnecter [dekɔnɛkte] *vt (fil)* to disconnect; *Fig* **déconnecté de la réalité** out of touch with the real world

déconner [dekɔne] *vi très Fam* **(a)** *(dire des bêtises)* to talk garbage; *(faire des bêtises)* to piss around; **faire qch pour d.** *(pour rire)* to do sth for a laugh; **sans d., c'était super** no kidding, it was great; **sans d.!** *(en réponse)* no kidding! **(b)** *(mal fonctionner)* to play up

déconneur, -euse [dekɔnœr, -øz] *nm,f très Fam* clown

déconseiller [dekɔseje] *vt* **d. qch à qn** to advise sb against sth; **d. à qn de faire qch** to advise sb against doing sth; **un livre à d. aux jeunes** an unsuitable book for young people; **il est déconseillé de faire qch** it is inadvisable to do sth

déconsidérer [34] [dekɔ̃sidere] **1** *vt* to discredit
2 se déconsidérer *vpr* to bring discredit on oneself

décontamination [dekɔ̃taminasjɔ̃] *nf* decontamination

décontaminer [dekɔ̃tamine] *vt* to decontaminate

décontenancer [16] [dekɔ̃tnɑ̃se] **1** *vt* to disconcert
2 se décontenancer *vpr* to become disconcerted

décontracté, -e [dekɔ̃trakte] *adj (ambiance, attitude, personne)* relaxed; *(vêtement)* casual; *Péj (désinvolte)* casual

décontraction [dekɔ̃traksjɔ̃] *nf* relaxation; **faire qch avec d.** to do sth casually

déconvenue [dekɔ̃vny] *nf Formel* disappointment; **quelle ne fut pas ma d. quand...** I was so disappointed when...

décor [dekɔr] *nm* **(a)** *(d'une maison, d'un restaurant)* décor **(b)** *Th, Cin & TV* décors set, scenery; **en d. naturel** on location; *Fam* **aller/envoyer qn dans le d.** *(en voiture)* to go/knock sb off the road **(c)** *(environnement)* surroundings; *Fig* **il aurait besoin d'un changement** *ou* **de changer de d.** he needs a change of scene

décorateur, -trice [dekɔratœr, -tris] *nm,f* **(a)** *(d'intérieur)* (interior) decorator **(b)** *Th* set designer

décoratif, -ive [dekɔratif, -iv] *adj* decorative; *(arbre)* ornamental; *Péj* **n'avoir qu'un rôle d.** to have a purely decorative role

décoration [dekɔrasjɔ̃] *nf* **(a)** *(d'une maison, d'un restaurant)* decoration; **faire de la d.** to decorate; **d. d'intérieur** interior decorating; **décorations de Noël** Christmas decorations **(b)** *(médaille)* decoration

décorer [dekɔre] *vt* **(a)** *(pièce, maison)* to decorate **(de** with**) (b)** *(médailler)* to decorate **(de** with**)**

décorticage [dekɔrtikaʒ] *nm (de crevettes, de noisettes)* shelling; *(de riz, d'orge)* hulling; *Fig (d'un texte, d'un auteur)* detailed analysis

décortiquer [dekɔrtike] *vt (crevettes, noisettes)* to shell; *(riz, orge)* to hull; *Fig (texte)* to analyse in detail

décorum [dekɔrɔm] *nm* decorum

découcher [dekuʃe] *vi* to stay out all night

découdre [21] [dekudr] **1** *vt (vêtement, poche, ourlet)* to unpick, to unstitch; *(bouton)* to take off
2 *vi* **en d.** to fight
3 se découdre *vpr (vêtement, poche, ourlet)* to come unstitched; *(bouton)* to come off

découler [dekule] *vi* to follow **(de** from**)**; **il en découle que...** it follows that...

découpage [dekupaʒ] *nm* **(a)** *(de gâteau)* cutting up; *(de viande)* carving; *(de métaux, du cuir)* punching; *Ordinat (de fichier, d'image)* splitting; *Pol* **d. électoral** division into constituencies **(b)** *(image découpée)* cutout; **faire du d.** *ou* **des découpages** to do some cutting out **(c)** *Fig (d'un texte)* division **(en** into**)**; *Cin (scénario)* shooting script

découpé, -e [dekupe] *adj (irrégulier)* jagged

découper [dekupe] **1** *vt* **(a)** *(gâteau, papier)* to cut up; *(viande)* to carve; *(métaux, cuir)* to punch; *Ordinat (fichier)* to split; *(disque dur)* to partition; **b. un article dans un journal** to cut an article out of a newspaper **(b)** *Fig (texte)* to divide **(en** into**)**

2 se découper *vpr* **se d. sur** to stand out against

décourageant, -e [dekuraʒɑ̃, -ɑ̃t] *adj (nouvelle, situation, travail)* disheartening; *(personne)* hopeless

découragement [dekuraʒmɑ̃] *nm* discouragement

décourager [45] **1** *vt* **(a)** *(démoraliser)* to discourage, to dishearten; **se laisser d.** to be discouraged or disheartened **(b)** *(dissuader)* to discourage; **d. qn de faire qch** to discourage sb from doing sth

2 se décourager *vpr* to get discouraged or disheartened

décousu, -e [dekuzy] *adj (ourlet, poche, vêtement)* unstitched; *Fig (phrases, idées)* disjointed; *(conversation)* rambling; *(travail)* unmethodical

découvert, -e [dekuver, -ert] **1** *adj (épaules)* bare; *(terrain)* open; **dormir d.** to sleep without any covers; **la tête découverte** bareheaded

2 *nm* **(a)** *Fin* **d.** *(bancaire)* overdraft; **être à d. (de 2000 francs)** *(personne, compte)* to be overdrawn (by 2,000 francs) **(b)** **agir à d.** to act openly; **s'avancer à d.** to move forward without cover

découverte [dekuvert] *nf* discovery; **aller** *ou* **partir à la d. de qch** to go off to explore sth; **faire une d.** to make a discovery; *Hum* **ce n'est pas une d.!** that's nothing new!

découvrir [52] [dekuvrir] **1** *vt* **(a)** *(trouver)* to discover **(b)** *(mettre à jour) (secret, complot)* to uncover; **d. qch à qn** *(projets, secrets)* to disclose or reveal sth to sb **(c)** *(apprendre à connaître) (domaine, art, sentiment)* to discover; *(personne)* to get to know **(d)** *(casserole, statue)* to uncover; *(dents, bras)* to bare; **une robe avec un décolleté qui découvre les épaules** an off-the-shoulder dress; *aussi Fig* **d. son jeu** to show one's hand **(e)** *(apercevoir)* to have a view of

2 se découvrir *vpr* **(a)** *(enlever son chapeau)* to take off one's hat **(b)** *(en dormant)* **le malade s'est découvert** the patient threw off his bedclothes **(c)** *(ciel)* to clear **(d)** *(se trouver)* to discover some distant relatives; **il s'est découvert une passion pour le jardinage** he discovered he had a passion for gardening

décrasser [dekrase] **1** *vt* to clean; *Fam Fig* **d. qn** to knock the rough edges off sb

2 se décrasser *vpr* to clean oneself up; *Fig (en faisant de l'exercice)* to clean out one's system

décrêper [dekrepe] *vt (cheveux)* to straighten

décrépit, -ite [dekrepi, -it] *adj (maison, mur, personne)* decrepit

décrépitude [dekrepityd] *nf* decrepitude; *(décadence)* decay

décret [dekrɛ] *nm* decree

décréter [34] [dekrete] *vt* **(a)** *Jur (état d'urgence, nomination)* to decree **(b)** *(décider)* **d. que** to vow (that)

décrié, -e [dekrije] *adj* disparaged

décrire [30] [dekrir] *vt* **(a)** *(représenter)* to describe **(b)** **d. un cercle** to circle; **d. une courbe** to curve

décrispation [dekrispasjɔ̃] *nf Pol* détente

décrisper [dekrispe] **1** *vt (personne)* to relax; *(atmosphère)* to lighten

2 se décrisper *vpr* to relax

décrocher [dekrɔʃe] **1** *vt* **(a)** *(détacher) (vêtement d'une patère, rideaux, tableau)* to take down **(de** from**)**; *(wagons)* to uncouple; *(combiné)* to pick up; **d. (le téléphone)** *(pour répondre)* to pick up the phone; *(pour ne pas être dérangé)* to take the phone off the hook; **décrochez** *(dans cabine téléphonique)* lift the receiver **(b)** *(recevoir) (poste, prix, contrat)* to land; *Fam* **d. la timbale** to hit the jackpot

2 *vi Fam* **(a)** *(ne plus se concentrer)* to switch off; *(être à la traîne)* to fail to keep up **(b)** *(arrêter de se droguer)* to kick the habit

3 se décrocher *vpr (rideau, tableau)* to come unhooked **(de** from**)**; *(vêtement)* to fall down **(de** from**)**; *(collier)* to come undone; *(wagon)* to come uncoupled **(de** from**)**; **se d. la mâchoire** to dislocate one's jaw

décrocheur, -euse [dekrɔʃœr, -øz] *nm,f Can* dropout

décroiser [dekrwaze] *vt (jambes, bras)* to uncross

décroissant, -e [dekrwasɑ̃, -ɑ̃t] *adj* decreasing; **par ordre d.** in descending order

décroître [4a] [dekrwatr] *vi (forces, population, nombre, intensité)* to decrease; *(journées)* to draw in, to get shorter; *(lune)* to wane; *(eaux)* to subside; **aller (en) décroissant** to be decreasing

décrotter [dekrote] *vt (chaussures, semelles)* to clean the mud off; *Fam Fig (personne)* to knock the rough edges off

décrue [dekry] *nf (de rivière)* drop in level

décrypter [dekripte] *vt* to decipher

déçu, -e [desy] **1** *pp voir* **décevoir**

2 *adj* disappointed; *Fig & Ironique* **elle ne va pas être déçue (du voyage)** she's in for a disappointment

déculottée [dekylɔte] *nf Fam* hammering

déculotter [dekylɔte] **1** *vt* **d. qn** *(enlever son slip)* to take sb's underpants off; *(enlever son pantalon)* to take sb's trousers off

2 se déculotter *vpr (enlever son slip)* to take one's underpants off; *(enlever son pantalon)* to take one's trousers; *Fig (s'abaisser)* to grovel **(devant** to**)**

déculpabiliser [dekylpabilize] **1** *vt* **d. qn** to stop sb feeling guilty

2 se déculpabiliser *vpr* to stop feeling guilty

décuple [dekypl] *nm* **le d. de qch** ten times sth

décupler [dekyple] **1** *vt* to increase tenfold; *Fig* **la terreur décupla ses forces** terror gave her the strength of ten people

2 *vi* to increase tenfold

dédaigner [dedɛɲe] *vt (offre)* to scorn; *(injure, conseil, gloire)* to disregard; *(personne)* to despise; **il ne dédaigne pas un cigare de temps en temps** he is not averse to the occasional cigar

dédaigneusement [dedɛɲøzmɑ̃] *adv* scornfully, disdainfully

dédaigneux, -euse [dedɛɲø, -øz] *adj* scornful, disdainful **(de** of**)**

dédain [dedɛ̃] *nm* scorn, disdain **(pour qn/de qch** for sb/sth**)**; **avec d.** scornfully, with disdain

dédale [dedal] *nm aussi Fig* maze

dedans [dədɑ̃] **1** *adv* inside; **la lettre est d.** the letter is inside; **c'est un bon film mais il y a trop de violence d.** it's a good film but there's too much violence in it; **de d.** *(depuis l'intérieur)* from inside; **en d.** *(d'un objet)* (on the) inside; *(en son for intérieur)* inwardly; **marcher les pieds en d.** to be pigeon-toed; **en d. de** inside

2 *nm (d'une maison, d'une boîte)* inside; **du d.** *(depuis l'intérieur)* from inside

dédicace [dedikas] *nf* (a) *(de livre, de photo)* dedication (b) *(à la radio)* dedication

dédicacer [16] [dedikase] *vt* (a) *(signer)* to sign (à for); *(écrire dans) (livre)* to write a dedication in (à to); *(photo)* to write a dedication on (à to) (b) *(chanson)* to dedicate (à to)

dédier [66] [dedje] *vt* to dedicate (à to)

dédire [27a] [dedir] **se dédire** *vpr* **se d. d'une déclaration** to retract or to withdraw a statement; **se d. d'une promesse** to go back on one's word

dédommagement [dedomaʒmɑ̃] *nm* compensation; **50 000 francs de d.** 50,000 francs (in) compensation; **en d. de qch** in compensation for sth

dédommager [45] [dedomaʒe] *vt (financièrement)* to compensate (de for); **pour me d., il m'a invité au restaurant** he took me out for a meal to make up for it

dédouanement [dedwanmɑ̃] *nm* clearance through customs

dédouaner [dedwane] **1** *vt (marchandise)* to clear (through customs), *Fig (personne)* to clear
2 se dédouaner *vpr* to clear one's name

dédoublement [dedublәmɑ̃] *nm* **d. de la personnalité** split personality

dédoubler [deduble] **1** *vt (partager)* to divide or split into two
2 se dédoubler *vpr Psy* to have a split personality; *Hum* **je ne peux pas me d.** I can't be in two places at once

dédramatiser [dedramatize] *vt* **d. qch** to make sth less dramatic

déductible [dedyktibl] *adj* deductible; **d. des impôts** tax-deductible

déduction [dedyksjɔ̃] *nf* (a) *(soustraction, abattement)* deduction; **d. faite des frais d'essence** after deduction of petrol costs (b) *(conclusion)* deduction

déduire [18] [dedɥir] *vt* (a) *(enlever)* to deduct (de from) (b) *(conclure)* to deduce (de from)

déesse [dees] *nf* goddess

défaillance [defajɑ̃s] *nf* (a) *(insuffisance) (morale)* failing; *(physique)* deficiency; *(d'une machine)* failure; **avoir des défaillances en** *(intellectuelles)* to have problems with; **courage sans d.** unfailing courage; **d. cardiaque** heart failure (b) *(évanouissement)* fainting fit; *(faiblesse)* feeling of weakness; **avoir une d.** *(s'évanouir)* to faint; *(se sentir faible)* to feel weak

défaillant, -e [defajɑ̃, -ɑ̃t] *adj* (a) *(forces, mémoire, santé)* failing; *(cœur)* weak; *(voix)* faltering (b) *(qui s'évanouit)* faint

défaillir [35] [defajir] *vi* (a) *(faiblir) (mémoire, forces)* to fail; **à cette nouvelle, son cœur défaillit** her heart sank at the news (b) *(s'évanouir)* to faint; **d. de faim/de bonheur** to feel faint with hunger/happiness

défaire [36] [defer] **1** *vt* (a) *(ouvrir, détacher)* to undo; *(valise)* to unpack; **d. le lit** *(enlever les draps)* to strip the bed; *(le mettre en désordre)* to rumple the bedclothes; **se cheveux** to let one's hair down (b) *(désassembler) (puzzle)* to take apart; *(ourlet)* to undo
2 se défaire *vpr* (a) *(se dénouer) (vêtement, nœud)* to come undone; *(cheveux)* to come down (b) *(se désagréger) (puzzle)* to come apart; *(ourlet)* to come undone; *Fig (alliance, mariage)* to break up (c) **se d. de qn/qch** to get rid of sb/sth; **je ne veux pas m'en d.** I don't want to part with it (d) *(s'altérer) (visage)* to drop

défait, -e [defɛ, -ɛt] *adj (traits, visage)* haggard; **il est arrivé à l'hôpital, complètement d.** he arrived at the hospital in total distress

défaite [defɛt] *nf* defeat

défaitisme [defetism] *nm* defeatism

défaitiste [defetist] *adj & nmf* defeatist

défalquer [defalke] *vt* to deduct (de from)

défausser [defose] **se défausser** *vpr (aux cartes)* to discard; **se d. à cœur** to discard a heart/some hearts; **se d. d'un dix** to discard a ten

défaut [defo] *nm* (a) *(imperfection) (d'une personne)* fault, shortcoming; *(d'une pierre précieuse, d'un verre, d'un tissu)* flaw; *(d'une machine)* defect; *(d'un raisonnement)* flaw; *(inconvénient)* drawback; **c'est là son moindre d.** that's the least of his faults; **sans d.** faultless, flawless; **prendre qn en d.** to catch sb napping; **d. de fabrication** manufacturing fault; **d. de prononciation** *ou* **d'élocution** speech impediment (b) *(manque)* lack; **le courage lui a fait d.** his courage failed him; **l'argent lui fait cruellement d.** she is very short of money; **le bon sens lui fait cruellement d.** he is sadly lacking in common sense; **ou à d.,...** or, failing that,...; **à d. de qch** for lack of sth; **à d. d'un salaire conséquent, elle a au moins un travail intéressant** she might not have a very good salary, but at least her work is interesting (c) *Jur* **faire d.** to default; **d. de paiement** default on payment (d) *Math* **total approché par d.** total rounded down; *Ordinat* **lecteur/clavier par d.** default drive/keyboard

défaveur [defavœr] *nf* **être en d. (auprès de qn)** to be in disfavour (with sb); **s'attirer la d. de qn** to incur sb's disfavour

défavorable [defavorabl] *adj* unfavourable (à to)

défavorisé, -e [defavorize] *adj (milieu, pays)* underprivileged

défavoriser [defavorize] *vt* to put at a disadvantage (**par rapport à** compared to)

défectif, -ive [defɛktif, -iv] *adj* defective

défection [defɛksjɔ̃] *nf* (a) *(d'un espion, d'un soldat)* defection (b) *(annulation)* cancellation

défectueux, -euse [defɛktɥø, -øz] *adj* defective, faulty

défendable [defɑ̃dabl] *adj* defensible

défendre [defɑ̃dr] **1** *vt* (a) *(soutenir)* to defend (**contre** against) (b) *(protéger) (personne, pays, propriété)* to defend (**contre** against *ou* from); *(intérêts)* to protect; **d. qn contre le froid** *ou* **du froid** to protect sb from the cold; *Fig* **d. son bifteck** to look after number one; *Sp* **Durant défendra les buts de l'équipe d'Aix** Durant will be in goal for Aix (c) *(interdire)* to forbid, to prohibit; **ce médicament est défendu aux enfants** this medicine must not be given to children; **d. à qn de faire qch** to forbid sb to do sth; **il m'est défendu de fumer** I'm not allowed to smoke; **il est défendu de fumer** smoking is prohibited
2 se défendre *vpr* (a) *(se protéger)* to defend oneself (**de** *ou* **contre** against); **se d. comme un beau diable** to fight like a mad thing (b) *Fam (se débrouiller)* **je me défends (en anglais/en tennis)** I can get by (in English/at tennis) (c) *(se justifier)* **ça se défend** there's something to be said for it (d) *(s'empêcher)* **se d. de faire qch** to refrain from doing sth; **on ne peut se d. de les aimer** you can't help liking them

défenestrer [defanɛstre] *vt* to defenestrate

défense¹ [defɑ̃s] nf (a) (soutien) (d'une théorie, d'une politique, d'un accusé) defence; **prendre la d. de qn** to come to sb's defence; **sans d.** defenceless; Jur **assurer la d. de qn** to defend sb; **qu'avez-vous à dire pour votre d.?** what do you have to say in your defence?; **d. des consommateurs** consumer protection (b) (protection) (d'une personne, d'un pays, en sport) defence; **d. aérienne/ nationale/passive** air/national/civil defence; Méd **défenses immunitaires** immune defences (c) (interdiction) **d. d'entrer/de fumer** (sur panneau) no entry/smoking; **et d. d'en parler à ton père!** don't go telling your father about it!

défense² nf (d'éléphant, de sanglier) tusk

défenseur [defɑ̃sœr] nm (a) (d'une personne, d'une ville, d'une cause, en sport) defender; **jouer les défenseurs de la veuve et de l'orphelin** to protect the weak and oppressed (b) Jur counsel for the defence

défensif, -ive [defɑ̃sif, -iv] 1 adj defensive
2 nf **être ou se tenir sur la défensive** to be on the defensive

déféquer [34] [defeke] vi to defecate

déférence [deferɑ̃s] nf deference (**pour** for)

déférer [34] [defere] vt Jur **d. une affaire à un tribunal** to refer a case to a court; **d. qn à la justice** to hand sb over to the police

déferlante [deferlɑ̃t] adj f & nf (vague) **d.** breaker

déferlement [deferləmɑ̃] nm (des vagues) breaking; Fig (de personnes) invasion; (d'enthousiasme, de violence, de racisme) wave

déferler [deferle] vi (vagues) to break; **la foule déferle dans les rues** the crowd is surging along the streets; **les vacanciers déferlent sur les routes** holiday-makers are taking to the roads in droves

défi [defi] nm (a) (acte de provocation) challenge (**à** to); **lancer** ou **jeter un d. à qn** to throw out a challenge to sb; **mettre qn au d. de faire qch** to defy sb to do sth; **relever un d.** to take up a challenge (b) (bravade) defiance

défiance [defjɑ̃s] nf mistrust

déficience [defisjɑ̃s] nf deficiency; **d. immu- nologique** immune deficiency

déficient, -e [defisjɑ̃, -ɑ̃t] 1 adj deficient; (raisonnement, théorie) weak
2 nm, f **d. moteur** person with motor deficiency; **d. mental** mentally deficient person

déficit [defisit] nm (a) Fin deficit; **être en d.** to be in deficit; **d. budgétaire/commercial** budget/trade deficit (b) Méd (mental) deficiency; **d. immunitaire** immunodeficiency

déficitaire [defisiter] adj (entreprise) loss-making; (compte) in debit; (budget) in deficit

défier [66] [defje] 1 vt (a) (provoquer) to challenge; **d. qn aux échecs** to challenge sb to a game of chess (b) (inciter) **d. qn de faire qch** to defy sb to do sth (c) (braver) (personne, danger, mort) to defy (d) (résister à) **d. l'imagination** to defy the imagination; **des prix qui défient toute concurrence** unbeatable prices
2 **se défier** vpr Litt **se d. de** to mistrust

défigurer [defigyre] vt (personne, paysage) to disfigure; Fig (vérité, sens) to distort; (pensée, intentions) to misrepresent

défilé [defile] nm (a) Géog (mountain) pass (b) (de manifestants) march; (de chars de carnaval) procession; Mil parade; **un d. ininterrompu de touristes/voitures** an endless stream of tourists/cars; **d. aérien** flypast; **d. de mode** fashion show

défilement [defilmɑ̃] nm Ordinat scrolling

défiler¹ [defile] **se défiler** vpr Fam (se dérober) to slope off

défiler² vi (a) (manifestants) to march; (chars de carnaval) to drive in procession; (touristes, voitures) to stream; Mil to parade (b) (avancer) (bande) to wind on; Ordinat **faire d. un document** to scroll through a document; Ordinat **d. vers le bas/le haut** to scroll down/up (c) (se succéder) (images, souvenirs) to pass; **le paysage défile à toute vitesse** the countryside is speeding past

défini, -e [defini] adj (a) (précis) definite; **bien d.** clearly defined; Ordinat **d. par l'utilisateur** user-defined (b) Gram definite

définir [definir] 1 vt to define
2 **se définir** vpr (a) (concept) **se d. comme** to be defined as (b) (soi-même) to describe oneself (**comme** as)

définissable [definisabl] adj definable

définitif, -ive [definitif, -iv] adj (a) (irrévocable) (jugement, décision, version) final (b) (pour toujours) (séparation, fermeture) permanent (c) (qui fait autorité) definitive (d) **en définitive** (à la fin) in the end

définition [definisjɔ̃] nf (a) (d'un mot, de conditions) definition; (de mots croisés) clue; **par d.** by definition (b) (d'une image sur écran) definition

définitivement [definitivmɑ̃] adv (décider) definitely; (partir, s'installer) for good; (nommé) permanently

défiscaliser [defiskalize] vt to exempt from tax

déflagration [deflagrasjɔ̃] nf (explosion) explosion

déflation [deflasjɔ̃] nf Écon deflation

déflecteur [deflektœr] nm (d'une voiture) Br quarterlight, Am vent

déflorer [deflore] vt (a) (vierge) to deflower (b) Fig (sujet) to spoil

défoliant [defɔljɑ̃] nm defoliant

défonce [defɔ̃s] nf Fam **la d.** getting high

défoncé, -e [defɔ̃se] adj (a) (chemin) bumpy (b) Fam (drogué) high

défoncer [16] [defɔ̃se] 1 vt (boîte, porte) to smash in; (matelas) to ruin; (mur) to knock down; (tonneau, bateau) to stave in; (chaussée) to break up
2 **se défoncer** vpr Fam (a) (se droguer) to get high (**à** on) (b) (faire un grand effort) to sweat blood (**pour faire qch** to do sth)

déforestation [defɔrestasjɔ̃] nf deforestation

déformant, -e [defɔrmɑ̃] adj (glace) distorting

déformation [defɔrmasjɔ̃] nf (d'un membre) deformation; (d'un vêtement, de chaussures) putting out of shape; (de métal) buckling; (de bois) warping; (des traits, d'une image, des faits) distortion; (de propos) twisting; **d. professionnelle** = habits acquired through the type of work one does

déformer [defɔrme] 1 vt (membre) to deform; (vêtement, chaussures) to put out of shape; (métal) to buckle; (bois) to warp; (traits, image, faits) to distort; (propos) to twist; (pensée) to misrepresent
2 **se déformer** vpr (corps, vêtement, chaussures) to get out of shape; (bois) to warp; (métal) to buckle

défoulement [defulmɑ̃] nm Fam letting off steam; **avoir besoin de d.** to need to let off steam

défouler [defule] *Fam* **1** *vt (agressivité)* to vent (**sur** on); **d. qn** to help sb let off steam; **ça défoule** it helps you let off steam

2 se défouler *vpr* to let off steam; **se d. sur qn** to take it out on sb

défraîchi, -e [defreʃi] *adj (fleur, beauté)* faded; *(vêtement)* shabby

défrayer [53] [defreje] *vt (rembourser)* **d. qn** to pay sb's expenses; **d. la chronique** to be widely talked about

défrichage [defriʃaʒ] *nm*, **défrichement** [defriʃmɑ̃] *nm (de terrain)* clearing

défricher [defriʃe] *vt* to clear; *Fig (domaine)* to open up; *Fig* **d. le terrain** to prepare the ground

défriser [defrize] *vt (cheveux)* to straighten; *Fam Fig (agacer)* to bug

défroisser [defrwase] *vt* to smooth out

défroqué, -e [defrɔke] *adj* defrocked

défunt, -e [defœ̃, -œ̃t] **1** *adj* **mon d. mari** my late husband; *Litt* **des amours défuntes** lost loves

2 *nm,f* deceased; **prier pour les défunts** to pray for the dead

dégagé, -e [degaʒe] *adj (ton, air)* casual; *(ciel, route)* clear; *(vue)* open; **une coupe avec la nuque très dégagée** a haircut that is very short at the back

dégagement [degaʒmɑ̃] *nm* **(a)** *(d'une route, des poumons)* clearing **(b)** *(au football)* clearance **(c)** *(de vapeur, de gaz, de chaleur)* emission

dégager [45] [degaʒe] **1** *vt* **(a)** *(libérer)* to free (**de** from); *(d'une voiture accidentée, de décombres)* to pull clear (**de** of); **une robe qui dégage les épaules** an off-the-shoulder dress **(b)** *(désencombrer)* (route, passage) to clear; *Fam* **dégage!** clear off! **(c)** *Fam (enlever)* to clear away; **tu vas me d. toutes ces bricoles de tes étagères** I want you to clear all these odds and ends off your shelves **(d)** *(laisser échapper)* (vapeur, odeur, chaleur) to emit; *Fig (impression)* to give off **(e)** *(au football)* **d. (le ballon) en touche** to kick the ball into touch **(f)** *Fin (crédits)* to release; *(profit)* to show

2 se dégager *vpr (se libérer)* to free oneself (**de** from); *(d'une situation difficile)* to extricate oneself (**de** from) **(b)** *(se débloquer)* (ciel, nez) to clear **(c)** *(gaz, odeur, chaleur)* to be given off (**de** by); *Fig* **le magnétisme qui se dégage d'elle** the magnetism she radiates

dégaine [degen] *nf Fam (démarche)* awkward way of walking; *(apparence)* strange appearance

dégainer [degene] *vt* to draw

dégarni, -e [degarni] *adj (personne)* balding; **avoir le front d.** to have a receding hairline

dégarnir [degarnir] **1** *vt (frigidaire, rayons)* to empty

2 se dégarnir *vpr (personne)* to go bald; *(arbre)* to lose its leaves; *Litt (salle)* to empty; *(rayons)* to be emptied

dégât [dega] *nm* damage; **faire du d. ou des dégâts** to cause damage; *Fig* **limiter les dégâts** to limit the damage; **dégâts des eaux** water damage; **dégâts matériels** material damage

dégel [deʒɛl] *nm Météo & Pol* thaw; *Écon (des prix, des salaires, des crédits)* unfreezing

dégeler [39] [deʒle] **1** *vt* **(a)** *(réchauffer)* to thaw; *(surgelé)* to defrost; *Fig (public)* to warm up; **d. l'atmosphère** to make the atmosphere less chilly **(b)** *Écon (prix, salaires, crédits)* to unfreeze

2 *vi (étang, surgelé)* to thaw; **faire d. qch** *(surgelé)* to defrost sth

3 *v impersonnel* to thaw

4 se dégeler *vpr* **(a)** *(étang)* to thaw **(b)** *Fig (atmosphère)* to become less chilly

dégénératif, -ive [deʒeneratif, -iv] *adj* degenerative

dégénéré, -e [deʒenere] **1** *adj* **(a)** *(arriéré)* mentally defective **(b)** *(dépravé)* degenerate

2 *nm,f* **(a)** *(arriéré)* mental defective **(b)** *(dépravé)* degenerate

dégénérer [34] [deʒenere] *vi (mal tourner)* (situation, conversation) to degenerate (**en** into); **son rhume a dégénéré en bronchite** his cold developed into bronchitis

dégénérescence [deʒeneresɑ̃s] *nf Méd & Fig* degeneration

dégingandé, -e [deʒɛ̃gɑ̃de] *adj* gangling, lanky

dégivrage [deʒivraʒ] *nm* **(a)** *(action)* (d'un pare-brise) de-icing; (d'un réfrigérateur) defrosting **(b)** *(dispositif)* (d'un pare-brise) de-icer; (d'un réfrigérateur) defroster

dégivrer [deʒivre] *vt (pare-brise)* to de-ice; *(réfrigérateur)* to defrost

déglacer [deglase] *vt Culin (poêle à frire)* to deglaze

déglinguer [deglɛ̃ge] *Fam* **1** *vt (appareil)* to bust; **ma moto est toute déglinguée** my motorbike is falling to pieces

2 se déglinguer *vpr (appareil)* to go wrong; *(véhicule)* to fall to pieces

déglutir [deglytir] *vi* to swallow

déglutition [deglytisjɔ̃] *nf* swallowing

dégobiller [degɔbije] *très Fam* **1** *vi* to puke

2 *vt* to puke up

dégonflé, -e [degɔ̃fle] **1** *adj* **(a)** *(pneu, ballon)* flat **(b)** *Fam (lâche)* chicken

2 *nm,f Fam* chicken

dégonfler [degɔ̃fle] **1** *vt (pneu, ballon)* to let the air out of, to deflate

2 *vi (partie du corps)* to go down

3 se dégonfler *vpr* **(a)** *(pneu, ballon)* to go flat **(b)** *Fam (personne)* to chicken out

dégorger [45] [degɔrʒe] **1** *vt* **(a)** *(évacuer)* to discharge; **la rue a dégorgé un flot de gens** a crowd of people surged from the street **(b)** *(passage, conduit, évier)* to unblock

2 *vi* **faire d. des concombres** = to remove water from cucumbers by sprinkling them with salt

dégot(t)er [degote] *vt Fam* to dig up

dégouliner [deguline] *vi (liquide)* to trickle; **je dégouline** I'm dripping wet

dégoupiller [degupije] *vt* to pull the pin out of

dégourdi, -e [degurdi] **1** *adj* smart, bright

2 *nm,f* **c'est un d.** he's a smart one

dégourdir [degurdir] **1** *vt (membres)* to remove the stiffness from; *Fig* **d. qn** to teach sb a thing or two

2 se dégourdir *vpr (membres)* **se d. les jambes** to stretch one's legs; *Fig* to learn a thing or two

dégoût [degu] *nm* **(a)** *(aversion)* disgust, distaste; **éprouver du d. pour qch** to be disgusted by sth; **prendre qch en d.** to take a strong dislike to sth **(b)** *(lassitude)* weariness; **le d. de la vie** world-weariness

dégoûtant, -e [degutɑ̃, -ɑ̃t] **1** *adj* disgusting

2 *nm,f* disgusting person; **un vieux d.** a dirty old man

dégoûté, -e [degute] **1** *adj* **(a)** *(écœuré)* (air) disgusted; *Ironique* **vous n'êtes pas d.!** you're not fussy! **(b)** *(choqué)* disgusted **(c)** *(las)* weary; **être d. de qch** to be sick of sth

2 *nm,f* **faire le d.** to turn up one's nose

dégoûter [degute] vt **d. qn** (physiquement) to turn sb's stomach; (moralement) to disgust sb, to make sb sick; **d. qn de qch** to put sb off sth; **c'est à vous d. de l'Espagne/des hommes!** it's enough to put you off Spain/men for life!

dégoutter [degute] **dégoutter de** vt ind (laisser couler) to drip with

dégradant, -e [degradɑ̃] adj degrading

dégradation [degradasjɔ̃] nf (d'un monument) defacement; (de matériel scolaire, de l'environnement) damage (**de** to); Fig (de la santé, de relations, d'une situation) deterioration

dégradé [degrade] nm (de couleurs) gradation; **se faire faire un d.** (chez le coiffeur) to have one's hair layered; Ordinat **d. de couleur** colour scale

dégrader [degrade] **1** vt (a) (abîmer) (monument) to deface; (matériel, maison) to damage; Ordinat (données) to corrupt (b) Fig (humilier) to degrade (c) Mil to demote
 2 se dégrader vpr (a) (se détériorer) (santé, relations, situation) to deteriorate; (bâtiment) to fall into disrepair (b) (s'abaisser) to degrade oneself

dégrafer [degrafe] **1** vt (vêtement, bracelet) to undo
 2 se dégrafer vpr (a) (vêtement, bracelet) to come undone (b) (femme) to undo one's dress

dégraissage [degresaʒ] nm (d'une entreprise) downsizing

dégraisser [degrese] **1** vt (bouillon) to skim the fat off; Fig (entreprise) to downsize; **d. les effectifs** to cut back on staff
 2 vi (entreprise) to downsize

degré [dəgre] nm (a) (d'un angle, de chaleur) degree; (de boisson alcoolisée) proof; **combien de degrés fait ce whisky?** what proof is this whisky?; **d. Celsius** degree Celsius; **d. Fahrenheit** degree Fahrenheit (b) (stade, niveau) stage; **d. de parenté** family relationship; **cousins au second d.** second cousins; **brûlure au deuxième/troisième d.** second/third degree burn; **au plus haut d.** (extrêmement) in the extreme; **jusqu'à un certain d.** up to a point; **par degrés** by degrees; **prendre une plaisanterie au premier d.** to take a joke seriously (c) (d'escalier) step; (d'échelle) rung

dégressif, -ive [degresif, -iv] adj **tarif d.** tapering rate; **impôt d.** degressive taxation

dégrèvement [degrɛvmɑ̃] nm **d.** (fiscal) tax relief

dégriffé, -e [degrife] **1** adj = with its designer label removed and reduced in price
 2 nm = reduced-price designer item with its label removed

dégringolade [degrɛ̃golad] nf Fam (chute) tumble; Fig (d'une entreprise) collapse; (des prix, des cours) slump (**de** in)

dégringoler [degrɛ̃gole] Fam **1** vt to rush down
 2 vi (personne) to tumble; Fig (entreprise) to collapse; (prix, cours) to slump

dégripper [degripe] vt (mécanisme) to unjam

dégriser [degrize] vt to sober up; Fig to bring down to earth

dégrossir [degrosir] vt (bois) to trim; (pierre) to roughhew; Fig (travail) to rough out; **d. qn** to knock the rough edges off sb; **être mal dégrossi** to be uncouth

dégrouper [degrupe] vt to divide into groups

déguenillé, -e [degɑnije] adj ragged

déguerpir [degɛrpir] vi to clear off; **faire d. qn** to chase sb away

dégueulasse [degœlas] très Fam **1** adj (sale) filthy; (mauvais, désagréable) disgusting; **c'est pas d.** (bon) it's not bad at all; **être d. avec qn** to be mean to sb; **se balader en d.** to go around in sloppy old clothes
 2 nmf **un gros d.** (sale) a filthy pig; (débauché) a filthy swine

dégueulasser [degœlase] vt très Fam to mess up

dégueuler [degœle] vi très Fam to puke

dégueulis [degœli] nm très Fam puke

déguisé, -e [degize] adj (pour tromper) disguised; (pour s'amuser) dressed up; **avec une joie non déguisée** with unconcealed delight

déguisement [degizmɑ̃] nm (pour tromper) disguise; (pour s'amuser) fancy dress

déguiser [degize] **1** vt (a) (costumer) to dress up; **d. qn en clown** to dress sb up as a clown (b) (voix, écriture, vérité, pensée) to disguise
 2 se déguiser vpr (pour tromper) to disguise oneself; (pour s'amuser) to dress up; **se d. en pompier** to dress up as a fireman

dégurgiter [degyrʒite] vt aussi Fig to regurgitate

dégustation [degystasjɔ̃] nf tasting; **d. de vin** wine tasting; **d. d'huîtres** (panneau devant un restaurant) oysters served here

déguster [degyste] vt (a) (tester) (vin, alcool) to taste (b) (savourer) (aliment, livre) to savour (c) très Fam **toute sa vie, elle a dégusté** (souffert) she's had a rough time of it all her life; **tu vas d.!** you're in for it!

déhanché, -e [deɑ̃ʃe] adj lopsided

déhanchement [deɑ̃ʃmɑ̃] nm (en marchant) swaying of the hips; (à l'arrêt) standing with one's weight on one foot

déhancher [deɑ̃ʃe] **se déhancher** vpr (en marchant) to sway one's hips; (à l'arrêt) to stand with one's weight on one foot

dehors [dəɔr] **1** adv (à l'extérieur) outside; (en plein air) out of doors; (pas chez soi) out; Fam **ficher** ou **foutre qn d.** to kick sb out; **ne pas mettre le nez** ou **les pieds d.** not to set foot outside; **en d.** (s'ouvrir, tourner) outwards; **marcher les pieds en d.** to walk with one's feet turned out; **en d. de** (à l'extérieur de) outside; (à part) apart from; **rester en d. d'une dispute** to keep out of an argument; **en d. du sujet** (remarque) irrelevant
 2 nm (a) (extérieur) outside; **au d.** on the outside; (se pencher, se répandre) out (b) (apparence) **une maison aux d. imposants** a house with an imposing exterior; **sous des d. aimables** under a pleasant exterior

déhoussable [deusabl] adj (canapé, siège) with loose covers

déjà [deʒa] adv (a) (dès maintenant) already; (si tôt) yet; **il est d. trois heures** it's already three o'clock; **faut-il que vous partiez d.?** do you have to go so soon?
 (b) (auparavant) before; **j'avais d. lu ce livre** I'd read that book before; **d. en 1900** as early as 1900
 (c) (intensif) **j'aurais dû le faire il y a d. trois jours** I should have done it three days ago; **c'est d. ça!**, **c'est d. pas mal!** that's not bad at all!; **vous avez d. trop de travail** you have too much work as it is; **d. que je n'en ai pas beaucoup, si tu m'en prends la moitié...** I haven't got much as it is, so if you take half...
 (d) (interrogatif) **qu'est-ce que vous faites, d.?** what did you say your job was?; **c'est quoi, d., ton nom?** what was your name again?

déjanter [deʒɑ̃te] **1** *vi très Fam (être fou)* to be off one's rocker; *(devenir fou)* to flip one's lid
2 se déjanter *vpr (pneu)* to come off the rim

déjà-vu [deʒavy] *nm inv* **une impression de d.** a feeling of déjà vu; **c'est du d.** *(ce n'est pas original)* it's the same old thing

déjeuner [deʒœne] **1** *nm* **(a)** *(repas de midi)* lunch; **prendre son d.** to have lunch; **d. d'affaires/de travail** business/working lunch **(b)** *(repas du matin)* **(petit) d.** breakfast **(c)** *(tasse et soucoupe)* breakfast cup and saucer
2 *vi* **(a)** *(le matin)* to have breakfast **(b)** *(à midi)* to have lunch; **nous avons les Dupont à d. dimanche** the Duponts are coming for lunch on Sunday; **d. d'un sandwich** to have a sandwich for lunch

déjouer [deʒwe] *vt (complot, plans)* to foil

délabré, -e [delabʁe] *adj (bâtiment, meuble)* dilapidated; *(santé)* ruined

délabrement [delabʁəmɑ̃] *nm (d'un bâtiment, d'un meuble)* dilapidated state; *(d'une entreprise)* ruin; **dans un état de grand d.** *(bâtiment)* in a state of total disrepair

délabrer [delabʁe] **se délabrer** *vpr (bâtiment)* to fall into disrepair; *(meuble)* to fall to pieces; *(entreprise)* to go to rack and ruin; *(santé)* to deteriorate

délacer [16] [delase] **1** *vt (chaussures)* to untie; *(corset)* to unlace
2 se délacer *vpr (chaussures)* to come untied; *(corset)* to come unlaced; *(femme)* to unlace one's corset

délai [delɛ] *nm* **(a)** *(laps de temps)* time allowed; **dans un d. de dix jours** within ten days; **il faut compter un d. de dix jours** you should allow ten days; **respecter** *ou* **tenir les délais** to meet the deadline; **dans les délais** on time; **dans les plus brefs délais** as soon as possible; **lundi dernier d.** by Monday at the very latest; **d. de livraison: un mois** delivery within one month; **d. de paiement** *(fixé par contrat)* term of payment **(b)** *(prolongation)* extension; **laisser à qn un d. de réflexion** to give sb time to think; **sans d.** without delay, immediately

délaisser [delese] *vt (abandonner)* to desert, to abandon; *(négliger)* to neglect

délassant, -e [delasɑ̃] *adj (bain, massage)* relaxing; *(lecture)* entertaining

délassement [delasmɑ̃] *nm* relaxation

délasser [delase] **1** *vt* to relax
2 se délasser *vpr* to relax

délateur, -trice [delatœʁ, -tʁis] *nm,f* informer

délation [delasjɔ̃] *nf* denouncement

délavé, -e [delave] *adj (tissu, jean)* faded; *(couleur)* watery

délayage [delɛjaʒ] *nm Péj* padding

délayer [53] [delɛje] *vt* **(a)** *(poudre)* to add water to; *(peinture)* to thin; *(liquide)* to water down; **d. de la farine dans du lait** to mix flour with milk **(b)** *Fig (discours, texte)* to pad out

Delco® [dɛlko] *nm Aut* distributor

délectable [delɛktabl] *adj* delectable

délecter [delɛkte] **se délecter** *vpr* **se d. de qch/à faire qch** to take delight in sth/in doing sth

délégation [delegasjɔ̃] *nf* **(a)** *(action de déléguer)* delegation; **agir par d.** to act on the authority invested in one; **d. de pouvoir** delegation of authority **(b)** *(groupe)* delegation

délégué, -e [delege] *nm,f* delegate; *Scol* **d. (de classe)** class representative *(at class meetings)*; **d. du personnel** staff representative; **d. syndical** union representative; *(d'usine)* shop steward

déléguer [34] [delege] *vt* **(a)** *(personne)* to delegate **(b)** *(transmettre) (pouvoirs)* to delegate (à to); **c'est un patron qui sait d.** he's a boss who knows how to delegate

délestage [delɛstaʒ] *nm (d'un navire, d'un ballon)* unballasting; **pour assurer le d. des grandes artères** to relieve congestion on the main roads

délester [delɛste] *vt (navire, ballon)* to unballast; *(voie de communication)* to relieve congestion on; *aussi Hum* **d. qn de qch** to relieve sb of sth

délibération [deliberasjɔ̃] *nf* **(a)** *(débat)* deliberation; **être en d.** to be under discussion **(b)** *(réflexion)* deliberation; **après mûre d.** after careful consideration

délibéré, -e [delibeʁe] **1** *adj (intentionnel)* deliberate
2 *nm Jur (de juges)* consultation

délibérément [delibeʁemɑ̃] *adv* deliberately

délibérer [34] [delibeʁe] *vi* **(a)** *(discuter)* to deliberate **(de** *ou* **sur** on); *Jur (jury)* to consider its verdict **(b)** *(réfléchir)* to deliberate

délicat, -e [delika, -at] *adj* **(a)** *(fragile, fin, difficile)* delicate; *(peau)* sensitive; *(travail)* fine **(b)** *(raffiné) (goûts)* refined; *(gestes)* graceful; *(plat)* sophisticated; **avoir le palais d.** to have a discerning palate **(c)** *(plein de tact)* tactful; **quelle attention délicate!** how thoughtful!; **peu d.** *(peu scrupuleux)* unscrupulous **(d)** *(exigeant)* fussy; **faire le d.** to turn up one's nose

délicatement [delikatmɑ̃] *adv (légèrement)* gently; *(finement)* finely

délicatesse [delikatɛs] *nf* **(a)** *(d'un objet)* fragility; *(d'une fleur, d'un tissu, d'un coloris)* delicacy; *(de la peau)* sensitivity; *(de la santé)* frailty **(b)** *(des goûts)* refinement; *(des gestes)* gracefulness; *(d'un plat)* sophistication; **avec d.** *(légèrement)* gently; *(finement)* finely **(c)** *(difficulté)* delicacy **(d)** *(tact)* tact; **avec d.** tactfully

délice [delis] *nm (plaisir)* delight; **cette tarte est un vrai d.** this tart is absolutely delicious

délices [delis] *nfpl Litt ou Hum* delights; **faire ses d. de qch** to delight in sth

délicieusement [delisjøzmɑ̃] *adv (agréablement)* delightfully; **d. bon** *(plat)* absolutely delicious

délicieux, -euse [delisjø, -øz] *adj (nourriture, sensation, chaleur)* delicious; *(personne, robe)* delightful

délictueux, -euse [deliktɥø, -øz] *adj Jur* **acte d.** offence

délié, -e [delje] **1** *adj (taille)* slim; *(doigts)* nimble
2 *nm (de l'écriture)* thin stroke

délier [66] [delje] **1** *vt* to untie; **d. qn d'une promesse** to release sb from a promise; *Fig* **le vin lui a délié la langue** the wine loosened his tongue
2 se délier *vpr (se défaire)* to come untied; *Fig* **sa langue s'est déliée** he/she found his/her tongue

délimiter [delimite] *vt (territoire)* to demarcate; *(responsabilité, sujet)* to define

délinquance [delɛ̃kɑ̃s] *nf* delinquency; **d. juvénile** juvenile delinquency; **la petite d. des banlieues** petty crime in the suburbs

délinquant, -e [delɛ̃kɑ̃, -ɑ̃t] **1** *adj* delinquent
2 *nm,f* offender; **d. juvénile** juvenile delinquent

déliquescence [delikesɑ̃s] *nf Péj (d'une civilisation, des mœurs)* decay; **tomber en d.** to fall into decay

déliquescent, -e [delikesɑ̃] adj Péj (civilisation, mœurs) decadent

délirant, -e [delirɑ̃, -ɑ̃t] adj Méd delirious; Fig (joie, imagination) frenzied; **c'est d. de leur demander de tout payer!** it's crazy asking them to pay for everything!

délire [delir] nm (a) Méd delirium; **avoir le d.** to be delirious; Fig **c'est du d.!** it's crazy!; **d. de grandeur** delusions of grandeur; **d. de persécution** persecution complex (b) (frénésie) frenzy; **foule en d.** frenzied crowd; Fam **cette soirée, c'est le d.!** it's a wild party!

délirer [delire] vi (être malade) to be delirious; (dire n'importe quoi) to rave

delirium tremens [delirjɔmtremɛ̃s] nm delirium tremens; **avoir le d.** to have delirium tremens

délit [deli] nm offence; **d. de fuite** failure to report an accident; **d. d'initié** insider dealing or trading

délivrance [delivrɑ̃s] nf (a) (soulagement) relief; **leur départ fut une vraie d.** it was a real relief when they left (b) (accouchement) delivery (c) (d'un certificat, d'un passeport, d'un permis) issue

délivrer [delivre] 1 vt (a) (libérer) (captif, otage) to rescue; (ville) to liberate; (peuple) to set free; **d. qn de ses liens** to free sb from his bonds (b) (soulager) **d. qn d'un secret trop lourd** to share the burden of a secret with sb; **d. qn d'un grand poids** to take a weight off sb's shoulders (c) (remettre) (marchandises) to deliver; (certificat, passeport, permis) to issue

2 **se délivrer** vpr to free oneself (**de** from)

délocalisation [delɔkalizasjɔ̃] nf relocation

déloger [45] [delɔʒe] vt (envahisseur) to drive out (**de** from); (locataire) to evict; (objet coincé) to dislodge (**de** from)

déloyal, -e, -aux, -ales [delwajal, -o] adj (ami) disloyal, unfaithful; (adversaire, pratique, concurrence, unfair; (coup) illegal

delta [dɛlta] nm (a) (d'un fleuve) delta (b) Av (aile) **d.** delta wing

deltaplane [dɛltaplan] nm hang-glider; **faire du d.** to go hang-gliding

déluge [delyʒ] nm (de pluie) downpour; (d'injures) torrent; (de larmes) flood; Rel **le D.** the Flood; **noyer qn sous un d. de compliments** to shower sb with compliments; **après moi le d.!** when I'm gone I don't care what happens!

déluré, -e [delyre] adj (vif) sharp, smart; Péj (provocant) forward

démagogie [demagɔʒi] nf demagogy

démagogique [demagɔʒik] adj demagogic

démagogue [demagɔg] nmf demagogue

demain [dəmɛ̃] 1 adv tomorrow; **d. soir** tomorrow evening; **d. en huit** a week tomorrow, tomorrow week; **à d.!** see you tomorrow!; **le journal de d.** tomorrow's paper; Fam **ce n'est pas pour d., ce n'est pas d. la veille** that won't happen for a long time yet; Fig **d. il fera jour** tomorrow is another day; Fig **de d.** (de l'avenir) of tomorrow

2 nm tomorrow; **tu as tout d. pour y réfléchir** you've got all tomorrow to think about it

demande [dəmɑ̃d] nf (a) (requête) request (**de** for); (formulaire) application form; **faire une d. de qch** (de permis, de prêt) to apply for sth; **faire qch à ou sur la d. de qn** to do sth at sb's request; **à la d. générale** by popular demand; **sur d.** on request; **demandes d'emploi** (titre de rubrique) situations wanted; **d. (en mariage)** proposal (of marriage); **faire sa d. (en mariage)** to propose; **d. de**

 rançon ransom demand (b) Écon demand; **d. des consommateurs** consumer demand (c) Jur **d. en divorce** divorce petition; **d. de dommages-intérêts** claim for damages (d) (besoin) (de soins, d'affection) need

demander [dəmɑ̃de] 1 vt (a) (réclamer) (augmentation, addition, preuves) to ask for; (dommages et intérêts) to claim; **d. qch à qn** to ask sb for sth; (service) to ask sb sth; **d. à qn de faire qch** to ask sb to do sth; **d. à manger/boire** to ask for something to eat/drink; **d. son avis à qn** to ask sb's opinion; **d. le divorce** to apply for a divorce; **d. la main de qn** to ask for sb's hand (in marriage); **d. qn en mariage** to propose to sb; **d. la parole** to ask to speak; **d. la permission de faire qch** to ask (for) permission to do sth; **combien demandez-vous de l'heure?** how much do you charge an hour?; **combien en demande-t-elle?** how much is she asking for it?; **je ne demande pas mieux que de vous aider** I'll be only too pleased to help you; **il ne demande que ça** he'd be only too pleased; Hum **que demande le peuple?** what more could I/he/etc ask?; **je ne demande qu'une seule chose: qu'on me laisse tranquille** all I ask is to be left alone; **on demande un maçon** (dans une petite annonce) builder wanted; **être très demandé** to be in great demand; **il n'y a qu'à** ou **il suffit de d.** you/he/etc only have/has to ask

(b) (nécessiter) (tact, réflexion, attention) to require; **ça demande de gros sacrifices** great sacrifices are called for

(c) (exiger) to demand; **en d. trop à qn** to ask too much of sb; **d. l'impossible** to ask the impossible

(d) (s'enquérir de) (prix, cause, raison) to ask; **d. qch à qn** to ask sb sth; **il m'a demandé de tes nouvelles** he asked after you; Fam **je ne t'ai rien demandé!** I didn't ask for your advice!; **je vous (le) demande, je vous demande un peu!** I ask you!

(e) (appeler) (médecin, prêtre) to ask for; **on vous demande** you're wanted; **on vous demande au téléphone** there's a call for you

2 **demander à** vt ind **d. à faire qch** to ask to do sth; **les suspects ne demandaient qu'à parler** the suspects were only too willing to speak; **demande à ce qu'on vienne te chercher** ask someone to come and collect you

3 **se demander** vpr to wonder, to ask oneself; **c'est à se d. si...** it makes you wonder whether...; **des choses comme ça, ça ne se demande pas!** you don't ask that sort of question!

demandeur, -euse [dəmɑ̃dœr, -øz] nm,f **d. d'asile** asylum seeker; **d. d'emploi** job seeker

démangeaison [demɑ̃ʒɛzɔ̃] nf itch; **avoir une d.** to have an itch, to be itching; **j'ai des démangeaisons dans les jambes** my legs are itchy

démanger [45] [demɑ̃ʒe] vi to itch; **l'épaule me démange** my shoulder's itching; Fig **méfie-toi, la main me démange!** (à un enfant) watch out or you'll feel the back of my hand!; **ça me démange de lui dire ce que je pense** I'm itching to tell him/her what I think

démantèlement [demɑ̃tɛlmɑ̃] nm breaking up

démanteler [39] [demɑ̃tle] vt to break up

démantibuler [demɑ̃tibyle] **Fam 1** vt to break up

2 **se démantibuler** vpr to come to pieces

démaquillage [demakijaʒ] nm removal of make-up

démaquillant, -e [demakijɑ̃] 1 adj cleansing

2 nm cleanser; **d. pour les yeux** eye make-up remover

démaquiller [demakije] **1** vt **d. qn** to remove sb's make-up
  2 se démaquiller vpr to remove one's make-up; **se d. les yeux** to remove one's eye make-up

démarcation [demarkasjɔ̃] nf demarcation

démarchage [demarʃaʒ] nm (porte-à-porte) door-to-door selling; **d. électoral** canvassing; **d. par téléphone** telesales

démarche [demarʃ] nf **(a)** (allure) gait, walk **(b)** (requête) step; **faire une d. auprès de qn** to approach sb; **faire les démarches nécessaires pour faire qch** to take the necessary steps to do sth **(c)** Fig (cheminement) process; **d. intellectuelle** thought process

démarcher [demarʃe] vt to canvass for

démarcheur, -euse [demarʃœr, -øz] nm,f door-to-door salesman, f saleswoman

démarque [demark] nf Com markdown; **la d. inconnue** shrinkage

démarquer [demarke] **1** vt (marchandises) to mark down
  2 se démarquer vpr Sp to lose one's marker; Fig **se d. de qn** (se distinguer) to distinguish oneself from sb

démarrage [demaraʒ] nm (d'un moteur) starting; (d'une entreprise) start-up; (d'un projet, d'une campagne publicitaire) start; **au d.** (d'un véhicule) when moving off; faire un d. (coureur) to put on a spurt; Ordinat **d. à chaud/froid** warm/cold start; **d. en côte** hill start

démarrer [demare] **1** vi **(a)** (véhicule) to move off; (moteur) to start; (conducteur) to drive off **(b)** (commencer) to start; **bien/mal d.** to get off to a good/bad start **(c)** (commencer à réussir) to take off
  2 vt to start; Ordinat to boot (up), to start up

démarreur [demarœr] nm Aut starter (motor)

démasquer [demaske] vt aussi Fig to unmask

démâter [demate] **1** vt to dismast
  2 vi to lose its mast

démêlant [demelɑ̃] adj m & nm **(produit) d.** conditioner

démêlé [demele] nm disagreement (avec with); **avoir des démêlés avec la justice** to be in trouble with the law

démêler [demele] **1** vt (fil, laine, cheveux) to untangle; (mystère) to unravel; **le vrai du faux** to disentangle the truth from the lies
  2 se démêler vpr **se d. de** to extricate oneself from

démembrement [demɑ̃brəmɑ̃] nm (d'un empire) breaking up; (d'une propriété agricole) division

démembrer [demɑ̃bre] vt (empire) to break up; (propriété agricole) to divide (up)

déménagement [demenaʒmɑ̃] nm move; **c'est pour quand le d.?** when are you/we/etc moving?

déménager [demenaʒe] **1** vi **(a)** (personne, entreprise) to move; **où déménage-t-il?** where's he moving to?; **d. à la cloche de bois** to do a moonlight flit; Fam **allez, déménagez!** beat it! **(b)** Fam Fig (musique) to be mind-blowing; (cocktail) to pack a punch
  2 vt (meubles) to move

déménageur [demenaʒœr] nm Br removal man, Am furniture mover; **avoir des épaules de d.** to have strong broad shoulders

démence [demɑ̃s] nf insanity; Méd dementia; Fam **c'est de la d.!** it's madness!

démener [46] [demne] **se démener** vpr **(a)** (s'agiter) to thrash about; **se d. comme un beau diable** (pour se libérer) to struggle like a madman **(b)** (se dépenser) to exert oneself

dément, -e [demɑ̃, -ɑ̃t] **1** adj (fou) insane; Fam (formidable) terrific; Fam **c'est d.!** it's unreal!
  2 nm,f lunatic; Méd demented person

démenti [demɑ̃ti] nm denial; Journ disclaimer; **opposer un d. formel à qch** to issue a firm denial of sth

démentiel, -elle [demɑ̃sjɛl] adj (idée, projet) insane; Fam (incroyable) crazy

démentir [64a] [demɑ̃tir] **1** vt to deny; (être en contradiction avec) to belie
  2 se démentir vpr (cesser) **leur honnêteté ne s'est jamais démentie** they've always been unfailing in their honesty

démerder [demerde] **se démerder** vpr très Fam to get by, to manage; **démerde-toi tout seul!** sort it out yourself!; **elle est assez grande pour se d. seule** she's old enough to take care of herself; **elle se démerde pas mal en cuisine/tennis** she's not a bad cook/tennis player; **se d. pour faire qch** to manage to do sth

démériter [demerite] vi to be at fault; **je ne vois pas en quoi il a démérité** I don't see how he is at fault

démesure [deməzyr] nf excess

démesuré, -e [deməzyre] adj (en taille) enormous; (orgueil, ambition) excessive

démesurément [deməzyremɑ̃] adv enormously

démettre[1] [demetr] **1** vt **il m'a démis l'épaule** he dislocated my shoulder
  2 se démettre vpr **se d. l'épaule/le genou** to dislocate one's shoulder/knee

démettre[2] vt **d. qn de ses fonctions** to remove sb from his/her post
  2 se démettre vpr **se d. de ses fonctions** to resign from one's post

demeurant [dəmœrɑ̃] **au demeurant** adv (malgré tout) for all that; (d'ailleurs) after all

demeure [dəmœr] nf **(a)** (château) mansion; Litt (résidence) (place of) residence; Euph **dernière d.** last resting place **(b)** **mettre qn en d. de faire qch** to instruct sb to do sth; Jur to give sb notice to do sth **(c)** **à d.** permanently

demeuré, -e [dəmœre] **1** adj Vieilli mentally retarded; Fam Péj halfwitted
  2 nm,f Vieilli mentally retarded person; Fam Péj halfwit

demeurer [dəmœre] vi **(a)** (aux être) (rester) to remain; **d. convaincu que...** to remain convinced that...; **d. fidèle à qn** to remain faithful to sb; **demeurons-en là** let's leave it at that; **il n'en demeure pas moins que...** the fact remains that... **(b)** Formel (aux avoir) (habiter) to reside

demi, -e [dəmi] **1** adj **(a)** (après un nom) **deux heures et demie** (durée) two and a half hours; (moment) half past two; **un litre/kilo et d.** a litre/kilo and a half; **il gagne trois fois et demie ce que je gagne** he earns three and a half times as much as I do **(b)** (avant un nom ou un adjectif) half; **une d.-cuillère de sucre** half a teaspoon of sugar
  2 nm **(a)** (moitié) half **(b)** (bière) **un d.** a beer, ≃ a half **(c)** Sp (au football) midfielder; **d. de mêlée** (au rugby) scrum half; **d. d'ouverture** (au rugby) fly half
  3 nf **demie** (heure) **il est la demie** it's half past; **à la demie** at half past

4 *adv* half; **d. plein** half full; **à d.** half; **à d. mort** half dead; **faire les choses à d.** to do things by halves; **croire qn à d.** to half believe sb; **ouvrir qch à d.** to half open sth

demiard [dəmjar] *nm Can* half pint

demi-cercle (*pl* **demi-cercles**) [dəmiserkl] *nm* semicircle, half circle; **en d.** in a semicircle

demi-dieu (*pl* **demi-dieux**) [dəmidjø] *nm* demigod

demi-douzaine (*pl* **demi-douzaines**) [dəmiduzɛn] *nf* half-dozen; **une d. d'œufs/de stylos** half a dozen eggs/pens

demi-droite (*pl* **demi-droites**) [dəmidrwat] *nf Math* half-line

demi-écrémé, -e (*mpl* **demi-écrémés**, *fpl* **demi-écrémées**) [dəmiekreme] *adj* semi-skimmed

demi-finale (*pl* **demi-finales**) [dəmifinal] *nf* semifinal

demi-fond [dəmifɔ̃] *nm inv Sp* **(course de) d.** middle-distance race

demi-frère (*pl* **demi-frères**) [dəmifrɛr] *nm* half-brother

demi-gros [dəmigro] *nm inv* **(commerce de) d.** cash and carry

demi-heure (*pl* **demi-heures**) [dəmijœr] *nf* **une d.** half an hour; **toutes les demi-heures** every half-hour

demi-jour (*pl* **demi-jours**) [dəmiʒur] *nm* half-light

demi-journée (*pl* **demi-journées**) [dəmiʒurne] *nf* half-day

démilitariser [demilitarize] *vt* to demilitarize

demi-litre (*pl* **demi-litres**) [dəmilitr] *nm* half-litre; **un d. de vin** half a litre of wine

demi-lune (*pl* **demi-lunes**) [dəmilyn] *nf* half-moon

demi-mesure (*pl* **demi-mesures**) [dəmiməzyr] *nf (compromis)* half-measure

demi-mort, -e (*mpl* **demi-morts**, *fpl* **demi-mortes**) [dəmimɔr, -mɔrt] *adj* half-dead

demi-mot [dəmimo] **à demi-mot** *adv* **comprendre à d.** to take the hint; **nous nous comprenons à d.** we don't have to spell everything out to each other

déminage [deminaʒ] *nm* mine clearance; *(en mer)* minesweeping

déminer [demine] *vt* to clear of mines

démineur [deminœr] *nm (personne)* bomb disposal expert; *(navire)* minesweeper

demi-pause (*pl* **demi-pauses**) [dəmipoz] *nf Mus Br* minim rest, *Am* half-note rest

demi-pension [dəmipɑ̃sjɔ̃] *nf (à l'hôtel) Br* half-board, *Am* breakfast and one meal; **sept jours en d.** seven days *Br* half-board or *Am* breakfast and one meal; *Scol* **être en d.** to be a *Br* day boarder or *Am* day student

demi-pensionnaire (*pl* **demi-pensionnaires**) [dəmipɑ̃sjɔnɛr] *nmf (écolier) Br* day boarder, *Am* day student

demi-portion (*pl* **demi-portions**) [dəmipɔrsjɔ̃] *nf Fam Péj* weed

demi-queue (*pl* **demi-queues**) [dəmikø] *adj & nm* **(piano) d.** baby grand (piano)

démis, -e [demi, -iz] *adj* dislocated

demi-saison (*pl* **demi-saisons**) [dəmisezɔ̃] *nf* spring or autumn; **vêtements de d.** spring or autumn clothes

demi-sel [dəmisɛl] *adj inv (beurre)* slightly salted; **fromage d.** slightly salted cream cheese

demi-sœur (*pl* **demi-sœurs**) [dəmisœr] *nf* half-sister

demi-sommeil (*pl* **demi-sommeils**) [dəmisɔmej] *nm* half-sleep

demi-soupir (*pl* **demi-soupirs**) [dəmisupir] *nm Mus Br* quaver rest, *Am* eighth-note rest

démission [demisjɔ̃] *nf* resignation; *Fig* renunciation; **donner sa d.** to hand in one's resignation

démissionnaire [demisjɔnɛr] *adj* resigning

démissionner [demisjɔne] *vi* to resign **(de** from); *Fig* to give up

demi-tarif [dəmitarif] **1** *nm* (*pl* **demi-tarifs**) half-price

2 *adj inv* **billet d.** *(de transports)* half-fare (ticket); *(de spectacle)* half-price ticket

demi-teinte (*pl* **demi-teintes**) [dəmitɛ̃t] *nf* halftone; *Fig* **être tout en demi-teintes** to be subtle in character

demi-ton (*pl* **demi-tons**) [dəmitɔ̃] *nm Mus Br* semitone, *Am* half step

demi-tour (*pl* **demi-tours**) [dəmitur] *nm* half-turn; *(en voiture)* U-turn; *Mil* about-turn; **faire d.** to turn back; **faire un d.** *(en voiture)* to do a U-turn; *Mil* **d. droite!** right about-turn!

démiurge [demjyrʒ] *nm* demiurge

demi-volée (*pl* **demi-volées**) [dəmivɔle] *nf (au tennis, au football)* half-volley

démobilisation [demɔbilizasjɔ̃] *nf* **(a)** *(de troupes)* demobilization **(b)** *Fig (désintérêt)* apathy

démobiliser [demɔbilize] *vt* **(a)** *(troupes)* to demobilize **(b)** *Fig (désintéresser)* to demotivate

démocrate [demɔkrat] **1** *adj* democratic

2 *nmf* democrat

démocrate-chrétien, -enne (*mpl* **démocrates-chrétiens**, *fpl* **démocrates-chrétiennes**) [demɔkratkretjɛ̃, -ɛn] *adj & nmf Pol* Christian Democrat

démocratie [demɔkrasi] *nf* democracy

démocratique [demɔkratik] *adj* democratic

démocratiquement [demɔkratikmɑ̃] *adv* democratically

démocratisation [demɔkratizasjɔ̃] *nf* democratization

démocratiser [demɔkratize] **1** *vt* to democratize

2 se démocratiser *vpr* to become (more) democratic

démodé, -e [demɔde] *adj* old-fashioned

démoder [demɔde] **se démoder** *vpr* to go out of fashion

démographie [demɔgrafi] *nf* demography

démographique [demɔgrafik] *adj* demographic

demoiselle [dəmwazɛl] *nf* **(a)** *(jeune fille)* young lady; **d. de compagnie** lady's companion; **d. d'honneur** *(d'une souveraine)* lady-in-waiting; *(d'une mariée)* bridesmaid **(b)** *(célibataire)* single woman; **c'est une vieille d.** she's never married **(c)** *(insecte)* dragonfly

démolir [demɔlir] *vt* **(a)** *(abattre)* to demolish, to pull down; *(mettre en pièces)* to demolish, to wreck; **d. une porte à coups de hache** to smash in a door with an axe; **l'alcool lui a démoli le foie** alcohol has ruined his/her liver **(b)** *Fig (théorie, adversaire)* to demolish; *(autorité)* to undermine; *(auteur, cinéaste, roman, film)* to slate **(c)** *Fam (battre)* to beat up; **le portrait à qn** to smash sb's face in; **se faire d. (le portrait)** to get beaten up

démolition [demɔlisjɔ̃] *nf* demolition; **chantier de d.** demolition site; **entreprise de d.** demolition contractors; **en d.** being demolished

démon [demɔ̃] *nm aussi Fig* demon, devil; **le d.** the Devil; **le d. de midi** the mid-life crisis

démoniaque [demɔnjak] *adj* demonic; *Fig (pervers)* fiendish

démonstratif, -ive [demɔ̃stratif, -iv] **1** *adj (affectueux) & Gram* demonstrative

2 *nm Gram* demonstrative

démonstration [demɔ̃strasjɔ̃] *nf* **(a)** *Math* demonstration; **d. par l'absurde** reductio ad absurdum; **faire la d. de qch** to demonstrate sth **(b)** *(d'appareil)* demonstration; **être en d.** to be a display model **(c)** *(manifestation)* show; **d. de force** show of force; **faire de grandes démonstrations d'amitié** to make a great show of friendship

démontable [demɔ̃tabl] *adj* that can be dismantled

démontage [demɔ̃taʒ] *nm* dismantling

démonté, -e [demɔ̃te] *adj (mer)* raging

démonter [demɔ̃te] **1** *vt* **(a)** *(machine, meuble, tente)* to dismantle; *(pneu)* to remove **(b)** *Fam (déconcerter)* to throw; **se laisser d.** to get thrown

2 se démonter *vpr* **(a)** *(machine, meuble)* to come apart **(b)** *Fam* **elle ne s'est pas démontée pour si peu** she wasn't so easily thrown

démontrable [demɔ̃trabl] *adj* demonstrable

démontrer [demɔ̃tre] *vt* to demonstrate; *Fam* **d. qch par A plus B** to prove sth conclusively

démoralisant, -e [demɔralizɑ̃, -ɑ̃t] *adj* demoralizing

démoralisation [demɔralizasjɔ̃] *nf* demoralization

démoraliser [demɔralize] **1** *vt* to demoralize

2 se démoraliser *vpr* to become demoralized

démordre [demɔrdr] **démordre de** *vt ind* **ne pas d. de qch** to stick to sth; **elle n'en démord pas** she's sticking to her guns

démotiver [demɔtive] *vt* to demotivate; **se laisser d. par qch** to be put off by sth

démoulage [demulaʒ] *nm (d'un moulage)* removal from the mould; *(d'un gâteau)* turning out

démouler [demule] *vt (moulage)* to remove from the mould; *(gâteau)* to turn out

démuni, -e [demyni] *adj* penniless

démunir [demynir] **1** *vt* **d. de qch** to deprive sb of sth

2 se démunir *vpr* **se d. de qch** to part with sth

démystification [demistifikasjɔ̃] *nf* demystification

démystifier [demistifje] *vt* to demystify

dénatalité [denatalite] *nf* fall in the birth rate

dénationaliser [denasjɔnalize] *vt* to denationalize

dénaturé, -e [denatyre] *adj* **(a)** *(parents, goût, mœurs)* unnatural **(b)** *Chim* denatured

dénaturer [denatyre] *vt (faits, propos)* to distort; *Chim* to denature

dénégation [denegasjɔ̃] *nf* denial

déneiger [45] [deneʒe] *vt* to clear the snow from

déneigeuse [deneʒøz] *nf Can* snowblower

déni [deni] *nm Jur* **d. de justice** denial of justice

déniaiser [denjeze] *vt Fam* **d. qn** *(dépuceler)* to initiate sb sexually; *(dégourdir)* to teach sb a thing or two

dénicher [denise] *vt Fam (objet)* to unearth; *(personne)* to track down

denier [dənje] *nm* **(a)** *(monnaie française)* denier; *Fig* **deniers** funds **(b)** *(de bas)* **bas de 30 deniers** 30-denier stockings

dénier [66] [denje] *vt* **(a)** *(nier) (faute, responsabilité)* to deny **(b)** *(refuser)* **d. à qn le droit de faire qch** to deny sb the right to do sth

dénigrement [denigrəmɑ̃] *nm* denigration; **une campagne de d.** a smear campaign

dénigrer [denigre] *vt* to denigrate

dénivelé [denivle] *nm* difference in level

dénivellation [denivelasjɔ̃] *nf* difference in level

dénombrable [denɔ̃brabl] *adj* countable

dénombrer [denɔ̃bre] *vt* to count

dénominateur [denɔminatœr] *nm Math* denominator; **le plus petit d. commun** the lowest common denominator

dénomination [denɔminasjɔ̃] *nf* designation

dénommé, -e [denɔme] *adj* **un d. Charles** someone by the name of Charles

dénoncer [16] [denɔ̃se] **1** *vt* **(a)** *(trahir) (malfaiteur)* to denounce (**à** to); *(tell on* (**à** to) **(b)** *(protester contre)* *(abus)* to denounce **(c)** *(annuler) (traité, contrat)* to terminate

2 se dénoncer *vpr (malfaiteur)* to give oneself up (**à** to); *(élève)* to own up (**à** to)

dénonciation [denɔ̃sjasjɔ̃] *nf* denunciation

dénoter [denɔte] *vt* to denote, to indicate

dénouement [denumɑ̃] *nm (d'un livre)* ending; *(d'une pièce)* dénouement; *(d'une affaire)* outcome

dénouer [denwe] **1** *vt (nœud)* to untie, to undo; *(cheveux)* to undo, to let down; *Fig (intrigue)* to unravel

2 se dénouer *vpr (nœud)* to come undone; *(cheveux)* to come down

dénoyauter [denwajote] *vt Br* to stone, *Am* to pit

denrée [dɑ̃re] *nf* foodstuff; **denrées alimentaires** foodstuffs; **denrées de consommation courante** staple foods; **denrées périssables** perishable goods

dense [dɑ̃s] *adj* dense

densité [dɑ̃site] *nf* **(a)** *(de population) & Phys* density **(b)** *Ordinat* **à double d.** double-density

dent [dɑ̃] *nf* **(a)** *(d'homme, d'animal)* tooth; **faire ses dents** *(enfant)* to be teething; **se faire les dents sur qch** *(chat, enfant)* to cut one's teeth on sth; **manger du bout des dents** to pick at one's food; **mordre à belles dents dans qch** to take a good bite out of sth; **parler entre ses dents** to mumble, to mutter; *Fig* **se casser les dents sur qch** to come a cropper over sth; *aussi Fig* **serrer les dents** to grit one's teeth; *Fig* **avoir les dents longues** to have great ambitions; *Fig* **avoir la d. dure** to have a sharp tongue; *Fig* **il n'a pas desserré les dents de la soirée** he hasn't opened his mouth all evening; *Fam* **être sur les dents** *(épuisé)* to be worn out; *(surmené)* to be overworked; *Fam* **avoir une d. contre qn** to have a grudge against sb; *Fam* **avoir la d.** to be starving; **d. de lait/de sagesse** milk/wisdom tooth **(b)** *(de peigne, de scie)* tooth; *(de roue)* cog; *(de fourchette)* prong; *(de timbre)* perforation; **en dents de scie** serrated; *Fig (évolution, progrès)* uneven

dentaire [dɑ̃ter] *adj* dental

denté, -e [dɑ̃te] *adj Tech* toothed; *(feuille)* jagged

dentelé, -e [dɑ̃tle] *adj (rivage, feuille)* jagged

dentelle [dɑ̃tɛl] *nf* lace; **robe de ou en d.** lace dress; **des crêpes d.** very thin pancakes; *Fam* **ne pas faire dans la d.** *(en paroles)* not to beat about the bush; *(en actions)* not to mess about

dentellière [dɑ̃taljer] *nf (personne)* lacemaker

dentelure [dɑ̃tlyr] *nf (d'un rivage, d'une feuille)* jagged outline; **dentelures** *(d'un timbre)* perforations

dentier [dɑ̃tje] *nm* (set of) false teeth, dentures

dentifrice [dɑ̃tifris] **1** *nm* toothpaste
2 *adj* **pâte d.** toothpaste

dentiste [dɑ̃tist] *nmf* dentist

dentition [dɑ̃tisjɔ̃] *nf* **(a)** *(croissance)* dentition **(b)** *(denture)* set of teeth

denture [dɑ̃tyr] *nf* set of teeth

dénudé, -e [denyde] *adj (campagne, arbre, fil)* bare

dénuder [denyde] **1** *vt (colline, arbre, fil)* to strip; **cette robe dénude le dos** this dress leaves the back bare
2 se dénuder *vpr* **(a)** *(colline)* to grow bare; *(arbre)* to lose its leaves **(b)** *(se déshabiller)* to strip (naked)

dénué, -e [denɥe] *adj* **d. de** *(intelligence, intérêt)* devoid of; **d. de tout fondement** totally without foundation

dénuement [denɥmɑ̃] *nm* destitution; **être dans le d.** to be destitute

déodorant [deɔdɔrɑ̃] *nm* deodorant

déodoriser [deɔdɔrize] *vt* to deodorize

déontologie [deɔ̃tɔlɔʒi] *nf* professional ethics

dépannage [depanaʒ] *nm (d'une machine)* (emergency) repairs; *(remorquage)* recovery; *Ordinat* trouble-shooting; **service de d.** breakdown service

dépanner [depane] *vt (machine)* to repair; *Fam (personne)* to help out **(de** with)

dépanneur [depanœr] *nm* **(a)** *(de voitures)* breakdown mechanic; *(de téléviseurs)* (television) repairman **(b)** *Can (magasin)* Br corner shop, Am convenience store

dépanneuse [depanøz] *nf* Br breakdown lorry, Am wrecker

dépareillé, -e [depareje] *adj (gant)* odd; *(service de table)* incomplete

déparer [depare] *vt* to spoil, to mar; **ce tableau ne dépare pas dans le salon** this painting looks pretty good in the living room

départ [depar] *nm* **(a)** *(d'une personne, d'un véhicule, d'un bateau)* departure; **les grands départs** the great holiday exodus; **être sur le d.** to be on the point of leaving; **excursions au d. de Nice** trips departing from Nice; **je regrette votre d.** I'm sorry you're leaving; **d. volontaire** *(d'employé)* voluntary redundancy **(b)** *(d'une course)* start; **ligne de d.** starting line; **faux d.** false start; **donner le d. (d'une course)** to give the starting signal (for a race); *aussi Fig* **prendre un bon/mauvais d.** to get off to a good/bad start **(c)** *(début)* start, beginning; **salaire de d.** starting salary; **au d.** at first, to start with

départager [45] [departaʒe] *vt* to decide between

département [departəmɑ̃] *nm* **(a)** *(de la France)* department *(division of local government)* **(b)** *(dans un ministère)* department; **le d. d'anglais** *(d'une faculté)* the English department

départemental, -e, -aux, -ales [departəmɑ̃tal, -o] **1** *adj* departmental
2 *nf* **départementale** secondary road, *Br* B road

départir [64a] [departir] **se départir** *vpr Litt* **il ne s'est jamais départi de son calme/sa bonne humeur** his calm/his good humour never deserted him

dépassé, -e [depase] *adj* **(a)** *(démodé)* *(vêtement, technique)* old-fashioned **(b)** *(perdu)* overwhelmed; **être d. par les événements** to be overtaken by events

dépassement [depasmɑ̃] *nm* **(a)** *(en voiture)* Br overtaking, Am passing **(b)** *Fin* **il y a un d. de crédit de plusieurs millions** the budget has been exceeded by several million

dépasser [depase] **1** *vt* **(a)** *(aller plus loin que)* to go past **(b)** *(doubler)* Br to overtake, Am to pass **(c)** *(excéder) (limite de vitesse, temps imparti, poids)* to exceed; **d. la date limite de vente** *(produit)* to be past its sell-by date; **d. dix minutes** to last longer than ten minutes; **ne pas d. la dose prescrite** *(sur notice)* do not exceed the stated dose; **cela dépasse l'entendement** it's beyond belief **(d)** *(surpasser)* to outstrip; **d. qn d'une tête** to stand a head taller than sb; **d. qn en beauté** to be more beautiful than sb; **d. les espérances de qn** to exceed sb's expectations **(e)** *(exagérer)* **d. les bornes** to overstep the mark; **cela me dépasse** it's beyond me
2 *vi* **(a)** *(en voiture)* Br to overtake, Am to pass **(b)** *(se voir)* to stick out **(de** of); *(jupon)* to show
3 se dépasser *vpr* to surpass oneself

dépassionner [depasjone] *vt (débat)* to take the heat out of

dépatouiller [depatuje] **se dépatouiller** *vpr Fam* to cope, to manage

dépaysé, -e [depeize] *adj* out of one's element

dépaysement [depeizmɑ̃] *nm (positif)* change of scene; *(négatif)* disorientation

dépayser [depeize] *vt (positivement)* to be a change of scene for; *(négativement)* to disorientate

dépecer [16/34] [depəse] *vt (sujet: boucher)* to cut up; *(sujet: animal)* to tear up

dépêche [depɛʃ] *nf* dispatch; **d. d'agence** agency news item

dépêcher [depeʃe] **1** *vt (messager)* to dispatch
2 se dépêcher *vpr* to hurry; **dépêchez-vous!** hurry up!; **se d. de faire qch** to hurry to do sth; **dépêche-toi de finir ton travail** hurry up and finish your work

dépeindre [54] [depɛ̃dr] *vt* to depict

dépenaillé, -e [depənaje] *adj* ragged

dépénalisation [depenalizasjɔ̃] *nf* decriminalization

dépénaliser [depenalize] *vt* to decriminalize

dépendance [depɑ̃dɑ̃s] *nf* **(a)** *(asservissement)* dependence (à on); **être sous la d. de qn** to be under sb's domination **(b)** *(bâtiment)* outbuilding

dépendant, -e [depɑ̃dɑ̃, -ɑ̃t] *adj* dependent **(de** on)

dépendre [depɑ̃dr] *vi* to depend **(de** on); **cela ne dépend pas de nous** it's not up to us; *Fam* **cela dépend (des fois)** it depends

dépens [depɑ̃] *nmpl* **(a)** **aux d. de** at the expense of; **apprendre qch à ses d.** to learn sth to one's cost **(b)** *Jur* **être condamné aux d.** to be ordered to pay costs

dépense [depɑ̃s] *nf* **(a)** *(frais)* expenditure, expense; **dépenses** spending; **les dépenses du ménage** household expenses; **faire des dépenses** to spend money; **pousser (les gens) à la d.** to encourage people to spend; **il ne regarde pas à la d.** he spares no expense **(b)** **d. physique** physical exertion

dépenser [depɑ̃se] **1** *vt (de l'argent)* to spend; *Fig* **d. toute son énergie (à faire qch)** to use up all one's energy (in doing sth)
2 *vi* to spend (money); **d. sans compter** to spend lavishly
3 se dépenser *vpr* to burn up energy

dépensier, -ère [depɑ̃sje, -er] *adj* extravagant

déperdition [deperdisjɔ̃] *nf (de chaleur, d'énergie)* loss

dépérir [deperir] *vi (personne)* to waste away; *(plante)* to wither; *(arbre)* to decay

dépêtrer [depetre] *Fam* **1** *vt* **d. qn de qch** to free sb from sth

2 se dépêtrer *vpr (se dégager)* to free oneself (**de** from); *Fig* **se d. de qch** to get oneself out of sth; *Fig* **se d. de qn** to get rid of sb

dépeuplement [depœpləmɑ̃] *nm (d'un pays)* depopulation

dépeupler [depœple] **1** *vt (pays)* to depopulate

2 se dépeupler *vpr (pays)* to become depopulated

déphasé, -e [defaze] *adj* (a) *Él* out of phase (b) *Fam (désorienté)* disorientated

dépiauter [depjote] *vt Fam (animal)* to skin; *Fig* **d. un texte** to pull a text to pieces

dépilatoire [depilatwar] *adj* **crème d.** hair-removing cream

dépistage [depistaʒ] *nm (d'une maladie)* screening; **d. du sida** AIDS screening

dépister [depiste] *vt (gibier, criminel)* to track down; *(maladie)* to detect

dépit [depi] *nm* (a) *(ressentiment)* spite; **par d.** out of spite (b) **en d. de** in spite of, despite; **en d. du bon sens** contrary to common sense

dépité, -e [depite] *adj* annoyed

déplacé, -e [deplase] *adj* (a) *(dérangé)* out of place; **avoir une vertèbre déplacée** to have a slipped disc (b) *(inconvenant) (observation)* uncalled-for

déplacement [deplasmɑ̃] *nm* (a) *(réarrangement)* moving; *(mutation)* transfer; **d. de vertèbre** slipped disc; *Ordinat* **d. du curseur** cursor movement; *Ordinat* **d. entre fichiers** movement between files (b) *(voyage)* trip; **déplacements** travel; **être en d.** to be on a (business) trip; *Fig* **valoir le d.** to be worth the trip

déplacer [16] [deplase] **1** *vt (objet)* to move; *(fonctionnaire, service)* to transfer; *Fig* **d. le problème** *(volontairement)* to avoid the issue; *(involontairement)* to miss the point

2 se déplacer *vpr (changer de place)* to move around (b) *(voyager)* to travel (c) **se d. une vertèbre** to slip a disc

déplafonner [deplafɔne] *vt (prix, crédit)* to remove the ceiling on

déplaire [55a] [depler] **1** *vi* **d. à qn** *(irriter)* to displease sb; **cet homme/cette maison me déplaît** I don't like that man/that house; **cela ne me déplairait pas** I wouldn't mind it; *Ironique* **ne vous/leur en déplaise** whether you/they like it or not

2 se déplaire *vpr* **il se déplaît à Paris** he doesn't like it in Paris; **elle ne se déplaît pas à Paris** she quite likes it in Paris

déplaisant, -e [deplezɑ̃, -ɑ̃t] *adj* unpleasant

déplaisir [deplezir] *nm* displeasure, annoyance; **à son grand d.** to his great annoyance

dépliant [deplijɑ̃] *nm* leaflet; *(d'un livre)* fold-out page

déplisser [deplise] **1** *vt* to take the creases out of

2 se déplisser *vpr* to lose its creases

déploiement [deplwamɑ̃] *nm (d'ailes)* spreading; *(de troupes)* deployment; *Fig (de force)* display

déplorable [deplɔrabl] *adj* deplorable

déplorer [deplɔre] *vt* to deplore; **nous devrons travailler plus, (et) je le déplore, mais...** we'll have to do more work, I'm sorry to say, but...; **d. la mort de qn** to mourn sb's death; **d. la perte de qch** to lament the loss of sth

déployer [32] [deplwaje] **1** *vt (journal, carte)* to unfold, to open out; *(voiles, ailes)* to spread; *(troupes, police)* to deploy; *Fig* to display

2 se déployer *vpr (voile)* to unfurl; *(troupes, police)* to deploy

déplumé, -e [deplyme] *adj* featherless; *Fam (chauve)* bald

déplumer [deplyme] **se déplumer** *vpr (oiseau)* to moult; *Fam (personne)* to go bald

dépoitraillé, -e [depwatraje] *adj Fam* with one's shirt open

dépoli, -e [depɔli] *adj (verre)* frosted

dépolitiser [depɔlitize] *vt* to depoliticize

dépolluer [depɔlɥe] *vt* to clean up

déportation [depɔrtasjɔ̃] *nf (en camp de concentration)* internment

déporté, -e [depɔrte] *nm,f (de camp de concentration)* internee

déporter [depɔrte] *vt* **d. qn** to send sb to a concentration camp

déposer [depoze] **1** *vt* (a) *(mettre à terre)* to put down; *aussi Fig* **d. les armes** to lay down one's arms (b) *(laisser) (personne)* to drop (off); **d. qch chez qn** to drop sth off at sb's house; **d. une gerbe sur une tombe** to lay a wreath on a grave; **d. un baiser sur le front de qn** to plant a kiss on sb's forehead; **d. la clé à la réception** to leave the key at reception; **d. une caution** to leave a deposit; **d. de l'argent (à la banque)** to deposit money (at the bank); *Jur* **d. une plainte (contre qn)** to lodge a complaint (against sb); *Pol* **d. un projet de loi** to introduce a bill (c) *(marque, brevet)* to register; **marque déposée** registered trademark (d) *(monarque)* to depose

2 *vi Jur* **d. (en justice)** to give evidence (**contre** against)

3 se déposer *vpr (substance)* to settle

dépositaire [depoziter] *nmf* (a) *(de papiers)* depositary; *Fig (d'un secret)* guardian (b) *Com (de produits)* agent

déposition [depozisjɔ̃] *nf Jur* statement *(made by witness)*; **faire/recueillir une d.** to make/take a statement (b) *(d'un monarque)* deposing

déposséder [34] [deposede] *vt* to dispossess, to deprive (**de** of)

dépôt [depo] *nm* (a) *(action)* depositing; *(somme)* deposit; **faire un d.** *(à la banque)* to make a deposit; **mettre qch en d.** to put sth into storage; *Fin* **d. d'espèces** cash deposit; *Jur* **d. légal** registration of copyright; *Fin* **d. à vue** cash deposit (b) *(entrepôt)* depot; *(de trains)* engine shed; *(prison)* prison; **d. de munitions** munitions depot; **d. d'ordures** *Br* rubbish dump, *Am* garbage dump (c) *(substance)* deposit; *(limon)* silt; *(de bouilloire)* fur

dépoter [depote] *vt (plantes)* to repot

dépotoir [depotwar] *nm (dépôt d'ordures)* dump; *Fam (chambre, classe)* dumping ground

dépôt-vente [*pl* dépôts-ventes] [depovɑ̃t] *nm* second-hand clothes shop *(where clothes are sold on commission)*

dépouille [depuj] *nf* (a) *(d'animal)* skin, hide; **d. (mortelle)** *(mortal)* remains (b) **dépouilles** *(trésor de guerre)* spoils, booty

dépouillé, -e [depuje] *adj (style)* bald; *(arbre)* bare

dépouillement [depujmã] nm (a) (examen) d. du scrutin counting of the votes; d. du courrier sorting through the mail (b) (pauvreté) poverty; (sobriété) austerity

dépouiller [depuje] 1 vt (a) (priver) to deprive (de of); d. qn de ses vêtements to strip sb; se faire d. (dans une affaire) to lose all one's money (b) (examiner) (courrier) to sort through; d. le scrutin to count the votes (c) (animal) to skin
  2 se dépouiller vpr se d. de qch to rid oneself of sth; les arbres se dépouillent de leurs feuilles the trees are shedding their leaves

dépourvu, -e [depurvy] adj (a) d. de qch devoid of sth (b) être pris au d. to be caught off (one's) guard

dépoussiérer [34] [depusjere] vt to dust; Fig (institution) to dust down

dépravation [depravasjõ] nf depravity

dépravé, -e [deprave] 1 adj depraved
  2 nm,f degenerate

dépraver [deprave] vt to deprave

dépréciation [depresjasjõ] nf depreciation

déprécier [66] [depresje] 1 vt to undervalue
  2 se déprécier vpr (valeurs, marchandises) to depreciate

déprédation [depredasjõ] nf depredation

dépressif, -ive [depresif, -iv] adj depressive

dépression [depresjõ] nf (a) (creux) depression; d. (atmosphérique) low, trough; Psy depression; faire de la d. to be suffering from depression; faire une d. to be depressed; d. nerveuse nervous breakdown

dépressurisation [depresyrizasjõ] nf depressurization

dépressuriser [depresyrize] vt (avion) to depressurize

déprimant, -e [deprimã, -ãt] adj depressing

déprime [deprim] nf Fam depression; avoir un (petit) coup de d. to be feeling (a bit) low

déprimé, -e [deprime] adj Psy depressed

déprimer [deprime] 1 vt (démoraliser) to depress
  2 vi Fam to be feeling low

déprogrammer [deprograme] vt (émission) to cancel; Ordinat to remove from a program

dépuceler [42] [depysle] vt Fam to deflower

depuis [depųi] 1 prép (a) (indiquant le point de départ) d. hier/ce matin/1995 since yesterday/this morning/1995; d. l'âge de cinq ans from the age of five; d. leur rencontre since they met; d. ce temps-là since then; d. quand êtes-vous ici? how long have you been here? (b) (durée) for; je suis ici d. trois jours I've been here for three days; d. combien de temps êtes-vous mariés? how long have you been married (for)?; il l'aime d. toujours he has always loved her; d. longtemps for a long time; d. la nuit des temps since the dawn of time
  (c) (lieu) from; il ne m'a pas parlé d. Rouen he hasn't spoken to me since (we left) Rouen
  2 adv since (then)
  3 conj d. que since; d. que le monde est monde since the world began

député [depyte] nm Pol deputy, Br ≃ MP, Am ≃ representative (de for); d. du Parlement européen Member of the European Parliament, MEP

déraciné, -e [derasine] 1 adj uprooted
  2 nm,f person who has been uprooted

déraciner [derasine] vt (arbre, personne) to uproot

déraillement [derajmã] nm derailment

dérailler [deraje] vi (a) (train, tram) to leave the rails; faire d. un train to derail a train (b) Fam (personne) to talk drivel

dérailleur [derajœr] nm (de bicyclette) derailleur (gears)

déraison [derɛzõ] nf Litt folly

déraisonnable [derɛzɔnabl] adj foolish

déraisonner [derɛzɔne] vi Litt to talk nonsense

dérangé, -e [derãʒe] adj (fou) deranged

dérangeant, -e [derãʒã, -ãt] adj (film, personnage) disturbing

dérangement [derãʒmã] nm (a) (gêne) trouble; je ne veux pas vous causer de d. I don't want to put you to any trouble; excusez-moi pour le d. I'm sorry to trouble you (b) (panne) la ligne est en d. the line is out of order

déranger [45] [derãʒe] 1 vt (a) (papiers, livres) to disturb; (pièce) to mess up (b) (gêner) (personne) to disturb; ne pas d. (sur panneau) do not disturb; cela vous dérange si j'ouvre la fenêtre? would you mind if I opened the window?; si cela ne vous dérange pas if that's all right by you; Ironique je ne te dérange pas trop? am I in your way?; Fam et alors, ça te dérange? what's it to you? (c) (perturber) to upset; avoir le cerveau dérangé to be deranged
  2 vi (choquer) to be disturbing
  3 se déranger vpr merci de vous être dérangé thank you for your trouble; ne vous dérangez pas pour moi please don't go to any trouble on my account

dérapage [derapaʒ] nm (en voiture) skid; (à skis) sideslip; Fig mistake; Fig le d. des prix spiralling prices

déraper [derape] vi (voiture) to skid; (à skis) to sideslip; Fig (prix) to be rising uncontrollably

dératé, -e [derate] nm,f Fam courir comme un d. to run flat out

dératiser [deratize] vt d. qch to clear sth of rats

derechef [dərəʃɛf] adv Litt once more

déréglé, -e [deregle] adj (mécanisme) not working properly

dérèglement [dereglamã] nm (d'un mécanisme) malfunctioning; d. hormonal hormone disorder

dérégler [34] [deregle] 1 vt (mécanisme) to cause to malfunction
  2 se dérégler vpr (mécanisme) to go wrong; elle s'est déréglé le système digestif she's ruined her digestive system

dérider [deride] 1 vt to cheer up
  2 se dérider vpr to cheer up

dérision [derizjõ] nf derision; tourner qch en d. to deride sth

dérisoire [derizwar] adj (salaire, somme) derisory; (prix) rock-bottom

dérivatif [derivatif] nm distraction (à from)

dérivation [derivasjõ] nf (a) (route, cours d'eau) diversion; Él monté en d. shunt connected (b) Math derivation

dérive [deriv] nf Naut & Av drift; à la d., en d. adrift; la d. des continents continental drift

dérivé, -e [derive] 1 adj (a) (sens, fonction) derived; produit d. Chim by-product; Fin derivative (b) Él courant d. shunt current
  2 nf Math dérivée derivative

dériver¹ [derive] 1 vt (a) (cours d'eau) to divert; Él (courant) to shunt (b) Math (fonction) to derive
  2 dériver de vt ind (mot) to be derived from

dériver² vi Naut & Av to drift

dériveur [derivœr] nm Naut sailing dinghy (with centreboard)

dermatite [dermatit] nf Méd dermatitis

dermato [dermato] nmf Fam dermatologist

dermatologie [dermatɔlɔʒi] nf dermatology

dermatologique [dermatɔlɔʒik] adj dermatological

dermatologiste [dermatɔlɔʒist], **dermatologue** [dermatɔlɔg] nmf dermatologist

derme [dɛrm] nm dermis

dernier, -ère [dɛrnje, -ɛr] 1 adj (a) (ultime) last; (marquant la fin) final; au d. moment at the last moment (b) (passé) last; (le plus récent) (livre, nouvelles, mode) latest; au cours des dernières années over the past or last few years
(c) (dans l'espace) last; le d. rang the back or last row; la dernière marche de l'escalier (en haut) the top step; (en bas) the bottom step; au d. étage on the top floor
(d) Litt (extrême) utmost; de la dernière importance of the utmost importance; c'est du d. chic it's the height of elegance
(e) (le pire) worst; de d. ordre very inferior; être reçu d. au concours to come last in the competition; c'était la dernière chose à faire that's the last thing you/he/etc should have done
2 nm,f (a) (dans un classement) last; les six derniers the last six; arriver dans les derniers to be one of the last to finish; il est arrivé le d. ou bon d. he came in last; c'est le d. de sa classe he's bottom of his class; Fam c'est le d. de mes soucis that's the least of my worries
(b) (dans une chronologie) (l'ultime) last; (le plus récent) latest; le d. en date the most recent; ce d. répondit... the latter answered...; c'est toujours le d. à sortir he's always last out; comment va la petite dernière? how's the little one?
(c) Péj on la traite comme la dernière des dernières they treat her like the lowest of the low; c'est vraiment le d. des menteurs he's the world's biggest liar
3 nf dernière (a) (spectacle) last night
(b) (nouveauté) tu as entendu la dernière de ton frère? have you heard your brother's latest?
4 adv en d. last (of all); il sort toujours en d. he's always last out

dernièrement [dɛrnjɛrmɑ̃] adv lately, recently

dernier-né, dernière-née (mpl derniers-nés, fpl dernières-nées) [dɛrnjene, dɛrnjɛrne] nm,f youngest (child)

dérobade [derɔbad] nf (a) (esquive) evasion (b) (d'un cheval) swerve

dérobé, -e [derɔbe] adj (a) (escalier, porte) hidden, secret (b) (volé) stolen

dérobée [derɔbe] à la dérobée adv secretly, on the sly; regarder qn à la d. to steal a glance at sb

dérober [derɔbe] 1 vt (a) (voler) to steal (à from) (b) (cacher) to hide (à from); d. qn à la curiosité des autres to keep sb away from prying eyes
2 se dérober vpr (a) (s'échapper) to slip away (à from); se d. à la curiosité de qn to avoid sb's prying eyes (b) (manquer) (sol, jambes) to give way (sous beneath) (c) (de cheval) to swerve

dérogation [derɔgasjɔ̃] nf exemption (à from); Jur waiver; (à une loi) derogation (à of)

déroger [45] [derɔʒe] vi d. à l'usage/à la loi to depart from custom/the law

dérouillée [deruje] nf très Fam belting

dérouiller [deruje] 1 vi très Fam (a) (être battu) to get a belting (b) (souffrir) to have a hard time of it
3 se dérouiller vpr Fam se d. les jambes to stretch one's legs

déroulement [derulmɑ̃] nm (d'événement) unfolding; pendant tout le d. de la cérémonie throughout the ceremony

dérouler [derule] 1 vt (rouleau) to unroll; (store) to let down; (câble) to unwind; Ordinat d. un menu to pull down a menu
2 se dérouler vpr (a) (rouleau) to unroll; (store) to come down; (câble) to unwind (b) Fig (événement) to unfold; la manifestation s'est déroulée dans le calme the demonstration passed off peacefully

déroutant, -e [derutɑ̃, -ɑ̃t] adj disconcerting

déroute [derut] nf aussi Fig rout; l'ennemi fut mis en d. the enemy was routed

dérouter [derute] vt (a) (navire, avion) to divert, to reroute (b) (égarer) (poursuivants) to throw off the scent (c) Fig (étonner) to throw

derrière [dɛrjɛr] 1 prép behind; les uns d. les autres one behind the other; sortir de d. un buisson to come out from behind a bush; aussi Fig les autres sont loin d. elle the others are way behind her; Fig il faut toujours être d. elle you always have to be at her back; Fig c'est lui qui est d. tout ça he's the one behind it all
2 adv behind; aller ou monter d. (en voiture) to sit in the back
3 nm (a) (de bâtiment) back, rear; le mur de d. the back wall (b) (de personne) behind, backside; (d'animal) hindquarters; recevoir des coups de pied dans le ou au d. to get kicked in the behind

des [de] voir de, un

dès [dɛ] prép (à partir de) from; d. 1840 as far back as 1840; d. le matin first thing in the morning; d. leur arrivée as soon as they arrive/arrived; d. maintenant, d. à présent from now on; d. que tu seras là as soon as you're here; d. lors (dans le temps) from then on; (par conséquent) consequently; d. lors que... since...

désabusé, -e [dezabyze] adj disillusioned

désaccord [dezakɔr] nm disagreement; être en d. avec qn (sur qch) to disagree with sb (about sth)

désaccordé, -e [dezakɔrde] adj out of tune

désaccoutumer [dezakutyme] se **désaccoutumer** vpr to get out of the habit (de of)

désaffecté, -e [dezafekte] adj disused

désaffection [dezafɛksjɔ̃] nf disaffection (à l'égard de with)

désagréable [dezagreabl] adj unpleasant

désagrégation [dezagregasjɔ̃] nf (désintégration) disintegration

désagréger [59] [dezagreʒe] 1 vt (désintégrer) to cause to disintegrate
2 se désagréger vpr to disintegrate

désagrément [dezagremɑ̃] nm (a) (gêne) trouble (b) (souci, aspect négatif) problem

désaltérant, -e [dezalterɑ̃, -ɑ̃t] adj thirst-quenching

désaltérer [34] [dezaltere] 1 vt d. qn to quench sb's thirst; c'est une boisson qui désaltère it's a thirst-quenching drink
2 se désaltérer vpr to quench one's thirst

désambiguïser [dezɑ̃bigɥize] vt (situation) to clarify; (mot) to disambiguate

désamorçage [dezamɔrsaʒ] nm (a) (d'une bombe, d'un conflit) defusing (b) (d'une pompe) draining

désamorcer [16] [dezamɔrse] vt (a) (bombe, conflit, querelle) to defuse (b) (pompe) to drain

désappointer [dezapwɛ̃te] vt Litt to disappoint

désapprobateur, -trice [dezaprɔbatœr, -tris] adj disapproving

désapprobation [dezaprɔbasjɔ̃] nf disapproval

désapprouver [dezapruve] vt to disapprove of

désarçonner [dezarsɔne] vt (a) (jeter bas) to unseat, to throw (b) Fig (déconcerter) to throw

désargenté, -e [dezarʒɑ̃te] adj Fam (personne) broke

désarmant, -e [dezarmɑ̃, -ɑ̃t] adj disarming

désarmé, -e [dezarme] adj (profondément touché) disarmed; (sans défenses) defenceless, helpless

désarmement [dezarməmɑ̃] nm (d'un pays, d'une région) disarmament; **d. multilatéral** multilateral disarmament (b) (de soldats) disarming

désarmer [dezarme] 1 vt (a) (malfaiteur) to disarm (b) Fig (toucher profondément) to disarm (c) (navire) to lay up 2 vi (a) (pays, région) to disarm (b) (cesser) **sa colère ne désarme pas** he is still angry

désarroi [dezarwa] nm confusion; **jeter qn dans le d.** to throw sb into confusion; **il est en plein d. ou dans un grand d.** he's in a state of utter confusion

désarticuler [dezartikyle] 1 vt to dislocate
2 **se désarticuler** vpr to contort oneself; **se d. l'épaule** to dislocate one's shoulder

désastre [dezastr] nm disaster

désastreux, -euse [dezastrø, -øz] adj disastrous

désavantage [dezavɑ̃taʒ] nm disadvantage; **avoir un d. par rapport à qn** to be at a disadvantage compared with sb; **voir qn à son d.** to see sb in an unfavourable light

désavantager [45] [dezavɑ̃taʒe] vt to put at a disadvantage, to disadvantage; **être désavantagé par rapport à qn** to be at a disadvantage compared with sb

désavantageux, -euse [dezavɑ̃taʒø, -øz] adj disadvantageous

désaveu [dezavø] nm (a) (reniement) disowning (b) (condamnation) disapproval

désavouer [dezavwe] vt (a) (renier) to disown (b) (condamner) to disapprove of (c) Jur (enfant) to disown

désaxé, -e [dezakse] nm,f unbalanced person

desceller [desele] vt (a) (pierre) to loosen (b) (acte, document) to unseal

descendance [desɑ̃dɑ̃s] nf (a) (filiation) descent (b) (postérité) descendants

descendant, -e [desɑ̃dɑ̃, -ɑ̃t] 1 adj (mouvement) downward
2 nm,f descendant

descendre [desɑ̃dr] 1 vi (aux être) (a) (en s'approchant) to come down; (en s'éloignant) to go down; **d. de qch** to come down from sth; **faire d. qn de qch** to get sb down from sth; **aider qn à d.** to help sb down; **d. à 150 m de profondeur** to go down to a depth of 150 m; **d. en dessous des dix secondes** to get below ten seconds; **d. à Marseille/dans le Midi** to go down to Marseilles/to the South; Fig **d. dans la rue** to take to the streets
(b) (d'un escalier) (en s'approchant) to come downstairs; (en s'éloignant) to go downstairs; **d. à la cave** to go down to the cellar
(c) (d'un véhicule) **d. d'un train/d'une voiture** to get off

a train/out of a car; **d. de cheval/de vélo/de moto** to dismount; **tout le monde descend!** (au terminus) all change!
(d) (baisser) (marée) to go out; **faire d. la fièvre** to reduce fever
(e) (tomber) (brouillard) to come down
(f) (s'étendre) to go down; (route, rue) to go downhill; **d. jusqu'à la taille/jusqu'aux chevilles** to come down to the waist/to the ankles; **ce chemin descend au village** this path goes down to the village
(g) (loger) **d. chez qn** to stay with sb; **d. à l'hôtel** to put up or stay at a hotel
(h) Fig (venir) **d. de** to be descended from
2 vt (aux avoir) (a) (dévaler) **d. un escalier/la rue/la rivière** (en s'éloignant) to go down a staircase/the street/the river; (en s'approchant) to come down a staircase/the street/the river
(b) (porter vers le bas) (en s'éloignant) to take down; (en s'approchant) to bring down; **d. la poubelle** to take the rubbish down; **peux-tu me d. mon pull?** can you bring me down my sweater?
(c) (abaisser) (store, étagère) to lower
(d) Fam (abattre) (avion, personne) to shoot down
(e) Fam (consommer) (repas, boisson) to put away; **qu'est-ce qu'il descend!** he's really putting it away!

descente [desɑ̃t] nf (a) (action de descendre) descent; **d. en rappel** abseiling
(b) (sortie) **accueillir qn à sa d. du train** to meet sb off the train
(c) (incursion) raid; **d. de police** police raid
(d) (route en pente) slope; **ralentir dans la d.** to slow down when going downhill
(e) (en ski) (course) downhill (race); **faire de la d.** to do downhill (skiing)
(f) **d. de lit** bedside rug
(g) (tuyau) downpipe
(h) Fam **il a une bonne d.** he can really put it away

descriptible [deskriptibl] adj describable

descriptif, -ive [deskriptif, -iv] 1 adj descriptive
2 nm description

description [deskripsjɔ̃] nf description; **faire la d.** to give a description of; **d. de poste** job description

désembourber [dezɑ̃burbe] vt to pull out of the mud

désembuage [dezɑ̃bɥaʒ] nm demisting

désemparé, -e [dezɑ̃pare] adj (personne) at a loss

désemparer [dezɑ̃pare] vi sans d. without stopping

désemplir [dezɑ̃plir] vi ne pas d. to be always full

désenchanté, -e [dezɑ̃ʃɑ̃te] adj (personne) disillusioned; (sourire) wistful

désenchantement [dezɑ̃ʃɑ̃tmɑ̃] nm disillusion

désenchanter [dezɑ̃ʃɑ̃te] vt to disillusion

désenclaver [dezɑ̃klave] vt (région) to open up

désencombrer [dezɑ̃kɔ̃bre] vt (passage) to clear (de of)

désendettement [dezɑ̃detmɑ̃] nm debt clearing

désenfler [dezɑ̃fle] vi to go down, to become less swollen

désengagement [dezɑ̃gaʒmɑ̃] nm disengagement

désengager [45] [dezɑ̃gaʒe] 1 vt to free (de from)
2 **se désengager** vpr to free oneself (de from)

désensabler [dezɑ̃sable] vt (a) (chenal, port) to clear of sand (b) (bateau) to get off the sand; (voiture) to dig out of the sand

désensibiliser [desɑ̃sibilize] vt aussi Fig to desensitize

désépaissir [dezepesir] vt (a) *(sauce)* to thin down (b) *(cheveux)* to thin out

déséquilibre [dezekilibr] nm imbalance; **être en d.** to be unsteady

déséquilibré, -e [dezekilibre] **1** adj unbalanced
2 nm,f unbalanced person

déséquilibrer [dezekilibre] vt (a) *(objet, personne)* to throw off balance (b) *Psy* to unbalance

désert, -e [dezer, -ert] **1** adj *(lieu)* deserted; *(pays, région)* uninhabited
2 nm desert; **d. culturel** cultural desert or wasteland; **le d. de Gobi** the Gobi Desert; **d. de sable** sandy desert

déserter [dezerte] **1** vt (a) *(lieu, fonction)* to desert; *Mil* **d. son poste** to desert one's post (b) *Fig (cause)* to desert, to abandon
2 vi *(soldat)* to desert

déserteur [dezertœr] nm deserter

désertification [dezertifikasjɔ̃] nf (a) *(transformation en désert)* desertification (b) *(dépeuplement)* depopulation

désertion [dezersjɔ̃] nf desertion

désertique [dezertik] adj desert

désespérant, -e [dezespera, -ɑ̃t] adj *(situation, personne)* hopeless; **être d'une lenteur/bêtise désespérante** to be incredibly slow/stupid

désespéré, -e [dezespere] **1** adj (a) *(qui ne laisse aucun espoir)* desperate; *(inconsolable)* in despair (b) *(exprimant le désespoir)* desperate (c) *(extrême) (mesure, solution)* desperate
2 nm,f desperate person

désespérément [dezesperema] adv desperately

désespérer [34] [dezespere] **1** vt *(personne)* to drive to despair
2 vi to despair
3 désespérer de vt ind to despair of; **d. de faire qch** to despair of doing sth; **il ne désespère pas d'y arriver** he hasn't given up hope of getting there
4 se désespérer vpr to despair

désespoir [dezespwar] nm despair; **être au d.** to be in despair; **être au d. de faire qch** to be extremely sorry to do sth; **faire ou être le d. de qn** *(personne)* to be the despair of sb; **réduire qn au d.** to drive sb to despair

déshabillé [dezabije] nm negligee

déshabiller [dezabije] **1** vt *(personne)* to undress; **d. qn du regard** to undress sb with one's eyes
2 se déshabiller vpr (a) *(pour être nu)* to undress, to take off one's clothes (b) *(ôter son manteau)* to take off one's coat

déshabituer [dezabitɥe] **1** vt **d. qn de qch/de faire qch** to get sb out of the habit of sth/of doing sth
2 se déshabituer vpr **se d. de qch/de faire qch** to get out of the habit of sth/of doing sth

désherbage [dezerbaʒ] nm weeding

désherbant [dezerbɑ̃] nm weedkiller

désherber [dezerbe] vt to weed

déshérité, -e [dezerite] **1** adj *(démuni)* deprived
2 nm,f les déshérités the underprivileged

déshériter [dezerite] vt to disinherit

déshonneur [dezonœr] nm dishonour

déshonorant, -e [dezonorã, -ɑ̃t] adj dishonourable

déshonorer [dezonore] **1** vt to disgrace; **se croire/sentir déshonoré de faire qch** to think/feel it beneath oneself to do sth
2 se déshonorer vpr to disgrace oneself

déshumaniser [dezymanize] vt to dehumanize

déshydratation [dezidratasjɔ̃] nf dehydration

déshydraté, -e [dezidrate] adj dehydrated

déshydrater [dezidrate] **1** vt to dehydrate
2 se déshydrater vpr to become dehydrated

desiderata [deziderata] nmpl desiderata

design [dizajn] **1** nm (a) *(stylique)* design; **d. industriel** industrial design (b) *(conception)* design
2 adj inv designer; **un intérieur d.** a designer interior

désignation [dezinasjɔ̃] nf (a) *(appellation)* designation (b) *(choix)* appointment

désigner [dezine] vt (a) *(montrer)* to point out; **d. qn/qch du doigt** to point to sb/sth (b) *(dénommer)* to refer to (c) *(choisir)* to designate, to appoint (d) **il est tout désigné pour le faire** he's just the man for the job

désillusion [dezilyzjɔ̃] nf disillusion

désillusionner [dezilyzjone] vt to disillusion

désincrustant, -e [dezɛ̃krystã, -ɑ̃t] **1** adj (a) *Tech (substance)* scaling (b) *(masque, savon)* cleansing
2 nm (a) *Tech* scale preventive (b) *(savon)* cleanser

désindustrialisation [dezɛ̃dystrijalizasjɔ̃] nf deindustrialization

désinence [dezinãs] nf *Gram* ending

désinfectant, -e [dezɛ̃fektã, -ɑ̃t] adj & nm disinfectant

désinfecter [dezɛ̃fekte] vt to disinfect

désinfection [dezɛ̃feksjɔ̃] nf disinfection

désinflation [dezɛ̃flasjɔ̃] nf *Écon* disinflation

désinformation [dezɛ̃formasjɔ̃] nf disinformation

désinformer [dezɛ̃forme] vt to disinform

désintégration [dezɛ̃tegrasjɔ̃] nf (a) *(des roches)* weathering (b) *(d'un groupe, de la famille)* break-up (c) *Phys (de matière)* disintegration

désintégrer [34] [dezɛ̃tegre] **1** vt (a) *(roches)* to weather (b) *(groupe, famille)* to break up (c) *Phys (matière)* to disintegrate; *(atome)* to split
2 se désintégrer vpr (a) *(roches)* to weather (b) *(groupe, famille)* to break up (c) *Phys (matière)* to disintegrate

désintéressé, -e [dezɛ̃terese] adj disinterested

désintéresser [dezɛ̃terese] **se désintéresser** vpr **se d. de qn/qch** *(ne pas s'y intéresser)* to have no interest in sb/sth; *(s'en détacher)* to lose interest in sb/sth

désintérêt [dezɛ̃tere] nm disinterest

désintoxication [dezɛ̃toksikasjɔ̃] nf *Méd* detoxification

désintoxiquer [dezɛ̃toksike] **1** vt *(alcoolique, drogué)* to treat for alcoholism/drug addiction
2 se désintoxiquer vpr (a) *(alcoolique, drogué)* to come off alcohol/drugs (b) *Fig (se remettre en forme)* to clean out one's system; *(perdre une habitude)* to get out of the habit

désinvolte [dezɛ̃volt] adj (a) *(négligeant)* casual, offhand (b) *(à l'aise) (manière)* unselfconscious; *(mouvements)* easy

désinvolture [dezɛ̃voltyr] nf (a) *(excès de liberté)* casualness; **avec d.** casually (b) *(naturel) (de manières)* unselfconsciousness; *(de mouvement)* ease

désir [dezir] nm (a) *(souhait)* desire; **selon le d. de qn** in accordance with sb's wishes; **prendre ses désirs pour des réalités** to indulge in wishful thinking; **tes désirs sont ses ordres** your wish is my command (b) **d. (sexuel)** (sexual) desire

désirable [dezirabl] adj desirable

désirer [dezire] vt (**a**) (souhaiter) to wish; **d. faire qch** to wish to do sth; **je désire qu'il vienne** I want him to come; **cela laisse à d.** it leaves a lot to be desired; **elle se fait d.** (elle n'arrive pas) she's keeping us waiting; **que désirez-vous?**, Fam **vous désirez?** (dans un magasin) can I help you?; (qu'est-ce que je vous sers?) what would you like? (**b**) (sexuellement) to desire

désireux, -euse [dezirø, øz] adj **être d. de faire qch** to be anxious to do sth

désistement [dezistəmã] nm withdrawal

désister [deziste] **se désister** vpr to withdraw

désobéir [dezɔbeir] vi to disobey; **d. à qn/qch** to disobey sb/sth

désobéissance [dezɔbeisãs] nf disobedience (à to)

désobéissant, -e [dezɔbeisã, -ãt] adj disobedient (à to)

désobligeant, -e [dezɔbliʒã, -ãt] adj disagreeable

désodorisant, -e [dezɔdɔrizã, -ãt] adj & nm deodorant

désodoriser [dezɔdɔrize] vt to deodorize

désœuvré, -e [dezœvre] adj idle

désœuvrement [dezœvrəmã] nm idleness; **par d.** for something to do

désolant, -e [dezɔlã, -ãt] adj (**a**) (affligeant) distressing (**b**) (contrariant) annoying

désolé, -e [dezɔle] adj (**a**) (navré) sorry; **je suis d. de vous déranger** I'm sorry to disturb you; **d., je n'ai pas le temps** sorry, I haven't got the time (**b**) (affligé) upset (**c**) (région) desolate

désoler [dezɔle] **1** vt (**a**) (navrer) to upset (**b**) (affliger) to distress
2 se désoler vpr to be upset

désolidariser [desɔlidarize] **se désolidariser** vpr **se d. de** to dissociate oneself from

désopilant, -e [dezɔpilã, -ãt] adj hilarious

désordonné, -e [dezɔrdɔne] adj (**a**) (chambre, bureau, personne) untidy (**b**) (désorganisé) (personne, article, pensées) disorganized; (mouvements) unco-ordinated (**c**) (vie) disorderly

désordre [dezɔrdr] nm (**a**) (manque d'ordre) untidiness, mess; **en d.** untidy; **mettre qch en d.** to make a mess of sth (**b**) (manque d'organisation) disorder (**c**) (trouble) commotion; **mettre le d. dans une réunion** to disrupt a meeting (**d**) (agitation) **désordres** disturbances (**e**) Méd disorder

désorganisation [dezɔrganizasjõ] nf disorganization

désorganiser [dezɔrganize] vt to disrupt

désorienté, -e [dezɔrjãte] adj (**a**) (égaré) disorientated (**b**) (déconcerté) bewildered

désorienter [dezɔrjãte] vt (déconcerter) to bewilder

désormais [dezɔrme] adv from now on, in future

désosser [dezɔse] **1** vt (viande, poisson) to bone
2 se désosser vpr to contort oneself

despote [despɔt] nm aussi Fig despot

despotique [despɔtik] adj despotic

desquamation [deskwamasjõ] nf peeling, Spéc desquamation

desquels, desquelles [dekɛl] voir **lequel**

DESS [deœsɛs] nm (abrév **diplôme d'études supérieures spécialisées**) = postgraduate diploma

dessaisir [desezir] **1** vt (**a**) (déposséder) **d. qn de qch** to confiscate sth from sb (**b**) **d. un juge d'une affaire** to withdraw a judge from a case
2 se dessaisir vpr **se d. de qch** to relinquish sth, to part with sth

dessaler [desale] **1** vt (**a**) (viande, poisson) to remove the salt from (by soaking); (eau de mer) to desalinate (**b**) Fam **d. qn** to teach sb a thing or two
2 vi (**a**) (voilier) to capsize (**b**) **mettre qch à d.** (viande, poisson) to soak sth to remove the salt
3 se dessaler vpr Fam to learn a thing or two

dessaouler [desule] Fam = **dessoûler**

dessèchement [desɛʃmã] nm (de la peau) drying up; (de la végétation) withering

dessécher [34] [deseʃe] **1** vt (déshydrater) (peau) to dry up; (végétation) to wither
2 se dessécher vpr (peau) to dry up; (végétation) to wither

dessein [desɛ̃] nm intention, purpose; **dans ce d.** with this intention; **à d.** intentionally; **dans le d. de faire qch** with the intention of doing sth

desseller [desele] vt (cheval) to unsaddle

desserrer [desere] **1** vt (**a**) (relâcher) (vis, ceinture, nœud) to loosen; (frein à main) to release (**b**) (décrisper) (poing) to unclench; (étreinte) to relax; Fig **il n'a pas desserré les dents** he didn't open his mouth
2 se desserrer vpr (**a**) (vis, ceinture, nœud) to come loose (**b**) (étreinte) to relax

dessert [desɛr] nm dessert; **qu'est-ce qu'il y a comme ou au d.?** what's for dessert?

desserte [desɛrt] nf (meuble) sideboard

desservir[1] [desɛrvir] vt (**a**) (passer par) (ville, localité) to serve; **ce train dessert les gares de...** (annonce) this train stops at...; **ville bien desservie** town with efficient public transport (**b**) (conduire à) (pièce) to lead to

desservir[2] vt (**a**) (débarrasser) (table) to clear (**b**) (nuire à) **d. qn** to do sb a disservice
2 vi (débarrasser la table) to clear away

dessiller [desije] vt Fig & Litt **d. les yeux de qn** to open sb's eyes

dessin [desɛ̃] nm (**a**) (technique, art) drawing; **faire du d.** to draw; **d. industriel** industrial drawing (**b**) (représentation) drawing; **faire un d.** to do a drawing; Fam Fig **faire un d. à qn** to spell it out for sb; Cin **d. animé** cartoon; **d. humoristique** cartoon (**c**) (motif) (sur tissu) design, pattern (**d**) (contour) (de la bouche, du visage) outline

dessinateur, -trice [desinatœr, -tris] nm,f (**a**) (artiste) drawer; **d. de bandes dessinées** cartoonist; **d. humoristique** cartoonist (**b**) (concepteur) designer (**c**) Tech **d. industriel** draughtsman

dessiner [desine] **1** vt (**a**) (faire un dessin de) to draw; **d. à l'encre/à la craie** to draw in ink/chalk (**b**) (concevoir) to design (**c**) Fig (tracer) (lignes) to outline; **vêtement qui dessine la taille** garment that shows off the waist; **visage bien dessiné** finely chiselled face
2 se dessiner vpr (**a**) (apparaître) to stand out; **se d. à l'horizon** to stand out on the horizon; **un sourire se dessine sur ses lèvres** a smile flickers over her lips (**b**) Fig (prendre forme) (changement, résultat) to become apparent; (projet) to take shape

dessoûler [desule] vt & vi Fam to sober up

dessous [dəsu] 1 *adv* (a) *(sous)* underneath (b) en d. underneath; **l'appartement d'en d.** the downstairs flat, the flat downstairs; **en d. de** below; **tu es très en d. de la vérité** you're not even close; *Fam* **être en d. de tout** to be worse than useless (c) **prendre/porter qch par (en) d.** to take hold of/carry sth from underneath; *Fig* **regarder qn par en d.** to look at sb furtively

  2 *nm (partie inférieure) (d'une assiette, d'une table)* underside; *(du pied)* bottom; **les gens du d.** the people below; **avoir le d.** to get the worst of it

  3 *nmpl* (a) *(partie cachée) (d'une affaire)* hidden side (b) *(sous-vêtements)* underwear

dessous-de-plat [dəsudpla] *nm inv* table mat

dessous-de-table [dəsudtabl] *nm inv* backhander; **verser un d. à qn** to give sb a backhander

dessous-de-verre [dəsudvɛr] *nm inv* coaster; *(en carton)* beer mat

dessus [dəsy] 1 *adv* on (it/them); **il a marché d.** he trod on it; **mais il n'y a pas l'adresse d.** but the address isn't on it

  2 *nm* (a) *(d'une table, du pied)* top; *(d'une assiette)* upper side; **l'étage du d.** the top floor (b) *Fig* **avoir le d.** to have the upper hand; **reprendre le d.** *(se remettre)* to get over it

dessus-de-lit [dəsydli] *nm inv* bedspread

déstabiliser [destabilize] *vt* to destabilize

destin [dɛstɛ̃] *nm* fate, destiny

destinataire [dɛstinatɛr] *nmf (d'une lettre)* addressee; *(de marchandises)* consignee; *(mandat postal)* payee

destination [dɛstinasjɔ̃] *nf* destination; **trains/vols à d. de Paris** trains/flights to Paris; **arriver à d.** to reach one's destination

destinée [dɛstine] *nf* (a) *(vie)* destiny (b) *Litt* **être promis à de grandes *ou* hautes destinées** to be destined for great things (c) *(fatalité)* fate, destiny

destiner [dɛstine] 1 *vt* (a) *(réserver)* **d. qch à qn** *(bien, somme d'argent, emploi)* to intend sth for sb (b) *(adresser)* **être destiné à qn** *(remarque, paquet)* to be meant for sb (c) *(assigner)* **d. une somme d'argent à qch** to allot or assign a sum of money to sth; **cet argent est destiné à la recherche contre le sida** this money is going towards AIDS research (d) *(concevoir pour)* **destiné à** (intended) for (e) *(vouer)* **d. qn à qch** to destine sb for sth; *Litt* **le sort les destinait à se rencontrer** they were destined to meet

  2 se destiner *vpr* **se d. à qch** to intend to take up sth

destituer [dɛstitɥe] *vt (renvoyer) (officier)* to discharge; *(fonctionnaire)* to remove from office; *(souverain)* to depose

destitution [dɛstitysjɔ̃] *nf (d'un officier)* discharge; *(d'un fonctionnaire)* removal from office; *(d'un souverain)* deposition

destructeur, -trice [dɛstryktœr, -tris] *adj* destructive

destruction [dɛstryksjɔ̃] *nf* destruction

désuet, -ète [desɥɛ, -ɛt] *adj* (a) *(dépassé)* obsolete (b) *(démodé)* old-fashioned

désuétude [desɥetyd] *nf* disuse; **tomber en d.** *(mot, expression)* to become obsolete

désuni, -e [dezyni] *adj (famille, amis, amants)* divided

désunir [dezynir] *vt (personnes, famille)* to divide

désynchronisé, -e [desɛ̃kronize] *adj* out of synch

détachable [detaʃabl] *adj* detachable

détachant, -e [detaʃɑ̃, -ɑ̃t] 1 *adj* stain-removing

  2 *nm* stain remover

détaché, -e [detaʃe] *adj* (a) *(ton, air, manière)* detached (b) *(fonctionnaire)* seconded

détachement [detaʃmɑ̃] *nm* (a) *(indifférence)* detachment (de from) (b) *(d'un fonctionnaire)* secondment; **être en d.** to be on secondment (c) *(troupes)* detachment

détacher¹ [detaʃe] 1 *vt* (a) *(défaire) (étiquette, page perforée)* to detach; *(ceinture, liens)* to undo; *(rideau)* to take down; *(wagon)* to uncouple; **d. ses yeux de qch** to take one's eyes off sth (b) *(libérer) (prisonnier, animal)* to untie (c) *(déléguer) (fonctionnaire)* to second; *(militaire)* to detach (d) *Fig* **d. qn de qch** to turn sb away from sth (e) *(faire sonner)* **d. les syllabes d'un mot** to pronounce each syllable of a word separately; *Mus* **d. les notes** to detach the notes

  2 se détacher *vpr (étiquette, bouton, page)* to come off; *(ceinture)* to come undone; *(écorce)* to peel off (b) *(se libérer) (animal)* to get loose (c) *Fig* **se d. de qn** *(en devenant adulte)* to break away from sb; *(par manque d'intérêt)* to grow apart from sb; **se d. de qch** to turn one's back on sth (d) *(se séparer) (groupe de coureurs)* to break away (e) *(ressortir)* to stand out **(sur** against)

détacher² *vt (nettoyer)* to remove the stains from

détail [detaj] *nm* (a) *(élément)* detail (b) *(énumération) (d'un compte, d'un inventaire)* items; *(d'une facture)* breakdown; **elle m'a fait le d. de sa soirée** she gave me a detailed account of her party; *Fam Fig* **il n'a pas fait de d.!** he didn't make any exceptions!; *Fam Fig* **il n'a pas fait dans le d.** he didn't go into detail; **en d.** in detail; **se perdre dans les détails** to get bogged down in detail (c) *Com* retail; **vendre/acheter au d.** to sell/buy retail

détaillant, -e [detajɑ̃, -ɑ̃t] *nm,f Com* retailer

détaillé, -e [detaje] *adj (récit, description)* detailed; *(facture)* itemized

détaler [detale] *vi Fam (personne)* to take off; **faire d. qn** to send sb packing

détartrage [detartraʒ] *nm* (a) *(de dents)* scaling; **se faire faire un d.** to have one's teeth scaled (b) *(de bouilloire, de cafetière, de chaudière)* descaling

détartrer [detartre] *vt* (a) *(dents)* to scale (b) *(bouilloire, cafetière, chaudière)* to descale

détaxe [detaks] *nf* tax refund

détaxer [detakse] *vt* to exempt from tax; **marchandises détaxées** duty-free goods

détectable [detɛktabl] *adj* detectable

détecter [detɛkte] *vt* to detect

détecteur, -trice [detɛktœr, -tris] 1 *adj* detecting

  2 *nm* detector; **d. de faux billets** forged banknote detector; **d. de fumée** smoke detector; **d. de mensonges** lie detector; **d. de mines** mine detector; *Ordinat* **d. virus** virus detector

détection [detɛksjɔ̃] *nf* detection; *Ordinat* **d. d'erreurs** error detection; *Ordinat* **d. virale** virus detection

détective [detɛktiv] *nm* detective; **d. privé** private detective

déteindre [54] [detɛ̃dr] *vi (tissu)* to run **(sur** over); **d. au lavage** to run in the wash; *Fig* **cela a déteint sur eux** it's rubbed off on them

dételer [42] [detle] 1 *vt (chevaux)* to unharness; *(bœufs)* to unyoke

  2 *vi Fam* to stop working; **sans d.** non-stop

détendre [detɑ̃dr] **1** vt **(a)** (relâcher) (corde) to slacken; (arc) to unbend; (ressort) to release **(b)** (décontracter) (personne) to relax; **le sport, ça détend** sport is relaxing **(c)** d. **l'atmosphère** to make the atmosphere less tense
2 se détendre vpr **(a)** (corde) to slacken; (arc) to unbend; (ressort) to lose its tension **(b)** (se relaxer) (personne, visage) to relax **(c)** (atmosphère, situation) to become less tense

détendu, -e [detɑ̃dy] adj (personne, conversation) relaxed

détenir [70] [detnir] vt **(a)** (avoir en sa possession) (passeport, titres, pouvoir, record du monde) to hold; (secret, preuve) to have **(b)** (garder prisonnier) to hold

détente [detɑ̃t] nf **(a)** (relaxation) relaxation **(b)** Pol détente **(c)** (d'une arme) trigger **(d)** (d'un athlète) spring; **avoir de la d.** to jump well **(e)** (d'un gaz) expansion **(f)** **être dur** ou **long à la d.** to be slow on the uptake

détenteur, -trice [detɑ̃tœr, -tris] nm,f (d'argent, de titres, de record) holder; (d'arme) possessor

détention [detɑ̃sjɔ̃] nf **(a)** (de titres) holding; (d'armes) possession **(b)** (incarcération) detention; **d. provisoire** detention pending trial

détenu, -e [detny] nm,f prisoner

détergent, -e [deterʒɑ̃, -ɑ̃t] adj & nm detergent

détérioration [deterjɔrasjɔ̃] nf deterioration

détériorer [deterjɔre] **1** vt to damage
2 se détériorer vpr to deteriorate

déterminant, -e [determinɑ̃, -ɑ̃t] **1** adj decisive
2 nm **(a)** Ling determiner **(b)** Math determinant

détermination [determinasjɔ̃] nf **(a)** (fermeté) determination **(b)** (d'une date, d'un lieu, d'un prix) determination, fixing; (du sang, d'un bactérie) typing

déterminé, -e [determine] adj **(a)** (résolu) determined; **être d. à faire qch** to be determined to do sth **(b)** (défini) specific

déterminer [determine] **1** vt **(a)** (définir) to determine, to fix; (sang, bactérie) to type **(b)** (décider) **d. qn à faire qch** to induce sb to do sth **(c)** (causer) (changement) to cause; (action, décision) to determine **(d)** Gram to determine
2 se déterminer vpr **se d. à faire qch** to make up one's mind to do sth

déterré, -e [detere] nm,f Fam **avoir une mine de d.** to look like death warmed up

déterrer [detere] vt aussi Fig to dig up

détestable [detestabl] adj foul

détester [deteste] **1** vt to detest, to hate; **je déteste être dérangé** I hate being disturbed; **ne pas d. faire qch** to quite like doing sth
2 se détester vpr (soi-même) to hate oneself; (l'un l'autre) to hate each other

détonant, -e [detɔnɑ̃, -ɑ̃t] **1** adj aussi Fig explosive
2 nm explosive

détonateur [detɔnatœr] nm detonator; Fig **servir de d. à** qch to spark sth off

détonation [detɔnasjɔ̃] nf (bruit) explosion; (bruit d'arme à feu) bang

détoner [detɔne] vi (explosif) to detonate; **faire d. qch** to detonate sth

détonner [detɔne] vi **(a)** (chanteur) to sing out of tune; (instrumentiste) to play out of tune **(b)** (trancher) (couleurs) to clash; **il détonne dans ce milieu** he's out of place in that environment

détordre [detɔrdr] vt (fil) to untwist

détour [detur] nm **(a)** (parcours) detour; **faire un d. (par)** to make a detour (via); **valoir le d.** (site) to be worth the trip **(b)** Fig (biais) roundabout means; **user de détours pour faire qch** to do sth in a roundabout way; **sans d.** without beating about the bush **(c)** (tracé) (d'une route, d'une rivière) bend; **faire un d.** to bend; Fig **au d. de la conversation** in the course of the conversation

détourné, -e [deturne] adj aussi Fig roundabout, indirect

détournement [deturnəmɑ̃] nm **(a)** **d. d'avion** hijacking **(b)** (d'un cours d'eau) diversion **(c)** **d. de fonds** embezzlement

détourner [deturne] **1** vt **(a)** (circulation, rivière) to divert; (avion) to hijack **(b)** (éloigner) **d. qn de** (ami, famille) to take sb away from; (préoccupation, engagement) to divert sb from; **d. qn du droit chemin** to lead sb astray; **d. l'attention de qn** to divert or distract sb's attention; **d. la conversation** to change the subject; **d. les soupçons** to avert suspicion **(c)** (voler) (fonds) to embezzle (à from) **(d)** (tourner) **d. la tête** to turn one's head away; **d. les yeux** ou **le regard** to look away
2 se détourner vpr aussi Fig to turn away from (**de** from)

détracteur, -trice [detraktœr, -tris] nm,f detractor

détraqué, -e [detrake] **1** adj (appareil) out of order; (estomac) upset; (temps) unsettled; Fam (personne) (psychologiquement) unhinged
2 nm,f Fam maniac

détraquer [detrake] **1** vt (appareil) to put out of order; (santé) to ruin; (estomac) to upset
2 se détraquer vpr (appareil, santé) to break down; (temps) to become unsettled; **se d. l'estomac** to upset one's stomach

détrempé, -e [detrɑ̃pe] adj (terre, sol) sodden, waterlogged

détresse [detres] nf **(a)** (angoisse) distress **(b)** (dénuement) financial difficulties **(c)** (perdition) **en d.** (navire) in distress; (voiture, avion) in difficulties

détriment [detrimɑ̃] nm **au d. de** to the detriment of; **je l'ai appris à mon d.** I found it out to my cost

détritus [detrity(s)] nm Br rubbish, Am garbage

détroit [detrwa] nm strait; **le d. de Béring** the Bering Strait; **le d. de Gibraltar** the Strait of Gibraltar

détromper [detrɔ̃pe] **1** vt **d. qn** to put sb right (**sur** about)
2 se détromper vpr to realize that one was wrong; **détrompez-vous!** think again!

détrôner [detrone] vt **(a)** (monarque) to dethrone **(b)** (théorie, méthode, produit) to supersede

détrousser [detruse] vt Hum **d. qn** to relieve sb of his valuables

détruire [18] [detrɥir] **1** vt **(a)** (anéantir) (espoir, mariage, santé) to ruin, to wreck **(b)** (démolir) (édifice, empire, avion) to destroy **(c)** (tuer) to kill
2 se détruire vpr (se faire du mal) to ruin one's health

dette [det] nf aussi Fig debt; **avoir des dettes** to be in debt; **être couvert** ou **criblé de dettes** to be crippled with debt; **d. extérieure** foreign debt; **la d. publique** ou **de l'État** the National Debt; **payer sa d. à la société** to pay one's debt to society

DEUG [dœg] nm (abrév **diplôme d'études universitaires générales**) = degree gained after a two-year course

deuil [dœj] *nm* (a) *(décès)* bereavement; **il y a eu un d. dans leur famille** there has been a death in their family (b) *(tristesse)* mourning; **être en d.** to be in mourning; **journée de d. national** day of national mourning (c) *(tenue)* **porter le d. (de qn)** to be in mourning (for sb); **prendre/quitter le d.** to go into/come out of mourning; *Fam Fig* **avoir les ongles en d.** to have dirty fingernails (d) **faire son d. de qch** to give sth up as lost

Deutsche Mark [dɔjtʃmark, dœtʃmark] *nm* Deutschmark

deux [dø] **1** *adj inv* (a) *(chiffre)* two; **d. fois** twice; **des d. côtés du fleuve** on either side *or* on both sides of the river; **tous (les) d.** both; **tous les d. jours** every other day, every two days; **nous/vous/eux** the two of us/you/them; **les ordinateurs et moi, ça fait d.** I know absolutely nothing about computers (b) *(peu de)* **c'est à d. pas d'ici** it's only a short distance away, it's two minutes away; **je reviens dans d. minutes** I'll be back in a minute; **tu peux venir? – d. secondes!** can you come here? – just a minute!

2 *nm inv* two; **casser qch en d.** to break sth in two; **marcher par d.** to walk in pairs *or* twos; *(dans une procession)* to march two abreast; *Fam* **en moins de d.** in next to no time; *voir aussi* **trois**

deuxième [døzjɛm] *adj & nmf* second; *voir aussi* **cinquième**

deuxièmement [døzjɛmmɑ̃] *adv* secondly

deux-mâts [døma] *nm* two-master

deux-pièces [døpjɛs] *nm* (a) *(maillot de bain)* two-piece (swimsuit) (b) *(tailleur)* two-piece (c) *(appartement)* two-room *Br* flat *or Am* apartment

deux-points [døpwɛ̃] *nm* colon

deux-roues [døru] *nm* two-wheeled vehicle

deux-temps [døtɑ̃] *nm (moteur)* two-stroke (engine)

deuzio [døzjo] *adv Fam* second

dévaler [devale] **1** *vt (escalier, pente)* to hurtle down
2 *vi (personne, pierres)* to hurtle down; *(eau, lave, boue)* to rush down

dévaliser [devalize] *vt* (a) *(cambrioler)* *(banque)* to rob; *(maison)* to burgle; *Fig (commerçant)* to clean out (b) *(vider)* *(réfrigérateur, placard)* to raid

dévalorisation [devalɔrizasjɔ̃] *nf* (a) *(action)* *(de la monnaie)* devaluation; *(de marchandises)* marking down; *(résultat)* *(de la monnaie)* depreciation; *(de marchandises)* mark-down (b) *Fig (d'une personne, d'une politique)* discrediting; *(d'un diplôme, d'une profession)* devaluation

dévaloriser [devalɔrize] **1** *vt* (a) *(monnaie)* to devalue (b) *(personne, politique)* to discredit; *(qualification, diplôme)* to devalue
2 se dévaloriser *vpr* (a) *(monnaie)* to depreciate (b) *(personne)* to put oneself down

dévaluation [devalyasjɔ̃] *nf Fin* devaluation

dévaluer [devalɥe] **1** *vt (monnaie)* to devalue
2 se dévaluer *vpr* to fall in value

devancer [16] [dəvɑ̃se] *vt* (a) *(être devant)* *(concurrent)* to be/get ahead of; **d. son époque** to be ahead of one's time (b) *(arriver avant)* to arrive before (c) *(prévoir)* *(personne, critiques)* to forestall; *(demande)* to anticipate (d) *(faire avant)* *Mil* **d. l'appel** to enlist before call-up; *Fin* **d. une échéance** to settle an account early

devant [dəvɑ̃] **1** *prép* (a) *(en face de, en avant de)* in front of; **assis d. moi** sitting in front of me; **marcher droit d. soi** to walk straight on; **regardez d. vous!** look where you're going!; **passer d. qn/qch** *(dans la rue)* to go past sb/sth; **passer d. qn** *(dans une file d'attente)* to go in front of sb; **avoir du temps/de l'argent d. soi** to have time/money to spare; **tu as la vie d. toi** you've got your whole life ahead of you; **d. derrière** back to front
(b) *(face à)* **d. le danger** in the face of danger; **égaux d. la loi** equal in the eyes of the law
2 *adv* (a) *(en face)* in front; **je cherchais la gare et j'étais juste d.** I was looking for the station when I was standing right in front of it; **où est Martin? – je crois qu'il est d.** where's Martin? – he's up ahead, I think
(b) *(en avant)* *(dans les premiers rangs)* at the front; *(en voiture)* in the front; **aller d.** to go in front; **marcher/courir d.** to walk on/run on ahead; **passez d.!** you go ahead of me!
3 *nm* front; *Fig* **prendre les devants** to make the first move

devanture [dəvɑ̃tyr] *nf (vitrine)* window; *(façade)* front

dévastateur, -trice [devastatœr, -tris] *adj* devastating

dévastation [devastasjɔ̃] *nf* devastation

dévaster [devaste] *vt* to devastate

déveine [devɛn] *nf Fam* bad luck; **être dans la d.** to be down on one's luck

développement [devlɔpmɑ̃] *nm* development; *(de pellicule)* developing; *(en cyclisme)* gear ratio; **en plein d.** *(entreprise, pays)* growing fast; **développements** *(d'une affaire)* developments; *Fig* **se lancer dans de grands développements** to go into detailed explanation

développer [devlɔpe] **1** *vt* to develop
2 se développer *vpr* to develop; *(s'étendre)* to spread

devenir¹ [dəvnir] *nm Litt* (a) *(évolution)* evolution; **être en perpétuel d.** to be constantly evolving (b) *(futur)* future

devenir² [70] *(aux être)* *vi* to become; **il devint général** he became a general; **il était devenu (un) homme** he had grown into a man; **ça devient difficile** it's getting difficult; **d. vieux** to get *or* grow old; **d. fou** to go mad; **c'est à d. fou!** it's enough to drive you mad!; **d. tout rouge** to go all red; **que devient-il?** how is he getting on?; **qu'est-il devenu?** what's become of him?

dévergondé, -e [devɛrgɔ̃de] **1** *adj* shameless
2 *nm,f* shameless person

dévergonder [devɛrgɔ̃de] **se dévergonder** *vpr* to get into bad ways

déversement [devɛrsmɑ̃] *nm (écoulement)* discharge; *(action)* pouring

déverser [devɛrse] **1** *vt* (a) *(eau)* to pour; *(sable, gravier, déchets)* to dump; *Fig (touristes, voyageurs)* to disgorge (b) **d. sa colère sur qn** to vent one's anger on sb; **d. des insultes sur qn** to shower sb with abuse
2 se déverser *vpr (rivière)* to empty (**dans** into)

dévêtir [71] [devetir] **1** *vt* to undress
2 se dévêtir *vpr* to undress

devez *voir* **devoir**

déviation [devjasjɔ̃] *nf* (a) *(itinéraire modifié)* *Br* diversion, *Am* detour (b) *(modification)* deviation (**par rapport à** from)

dévier [66] [devje] **1** vt **(a)** *(circulation)* to divert **(b)** *(balle, coup)* to deflect

2 vi *(véhicule, missile)* to veer **(vers** towards); *(balle)* to deflect **(vers** towards); **d. de sa route** *(véhicule, missile)* to veer off course; *Fig* **d. de son sujet** to digress

devin [dəvɛ̃] nm soothsayer; *Fam* **je ne suis pas d.!** I'm not a mind-reader!

deviner [dəvine] vt *(énigme, secret)* to guess; *(futur)* to predict; *(pensée)* to read; **devine qui j'ai vu** guess who I saw; *Fam* **je ne pouvais pas d.!** how was I supposed to know?

devinette [dəvinɛt] nf riddle; **poser une d. à qn** to ask sb a riddle

devis [dəvi] nm estimate, quote; **faire faire un d. pour qch** to get an estimate *or* a quote for sth

dévisager [45] [devizaʒe] vt to stare at

devise [dəviz] nf **(a)** *(d'une personne)* motto **(b)** *(monnaie)* currency; **devises étrangères** foreign currency; **d. forte** hard currency **(c)** *(en héraldique)* device

deviser [dəvize] vi *Litt* to converse

dévisser [devise] **1** vt to unscrew

2 vi *(alpiniste)* to fall

3 se dévisser vpr to unscrew; *(par accident)* to come unscrewed; *Fig* **se d. la tête** *ou* **le cou** to screw one's head round

de visu [devizy] adv with one's own eyes

dévitaliser [devitalize] vt *(dent)* to remove the nerve from

dévoiler [devwale] **1** vt *(visage, statue, plaque)* to unveil; *Fig (nom, secret, complot)* to disclose

2 se dévoiler vpr *(secret, complot)* to come to light

devoir¹ [dəvwar] nm **(a)** *(obligation)* duty; **faire qch par d.** to do sth out of a sense of duty; **un homme/une femme de d.** a man/a woman with a sense of duty; **faire ou remplir son d. (envers)** to do one's duty (by); **il est de mon d. de vous le dire** it is my duty to tell you **(b)** *(exercices)* in class) test; **devoirs** *(à la maison)* homework; **faire ses devoirs** to do one's homework; **devoirs de vacances** holiday homework **(c)** *Formel* **rendre les derniers devoirs à qn** to pay one's last respects to sb

devoir² [26] **1** vt *(être redevable de)* **d. qch à qn** to owe sb sth, to owe sth to sb; **il me doit mille francs** he owes me a thousand francs; **je lui dois bien cela** it's the least I can do for him, I owe him that at least

2 v aux **(a)** *(indique l'obligation)* **d. faire qch** to have to do sth; **vous devez être là à trois heures** you must *or* you have to be there by three o'clock; **elle a cru d. refuser** she thought it advisable to refuse; **les commandes doivent être adressées à...** orders should be sent to...; **vous devriez rester** you should stay, you ought to stay; **il aurait dû m'avertir** he should have warned me, he ought to have warned me **(b)** *(indique la nécessité)* **tu dois absolument lui en parler** you really must talk to him about it; **finalement, j'ai dû céder** I had to give way in the end; **il ne devait plus le revoir** *(il ne le reverrait plus!)* he was (destined) never to see them again; **cela devait arriver!** it was bound to *or* it had to happen!

(c) *(indique l'intention)* **je devais partir lundi, mais...** I was meant to leave on Monday, but...; **le train doit arriver à midi** the train is due (to arrive) at twelve o'clock **(d)** *(indique la supposition)* **vous devez avoir faim** you must be hungry; **il ne doit pas avoir plus de 40 ans** he can't be more than 40; **il a dû me prendre pour un**

autre he must have mistaken me for someone else; **la pollution devrait s'accroître d'ici la fin du siècle** pollution is expected to increase by the end of the century

3 se devoir vpr **je me dois à ma famille/mon travail** I must devote myself to my family/my work; **je me dois de le faire** it's my duty to do it; **comme il se doit** as is (only) right and proper

dévolu, -e [devoly] **1** adj *(somme, responsabilités)* assigned (à to)

2 nm **jeter son d. sur** to set one's heart on

devons voir **devoir**

dévorant, -e [devɔrɑ̃, -ɑ̃t] adj *(jalousie, passion)* consuming; *(envie)* overwhelming; *(curiosité)* burning; **avoir une faim dévorante** to be ravenous

dévorer [devɔre] vt **(a)** *(proie, nourriture, livre)* to devour; **être dévoré by les moustiques** to be eaten alive by mosquitoes; **d. qn des yeux ou du regard** to devour sb with one's eyes **(b)** *Fig (détruire)* **l'ambition/la jalousie la dévore** she is consumed by ambition/jealousy; **dévoré de remords** consumed with remorse **(c)** *Fig (fortune, kilomètres)* to eat up

dévot, -e [devo, -ɔt] **1** adj devout

2 nm,f devout person

dévotion [devosjɔ̃] nf **(a)** *(ferveur)* devoutness **(b)** *(adoration)* devotion; **avoir une d. pour** to be devoted to **(c)** **dévotions** *(prières)* devotions

dévoué, -e [devwe] adj devoted (à to)

dévouement [devumɑ̃] nm **(a)** *(abnégation)* devotion to duty **(b)** *(amour)* devotion (à to); **avec d.** devotedly

dévouer [devwe] **se dévouer** vpr *(se sacrifier)* to volunteer **(pour faire qch** to do sth); *(se consacrer)* to devote oneself (à to); **il faut que quelqu'un se dévoue** somebody has to do it

dévoyé, -e [devwaje] adj & nm,f delinquent

dévoyer [32] [devwaje] **se dévoyer** vpr *Litt* to go astray

devra etc voir **devoir**

dextérité [deksterite] nf dexterity, skill; **avec d.** skilfully

DGSE [deʒeɛse] nf *(abrév* **direction générale de la sécurité extérieure)** = French military intelligence service, Br ≃ MI6

diabète [djabɛt] nm diabetes; **avoir du d.** to have diabetes

diabétique [djabetik] adj & nmf diabetic

diable [djabl] nm **(a)** *(démon)* devil; **le d.** the Devil; **un petit d.** *(enfant)* a little devil; **avoir une faim de tous les diables** to be absolutely ravenous; **un bruit de tous les diables** a hell of a din; *Fig* **avoir le d. au corps** to be possessed; *Fig* **tirer le d. par la queue** to live from hand to mouth; **au d. l'avarice!** to hell with the expense!; **allez au d.!** go to hell!, **au d. vauvert** miles away; **que le d. l'emporte!** he can go to hell!; **c'est bien le d. si...** it would be surprising if...; **(b)** *(marque la surprise, l'agacement)* **d.!** goodness me!; **où d. est-elle allée?** where the devil has she gone?; **que d.!** for goodness sake! **(c)** *(chariot)* (two-wheeled) trolley **(d)** *(jouet)* jack-in-the-box

diablement [djabləmɑ̃] adv *Fam* damned

diablesse [djablɛs] nf *(démon, méchante femme)* she-devil; *Vieilli (jeune fille)* devil

diablotin [djablɔtɛ̃] nm imp

diabolique [djabɔlik] adj diabolical

diabolo [djabolo] *nm (boisson)* **d. menthe/fraise** mint/strawberry syrup and lemonade

diadème [djadɛm] *nm* tiara

diagnostic [djagnɔstik] *nm* diagnosis; **faire un d.** to make a diagnosis; **ce médecin a un d. très sûr** this doctor makes very reliable diagnoses; *Ordinat* **d. d'autotest** self-test diagnosis

diagnostiquer [djagnɔstike] *vt* to diagnose

diagonal, -e, -aux, -ales [djagɔnal, -o] **1** *adj* diagonal
2 *nf* **diagonale** diagonal; **en diagonale** diagonally; *Fig* **lire qch en diagonale** to skim through sth

diagonalement [djagɔnalmɑ̃] *adv* diagonally

diagramme [djagram] *nm* diagram

dialecte [djalɛkt] *nm* dialect

dialectique [djalɛktik] **1** *adj* dialectical
2 *nf* dialectics *(singulier)*

dialogue [djalɔg] *nm* dialogue; *(conversation)* conversation; **c'est un d. de sourds** it's a dialogue of the deaf; *Ordinat* **mode de d.** interactive mode

dialoguer [djalɔge] *vi* to communicate; *(avec un ordinateur)* to interact

dialyse [djaliz] *nf Méd* dialysis

diamant [djamɑ̃] *nm* diamond

diamantaire [djamɑ̃tɛr] *nm (tailleur)* diamond cutter; *(vendeur)* diamond merchant

diamétralement [djametralmɑ̃] *adv* **d. opposés** diametrically opposed

diamètre [djamɛtr] *nm* diameter

diapason [djapazɔ̃] *nm Mus* **(a)** *(note)* pitch; *Fig* **se mettre au d.** to fall in with the others **(b)** *(appareil)* tuning fork

diaphane [djafan] *adj* diaphanous

diaphragme [djafragm] *nm* diaphragm

diapo [djapo] *nf Fam* slide

diapositive [djapozitiv] *nf* slide

diarrhée [djare] *nf* diarrhoea; **avoir la d.** to have diarrhoea

diaspora [djaspora] *nf* diaspora

diatonique [djatɔnik] *adj* diatonic

diatribe [djatrib] *nf* diatribe *(contre against)*

dichotomie [dikɔtɔmi] *nf* dichotomy

dico [diko] *nm Fam* dictionary

Dictaphone® [diktafɔn] *nm* Dictaphone®

dictateur [diktatœr] *nm* dictator

dictatorial, -e, -aux, -ales [diktatɔrjal, -o] *adj* dictatorial

dictature [diktatyr] *nf* dictatorship

dictée [dikte] *nf (dictation)*; **écrire qch sous la d. de qn** to write sth at sb's dictation; **d. musicale** musical dictation

dicter [dikte] *vt* to dictate

diction [diksjɔ̃] *nf* diction

dictionnaire [diksjɔnɛr] *nm* dictionary; **d. électronique** electronic dictionary; **d. de langue** language dictionary

dicton [diktɔ̃] *nm* saying

didactique [didaktik] **1** *adj* **(a)** *(ouvrage, voyage)* educational **(b)** *(terme, langage)* technical
2 *nf* didactics *(singulier)*

dièse [djɛz] *Mus* **1** *nm* sharp
2 *adj* sharp; **fa d.** F sharp

diesel [djezɛl] **1** *adj* **moteur d.** diesel engine
2 *nm (carburant)* diesel
3 *nf (voiture)* diesel

diète [djɛt] *nf (partielle)* diet; *(totale)* fast; **être à la d.** *(partielle)* to be on a diet; *(totale)* to be fasting

diététicien, -enne [djetetisjɛ̃, -ɛn] *nm,f* dietitian

diététique [djetetik] **1** *adj (menu, repas)* diet; *(magasin, restaurant)* health food
2 *nf* dietetics *(singulier)*

dieu, -x [djø] *nm* **(a)** *(divinité)* god; *Fam* **comme un d.** *(chanter, jouer)* like a god **(b)** *(dans la religion chrétienne)* D. God; **le bon D.** God; **D. merci!, D. soit loué!** thank God!; **D. sait si j'ai travaillé** God knows I've worked hard enough; **D. seul le sait** God only knows
2 *exclam* **mon D.!** (good) God!; **D. qu'elle est petite!** God, she's small!; *Fam* **c'est pas D. possible!** it's just not possible!; *Fam* **bon D.!** for God's sake!; **très** *Fam* **nom de D.!** Christ almighty!

diffamation [difamasjɔ̃] *nf (paroles)* slander; *(écrits)* libel; **procès en d.** slander/libel trial

diffamatoire [difamatwar] *adj (paroles)* slanderous; *(écrits)* libellous

différé, -e [difere] **1** *adj Ordinat* **traitement d.** off-line processing
2 *nm* **en d.** *(émission)* pre-recorded

différemment [diferamɑ̃] *adv* differently

différence [diferɑ̃s] *nf* difference *(entre between)*; **d. d'âge/de prix** age/price difference; **faire la d. (entre)** to make a distinction (between); **cela ne fait aucune** *ou* **pas de d.** it makes no difference; **à la d. de** unlike

différenciation [diferɑ̃sjasjɔ̃] *nf* differentiation

différencier [66] [diferɑ̃sje] **1** *vt* to differentiate **(de** *ou* **d'avec** from)
2 se différencier *vpr* **(a)** *(être différent)* to differ **(de/par** from/in) **(b)** *(chercher à être différent)* to differentiate oneself **(de** from)

différend [diferɑ̃] *nm* difference of opinion, disagreement *(entre between)*; *Jur* dispute; **avoir un d. avec qn** to have a disagreement with sb

différent, -e [diferɑ̃, -ɑ̃t] *adj* different **(de** from); **différents cas** *(plusieurs)* various cases

différentiel, -elle [diferɑ̃sjɛl] **1** *adj & nm* differential
2 *nf* **différentielle** *Math* differential

différer [34] [difere] **1** *vt (jugement, paiement)* to defer; *(décision, départ)* to postpone
2 *vi (être différent)* to differ **(par** in)

difficile [difisil] **1** *adj* difficult; *(exigeant)* fussy; **le plus d. est fait** the most difficult part is over; **il est d. de le joindre** it's difficult to contact him; **il m'est d. d'accepter** it's difficult for me to accept; **être d. à vivre** to be difficult to get on with; **être d. sur qch** to be particular about sth
2 *nmf* **faire le d.** to be fussy

difficilement [difisilmɑ̃] *adv* with difficulty, not easily; **on peut d. le lui dire** you can hardly tell him that

difficulté [difikylte] *nf* difficulty; **être en d.** to be in difficulty *or* trouble; **faire des difficultés** to create difficulties; **avoir de la d. à faire qch** to have difficulty (in) doing sth; **avoir des difficultés en anglais** to have difficulties with English

difforme [difɔrm] *adj* deformed, misshapen

difformité [difɔrmite] nf deformity

diffus, -e [dify, -yz] adj (lumière, diffuse; (impression, souvenir) vague

diffuser [difyze] vt (a) (lumière, chaleur) to diffuse; (livres) to distribute; (idée, nouvelle) to spread (b) (émission) to broadcast

diffuseur [difyzœr] nm (de lumière, de chaleur) diffuser; **d. de parfum** room freshener

diffusion [difyzjɔ̃] nf (a) (de lumière, de chaleur) diffusion; (de livres) distribution; (d'une idée, d'une nouvelle) spreading (b) (d'une émission) broadcasting

digérer [34] [diʒere] vt (a) (aliment) to digest; **je ne digère pas le lait** I can't digest milk (b) (assimiler intellectuellement) to digest; Fam (accepter) to swallow

digeste [diʒɛst] adj Fam aussi Fig easily digestible

digestif, -ive [diʒɛstif, -iv] **1** adj digestive
2 nm liqueur

digestion [diʒɛstjɔ̃] nf digestion; **avoir une d. difficile** to have problems with one's digestion

digital¹, -e, -aux, -ales [diʒital, -o] adj (numérique) digital

digital², -e, -aux, -ales [diʒital] adj voir **empreinte**
2 nf digitale Bot digitalis

digne [diɲ] adj (a) (méritant) **d. de** worthy of; **d. d'éloges** praiseworthy; **d. de foi** reliable; **être d. de faire qch** to be fit to do sth (b) (approprié) **d. de** worthy of; **peu d. de qn** unworthy of sb; **d. de ce nom** worthy of the name; Hum **tu es bien le d. fils de ton père** you're your father's son all right (c) (grave) dignified

dignement [diɲamã] adv (a) (avec dignité) with dignity (b) (de façon appropriée) fittingly; **être d. récompensé** to be justly rewarded

dignitaire [diɲiter] nm dignitary

dignité [diɲite] nf dignity

digression [digrɛsjɔ̃] nf digression; **faire une d.** to digress

digue [dig] nf (dans un port) dike; (contre l'érosion) sea wall

dilapider [dilapide] vt (fortune) to squander; (fonds publics) to embezzle

dilatation [dilatasjɔ̃] nf (a) (des pupilles) dilation; (de l'estomac) distension (b) (d'un gaz) expansion

dilater [dilate] **1** vt (a) (pupilles) to dilate; (estomac) to distend (b) (gaz) to expand
2 se dilater vpr (a) (pupilles) to dilate; (estomac) to distend (b) (gaz) to expand

dilemme [dilɛm] nm dilemma

dilettante [diletãt] nmf dilettante; **faire qch en d.** to dabble in sth

diligence [diliʒãs] nf (a) (véhicule) (stage)coach (b) Litt (soin) diligence

diligent, -e [diliʒã, -ãt] adj Litt (zélé) diligent

diluant [dilɥã] nm thinner

diluer [dilɥe] vt (boisson) to dilute; (peinture) to thin down; Fig (discours, dissertation) to pad out

dilution [dilysjɔ̃] nf (de peinture) thinning down; (d'une boisson) dilution

diluvien, -enne [dilyvjɛ̃, -ɛn] adj (pluies) torrential

dimanche [dimãʃ] nm Sunday; **le d. des Rameaux/de Pâques** Palm/Easter Sunday; Fig **conducteur du d.** Sunday driver; voir aussi **samedi**

dîme [dim] nf Hist tithe

dimension [dimãsjɔ̃] nf (a) (grandeur) dimension, size; **à deux/trois dimensions** two-/three-dimensional; **prendre les dimensions de qch** (objet) to take the measurements of sth (b) (importance) magnitude (c) (aspect) dimension

diminué, -e [diminɥe] adj **être d.** to have gone downhill

diminuer [diminɥe] **1** vt (a) (réduire) to reduce, to decrease (b) (affaiblir) to weaken (c) (dénigrer) (personne) to belittle; (action) to undermine
2 vi to decrease; (fièvre) to drop
3 se diminuer vpr to belittle oneself

diminutif, -ive [diminytif, -iv] adj & nm diminutive

diminution [diminysjɔ̃] nf reduction, decrease

dinar [dinar] nm dinar

dinde [dɛ̃d] nf (a) (volaille, viande) turkey (b) Fam (femme sotte) silly goose

dindon [dɛ̃dɔ̃] nm turkey (cock); Fig **être le d. de la farce** to be made a fool of

dindonneau, -x [dɛ̃dɔno] nm turkey poult

dîner¹ [dine] nm (a) (repas du soir) dinner; (soirée) dinner party; **il y a des pâtes pour le ou au ou à d.** it's pasta for dinner (b) (repas de midi) lunch

dîner² vi (a) (le soir) to have dinner, to dine; **il dîna d'une tranche de jambon** he had a slice of ham for dinner (b) (à midi) to have lunch

dînette [dinɛt] nf (service) doll's teaset; **jouer à la d.** to have a dolls' tea party

dingo [dɛ̃go] adj Fam crazy

dingue [dɛ̃g] Fam **1** adj (a) (fou) crazy; **être d. de qn/ qch** to be crazy about sb/sth (b) (incroyable) incredible
2 nmf (fou) nutcase; **être un d. de moto/cinéma** to be a motorbike/film nut

dinguer [dɛ̃ge] vi Fam **aller d. contre qch** to go crashing into sth; **envoyer d. qn** (éconduire) to send sb packing; **envoyer d. qch** to send sth flying

dinosaure [dinozor] nm aussi Fig dinosaur

diocèse [djɔsɛz] nm Rel diocese

diode [djɔd] nf Él diode; **d. électroluminescente** light-emitting diode

dioxyde [diɔksid] nm Chim dioxide; **d. de carbone** carbon dioxide

diphtérie [difteri] nf Méd diphtheria; **avoir la d.** to have diphtheria

diphtongue [diftɔ̃g] nf Ling diphthong

diplomate [diplɔmat] **1** adj diplomatic
2 nm Culin ≃ trifle
3 nmf diplomat

diplomatie [diplɔmasi] nf (a) (habileté) diplomacy; **user de d.** to be diplomatic (b) (service) diplomatic service

diplomatique [diplɔmatik] adj diplomatic

diplomatiquement [diplɔmatikmã] adv diplomatically

diplôme [diplom] nm diploma; Univ degree; **avoir des diplômes** to have qualifications

diplômé, -e [diplome] adj qualified; Univ graduate; **un ingénieur d. de l'École polytechnique** an engineering graduate of the École Polytechnique
2 nmf holder of a diploma; Univ graduate

dire¹ [dir] nm **au d. de qn** according to sb; **selon ses dires** according to him/her

dire² [27a] **1** vt (a) (exprimer) to say; **comment dit-on 'soleil' en anglais?** how do you say 'soleil' in English?; **il ne savait plus quoi d.** he didn't know what to say; **je sais ce que je dis!** I know what I'm talking about!; **laisse-les d., ils sont stupides!** let them talk, they're stupid!; **elle a dit qu'elle arriverait en retard** she said she would be late; **comment dirais-je?** how shall I put it?; **comme on dit** as the saying goes; **cela dit...** having said that...; **il est un peu lent, pour ne pas d. complètement idiot** he's a bit slow, or to put it bluntly he's a complete idiot; **qui dit mieux?** (à une vente aux enchères) any advance?; **c'est vite dit** it's easier said than done

(b) (communiquer) **d. qch à qn** to tell sb sth; **d. à qn que...** to tell sb (that)...; **je t'ai déjà dit que oui!** I've already said yes!; **je vous l'avais bien dit!** I told you so!; **Fam c'est elle, je te dis** it's her, I tell you; **je lui ai fait d. de venir** I sent for him; **elle ne se le fit pas d. deux fois** she didn't wait to be told twice

(c) (ordonner) **d. à qn de faire qch** to tell sb to do sth; **faites ce qu'on vous dit** do as you're told; **taisez-vous, j'ai dit!** be quiet, I said!

(d) (prétendre) to say; **à ce qu'elle dit** according to her; **on le dit mort** he is said to have died

(e) (langage enfantin) (rapporter) to tell; **je vais le d. à ma mère** I'm going to tell my mum on you

(f) (décider) **disons à quatre heures** let's say four o'clock; **il est dit que je resterai célibataire** I'm destined to stay single

(g) (penser) **alors, qu'est-ce que tu en dis?** well, what do you think?; **qu'est-ce que tu dirais d'aller au cinéma?** how about going to the cinema?; **on dirait qu'il pleut** it looks as if it's raining; **on dirait du Mozart** it sounds like Mozart; **on dirait du gin** (au goût) it tastes like gin; **on aurait dit qu'elle était hypnotisée** it looked as if she was hypnotized; **et d. que...!** and to think (that)...!

(h) (objecter) **j'ai eu une augmentation conséquente, je n'ai rien à d.** I got a decent rise, I can't complain; **vous avez beau d.,...** you can say what you like, but...; **ce n'est pas pour d., mais...** I don't want to be rude, but...

(i) (indiquer) (sujet: statistiques) to show; **que dit le baromètre?** what does the barometer say?; **qu'est-ce qui vous dit qu'il viendra?** what makes you think he'll come?; **ce nom ne me dit rien** the name doesn't ring a bell; **quelque chose me dit que...** something tells me (that)...

(j) (plaire) **ça te dit de partir en vacances avec nous?** do you fancy coming on holiday with us?; **ça ne me dit trop rien de manger chinois** I don't really fancy Chinese food; **ça ne me dit rien qui vaille** I don't like the look of it

(k) (prière, messe) to say; (poésie) to recite

(l) (signifier) **qui dit bordeaux dit bon vin** Bordeaux is synonymous with good wine

(m) (locutions) **c'est (tout) d.** need I say more?; **c'est d. s'il t'aime** that shows how much he loves you; **c'est beaucoup d.** that's saying (quite) a lot; **c'est peu d.** that's putting it mildly; **il n'y a pas à d.,...** there are no two ways about it,...; **pour ainsi d.** so to speak, as it were; **pour tout (vous) d.,...** to be honest (with you),...; **quelques jours, je ne dis pas, mais un mois!** a few days, that's fair enough, but a whole month!; **Fam je te dis pas la tête qu'il a faite!** you should have seen his face!; **Fam je ne te dis que ça** say no more, enough said; **c'est moi qui vous le dis** let me tell you, believe me;

Fam à qui le dites-vous! you're telling ME!; **vous m'en direz tant!** you don't say!; **Fam je ne te le fais pas d.!** tell me something I don't know!; **Fam tu l'as dit (, bouffi)!** you can say that again!; **cela va sans d.** that goes without saying; **dis donc!** (au fait) hey!; (marque la surprise) gosh!; (marque l'indignation) do you mind!; **tu me le donnes, dis?** give it to me, yeah?

2 se dire vpr (a) (l'un à l'autre) **on se dit bonjour** we say hello

(b) (penser) **se d. que...** to think that...; **dis-toi bien que ça aurait pu être plus grave** it could have been worse, you know; **je me disais bien que je l'avais déjà vu quelque part** I knew I'd seen him somewhere before

(c) (être exprimé) **comment ça se dit en anglais?** how do you say that in English?; **ça se dit en français?** can you say that in French?

(d) (se prétendre) **elle se dit écossaise** she says she's Scottish

direct, -e [dirɛkt] **1** adj direct

2 nm (a) (à la radio, à la télévision) live broadcasting; **en d. de l'Opéra de Paris** live from the Paris Opera House (b) (en boxe) jab; **d. du droit/du gauche** straight right/left (c) (train) direct train (**pour** to)

3 adv Fam straight

directement [dirɛktəmɑ̃] adv (a) (sans détour) straight (b) (sans intermédiaire) directly

directeur, -trice [dirɛktœr, -tris] **1** nm,f (d'un magasin, d'un service) manager; **d. artistique** (d'un film) artistic director; (à la télévision) production designer; (d'un journal) art editor; **d. commercial** sales director; **d. général** (d'une entreprise) managing director; **d. de la rédaction** editorial director; **d. des ressources humaines** ou **du personnel** personnel manager (b) (d'une école) Br headmaster, f headmistress, Am principal (c) (d'une prison) Br governor, Am warden (d) Univ **d. de thèse** thesis supervisor

2 adj (équipe, instances) management; (idée) main; (principe, force) guiding

direction [dirɛksjɔ̃] nf (a) (d'une entreprise, d'un théâtre) management; (d'une école) running; (d'un parti, d'un pays) leadership; **sous la d. de qn** under the supervision of sb; (orchestre) conducted by sb (b) (ensemble des cadres) management; **d. générale** general management; **d. des ressources humaines** ou **du personnel** (service) personnel department (c) (orientation) direction; **toutes/ autres directions** (sur panneau) all/other directions; **quelle d. ont-ils prise?** which way did they go?; **le train en d. de Strasbourg** the train to Strasbourg, the Strasbourg train (d) (d'un véhicule) steering; **d. assistée** power steering

directive [dirɛktiv] nf directive

directoire [dirɛktwar] nm (d'une société anonyme) board of directors

dirham [diram] nm dirham

dirigeable [diriʒabl] adj & nm (**ballon**) **d.** dirigible, airship

dirigeant, -e [diriʒã, ãt] **1** adj voir **classe**

2 nm,f (d'un parti, d'un pays) leader; (d'une entreprise) manager; **d. syndical** union leader

diriger [45] [diriʒe] **1** vt (a) (entreprise, équipe, projet) to manage, to run; (pays, parti) to lead; (séance) to conduct; (travaux) to supervise; (acteurs) to direct; (orchestre) to conduct (b) (arme, télescope, lumière) to point (**sur** at) (c) (pas) to direct (**vers** towards); (regard) to turn (**vers** to); (attention) to turn (**sur** to); (conversation) to steer (**sur** onto) (d) (orienter professionnellement) to steer (**sur** ou **vers**

towards;

2 se diriger *vpr* (**a**) *(aller)* **se d. vers** *(endroit)* to head for; *(personne)* to go up to; *(carrière, secteur)* to go into (**b**) *(s'orienter)* to find one's way around

dirigisme [diriʒism] *nm* state control

disais *etc voir* **dire**

discernement [disɛrnəmɑ̃] *nm (jugement)* discernment; **sans d.** rashly

discerner [disɛrne] *vt* (**a**) *(percevoir)* to make out (**b**) *(différencier)* **d. qch de** to distinguish sth from (**c**) *(deviner)* to discern

disciple [disipl] *nmf* disciple

disciplinaire [disipliner] *adj* disciplinary

discipline [disiplin] *nf (ordre, matière)* discipline

discipliné, -e [disipline] *adj* disciplined

discipliner [disipline] **1** *vt (enfant)* to control

2 se discipliner *vpr* to discipline oneself

disc-jockey *(pl* **disc-jockeys)** [diskʒɔke] *nm* disc jockey

discographie [diskɔgrafi] *nf* discography

discontinu, -e [diskɔ̃tiny] *adj* intermittent; *(ligne)* broken

discontinuer [diskɔ̃tinɥe] **sans discontinuer** *adv* without stopping

disconvenir [70] [diskɔ̃vnir] *vi Litt* **ne pas d. de qch** not to deny sth

discordant, -e [diskɔrdɑ̃, -ɑ̃t] *adj* (**a**) *(son, bruit)* discordant (**b**) *(couleurs)* clashing; *(opinions)* conflicting

discorde [diskɔrd] *nf* discord; **semer la d.** to make trouble

discothèque [diskɔtɛk] *nf* (**a**) *(boîte de nuit)* disco (**b**) *(organisme)* record library; *(collection)* record collection

discount [diskunt] *nm (rabais)* discount

discourir [22] [diskurir] *vi* **d. sur qch** to discourse on sth; *Péj* to air one's opinions on sth

discours [diskur] *nm* (**a**) *(allocution)* speech; **prononcer** *ou* **faire un d.** to make a speech; **d. de clôture/ d'ouverture** closing/opening speech (**b**) *Gram* speech; **d. indirect/direct** reported *or* indirect/direct speech (**c**) *(paroles)* talk; **il m'a tenu un grand d. sur la tolérance** he gave me a great long speech about tolerance; **tous ces beaux d. ne nous avancent à rien** all this talking isn't getting us anywhere

discrédit [diskredi] *nm* discredit; **jeter le d. sur qn** to bring discredit on sb

discréditer [diskredite] **1** *vt* to discredit

2 se discréditer *vpr (personne)* to discredit oneself; **se d. auprès de** *ou* **aux yeux de qn** to discredit oneself with sb

discret, -ète [diskrɛ, -ɛt] *adj* (**a**) *(plein de retenue)* discreet; **tu sauras rester d.?** you'll keep it to yourself, won't you? (**b**) *(sobre) (personne)* unassuming; *(vêtements)* simple; *(maquillage)* natural (**c**) *(endroit)* quiet

discrètement [diskrɛtmɑ̃] *adv* (**a**) *(avec retenue)* discreetly; **il lui a parlé d.** he had a quiet word with him/her (**b**) *(sobrement) (habillé)* simply; **être d. maquillée** to be wearing natural make-up

discrétion [diskresjɔ̃] *nf* (**a**) *(retenue)* discretion (**b**) *(sobriété)* simplicity; **avec d.** *(s'habiller)* simply; *(se maquiller)* discreetly (**c**) **champagne à d.** unlimited champagne

discrimination [diskriminasjɔ̃] *nf* discrimination; **d. raciale/sexuelle** racial/sexual discrimination

discriminatoire [diskriminatwar] *adj* discriminatory

disculper [diskylpe] **1** *vt* to exonerate (**de** from)

2 se disculper *vpr* to exonerate oneself (**de** from)

discussion [diskysjɔ̃] *nf* discussion; **avoir une d. (sur** *ou* **à propos de** *)* to have a discussion (about); **pas de d., au travail!** don't argue, get to work!

discutable [diskytabl] *adj* questionable

discutailler [diskytaje] *vi Fam Péj* to quibble

discuté, -e [diskyte] *adj (question)* disputed; *(livre, sujet)* much discussed

discuter [diskyte] **1** *vt (examiner)* to discuss; *(contester)* to question; *Fam* **d. le coup, d. le bout de gras** to have a chat

2 *vi* (**a**) *(parler)* to discuss; **d. avec qn sur** *ou* **de qch** to discuss sth with sb (**b**) *(protester)* to argue

3 se discuter *vpr* **ça se discute** that's debatable

dise *etc voir* **dire**

disette [dizɛt] *nf* food shortage

diseuse [dizøz] *nf* **d. de bonne aventure** fortune teller

disgrâce [disgrɑs] *nf* **tomber en d.** to fall into disfavour

disgracieux, -euse [disgrasjø, -øz] *adj (personne)* ungainly; *(visage, moue)* ugly

disjoindre [43] [disʒwɛ̃dr] **1** *vt* to separate

2 se disjoindre *vpr* to come apart

disjoint, -e [disʒwɛ̃, -ɛ̃t] *adj (pièces)* separated

disjoncter [disʒɔ̃kte] **1** *vt (circuit électrique)* to break

2 *vi (circuit électrique)* to fuse; *Fam Fig* to crack up

disjoncteur [disʒɔ̃ktœr] *nm* circuit breaker

dislocation [dislokasjɔ̃] *nf (d'une articulation)* dislocation

disloquer [disloke] **1** *vt* (**a**) *(épaule, genou)* to dislocate (**b**) *(empire, État)* to break up

2 se disloquer *vpr (empire, État)* to break up; **se d. l'épaule** to dislocate one's shoulder

disparaître [20] [disparɛtr] *vi* (**a**) *(devenir invisible)* to disappear, to vanish; **d. dans la foule** to disappear into the crowd; *Fam* **d. de la circulation** to drop out of circulation; *Fam* **disparais!** clear off! (**b**) *(mourir)* to die (**c**) *(douleur, sentiment)* to disappear; *(maladie, tradition)* to die out; **faire d. qch** to get rid of sth

disparate [disparat] *adj (éléments)* disparate; *(couleurs, objets, mobilier)* ill-matched

disparité [disparite] *nf (d'éléments)* disparity; *(de couleurs, d'objets, de mobilier)* mismatch; *(des salaires, des revenus)* inequality

disparition [disparisjɔ̃] *nf* (**a**) *(absence)* disappearance (**b**) *(décès)* death

disparu, -e [dispary] **1** *adj (personne)* missing; **être porté d.** to be reported missing

2 *nm,f (mort)* dead person; *(absent)* missing person

dispensaire [dispɑ̃ser] *nm* community health centre

dispense [dispɑ̃s] *nf* (**a**) *(d'une obligation)* exemption (**b**) *(certificat)* certificate of exemption

dispenser [dispɑ̃se] **1** *vt* (**a**) **d. qn de qch/de faire qch** to exempt sb from sth/from doing sth; **se faire d. de qch** to be excused or let off sth; *Euph* **je vous dispense de vos commentaires** you can keep your remarks to yourself (**b**) *(soins, charité, faveurs)* to dispense

2 se dispenser *vpr* **se d. de qch/de faire qch** to get out of sth/of doing sth; **tu pourrais te d. de ce genre de commentaire!** you can keep that sort of remark to yourself!

dispersé, -e [disperse] *adj (épars)* scattered

disperser [disperse] **1** vt *(foule, famille, feuilles)* to scatter
2 se disperser vpr *(nuages, foule, famille)* to scatter, to disperse; *Fig (intellectuellement)* to spread oneself too thinly

dispersion [dispersjɔ̃] nf *(de manifestants, de nuages, d'une armée)* scattering, dispersal; *Fig (inattention)* lack of focus

disponibilité [disponibilite] nf **(a)** *(d'une personne, de places, d'un capital)* availability; **d. d'esprit** receptiveness **(b)** *(d'un fonctionnaire)* leave of absence; **être en d.** to be on leave of absence **(c)** *Fin* **disponibilités** available funds

disponible [disponibl] adj **(a)** *(personne, place, capital)* available; **êtes-vous d. ce soir?** are you free tonight? **(b)** *(fonctionnaire)* on leave of absence

dispos, -e [dispo, -oz] adj *(personne)* fit and well

disposé, -e [dispoze] adj *(personne)* **être bien/mal d.** to be in a good/bad mood; **être bien d. envers qn** to be well disposed towards sb; **être d. à faire qch** to feel disposed or willing to do sth

disposer [dispoze] **1** vt **(a)** *(objets, fleurs)* to arrange; *(table)* to lay, to set **(b)** **d. qn à (faire) qch** to dispose or incline sb to (do) sth
2 vi **(a)** *Formel* **vous pouvez d.** you may go **(b)** *(décider)* *Prov* **l'homme propose, Dieu dispose** man proposes, God disposes
3 disposer de vt ind to have at one's disposal; **les renseignements dont je dispose** the information at my disposal; **le droit des peuples à d. d'eux-mêmes** the right of people to self-determination
4 se disposer vpr **se d. à faire qch** to get ready to do sth

dispositif [dispozitif] nm **(a)** *(appareil)* device **(b)** *(ensemble de moyens)* system; **d. policier** police presence **(c)** *Ordinat* **d. d'alimentation** power unit; *(pour papier)* sheet feed; **d. d'alimentation papier** *(d'une imprimante)* sheet feed, paper feed

disposition [dispozisjɔ̃] nf **(a)** *(arrangement)* arrangement **(b)** *(disponibilité)* **à la d. de qn** at sb's disposal **(c)** *(tendance)* tendency **(à to) (d)** *(intentions)* **être dans de bonnes/mauvaises dispositions** to be in a good/bad mood; **être dans de bonnes dispositions à l'égard de qn** to be favourably disposed towards sb **(e)** *(dons)* **avoir des dispositions pour qch** to have an aptitude for sth **(f)** **dispositions** *(préparatifs)* arrangements; **prendre des dispositions pour faire qch** to make arrangements to do sth; **prendre ses dispositions** to make arrangements **(g)** *Jur* **dispositions** *(d'une loi)* clauses

disproportion [dispropɔrsjɔ̃] nf disproportion **(entre** between**)**

disproportionné, -e [dispropɔrsjɔne] adj disproportionate **(par rapport à** to**)**

dispute [dispyt] nf quarrel, argument

disputé, -e [dispyte] adj *(question)* controversial; *(match)* hard-fought; **ce poste sera très d.** there will be a lot of competition for this post

disputer [dispyte] **1** vt **(a)** *(match)* to play; *(combat)* to fight **(b)** *(se battre pour)* **d. qch à qn** to fight with sb over sth **(c)** *Fam (réprimander)* to tell off; **se faire d.** to get told off
2 se disputer vpr **(a)** *(se quereller)* to quarrel, to argue **(pour/avec** over/with**) (b)** *(avoir lieu)* **le match se disputera à Wimbledon** the match will be played at Wimbledon **(c)** *(se battre pour)* **se d. qch** to fight over sth

disquaire [disker] nmf record dealer

disqualification [diskalifikasjɔ̃] nf disqualification

disqualifier [66] [diskalifje] vt *(sportif)* to disqualify

disque [disk] nm **(a)** *(enregistrement)* record; **mettre un d.** to play a record; **d. audionumérique** compact disc; **d. compact** compact disc, CD; **d. compact vidéo** video compact disc; **d. laser** laser disc **(b)** *Ordinat* disk; **d. amovible** removable disk; **d. dur** hard disk; **d. fixe** fixed disk **(c)** *(cartilage)* disc **(d)** *(objet rond)* disc; **d. de stationnement** parking disc **(e)** *(en sport)* discus **(f)** *Tech* disc; **d. d'embrayage** clutch plate

disquette [disket] nf *Ordinat* diskette, floppy (disk); **sur d.** on diskette, on floppy; **d. de démonstration**, *Fam* **d. démo** demo disk; **d. haute densité** high-density disk; **d. optique** optical disk, floptical disk

dissection [diseksjɔ̃] nf aussi *Fig* dissection

dissemblable [disɑ̃blabl] adj dissimilar

dissémination [diseminasjɔ̃] nf *(de graines, de peuple)* scattering; *(de germes)* spreading

disséminer [disemine] **1** vt *(graines, peuple)* to scatter; *(germes)* to spread; **les écoles sont très disséminées** the schools are very thin on the ground
2 se disséminer vpr to be scattered

dissension [disɑ̃sjɔ̃] nf dissension

disséquer [34] [diseke] vt aussi *Fig* to dissect

dissertation [disertasjɔ̃] nf essay

disserter [diserte] vi *(parler)* **d. sur qch** to discourse on sth, *Péj* to hold forth on sth; *(écrire)* to write about sth

dissidence [disidɑ̃s] nf dissidence; **la d.** *(les opposants)* the dissidents

dissident, -e [disidɑ̃, -ɑ̃t] **1** adj *(en politique)* dissident; *(en religion)* dissenting
2 nm,f *(en politique)* dissident; *(en religion)* dissenter

dissimulateur, -trice [disimylatœr, -tris] **1** adj dissembling
2 nm,f dissembler

dissimulation [disimylasjɔ̃] nf **(a)** *(hypocrisie)* dissembling, deceit; **agir avec d.** to act in an underhand way **(b)** *(des sentiments, de la vérité)* concealment

dissimuler [disimyle] **1** vt to cover up, to conceal; *(sujet: rideau)* to screen off; **d. qch à qn** to conceal sth from sb; **avec un plaisir non dissimulé** with unconcealed delight
2 se dissimuler vpr to be hidden

dissipation [disipasjɔ̃] nf **(a)** *(de craintes, de soupçons)* dispelling; *(d'un malentendu)* clearing up; **après d. des brouillards matinaux** after the early fog has cleared **(b)** *(à l'école)* unruly behaviour **(c)** *Litt (débauche)* dissipation

dissipé, -e [disipe] adj **(a)** *(élève)* unruly **(b)** *Litt (débauché)* dissipated

dissiper [disipe] **1** vt **(a)** *(nuages)* to disperse; *(brouillard)* to clear; *(malentendu)* to clear up; *(craintes, soupçons)* to dispel **(b)** *(distraire)* to lead astray
2 se dissiper vpr **(a)** *(nuages)* to disperse; *(brouillard)* to clear; *(craintes, soupçons)* to vanish **(b)** *(se laisser distraire)* to be unruly

dissociable [disɔsjabl] adj separable

dissocier [66] [disɔsje] **1** vt to separate
2 se dissocier vpr **se d. de qch** to dissociate oneself from sth

dissolu, -e [disɔly] adj *Litt* dissolute

dissolution [disɔlysjɔ̃] nf **(a)** *(d'un parlement, d'un mariage)* dissolution; *(d'une association)* breaking up **(b)** *(dans un liquide)* dissolving

dissolvais etc voir **dissoudre**

dissolvant, -e [disɔlvã, -ãt] *adj & nm* (produit) d. solvent; *(pour ongles)* nail polish remover

dissonant, -e [disɔnã, -ãt] *adj (sons)* dissonant; *Fig* clashing

dissoudre [3a] [disudr] **1** *vt* (a) *(substance)* to dissolve (b) *(parlement, mariage)* to dissolve; *(association)* to break up
2 se dissoudre *vpr (substance)* to dissolve; *(association)* to break up

dissuader [disɥade] *vt* **d. qn de faire qch** to dissuade sb from doing sth

dissuasif, -ive [disɥazif, -iv] *adj* deterrent; *(prix)* prohibitive; **avoir un effet d.** to be a deterrent

dissuasion [disɥazjɔ̃] *nf* dissuasion; *Mil* **force de d.** deterrent

dissymétrie [disimetri] *nf* asymmetry

distance [distãs] *nf* distance; **suivre qn à d.** to follow sb at a distance; **à quelle d. sommes-nous de la ville?** how far are we from the town?; **à une courte d. (de)** a short distance away (from); **à d.** *(déclencher)* by remote control; *(rester, observer)* at a distance; *aussi Fig* **tenir qn à d.** to keep sb at a distance; **conserver ou garder ses distances, se tenir à d.** to hold oneself aloof; **prendre ses distances, prendre de la d.** to stand back; *Sp & Fig* **tenir la d.** to go the distance

distancer [16] [distãse] *vt aussi Fig* to outstrip, to outdistance; **se laisser d.** to fall *or* lag behind; **d. qn de deux points/de 10 mètres** to go two points/10 metres ahead of sb

distant, -e [distã, -ãt] *adj* (a) *(éloigné)* distant; **nos deux maisons sont distantes d'un kilomètre** our two houses are a kilometre apart (b) *Fig (froid)* distant, standoffish (**avec qn**)

distendre [distãdr] **1** *vt (corde, élastique, vêtement)* to stretch; *(muscle)* to strain
2 se distendre *vpr (corde, élastique, vêtement)* to stretch; *(muscle)* to slacken

distillation [distilasjɔ̃] *nf* distillation

distiller [distile] *vt* (a) *(alcool, pétrole)* to distil; **eau distillée** distilled water (b) *(poison)* to distil; *Fig (colère, ennui)* to exude

distillerie [distilri] *nf (lieu)* distillery; *(procédé)* distilling

distinct, -e [distɛ̃, -ɛ̃kt] *adj* (a) *(séparé)* distinct, separate (**de** from) (b) *(clair) (silhouette, voix)* distinct, clear

distinctement [distɛ̃ktəmã] *adv* distinctly, clearly

distinctif, -ive [distɛ̃ktif, -iv] *adj* distinctive

distinction [distɛ̃ksjɔ̃] *nf* (a) *(différence)* distinction; **faire une d. entre deux choses** to make a distinction between two things; **sans d.** without distinction, indiscriminately; **sans d. de race ou de couleur** regardless of race or colour (b) *(élégance)* distinction; **avoir de la d.** to be distinguished

distingué, -e [distɛ̃ge] *adj* distinguished

distinguer [distɛ̃ge] **1** *vt* (a) *(différencier)* to distinguish (**de** from); **il a appris à d. les champignons** he has learnt how to tell the various kinds of mushroom apart; **on peut à peine les d. l'un de l'autre** you can hardly tell them apart (b) *(discerner) (objet, silhouette)* to make out; *(personne)* to pick out; **d. une nuance d'amertume dans la voix de qn** to detect a trace of bitterness in sb's voice
2 se distinguer *vpr* (a) *(s'illustrer)* to distinguish oneself (**par** by); **on ne peut vraiment pas dire qu'il se distingue par son intelligence** he hardly stands out as being very intelligent (b) *(se différencier)* **se d. de qn/qch** to be distinguishable from sb/sth (**by**) (c) *(être perçu)* **au loin se distinguait la côte** the coastline could be made out in the distance

distinguo [distɛ̃go] *nm* distinction; **faire un d. entre** to make a distinction between

distordre [distɔrdr] *vt* to distort

distorsion [distɔrsjɔ̃] *nf* distortion; *(entre deux facteurs, deux salaires)* imbalance

distraction [distraksjɔ̃] *nf* (a) *(inattention)* absent-mindedness; **par d.** inadvertently, absent-mindedly (b) *(loisir)* activity; **ça manque de distractions, ici** there's nothing to do here

distraire [28] [distrer] **1** *vt* (a) *(détourner)* to distract (**de** from) (b) *(divertir)* to entertain, to amuse
2 se distraire *vpr (s'occuper)* to amuse oneself; *(se détendre)* to enjoy oneself

distrait, -e [distre, -et] *adj* (a) *(étourdi)* absent-minded; **d'un air d.** absent-mindedly (b) *(inattentif)* inattentive; **d'une oreille distraite** with only half an ear

distraitement [distretmã] *adv* absent-mindedly

distrayais *etc voir* **distraire**

distrayant, -e [distrejã, -ãt] *adj* entertaining

distribuer [distribɥe] *vt* (a) *(donner) (prix, bonbons, provisions, vivres)* to distribute (**à** to); *(dividendes)* to pay (**à** to); *(cartes)* to deal (**à** to); *(courrier)* to deliver (**à** to); *(eau, gaz, électricité)* to supply (**à** to); *(sourires, compliments)* to bestow (**à** on); **d. des coups** to lash out with one's fists (b) *(répartir) (tâches)* to allocate; **d. les rôles** to cast a play (c) *(commercialiser)* to distribute

distributeur, -trice [distribɥtœr, -tris] **1** *nm,f Com* distributor; **d. agréé** authorized distributor
2 *nm (appareil) (vending)* machine; **d. (automatique) de billets** cash dispenser *or* machine; **d. (automatique) de boissons/de cigarettes** drinks/cigarette machine

distribution [distribɥsjɔ̃] *nf* (a) *(remise)* distribution; *(de lettres, de marchandises)* delivery; **la d. des prix** *(à l'école)* prizegiving (b) *(répartition) (de tâches)* allocation; *(d'une maison, d'un appartement)* layout; *(d'un film, d'une pièce) (action)* casting; *(acteurs)* cast (c) *Com* distribution; **grande d.** large-scale distribution (d) *(approvisionnement)* supply; **d. des eaux** water supply

district [distrikt] *nm* district

dit, -e [di, dit] **1** *pp voir* **dire**
2 *adj* (a) *(décidé)* **à l'heure dite** at the agreed time (b) *(appelé)* known as

dithyrambique [ditirãbik] *adj* eulogistic

diurétique [djyretik] *adj & nm* diuretic

diurne [djyrn] *adj* diurnal

diva [diva] *nf* diva

divagations [divagasjɔ̃] *nfpl* raving

divaguer [divage] *vi* to rave

divan [divã] *nm* divan, couch

divergence [diverʒãs] *nf (de lignes, de rayons)* divergence; *(d'opinions)* difference

divergent, -e [diverʒã, -ãt] *adj (lignes)* divergent; *(opinions)* differing

diverger [45] [diverʒe] *vi (opinions, lignes, rayons)* to diverge (**de** from)

divers, -e [diver, -ers] *adj* (a) *(différents)* varied; **d.** *(rubrique)* miscellaneous (b) *(plusieurs)* various; **diverses solutions sont possibles** there are various possible solutions

diversement [diversəmã] *adv* in various ways

diversification [divɛʁsifikasjɔ̃] *nf* diversification

diversifier [66] [divɛʁsifje] **1** *vt (économie, cultures, activités)* to diversify; *(intérêts, couleurs)* to vary

2 se diversifier *vpr (entreprise, activités)* to diversify

diversion [divɛʁsjɔ̃] *nf* diversion; **faire d.** to create a diversion

diversité [divɛʁsite] *nf (variété)* variety, diversity

divertir [divɛʁtiʁ] **1** *vt (amuser)* to entertain, to amuse

2 se divertir *vpr* to enjoy oneself; **se d. de qch** to laugh at sth

divertissant, -e [divɛʁtisɑ̃, -ɑ̃t] *adj* amusing, entertaining

divertissement [divɛʁtismɑ̃] *nm* **(a)** *(amusement)* entertainment, amusement **(b)** *Mus* divertimento

dividende [dividɑ̃d] *nm Math & Fin* dividend

divin, -e [divɛ̃, -in] *adj aussi Fig* divine; **le d. Enfant** the Holy Child

divinement [divinmɑ̃] *adv* divinely

divinité [divinite] *nf (a) (nature de Dieu)* divinity **(b)** *(dieu)* deity

diviser [divize] **1** *vt* **(a)** *(partager)* to divide **(en/entre** into/among); **d. 15 par 3** to divide 15 by 3 **(b)** *(opposer)* to divide; **l'opinion est divisée au sujet de cette affaire** opinion on the matter is divided; **d. pour mieux régner** divide and rule

2 se diviser *vpr* to divide **(en** into); **l'examen se divise en trois parties** the examination is divided into three parts; **le chemin se divise en deux** the road divides or forks

diviseur [divizœʁ] *nm Math* divisor

divisible [divizibl] *adj* divisible

division [divizjɔ̃] *nf* **(a)** *(séparation)* & *Math* division **(en** into); **faire une d.** to do a division; *Biol* **d. cellulaire** cell division; **d. du travail** division of labour **(b)** *(partie)* part, section; *Mil* division; **d. blindée** armoured division **(c)** *(désaccord)* division

divisionnaire [divizjɔnɛʁ] *nm* (police) superintendent

divorce [divɔʁs] *nm* divorce; *Fig (désaccord)* gulf; **demander le d.** to ask for a divorce; **obtenir le d.** to get a divorce

divorcé, -e [divɔʁse] **1** *adj* divorced

2 *nm,f* divorcee

divorcer [16] [divɔʁse] *vi* to get divorced, to get a divorce; **d. d'avec** *ou* **de qn** to divorce sb

divulgation [divylgasjɔ̃] *nf* disclosure **(de** of)

divulguer [divylge] *vt* to divulge, to disclose

dix [dis] *adj & nm inv* ten; *voir aussi* **trois**

dix-huit [dizɥit] *adj & nm inv* eighteen; *voir aussi* **trois**

dix-huitième [dizɥitjɛm] *nmf, nm & adj* eighteenth; *voir aussi* **cinquième**

dixième [dizjɛm] *nmf, nm & adj* tenth; *voir aussi* **cinquième**

dixit [diksit] **d. Paul** so Paul says

dix-neuf [diznœf] *adj & nm inv* nineteen; *voir aussi* **trois**

dix-neuvième [diznœvjɛm] *nmf, nm & adj* nineteenth; *voir aussi* **cinquième**

dix-sept [dis(s)ɛt] *adj & nm inv* seventeen; *voir aussi* **trois**

dix-septième [dis(s)ɛtjɛm] *nmf, nm & adj* seventeenth; *voir aussi* **cinquième**

dizaine [dizɛn] *nf* **une d. (de)** about ten, ten or so; *Math* **la colonne des dizaines** the tens column

Djibouti [dʒibuti] *n* Djibouti

do [do] *nm inv (note)* C; *(chantée)* doh

doberman [dɔbɛʁman] *nm* doberman

docile [dɔsil] *adj (enfant, animal)* docile

docilement [dɔsilmɑ̃] *adv* docilely

docilité [dɔsilite] *nf* docility

dock [dɔk] *nm* **(a)** *(bassin)* dock **(b)** *(entrepôt)* warehouse

docker [dɔkɛʁ] *nm* docker

docte [dɔkt] *adj Litt* learned

docteur [dɔktœʁ] *nm* **(a)** *(médecin)* doctor **(b)** *Univ* **être d. ès lettres/ès sciences** ≃ to have a PhD in arts/science; **être d. en droit** ≃ to have an LLD

doctoral, -e, -aux, -ales [dɔktɔʁal, -o] *adj Péj (air, ton)* pompous

doctorat [dɔktɔʁa] *nm Univ* doctorate; **d. d'État** = highest postgraduate research degree; **d. de 3ᵉ cycle** ≃ PhD

doctoresse [dɔktɔʁɛs] *nf Vieilli* lady doctor

doctrine [dɔktʁin] *nf* doctrine

document [dɔkymɑ̃] *nm* document

documentaire [dɔkymɑ̃tɛʁ] *adj & nm* documentary

documentaliste [dɔkymɑ̃talist] *nmf (d'archives)* archivist; *(dans les écoles)* librarian

documentation [dɔkymɑ̃tasjɔ̃] *nf (action)* research; *(documents)* documentation **(sur** on)

documenté, -e [dɔkymɑ̃te] *adj (personne)* well-informed; *(étude, thèse)* documented

documenter [dɔkymɑ̃te] **se documenter** *vpr* to gather information or material **(sur** on)

dodeliner [dɔdline] *vi* **il dodelinait de la tête** his head kept nodding

dodo [dodo] *nm (langage enfantin)* **faire d.** to sleep; **aller au d.** to go to bye-byes

dodu, -e [dɔdy] *adj* plump, chubby

doge [dɔʒ] *nm Hist* doge

dogmatique [dɔgmatik] *adj* dogmatic

dogmatisme [dɔgmatism] *nm* dogmatism

dogme [dɔgm] *nm* dogma

dogue [dɔg] *nm* mastiff

doigt [dwa] *nm* **(a)** *(de la main)* finger; **d. de pied** toe; **le petit d.** the little finger; **lever le d.** *(en classe)* to put one's hand up; **porter une bague au d.** to wear a ring on one's finger; **faire signe à qn du d.** to beckon to sb; **être comme les (deux) doigts de la main** to be very close; **on peut les compter sur les doigts de la main** you can count them on the fingers of one hand; *Fig* **se faire taper sur les doigts** to get a rap over the knuckles; **filer** *ou* **glisser entre les doigts de qn** to slip through sb's fingers; **vous avez mis le d. dessus** you've put your finger on it; **obéir à qn au d. et à l'œil** to obey sb blindly; **savoir qch sur le bout des doigts** to have sth at one's fingertips; **mon petit d. me l'a dit** a little bird told me; **avoir des doigts de fée** to have nimble fingers; *Fig* **ne pas lever** *ou* **bouger le petit d.** not to lift a finger; *Fam* **tu te mets le d. dans l'œil (jusqu'au coude)** you couldn't be more wrong (if you tried); *Fam* **faire qch les doigts dans le nez** to do sth standing on one's head; *Fam* **gagner les doigts dans le nez** to win hands down **(b)** *(petite quantité)* *(d'alcool)* drop; **être à deux doigts de**

qch/de faire qch to be within a hair's breadth of sth/of doing sth

doigté [dwate] *nm* (a) *Mus (d'un morceau de musique)* fingering (b) *Fig (adresse)* dexterity; *(tact)* tact

dois, doive *etc voir* **devoir**

doléances [doleɑ̃s] *nfpl* complaints

dollar [dɔlar] *nm* dollar

dolmen [dɔlmɛn] *nm* dolmen

domaine [dɔmɛn] *nm* (a) *(propriété)* estate, property; **être du d. public** to be in the public domain; **d. skiable** skiing area (b) *(matière)* field, domain; **c'est du d. du possible** it's within the realms of possibility

domanial, -e, -aux, -ales [dɔmanjal, -o] *adj* state-owned

dôme [dom] *nm Archit & Géog* dome

domestication [dɔmɛstikasjɔ̃] *nf* domestication

domestique [dɔmɛstik] **1** *adj (vie, soucis, querelle)* domestic; *(tâches, déchets)* household; **accidents domestiques** accidents in the home
2 *nmf* servant

domestiquer [dɔmɛstike] *vt (animal)* to domesticate; *(éléments)* to harness

domicile [dɔmisil] *nm* (place of) residence, home; **sans d. fixe** of no fixed abode; **travailler à d.** to work from home; **livrer à d.** to do home deliveries; *Jur* **d. conjugal** marital home

domicilié, -e [dɔmisilje] *adj* **d. à** resident at

dominant, -e [dɔminɑ̃, -ɑ̃t] **1** *adj (opinion)* prevailing; *(couleur, trait, idée)* dominant; *Biol* **caractère d.** dominant characteristic
2 *nf* **dominante** *(ce qui domine)* chief characteristic; **une tenue pâle, avec une dominante de rose** a pale, mainly pink outfit

dominateur, -trice [dɔminatœr, -tris] *adj (personne, ton, attitude)* domineering

domination [dɔminasjɔ̃] *nf* domination **(sur** over); **être sous la d. de qn** to be dominated by sb

dominer [dɔmine] **1** *vt* (a) *(assujettir) (personne)* to dominate; *(empire)* to rule over (b) *(surpasser) (adversaire, concurrent)* to surpass (c) *(prédominer dans)* to be the dominant feature of (d) *(maîtriser) (timidité, passions, larmes, sujet)* to master; *(paresse, envie)* to overcome; *(match)* to dominate; **d. la situation** to keep the situation under control (e) *(surplomber)* to dominate; **de leur terrasse, on domine la mer** their balcony overlooks the sea
2 *vi* (a) *(l'emporter)* to be dominant (b) *(prédominer)* to predominate
3 se dominer *vpr* to control oneself

dominicain, -e [dɔminikɛ̃, -ɛn] **1** *adj* Dominican
2 *nm,f* (a) *Rel* Dominican (b) *(de la République Dominicaine)* D. Dominican

dominical, -e, -aux, -ales [dɔminikal, -o] *adj* Sunday; **repos d.** day of rest; **ouverture dominicale des magasins** Sunday opening

Dominique [dɔminik] *nf* **la D.** Dominica

domino [dɔmino] *nm (plaquette)* domino; **jouer aux dominos** to play dominoes

dommage [dɔmaʒ] *nm* (a) *(préjudice)* harm; **causer un d. à qn** to do sb harm; **d. corporel** physical injury; **dommages et intérêts, dommages-intérêts** damages; **d. matériel** material damage (b) **dommages** *(dégâts matériels)* damage (c) *(quel)* **d.!** what a pity!, what a shame!; **c'est (bien) d. qu'elle ne soit pas venue** it's a (great) pity that she didn't come

dommageable [dɔmaʒabl] *adj* detrimental **(à** to)

dompter [dɔ̃(p)te] *vt (fauve, fleuve, nature)* to tame; *(sentiments, passions, personne)* to subdue

dompteur, -euse [dɔ̃(p)tœr, -øz] *nm,f* tamer

DOM-TOM [dɔmtɔm] *nmpl (abrév* **départements et territoires d'outre-mer)** = French overseas departments and territories

DON [dɔœ̃] *nm Ordinat (abrév* **disque optique numérique)** CD

don [dɔ̃] *nm* (a) *(cadeau)* gift; *(à un musée, une œuvre)* donation; **faire d. à qn de qch** to make a gift of sth to sb; **d. du sang/de sperme** blood/sperm donation; *Fig* **d. du ciel** godsend; **le d. de soi** self-sacrifice (b) *(aptitude)* gift, talent; *aussi Ironique* **avoir le d. de faire qch** to have a knack for doing sth

donateur, -trice [dɔnatœr, -tris] *nm,f* donor

donation [dɔnasjɔ̃] *nf* donation

donc [dɔ̃k] *conj* (a) *(marque la conséquence)* so (b) *(emphatique)* **tu le savais d. depuis le début?** so you knew from the start?; **que voulez-vous d.?** whatever do you want?; **mais taisez-vous d.!** do be quiet!; **allons d.!** come on! (c) *(après interruption ou digression)* **je disais d. que...** I was saying, then, that...

dondon [dɔ̃dɔ̃] *nf Fam Péj* **grosse d.** great lump of a woman/girl

donjon [dɔ̃ʒɔ̃] *nm* keep

don Juan *(pl* **dons Juans)** [dɔ̃ʒɥɑ̃] *nm* Don Juan

donne [dɔn] *nf (aux cartes)* deal

donné, -e [dɔne] *adj* (a) *(offert)* given; *Fam* **c'est d.** it's dirt cheap; *Fam* **ce n'est pas d.** it doesn't come cheap (b) *(défini)* given; **à un moment d.** *(dans le passé)* at one point; *(dans le futur)* at some point; **étant d. la situation** given the situation; **étant d. que...** seeing that...

donnée [dɔne] *nf* (a) *(élément)* piece of information; **avoir toutes les données du problème** to have all the data or information on the problem (b) *Ordinat* **données data; données numériques** digital data

donner [dɔne] **1** *vt* (a) *(offrir, distribuer)* to give; **d. qch à qn** to give sth to sb, to give sb sth; **d. à boire à qn** to give sb something to drink; **d. à manger à** *(animal)* to feed; **c'est à qui de d.?** *(aux cartes)* whose deal is it?
(b) *(faire don de) (temps, vie)* to give; *(corps, organe)* to donate; **d. son sang** to give blood
(c) *(céder)* to give; *Fam (dénoncer)* to grass on **(à** to); **en d. à qn pour son argent** to give sb their money's worth
(d) *(payer)* **je lui donne 40 francs de l'heure** I pay him 40 francs an hour; **je vous en donne 10 francs** I'll give you 10 francs for it
(e) *(confier)* **d. à qn qch à garder** to give sb sth to look after; **d. un vêtement à nettoyer** to hand in a garment to be dry-cleaned
(f) *(avis, ordre, conseil)* to give; **d. l'heure à qn** to tell sb the time; **tu lui donneras le bonjour de ma part** say hello to her for me; **d. des ou de ses nouvelles à qn** to keep in touch with sb
(g) *(chance, délai, occasion)* to give; **je vous donne une semaine, pas plus** I'll give you a week and no more

(h) *(causer)* **d. de l'appétit à qn** to give sb an appetite; **d. des boutons à qn** to bring sb out in a rash; **d. mal à la tête à qn** to give sb a headache; **d. faim/sommeil/ chaud à qn** to make sb hungry/sleepy/hot; **d. du souci à qn** to cause sb worry; **toute cette histoire m'a donné à réfléchir** the whole business made me think again

(i) *(produire) (récoltes)* to yield; *(fruits)* to bear; **les blés vont d. cette année** there will be a good crop of wheat this year; **ça n'a rien donné** nothing came of it; **qu'est-ce que ça donne?** *(comment ça se présente?)* how does it look?

(j) *(administrer)* to give; **d. un baiser/une gifle à qn** to give sb a kiss/a slap in the face; **tu peux d. un coup de balai dans la cuisine?** can you give the kitchen a sweep?

(k) *(bal, dîner, conférence)* to give; *(pièce de théâtre)* to put on, to perform; **qu'est-ce qu'on donne au cinéma?** what's on at the cinema?

(l) *(attribuer)* **je lui donne vingt ans** I'd say she's twenty; **les médecins lui donnent deux jours (à vivre)** the doctors give him two days (to live)

(m) *(maladie)* to give

2 *vi (cogner)* **d. de la tête contre qch** to hit one's head against sth; *Fig* **je ne savais pas où d. de la tête** I didn't know where to start

3 *v impersonnel* **le spectacle le plus épouvantable qu'il m'ait été donné de voir** the most horrifying sight I've ever been unfortunate enough to witness; **il n'est pas donné à tout le monde d'être écrivain** not everyone can be a writer

4 donner dans *vt ind* (a) *(tomber)* **d. dans le piège** *ou* **le panneau** to fall into the trap

(b) *(avoir un penchant pour)* to have a tendency to

5 donner sur *vt ind (sujet: fenêtre)* to look onto; *(sujet: porte)* to lead into

6 se donner *vpr* (a) *(faire don de soi)* to give of oneself; **se d. à qch** to devote oneself to sth; **se d. en spectacle** to make an exhibition of oneself

(b) *(à soi-même)* **se d. un coup de peigne/brosse** to give one's hair a quick comb/brush; **se d. un coup de marteau sur le pouce** to hit one's thumb with a hammer; **se d. le temps de réfléchir** to give oneself time to think; **se d. pour tâche de faire qch** to set oneself the task of doing sth

(c) *Litt (sexuellement)* to give oneself (à to)

(d) *(l'un l'autre)* **se d. des coups** to exchange blows; **se d. des baisers** to kiss (each other)

donneur, -euse [dɔnœr, -øz] *nm, f* (a) *(d'organe)* donor; **d. de sang** blood donor (b) *(aux cartes)* dealer

dont [dɔ̃] *pron relatif* (a) *(introduit le complément du verbe)* **la famille d. je descends** the family I'm descended from; **la façon d. il me regardait** the way (in which) he looked at me; **le livre d. j'ai besoin** the book (that) I need; **un film d. on parle beaucoup** a film that is being talked about a lot; **l'homme d. elle se moque** the man she's making fun of

(b) *(introduit le complément du nom)* **la dame d. je connais le fils** the woman whose son I know; **la maison d. on voit le toit** the house whose roof can be seen; **un film d. voici le résumé** a film of which this is a summary; **quelques-uns étaient là, d. votre frère** there were a few people there, including your brother

(c) *(introduit le complément de l'adjectif)* **la femme d. il est amoureux** the woman he is in love with; **le groupe d'enfants d. vous êtes responsable** the group of children you are responsible for; **le souvenir d. elle est si honteuse** the memory she is so ashamed of

dopage [dɔpaʒ] *nm* doping; *(de sportif)* drug-taking

doper [dɔpe] **1** *vt (droguer)* to dope

2 se doper *vpr* to take drugs

dorade [dɔrad] *nf* sea bream

doré, -e [dɔre] **1** *adj* (a) *(recouvert d'or)* gilded, gilt; **d. sur tranche** gilt-edged (b) *(couleur d'or) (blé, lumière, peau, cheveux)* golden; *(gâteau passé au jaune d'œuf)* glazed; *(viande, pommes de terre, gâteau cuit)* browned

2 *nm Can (poisson)* wall-eyed pike, yellow pike

dorénavant [dɔrenavɑ̃] *adv* from now on

dorer [dɔre] **1** *vt* (a) *(recouvrir d'or)* to gild; *Fig* **d. la pilule à qn** to sweeten the pill for sb (b) *(donner une couleur dorée à) (peau)* to turn golden; *(gâteau)* to glaze; *(viande, pommes de terre)* to brown

2 *vi (plat, gâteau)* to brown

3 se dorer *vpr* **se d. au soleil** to sunbathe; *Fig* **se d. la pilule** to catch some rays

dorloter [dɔrlɔte] *vt* to pamper, to coddle

dormant, -e [dɔrmɑ̃, -ɑ̃t] *adj* **eaux dormantes** stagnant water

dormeur, -euse [dɔrmœr, -øz] *nm, f (personne endormie)* sleeper; **être un gros d.** to need a lot of sleep

dormir [29] [dɔrmir] *vi* (a) *(sommeiller)* to sleep; **elle dort** she's sleeping, she's asleep; **d. profondément** to be fast asleep; **je n'ai pas dormi de la nuit** I didn't sleep a wink (all night); **le café m'empêche de d.** coffee keeps me awake; *Fam* **ce n'est pas ça qui va m'empêcher de d.** I won't lose any sleep over it; **d. à poings fermés**, **comme un loir** to sleep like a log; **ne d. que d'un œil** to sleep with one eye open; **vous pouvez d. tranquille** *ou* **sur vos deux oreilles** you can rest easy; **avoir envie de d.** to be or feel sleepy; **d. debout** to be asleep on one's feet; *Prov* **qui dort, dîne** he who sleeps forgets his hunger (b) *Fig (ville, forêt)* to be sleeping; *(capitaux)* to lie idle

dorsal, -e, -aux, -ales [dɔrsal, -o] *adj* dorsal

dortoir [dɔrtwar] *nm* dormitory

dorure [dɔryr] *nf* (a) *(couche d'or)* gilding (b) *(ornement)* gilt

doryphore [dɔrifɔr] *nm* Colorado beetle

DOS [dɔs] *nm Ordinat* DOS

dos [do] *nm* (a) *(d'une personne, d'un animal)* back; **sur le d.** on one's back; **je n'ai rien à me mettre sur le d.** I haven't a thing to wear; **à d. d'âne** on a donkey; **je ne l'ai vu que de d.** I only saw him from the back; **d. à d.** back to back; **faire le gros d.** *(chat)* to arch its back; **faire qch derrière** *ou* **dans le d. de qn** to do sth behind sb's back; *Fam* **je lui ai tout le temps sur le d.** she's always on my back; **s'enrichir sur le d. de qn** to get rich off sb; **avoir bon d.** *(personne)* to have a broad back; **elle a bon d., la grève des postes, dis plutôt que tu n'as pas écrit** why don't you admit you haven't written instead of blaming it on the postal strike?; *Fam* **en avoir plein le d.** to be sick of it, to be fed up with it; **se mettre qn à d.** to get sb's back up; **tourner le d. à qn** *(debout)* to stand with one's back to sb; *(assis)* to sit with one's back to sb; *(volontairement)* to turn one's back on sb; **dès qu'il a le d. tourné** as soon as his back is turned

(b) *(d'une chaise, d'une page, d'un chèque, de la main)* back; *(d'un livre)* spine; **voir au d.** (please) turn over, PTO

(c) **d.** *(crawlé)* backstroke

dosage [dozaʒ] *nm (d'ingrédients)* proportioning; *(de médicaments)* dosage

dos-d'âne [dodan] *nm inv* bump; **pont en d.** humpbacked bridge

dose [doz] *nf* (*d'un élément dans un mélange*) proportion; (*de médicament*) dose; *Fig* **à petites doses** in small doses; *Fam* **il faut une sacrée d. de culot pour faire cela** it takes a hell of a nerve to do that; **forcer la d.** to overdo it; *Fam* **avoir sa d. (de qch)** to have had more than enough (of sth)

doser [doze] *vt* (*médicament, ingrédient*) to measure out

doseur [dozœr] *nm* measure

dossard [dosar] *nm* number (*worn by competitor*)

dossier [dosje] *nm* (**a**) (*d'un siège*) back (**b**) (*documents*) file, dossier; (*d'un prisonnier, d'un malade, d'un élève*) record; (*chemise*) folder, file; *Ordinat* file; **constituer un d. sur qn/qch** to build up a file on sb/sth; *Ordinat* **d. système** system folder (**c**) *Fig* (*sujet*) question

dot [dɔt] *nf* dowry

dotation [dɔtasjɔ̃] *nf* (*fonds*) (*d'hôpital, de collège*) endowment; (*versés à un chef d'Etat*) allowance

doter [dɔte] *vt* (*équiper*) to equip (de with); **elle est dotée d'une intelligence remarquable** she is endowed with great intelligence

douairière [dwerjer] *adj & nf* dowager

douane [dwan] *nf* customs; **passer à la d.** to go through customs; **droits de d.** customs duty

douanier, -ère [dwanje, -er] **1** *adj* customs; **union douanière** customs union; **barrières douanières** tariff barriers
  2 *nm* customs officer

doublage [dublaʒ] *nm* (**a**) (*d'un vêtement*) lining (**b**) (*d'un film, d'une voix*) dubbing; (*par une doublure*) doubling

double [dubl] **1** *adj* (**a**) (*quantité, lit, chambre*) double; **en d. exemplaire** in duplicate; **fermer une porte à d. tour** to double-lock a door; **avoir la d. nationalité** to have dual nationality; *Mus* **d. croche** *Br* semi-quaver, *Am* sixteenth note; *Ordinat* **d. densité** double density; **d. mètre** 2-metre rule; **d. vitrage** double glazing (**b**) (*ambigu*) **mener une d. vie** to lead a double life; **mot à d. sens** ambiguous word
  2 *adv* double
  3 *nm* (**a**) **le d. (de)** (*quantité, prix*) twice as much (as); (*nombre*) twice as many (as); **dix est le d. de cinq** ten is two times five; **mettre qch en d.** to fold sth in two or half (**b**) (*exemplaire*) duplicate, copy; (*d'une clef*) duplicate; *Ordinat* backup; **avoir qch en d.** to have two of sth; **faire qch en d.** (*lettre, devoir*) to make two copies of sth (**c**) (*personne*) double (**d**) (*au tennis*) doubles; **d. messieurs/dames/mixte** men's/ladies'/mixed doubles

doublé, -e [duble] **1** *adj* (**a**) (*veste, gants*) lined (de with) (**b**) (*film*) dubbed
  2 *nm* (*victoires*) double

doublement¹ [dubləmɑ̃] *adv* doubly

doublement² [dubləmɑ̃] *nm* (*d'un nombre, d'une somme, d'une lettre*) doubling

doubler [duble] **1** *vt* (**a**) (*multiplier par deux*) to double (**b**) (*plier*) to fold in two or in half (**c**) (*vêtement*) to line (**d**) (*film, voix*) to dub; (*sujet: acteur*) to dub the voice of; (*sujet: cascadeur*) to stand in for (**e**) (*passer*) (*véhicule*) *Br* to overtake, *Am* to pass (**f**) *Fam* (*trahir*) to double-cross
  2 *vi* (**a**) (*population, salaire*) to double; **d. de valeur** to double in value (**b**) (*véhicule*) *Br* to overtake, *Am* to pass
  3 **se doubler** *vpr* **se doubler de** to be coupled with

doublure [dublyr] *nf* (**a**) (*d'un vêtement, d'un sac*) lining (**b**) (*au théâtre*) understudy; (*au cinéma*) stand-in

douce [dus] *voir* **doux**

douceâtre [dusatr] *adj* (*saveur*) sickly sweet; (*ton*) smarmy

doucement [dusmɑ̃] *adv* (*délicatement*) gently; (*bas*) softly; **allez-y d.!** gently does it!; *Fam* (**allez-y**) **d. avec le vin!** go easy on the wine!

doucereux, -euse [dusrø, -øz] *adj* (*personne, voix, ton*) smarmy

douceur [dusœr] *nf* (**a**) (*d'un son, d'une matière*) softness; (*d'un climat*) mildness; (*du miel, d'un parfum*) sweetness (**b**) (*de caractère*) gentleness; (*d'un sourire*) sweetness; **traiter qn avec d.** to treat sb gently; **en d.** gently; **la voiture a démarré en d.** the car started smoothly (**c**) **douceurs** (*sucreries*) *Br* sweets, *Am* candy

douche [duʃ] *nf* shower; **prendre une d.** to have *or* take a shower; *Fig* **avec lui, c'est la d. écossaise** you never know where you are with him; *Fig* **d. froide** terrible disappointment

doucher [duʃe] **1** *vt* (*pour laver*) **d. qn** to give sb a shower
  2 **se doucher** *vpr* to have *or* take a shower

doudoune [dudun] *nf* (*anorak*) padded jacket

doué, -e [dwe] *adj* gifted, talented; **être d. pour** to have a gift for

douille [duj] *nf* (*d'une ampoule*) lamp socket; (*d'une cartouche*) case

douillet, -ette [duje, -et] *adj* (**a**) (*lit*) cosy (**b**) (*délicat*) **ne sois pas si d.!** don't be such a baby!

douillettement [dujetmɑ̃] *adv* (*confortablement*) cosily

douleur [dulœr] *nf* (*physique*) pain; (*morale*) sorrow, grief; **nous avons la d. de vous faire part de…** we regret to inform you of…; *Fam* **j'ai compris ma d.** my worst fears came true

douloureux, -euse [dulurø, -øz] *adj* (**a**) (*coup, maladie, opération*) painful; (*au contact*) sore, tender; **mon dos est d.** my back is aching (**b**) (*perte, événement*) sad; (*séparation, circonstances*) painful

doute [dut] *nm* (**a**) (*incertitude*) doubt; **être dans le d. (au sujet de qch)** to be doubtful (about sth); **mettre qch en d.** to question sth, to cast doubt on sth; **mettre en d. la parole de qn** to doubt sb's word; **il n'y a pas de ou aucun d.** there's no doubt about it; **sans d.** no doubt, probably; **sans aucun d.** without (any) doubt (**b**) (*soupçon*) doubt; **avoir des doutes sur ou au sujet de qn/qch** to have doubts about sb/sth

douter [dute] **1** *vi* to doubt; **d. de qn/qch** to doubt sb/sth; **elle ne doute de rien** she isn't backward in coming forward; **j'en doute** I doubt it
  2 *vt* **je doute qu'il soit assez fort** I doubt whether he's strong enough; **je n'ai jamais douté que tu viendrais** I never doubted that you'd come
  3 **se douter** *vpr* **se d. de qch** to suspect sth; **je m'en doutais (bien)** I thought as much; *Fam* **on s'en serait douté!** I might have known!

douteux, -euse [dutø, -øz] *adj* (**a**) (*incertain*) doubtful (**b**) (*suspect*) dubious; **vêtements d. ou d'une propreté douteuse** dubious clothes; **d'un goût d.** (*plaisanteries, vêtements*) in dubious taste

douve [duv] *nf* (*d'un château*) moat

Douvres [duvr] *n* Dover

doux, douce [du, dus] **1** *adj* (a) *(au toucher)* soft; *(au goût)* mild (b) *(couleur, son, lumière)* soft; *(climat, hiver, tabac)* mild; *(vin, cidre)* sweet; *(pente)* gentle; **les médecines douces** alternative forms of medicine (c) *(nature, regard, voix)* gentle; **faire les yeux d. à qn** to make sheep's eyes at sb; **d. comme un agneau** as gentle as a lamb
2 *adv Fam* **filer d.** to toe the line
3 *nf* **douce** Fam **en d.** on the quiet

douzaine [duzɛn] *nf* **une d. (de)** *(environ)* around a dozen, a dozen or so; **trois douzaines d'œufs** three dozen eggs

douze [duz] *adj & nm inv* twelve; *voir aussi* **trois**

douzième [duzjɛm] *nmf, nm & adj* twelfth; *voir aussi* **cinquième**

doyen, -enne [dwajɛ̃, -ɛn] *nm,f* (a) *(personne la plus âgée)* most senior member (b) *(d'une faculté)* dean

drachme [drakm] *nf* drachma

draconien, -enne [drakɔnjɛ̃, -ɛn] *adj* *(règlement)* draconian; *(régime)* very strict

dragage [draga3] *nm* *(nettoyage)* dredging

dragée [draʒe] *nf* *(confiserie)* sugared almond; *(médicament)* sugar-coated pill

dragon [dragɔ̃] *nm* (a) *(animal mythologique, femme acariâtre)* dragon (b) *(soldat)* dragoon

draguer [drage] **1** *vt* *(nettoyer)* to dredge (b) *Fam (hommes, femmes)* to chat up, *Am* to hit on
2 *vi Fam* to go on the pull

dragueur, -euse [dragœr, -øz] **1** *nm* *(bateau)* dredger; **d. de mines** minesweeper
2 *nm,f Fam* chat-up merchant

drain [drɛ̃] *nm* (a) *(conduit)* drain (b) *Méd* drainage tube

drainage [drɛnaʒ] *nm* *(d'un champ, d'une plaie)* draining

drainer [drɛne] *vt* *(sol, abcès)* to drain

dramatique [dramatik] **1** *adj* (a) *(de théâtre)* dramatic; **auteur d.** playwright (b) *(grave)* tragic
2 *nf* TV drama

dramatiser [dramatize] *vt* to dramatize

dramaturge [dramatyrʒ] *nm* dramatist, playwright

drame [dram] *nm* (a) *(genre littéraire, pièce)* drama (b) *Fig* tragedy; **faire un d. de qch** to make a drama out of sth

drap [dra] *nm* (a) *(linge)* **d. (de lit)** sheet; **d. de dessous/dessus** bottom/top sheet; *Fig* **être dans de beaux draps** to be in a real mess; **d. de bain** bath sheet (b) *(tissu)* cloth (c) *Belg (serviette)* towel

drapeau, -x [drapo] *nm* flag; *Fig* **être sous les drapeaux** to serve in the armed forces; **d. blanc** white flag; **d. tricolore** tricolour

draper [drape] **1** *vt* *(étoffe)* to drape
2 se draper *vpr* **se d. dans** to drape oneself in

draperie [drapri] *nf* *(tenture)* drapery

drap-housse [*pl* draps-housses] [draus] *nm* fitted sheet

drapier, -ère [drapje, -ɛr] **1** *nm,f* *(marchand)* draper; *(fabricant)* cloth manufacturer
2 *adj* cloth

drastique [drastik] *adj* drastic

drave [drav] *nf Can (de rondins)* drive

draver [drave] *vt Can (rondins)* to float, to drive

draveur [dravœr] *nm Can* driver, raftsman

Dresde [drɛzd] *n* Dresden

dressage [drɛsaʒ] *nm (d'un animal)* training; *(d'un cheval)* breaking in

dresser [drese] **1** *vt* (a) *(élever)* to put up, to erect; **d. la tête** to raise or lift one's head; *(pour regarder)* to look up; **d. les oreilles** to prick up or cock its ears; *Fig* **d. l'oreille** to prick up one's ears (b) *(plan, rapport, liste)* to prepare, to draw up (c) *(animal)* to train (**à faire qch** to do sth); *(cheval)* to break in; *Fam* **ça va le d.!** that'll put him in his place! (d) *(exciter)* **d. qn contre qn** to set sb against sb
2 se dresser *vpr* (a) *(se lever)* to stand up, to rise (b) *(monument)* to stand; *(montagne)* to rise up; *Fig* **les obstacles qui se dressent sur notre chemin** the obstacles that stand in our way

dresseur, -euse [drɛsœr, -øz] *nm,f (d'animaux)* trainer

dribble [dribl] *nm* dribble

dribbler [drible] **1** *vi* to dribble
2 *vt (joueur)* to dribble round

drille [drij] *nm Fam* **c'est un joyeux d.** he's always good for a laugh

drogue [drɔg] *nf* (a) *(stupéfiant)* drug; **d. dure/douce** hard/soft drug (b) *Vieilli (médicament)* medicine

drogué, -e [drɔge] *nm,f* drug addict

droguer [drɔge] **1** *vt* (a) *(victime)* to drug; *(cheval)* to dope (b) *(malade)* to dose with drugs
2 se droguer *vpr* to take drugs; **se d. à qch** to be on sth

droguerie [drɔgri] *nf* hardware *Br* shop or *Am* store

droguiste [drɔgist] *nmf* hardware dealer

droit¹, -e [drwa, drwat] **1** *adj* (a) *(rectiligne, vertical)* straight; **se tenir d.** *(debout)* to stand (up) straight; *(assis)* to sit (up) straight; **d. comme un i** *ou* **un piquet** as straight as a poker (b) *(honnête)* upright
2 *nf* **droite** straight line
3 *adv* **écrire/marcher d.** to write/walk straight; **aller d. devant soi** to go straight ahead; **aller d. au but** to get to the point; **aller d. à la catastrophe** to be heading straight for disaster; **c'est tout d.** it's straight ahead

droit², -e [drwa, drwat] **1** *adj (main, jambe, gant)* right; **du côté d.** on the right-hand side
2 *nf* **droite** (a) *(côté)* right; **tourner à droite** to turn (to the) right; **rouler à droite** to drive on the right; **le placard de droite** the right-hand cupboard, the cupboard on the right; **à ma droite, le château** to or on my right is the castle; *Fig* **courir à droite et à gauche** to run about all over the place (b) *Pol* **la droite** the right (wing); **de droite** *(candidat, journal)* right-wing; **voter à droite** to vote for the right

droit³ *nm* (a) *(prérogative)* right; **avoir d. à qch** to have a right to sth; **avoir le d. de faire qch** to have the right to do sth; **être dans son (bon) d.** to be within one's rights; **avoir des droits sur qn/qch** to have rights over sb/sth; **tous droits (de reproduction) réservés** *(sur livre)* all rights reserved; **de quel d. me critiques-tu?** what gives you the right to criticize me?; **d. d'aînesse** birthright; **d. d'asile** right of asylum; **avoir un d. de regard sur qch** to have the right to know about sth; **d. de réponse** right of reply; **d. de visite** *(d'un parent)* visiting rights; **d. de vote** right to vote; **les droits de l'homme** human rights (b) *(en argent)* fee; *(imposition)* duty; *(taxe)* tax; **droits d'auteur** royalties; **droits de douane** (customs) duty; **d. d'entrée** admission fee; **droits d'inscription** registration fee; **droits de succession** death duties; **d. de timbre** stamp duty (c) *Jur* law; **faire son d.** to study or read law; **d. administratif** administrative law; **d. des affaires** business law; **d. canon** canon law; **d. civil** civil law; **d. commercial** commercial law; **d. commun** common law; **d. communautaire** Community law; **d. constitutionnel** constitutional law; **d. international**

international law; **d. pénal** criminal law; **d. privé** private law; **d. public** public law; **d. du travail** labour laws

droitier, -ère [drwatje, -er] **1** *adj* right-handed
2 *nm,f* right-handed person

droiture [drwatyr] *nf* rectitude

drôle [drol] *adj* (a) (*amusant*) funny (b) (*étrange*) funny; **un d. de type** a funny sort; **faire une d. de tête** to pull a face; **Fam ça me fait tout d. de te voir ici** it feels really funny seeing you here

drôlement [drolmã] *adv* Fam (*très*) awfully; Fam **les prix ont d. augmenté** prices have gone up an awful lot; Fam **elle est d. bien** (*remarquable*) she's a terrific person; (*belle*) she's great-looking

drôlerie [drolri] *nf* funniness

dromadaire [dromader] *nm* dromedary

dru, -e [dry] **1** *adj* (*herbe, blé, cheveux, barbe*) thick; (*pluie*) heavy
2 *adv* **pousser d.** to grow thickly; **tomber d.** (*pluie*) to fall heavily

druide [drɥid] *nm* druid

DST [deeste] *nf* (*abrév* **Direction de la surveillance du territoire**) = French Secret Service

DTP [detepe] *nm* (*abrév* **diphtérie, tétanos, polio**) diphtheria, tetanus and polio vaccination

du [dy] *voir* **de**

dû, due (*mpl* **dus**, *fpl* **dues**) [dy] **1** *pp voir* **devoir**
2 *adj* (a) (*que l'on doit*) due, owed; **en port dû** carriage forward (b) (*causé*) **être dû à qch** to be due to sth (c) **en bonne et due forme** in due form
3 *nm* due

dualisme [dɥalism] *nm* dualism

dualité [dɥalite] *nf* duality

dubitatif, -ive [dybitatif, -iv] *adj* doubtful

Dublin [dyblɛ̃] *n* Dublin

dublinois, -e [dyblinwa, -az] **1** *adj* of Dublin
2 *nm,f* **D.** Dubliner

duc [dyk] *nm* duke

ducal, -e, -aux, -ales [dykal, -o] *adj* ducal

duché [dyʃe] *nm* duchy

duchesse [dyʃɛs] *nf* (a) (*femme*) duchess (b) **pommes (de terre) d.** duchesse potatoes (*mashed, shaped and baked*)

due *voir* **dû**

duel [dɥɛl] *nm* duel; **se battre en d.** to fight a duel

dulcinée [dylsine] *nf* Litt ou Hum ladylove

dûment [dymã] *adv* duly

dumping [dœmpiŋ] *nm* dumping; **faire du d.** to dump

dune [dyn] *nf* dune

Dunkerque [dœkerk] *n* Dunkirk

duo [dɥo] *nm* (*chanson*) duet; (*de comiques, de musiciens*) duo

duodénum [dɥɔdenom] *nm* duodenum

dupe [dyp] **1** *nf* dupe
2 *adj* **être d. (de)** to be taken in (by)

duper [dype] *vt* to dupe, to fool

duperie [dypri] *nf* deception

duplex [dyplɛks] *nm* (a) (*émission en*) **d.** link-up (b) (*appartement*) Br maisonette, Am duplex

duplicata [dyplikata] *nm* duplicate

duplication [dyplikasjɔ̃] *nf* (a) Biol doubling (b) Ordinat **d. de logiciel** software copying

duplicité [dyplisite] *nf* duplicity

dur, -e [dyr] **1** *adj* (a) (*rigide*) hard; (*viande*) tough; (*pain*) stale (b) (*difficile, pénible*) (*travail, hiver*) hard; (*scène, film*) distressing (c) (*sévère, cruel*) harsh (**avec** with) (d) Fam **être d. de la feuille** to be hard of hearing
2 *nm,f* Fam (*personne*) tough type; Pol hard liner; **un d. à cuire** a hard-boiled type; **jouer les durs** to act tough
3 *nm* **bâtiment en d.** permanent building
4 *nf* Fam **élever qn à la dure** to bring sb up the hard way
5 *adv* (*travailler*) hard

durable [dyrabl] *adj* lasting

durablement [dyrabləmã] *adv* for a long time

duraille [dyraj] *adj* Fam hard

durant [dyrã] *prép* **d. le mois de mai** during May; **d. plusieurs années** for several years; **d. toute sa vie, sa vie d.** throughout his life; **parler des heures d.** to talk for hours on end

durcir [dyrsir] **1** *vt aussi Fig* to harden
2 *vi* to harden
3 **se durcir** *vpr aussi Fig* to harden

durcissement [dyrsismã] *nm aussi Fig* hardening

durée [dyre] *nf* (*d'un règne, d'une guerre, d'un séjour*) duration, length; (*d'une note*) length, value; **de courte d.** (*bonheur, soulagement*) short-lived; **d. de projection** (*d'un film*) running time; **d. de validité** (*d'un billet*) period of validity; **d. de vie** (*de personne*) lifespan; (*d'une pile*) life; (*d'une machine*) useful life; **d. de vol** flight time

durement [dyrmã] *adv* (*répondre, parler*) harshly; **d. éprouvé** sorely tried

durer [dyre] *vi* to last; **voilà trois ans que cela dure** it's been going on for three years; **ça ne peut pas d.** this can't go on; Hum **faire d. le plaisir** to prolong the agony

dureté [dyrte] *nf* (a) (*rigidité*) hardness; (*d'une viande*) toughness (b) (*d'un hiver*) severity (c) (*cruauté*) (*d'une personne*) harshness; **parler avec d.** to speak harshly

durillon [dyrijɔ̃] *nm* (*de la main*) callus; (*du pied*) corn

Durit® [dyrit] *nf* hose (connection)

DUT [deyte] *nm* (*abrév* **diplôme universitaire de technologie**) = post-baccalauréat technical qualification awarded after two years

duvet [dyvɛ] *nm* (a) (*poil*) down (b) (*sac de couchage*) sleeping bag (c) Suisse duvet, continental quilt

duveteux, -euse [dyvtø, -øz] *adj* downy

dynamique [dinamik] **1** *adj* dynamic
2 *nf* (a) (*science*) dynamics (*singulier*) (b) (*progrès*) dynamic

dynamiser [dinamize] *vt* to energize

dynamisme [dinamism] *nm* dynamism

dynamite [dinamit] *nf* dynamite

dynamiter [dinamite] *vt* to dynamite

dynamo [dinamo] *nf* dynamo

dynastie [dinasti] *nf* dynasty

dysenterie [disãtri] *nf* dysentery

dysfonctionnement [disfɔ̃ksjɔnmã] *nm* dysfunction

dyslexie [disleksi] *nf* dyslexia

dyslexique [disleksik] *adj* dyslexic

E

E, e [ə] *nm inv* E, e

E (*abrév* **Est**) E

EAO [aao] *nm inv* (*abrév* **enseignement assisté par ordinateur**) CAL

eau, -x [o] *nf* (**a**) (*liquide*) water; **laver qch à grande e.** to wash sth down; **prendre l'e.** to let in water; **avoir l'e. courante** to have running water; *Fig* **mettre de l'e. dans son vin** to tone it down a bit; *Fig* **apporter de l'e. au moulin de qn** to strengthen sb's case; *Fig* **dans ces eaux-là** or thereabouts; *Fam* **s'en aller en e. de boudin** to go down the tubes; *Fam* **il y a de l'e. dans le gaz** there's trouble brewing; **e. bénite** holy water; **e. de Cologne** eau de Cologne; **e. douce** fresh water; **e. de Javel** bleach; **e. lourde** heavy water; **e. de mer** *ou* **salée** salt water; **e. minérale** mineral water; **e. oxygénée** hydrogen peroxide; **e. de pluie** rainwater; **e. du robinet** tap water; *Fig* **roman/film à l'e. de rose** sentimental novel/film; **e. de source** spring water; **eaux thermales** hot springs; **e. de toilette** toilet water; *aussi Fig* **e. de vaisselle** dishwater

(**b**) (*étendue*) water; **au bord de l'e.** by the water's edge; **tomber à l'e.** to fall into the water; *Fig* to fall through; *Fig* **se jeter à l'e.** to take the plunge; **les eaux territoriales françaises** French waters

(**c**) (*sécrétion*) **être tout en e.** to be dripping with perspiration; **j'en ai l'e. à la bouche!** my mouth's watering!; **elle a perdu les eaux** her waters have broken

(**d**) **un diamant de la plus belle e.** a diamond of the first water

eau-de-vie (*pl* **eaux-de-vie**) [odvi] *nf* brandy

eau-forte (*pl* **eaux-fortes**) [ofort] *nf* (*estampe*) etching

ébahi, -e [ebai] *adj* astounded

ébats [eba] *nmpl* frolicking; **é. amoureux** lovemaking

ébattre [11] [ebatr] **s'ébattre** *vpr* to frolic

ébauche [eboʃ] *nf* (*dessin*) rough sketch; (*d'un roman*) outline; (*d'une lettre*) draft; *Fig* **l'é. d'un sourire** the ghost of a smile

ébaucher [eboʃe] *vt* (*tableau, roman*) to rough out; (*lettre*) to draft; *Fig* **é. un sourire** to give a faint smile; *Fig* **é. un geste** to make a movement

ébène [eben] *nf* ebony; (**d'un noir**) **d'é.**, (**noir**) **é.** jet black

ébéniste [ebenist] *nmf* cabinet maker

éberlué, -e [eberlye] *adj* flabbergasted

éblouir [ebluir] *vt aussi Fig* to dazzle

éblouissant, -e [ebluisã, -ãt] *adj aussi Fig* dazzling; **d'une beauté éblouissante** dazzlingly beautiful

éblouissement [ebluismã] *nm* dazzle, glare; (*malaise*) fit of dizziness; *Fig* **ce fut un é.** it was dazzling

éborgner [eborɲe] *vt* **é. qn** to put sb's eye out

éboueur [ebwœr] *nm Br* dustman, *Am* garbage man

ébouillanter [ebujãte] **1** *vt* to scald
 2 s'ébouillanter *vpr* to scald oneself

éboulement [ebulmã] *nm* (**a**) (*écroulement*) collapse; (*de mine*) cave-in; **deux personnes sont mortes dans l'é. de la falaise** two people were killed when the cliff collapsed (**b**) (*gravats*) mass of fallen rocks

ébouler [ebule] **s'ébouler** *vpr* (*falaise, remblai*) to collapse; (*tunnel*) to cave in

éboulis [ebuli] *nm* mass of fallen rocks

ébouriffé, -e [eburife] *adj* (*cheveux, personne*) dishevelled

ébouriffer [eburife] *vt* (*cheveux*) to ruffle; **é. qn** to ruffle sb's hair

ébranler [ebrãle] **1** *vt aussi Fig* to shake
 2 s'ébranler *vpr* to move off

Èbre [ebr] *nm* **l'È.** the Ebro

ébrécher [34] [ebreʃe] *vt* (*verre, porcelaine*) to chip; (*lame*) to nick

ébriété [ebriete] *nf* **en état d'é.** in a state of inebriation

ébrouer [ebrue] **s'ébrouer** *vpr* (**a**) (*cheval*) to snort (**b**) (*chien*) to shake itself

ébruiter [ebrɥite] **1** *vt* (*secret*) to give away; (*nouvelle*) to spread
 2 s'ébruiter *vpr* (*nouvelle*) to spread

EBS [ebɛs] *nf* (*abrév* **encéphalite bovine spongiforme**) BSE

ébullition [ebylisjɔ̃] *nf* boiling; **arriver à é.** to come to the boil; **amener qch à é.** to bring sth to the boil; *Fig* **en é.** in turmoil

écaille [ekaj] *nf* (*de poisson*) scale; (*de tortue, d'huître*) shell; (*de peinture*) flake; **peigne en é.** tortoiseshell comb; **des lunettes d'é.** *ou* **en é.** tortoiseshell-rimmed glasses

écailler [ekaje] **1** *vt* (**a**) (*poisson*) to scale (**b**) (*huître*) to open
 2 s'écailler *vpr* (*émail*) to chip (off); (*peinture*) to peel (off)

écarlate [ekarlat] *adj* scarlet; *Fig* **devenir é.** to go bright red

écarquiller [ekarkije] *vt* **é. les yeux** to open one's eyes wide

écart [ekar] *nm* (**a**) (*entre deux chiffres*) difference (**entre** between); (*en distance, en temps, dans un classement*) gap (**entre** between); **ils ont trois ans d'é.** there's a three-year gap between them; **é. de niveau** (*dans une classe*) difference in level; **é. de salaires** wage differential (**b**) **faire le grand é.** to do the splits (**c**) (*déviation*) **faire un é.** (*personne*) to jump aside; (*cheval*) to shy; (*voiture*) to swerve; *Fig* **écarts de conduite** misbehaviour; *Fig* **écarts de langage** bad language (**d**) **mettre qn à l'é.** to keep sb out of things; **tenir qn à l'é. de qch** to keep sb out of sth; **se tenir à l'é.** to keep out of things; **un terrain à l'é. de la ville** a piece of land away from the town

écarté, -e [ekarte] *adj (bras, pieds)* apart; *(yeux)* widely spaced; **avoir les dents écartées** to be gap-toothed

écarteler [39] [ekartale] *vt* to quarter; *Fig* **être écartelé (entre)** to be torn (between)

écartement [ekartəmã] *nm (distance)* space, gap

écarter [ekarte] **1** *vt* (a) *(séparer) (doigts, bras, jambes)* to spread; *(rideaux)* to draw (back); *(personnes, objets)* to move apart (b) *(repousser) (objet, branches)* to move aside; *(danger, soupçons)* to avert; **é. qn/qch de** to move sb/sth away from; **é. qn de son chemin** to push sb out of one's way (c) *(exclure) (candidat, proposition)* to turn down

2 s'écarter *vpr* (a) *(se séparer) (personnes)* to move apart; *(foule)* to part; *(routes)* to diverge (b) *(s'éloigner) (piéton)* to move away (**de** from); *(voiture)* to swerve (**de** from); *Fig* **s'é. du sujet** to wander from the subject

ecchymose [ekimoz] *nf* bruise

ecclésiastique [eklezjastik] **1** *adj* ecclesiastical
2 *nm* clergyman

écervelé, -e [eservəle] **1** *adj* scatterbrained
2 *nm,f* scatterbrain

ECG [əseʒe] *nm Méd (abrév* **électrocardiogramme)** ECG

échafaud [eʃafo] *nm* scaffold; *Fig* **monter à l'é.** to go to the scaffold

échafaudage [eʃafodaʒ] *nm* scaffolding; **des échafaudages** scaffolding

échafauder [eʃafode] *vt (empiler)* to pile up; *Fig (système, argumentation)* to put together

échalas [eʃala] *nm Fam* **grand é.** beanpole

échalote [eʃalɔt] *nf* shallot

échancré, -e [eʃɑ̃kre] *adj* low-cut

échancrer [eʃɑ̃kre] *vt* to cut the neckline of

échancrure [eʃɑ̃kryr] *nf (décolleté)* low neckline

échange [eʃɑ̃ʒ] *nm* (a) *(d'objets, de prisonniers, d'idées)* exchange; **voulez-vous (me) faire l'é.?** could you exchange it/them (for me)?; **recevoir/donner qch en é.** (**de** qch) to receive/give sth in exchange (for sth); **de violents échanges** *(physiques)* violent clashes; *(verbaux)* violent exchanges; **échanges culturels** cultural exchanges (b) **échanges commerciaux** trade; **échanges internationaux** international trade (c) *(au tennis)* rally; **faire des échanges** to knock up (d) *Ordinat* **é. de données** data exchange; **é. de données informatisé** electronic data interchange

échanger [45] [eʃɑ̃ʒe] *vt (objets, articles)* to exchange, to swap (**contre** for); *Fig (coups, idées)* to exchange; *(injures)* to trade

échangeur [eʃɑ̃ʒœr] *nm* interchange

échantillon [eʃɑ̃tijɔ̃] *nm* sample; **prélever un é. de qch** to take a sample of sth; **é. gratuit** free sample

échantillonnage [eʃɑ̃tijɔnaʒ] *nm* (a) *(action)* sampling (b) *(échantillons)* selection of samples

échantillonner [eʃɑ̃tijɔne] *vt (pour sondage)* to sample

échappatoire [eʃapatwar] *nf* way out

échappée [eʃape] *nf* (a) *(de coureurs)* breakaway; **être dans l'é.** to be part of the breakaway group (b) *(espace libre)* **une é. sur la mer** a sea view

échappement [eʃapmã] *nm* (a) *(de voiture)* exhaust; **les gaz d'é.** exhaust fumes (b) *Ordinat* escape

échapper [eʃape] **1 échapper à** *vt ind* **é. à qn** *(sujet: personne)* to get away from sb; **é. à qch** *(punition, mort)* to escape sth; *(corvée)* to get out of sth; **son nom m'échappe** her name escapes me; **ça m'échappe** it escapes me; **rien ne lui échappe** he doesn't miss a thing; **la victoire nous a échappé** victory eluded us; **le vase m'a échappé des mains** the vase slipped out of my hands

2 *vi* **laisser é.** *(personne, animal)* to let escape; *(objet)* to drop; *(de l'air)* to let out; *(de la vapeur)* to let off; *(larme)* to let fall; *(secret, soupir, cri)* to let out; *(détail)* to overlook

3 *vt* **il l'a échappé belle** he had a narrow escape

4 s'échapper *vpr* (a) *(s'évader)* to escape (**de** from) (b) *(sortir) (eau, gaz)* to escape (**de** from); **un cri s'échappa de ses lèvres** she let out a cry

écharde [eʃard] *nf* splinter

écharpe [eʃarp] *nf* scarf; **l'é. tricolore** the tricolour sash; **avoir le bras en é.** to have one's arm in a sling

écharper [eʃarpe] *vt Fam* **se faire é.** to get torn to pieces

échasse [eʃas] *nf* (a) *(bâton)* stilt; **être monté sur des échasses** to be on stilts (b) *(oiseau)* stilt

échassier [eʃasje] *nm* wader

échaudé, -e [eʃode] *adj Fig* **être é.** to get one's fingers burnt

échauffement [eʃofmã] *nm* (a) *(d'un moteur)* overheating (b) *(excitation)* overexcitement (c) *(d'athlète)* warm-up

échauffer [eʃofe] **1** *vt* (a) *(moteur)* to overheat (b) *(exciter)* **é. les esprits** to get people worked up; *Fam* **é. les oreilles à qn** to get up sb's nose (c) *(athlète)* to warm up

2 s'échauffer *vpr* (a) *(moteur)* to get overheated (b) *(athlète)* to warm up

échauffourée [eʃofure] *nf* brawl; *Mil* skirmish

échéance [eʃeɑ̃s] *nf (de dette, de facture)* date of payment; **à courte/longue é.** *(prêt)* short-/long-term; **venir à é.** to fall due; **faire face à ses échéances** to meet one's financial obligations; *Fig* **une é. électorale** an election

échéancier [eʃeɑ̃sje] *nm* (a) *(livre)* billbook (b) *(calendrier)* timetable

échéant [eʃeɑ̃] *adj m voir* **cas**

échec [eʃɛk] *nm* (a) *(défaite)* failure; *(revers)* setback; **subir un é.** *(défaite)* to fail; *(revers)* to suffer a setback; *Can* **mettre en é.** *(au hockey)* to check; **faire é. à qch** to foil sth; **faire é. à qn** to frustrate sb; *Fig* **é. scolaire** doing badly at school (b) *(jeu)* **échecs** chess; **é.!** check!; **é. et mat!** checkmate!

échelle [eʃɛl] *nf* (a) *(pour grimper)* ladder; **l'é. des pompiers** the fireman's ladder; *Fig* **l'é. sociale** the social ladder; *Fig* **é. des valeurs** scale of values; **faire la courte é. à qn** to give sb *Br* a leg up *or Am* a boost; **5 sur l'é. de Richter** 5 on the Richter scale (b) *(d'une carte)* scale; **l'é. est de 1/10 000** the scale is 1:10,000; *Fig* **sur une grande é.** on a large scale; **à l'é. nationale** on a national scale; *Ordinat* **intégration à grande/petite é.** large-/small-scale integration (c) *(dans un collant) Br* ladder, *Am* run; **faire une é. à son collant** *Br* to ladder one's tights, *Am* to get a run in one's pantyhose

échelon [eʃlɔ̃] *nm* (a) *(d'une échelle)* rung (b) *(d'une hiérarchie)* grade; **gravir tous les échelons** to climb to the top of the ladder (c) *(niveau)* level; **à l'é. national** on a national level; **à tous les échelons** at every level

échelonnement [eʃlɔnmɑ̃] *nm* (a) *(de paiements)* spreading; *(de vacances)* staggering (b) *(d'objets)* spacing

échelonner [eʃlɔne] **1** *vt* (a) *(paiements)* to spread; *(vacances)* to stagger (b) *(objets)* to space out
2 s'échelonner *vpr* (a) **les paiements s'échelonnent sur deux ans** the payments are spread over two years (b) *(objets)* to be spaced out

écheveau, -x [eʃvo] *nm (de fil)* skein; *Fig* **démêler l'é. d'une affaire compliquée** to untangle a complicated business

échevelé, -e [eʃəvle] *adj (personne)* dishevelled; *Fig (course)* mad

échevin [eʃəvɛ̃] *nm Belg* deputy mayor

échine [eʃin] *nf* (a) *(colonne vertébrale)* spine, backbone (b) *(de porc)* loin

échiner [eʃine] **s'échiner** *vpr* **s'é. à faire qch** to wear oneself out doing sth

échiquier [eʃikje] *nm (d'échecs)* chessboard

écho [eko] *nm* (a) *(bruit)* echo; **il y a de l'é.** there's an echo; *Fig* **trouver un é.** to get a response; *Fig* **se faire l'é. de qch** to echo sth; *Fig* **j'en ai eu de très bons échos** I've had some very good feedback (b) **les échos** *(de journal)* gossip column

échographie [ekografi] *nf* (ultrasound) scan; **passer une é.** to have a scan

échoir [14] [eʃwar] **1** *vi (dette)* to fall due; *(investissement)* to mature
2 échoir à *vt ind* to fall to

échoppe [eʃɔp] *nf* shop

échotier, -ère [ekɔtje, -ɛr] *nm,f* gossip columnist

échouer [eʃwe] **1** *vi* (a) *(navire)* to run aground; *(baleine)* to get stranded; **navire échoué** stranded ship; *Fam* **é. dans un bar** to land up in a bar (b) *(rater) (projet, personne)* to fail; **é. à un examen** to fail an exam; **faire é.** *(projet)* to wreck; *(complot)* to foil
2 *vt (navire)* to beach
3 s'échouer *vpr (navire)* to run aground; *(baleine)* to get stranded

éclabousser [eklabuse] *vt* to splash, to spatter (**avec** with)

éclaboussure [eklabusyr] *nf* splash

éclair [eklɛr] **1** *nm* (a) *(lumière)* flash; *(pendant un orage)* flash of lightning; **éclairs** lightning; **être rapide comme l'é.** to be as quick as a flash; *Fig* **en un é.** in a flash (b) *Fig (de lucidité, de génie)* flash; **lancer des éclairs** *(yeux)* to flash (c) *(gâteau)* éclair
2 *adj inv (visite, attaque)* lightning

éclairage [eklɛraʒ] *nm* lighting; *(par projecteurs)* floodlighting

éclairagiste [eklɛraʒist] *nmf (de cinéma, de théâtre)* lighting technician

éclaircie [eklɛrsi] *nf* sunny spell

éclaircir [eklɛrsir] **1** *vt* (a) *(rendre plus clair) (couleur, cheveux)* to lighten; *(teint)* to clear (b) *(rendre moins épais) (sauce)* to thin (c) *Fig (élucider) (mystère)* to clear up
2 s'éclaircir *vpr* (a) *(temps, ciel)* to clear; *(visage)* to brighten up (b) *(se dissiper) (brouillard)* to clear; *Fig (mystère)* to be cleared up (c) *(cheveux)* to thin (d) **s'é. la voix** to clear one's throat

éclaircissement [eklɛrsismɑ̃] *nm* (a) *(explication)* explanation; **demander (à qn) des éclaircissements sur qch** to ask (sb) for an explanation of sth (b) *(de cheveux)* lightening

éclairé, -e [eklere] *adj* lit; *Fig* enlightened

éclairer [eklere] **1** *vt* (a) *(pièce, vitrine)* to light; **e. qn** to give sb some light; **éclairé au néon** neon-lit; *Fig* **é. qch d'un jour nouveau** to shed *or* throw new light on sth; *Fig* **un sourire éclairait son visage** a smile lit up her face (b) *Fig (informer)* to enlighten; *Fam* **é. la lanterne de qn** *(sur qch)* to put sb in the picture (about sth)
2 *vi* **cette lampe éclaire mal** this lamp doesn't give much light
3 s'éclairer *vpr* (a) *(personne)* **s'é. au pétrole/gaz** to use oil lamps/gaslight; **s'é. à la bougie** to use candles for lighting (b) *(devenir lumineux) (bâtiment, visage)* to light up (c) *Fig* **tout s'éclaire!** everything's becoming clear!

éclaireur, -euse [eklɛrœr, -øz] **1** *nm Mil* scout; *Mil & Fig* **partir en é.** to go off for a scout around
2 *nm,f (boy)* scout, *f (girl)* guide

éclat [ekla] *nm* (a) *(fragment) (de bois, de verre)* splinter; *(de pierre)* chip; **é. d'obus** piece of shrapnel; **des éclats d'obus** shrapnel; **des éclats de verre** *(bris)* broken glass; *(projeté)* flying glass; **voler en éclats** to shatter (b) *(son)* **é. de rire** burst of laughter; **partir d'un grand é. de rire** to burst out laughing; **rire aux éclats** to roar with laughter; **un é. de voix** loud voices (c) *Fig (scandale)* scandal (d) *(du soleil)* glare; *(d'un diamant)* flash; *(de couleurs)* brilliance; **l'é. de ses yeux** the sparkle in his/her eyes; *Fig* **l'é. de la jeunesse** the bloom of youth (e) *(d'une cérémonie, d'une époque)* splendour; **action** *ou* **coup d'é.** brilliant feat

éclatant, -e [eklatɑ̃, -ɑ̃t] *adj* (a) *(lumière, couleur, succès)* brilliant; *(teint)* glowing; *(preuve)* striking; **être é. de santé** to be glowing with health; **être dans une forme éclatante** to be on brilliant form (b) *(son, rire)* loud

éclaté, -e [eklate] *adj (vision)* fragmented

éclatement [eklatmɑ̃] *nm (d'un obus, d'un pneu)* bursting; *(d'un verre)* shattering; *(d'un groupe)* break-up

éclater [eklate] **1** *vi* (a) *(exploser) (obus, pneu, ballon)* to burst; *(verre)* to shatter; *Fig (groupe)* to break up; **faire é. qch** to burst/shatter sth; **faire é. un pétard** to let off a firework (b) *Fig* **é. de rire** to burst out laughing; **é. en sanglots** to burst into tears; **é. en applaudissements** to burst into applause (c) *(se déclencher) (guerre, incendie)* to break out; *(orage, scandale)* to break
2 *vt Fam* **é. la tête à qn** to smash sb's head in
3 s'éclater *vpr Fam* to have a really good time

éclectique [eklektik] *adj* eclectic

éclipse [eklips] *nf (de soleil, de lune)* eclipse

éclipser [eklipse] **1** *vt aussi Fig* to eclipse
2 s'éclipser *vpr Fam (s'esquiver)* to slip away

éclopé, -e [eklɔpe] **1** *adj* lame
2 *nm,f* lame person

éclore [15] [eklɔr] *vi* (a) *(œuf, poussin)* to hatch (b) *(fleur)* to open

éclosion [eklozjɔ̃] *nf* (a) *(d'œuf, de poussin)* hatching (b) *(de fleurs)* opening

écluse [eklyz] *nf* lock; **(porte d')é.** lock gate

éclusier, -ère [eklyzje, -ɛr] *nm,f* lock keeper

écœurant, -e [ekœrɑ̃, -ɑ̃t] *adj* (a) *(nourriture)* nauseating; *Fig (révoltant)* disgusting (b) *Fam (décourageant)* sickening

écœurement [ekœrmɑ̃] *nm (nausée)* nausea; *Fig (indignation)* disgust; **manger qch jusqu'à l'é.** to eat sth until one feels sick (b) *Fam (découragement)* discouragement

écœurer [ekœre] vt (a) é. qn (donner la nausée à) to make sb feel sick; Fig (indigner) to disgust sb (b) Fam (décourager) to sicken

école [ekɔl] nf (a) (établissement, enseignement) school; être à l'é. to be at school; aller à l'é. to go to school; reprendre l'é. to go back to school; faire l'é. buissonnière to play Br truant or Am hookey; Fig être à bonne é. to be in good hands; Fam je n'ai pas é. aujourd'hui I don't have any classes today; les grandes écoles = university-level colleges specializing in professional training; É. des beaux-arts = art school in Paris; é. de commerce business school; é. de conduite driving school; é. de danse dancing school; é. de dessin art school; é. hôtelière hotel school; é. libre independent or private school; é. maternelle nursery school; é. militaire military academy; é. de musique music school; É. nationale d'administration = university-level college preparing students for senior posts in law and economics; Anciennement É. normale teacher training college; É. normale supérieure = university-level college preparing students for senior posts in teaching; é. primaire (bâtiment) primary school; (enseignement) primary education; é. privée private school; é. publique Br state or Am public school (b) (de pensée, d'art) school; faire é. to win a following

écolier, -ère [ekɔlje, -er] nm,f schoolchild, schoolboy, f schoolgirl (at primary school)

écolo [ekɔlo] adj & nmf Fam green

écologie [ekɔlɔʒi] nf ecology

écologique [ekɔlɔʒik] adj ecological

écologiste [ekɔlɔʒist] adj & nmf environmentalist

écomusée [ekɔmyze] nm living museum (showing man in his natural and social environment)

éconduire [18] [ekɔ̃dɥir] vt (a) (congédier) to dismiss (b) (refuser) (prétendant) to reject

économat [ekɔnɔma] nm (a) (fonction) bursarship (b) (bureau) bursar's office

économe [ekɔnɔm] 1 adj economical, thrifty
2 nmf (de collège) bursar
3 nm (couteau) é. potato peeler

économie [ekɔnɔmi] nf (a) (système) economy; é. dirigée planned economy; é. libérale open market economy; é. de marché market economy (b) (gain) saving; (vertu) economy, thrift; avoir le sens de l'é. to be thrifty; faire une é. de temps/de 20% to save time/20%; faire l'é. d'un coup de fil to save oneself a phone call (c) économies savings; faire des économies to save money; faire des économies de chauffage to save money on heating; faire des économies d'énergie to save energy; prendre sur ses économies to dip into one's savings; il n'y a pas de petites économies every little helps

économique [ekɔnɔmik] adj (a) (relatif à l'économie) economic (b) (avantageux) economical

économiser [ekɔnɔmize] vt (argent, temps, énergie) to save; (électricité, nourriture) to economize on, to save on; é. ses forces to conserve one's strength; é. sa salive to save one's breath; é. pour ses vacances to save up for one's holidays

économiste [ekɔnɔmist] nmf economist

écoper [ekɔpe] 1 vt (barque) to bale (out); nous avons dû é. we had to bale out
2 écoper de vt ind Fam (être puni) é. d'une amende/de cinq ans de prison to get a fine/five years in prison; c'est encore moi qui vais é. I'm going to get the blame again

écorce [ekɔrs] nf (a) (d'arbre) bark; (d'orange) peel (b) é. terrestre the earth's crust

écorché, -e [ekɔrʃe] 1 nm anatomical model
2 nm,f Fig é. (vif) tortured soul

écorcher [ekɔrʃe] 1 vt (a) (animal) to skin; (criminel) to flay (b) (énafler) to graze; Fig (nom) to mispronounce; Fig é. les oreilles à qn to grate on sb's ears
2 s'écorcher vpr to graze oneself; s'é. le genou to graze one's knee

écorchure [ekɔrʃyr] nf graze

écorner [ekɔrne] vt (meuble) to damage the corner(s) of; (livre) to dog-ear

écossais, -e [ekɔse, -ez] 1 adj Scottish; (whisky) Scotch; une jupe écossaise a tartan skirt
2 nm,f É. Scot
3 nm (tissu) tartan

Écosse [ekɔs] nf l'É. Scotland

écosser [ekɔse] vt to shell

écosystème [ekɔsistem] nm ecosystem

écot [eko] nm payer son é. to pay one's share

écoulement [ekulmɑ̃] nm (a) (de liquide) flow (b) (de blessure) discharge (c) (de marchandises) sale (d) (du temps) passage

écouler [ekule] 1 vt (marchandises, faux billets) to dispose of
2 s'écouler vpr (a) (liquide) to flow out, to run out (de of) (b) (marchandises) to sell (c) (temps) to pass

écourter [ekurte] vt (robe, texte) to shorten; (visite, discours) to cut short

écoute [ekut] nf (a) (d'une radio) être à l'é. (de) to be listening in (to); rester à l'é. to stay tuned; heure de grande é. Rad peak listening time; TV peak viewing time; indice d'é. ratings; écoutes téléphoniques telephone tapping (b) être à l'é. des autres to be willing to lend a sympathetic ear

écouter [ekute] 1 vt (a) (entendre) to listen to; é. qn jusqu'au bout to hear sb out; savoir é. to be a good listener; é. aux portes to listen at doors; faire é. qch à qn to play sb sth; écoutez! listen! (b) (suivre) (personne) to listen to; é. sa conscience to listen to one's conscience
2 s'écouter vpr il s'écoute trop he coddles himself; si je m'écoutais if I did what I wanted; s'é. parler to like the sound of one's own voice

écouteur [ekutœr] nm (du téléphone) earpiece; écouteurs (casque) headphones

écoutille [ekutij] nf Naut hatchway

écouvillon [ekuvijɔ̃] nm (pour bouteille, biberon) bottle brush

écrabouiller [ekrabuje] vt Fam to squash, to crush; se faire é. par une voiture to get flattened by a car

écran [ekrɑ̃] nm (a) (de télévision, de cinéma) screen; porter une pièce à l'é. to adapt a play for the screen; prochainement sur vos écrans coming soon to a cinema near you; le grand/petit é. the big/small screen; é. panoramique wide screen; é. plat flat screen (b) Ordinat screen, display; à l'é. on screen; é. d'accueil logo screen; é. d'aide help screen; é. couleur colour screen or display; é. à cristaux liquides liquid crystal screen; **é. à fenêtres** split screen; **é. monochrome** monochrome screen; **é. rétro-éclairé** back-lit screen; **é. tactile** touch-sensitive screen **(c)** *(pour protéger)* screen; **on ne peut pas voir le lac car les arbres font é.** you can't see the lake because it's screened by the trees; **é. de fumée** smoke screen; **é. total** sun block

écrasant, -e [ekrazɑ̃, -ɑ̃t] *adj (poids, défaite, responsabilité)* crushing; *(majorité, victoire)* overwhelming

écrasé, -e [ekraze] *adj (nez)* flat

écraser [ekraze] **1** *vt (fruit, ail, membre)* to crush; *(insecte)* to squash; *(cigarette)* to stub out; *(piéton, chien)* to run over; **se faire é.** *(par une voiture)* to get run over; *Fam* **é. l'accélérateur** *ou* **le champignon** to put one's foot down **(b)** *(vaincre) (adversaire, troupes)* to crush **(c)** *Fam* **en é.** to sleep like a log **(d)** *très Fam* **écrase!** shut it!
2 s'écraser *vpr (a)* (avion) to crash **(b)** *Fam (ne rien dire)* to keep quiet

écrémage [ekremaʒ] *nm (sélection)* creaming off

écrémer [34] [ekreme] *vt (lait)* to skim; *Fig (sélectionner)* to cream off the best of

écrevisse [ekravis] *nf* crayfish

écrier [66] [ekrije] **s'écrier** *vpr* to cry out, to exclaim

écrin [ekrɛ̃] *nm (jewel)* case

écrire [30] [ekrir] **1** *vt (lettre, livre, chanson)* to write; *(noter)* to write down; **é. à qn** to write to sb; **é. un mot à qn** to drop sb a line; **je leur ai écrit de venir** I've written asking them to come; **il écrit bien** his handwriting is good; *(écrivain)* he writes well; **ce stylo écrit très bien** this pen writes very well
2 s'écrire *vpr (a)* (s'orthographier) to be spelt; **comment ça s'écrit?** how do you spell it? **(b)** *(correspondre)* to write to each other

écrit [ekri] *nm (a)* **mettre qch par é.** to put sth down in writing **(b)** *(texte)* (written) document; **écrits** *(œuvre)* writings **(c)** *(examen)* written examination

écriteau, -x [ekrito] *nm* notice

écritoire [ekritwar] *nf* writing case

écriture [ekrityr] *nf (a)* (système, caractères) writing; *Ordinat* write **(b)** *(façon d'écrire)* (hand)writing; **elle a une belle é.** she has good handwriting **(c)** *(littérature)* writing; *TV & Cin* **é. de scénarios** scriptwriting **(d)** **écritures** *(comptabilité)* accounts; **tenir les écritures** to keep the accounts **(e)** *Rel* **l'É. sainte, les saintes Écritures** the Scriptures

écrivain [ekrivɛ̃] *nm* writer; **é. public** (public) letter writer

écrivais *etc ou* **écrire**

écrou [ekru] *nm (de boulon)* nut

écrouer [ekrue] *vt Jur* to imprison

écroulé, -e [ekrule] *adj Fam* **é. (de rire)** doubled up with laughter

écroulement [ekrulmɑ̃] *nm* collapse

écrouler [ekrule] **s'écrouler** *vpr (bâtiment, prix, empire)* to collapse; *(espoirs)* to crumble away; **s'é. sur une chaise** to flop onto a chair; **s'é. de fatigue** to collapse with exhaustion

écru [ekry] *adj (beige)* ecru; *(naturel)* unbleached

ecstasy [ekstazi] *nf* ecstasy

ECU, ÉCU [eky] *nm (abrév **European Currency Unit**)* ECU

écu [eky] *nm (a)* Hist crown **(b)** *(bouclier)* shield

écueil [ekœj] *nm (rocher)* reef; *Fig (danger)* pitfall

écuelle [ekɥɛl] *nf* bowl

éculé, -e [ekyle] *adj (chaussure)* down-at-heel; *Fig (plaisanterie, argument)* hackneyed

écume [ekym] *nf (bave, sur la mer)* foam; *(sur la soupe, la confiture)* scum; **avoir l'é. à la bouche** to be foaming at the mouth; **é. (de mer)** *(magnésite)* meerschaum

écumer [ekyme] **1** *vt (a)* (soupe, confiture) to skim **(b)** *(piller)* to plunder; *Fig (parcourir)* to scour; **é. les mers** *(pirates)* to scour the seas
2 *vi* **é. (de rage)** to foam (with rage)

écumoire [ekymwar] *nf* skimmer; *Fig* **troué comme une é.** riddled with holes

écureuil [ekyrœj] *nm* squirrel

écurie [ekyri] *nf* stable; **é. (de courses)** *(de chevaux, de voitures)* (racing) stable

écusson [ekysɔ̃] *nm (a)* (armoiries) escutcheon **(b)** *(de tissu)* badge

écuyer, -ère [ekɥije, -er] **1** *nm Hist (gentilhomme)* squire
2 *nm,f* rider; **é. de cirque** circus rider

eczéma [egzema] *nm* eczema; **avoir** *ou* **faire de l'é.** to have eczema

édam [edam] *nm* Edam

edelweiss [edɛlves] *nm* edelweiss

Éden [edɛn] *nm* **l'É.** Eden; *Fig* **un é.** a paradise

édenté, -e [edɑ̃te] *adj* toothless

EDF [ødeɛf] *nf (abrév **Électricité de France**)* French electricity company

EDI [ødei] *nm Ordinat (abrév **échange de données informatisé**)* EDI

édifiant, -e [edifjɑ̃, -ɑ̃t] *adj* edifying

édification [edifikasjɔ̃] *nf (a)* (d'un monument) erection; *Fig (d'un empire, d'une fortune)* building up **(b)** *(instruction morale)* edification

édifice [edifis] *nm* building; *Fig* **apporter sa pierre à l'é.** to make a contribution; *Fig* **l'é. social** the social fabric

édifier [66] [edifje] *vt (a)* (monument) to erect; *Fig (empire, fortune)* to build up **(b)** *(instruire)* to edify

Édimbourg [edɛ̃bur] *n* Edinburgh

édimbourgeois, -e [edɛ̃burʒwa, -az] **1** *adj* of Edinburgh
2 *nm,f* **É.** person from Edinburgh

édit [edi] *nm Hist* edict

éditer [edite] *vt (a)* (publier) to publish **(b)** *(commenter) (texte)* to edit **(c)** *Ordinat* to edit; **pouvant être édité** editable

éditeur, -trice [editær, -tris] **1** *nm,f (a)* (d'une maison d'édition) publisher **(b)** *(commentateur)* editor
2 *nm Ordinat (de programme)* editor; **é. d'icônes** icon editor; **é. de logiciel** software company; **é. de texte** text editor

édition [edisjɔ̃] *nf (a)* (activité) publishing **(b)** *(texte, exemplaire)* edition; *Hum* **où est le sucre? – dans le placard, troisième é.!** where's the sugar? - for the third time, it's in the cupboard!; **é. originale** first edition **(c)** *(d'un journal)* edition; **dernière é.** final edition; **é. spéciale** special edition **(d)** *Ordinat* editing; **é. de liens** linking; **é. pleine page** full page editing; **é. électronique** electronic publishing

édito [edito] *nm Fam* editorial, *Br* leader

éditorial, -e, -aux, -ales [editɔrjal, -o] **1** *adj* editorial
2 *nm* editorial, *Br* leader

éditorialiste [editɔrjalist] *nmf* editorial writer, *Br* leader writer

édredon [edredɔ̃] *nm* eiderdown

éducateur, -trice [edykatœr, -tris] *nm,f* teacher; **é. spécialisé** special needs teacher

éducatif, -ive [edykatif, -iv] *adj* educational

éducation [edykasjɔ̃] *nf* (a) *(enseignement)* education; *(par les parents)* upbringing; **faire l'é. de qn** to educate sb; **é. manuelle et technique** handicraft classes; **l'É. nationale** the Department of Education; **é. physique** physical training *or* education; **é. religieuse** religious instruction; **é. sexuelle** sex education (b) *(savoir-vivre)* good manners; **avoir de l'é.** to have good manners; **manquer d'é.** to have no manners (c) *Fig (des réflexes, du goût)* training

édulcorant, -e [edylkɔrɑ̃, -ɑ̃t] 1 *adj* sweetening
2 *nm* sweetener; **é. de synthèse** artificial sweetener

édulcorer [edylkɔre] *vt (discours, compte rendu)* to water down; *(roman pornographique)* to tone down

éduquer [edyke] *vt* (a) *(donner un enseignement à)* (enfant, peuple) to educate; *(élever)* to bring up; **mal éduqué** ill-mannered (b) *Fig (réflexes, goût)* to train

EEG *(abrév* **électroencéphalogramme)** EEG

effaçable [efasabl] *adj* erasable

effacé, -e [efase] *adj* (a) *(personne, manières)* self-effacing (b) *(menton)* receding

effacement [efasmɑ̃] *nm* (a) *(d'un mot, d'un message, d'une bande)* erasing; *Ordinat* deletion; *(d'une tache)* removal; *(par le temps)* *(d'une inscription)* wearing away; *(des souvenirs)* fading (b) *(d'une personne)* self-effacement

effacer [efase] 1 *vt* (a) *(mot, enregistrement, bande)* to erase; *(tableau)* to clean; *Ordinat (données)* to erase, to delete; *(écran)* to clear; *(tache, traces)* to remove; *(sujet: temps)* *(inscription)* to wear away (b) *Fig* **e. qch de sa mémoire** to erase sth from one's memory; **on efface tout et on recommence** we'll wipe the slate clean and make a fresh start
2 **s'effacer** *vpr* (a) *(disparaître)* *(inscription)* to wear away; *Fig (sentiment, souvenir)* to fade (away) (b) *(s'écarter)* to move aside; *Fig (se faire discret)* to keep in the background

effaceur [efasœr] *nm* **e. (d'encre)** ink eraser

effarant, -e [efarɑ̃, -ɑ̃t] *adj* astounding

effaré, -e [efare] *adj* astounded

effarement [efarmɑ̃] *nm* astonishment

effarer [efare] *vt* to astound

effaroucher [efaruʃe] 1 *vt* (a) *(effrayer)* to scare; *(faire reculer)* to scare away (b) *(choquer)* to shock
2 **s'effaroucher** *vpr* (a) *(s'effrayer)* to take fright (**de** at) (b) *(s'offusquer)* to be shocked (**de** by)

effectif, -ive [efɛktif, -iv] 1 *adj* (*réel)* effective
2 *nm* *(employés)* staff; *(d'un club, d'un bataillon)* strength; *(d'une classe)* size

effectivement [efɛktivmɑ̃] *adv* (a) *(en effet)* actually; **c'est pratique, hein? – e.!** it's practical, isn't it? – yes it is! (b) *(réellement, de manière effective)* actually

effectuer [efɛktɥe] 1 *vt* *(mouvement, opération)* to perform; *(paiement, parcours, calcul, réservation)* to make; *(démarches)* to take; *(commande)* to place
2 **s'effectuer** *vpr* *(mouvement, opération)* to be performed; *(paiement, parcours)* to be made

efféminé, -e [efemine] *adj* effeminate

effervescence [efɛrvesɑ̃s] *nf* excitement; **être en e.** *(ville, bureau)* to be buzzing with excitement

effervescent, -e [efɛrvesɑ̃, -ɑ̃t] *adj (médicament)* effervescent

effet [efɛ] *nm* (a) *(résultat, conséquence)* effect (**sur** on); **avoir pour e. de faire qch** to have the effect of doing sth; **faire e.** to take effect; **à cet e.** with that in mind; **rester** *ou* **demeurer sans e.** to have no effect; **sous l'e. de l'alcool/la drogue** under the influence of alcohol/drugs; **les feuilles sont tombées sous l'e. de la chaleur** the heat caused the leaves to drop off; **e. pervers** undesired effect; *Méd* side effect; **e. de serre** greenhouse effect; **e. secondaire** side effect; *Ordinat* **e. de transition** melt
(b) *(impression)* impression; **quel e. ça te fait qu'elle revienne?** how do you feel about her coming back?; **ne faire aucun e. à qn** to make no impression on sb; **elle me fait l'e. d'une fille plutôt équilibrée** she strikes me as being a fairly well-balanced girl; **il me fait de l'e.** he does something for me; **faire un drôle d'e. à qn** to give sb a funny feeling; **faire bon/mauvais e. (à qn)** to make a good/bad impression (on sb)
(c) *(but recherché)* **manquer son e.** *(plaisanterie)* to fall flat; **faire des effets de voix** to make striking use of one's voice; *Cin* **effets spéciaux** special effects; **e. de style** stylistic effect
(d) *(application)* **prendre e.** to take effect
(e) *(au tennis)* spin; **donner de l'e. à une balle** to put spin on a ball
(f) *Fin* bill; **e. de commerce** bill of exchange
(g) **effets (personnels)** *(affaires)* belongings
(h) **en e., je m'en souviens** yes, I do remember; **en e., c'est ce que je me suis dit** that's just what I thought; **mais c'est monstrueux! – en e.!** it's abominable! – isn't it just!; **j'ai dû partir, e. en. j'étais pressé** I had to leave because I was in a hurry

effeuiller [efœje] *vt (fleur)* to pull the petals off; *(sujet: vent)* *(arbre)* to blow the leaves off; *Fig* **e. la marguerite** to play "he/she loves me, he/she loves me not"

efficace [efikas] *adj (méthode, remède)* effective; *(personne)* efficient

efficacement [efikasmɑ̃] *adv (avec succès)* effectively; *(de façon productive)* efficiently

efficacité [efikasite] *nf (d'une méthode, d'un remède)* effectiveness; *(d'une personne)* efficiency

effigie [efiʒi] *nf* effigy; **à l'e. de qn** bearing the image of sb

effilé, -e [efile] *adj (frange)* ragged; *(doigts)* tapering; *(outil, lame)* tapered; *(amandes)* slivered

effilocher [efilɔʃe] **s'effilocher** *vpr* to fray

efflanqué, -e [eflɑ̃ke] *adj* skinny

effleurement [eflœrmɑ̃] *nm* light touch

effleurer [eflœre] *vt (frôler)* to touch lightly; *(accidentellement)* to brush (against); *(surface de l'eau)* to skim; *Fig (sujet)* to touch on; **cette idée ne m'a jamais effleuré** the idea never crossed my mind

effluent [eflyɑ̃] *nm* **e. urbain** (sewage) effluent; **effluents radioactifs** radioactive waste

effluve [eflyv] *nm* emanation

effondré, -e [efɔ̃dre] *adj (peiné)* grief-stricken; *(déçu)* shattered

effondrement [efɔ̃drəmɑ̃] *nm (d'un bâtiment, d'un mur, d'un toit)* collapse; *Fig (d'un plan)* falling through; *(d'un empire, des prix)* collapse; *(d'une personne)* dejection

effondrer [efɔ̃dre] **s'effondrer** *vpr (bâtiment, mur, toit)* to collapse; *Fig (plan)* to fall through; *(empire, prix)* to collapse; *(personne)* to go to pieces

efforcer [16] [eforse] **s'efforcer** *vpr* **s'e. de faire qch** to do one's best to do sth

effort [efor] *nm* (a) *(physique, intellectuel)* effort; **allons, encore un (petit) e.** come on, try again; **son médecin lui a interdit tout e.** her doctor has forbidden any exertion; **sans e.** effortlessly; **faire un e. (pour faire qch)** to make an effort (to do sth); **faire des efforts to** make an effort; **faire l'e. de faire qch** to make the effort to do sth; **après l'e., le réconfort** I/you/*etc* deserve this; **il est partisan du moindre e.** he doesn't believe in exerting himself (b) *Tech* strain, stress

effraction [efraksjɔ̃] *nf Jur* breaking and entering; **entrer par e.** to break in

effraie [efre] *nf (oiseau)* barn owl

effranger [45] [efrãʒe] **1** *vt* to fray
2 s'effranger *vpr* to fray

effrayant, -e [efrejã, -ãt] *adj* frightening; *(chaleur, appétit)* tremendous

effrayer [53] [efreje] **1** *vt (faire peur à)* to frighten, to scare; *(inquiéter)* to alarm
2 s'effrayer *vpr* to be frightened (**de** at); **elle s'effraie pour un rien** the least little thing frightens her

effréné, -e [efrene] *adj (passion, luxe)* unbridled; *(galop, course)* frantic

effritement [efritmã] *nm (d'un mur, d'un revêtement)* crumbling; *(de la roche)* weathering; *Fig (de l'autorité, d'une majorité, de fonds)* erosion

effriter [efrite] **1** *vt (pain, fromage)* to crumble; *(roche)* to weather
2 s'effriter *vpr (mur, revêtement)* to crumble; *(roche)* to weather; *Fig (autorité, majorité, fonds)* to be eroded

effroi [efrwa] *nm Litt* dread

effronté, -e [efrɔ̃te] *adj (personne, manières)* impudent; *(mensonge, menteur)* brazen

effrontément [efrɔ̃temã] *adv* impudently; *(mentir)* brazenly

effronterie [efrɔ̃tri] *nf (d'une personne, de manières)* impudence; *(d'un mensonge)* brazenness

effroyable [efrwajabl] *adj* dreadful

effroyablement [efrwajabləmã] *adv* dreadfully

effusion [efyzjɔ̃] *nf* (a) **e. de sang** bloodshed (b) *(exubérance)* effusiveness; **avec e.** effusively

égailler [egaje] **s'égailler** *vpr* to disperse

égal, -e, -aux, -ales [egal, -o] **1** *adj* (a) *(équivalent)* equal (**à** to); **la partie n'est pas égale** they/we/you are not evenly matched; **ils sont de force/d'intelligence égale** they are equally strong/intelligent; **à surface égale, je préfère mon appartement au leur** square foot for square foot, I prefer my flat to theirs (b) *(constant)* *(respiration, son)* even; *(allure, pouls)* steady; *(sol)* level; *(climat)* equable; **être d'humeur égale** to be even-tempered; **rester é. à soi-même** to be still one's old self (c) **cela m'est é.** it's all the same to me; *(cela ne m'intéresse pas)* I don't care
2 *nmf,* equal; **être l'é. de qn** to be sb's equal; **traiter qn d'é. à é.** to treat sb as an equal; **sans é.** unequalled

également [egalmã] *adv (aussi)* as well, too

égaler [egale] *vt (personne, score, record)* to equal; **deux et deux égalent quatre** two and two equal four

égalisation [egalizasjɔ̃] *nf* (a) *(équilibrage)* equalization; *Sp* **(but/point d')é.** equalizer (b) *(d'une surface)* levelling

égaliser [egalize] **1** *vt (salaires, pression)* to equalize; *(cheveux)* to trim (b) *(sol)* to level
2 *vi Sp* to equalize

égalitaire [egaliter] *adj* egalitarian

égalité [egalite] *nf* (a) *(entre des quantités, des personnes)* equality; *(au tennis)* deuce; **être à é.** *(équipes)* to be level; **é. des chances** equal opportunities; **é. des salaires** equal pay (b) *(constance)* (de la respiration, d'un son) evenness; *(de l'allure, du pouls)* steadiness; *(du sol)* levelness; *(du climat)* equability; **é. d'humeur** even-temperedness

égard [egar] *nm* (a) *(respect)* consideration; **par é. pour qn** out of consideration for sb; **égards** *(attentions)* consideration (b) *(aspect)* à **cet é.,...** in this respect,...; **je n'ai pas d'opinion à cet é.** I've no opinion on that score; **à certains/tous les égards** in some/all respects (c) *(locutions)* **à l'é. de qn** towards sb; **eu é. à** considering

égaré, -e [egare] *adj* (a) *(personne, animal)* lost (b) *(hagard)* (air, regard) distraught

égarement [egarmã] *nm (folie)* distraction (b) **égarements** *(dérèglements de conduite)* wild behaviour

égarer [egare] **1** *vt (objet)* to mislay; *(personne)* *(volontairement)* to mislead; *(soupçons)* to avert
2 s'égarer *vpr* (a) *(se perdre)* (personne, lettre) to get lost (b) *(sortir du sujet)* to wander from the point

égayer [53] [egeje] **1** *vt (personne)* to cheer up; *(conversation)* to liven up; *(pièce, vêtement)* to brighten up
2 s'égayer *vpr (s'animer)* to cheer up

Égée [eʒe] *n voir* **mer**

égérie [eʒeri] *nf* muse

égide [eʒid] *nf* **sous l'é. de** under the aegis of

églantier [eglãtje] *nm* wild rose (bush)

églantine [eglãtin] *nf* wild rose

églefin [egləfɛ̃] *nm* haddock

église [egliz] *nf* (a) *(bâtiment)* church; **aller à l'é.** *(à la messe)* to go to church; **se marier à l'é.** to get married in church, to have a church wedding (b) **l'É.** the Church; **l'É. catholique** the Catholic Church; **l'É. anglicane** the Church of England, the Anglican Church

ego [ego] *nm inv* ego

égocentrique [egosãtrik] **1** *adj* self-centred, egocentric
2 *nmf* self-centred person

égoïsme [egoism] *nm* selfishness, egoism

égoïste [egoist] **1** *adj* selfish, egoistic
2 *nmf* selfish person, egoist

égorger [45] [egorʒe] *vt* to cut the throat of

égosiller [egozije] **s'égosiller** *vpr (en parlant)* to shout oneself hoarse; *(en chantant)* to sing at the top of one's voice

égout [egu] *nm* sewer

égoutier [egutje] *nm* sewerman

égoutter [egute] **1** *vt* to drain
2 *vi* **laisser é. qch** to leave sth to drain
3 s'égoutter *vpr* to drain

égouttoir [egutwar] *nm* (a) *(dans l'évier)* draining board; *(mobile)* drainer (b) *(passoire)* colander

égratigner [egratiɲe] **1** *vt* to scratch; *Fig* to have a dig at
2 s'égratigner *vpr* to scratch oneself; **s'é. la joue** to scratch one's cheek

égratignure [egratiɲyr] *nf* scratch; *Fig* dig

égrener [46] [egrəne] vt (a) (maïs, pois) to shell; (grappe) to pick the grapes off (b) Fig é. son chapelet to tell one's beads

égrillard, -e [egrijar, -ard] adj bawdy

Égypte [eʒipt] nf l'É. Egypt

égyptien, -enne [eʒipsjɛ̃, -ɛn] 1 adj Egyptian 2 nm,f É. Egyptian

eh [e] exclam hey!; **eh bien** well; **eh oui!** that's right!

éhonté, -e [eɔ̃te] adj shameless

éjaculation [eʒakylasjɔ̃] nf ejaculation; **é. précoce** premature ejaculation

éjaculer [eʒakyle] vi to ejaculate

éjectable [eʒɛktabl] adj **siège é.** ejector seat

éjecter [eʒɛkte] vt (cartouche, pilote) to eject; Fam (expulser) to throw out (de of)

éjection [eʒɛksjɔ̃] nf (d'une cartouche, du pilote) ejection; Fam (expulsion) throwing out

élaboration [elaborasjɔ̃] nf (d'un plan, d'une idée) development; (d'une constitution, d'une loi) drawing up

élaboré, -e [elabore] adj (technique, machine) sophisticated; (plan) elaborate

élaborer [elabore] vt (plan, idée) to develop; (constitution, loi) to draw up

élagage [elagaʒ] nm aussi Fig pruning

élaguer [elage] vt aussi Fig to prune

élan¹ [elɑ̃] nm (a) (course) run-up; (vitesse) momentum; Fig (impulsion) boost; **prendre de l'é.** ou **son é.** to take a run-up; **saut sans/avec é.** standing/running jump; Fig **d'un seul é.** all in one go; Fig **emporté par son é.** carried away (b) (transport) (d'enthousiasme) burst; (de tendresse, de passion) surge (c) (ferveur) fervour

élan² nm (cerf) elk

élancé, -e [elɑ̃se] adj slim, slender

élancement [elɑ̃smɑ̃] nm (douleur) shooting pain

élancer [16] [elɑ̃se] 1 vi **la jambe m'élance** I've got shooting pains in my leg 2 **s'élancer** vpr (se précipiter) to rush forward; Sp to take a run-up

élargir [elarʒir] 1 vt (a) (route, rue) to widen; (vêtement) to let out; (trou) to enlarge (b) Fig (groupe, gamme de produits) to expand; (connaissances, débat) to broaden (c) Jur (prisonnier) to release 2 vi Fam (personne) to get bigger 3 **s'élargir** vpr (a) (route, rue) to widen; (chaussures, vêtement) to stretch; (trou) to enlarge (b) Fig (groupe, gamme de produits) to expand; (connaissances, débat) to broaden

élargissement [elarʒismɑ̃] nm (a) (d'une route, d'une rue) widening; (d'un trou) enlargement (b) Fig (d'un groupe, d'une gamme de produits) expansion; (des connaissances, d'un débat) broadening (c) Jur (d'un prisonnier) release

élastique [elastik] 1 adj (corps, matière) elastic; Fig (démarche) springy; (règlement, principes) flexible; (conscience) accommodating 2 nm (a) (pour la couture) elastic (b) (de bureau) elastic or rubber band (c) (jeu) **jouer à l'é.** to play elastics

électeur, -trice [elɛktœr, -tris] nm,f voter, elector; **mes électeurs** the people who voted for me

élection [elɛksjɔ̃] nf (a) (d'un candidat) election; **élections législatives** general election; **élections municipales** local elections; **é. présidentielle, élections présidentielles** presidential election (b) (choix) **mon pays d'é.** my adopted country

électoral, -e, -aux, -ales [elɛktɔral, -o] adj (campagne, comité, promesses) election

électorat [elɛktɔra] nm voters, electorate; **l'é. communiste/féminin** communist/female voters

électricien, -enne [elɛktrisjɛ̃, -ɛn] nm,f electrician

électricité [elɛktrisite] nf electricity; (installation) wiring; Fig **il y a de l'é. dans l'air** the atmosphere is electric; **é. statique** static (electricity)

électrifier [66] [elɛktrifje] vt (chemin de fer) to electrify; (village) to bring electricity to

électrique [elɛktrik] adj aussi Fig electric

électrisant, -e [elɛktrizɑ̃, -ɑ̃t] adj (exaltant) electrifying

électriser [elɛktrize] vt aussi Fig to electrify

électroaimant [elɛktroɛmɑ̃] nm electromagnet

électrocardiogramme [elɛktrokardjɔgram] nm electrocardiogram

électrochoc [elɛktroʃɔk] nm electric shock; **traitement par électrochocs** electric shock treatment; **faire des électrochocs à qn** to give sb electric shock treatment

électrocuter [elɛktrokyte] 1 vt to electrocute; **se faire é.** to be electrocuted 2 **s'électrocuter** vpr to electrocute oneself

électrocution [elɛktrokysjɔ̃] nf electrocution

électrode [elɛktrɔd] nf electrode

électroencéphalogramme [elɛktroɑ̃sefalɔgram] nm electroencephalogram

électrogène [elɛktroʒɛn] adj **groupe é.** generating unit

électrolyse [elɛktroliz] nf electrolysis

électroménager [elɛktromenaʒe] 1 adj m **appareils électroménagers** household appliances 2 nm household appliances

électron [elɛktrɔ̃] nm electron

électronicien, -enne [elɛktrɔnisjɛ̃, -ɛn] nm,f electronics engineer

électronique [elɛktrɔnik] 1 adj (composant, jeu) electronic; (microscope, télescope) electron; (industrie) electronics 2 nf electronics (singulier)

électrophone [elɛktrofɔn] nm record player

élégamment [elegamɑ̃] adv (vêtu, maquillée) elegantly, smartly

élégance [elegɑ̃s] nf (d'une personne, d'un restaurant, d'un style) elegance, smartness; (d'un geste, d'un comportement) courtesy; (d'une méthode, d'une solution) neatness; **habillé avec é.** elegantly or smartly dressed; **savoir perdre avec é.** to be a good loser

élégant, -e [elegɑ̃, -ɑ̃t] adj (vêtements, restaurant, style) elegant, smart; (geste, comportement) courteous; (méthode, solution) neat; **un procédé peu é.** callous behaviour

élégie [eleʒi] nf elegy

élément [elemɑ̃] nm (a) (partie) (d'une structure, d'un problème) element; (meuble) unit; Ordinat **é. de menu** menu item (b) (personne) element; **j'ai de bons éléments dans ma classe** I've got some good pupils in my class (c) (naturel) element; **les quatre éléments** the four elements; Fig **être dans son é.** to be in one's element (d) Chim element (e) (d'une batterie, d'un accumulateur) cell

élémentaire [elemɑ̃ter] *adj* **(a)** *(de base)* *(connaissance, cours, problème)* elementary; *(minimal)* *(habitation)* basic; **c'est é.!** *(évident)* it's elementary! **(b)** *Chim & Phys* elementary

éléphant [elefɑ̃] *nm* elephant; **é. mâle/femelle** bull/cow elephant; **é. de mer** sea elephant; **é. d'Afrique/d'Asie** African/Indian elephant

éléphanteau, -x [elefɑ̃to] *nm* baby elephant

élevage [elvaʒ] *nm* **(a)** *(production)* breeding; *(d'abeilles, de volaille)* keeping; **faire de l'é.** *(de bétail)* to breed cattle; **é. intensif/en batterie** intensive/battery farming **(b)** *(ferme)* cattle farm

élévateur, -trice [elevatœr, -tris] **1** *adj* **chariot é.** fork-lift truck
  2 *nm (appareil)* elevator

élévation [elevasjɔ̃] *nf* **(a)** *(action d'élever)* *(du niveau d'eau, de la voix, des prix, de la température)* raising; *(d'une statue)* erection; *Rel (de l'hostie)* elevation **(b)** *(dans l'air)* rising (up) **(c)** *(augmentation)* rise (**de** in) **(d)** *Litt (des sentiments)* nobility **(f)** *Archit (projection)* elevation **(f)** *(relief)* rise

élevé, -e [elve] *adj* **(a)** *(haut, important)* high; *(rythme, pouls)* rapid; *Fig (style, esprit)* elevated **(b)** *(éduqué)* **bien/mal é.** well-/ill-mannered; **c'est très mal é. de parler la bouche pleine** it's very bad manners to speak with your mouth full

élève [elev] *nmf* student, pupil; **é. infirmière** student nurse; *Mil* **é. officier** cadet

élever¹ [46] [elve] *vt* **(a)** *(éduquer)* to bring up, to raise; **bébé élevé au sein/au biberon** breast-/bottle-fed baby **(b)** *(faire l'élevage de)* to breed; *(abeilles, volaille)* to keep

élever² **1** *vt* **(a)** *(faire monter)* *(niveau d'eau, voix, prix, température)* to raise; **é. un nombre au carré/au cube** to square/cube a number; **é. un nombre à la puissance 4** to raise a number to the power of 4 **(b)** *(dresser)* *(monument, statue)* to erect; *(bras, poing, yeux)* to raise; *Fig (objection)* to raise **(c)** *(rehausser)* *(plafond, plancher)* to raise; **é. qch de 20 cm** to raise sth by 20 cm **(d)** *(promouvoir)* to promote **(au rang de)** to **(e)** *(édifier)* *(esprit)* to improve; **é. le débat** to raise the tone of the debate
  2 s'élever *vpr* **(a)** *(avec mouvement)* to rise (up); *(cri)* to go up **(b)** *(se dresser)* *(bâtiment, montagnes)* to stand **(c)** *(monter)* *(température, prix)* to rise **(d)** *(protester)* **s'é. contre** to rise up against **(e)** **s'é. à** *(atteindre)* to amount to

éleveur, -euse [elvœr, -øz] *nm,f (de bovins)* cattle farmer; **é. de chevaux/chiens** horse/dog breeder; **é. de moutons/poulets** sheep/poultry farmer

elfe [elf] *nm* elf

éligibilité [eliʒibilite] *nf* eligibility

éligible [eliʒibl] *adj* eligible

élimé, -e [elime] *adj* worn, threadbare

élimination [eliminasjɔ̃] *nf* elimination; **procéder par é.** to use a process of elimination

éliminatoire [eliminatwar] *adj* **5 est une note é.** 5 counts as a fail; **il a eu une note é.** he didn't get a pass mark; *(épreuve)* **é.** qualifying heat

éliminer [elimine] *vt* *(candidat, suspect, toxines)* to eliminate **(de** from); *Sp (pour faute, dopage)* to disqualify; *(possibilité, éventualité)* to rule out; **faites de l'exercice pour é.** do some exercise to clear your system

élire [44] [elir] *vt* **(a)** *(candidat, représentant)* to elect **(b)** **é. domicile** to take up residence

élision [elizjɔ̃] *nf Ling* elision

élite [elit] *nf* elite; **d'é.** *(personnel)* top; *(régiment)* crack

élitisme [elitism] *nm* elitism

élitiste [elitist] *adj & nmf* elitist

élixir [eliksir] *nm* elixir

elle [el] *pron personnel* **(a)** *(sujet)* *(personne)* she; *(chose, animal)* it; **ton amie viendra-t-e.?** is your friend coming?; e., e. n'aurait pas levé le petit doigt SHE wouldn't have raised a finger; **la France, e., a exprimé clairement sa position** France, for its part, has clearly expressed its position; **si j'étais e., je me méfierais** if I were her, I'd be careful **(b)** *(objet direct)* *(personne)* her; *(chose)* it; **et e., tu l'oublies?** and what about her, have you forgotten her? **(c)** *(avec préposition)* *(personne)* her; *(chose, animal)* it; **dis-le-lui, à e.** tell HER; **ce n'est pas à moi, c'est à e.** it's not mine, it's hers; **elle possède une entreprise à e.** she has her own company; *Fam* **une relation à e.** a relation of hers; **e. ne pense qu' à e.** she only thinks about herself **(d)** *(dans les comparaisons)* her; **il boit plus qu'e.** he drinks more than she does *or* than her

elle-même [elmem] *pron personnel* *(personne)* herself; *(chose, animal)* itself

elles [el] *pron personnel* **(a)** *(sujet)* they; **nos chambres sont-e. prêtes?** are our rooms ready?; e., e. seraient déjà parties THEY would have left by now; **mes filles, e., ont fait des études** my daughters, for their part, have been to university; **si j'étais e., je me méfierais** if I were them, I'd be careful **(b)** *(objet direct)* them; **et e., tu les oublies?** and what about them, have you forgotten them? **(c)** *(avec préposition)* them; *(réfléchi)* themselves; **dis-le-leur, à e.** tell THEM; **cette voiture est à e.** this car is theirs; **e. ont un appartement à e.** they have their own flat; *Fam* **un parent à e.** a relative of theirs **(d)** *(dans les comparaisons)* them; **je mange plus qu'e.** I eat more than they do *or* than them

elles-mêmes [elmem] *pron personnel* themselves

ellipse [elips] *nf* **(a)** *Gram* ellipsis **(b)** *(courbe)* ellipse

elliptique [eliptik] *adj* elliptical

élocution [elɔkysjɔ̃] *nf* diction

éloge [elɔʒ] *nm* **(a)** *(louange)* praise; **faire l'é. de qn/qch** to praise sb/sth; **digne d'éloges** praiseworthy **(b)** *(discours)* eulogy; **é. funèbre** funeral oration

élogieux, -euse [elɔʒjø, -øz] *adj* *(discours, article)* complimentary; **parler de qn/qch en termes é.** to speak very highly of sb/sth

éloigné, -e [elwaɲe] *adj* *(dans l'espace, dans le temps)* distant, remote; *(parent)* distant; **ils sont éloignés d'un kilomètre** they're one kilometre apart; **être é. de qch** to be a long way (away) from sth; **se tenir é. de** to keep away from

éloignement [elwaɲmɑ̃] *nm* **(a)** *(séparation)* separation; **l'é. est difficile à vivre** being apart is difficult **(b)** *(distance)* *(dans l'espace, dans le temps)* distance, remoteness

éloigner [elwaɲe] **1** *vt* **(a)** *(dans l'espace)* *(personne, objet)* to move away (**de** from); *(moustiques)* to keep away; **ce trajet nous éloigne du centre-ville** this route takes us away from the centre of town **(b)** *(distraire, détourner)* *(crainte, pensée)* to dismiss; *(soupçons)* to avert; *(personne)* (**de** son travail, d'une autre personne) to keep away (**de** from)
  2 s'éloigner *vpr* **(a)** *(s'écarter)* to move away (**de** from); *(partir)* to go away (**de** from); *(orage)* to pass **(b)** **s'é.** distraire, se détourner) **s'é. de** *(vérité, sujet)* to wander from; *(famille, amis)* to distance oneself from; *(dans un couple)* to grow away from

élongation [elɔ̃gasjɔ̃] nf pulled muscle; **se faire une é.** to pull a muscle

éloquence [elɔkɑ̃s] nf (expressivité) eloquence

éloquent, -e [elɔkɑ̃, -ɑ̃t] adj aussi Fig eloquent; **ces chiffres sont éloquents** these figures speak for themselves

élu, -e [ely] 1 adj (à un poste) elected; Rel chosen 2 nm,f (a) Rel **les élus** the chosen ones (b) (responsable) elected representative (c) Hum **qui est l'heureuse élue?** who's the lucky lady?; **l'é. de son cœur** her beloved

élucider [elyside] vt to elucidate

élucubrations [elykybrasjɔ̃] nfpl Péj flights of fancy

éluder [elyde] vt to evade

Élysée [elize] nm **(le palais de) l'É.** the Élysée Palace (residence of the President of the French Republic)

émacié, -e [emasje] adj emaciated

émail, -aux [emaj, -o] nm enamel; (sur porcelaine) glaze; **en é.** (ustensile de cuisine) enamel

émaillé, -e [emaje] adj (a) (métal, ustensile de cuisine) enamelled (b) (porcelaine) glazed (c) Fig **é. de** (plein de) studded with

émanation [emanasjɔ̃] nf **émanations** emanations; **émanations toxiques** toxic fumes; Fig **être l'é. de qch** to emanate from sth

émancipation [emɑ̃sipasjɔ̃] nf emancipation; Fig (de l'esprit, de la pensée) liberation

émancipé, -e [emɑ̃sipe] adj emancipated

émanciper [emɑ̃sipe] 1 vt to emancipate 2 **s'émanciper** vpr to become emancipated

émaner [emane] **émaner de** vt ind aussi Fig to emanate from

émarger [45] [emarʒe] 1 vi to draw one's salary 2 vt (apposer ses initiales sur) to initial; (signer) to sign

émasculation [emaskylasjɔ̃] nf emasculation

émasculer [emaskyle] vt to emasculate

emballage [ɑ̃balaʒ] nm (a) (action) packing; (dans du papier) wrapping; **e. sous vide** vacuum-packing (b) (contenant) packaging; (papier) wrapping

emballé, -e [ɑ̃bale] adj Fam (enthousiaste) mad keen (par on)

emballer [ɑ̃bale] 1 vt (a) (empaqueter) to pack; (dans du papier) to wrap; (pour la vente) to package (b) (moteur) to race (c) Fam (enthousiasmer) to grab 2 **s'emballer** vpr (a) (moteur) to race; (cheval) to bolt (b) Fam (s'enthousiasmer) to get carried away (c) (cours, monnaie) to spiral out of control

embarcadère [ɑ̃barkader] nm landing stage

embarcation [ɑ̃barkasjɔ̃] nf (small) boat

embardée [ɑ̃barde] nf (d'une voiture) swerve; (d'un bateau) yaw; **faire une e.** (voiture) to swerve; (bateau) to yaw

embargo [ɑ̃bargo] nm embargo; **mettre l'e. sur** to put an embargo on; **lever l'e. sur** to lift the embargo on

embarquement [ɑ̃barkəmɑ̃] nm (de passagers) boarding; (de marchandises) loading; **e. immédiat porte 5** (annonce) now boarding at gate 5

embarquer [ɑ̃barke] 1 vt (a) (passagers) to take on board; (marchandises) to load (b) Fam (emporter) to take (with one) (c) Fam (entraîner) (en week-end, au cinéma) to take off; (arrêter) to nick; **se laisser e. dans** (affaire, discussion) to get caught up in 2 vi (sur un bateau) (monter) to go on board, to board; (pour une destination) to embark 3 **s'embarquer** vpr (a) (sur un bateau) (monter) to go on board, to board; (pour une destination) to embark (b) Fam Fig **s'e. dans** (entreprise, discussion) to embark on

embarras [ɑ̃bara] nm (a) (situation difficile) mettre qn **dans l'e.** to put sb in an awkward situation; **tirer qn d'e.** to get sb out of an awkward situation; **n'avoir que l'e. du choix** to be spoilt for choice (b) (difficulté financière) **être dans l'e.** to be in financial difficulties (c) (gêne) embarrassment (d) (obstacle) **être un e. pour qn** to be a bother to sb (e) Méd **e. gastrique** upset stomach

embarrassant, -e [ɑ̃barasɑ̃, -ɑ̃t] adj (a) (qui gêne) (question, situation) embarrassing (b) (qui encombre) cumbersome

embarrassé, -e [ɑ̃barase] adj (a) (gêné) embarrassed; **je suis très e. de devoir leur dire** I'm very embarrassed about having to tell them (b) (encombré) (table, pièce) cluttered (de with); **avoir les mains embarrassées** to have one's hands full

embarrasser [ɑ̃barase] 1 vt (a) (gêner) to embarrass (b) (encombrer) (table, pièce) to clutter up (de with); **e. qn** (vêtement, achats) to hamper sb; (empêcher le passage de) to be in sb's way 2 **s'embarrasser** vpr (s'encombrer) **s'e. de** to burden oneself with; Fig **elle ne s'embarrasse pas de douceur** she doesn't worry about being gentle

embauche [ɑ̃boʃ] nf (a) (action) taking on, hiring (b) (emploi) employment

embaucher [ɑ̃boʃe] 1 vt to take on, to hire; **son entreprise embauche en ce moment** the company is currently recruiting people 2 **s'embaucher** vpr to get taken on

embaumer [ɑ̃bome] vt (a) (corps) to embalm (b) (répandre une odeur de) to be fragrant with; **son parfum embaumait la pièce** the scent of her perfume filled the room; **le chèvrefeuille embaumait** there was a fragrant smell of honeysuckle

embaumeur [ɑ̃bomœr] nm (de corps) embalmer

embellie [ɑ̃beli] nf (éclaircie) bright spell; Naut calm spell, lull; Fig (de l'économie, d'une situation etc) improvement; **courte e.** bright interval

embellir [ɑ̃belir] 1 vt (pièce, parc, personne) to make more attractive; Fig (histoire, vérité) to embellish 2 vi to grow more attractive

embellissement [ɑ̃belismɑ̃] nm (d'un lieu) improvement; (d'un récit) embellishment

emberlificoter [ɑ̃berlifikɔte] Fam 1 vt (a) (fil) to tangle up (b) (duper) to take in 2 **s'emberlificoter** vpr **s'e. dans** (vêtements, mensonges) to get tangled up in

embêtant, -e [ɑ̃betɑ̃, -ɑ̃t] adj Fam annoying

embêtement [ɑ̃betmɑ̃] nm Fam problem; **faire des embêtements à qn** to make trouble for sb

embêter [ɑ̃bete] Fam 1 vt (contrarier, agacer) to annoy; (ennuyer) to bore 2 **s'embêter** vpr (s'ennuyer) to be bored; Ironique **tu ne t'embêtes pas!** you don't do badly for yourself!; **s'e. à faire qch** (prendre la peine de le faire) to bother doing sth

emblée [āble] **d'emblée** *adv* right away, straight away

emblématique [āblematik] *adj* emblematic; *Fig* symbolic

emblème [ɑ̃blɛm] *nm aussi Fig* emblem

embobiner [āobine] *vt Fam (duper)* to take in

emboîter [ɑ̃bwate] **1** *vt (assembler)* to fit together; **e. qch dans qch** to fit sth into sth; **e. le pas à qn** to follow close on sb's heels; *Fig* to follow sb's lead
2 s'emboîter *vpr* to fit together

embolie [āboli] *nf* embolism; **e. gazeuse/pulmonaire** air/pulmonary embolism; **e. cérébrale** clot on the brain, *Spéc* cerebral embolism

embonpoint [āboⁿpwɛ̃] *nm* stoutness; **avoir/prendre de l'e.** to be/get stout

embouché, -e [ɑ̃buʃe] *adj Fam* **mal e.** foul-tempered

embouchure [ɑ̃buʃyr] *nf* (a) *(d'un instrument à vent)* mouthpiece (b) *(d'un cours d'eau)* mouth

embourber [āburbe] **s'embourber** *vpr* (a) *(véhicule)* to get stuck in the mud (b) *Fig & Péj* to get bogged down

embourgeoisement [āburʒwazmā] *nm (d'une personne)* attainment of middle-class respectability; *(d'un quartier)* gentrification

embourgeoiser [āburʒwaze] **s'embourgeoiser** *vpr (personne)* to become middle-class; *(quartier)* to become gentrified

embout [ābu] *nm (d'un parapluie, d'une canne)* tip; *(d'un tuyau)* nozzle

embouteillage [ābutejaʒ] *nm* traffic jam, hold-up

embouteiller [ābuteje] *vt* to clog up

emboutir [ābutir] *vt* (a) *(véhicule)* to crash into (b) *(métal)* to stamp

embranchement [ɑ̃brɑ̃mɑ̃] *nm* (a) *(croisement)* junction; *(d'une route)* fork (b) *(voie secondaire) (de route)* side road; *(de chemin de fer)* branch line (c) *Bot & Zool* subkingdom

embraser [ɑ̃braze] *Litt* **1** *vt* (a) *(incendier)* to set ablaze (b) *(éclairer)* to set aglow (c) *Fig (exalter) (foule)* to set alight
2 s'embraser *vpr* (a) *(prendre feu)* to blaze up (b) *(rougeoyer)* to glow

embrassade [ɑ̃brasad] *nf* embrace, hug

embrasser [ɑ̃brase] **1** *vt* (a) *(donner un baiser à)* to kiss (b) *(étreindre)* to embrace, to hug; **qui trop embrasse mal étreint** one shouldn't spread oneself too thinly (c) *(adopter) (religion, doctrine, cause)* to embrace; *(carrière)* to take up (d) *(englober) (sujets, questions)* to embrace, to take in; **e. qch du regard** to take in at a glance
2 s'embrasser *vpr* to kiss (each other)

embrasure [ɑ̃brazyr] *nf Constr* aperture; **se tenir dans l'e. de la porte** to stand in the doorway

embrayage [ɑ̃brɛjaʒ] *nm* (a) *(mécanisme)* clutch (b) *(action)* engaging the clutch

embrayer [53] [ɑ̃brɛje] *vi* (a) *Aut* to engage the clutch (b) *Fam (commencer)* to get going (**sur** on)

embrigadement [ɑ̃brigadmɑ̃] *nm* dragooning (**dans** into)

embrigader [ɑ̃brigade] *vt* to dragoon (**dans** into)

embringuer [ɑ̃brɛ̃ge] *Fam* **1** *vt* **e. qn dans qch** to get sb mixed up in sth
2 s'embringuer *vpr* **s'e. dans qch** to get mixed up in sth

embrocher [ɑ̃brɔʃe] *vt* (a) *Culin (viande)* to put on a spit (b) *Fam (transpercer)* **e. qn** to skewer sb

embrouillamini [ābrujamini] *nm Fam* muddle

embrouillé, -e [ābruje] *adj* (a) *(fils)* tangled (b) *(idées, raisonnement, esprit)* muddled; *(affaire)* complicated

embrouiller [ābruje] **1** *vt* (a) *(fils)* to tangle (up) (b) *Fig (personne, situation, idées)* to muddle (up)
2 s'embrouiller *vpr (personne, idées)* to get muddled (up)

embroussaillé, -e [ābrusaje] *adj (allée, jardin)* overgrown; *(cheveux)* messed up

embrumé, -e [ābryme] *adj (horizon)* hazy; *(esprit)* fuddled

embruns [ābrœ̃] *nmpl* spray

embryologie [ābrijɔlɔʒi] *nf* embryology

embryon [ābrijɔ̃] *nm* embryo

embryonnaire [ābrijɔnɛr] *adj* embryonic

embûches [ɑ̃byʃ] *nfpl* traps; **semé d'e.** full of pitfalls

embuer [ābɥe] *vt (miroir, vitre)* to mist up; **yeux embués de larmes** eyes misted over with tears

embuscade [ābyskad] *nf* ambush; **tendre une e. à qn** to set an ambush for sb; **tomber dans une e.** to be ambushed

embusquer [ābyske] **s'embusquer** *vpr* (a) *(se mettre en embuscade)* to lie in ambush (b) *(se faire affecter loin du front)* to get a cushy posting

éméché, -e [emeʃe] *adj Fam* tipsy

émeraude [emrod] **1** *nf (pierre)* emerald
2 *nm & adj inv* emerald green

émergence [emɛrʒɑ̃s] *nf (apparition)* emergence

émerger [45] [emɛrʒe] *vi* (a) *(apparaître)* to emerge (**de** from) (b) *(se lever)* to surface

émeri [emri] *nm* emery; **papier ou toile é.** emery paper

émérite [emerit] *adj* (a) *(expert)* highly skilled (b) *(professeur)* emeritus

émerveillement [emɛrvɛjmɑ̃] *nm* wonder

émerveiller [emɛrveje] **1** *vt (enchanter)* to fill with wonder; **être émerveillé par** to marvel at
2 s'émerveiller *vpr* **s'é. de ou devant** *(s'enchanter de)* to marvel at

émetteur, -trice [emɛtœr, -tris] **1** *adj* (a) *Fin (banque, organisme)* issuing (b) *Rad* **poste é.** transmitter; **station émettrice** transmitting station
2 *nm* transmitter

émettre [47] [emɛtr] **1** *vt* (a) *(cri, rot, soupir)* to give; *(son, lumière)* to give out, to emit; *(fumée, chaleur)* to give off, to emit (b) *Fig (opinion, objection, idée)* to voice (c) *Rad & TV* to transmit, to broadcast (d) *(billets de banque, actions, timbres-poste)* to issue
2 *vi Rad & TV* to transmit, to broadcast

émeu [emø] *nm* emu

émeus, émeut *voir* **émouvoir**

émeute [emøt] *nf* riot

émeutier, -ère [emøtje, -ɛr] *nm, f* rioter

émeuve *etc voir* **émouvoir**

émietter [emjete] **1** *vt* (a) *(pain)* to crumble (b) *Fig (domaine, empire)* to break up
2 s'émietter *vpr (pain, roche)* to crumble

émigrant, -e [emigrɑ̃, -ɑ̃t] *nm, f* emigrant

émigration [emigrasjɔ̃] *nf* emigration

émigré, -e [emigre] **1** *nm, f* emigrant; *Hist* émigré
2 *adj (travailleur, population)* migrant

émigrer [emigre] *vi* to emigrate

émincer [16] [emɛ̃se] *vt (viande, légumes)* to slice thinly

éminemment [eminamã] *adv* eminently

éminence [eminãs] *nf* (a) *(de relief)* hill (b) *Rel* É. Eminence; *Fig* l'é. grise the éminence grise

éminent, -e [eminã, -ãt] *adj (personne)* eminent; **il nous a rendu d'éminents services** he rendered us outstanding service

émir [emir] *nm* emir

émirat [emira] *nm* emirate; **les Émirats arabes unis** the United Arab Emirates

émissaire [emiser] *nm (envoyé)* emissary

émission [emisjõ] *nf* (a) *(de son, de substance)* emission (b) *Rad & TV (action)* transmission, broadcasting; *(ce qui est diffusé)* programme (c) *(de billets de banque, d'actions, de timbres-poste)* issue

emmagasiner [ãmagazine] *vt (marchandises)* to store; *(électricité, chaleur, connaissances)* to store up

emmailloter [ãmajote] *vt (nourrisson)* to swaddle

emmancher [ãmãʃe] 1 *vt* (a) *(outil)* to fit a handle on (b) *(tuyaux)* to fit together; *(pièce)* to fit (dans into)
2 **s'emmancher** *vpr (pièces)* to fit together; *Fam Fig* **bien/mal s'e.** to get off to a good/bad start

emmanchure [ãmãʃyr] *nf* armhole

emmêler [ãmele] 1 *vt (fils, cheveux)* to tangle
2 **s'emmêler** *vpr (fils, cheveux)* to get tangled; *Fam* **s'e. les pédales** *ou* **les pinceaux** to get all muddled up

emménager [45] [ãmenaʒe] *vi* to move in

emmener [46] [ãmne] *vt* (a) *(prendre avec soi) (personne)* to take; *(prisonnier)* to take away; *Fam (objet)* to take; **e. qn en voiture** to give sb a *Br* lift *or Am* ride (b) *(entraîner) (équipier, peloton, sprint)* to lead

emmental [emɛ̃tal] *nm* Emmenthal

emmerdant, -e [ãmerdã, -ãt] *adj très Fam* bloody annoying

emmerdement [ãmerdəmã] *nm très Fam* bloody nuisance; **avoir des emmerdements** to have a hell of a lot of trouble

emmerder [ãmerde] 1 *vt très Fam* **e. qn** *(contrarier, agacer)* to get on sb's nerves; *(ennuyer)* to bore sb stiff; **je l'emmerde!** sod him!
2 **s'emmerder** *vpr très Fam* to be bored stiff; **s'e. à faire qch** *(prendre la peine de le faire)* to bother doing sth; *Ironique* **tu ne t'emmerdes pas!** you're not doing badly for yourself!; *(tu as du culot)* you've got a bloody nerve!

emmerdeur, -euse [ãmerdœr, -øz] *nm,f très Fam* pain in the arse

emmitoufler [ãmitufle] 1 *vt* to wrap up (dans in)
2 **s'emmitoufler** *vpr* to wrap oneself up (dans in)

emmurer [ãmyre] *vt* to wall up

émoi [emwa] *nm (trouble)* emotion; *(plaisir)* excitement; **être (tout) en é.** *(troublé)* to be in a flutter

émollient, -e [emɔljã, -ãt] *adj & nm* emollient

émoluments [emɔlymã] *nmpl* remuneration

émonder [emõde] *vt (arbre, texte)* to prune

émotif, -ive [emotif, -iv] 1 *adj* emotional
2 *nm,f* emotional person

émotion [emosjõ] *nf* emotion; *(frayeur)* fright; **donner des émotions à qn** to give sb a real fright

émotivité [emotivite] *nf* **être d'une grande é.** to be highly emotional

émoulu, -e [emuly] *adj* **frais é. de l'université** fresh from university

émoussé, -e [emuse] *adj (pointe, lame)* blunt; *Fig (sentiment, intérêt)* blunted

émoustiller [emustije] *vt* to arouse

émouvant, -e [emuvã, -ãt] *adj* moving

émouvoir [31a] [emuvwar] 1 *vt (toucher)* to move, to touch; *(troubler)* to upset
2 **s'émouvoir** *vpr (être touché)* to be moved *or* touched; **s'é. de qch** *(s'en inquiéter)* to be concerned about sth

empailler [ãpaje] *vt* (a) *(animal)* to stuff (b) **e. une chaise** to bottom a chair with straw

empaler [ãpale] 1 *vt* to impale
2 **s'empaler** *vpr* to impale oneself

empaqueter [42] [ãpakte] *vt* to pack

emparer [ãpare] **s'emparer** *vpr* **s'e. de** *(lieu, personne, objet)* to seize; *(sujet: sentiment, doute)* to take hold of

empâter [ãpate] **s'empâter** *vpr* to become bloated

empattement [ãpatmã] *nm* (a) *(d'une voiture)* wheelbase (b) *Typ* serif

empêché, -e [ãpeʃe] *adj (retenu)* held up, detained

empêchement [ãpeʃmã] *nm* hitch; **il a eu un e.** something came up

empêcher [ãpeʃe] 1 *vt (action, événement)* to prevent, to stop; *(mouvement, passage)* to obstruct; **e. qn de faire qch** to prevent *or* stop sb (from) doing sth; *Fam* **ça ne m'empêchera pas de dormir** I won't lose any sleep over it; **il n'y a rien qui t'en empêche** there's nothing stopping you; **cela n'empêche que..., il n'empêche que...,** all the same,...; *Fam* **(il) n'empêche all the same** 2 **s'empêcher** *vpr* **je ne peux pas m'en e.** I can't help it; **je ne pouvais pas m'e. de rire** I couldn't help laughing

empêcheur, -euse [ãpeʃœr, -øz] *nm,f Fam* **e. de tourner en rond** spoilsport

empennage [ãpenaʒ] *nm (de flèche)* feathering, feathers; *(d'avion)* tail section

empereur [ãprœr] *nm* emperor

empesé, -e [ãpəze] *adj* (a) *(col, chemise)* starched (b) *Fig (personne, air, style)* stiff

empester [ãpeste] 1 *vt (frigo, pièce)* to stink out; **e. l'alcool/le parfum/le fromage** to stink of alcohol/perfume/cheese
2 *vi* to stink

empêtrer [ãpetre] **s'empêtrer** *vpr* to get entangled; **s'e. les pieds dans qch** to get one's feet caught in sth; *Fig* **s'e. dans** *(explications, mensonges)* to get tangled up in; *Fig* **s'e. dans une affaire** to get mixed up in a business; **s'e. de qn** to land oneself with sb

emphase [ãfaz] *nf* pomposity; **avec e.** pompously

emphatique [ãfatik] *adj* pompous

emphysème [ãfizem] *nm* emphysema

empièccement [ãpjɛsmã] *nm (d'un vêtement)* yoke

empiétement [ãpjetmã] *nm* encroachment (sur on)

empiéter [34] [ãpjete] *vi* **e. sur** *(terrain, horaire, vie privée)* to encroach on

empiffrer [ãpifre] **s'empiffrer** *vpr Fam* to stuff oneself (de with)

empiler [ãpile] 1 *vt (livres, bois, boîtes)* to stack, to pile (up)
2 **s'empiler** *vpr* (a) *(livres, dossiers)* to pile up (b) *(passagers)* **s'e. dans** to cram into

empire [ɑ̃pir] *nm* (a) *Hist & Fig* empire; **un e. commercial** a business empire; **pas pour un e.!** not for all the tea in China!; **le premier E., l'E.** the First Empire; **le second E.** the Second Empire; **style/meubles E.** Empire style/furniture (b) *Litt (influence)* influence; **avoir de l'e. sur qn** to have influence over sb; **faire qch sous l'e. de la boisson/de la colère** to do sth under the influence of drink/in a fit of anger

empirer [ɑ̃pire] *vi* to worsen, to get worse

empirique [ɑ̃pirik] *adj* empirical

emplacement [ɑ̃plasmɑ̃] *nm* (a) *(endroit)* site, location; *(sur un marché, dans un parking)* space (b) *Ordinat* slot; **e. pour carte d'extension** expansion slot; **e. (pour) périphériques** extension slot

emplafonner [ɑ̃plafɔne] *vt Fam* to crash into

emplâtre [ɑ̃plɑtr] *nm* (a) *(pansement)* plaster (b) *Fam (personne)* drip

emplette [ɑ̃plɛt] *nf* purchase; **faire ses emplettes** to go shopping; **faire l'e. de qch** to purchase sth

emplir [ɑ̃plir] **1** *vt* to fill (**de** with)
2 s'emplir *vpr* to fill (up) (**de** with)

emploi [ɑ̃plwa] *nm* (a) *(utilisation)* use; **prêt à l'e.** ready to use; **e. du temps** timetable, schedule; **faire double e.** to be redundant (b) *(situation)* job; *(embauche)* employment; **être sans e.** to be out of work, to be unemployed; **la crise/situation de l'e.** the employment crisis/situation; *Fig* **il a le physique ou la tête ou Fam la gueule de l'e.** he looks the part

employé, -e [ɑ̃plwaje] *nm,f* employee; **e. de banque** bank clerk; **e. de bureau** office worker; **e. de maison** domestic employee

employer [32] [ɑ̃plwaje] **1** *vt* (a) *(utiliser)* (outil, mot, technique, force) to use; **e. les grands moyens** to take drastic measures; **e. son temps à faire qch** to spend one's time doing sth (b) *(faire travailler)* (personne) to employ; **elle l'emploie comme secrétaire** she employs her as a secretary
2 s'employer *vpr* (a) *(personne)* **s'e. à faire qch** to work on doing sth; **je m'y emploie** I'm working on it (b) *(être utilisé)* to be used

employeur, -euse [ɑ̃plwajœr, -øz] *nm,f* employer

empocher [ɑ̃pɔʃe] *vt* to pocket

empoignade [ɑ̃pwaɲad] *nf Fam* dust-up

empoigne [ɑ̃pwaɲ] *nf voir* **foire**

empoigner [ɑ̃pwaɲe] **1** *vt* to grab (hold of)
2 s'empoigner *vpr* to have a dust-up

empoisonnant, -e [ɑ̃pwazɔnɑ̃, -ɑ̃t] *adj Fam* irritating

empoisonnement [ɑ̃pwazɔnmɑ̃] *nm* (a) *(par une substance nocive)* poisoning (b) *Fam (ennui)* problem

empoisonner [ɑ̃pwazɔne] **1** *vt* (a) *(avec une substance nocive)* (personne, nourriture, lieu) to poison; *Fig* **empoisonné** (paroles) poisonous (b) *(empester)* (lieu) to stink out (c) *Fam (irriter)* **e. qn** to get on sb's nerves (d) *(altérer)* (existence, relations) to poison; **e. la vie de qn** to make sb's life a misery
2 s'empoisonner *vpr* to poison oneself

emporté, -e [ɑ̃pɔrte] *adj* quick-tempered

emportement [ɑ̃pɔrtəmɑ̃] *nm* anger

emporte-pièce [ɑ̃pɔrtəpjɛs] **à l'emporte-pièce** *adj (jugement, style)* incisive

emporter [ɑ̃pɔrte] **1** *vt* (a) *(prendre avec soi)* to take; **plats à e.** take-away meals (b) *(transporter)* to take away (c) *(entraîner)* (sujet: courant) to sweep away; (sujet: vent) to blow off; **il a eu une jambe emportée par un obus** a shell took one of his legs off; **e. qn** (maladie) to carry sb off; **e. la bouche** ou *Fam* **la gueule** (moutarde, plat épicé) to take the roof of your mouth off; *Fig* **se laisser e. par la colère/son imagination** to let one's anger/one's imagination get the better of one (d) *(conquérir)* (position) to take (e) **l'e.** *(gagner)* to win; *(prédominer)* to prevail; **l'e. sur qn** to beat sb; **l'e. sur qch** to prevail over sth
2 s'emporter *vpr* to lose one's temper (**contre qn** with sb)

empoté, -e [ɑ̃pɔte] *Fam* **1** *adj* cack-handed
2 *nm,f* cack-handed idiot

empourprer [ɑ̃purpre] **1** *vt* to tinge with crimson
2 s'empourprer *vpr* to turn crimson

empoussiéré, -e [ɑ̃pusjere] *adj* dusty

empreinte [ɑ̃prɛ̃t] *nf* (a) *(trace)* (de pas) footprint; (d'animal) track; **e. digitale** fingerprint; **e. génétique** genetic fingerprint (b) *Fig (de l'éducation, du milieu)* stamp, mark

empressé, -e [ɑ̃prese] **1** *adj (prévenant)* attentive
2 *nm,f Péj* **faire l'e. auprès de qn** to dance attendance on sb

empressement [ɑ̃presmɑ̃] *nm* (a) *(prévenance)* attentiveness (b) *(hâte)* eagerness (**à faire qch** to do sth); **il montre peu d'e. à faire les travaux** he doesn't seem very eager to do the work; **avec e.** eagerly; **mettre beaucoup d'e. à faire qch** to hasten to do sth

empresser [ɑ̃prese] **s'empresser** *vpr* (a) *(se dépêcher)* **s'e. de faire qch** to hasten to do sth (b) *(être prévenant)* **s'e. auprès de qn** to be attentive to sb

emprise [ɑ̃priz] *nf* hold (**sur** over); **sous l'e. de la colère** in a fit of anger

emprisonnement [ɑ̃prizɔnmɑ̃] *nm* imprisonment; **peine d'e.** prison sentence

emprisonner [ɑ̃prizɔne] *vt* to imprison

emprunt [ɑ̃prœ̃] *nm* (a) *(action)* borrowing (b) *(somme)* loan; **faire un e.** *(auprès d'une banque)* to take out a loan; **e. d'État** government loan; **lancer un e.** to issue a bond (c) *Ling* borrowing

emprunté, -e [ɑ̃prœ̃te] *adj* self-conscious, awkward

emprunter [ɑ̃prœ̃te] *vt* (a) *(objet, argent)* to borrow (**à** from) (b) *(route, chemin)* to take

emprunteur, -euse [ɑ̃prœ̃tœr, -øz] *nm,f* borrower

empuantir [ɑ̃pɥɑ̃tir] *vt (lieu)* to stink out

ému, -e [emy] **1** *pp voir* **émouvoir**
2 *adj (touché)* moved, touched; *(intimidé)* nervous; **voix émue** voice filled with emotion; **garder un souvenir é. de qch** to have fond memories of sth

émulation [emylasjɔ̃] *nf aussi Ordinat* emulation

émule [emyl] *nmf* emulator; **j'ai fait des émules** people followed my example

émuler [emyle] *vt Ordinat* to emulate

émulsifiant [emylsifjɑ̃] *nm* emulsifier

émulsion [emylsjɔ̃] *nf* emulsion

en¹ [ɑ̃] *prép* **(a)** *(indique la date ou la durée)* in; **en 1800** in 1800; **en hiver/été** in winter/summer; **en une minute/ trois jours** in a minute/three days

(b) *(indique la destination)* to; **aller en Allemagne** to go to Germany; **partir en vacances** to go on *Br* holiday *or Am* vacation

(c) *(indique le lieu)* in; **vivre en France** to live in France; **en altitude** at altitude; **se promener en forêt** to walk in the forest; **en pleine mer** out at sea; **il y a quelque chose en lui qui me déplaît** there's something about him I don't like

(d) *(indique le moyen)* by; **en voiture/avion/train** by car/plane/train

(e) *(décrit un état)* in; **écrit en français** written in French; **en ruines** ruined; **être en colère/en larmes** to be angry/crying; **être en transe/en danger** to be in a trance/in danger; **être en arrêt maladie** to be on sick leave; **en trois parties** in three parts; **montre en or/en argent** gold/silver watch; **disponible en rouge/38** available in red/in size 38; **être bon en physique** to be good at physics; **payer en francs** to pay in francs; **la même chose en mieux/en moins bien** the same thing but better/but not as good

(f) *(indique une transformation, une progression)* into; **traduire qch en français** to translate sth into French; **transformer une chambre en bureau** to convert a bedroom into an office; **casser qch en deux** to break sth in two *or* in half; **peindre qch en rouge** to paint sth red; **réduire qch en poudre** to reduce sth to a powder; **se mettre en colère** to get angry; **aller de ville en ville** to go from town to town; **de jour en jour** by the day; **changer en bien/mal** to change for the better/for the worse

(g) *(en tant que)* as; **parler à qn en ami** to speak to sb as a friend; **parler en connaisseur** to speak as an expert; **agir en traître** to be disloyal

(h) *(avec un participe présent)* **entrer en criant** to come in shouting; **il s'est coupé en se rasant** he cut himself shaving; **c'est impoli de lire en mangeant** it's rude to read while you're eating; **traverser en courant** to run across; **répondre en maugréant** to grumble in reply; **dire qch en plaisantant** to say sth as a joke; **elle s'est cassé la jambe en tombant** she fell and broke her leg; **c'est en s'entraînant qu'il s'améliorera** he'll only get better if he practices

en² *pron* **(a)** *(avec les adjectifs construits avec de)* **il en est bien capable** he's quite capable of it; **et ta voiture?** - **j'en suis très content** how's your car? - I'm very pleased with it

(b) *(avec les verbes construits avec de)* **qu'en penses-tu?** what do you think of it?; **je ne m'en souviens plus** I can't remember; **on en reparlera** we'll talk about it later; **j'espère en tirer 200 francs** I hope to get 200 francs for it

(c) *(remplace le complément du nom)* **nous en avons la possibilité** we can do it; **elle en a mangé un morceau** she ate a piece of it; **j'en ai acheté 3 kilos** I bought 3 kilos

(d) *(remplace le nom)* **il y en a plusieurs** there are several of them; **elle en a cassé deux** she broke two of them; **est-ce que tu en veux?** do you want some?; **je n'en ai jamais** vu I've never seen one/any; **est-ce de l'or?** - **non, ce n'en est pas** is it gold? - no, it's not

(e) *(indique la cause)* **il en a perdu la raison** it made him lose his mind; **il en est tout retourné** I'm really upset about it

(f) *Fam (pour insister)* **il en a fait une histoire!** he made a real song and dance about it; **des balayeurs, il en faut** someone has to sweep the streets

(g) *(indique la provenance)* from there; **justement, j'en viens** I've just come from there

ENA [ena] *nf (abrév* **École nationale d'administration)** = university-level college preparing students for senior posts in law and economics

énamourer [ɑ̃namure] **s'énamourer** *vpr* **s'é. de** to become enamoured of

énarque [enark] *nmf* = graduate of the ENA

encabaner [ɑ̃kabane] **s'encabaner** *vpr Can* to shut oneself away

encadré [ɑ̃kɑdre] *nm (dans un texte)* box; **Ordinat e. graphique** graphics box; **Ordinat e. texte** text box

encadrement [ɑ̃kɑdrəmɑ̃] *nm* **(a)** *(cadre)* frame; **dans l'e. de la porte** in the doorway **(b)** *(fonction) (de personnel)* management; *(d'élèves, d'enfants)* supervision; *(personnes qui encadrent) (du personnel)* management; *Mil* officers **(c)** *Écon* **e. du crédit** credit squeeze

encadrer [ɑ̃kɑdre] *vt* **(a)** *(tableau, photo)* to frame **(b)** *(entourer) (mots, paragraphe)* to circle; **encadré par deux gendarmes** flanked by two policemen **(c)** *(guider) (personnel, équipe)* to manage; *(enfants, handicapés)* to supervise; *Mil (soldats)* to officer **(d)** *Fam (supporter)* **je ne peux pas l'e.** I can't stand him/her

encadreur, -euse [ɑ̃kɑdrœr, -øz] *nm,f* picture framer

encaissé, -e [ɑ̃kese] *adj (vallée)* deep; *(rivière)* with steep sides; *(route)* cut into the hillside

encaissement [ɑ̃kɛsmɑ̃] *nm* **(a)** *(d'un chèque)* cashing; *(d'argent)* collection **(b)** *(d'une vallée)* depth

encaisser [ɑ̃kese] *vt* **(a)** *(chèque)* to cash; *(argent)* to collect **(b)** *Fam (supporter) (coups, critiques)* to take; **je ne peux pas l'e.** I can't stand her; **il sait e.** he can take it; **qu'est-ce qu'il a encaissé!** he took a lot of punishment!

encanailler [ɑ̃kanaje] **s'encanailler** *vpr* to slum it

encart [ɑ̃kar] *nm (feuille)* insert; **e. publicitaire** advertising insert

en-cas [ɑ̃kɑ] *nm inv* snack

encastrable [ɑ̃kastrabl] *adj (machine à laver, cuisinière)* that can be built in

encastré, -e [ɑ̃kastre] *adj* built-in

encastrer [ɑ̃kastre] **1** *vt* to build in

2 s'encastrer *vpr (éléments)* to fit together; *(machine à laver, cuisinière)* to fit (**dans** into); **la voiture s'est encastrée sous un camion** the car embedded itself under a lorry

encaustique [ɑ̃kostik] *nf* wax, polish

enceinte¹ [ɑ̃sɛ̃t] *nf* **(a)** *(mur)* (surrounding) wall; *(palissade)* fence **(b)** *(espace)* enclosure; *(d'église, de couvent)* precinct(s); **dans l'e. du parc** within the park **(c)** *(baffle)* **e. (acoustique)** speaker

enceinte² *adj f* pregnant; **e. de cinq mois** five months pregnant; **être e. de jumeaux** to be expecting twins; **elle est e. de Marc** she's pregnant by Marc

encens [ɑ̃sɑ̃] *nm* incense

encenser [ɑ̃sɑ̃se] *vt* **e. qn** to praise sb to the skies

encensoir [ɑ̃sɑ̃swar] *nm* censer

encéphalite [ɑ̃sefalit] *nf* encephalitis; **e. bovine spongiforme** bovine spongiform encephalopathy

encéphalogramme [ɑ̃sefalogram] *nm* encephalogram

encercler [ɑ̃serkle] *vt* **(a)** *(ennemi, lieu)* to encircle, to surround **(b)** *(mot)* to circle, to ring

enchaînement [ɑ̃ʃɛnmɑ̃] nm (a) *(série) (d'événements, de circonstances)* series, chain (b) *(liaison) (d'idées, de séquences)* linking (c) *(en danse)* sequence (of steps); *(en ballet)* enchaînement (d) *Ordinat* concatenation

enchaîner [ɑ̃ʃene] **1** vt (a) *(animal, prisonnier)* to chain up; *Fig (peuple)* to enslave; *(presse)* to curb; **e. qn à** to chain sb (up) to (b) *(lier) (épisodes, séquences)* to link (up)

2 vi to move on; **e. sur un sujet** to move on to a subject **3 s'enchaîner** vpr (a) *(personne)* **s'e. à** to chain oneself (up) to (b) *(séquences, épisodes)* to be linked together; **les événements se sont enchaînés rapidement** events happened very quickly

enchanté, -e [ɑ̃ʃɑ̃te] adj (a) *(ravi)* delighted (**de** with); **e. (de faire votre connaissance)!** pleased to meet you! (b) *(magique)* enchanted

enchantement [ɑ̃ʃɑ̃tmɑ̃] nm (a) *(sortilège)* (magic) spell; **comme par e.** as if by magic (b) *(ravissement, merveille)* delight

enchanter [ɑ̃ʃɑ̃te] vt (a) *(ravir)* to delight; **cette idée ne l'enchante pas** she's not keen on the idea (b) *(ensorceler)* to bewitch

enchanteur, -eresse [ɑ̃ʃɑ̃tœr, -trɛs] **1** adj *(sourire)* bewitching; *(spectacle, endroit)* enchanting, delightful **2** nm (a) *(sorcier)* sorcerer (b) *Fig (charmeur)* charmer **3** nf **enchanteresse** sorceress

enchâsser [ɑ̃ʃase] vt (a) *(bijou)* to set (b) *(relique)* to enshrine

enchère [ɑ̃ʃɛr] nf bid; **les enchères** the bidding; **vente aux enchères** auction; **faire monter les enchères** to up the bidding; *Fig* to raise the stakes; **vendre qch aux enchères** to sell sth at auction

enchérir [ɑ̃ʃerir] vi to make a higher bid; **e. sur qn** to outbid sb; *Fig* to go one better than sb

enchevêtré, -e [ɑ̃ʃəvetre] adj *(branchages, fils, explications)* tangled

enchevêtrement [ɑ̃ʃəvetrəmɑ̃] nm *(de fils, branchages)* tangle

enchevêtrer [ɑ̃ʃəvetre] **1** vt *(fils, branchages)* to tangle (up) **2 s'enchevêtrer** vpr *(fils)* to get tangled (up)

enclave [ɑ̃klav] nf enclave

enclenchement [ɑ̃klɑ̃ʃmɑ̃] nm *(d'une vitesse, d'un mécanisme)* engaging

enclencher [ɑ̃klɑ̃ʃe] **1** vt *(vitesse, mécanisme)* to engage; *Fig (processus)* to get under way **2 s'enclencher** vpr *(vitesse, mécanisme)* to engage; *Fig (processus)* to get under way

enclin, -e [ɑ̃klɛ̃, -in] adj **être e. à faire qch** to be inclined to do sth; **être e. à la paresse/la méfiance** to be inclined to be lazy/distrustful

enclos [ɑ̃klo] nm *(espace)* enclosure; *(pour chevaux)* paddock

enclume [ɑ̃klym] nf anvil; *Fig* **être entre le l'e. et marteau** to be between the devil and the deep blue sea

encoche [ɑ̃kɔʃ] nf notch; *Ordinat* **e. de protection contre l'écriture** write-protect notch

encodage [ɑ̃kɔdaʒ] nm *Ling & Ordinat* encoding

encoder [ɑ̃kɔde] vt *Ling & Ordinat* to encode

encoignure [ɑ̃kwaɲyr] nf (a) *(d'une pièce)* corner (b) *(meuble)* corner cupboard

encoller [ɑ̃kɔle] vt *(papier peint)* to paste

encolure [ɑ̃kɔlyr] nf (a) *(d'animal)* neck; **gagner d'une e.** to win by a neck (b) *(tour de cou)* collar size (c) *(d'un vêtement)* neck

encombrant, -e [ɑ̃kɔ̃brɑ̃, -ɑ̃t] adj *(meuble, valise, paquet)* cumbersome, bulky; *Fig (personne, témoin)* undesirable

encombre [ɑ̃kɔ̃br] nm **sans e.** without mishap

encombrement [ɑ̃kɔ̃brəmɑ̃] nm (a) *(état) (d'une pièce)* clutter; *(de lignes téléphoniques)* jamming; *(embouteillage)* traffic jam (b) *(volume) (d'un objet)* (overall) dimensions (c) *Ordinat* **faible e. sur le disque dur** low use of hard disk space

encombrer [ɑ̃kɔ̃bre] **1** vt *(pièce)* to clutter (up); *(passage, route)* to block; *(lignes téléphoniques)* to jam; **tu m'encombres, sors d'ici!** you're getting under my feet, get out! **2 s'encombrer** vpr **s'e. de** *(colis, équipement)* to load oneself down with; *Fig (obligations, personne)* to saddle oneself with

encontre [ɑ̃kɔ̃tr] **à l'encontre de** prép **aller à l'e. de** to go against

encorbellement [ɑ̃kɔrbɛlmɑ̃] nm corbelled structure

encorder [ɑ̃kɔrde] **s'encorder** vpr to rope up

encore [ɑ̃kɔr] adv (a) *(toujours)* still; **pas e.** not yet; **elle n'est pas e. arrivée** she hasn't arrived yet; **je n'avais e. jamais vu ça** I'd never seen that before; **qu'il m'appelle par mon prénom, passe e., mais...** his calling me by my Christian name is one thing, but...; **e. heureux que les enfants n'aient pas été là!** it's just as well the children weren't there!

(b) *(davantage)* more; **en voulez-vous e.?** would you like some more?; **e. une tasse de café** another cup of coffee; **e. trois mois** three more months, another three months; **e. plus/moins** even more/less; **e. plus froid** even colder; **c'est e. pire/mieux** it's even worse/better; **mais e.?** and apart from that?

(c) *(de nouveau)* again; **il a e. cassé un verre** he's broken another glass; **qu'est-ce qu'il a e. fait?** what's he done this time?; **quoi e.?** now what?; **et puis quoi e.?** is that all?; **e. une fois** once more, once again; **e. vous!** you again!

(d) *(restrictif)* **si e....** if only...; **il vous en donnera 10 francs, et e.!** he'll give you 10 francs for it, if that!; **et e., ce n'est même pas sûr** even then, it's not certain; **e. faudrait-il qu'elle accepte/qu'il le sache!** she has to agree/he has to know about it first!

(e) *(seulement)* only; **hier e. elle me disait que...** only yesterday she was telling me that...

(f) **e. que** although, even though

encorner [ɑ̃kɔrne] vt to gore

encourageant, -e [ɑ̃kuraʒɑ̃, -ɑ̃t] adj encouraging

encouragement [ɑ̃kuraʒmɑ̃] nm encouragement; **des encouragements** encouragement

encourager [45] [ɑ̃kuraʒe] vt (a) *(personne)* to encourage; *(athlète, équipe)* to cheer on; **e. qn à faire qch** to encourage sb to do sth (b) *(promouvoir) (arts)* to encourage

encourir [22] [ɑ̃kurir] vt to incur

encrasser [ɑ̃krase] **1** vt *(vêtements, mains)* to dirty; *Aut (bougie)* to soot up; *(moteur)* to clog **2 s'encrasser** vpr to get dirty; *Aut (bougie)* to soot up; *(moteur)* to get clogged

encre [ɑ̃kr] nf ink; *Fig* **nuit d'e.** inky black night; **e. de Chine** Indian ink; **e. sympathique** invisible ink

encrier [ākrije] *nm* inkpot; *(de pupitre)* inkwell

encroûter **s'encroûter** *vpr Fam (personne)* to get into a rut

enculé, -e [ākyle] *nm,f Vulg Br* arsehole, *Am* asshole

enculer [ākyle] *vt Vulg* to bugger; **va te faire e.!** fuck off!; *Fig* **e. les mouches** to nit-pick

encyclique [āsiklik] *nf Rel* encyclical

encyclopédie [āsiklɔpedi] *nf* encyclopedia

encyclopédique [āsiklɔpedik] *adj* encyclopedic

endémie [ādemi] *nf* endemic disease

endémique [ādemik] *adj* endemic

endetté, -e [ādete] *adj* in debt; **très e.** heavily in debt

endettement [ādetmā] *nm* debt

endetter [ādete] **1** *vt* **e. qn** to get sb into debt
2 s'endetter *vpr* to get into debt

endeuiller [ādœje] *vt (famille, nation)* to plunge into mourning; *(événement)* to cast a gloom over

endiablé, -e [ādjable] *adj (personne, musique, rythme)* wild

endiguer [ādige] *vt* **(a)** *(cours d'eau)* to dyke (up) **(b)** *Fig (révolte, inflation, chômage)* to contain

endimanché, -e [ādimāʃe] *adj* in one's Sunday best

endive [ādiv] *nf* chicory

endocrine [ādɔkrin] *adj (glande)* endocrine

endoctrinement [ādɔktrinmā] *nm* indoctrination

endoctriner [ādɔktrine] *vt* to indoctrinate

endolori, -e [ādɔlɔri] *adj* painful

endommager [45] [ādɔmaʒe] *vt* **(a)** *(abîmer)* to damage **(b)** *Ordinat* to corrupt

endormi, -e [ādɔrmi] **1** *adj* **(a)** *(qui dort) (personne)* sleeping; *(voix, village)* sleepy; **être e.** *(personne)* to be asleep *or* sleeping; **avoir l'air e.** to look sleepy **(b)** *(inerte, lent) (personne)* sluggish **(c)** *Fig (passion, intérêt)* dormant
2 *nm,f (personne inerte, lente)* slowcoach

endormir [29] [ādɔrmir] **1** *vt* **(a)** **e. qn** *(bébé)* to send sb to sleep; *(anesthésier)* to put sb to sleep; *(ennuyer)* to send sb to sleep **(b)** *(apaiser) (douleur)* to deaden
2 s'endormir *vpr* to fall asleep, to go to sleep

endossable [ādosabl] *adj (chèque)* endorsable

endossement [ādosmā] *nm (d'un chèque)* endorsement

endosser [ādose] *vt* **(a)** *(vêtement)* to put on **(b)** *(responsabilité)* to assume **(c)** *(chèque)* to endorse

endroit [ādrwa] *nm* **(a)** *(lieu)* place, spot; **à quel e.?** where?; **c'est à cet e. que...** this is where...; **par endroits** here and there, in places **(b)** *(d'un vêtement)* right side; **à l'e.** the right way round

enduire [18] [āduir] **1** *vt* **e.** qch **de** to coat, to cover **(de with)**
2 s'enduire *vpr* **s'e. de** to cover oneself with

enduit [ādɥi] *nm* coating; *(pour boucher)* filler

endurance [ādyrās] *nf* **(a)** *(physique)* stamina **(b)** *Sp* **épreuve/course d'e.** endurance race

endurant, -e [ādyrā, -āt] *adj* tough

endurci, -e [ādyrsi] *adj* **(a)** *(dur) (personne)* hard **(b)** *(invétéré) (criminel)* hardened; *(célibataire)* confirmed

endurcir [ādyrsir] **1** *vt* **(a)** *(moralement)* to harden **(b)** *(physiquement)* to toughen (up)
2 s'endurcir *vpr* **(a)** *(moralement)* to become hard **(b)** *(physiquement)* to toughen up

endurer [ādyre] *vt* to endure, to bear

enduro [ādyro] *nm Sp* enduro

énergétique [enɛrʒetik] *adj* **(a)** *(nourriture)* energy-giving **(b)** *(ressources, besoins)* energy

énergie [enɛrʒi] *nf* **(a)** *(dynamisme)* energy; **mettre toute son é. à qch/à faire qch** to devote all one's energy to sth/to doing sth; **avec é.** *(nier)* strongly; *(refuser, répondre)* forcefully; **sans é.** *(enfant)* listless; *(jouer)* listlessly **(b)** *(force)* energy, power; **é. hydroélectrique** hydroelectric power; **é. nucléaire** *ou* **atomique** nuclear power; **é. solaire** solar power *or* energy

énergique [enɛrʒik] *adj (personne)* energetic, dynamic; *(geste)* brisk; *(visage)* strong **(b)** *(mesures)* strong; *(remède)* powerful

énergiquement [enɛrʒikmā] *adv (nier)* strongly; *(refuser)* forcefully; **serrer é. la main à qn** to shake sb's hand warmly

énergumène [enɛrgymɛn] *nmf* eccentric

énervant, -e [enɛrvā, -āt] *adj* irritating

énervé, -e [enɛrve] *adj (agacé)* irritated; *(excité)* edgy, agitated

énervement [enɛrvəmā] *nm (agacement)* irritation; *(excitation)* agitation

énerver [enɛrve] **1** *vt* **é. qn** *(agacer)* to get on sb's nerves, to irritate sb; *(exciter)* to make sb nervous
2 s'énerver *vpr* to get worked up

enfance [āfās] *nf (jeunesse)* childhood; *(de garçon)* boyhood; *(de fille)* girlhood; **la petite e.** early childhood; *Fam* **c'est l'e. de l'art** it's child's play

enfant [āfā] *nmf* child; **faire l'e.** to act like a child; **je l'ai connu e.** I knew him when he was a child; **il lui a fait un e.** she had a child by him; **viens ici, mon e.** come here, my child; *Fam* **il n'y a plus d'enfants!** honestly, kids nowadays!; **e. en bas âge** infant; **e. bleu** blue baby; *Rel* **e. de chœur** altar boy; *Fig* **ce n'est pas un e. de chœur** he's no angel; **e. terrible** enfant terrible; **e. trouvé** foundling; **e.unique** only child

enfantement [āfātmā] *nm Litt* childbirth

enfanter [āfāte] *vt Litt* to give birth to

enfantillages [āfātijaʒ] *nmpl* childish behaviour; **faire des e.** to be childish

enfantin, -e [āfātɛ̃, -in] *adj (voix)* child's; *(littérature)* children's; *(très facile)* childishly simple; *Péj (remarque, conduite)* childish

enfariné, -e [āfarine] *adj (visage, cheveux)* covered with flour; *Fam* **arriver la gueule enfarinée** to arrive blithely ignorant of the facts

enfer [āfɛr] *nm aussi Fig* l'e. hell; **aller à un train d'e.** to go like a bat out of hell; *Fig* **elle a vécu un véritable e.** she's been through sheer hell; *Fam* **c'est l'e. pour se garer ici** it's hell trying to park here; *Fam* **une soirée d'e.** one hell of a party; **l'e. est pavé de bonnes intentions** the road to hell is paved with good intentions

enfermement [āfɛrməmā] *nm* imprisonment

enfermer [āfɛrme] **1** *vt (personne, chose)* to shut up; **e. qn/qch à clef** to lock sb/sth up; **je suis enfermé toute la journée** I'm cooped up all day; *Fam* **elle est bonne à e.** she should be locked up
2 s'enfermer *vpr* to shut oneself up; **s'e. à clef** to lock oneself in; *Fig* **s'e. dans le silence** to retreat into silence

enferrer [āfere] **s'enferrer** *vpr Fig* to get tangled up **(dans in)**

enfiévré, -e [āfjevre] *adj (front, imagination)* fevered

enfiévrer [34] [ãfjevre] **1** vt (personne, imagination) to excite

2 s'enfiévrer vpr to get excited

enfilade [ãfilad] nf (de portes, de pièces) series; **être en e.** to be adjoining

enfiler [ãfile] **1** vt (a) (aiguille, perles) to thread (b) (vêtements) to slip on

2 s'enfiler vpr (a) (gants, bottes) to go on (b) Fam (boisson, nourriture) to put away

enfin [ãfɛ̃] adv (a) (en dernier lieu) finally, lastly (b) (à la fin) at last, finally (c) (de résignation) e., **n'en parlons plus!** look, let's forget about it!; **e., ce qui est fait est fait!** what's done is done! (d) (d'exaspération) **e. quoi, tu n'as plus dix ans!** for God's sake, you're not ten any more!; **mais e., je te l'avais dit!** but I told you, for God's sake! (e) (d'hésitation, pour résumer) well; **e., je ne dis pas non, mais…** well, I'm not saying no, but…; **elle n'est pas mal, e. pour son âge** she's not bad, for her age that is; **e. (bref), c'était la panique!** in short, it was panic!

enflammé, -e [ãflame] adj (a) (brindille, torche, allumette) burning (b) (joues) (de froid) glowing; (de fièvre, de gêne) burning (c) Fig (discours) fiery, passionate

enflammer [ãflame] **1** vt (a) (mettre le feu à) to set light to; (allumette) to strike (b) Fig (imagination) to stir; **la colère enflammait son regard** her eyes were blazing with anger

2 s'enflammer vpr (a) (prendre feu) to catch fire (b) Fig (imagination) to be stirred

enflé, -e [ãfle] adj (rivière, membre) swollen

enfler [ãfle] **1** vt (a) (rivière, membre) to swell; **e. les joues** to puff out one's cheeks (b) Fig (exagérer) (histoire, succès) to exaggerate

2 vi (membre) to swell (up)

enflure [ãflyr] nf (a) (d'un membre) swelling (b) très Fam (imbécile) jerk, Br git

enfoiré, -e [ãfware] nm,f Vulg bugger, bastard

enfoncé, -e [ãfõse] adj (yeux) deep-set

enfoncement [ãfõsmã] nm (dans le sol) dip; (dans un mur) recess

enfoncer [16] [ãfõse] **1** vt (a) (clou) to bang in; (pieu) to drive in; (aiguille) to stick in, to push in; **e. un couteau dans qch** to stick a knife into sth; **e. la main dans sa poche** to thrust one's hand into one's pocket; **e. son chapeau sur sa tête** to jam one's hat on one's head (b) (porte) to break down (c) Fam (personne) to humiliate

2 s'enfoncer vpr (clou, couteau) to go in; (bateau) to sink; **s'e. dans son fauteuil** to sink into one's armchair; **s'e. dans un bois** to go into the depths of a wood; Fam **enfonce-toi ça dans le crâne!** can't you get it into your thick head?

enfouir [ãfwir] **1** vt to bury (**dans/sous** in/under)

2 s'enfouir vpr to bury oneself

enfourcher [ãfurʃe] vt (cheval, vélo) to get on, to mount

enfourner [ãfurne] vt (pain) to put in the oven; (poteries, briques) to put in the kiln; Fam (manger) to stuff down

enfreindre [54] [ãfrɛ̃dr] vt to infringe, to break

enfuir [38] [ãfɥir] **s'enfuir** vpr to run away (**de** from); (d'une prison) to escape (**de** from)

enfumé, -e [ãfyme] adj (pièce, atmosphère) smoky

enfumer [ãfyme] vt (a) (pièce) to fill with smoke (b) (personne, abeilles) to smoke out

enfuyais etc voir **enfuir**

engagé, -e [ãgaʒe] **1** adj (littérature, écrivain) committed

2 nm (soldat) e. **(volontaire)** enlisted man

engageant, -e [ãgaʒã, -ãt] adj (manière, sourire) engaging

engagement [ãgaʒmã] nm (a) (promesse) undertaking, commitment; **prendre un e.** to enter into an undertaking; **prendre l'e. de faire qch** to undertake to do sth; **tenir ses engagements** to honour one's commitments; **sans e. (de votre part)** without obligation (on your part) (b) (à une cause) commitment (c) (coup d'envoi) (au football, au rugby) kick-off; (au hockey) bully-off; (au basket) tip-off (d) (commencement) start; (de poursuites) institution (e) (d'un employé) appointment; (d'un soldat) enlistment

engager [45] [ãgaʒe] **1** vt (a) (lier) to commit; **e. sa parole** to give one's word; **cela ne vous engage à rien** it doesn't commit you to anything; **cela n'engage que moi** that's just my opinion (b) (mettre en gage) to pawn (c) (embaucher) (employé) to appoint; (soldat) to enlist (d) (commencer) (conversation, négociations) to begin, to start; (poursuites) to institute; **e. la partie** to start the match; **la partie est maintenant bien engagée** the match is now well under way (e) (introduire) (clef) to insert (f) (inciter) **e. qn à faire qch** to urge sb to do sth

2 s'engager vpr (a) (promettre) **s'e. à faire qch** to promise to do sth, to undertake to do sth (b) (prendre position) to commit oneself (c) (se lancer) **s'e. dans une aventure** to get involved in an adventure (d) (soldat) to enlist, to join up (e) (pénétrer) **s'e. dans une rue** to turn into a street; **s'e. dans une forêt** to enter a forest (f) (commencer) (négociations, conversation) to begin

engeance [ãʒãs] nf Fam crew, bunch

engelure [ãʒlyr] nf chilblain

engendrer [ãʒãdre] vt to father; Fig (maladie, pauvreté) to cause

engin [ãʒɛ̃] nm (machine) machine; (outil) device; Fam (objet) thing; **e. blindé** armoured vehicle; **e. de mort** deadly weapon; **e. spatial** spacecraft

englober [ãglɔbe] vt to include (**dans** in)

engloutir [ãglutir] vt (a) (avaler) (boisson) to gulp down; (nourriture) to wolf down (b) (submerger) (bateau, village) to submerge; Fig (fortune) to swallow up

engoncé, -e [ãgõse] adj **il avait l'air e. dans son manteau** his coat looked too tight for him

engorgement [ãgɔrʒəmã] nm (blocage) blocking; (d'un marché) glutting

engorger [45] [ãgɔrʒe] **1** vt (bloquer) to block, to clog; (marché) to glut

2 s'engorger vpr (tuyau) to be blocked or clogged

engouement [ãgumã] nm craze (**pour** for)

engouffrer [ãgufre] **1** vt Fam (nourriture) to devour

2 s'engouffrer vpr **s'e. dans** to rush in to; **le vent s'engouffra par la porte** the wind rushed in through the door

engourdi, -e [ãgurdi] adj numb (**par** with)

engourdir [ãgurdir] **1** vt (a) (membre) to numb (b) (douleur) to dull

2 s'engourdir vpr to go numb, to go to sleep

engourdissement [ãgurdismã] nm numbness

engrais [ãgrɛ] nm fertilizer

engraisser [ãgrese] **1** vt (animaux, personne) to fatten up

2 vi Fam to get fatter

engranger [45] [ãgrãʒe] vt (céréales) to bring in; Fig to build up

engrenage [ãgrənaʒ] *nm* (a) *(roues dentées)* gears (b) *Fig (d'événements)* chain; **l'e. de la violence** the cycle of violence; **être pris dans un e.** to get caught up in a system; **mettre le doigt dans l'e.** to get caught up in it

engrosser [ãgrose] *vt très Fam (femme)* to knock up; **se faire e. (par)** to get knocked up (by)

engueulade [ãgœlad] *nf Fam (réprimande)* earbashing; *(querelle)* row, *Br* slanging match

engueuler [ãgœle] *Fam* **1** *vt* **e. qn** to give sb an earbashing; **se faire e.** to get an earbashing; **e. qn comme du poisson pourri** to call sb every name under the sun
  2 s'engueuler *vpr* to have a row or *Br* slanging match

enguirlander [ãgirlãde] *vt* (a) *Fam* **e. qn** to give sb an earbashing; **se faire e.** to get an earbashing (b) *(décorer)* to garland (**de** with)

enhardir [ãardir] **1** *vt* to embolden
  2 s'enhardir *vpr* to become bolder; **s'e. à faire qch** to pluck up the courage to do sth

énième [enjɛm] *adj* **après une é. tentative** after countless attempts; **pour la é. fois** for the umpteenth time

énigmatique [enigmatik] *adj* enigmatic

énigme [enigm] *nf (mystère)* enigma, mystery; *(devinette)* riddle

enivrant, -e [ãnivrã, -ãt] *adj (parfum)* heady; *(vitesse)* exhilarating

enivrement [ãnivrəmã] *nm* (a) *(par l'alcool)* intoxication (b) *Fig* exhilaration

enivrer [ãnivre] **1** *vt* (a) *(soûler)* to intoxicate, to make drunk (b) *Fig (exalter)* to exhilarate; **enivré par le succès** intoxicated with success
  2 s'enivrer *vpr (se soûler)* to become intoxicated (**de** with), to get drunk (**de** on)

enjambée [ãʒãbe] *nf* stride; **marcher à grandes enjambées** to stride along

enjambement [ãʒãbmã] *nm* enjambment

enjamber [ãʒãbe] *vt (obstacle)* to step over; *(sujet: pont) (rivière)* to span

enjeu, -x [ãʒø] *nm (au jeu)* stake; *Fig (d'une guerre)* stakes; **quel est l'e. de cette élection?** what's at stake in this election?

enjoignais *etc voir* **enjoindre**

enjoindre [ãʒwɛdr] *vt Litt* **e. à qn de faire qch** to enjoin sb to do sth

enjôler [ãʒole] *vt* to cajole

enjôleur, -euse [ãʒolœr, -øz] **1** *adj* cajoling
  2 *nm,f* charmer

enjoliver [ãʒolive] *vt* to embellish

enjoliveur [ãʒolivœr] *nm* hubcap

enjoué, -e [ãʒwe] *adj* playful

enjouement [ãʒumã] *nm* playfulness

enlacement [ãlasmã] *nm* (a) *(de rubans, de branches)* intertwining (b) *(étreinte)* embrace

enlacer [ãlase] **1** *vt* (a) *(rubans, branches)* to intertwine (b) *(étreindre)* to embrace
  2 s'enlacer *vpr (s'étreindre)* to embrace

enlaidir [ãledir] **1** *vt (personne)* to make ugly, to disfigure; *(paysage, ville)* to disfigure
  2 s'enlaidir *vpr* to make oneself look ugly

enlevé, -e [ãlve] *adj (style)* lively

enlèvement [ãlevmã] *nm* (a) *(de meubles, d'une tache)* removal, removing; *(de bagages)* collection; **e. des ordures** *Br* rubbish *or Am* garbage collection (b) *(kidnapping)* kidnapping, abduction

enlever [46] [ãlve] **1** *vt* (a) *(vêtements, couvercle)* to remove, to take off; *(meubles)* to remove, to take away; *(tapis)* to take up; *(rideaux)* to take down; *(papier peint, étiquette, tache)* to remove; **e. qch à qn** to take sth away from sb; **elle me l'a enlevé des mains** she took it from me; **e. à qn la garde d'un enfant** to remove a child from sb's care; **e. à qn le goût de qch** to take away sb's taste for sth (b) *(kidnapper)* to kidnap, to abduct (c) *(remporter) (prix)* to carry off; *(victoire, contrat)* to win
  2 s'enlever *vpr (couvercle, peinture)* to come off; *(tache)* to come out

enlisement [ãlizmã] *nm* sinking

enliser [ãlize] **1** *vt* **e. une voiture** to get a car stuck
  2 s'enliser *vpr (personne, voiture)* to get stuck; *Fig* **s'e. dans ses explications** to get bogged down in explanations

enluminure [ãlyminyr] *nf* illumination

enneigé, -e [ãneʒe] *adj (montagne, champ, route)* snow-covered; *(village)* snowbound

enneigement [ãneʒmã] *nm* snow cover

ennemi, -e [ɛnmi] **1** *nm,f* enemy; **se faire un e. de qn** to make an enemy of sb; **passer à l'e.** to defect; *Prov* **le mieux est l'e. du bien** it's better to leave well alone; **e. public numéro un** public enemy number one
  2 *adj* **en pays e.** in enemy country

ennui [ãnɥi] *nm* (a) *(souci)* worry; *(problème)* problem; **avoir des ennuis** *(soucis)* to be worried; *(problèmes)* to have problems; **avoir des ennuis de santé** to have health problems; **avoir des ennuis avec la police** to be in trouble with the police; **attirer des ennuis à qn** to get sb into trouble; **faire des ennuis à qn** to bother sb (b) *(lassitude)* boredom; **il est d'un e.!** his conversation is so boring!

ennuyé, -e [ãnɥije] *adj* (a) *(contrarié)* annoyed (**de** about) (b) *(las)* bored

ennuyer [32] [ãnɥije] **1** *vt* (a) *(contrarier)* to bother; **cela vous ennuierait-il d'attendre?** would you mind waiting? (b) *(agacer)* to annoy, to irritate (c) *(lasser)* to bore (**avec** with)
  2 s'ennuyer *vpr* to be bored; **qu'est-ce qu'on s'ennuie ici!** it's so boring here!; **s'e. à cent sous de l'heure** to be bored to death

ennuyeux, -euse [ãnɥijø, -øz] *adj* (a) *(contrariant)* annoying, irritating; **comme c'est e.!** it's so annoying! (b) *(lassant)* boring

énoncé [enõse] *nm* (a) *(des faits)* statement; *(d'une sentence)* pronouncement (b) *(d'une question)* wording

énoncer [16] [enõse] *vt (opinion, conditions)* to state

énonciation [enõsjasjõ] *nf (de faits)* statement

enorgueillir [ãnorgœjir] **1** *vt* to make proud
  2 s'enorgueillir *vpr* **s'e. de qch/de faire qch** to pride oneself on sth/on doing sth

énorme [enorm] *adj* enormous, huge

énormément [enormemã] *adv (lire, travailler, pleurer)* an awful lot; **je le regrette é.** I'm extremely sorry; **s'amuser é.** to have a great time; **il n'a pas é. d'argent** he hasn't got a huge amount of money

énormité [enɔrmite] *nf* (a) *(d'une demande, d'un crime)* enormity, outrageousness (b) *(d'une personne, d'une somme)* huge size (c) *(erreur)* glaring mistake; *(propos choquants)* outrageous statement

enquérir [7] [ākerir] **s'enquérir** *vpr* to inquire (de about)

enquête [āket] *nf* (a) *(recherches)* inquiry; *(de journalistes, de policiers)* investigation (sur into); *Fam* **faire sa petite e.** to do a bit of investigating (b) *(sondage)* survey

enquêter [ākete] *vi* (a) *(faire des recherches)* to hold an inquiry; *(police, journaliste)* to investigate; **e. sur qch** to investigate sth (b) *(faire un sondage)* to conduct a survey (sur/auprès de into/among)

enquêteur, -trice [āketœr, -tris] *nm,f* (a) *(policier)* investigator (b) *(sondeur)* researcher

enquiers, enquiert *voir* **enquérir**

enquiquinant, -e [ākikinā, -āt] *adj Fam (agaçant)* irritating, annoying

enquiquiner [ākikine] *vt Fam (agacer)* to irritate, to annoy

enquiquineur, -euse [ākikinœr, -øz] *nm,f Fam* nuisance, pain

enquis, -e *voir* **enquérir**

enraciné, -e [ārasine] *adj (habitude, haine)* deep-rooted, deep-seated

enraciner [ārasine] **s'enraciner** *vpr aussi Fig* to take root

enragé, -e [āraʒe] **1** *adj (animal)* rabid
  2 *nm,f Fam* fanatic

enrager [45] [āraʒe] *vi* to be furious; **e. de devoir faire qch** to be really angry at having to do sth; **faire e. qn** *(taquiner)* to tease sb

enrayer [āreje] [53] **1** *vt (machine)* to jam; *Fig (épidémie)* to check; *(inflation)* to curb
  2 s'enrayer *vpr (machine)* to jam

enrégimenter [āreʒimāte] *vt Péj (dans une organisation)* to enrol

enregistrement [ārəʒistrəmā] *nm* (a) *(d'une naissance, d'un acte)* registration; *(de bagages)* check-in (b) *(disque)* recording; **e. vidéo** video recording; **e. sur bande/cassette** tape/cassette recording (c) *Ordinat (de données)* logging, recording; **e. de transactions** transaction logging

enregistrer [ārəʒistre] **1** *vt* (a) *(naissance, acte)* to register; *(bagages)* to check in; **les meilleures ventes jamais enregistrées** the best sales ever recorded (b) *(disque, émission)* to record, to tape; *(données)* to store; *Ordinat* **programme enregistré** stored programme (c) *Fam (mémoriser)* to note, to register
  2 s'enregistrer *vpr (personne)* to record oneself

enregistreur, -euse [ārəʒistrœr, -øz] *adj (appareil)* recording

enrhumé, -e [āryme] *adj* **être e.** to have a cold

enrhumer [āryme] **s'enrhumer** *vpr* to catch a cold

enrichi, -e [āriʃi] *adj* (a) *(personne)* wealthy (b) *(céréales)* enriched (en with)

enrichir [āriʃir] **1** *vt (personne, pays)* to make richer; *Fig (collection)* to enhance (de with)
  2 s'enrichir *vpr* (a) *(personne, pays)* to get richer; *Fig (collection)* to be enhanced (de by) (b) **s'e. l'esprit** to improve one's mind

enrichissant, -e [āriʃisā, -āt] *adj (expérience)* rewarding

enrichissement [āriʃismā] *nm (en argent)* acquiring of wealth

enrober [ārɔbe] *vt* (a) *(bonbon)* to coat (de with) (b) *Hum* **il est un peu enrobé** he's a bit chubby

enrôlement [ārolmā] *nm* enrolment; *(d'un soldat)* enlistment

enrôler [ārole] **1** *vt* to enrol, to recruit; *(soldat)* to enlist
  2 s'enrôler *vpr* to enrol; *(soldat)* to enlist

enroué, -e [ārwe] *adj* hoarse, husky; **avoir la voix enrouée** to have a husky voice

enrouer [ārwe] **1** *vt (voix, personne)* to make hoarse
  2 s'enrouer *vpr* to get hoarse

enrouler [ārule] **1** *vt* (a) *(rouler)* (carte, tapis) to roll up; *(câble, ruban)* to wind (b) *(envelopper)* to wrap up (dans in)
  2 s'enrouler *vpr* (a) *(serpent)* to coil up; *(fil)* to wind (b) **s'e. dans une couverture** to wrap oneself up in a blanket

ENS [øɛnɛs] *nf (abrév* **École normale supérieure)** = university-level college preparing students for senior posts in teaching

ensablement [āsabləmā] *nm* (a) *(d'un port)* silting up (b) *(dépôt) (dû à l'eau)* sandbank; *(dû au vent)* sand dune

ensabler [āsable] **1** *vt (port)* to silt up
  2 s'ensabler *vpr* (a) *(véhicule)* to get stuck in the sand (b) *(port)* to silt up

ensanglanter [āsāglāte] *vt* to cover with blood; **des mains ensanglantées** bloodstained *or* bloody hands; **un festival ensanglanté par un attentat** a festival marred by an attempted murder

enseignant, -e [āsɛɲā, -āt] **1** *nm,f* teacher
  2 *adj* **le corps e.** the teaching profession

enseigne [āsɛɲ] **1** *nf* (a) *(panonceau)* sign; **e. lumineuse** illuminated sign; *Fig* **nous sommes tous logés à la même e.** we're all in the same boat; *Litt* **à telle e. que...** so much so that...
  2 *nm* **e. (de vaisseau)** *Br* sub-lieutenant, *Am* ensign

enseignement [āsɛɲmā] *nm* (a) *(profession)* teaching; **être dans l'e.** to be a teacher (b) *(formation)* education; *Fig* **tirer un e. de qch** to learn a lesson from sth; **e. assisté par ordinateur** computer-aided learning; **e. par correspondance** distance learning; **e. primaire/secondaire** primary/secondary education; **e. professionnel/technique** vocational/technical education; **e. supérieur** higher education

enseigner [āsɛɲe] **1** *vt* to teach; **e. qch à qn** to teach sb sth
  2 *vi* to be a teacher, to teach

ensemble [āsābl] **1** *adv* together; **aller bien e.** *(personnes)* to be well matched; *(couleurs)* to go together; **ils sont partis tous e.** they left en masse; *Hum* **ne répondez pas tous e.** don't all answer at once
  2 *nm* (a) *(totalité)* **l'e. des personnes présentes** all the people present; **l'e. de sa fortune** his whole fortune; **dans l'e.** on the whole (b) *(unité)* unity; **avec un parfait e.** *(répondre)* as one; *(danser)* in unison (c) *(groupe) (de gens)* group; *(d'objets, de faits)* set; *(de services)* package (d) *(tenue)* outfit; **e. pantalon** *Br* trouser suit, *Am* pant suit (e) *(immeubles)* block; **grand e.** residential estate (f) *Math* set

ensemblier [āsāblije] *nm* interior designer; *(pour la télévision)* set designer

ensemencer [16] [āsəmāse] *vt* (a) *(champ)* to sow (b) *Biol* to culture

ensevelir [āsəvlir] *vt Litt* to bury

ensoleillé, -e [āsɔleje] *adj* sunny

ensoleillement [ɑ̃sɔlɛjmɑ̃] *nm* **en raison de l'e. d'une pièce** because the room gets a lot of sun; **cinq heures d'e. par jour** five hours of sunshine a day; **jouir d'un e. exceptionnel** to get a lot of sun

ensommeillé, -e [ɑ̃sɔmeje] *adj* sleepy

ensorceler [42] [ɑ̃sɔrsəle] *vt* to cast or put a spell on; *Fig* to bewitch, to captivate

ensorcellement [ɑ̃sɔrsɛlmɑ̃] *nm (action)* bewitching; *(état)* bewitchment; *Fig (charme)* charm

ensuite [ɑ̃sɥit] *adv (plus tard)* later; *(puis)* then, next; **et e., qu'est-ce qu'on fait?** what do you do next?; *Fam* **d'abord, c'est très cher, et e. ça ne te va pas du tout** for one thing it's very expensive, and for another it doesn't suit you at all

ensuivre [65] [ɑ̃sɥivr] **s'ensuivre** *vpr* **jusqu'à ce que mort s'ensuive** until dead; **il s'ensuit que... il** follows that...; **et tout ce qui s'ensuit** and all that goes with it

entacher [ɑ̃taʃe] *vt (réputation)* to sully

entaille [ɑ̃taj] *nf* **(a)** *(dans du bois)* notch; *(longue)* groove **(b)** *(blessure)* gash; **se faire une e. au doigt** to cut one's finger open

entailler [ɑ̃taje] *vt (blesser)* to gash

entame [ɑ̃tam] *nf* **(a)** *(de pain, de jambon)* first slice **(b)** *(aux cartes)* lead

entamer [ɑ̃tame] *vt* **(a)** *(blesser)* to cut into; *Fig (conviction, détermination)* to undermine **(b)** *(commencer) (pain, jambon)* to start on; *(bouteille, pot de confiture)* to open; *(travail, recherches, conversation, négociations)* to start; *(démarches)* to initiate; *(poursuites)* to institute **(c)** *(aux cartes)* **e. à trèfle** to open clubs

entartrer [ɑ̃tartre] **1** *vt (chaudière)* to fur (up)
2 s'entartrer *vpr (chaudière)* to fur (up); *(dents)* to scale up

entassement [ɑ̃tasmɑ̃] *nm* **(a)** *(de pierres) (action)* piling up; *(tas)* pile **(b)** *(de passagers, du bétail)* crowding together

entasser [ɑ̃tase] **1** *vt* **(a)** *(pierres, livres, vêtements)* to pile up **(b)** *(passagers, bétail)* to crowd together
2 s'entasser *vpr* **(a)** *(objets)* to pile up **(b)** *(personnes)* to crowd together

entendement [ɑ̃tɑ̃dmɑ̃] *nm* **dépasser l'e.** to be beyond comprehension

entendeur [ɑ̃tɑ̃dœr] *nm* **à bon e., salut!** mark my words!

entendre [ɑ̃tɑ̃dr] **1** *vt* **(a)** *(ouïr)* to hear; **je n'entends rien (de ce que tu dis)** I can't hear a thing (you're saying); **je l'entends rire** I can hear him laughing; **e. dire que...** to hear that...; **e. qn dire qch** to hear sb say sth; **e. parler de** *(connaître l'existence de)* to hear of; *(être au courant de)* to hear about; **elle ne veut pas en e. parler!** she doesn't want to hear another word about it!; **il va m'e.!** I'll give him a talking-to!; **elle répétait à qui voulait l'e. que...** she'd tell anyone who'd listen that...; *Fam* **ce qu'il ne faut pas e.!** I've heard it all now!
(b) *(écouter) (témoin, suppliant)* to hear; **e. qn en confession** to hear sb's confession; **à vous e., il a eu tort** from what you say, he was in the wrong; **il n'a rien voulu e.** he wouldn't listen; **que Dieu vous entende** may God answer your prayers
(c) *(comprendre)* to understand; **laisser e. qch** to imply sth; **elle m'a laissé e. que...** she gave me to understand that...; **ce n'est pas ainsi qu'il l'entend** he doesn't see it like that
(d) *(vouloir dire)* to mean; **qu'entendez-vous par là?** what do you mean by that?

(e) *(vouloir)* **e. faire qch** to intend or mean to do sth; **faites comme vous l'entendez** do as you think best; **il ne l'entendait pas ainsi** he wouldn't hear of it

2 *vi* to hear; **e. mal** to be hard of hearing; **j'ai mal entendu!** *(je n'ai pas entendu)* I didn't hear you properly!; *(je suis choqué)* I don't think I heard you right!; **tu entends?** *(menace)* got it?

3 s'entendre *vpr* **(a)** *(sympathiser)* to get on *(avec* with**) (b)** *(se mettre d'accord)* to agree; **entendons-nous bien!** let's be clear about this!
(c) *(être entendu)* to be heard; **on ne s'entend plus ici** you can't hear yourself think in here
(d) *(être compris)* to be understood
(e) s'e. aux affaires to have a good head for business; **il s'y entend** he knows what he's talking about

entendu, -e [ɑ̃tɑ̃dy] *adj* **(a)** *(complice) (sourire)* knowing; **d'un air e.** knowingly **(b)** *(décidé) (c'est) e.!** fine!, all right! **(c) bien e.** of course

entente [ɑ̃tɑ̃t] *nf* **(a)** *(accord)* agreement, understanding **(entre** between**) (b)** *(harmonie)* **bonne e.** harmony

entériner [ɑ̃terine] *vt* to ratify

entérite [ɑ̃terit] *nf Méd* enteritis

enterrement [ɑ̃tɛrmɑ̃] *nm* **(a)** *(mise en terre)* burial **(b)** *(cérémonie)* funeral; *Fam* **faire une tête d'e.** to look miserable **(c)** *(cortège)* funeral procession

enterrer [ɑ̃tere] **1** *vt* **(a)** *(trésor, corps)* to bury; *Hum* **il nous enterrera tous** he'll outlive us all **(b)** *Fig (projet)* to scrap; *(affaire)* to bury; **e. sa vie de garçon** to have a stag party
2 s'enterrer *vpr Fig* to hide oneself away

entêtant, -e [ɑ̃tɛtɑ̃, -ɑ̃t] *adj (parfum, musique)* heady

en-tête *(pl* **en-têtes)** [ɑ̃tɛt] *nm* heading; *Ordinat* header

entêté, -e [ɑ̃tete] **1** *adj* obstinate, stubborn
2 *nm,f* obstinate or stubborn person

entêtement [ɑ̃tɛtmɑ̃] *nm* obstinacy, stubbornness; **e. à faire qch** persistence in doing sth

entêter [ɑ̃tete] **s'entêter** *vpr* to persist; **s'e. à faire qch** to persist in doing sth

enthousiasmant, -e [ɑ̃tuzjasmɑ̃, -ɑ̃t] *adj* exciting

enthousiasme [ɑ̃tuzjasm] *nm* enthusiasm *(pour* for**); avec e.** enthusiastically; **sans e.** unenthusiastically

enthousiasmer [ɑ̃tuzjasme] **1** *vt (personne)* to fill with enthusiasm
2 s'enthousiasmer *vpr* to get enthusiastic *(pour* about**)**

enthousiaste [ɑ̃tuzjast] **1** *adj* enthusiastic
2 *nmf* enthusiast

enticher [ɑ̃tiʃe] **s'enticher** *vpr* **s'e. de qn/qch** to become infatuated with sb/sth

entier, -ère [ɑ̃tje, -ɛr] **1** *adj* **(a)** *(complet)* whole, entire; **la France entière** the whole of France; **il a mangé le gâteau tout e.** he ate the whole cake; **des heures entières** for hours on end; **le mystère reste e.** the mystery remains unsolved **(b)** *(responsable)* full; *(confiance)* complete; **jouir d'une entière liberté** to have absolute freedom; **donner entière satisfaction à qn** *(produit)* to give sb complete satisfaction **(c)** *(sans compromis) (personne)* uncompromising
2 *nm* **(a) j'ai écouté le disque en e.** I listened to the whole record; **elle a lu le livre en e.** she read the whole book; **le pays dans son e.** the whole country **(b)** *Math (nombre)* integer, whole number

entièrement [ɑ̃tjɛrmɑ̃] *adv* entirely; **je ne l'ai pas lu e.** I didn't read all of it

entité [ɑ̃tite] *nf* entity

entonner [ɑ̃tɔne] *vt* to start singing

entonnoir [ɑ̃tɔnwar] *nm* funnel

entorse [ɑ̃tɔrs] *nf* sprain, wrench; **se faire une e. au poignet** to sprain one's wrist; *Fig* **faire une e. au règlement** to stretch the rules

entortiller [ɑ̃tɔrtije] **1** *vt* (*envelopper*) to wrap (**dans** in); (*enrouler*) to wind (**autour de** round)
   2 s'entortiller *vpr* (**a**) (*serpent, lierre*) to coil (**autour de** round) (**b**) (*s'empêtrer*) to get tangled up (**dans** in) (**c**) (*s'enrouler*) to wrap oneself up (**dans** in)

entour [ɑ̃tur] *nm* **à l'e. de** round

entourage [ɑ̃turaʒ] *nm* (*amis*) circle (of friends); (*de ministre, de souverain*) entourage; **dans son e. proche** amongst those close to him

entourer [ɑ̃ture] **1** *vt* (**a**) (*border, enceindre*) to surround (**de** with) (**b**) (*être autour de*) to surround; **les gens qui vous entourent** the people around or about you; **le monde qui nous entoure** the world about us; **entouré de mystère** shrouded in mystery; **un rang de perles entourait son cou** she had a string of pearls round her neck (**c**) (*soutenir*) (*personne*) to rally round; **elle est très entourée** she has a lot of people she can turn to for support
   2 s'entourer *vpr* **s'e. d'amis/de belles choses** to surround oneself with friends/with beautiful things

entourloupe [ɑ̃turlup], **entourloupette** [ɑ̃turlupet] *nf Fam* dirty trick; **faire une e. à qn** to play a dirty trick on sb

entournure [ɑ̃turnyr] *nf Fam* **être gêné aux entournures** (*mal à l'aise*) to feel awkward; (*financièrement*) to feel the pinch

entracte [ɑ̃trakt] *nm* intermission, *Br* interval

entraide [ɑ̃trɛd] *nf* mutual aid

entraider [ɑ̃trɛde] **s'entraider** *vpr* to help one another

entrailles [ɑ̃trɑj] *nfpl* entrails

entrain [ɑ̃trɛ̃] *nm* get-up-and-go; **être plein d'e.** to be full of life; **travailler avec e.** to beaver away; **faire qch sans e.** to do sth half-heartedly

entraînant, -e [ɑ̃trɛnɑ̃, -ɑ̃t] *adj* (*air, rythme*) lively

entraînement [ɑ̃trɛnmɑ̃] *nm* (**a**) (*en sport*) training; **un e.** a training session; **à l'e.** in training; **avoir de l'e.** to be well trained; **manquer d'e.** to be out of practice (**b**) *Tech* drive

entraîner [ɑ̃trɛne] **1** *vt* (**a**) (*sujet: rivière*) to carry away; (*sujet: locomotive*) to pull; **e. qn quelque part** to take sb off somewhere; **il l'a entraîné dans sa chute** he dragged him down with him (**b**) (*exercer une influence sur*) to influence; **e. qn à faire qch** to lead sb to do sth; **e. qn dans un piège** to lure sb into a trap; **se laisser e.** to allow oneself to be led astray (**c**) (*causer*) (*dépense, modification*) to entail, to lead to; **e. un retard** to result in a delay (**d**) (*athlète, équipe*) to coach, to train; (*cheval*) to train; **e. qn à faire qch** to train sb to do sth (**e**) *Tech* to drive
   2 s'entraîner *vpr* (*athlète*) to train; **s'e. à faire qch** to practise doing sth

entraîneur [ɑ̃trɛnœr] *nm* (*d'un athlète, d'une équipe*) coach; (*d'un cheval*) trainer

entraîneuse [ɑ̃trɛnøz] *nf* (**a**) (*de boîte de nuit*) hostess (**b**) (*d'un athlète, d'une équipe*) coach; (*d'un cheval*) trainer

entrapercevoir [60] [ɑ̃trapɛrsɔvwar] *vt* to catch a fleeting glimpse of

entrave [ɑ̃trav] *nf* (*obstacle*) hindrance, impediment (**à** to)

entraver [ɑ̃trave] *vt* (**a**) (*mouvement, processus*) to hinder, to impede (**b**) *Fam* **j'y entrave que dalle** it beats me

entre [ɑ̃tr] *prép* (**a**) (*au milieu de*) between; *Fig* **e. les deux** (*ni l'un ni l'autre*) in between; **être e. la vie et la mort** to hover between life and death; **être e. deux âges** to be middle-aged; *Fig* **faire qch e. deux portes** to do sth in passing
   (**b**) (*parmi*) among(st); **hésiter e. plusieurs solutions** to hesitate between several solutions; **plusieurs d'e. nous** several of us; **être dangereux e. tous** to be extremely dangerous; **e. autres** among others
   (**c**) (*rapport réciproque*) (*deux personnes*) between; (*plus de deux personnes*) among(st); **se marier e. cousins** to intermarry with cousins; **ils se battent e. eux** they fight with each other; **qu'y a-t-il e. eux exactement?** what exactly is going on between them?; **soit dit e. nous** between you and me; *Fam* **il faut que je te parle e. quat'z'yeux** I've got to talk to you in private
   (**d**) (*dans*) **tenir qch e. ses mains** to hold sth in one's hands; **e. ces murs** within these walls
   (**e**) (*à travers*) through; **se faufiler e. les arbres** to thread one's way through the trees

entrebâillement [ɑ̃trəbɑjmɑ̃] *nm* **par l'e. de la porte** through the half-open door

entrebâiller [ɑ̃trəbɑje] *vt* (*porte, fenêtre*) to half-open; **la porte était entrebâillée** the door was ajar

entrechat [ɑ̃trəʃa] *nm* (*pas de danse*) entrechat

entrechoquer [ɑ̃trəʃɔke] **1** *vt* to knock together; **e. des verres** to chink glasses
   2 s'entrechoquer *vpr* to knock against one another; (*verres*) to chink

entrecôte [ɑ̃trəkot] *nf* rib steak

entrecouper [ɑ̃trəkupe] *vt* to interrupt (**de** with)

entrecroiser [ɑ̃trəkrwaze] **1** *vt* (*ligne*) to intersect; (*fils*) to interlace
   2 s'entrecroiser *vpr* (*lignes, routes*) to intersect; (*fils*) to interlace

entre-déchirer [ɑ̃trədeʃire] **s'entre-déchirer** *vpr* to tear each other to pieces

entre-deux-guerres [ɑ̃trədøgɛr] *nm inv* **l'e.** the inter-war period

entre-dévorer [ɑ̃trədevɔre] **s'entre-dévorer** *vpr* to devour one another or each other

entrée [ɑ̃tre] *nf* (**a**) (*action*) entry, entrance; (*de marchandises*) import; **faire son e.** to make one's entrance; **l'e. de la Norvège dans la CE** Norway's entry into the EC; **avant mon e. à l'université** before I went to university; **e. en scène** entrance (on to the stage); **e. en fonction** assumption of one's duties; **e. en matière** introduction; **e. en vigueur** coming into force; *Fig* **à l'e. de l'hiver** at the beginning of winter; *Fig* **d'e. (de jeu)** from the outset (**b**) (*accès*) admission, admittance (**dans** ou **de** to); **avoir ses entrées dans un lieu** to have contacts in a place; **e. à l'hôpital** admission into hospital; **e. interdite** (*sur panneau*) no admittance, no entry; **e. libre** (*dans un musée*) admission free; (*dans une boutique*) browsers welcome (**c**) (*voie d'accès*) way in, entrance (**de** to); (*vestibule*) entrance hall; **e. des artistes** stage door; **e. principale** main entrance; **e. de service** service entrance (**d**) (*hors-d'œuvre*) starter (**e**) **faire 1000 entrées** (*film*) to sell 1,000 tickets (**f**) *Ordinat* (*processus*) input, entry; (*information*) entry; (*touche*) enter (key); **données d'e.** input (data); **e. (par le) clavier** keyboard input; **e. de gamme** entry level; **e. de papier** paper input; **e./sortie** input/output; **e./sortie parallèles** parallel input/output

entrefaites [ɑ̃trəfɛt] *nfpl* **sur ces e.** at that moment

entrefilet [ɑ̃trəfilɛ] *nm* short (news) item

entrejambe [ɑ̃trəʒɑ̃b] *nm* crotch

entrelacer [16] [ɑ̃trəlase] **1** *vt* (*rubans, branches*) to intertwine; *Ordinat* **écran entrelacé** interlaced screen **2 s'entrelacer** *vpr* to intertwine

entrelacs [ɑ̃trəla] *nm* interlaced design, tracery

entrelarder [ɑ̃trəlarde] *vt Culin* (*viande*) to lard; *Fig* **e. un discours de citations** to lace a speech with quotations

entremêler [ɑ̃trəmele] **1** *vt* to interweave (**de** with) **2 s'entremêler** *vpr* to be interwoven

entremets [ɑ̃trəmɛ] *nm* dessert, *Br* sweet

entremetteur, -euse [ɑ̃trəmɛtœr, -øz] *nm,f* go-between

entremise [ɑ̃trəmiz] *nf* intervention; **par l'e. de qn** through sb

entrepont [ɑ̃trəpɔ̃] *nm* 'tweendecks; (*pour voyageurs*) steerage

entreposer [ɑ̃trəpoze] *vt* to store; (*marchandises*) to warehouse

entrepôt [ɑ̃trəpo] *nm* warehouse

entreprenant, -e [ɑ̃trəprənɑ̃, -ɑ̃t] *adj* enterprising; (*auprès des femmes*) forward

entreprendre [58] [ɑ̃trəprɑ̃dr] *vt* (**a**) (*commencer*) to undertake; **e. des démarches** to take steps; **e. de faire qch** to undertake to do sth (**b**) (*entretenir*) **e. qn sur qch** to engage sb in conversation about sth

entrepreneur, -euse [ɑ̃trəprənœr, -øz] *nm,f* (**a**) (*dans le bâtiment*) contractor (**b**) (*patron*) entrepreneur (**c**) **e. de pompes funèbres** *Br* undertaker, *Am* mortician

entrepris, -e *voir* **entreprendre**

entreprise [ɑ̃trəpriz] *nf* (**a**) (*action, initiative*) enterprise, undertaking; **la libre e.** free enterprise (**b**) (*firme*) company, firm; **e. privée** private company; **e. publique** public corporation

entrer [ɑ̃tre] **1** *vi* (*aux* **être**) (**a**) (*aller*) to go in, to enter; (*venir*) to come in, to enter; **e. dans qch** to go/come into sth, to enter sth; **e. dans une voiture/un ascenseur** to get into a car/lift; **e. par la fenêtre** to get in *or* enter through the window; **e. en courant** to run in; **e. sans payer** to get in without paying; **e. au port** to come into harbour; **laisser e. qn/qch** to let sb/sth in; **empêcher qn d'e.** to keep sb out; **faire e. qn** to let sb in; (*sujet: secrétaire, majordome*) to show sb in; **faire e. qch dans une pièce** to get sth into a room; *Th* **Hamlet entre en scène** enter Hamlet; **entrez!** come/go in!

(**b**) (*pénétrer*) (*eau, air*) to go/come in; **le clou entra dans le mur** the nail went into the wall; **la clef n'entre pas dans la serrure** the key won't go in the lock

(**c**) (*heurter*) **e. dans qch** to go into sth, to run into sth; *Fam* **e. dans le décor** to go off the road

(**d**) (*faire tenir*) **faire e. qch dans qch** to insert sth in sth; **on n'y entrera jamais à vingt** we'll never get twenty people in; **il n'entre pas dans le carton** it won't go in the box

(**e**) (*devenir membre*) **e. dans l'armée** to join the army; **e. en religion** to take (holy) orders; **e. aux PTT/chez Renault** to start working for the Post Office/for Renault; **e. au service de qn** to enter sb's service; **e. dans la**

Communauté européenne to join the European Community

(**f**) (*être admis*) **e. à l'université** to go to university; **e. à l'hôpital** to go into hospital; **e. en maternelle** to start nursery school

(**g**) (*faire partie de*) **e. dans une catégorie** to fall into a category; **e. dans la légende** to become a legend; **e. dans l'histoire** to go down in history; **e. en ligne de compte** to be taken into account; **e. dans les projets de qn** to be part of sb's plans; **e. dans la vie de qn** to come into sb's life; **e. dans la composition de qch** to go into the making of sth; **cela n'entre pas dans mes idées** I don't go along with that

(**h**) (*commencer*) **e. dans une colère terrible** to get extremely angry; **e. en campagne** *Mil* to take the field; *Pol* to go on the campaign trail; **e. en guerre** to enter the war; **e. en fonction** to take up one's duties; **e. en vigueur** to come into force *or* effect; **e. dans la vie active** to start one's working life; **e. dans une ère nouvelle** to enter a new era; **e. dans les détails** to go into detail; **on entre dans l'hiver** winter is just beginning

(**i**) *Fam* (*se concentrer*) **e. dans un match** to get into a match

(**j**) *Ordinat* to log in or on

2 *vt* (*aux* **avoir**) (**a**) (*introduire*) **e. des marchandises en fraude** to smuggle in goods

(**b**) (*enfoncer*) **e. ses ongles dans le cou de qn** to sink one's nails into sb's neck

(**c**) *Ordinat* (*données*) to enter, to input; (*au clavier*) to key in

3 *v impersonnel* **il n'entre pas dans mes projets de le faire** it's not part of my plans to do it

entresol [ɑ̃trəsɔl] *nm* mezzanine (floor)

entre-temps [ɑ̃trətɑ̃] *adv* meanwhile, in the meantime

entretenir [70] [ɑ̃trətənir] **1** *vt* (**a**) (*soigner*) (*maison, jardin, routes, machine*) to maintain; **une moquette facile à e.** a carpet which is easy to look after; **e. sa forme** to keep fit (**b**) (*payer pour*) (*famille, maîtresse*) to maintain, to support (**c**) (*maintenir*) **e. une correspondance avec qn** to keep up a correspondence with sb; **e. de bonnes relations avec qn** to remain on good terms with sb (**d**) (*parler à*) **e. qn de qch** to converse with sb about sth

2 s'entretenir *vpr* **s'e. avec qn** (**de qch**) to converse with sb (about sth)

entretenu, -e [ɑ̃trətny] *adj* (**a**) **bien/mal e.** (*maison, jardin*) well-kept/badly kept (**b**) **une femme entretenue** a kept woman

entretien [ɑ̃trətjɛ̃] *nm* (**a**) (*soins*) (*d'une maison, d'un jardin, des routes, d'une machine*) maintenance; **facile/difficile d'e., d'e.** facile/difficile easy/difficult to maintain; **produits d'e.** (household) cleaning materials (**b**) (*subsistance*) (*d'une famille, d'une armée*) support, maintenance (**c**) (*conversation*) conversation; (*audience*) interview; **entretiens** (*négociations*) discussions, talks

entre-tuer [ɑ̃trətɥe] **s'entre-tuer** *vpr* to kill each other

entreverrai *etc voir* **entrevoir**

entrevoir [73a] [ɑ̃trəvwar] *vt* (*rapidement*) to catch sight of, to catch a glimpse of; (*indistinctement*) to make out; **e. des difficultés** to foresee difficulties

entrevoyons *etc voir* **entrevoir**

entrevu, -e *voir* **entrevoir**

entrevue [ɑ̃trəvy] *nf* (*rendez-vous*) interview; (*réunion*) meeting

entrouvert, -e [ɑ̃truvɛr, -ɛrt] *adj* half-open

entrouvrir [52] [ɑ̃truvrir] **1** vt to half-open
2 s'entrouvrir vpr to half-open

entuber [ɑ̃tybe] vt Fam (duper) to con; **se faire e.** to be conned

énumération [enymerasjɔ̃] nf listing

énumérer [34] [enymere] vt to list

envahir [ɑ̃vair] vt (pays) to invade; (marché) to flood; **un jardin envahi par les mauvaises herbes** a garden overgrown with weeds; Fig **un doute m'a envahi** I was overcome with doubt; Fam **e. qn** (sujet: personne) to intrude on sb

envahissant, -e [ɑ̃vaisɑ̃, -ɑ̃t] adj (plantes) invasive; (odeur) overwhelming; Fam (personne) intrusive

envahisseur [ɑ̃vaisœr] nm invader

enveloppant, -e [ɑ̃vlɔpɑ̃, -ɑ̃t] adj (a) (couvrant) **regard e.** look that takes/took everything in (b) Fig (séduisant) (manières) captivating

enveloppe [ɑ̃vlɔp] nf (a) (de lettre) envelope; **e. à fenêtre** window envelope; **envoyer qch sous e.** to send sth under cover; Fig **e. budgétaire** budget; Fig **l'e. de la recherche** the research budget (b) (de paquet) wrapping (c) (de graines) husk (d) Fig (apparence) **sous une e. de rudesse** beneath a rough exterior

enveloppé, -e [ɑ̃vlɔpe] adj Fam **bien e.** (personne) well-padded

envelopper [ɑ̃vlɔpe] **1** vt (a) (marchandises, bébé) to wrap (up); **enveloppé dans des bandages** swathed in bandages (b) (entourer) **e. qch du regard** to take sth in with one's gaze; **la nuit nous enveloppa** darkness closed in on us; **enveloppé de mystère/brume** shrouded in mystery/mist
2 s'envelopper vpr **s'e. dans une couverture** to wrap oneself up in a blanket

envenimer [ɑ̃vnime] **1** vt (plaie) to make septic; Fig (querelle, discussion) to embitter
2 s'envenimer vpr (plaie) to turn septic; Fig (querelle, discussion) to get acrimonious

envergure [ɑ̃vɛrgyr] nf (a) (d'un oiseau, d'un avion) wingspan (b) Fig (ampleur) scope; **de grande e., d'e.** (réforme) far-reaching; (opération) large-scale (c) (personne) calibre; **manquer d'e.** to be of a low calibre

enverrai etc voir **envoyer**

envers[1] [ɑ̃vɛr] nm (d'un document, d'une assiette) back; (d'une médaille, d'une feuille) reverse; **à l'e.** (l'extérieur à l'intérieur) inside out; (de haut en bas) the wrong way up, upside down; (devant derrière) the wrong way round, back to front; Fig **l'e. du décor** the other side of the picture; Fam **c'est le monde à l'e.!** what's the world coming to!

envers[2] prép towards; **e. et contre tous** in the face of all opposition

envi [ɑ̃vi] **à l'envi** adv **faire qch à l'e.** to vie with one another in doing sth

enviable [ɑ̃vjabl] adj enviable

envie [ɑ̃vi] nf (a) (désir) desire; (caprice) craving (**de** for); **avoir (très) e. de qch/de faire qch** to (really) want sth/to do sth; **avoir e. de dormir** to feel sleepy; **être pris d'une terrible e. de rire** to have a terrible urge to laugh; **donner à qn l'e. de faire qch** to make sb want to do sth; **il a e. que je le fasse** he wants me to do it; **je vais lui ôter l'e. de s'amuser** I'll stop her messing around; **ce gâteau me fait e.** that cake is tempting; **faire e. à qn** (sujet: personne) to tempt sb; Fam **ça lui a pris comme une e. de pisser** he just got a sudden urge (b) (jalousie)

envy; **regarder qch avec e.** to look enviously at sth (c) (au doigt) hangnail; (sur la peau) birthmark

envier [66] [ɑ̃vje] vt to envy; **e. qch à qn** to envy sb sth; **n'avoir rien à e. à personne** to have no cause to be envious of anyone

envieux, -euse [ɑ̃vjø, -øz] **1** adj envious (**de** of)
2 nm,f envious person; **faire des e.** to make people envious

environ [ɑ̃virɔ̃] **1** adv (à peu près) about, around
2 environs nmpl (alentours) surrounding area; **aux ou dans les environs de Paris** in the vicinity of Paris; **aux environs de cinq heures** round about five o'clock

environnant, -e [ɑ̃vironɑ̃, -ɑ̃t] adj surrounding

environnement [ɑ̃vironmɑ̃] nm (a) (milieu) environment (b) Ordinat environment; **e. partagé** shared environment

environner [ɑ̃virone] **1** vt to surround; **environné de qch** surrounded by sth
2 s'environner vpr **s'e. de** to surround oneself with

envisageable [ɑ̃vizaʒabl] adj conceivable

envisager [45] [ɑ̃vizaʒe] vt (considérer) (question, situation, solution) to consider; (projeter) (conséquence, événement) to envisage; **e. l'avenir** to foresee the future; **e. de faire qch** to consider doing sth

envoi [ɑ̃vwa] nm (a) (action) sending; **e. recommandé** recorded delivery (b) (colis) parcel; (lettre) letter; (marchandises) consignment (**de** of)

envol [ɑ̃vɔl] nm (d'avion) take-off; (d'oiseau) taking off

envolée [ɑ̃vɔle] nf (a) (vol) flight; Fig **e. lyrique** flight of fancy; Fig **l'e. du dollar** the soaring price of the dollar

envoler [ɑ̃vɔle] **s'envoler** vpr (a) (oiseau) to fly away; (avion) to take off; **je m'envole dans une heure** my plane leaves in an hour; Fig **s'e. dans les sondages** to shoot up the opinion polls (b) (emporté par le vent) (chapeau) to blow off; (papiers) to blow away (c) Fam (disparaître) (personne, sac) to vanish

envoûtant, -e [ɑ̃vutɑ̃, -ɑ̃t] adj (fascinant) bewitching

envoûtement [ɑ̃vutmɑ̃] nm aussi Fig bewitchment

envoûter [ɑ̃vute] vt aussi Fig to bewitch

envoyé, -e [ɑ̃vwaje] nm,f (messager) messenger; (d'un gouvernement) envoy; **e. spécial** (journaliste) special correspondent

envoyer [33] [ɑ̃vwaje] **1** vt to send; (lancer) to throw; **e. qch par courrier** to mail sth, Br to post sth; **e. qch à qn** to send sb sth; (lancer) to throw sth to sb; **e. un baiser à qn** to blow sb a kiss; **e. chercher qn** to send for sb; **e. qn faire qch** to send sb to do sth; Fam **e. promener ou balader ou paître qn, e. qn sur les roses** to send sb packing; Fam **je vais tout e. promener** I'm going to chuck it all in; Fig **e. des fleurs à qn** to pat sb on the back
2 s'envoyer vpr (a) (l'un l'autre) **ils s'envoient des cartes postales** they send postcards to each other (b) Fam **s'e. un verre de vin** to knock back a glass of wine; très Fam **s'e. qn** Br to have it off with sb, Am to make it with sb; très Fam **s'e. en l'air** Br to have it off, Am to make it

envoyeur, -euse [ɑ̃vwajœr, -øz] nm,f sender; **retour à l'e.** return to sender

enzyme [ɑ̃zim] nf enzyme; **lessive aux enzymes** biological washing powder

éolien, -enne [eɔljɛ̃, -ɛn] **1** adj **énergie éolienne** wind energy; **moteur é.** wind-powered engine
2 nf **éolienne** wind turbine

épagneul, -e [epaɲœl] nm,f spaniel; **é. breton** Brittany spaniel

épais, -aisse [epɛ, -ɛs] **1** adj thick; **é. de 2 mètres** 2 metres thick; *Fam* **elle n'est pas bien épaisse** she hasn't got much on her

2 adv **(a)** *(pousser)* thick(ly) **(b)** *Fam (beaucoup)* **il n'y en a pas é.** there's not much of it

3 nm **au plus é. de la forêt** in the depths of the forest

épaisseur [epesœr] nf thickness; *Fig (d'une personne)* depth; **avoir 2 mètres d'é.** to be 2 metres thick

épaissir [epesir] **1** vt *(sauce, peinture)* to thicken; *(ombre, mystère)* to deepen

2 vi *(sauce)* to thicken; *(personne)* to fill out

3 s'épaissir vpr *(cheveux, brouillard, sauce)* to thicken; *(personne)* to fill out; *(ombre, mystère)* to deepen

épaississant [epesisɑ̃] nm *(substance)* thickener

épaississement [epesismɑ̃] nm *(du brouillard, d'une sauce)* thickening

épanchement [epɑ̃ʃmɑ̃] nm **(a)** **é. de synovie** water on the knee **(b)** *Fig (de sentiments)* outpouring

épancher [epɑ̃ʃe] **1** vt **é. sa bile** to vent one's spleen; **é. son cœur** to pour out one's heart

2 s'épancher vpr *(personne)* to pour out one's heart

épandre [epɑ̃dr] **s'épandre** vpr *Litt* to spread **(sur** over)

épanoui, -e [epanwi] adj *(fleur)* in full bloom; *(visage, sourire)* beaming; *(personne)* well-adjusted

épanouir [epanwir] **1** vt *(fleur, pétales)* to open out

2 s'épanouir vpr **(a)** *(fleur)* to bloom **(b)** *(visage)* to light up **(c)** *(personne)* to blossom

épanouissant, -e [epanwisɑ̃, -ɑ̃t] adj *(travail, vie)* fulfilling

épanouissement [epanwismɑ̃] nm **(a)** *(action) (d'une fleur)* blooming; *(d'un visage)* lighting up; *(d'une personne)* blossoming **(b)** *(plénitude)* full bloom

épargnant, -e [eparɲɑ̃, -ɑ̃t] nm,f saver

épargne [eparɲ] nf **(a)** *(action, vertu)* saving **(b)** *(sommes)* savings *(c)* *(épargnants)* l'é. private investors

épargner [eparɲe] **1** vt **(a)** *(argent, provisions)* to save **(b)** *(énergie, temps)* to save; **é. à qn la peine de faire qch** to save sb the trouble of doing sth; **épargne-moi les détails!** spare me the details! **(c)** *(prisonnier)* to spare

2 vi to save **(sur** on)

3 s'épargner vpr **s'é. la peine de faire qch** to save oneself the trouble of doing sth

éparpiller [eparpije] **1** vt *(objets, foule)* to scatter

2 s'éparpiller vpr *(objets, foule)* to scatter; *Fig (personne)* to take on too much

épars, -e [epar, -ars] adj *(maisons)* scattered; *(végétation, population, informations)* sparse; *(cheveux)* thin

épatant, -e [epatɑ̃, -ɑ̃t] adj *Fam* splendid

épaté, -e [epate] adj *Fam* dumbfounded

épater [epate] vt *Fam* to astound

épaule [epol] nf shoulder; **être large d'épaules** to be broad-shouldered; *Culin* **é. d'agneau** shoulder of lamb

épauler [epole] **1** vt **(a)** *(fusil)* to raise to one's shoulder **(b)** *(aider)* **é. qn** to back sb up

2 vi to take aim

épaulette [epolɛt] nf **(a)** *(rembourrage)* shoulder pad **(b)** *(bretelle)* shoulder strap

épave [epav] nf aussi Fig wreck

épée [epe] nf sword; *Sp* épée; **coup d'é.** swordthrust; *Fig* **un coup d'é. dans l'eau** a wasted effort; *Fig* **une é. de Damoclès** a Sword of Damocles

épeler [42] [eple] vt & vi to spell

éperdu, -e [eperdy] adj *(regard)* distraught; *(amour)* passionate

éperdument [eperdymɑ̃] adv *(aimer)* madly; **é. amoureux** head over heels in love, madly in love; *Fam* **je m'en fiche é.** I couldn't care less

éperlan [eperlɑ̃] nm smelt

éperon [eprɔ̃] nm spur

éperonner [eprɔne] vt to spur on

épervier [epɛrvje] nm sparrowhawk

éphèbe [efɛb] nm Adonis

éphémère [efemer] **1** adj short-lived, ephemeral

2 nm mayfly

épi [epi] nm **(a)** *(de grain)* ear; *(de fleur)* spike; **é. de maïs** corncob **(b)** *(de cheveux)* tuft of hair

épice [epis] nf spice; **quatre épices** allspice

épicé, -e [epise] adj spicy

épicéa [episea] nm spruce

épicentre [episɑ̃tr] nm epicentre

épicer [epise] vt to spice

épicerie [episri] nf **(a)** *(magasin)* grocer's (shop); **é. fine** delicatessen **(b)** *(produits)* groceries **(c)** *Can Fig* **liste d'é.** *(de griefs)* shopping list

épicier, -ère [episje, -ɛr] nm,f grocer

épicurien, -enne [epikyrjɛ̃, -ɛn] **1** adj epicurean; *Phil* Epicurean

2 nm,f epicure; *Phil* Epicurean

épidémie [epidemi] nf epidemic

épidémique [epidemik] adj epidemic

épiderme [epidɛrm] nm skin; *Spéc* epidermis

épidermique [epidɛrmik] adj epidermal; *Fig* **une réaction é.** a kneejerk reaction

épier [66] [epje] vt *(espionner) (personne, activités)* to spy on; *(observer) (signe, occasion)* to watch out for

épilation [epilasjɔ̃] nf *(des jambes)* removal of unwanted hair; *(des sourcils)* plucking

épilatoire [epilatwar] adj *(crème)* hair-removing

épilepsie [epilepsi] nf epilepsy; *crise* **d'é.** epileptic fit

épileptique [epileptik] adj & nmf epileptic

épiler [epile] **1** vt *(jambes)* to remove the unwanted hair from; *(sourcils)* to pluck

2 s'épiler vpr **s'é. les jambes** to remove the unwanted hair from one's legs; **s'é. les sourcils** to pluck one's eyebrows; **s'é. les jambes à la cire** to wax one's legs

épilogue [epilog] nm epilogue

épiloguer [epiloge] vi to hold forth **(sur** about)

épinard [epinar] nm *(plante)* spinach; **épinards** spinach; **épinards en branches** leaf spinach

épine [epin] nf **(a)** *(piquant)* thorn; *(d'un animal)* spine, prickle; *Fig* **tirer une é. du pied à qn** *(tirer d'embarras)* to get sb out of a mess; *(soulager)* to relieve sb's mind; **é. dorsale** backbone

épinette [epinɛt] nf **(a)** *Can Bot* spruce **(b)** *(instrument)* spinet

épineux, -euse [epinø, -øz] adj *(arbuste, problème)* thorny; *(poisson)* spiny

épingle [epɛ̃gl] *nf* pin; **attacher qch avec des épingles** *(cheveux)* to pin sth up; *(tissu, feuilles)* to pin sth together; *Fig* **tirer son é. du jeu** to extricate oneself; *Fig* **être tiré à quatre épingles** to be dressed up to the nines; *Fig* **chercher une é. dans une botte de foin** to look for a needle in a haystack; *Fig* **monter qch en é.** to make too much of sth; **é. à chapeau** hatpin; **é. à cheveux** hairpin; **virage en é. à cheveux** hairpin *Br* bend *or Am* turn; **é. à linge** clothes *Br* peg *or Am* pin; **é. de ou à nourrice, é. de sûreté** safety pin

épingler [epɛ̃gle] *vt* (a) *(attacher)* to pin (à/sur to/on) (b) *Fam (arrêter)* to nab; **se faire é.** to get nabbed

épinoche [epinɔʃ] *nf* stickleback

Épiphanie [epifani] *nf Rel* **l'É.** Epiphany

épique [epik] *adj* epic

épiscopal, -e, -aux, -ales [episkɔpal, -o] *adj* episcopal

épiscopat [episkɔpa] *nm (fonction, évêques)* episcopate

épisode [epizɔd] *nm aussi Fig* episode

épisodique [epizɔdik] *adj (intermittent)* occasional; *(accessoire)* minor

épisodiquement [epizɔdikmã] *adv* occasionally

épistémologie [epistemɔlɔʒi] *nf* epistemology

épistolaire [epistɔlɛr] *adj* epistolary; **être en relation é. avec qn** to correspond with sb

épitaphe [epitaf] *nf* epitaph

épithélium [epiteljɔm] *nm* epithelium

épithète [epitɛt] *nf* epithet; *Gram* attribute

épître [epitr] *nf* epistle

éploré, -e [eplɔre] *adj* tearful

épluchage [eplyʃaʒ] *nm* peeling; *Fig* detailed examination

épluche-légumes [eplyʃlegym] *nm inv* potato peeler

éplucher [eplyʃe] *vt (peler)* to peel; *Fig (texte, journal)* to go through in detail

épluchette [eplyʃɛt] *nf Can* **é. de blé d'Inde** cornhusking party

épluchure [eplyʃyr] *nf (pelure)* peeling

éponge [epɔ̃ʒ] **1** *nf* sponge; **donner un coup d'é. à qch** to wipe sth with a sponge; **d'un coup d'é.** with a sponge; **jeter l'é.** *(à la boxe)* to throw in the towel; *Fig* **passer l'é.** to forget all about it
2 *adj inv* **tissu é.** (terry) towelling; **serviette é.** terry towel

éponger [45] [epɔ̃ʒe] **1** *vt* (a) *(liquide)* to mop up (b) *(surface)* to sponge (down); *(le front de quelqu'un)* to mop (c) *Fig (déficit)* to mop up
2 s'éponger *vpr* **s'é. le front** to mop one's brow

épopée [epope] *nf aussi Fig* epic

époque [epɔk] *nf* (a) *(historique)* era, age; *Géol* period; **la Belle É.** ≃ the Edwardian era; **quelle é. (nous vivons)!** what times we live in!; **être de son é.** to be in tune with the times; **meubles d'é.** period furniture (b) *(moment précis)* time; **à l'é.** at the time

épouiller [epuje] *vt* to delouse

époumoner [epumone] **s'époumoner** *vpr (en criant)* to shout oneself hoarse; *(en chantant)* to sing oneself hoarse

épouse [epuz] *nf* wife

épouser [epuze] *vt* to marry; *Fig (cause)* to espouse; *Fig* **é. la forme de qch** to take on the exact shape of sth

épousseter [42] [epuste] *vt* to dust

époustouflant, -e [epustuflã, -ãt] *adj Fam* astounding

époustoufler [epustufle] *vt Fam* to astound

épouvantable [epuvãtabl] *adj* dreadful, appalling

épouvantail [epuvãtaj] *nm (de jardin)* scarecrow; *Péj (personne laide)* fright; *(personne terrifiante)* bogy

épouvante [epuvãt] *nf* terror

épouvanté, -e [epuvãte] *adj* terror-stricken

épouvanter [epuvãte] *vt* to terrify

époux [epu] *nm* husband; **les é.** the married couple; **les é. Thomas** Mr and Mrs Thomas

éprendre [58] [eprɑ̃dr] **s'éprendre** *vpr* **s'é. de qn** to fall in love with sb

épreuve [eprœv] *nf* (a) *(essai)* test; **mettre qn/qch à l'é.** to put sb/sth to the test; **à l'é. du feu** fireproof; **à l'é. des balles** bulletproof; **un courage à toute é.** unfailing courage; **être mis à rude é.** *(personne, patience)* to be severely tested; **les bateaux furent mis à rude é. par la tempête** the boats took a battering from the storm; *Fig* **é. de force** trial of strength (b) *(examen) (écrit)* (examination) paper; *(oral)* test (c) *(d'athlétisme)* event; **é. contre la montre** time trial; **é. éliminatoire** heat (d) *(adversité)* trial, ordeal; **dans l'é.** in adversity (e) *Typ* proof (f) *Phot* print

épris, -e [epri, -iz] *adj* (a) **é. de qn** in love with sb (b) **é. de qch** passionate about sth

éprouvant, -e [epruvã, -ãt] *adj* trying

éprouvé, -e [epruve] *adj* (a) *(testé) (remède)* proven, well-tried; *(matériaux)* tested (b) *(famille)* sorely tried; *(région)* hard-hit

éprouver [epruve] *vt* (a) *(essayer) (méthode, personne, courage)* to test (b) *(ressentir) (sensation, sentiment, douleur)* to feel (c) *(subir) (perte)* to suffer; *(difficultés)* to meet with

éprouvette [epruvɛt] **1** *nf* test tube
2 *adj* **bébé é.** test-tube baby

EPS [əpees] *nf (abrév* **éducation physique et sportive**) PE

épuisant, -e [epɥizɑ̃, -ãt] *adj* exhausting

épuisé, -e [epɥize] *adj* (a) *(très fatigué)* exhausted (b) *(sol)* exhausted (c) *(livre, édition)* out of print; *(marchandises)* sold out

épuisement [epɥizmɑ̃] *nm* (a) *(fatigue)* exhaustion; **danser jusqu'à l'é.** to dance till one drops (b) *(d'un sol, d'un stock, de ressources)* exhaustion; **jusqu'à. é. des stocks** while stocks last

épuiser [epɥize] **1** *vt* (a) *(fatiguer)* to exhaust (b) *(sol, stock, ressources, sujet)* to exhaust
2 s'épuiser *vpr* (a) *(se fatiguer)* to exhaust oneself, to wear oneself out; **s'é. à faire qch** to wear oneself out doing sth (b) *(source)* to dry up; *(stock, ressources)* to run out

épuisette [epɥizɛt] *nf* landing net

épuration [epyrasjɔ̃] *nf (de l'eau, du gaz)* purification; *(du pétrole, d'un minerai)* refining; *Fig (d'une langue)* refining; *Pol* purge

épurer [epyre] *vt (eau, gaz)* to purify; *(pétrole, minerai)* to refine; *Fig (langue)* to refine; *Pol (parti)* to purge

équarrir [ekarir] *vt* (a) *(bois, pierre)* to square (b) *(animal)* to quarter

équarrissage [ekarisaʒ] *nm* (a) *(du bois, de la pierre)* squaring (b) *(d'animaux)* quartering

Équateur [ekwatœr] *nm* **l'É.** Ecuador

équateur [ekwatœr] *nm* equator; **sous l'é.** at the equator

équation [ekwasjɔ̃] *nf* equation; **é. du premier/deuxième degré** simple/quadratic equation

équatorial, -e, -aux, -ales [ekwatɔrjal, -o] *adj* equatorial

équatorien, -enne [ekwatɔrjɛ̃, -ɛn] **1** *adj* Ecuadorian **2** *nm,f* É. Ecuadorian

équerre [ekɛr] *nf* **é. (à dessin)** set square; **en é., à l'é.** at right angles; **d'é.** square, straight

équestre [ekɛstr] *adj (statue, sports)* equestrian; *(exercices)* horseriding

équidés [ekɥide, ekide] *nmpl* horse family, *Spéc* Equidae

équidistant, -e [ekɥidistɑ̃, -ɑ̃t] *adj* equidistant **(de** from)

équilatéral, -e, -aux, -ales [ekɥilateral, -o] *adj* equilateral

équilibrage [ekilibraʒ] *nm* balancing

équilibre [ekilibr] *nm* **(a)** *(d'un corps, d'un objet)* balance; **mettre qch en é.** to balance sth; **perdre l'é.** to lose one's balance; **faire perdre l'é. à qn** to throw sb off balance; **faire de l'é. sur qch** to balance on sth; **être en é. instable** to be precariously balanced **(b)** *(mental)* (mental) balance, equilibrium **(c)** *(budget)* **é. budget en é.** balanced budget; **é. budgétaire** balanced budget **(d)** *(d'un ensemble)* balance

équilibré, -e [ekilibre] *adj (chargement, alimentation)* balanced; *(personne)* well-balanced; *(vie)* stable

équilibrer [ekilibre] **1** *vt (charge, composition)* to balance; *(bateau, avion)* to trim; **é. un budget** to balance a budget **2 s'équilibrer** *vpr (l'un l'autre)* to balance each other out

équilibriste [ekilibrist] *nmf (funambule)* tightrope walker

équinoxe [ekinɔks] *nm* equinox

équipage [ekipaʒ] *nm* **(a)** *(d'un navire, d'un avion)* crew; **les hommes d'é.** the crew; **les membres de l'é.** the crew **(b)** *(voiture et chevaux)* equipage

équipe [ekip] *nf* **(a)** *Sp* team; **une é. de football** a football team **(b)** *(de chercheurs, de médecins)* team; *(d'ouvriers)* gang; *(à l'usine)* shift; *Mil* working party; **faire é. avec qn** to team up with sb; **é. dirigeante** management team; **é. de jour/nuit** day/night shift; **é. de secours** rescue team

équipée [ekipe] *nf (frasque)* escapade; *(promenade, voyage)* jaunt

équipement [ekipmɑ̃] *nm* **(a)** *(action)* *(d'un atelier, d'une cuisine)* equipping, fitting out **(de** with) **(b)** *(matériel)* equipment; *(de soldat)* kit **(c)** *(installations)* facilities; **équipements collectifs** public facilities; *Ordinat* **é. informatique** computer equipment

équiper [ekipe] **1** *vt (atelier, cuisine)* to equip, to fit out **(de** with); *(sportif, armée)* to equip, *Br* to kit out **(de** with); **appartement avec cuisine équipée** flat with cooking facilities **2 s'équiper** *vpr* to equip oneself **(de** with)

équipier, -ère [ekipje, -ɛr] *nm,f* team member

équitable [ekitabl] *adj* fair

équitablement [ekitablmɑ̃] *adv* fairly

équitation [ekitasjɔ̃] *nf* (horse)riding; **faire de l'é.** to go (horse)riding

équivalence [ekivalɑ̃s] *nf* equivalence; *Univ* **avoir/obtenir une é.** to have/get an equivalent diploma

équivalent, -e [ekivalɑ̃, -ɑ̃t] **1** *adj* equivalent **(à** to) **2** *nm* equivalent; **sans é.** without equal

équivaloir [69] [ekivalwar] *vi* **é. à qch** *(valoir)* to be equivalent to sth; *(revenir à)* to amount to sth

équivaut *voir* **équivaloir**

équivoque [ekivɔk] **1** *adj* **(a)** *(ambigu)* *(terme, attitude)* equivocal, ambiguous **(b)** *(douteux)* *(conduite, passé)* dubious **2** *nf* ambiguity; **sans é.** *(réponse, situation)* unequivocal; *(répondre)* unequivocally

érable [erabl] *nm (arbre, bois)* maple; **sirop d'é.** maple syrup

érablière [erablijɛr] *nf Can* maple grove

éradication [eradikasjɔ̃] *nf* eradication

éradiquer [eradike] *vt* to eradicate

érafler [erafle] **1** *vt (genou)* to graze; *(cuir)* to scuff; *(bois, meuble)* to scratch **2 s'érafler** *vpr* **s'é.** **le coude** to graze one's elbow

éraflure [eraflyr] *nf (au genou)* graze; *(sur cuir)* scuff mark; *(sur bois, sur meuble)* scratch

éraillé, -e [eraje] *adj* **(a)** *(voix)* hoarse **(b)** *(surface)* scratched

ère [ɛr] *nf* era; **en l'an 1150 de notre è.** in the year 1150 AD; **avant notre è.** BC

érection [erɛksjɔ̃] *nf* **(a)** *(construction)* erection **(b)** *(gonflement)* erection; **être en é.** *(personne)* to have an erection; *(verge)* to be erect

éreintant, -e [erɛ̃tɑ̃, -ɑ̃t] *adj Fam* exhausting

éreinté, -e [erɛ̃te] *adj Fam* exhausted

éreinter [erɛ̃te] **1** *vt* **(a)** *(fatiguer)* *(personne, animal)* to exhaust, to wear out **(b)** *(critiquer)* *(livre, auteur)* to pull to pieces **2 s'éreinter** *vpr* **s'é. à faire qch** to wear oneself out doing sth

érémiste [eremist] = **RMiste**

Erevan [erevan] *n* Yerevan

ergot [ɛrgo] *nm* **(a)** *(d'un coq)* spur **(b)** *(d'un chien)* dewclaw **(c)** *Tech* pin

ergoter [ɛrgɔte] *vi* to quibble **(sur** about)

Érié [erje] *n voir* **lac**

ériger [45] [eriʒe] **1** *vt* **(a)** *(dresser)* *(statue, temple, mât)* to erect **(b)** *(créer)* *(tribunal)* to establish, to set up **(c)** *Fig* **é. qn en qch** to set sb up as sth; **é. qch en qch** to elevate sth to the status of sth **2 s'ériger** *vpr* **s'é. en qch** to set oneself up as sth

ermitage [ɛrmitaʒ] *nm* hermitage

ermite [ɛrmit] *nm* hermit; **vivre en e.** to live the life of a recluse

érogène [erɔʒɛn] *adj* erogenous

érosion [erozjɔ̃] *nf* erosion

érotique [erɔtik] *adj* erotic

érotisme [erɔtism] *nm* eroticism

errance [erɑ̃s] *nf Litt* roving, wandering

errant, -e [erɑ̃, -ɑ̃t] *adj (vie)* roving, wandering; **chevalier e.** knight-errant; **chien e.** stray dog

errata [erata] *nmpl voir* **erratum**

erratique [eratik] *adj* erratic

erratum [eratɔm] *(pl* **errata** [erata]) *nm* erratum

errements [ermɑ̃] *nmpl* bad ways; **retomber dans ses e.** passés to fall back into one's bad old ways

errer [ere] *vi (marcher)* to wander; **e. par les rues** to roam the streets; **e. comme une âme en peine** to wander about like a lost soul

erreur [erœr] *nf* (a) *(faute)* mistake, error; **faire** *ou* **commettre une e.** to make a mistake; **faire e.** to be mistaken; **être dans l'e.** to be mistaken; **induire qn en e.** to mislead sb; **par e.** by mistake; **sauf e. de ma part** if I'm not mistaken; **il y a e. sur la personne** you've/they've/*etc* got the wrong person; **il n'y a pas d'e. (possible)** there's no doubt about it; **l'e. est humaine** to err is human; **e. de calcul** miscalculation; **e. de jeunesse** youthful indiscretion; **e. judiciaire** miscarriage of justice; **e. de jugement** error of judgement (b) *Ordinat* error; **message d'e.** error message; **correction des erreurs** error correction; **e. d'analyse (syntaxique)** parse error; **e. disque** disk error; **e. d'échantillonnage** sampling error; **e. d'écriture** write error; **e. de lecture** read error; **e. de logiciel** software *or* system error; **e. de programmation** programming error; **e. de saisie** keying error

erroné, -e [ɛrɔne] *adj* erroneous

ersatz [ɛrzats] *nm inv* ersatz, substitute

éructer [erykte] **1** *vi* to belch
 2 *vt Fig* **é. des injures** to hurl abuse

érudit, -e [erydi, -it] **1** *adj* erudite, scholarly
 2 *nm,f* scholar

érudition [erydisjɔ̃] *nf* erudition, scholarship

éruption [erypsjɔ̃] *nf* (a) *(d'un volcan)* eruption; **entrer en é.** to erupt (b) *(de boutons)* rash

érythème [eritɛm] *nm Méd* rash; **é. fessier** *Br* nappy *or Am* diaper rash; **é. solaire** sunburn

Érythrée [eritre] *nf* l'É. Eritrea

érythréen, -enne [eritreɛ̃, -ɛn] **1** *adj* Eritrean
 2 *nm,f* É. Eritrean

E/S *Ordinat (abrév* **entrée/sortie**) I/O

es *voir* **être²**

ès [ɛs] *prép* **docteur ès lettres/sciences** ≃ PhD; **licencié ès lettres** ≃ BA; **licencié ès sciences** ≃ BSc

esbroufe [ɛzbruf] *nf Fam* bluffing; **faire de l'e.** to bluff

escabeau, -x [ɛskabo] *nm* (a) *(tabouret)* stool (b) *(marchepied)* stepladder

escadre [ɛskadr] *nf Naut* squadron; *Av* **e. aérienne** wing; **chef d'e.** *Naut* squadron commander; *Av* wing commander

escadrille [ɛskadrij] *nf* (a) *Naut* flotilla (b) *Av (unité)* flight

escadron [ɛskadrɔ̃] *nm* (a) *Mil* squadron; **chef d'e. major** (b) *Av* squadron (c) *Fig (groupe) (de journalistes)* troop, band

escalade [ɛskalad] *nf* (a) *(d'un mur, d'une falaise)* climbing, scaling; *Sp* climbing; **faire de l'e.** to go climbing (b) *Fig (d'une guerre, des prix, de la violence)* escalation

escalader [ɛskalade] *vt* to climb, to scale

escalator® [ɛskalatɔr] *nm* escalator

escale [ɛskal] *nf* (a) *(arrêt)* stopover; **faire e.** *(en bateau)* to put into port; *(en avion)* to touch down; **faire e. à Athènes** *(en bateau)* to put in at Athens; *(en avion)* to stop over at Athens; **vol sans e.** nonstop flight; **e. technique** refuelling stop (b) *(lieu) (pour bateau)* port of call; *(pour avion)* stopover

escalier [ɛskalje] *nm (marches)* stairs; *(cage)* staircase; **dans l'e., dans les escaliers** on the stairs; **monter en e.** *(en ski)* to sidestep; **e. en colimaçon** spiral staircase; **e. mécanique, e. roulant,** *Can* **e. mobile** escalator; **e. de secours** fire escape; **e. de service** backstairs

escalope [ɛskalɔp] *nf* escalope

escamotable [ɛskamɔtabl] *adj (antenne, train d'atterrissage, phares)* retractable; *(meuble)* foldaway

escamotage [ɛskamɔtaʒ] *nm* (a) *(par un illusionniste)* vanishing (b) *(d'un train d'atterrissage)* retraction (c) *Fig (d'un problème)* dodging

escamoter [ɛskamɔte] *vt* (a) **e. qch** *(sujet: illusionniste)* to make sth vanish (b) *(voler)* to sneak off with (c) *(train d'atterrissage)* to retract (d) *Fig (problème)* to dodge

escampette [ɛskɑ̃pɛt] *nf Fam* **prendre la poudre d'e.** to make off

escapade [ɛskapad] *nf* jaunt; **faire une e.** to go on a jaunt

escarbille [ɛskarbij] *nf* cinder

escargot [ɛskargo] *nm* snail; **aller à une allure d'e.** *ou* **à la vitesse d'un e.** to go at a snail's pace; **marcher comme un e.** to walk at a snail's pace; *Fig* **opération e.** = slowing down of traffic by protesting truck drivers

escarmouche [ɛskarmuʃ] *nf* skirmish

escarpé, -e [ɛskarpe] *adj (route, montagne)* steep

escarpement [ɛskarpəmɑ̃] *nm (versant)* steep slope; *Géog* escarpment

escarpin [ɛskarpɛ̃] *nm* pump, *Br* court shoe

escarpolette [ɛskarpɔlɛt] *nf Vieilli (balançoire)* swing

escarre [ɛskar] *nf Méd* scab; *(dû aux draps)* bedsore

escient [ɛsjɑ̃] *nm* **à bon e.** wisely; **à mauvais e.** unwisely

esclaffer [ɛsklafe] **s'esclaffer** *vpr* to burst out laughing, to roar with laughter

esclandre [ɛsklɑ̃dr] *nm (scandale, tapage)* scene; **faire** *ou* **causer un e.** to make a scene

esclavage [ɛsklavaʒ] *nm* slavery; **réduire qn en e.** to enslave sb

esclavagisme [ɛsklavaʒism] *nm* slavery; *(doctrine)* proslavery

esclave [ɛsklav] **1** *nmf* slave; **être vendu comme e.** to be sold into slavery; *Fig* **être l'e. de qn/qch** to be a slave to sb/sth
 2 *adj Fig* **être e. de ses habitudes** to be a slave to one's habits

escogriffe [ɛskɔgrif] *nm (grand)* **e.** beanpole

escompte [ɛskɔ̃t] *nm* discount; *Fin* **taux d'e.** (bank) discount rate

escompter [ɛskɔ̃te] *vt (espérer)* to expect, to anticipate *(que* that); **e. faire qch** to expect to do sth

escorte [ɛskɔrt] *nf* escort; **sous (bonne) e.** under escort

escorter [ɛskɔrte] *vt* to escort

escouade [ɛskwad] *nf Mil* squad

escrime [ɛskrim] *nf Sp* fencing; **faire de l'e.** to fence

escrimer [ɛskrime] **s'escrimer** *vpr* to fight; **s'e. à faire qch** to struggle to do sth

escrimeur, -euse [ɛskrimœr, -øz] *nm,f* fencer

escroc [ɛskro] *nm* crook, swindler

escroquer [ɛskrɔke] *vt (personne)* to swindle, to cheat; **e. qch à qn, e. qn de qch** to swindle *or* to cheat sb out of sth

escroquerie [ɛskrɔkri] nf (action) swindling; (résultat) swindle; (délit) fraud; Fam **mais c'est de l'e.!** it's a rip-off!

escudo [ɛskydo] nm escudo

eskimo [ɛskimo] = **esquimau**

ésotérique [ezɔterik] adj esoteric

espace [ɛspas] nm (a) (étendue, distance) space; **laisser de l'e.** to leave space; **e. blanc** space; **E. économique européen** European economic area; **e. publicitaire** advertising space; **e. de rangement** storage space; **e. vital** living space; **espaces verts** green spaces (b) (durée) **en l'e. d'une semaine** within a week (c) (atmosphère) space; **e. aérien** airspace (d) Math space; **e. à trois/quatre dimensions** three-/four-dimensional space (e) Ordinat **e. disque** disk space; **e. mémoire** memory space; **e. de stockage** storage space

espacement [ɛspasmã] nm (action) spacing out; (résultat) spacing; (distance) space; Ordinat **e. arrière** backspace

espacer [16] [ɛspase] 1 vt (objets, paiements, visites) to space out

2 s'espacer vpr (a) (visites, lettres) to become less frequent (b) (personnes) **espacez-vous** space yourselves out

espace-temps (pl **espaces-temps**) [ɛspastã] nm Math & Phys space-time (continuum)

espadon [ɛspadɔ̃] nm swordfish

espadrille [ɛspadrij] nf espadrille

Espagne [ɛspaɲ] nf l'E. Spain

espagnol, -e [ɛspaɲɔl] 1 adj Spanish

2 nm,f E. Spaniard; **les Espagnols** the Spanish

3 nm (langue) Spanish

espagnolette [ɛspaɲɔlɛt] nf window fastener (long vertical bar with pivoting central catch)

espalier [ɛspalje] nm (a) (mur) espalier wall (b) (de gymnase) wall bars

espèce [ɛspɛs] nf (a) (sorte) kind, sort; **les gens de son e.** people like her, people of her kind; **de la pire e.** of the worst sort; **cela n'a aucune e. d'importance** that's of no importance whatsoever; Fam **cette e. d'idiot** that stupid idiot!; Fam **e. d'idiot!** you idiot! (b) Jur **cas d'e.** specific case; **la loi applicable en l'e.** the law applicable to the case in point (c) **espèces** (argent) cash; **payer en espèces** to pay in cash; **espèces sonnantes et trébuchantes** hard cash (d) Bot & Zool species; **l'e. humaine** the human race, mankind

espérance [ɛsperɑ̃s] nf hope; **dans l'e. de faire qch** in the hope of doing sth; **dans l'e. que...** in the hope that...; **au-delà de nos espérances** beyond our expectations; **répondre aux espérances de qn** to live up to sb's expectations; **e. de vie** life expectancy

espérer [34] [ɛspere] 1 vt to hope for; **e. faire qch** to hope to do sth; **e. que** to hope that; **je ne vous espérais plus** I'd given you up

2 vi **j'espère bien** I hope so; **espérons!** let's hope so!

espiègle [ɛspjɛgl] adj mischievous

espion, -onne [ɛspjɔ̃, -ɔn] nm,f spy

espionnage [ɛspjɔnaʒ] nm espionage, spying; **faire de l'e.** to spy; **l'e. industriel** industrial espionage

espionner [ɛspjɔne] 1 vt to spy on

2 vi to spy

esplanade [ɛsplanad] nf esplanade

espoir [ɛspwar] nm (a) (espérance) hope; **avoir l'e. de faire qch** to have hopes of doing sth; **avoir bon e.** to be full of hope; **reprendre e.** to become hopeful again; **nourrir l'e. de faire qch** to live in hope of doing sth; **tous les espoirs sont permis** things look hopeful; Ironique **l'e. fait vivre** hope springs eternal (b) (personne) hope; **un e. du tennis français** one of the most promising French tennis players

esprit [ɛspri] nm (a) (intellectuel) mind; **avoir l'e. large/étroit** to be broad-/narrow-minded; **avoir l'e. tranquille** to be easy in one's mind; **avoir l'e. mal tourné** to have a dirty mind; **avoir l'e. d'analyse/scientifique** to have an analytical/a scientific (turn of) mind; **perdre l'e.** to go out of one's mind; **reprendre ses esprits** to regain consciousness; **elle avait l'e. ailleurs** her thoughts were elsewhere; **elle n'a pas l'e. à ce qu'elle fait** her mind isn't on what she's doing; **je n'ai pas l'e. à plaisanter** I'm not in the mood for joking; **une pareille idée ne me serait jamais venue à l'e.** such an idea would never have crossed my mind; **qu'avez-vous à l'e.?** what are you thinking about? (b) (attitude mentale) spirit; **avoir mauvais e.** to be a malicious sort; **faire du mauvais e.** to be malicious; **e. de caste** class-consciousness; **e. de clocher** parochialism; **e. de compétition** competitive spirit; **e. de corps** esprit de corps; **e. d'entreprise** enterprise spirit; **e. d'équipe** team spirit; **e. de famille** family feeling (c) (humour) wit; **avoir de l'e.** to be witty; **mots ou traits d'e.** witticisms; **faire de l'e.** to display one's wit (d) (personne) person; **un e. fort** a freethinker; Prov **les grands esprits se rencontrent** great minds think alike (e) (sens) spirit; **l'e. de la loi** the spirit of the law (f) (fantôme) spirit; **e., es-tu là?** (dans une séance de spiritisme) is there anybody there?; **e. frappeur** poltergeist (g) Chim (volatile) spirit

esquif [ɛskif] nm skiff; **un frêle e.** a frail barque

esquimau, -aude, -x, -audes [ɛskimo, -od] 1 adj Eskimo, Am Inuit

2 nm,f E. Eskimo, Am Inuit

3 nm (glace) E.® Br ≃ choc-ice (on a stick), Am ≃ ice-cream bar

esquinté, -e [ɛskɛ̃te] adj Fam (abîmé) knackered

esquinter [ɛskɛ̃te] Fam 1 vt (abîmer) to damage; (blesser) to hurt

2 s'esquinter vpr (s'abîmer) **s'e. la jambe** to hurt one's leg; **s'e. la santé/les yeux (à faire qch)** to ruin one's health/eyes (doing sth)

esquisse [ɛskis] nf (dessin) sketch; Fig (d'un projet, d'un roman) outline; (d'une suggestion) suggestion

esquisser [ɛskise] 1 vt (dessiner) to sketch; Fig (plan, roman) to outline; Fig **e. un sourire** to give a slight smile

2 s'esquisser vpr (idée, projet) to take shape

esquiver [ɛskive] 1 vt aussi Fig to dodge, to evade

2 s'esquiver vpr to slip away

essai [ɛse] nm (a) (tentative) try; **faire un e.** to have a try (b) (test) (d'un produit, d'une voiture) test, trial; **à l'e.** on a trial basis; Ordinat **e. approfondi** beta test; **e. nucléaire** nuclear test; Ordinat **e. de performance** benchmark (c) (ouvrage) essay (d) (au rugby) try

essaim [ɛsɛ̃] nm aussi Fig swarm

essaimer [ɛseme] vi (abeilles) to swarm; Fig (population, famille) to spread; (entreprise) to expand

essayage [ɛsejaʒ] nm fitting

essayer [53] [eseje] **1** *vt* **(a)** *(pour la première fois) (gadget, restaurant)* to try (out); *(voiture)* to test-drive; *(vin, plat)* to try, to taste; *(vêtement, chaussures)* to try on **(b)** *(tester) (machine, produit)* to test **(c)** *(tenter)* e. de faire qch to try to do sth

2 s'essayer *vpr* s'e. à qch/à faire qch to try one's hand at sth/at doing sth

ESSEC [esɛk] *nf* (*abrév* **École supérieure des sciences économiques et commerciales**) = university-level business school

essence [esɑ̃s] *nf* **(a)** *(combustible)* Br petrol, Am gas(oline); **e. ordinaire** Br two-star petrol, Am regular gas; **e. sans plomb** unleaded (Br petrol or Am gas) **(b)** *(extrait) (de plantes, de café)* essence; **e. de térébenthine** spirits of turpentine **(c)** *(caractère fondamental)* essence; **par e.** essentially **(d)** *(espèce)* species

essentiel, -elle [esɑ̃sjɛl] **1** *adj* **(a)** *(nécessaire)* essential, necessary (à/pour for); **(b)** *(principal) (condition, caractère)* essential; *(raison)* basic, main

2 *nm* **l'e.** *(le plus important)* the main thing; *(le minimum)* the essentials; **l'e. de** *(la majeure partie de)* the majority of

essentiellement [esɑ̃sjɛlmɑ̃] *adv* **(a)** *(principalement)* essentially, mainly **(b)** *(par nature)* essentially

esseulé, -e [esœle] *adj* isolated

essieu, -x [esjø] *nm* axle

essor [esɔr] *nm* **(a)** *(d'un oiseau)* flight; **prendre son e.** to fly off **(b)** *Fig (d'une industrie, d'une économie)* (rapid) growth; **en plein e.** booming; **prendre son e.** to take off

essorage [esɔraʒ] *nm* *(à la machine)* spin-drying; *(à la main)* wringing

essorer [esɔre] *vt* *(vêtements) (à la machine)* to spin(-dry); *(à la main)* to wring out; *(salade)* to spin

essoreuse [esɔrøz] *nf* *(à tambour)* spin-drier

essoufflé, -e [esufle] *adj* out of breath

essoufflement [esuflɔmɑ̃] *nm* breathlessness; *Fig (de l'économie, d'une activité)* running down

essouffler [esufle] **1** *vt* to make out of breath

2 s'essouffler *vpr* to get out of breath; *Fig (économie, activité)* to run down

essuie-glace (*pl* **essuie-glaces**) [esɥiglas] *nm* Br windscreen *or* Am windshield wiper

essuie-mains [esɥimɛ̃] *nm inv* hand towel

essuie-tout [esɥitu] *nm inv* kitchen paper

essuyer [32] [esɥije] **1** *vt* **(a)** *(surface)* to wipe; *(liquide)* to wipe up; *(larmes)* to wipe away; **e. la vaisselle** to dry the dishes, to dry up **(b)** *(subir) (défaite, perte, insultes)* to suffer; *(refus)* to meet with; *(tempête)* to run into

2 s'essuyer *vpr* to wipe oneself; *(après un bain)* to dry oneself; **s'e. la bouche/les yeux** to wipe one's mouth/eyes

est¹ [e] *voir* **être²**

est² [est] *nm* east; **un vent d'e.** an easterly wind; **le vent d'e.** the east wind; **à l'e.** in the east; **à l'e. de** (to the) east of; *Géog & Pol* **l'E.** the East

2 *adj inv (côte, face, régions)* eastern

estafilade [estafilad] *nf* gash

estaminet [estamine] *nm Belg* (small) café

estampe [estɑ̃p] *nf* print

estampille [estɑ̃pij] *nf (sur un document)* stamp; *(sur un produit)* mark

est-ce que [eskə] *adv interrogatif* **e. je peux entrer?** can I come in?; **est-ce qu'il est là?** is he here?; **e. tu la connais?** do you know her?

esthète [estɛt] *nmf* aesthete

esthéticien, -enne [estetisjɛ̃, -ɛn] *nm,f* beautician

esthétique [estetik] **1** *adj* aesthetic; *(beau)* aesthetically pleasing

2 *nf (beauté)* aesthetic quality

estimable [estimabl] *adj* **(a)** *(digne de respect)* estimable **(b)** *(assez bon)* fairly good

estimation [estimasjɔ̃] *nf* **(a)** *(détermination) (d'un prix, d'une distance, d'un poids)* estimation; *(de marchandises, d'une œuvre d'art)* valuation; *(de dommages, de besoins)* assessment **(b)** *(valeur, quantité estimée)* estimate

estime [estim] *nf* **(a)** *(respect)* esteem, regard; **avoir de l'e. pour qn/qch** to esteem sb/sth; **baisser/remonter dans l'e. de qn** to go down/up in sb's estimation; **avoir un succès d'e.** to be a critical (though not a popular) success **(b)** *Naut* **à l'e.** by dead reckoning

estimer [estime] **1** *vt* **(a)** *(déterminer) (prix, distance, poids)* to estimate; *(marchandises, œuvre d'art)* to value; *(dommages, besoins)* to assess **(b)** *(considérer)* to consider, to think (que that); **il n'a pas estimé nécessaire de me prévenir** he didn't consider it necessary to warn me **(c)** *(respecter) (personne)* to have a high opinion of; **e. qn à sa juste valeur** to value sb

2 s'estimer *vpr* **s'e. satisfait/heureux** to consider oneself satisfied/lucky

estival, -e, -aux, -ales [estival, -o] *adj* summer

estivant, -e [estivɑ̃, -ɑ̃t] *nm,f* Br holidaymaker, Am vacationer

estocade [estɔkad] *nf aussi Fig* death-blow; **donner l'e. à** to deal the death-blow to

estomac [estɔma] *nm* **(a)** *(ventre)* stomach; **avoir l'e. vide** to have an empty stomach; **avoir l'e. dans les talons** to be starving **(b)** *Fam Fig (courage)* guts

estomaquer [estɔmake] *vt Fam* to flabbergast

estomper [estɔ̃pe] **1** *vt Art (dessin)* to shade off; *Fig (paysage, contour, souvenir)* to blur

2 s'estomper *vpr (paysage, contour, souvenir)* to become blurred; *(peine)* to ease; *(rides)* to be smoothed out

Estonie [estɔni] *nf* **l'E.** Estonia

estonien, -enne [estɔnjɛ̃, -ɛn] **1** *adj* Estonian

2 *nm,f* **E.** Estonian

3 *nm (langue)* Estonian

estourbir [esturbir] *vt Fam* **(a)** *(tuer)* to bump off **(b)** *(étonner)* to astound

estrade [estrad] *nf* platform

estragon [estragɔ̃] *nm* tarragon

estropié, -e [estrɔpje] **1** *adj* crippled

2 *nm,f* cripple

estropier [66] [estrɔpje] *vt* **(a)** *(personne)* to cripple, to maim **(b)** *Fig (morceau de musique, langue étrangère)* to murder; *(mot, nom)* to mispronounce; *(texte)* to mutilate

estuaire [estɥɛr] *nm* estuary

estudiantin, -e [estydjɑ̃tɛ̃, -in] *adj* student

esturgeon [estyrʒɔ̃] *nm* sturgeon

et [e] **1** *conj* **(a)** *(exprime l'addition, la simultanéité)* and; **et son frère et sa sœur** both his brother and his sister; **et d'un, il pleut, et de deux, je n'ai pas envie d'y aller** in the first place it's raining, and in the second place I don't want to go; **j'aime le café, et vous?** I like coffee, do you?; **et moi, alors?** what about me? **(b)** *(dans les nombres, les heures)* **vingt/trente et un** twenty-/thirty-one; **une livre et demie** a pound and a half; **il est quatre heures et demie/et quart** it's half/quarter past four

2 *nm (symbole)* **et commercial** ampersand

ETA [atea] *nf (abrév* **Euskadi ta Askatasuna)** ETA

étable [etabl] *nf* cowshed

établi [etabli] *nm* workbench

établi², **-e** *adj* established; **considérer qch comme une chose établie** to take sth for granted

établir [etablir] **1** *vt* **(a)** *(paix, relations, principe)* to establish; *(agence)* to set up; *(camp)* to pitch; *(prix)* to fix; *(devis, liste)* to draw up; *(record)* to set **(b)** *(démontrer)* to establish, to prove **(c)** *(autorité, réputation)* to establish **(sur** on)

2 s'établir *vpr* **(a)** *(dans une ville, un pays)* to settle **(b)** *(pour exercer un métier)* to set up in business **(c)** *(s'instaurer)* to become established

établissement [etablismã] *nm* **(a)** *(de la paix, de relations, d'un principe)* establishment; *(d'une agence)* setting up; *(d'un camp)* pitching; *(d'un prix)* fixing; *(d'un devis, d'une liste)* drawing up **(b)** *(démonstration)* establishment **(c)** *(installation)* *(d'une personne)* settlement **(d)** *(institution)* establishment, institution; **é. bancaire** bank; **é. de crédit** credit institution; **é. financier** financial institution; **é. hospitalier** hospital; **é. scolaire** school **(e)** *(entreprise)* business, firm; **les établissements Martin** Martin & Co

étage [etaʒ] *nm* **(a)** *(d'un bâtiment)* floor, storey; **à deux étages** two-storeyed; **au troisième é.** on the *Br* third or *Am* fourth floor; **à l'é.** upstairs **(b)** *(d'un terrain)* level; *(d'un gâteau)* tier **(c)** *(d'une fusée)* stage

étager [45] [etaʒe] **s'étager** *vpr* to rise in tiers

étagère [etaʒɛr] *nf (meuble)* (set of) shelves; *(planche)* shelf

étai [etɛ] *nm Constr* prop

étain [etɛ̃] *nm* **(a)** *(métal)* tin **(b)** *(matériau pour vaisselle)* pewter; **un é.** a piece of pewter

étais, était *voir* **être²**

étal *(pl* **étals)** [etal] *nm* **(a)** *(au marché)* stall **(b)** *(de boucher)* butcher's block

étalage [etalaʒ] *nm* **(a)** *(vitrine)* window display **(b)** *Fig (ostentation)* display; **faire é. de son savoir/sa richesse** to show off one's knowledge/wealth

étalagiste [etalaʒist] *nmf* window dresser

étalement [etalmã] *nm (dans le temps)* staggering **(sur** over)

étaler [etale] **1** *vt* **(a)** *(étendre)* *(journal, papiers)* to spread out; *(nappe, beurre)* to spread; *(peinture, pommade)* to apply **(sur** to); *(cartes)* to lay down **(b)** *Fig (montrer)* *(richesse, connaissances)* to show off; *(vie privée)* to make a display of; **é. une affaire au grand jour** to make a matter public **(c)** *(dans le temps)* to stagger **(sur** over)

2 s'étaler *vpr* **(a)** *(village, parc)* to spread out **(b)** *(dans le temps)* to be spread **(sur** over) **(c)** *(se vautrer)* to sprawl **(d)** *Fam (tomber)* to fall flat on the ground; **s'é. de tout son long** to fall flat on one's face

étalon¹ [etalɔ̃] *nm (cheval)* stallion

étalon² *nm (de mesure, monétaire)* standard; *Fig (modèle)* yardstick; *Écon* **l'é.-or** the gold standard

étamine [etamin] *nf Bot* stamen

étanche [etɑ̃ʃ] *adj (bateau, récipient)* watertight; *(montre, bottes)* waterproof

étanchéité [etɑ̃ʃeite] *nf (d'un bateau, d'un récipient)* watertightness; *(d'une montre, de bottes)* waterproofness

étancher [etɑ̃ʃe] *vt* **(a)** *(liquide)* to stop the flow of; *(sang)* to staunch; *(larmes)* to dry **(b)** *(soif)* to quench

étang [etɑ̃] *nm* pond, pool

étant *voir* **être²**

étape [etap] *nf* **(a)** *(lieu)* stopover; **faire é.** to stop; *Fig* **brûler les étapes** *(dans la hiérarchie)* to shoot to the top; *(dans une tâche)* to cut corners **(b)** *(distance)* stage **(c)** *Fig (phase)* stage, step; **par étapes** in stages

état [eta] *nm* **(a)** *(façon d'être)* state, condition; *Phys* state; **l'é. des routes** road conditions; **à l'é. solide/naturel** in its solid/natural state; **à l'é. neuf** as good as new; **à l'é. pur** *(substance)* unalloyed; *Fig (bêtise, incompétence)* sheer, downright; **dans l'é. actuel des choses** as things stand; **être dans un triste é.** to be in a sorry state; **être dans tous ses états** to be in a state; **en bon/mauvais é.** in good/bad condition; **remettre qch en é.** to repair sth; *(moteur)* to overhaul sth; **laisser les choses en l'é.** to leave things as they are; **être en é. de marche** to be in working order; *(voiture)* to be roadworthy; **être/se sentir en é. de faire qch** to be/feel up to doing sth; **é. d'alerte** state of alert; **faire qch sans états d'âme** *(sans scrupules)* to have no qualms about doing sth; **é. de choses** state of affairs; **é. d'esprit** state of mind; **c'est un é. de fait** it's an undeniable fact; **l'é. de guerre a été déclaré** a state of war has been declared; **é. de santé** state of health; **être dans un é. second** to be spaced out; **é. de siège** martial law; **é. d'urgence** state of emergency **(b)** *Vieilli ou Hum (profession)* **épicier de son é.** grocer by trade **(c)** *(autorité centrale)* **l'É.** the State; **É. membre** member state **(d)** *(inventaire)* *(des dépenses, des ventes)* statement; **faire é. de qch** to mention sth; **é. civil** *(à la mairie)* register office; **é. des lieux** inventory of fixtures *(in rented premises)*; **états de service** service record **(e)** *Hist* **les États généraux** the States General **(f)** *Ordinat* **é. d'attente** wait state; **en é. de veille** in standby mode

étatique [etatik] *adj* state

étatiser [etatize] *vt* to bring under state control

état-major *(pl* **états-majors)** [etamaʒɔr] *nm* **(a)** *Mil (officiers)* general staff; *(lieu)* headquarters **(b)** *(d'une firme)* management; *(d'un parti politique)* leadership

États-Unis [etazyni] *nmpl* **les É. (d'Amérique)** the United States (of America)

étau, -x [eto] *nm* **(a)** *Tech* vice **(b)** *Fig (restrictions)* stranglehold; **l'é. se resserre** the net is closing in

étayer [53] [eteje] *vt* **(a)** *(mur, plafond)* to shore up **(b)** *Fig (argumentation, théorie)* to support

etc [ɛtsetera] *adv* etc

et cætera, et cetera [ɛtsetera] *adv* et cetera

été¹ [ete] *nm* summer; **en é.** in (the) summer; **un jour d'é.** a summer's day; **é. indien** Indian summer

été² *voir* **être²**

éteindre [54] [etɛ̃dr] **1** vt (incendie, bougie, cigarette) to put out, to extinguish; (gaz) to turn off; (lumière, radio, radiateur) to switch off, to turn off; **éteins dans le salon, s'il te plaît** can you switch the light off in the lounge, please

2 s'éteindre vpr **(a)** (incendie, cigarette, lampe) to go out **(b)** (passion) to fade; (son, rires, voix) to die away **(c)** (disparaître) to pass away; (race) to die out

éteint, -e [etɛ̃, -ɛ̃t] adj **(a)** être é. (incendie, cigarette) to be out; (lampe, électricité, radio) to be off **(b)** (race, famille, volcan) extinct **(c)** (terne) (couleur) dull; (regard) blank; (voix) faint; (personne) subdued

étendard [etɑ̃dar] nm **(a)** (drapeau) standard **(b)** Fig (symbole) **lever l'é. de la révolte** to raise the standard of revolt; **se ranger sous l'é. de qn** to join sb's camp

étendoir [etɑ̃dwar] nm (à linge) clothes-line

étendre [etɑ̃dr] **1** vt **(a)** (déployer) (carte, nappe) to spread out; (linge) to hang up; (beurre, pommade, ailes) to spread; (pâte) to roll out; **é. les bras** to open one's arms wide; Fam **se faire é.** (être assommé) to be knocked out; (à un examen) to fail **(b)** (coucher) to lay down **(c)** (influence, pouvoir, connaissances) to extend (à to) **(d)** (diluer) to dilute **(e)** Ordinat (mémoire) to upgrade

2 s'étendre vpr **(a)** (s'allonger) to lie down **(b)** (aller) to stretch **(c)** (incendie, épidémie, grève) to spread; (pouvoir, influence, connaissances) to grow **(d)** (s'attarder) **s'é. sur un sujet** to dwell on a subject

étendu, -e [etɑ̃dy] **1** adj **(a)** (large, important) (plaine, connaissances) extensive; (pouvoirs) far-reaching **(b)** (bras, jambes) outstretched **(c)** (personne) lying **(d)** (dilué) diluted (de with)

2 nf **étendue** (d'un champ, d'une région) area; (d'une grève, d'une épidémie, d'une catastrophe) scale, extent; (d'eau, de sable, de terre) expanse; (des connaissances, du vocabulaire, des pouvoirs) range

éternel, -elle [etɛrnɛl] **1** adj eternal; (discussion, bavardages) never-ending; **tu es un é. mécontent** you're never satisfied

2 nm **(a) l'É.** (Dieu) the Lord; Hum **c'est un grand fumeur/paresseux devant l'É.** he's an incurable smoker/incurably lazy **(b) l'é. féminin** the archetypal female

éternellement [etɛrnɛlmɑ̃] adv for ever; (reconnaissant) eternally; **elle est é. mécontente** she's never satisfied

éterniser [etɛrnize] **s'éterniser** vpr (durer) to drag on (for ever); (chez quelqu'un) to outstay one's welcome

éternité [etɛrnite] nf eternity; **il y a une é. ou des éternités que je ne vous ai vu** I haven't seen you for ages

éternuement [etɛrnymɑ̃] nm sneeze

éternuer [etɛrnɥe] vi to sneeze

êtes voir **être²**

éther [etɛr] nm ether

éthéré, -e [etere] adj ethereal

Éthiopie [etjɔpi] nf **l'É.** Ethiopia

éthiopien, -enne [etjɔpjɛ̃, -ɛn] **1** adj Ethiopian

2 nmf **É.** Ethiopian

éthique [etik] **1** adj ethical

2 nf ethics (singulier)

ethnie [ɛtni] nf ethnic group

ethnique [ɛtnik] adj ethnic

ethnologie [ɛtnɔlɔʒi] nf ethnology

ethnologique [ɛtnɔlɔʒik] adj ethnological

ethnologue [ɛtnɔlɔg] nmf ethnologist

éthylique [etilik] adj **alcool é.** ethyl alcohol; **coma é.** alcohol-induced coma

éthylisme [etilism] nm Méd alcoholism

étiez voir **être²**

étincelant, -e [etɛ̃slɑ̃, -ɑ̃t] adj sparkling; (étoile) twinkling

étinceler [42] [etɛ̃sle] vi (diamant, métal, lac) to sparkle; (étoile) to twinkle; (yeux) (de joie) to sparkle (de with); (de colère) to glint (de with)

étincelle [etɛ̃sɛl] nf aussi Fig spark; **lancer des étincelles** to throw out sparks; (diamant, yeux) to sparkle; Fig **ça va faire des étincelles** sparks will fly; **avoir une é. de génie** to have a stroke of genius

étioler [etjole] **s'étioler** vpr (plante) to wilt; (personne) to grow sickly; (esprit, mémoire) to deteriorate

étions voir **être²**

étiqueter [42] [etikte] vt aussi Fig to label (comme as)

étiquette [etiket] nf **(a)** (sur une valise, un produit) label **(b)** Fig (d'une personne) label; **coller une é. à qn** to label sb; **é. politique** political affiliation **(c)** (protocole) **l'é. etiquette**

étirer [etire] **1** vt to stretch

2 s'étirer vpr (personne, tissu, vêtement) to stretch; (journée, réunion) to drag on (for ever)

étoffe [etɔf] nf material, fabric; Fig **avoir l'é. d'un chef d'État** to have the makings of a statesman; **avoir l'é. d'un héros** to be the stuff heroes are made of

étoffer [etɔfe] **1** vt (discours, livre, personnage) to flesh out

2 s'étoffer vpr (personne) to fill out

étoile [etwal] nf **(a)** (astre) star; **un ciel sans étoiles** a starless sky; **coucher ou dormir à la belle é.** to sleep out (in the open); **né sous une bonne/mauvaise é.** born under a lucky/an unlucky star; **l'é. du berger** (vue le matin) the morning star; (vue le soir) the evening star; **é. filante** shooting star; **l'É. Polaire** the Pole star **(b)** (ornement, objet) star; (astérisque) asterisk; **hôtel trois étoiles** three-star hotel; **é. de David** Star of David **(c)** (vedette) star **(d)** **é. de mer** starfish **(e)** Ordinat **connecté en é.** in a star configuration

étoilé, -e [etwale] adj **(a)** (ciel, nuit) starry **(b)** (pare-brise) starred

étonnamment [etɔnamɑ̃] adv surprisingly

étonnant, -e [etɔnɑ̃, -ɑ̃t] adj surprising; **ce n'est pas é. qu'il soit malade** it's not surprising that he's ill; **chose étonnante, elle est arrivée à l'heure** amazingly enough, she arrived on time

étonné, -e [etɔne] adj surprised (de at)

étonnement [etɔnmɑ̃] nm surprise; **à mon grand é.** to my amazement

étonner [etɔne] **1** vt to surprise; **elle n'est pas venue? ça m'étonne** she didn't come? I'm surprised; Fam **alors ça, ça m'étonnerait!** that'll be the day!; **ça m'étonne de toi** I'm surprised at you; Fam **tu m'étonnes!** you don't say!; **tu m'étonneras toujours!** you never cease to amaze me!

2 s'étonner vpr to be surprised (de at); **je ne m'étonne plus de rien** nothing surprises me any more

étouffant, -e [etufɑ̃, -ɑ̃t] adj (air, chaleur, atmosphère) stifling; (temps) oppressive

étouffe-chrétien [etufkretjɛ̃] Fam **1** adj inv stodgy

2 nm inv **c'est de l'é., cette tarte** this tart is pure stodge

étouffée [etufe] **à l'étouffée 1** *adj* braised
2 *adv* **cuire qch à l'é.** to braise sth

étouffement [etufmɑ̃] *nm (asphyxie)* suffocation

étouffer [etufe] **1** *vt* **(a)** *(personne)* to suffocate; *Euph* **ce ne sont pas les scrupules qui l'étouffent** she's not exactly overscrupulous **(b)** *Fig (cri, bâillement, rire)* to stifle; *(son)* to muffle; *(feu)* to smother; *(révolte)* to suppress; *(scandale, affaire)* to hush up
2 *vi* to suffocate; **é. de rire/colère** to choke with laughter/anger; **on étouffe ici** it's stuffy in here
3 s'étouffer *vpr* to suffocate; *(en mangeant)* to choke (**avec** on)

étourderie [eturdəri] *nf* **(a)** *(caractère)* absent-mindedness **(b)** *(faute)* careless mistake

étourdi, -e [eturdi] **1** *adj (distrait)* scatterbrained
2 *nm,f* scatterbrain

étourdir [eturdir] *vt (assommer)* to stun, to daze; *Fig (sujet: vin, éloges)* to make dizzy

étourdissant, -e [eturdisɑ̃, -ɑ̃t] *adj (bruit)* deafening; *(nouvelles, succès)* staggering; *(beauté)* stunning

étourdissement [eturdismɑ̃] *nm* **avoir un é.** to feel dizzy

étourneau, -x [eturno] *nm* starling

étrange [etrɑ̃ʒ] *adj* strange, odd; **chose é., il est revenu** strangely enough, he came back

étrangement [etrɑ̃ʒmɑ̃] *adv* strangely, oddly; **ressembler é. à qch** to look suspiciously like sth

étranger, -ère [etrɑ̃ʒe, -ɛr] **1** *adj* **(a)** *(d'un autre pays)* foreign **(b)** *(inconnu)* strange, unfamiliar **(à** to) **(c)** *(extérieur)* **des éléments étrangers** outsiders; **elle est étrangère à cette société/au projet** she isn't involved with this company/the plan
2 *nm,f* **(a)** *(d'un autre pays)* foreigner **(b)** *(d'un autre groupe)* stranger, outsider
3 *nm* **l'é.** *(pays étrangers)* foreign countries; **aller/vivre à l'é.** to go/live abroad

étrangeté [etrɑ̃ʒte] *nf* strangeness, oddness

étranglé, -e [etrɑ̃gle] *adj (passage, vallée)* narrow; *(voix)* choked; *Méd (hernie)* strangulated

étranglement [etrɑ̃gləmɑ̃] *nm* **(a)** *(d'une personne)* strangling, strangulation; **mourir par é.** to be strangled **(b)** *(partie resserrée) (d'une rivière)* narrow part; *(d'une route)* bottleneck

étrangler [etrɑ̃gle] **1** *vt* **(a)** *(personne)* to strangle; *Fig (ruiner)* to cripple **(b)** *(resserrer) (taille, tube)* to constrict
2 s'étrangler *vpr* **(a)** *(en mangeant)* to choke (**avec** on); **s'é. de colère/rire** to choke with anger/laughter; *(voix)* to choke; **les mots s'étranglèrent dans sa gorge** the words stuck in her throat

étrave [etrav] *nf Naut* stem

être¹ [etr] *nm (personne, âme)* being; **un é. cher** a loved one; **c'est un é. méprisable** he's a despicable creature; **é. humain** human being; **é. vivant** living creature

être² [2] **1** *vi* **(a)** *(indique la nature)* to be; **ê. professeur/informaticien** to be a teacher/computer expert; **ceci est un reptile** this is a reptile
(b) *(indique l'état)* to be; **ê. bien/mal** *(en bonne/mauvaise santé)* to be well/ill; **le temps est à l'orage** there's a storm brewing
(c) *(indique le lieu)* to be; **elle est chez elle** she's at home; **Rabat est au Maroc** Rabat is in Morocco; **j'en suis au chapitre IV** I'm on chapter IV; **où en es-tu dans ton travail?** how far have you got with your work?; **je ne sais plus où j'en suis** I don't know what I'm doing any

more; **j'en suis à me demander si...** I'm beginning to wonder whether...
(d) *(indique le moment)* **nous sommes mercredi/le 16** it's Wednesday/the 16th today
(e) *(indique l'appartenance)* **ê. à qn** to belong to sb; *Fig* **je suis à vous** I'm all yours; **elle est de la famille** she's one of the family
(f) *(indique la provenance)* to be; **je suis de Lyon/du sud** I'm from Lyons/from the South; **l'enfant n'est pas de lui** it's not his child; **ce tableau est de Cézanne** this picture is by Cézanne
(g) *(indique l'obligation)* **ceci est à lire pour demain** this has to be read for tomorrow; **ce film est à voir absolument** this film is unmissable
(h) *(aller)* to go; **as-tu déjà été à Brighton?** have you ever been to Brighton?; *Fam* **ça a été** it went OK
(i) *(exister)* to be; **la plus belle voiture qui soit** the most beautiful car in the world; *Litt* **elle n'est plus** she is no longer with us
(j) *(locutions)* **ê. tout le temps à se plaindre/à médire** to be always complaining/criticizing; **ne serait-ce que** if only
2 *v aux* **(a)** *(avec des verbes à l'actif)* to have/to be; **je suis sorti hier soir** I went out last night; **es-tu déjà allé en Chine?** have you ever been to China?; **elle est née en 1967** she was born in 1967; **j'étais parti très tôt** I had left very early; **il serait mieux avec les cheveux courts** he would look better with short hair; **ils se sont aimés** they loved each other; **nous nous étions trompés** we had made a mistake
(b) *(avec des verbes au passif)* to be; **nous y sommes/étions toujours bien reçus** we are/were always warmly welcomed
3 *v impersonnel* to be; **il est cinq heures** it's five (o'clock); **il est difficile de juger** it's hard to tell; **il m'est impossible de vous répondre** it's impossible for me to give you an answer

étreindre [54] [etrɛ̃dr] *vt* to embrace; *(sujet: peur, douleur)* to grip

étreinte [etrɛ̃t] *nf (embrassade)* embrace; *(sexuelle)* coupling

étrenner [etrene] *vt (objet)* to use for the first time, to christen; *(vêtement)* to wear for the first time

étrennes [etren] *nfpl* New Year's gift; *(pour facteur, éboueur) Br* ≃ Christmas box

étrier [etrije] *nm* **(a)** *(en équitation)* stirrup; **vider les étriers** to be thrown; *Fig* **mettre le pied à l'é. à qn** to give sb a helping hand **(b)** *(sur table d'examen)* stirrup

étriller [etrije] *vt* **(a)** *(cheval)* to curry **(b)** *Fig (critiquer)* to pan

étriper [etripe] **1** *vt (poisson, volaille)* to gut; *Fam Fig* **je vais l'é.!** I'll murder him!
2 s'étriper *vpr Fam (se battre)* to tear each other apart

étriqué, -e [etrike] *adj* **(a)** *(vêtement)* tight **(b)** *Fig (esprit, vie)* narrow

étroit, -e [etrwa, -at] *adj* **(a)** *(peu large)* narrow; *Fig* **avoir l'esprit é.** to be narrow-minded **(b)** *(serré)* tight; *Fig (liens, collaboration, surveillance)* close **(c)** *(logement, pièce)* poky; **être à l'é.** to be cramped for room

étroitement [etrwatmɑ̃] *adv (nouer, tenir)* tightly; *Fig (unir, collaborer, surveiller)* closely

étroitesse [etrwates] *nf* narrowness; *(d'un logement, d'une pièce)* pokiness; *Fig* **é. d'esprit** narrow-mindedness

étron [etrɔ̃] *nm* piece of excrement

étrusque [etrysk] **1** adj Etruscan
2 nmf É. Etruscan

étude [etyd] nf (a) (examen) study, survey; **mettre qch à l'é.** to study or investigate sth; **é. de cas** case study; **é. de faisabilité** feasibility study; **faire une é. de marché** to do market research (b) études (éducation) studies; **j'ai arrêté mes études à seize ans** I left school when I was sixteen; **faire des études (de français/de droit)** to study French/law; **elle a fait ses études à Oxford** she studied at Oxford (c) Scol (heure) study period; (salle) study room (d) (morceau de musique, peinture) study (e) (bureau) office

étudiant, -e [etydjã, -ãt] **1** nm,f student; **é. en médecine/en droit** medical/law student; **é. de première/seconde année** first-/second-year student, Am freshman/sophomore
2 adj (vie, mouvement) student

étudié, -e [etydje] adj (a) (recherché) (tenue) carefully chosen (b) Péj (affecté) studied (c) Com **prix très étudiés** very reasonable prices

étudier [66] [etydje] **1** vt to study; (leçon) to prepare
2 vi to study
3 s'étudier vpr (l'un l'autre) to study each other

étui [etɥi] nm case; (de revolver) holster; **é. à lunettes** glasses case

étuve [etyv] nf (a) (aux thermes) steam room; Fig oven (b) (pour sécher) drying oven; (pour stériliser) sterilizer

étuvée [etyve] à **l'étuvée 1** adj braised
2 adv **cuire qch à l'é.** to braise sth

étymologie [etimɔlɔʒi] nf etymology

EU [əy] nmpl (abrév États-Unis) USA

eu, -e pp voir **avoir¹**

eucalyptus [økaliptys] nm eucalyptus

eucharistie [økaristi] nf Rel **l'e.** the Eucharist

euh [ø] exclam er!

eunuque [ønyk] nm eunuch

euphémisme [øfemism] nm euphemism

euphorie [øfɔri] nf euphoria

euphorique [øfɔrik] adj euphoric

euphorisant, -e [øfɔrizã, -ãt] **1** adj (effet, atmosphère) exhilarating; (médicament) antidepressant; (drogue) that produces a feeling of euphoria
2 nm antidepressant; (drogue) drug that produces a feeling of euphoria

Euphrate [øfrat] nm **l'E.** the Euphrates

eurasien, -enne [ørazjɛ̃, -ɛn] **1** adj Eurasian
2 nm,f E. Eurasian

eurêka [øreka] exclam eureka!

euro [øro] nm (monnaie) Euro

euro- [øro] préf Euro-

eurocrate [ørokrat] nmf Eurocrat

eurodevise [ørodəviz] nf Eurocurrency

eurodollar [ørodolar] nm Eurodollar

Europe [ørɔp] nf **l'E.** Europe; **l'E. centrale** central Europe; **l'E. de l'Est/de l'Ouest** Eastern/Western Europe; **l'E. du Nord** Northern Europe; **l'E. occidentale** Western Europe; **l'E. verte** European Community agriculture

européen, -enne [ørɔpeɛ̃, -ɛn] **1** adj European
2 nm,f E. European

eurosceptique [øroseptik] nmf Pol Eurosceptic

Eurovision [ørovizjõ] nf Eurovision

eut voir **avoir¹**

euthanasie [øtanazi] nf euthanasia

eux [ø] pron personnel (a) (sujet) they; **ils apprécient mon travail, e.!** THEY like my work!; **les enfants, e., se sont amusés** the children, for their part, enjoyed themselves; **si j'étais e., je me méfierais** if I were them, I'd be careful
(b) (objet direct) them; **et e., tu les oublies?** and what about them, have you forgotten them?
(c) (avec préposition) them; (réfléchi) themselves; **dis-le-leur, à e.** tell THEM; **les deux maisons sont à e.** both houses are theirs; **ils ont leurs méthodes à e.** they have their own methods; Fam **un copain à e.** a friend of theirs
(d) (dans les comparaisons) them; **je dépense plus qu'e.** I spend more than they do or than them

eux-mêmes [ømɛm] pron personnel themselves

évacuation [evakɥasjõ] nf (a) (de matières du corps) discharge; (des eaux de pluie, des eaux usées) drainage (b) (de personnes, d'un lieu) evacuation

évacuer [evakɥe] vt (a) (matières du corps) to discharge; (eaux de pluie, eaux usées) to drain off (b) (personnes, lieu) to evacuate; **faire é. une salle** to evacuate a hall (c) Fig (problème) to solve

évadé, -e [evade] nm,f escaped prisoner

évader [evade] **s'évader** vpr aussi Fig to escape (de from)

évaluation [evalɥasjõ] nf (d'une propriété, d'un bien) valuation; (de dommages) assessment; (d'un poids, d'un nombre, des risques) estimation

évaluer [evalɥe] vt (propriété, bien) to value; (dommages) to assess; (poids, nombre, risques) to estimate

évangéliser [evãʒelize] vt to evangelize

évangéliste [evãʒelist] nm (prédicateur) evangelist; (de la Bible) Evangelist

évangile [evãʒil] nm Rel **l'É.** the Gospel; Fig **prendre qch pour parole d'é.** to take sth as gospel (truth)

évanoui, -e [evanwi] adj unconscious; **tomber é.** to fall down in a faint

évanouir [evanwir] **s'évanouir** vpr (a) (perdre conscience) to faint (b) (disparaître) to fade (away)

évanouissement [evanwismã] nm (syncope) fainting fit

évaporation [evaporasjõ] nf evaporation

évaporé, -e [evapore] Péj **1** adj scatterbrained
2 nm,f airhead

évaporer [evapore] **s'évaporer** vpr (a) (liquide) to evaporate (b) Fig (disparaître) to vanish (into thin air)

évasé, -e [evaze] adj (récipient) wide-mouthed; (jupe) flared

évaser [evaze] **s'évaser** vpr to widen; (jupe) to be flared

évasif, -ive [evazif, -iv] adj evasive

évasion [evazjõ] nf (a) (fuite) escape (de from); **é. de capitaux** flight of capital; **é. fiscale** tax evasion (b) Fig (distraction) escapism; **avoir besoin d'é.** to need to escape

Ève [ɛv] npr Eve; Fam **je ne le connais ni d'È. ni d'Adam** I don't know him from Adam

évêché [eveʃe] nm (diocèse) bishopric; (palais) bishop's palace

éveil [evɛj] nm awakening; **être en é.** to be alert

éveillé, -e [eveje] adj (a) (non endormi) awake (b) (vif) alert

éveiller [eveje] **1** vt (a) (curiosité, soupçons, jalousie) to arouse; (intelligence, imagination) to stimulate (b) Litt (personne) to wake
2 s'éveiller vpr (a) Litt (personne) to awake (b) Fig (curiosité, soupçons, jalousie) to be aroused; (intelligence, imagination) to develop

événement [evɛnmɑ̃] nm event; attendre la suite des événements to wait and see what happens; créer l'é. to make big news; Hum quand il fait la vaisselle, c'est (tout) un é. it's a major event when he does the washing-up

éventail [evɑ̃taj] nm (a) (pour se rafraîchir) fan; en é. fan-shaped (b) (choix) range

éventaire [evɑ̃tɛr] nm (a) (étal) stall (b) (d'un marchand ambulant) tray

éventé, -e [evɑ̃te] adj (vin, parfum) stale; (bière) flat

éventer [evɑ̃te] **1** vt (a) (avec un éventail) to fan (b) (secret, complot) to discover
2 s'éventer vpr (a) (avec un éventail) to fan oneself (b) (vin, parfum) to go stale; (bière) to go flat

éventrer [evɑ̃tre] vt (personne, animal) to disembowel; (colis, matelas) to rip open; (fût, boîte) to break open

éventualité [evɑ̃tɥalite] nf (a) (circonstance) eventuality; parer à toute é. to be prepared for all eventualities; dans l'é. de in the event of (b) (possibilité) possibility

éventuel, -elle [evɑ̃tɥɛl] adj possible

éventuellement [evɑ̃tɥɛlmɑ̃] adv possibly; j'aurais é. besoin de votre concours I may need your help

évêque [evɛk] nm bishop

Everest [evərɛst] nm l'E., le mont E. (Mount) Everest

évertuer [evɛrtɥe] s'évertuer vpr s'é. à faire qch to endeavour to do sth

éviction [eviksjɔ̃] nf (d'un rival, d'une tête de parti) ousting; (d'un locataire) eviction

évidemment [evidamɑ̃] adv of course, obviously

évidence [evidɑ̃s] nf (a) (d'un fait, de la vérité) obviousness; c'est une é.! obviously!; nier l'é. to deny the obvious; se rendre à l'é. to face facts; de toute é., à l'é. obviously (b) en é. (visible) in a prominent position; mettre qch en é. (phénomène) to highlight sth; se mettre en é. to try to get oneself noticed

évident, -e [evidɑ̃, -ɑ̃t] adj obvious; tu crois qu'on va réussir? – c'est é.! do you think we'll succeed? – of course (we will)!; elle va se rendre compte, c'est é. she's bound to notice; Fam c'est pas é.! (pas facile) it's not so easy!

évider [evide] vt to hollow out

évier [evje] nm sink

évincer [evɛ̃se] vt (rival) to oust (de from)

éviter [evite] **1** vt (a) (s'écarter de) to avoid; é. de faire qch to avoid doing sth; il faut é. qu'il le voie he mustn't be allowed to see it; évite que ça se sache don't let it get out (b) (épargner) é. qch à qn to save or spare sb sth; ça m'évitera d'avoir à le faire il will save me having to do it
2 s'éviter vpr (a) s'é. qch to avoid sth (b) (se fuir mutuellement) to avoid each other

évocateur, -trice [evokatœr, -tris] adj evocative (de of)

évocation [evokasjɔ̃] nf evocation

évolué, -e [evolɥe] adj (société) advanced; (personne) broadminded; Ordinat (langage) high-level

évoluer [evolɥe] vi (a) (se déplacer) to move around; Fig é. dans le milieu des artistes to move in artistic circles (b) (se développer) to develop (c) Ordinat faire é. to upgrade

évolutif, -ive [evolytif, -iv] adj progressive; Ordinat upgradeable

évolution [evolysjɔ̃] nf (a) (développement) development (b) Biol evolution (c) évolutions (déplacements) movements

évoquer [evoke] vt (a) (se remémorer) (passé) to recall, to evoke (b) (faire penser à) to be reminiscent of; son nom ne m'évoque rien her name means nothing to me (c) (aborder) to touch on, to mention (d) (par la magie) to call up, to invoke

ex [ɛks] nmf Fam ex

ex- [ɛks] préf ex-; ex-femme/-ministre ex-wife/-minister

exacerbation [ɛgzasɛrbasjɔ̃] nf exacerbation

exacerber [ɛgzasɛrbe] **1** vt to exacerbate
2 s'exacerber vpr to become acute

exact, -e [ɛgzakt] adj (a) (quantité, poids, nombre) exact, precise; (rapport, description) exact, accurate; (mot, réponse, heure, date) right, correct; c'est e. (vrai) it's quite true; il s'appelle bien Martin? – e.! his name's Martin? – that's right! (b) (ponctuel) punctual, on time

exactement [ɛgzaktəmɑ̃] adv exactly

exactions [ɛgzaksjɔ̃] nfpl atrocities

exactitude [ɛgzaktityd] nf (a) (précision, fidélité) exactness; (justesse) correctness (b) (ponctualité) punctuality; Prov l'e. est la politesse des rois punctuality is the politeness of kings

ex æquo [ɛgzeko] **1** adj inv être e. to tie, to be equally placed (avec with)
2 nmf inv il y a deux e. there's a two-way tie; départager les e. to break the tie
3 adv être troisième e. to tie for third place

exagération [ɛgzaʒerasjɔ̃] nf exaggeration

exagéré, -e [ɛgzaʒere] adj (récit, geste) exaggerated; (prix, salaire, pessimisme) excessive; il n'est pas e. de dire que... it's no exaggeration to say that...

exagérément [ɛgzaʒeremɑ̃] adv excessively

exagérer [34] [ɛgzaʒere] **1** vt to exaggerate; il ne faut rien e., n'exagérons rien let's not exaggerate
2 vi (amplifier) to exaggerate; (abuser) to go too far

exaltant, -e [ɛgzaltɑ̃, -ɑ̃t] adj stirring

exaltation [ɛgzaltasjɔ̃] nf (excitation) intense excitement

exalté, -e [ɛgzalte] **1** adj (discours, sentiment) impassioned; (personne) fanatical
2 nm,f fanatic

exalter [ɛgzalte] vt (a) (exciter) (imagination) to stir; (ressentiment, orgueil) to intensify (b) (louer) (personne) to exalt

exam [ɛgzam] nm Fam exam

examen [ɛgzamɛ̃] nm (a) (d'un document, de faits) examination; (d'une machine) checking; (d'un local) inspection; (d'une demande) consideration; e. de conscience soul-searching (b) e. (médical) (medical) examination; e. de la vue sight or eye test (c) Scol & Univ exam, examination; e. blanc mock exam; e. d'entrée entrance exam; e. de passage Br end-of-year exam, Am final exam

examinateur, -trice [ɛgzaminatœr, -tris] nm,f examiner

examiner [ɛgzamine] **1** vt **(a)** (étudier) (document, faits) to examine; (machine) to check; (local) to inspect; (demande) to consider **(b)** (observer) to examine; (horizon) to scan; **e. qn de la tête aux pieds** to eye sb up and down **(c)** (patient) to examine; **se faire e. par un médecin** to be examined by a doctor
2 s'examiner vpr **(a)** (dans une glace) to examine oneself **(b)** (l'un l'autre) to examine each other

exaspérant, -e [ɛgzasperɑ̃, -ɑ̃t] adj exasperating

exaspération [ɛgzasperasjɔ̃] nf exasperation

exaspérer [34] [ɛgzaspere] vt **(a)** (personne) to exasperate **(b)** Litt (douleur, sentiment) to aggravate

exaucement [ɛgzosmɑ̃] nm granting

exaucer [16] [ɛgzose] vt **(a)** (souhait) to grant **(b)** **e. qn** to grant sb's wish

excavateur [ɛkskavatœr] nm excavator, (mechanical) digger

excavation [ɛkskavasjɔ̃] nf **(a)** (trou) excavation; (creusée par une bombe) crater **(b)** (action) excavation

excavatrice [ɛkskavatris] nf = **excavateur**

excédant, -e [ɛksedɑ̃, -ɑ̃t] adj exasperating

excédent [ɛksedɑ̃] nm surplus; **budget en e.** surplus budget; **e. de poids** excess weight; **e. de bagages** excess baggage; **être en e.** to show a surplus

excédentaire [ɛksedɑ̃tɛr] adj (production, poids) excess; (budget) surplus; **balance commerciale e.** trade surplus

excéder [34] [ɛksede] vt **(a)** (quantité, somme, limite) to exceed; (forces, compétences) to be beyond; **e. ses pouvoirs** to exceed one's powers **(b)** (irriter) to exasperate

excellence [ɛkselɑ̃s] nf excellence; Scol **prix d'e.** class prize (for all-round standard); **par e.** par excellence; **Son/Votre E.** (titre) His/Her/Your Excellency

excellent, -e [ɛkselɑ̃, -ɑ̃t] adj excellent (**en** at)

exceller [ɛksele] vi to excel (**en** at)

excentré, -e [ɛksɑ̃tre] adj **(a)** (quartier) outlying **(b)** Tech off centre

excentricité [ɛksɑ̃trisite] nf (de caractère, acte bizarre) eccentricity

excentrique [ɛksɑ̃trik] **1** adj (bizarre) eccentric
2 nmf (personne) eccentric

excepté, -e [ɛksɛpte] **1** prép except, apart from
2 adj **les femmes exceptées** except for or apart from the women

excepter [ɛksɛpte] vt to except (**de** from); **sans e. les enfants** not forgetting the children

exception [ɛksɛpsjɔ̃] nf exception (**à** to); **c'est l'e. qui confirme la règle** it's the exception that proves the rule; **à quelques exceptions près** with a few exceptions; **un être d'e.** an exceptional person

exceptionnel, -elle [ɛksɛpsjɔnɛl] adj exceptional; **ne rien avoir d'e.** to be nothing special

exceptionnellement [ɛksɛpsjɔnɛlmɑ̃] adv exceptionally

excès [ɛksɛ] nm **(a)** (excédent) excess; **pécher par e. de zèle** to be overzealous; **avec e.** excessively, to excess; **sans e.** in moderation; **jusqu'à l'e.** to excess, excessively; **tomber dans l'e. inverse** to go to the other extreme; **e. de vitesse** speeding; **faire un e. de vitesse** to speed **(b)** (abus) excess; **faire des e.** to overindulge

excessif, -ive [ɛksesif, -iv] adj excessive; **il est e.** he does things to excess

excessivement [ɛksesivmɑ̃] adv (extrêmement) extremely; (avec excès) excessively

excision [ɛksizjɔ̃] nf excision

excitant, -e [ɛksitɑ̃, -ɑ̃t] **1** adj (fascinant, provocant) exciting; (tonique) stimulating
2 nm stimulant

excitation [ɛksitasjɔ̃] nf **(a)** (incitation) incitement (**à** to) **(b)** (état) excitement **(c)** Méd excitation

excité, -e [ɛksite] **1** adj excited
2 nm,f (personne) hothead

exciter [ɛksite] **1** vt **(a)** (attiser) (curiosité, jalousie, pitié) to arouse **(b)** (encourager) to urge on; **e. qn à la révolte** to incite sb to revolt **(c)** (énerver) to excite **(d)** (nerf, muscle) to excite
2 s'exciter vpr to get excited

exclamation [ɛksklamasjɔ̃] nf exclamation

exclamer [ɛksklame] **s'exclamer** vpr **s'e. de qch** (joie, douleur) to cry out with sth; **"jamais!" s'exclama-t-il** "never!" he exclaimed

exclu, -e [ɛkskly] **1** adj **(a)** (non compris) TVA **exclue** excluding VAT **(b)** (impensable) out of the question; **il est e. qu'elle vienne avec nous** there's no question of her coming with us
2 nm,f outcast

exclure [17] [ɛksklyr] vt **(a)** (expulser) **e. qn de qch** (parti, école) to expel sb from sth; (fonction publique) to remove sb from sth; (salle, réunion) to eject sb from sth **(b)** (mettre à l'écart) **e. qn de qch** to exclude sb from sth **(c)** (ne pas considérer) (hypothèse, solution) to rule out; **cela n'exclut pas que vous puissiez enseigner** that doesn't rule out the possibility of your teaching

exclusif, -ive [ɛksklyzif, -iv] adj exclusive; (but, mission) sole; **être e. dans ses amitiés** to be selective in one's choice of friends

exclusion [ɛksklyzjɔ̃] nf **(a)** (d'un parti, d'une école) expulsion; (d'une fonction publique) removal; (d'une salle, d'une réunion) ejection (**de** from) **(b)** **à l'e. de** with the exception of

exclusivement [ɛksklyzivmɑ̃] adv exclusively

exclusivité [ɛksklyzivite] nf **(a)** (droit) exclusive rights (**de** to); **en e.** exclusively; **film en première e.** recent release; Fig **ne pas avoir l'e. de l'intelligence** not to have a monopoly on intelligence **(b)** (information) exclusive, scoop

excommunier [66] [ɛkskɔmynje] vt to excommunicate

excréments [ɛkskremɑ̃] nmpl excrement

excrétion [ɛkskresjɔ̃] nf **(a)** (action) excretion **(b)** **excrétions** (déchets) excreta

excroissance [ɛkskrwasɑ̃s] nf excrescence

excursion [ɛkskyrsjɔ̃] nf (en car, en voiture) excursion, trip; (d'une journée) day trip; (de plusieurs jours) tour; **faire une e., partir en e.** to go on a trip/a tour

excursionniste [ɛkskyrsjɔnist] nmf Br day-tripper, Am excursionist

excusable [ɛkskyzabl] adj excusable, forgivable

excuse [ɛkskyz] nf **(a)** (raison) excuse; **trouver des excuses à qn** to find excuses for sb; **ce n'est pas une e.!** that's no excuse! **(b)** **excuses** (regrets) apology; **faire ou présenter ses excuses à qn** to make one's apologies to sb

excuser [ɛkskyze] **1** vt (a) *(justifier) (personne, action)* to excuse; **e. qn auprès de qn** to apologize for sb to sb (b) *(pardonner) (personne, erreur, colère)* to excuse; **excusez-moi** *(j'ai fait une faute)* I'm sorry; *(pour attirer l'attention)* excuse me; **excuse-moi de te déranger** I'm sorry to disturb you; **excuse-moi de ne pas t'avoir téléphoné** I'm sorry I didn't phone you; *Formel* **je vous prie de m'e.** I do beg your pardon; **tu es tout excusé** there's no need to apologize; *Hum* **excusez du peu!** if you please! (c) *(dispenser)* to excuse; **se faire e.** to ask to be excused

2 s'excuser vpr to apologize; **s'e. auprès de qn** to apologize to sb; **s'e. de qch/de faire qch** to apologize for sth/for doing sth; **je m'excuse!** I'm sorry!

exécrable [ɛgzekrabl] adj atrocious

exécrer [34] [ɛgzekre] vt Litt to loathe

exécutable [ɛgzekytabl] adj executable

exécutant, -e [ɛgzekytɑ̃, -ɑ̃t] nm,f (a) *(employé)* subordinate; **ce n'est qu'un simple e.** he just carries out orders (b) *(musicien)* performer

exécuter [ɛgzekyte] **1** vt (a) *(effectuer) (travail, ordres)* to carry out; *(danse, morceau de musique)* to perform; *(peinture)* to execute (b) *Ordinat (programme)* to run; *(commande)* to execute (c) *(mettre à mort)* to execute; *Fam (battre)* to slaughter; *Fam (critiquer)* to savage

2 s'exécuter vpr to comply

exécuteur, -trice [ɛgzekytœr, -tris] nm,f Jur **e. testamentaire** executor; **exécutrice testamentaire** executrix

exécutif, -ive [ɛgzekytif, -iv] **1** adj *(pouvoir)* executive

2 nm **l'e.** the executive

exécution [ɛgzekysjɔ̃] nf (a) *(d'un travail, d'ordres)* carrying out; *(d'une danse, d'un morceau de musique)* performance; *(d'une peinture)* execution; **mettre qch à e.** to carry sth out (b) *Ordinat* execution (c) *(mise à mort)* execution

exécutoire [ɛgzekytwar] adj (a) **jugement e.** enforceable decision (b) **formule e.** executory formula

exégèse [ɛgzeʒɛz] nf exegesis

exemplaire¹ [ɛgzɑ̃plɛr] adj (a) *(comportement, courage)* exemplary (b) *(punition)* exemplary

exemplaire² nm *(livre, gravure)* copy; **en deux/trois exemplaires** in duplicate/triplicate; **photocopier qch en vingt exemplaires** to make twenty photocopies of sth; **le livre a été tiré à dix mille exemplaires** ten thousand copies of the book were printed

exemple [ɛgzɑ̃pl] nm (a) *(modèle)* example **(pour** for); **donner l'e. (à qn)** to set (sb) an example; **suivre l'e. de qn** to follow sb's example; **prendre qn en e.** to model oneself on sb; **citer qn/qch en e.** to quote sb/sth as an example; **faire un e.** *(en punissant)* to set an example (b) *(cas, mot, phrase)* example; **être l'e. même de la bêtise** to be stupidity itself (c) **par e.** for example, for instance; *Fam* **ah ça par e.!** *(stupeur)* oh no!

exempt, -e [ɛgzɑ̃, -ɑ̃t] adj **e. de** *(service militaire)* exempt from; *(danger, problème)* free from; **e. de droits de douane** duty-free; **sa remarque n'était pas exempte d'une certaine amertume** her remark wasn't without a trace of bitterness

exempter [ɛgzɑ̃te] vt *(dispenser)* to exempt **(de** from)

exemption [ɛgzɑ̃psjɔ̃] nf exemption **(de** from)

exercé, -e [ɛgzɛrse] adj *(œil, oreille)* trained; *(main)* practised

exercer [16] [ɛgzɛrse] **1** vt (a) *(entraîner) (corps, esprit, mémoire)* to train; **e. qn à qch/à faire qch** to train sb in sth/to do sth (b) *(user de) (autorité, talent, droit)* to exercise; **e. une influence sur qn** to exert an influence on sb; **e. une pression sur qn/qch** to exert pressure on sb/sth; **e. un contrôle sur qch** to exercise control over sth (c) *(profession)* to practise; **e. ses fonctions** to carry out one's duties; **e. le métier de journaliste** to work as a journalist

2 vi *(médecin, juriste)* to practise

3 s'exercer vpr (a) *(s'entraîner)* to practise; **s'e. à qch/à faire qch** to practise sth/doing sth (b) *(se manifester) (autorité, pouvoir)* to make itself felt

exercice [ɛgzɛrsis] nm (a) *(entraînement sportif ou scolaire)* exercise; **faire des exercices** to do (some) exercises; **prendre de l'e.** to (take) exercise (b) *Mil* drill; **être à l'e.** to be on parade (c) *(du pouvoir, d'un droit)* exercise (d) *(d'une profession)* practice; **dans l'e. de ses fonctions** in the exercise of one's duties; **être en e.** *(avocat, médecin)* to be in practice; *(président)* to be in office; **le président en e.** the incumbent president (e) **l'e. du culte** public worship (f) *(en comptabilité) Br* financial year, *Am* fiscal year

exergue [ɛgzɛrg] nm *(de médaille)* inscription; *(d'un texte)* epigraph; **en e.** *(citation)* as an epigraph

exfoliant, -e [ɛksfɔljɑ̃, -ɑ̃t] **1** adj exfoliating

2 nm exfoliant

exhaler [ɛgzale] **1** vt *(odeur)* to give off; *Fig (joie, colère)* to give vent to; *Fig* **cette maison exhale la tristesse** sadness pervades this house

2 s'exhaler vpr *(odeur)* to be given off

exhausser [ɛgzose] vt *(mur, édifice)* to heighten; **e. une maison d'un étage** to add a storey to a house

exhaustif, -ive [ɛgzostif, -iv] adj exhaustive

exhiber [ɛgzibe] **1** vt (a) *(documents, passeport)* to produce (b) *Péj (savoir, richesses)* to show off, to flaunt

2 s'exhiber vpr to flaunt oneself

exhibition [ɛgzibisjɔ̃] nf Péj *(de savoir, de richesses)* flaunting

exhibitionniste [ɛgzibisjɔnist] nmf exhibitionist

exhortation [ɛgzɔrtasjɔ̃] nf exhortation **(à** to)

exhorter [ɛgzɔrte] vt **e. qn à qch/à faire qch** to exhort sb to sth/to do sth

exhumation [ɛgzymasjɔ̃] nf *(d'un corps)* exhumation; *(d'un trésor, de vestiges)* excavation

exhumer [ɛgzyme] vt *(corps)* to exhume; *(trésor, vestiges)* to excavate

exigeant, -e [ɛgziʒɑ̃, -ɑ̃t] adj *(personne, travail)* exacting

exigence [ɛgziʒɑ̃s] nf (a) *(caractère)* exacting nature (b) *(condition)* demand

exiger [45] [ɛgziʒe] vt (a) *(demander en insistant)* to demand **(de** from); **e. que qch soit fait** to demand that sth be done (b) *(nécessiter) (soin, action)* to require

exigible [ɛgziʒibl] adj *(dette, impôt)* payable

exigu, -ë [ɛgzigy] adj cramped, tiny

exiguïté [ɛgziguite] nf crampedness

exil [ɛgzil] nm exile; **envoyer qn en e.** to send sb into exile; **être en e.** to be in exile

exilé, -e [ɛgzile] nm,f exile

exiler [ɛgzile] **1** vt to exile **(de** from)

2 s'exiler vpr to go into exile; *Fig* **s'e. de la ville** to cut oneself off from the town

existant, -e [ɛgzistɑ̃, -ɑ̃t] adj existing

existence [egzistãs] *nf* (a) *Phil (être)* existence (b) *(vie)* life; **mener une e. tranquille** to lead a quiet life; **dans l'e.** in life (c) *(présence)* existence (**de** of) (d) *(durée) (d'une institution)* life

existentialisme [egzistãsjalism] *nm Phil* existentialism

existentiel, -elle [egzistãsjel] *adj* existential

exister [egziste] **1** *vi* to exist; **rien n'existe pour lui que l'art** art is all that matters to him; **et l'amitié, cela existe, non?** there's such a thing as friendship, isn't there?
  2 *v impersonnel* **il existe** there is/are

exode [egzɔd] *nm* exodus; **e. rural** rural depopulation

exonération [egzɔnerasjɔ̃] *nf* exemption; **e. fiscale** tax exemption

exonérer [34] [egzɔnere] *vt (personne)* to exempt; *(marchandises)* to exempt from tax; **être exonéré d'impôts** to be exempt from tax

exorbitant, -e [egzɔrbitã, -ãt] *adj (prix, demande)* exorbitant

exorbité, -e [egzɔrbite] *adj (yeux)* protruding; *Fig* **ils regardaient, les yeux exorbités** they watched with bulging eyes

exorciser [egzɔrsize] *vt aussi Fig* to exorcize

exorcisme [egzɔrsism] *nm* exorcism

exotique [egzɔtik] *adj* exotic; **poisson e.** tropical fish

expansé, -e [ekspãse] *adj (polystyrène)* expanded

expansif, -ive [ekspãsif, -iv] *adj (exubérant)* expansive

expansion [ekspãsjɔ̃] *nf* (a) *(de gaz, de l'univers)* expansion; **l'univers en e.** the expanding universe (b) *(développement) (d'une ville, d'une industrie)* expansion; **taux d'e.** growth rate; **être en pleine e.** *(d'une économie, d'une entreprise)* to be booming

expansionnisme [ekspãsjɔnism] *nm* expansionism

expatriation [ekspatrijasjɔ̃] *nf* expatriation

expatrié, -e [ekspatrije] *adj & nm,f* expatriate

expatrier [66] [ekspatrije] **1** *vt (personne)* to expatriate
  2 s'expatrier *vpr* to leave one's country

expectative [ekspektativ] *nf* **être dans l'e.** to be waiting to see what happens

expectorant, -e [ekspektɔrã, -ãt] *adj & nm* expectorant

expectorer [ekspektɔre] *vt* to expectorate

expédient [ekspedjã] *nm* expedient; **vivre d'expédients** to live by one's wits

expédier [66] [ekspedje] *vt* (a) *(envoyer)* to send, to dispatch; **e. qch par bateau/par avion/par le train** to send sth by sea/air/rail (b) *(se débarrasser de)* to dispose of; **elle les a expédiés en colonie de vacances** she packed them off to camp (c) *(faire rapidement) (tâche)* to deal promptly with; *(devoirs, dissertation)* to dash off; **e. les affaires courantes** to deal with the day-to-day matters

expéditeur, -trice [ekspeditœr, -tris] **1** *nm,f* sender
  2 *adj (bureau, gare)* dispatching

expéditif, -ive [ekspeditif, -iv] *adj* hasty

expédition [ekspedisjɔ̃] *nf* (a) *(envoi)* dispatch, sending (b) *(marchandises)* consignment (c) *(voyage, opération militaire) & Fig* expedition; **partir en e.** to go on an expedition

expéditionnaire [ekspedisjɔner] *adj Mil* expeditionary

expérience [eksperjãs] *nf* (a) *(pratique)* experience; **avoir de l'e.** to have experience; **avoir l'e. de qch** to have experience of sth; **savoir qch par e.** to know sth from experience; **faire l'e. de qch** to experience sth; **tenter l'e.** to give it a try (b) *(test scientifique)* experiment; **e. en laboratoire** laboratory experiment; **faire une e. (sur)** to carry out an experiment (on)

expérimental, -e, -aux, -ales [eksperimãtal, -o] *adj* experimental

expérimentalement [eksperimãtalmã] *adv* experimentally

expérimentation [eksperimãtasjɔ̃] *nf* experimentation; **e. sur l'homme** human experiments

expérimenté, -e [eksperimãte] *adj* experienced

expérimenter [eksperimãte] *vt (remède, vaccin)* to test, to try out (**sur** on)

expert, -e [eksper, -ert] **1** *adj* expert, skilled (**en/dans** in); **être e. en la matière** to be an expert on the subject
  2 *nm* expert; *(d'assurance)* valuer

expert-comptable (*pl* **experts-comptables**) [eksperkɔ̃tabl] *nm Br* ≃ chartered accountant, *Am* ≃ certified public accountant, CPA

expertise [ekspertiz] *nf* (a) *(évaluation) (d'une œuvre d'art)* valuation; *(de dommages)* assessment (b) *(rapport)* expert's report (**de** on) (c) *(compétence)* expertise

expertiser [ekspertize] *vt (œuvre d'art)* to value; *(dommages)* to assess

expiation [ekspjasjɔ̃] *nf* expiation (**de** of)

expiatoire [ekspjatwar] *adj* expiatory

expier [66] [ekspje] *vt* to atone for, to expiate

expiration [ekspirasjɔ̃] *nf* (a) *(respiration)* breathing out (b) *(d'un contrat, d'un bail) Br* expiry, *Am* expiration; **venir ou arriver à e.** to expire

expirer [ekspire] **1** *vi* (a) *Litt (mourir)* to expire (b) *(contrat, bail)* to expire (c) *(respirer)* to breathe out
  2 *vt* to breathe out

explicatif, -ive [eksplikatif, -iv] *adj* explanatory; **notice explicative** directions for use

explication [eksplikasjɔ̃] *nf* explanation; **donner une e. à qch** to give an explanation for sth; **exiger des explications** to demand an explanation; **avoir une e. avec qn** *(discuter)* to talk things over with sb; *(se disputer)* to have it out with sb; **e. de textes** textual analysis

explicite [eksplisit] *adj* explicit

explicitement [eksplisitmã] *adv* explicitly

expliquer [eksplike] **1** *vt* to explain; *(texte)* to analyse
  2 s'expliquer *vpr* (a) *(communiquer ses idées, se justifier)* to explain oneself; **je m'explique** let me explain (b) *(comprendre)* **je ne m'explique pas pourquoi il...** I can't understand why he... (c) *(être explicable)* **cela s'explique facilement** that's easily explained; **tout s'explique!** there's a reason for everything! (d) *(se parler)* to talk things over; **s'e. avec qn** *(discuter)* to talk things over with sb; *(se disputer)* to have it out with sb

exploit [eksplwa] *nm* feat

exploitant, -e [eksplwatã, -ãt] *nm,f* (a) **e. (agricole)** farmer; **petits exploitants** small farmers (b) *Cin* exhibitor

exploitation [ɛksplwatasjɔ̃] nf (a) (d'une mine, d'une forêt) working; (d'une ligne de chemin de fer, d'une ferme) running; (d'une terre) farming; (des ressources naturelles, d'un brevet) & Fig Péj exploitation; Ordinat **système d'e.** operating system; Fig **c'est de l'e.!** it's exploitation! (b) (entreprise) concern; **e. agricole** farm; **e. minière** mine

exploiter [ɛksplwate] vt (a) (mine, forêt) to work; (ressources naturelles, brevet) to exploit; (ligne de chemin de fer, ferme) to run; (terre) to farm; Fig (situation, talent, idée) to exploit (b) Péj (abuser de) (personne) to exploit

exploiteur, -euse [ɛksplwatœr, -øz] nm,f Péj exploiter

explorateur, -trice [ɛksplɔratœr, -tris] nm,f (personne) explorer

exploration [ɛksplɔrasjɔ̃] nf exploration; **partir en e.** to go off exploring

exploratoire [ɛksplɔratwar] adj exploratory

explorer [ɛksplɔre] vt to explore

exploser [ɛksploze] vi (a) (bombe, avion, chaudière) to explode; **faire e. une bombe** to explode a bomb (b) Fig (se mettre en colère) to explode

explosif, -ive [ɛksplozif, -iv] **1** adj aussi Fig explosive **2** nm explosive

explosion [ɛksplozjɔ̃] nf aussi Fig explosion; **une e. de joie** an outburst of joy; **e. démographique** population explosion

exponentiel, -elle [ɛksponɑ̃sjɛl] **1** adj exponential **2** nf **exponentielle** exponential

export [ɛkspɔr] nm export; Ordinat **e. de données** data export

exportateur, -trice [ɛkspɔrtatœr, -tris] **1** adj exporting; **pays e. de vin** wine-exporting country **2** nm,f exporter

exportation [ɛkspɔrtasjɔ̃] nf (action) export(ation); (produit) export; Ordinat (d'un fichier) exporting; Ordinat (données exportées) exported data

exporter [ɛkspɔrte] vt aussi Ordinat to export (**vers** to)

exposant, -e [ɛkspozɑ̃, -ɑ̃t] **1** nm,f (artiste, firme) exhibitor **2** nm (a) Math exponent (b) Typ (chiffre, lettre) superscript; **3 en e.** superscript 3

exposé [ɛkspoze] nm (de faits, d'une situation) account; Scol & Univ talk; **après un bref e. de la situation** after outlining the situation; **faire un e.** to give a talk

exposer [ɛkspoze] **1** vt (a) (montrer) (marchandises) to display; (œuvres d'art) to exhibit (b) (expliquer) (raisons, projet) to set out; (griefs, point de vue) to air; **je leur ai exposé ma situation** I explained my situation to them (c) (présenter) **e. qch à la lumière/au soleil** to expose sth to the light/to the sun; **e. un film** to expose a film; **e. qn à la critique/au danger** to expose sb to criticism/to danger; **exposé au nord** facing north **2 s'exposer** vpr **s'e. au danger** to put oneself in danger; **s'e. à la critique/à des poursuites** to lay oneself open to criticism/to prosecution; **ne t'expose pas trop longtemps** don't stay in the sun too long

exposition [ɛkspozisjɔ̃] nf (a) (action) (de marchandises, de fleurs) display; (d'œuvres d'art) exhibition (b) (de musée) exhibition (c) (salon, foire) exhibition, show; **l'E. universelle** the World Fair (d) (de faits, de raisons) exposition (e) (au froid, au danger) exposure (à to); (d'une maison) aspect; Phot exposure

exprès¹, -esse [ɛksprɛs] adj (explicite) express

exprès² adj inv **lettre/paquet e.** special delivery letter/parcel; **en e.** by special delivery

exprès³ [ɛksprɛ] adv (à dessein) on purpose, deliberately; (spécialement) specially; **je l'ai allumé sans le faire e.** I switched it on without meaning to; **c'est fait e.** it's deliberate; **on dirait un fait e.** you'd think it was done on purpose; **comme (par) un fait e., il pleuvait** and wouldn't you know it, it was raining

express [ɛksprɛs] **1** adj (train) express **2** nm (a) (train) express (b) (café) espresso

expressément [ɛkspresemɑ̃] adv (a) (catégoriquement) expressly (b) (spécialement) specially

expressif, -ive [ɛkspresif, -iv] adj expressive

expression [ɛkspresjɔ̃] nf (a) (d'un sentiment, d'une opinion) expression; (du visage) expression, look; **l'e. de son visage** the expression or look on her face; **sans e.** expressionless; **e. corporelle** self-expression through movement (b) (locution) expression (c) Math expression; Fig **réduit à sa plus simple e.** reduced to its simplest form; Ordinat **e. logique** logical expression

expressionnisme [ɛkspresjonism] nm expressionism

exprimable [ɛksprimabl] adj expressible

exprimer [ɛksprime] **1** vt (a) (sentiment, opinion) & Math to express (b) (jus) to squeeze (**de** from) **2 s'exprimer** vpr (en parlant, en agissant) to express oneself; **s'e. par gestes** to use sign language; **si je peux m'e. ainsi** if I can put it like that; **le président ne s'est pas encore exprimé sur ce sujet** the president has yet to voice an opinion on the matter

expropriation [ɛksproprijasjɔ̃] nf expropriation

exproprier [66] [ɛksproprije] vt to expropriate

expulser [ɛkspylse] vt (étranger) to deport, to expel (**de** from); (locataire) to evict (**de** from); (élève, membre de parti) to expel (**de** from); (joueur) to send off

expulsion [ɛkspylsjɔ̃] nf (d'un étranger) deportation (**de** from); (d'un locataire) eviction (**de** from); (d'un élève, d'un membre de parti) expulsion (**de** from); (d'un joueur) sending off

expurger [45] [ɛkspyrʒe] vt to expurgate

exquis, -e [ɛkski, -iz] adj exquisite; (personne, sourire, temps) delightful

exsangue [ɛksɑ̃g, ɛgzɑ̃g] adj (patient, visage) anaemic; Fig (pays, région) bled white

extase [ɛkstaz] nf (a) Rel & Psy ecstasy (b) (admiration) rapture, ecstasy; **être en e. devant qn/qch** to be in raptures over sb/sth

extasier [66] [ɛkstazje] s'extasier vpr (s'exclamer) to go into raptures (**sur/devant** about/over); (être en extase) to be in raptures (**sur/devant** about/over)

extatique [ɛkstatik] adj ecstatic

extenseur [ɛkstɑ̃sœr] **1** adj m (muscle) extensor **2** nm (appareil) chest expander

extensible [ɛkstɑ̃sibl] adj (a) (métal) tensile; (vêtement, tissu) stretch (b) Ordinat upgradeable

extensif, -ive [ɛkstɑ̃sif, -iv] adj **culture extensive** extensive farming

extension [ɛkstɑ̃sjɔ̃] nf (a) (d'un muscle, d'un ressort) stretching; **être en e.** (ressort) to be released; (gymnaste) to be fully stretched (b) Fig (d'un territoire, d'une firme) expansion; (d'un contrat) extension; (d'une maladie, d'une langue) spread; **prendre de l'e.** (entreprise) to expand; (maladie, incendie) to spread (c) **par e.** by extension (d) Ordinat expansion; **e. mémoire** memory upgrade

exténuer [ekstenɥe] **1** *vt* to exhaust
2 s'exténuer *vpr* **s'e. à faire qch** to exhaust oneself doing sth

extérieur, -e [eksterjœr] **1** *adj* (**a**) (*surface, partie*) outer, external; (*escalier, éclairage, intérêts*) outside; (*signe, fragilité*) outward; (*facteur, cause*) external; **le monde e.** the outside world; **sans aide extérieure** without outside help (**b**) (*étranger*) (*commerce, politique*) foreign, external
2 *nm* (**a**) (*d'un bâtiment, d'une boîte*) outside, exterior; **vu de l'e.** seen from the outside; **à l'e.** (*d'un bâtiment*) outside; (*d'une boîte*) on the outside; **à l'e. de la gare/ville** outside the station/town; *Fig* **juger de l'e.** to judge by appearances; **match à l'e.** away match; **jouer à l'e.** to play away (**b**) **l'e.** (*pays étrangers*) foreign countries; **à l'e.** abroad; **de l'e.** from abroad (**c**) *Cin* location shot; **tourner en e.** to film on location

extérieurement [eksterjœrmɑ̃] *adv* (**a**) (*dehors*) on the outside, externally (**b**) (*en apparence*) outwardly

extérioriser [eksterjɔrize] **1** *vt* (*sentiment*) to express; *Psy* to externalize
2 s'extérioriser *vpr* (*sentiment*) to express itself; (*personne*) to express oneself

exterminateur, -trice [eksterminatœr, -tris] **1** *adj* (*rage*) destructive
2 *nm,f* exterminator

extermination [eksterminasjɔ̃] *nf* extermination

exterminer [ekstermine] *vt* to exterminate

externat [eksterna] *nm* (**a**) (*école*) day school (**b**) (*élèves*) day pupils (**c**) (*à l'hôpital*) non-resident (medical) studentship

externe [ekstern] **1** *adj* (**a**) (*surface, partie*) external, outer; (*cause*) external; *Ordinat* **dispositif e.** external device; **à usage e.** (*médicament*) for external use only (**b**) **élève e.** day pupil
2 *nmf* (**a**) (*élève*) day pupil (**b**) (*étudiant en médecine*) **e.** (*des hôpitaux*) non-resident medical student, *Am* extern

extincteur [ekstɛ̃ktœr] *nm* fire extinguisher

extinction [ekstɛ̃ksjɔ̃] *nf* (**a**) **e. des feux** lights out (**b**) (*d'une espèce*) extinction (**c**) **e. de voix** loss of voice; **avoir une e. de voix** to have lost one's voice

extirper [ekstirpe] **1** *vt* (*plante*) to root up; *Fig* (*vices*) to eradicate, to root out; **e. qn de son lit** to drag sb out of bed; **je n'ai pas pu lui e. le moindre renseignement** I couldn't get a single piece of information out of him
2 s'extirper *vpr* **s'e. de qch** to extricate oneself from sth; **s'e. de son lit** to drag oneself out of bed

extorquer [ekstɔrke] *vt* (*argent, promesse*) to extort (**à** from)

extorsion [ekstɔrsjɔ̃] *nf* extortion; **e. de fonds** extortion of funds

extra [ekstra] **1** *adj inv* (**a**) (*de qualité supérieure*) top-quality (**b**) *Fam* (*remarquable*) great, neat
2 *nm inv* (**a**) (*gâterie*) (special) treat; **s'offrir un e.** to treat oneself (**b**) (*serviteur*) extra hand; **faire des e. chez qn** to do occasional work for sb

extra- [ekstra] *préf* extra-

extraconjugal, -e, -aux, -ales [ekstrakɔ̃ʒygal, -o] *adj* extramarital

extracteur [ekstraktœr] *nm* extractor

extraction [ekstraksjɔ̃] *nf aussi Math* extraction; (*d'une balle*) removal; *Fig* **de haute/basse e.** of noble/humble extraction

extrader [ekstrade] *vt* to extradite

extradition [ekstradisjɔ̃] *nf* extradition

extrafin, -e [ekstrafɛ̃, -in] *adj* (*petit pois*) extra-fine (**b**) (*de qualité supérieure*) top-quality

extrafort, -e [ekstrafɔr, -ɔrt] **1** *adj* extra-strong
2 *nm* bias binding

extraire [28] [ekstrɛr] **1** *vt aussi Math* to extract (**de** from); (*balle*) to remove (**de** from); (*épingle, clou*) to pull out (**de** of); (*personne*) to free (**de** from); **cette citation est extraite de...** this quotation is taken from...
2 s'extraire *vpr* **s'e. de qch** to extricate oneself from sth

extrait [ekstrɛ] *nm* (**a**) (*essence*) extract (**b**) (*de texte, de film*) extract; (*d'un acte*) abstract; **e. de casier judiciaire** = documentary evidence showing whether one has a criminal record; **e. de naissance** birth certificate

extralucide [ekstralysid] *adj & nmf* (**voyante**) **e.** clairvoyant

extraordinaire [ekstraɔrdinɛr] *adj* (**a**) (*spécial*) (*mesures, message, mission*) special (**b**) (*étonnant, remarquable*) extraordinary; *Fam* (*excellent*) fantastic; **cela n'a rien d'e.** that's nothing out of the ordinary; **si par e.** if by some remote chance

extraordinairement [ekstraɔrdinɛrmɑ̃] *adv* extraordinarily

extraplat, -e [ekstrapla, -at] *adj* (*montre, calculette*) slimline

extrapoler [ekstrapɔle] *vt* to extrapolate

extrascolaire [ekstraskɔlɛr] *adj* (*activités*) extra-curricular

extraterrestre [ekstraterɛstr] *adj & nmf* extraterrestrial

extra-utérin, -e [ekstrayterɛ̃, -in] *adj voir* **grossesse**

extravagance [ekstravagɑ̃s] *nf* (**a**) (*d'un comportement, de vêtements*) extravagance; (*d'une personne*) eccentricity; **des idées d'une telle e.** such extravagant ideas (**b**) (*action, remarque*) piece of nonsense

extravagant, -e [ekstravagɑ̃, -ɑ̃t] *adj* (*idée, comportement, vêtements*) extravagant; (*personne*) eccentric

extraverti, -e [ekstravɛrti] *adj & nmf* extrovert

extrême [ekstrɛm] **1** *adj* (**a**) (*point, limite*) furthest; (*jeunesse, vieillesse, froid, plaisir*) extreme; **en cas d'e. urgence** if it's extremely urgent; **d'une maigreur e.** extremely thin; *Pol* **e. droite/gauche** far *or* extreme right/left (**b**) (*excessif*) extreme
2 *nm* extreme; **passer d'un e. à l'autre** to go from one extreme to the other; **prudent à l'e.** cautious in the extreme

extrêmement [ekstrɛmmɑ̃] *adv* extremely

extrême-onction [ekstrɛmɔ̃ksjɔ̃] (*pl* **extrêmes-onctions**) *nf Rel* extreme unction

Extrême-Orient [ekstrɛmɔrjɑ̃] *nm* **l'E.** the Far East

extrémisme [ekstremism] *nm* extremism

extrémité [ekstremite] *nf* (**a**) (*bout*) (*d'une jambe, d'une corde*) end; (*d'un doigt*) tip; (*d'une aiguille, d'une épée*) point; **les extrémités** (*pieds et mains*) the extremities (**b**) (*acte désespéré*) **se livrer à une e.** to do something desperate (**c**) (*situation désespérée*) extremity; **être à la dernière e.** to be on the point of death

exubérance [egzyberɑ̃s] *nf* (*d'une personne*) exuberance; (*d'une végétation*) lushness; **avec e.** exuberantly

exubérant, -e [egzyberɑ̃, -ɑ̃t] *adj* (*personne, joie*) exuberant; (*végétation*) lush

exultation [egzyltasjɔ̃] *nf* exultation

exulter [egzylte] *vi* to exult, to rejoice

exutoire [egzytwar] *nm* outlet (**à** for)

ex-voto [eksvoto] *nm inv Rel* votive offering

F

F, f [ɛf] *nm inv* F, f; **un F2/F3** *(appartement)* a two-/three-roomed *Br* flat *or Am* apartment

F (a) *(abrév* **franc(s))** F, fr (b) *(abrév* **Fahrenheit)** F

fa [fa] *nm inv (note de musique)* F; *(chantée)* fa

fable [fabl] *nf* (a) *(récit)* fable (b) *(invention)* story

fabricant, -e [fabrikɑ̃, -ɑ̃t] *nm,f* manufacturer

fabrication [fabrikasjɔ̃] *nf (industrielle)* manufacture; *(manuelle)* making; **f. artisanale** production by craftsmen; **bombe de f. artisanale** home-made bomb; **f. assistée par ordinateur** computer-aided manufacture; **de f. française** French-made

fabrique [fabrik] *nf* factory

fabriquer [fabrike] *vt* (a) *(industriellement)* to manufacture; *(manuellement)* to make; *Fam* **qu'est-ce qu'elle fabrique?** what's she up to? (b) *(inventer)* to make up, to fabricate

fabulation [fabylasjɔ̃] *nf* fantasizing

fabuleusement [fabyløzmɑ̃] *adv* fabulously

fabuleux, -euse [fabylø, -øz] *adj* fabulous

fac [fak] *nf Fam* uni; **être en f. d'allemand** to be studying German at uni

façade [fasad] *nf aussi Fig* façade

face [fas] *nf (visage)* face; *Fig* **perdre/sauver la f.** to lose/save face

(b) *(côté) (d'un disque)* side; *(d'une pièce de monnaie)* head (side); **changer un disque de f.** to turn a record over

(c) *Fig (aspect)* side; **changer la f. des choses** to change the face of things

(d) *(locutions)* **f. à** *(dans l'espace)* facing; *(difficultés, situation)* faced with; *(adversaire)* confronted with; **f. à f.** *(avec)* face to face (with); **faire f. à** *(lieu, personne)* to face, to be opposite; *(responsabilités, dépenses)* to meet; *(situation, difficultés)* to face up to; **de f.** face on; *(attaquer)* from the front; **en f.** opposite; *(de l'autre côté de la rue)* across the road; **regarder qn en f.** to look sb in the face; **dire à qn qch en f.** to tell sb sth to his face; **la maison (d')en f.** the house across the road; **en f. de** opposite, facing; **l'un en f. de l'autre** opposite *or* facing each other

face-à-face [fasafas] *nm inv (public)* face-to-face debate; *(privé)* one-to-one meeting

facétie [fasesi] *nf Litt* joke

facétieux, -euse [fasesjø, -øz] *adj Litt (personne)* mischievous

facette [fasɛt] *nf aussi Fig* facet; **à facettes** facetted; *(personnalité)* multi-faceted

fâché, -e [faʃe] *adj* (a) *(en colère)* angry **(contre** with); (b) *(brouillé)* on bad terms **(avec** with); *Fam* **elle est fâchée avec les maths** she's hopeless at maths (c) *(contrarié)* sorry; **je ne suis pas f. que ça soit terminé** I'm not sorry that it's finished

fâcher [faʃe] **1** *vt (mettre en colère)* to make angry, to anger

2 se fâcher *vpr* (a) *(se mettre en colère)* to get angry **(contre** with); (b) *(se brouiller)* to fall out **(avec** with)

fâcheux, -euse [faʃø, -øz] *adj* unfortunate

facho [faʃo] *adj & nmf Fam* fascist

faciès [fasjɛs] *nm* features

facile [fasil] **1** *adj* (a) *(simple)* easy; **être f. à faire** to be easy to do; **c'est f. à dire** that's easily said; **f. d'emploi** easy to use (b) *(agréable)* easy-going; **être f. à vivre** to be easy to get on with (c) *Péj (superficiel)* facile (d) *Péj (femme, fille)* easy

2 *adv Fam (au moins)* easily

facilement [fasilmɑ̃] *adv* easily

facilité [fasilite] *nf* (a) *(simplicité)* easiness; **choisir la f.** to take the easy way out (b) *(aisance)* ease; **avoir des facilités pour qch** to have a talent for sth (c) **facilités de paiement** payment facilities

faciliter [fasilite] *vt* to make easier; **f. qch à qn** to make sth easier for sb

façon [fasɔ̃] *nf* (a) *(manière)* way, manner; **faire qch à sa f.** to do sth (in) one's own way; **de cette f.** (in) this way; **de f. à faire qch** so as to do sth; **de f. à ce qu'il t'entende** so that he hears you; **de telle f. que** in such a way that; **d'une ou de f. générale** generally speaking; **d'une f. ou d'une autre** one way or another; **de toute f.** anyway, in any case; *Fam* **vous ne me dérangez en aucune f.** you're not disturbing me in the least; **c'est une f. de parler** in a manner of speaking; **je ne tolère pas ces façons de parler!** I won't tolerate that sort of language! (b) *(imitation)* **f. cuir** imitation leather (c) *(comportement)* manners, behaviour; **en voilà des façons!** what a way to behave!; **faire des façons** *(minauder)* to put on airs; **faire des façons pour accepter qch** to make a fuss about accepting sth; **sans façons** *(personne, repas)* unpretentious; **non merci, sans façons!** no thanks, really!

façonner [fasɔne] *vt* (a) *(travailler)* to shape (b) *(fabriquer)* to make (c) *Fig (personne, caractère)* to mould

fac-similé [faksimile] *(pl* **fac-similés)** *nm* facsimile

facteur¹, -trice [faktœr, -tris] **1** *nm,f (employé des Postes) Br* postman, *Am* mailman

2 *nm (de pianos, de clavecins)* maker; *(d'orgues)* builder

facteur² *nm* (a) *(élément)* factor; **le f. temps** the time factor (b) *Math* factor

factice [faktis] *adj* (a) *(faux)* imitation (b) *Fig (sourire)* forced; *(gaieté)* false

faction [faksjɔ̃] *nf* (a) *(groupe)* faction (b) *Mil* guard duty; **être de** *ou* **en f.** to be on guard duty

factotum [faktɔtɔm] *nm* factotum

factuel, -elle [faktɥɛl] *adj* factual

facturation [faktyrasjɔ̃] *nf* invoicing, billing

facture¹ [faktyr] nf (a) (style) (d'une œuvre) construction; (d'un artiste) style (b) (de pianos, de clavecins) making; (d'orgues) building

facture² (document) invoice, bill; **faire** ou **dresser une f.** to make out an invoice; **f. d'électricité/de gaz** electricity/gas bill; **f. détaillée** itemized invoice

facturer [faktyre] vt to invoice

facturette [faktyrɛt] nf credit card sales slip

facultatif, -ive [fakyltatif, -iv] adj optional

faculté [fakylte] nf (a) (de médecine, de droit) faculty (b) (pouvoir) capacity (de for) (c) **facultés mentales** faculties; **ne plus avoir toutes ses facultés** to no longer have all one's faculties

fada [fada] Fam 1 adj crazy
2 nmf nutcase

fadaise [fadɛz] nf silly remark; **dire des fadaises** to talk nonsense

fadasse [fadas] adj Fam insipid

fade [fad] adj insipid

fadeur [fadœr] nf insipidness

fagot [fago] nm bundle of firewood; Fig **de derrière les fagots** (bouteille de vin) for special occasions; (compliment, idée) remarkable

fagoté, -e [fagote] adj Péj **mal/bizarrement f.** badly/oddly dressed

faiblard, -e [feblar, -ard] adj Fam a bit weak

faible [fɛbl] 1 adj (a) (physiquement, moralement) weak; (b) (raisonnement, plaisanterie) weak; **être f. en qch** (élève) to be weak at sth (c) (voix, odeur, lumière) faint; (vent) light; **et le terme est f.!** and that's putting it mildly! (d) (quantité) small; (prix, revenu) low; (avantage, chance, espoir) slight; (vitesse) low; **à une f. hauteur/profondeur** not very high up/deep down
2 nmf weakling; **les faibles d'esprit** the feeble-minded
3 nm avoir un **f. pour qn/qch** to have a soft spot for sb/a weakness for sth

faiblement [feblǝmɑ̃] adv (résister, protester) weakly, feebly; (éclairer) faintly

faiblesse [feblɛs] nf (a) (physique, morale) weakness; **avoir la f. de faire qch** to be weak enough to do sth; **donner des signes de f.** (appareil) to be showing signs of wear and tear; (personne) to be looking weak (b) (médiocrité) weakness (en at) (c) (malaise) **avoir une f.** to feel faint

faiblir [feblir] vi (a) (devenir faible) (personne, monnaie) to weaken; (lumière) to grow weaker; (vent) to drop (b) (niveau scolaire) to decrease; (élève) to get weaker

faïence [fajɑ̃s] nf (a) (matière) earthenware (b) (objet) piece of earthenware; **faïences** earthenware

faïencerie [fajɑ̃sri] nf (a) (articles) earthenware (b) (fabrique) pottery (works) (c) (commerce) pottery (trade)

faille [faj] nf (a) (dans un raisonnement) flaw; (dans une amitié) rift; **sans f.** (raisonnement) flawless; (fidélité) unwavering (b) Géol fault

faillir [35] [fajir] 1 vi **j'ai failli tomber** I nearly or almost fell; **j'ai bien failli me noyer** I very nearly drowned
2 **faillir à** vt ind Litt (réputation) not to live up to; (devoir) to fail in

faillite [fajit] nf (a) (d'entreprise) bankruptcy; **être en f.** to be bankrupt; **faire f.** to go bankrupt (b) (échec) failure

faim [fɛ̃] nf hunger; **avoir f.** to be hungry; Fig **avoir f. de qch** to hunger for sth; Fam **avoir une grosse/petite f.** to be very hungry/a bit hungry; **avoir une f. de loup** to be ravenous; **rester sur sa f.** to remain hungry; Fig to be left unsatisfied

fainéant, -e [feneɑ̃, -ɑ̃t] 1 adj lazy, idle
2 nm, f idler

fainéanter [feneɑ̃te] vi to idle about

fainéantise [feneɑ̃tiz] nf laziness, idleness

faire [36] [fɛr] 1 vt (a) (fabriquer, produire) to make; (tache, trace) to leave; (de la fumée, de la poussière) to make; **f. de la fumée** to give off smoke; **f. une erreur** to make a mistake; **f. de la betterave/du colza** to grow beetroot/rape; Fam **des femmes comme ça, on n'en fait plus** they don't make women like that any more; **f. un enfant à qn** to make sb pregnant; **f. des compliments à qn** to compliment sb; **je ferai de lui un homme/un avocat** I'll make a man/a lawyer of him; **qu'est-ce que je vais f. de lui?** what am I going to do with him?; **qu'est-ce que tu vas f. de ce vieux bidon?** what are you going to do with that old can?; **qu'est-ce que j'ai fait de mes lunettes?** what have I done with my glasses?
(b) (effectuer) (changements, effort, grimace, mouvement) to make; **f. le ménage/la vaisselle** to do the housework/the washing-up; **f. un pas en avant** to step forward; **faire demi-tour** to turn round; **f. une école de commerce** to study at a business school; **f. une licence** to study for a degree; **c'est moi qui fais tout ici** I have to do everything round here; **voilà une bonne chose de faite** that's one thing out of the way; **ce qui est fait est fait** what's done is done; **c'est bien fait pour elle** it serves her right
(c) (occasionner) **f. de la peine à qn** to hurt sb; **qu'est-ce que tu lui as fait?** what have you done to her? Fam **f. des ennuis à qn** to make trouble for sb; **ça m'a fait quelque chose/un choc** it upset/shocked me; **ça a fait du scandale** it caused a scandal; **ça ne fait rien** it doesn't matter; **qu'est-ce que ça peut faire?** what difference does it make?; **ça fait mauvais effet** it gives a bad impression; **le médicament n'a pas fait effet** the medicine didn't take effect
(d) (changer) **on ne peut rien y f.** nothing can be done about it; Fam **rien à f.!** nothing doing!
(e) (subir) to have; **f. une dépression** to have depression; Fam **f. une pneumonie/une grippe** to have pneumonia/flu; Fam **il m'a encore fait une grippe!** he's gone and got the flu again!
(f) (pratiquer) **f. du tennis/football** to play tennis/football; **f. de la voile** to sail; **f. du violon/piano** to play the violin/the piano; **f. du russe/de l'espagnol** to do Russian/Spanish
(g) (constituer) to make; **il ferait un excellent mari/pompier** he would make an excellent husband/fireman; **f. l'affaire** to do the trick; **c'est cela qui fait ton charme** that's what gives you your charm; **cette chambre fait aussi bureau** this bedroom also serves as an office
(h) (s'occuper à) to do; **qu'est-ce qu'il fait dans la vie?** what does he do for a job?; **qu'est-ce que tu fais demain?** what are you doing tomorrow?; **f. des études** to study; **qu'est-ce que tu fais ici?** what are you doing here?
(i) (parcourir) to do; **f. 100 kilomètres par jour** to do 100 kilometres a day; **il a fait toute la ville pour la retrouver** he searched the whole town for her; **f. du cent à l'heure** to do 100 km/h

(j) *(indique une mesure, une quantité)* to be; **la table fait 1 mètre de long** the table is 1 metre long; **deux et deux font quatre** two and two are *or* make four; **combien ça fait en dollars?** how much is that in dollars?; **le bébé fait 5 kilos** the baby weighs 5 kilos

(k) *(agir comme)* **f. l'imbécile** to play the fool; **f. l'innocent** to play the innocent; **f. l'important** to act important; **il fait celui qui n'a pas entendu** he pretends he hasn't heard

(l) *(sembler)* to look; **il fait jeune/anglais** he looks young/English

(m) *(dire)* to say; **"à bientôt!", fit-elle** "see you soon!", she said; **ça a fait plouf** it went splash

(n) *(suivi d'un infinitif)* **f. voir qch à qn** to show sb sth; **f. traverser qn** to help sb across; **f. faire qch à qn** to make sb do sth; **elle m'a fait ranger ma chambre** she made me tidy up my bedroom; **f. réparer qch** to get *or* have sth repaired; **f. construire une maison** to have a house built; **elle ne fait que se plaindre** she's always complaining; **je ne fais que répéter ses paroles** I'm just repeating what she said

(o) *(pour remplacer un verbe)* **il devait arroser les plantes mais il ne l'a pas fait** he was meant to water the plants but he didn't; **mais faites donc!** please do!

2 *vi* **(a)** *(agir)* to do; **f. vite** to be quick; **fais comme tu voudras** do as you like; **f. pour le mieux** to do one's best; **f. comme chez soi** to make oneself at home; **comment f.?** how can I/we do it?; *Fam* **il faut f. avec** it'll have to do

(b) *Fam (faire ses besoins)* to go to the toilet

3 *v impersonnel* **(a)** *(indique un état)* to be; **il fait froid/chaud** it's cold/hot; **il fait beau** it's fine; **il fait 20 degrés** it's 20 degrees; **il fait jour/nuit** it's light/night

(b) *(indique la distance, la durée)* **ça fait un mois qu'il est parti** he's been gone for a month; **ça fait une heure que je t'attends** I've been waiting for you for an hour; **ça fait 200 kilomètres que nous roulons** we've been driving for 200 kilometres

4 se faire *vpr* **(a)** *(avoir lieu)* **finalement ça ne s'est jamais fait** nothing happened in the end; **comment se fait-il que...?** how is it that...?

(b) *(être pratiqué)* to be done; **ça se fait beaucoup cette année** it's the in thing this year

(c) *(être acceptable)* **ça se fait** it's the done thing; **ça ne se fait pas** it's not the done thing

(d) *(être fabriqué)* to be made

(e) *(se confectionner)* **se f. un lit** to make a bed for oneself; **se f. une bibliothèque** to build up a library; **se f. un œuf sur le plat** to make oneself a fried egg; **se f. les ongles** to do one's nails

(f) *(fromage, vin)* to mature; *(chaussures)* to wear in

(g) *(provoquer)* **se f. mal** to hurt oneself; **se f. une entorse au poignet** to sprain one's wrist; **se f. du souci** to worry; **se f. une opinion** to form an opinion; **se f. des amis/des ennemis** to make friends/enemies; *Fam* **s'en f.** to worry; **elle ne s'en fait pas celle-là!** *(elle a du culot)* she's got a nerve!; *(elle a beaucoup d'argent)* she hasn't got a care in the world!

(h) *(s'ériger en)* **se f. le défenseur des opprimés** to become established as a defender of the oppressed

(i) *(devenir)* **se f. vieux** to get old; **se f. beau** to do oneself up; **se f. moine** to become a monk; **il se fait tard** it's getting late

(j) *(avec un infinitif)* **se f. insulter** to get abused; **se f. couper les cheveux** to have one's hair cut; **se f. prêter qch** to borrow sth; **se f. refaire le nez** to have a nose job

(k) *(s'habituer)* **se f. à qch** to get used to sth

(l) *(l'un l'autre)* **se f. des cadeaux** to give each other presents; **se f. des reproches** to blame each other

(m) *Fam* **il faut se le f. celui-là!** what a pain in the neck!

faire-part [ferpar] *nm inv* announcement

faire-valoir [fervalwar] *nm inv (personne)* foil

fair-play [ferplɛ] **1** *adj inv* **être f.** to play fair
2 *nm* fair play

fais *voir* **faire**

faisabilité [fəzabilite] *nf* feasibility

faisable [fəzabl] *adj* feasible

faisan [fəzɑ̃] *nm* pheasant

faisandé, -e [fəzɑ̃de] *adj (gibier)* high

faisane [fazan] *adj f & nf (poule)* **f.** hen pheasant

faisceau, -x [feso] *nm* **(a)** *(rayons)* beam; **f. hertzien** electromagnetic wave; **f. lumineux** beam of light **(b)** *Fig (de preuves)* body

faiseur, -euse [fazœr, -øz] **1** *nm,f* maker; **f. d'embarras** fusspot; **f. de miracles** miracle worker
2 *nf* **faiseuse d'anges** backstreet abortionist

faisons *voir* **faire**

faisselle [fesɛl] *nf (fromage)* = type of soft white cheese; *(récipient)* cheese drainer

fait¹, -e *pp voir* **faire**

fait², -e [fɛ, fɛt] *adj* **(a)** *(fabriqué)* **tout f.** *(idée, expression)* fixed

(b) *(adapté)* **être f. pour qn/qch** to be made for sb/sth; **ils sont faits l'un pour l'autre** they're made for each other; **être f. pour faire qch** *(personne)* to be cut out to do sth

(c) *(bâti)* *Litt ou Hum* **être bien f. de sa personne** to be good-looking

(d) *(maquillé)* **avoir les ongles/les yeux faits** to be wearing nail polish/eye make-up

(e) *(fromage)* ripe

fait³ *nm* **(a)** *(acte)* act; **les faits et gestes de qn** sb's every move; **prendre qn sur le f.** to catch sb in the act *or* red-handed; **prendre f. et cause pour qn** to stand up for sb

(b) *(réalité)* fact; **le f. d'habiter en ville** living in town; **mettre qn devant le f. accompli** to present sb with a fait accompli; **c'est un f. acquis** it's an established fact

(c) *(point précis)* **aller droit au f.** to get straight to the point; **en venir au f.** to come to the point

(d) *(événement)* event; **un f. nouveau s'est produit** there was a new development; **un f. divers** a news item; **faits divers** *(rubrique)* ≃ news in brief

(e) *(locutions)* **au f.** by the way; **en f., de f.** in fact, as a matter of fact; **de ce f.** for that reason

faîte [fɛt] *nm* **(a)** *(d'un toit)* ridge; *(d'un arbre, d'une maison)* top; *(d'une montagne)* summit **(b)** *Fig* **le f. de la gloire** the height of glory

faites *voir* **faire**

faitout *nm*, **fait-tout** *nm inv* [fɛtu] stewpot

fakir [fakir] *nm* fakir

falaise [falɛz] *nf* cliff

fallacieux, -euse [falasjø, -øz] *adj (prétexte)* false; *(argument, raisonnement)* specious; *(apparence)* misleading

falloir [37] [falwar] **1** *v impersonnel* **(a)** *(être nécessaire)* **faut-il tout cela?** is all that necessary?; **je l'ai fait parce qu'il le fallait** I did it because I had to; **il lui faut un nouveau pardessus** he needs a new coat; **il me faudrait un kilo de pommes** I need a kilo of apples; **je lui ai tout donné, qu'est-ce qu'il lui faut de plus!** I've given him everything, what more does he want!; **il m'a fallu trois jours pour le faire** it took me three days to do it; **il faut partir** I/we/you/*etc* must go or have to go; **il lui faut se dépêcher** she has to hurry; **il fallait le dire!** why didn't you say so?; **je vous en prie, il ne fallait pas!** you shouldn't have!; **il faudrait qu'elle reste** she ought to stay; **il ne faudrait pas que je vous mette en retard** I'd better not make you late; **il faut toujours que tu fasses des histoires** why do you always have to cause such a fuss!; **il a fallu qu'elle le raconte à tout le quartier!** she had to go and tell the whole neighbourhood! **(b)** *(locutions)* *Fam* **il faut ce qu'il faut!** you might as well do things in style; **il faut voir** *(il faut attendre)* we'll have to wait and see; *(il faut réfléchir)* I/we will have to think about it; *Fam* **elle lui a répondu, faut voir comment!** you wouldn't believe the way she answered him!

2 s'en falloir *vpr* **il s'en est fallu de peu** *ou* **peu s'en est fallu qu'elle ne meure** she very nearly died; **5 livres ou peu s'en faut** the best part of £5; **loin** *ou* **tant s'en faut** far from it

fallu *voir* **falloir**

falot¹ [falo] *nm (lanterne)* lantern

falot², **-e** [falo, -ɔt] *adj* dreary, drab

falsification [falsifikasjɔ̃] *nf (de documents, de comptes)* falsification; *(d'une signature)* forging

falsifier [66] [falsifje] *vt (document, comptes)* to falsify; *(signature)* to forge

falzar [falzar] *nm Fam Br* trousers, *Am* pants

famé, -e [fame] *adj* **mal f.** disreputable

famélique [famelik] *adj* half-starved

fameusement [faməzmɑ̃] *adv Fam (très)* incredibly

fameux, -euse [famø, -øz] *adj* **(a)** *(célèbre)* famous *(pour* for); **c'est donc ça, ton f. régime!** so this is your famous diet! **(b)** *Fam (excellent)* brilliant; **pas f.** not much good

familial, -e, -aux, -ales [familjal, -o] **1** *adj (vie, atmosphère)* family; *(entreprise, hôtel)* family-run; *(paquet, format)* family-size

2 *nf* **familiale** *(auto) Br* estate car, *Am* station wagon

familiariser [familjarize] **1** *vt* **f. qn avec qch** to familiarize sb with sth, to get sb used to sth

2 se familiariser *vpr* **se f. avec qch** *(en le pratiquant)* to familiarize oneself with sth; *(en s'y habituant)* to get used to sth; *(lieu)* to get to know sth

familiarité [familjarite] *nf* **(a)** *(désinvolture)* informality **(b)** **familiarités** *(libertés)* familiarities

familier, -ère [familje, -ɛr] **1** *adj* **(a)** *(désinvolte)* informal **(avec** with) **(b)** *(langage, expression)* colloquial **(c)** *(connu)* familiar *(à* to)

2 *nm,f (client)* regular visitor **(de** to)

familièrement [familjɛrmɑ̃] *adv* familiarly; **parler f. à qn** to be familiar with sb

famille [famij] *nf* **(a)** *(proches)* family; **de bonne f.** from a good family; **en f.** with one's family; **c'est de f.** it runs in the family; *Fam* **un repas des familles** a cosy little meal; **f. monoparentale** one-parent family; **f. nombreuse** large family **(b)** *(d'animaux, de langues, de plantes)* family; **f. littéraire/politique** literary/political circle

famine [famin] *nf* famine; **crier f.** to be starving

fan [fan], **fana** [fana] *nmf Fam* fan

fanal, -aux [fanal, -o] *nm (lanterne)* lantern

fanatique [fanatik] **1** *adj* fanatical **(de** about)

2 *nmf* fanatic; **f. de football** football fanatic

fanatiser [fanatize] *vt* to make fanatical

fanatisme [fanatism] *nm* fanaticism

faner [fane] **1** *vi (fleur)* to wither; *Fig (beauté, teint)* to fade

2 se faner *vpr (fleur)* to wither; *Fig (beauté, teint)* to fade

fanes [fan] *nfpl (de carottes, de radis)* tops

fanfare [fɑ̃far] *nf (orchestre)* brass band; **réveil en f.** brutal awakening

fanfaron, -onne [fɑ̃farɔ̃, -ɔn] **1** *adj* boastful

2 *nm,f* braggart; **faire le f.** to brag, to boast

fanfaronnades [fɑ̃faronad] *nfpl* bragging, boasting

fanfaronner [fɑ̃farone] *vi* to brag, to boast

fanfreluches [fɑ̃frəlyʃ] *nfpl Péj* frills

fange [fɑ̃ʒ] *nf Litt* mire

fanion [fanjɔ̃] *nm (d'un club)* pennant; *(balise)* flag; **fanions** *(guirlandes)* bunting

fanon [fanɔ̃] *nm (de baleine)* whalebone

fantaisie [fɑ̃tezi] **1** *adj inv* **collants f.** patterned tights; **kirsch f.** kirsch-flavoured liqueur

2 *nf* **(a)** *(envie)* whim; **faire qch à sa f.** to do sth as the fancy takes one **(b)** *(créativité)* imagination **(c)** *(œuvre musicale)* fantasia

fantaisiste [fɑ̃tezist] **1** *adj (personne)* eccentric; *(interprétation)* fanciful; *(horaires, mode de vie)* unorthodox

2 *nmf (comédien)* variety artist

fantasmagorique [fɑ̃tasmagorik] *adj* phantasmagorical

fantasme [fɑ̃tasm] *nm* fantasy

fantasmer [fɑ̃tasme] *vi* to fantasize **(sur** about)

fantasque [fɑ̃task] *adj* whimsical

fantassin [fɑ̃tasɛ̃] *nm* foot soldier, infantryman

fantastique [fɑ̃tastik] **1** *adj (littérature, conte, film)* fantasy **(b)** *Fam (excellent)* fantastic **(c)** *(créature)* fantastic

2 *nm* **le f.** the fantastic; *(littérature)* fantasy literature

fantoche [fɑ̃tɔʃ] **1** *nm* puppet

2 *adj* **gouvernement f.** puppet government

fantomatique [fɑ̃tɔmatik] *adj* ghostly

fantôme [fɑ̃tom] **1** *nm* ghost, phantom

2 *adj (ville, train)* ghost

fanzine [fɑ̃zin] *nm* fanzine

faon [fɑ̃] *nm* fawn

far [far] *nm* **f. breton** custard flan with prunes

faramineux, -euse [faraminø, -øz] *adj Fam* phenomenal

farandole [farɑ̃dɔl] *nf* farandole

farce [fars] *nf* **(a)** *(tour)* (practical) joke, prank; **faire une f. à qn** to play a (practical) joke on sb; **magasin de farces et attrapes** joke shop **(b)** *(préparation culinaire)* stuffing **(c)** *(pièce de théâtre)* farce

farceur, -euse [farsœr, -øz] **1** *adj* mischievous **2** *nm,f* (*practical*) joker, prankster

farcir [farsir] **1** *vt* (**a**) (*volaille, légume*) to stuff (**b**) *Fam* (*remplir*) to cram (de with) **2 se farcir** *vpr Fam* **se f. qch** (*corvée*) to get landed with sth; **se f. qn** (*supporter*) to put up with sb

fard [far] *nm* make-up; *Fam* **piquer un f.** to go red; **f. à joues** blusher; **f. à paupières** eye shadow

fardeau, -x [fardo] *nm* load; *Fig* burden

farder [farde] **1** *vt* (*maquiller*) to make up **2 se farder** *vpr* to put on one's make-up; **se f. les yeux** to put eye shadow on

farfadet [farfadɛ] *nm* goblin

farfelu, -e [farfɛly] *Fam* **1** *adj* (*personne, idée*) weird **2** *nm,f* weirdo

farfouiller [farfuje] *vi Fam* to rummage (**dans** through)

farine [farin] *nf* flour; **f. de blé** wheat flour; **f. de maïs** *Br* cornflour, *Am* cornstarch

farineux, -euse [farinø, -øz] **1** *adj* (**a**) (*pommes de terre, banane*) floury (**b**) (*contenant de la fécule*) starchy **2** *nmpl* starchy food

farniente [farnjɛnte] *nm* idleness

farouche [faruʃ] *adj* (**a**) (*animal*) timid; (*personne*) shy (**b**) (*haine, air, regard*) fierce

farouchement [faruʃmɑ̃] *adv* fiercely

fart [fart] *nm* (ski) wax

fascicule [fasikyl] *nm* (*d'une publication*) instalment; (*brochure*) brochure

fascinant, -e [fasinɑ̃, -ɑ̃t] *adj* fascinating

fascination [fasinasjɔ̃] *nf* fascination

fasciner [fasine] *vt* (**a**) (*impressionner*) to fascinate (**b**) (*charmer*) to captivate

fascisme [faʃism] *nm* fascism

fasciste [faʃist] *adj & nmf* fascist

fasse *etc voir* **faire**

faste¹ [fast] *nm* splendour

faste² *adj* (*jour*) lucky; (*période*) good

fast-food (*pl* **fast-foods**) [fastfud] *nm* fast-food restaurant

fastidieux, -euse [fastidjø, -øz] *adj* tedious

fastoche [fastɔʃ] *adj Fam* dead easy

fastueux, -euse [fastɥø, -øz] *adj* sumptuous

fat [fa(t)] *nm* conceited person

fatal, -e, -als, -ales [fatal] *adj* (**a**) (*mortel*) fatal; *Fig* fatal (à for); **le choc lui a été f.** the shock killed him; *Ordinat* **erreur fatale** fatal error (**b**) (*inévitable*) inevitable

fatalement [fatalmɑ̃] *adv* inevitably

fatalisme [fatalism] *nm* fatalism

fataliste [fatalist] **1** *adj* fatalistic **2** *nmf* fatalist

fatalité [fatalite] *nf* (**a**) (*malédiction*) bad luck (**b**) (*inévitabilité*) inevitability

fatidique [fatidik] *adj* fateful

fatigant, -e [fatigɑ̃, -ɑ̃t] *adj* (**a**) (*épuisant*) tiring; **c'est f. pour le cœur/les yeux** it's a strain on the heart/the eyes (**b**) (*ennuyeux*) tiresome

fatigue [fatig] *nf* tiredness; **tomber** *ou* **être mort de f.** to be dead tired; **f. nerveuse** nervous exhaustion; **f. oculaire** eyestrain

fatigué, -e [fatige] *adj* (**a**) (*las*) tired; **f. par sa promenade** tired from one's walk; **f. par le voyage** travel-worn; **f. de qn/qch** tired of sb/sth; **f. de faire qch** tired *or* weary of doing sth (**b**) (*estomac, foie*) upset; (*cœur*) strained

fatiguer [fatige] **1** *vt* (**a**) (*personne*) to tire (out); (*yeux, cœur*) to strain; (*estomac, foie*) to upset; *Ironique* **si ça ne te fatigue pas trop** if it's not too much of an effort (**b**) (*ennuyer*) to wear out (**c**) *Fam* **f. la salade** to toss the salad **2** *vi* (*personne*) to get tired; (*moteur, voiture*) to labour **3 se fatiguer** *vpr* (**a**) (*s'épuiser*) to get tired; **se f. à faire qch** to tire oneself out doing sth; **se f. les yeux/le cœur** to strain one's eyes/heart; *Ironique* **tu ne t'es pas fatigué** you didn't exactly strain yourself; **ne te fatigue pas, je m'en charge** don't bother, I'll see to it (**b**) (*se lasser*) **se f. de qn/qch** to get tired of sb/sth

fatras [fatra] *nm* jumble, muddle

faubourg [fobur] *nm* suburb

fauche [foʃ] *nf Fam* thieving; **il y a de la f.** there are thieves about

fauché, -e [foʃe] *adj Fam* **f. (comme les blés)** (*flat*) broke

faucher [foʃe] *vt* (**a**) (*herbe, champ*) to mow; (*blé*) to reap (**b**) (*piéton*) to mow down; **se faire f. par une voiture** to be mown down by a car (**c**) *Fam* (*voler*) to pinch; **se faire f. qch** to get sth pinched

faucheur, -euse [foʃœr, -øz] **1** *nm,f* (*de blé*) reaper; (*d'herbe*) mower **2** *nm* (*insecte*) *Br* harvestman, *Am* daddy-long-legs **3** *nf* **faucheuse** (*machine*) (*pour le blé*) reaper; (*pour l'herbe*) mower; **la Faucheuse** (*la Mort*) the Grim Reaper

faucheux [foʃø] *nm Br* harvestman, *Am* daddy-long-legs

faucille [fosij] *nf* sickle; **la f. et le marteau** the hammer and sickle

faucon [fokɔ̃] *nm* falcon, hawk; **f. pèlerin** peregrine falcon

faudra *etc voir* **falloir**

faufiler [fofile] **1** *vt* to tack, to baste **2 se faufiler** *vpr* (*à travers la foule*) to work one's way (**à travers** through); **il s'était faufilé parmi les invités** he had slipped in with the guests

faune [fon] *nf* (*animaux*) fauna, animal life; *Fig & Péj* **la f. des boîtes de nuit** the nightclub set; **elle fréquente une f. bizarre** she mixes with a funny crowd

faussaire [fosɛr] *nmf* forger

fausse [fos] *adj voir* **faux¹**

faussement [fosmɑ̃] *adv* (**a**) (*injustement*) wrongly, falsely (**b**) (*de façon hypocrite*) deceptively

fausser [fose] **1** *vt* (**a**) (*clef, axe*) to buckle, to bend (**b**) (*réalité, résultat*) to distort (**c**) **f. compagnie à qn** to give sb the slip **2 se fausser** *vpr* (**a**) (*voix*) to become strained (**b**) (*clef, axe*) to buckle, to bend

fausset [fosɛ] *nm Mus* falsetto

fausseté [foste] *nf* (**a**) (*d'une information, d'un raisonnement*) falseness (**b**) (*hypocrisie*) duplicity

faut *voir* **falloir**

faute [fot] *nf* (a) *(erreur)* mistake, error; *(au football)* foul; *(au tennis)* fault; **faire une f.** to make a mistake or an error; **être en f.** to be at fault; **prendre qn en f.** to catch sb out; **c'est de ma f.** it's my fault; **f. d'étourderie** *ou* **d'inattention** careless mistake; **f. de français** grammatical mistake; **f. de frappe** typing mistake; **f. d'orthographe** spelling mistake; **f. professionnelle** professional misconduct (b) *(manque)* **sans f.** without fail; **f. de temps** for lack of time; **f. de mieux** for lack *or* want of anything better; **f. de quoi** failing which, otherwise; **ce n'est pas f. d'avoir essayé** it's not for want of trying

fauteuil [fotœj] *nm* (a) *(siège)* armchair, easy chair; **f. à bascule** rocking chair; **f. d'orchestre** seat in the *Br* stalls *or Am* orchestra; **f. pivotant** swivel chair; **f. roulant** wheelchair (b) *Fig (à l'Académie française)* seat

fauteur [fotœr] *nm* **f. de troubles** troublemaker

fautif, -ive [fotif, -iv] **1** *adj* (a) *(coupable)* at fault, in the wrong (b) *(incorrect)* faulty
2 *nm,f (coupable)* person at fault *or* in the wrong

fauve [fov] **1** *adj* (a) *(roux)* fawn (b) *(odeur)* musky *(en peinture)* Fauvist
2 *nm* (a) *(grand félin)* big cat; **sentir le f.** to smell of sweat (b) *(couleur)* fawn (c) *(en peinture)* Fauvist

fauvette [fovet] *nf* warbler

fauvisme [fovism] *nm* Fauvism

faux¹, fausse [fo, fos] **1** *adj* (a) *(incorrect)* wrong; **c'est un f. problème** that's not the real problem; **f. ami** false friend; **faire une fausse couche** to have a miscarriage; **faire une fausse note** to hit a wrong note; **faire fausse route** to take the wrong road; *Fig* to be on the wrong track; **faire un f. sens** *(en traduisant)* to give an inaccurate translation; *(en français)* to give an inaccurate definition (b) *(mensonger)* false, untrue; *Fam* **c'est un f. jeton** *ou* **cul** he's two-faced; **f. témoignage** perjury (c) *(injustifié)* *(alerte, espoirs)* false (d) *(postiche)* false (e) *(billet, pièce, document)* forged; *(tableau, bijoux)* fake; *(plafond)* false (f) *Péj (hypocrite)* false
2 *adv (chanter, sonner)* out of tune, off key; *Fig* **sonner f.** not to ring true
3 *nm* (a) *(tableau, sculpture)* fake (b) *(document)* forgery; **f. en écriture** forgery

faux² *nf* scythe

faux-filet *(pl* **faux-filets)** [fofile] *nm* sirloin

faux-fuyant *(pl* **faux-fuyants)** [fofɥijɑ̃] *nm* *(prétexte)* subterfuge

faux-monnayeur *(pl* **faux-monnayeurs)** [fomɔnɛjœr] *nm* forger, counterfeiter

faux-semblant *(pl* **faux-semblants)** [fosɑ̃blɑ̃] *nm* pretence, sham

faveur [favœr] *nf* (a) *(considération)* favour; **avoir la f. de qn** to be in favour with sb; **de f.** *(marques)* of favour; *(régime, traitement)* special (b) *(privilège)* favour; **faire une f. à qn** to do sb a favour (c) **être en f. de qch** *(être favorable à)* to be in favour of sth; **en ma/sa f.** *(à mon/son avantage)* in my/her favour, to my/her advantage (d) *(ruban)* favour

favorable [favorabl] *adj* favourable (à to)

favorablement [favorabləmɑ̃] *adv* favourably

favori, -ite [favori, -it] *adj & nm,f* favourite

favoris [favori] *nmpl* sideburns

favorisé, -e [favorize] *adj (milieu, famille)* fortunate

favoriser [favorize] *vt* (a) *(avantager)* *(personne)* to favour (b) *(encourager)* *(croissance, emploi)* to encourage, to promote

favoritisme [favoritism] *nm* favouritism

fax [faks] *nm (appareil)* fax (machine); *(message)* fax; **envoyer qch par f.** to send sth by fax; **f. modem** fax modem

faxer [fakse] *vt* to fax

fayot [fajo] *nm Fam* (a) *(haricot sec)* bean (b) *(élève)* crawler

fayotage [fajotaʒ] *nm Fam* crawling

fayoter [fajote] *vi Fam* to crawl

fébrile [febril] *adj aussi Fig* feverish

fébrilement [febrilmɑ̃] *adv* feverishly

fébrilité [febrilite] *nf* feverishness

fécond, -e [fekɔ̃, -ɔ̃d] *adj (femme, femelle, terre, imagination)* fertile; *(écrivain)* prolific; *Fig* **f. en qch** *(période, moment)* full of sth

fécondation [fekɔ̃dasjɔ̃] *nf (d'une femme, d'une femelle)* impregnation; *(d'un œuf, d'un ovule)* fertilization; **f. artificielle** artificial insemination; **f. in vitro** in vitro fertilization

féconder [fekɔ̃de] *vt (femme, femelle)* to impregnate; *(œuf, ovule)* to fertilize

fécondité [fekɔ̃dite] *nf* (a) *(d'une femme, d'une femelle)* fertility (b) *(d'un écrivain)* productivity

fécule [fekyl] *nf* starch

féculent, -e [fekylɑ̃, -ɑ̃t] **1** *adj* starchy
2 *nm* starchy food

FED [eføde] *nm (abrév* **Fonds européen de développement)** EDF

FEDER [fedɛr] *nm (abrév* **Fonds européen de développement régional)** ERDF

fédéral, -e, -aux, -ales [federal, -o] *adj* federal

fédéralisme [federalism] *nm* federalism

fédéraliste [federalist] *adj & nmf* federalist

fédérateur, -trice [federatœr, -tris] *adj* federal

fédération [federasjɔ̃] *nf* federation

fédéré, -e [federe] *adj* federate

fée [fe] *nf* fairy; *Hum* **f. du logis** ideal homemaker

feed-back [fidbak] *nm* feedback

féerie [feri, feeri] *nf (spectacle magnifique)* enchanting display

féerique [ferik, feerik] *adj (personnage, monde)* fairy; *(vision)* enchanting

feignais *etc voir* **feindre**

feignant, -e [fɛɲɑ̃, -ɑ̃t] *Fam* **1** *adj* bone idle
2 *nm,f* idler

feindre [54] [fɛ̃dr] *vt (maladie, sentiment)* to feign; **inutile de f.** it's no use pretending; **f. de faire qch** to pretend to do sth

feint, -e [fɛ̃, fɛ̃t] *adj (maladie, joie)* feigned

feinte [fɛ̃t] *nf* (a) *(ruse)* ruse (b) *(au football, au rugby)* dummy

feinter [fɛ̃te] **1** *vt Fam (duper)* to take in
2 *vi (au football, au rugby)* to dummy

fêlé, -e [fele] *adj* (a) *(verre, voix)* cracked (b) *Fam (fou)* cracked, bonkers

fêler [fele] *vt* to crack

félicitations [felisitasjɔ̃] *nfpl* congratulations **(pour** on)

féliciter [felisite] **1** *vt* to congratulate (**de/pour** on); **f. qn d'avoir fait qch** to congratulate sb on having done sth

2 se féliciter *vpr* **se f. de qch/d'avoir fait qch** to congratulate oneself on sth/on having done sth

félin, -e [felɛ̃, -in] *adj & nm* feline

fêlure [felyr] *nf* crack

femelle [fəmɛl] *adj & nf* female

féminin, -e [feminɛ̃, -in] **1** *adj* (*personne, charme, visage*) feminine; (*hormone, population, sexe*) female; (*équipe, magazine, mode*) women's

2 *nm* feminine; **au f.** in the feminine

féminiser [feminize] **1** *vt* **(a)** (*ouvrir aux femmes*) to increase the number of women in **(b)** (*rendre efféminé*) to make effeminate

2 se féminiser *vpr* **(a)** (*profession, institution, carrière*) to attract more women **(b)** (*homme*) to become effeminate

féminisme [feminism] *nm* feminism

féministe [feminist] *adj & nmf* feminist

féminité [feminite] *nf* femininity

femme [fam] *nf* **(a)** (*adulte de sexe féminin*) woman; **des femmes, de la f.** (*libération, émancipation, droits*) women's; **la f. de ma vie** the love of my life; **elle est très f.** she's very feminine; *Fam* **une bonne f.** a woman; **f. d'affaires** businesswoman; **f. de chambre** (*dans un hôtel*) (chamber)maid; **f. fatale** femme fatale; **f. au foyer** housewife; **f. de ménage** cleaning lady; **f. du monde** society woman; **f. de tête** forceful woman **(b)** (*épouse*) wife

femmelette [famlɛt] *nf Péj* (*homme*) weakling

fémur [femyr] *nm* thighbone, *Spéc* femur

FEN [fɛn] *nf* (*abrév* **Fédération de l'Éducation Nationale**) = largest French teachers' union

fenaison [fənɛzɔ̃] *nf* haymaking

fendant, -e [fɑ̃dɑ̃, -ɑ̃t] *adj Fam* hilarious

fendiller [fɑ̃dije] **1** *vt* (*bois, vernis*) to crack; (*peau, lèvres*) to chap

2 se fendiller *vpr* (*bois, vernis*) to crack; (*peau, lèvres*) to chap

fendre [fɑ̃dr] **1** *vt* **(a)** (*bois*) to split; (*pierre, sol*) to crack; **f. le cœur à qn** to break sb's heart **(b)** (*traverser*) (*flots, mer*) to plough through; (*air*) to cut through

2 se fendre *vpr* **(a)** (*bois*) to split; (*pierre, sol*) to crack **(b)** *Fam* **se f. de qch** (*d'une somme*) to fork out sth; (*d'un cadeau*) to fork out on sth; **tu ne t'es pas fendu** (*ce n'était pas cher*) it didn't break the bank; (*tu ne t'es pas fatigué*) you didn't strain yourself **(c)** *Fam* **se f. la pipe** *ou* **la pêche** *ou* **la poire** to split one's sides (laughing)

fendu, -e [fɑ̃dy] *adj* (*jupe*) slit

fenêtre [fənɛtr] *nf* **(a)** (*ouverture*) window; **f. à guillotine** sash window **(b)** *Ordinat* window; **f. d'aide** help window; **f. déroulante** pull-down window

fennec [fenɛk] *nm* fennec

fenouil [fənuj] *nm* fennel

fente [fɑ̃t] *nf* **(a)** (*dans le bois*) split; (*dans le sol, dans un mur*) crack **(b)** (*d'une tirelire, d'une boîte aux lettres*) slot

féodal, -e, -aux, -ales [feodal, -o] *adj* feudal

féodalité [feodalite] *nf* feudalism

fer [fɛr] *nm* **(a)** (*métal*) iron; *Fig* **de f.** (*discipline, volonté*) iron; (*santé*) cast-iron; **croire qch dur comme f.** to believe very firmly in sth; **f. forgé** wrought iron **(b)** (*objet en fer*) **f. à cheval** horseshoe; *Fam* **les quatre fers en l'air** flat on one's back; *Fig* **f. de lance** spearhead **(c)** (*outil*) **f. à repasser** iron; **donner un coup de f. à qch** to iron sth; **marquer qch au f. rouge** to brand sth; **f. à souder** soldering iron **(d)** **fers** (*chaînes*) irons

ferai *etc voir* **faire**

fer-blanc (*pl* **fers-blancs**) [fɛrblɑ̃] *nm* tin(plate); **en f.** tin

ferblanterie [fɛrblɑ̃tri] *nf* **(a)** (*commerce*) tinplate trade **(b)** (*articles*) tinware

férié, -e [ferje] *adj* **lundi prochain est f.** next Monday is a (public) holiday

férir [ferir] *vt* **sans coup f.** without any difficulty

ferme¹ [fɛrm] **1** *adj* **(a)** (*dur*) firm **(b)** *Jur* **trois ans de prison f., trois ans fermes** three years' imprisonment

2 *adv* (*travailler*) hard; (*discuter*) keenly; **s'ennuyer f.** to be bored stiff

ferme² *nf* farm; **produits de la f.** farm produce

fermé, -e [fɛrme] *adj* **(a)** (*porte, récipient, boutique*) closed, shut; (*route*) closed **(b)** (*expression, visage*) impassive; **être f. à qch** (*ne pas être sensible à*) to have no appreciation of sth **(c)** (*société, club, milieu*) exclusive, select

fermement [fɛrməmɑ̃] *adv* firmly

ferment [fɛrmɑ̃] *nm aussi Fig* ferment

fermentation [fɛrmɑ̃tasjɔ̃] *nf* fermentation

fermenter [fɛrmɑ̃te] *vi* to ferment

fermer [fɛrme] **1** *vt* **(a)** (*porte, boîte, livre*) to close, to shut; (*maison*) to shut up; (*rideaux*) to draw; (*vêtement*) to fasten, to do up; (*parenthèse*) to close; (*enveloppe*) to seal; **f. sa porte à qn** to close one's door to sb; **f. les yeux/la bouche** to close one's eyes/one's mouth; *Fig* **f. les yeux sur qch** to turn a blind eye to sth; *Fam* **je n'ai pas fermé l'œil** I didn't sleep a wink; *Fam* **f. sa gueule, la f.** to shut up, to shut one's mouth **(b)** (*frontière, pays*) to close off **(c)** (*robinet, eau, électricité*) to turn off **(d)** (*compte bancaire*) to close **(e)** (*entreprise*) (*temporairement*) to close, to shut; (*définitivement*) to close down; **f. boutique** to shut up shop **(f)** *Ordinat* (*fichier, fenêtre*) to close; (*commande*) to end

2 *vi* **(a)** (*porte, boîte*) to close, to shut; **f. bien/mal** to close/not to close properly **(b)** (*entreprise, magasin*) (*temporairement*) to close, to shut; (*définitivement*) to close down

3 se fermer *vpr* **(a)** (*porte, boîte, yeux*) to close, to shut; (*vêtement*) to fasten, to do up **(b)** (*visage*) to freeze; (*personne*) to clam up

fermeté [fɛrməte] *nf* firmness; **avec f.** firmly

fermeture [fɛrmatyr] *nf* **(a)** (*d'une porte*) closing, shutting; (*d'une route, d'une frontière, d'un débat*) closing **(b)** (*cessation d'activité*) closing; **heure de f.** closing time **(c)** (*d'un compte bancaire*) closing **(d)** **f. Éclair®** *ou* **f. à glissière** *Br* zip, *Am* zipper **(e)** *Ordinat* (*d'un fichier, d'une fenêtre*) closing; (*d'une commande*) ending

fermier, -ère [fɛrmje, -ɛr] **1** *adj* (*poulet*) free-range; (*beurre*) dairy

2 *nm,f* farmer

fermoir [fɛrmwar] *nm* clasp

féroce [ferɔs] *adj* (*animal, personne, critique*) ferocious; (*joie, moquerie*) savage; (*appétit*) ravenous

férocement [ferɔsmɑ̃] *adv* ferociously

férocité [ferosite] *nf* ferocity

Féroé [feroe] *nfpl* **les (îles) F.** the Faroe Islands, the Faroes

ferraille [feraj] *nf* (a) *(débris de fer)* scrap (iron); **mettre qch à la f.** to put sth on the scrap heap (b) *Fam (petite monnaie)* small change

ferré, -e [fere] *adj* (a) *(chaussure)* hobnailed; *(canne)* metal-tipped (b) *(calé)* **être f. en qch** to be well up in sth

ferrer [fere] *vt* (a) *(cheval)* to shoe (b) *(poisson)* to strike

ferreux, -euse [ferø, -øz] *adj* ferrous

ferronnerie [feronri] *nf* (a) *(objets)* **f. (d'art)** (decorative) ironwork (b) *(travail)* ironwork (c) *(atelier)* ironworks *(singulier)*

ferronnier, -ère [feronje, -ɛr] *nm,f* **f. (d'art)** worker in wrought iron

ferroviaire [ferovjɛr] *adj (réseau, trafic, ligne) Br* railway, *Am* railroad; *(transports)* rail

ferrugineux, -euse [feryʒinø, -øz] *adj* ferruginous

ferrure [feryr] *nf* (a) *(garniture)* fitting (b) *(d'un cheval)* shoeing

ferry [feri] *nm* ferry

ferry-boat *(pl ferry-boats)* [feribot] *nm* ferry

fertile [fertil] *adj aussi Fig* fertile; *Fig* **f. en qch** *(période)* full of sth

fertilisation [fertilizasjɔ̃] *nf* fertilization

fertiliser [fertilize] *vt* to fertilize

fertilité [fertilite] *nf* fertility

féru, -e [fery] *adj* **f. de qch** passionately interested in sth

férule [feryl] *nf Litt* **être sous la f. de qn** to be under sb's sway

fervent, -e [fervã, -ãt] **1** *adj* fervent; *(Catholique)* devout **2** *nm,f* devotee *(de* of)

ferveur [fervœr] *nf* fervour; **avec f.** fervently

fesse [fɛs] *nf* buttock; **fesses** *Br* bottom, *Am* butt

fessée [fese] *nf* spanking; **donner une f. à qn** to give sb a spanking

fessier, -ère [fesje, -ɛr] **1** *adj (muscle)* buttock, *Spéc* gluteal **2** *nm (muscle)* gluteal muscle

festif, -ive [festif, -iv] *adj* festive

festin [festɛ̃] *nm* feast, banquet

festival, -als [festival] *nm* festival; **le f. d'Avignon** = theatre festival held in Avignon; **le f. de Cannes** the Cannes film festival

festivités [festivite] *nfpl* festivities

feston [festɔ̃] *nm* (a) *(en broderie)* scallop; **à festons** scalloped (b) *(guirlande) & Archit* festoon

festoyer [32] [festwaje] *vi* to feast

feta [feta] *nf* feta cheese

fêtard, -e [fetar, -ard] *nm,f Fam* party animal

fête [fɛt] *nf* (a) *(célébration publique)* fête, fair; *(événement culturel)* festival; **f. foraine** funfair; **la f. des Mères/ Pères** Mother's/Father's Day; **la f. de la Musique** = annual music festival held on 21 June; **la f. des Rois** Twelfth Night (b) *(soirée)* party; **organiser ou faire une f.** to have a party (c) *(manifestation de joie)* **en f.** in a festive mood; **avoir le cœur en f.** to be over the moon; *Fam* **faire la f.** to party; **être de la f.** to be one of the party; **faire f. à qn** to make a fuss of sb (d) *(du saint dont on porte le nom)* saint's day; *Ironique* **ça va être ta f.!** you're in for it! (e) *(jour chômé)* holiday; **les fêtes (de fin d'année)** the Christmas and New Year holidays; **f. légale** *Br* bank holiday, *Am* legal holiday; **f. nationale** national holiday; **la f. du Travail** Labour Day

Fête-Dieu *(pl Fêtes-Dieu)* [fɛtdjø] *nf* **la F.** Corpus Christi

fêter [fete] *vt* (a) *(anniversaire, événement)* to celebrate (b) *(personne)* to fête

fétiche [fetiʃ] **1** *adj* lucky **2** *nm (objet de culte)* fetish; *(mascotte)* mascot

fétichisme [fetiʃism] *nm* fetishism

fétide [fetid] *adj* fetid

fétu [fety] *nm* **f. (de paille)** wisp of straw

feu¹, -x [fø] **1** *nm* (a) *(élément, flammes, incendie)* fire; **mettre (le) f. à qch** to set fire to sth; **prendre f.** to catch fire; **allumer ou faire un f.** to make a fire; **au f.!** fire!; **en f.** *(lieu)* on fire; *Fig (joues, visage)* burning; **mettre une ville à f. et à sang** to ransack a town; **être tout f. tout flamme** to be burning with enthusiasm; **faire f. de tout bois** to use every available means; **ne pas faire long f.** not to last long; **dans le f. de l'action** in the heat of the action; *Fig* **sous le f. des projecteurs** in the limelight; *Vulg* **avoir le f. au cul** *(être pressé)* to be in a mad rush; *(sexuellement)* to be always gagging for it; **f. d'artifice** *(spectacle)* fireworks display; **f. de Bengale** Bengal light; **f. de camp** campfire; **f. de cheminée** fire in the hearth; **f. follet** will-o'-the-wisp; **f. de forêt** forest fire; **f. de joie** bonfire; *Fig* **f. de paille** flash in the pan

(b) *(pour allumer une cigarette)* **avez-vous du f.?** have you got a light?

(c) *(brûleur)* burner; **à f. doux** *ou* **à petit f.** over a low heat; **à f. vif** over a high heat

(d) *(sur la chaussée)* **f. rouge/vert** red/green light; **feux de signalisation** *ou* **tricolores** traffic lights; *Fig* **donner le f. vert à qn** to give sb the green light

(e) *(phare)* **feux de brouillard** *ou* **antibrouillard** fog lamps; **feux de croisement** dipped headlights, *Am* low beams; **feux de détresse** hazard (warning) lights; **feux de position** sidelights; **feux de stationnement** parking lights

(f) *(tirs)* **faire f.** to fire, to shoot; **ouvrir le f.** to open fire; *Fig* **être pris entre deux feux** to be caught in the crossfire

2 *adj inv* **noir et f.** black-and-tan

feu², -e *adj* **f. M. Perrin** the late Mr Perrin; **f. mon mari** my late husband

feuillage [fœjaʒ] *nm* leaves, foliage

feuille [fœj] *nf* (a) *(de plante, d'arbre)* leaf; **f. morte** dead leaf; **f. de vigne** fig leaf (b) *(de papier)* sheet; **f. volante** loose sheet (c) *(journal) Péj* **f. de chou** rag (d) *(document)* **f. d'impôt** tax return; **f. de maladie** = form given by doctor to patient for claiming reimbursement from Social Security; **f. de paie** *ou* **paye** payslip; **f. de soins** medical expenses claim form (e) *Ordinat* **f. de calcul** spreadsheet

feuillet [fœjɛ] *nm* leaf

feuilleté, -e [fœjte] **1** *adj* (a) *(pâte)* flaky (b) *(verre)* laminated **2** *nm* **f. au jambon/au fromage** ham/cheese pasty

feuilleter [42] [fœjte] *vt* (a) *(livre)* to leaf through (b) *Ordinat* **f. en arrière** to page up; **f. en avant** to page down

feuilleton [fœjtɔ̃] *nm* serial; **f. télévisé** television serial

feuillu, -e [fœjy] **1** *adj* (a) *(ayant beaucoup de feuilles)* leafy (b) *Bot* broad-leaved **2** *nm Bot* broad-leaved tree

feutre [føtʀ] nm (a) (matière) felt (b) (chapeau) felt hat (c) (stylo) felt-tip (pen)

feutré, -e [føtʀe] adj (a) (garni de feutre) felt(-covered) (b) (assourdi) muffled; **à pas feutrés** stealthily (c) (vêtement) matted

feutrer [føtʀe] 1 vt (a) (garnir de feutre) to cover with felt (b) (assourdir) to muffle (c) (vêtement) to mat
2 vi (vêtement) to felt
3 **se feutrer** vpr (vêtement) to felt

feutrine [føtʀin] nf felt

fève [fɛv] nf (a) (plante, graine) broad bean (b) (dans la galette des Rois) charm (c) Can (haricot) bean

février [fevʀije] nm February; voir aussi **janvier**

FF nm (abrév **franc(s) français**) FF

FFI [ɛfɛfi] nfpl Hist (abrév **Forces françaises de l'intérieur**) = French Resistance forces in France during World War Two

FFL [ɛfɛfɛl] nfpl Hist (abrév **Forces françaises libres**) Free French Army

fiabilité [fjabilite] nf reliability

fiable [fjabl] adj reliable

fiacre [fjakʀ] nm hackney carriage

fiançailles [fjɑ̃saj] nfpl engagement

fiancé, -e [fjɑ̃se] nm,f fiancé, f fiancée

fiancer [16] [fjɑ̃se] **se fiancer** vpr to get engaged (**avec** to); **être fiancés** to be engaged

fiasco [fjasko] nm fiasco

fibre [fibʀ] nf fibre; Fig **avoir la f. maternelle** to be the maternal sort; **f. optique** fibre optics (singulier); **f. de verre** fibreglass

fibreux, -euse [fibʀø, -øz] adj (tissu) fibrous; (viande) stringy

fibrome [fibʀom] nm fibroma

fibroscopie [fibʀɔskɔpi] nf Méd fibre-optic endoscopy

ficelé, -e [fisle] adj Fam (a) (construit) **bien/mal f.** (scénario) well/poorly put together (b) (habillé) got up

ficeler [42] [fisle] vt (a) (attacher) to tie up (b) Fam (construire) to put together

ficelle [fisɛl] nf (a) (cordelette) string; Fig **les ficelles du métier** the tricks of the trade (b) (pain) small French stick

fiche¹ [fiʃ] nf (a) (formulaire) form; **f. d'état civil** = administrative record of birth details and marital status; **f. de paie** payslip; **f. signalétique** personal details card (b) (carte) (index) card; **mettre qch sur fiches** to card-index sth; **f. cartonnée** index card; **f. cuisine** (dans un magazine) recipe card (c) (prise) plug; (broche) pin (d) Ordinat **f. d'état** report form

fiche² = **ficher³**

ficher¹ [fiʃe] vt (mettre sur fiches) (informations) to file; (personne) to put on file

ficher² 1 vt (enfoncer) **f. qch dans qch** to stick sth into sth
2 **se ficher** vpr (balle, clou) **se f. dans qch** to go into sth

ficher³ Fam 1 vt (a) (mettre) **f. qn par terre** to send sb sprawling; **f. qch par terre** (exprès) to chuck sth on the floor; (accidentellement) to knock sth over; Fig **to** mess sth up; **f. qn à la porte** to kick sb out; **f. une gifle à qn** to give sb a slap in the face (b) Fam (faire) to do; **qu'est-ce que tu fiches?** what are you up to? (c) Fam **f. le camp** to clear off
2 **se ficher** vpr (a) (se mettre) **se f. un coup** to wallop oneself; **se f. par terre** to go sprawling; **se f. dedans** to

screw up (b) (se moquer) **se f. de qn** to poke fun at sb; **se f. du monde** to take the piss; **se f. de qch** not to give a damn about sth; **je m'en fiche** I don't give a damn

fichier [fiʃje] nm (a) (ensemble de fiches) (card-index) file (b) (boîte) card-index box; (meuble) card-index cabinet (c) Ordinat file

fichu¹, -e [fiʃy] adj Fam (a) (insupportable) damn; (caractère) rotten (b) (abîmé) **être f.** to have had it; **c'est f. maintenant!** (c'est raté) we can forget it!; **c'est f. pour dimanche** we can forget Sunday (c) (être) **être bien/mal f.** (bien/mal bâti) to have/not to have a nice body; (bien/mal conçu) to be well/badly designed; **être mal f.** (malade) to be under the weather (d) (capable) **être f. de faire qch** to be capable of doing sth

fichu² nm headscarf

fictif, -ive [fiktif, -iv] adj fictitious

fiction [fiksjɔ̃] nf fiction

ficus [fikys] nm ficus

fidèle [fidɛl] 1 adj (a) (ami, époux) faithful; (lecteur, auditeur, client) regular; **être f. à qn** to be faithful to sb; **être f. à qch** to be loyal or true to sth; Fig **être f. au poste** to be always there (b) (copie, traduction, récit) faithful (**à** to); (mémoire, souvenir) reliable
2 nm (a) (croyant) believer; **les fidèles** the faithful; (à l'église) the congregation (b) (partisan) loyal supporter (**de** of) (c) (d'un programme télévisé) regular viewer (**de** of); (d'un programme radio) regular listener (**de** to)

fidèlement [fidɛlmɑ̃] adv faithfully

fidélisation [fidelizasjɔ̃] nf **f. de la clientèle** building of customer loyalty

fidéliser [fidelize] vt to win the loyalty of; **f. la clientèle** to create customer loyalty

fidélité [fidelite] nf (a) (d'un époux, d'un ami) faithfulness (**à** to); (d'un client, à un principe) loyalty (**à** to) (b) (d'une traduction, d'une reproduction) faithfulness

Fidji [fidʒi] nfpl **les îles F.** Fiji

fiduciaire [fidysjɛʀ] adj Fin **monnaie f.** paper money

fief [fjɛf] nm fief; Fig **un f. du parti socialiste** a safe Socialist seat

fieffé, -e [fjefe] adj inveterate

fiel [fjɛl] nm aussi Fig gall

fier¹, fière [fjɛʀ] 1 adj (a) (satisfait) proud (**de** of); **être f. de faire qch** to be proud to do sth; **f. comme un paon** proud as a peacock (b) (hautain, noble) proud
2 nm,f Péj **faire le f.** to put on airs

fier² [66] [fje] **se fier** vpr **se f. à qn/qch** (avoir confiance en) to trust sb/sth; (compter sur) to rely on sb/sth

fièrement [fjɛʀmɑ̃] adv proudly

fierté [fjɛʀte] nf (a) (satisfaction) pride; **tirer f. de qch** to take pride in sth (b) (amour-propre) pride

fiesta [fjɛsta] nf Fam wild party

fièvre [fjɛvʀ] nf (a) (élévation de la température) fever; **avoir de la f.** to have a fever or a temperature; **elle a 40 de f.** she's got a temperature of 40 degrees; **avoir une f. de cheval** to have a raging fever (b) (excitation) frenzy

fiévreusement [fjevʀøzmɑ̃] adv feverishly

fiévreux, -euse [fjevʀø, -øz] adj aussi Fig feverish

fifre [fifʀ] nm (instrument) fife

figé, -e [fiʒe] adj (a) (locution) set (b) (sourire) fixed (c) (sauce) congealed

figer [45] [fiʒe] 1 *vt* (a) *(immobiliser)* to paralyse; **figé sur place** rooted to the spot (b) *(solidifier)* to congeal
2 **se figer** *vpr* *(huile, sauce)* to congeal; *(regard, traits, sourire)* to freeze

fignoler [fiɲɔle] *vt* *Fam* to put the finishing touches to; **il ne reste plus qu'à f.** it's just a matter now of adding the finishing touches

figue [fig] *nf* fig; **f. de Barbarie** prickly pear

figuier [figje] *nm* fig tree; **f. de Barbarie** prickly pear

figurant, -e [figyrã, -ãt] *nm,f* *(dans une pièce de théâtre)* walk-on; *(dans un film)* extra

figuratif, -ive [figyratif, -iv] *adj* figurative

figuration [figyrasjõ] *nf* **faire de la f.** to play bit parts

figure [figyr] *nf* (a) *(visage)* face; **faire bonne f.** to make a good impression; **faire f. d'intellectuel/de patriarche** to be seen as an intellectual/a patriarchal figure (b) *(représentation)* figure; *aussi Fig* **f. de proue** figurehead (c) *(personnage)* figure (d) *(en danse, en patinage artistique)* figure; **figures imposées** compulsory figures; **figures libres** freestyle (e) *Ling* **f. de rhétorique** figure of speech; **f. de style** stylistic device

figuré, -e [figyre] 1 *adj* *(sens)* figurative
2 *nm* **au f.** in the figurative sense

figurer [figyre] 1 *vt* to represent
2 *vi* (a) *(apparaître)* to appear **(sur/dans** on/in) (b) *(faire partie)* to figure **(parmi** among)
3 **se figurer** *vpr* **se f. que** to imagine that

figurine [figyrin] *nf* figurine

fil [fil] *nm* (a) *(brin, de toile d'araignée)* thread; **de f. en aiguille** little by little, bit by bit; **f. ne tenir qu'à un f.** to hang by a thread; **f. conducteur** unifying thread; **f. à coudre** (sewing) thread; **f. dentaire** dental floss; **f. d'Écosse** lisle thread; **f. à plomb** plumb line (b) *(métallique, électrique)* wire; *Fig* **donner du f. à retordre à qn** to give sb trouble; **f. de fer** wire; **f. de fer barbelé** barbed wire (c) *Fam* *(téléphone)* **au bout du f.** on the line; **coup de f.** call; **donner ou passer un coup de f. à qn** to give sb a call, to call sb (up) (d) *(cours)* **au f. de l'eau** with the current; **au f. des jours/semaines** with the passing days/weeks; **perdre/reprendre le f. de qch** to lose/pick up the thread of sth (e) *(tissu)* linen (f) *(tranchant)* edge

filament [filamã] *nm* (a) *(d'une ampoule électrique)* filament (b) *(de viande)* fibre (c) *Biol* filament

filandreux, -euse [filãdrø, -øz] *adj* *(viande, légumes)* stringy

filant, -e [filã, -ãt] *adj* voir **étoile**

filasse [filas] 1 *nf* tow
2 *adj inv* tow-coloured

filature [filatyr] *nf* (a) *(fabrique)* (spinning) mill (b) *(surveillance)* shadowing; **prendre qn en f.** to shadow sb

file [fil] *nf* (a) *(queue)* *Br* queue, *Am* line; **en f. indienne** in single file; **trois jours à la f.** three days in a row; **f.** **(d'attente)** *Br* queue, *Am* line (b) *(sur la route)* lane; **se garer en double f.** to double-park (c) *Ordinat* **f. d'attente** print queue

filé, -e [file] *adj* (a) *(bas, collant)* with a run, *Br* laddered (b) *(verre)* spun

filer [file] 1 *vt* (a) *(coton, verre)* to spin (b) *Fam* *(donner)* **f. qch à qn** to give sb sth (c) *(surveiller)* *(suspect)* to shadow, to tail (d) *(bas, collant)* to put a run in, *Br* to ladder (e) **f. le parfait amour** to live love's dream
2 *vi* (a) *(passer vite)* *(temps)* to fly; *(véhicule)* to speed along; **f. entre les mains ou les doigts à qn** *(argent)* to run through sb's fingers like water; *(personne)* to slip through sb's fingers (b) *Fam* *(partir)* **il faut que je file** I must dash; **allez, file!** off you go!; *(bas, collant)* to run, *Br* to ladder

filet¹ [file] *nm* (a) *(de lumière)* thin streak; *(d'air)* thin stream; *(d'eau)* trickle (b) *(petite quantité)* dash (c) *(d'une vis)* thread (d) *(de viande, de poisson)* fillet; **f. mignon** filet mignon *(small fillet steak)*

filet² *nm* (a) *(en mailles)* net; **f. à bagages** luggage rack; **f. à papillons** butterfly net; **f. de pêche** fishing net; **f. à provisions** string bag (b) *(au cirque)* (safety) net; **travailler sans f.** *(trapéziste)* to work without a net; *Fig* to take risks (c) *(au tennis)* net

filial, -e, -aux, -ales [filjal, -o] 1 *adj* filial
2 *nf* **filiale** subsidiary (company)

filiation [filjasjõ] *nf* (a) *(lien de parenté)* filiation (b) *Fig* *(relation)* relationship **(avec** to)

filière [filjɛr] *nf* (a) *(voie obligée)* channels (b) *(domaine d'études)* field of study; **suivre une f. scientifique/ commerciale** to study scientific/business subjects (c) *(organisation clandestine)* network

filiforme [filifɔrm] *adj* spindly

filigrane [filigran] *nm* *(dessin)* watermark; *Fig* **en f.** implicit

filin [filɛ̃] *nm* rope

fille [fij] *nf* (a) *(descendante)* daughter (b) *(enfant)* girl; **petite f.** little girl (c) *(femme)* **salut les filles!** hi, girls!; **f. de joie** prostitute; **jeune f.** girl; **vieille f.** old maid

fillette [fijɛt] *nf* little girl

filleul, -e [fijœl] *nm,f* godson, *f* goddaughter

film [film] *nm* (a) *(œuvre)* film, movie; **f. d'action** action film; **f. d'animation** animated film; **f. d'aventures** adventure film; **f. d'épouvante ou d'horreur** horror film; **f. policier** detective film (b) *(déroulement)* **revoir le f. de sa vie** to see one's life flashing before one's eyes (c) *(emballage)* film; **f. alimentaire** clingfilm

filmer [filme] *vt* to film

filmographie [filmɔgrafi] *nf* filmography

filon [filõ] *nm* (a) *(de minéraux)* vein, seam (b) *Fam* **trouver le f.** to strike it rich

filou [filu] *nm* *(escroc)* rogue; *(enfant)* rascal

fils [fis] *nm* son; **f. de famille** young man of good social standing; *Péj* **f. à papa** daddy's boy

filtrage [filtraʒ] *nm* (a) *(contrôle)* screening (b) *(d'un liquide)* filtering

filtrant, -e [filtrã, -ãt] *adj* *(pouvoir)* filtering; *(verres, papier)* filter

filtre [filtr] 1 *adj* *(cigarette, café, papier)* filter
2 *nm* filter; **f. à air** air filter; **f. à café** coffee filter; *Phot* **f. coloré** colour filter; *Ordinat* **f. écran** screen filter

filtrer [filtre] 1 *vt* (a) *(liquide, son, lumière)* to filter (b) *(informations, visiteurs)* to screen
2 *vi* *(liquide)* to filter **(à travers** through); *(nouvelle)* to leak out; **laisser f. qch** to let sth filter through; *Fig* to leak sth

fin¹ [fɛ̃] *nf* (a) *(conclusion)* end; **f. juillet** at the end of July; **à la f.** in the end; *Fam* **tu m'ennuies à la f.!** you're really annoying me!; **en f. de qch, à la f. de qch** at the end of sth; **chômeur en f. de droits** = unemployed person about to lose their entitlement to benefit; **mettre f. à qch** to put an end to sth; **prendre f.** to come to an end; **toucher** *ou* **tirer à sa f.** to draw to a close; **avoir des fins de mois difficiles** to be always short of money at the end of the month; **f. de série** discontinued line (b) *(mort)* end, death (c) *(but)* end, aim; **arriver** *ou* **parvenir à ses fins** to achieve one's ends; **à cette f.** to this end; **à toutes fins utiles** just in case (d) *Ordinat* **f. de ligne** line end; **f. de page** pagebreak; **f. de session** logoff

fin², **fine** [fɛ̃, fin] **1** *adj* (a) *(papier, tranche, taille)* thin; *(cheveux, sable, pointe)* fine; **une petite pluie fine** drizzle (b) *(traits)* fine (c) *(de première qualité)* **fines herbes** mixed herbs (e) **un f. connaisseur** a connoisseur *(vue, odorat)* keen; **avoir l'ouïe fine** to have keen hearing (g) *(subtil)* subtle (h) **le f. mot de l'histoire** the truth of the matter

2 **le f. du f.** the ultimate

3 *adv* (a) **f. prêt** all ready (b) *(finement)* finely

final, **-e**, **-als** *ou* **-aux**, **-ales** [final, -o] *adj* final

finale [final] **1** *nf* (a) *(compétition sportive)* final; **aller/être en f.** to go through to/to be in the finals (b) *(de mot)* final syllable

2 *nm (d'un morceau de musique)* finale

finalement [finalmɑ̃] *adv* in the end, finally

finaliser [finalize] *vt* to finalize

finaliste [finalist] *adj & nmf* finalist

finalité [finalite] *nf* (a) *(objectif)* aim (b) *(en biologie)* finality

finance [finɑ̃s] *nf* (a) *(profession)* finance; **la haute f.** high finance (b) *(argent)* **moyennant f.** for a fee; **finances** finances

financement [finɑ̃smɑ̃] *nm* financing

financer [16] [finɑ̃se] *vt* to finance

financier, **-ère** [finɑ̃sje, -er] **1** *adj* financial

2 *nm* financier

financièrement [finɑ̃sjermɑ̃] *adv* financially

finasser [finase] *vi Fam* to resort to trickery

finaud, **-e** [fino, -od] **1** *adj* crafty

2 *nm,f* crafty devil

fine [fin] *nf* liqueur brandy

finement [finmɑ̃] *adv* (a) *(adroitement)* cleverly (b) *(délicatement)* finely

finesse [fines] *nf* (a) *(minceur)* fineness; *(de la taille)* slenderness, slimness (b) *(d'un visage)* fineness; *(d'un travail fait à la main)* delicacy (c) *(subtilité)* subtlety

fini, **-e** [fini] **1** *adj* (a) *(usé, à bout)* finished (b) *Péj (imbécile, escroc)* absolute (c) *(espace, temps, nombre)* finite

2 *nm (d'un objet manufacturé)* finish

finir [finir] **1** *vt* to finish; *(vie)* to end; **f. son assiette** to finish what's on one's plate

2 *vi* to end, to finish; **f. bien/mal** to end well/badly; *(film, roman)* to have a happy/sad ending; **mal f.** *(personne)* to come to a bad end; **f. de faire qch** to finish doing sth; **f. par faire qch** to end up doing sth; **en f. avec qn/qch** to have done with sb/sth; **à n'en plus f.** endless; **pour f.** *(en résumé)* to cut a long story short; *(finalement)* in the end

finish [finiʃ] *nm inv* finish

finition [finisjɔ̃] *nf* finishing touch; **travail de f.** finishing touches; **les finitions de cette robe sont mal faites** this dress is badly finished

finlandais, **-e** [fɛ̃lɑ̃de, -ez] **1** *adj* Finnish

2 *nm,f* **F.** Finn

Finlande [fɛ̃lɑ̃d] *nf* **la F.** Finland

finnois, **-e** [finwa, -az] **1** *adj* Finnish

2 *nm (langue)* Finnish

fiole [fjɔl] *nf (flacon)* phial

fioriture [fjərityr] *nf (dessin)* flourish

fioul [fjul] *nm* fuel oil

firmament [firmamɑ̃] *nm Litt* firmament

firme [firm] *nf* firm

FIS [fis] *nm (abrév* **Front islamique du salut)** **le F.** the Islamic Salvation Front

fisc [fisk] *nm Br* ≃ Inland Revenue, *Am* ≃ Internal Revenue

fiscal, **-e**, **-aux**, **-ales** [fiskal, -o] *adj* tax

fiscaliser [fiskalize] *vt* to tax

fiscalité [fiskalite] *nf* tax system

fissure [fisyr] *nf aussi Fig* crack

fissurer [fisyre] **1** *vt* to crack; *Fig* to split

2 se fissurer *vpr* to crack; *Fig* to split

fiston [fistɔ̃] *nm Fam* son, lad

FIV [efive] *nf (abrév* **fécondation in vitro)** IVF

fivete [fivet] *nf (abrév* **fécondation in vitro et transfert embryonnaire)** GIFT

fixateur, **-trice** [fiksatœr, -tris] *Phot* **1** *adj* fixing

2 *nm* fixer

fixatif [fiksatif] *nm* fixative

fixation [fiksasjɔ̃] *nf* (a) *(action)* fixing (b) *(de skis)* (ski) binding (c) *(obsession)* fixation; **faire une f. sur qn/qch** to become fixated on sb/sth

fixe [fiks] **1** *adj* (a) *(immobile) (étagère, planche, regard)* fixed (b) *(arrêté) (prix, frais)* fixed

2 *nm* fixed salary

fixement [fiksəmɑ̃] *adv* fixedly; **regarder f. qn/qch** to stare at sb/sth

fixer [fikse] **1** *vt* (a) *(immobiliser)* to fix; **f. son attention/son regard sur qch** to focus one's attention/one's gaze on sth; **f. qn (du regard)** to stare at sb (b) *(déterminer) (date, heure, rendez-vous)* to fix; *(prix, salaire)* to fix, to set (à at); **f. son choix sur qch** to decide on sth (c) *(informer)* **maintenant, tu es fixé** now you know

2 se fixer *vpr* (a) *(s'installer)* to settle down (b) **son choix s'est fixé sur celui-ci** she decided on this one (c) **se f. un objectif** to set oneself a target

fixité [fiksite] *nf (du regard)* fixedness

fjord [fjɔrd] *nm* fjord

flacon [flakɔ̃] *nm (small)* bottle

flagada [flagada] *adj inv Fam* washed-out

flageller [flaʒele] *vt* to flog, to whip

flageoler [flaʒɔle] *vi (jambes)* to shake, to tremble

flageolet [flaʒɔle] *nm (haricot)* flageolet (bean)

flagornerie [flagɔrnəri] *nf Péj* fawning, toadying

flagrant, **-e** [flagrɑ̃, -ɑ̃t] *adj* flagrant, blatant; **en f. délit** red-handed; **être pris en f. délit d'adultère** to be caught in flagrante

flair [fler] *nm* sense of smell; **avoir du f.** to have a good sense of smell; *Fig* to have good intuition

flairer [flere] *vt aussi Fig* to smell

flamand, -e [flamɑ̃, -ɑ̃d] **1** *adj* Flemish
2 *nm,f* F. Fleming
3 *nm (langue)* Flemish

flamant [flamɑ̃] *nm* f. rose flamingo

flambant [flɑ̃bɑ̃] *adv* f. neuf brand new

flambeau, -x [flɑ̃bo] *nm (torche)* torch; *Fig* passer le f. à qn to pass the torch on to sb

flambée [flɑ̃be] *nf (a) (feu)* blaze **(b)** *(de violence)* flare-up; *(des prix)* upsurge

flamber [flɑ̃be] **1** *vi (a) (brûler)* to blaze **(b)** *Fam (parier)* to gamble for big money
2 *vt (a) (volaille)* to singe **(b)** *(crêpes)* to flambé

flambeur, -euse [flɑ̃bœr, -øz] *nm,f Fam* big-time gambler

flamboyant, -e [flɑ̃bwajɑ̃, -ɑ̃t] *adj (a) (regard)* blazing; d'un rouge f. flaming red **(b)** *Archit* flamboyant

flamboyer [32] [flɑ̃bwaje] *vi* to blaze

flamme [flam] *nf (a) (feu)* flame; en flammes on fire, ablaze, *Fig* descendre qn/qch en flammes to shoot sb/ sth down in flames **(b)** *Fig (enthousiasme)* fire **(c)** *Litt (amour)* passion

flammèche [flameʃ] *nf* spark

flan [flɑ̃] *nm (dessert)* baked custard

flanc [flɑ̃] *nm* side; *(d'une armée)* flank; être sur le f. *(malade)* to be laid up; *(épuisé)* to be worn out; *Fam* tirer au f. to shirk, *Br* to skive

flancher [flɑ̃ʃe] *vi Fam* to give in

Flandre [flɑ̃dr] *nf* la F., les Flandres Flanders

flanelle [flanɛl] *nf (tissu)* flannel

flâner [flane, flɑne] *vi (a) (se promener)* to stroll, to saunter **(b)** *(perdre son temps)* to hang about

flânerie [flɑnri, flanri] *nf (promenade)* stroll

flâneur, -euse [flɑnœr, flanœr, -øz] *nm,f (promeneur)* stroller

flanquer¹ [flɑ̃ke] *vt (accompagner)* flanqué de flanked by

flanquer² *Fam* **1** *vt (a) (jeter)* to chuck; f. qn à la porte ou dehors to kick sb out; *(licencier)* to fire sb, *Br* to sack sb **(b)** f. qch à qn *(coup de pied, gifle)* to give sb sth; f. la trouille *ou* les jetons à qn to put the wind up sb
2 se flanquer *vpr* se f. par terre to go sprawling

flapi, -e [flapi] *adj Fam* dead beat

flaque [flak] *nf (d'huile, de sang)* pool; f. (d'eau) puddle

flash [flaʃ] *nm (a) (sur un appareil photo)* flash **(b)** *(à la radio, à la télévision)* flash; f. d'information newsflash; f. publicitaire commercial

flash-back [flaʃbak] *nm inv* flashback

flasher [flaʃe] *vi Fam* f. sur qn/qch to fall for sb/sth in a big way

flasque¹ [flask] *adj (chair)* flabby

flasque² *nf* flask

flatter [flate] **1** *vt (a) (complimenter)* to flatter **(b)** *(avantager)* to flatter **(c)** *(caresser) (animal)* to stroke
2 se flatter *vpr* to flatter oneself; se f. de faire qch to pride oneself on doing sth; je ne m'en flatterai pas it's not something I'd be proud of

flatterie [flatri] *nf* flattery

flatteur, -euse [flatœr, -øz] **1** *adj (remarque, portrait, couleur)* flattering; *(personne)* full of flattery
2 *nm,f* flatterer

flatulence [flatylɑ̃s] *nf* flatulence

FLE [fla] *nm (abrév* français langue étrangère*)* French as a foreign language

fléau, -x [fleo] *nm (a) (calamité)* scourge; *Fig (chose pénible)* pain **(b)** *(à céréales)* flail **(c)** *(d'une balance à plateaux)* beam

fléchage [fleʃaʒ] *nm* signposting

flèche [flɛʃ] *nf (a) (projectile, signe)* arrow; partir comme une f. to shoot off; monter en f. *(avion, prix)* to shoot up **(b)** *(attaque verbale)* jibe **(c)** *(d'une église)* spire **(d)** *Ordinat* f. de défilement scroll arrow; flèches verticales up and down arrow keys

flécher [34] [fleʃe] *vt (route, direction)* to arrow; itinéraire fléché signposted route

fléchette [fleʃɛt] *nf* dart; jouer aux fléchettes to play darts

fléchir [fleʃir] **1** *vt (bras, jambe, genou)* to bend **(b)** *(émouvoir)* to sway
2 *vi (a) (ployer) (branche)* to bend; *(jambes)* to give way; *(poutre)* to sag **(b)** *(faiblir)* to weaken **(c)** *(baisser) (prix, devises)* to fall

fléchissement [fleʃismɑ̃] *nm (a) (du genou)* bending; *(d'une poutre)* sagging **(b)** *(de prix, de devises, de résultats)* drop **(c)** *(de)* in

flegmatique [flɛgmatik] *adj* phlegmatic

flegme [flɛgm] *nm* phlegm

flemmard, -e [flemar, -ard] *Fam* **1** *adj* lazy
2 *nm,f* lazybones

flemmarder [flemarde] *vi Fam* to laze about

flemmardise [flemardiz] *nf Fam* laziness

flemme [flɛm] *nf Fam* laziness; j'ai la f. (de le faire) I can't be bothered (to do it)

flétan [fletɑ̃] *nm* halibut

flétri, -e [fletri] *adj* withered

flétrir [fletrir] **1** *vt (peau, plantes)* to wither
2 se flétrir *vpr (visage, plantes)* to wither

fleur [flœr] *nf (a) (plante)* flower; à fleurs *(tissu)* floral; en fleurs *(arbre)* in flower; être f. bleue to be a romantic; *Fam* faire une f. à qn to do sb a favour; fleurs des champs wild flowers **(b)** *(locutions)* dans la f. de l'âge in the prime of life; la fine f. de qch the cream of sth; à f. d'eau just above the surface of the water; avoir les nerfs à f. de peau to be all on edge

fleurdelisé [flœrdəlize] *nm Can (drapeau du Québec)* flag of Quebec

fleurer [flœre] *vt Litt* to smell of

fleuret [flœrɛ] *nm (épée)* foil

fleurette [flœrɛt] *nf Vieilli* conter f. à qn to whisper sweet nothings to sb

fleuri, -e [flœri] *adj (a) (couvert de fleurs) (arbre)* in flower **(b)** *(orné de fleurs) (tissu, robe)* floral; *(vaisselle)* flower-patterned **(c)** *(style)* flowery

fleurir [flœrir] **1** *vi (a) (plantes)* to flower **(b)** *(art, commerce)* to flourish
2 *vt (table)* to decorate with flowers; *(tombe)* to lay flowers on

fleuriste [flœrist] *nmf (commerçant)* florist

fleuron [flœrɔ̃] *nm (d'une collection)* jewel

fleuve [flœv] *nm* river; le f. Jaune the Yellow River

flexibilité [flɛksibilite] *nf aussi Fig* flexibility

flexible [flɛksibl] **1** *adj aussi Fig* flexible
2 *nm (tuyau)* hose(pipe)

flexion [flɛksjɔ̃] *nf (fléchissement)* bending

flibustier [flibystje] *nm* buccaneer

flic [flik] *nm Fam* cop

flingue [flɛ̃g] *nm Fam* shooter

flinguer [flɛ̃ge] *Fam* **1** *vt* to gun down
2 se flinguer *vpr* to blow one's brains out

flippant, -e [flipɑ̃, -ɑ̃t] *adj Fam (déprimant)* grim; *(effrayant)* creepy

flipper¹ [flipœr] *nm (appareil)* pinball machine; *(jeu)* pinball; **jouer au f.** to play pinball

flipper² [flipe] *vi Fam (déprimer)* to feel down

flirt [flœrt] *nm* **(a)** *(amourette)* flirtation **(b)** *(personne)* boyfriend, *f* girlfriend

flirter [flœrte] *vi* to flirt *(avec with)*

FLN [ɛfɛlɛn] *nm (abrév* **Front de libération nationale)** National Liberation Front *(in Algeria)*

FLNC [ɛfɛlɛnse] *nm (abrév* **Front de libération nationale de la Corse)** Corsican liberation front

FLNKS [ɛfɛlɛnkaɛs] *nm (abrév* **Front de libération nationale kanak et socialiste)** Kanak national liberation front *(in New Caledonia)*

flocon [flɔkɔ̃] *nm* flake; **flocons d'avoine** oat flakes; **f. de neige** snowflake

floconneux, -euse [flɔkɔnø, -øz] *adj* fluffy

flonflons [flɔ̃flɔ̃] *nmpl* tiddly-om-pom-pom

flop [flɔp] *nm Fam* flop; **faire un f.** to flop

flopée [flɔpe] *nf Fam* **une f. ou des flopées de qch** loads of sth, masses of sth

floraison [flɔrɛzɔ̃] *nf* flowering

floral, -e, -aux, -ales [flɔral, -o] *adj* floral

floralies [flɔrali] *nfpl* flower show

flore [flɔr] *nf* flora; **f. intestinale** intestinal flora

Floride [flɔrid] *nf* **la F.** Florida

florilège [flɔrilɛʒ] *nm* anthology

florin [flɔrɛ̃] *nm* florin

florissant, -e [flɔrisɑ̃, -ɑ̃t] *adj (affaire)* flourishing; *(santé)* blooming

flot [flo] *nm* **(a)** *(marée)* flood (tide) **(b)** *(quantité importante)* stream (**de** of) **(c)** *Litt* **les flots** *(la mer)* the waves **(d)** *(locutions)* **couler à flots** to flow freely; **être à f.** *(bateau)* to be afloat; *Fig (personne)* to have one's head above water

flottaison [flɔtɛzɔ̃] *nf* floating

flotte [flɔt] *nf* **(a)** *(bateaux)* fleet **(b)** *Fam (pluie)* rain **(c)** *Fam (eau)* water

flottement [flɔtmɑ̃] *nm* **(a)** *(d'un drapeau)* fluttering **(b)** *(d'une monnaie)* fluctuation **(c)** *(hésitation)* wavering

flotter [flɔte] **1** *vi* **(a)** *(embarcation)* to float; *Fig* **il flotte dans sa veste** his jacket is far too baggy for him **(b)** *(drapeau)* to flutter; **f. au ou dans le vent** *(cheveux)* to stream in the wind
2 *v impersonnel Fam* **il flotte** it's raining

flotteur [flɔtœr] *nm* float

flottille [flɔtij] *nf (de bateaux)* flotilla

flou, -e [flu] **1** *adj* **(a)** *(contour, photographie)* blurred, fuzzy **(b)** *(idée, réponse)* vague
2 *nm (d'un contour, d'une photographie)* fuzziness; *(d'une idée, d'une réponse)* vagueness; **f. artistique** *(en photographie)* soft-focus effect; *Fig* deliberate vagueness

flouer [flue] *vt Fam* to swindle

flouse, flouze [fluz] *nm Fam (argent)* bread

fluctuant, -e [flyktɥɑ̃, -ɑ̃t] *adj* fluctuating

fluctuation [flyktɥasjɔ̃] *nf* fluctuation

fluctuer [flyktɥe] *vi* to fluctuate

fluet, -ette [flɥɛ, -ɛt] *adj* thin

fluide [flɥid] **1** *adj (liquide)* fluid; *(circulation)* flowing freely; *(style, pensée)* flowing
2 *nm* **(a)** *(substance)* fluid **(b)** *(pouvoir surnaturel)* occult power

fluidifier [66] [flɥidifje] *vt (sang)* to thin

fluidité [flɥidite] *nf (d'un corps)* fluidity; *(de la circulation)* free flow

fluo [flyo] *adj inv Fam* fluorescent

fluor [flyɔr] *nm* fluorine

fluorescent, -e [flyɔresɑ̃, -ɑ̃t] *adj* fluorescent

flûte [flyt] **1** *nf* **(a)** *(instrument)* flute; **f. à bec** recorder; **f. de Pan** panpipes; **f. traversière** concert flute **(b)** *(pain)* small French stick **(c)** *(verre)* **f. à champagne** champagne flute
2 *exclam Fam* damn!

flûtiste [flytist] *nmf Br* flautist, *Am* flutist

fluvial, -e, -aux, -ales [flyvjal, -o] *adj* river; *(alluvions)* fluvial

flux [fly] *nm* **(a)** *(de paroles)* flow **(b)** *(marée montante)* flow; **le f. et le reflux** the ebb and flow; **f. migratoire** flow of migrants **(c)** *(électrique, magnétique)* flux

fluxion [flyksjɔ̃] *nf* inflammation; **f. de poitrine** pneumonia

FM [ɛfɛm] *nf (abrév* **frequency modulation)** FM

FMI [ɛfɛmi] *nm (abrév* **Fonds monétaire international)** IMF

FN [ɛfɛn] *nm (abrév* **Front national)** = French political party of the extreme right

FNSEA [ɛfɛnɛsəa] *nf (abrév* **Fédération nationale des syndicats d'exploitants agricoles)** = French farmers' union

FO [ɛfo] *nf (abrév* **Force ouvrière)** = French trade union

foc [fɔk] *nm* jib

focal, -e, -aux, -ales [fɔkal, -o] *adj* focal

focaliser [fɔkalize] **1** *vt* to focus *(sur on)*
2 se focaliser *vpr* to focus *(sur on)*

fœtal, -e, -aux, -ales [fetal, -o] *adj* foetal

fœtus [fetys] *nm* foetus

fofolle [fɔfɔl] *adj voir* **foufou**

foi [fwa] *nf* **(a)** *(confiance)* faith, trust; **avoir f. en qn/qch** to have faith in sb/sth; **les candidatures devront nous parvenir avant le 1ᵉʳ mars, le cachet de la poste faisant f.** ≃ applications should be postmarked no later than 1 March **(b)** *(croyance religieuse)* faith; **avoir/perdre la f.** to have/lose faith **(c)** *(locutions)* **bonne f.** sincerity; **mauvaise f.** insincerity; **être de bonne/mauvaise f.** to be sincere/insincere; **ma f., oui!** yes indeed!

foie [fwa] *nm* liver; *très Fam* **avoir les foies** to be scared shitless; **f. gras** foie gras; **f. de veau/volaille** calf's/chicken liver

foin [fwɛ̃] *nm (fourrage)* hay; **faire les foins** to make hay; *Fam* **faire du f.** *(causer un scandale)* to kick up a fuss; *(faire du bruit)* to make a din

foire [fwar] *nf* **(a)** *(fête foraine)* funfair; *Fam* **faire la f.** to muck about; **c'est la f. ici** it's bedlam in here; **f. d'empoigne** free-for-all **(b)** *(salon international, professionnel)* (trade) fair

foirer [fware] *vi très Fam* to be a cock-up

foireux, -euse [fwarø, -øz] *adj très Fam (projet, affaire)* hopeless

fois [fwa] *nf* time; **une f.** once; **il était une f. un roi** once upon a time there was a king; **deux f.** twice; **deux f. par jour/mois** twice a day/month; **ça coûte trois f. rien** it costs next to nothing; **trois f. quatre douze** three times four is twelve; **trois f. plus grand** three times as big; **neuf f. sur dix** nine times out of ten; **combien de f.?** how many times?, how often?; **toutes les f. ou chaque f.** que every time (that), whenever; **encore une f.** once more, once again; **une (bonne) f. pour toutes** once and for all; **une f.** que once, as soon as; **pour cette f.** this once; **pour une f.** for once; **pour une f. que j'étais à l'heure, personne n'était là** the one time I was on time and no one was there; **à la f. utile et pas cher** both useful and inexpensive; **une chose à la f.** one thing at a time; **l'autre f.** *(il y a peu)* the other day; *Fam* **des f.** *(parfois)* sometimes; *Fam* **des f. qu'il viendrait** in case he comes; *Fam* **non, mais des f.!** really now!

foison [fwazɔ̃] *nf* **à f.** in abundance

foisonnement [fwazɔnmɑ̃] *nm (abondance)* abundance

foisonner [fwazɔne] *vi* to abound **(de** *ou* **en** in); **f. d'idées** *(personne)* to have plenty of ideas

fol [fɔl] *voir* **fou**

folâtre [fɔlɑtr] *adj (personne)* playful

folâtrer [fɔlɑtre] *vi (personne)* to romp, to frolic

foldingue [fɔldɛ̃g] *adj Fam* nutty

folichon, -onne [fɔliʃɔ̃, -ɔn] *adj Fam* **ce n'est pas f.** it's not much fun

folie [fɔli] *nf* madness; **aimer qn à la f.** to be madly in love with sb; **aimer qch à la f.** to adore sth; **faire des folies** *(faire des achats extravagants)* to go mad; **c'est de la f.!** it's madness!; **c'est de la f. douce** it's sheer madness; **la f. des grandeurs** delusions of grandeur

folio [fɔljo] *nm* folio

folk [fɔlk] *adj & nm* folk

folklo [fɔlklo] *adj inv Fam (personne)* eccentric; *(endroit, soirée)* bizarre

folklore [fɔlklɔr] *nm* folklore

folklorique [fɔlklɔrik] *adj (a) (costume)* traditional; *(danse)* folk **(b)** *Fam (personne)* eccentric; *(endroit, soirée)* bizarre

folle [fɔl] *adj voir* **fou**

follement [fɔlmɑ̃] *adv* madly

follet [fɔlɛ] *adj m voir* **feu**

fomenter [fɔmɑ̃te] *vt* to foment

foncé, -e [fɔ̃se] *adj* dark

foncer [16] [fɔ̃se] **1** *vt* to darken **2** *vi* **(a)** *(s'assombrir)* to darken **(b)** *(se hâter)* to get a move on; **f. sur qn/qch** *(se précipiter sur)* to swoop on sb/sth **(c)** *Fam (s'y mettre)* to get one's head down

fonceur, -euse [fɔ̃sœr, -øz] *Fam* **1** *adj* go-getting **2** *nm,f* go-getter

foncier, -ère [fɔ̃sje, -ɛr] *adj (a) (impôt, crédit)* land **(b)** *(fondamental)* fundamental, basic

foncièrement [fɔ̃sjɛrmɑ̃] *adv* fundamentally, basically

fonction [fɔ̃ksjɔ̃] *nf* **(a)** *(poste)* office; **entrer en fonctions, prendre ses fonctions** to take up one's duties; **être en f.** to be in office; **de f.** *(voiture, appartement)* company; **la f. publique** the civil service **(b)** *(rôle)* function; **faire f. de qch** to act as sth **(c)** *Ordinat* **f. de comptage de mots** word count facility; **f. d'éditeur de texte** text editing feature; **f. multimédia** multimedia

facility; **f. recherche et remplacement** search and replace function; **f. de sauvegarde** save function **(d) en f. de** according to

fonctionnaire [fɔ̃ksjɔnɛr] *nmf* civil servant; **haut f.** senior civil servant

fonctionnel, -elle [fɔ̃ksjɔnɛl] *adj* functional

fonctionnement [fɔ̃ksjɔnmɑ̃] *nm (d'une machine)* working, functioning; **en état de f.** in (good) working order; *Ordinat* **f. en réseau** networking

fonctionner [fɔ̃ksjɔne] *vi (machine, mécanisme)* to work, to function; *Ordinat* to run; **faire f. qch** to operate sth

fond [fɔ̃] *nm* **(a)** *(d'un récipient, de la mer, de l'océan)* bottom; *(d'un espace clos, de la gorge)* back; **la pièce du f.** the room at the end, the far room; **au fin f. de qch** in the depths of sth; **il n'en reste qu'un f.** there's only a drop left; **du f. du cœur** from the bottom of one's heart; **tu connais le f. de ma pensée** you know what my feelings really are; **à f.** *(à bloc)* all the way; *(complètement)* thoroughly; *(totalement)* totally; **à f. de train** at full tilt; *Fam* **à f. la caisse** *(très vite)* hell for leather; **au f., dans le f.** when it comes down to it; **de f. en comble** from top to bottom; **f. d'artichaut** artichoke heart; **f. de bouteille** *(contenu)* dregs; **f. de teint** foundation (cream)
(b) *(substance essentielle)* **le f. du problème** the heart of the problem; **avoir un bon/mauvais f.** to be basically a good/bad person; **le f. et la forme** form and content
(c) *(arrière-plan)* background; **f. sonore** background music

fondamental, -e, -aux, -ales [fɔ̃damɑ̃tal, -o] *adj* basic, fundamental

fondamentalement [fɔ̃damɑ̃talmɑ̃] *adv* fundamentally, basically

fondamentalisme [fɔ̃damɑ̃talism] *nm* fundamentalism

fondamentaliste [fɔ̃damɑ̃talist] *nmf* fundamentalist

fondant, -e [fɔ̃dɑ̃, -ɑ̃t] **1** *adj* **(a)** *(neige)* melting **(b)** *(poire)* that melts in the mouth; *(viande)* very tender **2** *nm (bonbon)* fondant

fondateur, -trice [fɔ̃datœr, -tris] **1** *adj (mythe)* underlying; **membre f.** founder member **2** *nm,f* founder

fondation [fɔ̃dasjɔ̃] *nf* **(a)** *(d'une ville, d'un hôpital)* founding **(b)** *(établissement)* foundation **(c) fondations** *(d'une construction)* foundations

fondé, -e [fɔ̃de] **1** *adj (reproches, doutes)* well-founded, justified; **être f. à faire qch** to have good reason to do sth **2** *nm,f* **f. de pouvoir** agent *(holding power of attorney)*; *(mandant)* proxy

fondement [fɔ̃dmɑ̃] *nm* foundation

fonder [fɔ̃de] **1** *vt* **a** *(créer)* *(ville, hôpital)* to found; *(société, journal)* to start, to set up; **f. un foyer** to start a family **(b)** *(baser)* **f. qch sur qch** to base sth on sth; **f. de grands espoirs sur qch** to pin one's hopes on sth **2 se fonder** *vpr* **se f. sur qch** *(sujet: remarque, théorie)* to be based on sth; **sur quoi se fonde-t-il pour le nier?** what are his grounds for denying it?; **pour son livre, elle s'est fondée sur plusieurs articles** she based her book on several articles

fonderie [fɔ̃dri] *nf (usine)* foundry

fondre [fɔ̃dr] **1** vt (a) (rendre liquide) (métal) to melt down; (sucre, sel) to dissolve; (neige, cire) to melt (b) (fabriquer) (cloche, arme) to cast (c) (combiner) (couleurs) to blend; (sociétés) to merge

2 vi (a) (se liquéfier) to melt; (sucre) to dissolve; **faire f. qch** to melt sth; (sucre) to dissolve sth; **f. dans la bouche** to melt in the mouth; **f. en larmes** to dissolve into tears; Fig **je fonds** my heart melts (b) Fig (diminuer) to melt away (c) Fam (maigrir) to lose weight

3 fondre sur vt ind to swoop on

4 se fondre vpr **se f. dans** to merge into

fonds [fɔ̃] **1** nm (a) (capital) funds; (organisme) fund; **prêter son argent à f. perdu** to lend one's money without security; **f. commun de placement** mutual fund; **F. européen de développement** European Development Fund; **F. européen de développement régional** European Regional Development Fund; **F. monétaire international** International Monetary Fund; **f. de roulement** working capital (b) (d'un musée, d'une bibliothèque) collection; (ressources) resource (c) **f. de commerce** business

2 nmpl (ressources financières) funds; **être en f.** to be in funds; **f. publics** government funds; (valeurs) government stocks

fondu [fɔ̃dy] nm (a) (de couleurs) blending (b) Cin fade-out; **f. enchaîné** dissolve

fondue [fɔ̃dy] nf **f.** (savoyarde) (cheese) fondue; **f. bourguignonne** fondue bourguignonne, = fondue consisting of cubes of raw beef cooked in hot oil

fongicide [fɔ̃ʒisid] **1** adj fungicidal
2 nm fungicide

font voir **faire**

fontaine [fɔ̃tɛn] nf (source naturelle) spring; (construction publique) fountain

fonte [fɔ̃t] nf (a) (de métaux) melting down; **la f. des neiges** the thaw (b) (alliage) cast iron; **poêle en f.** cast-iron stove (c) Typ font

fonts [fɔ̃] nmpl **f. baptismaux** font

foot [fut] nm Fam Br football, Am soccer

football [futbol] nm Br football, Am soccer

footballeur, -euse [futbolœr, -øz] nm,f Br footballer, Am soccer player

footing [futiŋ] nm jogging; **faire du f.** to go jogging

for [fɔr] nm **dans** ou **en son f. intérieur** in one's heart of hearts, deep (down) inside

forage [fɔraʒ] nm drilling, boring

forain, -e [fɔrɛ̃, -ɛn] **1** adj voir **fête, marchand**
2 nm fairground stallholder

forçat [fɔrsa] nm (prisonnier) convict

force [fɔrs] nf (a) (vigueur) strength; **ne pas se sentir/ne pas être de f. à faire qch** not to feel/not to be up to doing sth; **de f. égale, de même f.** equally matched; **dans la f. de l'âge** in the prime of life; **être à bout de forces** to have no strength left; **c'est au-dessus de ses forces** it's too much for him; **de toutes ses forces** (pousser, frapper) with all one's strength; (vouloir) with all one's heart; **de caractère** strength of character; **c'est une f. de la nature** (personne) she's a force to be reckoned with; **les forces vives du pays** the country's resources (b) (violence) force; **faire qch de force** ou **par la f.** to do sth by force; **par la f. des choses** through force of circumstance (c) (puissance) **f. centrifuge/centripète** centrifugal/centripetal force; aussi Fig **f. d'inertie** inertia; **f. motrice** motive power; Fig driving force (d)

(organisation) **les forces armées** the armed forces; **les forces aériennes** the airforce; **f. de dissuasion** deterrent; **f. de frappe** strike force; **les forces de police** ou **de l'ordre** the police (force) (e) (locutions) **à f.** in the end; **à f. de volonté** through sheer willpower; **à f. d'insister, tu vas finir par m'agacer** if you keep going on about it, I'm going to get annoyed; **en f.** in force

forcé, -e [fɔrse] adj forced; Fam **c'est f.!** it's inevitable!

forcément [fɔrsemɑ̃] adv inevitably; **elle sera f. déçue** she's bound to be disappointed; **pas f.** not necessarily

forcené, -e [fɔrsəne] **1** adj (partisan, individualisme) fanatical; (haine, lutte) frenzied
2 nm,f maniac

forceps [fɔrsɛps] nm forceps

forcer [16] [fɔrse] **1** vt (a) (obliger) to force; **f. qn à faire qch** to force sb to do sth; **f. la main à qn** to force sb's hand; **f. le respect/l'admiration** to command respect/admiration (b) (faire céder) (porte) to force (open) (c) (voix) to strain; Fig **f. la dose** to overdo it

2 vi (appuyer, tirer) to force it; (se surmener) to overdo it; Fam **f. sur qch** to overdo sth

3 se forcer vpr (s'obliger) to force oneself (**à faire qch** to do sth)

forcing [fɔrsiŋ] nm Fam sustained pressure; **faire du f.** to put on a lot of pressure

forcir [fɔrsir] vi (vent, tempête) to get stronger

forer [fɔre] vt to drill, to bore

forestier, -ère [fɔrɛstje, -ɛr] **1** adj (zone, chemin) forest; **exploitation forestière** (activité) forestry
2 nm forester

forêt [fɔrɛ] nf forest; **F.-noire** (gâteau) Black Forest gateau; **f. vierge** virgin forest

foreuse [fɔrøz] nf drill

forfait[1] [fɔrfɛ] nm (crime) heinous crime

forfait[2] nm (a) (contrat) fixed-price contract; **travailler au f.** to do fixed-price work (b) **être au f.** (fiscalement) to pay an estimated amount of tax (c) (prix global) all-in price; **f. week-end** weekend package (d) (de ski) pass

forfait[3] nm voir **déclarer**

forfaitaire [fɔrfɛter] adj (indemnités) basic; (prix) all-in

forfanterie [fɔrfɑ̃tri] nf bragging

forge [fɔrʒ] nf forge

forger [45] [fɔrʒe] **1** vt (a) (métal) to forge; Fig (caractère) to form (b) (inventer) (histoire, excuse) to make up
2 se forger vpr **se f. une réputation** to carve out a reputation for oneself

forgeron [fɔrʒərɔ̃] nm (black)smith

formaliser [fɔrmalize] **1** vt to formalize
2 se formaliser vpr to take offence (**de** at)

formalisme [fɔrmalism] nm formalism

formalité [fɔrmalite] nf formality; **les formalités d'usage** the usual formalities

format [fɔrma] nm format; Ordinat **f. d'écran** screen format; Ordinat **f. de fichier** file format; Ordinat **f. d'impression** print format; **f. de papier** paper format; **f. de poche** pocket format

formatage [fɔrmataʒ] nm Ordinat formatting

formater [fɔrmate] vt Ordinat to format

formateur, -trice [fɔrmatœr, -tris] **1** adj formative
2 nm,f trainer

formation [fɔrmasjɔ̃] *nf* (a) *(de roches, d'un mot)* formation; *(du caractère)* forming (b) *(éducation)* training; **f. continue** *ou* **permanente** continuing education; **f. professionnelle** vocational training; **être en f.** to be undergoing training (c) *(groupe)* group

forme [fɔrm] *nf* (a) *(configuration)* shape, form; **formes** *(d'une femme)* curves; **en f. de qch** in the shape of sth; **en f. de L** L-shaped; **sous f. de qch** in the form of sth; **sous toutes ses formes** in all its forms; **sans f.** shapeless; **prendre f.** to take shape (b) *(manière)* form; **en bonne et due f.** in due form; **sans autre f. de procès** without further ado (c) *(convention)* **de pure f.** purely formal; **pour la f.** as a matter of form; **dans les formes** in the accepted way (d) *(bonne santé physique)* form; **être en (pleine) f.** to be on (top) form

formel, -elle [fɔrmel] *adj* (a) *(personne)* positive; *(ordre)* express; *(démenti, refus)* flat; *(interdiction)* strict (b) *(apparent)* formal (c) *(soutenu)* formal

formellement [fɔrmelmã] *adv* (a) *(interdire)* strictly; *(affirmer)* categorically; *(identifier)* positively (b) *(du point de vue de la forme)* formally

former [fɔrme] **1** *vt* (a) *(créer)* *(gouvernement, projet)* to form (b) *(constituer)* to form; **ils forment une bonne équipe/un beau couple** they make a good team/a lovely couple (c) *(tracer)* *(lettre)* to form (d) *(entraîner)* to train (e) *(développer)* *(caractère)* to form; *(esprit, goût, jugement)* to develop
2 se former *vpr* (a) *(apparaître)* to form; *(association, liens)* to be formed (b) *(mûrir)* *(goût)* to develop (c) *(apprendre un métier)* to train oneself

Formica® [fɔrmika] *nm* Formica®; **en F.** Formica®

formidable [fɔrmidabl] *adj* (a) *(fantastique)* great, fantastic (b) *(gigantesque)* tremendous

formol [fɔrmɔl] *nm* formalin

formulaire [fɔrmylɛr] *nm* form; **remplir un f.** to fill in *ou* out a form; *Ordinat* **f. de saisie** input form

formulation [fɔrmylasjɔ̃] *nf* formulation, wording

formule [fɔrmyl] *nf* (a) *(expression)* phrase; **selon la f. consacrée** as the expression goes; **f. magique** magic formula; **f. de politesse** polite phrase; *(au début d'une lettre)* standard opening; *(à la fin d'une lettre)* standard ending (b) *(solution)* method; **nouvelle f.** *(menu, abonnement)* new-style (c) *(en mathématique, en chimie)* formula (d) *(automobile)* **f. 1/2** Formula 1/2

formuler [fɔrmyle] *vt* to formulate

forniquer [fɔrnike] *vi* to fornicate

FORPRONU [fɔrprɔny] *nf* (*abrév* **Forces de protection des Nations unies**) **la F.** UNPROFOR

forsythia [fɔrsisja] *nm* forsythia

fort, -e [fɔr, fɔrt] **1** *adj* (a) *(vigoureux)* strong; **f. comme un Turc** *ou* **un bœuf** as strong as an ox; **f. une forte tête** she's very strong-minded; **c'est plus f. que moi!** I can't help it!; *Fam* **c'est un peu f.!** that's a bit much!; **le plus f., c'est que...** the best of it is,... (b) *(doué)* **être f. en qch** to be good at sth (c) *(boisson, odeur, vent, lumière, accent)* strong; *(mer)* heavy; *(voix)* loud (d) *(robuste)* *(personne)* large (e) *(considérable)* *(somme d'argent)* large; *(pente)* steep; **il y a de fortes chances (pour) que ça réussisse** there's a good chance it will work
2 *adv* (a) *(parler, crier, chanter)* loud, loudly; *(frapper, taper)* hard; *(sentir)* strong; *Fam* **y aller f.** to overdo it; *Fam* **faire (très) f.** to do (really) brilliantly (b) *(très)* very (c) *(beaucoup)* very much; **avoir f. à faire (avec qn/qch)** to have one's work cut out (with sb/sth)
3 *nm* (a) *(spécialité)* strong point (b) *(citadelle)* fort (c) **au**

plus f. de qch *(hiver)* in the depths of sth; *(été, épidémie, tempête)* at the height of sth

fortement [fɔrtəmã] *adv* (a) *(avec force)* *(tirer, pousser)* hard (b) *(intensément)* *(désirer, souhaiter, influencer)* strongly; *(impressionner, irriter)* greatly; *(insister)* firmly (c) *(très)* *(épicé)* highly; *(conseillé)* strongly

forteresse [fɔrtərɛs] *nf* fortress

fortifiant, -e [fɔrtifjã, -ãt] **1** *adj* *(nourriture, boisson)* fortifying
2 *nm* tonic

fortification [fɔrtifikasjɔ̃] *nf* fortification

fortifier [66] [fɔrtifje] *vt* *(ville, mur)* to fortify; *(muscles, corps, sentiment)* to strengthen

fortuit, -e [fɔrtɥi, -it] *adj* chance, fortuitous

fortune [fɔrtyn] *nf* (a) *(richesse)* fortune; **faire f.** to make one's fortune (b) *(hasard)* fortune, chance; **de f.** *(moyens, installation)* makeshift; **faire contre mauvaise f. bon cœur** to make the best of it

fortuné, -e [fɔrtyne] *adj* *(riche)* wealthy

forum [fɔrɔm] *nm* forum

fosse [fos] *nf* (a) *(creux)* pit; **f. d'aisances** cesspool; **f. aux lions** lions' den; **f. d'orchestre** orchestra pit; **f. septique** septic tank (b) *(tombe)* grave; **f. commune** mass grave

fossé [fose] *nm* (le long de la route) ditch; *(autour d'un château)* moat; *Fig* *(entre personnes)* gulf

fossette [fosɛt] *nf* dimple

fossile [fosil] **1** *adj* fossil
2 *nm Fam aussi Fig* fossil

fossoyeur [foswajœr] *nm* gravedigger; *Fig* destroyer

fou, folle [fu, fɔl]

> **fol** is used before masculine singular nouns beginning with a vowel or h mute.

1 *adj* (a) *(dément)* mad, insane; **f. de joie** beside oneself with joy; **f. à lier** raving mad; **être f.** *(amoureux)* **de qn/qch** to be mad about sb/sth (b) *(énorme)* tremendous; *(prix)* exorbitant (c) *(incroyable)* incredible (d) *(train)* runaway; *(boussole, aiguille)* crazy; **f. rire** uncontrollable giggling; **avoir un** *ou* **le f. rire** to have the giggles
2 *nm, f* madman, *f* madwoman; *Fam* **comme un f.** like mad; **entrer/sortir comme un f.** to storm in/out; **faire le f.** to play *or* act the fool; **un f. furieux** a maniac; **un f. du volant** a reckless driver; *Prov* **plus on est de fous, plus on rit** the more the merrier
3 *nm* (a) *(aux échecs)* bishop (b) *(bouffon)* jester (c) **f. de Bassan** gannet

foudre [fudr] **1** *nf* lightning; *Litt* **s'attirer les foudres de qn** to bring down sb's wrath on one
2 *nm* **un f. de guerre** a great warrior; *Fig* **ce n'est pas un f. de guerre** he's no bright spark

foudroyant, -e [fudrwajã, -ãt] *adj* *(maladie)* violent; *(crise cardiaque)* massive; *(révélation, nouvelle)* devastating; *(succès)* stunning; *(vitesse, progrès)* lightning; *(regard)* withering

foudroyer [32] [fudrwaje] *vt* to strike; **être foudroyé** to be struck by lightning; **f. qn du regard** to give sb a withering look

fouet [fwɛ] *nm* *(pour punir)* whip; *(de cuisine)* whisk; **de plein f.** head-on

fouetter [fwete] **1** *vt* (**a**) *(punir)* to whip; *Fam* il n'y a pas de quoi f. un chat it's nothing to make a fuss about; *Fam* avoir d'autres chats à f. to have other fish to fry (**b**) *(cingler)* to lash (against) (**c**) *(battre) (œufs)* to beat, to whisk; *(crème)* to whip
 2 *vi Fam (puer)* to stink

foufou, fofolle [fufu, fɔfɔl] *adj Fam* daft

fougasse [fugas] *nf* = type of flat bread often made with olives, herbs, bacon etc

fougère [fuʒɛʀ] *nf* fern

fougue [fug] *nf* fire, spirit

fougueusement [fugøzmɑ̃] *adv (s'élancer)* impetuously; *(s'embrasser)* passionately

fougueux, -euse [fugø, -øz] *adj (personne, tempérament)* fiery, ardent; *(cheval)* spirited

fouille [fuj] *nf* (**a**) *(search)* faire une f. to make a search (**b**) fouilles *(archéologiques)* excavations, dig (**c**) *Fam (poche)* pocket

fouillé, -e [fuje] *adj (approfondi)* detailed

fouiller [fuje] **1** *vt* (**a**) *(maison, personne)* to search (**b**) *(problème)* to go thoroughly into
 2 *vi* to search (**dans** in)

fouillis [fuji] *nm* jumble, muddle

fouine [fwin] *nf* stone marten

fouiner [fwine] *vi* to nose about (**dans** in)

foulard [fular] *nm* scarf

foule [ful] *nf (de gens)* crowd; il ne supporte pas la f. he can't stand crowds; *Fig* une f. de qch lots of sth

foulée [fule] *nf (d'un coureur)* stride; *Fig* dans la f., j'ai vérifié les comptes while I was at it, I checked the accounts

fouler [fule] **1** *vt (sol)* to tread; *(raisins)* to press; *Fig* f. qch aux pieds to trample sth underfoot
 2 se fouler *vpr* (**a**) se f. la cheville to sprain one's ankle (**b**) *Fam (se fatiguer)* to strain oneself

foulure [fulyr] *nf* sprain

four [fur] *nm* (**a**) *(de cuisine)* oven; f. à gaz/électrique/à micro-ondes gas/electric/microwave oven; cuit au f. *(pain)* baked; *(viande)* roasted; il fait noir comme dans un f. it's pitch black; on ne peut être à la fois au f. et au moulin you can't be in two places at once (**b**) petits fours *(gâteaux)* petits fours (**c**) *(industriel)* kiln; *Hist* les fours crématoires the gas ovens (**d**) *Fam (fiasco)* flop; faire un f. to flop

fourbe [furb] **1** *adj* deceitful
 2 *nmf* cheat

fourbi [furbi] *nm Fam* (**a**) *(désordre)* mess (**b**) *(truc)* thingy

fourbu, -e [furby] *adj* exhausted

fourche [furʃ] *nf* (**a**) *(outil)* fork (**b**) *(de bicyclette, sur une route)* fork; *(des cheveux)* split end; faire une f. to fork

fourcher [furʃe] *vi* sa langue a fourché she made a slip of the tongue

fourchette [furʃɛt] *nf* (**a**) *(ustensile)* fork; *Fam* avoir un joli ou bon coup de f. to have a hearty appetite (**b**) *(écart)* bracket; f. de prix price bracket

fourchu, -e [furʃy] *adj* forked; avoir les cheveux fourchus to have split ends

fourgon [furgɔ̃] *nm* (**a**) *(véhicule)* van; f. cellulaire *Br* police van, *Am* patrol wagon; f. funèbre ou funéraire hearse (**b**) *(d'un train)* f. à bétail cattle truck

fourgonnette [furgɔnɛt] *nf* small van

fourguer [furge] *vt Fam* f. qch à qn to unload sth onto sb

fourmi [furmi] *nf* ant; *Fig (personne travailleuse)* busy bee; avoir des fourmis *(dans les jambes)* to have pins and needles (in one's legs)

fourmilière [furmiljɛr] *nf* anthill

fourmillement [furmijmɑ̃] *nm* (**a**) *(sensation)* pins and needles (**b**) *(agitation)* swarming

fourmiller [furmije] **1** *vi* to swarm, to teem
 2 fourmiller de *vt ind* to swarm with, to teem with

fournaise [furnɛz] *nf* furnace

fourneau, -x [furno] *nm* (**a**) *(de cuisine)* stove; être aux fourneaux to be cooking (**b**) *(de verrier, de fondeur)* furnace (**c**) *(d'une pipe)* bowl

fournée [furne] *nf aussi Fig* batch

fourni, -e [furni] *adj* (**a**) *(magasin)* bien/mal f. well/poorly stocked (**b**) *(barbe, sourcils)* bushy; peu f. sparse

fournil [furni] *nm* bakehouse

fournir [furnir] **1** *vt* (**a**) *(approvisionner)* to supply (**en** with) (**b**) *(procurer)* f. qch à qn to provide sb with sth (**c**) *(présenter) (preuve, alibi)* to provide; *(documents)* to provide; pièces à f. required documents (**d**) *(effort)* to make
 2 se fournir *vpr* se f. en qch to get in supplies of sth; se f. chez qn to get one's supplies from sb

fournisseur, -euse [furnisœr, -øz] *nm,f* supplier; *Ordinat* f. d'accès access provider

fournitures [furnityr] *nfpl* f. de bureau office supplies; f. scolaires educational stationery

fourrage [furaʒ] *nm* fodder

fourrager¹ [45] [furaʒe] *vi Fam (fouiller)* to rummage (**dans** in)

fourrager², -ère [furaʒe, -ɛr] *adj (plante)* fodder

fourreau, -x [furo] *nm* (**a**) *(d'épée)* sheath, scabbard; *(de parapluie)* cover (**b**) *(robe)* f. sheath dress; jupe f. pencil skirt

fourrer [fure] **1** *vt* (**a**) *(gâteau, bonbon)* to fill (**à** with); bonbon fourré *Br* soft-centred sweet, *Am* soft-centered candy (**b**) *Fam (mettre)* to stick
 2 se fourrer *vpr Fam* où est-il allé se f.? where's he got to?; ne pas savoir où se f. not to know where to put oneself; se f. dans une sale affaire to get involved in a nasty business

fourre-tout [furtu] **1** *adj inv (placard)* junk; un texte/une loi f. a ragbag of a text/a law
 2 *nm inv* (**a**) *(pièce)* junk room; *(placard)* junk cupboard (**b**) *(sac) Br* holdall, *Am* carryall

fourreur [furœr] *nm* furrier

fourrière [furjɛr] *nf* pound; mettre en f. ou à la f. *(voiture)* to impound; *(chien)* to put into the pound

fourrure [furyr] *nf* fur; de ou en f. fur

fourvoyer [32] [furvwaje] *Litt* se fourvoyer *vpr* to lose one's way; *Fig* to go astray

foutaise [futɛz] *nf Fam* bullshit

foutoir [futwar] *nm Fam* dump

foutre [futr] *très Fam* **1** *vt* (**a**) *(mettre)* to stick; f. qch par terre to chuck sth on the ground; f. qn à la porte to kick sb out; f. qch en l'air *(le faire échouer)* to screw sth up (**b**) *(faire)* to do; ne rien f. to do damn all; je n'en ai rien à f.! I couldn't give a damn!; qu'est-ce que ça peut f.? what the hell does it matter? (**c**) *(donner) (correction, gifle)* to give; f. la trouille à qn to put the wind up sb (**d**) *(locutions)* f. le camp to piss off; fous(-moi) le camp! piss off!; je t'en foutrais, du champagne! champagne, you'll be bloody lucky!; *Vulg* **va te faire f.!** fuck off!

2 se foutre *vpr* (**a**) (*se mettre*) **se f. un coup** to bang oneself; **se f. par terre** to go sprawling; **se f. dedans** to screw up (**b**) **se f. de (la gueule de) qn** (*se moquer de*) to take the piss out of sb; **se f. du monde** to take the piss (**c**) **se f. de qch** (*être indifférent à*) not to give a damn about sb/sth; **je m'en fous** I don't give a damn

foutu, -e [futy] *adj Fam* (**a**) (*maudit*) damn (**b**) (*en mauvais état, perdu*) **être f.** to have had it; **c'est f.!** forget it! (**c**) **être bien/mal f.** (*bien/mal bâti*) to have/not to have a nice body; (*bien/mal conçu*) to be well/badly designed; **être mal f.** (*malade*) to be under the weather (**d**) (*capable*) **être f. de faire qch** to be quite likely to do sth

fox [fɔks], **fox-terrier** (*pl* **fox-terriers**) [fɔksterje] *nm* fox terrier

foyer [fwaje] *nm* (**a**) (*domicile*) home; **le f. conjugal** the marital home (**b**) (*famille*) family (**c**) (*résidence*) (*d'étudiants*) residence; (*de travailleurs, de délinquants*) hostel (**d**) (*de chaleur, d'infection*) source; (*d'incendie, de conflits*) seat (**e**) (*âtre*) hearth (**f**) (*de lunettes*) focus

fracas [fraka] *nm* crash

fracassant, -e [frakasɑ̃, -ɑ̃t] *adj* (*bruit*) deafening; (*nouvelle, révélation*) shattering; (*succès*) resounding

fracasser [frakase] **1** *vt* to smash
  2 se fracasser *vpr* to smash

fraction [fraksjɔ̃] *nf* (**a**) (*partie*) part (**b**) *Math* fraction

fractionnement [fraksjɔnmɑ̃] *nm* splitting up

fractionner [fraksjɔne] **1** *vt* to split up
  2 se fractionner *vpr* to split up

fracture [fraktyr] *nf* fracture; **f. du crâne** fractured skull; *Fig* **la f. sociale** social fracture

fracturer [fraktyre] **1** *vt* (**a**) (*serrure, porte*) to break open (**b**) (*os*) to fracture
  2 se fracturer *vpr* **se f. le tibia** to fracture one's tibia

fragile [fraʒil] *adj* (*matériau, objet*) fragile; (*santé, estomac, équilibre*) delicate; (*personne*) (*physiquement*) frail; (*mentalement*) sensitive; (*bonheur*) precarious; (*hypothèse*) shaky

fragiliser [fraʒilize] *vt* to weaken

fragilité [fraʒilite] *nf* (*d'un matériau, d'un objet*) fragility; (*d'une personne*) (*physique*) frailty; (*mentale*) sensitivity; (*du bonheur*) precariousness; (*d'une hypothèse*) shakiness; (*de la santé, de l'estomac, d'un équilibre*) delicacy

fragment [fragmɑ̃] *nm* (*d'un objet, de conversation*) fragment; (*d'un livre*) extract; (*de vérité*) shred

fragmentaire [fragmɑ̃ter] *adj* fragmentary

fragmenter [fragmɑ̃te] *vt* to fragment

fraîche [frɛʃ] *adj voir* **frais¹**

fraîchement [frɛʃmɑ̃] *adv* (**a**) (*recevoir, accueillir*) coolly (**b**) (*récemment*) newly

fraîcheur [frɛʃœr] *nf* (*de la température, d'un accueil*) coolness; (*d'aliments, du teint*) freshness

fraîchir [frɛʃir] *vi* (*temps*) to freshen

frais¹, fraîche [frɛ, frɛʃ] **1** *adj* (**a**) (*vent, air, accueil*) cool (**b**) (*aliments, fleurs, teint*) fresh; **f. et dispos** hale and hearty (**c**) (*souvenir, nouvelles*) recent; (*encre, peinture*) wet
  2 *adv* **servir/boire f.** (*sur étiquette*) serve/drink chilled; **f. émoulu de** fresh out of
  3 *nm* **prendre le f.** to get a breath of fresh air; **mettre/conserver qch au f.** to put/keep sth in a cool place; **il fait f.** it's cool
  4 *nf* **à la fraîche** in the cool part of the day

frais² *nmpl* expenses, costs; **faire de gros f.** to go to great expense; **tous f. payés** all expenses paid; **rentrer dans ses f.** to cover one's expenses; *Fig* **faire les f. de qch** (*être victime de*) to pay the price for sth; **faire les f. de la conversation** to keep the conversation going; **faire qch à ses f.** to do sth at one's own expense; **aux f. de la société** at the company's expense; **aux f. de la princesse** at the firm's/government's/etc expense; **à grands/peu de f.** at great/little cost; **se mettre en f.** to go to great expense; **en être pour ses f.** to have been wasting one's time; **f. de déplacement** travelling expenses; **f. généraux** overheads; **f. d'inscription** membership fee; **f. de port** postage and packing; **f. de scolarité** school fees; **faux f.** incidental expenses

fraise¹ [frɛz] *nf* (*fruit*) strawberry; **f. des bois** wild strawberry

fraise² *nf* (*de dentiste*) drill

fraise³ *nf* (*collerette*) ruff

fraisier [frɛzje] *nm* (**a**) (*plante*) strawberry plant (**b**) (*gâteau*) strawberry cream cake

framboise [frɑ̃bwaz] *nf* raspberry

framboisier [frɑ̃bwazje] *nm* raspberry bush

franc¹ [frɑ̃] *nm* franc; **f. français/suisse/belge** French/Swiss/Belgian franc; **f. CFA** CFA franc; **ancien/nouveau f.** old/new franc; **f. symbolique** nominal sum

franc², franche [frɑ̃, frɑ̃ʃ] **1** *adj* (**a**) (*sincère*) frank (**b**) (*zone, ville, port*) free (**c**) (*net*) (*couleur*) pure; (*rupture*) clean
  2 *adv* (*parler*) frankly

français, -e [frɑ̃sɛ, -ɛz] **1** *adj* French
  2 *nm,f* **F.** Frenchman, *f* **Frenchwoman**; **les F.** the French
  3 *nm* (*langue*) French; **parler f.** to speak French; (*correctement*) to speak properly; *Fam* **tu ne comprends pas le f.?** don't you understand plain English?

France [frɑ̃s] *nf* la F. France; *TV* **F. 2/3** = second/third French state-owned TV channel

Francfort [frɑ̃kfɔr] *n* Frankfurt

franche [frɑ̃ʃ] *adj voir* **franc**

franchement [frɑ̃ʃmɑ̃] *adv* (**a**) (*sincèrement*) frankly (**b**) (*tout à fait, vraiment*) really (**c**) (*carrément*) **y aller f.** to get on with it

franchir [frɑ̃ʃir] *vt* (*obstacle, difficulté*) to get over; (*porte*) to go through; (*fossé*) to jump (over); (*ligne d'arrivée, rivière, frontière*) to cross; *Fig* (*cap, seuil, niveau*) to pass

franchise [frɑ̃ʃiz] *nf* (**a**) (*sincérité*) frankness; **en toute f.** quite frankly (**b**) (*exonération*) exemption; **f. postale** ≃ postage paid (**c**) (*d'assurance*) *Br* excess, *Am* deductible (**d**) *Com* franchise

franchouillard, -e [frɑ̃ʃujar, -ard] *adj Fam* typically French

franciscain, -e [frɑ̃siskɛ̃, -ɛn] *adj & nm,f* Franciscan

franciser [frɑ̃size] *vt* to gallicize

franc-maçon (*pl* **francs-maçons**) [frɑ̃masɔ̃] *nm* freemason

franc-maçonnerie [frɑ̃masɔnri] *nf* freemasonry

franco [frɑ̃ko] *adv* (**a**) *Fam* (*franchement*) **y aller f.** to get on with it (**b**) *Com* **f. (de port)** postage paid; **f. à bord** free on board

francophile [frɑ̃kɔfil] *adj & nmf* Francophile

francophobe [frɑ̃kɔfɔb] *adj & nmf* Francophobe

francophone [frɑ̃kɔfɔn] **1** *adj* French-speaking
  2 *nmf* French speaker

francophonie [frãkɔfɔni] *nf* French-speaking world

franc-parler [frãparle] *nm* outspokenness; **avoir son f.** to speak one's mind

franc-tireur (*pl* **francs-tireurs**) [frãtirœr] *nm* (*combattant*) irregular (soldier); *Fig* maverick

frange [frãʒ] *nf* fringe

frangin, -e [frãʒɛ̃, -in] *nm,f Fam* brother, *f* sister

frangipane [frãʒipan] *nf* = almond-flavoured confectioner's custard

franglais [frãglɛ] *nm* Franglais

franquette [frãkɛt] *nf* **à la bonne f.** without ceremony

frappant, -e [frapã, -ãt] *adj* striking

frappe [frap] *nf* (**a**) (*sur un clavier d'ordinateur*) keying; (*sur une machine à écrire*) typing; *Ordinat* **f. en continu** typeahead; *Ordinat* **f. au kilomètre** continuous input (**b**) (*de monnaie*) minting (**c**) (*au base-ball*) hit; (*au football*) kick; (*en boxe*) punch (**d**) *Fam* (*voyou*) hoodlum

frappé, -e [frape] *adj* (**a**) (*champagne*) chilled; (*café*) iced (**b**) *Fam* (*fou*) crazy

frapper [frape] **1** *vt* (**a**) (*donner un ou des coups à*) to hit, to strike; *Fig* (*faire une forte impression sur*) to strike (**b**) (*monnaie*) to mint (**c**) (*champagne*) to put on ice
2 *vi* (*donner un coup*) to strike, to hit; **f. du poing sur la table** to bang (on) the table; **f. des mains** *ou* **dans ses mains** to clap (one's hands); **f. à la porte** to knock on or at the door; *Fig* **tu frappes à la bonne/mauvaise porte** you've come to the right/wrong place; **entrez sans f.** (*sur écriteau*) go straight in (**b**) *Fam* (*agir*) to strike
3 se frapper *vpr Fam* (*se faire du souci*) to get oneself worked up

frasques [frask] *nfpl* carryings-on

fraternel, -elle [fraternel] *adj* fraternal, brotherly

fraterniser [fraternize] *vi* to fraternize

fraternité [fraternite] *nf* fraternity, brotherhood

fratricide [fratrisid] **1** *adj* fratricidal
2 *nmf* (*personne*) fratricide
3 *nm* (*crime*) fratricide

fraude [frod] *nf* fraud; **passer qch en f.** to smuggle sth in; **f. électorale** electoral fraud; **f. fiscale** tax evasion

frauder [frode] **1** *vt* (*douane*) to defraud; **f. le fisc** to evade tax
2 *vi* to cheat (**sur** on)

fraudeur, -euse [frodœr, -øz] *nm,f* defrauder

frauduleux, -euse [frodylø, -øz] *adj* fraudulent

frayer [53] [freje] **1** *vi* (*poisson*) to spawn; *Fig* **f. avec qn** to mix with sb
2 se frayer *vpr* **se f. un chemin** to clear a way (for oneself)

frayeur [frejœr] *nf* fright; **faire une f. à qn** to give sb a fright

fredaines [frɔden] *nfpl* pranks, escapades

fredonner [frɔdɔne] *vt & vi* to hum

free-lance [frilɑ̃s] **1** *adj inv* freelance
2 *nm* (*travail*) freelance work; **travailler en f.** to work freelance
3 *nmf* (*pl* **free-lances**) freelance, freelancer

freezer [frizœr] *nm* freezer compartment

frégate [fregat] *nf* (**a**) (*oiseau*) frigate bird (**b**) (*navire*) frigate

frein [frɛ̃] *nm* (**a**) (*de voiture*) brake; **donner un coup de f.** to put on the brakes; *Fig* **mettre un f. à qch** to curb sth; **freins à disque** disc brakes; **f. à main** *Br* handbrake, *Am* parking brake; **f. moteur** engine brake (**b**) (*mors*) bit

freinage [frenaʒ] *nm* braking

freiner [frene] **1** *vt* (**a**) (*véhicule, processus*) to slow down; (*chute*) to break; (*inflation, production*) to curb (**b**) (*personne*) to restrain
2 *vi* to brake

frelaté, -e [frɔlate] *adj* (*vin*) adulterated

frelater [frɔlate] *vt* to adulterate

frêle [frɛl] *adj* frail

frelon [frɔlɔ̃] *nm* hornet

freluquet [frɔlykɛ] *nm Fam* whippersnapper

frémir [fremir] *vi* (**a**) (*personne*) to tremble (**de** with) (**b**) (*eau chaude*) to simmer; (*feuillage*) to rustle

frémissant, -e [fremisã, -ãt] *adj* (*eau*) simmering; (*voix*) trembling; (*feuillage*) rustling

frémissement [fremismã] *nm* (**a**) (*de peur*) shudder; (*de plaisir, de joie*) thrill; (*de colère, d'impatience*) quiver (**b**) (*de l'eau*) simmering; (*des feuilles*) rustle

french cancan (*pl* **french cancans**) [frenʃkɑ̃kɑ̃] *nm* cancan

frêne [fren] *nm* ash

frénésie [frenezi] *nf* frenzy

frénétique [frenetik] *adj* frenzied

frénétiquement [frenetikmã] *adv* frenziedly

fréquemment [frekamã] *adv* frequently

fréquence [frekãs] *nf* frequency; **basse/haute f.** low/high frequency

fréquent, -e [frekã, -ãt] *adj* frequent

fréquentable [frekãtabl] *adj* **des gens peu fréquentables** people you wouldn't want to associate with

fréquentation [frekãtasjɔ̃] *nf* (**a**) (*d'un lieu*) frequenting; **la f. de qn** seeing sb regularly (**b**) **fréquentations** (*relations*) company; **avoir de mauvaises fréquentations** to keep bad company

fréquenté, -e [frekãte] *adj* **très f.** very busy; **bien/mal f.** of good/ill repute

fréquenter [frekãte] **1** *vt* (**a**) (*lieu*) to frequent (**b**) (*personne*) (*voir régulièrement*) to see regularly; (*sortir avec*) to go out with
2 se fréquenter *vpr* (*se voir régulièrement*) to see each other regularly; (*sortir ensemble*) to go out with each other

frère [frer] **1** *adj* (*pays, peuple*) fellow
2 *nm* brother; **faux f.** false friend; **frères d'armes** brothers-in-arms

frérot [frero] *nm Fam* kid brother

fresque [fresk] *nf* fresco

fret [frɛ, frɛt] *nm* freight

frétillant, -e [fretijã, -ãt] *adj* (*poisson*) wriggling; (*personne*) (*de joie*) quivering (**de** with)

frétiller [fretije] *vi* (*poisson, personne*) to wriggle; **f. de joie** to quiver with joy

fretin [frɔtɛ̃] *nm aussi Fig* **menu f.** small fry

freudien, -enne [frødjɛ̃, -en] *adj* Freudian

freux [frø] *nm* rook

FRF (*abrév* **franc(s) français**) FF

friable [frijabl] *adj* crumbly

friand, -e [frijɑ̃, -ɑ̃d] **1** adj être f. de qch to be fond of sth
2 nm (salé) = small savoury pastry; (sucré) = small almond cake

friandise [frijɑ̃diz] nf titbit, delicacy

fric [frik] nm Fam dough

fricassée [frikase] nf (ragoût) fricassee; Belg fried egg and bacon

friche [friʃ] nf fallow land; **en f.** fallow; **f. industrielle** industrial wasteland

frichti [friʃti] nm Fam grub

fricot [friko] nm Fam grub; **faire le f.** to do the cooking

fricoter [frikote] Fam **1** vt (a) (manigancer) to cook up (b) (plat) to cook
2 vi (avoir des activités suspectes) to be on the fiddle

friction [friksjɔ̃] nf (a) (massage) rubdown; (du cuir chevelu) scalp massage (b) (heurt) friction

frictionner [friksjɔne] vt (partie du corps) to rub; (personne) to rub down

Frigidaire® [friʒidɛr] nm fridge

frigide [friʒid] adj frigid

frigidité [friʒidite] nf frigidity

frigo [frigo] nm Fam fridge

frigorifié, -e [frigɔrifje] adj Fam (personne) frozen stiff

frigorifier [66] [frigɔrifje] vt (aliment) to refrigerate

frigorifique [frigɔrifik] adj voir **camion**

frileux, -euse [frilø, -øz] adj (personne) sensitive to the cold; (attitude, réponse) timid

frime [frim] nf Fam show

frimer [frime] vi Fam to show off

frimeur, -euse [frimœr, -øz] nm,f Fam show-off

frimousse [frimus] nf Fam sweet little face

fringale [frɛ̃gal] nf Fam (faim) hunger; Fig (envie) craving (de for); **avoir la f.** to be starving

fringant, -e [frɛ̃gɑ̃, -ɑ̃t] adj (personne) dashing

fringuer [frɛ̃ge] Fam **1** vt to dress
2 se fringuer vpr to get dressed

fringues [frɛ̃g] nfpl Fam gear

fripé, -e [fripe] adj crumpled

friper [fripe] **1** vt to crumple
2 se friper vpr to get crumpled

friperie [fripri] nf second-hand clothes shop

fripes [frip] nfpl second-hand clothes

fripier, -ère [fripje, -ɛr] nm,f second-hand clothes dealer

fripon, -onne [fripɔ̃, -ɔn] Fam **1** adj mischievous
2 nm,f rascal

fripouille [fripuj] nf Fam rogue

friqué, -e [frike] adj Fam loaded

frire [19a] [frir] **1** vt to fry
2 vi to fry; **faire f. qch** to fry sth

Frisbee® [frizbi] nm Frisbee®

frise [friz] nf frieze

frisé, -e [frize] **1** adj (cheveux) curly; (personne) curly-haired
2 nf frisée (salade) curly endive

friser [frize] **1** vt (a) (cheveux) to curl (b) (approcher) **f. la catastrophe** to come within an inch of disaster
2 vi (cheveux) to curl; (personne) to have curly hair

frisette [frizɛt] nf (de cheveux) small curl

frisotter [frizɔte] **1** vt (cheveux) to frizz
2 vi to be frizzy

frisquet, -ette [friskɛ, -ɛt] adj Fam chilly; **il fait f.** it's chilly

frisson [frisɔ̃] nm (de froid, de peur) shiver; (de plaisir) thrill; **avoir des frissons** to shiver; **donner des frissons** ou **le f. à qn** (de peur) to give sb the shivers

frissonner [frisɔne] vi (a) (personne) (de froid, de peur) to shiver (b) Litt (feuillage) to quiver; (eau) to ripple

frit, -e [fri, frit] **1** adj fried
2 nf frite (a) (de pomme de terre) Br chip, Am (French) fry (b) Fam **avoir la frite** to be on form

friteuse [fritøz] nf deep frier, Br chip pan; **f. électrique** electric frier

friture [frityr] nf (a) (mode de cuisson) frying (b) (corps gras) frying fat (c) (aliments) fried food; **f. (de poissons)** fried fish (d) Rad & Tél crackling (e) Belg (friterie) Br chip stall, Am French fry vendor

frivole [frivol] adj frivolous

frivolité [frivolite] nf frivolity

froc [frok] nm (a) Fam (pantalon) Br trousers, Am pants (b) (habit religieux) habit

froid, -e [frwa, frwad] **1** adj aussi Fig cold
2 adv **boire/manger qch f.** to drink/eat sth cold
3 nm cold; **les grands froids** the coldest part of the winter; **il fait f.** it's cold; Fam **il fait un f. de canard** it's freezing (cold); Fig **ça fait f. dans le dos** it sends a shiver down your spine; **avoir f.** to be cold; **j'ai f. aux mains** my hands are cold, I've got cold hands; Fig **ne pas avoir f. aux yeux** to be brave; Fig **à f.** (répondre) off the top of one's head; (humour) deadpan; **être en f. (avec qn)** to be on bad terms (with sb); **prendre f.** to catch cold

froidement [frwadmɑ̃] adv (accueillir, recevoir) coldly; (abattre) cold-bloodedly; (répondre) coolly

froideur [frwadœr] nf coldness; Fig (de réponse) coldness

froissement [frwasmɑ̃] nm (a) (bruit) rustle (b) (de muscle) straining

froisser [frwase] **1** vt (a) (tissu, papier) to crumple, to crease (b) Fig (sentiment, personne) to offend
2 se froisser vpr (a) (tissu) to crease, to crumple (b) **se f. un muscle** to strain a muscle (c) Fig (personne) to take offence (**de** at)

frôlement [frolmɑ̃] nm (contact) brushing (**contre** against); (son) rustle

frôler [frole] **1** vt (a) (effleurer) to brush (against), to touch lightly (b) Fig (la mort, la catastrophe) to come close to; (le ridicule) to border on
2 se frôler vpr to brush (against) each other

fromage [frɔmaʒ] nm (a) (produit laitier) cheese; Fam Fig **faire tout un f. de qch** to make a great fuss about sth; **f. blanc** fromage frais; **f. de chèvre** goat's cheese; **f. frais** soft cheese; **f. à pâte molle/dure** soft/hard cheese; **f. à tartiner** cheese spread (b) **f. de tête** Br brawn, Am headcheese

fromager, -ère [frɔmaʒe, -ɛr] **1** adj cheese
2 nm,f (commerçant) cheese seller; (fabricant) cheesemaker

fromagerie [frɔmaʒri] nf (lieu de fabrication) cheese dairy; (magasin) cheese shop

froment [frɔmɑ̃] nm wheat

fronce [frɔ̃s] nf gather

froncement [frɔ̃smɑ̃] nm **f. de(s) sourcils** frown

froncer [16] [frɔ̃se] vt (nez, front) to wrinkle; **f. les sourcils** to frown (b) (tissu) to gather

fronde [frɔ̃d] nf (a) (arme) sling; (jouet) Br catapult, Am slingshot (b) (révolte) rebellion

frondeur, -euse [frɔ̃dœr, -øz] **1** adj rebellious
2 nf, f rebel

front [frɔ̃] nm (a) (partie du visage) forehead (b) (avant) front; **faire f.** to face up to things; **faire f. à qn/qch** to face up to sb/sth; **de f.** (marcher, avancer) side by side; (heurter, aborder un problème) head-on; **mener plusieurs choses de f.** to have several things on the go at once; **f. de mer** seafront (c) (audace) **avoir le f. de faire qch** to have the nerve to do sth (d) Mil & Météo front

frontal, -e, -aux, -ales [frɔ̃tal, -o] adj (a) (attaque, choc) head-on; **machine à laver à chargement f.** front-loading washing machine (b) Ordinat front-end; **ordinateur f.** front end (c) (os) frontal

frontalier, -ère [frɔ̃talje, -er] **1** adj (région) border, frontier
2 nm, f (habitant) person living near the border; (travailleur) cross-border commuter

frontière [frɔ̃tjer] **1** adj (ville, poste) border, frontier
2 nf (entre pays) border, frontier; Fig (des langues) boundary; (de la connaissance) frontier

frontispice [frɔ̃tispis] nm frontispiece

fronton [frɔ̃tɔ̃] nm (a) (sur monument) pediment (b) (de pelote basque) fronton

frottement [frɔtmã] nm (a) (d'une chose contre une autre) rubbing; Tech friction (b) (heurt) friction

frotter [frɔte] **1** vt to rub; (allumette) to strike; (parquet) to scrub
2 vi to rub (contre against)
3 se frotter vpr to rub oneself; aussi Fig **se f. les mains** to rub one's hands; Fig **se f. à qn/qch** to be in contact with sb/sth; Fig **se f. à qn** (l'attaquer) to meddle with sb

frottis [frɔti] nm Méd smear; **f. vaginal** cervical smear

froufrou [frufru] nm (a) (bruit) rustling (b) froufrous (vêtements) frills

froufrouter [frufrute] vi to rustle

froussard, -e [frusar, -ard] adj & nm, f Fam chicken

frousse [frus] nf Fam fear; **avoir la f.** to be scared

fructifier [66] [fryktifje] vi (arbres, idée) to bear fruit; (terre) to be productive; (placements, capital) to yield a profit; **faire f. qch** (idée, projet) to bring sth to fruition

fructose [fryktoz] nm fructose

fructueux, -euse [fryktɥø, -øz] adj fruitful, profitable

frugal, -e, -aux, -ales [frygal, -o] adj frugal

frugalité [frygalite] nf frugality

fruit [frɥi] nm aussi Fig fruit; **des fruits** (some) fruit; **un f.** some fruit, a piece of fruit; **fruits confits** crystallized fruit; Fig **le f. défendu** the forbidden fruit; **fruits de mer** seafood; **f. de la passion** passion fruit; **fruits rouges** red berries and currants; **fruits secs** dried fruit

fruité, -e [frɥite] adj fruity

fruitier, -ère [frɥitje, -er] **1** adj voir **arbre**
2 nm, f fruit seller, Br fruiterer

frusques [frysk] nfpl Fam gear

fruste [fryst] adj (style, personne) rough

frustrant, -e [frystrã, -ãt] adj frustrating

frustration [frystrasjɔ̃] nf frustration

frustré, -e [frystre] **1** adj frustrated
2 nm, f frustrated person

frustrer [frystre] vt (a) (décevoir) to frustrate (b) (priver) **f. qn de qch** to deprive sb of sth

FTP [eftepe] nmpl (abrév **Francs-tireurs et partisans**) = French Communist resistance group in the Second World War

fuchsia [fyʃja] **1** adj inv (rose) f. fuchsia
2 nm (fleur, couleur) fuchsia

fuel [fjul] nm fuel oil

fugace [fygas] adj fleeting

fugitif, -ive [fyʒitif, -iv] **1** adj (fugace) fleeting
2 nm, f fugitive, runaway

fugue [fyg] nf (a) (composition musicale) fugue (b) (d'un enfant) **faire une f.** to run away

fuguer [fyge] vi to run away

fugueur, -euse [fygœr, -øz] **1** adj who runs away a lot
2 nm, f runaway

fui voir **fuir**

fuir [38] [fɥir] **1** vt (pays) to flee; (personne) to run away from; (guerre) to escape; (responsabilités) to shirk
2 vi (a) (s'échapper) to run away; to flee (devant from); **f. de son pays** to flee one's country (b) (robinet, gaz, eau) to leak (c) (s'écouler rapidement) to fly by

fuis, fuit voir **fuir**

fuite [fɥit] nf (a) (escapade) flight (devant from); Fig (devant des difficultés, des problèmes) avoidance (devant of); **prendre la f.** to take flight; **être en f.** to be on the run; **mettre qn en f.** to put sb to flight; **la f. des capitaux** the flight of capital; **la f. des cerveaux** the brain drain (b) (de liquide, de gaz, d'information) leak

fulgurant, -e [fylgyrã, -ãt] adj (a) (attaque, changement, rapidité) lightning; (succès) spectacular (b) (douleur) searing

fulminer [fylmine] vi to fulminate (contre against)

fumant, -e [fymã, -ãt] adj (a) (âtre, cendres) smoking; (potage) steaming (b) Fam (remarquable) **faire un coup f.** to pull off a masterstroke

fumé, -e [fyme] adj (a) (poisson, viande) smoked (b) (verres) tinted

fume-cigare [fymsigar] nm inv cigar holder

fumée [fyme] nf (de feu, de cigarette) smoke; (d'un liquide chaud) steam

fumer [fyme] **1** vt (a) (poisson, viande) to smoke (b) (tabac, cigarette) to smoke; **f. la pipe** to smoke a pipe
2 vi (a) (feu, moteur) to smoke; (liquide, plat) to steam (b) (fumeur) to smoke; **f. comme un pompier** ou **un sapeur** to smoke like a chimney

fumet [fyme] nm (d'un mets) aroma

fumeur, -euse [fymœr, -øz] nm, f smoker; **fumeurs** (sur panneau) smoking

fumeux, -euse [fymø, -øz] adj (idées, explications, projets) hazy

fumier [fymje] nm (a) (engrais) manure, dung (b) très Fam (injure) bastard

fumigation [fymigasjɔ̃] nf fumigation; Méd inhalation

fumiste [fymist] **1** nmf Fam (sur qui on ne peut compter) clown
2 nm (technicien) heating engineer
3 adj Fam unreliable

fumisterie [fymistəri] nf (a) (métier) heating engineering (b) Fam (farce) con

fumoir [fymwar] nm smoking room

funambule [fynãbyl] nmf tightrope walker

funboard [fœnbord] nm funboard

funèbre [fynɛbr] adj (a) (cérémonie, marche) funeral; **hymne** ou **chant f.** dirge (b) (lugubre) funereal

funérailles [fyneraj] *nfpl* funeral; **f. nationales** state funeral

funéraire [fynerɛr] *adj (dépenses, urne)* funeral; **pierre f.** tombstone, gravestone

funeste [fynɛst] *adj* (a) *(erreur, conséquences, influence)* disastrous (b) *Litt (accident)* fatal

funiculaire [fynikylɛr] *nm* funicular (railway)

fur [fyr] *nm* **au f. et à mesure** as one goes along, bit by bit; **au f. et à mesure de leurs recherches** as they progressed with their research

furax [fyraks] *adj inv Fam* livid

furet [fyrɛ] *nm* ferret

fureter [39] [fyrte] *vi (chercher)* to ferret about

fureur [fyrœr] *nf* (a) *(colère)* fury, rage (b) *(passion)* passion; **faire f.** to be all the rage

furibard, -e [fyribar, -ard] *adj Fam* livid

furibond, -e [fyribɔ̃, -ɔ̃d] *adj* furious

furie [fyri] *nf* (a) *(rage)* fury; **en f.** infuriated; **la f. du jeu** a passion for gambling (b) *Fig (femme)* shrew; **comme une f.** like a wild thing

furieux, -euse [fyrjø, -øz] *adj* (a) *(en colère)* furious (contre with); *Fig (tempête)* raging; *(combat)* violent (b) *Fam (intense) (envie)* tremendous

furoncle [fyrɔ̃kl] *nm* boil

furtif, -ive [fyrtif, -iv] *adj* furtive, stealthy

furtivement [fyrtivmɑ̃] *adv* furtively, stealthily; **entrer f.** to sneak in

fusain [fyzɛ̃] *nm (crayon, dessin)* charcoal

fuseau, -x [fyzo] *nm* (a) *(pantalon)* ski pants (b) *(pour filer la laine)* spindle; *(pour faire de la dentelle)* bobbin (c) **f. horaire** time zone

fusée [fyze] *nf* (a) *(projectile)* rocket **il est parti comme une f.** he shot off like a rocket; **f. éclairante** flare (b) *(d'axe)* spindle; *Aut* stub axle

fuselage [fyzlaʒ] *nm (d'un avion)* fuselage

fuselé, -e [fyzle] *adj (colonne, doigts)* tapering; *(voiture)* streamlined

fuser [fyze] *vi* **des rires/cris fusèrent de toutes parts** laughter was/cries were suddenly heard from all sides

fusible [fyzibl] *nm* fuse

fusil [fyzi] *nm* (a) *(arme)* gun, rifle; **f. à air comprimé** air gun; **f. de chasse** shotgun; **f. à lunette** rifle with telescopic sight; *Fig* **changer son f. d'épaule** to change tack; **coup de f.** gunshot; *Fam* **c'est le coup de f. dans ce restaurant** the prices in this restaurant are extortionate (b) *(personne)* shot (c) *(pour aiguiser)* steel

fusilier [fyzilje] *nm* fusilier; **f. marin** marine

fusillade [fyzijad] *nf (tir)* gunfire

fusiller [fyzije] *vt* (a) *(par un peloton d'exécution)* to shoot *Fig* **f. qn du regard** to look daggers at sb (b) *Fam (abîmer)* to wreck

fusil-mitrailleur *(pl* **fusils-mitrailleurs)** [fyzimitrajœr] *nm* light machine-gun

fusion [fyzjɔ̃] *nf* (a) *(par la chaleur)* melting, *Spéc* fusion; *(en métallurgie)* smelting; **point de f.** melting point; **métal/roche en f.** molten metal/rock (b) *(de sociétés)* merger; *Ordinat* **f. de fichiers** file merge

fusionner [fyzjone] *vi & vt aussi Ordinat* to merge

fustiger [45] [fystiʒe] *vt (critiquer)* to castigate

fût [fy] *nm* (a) *(tonneau)* cask, barrel (b) *(d'arbre)* bole (c) *(de colonne)* shaft (d) *(de fusil)* stock

futaie [fytɛ] *nf* forest *(producing timber from full-grown trees)*

futal, -als [fytal] *nm*, **fute** [fyt] *nm Fam Br* trousers, *Am* pants

futé, -e [fyte] **1** *adj* crafty
2 *nmf* crafty devil

futile [fytil] *adj (argument, occupation, prétexte)* trivial, trifling; *(personne)* frivolous

futilement [fytilmɑ̃] *adv* frivolously

futilité [fytilite] *nf* triviality

futur, -e [fytyr] **1** *adj* future; **un f. artiste** a budding artist; **mon f. emploi/appartement** my next job/flat; **mon f. mari** my husband-to-be
2 *nmf Hum* **mon f./ma future** my intended
3 *nm* (a) *(avenir)* future (b) *Gram* future (tense); **au f.** in the future (tense); **f. antérieur** future perfect

futurisme [fytyrism] *nm* futurism

futuriste [fytyrist] **1** *adj* futuristic
2 *nmf* futurist

fuyant, -e [fɥijɑ̃, -ɑ̃t] *adj* (a) *(ligne, menton)* receding; **lignes fuyantes** perspective lines (b) *(personne, attitude)* evasive; *(yeux)* shifty

fuyard, -e [fɥijar, -ard] *nm,f* fugitive, runaway

fuyez *etc voir* **fuir**

G

G, g [ʒe] *nm inv* G, g; **le G7** the G7

g. (a) (*abrév* **gauche**) L (b) (*abrév* **gramme(s)**) g

gabardine [gabardin] *nf* gabardine

gabarit [gabari] *nm* (a) (*dimension*) size (b) *Fam* (*corpulence*) **un grand/petit g.** a huge/tiny man, *f* woman (c) (*valeur*) calibre (d) (*instrument*) gauge (e) *Ordinat* template

Gabon [gabɔ̃] *nm* **le G.** Gabon

gabonais, -e [gabɔnɛ, -ɛz] **1** *adj* Gabonese
2 *nm,f* G. Gabonese

gâcher [gaʃe] *vt* (a) (*gaspiller*) to waste (b) (*gâter*) (*plaisir, soirée*) to spoil (c) (*mélanger*) (*mortier, plâtre*) to mix

gâchette [gaʃɛt] *nf* trigger; *Fam* **avoir la g. facile** to be trigger-happy; **appuyer sur la g.** to pull the trigger

gâchis [gaʃi] *nm* waste

gadget [gadʒɛt] *nm* gadget

gadoue [gadu] *nf* mud

gaélique [gaelik] *adj & nm* Gaelic

gaffe [gaf] *nf* (a) *Fam* (*maladresse*) blunder; **faire une g.** to put one's foot in it (b) (*perche*) boathook (c) *Fam* **faire g.** to pay attention

gaffer [gafe] **1** *vt* (*objet flottant*) to hook; (*poisson*) to gaff
2 *vi Fam* to put one's foot in it

gaffeur, -euse [gafœr, -øz] *nm,f Fam* blunderer

gag [gag] *nm* gag

gaga [gaga] *adj Fam* gaga

gage [gaʒ] *nm* (a) (*chez le prêteur sur gages*) pledge; *Fig* (*garantie*) guarantee; **laisser qch en g.** to leave sth as security; **mettre qch en g.** to pawn sth (b) (*preuve*) token; **en g. de notre amitié** as a token of our friendship (c) (*dans un jeu*) forfeit (d) *Vieilli* (*salaire*) **gages** wages

gager [45] [gaʒe] *vt Litt* **g. que...** to wager that...

gageure [gaʒyr] *nf* (a) (*action difficile*) challenge (b) *Litt* (*pari*) wager

gagnant, -e [gaɲɑ̃, -ɑ̃t] **1** *adj* winning
2 *nm,f* winner; **partir g.** to have a strong probability of winning

gagne-pain [gaɲpɛ̃] *nm inv* livelihood

gagne-petit [gaɲpəti] *nm,f inv* low wage earner

gagner [gaɲe] **1** *vt* (a) (*remporter*) (*course, prix, guerre*) to win; **rien n'est encore gagné** it's not in the bag yet! (b) (*comme rémunération*) to earn; **g. sa vie** to earn one's living (c) (*obtenir*) to gain; **g. du temps** (*aller plus vite*) to save time; (*temporiser*) to gain time; **g. de l'espace** to save space; **chercher à g. du temps** to play for time; **c'est toujours ça de gagné** that's something, anyway; **tu as tout à g.** you've got everything to gain; **et moi, qu'est-ce que j'y gagne?** and what do I get out of it? (d) (*se*

concilier) **g. qn à une cause** to win sb over to a cause; **g. la confiance/l'estime de qn** to win *or* gain sb's confidence/respect (e) (*atteindre*) (*ville, sortie, porte*) to reach, to get to; (*sujet: maladie, infection*) to spread to; (*sujet: sentiment, sommeil*) to overcome; **le rire gagna l'assemblée tout entière** laughter spread through the whole audience (f) (*s'étendre à*) (*sujet: feu, épidémie*) to spread to; **g. du vitesse** to outstrip sb

2 *vi* (a) (*être vainqueur*) to win; **g. haut la main** to win hands down (b) (*profiter*) **g. à qch/à faire qch** to benefit from sth/from doing sth; **g. à être connu** to improve with acquaintance; **j'ai gagné au change** I got the best of the deal (c) (*croître*) to increase; **g. en intensité/en vigueur** to increase in intensity/in strength

gagneur, -euse [gaɲœr, -øz] *nm,f* winner

gai, -e [ge] *adj* cheerful; **g. comme un pinson** happy as a lark; *Fam* **être un peu g.** (*ivre*) to be tipsy; *Ironique* **ça va être g.!** that'll be fun!

gaiement [gemɑ̃] *adv* cheerfully; *Ironique* **allons-y g.!** let's get on with it!

gaieté [gete] *nf* cheerfulness, gaiety; **je ne le fais pas de g. de cœur** I don't enjoy doing it

gaillard, -e [gajar, -ard] **1** *adj* (a) (*vigoureux*) (*personne*) strong; (*vieillard*) sprightly (b) (*jovial*) (*humeur*) merry; (*grivois*) (*histoire, commentaire*) bawdy
2 *nm* (a) (*homme*) hearty type; **un grand et solide g.** a great strapping man; **toi mon g., tu ne perds rien pour attendre!** just you wait, chum! (b) *Naut* **g. d'avant** forecastle; **g. d'arrière** poop

gaiment [gemɑ̃] = **gaiement**

gain [gɛ̃] *nm* (a) (*succès*) winning; **avoir *ou* obtenir g. de cause** to win one's case; **donner g. de cause à qn** to decide in favour of sb (b) (*profit*) gain, profit; **l'appât du g.** the lure of money (c) (*économie*) **ça fait un sacré g. de temps/de place** that saves an awful lot of time/space (d) (*au jeu*) **gains** winnings; (*à la Bourse*) profit

gaine [gɛn] *nf* (a) (*étui*) sheath (b) *Anat & Bot* sheath (c) (*sous-vêtement*) girdle

gainer [gene] *vt* to sheathe (**de** in)

Gal *Mil* (*abrév* **Général**) Gen

gala [gala] *nm* gala; **en habit *ou* tenue de g.** in gala dress; *Fig* in one's best clothes

galamment [galamɑ̃] *adv* gallantly

galant, -e [galɑ̃, -ɑ̃t] **1** *adj* (*homme*) gallant; **rendez-vous g.** romantic rendezvous
2 *nm Vieilli & Litt* gallant

galanterie [galɑ̃tri] *nf* gallantry; **dire des galanteries à qn** to pay sb compliments

Galapagos [galapagos] *nfpl* **les (îles) G.** the Galapagos (Islands)

galaxie [galaksi] *nf* galaxy

galbe [galb] *nm* curve

galbé, -e [galbe] *adj* shapely

gale [gal] *nf* (a) *Méd* scabies; *Fig* **je n'ai pas la g.!** I haven't got the plague! (b) *(de chien, de chat)* mange (c) *Bot* scab

galère [galɛr] *nf* (a) *(navire)* galley (b) *Fam (situation pénible)* hassle; **je me suis mis dans une g. pas possible** I got myself into a terrible mess; **être dans la même g.** to be in the same boat

galérer [34] [galere] *vi Fam* to have a hard time

galerie [galri] *nf* (a) *(passage, salle)* gallery; *Can (véranda)* porch; **g. d'art/de portraits** art/portrait gallery; **g. marchande** shopping arcade, *Am* mall (b) *(dans une mine)* gallery; *(de taupe)* tunnel (c) *(de voiture)* roof rack (d) *(de théâtre)* balcony; *Fig* **c'est pour (épater) la g.** it's just showing off

galérien [galerjɛ̃] *nm* galley slave

galet [galɛ] *nm* (a) *(caillou)* pebble; **plage de galets** shingle beach (b) *Tech* roller

galette [galɛt] *nf* (a) *(crêpe de blé noir)* buckwheat pancake; **g. des Rois** Twelfth Night cake (b) *(biscuit rond sablé)* butter biscuit (c) *Fam (argent)* dough

galeux, -euse [galø, -øz] *adj (chien)* mangy; *(mur)* peeling

Galice [galis] *nf* **la G.** Galicia

galicien, -enne [galisjɛ̃, -ɛn] **1** *adj* Galician **2** *nm,f* **G.** Galician

Galilée¹ [galile] *nf (région)* **la G.** Galilee

Galilée² *npr* Galileo

galimatias [galimatja] *nm* gibberish

galion [galjɔ̃] *nm* galleon

galipette [galipɛt] *nf Fam* somersault; **faire des galipettes** to do somersaults; *(ébats amoureux)* to have a bit of slap and tickle

galipote [galipɔt] *nf Can* **courir la g.** to chase women

Galles [gal] *voir* **pays**

gallicisme [galisism] *nm* Gallicism

gallois, -e [galwa, -az] **1** *adj* Welsh **2** *nm,f* **G.** Welshman, *f* Welshwoman; **les G.** the Welsh **3** *nm (langue)* Welsh

gallon [galɔ̃] *nm* gallon

gallo-romain, -e [galoromɛ̃, -ɛn] *(mpl* **gallo-romains,** *fpl* **gallo-romaines)** [galorɔmɛ̃, -ɛn] *adj* Gallo-Roman

galoche [galɔʃ] *nf* clog *(with leather upper)*

galon [galɔ̃] *nm (en couture)* braid (b) *(de militaire)* stripe; *Fam* **prendre du g.** to get promoted

galop [galo] *nm* gallop; **au g.** at a gallop; *Fig* **allez, au travail et au g.!** come on, to work, and be quick about it!; **g. d'essai** trial run

galopade [galopad] *nf* (a) *(de cheval)* gallop (b) *(de personnes)* stampede

galopant, -e [galopã, -ãt] *adj (inflation)* galloping; **phtisie galopante** galloping consumption

galoper [galope] *vi* to gallop

galopin [galopɛ̃] *nm Fam* urchin; **espèce de petit g.!** you little rascal!

galure [galyr] *nm,* **galurin** [galyrɛ̃] *nm Fam* hat

galvaniser [galvanize] *vt* to galvanize

galvauder [galvode] **1** *vt (nom, réputation)* to bring into disrepute; *(talents, dons)* to prostitute; *(mot)* to overuse **2 se galvauder** *vpr* to damage one's reputation

gambade [gãbad] *nf* leap

gambader [gãbade] *vi* to leap *or* frisk about

gambas [gãbas] *nfpl* large prawns

gamberger [45] [gãbɛrʒe] *vi Fam* to think hard

gambette [gãbɛt] *nf Fam (jambe)* pin

Gambie [gãbi] *nf* **la G.** the Gambia

gamelle [gamɛl] *nf (de soldat)* mess tin; *(d'ouvrier)* billy(can); *(d'animal)* bowl; *Hum (assiette)* plate; *Fam aussi* **Fig (se) ramasser** *ou* **(se) prendre une g.** to come a cropper

gamète [gamɛt] *nm* gamete

gamin, -e [gamɛ̃, -in] **1** *nm,f (enfant)* kid; **une gamine de dix ans** a girl of ten **2** *adj* (a) *(jeune)* **elle était encore toute gamine** she was still just a child (b) *(puéril)* childish

gaminerie [gaminri] *nf (acte)* childish prank; *(comportement)* childishness

gamme [gam] *nf* (a) *(de couleurs, de prix, d'articles)* range; **produit bas/haut de g.** bottom-of-the-range/top-of-the-range product (b) *Mus* scale

gammée [game] *adj f voir* **croix**

ganache [ganaʃ] *nf* (a) *Fam (imbécile)* **vieille g.** old fool (b) *(d'un cheval)* lower jaw

Gand [gãd] *n* Ghent

gang [gãg] *nm* gang

Gange [gãʒ] *nm* **le G.** the Ganges

ganglion [gãglijɔ̃] *nm* ganglion; **j'ai des ganglions** I've got swollen glands

gangrène [gãgrɛn] *nf* (a) *Méd* gangrene (b) *Fig* canker

gangrener [46] [gãgrəne] **1** *vt* (a) *Méd* to turn gangrenous (b) *Fig* to corrupt **2 se gangrener** *vpr* (a) *Méd* to go gangrenous (b) *Fig* to become corrupt

gangster [gãgstɛr] *nm* gangster

gangstérisme [gãgsterism] *nm* gangsterism

gangue [gãg] *nf (de minerai)* gangue; *(couche) (de boue, de glace)* layer; *Fig (carcan)* straitjacket

gant [gã] *nm* glove; **g. de boxe** boxing glove; **gants de caoutchouc** rubber gloves; **g. de toilette** ≃ facecloth; *Fig* **cela vous va comme un g.** it fits you like a glove; **prendre** *ou* **mettre des gants avec qn** to handle sb with kid gloves; **jeter le g. à qn** to throw down the gauntlet to sb; **relever le g.** to take up the gauntlet

ganté, -e [gãte] *adj (personne)* wearing gloves; *(main)* gloved

gantelet [gãtlɛ] *nm* gauntlet

garage [garaʒ] *nm (pour se garer, pour les réparations)* garage; **g. de ou à bicyclettes** bicycle shed; **g. d'autobus** bus depot; *Can* **vente de g.** garage sale

garagiste [garaʒist] *nmf (propriétaire)* garage owner; *(mécanicien)* garage mechanic

garant, -e [garã, -ãt] *nm,f* guarantor; **se porter g. de qn** *(à la banque)* to stand guarantor for sb; **se porter g. de qch** to vouch for sth

garantie [garãti] *nf* (a) *(précaution)* guarantee, safeguard **(contre** against) (b) *(de produit)* guarantee; **être sous g.** to be under guarantee (c) *(certitude)* guarantee

garantir [garãtir] vt (a) (*promettre*) to guarantee; **g. à qn que** to give sb a guarantee that; **je te le garantis** I can vouch for it (b) *Fin* (*émission d'actions*) to underwrite; (*emprunt*) to secure (c) (*protéger*) to protect (de from)

garce [gars] nf *Fam* bitch

garçon [garsõ] nm (a) (*enfant mâle, fils*) boy; (*jeune homme*) young man; **un mauvais g.** a bad sort; **vieux g.** confirmed bachelor; **g. manqué** tomboy (b) (*serveur*) waiter; **g. d'ascenseur** *Br* lift attendant, *Am* elevator operator; **g. de café** waiter; **g. d'honneur** best man

garçonne [garson] nf **être coiffée à la g.** to have an urchin cut

garçonnet [garsonɛ] nm little boy

garçonnière [garsonjɛr] nf bachelor *Br* flat or *Am* apartment

garde¹ [gard] nf (a) (*protection*) care; *Jur* **g. des enfants** (*après un divorce*) custody of the children (b) (*surveillance*) guarding; **être de g.** to be on duty; **monter la g.** to mount guard; **médecin de g.** duty doctor; **pharmacie de g.** emergency chemist (c) (*méfiance*) **mettre qn en g. contre qn/qch** to warn sb against sb/sth; **être ou se tenir sur ses gardes** to be on one's guard; **prendre g. à qn/qch** to watch out for sb/sth; **prendre g. que... (ne) + subjunctive** to be careful that...; **prendre g. de ne pas faire qch** to be careful not to do sth (d) (*groupe de soldats*) **la g.** the guard; **g. d'honneur** guard of honour; **la G. républicaine** the Republican Guard (*of Paris*) (e) *Jur* **g. à vue** police custody; **il a été mis/est resté en g. à vue** he was put/was held in police custody (f) (*en boxe, en escrime*) guard; **se mettre en g.** to take one's guard; **en g.!** on guard! (g) *Aut* **g. au sol** ground clearance (h) (*d'une épée*) hilt

garde² 1 nm (a) (*soldat*) (*sentinelle*) guard; (*dans une garde*) guardsman; **g. mobile** = member of the security police (b) (*dans un domaine particulier*) **g. champêtre** rural policeman; **g. du corps** bodyguard; **g. forestier** *Br* forest warden, *Am* ranger (c) **le g. des Sceaux** the (French) Minister of Justice

2 nmf **g. de nuit** (*pour un malade*) night nurse (*privately employed*); **g. d'enfants** childminder

garde-à-vous [gardavu] nm inv *Mil* (position of) attention; **se mettre/être au g.** to stand to attention; **g.! attention!**

garde-barrière (*pl* gardes-barrière(s)) [gardəbarjɛr] nmf *Br* level-crossing or *Am* grade-crossing keeper

garde-boue [gardəbu] nm inv mudguard

garde-chasse (*pl* gardes-chasse(s)) [gardəʃas] nm gamekeeper

garde-chiourme (*pl* gardes-chiourme(s)) [gardəʃjurm] nm (*personne autoritaire et brutale*) martinet

garde-côte (*pl* garde-côtes) [gardəkot] nm (*bateau*) coastguard vessel

garde-feu [gardəfø] nm inv fireguard

garde-fou (*pl* garde-fous) [gardəfu] nm (*mur*) parapet; (*rambarde*) railing; *Fig* safeguard

garde-malade (*pl* gardes-malade(s)) [gardəmalad] nmf nurse

garde-manger [gardəmãʒe] nm inv larder

garde-meuble (*pl* garde-meubles) [gardəmœbl] nm furniture repository; **mettre une table au g.** to put a table into storage

gardénia [gardenja] nm gardenia

garder [garde] 1 vt (a) (*conserver*) to keep; **g. qn à dîner** to get sb to stay for dinner; **g. la chambre** to keep to or stay in one's room; **devoir g. le lit** to be confined to bed; **g. la tête froide** to keep a cool head (b) (*surveiller*) (*maison, sac, enfants*) to look after, to mind; *Jur* **g. qn à vue** to hold sb in custody (c) (*protéger*) to protect (de from); **que Dieu nous garde!** God protect us!

2 **se garder** vpr (a) (*se méfier*) **se g. de qn/qch** to beware of sb/sth (b) (*s'abstenir*) **se g. de faire qch** to be careful not to do sth (c) *Fam* (*conserver*) **tes réflexions, tu peux te les g.!** you can keep your thoughts to yourself! (d) (*se conserver*) (*denrées*) to keep

garderie [gardəri] nf *Br* day nursery, *Am* daycare center; (*dans un magasin, une université*) *Br* crèche, *Am* baby-sitting service; (*le soir, après l'école*) childminding service

garde-robe (*pl* garde-robes) [gardərob] nf (*armoire, vêtements*) wardrobe

gardien, -enne [gardjɛ̃, -ɛn] nm, f (*concierge*) caretaker, *Am* janitor; (*de musée, de parking*) attendant; *Fig* (*de libertés, traditions*) guardian; **g. de but** goalkeeper; **g. de nuit** night watchman; **g. de la paix** policeman; **g. de prison** prison *Br* warder or *Am* guard; **gardienne d'enfants** childminder

gardiennage [gardjɛnaʒ] nm (*d'un bâtiment*) caretaking; (*de locaux*) guarding; **société de g.** security firm

gardon [gardõ] nm roach; *Fig* **frais comme un g.** fresh as a daisy

gare¹ [gar] nf station; **g. maritime** harbour station; **g. de marchandises** goods station; **g. routière** bus station; **g. de triage** marshalling yard

gare² exclam (a) (*menace*) **g. à toi si on l'apprend** woe betide you if anyone finds out; *Fam* **si je te reprends à voler du gâteau, g. à tes fesses!** if I catch you stealing cake again, you've had it! (b) (*attention*) **g. aux orties!** mind the nettles!; **sans crier g.** without warning

garer [gare] 1 vt (*voiture*) to park

2 **se garer** vpr (a) (*automobiliste*) to park (b) **se g. de qn/qch** to steer clear of sb/sth; *Fam* **garez-vous!** get out of the way!

gargariser [gargarize] **se gargariser** vpr to gargle; *Fam Péj* **se g. de qch** to revel in sth

gargarisme [gargarism] nm (*produit*) mouthwash; (*action*) gargling

gargote [gargot] nf *Péj* cheap restaurant

gargouillement [gargujmã] nm gurgling; (*d'estomac*) rumbling

gargouiller [garguje] vi (a) (*eau*) to gurgle (b) (*estomac*) to rumble

gargouillis [garguji] = **gargouillement**

garnement [garnəmã] nm scamp, rascal

garni, -e [garni] adj (a) **bien g.** (*bourse*) well-lined (b) (*plat, viande*) with vegetables

garnir [garnir] vt (a) (*munir*) to fit out (de with); (*commode, tiroir*) to line; (*siège*) (*rembourrer*) to stuff; (*couvrir*) to cover (b) (*embellir*) (*robe, chapeau*) to trim (de with) (c) *Culin* (*plat*) to garnish (d) (*remplir*) to fill (de with); (*cave*) to stock (de with)

garnison [garnizõ] nf garrison; **ville de g.** garrison town

garniture [garnityr] *nf* **(a)** *(ornement)* *(d'un chapeau, d'une robe)* trimming; **g. de lit** bedding; **g. de cheminée** mantelpiece ornaments **(b)** *(d'un plat)* garnish; *(légumes)* vegetables; *(d'un vol-au-vent)* filling **(c)** *Aut* **g. d'embrayage** clutch lining; **g. de frein** brake lining; *(de disque de frein)* brake pad

Garonne [garon] *nf* **la G.** the Garonne

garrigue [garig] *nf* scrubland *(typical of southern France)*

garrocher [garɔʃe] *vt Can très Fam* to throw

garrot[1] [garo] *nm* **(a)** *Méd* tourniquet **(b)** *(supplice)* garrotte

garrot[2] *nm* *(de quadrupède)* withers; **mesurer 1,20 m au g.** to be 12 hands high

garrotter [garɔte] *vt (prisonnier)* to tie up; *Fig (opposants)* to muzzle

gars [ga] *nm Fam (jeune homme)* lad; *(homme)* guy

Gascogne [gaskɔɲ] *nf* **la G.** Gascony

gas-oil, gasoil [gazɔjl, gazwal] *nm* diesel oil

gaspillage [gaspijaʒ] *nm (d'argent, de nourriture, de temps)* wasting; **c'est du g.** it's a waste; **quel g.!** what a waste!

gaspiller [gaspije] *vt* to waste

gastéropode [gasterɔpɔd] *nm Zool* gastropod

gastrique [gastrik] *adj* gastric; **embarras g.** upset stomach

gastrite [gastrit] *nf Méd* gastritis

gastro-entérite [pl **gastro-entérites**] [gastroɑ̃terit] *nf Méd* gastroenteritis

gastro-entérologue [pl **gastro-entérologues**] [gastroɑ̃terɔlɔg] *nmf Méd* gastroenterologist

gastro-intestinal, -e, -aux, -ales [gastroɛ̃testinal, -o] *adj Méd* gastrointestinal

gastronome [gastrɔnɔm] *nmf* gastronome, gourmet

gastronomie [gastrɔnɔmi] *nf* gastronomy

gastronomique [gastrɔnɔmik] *adj* gastronomic

gastropode [gastrɔpɔd] *nm Zool* gastropod

gâté, -e [gate] *adj* **(a)** *(pourri) (fruit, dents)* bad **(b)** *Fig (enfant)* spoilt

gâteau, -x [gato] *nm* cake; **faire un g.** to make or bake a cake; *Fam* **c'est du g.** it's a piece of cake; *Fam* **ce n'est pas du g.** it's no easy thing; *Fam* **se partager le g.** to share out the cake; **g. d'anniversaire** birthday cake; **g. de riz** rice pudding; **g. sec** *Br* biscuit, *Am* cookie

gâter [gate] **1** *vt* **(a)** *(gâcher)* to spoil **(b)** *(choyer) (personne)* to spoil; **on n'est pas gâtés!** just our luck!

2 se gâter *vpr (affaires, temps)* to take a turn for the worse; *(aliment)* to go bad

gâterie [gatri] *nf (petit cadeau, friandise)* treat

gâteux, -euse [gatø, -øz] *Fam* **1** *nm,f* old dodderer

2 *adj (sénile)* senile; **avec leurs petits-enfants, ils sont complètement g.** they're totally besotted with their grandchildren

gâtisme [gɑtism] *nm* senility

GATT [gat] *nm Écon (abrév* **General Agreement on Tariffs and Trade)** **le G.** GATT

gauche[1] [goʃ] **1** *adj* **(a)** *(par opposition à droit)* left **(b)** *(maladroit) (personne, attitude, démarche, style)* awkward, clumsy **(c)** *Tech (déformé)* warped

2 *nf* **(a)** *(côté)* left; **à ma g.** on my left; **le tiroir de g.** the left-hand drawer; **à g. (de)** on the left (of); **tournez à g.** turn left; **conduire à g.** to drive on the left; *Fam* **mettre de l'argent à g.** to put some money away **(b)** *Pol* **la g.** the left; **politique/gouvernement de g.** left-wing politics/

government; **voter à g.** to vote for the left

3 *nm (en boxe)* left; **un crochet du g.** a left hook; **un direct du g.** a straight left

gaucher, -ère [goʃe, -er] **1** *adj* left-handed

2 *nm,f* left-hander

gauchisant, -e [goʃizɑ̃, -ɑ̃t] *adj* leftish

gauchisme [goʃism] *nm* leftism

gauchiste [goʃist] *adj & nmf* leftist

gaufre [gofr] *nf* waffle

gaufrette [gofret] *nf* wafer (biscuit)

Gaule [gol] *nf* **la G.** Gaul

gaule [gol] *nf* pole; *(pour pêcher)* fishing rod

gauler [gole] *vt* **(a)** *(arbre fruitier, noyer)* to beat; *(fruits, noix)* to bring down *(using a pole)* **(b)** *Fam (attraper)* to nab; **se faire g.** to get nabbed

gaullisme [golism] *nm* Gaullism

gaulliste [golist] *adj & nmf* Gaullist

gaulois, -e [golwa, -az] **1** *adj* Gallic; **esprit g.** bawdy humour

3 *nm,f* **les G.** the Gauls

4 *nf* **Gauloise®** Gauloise *(popular brand of cigarette)*

gauloiserie [golwazri] *nf (plaisanterie)* bawdy joke; *(caractère)* bawdiness

gausser [gose] **se gausser** *vpr Litt* **se g. de qn** to mock sb; **vous vous gaussez!** you jest!

gaver [gave] **1** *vt (engraisser) (volaille)* to force-feed; *(personne) (de nourriture)* to stuff (with); *Fig* **g. qn de qch** to force-feed sb sth

2 se gaver *vpr Fam* to stuff oneself (**de** with); *Fig* **se g. de romans policiers/jeux vidéo** to read detective novels/play video games till they're coming out of one's ears

gaz [gaz] *nm* gas; *Fam* **il y a de l'eau dans le g.** things aren't going too well; *Fam* **mettre les g.** *Br* to put one's foot down, *Am* to step on the gas; *Av* to open up the throttle; **avoir des g.** to have wind; **g. carbonique** carbon dioxide; **g. de combat** poison gas; **g. d'échappement** exhaust fumes; **g. à effet de serre** greenhouse gas; **g. hilarant** laughing gas; **g. lacrymogène** tear gas; **g. naturel** natural gas; **g. de ville** town gas; **avoir le g. de ville** to be connected to the gas supply

Gaza [gaza] *n* **la bande de G.** the Gaza Strip

gaze [gaz] *nf* gauze

gazé, -e [gaze] **1** *adj* gassed

2 *nm,f (poison)* gas victim

gazéifier [66] [gazeifje] *vt* to gasify; *(boissons)* to carbonate

gazelle [gazɛl] *nf* gazelle

gazer [gaze] **1** *vt (asphyxier)* to gas

2 *vi Fam* **ça gaze!** everything's OK!; **ça gaze?** how's things?

gazette [gazɛt] *nf (journal)* newspaper

gazeux, -euse [gazø, -øz] *adj (a) (eau, boisson)* fizzy **(b)** *Chim* gaseous

gazinière [gazinjer] *nf* gas cooker

gazoduc [gazɔdyk, gazadyk] *nm* gas pipeline

gazole [gazɔl] *nm* diesel oil

gazomètre [gazɔmetr] *nm* gasometer

gazon [gazɔ̃] *nm* **(a)** *(herbe)* grass, turf **(b)** *(surface)* lawn

gazonner [gazɔne] *vt* to turf

gazouillement [gazujmɑ̃] nm (des oiseaux) twittering, chirping; (d'un bébé) gurgling; (d'un ruisseau) babbling

gazouiller [gazuje] vi (oiseau) to twitter, to chirp; (bébé) to gurgle; (eau) to babble

gazouillis [gazuji] = **gazouillement**

GDF [ʒedeɛf] nm (abrév Gaz de France) = French gas company

geai [ʒɛ] nm jay

géant, -e [ʒeɑ̃, -ɑ̃t] 1 adj (a) (arbre, écran) giant, gigantic; (paquet) giant(-size) (b) Fam (formidable) c'est g.! it's fantastic!
2 nm,f giant; Fig avancer ou aller à pas de g. to make great strides

geignard, -e [ʒɛɲar, -ard] Fam 1 adj whining
2 nm,f whiner

geindre [54] [ʒɛ̃dr] vi (a) (gémir) to moan, to groan (de with) (b) Fam (se plaindre constamment) to whine

gel [ʒɛl] nm (a) (verglas) frost; Fig g. des négociations suspension of negotiations; g. des prix/salaires price/wage freeze (b) (produit cosmétique) gel; g. douche shower gel

gélatine [ʒelatin] nf gelatine

gélatineux, -euse [ʒelatinø, -øz] adj gelatinous

gelé, -e [ʒale] adj (a) (lac, rivière) frozen; (plante) frost-nipped (b) Méd (orteil, doigt) frostbitten (c) (très froid) frozen; j'ai les pieds gelés/les mains gelées my feet/hands are frozen (d) (bloqué) (fonds) frozen; (négociations) suspended

gelée [ʒale] nf (a) (gel) frost; g. blanche hoarfrost (b) Culin jelly; g. royale royal jelly

geler [39] [ʒale] 1 vt (a) (lac, rivière, liquide) to freeze; fleurs/salades gelées par le froid flowers/lettuces nipped by the frost (b) Fin (bloquer) (crédits, capital) to freeze
2 vi (lac, rivière) to freeze (over); on gèle dans cette salle it's freezing in this room
3 v impersonnel il gèle it's freezing; il gèle à pierre fendre it's freezing hard; il a gelé blanc cette nuit there was a frost last night
4 se geler vpr Fam to freeze

gélifiant [ʒelifjɑ̃] nm gelling agent

gélule [ʒelyl] nf capsule

gelure [ʒalyr] nf frostbite

Gémeaux [ʒemo] nmpl Astron & Astrol Gemini; être G. to be (a) Gemini

gémir [ʒemir] vi (personne) to groan, to moan (de with); (vent) to moan

gémissant, -e [ʒemisɑ̃, -ɑ̃t] adj (personne) groaning; (voix) wailing

gémissement [ʒemismɑ̃] nm (d'une personne) groan, moan; (de vent) moaning

gemme [ʒɛm] nf (a) (pierre) gem(stone) (b) (résine) pine resin

gênant, -e [ʒɛnɑ̃, -ɑ̃t] adj (a) (témoin, situation, silence) awkward; (bruit, lumière) irritating (b) (encombrant) (objet) cumbersome

gencive [ʒɑ̃siv] nf gum

gendarme [ʒɑ̃darm] nm gendarme, policeman; jouer aux gendarmes et aux voleurs to play cops and robbers; Fam faire le g. to lay down the law; g. couché sleeping policeman; g. mobile = member of the flying squad

gendarmerie [ʒɑ̃darməri] nf (a) (corps) (en France) gendarmerie, police force; g. mobile = flying squad; g. nationale national police force; la G. royale du Canada the Royal Canadian Mounted Police (b) (lieu) gendarmes' headquarters

gendre [ʒɑ̃dr] nm son-in-law

gène [ʒɛn] nm gene

gêne [ʒɛn] nf (a) (confusion) embarrassment; ressentir de la g. to feel embarrassed; où (il) y a de la g., (il n')y a pas de plaisir we don't need to stand on ceremony (b) (dérangement) inconvenience (c) (difficulté physique) discomfort; g. respiratoire difficulty in breathing (d) (manque d'argent) être dans la g. to be in financial difficulties

gêné, -e [ʒene] adj (a) (embarrassé) embarrassed; Fam il n'est pas g., lui! he's got a nerve! (b) (serré) être g. dans un vêtement to be uncomfortable in a garment (c) (qui manque d'argent) in financial difficulties

généalogie [ʒenealɔʒi] nf genealogy

généalogique [ʒenealɔʒik] adj genealogical; arbre g. family tree

gêner [ʒene] 1 vt (a) (perturber) (sujet: bruit, fumée, chaleur) to bother; (opérations, déroulement) to hamper; g. la circulation to hold up the traffic; g. le passage to be in the way; pousse-toi, tu me gênes! move over, you're in my way!; ça te gêne si je fume? do you mind if I smoke?; cela ne te gênerait pas de me prêter ta voiture? would you mind lending me your car?; ce qui me gêne, c'est que... what bothers me is that...; sa présence me gêne I feel awkward in her presence (b) (être source d'inconfort) cette ceinture/ce col me gêne this belt/this collar is uncomfortable (c) (embarrasser) to embarrass; ça me gênerait de le rencontrer I'd feel uncomfortable meeting him; Fam et alors, ça te gêne? what's it to you?
2 se gêner vpr (a) je ne me suis pas gêné pour le lui dire I didn't hesitate to tell him so; elle aurait tort de se g. she shouldn't feel bad about it; aussi Ironique ne vous gênez pas pour moi! don't mind me! (b) (dans un lieu) to be in each other's way

général, -e, -aux, -ales [ʒeneral, -o] 1 adj general; assemblée/amnistie générale general assembly/amnesty; l'intérêt g. the general interest; à la surprise générale to everyone's surprise; à la demande générale by popular request; d'une façon générale generally speaking; en g. (globalement) in general; (habituellement) as a rule, generally
2 nm Mil general (b) (ce qui est universel) passer du g. au particulier to go from the general to the particular
3 nf générale (a) Th dress rehearsal (b) (femme de général) general's wife

généralement [ʒeneralmɑ̃] adv generally

généralisation [ʒeneralizasjɔ̃] nf generalization

généraliser [ʒeneralize] 1 vt to generalize; Méd un cancer généralisé a generalized cancer
2 vi to generalize
3 se généraliser vpr (utilisation, usage, phénomène) to become widespread; (conflit, grève) to spread

généraliste [ʒeneralist] adj & nmf (médecin) general practitioner, GP

généralité [ʒeneralite] nf (a) (notion générale) generality; s'en tenir à des généralités to confine oneself to generalities (b) (majorité) la g. de the majority of

générateur, -trice [ʒeneratœr, -tris] **1** *adj (machine)* generating; *(organe)* generative; **être g. de** to generate **2** *nm* generator; *Ordinat* **g. de caractères** character generator; **g. d'effets numériques** digital effects generator; **g. d'effets spéciaux** (special) effects generator; **g. graphique** graphics generator **3** *nf* **génératrice** generator

génération [ʒenerasjɔ̃] *nf* **(a)** *(classe d'âge, degrés de filiation)* generation **(b)** *(action de produire)* generation; *Biol* **g. spontanée** spontaneous generation

générer [34] [ʒenere] *vt* to generate

généreusement [ʒenerøzmɑ̃] *adv* generously

généreux, -euse [ʒenerø, -øz] *adj* generous; **une terre généreuse** a fertile soil; **elle a des formes généreuses** she has generous curves

générique [ʒenerik] **1** *adj* generic **2** *nm* *Cin & TV* credits; **g. de fin** closing credits

générosité [ʒenerozite] *nf* generosity; **avec g.** generously

Gênes [ʒɛn] *n* Genoa

genèse [ʒənɛz] *nf* genesis; **la G.** Genesis

genêt [ʒənɛ] *nm* broom

généticien, -enne [ʒenetisjɛ̃, -ɛn] *nm,f* geneticist

génétique [ʒenetik] **1** *adj* genetic **2** *nf* genetics *(singulier)*

gêneur, -euse [ʒɛnœr, -øz] *nm,f* nuisance

Genève [ʒənɛv] *n* Geneva

genevois, -e [ʒənvwa, -az] **1** *adj* Genevan **2** *nm,f* **G.** Genevan

genévrier [ʒənevrije] *nm* juniper

génial, -e, -aux, -ales [ʒenjal, -o] *adj* **(a)** *(invention, œuvre, artiste)* brilliant **(b)** *Fam (extraordinaire)* fantastic, great

génialement [ʒenjalmɑ̃] *adv* brilliantly

génie¹ [ʒeni] *nm* **(a)** *(qualité, personne)* genius; **avoir du g.** to be a genius; **une idée/invention de g.** a brilliant idea/invention; **un trait de g.** a stroke of genius; **avoir le g. de qch/pour faire qch** to have a genius for sth/for doing sth **(b)** *(être mythique)* genie; **son bon/mauvais g.** his good/evil genius

génie² *nm* *Mil* **le (corps du) g.** ≃ the Engineers; **g. civil** civil engineering; *(corps)* civil engineers; **g. génétique** genetic engineering

genièvre [ʒənjɛvr] *nm (fruit)* juniper berry; *(arbre)* juniper (tree)

génique [ʒenik] *adj* *Méd* **thérapie g.** gene therapy

génisse [ʒenis] *nf* heifer

génital, -e, -aux, -ales [ʒenital, -o] *adj (glandes, hormones)* genital

géniteur, -trice [ʒenitœr, -tris] *nm,f* *Hum* parent

génocide [ʒenɔsid] *nm* genocide

génoise [ʒenwaz] *nf (gâteau)* sponge cake

génome [ʒenɔm] *nm* *Biol* genome

génotype [ʒenotip] *nm* *Biol* genotype

genou, -x [ʒənu] *nm* knee; **enfoncé jusqu'aux genoux dans la boue** knee-deep in mud; **avoir les genoux en dedans** to be knock-kneed; **être à genoux** to be kneeling (down), to be on one's knees; **se mettre à genoux** to kneel (down); *Fig* **être à genoux devant qn** to worship sb; *Fig* **demander qch à genoux** to ask for sth on bended knee; *Fig* **être sur les genoux** to be on

one's last legs; **tenir un enfant sur ses genoux** to hold a child on one's knee *or* one's lap

genouillère [ʒənujɛr] *nf (protection du genou)* kneepad; *Méd* knee bandage

genre [ʒɑ̃r] *nm* **(a)** *(sorte)* kind, sort; **en tout g., en tous genres** of all kinds; **en tout g.** in its own way; **c'est ce qu'on fait de mieux dans le g.** it's the best of its kind; **c'est tout à fait son g. d'arriver en retard** it's just like him to be late; **ce n'est pas le g. (de femme) à se plaindre** she's not the sort (of woman) to complain; **tu vois le g.** you know the sort; **un vin blanc g. sauternes** a white wine similar to Sauternes **(b)** *(artistique, littéraire)* genre; **le g. comique** comedy **(c)** *(race)* **le g. humain** the human race **(d)** *(goût)* **ça fait bon/mauvais g.** it's in good/bad taste **(e)** *Gram* gender

gens [ʒɑ̃] *nmpl (individus)* people; **les g. du pays** *ou* **du coin** the local people; **jeunes g.** *(garçons et filles)* young people; *(jeunes hommes)* young men; **g. de lettres** men and women of letters; **g. du voyage** travelling people

gent [ʒɑ̃] *nf* *Vieilli ou Hum* **la g. féminine/masculine** the fair/male sex

gentiane [ʒɑ̃sjan] *nf (plante)* gentian

gentil, -ille [ʒɑ̃ti, -ij] *adj* **(a)** *(aimable)* kind, nice (avec to); *(sage)* good; **sois g., ferme la fenêtre** do me a favour and close the window **(b)** *(considérable)* **une gentille somme** a nice little sum

gentilhomme [ʒɑ̃tijɔm] *(pl* **gentilshommes** [ʒɑ̃tizɔm])* *nm* gentleman

gentillesse [ʒɑ̃tijɛs] *nf (bonté)* kindness; **auriez-vous la g. de...?** would you be so kind as to...?; **elle a eu la g. de venir elle-même** she was kind enough to come herself; **dire des gentillesses à qn** to say kind things to sb

gentillet, -ette [ʒɑ̃tijɛ, -ɛt] *adj* *Péj (roman, film)* pleasant enough

gentiment [ʒɑ̃timɑ̃] *adv (aimablement)* kindly; *(sagement)* nicely

génuflexion [ʒenyflɛksjɔ̃] *nf* genuflexion; **faire une g.** to genuflect

géo [ʒeo] *nf* *Fam Scol* geog

géographe [ʒeɔɡraf] *nmf* geographer

géographie [ʒeɔɡrafi] *nf* geography

géographique [ʒeɔɡrafik] *adj* geographic(al)

geôle [ʒol] *nf* *Litt* jail, *Br* gaol

geôlier, -ère [ʒolje, -ɛr] *nm,f* *Litt* jailer, *Br* gaoler

géologie [ʒeɔlɔʒi] *nf* geology

géologique [ʒeɔlɔʒik] *adj* geological

géologue [ʒeɔlɔɡ] *nmf* geologist

géomètre [ʒeɔmɛtr] *nm* **(arpenteur) g.** (land) surveyor

géométrie [ʒeɔmetri] *nf* geometry; **g. dans l'espace** solid geometry; **à g. variable** *(avion)* swing-wing; *Fig* that varies according to circumstances

géométrique [ʒeɔmetrik] *adj* geometric(al)

géophysicien, -enne [ʒeofizisjɛ̃, -ɛn] *nm,f* geophysicist

géophysique [ʒeofizik] **1** *adj* geophysical **2** *nf* geophysics *(singulier)*

géopolitique [ʒeopolitik] **1** *adj* geopolitical **2** *nf* geopolitics *(singulier)*

Géorgie [ʒeɔrʒi] *nf* **la G.** *(aux États-Unis, dans le Caucase)* Georgia

géorgien, -enne [ʒeɔrʒjɛ̃, -ɛn] **1** adj Georgian **2** nmf G. Georgian

géostationnaire [ʒeostasjɔner] adj voir **satellite**

géothermie [ʒeotermi] nf geothermics (singulier)

géothermique [ʒeotermik] adj geothermal

gérance [ʒerɑ̃s] nf management; **prendre un commerce en g.** to take over the management of a business

géranium [ʒeranjɔm] nm geranium

gérant, -e [ʒerɑ̃, -ɑ̃t] nm,f manager, f manageress

gerbe [ʒerb] nf (de blé) sheaf; (d'étincelles) shower; (d'eau) spray; **g. (de fleurs)** spray of flowers

gerber [ʒerbe] vi Vulg (vomir) to puke, to barf

gercé, -e [ʒerse] adj chapped

gercer [16] vt & vi to chap **2 se gercer** vpr to chap

gerçure [ʒersyr] nf **avoir des gerçures (aux mains/ lèvres)** to have chapped hands/lips

gérer [34] [ʒere] vt to manage

gériatrie [ʒerjatri] nf Méd geriatrics (singulier)

gériatrique [ʒerjatrik] adj Méd geriatric

germain, -e [ʒermɛ̃, -ɛn] adj voir **cousin**

germanique [ʒermanik] adj **(a)** Hist (relatif aux Germains) Germanic **(b)** (allemand) German **(c)** (langue) Germanic

germanophone [ʒermanɔfɔn] **1** adj German-speaking **2** nmf German speaker

germe [ʒerm] nm (embryon, virus) germ; (de pomme de terre) eye; Fig **les germes de** (origine) the seeds of; **germes de soja** bean sprouts

germer [ʒerme] vi (plante, idée) to germinate; (pommes de terre) to sprout

germination [ʒerminasjɔ̃] nf Biol germination

gérondif [ʒerɔ̃dif] nm Gram gerund; (cas latin) gerundive

gérontologie [ʒerɔ̃tɔlɔʒi] nf Méd gerontology

gérontologue [ʒerɔ̃tɔlɔg] nmf Méd gerontologist

gésier [ʒezje] nm gizzard

gésir [40] [ʒezir] vi Litt to lie; **ci-gît...** (sur une tombe) here lies...

gestation [ʒestasjɔ̃] nf Biol gestation; Fig **en g.** in preparation

geste [ʒest] nm **(a)** (mouvement) gesture; **faire un g.** to make a gesture; **pas un g. ou je tire!** one move and I'll shoot!; **il lui montra la porte d'un g.** he motioned her towards the door; **d'un g. de la main** with a wave of the hand; **écarter qn d'un g.** to wave sb aside; **joindre le g. à la parole** to suit the action to the word **(b)** (action) gesture; **un beau g.** a fine gesture; **faire un g.** to make a gesture

gesticuler [ʒestikyle] vi to gesticulate

gestion [ʒestjɔ̃] nf management; **g. de bases de données** database management; Ordinat **g. des couleurs** colour management; **g. d'entreprise** business management; Ordinat **g. de fichiers** file management; Ordinat **g. de mémoire** memory management; Ordinat **g. sonore** sound handling, sound management; **g. des stocks** stock control

gestionnaire [ʒestjɔner] **1** nmf (dirigeant) administrator **2** nm Ordinat manager, driver; **g. de fichiers** file manager; **g. de périphérique** device driver; **g. de projets** project management package; **g. de réseau** network manager

gestuel, -elle [ʒestɥel] **1** adj gestural **2** nf **gestuelle** body language

geyser [ʒezer] nm geyser

Ghana [gana] nm **le G.** Ghana

ghanéen, -enne [ganeɛ̃, -ɛn] **1** adj Ghanaian **2** nm,f G. Ghanaian

ghetto [geto] nm ghetto

gibecière [ʒibsjer] nf (de chasseur) game bag

gibelotte [ʒiblɔt] nf Culin **g. (de lapin)** fricassee of rabbit cooked in white wine

gibet [ʒibe] nm gibbet, gallows (singulier)

gibier [ʒibje] nm game; aussi Fig **gros g.** big game; **g. à plumes** game birds; **g. à poil** game animals; Fig **g. de potence** gallows bird

giboulée [ʒibule] nf sudden shower; **giboulées de mars** ≃ April showers

Gibraltar [ʒibraltar] n Gibraltar

giclée [ʒikle] nf (d'eau, de sang) spurt

gicler [ʒikle] vi (eau, sang) to spurt out; (boue) to splash up

gicleur [ʒiklœr] nm Aut jet

gifle [ʒifl] nf aussi Fig slap in the face; **donner une g. à qn** to give sb a slap in the face

gifler [ʒifle] vt (sujet: personne) to slap in the face; (sujet: vent) to lash

gigahertz [ʒigaerts] nm Phys gigahertz

gigantesque [ʒigɑ̃tesk] adj gigantic

gigaoctet [ʒigaɔkte] nm Ordinat gigabyte

GIGN [ʒeiʒeen] nm (abrév **Groupe d'intervention de la gendarmerie nationale**) = special task force of the gendarmerie

gigogne [ʒigɔɲ] adj **tables gigognes** nest of tables; **lits gigognes** beds that fit one underneath the other; **poupées gigognes** nest of (Russian) dolls

gigolo [ʒigolo] nm Fam gigolo

gigot [ʒigo] nm (d'agneau, de mouton) leg

gigoter [ʒigɔte] vi to wriggle, to fidget

gigue¹ [ʒig] nf (danse) jig

gigue² nf Fam **une grande g.** (fille) a beanpole (of a girl)

gilet [ʒile] nm (sans manches) Br waistcoat, Am vest; (veste en laine) cardigan; **g. pare-balles** bulletproof jacket; **g. de sauvetage** life jacket

gin [dʒin] nm gin; **g. tonic** gin and tonic

gingembre [ʒɛ̃ʒɑ̃br] nm ginger

gingivite [ʒɛ̃ʒivit] nf Méd gingivitis

ginseng [ʒɛ̃sɛ̃, ʒinsɑ̃g] nm ginseng

girafe [ʒiraf] nf giraffe; Fig (personne) beanpole

giratoire [ʒiratwar] adj (mouvement) gyratory

girofle [ʒirɔfl] nm voir **clou**

giroflée [ʒirɔfle] nf stock

girolle [ʒirɔl] nf chanterelle (mushroom)

giron [ʒirɔ̃] nm (partie du corps) lap; Fig bosom

gironde [ʒirɔ̃d] adj f Fam curvy; Péj on the plump side

girondin, -e [ʒirɔ̃dɛ̃, -in] **1** adj of the Gironde **2** nm,f G. person from the Gironde

girouette [ʒirwet] nf aussi Fig weathercock

gisais etc voir **gésir**

gisement [ʒizmɑ̃] nm (de minerai) deposit; **g. de pétrole** oilfield

gît voir **gésir**

gitan, -e [ʒitã, -an] **1** *adj* gypsy

2 *nm,f* gypsy

3 *nf* **Gitane®** Gitane® *(popular brand of cigarette)*

gîte¹ [ʒit] *nm* **(a)** *(logement)* lodging; **offrir le g. et le couvert à qn** to offer sb board and lodging **(b)** *(en montagne, à la campagne)* **g. d'étape** = transit accommodation for hikers, cyclists etc; **g. rural** gîte, = self-catering holiday cottage or apartment **(c)** *(du lièvre)* form **(d)** *Culin* shank

gîte² *nf Naut* list; **donner de la g.** to list

gîter [ʒite] *vi Naut* to list

givre [ʒivr] *nm* frost

givré, -e [ʒivre] *adj* **(a)** *(couvert de givre)* covered with frost **(b)** *Fam (fou)* barmy

glabre [glabr] *adj (rasé)* clean-shaven; *(imberbe) (personne)* smooth-chinned; *(visage)* hairless

glaçage [glasaʒ] *nm (d'un gâteau)* icing

glaçant, -e [glasã, -ãt] *adj (manières, accueil)* frosty

glace [glas] *nf* **(a)** *(eau à l'état solide)* ice; *Fig* **rester de g.** to remain impassive; *Fig* **rompre la g.** to break the ice; **g. pilée** crushed ice **(b)** *(de voiture)* window **(c)** *(miroir)* mirror; **g. sans tain** two-way mirror **(d)** *(crème congelée)* ice cream; **g. à la vanille/à la fraise** vanilla/strawberry ice cream; **g. à l'italienne** soft ice cream

glacé, -e [glase] *adj* **(a)** *(rivière, lac)* frozen **(b)** *(très froid) (pièce, eau, personne)* freezing (cold); *(avec des glaçons) (café)* iced; **j'ai les pieds glacés** my feet are freezing **(c)** *(accueil, politesse, regard)* frosty **(d)** *(brillant) (papier, épreuve)* glossy **(e)** *Culin (fruits)* glacé

glacer [16] [glase] **1** *vt* **(a)** *(refroidir, intimider)* to chill; *Fig* **à vous g. le sang** spine-chilling **(b)** *(gâteau)* to ice

2 se glacer *vpr (sang)* to run cold

glaciaire [glasjɛr] *adj Géol (vallée)* glacial; **période g.** Ice Age

glacial, -e, -als *ou* **-aux, -ales** [glasjal, -o] *adj (température, froid, air, vent)* freezing, icy; *Fig (ton, accueil, sourire)* frosty; *(personne)* cold

glacier¹ [glasje] *nm (étendue de glace)* glacier

glacier² *nm (vendeur)* ice-cream seller; *(fabricant)* ice-cream maker

glacière [glasjɛr] *nf (de pique-nique)* cool box; **cette chambre est une vraie g.!** this room's like an icebox!

glaçon [glasɔ̃] *nm (pour rafraîchir une boisson)* ice cube; *(pendant)* icicle; *Fig (personne)* cold fish; **glaçons** *(sur une rivière)* drift ice; **avec ou sans glaçons?** with or without ice?; **un whisky avec des glaçons** a whisky on the rocks; **j'ai les pieds comme des glaçons** my feet are like blocks of ice

gladiateur [gladjatœr] *nm* gladiator

glaïeul [glajœl] *nm* gladiolus; **des glaïeuls** gladioli

glaire [glɛr] *nf (crachat)* phlegm; **g. cervicale** cervical mucus

glaise [glɛz] *nf (terre)* **g.** clay

glaive [glɛv] *nm (épée)* broadsword; *Fig (symbole)* sword

gland [glɑ̃] *nm* **(a)** *(de chêne)* acorn **(b)** *(de passementerie)* tassel **(c)** *Anat* glans **(d)** *très Fam (personne) Br* prat, *Am* jerk

glande [glɑ̃d] *nf (organe)* gland; *très Fam* **foutre les glandes à qn** *(énerver)* to piss sb off; *(mettre mal à l'aise)* to put the wind up sb; **glandes lacrymales** tear glands

glander [glɑ̃de] *vi très Fam (ne rien faire)* to loaf about; *(attendre)* to hang around; **mais qu'est-ce qu'il glande?** *(que fait-il?)* what the hell's he up to?; **j'en ai rien à g.** I don't give a shit

glandeur, -euse [glɑ̃dœr, -øz] *nm,f très Fam* layabout

glandouiller [glɑ̃duje] *vi très Fam (ne rien faire)* to loaf around; *(attendre)* to hang around

glandulaire [glɑ̃dylɛr], **glanduleux, -euse** [glɑ̃dylø, -øz] *adj* glandular

glaner [glane] *vt aussi Fig* to glean

glapir [glapir] *vi (chien)* to yap; *(renard)* to bark; *(personne, radio)* to shriek

glapissements [glapismɑ̃] *nmpl (d'un chien)* yapping; *(d'un renard)* barking; *(d'une personne, de la radio)* shrieking

glas [glɑ] *nm* knell; **sonner le g.** to toll the knell; *Fig* **sonner le g. de qch** to sound the death knell for sth

glaucome [glokom] *nm Méd* glaucoma

glauque [glok] *adj (eau)* murky; *(ambiance, personne)* creepy

glissade [glisad] *nf* sliding; *(de patineur)* gliding; *(pas de danse)* glissade; **faire une g./des glissades** to slide

glissant, -e [glisã, -ãt] *adj* slippery; *Fig* **être sur un terrain g.** to be on dangerous ground

glisse [glis] *nf* **sports de g.** = sports involving sliding motion, e.g. skiing, surfing, windsurfing

glissement [glismɑ̃] *nm (action)* sliding; *(variation électorale)* swing (**à** to); **g. de sens** shift in meaning; **g. de terrain** landslide; *(moins important)* landslip

glisser¹ [glise] **1** *vi* **(a)** *(par accident)* to slip; *(roue)* to skid; **le couteau lui a glissé des mains** the knife slipped out of her hands; *Avg* **sur l'aile** to sideslip **(b)** *(volontairement)* to slide; **se laisser g. le long d'une corde** to slide down a rope; *Ordinat* **faire g.** *(pointeur)* to drag **(c)** *(avancer régulièrement)* to glide; **g.** *(dans le sommeil, vers le désespoir)* to slip **(d)** **g. sur** *(sujet)* to skip over **(e)** *(avoir une surface glissante)* to be slippery

2 *vt (introduire)* to slip; **g. un mot à l'oreille de qn** to drop a word in sb's ear

3 se glisser *vpr* to slip (**dans** into)

glisser² *nm Ordinat* **g. d'icônes** icon drag

glissière [glisjɛr] *nf (a) Tech* runner, slide; **à g.** sliding **(b)** **g. de sécurité** crash barrier **(c)** *Ind (pour le charbon)* chute

global, -e, -aux, -ales [glɔbal, -o] *adj (somme)* total; *(paiement)* lump; *(vision)* overall; *Scol* **méthode globale** word recognition method

globalement [glɔbalmɑ̃] *adv* overall

globalité [glɔbalite] *nf* **prendre un problème dans sa g.** to tackle a problem as a whole

globe [glɔb] *nm* **(a)** *(sphère)* globe; **g. oculaire** eyeball **(b)** *(terre)* globe; **faire le tour du g.** to go round the world; **g. terrestre** *(terre)* earth; *(mappemonde)* globe **(c)** *(en verre) (d'une pendule)* glass dome

globe-trotter *(pl* **globe-trotters)** [glɔbtrɔtœr] *nmf* globetrotter

globulaire [glɔbylɛr] *adj Méd* **numération g.** blood count

globule [glɔbyl] *nm (du sang)* corpuscle; **globules blancs/rouges** white/red corpuscles

globuleux, -euse [glɔbylø, -øz] *adj (yeux)* protruding

gloire [glwar] *nf* **(a)** *(renom)* glory; **tirer g. de qch** to glory in sth **(b)** *(personne célèbre)* celebrity; **il est la g. de notre école** he is the pride of our school **(c)** *(manifestation de respect)* **rendre g. à** to glorify; **g. à...!** glory to...!; **à la g. de qn** in praise of sb

glorieux, -euse [glɔrjø, -øz] adj glorious; être promis à un avenir g. to have a glorious future ahead of one; Fam ce n'est pas très g. (pas très bon) it's not exactly brilliant

glorifier [66] [glɔrifje] **1** vt to glorify

2 se glorifier vpr se g. de (faire) qch to glory in (doing) sth

gloriole [glɔrjɔl] nf Fam faire qch par g. to do sth in order to show off

glose [gloz] nf (explication) gloss

gloser [gloze] gloser sur vt ind (discourir sur) to ramble on about

glossaire [glɔsɛr] nm (ouvrage) glossary

glotte [glɔt] nf Anat glottis

glouglou [gluglu] nm (a) (bruit d'un liquide) gurgle; faire g. to gurgle (b) (cri de la dinde) gobble

gloussements [glusmɑ̃] nmpl (d'une poule) clucking; (d'une dinde) gobbling; (d'une personne) chuckling

glousser [gluse] vi (poule) to cluck; (dinde) to gobble; (personne) to chuckle

glouton, -onne [glutɔ̃, -ɔn] **1** adj greedy, gluttonous

2 nm,f glutton

3 nm (animal) wolverine

gloutonnement [glutɔnmɑ̃] adv greedily

gloutonnerie [glutɔnri] nf gluttony, greed

glu [gly] nf (colle) glue

gluant, -e [glyɑ̃, -ɑ̃t] adj slimy

glucide [glysid] nm carbohydrate

glucose [glykoz] nm glucose

gluten [glytɛn] nm gluten

glycémie [glisemi] nf Méd glycaemia

glycérine [gliserin] nf glycerine

glycine [glisin] nf (plante) wisteria

gnangnan [nɑ̃nɑ̃] adj inv Fam (personne) drippy; (livre, film) soppy

gnognot(t)e [nɔɲɔt] nf Fam (mauvaise qualité) c'est de la g. it's a load of rubbish; c'est pas de la g., cette voiture that car's quite something

gnole, gnôle [nɔl] nf Fam hooch

gnome [gnom] nm gnome; Fig & Péj (homme) midget

gnon [nɔ̃] nm Fam (coup de poing) thump; se prendre un g. to get thumped

GO 1 Rad (abrév grandes ondes) LW

2 [ʒeo] nm (abrév gentil organisateur) activity organizer (at Club Méditerranée holiday villages)

Go nm Ordinat (abrév gigaoctet(s)) GB

go [go] tout de go adv straight away

goal [gol] nm goalkeeper

gobelet [gɔblɛ] nm (en argent, en étain) tumbler; g. en plastique/carton plastic/paper cup

gober [gɔbe] vt (nourriture) to gulp down; Fig (croire) to swallow

goberger [gɔbɛrʒe] se goberger vpr Fam to have a good time

Gobi [gɔbi] n voir désert

godasse [gɔdas] nf Fam shoe

godelureau, -x [gɔdlyro] nm Péj & Vieilli popinjay

godet [gɔdɛ] nm (a) (récipient) pot; Fam boire un g. to have a jar (b) (d'une noria) scoop; (d'un excavateur, d'une roue à eau) bucket (c) (d'une jupe) à godets flared

godiche [gɔdiʃ] Fam **1** adj clumsy

2 nf clumsy oaf

godille [gɔdij] nf (a) Naut scull; avancer à la g. to scull (b) (en ski) wedeln; faire de la g. to wedeln

godiller [gɔdije] vi (a) Naut to scull (b) (en ski) to wedeln

godillot [gɔdijo] nm Mil boot; Fam (gros soulier) clodhopper

goéland [gɔelɑ̃] nm gull

goélette [gɔelɛt] nf (navire) schooner

goémon [gɔemɔ̃] nm wrack

gogo¹ [gogo] à gogo adv Fam galore

gogo² [gogo] nm Fam sucker, mug

goguenard, -e [gɔgnar, -ard] adj mocking

goguette [gɔgɛt] nf Fam être en g. (faire la noce) to be out for a good time

goinfre [gwɛ̃fr] Fam **1** nmf pig

2 adj piggish

goinfrer [gwɛ̃fre] se goinfrer vpr Fam to pig oneself (de on)

goinfrerie [gwɛ̃frəri] nf piggishness

goitre [gwatr] nm Méd goitre

golden [gɔldɛn] nf Golden Delicious (apple)

golf [gɔlf] nm golf; (terrain de) g. golf course; g. miniature miniature golf

golfe [gɔlf] nm gulf, bay; le G. the Gulf; le g. Persique the Persian Gulf; les États ou les pays du G. the Gulf States; le g. du Bengale the Bay of Bengal; le g. de Gascogne the Bay of Biscay; le g. du Mexique the Gulf of Mexico

golfeur, -euse [gɔlfœr, -øz] nm,f golfer

Gomina® [gɔmina] nf hair cream

gominé, -e [gɔmine] adj plastered-down

gommage [gɔmaʒ] nm (a) (pour effacer) rubbing out, erasing (b) (nettoyage de la peau) face scrub; se faire un g. to give oneself a face scrub

gomme [gɔm] nf (a) (pour effacer) eraser, Br rubber (b) (substance) gum; g. à mâcher chewing gum (c) Fam (locutions) mettre (toute) la g. to get a move on; (en voiture) to step on it; à la g. useless

gommé, -e [gɔme] adj (papier, enveloppe) gummed

gommer [gɔme] vt (effacer) to rub out, to erase; Fig (souvenir) to erase

gond [gɔ̃] nm (de porte) hinge; sortir de ses gonds (porte) to come off its hinges; Fig to fly off the handle

gondole [gɔ̃dɔl] nf (barque, présentoir) gondola

gondoler [gɔ̃dɔle] **1** vi (bois, disque) to warp; (papier) to crinkle

2 se gondoler vpr (a) (bois, disque) to warp; (papier) to crinkle (b) Fam (rire) to fall about laughing

gondolier [gɔ̃dɔlje] nm gondolier

gonflable [gɔ̃flabl] adj inflatable

gonflage [gɔ̃flaʒ] nm g. (des pneus) tyre pressure

gonflant, -e [gɔ̃flɑ̃, -ɑ̃t] adj (a) (coiffure) bouffant (b) très Fam (énervant) maddening

gonflé, -e [gɔ̃fle] adj (a) (ballon) swollen (b) Fam être g. (personne) to have a lot of nerve; c'est g., ce qu'il a fait là what he did took some nerve; g. à bloc (sûr de soi) raring to go

gonflement [gɔ̃fləmɑ̃] nm (d'une partie du corps) swelling

gonfler [gɔ̃fle] **1** vt (a) (pneu, ballon, matelas pneumatique) to blow up, to inflate; (ses joues) to puff out; (sujet: vent) (voiles) to fill (b) (faire augmenter de volume) to swell (c) Fig (grossir) (résultats, conséquences) to exaggerate; Fam (moteur) to soup up (d) très Fam (énerver) **g. qn** to get up sb's nose or Br on sb's tits

2 vi to swell; (gâteau, pâte) to rise

3 se gonfler vpr (voiles, poumons) to fill; Fig **se g. de joie** (cœur) to fill with joy

gonflette [gɔ̃flɛt] nf Fam Péj pumping iron; **faire de la g.** to pump iron

gong [gɔ̃g] nm (a) (percussion) gong (b) (en boxe) bell; Fig **sauvé par le g.** saved by the bell

gonzesse [gɔ̃zɛs] nf très Fam chick, Br bird

goret [gɔrɛ] nm piglet; Fam (enfant malpropre) little pig

gorge [gɔrʒ] nf (a) (gosier, cou) throat; **avoir mal à la g.** to have a sore throat; **avoir la g. serrée** to have a lump in one's throat; Fig **cela m'est resté en travers de la g.** it stuck in my throat; **trancher la g. à qn** to cut sb's throat; Fig **être pris à la g.** to be in a stranglehold; **faire des gorges chaudes de qch** to laugh sth to scorn; **rire à g. déployée** to roar with laughter (b) Litt (poitrine) bosom (c) (vallée) gorge (d) (d'une poulie) groove

gorgé, -e [gɔrʒe] adj **une éponge gorgée d'eau** a sponge full of water; **sol g. d'eau** waterlogged earth

gorgée [gɔrʒe] nf mouthful; **boire qch à petites gorgées** to sip sth; **avaler qch d'une g.** to swallow sth in one gulp

gorger [45] [gɔrʒe] **se gorger** vpr to gorge oneself (de on or with); **se g. d'eau** (sol) to get waterlogged

gorgonzola [gɔrgɔzɔla] nm Gorgonzola

gorille [gɔrij] nm (animal) gorilla; Fam (garde du corps) gorilla

gosier [gozje] nm throat; Fam **avoir le g. sec** to be parched

gosse [gɔs] nmf (a) Fam (enfant) kid (b) Fam **être beau g.** to be good-looking (c) Can Fam **gosses** balls

gosser [gɔse] vt Can Fam to whittle

gotha [gɔta] nm **le g. du show-business/de la finance** the show-business/financial elite

gothique [gɔtik] **1** adj Gothic; **écriture g.** Gothic script

2 nm (style) Gothic

gouache [gwaʃ] nf gouache

gouailleur, -euse [gwajœr, -øz] adj (ton) bantering

gouda [guda] nm Gouda

goudron [gudrɔ̃] nm tar; **goudrons** (dans les cigarettes) tar

goudronner [gudrone] vt to tar

gouffre [gufr] nm abyss; Géol sinkhole, Br swallow hole; Fig **être au bord du g.** to be on the edge of the abyss; Fig **cette voiture est un g.** this car just swallows up money

gougère [guʒɛr] nf Culin gougère (choux pastry with cheese)

gouine [gwin] nf très Fam dyke, = offensive term used to refer to a lesbian

goujat [guʒa] nm boor

goujon [guʒɔ̃] nm (poisson) gudgeon

goulache, goulasch [gulaʃ] nm goulash

goulée [gule] nf (de liquide) gulp; (d'air) lungful

goulet [gule] nm (défilé) gully; **g. d'étranglement** bottleneck

gouleyant, -e [gulejã, -ãt] adj (vin) easy-drinking

goulot [gulo] nm (d'une bouteille) neck; **boire au g.** to drink straight from the bottle

goulu, -e [guly] **1** adj greedy, gluttonous

2 nm,f glutton

goulûment [gulymã] adv greedily

goupille [gupij] nf (d'une grenade) pin

goupiller [gupije] Fam **1** vt (arranger) to fix (up)

2 se goupiller vpr **bien se g.** to work out well; **ça s'est mal goupillé** it didn't work out

goupillon [gupijɔ̃] nm (a) (pour eau bénite) sprinkler (b) (pour biberons, bouteilles) bottle brush

gourd, -e [gur, gurd] adj numb (with cold)

gourde [gurd] **1** nf (a) (récipient) flask (b) Fam (femme niaise) dope

2 adj Fam dopey

gourdin [gurdɛ̃] nm club, cudgel

gourer [gure] **se gourer** vpr Fam Br to boob, Am to goof; **se g. d'adresse/de jour** to get the wrong address/day

gourgane [gurgan] nf Can broad bean

gourmand, -e [gurmã, -ãd] **1** adj (personne) who likes his/her food; Fig (intéressé, regard) greedy

2 nm,f person who likes his/her food; **quel g.!** he certainly likes his food!

gourmandise [gurmãdiz] nf (a) (d'une personne) love of food; Fig **avec g.** greedily (b) **gourmandises** (sucreries) delicacies

gourmet [gurmɛ] nm gourmet; **un fin g.** a great gourmet

gourmette [gurmɛt] nf (bracelet) chain (bracelet)

gourou [guru] nm aussi Fig guru

gousse [gus] nf (de haricot, de petit pois) pod; **g. d'ail** clove of garlic; **g. de vanille** vanilla pod

gousset [gusɛ] nm (poche) fob (pocket)

goût [gu] nm (a) (saveur) taste; **avoir un g. de banane/d'alcool** to taste of banana/alcohol; **manquer de g.**, **ne pas avoir de g.** to be tasteless (b) (sens) taste (c) (préférence, convenance) taste; **avoir des goûts de luxe** to have expensive tastes; **trouver qn/qch à son g.** to find sb/sth to one's taste; **avoir du g. pour ou le g. de qch** to have a taste for sth; **elle n'a plus g. à rien** she doesn't want to do anything any more; **faire qch par g.** to do sth because one likes to; **prendre g. à qch** to acquire a taste for sth; **chacun ses goûts** each to his own; **des goûts et des couleurs on ne discute pas**, **tous les goûts sont dans la nature** there's no accounting for taste (d) (discernement, jugement) taste; **s'habiller avec g.** to have good dress sense; **de bon g.** tasteful; **d'un g. douteux** in doubtful taste; **de mauvais g.** in bad taste (e) (style) **quelque chose dans ce g.-là** something of that sort

goûter¹ [gute] nm (afternoon) tea; **l'heure du g.** teatime

goûter² [gute] **1** vt (a) (essayer) (nourriture, boisson) to taste, to try (b) (apprécier) to enjoy, to appreciate

2 vi (à quatre heures) to have tea

3 goûter à vt ind (aliment) to taste, to try; Fig to have a taste of

goûteur, -euse [gutœr, -øz] nm,f taster

goutte [gut] **1** *nf* (a) *(de liquide)* drop; **couler g. à g.** to drip; **il suait à grosses gouttes** the sweat was pouring off him; *Fig* **c'est la g. d'eau qui fait déborder le vase** it's the straw that breaks/broke the camel's back; *Fam* **avoir la g. au nez** to have a runny nose; **se ressembler comme deux gouttes d'eau** to be as like as two peas in a pod (b) *(petite quantité)* drop; **encore une g. de café?** a drop more coffee?; *Fam* **boire la g.** to have a nip (c) *Méd* gout; **gouttes** *(pour les yeux, les oreilles)* drops
2 *Vieilli* **je n'y vois/entends g.** I can't see/understand anything

goutte-à-goutte [gutagut] *nm inv Méd* drip; **on lui a mis un g.** she was put on a drip

gouttelette [gutlɛt] *nf* droplet

goutter [gute] *vi* to drip

gouttière [gutjɛr] *nf* (a) *(le long du toit)* gutter (b) *(le long du mur)* drainpipe

gouvernail [guvɛrnaj] *nm Naut* rudder; **tenir le g.** to be at the helm

gouvernant, -e [guvɛrnɑ̃, -ɑ̃t] **1** *adj (classe, parti)* governing, ruling
2 *nm* **les gouvernants** those in power

gouvernante [guvɛrnɑ̃t] *nf (d'enfants)* governess; *(d'une personne, d'un hôtel)* housekeeper

gouverne [guvɛrn] *nf* (a) *Av* **gouvernes** control surfaces (b) **pour votre g.** for your guidance

gouvernement [guvɛrnəmɑ̃] *nm* government; **sous le g.** Giscard during Giscard's term of office

gouvernemental, -e, -aux, -ales [guvɛrnəmɑ̃tal, -o] *adj* government; *(parti)* governing

gouverner [guvɛrne] **1** *vt* (a) *(diriger) (pays)* to govern, to rule; **un parti qui gouverne depuis des années** a party which has been in power for years (b) *(bateau)* to steer
2 se gouverner *vpr* **le droit des peuples à se g. eux-mêmes** the right of peoples to self-government

gouverneur [guvɛrnœr] *nm* governor; *Can* **G. Général** governor-general; *Can* **Lieutenant-G.** lieutenant-governor

goyave [gɔjav] *nf* guava

GR [ʒeɛr] *nm (abrév* **(sentier de) grande randonnée)** = designation for long-distance footpath

grabat [graba] *nm* pallet

grabataire [grabatɛr] **1** *adj* bedridden
2 *nmf* bedridden invalid

grabuge [grabyʒ] *nm Fam* rumpus; **il va y avoir du g.** there'll be a rumpus

grâce [grɑs] *nf* (a) *(charme)* grace; **avec g.** gracefully (b) **g. à qn/qch** *(avec l'aide de)* thanks to sb/sth (c) *Litt (bienveillance, faveur)* favour; **faites-moi la g. d'oublier cette histoire** do me the favour of forgetting this matter; **trouver g. aux yeux de qn** to find favour in sb's eyes; **de g.!** for pity's sake! (d) *(volonté)* **de bonne g.** willingly, readily; **de mauvaise g.** unwillingly, grudgingly (e) *(acquittement)* pardon; **demander *ou* crier g.** to beg for mercy; **faire g. à qn de qch** *(dette, tâche)* to let sb off sth; **je vous fais g. des détails** I'll spare you the details; **g. présidentielle** presidential pardon (f) *(remerciements)* **rendre g. à** to give thanks to (g) *Rel* grace

gracier [66] [grasje] *vt* to pardon

gracieusement [grasjøzmɑ̃] *adv* (a) *(avec grâce)* gracefully (b) *(aimablement)* graciously (c) *(gratuitement)* free of charge

gracieux, -euse [grasjø, -øz] *adj* (a) *(qui a du charme)* graceful (b) *(aimable)* gracious (c) *(gratuit)* **à titre g.** free of charge

gracile [grasil] *adj* slender

gradation [gradasjɔ̃] *nf* gradation

grade [grad] *nm (dans l'armée, dans l'administration)* rank; **monter en g.** to be promoted; *Fam* **en prendre pour son g.** to be hauled over the coals

gradé, -e [grade] *nm,f Mil* non-commissioned officer, NCO

gradin [gradɛ̃] *nm (d'amphithéâtre, de stade)* row of seats; **les gradins** *(d'un stade) Br* the terraces, *Am* the bleachers

graduation [graduasjɔ̃] *nf* graduation

gradué, -e [gradɥe] *adj* (a) *(qui porte une graduation)* graduated (b) *(progressif) (exercices, problèmes)* graded

graduel, -elle [gradɥɛl] *adj* gradual

graduellement [gradɥɛlmɑ̃] *adv* gradually

graduer [gradɥe] *vt* (a) *(diviser en degrés)* to graduate (b) *(augmenter)* to increase gradually

graffiti [grafiti] *nm* piece of graffiti; **des graffitis** graffiti

graillé, -e [graje] *adj Can (pour faire qch)* well-equipped; *Fam (bien monté)* well-hung

grailler [graje] *vi très Fam (manger)* to eat

graillon [grajɔ̃] *nm* **sentir le g.** to smell of burnt fat

grain¹ [grɛ̃] *nm* (a) *(graine, fruit, céréales)* grain; **g. de café** coffee bean; **g. de poivre** peppercorn; **g. de raisin** grape (b) *(de sable, de poudre)* grain; *(de poussière)* speck; *(de chapelet)* bead; *Fig* **un g. de qch** *(un peu de)* a hint of sth; **pas un g. de bon sens/de vérité** not a grain of common sense/of truth; *Fam* **il a un g.** he's not quite right in the head; **mettre son g. de sel** to stick one's oar in; **g. de beauté** mole (c) *(d'un tissu, d'une photographie)* grain; *(de la peau)* rough side

grain² *nm Naut* squall; *Fig* **veiller au g.** to keep a weather eye open

graine [grɛn] *nf* seed; **monter en g.** to run to seed; *Fig (personne)* to shoot up; **regarde un peu ce qu'a fait ton cousin et prends-en de la g.!** just look at what your cousin's done and take a leaf out of his book!; **c'est de la mauvaise g.** he's a bad lot; **g. de voyou/voleur** little lout/thief

graissage [grɛsaʒ] *nm (d'une machine, d'un engrenage)* greasing

graisse [grɛs] *nf (d'animal, de personne)* fat; *(lubrifiant)* grease; **graisses animales/végétales** animal/vegetable fat

graisser [grese] *vt (machine, engrenage)* to grease; *(bottes)* to oil, *Br* to dubbin; **g. la patte à qn** to grease sb's palm

graisseux, -euse [grese, -øz] *adj (taché de graisse)* greasy (b) *(tumeur, tissu)* fatty

grammaire [gramɛr] *nf* (a) *(science, règles)* grammar; **faute/règle de g.** grammatical error/rule (b) *(livre)* grammar (book)

grammairien, -enne [gramɛrjɛ̃, -ɛn] *nm,f* grammarian

grammatical, -e, -aux, -ales [gramatikal, -o] *adj* grammatical

gramme [gram] *nm* gram; *aussi Fig* **pas un g. de** not an ounce of

grand, -e [grã, grãd] **1** *adj* **(a)** *(en taille)* big, large; *(en hauteur)* tall; *(en longueur)* long; *Phot* **g. angle** wide-angle lens

(b) *(principal)* chief, main; **grandes lignes** *(de train)* main lines

(c) *(adulte, plus âgé)* big

(d) *(en quantité, en intensité) (bruit)* loud; *(coup)* heavy; *(froid)* severe; *(différence, catastrophe)* big; **le g. amour** true love; **un acteur sans g. talent** a rather untalented actor; **il fait g. jour** it's broad daylight; **c'est un g. buveur** he's a big drinker; **les grands blessés** the seriously wounded

(e) *(puissant, prestigieux)* great; **une grande dame de la littérature** a great literary lady

(f) *(dans un titre, un grade)* grand; **g. prêtre** high priest; **g. reporter** chief reporter

2 *adv* **ouvrir g. la bouche/la fenêtre** to open one's mouth/the window wide; **g. ouvert** wide open

3 *nm,f* **les grands** *(enfants)* the older ones; **grands et petits** old and young, grown-ups and children; **les grands de ce monde** those in high places; **les grands du pétrole** the oil giants; **mon g.** mate, pal; **ma grande** dear

grand-chose [grãʃoz] **1** *pron indéfini* **pas g.** not much; **ce ne sont que quelques fleurs, ce n'est pas g.** it's just a few flowers, nothing much

2 *nmf inv Fam (personne)* **un pas g.** a dead loss

grand-duc *(pl* **grands-ducs**) [grãdyk] *nm (noble)* grand duke; *Fam* **faire la tournée des grands-ducs** to go out on the town

grand-duché *(pl* **grands-duchés**) [grãdyʃe] *nm* grand duchy

Grande-Bretagne [grãdbrətaɲ] *nf* **la G.** Great Britain

grande-duchesse *(pl* **grandes-duchesses**) [grãddyʃes] *nf* grand duchess

grandement [grãdmã] *adv (beaucoup)* greatly; **se tromper g.** to be greatly mistaken; **avoir g. le temps** to have ample time; **avoir g. de quoi vivre** to have plenty to live on

grandeur [grãdœr] *nf (a) (taille)* size; *(d'un arbre)* height, size; **g. nature** life-size **(b)** *(importance)* importance **(c)** *Math* magnitude **(d)** *(gloire)* greatness, grandeur; **g. et décadence d'un empire** rise and fall of an empire **(e)** *(des sentiments)* nobility; **g. d'âme** magnanimity

grand-guignol [grãgiɲɔl] *nm Péj* **c'est du g.** it's all blood and gore

grandiloquence [grãdilɔkãs] *nf* grandiloquence

grandiloquent, -e [grãdilɔkã, -ãt] *adj* grandiloquent

grandiose [grãdjoz] *adj* imposing

grandir [grãdir] **1** *vi (en taille)* to grow; *(en âge)* to grow up; *(en importance)* to increase, to grow

2 *vt* **g. qn** *(sujet: talons)* to make sb look taller; *Fig (sujet: expérience, épreuve)* to improve sb's standing

3 se grandir *vpr (en taille)* to make oneself taller

grandissant, -e [grãdisã, -ãt] *adj* growing

grand-mère *(pl* **grand-mères** *ou* **grands-mères**) [grãmer] *nf* grandmother; *Fam (vieille femme)* old granny

grand-oncle [grãtõkl] *(pl* **grands-oncles** [grãzõkl]) *nm* great-uncle

grand-peine [grãpɛn] **à grand-peine** *adv* with great difficulty

grand-père *(pl* **grands-pères**) [grãper] *nm* grandfather; *Fam (vieil homme)* granddad

grand-route *(pl* **grand-routes**) [grãrut] *nf* main road

grand-rue *(pl* **grand-rues**) [grãry] *nf* high street, main street

grands-parents [grãparã] *nmpl* grandparents

grand-tante *(pl* **grand-tantes** *ou* **grands-tantes**) [grãtãt] *nf* great-aunt

grand-voile *(pl* **grand-voiles** *ou* **grands-voiles**) [grãvwal] *nf* mainsail

grange [grãʒ] *nf* barn

granit(e) [granit] *nm* granite

granule [granyl] *nm* granule

granulé [granyle] *nm* granule

granuleux, -euse [granylø, -øz] *adj* granular

graphe [graf] *nm* graph

graphie [grafi] *nf* Ling written form

graphique [grafik] **1** *adj* graphic

2 *nm* diagram; *(sur un axe)* graph; *Ordinat* graphic; *Ordinat* **g. de gestion** management chart; **g. à** *ou* **en barres** bar chart

graphisme [grafism] *nm (a) (écriture)* handwriting **(b)** *Art (style)* style of drawing

graphiste [grafist] *nmf* graphic designer

graphite [grafit] *nm* graphite

graphologie [grafɔlɔʒi] *nf* graphology

graphologue [grafɔlɔg] *nmf* graphologist

grappe [grap] *nf (de raisin)* bunch; *(de fleurs, de gens)* cluster; *Vulg* **lâche-moi la g.!** piss off!

grappiller [grapije] *vt (renseignements)* to glean; *(argent)* to make on the side

grappin [grapɛ̃] *nm Naut* grappling hook or iron; *Fam Fig* **mettre le g. sur qn/qch** to get one's hands on sb/sth

gras, grasse [grɑ, grɑs] **1** *adj (a) (nourriture, tissu)* fatty **(b)** *(gros) (personne, animal)* fat; *(poulet)* plump **(c)** *(graisseux) (chiffon, cheveux, peau)* greasy **(d)** *(épais) (terre)* heavy, clayey; *(crayon)* soft lead; *(toux)* loose; *(rire)* throaty **(e)** *Typ* bold; **caractères g.** bold type **(f)** *Fig (bénéfices, récompense)* handsome; **faire la grasse matinée** to have a lie-in **(g)** *(graveleux) (histoire)* dirty, smutty

2 *adv* **manger g.** to eat fatty food

3 *nm (a) (de la jambe, du bras)* fleshy part **(b)** *(du jambon, de la viande)* fat **(c)** *Typ* bold; **en g.** in bold

gras-double *(pl* **gras-doubles**) [grɑdubl] *nm* tripe

grassement [grɑsmã] *adv (récompenser, payer)* handsomely

grasseyer [graseje] *vi* to pronounce one's r's at the back of the throat

grassouillet, -ette [grɑsuje, -et] *adj* plump, chubby

gratifiant, -e [gratifjã, -ãt] *adj* rewarding, gratifying

gratification [gratifikasjõ] *nf (a) (prime)* bonus **(b)** *(satisfaction)* gratification

gratifier [66] [gratifje] *vt* **g. qn de qch** *(récompense)* to present sb with sth; *Ironique (sourire)* to bestow sth on sb **(b)** *(valoriser)* to gratify

gratin [gratɛ̃] *nm (a) (plat)* gratin *(baked dish with a topping of grated cheese and sometimes breadcrumbs)*; **au g. au gratin; chou-fleur au g.** cauliflower cheese; **g. dauphinois** = sliced potatoes baked with cream and browned on top **(b)** *Fam Fig* **le g.** *(le beau monde)* the upper crust

gratiné, -e [gratine] **1** *adj (a) (au gratin)* au gratin *(topped with grated cheese and sometimes breadcrumbs)* **(b)** *Fam Fig (addition)* huge; *(examen, problème)* tough

2 *nf* **gratinée** *Culin* onion soup au gratin

gratiner [gratine] **1** *vt* to brown
 2 *vi* **faire g. qch** to brown sth

gratis [gratis] **1** *adv* free (of charge)
 2 *adj* free

gratitude [gratityd] *nf* gratitude

gratouiller [gratuje] *vt Fam (démanger)* **ça (me) gratouille** it makes me itch

gratte [grat] *nf Can* snowplough

gratte-ciel [gratsjɛl] *nm inv* skyscraper

gratte-papier [gratpapje] *nm inv Péj* pen-pusher

gratter [grate] **1** *vt (avec les ongles)* to scratch; *(avec un objet)* to scrape; *(effacer) (mot, inscription)* to scratch out; *(tache)* to scrape off; **ça me gratte** it makes me itch; **pull qui gratte** scratchy jumper; *Fig* **g. les fonds de tiroir** to scrape around for money
 2 *vi* **g. à la porte** to tap lightly at the door
 3 se gratter *vpr* to scratch oneself; **se g. jusqu'au sang** to scratch oneself raw; **se g. la tête/l'oreille** to scratch one's head/ear; *très Fam* **tu peux toujours te g.!** you can take a running jump!

grattoir [gratwar] *nm* scraper; *(de boîte d'allumettes)* striking surface

grattouiller [gratuje] = **gratouiller**

gratuit, -e [gratɥi, -it] *adj* **(a)** *(billet, entrée, échantillon)* free; **à titre g.** free of charge **(b)** *(acte, violence)* gratuitous

gratuité [gratɥite] *nf* **(a)** *(fait de ne pas payer)* **la g. de l'enseignement/des soins hospitaliers** free education/hospital care **(b)** *(d'un acte, de la violence)* gratuitousness

gratuitement [gratɥitmã] *adv* **(a)** *(sans payer)* free (of charge) **(b)** *(sans motif)* gratuitously

gravats [grava] *nmpl* rubble

grave [grav] **1** *adj* **(a)** *(sérieux, dramatique)* serious; **ce n'est pas g.** *(ça n'a pas d'importance)* it doesn't matter; **un accident qui a fait deux blessés graves** an accident in which two people were seriously injured **(b)** *(solennel) (visage, ton, expression)* grave, solemn **(c)** *(note, voix)* low, deep
 2 *nm* **le g., les graves** *(notes)* the low notes; **les graves** *(sur une chaîne stéréo)* the bass

graveleux, -euse [gravlø, -øz] *adj* **(a)** *(histoire, chanson)* smutty, dirty **(b)** *(terre)* gravelly

gravement [gravmã] *adv* **(a)** *(malade, blessé)* seriously **(b)** *(avec dignité)* gravely, solemnly

graver [grave] *vt (matériau, motif)* to engrave; *(sur bois)* to carve; *(disque)* to make; *Fig* **rester gravé dans la mémoire de qn** to be engraved on sb's memory

graveur, -euse [gravœr, -øz] *nm,f* engraver; **g. sur bois** woodcarver

gravier [gravje] *nm* gravel

gravillon [gravijɔ̃] *nm (caillou)* piece of gravel; **du g., des gravillons** gravel; **gravillons** *(sur panneau)* loose chippings

gravir [gravir] *vt* to climb; *Fig* **g. les échelons** to climb the ladder

gravissime [gravisim] *adj* extremely serious

gravitation [gravitasjɔ̃] *nf* gravitation

gravité [gravite] *nf* **(a)** *Phys* gravity **(b)** *(solennité)* gravity **(c)** *(importance)* seriousness; **sans g.** *(blessure, problème)* minor

graviter [gravite] *vi* **g. autour de qch** to orbit sth; *Fig* **g. autour de qn** to hover around sb

gravure [gravyr] *nf* **(a)** *(action)* engraving; **g. sur bois** woodcarving **(b)** *(ouvrage)* engraving; **g. sur bois** woodcut; *Fig* **c'est une vraie g. de mode** she dresses like a fashion model

gré [gre] *nm* **(a)** *(goût)* **à mon/son g.** for my/his/her liking **(b)** *(volonté)* **contre son g.** against one's will; **de son propre g., de son plein g.** of one's own free will; **de bon g.** willingly, gladly; **bon g. mal g.** whether we/you/*etc* like it or not; **faites-le venir de g. ou de force** make him come whether he wants to or not; **au g. des flots** at the mercy of the waves; **au g. des événements/des circonstances** *(agir, changer d'avis)* according to how events turn out/to the circumstances **(c)** *Formel (gratitude)* **nous vous saurions g. de bien vouloir...** we would be grateful if you would kindly...

grec, grecque [grɛk] **1** *adj* Greek
 2 *nm,f* **G.** Greek
 3 *nm (langue)* Greek; **g. ancien/moderne** ancient/modern Greek
 4 *nf* **grecque (a)** *Culin* **à la grecque** *(légumes)* = marinated in olive oil, lemon juice and herbs and served cold **(b)** *(motif)* Greek key pattern

Grèce [grɛs] *nf* **la G.** Greece

gredin, -e [grədɛ̃, -in] *nm,f Fam Vieilli* rascal

gréement [gremã] *nm Naut* rigging

greffe¹ [grɛf] *nf* **(a)** *(de peau, de tissu)* graft; *(d'organe)* transplant; **g. du cœur/du rein** heart/kidney transplant **(b)** *Bot (action)* grafting; *(bouture)* graft

greffe² [grɛf] *nm Jur* clerk of the court's office

greffé, -e [grefe] *nm,f Méd* **g. cardiaque** *ou* **du cœur** heart transplant patient

greffer [grefe] *vt (peau, tissu, bouture)* to graft; *(organe)* to transplant

greffier, -ère [grefje, -ɛr] *nm Jur* clerk (of the court)

greffon [grefɔ̃] *nm (de tissu, de peau)* graft; *(d'organe)* transplant; *(bouture)* graft

grégaire [greger] *adj* gregarious; **l'instinct g.** the herd instinct

grège [grɛʒ] *adj* *(beige)* whitish-beige

grégorien, -enne [gregorjɛ̃, -ɛn] *adj* Gregorian

grêle¹ [grɛl] *adj (jambes, mains)* skinny; *(tige, silhouette)* slender; *(voix, son)* shrill

grêle² *nf aussi Fig* hail

grêlé, -e [grele] *adj (peau)* pockmarked

grêler [grele] *v impersonnel* to hail

grêlon [grelɔ̃] *nm* hailstone

grelot [grəlo] *nm (small)* bell

grelotter [grəlɔte] *vi* to shiver **(de** with)

Grenade [grənad] *nf (aux Antilles)* **la G.** Grenada

grenade [grənad] *nf* **(a)** *(projectile)* grenade; **g. lacrymogène** tear-gas grenade **(b)** *(fruit)* pomegranate

grenadine [grənadin] *nf* grenadine

grenaille [grənaj] *nf* **(a)** *(plombs)* shot **(b)** *Belg* **grenailles errantes** *(sur panneau)* loose chippings

grenat [grəna] **1** *nm* garnet
 2 *adj inv* dark red

grenier [grənje] *nm* **(a)** *(sous les combles)* attic **(b)** *(pour grain, fourrage)* granary; **g. à blé** wheat loft; **g. à foin** hayloft

grenouille [grənuj] *nf (animal)* frog; *Fig & Péj* **g. de bénitier** Bible basher

grenouillère [grənujer] *nf (pour bébé)* Babygro®

grès [grɛ] nm (a) (pierre) sandstone (b) (céramique) stoneware; **cruche en g.** stoneware jug

grésil [grezil, grezi] nm fine hail

grésillement [grezijmɑ̃] nm (du feu, d'une radio) crackling; (de l'huile) sizzling

grésiller [grezije] vi (feu, radio) to crackle; (huile) to sizzle

gressin [gresɛ̃] nm bread stick

grève¹ [grɛv] nf (arrêt du travail) strike; **se mettre en g.** to go out on strike, to strike; **être en g., faire g.** to be on strike; **g. des Postes** postal strike; **g. de la faim** hunger strike; **g. générale** general strike; **g. sauvage** wildcat strike; **g. sur le tas** sit-down strike; **g. tournante** staggered strike; **g. du zèle** work-to-rule, go-slow

grève² nf (le long de la mer) shore; (d'un fleuve) bank

grever [46] [grəve] vt (pouvoir d'achat) to restrict; (budget) to put a strain on

gréviste [grevist] nmf striker; **g. de la faim** hunger striker

gribouillage [gribujaʒ] nm (écriture) scribble, scrawl; (dessin) doodle

gribouiller [gribuje] vt & vi (écrire) to scrawl, to scribble; (dessiner) to doodle

gribouillis [gribuji] = **gribouillage**

grief [grijɛf] nm grievance, ground for complaint; **faire ou tenir g. à qn de qch** to hold sth against sb

grièvement [grijɛvmɑ̃] adv seriously, badly

griffe [grif] nf (a) (d'animal) claw; **faire ses griffes** (chat) to sharpen its claws; Fig **montrer les griffes** to show one's claws; **arracher qn des griffes de qn** to snatch sb out of sb's clutches (b) (sur un bijou) claw (c) (sur vêtements) label; Fig (style) stamp

griffé, -e [grife] adj (vêtement) designer

griffer [grife] vt to scratch

griffon [grifɔ̃] nm (a) (chien) griffon (b) (créature mythique) griffin

griffonner [grifɔne] vt & vi (écrire) to scrawl, to scribble; (dessiner) to sketch quickly

griffure [grifyr] nf scratch

grignoter [grijɔte] 1 vt to nibble; Fig (libertés) to erode; (capital, économies) to eat into
2 vi to nibble

gril [gril] nm (de cuisine) Br grill, Am broiler; **faire cuire qch sur le g.** to grill sth; Fig **être sur le g.** to be on tenterhooks

grillade [grijad] nf (viande) piece of grilled meat; (poisson) piece of grilled fish; **faire des grillades** to have a barbecue

grillage [grijaʒ] nm (de fenêtre, de porte) wire mesh; (clôture) wire netting

grillagé, -e [grijaʒe] adj (fenêtre) covered with wire mesh; (jardin) surrounded with wire netting

grille [grij] nf (a) (à l'entrée d'un parc, d'un jardin) gate; (clôture basse) railings (b) (d'une cage, d'une fenêtre) screen, netting; Aut **g. de radiateur** radiator grille (c) (d'un évier, d'un égout) grating, grate (d) (tableau) (de mots croisés) grid; Rad & TV **g. des programmes** programme schedule; **g. des salaires** salary scale

grille-pain [grijpɛ̃] nm inv toaster

griller [grije] 1 vt (a) (rôtir) (viande) to grill; (pain) to toast; (café, marrons) to roast (b) (brûler) to scorch, to burn; (ampoule, fusible) to blow; Fam (cigarette) to smoke (c) Fam (dépasser) **g. un concurrent** to leave a competitor standing; **g. un feu rouge** to jump the lights (d) Fam (discréditer) **il est grillé** his game's up
2 vi (a) (viande) to grill; (pain) to toast; (marrons) to roast; Fig **g. d'impatience** to be burning with impatience (b) (ampoule, fusible) to blow
3 **se griller** vpr **se g. au soleil** to roast in the sun; Fam **se g. auprès de qn** to blot one's copybook with sb

grillon [grijɔ̃] nm cricket

grimaçant, -e [grimasɑ̃, -ɑ̃t] adj grimacing

grimace [grimas] nf grimace; **faire une g. (à qn)** to make or pull a face (at sb); **faire la g.** to make or pull a face; **faire une g. de douleur** to wince with pain

grimacer [16] [grimase] vi to make or pull a face; **g. de douleur** to wince with pain

grimer [grime] 1 vt to make up
2 **se grimer** vpr to put on's make-up on

grimpant, -e [grɛ̃pɑ̃, -ɑ̃t] adj (plante) climbing

grimpe [grɛ̃p] nf Fam rock-climbing; **faire de la g.** to go rock-climbing

grimpée [grɛ̃pe] nf (stiff) climb

grimper [grɛ̃pe] 1 vi aussi Fig to climb; **g. aux arbres** to climb trees; Fam **ça grimpe** it's steep
2 vt (montagne, escalier) to climb; Fig **g. les échelons** to climb the ladder

grimpeur, -euse [grɛ̃pœr, -øz] nm,f climber

grinçant, -e [grɛ̃sɑ̃, -ɑ̃t] adj (qui grince) creaking; Fig (caustique) caustic

grincement [grɛ̃smɑ̃] nm (d'une porte, de roues) creaking; **grincements de dents** grinding of teeth; Fig gnashing of teeth

grincer [16] [grɛ̃se] vi (porte, roues) to creak; **g. des dents** to grind one's teeth

grincheux, -euse [grɛ̃ʃø, -øz] 1 adj grumpy
2 nm,f grumpy person

gringalet [grɛ̃gale] 1 nm weakling
2 adj m puny

griotte [grijɔt] nf morello (cherry)

grippal, -e, -aux, -ales [gripal, -o] adj **soulage les états grippaux** (sur médicament) relieves flu symptoms

grippe [grip] nf (a) (maladie) flu; **avoir la g.** to have (the) flu; **g. intestinale** gastric flu (b) **prendre qn/qch en g.** to take a dislike to sb/sth

grippé, -e [gripe] adj (a) (malade) **être g.** to have (the) flu (b) (moteur, mécanisme) seized-up

grippe-sou [gripsu] (pl **grippe-sous** ou **grippe-sou**) nm skinflint, miser

gris, -e [gri, griz] 1 adj (a) (couleur, temps) grey; **il fait g. ce matin** it's a grey or dull morning; **g. ardoise** slate grey; **g. perle** pearl grey; (ivre) tipsy
2 nm (a) (couleur) grey; Ordinat **tons de g.** shades of grey; **s'habiller en g.** to wear grey (b) (tabac) shag

grisaille [grizaj] nf (caractère morne) dreariness

grisant, -e [grizɑ̃, -ɑ̃t] adj (succès, atmosphère) intoxicating; (aventure, soirée) exhilarating

grisâtre [grizɑtr] adj greyish

grisé [grize] nm Ordinat grey tone

griser [grize] **1** vt (a) (enivrer) to make tipsy; Fig to intoxicate (b) Ordinat to shade

2 se griser vpr **se g. de qch** (air pur) to get drunk on sth; (paroles) to get carried away by sth

grisonnant, -e [grizɔnɑ̃, -ɑ̃t] adj (cheveux, personne) greying; **avoir les tempes grisonnantes** to be greying at the temples

grisonner [grizɔne] vi (cheveux, personne) to go grey

grisou [grizu] nm firedamp; **coup de g.** firedamp explosion

grive [griv] nf thrush

grivois, -e [grivwa, -az] adj bawdy

grivoiserie [grivwazri] nf (plaisanterie) bawdy joke; (histoire) bawdy story; (acte) rude gesture

grizzli, grizzly [grizli] nm grizzly (bear)

Groenland [grɔenlɑ̃d] nm **le G.** Greenland

grog [grɔg] nm hot toddy

groggy [grɔgi] adj inv Fam groggy

grogne [grɔɲ] nf Fam discontent

grognement [grɔɲmɑ̃] nm (d'un cochon) grunt; (d'un chien, d'un ours, d'une personne) growl; **pousser des grognements** to grunt/to growl

grogner [grɔɲe] vi (a) (gronder) (cochon) to grunt; (chien, personne) to growl (b) (protester) to grumble

grognon [grɔɲɔ̃] adj grumpy

groin [grwɛ̃] nm snout

grol(l)e [grɔl] nf très Fam shoe

grommeler [42] [grɔmle] vt & vi to mutter

grommellements [grɔmelmɑ̃] nmpl muttering

grondement [grɔ̃dmɑ̃] nm (a) (d'un chien) growl (b) (du tonnerre) rumble; (d'un torrent, des vagues, d'un moteur) roar; (des canons) booming

gronder [grɔ̃de] **1** vi (a) (chien) to growl (b) (tonnerre) to rumble; (torrent, vagues, moteur) to roar; (canons) to boom; **la révolte/le mécontentement gronde** there are rumblings of rebellion/discontent

2 vt (réprimander) to scold, to tell off

groom [grum] nm Br page, Am bellhop

gros, grosse [gro, gros] **1** adj (a) (corpulent) big, fat (b) (important, abondant) big; (rhume) bad; (dépenses, averse, mer) heavy; (somme) large; (faute) serious; **g. buveur/mangeur** big drinker/eater; **avoir un g. chagrin** to be very upset; **la plus grosse partie de qch** the majority of sth; **un mensonge g. comme une maison** a whopper of a lie; très Fam **g. lard** big fat slob; Fam **g. nigaud** ou **bêta!** you great twit!; Fam **g. bonnet, grosse légume** big shot, bigwig

(c) (épais) (morceau, caractères) big, large; (toile) coarse; (pull, chaussettes, corde) thick; (chaussures) strong, stout

(d) (peu subtil) (voix) gruff; (rire) coarse; **c'est un peu g.!** that's a bit much!; **g. mot** swearword

(e) Mus **grosse caisse** bass drum

2 adv (beaucoup) (gagner, rapporter, risquer) a lot; **je donnerais g. pour savoir qui a fait ça** I'd give a lot to know who did that

3 nm,f fat man, f fat woman

4 nm (a) (partie la plus importante) bulk; **le g. de** the majority of; **le plus g. est fait** the bulk of the work has been done

(b) Com wholesale (trade); **faire du g.** to sell wholesale; **de g.** (commerce, boucher) wholesale

(c) **en g.** (en grosses lettres) in big or large letters; (approximativement) roughly; Com wholesale

groseille [grozej] nf **g. (rouge)** redcurrant; **g. à maquereau** gooseberry

groseillier [grozeje] nm redcurrant bush; **g. à maquereau** gooseberry bush

grosse [gros] voir **gros**

grossesse [groses] nf pregnancy; **g. extra-utérine** ectopic pregnancy; **g. nerveuse** phantom pregnancy; **g. à risque** high-risk pregnancy

grosseur [grosœr] nf (a) (taille, volume) size (b) Méd lump

grossier, -ère [grosje, -ɛr] adj (a) (impoli) (personne) rude (**envers** to); (langage, plaisanterie) crude; **un g. personnage** an uncouth individual (b) (peu raffiné) (nourriture, tissu) coarse, rough; (dessin) rough; (goûts, traits du visage) coarse; (ruse) crude (c) (important) (erreur) gross

grossièrement [grosjɛrmɑ̃] adv (a) (de façon impolie) rudely (b) (sans raffinement) crudely (c) (approximativement) roughly

grossièreté [grosjɛrte] nf (a) (incorrection) coarseness (b) (parole grossière) rude word (c) (caractère rudimentaire) (d'un dessin) crudeness; (d'un tissu, des goûts) coarseness

grossir [grosir] **1** vi (personne, animal) to put on weight, to get fatter; (mer) to get rough; (rivière) to swell; **g. de 2 kilos** (personne) to put on 2 kilos

2 vt (sujet: loupe, microscope) to magnify; Fig (exagérer) to exaggerate; **g. qn** (sujet: vêtement) to make sb look fat; **g. les rangs de qch** to swell the ranks of sth

grossissant, -e [grosisɑ̃, -ɑ̃t] adj **miroir g.** distorting mirror

grossissement [grosismɑ̃] nm (a) (augmentation de taille) increase in size (b) (pouvoir grossissant) magnification

grossiste [grosist] nmf wholesaler

grosso modo [grosomodo] adv roughly; **g. c'est une comédie** broadly speaking it's a comedy

grotesque [grɔtɛsk] adj ludicrous, ridiculous

grotte [grɔt] nf cave; **g. artificielle** grotto

grouillant, -e [grujɑ̃, -ɑ̃t] adj swarming (**de** with)

grouiller [gruje] **1** vi (se presser) to swarm around; **g. de** to swarm with

2 se grouiller vpr Fam to get a move on

groupe [grup] nm (a) (de gens, de choses) group; (de musiciens) group, band; **en g.** in a group; **se mettre par groupes de trois** to get into or form groups of three; Pol **le G. des 7** the Group of Seven; **g. d'âge** age group; Ordinat **g. de discussion** discussion group; Scol **g. de niveau** stream; Pol **g. de pression** pressure group (b) (industriel, de presse) group; (hospitalier, scolaire) complex (c) Gram **g. verbal/nominal** verbal/nominal group (d) Mil **g. de combat** unit (e) Méd **g. sanguin** blood group (f) Él **g. électrogène** generator

groupement [grupmɑ̃] nm (association) group; **g. d'achat** purchasing co-operative; **g. de consom-mateurs** consumer group

grouper [grupe] **1** vt to group (together); (moyens, ressources) to pool

2 se grouper vpr (dans une association) to form a group; (dans un lieu) to gather; **rester groupés** to keep together

groupie [grupi] nf Fam groupie

groupuscule [grupyskyl] nm small group

gruau [gryo] nm **g. (d'avoine)** groats; **(farine de) g.** (fine) wheat flour

grue [gry] *nf* (a) *(oiseau)* crane; **faire le pied de g.** to hang about (b) *(machine)* crane; *TV & Cin* cherry picker (c) *très Fam Vieilli (prostituée)* tart

gruger [45] [gryʒe] *vt (rouler)* to swindle

grumeau, -x [grymo] *nm (dans une sauce, une pâte)* lump

grumeleux, -euse [grymlø, -øz] *adj (sauce, pâte)* lumpy

gruyère [gryjɛr] *nm* Gruyère (cheese)

Guadeloupe [gwadlup] *nf* **la G.** Guadeloupe

guadeloupéen, -enne [gwadlupeɛ̃, -ɛn] **1** *adj* of Guadeloupe
2 *nmf* **G.** person from Guadeloupe

Guatemala [gwatemala] *nm* **le G.** Guatemala

guatémaltèque [gwatemaltɛk] **1** *adj* Guatemalan
2 *nmf* **G.** Guatemalan

gué [ge] *nm* ford; **passer une rivière à g.** to ford a river

guéguerre [gegɛr] *nf Fam* squabble

guenilles [gənij] *nfpl* (old) rags; **en g.** in rags

guenon [gənɔ̃] *nf* female monkey

guépard [gepar] *nm* cheetah

guêpe [gɛp] *nf* wasp; *Fam* **pas folle, la g.!** she's nobody's fool!

guêpier [gepje] *nm* wasps' nest; *Fig (situation)* sticky situation

guêpière [gepjɛr] *nf* basque

guère [gɛr] *adv* **ne... g.** (pas beaucoup) not much; *(pas longtemps)* hardly, scarcely; **il n'a g. d'argent/d'amis** he hasn't got much money/many friends; **il n'y a g. que lui qui soit au courant** he's about the only one who knows what's going on; **il ne mange g. que du pain** he eats hardly anything but bread; **il n'y a g. plus de six ans** just over six years ago; **et celui-là, comment le trouvez-vous? - g. mieux!** and what do you think of that one? - not much better!

guéri, -e [geri] *adj aussi Fig* cured **(de** of)

guéridon [geridɔ̃] *nm* pedestal table

guérilla [gerija] *nf* guerrilla warfare

guérillero [gerijero] *nm* guerrilla

guérir [gerir] **1** *vt (personne, maladie)* to cure; *Fig* **g. qn de qch** *(timidité, habitude)* to cure sb of sth
2 *vi (personne)* to get better, to recover; *(blessure)* **g.** to heal
3 se guérir *vpr (soi-même)* to cure oneself; *Fig* **se g. de qch** *(timidité, habitude)* to cure oneself of sth

guérison [gerizɔ̃] *nf (rétablissement)* recovery

guérissable [gerisabl] *adj* curable

guérisseur, -euse [gerisœr, -øz] *nm,f* healer
2 *nm (d'une tribu)* medicine man

guérite [gerit] *nf Mil* sentry box

guerre [gɛr] *nf* (a) *(conflit)* war; *(technique)* warfare; **en temps de g.** in wartime; **être en g. (contre)** to be at war (with); **faire la g. (soldat)** to fight; **la drôle de g.** the phoney war; **la Grande G.** the Great War; **la Première/la Seconde G. mondiale** the First/Second World War, World War One/Two; **la g. de 14** the 1914–18 War; **la g. de 70** the Franco-Prussian War; **la g. d'Algérie** the Algerian War of Independence; **la g. de Cent Ans** the Hundred Years' War; **la g.** civile civil war; **la g. de Corée** the Korean War; **g. éclair** blitzkrieg; **la g. d'Espagne** the Spanish Civil War; **la g. froide** the cold war; **la g. du Golfe** the Gulf War; **la g. d'Indochine** the first Indo-Chinese War *(1946–1954)*; **g. sainte** holy war; **la g. de Sécession** the American Civil War; **la g. du Viêt Nam** the Vietnam War (b) *(locutions)* **elle fait la g. à son fils pour qu'il ne fume pas** she's fighting a running battle with her son about smoking; **faire la g. à qch** to wage war on sth; **partir en g. contre qch** to declare war on sth; **il est en g. ouverte contre sa hiérarchie** there's open war between him and his superiors; **à la g. comme à la g.** we'll/you'll/*etc* have to do the best we/you/*etc* can; **c'est de bonne g.** that's fair enough; **de g. lasse** for the sake of peace and quiet

guerrier, -ère [gɛrje, -ɛr] **1** *adj* warlike; *(chant)* war
2 *nm,f* warrior

guerroyer [32] [gɛrwaje] *vi Litt* to wage war **(contre** on)

guet [gɛ] *nm* **poste de g.** lookout post; **faire le g.** to be on the lookout

guet-apens *(pl* **guets-apens)** [gɛtapɑ̃] *nm (piège)* ambush; *Fig* trap; **tomber dans un g.** to be ambushed; *Fig* to fall into a trap

guêtre [gɛtr] *nf* gaiter

guetter [gete] *vt (occasion)* to watch out for; *(proie)* to lie in wait for; **le surmenage/la dépression le guette** overwork/depression will get him in the end

gueulante [gœlɑ̃t] *nf* **pousser une g.** to kick up a stink

gueulard, -e [gœlar, -ard] *très Fam* **1** *adj (personne)* loudmouthed, *Br* gobby; *(bébé)* screaming; *(couleur)* garish
2 *nm,f (personne)* loudmouth; *(bébé)* screaming kid

gueule [gœl] *nf* (a) *(d'un animal)* mouth; *Fig* **se jeter dans la g. du loup** to put one's head in the lion's mouth (b) *très Fam (bouche)* mouth; **ça emporte ou arrache la g.** it takes the roof of your mouth off; **une grande g.** *(personne)* a loudmouth; *(ferme)* **ta g.!** shut your mouth or face!, shut it!; **avoir la g. de bois** to have a hangover (c) *très Fam (visage)* mug, face; **avoir une sale g.** *(mine patibulaire)* to look shady; *(mauvaise mine)* to look rotten; **faire la g.** to sulk; **faire la g. à qn** to be in a huff with sb; **faire une g. d'enterrement** to look really pissed off; **se foutre de ou se payer la g. de qn** to take the piss out of sb; **(s')en prendre plein la g.** to get a right mouthful (of abuse) (d) *Fam (allure)* **avoir une drôle de g.** to look odd; **ce tableau a de la g.** that's some picture

gueuler [gœle] *très Fam* **1** *vi* to yell, to bawl; *(radio, télévision)* to blare; *(protester)* to kick up a fuss; **si je suis en retard, ça va g. à la maison** if I'm late, I'll get an earbashing when I get home
2 *vt* to bawl out, to yell out

gueuleton [gœltɔ̃] *nm Fam* blowout; **faire un g.** to have a blowout

gueux, gueuse [gø, gøz] *nm,f Vieilli (mendiant)* beggar

gueuze, gueuse [gøz] *nf* = type of strong double-fermented Belgian beer

gugusse [gygys] *nm Fam* twit; **faire le g.** to act the fool

gui [gi] *nm* mistletoe

guibol(l)e [gibol] *nf Fam (jambe)* pin, leg

guichet [giʃɛ] *nm* (a) *(de gare, de poste, de banque)* window; *(de théâtre)* box office; **on joue à guichets fermés** the performance is sold out; **g. automatique** *(de banque)* cash dispenser (b) *(de porte de prison)* hatch; *(de confessionnal)* grille (c) *(au cricket)* wicket

guichetier, -ère [giʃtje, -ɛr] *nm,f (de gare)* ticket clerk; *(de poste, de banque)* counter clerk

guide [gid] **1** *nm* (a) *(personne)* guide; **g. de haute montagne** mountain guide; **g.-interprète** bilingual tour guide (b) *(manuel)* guide (book); **g. de conversation** phrase book; **g. gastronomique** restaurant guide; **g. touristique** tourist guide
2 *nf (scout) Br* (Girl) Guide, *Am* Girl Scout

guider [gide] *vt* to guide; **se laisser g. par son intuition** to be guided by one's intuition

guidon [gidɔ̃] *nm* handlebars

guigne¹ [giɲ] *nf (cerise)* sweet cherry; *Fam* **se soucier de qn/qch comme d'une g.** not to give a fig about sb/sth

guigne² *nf Fam (malchance)* bad luck; **avoir la g.** to be out of luck

guigner [giɲe] *vt Fam (avoir des vues sur)* to have one's eye on

guignol [giɲɔl] *nm* (a) G. *(personnage)* ≃ Punch (b) *Péj (personne)* clown, joker; **faire le g.** to clown around (c) *(spectacle)* ≃ Punch and Judy show

Guillaume [gijom] *npr* **G. le Conquérant** William the Conqueror

guillemets [gijmε] *nmpl* inverted commas, quotation marks; **entre g.** in inverted commas, in quotation marks

guilleret, -ette [gijrε, -εt] *adj* jaunty, lively

guillotine [gijɔtin] *nf* guillotine

guillotiner [gijɔtine] *vt* to guillotine

guimauve [gimov] *nf (confiserie)* marshmallow; *Fig & Péj* **c'est de la g.** it's pure schmaltz

guimbarde [gɛ̃bard] *nf* (a) *Fam (vieille voiture)* jalopy (b) *(instrument de musique)* Jew's harp

guindé, -e [gɛ̃de] *adj (personne, air)* stiff; *(atmosphère)* strained; *(style)* stilted; *(réception)* posh

Guinée [gine] *nf* **la G.** Guinea; **la G. équatoriale** Equatorial Guinea

Guinée-Bissau [ginebiso] *nf* **la G.** Guinea-Bissau

guinéen, -enne [gineɛ̃, -εn] **1** *adj* Guinean
2 *nm,f* **G.** Guinean

guingois [gɛ̃gwa] **de guingois** *adv* askew, lopsided

guinguette [gɛ̃gεt] *nf* riverside café

guirlande [girlɑ̃d] *nf (de fleurs)* garland; **g. lumineuse** string of lights; **g. de Noël** piece of tinsel; **g. de papier** paper chain

guise [giz] *nf* **faire qch à sa g.** to do sth as one likes; **n'en faire qu'à sa g.** to do just as one likes; **en g. de** by way of

guitare [gitar] *nf* guitar; **g. basse** bass guitar; **g. électrique** electric guitar; **g. sèche** acoustic guitar

guitariste [gitarist] *nmf* guitarist

gus [gys] *nm Fam* guy

gustatif, -ive [gystatif, -iv] *adj* **papilles gustatives** taste buds

guttural, -e, -aux, -ales [gytyral, -o] *adj* guttural

Guyana [gɥijana] *nm* **le G.** Guyana

guyanais, -e [gɥijanε, -εz] **1** *adj* Guianese
2 *nm,f* **G.** Guianese

Guyane [gɥijan] *nf* **la G.** Guiana; **la G. française** French Guiana

gym [ʒim] *nf Fam* gym

gymkhana [ʒimkana] *nm* rally

gymnase [ʒimnɑz] *nm* gymnasium

gymnaste [ʒimnast] *nmf* gymnast

gymnastique [ʒimnastik] *nf* gymnastics; *Fig* **il faut faire toute une g. pour sortir de cette auto** you have to be a contortionist to get out of this car; **g. respiratoire** breathing exercises; **g. rythmique** eurhythmics *(singulier)*

gynécologie [ʒinekɔlɔʒi] *nf* gynaecology

gynécologique [ʒinekɔlɔʒik] *adj* gynaecological

gynécologue [ʒinekɔlɔg] *nmf* gynaecologist

gypse [ʒips] *nm* gypsum

gyrophare [ʒirofar] *nm* flashing light

H

H, h [aʃ] *nm inv* H, h; **h. aspiré** aspirate h; **h muet** mute h

*ha [ɑ] *exclam* ah!; **ha, ha!** *(rire)* ha-ha!

habile [abil] *adj* **(a)** *(personne)* skilful; *(manœuvre, film, roman)* clever; **être h. de ses mains** to be good with one's hands; **être h. en affaires** to be a good businessman/businesswoman **(b)** *Jur* **h. à faire qch** able to do sth

habilement [abilmɑ̃] *adv* skilfully

habileté [abilte] *nf* skill

habiliter [abilite] *vt* **Jur h. qn à faire qch** to enable sb to do sth

habillage [abijaʒ] *nm* **(a)** *(d'une personne)* dressing **(b)** **h. intérieur** *(d'une voiture)* trim **(c)** *TV & Rad* station identification

habillé, -e [abije] *adj* **(a)** *(vêtu)* dressed; **h. en femme/cosmonaute** dressed (up) as a woman/spaceman; **s'endormir tout h.** to go to sleep with one's clothes on **(b)** *(élégant) (personne, tenue)* smart; **soirée habillée** formal occasion

habillement [abijmɑ̃] *nm* **(a)** *(vêtements)* clothes **(b)** *(industrie)* clothing industry

habiller [abije] **1** *vt* **(a)** *(vêtir)* to dress; **h. qn en soldat/cow-boy** to dress sb up as a soldier/cowboy **(b)** *(fournir en vêtements)* to clothe **(c)** *(garnir)* to cover **(d)** *(aller à)* **un rien t'habille** you look good in anything
2 s'habiller *vpr* **(a)** *(se vêtir)* to get dressed, to dress; **elle s'habille n'importe comment** she wears any old thing; **comment vous habillez-vous pour la soirée?** what are you wearing to the party?; **s'h. en femme/cosmonaute** to dress up as a woman/spaceman **(b)** *(se fournir)* **elle s'habille chez Dior** she buys her clothes from Dior **(c)** *(élégamment)* to dress up

habilleur, -euse [abijœr, -øz] *nm,f* dresser

habit [abi] *nm* **(a)** *(vêtement)* **habits** clothes; **habits du dimanche** Sunday best **(b)** *(tenue)* **h. (de soirée)** evening dress, tails; **l'h. vert** = the green coat worn by a member of the Académie française **(c)** *(religieux)* habit; *Prov* **l'h. ne fait pas le moine** appearances can be deceptive

habitable [abitabl] *adj* (in)habitable

habitacle [abitakl] *nm (d'un avion)* cockpit; *(d'une voiture)* passenger compartment

habitant, -e [abitɑ̃, -ɑ̃t] **1** *nm,f* **(a)** *(d'une ville)* inhabitant, resident; *(d'une maison)* occupant; **loger chez l'h.** *(en voyage)* to stay with local people **(b)** *Can (fermier)* small-scale farmer
2 *adj Can Péj* **il est un peu h.** he's a bit of a country bumpkin

habitat [abita] *nm (d'un animal, d'une plante)* habitat; *(de personnes) (mode de peuplement)* settlement; *(conditions de logement)* housing conditions

habitation [abitasjɔ̃] *nf* **(a)** *(fait de résider)* living; **locaux à usage d'h.** premises for residential use **(b)** *(lieu)* dwelling; **h. à loyer modéré** *Br* ≃ council flat/house, *Am* ≃ public housing unit

habiter [abite] **1** *vt (maison, lieu)* to live in; *Fig (âme, personne)* to possess; **la région n'est pas habitée** the area is uninhabited
2 *vi* to live (**à/en** in)

habitude [abityd] *nf* **(a)** *(comportement répété)* habit; **avoir l'h.** *ou* **avoir pour h. de faire qch** to be in the habit of doing sth; **ça ne la gênera pas, elle a l'h.** that won't bother her, she's used to it; **avoir l'h. de qch** to be used to sth; **prendre l'h. de faire qch** to get into the habit of doing sth; **faire qch par h.** to do sth out of habit; **ce n'est pas dans mes habitudes** I don't make a habit of it; **d'h.** usually; **meilleur/plus tôt que d'h.** better/earlier than usual; **comme d'h.** as usual **(b)** **habitudes** *(coutumes)* customs

habitué, -e [abitye] *nm,f (d'une maison)* regular visitor; *(d'un restaurant, d'un magasin)* regular (customer)

habituel, -elle [abityɛl] *adj* usual, customary

habituellement [abityɛlmɑ̃] *adv* usually

habituer [abitye] **1** *vt* **h. qn à qch/à faire qch** to get sb used to sth/to doing sth; **être habitué à qn/à qch/à faire qch** to be used or accustomed to sb/to sth/to doing sth
2 s'habituer *vpr* **s'h. à qn/à qch/à faire qch** to get used or accustomed to sb/to sth/to doing sth

*hâbleur, -euse [ablœr, -øz] *adj* boastful

*hache [aʃ] *nf* axe; *Fig* **enterrer la h. de guerre** to bury the hatchet

*haché, -e [aʃe] **1** *adj* **(a)** *(viande)* *Br* minced, *Am* ground; *(légumes, herbes)* chopped **(b)** *(style, phrases)* jerky
2 *nm Br* mince, *Am* ground meat

*hacher [aʃe] *vt* to chop (up); *(viande) (dans un hachoir)* *Br* to mince, *Am* to grind; **h. menu qch** to chop sth (up) finely; *Fig* **h. qn menu** *(comme chair à pâté)* to make mincemeat of sb; *Fig* **se faire h.** *(se faire battre)* to be massacred

*hachette [aʃɛt] *nf* hatchet

*hachis [aʃi] *nm* **h. d'herbes** chopped herbs; **h. Parmentier** ≃ cottage pie; **h. de viande** *Br* mince, *Am* ground meat

*hachisch [aʃiʃ] *nm* hashish

*hachoir [aʃwar] *nm* **(a)** *(couteau)* chopper **(b)** *(machine)* *Br* mincer, *Am* grinder

*hachurer [aʃyre] *vt* to hatch

*hachures [aʃyr] *nfpl* hatching

*hagard, -e [agar, -ard] *adj (visage)* haggard; *(expression, regard, yeux)* wild

---

The symbol ***** indicates that the initial **h** is aspirate and that hence there is no liaison

*haie [ε] nf (a) (clôture) hedge; h. vive quickset hedge (b) (en athlétisme) hurdle; (en équitation) fence; 400 mètres haies 400 metre hurdles (c) (d'arbres, de pieux, de curieux) line, row; h. d'honneur guard of honour

*haillons [ɔjɔ̃] nmpl (vêtements) rags; en h. in rags (and tatters)

*haine [ɛn] nf hate, hatred; sa h. de/pour his hatred of/for; très Fam avoir la h. (être révolté) to be full of rage; (être furieux) to be bloody furious

*haineux, -euse [ɛnø, -øz] adj full of hatred

*haïr [41] [air] 1 vt to hate
2 se haïr vpr (soi-même) to hate oneself; (l'un l'autre) to hate each other

*hais voir haïr

*haïssable [aisabl] adj hateful

*hait voir haïr

Haïti [aiti] n Haiti

haïtien, -enne [aisjɛ̃, -ɛn] 1 adj Haitian
2 nm,f H. Haitian

*halage [alaʒ] nm towing

*hâle [al] nm (sun)tan

*hâlé, -e [ale] adj (sun)tanned

haleine [alɛn] nf breath; avoir mauvaise h. to have bad breath; courir à perdre h. to run until one is out of breath; reprendre h. to get one's breath (back); tenir qn en h. to keep sb in suspense; hors d'h. out of breath, breathless; travail de longue h. long job

*haler [ale] vt to tow

*haletant, -e [alatɑ̃, -ɑ̃t] adj (coureur, malade, voix) panting, gasping; Fig (suspense) unbearable; respiration haletante panting, gasping

*halètement [alɛtmɑ̃] nm (d'un coureur, d'un malade) panting, gasping

*haleter [alte] vi (coureur, malade) to pant, to gasp

*hall [ol] nm (d'une maison) entrance hall; (d'un hôtel) foyer, lobby; (d'un aéroport) lounge; h. d'accueil reception hall; h. d'entrée entrance hall; h. de gare station concourse; Péj littérature/roman de h. de gare trashy literature/novel

*halle [al] nf (covered) market; h. au poisson fish market

*hallebarde [albard] nf halberd; Fam il pleut ou tombe des hallebardes it's raining cats and dogs

hallucinant, -e [alysinɑ̃, -ɑ̃t] adj (extraordinaire) striking; (incroyable) incredible

hallucination [alysinasjɔ̃] nf hallucination; avoir des hallucinations (malade, ivrogne) to have hallucinations; Fig (se tromper) to see things

halluciner [alysine] vi (avoir des hallucinations) to hallucinate; Fam Fig j'hallucine! I don't believe it!

hallucinogène [alysinɔʒɛn] 1 adj hallucinogenic
2 nm hallucinogen

*halo [alo] nm aussi Fig halo

halogène [alɔʒɛn] nm Chim halogen; (lampe à) h. halogen lamp

*halte [alt] nf (a) (arrêt) stop; faire h. to stop; h.(-là)! stop!; Fig h.-là, je ne suis pas d'accord! hold on, I don't agree!; h. à l'armement! stop the arms build-up! (b) (lieu) stopping place

*halte-garderie [pl haltes-garderies] [altəgardəri] nf crèche

haltère [altɛr] nm dumbbell

haltérophile [altɛrɔfil] nmf weightlifter

haltérophilie [altɛrɔfili] nf weightlifting

*hamac [amak] nm hammock

*Hambourg [ɑ̃bur] n Hamburg

*hamburger [ɑ̃burgœr] nm burger

*hameau, -x [amo] nm hamlet

hameçon [amsɔ̃] nm (fish-)hook; Fig mordre à l'h. to swallow the bait

*hammam [amam] nm Turkish baths

*hampe [ɑ̃p] nf (d'un drapeau) pole

*hamster [amster] nm hamster

*hanche [ɑ̃ʃ] nf hip

*hand [ɑ̃d] nm Fam handball

*handball [ɑ̃dbal] nm handball

*handballeur, -euse [ɑ̃dbalœr, -øz] nm,f handball player

*handicap [ɑ̃dikap] nm (physique, mental) disability; Fig handicap; Fig partir avec un h. to start at a disadvantage

*handicapé, -e [ɑ̃dikape] 1 adj disabled
2 nm,f disabled person; les handicapés the disabled; h. mental mentally handicapped person; h. moteur person with motor impairment

*handicaper [ɑ̃dikape] vt (physiquement, mentalement) to disable; Fig to handicap

*hangar [ɑ̃gar] nm shed; (pour les trains, les bus) depot; (pour les avions) hangar; h. à bateaux boathouse

*hanneton [antɔ̃] nm cockchafer; Fam pas piqué des hannetons (difficile) tough; (bon, beau) incredible

Hanoi [anɔj] n Hanoi

Hanovre [anɔvr] n Hanover

*hanté, -e [ɑ̃te] adj haunted

*hanter [ɑ̃te] vt (sujet: fantôme, pensée) to haunt; Fig (bars, musées) to hang round

*hantise [ɑ̃tiz] nf obsession; avoir la h. de qch to really dread sth

*happer [ape] vt (dans sa gueule, son bec) to snap up; (sujet: véhicule) to hit

*hara-kiri [arakiri] nm hara-kiri; (se) faire h. to commit hara-kiri

*harangue [arɑ̃g] nf harangue

*haranguer [arɑ̃ge] vt to harangue

*haras [ara] nm stud farm

*harassant, -e [arasɑ̃, -ɑ̃t] adj exhausting

*harassé, -e [arase] adj exhausted

*harasser [arase] vt to exhaust

*harcèlement [arsɛlmɑ̃] nm harassment; h. sexuel sexual harassment

*harceler [39/42] [arsəle] vt (importuner) to harass; (insister auprès de) to pester; h. qn de questions to pester sb with questions; être harcelé de remords/regrets to be plagued by remorse/regrets

*harde [ard] nf (de cerfs) herd

*hardes [ard] nfpl (haillons) rags

*hardi, -e [ardi] adj (audacieux, original) bold; (osé) brazen

*hardiesse [ardjɛs] nf (audace, originalité) boldness; (caractère osé) brazenness

*hardiment [ardimɑ̃] adv (avec audace) boldly

*hard-rock [ardrɔk] nm hard rock

*harem [arɛm] nm harem

eg les haricots [leariko] and not [lezariko], or contraction in spelling, eg la haine and not l'haine.

*hareng [arɑ̃] *nm* herring; **h. saur** smoked herring

*harfang [arfɑ̃] *nm Can* snowy owl

*hargne [arɲ] *nf* bad temper; **avec h.** bad-temperedly

*hargneux, -euse [arɲø, -øz] *adj (personne)* bad-tempered; **d'un ton h.** bad-temperedly

*haricot [ariko] *nm* **(a)** *(légume)* bean; **haricots en grains** dried beans; *Fam* **c'est la fin des haricots** we've/they've/*etc* had it now; *Fam* **courir sur le h. à qn** *Br* to get up sb's nose, *Am* to tee sb off; **h. beurre** butter bean; **h. blanc** haricot bean; **h. rouge** red kidney bean; **h. vert** green bean **(b)** *Culin* **h. de mouton** mutton stew

*harissa [arisa] *nf Culin* harissa *(hot pepper purée)*

*harki [arki] *nm* harki *(Algerian soldier who fought on the French side during the Franco-Algerian War)*

harmonica [armɔnika] *nm* harmonica, mouth organ

harmonie [armɔni] *nf* **(a)** *(accord)* & *Mus* harmony; **être en h. avec qch** to be in harmony with sth; **vivre en h.** to live in harmony **(b)** *(fanfare)* brass band

harmonieux, -euse [armɔnjø, -øz] *adj* harmonious

harmonique [armɔnik] *adj Mus* harmonic

harmonisation [armɔnizasjɔ̃] *nf* harmonization

harmoniser [armɔnize] **1** *vt* to harmonize **(avec** with)
2 s'harmoniser *vpr* to go well together

harmonium [armɔnjɔm] *nm* harmonium

*harnachement [arnaʃmɑ̃] *nm* **(a)** *(action)* harnessing **(b)** *(harnais)* harness; *Fig (vêtements)* get-up

*harnacher [arnaʃe] *vt (cheval)* to harness; *Fig* **il fallait voir comment elle était harnachée** you should have seen the get-up she was wearing

*harnais [arnɛ] *nm* **(a)** *(de cheval)* harness **(b)** **h. de sécurité** *(d'alpiniste, d'élagueur)* safety harness

*haro [aro] *nm* **crier h. sur** to rail against; **crier h. sur le baudet** to scream for blood

*harpe [arp] *nf* harp

*harpie [arpi] *nf aussi Fig* harpy

*harpiste [arpist] *nmf* harpist

*harpon [arpɔ̃] *nm* harpoon; **pêche au h.** harpoon fishing

*harponner [arpɔne] *vt* **(a)** *(poisson)* to harpoon **(b)** *Fam (sujet: police)* to nab; *(sujet: importun)* to corner

*hasard [azar] *nm* **(a)** *(sort)* chance, luck; **coup de h.** stroke of luck; **par un heureux h.** by a happy coincidence; **ne rien laisser au h.** to leave nothing to chance; **le h. fait bien les choses!** what a stroke of luck!; **au h.** *(choisir, répondre)* at random; *(marcher)* aimlessly; **au h. de ses voyages/lectures** in the course of her travels/reading; **à tout h.** *(par précaution)* just in case; *(pour voir)* on the off chance; **par h.** by accident, by chance; **si par h. vous le voyez** if you (should) happen to see him; **comme par h.** as if by chance **(b)** **hasards** *(dangers)* hazards

*hasarder [azarde] **1** *vt (opinion, remarque)* to venture
2 se hasarder *vpr (dans l'obscurité, dans la jungle)* to venture; **se h. à faire qch** to risk doing sth

*hasardeux, -euse [azardø, -øz] *adj* risky, hazardous

*hasch [aʃ] *nm Fam* hash, pot

*haschisch [aʃiʃ] *nm* hashish

*hâte [ɑt] *nf* haste; **avoir h. de faire qch** *(avoir envie)* to be eager to do sth; **à la h.** hastily; **en h.** in a hurry, hurriedly

*hâter [ɑte] **1** *vt (accélérer)* to hasten; *(avancer)* to bring forward
2 se hâter *vpr* to hurry; **se h. de faire qch** to hurry to do sth

*hâtif, -ive [ɑtif, -iv] *adj (trop rapide)* hasty

*hâtivement [ɑtivmɑ̃] *adv* hastily

*hauban [obɑ̃] *nm* **(a)** *Naut* shroud **(b)** *(d'un pont)* stay

*hausse [os] *nf* rise, increase **(de** in); **être en h.** to be rising; **être à la h.** *(marché)* to be rising; **jouer à la h.** *(en Bourse)* to speculate on a rising market

*haussement [osmɑ̃] *nm* **h. d'épaules** shrug; **avec un h. de sourcils** with raised eyebrows

*hausser [ose] **1** *vt* to raise; **h. la voix/les sourcils** to raise one's voice/eyebrows; **h. les épaules** to shrug (one's shoulders)
2 se hausser *vpr* to raise oneself (up); **se h. sur la pointe des pieds** to stand on tiptoe

*haussier [osje] *adj m voir* **marché**

*haut, -e [o, ot] **1** *adj* **(a)** *(dans l'espace, en quantité, en intensité)* high; **une femme de haute taille** a tall woman; **un mur h. de 3 mètres** a 3-metre high wall **(b)** *(dans une hiérarchie)* high; **la haute couture** high fashion; **les hauts salaires** the highly paid; **un athlète de h. niveau** a top-ranking athlete; **une montre de haute précision** a high-precision timepiece; **de hauts faits** daring deeds **(c)** *(note)* high **(d)** *(dans le temps)* early; **le h. Moyen Âge** the early Middle Ages **(e)** **h. en couleur** *(récit, personnage)* colourful

2 *adv* **(a)** *(dans l'espace)* high; **comme il est dit plus h.** as mentioned above; **h. les mains!** hands up! **gagner h. la main** to win hands down; **h. les cœurs!** cheer up! **(b)** *(dans une hiérarchie)* highly **(c)** *(dans la gamme)* high **(d)** *(fort)* **dire qch tout h.** to say sth out loud; **dire tout h. ce que tout le monde pense tout bas** to say what everyone is thinking (but is too afraid to say) **(e)** **en h.** at the top; *(à l'étage supérieur)* upstairs; **les gens d'en h.** the people above *or* upstairs; **en h. de** at the top of **3** *nm* **(a)** *(hauteur)* **le mur fait 3 mètres de h.** the wall is 3 metres high **(b)** *(partie supérieure)* top; **l'étagère du h.** the top shelf; **regarder qn de h. en bas** to look sb up and down; **connaître des hauts et des bas** to have one's ups and downs **(c)** *(corsage)* top

4 *nf Fam* **haute** upper crust

*hautain, -e [otɛ̃, -ɛn] *adj* haughty

*hautbois [obwa] *nm* oboe

*haut-commissariat *(pl* **hauts-commissariats** [okomisarja] *nm* high commission

*haut-de-chausses *(pl* **hauts-de-chausses** [odəʃos] *nm* breeches

*haut-de-forme *(pl* **hauts-de-forme** [odəfɔrm] *nm* top hat

*haute-contre *(pl* **hautes-contre** [otkɔ̃tr] *nm* counter tenor

*haute-fidélité [otfidelite] *nf* hi-fi; **chaîne h.** hi-fi (system)

*hautement [otmɑ̃] *adv (très)* highly

*hauteur [otœr] *nf* (a) *(dimension)* height (b) *(altitude)* altitude; prendre de la h. to climb, to gain height; à la h. de qch *(dans l'espace)* level with sth; à la h. du Mans near Le Mans; *Fig* être *ou* se montrer à la h. de qch to be equal to *or* up to sth; être à la h. to be up to it; à h. des yeux at eye level; l'eau nous arrivait à h. des épaules the water came up to our shoulders; contribuer à h. de deux millions to contribute two million (c) *(d'une note de musique)* pitch

*haut-fond (*pl* hauts-fonds) [ofõ] *nm* shallow

*haut-fourneau (*pl* hauts-fourneaux) [ofurno] *nm* blast furnace

*haut-le-cœur [olɔkœr] *nm inv* avoir un h. to retch; cette vision me donna un h. the sight of it made me feel sick

*haut-parleur (*pl* haut-parleurs) [oparlœr] *nm* (loud)speaker

*Havane [avan] 1 *voir* La Havane
2 *nm* h. Havana (cigar)

*hâve [av] *adj* *(visage)* gaunt; *(joues)* sunken

*havre [avr] *nm Litt* haven

Hawaii [awai] *n* Hawaii

hawaiien, -enne [awajɛ̃, -ɛn] 1 *adj* Hawaiian
2 *nm,f* H. Hawaiian

*Haye [ɛ] *voir* La Haye

*hayon [ajõ] *nm* *(d'une voiture)* hatchback

HCR [aʃœr] *nm (abrév* Haut-Commissariat des Nations unies pour les réfugiés) UNHCR

*hé [e] *exclam (pour interpeller)* hey!

hebdo [ɛbdo] *nm Fam* weekly; h. télé TV magazine programme

hebdomadaire [ɛbdomadɛr] *adj & nm* weekly

hébergement [ebɛrʒəmã] *nm (d'un ami)* putting up; *(d'un sans-abri, d'un réfugié)* taking in; *(d'un fugitif)* harbouring

héberger [45] [ebɛrʒe] *vt (ami)* to put up; *(sans-abri, réfugié)* to take in; *(fugitif)* to harbour

hébété, -e [ebete] *adj* dazed

hébreu, -x [ebrø] 1 *adj m* Hebrew
2 *nm (langue)* Hebrew; *Fam* c'est de l'h. pour moi it's all Greek to me
3 *nmpl* les Hébreux the Hebrews

Hébrides [ebrid] *nfpl* les H. the Hebrides

HEC [aʃœk] *nf (abrév* Hautes études commerciales) = prestigious business school in Paris

hécatombe [ekatõb] *nf (tuerie)* slaughter, massacre; *Fig* ça a été une h. cette année à l'examen! the exam results were disastrous this year!

hectare [ɛktar] *nm* hectare

hectogramme [ɛktogram] *nm* hectogram

hectolitre [ɛktolitr] *nm* hectolitre

hectomètre [ɛktometr] *nm* hectometre

hédonisme [edɔnism] *nm* hedonism

hédoniste [edɔnist] 1 *adj* hedonistic
2 *nmf* hedonist

hégémonie [eʒemɔni] *nf* hegemony

*hein [ɛ̃] *exclam Fam* (a) *(pour faire répéter)* eh?, what? (b) *(pour insister)* il fait beau aujourd'hui, h.? it's a nice day, isn't it?; ne refais jamais ça, h.! don't ever do that again, OK?; h. qu'il fait bien la cuisine! he does cook well, doesn't he?

*hélas [elɑs] *exclam* unfortunately

*hêler [34] [ele] *vt* to hail

hélice [elis] *nf* (a) *(d'un hélicoptère, d'un bateau)* propeller (b) *Math & Biol* helix

hélico [eliko] *nm Fam* chopper

hélicoïdal, -e, -aux, -ales [elikoidal, -o] *adj* helical

hélicoptère [elikɔptɛr] *nm* helicopter

héliomarin, -e [eljomarɛ̃, -in] *adj Méd* cure héliomarine = course of treatment based on sun and sea air; centre h. = seaside convalescent home where heliotherapy is used

héliothérapie [eljoterapi] *nf Méd* heliotherapy

héliport [elipɔr] *nm* heliport

héliporté, -e [elipɔrte] *adj (matériel)* transported by helicopter; *(troupes)* airborne

hélium [eljɔm] *nm* helium

*Helsinki [ɛlsinki] *n* Helsinki

helvétique [ɛlvetik] *adj* Swiss

hématie [emasi] *nf Biol* red blood corpuscle

hématologie [ematɔlɔʒi] *nf Méd* haematology

hématome [ematom] *nm* bruise, *Spéc* haematoma; se faire un h. to bruise oneself

hémicycle [emisikl] *nm* l'h. *(de l'Assemblée nationale)* the chamber

hémiplégie [emipleʒi] *nf Méd* hemiplegia

hémiplégique [emipleʒik] *adj & nmf Méd* hemiplegic

hémisphère [emisfɛr] *nm* hemisphere; l'h. Nord/Sud the Northern/Southern hemisphere

hémisphérique [emisferik] *adj* hemispheric(al)

hémistiche [emistiʃ] *nm* hemistich

hémoglobine [emoglɔbin] *nf* haemoglobin; *Fig (dans un film)* blood and gore

hémophile [emofil] *Méd* 1 *adj* haemophilic
2 *nm* haemophiliac

hémophilie [emofili] *nf Méd* haemophilia

hémorragie [emoraʒi] *nf* haemorrhage, bleeding; *Fig (des capitaux)* drain; h. interne internal bleeding

hémorroïdes [emorɔid] *nfpl* haemorrhoids, piles

*henné [ene] *nm* henna; se faire un h. to henna one's hair

*hennir [enir] *vi* to neigh, to whinny; *Fig (personne)* to bray

*hennissement [enismã] *nm* neigh, whinny; *Fig (d'une personne)* braying; hennissements neighing, whinnying; *Fig* braying

*hep [ɛp] *exclam* hey!

hépatique [epatik] *adj Méd* hepatic

hépatite [epatit] *nf* hepatitis

héraldique [eraldik] 1 *adj* heraldic
2 *nf* heraldry

herbage [ɛrbaʒ] *nm* pasture

herbe [ɛrb] *nf* (a) *(de gazon)* grass; *Fig* couper l'h. sous le pied à qn to cut the ground from under sb's feet; en h. *(céréale)* green; *Fig (débutant)* budding (b) *(plante)* herb; fines herbes mixed herbs; omelette/fromage aux fines herbes omelette/cheese with herbs; mauvaise h. weed; herbes folles wild grass; *Can* h. à la puce poison ivy (c) *Fam (drogue)* grass

herbeux, -euse [ɛrbø, -øz] *adj* grassy

herbicide [ɛrbisid] *adj & nm (produit)* h. weedkiller

herbier [ɛrbje] *nm (collection)* herbarium

herbivore [ɛrbivɔr] *Zool* **1** *adj* herbivorous
 2 *nm* herbivore

herboriser [ɛrbɔrize] *vi* to collect plants

herboriste [ɛrbɔrist] *nmf* herbalist

herboristerie [ɛrbɔristəri] *nf* (*boutique*) herbalist's (shop); (*commerce*) herb trade

herbu, -e [ɛrby] *adj* grassy

herculéen, -enne [ɛrkyleẽ, -ɛn] *adj* Herculean

*****here** [ɛr] *nm* **pauvre h.** poor creature

héréditaire [ereditɛr] *adj* (*maladie, titre*) hereditary; **c'est h.!** it runs in the family!

hérédité [eredite] *nf Biol* heredity; **avoir une lourde h.** to come from a family with a history of mental/physical illness

hérésie [erezi] *nf* heresy; *Fig* **c'est une h. ou de l'h.!** that's sacrilege!

hérétique [eretik] **1** *adj* heretical
 2 *nmf* heretic

*****hérissé, -e** [erise] *adj* (**a**) (*cheveux*) spiky; (*moustache*) bristly (**b**) (*garni*) **h. de** bristling with

*****hérisser** [erise] **1** *vt* (**a**) (*ses plumes*) to ruffle up; **h. ses poils** to bristle (**b**) *Fig* (*mettre en colère*) **h. qn** to get sb's back up
 2 se hérisser *vpr* (*animal*) to bristle; (*poils, cheveux*) to stand on end; *Fig* (*personne*) to bristle

*****hérisson** [erisɔ̃] *nm* hedgehog

héritage [eritaʒ] *nm* inheritance; *Fig* (*spirituel, intellectuel*) heritage; **faire un h.** to come into an inheritance

hériter [erite] **1** *vt* to inherit (**de** from)
 2 hériter de *vt ind* (*fortune, objet, qualité*) to inherit; **h. de qn** to receive an inheritance from sb; *Fig* **h. de qn/qch** (*se retrouver avec*) to be landed with sb/sth

héritier, -ère [eritje, -ɛr] *nm,f* heir, *f* heiress (**de** to)

hermaphrodite [ɛrmafrɔdit] *nm & adj* hermaphrodite

hermétique [ɛrmetik] *adj* (**a**) (*récipient*) hermetically sealed; (*joint*) (*à l'air*) airtight; (*à l'eau*) watertight (**b**) *Fig* (*abscons*) abstruse; (*visage*) impenetrable; **être h. à qch** to be impervious to sth

hermétiquement [ɛrmetikmɑ̃] *adv* hermetically

hermine [ɛrmin] *nf* (*animal*) stoat; (*fourrure*) ermine

*****hernie** [ɛrni] *nf* hernia; **h. discale** slipped disc

héroïne¹ [erɔin] *nf* (*personnage*) heroine

héroïne² (*drogue*) heroin

héroïnomane [erɔinɔman] *nmf* heroin addict

héroïque [erɔik] *adj* heroic

héroïquement [erɔikmɑ̃] *adv* heroically

héroïsme [erɔism] *nm* heroism

*****héron** [erɔ̃] *nm* heron; **h. cendré** grey heron

*****héros** [ero] *nm* hero; **mourir en h.** to die a hero's death

herpès [ɛrpɛs] *nm Méd* herpes; (*buccal*) cold sore

*****herse** [ɛrs] *nf* (**a**) (*pour labourer*) harrow (**b**) (*de forteresse*) portcullis

hertz [ɛrts] *nm* hertz

hésitant, -e [ezitɑ̃, -ɑ̃t] *adj* hesitant

hésitation [ezitasjɔ̃] *nf* hesitation; **avec h.** hesitatingly; **sans h.** without hesitation

hésiter [ezite] *vi* to hesitate (**sur/entre** over/between); **je ne sais pas, j'hésite** I don't know, I can't make up my mind; **h. à faire qch** to hesitate to do sth

hétéro [etero] *adj & nmf Fam* straight, hetero

hétéroclite [eterɔklit] *adj* motley

hétérogène [eterɔʒɛn] *adj* mixed

hétérogénéité [eterɔʒeneite] *nf* heterogeneity

hétérosexualité [eterɔsɛksɥalite] *nf* heterosexuality

hétérosexuel, -elle [eterɔsɛksɥɛl] *adj & nm,f* heterosexual

*****hêtre** [ɛtr] *nm* beech

*****heu** [ø] *exclam* er

heure [œr] *nf* (**a**) (*soixante minutes*) hour; **30 francs l'h. ou de l'h.** 30 francs an hour; *Scol* **h. de cours** period; **heures supplémentaires** overtime
 (**b**) (*de la journée*) time; **à h. fixe** at regular intervals; **à toute h.** at any time; **à toute h. du jour ou de la nuit** at any hour of the day or night; **quelle h. est-il?** what time is it?, what's the time?; **quelle h. avez-vous?** what time do you make it?; **il est deux heures** it's two o'clock; **cinq heures moins dix** ten to five; **trois heures vingt** twenty past three; **vingt heures quarante** eight forty pm; **à quelle h....?** what time...?; **ils devraient être arrivés à l'h.** qu'il est they ought to have arrived by now; **être à l'h.** (*personne*) to be on time; (*montre*) to be right; **mettre sa montre à l'h.** to set one's watch; **à la bonne h.!** marvellous!; **de bonne h.** early; **heures d'affluence** peak hours; **heures de bureau** office hours; **h. d'été** *Br* summer opening, *Am* daylight-saving time; **heures d'ouverture** opening hours; **heures de pointe** rush hour
 (**c**) (*moment précis*) time; **l'h. du dîner/déjeuner** dinner/lunch time; **il est ou c'est l'h. (de faire qch)** it's time (to do sth); **son h. est venue** his time has come; **avoir son h. de gloire** to have one's moment of glory; **l'h. H** zero hour
 (**d**) (*moment présent*) **l'h. est grave** these are difficult times; **à l'h. actuelle** currently; **pour l'h.** for the present, for the time being; *Litt* **sur l'h.** at once

heureusement [œrøzmɑ̃] *adv* (**a**) (*par bonheur*) fortunately, luckily; **h. que j'étais là** it's a good thing I was there (**b**) (*avec succès*) successfully

heureux, -euse [œrø, -øz] **1** *adj* (**a**) (*satisfait*) happy (**de** with); **être h. en ménage** to be happily married; **vivre h.** to live happily; **être h. de faire qch** to be happy to do sth; **h. anniversaire!** happy birthday! (**b**) (*favorable*) successful; (*juste*) (*formule, style*) apt; (*choix*) happy (**c**) (*favorisé*) lucky; **h. au jeu/en amour** lucky at cards/in love; **s'estimer h. (de faire qch)** to consider oneself lucky (to do sth) (**d**) (*situation*) **c'est h. que vous soyez libre** it's a good thing you're free; *Fam* **encore h. (qu'il ait gardé le ticket de caisse)!** it's just as well (he held on to the receipt)!
 2 *nm,f* **si tu le lui donnes, tu vas faire un h.** if you give it to him, you'll make him a happy man; **faire des h.** to make some people happy

*****heurt** [œr] *nm* (*choc*) collision; *Fig* (*conflit*) clash; **sans heurts** smoothly, without a hitch

*****heurter** [œrte] **1** *vt* (**a**) (*cogner*) to hit; (*entrer en collision avec*) to collide with (**b**) (*choquer*) to offend
 2 *vi* **h. contre qch** to hit sth
 3 se heurter *vpr* (**a**) (*se cogner*) to collide (**à** *ou* **contre** with); *Fig* **se h. à qch** to meet with sth (**b**) (*couleurs, intérêts, personnes*) to clash

*****heurtoir** [œrtwar] *nm* (*door*) knocker

hévéa [evea] *nm* rubber tree

hexagonal, -e, -aux, -ales [ɛgzagɔnal, -o] *adj* hexagonal; *Fig* French

hexagone [ɛgzagɔn] *nm* hexagon; *Fig* **l'H.** France

The symbol * indicates that the initial **h** is aspirate and that hence there is no liaison

hiatus [jatys] *nm* (a) *Ling & Anat* hiatus (b) *(décalage)* gap

hibernation [ibɛrnasjɔ̃] *nf* hibernation

hiberner [ibɛrne] *vi* to hibernate

*****hibou, -x** [ibu] *nm* owl

*****hic** [ik] *nm inv Fam* **voilà le h.!** that's the snag!; **le h., c'est que...** the snag is...

*****hideusement** [idøzmɑ̃] *adv* hideously

*****hideux, -euse** [idø, -øz] *adj* hideous

hier [jɛr] *adv* yesterday; **h. matin/soir** yesterday morning/evening; **je m'en souviens comme si c'était h.** I remember it as if it were yesterday; **le journal d'h.** yesterday's paper; **cela ne date pas d'h.** that's nothing new; **je ne suis pas né d'h.** I wasn't born yesterday

*****hiérarchie** [jerarʃi] *nf* hierarchy

*****hiérarchique** [jerarʃik] *adj* hierarchical; **c'est mon supérieur h.** he's immediately above me in rank; **par la voie h.** through the official channels

*****hiérarchisé, -e** [jerarʃize] *adj* hierarchical

*****hiéroglyphe** [jeroglif] *nm* hieroglyph

*****hi-fi** [ifi] *adj inv & nf inv* hi-fi

*****hi-han** [iɑ̃] *exclam* hee-haw!

hilarant, -e [ilarɑ̃, -ɑ̃t] *adj* hilarious

hilare [ilar] *adj* grinning

hilarité [ilarite] *nf* hilarity, mirth; **provoquer l'h. générale** to be the source of much hilarity

Himalaya [imalaja] *nm* **l'H.** the Himalayas

*****hindi** [indi] *nm* Hindi

hindou, -e [ɛ̃du] **1** *adj* Hindu
  2 *nm,f* **H.** Hindu

hindouisme [ɛ̃duism] *nm* Hinduism

*****hippie** [ipi] *adj & nmf* hippy

hippique [ipik] *adj* **concours h.** horse show; **sport h.** equestrianism

hippisme [ipism] *nm* horse riding; *(courses)* horse racing

hippocampe [ipokɑ̃p] *nm* sea horse

hippodrome [ipodrom] *nm Br* racecourse, *Am* racetrack

hippopotame [ipopotam] *nm* hippopotamus

*****hippy** [ipi] = **hippie**

hirondelle [irɔ̃dɛl] *nf* swallow; *Prov* **une h. ne fait pas le printemps** one swallow doesn't make a summer; **h. de mer** tern

hirsute [irsyt] *adj (personne)* hairy; *(barbe)* shaggy; *(cheveux)* unkempt

hispanique [ispanik] *adj* Hispanic

hispano-américain, -e *(mpl* **hispano-américains,** *fpl* **hispano-américaines)** [ispanoamerikɛ̃, -ɛn] **1** *adj* Spanish-American
  2 *nm,f* **H.** Spanish-American, Hispanic

hispanophone [ispanofɔn] **1** *adj* Spanish-speaking
  2 *nmf* Spanish speaker

*****hisser** [ise] **1** *vt* to hoist (up); **ho! hisse!** heave-ho!
  2 se hisser *vpr* to heave oneself up; **se h. sur la pointe des pieds** to stand on tiptoe; *Fig* **se h. jusqu'au pouvoir** to rise to power

histogramme [istogram] *nm* bar chart, histogram

histoire [istwar] *nf* (a) *(discipline)* history; **l'h. de France** French history; **h. de l'art** history of art; **sachez, pour la petite h., que...** let me tell you in passing that...; *Fig* **c'est de l'h. ancienne** that's all ancient history

(b) *(récit)* story; *Fam (mensonge)* fib, story; **raconter des histoires** *(mentir)* to tell fibs; **c'est toujours la même h.** it's always the same old story; **c'est une autre h.** it's quite a different matter; **il m'est arrivé une drôle d'h.** a funny thing happened to me; **elle l'a dit, h. de dire quelque chose** she said it just for the sake of saying something; **c'est toute une h.** *(à raconter)* it's a long story; **c'est une h. de fous!** it's crazy!

(c) *(problème)* fuss; **c'est toute une h. pour lui faire prendre son bain** it's quite a business getting her to have a bath; *Fam* **en voilà une h.!** what a fuss!, what a song and dance!; **faire des histoires** to make a fuss; **s'attirer des histoires** to get oneself into trouble; **faire des histoires à qn** to make trouble for sb; **au lit, et pas d'histoires!** off to bed now, and no fuss!

histologie [istolɔʒi] *nf* histology

historien, -enne [istorjɛ̃, -ɛn] *nm,f* historian

historique [istorik] **1** *adj (qui concerne l'histoire)* historical; *(important)* historic
  2 *nm* historical account; *Ordinat (de document)* log; **faire l'h. des événements** to give a chronological account of events

historiquement [istorikmɑ̃] *adv* historically

*****hit-parade** *(pl* **hit-parades)** [itparad] *nm* charts

HIV [aʃive] *nm* HIV

hiver [ivɛr] *nm* winter; **en h.** in winter; **une soirée d'h.** a winter's night; **h. nucléaire** nuclear winter

hivernal, -e, -aux, -ales [ivɛrnal, -o] *adj* winter; *(temps)* wintry

hiverner [ivɛrne] *vi* to overwinter

*****HLM** [aʃɛlɛm] *nm ou nf (abrév* **habitation à loyer modéré)** *Br* ≃ block of council flats, *Am* ≃ low-rent apartment building

*****hochement** [ɔʃmɑ̃] *nm* **h. de tête** *(négatif)* shake of the head; *(affirmatif)* nod

*****hocher** [ɔʃe] *vt* **h. la tête** *(pour dire non)* to shake one's head; *(pour dire oui)* to nod

*****hochet** [ɔʃe] *nm* (child's) rattle

*****hockey** [ɔkɛ] *nm* (a) *(sport)* hockey; **h. sur gazon** *Br* hockey, *Am* field hockey; **h. sur glace** ice hockey, *Am* hockey (b) *Can (crosse)* ice hockey stick

*****holà** [ɔla] **1** *exclam (pour appeler)* stop!, hold on!; **h., on se calme, hein!** hey, cool it, OK?
  2 *nm* **mettre le h. à qch** to put a stop to sth

*****holding** [ɔldiŋ] *nm* holding company

*****hold-up** [ɔldœp] *nm inv Fam* hold-up

*****hollandais, -e** [ɔlɑ̃dɛ, -ɛz] **1** *adj* Dutch
  2 *nm,f* **H.** Dutchman, *f* Dutchwoman; **les H.** the Dutch
  3 *nm (langue)* Dutch

*****Hollande** [ɔlɑ̃d] *nf* **la H.** Holland

holocauste [ɔlokost] *nm* holocaust

hologramme [ɔlogram] *nm* hologram

holographie [ɔlografi] *nf* holography

*****homard** [ɔmar] *nm* lobster

homélie [ɔmeli] *nf* homily

homéopathe [ɔmeopat] *nmf* homeopath

homéopathie [ɔmeopati] *nf* homeopathy

homéopathique [ɔmeɔpatik] *adj* homeopathic

Homère [ɔmɛr] *npr* Homer

homicide [ɔmisid] **1** *adj* homicidal
2 *nm* homicide; **h. involontaire** *ou* **par imprudence** manslaughter *(through negligence)*

hommage [ɔmaʒ] *nm* homage; **rendre h. à qn** to pay homage to sb; **hommages** respects; **mes hommages!** how do you do!

hommasse [ɔmas] *adj Péj* mannish

homme [ɔm] *nm* **(a)** *(adulte)* man; **rayon hommes** men's department; **parler à qn d'h. à h.** to have a man-to-man talk with sb; **il n'est pas h. à laisser passer cela** he's not the sort of man to let something like that happen; **comme un seul h.** in unison; *Fam* **mon h.** my man; **jeune h.** young man; **h. d'affaires** businessman; **h. de barre** helmsman; **h. de confiance** right-hand man; **h. d'église** man of the church; **h. d'équipage** crewman; **h. d'État** statesman; **h. à femmes** ladies' man; **h. de loi** lawyer; **h. de main** henchman; **h. du monde** gentleman; **h. de paille** figurehead; **h. de peine** labourer; **h. politique** politician; **h. à tout faire** handyman; **h. de troupe** private **(b)** *(genre humain)* man, mankind; **de mémoire d'h.** within living memory

homme-grenouille *(pl* **hommes-grenouilles** [ɔmgrənuj] *nm* frogman

homme-orchestre *(pl* **hommes-orchestres** [ɔmɔrkɛstr] *nm* one-man band

homme-sandwich *(pl* **hommes-sandwichs** [ɔmsɑ̃dwitʃ] *nm* sandwich man

homo [ɔmo] *adj & nmf* gay

homogène [ɔmɔʒɛn] *adj* homogeneous

homogénéisation [ɔmɔʒeneizasjɔ̃] *nf* homogenization

homogénéiser [ɔmɔʒeneize] *vt* to homogenize

homogénéité [ɔmɔʒeneite] *nf* homogeneity

homologue [ɔmɔlɔg] *nmf* counterpart, opposite number

homologuer [ɔmɔlɔge] *vt (accord, décision, record)* to ratify; *(testament)* to prove

homonyme [ɔmɔnim] **1** *nm (mot)* homonym
2 *nmf (personne)* namesake

homosexualité [ɔmɔseksɥalite] *nf* homosexuality

homosexuel, -elle [ɔmɔseksɥɛl] *adj & nm,f* homosexual

***Honduras** [ɔ̃dyras] *nm* le H. Honduras

***hondurien, -enne** [ɔ̃dyrjɛ̃, -ɛn] **1** *adj* Honduran
2 *nm,f* H. Honduran

***Hongrie** [ɔ̃gri] *nf* la H. Hungary

***hongrois, -e** [ɔ̃grwa, -az] **1** *adj* Hungarian
2 *nm,f* H. Hungarian
3 *nm (langue)* Hungarian

honnête [ɔnɛt] *adj* **(a)** *(intègre) (personne, conduite)* honest; **peu h.** dishonest; **être h. avec soi-même** to be honest with oneself **(b)** *(décent) (vie, gens)* decent; *(intentions)* honourable **(c)** *(acceptable) (prix, note, résultat)* fair; **un repas/film h. sans plus** an OK meal/film, but nothing to write home about

honnêtement [ɔnɛtmɑ̃] *adv* **(a)** *(avec intégrité) (agir, se comporter)* honestly **(b)** *(franchement)* to be honest; **h., qu'est-ce que tu en penses?** be honest, what do you think? **(c)** *(raisonnablement)* decently

honnêteté [ɔnɛtte] *nf* **(a)** *(intégrité)* honesty **(b)** *(décence)* decency

honneur [ɔnœr] *nm* honour; **mettre un point d'h. à faire qch** to make it a point of honour to do sth; **déclarer/jurer sur l'h. que...** to state/swear on one's honour that...; **sauver l'h.** to save one's honour; **en tout bien tout h.** with no ulterior motive; **en l'h. de qn** in sb's honour; **à qui ai-je l'h.?** to whom have I the honour (of speaking)?; *Fam* **en quel h. devrais-je t'aider?** give me one good reason why I should help you; **à vous l'h.** after you; **être à l'h.** to have pride of place; **c'est tout à ton h.** it's to your credit; **faire h. à qn/qch** to be a credit to sb/sth; **faire h. à un repas** to do justice to a meal; **rechercher les honneurs** to court fame

***honnir** [ɔnir] *vt* to disgrace

honorable [ɔnɔrabl] *adj* **(a)** *(profession, personne, intentions)* honourable **(b)** *(performance, résultat)* creditable, respectable

honorablement [ɔnɔrabləmɑ̃] *adv* **(a)** *(de façon respectable)* honourably **(b)** *(correctement)* **il s'en est h. tiré** he did quite creditably; **gagner h. sa vie** to earn a good living

honoraire [ɔnɔrɛr] **1** *adj (fonction, membre)* honorary
2 *nmpl* **honoraires** fee, fees

honorer [ɔnɔre] **1** *vt* **(a)** *(rendre hommage à)* to honour; **h. qn de sa confiance** to put one's trust in sb **(b)** *(acquitter) (facture, dette, engagements)* to honour **(c)** *(valoir de l'estime à) (personne, chose)* to be a credit to **(d)** *Hum (sexuellement)* to service
2 **s'honorer** *vpr* **s'h. de qch/d'avoir fait qch** to pride oneself on sth/on having done sth

honorifique [ɔnɔrifik] *adj* honorary

***honoris causa** [ɔnɔriskoza] *adj* honoris causa; **docteur h.** doctor honoris causa, honorary doctor

***honte** [ɔ̃t] *nf* **(a)** *(sentiment)* shame; **à ma grande h.** to my shame; **sans h.** shamelessly; **avoir h. (de)** to be ashamed (of); **avoir h. pour qn** to feel embarrassed for sb; **faire h. à qn** to make sb ashamed **(b)** *(chose scandaleuse)* disgrace; **c'est une h.!** it's a disgrace!

***honteux, -euse** [ɔ̃tø, øz] *adj* **(a)** *(personne)* ashamed **(b)** *(conduite, acte)* shameful, disgraceful; **c'est h.!** it's a disgrace!

***hop** [ɔp] *exclam* **allez h., saute!** go on, jump!; **allez h., tout le monde dehors!** come on, everybody out!; **h.-là!** oops(-a-daisy)!

hôpital, -aux [ɔpital, -o] *nm* hospital; **h. de campagne** field hospital; **h. de jour** day hospital; **h. militaire** military hospital; **h. psychiatrique** psychiatric hospital

***hoquet** [ɔkɛ] *nm* hiccup; **avoir le h.** to have the hiccups

***hoqueter** [42] [ɔkte] *vi* to hiccup

horaire [ɔrɛr] **1** *adj* hourly
2 *nm* **(a)** *(des services de transport)* timetable, schedule; **être en retard sur l'h.** to be running late **(b)** *(emploi du temps)* timetable, schedule; **h. variable** *ou* **flexible** flexible hours, flexitime; **horaires de travail** working hours

***horde** [ɔrd] *nf* horde

horizon [ɔrizɔ̃] *nm aussi Fig* horizon; **à l'h.** on the horizon; **à l'h. 2000** in the year 2000; **h. intellectuel** intellectual horizons

horizontal, -e, -aux, -ales [ɔrizɔ̃tal, -o] **1** *adj* horizontal
2 *nf* **horizontale** horizontal line; **à l'horizontale** horizontal

---

The symbol * indicates that the initial **h** *is aspirate and that hence there is no liaison*

horizontalement [ɔrizɔtalmɑ̃] *adv* horizontally; *(dans les mots croisés)* across

horloge [ɔrlɔʒ] *nf* clock; **réglé comme une h.** as regular as clockwork; **h. biologique** biological clock; **l'h. parlante** the speaking clock; *Ordinat* **h. du système** system clock; *Ordinat* **h. en temps réel** real-time clock

horloger, -ère [ɔrlɔʒe, -ɛr] **1** *adj* **l'industrie horlogère** the watchmaking industry

2 *nm,f* watchmaker

horloger-bijoutier (*pl* **horlogers-bijoutiers**) [ɔrlɔʒebiʒutje] *nm* jeweller and watchmaker

horlogerie [ɔrlɔʒri] *nf (industrie)* watchmaking; *(magasin)* watchmaker's (shop); **l'h.** *(ouvrages)* clocks and watches

*****hormis** [ɔrmi] *prép Litt* except, save

hormonal, -e, -aux, -ales [ɔrmɔnal, -o] *adj* hormonal

hormone [ɔrmɔn] *nf* hormone

hormonothérapie [ɔrmɔnoterapi] *nf* hormone therapy

horodateur [ɔrɔdatœr] *nm* time and date stamping machine; *(de stationnement)* pay and display machine

horoscope [ɔrɔskɔp] *nm* horoscope

horreur [ɔrœr] *nf* (a) *(effroi)* horror (b) *(répugnance)* disgust; **avoir h. de qn/qch** to hate sb/sth; **avoir h. de faire qch** to hate doing sth; **avoir qn/qch en h.** to loathe sb/sth; **faire h. à qn** to disgust sb (c) *(caractère horrible)* horror; **quelle h.!** how horrible!, how awful! (d) *(chose ou personne exécrable)* **être une h.** to be a nightmare (e) **horreurs** *(atrocités)* horrors; *(calomnies)* horrible things

horrible [ɔribl] *adj* (a) *(effrayant)* horrible (b) *(très laid)* hideous

horriblement [ɔribləmɑ̃] *adv (brûlé, défiguré)* horribly; *(cher, froid)* terribly

horrifiant, -e [ɔrifjɑ̃, -ɑ̃t] *adj* horrifying

horrifier [66] [ɔrifje] *vt* to horrify

horripilant, -e [ɔripilɑ̃, -ɑ̃t] *adj* exasperating

horripiler [ɔripile] *vt* to exasperate

*****hors** [ɔr] *prép* (a) *(dehors)* **h. de** outside; **h. d'ici!** get out (of here)!; **ça l'a mise h. d'elle** that infuriated her; **être h. de soi** to be beside oneself (b) *Litt (sauf)* except, save (c) *(en conjonction avec un nom)* **h. antenne** off-air; **h. d'atteinte** out of reach; **h. de combat** out of action; **h. pair** unrivalled; **h. piste** off piste; **h. de prix** extortionate; **h. de question** out of the question; **h. saison** off-season; **numéro h. série** special issue; **h. service** out of order; **h. sujet** not relevant; **h. taxe** net of tax; *(exempt de taxe)* tax-free; **boutique h. taxe** duty-free shop; **h. d'usage** *(vêtement)* worn out; *(machine)* beyond repair

*****hors-bord** [ɔrbɔr] *nm inv* speedboat; **moteur h.** outboard motor

*****hors-d'œuvre** [ɔrdœvr] *nm inv* (a) *(plat)* hors d'œuvre, starter (b) *Fig* starter, taster

*****hors-jeu** [ɔrʒø] *nm inv* offside

*****hors-la-loi** [ɔrlalwa] *nm inv* outlaw

*****hors-piste** [ɔrpist] *nm inv (en ski)* off-piste skiing; **faire du h.** to ski off piste

hortensia [ɔrtɑ̃sja] *nm* hydrangea

horticole [ɔrtikɔl] *adj* horticultural; **exposition h.** flower show

horticulteur [ɔrtikyltœr] *nm* nurseryman

horticulture [ɔrtikyltyr] *nf* horticulture

hospice [ɔspis] *nm* (a) *(asile)* home (b) *(monastère)* hospice

hospitalier[1], -ère [ɔspitalje, -ɛr] *adj (accueillant)* hospitable

hospitalier[2], -ère *adj (relatif aux hôpitaux)* hospital; **personnel h.** hospital staff

hospitalisation [ɔspitalizasjɔ̃] *nf* hospitalization; **h. à domicile** home care

hospitaliser [ɔspitalize] *vt* to hospitalize; **faire h. qn** to have sb hospitalized

hospitalité [ɔspitalite] *nf* hospitality

hospitalo-universitaire [ɔspitaloyniversiter] *adj* **centre h.** teaching hospital

hostie [ɔsti] *nm Rel* host

hostile [ɔstil] *adj* hostile (**à** towards)

hostilité [ɔstilite] *nf* hostility (**contre** *ou* **envers** towards); **hostilités** hostilities

hosto [ɔsto] *nm Fam* hospital

hôte [ot] *nm* (a) *(personne qui invite)* host (b) *(invité)* guest, visitor; **h. payant** paying guest (c) *Biol* host

hôtel [otel] *nm* (a) *(pour l'hébergement)* hotel; **h. de passe** = hotel used as a brothel (b) *(bâtiment)* **h. des impôts** tax office; **l'h. de la Monnaie** ≃ the Royal Mint; **h. (particulier)** mansion, town house; **h. des ventes** saleroom; **h. de ville** town hall

hôtelier, -ère [otalje, -ɛr] **1** *adj* **l'industrie hôtelière** the hotel industry

2 *nm,f* hotel keeper, hotelier

hôtellerie [otelri] *nf* (a) *(hôtel)* inn (b) *(secteur)* **l'h.** the hotel industry

hôtel-restaurant (*pl* **hôtels-restaurants**) [otelrestɔrɑ̃] *nm* hotel and restaurant

hôtesse [otɛs] *nf* (a) *(personne qui reçoit)* hostess (b) *(dans un avion)* hostess, stewardess; **h. d'accueil** receptionist; **h. de l'air** air hostess

*****hotte** [ɔt] *nf* (a) *(panier)* basket; **h. du Père Noël** Santa Claus's sack (b) *(pour la ventilation)* hood; **h. aspirante** extractor hood

*****hou** [u] *exclam* boo!; **h.! la vilaine!** tut-tut, you naughty girl!

*****houblon** [ublɔ̃] *nm* hops

*****houe** [u] *nf* hoe

*****houille** [uj] *nf* coal; **h. blanche** hydroelectric power

*****houiller, -ère** [uje, -ɛr] **1** *adj (terrain)* rich in coal; **bassin h.** coalfield; **production houillère** coal output

2 *nf* **houillère** coalmine, colliery

*****houle** [ul] *nf* swell

*****houlette** [ulɛt] *nf* (a) *(de berger)* crook; *Fig* **sous la h. de** under the leadership of (b) *(petite bêche)* trowel

*****houleux, -euse** [ulø, -øz] *adj (mer)* choppy; *Fig (réunion)* stormy

*****houppette** [upɛt] *nf (de plumes)* small tuft; *(de cheveux)* quiff; *(à poudre)* powder puff

*****hourra** [ura] **1** *exclam* hurrah!; **hip, hip, hip, h.!** hip, hip, hooray!

2 *nm* hurrah; **pousser des hourras** to cheer

*****houspiller** [uspije] *vt* to tell off

*****housse** [us] *nf* cover; *(contre la poussière)* dust sheet; *(dans une voiture)* seat cover

*****houx** [u] *nm* holly

---

eg **les haricots** [leariko] and not [lezariko], or contraction in spelling, eg **la haine** and not **l'haine**.

hovercraft [ɔvœrkraft] *nm* hovercraft

HT (a) *(abrév* **haute tension**) HT (b) *(abrév* **hors taxe**) exclusive of tax

*****hublot** [yblo] *nm (de bateau)* porthole; *(dans un avion, une machine à laver)* window

*****huche** [yʃ] *nf* chest; **h. à pain** bread bin

*****hue** [y, hy] *exclam (à un cheval)* gee up!; **tirer à h. et à dia** to pull in opposite directions

*****huées** [ɥe] *nfpl* booing; **quitter la scène sous les h.** to be booed off the stage

*****huer** [ɥe] **1** *vt* to boo
2 *vi (hibou, chouette)* to hoot

huile [ɥil] *nf* (a) *(liquide)* oil; *Fig* **jeter de l'h. sur le feu** to add fuel to the fire; **une mer d'h.** a glassy sea; **h. d'amandes douces** almond oil; **h. d'arachide** groundnut oil; *Can* **h. de chauffage** heating oil; *Fig* **h. de coude** elbow grease; **h. essentielle** essential oil; **h. de foie de morue** cod liver oil; **h. de moteur** engine oil; **h. d'olive** olive oil; **h. de ricin** castor oil; **h. solaire** suntan oil; **h. de tournesol** sunflower oil; **h. végétale** vegetable oil; **h. de vidange** sump oil (b) *(peinture)* oil painting (c) *Fam (personne importante)* big shot

huiler [ɥile] *vt* to oil

huileux, -euse [ɥilø, -øz] *adj* oily

huis [ɥi] *nm* **à h. clos** behind closed doors; *Jur* in camera

huissier [ɥisje] *nm* (a) *Jur* bailiff (b) *(portier)* usher

*****huit** [ɥit] *adj & nm inv* eight; **h. jours** a week; **aujourd'hui/demain en h.** a week today/tomorrow; **donner ses h. jours à qn** to give sb a week's notice; *voir aussi* **trois**

*****huitaine** [ɥiten] *nf* (a) *(environ huit)* (about) eight (b) *(semaine)* week; **dans une h. de jours** in a week or so

*****huitante** [ɥitɑ̃t] *adj inv Suisse* eighty

*****huitième** [ɥitjem] *adj, nm & nmf* eighth; *voir aussi* **cinquième**

huître [ɥitr] *nf* oyster; **h. perlière** pearl oyster

*****hulotte** [ylɔt] *nf* tawny owl

*****hululement** [ylylmɑ̃] *nm* hoot; **des hululements** hooting

*****huluter** [ylyle] *vi* to hoot

*****hum** [œm] *exclam* hm!

humain, -e [ymɛ̃, -ɛn] **1** *adj* (a) *(relatif à l'homme)* human; **c'est h.** it's only human; **des pertes humaines énormes** a huge loss of life (b) *(compatissant)* humane
2 *nm* human (being)

humainement [ymɛnmɑ̃] *adv* (a) *(relatif à l'homme)* in human terms; **h. possible** humanly possible (b) *(avec bonté)* humanely

humaniser [ymanize] *vt* to make more human

humanisme [ymanism] *nm* humanism

humaniste [ymanist] *adj & nmf* humanist

humanitaire [ymaniter] *adj* humanitarian

humanité [ymanite] *nf* (a) *(genre humain)* humanity, mankind (b) *(bonté)* humanity; **avec h.** humanely

humanoïde [ymanoid] *nm* humanoid

humble [œbl] *adj* humble; **à mon h. avis** in my humble opinion

humblement [œblǝmɑ̃] *adv* humbly

humecter [ymɛkte] *vt* to moisten

*****humer** [yme] *vt (air)* to breathe in; *(parfum)* to smell

humérus [ymerys] *nm* humerus

humeur [ymœr] *nf* (a) *(disposition)* mood; **être de bonne/mauvaise h.** to be in a good/bad mood; **mettre qn de bonne/mauvaise h.** to put sb in a good/bad mood; **être d'une h. massacrante** to be in a foul mood; **plein de bonne h.** good-humoured; **être/ne pas être d'h. à faire qch** to be/not be in the mood to do sth (b) *(caractère)* temper, temperament; **d'h. égale** even-tempered; **d'humeur inégale** *ou* **changeante** temperamental (c) *Litt (mauvaise humeur)* bad mood; **geste d'h.** ill-tempered gesture; **avec h.** irritably (d) *Anat* **h. aqueuse** aqueous humour; **h. vitrée** vitreous humour

humide [ymid] *adj (maison, linge)* damp, wet; *(climat)* humid; **les yeux humides (de larmes)** eyes moist with tears

humidificateur [ymidifikatœr] *nm* humidifier

humidifier [66] [ymidifje] *vt* to dampen; *(air)* to humidify

humidité [ymidite] *nf (d'une maison)* dampness; *(du climat, d'une région)* humidity; **il faut beaucoup d'h. à cette plante** this plant needs a lot of moisture; **craint l'h.** *(sur un paquet)* store in a dry place

humiliant, -e [ymiljɑ̃, -ɑ̃t] *adj* humiliating

humiliation [ymiljasjɔ̃] *nf* humiliation

humilier [66] [ymilje] **1** *vt* to humiliate
2 s'humilier *vpr* to humiliate oneself

humilité [ymilite] *nf* humility

humoriste [ymɔrist] *nmf* humorist

humoristique [ymɔristik] *adj* humorous; **dessin h.** cartoon

humour [ymur] *nm* humour; **avoir (le sens) de l'h.** to have a (good) sense of humour; **h. noir** black humour

*****huppe¹** [yp] *nf (oiseau)* hoopoe

*****huppe²** *nf (d'un oiseau)* crest

*****huppé, -e** [ype] *adj* (a) *Fam (gens, endroit, quartier)* smart (b) *(oiseau)* crested

*****hurlement** [yrlǝmɑ̃] *nm (d'un loup, d'un chien)* howl; *(d'une personne)* scream; *(du vent)* roaring; *(d'une sirène)* wail

*****hurler** [yrle] **1** *vi (loup, chien)* to howl; *(personne)* to howl, to scream; *(vent, tempête)* to roar; *(sirène)* to wail; *(radio)* to blare; **h. de douleur/rage** to howl with pain/rage; **c'est à h. de rire** it's screamingly funny; **h. à la lune** to bay at the moon; **il faut h. avec les loups** if you can't beat them join them
2 *vt (insultes, instructions)* to yell

hurluberlu [yrlybɛrly] *nm* oddball

*****Huron** [yrɔ̃] *n voir* **lac**

*****husky** *(pl* **huskies)** [œski] *nm* husky

*****hussard** [ysar] *nm* hussar

*****hussarde** [ysard] *nf* **à la h.** roughly

*****hutte** [yt] *nf* hut

hybride [ibrid] *adj & nm* hybrid

hydratant, -e [idratɑ̃, -ɑ̃t] *adj* moisturizing

hydratation [idratasjɔ̃] *nf (de la peau)* moisturizing

hydrate [idrat] *nm* hydrate; **h. de carbone** carbohydrate

hydrater [idrate] **1** *vt (peau)* to moisturize; *(organisme)* to hydrate
2 s'hydrater *vpr* to take in water

hydraulique [idrolik] **1** *adj* hydraulic
2 *nf (science)* hydraulics *(singulier)*

hydravion [idravjɔ̃] *nm* seaplane

The symbol * indicates that the initial **h** is aspirate and that hence there is no liaison

hydre [idr] *nf* hydra

hydrocarbure [idrɔkarbyr] *nm* hydrocarbon

hydrocution [idrɔkysjɔ̃] *nf* = loss of consciousness caused by immersion in cold water

hydroélectricité [idrɔelektrisite] *nf* hydroelectricity

hydroélectrique [idrɔelektrik] *adj* hydroelectric

hydrogène [idrɔʒɛn] *nm* hydrogen

hydroglisseur [idrɔglisœr] *nm* jetfoil

hydrographie [idrɔgrafi] *nf* hydrography

hydrolyse [idrɔliz] *nf* hydrolysis

hydromel [idrɔmɛl] *nm* mead

hydrophile [idrɔfil] *adj* (*coton*) absorbent

hydrothérapie [idrɔterapi] *nf* hydrotherapy

hydroxyde [idrɔksid] *nm* hydroxide

hyène [jɛn] *nf* hyena

Hygiaphone® [iʒjafɔn] *nm* (*au guichet*) grille; **parlez dans l'H.** speak into the grille

hygiène [iʒjɛn] *nf* hygiene; **par mesure d'h.** for hygiene reasons; **h. alimentaire** diet; **h. mentale** mental health

hygiénique [iʒjenik] *adj* (a) (*propre*) hygienic; **peu h.** unhygienic (b) (*bon pour la santé*) healthy; **une promenade h.** a bracing walk

hymne [imn] *nm* hymn; **h. national** national anthem

hyper- [iper] *préf Fam* very, *Br* dead, *Am* real

hyperbole [iperbɔl] *nf* (a) (*figure de style*) hyperbole (b) *Math* hyperbola

hyperbolique [iperbɔlik] *adj* hyperbolic

hyperglycémie [iperglisemi] *nf* hyperglycemia

hypermarché [ipermarʃe] *nm* hypermarket, superstore

hypermétrope [ipermetrɔp] *adj* longsighted

hypernerveux, -euse [ipernervø, -øz] **1** *adj* highly-strung
2 *nm,f* highly-strung person

hypersensibilité [ipersãsibilite] *nf* hypersensitivity

hypersensible [ipersãsibl] *adj* hypersensitive

hypertendu, -e [ipertãdy] *adj* **être h.** to have high blood pressure

hypertension [ipertãsjɔ̃] *nf* high blood pressure, *Spéc* hypertension

hypertexte [ipertekst] *nm Ordinat* hypertext

hypertrophie [ipertrɔfi] *nf* enlargement, *Spéc* hypertrophy

hypertrophié, -e [ipertrɔfje] *adj* enlarged, *Spéc* hypertrophied

hypnose [ipnoz] *nf* hypnosis; **être en état d'h.** to be in a trance

hypnotique [ipnɔtik] *adj* hypnotic

hypnotiser [ipnɔtize] *vt* to hypnotize

hypnotisme [ipnɔtism] *nm* hypnotism

hypoallergénique [ipoalerʒenik] *adj* hypoallergenic

hypocalorique [ipokalɔrik] *adj* (*régime, aliment*) low-calorie

hypocondriaque [ipokɔ̃drijak] *adj & nmf* hypochondriac

hypocrisie [ipokrizi] *nf* hypocrisy

hypocrite [ipokrit] **1** *adj* hypocritical
2 *nmf* hypocrite

hypocritement [ipokritmã] *adv* hypocritically

hypodermique [ipodermik] *adj* hypodermic

hypoglycémie [ipoglisemi] *nf* hypoglycemia

hypokhâgne [ipokɑɲ] *nf* = first-year arts class preparing students for the entrance examination for the "École normale supérieure"

hypophyse [ipofiz] *nf* pituitary gland

hypotendu, -e [ipotãdy] *adj* **être h.** to have low blood pressure

hypotension [ipotãsjɔ̃] *nf* low blood pressure, *Spéc* hypotension

hypoténuse [ipotenyz] *nf* hypotenuse

hypothalamus [ipotalamys] *nm* hypothalamus

hypothécaire [ipoteker] *adj* **contrat h.** mortgage deed; **prêt h.** mortgage (loan)

hypothèque [ipotek] *nf* mortgage

hypothéquer [34] [ipoteke] *vt* (*propriété*) to mortgage; *Fig* **h. son avenir** to sign away one's future

hypothermie [ipotermi] *nf* hypothermia

hypothèse [ipotez] *nf* hypothesis; **dans l'h. où nous échouerions** should we fail; **ils ont écarté l'h. du suicide** they have ruled out the possibility of suicide

hypothétique [ipotetik] *adj* hypothetical

hystérectomie [isterektɔmi] *nf* hysterectomy

hystérie [isteri] *nf* hysteria; **h. collective** mass hysteria

hystérique [isterik] **1** *adj* hysterical
2 *nmf* hysterical person

---

eg **les haricots** [leariko] and not [lezariko], or contraction in spelling, eg **la haine** and not **l'haine**.

I, i [i] *nm inv* I, i

ibère [iber] **1** *adj* Iberian
2 *nmf* I. Iberian

ibérique [iberik] *adj* Iberian

ibis [ibis] *nm* ibis

iceberg [ajsberg, isberg] *nm* iceberg; *Fig* **la partie visible de l'i.** the tip of the iceberg

ichtyologie [iktjɔlɔʒi] *nf* ichthyology

ici [isi] *adv* **(a)** *(dans l'espace)* here; **i. et là** here and there; **i. même** on this very spot; **les gens d'i.** the people from round here, the locals; **c'est i.** this is the place; **c'est i. que ça s'est passé** this is where it happened; *Fig* **je reprends i. ses propres paroles** and here I'm using her own words; **i. Thomas** *(au téléphone)* this is Thomas
(b) *(dans le temps)* **jusqu'i.** until now, up to now; **d'i. lundi/demain** by Monday/tomorrow; **d'i. là** by that time, by then; **d'i. peu** before long; **d'i. à ce que vous ayez fini, je serai parti** by the time you've finished, I'll have gone; **d'i. à ce qu'il la quitte, il n'y a pas loin** he will have left her before long

icône [ikon] *nf Rel & Ordinat* icon; *Ordinat* **i. de la corbeille** wastebasket icon, *Am* trash icon

iconoclaste [ikonoklast] **1** *adj* iconoclastic
2 *nmf* iconoclast

iconographie [ikɔnɔgrafi] *nf* **(a)** *(dans un domaine particulier)* iconography **(b)** *(dans l'édition)* illustrations, art work

iconographique [ikɔnɔgrafik] *adj* iconographic

idéal, -e, -als *ou* **-aux, -ales** [ideal, -o] *adj* ideal
2 *nm* ideal; **l'i.** the ideal thing; **dans l'i.** ideally; **l'i. serait que tu y ailles tout seul** it would be best if you went alone

idéalement [idealmã] *adv* ideally

idéalisation [idealizasjɔ̃] *nf* idealization

idéaliser [idealize] *vt* to idealize

idéalisme [idealism] *nm* idealism

idéaliste [idealist] **1** *adj* idealistic
2 *nmf* idealist

idée [ide] *nf* **(a)** *(inspiration)* idea; **i. de génie, i. lumineuse** brilliant idea; **avoir la bonne i. de faire qch** to have the bright idea of doing sth; **avoir une i. derrière la tête** to be up to something; **donner des idées à qn** to put ideas into sb's head; **quelle drôle d'i.!, en voilà une i.!** the very idea!; **se faire des idées** to imagine things; **i. fixe** obsession; **idées noires** black thoughts; **i. reçue** generally accepted idea **(b)** *(notion)* idea; **pour vous donner une i.** to give you an idea; **as-tu une i. du prix que ça coûte?** have you any idea how much it costs?; **je n'en ai pas la moindre i.** I haven't got the faintest idea; *Fam* **on n'a pas i. de faire des choses pareilles!** whoever heard of such a thing! **(c)** *(opinion)*

view, opinion; **avoir une haute i. de qn/qch** to have a high opinion of sb/sth; **se faire une i. de qn/qch** to get an idea of sb/sth; **avoir sa petite i. sur qch** to have one's pet theory about sth; **avoir les idées larges** to be broad-minded; **fais à ton i.** do as you like; **changer d'i.** to change one's mind **(d)** *(esprit)* **ça ne m'est jamais venu à l'i.** it's never occurred to me; **je ne peux pas lui ôter cela de l'i.** I can't get her to change her mind about it; **se mettre dans l'i. que/de faire qch** to get it into one's head that/to do sth; **cela m'était sorti de l'i.** it had slipped my mind

idem [idɛm] *adv* ditto

identification [idãtifikasjɔ̃] *nf* identification (**avec** *ou* **à** with); *Ordinat* **i. de l'utilisateur** user identification

identifier [66] [idãtifje] **1** *vt* to identify
2 s'identifier *vpr* to identify (**avec** *ou* **à** with)

identique [idãtik] *adj* identical (**à** to)

identité [idãtite] *nf* identity; **papiers** *ou* **pièces d'i.** identity papers

idéogramme [ideogram] *nm* ideogram

idéologie [ideɔlɔʒi] *nf* ideology

idéologique [ideɔlɔʒik] *adj* ideological

idiomatique [idjɔmatik] *adj* idiomatic; **expression i.** idiom

idiome [idjom] *nm* idiom

idiot, -e [idjo, -ɔt] **1** *adj* *(stupide)* idiotic, stupid; *(regrettable)* stupid, silly; **ce système n'est pas i.** this system is pretty smart
2 *nm,f* *Fam* **l'i. du village** the village idiot; **faire l'i.** *(faire des bêtises)* to act the fool; *(feindre de ne pas comprendre)* to act dumb

idiotie [idjɔsi] *nf* *(chose, parole idiote)* stupid thing; *(caractère stupide)* stupidity; **ne dites pas d'idioties!** don't talk rubbish!

idolâtrer [idolatre] *vt* to idolize

idolâtrie [idolatri] *nf* idolatry

idole [idɔl] *nf* idol; **i. des jeunes** teenage idol

idylle [idil] *nf* **(a)** *(aventure)* romance **(b)** *(poème)* idyll

idyllique [idilik] *adj* idyllic

IEP [iəpe] *nm* (*abrév* **Institut d'études politiques**) = higher education establishment for political science students

if [if] *nm* yew

IGF [iʒeɛf] *nm inv* (*abrév* **impôt sur les grandes fortunes**) wealth tax

igloo, iglou [iglu] *nm* igloo

IGN [iʒeɛn] *nm* (*abrév* **Institut géographique national**) *Br* ≃ Ordnance Survey, *Am* ≃ United States Geological Survey

ignare [iɲar] **1** adj ignorant
2 nmf ignoramus

ignifuge [ignifyʒ] **1** adj fireproof
2 nm fireproofing material

ignifugé, -e [ignifyʒe] adj fireproofed

ignoble [iɲɔbl] adj **(a)** (personne, conduite) vile **(b)** (habitation, quartier) filthy; (nourriture) disgusting

ignominie [iɲɔmini] nf **(a)** (caractère) ignominy; **se couvrir d'i.** to bring shame upon oneself **(b)** (action) shameful thing; **c'est une i.!** it's a disgrace!

ignorance [iɲɔrɑ̃s] nf ignorance; **être/tenir qn dans l'i.** to be/keep sb in the dark

ignorant, -e [iɲɔrɑ̃, -ɑ̃t] **1** adj ignorant (**de** of)
2 nm,f ignoramus; **faire l'i.** to pretend one doesn't know

ignoré, -e [iɲɔre] adj unknown; (négligé) ignored; **vivre i.** to live in obscurity

ignorer [iɲɔre] **1** vt **(a)** (ne pas savoir) not to know (about); **il en ignore tout de cela** he knows nothing about it; **ne rien i. de qch** to know all about sth; **personne n'ignore que...** everybody knows that...; **i. la peur/la jalousie** to feel no fear/jealousy **(b)** (mépriser) (personne, conseil, interdiction) to ignore
2 s'ignorer vpr **(a)** (se mépriser l'un l'autre) to ignore each other **(b)** (se méconnaître) **c'est un artiste qui s'ignore** he's an artist but he doesn't know it

iguane [igwan] nm iguana

il [il] pron personnel **(a)** (personne) he; (chose, animal) it; **ton père est-il toujours à l'hôpital?** is your father still in hospital?
(b) (impersonnel) it; **il est six heures** it's six o'clock; **il pleut** it's raining; **il existe de nombreuses possibilités** there are many possibilities

île [il] nf island; **dans une î.** on an island; **î. déserte** desert island; **les îles Anglo-Normandes** the Channel Islands; Culin **î. flottante** floating island (beaten egg whites served on custard); **les îles Salomon** the Solomon Islands; **les îles de la Société** the Society Islands; **les îles Sous-le-Vent** the Leeward Islands

Île-de-France [ildəfrɑ̃s] nf **l'Î.** = administrative region including Paris

iliaque [iljak] adj Anat iliac; **os i.** ilium

illégal, -e, -aux, -ales [ilegal, -o] adj illegal

illégalement [ilegalmɑ̃] adv illegally

illégalité [ilegalite] nf illegality; **vivre dans l'i.** to live outside the law; **être dans l'i.** to break the law

illégitime [ileʒitim] adj (enfant) illegitimate; (union) unlawful; (demande) unwarranted

illettré, -e [iletre] adj & nm,f illiterate

illettrisme [iletrism] nm illiteracy

illicite [ilisit] adj illicit, unlawful

illico [iliko] adv Fam **i.** (presto) pronto

illimité, -e [ilimite] adj (pouvoirs, moyens, crédit) unlimited; (confiance) boundless

illisible [ilizibl] adj **(a)** (indéchiffrable) illegible; Ordinat (fichier, disquette) unreadable **(b)** (incompréhensible) unreadable

illogique [ilɔʒik] adj illogical

illumination [ilyminasjɔ̃] nf **(a)** (action d'illuminer) illumination; (par projecteurs) floodlighting **(b)** (lumière) **illuminations** illuminations **(c)** (inspiration) flash of inspiration

illuminé, -e [ilymine] **1** adj (éclairé) lit up, illuminated; (par projecteurs) floodlit
2 nm,f Péj fanatic

illuminer [ilymine] **1** vt (éclairer) to light up, to illuminate; (par projecteurs) to floodlight; Fig (visage, yeux) to light up
2 s'illuminer vpr aussi Fig to light up (**de** with)

illusion [ilyzjɔ̃] nf illusion; **se faire des illusions** to delude oneself; **je ne me fais aucune i. sur ses intentions** I have no illusions about her intentions; **perdre ses illusions** to become disillusioned; **enlever ou faire perdre ses illusions à qn** to disillusion sb; **faire i.** to take people in; **i. d'optique** optical illusion

illusionner (s') [ilyzjone] **s'illusionner** vpr to delude oneself (**sur** about)

illusionniste [ilyzjonist] nmf conjurer

illusoire [ilyzwar] adj illusory

illustrateur, -trice [ilystratœr, -tris] nm,f illustrator

illustration [ilystrasjɔ̃] nf illustration

illustre [ilystr] adj illustrious; Hum **un i. inconnu** a famous person no one has ever heard of

illustré, -e [ilystre] **1** adj illustrated
2 nm Vieilli (pour enfants) comic

illustrer [ilystre] **1** vt (livre, récit) to illustrate (**de** with)
2 s'illustrer vpr to distinguish oneself (**par** by)

îlot [ilo] nm (île) small island; (groupe d'immeubles) block; Fig **î. de verdure** island of greenery

îlotage [ilotaʒ] nm community policing

ils [il] pron personnel they; **les magasins sont-i. ouverts le dimanche?** are the shops open on Sunday?

image [imaʒ] nf **(a)** (dans un miroir) reflection, image; (à la télévision) picture; **vingt-quatre images par seconde** twenty-four frames a second; **être à l'i.** to be on camera; **nous n'avons plus d'i.** the picture's gone; **i. d'archives** stock shot; Ordinat **i. bitmap** bitmap image; **images de synthèse** computer-generated images; Ordinat **i. vectorielle** outline image **(b)** Fig image; **soigner son i.** to cultivate one's image; **donner une bonne/mauvaise i. de** to present a good/bad image of; **i. de marque** (d'un produit) brand image; (d'un homme politique, d'une entreprise) public image **(c)** (dessin) picture; (récompense scolaire) ≃ gold star

imagé, -e [imaʒe] adj vivid

imagerie [imaʒri] nf imagery; Méd **i. médicale** medical imaging; Méd **i. par résonance magnétique** magnetic resonance imaging

imaginable [imaʒinabl] adj imaginable

imaginaire [imaʒinɛr] **1** adj (personnage, pays, animal) imaginary
2 nm **l'i.** the imagination

imaginatif, -ive [imaʒinatif, -iv] adj imaginative

imagination [imaʒinasjɔ̃] nf imagination; **avoir de l'i.** to be imaginative

imaginer [imaʒine] **1** vt **(a)** (inventer) to devise **(b)** (se figurer) to imagine; **tu l'imagines avec des enfants!** just imagine him with children!; **j'imagine qu'elle viendra vers neuf heures** she'll come about nine o'clock, I should imagine
2 s'imaginer vpr **(a)** (croire) **s'i. que** to think that; **il s'imagine tout savoir** he thinks he knows it all **(b)** (se figurer) to imagine; (soi-même) to picture oneself; **tu t'imagines la tête qu'elle va faire** you can imagine how she'll take it; **je me l'imaginais bien plus grand** I imagined him much taller

imam [imam] *nm* imam

imbattable [ɛ̃batabl] *adj* unbeatable

imbécile [ɛ̃besil] **1** *adj* idiotic, stupid
2 *nmf* idiot, fool; **c'est un i. heureux** he's living in blissful ignorance; **faire l'i.** *(faire des bêtises)* to play or act the fool; *(feindre de ne pas comprendre)* to act stupid

imbécillité [ɛ̃besilite] *nf* (a) *(caractère stupide)* idiocy, stupidity (b) *(parole, chose stupide)* idiotic thing; **dire des imbécillités** to talk nonsense

imberbe [ɛ̃bɛrb] *adj* beardless

imbiber [ɛ̃bibe] **1** *vt* **i. qch de qch** to soak sth in sth; **imbibé d'eau** *(coton, éponge)* saturated (with water); *(terrain)* waterlogged
2 **s'imbiber** *vpr* **s'i. de qch** to become soaked with sth

imbrication [ɛ̃brikasjɔ̃] *nf* overlapping; *Fig (ensemble complexe)* web; *Ordinat* embedding; *(de commandes)* nesting

imbriquer [ɛ̃brike] **1** *vt* to overlap; *Ordinat* to embed; *(commandes)* to nest
2 **s'imbriquer** *vpr (s'emboîter)* to overlap; *Fig (problèmes, situations)* to be interwoven

imbroglio [ɛ̃broljo] *nm* imbroglio

imbu, -e [ɛ̃by] *adj* **i. de sa personne** *ou* **de soi-même** full of oneself

imbuvable [ɛ̃byvabl] *adj* undrinkable; *Fig (personne)* insufferable

imitateur, -trice [imitatœr, -tris] *nm,f (amateur)* mimic; *(professionnel)* impersonator, impressionist

imitation [imitasjɔ̃] *nf* (a) *(d'une personne)* impersonation, impression; *(d'un produit, d'un style)* imitation; *(d'une signature, d'un billet)* forgery (b) *(copie)* imitation; **bijoux en i. argent** imitation silver jewellery

imiter [imite] *vt (personne) (singer)* to imitate; *(faire une imitation de)* to impersonate; *(produit, style)* to imitate; *(signature)* to forge; *(billet, pièce de monnaie)* to counterfeit; **il leva son verre et tout le monde l'imita** he raised his glass and everyone did the same

immaculé, -e [imakyle] *adj (draps, linge, réputation)* spotless; **d'un blanc i.** spotlessly white; *Rel* **l'Immaculée Conception** the Immaculate Conception

immangeable [ɛ̃mɑ̃ʒabl] *adj* inedible

immanquablement [ɛ̃mɑ̃kabləmɑ̃] *adv* inevitably

immatériel, -elle [imaterjɛl] *adj Phil* immaterial; *Fin (actif)* intangible; *Litt (pâleur, minceur)* ethereal

immatriculation [imatrikylasjɔ̃] *nf* registration (à with); **(numéro d')i.** *Br* registration number, *Am* license number

immatriculer [imatrikyle] *vt* to register (à with); **la voiture est immatriculée en Dordogne** the car has a Dordogne *Br* number plate *or Am* license plate

immature [imatyr] *adj* immature

immaturité [imatyrite] *nf* immaturity

immédiat, -e [imedja, -at] **1** *adj* immediate; *(contact)* direct; *(mort)* instantaneous
2 *nm* **dans l'i.** for the time being

immédiatement [imedjatmɑ̃] *adv* immediately

immémorial, -e, -aux, -ales [imemɔrjal, -o] *adj Litt* age-old; **en des temps immémoriaux** in ancient times

immense [imɑ̃s] *adj* immense

immensément [imɑ̃semɑ̃] *adv* immensely

immensité [imɑ̃site] *nf* immensity

immerger [45] [imɛrʒe] *vt* to immerse (**dans** in)

immérité, -e [imerite] *adj* unmerited, undeserved

immersion [imɛrsjɔ̃] *nf* immersion (**dans** in)

immettable [ɛ̃mɛtabl] *adj* unwearable

immeuble [imœbl] **1** *nm (bâtiment)* building; *(d'appartements)* Br block of flats, *Am* apartment block
2 *adj voir* **bien**

immigrant, -e [imigrɑ̃, -ɑ̃t] *adj & nm,f* immigrant

immigration [imigrasjɔ̃] *nf* immigration

immigré, -e [imigre] *adj & nm,f* immigrant

immigrer [imigre] *vi* to immigrate

imminence [iminɑ̃s] *nf* imminence

imminent, -e [iminɑ̃, -ɑ̃t] *adj* imminent

immiscer [16] [imise] **s'immiscer** *vpr* to interfere (**dans** in)

immobile [imɔbil] *adj* motionless, still; *Fig (figé)* unchanging

immobilier, -ère [imɔbilje, -ɛr] **1** *adj Br* property, *Am* real-estate
2 *nm* **l'i.** *Br* property, *Am* real estate

immobilisation [imɔbilizasjɔ̃] *nf* (a) *(fait de ne plus bouger)* immobilization (b) *Fin* **immobilisations** fixed assets

immobiliser [imɔbilize] **1** *vt* (a) *(blessé)* to immobilize; *(train)* to bring to a standstill; *(véhicule) (avec un sabot)* to clamp (b) *(capital)* to tie up
2 **s'immobiliser** *vpr* to come to a stop

immobilisme [imɔbilism] *nm* opposition to change

immobilité [imɔbilite] *nf* stillness; *(d'un visage)* immobility

immodéré, -e [imɔdere] *adj* immoderate

immodérément [imɔderemɑ̃] *adv* immoderately

immoler [imɔle] *Litt* **1** *vt aussi Fig* to sacrifice (à to)
2 **s'immoler** *vpr* to sacrifice oneself; **s'i. par le feu** to die by setting fire to oneself

immonde [imɔ̃d] *adj (sale)* foul; *(ignoble, laid)* vile

immondices [imɔ̃dis] *nfpl* refuse

immoral, -e, -aux, -ales [imɔral, -o] *adj* immoral

immoralité [imɔralite] *nf* immorality

immortaliser [imɔrtalize] *vt* to immortalize

immortalité [imɔrtalite] *nf* immortality

immortel, -elle [imɔrtɛl] **1** *adj (dieu, être)* immortal; *(amour)* everlasting
2 *nm,f (membre de l'Académie française)* member of the Académie Française
3 *nf* **immortelle** *(plante)* everlasting flower

immuable [imɥabl] *adj (vérité)* unchanging, immutable; *(opinion, sourire)* fixed

immunisation [imynizasjɔ̃] *nf* immunization (**contre** against)

immuniser [imynize] *vt* to immunize (**contre** against)

immunitaire [imyniter] *adj (système, réactions, défenses)* immune

immunité [imynite] *nf* immunity; **i. parlementaire/diplomatique** parliamentary/diplomatic immunity

immunodéficitaire [imynodefisiter] *adj Méd* immunodeficient

immunodépresseur [imynodepresœr] *adj m & nm Méd* immunosuppressive

immunologie [imynɔlɔʒi] *nf* immunology

immunologique [imynɔlɔʒik] *adj* immunological

immunosuppresseur [imynɔsypresœr] *adj m & nm Méd* immunosuppressive

impact [ɛpakt] *nm* impact; **avoir un i. sur qch** to have an impact on sth

impair, -e [ɛper] **1** *adj (nombre, jours)* odd; *(côté d'une rue)* odd-numbered
2 *nm* **(a)** *(à la roulette)* odd numbers **(b)** *(maladresse)* blunder; **faire** *ou* **commettre un i.** to make a blunder

impalpable [ɛpalpabl] *adj* impalpable

imparable [ɛparabl] *adj (coup)* unstoppable; *Fig (argument, logique)* irrefutable

impardonnable [ɛpardɔnabl] *adj* unforgivable; **j'ai encore payé votre parapluie, je suis i.** I've taken your umbrella again, how unforgivable of me!

imparfait, -e [ɛparfɛ, -ɛt] **1** *adj* **(a)** *(qui a des défauts)* imperfect **(b)** *(inachevé)* unfinished
2 *nm Gram* imperfect (tense); **à l'i.** in the imperfect (tense)

impartial, -e, -aux, -ales [ɛparsjal, -o] *adj* impartial, unbiased

impartialité [ɛparsjalite] *nf* impartiality

impartir [ɛpartir] *vt Littr* **i. qch à qn** *(droit)* to grant sth to sb; *(tâche)* to assign sth to sb; **dans le délai imparti** within the time allowed; **le temps qui vous est imparti** the time allotted to you

impasse [ɛpas] *nf* **(a)** *(cul-de-sac)* dead end, cul-de-sac; *Fig* impasse, deadlock; *Fig* **être dans une i.** to be deadlocked; **sortir de l'i.** to break the deadlock **(b)** **faire une i.** *(en révisant)* = to miss out part of a subject when revising

impassibilité [ɛpasibilite] *nf* impassiveness

impassible [ɛpasibl] *adj* impassive

impatiemment [ɛpasjamã] *adv* impatiently

impatience [ɛpasjãs] *nf* impatience; **avec i.** impatiently

impatient, -e [ɛpasjã, -ãt] **1** *adj* impatient; **d'un air i.** impatiently; **être i. de faire qch** to be impatient to do sth
2 *nf* **impatiente** *(plante)* Busy Lizzie

impatienter [ɛpasjãte] **1** *vt* to annoy, to irritate
2 **s'impatienter** *vpr* to get impatient **(de/contre** at/with)

impavide [ɛpavid] *adj Litt* impassive

impayable [ɛpejabl] *adj Fam (histoire, personne)* priceless

impayé, -e [ɛpeje] **1** *adj* unpaid
2 *nm* outstanding payment

impec [ɛpek] *adj Fam* spotless; **i.!** *(parfait)* great!

impeccable [ɛpekabl] *adj* impeccable; **d'une propreté i.** impeccably clean; **Fam i.!** *(parfait)* great!

impeccablement [ɛpekabləmã] *adv* impeccably

impénétrable [ɛpenetrabl] *adj* **(a)** *(forêt, citadelle)* impenetrable **(b)** *(visage, caractère, air)* inscrutable; *(mystère, texte)* impenetrable; **les voies du Seigneur sont impénétrables** God works in mysterious ways

impénitent, -e [ɛpenitã, -ãt] *adj* unrepentant

impensable [ɛpãsabl] *adj* unthinkable; **il est i. que vous ne soyez pas remplacé** it's unthinkable that they're not going to replace you

imper [ɛper] *nm Fam* raincoat, *Br* mac

impératif, -ive [ɛperatif, -iv] *adj* **(a)** *(ton, geste)* imperious **(b)** *(nécessité, besoin)* imperative; **il est i. de connaître l'anglais** it is imperative to know English
2 *nm* **(a)** *(exigence)* requirement; **savoir nager est un i.** it is essential to be able to swim; **les impératifs de la mode** the dictates of fashion **(b)** *Gram* imperative (mood); **à l'i.** in the imperative (mood)

impérativement [ɛperativmã] *adv* **il faut i. que je la voie** it is imperative that I see her

impératrice [ɛperatris] *nf* empress

imperceptible [ɛperseptibl] *adj* imperceptible **(à** to)

imperceptiblement [ɛperseptibləmã] *adv* imperceptibly

imperdable [ɛperdabl] *adj* **le match/le procès est i.** the match/the case can't be lost

imperfectible [ɛperfektibl] *adj* imperfectible

imperfection [ɛperfeksjõ] *nf* imperfection

impérial, -e, -aux, -ales [ɛperjal, -o] *adj aussi Fig* imperial
2 *nf* **impériale** *(d'un bus)* top deck

impérialisme [ɛperjalism] *nm* imperialism

impérialiste [ɛperjalist] *adj & nmf* imperialist

impérieux, -euse [ɛperjø, -øz] *adj* **(a)** *(autoritaire)* imperious **(b)** *(nécessité, désir, besoin)* urgent, pressing

impérissable [ɛperisabl] *adj (œuvre, souvenir)* enduring; **ça ne m'a pas laissé un souvenir i.** it didn't make a lasting impression on me

imperméabilisant, -e [ɛpermeabilizã, -ãt] **1** *adj* waterproofing
2 *nm* waterproofing agent

imperméabiliser [ɛpermeabilize] *vt* to waterproof

imperméable [ɛpermeabl] **1** *adj* impermeable; *(à l'eau)* waterproof; *Fig* **être i. à qch** to be impervious to sth
2 *nm* raincoat, *Br* mackintosh

impersonnel, -elle [ɛpersɔnɛl] *adj* impersonal

impertinemment [ɛpertinamã] *adv* impertinently

impertinence [ɛpertinãs] *nf* impertinence; **avec i.** impertinently

impertinent, -e [ɛpertinã, -ãt] **1** *adj* impertinent
2 *nm,f* impertinent person; **un petit i.** an impertinent little boy

imperturbable [ɛpertyrbabl] *adj (personne)* imperturbable; *(optimisme)* unshakeable

imperturbablement [ɛpertyrbabləmã] *adv* imperturbably

impétigo [ɛpetigo] *nm* impetigo

impétueusement [ɛpetɥøzmã] *adv* impetuously

impétueux, -euse [ɛpetɥø, -øz] *adj* **(a)** *(personne)* impetuous; *(tempérament)* fiery **(b)** *Litt (torrent)* raging

impétuosité [ɛpetɥozite] *nf (fougue)* impetuosity

impie [ɛpi] *adj Litt* **1** *adj* impious
2 *nmf* impious person

impitoyable [ɛpitwajabl] *adj* merciless

impitoyablement [ɛpitwajabləmã] *adv* mercilessly

implacable [ɛplakabl] *adj (personne, vengeance, logique)* implacable; *(avancée)* relentless

implant [ɛplã] *nm* implant; **i. mammaire** breast implant; **implants (capillaires)** hair graft

implantation [ɛplãtasjõ] *nf* **(a)** *(installation)* establishment **(b)** *(des cheveux)* line; *(des dents)* arch

implanter [ɛplãte] **1** *vt* **(a)** *(installer)* to establish **(b)** *(chirurgicalement)* to implant
2 **s'implanter** *vpr* to become established

implication [ɛplikasjõ] *nf* **(a)** *(engagement)* involvement **(b)** **implications** *(conséquences)* implications

implicite [ɛplisit] *adj* implicit

implicitement [ɛplisitmã] *adv* implicitly

impliquer [ɛ̃plike] **1** vt (a) (compromettre) to implicate (dans in) (b) (supposer) to imply; **i. que** to imply that **2 s'impliquer** vpr to get involved (dans in)

implorer [ɛ̃plɔre] vt to implore, to beseech; **i. le pardon de qn** to beg sb's forgiveness; **i. qn de faire qch** to implore or beseech sb to do sth

imploser [ɛ̃ploze] vi to implode

implosion [ɛ̃plozjɔ̃] nf implosion

impoli, -e [ɛ̃pɔli] adj impolite, rude

impoliment [ɛ̃pɔlimɑ̃] adv impolitely, rudely

impolitesse [ɛ̃pɔlites] nf (a) (d'une personne, d'une remarque) impoliteness, rudeness (b) (acte) impolite act; (remarque) rude remark

impondérable [ɛ̃pɔ̃derabl] adj & nm imponderable

impopulaire [ɛ̃pɔpyler] adj unpopular

import [ɛ̃pɔr] nm import; Ordinat **i. de données** data import

importable [ɛ̃pɔrtabl] adj (vêtement) unwearable

importance [ɛ̃pɔrtɑ̃s] nf (a) (d'un événement, d'un acte, d'une personne) importance; **avoir de l'i. (pour)** to be important (to); **sans i.** unimportant; **cela n'a aucune i.** it's of no importance; **c'est d'une i. capitale** it's extremely important; **de la première ou de la plus haute i.** extremely important; **attacher ou donner de l'i. à qch** to attach importance to sth; **et alors, quelle i.?** well, so what? (b) (d'une ville, d'une somme, d'un projet) size; (de dégâts, d'une catastrophe) extent; **prendre de l'i.** (société) to expand; (mouvement, parti) to gain ground

important, -e [ɛ̃pɔrtɑ̃, -ɑ̃t] **1** adj (a) (événement, acte, personne) important (pour to); **il est i. que vous le sachiez** it's important for you to know; **peu i.** unimportant; **se donner des airs importants** to give oneself airs (b) (ville, projet) large; (somme d'argent, dégâts, retard) considerable; (chiffre) high
2 nm,f Péj **faire l'i.** to act important
3 nm **l'i., c'est que tu sois satisfait** the important thing is that you're satisfied

importateur, -trice [ɛ̃pɔrtatœr, -tris] **1** nm,f importer **2** adj importing; **les pays importateurs de pétrole** oil-importing countries

importation [ɛ̃pɔrtasjɔ̃] nf (a) (de marchandises) importing; **articles ou produits d'i.** imports; **licence d'i.** import licence (b) (produit) import

importer¹ [ɛ̃pɔrte] vt (a) (marchandises) to import (b) Ordinat to download

importer² **1** vi (compter) to matter (à to); **ce qui importe, c'est que tu viennes** the important thing is that you come
2 v impersonnel (a) (être important) **il importe que vous y soyez** it's important that you're there; **peu importe** it doesn't matter; **peu m'importe** I don't mind; **qu'importe?** what does it matter? (b) **faire qch n'importe où/quand/comment** to do sth anywhere/any time/anyhow; **c'est trop tard anyway, it's too late; n'importe comment,** c'est trop tard anyway, it's too late; **n'importe** never mind; **n'importe quel gamin** any child; **n'importe qui** anyone, anybody; **n'importe qui d'autre** anyone else; **n'importe quoi** anything; Péj **dire/écrire n'importe quoi** to talk/write nonsense; Fam **n'importe quoi!** rubbish!

import-export [ɛ̃pɔrɛkspɔr] nm import-export business

importun, -e [ɛ̃pɔrtœ̃, -yn] **1** adj (personne, visiteur, question) importunate; (arrivée, remarque) ill-timed
2 nm,f (personne) nuisance

importuner [ɛ̃pɔrtyne] vt Formel to bother

imposable [ɛ̃pozabl] adj taxable

imposant, -e [ɛ̃pozɑ̃, -ɑ̃t] adj imposing

imposé, -e [ɛ̃poze] adj (taxé) taxed; **être i. à la source** to be taxed at source

imposer [ɛ̃poze] **1** vt (a) (une condition) to impose (à on); **i. une tâche à qn** to set sb a task; **i. le respect** to command respect; **i. sa loi** to lay down the law; **i. le silence à qn** to make sb be quiet; **i. sa présence à qn** to impose on sb (b) (soumettre à l'impôt) to tax
2 vi **en i.** to be impressive; **en i. à qn** to impress sb
3 s'imposer vpr (a) (faire reconnaître sa valeur) to assert oneself; (gagner) to win (b) (déranger) **je ne voulais pas m'i.** I didn't want to impose (c) (être nécessaire) to be essential; **prendre les mesures qui s'imposent** to take the necessary steps (d) (se contraindre) **s'i. un sacrifice** to force oneself to make a sacrifice; **s'i. de faire qch** to make it a rule to do sth

imposition [ɛ̃pozisjɔ̃] nf (taxation) taxation

impossibilité [ɛ̃pɔsibilite] nf impossibility; **être ou se trouver dans l'i. de faire qch** to find it impossible to do sth

impossible [ɛ̃pɔsibl] **1** adj impossible; **i. à lire** impossible to read; **il est i. qu'il revienne avant lundi** he can't possibly be back before Monday; **il m'est i. de le faire** it's impossible for me to do it; **i. n'est pas français** there's no such word as can't; **rendre la vie i. à qn** to make life impossible for sb; **tu es i.!** you're impossible!
2 nm **tenter/demander l'i.** to attempt/to ask the impossible; **faire l'i. pour faire qch** to do everything possible to do sth

imposteur [ɛ̃pɔstœr] nm impostor

imposture [ɛ̃pɔstyr] nf deception

impôt [ɛ̃po] nm tax; **payer 1000 francs d'impôts** to pay 1,000 francs in tax; Fam **les impôts m'ont envoyé une lettre** the tax man has sent me a letter; **i. direct/indirect** direct/indirect tax; **i. foncier** land tax; **i. sur les grandes fortunes** wealth tax; **impôts locaux** local taxes; **i. sur le revenu** income tax; **i. sur les sociétés** corporation tax

impotence [ɛ̃pɔtɑ̃s] nf (infirmité) disability; (due à la vieillesse) infirmity

impotent, -e [ɛ̃pɔtɑ̃, -ɑ̃t] **1** adj (infirme) disabled; (à cause de la vieillesse) infirm
2 nm,f (infirme) disabled person; (vieillard) infirm person

impraticable [ɛ̃pratikabl] adj (a) (où l'on ne peut pas passer) impassable (b) (terrain de sport) unfit for play (c) (irréalisable) impracticable

imprécation [ɛ̃prekasjɔ̃] nf Litt imprecation

imprécis, -e [ɛ̃presi, -iz] adj imprecise

imprécision [ɛ̃presizjɔ̃] nf imprecision

imprégner [34] [ɛ̃preɲe] **1** vt (a) (sujet: eau, odeur) to impregnate (b) Fig (influencer) **être imprégné de qch** to be full of sth
2 s'imprégner vpr (a) (s'imbiber) to become impregnated (de with); **s'i. d'eau** to become soaked with water (b) Fig **s'i. d'un auteur** to immerse oneself in an author

imprenable [ɛ̃prənabl] adj (a) (forteresse, ville) impregnable (b) (vue) unobstructed

imprésario [ɛ̃presarjo] nm manager

imprescriptible [ɛ̃preskriptibl] *adj Jur* imprescriptible

impression [ɛ̃presjɔ̃] *nf* (a) (*sensation*) impression; **donner à qn l'i. que** to give sb the impression that; **faire bonne/mauvaise/forte i. (à qn)** to make a good/bad/strong impression (on sb); **ça m'a fait une drôle d'i.** it gave me a funny feeling; **j'ai l'i. de l'avoir déjà vue** I've a feeling that I've seen her before; **j'ai l'i. qu'elle est timide** I have the impression that she's shy (b) (*action d'imprimer*) printing; (*copie*) printout; *Ordinat* **i. écran** screen dump; **i. laser** laser printing; (*copie*) laser printout (c) (*motif*) **tissu à impressions florales** material with a floral pattern

impressionnable [ɛ̃presjɔnabl] *adj* (*personne*) impressionable

impressionnant, -e [ɛ̃presjɔnɑ̃, -ɑ̃t] *adj* (*imposant*) impressive; (*bouleversant*) upsetting

impressionner [ɛ̃presjɔne] *vt* (a) (*frapper*) to impress; (*bouleverser*) to upset; **se laisser i.** to let oneself be overawed (b) *Phot* (*pellicule*) to expose

impressionnisme [ɛ̃presjɔnism] *nm* impressionism

impressionniste [ɛ̃presjɔnist] *adj & nmf* impressionist

imprévisible [ɛ̃previzibl] *adj* (*temps, réaction, personne*) unpredictable; (*événement*) unforeseeable

imprévoyance [ɛ̃prevwajɑ̃s] *nf* lack of foresight

imprévoyant, -e [ɛ̃prevwajɑ̃, -ɑ̃t] *adj* lacking in foresight

imprévu, -e [ɛ̃prevy] **1** *adj* unexpected, unforeseen
2 *nm* (a) (*surprise*) **aimer l'i.** to like the unexpected; **un voyage plein d'i.** a journey full of surprises (b) (*incident*) unexpected *or* unforeseen event; **sauf i., à moins d'un i.** unless something unexpected happens

imprimable [ɛ̃primabl] *adj* printable

imprimante [ɛ̃primɑ̃t] *nf* printer; **i. à aiguilles** 24 pin printer; **i. à feuille à feuille** sheet-fed printer; **i. graphique** graphics printer; **i. à jet d'encre** ink-jet printer; **i. (à) laser** laser printer

imprimé, -e [ɛ̃prime] **1** *adj* printed
2 *nm* (a) (*formulaire*) form; **imprimés** (*journaux, prospectus*) printed matter (b) (*sur un tissu*) print; **un i. à fleurs/à motifs géométriques** a floral/geometric print

imprimer [ɛ̃prime] *vt* (a) (*livre*) to print; *Ordinat* to print (out); *Ordinat* **i. un écran** to do a print screen (b) (*motif, empreinte, tissu*) to print (c) (*mouvement*) to impart (à to)

imprimerie [ɛ̃primri] *nf* (*technique*) printing (b) (*atelier, usine*) printing works; **l'I. nationale** = French government printing office, *Br* ≃ Her Majesty's Stationery Office

imprimeur [ɛ̃primœr] *nm* printer

improbable [ɛ̃prɔbabl] *adj* improbable, unlikely

improductif, -ive [ɛ̃prɔdyktif, -iv] *adj* unproductive

impromptu, -e [ɛ̃prɔ̃pty] *adj & nm* impromptu

imprononçable [ɛ̃prɔnɔ̃sabl] *adj* unpronounceable

impropre [ɛ̃prɔpr] *adj* (a) (*incorrect*) incorrect (b) (*inadapté*) **i. à qch** unfit for sth; **i. à la consommation** unfit for human consumption

improprement [ɛ̃prɔprəmɑ̃] *adv* incorrectly

improvisation [ɛ̃prɔvizasjɔ̃] *nf* improvisation; **faire une i.** to improvise

improvisé, -e [ɛ̃prɔvize] *adj* improvised
2 s'improviser *vpr* **un départ en vacances, ça ne s'improvise pas** going on holiday isn't something you can do just like that

improviste [ɛ̃prɔvist] **à l'improviste** *adv* unexpectedly

imprudemment [ɛ̃prydamɑ̃] *adv* (*parler, agir*) rashly; (*conduire*) recklessly

imprudence [ɛ̃prydɑ̃s] *nf* (a) (*d'un acte, d'une personne*) rashness (b) (*acte*) **commettre une i.** to act rashly

imprudent, -e [ɛ̃prydɑ̃, -ɑ̃t] **1** *adj* rash; (*conducteur*) reckless
2 *nm,f* rash person

impubliable [ɛ̃pyblijabl] *adj* unpublishable

impudence [ɛ̃pydɑ̃s] *nf* impudence

impudent, -e [ɛ̃pydɑ̃, -ɑ̃t] *adj* impudent

impudeur [ɛ̃pydœr] *nf* shamelessness

impudique [ɛ̃pydik] *adj* shameless

impuissance [ɛ̃pyisɑ̃s] *nf* (a) (*incapacité*) powerlessness (à faire qch to do sth) (b) (*sexuelle*) impotence

impuissant, -e [ɛ̃pyisɑ̃, -ɑ̃t] **1** *adj* (a) (*désarmé*) powerless (b) (*sexuellement*) impotent
2 *nm* impotent man

impulsif, -ive [ɛ̃pylsif, -iv] **1** *adj* impulsive
2 *nm,f* impulsive person

impulsion [ɛ̃pylsjɔ̃] *nf* (a) *Tech* impulse (b) *Fig* (*élan*) impulse; **faire qch sous l'i. de la colère** to do sth in a fit of anger (c) (*essor*) impetus

impulsivité [ɛ̃pylsivite] *nf* impulsiveness

impunément [ɛ̃pynemɑ̃] *adv* with impunity

impuni, -e [ɛ̃pyni] *adj* unpunished

impunité [ɛ̃pynite] *nf* impunity; **agir en toute i.** to act with impunity

impur, -e [ɛ̃pyr] *adj* impure

imputable [ɛ̃pytabl] *adj* (a) (*erreur*) attributable (à to) (b) *Fin* chargeable (sur to)

imputer [ɛ̃pyte] *vt* (a) (*crime, erreur*) **i. qch à qn** to attribute sth to sb (b) *Fin* **i. des frais sur un compte** to charge expenses to an account

inabordable [inabɔrdabl] *adj* (*endroit*) inaccessible; (*prix, marchandises*) unaffordable; (*personne*) unapproachable

inacceptable [inaksɛptabl] *adj* unacceptable

inaccessible [inaksesibl] *adj* (a) (*lieu*) inaccessible; (*objectif*) unattainable (b) (*personne*) unapproachable (c) (*insensible*) **i. à la pitié** incapable of pity; **i. à la flatterie** impervious to flattery

inachevé, -e [inaʃəve] *adj* unfinished

inactif, -ive [inaktif, -iv] **1** *adj* (a) (*personne*) inactive; *Écon* **la population inactive** the non-working population (b) (*remède*) ineffective
2 *nm,f* **un i.** a person without paid employment; **les inactifs** the non-working population

inaction [inaksjɔ̃] *nf* inaction

inactivité [inaktivite] *nf* inactivity

inadapté, -e [inadapte] **1** *adj* (*personne*) (*socialement*) maladjusted; (*physiquement, mentalement*) handicapped; (*matériel*) unsuitable (à for)
2 *nm,f* (*socialement*) maladjusted person; (*physiquement, mentalement*) handicapped person; **les inadaptés** the maladjusted/handicapped

inadéquation [inadekwasjɔ̃] *nf* inadequacy

inadmissible [inadmisibl] *adj* inadmissible

inadvertance [inadvertɑ̃s] **par inadvertance** *adv* inadvertently

inaliénable [inaljenabl] *adj Jur* (*droit*) inalienable

inaltérable [inalterabl] adj (a) (métal, revêtement) stable (b) Fig (constant) unwavering

inamical, -e, -aux, -ales [inamikal, -o] adj unfriendly

inamovible [inamovibl] adj (a) (four, autoradio) built-in (b) (juge, magistrat) permanent

inanimé, -e [inanime] adj (a) (mort) lifeless; (inconscient) unconscious; **tomber i.** to fall down in a faint (b) (objet) inanimate

inanité [inanite] nf (d'un effort) futility; (d'une conversation) inanity

inanition [inanisjɔ̃] nf starvation; **mourir d'i.** to die of starvation

inaperçu, -e [inapersy] adj **passer i.** to go unnoticed

inapplicable [inaplikabl] adj (réforme, loi) unenforceable; (théorie) inapplicable

inappréciable [inapresjabl] adj (précieux) invaluable

inapte [inapt] adj (pour raisons médicales) unfit; (intellectuellement) unsuited; **être i. à qch/à faire qch** (pour raisons médicales) to be unfit for sth/to do sth; (intellectuellement) to be unsuited for sth/to do sth; **être i. (au service)** (appelé) to be unfit (for service)

inaptitude [inaptityd] nf (intellectuelle) inaptitude; (médicale, militaire) unfitness (à for)

inarticulé, -e [inartikyle] adj (son, cris) inarticulate

inassouvi, -e [inasuvi] adj (faim, désir, vengeance) unsatisfied; (soif) unquenched

inattaquable [inatakabl] adj unassailable

inattendu, -e [inatɑ̃dy] adj unexpected

inattentif, -ive [inatɑ̃tif, -iv] adj (distrait) inattentive; **i. à qch** (indifférent) heedless of sth

inattention [inatɑ̃sjɔ̃] nf lack of attention; **un moment d'i.** a lapse of concentration

inaudible [inodibl] adj inaudible

inaugural, -e, -aux, -ales [inogyral, -o] adj (discours, séance) inaugural

inauguration [inogyrasjɔ̃] nf (d'un bâtiment, d'une route) (official) opening, inauguration; (d'une statue, d'un monument) unveiling

inaugurer [inogyre] vt (bâtiment, route) to officially open, to inaugurate; (statue, monument) to unveil; Fig (politique, méthode) to implement; (époque) to usher in

inavouable [inavwabl] adj shameful

inavoué, -e [inavwe] adj unconfessed

INC [iɛnse] nm (abrév **Institut national de la consommation**) = national institute for consumer advice, Br ≃ National Consumer Council

inca [ɛ̃ka] 1 adj Inca
2 nmf **I.** Inca

incalculable [ɛ̃kalkylabl] adj incalculable; **un nombre i. de fois** countless times

incandescence [ɛ̃kɑ̃desɑ̃s] nf incandescence

incandescent, -e [ɛ̃kɑ̃desɑ̃, -ɑ̃t] adj incandescent

incantation [ɛ̃kɑ̃tasjɔ̃] nf incantation

incantatoire [ɛ̃kɑ̃tatwar] adj incantatory

incapable [ɛ̃kapabl] 1 adj (a) (personne) incapable, incompetent; Jur incompetent (b) **être i. de faire qch** to be incapable of doing sth; **i. de lâcheté** incapable of cowardice
2 nmf (a) (incompétent) incompetent (b) Jur incompetent person

incapacité [ɛ̃kapasite] nf (a) (impossibilité) **i. à faire qch** inability to do sth; **être dans l'i. de faire qch** to be unable to do sth (b) (incompétence) incompetence (c) (invalidité) disability; **i. de travail** unfitness for work (d) Jur incompetence

incarcération [ɛ̃karserasjɔ̃] nf incarceration

incarcérer [34] [ɛ̃karsere] vt to incarcerate

incarnation [ɛ̃karnasjɔ̃] nf aussi Fig incarnation

incarné, -e [ɛ̃karne] adj (a) Rel & Fig incarnate (b) (ongle) ingrowing

incarner [ɛ̃karne] 1 vt (a) (représenter) to embody (b) Th & Cin **i. (le rôle de) qn** to play (the part of) sb
2 **s'incarner** vpr (a) Rel to become incarnate (b) (ongle) to become ingrown

incartade [ɛ̃kartad] nf indiscretion

incassable [ɛ̃kasabl] adj unbreakable

incendiaire [ɛ̃sɑ̃djɛr] 1 adj (bombe) incendiary; Fig (discours) inflammatory
2 nmf (personne) arsonist, fire-raiser

incendie [ɛ̃sɑ̃di] nm fire; **i. de forêt** forest fire; **un i. criminel** arson

incendier [66] [ɛ̃sɑ̃dje] vt (a) (mettre le feu à) to set on fire (b) Fam (accabler de reproches) **i. qn** to haul sb over the coals; **se faire i.** to get hauled over the coals

incertain, -e [ɛ̃sertɛ̃, -ɛn] adj (fait, donnée, résultat) uncertain; (temps) unsettled; (mémoire) unreliable; (personne) indecisive; (démarche, pas) unsteady; (couleur) vague

incertitude [ɛ̃sertityd] nf uncertainty; **être dans l'i. (quant à)** to be uncertain (about)

incessamment [ɛ̃sesamɑ̃] adv very soon

incessant, -e [ɛ̃sesɑ̃, -ɑ̃t] adj incessant, constant

incessible [ɛ̃sesibl] adj (pension, titre de propriété) non-transferable; (droit) inalienable

inceste [ɛ̃sɛst] nm incest

incestueux, -euse [ɛ̃sɛstɥø, -øz] adj incestuous; **enfant i.** child of an incestuous relationship

inchangé, -e [ɛ̃ʃɑ̃ʒe] adj unchanged

incidemment [ɛ̃sidamɑ̃] adv in passing

incidence [ɛ̃sidɑ̃s] nf (a) (répercussion) impact (**sur** on) (b) Méd & Phys incidence

incident, -e [ɛ̃sidɑ̃, -ɑ̃t] 1 nm (a) (événement sans conséquence) hitch; **se dérouler sans i.** to go off without incident; **i. de parcours** minor setback; **i. technique** technical hitch (b) (événement plus grave) incident; **i. diplomatique** diplomatic incident
2 adj (question, remarque) incidental

incinérateur [ɛ̃sineratœr] nm incinerator

incinération [ɛ̃sinerasjɔ̃] nf (de déchets) incineration; (d'une personne) cremation

incinérer [34] [ɛ̃sinere] vt (déchets) to incinerate; (personne) to cremate

inciser [ɛ̃size] vt (peau) to make an incision in; (abcès) to lance

incisif, -ive [ɛ̃sizif, -iv] 1 adj (remarque, personne, style) incisive
2 nf **incisive** incisor

incision [ɛ̃sizjɔ̃] nf incision

incitation [ɛ̃sitasjɔ̃] nf (à la violence, l'émeute) incitement; (encouragement) incentive; **i. fiscale** tax incentive; **i. à l'achat** incentive to buy; **i. de mineurs à la débauche** corruption of minors

inciter [ɛ̃site] *vt* i. qn à faire qch to encourage sb to do sth; i. qn à la prudence/la clémence *(sujet: événement)* to incline sb to be cautious/merciful

inclassable [ɛ̃klasabl] *adj* unclassifiable; **un film/ peintre i.** a film/painter that cannot be pigeonholed

inclinable [ɛ̃klinabl] *adj (siège, dossier)* reclining

inclinaison [ɛ̃klinɛzɔ̃] *nf (d'un toit)* slope; *(d'une pente)* incline; *(de la tête, d'un chapeau)* tilt

inclination [ɛ̃klinasjɔ̃] *nf* (a) i. de la tête *(pour saluer)* nod (b) *(tendance)* inclination (pour for)

incliné, -e [ɛ̃kline] *adj (mât, toit)* sloping; *(table à dessin, dossier)* tilted

incliner [ɛ̃kline] 1 *vt* (a) *(pencher)* to tilt; i. la tête *(en avant)* to bow one's head; *(en signe de salut)* to nod; *(sur le côté)* to tilt one's head to one side (b) *(pousser)* i. qn à faire qch to incline sb to do sth; i. qn à la prudence/la clémence to incline sb to be cautious/merciful

2 s'incliner *vpr* (a) *(terrain)* to slant, to slope; *(bateau)* to heel or keel over; *(avion)* to bank (b) *(se pencher) (en avant)* to lean forward; *(sur le côté)* to lean to one side; *(pour saluer)* to bow; *Fig* s'i. devant qch to bow to sth (c) *(se soumettre)* to give in (devant to) (d) *(être battu)* to lose (devant to)

inclure [17] [ɛ̃klyr] *vt (dans un courrier)* to enclose (dans with) (b) *(englober, insérer) & Math* to include

inclus, -e [ɛ̃kly, -yz] *adj (compris)* jusqu'à la page 5 inclus(e) up to and including page 5; jusqu'au mardi i. *Br* up to and including Tuesday; *Am* through Tuesday; du 7 au 18 i. from the 7th to the 18th inclusive; ils seront trente-cinq, professeurs i. there will be thirty-five of them, including the teachers (b) *(dent)* impacted

inclusion [ɛ̃klyzjɔ̃] *nf* (a) *(dans un courrier)* enclosure (dans with) (b) *(insertion)* insertion (c) *(objet décoratif)* = flower, shell etc set into plastic and used as a paperweight, an ornament, jewellery etc (d) *(d'une dent)* impacting (e) *Ordinat (de fichier)* insertion

incognito [ɛ̃kɔɲito] 1 *adv* incognito
2 *nm* garder l'i. to remain incognito

incohérence [ɛ̃kɔerɑ̃s] *nf (d'une personne, dans un film, une histoire)* inconsistency; *(d'un discours, d'idées)* incoherence

incohérent, -e [ɛ̃kɔerɑ̃, -ɑ̃t] *adj (personne, histoire, attitude)* inconsistent; *(idées, argumentation, discours)* incoherent; tenir des propos incohérents to talk incoherently

incollable [ɛ̃kɔlabl] *adj* (a) *(riz)* non-stick (b) *Fam (personne)* elle est i. sur la question/en histoire you can't catch her out on the subject/on history

incolore [ɛ̃kɔlɔr] *adj* colourless

incomber [ɛ̃kɔ̃be] **incomber à** *vt ind (responsabilité)* to lie with; *(devoirs)* to fall to; il m'incombe/il lui incombe de... it falls to me/to him to...

incombustible [ɛ̃kɔ̃bystibl] *adj* incombustible

incommensurable [ɛ̃kɔmɑ̃syrabl] *adj (richesse)* immeasurable; *(espace)* boundless; *Hum* être d'une bêtise i. to be incredibly stupid

incommodant, -e [ɛ̃kɔmɔdɑ̃, -ɑ̃t] *adj* discomforting

incommode [ɛ̃kɔmɔd] *adj (horaire, arrangement)* inconvenient; *(situation)* awkward

incommoder [ɛ̃kɔmɔde] *vt* to bother

incomparable [ɛ̃kɔ̃parabl] *adj (sans pareil)* beyond compare, matchless

incomparablement [ɛ̃kɔ̃parabləmɑ̃] *adv* incomparably

incompatibilité [ɛ̃kɔ̃patibilite] *nf* incompatibility; i. d'humeur *ou* de caractère mutual incompatibility

incompatible [ɛ̃kɔ̃patibl] *adj* incompatible (avec with)

incompétence [ɛ̃kɔ̃petɑ̃s] *nf* incompetence

incompétent, -e [ɛ̃kɔ̃petɑ̃, -ɑ̃t] *adj* incompetent

incomplet, -ète [ɛ̃kɔ̃plɛ, -ɛt] *adj* incomplete

incompréhensible [ɛ̃kɔ̃preɑ̃sibl] *adj* incomprehensible

incompréhension [ɛ̃kɔ̃preɑ̃sjɔ̃] *nf* incomprehension

incompressible [ɛ̃kɔ̃presibl] *adj* (a) *(matériau)* incompressible (b) *Jur (peine)* to be served in full (c) *(dépenses)* which cannot be reduced

incompris, -e [ɛ̃kɔ̃pri, -iz] 1 *adj* misunderstood
2 *nm,f* être un i. to be misunderstood

inconcevable [ɛ̃kɔ̃səvabl] *adj* inconceivable

inconciliable [ɛ̃kɔ̃siljabl] *adj (théorie)* irreconcilable (avec with); *(mode de vie, activité)* incompatible (avec with)

inconditionnel, -elle [ɛ̃kɔ̃disjɔnɛl] 1 *adj (soutien, retrait)* unconditional; *(obéissance)* unquestioning, unconditional; *(supporter)* staunch
2 *nm,f* fan; c'est un i. de la pêche/du hard rock he's absolutely mad about fishing/hard rock

inconfort [ɛ̃kɔ̃fɔr] *nm (matériel)* discomfort; *(moral)* awkwardness

inconfortable [ɛ̃kɔ̃fɔrtabl] *adj aussi Fig* uncomfortable

incongru, -e [ɛ̃kɔ̃gry] *adj* inappropriate; *(bruit)* rude

incongruité [ɛ̃kɔ̃gryite] *nf* (a) *(manque d'à-propos)* inappropriateness (b) *(remarque déplacée)* inappropriate remark

inconnu, -e [ɛ̃kɔny] 1 *adj (auteur, civilisation, destination)* unknown (de to); *(lieu, visage)* strange; il m'est i. I've never heard of him/it; né de père i. *(sur document administratif)* father unknown; i. à cette adresse not known at this address; *Fam* Durand? i. au bataillon! Durand? never heard of him!
2 *nm,f (étranger)* stranger; *(personne non célèbre)* unknown
3 *nm* la peur de l'i. the fear of the unknown
4 *nf* inconnue *Math & Fig* unknown (quantity)

inconsciemment [ɛ̃kɔ̃sjamɑ̃] *adv* (a) *(sans réfléchir)* without thinking (b) *(dans l'inconscient)* subconsciously

inconscience [ɛ̃kɔ̃sjɑ̃s] *nf* (a) *(perte de connaissance)* unconsciousness; sombrer *ou* tomber dans l'i. to lose consciousness (b) *(manque de jugement)* recklessness; c'est de l'i.! it's sheer madness!

inconscient, -e [ɛ̃kɔ̃sjɑ̃, -ɑ̃t] 1 *adj* (a) *(évanoui)* unconscious (b) *(acte)* unconscious; i. du danger oblivious to the danger (c) *(irréfléchi) (personne)* reckless
2 *nm* l'i. the unconscious, the subconscious; l'i. collectif the collective unconscious

inconséquence [ɛ̃kɔ̃sekɑ̃s] *nf (caractère)* recklessness; *(acte)* reckless act

inconséquent, -e [ɛ̃kɔ̃sekɑ̃, -ɑ̃t] *adj* (a) *(irréfléchi)* reckless (b) *(illogique)* inconsistent

inconsidéré, -e [ɛ̃kɔ̃sidere] *adj (acte, remarque)* ill-considered; *(dépenses)* reckless

inconsistance [ɛ̃kɔ̃sistɑ̃s] *nf* (a) *(d'une pâte, d'une soupe)* thinness (b) *(d'une personne, d'une conduite)* inconsistency (c) *(d'une intrigue, d'un film, d'un roman)* thinness

inconsistant, -e [ɛ̃kɔ̃sistɑ̃, -ɑ̃t] *adj* (a) *(pâte, crème, soupe)* thin (b) *(conduite, personne)* inconsistent (c) *(intrigue, film, roman)* thin

inconsolable [ɛ̃kɔ̃sɔlabl] *adj* inconsolable

inconstance [ɛ̃kɔ̃stɑ̃s] nf (instabilité) changeableness; (infidélité) fickleness

inconstant, -e [ɛ̃kɔ̃stɑ̃, -ɑ̃t] adj (instable) changeable; (infidèle) fickle

inconstitutionnel, -elle [ɛ̃kɔ̃stitysjɔnɛl] adj unconstitutional

incontestable [ɛ̃kɔ̃tɛstabl] adj indisputable

incontestablement [ɛ̃kɔ̃tɛstabləmɑ̃] adv indisputably

incontesté, -e [ɛ̃kɔ̃tɛste] adj undisputed

incontinence [ɛ̃kɔ̃tinɑ̃s] nf Méd incontinence; **i. verbale** verbal diarrhoea

incontinent, -e [ɛ̃kɔ̃tinɑ̃, -ɑ̃t] adj Méd incontinent

incontournable [ɛ̃kɔ̃turnabl] adj (film, artiste) that cannot be ignored; **son argument était i.** there was no getting away from her argument

incontrôlable [ɛ̃kɔ̃trolabl] adj (a) (incendie, bâillements) uncontrollable; **des éléments incontrôlables** rowdy elements (b) (affirmation) unverifiable

incontrôlé, -e [ɛ̃kɔ̃trole] adj (éléments, bande) uncontrolled

inconvenance [ɛ̃kɔ̃vənɑ̃s] nf (indécence) impropriety; **dire/commettre une i.** to say/to do something improper

inconvenant, -e [ɛ̃kɔ̃vənɑ̃, -ɑ̃t] adj (propos, remarque, acte) improper

inconvénient [ɛ̃kɔ̃venjɑ̃] nm drawback, disadvantage; **je n'y vois pas d'i.** I have no objection

inconvertible [ɛ̃kɔ̃vɛrtibl] adj (monnaie) non-convertible

incorporation [ɛ̃kɔrpɔrasjɔ̃] nf (a) (mélange) blending, mixing (de qch dans qch of sth into sth) (b) Mil conscription

incorporé, -e [ɛ̃kɔrpɔre] adj (flash, micro) built-in

incorporer [ɛ̃kɔrpɔre] 1 vt (a) (mélanger) i. qch à qch to blend or mix sth into sth (b) (insérer) to insert (à in) (c) (troupes) to draft
2 **s'incorporer** vpr **s'i. dans un groupe** to join a group

incorrect, -e [ɛ̃kɔrɛkt] adj (a) (erroné) incorrect, wrong (b) (personne) impolite; (attitude) improper (c) (tenue) (déplacée) unsuitable; (indécente) improper

incorrectement [ɛ̃kɔrɛktəmɑ̃] adv (a) (en faisant des erreurs) incorrectly, wrongly (b) (impoliment) impolitely (c) (habillé) (de façon déplacée) unsuitably; (de façon indécente) improperly

incorrection [ɛ̃kɔrɛksjɔ̃] nf (a) (impolitesse) impoliteness (b) (action) impolite action; (propos) impolite remark (c) (grammaticale) mistake

incorrigible [ɛ̃kɔriʒibl] adj incorrigible

incorruptible [ɛ̃kɔryptibl] 1 adj incorruptible
2 nmf incorruptible person

incrédule [ɛ̃kredyl] adj (sceptique) incredulous; **d'un air i.** with a look of disbelief

incrédulité [ɛ̃kredylite] nf incredulity

increvable [ɛ̃krəvabl] adj (a) (pneu) puncture-proof (b) Fam (personne) tireless; (voiture, moteur) indestructible

incriminer [ɛ̃krimine] vt (personne) to accuse; (sujet: événement) to condemn; (comportement, décision) to condemn

incrochetable [ɛ̃krɔʃtabl] adj unpickable

incroyable [ɛ̃krwajabl] adj incredible; **c'est i., ça!** I don't believe it!

incroyablement [ɛ̃krwajabləmɑ̃] adv incredibly

incroyance [ɛ̃krwajɑ̃s] nf unbelief

incroyant, -e [ɛ̃krwajɑ̃, -ɑ̃t] 1 adj unbelieving
2 nm,f unbeliever

incrustation [ɛ̃krystasjɔ̃] nf (a) (ornement) inlay (b) (dépôt calcaire) fur, scale (c) TV (image) inset

incruster [ɛ̃kryste] 1 vt (a) (bois, métal) to inlay (de with) (b) (entartrer) to scale, to fur up
2 **s'incruster** vpr (a) (adhérer) to become encrusted (b) (chaudière, bouilloire) to fur up (c) Fam (s'imposer) **quand on l'invite, il s'incruste** once you invite him you can't get rid of him

incubateur [ɛ̃kybatœr] nm incubator

incubation [ɛ̃kybasjɔ̃] nf incubation; **période d'i.** incubation period

incuber [ɛ̃kybe] vt to incubate, to hatch

inculpation [ɛ̃kylpasjɔ̃] nf indictment; **sous l'i. d'assassinat** charged with murder

inculpé, -e [ɛ̃kylpe] nm,f l'i. the accused

inculper [ɛ̃kylpe] vt to indict, to charge (de with)

inculquer [ɛ̃kylke] vt to instil (à qn in sb)

inculte [ɛ̃kylt] adj (terre, personne) uncultivated

incultivable [ɛ̃kyltivabl] adj untillable

inculture [ɛ̃kyltyr] nf lack of culture

incurable [ɛ̃kyrabl] 1 adj incurable; **d'une paresse i.** incurably lazy
2 nmf person with an incurable disease

incurie [ɛ̃kyri] nf Formel negligence

incursion [ɛ̃kyrsjɔ̃] nf (a) (invasion) raid, incursion (b) Fig (entrée soudaine) intrusion; **faire une i. dans une pièce/une réunion** to burst into a room/a meeting

incurvé, -e [ɛ̃kyrve] adj bent, curved

indatable [ɛ̃databl] adj that cannot be dated

Inde [ɛ̃d] nf l'I. India

indécence [ɛ̃desɑ̃s] nf indecency

indécent, -e [ɛ̃desɑ̃, -ɑ̃t] adj indecent

indéchiffrable [ɛ̃deʃifrabl] adj (a) (illisible) indecipherable (b) (incompréhensible) impenetrable

indéchirable [ɛ̃deʃirabl] adj tearproof

indécis, -e [ɛ̃desi, -iz] 1 adj (a) (personne) (de caractère) indecisive; (ponctuellement) undecided; **je suis encore indécise** I haven't made my mind up yet (b) (peu net) (victoire, bataille) inconclusive; (contour) vague
2 nm,f indecisive person; Pol **les i.** the floating voters

indécision [ɛ̃desizjɔ̃] nf (de caractère) indecisiveness; (ponctuelle) indecision

indécrottable [ɛ̃dekrɔtabl] adj Fam (incorrigible) hopeless; **être d'une bêtise i.** to be hopelessly stupid

indéfendable [ɛ̃defɑ̃dabl] adj indefensible

indéfini, -e [ɛ̃defini] adj (a) (illimité) indefinite (b) (imprécis) (tristesse, malaise) vague, undefined (c) Gram (pronom, article) indefinite

indéfiniment [ɛ̃definimɑ̃] adv indefinitely

indéfinissable [ɛ̃definisabl] adj indefinable

indéformable [ɛ̃deformabl] adj that keeps its shape

indélébile [ɛ̃delebil] adj indelible

indélicat, -e [ɛ̃delika, -at] adj (a) (sans tact) tactless, insensitive (b) (malhonnête) dishonest

indélicatesse [ɛ̃delikatɛs] *nf* **(a)** *(manque de tact)* tactlessness **(b)** *(malhonnêteté)* dishonesty; *(acte malhonnête)* dishonest act; **commettre une i.** to behave dishonestly

indemne [ɛ̃dɛmn] *adj* unharmed, unscathed

indemnisation [ɛ̃dɛmnizasjɔ̃] *nf* compensation

indemniser [ɛ̃dɛmnize] *vt* to compensate (**de** for)

indemnité [ɛ̃dɛmnite] *nf* **(a)** *(pour perte encourue)* compensation; *(pour délai, non-livraison)* penalty **(b)** *(allocation)* allowance; **i. journalière** daily allowance; **i. de licenciement** severance pay, redundancy payment; **i. parlementaire** = salary paid to member of French parliament; **i. de transport** travel allowance

indémodable [ɛ̃demɔdabl] *adj* perennially fashionable

indémontrable [ɛ̃demɔ̃trabl] *adj* unprovable

indéniable [ɛ̃denjabl] *adj* undeniable

indéniablement [ɛ̃denjablamɑ̃] *adv* undeniably

indépendamment [ɛ̃depɑ̃damɑ̃] *adv* independently; **i. de** apart from

indépendance [ɛ̃depɑ̃dɑ̃s] *nf* independence; **accéder à l'i.** to gain independence

indépendant, -e [ɛ̃depɑ̃dɑ̃, -ɑ̃t] **1** *adj* **(a)** *(personne, pays, vie)* independent (**de** of); *(travailleur)* self-employed, freelance; *(appartement)* self-contained; **i. de ma volonté** beyond my control **(b)** *Gram* **proposition indépendante** main clause
2 *nm, f (travailleur)* self-employed person, freelancer

indépendantisme [ɛ̃depɑ̃dɑ̃tism] *nm* independence movement

indépendantiste [ɛ̃depɑ̃dɑ̃tist] *nmf Pol (partisan de l'indépendance)* supporter of independence; *(activiste)* freedom fighter

indéracinable [ɛ̃derasinabl] *adj (préjugés)* deep-rooted

indescriptible [ɛ̃deskriptibl] *adj* indescribable

indésirable [ɛ̃dezirabl] *adj & nmf* undesirable

indestructible [ɛ̃destryktibl] *adj* indestructible

indétectable [ɛ̃detɛktabl] *adj* undetectable

indéterminé, -e [ɛ̃detɛrmine] *adj* **(a)** *(date, heure)* unspecified; *(raison)* unknown **(b)** *(personne)* undecided

index [ɛ̃dɛks] *nm* **(a)** *(doigt)* forefinger, index finger **(b)** *(de livre)* index; *Fig* **mettre qn/qch à l'i.** to blacklist sb/sth **(c)** *Ordinat* index

indexation [ɛ̃dɛksasjɔ̃] *nf Écon* index-linking; *Ordinat* indexing

indexer [ɛ̃dɛkse] *vt* **(a)** *Écon* to index-link (**sur** to) **(b)** *aussi Ordinat (ajouter un index à)* to index

indic [ɛ̃dik] *nm Fam* grass, informer

indicateur, -trice [ɛ̃dikatœr, -tris] **1** *adj voir* **panneau, poteau**
2 *nm* **(a)** *(livre)* **i. des rues de Paris** Paris street finder; **i. des chemins de fer** railway timetable **(b)** *(instrument)* indicator, gauge; *Av* **i. d'altitude** altimeter; **i. de niveau de carburant** fuel gauge **(c)** *(informateur)* informer **(d)** *Écon* indicator

indicatif, -ive [ɛ̃dikatif, -iv] **1** *adj* indicative (**de** of); **à titre i.** as a guide
2 *nm* **(a)** *Gram* indicative (mood); **à l'i.** in the indicative **(b)** *Tél* dialling code; *TV & Rad* theme tune

indication [ɛ̃dikasjɔ̃] *nf* **(a)** *(action)* indication **(b)** *(renseignement)* (piece of) information **(c)** *(directive)* instruction, direction; **sauf i. contraire** unless otherwise specified; *Th* **indications scéniques** stage directions **(d)** *(sur notice pharmaceutique)* **indications:... suitable for...**

indice [ɛ̃dis] *nm* **(a)** *(signe)* sign, indication (**de** of); *(dans une enquête)* clue (**de** to) **(b)** *(chiffre indicateur) & Math* index; *Typ* subscript; *Aut* **i. d'octane** octane rating; **i. des prix** price index; **i. de protection** *(d'une crème solaire)* protection factor

indicible [ɛ̃disibl] *adj Litt* indescribable

indien, -enne [ɛ̃djɛ̃, -ɛn] **1** *adj* Indian
2 *nm, f* **I.** *(d'Inde, d'Amérique)* Indian

indifféremment [ɛ̃diferamɑ̃] *adv (sans distinction)* equally

indifférence [ɛ̃diferɑ̃s] *nf* indifference

indifférencié, -e [ɛ̃diferɑ̃sje] *adj* undifferentiated

indifférent, -e [ɛ̃diferɑ̃, -ɑ̃t] *adj* **(a)** *(peu ou pas intéressé)* indifferent (**à** to); **laisser qn i.** to leave sb cold; **il m'est i.** I'm indifferent to him **(b)** *(sans importance)* irrelevant; **cela m'est i.** it makes no difference to me; **parler de choses indifférentes** to chat about nothing in particular

indifférer [34] [ɛ̃difere] *vt* **cela m'indiffère** it's a matter of complete indifference to me

indigence [ɛ̃diʒɑ̃s] *nf* destitution

indigène [ɛ̃diʒɛn] *adj & nmf* native

indigent, -e [ɛ̃diʒɑ̃, -ɑ̃t] **1** *adj* destitute
2 *nm, f* pauper; **les indigents** the poor

indigeste [ɛ̃diʒɛst] *adj aussi Fig* indigestible

indigestion [ɛ̃diʒɛstjɔ̃] *nf* **avoir une i.** to have a stomach upset; **faire une i. de chocolat** to make oneself sick from eating chocolate; *Fig* **j'en ai une i.** I'm fed up with it

indignation [ɛ̃diɲasjɔ̃] *nf* indignation

indigne [ɛ̃diɲ] *adj (personne)* unworthy (**de** of); *(action, conduite)* shameful

indigner [ɛ̃diɲe] **1** *vt* to outrage
2 **s'indigner** *vpr* to be indignant (**de** at)

indignité [ɛ̃diɲite] *nf* **(a)** *(d'une personne)* unworthiness; *(d'une action)* shamefulness **(b)** *(action)* shameful act

indigo [ɛ̃digo] *nm & adj inv* indigo

indiqué, -e [ɛ̃dike] *adj (recommandé)* advisable; **il est tout à fait i. pour ce poste** he's the right person for the job

indiquer [ɛ̃dike] *vt* **(a)** *(montrer) (sujet: personne)* to point out; **i. qch du doigt** to point to or at sth; **i. le chemin à qn** to tell sb the way, to direct sb **(b)** *(marquer) (sujet: panneau, étiquette, carte)* to show, to indicate; *(sujet: compteur)* to show, to read **(c)** *(donner) (date, adresse)* to give; **à l'heure indiquée** at the agreed time; **pourriez-vous m'i. le prix de ce vase?** could you tell me how much this vase costs? **(d)** *(recommander)* to recommend; **elle m'a indiqué un excellent dentiste/hôtel** she recommended an excellent dentist/hotel to me **(e)** *(dénoter)* to point to, to indicate

indirect, -e [ɛ̃dirɛkt] *adj aussi Gram* indirect

indirectement [ɛ̃dirɛktamɑ̃] *adv* indirectly

indiscipline [ɛ̃disiplin] *nf* indiscipline

indiscipliné, -e [ɛ̃disipline] *adj* undisciplined; *(cheveux)* unmanageable

indiscret, -ète [ɛ̃diskrɛ, -ɛt] 1 *adj* (a) *(qui parle trop)* indiscreet (b) *(curieux)* inquisitive; **à l'abri des regards indiscrets** safe from prying eyes

2 *nm,f* (a) *(qui parle trop)* indiscreet person (b) *(curieux)* inquisitive person

indiscrétion [ɛ̃diskresjɔ̃] *nf* (a) *(manque de discrétion)* indiscretion (b) *(curiosité)* inquisitiveness; **sans i., combien l'avez-vous payé?** if you don't mind me asking, how much did you pay for it? (c) *(remarque)* indiscreet remark

indiscutable [ɛ̃diskytabl] *adj* indisputable

indiscutablement [ɛ̃diskytabləmɑ̃] *adv* indisputably

indispensable [ɛ̃dispɑ̃sabl] 1 *adj* indispensable, essential (**à qch** for sth); **i. à qn** indispensable to sb; **il est i. que tu y ailles** it is essential that you go

2 *nm* **l'i.** the essentials

indisponibilité [ɛ̃disponibilite] *nf* unavailability

indisponible [ɛ̃disponibl] *adj* unavailable

indisposé, -e [ɛ̃dispoze] *adj* indisposed, unwell; *Euph* **elle est indisposée** it's her time of the month

indisposer [ɛ̃dispoze] *vt* (a) *(rendre malade)* **i. qn** *(odeur, climat)* to make sb feel ill; *(nourriture)* to disagree with sb (b) *(contrarier)* to annoy

indisposition [ɛ̃dispozisjɔ̃] *nf* indisposition, slight illness

indissociable [ɛ̃disɔsjabl] *adj* indissociable

indissoluble [ɛ̃disɔlybl] *adj* indissoluble

indistinct, -e [ɛ̃distɛ̃, -ɛkt] *adj* indistinct

indistinctement [ɛ̃distɛ̃ktəmɑ̃] *adv* (a) *(voir, parler)* indistinctly (b) *(indifféremment)* equally

individu [ɛ̃dividy] *nm* (a) *(être humain)* individual (b) *Péj (homme)* individual, character; **un drôle d'i.** a strange individual *or* character

individualiser [ɛ̃dividɥalize] *vt* (a) *(différencier)* to make individual (b) *(adapter)* to adapt to individual circumstances

individualisme [ɛ̃dividɥalism] *nm* individualism

individualiste [ɛ̃dividɥalist] 1 *adj* individualistic

2 *nmf* individualist

individualité [ɛ̃dividɥalite] *nf* individuality

individuel, -elle [ɛ̃dividɥɛl] *adj* individual; *(liberté, responsabilité)* personal; *(maison)* detached; *(chambre)* single

individuellement [ɛ̃dividɥɛlmɑ̃] *adv* individually

indivisible [ɛ̃divizibl] *adj* indivisible

Indochine [ɛ̃dɔʃin] *nf* **l'I.** Indochina

indocile [ɛ̃dɔsil] *adj* disobedient

indo-européen, -enne *(mpl* **indo-européens,** *fpl* **indo-européennes)** [ɛ̃dɔørɔpeɛ̃, -ɛn] 1 *adj* Indo-European

2 *nm,f* **I.** Indo-European

3 *nm (langue)* Indo-European

indolence [ɛ̃dɔlɑ̃s] *nf* laziness

indolent, -e [ɛ̃dɔlɑ̃, -ɑ̃t] *adj* lazy

indolore [ɛ̃dɔlɔr] *adj* painless

indomptable [ɛ̃dɔ̃tabl] *adj* (a) *(animal)* untamable (b) *Fig (orgueil, caractère)* indomitable; *(passion)* uncontrollable

indompté, -e [ɛ̃dɔ̃te] *adj* (a) *(animal)* untamed (b) *Fig (passion, orgueil)* uncontrolled

Indonésie [ɛ̃dɔnezi] *nf* **l'I.** Indonesia

indonésien, -enne [ɛ̃dɔnezjɛ̃, -ɛn] 1 *adj* Indonesian

2 *nm,f* **I.** Indonesian

indu, -e [ɛ̃dy] *adj* **à une heure indue** at an ungodly hour; **il rentre à des heures indues** he comes home at all hours of the night

indubitable [ɛ̃dybitabl] *adj* indisputable, indubitable; **c'est i.** there's no doubt about it

indubitablement [ɛ̃dybitabləmɑ̃] *adv* undoubtedly

induire [18] [ɛ̃dɥir] *vt* (a) *(entraîner)* **i. qn à faire qch** to induce sb to do sth; **i. qn en erreur** to mislead sb (b) *(conclure)* to infer (**de** from)

indulgence [ɛ̃dylʒɑ̃s] *nf* (a) *(bienveillance)* indulgence, leniency; **faire preuve d'i. envers qn** to be indulgent towards sb; **rires sans i.** merciless laughter; **faire de qn un portrait sans i.** to describe sb warts and all (b) *Rel* indulgence

indulgent, -e [ɛ̃dylʒɑ̃, -ɑ̃t] *adj* indulgent

indûment [ɛ̃dymɑ̃] *adv* unduly

industrialisation [ɛ̃dystrijalizasjɔ̃] *nf* industrialization

industrialiser [ɛ̃dystrijalize] 1 *vt* to industrialize

2 **s'industrialiser** *vpr* to become industrialized

industrie [ɛ̃dystri] *nf* industry; **travailler dans l'i.** to work in industry; **l'i. alimentaire** the food industry; **l'i. automobile** the car industry; **l'i. lourde** heavy industry; **l'i. pharmaceutique** the pharmaceutical industry

industriel, -elle [ɛ̃dystrijɛl] 1 *adj* industrial; *Fam* **des magazines en quantité industrielle** vast quantities of magazines

2 *nm* manufacturer, industrialist

industriellement [ɛ̃dystrijɛlmɑ̃] *adv* industrially

industrieux, -euse [ɛ̃dystrijø, -øz] *adj Litt (habile)* skilful, ingenious; *(travailleur)* industrious

inébranlable [inebrɑ̃labl] *adj (mur, rocher)* immovable; *Fig* unshakeable

inédit, -e [inedi, -it] 1 *adj* (a) *(livre)* previously unpublished; *(disque)* previously unreleased (b) *(spectacle, projet, idée)* new, original

2 *nm (texte)* previously unpublished work; *(disque)* previously unreleased record

ineffable [inefabl] *adj* ineffable, unutterable

ineffaçable [inefasabl] *adj aussi Fig* indelible

inefficace [inefikas] *adj (personne)* inefficient; *(remède, méthode, loi)* ineffective

inefficacité [inefikasite] *nf (de personne)* inefficiency; *(d'un remède, d'une méthode, d'une loi)* ineffectiveness

inégal, -e, -aux, -ales [inegal, -o] *adj* (a) *(non égal)* *(parts, partage, force, lutte)* unequal (b) *(irrégulier)* *(sol)* uneven; *(pouls)* irregular; *Fig (travail, écrivain, style, qualité)* inconsistent; *(humeur)* changeable

inégalable [inegalabl] *adj* incomparable, matchless

inégalé, -e [inegale] *adj (qualité, personne)* unequalled; *(record)* unbeaten

inégalement [inegalmɑ̃] *adv* (a) *(injustement)* unequally (b) *(irrégulièrement)* unevenly

inégalité [inegalite] *nf* (a) *(injustice)* inequality (**entre** between) (b) *(différence)* disparity (**de** in) (c) *(du sol)* unevenness; *Fig* **i. d'humeur** moodiness

inélégant, -e [inelegɑ̃, -ɑ̃t] *adj Litt (mal habillé)* inelegant; *(discourtois)* discourteous

inéligible [ineliʒibl] *adj* ineligible

inéluctable [inelyktabl] *adj* inescapable

inemployable [inɑ̃plwajabl] *adj* unusable

inemployé, -e [inɑ̃plwaje] *adj (objet, machine, talent)* unused; *(ressources)* untapped; *(forces)* unchannelled

inénarrable [inenarabl] *adj* comical

inepte [inεpt] *adj (remarque, réponse, histoire)* inane; *(personne)* inept

ineptie [inεpsi] *nf (a) (d'un comportement, d'un film)* inanity **(b)** *(action)* stupid thing; *(remarque)* stupid comment

inépuisable [inepɥizabl] *adj (réserves, sujet, curiosité)* inexhaustible; *(imagination)* limitless; **sur ce sujet-là, elle est i.** you can never get her off the subject

inerte [inεrt] *adj (a) (masse, corps, matière)* inert **(b)** *(personne) (inanimé)* lifeless; *(passif)* apathetic

inertie [inεrsi] *nf (a)* Phys inertia **(b)** *(manque de réaction)* apathy

inespéré, -e [inεspere] *adj* unexpected, unhoped-for

inesthétique [inεstetik] *adj* unaesthetic

inestimable [inεstimabl] *adj (dégâts, coût, richesse)* incalculable; *(aide, chance)* invaluable; *(œuvre d'art)* priceless; **d'une valeur i.** priceless

inévitable [inevitabl] *adj* inevitable, unavoidable

inévitablement [inevitabləmɑ̃] *adv* inevitably, unavoidably

inexact, -e [inεgzakt] *adj (a) (incorrect) (réponse, description, détail)* inaccurate; *(somme, calcul)* wrong, incorrect **(b)** *(manque de ponctualité)* unpunctual

inexactitude [inεgzaktityd] *nf (a) (caractère erroné, erreur)* inaccuracy **(b)** *(manque de ponctualité)* unpunctuality

inexcusable [inεkskyzabl] *adj* inexcusable, unforgivable

inexhaustible [inεgzostibl] *adj* Litt inexhaustible

inexistant, -e [inεgzistɑ̃, -ɑ̃t] *adj* non-existent; Hum **il est totalement i.** he's a complete nonentity

inexistence [inεgzistɑ̃s] *nf* non-existence

inexorable [inεgzɔrabl] *adj (destin)* inexorable; *(juge)* pitiless; *(volonté)* inflexible

inexorablement [inεgzɔrabləmɑ̃] *adv* inexorably

inexpérience [inεkspeʀjɑ̃s] *nf* inexperience

inexpérimenté, -e [inεksperimɑ̃te] *adj* inexperienced

inexplicable [inεksplikabl] *adj* inexplicable

inexpliqué, -e [inεksplike] *adj* unexplained

inexploité, -e [inεksplwate] *adj (mine)* unworked; *(terre)* undeveloped; *(ressources)* untapped

inexploré, -e [inεksplɔre] *adj* unexplored

inexpressif, -ive [inεkspresif, -iv] *adj* inexpressive, expressionless

inexprimable [inεksprimabl] *adj* inexpressible

inexprimé, -e [inεksprime] *adj* unexpressed

in extenso [inεkstɛ̃so] *adv* in full

in extremis [inεkstremis] *adv* at the last minute

inextricable [inεkstrikabl] *adj* inextricable

inextricablement [inεkstrikabləmɑ̃] *adv* inextricably

infaillibilité [ɛ̃fajibilite] *nf* infallibility

infaillible [ɛ̃fajibl] *adj* infallible

infailliblement [ɛ̃fajibləmɑ̃] *adv* infallibly

infaisable [ɛ̃fəzabl] *adj* not feasible, impossible

infamant, -e [ɛ̃famɑ̃, -ɑ̃t] *adj (déclaration, accusation)* defamatory, slanderous **(b)** Jur *(peine)* involving loss of civil rights

infâme [ɛ̃fɑm] *adj (mensonge, personne)* despicable; *(acte, crime)* unspeakable; *(taudis)* squalid; *(odeur, nourriture)* revolting

infamie [ɛ̃fami] *nf (a) (caractère infâme)* infamy **(b)** *(action)* unspeakable act; *(remarque)* slanderous remark

infant, -e [ɛ̃fɑ̃, -ɑ̃t] *nm,f* infante, infanta

infanterie [ɛ̃fɑ̃tri] *nf* infantry; **i. de marine** marine corps, marines

infanticide [ɛ̃fɑ̃tisid] **1** *adj* infanticidal
2 *nmf (personne)* child-killer, infanticide
3 *nm (crime)* infanticide

infantile [ɛ̃fɑ̃til] *adj (a) (maladie)* childhood **(b)** Péj *(comportement, personne)* childish, infantile

infantiliser [ɛ̃fɑ̃tilize] *vt* Péj **la télévision infantilise les gens** television makes people behave like children

infarctus [ɛ̃farktys] *nm* heart attack; **i. du myocarde** myocardial infarction, coronary thrombosis

infatigable [ɛ̃fatigabl] *adj* tireless

infatué, -e [ɛ̃fatɥe] *adj* conceited; **i. de soi-même** full of oneself

infécond, -e [ɛ̃fekɔ̃, -ɔ̃d] *adj* infertile

infect, -e [ɛ̃fεkt] *adj* foul

infecter [ɛ̃fεkte] **1** *vt (a) (plaie, blessure)* to infect **(b)** *(atmosphère, eau, sol)* to contaminate
2 s'infecter *vpr* to become infected, to go septic

infectieux, -euse [ɛ̃fεksjø, -øz] *adj* infectious

infection [ɛ̃fεksjɔ̃] *nf (a)* Méd & Ordinat infection **(b)** *(puanteur)* stench, stink; **quelle i. dans cette pièce!** this room stinks!

inférieur, -e [ɛ̃ferjœr] **1** *adj (a) (qui est en bas) (étagère, niveau)* bottom; *(étages, lèvre, paupière, membres, mâchoire)* lower; **partie inférieure** bottom (part); **allez voir à l'étage i.** go and look on the floor below **(b)** *(dans une hiérarchie) (qualité, marchandises, intelligence)* inferior; **d'un rang i.** of a lower rank; **être rétrogradé à l'échelon i.** to be demoted to the grade below **(c)** *(dans une comparaison)* **i. à** *(qualité)* inferior to; *(quantité)* less than; **i. ou égal à** less than or equal to; **note inférieure à douze** mark below twelve; **i. en nombre** fewer in number; **i. à la moyenne** below average
2 *nm,f* inferior

infériorité [ɛ̃ferjɔrite] *nf* inferiority

infernal, -e, -aux, -ales [ɛ̃fεrnal, -o] *adj (a) (de l'enfer)* infernal; Fig *(cruauté, méchanceté)* diabolical **(b)** Fam *(insupportable) (chaleur, bruit)* infernal; **à une vitesse infernale** at breakneck speed; **des cadences infernales** an impossible rate of work; **cet enfant est i.** this child's a little devil

infertile [ɛ̃fεrtil] *adj* infertile

infertilité [ɛ̃fεrtilite] *nf* infertility

infester [ɛ̃fεste] *vt (sujet: vermine)* to infest; Fig *(sujet: personnes)* to overrun; **infesté de** infested/overrun with

infidèle [ɛ̃fidεl] **1** *adj (a) (déloyal)* unfaithful (à to) **(b)** *(inexact) (traduction, rapport)* inaccurate **(c)** Rel infidel
2 *nmf* Rel infidel

infidélité [ɛ̃fidelite] *nf (a) (déloyauté)* unfaithfulness (à to); **faire des infidélités à** to be unfaithful to **(b)** *(manque d'exactitude) (dans une traduction, un compte rendu)* inaccuracy

infiltration [ɛ̃filtrasjɔ̃] *nf (a) (d'un liquide)* infiltration; **il y a des infiltrations dans le plafond** there are some leaks in the ceiling **(b)** *(d'espions)* infiltration **(c)** *(piqûre)* **faire des infiltrations à qn** to give sb injections

infiltrer [ɛ̃filtre] **1** *vt (noyauter) (parti, pays)* to infiltrate
2 s'infiltrer *vpr (a) (fluide)* to infiltrate; **s'i. dans** to seep into **(b)** *(espion)* **s'i. dans** to infiltrate

infime [ɛ̃fim] *adj* tiny

infini, -e [ɛ̃fini] **1** *adj* infinite; **ça prend un temps i.** it takes an eternity
2 nm l'i. infinity; **à l'i.** *(s'étendre, se refléter)* to infinity; *(discutailler)* ad infinitum

infiniment [ɛ̃finimɑ̃] *adv (énormément)* infinitely; **i. petit** infinitesimal; **i. reconnaissant** extremely grateful; **je regrette i.** I'm extremely sorry

infinité [ɛ̃finite] *nf* infinity; **une i. de** an infinite number of

infinitésimal, -e, -aux, -ales [ɛ̃finitezimal, -o] *adj* infinitesimal

infinitif, -ive [ɛ̃finitif, -iv] **1** *adj* infinitive
2 nm infinitive; **à l'i.** in the infinitive

infirmation [ɛ̃firmasjɔ̃] *nf Jur* invalidation

infirme [ɛ̃firm] **1** *adj* disabled
2 nmf disabled person; **les infirmes** the disabled

infirmer [ɛ̃firme] *vt* to invalidate

infirmerie [ɛ̃firməri] *nf (d'une prison, d'une caserne)* infirmary; *(à l'école, dans un bateau)* sick bay

infirmier [ɛ̃firmje] *nm* (male) nurse

infirmière [ɛ̃firmjɛr] *nf* nurse; **i. de jour/nuit** day/ night nurse

infirmité [ɛ̃firmite] *nf* disability

inflammable [ɛ̃flamabl] *adj* inflammable, flammable

inflammation [ɛ̃flamasjɔ̃] *nf Méd* inflammation

inflation [ɛ̃flasjɔ̃] *nf* inflation

inflationniste [ɛ̃flasjonist] *adj* inflationary

infléchir [ɛ̃fleʃir] **1** *vt* (a) *(rayon)* to bend (b) *(politique)* to change the direction of; **i. le cours des événements** to change the course of events
2 s'infléchir *vpr* (a) *(dévier) (route, ligne)* to bend (b) *(changer) (politique)* to change direction

inflexibilité [ɛ̃fleksibilite] *nf* inflexibility

inflexible [ɛ̃fleksibl] *adj* inflexible

inflexion [ɛ̃fleksjɔ̃] *nf* (a) *(mouvement)* **i. du corps** bend of the body; *(pour saluer)* bow; **i. de (la) tête** tilt of the head; *(pour saluer, acquiescer)* nod (b) *(de la voix)* inflection (c) *(de courbe, rayon)* inflection

infliger [45] [ɛ̃fliʒe] *vt* **i. qch à qn** *(correction, punition)* to inflict sth on sb; *(peine, amende)* to impose sth on sb

influençable [ɛ̃flyɑ̃sabl] *adj* easily influenced

influence [ɛ̃flyɑ̃s] *nf* influence (**sur** on); **trafic d'i.** corruption *(involving a public official)*

influencer [16] [ɛ̃flyɑ̃se] *vt* to influence; **il ne faut pas te laisser i.** you mustn't let yourself be influenced; **il se laisse facilement i.** he's easily influenced

influent, -e [ɛ̃flyɑ̃, -ɑ̃t] *adj* influential

influer [ɛ̃flye] *vi* **i. sur** to influence

influx [ɛ̃fly] *nm* **i. nerveux** nerve impulse

info [ɛ̃fo] *nf Fam (nouvelle)* news item; **les infos** the news *(singulier)*

Infographie® [ɛ̃fografi] *nf* computer graphics

informateur, -trice [ɛ̃formatœr, -tris] *nm,f* informant; *(de police)* informer

informaticien, -enne [ɛ̃formatisjɛ̃, -ɛn] **1** *nm,f* computer scientist
2 *adj* **ingénieur i.** computer engineer

information [ɛ̃formasjɔ̃] *nf* (a) *(renseignement)* (piece of) information; **informations** information; **pour votre i.** for your information; **à titre d'i.** for information; **assurer l'i. du public en matière de santé** to ensure that the public is kept informed about health matters; **le droit à l'i.** freedom of information (b) *(nouvelle)* news item; **une i. de dernière minute** some late news; **les informations** the news *(singulier)* (c) *(médias)* **l'i.** the media (d) *Ordinat* data, information; **traitement de l'i.** data processing; **théorie de l'i.** information theory (e) *Jur (enquête)* inquiry; *(instruction préparatoire)* preliminary investigation; **ouvrir une i.** to begin legal proceedings

informatique [ɛ̃formatik] *nf (traitement de l'information)* data processing; *(science)* computer science, computing; **travailler dans l'i.** to work in computers; **société/ magazine/cours d'i.** computer company/magazine/ course

informatisation [ɛ̃formatizasjɔ̃] *nf* computerization

informatiser [ɛ̃formatize] *vt* to computerize

informe [ɛ̃form] *adj (masse, objet, vêtement)* shapeless; *(monstre, être)* misshapen

informé, -e [ɛ̃forme] **1** *adj* informed; **bien i.** well-informed; **mal i.** ill-informed; **dans les milieux informés** in informed circles
2 nm *Jur* inquiry; **jusqu'à plus ample i.** until we have further information

informel, -elle [ɛ̃formɛl] *adj* informal

informer [ɛ̃forme] **1** *vt* to inform (**de** of); **i. qn que...** to inform sb that...; **nous informons les voyageurs que...** we would like to inform passengers that...
2 s'informer *vpr (se renseigner)* to inquire, to ask (**de/au sujet de** about); *(se tenir au courant)* to keep oneself informed

infortune [ɛ̃fortyn] *nf* misfortune; **compagnons d'i.** companions in adversity

infortuné, -e [ɛ̃fortyne] **1** *adj* unfortunate
2 nm,f unfortunate wretch

infoutu, -e [ɛ̃futy] *adj Fam* downright incapable (**de** of)

infraction [ɛ̃fraksjɔ̃] *nf (à un règlement, à la loi)* infringement; *(délit)* offence; **être en i.** to be committing an offence

infranchissable [ɛ̃frɑ̃ʃisabl] *adj (rivière, col, gouffre)* impassable; *(obstacle, difficulté)* insurmountable

infrarouge [ɛ̃fraruʒ] *adj & nm* infrared

infrastructure [ɛ̃frastryktyr] *nf* (a) *Constr* substructure (b) *(d'équipements)* infrastructure; **i. routière/touris-tique** road/tourist infrastructure

infructueux, -euse [ɛ̃fryktɥø, -øz] *adj* fruitless

infumable [ɛ̃fymabl] *adj* unsmokable

infuse [ɛ̃fyz] *adj f voir* **science**

infuser [ɛ̃fyze] **1** *vi* (a) *(thé)* to brew; *(tisane)* to infuse
2 vt (a) *(faire pénétrer)* to instil (**dans** into) (b) *(herbes)* to infuse; *(thé)* to brew

infusion [ɛ̃fyzjɔ̃] *nf* (a) *(boisson)* herb tea; **une i. de camomille** some camomile tea (b) *(processus)* infusion; *(de thé)* brewing

ingénier [56] [ɛ̃ʒenje] **s'ingénier** *vpr* **s'i. à faire qch** to strive to do sth; **il s'ingénie à me contredire** he goes out of his way to contradict me

ingénierie [ɛ̃ʒeniri] *nf* engineering

ingénieur [ɛ̃ʒenjœr] *nm* engineer; **i. agronome** agricultural engineer; **i. électronicien** electronics engineer; **i. des mines** mining engineer; **i. du son** sound engineer; **i. des travaux publics** civil engineer

ingénieur-conseil (*pl* **ingénieurs-conseils**) [ɛ̃ʒenjœrkɔ̃sɛj] *nm* consultant engineer

ingénieusement [ɛ̃ʒenjøzmɑ̃] *adv* ingeniously

ingénieux, -euse [ɛ̃ʒenjø, -øz] *adj* ingenious

ingéniosité [ɛ̃ʒenjozite] *nf* ingenuity

ingénu, -e [ɛ̃ʒeny] **1** *adj* ingenuous **2** *nm,f* ingenuous person

ingénuité [ɛ̃ʒenyite] *nf* ingenuousness

ingérence [ɛ̃ʒerɑ̃s] *nf* interference (**dans** in)

ingérer [34] [ɛ̃ʒere] *vt* to ingest

ingestion [ɛ̃ʒɛstjɔ̃] *nf* ingestion

ingrat, -e [ɛ̃gra, -at] **1** *adj (personne)* ungrateful (**envers** to); *(sol, terre)* barren; *(tâche)* thankless; *(travail, sujet)* unrewarding; *(physique, visage)* unattractive **2** *nm,f* ungrateful person

ingratitude [ɛ̃gratityd] *nf* ingratitude

ingrédient [ɛ̃gredjɑ̃] *nm* ingredient

inguérissable [ɛ̃gerisabl] *adj* incurable

ingurgiter [ɛ̃gyrʒite] *vt (aliment, boisson)* to gulp down; *Fam Fig (connaissances)* to cram into one's head

inhabitable [inabitabl] *adj* uninhabitable

inhabité, -e [inabite] *adj* uninhabited

inhabituel, -elle [inabituɛl] *adj* unusual

inhalation [inalasjɔ̃] *nf* inhalation; *Méd* **faire des inhalations** to inhale

inhaler [inale] *vt* to inhale

inhérent, -e [inerɑ̃, -ɑ̃t] *adj* inherent (**à** in)

inhiber [inibe] *vt* to inhibit

inhibition [inibisjɔ̃] *nf* inhibition

inhospitalier, -ère [inɔspitalje, -ɛr] *adj* inhospitable

inhumain, -e [inymɛ̃, -ɛn] *adj* inhuman

inhumanité [inymanite] *nf* inhumanity

inhumation [inymasjɔ̃] *nf* burial

inhumer [inyme] *vt* to bury

inimaginable [inimaʒinabl] *adj* unimaginable

inimitable [inimitabl] *adj* inimitable

inimitié [inimitje] *nf* enmity

ininflammable [inɛ̃flamabl] *adj* non-flammable

inintelligent, -e [inɛ̃teliʒɑ̃, -ɑ̃t] *adj* unintelligent

inintelligible [inɛ̃teliʒibl] *adj* unintelligible

inintéressant, -e [inɛ̃teresɑ̃, -ɑ̃t] *adj* uninteresting

ininterrompu, -e [inɛ̃terɔ̃py] *adj* continuous

inique [inik] *adj* iniquitous

iniquité [inikite] *nf* iniquity

initial, -e, -aux, -ales [inisjal, -o] **1** *adj* initial **2** *nf* initiale initial

initialement [inisjalmɑ̃] *adv* initially

initialisation [inisjalizasjɔ̃] *nf Ordinat* initialization

initialiser [inisjalize] *vt Ordinat (disque)* to initialize; *(ordinateur)* to boot (up)

initiateur, -trice [inisjatœr, -tris] **1** *nm,f (d'un projet, d'une réforme)* initiator **2** *adj* initiatory

initiation [inisjasjɔ̃] *nf* **(a)** *(formation)* introduction (**à** to) **(b)** *(rituels)* initiation (**à** into)

initiatique [inisjatik] *adj* initiatory

initiative [inisjativ] *nf* initiative; **à l'i. de qn** on sb's initiative; **prendre l'i. de faire qch** to take the initiative in doing sth; **faire qch de sa propre i.** to do sth on one's own initiative; **il n'a aucune i.** he's got no initiative

initié, -e [inisje] *nm,f* initiate

initier [66] [inisje] **1** *vt* **(a)** *(former)* to introduce (**à** to) **(b)** *(rituellement)* to initiate (**à** into) **2** s'initier *vpr* **s'i. à qch** to start learning sth

injectable [ɛ̃ʒɛktabl] *adj* injectable

injecté, -e [ɛ̃ʒɛkte] *adj* **yeux injectés de sang** bloodshot eyes

injecter [ɛ̃ʒɛkte] *vt (substance, capitaux)* to inject (**dans** into)

injection [ɛ̃ʒɛksjɔ̃] *nf (de substance, de capital)* injection; **moteur à i.** fuel-injection engine

injonction [ɛ̃ʒɔ̃ksjɔ̃] *nf* injunction; **recevoir l'i. de faire qch** to get the order to do sth

injure [ɛ̃ʒyr] *nf* insult; **injures** abuse, insults; **faire i. à qn** to insult sb

injurier [66] [ɛ̃ʒyrje] *vt* to insult, to abuse

injurieux, -euse [ɛ̃ʒyrjø, -øz] *adj* insulting, abusive

injuste [ɛ̃ʒyst] *adj* unfair (**envers** *ou* **avec** to or towards)

injustement [ɛ̃ʒystəmɑ̃] *adv* unjustly, unfairly

injustice [ɛ̃ʒystis] *nf* **(a)** *(iniquité)* injustice, unfairness (**envers** towards); **i. sociale** social injustice **(b)** *(acte, parole)* injustice

injustifiable [ɛ̃ʒystifjabl] *adj* unjustifiable

injustifié, -e [ɛ̃ʒystifje] *adj* unjustified

inlassable [ɛ̃lɑsabl] *adj* untiring

inlassablement [ɛ̃lɑsabləmɑ̃] *adv* untiringly; *(répéter)* ceaselessly

inné, -e [ine] *adj* innate, inborn

innocemment [inɔsamɑ̃] *adv* innocently

innocence [inɔsɑ̃s] *nf* innocence; **en toute i.** in all innocence

innocent, -e [inɔsɑ̃, -ɑ̃t] **1** *adj* innocent (**de** of) **2** *nm,f (non coupable)* innocent person; *(idiot)* simpleton; **ne fais pas l'i.!** don't act the innocent!; *Prov* **aux innocents les mains pleines** fortune favours fools

innocenter [inɔsɑ̃te] *vt* to clear (**de** of)

innocuité [inɔkɥite] *nf* harmlessness

innombrable [inɔ̃brabl] *adj* innumerable, countless; *(foule)* huge

innommable [inɔmabl] *adj Péj (conduite, actes)* unspeakable; *(nourriture, odeur)* vile

innovateur, -trice [inɔvatœr, -tris] **1** *adj* innovative **2** *nm,f* innovator

innovation [inɔvasjɔ̃] *nf* innovation

innover [inɔve] *vi* to innovate

inoccupé, -e [inɔkype] *adj* unoccupied

inoculation [inɔkylasjɔ̃] *nf Méd* inoculation

inoculer [inɔkyle] *vt* **(a)** **i. un virus/un vaccin à qn** to inoculate sb with a virus/a vaccine; **i. une maladie à qn** to infect sb with a disease; *Fig* **elle nous a inoculé sa gaieté** she infected us with her cheerfulness **(b)** **i. qn (contre une maladie)** to inoculate sb (against a disease)

inodore [inɔdɔr] *adj* odourless

inoffensif, -ive [inɔfɑ̃sif, -iv] *adj* harmless

inondation [inɔ̃dasjɔ̃] *nf* flood; *(action)* flooding

inondé, -e [inɔ̃de] *adj (lieu)* flooded; **populations inondées** flood victims; **visage i. de larmes** face streaming with tears; **i. de lumière** flooded with light

inonder [inɔ̃de] *vt (lieu)* to flood; *Fig (marché)* to flood, to inundate (**de** with); **être inondé de réclamations** to be inundated with complaints

inopérable [inɔperabl] *adj* inoperable

inopérant, -e [inɔperɑ̃, -ɑ̃t] *adj* ineffective

inopiné, -e [inɔpine] *adj* unexpected

inopportun, -e [inɔpɔrtœ̃, -yn] *adj* inopportune

inoubliable [inublijabl] *adj* unforgettable

inouï, -e [inwi] *adj* (a) *(ahurissant)* incredible; **il leur est arrivé une histoire inouïe** something incredible happened to them; **c'est/vous êtes i.!** it's/you're incredible! (b) *(nouveau)* unheard-of

inox® [inɔks] *nm* stainless steel

inoxydable [inɔksidabl] *adj (métal)* rustproof; **acier i.** stainless steel

inqualifiable [ɛ̃kalifjabl] *adj* unspeakable

inquiet, -ète [ɛ̃kjɛ, -ɛt] **1** *adj (anxieux) (personne, air, voix)* worried, anxious (**au sujet de** about); *(attente)* anxious
2 *nm,f* worrier

inquiétant, -e [ɛ̃kjetɑ̃, -ɑ̃t] *adj* (a) *(alarmant)* worrying (b) *(qui effraie) (air, sourire)* frightening

inquiéter [34] [ɛ̃kjete] **1** *vt* to worry; **être inquiété par la police** to be bothered by the police
2 s'inquiéter *vpr* (a) *(se faire du souci)* to worry; **il n'y a pas de quoi s'i.** there's nothing to worry about; **s'i. pour qn** to be worried about sb (b) **s'i. de** *(se faire du souci pour)* to bother about; *(s'informer de)* to inquire about; **sans s'i. de rien** without a care in the world

inquiétude [ɛ̃kjetyd] *nf* anxiety, worry; **sujet d'i.** cause for anxiety; **éprouver quelques inquiétudes** to feel a bit worried

inquisiteur, -trice [ɛ̃kizitœr, -tris] **1** *adj (regard)* inquisitive
2 *nm* inquisitor

inquisition [ɛ̃kizisjɔ̃] *nf* inquisition; **l'I.** the Inquisition

insaisissable [ɛ̃sezisabl] *adj* (a) *(personne)* elusive (b) *(son, différence, nuance)* imperceptible

insalubre [ɛ̃salybr] *adj (climat, habitation, pays)* insalubrious; *(occupation)* unhealthy

insanité [ɛ̃sanite] *nf (de raisonnement, de propos)* insanity; **des insanités** complete nonsense

insatiable [ɛ̃sasjabl] *adj* insatiable

insatisfait, -e [ɛ̃satisfɛ, -ɛt] **1** *adj (personne)* dissatisfied; *(désir)* unsatisfied
2 *nm,f* **c'est un éternel i.** he's never satisfied

inscription [ɛ̃skripsjɔ̃] *nf* (a) *(action) (dans un journal, un registre)* entering; *(immatriculation)* registration (b) *(sur une tombe, un mur)* inscription; *(dans un livre de comptes)* entry

inscrire [30] [ɛ̃skrir] **1** *vt* (a) *(renseignements, date)* to write down; *(dans un journal, dans un registre)* to enter (b) *(pour participer)* **i. qn à un club/à une activité** to enrol sb in a club/for an activity; **i. un enfant dans une école** to enrol a child at a school (c) *(dans la pierre)* to inscribe
2 s'inscrire *vpr (à l'université)* Br to matriculate, Am to register (**à** at); *(à un tournoi, à un concours)* to enter (**à** for); *(à une activité)* to enrol (**à** for); *(dans une école)* to enrol (**dans** at); **s'i. dans un club/à un parti** to join a club/party; **s'i. sur les listes électorales** to register to vote; **s'i. en**

faux contre qch to deny sth; **s'i. dans le cadre de** to come within the framework of

inscrit, -e [ɛ̃skri, -it] **1** *adj (électeur, candidat)* registered
2 *nm,f (à l'université)* registered student; *(à un concours)* registered entrant; *(électeur)* registered voter

insécable [ɛ̃sekabl] *adj* indivisible

insecte [ɛ̃sɛkt] *nm* insect

insecticide [ɛ̃sɛktisid] **1** *adj* insecticidal
2 *nm* insecticide

insectivore [ɛ̃sɛktivɔr] **1** *adj* insectivorous
2 *nm* insectivore

insécurité [ɛ̃sekyrite] *nf* insecurity

insémination [ɛ̃seminasjɔ̃] *nf* insemination; **i. artificielle** artificial insemination

inséminer [ɛ̃semine] *vt* to inseminate

insensé, -e [ɛ̃sɑ̃se] **1** *adj (projet, idée)* crazy; *(action, espoir, dépenses)* wild; **c'est i.!** it's crazy!
2 *nm,f* madman, *f* madwoman

insensibilité [ɛ̃sɑ̃sibilite] *nf* insensitivity (**à** to)

insensible [ɛ̃sɑ̃sibl] *adj (à la douleur, au froid)* insensitive (**à** to); **i. à la critique** impervious to criticism; **elle demeura i. à leurs larmes** she remained unmoved by their tears

insensiblement [ɛ̃sɑ̃sibləmɑ̃] *adv* imperceptibly

inséparable [ɛ̃separabl] *adj* inseparable

insérer [34] [ɛ̃sere] **1** *vt* to insert (**dans** in); **i. une annonce dans un journal** to put an advertisement in a paper
2 s'insérer *vpr* (a) *(s'attacher)* to be attached (**sur** to) (b) *(s'intégrer)* **s'i. dans** *(réformes, politique)* to fit into

insertion [ɛ̃sersjɔ̃] *nf* insertion; **i. sociale** (social) integration; **i. professionnelle** integration into the job market; *Ordinat* **mode d'i.** insert mode; *Ordinat* **i. de ligne** line insert; **i. publicitaire** advertisement

insidieusement [ɛ̃sidjøzmɑ̃] *adv* insidiously

insidieux, -euse [ɛ̃sidjø, -øz] *adj* insidious

insigne¹ [ɛ̃siɲ] *nm* badge; **insignes de la royauté** insignia of royalty

insigne² *adj* (a) *Formal (remarquable)* signal (b) *Hum (indiscrétion, maladresse)* remarkable

insignifiant, -e [ɛ̃siɲifjɑ̃, -ɑ̃t] *adj* insignificant

insinuation [ɛ̃sinɥasjɔ̃] *nf* insinuation

insinuer [ɛ̃sinɥe] **1** *vt* to insinuate; **que voulez-vous i.?** what are you insinuating?
2 s'insinuer *vpr* **s'i. dans** *(froid, odeur)* to creep into; *(personne)* to worm one's way into; **le doute/l'idée qui s'insinue dans mon esprit** the doubt/the idea that is creeping into my mind

insipide [ɛ̃sipid] *adj* insipid

insistance [ɛ̃sistɑ̃s] *nf* insistence; **avec i.** insistently

insistant, -e [ɛ̃sistɑ̃, -ɑ̃t] *adj* insistent

insister [ɛ̃siste] *vi* (a) *(persévérer)* to insist; **elle a beaucoup insisté** she was very insistent; **i. pour faire qch** to insist on doing sth; **elle a essayé la planche à voile mais elle n'a pas insisté** she tried windsurfing but soon gave it up; **j'ai dit non, n'insistez pas!** *ou* **inutile d'i.!** I said no, don't go on about it!; **ça ne répond pas – insiste encore un peu** there's no answer – hang on a bit (b) *(mettre l'accent sur)* **i. sur qch** to stress sth; **nous insistons particulièrement sur la ponctualité** we lay particular stress on punctuality

insolation [ɛ̃sɔlasjɔ̃] *nf* (a) *Méd* sunstroke; **attraper une i.** to get sunstroke (b) *(ensoleillement)* sunshine

insolence [ɛ̃sɔlɑ̃s] *nf* (a) *(impertinence)* insolence (b) *(remarque, action)* impertinence

insolent, -e [ɛ̃sɔlɑ̃, -ɑ̃t] 1 *adj* (a) *(impertinent)* insolent (envers *ou* avec to) (b) *(dans la victoire)* haughty (c) *(succès)* outrageous; *(luxe)* unashamed
2 *nm,f* insolent person

insolite [ɛ̃sɔlit] 1 *adj* unusual, strange
2 *nm* **l'i.** the unusual

insoluble [ɛ̃sɔlybl] *adj* insoluble

insolvable [ɛ̃sɔlvabl] *adj* insolvent

insomniaque [ɛ̃sɔmnjak] *adj & nmf* insomniac

insomnie [ɛ̃sɔmni] *nf* insomnia

insondable [ɛ̃sɔ̃dabl] *adj (océan, gouffre, mystère)* unfathomable; *(bêtise)* immense

insonorisation [ɛ̃sɔnɔrizasjɔ̃] *nf* soundproofing

insonoriser [ɛ̃sɔnɔrize] *vt* to soundproof

insouciance [ɛ̃susjɑ̃s] *nf* carefree attitude; **vivre dans l'i.** to live a carefree life

insouciant, -e [ɛ̃susjɑ̃, -ɑ̃t] *adj* carefree; **i. de son avenir** unconcerned about his future

insoumis, -e [ɛ̃sumi, -iz] 1 *adj* (a) *(peuple, tribus)* unsubdued (b) *(personne)* rebellious (c) *Mil (soldat)* absentee
2 *nm Mil* absentee

insoupçonnable [ɛ̃supsɔnabl] *adj (personne)* beyond suspicion

insoupçonné, -e [ɛ̃supsɔne] *adj* unsuspected (de by)

insoutenable [ɛ̃sutnabl] *adj* (a) *(spectacle, odeur)* unbearable (b) *(opinion, position)* untenable

inspecter [ɛ̃spɛkte] *vt* to inspect

inspecteur, -trice [ɛ̃spɛktœr, -tris] *nm,f* inspector; **i. d'Académie** school inspector; **i. de police** police inspector; **i. du travail** factory inspector; *Hum* **i. des travaux finis** idler, *Br* skiver *(who arrives after the work has been done)*

inspection [ɛ̃spɛksjɔ̃] *nf* (a) *(examen)* inspection; **faire l'i. de** to inspect (b) *(service)* inspectorate; **i. académique** school inspectorate; **i. du travail** factory inspectorate

inspiration [ɛ̃spirasjɔ̃] *nf* (a) *(créatrice)* inspiration; **avoir de l'i.** to be inspired; **un poème d'i. romantique** a poem in the romantic style (b) *(idée)* inspiration (c) *(d'air)* breathing in

inspiré, -e [ɛ̃spire] *adj (style, poète, artiste, air)* inspired (de by); **être bien/mal i. de faire qch** to do the right/wrong thing in doing sth

inspirer [ɛ̃spire] 1 *vt* (a) *(donner de l'inspiration à)* to inspire; **ça m'a inspiré une chanson** it inspired me to write a song; *Hum* **ça ne m'inspire pas** it doesn't exactly inspire me (b) *(susciter)* **i. confiance à qn** to inspire confidence in sb; **ça m'inspire la plus grande inquiétude** it gives me great cause for concern (c) *(air)* to breathe in
2 *vi* to breathe in
3 **s'inspirer** *vpr* **s'i. de** to be inspired by

instabilité [ɛ̃stabilite] *nf* instability; *(du temps)* changeability

instable [ɛ̃stabl] *adj* unstable; *(temps)* changeable

installateur, -trice [ɛ̃stalatœr, -tris] *nm,f* fitter

installation [ɛ̃stalasjɔ̃] *nf* (a) *(fait d'installer)* (d'une machine, du chauffage, d'un ascenseur) installation; *(d'une cuisine)* fitting out; *(de rideaux)* putting up (b) *(emménagement)* move; **prévoir son i. dans une région** to plan to settle in an area (c) *(d'un ecclésiastique, d'un magistrat)* installation (d) *Ordinat* **programme d'i.** installation program; **i. en réseau** network installation (e) **installations** *(d'une maison, d'un atelier)* fittings; **l'i. électrique** the wiring; **installations sanitaires** sanitary fittings; **installations touristiques** tourist facilities

installer [ɛ̃stale] 1 *vt* (a) *(mettre en place)* (machine, chauffage, ascenseur) to install, to put in; *(cuisine)* to fit out; *(rideaux)* to put up (b) *(placer)* **i. qn dans un fauteuil/devant la télévision** to settle sb down in an armchair/in front of the television; **je les ai installés dans la chambre bleue** I've put them in the blue room (c) *(aménager)* **les nouveaux bureaux sont très bien installés** the new offices are very well fitted out; **il a installé son bureau au grenier** he set up his office in the attic (d) *(dans une fonction)* (ecclésiastique, magistrat) to install
2 **s'installer** *vpr (supermarché, cirque)* to be set up; *(personne) (dans un fauteuil)* to settle down; *(dans un bureau)* to install oneself; **confortablement installé dans un fauteuil** comfortably installed in an armchair; **s'i. à la campagne** to settle in the country; **des bourgeois bien installés** comfortably off middle-class people; **s'i. comme médecin** to set up as a doctor; **un climat d'insécurité s'est installé dans le pays** a climate of insecurity has taken hold of the country

instamment [ɛ̃stamɑ̃] *adv* earnestly

instance [ɛ̃stɑ̃s] *nf* (a) *(insistance)* plea; **demander à qn de faire qch avec i.** to plead with sb to do sth (b) *Jur* proceedings; **en seconde i.** on appeal (c) *(autorité)* authority; **les instances internationales** the international authorities; **l'i. compétente** the relevant authority (d) *(cours)* **être en i. de divorce** to be waiting for a divorce; **courrier en i.** mail waiting to go out; **être en i.** *(affaire)* to be pending

instant [ɛ̃stɑ̃] *nm* moment, instant; **à chaque** *ou* **tout i.** all the time; **pendant un i.** for a moment; **un i.!** one moment!; **sans perdre un i.** without wasting a second; **d'un i. à l'autre** at any moment; **à l'i.** (just) a moment ago; **à l'i. même où** at the very moment that; **j'en reviens à l'i.** I've just come back from there; **pour l'i.** for the moment; **dans un i.** in a moment; **en un i.** in no time at all

instantané, -e [ɛ̃stɑ̃tane] 1 *adj (mort, riposte)* instantaneous; *(café, soupe)* instant
2 *nm (photo)* snap

instantanément [ɛ̃stɑ̃tanemɑ̃] *adv* instantaneously

instar [ɛ̃star] **à l'instar de** *prép* following the example of

instauration [ɛ̃stɔrasjɔ̃] *nf* establishment

instaurer [ɛ̃stɔre] 1 *vt* to establish
2 **s'instaurer** *vpr* to be established

instigateur, -trice [ɛ̃stigatœr, -tris] *nm,f* instigator

instigation [ɛ̃stigasjɔ̃] *nf* instigation; **à l'i. de qn** at sb's instigation

instinct [ɛ̃stɛ̃] *nm* instinct; **faire qch d'i.** to do sth by instinct

instinctif, -ive [ɛ̃stɛ̃ktif, -iv] *adj* instinctive

instinctivement [ɛ̃stɛ̃ktivmɑ̃] *adv* instinctively

instit [ɛ̃stit] *nmf Fam* (primary school) teacher

instituer [ɛ̃stitɥe] *vt* to establish

institut [ɛ̃stity] *nm* institute; **i. de beauté** beauty salon; **i. médico-légal** mortuary

instituteur, -trice [ɛ̃stitytœr, -tris] *nm,f* (primary school) teacher

institution [ɛ̃stitysjɔ̃] *nf* **(a)** *(création)* establishment **(b)** *(école)* private school **(c)** *(coutume)* institution **(d)** *Pol* **institutions** institutions

institutionnaliser [ɛ̃stitysjɔnalize] *vt* to institutionalize

institutionnel, -elle [ɛ̃stitysjɔnel] *adj* institutional

instructeur [ɛ̃stryktœr] **1** *nm* instructor
2 *adj m* *Jur* **juge i.** examining magistrate

instructif, -ive [ɛ̃stryktif, -iv] *adj* instructive

instruction [ɛ̃stryksjɔ̃] *nf* **(a)** *(éducation)* education; *Mil* training; **avoir de l'i.** to be well educated; **sans i.** uneducated; **i. civique** civics *(singulier)*; **i. musicale** musical training; **i. religieuse** religious instruction **(b)** *Ordinat* instruction **(c)** *(circulaire)* memo **(d)** *Jur (d'une affaire)* preliminary investigation **(e)** **instructions** instructions

instruire [18] [ɛ̃strɥir] **1** *vt* **(a)** *(enseigner à)* to teach, to educate; **i. par le jeu** to teach through play **(b)** *(soldats)* to train **(c)** *(informer)* **i. qn de qch** to inform sb of sth **(d)** *Jur (affaire)* to investigate
2 s'instruire *vpr* to educate oneself; **s'i. de** to find out about

instruit, -e [ɛ̃strɥi, -it] *adj* educated

instrument [ɛ̃strymɑ̃] *nm* **(a)** *(outil)* instrument; **i. de mesure/de précision** measuring/precision instrument; *Fig* **il n'a été qu'un i.** he was merely a tool **(b)** **i. (de musique)** (musical) instrument; **i. à vent/cordes** wind/string instrument

instrumental, -e, -aux, -ales [ɛ̃strymɑ̃tal, -o] *adj* instrumental

instrumentiste [ɛ̃strymɑ̃tist] *nmf* instrumentalist

insu [ɛ̃sy] **à l'insu de** *prép* without the knowledge of; **à leur i.** without their knowing; **je l'ai fait à mon i.** I did it without realizing

insubmersible [ɛ̃sybmersibl] *adj* unsinkable

insubordination [ɛ̃sybɔrdinasjɔ̃] *nf* insubordination

insuccès [ɛ̃syksɛ] *nm* failure

insuffisamment [ɛ̃syfizamɑ̃] *adv* insufficiently, inadequately

insuffisance [ɛ̃syfizɑ̃s] *nf* **(a)** *(manque)* insufficiency; *(de personnel, de réserves)* shortage; *(de moyens)* inadequacy **(b)** *Méd (d'un organe)* insufficiency; **i. respiratoire/cardiaque** respiratory/cardiac insufficiency **(c)** **insuffisances** *(faiblesses)* shortcomings

insuffisant, -e [ɛ̃syfizɑ̃, -ɑ̃t] *adj (quantité)* insufficient; *(moyens, mesures)* inadequate; **tes résultats sont insuffisants** your results are not good enough

insuffler [ɛ̃syfle] *vt* *Méd* to insufflate (dans into); **ce succès a insufflé un nouvel élan à l'entreprise** this success breathed new life into the company

insulaire [ɛ̃syler] **1** *adj* island; *Péj (mentalité)* insular
2 *nmf* islander

insuline [ɛ̃sylin] *nf* insulin

insulte [ɛ̃sylt] *nf* insult; **faire i. à qn** to insult sb

insulter [ɛ̃sylte] *vt* to insult

insupportable [ɛ̃sypɔrtabl] *adj* unbearable

insurgé, -e [ɛ̃syrʒe] *adj & nm,f* insurgent

insurger [45] [ɛ̃syrʒe] **s'insurger** *vpr* to rise up (**contre** against)

insurmontable [ɛ̃syrmɔ̃tabl] *adj (difficulté, obstacle)* insurmountable; *(aversion, dégoût)* unconquerable

insurrection [ɛ̃syreksjɔ̃] *nf* uprising, rebellion; **en état d'i.** in a state of rebellion

insurrectionnel, -elle [ɛ̃syreksjɔnel] *adj* insurrectionary

intact, -e [ɛ̃takt] *adj* intact

intangible [ɛ̃tɑ̃ʒibl] *adj (loi, institution)* sacred

intarissable [ɛ̃tarisabl] *adj* inexhaustible

intégral, -e, -aux, -ales [ɛ̃tegral, -o] *adj* **(a)** *(paiement, remboursement)* full; *(texte)* unabridged; *Fam* **un fumiste/crétin/menteur i.** a complete clown/idiot/liar **(b)** *Math* **calcul i.** integral calculus

intégrale [ɛ̃tegral] *nf* **(a)** *Math* integral **(b)** *(totalité)* **l'intégrale des symphonies de Beethoven/des œuvres de Shakespeare** the complete Beethoven symphonies/works of Shakespeare

intégralement [ɛ̃tegralmɑ̃] *adv (citer, rembourser)* fully, in full

intégralité [ɛ̃tegralite] *nf* **l'i.** the whole (**de** of); **dans son i.** in its entirety

intégrante [ɛ̃tegrɑ̃t] *adj f* **une partie i. de** an integral part of; **faire partie i. de** to be an integral part of

intégration [ɛ̃tegrasjɔ̃] *nf (au sein d'un groupe) & Math* integration; *(dans une grande école)* admission

intègre [ɛ̃tegr] *adj* upright, honest

intégrer [34] [ɛ̃tegre] **1** *vt (incorporer)* to integrate (**à/dans** into)
2 s'intégrer *vpr* to become integrated (**à/dans** into); **cette sculpture s'intègre bien au paysage** this sculpture blends in well with the countryside

intégrisme [ɛ̃tegrism] *nm* fundamentalism

intégriste [ɛ̃tegrist] *adj & nmf* fundamentalist

intégrité [ɛ̃tegrite] *nf* integrity; *Ordinat* **i. des données** data integrity

intellect [ɛ̃telɛkt] *nm* intellect

intellectuel, -elle [ɛ̃telɛktɥel] **1** *adj* intellectual; *(fatigue)* mental; *(travail)* non-manual
2 *nm,f* intellectual

intelligemment [ɛ̃teliʒamɑ̃] *adv* intelligently

intelligence [ɛ̃teliʒɑ̃s] *nf* **(a)** *(intellect)* intelligence; **avoir l'i. de faire qch** to have the intelligence to do sth; **i. artificielle** artificial intelligence **(b)** *(compréhension)* understanding **(c)** *(entente)* **vivre en bonne/mauvaise i. avec qn** to be on good/bad terms with sb **(d)** *(connivence)* **un regard/sourire d'i.** a knowing look/smile; **faire des signes d'i. à qn** to signal to sb

intelligent, -e [ɛ̃teliʒɑ̃, -ɑ̃t] *adj* intelligent, clever; *Ordinat* smart, intelligent

intelligentsia [ɛ̃teliʤɛnsja] *nf* **l'i.** the intelligentsia

intelligible [ɛ̃teliʒibl] *adj (compréhensible)* intelligible; *(clair)* clear; **à haute et i. voix** in a loud, clear voice

intello [ɛ̃telo] *nmf* *Fam souvent Péj* intellectual, highbrow

intempéries [ɛ̃tɑ̃peri] *nfpl* bad weather; **exposé aux i.** exposed to the elements

intempestif, -ive [ɛ̃tɑ̃pestif, -iv] *adj* untimely, ill-timed

intemporel, -elle [ɛ̃tɑ̃pɔrel] *adj (hors du temps)* timeless

intenable [ɛ̃tənabl] *adj (chaleur, situation)* intolerable, unbearable; *(position)* untenable; *Fam (enfant)* uncontrollable

intendance [ɛ̃tɑ̃dɑ̃s] *nf* (a) *Scol* bursary; *(bureau)* bursar's office (b) *Mil* commissariat (c) *(d'un domaine)* stewardship (d) *Fig (questions matérielles)* practical matters

intendant [ɛ̃tɑ̃dɑ̃] *nm* (a) *Scol* bursar (b) *Mil* quartermaster (c) *(d'un domaine)* steward

intendante [ɛ̃tɑ̃dɑ̃t] *nf* (a) *Scol* (woman) bursar (b) *(d'une maison)* housekeeper

intense [ɛ̃tɑ̃s] *adj* intense

intensément [ɛ̃tɑ̃semɑ̃] *adv* intensely

intensif, -ive [ɛ̃tɑ̃sif, -iv] *adj* intensive

intensification [ɛ̃tɑ̃sifikɑsjɔ̃] *nf* intensification

intensifier [66] [ɛ̃tɑ̃sifje] **1** *vt* to intensify
2 s'intensifier *vpr* to intensify

intensité [ɛ̃tɑ̃site] *nf* intensity

intenter [ɛ̃tɑ̃te] *vt* **i. une action contre qn** to bring an action against sb; **i. un procès à** *ou* **contre qn** to institute proceedings against sb

intention [ɛ̃tɑ̃sjɔ̃] *nf (projet)* intention; *Jur* intent; **avoir l'i. de faire qch** to intend to do sth; **dans l'i. de faire qch** with a view to *or* with the intention of doing sth; **elle a de bonnes intentions** she means well; **c'est l'i. qui compte** it's the thought that counts; **à l'i. de...** *(pour)* for...; *(en l'honneur de)* in honour of...; *(sur une lettre)* for the attention of...

intentionné, -e [ɛ̃tɑ̃sjɔne] *adj* **bien/mal i.** well-/ill-intentioned; **bien/mal i. envers qn** well-/ill-disposed towards sb

intentionnel, -elle [ɛ̃tɑ̃sjɔnɛl] *adj* intentional, deliberate

intentionnellement [ɛ̃tɑ̃sjɔnɛlmɑ̃] *adv* intentionally, deliberately

interactif, -ive [ɛ̃tɛraktif, -iv] *adj Ordinat* interactive

interaction [ɛ̃tɛraksjɔ̃] *nf* interaction

interallié, -e [ɛ̃tɛralje] *adj* allied

interbancaire [ɛ̃tɛrbɑ̃kɛr] *adj* interbank

intercalaire [ɛ̃tɛrkaler] **1** *adj (jour)* intercalary; **feuillet i.** insert
2 *nm (feuillet)* insert; *(dans un classeur)* divider

intercaler [ɛ̃tɛrkale] **1** *vt (dans un texte, un film)* to insert, to include; *(dans un programme, entre deux événements)* to slot in
2 s'intercaler *vpr* to come in between

intercéder [34] [ɛ̃tɛrsede] *vi* to intercede **(en faveur de/auprès de** on behalf of/with)

intercepter [ɛ̃tɛrsɛpte] *vt (lettre, avion, ballon, personne)* to intercept; *(bruit, lumière)* to shut out

interchangeable [ɛ̃tɛrʃɑ̃ʒabl] *adj* interchangeable

interclasse [ɛ̃tɛrklas] *nm* = short break between classes

intercontinental, -e, -aux, -ales [ɛ̃tɛrkɔ̃tinɑtal, -o] *adj* intercontinental

interdépartemental, -e, -aux, -ales [ɛ̃tɛr-departamɑ̃tal, -o] *adj* = shared by several French départements

interdépendant, -e [ɛ̃tɛrdepɑ̃dɑ̃, -ɑ̃t] *adj* interdependent

interdiction [ɛ̃tɛrdiksjɔ̃] *nf* (a) *(défense)* ban, banning; **i. de fumer/stationner** *(sur panneau)* no smoking/parking (b) *(suspension)* banning; **i. de séjour** = order banning former prisoner from certain areas

interdire [27b] [ɛ̃tɛrdir] **1** *vt* (a) *(défendre) (stationnement, port d'armes)* to ban; **i. qch à qn** to forbid sb sth; **le centre-ville est interdit aux camions** lorries are not allowed in the town centre; **i. à qn de faire qch** to forbid sb to do sth, to ban sb from doing sth; **il nous est interdit de révéler...** we are not allowed to reveal... (b) *(empêcher)* to prevent, to stop **(de faire qch** from doing sth)
2 s'interdire *vpr* **s'i. l'alcool** to abstain from drinking; **il s'interdit d'y penser** he doesn't let himself think about it

interdit, -e [ɛ̃tɛrdi, -it] **1** *adj* (a) *(défendu)* forbidden; **il est i. de fumer** smoking is not allowed; **i. au public** *(sur un écriteau)* no unauthorized entry; **un film i. aux moins de 18 ans** an 18 film; **i. de séjour** = banned from living in certain areas; **être i. de chéquier** to have (had) one's chequebook facilities withdrawn; *Ordinat* **i. d'écriture** *(disquette)* write-protected (b) *(déconcerté)* disconcerted, taken aback
2 *nm,f Jur* **i. de séjour** = former prisoner banned from certain areas
3 *nm (social)* taboo; *(religieux)* interdict; **frapper qn/qch d'i.** to impose a ban on sb/sth

intéressant, -e [ɛ̃teresɑ̃, -ɑ̃t] **1** *adj* (a) *(attirant)* interesting (b) *(avantageux)* worthwhile; *(prix)* attractive; *(lucratif)* profitable
2 *nm,f Fam* **faire l'i.** to show off

intéressé, -e [ɛ̃terese] **1** *adj (concerné)* **les parties intéressées** the interested parties, the persons concerned (b) *(égoïste) (personne)* self-seeking; *(sentiment)* self-interested; *(conseil)* biased; **agir dans un but i.** to have an axe to grind
2 *nm,f* **l'i.** the person concerned

intéresser [ɛ̃terese] **1** *vt* (a) *(captiver)* to interest; **l'art m'intéresse beaucoup** I'm very interested in art; **est-ce que ça t'intéresse d'aller au cinéma?** would you like to go to the cinema? (b) *Ind & Com* **i. les employés (aux bénéfices)** to operate a profit-sharing scheme; **être intéressé dans une affaire** to have a financial interest in a business (c) *(concerner)* to concern, to affect
2 s'intéresser *vpr* **s'i. à qn/qch** to take an interest in sb/sth, to be interested in sb/sth

intérêt [ɛ̃terɛ] *nm* (a) *(avantage)* interest; **c'est mon i. de le faire** it's in my interest to do it; **on a i. à réserver si on veut avoir des places** we'd better book if we want seats; *Fam* **tu n'as pas i. à recommencer!** you'd better not do it again!; **agir dans/contre l'i. de qn** to act in/against sb's interest(s); **agir par i. personnel** to act out of self-interest; **faire un mariage d'i.** to marry for money; **l'i. des vacances en groupe, c'est de faire des rencontres** the advantage of group holidays is that you meet people; *Fam* **tu viens à la réunion du syndicat? – y a i.!** are you coming to the union meeting? – you bet (I am)! (b) *(attrait)* interest; **sans i.** uninteresting (c) *(curiosité)* interest **(pour** in) (d) *Fin* interest; **i. fixe** fixed interest; **i. variable** variable-rate interest

interface [ɛ̃tɛrfas] *nf Ordinat* interface; **i. graphique** graphic interface; **i. d'imprimante** printer interface; **i. numérique** digital interface; **i. parallèle** parallel interface; **i. utilisateur** user interface; **i. vidéo numérique** digital video interface

interférence [ɛ̃tɛrferɑ̃s] *nf (d'ondes)* interference; *Fig (d'événements)* combination

interférer [34] [ɛ̃tɛrfere] *vi aussi Fig* to interfere

intergouvernemental, -e, -aux, -ales [ɛ̃ter-guvɛrnəmɑ̃tal, -o] *adj* intergovernmental

intérieur, -e [ɛ̃terjœr] **1** *adj* (**a**) *(dans l'espace) (escalier)* interior, inside; *(cour)* inner; *(poche)* inside; *(partie)* inside, internal; *(mer)* inland (**b**) *(national)* domestic (**c**) *(vie, sentiments, force)* inner

2 *nm* (**a**) *(dedans)* inside, interior; **à l'i.** inside; **à l'i. de la gare** inside the station; **fermé de l'i.** locked from the inside; **tourné en i.** *(film)* shot indoors (**b**) *(d'un pays)* interior; **dans l'i. du pays** inland (**c**) *(maison)* home; **femme d'i.** houseproud housewife

intérieurement [ɛ̃terjœrmɑ̃] *adv* inwardly

intérim [ɛ̃terim] *nm (travail intérimaire)* temporary work, temping; **faire de l'i.** to temp; **par i.** acting; **assurer l'i. (de qn)** to stand in (for sb)

intérimaire [ɛ̃terimɛr] **1** *adj (fonction, employé)* temporary; *(directeur, ministre)* acting; *(cabinet, gouvernement)* caretaker

2 *nmf (travailleur)* temporary worker; *(secrétaire)* temp

intérioriser [ɛ̃terjɔrize] *vt* to internalize

interjection [ɛ̃terʒɛksjɔ̃] *nf* interjection

interligne [ɛ̃terliɲ] *nm* line spacing; **dans l'i.** in the space between the lines; **simple/double i.** single/double spacing

interlocuteur, -trice [ɛ̃terlɔkytœr, -tris] *nm,f* (**a**) *(dans une conversation)* speaker; **mon i.** the person I was/am speaking to (**b**) *(dans une négociation)* discussion partner

interloqué, -e [ɛ̃terlɔke] *adj* taken aback

interlude [ɛ̃terlyd] *nm* interlude

intermède [ɛ̃termɛd] *nm aussi Fig* interlude

intermédiaire [ɛ̃termedjɛr] **1** *adj* intermediate; **i. entre** halfway between; **trouver une solution i.** to find a compromise solution; **pointure i.** size in-between

2 *nm (personne)* intermediary, go-between; *Com* middleman; **sans i.** directly

3 *nm* **par l'i. de** through; **sans l'i. de** without

interminable [ɛ̃terminabl] *adj* interminable

interministériel, -elle [ɛ̃terministerjɛl] *adj* interministerial

intermittence [ɛ̃termitɑ̃s] *nf* **par i.** intermittently, on and off

intermittent, -e [ɛ̃termitɑ̃, -ɑ̃t] **1** *adj (lumière, bruit, tir)* intermittent, sporadic; *(travail)* casual

2 *nm,f* casual worker

internat [ɛ̃terna] *nm* (**a**) *Scol (système)* boarding; *(pensionnat)* boarding school (**b**) *Méd (concours)* entrance examination for *Br* a housemanship or *Am* an internship; *(formation) Br* clinicals, *Am* internship

international, -e, -aux, -ales [ɛ̃tɛrnasjɔnal, -o] **1** *adj & nm,f* international

2 *nf* **l'Internationale** *(groupement)* the International; *(chant)* the Internationale

internationalisation [ɛ̃tɛrnasjɔnalizasjɔ̃] *nf* internationalization

internationaliser [ɛ̃tɛrnasjɔnalize] **1** *vt* to internationalize

2 **s'internationaliser** *vpr* to become international

internaute [ɛ̃tɛrnot] *nmf* Internet surfer

interne [ɛ̃tɛrn] **1** *adj (structure, paroi, hémorragie)* internal; *(côté)* inner; *(de l'entreprise)* in-house

2 *nmf (élève)* boarder; **i. (des hôpitaux)** *Br* house doctor, *Am* intern

internement [ɛ̃tɛrnəmɑ̃] *nm (emprisonnement)* internment; *(hospitalisation)* confinement

interner [ɛ̃tɛrne] *vt (emprisonner)* to intern; *(hospitaliser)* to commit

Internet [ɛ̃tɛrnɛt] *nm* **l'I.** the Internet; **sur I.** on the Internet

interparlementaire [ɛ̃tɛrparləmɑ̃tɛr] *adj (réunion)* interparliamentary; *(commission)* joint

interpellation [ɛ̃tɛrpelasjɔ̃] *nf (appel)* calling out; *(au Parlement)* question; **la police a procédé à plusieurs interpellations** the police took several people in for questioning

interpeller [ɛ̃tɛrpele] **1** *vt* (**a**) *(appeler)* to call (out) to; *(sujet: police)* to take in for questioning; *(ministre)* to question; *(à une réunion, un spectacle)* to heckle; *(sujet: sentinelle)* to challenge (**b**) *(toucher)* **ce roman m'a interpellé** I can really relate to this novel

2 **s'interpeller** *vpr (s'appeler)* to call (out) to each other; *(s'insulter)* to shout insults at each other

Interphone® [ɛ̃tɛrfɔn] *nm (de bureau)* intercom; *(d'immeuble)* Entryphone®; **à l'I.** on the intercom/Entryphone®

interplanétaire [ɛ̃tɛrplanetɛr] *adj* interplanetary

interpolation [ɛ̃tɛrpɔlasjɔ̃] *nf* interpolation

interpoler [ɛ̃tɛrpɔle] *vt* to interpolate

interposé, -e [ɛ̃tɛrpoze] *adj* **par personne interposée** through an intermediary

interposer [ɛ̃tɛrpoze] **1** *vt* to interpose (**entre** between)

2 **s'interposer** *vpr (intervenir)* to intervene

interprétariat [ɛ̃tɛrpretarja] *nm* interpreting

interprétation [ɛ̃tɛrpretasjɔ̃] *nf* (**a**) *(d'un texte, d'un rêve, d'un rôle)* interpretation (**b**) *(traduction)* interpreting

interprète [ɛ̃tɛrprɛt] *nmf (dans une autre langue)* interpreter; *(d'un rôle, d'une œuvre musicale)* performer; *(porte-parole)* spokesman, *f* spokeswoman; **i. de conférence** conference interpreter

interpréter [34] [ɛ̃tɛrprete] *vt* (**a**) *(rôle, œuvre musicale)* to perform, to interpret (**b**) *(texte, paroles, geste, rêve)* to interpret; **mal i. les paroles de qn** to misinterpret sb's words

interrogateur, -trice [ɛ̃terɔgatœr, -tris] **1** *adj* questioning

2 *nm,f (examinateur)* (oral) examiner

interrogatif, -ive [ɛ̃terɔgatif, -iv] **1** *adj* (**a**) *(air, ton)* inquiring, questioning (**b**) *(pronom, phrase)* interrogative

2 *nm* interrogative

3 *nf* **interrogative** interrogative (clause)

interrogation [ɛ̃terɔgasjɔ̃] *nf* (**a**) *(question)* question; **i. directe/indirecte** direct/indirect question; **i. écrite/orale** written/oral test (**b**) *(d'un suspect)* questioning, interrogation (**c**) *Ordinat (d'une base de données)* inquiry, query; *(activité)* interrogation; **i. à distance** remote interrogation

interrogatoire [ɛ̃terɔgatwar] *nm* questioning

interroger [45] [ɛ̃terɔge] **1** *vt* (**a**) *(personne)* to question; *(candidat, élève)* to test; **i. qn du regard** to look at sb questioningly (**b**) *Ordinat (base de données)* to query, to interrogate

2 **s'interroger** *vpr* to ask oneself, to wonder (**sur** about)

interrompre [ɛ̃terɔ̃pr] **1** *vt* to interrupt; *(trafic)* to hold up; *(grossesse)* to terminate

2 **s'interrompre** *vpr* to break off

interrupteur [ɛteryptœr] *nm* switch; **i. à bascule** toggle switch; *Ordinat* **i. DIP** *ou* **à plusieurs positions** DIP switch

interruption [ɛterypsjɔ̃] *nf* (*arrêt*) interruption; (*de négociations*) breaking off; **sans i.** non-stop, continuously; *Ordinat* **fonction d'i.** interrupt function; **i. volontaire de grossesse** termination (of pregnancy)

intersection [ɛtersɛksjɔ̃] *nf* intersection, junction

intersidéral, -e, -aux, -ales [ɛtersideral, -o] *adj* interstellar

interstice [ɛterstis] *nm* chink, crack

intersyndical, -e, -aux, -ales [ɛtersɛ̃dikal, -o] **1** *adj* interunion
2 *nf* **intersyndicale** (*association*) interunion group

intertitre [ɛtertitr] *nm Journ* subheading; *Cin* subtitle

interurbain, -e [ɛteryrbɛ̃, -en] **1** *adj* interurban; *Vieilli Tél* **appel i.** trunk call
2 *nm Vieilli Tél* long-distance service

intervalle [ɛterval] *nm* (**a**) (*dans le temps, en musique*) interval; **un i. d'une heure** a one-hour interval; **à deux mois d'i.** two months apart; **par intervalles** at intervals, now and then; **dans l'i.** in the meantime, meanwhile (**b**) (*dans l'espace*) gap, space; **à 2 mètres d'i.** 2 metres apart (**c**) *Math* interval

intervenant, -e [ɛtervənɑ̃, -ɑ̃t] *nm,f* (*dans une conférence, un débat*) speaker, contributor

intervenir [70] [ɛtervənir] *vi* (**a**) (*agir, prendre la parole*) to intervene (**dans** in); **i. pour faire qch** to intervene or step in to do sth; **i. en faveur de qn** to intervene on sb's behalf; **i. auprès de qn** to intercede with sb; **faire i. qn** to bring sb in (**b**) (*arriver*) (*événement, changement*) to occur; (*accord*) to be reached (**c**) (*jouer un rôle*) to play a part (**dans** in)

intervention [ɛtervɑ̃sjɔ̃] *nf* (**a**) (*intercession, ingérence*) intervention (**en faveur de/auprès de** on behalf of/ with) (**b**) (*prise de parole*) intervention; (*discours*) speech (**c**) (*opération*) **i. (chirurgicale)** operation

interventionniste [ɛtervɑ̃sjɔnist] *adj & nmf* interventionist

interversion [ɛterversjɔ̃] *nf* inversion, reversal

intervertir [ɛtervertir] *vt* (*l'ordre de qch*) to invert, to reverse; (*objets, éléments*) to switch (round); (*rôles*) to reverse

intervienne *voir* **intervenir**

interview [ɛtervju] *nm ou nf* interview

interviewer [ɛtervjuve] *vt* to interview

intestin[1], -e [ɛtɛstɛ̃, -in] *adj Litt* internal

intestin[2] *nm* intestine; **intestins** intestines, bowels; **gros i.** large intestine; **i. grêle** small intestine

intestinal, -e, -aux, -ales [ɛtɛstinal, -o] *adj* intestinal

intime [ɛtim] **1** *adj* intimate; (*hygiène, toilette*) personal; **être i. avec qn** to be close to sb; **avoir l'i. conviction que...** to be thoroughly convinced that...
2 *nmf* close friend; **pour les intimes** to my/her/*etc* friends

intimement [ɛtimmɑ̃] *adv* intimately; **i. liés** (*amis*) very close; (*phénomènes*) closely linked; **être i. persuadé que...** to be thoroughly convinced that...

intimer [ɛtime] *vt* (**a**) (*ordonner*) **i. à qn l'ordre de faire qch** to order sb to do sth (**b**) *Jur* to summon before the Court of Appeal

intimidant, -e [ɛtimidɑ̃, -ɑ̃t] *adj* intimidating

intimidation [ɛtimidasjɔ̃] *nf* intimidation

intimider [ɛtimide] *vt* to intimidate

intimité [ɛtimite] *nf* (*vie privée*) privacy; (*familiarité*) intimacy, closeness; **dans l'i.** in private; **le mariage a eu lieu dans la plus stricte i.** only close family and friends attended the wedding

intitulé [ɛtityle] *nm* (*de livre*) title; (*de chapitre*) heading, title

intituler [ɛtityle] **1** *vt* (*livre, chanson*) to give a title to; **un livre intitulé...** a book entitled or called...
2 s'intituler *vpr* (*livre, chanson*) to be entitled, to be called; (*personne*) to call oneself

intolérable [ɛtolerabl] *adj* intolerable

intolérance [ɛtolerɑ̃s] *nf* intolerance; *Méd* **i. à qch** intolerance to sth

intolérant, -e [ɛtolerɑ̃, -ɑ̃t] *adj* intolerant

intonation [ɛtonasjɔ̃] *nf* intonation

intouchable [ɛtuʃabl] *adj & nmf* untouchable

intox [ɛtoks] *nf Fam* brainwashing

intoxication [ɛtoksikasjɔ̃] *nf* (*empoisonnement*) poisoning; *Fig* brainwashing; **i. alimentaire** food poisoning

intoxiquer [ɛtoksike] **1** *vt* (*empoisonner*) to poison; *Fig* to brainwash
2 s'intoxiquer *vpr* to poison oneself

intradermique [ɛtradermik] *Méd* **1** *adj* intradermal
2 *nf* intradermal injection

intraduisible [ɛtradɥizibl] *adj* untranslatable

intraitable [ɛtretabl] *adj* uncompromising, inflexible (**sur** about)

intra-muros [ɛtramyros] **1** *adj inv* **Londres/Paris i.** inner London/Paris
2 *adv* within the city

intramusculaire [ɛtramyskyler] **1** *adj* intramuscular
2 *nf* intramuscular injection

intransigeance [ɛtrɑ̃ziʒɑ̃s] *nf* intransigence

intransigeant, -e [ɛtrɑ̃ziʒɑ̃, -ɑ̃t] *adj* (*personne*) intransigent, uncompromising (**envers/sur** with/ about); (*morale*) uncompromising

intransitif, -ive [ɛtrɑ̃zitif, -iv] *adj & nm Gram* intransitive

intransmissible [ɛtrɑ̃smisibl] *adj* untransferable

intransportable [ɛtrɑ̃sportabl] *adj* (*objet*) un-transportable; (*blessé*) unfit to travel

intraveineux, -euse [ɛtravɛnø, -øz] **1** *adj* intravenous
2 *nf* intraveineuse intravenous injection

intrépide [ɛtrepid] *adj* intrepid, fearless

intrépidité [ɛtrepidite] *nf* fearlessness

intrigant, -e [ɛtrigɑ̃, -ɑ̃t] **1** *adj* scheming, plotting
2 *nm,f* schemer

intrigue [ɛtrig] *nf* (*machination*) intrigue; (*liaison amoureuse*) (love) affair; (*d'un roman, d'un film*) plot

intriguer [ɛtrige] **1** *vt* to intrigue
2 *vi* to scheme, to intrigue

intrinsèque [ɛtrɛ̃sɛk] *adj* intrinsic

intrinsèquement [ɛtrɛ̃sɛkmɑ̃] *adv* intrinsically

intro [ɛtro] *nf Fam* intro; (*musicale*) theme tune

introductif, -ive [ɛtrɔdyktif, -iv] *adj* (**a**) (*discours, exposé*) introductory, opening (**b**) *Jur* introductory

introduction [ɛ̃trɔdyksjɔ̃] *nf* introduction; *(insertion)* insertion, introduction (**dans** into); *(au rugby)* put-in; **i. en Bourse** listing on the stock market

introduire [18] [ɛ̃trɔdɥir] **1** *vt (dans une serrure, dans un trou)* to insert (**dans** into); *(marchandises)* to bring in; *(coutume, réforme, mesures, mode)* to introduce; *(étranger, visiteur)* to show in; **i. qn auprès de qn** *(faire entrer)* to show sb in to see sb; *(présenter)* to introduce sb to sb; **i. en Bourse** to list on the stock market; **i. sur le marché** to launch onto the market

2 s'introduire *vpr* **s'i. dans une maison** to get into a house; **l'eau s'introduit partout** there's water coming in everywhere

intronisation [ɛ̃trɔnizasjɔ̃] *nf* enthronement; *Fig* establishment

introniser [ɛ̃trɔnize] *vt* to enthrone; *Fig* to establish

introspection [ɛ̃trɔspɛksjɔ̃] *nf* introspection

introuvable [ɛ̃truvabl] *adj (produit, denrées)* unobtainable; *(personne)* nowhere to be found

introversion [ɛ̃trɔvɛrsjɔ̃] *nf* introversion

introverti, -e [ɛ̃trɔvɛrti] **1** *adj* introverted
2 *nm,f* introvert

intrus, -e [ɛ̃try, -yz] *nm,f aussi Ordinat* intruder

intrusion [ɛ̃tryzjɔ̃] *nf* intrusion (**dans** into)

intuitif, -ive [ɛ̃tɥitif, -iv] *1 adj* intuitive
2 *nm,f* **c'est un i.** he's an intuitive sort

intuition [ɛ̃tɥisjɔ̃] *nf* intuition; **avoir l'i. de qch/que** to sense sth/that

intuitivement [ɛ̃tɥitivmɑ̃] *adv* intuitively

inusable [inyzabl] *adj aussi Fig* hard-wearing

inusité, -e [inyzite] *adj (mot)* uncommon

inutile [inytil] *adj (qui ne sert à rien)* useless; *(effort)* vain, pointless; *(précautions, démarche, bagages)* unnecessary; **c'est i.!** *(ça ne sert à rien)* it's pointless!; *(ce n'est pas nécessaire)* you/he/*etc* needn't bother!; **i. de dire que...** needless to say,...; **c'est i. d'attendre** there's no point in waiting; **i. d'insister, je ne viens pas** don't go on about it, I'm not coming

inutilement [inytilmɑ̃] *adv* needlessly, unnecessarily

inutilisable [inytilizabl] *adj* unusable

inutilisé, -e [inytilize] *adj* unused

inutilité [inytilite] *nf (d'un objet)* uselessness; *(d'un effort, d'un argument)* pointlessness

invaincu, -e [ɛ̃vɛ̃ky] *adj* undefeated

invalidant, -e [ɛ̃validɑ̃, -ɑ̃t] *adj* disabling

invalidation [ɛ̃validasjɔ̃] *nf Jur* invalidation

invalide [ɛ̃valid] **1** *adj* disabled
2 *nmf* disabled person, invalid; **i. de guerre** disabled ex-serviceman/ex-servicewoman

invalider [ɛ̃valide] *vt Jur* to invalidate

invalidité [ɛ̃validite] *nf* disability

invariable [ɛ̃varjabl] *adj* invariable

invariablement [ɛ̃varjabləmɑ̃] *adv* invariably

invasion [ɛ̃vazjɔ̃] *nf aussi Fig* invasion

invective [ɛ̃vɛktiv] *nf* invective; **invectives** abuse

invectiver [ɛ̃vɛktive] *vt* to hurl abuse at
2 s'invectiver *vpr* to hurl abuse at each other

invendable [ɛ̃vɑ̃dabl] *adj* unsellable

invendu, -e [ɛ̃vɑ̃dy] **1** *adj* unsold
2 *nm* **invendus** unsold goods; *(journaux, livres)* unsold copies; *(revendus moins cher)* remainders

inventaire [ɛ̃vɑ̃tɛr] *nm* **(a)** *(liste)* inventory **(b)** *(de marchandises)* stocklist; **faire** *ou* **dresser l'i. (des stocks)** to stocktake; **fermé pour cause d'i.** *(sur un écriteau)* closed for stocktaking **(c)** *Fig (de peintures, de richesses artistiques)* survey

inventer [ɛ̃vɑ̃te] **1** *vt (machine)* to invent; *(concept, moyen)* to think up; *(histoire, excuse)* to make up; *(expression)* to coin; **qu'est-ce qu'il va encore i.?** what's he going to come out with next?; *Fam* **il n'a pas inventé la poudre** *ou* **le fil à couper le beurre** he'll never set the Thames on fire

2 s'inventer *vpr* **ça ne s'invente pas** you can't make something like that up; **s'i. un passé** to invent a past for oneself

inventeur, -trice [ɛ̃vɑ̃tœr, -tris] *nm,f* **(a)** *(d'une machine, d'un procédé)* inventor **(b)** *Jur (d'un trésor)* finder

inventif, -ive [ɛ̃vɑ̃tif, -iv] *adj* inventive

invention [ɛ̃vɑ̃sjɔ̃] *nf* **(a)** *(action)* invention; *(faculté)* inventiveness **(b)** *(chose découverte, mensonge)* invention **(c)** *Jur (d'un trésor)* finding

inventorier [66] [ɛ̃vɑ̃tɔrje] *vt* to make an inventory of; *(marchandises)* to make a stocklist of

invérifiable [ɛ̃verifjabl] *adj* unverifiable

inverse [ɛ̃vɛrs] **1** *adj aussi Math* inverse; **en sens i.** in the opposite direction (to); **dans l'ordre i.** in reverse order; **dans le sens i. des aiguilles d'une montre** *Br* anticlockwise, *Am* counterclockwise

2 *nm* **l'i.** the opposite, the reverse; **faire l'i. (de)** to do the opposite (of); **à l'i. de** contrary to

inversement [ɛ̃vɛrsəmɑ̃] *adv* et **i.** and vice versa; **i., on peut dire que...** conversely, one can say that...; **i. proportionnel (à)** inversely proportional (to)

inverser [ɛ̃vɛrse] *vt (ordre, tendance)* to reverse; *(deux mots)* to invert

inversion [ɛ̃vɛrsjɔ̃] *nf (d'ordre, de mots)* inversion; *Ordinat* **i. vidéo** reverse video

invertébré, -e [ɛ̃vɛrtebre] *adj & nm* invertebrate

inverti, -e [ɛ̃vɛrti] *adj (sucre)* invert

investigateur, -trice [ɛ̃vɛstigatœr, -tris] **1** *adj (regard)* searching
2 *nm,f* investigator

investigation [ɛ̃vɛstigasjɔ̃] *nf* investigation

investir [ɛ̃vɛstir] **1** *vt (argent, temps, énergie)* to invest (**dans** in) **(b)** *(ville, édifice)* to besiege **(c)** *(charger)* **i. qn d'une mission** to entrust sb with a mission
2 *vi* to invest (**dans** in)
3 s'investir *vpr* **s'i. dans qch** to put a lot into sth

investissement [ɛ̃vɛstismɑ̃] *nm* investment; **i. à court/long terme** short-/long-term investment

investisseur [ɛ̃vɛstisœr] *nm* investor

investiture [ɛ̃vɛstityr] *nf (d'un candidat)* nomination; *(d'un gouvernement)* voting in; *(d'un évêque)* investiture

invétéré, -e [ɛ̃vetere] *adj* inveterate

invincible [ɛ̃vɛ̃sibl] *adj (armée, adversaire)* invincible; *(peur)* unconquerable

inviolabilité [ɛ̃vjɔlabilite] *nf Jur* inviolability; *(d'un parlementaire)* immunity; **i. diplomatique** diplomatic immunity

inviolable [ɛ̃vjɔlabl] *adj (coffre)* burglarproof; *(droit, asile)* inviolable; *(parlementaire)* immune

invisibilité [ɛ̃vizibilite] *nf* invisibility

invisible [ɛ̃vizibl] *adj* invisible

invitation [ɛ̃vitasjɔ̃] *nf* invitation; **venir à** *ou* **sur l'i. de qn** to come at sb's invitation; **sur i.** by invitation

invite [ɛ̃vit] *nf* (a) *(invitation)* invitation (b) *Ordinat* prompt; **i. du DOS** DOS prompt; **i. du système** system prompt

invité, -e [ɛ̃vite] *nm,f* guest

inviter [ɛ̃vite] 1 *vt* (a) *(convier)* to invite; **i. qn à dîner** to invite *or* ask sb to dinner (b) **i. qn à faire qch** *(inciter)* to urge sb to do sth; *(prier)* to request sb to do sth; **je vous invite à me suivre** would you be so kind as to follow me
2 *vi (payer)* **ce soir, c'est moi qui invite!** it's my treat tonight!
3 **s'inviter** *vpr* to invite oneself

in vitro [invitro] *adj inv & adv* in vitro

invivable [ɛ̃vivabl] *adj* unbearable

in vivo [invivo] *adj inv & adv* in vivo

invocation [ɛ̃vɔkasjɔ̃] *nf* invocation

involontaire [ɛ̃vɔlɔ̃tɛr] *adj (mouvement, geste)* involuntary; *(erreur, réaction)* unintentional; *(témoin)* unwilling

involontairement [ɛ̃vɔlɔ̃tɛrmɑ̃] *adv* involuntarily, unintentionally

invoquer [ɛ̃vɔke] *vt* (a) *(raison, argument)* to put forward; *(prétexte, excuse)* to plead; *(loi, texte)* to refer to (b) *(Dieu, divinité, esprit)* to invoke; **i. l'aide de qn** to call upon sb's help

invraisemblable [ɛ̃vrɛsɑ̃blabl] *adj* (a) *(hypothèse)* unlikely (b) *(excuses, alibi)* implausible (c) *(extraordinaire)* incredible

invraisemblance [ɛ̃vrɛsɑ̃blɑ̃s] *nf (improbabilité)* unlikelihood; *(d'un récit, d'une excuse)* implausibility; **des invraisemblances** implausibilities

invulnérabilité [ɛ̃vylnerabilite] *nf* invulnerability

invulnérable [ɛ̃vylnerabl] *adj* invulnerable

iode [jɔd] *nm* iodine

iodé, -e [jɔde] *adj (eau, air)* iodized

ion [jɔ̃] *nm* ion

iota [jɔta] *nm inv* iota; **ça n'a pas changé d'un i.** it hasn't changed one iota; **ne pas bouger d'un i.** not to budge an inch

ipso facto [ipsofakto] *adv* ipso facto

ira, irai *etc voir* **aller**

Irak [irak] *nm* **l'I.** Iraq

irakien, -enne [irakjɛ̃, -ɛn] 1 *adj* Iraqi
2 *nm,f* **I.** Iraqi

Iran [irɑ̃] *nm* **l'I.** Iran

iranien, -enne [iranjɛ̃, -ɛn] 1 *adj* Iranian
2 *nm,f* **I.** Iranian
3 *nm (langue)* Iranian

Iraq [irak] = **Irak**

iraquien, -enne [irakjɛ̃, -ɛn] = **irakien**

irascible [irasibl] *adj Litt* irascible

iriez *etc voir* **aller**

iris [iris] *nm* (a) *(de l'œil)* iris (b) *(fleur)* iris

irisé, -e [irize] *adj* iridescent

irlandais, -e [irlɑ̃dɛ, -ɛz] 1 *adj* Irish
2 *nm,f* **I.** Irishman, *f* Irishwoman; **I. du Nord** person from Northern Ireland; **les I.** the Irish
3 *nm (langue)* Irish

Irlande [irlɑ̃d] *nf* **l'I.** Ireland, Eire; **l'I. du Nord** Northern Ireland, Ulster

IRM [iɛrɛm] *nf Méd (abrév* **imagerie par résonance magnétique)** MRI

ironie [irɔni] *nf* irony; **l'i. du sort a voulu que...** as fate would have it,...

ironique [irɔnik] *adj* ironic(al)

ironiquement [irɔnikmɑ̃] *adv* ironically

ironiser [irɔnize] *vi* to be ironical *(sur* about)

irradiation [iradjasjɔ̃] *nf Phys & Méd* irradiation

irradier [66] [iradje] 1 *vi (rayons)* to radiate; *(douleur)* to spread
2 *vt* to irradiate

irraisonné, -e [irɛzɔne] *adj* irrational

irrationnel, -elle [irasjɔnɛl] *adj* irrational

irrattrapable [iratrapabl] *adj (retard)* that cannot be made up; *(erreur)* irredeemable

irréalisable [irealizabl] *adj (rêve)* unrealizable; *(projet)* impracticable

irréaliste [irealist] *adj* unrealistic

irréalité [irealite] *nf* unreality

irrecevable [irsəvabl] *adj (inacceptable)* unacceptable; *Jur (preuve, demande)* inadmissible

irrécupérable [irekyperabl] *adj (argent)* irrecoverable; *(personne)* irredeemable; *(appareil, voiture)* beyond repair

irrécusable [irekyzabl] *adj* (a) *(indéniable) (preuve, signe)* indisputable (b) *Jur (témoignage, juge)* unimpeachable

irréductible [iredyktibl] 1 *adj* (a) *(volonté, optimisme)* indomitable, invincible; *(attachement, fidélité)* unshakeable; *(opposition, ennemi)* implacable (b) *(fracture, fraction)* irreducible
2 *nmf* die-hard

irréel, -elle [ireɛl] 1 *adj* unreal
2 *nm* **l'i.** the unreal; *Gram* **l'i. du présent/passé** the hypothetical present/past

irréfléchi, -e [irefleʃi] *adj* rash

irréfutable [irefytabl] *adj* irrefutable

irrégularité [iregylarite] *nf* (a) *(du sol, d'un terrain)* unevenness; *(du pouls, de traits, d'horaires)* irregularity (b) *(acte)* irregularity

irrégulier, -ère [iregylje, -ɛr] *adj* (a) *(sol, terrain)* uneven; *(rythme, respiration, traits, verbe)* irregular; *(résultats, athlète)* inconsistent (b) *(malhonnête) (procédure, situation)* irregular; **être en situation irrégulière** *(étranger)* not to have one's residence papers in order; *(voyageur)* not to hold a valid ticket

irrégulièrement [iregyljɛrmɑ̃] *adv* irregularly

irréligieux, -euse [ireliʒjø, -øz] *adj* irreligious

irrémédiable [iremedjabl] *adj (préjudice, perte, problème)* irreparable; *(désastre)* irreversible

irrémissible [iremisibl] *adj Litt* (a) *(impardonnable)* unpardonable (b) *(irrémédiable)* irreversible

irremplaçable [irɑ̃plasabl] *adj* irreplaceable

irréparable [ireparabl] 1 *adj (tort, perte, erreur)* irreparable; *(affront)* unpardonable; *(vêtement, voiture, télévision)* beyond repair
2 *nm* **commettre l'i.** to go beyond the point of no return

irrépressible [irepresibl] *adj* irrepressible

irréprochable [ireprɔʃabl] *adj (personne, conduite)* irreproachable; *(tenue, travail)* impeccable; **d'une propreté i.** impeccably clean

irrésistible [irezistibl] *adj (personne, charme)* irresistible; *(envie, besoin)* compelling

irrésolu, -e [irezɔly] *adj* **(a)** *(personne)* indecisive; *(pas)* uncertain **(b)** *(problème)* unresolved

irrespect [irɛspɛ] *nm* disrespect (**envers** towards)

irrespectueux, -euse [irɛspɛktɥø, -øz] *adj* disrespectful (**envers** towards)

irrespirable [irɛspirabl] *adj (air)* unbreathable; Fig *(atmosphère)* unbearable

irresponsable [irɛspɔ̃sabl] **1** *adj* irresponsible
2 *nmf* irresponsible person

irrévérence [ireverɑ̃s] *nf* irreverence

irrévérencieux, -euse [ireverɑ̃sjø, -øz] *adj* irreverent

irréversible [irevɛrsibl] *adj* irreversible

irrévocabilité [irevɔkabilite] *nf* irrevocability

irrévocable [irevɔkabl] *adj* irrevocable

irrévocablement [irevɔkabləmɑ̃] *adv* irrevocably

irrigation [irigasjɔ̃] *nf* irrigation; **l'i. du cerveau** the blood supply to the brain

irriguer [irige] *vt* to irrigate; **le cerveau n'est plus irrigué** the brain is no longer being supplied with blood

irritable [iritabl] *adj* irritable

irritant, -e [iritɑ̃, -ɑ̃t] *adj* **(a)** *(personne, comportement)* irritating **(b)** *(substance)* irritant (**pour** to)

irritation [iritasjɔ̃] *nf aussi Méd* irritation

irrité, -e [irite] *adj* **(a)** *(énervé)* irritated (**contre** with) **(b)** *(enflammé)* irritated, inflamed

irriter [irite] **1** *vt* **(a)** *(énerver, enflammer)* to irritate
2 *s'irriter vpr* **(a)** *(s'énerver)* **s'i. contre qn/de qch** to get irritated with sb/at sth **(b)** *(s'enflammer)* to become irritated or inflamed

irruption [irypsjɔ̃] *nf* **(a)** *(entrée)* irruption; **faire i. dans** to burst into **(b)** *(invasion)* invasion **(c)** *(émergence)* upsurge

islam [islam] *nm* **l'i.** Islam

islamique [islamik] *adj* Islamic

islamiste [islamist] *nmf* Islamic fundamentalist

islandais, -e [islɑ̃dɛ, -ɛz] **1** *adj* Icelandic
2 *nm,f* **I.** Icelander
3 *nm (langue)* Icelandic

Islande [islɑ̃d] *nf* **l'I.** Iceland

isobare [izɔbar] **1** *adj* isobaric
2 *nf* isobar

isocèle [izɔsɛl] *adj* isosceles

isolant, -e [izɔlɑ̃, -ɑ̃t] **1** *adj (contre le froid, en électricité)* insulating; *(contre le bruit)* soundproofing
2 *nm (contre le froid, en électricité)* insulating material; *(contre le bruit)* soundproofing (material)

isolation [izɔlasjɔ̃] *nf (électrique)* insulation; **i. acoustique** *ou* **phonique** soundproofing; **i. thermique** (thermal) insulation

isolationniste [izɔlasjɔnist] *adj & nmf* isolationist

isolé, -e [izɔle] *adj* **(a)** *(personne, cas, endroit, maison)* isolated **(b)** *(protégé)* (en électricité, du froid) insulated; *(du bruit)* soundproofed

isolement [izɔlmɑ̃] *nm* **(a)** *(d'une personne, d'une maison)* isolation **(b)** *(isolation)* insulation

isolément [izɔlemɑ̃] *adv (agir)* in isolation; *(interroger des gens)* individually

isoler [izɔle] **1** *vt* **(a)** *(séparer)* to isolate (**de** from) **(b)** *(protéger) (du froid, d'un courant électrique)* to insulate; *(du bruit)* to soundproof
2 *s'isoler vpr* to isolate oneself

isoloir [izɔlwar] *nm* polling booth

isotherme [izɔtɛrm] **1** *adj* maintained at a constant temperature; **boîte/sac i.** cool box/bag; **bouteille i.** vacuum flask
2 *nf* isotherm

Israël [israɛl] *n* Israel

israélien, -enne [israeljɛ̃, -ɛn] **1** *adj* Israeli
2 *nm,f* **I.** Israeli

israélite [israelit] **1** *adj* Jewish
2 *nmf* Jew

issu, -e [isy] *adj* **être i. de** *(être originaire de)* to come from; *(résulter de)* to stem from

issue [isy] *nf* **(a)** *(sortie)* exit; Fig *(solution)* way out; **i. de secours** emergency exit **(b)** *(fin)* outcome; **à l'i. de** at the end of

Istanbul [istɑ̃bul] *n* Istanbul

isthme [ism] *nm* isthmus

Italie [itali] *nf* **l'I.** Italy

italien, -enne [italjɛ̃, -ɛn] **1** *adj* Italian
2 *nm,f* **I.** Italian
3 *nm (langue)* Italian
4 *nf* **italienne** *Ordinat* **imprimer à l'italienne** to print landscape

italique [italik] **1** *adj* italic
2 *nm* **en italique(s)** in italics

Ithaque [itak] *nf* Ithaca

itinéraire [itinerɛr] *nm* route, itinerary; **i. bis =** alternative route recommended when roads are highly congested, especially at peak holiday times; **i. touristique** tourist route

itinérant, -e [itinerɑ̃, -ɑ̃t] *adj (comédiens, exposition)* travelling; *(ambassadeur)* roving

itou [itu] *adv Fam Vieilli* likewise, too; **et moi i.!** me too!

IUFM [iyefɛm] *nm (abrév* **Institut universitaire de formation des maîtres)** ≃ teacher training college

IUT [iyte] *nm (abrév* **Institut universitaire de technologie)** = vocational higher education college

IVG [iveʒe] *nf (abrév* **interruption volontaire de grossesse)** termination (of pregnancy)

ivoire [ivwar] *nm* ivory

ivoirien, -enne [ivwarjɛ̃, -ɛn] **1** *adj* of the Ivory Coast
2 *nm, f* **I.** person from the Ivory Coast

ivre [ivr] *adj* drunk; **i. mort** blind drunk; **i. de joie** beside oneself with joy

ivresse [ivrɛs] *nf (ébriété)* drunkenness; *(extase)* exhilaration; **conduite en état d'i.** drink-driving

ivrogne [ivrɔɲ] *nmf* drunkard

ivrognerie [ivrɔɲri] *nf* drunkenness

J

J, j [ʒi] *nm inv* J, j

j' [ʒ] *voir* **je**

jabot [ʒabo] *nm* (a) *(d'oiseau)* crop (b) *(de chemise)* frill, ruffle

jacassements [ʒakasmɑ̃] *nmpl (d'une pie, d'une personne)* chattering

jacasser [ʒakase] *vi (pie, personne)* to chatter

jachère [ʒaʃɛr] *nf* leaving land fallow; **laisser en j.** *(champ)* to leave fallow; *Fig (talent)* to leave undeveloped

jacinthe [ʒasɛ̃t] *nf* hyacinth

jacquard [ʒakar] *adj (pull)* argyle

jacquet [ʒakɛ] *nm* backgammon

jacter [ʒakte] *vi Fam* to gab

Jacuzzi® [ʒakyzi] *nm* Jacuzzi®

jade [ʒad] *nm* (a) *(pierre)* jade (b) *(objet)* jade object

jadis [ʒadis] *Litt* **1** *adv* in times past, formerly; **les chevaliers de j.** the knights of old
2 *adj* **au temps j.** in the olden days

jaguar [ʒagwar] *nm* jaguar

jaillir [ʒajir] *vi* (a) *(source, liquide)* to gush out; *(étincelles, flammes, foule)* to shoot out; *(lumière)* to flash (b) *(rires, cris)* to burst out

jais [ʒɛ] *nm* jet; *(d'un noir)* **de j.** jet-black

Jakarta [dʒakarta] *n* Jakarta

jalon [ʒalɔ̃] *nm* ranging pole; *Fig* **poser des jalons** to prepare the ground

jalonner [ʒalɔne] *vt (marquer) (parcelle, piste d'atterrissage)* to mark out; *(ponctuer) (route, côte)* to line (**de** with); *Fig* to punctuate

jalousement [ʒaluzmɑ̃] *adv* jealously

jalouser [ʒaluze] *vt* to be jealous of

jalousie [ʒaluzi] *nf* (a) *(sentiment)* jealousy; **éprouver de la j. envers qn** to feel jealous of sb; **être malade de j.** to be green with envy (b) *(store)* Venetian blind

jaloux, -ouse [ʒalu, -uz] **1** *adj* jealous (**de** of); **j. comme un tigre** wildly jealous
2 *nm,f* **c'est un j.** he's a jealous man; **faire des j.** to make people jealous

jamaïcain, -e, jamaïquain, -e [ʒamaikɛ̃, -ɛn] **1** *adj* Jamaican
2 *nm,f* J. Jamaican

Jamaïque [ʒamaik] *nf* **la J.** Jamaica

jamais [ʒamɛ] *adv* (a) *(positif)* ever; **plus que j.** more than ever; **à (tout) j.** for good, for ever; **si j. elle revenait** she ever came back; **le film le plus drôle que j'aie j. vu** the funniest film I've ever seen (b) *(négatif)* never; **je ne l'ai j. vu** I've never seen him; **il a passé toute sa vie sans j. boire un verre d'alcool** he's spent all his life without ever touching a drop of alcohol; **j. plus**

never again; **j., au grand j., je ne le dirai** I shall never ever tell; **elle n'a j. que dix minutes de retard** she's only ten minutes late; *Fam* **j. de la vie!** not on your life!; *Prov* **j. deux sans trois** things come in threes

jambe [ʒɑ̃b] *nf* leg; **jambes nues** bare-legged; **traîner la j.** *(de fatigue)* to drag one's feet; *(en boitant)* to drag one foot behind one; **à toutes jambes** as fast as one can; **prendre ses jambes à son cou** to take to one's heels; **être dans les jambes de qn** to be under sb's feet; **traiter qn par-dessous** *ou* **par-dessus la j.** to treat sb in an offhand manner; *Fam* **ça me fait une belle j.!** a fat lot of good that does me!; *Fam* **tenir la j. à qn** to drone on and on at sb; **j. de bois** wooden leg

jambière [ʒɑ̃bjɛr] *nf* (a) *(de sport)* (shin) pad (b) *(pour tenir chaud)* legwarmer

jambon [ʒɑ̃bɔ̃] *nm* ham; **j. blanc** boiled ham; **j. cru** raw ham; **j. fumé** smoked ham; **j. de Parme** Parma ham

jambonneau, -x [ʒɑ̃bɔno] *nm* knuckle of ham

jante [ʒɑ̃t] *nf* rim

janvier [ʒɑ̃vje] *nm* January; **en j., au mois de j.** in January; **nous sommes le 7 j.** it's the 7th of January, it's January the 7th; **j'y vais le 7 j.** I'm going on the 7th of January *or* January the 7th

Japon [ʒapɔ̃] *nm* **le J.** Japan

japonais, -e [ʒapɔnɛ, -ɛz] **1** *adj* Japanese
2 *nm,f* J. Japanese; **les J.** the Japanese
3 *nm (langue)* Japanese

jappement [ʒapmɑ̃] *nm* yap, yelp; **jappements** yapping, yelping

japper [ʒape] *vi* to yap, to yelp

jaquette [ʒakɛt] *nf* (a) *(d'homme)* morning coat; *(de femme)* jacket; *Can (chemise de nuit)* nightdress (b) *(de livre) (dust)* jacket, (dust) cover

jardin [ʒardɛ̃] *nm* garden; *Fig* **c'est mon j. secret** I keep it very much to myself; **j. botanique** botanical garden(s); **j. d'enfants** kindergarten; **j. potager** vegetable garden; **j. public** gardens; **j. zoologique** zoological gardens

jardinage [ʒardinaʒ] *nm* gardening

jardiner [ʒardine] *vi* to do some gardening

jardinet [ʒardinɛ] *nm* small garden

jardinier, -ère [ʒardinje, -ɛr] **1** *nm,f* gardener
2 *nf* **jardinière** (a) *(pour balcon)* window box; *(intérieure)* jardinière (b) *Culin* **jardinière (de légumes)** mixed vegetables

jargon [ʒargɔ̃] *nm* (a) *(argot, de métier)* jargon (b) *(langage incompréhensible)* gibberish

jarre [ʒar] *nf (earthenware)* jar

jarret [ʒarɛ] *nm* (a) *(de personne)* back of the knee; *(de cheval)* hock (b) *(pièce de viande) (de veau)* knuckle; *(de bœuf)* shin

jarretelle [ʒartɛl] *nf Br* suspender, *Am* garter

jarretière [ʒartjɛr] *nf* garter

jaser [ʒɑze] *vi* (a) *(médire)* to gossip; **cela va faire j.** that'll set tongues wagging (b) *Can (bavarder)* to chatter (de about)

jasmin [ʒasmɛ̃] *nm* jasmine

jatte [ʒat] *nf* bowl

jauge [ʒoʒ] *nf* (a) *(instrument de mesure)* gauge; **j. d'essence** *Br* petrol or *Am* gas gauge; **j. de niveau d'huile** oil-level indicator; *(manuelle)* dipstick (b) *(de navire)* tonnage

jauger [45] [ʒoʒe] **1** *vt* (a) *(mesurer) (tonneau, réservoir)* to measure the capacity of; *(navire)* to measure the tonnage of (b) *Fig (personne, situation)* to size up
2 *vi* **j. 300 tonneaux** to be of 300 tons burden

jaunâtre [ʒonɑtr] *adj* yellowish

jaune [ʒon] **1** *adj (couleur, objet)* yellow; *(teint)* sallow; **j. canari** canary yellow; **j. citron** lemon yellow; **j. moutarde** mustard yellow; **j. d'or** golden yellow; **j. paille** straw-coloured
2 *nm* (a) *(couleur)* yellow (b) **j. d'œuf** (egg) yolk (c) *Can (lâche)* yellowbelly
3 *adv* **rire j.** to give a forced laugh

jauni, -e [ʒoni] *adj* yellowed

jaunir [ʒonir] *vt & vi* to turn yellow

jaunisse [ʒonis] *nf* jaundice; *Fam Fig* **en faire une j.** to get into a state about it

java [ʒava] *nf* (a) *(danse)* = type of popular waltz (b) *Fam (fête)* **faire la j.** to live it up

Javel [ʒavɛl] *n voir* **eau**

javelot [ʒavlo] *nm* javelin

jazz [dʒaz] *nm* jazz

J.-C. *(abrév* **Jésus-Christ)** JC; **av. J.-C.** BC; **ap. J.-C.** AD

je [ʒə]

> **j'** is used before a word beginning with a vowel or h mute.

pron personnel I

jean [dʒin] *nm (pantalon)* jeans; *(tissu)* denim; **un j.** a pair of jeans; **veste en j.** denim jacket

Jeanne [ʒan] *npr* **J. d'Arc** Joan of Arc

Jeep® [dʒip] *nf* Jeep®

Jéhovah [ʒeova] *npr* Jehovah

je-m'en-foutisme [ʒmɑ̃futism] *nm très Fam* couldn't-care-less attitude

je-m'en-foutiste *(pl* **je-m'en-foutistes)** [ʒmɑ̃futist] *nmf très Fam* couldn't-care-less type

je-ne-sais-quoi [ʒənsɛkwa] *nm inv* **un j.** a certain something

jérémiades [ʒeremjad] *nfpl* whining

jerrican(e), jerrycan [dʒerikan, ʒerikan] *nm* jerry can

Jérusalem [ʒeryzalɛm] *n* Jerusalem

jésuite [ʒezɥit] **1** *adj* Jesuit; *Fig & Péj* jesuitical
2 *nm* Jesuit

Jésus(-Christ) [ʒezy(kri)] *npr* Jesus (Christ)

jet¹ [ʒɛ] *nm* (a) *(lancer) (de pierre)* throwing; *Fig* **faire qch d'un seul j.** to do sth in one go (b) *(de liquide, de vapeur)* jet; **premier j.** *(d'un roman)* first draft; **j. d'eau** *(fontaine)* fountain

jet² [dʒɛt] *nm (avion)* jet

jetable [ʒətablə] *adj* disposable

jeté, -e [ʒəte] **1** *nm* (a) *(en danse)* jeté (b) **j. de lit** bedspread
2 *adj très Fam* barking (mad)

jetée [ʒəte] *nf* jetty, pier

jeter [42] [ʒəte] **1** *vt* (a) *(lancer)* to throw; *(plus fort)* to fling, to hurl; *(filets)* to cast; **j. qch à qn** to throw sth to sb, to throw sth to sb; **j. qn à terre** to throw sb to the ground; **j. qch à terre** *ou* **par terre** to throw sth on the ground; **j. qn en prison** to throw sb in prison; **j. les bras autour de qn** to throw one's arms around sb; **j. quelques idées sur le papier** to jot down a few ideas; **j. le trouble dans l'esprit de qn** to trouble sb; **ça a jeté un froid** it cast a chill
(b) *(se défaire de)* to throw away or out; **j. son argent par les fenêtres** to throw one's money down the drain; *Fam* **se faire j. (de)** to get chucked out (of)
(c) *(émettre) (cri)* to utter; **j. un regard à qn** to glance at sb; **j. un coup d'œil (sur qch)** to have a quick glance (at sth)
(d) *(établir)* **j. les fondements de qch** to lay the foundations for sth
(e) *Fam* **ça (en) jette!** it's really something!
3 se jeter *vpr* (a) *(fleuve, rivière)* **se j. dans** to flow into
(b) *(personne)* to throw oneself; **se j. sur qn** to throw oneself at sb; *Fig* to pounce on sb; **se j. sur** *(nourriture)* to pounce on; *(occasion)* to jump at; **se j. à l'eau** to plunge into the water; *Fig* to take the plunge; **se j. par la fenêtre** to throw oneself out of the window; **se j. aux pieds de qn** to throw oneself at sb's feet; *Fig* **se j. à la tête de qn** *(le draguer)* to throw oneself at sb

jeton [ʒətɔ̃] *nm* (a) *(au jeu)* chip; *(pour téléphone, machine)* token; **j. de présence** *(objet)* token *(issued as voucher for attendance at meeting)*; *(honoraires)* director's fees (b) *Fam* **avoir les jetons** to have the jitters

jeu, -x [ʒø] *nm* (a) *(amusement)* play; **faire qch par j.** to do sth for fun; **entrer en j.** to come into play; *Fig* **c'est un j. d'enfant** it's child's play; *Prov* **jeux de mains, jeux de vilains** all this fooling around is going to end in tears; **j. de mots** play on words, pun; **j. de rôles** role-playing
(b) *(activité)* game; **mettre la balle en j.** to bring the ball into play; *Fig* **jouer le j.** to play the game; *Fig* **jouer franc j.** *(avec qn)* to play fair (with sb); *Fig* **se prendre au j.** to get caught up in it; *Fig* **faire le j. de qn** to play into sb's hands; **on aurait beau j. de répondre** it would be quite easy to answer; **j. d'adresse** game of skill; **j. de cartes** card game; **j. électronique** computer game; **le j. de l'oie** = board game similar to snakes and ladders; **les jeux Olympiques** the Olympic Games, the Olympics; **jeux de société** *(charades, devinettes)* parlour games; *(petits chevaux, jeu de l'oie)* board games; **j. télévisé** (television) game show; *(avec questions)* (television) quiz show; **j. vidéo** video game
(c) *(au casino)* **le j.** gambling; **se ruiner au j.** to bankrupt oneself gambling; **mettre qch en j.** *(argent, voiture, carrière)* to stake sth; *Fig* **être en j.** to be at stake; **les jeux sont faits** *(à la roulette)* les jeux sont faits; **faites vos jeux!** place your bets!; **jeux de hasard** games of chance
(d) *(cartes en main)* hand; **avoir du j.** to have a good hand; **cacher son j.** to hide one's hand; *Fig* to keep one's cards close to one's chest; *Fig* **sortir le grand j.** to pull out all the stops
(e) *(au tennis)* game; **j., set et match** game, set and match; **j. Noah** game (to) Noah; **j. blanc** love game
(f) *(d'un danseur)* acting; *(d'un musicien)* playing; **j. de jambes** *(d'un boxeur, d'un tennisman)* footwork
(g) *(d'outils, de clefs)* set; **j. de boules/quilles** set of bowls/skittles; **j. de cartes** *Br* pack or *Am* deck of cards; **j.**

d'échecs chess set
(h) il y a du j. *(ça bouge)* there's a bit of play
(i) *(mécanisme)* **le j. de l'offre et de la demande** the system of supply and demand

jeu-concours *(pl* **jeux-concours** *[ʒøkɔ̃kur] nm* competition

jeudi *[ʒødi] nm* Thursday; **le j. saint** Maundy Thursday; *Fam* **la semaine des quatre jeudis** when pigs fly; *voir aussi* **samedi**

jeun *[ʒœ̃]* **à jeun 1** *adj* **être à j.** *(sans avoir mangé ni bu)* not to have eaten or drunk anything; *(pas ivre)* to be sober
2 *adv* **prendre qch à j.** to take sth on an empty stomach

jeune *[ʒœn]* **1** *adj (personne, vin, pays)* young; *(apparence, allure)* youthful; *(coiffure, vêtement)* that makes one look young; **être j. d'esprit** to have a youthful outlook; **faire plus j. que son âge** to look younger than one's age; **elle n'est plus toute j.** she's not as young as she was
2 *nmf* **un j.** a youngster; **une j.** a girl; *Fam* **un petit j.** a young guy; **les jeunes** young people
3 *adv* **s'habiller j.** to dress in a youthful style; **ça fait j.** it makes you/her/*etc* look young

jeûne *[ʒøn] nm* **(a)** *(période)* fast; **rompre le j.** to break one's fast **(b)** *(pratique)* fasting

jeûner *[ʒøne] vi* to fast

jeunesse *[ʒœnɛs] nf* **(a)** *(période)* youth **(b)** *(d'apparence, d'esprit)* youthfulness **(c)** *(jeunes gens)* young people

jeunot, -otte *[ʒœno, -ɔt] Fam* **1** *adj* youngish
2 *nmf Péj* youngster; **un petit j.** a young little fellow

JF **(a)** *(abrév* **jeune fille)** girl **(b)** *(abrév* **jeune femme)** young woman

JH *(abrév* **jeune homme)** young man

jingle *[dʒingəl] nm* jingle

JO *[ʒio]* **1** *nm (abrév* **Journal officiel)** = French government publication giving information to the public about new laws, government business, new companies etc
2 *nmpl (abrév* **jeux Olympiques)** Olympic Games

joaillerie *[ʒɔajri] nf* **(a)** *(magasin)* jeweller's shop **(b)** *(bijoux)* jewellery

joaillier, -ère *[ʒɔaje, -ɛr] nm,f* jeweller

job *[dʒɔb] nm Fam* job

jockey *[ʒɔkɛ] nm* jockey

Joconde *[ʒɔkɔ̃d] nf* **la J.** the Mona Lisa

joggeur, -euse *[dʒɔgœr, -øz] nm,f* jogger

jogging *[dʒɔgiŋ] nm* **(a)** *(vêtement)* jogging suit **(b)** *(activité)* jogging; **faire du j.** to go jogging, to jog

Johannesburg *[ʒɔanɛsburg] n* Johannesburg

joie *[ʒwa] nf* joy, delight; **avec j.** with pleasure, gladly; *Fam* **c'est pas la j.!** it's no fun!; **faire la j. de qn** to make sb happy; **se faire une j. de faire qch** *(envisager)* to look forward to doing sth; *(faire avec plaisir)* to be delighted to do sth; **faire une fausse j. à qn** to falsely raise sb's hopes; **j. de vivre** joie de vivre

joignable *[ʒwaɲabl] adj* contactable

joignais *etc voir* **joindre**

joindre *[43] [ʒwɛ̃dr]* **1** *vt* **(a)** *(réunir)* to join; **j. les mains** to put one's hands together; *Fam* **Fig j. les deux bouts** to make ends meet **(b)** *(ajouter)* to add *(à* to); *(dans une lettre, un colis)* to enclose *(à* with); **j. le geste à la parole** to suit the action to the word; **j. l'utile à l'agréable** to combine business with pleasure **(c)** *(contacter)* to contact
2 *se* **joindre** *vpr* **se j. à qn** to join sb; **se j. à qch** to join in sth

joint, -e *[ʒwɛ̃, -ɛt]* **1** *pp de* **joindre**
2 *adj* **sauter à pieds joints** to jump from a standing position; **les mains jointes** with hands together; **pièces jointes** *(dans une lettre)* enclosures
3 *nm* **(a)** *(d'étanchéité)* seal; *(articulation)* joint; **j. de culasse** cylinder head gasket; **j. de dilatation** expansion joint **(b)** *Fam (à fumer)* joint

jointure *[ʒwɛ̃tyr] nf (articulation)* joint

jojo *[ʒɔʒo] Fam* **1** *nm voir* **affreux**
2 *adj inv* **ne pas être j.** *(physiquement)* not to look very nice; *(moralement)* not to be very nice

jojoba *[ʒɔʒɔba] nm* jojoba

joker *[ʒɔkɛr] nm (aux cartes)* joker; *Ordinat* wild-card

joli, -e *[ʒɔli]* **1** *adj* **(a)** *(personne, ville, voix)* pretty, attractive; **il est j. garçon** he's good-looking; **j. comme un cœur** pretty as a picture; **faire le j. cœur** to flirt **(b)** *(situation, somme)* nice; **c'est bien j., tout ça mais...** that's all well and good but...; *Fam* **c'est pas j.** *(blâmable)* that's not very nice; *(laid)* it's not a pretty sight
2 *nm Ironique* **c'est du j.!** marvellous!

joliment *[ʒɔlimɑ̃] adv* **(a)** *(bien)* nicely; **c'est j. dit** that's nicely put; *Ironique* **te voilà j. arrangé!** you're in a right mess! **(b)** *Fam (extrêmement)* really; **elle s'est j. fait engueuler** she got a telling-off

jonc *[ʒɔ̃] nm (plante)* rush

joncher *[ʒɔ̃ʃe] vt* to strew *(de* with)

jonction *[ʒɔ̃ksjɔ̃] nf* junction

jongler *[ʒɔ̃gle] vi* to juggle *(avec* with)

jongleur, -euse *[ʒɔ̃glœr, -øz] nm,f* juggler

jonquille *[ʒɔ̃kij] nf* daffodil

Jordanie *[ʒɔrdani] nf* **la J.** Jordan

jordanien, -enne *[ʒɔrdanjɛ̃, -ɛn]* **1** *adj* Jordanian
2 *nm,f* **J.** Jordanian

jouable *[ʒwabl] adj* playable

joual *[ʒwal] Can1 nm* joual (French-Canadian dialect)
2 *adj* **langue jouale** joual

joue *[ʒu] nf (de personne, d'animal)* cheek; **mettre qn en j.** to take aim at sb; **tenir qn en j.** to keep sb in one's sights

jouer *[ʒwe]* **1** *vt (parier)* to stake *(sur* on); *(cheval)* to back, to bet on
(b) *(participer à)* **j. la finale** to play in the final
(c) *(carte)* to play; *(pion, pièce)* to move
(d) *(rôle)* to act, to play; **j. la surprise** to pretend to be surprised; **j. les héros** to play the hero; *Hum* **j. la fille de l'air** to vanish into thin air
(e) *(air)* to play; **j. du Bach** to play (some) Bach
2 *vi* **(a)** *(s'amuser)* to play; *Fig* **j. sur les mots** to play with words; *Fig* **j. avec les sentiments de qn** to play with sb's feelings; *Fig* **j. avec son avenir** to risk one's future; *Fig* **j. avec le feu** to play with fire; **c'est à qui de j.?** whose turn is it?; *(aux échecs, aux dames)* whose move is it?; *Fig* **maintenant à vous de j.** now it's your turn
(b) *(acteur)* to act; *(troupe)* to perform; **il joue très mal** he's a very bad actor
(c) *(parier)* to gamble; **j. en Bourse** to speculate on the stock market
(d) *(fonctionner)* **j. en faveur/défaveur de qn** to work in sb's favour/against sb; **faire j. un ressort** to release a spring; *Fig* **faire j. ses relations pour obtenir qch** to pull a few strings to get sth
(e) *(bois)* to warp; *(pièce)* to work loose
3 jouer à *vt ind* **(a)** *(pratiquer)* to play; **j. au tennis/aux cartes** to play tennis/cards; **j. aux gendarmes et aux voleurs** to play cops and robbers; **j. à la marchande** to

play shops; *Fig* **j. au plus fin** to try to outwit each other
(b) *(parier sur)* **j. aux courses** to bet on *or* back horses

4 jouer de *vt ind* **j. du piano/de la harpe** to play the piano/the harp; *Fig* **j. des coudes** to elbow one's way through

5 se jouer *vpr* **(a)** *(match)* to be played
(b) *(se décider)* **son sort est en train de se j.** his/her fate is hanging in the balance
(c) se j. de qn to trifle with sb; **se j. des lois** to make a mockery of the law; **se j. des difficultés** to make light of difficulties
(d) *(pièce de théâtre, film)* to be on

jouet [ʒwε] *nm* toy; *Fig* **être le j. de** to be the victim of

joueur, -euse [ʒwœr, -øz] **1** *nm,f (d'un jeu, d'un sport, d'un instrument de musique)* player; **j. de tennis/cartes** tennis/card player; **être beau/mauvais j.** to be a good/bad loser **(b)** *(au casino)* gambler
2 *adj (enfant, chien)* playful

joufflu, -e [ʒufly] *adj (bébé, angelot)* chubby-cheeked; *(visage)* chubby

joug [ʒu] *nm aussi Fig* yoke

jouir [ʒwir] *vi* **(a)** *(profiter)* **j. de qch** to enjoy sth **(b)** *(sexuellement)* to come **(c)** *(être en possession)* **j. d'une bonne réputation** to have a good reputation; **j. d'une bonne santé** to enjoy good health

jouissance [ʒwisɑ̃s] *nf* **(a)** *(plaisir)* enjoyment; *(sexuel)* orgasm **(b)** *Jur (usage)* use

jouisseur, -euse [ʒwisœr, -øz] *nm,f* sensualist

jouissif, -ive [ʒwisif, -iv] *adj très Fam* orgasmic

joujou, -x [ʒuʒu] *nm (langage enfantin)* toy; **faire j.** to play

joule [ʒul] *nm* joule

jour [ʒur] *nm* **(a)** *(clarté)* daylight; **au petit j.** at daybreak; **en plein j.** in broad daylight; *Fig* **au grand j.** publicly; **travailler le** *ou* **de j.** to work days; **j. et nuit** day and night; *Fig* **elle et son mari, c'est le j. et la nuit** she and her husband are like chalk and cheese; **elle est belle comme le j.** she's a real beauty; **il fait j.** it's light
(b) *(journée)* day; **huit jours** a week; **quinze jours** two weeks, *Br* a fortnight; **un j. ou l'autre** one day; **de j. en j.** day by day; **du j. au lendemain** overnight; **nous l'attendons d'un j. à l'autre** we're expecting him any day (now); **un de ces jours** one of these days; **un beau j., elle décida de...** one day, she decided to...; **vivre au j. le j.** *(sans faire de projets)* to live from day to day; *(financièrement)* to live from hand to mouth; **mettre qch à j.** to update sth, to bring sth up to date; **tenir qch à j.** to keep sth up to date; **décidément, ce n'est pas mon j.!** it just isn't my day today!; **il y a des jours avec et les jours sans** there are good days and bad days; **le j. de l'an** New Year's Day; **j. de congé** day off; **j. férié** public holiday, *Br* bank holiday; **le jour J** D-day; **le j. de Noël** Christmas Day; **j. ouvrable** working day; **j. de repos** day off
(c) *(date)* day; **quel j. sommes-nous?** what's the date (today)?; **le j. de mes vingt ans** my twentieth birthday; **il y a six ans j. pour j.** six years ago to the day; **à ce j., nous n'avons toujours pas reçu votre lettre** as of this date we still have not received your letter
(d) *(époque)* **de nos jours** these days, nowadays; **les beaux jours** the fine days of summer; **pour mes vieux jours** for my old age
(e) *(vie)* **donner le j. à un enfant** to give birth to a child; **mettre fin à ses jours** to put an end to one's life; **il vit le j. à Paris** he was born in Paris; **jusqu'à mon dernier j.** to my dying day

(f) *(éclairage)* light; *Fig* **voir qch sous un j. nouveau/sous son vrai j.** to see sth in a new light/in its true light; *Fig* **présenter qch sous un j. favorable** to present sth in a favourable light
(g) *(ouverture)* gap

Jourdain [ʒurdɛ̃] *nm* **le J.** the River Jordan

journal, -aux [ʒurnal, -o] *nm* **(a)** *(publication)* paper, newspaper; **j. (télévisé)** (television) news **(b)** *(récit d'événements, d'expériences)* journal; *Ordinat* log; **tenir un j.** to keep a journal; **j. de bord** log (book); **j. intime** diary; **J. officiel** = French government publication giving information to the public about new laws, government business, new companies etc

journalier, -ère [ʒurnalje, -εr] **1** *adj* daily
2 *nm,f (ouvrier agricole)* day labourer

journalisme [ʒurnalism] *nm* journalism

journaliste [ʒurnalist] *nmf* journalist; **elle est j. au Monde** she's a journalist with Le Monde; **j. sportif** sports journalist

journalistique [ʒurnalistik] *adj* journalistic

journée [ʒurne] *nf* **(a)** *(par opposition à nuit)* day(time); **pendant la j.** in the daytime, during the day; **dans la j.** in the course of the day; **toute la j.** all day **(b)** *(unité de temps)* day; **j. de travail** *(jour non chômé)* working day; *(quantité de travail)* day's work; **faire la j. continue** *(personne)* to work through lunch; **j. portes ouvertes** *Br* open day, *Am* open house

journellement [ʒurnεlmɑ̃] *adv* daily

joute [ʒut] *nf (combat médiéval)* joust; *Fig* **joutes oratoires** verbal sparring

jouvence [ʒuvɑ̃s] *nf Litt* **cela a été un bain** *ou* **une cure de j.** it has rejuvenated me

jouvenceau, -x [ʒuvɑ̃so] *nm Hum* stripling

jouvencelle [ʒuvɑ̃sεl] *nf Hum* maiden

jouxter [ʒukste] *vt* to adjoin

jovial, -e, -als *ou* **-aux, -ales** [ʒɔvjal, -o] *adj* jovial, jolly

jovialité [ʒɔvjalite] *nf* joviality, jolliness

joyau, -x [ʒwajo] *nm aussi Fig* jewel

joyeusement [ʒwajøzmɑ̃] *adv* joyfully

joyeux, -euse [ʒwajø, -øz] *adj* joyful; **j. anniversaire!** happy birthday!; **j. Noël!** Happy *or* Merry Christmas!

JT [ʒite] *nm (abrév* **journal télévisé)** TV news

jubilation [ʒybilasjɔ̃] *nf* jubilation

jubilé [ʒybile] *nm* jubilee

jubiler [ʒybile] *vi* to be jubilant; *(méchamment)* to gloat

jucher [ʒyʃe] **1** *vt* to perch **(sur** on)
2 se jucher *vpr* to perch **(sur** on)

judaïque [ʒydaik] *adj* Jewish; *(loi)* Judaic

judaïsme [ʒydaism] *nm* Judaism

judas [ʒyda] *nm (ouverture)* peephole

judéo-chrétien, -enne *(mpl* **judéo-chrétiens,** *fpl* **judéo-chrétiennes)** [ʒydeokretjɛ̃, -εn] *adj* Judaeo-Christian

judiciaire [ʒydisjεr] *adj (pouvoir, enquête, acte)* judicial; *(aide, autorité)* legal

judicieusement [ʒydisjøzmɑ̃] *adv* judiciously

judicieux, -euse [ʒydisjø, -øz] *adj* judicious; **peu j.** injudicious

judo [ʒydo] *nm* judo

judoka [ʒydoka] *nmf Sp* judoka

juge [ʒyʒ] *nm* judge; **Monsieur le J.** Your Honour; **les juges** the bench; **je vous laisse j.** I'll let you be the judge; *Fig* être à la fois j. et partie to sit in judgement on oneself; **j. d'instruction** examining magistrate; **j. de ligne** line judge; **j. de touche** *(au football)* linesman; *(au rugby)* touch judge

jugé [ʒyʒe] **au jugé** *adv (tirer)* blind; *(calculer)* roughly

jugement [ʒyʒmã] *nm* **(a)** *Jur (d'une affaire)* trial; **passer en j.** to stand trial **(b)** *Jur (décision)* decision; *(dans les affaires criminelles)* sentence **(c)** *(opinion)* judgement; **porter un j. sur qch** to pass judgement on sth; **j. de valeur** value judgement **(d)** *(discernement)* judgement

jugeote [ʒyʒɔt] *nf Fam* common sense

juger¹ [45] [ʒyʒe] **1** *vt* **a** *(affaire, prévenu)* to try; *(demande, litige)* to adjudicate. **b** *(évaluer, condamner)* to judge *(sur* by); **à toi de j.** it's for you to judge **(c)** *(croire)* **j. que** to consider that; **on le jugeait fou** people considered him mad; **j. superflu de faire qch** to consider it superfluous to do sth

2 juger *vti ind* to judge; **jugez de ma surprise!** imagine my surprise!; **à en j. par...** judging by...

juger² = jugé

jugulaire [ʒygylɛr] *nf* **(a)** *(veine)* jugular (vein) **(b)** *(de casque)* chin strap

juguler [ʒygyle] *vt (rébellion)* to quell; *(inflation, épidémie)* to check

juif, -ive [ʒɥif, -iv] **1** *adj* Jewish

2 *nm,f* J. Jew

juillet [ʒɥijɛ] *nm* July; **le 14-J.** Bastille Day *(day of national celebration in France)*; *voir aussi* **janvier**

juin [ʒɥ̃ɛ] *nm* June; *voir aussi* **janvier**

juke-box [dʒykbɔks, ʒykbɔks] *nm inv* jukebox

Jules [ʒyl] *npr* J. César Julius Caesar

jules [ʒyl] *nm Fam (mari, petit ami)* guy

julienne [ʒyljɛn] *nf* j. de légumes vegetables julienne *(cut into thin strips)*

jumbo [dʒœmbo], **jumbo-jet** *(pl* **jumbo-jets** [dʒœmbodʒɛt] *nm* jumbo (jet)

jumeau, -elle, -x, -elles [ʒymo, -ɛl] **1** *adj (frère, sœur)* twin

2 *nm,f* twin; *(sosie)* double; **vrais/faux jumeaux** identical/fraternal twins

jumelage [ʒymlaʒ] *nm (de villes)* twinning

jumelé, -e [ʒymle] *adj (villes)* twinned; *(maisons)* semi-detached

jumelles [ʒymɛl] *nfpl (paire de)* **j.** (pair of) binoculars; **j. de théâtre** opera glasses

jument [ʒymã] *nf* mare

jungle [ʒɔ̃gl, ʒœ̃gl] *nf aussi Fig* jungle

junior [ʒynjɔr] **1** *adj (mode, taille)* junior

2 *nmf Sp* junior *(9 to 20 years old)*

junte [ʒœ̃t] *nf* junta

jupe [ʒyp] *nf* skirt; *Fam* être dans les *ou* pendu aux jupes de sa mère to be clinging to one's mother's skirts; **j. droite** straight skirt

jupe-culotte *(pl* **jupes-culottes** [ʒypkylɔt] *nf* culottes

jupette [ʒypet] *nf* skirt

Jupiter [ʒypiter] *npr (dieu, planète)* Jupiter

jupon [ʒypɔ̃] *nm* underskirt, petticoat

Jura [ʒyra] *nm* **le J.** the Jura (Mountains)

jurassique [ʒyrasik] *Géol* **1** *adj* Jurassic

2 *nm* **le J.** the Jurassic period

juré, -e [ʒyre] **1** *adj* **ennemi j.** sworn enemy

2 *nm,f* juror; **les jurés** the jury

jurer [ʒyre] **1** *vt* to swear; **je le jure** I swear; **j. qch sur la tête de qn** to swear sth on sb's grave; **j'aurais juré qu'il était là** I could have sworn that it was there; **j. de faire qch** to swear to do sth; **ne j. que par** to swear by; *Prov* **il ne faut j. de rien** you never can tell

2 *vi* **(a)** *(dire des gros mots)* to swear **(b)** *(couleurs, vêtements)* to clash *(avec* with)

3 se jurer *vpr* **(a)** *(l'un à l'autre)* **se j. fidélité** to swear to be faithful to each other **(b)** *(à soi-même)* **se j. que** to swear *(to oneself)* that; **se j. de faire qch** to swear to do sth

juridiction [ʒyridiksjɔ̃] *nf (compétence)* jurisdiction; *(tribunaux)* courts

juridique [ʒyridik] *adj* legal

jurisprudence [ʒyrisprydãs] *nf* case law; **faire j.** to set a precedent

juriste [ʒyrist] *nmf* legal expert

juron [ʒyrɔ̃] *nm* swearword

jury [ʒyri] *nm* **(a)** *(d'un tribunal)* jury **(b)** *(pour l'attribution d'un prix)* (panel of) judges; *(d'examen)* board of examiners

jus [ʒy] *nm* **(a)** *(de fruits, de légumes)* juice; *(de viande)* juices; **j. d'orange/de fruit** orange/fruit juice; *Fam Hum* **j. de chaussettes** *(café)* dishwater **(b)** *Fam (courant électrique)* juice; **prendre le j.** to get an electric shock

jusant [ʒyzã] *nm* ebb tide

jusque [ʒysk, ʒyskə] *prép* **(a)** *(délimite un espace)* **jusqu'à** as far as; *(délimite une mesure)* up to; **jusqu'ici** as far as here; **j.-là** as far as there; *Fam* **s'en mettre j.-là** to stuff oneself; **jusqu'où?** how far?; **avoir de l'eau jusqu'à la taille** to have water right up to one's waist; **compter jusqu'à dix** to count (up) to ten; **jusqu'au bout (de la rue)** to the end (of the street); **j. dans les campagnes** right into the countryside; *Fig* **aller jusqu'au bout d'un raisonnement** to follow an argument through; **aller jusqu'à faire qch** to go so far as to do sth

(b) *(indique le temps)* until, till; **jusqu'ici, jusqu'à maintenant, jusqu'à présent** until now, up to now; **j.-là, jusqu'alors** until then, up to then; **jusqu'à ce que** + *subjunctive* until, till; **jusqu'à (l'âge de) quinze ans** up to the age of fifteen; **jusqu'à nouvel ordre** until further notice; **jusqu'au jour** *ou* **moment où...** until the time when...; **si nous remontons jusqu'en** *ou* **jusqu'à 1800** if we go right back to 1800

(c) *(également)* **jusqu'à** even

justaucorps [ʒystokɔr] *nm (de sport)* leotard

juste [ʒyst] **1** *adj (a)* *(équitable)* fair *(avec ou envers* to); **à j. titre** rightly

(b) *(exact)* *(calcul, réponse)* right, correct; *(raisonnement)* sound; *(note)* right; **arriver à l'heure j.** to arrive right on time; **avez-vous l'heure j.?** do you have the right time?

(c) *(trop petit)* *(chaussures, vêtement)* tight; **une bouteille pour six, c'est un peu j.** one bottle isn't quite enough for six people

(d) *Fam (financièrement)* être (un peu) j. to be (a bit) strapped for cash

2 *adv* **(a)** *(avec exactitude)* *(viser, parler)* accurately; *(chanter)* in tune; *Fam* **tomber j.** to guess right; **tout j.!** that's right!

(b) *(précisément)* just; **à dix heures j.** on the stroke of ten; **j. au coin/en face/à côté** just *or* right on the corner/opposite/next door; **arriver j. à temps** to arrive just in time; **ça fait 10 francs tout j.** that's 10 francs exactly

(c) *(à peine)* just; **c'est tout j. s'il sait lire** he can barely

read; **avoir j. le temps (de faire qch)** to have just enough time (to do sth); **ils ont tout j. fini de manger** they've only just finished eating
(d) *(trop peu)* **calculer trop j. (pour)** not to allow enough (for)
(e) **au j.** *(exactement)* exactly

justement [ʒystəmɑ̃] *adv* (a) *(précisément)* exactly; **j'allais j. t'appeler** I was just going to ring you (b) *(avec justesse)* rightly (c) *(avec justice)* justly

justesse [ʒystɛs] *nf* (a) *(précision) (d'une expression, d'une remarque)* aptness (b) **de j.** (only) just; **j'ai eu mon train de j.** I (only) just caught my train

justice [ʒystis] *nf* (a) *(équité)* justice; **faire** *ou* **rendre j. à qn** to do justice to sb; **se faire j.** *(se venger)* to take the law into one's own hands; *(se tuer)* to take one's own life (b) *Jur* **la j.** the law; **aller en j.** to go to law

justicier, -ère [ʒystisje, -ɛr] *nm,f* righter of wrongs

justifiable [ʒystifjabl] *adj* justifiable

justificatif, -ive [ʒystifikatif, -iv] 1 *adj* justificatory; **pièces justificatives** *(d'un dossier)* supporting documents

2 *nm* written proof

justification [ʒystifikasjɔ̃] *nf* (a) *(explication)* justification (**de** for *or* of) (b) *(preuve)* proof (c) *Typ & Ordinat* justification

justifié, -e [ʒystifje] *adj* (a) *(légitime)* justified; **peu j.** unjustified (b) *Typ & Ordinat* justified; **j. à droite/à gauche** right-/left-justified

justifier [66] [ʒystifje] 1 *vt* (a) *(légitimer, démontrer)* to justify (b) *Typ & Ordinat* to justify; **j. à droite/gauche** to right-/left-justify
2 **se justifier** *vpr* to justify oneself

jute [ʒyt] *nm* jute; **(toile de) j.** hessian

juter [ʒyte] *vi* to be juicy

juteux, -euse [ʒytø, -øz] *adj aussi Fam Fig* juicy

juvénile [ʒyvenil] *adj* youthful

juxtaposer [ʒykstapoze] *vt* to juxtapose

juxtaposition [ʒykstapozisjɔ̃] *nf* juxtaposition

K

K, k [kα] *nm inv* K, k

k (*abrév* **kilo(s)**) k

K7 [kaset] *nf* (*abrév* **cassette**) tape

Kaboul [kabul] *n* Kabul

kaki¹ [kaki] *adj inv & nm inv (couleur)* khaki

kaki² *nm (arbre, fruit)* persimmon

kaléidoscope [kaleidoskɔp] *nm aussi Fig* kaleidoscope

kamikaze [kamikaz] *nm* kamikaze; *Fig* **être k.** to have a death wish

kanak, -e [kanak] = **canaque**

kangourou [kɑ̃guru] *nm* kangaroo

kapok [kapɔk] *nm* kapok

karaoké [karaɔke] *nm* karaoke

karaté [karate] *nm* karate

karatéka [karateka] *nmf* karate expert

karma [karma] *nm* karma

kart [kart] *nm* (go-)kart

karting [kartiŋ] *nm* karting, go-kart racing; **faire du k.** to go karting

kasher [kaʃer] *adj inv Rel* kosher

Katmandou [katmɑ̃du] *n* Katmandu

kayak [kajak] *nm* **(a)** (*embarcation de sport*) canoe, kayak; **faire du k.** to go canoeing **(b)** (*esquimau*) kayak

kayakiste [kajakist] *nmf* canoeist

kazakh, -e [kazak] **1** *adj* Kazakh

2 *nm,f* **K.** Kazakh

Kazakhstan [kazakstɑ̃] *nm* le K. Kazakhstan

keffieh [kefje] *nm* kaffiyeh

kendo [kɛndo] *nm* kendo

Kenya [kenja] *nm* le K. Kenya

kenyan, -e [kenjɑ̃, -an] **1** *adj* Kenyan

2 *nm,f* **K.** Kenyan

képi [kepi] *nm* kepi

kératine [keratin] *nf* keratin

kermesse [kermes] *nf* **(a)** (*dans les Flandres*) village fair **(b)** (*fête de bienfaisance*) (charity) fête

kérosène [kerozen] *nm* kerosine

ketchup [ketʃœp] *nm* (tomato) ketchup

keuf [kœf] *nm très Fam* cop

kF [kaef] *nm* (*abrév* **kilofranc(s)**) thousand francs

kg (*abrév* **kilogramme(s)**) kg

KGB [kαɡebe] *nm* le K. the KGB

khâgne [kɑɲ] *nf* = second-year arts class preparing students for the entrance examination for the "École normale supérieure"

khâgneux, -euse [kɑɲø, -øz] *nm,f* = student in the "khâgne"

Khartoum [kartum] *n* Khartoum

khmer, -ère [kmer] **1** *adj* Khmer

2 *nm,f* **K.** Khmer; **les Khmers rouges** the Khmer Rouge

khôl [kol] *nm* kohl

kibboutz [kibuts] *nm inv* kibbutz

kidnapper [kidnape] *vt* to kidnap

kidnappeur, -euse [kidnapœr, -øz] *nm,f* kidnapper

kidnapping [kidnapiŋ] *nm* kidnapping

kif-kif [kifkif] *adj inv Fam* **c'est k. (bourricot)** it's six and half a dozen

kiki [kiki] *nm Fam* **(a)** *(cou)* **serrer le k. à qn** to wring sb's neck **(b)** (*langage enfantin*) (*pénis*) willy **(c)** **c'est parti mon k.!** here we go!

kilo [kilo] *nm* kilo

kilobaud [kilɔbo] *nm Ordinat* kilobaud

kilocalorie [kilɔkalɔri] *nf* kilocalorie

kilofranc [kilɔfrɑ̃] *nm* thousand francs

kilogramme [kilɔgram] *nm* kilogram(me)

kilohertz [kilɔɛrts] *nm* kilohertz

kilojoule [kilɔʒul] *nm* kilojoule

kilométrage [kilometraʒ] *nm* (*distance*) ≃ mileage; **k. illimité** (*de voiture de location*) unlimited mileage

kilomètre [kilometr] *nm* kilometre; **100 kilomètres à l'heure, 100 kilomètres-heure** 100 kilometres per *or* an hour; **taper du texte au k.** to type text straight in (*and leave the formatting etc until later*)

kilométrique [kilometrik] *adj voir* **borne**

kilo-octet (*pl* **kilo-octets**) [kilɔɔkte] *nm Ordinat* kilobyte

kilovolt [kilɔvolt] *nm* kilovolt

kilowatt [kilɔwat] *nm* kilowatt

kilowattheure [kilɔwatœr] *nm Phys* kilowatt-hour

kilt [kilt] *nm* kilt

kimono [kimono] *nm* kimono

kiné [kine] *Fam* **1** *nmf* (*médecin*) physio

2 *nf* (*discipline*) physio

kinésithérapeute [kineziterapøt] *nmf Br* physiotherapist, *Am* physical therapist

kinésithérapie [kineziterapi] *nf Br* physiotherapy, *Am* physical therapy

Kinshasa [kinʃasa] *n* Kinshasa

kiosque [kjɔsk] *nm* **(a)** (*pavillon*) pavilion; (*point de vente*) kiosk; **k. à journaux** newspaper kiosk, newsstand; **k. à musique** bandstand **(b)** (*sur Minitel®*) **K.®** = service accessible on the Minitel® information network

kippa [kipa] *nf* kippa

kir [kir] *nm* kir

kirghiz, -e [kirgiz] **1** *adj* Kirg(h)iz
2 *nmf* K. Kirg(h)iz
3 *nm (langue)* Kirg(h)iz

Kirghizistan [kirgizistɑ̃] *nm* le K. Kirg(h)izia, Kirg(h)izstan

kirsch [kirʃ] *nm* kirsch

kit [kit] *nm* (self-assembly) kit; **en k.** in kit form; *Ordinat* k. d'extension *ou* d'évolution upgrade kit

kitch [kitʃ] = **kitsch**

kitchenette [kitʃanɛt] *nf* kitchenette

kitsch [kitʃ] *adj inv & nm inv* kitsch

kiwi [kiwi] *nm* **(a)** *(fruit)* kiwi fruit **(b)** *(oiseau)* kiwi

Klaxon® [klaksɔn] *nm* horn; **donner un coup de K.** to sound one's horn

klaxonner [klaksɔne] **1** *vi* to sound one's horn
2 *vt* to sound one's horn at

klebs [klɛps] = **clebs**

Kleenex® [klineks] *nm inv* tissue, Kleenex®

kleptomane [klɛptɔman] *adj & nmf* kleptomaniac

kleptomanie [klɛptɔmani] *nf* kleptomania

km *(abrév* **kilomètre(s))** km

km/h *(abrév* **kilomètres à l'heure, kilomètres-heure)** kph

Ko *nm (abrév* **kilo-octet(s))** K, KB

K-O [kao] **1** *nm inv* knockout
2 *adj inv* **(a)** *(assommé)* knocked out; **mettre qn K.** to knock sb out **(b)** *Fam (fatigué)* shattered

koala [kɔala] *nm* koala (bear)

kopeck [kɔpɛk] *nm* kopeck; *Fam* **ça ne vaut pas un k.** it's not worth a bean

kouglof [kuglɔf] *nm* kugelhopf

Koweït [kɔwɛjt, kɔwɛt] *nm* le K. Kuwait

koweïtien, -enne [kɔwɛjtjɛ̃, kɔwɛtjɛ̃, -ɛn] **1** *adj* Kuwaiti
2 *nm,f* K. Kuwaiti

krach [krak] *nm* k. **(boursier)** (stock market) crash

kraft [kraft] *nm voir* **papier**

Kremlin [krɛmlɛ̃] *nm* le K. the Kremlin

kumquat [kɔmkwat, kumkwat] *nm (fruit)* kumquat

kung-fu [kuŋfu] *nm inv* kung fu

kurde [kyrd] **1** *adj* Kurdish
2 *nmf* K. Kurd
3 *nm (langue)* Kurdish

Kurdistan [kyrdistɑ̃] *nm* le K. Kurdistan

kW *(abrév* **kilowatt(s))** kW

K-way® [kawe] *nm inv* cagoule

kWh *(abrév* **kilowattheure(s))** kWh

kyrielle [kirjɛl] *nf (de mots, de fautes)* string; *(d'insultes)* stream; *(d'enfants)* crowd; **elle a toute une k. d'amis** she has masses of friends

kyste [kist] *nm* cyst

L

L, I [ɛl] *nm inv* L, l

l (*abrév* **litre(s)**) l

l' [l] **1** *art défini voir* **le¹**
2 *pron personnel voir* **le², la²**

la¹ [la] *art défini voir* **le¹**

la² [la]

> **l'** is used before a word beginning with a vowel or h mute.

pron personnel (femme, fille) her; *(chose, idée)* it; *(animal)* her; **je la connais bien** I know her well; **il te la rendra demain** he'll give it back to you tomorrow; **et ta cousine, tu l'as vue?** have you seen your cousin?; **la voilà** here she/it is

la³ *nm inv (note)* A; *(chantée)* la

là [la] **1** *adv* **(a)** *(là-bas)* there; *(ici)* here; **il est là** *(présent)* he's in; *(près d'ici)* he's here; *(là-bas)* he's there; **est-ce que Paul est là?** *(au téléphone)* is Paul there?; **je suis là pour ça** that's what I'm here for; **à quelques mètres de là** a few metres away; **de là à Paris, il n'y a que quelques kilomètres** it's only a few kilometres (away) from Paris; **là en bas/haut** down/up there; **qui va là?** who goes there?
(b) *(à ce point)* **restons-en là** let's leave it at that; **la question n'est pas là** that's not the point; **c'est bien là le problème** that's the problem; **je sais bien qu'il est bizarre mais de là à dire qu'il est fou...** I know he's strange, but to say he's mad...; **je ne vois là aucune raison de s'inquiéter** I can't see any cause for concern; **de là sa réaction** hence his/her reaction
(c) *(avec un relatif)* **c'est là que j'habite** that's where I live; **c'est là que j'ai compris** that's when I understood
(d) ce vin-là that wine; **ces vins-là** those wines
2 *exclam* **oh là là!** my goodness!; **alors là, je n'aurais jamais cru!** I'd never have expected that!

là-bas [laba] *adv* over there; *(dans cette région, dans ce pays)* there

label [label] *nm* **(a)** *Com* quality label **(b)** *Ordinat* **l. de volume** volume label

labeur [labœr] *nm Litt* labour

labo [labo] *nm Fam* lab; **l. photo** darkroom

laborantin, -e [labɔrɑ̃tɛ̃, -in] *nm,f* laboratory assistant

laboratoire [labɔratwar] *nm* laboratory; **l. d'analyses (médicales)** pathology laboratory

laborieusement [labɔrjøzmɑ̃] *adv* laboriously

laborieux, -euse [labɔrjø, -øz] *adj* **(a)** *(difficile)* laborious; *Péj (style)* laboured; *Fam* **il n'a pas encore fini? c'est l.!** hasn't he finished yet? he's making heavy weather of it! **(b)** *Litt* **les masses laborieuses** the toiling masses

labour [labur] *nm* **(a)** *(labourage)* ploughing **(b)** **labours** *(champs)* ploughed land

labourage [laburaʒ] *nm* ploughing

labourer [labure] *vt* **(a)** *(terre)* to plough *Fig (griffer)* to claw; **visage labouré de rides** face furrowed with wrinkles

laboureur [laburœr] *nm* ploughman

labrador [labradɔr] *nm* labrador

labyrinthe [labirɛ̃t] *nm* maze, labyrinth

lac [lak] *nm* lake; **les Grands Lacs** the Great Lakes; **le l. Baïkal** Lake Baikal; **le l. Érié** Lake Erie; **le l. Huron** Lake Huron; **le l. Léman** *ou* **de Genève** Lake Geneva; **le l. Michigan** Lake Michigan; **le l. Ontario** Lake Ontario; **le l. Supérieur** Lake Superior

lacer [16] [lase] **1** *vt (chaussures)* to tie (up); *(corset)* to lace up
2 se lacer *vpr (chaussures)* to tie (up); *(corset)* to lace up

lacérer [34] [lasere] *vt (déchirer)* to tear to shreds; *(blesser)* to lacerate

lacet [lase] *nm* **(a)** *(de chaussure, de corset)* lace; **faire ses lacets** to tie one's laces **(b)** *(tournant)* sharp bend; **faire des lacets** to twist and turn **(c)** *(collet)* snare

lâche [lɑʃ] **1** *adj* **(a)** *(ressort, nœud)* loose; *(vêtement)* loose-fitting; *(discipline)* lax **(b)** *Péj (personne, acte, attitude)* cowardly
2 *nmf* coward

lâchement [lɑʃmɑ̃] *adv (sans courage)* in a cowardly way

lâcher [lɑʃe] **1** *vt* **(a)** *(desserrer) (corde, ceinture)* to loosen **(b)** *(ne plus tenir)* to let go of; *(laisser tomber)* to drop; *Fam Fig (cesser d'importuner)* to leave alone; **l. prise** to let go; *Fam* **il ne m'a pas lâché d'une semelle** he stuck to me like a leech; *Fam* **lâche-moi les baskets** *ou* **la grappe!** get off my back! **(c)** *Fam (abandonner) (associé)* to walk out on; *(ami)* to let down; *(amant)* to chuck, to dump; *(emploi)* to chuck in; **la voiture nous a lâchés** the car died on us **(d)** *(distancer) (poursuivant)* to shake off; *(dans une course)* to leave behind **(e)** *(libérer)* to release; **l. un chien sur qn** to set a dog on sb **(f)** *(laisser échapper) (juron, cri, pet)* to let out; *(sottise, plaisanterie)* to come out with; *Fam* **l. le morceau** to spill the beans
2 *vi (corde, câble)* to break; *(mécanisme, pièce)* to go; *(moteur)* to die; *(freins)* to fail; *Fig* **ses nerfs ont lâché** he/she broke down
3 *nm (de colombes, de ballons)* release

lâcheté [lɑʃte] *nf* cowardice

lâcheur, -euse [lɑʃœr, -øz] *nm,f Fam* unreliable person

lacis [lasi] *nm (de nerfs, de fils)* network; *(de ruelles)* maze

laconique [lakɔnik] *adj* laconic

laconiquement [lakɔnikmɑ̃] *adv* laconically

lacrymal, -e, -aux, -ales [lakrimal, -o] *adj* tear, *Spéc* lachrymal

lacrymogène [lakrimɔʒɛn] *adj voir* **gaz, grenade**

lacté, -e [lakte] *adj* (*produit*) which contains milk; (*régime*) milk

lactique [laktik] *adj Chim* lactic

lactose [laktoz] *nm Chim* lactose

lacune [lakyn] *nf* (*dans une liste, ses connaissances, ses souvenirs*) gap; **avoir des lacunes en qch** to have a patchy knowledge of sth

lacustre [lakystr] *adj* lakeside

lad [lad] *nm* stable lad

là-dedans [ladədã] *adv* inside, in there; **il y a l. quelque chose que je ne comprends pas** there's something here I don't understand; **elle n'a rien à voir l.!** she's got nothing to do with it

là-dessous [latsu] *adv* underneath, under there; *Fig* **il y a quelque chose l.** there's something behind it

là-dessus [latsy] *adv* on there; (*sur ces mots*) with that; **tout le monde est d'accord l.** everybody agrees about it; **c'est l. que tu dois te concentrer** that's what you have to concentrate on

lagon [lagɔ̃] *nm* lagoon

lagopède [lagoped] *nm* **l. d'Écosse** grouse

lagune [lagyn] *nf* lagoon

là-haut [lao] *adv* up there; (*à un étage supérieur*) upstairs

La Havane [laavan] *n* Havana

La Haye [lae] *n* The Hague

laïc [laik] = **laïque**

laïciser [laisize] *vt* to secularize

laïcité [laisite] *nf* (*des écoles*) secularity; *Pol* secularism

laid, -e [lɛ, lɛd] (**a**) *adj* (*personne, visage, bâtiment*) ugly; **l. comme un pou** *ou* **à faire peur** as ugly as sin (**b**) (*langage enfantin*) (*méprisable*) not nice

laideron [lɛdrɔ̃] *nm Péj* (*fille*) ugly girl; (*femme*) ugly woman

laideur [lɛdœr] *nf* (**a**) (*d'une personne, d'un visage, d'un bâtiment*) ugliness (**b**) (*bassesse*) meanness

laie [lɛ] *nf* (*animal*) wild sow

lainage [lɛnaʒ] *nm* (**a**) (*étoffe*) woollen fabric (**b**) (*vêtement en laine*) jumper; **lainages** woollens

laine [lɛn] *nf* (**a**) (*tissu*) wool; **en l.** woollen; **l. d'agneau** lambswool; **l. vierge** new wool; (**en**) **pure l.** pure wool (**b**) (*vêtement*) **mettre une petite l.** to put a woolly on (**c**) **l. de verre** glass wool

laineux, -euse [lɛnø, -øz] *adj* (*tissu*) fleecy; (*mouton, cheveux*) woolly

lainier, -ère [lɛnje, -ɛr] *adj* wool

laïque [laik] 1 *adj* (*État*) secular; (*école, enseignement*) non-religious
2 *nmf* layman, *f* laywoman

laisse [lɛs] *nf* (*pour chien*) lead, leash; **tenir un chien en l.** to keep a dog on a lead

laissé-pour-compte, laissée-pour-compte (*mpl* **laissés-pour-compte**, *fpl* **laissées-pour-compte**) [lesepurkɔ̃t] *nm,f* reject

laisser [lese] 1 *vt* (**a**) (*permettre à*) **l. qn faire qch** to let sb do sth; **laissez-le faire!** leave him alone!; **le toit laissait passer la pluie** the roof let the rain in; **l. sécher la peinture** to let the paint dry; *Fig* **laissez-moi rire!** don't make me laugh!; *aussi Fig* **l. tomber qn/qch** to drop sb/sth; *Fam* **l. courir** to leave things alone; **l. dire** to let people talk; **laisse faire!** never mind!

(**b**) (*quitter*) (*mari, femme*) to leave; **l. qn tout seul** to leave sb all on their own; **bon, je vous laisse!** well, I'll be off; **il a laissé une veuve et trois enfants** he left a widow and three children

(**c**) (*ne pas prendre*) to leave; **l. qch à qn** (*le lui réserver*) to leave sth for sb

(**d**) (*maintenir*) **l. qch ouvert/fermé** to leave sth open/closed

(**e**) (*oublier*) to leave

(**f**) (*traces, impression, souvenir*) to leave

(**g**) (*ne pas s'occuper de*) (*personne*) to leave; **laisse, je m'en occupe** don't bother about that, I'll see to it

(**h**) (*donner*) **l. qch à qn** (*en héritage*) to leave sb sth; (*pour qu'il s'en occupe*) to leave sth to sb; **l. le choix à qn** to give sb a choice; **cela nous laisse le temps de...** that leaves us time to...; **ils ont laissé les enfants à la grand-mère** they left the children with their grandmother; **je vous le laisse pour 100 francs** I'll let you have it for 100 francs

(**i**) (*perdre*) (*fortune, vie, membre*) to lose

(**j**) *Formel* **cela n'a pas laissé de le surprendre** it could not fail to surprise him

2 **se laisser** *vpr* **se l. décourager/embrasser** to let oneself be discouraged/kissed; **ne te laisse pas faire!** don't let him/her walk all over you; **se l. aller** to let oneself go; **se l. aller au découragement** to let oneself get discouraged; **ce vin se laisse boire** this wine is very drinkable; **je me suis laissé dire que...** I hear that...; **se l. vivre** to take life as it comes

laisser-aller [leseale] *nm inv* (*relâchement*) carelessness

laissez-passer [lesepase] *nm inv* pass

lait [lɛ] *nm* (**a**) (*aliment*) milk; **petit l.** whey; *Fig* **boire du petit l.** to lap it up; **l. de brebis/de chèvre/de vache** sheep's/goat's/cow's milk; **l. caillé** curd; **l. condensé** condensed milk; **l. cru** unpasteurized milk; **l. demi-écrémé** semi-skimmed milk; **l. écrémé** skimmed milk; **l. entier** whole milk; **l. longue conservation** long-life milk; **l. maternel** mother's milk; **l. en poudre** powdered milk; **l. de soja** soya milk (**b**) (*cosmétique*) **l. après-soleil** after-sun (lotion); **l. bronzant** suntan lotion; **l. démaquillant** *ou* **de toilette** cleansing lotion

laitage [lɛtaʒ] *nm* dairy product

laitance [lɛtãs] *nf* (*de poisson*) milt; *Culin* soft roe

laiterie [lɛtri] *nf* dairy

laiteux, -euse [lɛtø, -øz] *adj* (*teint*) creamy; (*couleur, lumière*) milky

laitier¹, -ère [lɛtje, -ɛr] 1 *adj* dairy
2 *nm,f* (*livreur*) milkman, *f* milkwoman
3 *nf* **laitière** (*vache*) dairy cow

laitier² *nm Ind* slag

laiton [lɛtɔ̃] *nm* brass

laitue [lɛty] *nf* lettuce

laïus [lajys] *nm* (*discours*) speech

lama¹ [lama] *nm Rel* lama; **le Grand l.** the dalai lama

lama² *nm* (*animal*) llama

lambda [lãbda] *adj inv* (*moyen*) average

lambeau, -x [lãbo] *nm (de tissu, de papier, de viande)* scrap; **vêtements en lambeaux** clothes in tatters; **tomber en lambeaux** to fall to pieces

lambin, -e [lãbɛ̃, -in] *Fam* 1 *adj* slow
2 *nm,f Br* slowcoach, *Am* slowpoke

lambiner [lãbine] *vi Fam* to dawdle

lambris [lãbri] *nm (en bois)* panelling; *(en marbre, en stuc)* lining

lambrissé, -e [lãbrise] *adj (de bois)* panelled; *(de marbre, de stuc)* lined

lambswool [lãbswul] *nm* lambswool; **en l.** lambswool

lame [lam] *nf* **(a)** *(d'épée, de couteau)* blade; *(épée)* sword; *Fig* **une fine l.** a fine swordsman; **visage en l. de couteau** hatchet face; **l. de rasoir** razor blade **(b)** *(bande) (de métal, de verre, de parquet)* strip; *(de store)* slat **(c)** *(vague)* wave; **l. de fond** groundswell

lamé, -e [lame] 1 *adj* lamé; **l. or** gold lamé
2 *nm* lamé; **en l.** lamé

La Mecque [lamɛk] *n* Mecca

lamelle [lamɛl] *nf* **(a)** *(de métal, de verre)* thin strip; *Bot (de champignon)* gill; *Culin* **couper en (fines) lamelles** to cut into (wafer-)thin slices **(b)** *(de microscope)* cover glass

lamentable [lamãtabl] *adj* appalling, awful; *(personne)* hopeless, pathetic

lamentablement [lamãtabləmã] *adv (échouer)* miserably

lamentations [lamãtasjõ] *nfpl* **(a)** *(cris, pleurs)* wailing **(b)** *Péj (plaintes)* moaning, complaining

lamenter [lamãte] **se lamenter** *vpr* to moan; **se l. sur qch** to bemoan sth

laminage [laminaʒ] *nm (du métal)* rolling; **l. à chaud/à froid** hot-/cold-rolling

laminer [lamine] *vt* **(a)** *(métal)* to roll **(b)** *Fig (revenus)* to erode; *(parti politique)* to annihilate

laminoir [laminwar] *nm* rolling mill

lampadaire [lãpadɛr] *nm* **(a)** *(d'intérieur) Br* standard lamp, *Am* floor lamp **(b)** *(réverbère)* lamppost

lampe [lãp] *nf* **(a)** *(appareil d'éclairage)* lamp; **l. à alcool** spirit lamp; **l. de bureau** desk lamp; **l. de chevet** bedside lamp; **l. à pétrole** oil lamp; **l. de poche** *Br* torch, *Am* flashlight **(b)** *Fam* **s'en mettre plein la l.** to have a good blowout

lampée [lãpe] *nf Fam* gulp

lampe-tempête *(pl* **lampes-tempête)** [lãptãpɛt] *nf* hurricane lamp

lampion [lãpjõ] *nm* paper lantern

lampiste [lãpist] *nm (subalterne)* underling

lamproie [lãprwa] *nf* lamprey

lance [lãs] *nf* **(a)** *(pique)* spear **(b)** *(tuyau)* **l. d'incendie** fire hose

lancée [lãse] *nf* **continuer sur sa l.** to keep going; **j'ai fait les exercices 5 et 6, et sur ma l. j'ai aussi fait le 7** I did exercises 5 and 6, and while I was at it I did 7 as well

lance-flammes [lãsflam] *nm inv* flamethrower

lancement [lãsmã] *nm* **(a)** *(d'une fusée, d'un projet, d'un produit)* launch(ing) **(b)** *Ordinat (d'impression)* start; *(de programme)* running

lance-missiles [lãsmisil] *nm inv* missile launcher

lance-pierre *(pl* **lance-pierres)** [lãspjɛr] *nm Br* catapult, *Am* slingshot; *Fam Fig* **manger avec un l.** to wolf one's food down

lancer [16] [lãse] 1 *vt* **(a)** *(projeter)* to throw (**à** to); *(flèche)* to shoot; *(fusée)* to launch; *(bombe)* to drop; *(étincelles)* to shoot out; *Fig (idée, proposition)* to throw out; *(remarque)* to come out with; *(plaisanterie)* to crack; *(juron)* to let out; **l. un coup d'œil à qn** to dart or shoot a glance at sb; **l. le poids** to put the shot
(b) *(envoyer) (signaux de détresse, SOS)* to send out
(c) *(projet, produit, artiste)* to launch; *(mode)* to start; *Fin* **l. un emprunt** to issue a bond
(d) *(faire démarrer) (moteur)* to start (up); **être lancé** *(dans une course, dans un travail)* to have got going; **l. qn sur un sujet** to start sb (off) on a subject
(e) *Ordinat (impression)* to start; *(programme)* to run, to start (up)
2 *nm* **(a)** *(pêche au)* **l.** rod-and-reel fishing
(b) *Sp* **l. du javelot/du disque/du marteau** throwing the javelin/the discus/the hammer; **l. du poids** putting the shot; *(au basket)* free throw
3 **se lancer** *vpr* **(a)** *(se jeter)* **l. dans le vide** to throw oneself off; **se l. en avant** to rush forward; **se l. à la poursuite de qn** to rush off in pursuit of sb
(b) *(s'engager)* **se l. dans** *(affaire, discussion, aventure)* to embark on; *(dépenses)* to get involved in; *(domaine)* to launch out into
(c) *(se faire connaître)* to make a name for oneself

lance-roquettes [lãsrokɛt] *nm inv* rocket launcher

lance-torpilles [lãstɔrpij] *nm inv* torpedo tube

lanceur, -euse [lãsœr, -øz] *nm,f (au cricket)* bowler; *(au base-ball)* pitcher; **l. de javelot/disque/marteau** javelin/discus/hammer thrower; **l. de poids** shot putter

lancinant, -e [lãsinã, -ãt] *adj (douleur)* shooting; *(souvenir, air, musique)* haunting; *(regret)* nagging

landau [lãdo] *nm (voiture d'enfant) Br* pram, *Am* baby carriage

lande [lãd] *nf* moor, heath

langage [lãgaʒ] *nm* **(a)** *(langue, vocabulaire)* language; *Fig* **changer de l.** to change one's tune; **l. chiffré** cipher, code **(b)** *Ordinat* language; **l. de description de page** page description language; **l. d'imprimante par pages** page printer language; **l. d'interrogation** query language; **l. machine** machine language; **l. naturel** natural language; **l. à objets** object-oriented language; **l. de programmation** programming language; **l. utilisateur** user language

lange [lãʒ] *nm (couche) Br* nappy, *Am* diaper; *Vieilli* **langes** swaddling clothes

langer [45] [lãʒe] *vt (mettre une couche à)* to put a *Br* nappy or *Am* diaper on; *Vieilli* to wrap in swaddling clothes

langoureusement [lãgurøzmã] *adv* languorously

langoureux, -euse [lãgurø, -øz] *adj* languorous

langouste [lãgust] *nf* crayfish

langoustine [lãgustin] *nf* Dublin Bay prawn

langue [lãg] *nf* **(a)** *(organe)* tongue; **tirer la l. à qn** to stick one's tongue out at sb; *Fig* **j'ai tiré la l.** *(peiné)* it was hard going; **avoir la l. bien pendue** to have the gift of the gab; **ne pas avoir la l. dans sa poche** never to be at a loss for words; **donner sa l. au chat** to give up; **tu as avalé ou perdu ta l.?** has the cat got your tongue?; *Culin* **l. de bœuf** ox tongue
(b) *(langage, style, jargon)* language; **peuples/pays de l. anglaise** English-speaking people/countries; **parler la l. de bois** to come out with clichés; **l. étrangère** foreign language; **l. maternelle** native language, mother tongue; **l. morte** dead language; **l. d'oc** = medieval French dialect spoken in Southern France; **l. d'oïl** = medieval French

dialect spoken in Northern France; **langues vivantes** (*matière*) modern languages **(c)** (*personne*) une mauvaise l. a backbiter; **une l. de vipère** a spiteful gossip **(d)** (*bande*) l. de terre strip of land

langue-de-chat (*pl* **langues-de-chat**) [lɑ̃gdəʃa] *nf* finger biscuit

languedocien, -enne [lɑ̃gdɔsjɛ̃, -ɛn] **1** *adj* of the Languedoc **2** *nm,f* L. person from the Languedoc

languette [lɑ̃gɛt] *nf* (*de bois, de métal, de chaussure*) tongue

langueur [lɑ̃gœr] *nf* **(a)** (*apathie*) listlessness **(b)** (*mélancolie, rêverie*) languor

languir [lɑ̃gir] *vi* **(a)** *Litt ou Hum* (*dépérir*) to languish **(b)** (*attendre avec impatience*) **ne nous faites pas l.** don't keep us in suspense; *Litt* **l. de faire qch** to long to do sth **(c)** (*conversation*) to be flagging

lanière [lanjɛr] *nf* (*de sac, de sandale*) strap; (*de fouet*) lash; **découper qch en lanières** to cut sth into strips

lanoline [lanɔlin] *nf* lanolin

La Nouvelle-Orléans [lanuvɛlɔrleɑ̃] *n* New Orleans

lanterne [lɑ̃tɛrn] *nf* **(a)** (*lampe*) lantern; *Fig* **éclairer la l. de qn** to enlighten sb; **l. chinoise** Chinese lantern **(b)** (*de véhicule*) *Br* sidelight, *Am* parking light

lanterner [lɑ̃tɛrne] *vi Fam* to dawdle; **faire l. qn** to keep sb hanging about

Laos [laɔs] *nm* le L. Laos

laotien, -enne [laɔsjɛ̃, -ɛn] **1** *adj* Laotian **2** *nm,f* L. Laotian

lapalissade [lapalisad] *nf* statement of the obvious

laper [lape] *vt* to lap up

lapidaire [lapidɛr] *adj* (*style, formule*) concise, succinct

lapidation [lapidasjɔ̃] *nf* stoning

lapider [lapide] *vt* (*mettre à mort*) to stone (to death); *Fig* (*critiquer*) to lambast

lapin [lapɛ̃] *nm* rabbit; **manteau en (peau de) l.** rabbitskin coat; **poser un l. à qn** to stand sb up; **mon petit l.** sweetheart; **l. de garenne** wild rabbit; *Fam* **un chaud l.** a randy devil

lapine [lapin] *nf* doe (rabbit)

lapis [lapis], **lapis-lazuli** [lapislazyli] *nm inv* lapis lazuli

lapon, -one *ou* **-onne** [lapɔ̃, -ɔn] **1** *adj* Lapp **2** *nm,f* L. Lapp, Laplander

Laponie [laponi] *nf* la L. Lapland

laps [laps] *nm* **un l. de temps** a period of time; **un l. de temps de trois heures** a period of three hours

lapsus [lapsys] *nm* (*oral*) slip of the tongue; (*écrit*) slip of the pen; **faire un l.** to make a slip (of the tongue/pen); **un l. révélateur** a Freudian slip

laquais [lakɛ] *nm* footman; *Fig & Péj* lackey

laque [lak] *nf* **(a)** (*vernis*) lacquer **(b)** (*pour les cheveux*) hair spray, lacquer **(c)** (*peinture*) gloss (paint)

laquelle [lakɛl] *voir* **lequel**

laquer [lake] *vt* **(a)** (*vernir*) to lacquer **(b)** (*cheveux*) to lacquer **(c)** (*peindre*) to paint with gloss

larbin [larbɛ̃] *nm Fam* flunkey

larcin [larsɛ̃] *nm* (*vol*) petty theft

lard [lar] *nm* **(a)** (*du porc*) (*viande*) bacon; (*gras*) fat; *Fig* **se demander si c'est du l. ou du cochon** to wonder what to make of it; **l. fumé** smoked bacon; **l. maigre** streaky bacon **(b)** *Fam* (*graisse*) **faire du l.** to sit around and get fat; **rentrer dans le l. à qn** to lay into sb

larder [larde] *vt Culin* to lard; *Fig* **l. qn de coups de couteau** to hack at sb with a knife; **l. un texte de citations** to pepper a text with quotations

lardon [lardɔ̃] *nm* **(a)** *Culin* piece of chopped bacon **(b)** *très Fam* (*enfant*) kid

large [larʒ] **1** *adj* **(a)** (*route, porte, chaussures*) wide; (*vêtement*) loose-fitting; (*visage, nez, geste*) broad; **l. d'épaules** broad-shouldered; **l. de 10 mètres** 10 metres wide; **terme employé dans son sens l.** term used in its broad sense; **avoir l'esprit l., être l. d'esprit** to be broad-minded **(b)** (*considérable*) large; (*ressources*) ample; **dans une l. mesure** to a large extent **(c)** (*généreux*) generous
2 *nm* **(a)** (*espace*) **être au l.** to have plenty of room **(b)** (*haute mer*) open sea; **au l. de** off; **prendre le l.** to take to the open sea; *Fig* (*s'enfuir*) to beat it **(c)** (*largeur*) **faire 10 mètres de l.** to be 10 metres wide
3 *adv* **compter l.** to allow for more

largement [larʒəmɑ̃] *adv* **(a)** (*répandu, critiqué*) widely **(b)** (*abondamment*) (*récompenser, payer, servir*) generously; (*dépasser*) by a long way; **avoir de quoi vivre** to have easily enough to live on; **avoir l. le temps** to have plenty of time; **c'est l. suffisant, ça suffit l.** it's more than enough

largesse [larʒɛs] *nf* **(a)** (*générosité*) generosity (**envers** towards) **(b)** **largesses** (*dons*) generous gifts

largeur [larʒœr] *nf* **(a)** (*dimension*) width, breadth; (*de voie ferrée*) gauge; **en l., dans la l.** widthwise; **les policiers barraient la rue sur toute sa l.** the policemen blocked off the whole width of the street; *Rad* **l. de bande** bandwidth; *Ordinat* **l. de papier** paper width **(b)** *Fig* **l. d'esprit** *ou* **de vues** broadmindedness

largué, -e [large] *adj Fam* (*qui ne comprend plus*) lost

larguer [large] *vt* **(a)** (*amarres*) to cast off; (*cordage*) to loose; (*voile*) to unfurl **(b)** (*par avion*) (*parachutiste, vivres, bombe*) to drop **(c)** *Fam* (*abandonner*) (*personne*) to chuck; **il a tout largué pour partir vivre aux Caraïbes** he chucked everything in and went to live in the Caribbean

larme [larm] *nf* **(a)** (*pleur*) tear; **larmes de joie** tears of joy; **avoir facilement la l. à l'œil** to be easily moved to tears; **avoir les larmes aux yeux** to have tears in one's eyes; **en larmes** in tears; **larmes de crocodile** crocodile tears **(b)** (*petite quantité*) drop

larmoyant, -e [larmwajɑ̃, -ɑ̃t] *adj* **(a)** (*pleurnicheur*) (*voix, ton*) tearful **(b)** *Péj* (*histoire, film, sentimentalité*) mawkish

larmoyer [32] [larmwaje] *vi* **(a)** (*yeux*) to water **(b)** *Péj* (*personne*) to snivel

larron [larɔ̃] *nm* **s'entendre comme larrons en foire** to be as thick as thieves

larve [larv] *nf* **(a)** (*de batracien, de poisson*) larva; (*d'insecte*) grub **(b)** *Fam* (*personne apathique*) wimp

larvé, -e [larve] *adj* (*guerre, conflit*) latent

laryngite [larɛ̃ʒit] *nf Méd* laryngitis

laryngologie [larɛ̃gɔlɔʒi] *nf Méd* laryngology

laryngologiste [larɛ̃gɔlɔʒist], **laryngologue** [larɛ̃gɔlɔg] *nmf Méd* throat specialist, *Spéc* laryngologist

larynx [larɛ̃ks] *nm Anat* larynx

las, lasse [lɑ, lɑs] *adj Litt* weary; **être l. de qch/de faire qch** to be weary of sth/of doing sth

lasagnes [lazaɲ] *nfpl* lasagne

lascar [laskar] *nm Fam* rascal

lascif, -ive [lasif, -iv] *adj* lascivious

lascivement [lasivmã] *adv* lasciviously

laser [lazɛr] *nm* laser

lassant, -e [lɑsɑ̃, -ɑ̃t] *adj* tiresome

lasser [lɑse] **1** *vt* to tire
 2 se lasser *vpr* se **l. (de qch/de faire qch)** to get tired (of sth/of doing sth)

lassitude [lasityd] *nf* weariness

lasso [laso] *nm* lasso; **prendre un animal au l.** to lasso an animal

latent, -e [latɑ̃, -ɑ̃t] *adj* latent; **à l'état l.** latent

latéral, -e, -aux, -ales [lateral, -o] *adj* (*entrée, rue, vent, choc*) side

latéralement [lateralmɑ̃] *adv* (*se déplacer*) sideways; (*être situé*) at the side

latex [latɛks] *nm* latex

latin, -e [latɛ̃, -in] **1** *adj* Latin; (*langue*) Romance
 2 *nm* Latin; **l. de cuisine** dog Latin; *Fig* **j'y perds mon l.** I can't make head or tail of it

latiniste [latinist] *nmf* (*spécialiste*) Latinist; (*étudiant*) Latin student

latino [latino] *nmf Fam* Latino

latino-américain, -e (*mpl* **latino-américains**, *fpl* **latino-américaines**) [latinoamerikɛ̃, -ɛn] **1** *adj* Latin-American
 2 *nm,f* L.-A. Latin-American

latitude [latityd] *nf* (*a*) *Géog* latitude; **à 30° de l. nord** at latitude 30° north; **sous ces latitudes** in these latitudes (*b*) (*liberté*) latitude, scope; **avoir/donner à qn toute l. pour agir** to have/to give sb total freedom of action

latrines [latrin] *nfpl* latrines

latte [lat] *nf* lath; *Fam* **donner un coup de l. à qn** to give sb a kick

lattis [lati] *nm* lathing

laudanum [lodanɔm] *nm* laudanum

lauréat, -e [lɔrea, -at] **1** *adj* (*prize*)winning
 2 *nm,f* (*prize*)winner

laurier [lɔrje] *nm* (*a*) (*plante*) laurel; *Culin* bay leaves (*b*) *Fig* (*gloire*) **lauriers** laurels; **se reposer** *ou* **s'endormir sur ses lauriers** to rest on one's laurels; **être couvert de lauriers** to be covered with glory

laurier-rose (*pl* **lauriers-roses**) [lɔrjeroz] *nm* oleander

lavable [lavabl] *adj* washable; **l. en machine/à la main** machine-/hand-washable

lavabo [lavabo] *nm* (*a*) (*cuvette*) washbasin (*b*) **lavabos** (*toilettes*) toilets

lavage [lavaʒ] *nm* washing; **l. de cerveau** brainwashing; **faire subir un l. de cerveau à qn** to brainwash sb; **faire un l. d'estomac à qn** to pump sb's stomach (out)

lavande [lavɑ̃d] **1** *nf* (*fleur*) lavender; (**eau de**) **l.** lavender water
 2 *adj inv* (**bleu**) **l.** lavender blue

lavandière [lavɑ̃djer] *nf* (*a*) (*blanchisseuse*) washer-woman (*b*) (*oiseau*) wagtail

lave [lav] *nf* lava

lave-autos [lavoto] *nm inv Can* carwash

lave-glace (*pl* **lave-glaces**) [lavglas] *nm Br* windscreen *or Am* windshield washer

lave-linge [lavlɛ̃ʒ] *nm inv* washing machine

lave-mains [lavmɛ̃] *nm inv* handbasin

lavement [lavmɑ̃] *nm* enema

laver [lave] **1** *vt* (*a*) (*nettoyer*) to wash; (*plaie*) to bathe; **l. qch à l'eau froide** to wash sth in cold water; **il faut l. son linge sale en famille** one shouldn't wash one's dirty linen in public (*b*) (*disculper*) **l. qn d'une accusation/de tout soupçon** to clear sb of an accusation/of all suspicion (*c*) (*venger*) **l'affront a été lavé dans le sang** the insult was paid for in blood
 2 se laver *vpr* (*a*) (*se nettoyer*) to wash (oneself), to have a wash; **se l. les dents** to clean *or* brush one's teeth; **se l. les cheveux/les mains** to wash one's hair/one's hands; *Fig* **je m'en lave les mains** I wash my hands of it (*b*) (*pouvoir être lavé*) **se l. à la main/à la machine** to be hand-/machine-washable

laverie [lavri] *nf* **l. automatique** *Br* launderette, *Am* Laundromat®

lavette [lavɛt] *nf* (*a*) (*de vaisselle*) dishcloth (*b*) *Belg & Suisse* (*gant de toilette*) *Br* face cloth, *Am* washcloth (*c*) *Fam* Fig (*homme*) drip

laveur, -euse [lavœr, -øz] *nm,f* washer; **l. de vitres** window cleaner

lave-vaisselle [lavvesɛl] *nm inv* dishwasher

lave-vitre (*pl* **lave-vitres**) [lavvitr] *nm Br* windscreen *or Am* windshield washer

lavis [lavi] *nm* (*a*) (*procédé*) washing (*b*) (*dessin*) wash drawing

lavoir [lavwar] *nm* (*a*) (*établissement*) **l. (public)** (public) washhouse (*b*) (*bassin*) washtub

lavomatic [lavomatik] *nm Br* launderette, *Am* Laundromat®

laxatif, -ive [laksatif, -iv] *adj & nm* laxative

laxisme [laksism] *nm* laxness

laxiste [laksist] **1** *adj* lax
 2 *nmf* lax person

layette [lejɛt] *nf* baby clothes

le¹, la, les [lə, la, le]

 l' is used instead of **le** or **la** before a word beginning with a vowel or h mute.

article défini (*a*) (*pour définir les noms*) the; **le soleil** the sun; **la lune** the moon; **l'étoile** the star; **les planètes** the planets; **le pull que je me suis acheté** the jumper I bought myself; **le Paris de 1900** Paris in 1900, the Paris of 1900; **oh, la jolie robe!** what a lovely dress!; **debout, les enfants!** get up, children!
 (*b*) (*avec des notions ou des généralités*) **le français** French; **la biologie** biology; **l'amour** love; **l'homme et la femme** man and woman; **le chien est l'ami de l'homme** a dog is a man's best friend; **aider les pauvres** to help the poor; **fumer la pipe** to smoke a pipe
 (*c*) (*avec les noms de lieux*) **la France** France; **les États-Unis** the United States; **le mont Blanc** Mont Blanc; **les Alpes** the Alps; **la Seine** the Seine
 (*d*) (*avec les noms de personnes*) **la reine d'Angleterre** the Queen of England; **le roi Henri IV** King Henry IV; **le Docteur Goron** Doctor Goron
 (*e*) (*avec les parties du corps*) **avoir les yeux verts** to have green eyes; **avoir mal à la gorge** to have a sore throat; **hausser les épaules** to shrug one's shoulders; **se**

laver les pieds to wash one's feet

(f) *(avec un adjectif)* **je préfère le rouge** I prefer the red one

(g) *(distributif)* **50 francs le mètre** 50 francs a metre; **35 francs de l'heure** 35 francs an hour

(h) *(dans un complément de temps)* **le dimanche, il ne travaille pas** he doesn't work on Sundays; **il va à l'école le matin** he goes to school in the mornings; **il y fait vraiment froid l'hiver** it's really cold there in the winter; **je n'ai rien mangé de la journée** I haven't eaten all day; **Londres, le 9 novembre 1997** *(dans une lettre)* 9 November 1997; **je suis arrivé le 10** I arrived on the 10th

le²

---

l' is used before a word beginning with a vowel or h mute.

---

pron personnel (a) *(homme, garçon)* him; *(chose, idée)* it; *(animal)* it, him; **elle l'admire** she admires him; **je te le rendrai demain** I'll give it back to you tomorrow; **et lui, tu le connais?** do you know him?; **le voici** here it/he is

(b) *(remplace une proposition)* **elle me l'a dit** she told me; **il me l'a confirmé** he confirmed it

(c) *(remplace un adjectif, un nom)* **est-ce qu'elle est disponible? – oui, je crois qu'elle l'est** is she available? – yes, I think she is; **jaloux, il l'est sans aucun doute** he's undoubtedly jealous; **son frère est médecin, il voudrait l'être aussi** his brother is a doctor and he'd like to be one too

leader [lidœr] *nm* leader

leasing [liziŋ] *nm* leasing; **acheter une auto en l.** to buy a car on a leasing basis

Le Caire [ləkɛr] *n* Cairo

Le Cap [ləkap] *n* Cape Town

lèche [lɛʃ] *nf très Fam* bootlicking; **faire de la l.** to be a bootlicker

lèche-bottes [lɛʃbɔt] *Fam* **1** *adj inv* **elle est l.** she's a bootlicker
2 *nmf inv* bootlicker

lèche-cul [lɛʃky] *nm inv Vulg Br* arse-licker, *Am* brown-nose

lécher [34] [leʃe] **1** *vt* (a) *(avec la langue)* to lick; *Fam* **les bottes à qn** to lick sb's boots (b) *(fignoler)* *(travail, style)* to polish (c) *(effleurer)* *(sujet: vagues)* to lap against; *(sujet: flammes)* to lick
2 se lécher *vpr* **se l. les doigts** to lick one's fingers

lèche-vitrines [lɛʃvitrin] *nm Fam* window-shopping; **faire du l.** to go window-shopping

leçon [ləsɔ̃] *nf* (a) *(cours, contenu)* lesson; **leçons de chant** singing lessons; **l. de choses** general science *(in primary school)*; **l. particulière** private lesson; **le bricolage en dix leçons** DIY in ten easy lessons (b) *(conseil)* **faire la l. à qn** to give sb a lecture; **donner une l. à qn** to teach sb a lesson; **je n'ai pas de l. à recevoir de toi** I don't need your advice; **que cela te serve de l.!** let that be a lesson to you!

lecteur, -trice [lɛktœr, -tris] **1** *nm, f* (a) *(personne qui lit)* reader (b) *(dans l'édition)* (publisher's) reader (c) *Univ* foreign language assistant
2 *nm* *(dispositif)* **l. de cassettes** cassette player; **l. de disques compacts** compact disc player, CD player; **l. optique** optical reader (b) *Ordinat* **l. de** (disquettes) (disk) drive, floppy (disk) drive; **l. de bandes** tape drive *or* reader; **l. de CD-ROM** *ou* **de disque optique** CD-ROM drive; **l. de disque dur** hard disk drive

---

lecteur-encodeur (*pl* **lecteurs-encodeurs**) [lɛktœr-ɑ̃kɔdœr] *nm Ordinat* reader-encoder

lectorat [lɛktɔra] *nm* (a) *Univ* assistantship (b) *(lecteurs)* readership

lecture [lɛktyr] *nf* (a) *(action de lire)* reading; **faire la l. à qn** to read aloud to sb; *Pol* **en deuxième l.** at the second reading (b) *(ce qu'on lit)* reading; **elle m'a apporté de la l.** she brought me something to read, reading; **avoir de mauvaises lectures** to read the wrong things; **livre de l.** reading book (c) *(interprétation)* reading (d) *Ordinat* read(ing); **l. optique** optical reading; **l. au scanneur** scan; **en l. seule** in read-only mode; **l. sur disque** reading to disk

ledit, ladite [lədi, ladit] (*mpl* **lesdits** [ledi], *fpl* **lesdites** [ledit]) *adj* the aforementioned

légal, -e, -aux, -ales [legal, -o] *adj* legal

légalement [legalmɑ̃] *adv* legally

légalisation [legalizasjɔ̃] *nf* legalization; *(de signature)* authentication

légaliser [legalize] *vt* *(rendre légal)* to legalize; *(authentifier)* to authenticate

légalité [legalite] *nf* (a) *(de mesure, décision)* legality (b) *(situation légale)* **la l.** the law; **agir en toute l.** to act within the law

légataire [legater] *nmf* legatee; **l. universel** sole legatee

légendaire [leʒɑ̃dɛr] *adj* legendary

légende [leʒɑ̃d] *nf* (a) *(histoire, fable)* legend; *Fig (mensonge)* fairy tale; **entrer dans la l.** to become a legend (b) *(d'un dessin, d'une photo)* caption; *(d'une carte)* key

léger, -ère [leʒe, -ɛr] **1** *adj* (a) *(de peu de poids)* light; **l. comme une plume** as light as a feather; **avoir le cœur l.** to be light-hearted (b) *(blessure, amélioration, nuance)* slight; *(brise, vin, parfum)* light; *(tabac)* mild; *(thé, café)* weak; **il y a eu quelques blessés légers** some people were slightly injured (c) *(insuffisant)* *(preuves, arguments)* lightweight; *Fam* **ses résultats sont un peu légers** his/her marks are a bit on the low side (d) *(désinvolte)* *(personne)* thoughtless; *(en amour)* fickle; **femme légère** *ou* **de mœurs légères** loose woman
2 *nf* **à la légère** *(agir, parler)* thoughtlessly; **prendre qch à la légère** to make light of sth
3 *adv* **je vais manger l.** I'll have a light meal; **s'habiller l.** to wear light clothes

légèrement [leʒɛrmɑ̃] *adv* (a) *(habillé)* lightly (b) *(un peu)* slightly; **ça sent le moisi** there's a slight smell of mildew; **pourrais-tu baisser le volume?** could you turn the volume down a bit? (c) *(avec désinvolture)* *(agir)* thoughtlessly

légèreté [leʒɛrte] *nf* (a) *(d'un objet, d'un danseur, d'une démarche)* lightness (b) *(faiblesse)* *(d'une blessure, d'une nuance)* slightness (c) *(désinvolture)* thoughtlessness; **avec l.** *(agir, parler)* thoughtlessly (d) *(en amour)* fickleness; *(des mœurs)* looseness

légiférer [34] [leʒifere] *vi* to legislate (**sur** on)

légion [leʒjɔ̃] *nf* legion; *Fig (multitude)* huge number; **ils sont l.** they are legion; **la L. (étrangère)** the Foreign Legion; **la L. d'honneur** the Legion of Honour

légionnaire [leʒjɔnɛr] *nm* (a) *Hist* legionary (b) *(à la Légion étrangère)* legionnaire

légismlateur, -trice [leʒislatœr, -tris] *Jur* **1** *nm, f* legislator
2 *nm* *(corps législatif)* legislature
3 *adj* legislative

législatif, -ive [leʒislatif, -iv] **1** *adj* legislative; **le pouvoir l.** the legislature
2 *nm* **le l.** legislative power
3 *nfpl* **les législatives** the parliamentary elections

législation [leʒislasjɔ̃] *nf* legislation

législature [leʒislatyr] *nf* (a) *(durée)* term of office (b) *(corps)* legislature

légiste [leʒist] *nm* jurist

légitime [leʒitim] *adj* (a) *(légal) (pouvoir, enfant)* legitimate; *(action)* lawful; *(propriétaire)* legal; *(héritier)* rightful (b) *(juste) (récompense, motif, désir)* legitimate (c) *(justifié) (colère, action)* justified; **l. défense** self-defence; **elle était en état de l. défense** she was acting in self-defence

légitimement [leʒitimmɑ̃] *adv* legitimately; *Jur* lawfully

légitimer [leʒitime] *vt* (a) *(enfant, union)* to legitimize (b) *(action, demande)* to justify (c) *(titre, pouvoir)* to recognize

légitimité [leʒitimite] *nf* legitimacy

legs [lɛ, lɛg] *nm* (a) *Jur* legacy, bequest; **faire un l. à qn** to leave sb a legacy (b) *Fig (héritage)* legacy

léguer [34] [lege] *vt* (a) *Jur* to bequeath (à to) (b) *(tradition, qualité)* to pass on (à to)

légume [legym] **1** *nm* (a) *(aliment)* vegetable; **légumes verts** green vegetables, greens; **légumes secs** pulses (b) *Fam Fig (personne végétative)* vegetable
2 *Fam* **grosse l.** bigwig

leitmotiv [lajtmotif, letmotif] *nm* leitmotiv

Léman [lemɑ̃] *nm* **le lac L.** Lake Geneva

lendemain [lɑ̃dmɛ̃] *nm* (a) *(jour suivant)* **le l.** the next day; **le l. matin/soir** the next morning/evening; **le l. de la bataille** the day after the battle (b) *(avenir)* **penser au l.** to think of the future; **des lendemains prometteurs** a promising future; **sans l.** *(succès, aventures)* short-lived (c) *(période qui suit)* **au l. de la guerre/de ce scandale** soon after the war/this scandal

lent, -e [lɑ̃, lɑ̃t] *adj* slow; **être l. à comprendre** to be slow to understand; **avoir l'esprit l.** to be slow-witted

lente [lɑ̃t] *nf* nit

lentement [lɑ̃tmɑ̃] *adv* slowly; **l. mais sûrement** slowly but surely

lenteur [lɑ̃tœr] *nf* slowness; **avec l.** slowly; **les lenteurs de la justice** the slowness of the law

lentille [lɑ̃tij] *nf* (a) *(plante)* lentil; **l. d'eau** duckweed (b) *(en optique)* lens; **lentilles de contact** contact lenses

léopard [leopar] *nm* *(animal)* leopard; *(fourrure)* leopard skin

LEP [ɛləp, lɛp] *nm Anciennement (abrév* **lycée d'enseignement professionnel)** ≃ technical college

lèpre [lɛpr] *nf* leprosy

lépreux, -euse [leprø, -øz] **1** *adj* leprous
2 *nm,f* leper

lequel, laquelle [ləkɛl, lakɛl] *(mpl* **lesquels** [lekɛl], *fpl* **lesquelles** [lekɛl])

lequel and **lesquel(le)s** contract with **à** to form **auquel** and **auxquel(le)s**, and with **de** to form **duquel** and **desquel(le)s**.

1 *pron relatif (personne)* who; *(après une préposition)* whom; *(chose)* which; **l'actrice à laquelle je pense** the actress (that) I'm thinking of *or* of whom I'm thinking; **le stylo avec l. j'écris** the pen I'm writing with *or* with which I'm writing
2 *pron relatif* **j'ai vu mon adversaire, l. adversaire est impressionnant** I've seen his opponent, he's/she's impressive; **auquel cas** in which case
3 *pron interrogatif* which (one)

les [le] **1** *art défini voir* **le**[1]
2 *pron personnel* them; **l. voilà** here they are

lesbienne [lɛsbjɛn] *nf* lesbian

lèse-majesté [lɛzmaʒɛste] *nf inv* high treason, lese-majesty

léser [34] [leze] *vt* (a) *(désavantager) (personne)* to wrong; *(intérêts)* to harm; **la partie lésée** the injured party (b) *Méd* to injure

lésiner [lezine] *vi* to skimp (**sur** on); **ne pas l. sur les moyens** not to spare any expense

lésion [lezjɔ̃] *nf* lesion

lesquels, lesquelles [lekɛl] *voir* **lequel**

lessivable [lesivabl] *adj* washable

lessivage [lesivaʒ] *nm* washing

lessive [lesiv] *nf* (a) *(produit) (en poudre)* washing powder; *(liquide)* liquid detergent (b) *(action de laver)* wash(ing); **faire la l.** to do the washing; **j'ai fait trois lessives ce matin** I've done three washes this morning (c) *(linge propre)* washing

lessivé, -e [lesive] *adj Fam* washed out

lessiver [lesive] *vt* (a) *(nettoyer)* to wash (b) *Fam (fatiguer)* to wear out

lessiveuse [lesivøz] *nf* boiler; *Fam Fig* **en faire une l.** to make a song and dance about it

lest [lɛst] *nm (de bateau, ballon)* ballast; **lâcher du l.** to discharge ballast; *Fig (faire des concessions)* to make concessions

leste [lɛst] *adj* (a) *(agile)* nimble (b) *(grivois)* risqué

lestement [lɛstəmɑ̃] *adv (avec agilité)* nimbly

lester [lɛste] *vt* (a) *(bateau, ballon)* to ballast (b) *Fam (poche, portefeuille)* to stuff

letchi [lɛtʃi] *nm* lychee

léthargie [letarʒi] *nf* lethargy

léthargique [letarʒik] *adj* lethargic

letton, -onne *ou* **-one** [letɔ̃, -ɔn] **1** *adj* Latvian
2 *nm,f* **L.** Latvian
3 *nm (langue)* Latvian

Lettonie [lɛtɔni] *nf* **la L.** Latvia

lettre [lɛtr] *nf* (a) *(de l'alphabet)* letter; **l. majuscule/minuscule** capital/small letter; **écrire qch en toutes lettres** to write sth out in full; **au pied de la l.** literally; **à la l. (suivre, exécuter)** to the letter; **il fut surréaliste avant la l.** he was a surrealist before the word had been invented; **rester l. morte** to remain a dead letter; **gagner ses lettres de noblesse** to prove one's/its worth
(b) *(missive)* letter; **l. de change** bill of exchange; **l. ouverte (à)** open letter (to); **l. recommandée** registered letter; *Fam* **c'est passé comme une l. à la poste** it went off without a hitch; *Fam* **la nouvelle est passée comme une l. à la poste** the news was received without any fuss
(c) **lettres** *(littérature)* literature; *(à l'université)* arts subjects; **homme/femme de lettres** man/woman of

letters; **avoir des lettres** to be well-read; **faculté de lettres** faculty of arts; **lettres classiques** classics; **lettres modernes** *(à l'université)* French

lettré, -e [letre] **1** *adj* well-read
  2 *nm,f* well-read person

leu [lø] *nm* **à la queue l.** in single file

leucémie [løsemi] *nf* leukaemia

leucocyte [løkɔsit] *nm* leucocyte

leur¹, leurs [lœr] **1** *adj possessif* their; **l. chien** *(il y a un chien)* their dog; *(chacun a son chien)* their dogs; **leurs enfants** their children; **l. père et l. mère** their mother and father; **un de leurs amis** one of their friends, a friend of theirs; *Fam* **ils ont eu l. vendredi** they got Friday off
  2 *pron possessif* **le l., la l., les leurs** theirs; *(en insistant)* their own; **ils te prêtent le l.** you can borrow theirs; **ils n'en ont pas besoin, ils ont le l.** they don't need it, they've got their own
  3 *nm* **il faut qu'ils y mettent du l.** they have to do their share
  4 *nmpl* **les leurs** *(leur famille)* their family; **nous serons des leurs ce soir** we'll be joining them tonight

leur² *pron personnel* to them; **donne-l. ta carte de visite** give them your business card; **je le l. ai montré** I showed it to them

leurre [lœr] *nm* **(a)** *(à la chasse)* decoy **(b)** *(illusion)* illusion

leurrer [lœre] **1** *vt (tromper)* to delude
  2 se leurrer *vpr* to delude oneself **(sur** about)

levage [ləvaʒ] *nm* lifting; **appareil de l.** lifting apparatus

levain [ləvɛ̃] *nm* leaven; **pain au/sans l.** leavened/unleavened bread

levant [ləvɑ̃] **1** *adj m* **soleil l.** rising sun; **au soleil l.** at sunrise
  2 *nm* **(a)** *Litt* **le l.** the east **(b) le L.** the Levant

levé, -e [ləve] **1** *adj* **(a)** *(en l'air) (main, poing)* raised **(b)** *(personne, soleil)* up
  2 *nm (de terrain)* survey

levée [ləve] *nf* **(a)** *(d'une interdiction, de sanctions)* lifting; *(d'une adresse)* close; *(d'un siège)* raising; *(de scellés)* breaking **(b)** *(de troupes)* levying **(c)** *(de lettres)* collection **(d)** *(aux cartes)* trick; **faire une l.** to take a trick **(e)** *(remblai)* levee **(f) l. de boucliers** general outcry; **l. du corps** = removal of the coffin; **l. d'écrou** release from prison

lever¹ [46] [ləve] **1** *vt* **(a)** *(objet)* to lift, to raise; **l. son verre (à qn/qch)** to raise one's glass to sb/sth
  (b) *(bras, main, jambe)* to raise, to lift; **l. la tête** to look up; **l. les yeux au ciel** to raise one's eyes to heaven; **l. les bras au ciel** to throw up one's hands; **l. la main sur qn** to raise one's hand to sb; **l. le doigt** to put one's hand up; **il n'a pas levé le petit doigt** he didn't lift a finger; *Fam* **l. le pied** *(ralentir)* to slow down
  (c) *(faire cesser) (embargo, peine, interdiction)* to lift; *(difficulté, doute, ambiguïté)* to remove; *(siège)* to raise; *(séance)* to close **(d)** *(débusquer) (perdrix)* to flush; *très Fam (femme)* to pull; **l. un lièvre** to start a hare; *Fig* to open a can of worms **(e)** *(faire sortir du lit) (enfant, malade)* to get up **(f)** *(collecter) (courrier, impôts)* to collect **(g)** *(enrôler) (troupes, armée)* to raise, to levy **(h)** *(plan)* to draw
  2 *vi* **(a)** *(blé, grain)* to shoot **(b)** *(pâte)* to rise
  3 se lever *vpr* **(a)** *(se mettre debout)* to stand up, to get up; **se l. de sa chaise** to get up from one's chair; **se l. de table** to leave the table
  (b) *(quitter le lit)* to get up; *Fam* **se l. du pied gauche** to

get out of bed on the wrong side
  (c) *(apparaître) (soleil, lune)* to rise; *(vent)* to get up; *(jour)* to break
  (d) *(s'éclaircir) (brouillard, brume)* to lift, to clear
  (e) *(monter) (rideau de théâtre)* to go up, to rise

lever² *nm* **(a)** *(du lit)* getting up; **demain, l. six heures trente** tomorrow, get up six thirty; **au l., buvez un jus d'orange** first thing in the morning, have a drink of orange juice **(b)** *(apparition)* **le l. du jour** daybreak; **le l. du soleil** sunrise **(c) l. de rideau** *(début du spectacle)* curtain up; *(première partie)* curtain raiser **(d)** *(de terrain)* survey

lève-tard [levtar] *nmf inv Fam* late riser

lève-tôt [levto] *nmf inv Fam* early riser

lève-vitre *(pl* **lève-vitres)** [levvitr] *nm* window winder

levier [ləvje] *nm aussi Fig* lever; **faire l.** to act as a lever; **l. de commande** control lever; *Fig* **être aux leviers de commande** to be in control; **l. (de changement) de vitesse** *Br* gear lever, *Am* gearshift

lévitation [levitasjɔ̃] *nf* levitation; **être en l.** to be levitating

lèvre [levr] *nf* **(a)** *(de la bouche)* lip; **un cigare aux lèvres** with a cigar in his mouth; **le sourire aux lèvres** with a smile on her lips; **manger du bout des lèvres** to pick at one's food; **rire du bout des lèvres** to force a laugh; **accepter du bout des lèvres** to accept grudgingly; *Fig* **nous étions tous suspendus à ses lèvres** we were all hanging on her every word **(b)** *(de la vulve)* **lèvres** labia; **les grandes/petites lèvres** the labia majora/minora **(c)** *(bord) (de plaie)* lip; *(de cratère)* rim

levrette [ləvret] *nf* greyhound bitch

lévrier [levrije] *nm* greyhound; **l. afghan** Afghan hound

levure [ləvyr] *nf* yeast; **l. chimique** baking powder

lexical, -e, -aux, -ales [lɛksikal, -o] *adj* lexical

lexicographe [lɛksikɔgraf] *nmf* lexicographer

lexicographie [lɛksikɔgrafi] *nf* lexicography

lexique [lɛksik] *nm* **(a)** *(dictionnaire)* lexicon; *(glossaire)* glossary **(b)** *(mots d'un auteur)* vocabulary

lézard [lezar] *nm* **(a)** *(animal)* lizard; *(cuir)* lizard skin

lézarde [lezard] *nf* crack

lézarder [lezarde] **1** *vt* to crack
  2 *vi Fam* to lounge in the sun
  3 se lézarder *vpr* to crack

liaison [ljezɔ̃] *nf* **(a)** *(dans les transports)* **l. aérienne/maritime/ferroviaire/routière** air/sea/rail/road link; **toutes les liaisons Paris-Téhéran sont suspendues** all services between Paris and Teheran have been suspended **(b)** *Tél* link; **l. radio/téléphonique** radio/telephone link; **l. par satellite** satellite link; **établir une l. radio** to establish radio contact; *Ordinat* **l. par modem** modem link; *Ordinat* **l. spécialisée** dedicated line **(c)** *(entre des personnes)* contact; **assurer la l. entre deux personnes/services** to liaise between two people/departments; **être en l. avec qn** to be in contact with sb; **travailler en l. (étroite) avec qn** to work (closely) with sb **(d)** *(relation amoureuse)* (love) affair **(e)** *(enchaînement logique)* connection **(f)** *Ling* liaison *(sounding of final consonant before initial vowel sound)* **faire la l.** to make the liaison

liane [ljan] *nf* creeper

liant, -e [ljɑ̃, -ɑ̃t] **1** *adj* sociable
  2 *nm Tech* binder

liasse [ljas] *nf (de lettres, papiers)* bundle; *(de billets)* wad

Liban [libɑ̃] nm le L. (the) Lebanon

libanais, -e [libanɛ, -ɛz] 1 adj Lebanese
2 nm,f L. Lebanese; les L. the Lebanese

libations [libasjɔ̃] nfpl libations

libellé [libele] nm wording

libeller [libele] vt (document, acte, contrat) to word; l. un chèque à l'ordre de to make out a cheque to

libellule [libelyl] nf dragonfly

libéral, -e, -aux, -ales [liberal, -o] adj & nm,f liberal

libéralisation [liberalizasjɔ̃] nf liberalization

libéraliser [liberalize] vt to liberalize

libéralisme [liberalism] nm liberalism

libéralité [liberalite] nf (a) (générosité) generosity (b) (cadeau) generous gift; **vivre des libéralités de ses amis** to live off the generosity of one's friends

libérateur, -trice [liberatœr, -tris] 1 adj liberating
2 nm,f liberator

libération [liberasjɔ̃] nf (a) (mise en liberté) (d'un prisonnier) release; (d'un soldat) discharge; l. **conditionnelle** (release on) parole (b) (affranchissement) liberation (c) (fin de l'Occupation) la L. the Liberation (from the Germans in 1944-45) (d) (d'énergie, d'une substance) release

libéré, -e [libere] 1 adj liberated; **jeune homme l. des obligations militaires** young man who has carried out his national service duties
2 nm,f released prisoner

libérer [34] [libere] 1 vt (a) (rendre sa liberté à) (otage, prisonnier) to free, to release; (pays, peuple) to liberate (b) (laisser partir) (élèves, étudiants) to let go; (soldat) to discharge (c) (soulager) l. qn d'un souci ou d'un poids to take a weight off sb's mind (d) (rendre disponible) (appartement, chambre d'hôtel) to vacate (e) (débloquer) (prix) to free; (cran de sûreté) to release; (instincts, passions) to unleash; l. le passage to clear the way (f) (décharger) l. qn de qch (dette) to free sb from sth; (engagement) to release sb from sth (g) (émettre) (substance, énergie) to release
2 se libérer vpr (a) (s'affranchir) to free oneself (de from) (b) (se rendre disponible) je tâcherai de me l. ce jour-là I'll try and be free that day; je n'ai pas pu me l. plus tôt I couldn't get away any earlier; il y a un poste qui vient de se l. a job vacancy has just come up

Liberia [liberja] nm le L. Liberia

libérien, -enne [liberjɛ̃, -ɛn] 1 adj Liberian
2 nm,f L. Liberian

libertaire [libertɛr] adj & nmf libertarian

liberté [liberte] nf (a) (condition) freedom, liberty; **en l.** (fugitif) at large; (animal) in the wild; **rendre sa l. à qn/un animal** to let sb/an animal go; **reprendre sa l.** to regain one's freedom; **mettre qn en l.** to set sb free; **(mise en) l. provisoire** ou **sous caution** (release on) bail; l. **conditionnelle** parole; l. **surveillée** probation; **mettre qn en l. provisoire/conditionnelle/ surveillée** to release sb on bail/parole/probation
(b) (droit de l'individu) freedom, liberty; l., **égalité, fraternité** liberty, equality, fraternity; l. **d'expression** freedom of expression or speech; l. **d'opinion** freedom of opinion; l. **de la presse** freedom of the press
(c) (absence de contrainte) freedom; l. **d'entreprise** free enterprise; **avoir toute l. d'action** to have complete freedom of action; **avoir toute l. pour faire qch** to have complete freedom to do sth; **en toute l.** (s'exprimer, agir) freely; **prendre la l. de faire qch** to take the liberty of doing sth

(d) (familiarités) **prendre** ou **se permettre des libertés avec** to take liberties with

libertin, -e [libertɛ̃, -in] 1 adj (personne) dissolute; (livre, propos) licentious
2 nm,f libertine

libertinage [libertinaʒ] nm licentiousness

libidineux, -euse [libidinø, -øz] adj lustful

libido [libido] nf libido

libraire [librɛr] nmf bookseller

librairie [librɛri] nf (magasin) bookshop; (activité) bookselling

librairie-papeterie (pl **librairies-papeteries**) [libreripaptri] nf bookshop and stationer's

libre [libr] adj (a) (non soumis) (personne, pays) free; **être l. de faire qch** to be free to do sth; l. **à vous de le faire** you're quite at liberty to do it; **donner l. cours à son enthousiasme/son imagination** to give one's enthusiasm/imagination free rein; l. **de** (souci, contrainte, préjugé) free from; l. **arbitre** free will; l. **pensée** free thinking; l. **penseur** free thinker
(b) (disponible) (personne, siège) free; (appartement, chambre) available; (toilettes) vacant; **je n'ai pas eu une minute de l. aujourd'hui** I haven't had a spare minute today; **être l. comme l'air** to be as free as a bird; **avoir les mains libres** to have one's hands free; Fig to have a free hand; l. **de suite** (dans une annonce) available immediately; **la ligne n'est pas l.** the line's Br engaged or Am busy
(c) (non bloqué) (route) clear; Fig **la voie est l.** the coast is clear
(d) (privé) **enseignement/école l.** independent Catholic education/school; **radio l.** independent radio
(e) (non réglementé) (prix) free; (honoraires) unrestricted; **la l. entreprise** free enterprise; **il pratique des honoraires libres** there are no restrictions on his fees

libre-échange [librēʃɑ̃ʒ] nm free trade

librement [librəmɑ̃] adv freely

libre-service (pl **libres-services**) [librəsɛrvis] nm (a) (principe) self-service; **station-service en l.** self-service Br petrol or Am gas station (b) (magasin) self-service shop; (restaurant) self-service restaurant

Libreville [librəvil] n Libreville

Libye [libi] nf la L. Libya

libyen, -enne [libjɛ̃, -ɛn] 1 adj Libyan
2 nm,f L. Libyan

lice [lis] nf **entrer en l.** to enter the fray

licence [lisɑ̃s] nf (a) Univ (bachelor's) degree; l. **ès** ou **de lettres/ès** ou **de sciences/en droit** arts/science/law degree; **faire une l.** to do a degree (b) (dans le commerce) licence (c) Sp permit (giving right of entry into competition) (d) (liberté) licence; l. **poétique** poetic licence (e) (dérèglement) licentiousness

licencié, -e [lisɑ̃sje] nm,f (a) Univ l. **ès lettres/ès** ou **en sciences/en droit** arts/science/law graduate (b) Sp permit holder

licenciement [lisɑ̃simɑ̃] nm (pour raisons économiques) redundancy; (pour faute professionnelle) dismissal; l. **collectif** mass redundancies; l. **économique** redundancy

licencier [66] [lisɑ̃sje] vt (pour raisons économiques) to make redundant; (pour faute professionnelle) to dismiss

lichen [liken] nm lichen

lichette [liʃɛt] nf Fam (de pain, fromage) tiny bit

licol [likɔl] nm halter

licorne [likɔrn] *nf* unicorn

licou [liku] *nm* halter

LICRA [likra] *nf* (*abrév* **Ligue internationale contre le racisme et l'antisémitisme**) = anti-racist movement

lie [li] *nf* dregs; *Fig* **la l. de la société** the dregs of society

lié, -e [lje] *adj* (a) (*attaché*) bound; **avoir les mains liées** to have one's hands tied; *Fig* **j'ai les mains liées** my hands are tied; *Fig* **être pieds et poings liés** to be bound hand and foot (b) (*en relation étroite*) **être (très) l. avec qn** to be (great) friends with sb

liège [ljɛʒ] *nm* cork; **bouchon de l.** cork

liégeois, -e [ljeʒwa, -az] **1** *adj* (a) of Liège (b) *Culin* **café/chocolat l.** coffee/chocolate ice cream topped with crème Chantilly

2 *nm,f* L. person from Liège

lien [ljɛ̃] *nm* (a) (*attache*) bond; *aussi Fig* **se libérer de ses liens** to free oneself from one's bonds (b) (*relation*) link, connection; **l. de parenté** *ou* **de famille** family relationship; **il y a un l. de parenté entre ces deux familles** the two families are related; **les liens du mariage** the bonds of marriage; **l. d'amitié** bond of friendship (c) *Ordinat* **l. hypertexte** hypertext link

lier [66] [lje] **1** *vt* (a) (*attacher*) to tie up; (*sujet: contrat, serment*) to be binding on (b) (*unir*) (*personnes*) to bind together (c) (*établir un rapport entre*) (*événements, paragraphes*) to connect, to link; **tout est lié** everything's connected (d) *Culin* (*sauce*) to thicken (e) **l. amitié/conversation avec qn** to strike up a friendship/conversation with sb

2 se lier *vpr* **se l. (d'amitié) avec qn** to strike up a friendship with sb

lierre [ljɛr] *nm* ivy

liesse [ljɛs] *nf* jubilation; **en l.** jubilant

lieu¹, -x [ljø] *nm* (a) (*endroit*) place; **en l. sûr** in a safe place; **un l. de passage** a busy place; **les lieux** (*local*) the premises; (*d'un accident, d'un crime*) the scene; **quitter les lieux** to vacate the premises; **un haut l. de** a mecca for; **en haut l.** in high places; **l. de naissance** place of birth; **l. de perdition** den of vice; **l. public** public place; **l. de rendez-vous** meeting place; **l. saint** holy place (b) (*pour indiquer un ordre*) **en premier l.** in the first place; **en dernier l.** last(ly) (c) **l. commun** commonplace (d) (*locutions*) **avoir l.** to take place; **il y a l. de supposer que...** there is reason to suppose that...; **il n'y a pas l. de s'inquiéter** there's no need to worry; **s'il y a l.** if necessary; **donner l. à qch** to give rise to sth; **tenir l. de qch** to take the place of sth; **au l. de** instead of; **au l. de te plaindre** instead of complaining; **au l. de cela** instead

lieu², -x (*pl* **lieus**) *nm* (*poisson*) **l. jaune** pollack; **l. noir** coalfish

lieu-dit (*pl* **lieux-dits**) [ljødi] *nm* locality

lieue [ljø] *nf* league; *Naut* **l. marine** marine league; **j'étais à cent** *ou* **mille lieues de penser que...** I never dreamt for a single moment that...

lieutenant [ljøtnɑ̃] *nm* (*dans l'armée de terre*) lieutenant; (*dans l'armée de l'air*) Br flying officer, Am first lieutenant; (*dans la marine marchande*) mate

lieutenant-colonel (*pl* **lieutenants-colonels**) [ljøtnɑ̃kɔlɔnɛl] *nm* (*dans l'armée de terre*) lieutenant-colonel; (*dans l'armée de l'air*) Br wing commander, Am lieutenant-colonel

lièvre [ljɛvr] *nm* hare; **courir deux lièvres à la fois** to try to do two things at once

lifter [lifte] *vt* (*balle*) to put topspin on

liftier, -ère [liftje, -ɛr] *nm,f* Br lift attendant, Am elevator operator

lifting [liftiŋ] *nm* face lift

ligament [ligamɑ̃] *nm* ligament

ligature [ligatyr] *nf* Méd ligature; **l. des trompes** tying of tubes

ligaturer [ligatyre] *vt* Méd to ligature

ligne [liɲ] *nf* (a) (*trait*) line; **l. droite** straight line; **lire les lignes de la main à qn** to read sb's palm; **l. d'arrivée** finishing line; **l. blanche** (*sur la route*) Br white line, Am yellow line; **l. continue** (*sur la route*) continuous line; **l. de démarcation** demarcation line; **l. de départ** starting line; **l. discontinue** (*sur la route*) broken line; **l. de flottaison** waterline; **l. d'horizon** horizon; **l. jaune** (*sur la route*) Br white line, Am yellow line; **l. de mire** line of sight; **l. de mire** to have **l. de mire** to have sb in one's sights; **l. de touche** touchline

(b) (*d'écriture*) line; **lire entre les lignes** to read between the lines; **aller à la l.** to begin a new paragraph; **à la l.** (*en dictant*) new paragraph; *Fig* **entrer en l. de compte** to be taken into consideration

(c) (*contour, silhouette, de voiture, d'objet*) line; (*de personne*) figure; **avoir la l.** to have a good figure

(d) (*rangée*) line; **se mettre en l.** to line up; *Mil & Fig* **en première l.** in the front line; *Mil* **les lignes ennemies** the enemy lines; *Fig* **sur toute la l.** completely

(e) (*orientation*) line; **l. d'action/de conduite** line of action/conduct; **la l. du parti** the party line; **l. directrice** guideline

(f) (*dans les transports*) **l. de chemin de fer** Br railway *or* Am railroad line; **grandes lignes** main lines; **l. maritime/aérienne** shipping/air route; **l. d'autobus** bus service; (*parcours*) bus route; **lignes de banlieue** suburban lines; **l. de métro** Br underground *or* Am subway line

(g) *Él* **l. électrique** power line; **l. à haute tension** high tension line

(h) *Tél* **l. (téléphonique)** (telephone) line; **rappelez plus tard, elle est en l.** call back later, her line's Br engaged *or* Am busy; **vous êtes en l.** you're through; **l. extérieure** outside line

(i) (*fil*) line; (*de pêche*) (fishing) line

(j) (*de produits*) line, range

(k) (*filiation*) **descendre en l. directe** *ou* **en droite l. de...** to be directly descended from...

(l) *Ordinat* **en l.** on line; **hors l.** off line; **changer de l.** to do a line feed; **l. d'état** status line

lignée [liɲe] *nf* descendants; *Fig* **dans la l. de** in the tradition of

lignite [liɲit] *nm* lignite

ligoter [ligɔte] *vt* to tie up (à to)

ligue [lig] *nf* league

liguer [lige] **1** *vt* **être ligués contre** to be lined up against

2 se liguer *vpr* (*États*) to form a league (**avec/contre** with/against); (*personnes*) to gang up (**avec/contre** with/against)

lilas [lila] *nm & adj inv* lilac

lilliputien, -enne [lilipysjɛ̃, -ɛn] *adj* (*minuscule*) Lilliputian

Lima [lima] *n* Lima

limace [limas] *nf* slug; *Fam (personne lente) Br* slowcoach, *Am* slowpoke

limaille [limaj] *nf* filings

limande [limɑ̃d] *nf* dab; **l.-sole** lemon sole

lime [lim] *nf (outil)* file; **l. à ongles** nail file

limer [lime] **1** *vt* to file; *(barreaux de cellule)* to file through **2 se limer** *vpr* **se l. les ongles** to file one's nails

limier [limje] *nm (chien)* bloodhound; *Fig* sleuth; **un l.** a supersleuth

limitatif, -ive [limitatif, -iv] *adj* restrictive

limitation [limitasjɔ̃] *nf* limitation; **l. des naissances** birth control; **l. de vitesse** speed limit

limite [limit] **1** *nf (a) (frontière)* boundary **(b)** *(maximum)* limit; **ma patience a des limites!** there are limits to my patience!; **mettre une l./des limites à qch** to set a limit/limits to sth; **c'est à la l. de la vulgarité/du supportable** it's bordering on vulgarity/the unacceptable; **dans la l. des stocks disponibles** while stocks last; **à la l., on pourrait changer d'hôtel** if it came to it, we could change hotels; **sans limites** unbounded, limitless
2 *adj* **cas l.** borderline case; **vitesse l.** maximum speed; *Fam* **je ne lui ai pas mis une claque, mais c'était l.** I didn't slap him, but it was touch and go; *Fam* **je suis un peu l. financièrement** I'm a bit short of cash

limité, -e [limite] *adj (réduit)* limited; *Fam Péj (obtus)* thick

limiter [limite] **1** *vt (a) (délimiter) (pays, territoire)* to bound **(b)** *(restreindre)* to limit, to restrict (à to); **l. les dégâts** to limit the damage
2 se limiter *vpr (personne)* to limit oneself; **se l. à qch/à faire qch** *(personne)* to limit or restrict oneself to sth/to doing sth; **son œuvre se limite à quelques essais** his works amount to no more than a few essays

limitrophe [limitrɔf] *adj* neighbouring; **être l. de** *(pays)* to border on; *(région)* to adjoin

limogeage [limɔʒaʒ] *nm* dismissal

limoger [45] [limɔʒe] *vt* to dismiss

limon [limɔ̃] *nm (alluvions)* silt

limonade [limɔnad] *nf (boisson gazeuse)* lemonade

limousine [limuzin] *nf* limousine

limpide [lɛ̃pid] *adj (eau, diamant, regard)* limpid; *(explication)* lucid

limpidité [lɛ̃pidite] *nf (de l'eau, d'un diamant, d'un regard)* limpidity; *(d'une explication)* lucidity

lin [lɛ̃] *nm (a) (tissu)* linen **(b)** *(plante)* flax

linceul [lɛ̃sœl] *nm* shroud

linéaire [lineɛr] *adj* **1 (a)** *(récit) & Math* linear **(b)** *(dessin)* line
2 *nm (dans un magasin)* shelf space

linge [lɛ̃ʒ] *nm (a) (draps, serviettes, nappes)* linen; **l. de maison** household linen; **l. de table** table linen **(b)** *(lessive)* washing **(c)** *(dessous)* **l. (de corps)** underwear; *Fam Fig* **du beau l.** top-drawer people **(d)** *(morceau de tissu)* cloth

lingerie [lɛ̃ʒri] *nf (a) (dessous)* underwear, lingerie **(b)** *(pièce)* linen room

lingot [lɛ̃go] *nm (de métal)* ingot; **l. (d'or)** gold bar or ingot

linguiste [lɛ̃gɥist] *nmf* linguist

linguistique [lɛ̃gɥistik] **1** *adj* linguistic
2 *nf* linguistics *(singulier)*

lino [lino] *nm Fam* lino

linoléum [linɔleɔm] *nm* linoleum

linotte [linɔt] *nf voir* **tête**

linteau, -x [lɛ̃to] *nm Constr* lintel

lion [ljɔ̃] *nm (a) (animal)* lion; **tourner comme un l. en cage** to prowl around **(b)** *Astron & Astrol* **le L.** Leo; **être L.** to be (a) Leo

lionceau, -x [ljɔ̃so] *nm* lion cub

lionne [ljɔn] *nf* lioness

lipide [lipid] *nm* lipid

liposome [lipozom] *nm Chim* liposome

liposuccion [liposysjɔ̃] *nf* liposuction

liquéfaction [likefaksjɔ̃] *nf* liquefaction

liquéfier [66] [likefje] **1** *vt* to liquefy
2 se liquéfier *vpr* to liquefy

liquette [liket] *nf* grandad shirt

liqueur [likœr] *nf (a) (spiritueux)* liqueur **(b)** *Can* **l. (douce)** soft drink

liquidation [likidasjɔ̃] *nf (a) Jur* liquidation; **l. judiciaire** official receivership **(b)** *(d'une dette, en Bourse)* settlement **(c)** *Com (de stocks)* selling off; **l. totale** *(sur une vitrine)* stock clearance **(d)** *Fam (meurtre)* liquidation

liquide [likid] **1** *adj (non solide)* liquid; *(trop fluide)* thin
2 *nm (a) (substance)* liquid, fluid; **l. correcteur** correction fluid; **l. de frein** brake fluid; **l. vaisselle** washing-up liquid **(b)** *(espèces)* cash; **payer en l.** to pay cash

liquider [likide] *vt (a) Jur (affaire)* to liquidate **(b)** *Fin (dette)* to settle **(c)** *Fam (tuer)* to liquidate **(d)** *Fam (travail, restes, bouteille)* to polish off **(e)** *(stocks)* to sell off; **on liquide** *(sur une vitrine)* stock clearance

liquidités [likidite] *nfpl Fin* liquid assets

liquoreux, -euse [likorø, -øz] *adj (vin)* syrupy

lire¹ [44] [lir] **1** *vt (a) (déchiffrer, interpréter)* to read; **l. qch à qn** to read sth to sb; **lu et approuvé** read and approved; **l. dans les pensées de qn** to read sb's thoughts **(b)** *Fig (deviner) (sur un visage, dans un regard)* to read
2 se lire *vpr (se deviner)* to show

lire² *nf (monnaie)* lira

lis [lis] *nm* lily; **l. blanc** white lily

lisais *etc voir* **lire**

Lisbonne [lizbɔn] *n* Lisbon

lise *etc voir* **lire**

liseré [lizre], **liséré** [lizere] *nm* border, edging

liseron [lizrɔ̃] *nm* bindweed, convolvulus

lisibilité [lizibilite] *nf (d'une écriture)* legibility; *(d'un roman, d'un fichier informatique)* readability

lisible [lizibl] *adj (écriture)* legible; *(roman, fichier informatique)* readable

lisiblement [lizibləmɑ̃] *adv* legibly

lisière [lizjɛr] *nf (d'un champ, d'une forêt)* edge

lisiez *etc voir* **lire**

lissage [lisaʒ] *nm Ordinat* **l. de courbes/des caractères** curve/character smoothing

lisse [lis] *adj (surface, peau, eau)* smooth; *(pneu)* bald; *(cheveux)* sleek

lisser [lise] *vt (cheveux)* to smooth down; *(vêtement)* to smooth out; *(sujet: oiseau) (plumes)* to preen

liste [list] *nf* list; **l. d'attente** waiting list; **l. électorale** electoral roll; *Ordinat* **l. de fichiers à imprimer** print list, print queue; **l. de mariage** wedding list; **l. noire** blacklist; **être sur (la) l. rouge** *(du téléphone) Br* to be ex-directory, *Am* to be unlisted

listing [listiŋ] *nm Ordinat* listing, printout

lit [li] *nm* (a) *(meuble)* bed; **être au l.** to be in bed; **aller au l.** to go to bed; **mettre qn au lit** to put sb to bed; **au l., les enfants!** bedtime, children!; **faire son l.** to make one's bed; **faire l. à part** to sleep in separate beds; **enfant d'un premier l.** child from a first marriage; **l. à baldaquin** four-poster (bed); **l. de camp** *Br* camp bed, *Am* cot; **l. conjugal** marital bed; **grand l.** double bed; **l. d'enfant** *Br* cot, *Am* crib; **lits jumeaux** twin beds; **être sur son l. de mort** to be on one's death bed; **une place/deux places** single/double bed; **lits superposés** bunk beds (b) *(couche) (d'argile, de pierres)* bed, layer; *Culin* **bed** (c) *(de rivière)* bed; **sortir de son l.** to burst its banks

litanie [litani] *nf aussi Fig* litany

litchi [litʃi] *nm* lychee

literie [litri] *nf* bedding

lithium [litjɔm] *nm Chim* lithium

lithographie [litɔgrafi] *nf* (a) *(technique)* lithography (b) *(œuvre)* lithograph

litière [litjɛr] *nf* (a) *(pour cheval, pour chat)* litter (b) *(palanquin)* litter

litige [litiʒ] *nm (conflit)* dispute; *(procès)* lawsuit

litigieux, -euse [litiʒjø, -øz] *adj (question, cas)* contentious

litote [litɔt] *nf* understatement, *Spéc* litotes

litre [litr] *nm* litre

litron [litrɔ̃] *nm Fam* bottle of wine

littéraire [literɛr] **1** *adj* literary
2 *nmf* (a) *(doué pour la littérature)* literary person (b) *(étudiant)* student of literature

littéral, -e, -aux, -ales [literal, -o] *adj (traduction, sens)* literal

littéralement [literalmɑ̃] *adv* literally

littérature [literatyr] *nf (œuvres, documentation)* literature; *(métier)* writing

littoral, -e, -aux, -ales [litoral, -o] **1** *adj* coastal
2 *nm* coast(line)

Lituanie [lituani] *nf* **la L.** Lithuania

lituanien, -enne [lituanjɛ̃, -ɛn] **1** *adj* Lithuanian
2 *nm,f* **L.** Lithuanian
3 *nm (langue)* Lithuanian

liturgie [lityrʒi] *nf* liturgy

liturgique [lityrʒik] *adj* liturgical

livide [livid] *adj (pâle)* pallid

living [liviŋ], **living-room** *(pl* **living-rooms)** [liviŋrum] *nm Vieilli* living room

livraison [livrɛzɔ̃] *nf* (a) *(de marchandises)* delivery; **payable à la l.** payable on delivery; **faire la l. de pain/ journaux** to deliver the bread/the newspapers; **prendre l. de qch** to take delivery of sth; **l. à domicile** home delivery (b) *(d'ouvrage publié en fascicules)* part

livre[1] [livr] *nm* (a) *(ouvrage, partie d'un ouvrage)* book; **l. d'histoire/d'anglais** history/English book; **l. de chevet** bedside book; **l. de classe** *ou* **scolaire** schoolbook; **l. de cuisine** *ou* **de recettes** cookery book, cookbook; **l. pour enfants** children's book; **l. d'images** picture book; **l. de poche** paperback; **l. de prières** prayer book (b) *(édition)* **l'industrie du l.** the book trade (c) *(registre)* **l. de bord** *Naut* log(book); *Scol* (teacher's) record book; **l. de comptes** account book; **l. d'or** visitors' book; **grand l.** ledger

livre[2] *nf* (a) *(unité de poids)* half kilo, $\simeq$ pound; *Can* pound (b) *(monnaie)* **l. (sterling)** pound (sterling); **l. irlandaise** Irish pound, punt

livre-cassette *(pl* **livres-cassettes)** [livrəkaset] *nm* audio book

livrée [livre] *nf (de domestique)* livery

livrer [livre] **1** *vt* **a** *(marchandises)* to deliver; **nous livrons à domicile** we deliver; **vous serez livré dès demain** you'll receive delivery tomorrow (b) *(abandonner)* **l. un village au pillage/un pays à l'anarchie** to abandon a village to pillage/a country to anarchy; **livré à soi-même** left to oneself (c) *(remettre)* **l. qn à qn** *(coupable, complice)* to hand sb over to sb; **l. un secret à qn** to reveal a secret to sb (d) *(locutions)* **l. bataille** to join battle; **l. passage à qn** to let sb pass
2 se livrer *vpr* (a) *(se rendre)* to give oneself up (à to) (b) *(se confier)* to open up; **se l. à qn** to confide in sb (c) *(s'abandonner)* **se l. à qch** *(vice, spéculations)* to indulge in sth; *(désespoir)* to give way to sth (d) *(s'occuper)* **se l. à qch** *(occupations, recherches)* to be engaged in sth; *(étude, lecture)* to devote oneself to sth

livret [livre] *nm* (a) *(petit livre)* booklet; **l. (de caisse) d'épargne** bankbook, passbook; **l. de famille** family record book *(for registration of births and deaths)*; **l. militaire** service record; **l. scolaire** (school) report book (b) *Mus (d'opéra)* libretto

livreur, -euse [livrœr, -øz] *nm,f* delivery man, *f* delivery woman

lob [lɔb] *nm* lob; **faire un l.** to hit a lob

lobe [lɔb] *nm* (a) *Anat & Bot* lobe (b) *Archit* foil

lober [lɔbe] *vt & vi* to lob

lobotomie [lɔbɔtɔmi] *nf Méd* lobotomy

local, -e, -aux, -ales [lɔkal, -o] **1** *adj aussi Méd* local; *(averses)* scattered
2 *nm* (a) *(lieu) (de société, d'organisation)* premises; *(sans usage précis)* place; **locaux commerciaux** business premises (b) *Can Tél* extension

localement [lɔkalmɑ̃] *adv* locally

localisation [lɔkalizasjɔ̃] *nf (repérage)* location; *(d'un appel téléphonique)* tracing

localisé, -e [lɔkalize] *adj (circonscrit)* localized

localiser [lɔkalize] *vt (repérer) (bruit, gène, personne)* to locate; *(appel téléphonique)* to trace

localité [lɔkalite] *nf (ville)* town; *(village)* village

locataire [lɔkatɛr] *nmf* tenant; *(chez le propriétaire)* lodger

locatif, -ive [lɔkatif, -iv] *adj voir* **charge**

location [lɔkasjɔ̃] *nf* (a) *(de voiture, d'équipement, de costume) (par le locataire)* renting, *Br* hiring; *(par le propriétaire)* renting out, *Br* hiring out; **prendre qch en l.** to rent sth, *Br* to hire sth; **donner qch en l.** to rent sth out, *Br* to hire sth out; **l. de voitures** car rental, *Br* car hire (b) *(de logement) (par le locataire)* renting; *(par le propriétaire)* renting out, *Br* letting (out) (c) *(appartement, maison)* rented accommodation (d) *(de places de spectacle)* booking

location-vente *(pl* **locations-ventes)** [lɔkasjɔ̃vɑ̃t] *nf Br* hire purchase, *Am* installment plan

loche [lɔʃ] *nf (poisson)* loach

locomoteur, -trice [lɔkɔmɔtœr, -tris] *adj* locomotor

locomotion [lɔkɔmɔsjɔ̃] *nf* locomotion; **moyen de l.** means of transport

locomotive [lɔkɔmɔtiv] *nf* (a) *(de train)* locomotive, engine; l. **à vapeur** steam engine (b) *Fig (leader)* pacemaker

locuteur, -trice [lɔkytœr, -tris] *nm,f Ling* speaker

locution [lɔkysjɔ̃] *nf* expression, phrase

loft [lɔft] *nm* converted loft

logarithme [lɔgaritm] *nm* logarithm

loge [lɔʒ] *nf* (a) *(d'artiste)* dressing room (b) *(sièges)* box; *Fig* **être aux premières loges** to have a ringside seat (c) *(maçonnique, de concierge)* lodge

logement [lɔʒmɑ̃] *nm* (a) *(habitation)* accommodation; *(maison)* house; *(appartement)* *Br* flat, *Am* apartment; l. **de fonction** accommodation that goes with the job; **logements sociaux** *Br* ≃ council flats, *Am* ≃ low rent housing (b) *(action)* housing; **la crise du l.** the housing shortage

loger [45] [lɔʒe] **1** *vi (en permanence)* to live; *(temporairement)* to stay; l. **chez l'habitant** *(en vacances)* to stay in a private house
2 *vt* (a) *(héberger)* to put up; **être logé et nourri** to have board and lodging (b) *(contenir) (sujet: hôtel, maison)* to accommodate (c) *(placer)* to put
3 se loger *vpr* (a) *(trouver à)* **se l.** *(permanent)* to find somewhere to live; *(temporaire)* to find accommodation (b) *(se placer)* to lodge itself

logeur, -euse [lɔʒœr, -øz] *nm,f* landlord, *f* landlady *(of furnished apartments)*

loggia [lɔdʒja] *nf Archit* loggia

logiciel [lɔʒisjɛl] *nm Ordinat* software; **un l.** a software package, a package; l. **d'application** application software; l. **bureautique** business software (package); l. **de communication** communications package, comms package, communications software; l. **de compression de données** data compression software; l. **de comptabilité** accounts package, accounts software; l. **de décompression** decompression software, decompressor; l. **de dessin** art package, drawing program; l. **d'exploitation** operating system software; l. **grapheur** graphics package, graphics software; l. **de jeu** games software; l. **de mise en page** desktop publishing package; l. **public** freeware; l. **de reconnaissance de caractères** OCR software, character recognition software; l. **de reconnaissance vocale** voice recognition software; l. **de réseau** network software; l. **de SGBD** DBMS software; l. **de télémaintenance** remote access software; **logiciels de traitement de texte** word-processing software, word-processing software packages

logique [lɔʒik] **1** *adj* logical
2 *nf* logic; **en toute l.,...** logically,...; *Ordinat* l. **câblée** wired logic; l. **floue** fuzzy logic

logiquement [lɔʒikmɑ̃] *adv* logically

logis [lɔʒi] *nm Litt (maison)* dwelling, abode

logistique [lɔʒistik] **1** *adj* logistic
2 *nf* logistics *(singulier)*

logo [logo] *nm* logo

loi [lwa] *nf* law; **nul n'est censé igorer la l.** ignorance of the law is no excuse; **faire la** *ou* **sa l.** to lay down the law; *Pol* l. **de finances** Finance Act; **la l. de la jungle** the law of the jungle; l. **martiale** martial law; **la l. de l'offre et de la demande** the law of supply and demand; **la l. du plus fort** the law of the strongest; **la l. du talion** an eye for an eye

loi-cadre (*pl* **lois-cadres**) [lwakadr] *nf* outline law

loin [lwɛ̃] **1** *adv* (a) *(dans l'espace)* far *(de* from); **la poste est l.** the post office is a long way away; **c'est encore l., le théâtre/Annecy?** is it far to the theatre/Annecy?; **il y a l. d'ici à Paris** it's a long way to Paris; **plus l.** further (on); **voir plus l.** *(dans un texte)* see below; **de l.** *(reconnaître, admirer)* from a distance; *Prov* l. **des yeux, l. du cœur** out of sight, out of mind
(b) *(dans le temps)* far away *(de* from); **comme c'est l., tout ça!** that all happened such a long time ago!; **ce jour est encore l.** that day is still a long way off; **d'aussi l.** *ou* **du plus l. qu'elle se souvienne** for as long as she can remember
(c) *Fig* **de là à l'accuser de mensonge il n'y a pas l.** it's practically calling him/her a liar; **aller l.** *(réussir)* to go far; **aller trop l.** *(exagérer)* to go too far; **nous étions l. de penser que...** we never thought for a moment that...; **elle est l. d'être bête** she's far from stupid; **je ne suis pas fâché, l. de là!** I'm not angry, far from it!; **l. de moi l'idée d'insinuer que...** far be it from me to insinuate that...; l. **de moi cette idée!** I wouldn't dream of it!, perish the thought!; **pas l. de** *(presque)* not far off; **de l.** *(de beaucoup)* by far; **de l. en l.** *(de temps en temps)* every now and then
2 *nm* **au l.** in the distance

lointain, -e [lwɛ̃tɛ̃, -ɛn] **1** *adj (dans l'espace, dans le temps)* distant; *(ressemblance)* vague; *(air, regard)* faraway; **dans un avenir l.** in the distant future
2 *nm* **dans le l., au l.** in the distance

loir [lwar] *nm* dormouse

Loire [lwar] *nf* **la L.** the Loire

loisir [lwazir] *nm* (a) *(temps libre)* leisure; **activités de l.** leisure *ou* spare-time activities; **loisirs** spare time; **avoir des loisirs** to have some spare time (b) *(activité)* pastime; **les loisirs** leisure *ou* spare-time activities (c) *Formel (possibilité, temps nécessaire)* **avoir le l. de faire qch** to have time to do sth; **donner** *,ou* **laisser à qn le l.** de **faire qch** to give sb the opportunity to do sth; *Litt* **à l.** at one's leisure

lolo [lolo] *nm Fam* (a) *(langage enfantin) (lait)* milk (b) *(sein)* boob

lombaire [lɔ̃bɛr] *Anat* **1** *adj* lumbar
2 *nf* lumbar vertebra

lombalgie [lɔ̃balʒi] *nf Méd* lumbago

lombric [lɔ̃brik] *nm* earthworm

Lomé [lɔme] *n* Lomé

londonien, -enne [lɔ̃dɔnjɛ̃, -ɛn] **1** *adj* London
2 *nm,f* **L.** Londoner

Londres [lɔ̃dr] *n* London

long, longue [lɔ̃, lɔ̃g] **1** *adj* (a) *(dans l'espace)* long; *(personne)* tall; l. **de 5 mètres** 5 metres long (b) *(dans le temps)* long; **dix jours, c'est l.** ten days is a long time; **ce ne sera pas l.** it won't take long; **pendant de longues années** for many years; **longue durée** *(pile)* long-life; *(cassette)* extended play; **de longue durée** *(chômage, chômeur)* long-term (c) *(lent)* slow; **être l. à faire qch** to be slow to do sth
2 *nm* (a) *(dans l'espace)* **faire 2 mètres de l.** to be 2 metres long; **(tout) le l. de** *(all)* along; **de tout son l.** *(être étendu)* at full length; *(tomber)* flat on one's face; **de l. en large** up and down, to and fro; **en l.** *(couper, fendre)* lengthwise; *Fam* **expliquer qch en l. et en large** *ou* **en l., en large et en travers** to explain sth in great detail (b) *(dans le temps)* **tout au l. de** throughout
3 *adv* (a) *(beaucoup)* **en dire l.** *(être révélateur)* to speak

volumes; **en savoir l. (sur)** to know a lot (about) (b) **s'habiller l.** to wear long clothes

long-courrier (*pl* **long-courriers**) [lɔ̃kurje] **1** *adj* (*navire*) ocean-going; (*avion*) long-haul
2 *nm* (*navire*) ocean-going ship; (*avion*) long-haul aircraft

longe¹ [lɔ̃ʒ] *nf* (*pour guider*) leading rein; (*pour attacher*) tether

longe² *nf Culin* (*de veau, de porc*) loin

longer [45] [lɔ̃ʒe] *vt* (a) (*sujet: personne, voiture*) (*route, rivière*) to go along; (*mur, côte*) to hug (b) (*sujet: sentier, canal, voie ferrée*) to run alongside

longévité [lɔ̃ʒevite] *nf* (*longue vie*) longevity; (*espérance de vie*) life expectancy

longiligne [lɔ̃ʒiliɲ] *adj* willowy

longitude [lɔ̃ʒityd] *nf Géog* longitude; **à 10° de l. ouest** at longitude 10° west

longitudinal, -e, -aux, -ales [lɔ̃ʒitydinal, -o] *adj* longitudinal, lengthwise

longtemps [lɔ̃tɑ̃] *adv* (a) (*attendre, rester*) (for) a long time; **ça ne durera pas l.** it won't last (for) long; *Fig* **tu peux attendre l.** you'll have a long wait (b) (*avec une préposition, avec "il y a"*) **avant l.** before long; **pas avant l.** not for a long time; **cela existe depuis l.** it has existed for a long time; **pendant l.** for a long time; **je n'en ai pas pour l.** I won't be long; **il n'en a plus pour l.** (*il va bientôt mourir*) he doesn't have much longer to live; **il y a l.** a long time ago; **il y a l. qu'il est mort** he's been dead for a long time; **il y a l. que je ne l'ai pas vue** it's a long time since I saw her; **l. avant/après** long before/after

longue [lɔ̃g] **1** *adj voir* **long**
2 *nf* **à la l.** in the end

longuement [lɔ̃gmɑ̃] *adv* (*attendre, réfléchir, s'attarder*) for a long time; (*parler, expliquer*) at length; **il a l. insisté pour que je vienne** he kept on insisting I should come

longuet, -ette [lɔ̃gɛ, -ɛt] *adj Fam* longish

longueur [lɔ̃gœr] *nf* (a) (*dimension, durée*) & *Sp* length; **jardin de 100 mètres de l.** *ou* **d'une l. de 100 mètres** garden 100 metres long; **en l., dans le sens de la l.** (*couper, fendre*) lengthwise; **avoir une l. d'avance sur** *Sp* to be one length ahead of; *Fig* to have a clear lead over; **à l. de journée/de semaine/d'année** all day/week/year long (b) *Péj* (*développement trop long*) **longueurs** drawn-out passages (c) *Rad* **l. d'ondes** wavelength; *Fig* **être sur la même l. d'ondes** to be on the same wavelength

longue-vue (*pl* **longues-vues**) [lɔ̃gvy] *nf* telescope

look [luk] *nm Fam* look; **avoir un l. d'enfer** to look out of this world

looping [lupiŋ] *nm Av* loop; **faire un l./des loopings** to loop the loop

lopin [lɔpɛ̃] *nm* **l. de terre** patch *or* plot of land

loquace [lɔkas] *adj* talkative

loque [lɔk] *nf* (a) (*vêtement*) rag; **être en loques** to be in rags; **tomber en loques** to fall to pieces (b) *Fig* (*personne*) wreck

loquet [lɔkɛ] *nm* latch

lordose [lɔrdoz] *nf Méd* hollow-back, *Spéc* lordosis

lorgner [lɔrɲe] *vt* (a) (*regarder indiscrètement*) to eye; (*avec concupiscence*) to eye up (b) (*convoiter*) to have one's eye on

lorgnette [lɔrɲɛt] *nf* opera glasses; *Fig* **regarder** *ou* **voir les choses par le petit bout de la l.** to take a narrow-minded view of things

lorgnon [lɔrɲɔ̃] *nm* (*avec tige*) lorgnette; (*avec ressort*) pince-nez

lorrain, -e [lɔrɛ̃, -ɛn] **1** *adj* of Lorraine
2 *nm,f* **L.** person from Lorraine

lors [lɔr] *adv* **l. de** (*pendant*) during; (*au moment de*) at the time of; *Litt* **depuis l.** from that time

lorsque [lɔrsk] *conj* when

losange [lɔzɑ̃ʒ] *nm* (*forme*) diamond; (*en géométrie*) rhombus

Los Angeles [lɔsɑ̃dʒəlɛs] *n* Los Angeles

lot [lo] *nm* (a) (*dans une loterie*) prize; **gros l.** jackpot; *Fam* *Fig* **tirer le gros l.** to hit the jackpot; **l. de consolation** consolation prize (b) *Com* (*de marchandises*) batch; (*de serviettes, de casseroles*) set; (*de chaussettes, de savonnettes*) pack; *Fig* **dans le l., il y en aura bien un de bon** (*choses, personnes*) at least one out of this lot should be some good; **se détacher** *ou* **être au-dessus du l.** to stand out from the crowd (c) (*de terrain*) plot (d) *Litt* (*sort*) lot (e) *Ordinat* **traitement par lots** batch processing

loterie [lɔtri] *nf* lottery; **gagner à la l.** to win on the lottery; **l. nationale** national lottery

loti, -e [lɔti] *adj* **être bien/mal l.** to be well/badly off

lotion [lɔsjɔ̃] *nf* lotion; **l. après-rasage** aftershave (lotion); **l. capillaire** hair lotion; **l. tonique** toner

lotissement [lɔtismɑ̃] *nm* (*ensemble résidentiel*) housing estate

loto [lɔto] *nm* (a) (*jeu de hasard*) lotto (b) (*jeu national*) national lottery; **jouer au l.** to do the lottery

lotte [lɔt] *nf* (*de rivière*) burbot; (*de mer*) monkfish

lotus [lɔtys] *nm* lotus; **fleur de l.** lotus; **position du l.** lotus position

louable [lwabl] *adj* (*admirable*) praiseworthy, laudable

louage [lwaʒ] *nm* **contrat de l.** rental agreement; **voiture de l.** hired carriage

louange [lwɑ̃ʒ] *nf* praise; **digne de louange(s)** praiseworthy; **chanter les louanges de qn** to sing sb's praises

loubard [lubar] *nm Fam* hooligan

louche¹ [luʃ] *adj* dodgy

louche² *nf* ladle

loucher [luʃe] *vi* (*volontairement*) to squint; (*être atteint de strabisme*) to have a squint; **l. de l'œil gauche** to have a squint in one's left eye; *Fig* **l. sur qch** (*regarder*) to eye sth; (*convoiter*) to have one's eye on sth

louer¹ [lwe] *vt* (a) (*donner en location*) (*logement*) to rent out, *Br* to let (out) (à to); (*équipement, véhicule, costume*) to rent out, *Br* to hire out (à to); **maison à l.** house *Br* to let *or Am* for rent (b) (*prendre en location*) (*logement*) to rent (à from); (*équipement, véhicule, costume*) to rent, *Br* to hire; (*place de spectacle*) to book

louer² **1** *vt* (*exalter*) to praise; **l. qn de** *ou* **pour qch** to praise sb for sth; **louons le Seigneur!** praise the Lord!
2 se louer *vpr* **se l. de qch** to be very satisfied with sth; **je n'ai qu'à me l. de lui/de ses services** I have nothing but praise for him/for his/her work; **se l. d'avoir fait qch** to congratulate oneself on having done sth

loufdingue [lufdɛ̃g] *adj Fam* bonkers

loufoque [lufɔk] *adj Fam* crazy

louis [lwi] *nm* **l. (d'or)** louis(-d'or)

Louisiane [lwizjan] *nf* **la L.** Louisiana

loukoum [lukum] *nm* piece of Turkish delight; **des loukoums** Turkish delight

loup [lu] *nm* (a) *(mammifère)* wolf; *Fig* **il est connu comme le l.** blanc everybody knows him; **quand on parle du l.** on en voit la queue talk of the devil; *Fig* **jeune l.** young go-getter; *(en politique)* Young Turk; *Fam* **mon petit l.**, **mon gros l.** darling, pet (b) *(poisson)* bass (c) *(demi-masque)* eye mask (d) **(vieux) l. de mer** *(marin)* old salt, sea dog

loupe [lup] *nf (instrument d'optique)* magnifying glass; **regarder qch à la l.** to look at sth through a magnifying glass; *Fig* to put sth under the microscope

louper [lupe] *Fam* **1** *vt* (a) *(ne pas réussir) (travail, plat)* to botch, to bungle; *(examen)* to flunk; **l. son entrée** *(au théâtre)* to fluff one's entrance; **loupé!** missed!; **la soirée est loupée** the party's a flop (b) *(ne pas prendre) (son tour, occasion, train)* to miss; **il n'en loupe pas une!** *(en actions)* it's one stupid thing after another!; *(en paroles)* he's always opening his big mouth!; **je ne vais pas le l.!** I won't let him get away with it!

2 *vi* **je lui ai dit qu'il attraperait froid et ça n'a pas loupé** I told him he'd catch cold and sure enough he did

3 se louper *vpr (manquer son suicide)* to bungle it; *Ironique* **il ne s'est pas loupé!** he made a proper job of it!

loup-garou [lugaru] *(pl* **loups-garous)** *nm* werewolf; *(pour faire peur aux enfants)* bogeyman

loupiote [lupjot] *nf Fam (lampe)* small light

lourd, -e [lur, lurd] **1** *adj* (a) *(pesant)* heavy; **j'ai la tête lourde** I've got a thick head; **avoir l'estomac l.** to feel bloated; **yeux lourds de fatigue** eyes heavy with tiredness (b) *(à l'aspect pesant) (personne)* heavily built; *(tentures)* heavy (c) *(peu subtil) (personne, plaisanterie)* unsubtle; *(mouvement, style)* heavy (d) *(perte, dépenses, responsabilité)* heavy (e) *(temps)* close; *(parfum)* heavy (f) *(plein)* **l. de conséquences** fraught with consequences; **l. de menaces** ominous

2 *adv* **peser l.** to weigh a lot, to be heavy; *Fam* **pas l.** not much

lourdaud, -e [lurdo, -od] **1** *adj* oafish

2 *nm,f* oaf

lourdement [lurdəmɑ̃] *adv* heavily; **se tromper l.** to be greatly mistaken; **insister l.** to keep on insisting

lourder [lurde] *vt Fam* **l. qn** to give sb the boot; **se faire l. (par qn)** to get the boot (from sb)

lourdeur [lurdœr] *nf (poids, manque de subtilité)* heaviness; *(de la bureaucratie)* unwieldiness; *(d'une responsabilité, d'une tâche)* weight; *(du temps)* closeness; **l. d'esprit** slow-wittedness; **j'ai des lourdeurs d'estomac** I feel bloated

lourdingue [lurdɛ̃g] *adj Fam (style)* heavy; *(personne, plaisanterie)* unsubtle

loustic [lustik] *nm Fam* **un drôle de l.** *(louche)* a dodgy character

loutre [lutr] *nf* otter; *(fourrure)* otter skin

louve [luv] *nf* she-wolf

louveteau, -x [luvto] *nm* (a) *(animal)* wolf cub (b) *(jeune scout)* Cub (Scout)

louvoyer [32] [luvwaje] *vi Naut* to tack; *Fig* to hedge

lover [love] **se lover** *vpr (serpent)* to coil up; *(personne)* to curl up

loyal, -e, -aux, -ales [lwajal, -o] **1** *adj* (a) *(honnête)* fair (b) *(fidèle) (serviteur, ami)* loyal; **après vingt-cinq ans de bons et loyaux services** after twenty-five years of good and faithful service

2 *nf* **loyale** *Fam* **se battre à la loyale** to fight cleanly

loyalement [lwajalmɑ̃] *adv* (a) *(honnêtement)* fairly (b) *(fidèlement)* loyally

loyaliste [lwajalist] *adj & nmf Pol* loyalist

loyauté [lwajote] *nf* (a) *(honnêteté)* fairness (b) *(fidélité)* loyalty *(envers* to)

loyer [lwaje] *nm* rent; **j'ai trois loyers de retard** I'm three months behind with the rent

LP [ɛlpe] *nm (abrév* **lycée professionnel)** technical college

LSD [ɛlɛsde] *nm* LSD

lu, -e *voir* **lire**

lubie [lybi] *nf* whim, fad

lubrifiant, -e [lybrifjɑ̃, -ɑ̃t] **1** *adj* lubricating

2 *nm* lubricant

lubrifier [66] [lybrifje] *vt* to lubricate

lubrique [lybrik] *adj* lustful, lecherous

lucarne [lykarn] *nf* (a) *(dans un toit)* skylight; *(en saillie)* dormer (window) (b) *(au football)* top corner

lucide [lysid] *adj* lucid

lucidement [lysidmɑ̃] *adv* lucidly

lucidité [lysidite] *nf* lucidity

Lucifer [lysifɛr] *npr* Lucifer

luciole [lysjɔl] *nf* firefly

lucratif, -ive [lykratif, -iv] *adj* lucrative; **à but l.** profit-making; **sans but l.** *Br* non-profit-making, *Am* not-for-profit

lucre [lykr] *nm Litt* lucre

ludique [lydik] *adj* play

ludothèque [lydotɛk] *nf* toy and game library

luette [lɥɛt] *nf Anat* uvula

lueur [lɥœr] *nf* (a) *(lumière faible)* glow; **à la l. d'une bougie/des étoiles** by candlelight/starlight; **à la l. des derniers événements** in the light of recent events (b) *Fig (de lucidité, de colère)* flash; *(d'intelligence, d'espoir)* glimmer

luge [lyʒ] *nf* toboggan, *Br* sledge, *Am* sled; **faire de la l.** to go tobogganing or *Br* sledging or *Am* sledding

lugubre [lygybr] *adj* gloomy; *(son, cri)* mournful

lui [lɥi] *pron personnel* (a) *(sujet) (personne)* he; *(chose, animal)* it; **l., il aurait fait un effort** HE would have made an effort; **mon frère, l., n'est pas venu** as for my brother, he didn't come; **si j'étais l., je me méfierais** if I were him I'd be careful

(b) *(objet direct) (personne)* him; *(chose, animal)* it; **et l., tu le connais?** and what about him, do you know him?

(c) *(objet indirect) (homme)* to him; *(femme)* to her; *(chose, animal)* to it; **donnez-le-l.** give it to him/her/it, give him/her/it it; **je l. ai serré la main** I shook his/her hand; **il l. jeta une pierre** he threw a stone at him/her/it

(d) *(avec préposition) (personne)* him; *(chose, animal)* it; **elle pense encore à l.** she still thinks about him/her/it; **dis-le-lui, à l.** tell HIM; **ce livre est à l.** this book is his

(e) *(réfléchi) (personne)* himself; *(chose, animal)* itself; **il ne pense qu'à l.** he thinks only of himself; **il a un appartement à l.** he's got his own flat; **un ami à l.** a friend of his

(f) *(dans les comparaisons)* him; **elle gagne plus que l.** she earns more than him *or* than he does

lui-même [lɥimɛm] *pron personnel (personne)* himself; *(chose, animal)* itself

luire [18] [lɥir] *vi (métal, astre, yeux)* to shine; *(surface de l'eau, trottoir mouillé)* to glisten; *(flamme, braises)* to glow

luisais *etc voir* **luire**

luisant, -e [lɥizɑ̃, -ɑ̃t] **1** *adj (étoile, métal, yeux)* shining; *(surface, pelage, peau)* shiny; *(braise)* glowing; **front l. de sueur** forehead glistening with sweat
  2 *nm* sheen

lumbago [lɔ̃bago] *nm* lumbago

lumière [lymjɛr] *nf* (a) *(clarté)* light; **à la l. de la lune** by moonlight; **il y a de la l. chez lui** there's a light on/there are lights on at his place; *Fig* **j'ai besoin de tes lumières** I need the benefit of your knowledge; **l. d'ambiance** subdued lighting (b) *(locutions)* **à la l. de son exposé,...** in the light of his account,...; **faire (toute) la l. sur qch** to get (right) to the bottom of sth; **mettre qch en l.** to bring sth out; *Fam* **ce n'est pas une l.** he's/she's not very bright

lumignon [lymiɲɔ̃] *nm* small light

luminaire [lyminɛr] *nm* **magasin de luminaires** lighting shop

luminescent, -e [lyminɛsɑ̃, -ɑ̃t] *adj* luminescent

lumineux, -euse [lyminø, -øz] *adj* (a) *(corps, cadran)* luminous; *(pièce, ciel)* bright (b) *(radieux) (regard)* radiant; *(teint)* glowing (c) *(explication, propos)* lucid; *(idée)* brilliant

luminosité [lyminozite] *nf* (a) *(du ciel)* brightness; *(d'un regard)* radiance; *Phot* **la l.** the amount of light available (b) *(d'un écran)* brightness

lump [lœp] *nm* **œufs de l.** lumpfish roe

lunaire [lynɛr] *adj* lunar; *Fig* **un visage l.** a moon face

lunatique [lynatik] *adj* quirky

lunch [pl **lunchs** ou **lunches**] [lœntʃ] *nm* buffet lunch

lundi [lœdi] *nm* Monday; **le l. de Pâques/de la Pentecôte** Easter/Whit Monday; *voir aussi* **samedi**

lune [lyn] *nf* (a) *(astre)* moon; *Fig* **je ne te demande pas la l.** I'm not asking for the moon; **être dans la l.** to be miles away; **la nouvelle/pleine l.** the new/full moon; **l. de miel** honeymoon (b) *Fam (derrière)* bottom

luné, -e [lyne] *adj Fam* **être bien/mal l.** to be in a good/bad mood

lunette [lynɛt] *nf* (a) *(pour la vue)* **lunettes** glasses, spectacles; **lunettes noires** dark glasses; **lunettes de soleil** sunglasses; **lunettes de vue** corrective glasses (b) *(instrument d'optique)* telescope (c) *(siège du W.-C.)* seat (d) *(de voiture)* **l. arrière** rear window

lupin [lypɛ̃] *nm* lupin

lurette [lyrɛt] *nf* **il y a belle l.** ages ago; **il y a belle l. que je ne l'ai pas vu** I haven't seen him for ages

luron [lyrɔ̃] *nm* **c'est un gai** ou **joyeux l.** he's a bit of a lad

lustre¹ [lystr] *nm* (a) *(lampe)* chandelier (b) *(brillant)* lustre (c) *(prestige)* lustre

lustre² *nm* **ça dure depuis des lustres** it's been going on for ages

lustrer [lystre] *vt (glace, meuble, voiture)* to polish; **lustré par l'usure** shiny with wear

lustrine [lystrin] *nf* cotton lustre

luth [lyt] *nm* lute

luthier [lytje] *nm* stringed-instrument maker

lutin [lytɛ̃] *nm* imp, elf

lutrin [lytrɛ̃] *nm (à la messe)* lectern; *(pour soutenir un livre, des feuilles)* reading stand

lutte [lyt] *nf* (a) *(combat)* fight, struggle; *(antagonisme)* conflict; *(contre une maladie, contre la pollution)* fight; **entrer/être en l. contre qn** to enter into/to be in conflict with sb; **gagner de haute l.** to win after a hard struggle; **l. armée** armed struggle; **la l. des classes** class struggle (b) *Sp* wrestling; **faire de la l.** to wrestle

lutter [lyte] *vi* (a) *(se battre)* to struggle, to fight; **l. contre** *(adversaire, oppresseur)* to fight against; *(maladie, incendie, tentation)* to fight; *(sommeil)* to fight off (b) *(rivaliser)* **l. de vitesse avec qn** to race sb (c) *Sp* to wrestle (**avec** ou **contre with**)

lutteur, -euse [lytœr, -øz] *nm,f Sp* wrestler

luxation [lyksasjɔ̃] *nf Méd* dislocation

luxe [lyks] *nm* (a) *(abondance, richesse)* luxury; *(d'une maison, de l'ameublement)* luxuriousness (b) *(qualité)* de l. *(produits)* luxury; *(voiture, édition)* de luxe; **boutique de l.** luxury goods shop (c) *(bien superflu)* luxury; *Fig* **s'offrir** ou **se payer le l. de faire qch** to give oneself the luxury of doing sth; **je vais faire nettoyer ce vieil imperméable, ce ne sera pas du l.** I'm going to have this old raincoat cleaned, and not before time (d) *(profusion)* **un l. de précautions/de détails** a wealth of precautions/details

Luxembourg [lyksɑ̃bur] **1** *n (ville)* Luxembourg
  2 *nm* **le L.** Luxembourg

luxembourgeois, -e [lyksɑ̃burʒwa, -az] **1** *adj* of Luxembourg
  2 *nm,f* **L.** Luxembourger

luxer [lykse] **se luxer** *vpr* **se l. l'épaule/le poignet** to dislocate one's shoulder/one's wrist

luxueux, -euse [lyksɥø, -øz] *adj* luxurious

luxure [lyksyr] *nf Litt* lust

luxuriant, -e [lyksyrjɑ̃, -ɑ̃t] *adj (végétation, forêt, chevelure)* luxuriant; *(imagination)* fertile

luzerne [lyzɛrn] *nf Br* lucerne, *Am* alfalfa

lycée [lise] *nm Br* ≃ secondary school, *Am* ≃ high school *(for pupils aged fifteen to eighteen)*; **l. professionnel** vocational school; **l. technique** technical school

lycéen, -enne [liseɛ̃, -ɛn] *nm,f Br* ≃ secondary school pupil, *Am* ≃ high school pupil

Lycra® [likra] *nm* Lycra®

lymphatique [lɛ̃fatik] *adj* (a) *Biol* lymphatic (b) *(personne)* lethargic

lymphe [lɛ̃f] *nf* lymph

lymphocyte [lɛ̃fɔsit] *nm Biol* lymphocyte

lyncher [lɛ̃ʃe] *vt* to lynch

lynx [lɛ̃ks] *nm* lynx; *Fig* **avoir des yeux de l.** to have eyes like a hawk

Lyon [ljɔ̃] *n* Lyons

lyonnais, -e [ljɔnɛ, -ɛz] **1** *adj* of Lyons
  2 *nm,f* **L.** person from Lyons

lyophilisé, -e [ljɔfilize] *adj* freeze-dried

lyre [lir] *nf* lyre

lyrique [lirik] *adj* (a) *(poème, poète)* lyric (b) *(passionné)* lyrical

lyrisme [lirism] *nm* lyricism; **parler de qch avec l.** to wax lyrical about sth

lys [lis] = **lis**

M

M, m [ɛm] *nm inv* M, m

m (a) M. (*abrév* **Monsieur**) Mr (b) (*abrév* **mètre(s)**) m; 1 m 50 1.5 m (c) *Gram* (*abrév* **masculin**) m

m' [m] *voir* **me**

ma [ma] *voir* **mon**

MA [ɛma] *nm* (*abrév* **maître auxiliaire**) *Br* supply *or Am* substitute teacher

maboule, -e [mabul] *Fam* **1** *adj* (*fou*) crazy, *Br* bonkers **2** *nmf* nutcase

mac [mak] *nm très Fam* (*maquereau*) pimp

macabre [makabr] *adj* (*découverte, histoire*) macabre, gruesome; (*humour*) macabre

macadam [makadam] *nm* (a) (*revêtement*) macadam; **m. goudronné** tarmac(adam) (b) (*route*) road

macaque [makak] **1** *nm* (*singe*) macaque; **m. rhésus** rhesus monkey **2** *nmf Fam* (*personne laide*) pig

macareux [makarø] *nm* puffin

macaron [makarɔ̃] *nm* (a) *Culin* macaroon (b) **macarons** (*coiffure*) coils (over the ears) (c) (*badge*) badge; (*décoration*) rosette; (*autocollant*) sticker; *Journ* **m. de presse** press badge

macaroni [makaroni] *nm* (a) (*pâte*) piece of macaroni; **des macaronis** macaroni (b) (*Italien*) *Br* Eyetie, = racist term used to refer to an Italian

Macédoine [masedwan] *nf* **la M.** Macedonia

macédoine [masedwan] *nf* **m. de fruits** fruit salad; **m. de légumes** mixed vegetables

macédonien, -enne [masedɔnjɛ̃, -ɛn] **1** *adj* Macedonian **2** *nm,f* **M.** Macedonian

macération [maserasjɔ̃] *nf* steeping

macérer [34] [masere] **1** *vt* to steep **2** *vi* to steep; **faire m. qch** to steep sth; *Fig* **laisser m. qn** to leave sb to stew

mâche [maʃ] *nf* lamb's lettuce

mâcher [maʃe] *vt* (*nourriture*) to chew; **ne pas m. ses mots** not to mince one's words

machette [maʃet] *nf* machete

machiavélique [makjavelik] *adj* Machiavellian

machin [maʃɛ̃] *nm Fam* (a) (*objet*) thingy, thingummy (b) (*personne*) what's-his-name, *f* what's-her-name; **monsieur M.** Mr What's-his-name; **madame M.** Mrs What's-her-name

machinal, -e, -aux, -ales [maʃinal, -o] *adj* (*action, geste, travail*) mechanical; (*réaction*) automatic

machinalement [maʃinalmã] *adv* (*agir*) mechanically; (*réagir, répondre*) automatically

machination [maʃinasjɔ̃] *nf* conspiracy

machine [maʃin] *nf* (a) (*appareil*) machine; **m. à café** coffee machine; **m. à calculer** calculator; (*plus grande*) calculating machine; **m. à coudre** sewing machine; **m. à écrire** typewriter; **écrire qch à la m.** to type sth; **m. à laver** washing machine; **m. à sous** slot machine, *Br* fruit machine; **m. à tricoter** knitting machine (b) (*dans un bateau*) **stopper les machines** to stop engines; **faire m. arrière** to reverse engines; *Fig* to backtrack (c) (*locomotive*) engine; *Fam* (*moto*) machine (d) (*organisation*) machinery

machine-outil (*pl* **machines-outils**) [maʃinuti] *nf* machine tool

machiner [maʃine] *vt* to plot

machinisme [maʃinism] *nm* mechanization

machiniste [maʃinist] *nmf* (a) (*dans un théâtre*) sceneshifter, stagehand; (*au cinéma, à la télévision*) grip (b) (*conducteur d'autobus*) driver

machisme [matʃism, maʃism] *nm* machismo

macho [matʃo] *adj & nm Fam* macho

mâchoire [maʃwar] *nf* (a) (*d'une personne, d'un animal*) jaw (b) (*d'une poulie*) flange (c) **mâchoires** (*d'un étau, d'une tenaille*) jaws; (*de frein*) shoes

mâchonner [maʃɔne] *vt* (a) (*mâcher*) to chew (b) (*marmonner*) to mutter

mâchouiller [maʃuje] *vt Fam* to chew away at

maçon [masɔ̃] *nm* (a) (*d'ouvrage en briques*) bricklayer; (*d'ouvrage en pierre*) (stone)mason (b) (*franc-maçon*) mason

maçonnerie [masɔnri] *nf* (a) (*de briques*) brickwork; (*de pierres*) masonry, stonework (b) (*franc-maçonnerie*) masonry

maçonnique [masɔnik] *adj* masonic

macramé [makrame] *nm* macramé

macrobiotique [makrɔbjɔtik] **1** *adj* macrobiotic **2** *nf* macrobiotics (*singulier*)

macro-commande (*pl* **macro-commandes**) [makrokɔmɑ̃d] *nf Ordinat* macro(-command)

macroéconomie [makroekɔnɔmi] *nf* macroeconomics (*singulier*)

macrolangage [makrolɑ̃gaʒ] *nm Ordinat* macrolanguage

maculer [makyle] *vt* to stain (**de** with)

Madagascar [madagaskar] *n* Madagascar

madame [madam] (*pl* **mesdames** [medam]) *nf* (a) (*titre*) Mrs; **M. Martin** Mrs Martin; **M. le Ministre** the Minister (b) (*en apostrophe*) madam; **M. le Ministre** Madam Minister; **au revoir, m.** goodbye; **M.,** (*dans une lettre*) Dear Madam; **par ici, mesdames** this way, ladies; **mesdames, messieurs** ladies and gentlemen

madeleine [madlɛn] *nf* (*gâteau*) madeleine

mademoiselle [madmwazɛl] (*pl* **mesdemoiselles** [medmwazɛl]) *nf* (a) (*suivi d'un nom*) Miss; **M.** Martin Miss Martin; **Mesdemoiselles Martin et Durand** the Misses Martin and Durand (b) (*en apostrophe*) **merci m.** thank you; **mesdemoiselles, un peu de silence je vous prie!** (*dans une classe*) let's have some quiet, girls, please! (c) (*dans une lettre*) **M.** Dear Madam (d) (*utilisé seul*) **M. se plaint que...** (*dans un magasin*) this young lady is complaining that...

Madère [madɛr] *n* Madeira

madère [madɛr] *nm* Madeira (wine)

madone [madɔn] *nf* Madonna

madras [madras] *nm* (*tissu*) madras (cotton)

Madrid [madrid] *n* Madrid

madrier [madrije] *nm* beam

madrilène [madrilɛn] **1** *adj* of Madrid
  2 *nmf* M. person from Madrid

maestria [maɛstrija] *nf* mastery

maf(f)ia [mafja] *nf* Mafia; **la M.** the Mafia

maf(f)ieux, -euse [mafjø, -øz] **1** *adj* Mafia
  2 *nm,f* Mafioso

maf(f)ioso [mafjozo] (*pl* **maf(f)iosi** [mafjozi]) *nm* Mafioso

maganer [magane] *vt* Can (*chose*) to spoil, to waste; (*personne*) to manhandle

magasin [magazɛ̃] *nm* (a) (*boutique*) Br shop, Am store; **avoir qch en m.** to have sth in stock; **courir ou faire les magasins** to go shopping; **grand m.** department store (b) (*entrepôt*) warehouse (c) (*d'un appareil photo, d'une arme*) magazine

magasinage [magazinaʒ] *nm* (a) (*mise en dépôt*) warehousing (b) (*droits*) warehouse charges (c) Can **faire du m.** to go shopping

magasiner [magazine] *vi* Can to go shopping

magasinier [magazinje] *nm* warehouseman

magazine [magazin] *nm* (a) (*journal*) magazine (b) (*émission à la radio ou à la télévision*) magazine programme

mage [maʒ] *nm* magus

Maghreb [magrɛb] *nm* **le M.** the Maghreb

maghrébin, -e [magrebɛ̃, -in] **1** *adj* of the Maghreb
  2 *nm,f* M. person from the Maghreb

magicien, -enne [maʒisjɛ̃, -ɛn] *nm,f* magician

magie [maʒi] *nf* magic; **m. blanche/noire** white/black magic

magique [maʒik] *adj* (a) (*surnaturel*) magic (b) (*extraordinaire*) magical

magiquement [maʒikmã] *adv* magically

magistère [maʒistɛr] *nm* (a) (*diplôme*) = post-graduate vocational qualification (b) (*autorité*) authority

magistral, -e, -aux, -ales [maʒistral, -o] *adj* (a) (*admirable*) (*interprétation, démonstration*) masterly; (*réussite*) brilliant (b) (*énorme*) (*correction, dispute*) proper; (*erreur*) colossal (c) (*docte*) (*ton*) magisterial

magistralement [maʒistralmã] *adv* authoritatively

magistrat [maʒistra] *nm* magistrate

magistrature [maʒistratyr] *nf* magistrature

magma [magma] *nm* (a) *Géol* magma (b) (*ensemble confus*) jumble

magnanime [maɲanim] *adj* magnanimous

magnanimité [maɲanimite] *nf* magnanimity

magnat [magna] *nm* magnate, tycoon; **m. de la presse** press baron

magner [maɲe] **se magner** *vpr Fam* to get a move on

magnésium [maɲezjɔm] *nm* magnesium

magnétique [maɲetik] *adj* magnetic

magnétiser [maɲetize] *vt* (a) (*matériau, corps*) to magnetize (b) (*personne, foule*) to hypnotize

magnétisme [maɲetism] *nm* (*d'un matériau, de la terre, d'une personne*) magnetism

magnéto [maɲeto] *nm Fam* tape recorder

magnétophone [maɲetɔfɔn] *nm* tape recorder

magnétoscope [maɲetɔskɔp] *nm* video(recorder)

magnificence [maɲifisãs] *nf* magnificence

magnifier [66] [maɲifje] *vt* to magnify, to glorify

magnifique [maɲifik] *adj* magnificent

magnifiquement [maɲifikmã] *adv* magnificently

magnitude [maɲityd] *nf* magnitude

magnolia [maɲɔlja] *nm* magnolia (tree)

magnum [magnɔm] *nm* magnum

magot [mago] *nm Fam* hoard

magouille [maguj] *nf Fam* scheming; **faire des magouilles** to scheme

magouiller [maguje] *vt & vi Fam* to scheme

magouilleur, -euse [magujœr, -øz] *nm,f Fam* schemer

magret [magrɛ] *nm* (*de canard*) fillet

Mahomet [maɔmɛ] *npr* Mohammed

mai [mɛ] *nm* May; **le premier m.** (*fête*) May Day; **le huit m.** (*fête*) VE day; *voir aussi* **janvier**

maigre [mɛgr] **1** *adj* (a) (*très mince*) (*personne, partie du corps*) thin (b) (*sans gras*) (*viande*) lean; (*fromage, yaourt*) low-fat (c) (*peu abondant*) (*filet d'eau*) thin; (*repas, salaire*) meagre; (*végétation, barbe*) sparse (d) (*peu conséquent*) (*conclusions, explication*) thin; (*succès*) very limited
  2 *nm* (*de viande*) lean part
  3 *nmf* thin person
  4 *adv* **faire m.** not to eat meat

maigrelet, -ette [mɛgrəlɛ, -ɛt] *adj* skinny

maigreur [mɛgrœr] *nf* (*d'une personne*) thinness

maigrichon, -onne [mɛgriʃɔ̃, -ɔn] *adj* skinny

maigrir [mɛgrir] *vi* to get thinner

mailing [meliŋ] *nm* mailshot

maillage [majaʒ] *nm* networking

maille [maj] *nf* (a) (*de tricot*) stitch; **m. à l'endroit/à l'envers** plain/purl stitch (b) (*de filet*) mesh; *Fig* **passer entre les mailles du filet** to slip through the net (c) (*tissu*) knitted fabric (d) (*de chaîne*) link (e) **avoir m. à partir avec qn** to have a set-to with sb

maillet [majɛ] *nm* mallet

maillon [majɔ̃] *nm* link

maillot [majo] *nm* (*de footballeur, de coureur cycliste*) shirt, jersey; **m. de bain** (*pour femmes*) swimsuit; (*pour hommes*) (swimming) trunks; **m. de corps** Br vest, Am undershirt; **m. jaune** yellow jersey (*in the Tour de France*)

main [mɛ̃] **1** *nf* hand; **avoir qch en m.** (*situation*) to have sth in hand; (*voiture*) to have the feel of sth; **avoir la m. heureuse** to be lucky; **avoir la m. leste** to be quick to raise one's hand; **avoir la m. lourde** (*être brutal*) to be heavy-handed; **il a eu la m. lourde avec le sel** he was a bit heavy-handed with the salt; **donner la m. à qn** to hold sb's hand; **faire m. basse sur qch** to get one's hands on sth; **mettre la m. sur qch** (*trouver ce que l'on cherchait*) to

lay one's hands on sth; **mettre la m. à la pâte** *ou* **à l'ouvrage** to lend a hand; **mettre la dernière m. à qch** to put the finishing touches to sth; **en mettre sa m. au feu** *ou* **à couper** to stake one's life on it; **ne pas y aller de m. morte** *(en frappant, en insultant)* not to pull one's punches; *(forcer une description, une action)* to overdo it; **prendre qn par la m.** to take sb's hand; *Fig* **se prendre par la m.** to take oneself in hand; **prendre qn/qch en m.** to take sb/sth in hand; **prendre qn/qch dans le sac** to catch sb red-handed; **à la m.** *(faire, fabriquer)* by hand; *(tenir, avoir)* in one's hand; **écrit à la m.** handwritten; **fait à la m.** *(pull, poterie)* handmade; **à deux mains** in both hands; **à quatre mains** *(morceau)* for four hands; *(jouer)* four-handed; **à m. armée** *(vol, attaque)* armed; **à main(s) nue(s)** with bare hands; **à pleines mains** by the handful; **de m. en m.** from hand to hand; **de la m. à la m.** cash in hand; **de m. de maître** with a master's hand; **de première m.** firsthand; **de seconde m.** secondhand; **en mains propres** in person; **haut les mains!**, **les mains en l'air!** hands up!; **les mains vides** empty-handed; *Fig* **les mains dans les poches** unprepared; **sous la m.** handy; **m. courante** handrail
2 *adv* **tricoté/fait/cousu m.** hand-knitted/-made/-sewn

main-d'œuvre [mɛ̃dœvr] *nf* labour

main-forte [mɛ̃fɔrt] *voir* **prêter**

mainmise [mɛ̃miz] *nf* seizure (**sur** of)

maint, -e [mɛ̃, mɛ̃t] *adj indéfini Litt* many a; **maintes et maintes fois**, **en maintes et maintes occasions** time and (time) again

maintenance [mɛ̃tnɑ̃s] *nf* maintenance

maintenant [mɛ̃tnɑ̃] *adv* now

maintenir [70] [mɛ̃tnir] **1** *vt* **(a)** *(soutenir)* to hold in position **(b)** *(empêcher d'avancer)* *(foule)* to hold back; **m. qn à distance** to keep sb at a distance **(c)** *(conserver)* *(tradition, paix)* to maintain, to keep; *(décision)* to abide by; **m. qn en vie** to keep sb alive **(d)** *(affirmer)* to maintain (**que** that)
2 se maintenir *vpr* to hold up

maintien [mɛ̃tjɛ̃] *nm* **(a)** *(conservation)* maintenance; *(de la loi)* upholding; **m. de l'ordre** maintenance of law and order **(b)** *(allure, posture)* bearing

maintiendrai *etc voir* **maintenir**

maire [mɛr] *nm* mayor

mairie [mɛri] *nf* *(lieu) Br* town hall; *Am* city hall; *(administration) Br* town council, *Am* city hall

mais [mɛ] **1** *conj* **(a)** *(marque l'opposition ou la transition)* but; **non seulement..., m. aussi** *ou* **encore... not** only... but also...; **m. qu'est-ce qui t'arrive?** whatever's the matter with you?; **m. j'y pense, je ne l'ai pas encore appelée!** I've just thought, I haven't rung her yet! **(b)** *(emphatique)* **m. oui!** of course!; **m. non!** of course not!; **m. enfin** well really; **elle ne fait rien, m. vraiment rien** she does nothing all day, and I mean nothing; **on a ri, m. ri!** we laughed, I mean laughed!
2 *nm* **il y a un m.** there's a but

maïs [mais] *nm Br* maize, *Am* corn

maison [mɛzɔ̃] **1** *nf* **(a)** *(habitation)* house; **m. de campagne** *(résidence secondaire)* house in the country; **m. individuelle** detached house; **m. de poupée** doll's house **(b)** *(foyer)* home; **à la m.** at home; **toute la m. dort** the whole house is asleep **(c)** *(entreprise)* company; **m. de couture** fashion house; **m. d'édition** publishing house; **m. mère** parent company **(c)** *(lignée)* house **(d)** *(institution)* **m. d'arrêt** remand centre; **m. close** *ou* **de passe** brothel; **m. de correction** *ou* **de redressement**

detention centre; **m. de la culture** arts centre; **m. des jeunes et de la culture** = youth club and arts centre; **m. de retraite** old people's home
2 *adj inv* **(a)** *(artisanal)* home-made **(b)** *(au sein de l'entreprise)* in-house **(c)** *Fam (énorme)* colossal

Maison-Blanche [mɛzɔ̃blɑ̃ʃ] *nf* **la M.** the White House

maisonnée [mɛzɔne] *nf* household

maisonnette [mɛzɔnɛt] *nf* small house

maître [mɛtr] **1** *nm* **(a)** *(de situation, de chien)* master; **m. de maison** host; **en m.** authoritatively; **être m. de son destin** to be master of one's own destiny; **être m. de soi** to have self-control; **il n'était plus m. de ses actes** he didn't know what he was doing
(b) *(dans des fonctions)* **m. (d'école)** *(Br* primary school *or Am* elementary school) teacher; **m. assistant** = assistant lecturer; **m. auxiliaire** *Br* supply or *Am* substitute teacher; **m. de conférence** *Br* (senior) lecturer, *Am* assistant professor; **m. d'hôtel** *(dans une maison)* butler; *(dans un restaurant)* head waiter; **m. nageur** swimming instructor; **m. d'œuvre** project manager
(c) *(titre octroyé à un peintre, à un musicien)* maestro; **les grands maîtres** the great masters; **être passé m. dans l'art de qch/de faire qch** to be a past master at sth/at doing sth
(d) *(titre donné à un avocat)* = form of address for lawyer
(e) **m. chanteur** blackmailer
2 *adj* **m.** key word word

maîtresse [mɛtrɛs] **1** *nf* mistress; **être m. de son destin** to be mistress of one's own destiny; **être m. de soi** to have self-control; **m. (d'école)** *(Br* primary school *or Am* elementary school) teacher; **m. de maison** hostess
2 *adj* main, principal; **m. femme** capable woman

maîtrise [mɛtriz] *nf* **(a)** *(diplôme universitaire)* ≃ master's degree (**de** in) **(b)** *(contrôle)* *(de ses passions)* mastery; **m. de soi** self-control **(c)** *(connaissance)* mastery **(d)** *(école de chant)* choir school

maîtriser [mɛtrize] **1** *vt* **(a)** *(soumettre)* *(agresseur)* to overpower; *(élèves, animal)* to control; *(flammes, opposition)* to subdue; *(incendie, épidémie)* to control **(b)** *(contrôler)* *(passion)* to control; *(peur)* to overcome **(c)** *(connaître parfaitement)* *(sujet, langue)* to master; **il ne maîtrise pas la langue** he hasn't mastered the language **(d)** *(rester maître de)* *(véhicule)* to have under control
2 se maîtriser *vpr* to control oneself

Maizena® [maizena] *nf Br* cornflour, *Am* cornstarch

majesté [maʒɛste] *nf* **(a)** *(noblesse)* majesty **(b)** *Sa M.* **(le Roi)** His Majesty (the King); *Sa M.* **(la Reine)** Her Majesty (the Queen)

majestueux, -euse [maʒɛstɥø, -øz] *adj* majestic

majeur, -e [maʒœr] **1** *adj* **(a)** *(principal)* major **(b)** *(personne)* of age **(c)** *Mus (mode, intervalle)* major
2 *nm (doigt)* middle finger

major [maʒɔr] *nm* **(a)** *(d'une promotion)* top student **(b)** *(officier)* regimental adjutant *(with administrative duties)*

majoration [maʒɔrasjɔ̃] *nf (d'une facture)* surcharge (**de** on); *(d'un prix)* increase (**de** in)

majordome [maʒɔrdɔm] *nm* major-domo

majorer [maʒɔre] *vt (facture)* to put a surcharge on; *(prix)* to increase

majorette [maʒɔrɛt] *nf* (drum) majorette

majoritaire [maʒɔritɛr] *adj* majority; **être m.** to be in the majority

majorité [maʒɔrite] *nf* (a) *(supériorité en nombre)* majority; **en m.** for the most part; **avoir la m.** to be in the majority (b) *(dans des élections)* majority; **m. relative/absolue** relative/absolute majority (c) *(parti politique)* majority party (d) **m. civile** majority, coming of age

Majorque [maʒɔrk] *n* Majorca

majorquin, -e [maʒɔrkɛ̃, -in] *1 adj* Majorcan **2** *nm,f* **M.** Majorcan

majuscule [maʒyskyl] *1 adj (lettre)* capital **2** *nf* capital letter

mal¹, maux [mal, mo] *nm* (a) *(douleur)* pain, ache; **avoir m. à l'estomac/à la tête/au dos** to have stomach ache/ a headache/backache; **avoir m. à la gorge** to have a sore throat; **j'ai m. au bras** my arm hurts, I have a sore arm; **avoir m. aux dents** to have toothache; **avoir des maux d'estomac/de tête** to get stomach ache/ headaches; **où avez-vous m.?** where does it hurt?; **faire m. à qn** to hurt sb; **mon genou/œil me fait m.** my knee/eye hurts; **se faire m.** to hurt oneself; *Fam* **attraper du m.** to catch cold; **ça fait m. au cœur de voir ça!** it's sickening to see things like that!; *Fam* **ça me ferait m.!** I'm not having it!; **être en m. de qch** to crave sth; **être en m. d'enfants** to be broody; **m. de cœur** sickness; **m. de dents** toothache; **m. de gorge** sore throat; **m. de mer** seasickness; **avoir le m. de mer** to be seasick; **du pays** homesickness; **avoir le m. du pays** to be homesick; *Litt* **du siècle** world-weariness; **m. de tête** headache; **m. des transports** travel-sickness; *Prov* **aux grands maux les grands remèdes** desperate situations call for desperate remedies

(b) *(préjudice)* harm; **faire du m. à qn** to harm sb; **ça n'a jamais fait de m. à personne!** it never did anyone any harm!; **vouloir du m. à qn** to mean to harm sb; **cela fera plus de m. que de bien** it will do more harm than good; **le m. est fait** the damage has been done; **un m. nécessaire** a necessary evil; **il n'y a pas de m. à cela** there's no harm in that; *Fam* **il n'y a pas de m.** there's no harm done; **dire du m. de qn** to speak ill of sb; **ne pas penser à m.** to mean well

(c) *(contraire du bien)* wrong; **le bien et le m.** right and wrong, good and evil; **voir le m. partout** to always see the bad side

(d) *(difficulté)* **avoir du m. à faire qch** to have difficulty or trouble doing sth; *Fam* **avoir un m. de chien à faire qch** to have a hell of a job doing sth; **non sans m.** not without difficulty; **se donner du m. pour faire qch** to take pains to do sth; **donner du m. à qn** to give sb trouble

mal² *1 adv* (a) *(médiocrement)* badly; *(incorrectement)* wrongly; **elle chante m.** she's a bad singer; **la porte est m. fermée** the door isn't closed properly; **il travaille m. à l'école** he's a poor student; **cette lampe éclaire m.** this lamp doesn't give much light; **m. comprendre** to misunderstand; **m. interpréter** to misinterpret; **m. choisir** to make the wrong choice; **ça va m. finir** it'll end in tears; **on y mange m.** the food's not very good there; **je ne pensais pas m. faire** I didn't think I was doing anything wrong; **aller de m. en pis** to go from bad to worse; **on voit m. d'ici** you can't see very well from here; *Fam* **se mettre m. avec qn** to fall out with sb; *Fam* **être m. avec qn** to be on bad terms with sb; **vous ne feriez pas m. de...** you would be wise to...

(b) *(en mauvaise santé)* **se sentir m.** to feel ill; **se trouver m.** to faint; **être m. en point** to be in a bad way

(c) *(une certaine quantité)* **pas m. de** quite a lot of; **il y en a**

pas m. there is/are quite a lot; **cela m'a pris pas m. de temps** it took me quite a while

2 *adj inv (contraire à la morale)* bad; **c'est très m. de faire ça** it's very naughty to do that; **c'est pas m.** it's not bad, it's quite good; **elle n'est pas m.** she's not bad; **on n'est pas m. ici** we've found a nice place here

malabar [malabar] *nm Fam* hulk

malade [malad] *1 adj* (a) *(souffrant)* ill, sick; **tomber m.** to fall or be taken ill; **être m. du cœur/du foie** to have heart/liver trouble; **être m. d'inquiétude/de jalousie** to be sick with worry/jealousy (b) *(qui fonctionne mal) (organe, dent)* bad; *Fig (industrie)* ailing (c) *(dérangé intellectuellement)* mad

2 *nmf* sick person; *(dans un hôpital)* patient; **un m. mental** a mentally ill person; *(dans un hôpital)* a mental patient; **un m. imaginaire** a hypochondriac

maladie [maladi] *nf* illness, disease; *Fig* **en faire une m.** to have a song and dance about it; **m. bleue** cyanosis; **m. sexuellement transmissible** sexually transmitted disesase; **m. de la vache folle** mad cow disease

maladif, -ive [maladif, -iv] *adj* (a) *(personne, teint)* sickly (b) *(curiosité, pensées)* morbid (c) *(susceptibilité, jalousie)* pathological

maladresse [maladrɛs] *nf* (a) *(manque d'habileté physique)* clumsiness, awkwardness (b) *(manque de tact)* tactlessness; *(bévue)* blunder

maladroit, -e [maladrwa, -at] *1 adj* (a) *(inhabile)* clumsy, awkward (b) *(manquant de tact)* tactless

2 *nm,f* (a) *(personne inhabile)* clumsy or awkward person (b) *(personne sans tact)* tactless person

maladroitement [maladrwatmɑ̃] *adv* (a) *(de façon gauche)* clumsily (b) *(sans tact)* tactlessly

malais, -e [malɛ, -ez] *1 adj* Malaysian **2** *nm,f* **M.** Malaysian **3** *nm (langue)* Malay

malaise [malɛz] *nm* (a) *(trouble physique)* feeling of sickness; *(étourdissement)* dizzy spell; **avoir un m.** to feel faint (b) *(inconfort moral)* uneasiness (c) *(état de crise)* unrest

malaisé, -e [maleze] *adj* difficult

Malaisie [malɛzi] *nf* la **M.** Malaysia

malaria [malarja] *nf* malaria; **avoir la m.** to have malaria

malavisé, -e [malavize] *adj Litt* unwise (**de faire qch** to do sth)

Malawi [malawi] *nm* le **M.** Malawi

malaxer [malakse] *vt* to knead

malchance [malʃɑ̃s] *nf* bad luck; **par m.** as bad luck would have it

malchanceux, -euse [malʃɑ̃sø, -øz] *1 adj* unlucky **2** *nm,f* unlucky person

malcommode [malkɔmɔd] *adj (appareil)* impractical; *(vêtement)* unsuitable

Maldives [maldiv] *nfpl* les **(îles) M.** the Maldives

maldonne [maldɔn] *nf* misdeal; *Fig* **il y a m.** something's gone wrong somewhere

mâle [mɑl] *1 adj* (a) *(du sexe masculin)* male (b) *(viril) (courage, assurance)* manly; *(style)* virile (c) **prise m.** plug **2** *nm* male

malédiction [malediksjɔ̃] *nf* curse

maléfice [malefis] *nm* evil spell

maléfique [malefik] *adj* evil

malencontreusement [malɑ̃kɔ̃trøzmɑ̃] *adv* unfortunately

malencontreux, -euse [malɑ̃kɔ̃trø, -øz] *adj* unfortunate

malentendant, -e [malɑ̃tɑ̃dɑ̃, -ɑ̃t] **1** *adj* hard of hearing
 2 *nm,f* person who is hard of hearing

malentendu [malɑ̃tɑ̃dy] *nm* misunderstanding

malfaçon [malfasɔ̃] *nf* defect

malfaisant, -e [malfəzɑ̃, -ɑ̃t] *adj* harmful

malfaiteur [malfɛtœr] *nm* criminal

malfamé, -e [malfame] *adj* disreputable

malformation [malfɔrmasjɔ̃] *nf* malformation

malfrat [malfra] *nm Fam* crook

malgache [malɡaʃ] **1** *adj* Madagascan
 2 *nmf* M. Madagascan
 3 *nm (langue)* Malagasy

malgré [malɡre] *prép (en dépit de)* in spite of, despite; **m. tout** *(en dépit de tout)* in spite of *or* despite everything; *(pourtant)* all the same

malhabile [malabil] *adj* clumsy, awkward

malheur [malœr] **1** *nm* (a) *(drame, catastrophe)* misfortune; **le m., c'est que...** the unfortunate thing is that...; **faire un m.** to be a big hit; **un m. n'arrive jamais seul** it never rains but it pours (b) *(chagrin, infortune)* misfortune; **faire le m. de qn** to cause sb a lot of unhappiness (c) *(malchance)* bad luck; **par m.** unfortunately; **porter m. à qn** to bring sb bad luck; **avoir le m. de faire qch** to make the big mistake of doing sth
 2 *exclam* hell!

malheureusement [malœrøzmɑ̃] *adv* unfortunately

malheureux, -euse [malœrø, -øz] **1** *adj* (a) *(triste)* unhappy, miserable (b) *(malchanceux) (personne)* unlucky; *(candidat, tentative)* unsuccessful; *(amour)* unrequited; **m. au jeu/en amour** unlucky at gambling/in love (c) *(regrettable)* unfortunate (d) *(négligeable)* miserable, wretched
 2 *nm,f* (a) *(personne infortunée)* poor wretch (b) *(indigent)* poor *or* needy person; **les m.** the poor, the needy

malhonnête [malɔnɛt] *adj* (a) *(personne, pratique)* dishonest (b) *(indécent) (proposition)* indecent

malhonnêteté [malɔnɛtte] *nf* dishonesty

Mali [mali] *nm* **le M.** Mali

malice [malis] *nf* (a) *(espièglerie)* mischief (b) *(méchanceté)* malice; **sans m.** without malice

malicieusement [malisjøzmɑ̃] *adv* mischievously

malicieux, -euse [malisjø, -øz] *adj (espiègle)* mischievous

malien, -enne [maljɛ̃, -ɛn] **1** *adj* Malian
 2 *nm,f* M. Malian

malignité [malinite] *nf* (a) *(méchanceté)* malice (b) *(d'une tumeur)* malignancy

malin, -igne [malɛ̃, -iɲ] **1** *adj* (a) *(rusé) (personne)* crafty; *(regard)* knowing; *Ironique* **c'est m.!** that's clever! (b) *(méchant) (plaisir)* perverse, malicious; **prendre un m. plaisir à faire qch** to take a perverse *or* malicious pleasure in doing sth (c) *(tumeur)* malignant
 2 *nm,f* crafty person; **faire le m.** to show off

malingre [malɛ̃gr] *adj* puny

malintentionné, -e [malɛ̃tɑ̃sjone] *adj* ill-intentioned

malle [mal] *nf* (a) *(valise)* trunk; *Fam* **se faire la m.** to clear off (b) *(de voiture) Br* boot, *Am* trunk (c) *Can* **mettre une lettre à la m.** to mail *or Br* post a letter

malléable [maleabl] *adj* malleable

mallette [malɛt] *nf (porte-documents)* briefcase

malmener [46] [malməne] *vt* (a) *(brutaliser) (personne)* to manhandle, to treat roughly; *(verbalement)* to attack; *(matériel, véhicule)* to mistreat (b) *(dominer)* **m. qn** to give sb a hard time

malnutrition [malnytrisjɔ̃] *nf* malnutrition

malodorant, -e [malɔdɔrɑ̃, -ɑ̃t] *adj* smelly

malotru, -e [malɔtry] *nm,f* lout

Malouines [malwin] *nfpl* **les (îles) M.** the Falkland Islands, the Falklands

malpoli, -e [malpɔli] *Fam* **1** *adj* rude
 2 *nm,f* rude person

malpropre [malprɔpr] *adj* (a) *(sale) (mains)* dirty; *(apparence, travail)* slovenly (b) *(inconvenant)* smutty (c) *(malhonnête)* despicable

malsain, -e [malsɛ̃, -ɛn] *adj* (a) *(dangereux pour la santé)* unhealthy (b) *(pernicieux)* unhealthy; *(personne)* unwholesome

malséant, -e [malseɑ̃, -ɑ̃t] *adj Litt* unseemly

malt [malt] *nm* malt

maltais, -e [maltɛ, -ɛz] **1** *adj* Maltese
 2 *nm,f* M. Maltese; **les M.** the Maltese
 3 *nm (langue)* Maltese

Malte [malt] *n* Malta

maltraitance [maltrɛtɑ̃s] *nf* ill-treatment

maltraiter [maltrɛte] *vt* (a) *(brutaliser)* to ill-treat (b) *(verbalement)* to attack

malus [malys] *nm* partial loss of no-claims bonus *(due to insurance claim)*

malveillance [malvejɑ̃s] *nf* spite

malveillant, -e [malvejɑ̃, -ɑ̃t] *adj* spiteful

malvenu, -e [malvəny] *adj* out of place, inappropriate

malversation [malvɛrsasjɔ̃] *nf* embezzlement

maman [mamɑ̃] *nf Br* mum, *Am* mom; *(langage enfantin) Br* mummy, *Am* mommy

mamelle [mamɛl] *nf (de vache)* udder; *(de chienne, de truie)* teat

mamelon [mamlɔ̃] *nm* (a) *(du sein)* nipple (b) *(colline)* hillock

mamie [mami] *nf* grandma, gran(ny)

mammaire [mamɛr] *adj* mammary

mammifère [mamifɛr] **1** *adj* mammalian
 2 *nm* mammal

mammographie [mamɔɡrafi] *nf* mammography

mammouth [mamut] *nm* mammoth

mamours [mamur] *nmpl Fam* kissing and cuddling; **faire des m. à qn** to kiss and cuddle sb

manager¹ [manadʒɛr] *nm* manager

manager² [45] [manadʒe] *vt* to manage

manant [manɑ̃] *nm* (a) *Hist (villageois)* villager; *(paysan)* peasant (b) *Litt (mufle)* churl, boor

Manche [mɑ̃ʃ] *nf* **la M.** the (English) Channel

manche¹ [mɑ̃ʃ] *nf* (a) *(de vêtement)* sleeve; **en manches de chemise** in one's shirtsleeves; **manches longues/courtes** long/short sleeves; **manches ballon/kimono/raglan** puff/kimono/raglan sleeves (b) *(de jeu, de compétition)* round; *(au tennis)* set (c) *Fam* **faire la m.** to beg

manche² *nm* (a) *(d'outil)* handle; **m. à balai** broomstick; *(d'avion)* joystick (b) *(de guitare)* neck

manchette [mɑ̃ʃɛt] *nf* (**a**) *(extrémité de la manche)* cuff (**b**) *(de journal)* headline (**c**) *(au catch)* forearm smash; *(au volley-ball)* dig

manchon [mɑ̃ʃɔ̃] *nm* (**a**) *(vêtement)* muff (**b**) *Tech* sleeve

manchot¹, -e [mɑ̃ʃo, -ɔt] **1** *adj (privé d'un bras)* one-armed; *Fam* **il n'est pas m.** *(adroit)* he's clever with his hands; *(il peut le faire lui-même)* he's got hands, hasn't he? **2** *nm,f* one-armed person

manchot² *nm (oiseau)* penguin

mandale [mɑ̃dal] *nf très Fam* clout, slap

mandarin [mɑ̃darɛ̃] *nm* (**a**) *(de Chine)* mandarin (**b**) *Fig & Péj (personnage influent)* mandarin (**c**) *(langue)* Mandarin (Chinese)

mandarine [mɑ̃darin] *nf (fruit)* mandarin (orange)

mandat [mɑ̃da] *nm* (**a**) *(mission) (de député)* mandate; *(de président)* term of office; *(ordre)* warrant; **m. d'amener** = summons; **m. d'arrêt** arrest warrant; **m. de dépôt** committal order; **m. de perquisition** search warrant (**c**) *(mode de paiement)* order; **m. postal** *Br* postal order, *Am* money order (**d**) *(autorité)* mandate (**e**) *(procuration)* power of attorney

mandataire [mɑ̃datɛr] *nmf (d'électeurs)* representative; *(dans une réunion)* proxy

mandat-carte (*pl* **mandats-cartes**) [mɑ̃dakart] *nm Br* postal order, *Am* money order *(in postcard form)*

mandater [mɑ̃date] *vt (représentant)* to commission; *(membre parlementaire)* to give a mandate to (**b**) *(frais)* to pay by order

mandat-lettre (*pl* **mandats-lettres**) [mɑ̃daletr] *nm Br* postal order, *Am* money order *(in letter-card form)*

mandibule [mɑ̃dibyl] *nf* mandible

mandoline [mɑ̃dɔlin] *nf* mandolin

mandrin [mɑ̃drɛ̃] *nm (pour percer)* punch; *(pour élargir un trou)* drift

manège [manɛʒ] *nm* (**a**) *(attraction foraine) Br* roundabout, merry-go-round, *Am* carousel (**b**) *(en équitation)* riding school (**c**) *(manigances)* game

manette [manɛt] *nf* lever

manganèse [mɑ̃ganɛz] *nm* manganese

mangeable [mɑ̃ʒabl] *adj* (**a**) *(comestible)* edible (**b**) *(médiocre)* eatable

mangeoire [mɑ̃ʒwar] *nf* manger

manger [45] [mɑ̃ʒe] **1** *vt* (**a**) *(aliments)* to eat; **m. qn/ qch des yeux** to look at sb/sth longingly; **m. ses mots** to mumble; **ça ne mange pas de pain** it doesn't cost anything; **je ne mange pas de ce pain-là** I don't go in for that sort of thing (**b**) *(attaquer)* to eat away (**c**) *(consommer)* to get through (**d**) *(dépenser)* to get through **2** *vi* to eat; **donner à m. à qn** to give sb something to eat; **m. comme quatre** *ou* **comme un ogre** to eat like a horse; **m. comme un oiseau** to eat like a sparrow; **m. à sa faim** to eat one's fill **3 se manger** *vpr* to be eaten

mange-tout [mɑ̃ʒtu] *nm inv (pois) Br* mangetout, *Am* snow pea; *(haricot) Br* runner bean, *Am* string bean

mangeur, -euse [mɑ̃ʒœr, -øz] *nm,f* **gros m.** big eater; **tigre/requin m. d'hommes** man-eating tiger/shark

mangue [mɑ̃g] *nf* mango

maniable [manjabl] *adj (outil)* handy; *(véhicule)* easy to handle

maniaque [manjak] **1** *adj* (**a**) *(pointilleux)* fussy (**b**) *(fou)* manic **2** *nmf* (**a**) *(pointilleux) Br* fusspot, *Am* fussbudget; **être un m. de qch** to be fanatical about *or* obsessed with sth (**b**) *(fou)* maniac

manichéen, -enne [manikeɛ̃, -ɛn] *adj* Manichean

manichéisme [manikeism] *nm* Manicheism

manie [mani] *nf* (**a**) *(habitude)* odd habit (**b**) *(idée fixe)* mania, obsession (**c**) *Méd* mania

maniement [manimɑ̃] *nm* handling

manier [66] [manje] *vt* (**a**) *(manipuler) (objet)* to handle (**b**) *(utiliser) (véhicule)* to handle; *(outil, ironie)* to use

manière [manjɛr] *nf (façon)* way, manner; **faire qch à sa m.** to do sth one's (own) way; **de m. à faire qch** so as to do sth; **de m. que** + *subjunctive* so that, in such a way that; **d'une** *ou* **de m. générale** generally speaking; **en aucune m.** under no circumstances; **de toute m.** in any case; **d'une certaine m.** in a manner of speaking, in a sense; **c'est sa m. d'être** that's the way he is; **la m. forte** strong-arm tactics (**b**) *(conduite)* **manières** manners; **faire des manières** *(agir de façon pompeuse)* to put on airs and graces; *(se faire prier)* to make a fuss (**c**) *(d'une œuvre)* **à la m. de** in the style of

maniéré, -e [manjere] *adj* affected

maniérisme [manjerism] *nm* mannerism

manif [manif] *nf Fam* demo

manifestant, -e [manifestɑ̃, -ɑ̃t] *nm,f* demonstrator

manifestation [manifestasjɔ̃] *nf* (**a**) *(de sentiments)* display (**b**) *(rassemblement politique)* demonstration (**c**) *(événement organisé)* event

manifeste¹ [manifest] *adj* obvious, manifest

manifeste² *nm* manifesto

manifestement [manifestəmɑ̃] *adv* obviously, manifestly

manifester [manifeste] **1** *vt (exprimer)* to show **2** *vi* to demonstrate **3 se manifester** *vpr* (**a**) *(personne)* to make oneself known (**b**) *(maladie)* to show *or* manifest itself (**par** in)

manigancer [16] [manigɑ̃se] *vt* to scheme

manigances [manigɑ̃s] *nfpl* scheming

Manille [manij] *n* Manila

manioc [manjɔk] *nm* manioc, cassava

manipulateur, -trice [manipylatœr, -tris] **1** *nm,f* (**a**) *(de machines)* operator (**b**) *Péj (de personnes)* manipulator **2** *nm (appareil de transmission)* (sending) key

manipulation [manipylasjɔ̃] *nf* (**a**) *(d'appareils, de produits)* handling; **m. génétique** genetic engineering (**b**) **manipulations** *(en science)* experiments, practical work (**c**) *Péj (de personnes)* manipulation (**d**) *Ordinat* **m. de colonnes** column handling

manipuler [manipyle] *vt* (**a**) *(appareils, produits)* to handle (**b**) *Péj (personnes)* to manipulate (**c**) *(statistiques)* to massage

manivelle [manivel] *nf* crank

manne [man] *nf (dans la Bible)* manna; *Fig (don inespéré)* godsend

mannequin [mankɛ̃] *nm* (**a**) *(personne)* model (**b**) *(de magasin, de couturier)* dummy

manœuvre¹ [manœvr] *nf* **(a)** *(conduite, direction) (de machines)* operation; *(de véhicules)* manoeuvring; **faire une m.** to (do a) manoeuvre; **faire une fausse m.** *(en voiture)* to manoeuvre badly; *Fig* to get it wrong **(b)** *(intrigue)* manoeuvre; **manœuvres** manoeuvring **(c)** *Mil (dans une bataille)* manoeuvre; **être en manœuvres** to be on manoeuvres **(d)** *(d'un bateau)* manoeuvre

manœuvre² *nm (ouvrier)* unskilled worker

manœuvrer [manœvre] **1** *vt* **(a)** *(faire fonctionner) (machine)* to operate; *(véhicule)* to manoeuvre **(b)** *(influencer)* to influence
2 *vi aussi Fig* to manoeuvre

manoir [manwar] *nm* manor house

manomètre [manɔmɛtr] *nm* pressure gauge, manometer

manquant, -e [mɑ̃kɑ̃, -ɑ̃t] *adj* missing

manque [mɑ̃k] **1** *nm* **(a)** *(insuffisance)* lack; **par m. de** through lack of; **m. de chance!** bad luck!; **m. à gagner** loss of earnings **(b)** *(lacune)* gap **(c)** *(d'un drogué)* withdrawal symptoms; **être en (état de) m.** to have withdrawal symptoms
2 *Fam* **à la m.** useless, pathetic

manqué, -e [mɑ̃ke] **1** *adj* **(a)** *(occasion, rendez-vous)* missed **(b)** *(tentative, expérience)* unsuccessful **(c)** *(personne)* **c'est un poète/un médecin m.** he should have been a poet/doctor
2 *nm (gâteau)* = sponge cake with almond-flavoured or fruit-flavoured icing

manquement [mɑ̃kmɑ̃] *nm* breach **(à of)**

manquer [mɑ̃ke] **1** *vt* **(a)** *(cible, train, occasion)* to miss **(b)** *(échouer à)* to fail
2 *vi* **(a)** *(faire défaut)* to be lacking; **le temps/la place me manque** I don't have enough time/room; **elle me manque** I miss her **(b)** *(échouer)* to fail; **ça n'a pas manqué, il est arrivé en retard** sure enough, he was late **(c)** *(être absent)* to be missing **(à** from)
3 *v impersonnel* **il ne manque personne** there's no one missing; **il manque quelques pages** there are a few pages missing; **il manque un bouton à ta veste** there's a button missing from your jacket; **il me manque 10 francs** I'm 10 francs short; **il ne manquait plus que cela!** that's all I/he/etc needed!
4 manquer à *vt ind (devoir, honneur)* to fail in; *(parole, promesses)* to break
5 manquer de *vt ind* **(a)** *(argent, main-d'œuvre)* to be short of, to lack; *(temps)* to be short of; *(courage, bon sens, charme)* to lack; **ne m. de rien** to have all that one needs; **m. de respect à qn** to show a lack of respect towards sb; **on manque d'air ici** there isn't enough air in here **(b)** *(faillir)* **m. (de) faire qch** to almost do sth **(c)** *(à la forme négative)* **ne pas m. de faire qch** to be sure to do sth; **je n'y manquerai pas** I certainly will
6 se manquer *vpr* to miss each other *(by not being in the same place at the same time)*

mansarde [mɑ̃sard] *nf* attic

mansardé, -e [mɑ̃sarde] *adj (chambre)* attic

mante [mɑ̃t] *nf* mantis; **m. religieuse** praying mantis

manteau, -x [mɑ̃to] *nm* coat; **m. de fourrure** fur coat; *Fig* **sous le m.** secretly

mantille [mɑ̃tij] *nf* mantilla

manucure [manykyr] **1** *nmf (personne)* manicurist
2 *nf (soin)* manicure

manuel¹, -elle [manɥɛl] **1** *adj (travail, activité)* manual; **être m.** *(personne)* to be good with one's hands
2 *nm,f* **(a)** *(travailleur)* manual worker **(b)** *(personne adroite de ses mains)* **c'est un m.** he's good with his hands

manuel² *nm (d'utilisation, d'entretien)* manual, handbook; *(scolaire)* textbook

manuellement [manɥɛlmɑ̃] *adv* manually

manufacture [manyfaktyr] *nf (usine)* factory

manufacturer [manyfaktyre] *vt* to manufacture

manu militari [manymilitari] *adv* by force

manuscrit, -e [manyskri, -it] **1** *adj* handwritten
2 *nm* manuscript

manutention [manytɑ̃sjɔ̃] *nf* handling

manutentionnaire [manytɑ̃sjɔnɛr] *nmf* warehouseman, *f* warehousewoman

maous, -ousse [maus] *adj Fam* enormous

mappemonde [mapmɔ̃d] *nf* **(a)** *(carte)* map of the world *(in two hemispheres)* **(b)** *(globe)* globe

maquereau¹, -x [makro] *nm (poisson)* mackerel

maquereau², -x *nm très Fam (souteneur)* pimp

maquerelle [makrɛl] *nf très Fam* madam

maquette [makɛt] *nf* **(a)** *(de livre)* dummy **(b)** *(d'une construction architecturale)* (scale) model; *(de mise en page)* paste-up **(c)** *(jouet)* model; **m. d'avion/de bateau** model plane/boat

maquettiste [makɛtist] *nmf* **(a)** *(dans une entreprise)* model maker **(b)** *(graphiste)* graphic designer

maquignon [makiɲɔ̃] *nm* **(a)** *(marchand de chevaux)* horse dealer **(b)** *Fig (entremetteur malhonnête)* crooked dealer

maquillage [makijaʒ] *nm* **(a)** *(de visage) (action)* making up; *(produits)* make-up **(b)** *(de documents)* forging; *(de photos)* faking; *(de comptes)* falsification

maquiller [makije] **1** *vt* **(a)** *(personne, visage)* to make up **(b)** *(documents)* to forge; *(photos)* to fake; *(comptes)* to falsify
2 se maquiller *vpr* to put one's make-up on

maquilleur, -euse [makijœr, -øz] *nm,f* make-up artist

maquis [maki] *nm* **(a)** *(végétation)* maquis **(b)** *Fig (d'une procédure, de l'administration)* jungle **(c)** *Hist* maquis *(Resistance movement in World War II)*; **prendre le m.** to take to the hills

maquisard [makizar] *nm Hist* member of the maquis, Resistance fighter *(in World War II)*

marabout [marabu] *nm* **(a)** *(sorcier)* witchdoctor **(b)** *(oiseau)* marabou

maracas [maraka] *nfpl* maracas

maraîcher, -ère [mareʃe, -ɛr] **1** *adj* **culture maraîchère** *Br* market gardening, *Am* truck farming; **produits maraîchers** *Br* market garden produce, *Am* truck
2 *nm,f Br* market gardener, *Am* truck farmer

marais [marɛ] *nm* marsh; **m. salant** saltern

marasme [marasm] *nm* **(a)** *(ralentissement)* stagnation **(b)** *(découragement)* depression

marathon [maratɔ̃] *nm* marathon

marathonien, -enne [maratɔnjɛ̃, -ɛn] *nm,f* marathon runner

marâtre [maratr] *nf* **(a)** *(belle-mère)* stepmother **(b)** *(mère cruelle)* cruel mother

maraude [marod] *nf* pilfering

marauder [marode] *vi* **(a)** *(voler)* to pilfer **(b)** *(taxi)* to cruise for fares **(c)** *(rôdeur)* to prowl around

maraudeur, -euse [maʀodœʀ, -øz] *nm,f* pilferer

marbre [maʀbʀ] *nm* (a) *(roche)* marble; **en** *ou* **de m.** marble; *Fig* **rester de m.** to remain impassive (b) *(statue)* marble (statue) (c) *(table de traçage)* faceplate (d) *(de presse)* bed

marbré, -e [maʀbʀe] *adj* (a) *(surface, couverture de livre)* marbled; *(pierre)* veined (b) *(peau)* blotchy (c) **gâteau m.** marble cake

marbrier [maʀbʀije] *nm* monumental mason

marbrière [maʀbʀijɛʀ] *nf* marble quarry

marbrure [maʀbʀyʀ] *nf* (a) *(sur un livre)* marbling (b) *(sur la peau)* mottling

marc [maʀ] *nm* (a) *(de raisins, d'olives)* marc (b) *(eau-de-vie)* marc (brandy) (c) *(de café)* grounds

marcassin [maʀkasɛ̃] *nm* young wild boar

marchand, -e [maʀʃɑ̃, -ɑ̃d] **1** *adj (prix)* trade **2** *nm,f (dans un magasin)* Br shopkeeper, Am storekeeper; *(de vin)* merchant; *(de meubles, de chevaux)* dealer; **m. ambulant** street vendor; **m. forain** travelling stallholder; **m. de glaces** ice cream seller; **m. de journaux** Br newsagent, Am newsdealer; **m. de légumes** greengrocer; **m. de tableaux** art dealer; **m. de tapis** carpet dealer

marchandage [maʀʃɑ̃daʒ] *nm* haggling

marchander [maʀʃɑ̃de] **1** *vt* to haggle over **2** *vi* to haggle

marchandisage [maʀʃɑ̃dizaʒ] *nm* merchandizing

marchandise [maʀʃɑ̃diz] *nf* commodity; **marchandises** goods, merchandise

marche [maʀʃ] *nf* (a) *(d'escalier)* step, stair (b) *(action de marcher)* walking; *(promenade)* walk; *(allure)* pace; **faire une m.** to go for a walk; **à deux heures de m.** two hours' walk away; **m. à pied** walking (c) *(défilé, manifestation)* march; **ouvrir la m.** to lead the way; **fermer la m.** to bring up the rear (d) *(morceau de musique)* march; **m. funèbre** funeral march (e) *(déplacement)* **être en m.** *(véhicule)* to be moving; *(mouvement, progrès)* to be on the march; **se mettre en m.** *(véhicule)* to move off; *(personne)* to set off *or* out; **dans le sens de la m.** *(en voyage)* facing forward; **dans le sens contraire de la m.** facing backwards; **m. avant/arrière** *(vitesse)* forward/reverse gear; **faire m. arrière** *(véhicule)* to reverse; *Fig* to backtrack (f) *(fonctionnement)* running, working; **mettre qch en m.** to start sth; **se mettre en m.** to start (g) *(des événements, de l'histoire)* course; *(du temps)* march; **m. à suivre** procedure

marché [maʀʃe] *nm* (a) *(accord)* deal, bargain; *(plus officiel)* contract; **m. conclu!** it's a deal!; **par-dessus le m.** into the bargain; **bon m.** cheap *(lieu public de vente)* market; **faire son m.** to go shopping; **M. commun** Common Market; **m. noir** black market; **m. aux puces** flea market; **M. unique (européen)** Single (European) Market (c) *(débouché économique)* market (d) *Fin* market; **m. des changes** foreign exchange market; **m. haussier/baissier** bull/bear market; **m. à terme** futures market

marchepied [maʀʃəpje] *nm* (a) *(de train)* step (b) *(escabeau)* steps (c) *Fig* stepping-stone

marcher [maʀʃe] *vi* (a) *(se déplacer à pied)* to walk; *(mettre le pied)* to step *(dans/sur* in/on); *aussi Fig* **m. sur les pieds de qn** to tread on sb's toes; *Fig* **m. droit** to keep on the straight and narrow (b) *(fonctionner) (machine)* to work, to run; *(plans)* to work; **faire m.** to work *or* operate sth; **comment ça marche?** how does it work?; *Fig* **les affaires marchent (bien)** business is doing well; **ça marche!** *(d'accord)* sure! (c) *(avancer)* to march *(vers/vers* towards/on) (d) *Fam (croire sans réserve)* to fall for it; **faire m. qn** to pull sb's leg (e) *Fam (accepter)* to go along with it

marcheur, -euse [maʀʃœʀ, -øz] *nm,f* walker

mardi [maʀdi] *nm* Tuesday; **M. gras** Shrove Tuesday; *voir aussi* **samedi**

mare [maʀ] *nf* (a) *(étendue d'eau)* pond (b) *(grande quantité)* pool

marécage [maʀekaʒ] *nm* marsh, bog

marécageux, -euse [maʀekaʒø, -øz] *adj* (a) *(terrain)* marshy, boggy (b) *(plante)* marsh

maréchal, -aux [maʀeʃal, -o] *nm* **m. (de France)** *(officier général)* field marshal; *(d'un roi)* marshal; **m. des logis** sergeant

maréchal-ferrant [maʀeʃalferɑ̃] *(pl* maréchaux-ferrants [maʀeʃoferɑ̃])* *nm* blacksmith

marée [maʀe] *nf* (a) *(de la mer)* tide; **à m. haute/basse** at high/low tide; **à la m. montante/descendante** when the tide comes in/goes out; **m. noire** oil slick (b) *Fig (de personnes)* surging mass (c) *(fruits de la pêche)* fresh seafood

marelle [maʀɛl] *nf* hopscotch

marémoteur, -trice [maʀemotœʀ, -tʀis] *adj (énergie)* tidal; **usine marémotrice** tidal power station

mareyeur, -euse [maʀejœʀ, -øz] *nm,f* fish wholesaler

margarine [maʀgaʀin] *nf* margarine

marge [maʀʒ] *nf* (a) *(de page)* margin; **en m. de** on the fringes of; **vivre en m. (de la société)** to live on the fringes of society (b) *(liberté d'action)* leeway; **avoir de la m.** to have some leeway; *(temps)* to have time to spare; **m. d'erreur** margin of error; **m. de négociation/manœuvre** room for negotiation/manoeuvre; **m. de sécurité** safety margin (c) *(commerciale)* **m. (bénéficiaire)** profit margin

margelle [maʀʒɛl] *nf (de puits)* coping, curb

marger [45] [maʀʒe] *vt (page)* to feed in; *Ordinat* to set the margins for

marginal, -e, -aux, -ales [maʀʒinal, -o] **1** *adj* (a) *(personne, mode de vie)* on the fringes of society (b) *(secondaire) (occupations, importance)* marginal **2** *nm,f* dropout

marginalisation [maʀʒinalizasjɔ̃] *nf* marginalization

marginaliser [maʀʒinalize] **1** *vt* to marginalize **2 se marginaliser** *vpr* to become marginalized

marguerite [maʀgəʀit] *nf (a) (fleur)* daisy (b) *(de machine à écrire)* daisy wheel

mari [maʀi] *nm* husband

mariage [maʀjaʒ] *nm* (a) *(cérémonie)* wedding; *(union)* marriage; **m. d'amour** love match; **m. blanc** marriage in name only *(primarily in order to acquire nationality)*; **m. civil** ≃ registry office wedding; **m. de raison** marriage of convenience (b) *(de choses)* combination, marriage; *(de couleurs)* blend(ing)

Marianne [maʀjan] *nf* ≃ young woman symbolizing the French Republic

marié, -e [marje] **1** adj married; **non m.** unmarried, single

2 nm,f groom, f bride; **les mariés** the bride and groom; **les jeunes mariés** the newly-weds

marier [66] [marje] **1** vt (a) (sujet: prêtre) to marry; (sujet: père) to marry off (b) (qualités) to combine; (sociétés) to merge; (couleurs) to blend; (styles) to harmonize

2 se marier vpr (a) (personnes) to get married, to marry; **se m. avec qn** to marry sb (b) (couleurs) to blend (avec with); (styles) to go together (avec with)

marieur, -euse [marjœr, -øz] nm,f Fam matchmaker

marihuana [marirwana], **marijuana** [mariʒwana] nf marijuana

marin, -e [marɛ̃, -in] **1** adj (a) (air, brise) sea; (plante, animal) marine (b) (carte) sea; (mille) nautical

2 nm seaman, sailor; **m. pêcheur** (deep-sea) fisherman; **m. d'eau douce** landlubber

marina [marina] nf marina

marinade [marinad] nf (mélange aromatique) marinade; **m. de poissons/de gibier** marinated fish/game

marine [marin] **1** nf (a) (flotte) navy; **la m. de guerre** the navy; **la m. marchande** the merchant navy; **la M. nationale** the French navy (b) (navigation) seamanship (c) (tableau) seascape

2 adj inv navy (blue)

3 nm (fusilier) Br (Royal) Marine, Am marine

mariner [marine] **1** vt to marinate

2 vi (a) (aliment) to marinate; **faire m. qch** to marinate sth; **harengs marinés** pickled herrings (b) Fam Fig (personne) to hang around; **faire ou laisser m. qn** (dans un lieu) to keep sb hanging around; (dans une situation) to leave sb to stew

maringouin [marɛ̃gwɛ̃] nm Can mosquito

marinier [marinje] nm Br bargee, Am bargeman

marinière [marinjɛr] nf blouse

mariole [marjɔl] nm Fam sly devil; **faire le m.** to try to be clever

marionnette [marjɔnɛt] nf puppet

marionnettiste [marjɔnetist] nmf puppeteer

marital, -e, -aux, -ales [marital, -o] adj marital

maritalement [maritalmɑ̃] adv **vivre m.** to cohabit

maritime [maritim] adj (a) (navigation, plante, trafic) maritime; (ville) seaside (b) Can **les Maritimes** the Maritimes

marivaudage [marivodaʒ] nm Litt light-hearted banter

marjolaine [marʒɔlɛn] nf marjoram

mark [mark] nm (German) mark

marketing [marketiŋ] nm marketing

marmaille [marmaj] nf Fam brood, kids

marmelade [marməlad] nf compote; **m. (d'oranges)** (orange) marmalade; Fig **en m.** reduced to a pulp

marmite [marmit] nf (cooking) pot; Fig **faire bouillir la m.** to bring home the bacon

marmonner [marmɔne] vt & vi to mumble, to mutter

marmot [marmo] nm Fam kid

marmotte [marmɔt] nf marmot

marmotter [marmɔte] vt to mumble, to mutter

marner [marne] vi Fam to slog

Maroc [marɔk] nm **le M.** Morocco

marocain, -e [marɔkɛ̃, -ɛn] **1** adj Moroccan

2 nm,f **M.** Moroccan

maronite [marɔnit] adj & nmf Maronite

maroquin [marɔkɛ̃] nm morocco (leather)

maroquinerie [marɔkinri] nf (a) (fabrication) leather tanning (b) (magasin) leather goods shop (c) (articles) leather goods

maroquinier [marɔkinje] nm (a) (fabricant) leather worker (b) (commerçant) dealer in leather goods

marotte [marɔt] nf (idée fixe) craze

marquant, -e [markɑ̃, -ɑ̃t] adj (incident, personne, journée) remarkable; (épisode) significant

marque [mark] nf (a) (signe, trace) mark (b) (de produits, d'appareils) brand; (de voiture) make; **de m.** (produits) branded; (vêtements) designer; **m. déposée** registered trademark (c) (preuve) (d'amitié) token; (de confiance) sign (d) (cachet) stamp; **porter la m. du génie** to bear the stamp of genius (e) Ordinat marker; **m. d'insertion** insertion marker (f) **de m.** (important) distinguished, prominent (g) **marques** (repères) marks; **à vos marques! prêts? partez!** on your marks! get set! go!

marqué, -e [marke] adj (a) (visage) lined; **il est très m.** his face is very lined (b) (différence, penchant) marked

marque-page (pl **marque-pages**) [markpaʒ] nm bookmark

marquer [marke] **1** vt (a) (faire un signe sur) to mark (b) (écrire) to write (c) (délimiter) to mark (d) (adversaire) to mark; (but, essai) to score (e) (indiquer) to show (f) (accentuer) to mark; **m. le pas** to mark time; Fig **m. le coup** to mark the occasion (g) (impressionner) to make an impression on (h) Ordinat to mark

2 vi (laisser une trace) to leave a mark

marqueterie [markɛtri] nf marquetry

marqueur [markœr] nm (a) (stylo) (felt-tip) marker (b) (biologique, génétique) marker

marquis [marki] nm marquis

marquise [markiz] nf (a) (auvent) canopy (b) (canapé) (two-seater) sofa (c) (personne) marchioness

Marquises [markiz] nfpl **les (îles) M.** the Marquesas Islands

marraine [marɛn] nf (a) (d'un enfant) godmother (b) (d'un bateau) = woman who launches a new boat

Marrakech [marakɛʃ] n Marrakesh

marrant, -e [marɑ̃, -ɑ̃t] adj Fam funny

marre [mar] adv Fam **en avoir m. (de qn/qch)** to be fed up (with sb/sth); **en avoir m. de faire qch** to be fed up with doing sth

marrer [mare] **se marrer** vpr Fam to have a good laugh

marron[1] [marɔ̃] **1** adj inv (couleur) brown

2 nm (a) (fruit) chestnut; **marrons chauds** roast chestnuts; **marrons glacés** marrons glacés; **m. d'Inde** horse chestnut (b) (couleur) brown (c) Fam (coup de poing) thump

marron[2], -onne [marɔ̃, -ɔn] adj (médecin, homme de loi) quack

marronnier [marɔnje] nm horse chestnut (tree)

Mars [mars] npr (dieu, planète) Mars

mars [mars] nm March; voir aussi **janvier**

marseillais, -e [marsejɛ, -ɛz] **1** adj of Marseilles

2 nm,f **M.** person from Marseilles

3 nf **la Marseillaise** the Marseillaise

Marseille [marsɛj] n Marseilles

marsouin [marswɛ̃] nm porpoise

marsupial, -e, -aux, -ales [marsypjal, -o] *adj & nm* marsupial

marteau, -x [marto] **1** *adj Fam* crazy
  2 *nm* (a) *(outil)* hammer; **m. piqueur** pneumatic drill; *Fig* **être entre le m. et l'enclume** to be between the devil and the deep blue sea (b) *(de porte)* (door) knocker (c) *(de piano)* hammer

martel [martel] *nm* **se mettre m. en tête** to worry oneself sick

martèlement [martelmɑ̃] *nm* hammering

marteler [39] [martale] *vt* (a) *(métal, pieu)* to hammer; **m. la table à coups de poing** to hammer on the table (b) *(mot, phrase)* to hammer out

martial, -e, -aux, -ales [marsjal, -o] *adj* martial

martien, -enne [marsjɛ̃, -ɛn] *adj & nm,f* Martian

martinet¹ [martine] *nm (fouet)* strap

martinet² *nm (oiseau)* swift

martingale [martɛ̃gal] *nf (sur un vêtement)* half belt

martiniquais, -e [martinike, ez] **1** *adj* Martinican
  2 *nm,f* M. Martinican

Martinique [martinik] *nf* **la M.** Martinique

martin-pêcheur [martɛ̃pɛʃœr] *nm* kingfisher
(pl **martins-pêcheurs)**

martyr, -e [martir] **1** *adj (enfant)* battered; *(peuple)* martyred
  2 *nm,f* martyr

martyre [martir] *nm* martyrdom

martyriser [martirize] *vt (maltraiter)* to batter; *(harceler)* to bully

marxisme [marksism] *nm* Marxism

marxiste [marksist] *adj & nmf* Marxist

mas [mɑ, mɑs] *nm (en Provence) (ferme)* farm; *(maison)* farmhouse

mascara [maskara] *nm* mascara

mascarade [maskarad] *nf* masquerade; *Fig* sham

mascotte [maskɔt] *nf* mascot

masculin, -e [maskylɛ̃, -in] **1** *adj* (a) *(sexe, mode, métier)* male; *(trait de caractère, femme)* masculine (b) *(nom, genre)* masculine (c) *(rime)* masculine
  2 *nm* masculine; **au m.** in the masculine

masculinité [maskylinite] *nf* masculinity

maskinongé [maskinɔ̃ʒe] *nm Can* muskellunge

maso [mazo] *Fam* **1** *adj* masochistic
  2 *nmf* masochist

masochisme [mazɔʒism] *nm* masochism

masochiste [mazɔʃist] **1** *adj* masochistic
  2 *nmf* masochist

masquage [maskaʒ] *nm Ordinat* masking

masque [mask] *nm* (a) *(déguisement)* mask; **m. à gaz/oxygène** gas/oxygen mask; **m. de plongée** diving mask (b) *(apparence)* façade; **lever le m.** to remove one's mask (c) *(soin cosmétique)* **m. (de beauté)** face pack (d) *Ordinat* mask; **m. d'entrée, m. de saisie** input mask

masqué, -e [maske] *adj (personne)* masked

masquer [maske] *vt* to mask

massacrante [masakrɑ̃t] *adj f voir* **humeur**

massacre [masakr] *nm* (a) *(tuerie)* massacre (b) *Fig (travail mal fait)* mess; **faire un m.** *(travailler mal)* to make a complete mess; *(remporter un grand succès)* to be a runaway success

massacrer [masakre] *vt* (a) *(tuer, exterminer)* to massacre (b) *Fam (abîmer) (travail)* to make a mess of; *(mal interpréter) (morceau de musique, texte)* to murder

massage [masaʒ] *nm* massage; **faire un m. à qn** to give sb a massage

masse¹ [mas] *nf* (a) *(volume)* mass; **m. d'air** air mass; **taillé/sculpté dans la m.** carved/sculpted from the block; **tomber comme une m.** to fall in a heap (b) *(grande quantité)* mass; **de m.** *(culture, communication)* mass; **en m.** en masse; **une m. de** masses of; *Fam* **pas des masses** not much; *(nombre)* not many; **m. monétaire** money supply; **m. salariale** wage bill (c) **les masses** *(le peuple)* the masses; **masses laborieuses** working masses (d) *Phys* mass (e) *Él Br* earth, *Am* ground; **mettre qch à la m.** *Br* to earth sth, *Am* to ground sth; *Fam Fig* **être à la m.** to be off one's head

masse² *nf (marteau)* sledgehammer

massepain [maspɛ̃] *nm* marzipan

masser¹ [mase] **1** *vt (rassembler)* to assemble; *(troupes)* to mass
  2 se masser *vpr* to assemble

masser² **1** *vt (faire un massage à)* to massage; **se faire m.** to have a massage
  2 se masser *vpr* to massage oneself; **se m. le pied** to massage one's foot

masseur, -euse [masœr, -øz] *nm,f* masseur, *f* masseuse

massicot [masiko] *nm* guillotine

massif, -ive [masif, -iv] **1** *adj* (a) *(formes, meuble, porte)* massive; *(personne)* heavily built (b) *(argent, or, bois)* solid (c) *(dose)* massive
  2 *nm* (a) *(de plantes, d'arbres)* clump; **m. de fleurs** flower bed (b) *(ensemble de montagnes)* massif; **le M. central** the Massif Central *(mountains in central France)*

massivement [masivmɑ̃] *adv (répondre, voter)* en masse

mass media [masmedja] *nmpl* mass media

massue [masy] **1** *adj inv (argument)* sledgehammer
  2 *nf* club

mastectomie [mastektɔmi] *nf* mastectomy

mastic [mastik] *nm (pour fenêtres)* putty; *(pour bois)* mastic

mastication [mastikasjɔ̃] *nf* chewing

mastiquer¹ [mastike] *vt (mâcher)* to chew

mastiquer² *vt (fissures)* to fill (in); *(vitre)* to put putty round

mastoc [mastɔk] *adj inv Fam (personne)* hulking; *(construction)* clumsy

mastodonte [mastodɔ̃t] *nm* (a) *Fam (personne)* colossus; *(objet)* hulking great thing (b) *(animal)* mastodon

masturbation [mastyrbasjɔ̃] *nf* masturbation

masturber [mastyrbe] **1** *vt* to masturbate
  2 se masturber *vpr* to masturbate

m'as-tu-vu [matyvy] *nmf inv Fam* show-off

masure [mazyr] *nf* hovel

mat¹, -e [mat] *adj (métal, couleur)* matt; *(teint)* darkish; *(son)* dull

mat² **1** *adj inv (aux échecs)* checkmated
  2 *nm* checkmate

mât [mɑ] *nm* (a) *(d'un voilier)* mast (b) *(poteau)* pole; **m. de cocagne** greasy pole

matador [matadɔr] *nm* matador

match (*pl* matchs *ou* matches) [matʃ] *nm Br* match, *Am* game; **m.** aller/retour first/return leg; **un m. amical** a friendly; **m. nul** draw; **faire m. nul** to draw

matelas [matla] *nm* mattress; **m. pneumatique** air bed

matelassé, -e [matlase] *adj* (*tissu, blouson*) quilted; (*enveloppe*) padded

matelot [matlo] *nm* sailor

mater¹ [mate] *vt* (*se rendre maître de*) (*personne*) to bring to heel; (*rébellion*) to put down

mater² *vt Fam* (*regarder*) to ogle

matérialisation [materjalizasjɔ̃] *nf* materialization

matérialiser [materjalize] **se matérialiser** *vpr* to materialize

matérialisme [materjalism] *nm* materialism

matérialiste [materjalist] **1** *adj* materialistic
2 *nmf* materialist

matériau, -x [materjo] *nm* (**a**) (*substance*) material (**b**) **matériaux** (*de construction*) material(s); (*documents*) material

matériel¹, -elle [materjɛl] *adj* (*confort, besoins, dégâts*) material; (*organisation, problème*) practical

matériel² *nm* (**a**) (*pour une activité, un sport*) equipment; **m. de bureau** office equipment; **m. pédagogique** teaching material; **m. agricole** farm equipment (**b**) (*d'une entreprise*) plant; **m. d'exploitation** working plant (**c**) *Ordinat* **m. (informatique)** (computer) hardware

matériellement [materjɛlmɑ̃] *adv* (**a**) (*sur le plan matériel*) materially (**b**) **c'est m. impossible** it's physically impossible

maternel, -elle [matɛrnɛl] *adj* (**a**) (*personne, attitude, gestes*) maternal (**b**) (*langue*) native

maternelle [matɛrnɛl] *nf* nursery (school)

materner [matɛrne] *vt* to mother

maternisé, -e [matɛrnize] *adj* **lait m.** milk suitable for infants

maternité [matɛrnite] *nf* (**a**) (*fait d'être mère*) motherhood (**b**) (*hôpital*) maternity hospital (**c**) (*tableau*) Madonna and Child

mathématicien, -enne [matematisjɛ̃, -ɛn] *nm,f* mathematician

mathématique [matematik] **1** *adj* (**a**) (*science*) mathematical (**b**) (*esprit*) logical; (*rigueur*) mathematical
2 *nfpl* **les mathématiques** mathematics (*singulier*)

mathématiquement [matematikmɑ̃] *adv* mathematically

matheux, -euse [matø, -øz] *nm,f Fam* mathematician

maths [mat] *nfpl Fam Br* maths, *Am* math; **M. Sup/Spé** = first/second year of classes preparing students for entrance to science-oriented "grandes écoles"

matière [matjɛr] *nf* (**a**) (*substance*) material; **matières grasses** fat; **m. grise** grey matter; *Fam* **faire fonctionner sa m. grise** to exercise one's grey matter; **m. plastique** plastic; **matières premières** raw materials (**b**) (*sujet*) (*scolaire*) subject; (*pour en faire un film, un livre, une étude*) material; **il n'y a pas m. à rire** it's no laughing matter; **donner m. à qch** to give cause for sth; **en m. de** as regards (**c**) (*d'un corps physique*) matter

Matignon [matiɲɔ̃] *n* (**l'hôtel**) **M.** = French Prime Minister's offices

matin [matɛ̃] *nm* morning; **ce m.** this morning; **quatre heures du m.** four o'clock in the morning, 4 am; **le jeudi 2 au m.** on the morning of Thursday the 2nd; **faire qch le m.** to do sth in the morning; **être du m.** to be a morning person; **tous les lundis m.** every Monday morning; **de grand** *ou* **bon m.** early in the morning, in the early morning; **au petit m.** in the small *or* early hours; **du m. au soir** from morning till night

matinal, -e, -aux, -ales [matinal, -o] *adj* (**a**) (*heure*) early; (*excursion, activité*) morning (**b**) (*personne*) **être m.** to be an early riser

mâtiné, -e [matine] *adj* crossbred; **m. de** crossed with; *Fig* mixed with

matinée [matine] *nf* (**a**) (*matin*) morning; **dans la m.** in (the course of) the morning; **en fin de m.** towards the end of the morning (**b**) (*au théâtre, cinéma*) matinée

maton, -onne [matɔ̃, -ɔn] *nm,f Fam* screw (*prison warder*)

matos [matos] *nm Fam* gear

matou [matu] *nm* tom (cat)

matraquage [matrakaʒ] *nm* (**a**) (*avec une matraque*) bludgeoning (**b**) (*insistance*) **m. publicitaire** hype

matraque [matrak] *nf* bludgeon; (*d'agent de police*) *Br* truncheon, *Am* nightstick

matraquer [matrake] *vt* (**a**) (*frapper*) to club (**b**) *Fig* (*harceler*) to bombard (**c**) *Fam* (*faire payer très cher*) to rip off, to fleece

matriarcal, -e, -aux, -ales [matrijarkal, -o] *adj* matriarchal

matrice [matris] *nf* (**a**) (*moule*) matrix, die; (*de disque*) matrix (**b**) *Math* matrix (**c**) *Ordinat* array; **m. d'aiguilles** dot matrix

matricide [matrisid] *nm* matricide

matriciel, -elle [matrisjɛl] *Ordinat* **1** *adj* **imprimante matricielle** dot matrix printer
2 *nf* **matricelle** dot matrix

matricule [matrikyl] **1** *nm* (*numéro*) number
2 *nf* (*registre*) register

matrimonial, -e, -aux, -ales [matrimɔnjal, -o] *adj* matrimonial

matrone [matron] *nf Péj* stout woman

mature [matyr] *adj* mature

mâture [matyr] *nf* masts

maturité [matyrite] *nf* (*de personne*) maturity; (*de fruit*) ripeness; **arriver** *ou* **venir à m.** (*fromage, vin*) to mature; (*fruit*) to ripen

maudire [modir] *vt* to curse

maudit, -e [modi, -it] *adj* (**a**) (*damné*) cursed (**b**) (*avant le nom*) (*insupportable*) damn(ed)

maugréer [24] [mogree] *vi* to grumble (**contre** about *or* at)

maure [mɔr] **1** *adj* Moorish
2 *nm* **M.** Moor

mauresque [moresk] **1** *adj* Moorish
2 *nf* **M.** Moorish woman

Maurice [moris] *n* **l'île M.** Mauritius

mauricien, -enne [morisjɛ̃, -ɛn] **1** *adj* Mauritian
2 *nm,f* **M.** Mauritian

Mauritanie [moritani] *nf* **la M.** Mauritania

mauritanien, -enne [moritanjɛ̃, -ɛn] **1** *adj* Mauritanian
2 *nm,f* **M.** Mauritanian

mausolée [mozɔle] *nm* mausoleum

maussade [mosad] *adj* (a) *(de mauvaise humeur)* sullen (b) *(temps, paysage)* gloomy

mauvais, -e [move, -ez] 1 *adj* (a) *(défectueux)* *(santé, vue, excuse)* poor (b) *(incompétent)* *(élève, professeur, mère)* bad (en at) (c) *(nuisible)* bad (pour for) (d) *(inapproprié)* *(clef, numéro, moment)* wrong (e) *(méchant)* *(personne)* bad, nasty; *(chien)* vicious (f) *(mer)* rough (g) *Fam* **je l'ai trouvée mauvaise** I didn't find it at all funny

2 *adv* (a) **sentir m.** to smell (bad) (b) **il fait m.** the weather's bad

mauve [mov] 1 *adj* mauve

2 *nm (couleur)* mauve

mauviette [movjet] *nf Fam* wimp

max [maks] *nm Fam* **un m. de gens** *(le plus possible)* as many people as possible; *(énormément)* loads of people

max. *(abrév* **maximum)** max

maxillaire [maksiler] *nm* jawbone, *Spéc* maxilla

maxima [maksima] *voir* **maximum**

maximal, -e, -aux, -ales [maksimal, -o] *adj* maximum

maxime [maksim] *nf* maxim

maximiser [maksimize] *vt* to maximize

maximum [maksimɔm] *(pl* **maximums** *ou* **maxima** [maksima])* 1 *adj* maximum

2 *nm* maximum; **faire le m. (pour faire qch)** to do one's very best (to do sth); **au m.** at the most; *Fam* **un m.** *(beaucoup)* loads; *Fam* **un m. de gens** *(le plus possible)* as many people as possible; *(énormément)* loads of people

maya [maja] 1 *adj* Maya, Mayan

2 *nmf* M. Maya, Mayan

3 *nm (langue)* Mayan

mayonnaise [majɔnez] *nf* mayonnaise

mazout [mazut] *nm (fuel)* oil

mazouté, -e [mazute] *adj (plage)* oil-polluted; *(oiseau)* covered in oil

Mbps *Ordinat (abrév* **mégabits par seconde)** mbps

me [mə]

> **m'** is used before a word beginning with a vowel or h mute.

pron personnel (a) *(objet direct)* me; **me voici** here I am (b) *(objet indirect)* to me; **elle m'a serré la main** she shook my hand; **ils m'ont lancé des cailloux** they threw stones at me (c) *(dans les réfléchis)* myself; **je vais me doucher** I'm going to have a shower (d) *(dans les pronominaux)* **je me suis trompé** I made a mistake

mea culpa [meakylpa] *nm inv* **faire son m.** to own up

méandre [meɑ̃dr] *nm (de rivière)* meander; *(de route)* bend; *Fig* **méandres** *(d'un raisonnement)* intricacies

mec [mɛk] *nm Fam (homme quelconque)* guy, *Br* bloke; *(amoureux)* man

mécanicien, -enne [mekanisjɛ̃, -ɛn] *nm,f* (a) *(garage ou motor)* mechanic (b) *(conducteur de train)* Br train driver, Am engineer

mécanique [mekanik] 1 *adj* mechanical

2 *nf* (a) *(science du mouvement)* mechanics *(singulier)* (b) *(des moteurs, des machines)* mechanical engineering (c) *(mécanisme)* mechanism

mécaniquement [mekanikmɑ̃] *adv* mechanically

mécanisation [mekanizasjɔ̃] *nf* mechanization

mécanisme [mekanism] *nm* (a) *(d'une machine, d'une montre, d'un moteur)* mechanism (b) *(de la pensée, de la parole)* mechanics

mécénat [mesena] *nm* sponsorship; **m. d'entreprise** corporate sponsorship

mécène [mesen] *nm* sponsor

méchamment [meʃamɑ̃] *adv* (a) *(avec méchanceté)* nastily (b) *Fam (en intensif)* **être m. déçu/embêté** to be terribly disappointed/annoyed

méchanceté [meʃɑ̃ste] *nf* (a) *(d'une personne, d'une remarque)* nastiness; *(d'un enfant)* naughtiness (b) *(action)* nasty action; *(parole)* nasty remark

méchant, -e [meʃɑ̃, -ɑ̃t] 1 *adj* (a) *(personne, remarque)* nasty; *(enfant)* naughty; *(animal)* vicious; **attention chien m.** *(sur panneau)* beware of the dog (b) *(désagréable)* *(affaire)* unpleasant; *(blessure, grippe)* nasty; *(humeur)* foul

2 *nm,f Fam* baddie, baddy

mèche¹ [mɛʃ] *nf* (a) *(de bougie, de lampe)* wick; *(de charge explosive)* fuse (b) *(de perceuse)* bit (c) *(de cheveux)* strand; *(boucle)* lock; **se faire des mèches** to get highlights (in one's hair)

mèche² *nf* **être de m. avec qn** to be in cahoots with sb

méchoui [meʃwi] *nm* spit-roasted lamb

méconnaissable [mekɔnɛsabl] *adj* unrecognizable

méconnaître [20] *nf* (a) *(faits)* to fail to take account of (b) *(talent, artiste)* to fail to recognize

méconnu, -e [mekɔny] *adj (talent, artiste)* unrecognized

mécontent, -e [mekɔ̃tɑ̃, -ɑ̃t] 1 *adj (insatisfait)* displeased (**de** with); *(contrarié)* annoyed

2 *nm,f* grumbler; *(électeur)* malcontent

mécontentement [mekɔ̃tɑ̃tmɑ̃] *nm (insatisfaction)* displeasure; *(contrariété)* annoyance

mécontenter [mekɔ̃tɑ̃te] *vt (ne pas satisfaire)* to displease; *(contrarier)* to annoy

Mecque [mɛk] *n voir* **La Mecque**

médaille [medaj] *nf* (a) *(prix, décoration)* medal; **la m. d'or/d'argent/de bronze** the gold/silver/bronze medal (b) *(bijou)* *(avec le nom)* pendant *(with name engraved on it)*; *(à l'effigie d'un saint)* medal (c) *(de chat, de chien)* identity disc

médaillé, -e [medaje] 1 *adj (sportif)* holding a medal; *(soldat)* decorated

2 *nm,f (sportif)* medallist; *(soldat)* medal-holder

médaillon [medajɔ̃] *nm* (a) *(bijou)* locket (b) *(de poisson, de viande)* medallion

médecin [medsɛ̃] *nm* doctor; **m. généraliste** general practitioner, GP; **m. légiste** *Br* forensic scientist, *Am* medical examiner; **m. traitant** consulting physician; **m. du travail** = doctor who carries out the annual medical examination, required by law, of a company's employees

médecine [medsin] *nf* medicine; **exercer la m.** to practise medicine; **m. douce** *ou* **parallèle** alternative medicine; **m. générale** general medicine; **m. du travail** industrial medicine

média [medja] *nm* medium; **les médias** the media

médian, -e [medjɑ̃, -an] 1 *adj* median

2 *nf* médiane median

médiateur, -trice [medjatœr, -tris] 1 *adj* mediating

2 *nm,f* mediator

3 *nm* **le M. (de la République)** ≃ Ombudsman, Parliamentary Commissioner for Administration

médiathèque [medjatɛk] *nf* media library

médiation [medjasjɔ̃] *nf* mediation

médiatique [medjatik] *adj* media

médiatisation [medjatizasjɔ̃] *nf* media coverage

médiatiser [medjatize] *vt* to give media coverage to

médiator [medjatɔr] *nm Mus* plectrum

médiatrice [medjatris] *nf* median

médical, -e, -aux, -ales [medikal, -o] *adj* medical

médicalisé, -e [medikalize] *adj* **logement m.** nursing home

médicaliser [medikalize] *vt* (a) *(région, pays, population)* to make medical care available to (b) *(grossesse)* to treat as a medical matter

médicament [medikamɑ̃] *nm* medicine; **m. de confort** = medication prescribed to relieve pain and symptoms rather than as a cure for the illness

médicinal, -e, -aux, -ales [medisinal, -o] *adj* medicinal

médico-légal, -e *(mpl* médico-légaux, *fpl* médico-légales*)* [medikolegal, -o] *adj* forensic

médico-social, -e *(mpl* médico-sociaux, *fpl* médico-sociales*)* [medikosɔsjal, -o] *adj* **centre m.** health centre

médiéval, -e, -aux, -ales [medjeval, -o] *adj* medieval

médiocre [medjɔkr] *adj* mediocre

médiocrement [medjɔkrəmɑ̃] *adv* indifferently

médiocrité [medjɔkrite] *nf* mediocrity

médire [27b] [medir] **médire de** *vi ind* to speak ill of

médisance [medizɑ̃s] *nf* (a) *(action)* scandalmongering, gossiping (b) *(propos)* piece of scandal *or* gossip; **médisances** scandal, gossip

médisant, -e [medizɑ̃, -ɑ̃t] *adj (paroles)* slanderous; *(personne)* scandalmongering

méditation [meditasjɔ̃] *nf* meditation

méditer [medite] **1** *vt* (a) *(considérer par une profonde réflexion)* to contemplate (b) *(préparer)* to mull over
2 *vi* to meditate
3 **méditer sur** *vt ind* to meditate on

Méditerranée [mediterane] *nf* **la (mer) M.** the Mediterranean (Sea)

méditerranéen, -enne [mediteraneɛ̃, -ɛn] **1** *adj* Mediterranean
2 *nm,f* **M.** person from a Mediterranean country

médium [medjɔm] *nmf (voyant)* medium

médius [medjys] *nm* middle finger

méduse [medyz] *nf* jellyfish

méduser [medyze] *vt* to dumbfound

meeting [mitiŋ] *nm* meeting; **m. aérien** air show

méfait [mefɛ] *nm* misdemeanour; **les méfaits du tabac** the damage caused by smoking

méfiance [mefjɑ̃s] *nf (manque de confiance)* distrust; *(suspicion)* mistrust, suspicion

méfiant, -e [mefjɑ̃, -ɑ̃t] *adj (n'ayant pas confiance)* distrustful; *(suspicieux)* suspicious **(à l'égard de** *ou* **avec** of)

méfier [66] [mefje] **se méfier** *vpr* to be careful; **se m. de qn** not to trust sb; **se m. de qch** to watch out for sth

méga¹ [mega] *nm Ordinat* megabyte, meg

méga² *adj inv Fam* mega

mégalo [megalo] *adj & nmf Fam* megalomaniac

mégalomane [megaloman] *adj & nmf* megalomaniac

mégalomanie [megalomani] *nf* megalomania

mégalopole [megalopɔl] *nf* megalopolis

méga-octet *(pl* méga-octets*)* [megaɔktɛ] *nm Ordinat* megabyte

mégaphone [megafɔn] *nm Br* megaphone, *Am* bullhorn

mégarde [megard] **par mégarde** *adv* inadvertently, accidentally

mégère [meʒɛr] *nf (femme)* shrew

mégot [mego] *nm* fag butt *or* end

mégoter [megote] *vi Fam* to skimp **(sur** on)

meilleur, -e [mejœr] **1** *adj* (a) *(comparatif de bon)* better *(que* than) (b) *(superlatif de bon)* **le m. élève** *(de la classe)* the best pupil; *(parmi deux élèves)* the better pupil
2 *nm,f (personne)* **le m.** *(de tous)* the best; *(des deux)* the better; *Fam* **alors ça, c'est la meilleure!** that's just great!
3 *nm (ce qu'il y a de mieux)* **le m.** the best; **pour le m. et pour le pire** for better and for worse
4 *adv* **il fait m.** it's warmer

méjuger [45] [meʒyʒe] **1** *vt Litt (mal juger)* to misjudge; *(sous-estimer)* to underestimate
2 **méjuger de** *vt ind (mal juger)* to misjudge; *(sous-estimer)* to underestimate

mélancolie [melɑ̃kɔli] *nf* melancholy

mélancolique [melɑ̃kɔlik] *adj* melancholy

Mélanésie [melanezi] *nf* **la M.** Melanesia

mélanésien, -enne [melanezjɛ̃, -ɛn] **1** *adj* Melanesian
2 *nm,f* **M.** Melanesian
3 *nm (langue)* Melanesian

mélange [melɑ̃ʒ] *nm* (a) *(action)* mixing (b) *(résultat)* mixture; **je ne fais jamais de mélanges** I never mix my drinks

mélanger [45] [melɑ̃ʒe] **1** *vt* (a) *(mettre ensemble)* to mix (b) *(confondre, déranger)* to mix up; **je mélange tout en français** I get everything in French mixed up (c) *(cartes)* to shuffle
2 **se mélanger** *vpr* (a) *(s'incorporer)* to mix (b) *(se confondre)* to get mixed up (c) *Fam* **se m. les pédales** *ou* **les pinceaux** to get into a muddle

mélangeur [melɑ̃ʒœr] *nm* **(robinet) m.** *Br* mixer tap, *Am* mixing faucet

mélanome [melanom] *nm Méd* melanoma

mêlant [mɛlɑ̃] *adj m Can* **c'est pas m.** there's no doubt about it

mélasse [melas] *nf Br (black)* treacle, *Am* molasses *(singulier)*; *Fam* **être dans la m.** to be in a mess

Melba [mɛlba] *adj inv* **pêche M.** peach Melba

mêlé, -e [mele] *adj* mixed **(de** with)

mêlée [mele] *nf* (a) *(conflit)* fray, mêlée (b) *(au rugby)* scrum, scrummage

mêler [mele] **1** *vt* (a) *(mettre ensemble)* to mix **(à** *ou* **avec** with) (b) *(impliquer)* **m. qn à qch** *(affaire, conversation)* to involve sb in sth
2 **se mêler** *vpr* (a) *(substances)* to combine (b) *(se joindre)* **se m. à qch** *(foule)* to mingle with sth; *(cortège)* to join sth; *(conversation)* to join in sth (c) *(s'occuper)* **se m. de qch** to get involved in sth; **mêle-toi de tes affaires!** mind your own business!

mélèze [melɛz] *nm* larch (tree)

méli-mélo *(pl* mélis-mélos*)* [melimelo] *nm Fam* jumble

mélo [melo] *Fam* **1** *adj* melodramatic
2 *nm* melodrama

mélodie [melɔdi] *nf* (a) *(composition musicale)* melody, tune (b) *(de vers, d'une langue)* melodiousness, tunefulness

mélodieusement [melɔdjøzmɑ̃] *adv* melodiously, tunefully

mélodieux, -euse [melɔdjø, -øz] *adj* melodious, tuneful

mélodique [melɔdik] *adj* melodic

mélodiste [melɔdist] *nmf* melody writer

mélodrame [melɔdram] *nm* melodrama

mélomane [melɔman] **1** *adj* music-loving
2 *nmf* music lover

melon [məlɔ̃] *nm* (a) (*fruit*) melon (b) (*chapeau*) *Br* bowler (hat), *Am* derby

membrane [mɑ̃bran] *nf* membrane

membre [mɑ̃br] **1** *adj* (*État, pays*) member
2 *nm* (a) (*partie du corps*) limb; **m. supérieur/inférieur** upper/lower limb; **m. viril** male member (b) (*d'une association, d'un groupe*) member

même [meme] *nf* (*grand-mère*) gran(ny), grandma; *Fam* (*vieille femme*) old dear

même [mem] **1** *adj indéfini* (a) (*avant le nom*) (*identique*) same; **j'ai la m. voiture que toi** I have the same car as you (do)
(b) (*après le nom, pour insister*) **je l'ai fait le jour m.** I did it that (very) same day; **c'est cela m.** that's it exactly; **c'est la gentillesse m.** she's kindness itself *or* personified
2 *pron indéfini* **le/la m.** the same (one); **j'ai les mêmes que lui** I have the same (ones) as him; **cela revient au m.** it comes *or* amounts to the same thing
3 *adv* (a) (*pour insister*) even; **il n'est m. pas beau** he's not even good-looking; **m. moi, je le sais!** even I know that!; **elle habite ici m.** she lives in this very place; **aujourd'hui m.** this very day; **je pense m. qu'il sera d'accord** I think he'll actually agree
(b) **être à m. de faire qch** to be able *or* in a position to do sth; **dormir à m. le sol** to sleep on the bare ground; **porter un pull-over à m. la peau** to wear a jumper next to one's bare skin; **de m.** likewise; **Joyeux Noël – vous de m.** Merry Christmas – same to you; **il en est de m. des autres** the same goes for the others; **faire de m.** to follow suit; **de m. que** as just like so; **de m. que qch** just like sth; (*aussi bien que qch*) as well as sth; **m. si je l'avais, je ne te le donnerais pas** even if I had it, I wouldn't give it to you; **tout de m., *Fam* quand m.** all the same; *Fam* **enfin, quand m.!** honestly!; *Fam* **m. que je te l'avais déjà dit!** but I already TOLD you!

mémento [meme̅to] *nm* (a) (*pour réviser*) revision notes; **m. de chimie** chemistry revision notes (b) (*carnet*) diary

mémère [memer] *nf Fam Péj* **une grosse m.** a fat old bag

mémo [memo] *nm* memo

mémoire¹ [memwar] *nf* (a) (*faculté*) memory; **avoir de la m.** to have a good memory; **avoir la m. des noms/ dates** to have a good memory for names/dates; **avoir la m. courte** to have a short memory; **se rafraîchir la m.** to refresh one's memory; **à la m. de qn** (*monument*) in memory of sb; **de m.** (*citer*) from memory; **de m. d'homme** within living memory; **pour m.** for the record; **si j'ai bonne m.** if I remember correctly; **avoir une m. d'éléphant** to have a memory like an elephant; **la m. collective** collective memory
(b) *Ordinat* memory; **mettre un dossier en m.** to write a file to memory; **carte d'extension de m.** memory expansion card; **m. cache** cache memory; **m. centrale** main memory; **m. à disque** disk memory, RAM disc; **m. étendue** extended memory; **m. expansée** expanded memory; **m. haute** high memory; **m. de masse** mass storage; **m. morte** read-only memory; **m. non**

effaçable non-erasable memory; **m. paginée** expanded memory; **m. permanente** permanent memory; **m. tampon** buffer (store *or* memory); **m. vidéo** video memory; **m. vive random access memory**, RAM; **m. vive dynamique** DRAM, dynamic random access memory; **m. vive statique** static RAM, static random access memory

mémoire² *nm* (a) (*thèse*) thesis, dissertation (b) (*rapport*) report (c) **Mémoires** (*chronique*) memoirs

mémorable [memɔrabl] *adj* memorable

mémorandum [memɔrɑ̃dɔm] *nm* (a) (*note*) memorandum (b) (*carnet*) notebook

mémorial, -aux [memɔrjal, -o] *nm* (*monument*) memorial

mémoriser [memɔrize] *vt* to memorize

menaçant, -e [mənasɑ̃, -ɑ̃t] *adj* threatening, menacing

menace [mənas] *nf* threat (**de** of); **menaces de mort** death threats

menacer [16] [mənase] **1** *vt* to threaten (**de** with); **m. qn du poing** to shake one's fist at sb; **m. de faire qch** to threaten to do sth
2 *vi* (*tempête, orage, révolution*) to be brewing; **la pluie menace** it's threatening to rain

ménage [menaʒ] *nm* (a) (*nettoyage*) **faire le m.** (*à la maison*) to do the housework; *Fig* to have a shake-up; **faire des ménages** to go out cleaning (b) (*couple*) couple; **se mettre en m.** to move in together; **se mettre en m. avec qn** to move in with sb; **faire bon/mauvais m.** (**avec qn**) to get on well/badly (with sb); **m. à trois** ménage à trois (c) *Écon* household

ménagement [menaʒmɑ̃] *nm* care, caution; (*tact*) consideration; **sans m.** (*annoncer*) bluntly

ménager¹, -ère [menaʒe, -ɛr] **1** *adj* (*équipement, appareils*) household
2 *nf* **ménagère** (*femme*) housewife

ménager² [45] **1** *vt* (a) (*utiliser avec parcimonie*) (*argent*) to use sparingly; (*forces*) to conserve, to save; (*santé*) to take care of; **ne pas m. sa peine** to put in a lot of effort (b) (*traiter avec soin*) to treat carefully; *Fig* **m. la chèvre et le chou** to keep everyone happy (c) (*arranger*) (*entrevue, réunion*) to arrange, to organize; (*sortie*) to provide; (*réconciliation*) to bring about
2 se ménager *vpr* (a) (*prendre soin de soi*) to look after oneself, to look after oneself (b) (*se réserver*) to set aside

ménagerie [menaʒri] *nf* menagerie

mendiant, -e [mɑ̃djɑ̃, -ɑ̃t] **1** *adj* (*moine, ordre*) mendicant
2 *nm,f* beggar

mendicité [mɑ̃disite] *nf* begging

mendier [66] [mɑ̃dje] **1** *vt* to beg for
2 *vi* to beg

mener [46] [məne] **1** *vt* (a) (*accompagner*) to take (à to) (b) (*cortège, course*) to lead; **m. qch à bien** to bring sth to a successful conclusion; *Fig* **m. la danse** to call the tune (c) (*vie*) to lead; **la vie dure à qn** to give sb a hard time (d) (*débat, enquête*) to lead (e) (*contrôler*) (*personne*) **m. qn à la baguette** to rule sb under one's thumb; **m. qn par le bout du nez** to lead sb by the nose
2 *vi* (*dans un match, une compétition*) to lead; **m. par 2 buts à 1** to lead by 2 goals to 1 (b) **m. à un lieu** to lead to a place; *Fig* **cela ne mène à rien** this is getting us nowhere (c) *Fam* **elle n'en menait pas large** her heart was in her mouth

meneur, -euse [mənœr, -øz] 1 *nm,f (de parti politique)* leader; *(agitateur)* ringleader; **m. d'hommes** born leader; **m. de jeu** question master, quiz master; *Sp* play maker 2 *nf* **meneuse de revue** principal chorus girl

menhir [menir] *nm* menhir

méninges [menɛʒ] *nfpl Fam* brains

méningite [menɛʒit] *nf* meningitis; **avoir une m.** to have meningitis

ménisque [menisk] *nm* meniscus

ménopause [menopoz] *nf* menopause

menotte [mənɔt] *nf* **(a)** *Fam (petite main)* little hand **(b)** **menottes** *(bracelets métalliques)* handcuffs; **mettre** *ou* **passer les menottes à qn** to handcuff sb, to put handcuffs on sb

mensonge [mɑ̃sɔ̃ʒ] *nm* **(a)** *(propos)* lie; **petit m., pieux m.** white lie **(b)** *(acte)* lying

mensonger, -ère [mɑ̃sɔ̃ʒe, -ɛr] *adj (propos)* untrue; *(publicité)* misleading

menstruation [mɑ̃stryasjɔ̃] *nf* menstruation

menstruel, -elle [mɑ̃stryɛl] *adj* menstrual

mensualiser [mɑ̃sɥalize] *vt* to pay monthly; **être mensualisé** *(pour les impôts)* ≃ to pay one's income tax in advance monthly instalments, the amount paid being an estimation based on previous years

mensualité [mɑ̃sɥalite] *nf* monthly payment

mensuel, -elle [mɑ̃sɥɛl] 1 *adj* monthly 2 *nm (publication)* monthly *(magazine)*

mensuellement [mɑ̃sɥɛlmɑ̃] *adv* monthly, every month

mensuration [mɑ̃syrasjɔ̃] *nf* **(a)** *(action)* measurement, measuring **(b)** **mensurations** *(dimensions)* measurements

mental, -e, -aux, -ales [mɑ̃tal, -o] 1 *adj* mental 2 *nm* mental attitude

mentalement [mɑ̃talmɑ̃] *adv* mentally

mentalité [mɑ̃talite] *nf* mentality

menteur, -euse [mɑ̃tœr, -øz] 1 *adj (personne)* untruthful, lying 2 *nm,f* liar

menthe [mɑ̃t] *nf (plante)* mint; **m. à l'eau** peppermint cordial

menthol [mɑ̃tɔl] *nm* menthol

mentholé, -e [mɑ̃tɔle] *adj* menthol, mentholated

mention [mɑ̃sjɔ̃] *nf* **(a)** *(fait de citer)* mention; **faire m. de qn/qch** to mention sb/sth **(b)** **rayer la m. inutile** *(sur formulaire)* delete where applicable **(c)** *(à un examen)* **m. passable** ≃ C; **m. assez bien** ≃ B; **m. bien/très bien** ≃ A

mentionner [mɑ̃sjɔne] *vt* to mention

mentir [64b] [mɑ̃tir] *vi* to lie (à to); **sans m.** honestly

menton [mɑ̃tɔ̃] *nm* chin; **m. en galoche** jutting-out chin; **m. fuyant** receding chin; **double m.** double chin

mentor [mɑ̃tɔr] *nm* mentor

menu[1], -e [məny] 1 *adj* **(a)** *(détail, monnaie)* small **(b)** *(taille)* slim; *(personne)* petite 2 *adv* small, fine

menu[2] *nm* **(a)** *(au restaurant)* set menu, fixed-price menu **(b)** *Ordinat* menu; **contrôlé par m.** menu-driven; **m. d'aide** help menu; **m. déroulant** pull-down menu; **m. fichier** file menu; **m. primaire/secondaire/principal** primary/secondary/main menu

menuet [mənɥɛ] *nm* minuet

menuiserie [mənɥizri] *nf* **(a)** *(atelier)* (joiner's) workshop **(b)** *(travail du bois, résultat)* joinery, woodwork

menuisier [mənɥizje] *nm* joiner, carpenter

méprendre [58] [meprɑ̃dr] **se méprendre** *vpr* to be mistaken (**sur** about); **elle te ressemble à s'y m.** she looks exactly like you

mépris[1], -e *voir* **méprendre**

mépris[2] [mepri] *nm* contempt, scorn; **avec m.** scornfully, contemptuously; **avoir du m. pour qn** to despise sb; **au m. de qch** regardless of sth

méprisable [meprizabl] *adj* contemptible, despicable

méprisant, -e [meprizɑ̃, -ɑ̃t] *adj* scornful, contemptuous

méprise [mepriz] *nf* mistake

mépriser [meprize] *vt* **(a)** *(dédaigner) (personne, argent)* to despise **(b)** *(ignorer) (conseil, offre, danger)* to disregard

mer [mer] *nf* **(a)** *(étendue d'eau)* sea; **en haute** *ou* **pleine m.** (out) at sea; **au bord de la m.** at the seaside; **aller à la m.** to go to the seaside; **prendre la m.** to set sail, to put (out) to sea; *Fam* **ce n'est pas la m. à boire** it's no big deal; **une m. d'huile** a sea as calm as a millpond; **la m. Adriatique** the Adriatic Sea; **la m. d'Aral** the Aral Sea; **la m. Caspienne** the Caspian Sea; **la m. de Chine** the China Sea; **la m. de Corail** the Coral Sea; **la m. Égée** the Aegean Sea; **la m. d'Irlande** the Irish Sea; **la m. Morte** the Dead Sea; **la m. Noire** the Black Sea; **la m. du Nord** the North Sea; **la m. Rouge** the Red Sea; **la m. des Sargasses** the Sargasso Sea **(b)** *(marée)* tide

mercantile [merkɑ̃til] *adj* mercenary

mercatique [merkatik] *nf* marketing

mercenaire [mersəner] *adj et nm* mercenary

mercerie [mersəri] *nf* **(a)** *(magasin)* Br haberdasher's (shop), Am notions store **(b)** *(articles)* Br haberdashery, Am notions

merchandising [merʃɑ̃dajziŋ] *nm* merchandizing

merci [mersi] 1 *exclam* thank you, thanks (**de** *ou* **pour** for); **(non) m.** no thank you, no thanks; **dire m. (à qn)** to say thank you *or* thanks (to sb); **m. bien, m. beaucoup** thank you *or* thanks very much 2 *nm* thank you 3 *nf* **être à la m. de qn/qch** to be at the mercy of sb/sth; **sans m.** merciless

mercier, -ère [mersje, -ɛr] *nm,f Br* haberdasher, Am notions dealer

mercredi [merkrədi] *nm* Wednesday; **le m. des Cendres** Ash Wednesday; *voir aussi* **samedi**

Mercure [merkyr] *npr (dieu, planète)* Mercury

mercure [merkyr] *nm* mercury

Mercurochrome® [merkyrokrom] *nm* Mercurochrome®

merde [merd] *Vulg* 1 *nf* shit, *Fig* **être dans la m.** to be in the shit; **ne pas se prendre pour de la m.** to think the sun shines out of one's arse; **c'est de la m.** *(c'est de la mauvaise qualité)* it's shit; **de m.** *(voiture, idée)* shitty 2 *exclam* shit! *Fig* **dire m. à qn** *(l'envoyer au diable)* to tell sb to bugger off; **je te dis m.!** *(bonne chance)* break a leg!; **m. alors!** oh shit!

merder [merde] *vi très Fam (mal fonctionner) (projet)* to go down the pan; **ça merde entre eux** things between them are really screwed up; **j'ai merdé à l'examen** I really screwed up in the exam

merdeux, -euse [mɛrdø, -øz] *très Fam* **1** *adj* **se sentir m.** to feel shitty
2 *nm,f (enfant)* **un petit m.** a little shit

merdier [mɛrdje] *nm Vulg* **être dans le m.** to be in the shit

merdique [mɛrdik] *adj très Fam* shitty

mère [mɛr] **1** *adj voir* **maison**
2 *nf* **(a)** *(parent)* mother; **elle est m. de trois enfants** she is the mother of three children; **m. célibataire** single mother; **être m. de famille** to be a wife and mother; **m. nourricière** foster mother; **m. patrie** mother country, motherland; **m. porteuse** surrogate mother; **m. poule** mother hen **(b)** *Fam (femme)* **la m. Martin** old Mrs Martin

merguez [mɛrgɛz] *nf* merguez *(spicy North African sausage)*

méridien, -enne [meridjɛ̃, -ɛn] **1** *adj (ligne)* meridian, meridional
2 *nm Géog* meridian
3 *nm f* méridienne *(canapé)* day bed

méridional, -e, -aux, -ales [meridjɔnal, -o] **1** *adj (du Sud)* southern; *(du sud de la France)* from the South of France
2 *nm,f (du Sud)* southerner; *(du sud de la France)* person from the South of France

meringue [mərɛ̃g] *nf* meringue

mérinos [merinos] *nm* merino

merisier [mərizje] *nm (arbre)* wild cherry (tree); *(bois)* cherry (wood)

méritant, -e [meritɑ̃, -ɑ̃t] *adj* deserving

mérite [merit] *nm (mot; honneur)* credit; **avoir du m. (à faire qch)** to deserve credit (for doing sth); **au moins, son livre a le m. de la clarté** at least her book has the merit of being clearly written; **tout le m. lui revient** he deserves all the credit

mériter [merite] *vt* **(a)** *(après une action)* to deserve; **m. d'être puni/récompensé** to deserve to be punished/rewarded; **elle mérite qu'on le lui dise** she deserves to be told **(b)** *(demander)* to be worth; **m. réflexion** to be worth thinking about; **ce livre mérite d'être lu** this book is worth reading

méritoire [meritwar] *adj* commendable, praiseworthy

merlan [mɛrlɑ̃] *nm* **(a)** *(poisson)* whiting **(b)** *très Fam (coiffeur)* hairdresser

merle [mɛrl] *nm* blackbird

merlu [mɛrly] *nm* hake

mérou [meru] *nm* grouper

mérovingien, -enne [merovɛ̃ʒjɛ̃, -ɛn] **1** *adj* Merovingian
2 *nmpl* **les Mérovingiens** the Merovingians

merveille [mɛrvɛj] *nf* **(a)** *(chose remarquable)* marvel, wonder; **à m.** wonderfully (well); **se porter à m.** to be in the best of health; *Fig* **faire des merveilles** to work wonders; **les Sept Merveilles du monde** the Seven Wonders of the World **(b)** *(gâteau)* = sweet fritter

merveilleusement [mɛrvɛjøzmɑ̃] *adv* marvellously, wonderfully

merveilleux, -euse [mɛrvɛjø, -øz] **1** *adj* marvellous, wonderful
2 *nm* **le m.** the supernatural

mes [me] *voir* **mon**

mésalliance [mezaljɑ̃s] *nf* unsuitable marriage; **faire une m.** to marry beneath oneself

mésallier [66] [mezalje] **se mésallier** *vpr* to marry beneath oneself

mésange [mezɑ̃ʒ] *nf* tit; **m. bleue** blue tit; **m. charbonnière** coal tit

mésaventure [mezavɑ̃tyr] *nf* misadventure

mesdames [medam] *nfpl voir* **madame**

mesdemoiselles [medmwazɛl] *nfpl voir* **mademoiselle**

mésentente [mezɑ̃tɑ̃t] *nf* disagreement

mésestimer [mezɛstime] *vt* to underestimate

mésothérapie [mezoterapi] *nf* = treatment consisting of injecting minute quantities of medication into the affected area

mesquin, -e [mɛskɛ̃, -in] *adj* mean, petty

mesquinement [mɛskinmɑ̃] *adv* meanly

mesquinerie [mɛskinri] *nf* **(a)** *(d'un caractère, d'un procédé)* meanness, pettiness **(b)** *(action)* mean *or* petty thing (to do)

mess [mɛs] *nm* mess

message [mesaʒ] *nm* message; *Ordinat* **m. d'accueil** welcome message; *Ordinat* **m. d'alerte** warning message, alert box; *Ordinat* **m. d'erreur** error message; *Ordinat* **m. d'invite** *(du système)* prompt; **m. publicitaire** advertisement

messager, -ère [mesaʒe, -ɛr] *nm,f* messenger

messagerie [mesaʒri] *nf* **(a)** *(service de transports)* courier company; **messageries aériennes** air freight company **(b)** *(service télématique)* **m. électronique** electronic mail service, e-mail **(c)** *(entreprise de routage)* **m. de presse** newspaper distributing service

messe [mɛs] *nf* *(office religieux, composition musicale)* mass; **aller à la m.** to go to mass; *Fig* **faire des messes basses** to whisper; **m. de minuit** midnight mass

messeigneurs [mesɛɲœr] *nmpl voir* **monseigneur**

Messie [mesi] *nm* **le M.** the Messiah

messieurs [mesjø] *nmpl voir* **monsieur**

mesurable [mazyrabl] *adj* measurable

mesure [mazyr] *nf* **(a)** *(dimension)* measurement; *(action)* measurement, measuring; **prendre les mesures de qn/qch** to measure sb/sth; *Fig* **prendre la m. de qn/qch** to size sb/sth up; **sur m.** *(costume)* made to measure; *(rôle, emploi)* ideal; **donner toute sa m.** to show what one is capable of; **être à la m. de qn/qch** to measure up to sb/sth; **être sans commune m. avec qch** to be out of proportion to sth; **elle a trouvé quelqu'un/un homme à sa m.** she met her match
(b) *(moyen)* measure; **prendre des mesures** to take measures; **m. de sécurité** safety measure *or* precaution; **par m. d'économie** as a way to save money
(c) *(quantité, unité)* measure; **sans commune m.** unrivalled
(d) *(modération)* moderation; **sans m.** *(ambition, jalousie)* limitless
(e) *Mus (temps)* time; *(division)* bar; **m. à quatre temps** four-four time, common time; **battre la m.** to beat time; **en m.** in time
(f) *(locutions)* **m. que** as; *(au fur et)* **à m.** as one goes along; **dans une certaine m.** to some *or* a certain extent; **dans la m. où** in so far as; **dans la m. du possible** as far as is possible; **être en m. de faire qch** to be in a position to do sth

mesuré, -e [mazyre] *adj (pas)* measured; *(langage, personne)* restrained

mesurer [məzyre] **1** vt (**a**) (dimensions, taille) to measure; (tissu) to measure off (**b**) (déterminer) to assess (**c**) (limiter) to limit; **m. l'argent à qn** to ration out money to sb (**d**) **m. ses paroles** to moderate one's language

2 vi to measure; **m. 2 mètres** (personne) to be 2 metres tall; (tour, colonne) to be 2 metres high

3 se mesurer vpr **se m. avec** ou **à qn** to pit oneself against sb

met voir **mettre**

métabolique [metabolik] adj metabolic

métabolisme [metabolism] nm metabolism

métairie [meteri] nf small farm (worked by share-cropper)

métal, -aux [metal, -o] nm metal

métallique [metalik] adj metallic

métallisé, -e [metalize] adj (peinture, couleur) metallic

métallo [metalo] nm Fam metalworker

métallurgie [metalyrʒi] nf (**a**) (industrie) metallurgical industry (**b**) (procédé) metallurgy

métallurgique [metalyrʒik] adj metallurgical

métallurgiste [metalyrʒist] nm (**a**) (ouvrier) metalworker (**b**) (chef d'entreprise) metallurgist

métamorphose [metamorfoz] nf aussi Fig metamorphosis

métamorphoser [metamorfoze] **1** vt to transform (**en** into)

2 se métamorphoser vpr Biol to metamorphose; Fig to be transformed (**en** into)

métaphore [metafor] nf metaphor

métaphorique [metaforik] adj metaphorical

métaphoriquement [metaforikmã] adv metaphorically

métaphysique [metafizik] **1** adj metaphysical

2 nf metaphysics (singulier)

métastase [metastaz] nf metastasis

métayer, -ère [meteje, -ɛr] nm,f sharecropper

météo [meteo] Fam **1** adj weather

2 nf (bulletin) weather forecast; (organisme) Br weather centre, Am weather bureau

météore [meteor] nm meteor

météorite [meteorit] nf meteorite

météorologie [meteorolɔʒi] nf meteorology

météorologique [meteorolɔʒik] adj (bulletin, prévisions) weather

météorologiste [meteorolɔʒist], **météorologue** [meteorolog] nmf meteorologist

métèque [metɛk] nm Br wog, = racist term used to refer to a coloured person

méthane [metan] nm methane

méthanol [metanol] nm methanol

méthode [metɔd] nf (**a**) (démarche) method; **m. pour faire qch** method of doing sth (**b**) (ordre) method; **avec m.** methodically (**c**) (livre) **m. d'anglais** English course book; **m. de piano** piano tutor

méthodique [metɔdik] adj methodical

méthodiquement [metɔdikmã] adv methodically

méthodiste [metɔdist] adj & nmf Methodist

méthodologie [metɔdolɔʒi] nf methodology

méthodologique [metɔdolɔʒik] adj methodological

méthylène [metilɛn] nm methylene

méticuleusement [metikyløzmã] adv meticulously

méticuleux, -euse [metikylø, -øz] adj meticulous

méticulosité [metikylozite] nf meticulousness

métier [metje] nm (**a**) (manuel, commercial) trade; (intellectuel) profession; **exercer un m.** to have a job; **j'exerce le m. de journaliste** I'm a journalist by profession; **quel m. veux-tu faire plus tard?** what do you want to be when you grow up?; **il n'est pas** ou **il n'y a pas de sot m.** a job's a job; **être du m.** to be in the business; **connaître son m.** to know what one is doing (**b**) (savoir-faire, expérience) experience; **avoir du m.** to have experience; **elle a plusieurs années de m.** she has several years' experience (**c**) (machine) **m. à tisser** loom

métis, -isse [metis] **1** adj (personne) half-caste

2 nm,f (personne) half-caste

3 nm (tissu) linen and cotton mixture

métissage [metisaʒ] nm crossbreeding

métisser [metise] vt to cross(breed)

métrage [metraʒ] nm (**a**) (action) measuring (**b**) (coupon de tissu) length (**c**) (longueur d'un film) footage, length; **long/moyen/court m.** feature/medium-length/short film

mètre¹ [mɛtr] nm (**a**) (unité de longueur) metre; **m. carré/cube** square/cubic metre (**b**) (pour mesurer) tape measure; (en bois, en métal) rule; **m. à ruban** tape measure

mètre² nm (en poésie) metre

métreur [metrœr] nm quantity surveyor

métrique¹ [metrik] adj (système) metric

métrique² **1** adj (en poésie) metrical

2 nf metrics (singulier)

métro [metro] nm Br underground, Am subway

métronome [metronom] nm metronome

métropole [metropol] nf (**a**) (grande ville) metropolis (**b**) (pays) mother country

métropolitain, -e [metropolitɛ̃, -ɛn] **1** adj (non insulaire) metropolitan

2 nm Vieilli (métro) Br underground, Am subway

mets¹ [mɛ] voir **mettre**

mets² nm dish

mettable [metabl] adj wearable

mette etc voir **mettre**

metteur [metœr] nm **m. en scène** director

mettre [47] [mɛtr] **1** vt (**a**) (placer) to put; **m. qch sur/ dans qch** to put sth on/in sth; **m. qn à mal** (verbalement) to berate sb; (physiquement) to beat sb up

(**b**) (vêtement, chaussures, lunettes, pansement) to put on

(**c**) (moquette) to lay; (papier peint, étagères) to put up

(**d**) (allumer) to put on, to switch on; **m. qch en marche** to turn sth on; **m. qch plus fort** to turn sth up; **m. de la musique** to put some music on; **m. le réveil (à cinq heures)** to set the alarm (for five o'clock); **faire m. le téléphone** to get the phone put in

(**e**) **elle y a mis beaucoup d'argent** she's spent a lot of money on it

(**f**) **elle a mis du temps/deux ans à le faire** it took her a while/two years to do it; **combien de temps met-on pour y aller?** how long does it take to get there?

(**g**) **ça va prendre, mettons, trois mois** it will take, (let's) say, three months; **mettons que je n'ai rien dit** pretend I didn't say anything

(**h**) (écrire) to put

(**i**) Fam **qu'est-ce qu'on leur a mis!** we really thrashed them!; **m. les bouts** ou **les voiles** to make a move

2 vi (**a**) **m. bas** to give birth

(b) *Vulg* va te faire m.! go fuck yourself!

3 se mettre *vpr* **(a)** *(se placer)* mets-toi là! *(va là-bas)* stand there!; *(assieds-toi là-bas)* sit there!; **se m. au soleil** *(s'asseoir)* to sit in the sun; *(s'allonger)* to lie in the sun; **se m. au lit** to get into bed; **se m. sur le dos/ventre** to lie on one's back/stomach; *(en se tournant)* to turn (over) onto one's back/stomach; *Fig* **se m. en avant** to push oneself forward; *Fig* **je ne savais plus où me m.** I didn't know where to put myself

(b) *(maquillage, vêtement)* to put on; **je n'ai plus rien à me m.** I haven't a thing to wear

(c) *(commencer)* **se m. à qch** *(activité)* to take sth up; **se m. au travail** to get (down) to work; **se m. à faire qch** to begin *or* to start doing sth; **le temps s'est mis à la pluie** it turned to rain; *Fam* **si tu t'y mets aussi!** don't YOU start!

(d) il a fallu se m. à trois pour le déplacer it took three of us to move it

(e) *Fam* **qu'est-ce qu'ils se sont mis!** they really laid into each other!

meuble [mœbl] **1** *adj* **(a)** *(sol, terre, roche)* soft **(b)** *(biens)* movable

2 *nm* piece of furniture; **meubles** furniture; **être dans ses meubles** to have a place of one's own; *Fam* **faire partie des meubles** to be part of the furniture

meublé, -e [mœble] **1** *adj* furnished; **non m.** unfurnished

2 *nm (chambre)* furnished room; *(appartement)* furnished *Br* flat *or Am* apartment

meubler [mœble] **1** *vt* **(a)** *(pièce, maison)* to furnish (de with) **(b)** *(remplir)* to fill (de with); **m. la conversation** to make conversation

2 se meubler *vpr* to furnish one's home

meuf [mœf] *nf très Fam Br* bird, *Am* chick

meuglement [møgləmã] *nm* moo; **des meuglements** mooing

meugler [møgle] *vi* to moo

meule [møl] *nf* **(a)** *(d'herbe, de céréales)* stack; **m. de foin** haystack **(b)** *(de moulin)* millstone **(c)** *(de fromage)* round

meunier, -ère [mønje, -ɛr] **1** *adj* **(a)** *(industrie)* flour-milling **(b)** *(à la)* **meunière** *(poisson)* = coated with flour and fried in butter

2 *nm,f* miller; *f* miller's wife

meurs, meurt *voir* **mourir**

meurtre [mœrtr] *nm* murder

meurtri, -e [mœrtri] *adj* bruised

meurtrier, -ère [mœrtrije, -ɛr] **1** *adj (guerre, attentat, colère)* murderous; *(arme, épidémie)* deadly

2 *nm,f* murderer

3 *nf* **meurtrière** *Archit* loophole

meurtrir [mœrtrir] *vt* to bruise

meurtrissure [mœrtrisyr] *nf* bruise

meute [møt] *nf aussi Fig* pack

MEV [mɛv] *nf Ordinat (abrév* **mémoire vive**) RAM

mexicain, -e [mɛksikɛ̃, -ɛn] **1** *adj* Mexican

2 *nm,f* M. Mexican

Mexico [mɛksiko] *n* Mexico City

Mexique [mɛksik] *nm* **le M.** Mexico

mézigue [mezig] *pron personnel Fam* yours truly

mezzanine [medzanin] *nf* **(a)** *(entre deux étages)* mezzanine *(floor)* **(b)** *(au théâtre) Br* dress circle, *Am* mezzanine

mezzo-soprano *(pl* **mezzo-sopranos)** [medzo-soprano] **1** *nm (voix)* mezzo-soprano

2 *nf (cantatrice)* mezzo-soprano

MF [emef] *nf Rad (abrév* **modulation de fréquence)** FM

mg *(abrév* **milligramme(s))** mg

Mgr *Rel (abrév* **Monseigneur)** Mgr

mi [mi] *nm inv (note)* E; *(chantée)* mi

mi- [mi] *adv* **la mi-avril** mid-April; **à mi-hauteur** *(en montant)* halfway up; *(en descendant)* halfway down; **elle avait de l'eau jusqu'à mi-jambe** the water was halfway up her legs; **mi-amusé, mi-intrigué** half-amused, half-puzzled; **mi-figue, mi-raisin** *(sourire)* half-hearted; *(plaisanterie)* half-serious

miam-miam [mjammjam] *exclam* yum yum!

miaou [mjau] *exclam* miaow!

miasme [mjasm] *nm* miasma

miaulement [mjolmã] *nm* miaowing

miauler [mjole] *vi* to miaow

mi-bas [miba] *nm inv (en laine)* knee sock; *(en voile)* popsock

mica [mika] *nm* mica

mi-carême *(pl* **mi-carêmes)** [mikarɛm] *nf* = third Thursday in Lent

miche [miʃ] *nf* **(a)** *(pain)* round loaf **(b)** *Fam* **miches** *(fesses) Br* bum, *Am* butt

Michel-Ange [mikɛlɑ̃ʒ] *npr* Michelangelo

micheline [miʃlin] *nf* railcar

mi-chemin [miʃmɛ̃] **à mi-chemin** *adv* halfway

Michigan [miʃigɑ̃] *n voir* **lac**

mi-clos, -e *(mpl* **mi-clos,** *fpl* **mi-closes)** [miklo, mikloz] *adj* half-closed

micmac [mikmak] *nm Fam* muddle

mi-côte [mikot] **à mi-côte** *adv* halfway up the hill

mi-course [mikurs] **à mi-course** *adv* at the halfway mark

micro [mikro] **1** *nm* **(a)** *(microphone)* mike **(b)** *Ordinat* micro(computer)

2 *nf Ordinat* microcomputing

microbe [mikrɔb] *nm* **(a)** *(germe)* microbe, germ **(b)** *Fam (personne chétive)* little squirt

microbien, -enne [mikrɔbjɛ̃, -ɛn] *adj* microbial

microbiologie [mikrɔbjɔlɔʒi] *nf* microbiology

microchirurgie [mikroʃiryrʒi] *nf* microsurgery

microcircuit [mikrosirkɥi] *nm Ordinat* microcircuit; **microcircuits** microcircuitry

microclimat [mikroklima] *nm* microclimate

microcosme [mikrɔkɔsm] *nm* microcosm

microéconomie [mikroekɔnɔmi] *nf* microeconomics *(singulier)*

microéconomique [mikroekɔnɔmik] *adj* micro-economic

microédition [mikroedisjɔ̃] *nf Ordinat* desktop publishing, DTP

microfiche [mikrofiʃ] *nf* microfiche

microfilm [mikrofilm] *nm* microfilm

micro-informatique [mikroɛ̃fɔrmatik] *nf Ordinat* microcomputing

micron [mikrɔ̃] *nm* micron

Micronésie [mikrɔnezi] *nf* **la M.** Micronesia

micro-ondes [mikroõd] *nm inv* microwave

micro-ordinateur (*pl* **micro-ordinateurs**) [mikroordinatœr] *nm Ordinat* microcomputer

micro-organisme (*pl* **micro-organismes**) [mikroorganism] *nm* micro-organism

microphone [mikrofɔn] *nm* microphone

micropilule [mikropilyl] *nf* mini pill

microprocesseur [mikroprɔsesœr] *nm Ordinat* microprocessor

microscope [mikrɔskɔp] *nm* microscope; **au m.** under a microscope; **m. électronique** electron microscope

microscopique [mikrɔskɔpik] *adj* microscopic

microsillon [mikrɔsijõ] *nm* (*de disque*) groove

midi [midi] *nm* (**a**) (*heure*) twelve o'clock, midday; **m. et demie** half past twelve; **entre m. et deux** at lunchtime (**b**) (*moment du déjeuner*) lunchtime (**c**) (*partie sud*) south; **le M. (de la France)** the South of France

midinette [midinet] *nf* silly young girl

mi-distance [midistãs] **à mi-distance** *adv* halfway (de in)

mie [mi] *nf* (*de pain*) soft part

miel [mjɛl] *nm* honey

mielleusement [mjɛløzmã] *adv* (*parler*) in honeyed tones

mielleux, -euse [mjɛlø, -øz] *adj* (*discours, sourire*) sugary; (*personne*) smooth

mien, mienne [mjɛ̃, mjɛn] **1** *pron possessif* **le m., la mienne, les miens, les miennes** mine; (*en insistant*) my own; **je te prête le m.** you can borrow mine; **je n'en ai pas besoin, j'ai le m.** I don't need it, I've got my own **2** *nm* **j'y ai mis du m.** I did my share **3** *nmpl* **les miens** (*ma famille*) my family

miette [mjɛt] *nf* (*de pain*) crumb; *Fig* **en miettes** in pieces; **mettre qch en miettes** (*briser*) to smash qch to pieces; **ne pas perdre une m. de qch** (*conversation*) not to miss a word of sth

mieux [mjø] **1** *adv* (**a**) (*comparatif*) better; **m. que** better than; **il vaut m. les surveiller** it's best to watch them; **vous feriez m. de m'écouter** you'd do better to listen to me; **elle va m.** she's (feeling) better; **c'est on ne peut m.** it couldn't be better; **j'espérais m. de votre part** I expected better of you; **plus on se voit et m. on s'apprécie** the more we see each other, the more we like each other; **de m. en m.** better and better; **faire qch à qui m. m.** to try to outdo each other in doing sth (**b**) (*superlatif*) **c'est elle qui s'exprime le m.** she expresses herself (the) best; **le plus tôt sera le m.** the sooner the better; **le m. serait de...** the best thing would be to...; **ils s'entendent le m. du monde** they get on extremely well; **être au m. avec qn** to be on the best of terms with sb; **un service des m. organisés** an extremely well-organized department **2** *adj* better; (*plus beau*) better-looking; **si tu n'as rien de m. à faire** if you've nothing better to do; **c'est le m. (de tous)** (*le plus beau*) he's the best-looking (of all) **3** *nm* **espérer m.** to hope for better things; **il y a un m. ou du m.** there's been a change for the better; **faire ou agir pour le m.** to act for the best; **faire de son m.** to do one's best; **fais du m. que tu peux** do the best you can

mièvre [mjɛvr] *adj* insipid

mièvrerie [mjɛvrəri] *nf* insipidness

mignon, -onne [miɲõ, -ɔn] **1** *adj* (**a**) (*joli, charmant*) cute (**b**) (*gentil*) nice **2** *nm* (*favori*) minion **3** *nm,f* **mon m.** darling

migraine [migren] *nf* (*douleur violente*) migraine; (*mal de tête*) headache

migraineux, -euse [migrenø, -øz] *nm,f* migraine sufferer

migrant, -e [migrã, -ãt] *adj & nm,f* migrant

migrateur, -trice [migratœr, -tris] *adj* (*animaux*) migratory

migration [migrasjõ] *nf* migration

migratoire [migratwar] *adj* migratory

migrer [migre] *vi aussi Ordinat* to migrate (**vers** to)

mijaurée [miʒɔre] *nf* (*jeune fille*) affected girl; **faire la ou sa m.** to give oneself airs

mijoter [miʒɔte] **1** *vt* (**a**) (*faire cuire*) to simmer; (*préparer avec soin*) to cook up (**b**) (*tramer*) to cook up **2** *vi* to simmer

mikado [mikado] *nm* (*jeu*) jack-straws, spillikins

mil¹ [mil] *adj inv* **l'an m.** the year one thousand

mil² [mij, mil] *nm* (*céréale*) millet

Milan [milã] *n* Milan

mildiou [mildju] *nm* (*des céréales*) mildew; (*de la vigne*) brown rot

mile [majl] *nm* mile

milice [milis] *nf* militia

milicien, -enne [milisjɛ̃, -ɛn] *nm,f* militiaman, *f* militiawoman

milieu, -x [miljø] *nm* (**a**) (*centre*) middle; **au m. de** in the middle of; **en plein ou au beau m. de qch** right in the middle of sth; **la table du m.** the middle table (**b**) (*environnement*) environment; (*social*) background; *Phys* medium; **le m. familial** the home environment; **dans les milieux autorisés** in official circles (**c**) (*position intermédiaire*) middle course; **le juste m.** the happy medium (**d**) (*pègre*) **le m.** the underworld

militaire [militer] **1** *adj* military; (*port*) naval **2** *nm* serviceman; **m. de carrière** professional soldier

militant, -e [militã, -ãt] *adj & nm,f* militant

militantisme [militãtism] *nm* militancy

militarisation [militarizasjõ] *nf* militarization

militariser [militarize] *vt* to militarize

militariste [militarist] **1** *adj* militaristic **2** *nmf* militarist

militer [milite] *vi* to campaign (**pour** ou **en faveur de/contre** for/against)

milk-shake (*pl* **milk-shakes**) [milkʃɛk] *nm* milk shake

mille¹ [mil] **1** *adj inv* (**a**) (*cardinal*) a ou one thousand; **deux m.** two thousand; **l'an m.** the year one thousand (**b**) *Fig* (*nombreux*) (*exemples, occasions*) countless; **je vous l'ai dit m. fois** I've told you a thousand times; **vous avez m. fois raison** you're absolutely right; **c'est m. fois trop grand** it's far too big **2** *nm inv* (**a**) (*nombre*) a ou one thousand; **plusieurs centaines de m.** several hundred thousand; **cinq pour m.** five per thousand (**b**) (*locutions*) **mettre (en plein) dans le m.** to hit the bull's-eye; **gagner des m. et des cents** to make a mint; *voir aussi* **trois**

mille² *nm* (**a**) (*marin* ou *nautique*) nautical mile

mille-feuille (*pl* **mille-feuilles**) [milfœj] *nm Br* ≃ vanilla slice, millefeuille, *Am* ≃ napoleon

millénaire [milenɛr] **1** *adj* thousand-year-old **2** *nm* millennium

mille-pattes [milpat] *nm inv* centipede, millipede

millepertuis [milpɛrtɥi] *nm* St John's wort

millésime [milezim] *nm (de vin, de voiture)* year; *(sur pièce de monnaie)* date

millésimé, -e [milezime] *adj (vin)* vintage; *(pièce de monnaie)* dated

millet [mijɛ] *nm* millet

milliard [miljar] *nm* billion

milliardaire [miljardɛr] *adj & nmf* billionaire

millibar [milibar] *nm* millibar

millième [miljɛm] *nmf, nm & adj* thousandth; *voir aussi* **cinquième**

millier [milje] *nm* thousand; **un m. de personnes** a thousand people; **des milliers de personnes** thousands of people; **par milliers** in thousands

milligramme [miligram] *nm* milligram(me)

millilitre [mililitr] *nm* millilitre

millimètre [milimɛtr] *nm* millimetre

millimétré, -e [milimetre], **millimétrique** [milimetrik] *adj voir* **papier**

million [miljɔ̃] *nm* million; **un m. de francs** a million francs; **quatre millions d'hommes** four million men; **par millions** in millions

millionnaire [miljonɛr] *adj & nmf* millionaire

millivolt [milivolt] *nm* millivolt

mime [mim] **1** *nm (art)* mime **2** *nmf (artiste)* mime (artist)

mimer [mime] *vt* (a) *(exprimer)* to mime (b) *(imiter)* to mimic

mimétisme [mimetism] *nm* mimicry

mimi [mimi] **1** *nm (langage enfantin)* kiss; **faire un m. à qn** to give sb a kiss **2** *adj inv Fam (mignon)* sweet

mimique [mimik] *nf* expression

mimolette [mimolɛt] *nf =* type of Dutch hard cheese

mimosa [mimoza] *nm* mimosa

min *(abrév* **minute(s)**) min

min. *(abrév* **minimum**) min

minable [minabl] **1** *adj* (a) *(mesquin, pauvre)* shabby (b) *(incompétent, insuffisant)* pathetic **2** *nmf* failure, loser

minaret [minarɛ] *nm* minaret

minauder [minode] *vi* to simper

minauderie [minodri] *nf* simpering; **faire des minauderies** to simper

mince [mɛ̃s] **1** *adj* (a) *(fin)* *(tranche, mur)* thin; *(taille, personne)* slim (b) *(insuffisant)* slight; **c'est un peu m., comme excuse!** it's a bit of a poor excuse! **2** *exclam Fam* **m. (alors)!** *(surprise)* well, blow me!; *(déception)* blast!

minceur [mɛ̃sœr] *nf* (a) *(d'une tranche, d'un tissu)* thinness; *(de la taille, d'une personne)* slimness (b) *(insuffisance)* slightness

mincir [mɛ̃sir] *vi* to get slimmer

mine¹ [min] *nf* (a) *(gisement)* mine; *Fig* **une m. de renseignements** a mine of information; **m. de charbon** coalmine; *aussi Fig* **m. d'or** goldmine (b) *(de crayon)* lead (c) *(explosif)* mine (d) **les Mines =** government department responsible for supervising all construction projects involving tunnelling; **École des Mines**, *Fam* **les Mines =** university-level institute for geological engineers

mine² *nf* (a) *(expression)* look; **avoir bonne/mauvaise m.** to look well/ill; **avoir une m. de papier mâché** to look like death warmed up; **faire ou avoir triste m.** to look down in the dumps; **faire grise m.** not to look pleased; **faire m. de faire qch** to make as if to do sth (b) *(allure)* appearance; **juger les gens sur la m.** to judge people by appearances; *Fam* **ne pas payer de m.** not to be much to look at; *Fam* **m. de rien, il n'est pas bête** you wouldn't think it to look at him, but he's not stupid (c) *Péj* **mines** *(simagrées)* faces

miner¹ [mine] *vt* (a) *(creuser)* to eat away (b) *(ruiner moralement)* to wear down

miner² *vt (poser des explosifs dans)* to mine

minerai [minrɛ] *nm* ore; **m. de fer** iron ore

minéral, -e, -aux, -ales [mineral, -o] *adj & nm* mineral

minéralogique [mineralɔʒik] *adj* **plaque m.** *Br* number *or Am* license plate (b) *Géol* mineralogical

minerve [minɛrv] *nf (surgical)* collar

minestrone [minɛstron] *nm* minestrone

minet, -ette [minɛ, -ɛt] *nm,f Fam* (a) *(chat)* pussy cat (b) *(personne coquette)* trendy

mineur¹ [minœr] *nm. (ouvrier)* miner; **m. de fond** underground worker

mineur², -e **1** *adj* (a) *(secondaire)* minor (b) *(qui n'a pas la majorité légale)* underage (c) *Mus* minor **2** *nm,f* minor

mini [mini] *Fam* **1** *adj inv (jupe, robe)* mini **2** *nm* (a) *(mode)* **le m.** miniskirts (b) *(mini-ordinateur)* mini

miniature [minjatyr] **1** *nf* miniature; **en m.** in miniature **2** *adj* miniature

miniaturiser [minjatyrize] *vt* to miniaturize

minibus [minibys] *nm* minibus

minichaîne [miniʃɛn] *nf* mini-hifi

minier, -ère [minje, -ɛr] *adj* mining

minigolf [minigolf] *nm* crazy golf

minijupe [miniʒyp] *nf* miniskirt

minima [minima] *voir* **minimum**

minimal, -e, -aux, -ales [minimal, -o] *adj* minimum; *(art)* minimal

minimaliste [minimalist] *adj & nmf* minimalist

minime [minim] **1** *adj* minimal **2** *nmf Sp* junior *(13 to 15 years old)*

minimiser [minimize] *vt* to minimize

minimum [minimɔm] *(pl* **minimums** *ou* **minima** [minima]) **1** *adj* minimum **2** *nm* minimum; **avec un m. d'efforts** with a minimum of effort; **en un m. de temps** in as short a time as possible; **réduire qch au m.** to minimize sth; **faire le m. (pour faire qch)** to do the bare minimum (to do sth); **c'est vraiment le m. que tu puisses faire pour elle** it's the very least you can do for her; **au m.** at the very least; **le m. vital** a minimum to live on; **le strict m.** the absolute minimum

mini-ordinateur (*pl* **mini-ordinateurs**) [mini-ordinatœr] *nm* minicomputer

minipilule [minipilyl] *nf* mini pill

ministère [ministɛr] *nm* (**a**) *(département)* government department, *Br* ministry; **m. des Affaires étrangères** *Br* ≃ Foreign Office, *Am* ≃ State Department; **m. de la Défense (nationale)** *Br* ≃ Ministry of Defence, *Am* ≃ Department of Defense; **m. de l'Éducation nationale** Department of Education (**b**) *(gouvernement)* government (**c**) *Jur* **le m. public** ≃ the Crown Prosecution Service (**d**) *Rel* ministry

ministériel, -elle [ministerjɛl] *adj* (*arrêté, décret, entourage*) ministerial; *(crise, remaniement)* cabinet

ministre [ministr] *nm* (**a**) *(homme d'État)* secretary, *Br* minister; **m. des Affaires étrangères** *Br* ≃ Foreign Secretary, *Am* ≃ Secretary of State; **m. de la Défense (nationale)** ≃ Secretary of State for Defence; **m. de l'Éducation nationale** ≃ Secretary of State for Education; **m. d'État** ≃ secretary of state, *Br* ≃ cabinet minister; **Premier m.** Prime Minister; *Can (d'une province)* Premier (**b**) *(pasteur)* minister

Minitel® [minitɛl] *nm* = consumer information network accessible via home computer terminal; **le M. rose** = dating and erotic entertainment service available on Minitel®

minitéliste [minitelist] *nmf* Minitel® user

minois [minwa] *nm* pretty face

minorer [minɔre] *vt* (**a**) *(minimiser)* to downplay (**b**) *(faire baisser)* to reduce

minoritaire [minɔritɛr] *adj* minority; **être m.** to be in the minority

minorité [minɔrite] *nf* (**a**) *(de choses, de personnes)* minority; **être en m.** to be in the minority; **m. ethnique** ethnic minority (**b**) *(avant la majorité légale)* minority

Minorque [minɔrk] *n* Minorca

minorquin, -e [minɔrkɛ̃, -in] **1** *adj* Minorcan
2 *nm,f* **M.** Minorcan

minoterie [minɔtri] *nf (moulin)* flour mill; *(activité)* flour-milling

minou [minu] *nm Fam (chat)* pussy cat

Minsk [minsk] *n* Minsk

minuit [minɥi] *nm* midnight, twelve o'clock

minuscule [minyskyl] **1** *adj* (**a**) *(très petit)* tiny, minute (**b**) *(lettre)* small
2 *nf* small letter

minute [minyt] **1** *nf* (**a**) *(unité de temps)* minute; **une m. de silence** a minute's silence; **de dernière m.** last-minute; **faire qch à la m.** to do sth this very minute; **d'une m. à l'autre** any minute (**b**) *(court moment)* minute, moment; **la m. de vérité** the moment of truth; **m.! I** hold on a minute! (**c**) *(de contrat)* minute; *(d'acte notarié, de jugement)* record
2 *adj (sur panneau)* **nettoyage m.** dry-cleaning while you wait; **talons m.** heel bar

minuter [minyte] *vt* to time

minuterie [minytri] *nf (pour l'éclairage)* time switch; *(d'un four)* timer

minuteur [minytœr] *nm* timer

minutie [minysi] *nf* meticulousness; **avec m.** meticulously

minutieusement [minysjøzmɑ̃] *adv* meticulously

minutieux, -euse [minysjø, -øz] *adj* meticulous

mioche [mjɔʃ] *nmf Fam* kid

MIPS [mips] *nm Ordinat (abrév* **million d'instructions par seconde)** MIPS

mirabelle [mirabɛl] *nf* mirabelle plum

miracle [mirakl] **1** *nm* miracle; **faire un m.** to perform a miracle; *(rescapé)* **faire des miracles** to work miracles; **par m.** by a miracle
2 *adj inv* miracle

miraculé, -e [mirakyle] **1** *adj (malade)* miraculously cured; *(rescapé)* miraculously saved
2 *nm,f (malade)* miraculously cured person; *(rescapé)* miraculous survivor

miraculeusement [mirakyløzmɑ̃] *adv* miraculously

miraculeux, -euse [mirakylø, -øz] *adj* miraculous

mirador [miradɔr] *nm* watchtower

mirage [miraʒ] *nm* mirage

mire [mir] *nf* test card

mirer [mire] **se mirer** *vpr Litt* (**a**) *(se regarder)* to gaze at oneself (**b**) *(se refléter)* to be reflected

mirettes [mirɛt] *nfpl Fam* eyes

mirifique [mirifik] *adj* wonderful

mirobolant, -e [mirɔbɔlɑ̃, -ɑ̃t] *adj* fabulous

miroir [mirwar] *nm* mirror; *Fig* **m. aux alouettes** lure; **m. de courtoisie** vanity mirror; **m. grossissant** magnifying mirror; **m. de poche** pocket mirror

miroiter [mirwate] *vi* to shimmer; *Fig* **faire m. qch à qn** to lure sb with the prospect of sth

miroton [mirɔtɔ̃] *nm* = beef boiled in sauce with onions

mis, -e *pp voir* **mettre**

misanthrope [mizɑ̃trɔp] **1** *adj* misanthropic
2 *nmf* misanthropist, misanthrope

mise [miz] *nf* (**a**) *(placement)* putting; **m. en accusation** committal (for trial); **m. en application** implementation; **m. en demeure** formal demand; **m. en disponibilité** leave of absence; *Can* layoff; **m. en examen** indictment; **m. à feu** *(d'une fusée)* launch; **m. de fonds** investment; **m. en garde** warning; **m. à jour** updating; **m. en liberté provisoire** release on bail; **m. à mort** killing; **m. en page(s)** page make-up; **m. à pied** suspension; *Can* layoff; **m. en place** putting into place; **m. en plis** set *(hairstyle)*; **m. au point** *(d'un objectif)* focusing; *(d'une technique)* perfecting; *(d'un moteur)* tuning; *(d'un document, d'un rapport)* finalization; *Fig* **faire une m. au point** to make things clear; **m. en route** start-up; **m. en scène** *(d'une pièce de théâtre)* production; *(d'un film)* direction; **m. en service** *(d'une machine)* commissioning; **m. en vigueur** implementation
(**b**) *(habillement)* attire
(**c**) *(au jeu)* stake; *(à une vente aux enchères)* bid; *Fig* **sauver la m. à qn** to get sb out of a tight spot
(**d**) **être de m.** to be acceptable
(**e**) *Ordinat* **m. en attente des fichiers à imprimer** printer spooling; **m. en forme** formatting; **m. en mémoire** saving; **m. à niveau** upgrade; **m. en relation** *(avec un service)* log-on; **m. en réseau** networking; **m. sous tension** power-up

miser [mize] *vt* to stake **(sur** on); **m. sur qn/qch** *(parier)* to bet on sb/sth; *(compter sur)* to count on sb/sth; **m. sur tous les tableaux** to hedge one's bets

misérabilisme [mizerabilism] *nm* sordid realism

misérabiliste [mizerabilist] *adj* sordidly realistic

misérable [mizerabl] **1** adj (a) (indigent) (personne) poor; (condition, existence) wretched (b) (pitoyable, insignifiant) miserable

2 nmf (a) (personne indigente) poor wretch (b) (coquin, fripouille) scoundrel

misérablement [mizerabləmã] adv (a) (pauvrement) wretchedly (b) (pitoyablement) miserably

misère [mizɛr] nf (a) (indigence) extreme poverty; **être dans la m.** to be poverty-stricken; **être dans une m. noire** to be destitute; **salaire de m.** starvation wage (b) (ennui) trouble; **faire des misères à qn** to give sb trouble (c) (vétille) **payer qch une m.** to pay next to nothing for sth

miséreux, -euse [mizerø, -øz] adj poverty-stricken

miséricorde [mizerikɔrd] **1** nf mercy

2 exclam Vieilli mercy!

miséricordieux, -euse [mizerikɔrdjø, -øz] adj merciful (envers to)

misogyne [mizɔʒin] **1** adj misogynous

2 nmf misogynist

misogynie [mizɔʒini] nf misogyny

miss (pl **miss** ou **misses**) [mis] nf (reine de beauté) beauty queen; **M. Monde/France** Miss World/France

missel [misɛl] nm missal

missile [misil] nm missile

mission [misjɔ̃] nf (a) (tâche) mission; (d'un employé) task; **partir en m.** (cadre) to go away on business; (diplomate) to go off on a mission (b) (groupe) delegation; **m. scientifique** scientific expedition (c) Rel (vocation, organisation) mission; (bâtiment) mission (station)

missionnaire [misjɔnɛr] adj & nmf missionary

Mississippi [misisipi] nm **le M.** the Mississippi

missive [misiv] nf Litt missive

mistral [mistral] nm mistral

mitaine [miten] nf fingerless glove; Can (moufle) mitten

mite [mit] nf moth

mité, -e [mite] adj moth-eaten

mi-temps [mitã] **1** nf inv (moitié) half; (pause) half-time

2 nm inv part-time job; **travailler** ou **être à m.** to work part-time

miteux, -euse [mitø, -øz] adj shabby

mitigé, -e [mitiʒe] adj (enthousiasme, accueil) lukewarm; (sentiments, impressions) mixed

mitigeur [mitiʒœr] nm mixer Br tap or Am faucet

mitonner [mitɔne] **1** vt (a) (cuire à feu doux) to simmer (b) Fig (projet) to concoct

2 vi to simmer

mitoyen, -enne [mitwajɛ̃, -ɛn] adj (mur) party

mitrailler [mitraje] vt to machine-gun; Fig **m. qn de questions** to bombard sb with questions

mitraillette [mitrajɛt] nf submachine gun

mitrailleuse [mitrajøz] nf machine gun

mitre [mitr] nf (a) (d'évêque) mitre (b) (de cheminée) cowl

mi-voix [mivwa] **à mi-voix** adv in a low voice

mixage [miksaʒ] nm mixing

mixer¹ [mikse] vt (a) (film) to mix (b) (ingrédients) (mélanger) to mix; (réduire à l'état liquide) to blend

mixer², mixeur [miksœr] nm (pour mélanger) mixer; (pour réduire à l'état liquide) blender

mixité [miksite] nf coeducation

mixte [mikst] adj (a) (des deux sexes) mixed; **double m.** (au tennis) mixed doubles (b) (combiné) (commission) joint; (mariage) mixed; (cuisinière) gas-and-electric

mixture [mikstyr] nf (a) (pharmaceutique) mixture (b) Fig concoction

MJC [emʒise] nf (abrév **maison des jeunes et de la culture**) community centre

ml (abrév **millilitre(s)**) ml

MLF [emɛlɛf] nm (abrév **Mouvement de libération des femmes**) ≃ Women's Liberation Movement

Mlle (abrév **Mademoiselle**) Miss

MM (abrév **Messieurs**) Messrs

mm (abrév **millimètre(s)**) mm

Mme (abrév **Madame**) Mrs

Mmes (abrév **Mesdames**) **M. Binoche et Huppert** Mrs Binoche and Mrs Huppert

Mo nm Ordinat (abrév **méga-octet(s)**) Mb

mobile [mɔbil] **1** adj (a) (cloison) movable; (feuillets) loose; (cible) moving (b) (expression, regard) shifting; (visage) lively (c) (personne âgée, main d'œuvre, population) mobile

2 nm (a) (motif) motive (de for) (b) (objet décoratif) mobile (c) (objet en mouvement) moving body

mobilier, -ère [mɔbilje, -er] **1** adj Jur movable

2 nm furniture

mobilisation [mɔbilizasjɔ̃] nf mobilization; **m. générale** general mobilization

mobiliser [mɔbilize] **1** vt to mobilize; Fig (énergie, courage) to summon up

2 se mobiliser vpr to mobilize (contre/en faveur de against/in support of)

mobilité [mɔbilite] nf mobility

Mobylette® [mɔbilɛt] nf moped

mocassin [mɔkasɛ̃] nm moccasin

moche [mɔʃ] adj Fam (a) (laid) ugly (b) (moralement) rotten

modal, -e, -aux, -ales [mɔdal, -o] adj modal

modalité [mɔdalite] nf (a) (manière) mode; **modalités de paiement** conditions of payment (b) (d'un acte juridique) clause

mode¹ [mɔd] **1** adj inv **c'est très m.** it's very fashionable

2 nf (a) (vestimentaire, de consommation) fashion; **à la m.** fashionable; **revenir à la m.** to come back into fashion (b) (manière) **à la m. de Lyon/Provence** Lyons/Provence style

mode² nm (a) (manière) **m. de** means of; **m. de cuisson** cooking instructions; **m. d'emploi** instructions; **m. de paiement** means of payment; **m. de transport** mode of transport; **m. de vie** way of life (b) Gram mood (c) Mus mode (d) Ordinat mode

modèle [mɔdɛl] **1** adj (parfait) model; (appartement, maison) show

2 nm (a) (exemple) model; **prendre qn pour m.** to take sb as one's model; **m. de lettre** standard letter (b) (personne) **m. de générosité/fidélité** model of generosity/fidelity; **m. de vertu** paragon of virtue (c) (exemplaire) (de voiture, d'appareil) model; (de robe) style; (de tricot) pattern; **vous n'auriez pas un plus grand m.?** do you have it in a larger size?; **m. déposé** registered design (d) (d'un peintre, d'un sculpteur) model (e) (maquette) **m. réduit** small-scale model

modeler [39] [mɔdle] 1 vt (argile, pot) to model; Fig (relief, caractère, destinée) to shape; **m. sa personnalité sur celle de qn** to model oneself on sb

2 **se modeler** vpr **se m. sur qn** to model oneself on sb

modélisme [mɔdelism] nm model-making

modem [mɔdɛm] nm Ordinat modem; **carte m. modem card**

modérateur, -trice [mɔderatœr, -tris] 1 adj moderating

2 nm (a) (personne) moderator (b) (de moteur) regulator

modération [mɔderasjɔ̃] nf (a) (retenue) moderation; **avec m.** in moderation; **à consommer avec m.** (dans les publicités) drink in moderation (health warning on all products advertising alcoholic drinks) (b) (réduction) reduction

modéré, -e [mɔdere] adj & nmf moderate

modérément [mɔderemã] adv moderately; Euph **j'ai m. apprécié sa remarque** I didn't much appreciate her remark

modérer [34] [mɔdere] 1 vt (a) (passions, désirs, envies) to moderate, to restrain; Hum **modère tes ardeurs!** control yourself!; **je te prie de m. ton langage!** please mind your language! (b) (prix, vitesse) to reduce

2 **se modérer** vpr (personne) to calm down

moderne [mɔdɛrn] 1 adj modern

2 nm **le m.** the modern style

modernisation [mɔdɛrnizasjɔ̃] nf modernization

moderniser [mɔdɛrnize] vt to modernize

modernisme [mɔdɛrnism] nm modernism

moderniste [mɔdɛrnist] adj & nmf modernist

modernité [mɔdɛrnite] nf modernity

modeste [mɔdɛst] 1 adj modest

2 nmf **faire le m.** to be modest

modestement [mɔdɛstəmã] adv modestly; **être m. logé** to live in modest surroundings

modestie [mɔdɛsti] nf modesty; **fausse m.** false modesty

modicité [mɔdisite] nf lowness

modifiable [mɔdifjabl] adj modifiable

modification [mɔdifikasjɔ̃] nf alteration, modification; **apporter** ou **faire une m. à qch** to make an alteration to sth

modifier [66] [mɔdifje] 1 vt to alter, to modify; Gram to modify

2 **se modifier** vpr to alter

modique [mɔdik] adj modest

modiste [mɔdist] nmf milliner

modulable [mɔdylabl] adj (horaires) flexible; (éclairage, chauffage) adjustable

modulaire [mɔdylɛr] adj modular

modulation [mɔdylasjɔ̃] nf (a) (des sons, de la voix) modulation (b) (adaptation) adjustment (**en fonction de** in relation to) (c) Rad modulation; **m. de fréquence** frequency modulation

module [mɔdyl] nm (a) (élément d'un tout) unit; m. (d'enseignement) module (b) (d'un vaisseau spatial) module; **m. lunaire/de commande** lunar/command module

moduler [mɔdyle] 1 vt (a) (sons, amplitude, voix) to modulate (b) (adapter) to adjust (**en fonction de** in relation to)

2 vi to modulate

modus vivendi [mɔdysvivɛ̃di] nm inv modus vivendi

moelle [mwal] nf marrow; Fig **jusqu'à la m.** to the core; **m. épinière** spinal cord; **m. osseuse** bone marrow

moelleusement [mwaløzmã] adv snugly

moelleux, -euse [mwalø, -øz] adj (a) (au toucher) soft (b) (fromage, vin) smooth; (gâteau) spongy

moellon [mwalɔ̃] nm quarry stone

mœurs [mœr, mœrs] nfpl (a) (coutumes) customs; **entrer** ou **passer dans les m.** to become part of everyday life (b) (d'animaux) habits (c) (sens moral) morals; **bonnes m.** morality; **contraire aux bonnes m.** contrary to accepted standards of behaviour; **femme de m. légères** ou **faciles** woman of easy virtue

mohair [mɔɛr] nm mohair

moi [mwa] 1 pron personnel (a) (sujet) I; **qui vient avec nous? – m.** who's coming with us? – I am or me; **m., quand je serai grand...** when I grow up,...; **m., je n'aurais pas fait comme ça** I wouldn't have done it like that

(b) (objet direct) me; **et m., tu m'oublies?** and what about me, have you forgotten me?

(c) (avec préposition) me; **fais-m. voir, à m.** show ME; **ce livre est à m.** this book is mine; **j'ai mes petits secrets à m.** I've got my own little secrets; **Fam un ami à m.** a friend of mine; **à m.! help!; je ne le fais pas que pour m.** I'm not doing it just for myself

(d) (dans les comparaisons) me; **elle boit plus que m.** she drinks more than me or than I do

2 nm ego, self

moignon [mwaɲɔ̃] nm stump

moi-même [mwamɛm] pron personnel myself

moindre [mwɛ̃dr] adj (a) (comparatif) lesser; (prix) lower; (quantité) smaller; (vitesse) slower; **c'est un m. mal** it's not as bad as it might have been (b) (superlatif) **le/la m.** the least; **pas la m. chance/idée** not the slightest chance/idea; **au m. reproche** at the slightest reproach; **dans les moindres détails** in the smallest detail; **c'est la m. des choses** it's the least I/he/etc can do; **on a fait venir un expert, et non des moindres** we called in an expert, and not just any old one

moine [mwan] nm monk

moineau, -x [mwano] nm sparrow

moins [mwɛ̃] 1 adv (a) (comparatif) less; **je gagne m. que vous** I earn less than you (do); **elle est m. intelligente que sa sœur** she's not as intelligent as her sister; **il n'est pas m. nerveux que toi** he's no less nervous than you (are); **m. de** (argent, patience) less; (hommes, occasions) fewer; (avec un nombre) less than; **elle a m. de vingt ans** she's under twenty; **m. tu feras d'exercice, plus tu grossiras** the less exercise you do, the fatter you'll get; **de m. en m.** less and less; **celui-ci coûte 10 francs de m. que l'autre** this one costs 10 francs less than the other one; **il y a eu 20% de visiteurs de m.** ou **en m.** there have been 20% fewer visitors; **il n'en est pas m. vrai que...** the fact remains that...

(b) (superlatif) **le m.** the least; **c'est celui qui me plaît le m.** that's the one I like (the) least; **les élèves les m. appliqués** the least industrious pupils; **pas le m. du monde** not in the least or slightest

(c) (locutions) **à m. d'un imprévu/d'un miracle** barring unforeseen circumstances/a miracle; **à m. de partir tout de suite** unless I/you/etc leave at once; **à m. que... + subjunctive** unless...; **au m., du m.** at least; **Fam tu as fait ton travail, au m.?** you've done your work, I hope?; **du m.** at least; **c'est pour le m. surprenant** it's surprising, to say the least; *Fam* **un m. que rien** a nobody

2 *prép (dans les calculs, les températures)* minus; **une heure m. cinq** five (minutes) to one; **il est m. vingt** it's twenty to; *Fam* **il était m. une** it was a close shave *or* a near thing

3 *nm (signe)* minus (sign)

moins-value (*pl* **moins-values**) [mwɛvaly] *nf Fin* depreciation; *(après une vente)* capital loss

moire [mwar] *nf* moire

moiré, -e [mware] *adj* **(a)** *(tissu)* watered, moiré **(b)** *(aux reflets changeants)* shimmering

mois [mwa] *nm* **(a)** *(période)* month; **au m. d'août** in August; **un m. de vacances/salaire** a month's holiday/ wages **(b)** *(paie mensuelle)* monthly salary; **treizième m.** extra month's salary *(paid as an annual bonus)*

Moïse [mɔiz] *npr* Moses

moisi, -e [mwazi] **1** *adj (aliment)* mouldy; *(mur, livre)* mildewed

2 *nm (sur un aliment)* mould; *(sur un mur, un tissu)* mildew

moisir [mwazir] *vi* **(a)** *(aliment)* to go mouldy; *(mur, livre)* to go mildewed **(b)** *(personne) (stagner)* to moulder away; *(attendre longtemps)* to hang about

moisissure [mwazisyr] *nf* mould

moisson [mwasɔ̃] *nf* **(a)** *(récolte, époque)* harvest; **faire la m.** *ou* **les moissons** to harvest **(b)** *Fig (de documents, d'idées)* wealth

moissonner [mwasone] *vt* **(a)** *(céréales)* to harvest; *(champ)* to reap **(b)** *Fig (informations, idées)* to collect, to gather

moissonneur, -euse [mwasonœr, -øz] **1** *nm,f* harvester

2 *nf* **moissonneuse** *(machine)* harvester

moissonneuse-batteuse (*pl* **moissonneuses-batteuses**) [mwasonøzbatøz] *nf* combine harvester

moite [mwat] *adj (mains, front, chaleur)* sticky; *(atmosphère, air)* muggy

moiteur [mwatœr] *nf (des mains, du front)* stickiness; *(d'atmosphère, d'air)* mugginess

moitié [mwatje] *nf* **(a)** *(d'un tout)* half; **la m. des livres/ de la journée** half (of) the books/the day; **m. anglais, m. écossais** half English, half Scottish; **c'est m. moins cher** it's half the price; *Fam* **m.-m.** fifty-fifty; **faire m.-m.** to go halves; **à m. plein/vide** half-full/-empty; **à m. mort** half-dead; **vendre qch à m. prix** to sell sth (at) half-price; **ne pas faire les choses à m.** not to do things by halves **(b)** *Fam (époux, épouse)* **ma m.** my better half

moka [mɔka] *nm* **(a)** *(café)* mocha **(b)** *(gâteau)* coffee cake

molaire [mɔlɛr] *nf* molar

moldave [mɔldav] **1** *adj* Moldavian

2 *nmf* **M.** Moldavian

Moldavie [mɔldavi] *nf* **la M.** Moldavia

mole [mɔl] *nf Phys* mole

moléculaire [mɔlekyler] *adj* molecular

molécule [mɔlekyl] *nf* molecule

moleskine [mɔlɛskin] *nf* imitation leather

molester [mɔlɛste] *vt* to manhandle

molette [mɔlɛt] *nf* **(a)** *(de briquet, de clé)* wheel; *(de jumelles)* focus wheel **(b)** *(pour couper le verre)* cutting wheel

Molières [mɔljɛr] *nmpl* **les M.** *(cérémonie)* = French theatre awards ceremony

mollard [mɔlar] *nm très Fam* gob of spit

mollasson, -onne [mɔlasɔ̃, -ɔn] *Fam* **1** *adj (personne)* lethargic

2 *nm,f* lazy lump

molle [mɔl] *voir* **mou**[1]

mollement [mɔlmɑ̃] *adv* **(a)** *(avec abandon)* languidly; *(avec lenteur)* gently **(b)** *(sans énergie)* feebly

mollesse [mɔlɛs] *nf* **(a)** *(d'un coussin, d'un matelas)* softness; *(de tissus, de muscles)* flabbiness **(b)** *(d'une personne)* lethargy; *(d'un gouvernement)* laxness; *(du style)* limpness

mollet[1] [mɔlɛ] *adj m (œuf)* soft-boiled

mollet[2] *nm* calf; **avoir des mollets de coq** to have spindly legs

molleton [mɔltɔ̃] *nm* **(a)** *(tissu) (en coton)* flannelette; *(en laine)* flannel **(b)** *(sous-nappe)* table felt

molletonné, -e [mɔltone] *adj* fleece-lined

mollir [mɔlir] *vi* **(a)** *(faiblir) (vent)* to die down; *(courage, enthousiasme)* to flag; **sentir ses jambes m.** to feel one's legs give way **(b)** *(devenir moins ferme) (matière)* to soften; *(sol)* to give way **(sous** beneath*)*

mollo [mɔlo] *adv Fam* **y aller m.** to take it easy

mollusque [mɔlysk] *nm* **(a)** *(animal)* mollusc **(b)** *Fam (personne)* lazy lump

molosse [mɔlɔs] *nm* big dog

môme [mom] *nmf Fam (enfant)* kid

moment [mɔmɑ̃] *nm* **(a)** *(point précis dans le temps)* moment; **arriver au bon m.** to arrive at just the right time; **le m. venu** *(dans le passé)* when the time came; *(dans l'avenir)* when the time comes; **c'est le m. ou jamais** it's now or never; **c'est le m. ou jamais de le faire** now's the time to do it; **au m. de qch** at the time of sth; **au m. où j'allais me coucher, le téléphone a sonné** just as I was going to bed, the phone rang; **à quel m. de sa vie?** at what point in his life?; **à un m. donné** at one point; **dans ces moments-là** at times like that; **d'un m. à l'autre** (at) any moment; **en ce m.** at the moment, just now; **jusqu'au m. où... until...;** par **moments** at times, now and again; **pour le m.** for the moment, for the time being; **sur le m.** at the time; **à tout m., à tous moments** *(sans cesse)* constantly; *(n'importe quand)* (at) any moment; **à ce m.-là** then; *(dans ces conditions)* in that case

(b) *(durée)* moment; **un m.!** just a moment!; **je suis à vous dans un m.** I'll be with you in a moment; **passer un bon m.** to have a good time; **ce n'est qu'un mauvais m. à passer** it'll soon be over with; **j'en ai pour un m.** I'll be a while; **ne pas avoir un m. à soi** not to have a moment to oneself; **dans un m. de bonté** in a moment of kindness

(c) *(temps présent)* **du m.** *(disque, star)* of the moment

(d) *(locutions)* **du m. que...** seeing that...

momentané, -e [mɔmɑ̃tane] *adj (bref)* brief; *(temporaire)* temporary

momentanément [mɔmɑ̃tanemɑ̃] *adv (brièvement)* briefly; *(temporairement)* temporarily

momie [mɔmi] *nf* mummy

momifier [66] [mɔmifje] **1** *vt* to mummify

2 se momifier *vpr* to become fossilised

mon, ma, mes [mɔ̃, ma, me]

ma becomes **mon** before a word beginning with a vowel or mute h.

adj possessif (a) *(marquant la possession)* my; **m. chien** my dog; **ma voiture** my car; **m. ami/amie** my friend; **mes enfants** my children; **mon père et ma mère** my mother and father; **un de mes amis** one of my friends, a friend of mine; *Fam* **j'ai eu m. vendredi** I got Friday off (b) *(en s'adressant à quelqu'un)* **non, m. général** no, General

monacal, -e, -aux, -ales [mɔnakal, -o] *adj* monastic

Monaco [monako] *n* Monaco

monarchie [mɔnarʃi] *nf* monarchy

monarchique [mɔnarʃik] *adj* monarchical

monarchiste [mɔnarʃist] *adj & nmf* monarchist

monarque [mɔnark] *nm* monarch

monastère [monaster] *nm* (*d'hommes*) monastery; *(de femmes)* convent

monastique [monastik] *adj* monastic

monceau, -x [mɔ̃so] *nm* heap, pile

mondain, -aine [mɔ̃dɛ̃, -ɛn] **1** *adj* (a) *(soirée, journaliste)* society (b) *Péj (personne)* **être très m.** to be a great socialite
   2 *nm,f* socialite
   3 *nf Fam Vieilli* **la mondaine** the drugs squad

mondanités [mɔ̃danite] *nfpl* (a) *(événements)* society life (b) *(politesses)* social niceties; *(conversations superficielles)* social chitchat

monde [mɔ̃d] *nm* (a) *(univers, humanité)* world; **l'autre m.** the next world; **dans le m. entier** *(connu, en vente)* worldwide, all over the world; **personne au m.** no one in the world; **pour rien au m.** not for anything in the world; **mettre un enfant au m.** to bring a child into the world; **venir au m.** to come into the world; *Litt* **il n'est plus de ce m.** he is no longer of this world; **les meilleurs amis du m.** the best friends in the world; **en ce bas m.** here on earth; *Fam* **c'est (quand même) un m.!** that's a bit much!; *Fam* **se faire un m. de qch** to get worked up about sth; **comme le m. est petit!** it's a small world!; **c'est le m. à l'envers** the world's gone mad (b) *(milieu)* world; **être du même m.** to belong to the same crowd; **le (beau) m.** (fashionable) society (c) *(gens)* people; **tout le m.** everyone, everybody; **il y a du m.** *(beaucoup de gens)* there are a lot of people; **peu de m., pas grand m.** not many people; **avoir du m. à dîner** to have people to dinner (d) *(vie séculière)* world

mondial, -e, -aux, -ales [mɔ̃djal, -o] *adj* world, global; **guerre mondiale** world war

mondialement [mɔ̃djalmɑ̃] *adv* throughout the world

mondialisation [mɔ̃djalizasjɔ̃] *nf* globalization

mondialiser [mɔ̃djalize] **1** *vt* to globalize
   2 se mondialiser *vpr* to become globalized

monégasque [monegask] **1** *adj* Monegasque
   2 *nmf* **M.** Monegasque

monétaire [moneter] *adj* *(unité, système, questions)* monetary; *(marché)* money

monétarisme [monetarism] *nm* monetarism

monétariste [monetarist] *adj & nmf* monetarist

mongol, -e [mɔ̃gɔl] **1** *adj* Mongolian
   2 *nm,f* **M.** Mongolian
   3 *nm (langue)* Mongolian

Mongolie [mɔ̃gɔli] *nf* **la M.** Mongolia

mongolien, -enne [mɔ̃gɔljɛ̃, -ɛn] **1** *adj* **être m.** to have Down's syndrome
   2 *nm,f (bébé)* Down's syndrome baby; *(personne)* person with Down's syndrome

mongolisme [mɔ̃gɔlism] *nm* Down's syndrome

moniteur, -trice [monitœr, -tris] **1** *nm,f* (a) *(d'activités sportives, d'auto-école)* instructor (b) *(dans une colonie de vacances)* Br assistant, Am (camp) counselor
   2 *nm aussi Ordinat* monitor; **m. cardiaque** heart monitor

monitoring [monitoriŋ] *nm* monitoring

monnaie [monɛ] *nf* (a) *(argent)* money; *(d'un pays)* currency; **m. électronique** plastic money; **fausse m.** counterfeit money; **c'est m. courante dans ce milieu** it's common in these circles; *Fam* **payer qn en m. de singe** to fob sb off (b) *(pièces)* change; **avoir la m. de 100 francs** to have change for 100 francs; **faire (de) la m.** to get some change; **faire la m. de 100 francs** to get change for 100 francs; **petite** *ou* **menue m.** small change

monnayable [monɛjabl] *adj* convertible into cash; *Fig* **être m.** *(expérience, information)* to be worth money

monnayer [53] [monɛje] **1** *vt* (a) *(terrains, biens)* to convert into cash (b) *(expérience, information)* to cash in on
   2 se monnayer *vpr* **ici tout se monnaye** money can buy you anything here

monnayeur [monɛjœr] *nm (appareil)* change machine

monochrome [monokrom] *adj* monochrome

monocle [monokl] *nm* monocle

monocoque [monokɔk] *nm* monohull

monocorde [monokɔrd] *adj* monotonous

monoculture [monokyltyr] *nf* monoculture

monogame [monogam] *adj* monogamous

monogamie [monogami] *nf* monogamy

monogramme [monogram] *nm* monogram

monoï [monoj] *nm inv* scented coconut oil

monokini [monokini] *nm* monokini; **faire du m.** to go topless

monolingue [monolɛ̃g] *adj* monolingual

monolithe [monolit] *nm* monolith

monolithique [monolitik] *adj aussi Fig* monolithic

monologue [monolog] *nm* monologue; **m. intérieur** interior monologue

monologuer [monologe] *vi* (a) *(monopoliser la parole)* to carry on a monologue (b) *(au théâtre)* to soliloquize

monôme [monom] *nm Math* monomial

mononucléose [mononykleoz] *nf* **m. (infectieuse)** glandular fever

monoparental, -e, -aux, -ales [monoparɑ̃tal, -o] *adj (famille)* single-parent, one-parent

monoplace [monoplas] *adj & nm* single-seater

monopole [monopol] *nm* monopoly; **avoir le m. de qch** to have a monopoly on sth; **m. d'État** state monopoly

monopoliser [monopolize] *vt* to monopolize

monoposte [monopost] *nm Ordinat* stand-alone

monoski [monoski] *nm* mono-ski; **faire du m.** to mono-ski

monosyllabe [monosilab] **1** *adj* monosyllabic
   2 *nm* monosyllable

monosyllabique [monosilabik] *adj* monosyllabic

mono-tâche [monotaʃ] *adj inv Ordinat* single-tasking

monothéisme [monoteism] *nm* monotheism

monotone [monoton] *adj* monotonous

monotonie [monotoni] *nf* monotony

monoxyde [monoksid] *nm* m. de carbone carbon monoxide

monseigneur [mɔ̃sɛɲœr] (*pl* messeigneurs [mesɛɲœr]) *nm* (a) (*titre*) (*d'un prince*) His Royal Highness; (*d'un cardinal*) His Eminence; (*d'un évêque*) His Lordship (b) (*en s'adressant au prince*) Your Royal Highness; (*au cardinal*) Your Eminence; (*à l'évêque*) Your Lordship

monsieur [məsjø] (*pl* messieurs [mesjø]) *nm* (a) (*titre*) M. Robert Marceau Mr Robert Marceau; M. le Ministre the Minister; *Fam* m. je-sais-tout Mr Know-it-all; m. météo the weatherman; m. tout-le-monde the man in the street (b) (*en apostrophe*) sir; M. le Ministre Minister; au revoir, m. goodbye; M., (*dans une lettre*) Dear Sir,; que prendront ces messieurs? what will you have, gentlemen?; bonsoir, messieurs-dames! good evening! (c) (*homme quelconque*) gentleman

monstre [mɔ̃str] **1** *adj Fam* huge
2 *nm* monster; m. d'ingratitude/d'égoïsme ungrateful/selfish monster; petit m.! you little monster!; m. sacré giant

monstrueusement [mɔ̃stryøzmɑ̃] *adv* monstrously

monstrueux, -euse [mɔ̃stryø, -øz] *adj* (a) (*malformé*) monstrous (b) (*énorme*) huge; être d'un égoïsme m. to be extremely selfish (c) (*scandaleux*) monstrous

monstruosité [mɔ̃stryozite] *nf* monstrosity

mont [mɔ̃] *nm* mountain; *Fig* être toujours par monts et par vaux to be always on the move; le m. Blanc Mont Blanc

montage [mɔ̃taʒ] *nm* (a) (*pose*) (*de bijou*) mounting; (*d'appareils*) assembling (b) (*d'un film*) editing; (*image truquée*) montage; m. vidéo video(tape) editing (c) *Écon* m. financier financial arrangement (d) (*d'installation électrique*) wiring (up)

montagnard, -e [mɔ̃taɲar, -ard] **1** *adj* mountain
2 *nm,f* mountain dweller

montagne [mɔ̃taɲ] *nf* (a) (*élévation*) mountain; (*région*) mountains; à la m. in the mountains; *Fig* se faire une m. de qch to make a great song and dance about sth; en haute m. in the high mountains (b) faire de la m. (*alpinisme*) to go mountain climbing; (*randonnée*) to go hill walking (c) *Fig* (*grande quantité*) une m. de a mountain of (d) montagnes russes (*attraction foraine*) big dipper, rollercoaster

montagneux, -euse [mɔ̃taɲø, -øz] *adj* mountainous

montant [mɔ̃tɑ̃] *nm* (a) (*somme*) amount; versement d'un m. de 500 francs payment of 500 francs; montants compensatoires subsidies (b) (*d'échelle*) upright; (*de lit*) post; (*de fenêtre*) jamb

mont-de-piété (*pl* monts-de-piété) [mɔ̃dpjete] *nm* pawnshop

monté, -e [mɔ̃te] *adj* (*équipé*) être bien m. (en qch) to be well stocked (with sth)

monte-charge (*pl* monte-charges) [mɔ̃tʃarʒ] *nm* goods *Br* lift *or Am* elevator

montée [mɔ̃te] *nf* (a) (*côte*) slope, hill (b) (*d'une côte*) climb; (*d'un avion*) ascent; la m. des eaux the rise in the water level (c) (*des prix*) rise (de in) (d) (*apparition*) (*du nationalisme, du fascisme*) rise, growth

monte-plats [mɔ̃tpla] *nm inv* dumb waiter

monter [mɔ̃te] **1** *vt* (*aux avoir*) (a) (*colline, escalier*) (*en s'éloignant*) to go up, to climb (up); (*en s'approchant*) to come up, to climb (up); m. la rue en courant to run up the street
(b) (*porter en haut*) (*en s'éloignant*) to take up; (*en s'approchant*) to bring up
(c) (*son, chauffage*) to turn up
(d) (*assembler*) (*meuble*) to assemble; (*tente*) to put up; (*bijou, photo*) to mount
(e) (*pièce de théâtre*) to put on, to stage
(f) (*film*) to edit
(g) (*créer*) (*entreprise, magasin*) to set up; (*complot*) to hatch; m. un coup to plan a job
(h) (*trousseau*) to put together
(i) (*en tricot*) m. les mailles to cast on
(j) (*cheval*) to ride
(k) (*locutions*) m. la garde to mount guard; m. (la tête à) qn contre qn to set sb against sb
2 *vi* (*aux être*) (a) (*aller vers le haut*) to go up; (*venir vers le haut*) to come up; (*oiseau*) to fly up; (*avion*) to climb; m. se coucher to go (up) to bed; faire m. qn to show sb up; m. sur qch to climb onto sth; m. à qch to climb (up) sth; m. à Paris (*y déménager*) to move up to Paris; (*en visite*) to go up to Paris; m. à la tête de qn (*sang*) to rush to sb's head; *Fig* ça va lui m. à la tête it'll go to his head; les larmes lui sont montées aux yeux his eyes filled with tears
(b) (*prendre place*) m. dans qch (*voiture, banque*) to get in sth; (*train, autobus, avion*) to get on sth; m. sur qch to get on sth; m. à bord to go on board; m. à bicyclette to ride a bicycle; m. à cheval to ride, to go riding; m. en voiture to get into a car
(c) (*route*) to climb
(d) (*prix, baromètre, marée*) to rise; m. en flèche (*prix*) to soar; faire m. les prix to put up prices; m. à (*s'élever à*) amount to, to come to
3 se monter *vpr* (a) (*s'élever*) se m. à to come to, to amount to
(b) (*s'équiper*) se m. en qch to provide oneself with sth
(c) *Fam* se m. la tête (*s'exalter*) to get carried away with oneself

monteur, -euse [mɔ̃tœr, -øz] *nm,f Cin* editor

Montevideo [mɔ̃tevideo] *n* Montevideo

montgolfière [mɔ̃ɡɔlfjɛr] *nf* hot-air balloon

monticule [mɔ̃tikyl] *nm* hillock, mound

montre [mɔ̃tr] *nf* (a) (*instrument*) watch; à ma m. il est midi by my watch it's twelve o'clock; m. en main exactly; m. de plongée diver's watch; m. à quartz quartz watch (b) (*preuve*) faire m. de qch to show sth

Montréal [mɔ̃real] *n* Montreal

montréalais, -e [mɔ̃reale, -ez] **1** *adj* of Montreal
2 *nm,f* M. Montrealer

montre-bracelet (*pl* montres-bracelets) [mɔ̃trabrasle] *nf* wristwatch

montrer [mɔ̃tre] **1** *vt* (a) (*révéler*) to show (à to); tu devrais m. ça au médecin you should let the doctor take a look at it; m. le chemin à qn to show sb the way; m. les dents to show or bare one's teeth (b) (*désigner*) to point out; m. qn/qch du doigt to point at sb/sth; *Fig* to point the finger at sb/sth (c) (*faire preuve de*) to show
2 se montrer *vpr* (a) (*se présenter*) (*personne*) to show oneself (b) (*s'avérer*) se m. gentil/courageux to be kind/courageous

montreur, -euse [mɔ̃trœr, -øz] *nm,f* m. d'ours bear leader

monture [mɔ̃tyr] nf (a) (de lunettes) frame; (de bijou) setting (b) (cheval) mount

monument [mɔnymã] nm (a) (statue) monument; m. funéraire monument (over a tomb); m. aux morts war memorial (b) (édifice public) monument; m. classé listed building; être classé m. historique to be a listed building (c) Fig (livre, film) masterpiece

monumental, -e, -aux, -ales [mɔnymãtal, -o] adj monumental

moquer [mɔke] **se moquer** vpr (a) (rire) se m. de qn/qch to make fun of sb/sth; Fig il se moque du monde who does he think he is? (b) (ignorer) se m. de qch not to care about sth; Fam se m. de qch comme de l'an quarante ou comme de sa première chemise not to give two hoots about sth

moquerie [mɔkri] nf mockery

moquette [mɔket] nf (fitted) carpet; **poser de la m.** to fit a carpet

moqueur, -euse [mɔkœr, -øz] adj (remarque, rires) mocking; (personne) given to mockery

moraine [mɔren] nf moraine

moral, -e, -aux, -ales [mɔral, -o] **1** adj moral
2 nm morale; **avoir le m.** to be in good spirits; **avoir le m. au beau fixe** to be in fine spirits; **avoir un m. d'acier** to be very resilient; **avoir le m. à zéro** to feel really down; **remonter le m. à qn** to cheer sb up

morale [mɔral] nf (a) (bien) morals; **contraire à la m.** immoral (b) (règles) morality; **faire une leçon de m. à qn, faire la m. à qn** to lecture sb (c) (d'une histoire) moral

moralement [mɔralmã] adv morally

moralisateur, -trice [mɔralizatœr, -tris] **1** adj (discours, personne) moralizing
2 nm,f moralizer

moraliste [mɔralist] **1** adj moralistic
2 nmf moralist

moralité [mɔralite] nf (a) (conduite, attitude) morality; être d'une m. irréprochable to have impeccable moral standards (b) (d'une histoire) moral; **m.: quand on veut, on peut** the moral of the story is, you can do anything if you put your mind to it

moratoire [mɔratwar] nm Jur moratorium

morbide [mɔrbid] adj morbid

morbidité [mɔrbidite] nf morbidness

morceau, -x [mɔrso] nm (a) (de nourriture) piece, bit; Fam **le gros m.** (le plus difficile) the big one; Fam **manger un m.** to have a bite to eat; Fam Fig **lâcher ou cracher le m.** to spill the beans; m. **de choix** choice morsel; **bas morceaux** (de viande) cheap cuts (b) (de savon, de tissu, de papier) piece, bit; (de sucre) lump; (de terre) piece; **en morceaux** in pieces; **mettre qch en morceaux** to tear sth to pieces; **tomber en morceaux** to fall to pieces (c) (de musique) piece (d) (extrait) m. **d'anthologie** anthology piece; m. **de bravoure** purple passage; **morceaux choisis** selected passages or extracts

morceler [42] [mɔrsəle] vt to divide up

morcellement [mɔrselmã] nm dividing up

mordant, -e [mɔrdã, -ãt] **1** adj (a) (esprit, remarque, ton) biting, caustic (b) (froid) biting
2 nm (causticité) bite

mordicus [mɔrdikys] adv Fam stubbornly

mordiller [mɔrdije] vt to nibble

mordoré, -e [mɔrdɔre] adj (couleur) bronze

mordre [mɔrdr] **1** vt (a) (sujet: personne, animal) to bite; m. **qn au bras** to bite sb's arm, to bite sb on the arm; **se faire m. par un chien** to be bitten by a dog (b) (entamer) (sujet: lime) to bite into; (sujet: acide) to eat into
2 vi (personne, chien) to bite; m. **dans une pomme** to bite into an apple; **ça mord?** (poissons) are the fish biting?
3 mordre à vt ind (a) (poisson) m. **à l'appât** ou à **l'hameçon** to rise to the bait (b) Fam (prendre goût à) to take to
4 mordre sur vt ind (déborder) m. **sur qch** to encroach (up)on sth; m. **sur la ligne** (sportif) to have one's foot over the line
5 se mordre vpr se m. **la langue** to bite one's tongue; Fig se m. **les doigts d'avoir fait qch** to kick oneself for doing sth; **vous vous en mordrez les doigts** you'll be sorry

mordu, -e [mɔrdy] Fam **1** adj (a) (amoureux) madly in love; (b) (passionné) être m. **de qch** to be mad on sth
2 nm,f fanatic; **un m. de bridge/cinéma** a bridge/film fanatic

morfal, -e, -als, -ales [mɔrfal] nm,f Fam greedy-guts

morfondre [mɔrfɔ̃dr] **se morfondre** vpr to mope

morgue¹ [mɔrg] nf (arrogance) haughtiness; **plein de m.** haughty

morgue² [mɔrg] nf (dans un hôpital) mortuary; (pour les corps non identifiés) morgue

moribond, -e [mɔribɔ̃, -ɔ̃d] **1** adj dying
2 nm,f dying man, f dying woman

morille [mɔrij] nf morel

mormon, -e [mɔrmɔ̃, -ɔn] adj & nm,f Mormon

morne [mɔrn] adj (personne, regard) glum; (silence) gloomy; (temps) dismal, dreary

morose [mɔroz] adj (personne, humeur) morose; (temps) miserable

morosité [mɔrozite] nf (d'une personne, de l'humeur) moroseness; (du temps) miserable nature

morphine [mɔrfin] nf morphine

morphologie [mɔrfɔlɔʒi] nf morphology

morphologique [mɔrfɔlɔʒik] adj morphological

morpion [mɔrpjɔ̃] nm (a) très Fam (pou) crab (b) Fam (enfant) kid (c) (jeu) Br noughts and crosses, Am tick-tack-toe

mors [mɔr] nm bit; Fig **prendre le m. aux dents** to take the bit between one's teeth

morse¹ [mɔrs] nm (animal) walrus

morse² nm (code) Morse (code)

morsure [mɔrsyr] nf bite

mort¹, -e [mɔr, mɔrt] **1** pp voir mourir
2 adj (a) (personne, feuille, langue) dead; **plus m. que vif** more dead than alive; m. **de peur/d'inquiétude/de froid** frightened/worried/frozen to death; Fam être m. **de rire** to fall about laughing; Fam être m. **(de fatigue)** to be dead tired (b) (hors d'usage) (pile) dead; Fam être m. **(voiture, chaussures)** to have had it
3 nm,f dead man, f dead woman; **les morts** the dead; Rel **le jour** ou **la fête des morts** All Souls' Day; **faire le m.** to pretend to be dead; Fig to lie low; **l'accident a fait trois morts** three people were killed in the accident
4 nm (aux cartes) dummy

mort² *nf* death; **trouver la m. dans un accident** to die in an accident; **se donner la m.** to take one's own life; **mettre qn à m.** to put sb to death; **en vouloir à qn à m.** to have a huge grudge against sb; **la m. dans l'âme** with a heavy heart; *Fam* **c'est pas la m.!** it won't kill you/him/etc!

mortadelle [mɔrtadɛl] *nf* mortadella

mortaise [mɔrtɛz] *nf* mortise

mortalité [mɔrtalite] *nf* mortality, death rate; **m. infantile** infant mortality

mort-aux-rats [mɔroRa] *nf inv* rat poison

mortel, -elle [mɔrtɛl] **1** *adj* (a) *(éphémère)* mortal (b) *(fatal) (maladie, accident)* fatal; *(dose)* lethal; *(champignon, poison)* deadly (c) *(péché, ennemi)* deadly; *(silence)* deathly; **d'une pâleur mortelle** deathly pale (d) *Fam (ennuyeux)* deadly boring
2 *nm,f* mortal

mortellement [mɔrtɛlmɑ̃] *adv (blessé)* fatally; *(ennuyeux)* deadly

morte-saison *(pl* **mortes-saisons)** [mɔrtsɛzɔ̃] *nf* off-season

mortier [mɔrtje] *nm* mortar; **tirs de m.** mortar fire

mortifiant, -e [mɔrtifjɑ̃, -ɑ̃t] *adj* mortifying

mortification [mɔrtifikasjɔ̃] *nf* mortification

mortifié, -e [mɔrtifje] *adj* mortified

mortifier [66] [mɔrtifje] **1** *vt* to mortify
2 se mortifier *vpr* to mortify oneself

mort-né, -e *(mpl* **mort-nés,** *fpl* **mort-nées)** [mɔrne] **1** *adj aussi Fig* stillborn
2 *nm,f* stillborn child

mortuaire [mɔrtɥɛr] *adj* death

morue [mɔry] *nf* (a) *(poisson)* cod (b) *très Fam (prostituée)* tart

morve [mɔrv] *nf* snot

morveux, -euse [mɔrvø, -øz] **1** *adj (enfant)* runny-nosed; *(nez)* runny
2 *nm,f Fam Péj (gamin)* brat; *(jeune prétentieux)* upstart

mosaïque [mɔzaik] *nf* (a) *(en décoration)* mosaic (b) *Fig (de couleurs)* kaleidoscope; *(de populations)* medley

Moscou [mɔsku] *n* Moscow

moscovite [mɔskɔvit] **1** *adj* Muscovite
2 *nmf* **M.** Muscovite

mosquée [mɔske] *nf* mosque

mot [mo] *nm* (a) *(parole)* word; **avoir son m. à dire** to have one's say; **avoir toujours le m. pour rire** to be always ready with a joke; **avoir des mots avec qn** to have words with sb; **avoir le dernier m.** to have the last word; **je n'ai pas dit mon dernier m.** I'm not finished yet; **dire un m.** *ou* **deux mots à qn** to have a word with sb; **se donner le m.** to pass the word around; **prendre qn au m.** to take sb at his/her word; **traduire m. à m.,** **faire du m. à m.** to translate word for word; **répéter qch m. pour m.** to repeat sth word for word; **sans m. dire** without (saying) a word; **sur ces mots** and with these words; **en un m.** in a word; **au bas m.** at least; **la mots couverts** in veiled terms; **mots doux, mots d'amour** sweet nothings; **mots croisés** crossword; **faire des mots croisés** to do crosswords; **m. d'ordre** watchword, slogan; **m. de passe** password; **bon m.** witty remark; **gros m.** swear word; **dire des gros mots** to swear
(b) *(message écrit)* note; **envoyer un m. à qn** to drop sb a line; **m. d'excuse** note *(explaining absence)*

(c) *Ordinat* **m. de 6 bits** 6-bit byte; **m. binaire** binary word

motard, -e [mɔtar, -ard] **1** *nm,f Fam (conducteur de moto)* biker
2 *nm (policier)* motorcycle policeman

mot-clef *(pl* **mots-clefs)** [mɔkle] *nm* keyword

motel [mɔtɛl] *nm* motel

moteur, -trice [mɔtœr, -tris] **1** *adj* (a) *(force, roue)* driving; **à deux/quatre roues motrices** two-/four-wheel drive (b) *(nerf, trouble)* motor
2 *nm* engine; *(électrique)* motor; *Fig* driving force; *Cin* **m.!** cameral; **à m.** motor(-driven); **m. à deux/quatre temps** two-/four-stroke engine; **m. à explosion** internal combustion engine; **m. à injection** fuel-injected engine; **m. à réaction** jet engine; *Ordinat* **m. de recherche** search engine
3 *nf Rail* **motrice** engine

motif [mɔtif] *nm* (a) *(raison)* reason (de for); **elle n'a aucun m. de mécontentement** she has no reason to be unhappy (b) *(dessin)* pattern, motif (c) *(dans un morceau de musique)* motif

motion [mɔsjɔ̃] *nf* motion; **m. de censure** motion of censure

motivant, -e [mɔtivɑ̃, -ɑ̃t] *adj (travail)* motivating; *(salaire, rémunération)* attractive

motivation [mɔtivasjɔ̃] *nf* motivation

motivé, -e [mɔtive] *adj* (a) *(personne)* motivated (b) *(action)* justified

motiver [mɔtive] *vt* (a) *(provoquer, stimuler)* to motivate (b) *(justifier)* to justify

moto [mɔto] *nf* motorbike; **faire de la m.** to ride a motorbike; **m. tout terrain** trial bike

motocross [mɔtokrɔs] *nm* motocross

motoculteur [mɔtokyltœr] *nm* motor cultivator

motocyclette [mɔtosiklɛt] *nf* motorcycle

motocycliste [mɔtosiklist] *nm* motorcyclist; *Mil* dispatch rider

motomarine [mɔtomarin] *nf Can* jet ski

motoneige [mɔtonɛʒ] *nf Can* snowmobile

motorisé, -e [mɔtɔrize] *adj* motorized; **être m.** *(personne)* to have transport

motrice [mɔtris] *voir* **moteur**

motricité [mɔtrisite] *nf* motor function

motte [mɔt] *nf* (a) *(de terre)* clod, clump (b) *(de beurre)* block

motus [mɔtys] *exclam* **m. (et bouche cousue)!** mum's the word!

mou¹, molle [mu, mɔl] **1** *adj (a) (matelas, substance)* soft; *(chair, ventre)* flabby; **j'ai les jambes molles** my legs are like jelly (b) *(personne, gouvernement)* spineless; *(protestation)* feeble; *(poignée de main)* limp
2 *nm,f Fam* wimp
3 *nm (dans un cordage, d'un câble)* slack

mou² *nm (abats)* lights, lungs

mouchard, -e [muʃar, -ard] *Fam* **1** *nm,f (informateur)* Br grass, *Am* fink; *(à l'école)* sneak
2 *nm (de camion)* tachograph

moucharder [muʃarde] *Fam* **1** *vt (personne)* to squeal or Br grass on; *(élève)* to sneak on
2 *vi (élève)* to sneak on people

mouche [muʃ] nf (a) (insecte) fly; **prendre la m.** to fly off the handle; **elle ne ferait pas de mal à une m.** she wouldn't hurt a fly; **quelle m. te pique?** what's got into you?; **m. tsé-tsé** tsetse fly; **fine m.** sharp customer (b) (de cible) bull's-eye; **faire m.** to hit the bull's-eye; Fig to hit home (c) (accessoire cosmétique) beauty spot

moucher [muʃe] 1 vt (a) (nez) to blow; **m. un enfant** to blow a child's nose (b) Fig **m. qn** to put sb in his/her place (c) (chandelle) to snuff out
 2 **se moucher** vpr to blow one's nose; Fam **ne pas se m. du coude** ou **du pied** to think one is the bee's knees

moucheron [muʃrɔ̃] nm midge

moucheté, -e [muʃte] adj (cheval) dappled; (tissu) speckled

mouchoir [muʃwar] nm handkerchief; **arriver dans un m.** to come in neck and neck; **grand comme un m. de poche** no bigger than a pocket handkerchief; **m. en papier** tissue; **m. en tissu** handkerchief

moudre [48] [mudr] vt to grind

moue [mu] nf pout; **faire la m.** to pout

mouette [mwɛt] nf (sea)gull

moufle [mufl] nf mitten, mitt

mouflet, -ette [muflɛ, -ɛt] nm,f Fam kid

mouflon [muflɔ̃] nm moufflon

mouillage [mujaʒ] nm (a) (de bateau) (manœuvre) anchoring; (emplacement) anchorage; **être au m.** to be riding at anchor (b) (du vin) watering down

mouillé, -e [muje] adj (a) (vêtement, personne, pieds) wet; **tout m.** soaking wet (b) (consonne) palatalized

mouiller [muje] 1 vt (a) (rendre humide) to wet; **se faire m.** to get wet; Fig **m. sa chemise** to work up a sweat (b) (vin, lait) to water down (c) (ancre) to drop (d) Fam (compromettre) to involve
 2 vi (bateau) to anchor
 3 **se mouiller** vpr (a) (personne) to get wet; **se m. les pieds** to get one's feet wet (b) Fam (prendre position) to stick one's neck out

mouillette [mujɛt] nf finger (of bread)

mouise [mwiz] nf très Fam **être dans la m.** to be hard up

moulage [mulaʒ] nm (a) (action) casting (b) (objet) plaster cast

moule[1] [mul] nm aussi Fig mould; Fig **être coulé dans le même m.** to be cast in the same mould; **m. à gâteaux** Br cake tin, Am cake pan; **m. à gaufres** waffle iron; **m. à tarte** flan dish

moule[2] nf mussel; **moules marinières** = mussels in white wine

mouler [mule] vt (a) (statue) to mould (b) (sujet: vêtement) to fit closely

moulin [mulɛ̃] nm (a) (bâtiment) mill; **on y entre comme dans un m.** anyone can just walk in; **m. à eau** watermill; Can **m. à scie** sawmill; **m. à vent** windmill (b) (appareil) **m. à café** coffee grinder; **m. à légumes** vegetable mill; Fig **m. à paroles** chatterbox; **m. à poivre** pepper mill

mouliner [muline] vt (aliment) to pass through a food mill

moulinet [mulinɛ] nm (a) (de canne à pêche) reel (b) (rotation) **faire des moulinets (avec les bras)** to circle one's arms

Moulinette® [mulinɛt] nf food mill

moult [mult] adv Hum ou Vieilli many

moulu, -e [muly] 1 pp voir moudre
 2 adj (a) (café, poivre) ground (b) Fig **être m. (de fatigue)** to be shattered

moulure [mulyr] nf (ornemental) moulding

mourant, -e [murɑ̃, -ɑ̃t] 1 adj dying
 2 nm,f dying man, f dying woman

mourir [49] [murir] (aux être) 1 vi (a) (personne, animal, plante) to die; **de sa belle mort** ou **de mort naturelle** to die a natural death; **m. de vieillesse** to die of old age; **m. assassiné** to be murdered; **m. d'inquiétude/de peur** to be worried/frightened to death; **m. de faim** to starve to death; Fam (avoir très faim) to be starving; **m. de soif/d'ennui** to die of thirst/boredom; **s'ennuyer à m.** to be bored to death; **aimer qn à m.** to be desperately in love with sb; **à m. d'ennui** deadly boring; **à m. de rire** hilarious, hysterical; **m. d'envie de faire qch** to be dying to do sth; Fig **tu ne vas pas en m.!** it won't kill you! (b) (coutume, industrie, civilisation) to die out; (feu, région) to die
 2 v impersonnel **il meurt des milliers d'enfants chaque jour** thousands of children die every day
 3 **se mourir** [murir] vpr Litt (personne) to be dying

mouroir [murwar] nm Fam Péj old people's home

mouron [murɔ̃] nm Fam **se faire du m.** to worry

mousquetaire [muskətɛr] nm musketeer

mousqueton [muskətɔ̃] nm (a) (anneau) snap clasp; (d'alpiniste) karabiner (b) (arme) carbine

moussaka [musaka] nf moussaka

moussant, -e [musɑ̃, -ɑ̃t] adj **être peu m.** not to produce a lot of lather; **bain m.** bubble bath

mousse[1] [mus] nf (a) (végétation) moss (b) (écume) foam; (sur un verre de bière) head; (de savon) lather; Fam **une m.** (bière) a beer; **m. à raser** shaving foam (c) (plat, dessert) mousse; **m. au chocolat/de saumon** chocolate/salmon mousse (d) (matériau synthétique) foam rubber

mousse[2] nm ship's boy

mousseline [muslin] nf (tissu) muslin; **m. de soie** chiffon

mousser [muse] vi (bière) to froth; (savon, lessive) to lather; (vin, eau gazeuse) to fizz; Fam Fig **se faire m.** to show off

mousseux, -euse [musø, -øz] 1 adj (a) (vin, cidre) sparkling (b) (lait, bière) frothy
 2 nm sparkling wine

mousson [musɔ̃] nf monsoon

moussu, -e [musy] adj mossy

moustache [mustaʃ] nf (a) (d'un homme) moustache; **porter la m.** to have a moustache (b) (de chat, de rongeur) whiskers

moustachu, -e [mustaʃy] 1 adj with a moustache; **être m.** to have a moustache
 2 nm man with a moustache

moustiquaire [mustikɛr] nf mosquito net

moustique [mustik] nm mosquito

moût [mu] nm (de raisins) must; (de bière) wort

moutard [mutar] nm Fam kid

moutarde [mutard] 1 adj inv (jaune) **m.** mustard (yellow)
 2 nf mustard; Fig **la m. me monte au nez** I'm beginning to lose my temper; **m. forte/de Dijon** strong/Dijon mustard

moutardier [mutardje] nm (pot) mustard pot

mouton [mutɔ̃] *nm* (a) *(animal)* sheep; **(peau de) m.** sheepskin; **être frisé comme un m.** to have curly hair; *Fig* **revenons à nos moutons** let's get back to the subject; **compter les moutons** *(pour s'endormir)* to count sheep; *Fig* **m. à cinq pattes** rare bird (b) *(viande)* mutton; (c) **moutons** *(écume)* white horses; *(poussière)* fluff

moutonner [mutɔne] *vi (mer)* to be flecked with foam

moutonneux, -euse [mutɔnø, -øz] *adj* (a) *(mer)* foam-flecked (b) *(ciel)* dotted with fleecy clouds

mouture [mutyr] *nf* (a) *(action de moudre)* grinding (b) *(d'un ouvrage, d'un livre)* version

mouvance [muvɑ̃s] *nf* **il faisait partie de la m. surréaliste** he moved in surrealist circles

mouvant, -e [muvɑ̃, ɑ̃t] *adj (terrain)* unstable; *(cible)* moving; *Fig (situation)* uncertain

mouvement [muvmɑ̃] *nm* (a) *(déplacement)* movement, motion; *(des marchandises, des capitaux)* movement; *(geste)* gesture; **faire un m.** to make a movement; **faire un faux m.** *(se faire mal)* to move the wrong way; **en m.** in motion; **ralentir le m.** to slow down; **suivre le m.** to go with the flow; **il y eut un m. de foule** a ripple ran through the crowd; **m. de tête** *(pour acquiescer)* nod; *(pour nier)* shake of the head (b) *(de gymnastique)* exercise (c) *(élan)* impulse; **m. d'humeur** outburst (of temper); **m. de colère** fit of anger (d) *(politique, artistique)* movement; **m. de grève** strike action (e) *(d'un concerto, d'une symphonie)* movement

mouvementé, -e [muvmɑ̃te] *adj (discussion, débat)* animated, lively; *(journée, voyage, vie)* eventful

mouvoir [31b] [muvwar] **1** *vt Litt (machine)* to drive; *(bateau)* to propel; **mû par la vapeur** steam-driven (b) *(pousser)* **mû par l'intérêt** prompted by self-interest **2 se mouvoir** *vpr* to move

moyen¹, -enne [mwajɛ̃, -ɛn] *adj (du milieu)* middle; **trouver un m. terme** to find a happy medium (b) *(coût, taille, vitesse)* average; **de taille moyenne** medium-sized; *(personne)* of average height (c) *(quelconque, médiocre)* average; **le Français m.** the average Frenchman

moyen² *nm* (a) *(façon, possibilité)* means, way; *aussi Hum* **trouver le m. de faire qch** to manage to do sth; **se donner les moyens de faire qch** to provide oneself with the means to do sth; **faire qch par ses propres moyens** to do sth on one's own; **employer les grands moyens** to take extreme measures; **au m. de qch** by means of sth; **par tous les moyens** any way I/you/etc can; **il n'y a pas m. de le lui faire comprendre** it's impossible to make him understand; **faire avec les moyens du bord** to make do with what one has; **moyens de communication/production/transport** means of communication/production/transport (b) **avoir des moyens** *(capacité mentale)* to be bright; **perdre tous ses moyens** to go to pieces (c) **moyens** *(financiers)* means; **j'en ai/je n'en ai pas les moyens** I can/can't afford it

Moyen Âge [mwajɛnɑʒ] *nm* **le M.** the Middle Ages

moyenâgeux, -euse [mwajɛnɑʒø, -øz] *adj* medieval

moyen-courrier *(pl* **moyen-courriers)** [mwajɛ̃kurje] *nm* **(avion)** m. medium-haul aircraft

moyennant [mwajɛnɑ̃] *prép* (in return) for; **faire qch m. finance** to do sth in return for payment; **m. quoi** in return for which

moyenne [mwajɛn] **1** *adj voir* **moyen¹**
2 *nf* (a) *(niveau le plus courant)* average; **en m.** on average (b) *(à un examen)* pass mark; *(sur une période)* average (mark); **avoir 10 sur 20 de m.** to average 10 out of 20

moyennement [mwajɛnmɑ̃] *adv* moderately, fairly

Moyen-Orient [mwajɛ̃nɔrjɑ̃] *nm* **le M.** the Middle East

moyeu [mwajø] *nm* hub

mozambicain, -e [mɔzɑ̃bikɛ̃, -ɛn] **1** *adj* Mozambican
2 *nm,f* **M.** Mozambican

Mozambique [mɔzɑ̃bik] *nm* **le M.** Mozambique

mozzarella [mɔdzarɛla], **mozzarelle** [mɔdzarɛl] *nf* mozzarella

MRAP [mrap] *nm (abrév* **Mouvement contre le racisme, l'antisémitisme et pour la paix)** = French anti-racist pressure movement

MRG [ɛmɛrʒe] *nm (abrév* **Mouvement des radicaux de gauche)** = French left-wing political party

MST¹ [ɛmɛste] *nf (abrév* **maladie sexuellement transmissible)** STD

MST² *nf (abrév* **maîtrise de sciences et techniques)** = Master's degree in science and technology

mû [my] *voir* **mouvoir**

mucoviscidose [mykovisidoz] *nf* cystic fibrosis

mucus [mykys] *nm* mucus

mue [my] **1** *pp voir* **mouvoir**
2 *nf* (a) *(d'oiseaux, de mammifères)* moulting; *(de reptiles)* sloughing (b) *(à la puberté)* breaking of the voice

muer [mɥe] **1** *vi* (a) *(mammifère)* to moult; *(serpent)* to slough (b) *(voix)* to break; **il commence à m.** his voice is breaking
2 se muer *vpr* **se m. en** to change into

muesli [mysli] *nm* muesli

muet, -ette [mɥɛ, -ɛt] **1** *adj* (a) *(personne)* dumb; *Fig (silencieux)* silent; **m. d'étonnement/de colère** speechless with astonishment/anger; **m. comme la tombe** as quiet as the grave; **il est resté m. comme une carpe** he didn't open his mouth (b) *(film, réprobation)* silent; *(rôle)* non-speaking (c) *Ling* silent
2 *nm,f* mute
3 *nm Cin* **le m.** silent films

muezzin [mɥedzin] *nm* muezzin

mufle [myfl] *nm* (a) *Fam (homme)* lout (b) *(du bœuf, du bison)* muffle; *(du lion, du taureau)* muzzle

muge [myʒ] *nm* mullet

mugir [myʒir] *vi* (a) *(vache)* to moo; *(taureau)* to bellow (b) *(vent)* to howl

mugissement [myʒismɑ̃] *nm* (a) *(de vache)* moo; *(de taureau)* bellow; **des mugissements** *(de vache)* mooing; *(de taureau)* bellowing (b) *(du vent)* howling

muguet [mygɛ] *nm (plante)* lily of the valley

mulâtre [mylɑtr] *adj & nm* mulatto

mulâtresse [mylɑtrɛs] *nf* mulatto

mule¹ [myl] *nf (animal)* mule

mule² *nf (chaussure)* mule

mulet¹ [mylɛ] *nm (équidé)* mule

mulet² *nm (poisson)* grey mullet

muletier, -ère [myltje, -ɛr] *nm,f* mule driver

mulot [mylo] *nm* field mouse

multicarte [myltikart] *adj (représentant)* for several companies

multicolore [myltikɔlɔr] *adj* multicoloured

multicoque [myltikɔk] *nm* multihull

multicritère [myltikritɛr] *nm Ordinat* multicriterion

multiculturel, -elle [myltikyltyrɛl] *adj* multicultural

multidisciplinaire [myltidisipliner] *adj* multi-disciplinary

multi-écran (*pl* **multi-écrans**) [myltiekrɑ̃] *nm* split screen

multifonctions [myltifɔ̃ksjɔ̃] *adj* multi-functional

multiforme [myltiform] *adj* multifaceted

multilatéral, -e, -aux, -ales [myltilateral, -o] *adj* multilateral

multimédia [myltimedja] *adj & nm* multimedia

multimilliardaire [myltimiljarder] *adj & nmf* multi-millionaire

multimillionnaire [myltimiljoner] *adj & nmf* multi-millionaire

multinational, -e, -aux, -ales [myltinasjonal, -o] *adj* multinational
  2 *nf* **multinationale** multinational (company)

multiple [myltipl] **1** *adj* (a) (*nombreux*) many, numerous; **à usages multiples** multipurpose; **à de multiples reprises** repeatedly; *Ordinat* **à accès m.** multi-access (b) (*divers*) many, multiple
  2 *nm Math* multiple; **le plus petit commun m.** the lowest common multiple

multiplex [myltiplɛks] *adj inv & nm inv* multiplex

multiplicateur, -trice [myltiplikatœr, -tris] **1** *adj* multiplying
  2 *nm* multiplier

multiplication [myltiplikasjɔ̃] *nf* (a) (*calcul*) multiplication (b) (*augmentation*) increase (**de** in)

multiplicité [myltiplisite] *nf* multiplicity

multiplier [66] [myltiplije] **1** *vt* (a) (*somme, chiffre*) to multiply (**par** by) (b) (*répéter*) **m. les mises en garde** to issue repeated warnings; **m. les erreurs** to make mistake after mistake
  2 se multiplier *vpr* (a) (*augmenter*) to increase (b) (*se reproduire*) to multiply

multiposte [myltipost] *adj Ordinat* multi-station

multiprocesseur [myltiprɔsɛsœr] *nm Ordinat* multiprocessor

multiprogrammation [myltiprɔgramasjɔ̃] *nf Ordinat* multiprogramming

multipropriété [myltiprɔprijete] *nf* time-share; **acheter un appartement en m.** to buy a time-share *Br* flat *or Am* apartment

multiracial, -e, -aux, -ales [myltirasjal, -o] *adj* multiracial

multirisque [myltirisk] *adj* comprehensive

multisalles [myltisal] *adj* **complexe m.** multiplex (cinema)

multitâche [myltitɑʃ] *adj Ordinat* multitasking

multitraitement [myltitrɛtmɑ̃] *nm Ordinat* multi-processing

multitude [myltityd] *nf* multitude (**de** of)

multi-utilisateurs [myltiytilizatœr] *adj inv Ordinat* multiuser

municipal, -e, -aux, -ales [mynisipal, -o] **1** *adj* municipal
  2 *nfpl* **les municipales** municipal *or* local (government) elections

municipalité [mynisipalite] *nf* (a) (*commune*) municipality (b) (*maire et conseillers*) (local) council

munir [mynir] **1** *vt* (*personne*) to supply, to provide (**de** with); (*voiture, chambre*) to fit, to equip (**de** with)
  2 se munir *vpr* **se m. de qch** to take sth

munitions [mynisjɔ̃] *nfpl* ammunition, munitions

munster [mœster] *nm* Munster (cheese)

muqueuse [mykøz] *nf* mucous membrane

mur [myr] *nm* (a) (*construction*) wall; **l'ennemi est dans nos murs** the enemy is within the gates; **le m. de Berlin** the Berlin Wall; **le M. des lamentations** the Wailing Wall; **m. porteur** load-bearing wall; **m. du son** sound barrier; **franchir le m. du son** to break the sound barrier; **m. de soutènement** retaining wall (b) *Fig* (*résistance*) brick wall

mûr, -e [myr] *adj* (a) (*fruit*) ripe; *Fig* **être m. pour qch** to be ripe for sth (b) (*personne, esprit*) mature (c) (*intense*) **après mûre réflexion** after careful consideration

muraille [myrɑj] *nf* wall; **la Grande M. de Chine** the Great Wall of China

mural, -e, -aux, -ales [myral, -o] *adj* wall

mûre [myr] *nf* mulberry; (*fruit de la ronce*) blackberry

mûrement [myrmɑ̃] *adv* **après avoir m. réfléchi** after careful consideration; **un projet m. réfléchi** a carefully thought-out plan

murène [myrɛn] *nf* moray (eel)

murer [myre] **1** *vt* (a) (*ville, jardin*) to wall in (b) (*porte, fenêtre, personne*) to wall up
  2 se murer *vpr* to shut oneself away; **se m. dans le silence/la solitude** to retreat into silence/solitude

muret [myrɛ] *nm*, **murette** [myrɛt] *nf* (*mur bas*) low wall; (*de pierres sèches*) dry-stone wall

mûrier [myrje] *nm* (a) (*arbre*) mulberry tree (b) (*roncier*) blackberry bush

mûrir [myrir] *vi* (a) (*fruit*) to ripen (b) (*projet, sentiment*) to evolve, to develop (c) (*personne*) to mature

murmure [myrmyr] *nm* murmur

murmurer [myrmyre] *vt & vi* to murmur

musaraigne [myzarɛɲ] *nf* shrew

musarder [myzarde] *vi* (*flâner*) to wander around; (*fainéanter*) to lounge around

musc [mysk] *nm* musk

muscade [myskad] *nf* **m., noix (de) m.** nutmeg

muscat [myska] *nm* (a) (*raisin*) muscat grape (b) (*vin*) muscatel (wine)

muscle [myskl] *nm* muscle; **être tout en m.** to be all muscle

musclé, -e [myskle] *adj* (a) (*personne, bras, jambes*) muscular (b) *Fig* (*campagne électorale, discours*) punchy; (*intervention*) forceful; (*politique, mesure*) tough

muscler [myskle] **1** *vt* to develop the muscles of
  2 se muscler *vpr* to develop one's muscles

muscu [mysky] *Fam* = **musculation**

musculaire [myskyler] *adj* (*système, tissu, force*) muscular; (*fibre*) muscle

musculation [myskylasjɔ̃] *nf* body-building; **faire de la m.** to do body-building

musculature [myskylatyr] *nf* musculature

muse [myz] *nf* muse

museau, -x [myzo] *nm* (a) (*d'animal*) muzzle, snout (b) *Fam* (*visage*) face

musée [myze] *nm* museum; **m. (de peinture)** art gallery; **m. des horreurs** chamber of horrors

museler [42] [myzle] *vt aussi Fig* to muzzle

muselière [myzljɛr] *nf* muzzle

musette [myzɛt] 1 *nf* **(a)** *(instrument de musique)* musette **(b)** *(sac)* bag; *(de soldat)* haversack; *(d'écolier)* satchel
  2 *nm Fam* **le m.** accordion music

muséum [myzeɔm] *nm* natural history museum

musical, -e, -aux, -ales [myzikal, -o] *adj* musical

musicalement [myzikalmɑ̃] *adv* musically

music-hall *(pl* **music-halls)** [myzikol] *nm (genre, salle)* music hall

musicien, -enne [myzisjɛ̃, -ɛn] 1 *adj* musical
  2 *nm,f* musician

musicologie [myzikɔlɔʒi] *nf* musicology

musicologue [myzikɔlɔg] *nmf* musicologist

musique [myzik] *nf* music; **mettre qch en m.** to set sth to music; **faire de la m.** to make music; *Fig* **connaître la m.** to have heard it all before; *Can* **faire face à la m.** to face the music; **m. d'ambiance** *ou* **de fond** background music; **m. de chambre** chamber music; **m. classique** classical music; **m. folklorique** folk music; **m. religieuse** religious music; **m. sacrée** sacred music

musqué, -e [myske] *adj (odeur)* musky

must [mœst] *nm Fam* must

mustang [mystɑ̃g] *nm* mustang

musulman, -e [myzylmɑ̃, -an] *adj & nm,f* Moslem, Muslim

mutant, -e [mytɑ̃, ɑ̃t] *adj & nm,f* mutant

mutation [mytasjɔ̃] *nf* **(a)** *(de personnel)* transfer **(b)** *(changement)* change, alteration

muter [myte] *vt* to transfer

mutilation [mytilasjɔ̃] *nf* mutilation

mutilé, -e [mytile] *nm,f* **mutilés de guerre** disabled ex-servicemen

mutiler [mytile] 1 *vt (personne)* to mutilate, to maim; *(partie du corps)* to badly injure; *(paysage)* to disfigure
  2 **se mutiler** *vpr* to mutilate oneself

mutin[1] [mytɛ̃] *nm* mutineer

mutin[2], **-e** [mytɛ̃, -in] *adj (espiègle)* mischievous

mutiner [mytine] **se mutiner** *vpr* to mutiny **(contre** against)

mutinerie [mytinri] *nf* mutiny

mutisme [mytism] *nm* silence; **observer un m. absolu** to maintain total silence

mutualité [mytɥalite] *nf* mutual insurance

mutuel, -elle [mytɥɛl] 1 *adj* mutual
  2 *nf* **mutuelle** mutual insurance company

mutuellement [mytɥɛlmɑ̃] *adv* each other, one another

Myanmar [mjanmar] *nm* **le M.** Myanmar

mycose [mikoz] *nf* fungal infection, *Spéc* mycosis

mygale [migal] *nf* trapdoor spider

myocarde [mjɔkard] *nm* myocardium

myopathe [mjɔpat] *nmf* person with muscular dystrophy

myopathie [mjɔpati] *nf* muscular dystrophy

myope [mjɔp] 1 *adj* shortsighted, *Spéc* myopic; *Fig* **m. comme une taupe** as blind as a bat
  2 *nmf* shortsighted person

myopie [mjɔpi] *nf* shortsightedness, *Spéc* myopia

myosotis [mjɔzɔtis] *nm* forget-me-not

myriade [mirjad] *nf* myriad **(de** of)

myrrhe [mir] *nf* myrrh

myrtille [mirtij] *nf Br* bilberry, *Am* blueberry

mystère [mistɛr] *nm* **(a)** *(énigme)* mystery; **faire des mystères** to be mysterious; **faire m. de qch** to make a secret of sth; **il n'y a pas de m.** it's quite simple; *Fam* **m. et boule de gomme!** search me! **(b)** *(pièce de théâtre)* mystery (play) **(c)** **Mystère®** *(dessert glacé)* = vanilla ice cream filled with meringue and coated with chopped nuts

mystérieusement [misterjøzmɑ̃] *adv* mysteriously

mystérieux, -euse [misterjø, -øz] *adj* mysterious; *(secret)* secret

mysticisme [mistisism] *nm* mysticism

mystification [mistifikasjɔ̃] *nf* hoax

mystifier [66] [mistifje] *vt* to take in

mystique [mistik] 1 *adj* mystical
  2 *nmf* mystic

mythe [mit] *nm* myth

mythique [mitik] *adj* mythical

mythologie [mitɔlɔʒi] *nf* mythology

mythologique [mitɔlɔʒik] *adj* mythological

mythomane [mitɔman] 1 *adj* **être m.** to be a pathological liar
  2 *nmf* pathological liar, *Spéc* mythomaniac

mythomanie [mitɔmani] *nf* mythomania

myxomatose [miksɔmatoz] *nf* myxomatosis

N

N, n [ɛn] *nm inv* N, n

N [ɛn] 1 (*abrév* **Nord**) N
  2 *nf* (*abrév* **route nationale**) = designation of major road

nabot, -e [nabo, -ɔt] *nm,f Péj* midget

nacelle [nasɛl] *nf* (**a**) (*de montgolfière*) basket; (*de dirigeable*) gondola (**b**) (*de landau*) (*détachable*) carrycot; (*fixe*) carriage

nacre [nakr] *nf* mother-of-pearl; **un collier de** *ou* **en n.** a mother-of-pearl necklace

nacré, -e [nakre] *adj* pearly

nage [naʒ] *nf* (**a**) (*activité*) swimming; (*manière*) stroke; **traverser une rivière à la n.** to swim across a river; **le 100 mètres quatre nages** the 4 x 100 metres relay; **n. indienne** sidestroke; **n. libre** freestyle (**b**) **être en n.** to be bathed in perspiration

nageoire [naʒwar] *nf* (*de poisson*) fin; (*de dauphin, de cétacé*) flipper

nager [45] [naʒe] 1 *vi* to swim; **aller n.** to go for a swim; **n. vers la côte** to swim for the shore; *Fig* **n. entre deux eaux** to sit on the fence; *Fig* **n. dans son sang** to be bathed in blood; *Fig* **n. dans le bonheur** to be on cloud nine; *Fam* **il nage dans ses vêtements** his clothes are far too baggy on him; *Fam* **je nage complètement!** I'm totally at sea!
  2 *vt* (**a**) (*la brasse, le crawl*) to do, to swim (**b**) (*disputer*) **n. le 100 mètres** to swim (in) the 100 metres

nageur, -euse [naʒœr, -øz] *nm,f* swimmer

naguère [nager] *adv Litt* not long ago; (*autrefois*) formerly

naïf, -ïve [naif, -iv] 1 *adj* naive
  2 *nm,f* (**a**) (*personne*) fool (**b**) (*peintre*) naive painter

nain, -e [nɛ̃, nɛn] 1 *adj* (*personne*) dwarf
  2 *nm,f* dwarf

Nairobi [nerobi] *n* Nairobi

naissance [nesɑ̃s] *nf* (**a**) *aussi Fig* birth; **sourd/ aveugle de n.** deaf/blind from birth, born deaf/blind; **français de n.** French by birth; **donner n. à un enfant** to give birth to a child; **donner n. à une rumeur** to give rise to a rumour; **il était blond à la n.** his hair was blond when he was born (**b**) (*d'ongle*) root; (*du cou*) base; **prendre n.** to originate; (*rivière*) to rise

naissant, -e [nesɑ̃, -ɑ̃t] *adj* (*jour*) dawning; (*beauté*) nascent; **une barbe naissante** stubble

naître [50a] [netr] *vi* (*aux* **être**) (**a**) (*personne, animal*) to be born; **enfant à n.** unborn child; **il naît plus de filles que de garçons** more girls are born than boys; **elle est née en 1880** she was born in 1880; *Fam* **je ne suis pas né d'hier** I wasn't born yesterday (**b**) (*espoir*) to arise; (*projet, idée*) to originate (**de** in); **faire n.** (*espoir, doute, soupçons*) to give rise to; (*sourire*) to raise

naïvement [naivmɑ̃] *adv* naively

naïveté [naivte] *nf* naivety; **avoir la n. de croire qch** to be naive enough to believe sth

Namibie [namibi] *nf* **la N.** Namibia

namibien, -enne [namibjɛ̃, -ɛn] 1 *adj* Namibian
  2 *nm,f* **N.** Namibian

nana [nana] *nf Fam* girl

nanisme [nanism] *nm* dwarfism

nano- [nano] *préf* nano-

nanti, -e [nɑ̃ti] 1 *adj* well-to-do
  2 *nm,f* well-to-do person; **les nantis** the well-to-do

nantir [nɑ̃tir] *vt* **n. qn de qch** to provide sb with sth

napalm [napalm] *nm* napalm

naphtaline [naftalin] *nf* naphthalene; **boules de n.** mothballs; *Can Fig* **sortir qch de la n.** to take sth out of mothballs

Napoléon [napoleɔ̃] 1 *npr* Napoleon
  2 *nm* **n.** (*pièce*) 20-franc piece (*bearing the likeness of Napoleon*)

nappage [napaʒ] *nm* coating

nappe [nap] *nf* (**a**) (*de table*) tablecloth; **mettre la n.** to put the tablecloth on; **ôter la n.** to take the tablecloth off (**b**) *Fig* **n. de brouillard** fog patch; **n. d'eau** expanse of water; **n. de pétrole** (*souterraine*) layer of oil; (*de marée noire*) oil slick; **n. phréatique** water table

napper [nape] *vt* to coat (**de** with)

napperon [naprɔ̃] *nm* mat

narcisse [narsis] *nm* (**a**) (*fleur*) narcissus (**b**) (*personne*) narcissist

narcissique [narsisik] *adj* narcissistic

narcissisme [narsisism] *nm* narcissism

narcodollars [narkodɔlar] *nmpl* drug money

narcotique [narkɔtik] *adj & nm* narcotic

narcotrafiquant, -e [narkotrafikɑ̃, -ɑ̃t] *nm,f* drug trafficker

narguer [narge] *vt* to taunt

narine [narin] *nf* nostril

narquois, -e [narkwa, -az] *adj* taunting

narquoisement [narkwazmɑ̃] *adv* tauntingly

narrateur, -trice [naratœr, -tris] *nm,f* narrator

narratif, -ive [naratif, -iv] *adj* narrative

narration [narasjɔ̃] *nf* (**a**) (*genre*) narration (**b**) (*récit*) narrative

narrer [nare] *vt Litt* to narrate

narval, -als [narval] *nm* narwhal

nasal, -e, -aux, -ales [nazal, -o] *adj* nasal

nase [naz] *adj Fam* (*personne*) shattered; (*machine, voiture*) kaput

naseau, -x [nazo] *nm* nostril

nasillard, -e [nazijar, -ard] *adj* nasal; *(vieux disque)* tinny

nasse [nas] *nf* pot

natal, -e, -als, -ales [natal] *adj* native

nataliste [natalist] *adj* **politique n.** pro-birth policy

natalité [natalite] *nf* **(taux de) n.** birth rate

natation [natasjɔ̃] *nf* swimming; **faire de la n.** to swim; **n. synchronisée** synchronized swimming

natif, -ive [natif, -iv] **1** *adj* native; **être n. de** to be a native of
2 *nm,f* native

nation [nasjɔ̃] *nf* nation; **les Nations unies** the United Nations

national, -e, -aux, -ales [nasjonal, -o] **1** *adj* national
2 *nmpl* **nationaux** nationals
3 *nf* **nationale** *(route) Br* ≃ A road, *Am* ≃ highway

nationalisation [nasjonalizasjɔ̃] *nf* nationalization

nationaliser [nasjonalize] *vt* to nationalize

nationalisme [nasjonalism] *nm* nationalism

nationaliste [nasjonalist] *adj & nmf* nationalist

nationalité [nasjonalite] *nf* nationality; **être de n. française** to be a French national

national-socialisme [nasjonalsosjalism] *nm Hist* National Socialism

nativité [nativite] *nf (Noël, peinture)* Nativity

natte [nat] *nf* **(a)** *(de cheveux) Br* plait, *Am* braid **(b)** *(de paille)* mat

natter [nate] *vt (cheveux, paille) Br* to plait, *Am* to braid

naturalisation [natyralizasjɔ̃] *nf* naturalization

naturaliser [natyralize] *vt* to naturalize; **se faire n.** to become naturalized

naturalisme [natyralism] *nm* naturalism

nature [natyr] **1** *nf* **(a)** *(univers)* nature; **contre n.** unnatural; **plus grand que n.** larger than life; **laisser faire la n.** to let nature take its course; *Fam* **elle n'est pas gâtée par la n.** nature hasn't been kind to her **(b)** *(campagne)* country; **en pleine n.** in the middle of the country; *Fig* **disparaître dans la n.** to vanish into thin air **(c)** *(caractère)* nature; **être timide de ou par n.** to be shy by nature; **être de n. à faire qch** to be likely to do sth; **chez elle, c'est une seconde n.** it's second nature to her; *Fam* **c'est une petite n.** he's a bit fragile **(d)** **payer en n.** to pay in kind **(e)** **n. morte** still life
2 *adj inv* **(a)** *(yaourt, omelette)* plain; **thé n.** tea without milk **(b)** *Fam (personne)* natural

naturel, -elle [natyrɛl] **1** *adj* natural; *(besoin)* bodily; **mort naturelle** death from natural causes; **mais c'est tout n.** don't mention it
2 *nm* **(a)** *(caractère)* nature; **être d'un n. peureux** to be timid by nature; *Prov* **chassez le n., il revient au galop** what's bred in the bone will come out in the flesh **(b)** *(simplicité)* naturalness; **avec (beaucoup de) n.** (very) naturally **(c)** **thon au n.** tuna in brine

naturellement [natyrɛlmɑ̃] *adv* naturally

naturisme [natyrism] *nm* naturism

naturiste [natyrist] *nmf & adj* naturist

naufrage [nofraʒ] *nm* (ship)wreck; *Fig (d'entreprise)* failure; **faire n.** *(bateau)* to be wrecked; *(marin)* to be shipwrecked; *Fig (entreprise)* to founder

naufragé, -e [nofraʒe] **1** *adj (bateau)* wrecked; *(marin)* shipwrecked
2 *nm,f* shipwrecked person

nauséabond, -e [nozeabɔ̃, -ɔ̃d] *adj (odeur)* nauseating; *(personne, pièce)* foul-smelling; *Fig (thèses)* sickening

nausée [noze] *nf* **(a)** *(envie de vomir)* nausea, sickness; **avoir la n., avoir des nausées** to feel sick **(b)** *Fig* disgust

nauséeux, -euse [nozeø, -øz] *adj* **se sentir n.** to feel sick *or* nauseous

nautique [notik] *adj* nautical

nautisme [notism] *nm* water sports

naval, -e, -als, -ales [naval] *adj* naval

navet [navɛ] *nm* turnip; *Fam* **c'est un n.** *(film, pièce)* it's a load of rubbish

navette [navɛt] *nf* **(a)** *(véhicule)* shuttle; **faire la n. entre deux endroits/services** to shuttle back and forth between two places/departments; **n. gratuite** courtesy bus **(b)** *(fusée)* **n. (spatiale)** (space) shuttle

navigable [navigabl] *adj* navigable

navigant, -e [navigɑ̃, -ɑ̃t] *adj voir* **personnel**

navigateur, -trice [navigatœr, -tris] **1** *nm,f (marin)* navigator; **n. solitaire** lone yachtsman
2 *nm Ordinat* browser

navigation [navigasjɔ̃] *nf* navigation; **après un mois de n.** after a month at sea

naviguer [navige] *vi* to sail **(vers)** to; **n. sur l'Internet** to surf the Net

navire [navir] *nm* ship; **n.-école** training ship; **n. de guerre** warship

navrant, -e [navrɑ̃, -ɑ̃t] *adj* appalling; **un film n. de bêtise** an appallingly stupid film

navré, -e [navre] *adj (personne, expression, ton)* distressed; **être n. (de qch)** to be terribly sorry (about sth)

navrer [navre] *vt* to appal

naze [naz] = **nase**

nazi, -e [nazi] *adj & nm,f Hist* Nazi

nazisme [nazism] *nm Hist* Nazism

NB *(abrév* **nota bene)** NB

NDLR *(abrév* **note de la rédaction)** Ed

NdT *(abrév* **note du traducteur)** translator's note

ne [nə] *adv* **(a)** *voir* **aucun, guère, jamais, pas, personne, plus, que, rien (b)** *(utilisé seul)* **je n'ai que faire de vos conseils** I have no need of your advice; **elle est plus vigoureuse qu'elle n'y paraît** she's stronger than she looks; **qui ne connaît cette œuvre?** who doesn't know this work?

né, -e [ne] **1** *pp voir* **naître**
2 *adj* born; **Mme Martin, née Dupond** Mrs Martin, née Dupond; **né de parents anglais/inconnus** of English/unknown parentage; **être bien né** to be of noble birth; *Fig* **être né coiffé** to be born with a silver spoon in one's mouth; **c'est un conteur né** he's a born storyteller

néanmoins [neɑ̃mwɛ̃] *adv* nevertheless

néant [neɑ̃] *nm* **(a)** *(ce qui n'existe pas)* nothingness; **réduire qch à n.** to reduce sth to nothing **(b)** *(sur formulaire)* none

nébuleux, -euse [nebylø, -øz] **1** *adj aussi Fig* hazy
2 *nf* **nébuleuse** *Astron* nebula

nécessaire [neseser] **1** *adj* necessary (à for); *n.* **pour faire qch** necessary to do sth; **il est n. que vous y alliez** you must go; **elles n'ont pas jugé n. de me le dire** they didn't think it necessary to tell me

2 *nm* **le n.** the necessities; **faire le n.** to do what's necessary; **n. de couture** sewing kit; **n. de toilette** toilet bag; **n. de voyage** overnight bag

nécessairement [nesesermã] *adv* necessarily

nécessité [nesesite] *nf* necessity; **être dans la n. de faire qch** to have no choice but to do sth; **quelle n. y avait-il de le faire?** what need was there to do it?; **faire de n. vertu** to make a virtue out of necessity; **produits de première n.** basic essentials; *Prov* **n. fait loi** needs must

nécessiter [nesesite] *vt* to require, to necessitate

nécessiteux, -euse [nesesitø, -øz] **1** *adj* needy

2 *nm,f* person in need; **les n.** the needy

nec plus ultra [nɛkplyzyltra] *nm inv* **le n.** the best there is

nécrologie [nekrɔlɔʒi] *nf (notice)* obituary; *(liste)* obituary column

nécrologique [nekrɔlɔʒik] *adj voir* **rubrique**

nécropole [nekrɔpɔl] *nf* necropolis

nécrose [nekroz] *nf* necrosis

nécroser [nekroze] **1** *vt* to necrose

2 se nécroser *vpr* to necrose

nectar [nɛktar] *nm* nectar

nectarine [nɛktarin] *nf* nectarine

néerlandais, -e [neɛrlãdɛ, -ɛz] **1** *adj* Dutch

2 *nm,f* **N.** Dutchman, *f* Dutchwoman; **les N.** the Dutch

3 *nm (langue)* Dutch

nef [nɛf] *nf (d'église)* n. **(centrale)** nave; **n. latérale** aisle

néfaste [nefast] *adj* harmful

nèfle [nɛfl] *nf* medlar; *Fam* **des nèfles!** no way!

négatif, -ive [negatif, -iv] **1** *adj* negative

2 *nm Phot* negative

négation [negasjõ] *nf* **(a)** *(fait de nier)* negation **(b)** *Gram* negative

négationniste [negasjɔnist] *adj & nmf* revisionist

négativement [negativmã] *adv (réagir)* negatively; *(répondre)* in the negative

négligé, -e [negliʒe] **1** *adj* **(a)** *(peu soigné)* slovenly **(b)** *(délaissé)* neglected

2 *nm (vêtement)* negligée

négligeable [negliʒabl] *adj* negligible; **un avantage non n.** a not inconsiderable advantage; **une quantité non n. de** a significant quantity of

négligemment [negliʒamã] *adv (habillé)* carelessly **(b)** *(répondre, lire)* casually

négligence [negliʒãs] *nf* **(a)** *(manque de soin)* carelessness, negligence; *(abandon)* neglect; **avec n.** carelessly **(b)** *(acte négligent)* act of carelessness; *(oubli)* oversight; **par n.** through carelessness

négligent, -e [negliʒã, -ãt] *adj* careless, negligent

négliger [45] [negliʒe] **1** *vt* **(a)** *(délaisser)* to neglect **(b)** *(omettre)* to disregard; **n. de faire qch** to neglect to do sth

2 se négliger *vpr* to neglect oneself

négoce [negɔs] *nm* trade

négociable [negɔsjabl] *adj* negotiable

négociant, -e [negɔsjã, -ãt] *nm,f* merchant, dealer

négociation [negɔsjasjõ] *nf* negotiation; **entamer des négociations sur qch** to enter into negotiations on sth; **être en n. avec qn** to be in negotiation with sb

négocier [66] [negɔsje] **1** *vt* **(a)** *(prêt, salaire, paix)* to negotiate; **prix à n.** price negotiable **(b)** *(virage)* to negotiate

2 *vi (discuter)* to negotiate **(avec** with)

nègre [nɛgr] **1** *nm* **(a)** *Injurieux* Negro **(b)** *Fig (écrivain)* ghost writer; **être le n. de qn** to ghost for sb

2 *adj* **(a)** *Injurieux* **l'art n.** Negro art **(b)** *Injurieux (personne)* Negro

négresse [negrɛs] *nf Injurieux* Negress

neige [nɛʒ] *nf* **(a)** *(flocons)* snow; *Can* **banc de n.** snow bank; **être bloqué par la n.** to be snowbound; **aller à la n.** to go on a skiing holiday; **fondre comme n. au soleil** to melt away; **être blanc comme n.** to be as white as snow; *Fig* to be as pure as the driven snow; **n. artificielle** artificial snow; **n. carbonique** dry ice; **neiges éternelles** perpetual snow; **n. fondue** *(qui tombe)* sleet; *(par terre)* slush **(b)** *très Fam (cocaïne)* snow

neiger [45] [neʒe] *v impersonnel* to snow

neigeux, -euse [neʒø, -øz] *adj (temps, blanc)* snowy; *(pic, pente)* snow-covered

nem [nɛm] *nm* spring roll

néné [nene] *nm Fam* tit, boob

nénette [nenɛt] *nf Fam* **(a)** *(jeune fille)* chick **(b)** *(petite amie)* girl **(c)** *(tête)* **se casser la n.** to rack one's brains

nénuphar [nenyfar] *nm* water lily

néo- [neo] *préf* neo-

néo-calédonien, -enne [neokaledɔnjɛ̃, -ɛn] **1** *adj* New Caledonian

2 *nm,f* **N.-C.** New Caledonian

néoclassique [neoklasik] *adj* neoclassical

néocolonialisme [neokolɔnjalism] *nm* neocolonialism

néolithique [neolitik] *Géol* **1** *adj* Neolithic

2 *nm* **le N.** the Neolithic period

néologisme [neolɔʒism] *nm* neologism

néon [neõ] *nm (gaz)* neon; *(tube)* neon tube; *(enseigne)* neon sign

néonazi, -e [neonazi] *adj & nm,f* neo-Nazi

néonazisme [neonazism] *nm* neo-Nazism

néophyte [neofit] *nmf (nouvel adepte)* novice

néo-zélandais, -e [neozelãdɛ, -ɛz] *(mpl* néo-zélandais, *fpl* néo-zélandaises) **1** *adj* New Zealand

2 *nm,f* **N.-Z.** New Zealander

Népal [nepal] *nm* **le N.** Nepal

népalais, -e [nepalɛ, -ɛz] **1** *adj* Nepalese

2 *nm,f* **N.** Nepalese; **les N.** the Nepalese

3 *nm (langue)* Nepali

néphrétique [nefretik] *adj voir* **colique**

népotisme [nepotism] *nm* nepotism

Neptune [nɛptyn] *npr (dieu, planète)* Neptune

nerf [nɛr] *nm* **(a)** *(optique, spinal)* nerve; **viande pleine de nerfs** meat full of gristle; **avoir les nerfs solides** to have strong nerves; **être malade des nerfs** to suffer from nerves; **être sur les nerfs** to live on one's nerves; **être à bout de nerfs** to be at the end of one's tether; **passer ses nerfs sur qn/qch** to take it out on sb/sth; *Fam* **avoir les nerfs en pelote ou en boule** to be all on edge; *Fam* **porter ou taper** *ou Can* **tomber sur les nerfs à qn** to get on sb's nerves; *Fam* **c'est un paquet ou une boule de nerfs** he's a bag of nerves **(b)** *(force)* **un peu de**

n.!, du n.! get stuck in!; l'argent est le n. de la guerre money is the sinews of war

nerveusement [nɛrvøzmɑ̃] *adv* nervously

nerveux, -euse [nɛrvø, -øz] **1** *adj* (a) *(système, maladie)* nervous (b) *(émotif) (personne, rire, toux)* nervous (c) *(dynamique) (personne, style)* dynamic; **une conduite nerveuse** a jerky way of driving (d) *(corps, main)* sinewy; *(viande)* stringy

2 *nmf* nervous person

nervosité [nɛrvozite] *nf (excitation)* nervousness; *(irritabilité)* irritability

nervure [nɛrvyr] *nf* (a) *(de feuille, d'aile d'insecte)* vein (b) *(de voûte)* rib

n'est-ce pas [nɛspa] *adv* tu viendras, n.? you'll come, won't you?; tu l'as, n.? you've got it, haven't you?; n. qu'elle est mignonne? she's cute, isn't she?; le problème, n., c'est qu'il est déjà tard the problem is that it's already late, don't you think?

net, nette [nɛt] **1** *adj* (a) *(propre)* clean; *Fig (conscience)* clear; **faire place nette** to clear everything out (b) *(précis) (contour)* sharp; *(différence, souvenir)* clear; *(écriture)* neat; *(cassure)* clean; **il fait plus froid, c'est très n.** it's noticeably colder (c) *(prix, salaire, profit)* net; **n. d'impôt** net of tax (d) *Fam* **il n'est pas n.** *(fou)* he's not all there; *(louche)* he's a bit dodgy

2 *adv* (a) *(brutalement)* **refuser (tout) n.** to refuse point-blank; **s'arrêter n.** to stop dead; **se casser n.** to break clean through; **tué n.** killed outright (b) *Com* **100 francs n.** 100 francs net; **n. à payer** net payable

nettement [nɛtmɑ̃] *adv* (a) *(avec précision)* clearly (b) *(incontestablement)* distinctly (c) *(beaucoup)* much; **il va n. mieux** he's much better; **il est n. moins bon qu'elle** he's not nearly as good as her

netteté [nɛtte] *nf* (a) *(propreté)* cleanness (b) *(précision) (de cassure)* cleanness (c) *(clarté) (de vision, d'objet)* distinctness; *(d'image)* sharpness; *(de refus)* flatness

nettoiement [nɛtwamɑ̃] *nm* cleaning; **service du n.** refuse collection service

nettoyage [nɛtwajaʒ] *nm* cleaning; **faire du n.** to do the cleaning; **faire le n. par le vide** to throw everything out; **grand n. de printemps** spring cleaning; **n. à sec** dry-cleaning

nettoyant, -e [nɛtwajɑ̃, -ɑ̃t] **1** *adj* cleaning

2 *nm* cleaning product

nettoyer [32] [nɛtwaje] **1** *vt* (a) *(rendre propre)* to clean; **n. à sec** to dry-clean (b) *Fam (sujet: cambrioleur) (maison)* to clean out; **se faire n. au jeu** to be cleaned out gambling

2 se nettoyer *vpr* (a) **se n. les oreilles/les mains** to clean one's ears/hands (b) **le four se nettoie automatiquement** the oven is self-cleaning

neuf¹ [nœf] *adj & nm inv* nine; *voir aussi* **trois**

neuf², neuve [nœf, nœv] **1** *adj* new; **tout n.** brand new; **comme n.** as good as new; **quoi de n.?** what's new?

2 *nm* **habillé de n.** wearing new clothes; **acheter du n.** *(dans l'immobilier)* to buy new; **remettre qch à n.** to make sth as good as new; *(machine)* to recondition sth

neurasthénie [nørasteni] *nf* depression

neurasthénique [nørastenik] *adj & nmf* depressive

neurochirurgie [nøroʃiryrʒi] *nf* neurosurgery

neurochirurgien, -enne [nøroʃiryrʒjɛ̃, -ɛn] *nm,f* neurosurgeon

neuroleptique [nørɔlɛptik] *adj & nm* neuroleptic

neurologie [nørɔlɔʒi] *nf* neurology

neurologue [nørɔlɔg] *nmf* neurologist

neurone [nøron, nørɔn] *nm* neuron

neutraliser [nøtralize] **1** *vt* to neutralize

2 se neutraliser *vpr* to neutralize each other

neutralité [nøtralite] *nf* neutrality; **sortir de sa n.** to abandon one's neutral position

neutre [nøtr] **1** *adj* (a) *(ni masculin ni féminin)* neuter (b) *(impartial)* neutral (c) *(ton de voix, couleur)* neutral (d) *Chim & Él* neutral

2 *nm* (a) *Gram* neuter (b) *Can Aut* neutral; **se mettre sur le n.** to go into neutral

neutron [nøtrɔ̃] *nm* neutron

neuvième [nœvjɛm] *nmf, nm & adj* ninth; *voir aussi* **cinquième**

névé [neve] *nm* névé, firn

neveu, -x [nəvø] *nm* nephew; *Fam* **un peu, mon n.!** not half!

névralgie [nevralʒi] *nf* neuralgia; **avoir des névralgies** to suffer from neuralgia

névralgique [nevralʒik] *adj* neuralgic

névrose [nevroz] *nf* neurosis; **n. post-traumatique** post-traumatic stress disorder

névrosé, -e [nevroze] *adj & nm,f* neurotic

New York [nujɔrk] *n* New York

new-yorkais, -e [njujɔrkɛ, -ɛz] **1** *adj* of New York

2 *nm,f* **N.-Y.** New Yorker

nez [ne] *nm* (a) *(organe)* nose; **n. en trompette** turned-up nose; **parler du n.** to speak through one's nose; **sentir qch à plein n.** to smell strongly of sth; **rire au n. de qn** to laugh in sb's face; **faire qch au n. et à la barbe de qn** to do sth right under sb's nose; **fermer ou claquer la porte au n. de qn** to shut the door in sb's face; **se trouver n. à n. avec qn** to find oneself face to face with sb; **avoir le n. dans son journal** to have one's nose in one's newspaper; **avoir le n. en l'air** to be looking up in the air; *Fig (rêvasser)* to have one's head in the clouds; *Fig* **mener qn par le bout du n.** to lead sb by the nose; *Fam* **fourrer ou mettre son n. dans les affaires de qn** to poke one's nose into sb's affairs; *Fam* **avoir un verre ou un coup dans le n.** to have had one too many; **je n'ai pas mis le n. dehors de toute la journée** I didn't set foot outside all day; **tu ne vois pas plus loin que le bout de ton n.** you can't see further than the end of your nose; *Fam* **elle nous a dans le n.** she can't stand us; **ça lui pend au n.** she's got it coming to her; **ça se voit comme le n. au milieu de la figure** it's as plain as the nose on your face; **où est-il? – il est sous ton n.** *ou* **tu as le n. dessus** where is it? – it's under your nose (b) *(odorat)* sense of smell; **avoir le n. fin** to have a good nose; *Fig* **avoir du n.** to be shrewd (c) *(de bateau, d'avion)* nose (d) *(parfumeur)* nose

ni [ni] *conj* **ni... ni...** neither... nor...; **ni Pierre ni Paul ne sont venus** neither Pierre nor Paul came; **sans argent ni bagages** without money or luggage; **il est parti sans manger ni boire** he left without eating or drinking; **ni l'un ni l'autre** neither (of them); **ni plus ni moins** neither more nor less

niais, -e [njɛ, -njɛz] **1** *adj* silly

2 *nm,f* fool

niaisage [njɛzaʒ] *nm Can* idleness

niaisement [njɛzmɑ̃] *adv* foolishly

niaiser [njeze] *Can* **1** *vt* **n. qn** *(faire tourner en bourrique)* to drive sb crazy; *(se moquer de)* to laugh at sb; *(raconter des histoires à)* to pull sb's leg
2 *vi (ne rien faire)* to hang around doing nothing

niaiserie [njezri] *nf* **(a)** *(caractère stupide)* silliness **(b)** *(acte, remarque)* silly thing

niaiseux, -euse [njezø, -øz] *Can Fam* **1** *adj* silly
2 *nm,f* fool

Nicaragua [nikaragwa] *nm* **le N.** Nicaragua

nicaraguayen, -enne [nikaragwajɛ̃, -ɛn] **1** *adj* Nicaraguan
2 *nm,f* **N.** Nicaraguan

niche [niʃ] *nf* **(a)** *(renfoncement)* niche, recess **(b)** *(de chien)* kennel

nichée [niʃe] *nf (d'oisillons)* brood; *(de souris, de chiots)* litter

nicher [niʃe] **1** *vi (oiseau)* to nest *(dans* in)
2 *vt* **n. sa tête au creux de l'épaule de qn** to nestle one's head against sb's shoulder
3 **se nicher** *vpr* **(a)** *(oiseau)* to nest **(b)** *Fam (se cacher)* **où est-elle allée se n.?** where's she hiding (herself)?

nichon [niʃɔ̃] *nm Fam* boob, tit

nickel [nikɛl] **1** *nm* nickel
2 *adj inv Fam (propre)* spotlessly clean

nicotine [nikɔtin] *nf* nicotine

nid [ni] *nm aussi Fig* nest; *Fig* **n. à poussière** dust trap; *Prov* **petit à petit, l'oiseau fait son n.** slow and steady wins the race

nid-de-poule [*pl* **nids-de-poule**] [nidpul] *nm* pothole

nièce [njɛs] *nf* niece

nier [66] [nje] **1** *vt* to deny; **je nie l'avoir vue** I deny having seen her; **on ne peut pas n. que...** there's no denying that...; **n. l'évidence** to deny the obvious
2 *vi (accusé)* to deny the charge

nigaud, -e [nigo, -od] *nm,f* ninny; **gros n.!** you big ninny!

Niger [niʒɛr] *nm* **le N.** *(pays)* Niger; *(fleuve)* the Niger

Nigeria [niʒerja] *nm* **le N.** Nigeria

nigérian, -e [niʒerjɑ̃, -an] **1** *adj* Nigerian
2 *nm,f* **N.** Nigerian

nigérien, -enne [niʒerjɛ̃, -ɛn] **1** *adj* Nigerien
2 *nm,f* **N.** Nigerien

nihilisme [niilism] *nm* nihilism

nihiliste [niilist] **1** *adj* nihilistic
2 *nmf* nihilist

Nil [nil] *nm* **le N.** the Nile

n'importe [nɛ̃pɔrt] *voir* **importer**

nipper [nipe] *Fam* **1** *vt* to dress; **bien nippé** dolled up
2 **se nipper** *vpr* to dress

nippes [nip] *nfpl Fam (vêtements)* gear, togs

nippon, -onne *ou* **-one** [nipɔ̃, -ɔn] **1** *adj* Japanese
2 *nm,f* **N.** Japanese; **les Nippons** the Japanese

nique [nik] *nf Fam* **faire la n. à qn** to cock a snook at sb

niquer [nike] *vt* **(a)** *très Fam (abîmer)* to knacker **(b)** *Vulg (sexuellement)* to shag, to screw **(c)** *très Fam (escroquer)* **se faire n.** to get shafted

nitrate [nitrat] *nm* nitrate

nitreux, -euse [nitrø, -øz] *adj* nitrous

nitrique [nitrik] *adj* nitric

nitroglycérine [nitrogliserin] *nf* nitroglycerine

niveau, -x [nivo] *nm* **(a)** *(hauteur, étage)* level; **n. de l'eau/de la mer** water/sea level; **au n. de la mer** at sea level; **au n. régional/local** at regional/local level; *Fam* **au n. sentimental** as far as one's love life is concerned; *aussi Fig* **se mettre au n. de qn** to put oneself on sb's level; **l'eau nous arrivait au n. de la taille** the water came up to our waists **(b)** *(degré)* level; *Scol* standard; **avoir le n. (requis), être au n.** to be up to standard; **ne pas avoir le n. pour passer un concours** not to be of a high enough standard to take an examination; **elle a un très bon n. en physique** her physics is of a very high standard; **ils sont d'un n. social différent** they are from different social backgrounds; *Ordinat* **n. d'accès** *(dans un réseau)* access level; *Ordinat* **n. de gris** grey scale; **n. de langue** register; **n. de vie** standard of living

niveler [42] [nivle] *vt* **(a)** *(sol)* to level **(b)** *(fortunes)* to even out

nivellement [nivɛlmɑ̃] *nm (de terrain, des classes sociales)* levelling; **n. par le bas** levelling down

nobiliaire [nɔbiljɛr] *adj* **titre n.** title; **particule n.** nobiliary particle

noble [nɔbl] **1** *adj* noble; **le n. art** *(boxe)* the noble art
2 *nmf* nobleman, *f* noblewoman; **les nobles** the nobility

noblement [nɔbləmɑ̃] *adv* nobly

noblesse [nɔblɛs] *nf* nobility; **la haute et la petite n.** the nobility and the gentry; **n. oblige** noblesse oblige

noce [nɔs] *nf* **(a)** *(cérémonie du mariage)* wedding; *(ensemble des invités)* wedding party; **noces d'argent/d'or/de diamant** silver/golden/diamond wedding; **il l'a épousée en secondes noces** she's his second wife **(b)** *Fam* **faire la n.** to live it up **(c)** *Fam* **je n'étais pas à la n.** it was no picnic

noceur, -euse [nɔsœr, -øz] *nm,f Fam* party animal, raver

nocif, -ive [nɔsif, -iv] *adj* harmful

nocivité [nɔsivite] *nf* harmfulness

noctambule [nɔktɑ̃byl] *nmf* night owl

nocturne [nɔktyrn] **1** *adj (animal)* nocturnal; *(attaque, visite)* night; **évasion n.** escape by night
2 *nm (musique)* nocturne
3 *nf* **(a)** *(de magasin)* late-night opening **(b)** **match** *(disputé)* **en n.** evening game

nodal, -e, -aux, -ales [nɔdal, -o] *adj* nodal

nodule [nɔdyl] *nm Géol & Méd* nodule

Noé [nɔe] *n* Noah

Noël [nɔɛl] *nm* **(a)** *(fête)* Christmas; **à N.** at Christmas (time); **le jour de N.** Christmas Day; **arbre** *ou* **sapin de N.** Christmas tree; **joyeux N.!** Happy *or* Merry Christmas! **(b)** *(chanson)* **n.** (Christmas) carol **(c)** *(cadeau)* **(petit) n.** Christmas present

nœud [nø] *nm* **(a)** *(entrecroisement)* knot; **faire un n.** (à **qch**) to make *or* tie a knot (in sth); **n. coulant** *(pour serrer)* slipknot; *(pour étrangler)* noose; **n. de vipères** nest of vipers **(b)** *(ornement)* bow; **n. de cravate** tie knot; **faire un n. de cravate** to knot a tie; *Fam* **n. pap** bow tie; **n. papillon** bow tie **(c)** *(de courbe) & Ordinat* node **(d)** *(sur bois)* knot **(e)** *Naut (vitesse)* knot; **filer** *ou* **faire 20 nœuds** to do *or* make 20 knots **(f)** *Vulg (pénis)* cock

noie *etc voir* **noyer**

noir, -e [nwar] **1** *adj* **(a)** *(couleur)* black; **la place était noire de monde** the square was swarming with people **(b)** *(très sombre)* dark; **il fait tout n.** it's pitch-black **(c)** *(sale)* black **(d)** *Fig (pensées, dessein, regard)* black; **être d'une humeur noire** to be in a black mood **2** *nm,f* N. Black (man), *f* Black (woman) **3** *nm* **(a)** *(couleur)* black; **en n. et blanc** *(film, photo)* black and white; **être en n.** to be dressed in black; **c'était écrit n. sur blanc** it was there in black and white **(b)** *(obscurité)* dark; **avoir peur du n.** to be afraid of the dark **(c)** *(salissure)* **avoir du n. sur le visage** to have a black mark on one's face **(d)** *(d'une cible)* bull's-eye **(e)** *(café)* **un (petit) n.** a (small) black coffee **(f)** *Fig* **voir tout en n.** to look on the black side of everything **(g)** *Fam* **le travail au n.** moonlighting; **travailler au n.** to moonlight **4** *nf* **noire** *(note de musique)* Br crotchet, Am quarter note

noirâtre [nwarɑtr] *adj* blackish

noirceur [nwarsœr] *nf* **(a)** *(couleur)* blackness; *Litt (d'un crime)* heinousness **(b)** *Can (obscurité)* dark, darkness; **dans la n.** in the dark or darkness; **avoir peur dans la n.** to be afraid of the dark

noircir [nwarsir] **1** *vt* to blacken; *Fig* **n. du papier** to write pages and pages; *Fig* **n. (la réputation de) qn** to blacken sb's reputation; *Fig* **n. le tableau** *ou* **la situation** to paint things blacker than they are **2** *vi* to turn or go black **3** *se noircir* *vpr* **(a)** *(ciel)* to darken **(b)** **se n. le visage** to black one's face; *Th* to black up

noise [nwaz] *nf* **chercher n.** *ou* **des noises à qn** to try to pick a quarrel with sb

noisetier [nwaztje] *nm (arbre)* hazel tree; *(bois)* hazel (wood)

noisette [nwazet] **1** *nf* **(a)** *(fruit)* hazelnut **(b)** *(petite quantité) (de beurre)* small knob; *(de gel)* small amount **2** *adj inv* **yeux n.** hazel eyes

noix [nwa] *nf* **(a)** *(fruit)* walnut; **n. de cajou** cashew nut; **n. de coco** coconut; **n. de pécan** pecan **(b)** *(petite quantité) (de beurre)* knob **(c)** **n. de veau** cushion of veal **(d)** *Fam* **à la n.** lousy

nom [nɔ̃] *nm* **(a)** *(de personne, de chose)* name; **un homme du n. de Pierre** a man by the name of Pierre; **n.... prénom...** *(sur formulaire)* surname... first name...; **vos n., prénoms et adresse** your full name and address; **porter le n. de sa mère** to be named after one's mother; **sous le n. de Leduc** under the name of Leduc; **se faire un n.** to make a name for oneself; **appeler les choses par leur n.** to call a spade a spade; **traiter qn de tous les noms** to call sb everything under the sun; **quelqu'un dont je tairai le n.** someone who shall remain nameless; **une impolitesse sans n.** unspeakable rudeness; **un grand n. de la musique** one of the great names in music; **au n. de la loi/de l'amitié** in the name of the law/of friendship; *Fam* **avoir un n. à coucher dehors** to have a totally unpronounceable name; **n. de baptême** Christian name; *Ordinat* **n. de champ** field name; **n. d'emprunt** assumed name; **n. de famille** surname; *Ordinat* **n. de fichier** file name; **n. de jeune fille** maiden name; **n. à particule** aristocratic name *(with a nobiliary particle)*; **n. de plume** nom de plume, pen name; *Fam* **n. à rallonges** *ou* **à tiroirs** long aristocratic name; **n. de scène** *ou* **de théâtre** stage name **(b)** *Gram* noun; **n.**

commun common noun; **n. composé** compound (noun); **n. propre** proper noun **(c)** *Fam* **n. d'une pipe!, n. d'un chien!** hell!

nomade [nɔmad] **1** *adj* nomadic **2** *nmf* nomad

nomadisme [nɔmadism] *nm* nomadism

nombre [nɔ̃br] *nm aussi Gram* number; **un grand/petit n. d'entre nous** many/a few of us; **le plus grand n.** the majority; **(bon) n. de** a good many; **supérieur en n.** superior in number(s); **nous sommes en n. suffisant** there are enough of us; **venir en n.** to come in large numbers; **ils sont au n. de huit** there are eight of them; **être au n. de** *ou* **du n. de** to be among; **faire n.** to make up the numbers; *Phys* **n. atomique** atomic number; *Math* **n. décimal** decimal (number); *Math* **n. entier** whole number, integer; *Math* **n. premier** prime number

nombreux, -euse [nɔ̃brø, -øz] *adj (membres, objets)* numerous, many; *(famille, armée, groupe)* large; **nous sommes peu n.** there aren't many of us; **venir (très) n.** to come in (very) large numbers

nombril [nɔ̃bri, nɔ̃bril] *nm* navel; **une chemise ouverte jusqu'au n.** a shirt open to the waist; **il se prend pour le n. du monde** he thinks the whole world revolves around him; *Fig* **se regarder le n.** to contemplate one's navel

nombrilisme [nɔ̃brilism] *nm* navel-gazing

nombriliste [nɔ̃brilist] *adj* self-absorbed

nomenclature [nɔmɑ̃klatyr] *nf (de termes techniques)* nomenclature; *(d'un dictionnaire)* word list

nominal, -e, -aux, -ales [nɔminal, -o] *adj* **(a)** *(prix, autorité) & Fin* nominal **(b)** *(par noms de famille)* **appel n.** roll call; **liste nominale** list of names **(c)** *Gram* noun

nominalement [nɔminalmɑ̃] *adv* **(a)** *(de nom seulement)* in name only **(b)** *Gram (employé)* as a noun

nominatif, -ive [nɔminatif, -iv] *adj (carte d'adhérent, billet)* nontransferable; *Fin (titre)* registered

nomination [nɔminasjɔ̃] *nf* **(a)** *(à un poste)* appointment (à to) **(b)** *(pour une remise de récompense)* nomination (à for)

nominativement [nɔminativmɑ̃] *adv* by name

nominé, -e [nɔmine] *adj* nominated (à for)

nommé, -e [nɔme] **1** *adj (personne, objet)* named **2** *nm,f* **un n. Bertrand a appelé** someone called Bertrand rang

nommément [nɔmemɑ̃] *adv* **(a)** *(par son nom)* by name **(b)** *(spécialement)* especially, in particular

nommer [nɔme] **1** *vt* **(a)** *(donner un prénom à)* to name, to call **(b)** *(donner un nom à)* **on nomme aumôniers les prêtres attachés à un régiment** priests attached to a regiment are called chaplains **(c)** *(désigner)* to name; *Hum* **M. Boivin, pour ne pas le n.** without mentioning any names, Mr Boivin **(d)** *(à un poste)* to appoint (à to); **être nommé à Lille** to be posted to Lille **2** *se nommer* *vpr* **(a)** *(avoir pour nom)* to be called **(b)** *(s'identifier)* to give one's name

non [nɔ̃] **1** *adv* **(a)** *(en réponse, exprime la surprise, l'indignation)* no; **je pense que n.** I don't think so; **faire signe que n.** *(de la tête)* to shake one's head; **n. mais!** honestly! **(b)** *(n'est-ce pas?)* **c'est dégoûtant, n.?** it's disgusting, isn't it?; **il est pas mal, n.?** he's not bad-looking, is he? **(c)** *(pas)* not; **n. loin** not far; **qu'elle vienne ou n.** whether she comes or not; **elle veut déménager, lui n.** she wants to move house but he doesn't; *Litt* **n. (pas) que je le craigne** not that I fear

him
 2 *nm inv* no

nonagénaire [nɔnaʒenɛr] *adj & nmf* nonagenarian

non-agression [nɔnagresjɔ̃] *nf voir* **pacte**

non-alcoolisé, -e [nɔnalkɔlize] *adj* non-alcoholic

non-aligné, -e [nɔnaliɲe] *adj Pol* non-aligned

nonante [nɔnɑ̃t] *adj & nm inv* Belg & Suisse ninety; *voir aussi* **trois**

non-assistance [nɔnasistɑ̃s] *nf* Jur **n. à personne en danger** = failure to assist injured people, for example at the scene of an accident

non-autorisé, -e [nɔnotorize] *adj* Ordinat (nom de fichier) illegal

non-belligérant, -e [nɔ̃beliʒerɑ̃, -ɑ̃t] *adj* non-belligerent

nonchalamment [nɔ̃ʃalamɑ̃] *adv* nonchalantly

nonchalance [nɔ̃ʃalɑ̃s] *nf* nonchalance

nonchalant, -e [nɔ̃ʃalɑ̃, -ɑ̃t] *adj* nonchalant

non-conformisme [nɔ̃kɔ̃fɔrmism] *nm* non-conformism

non-conformiste [nɔ̃kɔ̃fɔrmist] *adj & nmf* non-conformist

non-conformité [nɔ̃kɔ̃fɔrmite] *nf* nonconformity

non-connecté, -e [nɔ̃kɔnekte] *adj* Ordinat off-line

non-dit [nɔ̃di] *nm* **le n.** what is unspoken; **un film riche en non-dits** a film full of meaningful silences

non-formaté, -e [nɔ̃fɔrmate] *adj* Ordinat unformatted

non-fumeur, -euse [nɔ̃fymœr, -øz] 1 *adj* non-smoking
 2 *nm,f* non-smoker

non-ingérence [nɔ̃nɛ̃ʒerɑ̃s] *nf* noninterference

non-initialisé, -e [nɔninisjalize] *adj* Ordinat uninitialized

non-initié, -e [nɔninisje] *nm,f* uninitiated person; **les non-initiés** the uninitiated

non-inscrit, -e [nɔnɛ̃skri, -it] *nm,f* Pol independent

non-intervention [nɔnɛ̃tɛrvɑ̃sjɔ̃] *nf* non-intervention

non-interventionniste [nɔnɛ̃tɛrvɑ̃sjɔnist] *adj* non-interventionist

non-lieu, -x [nɔ̃ljø] *nm* Jur **bénéficier d'un n.** to be discharged through lack of evidence

nonne [nɔn] *nf* nun

nono, -ote [nono, -ɔt] *nm,f* Can Fam idiot

non-paiement [nɔ̃pɛmɑ̃] *nm* non-payment

non-polluant, -e [nɔ̃pɔlɥɑ̃, -ɑ̃t] *adj* environmentally friendly

non-prolifération [nɔ̃proliferasjɔ̃] *nf* nonproliferation

non-remboursable [nɔ̃rɑ̃bursabl] *adj* non-refundable

non-respect [nɔ̃rɛspɛ] *nm* (d'une loi) non-observance

non-retour [nɔ̃rətur] *nm* **point de n.** point of no return

non-salarié, -e [nɔ̃salarje] *nm,f* self-employed person

non-sens [nɔ̃sɑ̃s] *nm inv* (a) (dans une traduction) meaningless phrase (b) (absurdité) **un n.** a nonsense

non-stop [nɔnstɔp] *adj inv & adv* Fam non-stop

non-syndiqué, -e [nɔ̃sɛ̃dike] 1 *adj* non-union
 2 *nm,f* non-union worker

non-violence [nɔ̃vjɔlɑ̃s] *nf* non-violence

non-violent, -e [nɔ̃vjɔlɑ̃, -ɑ̃t] *adj* non-violent

non-voyant, -e [mpl **non-voyants,** fpl **non-voyantes**) [nɔ̃vwajɑ̃, -ɑ̃t] *nm,f* unsighted person; **les non-voyants** the unsighted

nord [nɔr] 1 *nm* north; **un vent du n.** a northerly or north wind; **le vent du n.** the north wind; **au n.** in the north; **au n. de** (to the) north of; Fig **il ne perd pas le n.** he's keeping a cool head; **le grand N.** the Frozen North
 2 *adj inv* (côte, face) north; (régions) northern

nord-africain, -e (mpl **nord-africains,** fpl **nord-africaines**) [nɔrafrikɛ̃, -ɛn] 1 *adj* North African
 2 *nm,f* **N.-A.** North African

nord-américain, -e (mpl **nord-américains,** fpl **nord-américaines**) [nɔramerikɛ̃, -ɛn] 1 *adj* North American
 2 *nm,f* **N.-A.** North American

nord-coréen, -enne (mpl **nord-coréens,** fpl **nord-coréennes**) [nɔrkɔreɛ̃, -ɛn] 1 *adj* North Korean
 2 *nm,f* **N.-C.** North Korean

nord-est [nɔrɛst] *nm & adj inv* northeast

nordique [nɔrdik] 1 *adj* Nordic, Scandinavian
 2 *nmf* N. Scandinavian

nordiste [nɔrdist] *adj & nmf* Unionist

nord-nord-est [nɔrnɔrɛst] *nm & adj inv* north-north-east

nord-nord-ouest [nɔrnɔrwɛst] *nm & adj inv* north-northwest

nord-ouest [nɔrwɛst] *nm & adj inv* northwest

nord-vietnamien, -enne (mpl **nord-vietnamiens,** fpl **nord-vietnamiennes**) [nɔrvjɛtnamjɛ̃, -ɛn] 1 *adj* North Vietnamese
 2 *nm,f* **N.-V.** North Vietnamese

noria [nɔrja] *nf* noria

normal, -e, -aux, -ales [nɔrmal, -o] 1 *adj* (a) (dans la norme, naturel) normal; **c'est tout à fait n. que la jeunesse se rebelle** it's only normal for young people to rebel; **ce n'est pas n.** (que + subjunctive) it's not right (that); **en temps n.** in normal circumstances (b) (moyen) (poids, taille) standard
 2 *nf* **normale** (a) **la normale** normal, the norm; **au-dessus/au-dessous de la normale** above/below average; **température au-dessous des normales saisonnières** temperature below the seasonal average (b) Fam Univ **Normale Sup** = university-level college preparing students for senior posts in teaching

normalement [nɔrmalmɑ̃] *adv* normally

normalien, -enne [nɔrmaljɛ̃, -ɛn] *nm,f* Univ = student or former student of the "École normale supérieure"

normalisation [nɔrmalizasjɔ̃] *nf* (a) (des relations diplomatiques) normalization (b) Ind standardization

normaliser [nɔrmalize] *vt* (a) (relations diplomatiques) to normalize (b) Ind to standardize

normalité [nɔrmalite] *nf* normality

normand, -e [nɔrmɑ̃, -ɑ̃d] *aussi* Hist 1 *adj* Norman
 2 *nm,f* N. Norman

Normandie [nɔrmɑ̃di] *nf* **la N.** Normandy

norme [nɔrm] *nf* (a) (règle) norm; **dans la n.** within the norm (b) Ind & Com standard

noroît [nɔrwa] *nm* north-wester

Norvège [nɔrvɛʒ] *nf* **la N.** Norway

norvégien, -enne [nɔrveʒjɛ̃, -ɛn] 1 *adj* Norwegian
 2 *nm,f* N. Norwegian
 3 *nm* (langue) Norwegian

nos [no] *voir* **notre**

nostalgie [nɔstalʒi] *nf* nostalgia; *(mal du pays)* homesickness; **avoir la n. de qch** to feel nostalgic for sth; **avoir la n. du pays** to be homesick

nostalgique [nɔstalʒik] *adj* nostalgic

nota bene [nɔtabene] *nm inv* nota bene

notable [nɔtabl] *adj & nm* notable

notablement [nɔtabləmɑ̃] *adv* notably

notaire [nɔtɛr] *nm* notary (public)

notamment [nɔtamɑ̃] *adv* notably

notarié, -e [nɔtarje] *adj Jur* **acte n.** notarized deed

notation [nɔtasjɔ̃] *nf* (a) *(d'un travail scolaire)* marking (b) *(par des symboles)* notation; *Ordinat* **n. hexadécimale** hex or hexadecimal code

note [nɔt] *nf* (a) *(annotation, communication écrite)* note; **prendre des notes** to take (down) notes; **prendre bonne n. de qch** to take due note of sth; *Typ & Ordinat* **n. de ou en bas de page** footnote; **n. de service** memo (b) *(appréciation)* Br mark, Am grade (c) *Mus* note (d) *(facture)* bill; *(dans un hôtel)* Br bill, Am check; **n. de frais** expenses; **n. de téléphone** phone bill (e) *(nuance)* touch, note

notebook [nɔtbuk] *nm Ordinat* notebook

noter [nɔte] *vt* (a) *(mettre par écrit)* to note down, to make a note of (b) *(remarquer)* to note; **note bien que**... mind you,...; *Fig* **c'est noté, je note** got it (c) *(travail scolaire, élève)* Br to mark, Am to grade

notice [nɔtis] *nf* *(mode d'emploi)* instructions; *(d'un médicament)* directions

notification [nɔtifikasjɔ̃] *nf Jur* notification

notifier [66] [nɔtifje] *vt* **n. qch à qn** to notify sb of sth

notion [nɔsjɔ̃] *nf* (a) *(concept)* notion, concept; **perdre la n. du temps/de la réalité** to lose track of time/all sense of reality (b) **notions** *(connaissances sommaires)* basics; **avoir des notions de qch** to know the basics of sth

notoire [nɔtwar] *adj* *(fait)* well-known; *(criminel, mesquinerie)* notorious

notoriété [nɔtɔrjete] *nf* *(d'une personne)* fame; **il est de n. publique que**... it's common knowledge that...

notre, nos [nɔtr, no] *adj possessif* our; **n. chien** *(il y a un chien)* our dog; *(chacun a son chien)* our dogs; **nos enfants** our children; **n. père et n. mère** our mother and father; **un de nos amis** one of our friends, a friend of ours; *Fam* **nous avons n. vendredi** we've got Friday off

nôtre [nɔtr] *pron possessif* **le n., la n., les nôtres** ours; *(en insistant)* our own; **nous le prêtons le n.** you can borrow ours; **nous n'en avons pas besoin, nous avons le n.** we don't need it, we've got our own; *Fam* **à la n.!** here's to us!

2 *nm* **il faut y mettre du n.** we have to do our share

3 *nmpl* **les nôtres** *(notre famille)* our family; **serez-vous des nôtres ce soir?** will you be joining us this evening?

nouba [nuba] *nf Fam* party; **faire la n.** to party

noué, -e [nwe] *adj* **avoir l'estomac n.** to have a knot in one's stomach; **avoir la gorge nouée** to have a lump in one's throat

nouer [nwe] 1 *vt* (a) *(ficelle, ruban, lacets)* to tie; *(cheveux)* to tie up; *(cravate)* to knot (b) *(relations)* to establish (avec with)

2 **se nouer** *vpr* (a) *(amitié)* to be formed (b) *(intrigue)* to take shape

noueux, -euse [nwø, -øz] *adj* *(bois)* knotty; *(tronc d'arbre, mains, doigts)* gnarled

nougat [nuga] *nm* nougat

nougatine [nugatin] *nf* nougatine

nouille [nuj] *nf* (a) *Culin* **nouilles** noodles; *(pâtes en général)* pasta (b) *Fam (personne) (molle)* drip; *(niaise)* dimwit

nounou [nunu] *nf (langage enfantin)* nanny

nounours [nunurs] *nm (langage enfantin)* teddy (bear)

nourri, -e [nuri] *adj (applaudissements)* prolonged; *(feu)* heavy

nourrice [nuris] *nf* (a) *(assistante maternelle)* child minder; **n. agréée** registered child minder (b) *Vieilli (qui allaite)* wet nurse

nourricier, -ère [nurisje, -ɛr] *adj Litt (terre)* nourishing

nourrir [nurir] 1 *vt* (a) *(personnes, animaux)* to feed (de with); **le lait nourrit** milk is nourishing (b) *(peau, visage, cuir)* to nourish; *(feu)* to feed (c) *Litt (entretenir) (idées de vengeance, illusion)* to harbour; *(espoir)* to cherish; *(projet)* to nurse

2 **se nourrir** *vpr (manger)* to eat; **se n. de qch** to live on sth; *Fig & Litt* to feed on sth

nourrissant, -e [nurisɑ̃, -ɑ̃t] *adj* nourishing

nourrisson [nurisɔ̃] *nm* infant

nourriture [nurityr] *nf* food

nous [nu] 1 *pron personnel* (a) *(sujet)* we; **n. deux/tous** both/all of us; **n. autres Français** we French; **n., n. n'aurions pas fait comme ça** WE wouldn't have done it like that

(b) *(objet direct)* us; **et n., tu n. oublies?** and what about us, have you forgotten us?

(c) *(objet indirect)* to us; **lisez-le-n.** read it to us; **il n. a serré la main** he shook our hands; **les enfants n. ont jeté des pierres** the children threw stones at us

(d) *(avec préposition)* us; **n. ne pensons pas qu'à n.** we're not just thinking of ourselves; **tu n. le montres, à n.?** can you show us?; **ce livre est à n.** this book is ours; **n. avons nos règles à n.** we have our own rules; *Fam* **un ami à n.** a friend of ours; **à n. deux** *(sur un ton menaçant)* I want a word with you; *Hum* I'm all yours

(e) *(dans les réfléchis)* ourselves; **n. n. sommes habillés** we got dressed

(f) *(dans les pronominaux)* **n. n. déciderons demain** we'll decide tomorrow

(g) *(réciproque)* each other

(h) *(dans les comparaisons)* us; **vous buvez plus que n.** you drink more than us *or* than we do

2 **se le n. de majesté** the royal we

nous-mêmes [numɛm] *pron personnel* ourselves

nouveau, -elle, -x, -elles [nuvo, -ɛl] 1 *adj*

┌───┐
│ **nouvel** is used before masculine singular nouns │
│ beginning with a vowel or h mute.   │
└───┘

(a) *(récent, moderne, autre)* new; *(mode)* latest; **les nouveaux pères** modern fathers; **tout est n. tout beau** it's all new and exciting; **le nouvel an** the New Year; **nouvelle cuisine** nouvelle cuisine; *Péj* **n. riche** nouveau riche (b) *(avec une fonction adverbiale)* **les nouveaux arrivants** the newcomers; **les nouveaux élus** those newly elected; **n. pays industrialisé** newly industrialized country (c) **à n., de n.** again

2 *nm* **il y a du n.** there's been a new development

3 *nm,f (personne)* new person; *(à l'école)* new pupil

Nouveau-Brunswick [nuvobrɛ̃zvik] *nm* **le N.** New Brunswick

Nouveau-Mexique [nuvomɛksik] *nm* **le N.** New Mexico

nouveau-né, -e (*mpl* **nouveau-nés,** *fpl* **nouveau-nées**) [nuvone] **1** *adj* newborn
2 *nm,f* newborn baby

nouveauté [nuvote] *nf* (**a**) (*caractère nouveau*) novelty (**b**) (*produit récent*) (*livre*) new publication; (*disque*) new release; *Fam* ce n'est pas une n.! that's nothing new!

nouvel [nuvɛl] *voir* **nouveau**

nouvelle [nuvɛl] *nf* (**a**) (*annonce d'un événement*) une n. a piece of news; je viens d'apprendre la n. I've just heard the news; *Fam* première n.! that's news to me! (**b**) (*information*) avoir des nouvelles de qn (*directement*) to have heard from sb; (*indirectement*) to have had news about sb; *Fig* vous aurez de mes nouvelles! you'll be hearing from me! demander *ou* prendre des nouvelles de qn to inquire or ask about sb; être sans nouvelles de qn to have no news from sb; aux dernières nouvelles,... the last I/we/*etc* heard,...; les nouvelles vont vite! (*good*) news travels fast!; goûtez cela, vous m'en direz des nouvelles taste this, you'll love it; pas de nouvelles, bonnes nouvelles no news is good news (**c**) *Journ* news item; les nouvelles the news (**d**) (*roman court*) short story

Nouvelle-Angleterre [nuvɛlɑ̃glətɛr] *nf* la N. New England

Nouvelle-Calédonie [nuvɛlkaledɔni] *nf* la N. New Caledonia

Nouvelle-Écosse [nuvɛlekɔs] *nf* la N. Nova Scotia

nouvellement [nuvɛlmɑ̃] *adv* newly, recently

Nouvelle-Orléans [nuvɛlɔrleɑ̃] *voir* **La Nouvelle-Orléans**

Nouvelles-Hébrides [nuvɛlzebrid] *nfpl* les N. the New Hebrides

Nouvelle-Zélande [nuvɛlzelɑ̃d] *nf* la N. New Zealand

novateur, -trice [nɔvatœr, -tris] **1** *adj* innovative
2 *nm,f* innovator

novembre [nɔvɑ̃br] *nm* November; le onze n. (*fête*) *Br* Armistice Day; *Am* Veterans Day; *voir aussi* **janvier**

novice [nɔvis] *nmf aussi Rel* novice

noyade [nwajad] *nf* drowning

noyau, -x [nwajo] *nm* (**a**) (*de fruit*) stone, *Am* pit (**b**) (*centre*) (*d'atome, de cellule*) nucleus; (*de la terre*) core (**c**) (*petit groupe*) small group; le n. dur the hard core (**d**) *Ordinat* node

noyauter [nwajote] *vt* to infiltrate

noyé, -e [nwaje] **1** *adj* (**a**) (*dans l'eau*) mourir n. to die by drowning; *Fig* être n. (*perdu*) to be out of one's depth (**b**) (*plein*) yeux noyés de larmes eyes brimming with tears (**c**) (*perdu*) le village était n. dans la brume the village was shrouded in mist; les points essentiels sont noyés dans le détail the essential points are buried in too many details
2 *nm,f* drowned person

noyer[1] [nwaje] *nm* (*arbre*) walnut (tree); (*bois*) walnut

noyer[2] [nwaje] **1** *vt* (**a**) (*personne, animal*) to drown; (*terres, champs*) to swamp; *Fig* n. une rébellion dans le sang to bloodily quash a rebellion; n. son chagrin (*dans l'alcool*) to drown one's sorrows (in drink); n. le poisson to confuse the issue deliberately (**b**) (*moteur*) to flood (**c**) (*diluer*) (*vin*) to drown
2 se noyer (**a**) (*accidentellement*) to drown; (*volontairement*) to drown oneself; *Fig* se n. dans les détails to get bogged down in details; se n. dans un verre d'eau to make a mountain out of a molehill

NPI [ɛnpei] *nm* (*abrév* **nouveau pays industrialisé**) NIC

nu, -e [ny] **1** *adj* (**a**) (*dévêtu*) (*personne*) naked; (*partie du corps*) bare; *Art* nude; être tout nu to be naked or in the nude; se baigner tout nu to go swimming in the nude; nu comme un ver stark naked; aller pieds nus to go barefoot; (**b**) *Fig* (*paysage, arbre, pièce*) bare; (*style*) plain
2 *nm Art* nude; mettre qch à nu (*surface*) to expose sth; (*fil électrique*) to strip sth

nuage [nɥaʒ] *nm* (**a**) (*dans le ciel*) cloud; sans nuages (*ciel*) cloudless; *Fig* (*vie, avenir*) uncloudied; (*bonheur*) perfect; *Fig* être dans les nuages to have one's head in the clouds; n. radioactif cloud of radioactive dust (**b**) (*de lait*) drop

nuageux, -euse [nɥaʒø, -øz] *adj* cloudy

nuance [nɥɑ̃s] *nf* (**a**) (*de couleur*) shade (**b**) (*légère trace*) touch, hint (**c**) (*subtilité*) nuance; (*légère différence*) slight difference; tout en nuances full of nuances; j'ai dit peut-être, pas oui, n.! I said perhaps, not yes, there's a slight difference!; être sans nuances (*personne*) to see everything in black and white

nuancé, -e [nɥɑ̃se] *adj* full of nuances

nuancer [16] [nɥɑ̃se] *vt* to qualify

nucléaire [nykleɛr] **1** *adj* nuclear
2 *nm* le n. nuclear power

nucléon [nykleɔ̃] *nm Phys* nucleon

nudisme [nydism] *nm* nudism

nudiste [nydist] *nmf* nudist

nudité [nydite] *nf* (*d'une personne*) nudity, nakedness; (*d'un mur, d'un paysage*) bareness; (*d'un style*) plainness

nue [ny] *nf* porter qn/qch aux nues to praise sb/sth to the skies; tomber des nues to be taken aback

nuée [nɥe] *nf* (**a**) (*d'insectes, de criquets*) cloud, swarm; (*de personnes*) horde (**b**) *Litt* (*dans le ciel*) cloud

nui *voir* **nuire**

nuire [18] [nɥir] **1** nuire à *vt ind* to harm; nuit gravement à la santé (*sur paquet de cigarettes*) tobacco seriously damages health; mettre qn hors d'état de n. (*en lieu sûr*) to put sb out of harm's way
2 se nuire *vpr* se n. (à soi-même) to do oneself harm

nuisais *etc voir* **nuire**

nuisance [nɥizɑ̃s] *nf* nuisance; nuisances acoustiques noise pollution

nuise *voir* **nuire**

nuisette [nɥizɛt] *nf* baby doll nightie

nuisible [nɥizibl] *adj* harmful (à to); animaux nuisibles vermin, pests

nuit [nɥi] *nf* night; cette n. (*ce soir*) tonight; (*passée*) last night; bonne n.! good night!; le train/bateau de n. the night train/boat; voyager de n. to travel by or at night; il commence à faire n. it's getting dark; il fait n. it's dark; il fait n. noire it's pitch-black; à la n. tombante at nightfall; *Fig* perdu dans la n. des temps lost in the mists of time; *Prov* la n. porte conseil it would be best to sleep on it; *Prov* la n., tous les chats sont gris all cats are grey in the dark; passer une n. blanche (*avoir une insomnie*) to have a sleepless night; (*volontairement*) to stay up all night; n. de noces wedding night

nuitée [nɥite] *nf* overnight stay

nul, nulle [nyl] **1** *adj* **(a)** *(inexistant) (différence, risques, écart)* nil **(b)** *(non valable) (bulletin de vote)* spoilt; *Jur* **n. et non avenu** null and void **(c)** *Fam (qui ne vaut rien) (réponse, personne)* useless; *(film, livre, chanson, blague)* rubbish; **être n. en qch** to be useless at sth; *Vulg* **c'est n. à chier!** it's a load of crap!

2 *nm, f Fam* useless idiot

3 *adj indéfini Litt* no

4 *pron indéfini Litt* no one, nobody

nullard, -e [nylar, -ard] *nm, f très Fam* useless idiot

nullement [nylmɑ̃] *adv* not at all

nulle part [nylpar] *adv* nowhere; **je ne les vois n.** I can't see them anywhere; **n. ailleurs** nowhere else

nullité [nylite] *nf (d'un contrat, d'un mariage)* nullity, invalidity

numéraire [nymerɛr] *nm* cash

numéral, -e, -aux, -ales [nymeral, -o] *adj & nm* numeral

numérateur [nymeratœr] *nm Math* numerator

numération [nymerasjɔ̃] *nf Math* numeration

numérique [nymerik] *adj* **(a)** *(valeur, supériorité)* numerical **(b)** *Ordinat (ordinateur, donnée)* digital; **balance à affichage n.** digital scales

numérisation [nymerizasjɔ̃] *nf Ordinat* digitization

numériser [nymerize] *vt Ordinat* to digitize

numériseur [nymerizœr] *nm Ordinat* digitizer; **n. d'image** image digitizer

numéro [nymero] *nm* **(a)** *(chiffre)* number; *Fig* **tirer le bon n.** to strike (it) lucky; **n. azur** = special telephone number for which users are charged at local rate irrespective of distance; **n. de compte** account number; **n. de fax** fax number; **n. d'immatriculation** *Br* registration number, *Am* license number; **n. de téléphone** telephone number; **n. vert** *Br* Freefone® number, *Am* toll-free number; **n. de vol** flight number **(b)** *(de périodique)* issue, number; **la suite au prochain n.** (to be) continued in the next issue; *Fig* watch this space; **n. spécial** special issue **(c)** *(spectacle)* act, number; *Fam Fig* **faire son petit n.** to do one's little act **(d)** *Fam (personne)* character

numérotation [nymerɔtasjɔ̃] *nf* numbering

numéroter [nymerɔte] *vt* to number

numismate [nymismat] *nmf* numismatist

numismatique [nymismatik] **1** *adj* numismatic

2 *nf* numismatics *(singulier)*

nunuche [nynyʃ] *adj Fam* twee

nu-pieds [nypje] **1** *nm inv* sandal

2 *adv* barefoot

nuptial, -e, -aux, -ales [nypsjal, -o] *adj (anneau, marche)* wedding; *(chambre, cortège)* bridal

nuque [nyk] *nf* nape, back of the neck

nurse [nœrs] *nf Vieilli* nanny

nu-tête [nytɛt] *adv* bareheaded

nutritif, -ive [nytritif, -iv] *adj* nutritious

nutrition [nytrisjɔ̃] *nf* nutrition

nutritionniste [nytrisjɔnist] *nmf* nutritionist

Nylon® [nilɔ̃] *nm* nylon

nymphe [nɛ̃f] *nf (déesse)* nymph

nymphette [nɛ̃fɛt] *nf* nymphet

nymphomane [nɛ̃fɔman] *adj & nf* nymphomaniac

nymphomanie [nɛ̃fɔmani] *nf* nymphomania

O

O, o [o] *nm inv* O, o

O (*abrév* **ouest**) W

ô [o] *exclam Litt* O!

OAS [oaes] *nf* (*abrév* **Organisation de l'armée secrète**) OAS (*terrorist group opposed to Algerian independence*)

oasis [oazis] *nf* oasis; *Fig* haven

obédience [obedjɑ̃s] *nf* **d'o. communiste/musulmane** of the Communist/Muslim persuasion

obéir [obeir] *vi* (**a**) (*personne*) to obey; **o. à qn/qch** to obey sb/sth; **o. à une impulsion** to act on an impulse; **o. à qn au doigt et à l'œil** to be at sb's beck and call; **se faire o.** to command obedience (**b**) (*freins, mécanisme*) to respond (**à** to)

obéissance [obeisɑ̃s] *nf* obedience (**à** to); **jurer o. à qn** to swear allegiance to sb

obéissant, -e [obeisɑ̃, -ɑ̃t] *adj* obedient

obélisque [obelisk] *nm* obelisk

obèse [obez] **1** *adj* obese
2 *nmf* obese person

obésité [obezite] *nf* obesity

objecter [obʒɛkte] *vt* (**a**) (*rétorquer*) **n'avoir rien à o.** à qch to have no objection to sth; **o. que...** to object that... (**b**) (*invoquer*) **on lui objecta sa jeunesse** his youth was held against him

objecteur [obʒɛktœr] *nm* **o. de conscience** conscientious objector

objectif, -ive [obʒɛktif, -iv] **1** *adj* objective
2 *nm* (**a**) (*but, cible*) objective (**b**) (*d'un appareil photo*) lens; (*d'un microscope*) objective; *Fig* **devant l'o.** in front of the camera

objection [obʒɛksjɔ̃] *nf aussi Jur* objection

objectivement [obʒɛktivmɑ̃] *adv* objectively

objectivité [obʒɛktivite] *nf* objectivity; **en toute o.** quite objectively

objet [obʒɛ] *nm* (**a**) (*chose*) object; (**bureau des**) **objets trouvés** *Br* lost-property office, *Am* lost and found; **femme-o.** sex object; **o. d'art** objet d'art; **objets de valeur** valuables; **o. volant non identifié** unidentified flying object
(**b**) *Gram* object; **o. direct/indirect** direct/indirect object
(**c**) (*sujet*) (*d'une dispute, d'une conversation*) subject; **être ou faire l'o. de qch** to be the object of sth; *Hum* **l'o. de ses désirs** the object of her desires
(**d**) (*but*) object, aim; **ma visite a pour o. de...** the object of my visit is to...; **sans o.** (*remarque, réclamation*) unjustified
(**e**) *Ordinat* object

obligataire [obligater] *Fin* **1** *nmf* bondholder, debenture holder
2 *adj* (*emprunt, marché*) debenture

obligation [obligasjɔ̃] *nf* (**a**) (*contrainte*) obligation; **tu viens si tu veux, mais ce n'est pas une o.** you can come if you want, but you're not obliged to; **avoir l'o. de faire qch** to be under an obligation to do sth; **être ou se voir dans l'o. de faire qch** to be obliged to do sth; **sans o. d'achat** no purchase necessary; **être dégagé des obligations militaires** to have done one's military service (**b**) *Fin* bond, debenture; **o. au porteur** bearer bond

obligatoire [obligatwar] *adj* obligatory, compulsory; *Fam* (*inévitable*) inevitable

obligatoirement [obligatwarmɑ̃] *adv* **vous devez o. montrer votre passeport** you are required to show your passport; **pas o.** not necessarily

obligé, -e [obliʒe] *adj* (**a**) *Fam* (*inévitable*) inevitable (**b**) *Formel* (*reconnaissant*) **être o. à qn de qch** to be obliged to sb for sth

obligeance [obliʒɑ̃s] *nf Formel* **avoir l'o. de faire qch** to be so kind as to do sth

obligeant, -e [obliʒɑ̃, -ɑ̃t] *adj* obliging, kind

obliger [45] [obliʒe] **1** *vt* (**a**) (*contraindre*) **o. qn à faire qch** to force sb to do sth; **son état de santé l'oblige au repos** the state of his health means he has to rest; **être obligé de faire qch** to be obliged to do sth; **ne te crois pas obligé de tout manger** don't feel you have to eat everything; **tu y es allé? – bien obligé!** did you go? – I had to! (**b**) *Formel* (*rendre service à*) **vous m'obligeriez en fermant la porte** I'd be obliged if you would close the door
2 s'obliger *vpr* **s'o. à faire qch** to force oneself to do sth

oblique [oblik] **1** *adj* (*ligne*) oblique; (*regard*) sidelong
2 *nf* oblique (line)

obliquement [oblikmɑ̃] *adv* obliquely

obliquer [oblike] *vi* **o. à gauche/à droite** to bear left/right

oblitérer [34] [oblitere] *vt* (**a**) (*timbre*) to cancel (**b**) *Litt* (*souvenirs, passé*) to obliterate

oblong, -ongue [oblɔ̃, -ɔ̃g] *adj* oblong

obnubiler [obnybile] *vt* to obsess

obole [obol] *nf* small contribution; **apporter ou verser son o. à qch** to make a small contribution to sth

obscène [opsɛn] *adj* obscene

obscénité [opsenite] *nf* obscenity

obscur, -e [opskyr] *adj* (**a**) (*sombre*) dark (**b**) (*difficile à comprendre*) obscure (**c**) (*pressentiment, impression*) vague (**d**) (*écrivain, peintre*) obscure

obscurantisme [opskyrɑ̃tism] *nm* obscurantism

obscurcir [ɔpskyrsir] **1** vt (a) (assombrir) to darken (b) (rendre confus) (faits, sens) to obscure; (jugement) to cloud
2 s'obscurcir vpr (pièce, ciel) to darken, to grow dark; (esprit, vue) to grow dim

obscurément [ɔpskyremã] adv vaguely

obscurité [ɔpskyrite] nf (a) (noirceur) darkness; **dans l'o.** in the dark (b) (anonymat) obscurity

obsédant, -e [ɔpsedã, -ãt] adj (souvenir, musique) haunting; (pensée) obsessive

obsédé, -e [ɔpsede] nm,f fanatic; **o. (sexuel)** sex maniac; **un o. du cinéma/du rangement** a film/tidiness fanatic

obséder [34] [ɔpsede] vt to obsess; **être obsédé par qch** to be obsessed by or with sth

obsèques [ɔpsek] nfpl funeral; **o. nationales** state funeral

obséquieux, -euse [ɔpsekjø, -øz] adj obsequious

observateur, -trice [ɔpservatœr, -tris] **1** adj observant
2 nm,f observer

observation [ɔpservasjɔ̃] nf (a) (étude, surveillance) observation; **être en o.** (à l'hôpital) to be under observation; **avoir l'esprit d'o.** to be very observant (b) (remarque) observation; (critique) remark (c) (respect) observance

observatoire [ɔpservatwar] nm (astronomique, météorologique) observatory; Mil observation post

observer [ɔpserve] **1** vt (a) (regarder) to watch, to observe; **se sentir observé** to feel one is being watched (b) (remarquer) to notice; **faire o. qch à qn** to point sth out to sb; **faire o. à qn que...** to point out to sb that... (c) (étudier) to observe (d) (respecter) to observe; **o. une minute de silence** to observe a minute's silence
2 s'observer vpr (a) (l'un l'autre) to watch or observe each other (b) (phénomène, attitude) to be seen

obsession [ɔpsesjɔ̃] nf obsession; **mais c'est une o. ou de l'o.!** you're/he's/etc obsessed!

obsessionnel, -elle [ɔpsesjɔnel] adj Psy obsessional

obsidienne [ɔpsidjen] nf obsidian

obsolète [ɔpsɔlet] adj obsolete

obstacle [ɔpstakl] nm aussi Fig obstacle; (aux courses) fence, jump; **faire o. à qch** to stand in the way of sth

obstétricien, -enne [ɔpstetrisjẽ, -en] nm,f obstetrician

obstétrique [ɔpstetrik] nf obstetrics (singulier)

obstination [ɔpstinasjɔ̃] nf obstinacy, stubbornness

obstiné, -e [ɔpstine] adj (personne, caractère) obstinate, stubborn; (résistance, efforts) dogged; (refus) stubborn

obstinément [ɔpstinemã] adv (travailler, avancer) doggedly; (refuser) stubbornly

obstiner [ɔpstine] **s'obstiner** vpr to persist; **s'o. à faire qch** (continuer) to persist in doing sth; (vouloir) to be set on doing sth; **s'o. dans ses convictions** to cling stubbornly to one's convictions

obstruction [ɔpstryksjɔ̃] nf obstruction; **faire de l'o.** Pol to be obstructive; Sp to obstruct

obstructionnisme [ɔpstryksjɔnism] nm Pol obstructionism

obstruer [ɔpstrye] vt to obstruct

obtempérer [34] [ɔptãpere] **obtempérer à** vt ind to comply with; Jur **refus d'o.** obstruction

obtenir [70] [ɔptanir] vt to get, to obtain; **o. qch de qn** to get sth from sb; **faire o. qch à qn** to get sth for sb; **o. de faire qch** to get permission to do sth; **j'ai obtenu qu'elle revienne** I got her to come back

obtention [ɔptãsjɔ̃] nf obtaining; **depuis l'o. de son diplôme** since obtaining her diploma

obtenu, -e voir obtenir

obtiendrai etc voir obtenir

obtienne voir obtenir

obturateur [ɔptyratœr] nm Phot shutter

obtus, -e [ɔpty, -yz] adj (angle, personne) obtuse

obus [ɔby] nm shell

OC nfpl (abrév ondes courtes) SW

oc [ɔk] voir langue

ocarina [ɔkarina] nm ocarina

occase [ɔkaz] nf Fam (a) (affaire) bargain (b) (article de seconde main) second-hand item; **d'o.** second-hand

occasion [ɔkazjɔ̃] nf (a) (circonstance favorable) opportunity, chance; **avoir l'o. de faire qch** to have the opportunity or chance to do sth; **Hum tu as encore perdu l'o. de te taire** why can't you keep your big mouth shut?; **c'est l'o. ou jamais** it's now or never; **c'est l'o. ou jamais d'essayer** now's the time to try; **venez boire un coup à l'o.** come for a drink when you get the chance; **à la première o.** at the first opportunity; Prov **l'o. fait larron** opportunity makes the thief (b) (moment) occasion; **à plusieurs occasions** on several occasions; **à l'o. de** (pour fêter) on the occasion of; **à l'o. d'une visite de routine** during a routine visit; **dans/pour les grandes occasions** on/for special occasions; **être l'o. de qch** to be the occasion of sth (c) (affaire) bargain (d) (article de seconde main) second-hand item; **le marché de l'o.** the second-hand market; **d'o.** second-hand

occasionnel, -elle [ɔkazjɔnel] adj occasional; (rencontre) chance; (aide) casual

occasionnellement [ɔkazjɔnelmã] adv occasionally

occasionner [ɔkazjɔne] vt to cause

occident [ɔksidã] nm west; Pol **l'O.** the West

occidental, -e, -aux, -ales [ɔksidãtal, -o] **1** adj western; **l'Europe occidentale** Western Europe
2 nm,f **O.** Westerner

occidentaliser [ɔksidãtalize] **1** vt to westernize
2 s'occidentaliser vpr to become westernized

occiput [ɔksipyt] nm back of the head

occire [ɔksir] vt to slay

occitan, -e [ɔksitã, -an] **1** adj of the langue d'oc
2 nm (langue) = language spoken in some parts of southern France

occlusion [ɔklyzjɔ̃] nf occlusion; **o. intestinale** intestinal obstruction

occulte [ɔkylt] adj (surnaturel) occult; (secret) secret; (cause) hidden; (rôle) clandestine

occulter [ɔkylte] vt Astron to occult; (signal lumineux) to block out; Fig (informations, intentions) to conceal

occupant, -e [ɔkypã, -ãt] **1** adj (armée) occupying
2 nm,f (d'une maison) occupier, occupant; Mil **l'o.** the occupying forces

occupation [ɔkypasjɔ̃] nf (a) (d'un lieu) & Mil occupation; Hist **l'O.** the Occupation; **grève avec o. des locaux** sit-down strike (b) (activité) occupation; **vaquer à ses occupations** to go about one's business

occupé, -e [ɔkype] *adj (personne)* busy; *(place)* taken; *(ligne téléphonique)* Br engaged, Am busy; *(toilettes)* engaged; **en territoire o.** in occupied territory

occuper [ɔkype] **1** *vt* (a) *(maison, lieu)* to occupy; *(place)* to take up, to occupy; **le magasin occupe le rez-de-chaussée** the shop takes up *or* occupies the ground floor (b) *(par la force)* to occupy (c) *(temps)* to fill, to occupy (d) *(poste, fonction)* to have, to hold (e) **o. qn** *(employer)* to employ sb; *(donner une activité à)* to keep sb busy, to occupy sb
2 s'occuper *vpr* (a) *(avoir une activité)* to keep oneself busy *or* occupied, to occupy oneself; **s'o. en lisant** to spend one's time reading; **on a toujours de quoi s'o.** there's always something to keep you busy (b) **s'o. de** *(s'intéresser à)* to be interested in; *(se charger de)* to take care of; **s'o. de faire qch** to see about doing sth; **je m'en occuperai** I'll see to it; *Fam* **occupe-toi de ce qui te regarde** *ou* **de tes affaires** *ou* **de tes oignons!** mind your own business!; *Fam* **t'occupe (pas)!** keep your nose out!; *Ironique* **je vais m'o. de lui** I'll take care of him; **est-ce qu'on s'occupe de vous?** *(dans un magasin)* are you being attended to?

occurrence [ɔkyrɑ̃s] *nf* (a) *(circonstance)* **en l'o.** in this case (b) *Ling* occurrence

OCDE [osede] *nf (abrév* **Organisation de coopération et de développement économiques)** OECD

océan [ɔseɑ̃] *nm* ocean; **l'O.** *(l'Atlantique)* the Atlantic; **l'O. Atlantique/Pacifique/Indien** the Atlantic/Pacific/Indian Ocean; **l'O. (Glacial) Arctique** the Arctic Ocean; *Fig* **un o. de fleurs/couleurs** a sea of flowers/colour

Océanie [ɔseani] *nf* **l'O.** Oceania

océanique [ɔseanik] *adj* oceanic

océanographie [ɔseanɔgrafi] *nf* oceanography

ocelot [ɔslo] *nm* ocelot

ocre [ɔkr] *nm & adj inv* ochre

octane [ɔktan] *nm* octane

octante [ɔktɑ̃t] *adj & nm inv Belg & Suisse* eighty; *voir aussi* **trois**

octave [ɔktav] *nf* octave

octet [ɔktɛ] *nm Ordinat* byte; **milliard d'octets** gigabyte

octobre [ɔktɔbr] *nm* October; *voir aussi* **janvier**

octogénaire [ɔktɔʒenɛr] *adj & nmf* octogenarian

octogonal, -e, -aux, -ales [ɔktɔgɔnal, -o] *adj* octagonal

octogone [ɔktɔgɔn] *nm* octagon

octroyer [32] [ɔktrwaje] **1** *vt* **o. qch à qn** to grant sb sth
2 s'octroyer *vpr* **s'o. qch** to grant oneself sth

oculaire [ɔkylɛr] **1** *adj* **hygiène o.** eye care; **témoin o.** eyewitness
2 *nm* eyepiece

oculiste [ɔkylist] *nmf* eye specialist

ode [ɔd] *nf* ode

odeur [ɔdœr] *nf* smell; **une o. de brûlé** a smell of burning; **sans o.** odourless; **bonne/mauvaise o.** pleasant/unpleasant smell; *Fig* **ne pas être en o. de sainteté auprès de qn** to be in sb's bad books; *Prov* **l'argent n'a pas d'o.** money has no smell

odieux, -euse [ɔdjø, -øz] *adj* odious

odorant, -e [ɔdɔrɑ̃, -ɑ̃t] *adj (agréable)* sweet-smelling, fragrant; *(désagréable)* strong-smelling

odorat [ɔdɔra] *nm* (sense of) smell

odyssée [ɔdise] *nf* odyssey; **l'O.** the Odyssey

œcuménique [ekymenik, økymenik] *adj* ecumenical

œdème [edɛm, ødɛm] *nm* oedema; **avoir un o. aux poumons** to have pulmonary oedema

œil [œj] *(pl* **yeux** [jø]*) nm* (a) *(organe)* eye; **avoir les yeux bleus** to have blue eyes; **o. de verre** glass eye; **un o. au beurre noir, un o. poché** a black eye; **j'ai le soleil dans les yeux** *ou* **dans l'o.** the sun's in my eyes; **visible à l'o. nu** visible to the naked eye; **voir qch de ses (propres) yeux** to see sth with one's own eyes; **je n'ai pas fermé l'o. de la nuit** I didn't sleep a wink all night; **faire qch les yeux fermés** to do sth with one's eyes closed; **ouvrir de grands yeux** to look surprised; **faire les gros yeux (à qn)** to glare (at sb); *Fam* **avoir de petits yeux** to look tired; **ouvrir des yeux ronds** to gape in amazement; *Fam* **entre quat'z'yeux** in private; **les yeux dans les yeux** gazing into each other's eyes; **o. pour o., dent pour dent** an eye for an eye, a tooth for a tooth; **je ne le fais pas pour ses beaux yeux** I'm not doing it just to please him; **tu as les yeux plus gros** *ou* **grands que le ventre** your eyes are bigger than your belly; **n'avoir plus que les** *ou* **ses yeux pour pleurer** to have nothing left but the clothes on one's back; *Fam* **mon o.!** my foot!; *Fam* **à l'o.** free; **faire les yeux doux à qn** to make eyes at sb; *Fam* **faire de l'o. à qn** to give sb the eye; **le mauvais o.** the evil eye; **sous mes/leurs yeux** right before my/their eyes; **avoir qch sous les yeux** to have sth right in front of one
(b) *(vue)* **yeux** (eye)sight, eyes; **avoir de bons/mauvais yeux** to have good/bad (eye)sight; **avoir des yeux de lynx** to be eagle-eyed
(c) *(attention)* **avoir l'o. sur qch** to keep an eye on sth; **avoir qn à l'o.** to keep an eye on sb; **avoir l'o. à tout** to keep an eye on everything; *Fam* **ouvrir l'o. (et le bon)** to keep one's eyes open or peeled; **ne pas avoir les yeux dans sa poche** to have sharp eyes; **fermer les yeux sur qch** to turn a blind eye to sth; **coup d'o.** glance; **au** *ou* **du premier coup d'o.** at a glance; **jeter un coup d'o. sur qch** to have a glance at sth; **avoir le coup d'o.** to have a good eye; **ça vaut** *ou* **ça mérite le coup d'o.** it's worth a look
(d) *(point de vue)* **voir qch d'un autre o.** to look at sth differently; **voir qch d'un bon/mauvais o.** to look favourably/unfavourably on sth; **aux yeux de la loi** in the eyes of the law; **à mes yeux** in my eyes
(e) *(dans la soupe)* speck of fat
(f) *(d'un cyclone)* eye

œil-de-bœuf *(pl* **œils-de-bœuf)** [œjdəbœf] *nm* bull's-eye (window)

œillade [œjad] *nf* wink; **lancer une o. à qn** to wink at sb

œillère [œjɛr] *nf Br* blinker, *Am* blinder; *Fig* **avoir des œillères** to wear *Br* blinkers or *Am* blinders

œillet [œjɛ] *nm* (a) *(fleur)* carnation (b) *(trou) (de vêtement, de chaussure)* eyelet (c) *(en papeterie)* reinforcement ring

œnologie [enɔlɔʒi, ønɔlɔʒi] *nf* oenology

œnologue [enɔlɔg, ønɔlɔg] *nmf* oenologist

œsophage [ezɔfaʒ, øzɔfaʒ] *nm* oesophagus

œstrogène [estrɔʒɛn, østrɔʒɛn] *adj & nm* oestrogen

œuf [œf, *pl* ø] *nm* egg; **œufs** *(de poisson)* spawn, hard roe; *Fig* **mettre tous ses œufs dans le même panier** to put all one's eggs in one basket; *Fam Fig* **marcher sur des œufs** *(avancer)* to walk carefully; *(être prudent)* to be walking on eggs; *Fam* **va te faire cuire un o.!** take a running jump!; **étouffer** *ou* **tuer qch dans l'o.** to nip sth in the bud; **œufs brouillés** scrambled eggs; **o. en chocolat** chocolate egg; **o. à la coque** boiled egg; **o. dur** hard-boiled egg; **o. mollet** soft-boiled egg; **œufs à la neige** floating islands *(beaten egg whites served on custard)*; **œufs en neige** beaten egg whites; **o. de Pâques** Easter egg; **o. au plat** *ou* **sur le plat** fried egg; **o. poché** poached egg; **o. à repriser** darning egg

œuvre [œvr] **1** *nf* **(a)** *(travail)* work; **être à l'o.** to be at work; **se mettre à l'o.** to get down to work; **mettre qch en o.** *(traité, loi, système)* to implement sth; **mettre tout en o.** to do everything possible; **les bonnes œuvres** charitable work **(b)** *(création)* work; *(ensemble de créations)* works; **o. d'art** work of art; **œuvres complètes/choisies** complete/selected works

2 *nm Constr* **gros o.** fabric; **à pied d'o.** on site; *Fig* ready to start work

œuvrer [œvre] *vi* to work *(pour* for)

offensant, -e [ɔfɑ̃sɑ̃, -ɑ̃t] *adj* offensive

offense [ɔfɑ̃s] *nf* **(a)** *(affront)* insult **(b)** *Rel* transgression

offenser [ɔfɑ̃se] **1** *vt* **(a)** *(insulter)* to offend; **sans vouloir vous o....** with all due respect... **(b)** *Litt (bon goût, délicatesse)* to offend against

2 s'offenser *vpr* to take offence *(de* at)

offensif, -ive [ɔfɑ̃sif, -iv] *adj* offensive

offensive [ɔfɑ̃siv] *nf* offensive; **passer à l'o.** to go on the offensive

offert, -e *voir* **offrir**

office [ɔfis] *nm* **(a)** *(charge)* office; **faire o. de secrétaire/témoin** to act as secretary/witness; **d'o.** without having any say in the matter; **être commis d'o.** to be appointed by the court **(b)** *(assistance)* **recourir aux bons offices de qn** to turn to sb for assistance **(c)** *Rel* service **(d)** *(pièce)* pantry **(e)** **o. du tourisme** tourist information centre

officialiser [ɔfisjalize] *vt* to make official

officiel, -elle [ɔfisjɛl] *adj & nm* official

officiellement [ɔfisjɛlmɑ̃] *adv* officially

officier¹ [ɔfisje] *nm* officer; **o. de réserve** reserve officer

officier² [66] *vi* to officiate

officieusement [ɔfisjøzmɑ̃] *adv* unofficially; *(en confidence)* off-the-record

officieux, -euse [ɔfisjø, -øz] *adj* unofficial; *(confidentiel)* off-the-record

off-line [ɔflajn] *adj Ordinat* off-line

offrande [ɔfrɑ̃d] *nf* offering; **en o.** as an offering

offrant [ɔfrɑ̃] *nm* **vendre au plus o.** to sell to the highest bidder

offre [ɔfr] *nf* offer; *(dans un appel d'offres)* tender; *(dans une vente aux enchères)* bid; **o. d'emploi** job offer; **o. spéciale** special offer; **o. publique d'achat** takeover bid; **faire** *ou* **lancer une o. publique d'achat (sur)** to make a takeover bid (for); **l'o. et la demande** supply and demand

offrir [52] [ɔfrir] **1** *vt* **(a)** *(cadeau)* to give *(à* to); **c'est pour o.** it's a gift; **je t'offre un verre** I'll buy you a drink; **o. la main de sa fille à qn** to offer sb one's daughter's hand in marriage to sb **(b)** *(proposer)* to offer; **o. de faire qch** to offer to do sth; **combien t'en a-t-elle offert?** how much did she offer you for it? **(c)** *(présenter)* *(avantage, garantie)* to offer; **o. une résistance acharnée** to put up stiff resistance

2 s'offrir *vpr* **(a)** *(se proposer)* **s'o. pour faire qch** to offer to do sth; **s'o. aux regards** *(spectacle, vue)* to meet our/your/*etc* eyes **(b)** *(se présenter)* *(occasion, possibilité)* to present itself **(c)** *(s'acheter)* **s'o. un bon cigare/une semaine de vacances** to treat oneself to a good cigar/a week's holiday; **je ne peux pas m'o. de vacances** I can't afford a holiday

offset [ɔfsɛt] *nm inv* offset

offusquer [ɔfyske] **1** *vt* to offend

2 s'offusquer *vpr* to take offence *(de* at)

ogive [ɔʒiv] *nf* **(a)** *Archit* (diagonal) rib **(b)** *Mil (d'un obus)* head; *(d'une roquette)* nose cone; **o. nucléaire** nuclear warhead

ogre [ɔgr] *nm* ogre

ogresse [ɔgrɛs] *nf* ogress

oh [o] *exclam* oh!; **oh! hisse!** heave-ho!

ohé [ɔe] *exclam* hey!

ohm [om] *nm* ohm

oie [wa] *nf* goose; **o. sauvage** wild goose; *Fig* **une o. blanche** an innocent young thing

oignon [ɔɲɔ̃] *nm* **(a)** *(légume)* onion; **petits oignons** *(pour les salades)* spring onions; *Fam* **aux petits oignons** first-rate; *Fam* **mêle-toi de tes oignons** mind your own business; *Fam* **ce ne sont pas tes oignons** it's none of your business **(b)** *Bot* bulb **(c)** *Méd* bunion

oindre [43] [wɛ̃dr] *vt* **(a)** *(enduire)* to oil **(b)** *Rel* to anoint

oiseau, -x [wazo] *nm* bird; *Fam* **l'o. c'est un drôle d'o.** he's an odd character; **o. de malheur, o. de mauvais augure** bird of ill omen; **o. marin** sea bird; **o. nocturne** nocturnal bird; *Fig* **o. de nuit** night owl; **o. de proie** bird of prey; **l'o. rare** the ideal person

oiseau-lyre *(pl* **oiseaux-lyres)** [wazolir] *nm* lyrebird

oiseau-mouche *(pl* **oiseaux-mouches)** [wazomuʃ] *nm* hummingbird

oiseleur [wazlœr] *nm* bird catcher

oiseux, -euse [wazø, -øz] *adj (conversation)* idle; *(débat)* pointless; *(explication)* unsatisfactory

oisif, -ive [wazif, -iv] *adj* idle

2 *nm,f* person of leisure

oisillon [wazijɔ̃] *nm* fledgling

oisiveté [wazivte] *nf* idleness; *Prov* **l'o. est (la) mère de tous les vices** the Devil finds work for idle hands to do

OIT [ɔite] *nf (abrév* **Organisation internationale du travail)** ILO

okapi [ɔkapi] *nm* okapi

oléagineux, -euse [ɔleaʒinø, -øz] **1** *adj* oil-yielding

2 *nmpl* oil-yielding plants

oléoduc [ɔleɔdyk] *nm* pipeline

olé olé [ɔleɔle] *adj inv Fam (propos, spectacle)* risqué; *(gens)* wild

olfactif, -ive [ɔlfaktif, -iv] *adj* olfactory

olibrius [ɔlibrijys] *nm Fam* oddball

oligarchie [ɔligarʃi] *nf* oligarchy

oligarchique [ɔligarʃik] *adj* oligarchic

oligoélément [oligoelemɑ̃] *nm* trace element

olivâtre [olivatr] *adj* olive-greenish; *(teint)* sallow

olive [oliv] **1** *nf* olive
2 *adj inv* olive (green)

oliveraie [olivrɛ] *nf* olive grove

olivier [olivje] *nm (arbre)* olive tree; *(bois)* olive (wood)

OLP [oɛlpe] *nf (abrév* **Organisation de libération de la Palestine)** PLO

olympiade [olɛ̃pjad] *nf* Olympiad

olympique [olɛ̃pik] *adj* Olympic

ombilical, -e, -aux, -ales [ɔ̃bilikal, -o] *adj* umbilical

omble [ɔ̃bl] *nm* o.(-chevalier) char

ombrage [ɔ̃braʒ] *nm* shade; **prendre o. de qch** to take umbrage at sth; **porter o. à qn** to give offence to sb

ombragé, -e [ɔ̃braʒe] *adj* shady

ombrageux, -euse [ɔ̃braʒø, -øz] *adj (personne)* touchy

ombre¹ [ɔ̃br] *nf* (a) *(forme)* shadow; **ombres chinoises** shadow play; *Fig* **jeter une o. sur qch** to cast a shadow over sth (b) *(zone sombre)* shade; **40 degrés à l'o.** 40 degrees in the shade; **faire de l'o. à qn** to be in sb's light; *Fig* **il y a une o. au tableau** there's a fly in the ointment (c) *(obscurité)* darkness; *Fig (anonymat)* obscurity; *Fig* **rester dans/sortir de l'o.** to remain in/emerge from obscurity; *Fig* **laisser qch dans l'o.** to keep sth dark; *Fig* **travailler dans l'o.** to work behind the scenes; *Fam* **mettre qn à l'o.** to put sb inside (d) *Litt (fantôme)* shade; *Fig* **n'être plus que l'o. de soi-même** to be a mere shadow of one's former self (e) *(trace)* hint; **vous n'avez pas l'o. d'une chance** you haven't the ghost of a chance; **il n'y a pas l'o. d'un doute** there isn't the shadow of a doubt; **pas l'o. d'un** not a single one (f) **o. à paupières** eye shadow

ombre² *nm (poisson)* char; **o. de rivière** grayling

ombré [ɔ̃bre] *nm Ordinat* shading

ombrelle [ɔ̃brɛl] *nf* sunshade, parasol

omelette [omlɛt] *nf* omelette; *Fig* **on ne fait pas d'o. sans casser des œufs** you can't make an omelette without breaking eggs; **o. norvégienne** baked Alaska

omettre [47] [omɛtr] *vt* to omit; **o. de faire qch** to omit to do sth

omis, -e *voir* **omettre**

omission [omisjɔ̃] *nf (d'un mot, d'un détail)* omission; *(oubli)* oversight

omnibus [omnibys] *nm* slow train

omnipotence [omnipotɑ̃s] *nf* omnipotence

omnipotent, -e [omnipotɑ̃, -ɑ̃t] *adj* omnipotent

omniprésence [omniprezɑ̃s] *nf* omnipresence

omniprésent, -e [omniprezɑ̃, -ɑ̃t] *adj* omnipresent

omniscience [omnisjɑ̃s] *nf* omniscience

omniscient, -e [omnisjɑ̃, -ɑ̃t] *adj* omniscient

omnisports [omnispɔr] *adj inv* **stade/centre o.** sports stadium/centre

omnivore [omnivɔr] **1** *adj* omnivorous
2 *nm* omnivore

omoplate [omoplat] *nf* shoulder blade, *Spéc* scapula

OMS [oɛmɛs] *nf (abrév* **Organisation mondiale de la santé)** WHO

on [ɔ̃] *pron indéfini* (a) *(indéterminé)* you, people; *(quelqu'un)* somebody, someone; **on ne sait jamais** you never know; **on nous prend parfois pour deux sœurs** people sometimes take us for sisters; **on dit qu'il est malade**, on le dit malade they say he's ill; **on sonne** there's somebody at the door; **dans tous les pays où l'on parle français** in every country where French is spoken; **on m'a volé mon sac** my bag's been stolen, someone's stolen my bag (b) *Fam (nous)* we; **on ne s'est plus jamais quittés** we've been together ever since

once [ɔ̃s] *nf aussi Fig* ounce

oncle [ɔ̃kl] *nm* uncle; **o. d'Amérique** rich uncle

onctueux, -euse [ɔ̃ktɥø, -øz] *adj aussi Fig & Péj* smooth

onctuosité [ɔ̃ktɥozite] *nf* smoothness

onde [ɔ̃d] *nf* (a) *Phys* wave; *Rad* **grandes ondes** long wave; *Rad* **ondes courtes/moyennes** short/medium wave; **o. de choc** shock wave; **sur les ondes** on the radio; **passer sur les ondes** to be on the radio; **o. sonore** sound wave (b) *Litt (eau)* waters

ondée [ɔ̃de] *nf* sudden downpour

on-dit [ɔ̃di] *nm inv* rumour, hearsay; **ce ne sont que des o.** it's only hearsay

ondoyant, -e [ɔ̃dwajɑ̃, -ɑ̃t] *adj Litt* undulating

ondoyer [32] [ɔ̃dwaje] *vi (blés)* to sway; *(drapeau)* to wave; *(surface de l'eau)* to ripple; *(flamme)* to flicker

ondulant, -e [ɔ̃dylɑ̃, -ɑ̃t] *adj (plaine)* rolling, undulating; *(vagues)* rippling; *(chevelure)* wavy; *(démarche)* swaying

ondulation [ɔ̃dylasjɔ̃] *nf (des vagues)* ripple; **les ondulations de la plaine** the rolling or undulating plain; **les ondulations de sa chevelure** her wavy hair

ondulé, -e [ɔ̃dyle] *adj (sol)* undulating; *(cheveux)* wavy; *(tôle, carton)* corrugated

onduler [ɔ̃dyle] *vi* to undulate; *(cheveux)* to be wavy

onduleur [ɔ̃dylœr] *nm Ordinat* uninterruptible power supply, UPS

onéreux, -euse [onerø, -øz] *adj* costly

ONF [oɛnɛf] *nm (abrév* **Office national des forêts)** *Br* ≃ Forestry Commission, *Am* ≃ National Forestry Service

ONG [oɛnʒe] *nf (abrév* **organisation non gouvernementale)** NGO

ongle [ɔ̃gl] *nm (finger)*nail; *(des orteils)* (toe)nail; *(d'un animal)* claw; *(d'un oiseau de proie)* talon; **se faire les ongles** to do one's nails; **o. incarné** ingrowing nail; *Fig* **jusqu'au bout des ongles** to one's fingertips

onglée [ɔ̃gle] *nf* **j'ai l'o.** my fingers are numb with cold

onglet [ɔ̃glɛ] *nm* (a) *(d'un répertoire)* tab; *(d'un canif)* thumbnail groove; **dictionnaire à onglets** thumb-indexed dictionary (b) *Culin* flank of beef

onguent [ɔ̃gɑ̃] *nm Litt* ointment

onirique [onirik] *adj* dreamlike

onomatopée [onomatope] *nf* onomatopoeia

ont *voir* **avoir**

Ontario [ɔ̃tarjo] *n voir* **lac**

ONU [ony, oɛny] *nf (abrév* **Organisation des Nations unies)** UN

onyx [oniks] *nm* onyx

onze [ɔ̃z] *adj & nm inv* eleven; *voir aussi* **trois**

onzième [ɔ̃zjɛm] *nmf, nm & adj* eleventh; *voir aussi* **cinquième**

OPA [ɔpea] *nf* (*abrév* **offre publique d'achat**) takeover bid; **lancer une O. (sur)** to make a takeover bid (for)

opacité [ɔpasite] *nf* opacity

opale [ɔpal] *nf* opal

opaque [ɔpak] *adj* (*voir aussi Fig*) opaque

OPEP [ɔpep] *nf* (*abrév* **Organisation des pays exportateurs de pétrole**) OPEC

opéra [ɔpera] *nm* (a) (*genre, œuvre*) opera (b) (*lieu*) opera house; **aller à l'o.** to go to the opera; **l'O. (de Paris)** the Paris Opera House; **o. bouffe** comic opera

opérable [ɔperabl] *adj* operable

opérateur, -trice [ɔperatœr, -tris] 1 *nm,f* (*personne*) operator; *Cin* cameraman
2 *nm* (a) *Math* operator (b) *Ordinat* **o. logique** logical operator; **o. de saisie** keyboarder

opération [ɔperasjɔ̃] *nf* (a) **o. (chirurgicale)** operation; **o. à cœur ouvert** open-heart surgery (b) *Math* operation; **faire des opérations** to do some calculations (c) (*transaction*) deal, transaction; **o. financière** financial transaction (d) (*action*) operation; **o. de police** police operation

opérationnel, -elle [ɔperasjɔnel] *adj* operational

opératoire [ɔperatwar] *adj* (*procédure*) operating

opérer [34] [ɔpere] 1 *vt* (a) (*réforme, restructuration*) to carry out; (*changement, distinction*) to make (b) (*patient*) to operate on; **se faire o.** to have an operation; **se faire o. des amygdales** to have one's tonsils (taken) out; **se faire o. du cœur/de la hanche** to have a heart/hip operation; **se faire o. d'une tumeur** to have an operation to remove a tumour
2 *vi* (a) (*être efficace*) to work (b) (*procéder*) to operate
3 **s'opérer** *vpr* (*changement, transformation*) to take place

opérette [ɔperet] *nf* operetta

ophtalmo [ɔftalmo] *nmf Fam* ophthalmologist

ophtalmologie [ɔftalmɔlɔʒi] *nf Méd* ophthalmology

ophtalmologiste [ɔftalmɔlɔʒist], **ophtalmologue** [ɔftalmɔlɔg] *nmf Méd* ophthalmologist

opiner [ɔpine] *vi* **o. du chef** *ou* **du bonnet** to nod one's assent

opiniâtre [ɔpinjɑtr] *adj* stubborn

opinion [ɔpinjɔ̃] *nf* opinion (**de/sur** of/about); **se faire une o. sur qch** to make up one's mind about sth, to form an opinion about sth; **sans o.** (*dans un sondage*) don't know; **avoir une bonne/mauvaise o. de qn/qch** to have a good/bad opinion of sb/sth; **o. publique** public opinion

opiomane [ɔpjɔman] *nmf* opium addict

opium [ɔpjɔm] *nm* opium

opossum [ɔpɔsɔm] *nm* opossum

opportun, -e [ɔpɔrtœ̃, -yn] *adj* (*arrivée*) timely, opportune; (*moment, jour*) right

opportunément [ɔpɔrtynemɑ̃] *adv* opportunely

opportunisme [ɔpɔrtynism] *nm* opportunism

opportuniste [ɔpɔrtynist] *adj & nmf* opportunist

opportunité [ɔpɔrtynite] *nf* (*d'une arrivée*) timeliness; (*d'un projet, d'une décision*) advisability

opposant, -e [ɔpozɑ̃, -ɑ̃t] 1 *adj* opposing
2 *nm,f* opponent (**à** of)

opposé, -e [ɔpoze] 1 *adj* (a) (*en contradiction*) (*armées, caractères, équipe*) opposing; (*intérêts*) conflicting (b) (*dans l'espace*) (*côtés, rivage, direction*) opposite (c) (*contre*) **être o. à qch** to be opposed to sth
2 *nm* (*contraire*) **l'o.** the opposite; **à l'o.** (*côté*) on the opposite side; (*direction*) in the opposite direction; *Fig* on the other hand; **à l'o. de** (*côté*) on the opposite side to; (*contrairement à*) unlike; **à l'o. de ce qu'elle dit** contrary to what she says

opposer [ɔpoze] 1 *vt* (a) (*mettre en conflit*) (*armées, pays*) to bring into conflict (with each other); (*équipes*) to pit against each other; **o. à** (*armée, pays*) to bring into conflict with; (*équipe*) to pit against (b) (*objecter*) (*argument*) to put forward (**à** against); (b) **une résistance vigoureuse** to put up stiff resistance (c) (*mettre en contraste*) (*théories, styles, conceptions*) to contrast
2 **s'opposer** *vpr* (a) (*théories, styles, conceptions*) to contrast; (*équipes, adversaires*) to confront each other (b) **s'o. à qch** to be opposed to sth

opposition [ɔpozisjɔ̃] *nf* (a) (*résistance*) opposition; *Pol* **l'o.** the Opposition; **faire o. à un chèque** to stop a cheque (b) (*contraste*) contrast; **tout cela est en o. totale avec ce que je pense** all that is the complete opposite of what I think; **par o. à qch** as opposed to sth

oppressant, -e [ɔpresɑ̃, -ɑ̃t] *adj* oppressive

oppresser [ɔprese] *vt* (*sujet: situation, atmosphère*) to oppress (b) *Litt* (*peuple, nation*) to oppress

oppresseur [ɔpresœr] 1 *nm* oppressor
2 *adj* oppressive

oppression [ɔpresjɔ̃] *nf* (a) (*asservissement*) oppression (b) *Méd* tightness of the chest

opprimé, -e [ɔprime] 1 *adj* oppressed
2 *nm,f* **les opprimés** the oppressed

opprimer [ɔprime] *vt* (*peuple, nation*) to oppress

opprobre [ɔprɔbr] *nm Litt* opprobrium; **jeter l'o. sur qn** to cast opprobrium on sb

opter [ɔpte] *vi* **o. pour qch** to opt for sth; **o. entre deux choses** to choose between two things

opticien, -enne [ɔptisjɛ̃, -en] *nm,f* optician

optimal, -e, -aux, -ales [ɔptimal, -o] *adj* optimum, optimal

optimiser [ɔptimize] *vt* to optimize

optimisme [ɔptimism] *nm* optimism; **avec o.** optimistically

optimiste [ɔptimist] 1 *adj* optimistic
2 *nmf* optimist

option [ɔpsjɔ̃] *nf* (a) (*choix*) option (b) (*chose facultative*) optional extra; *Scol* (*matière*) option; **le flash est en o.** the flash is an optional extra; *Scol* **matières à o.** optional subjects (c) (*d'achat*) **prendre une o. sur qch** to take (out) an option on sth (d) *Ordinat* **o. d'impression** print option; **o. de menu** menu option

optionnel, -elle [ɔpsjɔnel] *adj* optional

optique [ɔptik] 1 *adj* (*nerf*) optic; (*verre*) optical
2 *nf* (a) (*science*) optics (*singulier*); **instruments d'o.** optical instruments (b) (*perspective*) perspective; **dans cette o.** from this perspective (c) (*d'un projecteur*) optical system

opulence [ɔpylɑ̃s] *nf* (a) (*richesse*) opulence (b) (*des formes*) fullness

opulent, -e [ɔpylɑ̃, -ɑ̃t] *adj* (*pays, personne*) opulent; (*pâturage*) abundant; (*poitrine*) full

opuscule [ɔpyskyl] *nm* opuscule

or¹ [ɔr] *nm* (a) *(métal)* gold; **montre/dent en or** gold watch/tooth; *Fam* **j'ai une femme en or** my wife is worth her weight in gold; **pour tout l'or du monde** for all the money in the world; *Fig* **c'est de l'or en barre** it's a safe investment; **le silence est d'or** silence is golden; **or fin** fine gold; **or massif** solid gold; **or noir** black gold; **or pur** pure gold (b) *(couleur)* gold; **cheveux d'or** golden hair

or² *conj (pour introduire une précision)* now; *(pour introduire une opposition)* well

oracle [ɔrakl] *nm* oracle

orage [ɔraʒ] *nm* (thunder)storm; *aussi Fig* **il y a de l'o. dans l'air** there's a storm brewing

orageux, -euse [ɔraʒø, -øz] *adj aussi Fig* stormy

oraison [ɔrezɔ̃] *nf* prayer; **o. funèbre** funeral oration

oral, -e, -aux, -ales [ɔral, -o] **1** *adj* oral; **par voie orale** orally
2 *nm* oral

oralement [ɔralmɑ̃] *adv* orally

orange [ɔrɑ̃ʒ] **1** *nf* orange; **o. givrée** = orange sorbet served inside the skin of a whole orange; **o. pressée** freshly-squeezed orange juice served with water and sugar; **o. sanguine** blood orange
2 *nm (couleur)* orange; **passer à l'o.** *(automobiliste)* to go through (the lights) on amber
3 *adj inv* orange

orangé, -e [ɔrɑ̃ʒe] *adj* orange-coloured

orangeade [ɔrɑ̃ʒad] *nf Br* orange squash, *Am* orangeade

oranger [ɔrɑ̃ʒe] *nm* orange tree

orangeraie [ɔrɑ̃ʒrɛ] *nf* orange grove

orangerie [ɔrɑ̃ʒri] *nf* orangery

orang-outan *(pl* **orangs-outans)**, **orang-outang** *(pl* **orangs-outangs)** [ɔrɑ̃utɑ̃] *nm* orang-outang, orang-utan

orateur, -trice [ɔratœr, -tris] *nm,f (personne éloquente)* orator; *(personne qui prend la parole)* speaker

oratoire¹ [ɔratwar] *adj* oratorical

oratoire² *nm (chapelle)* oratory

oratorio [ɔratɔrjo] *nm* oratorio

orbite [ɔrbit] *nf* (a) *Astron & Fig* orbit; **en** *ou* **sur o.** in orbit; **mettre** *ou* **placer un satellite en** *ou* **sur o.** to put a satellite into orbit (b) *(de l'œil)* socket

Orcades [ɔrkad] *nfpl* **les (îles) O.** the Orkneys, the Orkney Islands

orchestral, -e, -aux, -ales [ɔrkɛstral, -o] *adj* orchestral

orchestration [ɔrkɛstrasjɔ̃] *nf aussi Fig* orchestration

orchestre [ɔrkɛstr] *nm* (a) *(de musiciens)* orchestra; **o. de chambre** chamber orchestra; **o. de jazz** jazz band (b) *(partie de la salle) Br* stalls, *Am* orchestra

orchestrer [ɔrkɛstre] *vt aussi Fig* to orchestrate

orchidée [ɔrkide] *nf* orchid

ordinaire [ɔrdinɛr] **1** *adj* (a) *(habituel)* ordinary, usual; **peu** *ou* **pas o.** unusual (b) *(commun)* ordinary
2 *nm* (a) *(habitude)* **d'o.** usually; **comme à l'o.** as usual; **moins/plus que d'o.** less/more than usual (b) *(moyenne)* **ça sort de l'o.** it's out of the ordinary (c) *(régime habituel)* standard fare; *Mil* (company) mess (d) *(essence) Br* two-star, *Am* regular

ordinal, -e, -aux, -ales [ɔrdinal, -o] *adj* ordinal

ordinateur [ɔrdinatœr] *nm* computer; **o. autonome** stand-alone (computer); **o. bloc-notes** notebook (computer); **o. central** mainframe (computer); **o. domestique** home computer; **o. individuel** personal computer; **o. portable** laptop (computer)

ordination [ɔrdinasjɔ̃] *nf* ordination

ordonnance [ɔrdɔnɑ̃s] *nf* (a) *(document)* prescription; **délivré seulement sur o.** available only on prescription (b) *(disposition)* arrangement (c) *Jur* order, ruling (d) *Mil* orderly

ordonné, -e [ɔrdɔne] *adj* (a) *(vie)* orderly (b) *(personne, armoire, bureau)* tidy
2 *nf* **ordonnée** *Math* ordinate; **axe des ordonnées** Y-axis

ordonner [ɔrdɔne] *vt* (a) *(mettre de l'ordre dans)* to organize (b) *(commander)* to order; **o. à qn de faire qch** to order sb to do sth (c) *Rel* to ordain

ordre [ɔrdr] *nm* (a) *(organisation)* order; **par o. alphabétique/chronologique** in alphabetical/chronological order; **procéder par o.** to do things in order; **par o. d'apparition à l'écran** in order of appearance; *Fig* **c'est dans l'o. des choses** it's in the nature of things (b) *(de pièce, de personne)* tidiness; **en o.** *(bureau, maison)* tidy; *(comptes)* in order; **mettre de l'o.** to tidy up (c) *(discipline)* order; **maintenir/rétablir l'o.** to maintain/restore order; **tout est rentré dans l'o.** everything has returned to normal; **l'o. établi** the established order; **l'o. public** law and order; **troubler l'o. public** to cause a breach of the peace (d) *(catégorie)* order; **de premier/second/troisième o.** first-/second-/third-rate; **renseignements/idées d'o. général** general information/ideas; **d'o. privé/pratique** of a private/practical nature; **du même o.** of the same order; **de l'o. de** in the order of (e) *(communauté)* order; **o. religieux** religious order; **entrer dans les ordres** to take holy orders; **l'o. des médecins** *Br* ≃ the British Medical Association, *Am* ≃ the American Medical Association (f) *(commandement)* order; **donner l'o. à qn de faire qch** to give sb the order to do sth; **je ne suis pas à tes ordres!** I don't take orders from you!; **à vos ordres, mon général!** yes sir!; **sur l'o. de qn** on the order of sb; **jusqu'à nouvel o.** until further notice (g) *Fin* order; **à l'o. de...** payable to (the order of)... (h) **o. du jour** *(d'un comité)* agenda; *Mil* order of the day

ordure [ɔrdyr] *nf* (a) *(saleté)* dirt, filth (b) **ordures** *(déchets) Br* rubbish, *Am* garbage; **ordures ménagères** household *Br* rubbish *ou Am* garbage; **jeter** *ou* **mettre qch aux ordures** to throw sth in the *Br* dustbin *ou Am* garbage can (c) *Fam (personne méprisable)* bastard

ordurier, -ère [ɔrdyrje, -ɛr] *adj* filthy

orée [ɔre] *nf* **à l'o. de la forêt/du bois** on the edge of the forest/wood

oreille [ɔrɛj] *nf* (a) *(d'une personne, d'un animal)* ear; **o. externe/interne** outer/inner ear; *Fam* **avoir les oreilles en feuilles de chou** to have big sticky-out ears; **il partit l'o. basse** he went off with his tail between his legs; **tirer les oreilles à qn** to pull sb's ears; *Fig* to give sb a telling off; **n'écouter qu'une o., écouter d'une o. distraite** to listen with half an ear; **dire qch à l'o. de qn** to whisper sth in sb's ear; **dresser** *ou* **tendre l'o.** to prick up one's ears; **je n'en crois pas mes oreilles** I can't believe my ears; **faire la sourde o.** to turn a deaf ear; **ce n'est pas tombé dans l'o. d'un sourd** it didn't fall on deaf ears; *Fig* **elle ne l'entend pas de cette o.** she won't hear of it; **être dur d'o.** to be hard of hearing; **avoir de**

l'o. to have a good ear **(b)** *(d'un fauteuil)* wing; *(d'un plat, d'un vase)* handle; *(d'une casquette)* ear flap; **écrou à oreilles** wing nut

oreiller [ɔreje] *nm* pillow; **sur l'o.** in bed; **confidences sur l'o.** pillow talk

oreillette [ɔrejet] *nf* **(a)** *(du cœur)* auricle **(b)** *(d'une casquette)* ear flap

oreillons [ɔrejɔ̃] *nmpl* mumps; **avoir les o.** to have mumps

Orénoque [ɔrenɔk] *nm* **l'O.** the Orinoco

ores [ɔr] **d'ores et déjà** *adv* already

orfèvre [ɔrfevr] *nm (d'or)* goldsmith; *(d'argent)* silversmith; *Fig* **être o. en la matière** to be an expert in the matter

orfèvrerie [ɔrfevrəri] *nf (travail de l'or)* goldsmith's trade; *(travail de l'argent)* silversmith's trade; *(objets)* plate

organe [ɔrgan] *nm* **(a)** *Anat* organ; **organes génitaux** genitals **(b)** *(d'une machine)* part; **organes de transmission** transmission system **(c)** *Fig (instrument)* organ; **o. de publicité** advertising agency; **l'o. officiel du parti** the official organ of the party **(d)** *Hum (voix)* voice

organigramme [ɔrganigram] *nm* organization chart; *Ordinat* (data) flow chart

organique [ɔrganik] *adj* organic

organisateur, -trice [ɔrganizatœr, -tris] **1** *adj* organizing
2 *nmf* organizer; **o. de conférences/de congrès** conference organizer; **o. de voyages** tour operator

organisation [ɔrganizasjɔ̃] *nf* **(a)** *(action, résultat)* organization **(b)** *(groupement)* organization; **o. à but non lucratif** *Br* non-profit-making *or Am* not-for-profit organization; **o. politique/syndicale** political/trade-union organization; **O. mondiale de la santé** World Health Organization; **O. des Nations unies** United Nations Organization; **O. du Traité de l'Atlantique Nord** North Atlantic Treaty Organization

organisé, -e [ɔrganize] *adj* organized

organiser [ɔrganize] **1** *vt* to organize
2 s'organiser *vpr* to get organized

organisme [ɔrganism] *nm* **(a)** *Biol & Zool* organism; *Anat* system **(b)** *(organisation)* organization, body; **o. de crédit** credit institution; **o. international** international organization

organiste [ɔrganist] *nmf* organist

orgasme [ɔrgasm] *nm* orgasm

orge [ɔrʒ] *nf* barley

orgeat [ɔrʒa] *nm* **sirop d'o.** barley water

orgelet [ɔrʒəle] *nm* sty

orgie [ɔrʒi] *nf* orgy

orgue [ɔrg] **1** *nm* organ; **o. de Barbarie** barrel organ
2 *nfpl* **(a)** *Mus* **orgues** organ **(b)** *Géol* **orgues de basalte** basalt columns

orgueil [ɔrgœj] *nm* pride

orgueilleux, -euse [ɔrgœjø, -øz] *Péj* **1** *adj* proud
2 *nm,f* proud person

orient [ɔrjã] *nm* east; **l'O.** the East, the Orient; **en O.** in the East

orientable [ɔrjãtabl] *adj (grue)* swivelling; *(lampe, antenne)* adjustable

oriental, -e, -aux, -ales [ɔrjãtal, -o] **1** *adj (région, côte)* eastern; *(langue)* oriental
2 *nm,f* **O.** Oriental

orientateur, -trice [ɔrjãtatœr, -tris] = **orienteur**

orientation [ɔrjãtasjɔ̃] *nf* **(a)** *(détermination de position)* orientation; **avoir le sens de l'o.** to have a good sense of direction **(b)** *Scol* careers guidance; **choisir une o.** to choose a course of study **(c)** *(d'une grue, d'une antenne)* positioning **(d)** *(d'une maison)* aspect **(e)** *(d'une politique, de recherches)* direction

orienté, -e [ɔrjãte] *adj* **(a)** *(disposé)* **maison/pièce orientée au sud** house/room facing south **(b)** *(peu objectif)* biased **(c)** *Ordinat* **o. ligne** line-orientated; **o. objet** object-orientated

orienter [ɔrjãte] **1** *vt* **(a)** *(bâtiment)* to orientate; *(canon, fusil, télescope)* to point **(vers ou sur at) (b)** *(voyageur)* to direct, to guide; *Scol* **on l'a bien/mal orientée** she was given good/bad careers advice; **o. la conversation sur** to steer the conversation to; **o. ses recherches vers** to direct one's research towards
2 s'orienter *vpr* **(a)** *(trouver sa route)* to get one's bearings **(b)** *Fig* **s'o. vers** *(sujet: étudiant)* to specialize in; *(sujet: recherches)* to be directed towards

orienteur, -euse [ɔrjãtœr, -øz] *nm,f Scol* careers adviser

orifice [ɔrifis] *nm* opening; *(du corps)* orifice; *Tech* port

oriflamme [ɔriflam] *nf* **(a)** *Hist* oriflamme **(b)** *(bannière)* banner

origan [ɔrigã] *nm* oregano

originaire [ɔriʒiner] *adj* **être o. de** *(sujet: personne)* to be a native of; *(sujet: coutume, plat)* to originate from

original, -e, -aux, -ales [ɔriʒinal, -o] **1** *adj* **(a)** *(premier, nouveau)* original **(b)** *(excentrique)* eccentric
2 *nm,f (excentrique)* eccentric
3 *nm (œuvre, document)* original; *(d'un fichier, d'une disquette)* master copy

originalité [ɔriʒinalite] *nf* **(a)** *(nouveauté)* originality **(b)** *(excentricité)* eccentricity **(c)** *(trait original)* original feature

origine [ɔriʒin] *nf* origin; **des origines à nos jours** from the earliest times to the present day; **à l'o.** originally; **être à l'o. de qch** to be at the origin of sth; **être d'o. modeste** to be of humble origin; **être d'o. anglaise, être anglais d'o.** to be of English origin

originel, -elle [ɔriʒinel] *adj* original

orignal, -aux [ɔriɲal, -o] *nm* moose

oripeaux [ɔripo] *nmpl* rags, tatters

ORL [ɔerel] *nmf Méd (abrév* **oto-rhino-laryngologiste)** ENT specialist

orme [ɔrm] *nm* elm

ormeau, -x [ɔrmo] *nm* **(a)** *(arbre)* young elm **(b)** *(mollusque)* abalone

ornement [ɔrnəmã] *nm aussi Mus* ornament

ornemental, -e, -aux, -ales [ɔrnəmãtal, -o] *adj* ornamental

orner [ɔrne] *vt* to decorate **(de** with); *(vêtement)* to trim **(de** with)

ornière [ɔrnjer] *nf* rut; *Fig* **sortir de l'o.** to get out of trouble

ornithologie [ɔrnitɔlɔʒi] *nf* ornithology

ornithologiste [ɔrnitɔlɔʒist], **ornithologue** [ɔrnitɔlɔg] *nmf* ornithologist

oronge [ɔrɔ̃ʒ] *nf* agaric

orphelin, -e [ɔrfəlɛ̃, -in] **1** *adj* orphan(ed); **o. de père** fatherless; **o. de mère** motherless

2 *nm,f* orphan

orphelinat [ɔrfəlina] *nm* orphanage

orque [ɔrk] *nf* killer whale

Orsay [ɔrse] *n voir* **quai**

ORSEC [ɔrsek] (*abrév* **organisation des secours**) **le plan O.** = disaster contingency plan

orteil [ɔrtɛj] *nm* toe; **gros/petit o.** big/little toe

orthodontiste [ɔrtɔdɔ̃tist] *nmf* orthodontist

orthodoxe [ɔrtɔdɔks] **1** *adj aussi Rel* orthodox; **peu o.** unorthodox

2 *nmf Rel (de stricte obédience)* person of orthodox beliefs; *(de l'Église orthodoxe)* member of the Orthodox Church

orthodoxie [ɔrtɔdɔksi] *nf* orthodoxy

orthogonal, -e, -aux, -ales [ɔrtɔgonal, -o] *adj* orthogonal

orthographe [ɔrtɔgraf] *nf* spelling; **avoir une bonne o.** to be good at spelling

orthographier [66] [ɔrtɔgrafje] *vt* to spell; **mal o. un mot** to misspell a word

orthographique [ɔrtɔgrafik] *adj* orthographic

orthopédie [ɔrtɔpedi] *nf* orthopaedics *(singulier)*

orthopédique [ɔrtɔpedik] *adj* orthopaedic

orthopédiste [ɔrtɔpedist] *nmf* **(a)** *(médecin)* orthopaedist **(b)** *(fabricant)* maker of orthopaedic apparatus

orthophonie [ɔrtɔfɔni] *nf* speech therapy

orthophoniste [ɔrtɔfɔnist] *nmf* speech therapist

ortie [ɔrti] *nf* nettle

ortolan [ɔrtɔlɑ̃] *nm* ortolan (bunting)

OS [oes] *nm* (*abrév* **ouvrier spécialisé**) semi-skilled worker

os [ɔs, *pl* o] *nm* bone; *Fam Fig (obstacle)* snag; **mouillé ou trempé jusqu'aux os** soaked to the skin; **il ne fera pas de vieux os** he won't make old bones; *Fam* **tomber sur un os** to hit a snag; *très Fam* **je l'ai dans l'os** I've had it; **os à moelle** marrowbone

oscar [ɔskar] *nm (récompense)* Oscar

oscillateur [ɔsilatœr] *nm Phys* oscillator

oscillation [ɔsilasjɔ̃] *nf* **(a)** *(d'un pendule)* swing; *(d'une aiguille)* flickering; *(d'un bateau)* rocking; *Phys* oscillation **(b)** *Fig (du marché, de l'opinion)* fluctuation

osciller [ɔsile] *vi* **(a)** *(pendule)* to swing; *(aiguille)* to flicker; *(bateau)* to rock; *Phys* to oscillate **(b)** *(hésiter)* **o. entre** to waver between

osé, -e [oze] *adj* daring

oseille [ozɛj] *nf* **(a)** *(plante)* sorrel **(b)** *Fam (argent)* dosh

oser [oze] *vt* **o. faire qch** to dare (to) do sth; **j'ose croire que...** I dare say that...; **si j'ose dire** if I may say so; **comment osez-vous!** how dare you!

osier [ozje] *nm* **(a)** *(arbre)* osier **(b)** *(en vannerie)* wicker

Oslo [oslo] *n* Oslo

osmose [ɔsmoz] *nf aussi Fig* osmosis

ossature [ɔsatyr] *nf* **(a)** *(d'un homme, d'un animal)* frame **(b)** *Fig (d'un bâtiment, d'un texte)* framework

osselets [ɔslɛ] *nmpl* **jouer aux o.** to play at knucklebones

ossements [ɔsmɑ̃] *nmpl* bones

osseux, -euse [ɔsø, -øz] *adj (visage, main)* bony; *(tissu, greffe)* bone

ossuaire [ɔsɥɛr] *nm* ossuary

ostensible [ɔstɑ̃sibl] *adj* open

ostensiblement [ɔstɑ̃sibləmɑ̃] *adv* openly

ostensoir [ɔstɑ̃swar] *nm Rel* monstrance

ostentation [ɔstɑ̃tasjɔ̃] *nf* ostentation; **sans o.** unostentatiously

ostéopathe [ɔsteopat] *nmf* osteopath

ostéoporose [ɔsteoporoz] *nf Méd* osteoporosis

ostracisme [ɔstrasism] *nm* ostracism

ostréiculteur, -trice [ɔstreikyltœr, -tris] *nm,f* oyster farmer

ostréiculture [ɔstreikyltyr] *nf* oyster farming

otage [ɔtaʒ] *nm* hostage; **prendre qn en o.** to take sb hostage

otalgie [ɔtalʒi] *nf Méd* earache, *Spéc* otalgia

OTAN [ɔtɑ̃] *nf* (*abrév* **Organisation du traité de l'Atlantique Nord**) **l'O.** NATO

otarie [ɔtari] *nf* sea lion

OTASE [ɔtaz] *nf* (*abrév* **Organisation du traité de l'Asie du Sud-Est**) **l'O.** SEATO

ôter [ote] **1** *vt* **(a)** *(enlever)* to take away, to remove; *(vêtement)* to take off; *(tache)* to remove; *(assiettes)* to clear away; **ô. qch à qn** to take sth away from sb; *(illusions)* to rid sb of sth; **cela lui a ôté l'appétit** it's made him lose his appetite; **je vais t'ô. l'envie de recommencer!** I'll teach you not to start that again!; **tu ne m'ôteras pas de l'idée que...** I'm quite convinced that... **(b)** *Math* **10 ôté de 30 égale 20** 10 from 30 leaves 20

2 s'ôter *vpr* **ôtez-vous de là!** move yourself!; **s'ô. une idée de la tête** to get an idea out of one's head

otite [ɔtit] *nf Méd* ear infection, *Spéc* otitis

oto-rhino (*pl* **oto-rhinos**) [ɔtorino] *nmf Fam* ENT specialist

oto-rhino-laryngologiste (*pl* **oto-rhino-laryngologistes**) [ɔtorinolarɛ̃gɔlɔʒist] *nmf* ear, nose and throat specialist

Ottawa [ɔtawa] *n* Ottawa

ou [u] *conj* or; **ou...** (**bien**)... either... or (else)...

où [u] **1** *adv* **(a)** *(interrogatif, relatif)* where; **d'où vient ce mot?** where does this word come from?; **par où est-il passé?** which way did he go?; **je ne sais pas où aller** I don't know where to go **(b)** *(indéfini)* **où que vous soyez** wherever you may be **(c)** *(exprime la conséquence)* **d'où sa tristesse** hence his sadness

2 *pron relatif* **(a)** *(dans l'espace)* where; **là où** where; **partout où** wherever **(b)** *(dans le temps)* when **(c)** *(dans lequel, auquel)* **dans l'état où elle est** in the state she's in; **au prix où est le champagne** with champagne the price it is

OUA [oya] *nf* (*abrév* **Organisation de l'unité africaine**) **l'O.** the OAU

ouache [waʃ] *nf Can* bear's den

ouah [wa] *exclam* **(a)** *(aboiement)* woof! **(b)** *(exprime l'admiration)* wow!

ouailles [waj] *nfpl Litt ou Hum* flock

ouais [wɛ] *exclam Fam* yeah!

ouananiche [wananiʃ] *nf Can* freshwater salmon

ouaouaron [wawarɔ̃] *nm Can* bullfrog

ouate [wat] *nf* **(a)** *(pour soins) Br* cotton wool, *Am* absorbent cotton **(b)** *(pour rembourrage)* padding

ouatine [watin] *nf* quilting (material)

ouatiné, -e [watine] *adj* quilted

oubli [ubli] nm (a) (trou de mémoire) oversight; (lacune) omission (b) (général) oblivion; **tomber dans l'o.** to sink into oblivion (c) (acte d'oublier) forgetting

oublier [66] [ublije] **1** vt to forget; (omettre) to leave out; **o. de faire qch** to forget to do sth

2 s'oublier vpr (a) (se relâcher) to forget oneself; Euph (chien) to make a mess (b) (sortir de la mémoire) to be forgotten; **c'est comme le vélo, ça ne s'oublie pas** it's like riding a bike, once you learn you never forget

oubliettes [ublijet] nfpl dungeon; Fig **mettre qch aux o.** to shelve sth

ouest [west] **1** nm west; **un vent d'o.** a westerly wind; **le vent d'o.** the west wind; **à l'o.** in the west; **à l'o. de** (to the) west of; Géog & Pol **l'O.** the West

2 adj inv (côte, face) west; (régions) western

ouf [uf] exclam phew!; Fam **elle n'a pas eu le temps de dire o.** she didn't even have time to catch her breath

Ouganda [ugɑ̃da] nm **l'O.** Uganda

ougandais, -e [ugɑ̃de, -ez] **1** adj Ugandan

2 nmf **O.** Ugandan

oui [wi] **1** adv yes; **répondre par o. ou par non** to answer yes or no; **je crois que o.** I think so; **faire signe que o.** to nod (one's head); **ah, o.?** really?; Fam **tu viens, o.?** are you coming?; Fam **tu viens, o. ou non?** are you coming or aren't you?

2 nm inv Pol aye; Fam **se quereller/pleurer pour un o., pour un non** to quarrel/cry over the slightest thing

ouï-dire [widir] nm hearsay; **par o.** by hearsay

ouïe [wi] nf (a) (sens) hearing; **avoir l'o. fine** to have sharp ears; Hum **être tout o.** to be all ears (b) (de poisson) **ouïes** gills (c) Mus **ouïes** sound holes

ouille [uj] exclam ouch!, ow!

ouistiti [wistiti] nm marmoset; Fam Fig **un drôle de o.** an odd character

ouragan [uragɑ̃] nm (a) hurricane; Fig (de protestations) storm; **entrer comme un o. dans une pièce** to burst into a room

Oural [ural] nm **l'O.** (montagnes) the Urals

ourler [urle] vt (a) (faire un ourlet à) to hem (b) (border) to edge (de with)

ourlet [urle] nm (a) (d'un vêtement) hem; **faire un o. à** to put a hem on (b) (de l'oreille) rim

ours [urs] nm aussi Fig bear; Prov **il ne faut pas vendre la peau de l'o. avant de l'avoir tué** don't count your chickens before they're hatched; **o. blanc** polar bear; **o. brun** brown bear; Fig **o. mal léché** boor; **o. en peluche** teddy bear; **o. polaire** polar bear

ourse [urs] nf she-bear; Astron **la Grande O.** the Great Bear; **la Petite O.** the Little Bear

oursin [ursɛ̃] nm sea urchin

ourson [ursɔ̃] nm bear cub

oust(e) [ust] exclam (pour presser) get a move on!; (pour chasser) scram!

outarde [utard] nf Can Canada goose

outil [uti] nm aussi Fig tool; **outils pédagogiques** teaching aids; **o. de travail** tool

outillage [utijaʒ] nm (a) (ensemble d'outils) (set of) tools (b) (industriel, agricole) equipment

outiller [utije] **1** vt to equip

2 s'outiller vpr (bricoleur) to equip oneself; (usine) to equip itself

outrage [utraʒ] nm (au bon goût, au bon sens) insult (à to); Euph & Litt **faire subir les derniers outrages à une femme** to violate a woman; Jur **o. aux bonnes mœurs** affront to public decency; **o. à magistrat** contempt of court; **o. à la pudeur** public indecency

outrageant, -e [utraʒɑ̃, -ɑ̃t] adj (proposition, refus) insulting; (plaisanterie, propos) offensive; (accusation) outrageous

outrageusement [utraʒøzmɑ̃] adv (excessivement) outrageously

outrance [utrɑ̃s] nf (d'une tenue, d'une attitude, de propos) extravagance; **à o.** excessively

outre¹ [utr] nf wine skin

outre² **1** prép (a) (en plus de) besides (b) **o. mesure** unduly

2 adv en o. besides; **passer o.** (malgré une interdiction) to carry on regardless; **passer o. à qch** to disregard sth

3 conj o. (le fait) **que...** apart from the fact that...

outré, -e [utre] adj (a) (indigné) outraged (de ou par by) (b) (excessif) overdone

outre-Atlantique [utratlɑ̃tik] adv across the Atlantic

outrecuidance [utrəkɥidɑ̃s] nf Litt (a) (insolence) impertinence; **avoir l'o. de faire qch** to have the impertinence to do sth (b) (orgueil) presumptuousness

outrecuidant, -e [utrəkɥidɑ̃, -ɑ̃t] adj (a) (insolent) impertinent (b) (orgueilleux) presumptuous

outre-Manche [utrəmɑ̃ʃ] adv across the Channel

outre-mer [utrəmɛr] adv overseas

outrepasser [utrəpase] vt to exceed, to go beyond

outre-Rhin [utrərɛ̃] adv across the Rhine

outre-tombe [utrətɔ̃b] **d'outre-tombe** adj (voix) sepulchral

ouvert, -e [uvɛr, -ɛrt] **1** pp voir **ouvrir**

2 adj (a) (porte, yeux, plaie, vêtement, magasin) open; **grand o.** wide open; **être o. à qn** (lieu, concours) to be open to sb (b) (gaz, robinet) on (c) Fig (franc, sans préjugés) open; **avoir l'esprit o.** to be open-minded; **être o. à toute proposition** to be open to suggestions

ouvertement [uvɛrtəmɑ̃] adv openly

ouverture [uvɛrtyr] nf (a) (d'une porte, d'une séance, d'un compte) opening; (des hostilités) outbreak; **l'o. de la chasse/de la pêche** the start of the hunting season/fishing season; **à l'o.** (de la Bourse) at the start of trading; Fig **o. d'esprit** open-mindedness; Ordinat **o. de session** log-on (b) (orifice) opening (c) **ouvertures** (avances) overtures; **faire des ouvertures à qn** to make overtures to sb (d) Mus overture (e) Phot aperture (f) Pol **politique d'o.** policy of conciliation (g) (aux échecs, aux cartes) opening

ouvrable [uvrabl] adj voir **jour**

ouvrage [uvraʒ] **1** nm (a) (travail) work; **se mettre à l'o.** to get down to work (b) (construction) **ouvrages d'art** civil engineering works (c) (livre) work; **o. de référence** reference work (d) (résultat d'un travail) piece of work; (tricot, broderie) work

2 nf Fam **c'est de la belle o.** that's a nice piece of work

ouvragé, -e [uvraʒe] adj elaborate

ouvrant, -e [uvrɑ̃, -ɑ̃t] adj voir **toit**

ouvre-boîtes [uvrəbwat] nm inv can opener

ouvre-bouteilles [uvrəbutej] nm inv bottle opener

ouvreur, -euse [uvrœr, -øz] nmf usher, f usherette

ouvrier, -ère [uvrije, -ɛr] **1** *adj (quartier, tradition)* working-class; *(agitation)* industrial

2 *nm,f* worker; **une famille d'ouvriers** a working-class family; **o. agricole** farm worker; **o. qualifié** skilled worker; **o. spécialisé** semi-skilled worker

3 *nm (dans les travaux publics, le bâtiment)* workman

4 *nf* **ouvrière** *(abeille, fourmi)* worker

ouvrir [52] [uvrir] **1** *vt* **(a)** *(porte, boîte, bouteille, rideaux)* to open; *(verrou)* to draw; *(avec une clef)* to unlock; *(robinet, gaz)* to turn on; *(électricité)* to switch on; **o. à qn** to let sb in; **ouvre, c'est moi** open the door, it's me **(b)** *Méd (abcès)* to open up **(c)** *(lancer)* *(boutique, compte, débat)* to open; **o. la marche** to lead the way; *Ordinat* **o. une session** to log in, to log on **(d)** *Fig* **cela ouvre l'appétit** it whets the appetite; **o. son cœur à qn** to open one's heart to sb; **o. l'esprit à qn** to broaden sb's mind; **o. qch à qn** *(domaine, profession, perspectives)* to open up sth to sb

2 *vi (magasin, porte)* to open

3 s'ouvrir *vpr* **(a)** *(porte, yeux, séance, fleur)* to open; *Fig* **s'o. à qn** *(perspectives, domaine)* to open up for sb **(b)** *(se couper)* **s'o. la main/le menton** to cut open one's hand/chin; **s'o. les veines** to slash one's wrists

ouzbek [uzbɛk] **1** *adj* Uzbek

2 *nmf* **O.** Uzbek

Ouzbékistan [uzbekistã] *nm* **l'O.** Uzbekistan

ovaire [ovɛr] *nm* ovary

ovale [oval] *adj & nm* oval

ovariectomie [ovarjɛktɔmi] *nf Méd* ovariectomy

ovarien, -enne [ovarjɛ̃, -ɛn] *adj* ovarian

ovation [ovasjɔ̃] *nf* ovation; **faire une o. à qn** to give sb an ovation

ovationner [ovasjone] *vt* **o. qn** to give sb an ovation

overdose [ovœrdoz] *nf aussi Fig* overdose; **faire une o. (de qch)** *(drogue)* to take an overdose (of sth); *Fig* to overdose (on sth)

ovin, -e [ovɛ̃, -in] *Zool* **1** *adj* ovine

2 *nm* sheep

ovni [ovni] *nm (abrév* **objet volant non identifié)** UFO

ovulation [ovylasjɔ̃] *nf* ovulation

ovule [ovyl] *nm* ovum

ovuler [ovyle] *vi* to ovulate

oxhydrique [oksidrik] *adj* oxyhydrogen

oxydant, -e [oksidã, -ãt] **1** *adj* oxidizing

2 *nm* oxidizer

oxydation [oksidasjɔ̃] *nf* oxidization

oxyde [oksid] *nm Chim* oxide; **o. de carbone** carbon monoxide

oxyder [okside] **1** *vt* to oxidize

2 s'oxyder *vpr* to oxidize

oxygéné, -e [oksiʒene] *adj Chim* oxygenated; *(cheveux)* peroxide blonde, bleached

oxygène [oksiʒɛn] *nm* oxygen; *Fig* **j'ai besoin d'o.** I need some fresh air

oxygéner [34] [oksiʒene] **1** *vt* **(a)** *Chim (liquide, tissu vivant)* to oxygenate; *(élément, produit chimique)* to oxidize **(b)** *(cheveux)* to bleach, to peroxide

2 s'oxygéner *vpr (respirer)* to get some fresh air

oyat [oja] *nm* marram grass

ozone [ozon] *nm* ozone

P

P, p [pe] *nm inv* P, p

PAC [pak] *nf* (*abrév* **politique agricole commune**) CAP

PACA [paka] *nf* (*abrév* **Provence-Alpes-Côte d'Azur**) = region of south-eastern France

pacage [pakaʒ] *nm* (*champ*) pasture

pacemaker [pesmɛkœr] *nm* pacemaker

pacha [paʃa] *nm* pasha; *Fig* **mener une vie de p.** to live like a lord

pachyderme [paʃidɛrm] *nm* pachyderm; *Fig* (*personne*) lumbering oaf

pacification [pasifikasjɔ̃] *nf* pacification

pacifier [66] [pasifje] *vt* to pacify

pacifique [pasifik] **1** *adj* (*sans violence, calme*) peaceful; (*qui aime la paix*) peace-loving
2 *nm* **le P.** (*océan*) the Pacific; **le P. sud** the South Pacific

pacifisme [pasifism] *nm* pacifism

pacifiste [pasifist] *adj & nmf* pacifist

pack [pak] *nm* (*lot*) & *Sp* pack; **vendu en p.** sold in packs

pacotille [pakɔtij] *nf* junk; **de p.** (*marchandise*) shoddy; (*bijoux*) paste; *Fig* third-rate

pacson [paksɔ̃] *nm Fam* (*argent*) packet

pacte [pakt] *nm* pact; **p. de non-agression** non-aggression pact; **le p. de Varsovie** the Warsaw Pact

pactiser [paktize] *vi* **p. avec l'ennemi** to make a pact with the enemy

pactole [paktɔl] *nm Fam* (*au loto*) jackpot; **un joli p.** a nice little sum

paddock [padɔk] *nm* paddock; *Fam* (*lit*) bed

paella [paɛla] *nf* paella

PAF [paf] *nm* (*abrév* **paysage audiovisuel français**) = French broadcasting

paf [paf] **1** *exclam* (*chute*) bang!; (*claque*) slap!; (*coup de poing*) wham!
2 *adj inv Fam* (*saoul*) plastered

pagaie [page] *nf* paddle

pagaïe, pagaille [pagaj] *nf Fam* **(a)** (*désordre*) mess; **en p. in a mess** **(b)** (*confusion*) chaos; **semer la p.** to cause chaos **(c) des cadeaux/des jouets en p.** loads of presents/toys

pagayer [53] [pageje] *vi* to paddle

page¹ [paʒ] *nf* **(a)** (*d'un livre, d'un cahier, sur l'Internet*) page; *Fig* (*extrait*) passage; (*de l'histoire, d'une vie*) chapter; **en première p.** (*des journaux*) on the front page (of the newspapers); *Typ* **mettre qch en page(s)** to make sth up; **perdre la p.** to lose one's place; *Fig* **tourner la p.** to make a fresh start; **p. centrale** (*d'un magazine*) centre pages; **p. de garde** flyleaf; **les pages jaunes** (*de l'annuaire*) the Yellow Pages®; *Ordinat* **p. précédente**

page up; *Rad & TV* **p. de publicité** commercial break; *Ordinat* **p. suivante** page down **(b) être à la p.** (*à la mode*) to be up to date

page² *nm* page(boy)

pagination [paʒinasjɔ̃] *nf* pagination

paginer [paʒine] *vt* to paginate

pagne [paɲ] *nm* loincloth; (*en paille*) grass skirt

pagode [pagɔd] *nf* pagoda

paie [pɛ] **1** *voir* **payer**
2 *nf* **(a)** (*salaire*) pay, wages **(b)** *Fam* **ça fait une p.** it's ages ago; **ça fait une p. que je ne l'ai pas vue** I haven't seen her for ages

paiement [pemɑ̃] *nm* payment; *aussi Fig* **en p. de qch** as payment for sth; **p. à la commande** cash with order; **p. à la livraison** cash on delivery

païen, -enne [pajɛ̃, -ɛn] *adj & nm,f* pagan, heathen

paiera *etc voir* **payer**

paillard, -e [pajar, -ard] *adj* bawdy

paillasse [pajas] *nf* **(a)** (*matelas*) straw mattress **(b)** (*de l'évier*) draining board; (*de laboratoire*) bench

paillasson [pajasɔ̃] *nm aussi Fig* doormat

paille [paj] **1** *nf* **(a)** (*de céréales*) straw; *Fig* **être sur la p.** to be down and out; **tirer à la courte p.** to draw lots; **p. de fer** steel wool **(b)** (*pour boire*) straw
2 *adj inv* (*jaune*) straw-coloured

paillé, -e [paje] *adj* (*chaise*) straw-bottomed

pailleté, -e [pajte] *adj* sequined

paillette [pajɛt] *nf* **(a)** (*sur vêtement*) sequin; **paillettes** (*pour se maquiller*) glitter; **à paillettes** sequined **(b)** (*d'or*) speck; (*de savon*) flake

paillote [pajɔt] *nf* straw hut

pain [pɛ̃] *nm* **(a)** (*aliment*) bread; (*miche*) loaf; *Fig* **avoir du p. sur la planche** to have a lot on one's plate; **gagner son p.** to earn one's living; **je ne mange pas de ce p.-là** I'm having nothing to do with that; **ça ne mange pas de p.** it won't cost you/him/*etc* anything; **ôter le p. de la bouche à qn** to take the bread out of sb's mouth; **petit p.** (*bread*) roll; *Fig* **partir** *ou* **se vendre comme des petits pains** to sell like hot cakes; **p. azyme** unleavened bread; **p. bénit** consecrated bread; **p. bis** brown bread; **p. de campagne** farmhouse bread; **p. au chocolat** chocolate-filled pastry; **p. complet** wholemeal bread; **p. d'épices** ≃ gingerbread; **p. grillé** toast; **p. au lait** sweet roll; **p. de mie** sliced white bread; **p. perdu** French toast; **p. aux raisins** currant bun; **p. de seigle** rye bread; **p. au** *ou* **de son** bran bread; **p. de sucre** sugarloaf **(b)** (*de savon*) bar **(c)** *Fam* (*coup de poing*) punch

pair, -e [pɛr] **1** *adj (nombre, jours)* even
2 *nm* **(a)** *(égal)* être jugé par ses pairs to be judged by one's peers; aller de p. avec qch to go hand in hand with sth **(b)** *(noble)* peer **(c)** jeune fille au p. au pair; être *ou* travailler au p. to work as an au pair **(d)** *(au jeu)* even numbers

paire [pɛr] *nf* pair; *(de gibier à plumes, de pistolets)* brace; **il a reçu une p. de claques** he got his face slapped; *Fam Fig* ça, c'est une autre p. de manches that's a different kettle of fish

paisible [pezibl] *adj* peaceful; *(personne)* quiet

paisiblement [pezibləmɑ̃] *adv* peacefully

paître [50b] [pɛtr] **1** *vt (herbe)* to crop; *(feuilles)* to feed on
2 *vi* to feed; *(manger de l'herbe)* to graze; *(manger des feuilles)* to browse; *Fam Fig* envoyer p. qn to send sb packing

paix [pɛ] *nf* **(a)** *(entre États)* peace; faire la p. (avec qn) to make peace (with sb); *Fig* to make it up (with sb); vivre en p. avec sa conscience to have a clear conscience **(b)** *Rel* p. à son âme may his soul rest in peace; allez en p. go in peace **(c)** *(tranquillité)* peace; avoir la p. to have some peace (and quiet); faire qch en p. to do sth in peace (and quiet); laisser qn en p. to leave sb in peace; *Fam* fiche-moi *ou* fous-moi la p.! get off my back!; *Fam* la p.! quiet!

Pakistan [pakistɑ̃] *nm* le P. Pakistan

pakistanais, -e [pakistane, -ɛz] **1** *adj* Pakistani
2 *nm,f* P. Pakistani

Pal [pal] *adj inv TV (abrév* **phase alternation line***)* PAL

palabres [palabr] *nfpl* endless discussion

palace [palas] *nm* luxury hotel

palais¹ [palɛ] *nm* **(a)** *(d'un roi, d'un noble)* palace; le p. Bourbon = home of the French parliament; le p. des congrès conference centre; le p. de l'Élysée the Élysée (Palace) *(official residence of the French President)*; le p. Garnier = the Paris Opera House; le p. du Luxembourg = home of the French Senate; p. des sports sports centre **(b)** *(tribunal)* le P. (de justice) the law courts

palais² *nm (partie de la bouche, goût)* palate

palan [palɑ̃] *nm* hoist

pale [pal] *nf* blade

pâle [pal] *adj* **(a)** pale; p. comme un linge as white as a sheet; p. comme la mort deathly pale; *Fam Mil* se faire porter p. to report sick **(b)** *Fig (sourire)* faint; *(style)* colourless; une p. imitation de qch a pale imitation of sth

palefrenier [palfrənje] *nm* groom

paléolithique [paleolitik] *Géol* **1** *adj* Palaeolithic
2 *nm* le P. the Palaeolithic period

paléontologie [paleɔ̃tɔlɔʒi] *nf* palaeontology

paléontologiste [paleɔ̃tɔlɔʒist], **paléontologue** [paleɔ̃tɔlɔg] *nmf* palaeontologist

Palerme [palɛrm] *n* Palermo

Palestine [palestin] *nf* la P. Palestine

palestinien, -enne [palestinjɛ̃, -ɛn] **1** *adj* Palestinian
2 *nm,f* P. Palestinian

palet [palɛ] *nm* **(a)** *(pour hockey)* puck **(b)** *(gâteau sec)* = round butter biscuit

paletot [palto] *nm (short)* overcoat; *Fam Fig* tomber sur le p. à qn *(l'attaquer)* to jump on sb; *(pour lui parler)* to buttonhole sb

palette [palɛt] *nf* **(a)** *(de peintre)* palette; *Fig (éventail)* range; *Ordinat* p. graphique graphics palette; *Ordinat* p. d'outils tool palette **(b)** *(pour la manutention)* pallet **(c)** *Culin (de mouton, de porc)* shoulder

palétuvier [paletyvje] *nm* mangrove

pâleur [palœr] *nf (d'une personne)* pallor; *(d'une couleur, de la lumière)* paleness; *(du style)* colourlessness; d'une p. mortelle deathly pale

pâlichon, -onne [paliʃɔ̃, -ɔn] *adj Fam* a bit pale

palier [palje] *nm* **(a)** *(d'escalier)* landing **(b)** *(dans une évolution)* plateau; par paliers in stages

palindrome [palɛ̃drom] *nm Ling* palindrome

pâlir [palir] *vi (personne)* to turn or go pale; *(lumière, couleur, souvenir)* to fade; *Fig* de rage to turn white with anger; *Fig* faire p. qn de jalousie to make sb green with envy

palissade [palisad] *nf* fence

palliatif, -ive [paljatif, -iv] **1** *adj* palliative
2 *nm Méd* palliative; *Fig* stopgap measure

pallier [66] [palje] **1** *vt (manque)* to compensate for; *(erreur, problème)* to lessen the impact of
2 pallier à *vt ind (manque)* to compensate for; *(erreur, problème)* to lessen the impact of

palmarès [palmarɛs] *nm (à un concours)* list of prize-winners; *(d'une compétition sportive)* list of winners; le p. (de la chanson) the charts; être *ou* figurer au p. *(d'un concours, d'une compétition)* to be among the (prize-)winners; *(de la chanson)* to be in the charts; avoir un p. impressionnant to have an impressive track record

palme [palm] *nf* **(a)** *(de palmier)* palm (branch) **(b)** *(récompense)* les palmes académiques = decoration awarded to teachers; la P. d'or *(du festival de Cannes)* the Palme d'or **(c)** *(pour nager)* flipper

palmé, -e [palme] *adj* **(a)** *(feuille)* palmate **(b)** *(pattes)* webbed

palmeraie [palmərɛ] *nf* palm grove

palmier [palmje] *nm* **(a)** *(arbre)* palm (tree); p. dattier date palm **(b)** *(gâteau sec)* = sweet heart-shaped pastry

palmipède [palmiped] *nm Zool* web-footed bird, *Spéc* palmiped

palombe [palɔ̃b] *nf* wood pigeon

pâlot, -otte [palo, -ɔt] *adj Fam* a bit pale

palourde [palurd] *nf* clam

palpable [palpabl] *adj* palpable

palpation [palpasjɔ̃] *nf Méd* palpation

palper [palpe] *vt* **(a)** *(objet)* to feel (with one's hands); *Méd* to palpate **(b)** *Fam (somme)* to be paid, to get

palpitant, -e [palpitɑ̃, -ɑ̃t] *adj* **(a)** *(cœur, pouls)* fluttering; *(plus fort)* throbbing; *(personne) (d'émotion)* quivering **(b)** *(passionnant)* thrilling
2 *nm très Fam (cœur)* ticker

palpitations [palpitasjɔ̃] *nfpl* palpitations

palpiter [palpite] *vi (cœur, pouls)* to flutter; *(plus fort)* to throb

paludisme [palydism] *nm* malaria

pâmer [pame] se pâmer *vpr Veilli* to swoon; *Fig & Hum* se p. d'aise to be blissfully happy; *Fig & Hum* se p. (devant) to swoon (over)

pamphlet [pɑ̃flɛ] *nm* satirical tract

pamplemousse [pɑ̃pləmus] *nm* grapefruit

pan¹ [pɑ̃] nm (a) (de chemise, de manteau) tail; (de jupe) panel (b) (morceau) section, piece; Fig (d'une époque) part; p. de mur section of wall

pan² exclam (coup de feu) bang!; (gifle) whack!; **et p., la voilà qui entre!** and lo and behold, in she walks!

panacée [panase] nf panacea

panachage [panaʃaʒ] nm mixing; (de liste électorale) = voting for candidates from more than one list

panache [panaʃ] nm (a) (plume) plume (b) (brio, éclat) panache

panaché, -e [panaʃe] 1 adj multicoloured; **p. de blanc** streaked with white, with white streaks
2 nm (boisson) shandy

panacher [panaʃe] vt to mix

panade [panad] nf Fam **être dans la p.** (avoir des ennuis) to be in a bit of a mess; (manquer d'argent) to be strapped for cash

panafricain, -e [panafrikɛ̃, -ɛn] adj Pan-African

panais [panɛ] nm parsnip

Panama [panama] nm **le P.** Panama

panama [panama] nm (chapeau) panama hat

Paname [panam] n Fam Paris

panaméen, -enne [panameɛ̃, -ɛn] 1 adj Panamanian
2 nm,f P. Panamanian

panaméricain, -e [panamerikɛ̃, -ɛn] adj Pan-American

panard [panar] nm Fam foot

panaris [panari] nm whitlow

pan-bagnat [pl pans-bagnats] [pɑ̃baɲa] nm = large bread roll filled with salade niçoise

pancarte [pɑ̃kart] nf (affiche) sign, notice; (pour manifestation) placard

pancréas [pɑ̃kreas] nm pancreas

panda [pɑ̃da] nm panda

pané, -e [pane] adj coated with breadcrumbs, breaded

panégyrique [panegirik] nm eulogy; **faire le p. de qn** to eulogize sb

panel [panɛl] nm (groupe) panel; (échantillon) sample (group)

paneuropéen, -enne [panørɔpeɛ̃, -ɛn] adj Pan-European

panier [panje] nm (a) (corbeille) basket; **mettre** ou **jeter qch au p.** to throw sth in the wastepaper basket; **le p. le dessus du p.** the pick of the bunch; Fig **c'est un p. de crabes** they're always at each other's throats; **p. à linge** linen basket; Fam **p. percé** spendthrift; **p. à provisions** shopping basket; **p. à salade** salad shaker; Fam (convoi cellulaire) Br black Maria, Am paddy wagon (b) (au basketball) basket (c) (pour diapositives) slide magazine (d) (de robe) hoop

panier-repas [pl paniers-repas] [panjerəpɑ] nm packed lunch

panique [panik] 1 nf panic; **être pris de p.** to panic; **ne pas céder à la p.** not to panic; **il y a eu un début de p.** people started to panic; **il y a eu un mouvement de p.** people panicked
2 adj peur p. panic

paniqué, -e [panike] adj Fam in a panic

paniquer [panike] vt & vi Fam to panic

panislamisme [panislamism] nm Pan-Islamism

panne [pan] nf breakdown; Ordinat failure, crash; **être en p.** (machine) to be out of order; (automobiliste) to have broken down; **tomber en p.** to break down; **tomber en p. d'essence, tomber en p. sèche** to run out of Br petrol or Am gas; Fam **il m'a fait le coup de la p.** he tried to pull the old "the car won't start" trick on me; **p. (de courant** ou **d'électricité)** power failure or cut; **p. de moteur** engine failure; **p. de secteur** power failure

panneau, -x [pano] nm (a) (pour afficher) board; **p. d'affichage** Br notice board, Am bulletin board; **p. indicateur** road sign; **p. publicitaire** Br hoarding, Am billboard (b) (sur la route) **p. (de signalisation routière), p. indicateur** road sign (c) (élément plan) panel (d) Fig **tomber** ou **donner dans le p.** to fall into the trap

panonceau, -x [panɔ̃so] nm (a) (de notaire) plaque (b) (pancarte) sign

panoplie [panɔpli] nf (a) (habit) outfit (b) (assortiment) set

panorama [panɔrama] nm panorama; Fig overview

panoramique [panɔramik] adj (vue) panoramic; (restaurant) with panoramic views; (écran) wide

panse [pɑ̃s] nf (a) (de ruminant) rumen (b) Fam (ventre) belly; **s'en mettre plein la p.** to stuff oneself

pansement [pɑ̃smɑ̃] nm dressing; **p. (adhésif)** (sticking) plaster, Am Band-aid®; **faire un p. à qn** to put a dressing on (sb); **refaire un p. à qn** to change sb's dressing

panser [pɑ̃se] vt (a) (blessure) to dress; (membre) to bandage; **p. qn** to dress sb's wounds; Fig **p. ses blessures** to lick one's wounds (b) (cheval) to groom

pantagruélique [pɑ̃tagryelik] adj gigantic

pantalon [pɑ̃talɔ̃] nm Br trousers, Am pants; **un p.** a pair of Br trousers or Am pants; **p. de golf** plus-fours; **p. à pattes d'éléphant** flares; **p. à pinces** pleated Br trousers or Am pants; **p. de pyjama** pyjama Br trousers or Am pants

pantalonnade [pɑ̃talɔnad] nf (spectacle) burlesque farce

pantelant, -e [pɑ̃tlɑ̃, -ɑ̃t] adj Litt (à bout de souffle) panting

panthère [pɑ̃tɛr] nf leopard; **p. noire** panther

pantin [pɑ̃tɛ̃] nm (jouet) jumping-jack; Péj (fantoche) puppet

pantois, -e [pɑ̃twa, -az] adj speechless; **en rester p.** to be speechless

pantomime [pɑ̃tɔmim] nf (art) mime; (spectacle) mime show

pantouflard, -e [pɑ̃tuflar, -ard] adj & nm,f Fam stay-at-home

pantoufle [pɑ̃tufl] nf slipper

pantoufler [pɑ̃tufle] vi Fam to join the private sector

PAO [peao] nf Ordinat (abrév **publication assistée par ordinateur**) DTP

paon [pɑ̃] nm peacock

papa [papa] nm dad; (langage enfantin) daddy; **p. gâteau** indulgent father; **p. poule** doting father; Fam Péj **de p.** old-fashioned; **jouer au p. et à la maman** to play mummies and daddies

papal, -e, -aux, -ales [papal, -o] adj papal

paparazzi [paparadzi] nmpl paparazzi

papauté [papote] nf papacy

papaye [papaj] nf papaya

pape [pap] *nm* pope; *Fam* **sérieux comme un p.** deadly serious

papelard [paplar] *nm Fam* piece of paper

paperasse [papras] *nf Péj* papers; *Br* bumf

paperasserie [paprasri] *nf Péj* (a) *(documents)* papers, *Br* bumf; faire **la p.** to do paperwork (b) *(d'un système bureaucratique)* red tape

papeterie [papetri] *nf (usine)* paper mill; *(magasin)* stationer's; *(articles)* stationery

papetier, -ère [papotje, -ɛr] *nm,f* (a) *(industriel)* paper manufacturer (b) *(commerçant)* stationer

papi [papi] *nm* grandpa, granddad

papier [papje] *nm* (a) *(pour écrire)* paper; **un p.** a piece of paper; *Fam* **être dans les petits papiers de qn** to be in sb's good books; *Fam* **p. alu** tinfoil; **p. avion** airmail paper; *Ordinat* **p. à bandes perforées** perforated paper; **p. de bonbon** sweet wrapper; **p. cadeau** gift wrap, wrapping paper; *Ordinat* **p. continu** continuous paper *or* stationery; *Ordinat* **p. continu plié en accordéon** fanfold paper; **p. crépon** crêpe paper; *très Fam* **p. cul** bog roll; **p. à dessin** drawing paper; **p. d'emballage** brown paper; **p. à en-tête** headed notepaper; **p. glacé** glazed paper; **papiers gras** litter; **p. hygiénique** toilet paper; **p. journal** newspaper; **p. kraft** brown paper; **p. à lettres** writing paper; *Ordinat* **p. listing** listing paper; **p. mâché** papier-mâché; *Fig* **avoir une mine de p. mâché** to look like death warmed up; **p. machine** typing paper; **p. millimétré** graph paper; **p. à musique** manuscript paper; *Fig* **être réglé comme du p. à musique** *(événement)* to be as regular as clockwork; **elle est réglée comme du p. à musique** you can set your watch by her; **p. peint** wallpaper; **p. de soie** tissue paper; **p. toilette** toilet paper; **p. de verre** sandpaper; **passer qch au p. de verre** to sandpaper sth (b) **papiers** *(documents officiels)* papers; **papiers (d'identité)** (identity) papers; *(d'un automobiliste)* *Br* driving licence, *Am* driver's license (c) *Fam (article de journal)* article

papilles [papij] *nfpl* **p. gustatives** taste buds

papillon [papijɔ̃] *nm* (a) *(insecte)* butterfly; **p. de nuit** moth; *Fam* **minute p.!** hold on a minute! (b) *(écrou)* wing nut (c) *(sur document)* flag (d) *Fam (contravention)* (parking) ticket (e) *(nage)* butterfly

papillonner [papijɔne] *vi* (a) *(paupières)* to flutter (b) *(d'une personne à une autre)* to flirt about

papillote [papijɔt] *nf* (a) *(en papier alu)* **cailles en papillotes** quails en papillotes *(cooked in tinfoil)* (b) *(de gigot)* frill (c) *Fam* **tu peux en faire des papillotes** you can chuck it away

papilloter [papijɔte] *vi (yeux)* to blink; *(lumière)* to flicker

papoter [papote] *vi Fam* to chat

papou, -e [papu] **1** *adj* Papuan
2 *nm,f* **P.** Papuan

Papouasie-Nouvelle-Guinée [papwazinuvɛlgine] *nf* **la P.** Papua New Guinea

papouille [papuj] *nf Fam* **faire des papouilles à qn** to tickle sb

paprika [paprika] *nm* paprika

papyrus [papirys] *nm* papyrus

paqson [paksɔ̃] = **pacson**

Pâque [pak] *nf* **P., la P. juive** Passover

paquebot [pakbo] *nm* liner

pâquerette [pakrɛt] *nf* daisy

pâques [pak] **1** *nfpl* **joyeuses p.!** Happy Easter!
2 *nm* **P.** Easter; *Fam* **à P. ou à la Trinité!** never in a month of Sundays!

paquet [pakɛ] *nm* (a) *(sac)* packet; *(de sucre)* bag; *(de cigarettes)* packet, *Am* pack; *(postal)* parcel, package; *Fam* **toucher un joli p.** to make a packet; *Fam* **mettre le p.** to pull out all the stops; *Fam* **c'est un p. de nerfs** she's a bundle *or* a bag of nerves; **p.-cadeau** gift-wrapped parcel; **je vous fais un p.-cadeau?** would you like it gift-wrapped?

paquetage [paktaʒ] *nm (soldier's)* pack; **faire son p.** to get one's kit ready

par [par] *prép* (a) *(à travers)* through; **p. la porte/le trou de la serrure** through the door/the keyhole; **regarder p. la fenêtre** *(de l'intérieur)* to look out (of) the window; *(de l'extérieur)* to look through the window; **passer p. Calais** to go via Calais; **p. ici/là** this/that way; **p. où est-il passé?** which way did he go?
(b) *(position)* **p. ici** round about here; **p. là** over there; **p. 200 mètres de fond** at a depth of 200 metres; **p. endroits** in places
(c) *(pendant)* **p. une belle journée d'automne** on a beautiful autumn day; **p. cette chaleur** in this heat; **p. le passé** in the past; *Litt* **p. deux fois** twice
(d) *(introduit le complément d'agent)* by; **c'est p. eux que je l'ai appris** I found out from them; **faire faire qch p. qn** to have sth done by sb
(e) *(indique la cause)* out of; **faire qch p. amitié/pitié** to do sth out of friendship/pity; **p. hasard/erreur** by chance/mistake; **p. malheur** unfortunately, as bad luck would have it; **p. pitié!** for pity's sake!
(f) *(au moyen de)* with, by; **retenu p. une corde** held by a rope; **fermé p. un cadenas** padlocked; **p. train/avion/voiture/bateau** by train/plane/car/boat; **conduire/prendre qn p. la main** to lead/take sb by the hand; **tenir qn p. la taille** to hold sb round the waist; **pendu p. les pieds** hanging by the feet; **envoyer qch p. la poste** to send sth by post; **répondre p. oui ou p. non** to answer yes or no; **se terminer p. un divorce/une dispute** to end in divorce/an argument; **p. tous les moyens** by every possible means; **il est monté p. l'escalier** he took the stairs up; **obtenir qch p. la force** to obtain sth by force; **appeler qn p. son nom** to call sb by his/her name
(g) *(selon)* according to; **p. ordre de grandeur** according to size
(h) *(distributif)* per, a; **deux p. deux** two by two; **p. groupes de six** in groups of six; **deux jours p. semaine** two days a week; **10 000 francs p. an** 10,000 francs a year; **un siège p. personne** one seat per person
(i) *(de. p. (à cause de)* due to; **de p. le monde** the world over

para [para] *nm Fam* para

parabole [parabɔl] *nf* (a) *(allégorie)* parable (b) *(courbe)* parabola (c) *(antenne)* (parabolic) dish

parabolique [parabɔlik] *adj* parabolic

paracétamol [parasetamɔl] *nm* paracetamol

parachever [46] [paraʃve] *vt* to complete, to finish off

parachutage [paraʃytaʒ] *nm* parachuting

parachute [paraʃyt] *nm* parachute; **faire du p.** to go parachuting; **p. ascensionnel** parascending

parachuter [paraʃyte] *vt (vivres, soldats)* to parachute in; *Fam (nommer)* to draft in

parachutisme [paraʃytism] *nm* parachuting

parachutiste [paraʃytist] *nmf* (a) *(sportif)* parachutist (b) *(soldat)* paratrooper

parade¹ [parad] *nf* (a) *(exhibition)* show, ostentation; **faire p. de qch** to show sth off (b) *(défilé)* parade

parade² [parad] *nf* (a) *(en escrime, boxe)* parry (b) *(réplique)* riposte; **Fig je n'ai pas encore trouvé la p.** I haven't come up with a way of handling him/it/*etc* yet

parader [parade] *vi* to show off

paradis [paradi] *nm* heaven; *Fig* paradise; **le p. terrestre** the Garden of Eden; *Fig* heaven on earth; **aller au p.** to go to heaven; **un p. fiscal** a tax haven; *Fam* **le p.** *(d'un théâtre)* the gods; *Fam* **il ne l'emportera pas au p.** he won't get away with it, he'll be sorry

paradisiaque [paradizjak] *adj* heavenly

paradoxal, -e, -aux, -ales [paradoksal, -o] *adj* paradoxical

paradoxalement [paradoksalmã] *adv* paradoxically

paradoxe [paradoks] *nm* paradox

parafe [paraf] = **paraphe**

parafer [parafe] = **parapher**

paraffine [parafin] *nf* paraffin

parafiscalité [parafiskalite] *nf* = taxes paid to the state and used for administration purposes

parages [paraʒ] *nmpl* (a) *Naut* waters (b) *(alentours)* **dans les p. de...** in the vicinity of...; *Fam* **est-ce qu'elle est dans les p.?** is she around?

paragraphe [paragraf] *nm* (a) paragraph (b) *Typ* paragraph (sign)

Paraguay [paragwe] *nm* **le P.** Paraguay

paraguayen, -enne [paragwejẽ, -ɛn] **1** *adj* Paraguayan
2 *nmf* **P.** Paraguayan

paraître [20] [parɛtr] **1** *vi* (a) *(apparaître)* to appear; *(étoile, lune)* to appear, to come out; **laisser p. sa déception** to let one's disappointment show; **un faible sourire parut sur ses lèvres** he/she smiled weakly; **elle ne pense qu'à p.** all she thinks about is showing off
(b) *(livre)* to come out, to be published
(c) *(sembler)* to seem, to appear; **cette décision me paraît bizarre** it seems a strange decision to me; **elle paraissait furieuse** *(à la voir)* she looked furious; *(à l'entendre)* she sounded furious
2 *v impersonnel* (a) **il me paraît utile de...** *(il semble utile de...)* I think it would be useful to...; **demain, il n'y paraîtra plus** there'll be no trace of it tomorrow; **sans qu'il y paraisse** without it being apparent
(b) **il paraît que...** *(on dit)* it seems *or* appears that...; **il paraît qu'elle s'en va, elle s'en va, paraît-il** it seems *or* appears that she's leaving, apparently she's leaving; **il paraît que ça fait maigrir** apparently it helps you lose weight; **il paraît que oui** so it would appear, apparently (so); **il paraît que non** it would appear not, apparently not; **à ce qu'il paraît** apparently
3 *nm* **le p.** appearance

parallèle [paralɛl] **1** *adj* parallel (**à** to *or* with); *(police, marché)* unofficial; **mener une vie p.** to lead a secret life; *Ordinat* **imprimante/interface p.** parallel printer/interface
2 *nf* parallel (line)
3 *nm* parallel; **mettre qch en p. avec qch** to draw a parallel between sth and sth

parallèlement [paralɛlmã] *adv* parallel (**à** to *or* with); *(simultanément)* at the same time (**à** as)

parallélépipède [paralelepiped] *nm* parallelepiped

parallélisme [paralelism] *nm* parallelism; **p. (des roues)** (wheel) alignment

parallélogramme [paralelogram] *nm* parallelogram

paralysant, -e [paralizã, -ãt] *adj* paralysing

paralysé, -e [paralize] *adj aussi Fig* paralysed

paralyser [paralize] *vt aussi Fig* to paralyse; **le froid lui paralyse les mains** his hands are numb with the cold

paralysie [paralizi] *nf aussi Fig* paralysis

paralytique [paralitik] *adj & nmf* paralytic

paramédical, -e, -aux, -ales [paramedikal, -o] **1** *adj* paramedical
2 *nm* **les emplois du p.** paramedical jobs

paramétrable [parametrabl] *adj Ordinat* configurable; **p. par l'utilisateur** user-definable

paramètre [parametr] *nm Math & Fig* parameter; *Ordinat* parameter, setting; *(du DOS)* switch

paramétrer [34] [parametre] *vt Ordinat* to configure

paramilitaire [paramilitɛr] *adj* paramilitary

parano [parano] *Fam* **1** *adj* paranoid
2 *nf* **faire de la p.** to be paranoid

paranoïa [paranɔja] *nf* paranoia

paranoïaque [paranɔjak] *adj & nmf* paranoiac

paranormal, -e, -aux, -ales [paranɔrmal, -o] *adj* paranormal

parapente [parapãt] *nm (activité)* paragliding; *(parachute)* paraglider; **faire du p.** to go paragliding

parapet [parapɛ] *nm* parapet

paraphe [paraf] *nm* initials

parapher [parafe] *vt* to initial

paraphrase [parafraz] *nf* paraphrase

paraphraser [parafraze] *vt* to paraphrase

paraplégie [parapleʒi] *nf* paraplegia

paraplégique [parapleʒik] *adj & nmf* paraplegic

parapluie [paraplɥi] *nm* umbrella

parapsychologie [parapsikɔlɔʒi] *nf* parapsychology

parascolaire [paraskɔlɛr] *adj* extra-curricular

parasite [parazit] **1** *nm aussi Fig* parasite; **parasites** *(à la radio)* interference
2 *adj (insecte, plante)* parasitic

parasol [parasɔl] *nm* parasol, sunshade; *(de plage)* beach umbrella

paratonnerre [paratɔnɛr] *nm* lightning conductor

paravent [paravã] *nm aussi Fig* screen; *Fig* **servir de p. à qch** to be a screen for sth

parbleu [parblø] *exclam Vieilli* good Lord!; *(évidemment)* good Lord, yes!

parc [park] *nm* (a) *(jardin)* park; *(d'un château)* grounds; **p. naturel** nature reserve; **p. zoologique** zoo (b) *(enclos)* *(pour enfant)* playpen; **p. d'attractions** theme park; **p. des expositions** exhibition centre; **p. à huîtres** oyster bed; **p. de stationnement** *Br* car park, *Am* parking lot (c) *(ensemble)* **le p. automobile français** the number of cars in France

parcelle [parsɛl] *nf* small piece; **p. de terrain** plot; *Fig* **pas la moindre p. d'intelligence** not an ounce of intelligence

parce que [parskə] *conj* because; **ce n'est pas parce qu'il fait froid qu'on doit rester à la maison** just because it's cold doesn't mean we have to stay in; **pourquoi ne viens-tu pas? – p.** why aren't you coming? – (just) because

parchemin [parʃəmɛ̃] nm parchment

parcimonie [parsimɔni] nf thrift; **avec p.** sparingly

parcimonieux, -euse [parsimɔnjø, -øz] adj thrifty

parcmètre [parkmɛtr] nm (parking) meter

parcourir [22] [parkurir] vt (a) (lieu) to walk round; (pays) to travel through; (rues) to walk through; (mer) to sail; **p. un lieu à la recherche de qn** to scour a place for sb; **p. la terre entière pour retrouver qn** to travel the world to find sb; **p. une distance de plusieurs kilomètres** to cover a distance of several kilometres; **il reste 2 mètres à p.** there are 2 kilometres to go; Fig **un frisson me parcourut l'échine** ou **le dos** a shiver ran down my spine; Fig **un murmure a parcouru la foule** a murmur ran through the crowd (b) (regarder) (texte, journal) to skim through; Ordinat to scroll through; **p. qch des yeux** ou **du regard** to glance at sth

parcours [parkur] nm (de défilé, de bus) route; (circuit automobile) circuit; (d'équitation, de golf, d'un fleuve) course; Mil **le p. du combattant** the assault course; **faire un p. sans faute** (cheval) to have a clear round; Fig (dans une carrière) to have a copybook career; **refaire le p. pour retrouver qch** to retrace one's steps to find sth; **elle fait plusieurs fois le p. dans la journée** she does the journey several times a day

par-delà [pardəla] prép & adv beyond

par-derrière [pardɛrjɛr] 1 prép behind
2 adv (attaquer) from behind; (se boutonner) at the back; **passer p.** to go in the back door; Fig **dire des choses de qn p.** to talk about sb behind his/her back

par-dessous [pardəsu] 1 prép under, underneath
2 adv underneath

pardessus [pardəsy] nm overcoat

par-dessus [pardəsy] 1 prép over; **p. tout** above all
2 adv over

par-devant [pardəvɑ̃] 1 prép Jur **acte signé p. notaire** deed signed in the presence of a lawyer
2 adv (attaquer) from the front; (se boutonner) at the front

pardi [pardi] exclam Fam of course!

pardon [pardɔ̃] nm (a) (grâce) forgiveness; **accorder p. à qn** to forgive sb; **demander p. à qn** to apologize to sb; **(je vous demande) p.!** (pour passer) excuse me!; (pour s'excuser) (I'm) sorry!; **(je vous demande) p.?** (je n'ai pas entendu) pardon?; (je suis indigné) I beg your pardon!; Fam **elle est intelligente, mais sa fille, p.!** she's pretty clever but you should see her daughter! (b) Rel **le Grand P.** the Day of Atonement, Yom Kippur

pardonnable [pardɔnabl] adj forgivable, excusable

pardonner [pardɔne] 1 vt to forgive; **p. qch à qn** to forgive sb sth; **elle m'a pardonné d'avoir oublié** she forgave me for forgetting; **pour me/te/etc faire p.** to make it up; **tu es tout pardonné** I'll let you off
2 vi (a) (oublier une faute) to forgive (b) **ça ne pardonne pas** it's fatal
3 **se pardonner** vpr **je ne me le pardonnerai jamais** I'll never forgive myself

paré, -e [pare] adj (a) (prêt) prepared (**contre** for) (b) (revêtu) adorned (**de** with)

pare-avalanches [paravalɑ̃ʃ] nm inv avalanche barrier

pare-balles [parbal] adj inv bullet-proof

pare-boue [parbu] nm inv mudflap

pare-brise [parbriz] nm inv Br windscreen, Am windshield

pare-chocs [parʃɔk] nm inv bumper

pare-feu [parfø] nm inv (a) (dans la forêt) fire-break (b) (de cheminée) fireguard

pareil, -eille [parɛj] 1 adj (a) (identique) the same; **elles sont presque pareilles** they're almost the same; **ce n'est pas p.** it's not the same (thing); Litt **à nul autre p.** unparalleled; **p. que** ou **à** the same as, just like; Fam **si ça ne te plaît pas, c'est p.** if you don't like it, too bad (b) (tel) such; **en p. cas** in such cases; **dans des moments pareils** at times like these; **mais je n'ai jamais dit une chose pareille!** but I never said any such thing!
2 nm,f **elle n'a pas sa pareille** she's second to none; **sans p.** unparalleled; **mes pareils** my equals
3 nf **rendre la pareille à qn** (se venger de qn) to get one's own back on sb, to pay sb back; (rendre un service à qn) to repay sb
4 nm Fam **c'est du p. au même** it's six of one and half a dozen of the other
5 adv Fam **faire p.** to do the same (thing)

pareillement [parɛjmɑ̃] adv (a) (de la même manière) in a similar manner, in the same way (b) (aussi) likewise

parement [parmɑ̃] nm (de manche, de col) facing

parent, -e [parɑ̃, -ɑ̃t] 1 adj related
2 nm,f (tante, oncle, cousin) relative, relation
3 nmpl **parents** (père et mère) parents; **parents adoptifs** adoptive parents; **parents biologiques** biological parents

parental, -e, -aux, -ales [parɑ̃tal, -o] adj parental

parenté [parɑ̃te] nf relationship; **avoir un lien de p. avec qn** to be related to sb

parenthèse [parɑ̃tɛz] nf bracket, parenthesis; Fig (dans un discours) digression; **entre parenthèses** in brackets

parer¹ [pare] 1 vt (a) aussi Fig (éviter) to parry (b) (protéger) to protect (**contre** against)
2 **parer à** vt ind (accident) to prevent; (problème) to avoid; **p. au plus pressé** to attend to the most urgent things first

parer² [pare] Litt 1 vt (vêtir) to adorn (**de** with); Fig **p. qn de toutes les vertus** to endow sb with every virtue
2 **se parer** vpr to get dressed up (**de** in)

pare-soleil [parsɔlɛj] nm inv (de voiture) sun visor

paresse [parɛs] nf (a) (indolence) laziness; **d'une p. incroyable** incredibly lazy (b) (lenteur) laziness; **p. intellectuelle** laziness of mind; **p. intestinale** sluggishness of the bowels

paresser [parɛse] vi to laze about or around

paresseux, -euse [parɛsø, -øz] 1 adj (a) (nonchalant) lazy (b) (intestin) sluggish
2 nm,f lazy person
3 nm (animal) sloth

parfaire [36] [parfɛr] vt (travail) to finish off, to complete; (technique) to perfect

parfait, -e [parfɛ, -ɛt] 1 adj (a) (sans fautes) perfect (b) (complet) (bonheur) perfect, complete; (ressemblance) exact; Fam **un p. imbécile** an utter fool
2 nm **p. au café** coffee parfait

parfaitement [parfɛtmɑ̃] adv (a) (sans fautes) perfectly; **parler p. l'anglais** to speak perfect English (b) (complètement) completely, thoroughly; (compréhensible, clair, heureux) perfectly; **ça m'est p. égal** it makes absolutely no difference to me; **j'ai p. conscience de...** I'm perfectly aware of... (c) (tout à fait) vous affirmez **que vous l'avez vu? – p.!** you say you saw it? – I certainly did!

parfois [parfwa] adv sometimes

parfum [parfœ̃] *nm* (a) *(essences)* perfume (b) *(senteur)* *(d'une fleur)* fragrance, scent; *(d'un vin)* bouquet; Fig **un p. de scandale** a whiff of scandal (c) *(de glace, de yaourt)* flavour (d) Fam **être au p.** to be in the know; **mettre qn au p.** to fill sb in

parfumer [parfyme] 1 *vt* (a) *(embaumer)* to scent (b) *(gâteau, glace)* to flavour (à with) (c) *(mouchoir)* to scent; **je vous parfume?** *(à une cliente)* would you like to try some perfume?
2 **se parfumer** *vpr* to put perfume on

parfumerie [parfymri] *nf (magasin)* perfumery; *(rayon)* perfume counter; *(produits)* perfumes; *(industrie)* perfume industry

parfumeur, -euse [parfymœr, -øz] *nm,f* perfumer

pari [pari] *nm* bet; **faire un p. avec qn** to make a bet with sb; **p. mutuel** Br ≃ tote, Am ≃ pari-mutuel

paria [parja] *nm Fig* pariah, (social) outcast

parier [66] [parje] 1 *vt* to bet; **il y a fort** *ou* **gros à p. que...** the odds are that...; **je te parie qu'elle viendra** I bet you she'll come; **je l'aurais parié** I thought as much
2 *vi* to bet; **p. avec qn/sur qch** to bet with sb/on sth; **je te dis qu'elle viendra – on parie?** she'll come I tell you – (do you) want a bet?

parieur, -euse [parjœr, -øz] *nm,f* better

parigot, -e [parigo, -ɔt] Fam 1 *adj* Parisian
2 *nm,f* **P.** Parisian

Paris [pari] *n* Paris

parisien, -enne [parizjɛ̃, -ɛn] 1 *adj* Parisian
2 *nm,f* **P.** Parisian

parité [parite] *nf aussi Ordinat* parity

parjure [parʒyr] 1 *nm (action)* perjury
2 *nmf (personne)* perjurer
3 *adj* treacherous

parjurer [parʒyre] **se parjurer** *vpr* to perjure oneself

parka [parka] *nm ou nf* parka

parking [parkiŋ] *nm Br* car park, *Am* parking lot; **p. payant** *Br* ≃ pay-and-display car park

parlant, -e [parlɑ̃, -ɑ̃t] *adj (geste)* eloquent, meaningful; *(description)* vivid

parlé, -e [parle] *adj* **le français p.** spoken French; **journal p.** news (programme)

parlement [parləmɑ̃] *nm* **le P.** Parliament; **le P. européen** the European Parliament

parlementaire [parləmɑ̃tɛr] 1 *adj* parliamentary
2 *nmf* member of parliament, *Am* Congressman, f Congresswoman

parlementarisme [parləmɑ̃tarism] *nm* parliamentary government

parlementer [parləmɑ̃te] *vi* to negotiate *(avec* with)

parler¹ [parle] 1 *vi* (a) *(s'exprimer)* to speak, to talk; *(avouer)* to talk; **elle parle bien** *(oratrice)* she's a good speaker; **p. par signes** to use sign language; **parlez-vous sérieusement?** are you serious?; **les résultats/faits parlent d'eux-mêmes** the results/facts speak for themselves; **p. pour ne rien dire** to talk for the sake of talking; **c'est comme si je parlais à un mur** it's like talking to a brick wall; **p. de qn/qch (à qn)** to talk (to sb) about sb/sth; **p. de** *(sujet: livre, film)* to be about; **on m'a beaucoup parlé de vous** I've heard a lot about you; **n'en parlons plus** let's drop the subject; **faire p. de soi** to be talked about; **p. de faire qch** to talk about doing sth
(b) *(locutions)* **je sais de quoi je parle** I know what I'm talking about; Fam **tu peux p.!** YOU can talk!; Fam **parle**

pour toi! speak for yourself!; Fam **tu parles!** you bet!; Fam **tu parles d'une occasion/d'un idiot!** talk about an opportunity/an idiot!; Fam **ses ambitions? parlons-en!** his ambitions? who are you kidding? *or* you've got to be joking!; Fam **ne m'en parlez pas!** you're telling me!; **sans p. de...** not to mention...; **trouver à qui p.** to get more than one bargains for
2 *vt (langue)* to speak; **p. (le) français** to speak French; **ici on parle anglais** *(dans un magasin)* English spoken; **p. chiffons/cuisine** to talk about clothes/cooking; **p. affaires/politique** to talk business/politics
3 **se parler** *vpr* (a) *(langue)* to be spoken
(b) *(l'un à l'autre)* to talk to each other

parler² *nm* speech; *(régional)* dialect; **il a un p. très rude** he has a very abrupt way of speaking

parleur, -euse [parlœr, -øz] *nm,f Péj* **beau p.** smooth talker

parloir [parlwar] *nm* visiting room

parlot(t)e [parlɔt] *nf Fam* chat

Parme [parm] *n* Parma

parmesan [parməzɑ̃] *nm* Parmesan (cheese)

parmi [parmi] *prép* among; **choisir p. plusieurs possibilités** to choose from several possibilities; **nous espérons vous revoir p. nous** we hope to see you back with us

parodie [parɔdi] *nf* parody

parodier [66] [parɔdje] *vt* to parody

parodique [parɔdik] *adj* parodic

paroi [parwa] *nf* (a) *(d'une falaise, d'une montagne)* face (b) *(d'une pièce, d'une caverne)* wall; *(d'un tunnel, de l'estomac)* lining

paroisse [parwas] *nf* parish

paroissial, -e, -aux, -ales [parwasjal, -o] *adj* parish

paroissien, -enne [parwasjɛ̃, -ɛn] *nm,f* parishioner

parole [parɔl] *nf* (a) *(mot)* word; **paroles** *(de chanson)* lyrics, words; **histoire sans paroles** short silent film; **une p. blessante** a hurtful remark; *Ironique* **de belles paroles** fine words; **ce ne sont que des paroles en l'air** they're just empty threats (b) Fig *(engagement)* promise, word; **tenir p.** to keep one's promise *or* word; **manquer à sa p.** to break one's promise *or* word; **il n'a qu'une p.** he's a man of his word; **donner sa p. (d'honneur) à qn que...** to give sb one's word that...; **(ma) p. d'honneur!** I give you my word! (c) **la p.** *(faculté de parler)* speech; *(diction)* delivery; **adresser la p. à qn** to speak to sb; **couper la p. à qn** to interrupt sb; **prendre la p.** to speak; **laisser la p. à qn** to let sb speak; **la p. est à M. Renant, M. Renant a la p.** Mr Renant has the floor; **la p. est d'argent mais le silence est d'or** speech is silver, silence is golden (d) *(aux cartes)* **p.!** pass!; *(au bridge)* no bid!

parolier, -ère [parɔlje, -ɛr] *nm,f* lyricist

paroxysme [parɔksism] *nm* **atteindre son p.** to reach its peak *or* climax; **être au p. de la joie** to be ecstatically happy

parpaing [parpɛ̃] *nm* breeze block

parquer [parke] *vt (bétail)* to pen in; *(prisonniers)* to confine

parquet [parke] *nm* (a) *(sol)* wooden floor; *(avec des motifs)* parquet floor (b) *Jur* public prosecutor's office

parrain [parɛ̃] *nm (pour un baptême, d'une organisation criminelle)* godfather; *(d'un sportif, d'un membre d'un club)* sponsor

parrainer [parene] *vt (sportif, nouveau membre)* to sponsor

parricide [parisid] **1** *adj* parricidal
   2 *nmf & nm* parricide

pars *voir* **partir**

parsemer [46] [parsəme] *vt* to scatter (**de** with)

part¹ [par] *voir* **partir**

part² *nf* (a) *(partie d'un tout)* part; *(d'un marché, de bénéfices, d'un héritage)* share; *(d'un gâteau, d'une pizza)* slice; **diviser qch en parts égales** to divide sth into equal parts; **ils viennent pour une bonne p. des environs de Lille** a good many of them come from the Lille area; **à p. entière** fully-fledged; **pour ma p.** personally, as for me; **faire la p. du feu** to cut one's losses; **la p. du lion** the lion's share
   (b) *(participation)* share, part; **prendre p. à qch** to take part in sth; *(joie, douleur)* to share sth; **faire p. de qch à qn** to inform sb of sth, to tell sb about sth; **faire la p. des choses** to get things in perspective
   (c) *(côté)* **de p. et d'autre** on both sides; **de p. en p.** right through; **d'une p...., d'autre p....** on the one hand..., on the other hand...; **de toutes parts** on all sides
   (d) **de la p. de qn** *(en provenance de)* from sb; *(à la place de)* on sb's behalf; **c'est de la p. de qui?** *(au téléphone)* who's calling?; **ce serait bien aimable de votre p.** that would be very kind of you; **cela m'étonne de sa p.** that surprises me, coming from him/her
   (e) *(locutions)* **prendre qn à p.** to take sb aside; **à p. lui/ quelques erreurs** apart from him/a few mistakes; **c'est un cas à p.** he's a special case; *Fam* **à p. que...** apart from the fact that...

partage [partaʒ] *nm* (a) *(action)* *(d'une fortune, d'un domaine)* dividing up; *(de tâches, de responsabilités)* sharing out; **faire le p. de qch** to divide sth up; **sans p.** *(amour)* total; *Ordinat* **p. d'imprimantes** printer sharing (b) *(lot)* **recevoir qch en p.** to be left sth *(in a will)*

partagé, -e [partaʒe] *adj* (a) *(entre plusieurs personnes)* shared; *(amour)* mutual; *Ordinat* **travail en temps p.** timesharing (b) *(indécis)* **être p.** to be torn; **les avis sont partagés** opinions are divided

partager [45] [partaʒe] **1** *vt* (a) *(répartir)* to divide (up); **p. son temps entre** to divide one's time between; **p. qch en deux** to divide sth in two (b) *(avoir en commun)* to share *(avec* with); **p. l'avis de qn** to share sb's opinion; **p. la joie de qn** to share (in) sb's joy
   2 *vi* to share
   3 se partager *vpr* (a) *(se répartir)* **ils se le sont partagé** they shared it between them (b) *(partager son temps)* to divide one's time *(entre* between)

partageur, -euse [partaʒœr, -øz] *adj* willing to share

partance [partɑ̃s] *nf* **en p.** about to depart; **en p. pour Bordeaux** for Bordeaux

partant¹ [partɑ̃] *conj Litt* consequently, therefore

partant², -e [partɑ̃, -ɑ̃t] **1** *adj Fam* **je suis p.!** count me in!
   2 *nm,f (coureur, cheval)* starter

partenaire [partənɛr] *nmf* partner; **les partenaires sociaux** workers and management

partenariat [partənarja] *nm* partnership

parterre [partɛr] *nm* (a) *(de fleurs)* flower bed; *(plate-bande)* border (b) *(au théâtre) Br* stalls, *Am* orchestra (c) *Fam (sol)* floor

parti¹ [parti] *nm* (a) *(camp)* side; **prendre le p. de qn** to take sb's side; **prendre p. pour qn** to side with sb; **prendre p. contre qn** to take sides against sb (b) **p. (politique)** (political) party; **le P. (communiste)** the Communist Party (c) *(personne)* **un beau p.** a good match (d) *(choix)* **prendre le p. de faire qch** to make up one's mind to do sth; **en prendre son p.** to resign oneself to the fact (e) *(profit)* **tirer p. de qch** to make good use of sth (f) **p. pris** bias

parti², -e *adj Fam (ivre)* tight; *(drogué)* high

partial, -e, -aux, -ales [parsjal, -o] *adj* biased

partialement [parsjalmɑ̃] *adv* in a biased way

partialité [parsjalite] *nf* bias *(envers/contre* in favour of/against)

participant, -e [partisipɑ̃, -ɑ̃t] **1** *adj* participating
   2 *nm,f (personne présente)* participant *(à* in); *(sportif)* competitor

participation [partisipasjɔ̃] *nf* (a) *(collaboration, en classe)* participation *(à* in); *(argent)* contribution *(à* towards); *(nombre de votants)* turnout *(à* at); **avec la p. de Jean Martin (dans le rôle de...)** with Jean Martin (as...); **p. aux frais** contribution towards costs; **p. aux bénéfices** profit-sharing (b) *Fin* interest *(à* in)

participe [partisip] *nm Gram* participle

participer [partisipe] **participer à** *vt ind* (a) *(assister à)* to take part in, to participate in; *(spectacle)* to appear in; **p. activement à qch** to take an active part in sth (b) *(financièrement)* to contribute to (c) **p. aux bénéfices** to share in the profits

particulariser [partikylarize] *vt* to particularize

particularisme [partikylarism] *nm* particularism

particularité [partikylarite] *nf* distinctive feature

particule [partikyl] *nf* particle

particulier, -ère [partikylje, -er] **1** *adj* (a) *(propre)* characteristic *(à* of) (b) *(remarquable)* unusual, exceptional; *(soin, intérêt)* particular (c) *Péj (bizarre)* peculiar (d) *(privé)* *(maison, voiture)* private; *(salle de bain)* en suite (e) **en p.** *(spécialement)* in particular; *(en privé)* in private
   2 *nm (individu)* private individual; **un simple p.** an ordinary person

particulièrement [partikyljɛrmɑ̃] *adv* particularly; **j'attire tout p. votre attention sur...** I would particularly like to draw your attention to...

partie [parti] *nf* (a) *(morceau)* part; **la plus grande p. de qch** the greatest part of sth; **en p.** partly, in part; **en grande** *ou* **majeure p.** for the most part; **être en p. remboursé** to be partially refunded; **faire p. de qch** to be part of sth; *Fam* **faire p. des meubles** to be part of the furniture; **les parties communes** the communal areas; *Fam* **les parties** the private parts; **les parties génitales** the genitals
   (b) *(domaine)* field, subject; **je ne suis pas de la p.** that's not my field
   (c) *(d'un chanteur, d'un instrument)* part
   (d) *(fête)* party; **ce n'est pas une p. de plaisir!** it's not my idea of fun!; **p. de campagne** day in the country; **p. de chasse** shooting party; *Fam* **p. de jambes en l'air** roll in the hay; *Can* **p. de sucre** sugaring-off party
   (e) *(jeu)* game; **faire une p. de cartes** to have a game of cards; *Fig* **ce n'est que p. remise** we'll do it another time
   (f) *Jur* party; **la p. adverse** the other side; **être p. prenante** to be an interested party; **p. civile** plaintiff; **se constituer** *ou* **se porter p. civile** to institute proceedings *(in a civil case)*
   (g) *(locutions)* **avoir affaire à forte p.** to have a tough

opponent on one's hands; **prendre qn à p.** to take sb to task; **avoir p. liée avec qn** to be hand in glove with sb

partiel, -elle [parsjɛl] **1** adj partial; **élection partielle** by-election; **travailler à temps p.** to work part-time

2 nm Univ end-of-term exam

3 nf **partielle** by-election

partiellement [parsjɛlmɑ̃] adv partially

partir [64a] [partir] vi (aux **être**) **(a)** (s'en aller) to go, to leave; (commencer un voyage) to set off; (sans destination particulière) to go off; (bateau, avion) to leave; (moteur) to start; (fusil, pétard) to go off; Euph (mourir) to pass away; **p. en vacances** to go (away) on holiday; **p. en promenade** to go for a stroll; **p. faire ses courses** to go out shopping; **p. en courant** to run off; **p. de rien** to start from nothing; **p. d'un éclat de rire** to burst out laughing; **être bien/mal parti** to have got off to a good/bad start; **faire p.** (fusil) to fire; (feux d'artifice) to let off; (moteur) to start; Fam **c'est parti, mon kiki!** here we go!

(b) (disparaître) (douleur, bleu) to go, to disappear; (tache) to come out; (peinture, vernis) to come off; **faire p. une tache** to get a stain out

(c) (sortir) (sujet: route, chemin) to start from; **en partant du principe que...** assuming that...; **ça partait d'un bon sentiment** the thought was there; **et, partant de là,...** on that assumption,...

(d) **à p. du village** from the village; **à p. d'aujourd'hui** from today (onwards); **à p. de maintenant** from now on; **à p. de 200 francs** from 200 francs (upwards)

partisan, -e [partizɑ̃, -an] nm **(a)** (fidèle) supporter **(b)** (combattant) partisan

2 adj (esprit) partisan; **querelles partisanes** sectarian quarrels; **être p. de qch/de faire qch** to be in favour of sth/of doing sth

partitif, -ive [partitif, -iv] adj & nm Gram partitive

partition [partisjɔ̃] nf (musique) score

partout [partu] adv **(a)** (en tous lieux) everywhere; **p. où je vais** everywhere I go; **un peu p.** all over the place; **j'ai mal p.** I'm aching all over; **un** **3 buts p.** (au football) 3 all; 15/30 **p.** (au tennis) 15/30 all; **40 p.** (au tennis) deuce

partouze [partuz] nf très Fam orgy

paru, -e voir **paraître**

parure [paryr] nf (ensemble) set; **p. de lit** set of bed linen

parution [parysjɔ̃] nf appearance, publication

parvenir [70] [parvənir] parvenir à vt ind (aux **être**) **(a)** (atteindre) (endroit, personne) to reach; **p. à ses fins** to achieve one's ends; **faire p. qch à qn** to send sth to sb **(b)** (réussir) **p. à faire qch** to manage to do sth

parvenu, -e [parvəny] nm, f Péj upstart

parvis [parvi] nm square (in front of a church)

pas¹ [pɑ] nm **(a)** (enjambée, de danse) step; (allure) pace; **p. à p.** step by step; **p. de loup** stealthily; **marcher à grands p.** to stride along; **marcher à petits p.** to toddle along; **marcher d'un p. hésitant** to walk hesitantly; **faire un faux p.** to trip; Fig to make a faux pas; **faire un p. (vers)** to take a step (towards); **faire un p. en avant/en arrière** to (take a) step forward/back; **faire les cent p.** to pace up and down; Fig **faire le premier p.** to take the first step; **marcher au p.** (soldat) to march in step; **rouler au p.** (en voiture) to crawl along; **ils habitent à deux p. d'ici** they live a few yards away; **j'y vais de ce p.** I'll be right away; **p. de deux** pas de deux; **p. de course** ou **gymnastique** jog trot

(b) (trace) footprint; **revenir** ou **retourner sur ses p.** to retrace one's steps

(c) (seuil) **p. de la porte** doorstep

(d) (passage) **le p. de Calais** the Straits of Dover

(e) (de vis, d'hélice) pitch

(f) (locutions) **prendre le p. sur qch** to take precedence over sth; **tirer qn d'un mauvais p.** to get sb out of a tight corner

pas² adv not; **je ne sais p.** I don't know; **je ne l'ai p. vue** I haven't seen her; **il est difficile de ne p. le lui dire** it's difficult not to tell him; **qu'elle vienne ou p.** whether she comes or not; **viendra? viendra p.?** will she come or won't she?; **p. mal** not bad; **une explication p.** claire an unclear explanation; **p. un n'a réagi** not one of them reacted; **p. de sucre/lecteurs** no sugar/readers; **p. du tout** not at all

pascal¹, -e, -als ou **-aux, -ales** [paskal, -o] adj Easter; (agneau) paschal

pascal², -als nm **(a)** Phys pascal **(b)** Fam (billet) 500-franc note

passable [pasabl] adj passable, fair

passablement [pasabləmɑ̃] adv fairly

passade [pasad] nf passing fancy

passage [pasaʒ] nm **(a)** (d'une route, d'une rivière) crossing; (d'un lieu) passing; **on sourit sur son p.** people smile as he goes by; **les soldats ont tout détruit sur leur p.** the soldiers destroyed everything in their path; **être de p. dans une ville** to be passing through a town; Fig **et au p., je te ferai remarquer que...** and incidentally, let me draw your attention to the fact that...; Fam **p. à tabac** beating up; Ordinat **p. automatique à la ligne suivante** wordwrap

(b) (chemin) passage; (ruelle) alley(way); (galerie commerciale) (shopping) arcade; **p. clouté** Br pedestrian crossing, Am crosswalk; **p. à niveau** Br level crossing, Am grade crossing; **p. pour piétons** Br pedestrian crossing, Am crosswalk; (souterrain) pedestrian subway; **p. souterrain** underpass

(c) (extrait) passage

(d) (moment) **p. nuageux/pluvieux** cloudy/rainy spell; Fam **avoir un p. à vide** to go through a bad patch

passager, -ère [pasaʒe, -er] **1** adj momentary; **des pluies passagères** occasional showers; **ils ont eu une petite brouille passagère** they fell out for a while

2 nm, f passenger; **p. clandestin** stowaway

passant¹ [pasɑ̃] nm (de ceinture) loop

passant², -e [pasɑ̃, -ɑ̃t] **1** adj (rue) busy

2 nm, f passer-by

passation [pasasjɔ̃] nf (d'un accord) signing; **p. de pouvoirs** transfer of power

passe¹ [pas] nf **(a)** (au football) pass; **p. en avant/en retrait** forward/back pass **(b)** (d'une prostituée) trick; **hôtel de p.** = hotel used by prostitutes and their clients; **maison de p.** brothel **(c)** (à la roulette) passe (any number above 18) **(d)** Fig **être en p. de faire qch** to be on the way to doing sth; **être dans une mauvaise p.** to be going through a bad patch

passe² nm Fam (clef) master key

passé, -e [pase] **1** adj **(a)** (écoulé) (temps) past; **la semaine passée** last week; **il est quatre heures passées** it's gone ou after four; **elle a quarante ans passés** she's over forty **(b)** (terminé) over; **penser à son enfance passée** to think about one's childhood **(c)** (décoloré) faded **(d)** **p. de mode** out of fashion

2 nm (a) (période) **le p.** the past; **par le p.** in the past; **tout ça, c'est du p.** that's all in the past **(b)** Gram past (tense); **p. antérieur** past anterior; **p. composé** perfect (tense); **p. simple** preterite, past historic; **au p.** in the past

(tense)

3 *prép* after

passe-droit (*pl* **passe-droits**) [pasdrwa] *nm* privilege

passéiste [paseist] *Péj* **1** *adj* living in the past
2 *nmf* person who lives in the past

passe-montagne (*pl* **passe-montagnes**) [pasmɔtaɲ] *nm* balaclava (helmet)

passe-partout [paspartu] **1** *nm inv* master key
2 *adj inv* all-purpose

passe-plat (*pl* **passe-plats**) [paspla] *nm* serving hatch

passeport [paspɔr] *nm aussi Fig* passport

passer [pase] **1** *vi* (*aux être*) (a) (*se déplacer*) to go past; **p. devant qn/qch** to go past sb/sth; **laisser p. qn** to let sb past; (*dans une queue*) to let sb in; **je ne peux pas p.** I can't get by or past; **p. sur les détails** to skip the details; **elle nous a fait p. dans son bureau** she showed us into her office; **mais où est-il passé?** where's he/it got to?; **dire qch en passant** to mention sth in passing; **soit dit en passant** incidentally

(b) (*évoluer*) **p. de qch à qch** to go from sth to sth; **p. dans la classe supérieure** to move up a class; **p. en première/seconde** (*en voiture*) to change into first/second; **p. capitaine** to be promoted to captain

(c) (*traverser*) **p. par le village/Paris** to go through the village/Paris; **par où est -il passé?** which way did he go?; **laisser p. qch** (*lumière, air*) to let sth in

(d) (*apparaître*) **p. à la radio/télévision** to be on the radio/television; **p. au cinéma** to be on at the cinema

(e) (*aller*) **je suis passé chez elle/à la boucherie** I went round to her house/to the butcher's; **le facteur est déjà passé** the postman's already been; **je ne fais que p.** I'm not staying

(f) (*disparaître*) to go; **laisser p. qch** (*occasion*) to pass up sth; (*erreur*) to miss sth; **le plus dur est passé** the worst is over; (*douleur*) **j'avais mal à la tête mais ça m'a passé** I had a headache but it's gone away; **il était amoureux d'elle mais ça lui a passé** he was in love with her but he's got over it

(g) (*année, temps*) to pass, to go by

(h) (*être considéré*) **p. pour un génie** to be considered a genius; **faire p. qn pour** to pass sb off as

(i) (*être adopté*) (*loi, proposition*) to be passed, to go through

(j) **passe!** (*aux cartes*) pass!

(k) *Fam* **il a bien failli y p.** (*mourir*) he nearly didn't make it; **toute sa fortune y est passée** she spent her entire fortune on it

2 *vt* (*aux avoir*) (a) (*pont, rivière, frontière*) to go over; (*porte, douane*) to go through; **il a passé la soixantaine** he's in his sixties

(b) (*donner*) (*ballon, témoin*) to pass; **p. qch à qn** to pass or give sth to sb; *Fam* **p. son rhume à qn** to give sb one's cold; **p. la parole à qn** to hand over to sb; **pourriez-vous me la p.?** (*au téléphone*) could you put me through to her?

(c) (*mettre*) (*vêtement*) to slip on; **p. un coup d'éponge sur qch** to give sth a sponge; **p. la tête par la fenêtre** to lean one's head out of the window; **p. le doigt sur qch** to run one's finger over sth; **p. la seconde/troisième** (*en voiture*) to change into second/third; *Fam* **qu'est-ce qu'il va nous p.!** he's going to make us wish we'd never been born!

(d) (*film*) to show; (*disque*) to play; (*vidéo*) to put on

(e) (*temps, vacances*) to spend; **p. son temps à faire qch** to spend one's time doing sth; **pour p. le temps** to pass the time

(f) (*pardonner*) **elle lui passe tout** she lets him get away

with everything

(g) (*omettre*) to leave out; **p. son tour** to miss a turn; **j'en passe et des meilleures** and that's not the half of it

(h) (*examen*) to take or sit; (*visite médicale*) to have; **faire p. un examen à qn** to take sb for an exam

(i) (*accord, contrat*) to enter into, to sign; (*commande*) to place (à with)

(j) (*liquide*) to strain; (*café*) to filter

3 se passer *vpr* (a) (*se produire*) to happen; **que se passe-t-il?, qu'est-ce qui se passe?** what's happening?; **ça s'est bien passé** it went well; **l'histoire se passe en 1900/en Normandie** the story takes place in 1900/in Normandy; *Fam* **ça ne se passera pas comme ça!** I'm not having it!

(b) (*mettre*) **se p. la main dans les cheveux** to run one's fingers through one's hair; **se p. de l'eau sur la figure** to splash one's face with water

4 se passer de *vt ind* (*se priver de*) to do without

passereau, -x [pasro] *nm* passerine

passerelle [pasrɛl] *nf* (a) (*au-dessus d'une rue, d'un ruisseau*) footbridge (b) (*de navire*) bridge; **p. de débarquement** *ou* **d'embarquement** (*de navire*) gangway; (*d'avion*) (*amovible*) steps (c) *Fig* (*intermédiaire*) link (d) *Ordinat* **p. (de connexion)** (*avec*) gateway (to)

passe-temps [pastɑ̃] *nm inv* pastime

passe-thé [paste] *nm inv* tea-strainer

passeur, -euse [pasœr, -øz] *nm,f* (*de bac*) ferryman, f ferrywoman; (*de frontière*) = person who helps wanted people across the border to safety

passible [pasibl] *adj* liable (**de** to)

passif, -ive [pasif, -iv] **1** *adj* passive
2 *nm* (a) *Gram* passive; **au p.** in the passive (b) *Fin* liabilities

passion [pasjɔ̃] *nf* (a) (*sentiment dévorant*) passion; **avoir une p. pour qn/qch** to have a passion for sb/sth; **vivre une p.** to have a passionate love affair; **avec p.** passionately (b) *Rel* **la P. selon saint Jean** the St John Passion

passionnant, -e [pasjɔnɑ̃, -ɑ̃t] *adj* fascinating

passionné, -e [pasjɔne] **1** *adj* passionate; **p. de qch** extremely keen on sth
2 *nm,f* enthusiast; **un p. de football** a football enthusiast

passionnel, -elle [pasjɔnɛl] *adj* passionate

passionnément [pasjɔnemɑ̃] *adv* passionately

passionner [pasjɔne] **1** *vt* (*sujet: livre, film*) to fascinate; **son métier la passionne** she finds her job fascinating
2 se passionner *vpr* **se p. pour qch** to have a passion for sth

passivement [pasivmɑ̃] *adv* passively

passivité [pasivite] *nf* passivity, passiveness

passoire [paswar] *nf* (*avec un grillage*) sieve; (*avec de petits trous*) colander

pastel [pastɛl] *nm & adj inv* pastel

pastèque [pastɛk] *nf* watermelon; *Fam* **j'ai la tête comme une p.** my head's throbbing

pasteur [pastœr] *nm* (a) *Litt* (*berger*) shepherd (b) (*religieux*) pastor, minister

pasteurisation [pastœrizasjɔ̃] *nf* pasteurization

pasteuriser [pastœrize] *vt* to pasteurize

pastiche [pastiʃ] *nm* pastiche

pastille [pastij] *nf (bonbon mou)* pastille; *(médicament)* lozenge; **p. contre la toux** cough sweet *or* lozenge; **p. de menthe** mint

pastis [pastis] *nm* (a) *(boisson)* pastis (b) *Fam* **être dans le p.** to be in a fix

pastoral, -e, -aux, -ales [pastɔral, -o] 1 *adj* pastoral 2 *nf* **pastorale** *(musique)* pastorale

patachon [pataʃɔ̃] *nm Fam* **mener une vie de p.** to lead a wild life

Patagonie [patagɔni] *nf* **la P.** Patagonia

patapouf [patapuf] 1 *exclam* flop! 2 *nm (langage enfantin)* **gros p.** fatty

pataquès [patakɛs] *nm (faute de langage)* malapropism

patate [patat] *nf Fam (pomme de terre)* spud; *Fig (imbécile)* clot; *Fig* **en avoir gros sur la p.** to be down in the mouth

patati [patati] *exclam Fam* **et p. et patata** and so on and so forth

patatras [patatra] *exclam Fam* crash!

pataud, -e [pato, -od] *adj Fam* clumsy

Pataugas® [patogas] *nm* canvas walking boot

pataugeoire [patoʒwar] *nf* paddling pool

patauger [45] [patoʒe] *vi (s'embourber)* to squelch (**dans** in); *(barboter)* to splash about (**dans** in); *Fam (s'embrouiller)* to flounder (**dans** in)

pâte [pɑt] *nf* 1 (a) *(pour une tarte)* pastry; *(pour le pain)* dough; *(pour un gâteau)* mixture; **p. brisée** shortcrust pastry; **p. à choux** choux pastry; **p. à crêpes** pancake batter; **p. feuilletée** puff *or* flaky pastry; **p. à frire** batter; **p. à pain** bread dough; **p. sablée** rich shortcrust pastry; **p. à tarte** pastry; **p. à tartiner** chocolate spread (b) *(mixture)* **p. d'amandes** marzipan; **p. de fruits** fruit jelly; **p. à modeler** modelling clay; **p. à papier** pulp 2 *nfpl* **pâtes (alimentaires)** pasta; **pâtes fraîches** fresh pasta

pâté [pate] *nm* (a) *(terrine)* pâté; **p. de campagne** pâté de campagne *(coarse pâté made with pork)*; **p. en croûte** ≃ pork pie; **p. de foie** liver pâté (b) **p. (de sable)** sandpie (c) **p. de maisons** block of houses (d) *(tache d'encre)* blot; **faire un p. sur qch** to get a blot on sth

pâtée [pate] *nf* (a) *(de chat)* cat food; *(de chien)* dog food (b) *Fam (défaite)* **prendre la p.** to get thrashed; **mettre la p. à qn** to thrash sb

patelin¹ [patlɛ̃] *nm Fam* village

patelin², -e [patlɛ̃, -in] *adj Litt & Péj* unctuous

patent, -e [patɑ̃, -ɑ̃t] *adj* (a) *(évident)* patent (b) **lettres patentes** letters patent

patente [patɑ̃t] *nf (impôt)* tax *(paid by self-employed people)*

patenté, -e [patɑ̃te] *adj* licensed

patère [patɛr] *nf (coat)* peg

paternaliste [patɛrnalist] *adj* paternalistic

paternel, -elle [patɛrnɛl] 1 *adj* paternal; *(ton)* fatherly; **du côté p.** on the father's side; **ma grand-mère paternelle** my grandmother on my father's side 2 *nm Fam* **le p.** the old man

paternité [patɛrnite] *nf* paternity, fatherhood; **recherche de p.** establishment of paternity

pâteux, -euse [patø, -øz] *adj* (a) *(nourriture)* doughy; **avoir la langue pâteuse** to have a furry tongue (b) *(sauce)* thick

pathétique [patetik] *adj* pathetic, moving

pathogène [patoʒɛn] *adj* pathogenic

pathologique [patɔlɔʒik] *adj aussi Fam Fig* pathological

patibulaire [patibylɛr] *adj* **avoir une mine p.** to have a sinister look

patiemment [pasjamɑ̃] *adv* patiently

patience [pasjɑ̃s] *nf* (a) *(qualité)* patience; **avoir de la p. (avec qn)** to be patient (with sb); **avoir une p. d'ange** to have the patience of a saint; **prendre son mal en p.** to suffer in silence; **perdre p.** to lose patience; *Prov* **p. et longueur de temps font plus que force ni que rage** all things take their time (b) *(jeu de cartes)* *Br* patience, *Am* solitaire

patient, -e [pasjɑ̃, -ɑ̃t] 1 *adj* patient 2 *nm,f (malade)* patient

patienter [pasjɑ̃te] *vi* to wait; **faire p. qn** to ask sb to wait

patin [patɛ̃] *nm* (a) *(de patineur)* skate; **patins à glace/à roulettes** ice/roller skates; **faire du p. à glace/à roulettes** to go ice-/roller-skating (b) *(pour parquet)* cloth pad (c) *Tech* shoe; **p. de frein** brake shoe

patinage [patinaʒ] *nm (sport)* skating; **p. artistique** figure skating; **p. de vitesse** speed skating

patine [patin] *nf* patina

patiner¹ [patine] *vi* (a) *(faire du patinage)* to skate (b) *(glisser) (voiture)* to skid; *(embrayage)* to slip; **ça patine!** it's like a skating rink!

patiner² *vt* to give a patina to

patinette [patinɛt] *nf* scooter

patineur, -euse [patinœr, -øz] *nm,f* skater

patinoire [patinwar] *nf* skating *or* ice rink

pâtir [patir] *vi* to suffer (**de** because of)

pâtisserie [patisri] *nf* (a) *(magasin)* cake shop; **p.-confiserie** confectioner's (b) *(gâteau)* pastry, cake (c) *(confection)* pastry-making; **faire de la p.** to make cakes

pâtissier, -ère [patisje, -ɛr] 1 *nm,f (artisan)* pastry cook; *(commerçant)* confectioner 2 *adj voir* **crème**

patois [patwa] *nm* patois

patraque [patrak] *adj Fam* out of sorts

patriarcal, -e, -aux, -ales [patriarkal, -o] *adj* patriarchal

patriarche [patriarʃ] *nm* patriarch

patrie [patri] *nf* homeland; **ma seconde p.** my second home; *Fig* **la p. des arts** the cradle of the arts

patrimoine [patrimwan] *nm* heritage; *(biens)* property; **p. culturel** cultural heritage; *Biol* **p. génétique** genotype

patriote [patrijɔt] 1 *adj* patriotic 2 *nmf* patriot

patriotique [patrijɔtik] *adj* patriotic

patriotisme [patrijɔtism] *nm* patriotism

patron, -onne [patrɔ̃, -ɔn] 1 *nm,f* (a) *(dirigeant)* boss; *(propriétaire)* owner (b) *Rel* patron saint (**de** of) 2 *nm* (a) *(médecin)* senior consultant (b) *(pour la couture)* pattern

patronage [patrɔnaʒ] *nm* (a) *(parrainage)* patronage; **placé sous le p. de...** sponsored by... (b) *(organisation)* youth club

patronal, -e, -aux, -ales [patrɔnal, -o] *adj* employers'

patronat [patrɔna] *nm* employers

patronnesse [patrɔnɛs] *adj f* **dame p.** patroness

patronyme [patrɔnim] *nm* patronymic

patrouille [patruj] *nf* patrol

patrouiller [patruje] *vi* to patrol

patte [pat] *nf* **(a)** *(de chien, de chat)* paw; *(d'oiseau)* foot; *(d'insecte)* leg; **pattes de devant** forelegs; *(partie griffue)* front paws; **pattes de derrière** hind legs; *(partie griffue)* back paws; **court/haut sur pattes** short-/long-legged; **marcher/se mettre à quatre pattes** to walk/get down on all fours; *Fig* **tirer dans les pattes à qn** to give sb a hard time; *Fig* **retomber sur ses pattes** to land on one's feet; *Fig* **montrer p. blanche** to show one's credentials; *Fam* **bas les pattes!** hands off!; *Fam* **pattes de mouche(s)** cramped handwriting **(b)** *(de cartable, de sac)* tab **(c)** *(de poche)* flap; *(d'épaule)* epaulette **(d)** **pattes** *(favoris)* sideburns

patte-d'oie *(pl* **pattes-d'oie)** [patdwa] *nf* **(a)** *(carrefour)* crossroads *(singulier)* **(b)** *(ride)* crow's foot

pattemouille [patmuj] *nf* damp cloth *(for ironing clothes)*

pâturage [patyraʒ] *nm (endroit)* pasture; **pâturages** pasture land

paume [pom] *nf* palm

paumé, -e [pome] *Fam* **1** *adj* lost
2 *nm,f* loser

paumer [pome] *Fam* **1** *vt* to lose
2 se paumer *vpr* to get lost

paupérisation [poperizasjɔ̃] *nf* impoverishment

paupière [popjɛr] *nf* eyelid

paupiette [popjɛt] *nf* (meat) olive; **paupiettes de veau** veal olives

pause [poz] *nf* **(a)** *(dans une activité)* break; *(en parlant)* pause; **faire une p.** to have a break; *(en parlant)* to pause; **p. de midi** lunch break; **p.-café** coffee break **(b)** *Mus Br* semibreve rest, *Am* whole rest

pauvre [povr] **1** *adj* **(a)** *(personne, sol)* poor; **p. en vitamine C** with a low vitamin C content; **p. de moi!** poor old me! **(b)** *(misérable, triste, meubles)* shabby; *(sourire)* weak; *(excuse)* poor (-) *Péj* sad, pathetic; *Fam* **p. mec!** you sad individual!
2 *nmf* poor man, *f* poor woman; **les pauvres** the poor; *Fig* **p. d'esprit** half-wit

pauvrement [povrəmã] *adv* poorly

pauvresse [povrɛs] *nf (fille)* poor girl; *(femme)* poor woman

pauvreté [povrəte] *nf aussi Fig* poverty

pavane [pavan] *nf Mus* pavane

pavaner [pavane] **se pavaner** *vpr* to strut about

pavé [pave] *nm* **(a)** *(morceau de grès)* paving stone; *Fam Péj (livre)* massive tome; *Fig* **un p. dans la mare** a bombshell **(b)** *(revêtement)* paving; *Fig* **tenir le haut du p.** to be at the top; *Fig* **battre le p.** to hang about the streets; *Fig* **être sur le p.** to be on the street **(c)** *Ordinat* keypad; **p. numérique** numeric keypad

paver [pave] *vt* to pave *(with small stones)*; *Fig* **l'enfer est pavé de bonnes intentions** the road to hell is paved with good intentions

pavillon [pavijɔ̃] *nm* **(a)** *(petite maison)* detached house; **p. de chasse** hunting lodge **(b)** *(d'hôpital)* wing **(c)** *(partie évasée)* *(d'un Klaxon®, d'un haut-parleur)* horn; *(d'une trompette)* bell; *(d'un entonnoir)* mouth; **p. de l'oreille** external ear **(d)** *(drapeau)* flag; **p. de complaisance** flag of convenience

pavillonnaire [pavijɔnɛr] *adj* **banlieue p.** suburb

pavoiser [pavwaze] *vi Fam* to gloat

pavot [pavo] *nm* poppy

payable [pɛjabl] *adj* payable; **p. comptant** payable in cash; **p. à la livraison** payable on delivery; **p. à vue** payable at sight

payant, -e [pɛjã, -ãt] *adj (qui paie)* *(hôte, élève)* paying; *(où il faut payer)* with a charge for admission; **l'entrée est payante** there is a charge for admission; *Fig* **ça s'est avéré p.** it turned out to be worth it

paye [pɛj] = **paie**

payement [pɛjmã] = **paiement**

payer [53] [pɛje] **1** *vt* **(a)** *(somme, dette, loyer, personne)* to pay; *(objet, service)* to pay for; **faire p. qch** *(service)* to charge for sth; *(somme)* to charge sth; **se faire p.** to get *or* be paid; **je le lui ai payé 100 francs** I paid her 100 francs for it; *Fam* **p. qch à qn** *(le lui offrir)* to buy sth for sb; *Fig* **p. les pots cassés** to carry the can **(b)** *Fig (expier)* to pay for; **il l'a payé de sa vie** he paid for it with his life; **tu me le paieras!** you'll pay for it!; *Fam* **j'en suis payé pour le savoir** I've learnt it the hard way

2 *vi* **(a)** *(verser de l'argent)* to pay; **p. en liquide/par carte (de crédit)/par chèque** to pay (in) cash/by credit card/by cheque; **p. de sa poche** to pay out of one's own pocket **(b)** *Fig* **p. de sa personne** to put oneself out; **il ne paie pas de mine, mais il est doué** he doesn't look it, but he's very clever **(c)** *Fam (rapporter)* to pay

3 se payer *vpr Fam (s'offrir)* **se p. qch** to treat oneself to sth; **se p. un arbre** to crash into a tree; **se p. la tête de qn** to take the mickey out of sb; **se p. le culot de faire qch** to have the nerve to do sth

payeur, -euse [pɛjœr, -øz] *nm,f* payer

pays [pɛi] *nm* **(a)** *(nation)* country; **p. en voie de développement** developing country; **les p. de l'Est** Eastern European countries **(b)** *(région)* region; **voir du p.** to travel around; **revenir au p.** to go back home; **p. de chasse/pêche** hunting/fishing country **(c)** **le P. basque** the Basque country; **le p. de Galles** Wales

paysage [pɛizaʒ] *nm* **(a)** *(site)* landscape; *(vue)* scenery; *Fig (ensemble)* scene; **le p. audiovisuel français** French broadcasting **(b)** *(peinture)* landscape (painting) **(c)** *Ordinat* mode **p.** landscape mode

paysager, -ère [pɛizaʒe, -ɛr] *adj (jardin)* landscaped; *(bureau)* open-plan

paysagiste [pɛizaʒist] *nmf* **(a)** *(peintre)* landscape painter **(b)** *(jardinier)* **p.** landscape gardener

paysan, -anne [pɛizã, -an] **1** *adj* country; *(syndicat)* farmers'; *Péj* peasant
2 *nm,f* farmer; *Péj* peasant

paysannerie [pɛizanri] *nf* **la p.** the peasantry

Pays-Bas [pɛiba] *nmpl* **les P.** the Netherlands

PC [pese] *nm* **(a)** *(abrév* **parti communiste)** CP **(b)** *(abrév* **personal computer)** PC

PCF [peseɛf] *nm (abrév* **parti communiste français)** French Communist Party

PCV [peseve] *nm* **(appel en) P.** *Br* reverse-charge call, *Am* collect call; **appeler en P.** *Br* to reverse the charges, *Am* to call collect

P-DG [pedeʒe] *nm inv (abrév* **président-directeur général)** *Br* chairman and managing director, *Am* chief executive officer

péage [peaʒ] *nm* **(a)** *(droit)* toll; **pont à p.** toll bridge **(b)** *(installation)* tollbooth **(c)** **chaîne (de télévision) à p.** pay channel

peau, -x [po] *nf* (**a**) *(derme)* skin; **avoir la p. grasse** to have greasy skin; **avoir la p. blanche/noire** to be white/black; **avoir une p. de pêche** to have velvety skin; *Fig* **faire p. neuve** *(personne)* to turn over a new leaf; *(entreprise, parti)* to get a new image; **entrer dans la p. d'un personnage** to get right inside a character; **n'avoir que la p. et les os** to be nothing but skin and bone; **diminuer comme une p. de chagrin** to dwindle away; *Fam* **avoir qch dans la p.** to feel/not to feel good about oneself; *Fam* **avoir qch dans la p.** to have sth in one's blood; *Fam* **avoir qn dans la p.** to be crazy about sb; *Fam* **tenir à sa p.** to value one's life; *Fam* **risquer sa p.** to risk one's neck; *Fam* **sauver sa p.** to save one's skin; *Fam* **avoir la p. de qn** to have sb's hide; *Fam* **prendre douze balles dans la p.** to be shot by a firing squad; *Fam* **p. de vache** *(femme)* bastard; *(femme)* cow (**b**) *(dépouille)* *(d'un animal)* skin; *(d'un animal à fourrure)* pelt (**c**) *(cuir)* hide, leather; *(d'un tambour)* skin; **p. de chamois** chamois (leather); **p. de mouton** sheepskin; **p. de serpent** snakeskin (**d**) *(de fruit, de légume)* skin; *(d'agrume, de pomme)* peel; **p. de banane** banana skin; **p. d'orange** orange peel; *Fig* orange-peel skin (**e**) *(du lait)* skin (**f**) *(des ongles)* hangnail

peaufiner [pofine] *vt* to polish *(with a chamois leather)*; *Fam Fig* *(fignoler)* to add the final touches to

Peau-Rouge *(pl* **Peaux-Rouges**) [poruʒ] *nmf* Red Indian

peausserie [posri] *nf* (**a**) *(commerce)* skin trade (**b**) *(marchandise)* leatherwear

pécari [pekari] *nm* peccary

peccadille [pekadij] *nf* peccadillo

péché [peʃe] *nm* sin; **les sept péchés capitaux** the seven deadly sins; **p. de jeunesse** youthful indiscretion; **p. mignon** weakness; **le p. originel** original sin

pêche¹ [pɛʃ] **1** *nf* (**a**) *(fruit)* peach; **p. blanche** white peach; **p. jaune** yellow peach (**b**) *Fam (coup)* clout (**c**) *Fam (forme)* **avoir la p.** to be on form
2 *adj inv* peach(-coloured)

pêche² [pɛʃ] *nf* (**a**) *(activité)* fishing; **aller à la p.** to go fishing; **p. à la ligne** angling; **p. à la mouche** fly fishing; *Can* **p. sous la glace** ice fishing (**b**) *(produits pêchés)* catch; **faire une bonne p.** to get a good catch

pécher [34] [peʃe] *vi* to sin; **il pèche par excès de timidité** he's painfully shy; **cette enquête pèche sur un point** the inquiry falls down on one point; **p. par omission** to sin by omission

pêcher¹ [peʃe] *nm* peach tree

pêcher² **1** *vt* (**a**) *(chercher à prendre)* to fish for; *(prendre)* to catch; **p. la baleine** to go whaling (**b**) *Fam (trouver)* **où avez-vous pêché cela?** where did you pick that up?
2 *vi* to fish; **p. à la ligne** to go angling; *Fig* **p. en eau trouble** to fish in troubled waters

pécheresse [peʃrɛs] *voir* **pêcheur**

pêcherie [peʃri] *nf* fishery, fishing ground

pêcheur, -eresse [peʃœr, peʃrɛs] *nmf* sinner

pêcheur, -euse [peʃœr, -øz] *nmf* fisherman, *f* fisherwoman; **p. à la ligne** angler; **p. de baleines** whaler; **p. de corail** coral fisher

pécore [pekɔr] *nmf Fam Péj* country bumpkin, yokel

pectoral, -e, -aux, -ales [pɛktɔral, -o] **1** *adj* pectoral
2 *nm* pectoral muscle

pécule [pekyl] *nm* savings, nest egg

pécuniaire [pekynjɛr] *adj* financial

pédagogie [pedagɔʒi] *nf* (**a**) *(discipline)* pedagogy (**b**) *(qualité du pédagogue)* teaching skills

pédagogique [pedagɔʒik] *adj (voyage, sortie)* educational; *(méthode)* teaching

pédagogue [pedagɔg] *nmf* (**a**) *(spécialiste)* educationalist (**b**) *(personne qui sait enseigner)* teacher

pédale [pedal] *nf* (**a**) *(de vélo, de voiture, de piano)* pedal; **p. d'accélérateur** accelerator pedal; **p. d'embrayage** clutch pedal; **p. de frein** brake pedal; *Fam Fig* **mettre la p. douce** to go easy; *Fam Fig* **perdre les pédales** *(s'affoler)* to lose one's head (**b**) *Fam Péj (homosexuel)* queer, = offensive term used to refer to a male homosexual

pédaler [pedale] *vi* to pedal; *Fam* **p. dans la choucroute** *ou* **la semoule** to be all at sea

pédalier [pedalje] *nm* (**a**) *(de vélo)* crank gear (**b**) *(clavier d'orgue)* pedal board

Pédalo® [pedalo] *nm* pedal boat, pedalo

pédant, -e [pedã, -ãt] **1** *adj* pedantic
2 *nm,f* pedant

pédé [pede] *nm très Fam* queer, = offensive term used to refer to a male homosexual

pédéraste [pederast] *nm* (**a**) *(homosexuel)* homosexual (**b**) *(pédophile)* pederast

pédestre [pedɛstr] *adj (voyage)* on foot; **chemin p.** footpath; **randonnée p.** hike

pédiatre [pedjatr] *nmf* paediatrician

pédiatrie [pedjatri] *nf* paediatrics *(singulier)*

pédicure [pedikyr] *nmf* chiropodist

pedigree [pedigre] *nm* pedigree

pédoncule [pedɔ̃kyl] *nm* peduncle

pédophile [pedɔfil] *nmf* paedophile

pègre [pɛgr] *nf* underworld

peignais, peigne *etc voir* **peindre**

peigne [pɛɲ] *nm* (**a**) *(pour les cheveux)* comb; **se donner un coup de p.** to give one's hair a comb; **p. fin** fine-tooth comb; *Fig* **passer qch au p. fin** to go through sth with a fine-tooth comb (**b**) *(pour la laine)* card

peigne-cul *(pl* **peigne-culs**) [pɛɲky] *nm très Fam Péj* creep

peignée [pɛɲe] *nf Fam* thrashing

peigner [pɛɲe] **1** *vt* (**a**) *(cheveux)* to comb; **p. un enfant** to comb a child's hair; *Fam* **p. la girafe** to waste one's time (**b**) *(laine)* to card
2 se peigner *vpr* to comb one's hair

peignoir [pɛɲwar] *nm* (**a**) *(vêtement d'intérieur)* housecoat; *(robe de chambre)* dressing gown; **p. (de bain)** bathrobe (**b**) *(chez le coiffeur)* cape

peinard, -e [pɛnar, -ard] *adj Fam (poste)* cushy; *(personne)* nice and comfortable

peindre [54] [pɛ̃dr] **1** *vt* (**a**) *(avec de la peinture)* to paint; **p. qch en vert** to paint sth green (**b**) *(décrire)* to depict
2 *vi* to paint
3 se peindre *vpr* **l'émotion/la consternation se peignit sur son visage** emotion/dismay was written on his face

peine [pɛn] nf (a) (sanction) punishment; **p. capitale** capital punishment; **p. de mort** death penalty; **p. de prison** prison sentence; **défense d'entrer sous p. d'amende** (sur panneau) trespassers will be prosecuted; **pour la ou ta p., tu vas descendre la poubelle** just for that, you can take the bin down
(**b**) (chagrin) sorrow, sadness; **avoir de la p.** to be upset; **faire de la p. à qn** to upset sb; **elle fait p. à voir** she's a pitiful sight; **p. de cœur** heartache
(**c**) (effort) trouble; **se donner de la p. pour faire qch** to go to a lot of trouble to do sth; **donnez-vous ou prenez la p. d'entrer** please come in; **c'est p. perdue** it's a waste of time; **elle n'est pas au bout de ses peines** her troubles aren't over yet; **en être pour sa p.** to have nothing to show for one's trouble; **ça vaut la p. d'essayer** it's worth a try; **ça ne vaut pas la p.** it's not worth it; **ce n'est pas la p. de débarrasser la table** there's no point (in) clearing the table; **est-ce que ça vaut la p. que je vienne?** do I need to come?; _Ironique_ **c'était bien la p. de se donner tout ce mal!** it was really worth going to all that trouble!
(**d**) (difficulté) difficulty; **avoir de la p. à faire qch** to have difficulty doing sth; **j'ai (de la) p. à croire que…** I find it hard to believe that…; **elle serait bien en p. de t'expliquer comment ça marche** she'd be hard put to explain to you how it works; **cela n'a pas été sans p.** it was no easy matter
(**e**) **à p.** hardly, scarcely; **c'est à p. si je le connais** I hardly know him; **il est à p. trois heures** it's only just three o'clock; **à p. étions-nous sortis que…** we'd only just gone out when…; **j'arrive à p.** I've only just arrived; **à p. arrivée, elle alluma une cigarette** no sooner had she arrived than she lit a cigarette

peiner [pene] **1** vt to upset, to sadden; **d'un ton peiné** in a sad voice
2 vi to labour

peint, -e voir **peindre**

peintre [pɛtr] nm (**a**) (artisan, artiste) painter; **p. en bâtiment** painter and decorator (**b**) Fig portrayer

peinture [pɛtyr] nf (**a**) (art, action) painting; **p. à l'eau** watercolour (painting); **p. à l'huile** oil painting (**b**) (tableau) painting, picture; Fig (description) depiction; Fig **je ne peux pas le voir en p.** I can't stand the sight of him; **p. murale** mural (**c**) (matière) paint; **p. fraîche** (sur écriteau) wet paint (**d**) (surface peinte) paintwork; **il faudra refaire les peintures** the paintwork will have to be done

peinturer [pɛtyre] vt Can to paint

peinturlurer [pɛtyrlyre] vt Fam to daub with paint; **se p. le visage** to plaster make-up on one's face

péjoratif, -ive [peʒɔratif, -iv] adj pejorative

Pékin [pekɛ̃] n Peking, Beijing

pékinois, -e [pekinwa, -az] **1** adj of Peking, of Beijing
2 nm,f person from Peking or Beijing
3 nm (**a**) (chien) pekin(g)ese (**b**) (langue) Pekingese

pelade [pəlad] nf alopecia

pelage [pəlaʒ] nm coat, fur

pelé, -e [pəle] **1** adj (personne, fourrure) bald; Fig (paysage) bare; (tissu) threadbare
2 nm Fam **il y avait trois pelés et un tondu** there was hardly a soul there

pêle-mêle [pɛlmɛl] adv higgledy-piggledy

peler [39] [pəle] **1** vt to peel
2 vi (peau) to peel; **j'ai le nez qui pèle** my nose is peeling; Fam Fig **je pèle (de froid)** I'm freezing (cold)
3 **se peler** vpr Fam **on se pèle (de froid)** it's freezing (cold)

pèlerin [pɛlrɛ̃] nm pilgrim

pèlerinage [pɛlrinaʒ] nm pilgrimage; **faire un p.** to go on a pilgrimage

pèlerine [pɛlrin] nf cape

pélican [pelikã] nm pelican

pelisse [pəlis] nf pelisse

pelle [pɛl] nf shovel; (d'enfant) spade; Fig **à la p.** by the bucketful; Fam **ramasser ou se prendre une p.** to fall flat on one's face; **p. mécanique** mechanical shovel; **p. à ordures** dustpan; **p. à tarte** cake slice

pelletée [pɛlte] nf shovelful

pelleteuse [pɛltøz] nf mechanical shovel

pellicule [pelikyl] nf (**a**) (de glace, de peinture) thin layer; (sur un liquide) film (**b**) Cin & Phot film (**c**) (dans les cheveux) **pellicules** dandruff; **avoir des pellicules** to have dandruff

pelote [pəlɔt] nf (**a**) (de laine, de ficelle) ball; Fig **avoir les nerfs en p.** to be on edge (**b**) (sport) **p. (basque)** pelota (**c**) **p. (à épingles)** pincushion

peloter [pəlɔte] vt Fam to pet

peloton [pəlɔtɔ̃] nm (**a**) (petite pelote) small ball (**b**) (en cyclisme) pack; aussi Fig **le p. de tête** the leaders (**c**) Mil platoon; **p. d'exécution** firing squad

pelotonner [pəlɔtɔne] **se pelotonner** vpr to curl up; (pour avoir chaud) to snuggle up

pelouse [pəluz] nf lawn

peluche [pəlyʃ] nf (**a**) (tissu) plush; **jouet en p.** soft or cuddly toy (**b**) (jouet) soft or cuddly toy (**c**) (bout d'étoffe) piece of fluff

pelucheux, -euse [pəlyʃø, -øz] adj fluffy

pelure [pəlyr] nf (**a**) (peau) (de fruit) peel; (de légumes) **peelings** (**b**) Fam (vêtement) coat

pelvis [pɛlvis] nm pelvis

pénal, -e, -aux, -ales [penal, -o] adj penal

pénaliser [penalize] vt to penalize

pénalité [penalite] nf penalty

penalty [penalti] nm penalty

pénates [penat] nmpl Fam **regagner ses p.** to return home

penaud, -e [pəno, -od] adj sheepish; **d'un air p.** sheepishly

penchant [pãʃã] nm (tendance) propensity (pour for); (préférence) penchant (pour for)

penché, -e [pãʃe] adj leaning; (écriture) sloping

pencher [pãʃe] **1** vt (récipient, meuble) to tilt; **p. la tête avant/en arrière** to lean forward/backwards; **p. la tête à droite** to lean one's head to the right
2 vi (s'écarter de la position verticale) to lean over; (bateau) to list; **pencher vers la droite** to lean to the right; Fig **p. pour qch** to incline towards sth
3 **se pencher** vpr to lean over; **se p. en avant/en arrière/sur le côté** to lean forward/backwards/to the side; **se p. par la fenêtre** to lean out of the window; Fig **se p. sur un problème** to look into a problem

pendaison [pãdɛzɔ̃] nf hanging; **p. de crémaillère** housewarming (party)

pendant¹, -e [pɑ̃dɑ̃, -ɑ̃t] 1 *adj* (a) *(qui pend)* hanging; *(jambes)* dangling; **le chien avait la langue pendante** the dog's tongue was hanging out (b) *(en attente)* pending
 2 *nm* (a) p. **(d'oreille)** drop earring (b) *(d'un tableau, d'un bibelot)* matching piece **(de** to); **se faire p.** to go together

pendant² 1 *prép* (a) *(au cours de)* during; **p. mon séjour** during my stay (b) *(pour une durée de)* **p. dix minutes/deux mois** for ten minutes/two months; **p. tout le trajet** throughout the journey, for the whole journey; **p. ce temps(-là)** in the meantime
 2 *conj* **p. que** while; **p. que vous y êtes** while you're at it

pendentif [pɑ̃dɑ̃tif] *nm (bijou)* pendant

penderie [pɑ̃dri] *nf Br* wardrobe, *Am* closet

pendouiller [pɑ̃duje] *vi Fam* to dangle

pendre [pɑ̃dr] 1 *vt* (a) *(accrocher)* to hang (up) (b) *(mettre à mort)* to hang; **p. qn haut et court** to string sb up; *Fam Fig* **qu'il aille se faire p. ailleurs** let him go hang; **Fig je veux bien être pendu si...** I'll be hanged if...
 2 *vi* to hang; *(cheveux)* to hang down; *(langue d'un animal)* to hang out; *(bras, jambes)* to dangle; **ton pan de chemise pend** your shirt's hanging out; *Fam* **ça lui pend au nez** she's got it coming to her
 3 **se pendre** *vpr* (a) *(se suicider)* to hang oneself (b) *(s'accrocher)* **se p. à qch** to hang from sth; **se p. au cou de qn** to throw one's arms round sb's neck

pendu, -e [pɑ̃dy] 1 *adj* (a) *(mort)* hanged (b) *(accroché)* hanging up; **p. à** hanging from; **p. aux jupes de sa mère** clinging to one's mother's skirts; *Fig* **avoir la langue bien pendue** to be a great talker; **elle est toujours pendue au téléphone** she's never off the phone
 2 *nm,f* hanged man, *f* hanged woman; **le p.** *(jeu)* hangman

pendule [pɑ̃dyl] 1 *nf* clock; *Fig* **remettre les pendules à l'heure** to get things straight
 2 *nm* pendulum

pendulette [pɑ̃dylɛt] *nf* small clock

pêne [pɛn] *nm* bolt

pénétrant, -e [penetrɑ̃, -ɑ̃t] *adj (vent, froid)* piercing; *(pluie)* soaking; *(odeur, regard, esprit)* penetrating

pénétration [penetrasjɔ̃] *nf* penetration

pénétré, -e [penetre] *adj (air, ton)* earnest; **p. d'un sentiment/d'une idée** imbued with a feeling/an idea; **il est p. de son importance** he's full of his own importance

pénétrer [34] [penetre] 1 *vi* to penetrate; **p. dans une maison** to get into a house
 2 *vt* (a) *(sujet: balle)* to penetrate; *(sujet: liquide)* to soak into; *Fig (pensée, intentions)* to fathom; *(marché)* to penetrate (b) *(sexuellement)* to penetrate
 3 **se pénétrer** *vpr* **se p. d'une idée** to become convinced of an idea

pénible [penibl] *adj* (a) *(tâche, voyage, vie)* hard; *(hiver, froid)* severe (b) *(spectacle, nouvelles)* painful (c) *Fam (personne)* **ce qu'il est p.!** he's such a pain!

péniblement [peniblǝmɑ̃] *adv* with difficulty; **avancer ou marcher p.** to struggle along

péniche [penif] *nf* barge

pénicilline [penisilin] *nf* penicillin

péninsule [penɛ̃syl] *nf* peninsula

pénis [penis] *nm* penis

pénitence [penitɑ̃s] *nf* (a) *Rel (repentir)* penitence; *(peine)* penance (b) *(punition)* punishment; **mettre un enfant en p.** to punish a child

pénitencier [penitɑ̃sje] *nm* prison, *Am* penitentiary

pénitent, -e [penitɑ̃, -ɑ̃t] *adj & nm,f* penitent

pénitentiaire [penitɑ̃sjɛr] *adj* prison

Pennsylvanie [pensilvani] *nf* **la P.** Pennsylvania

pénombre [penɔ̃br] *nf* half-light

pensable [pɑ̃sabl] *adj* **ce n'est pas p.** it's unthinkable

pensant, -e [pɑ̃sɑ̃, -ɑ̃t] *adj* thinking; **bien p.** conformist

pense-bête *(pl* **pense-bêtes)** [pɑ̃sbɛt] *nm Fam* reminder

pensée¹ [pɑ̃se] *nf (fleur)* pansy

pensée² *nf (idée)* thought; *(activité)* thinking; **perdu dans ses pensées** lost in thought; **deviner les pensées de qn** to guess what sb is thinking; **dire le fond de sa p.** to say what one really thinks; **à la p. des vacances,...** at the thought of the holidays,...; **la seule p. de ce repas me met l'eau à la bouche** just thinking about this meal makes my mouth water; **la p. marxiste/bouddhiste** Marxist/Buddhist thought *or* thinking; **je suis avec vous en p.** *ou* **par la p.** you're in my thoughts; **avoir une p. pour qn** to think of sb

penser [pɑ̃se] 1 *vi (songer, réfléchir)* to think; **p. à qn/qch** to think of or about sb/sth; **pensez-vous!** what an ideal; **vous n'y pensez pas!** you're not serious!; **n'y pensons plus** let's forget (about) it; **ce n'est même pas la peine d'y p.** it's not even worth thinking about; **ah, j'y pense!** by the way!; **rien que d'y p., ça me donne des frissons** just thinking about it gives me the shivers; **elle l'a fait sans p. à mal** she didn't mean any harm by it (b) *(se souvenir)* **p. à faire qch** to remember to do sth; **fais-moi p. à vérifier que...** remind me to check that...; **elle me fait p. à ma sœur** she reminds me of my sister
 2 *vt (estimer)* to think; **c'est bien ce que je pensais** I thought as much; **je pense que oui/non** I think/don't think so; *Fam* **pensez si j'étais furieux** you can imagine how angry I was; **p. du bien/du mal de qn** to think a lot/not much of sb
 (b) **p. faire qch** *(espérer)* to hope to do sth; *(avoir l'intention)* to be thinking of doing sth
 (c) *(croire à)* to mean; **elle ne pense pas ce qu'elle dit** she doesn't mean what she says; *(concevoir)* **c'est bien/mal pensé** it's well/badly thought out

penseur, -euse [pɑ̃sœr, -øz] *nm,f* thinker

pensif, -ive [pɑ̃sif, -iv] *adj* pensive, thoughtful

pension [pɑ̃sjɔ̃] *nf* (a) *(allocation)* pension; **p. alimentaire** maintenance, alimony; **p. de retraite** *(retirement or old age)* pension (b) *(pensionnat)* boarding school; **mettre un enfant en p.** to send a child to boarding school (c) *(hôtel)* **p. (de famille)** boarding house; **être en p. chez qn** to board with sb; **prendre qn en p.** to take sb in as a lodger; **p. complète** *Br* full board, *Am* American plan

pensionnaire [pɑ̃sjɔnɛr] *nmf (dans une pension de famille, à l'école)* boarder; *(dans une maison privée)* lodger; *Fam (d'une prison)* inmate

pensionnat [pɑ̃sjɔna] *nm* boarding school

pensionné, -e [pɑ̃sjɔne] *nm,f* pensioner

pensionner [pɑ̃sjɔne] *vt* to pension

pensivement [pɑ̃sivmɑ̃] *adv* thoughtfully, pensively

pensum [pɛ̃sɔm] *nm* (a) *(travail ennuyeux)* chore (b) *Vieilli Scol* imposition

pentagone [pɛ̃tagɔn] nm (a) (figure) pentagon (b) le P. (aux États-Unis) the Pentagon

pente [pɑ̃t] nf slope; **en p.** sloping; Fig **être sur une mauvaise p.** to be going downhill; Fig **remonter la p.** to get back on one's feet

Pentecôte [pɑ̃tkot] nf Rel Pentecost; (jours fériés) Whit(sun)

pentu, -e [pɑ̃ty] adj sloping

pénultième [penyltjɛm] adj & nf penultimate

pénurie [penyri] nf shortage, scarcity

pépé [pepe] nm (grand-père) grandpa, grandad; Fam (vieux monsieur) grandad

pépée [pepe] nf Fam chick

pépère [pepɛr] Fam 1 nm (a) **c'est un gros p.** (enfant) he's a chubby little fellow (b) (grand-père) grandad
2 adj (endroit) quiet; (tranquille) cushy; **un petit coin p.** a nice quiet little spot; **être p.** (dans une situation confortable) to have it easy

pépie [pepi] nf Fam **avoir la p.** to be parched

pépiement [pepimɑ̃] nm cheeping, chirping

pépier [66] [pepje] vi to cheep, to chirp

pépin [pepɛ̃] nm (a) (de fruit) seed, Br pip; **sans pépins** seedless (b) Fam (ennui) hitch (c) Fam (parapluie) umbrella, Br brolly

pépinière [pepinjɛr] nf (a) (d'arbustes) nursery (b) Fig training ground (de for)

pépite [pepit] nf (d'or) nugget; **pépites de chocolat** chocolate chips

péquenaud, -e [pekno, -od] nm,f Fam peasant, yokel

péquiste [pekist] 1 adj of the Parti Québécois
2 nmf (membre) member of the Parti Québécois; (partisan) supporter of the Parti Québécois

percale [pɛrkal] nf percale

perçant, -e [pɛrsɑ̃, -ɑ̃t] adj (regard, cri) piercing; (voix) penetrating; (vue) sharp

percée [pɛrse] nf (a) (ouverture) opening (b) Mil, Sp & Fig breakthrough

percement [pɛrsəmɑ̃] nm (d'un trou, d'un passage, d'un tunnel) boring; (d'une avenue) opening; (d'un canal) cutting

perce-neige [pɛrsənɛʒ] nm ou nf inv snowdrop

perce-oreille (pl perce-oreilles) [pɛrsɔrɛj] nm earwig

percepteur [pɛrsɛptœr] nm tax collector

perceptible [pɛrsɛptibl] adj (a) (que l'on peut percevoir) perceptible (b) (impôt) collectable

perception [pɛrsɛpsjɔ̃] nf (a) (par les sens) perception (b) (d'impôts, de droits, de loyer) collection (c) (bureau) tax office

percer [16] [pɛrse] 1 vt (a) (transpercer) (corps, surface, armure) to pierce; (abcès) to lance; **le soleil perce les nuages** the sun's breaking through the clouds (b) (découvrir) (complot, secret) to uncover; (mystère, énigme) to solve; **p. qch à jour** to see through sth (c) (trouer) to make a hole in; (trou) to make; (avec une perceuse) to drill, to bore; (tunnel) to bore; (avenue) to open; (canal, fenêtre) to cut; (tonneau) to broach; (coffre-fort) to crack; **se faire p. les oreilles** to have one's ears pierced
2 vi (a) (apparaître) (soleil) to break through; (dents) to come through (b) (être révélé) to get out; **rien n'a percé de leur entretien** nothing's got out about their meeting (c) (devenir célèbre) to make a name for oneself

perceuse [pɛrsøz] nf drill

percevable [pɛrsəvabl] adj (impôt) collectable

percevoir [60] [pɛrsəvwar] vt (a) (par les sens, l'intellect) to perceive; (bruit) to hear; **être bien/mal perçu** to be well/badly received (b) (impôts, loyers) to collect; (intérêts, allocation, commission) to receive

perchaude [pɛrʃod] nf Can yellow perch

perche[1] [pɛrʃ] nf (tige) pole; (pour micro) boom; Fam Fig **une grande p.** (personne) a beanpole; Fig **tendre la p. à qn** to throw sb a line

perche[2] nf (poisson) perch

percher [pɛrʃe] 1 vi (a) (oiseaux) to perch; (poules) to roost (b) Fam (personne) to live
2 vt Fam (mettre) to perch
3 se percher vpr to perch

percheron [pɛrʃərɔ̃] nm percheron

perchiste [pɛrʃist] nmf Sp pole vaulter; Cin & TV boom operator

perchman [pɛrʃman] nm ski-lift attendant; Cin & TV boom operator

perchoir [pɛrʃwar] nm aussi Fig perch; (pour les volailles) roost

perclus, -e [pɛrkly, -yz] adj **p. de rhumatismes** crippled with rheumatism

percolateur [pɛrkɔlatœr] nm percolator

perçu, -e voir **percevoir**

percussion [pɛrkysjɔ̃] nf percussion

percussionniste [pɛrkysjɔnist] nmf percussionist

percutant, -e [pɛrkytɑ̃, -ɑ̃t] adj forceful

percuter [pɛrkyte] 1 vt to crash into
2 vi **p. contre qch** to crash into sth
3 se percuter vpr to crash into each other

percuteur [pɛrkytœr] nm firing pin

perdant, -e [pɛrdɑ̃, -ɑ̃t] 1 adj losing; **partir p.** to start out with low hopes
2 nm,f loser; **être bon/mauvais p.** to be a good/bad loser

perdition [pɛrdisjɔ̃] nf (a) Rel perdition; **lieu de p.** den of iniquity (b) Naut **navire en p.** ship in distress; Fig **entreprise en p.** company in difficulties

perdre [pɛrdr] 1 vt (a) (égarer) to lose; (habitude) to get out of; (occasion) to miss; aussi Fig **p. qn/qch de vue** to lose sight of sb/sth; **p. de son assurance/sa souplesse** to lose some of one's confidence/suppleness; **il perd son pantalon** his trousers keep slipping down; **tu ne perds rien pour attendre!** just you wait!; **p. son temps** to waste one's time; **il n'y a pas de temps à p.** there's no time to lose; **tu n'as rien perdu en ne venant pas** you didn't miss anything by not coming; **y p.** (dans un échange) to lose out; (dans une vente) to make a loss; **p. au change** to lose out on the deal (b) (ruiner) **ta générosité/ton ambition te perdra** your generosity/ambition will be the ruin of you
2 se perdre vpr (a) (s'égarer) to get lost; Fig **se p. de vue** to lose touch with each other; **se p. en conjectures/dans les détails** to get lost in conjecture/details; Fam **je m'y perds** I'm lost (b) (denrée) (nourriture, récolte) to go to waste; **il y a des claques qui se perdent** you/they/etc need a good slap (c) (disparaître) (usage, tradition) to die out

perdreau, -x [pɛrdro] nm young partridge

perdrix [pɛrdri] nf partridge; **p. des neiges** ptarmigan

perdu, -e [perdy] *adj* (*égaré*) lost; (*vêtement, récolte*) ruined; (*endroit*) out-of-the-way; (*emballage*) non-returnable; **p. dans ses pensées** lost in thought; **il est p.** (*d'un malade*) there's no hope for him; **à mes moments perdus, à mes heures perdues** in my spare time; **un de p., dix de retrouvés** there are plenty more fish in the sea

perdurer [perdyre] *vi Litt* to continue

père [pɛr] *nm* (**a**) (*géniteur*) father; **p. de famille** father; **de p. en fils** from father to son; *Prov* **tel p., tel fils** like father, like son; **nos pères** our forefathers, our ancestors; *Fig* **le p. du cubisme** the father of cubism; *Fam* (**mon**) **petit p.** *Br* old chap, *Am* old buddy; **le p. Paul** old Paul; **le p. Noël** Father Christmas, Santa Claus; *aussi Fam Fig* **croire au p. Noël** to believe in Father Christmas (**b**) *Rel* father; **le (révérend) p. Martin** Father Martin; **mon p.** father

pérégrinations [peregrinasjɔ̃] *nfpl* peregrinations

péremption [perɑ̃psjɔ̃] *nf* **date de p.** use-by date

péremptoire [perɑ̃ptwar] *adj* peremptory

pérennité [perenite] *nf* permanence

péréquation [perekwasjɔ̃] *nf* equalization

perestroïka [perɛstrɔjka] *nf* perestroika

perfectif, -ive [pɛrfɛktif, -iv] *adj & nm* perfective

perfection [pɛrfɛksjɔ̃] *nf* perfection; **à la p.** to perfection

perfectionné, -e [pɛrfɛksjɔne] *adj* sophisticated

perfectionnement [pɛrfɛksjɔnmɑ̃] *nm* (**a**) (*action*) perfecting, improving; (*formation*) further training; **cours de p.** proficiency course (**b**) (*résultat*) improvement

perfectionner [pɛrfɛksjɔne] **1** *vt* to perfect, to improve **2 se perfectionner** *vpr* to improve; **se p. en allemand** to improve one's German

perfectionnisme [pɛrfɛksjɔnism] *nm* perfectionism

perfectionniste [pɛrfɛksjɔnist] *nmf* perfectionist

perfide [pɛrfid] *adj* perfidious; **la p. Albion** perfidious Albion

perfidie [pɛrfidi] *nf Litt* (**a**) (*déloyauté*) perfidiousness (**b**) (*action*) perfidy

perforation [pɛrfɔrasjɔ̃] *nf* (**a**) (*action*) perforation; *Ordinat* punching (**b**) (*trou*) & *Méd* perforation; *Ordinat* punch (hole)

perforatrice [pɛrfɔratris] *nf* (*pour papier*) (hole) punch

perforer [pɛrfɔre] *vt* (**a**) (*papier, organe*) to perforate; (*cuir*) to punch; (*sujet: missile*) to pierce (**b**) *Ordinat* (*carte, bande*) to punch; **bande perforée** punched tape; **carte perforée** punch card

perforeuse [pɛrfɔrøz] *nf* hole punch

performance [pɛrfɔrmɑ̃s] *nf* (*en sport*) performance; *Fig* (*exploit*) feat, achievement; **performances** (*d'une voiture, d'un ordinateur*) performance

performant, -e [pɛrfɔrmɑ̃, -ɑ̃t] *adj* (*machine*) high-performance; (*personne*) highly efficient

perfusion [pɛrfyzjɔ̃] *nf* drip; **être sous p.** to be on a drip

péricliter [periklite] *vi* to collapse

péridurale [peridyral] *nf* epidural

Périgord [perigɔr] *nm* **le P.** Périgord

périgourdin, -e [perigurdɛ̃, -in] **1** *adj* of Périgord **2** *nm,f* **P.** person from Périgord

péril [peril] *nm* peril, danger; **au p. de sa vie** at the risk of one's life; **en p.** in peril; **mettre qch en p.** to imperil *or* endanger sth; **à ses risques et périls** at one's own risk; **il n'y a pas p. en la demeure** it's not a matter of urgency

périlleux, -euse [perijø, -øz] *adj* perilous, dangerous

périmé, -e [perime] *adj* (*billet, passeport, coupon*) out of date; (*nourriture, article*) past its sell-by date; (*idée, conception*) outdated

périmètre [perimɛtr] *nm* perimeter; **dans un p. de 50 km** within a 50-km radius

périnée [perine] *nm* perineum

période [perjɔd] *nf* period; **p. bleue/blanche/rouge** (*de trains*) = off-peak/peak/high-peak periods of rail schedules during which ticket prices vary accordingly; **p. d'essai** trial period

périodique [perjɔdik] **1** *adj* (**a**) (*cyclique*) periodic (**b**) (*hygiénique*) **serviette p.** sanitary *Br* towel *or Am* napkin **2** *nm* periodical

périodiquement [perjɔdikmɑ̃] *adv* periodically

péripétie [peripesi] *nf Litt* event

périph [perif] *nm Fam Br* ring road, *Am* beltway

périphérie [periferi] *nf* periphery; (*banlieue*) outskirts

périphérique [periferik] **1** *adj aussi Ordinat* peripheral; **boulevard p.** *Br* ring road, *Am* beltway; **radio** *ou* **station p.** = private radio station broadcasting from outside national territory **2** *nm* (**a**) (*route*) *Br* ring road, *Am* beltway (**b**) *Ordinat* peripheral; **p. d'impression** printer peripheral; **p. de sortie** output device

périphrase [perifraz] *nf* circumlocution, *Spéc* periphrasis

périple [peripl] *nm* (*voyage*) tour, journey; (*par mer*) voyage

périr [perir] *vi* to perish

périscolaire [periskɔlɛr] *adj* extracurricular

périscope [periskɔp] *nm* periscope

périssable [perisabl] *adj* (*denrées, produit*) perishable; *Fig* (*sentiment*) transient

péristyle [peristil] *nm* peristyle

péritonite [peritɔnit] *nf* peritonitis

perle [pɛrl] *nf* (**a**) (*naturelle*) pearl; (*de verre, de métal*) & *Fig* (*de sueur*) bead; **p. fine/de culture** real/cultured pearl; *Fig* **jeter des perles aux pourceaux** to cast pearls before swine; *Fam Fig* **enfiler des perles** to waste one's time on trivia (**b**) (*personne*) gem, treasure; **c'est la p. des sœurs** she's the best sister in the world; **ma bonne est une p.** rare my maid is a real gem (**c**) *Hum* (*erreur*) howler

perlé, -e [pɛrle] *adj* (*orné de perles*) set with pearls; (*de perles de verre*) beaded; **grève perlée** *Br* go-slow, *Am* slowdown

perler [pɛrle] *vi* (*larmes, sueur*) to form in beads

perlimpinpin [pɛrlɛ̃pɛ̃pɛ̃] *nm* **poudre de p.** magic powder

perm [pɛrm] *nf Fam* (**a**) *Mil* leave (**b**) *Scol* study room; **avoir deux heures de p.** to have two hours' private study

permanence [pɛrmanɑ̃s] *nf* (**a**) (*continuité*) permanence; **en p.** permanently (**b**) (*lieu*) duty office; **la p. est assurée le dimanche** there's someone on duty on Sundays; **être de p.** to be on duty (**c**) *Scol* study room; **avoir deux heures de p.** to have two hours' private study

permanent, -e [pɛrmanɑ̃, -ɑ̃t] **1** *adj (commission)* standing; *(spectacle)* continuous; *(tribunal)* permanent; **cinéma p.** cinema with continuous showings
2 *nm,f Pol* official
3 *nf* **permanente** perm

perméable [pɛrmeabl] *adj* permeable (**à** to); *Fig* susceptible (**à** to)

permettre [47] [pɛrmɛtr] **1** *vt* (a) *(autoriser)* to allow, to permit; **p. à qn de faire qch** to allow *or* permit sb to do sth; **p. qch à qn** to allow sb sth; **permettez-moi de...** allow me to..; **permettez!** excuse me!; **vous permettez?** may I?; **il se croit tout permis** he thinks he can do whatever he likes; *Fam* **il est égoïste comme ce n'est pas permis!** he's incredibly selfish! (b) *(rendre possible)* to allow; **p. à qn de faire qch** to allow sb to do sth; **mes moyens ne me le permettent pas** I can't afford it; **si le temps le permet** weather permitting; **si mon emploi du temps le permet** if my schedule allows it
2 se permettre *vpr* **se p. qch** to allow oneself sth; **se p. de faire qch** to take the liberty of doing sth; **je me permets d'attirer votre attention sur...** may I draw your attention to...

permis, -e [pɛrmi, -iz] **1** *adj* allowed, permitted
2 *nm* permit, licence; **p. de chasse** hunting permit; **p. de conduire** *Br* driving licence, *Am* driver's license; *(examen)* driving test; **p. de construire** planning permission; **p. de séjour** residence permit; **p. de travail** work permit

permissif, -ive [pɛrmisif, -iv] *adj* permissive

permission [pɛrmisjɔ̃] *nf* (a) *(autorisation)* permission; **demander/donner la p. à qn de faire qch** to ask/give sb permission to do sth (b) *Mil (congé)* leave; *(certificat)* pass; **en p.** on leave

permissionnaire [pɛrmisjɔnɛr] *nmf* person on leave

permutation [pɛrmytasjɔ̃] *nf* (a) *(échange)* exchange of posts; *Mil* transfer (b) *(de lettres, de chiffres)* transposition; *Math* permutation

permuter [pɛrmyte] **1** *vt (lettres, chiffres)* to transpose; *Math* to permute
2 *vi* to exchange posts

pernicieux, -euse [pɛrnisjø, -øz] *adj* pernicious

péroné [peɾɔne] *nm* fibula

péroraison [peɾɔɾɛzɔ̃] *nf* peroration

pérorer [peɾɔɾe] *vi Péj* to hold forth

Pérou [peɾu] *nm* **le P.** Peru; *Fig* **ce n'est pas le P.** *(pas extraordinaire)* it's no great shakes; *(peu d'argent)* it's not a fortune

peroxyde [peɾɔksid] *nm* peroxide

perpendiculaire [pɛrpɑ̃dikylɛr] *adj & nf* perpendicular (**à** to)

perpète [pɛrpɛt] *nf Fam* (a) *(perpétuité)* **condamné à p.** sentenced to life; **prendre p.** to get life; **jusqu'à p.** for ever (b) *(distance)* **à p.** miles away

perpétrer [34] [pɛrpetre] *vt* to perpetrate

perpète [pɛrpɛt] = **perpète**

perpétuel, -elle [pɛrpetɥɛl] *adj* perpetual; *(secrétaire, membre)* permanent

perpétuellement [pɛrpetɥɛlmɑ̃] *adv* perpetually

perpétuer [pɛrpetɥe] **1** *vt* to perpetuate
2 se perpétuer *vpr* to be perpetuated

perpétuité [pɛrpetɥite] *nf* perpetuity; **à p.** *(concession)* in perpetuity; *(emprisonnement)* for life; **être condamné (à la réclusion) à p.** to be sentenced to life (imprisonment)

perplexe [pɛrplɛks] *adj* perplexed, puzzled; **laisser qn p.** to perplex *or* puzzle sb

perplexité [pɛrplɛksite] *nf* perplexity

perquisition [pɛrkizisjɔ̃] *nf* search; **faire une p.** to make a search

perquisitionner [pɛrkizisjɔne] **1** *vi* to make a search
2 *vt* to search

perron [peɾɔ̃] *nm* steps *(leading to a building)*

perroquet [peɾɔkɛ] *nm* (a) *(oiseau)* parrot; **p. de mer** puffin (b) *(voile)* topgallant

perruche [peɾyʃ] *nf* budgerigar

perruque [peɾyk] *nf* wig

perruquier, -ère [peɾykje, -ɛr] *nm,f* wig maker

pers [pɛr] *adj m Litt* blue-green

persan, -e [pɛrsɑ̃, -an] **1** *adj* Persian
2 *nm,f* **P.** Persian
3 *nm (langue)* Persian

perse [pɛrs] **1** *adj* Persian
2 *nm,f* **P.** Persian
3 *nm (langue)* Persian
4 *nf* **la P.** Persia

persécuter [pɛrsekyte] *vt* to persecute

persécution [pɛrsekysjɔ̃] *nf* persecution; **manie** *ou* **délire de p.** persecution mania

persévérance [pɛrseveɾɑ̃s] *nf* perseverance

persévérant, -e [pɛrseveɾɑ̃, -ɑ̃t] *adj* persevering

persévérer [34] [pɛrseveɾe] *vi* to persevere (**dans** in)

persienne [pɛrsjɛn] *nf* shutter

persifler [pɛrsifle] *vt* to mock, to ridicule

persil [pɛrsi] *nm* parsley

persillé, -e [pɛrsije] *adj (viande)* marbled; *(assaisonné de persil)* sprinkled with chopped parsley; *(fromage)* veined

Persique [pɛrsik] *adj voir* **golfe**

persistance [pɛrsistɑ̃s] *nf* persistence (**à faire qch** in doing sth); **avec p.** persistently; **p. dans le mensonge** persistent lying

persistant, -e [pɛrsistɑ̃, -ɑ̃t] *adj* persistent; **à feuillage p.** evergreen

persister [pɛrsiste] *vi* (a) *(persévérer)* to persist (**dans** in); **p. à faire qch** to persist in doing sth (b) *(continuer)* to persist; **il persiste un doute** there remains a doubt

personnage [pɛrsɔnaʒ] *nm* (a) *(de fiction)* character; *aussi Fig* **jouer un p.** to play a part *or* a role (b) *(individu)* character (c) *(image publique)* image, persona (d) *(personnalité)* important person; **p. célèbre** celebrity; **p. officiel** VIP; **un grand p. de l'État** a state dignitary

personnalisation [pɛrsɔnalizasjɔ̃] *nf* personalization

personnalisé, -e [pɛrsɔnalize] *adj* personalized; *(voiture, crédit)* customized

personnaliser [pɛrsɔnalize] *vt* to personalize; *(voiture)* to customize

personnalité [pɛrsɔnalite] *nf* (a) *(caractère)* personality; **avoir de la p.** to have lots of personality; **manquer de p.** to have no personality (b) *(personnage important)* personality (c) *Jur* **p. juridique** legal personality

personne [pɛrsɔn] 1 *nf* (a) *(individu)* person; **deux personnes** two people; **les personnes intéressées** those interested; **les personnes âgées** the elderly, elderly people; **une grande p.** a grown-up; **une jeune p.** a young lady (b) *(soi-même)* **en p.** in person, personally; **être bien de sa p.** to be good-looking; **une petite p.** to be satisfied of sa petite p. to be pleased with oneself (c) *Jur* **p. morale** legal entity; **p. physique** natural person (d) *Gram* person
2 *pron indéfini* (a) *(quiconque)* anyone, anybody; **elle le sait mieux que p.** she knows better than anyone (b) *(aucune personne)* no one, nobody; **p. n'est venu** no one has come; **il n'y a p. de blessé** no one has been injured; **p. d'autre** no one else, nobody else; **je n'y suis pour p.** I'm not at home to anyone; **ne connaissez-vous p. qui puisse nous aider?** don't you know anyone who could help us?; *Fam* **dès qu'il s'agit de travailler, il n'y a plus p.** as soon as there's work to be done, you can't see anyone for dust

personnel, -elle [pɛrsɔnɛl] 1 *adj* (a) *(à soi)* personal (b) *(égoïste)* selfish; *(intérêt)* vested
2 *nm (d'une firme, d'une école)* staff; *(d'une usine)* workforce; *(dans l'armée)* personnel; **faire partie du p. de...** to be on the staff of...; **manquer de p.** to be understaffed; **un membre du p.** a member of staff; **p. de bureau** office *or* clerical staff; **p. navigant** flight personnel; **p. au sol** ground personnel

personnellement [pɛrsɔnɛlmã] *adv* personally

personnifier [66] [pɛrsɔnifje] *vt* to personify; **il est la bêtise personnifiée** he's stupidity personified

perspective [pɛrspɛktiv] *nf* (a) *(de dessin)* perspective (b) *(idée)* prospect; **à la p. de faire qch** at the prospect of doing sth; **en p.** in prospect; **des perspectives de reprise** outlook for recovery; **des perspectives d'avenir** future prospects (c) *(point de vue)* viewpoint, point of view

perspicace [pɛrspikas] *adj* shrewd

perspicacité [pɛrspikasite] *nf* shrewdness

persuader [pɛrsɥade] 1 *v* **p. qn (de qch)** to persuade *or* convince sb (of sth); **p. qn de faire qch** to persuade sb to do sth; **être persuadé de qch/que...** to be convinced of sth/that...
2 **se persuader** *vpr* **se p. de qch/que...** to convince oneself of sth/that...

persuasif, -ive [pɛrsɥazif, -iv] *adj* persuasive

persuasion [pɛrsɥazjõ] *nf* persuasion

perte [pɛrt] *nf* (a) *(d'un objet, d'une personne, d'un procès)* loss; **de lourdes pertes en hommes et en matériel** heavy losses of men and equipment; **à p. de vue** as far as the eye can see; **vendre qch à p.** to sell sth at a loss; *aussi Fig* **passer qch par pertes et profits** to write sth off; **p. sèche** dead loss; **ce n'est pas une grosse p.** it's no great loss (b) *(gaspillage)* **une p. de temps** a waste of time; **en pure p.** to no purpose (c) *(déperdition)* loss; **être en p. de vitesse** to be losing speed; *Fig* to be running out of steam; **pertes blanches** vaginal discharge; **p. de chaleur** heat loss; **p. de connaissance** loss of consciousness; *Ordinat* **p. de données irréparable** irretrievable data loss (d) *(destruction)* ruin; **jurer la p. de qn** to swear to ruin sb; **courir à sa p.** to be heading for disaster

pertinemment [pɛrtinamã] *adv* **savoir qch p.** to know sth for a fact

pertinence [pɛrtinãs] *nf* pertinence, relevance

pertinent, -e [pɛrtinã, -ãt] *adj* pertinent, relevant

perturbant, -e [pɛrtyrbã, -ãt] *adj* disturbing, upsetting

perturbateur, -trice [pɛrtyrbatœr, -tris] 1 *adj* disruptive
2 *nm,f* troublemaker

perturbation [pɛrtyrbasjõ] *nf* disruption; **p. (atmosphérique)** (atmospheric) disturbance

perturber [pɛrtyrbe] *vt* *(services publics, circulation)* to disrupt; *(personne)* to perturb, to upset

péruvien, -enne [peryvjɛ̃, -ɛn] 1 *adj* Peruvian
2 *nm,f* **P.** Peruvian

pervenche [pɛrvãʃ] *nf* (a) *(plante)* periwinkle; **(bleu) p.** periwinkle blue (b) *Fam (contractuelle)* *Br* (female) traffic warden, *Am* meter maid

pervers, -e [pɛrvɛr, -ɛrs] 1 *adj* perverse
2 *nm,f* pervert

perversion [pɛrvɛrsjõ] *nf* perversion

perversité [pɛrvɛrsite] *nf* perversity

pervertir [pɛrvɛrtir] 1 *vt* to pervert
2 **se pervertir** *vpr* to become perverted

pesamment [pəzamã] *adv* heavily

pesant, -e [pəzã, -ãt] 1 *adj* heavy; *(sommeil)* deep; *(ambiance)* oppressive; **marcher à pas pesants** to walk heavily
2 *nm* **valoir son p. d'or** to be worth one's/its weight in gold

pesanteur [pəzãtœr] *nf* (a) *(attraction terrestre)* gravity (b) *(lourdeur)* heaviness

pesée [pəze] *nf* (a) *(pour connaître le poids)* weighing; *(de boxeur, de chevaux)* weigh-in (b) *(pression)* force

pèse-lettre *(pl* **pèse-lettres**) [pɛzlɛtr] *nm* letter scales

pèse-personne *(pl* **pèse-personnes**) [pɛzpɛrsɔn] *nm* scales

peser [46] [pəze] 1 *vt* to weigh; *Fig* **p. le pour et le contre** to weigh up the pros and cons; *Fig* **p. ses mots** to weigh one's words; *Fig* **tout bien pesé** all things considered
2 *vi* *(être lourd)* to weigh; **p. 2 kilos** to weigh 2 kilos; **p. sur qch** to press on sth; *Fig* **p. sur la conscience** to lie heavy on one's conscience; *Fig* **p. sur l'estomac** to lie heavy on the stomach; *Fig* **p. sur** *ou* **dans une décision** to carry weight in a decision; **la solitude me pèse** the solitude is getting me down
3 **se peser** *vpr* to weigh oneself

peseta [pezeta] *nf* peseta

peso [pezo] *nm* peso

pessimisme [pesimism] *nm* pessimism

pessimiste [pesimist] 1 *adj* pessimistic
2 *nmf* pessimist

peste [pɛst] *nf* (a) *(maladie)* plague; *Fig* **je me méfie de lui comme de la p.** I don't trust him as far as I could throw him; **la p. bubonique** the bubonic plague; *Hist* **la p. noire** the Black Death (b) *Fig & Péj (personne)* pest

pester [pɛste] *vi* **p. contre qn/qch** to curse sb/sth

pesticide [pɛstisid] 1 *adj* pesticidal
2 *nm* pesticide

pestiféré, -e [pɛstifere] 1 *adj* plague-stricken
2 *nm,f* plague victim

pestilentiel, -elle [pɛstilãsjɛl] *adj* stinking

pet [pɛ] *nm* *Fam (gaz)* fart; **lâcher un p.** to fart; **ça ne vaut pas un p. (de lapin)** it isn't worth a monkey's fart; **il a toujours un p. de travers** there's always something up with him

pétale [petal] *nm* petal

pétanque [petɑ̃k] nf ≃ bowls (played in the South of France)

pétant, -e [petɑ̃, -ɑ̃t] adj Fam **à une heure pétante** at one o'clock on the dot

pétarade [petarad] nf (a) (de feux d'artifice, d'armes à feu) crackling (b) (de véhicule) backfiring

pétarader [petarade] vi (a) (feux d'artifice, armes à feu) to crackle (b) (véhicule) to backfire

pétard [petar] nm (a) (feu d'artifice) (fire)cracker, Br banger (b) Fam (pistolet) shooter (c) Fam (joint) joint (d) Fam **être en p.** (contre) to be raging (at)

pétasse [petas] nf Vulg slag

pétaudière [petodjɛr] nf Fam bedlam

pété, -e [pete] adj Fam (ivre) smashed

péter [34] [pete] Fam 1 vi (a) (bois qui brûle) to crackle; (bouchon) to pop; Fam (personne) to fart; Vulg **il pète plus haut que son cul** he thinks he's God's gift to humanity (b) (exploser) to blow up; Fig **je veux que ça pète!** get your finger out! (c) (casser) to bust
2 vt (a) p. **le feu** ou **la forme** to be full of beans; p. **les plombs** to blow one's top (b) (casser) to bust
3 se **péter** vpr (se casser) to bust; se p. **la gueule** to get wasted

pète-sec [petsɛk] adj inv Fam curt

péteux, -euse [petø, -øz] Fam Péj 1 adj (honteux) sheepish
2 nm,f (a) (lâche) yellowbelly (b) (prétentieux) upstart

pétillant, -e [petijɑ̃, -ɑ̃t] adj (vin, yeux) sparkling; (eau) fizzy

pétillement [petijmɑ̃] nm (du vin, des yeux) sparkling

pétiller [petije] vi (vin, yeux) to sparkle; p. **d'intelligence** (yeux) to sparkle with intelligence

petit, -e [pəti, -it] 1 adj (a) (de taille réduite) small, little; (distance, séjour) short; (somme) small; **tout p.** tiny; **un p. moment** a little while; Fam **une petite demi-heure** barely half an hour; Fig **se faire tout p.** to make oneself as inconspicuous as possible; **petites et moyennes entreprises** small and medium-sized businesses
(b) (peu grave) (problème, erreur) small; (accident) minor; (rhume) slight
(c) (jeune) little, young; **mon p. frère** my little brother; **p. cousin** first cousin once removed; **un p. Anglais** an English boy
(d) (faible) (voix) small; (bruit) little; **avoir une petite santé** to be delicate
(e) (de niveau inférieur) Scol **les petites classes** the lower classes; **petite route** minor road; **p. commerçant/ artisan** small trader/craftsman
(f) (pour insister) little; **p. crétin/con!** little idiot/ bastard!; **mon p. ange** my little angel; **je fumerais bien une petite cigarette** I'd love a cigarette; Fam **p. nom** first name
(g) (mesquin) petty
2 nm,f (a) (enfant) (little) boy, f (little) girl; **les petits** the little ones; Fam **mon p.** my dear; **pauvre p.!** poor little thing!
(b) (en taille) **les petits devant, les grands derrière** small people in front and the tall ones behind
3 nm (d'un chien) puppy; (d'un chat) kitten; **faire** ou **avoir des petits** to have puppies/kittens/etc; Fam **faire des petits** (argent) to multiply
4 adv (écrire) small; **p. à p.** little by little

petit-beurre (pl **petits-beurre**) [pətibœr] nm butter Br biscuit or Am cookie

petit-bourgeois, petite-bourgeoise (mpl **petits-bourgeois**, fpl **petites-bourgeoises**) [pətiburʒwa, pətitburʒwaz] aussi Péj 1 adj lower middle class
2 nm,f member of the lower middle class

petite-fille (pl **petites-filles**) [pətitfij] nf grand-daughter

petitesse [pətites] nf (d'un objet) smallness; Péj (mesquinerie) pettiness

petit-fils (pl **petits-fils**) [pətifis] nm grandson

pétition [petisjɔ̃] nf petition

petit-lait (pl **petits-laits**) [pətilɛ] nm whey; Fam **se boire comme du p.** to go down a treat

petit-nègre [pətinɛgr] nm Fam (mauvais français) pidgin French; **c'est du p.** (mal écrit) it's gibberish

petits-enfants [pətizɑ̃fɑ̃] nmpl grandchildren

petit-suisse (pl **petits-suisses**) [pətisчis] nm = small dessert of thick fromage frais

pétoche [petɔʃ] nf Fam jitters; **avoir la p.** to have the jitters; **flanquer la p. à qn** to give sb the jitters

pétoire [petwar] nf Fam (fusil) popgun

pétri, -e [petri] adj **p. de qch** (orgueil) puffed up with sth; (contradictions) riddled with sth

pétrifier [66] [petrifje] vt aussi Fig to petrify

pétrin [petrɛ̃] nm kneading trough; Fam **être dans le p.** to be in a mess

pétrir [petrir] vt (pâte à pain, argile) to knead

pétrochimique [petrɔʃimik] adj petrochemical

pétrodollar [petrɔdɔlar] nm Fin petrodollar

pétrole [petrɔl] nm oil, petroleum

pétrolette [petrɔlɛt] nf Fam moped

pétrolier, -ère [petrɔlje, -ɛr] 1 adj **l'industrie pétro-lière** the oil industry
2 nm (oil) tanker

pétrolifère [petrɔlifɛr] adj oil-bearing; **gisement p.** oilfield

pétulant, -e [petylɑ̃, -ɑ̃t] adj exuberant

pétunia [petynja] nm petunia

peu [pø] 1 adv (a) (avec un verbe) not much; **elle mange/ parle p.** she doesn't eat/talk much
(b) (avec un adjectif ou un adverbe) not very; **il a agi p. honorablement** he didn't behave very honourably; **très/trop p.** very/too little
(c) (avec un nom) **p. de** (temps, courage, vin) little, not much; (amis, lettres, illusions) few, not many; **ne te fâche pas pour si p.** don't get angry over such a small thing; **c'est p. de chose** it's nothing; Fam **très p. pour moi!** not for me!
(d) (un petit nombre) few; **p. ont compris** few (people) understood
(e) (indique la durée) **sous p.**, **avant p.**, **d'ici p.** soon, shortly; **p. après** shortly afterwards; **depuis p.** lately, recently; **c'est ouvert depuis p.** it hasn't been open long; **j'ai manqué le train de p.** I (only) just missed the train; **il y a p.** not very long ago, recently; **p. à p.** little by little, gradually
(f) **pour p. que** + subjunctive if by chance; **pour p. qu'il ait oublié la clé,...** if by chance he's forgotten the key,...
2 nm (a) (petite quantité) **le p. que je sais d'elle** the little I know about her; **le p. d'argent qu'il me reste** what little money I have left; **son p. d'instruction** what little education he/she has had
(b) **un p.** a little or a bit; **un peu grand/ennuyeux** a little or a bit big/boring; **un p. de temps/sucre** a bit of or

a little time/sugar; **je le connais un p.** I know him slightly *or* a little; **un p. plus/moins** a little *or* a bit more/less; **un tout petit p.** a tiny bit; **il est un p. artiste** he's a bit of an artist; **un p. plus et elle tombait** she very nearly fell; **pour un p. je l'aurais jeté dehors** I all but *or* I very nearly threw him out; **écoutez un p.** just listen; **viens un p. ici** come here a minute; *Fam* **tu ferais ça? – un p.!** you'd do that? – you bet!

(c) *(de temps)* **un p.** a bit, a little while; **restez encore un p.** stay a bit longer, stay a little (while) longer

peuchère [pøʃɛr] *exclam* heavens!

peuh [pø] *exclam* bah!

peuplade [pøplad] *nf* tribe

peuple [pøpl] *nm* **(a)** *(nation)* people; **le p. français** the French people **(b)** *(citoyens)* people; **les gens du p.** ordinary people **(c)** *Fam (foule)* crowd

peuplé, -e [pøple] *adj* inhabited (de by); **très/peu p.** densely/sparsely populated

peuplement [pøpləmã] *nm (d'une région)* populating

peupler [pøple] **1** *vt* **(a)** *(installer une population dans)* to populate **(b)** *(habiter)* to inhabit; *Fig* **peuplé de qch** full of sth

2 se peupler *vpr* to become populated

peuplier [pøplije] *nm* poplar

peur [pœr] *nf* fear; *(subite)* fright; **avoir p. (de)** to be afraid *or* frightened (of); *Fam* **avoir une p. bleue de qn/qch** to be frightened *or* scared to death of sb/sth; **faire p. à qn** to frighten *or* scare sb; **par p. de qch** through fear of sth; **de p. de faire qch** for fear of doing sth; **de p. qu'il ne le fasse** for fear that he would do it; **j'ai bien p. qu'il (ne) soit en retard** I'm very much afraid he's going to be late

peureux, -euse [pœrø, -øz] **1** *adj* fearful
2 *nm,f* fearful person

peut *voir* **pouvoir**

peut-être [pøtɛtr] *adv* perhaps, maybe; **p. que oui, p. que non** perhaps, perhaps not; **p. (bien) qu'elle viendra, p. viendra-t-elle** perhaps she'll come; **je ne suis p. pas riche, mais...** I may not be rich, but...; *Ironique* **tu le sais mieux que moi, p.?** you think you know better, do you?

peux *voir* **pouvoir**

pèze [pez] *nm très Fam (argent)* dosh

pH [peaʃ] *nm Chim* pH

phacochère [fakoʃɛr] *nm* warthog

phagocyter [fagosite] *vt Biol* to phagocytose; *Fig* to swallow up

phalange [falɑ̃ʒ] *nf (du doigt)* phalanx

phallique [falik] *adj* phallic

phallocrate [falokrat] *nm Péj* male chauvinist

phalloïde [faloid] *adj voir* **amanite**

phallus [falys] *nm* phallus

phantasme [fɑ̃tasm] *nm* = **fantasme**

pharamineux, -euse [faraminø, -øz] = **faramineux**

pharaon [faraɔ̃] *nm* Pharaoh

phare [far] **1** *nm* **(a)** *(pour navires)* lighthouse; *(pour avions)* beacon **(b)** *(de voiture)* headlight; **faire un appel de phares** to flash one's headlights; **se mettre en phares** *Br* to dip *or Am* to dim one's headlights; **p. antibrouillard** foglight
2 *adj* **film-p.** seminal film; **épreuve-p.** star event

pharmaceutique [farmasøtik] *adj* pharmaceutical

pharmacie [farmasi] *nf* **(a)** *(science)* pharmacy **(b)** *(magasin) Br* chemist's, *Am* drugstore **(c)** *(médicaments)* pharmaceuticals; **(armoire à) p.** medicine cabinet

pharmacien, -enne [farmasjɛ̃, -ɛn] *nm,f (vendeur) Br* chemist, *Am* druggist; *(chercheur)* pharmacist, *Br* chemist

pharmacologie [farmakɔlɔʒi] *nf* pharmacology

pharyngite [farɛ̃ʒit] *nf Méd* pharyngitis

pharynx [farɛ̃ks] *nm Anat* pharynx

phase [faz] *nf* phase; **cancer en p. terminale** terminal cancer; **être en p.** *Phys* to be in phase; *Fam* to be on the same wavelength

phénicien, -enne [fenisjɛ̃, -ɛn] *Hist* **1** *adj* Phoenician
2 *nm,f* P. Phoenician

phénix [feniks] *nm (animal mythologique)* phoenix; *Fig & Litt* paragon

phénoménal, -e, -aux, -ales [fenomenal, -o] *adj Fam* phenomenal

phénomène [fenomɛn] *nm* phenomenon; *Fam (personne)* character; **un p. de foire** a freak

Philadelphie [filadɛlfi] *n* Philadelphia

philanthrope [filɑ̃trɔp] *nmf* philanthropist

philanthropique [filɑ̃trɔpik] *adj* philanthropic

philatélie [filateli] *nf* philately, stamp collecting

philatéliste [filatelist] *nmf* philatelist, stamp collector

philharmonique [filarmɔnik] *adj* philharmonic

philippin, -e [filipɛ̃, -in] **1** *adj* Filipino
2 *nm,f* P. Filipino

Philippines [filipin] *nfpl* **les P.** the Philippines

philosophale [filozofal] *adj f voir* **pierre**

philosophe [filozof] **1** *nmf* philosopher
2 *adj* philosophical

philosopher [filozofe] *vi* to philosophize

philosophie [filozofi] *nf* philosophy; *Fig* **avec p.** philosophically

philosophique [filozofik] *adj* philosophical

philtre [filtr] *nm* philtre; **p. d'amour** love potion

phlébite [flebit] *nf Méd* phlebitis

phlébologue [flebɔlɔg] *nmf Méd* vein specialist; *Spéc* phlebologist

Phnom Penh [pnɔmpɛn] *n* Phnom Penh

phobie [fɔbi] *nf* phobia; **avoir la p. de qch** to have a phobia about sth

phonème [fɔnɛm] *nm* phoneme

phonétique [fɔnetik] **1** *adj* phonetic
2 *nf* phonetics *(singulier)*

phonographe [fɔnɔgraf] *nm Vieilli Br* gramophone, *Am* phonograph

phoque [fɔk] *nm* **(a)** *(animal)* seal; *très Fam* **il est pédé comme un p.** he's a screaming queen **(b)** *(fourrure)* sealskin

phosphate [fɔsfat] *nm* phosphate; **sans phosphates** phosphate-free

phosphore [fɔsfɔr] *nm* phosphorus

phosphorescent, -e [fɔsfɔresɑ̃, -ɑ̃t] *adj* phosphorescent photo 389 pièce

photo [foto] 1 *nf* (a) *(cliché)* photo; **prendre qn/qch en p.** to take a photo of sb/sth; *Fam* **tu veux ma p.?** who do you think you're staring at?; **p. d'identité** passport-sized photograph; **p. de mode** fashion photo; **p. souvenir** souvenir photo (b) *(activité)* **faire de la p.** *(en amateur)* to take photographs; *(en professionnel)* to be a photographer 2 *adj inv voir* **appareil**

photocomposition [fotokɔ̃pozisjɔ̃] *nf* photosetting

photocopie [fotokɔpi] *nf* photocopy

photocopier [66] [fotokɔpje] *vt* to photocopy

photocopieur [fotokɔpjœr] *nm,* **photocopieuse** [fotokɔpjøz] *nf* photocopier

photoélectrique [fotoelektrik] *adj* photoelectric

photo-finish *(pl* **photos-finish)** [fotofiniʃ] *nf* photo finish; *(appareil)* photo-finish camera

photogénique [fotoʒenik] *adj* photogenic

photographe [fotograf] *nmf* (a) *(professionnel)* photographer; **p. de mode** fashion photographer; **p. de presse** press photographer (b) *(commerçant)* **chez le p.** at the photo shop

photographie [fotografi] *nf* (a) *(technique)* photography; **faire de la p.** to take photographs (b) *(cliché)* photograph; **prendre une p. de** to take a photograph of; **p. aérienne** aerial photograph

photographier [66] [fotografje] *vt* to photograph; **se faire p.** to have one's photograph taken

photographique [fotografik] *adj* photographic

photogravure [fotogravyr] *nf* photogravure

Photomaton® [fotomatɔ̃] *nm* photo booth

photomontage [fotomɔ̃taʒ] *nm* photomontage

photon [fotɔ̃] *nm Phys* photon

photoreportage [fotorəportaʒ] *nm* photo report

photosensible [fotosɑ̃sibl] *adj* photosensitive

photostyle [fotostil] *nm Ordinat* light pen

photosynthèse [fotosɛ̃tɛz] *nf Biol* photosynthesis

phrase [fraz] *nf* sentence; *(musicale)* phrase; *Fig* **faire de grandes phrases** to use flowery language

phrasé [fraze] *nm Mus* phrasing

phraséologie [frazeɔlɔʒi] *nf* phraseology; *Péj* flowery language

phréatique [freatik] *adj voir* **nappe**

phrygien, -enne [friʒjɛ̃, -ɛn] *adj Hist* **bonnet p.** Phrygian cap *(in French Revolution)*

phtisie [ftizi] *nf Vieilli* consumption

phylloxéra, phylloxera [filɔksera] *nm* phylloxera

physicien, -enne [fizisjɛ̃, -ɛn] *nm,f* physicist

physiologie [fizjɔlɔʒi] *nf* physiology

physiologique [fizjɔlɔʒik] *adj* physiological

physionomie [fizjɔnɔmi] *nf* (a) *(traits du visage)* features; **juger les gens à leur p.** to judge people by appearances (b) *(aspect)* face

physionomiste [fizjɔnɔmist] *adj* **être p.** to have a good memory for faces

physiothérapie [fizjɔterapi] *nf* natural medicine

physique [fizik] 1 *adj* physical; *Fam* **je ne le supporte pas, c'est p.** he absolutely repulses me 2 *nf (science)* physics *(singulier)*; **p. nucléaire** nuclear physics 3 *nm (d'une personne)* physique; **avoir un p. avantageux** to have a good physique; **avoir le p. de l'emploi** to look the part

physiquement [fizikmɑ̃] *adv* physically

phytoplancton [fitoplɑ̃ktɔ̃] *nm* phytoplankton

phytothérapie [fitoterapi] *nf* herbal medicine

piaf [pjaf] *nm Fam* sparrow

piaffer [pjafe] *vi (cheval)* to paw the ground; *Fig* **p. d'impatience** to fidget impatiently

piaillement [pjajmɑ̃] *nm (d'un oiseau)* cheeping; *Fam (d'un enfant)* squealing

piailler [pjaje] *vi (oiseau)* to cheep; *Fam (enfant)* to squeal

pianiste [pjanist] *nmf* pianist

piano¹ [pjano] *nm* piano; **jouer** *ou* **faire du p.** to play the piano; **p. demi-queue** baby grand; **p. droit** upright piano; **p. à queue** grand piano

piano² *adv Mus* piano; *Fig* gently

pianoter [pjanɔte] *vi Fam* (a) *(mal jouer)* to tinkle away (b) *(tapoter)* **p. sur qch** *(table)* to drum one's fingers on sth; *Fam (clavier)* to tap away at sth

piastre [pjastr] *nf* piastre; *Can Fam (dollar)* buck

piaule [pjol] *nf Fam* pad

piauler [pjole] *vi (poussins)* to cheep

PIB [peibe] *nm Écon (abrév* **produit intérieur brut)** GDP

pic [pik] *nm* (a) *(pioche)* pick(axe); **p. à glace** ice pick (b) *(sommet)* peak; **couler à p.** to sink like a stone; **tomber à p.** *(falaise)* to go straight down; *Fam* to come at just the right moment

picard, -e [pikar, -ard] 1 *adj* of Picardy 2 *nm,f* **P.** person from Picardy

Picardie [pikardi] *nf* **la P.** Picardy

picaresque [pikaresk] *adj* picaresque

pichenette [piʃnɛt] *nf* flick

pichet [piʃe] *nm Br* jug, *Am* pitcher

pickpocket [pikpɔkɛt] *nm* pickpocket

pick-up [pikœp] *nm inv* (a) *Vieilli (électrophone)* record player (b) *(véhicule)* pick-up (truck)

picoler [pikɔle] *vi Fam* to booze

picorer [pikɔre] 1 *vt (sujet: oiseau)* to peck (at); *(sujet: personne)* to nibble 2 *vi (oiseau)* to pick about; *(personne)* to pick at one's food

picotement [pikɔtmɑ̃] *nm (dans la gorge, dans le nez)* tickling; *(dans les yeux)* stinging; *(sur la peau)* prickling

picoter [pikɔte] *vt* **j'ai la gorge qui (me) picote** I've got a tickle in my throat; **la fumée me picotait les yeux** the smoke made my eyes sting; **j'ai la peau qui (me) picote** my skin's prickling

Pictes [pikt] *nmpl* **les P.** the Picts

pictogramme [piktɔgram] *nm* pictogram

pictural, -e, -aux, -ales [piktyral, -o] *adj* pictorial

pic-vert *(pl* **pics-verts)** [piver] = **pivert**

pie [pi] 1 *nf* magpie; *Fam (personne)* chatterbox; *Fam* **être bavard comme une p.** to be a real chatterbox 2 *adj inv (cheval)* piebald; *(vache)* black-and-white

pièce [pjɛs] *nf* (a) *(salle)* room (b) *(élément)* piece; *(d'un mécanisme)* part; **un service complet de trente-six pièces** a complete thirty-six piece service; **coûter 10 francs p.** to cost 10 francs each; **travailler à la p.** to do piecework; *Fig* **être tout d'une p.** to be straightforward; *Fig* **une histoire fabriquée de toutes pièces** a completely made-up story; **mettre qch en pièces** to tear sth to pieces; **p. de bœuf** cut *or* piece of beef; **p. de collection** collector's item; **p. d'eau** ornamental lake; *(plus petite)* ornamental pond; **p. montée** = large tiered cake served at weddings, baptisms etc; **p. de musée** museum piece; **pièces de rechange, pièces détachées** spare parts, spares; **p. de résistance** main dish; *Fig* pièce de résistance

  (c) *(argent)* **p. (de monnaie)** coin; **p. de 10 francs** 10-franc piece

  (d) **p. (de théâtre)** play

  (e) *(raccord)* patch; **mettre une p. à qch** to put a patch on sth

  (f) *(document)* document; **juger sur pièces** to judge on the evidence; **p. à conviction** exhibit *(in criminal case)*; **p. d'identité** proof of identity; **p. jointe** *(à une lettre)* enclosure

  (g) *(aux échecs)* piece; *(aux dames)* Br draught, Am checker

piécette [pjesɛt] *nf* small coin

pied [pje] *nm* (a) *(d'une personne)* foot; **avoir les pieds plats** to have flat feet; **avoir un p. bot** to have a club foot; **se prendre les pieds dans qch** to get one's feet caught in sth; **avoir p.** to be within one's depth; **perdre p.** to get out of one's depth; **mettre p. à terre** *(de cheval, de vélo)* to dismount; **de p. en cap** from head to toe

  (b) *(de cheval)* hoof; *Culin* **p. de porc** pig's trotter

  (c) *(de vigne)* stock; *(de céleri, de salade)* head

  (d) *(de chaise, de table)* leg; *(de verre)* stem; *(d'appareil photo, de lampadaire)* stand

  (e) *(base)* foot

  (f) **à p.** on foot; **j'y suis allé à p.** I walked there, I went there on foot; **faire 2 kilomètres à p.** to walk 2 kilometres; **tu en as pour dix minutes à p.** it'll take you ten minutes to walk (there)

  (g) *(mesure)* foot; *Fig* **six pieds sous terre** six foot under

  (h) *(locutions)* **mettre qch sur p.** to set sth up; **être sur p.** *(personne)* to be up and about; **être à p. d'œuvre** to be ready to get on with the job; **être sur un p. d'égalité avec qn** to be on an equal footing with sb; *Fig* **être sur le p. de guerre** to be ready for action; **avoir bon p. bon œil** to be hale and hearty; **avoir un p. dans la tombe** to have one foot in the grave; **avoir le p. marin** to be a good sailor; **mettre qn au p. du mur** to get sb with his/her back to the wall; **attendre qn de p. ferme** to be ready and waiting for sb; **se lever du p. gauche** to get out of bed on the wrong side; **faire qch au p. levé** to do sth at a moment's notice; **faire un p. de nez à qn** to cock a snook at sb; *Fam* **il chante/conduit comme un p.** he can't sing/drive to save his life; *Fam* **s'y prendre comme un p.** to make a real mess of it; *Fam* **mettre les pieds dans le plat** to put one's foot in it; *Fam* **je ne remettrai jamais les pieds chez lui** I'll never set foot in his house again; *Fam* **faire des pieds et des mains pour obtenir qch** to move heaven and earth to get sth; *Fam* **faire du p. à qn** to play footsie with sb; *Fam* **ça lui fera les pieds!** that'll teach him a lesson; *Fam* **prendre son p.** to get one's kicks; *Fam* **c'est le p.!** it's fantastic!

pied-à-terre [pjetatɛr] *nm inv* pied-à-terre

pied-bot *(pl* pieds-bots*)* [pjebo] *nm* club-footed person

pied-de-biche *(pl* pieds-de-biche*)* [pjedbiʃ] *nm (outil)* nail claw

pied-de-poule *(pl* pieds-de-poule*)* [pjedpul] *adj inv & nm* hound's-tooth

piédestal, -aux [pjedɛstal, -o] *nm* pedestal

pied-noir *(pl* pieds-noirs*)* [pjenwar] *nmf Fam* = French settler in North Africa

piège [pjɛʒ] *nm aussi Fig* trap; **tendre un p. (à)** to set a trap (for); **prendre un animal au p.** to catch an animal in a trap; **tomber dans un p.** to fall into a trap; *Fam* **p. à cons**

piéger [59] [pjeʒe] *vt* (a) *aussi Fig (attraper)* to trap; **se faire p.** to be trapped; **se laisser p.** to fall into a trap (b) *(placer une bombe dans)* to booby-trap; **colis piégé** parcel bomb; **lettre piégée** letter bomb; **voiture piégée** car bomb

Piémont [pjemɔ̃] *nm* **le P.** Piedmont

piémontais, -e [pjemɔ̃tɛ, -ɛz] **1** *adj* Piedmontese
 2 *nm,f* **P.** Piedmontese
 3 *nm (langue)* Piedmontese

pierraille [pjɛraj] *nf* loose stones

pierre [pjɛr] *nf* (a) *(matière, caillou)* stone; *(rocher)* rock; **mur de p.** stone wall; **maison en p.** stone(-built) house; **investir dans la p.** to invest in bricks and mortar; **poser la première p.** to lay the foundation stone for sth; *Fig* **jeter la p. à qn** to reproach sb; *Fig* **faire d'une p. deux coups** to kill two birds with one stone; *Fig* **être malheureux comme les pierres** to be extremely unhappy; *Prov* **p. qui roule n'amasse pas mousse** a rolling stone gathers no moss; **p. d'achoppement** stumbling block; *aussi Fig* **p. angulaire** cornerstone; **p. à briquet** flint *(for lighter)*; **p. philosophale** philosopher's stone; **p. ponce** pumice stone; **p. de taille** dressed stone; **p. tombale** tombstone; *aussi Fig* **p. de touche** touchstone (b) *(en bijouterie)* stone; **p. précieuse** precious stone, gem; **p. fine** *ou* **semi-précieuse** semi-precious stone

pierreries [pjɛrəri] *nfpl* precious stones, gems

pierreux, -euse [pjɛrø, -øz] *adj (sol, route)* stony; *(lit de rivière)* gravelly

piétaille [pjetaj] *nf Péj* rank and file

piété [pjete] *nf* (a) *(ferveur religieuse)* piety (b) *(affection)* **p. filiale** filial devotion

piétinement [pjetinmɑ̃] *nm (bruit)* stamping; *(marche sur place)* standing around; *Fig (stagnation)* lack of progress

piétiner [pjetine] **1** *vt* **p. qch** *(en trépignant)* to stamp on sth; *(en marchant)* to trample on sth; *(écraser)* to trample sth underfoot; **ils sont morts piétinés par la foule** they were trampled to death by the crowd
 2 *vi* (a) **p. d'impatience** to stamp (one's feet) impatiently (b) *(faire du surplace)* to stand around; *Fig* to make no progress

piéton, -onne [pjetɔ̃, -ɔn] **1** *nm,f* pedestrian
 2 *adj* **rue piétonne** pedestrianized street; **zone piétonne** pedestrian precinct

piétonnier, -ère [pjetɔnje, -ɛr] *adj* pedestrian; **rue piétonnière** pedestrianized street; **zone piétonnière** pedestrian precinct

piètre [pjɛtr] *adj Litt (compagnon)* wretched; *(excuse)* paltry; *(consolation)* small

pieu[1], -x [pjø] *nm (piquet)* stake

pieu[2], -x *nm Fam (lit)* bed; **se mettre au p.**, **aller au p.** to hit the sack

pieuter [pjøte] **se pieuter** *vpr Fam* to hit the sack

pieuvre [pjœvr] *nf* octopus

pieux, -euse [pjø, -øz] *adj* pious, devout

pif [pif] *nm Fam (nez)* conk, *Br* hooter; *Fig* **faire qch au p.** to do sth by guesswork; **répondre au p.** to hazard a guess; **au p., je dirais...** at a rough guess, I'd say...

pif(f)er [pife] vt Fam **je ne peux pas le p.** I can't stomach him

pifomètre [pifɔmɛtr] nm Fam **faire qch au p.** to do sth by guesswork; **répondre au p.** to hazard a guess; **au p., je dirais…** at a rough guess, I'd say…

pige [piʒ] nf (a) (article) freelance contribution; **faire des piges** to do freelance work (b) Fam (année) **elle a quarante-cinq piges** she's forty-five; **à soixante piges** at sixty

pigeon [piʒɔ̃] nm (a) (oiseau) pigeon; **p. d'argile** clay pigeon; **p. ramier** wood pigeon; **p. vole** = children's game with forfeits, ≃ Simon says; **p. voyageur** carrier pigeon, homing pigeon (b) Fam (personne) sucker

pigeonnant, -e [piʒɔnɑ̃, -ɑ̃t] adj Fam **poitrine pigeonnante** high bust; **soutien-gorge p.** uplift bra

pigeonnier [piʒɔnje] nm dovecot

piger [45] [piʒe] Fam **1** vt to get; **ne rien p. à qch** (maths, anglais) not to have a clue about sth; **je n'ai rien pigé à ce qu'il a dit** I didn't get any of what he said
2 vi to get it

pigiste [piʒist] nmf freelance journalist

pigment [pigmɑ̃] nm pigment

pigmentation [pigmɑ̃tasjɔ̃] nf pigmentation

pignon¹ [piɲɔ̃] nm (de mur) gable; **avoir p. sur rue** to be of some standing

pignon² nm (petite roue) pinion

pignon³ nm (graine) pine nut

pilage [pilaʒ] nm crushing

pile¹ [pil] nf (a) (tas) pile; **en p.** in a pile (b) (électrique) battery; **marcher avec des piles** to work off batteries; **p. atomique** atomic pile

pile² **1** nf (d'une pièce) reverse; **p. ou face?** heads or tails?; **tirer à p. ou face** to toss for it
2 adv Fam **s'arrêter p.** to stop dead; **tomber p.** to come at just the right time; **à six heures p.** at six on the dot; **nous étions p. dix à table** there were exactly ten of us at the table; **elle est arrivée p. le même jour que moi** she arrived on exactly the same day as I did

piler [pile] **1** vt (a) (broyer) to crush; (amandes) to grind (b) Fam (battre) to thrash
2 vi Fam to slam on the brakes

pileux, -euse [pilø, -øz] adj Fam hair; **système p.** body hair

pilier [pilje] nm (a) (colonne) pillar (b) (au rugby) prop (forward) (c) Fam Péj **c'est un p. de bar** he's always propping up the bar

pillage [pijaʒ] nm pillaging, looting; (lors d'une émeute) looting

pillard, -e [pijar, -ard] **1** adj pillaging, looting; (lors d'une émeute) looting
2 nm,f pillager; (lors d'une émeute) looter

piller [pije] vt to pillage, to loot; (lors d'une émeute) to loot

pilleur, -euse [pijœr, -øz] nm,f pillager; (lors d'une émeute) looter; **p. d'épaves** looter of wrecks

pilon [pilɔ̃] nm (a) (de pharmacien) pestle; Fig **mettre un livre au p.** to pulp a book (b) (de poulet) drumstick (c) (jambe de bois) wooden leg

pilonnage [pilɔnaʒ] nm (bombardement) bombardment

pilonner [pilɔne] vt (bombarder) to bombard

pilori [pilɔri] nm pillory; aussi Fig **mettre qn au p.** to pillory sb

pilosité [pilozite] nf hairiness

pilotage [pilɔtaʒ] nm (a) (d'un navire, d'un avion) piloting; **p. automatique** automatic piloting (b) Ordinat control

pilote [pilɔt] **1** nm (a) (de navire, d'avion) pilot; (de voiture de course) driver; (de moto de course) rider; Fig **servir de p. à qn** to show sb round; **p. automatique** automatic pilot, autopilot; **p. de chasse** fighter pilot; **p. d'essai** test pilot; **p. de ligne** airline pilot (b) Ordinat driver; **p. d'affichage** display driver; **p. d'imprimante** printer driver
2 adj **installation(-)p.** pilot plant; **université(-)p.** experimental university

piloter [pilɔte] vt (a) (navire) to pilot; (avion) to pilot, to fly; (voiture) to drive; (moto) to ride; Fig (projet) to be in charge of; (touriste) to show round (b) Ordinat to drive; **piloté par menu** menu-driven

pilotis [pilɔti] nmpl stilts

pilule [pilyl] nf pill, tablet; **la p.** (contraceptif) the pill; **prendre la p.** to be on the pill; **p. abortive** abortion pill; **p. du lendemain** morning-after pill

pimbêche [pɛ̃bɛʃ] **1** nf (fille) stuck-up girl; (femme) stuck-up woman
2 adj stuck-up

piment [pimɑ̃] nm (a) (piquant) chilli; **p. doux** (sweet) pepper (b) Fig spice

pimenter [pimɑ̃te] vt aussi Fig to spice up

pimpant, -e [pɛ̃pɑ̃, ɑ̃t] adj smart

pin [pɛ̃] nm pine; **p. maritime** maritime pine; **p. parasol** umbrella pine; **p. sylvestre** Scots pine

pinacle [pinakl] nm **être au p.** to be at the top; **porter qn au p.** to praise sb to the skies

pinailler [pinaje] vi Fam to nitpick (sur over)

pinailleur, -euse [pinajœr, -øz] Fam **1** adj nitpicking
2 nm,f nitpicker

pinard [pinar] nm Fam wine, Br plonk

pince [pɛ̃s] nf (a) (outil) pliers; (de forgeron) tongs; **p. à cheveux** hair clip; **p. crocodile** crocodile clip; **p. à épiler** tweezers; **p. à linge** clothes peg; **p. à sucre** sugar tongs; **p. à vélo** bicycle clip (b) (des crustacés) pincer, claw (c) (sur un vêtement) dart (d) Fam **serrer la p. à qn** to shake hands with sb (e) Fam **à pinces** on foot

pincé, -e [pɛ̃se] adj (air) stiff, starchy; (sourire) tight-lipped; (lèvres) pursed

pinceau, -x [pɛ̃so] nm (brosse) brush, paintbrush; **avoir un bon coup de p.** to be a good painter

pincée [pɛ̃se] nf pinch

pincement [pɛ̃smɑ̃] nm (a) **avoir un p. au cœur** (être ému) to feel a pang of sadness (b) (fait de pincer) pinching; (des cordes d'un instrument) plucking

pince-monseigneur [pɛ̃smɔ̃seɲœr] nf (pl pinces-monseigneur) jemmy

pince-nez [pɛ̃sne] nm inv pince-nez

pincer [16] [pɛ̃se] **1** vt (a) (serrer) to pinch, to nip; (lèvres) to purse; (cordes d'un instrument) to pluck (b) Fam (attraper) to catch; **se faire p.** to get caught (c) Fam **en p. pour qn** to be crazy about sb (d) Fam **ça pince** it's freezing
2 se pincer vpr **se p. le doigt** to catch one's finger; **se p. le nez** to hold one's nose

pince-sans-rire [pɛ̃ssɑ̃rir] **1** nmf inv person with a dry sense of humour
2 adj inv dry, deadpan

pincette [pɛ̃sɛt] nf (petite pince) tweezers; **pincettes** (à feu) (fire) tongs; Fig **il n'est pas à prendre avec des pincettes** he's like a bear with a sore head

pinçon [pɛ̃sɔ̃] nm pinch mark

pinède [pinɛd] *nf* pine wood

pingouin [pɛ̃gwɛ̃] *nm* auk; *(manchot)* penguin

ping-pong [piŋpɔ̃g] *nm* table tennis, Ping-Pong®

pingre [pɛ̃gr] *adj* stingy

pingrerie [pɛ̃grəri] *nf* stinginess

pin's [pinz] *nm inv* badge

pinson [pɛ̃sɔ̃] *nm* chaffinch

pintade [pɛ̃tad] *nf* guinea fowl

pinte [pɛ̃t] *nf (ancienne mesure)* pint (0.93 litres); *(au Royaume-Uni, aux États-Unis)* pint; *Can* quart

pinter [pɛ̃te] *très Fam* **1** *vi* to booze
2 se pinter *vpr* to get sozzled

pin-up [pinœp] *nf inv* pin-up

pioche [pjɔʃ] *nf (a) (outil)* pick, pickaxe **(b)** *(aux cartes, aux dominos)* stock, pile

piocher [pjɔʃe] **1** *vt (creuser)* to dig *(with a pick)*
2 *vi (aux cartes, aux dominos)* to pick up; *Fig* **p. dans qch** *(tas)* to plunge one's hand into sth; *(économies, réserves)* to dip into sth

piolet [pjɔlɛ] *nm* ice axe

pion¹ [pjɔ̃] *nm (de jeu de société)* piece; *(aux échecs)* pawn; *(aux dames)* Br draught, Am checker; *Fig* **n'être qu'un p. (sur l'échiquier)** to be only a pawn in the game

pion², pionne [pjɔ̃, pjɔn] *nm,f Fam (surveillant)* supervisor *(paid to supervise pupils outside school hours)*

pioncer [16] [pjɔ̃se] *vi Fam* to sleep

pionnier, -ère [pjɔnje, -ɛr] *nm,f aussi Fig* pioneer

pipe [pip] *nf (à fumeur)* pipe; *Fam Fig* **casser sa p.** to kick the bucket **(b)** *Vulg* **faire** *ou* **tailler une p. à qn** to give sb a blowjob

pipeau, -x [pipo] *nm Mus* (reed) pipe; *Fam* **c'est du p.** it's all claptrap

pipelette [piplɛt] *nf Fam* gossip

pipeline, pipe-line *(pl pipe-lines)* [piplin, pajplajn] *nm* pipeline

piper [pipe] *vt (dés)* to load; *(cartes)* to mark; *Fig* **les dés sont pipés** the dice are loaded **(b)** **ne pas p. (mot)** to keep mum

pipette [pipɛt] *nf* pipette

pipi [pipi] *nm Fam* pee; **faire p. au lit** to wet the bed; *Fam Péj* **c'est du p. de chat** *(boisson)* it's dishwater

piquant, -e [pikɑ̃, ɑ̃t] **1** *adj (a) (au goût)* spicy, hot; *(moutarde)* hot **(b)** *(plante)* prickly, thorny; *(barbe)* prickly; *(vent)* biting **(c)** *Fig (détail, style, situation)* piquant; *(histoire)* spicy; **une petite brune piquante** a striking little brunette
2 *nm (a) (d'une plante)* thorn; *(d'un porc-épic, d'un hérisson)* spine; *(de barbelé)* spike, barb **(b)** *(d'un style, d'une situation)* piquancy; *(d'une histoire)* spice; **avoir du p.** *(femme)* to be striking

pique¹ [pik] **1** *nf (arme)* pike; *(d'un picador)* lance
2 *nm (carte)* spade; *(couleur)* spades

pique² *nf (méchanceté)* spiteful remark; **envoyer** *ou* **lancer des piques à qn** to have a go at sb

piqué, -e [pike] **1** *adj (a) (bois)* wormeaten; *(livre)* foxed; *(miroir)* tarnished; *(métal)* pitted; *Fam* **une histoire/ angine pas piquée des hannetons** *ou* **des vers** one heck of a story/sore throat **(b)** *(vin)* sour **(c)** *Fam (fou)* bonkers **(d)** *Mus (note)* staccato
2 *nm (a) Av* **descente en p.** nose dive **(b)** *(tissu)* piqué

pique-assiette *(pl pique-assiettes)* [pikasjɛt] *nmf Fam* scrounger, sponger

pique-feu [pikfø] *nm inv* poker

pique-nique *(pl pique-niques)* [piknik] *nm* picnic; **faire un p.** to have a picnic

pique-niquer [piknike] *vi* to have a picnic, to picnic

piquer [pike] **1** *vt (a) (avec une pointe)* to prick; *(sujet: guêpe)* to sting; *(sujet: puce, moustique)* to bite; *(cheval)* to spur on; *(bœuf)* to goad; **la fumée me pique les yeux** the smoke is making my eyes sting; **ça me pique la gorge/le nez** it tickles my throat/nose **(b)** *Fam (faire une piqûre à)* **p. qn** to give sb an injection; **p. un chien** to put a dog down, to put a dog to sleep **(c)** *Fam (voler)* to pinch, Br to nick *(à from)*; **je me suis fait p. mon stylo** my pen got pinched *or* Br nicked **(d)** *(coudre)* to stitch **(e)** *(enfoncer)* to stick *(dans into)* **(f)** *Fam* **p. une crise** to throw a fit; **p. une tête** to dive **(g)** *(vexer)* **p. qn au vif** to cut sb to the quick **(h)** *(exciter)* **p. la curiosité de qn** to arouse or excite sb's curiosity **(i)** *(sujet: acide, vers)* to eat into; *(sujet: humidité)* to spot, to mark **(j)** *Culin* **p. qch d'ail** to stick garlic into sth
2 *vi (a)* *Av* **p. (du nez)** to nosedive; *Fig* **p. du nez** *(s'assoupir)* to nod off; *(baisser les yeux)* to look down **(b)** *(plat)* to be spicy or hot; *(vin)* to be sour **(c)** *(guêpe)* to sting; *(puce, moustique)* to bite; *(plante)* to be prickly; **tu piques!** *(à un homme mal rasé)* you're all bristly!
3 se piquer *vpr (a) (se blesser)* to prick oneself; **se p. le doigt** to prick one's finger **(b)** *(se faire une piqûre)* to give oneself an injection; *Fam (se droguer)* to shoot up **(c)** *(se vexer)* to take offence **(d)** *(vin)* to turn sour **(e)** *(locutions)* **se p. au jeu** to get into it; *Litt* **se p. de faire qch** to pride oneself on doing sth

piquet [pikɛ] *nm (a) (pieu)* stake, post; *(de tente)* peg **(b)** *Vieilli Scol* **mettre** *ou* **envoyer qn au p.** to send sb to stand in the corner **(c)** **p. de grève** picket

piquette [pikɛt] *nf (a) Péj (vin)* cheap wine, Br plonk **(b)** *Fam (défaite)* **prendre une** *ou* **la p.** to get a hammering

piqûre [pikyr] *nf (a) (de guêpe)* sting; *(de puce, de moustique)* bite; **p. d'épingle** pinprick **(b)** *Méd* injection, shot; **faire une p. à qn** to give sb an injection **(c)** *(piqûres* **(c)** *(d'un tissu, du cuir)* stitching **(d)** *(de rouille, de moisi)* spot, speck

piranha [pirana] *nm* piranha

piratage [pirataʒ] *nm* pirating; **p. informatique** hacking

pirate [pirat] **1** *nm (a) (des mers)* pirate; **p. de l'air** hijacker, skyjacker; **p. informatique** hacker **(b)** *(escroc)* crook
2 *adj (radio, enregistrement)* pirate

pirater [pirate] *vt (enregistrement, cassette)* to pirate; *Ordinat* to hack

piraterie [piratri] *nf (a) (sur les mers)* piracy **(b)** *Fig (escroquerie)* swindling

pire [pir] **1** *adj (a) (comparatif)* worse; **c'est de p. en p.** it's getting worse and worse **(b)** *(superlatif)* worst
2 *nm* **le p., c'est que...** the worst thing about it is...; **craindre le/s'attendre au p.** to fear/to expect the worst; **au p....** if the worst comes to the worst...

pirogue [pirɔg] *nf* dugout (canoe)

pirouette [pirwɛt] *nf (tour sur soi-même)* pirouette; *(saut périlleux)* somersault; *Fig (dérobade)* flippant answer

pis¹ [pi] *nm (mamelle)* udder

pis[1] [pi] **1** *adv* **aller de mal en p.** to go from bad to worse **2** *adj Litt* worse **3** *nm* (**a**) *Litt (comparatif)* worse; **il y a p.** there is/are worse (**b**) *Litt (superlatif)* worst; **au p.** if the worst comes to the worst; **au p. que** at the very worst (**c**) **dire p. que pendre de qn** to call sb every name under the sun

pis-aller [pizale] *nm inv* stopgap (solution)

pisciculture [pisikyltyr] *nf* fish farming

piscine [pisin] *nf* (swimming) pool; **p. couverte/en plein air** indoor/outdoor pool

Pise [piz] *n* Pisa

pisse [pis] *nf très Fam* piss, pee

pisse-froid [pisfrwa] *nm inv Fam* wet blanket

pissenlit [pisɑ̃li] *nm* dandelion; *Fam* **manger les pissenlits par la racine** to be pushing up the daisies

pisser [pise] **1** *vi* (**a**) *très Fam (uriner)* to piss; **c'est comme si je pissais dans un violon** it's like pissing in the wind; **laisse p.!** forget it!; **c'était à p. de rire** we were wetting ourselves (**b**) *Fam (fuir)* to leak **2** *vt* (**a**) *très Fam* **p. du sang** to piss blood (**b**) *Fam* **son bras pissait le sang** blood was pouring from his/her arm

pisseux, -euse [pisø, -øz] *adj Fam (couleur)* washed out

pissotière [pisotjɛr] *nf Fam* (public) urinal

pistache [pistaʃ] **1** *nf (graine)* pistachio (nut); **glace à la p.** pistachio ice cream **2** *adj inv (couleur)* pistachio (green)

piste [pist] *nf* (**a**) *(trace)* track, trail; *(indices)* lead; **être sur la p. de qn** to be on sb's track; **suivre une fausse p.** to be on the wrong track (**b**) *Sp (de courses de chevaux)* Br racecourse, *Am* racetrack; *(de course automobile)* racetrack; *(de ski)* run, piste; *(de cirque)* ring; **p. artificielle** *(de ski)* artificial or dry ski slope; **p. de danse** dance floor (**c**) *Av* runway; **p. d'atterrissage** landing strip; *(dans la brousse, dans la forêt)* airstrip (**d**) *(chemin)* track, trail; **p. cyclable** cycle path (**e**) *(de magnétophone, de disque)* track; *Ordinat* **p. d'amorçage** boot track; *Ordinat* **p. magnétique** magnetic stripe

pister [piste] *vt (animal)* to track; *(personne)* to tail

pistil [pistil] *nm Bot* pistil

pistolet [pistolɛ] *nm* (**a**) *(arme à feu)* pistol, gun; **p. à air comprimé** air pistol; **p. à eau** water pistol (**b**) *(à peinture)* paint gun

pistolet-mitrailleur *(pl* **pistolets-mitrailleurs)** [pistolɛmitrajœr] *nm* submachine-gun

piston [pistɔ̃] *nm* (**a**) *Tech* piston (**b**) *Fam Fig (recommandation)* string-pulling; **il a eu la place par p.** someone pulled some strings to get him the job (**c**) *(d'instrument à vent)* valve

pistonner [pistone] *vt Fam* to pull strings for; **elle s'est fait p.** she got someone to pull strings for her

pistou [pistu] *nm (sauce)* pesto; *(soupe)* vegetable soup with pesto

pitance [pitɑ̃s] *nf Vieilli (nourriture)* sustenance

pit-bull *(pl* **pit-bulls)** [pitbul] *nm* pit bull (terrier)

piteux, -euse [pitø, -øz] *adj* (**a**) *(mauvais) (résultat)* poor, pitiful; **en p. état** in a sorry state (**b**) *(honteux)* shamefaced

pithiviers [pitivje] *nm Culin* = cake made of puff pastry containing rum and almond-flavoured cream

pitié [pitje] *nf* (**a**) *(compassion)* pity; **avoir p. de qn** to pity sb; **il me faisait p.** I felt sorry for him; **faire p. (à voir)** to be a pitiful sight; **être sans p.** to be ruthless; *(par) p.!* *(pour demander grâce)* (have) mercy!; *(exprime l'agacement)* for pity's sake! (**b**) *(tristesse)* **quelle p.!** what a terrible shame!

piton [pitɔ̃] *nm* (**a**) *Tech* eye bolt; *(d'alpiniste)* piton (**b**) *(sommet)* **p. (rocheux)** (rocky) peak

pitoyable [pitwajabl] *adj* (**a**) *(digne de pitié)* pitiful (**b**) *Péj (excuse, plaisanterie)* pathetic

pitre [pitr] *nm* clown; **faire le p.** to clown around

pitrerie [pitrəri] *nf* piece of clowning; **pitreries** clowning

pittoresque [pitorɛsk] *adj (lieu)* picturesque; *(description, style)* vivid

pivert [pivɛr] *nm* green woodpecker

pivoine [pivwan] *nf* peony

pivot [pivo] *nm* (**a**) *(axe)* pivot; *(de levier)* fulcrum; *(de compas, de boussole)* centre pin; *(en dentisterie)* post (**b**) *Fig (d'un drame, d'une argumentation)* pivot (**c**) *(au basket)* pivot, post

pivotant, -e [pivotɑ̃, ɑ̃t] *adj (grue, lampe)* swivelling; *(présentoir)* revolving

pivoter [pivote] *vi* to pivot, to swivel (**sur** on); **faire p. qch** to swivel sth round

pixel [piksɛl] *nm Ordinat* pixel

pixélisé, -e [pikselize] *adj Ordinat* bit-mapped

pizza [pidza] *nf* pizza

pizzeria [pidzerja] *nf* pizzeria

PJ [peʒi] *nf Fam (abrév* **police judiciaire)** *Br* ≃ CID, *Am* ≃ FBI

placage [plakaʒ] *nm* (**a**) *(bois)* veneer; *(métal)* plating (**b**) *(au rugby)* tackle

placard [plakar] *nm* (**a**) *(armoire)* cupboard; *Fam Fig* **mettre qn au p.** to sideline sb; *Fam Fig* **mettre qch au p.** to put sth on ice, to shelve sth (**b**) *(affiche)* poster

placarder [plakarde] *vt (affiche)* to stick up, to put up; **un mur d'affiches** to cover a wall with posters

place [plas] *nf* (**a**) *(endroit, rôle)* place; **changer qch de p.** to move sth; *Fig* **se mettre à la p. de qn** to put oneself in sb's position; **mettre qch en p.** to put sth in place; **être en p.** *(objet)* to be in place; *(au pouvoir)* to be in office; **les gens en p.** people in high places; *Fig* **remettre qn à sa p.** to put sb in his/her place; **il ne tient pas en p.** he can't keep still; **à la p. de qn** *(au lieu de)* instead of sb; **à votre p....** if I were you...; **sur p.** on the spot; **faire p. nette** to have a clearout; **p. de parking** parking place or space (**b**) *(espace)* room, space; **prendre beaucoup de p.** to take up a lot of room or space; **faire de la p. à qn** to make room for sb; *Fig* **faire p. à qn/qch** to make way for sb/sth (**c**) *(siège)* seat; **(voiture à) deux/quatre places** two-/four-seater (car); **prendre p.** to take a seat; **p. assise** seat; **p. debout** *(billet)* standing ticket; **la p. du mort** the passenger seat (**d**) *(poste)* job, post (**e**) *(lieu public)* square; **p. du marché** market place (**f**) *(rang)* place (**g**) *Mil* **p. forte** fortified town (**h**) *Com & Fin* market; **sur la p. de Paris** on the Paris market; **p. financière** financial market

placé, -e [plase] *adj* **être bien/mal p. pour faire qch** to be well/badly placed to do sth

placebo [plasebo] *nm* placebo

placement [plasmɑ̃] *nm* (**a**) *(d'argent)* investment; **faire des placements** to invest (money) (**b**) *(à un emploi)* placement, placing

placenta [plaseta] nm placenta

placer [16] [plase] **1** vt (a) (mettre à sa place) to place, to put; (faire asseoir) to seat (b) (procurer un emploi à) to find a job for, to place; **p. qn comme apprenti chez qn** to apprentice sb to sb (c) (vendre) to sell (d) (dans la conversation) to get in; Fam **avec elle, on ne peut pas en p. une!** you can't get a word in edgeways with her! (e) (argent) to invest
2 se placer vpr (a) (debout) to stand; (assis) to sit (b) **se p. sous la protection de qn** to place oneself under sb's protection; **il faut se p. dans son optique** you have to look at things from her point of view (c) (trouver un emploi) to find a job

placide [plasid] adj placid, calm

placoter [plakɔte] vi Can Fam to chat

plafond [plafɔ̃] nm aussi Fig ceiling; **être haut/bas de p.** to have a high/low ceiling; **prix/vitesse p.** maximum price/speed

plafonner [plafɔne] vi (quantité, salaire) to have reached a ceiling (à of)

plafonnier [plafɔnje] nm ceiling light

plage [plaʒ] nf (a) (grève) beach; **aller en vacances à la p.** to go on holiday to the seaside; **p. de sable/de galets** sandy/pebble beach (b) (surface) area (c) (dans un emploi du temps, à la télé, à la radio) slot; **p. horaire** time slot (d) (d'un disque) track (e) **p. arrière** (d'une voiture) back shelf

plagiaire [plaʒjɛr] nmf plagiarist

plagiat [plaʒja] nm plagiarism

plagier [66] [plaʒje] vt to plagiarize

plaid [plɛd] nm travelling rug

plaider [plede] **1** vt to plead; **p. coupable/non coupable** to plead guilty/not guilty; **p. la cause de qn** Jur to plead sb's case; Fig to plead sb's cause
2 vi (avocat) to plead; **p. pour/contre qn** to defend/prosecute sb; Fig **p. en faveur de qn/qch** to speak for sb/sth, to defend sb/sth

plaidoirie [pledwari] nf Jur speech for the defence

plaidoyer [pledwaje] nm Jur speech for the defence; Fig plea

plaie [plɛ] nf (a) aussi Fig wound (b) (fléau) affliction, scourge; (personne, chose) pest, nuisance

plaignant, -e [plɛɲɑ̃, -ɑ̃t] nm,f Jur plaintiff

plaindre [23] [plɛ̃dr] **1** vt to pity, to feel sorry for; **je vous plains de voyager dans ces conditions** I feel sorry for you having to travel in these conditions; **elle n'est pas à p.** she's got nothing to worry about
2 se plaindre vpr (a) (protester) to complain; **se p. de** to complain about; (douleur) to complain of (b) (gémir) to moan

plaine [plɛn] nf plain

plain-pied [plɛ̃pje] **de plain-pied** adv (pièce) on the same level (avec as); (maison) single-storey

plainte [plɛ̃t] nf (a) (protestation) complaint (b) (gémissement) moan (c) Jur complaint; **porter p. contre qn (auprès de)** to lodge a complaint against sb (with); **p. contre X** complaint against person or persons unknown

plaintif, -ive [plɛ̃tif, -iv] adj plaintive

plaire [55a] [plɛr] **1** vi (a) (être apprécié) **cet homme me plaît** I like this man; **ce livre/film m'a plu** I liked or enjoyed the book/film; **cette offre devrait lui p.** the offer should appeal to him; **ça plaît beaucoup** it's very popular; **je fais ce qui me plaît** I do whatever I want; **que cela te plaise ou non** whether you like it or not (b) (se rendre agréable) to please; **rien à faire, elle ne plaît pas** no matter what she does, no one finds her attractive
2 v impersonnel **s'il te/vous plaît** please; **et pas n'importe qui, s'il vous plaît** and not just anybody, if you please; **comme il vous plaira** just as you like
3 se plaire vpr (a) (soi-même) **elle se plaît dans cette robe** she likes herself in that dress (b) (l'un l'autre) to like each other (c) (se trouver bien) **je me plais beaucoup à Paris** I'm very happy in Paris; **se p. à faire qch** to enjoy or like doing sth

plaisance [plɛzɑ̃s] nf **la (navigation de) p.** boating

plaisancier, -ère [plɛzɑ̃sje, -ɛr] nm,f (amateur) yachtsman, f yachtswoman

plaisant, -e [plɛzɑ̃, -ɑ̃t] **1** adj (a) (agréable) pleasant, agreeable (b) (drôle) funny, amusing
2 nm **mauvais p.** malicious joker

plaisanter [plɛzɑ̃te] **1** vi to joke; **dire qch en plaisantant** to say sth as a joke; **vous plaisantez!** you're joking!; **on ne plaisante pas avec la santé** health is a serious matter
2 vt to tease, to poke fun at (sur about)

plaisanterie [plɛzɑ̃tri] nf (acte, propos) joke; **elle ne comprend pas la p.** she can't take a joke; **par p.** for a joke; **tourner qch en p.** to make a joke out of sth; **les plaisanteries les plus courtes sont les meilleures** brevity is the soul of wit

plaisantin [plɛzɑ̃tɛ̃] nm joker

plaise etc voir plaire

plaisir [plezir] nm (a) (sensation agréable) pleasure; **j'ai le p. de vous apprendre que...** I'm pleased to be able to tell you that...; **faire qch pour le p.** to do sth for fun; Ironique **je vous souhaite bien du p.!** the best of luck!; **ça m'a fait p. de te revoir** I was pleased to see you again; **ça me ferait p. que tu viennes** I'd be pleased if you came; **fais-moi p., viens danser** do me a favour, come and dance; **si cela peut te faire p.** if it makes you happy; **il va se faire un p. de te téléphoner demain** he'll be only too pleased to phone you tomorrow; **cela fait p. à voir** it's good to see; **prendre p. à qch/à faire qch** to enjoy sth/doing sth; **les plaisirs de la table** fine food and wine (b) (distraction) pleasure; **c'est son plus grand p.** it's his greatest pleasure

plan¹, -e [plɑ̃, plan] **1** adj (terrain, surface) flat; Math plane
2 nm (a) Math plane (b) (surface) de cuisson hob; **p. d'eau** lake; **p. incliné** inclined plane; **p. de travail** (d'une cuisine) worktop (c) Cin, Phot & Fig au premier p. in the foreground; **au second p.** in the background; **un artiste de premier p.** a leading artist; **sur le même p. (que)** on the same level (as); **sur le p. politique/économique** from a political/an economic point of view; **gros p.** close-up; **en gros p.** in close-up

plan² nm (a) (relevé) plan; (carte) (de ville) map; **p. d'occupation des sols** land-use map (b) (projet) plan; Fam **un bon p.** (combine) a good trick; **p. social** = corporate restructuring plan, usually involving job losses (c) (d'un roman, d'un devoir) plan, framework (d) Fin **p. d'épargne** savings plan; **p. d'épargne en actions** personal equity plan, PEP; **p. d'épargne-logement** = savings plan entitling savers to low mortgages; **p. d'épargne-retraite** personal pension plan

plan³ *nm Fam* **laisser qn en p.** to leave sb in the lurch; **tout laisser en p.** to drop everything

planant, -e [planɑ̃, ɑ̃t] *adj Fam* mind-blowing

planche [plɑ̃ʃ] *nf* (a) *(pièce de bois)* plank; *(plus large)* board; **faire la p.** *(flotter)* to float on one's back; *Fam* **c'est une vraie p. à pain** she's as flat as a pancake; **p. à découper** chopping board; **p. à dessin** drawing board; **p. à repasser** ironing board; **p. de salut** last hope (b) *Th* **monter sur les planches** to go on the stage, to tread the boards (c) *(d'imprimerie, de gravure)* plate, block (d) *Sp* **p. (de surf)** surfboard; **p. (à voile)** windsurfer; *Can* **p. à neige** snowboard; **p. à roulettes** skateboard; **faire de la p. à roulettes** to skateboard; **faire de la p. à voile** to go windsurfing

plancher¹ [plɑ̃ʃe] *nm* (a) *(sol)* floor; *Fam* **le p. des vaches** dry land, terra firma; *Fig* **mettre le pied au p.** to put one's foot down (b) *Fig (minimum)* minimum; **prix p.** bottom price

plancher² 1 *vi Fam Scol* to have an exam
2 **plancher sur** *vt ind* **p. sur un problème** to work on a problem

plancton [plɑ̃ktɔ̃] *nm* plankton

plané, -e [plane] *adj* *nv voir* **vol**

planer [plane] *vi* (a) *(oiseau, planeur)* to glide; *(brume, fumée)* to hang; *Fig* **p. sur qn/qch** *(danger)* to hang over sb/sth (b) *Fam (se sentir bien)* to be floating on air, to be on a high; *(après s'être drogué)* to be high; *(rêver)* to dream

planétaire [planeter] *adj* (a) *Astron* planetary (b) *(expansion, action)* worldwide

planétarium [planetarjɔm] *nm* planetarium

planète [planɛt] *nf* planet

planeur [planœr] *nm (avion)* glider

planification [planifikasjɔ̃] *nf Écon* planning

planifier [66] [planifje] *vt* to plan

planisphère [planisfɛr] *nm* planisphere

planning [planiŋ] *nm* schedule; **p. familial** family planning; *(lieu)* family planning clinic

planque [plɑ̃k] *nf Fam* (a) *(d'un gangster)* hideout; *(pour un butin)* hiding place (b) *(travail facile)* cushy job

planqué, -e [plɑ̃ke] *nm,f Fam* person with a cushy job; *Mil* draft dodger

planquer [plɑ̃ke] *Fam* 1 *vt* to hide
2 **se planquer** *vpr* to hide

plant [plɑ̃] *nm (d'arbre)* sapling; *(de plante)* seedling

plantaire [plɑ̃ter] *adj Anat* plantar

plantation [plɑ̃tasjɔ̃] *nf (exploitation agricole)* plantation

plante¹ [plɑ̃t] *nf* **p. du pied** sole (of the foot)

plante² *nf (végétal)* plant; *Fam Fig* **une belle p.** *(femme)* a voluptuous woman; **p. d'appartement** house plant; **p. grasse** succulent (plant); **p. potagère** plant grown for food; **p. verte** house plant

planté, -e [plɑ̃te] *adj (debout)* standing; *Fam* **rester p. (comme un piquet)** *(immobile)* to stand there doing nothing, *Br* to stand there like a lemon (b) **bien p.** *(robuste)* sturdy

planter [plɑ̃te] 1 *vt* (a) *(graines, fleurs, arbre)* to plant; **une colline plantée d'arbres** a hill planted with trees (b) *(clou)* to hammer in; *(tente)* to put up, to pitch; **p. un clou dans qch** to hammer a nail into sth; *Fig* **p. un baiser sur la joue à qn** to plant a kiss on sb's cheek (c) *Fam* **p. là qn** to dump sb; **il veut tout p. là** he wants to pack it all in
2 **se planter** *vpr* (a) *(se tenir immobile)* to stand (b) *Fam (se tromper)* to get it wrong (c) *Fam (tomber)* to come a cropper (d) *Fam (en voiture)* to crash

planteur [plɑ̃tœr] *nm* (a) *(exploitant)* planter (b) *(cocktail)* planter's punch

plantigrade [plɑ̃tigrad] *nm Zool* plantigrade

planton [plɑ̃tɔ̃] *nm Mil* orderly

plantureux, -euse [plɑ̃tyrø, -øz] *adj (femme)* buxom; *(poitrine)* ample

plaquage [plakaʒ] = **placage** (b)

plaque [plak] *nf* (a) *(de métal)* plate, sheet; *(de marbre)* slab; *(de chocolat)* bar; *(de beurre)* pack; *(de verglas)* sheet; **p. chauffante** hotplate; **p. d'égout** manhole cover; *Fig* **p. minéralogique** *Br* number plate, *Am* license plate; **p. de rue** street sign (c) *(sur la peau)* patch; **p. (dentaire)** *(dental)* plaque (d) *Fam* **être à côté de la p.** to be wide of the mark

plaqué, -e [plake] 1 *adj* **p. or/argent** gold-/silver-plated
2 *nm* (a) **p. or/argent** gold/silver plate; **montre en p. or** gold-plated watch (b) *(bois)* veneered wood

plaquer [plake] 1 *vt* (a) *(cheveux)* to plaster down; **p. qn contre un mur** to pin sb against a wall (b) *Fam (petit ami)* to ditch, to chuck; **tout p.** to chuck it all in (c) *(au rugby)* to tackle (d) *Mus (accord)* to play (e) *(bois)* to veneer; *(métal)* to plate
2 **se plaquer** *vpr* **se p. au sol** to lie flat on the ground; **se p. contre un mur** to flatten oneself against a wall

plaquette [plaket] *nf* (a) *(de métal)* (small) plate; *(portant une inscription)* (small) plaque; *Ordinat* circuit board; *Aut* **p. de frein** brake pad (b) *(de chocolat)* bar; *(de beurre)* pack (c) *(petit livre)* booklet (d) *Méd* **plaquettes** (blood) platelets

plasma [plasma] *nm Biol & Phys* plasma

plastic [plastik] *nm* plastic explosive

plasticage [plastikaʒ] *nm* bombing (**de** of)

plastifier [66] [plastifje] *vt* to laminate

plastiquage [plastikaʒ] = **plasticage**

plastique [plastik] 1 *adj & nm* plastic
2 *nf* (a) *(art)* art of modelling (b) *(du corps)* figure

plastiquer [plastike] *vt* to bomb

plastron [plastrɔ̃] *nm* (a) *(de chemise)* shirt front (b) *(d'escrimeur)* plastron

plat, -e [pla, plat] 1 *adj* (a) *(sans relief)* flat, level; *(chaussure)* flat; *(mer)* smooth; *(eau)* still; *Fam* **plate comme une limande** *(femme)* as flat as a pancake (b) *Fig (ennuyeux)* flat, dull (c) **à p.** *(pneu, batterie)* flat; *Fam* **être à p.** *(épuisé)* to be worn down; **mettre qch à p.** to lay sth (down) flat; *Fig* **tomber à p.** *(proposition, plaisanterie)* to fall flat; **se mettre à p. ventre** to lie face down; *Fig* **se mettre à p. ventre devant qn** to grovel to sb
2 *nm* (a) *(assiette)* dish; *Fig* **mettre les petits plats dans les grands** to put on a marvellous spread (b) *(mets)* dish; *(partie du menu)* course; *Fam* **en faire tout un p.** to make a song and dance about it; **p. cuisiné** ready meal; **p. du jour** today's special, dish of the day; **p. principal** *ou* **de résistance** main course (c) *(de la main, d'un épée)* flat (d) *(en cyclisme, en hippisme)* **sur le p.** on the flat (e) **faire un p.** *(en plongeant)* to do a bellyflop (f) *Fam* **faire du p. à qn** *Br* to chat sb up, *Am* to hit on sb

platane [platan] *nm* plane tree

plateau, -x [plato] *nm* (a) *(plat)* tray; **p. à fromages** cheeseboard; **p. de fruits de mer** seafood platter (b) *(d'une balance)* pan; *(d'une platine, d'un four micro-ondes)* turntable (c) *Géog* plateau; **haut p.** high plateau (d) *TV & Cin* set (e) *(de vélo)* chain wheel

plateau-repas (*pl* **plateaux-repas**) [platoʀəpa] *nm* meal on a tray

plate-bande (*pl* **plates-bandes**) [platbɑ̃d] *nf* flower bed; *Fam* **marcher sur les plates-bandes de qn** to tread on sb's toes

plate-forme (*pl* **plates-formes**) [platfɔʀm] *nf* (a) *(surface plane)* platform; **p. pétrolière** *ou* **de forage** oil rig (b) *Géog* **p. continentale** continental shelf (c) *Ordinat* platform

platement [platmɑ̃] *adv* (a) *(s'exprimer, écrire)* dully (b) *(s'excuser)* humbly

platine¹ [platin] *nf (tourne-disque)* turntable; **p. cassettes** cassette *ou* tape deck; **p. laser** CD player

platine² 1 *nm* platinum
2 *adj inv* **cheveux (blonds)** platinum blond hair

platiné, -e [platine] *adj* (a) *(recouvert de platine)* platinum-plated (b) *(cheveux)* platinum blond; **une blonde platinée** a platinum blonde

platitude [platityd] *nf* (a) *(manque d'intérêt)* dullness (b) *(propos)* platitude

Platon [platɔ̃] *npr* Plato

platonique [platɔnik] *adj (amour)* platonic

plâtras [plɑtʀa] *nmpl (plâtre)* rubble

plâtre [plɑtʀ] *nm* plaster; *(sculpture)* plaster cast; *(pour jambe cassée)* plaster (cast); **avoir la jambe dans le p.** to have one's leg in plaster; *Fig* **essuyer les plâtres** to put up with the teething problems

plâtrer [plɑtʀe] *vt* (a) *(mur, plafond)* to plaster; *(trou, fissure)* to plaster over (b) *(jambe, bras)* to put in plaster

plâtreux, -euse [plɑtʀø, -øz] *adj (fromage)* chalky

plâtrier [plɑtʀije] *nm* plasterer

plausible [plozibl] *adj* plausible

play-back [plɛbak] *nm inv* miming; **chanter en p.** to mime

play-boy (*pl* **play-boys**) [plɛbɔj] *nm* playboy

plèbe [plɛb] *nf* **la p.** the plebs

plébéien, -enne [plebejɛ̃, -ɛn] *adj & nm,f* plebeian

plébiscite [plebisit] *nm* plebiscite

plébisciter [plebisite] *vt* (a) *(élire)* **p. qn/qch** to vote for sb/sth by plebiscite (b) *Fig* to endorse

pléiade [plejad] *nf* **une p. de** a host of

plein, -e [plɛ̃, plɛn] 1 *adj* (a) *(rempli)* full (**de** of); **il a les doigts pleins d'encre** his fingers are covered with ink; **p. à craquer** full to bursting; **p. comme un œuf** chock-full (b) *(complet) (accord, pouvoirs)* full; **pleine lune** full moon; **pleine mer** high tide; **p. tarif** full price; *(de transports)* full fare; **travailler à p. temps** to work full-time (c) *(solide)* solid (d) *(en intensif)* **une pleine bouteille** a whole bottle; **p. sud** due south; **en p.** (milieu du) **désert/village** right in the middle of the desert/village; **en p. dans/devant/sur** right in/in front of/on; **en pleine figure/poitrine** right in the face/chest; **être en p. travail** to be hard at work; **en p. hiver** in the depths of winter; **en p. soleil** in the full heat of the sun (e) *(animal)* pregnant (f) *Fam (soûl)* plastered
2 *adv* **il avait des larmes p. les yeux** his eyes were full of tears; **elle avait de la colle p. les mains** her hands were covered with glue; **à p.** *(fonctionner)* at full capacity;

Fam **gentil tout p.** really kind; *Fam* **p. de** *(beaucoup de)* lots *ou* loads of
3 *nm* (a) *(d'essence)* **faire le p. (d'essence)** to fill up (with *Br* petrol *ou* *Am* gas); **le p., s'il vous plaît** fill her up, please; *Fig* **faire le p. d'air pur/de soleil** to get a good dose of fresh air/of sunshine (b) *(trait)* downstroke (c) **battre son p.** to be in full swing

pleinement [plɛnmɑ̃] *adv* fully; **profiter p. de qch** to take full advantage of sth

plein-emploi [plɛnɑ̃plwa] *nm* full employment

plénier, -ère [plenje, -ɛʀ] *adj* plenary

plénipotentiaire [plenipɔtɑ̃sjɛʀ] *adj & nm* plenipotentiary

plénitude [plenityd] *nf* fullness

pléonasme [pleɔnasm] *nm* pleonasm

pléthore [pletɔʀ] *nf* plethora (**de** of)

pleurer [plœʀe] 1 *vi* (a) *(verser des larmes)* to cry, to weep (**sur/pour** over/for); **p. sur son sort** to bewail one's fate; **p. de joie** to weep for joy; **p. de rage** to cry with rage; **p. à chaudes larmes**, *Fam* **p. comme une madeleine** *ou* **comme un veau** to cry one's eyes out; **bête/triste à p.** terribly stupid/sad; **j'ai les yeux qui pleurent** my eyes are watering (b) *Fig & Péj (réclamer plaintivement)* to beg; **aller p. auprès de qn** to go begging to sb
2 *vt* (a) *(regretter) (personne disparue)* to mourn (for) (b) **p. toutes les larmes de son corps** to cry one's eyes out

pleurésie [plœʀezi] *nf* pleurisy

pleureur [plœʀœʀ] *adj m voir* **saule**

pleureuse [plœʀøz] *nf (hired)* mourner

pleurnichard, -e [plœʀniʃaʀ, -aʀd] = **pleurnicheur**

pleurnicher [plœʀniʃe] *vi Fam* to whine

pleurnicheur, -euse [plœʀniʃœʀ, -øz] *Fam* 1 *nm,f* whine
2 *adj* whining

pleurote [plœʀɔt] *nm* oyster mushroom

pleurs [plœʀ] *nmpl* **en p.** in tears

pleut *voir* **pleuvoir**

pleutre [pløtʀ] *adj & nm Litt* craven

pleuvoir [56] [pløvwaʀ] 1 *v impersonnel* to rain; **il pleut** it's raining; **il pleut à verse** it's pouring (down); *Fam* **il pleut des cordes** it's coming down in buckets; *Fam* **il pleut comme vache qui pisse** it's chucking it down; **des cadeaux comme s'il en pleuvait** presents galore
2 *vi (obus, coups, insultes)* to rain down (**sur** on)

plèvre [plɛvʀ] *nf* pleura

Plexiglas® [plɛksiglas] *nm Br* Perspex®, *Am* Plexiglass®

plexus [plɛksys] *nm* plexus; **p. solaire** solar plexus

pli [pli] *nm* (a) *(de rideaux, de tissu, de papier)* fold; *(en couture)* pleat; *(faux)* crease; *Fig* **ça ne fait pas un p.** there's no doubt about it; *Fig* **prendre le p. (de faire qch)** to get into the habit (of doing sth); *Fig* **prendre un mauvais p.** to get into a bad habit (b) *(de la peau) (du ventre, du cou, du menton)* fold; *(de la bouche, des yeux)* wrinkle; *(du front)* line (c) *(enveloppe)* envelope; *(lettre)* letter; **sous p. séparé** under separate cover; **p. cacheté** sealed envelope; **envoyer qch sous p. cacheté** to send sth in a sealed envelope (d) *(aux cartes)* trick; **faire un p.** to take a trick (e) *Géol* fold

pliage [plijaʒ] *nm* folding

pliant, -e [plijɑ̃, -ɑ̃t] 1 *adj (chaise, table)* folding
2 *nm* folding stool

plie [pli] *nf* plaice

plier [66] [plije] 1 vt (a) (draps, vêtements) to fold; (page) to turn down; (voile) to furl; (parapluie, pliant) to fold up; Fig **p. bagage** to pack one's bags (b) (courber) (branche, genou) to bend; Fam Fig **être plié de rire/de douleur** to be doubled up with laughter/with pain; **être plié en deux** ou **en quatre** (de rire) to be doubled up or bent double; **être plié en deux** (de douleur) to be doubled up or bent double; **p. qn à la discipline/une règle** to impose discipline/a rule on sb

2 vi (a) (se courber) to bend (over); **p. sous le poids de qch** (poutre, branches) to bend under the weight of sth (b) (se soumettre) **se p. à la discipline** to submit to discipline; se p. **aux lois** to obey the law; se p. **aux caprices/volontés de qn** to give in to sb's whims/wishes

plinthe [plɛ̃t] nf (a) (de mur) Br skirting (board), Am baseboard (b) (de colonne) plinth

plissé, -e [plise] 1 adj (a) (visage, front) wrinkled (b) jupe **plissée** pleated skirt
2 nm pleats

plissement [plismɑ̃] nm (a) (des yeux) screwing up (b) Géol fold

plisser [plise] 1 vt (a) (front) to wrinkle; (lèvres) to pucker; (yeux) to screw up (b) (tissu, jupe) to pleat
2 vi (vêtement) to crease
3 se plisser vpr (étoffe) to crease; (bouche) to pucker; (yeux) to wrinkle up; **son front se plissa** the frowned

pliure [plijyr] nf (d'un tissu) fold; (de papier) folding; (du genou) bend

plomb [plɔ̃] nm (a) (métal) lead; **ciel de p.** leaden sky; **soleil de p.** blazing sun; Fig **n'avoir pas de p. dans la tête** to be scatterbrained; **cela lui mettra un peu de p. dans la tête** ou **dans la cervelle** that'll knock some sense into him (b) (de chasse) shot; Fam Fig **avoir du p. dans l'aile** to be in a bad way (c) Él (fusible) fuse; **faire sauter les plombs** to blow the fuses; très Fam **j'ai pété les plombs** I blew my top (d) (pour la pêche) sinker (e) (sceau) lead seal

plombage [plɔ̃baʒ] nm (a) (fait de mettre des plombs) weighting with lead (b) (d'une dent) filling

plombe [plɔ̃b] nf Fam hour

plombé, -e [plɔ̃be] adj (toit) lead(-covered); Fig (teint) livid; (ciel) leaden

plomber [plɔ̃be] 1 vt (a) (couvrir de plomb) to cover with lead (b) (mettre des plombs à) to weight with lead (c) (dent) to fill
2 se plomber (visage, ciel) to become leaden

plomberie [plɔ̃bri] nf (installations, métier) plumbing

plombier [plɔ̃bje] nm plumber

plonge [plɔ̃ʒ] nf Fam dishwashing, Br washing up; **faire la p.** to wash dishes

plongeant, -e [plɔ̃ʒɑ̃, -ɑ̃t] adj (tir, décolleté) plunging; **vue plongeante** (sur) bird's-eye view (onto)

plongée [plɔ̃ʒe] nf (a) (discipline) diving; **faire de la p.** to dive; **p. sous-marine** skin or scuba diving (b) (de sous-marin) dive (c) Cin & TV elevated shot; (verticale) bird's-eye view

plongeoir [plɔ̃ʒwar] nm diving board

plongeon [plɔ̃ʒɔ̃] nm (a) (fait de plonger) dive; **faire un p.** (nageur, gardien de but) to dive; Fam Fig **faire le p.** to hit the rocks (b) (oiseau) Br diver, Am loon

plonger [45] [plɔ̃ʒe] 1 vi (a) (nageur, sous-marin) to dive (dans into) (b) (avion, oiseau) to dive (sur onto)
2 vt aussi Fig to plunge (dans into)
3 se plonger vpr **se p. dans l'étude** to immerse oneself in one's studies; **plongé dans ses pensées** lost or deep in thought; **être plongé dans le silence** to be plunged in silence

plongeur, -euse [plɔ̃ʒœr, -øz] 1 nm,f (a) (dans l'eau) diver; **p. sous-marin** skin or scuba diver (b) Fam (dans un restaurant) dishwasher, Br washer-up
2 nm (oiseau) diver

plot [plɔ] nm (a) Él contact (b) **p. de départ** starting block

plouc [pluk] Péj 1 nm yokel, peasant
2 adj Fam naff; **ça fait p.!** that's really naff!

plouf [pluf] exclam & nm (a) (objet plus lourd) splash!

ploutocratie [plutokrasi] nf plutocracy

ployer [32] [plwaje] 1 vi (courber) to bend; (plancher, poutre) to sag; (sous un joug, un fardeau) to bend
2 vt to bend

plu voir **plaire, pleuvoir**

pluie [plɥi] nf (a) (précipitations) rain; **pluies acides** acid rain; **p. battante** driving rain; **p. fine** drizzle; **temps de p.** rainy or wet weather; **sous la p.** in the rain; **parler de la p. et du beau temps** to talk of this and that; **il n'est pas tombé** ou **né de la dernière p.** he wasn't born yesterday; Fam **faire la p. et le beau temps** to rule the roost; Prov **après la p., le beau temps** it's a long road that has no turning (b) Fig (de coups, de projectiles) hail, shower; (d'injures, de compliments) stream

plumage [plymaʒ] nm plumage

plumard [plymar] nm Fam bed

plume [plym] nf (a) (d'oiseau) feather; Fam Fig **il y a laissé des plumes** he didn't come out of it unscathed; Fam Fig **on lui a volé dans les plumes** they laid into him; **léger comme une p.** as light as a feather; Hum **perdre ses plumes** to go thin on top (b) (de stylo) nib; **p. (d'oie)** quill (pen); **écrire au fil de la p.** to write just what comes into one's head; **dessin à la p.** pen(-and-ink) drawing; **prendre la p.** to put pen to paper; **vivre de sa p.** to live by one's pen; **avoir la p. facile** to have a gift for writing

plumeau, -x [plymo] nm feather duster

plumer [plyme] vt (volaille) to pluck; Fam (personne) to fleece

plumier [plymje] nm pencil box

plupart [plypar] nf la p. most; **la p. des gens/des cas** most people/cases; **la p. d'entre eux** most of them; **la p. du temps** most of the time; (en général) in most cases; **pour la p.** for the most part, mostly

pluralisme [plyralism] nm pluralism

pluridisciplinaire [plyridisipliner] adj multi-disciplinary

pluriel, -elle [plyrjɛl] 1 adj plural
2 nm plural; **au p.** in the plural

plus 1 adv [ply] (a) (comparatif) more; **je gagne p. que vous** I earn more than you (do); **il est p. grand que moi** he's taller than I am or than me; **elle est p. jolie que belle** she is pretty rather than beautiful; **p. de** (temps, hommes) more; (avec un nombre) more than; **il a p. de vingt ans** he's over twenty; **p.... p....** the more... the more...; **p.... moins...** the more... the less...; **p. on va vers le sud, p. les jours allongent** the further south you go, the longer the days get; **de p. en p.** more and more; **de p.**

en p. froid colder and colder; **celui-ci coûte 10 francs de p. que l'autre** this one costs 10 francs more than the other one; **cette année, il y a trois élèves de** *ou* **en p.** this year there are three more *or* extra pupils; **le vin est en p.** the wine is extra; **de p.** *(aussi)* furthermore; **en p.** *(aussi)* what's more; **en p. de** besides; **sans p. attendre** without further ado

(b) *(superlatif)* **le p.** the most; **la p. longue rue** *ou* **la rue la p. longue de la ville** the longest street in the town; **c'est tout ce qu'il y a de p. simple** nothing could be simpler; **une soirée des p. réussies** a most successful evening; **qui peut le p. peut le moins** you've/he's/*etc* done more difficult things than that before

(c) *(indique la négation)* **ne… p.** no more, no longer; **je ne les vois p.** I don't see them any more, I no longer see them; **je ne le ferai p.** I won't do it again; **il n'y a p. rien** there's nothing left; **p. que dix minutes!** only ten minutes left!; **non p.** neither; **je ne suis jamais allé en Afrique – moi non p.** I've never been to Africa – neither or nor have I

(d) *(locutions)* **p. ou moins** more or less; **ni p. ni moins** no more no less; **sans p.** but no more than that

2 *conj* [plys] *(dans les calculs, dans les températures)* plus

3 *nm* [plys] **(a)** *(signe)* plus (sign)

(b) *Fig (atout)* plus

plusieurs [plyzjœr] *adj indéfini & pron indéfini* several

plus-que-parfait (*pl* **plus-que-parfaits**) [plyskəparfɛ] *nm* pluperfect, past perfect

plus-value (*pl* **plus-values**) [plyvaly] *nf (bénéfice)* profit; *(augmentation de valeur)* appreciation; *(excédent) (d'impôts)* surplus; **impôt sur les plus-values** capital gains tax

Pluton [plytɔ̃] *npr (dieu, planète)* Pluto

plutonium [plytɔnjɔm] *nm* plutonium

plutôt [plyto] *adv* rather; **p. que de faire qch** rather than doing sth

pluvial, -e, -aux, -ales [plyvjal, -o] *adj* pluvial; **eau pluviale** rainwater

pluvieux, -euse [plyvjø, -øz] *adj* rainy, wet

PME [peɛmə] *nf (abrév* **petite et moyenne entreprise)** small business

PMI [peɛmi] *nf (abrév* **petite et moyenne industrie)** small industrial firm

PMU [peɛmy] *nm (abrév* **Pari mutuel urbain)** = state-run betting system

PNB [peɛnbe] *nm (abrév* **produit national brut)** GNP

pneu [pnø] *nm* **(a)** *(de véhicule)* tyre; **avoir un p. à plat/crevé** to have a flat/a puncture; **p. à clous, p. clouté** studded tyre; *Can* **p. d'hiver** winter tyre; **p. neige** snow tyre; **p. pluie** wet-weather tyre; *Can* **p. quatre-saisons** all-season tyre **(b)** *(lettre)* express letter *(sent through a pneumatic dispatch system)*

pneumatique [pnømatik] **1** *adj (qui fonctionne à l'air)* pneumatic; *(gonflable)* inflatable

2 *nm* = **pneu**

pneumonie [pnømɔni] *nf* pneumonia

pneumothorax [pnømɔtɔraks] *nm* pneumothorax

poche [pɔʃ] *nf* **(a)** *(de vêtement)* pocket; **p. revolver** hip pocket; *Fam* **faire les poches à qn** to go through sb's pockets; **de p.** pocket; **en être de sa p.** to be out of pocket; **payer de sa p.** to pay out of one's own pocket; *Fig* **connaître un endroit comme sa p.** to know a place like the back of one's hand; *Fam Fig* **se remplir les poches, s'en mettre plein les poches** to make a

packet; **sans un sou en p.** without a penny in one's pocket; *Fam* **c'est dans la p.** it's in the bag **(b)** *(sac)* bag; **p. de glace** ice pack **(c)** *(amas de substance)* pocket; **p. de pétrole/gaz** pocket of oil/gas **(d)** *(déformation)* poches **sous les yeux** bags under the eyes; **son pantalon fait des poches aux genoux** his trousers are baggy at the knees **(e)** *(de kangourou)* pouch **(f)** *(zone)* **p. de résistance/pauvreté** pocket of resistance/deprivation

pocher [pɔʃe] *vt* **(a)** *(œuf, poisson)* to poach **(b)** *Fam* **p. l'œil à qn** to give sb a black eye

pochette [pɔʃɛt] *nf* **(a)** *(petit sac)* (small) bag; *(d'un disque)* sleeve; *(de photos)* wallet; **p. d'allumettes** book of matches **(b)** *(mouchoir)* pocket handkerchief

pochette-surprise (*pl* **pochettes-surprises**) [pɔʃɛtsyrpriz] *nf* lucky bag; *Fam* **il a eu son permis dans une p.** it's a wonder he passed his test

pochoir [pɔʃwar] *nm* stencil

podium [pɔdjɔm] *nm* podium; **monter sur le p.** to mount the podium

poêle¹ [pwal] *nf* frying pan; **passer qch à la p.** to fry sth

poêle² [pwal] *nm (appareil de chauffage)* stove; **p. à mazout** oil stove

poêlon [pwalɔ̃] *nm* casserole (dish)

poème [pɔɛm] *nm* poem

poésie [pɔezi] *nf* **(a)** *(art)* poetry **(b)** *(poème)* poem

poète [pɔɛt] *nm aussi Fig* poet

poétesse [pɔetɛs] *nf* poetess

poétique [pɔetik] *adj* poetic

poétiquement [pɔetikmɑ̃] *adv* poetically

pogne [pɔɲ] *nf Fam* paw

pognon [pɔɲɔ̃] *nm Fam* dough

pogrom(e) [pɔgrɔm] *nm* pogrom

poids [pwa] *nm* **(a)** *(masse)* weight; **de tout son p.** with all one's weight; **perdre/prendre du p.** to lose/gain weight; **vendre au p.** to sell by weight; *Fam* **il ne fait pas le p.** he's not up to scratch; **p. net/brut** net/gross weight; **p. léger** *(en boxe)* lightweight; **p. lourd** *(camion)* *Br* lorry, *Am* truck; *(en boxe)* heavyweight; **p. mouche** flyweight; **p. plume** *(en boxe)* featherweight; **p. lightweight** *Fig (charge pénible)* burden; *Litt* **le p. des ans** the weight of the years; **le p. des impôts** the burden of taxation **(c)** *Fig (importance)* weight; **donner du p. à qch** to give weight to sth; **avoir du p.** to carry weight; **faire deux poids deux mesures** to apply double standards **(d)** *(sport)* shot; **lancer le p.** to put the shot

poignant, -e [pwaɲɑ̃, -ɑ̃t] *adj* poignant

poignard [pwaɲar] *nm* dagger

poignarder [pwaɲarde] *vt* to stab

poigne [pwaɲ] *nf* grip; **avoir de la p.** to have a strong grip; *Fig* to be firm

poignée [pwaɲe] *nf* **(a)** *(quantité, petit nombre)* handful **(b)** *(de porte, sac)* handle; *(d'épée)* hilt **(c)** **p. de main** handshake

poignet [pwaɲɛ] *nm* **(a)** *(du bras)* wrist; *Fig* **faire qch à la force du p.** to do sth by sheer hard work **(b)** *(de chemise)* cuff

poil [pwal] *nm* **(a)** *(d'un animal, d'une personne, d'une plante)* hair; *(pelage)* coat; *(d'une brosse, d'un pinceau)* bristle; à p. long/ras long/short-haired; *Fam* caresser qn dans le sens du p. to rub sb up the right way; *Fam* tomber sur le p. à qn to lay into sb; *Fam* à p. stark naked; *Fam* se mettre à p. to strip off; *Fam* avoir un p. dans la main to be bone idle; *Fam* reprendre du p. de la bête to pick up again; *Fam* Fig de tous poils of all sorts; *Fam* être de bon/mauvais p. to be in a good/bad mood; *Fam* au quart de p. perfectly; *Fam* à un p. près very nearly; *Fam* un p. plus haut/moins vite a touch higher/slower; *Fam* au p. great **(b)** p. à gratter itching powder

poiler [pwale] **se poiler** *vpr Fam* to kill oneself laughing

poilu, -e [pwaly] **1** *adj* hairy
2 *nm Fam* poilu (French soldier 1914-1918)

poinçon [pwɛ̃sɔ̃] *nm* *(de graveur)* style; *(de cordonnier)* awl; *(marque)* hallmark

poinçonner [pwɛ̃sɔne] *vt* *(perforer)* to punch; *(or, argent)* to hallmark

poinçonneur, -euse [pwɛ̃sɔnœr, -øz] **1** *nm,f* *(personne)* ticket puncher
2 *nf* poinçonneuse punching machine

poindre [43] [pwɛ̃dr] *vi* *(jour)* to dawn, to break; *(plantes, étoiles)* to appear

poing [pwɛ̃] *nm* fist; **sabre/revolver au p.** sword/revolver in hand; **les poings sur les hanches** hands on hips, arms akimbo; **dormir à poings fermés** to sleep like a log

point¹ [pwɛ̃] *nm* **(a)** *(endroit)* point, spot; *(en géométrie)* point; **les quatre points cardinaux** the (four) points of the compass; *Ordinat* p. de césure breakpoint, hyphenation point; *Fig* p. chaud *(zone de conflits)* hot spot, trouble spot; **p. de côté** *(douleur)* stitch; *aussi Fig* **p. de départ** starting point; **p. d'eau** *(dans la nature)* waterhole; **p. de mire** target; *Fig* focus; *Aut* **p. mort** neutral; *Fig* être au p. mort to be at a standstill; **p. noir** *(comédon)* blackhead; *(embouteillage)* blackspot; **p. de rencontre** meeting point; **p. de vente** *(magasin)* point of sale, sales outlet; **p. de vue** *(panorama)* viewpoint; *(opinion)* point of view; **du p. de vue international/économique** from an international/economic point of view

(b) *(marque)* dot; *(en fin de ligne)* Br full stop, Am period; *Fig* mettre les points sur les i (à qn) to make oneself perfectly clear (to sb); *Typ & Ordinat* points par pouce dots per inch; **deux points** colon; **p. d'exclamation** exclamation Br mark or Am point; *Br* full stop, Am period; *Fam* un p., c'est tout!, p. final! and that's that!; *aussi Fig* **p. d'interrogation** question mark; **points de suspension** suspension points; *Ordinat* **p. de tabulation** tab marker

(c) *(aspect, question)* point; **en tous points** in every way, in all respects; **p. faible/fort** weak/strong point

(d) *(de couture, de tricot)* stitch; **p. de croix** cross-stitch; **p. mousse** garter stitch

(e) *(phase, degré)* point, stage; **traiter un problème en trois points** to deal with a problem in three stages; **(cuit)** à p. done to a turn; *(steak)* medium-rare; **jusqu'à un certain p.** to a certain extent, up to a (certain) point; **au p. où j'en suis...** at the stage I've reached...; à **tel p. que..., au p. que...** to such an extent that..., so much so that...; **vous n'êtes pas malade à ce p.-là** you're not as ill as all that; **au plus haut p.** extremely

(f) *(dans le temps)* point; **être sur le p. de faire qch** to be about to do sth, to be on the point of doing sth; **arriver à p. nommé** to arrive just at the right moment

(g) *(dans un score, dans un pourcentage)* point; *(dans une notation)* mark; *Scol* bon p. ≃ gold star

(h) mettre au p. *(objectif)* to focus; *(moteur)* to tune; *(technique)* to perfect; *(stratégie)* to finalize; être au p. to be up to scratch

(i) *Naut & Av* faire le p. to take one's bearings; *Fig* to take stock; *Fig* faire le p. sur qch to take stock of sth

point² *adv Vieilli* = **pas²**

pointage [pwɛ̃taʒ] *nm* **(a)** *(contrôle)* *(de noms sur une liste)* ticking off; *(de votes)* counting; *(au travail)* *(à l'arrivée)* clocking in; *(au départ)* clocking out **(b)** *(d'un télescope)* pointing; *(de fusil)* aiming

pointe [pwɛ̃t] *nf* **(a)** *(extrémité)* *(d'aiguille, de couteau)* point; *(de flèche)* tip; *(de balle)* nose; *(de chaussure)* toe; *(de sein)* nipple; **p. d'asperge** asparagus tip; **p. en p.** pointed; **sur la p. des pieds** on tiptoe; **entrer sur la p. des pieds** to tiptoe in; **faire des pointes** *(en danse)* to go up on points **(b)** *(maximum)* peak; **p. de vitesse** burst of speed; **faire une p. de vitesse** to put on a burst of speed; **vitesse de p.** top speed **(c)** *(summum)* être à la p. de la technique/de la recherche to be in the forefront of technology/of research; **de p.** *(secteur, industrie, technique)* state-of-the-art **(d)** *(petite quantité)* *(d'accent, d'ironie)* hint; *(d'ail, de vanille)* dash **(e)** *(naillerie)* dig; **lancer des pointes à qn** to make digs at sb **(f)** *(clou)* nail; *(pour tapis)* tack; *(sur une chaussure de sport)* spike; **chaussures à pointes** spiked shoes

pointer¹ [pwɛ̃te] **1** *vt* **(a)** *(vérifier)* *(noms sur une liste)* to tick off; *(votes)* to count **(b)** *(dresser)* **p. les oreilles** to prick up its ears **(c)** *(diriger)* *(télescope)* to point *(sur* at*)*; *(fusil)* to aim *(sur* at*)*; *Ordinat* *(curseur)* to position *(sur* on*)*; **j'ai pointé le doigt vers lui** I pointed (my finger) at him
2 *vi* **(a)** *(au travail)* *(à l'arrivée)* to clock in; *(à la sortie)* to clock out **(b)** *(apparaître)* *(jour)* to come up; *(jour)* to dawn **(c)** *(se dresser)* *(clocher, tour, arbre)* to rise **(d)** *(au jeu de boules)* to get one's ball nearest to the jack
3 se pointer *vpr Fam* to show up

pointer² [pwɛ̃ter] *nm* *(chien)* pointer

pointeur, -euse [pwɛ̃tœr, -øz] **1** *nm,f* *(contrôleur)* timekeeper; *(en sport)* scorer
2 *nm Ordinat* pointer
3 *nf* pointeuse *(machine)* timeclock

pointillé [pwɛ̃tije] *nm* **(a)** *(trait)* dotted line; *(sur une feuille détachable)* perforations; **découper suivant les pointillés** cut along the dotted line **(b)** *(technique de dessin)* stippling

pointilleux, -euse [pwɛ̃tijø, -øz] *adj* particular, fussy *(sur* about*)*

pointu, -e [pwɛ̃ty] **1** *adj* **(a)** *(en forme de pointe)* pointed; *(voix)* shrill; *Fig* *(susceptible)* *(ton de la voix, humeur)* touchy **(c)** *Fig* *(spécialisé)* specialized
2 *adv* parler p. to speak with a Parisian accent

pointure [pwɛ̃tyr] *nf* size; *Fam Fig* une (grosse) p. du cinéma français a major name in French cinema

point-virgule *(pl* points-virgules*)* [pwɛ̃virgyl] *nm* semicolon

poire [pwar] *nf* **(a)** *(fruit)* pear; *Fig* couper la p. en deux to meet each other halfway; *(faire la moyenne entre deux quantités)* to split the difference **(b)** *(objet en forme de poire)* *(d'un appareil photo)* bulb; *(interrupteur)* switch **(c)** *Fam* *(tête)* mug; **en pleine p.** right in the face **(d)** *Fam* *(idiot)* sucker, mug; **et moi, bonne p., j'ai accepté** and like the sucker or mug I am, I accepted

poireau, -x [pwaro] *nm* leek; *Fam* faire le p. to hang around

poireauter [pwarote] *vi Fam* to hang around

poirier [pwarje] *nm* (a) *(arbre)* pear tree; **faire le p.** to do a headstand, to stand on one's head (b) *(bois)* pear-tree wood

pois [pwa] *nm* (a) *(plante)* pea; **petit p.** (garden) pea; **p. cassés** split peas; **p. chiche** chickpea; **p. de senteur** sweet pea (b) *(rond)* (polka) dot; **à p.** polka-dot

poison [pwazɔ̃] 1 *nm* poison
2 *nmf Fam (personne)* pest

poisse [pwas] *nf Fam* bad luck

poisseux, -euse [pwasø, -øz] *adj* sticky

poisson [pwasɔ̃] *nm* (a) *(animal)* fish; **p. d'eau douce/ de mer** freshwater/saltwater fish; *Prov* **petit p. deviendra grand** great oaks from little acorns grow; **p. d'argent** silverfish; **p. d'avril** April fool; **p. rouge** goldfish; **p. volant** flying fish (b) *Astron & Astrol* **les Poissons** Pisces; **être Poissons** to be (a) Pisces

poisson-chat (*pl* **poissons-chats**) [pwasɔ̃ʃa] *nm* catfish

poissonnerie [pwasɔnri] *nf* fish shop, *Br* fishmonger's

poissonneux, -euse [pwasɔnø, -øz] *adj* full of fish

poissonnier, -ère [pwasɔnje, -ɛr] *nm,f Br* fishmonger, *Am* fish merchant

poitevin, -e [pwatvɛ̃, -in] *adj (de Poitiers)* of Poitiers; *(du Poitou)* of Poitou

poitrail [pwatraj] *nm (d'animal)* breast; *Fam (poitrine)* chest

poitrinaire [pwatriner] *adj & nmf Vieilli* consumptive

poitrine [pwatrin] *nf* (a) *(thorax)* chest; *(seins)* bust; **serrer qn contre sa p.** to hold sb to one's breast; **ne pas avoir beaucoup de p.** to have a small bust (b) *Culin (de veau)* breast; *(de bœuf)* brisket; *(de porc)* belly

poivre [pwavr] *nm* pepper; **p. en grains** peppercorns; **p. et sel** *(cheveux, barbe)* pepper-and-salt

poivré, -e [pwavre] *adj* (a) *(nourriture, odeur)* peppery (b) *Fig (histoire)* spicy

poivrer [pwavre] 1 *vt* to put pepper on/in
2 **se poivrer** *vpr Fam* to get plastered

poivrier [pwavrije] *nm* (a) *(plante)* pepper plant (b) *(petit pot)* pepper pot; *(moulin)* pepper mill

poivron [pwavrɔ̃] *nm* pepper

poivrot, -e [pwavro, -ɔt] *nm,f Fam* drunk

poix [pwa] *nf* pitch

poker [pɔkɛr] *nm* poker

polaire [pɔlɛr] *adj (faune, expédition)* polar; *(froid)* Arctic

polar [pɔlar] *nm Fam* whodunnit

polarisation [pɔlarizasjɔ̃] *nf* (a) *Phys* polarization (b) *Fig (focalisation)* focusing

polariser [pɔlarize] 1 *vt Phys* to polarize; *Fig (attention)* to focus
2 **se polariser** *vpr* **se p. sur** to focus on

Polaroid® [pɔlarɔid] *nm* Polaroid® (camera)

pôle [pol] *nm* (a) *Géog* pole; **p. Nord/Sud** North/South Pole (b) *Fig* **p. d'intérêt** focus of interest; **p. d'attraction** centre of attention

polémique [pɔlemik] 1 *adj* polemical
2 *nf* heated debate

polémiquer [pɔlemike] *vi* to debate

poli¹, -e [pɔli] *adj (lisse)* polished

poli², -e *adj (courtois)* polite (**avec** to)

police¹ [pɔlis] *nf* (a) *(maintien de l'ordre)* policing; **faire la p.** to keep order (b) *(institution)* **la p.** the police; **appeler p. secours** to call the police *(in an emergency)*; **être de** *ou* **dans la p.** to be in the police; **p. de l'air et des frontières** airport and border police; **p. judiciaire** police investigation department; **p. mondaine** *ou* **des mœurs** vice squad; **p. montée** mounted police; **p. municipale** local police; **la p. nationale** the national police force; **p. secrète** secret police

police² *nf* (a) *(d'assurance)* policy; **p. d'assurance** insurance policy (b) *Ordinat* **p.** (**de caractères**) font; **p. bitmap** *ou* **pixélisée** bitmap font; **p. de taille variable** scalable font; **p. vectorielle** outline font

polichinelle [pɔliʃinɛl] *nm (marionnette)* Punch (b) *Fig & Péj* buffoon

policier, -ère [pɔlisje, -ɛr] 1 *adj (enquête, État, régime)* police; *(roman, film)* detective
2 *nm* (a) *(personne)* policeman, police officer; **femme p.** policewoman, woman police officer (b) *(roman)* detective novel; *(film)* detective film

policlinique [pɔliklinik] *nf* outpatients' clinic

poliment [pɔlimɑ̃] *adv* politely

polio [pɔljo] 1 *nf* polio
2 *nmf* polio victim

poliomyélite [pɔljɔmjelit] *nf* poliomyelitis

polir [pɔlir] *vt* to polish

polisson, -onne [pɔlisɔ̃, -ɔn] 1 *nm,f (enfant espiègle)* rascal
2 *adj* (a) *(espiègle)* naughty (b) *(grivois)* saucy

politesse [pɔlitɛs] *nf* politeness; **par p.** out of politeness; **ce serait la moindre des politesses de le prévenir** it's only polite to warn him; **rendre la p. à qn** to return sb's favour

politicien, -enne [pɔlitisjɛ̃, -ɛn] 1 *nm,f* politician
2 *adj Péj* **politique politicienne** politicking

politique [pɔlitik] 1 *adj* political
2 *nf* (a) *(de gouvernement, d'entreprise)* policy; **p. intérieure/extérieure** domestic/foreign policy; **la p. du pire** = the policy of presenting one's situation in the worst possible light in order to achieve one's objectives; **la p. agricole commune** the Common Agricultural Policy (b) *(affaires publiques)* politics; **faire de la p.** *(en tant que politicien)* to be in politics; *(en tant que militant)* to be involved in politics
3 *nm (personne)* politician

politiquement [pɔlitikmɑ̃] *adv* politically

politisation [pɔlitizasjɔ̃] *nf* politicization

politiser [pɔlitize] *vt* to politicize

politologue [pɔlitɔlɔg] *nmf* political scientist

polka [pɔlka] *nf* polka

pollen [pɔlɛn] *nm* pollen

polluant, -e [pɔlɥɑ̃, -ɑ̃t] 1 *adj* polluting; **produit p.** pollutant
2 *nm* pollutant

pollué, -e [pɔlɥe] *adj* polluted

polluer [pɔlɥe] *vt* to pollute

pollueur, -euse [pɔlɥœr, -øz] 1 *nm,f* polluter
2 *adj* polluting

pollution [pɔlysjɔ̃] *nf* pollution

polo [pɔlo] *nm* (a) *(sport)* polo (b) *(chemise)* polo shirt

polochon [pɔlɔʃɔ̃] *nm Fam* bolster; **bataille de polochons** pillow fight

Pologne [pɔlɔɲ] *nf* **la P.** Poland

polonais, -e [polɔnɛ, -ɛz] **1** *adj* Polish
2 *nm,f* P. Pole
3 *nm (langue)* Polish
4 *nf* **polonaise** *(danse)* polonaise

poltron, -onne [poltrõ, -ɔn] **1** *adj* cowardly
2 *nm,f* coward

polyamide [poliamid] *nm* polyamide

polychrome [polikrom] *adj* polychrome

polyclinique [poliklinik] *nf* polyclinic

polycopie [polikɔpi] *nf (procédé)* duplication; *(document)* duplicate

polycopié, -e [polikɔpje] **1** *adj* duplicated
2 *nm* duplicate; *Scol & Univ* duplicated course material

polycopier [66] [polikɔpje] *vt* to duplicate

polyculture [polikyltyr] *nf* mixed farming

polyester [poliɛstɛr] *nm* polyester

polygame [poligam] **1** *adj* polygamous
2 *nmf* polygamist

polygamie [poligami] *nf* polygamy

polyglotte [poliglɔt] *adj & nmf* polyglot

polygone [poligon, poligõn] *nm* **(a)** *(figure)* polygon **(b)** *Mil* shooting range

polymère [polimɛr] **1** *adj* polymeric
2 *nm* polymer

Polynésie [polinezi] *nf* **la P.** Polynesia; **la P. française** French Polynesia

polynésien, -enne [polinezjɛ̃, -ɛn] **1** *adj* Polynesian
2 *nm,f* P. Polynesian

polype [polip] *nm* polyp

polyphonie [polifɔni] *nf* polyphony

polysémique [polisemik] *adj* polysemous

polystyrène [polistirɛn] *nm* polystyrene

polytechnicien, -enne [politɛknisjɛ̃, -ɛn] *nm,f* graduate of the 'École polytechnique'

Polytechnique [politɛknik] *nf* **(l'École) p.**, **P.** = 'grande école' specializing in technology

polythéisme [politeism] *nm* polytheism

polyvalence [polivalɑ̃s] *nf (en chimie)* polyvalency; *Fig (d'une personne)* versatility

polyvalent, -e [polivalɑ̃, -ɑ̃t] **1** *adj* **(a)** *(en chimie)* polyvalent **(b)** *(salle)* multi-purpose; *(outil, personne)* versatile
2 *nm* tax inspector

pomélo [pomelo] *nm* pomelo

pommade [pomad] *nf* ointment; *Fam* **passer de la p. à qn** to butter sb up

pomme [pom] *nf* **(a)** *(fruit)* apple; *Fam* **haut comme trois pommes** knee-high to a grasshopper; *Fam* **tomber dans les pommes** to pass out; **p. être dans les pommes** to be out for the count; **p. d'Adam** Adam's apple; **p. de discorde** bone of contention; **p. de pin** pine cone; *(de sapin)* fir cone **(b)** *(partie arrondie) (de bois de lit, de canne)* knob; *(d'arrosoir)* rose; **p. de douche** shower head **(c)** *(pomme de terre)* **pommes allumettes** matchstick *Br* chips or *Am* potatoes; **pommes chips** (potato) *Br* crisps or *Am* chips; **pommes dauphine** dauphine potatoes; **p. de terre** potato; **pommes (de terre) à l'eau** boiled potatoes; **pommes (de terre) frites** *Br* chips, *Am* (French) fries; **pommes (de terre) sautées** sauté potatoes; **pommes vapeur** steamed potatoes **(d)** *Fam (personne)* **ma p.** yours truly; **ta p.** you; **sa p.** him/her **(d)** *Fam (idiot)* mug

pommeau, -x [pomo] *nm (d'un sabre, d'une selle)* pommel; *(d'une canne, d'un levier de vitesse)* knob

pommelé, -e [pomle] *adj* dappled; **gris p.** *(cheval)* dapple-grey; **ciel p.** mackerel sky

pommer [pome] *vi (chou, salade)* to form a heart

pommeraie [pomrɛ] *nf* apple orchard

pommette [pomɛt] *nf* cheekbone

pommier [pomje] *nm* apple tree; **p. sauvage** crab-apple tree

pompage [põpaʒ] *nm* pumping

pompe¹ [põp] *nf (cérémonie)* pomp, ceremony; **en grande p.** with great (pomp and) ceremony

pompe² [põp] *nf* **(a)** *(machine)* pump; **p. à essence** *(distributeur)* *Br* petrol or *Am* gas pump; *(station-service)* *Br* petrol or *Am* gas station; **p. à incendie** water pump *(on a fire engine)*; **p. à vélo** bicycle pump; *Fam* **à toute p.** like lightning; *Fam* **faire des pompes** to do *Br* press-ups or *Am* push-ups **(b)** *Fam* **pompes** *(chaussures)* shoes; *Fig* **il est à côté de ses pompes** he's not with it **(c)** **pompes funèbres** undertaker's

pomper [põpe] **1** *vt* **(a)** *(puiser) (eau, air)* to pump; *(faire monter)* to pump up; *(évacuer)* to pump out; *Fam Fig* **p. qn** *(épuiser)* to do sb in; *Fam* **être pompé** to be done in; *Fam* **tu me pompes l'air** you're getting on my nerves **(b)** *Fam (boisson)* to knock back; *Fam Scol* to crib *(sur* from)
2 *vi* **(a)** *(faire marcher une pompe)* to pump **(b)** *Fam Scol* to crib *(sur* from)

pompette [põpɛt] *adj Fam* tipsy

pompeux, -euse [põpø, -øz] *adj Péj* pompous

pompier¹ [põpje] *nm* fireman; **appeler les pompiers** to call the fire *Br* brigade or *Am* department

pompier², -ère [põpje, -ɛr] *adj (art, style)* pompous

pompiste [põpist] *nmf* pump attendant

pompon [põpõ] *nm* pompom, bobble; **bonnet à p.** bobble hat; *Fam* **c'est le p.!** that's the limit!

pomponner [põpone] **se pomponner** *vpr Fam* to doll oneself up

ponce [põs] *adj voir* **pierre**

poncer [16] [põse] *vt* **(a)** *(au papier de verre, avec une ponceuse)* to sand (down) **(b)** *(passer à la pierre ponce)* to pumice

ponceuse [põsøz] *nf* sander

poncho [põtʃo] *nm* poncho

poncif [põsif] *nm* cliché, commonplace

ponction [põksjõ] *nf Méd (ponction) (de poumon)* tapping; **p. lombaire** lumbar puncture; *Fig* **faire des ponctions dans ses économies** to draw on one's savings; **p. fiscale** taxation

ponctualité [põktyalite] *nf* punctuality

ponctuation [põktyasjõ] *nf* punctuation

ponctuel, -elle [põktyɛl] *adj* **(a)** *(à l'heure)* punctual **(b)** *(unique)* *Br* one-off, *Am* one-of-a-kind; *(isolé)* selective

ponctuellement [põktyɛlmã] *adv (de façon limitée)* on a *Br* one-off or *Am* one-of-a-kind basis

ponctuer [põktɥe] *vt aussi Fig* to punctuate *(de* with)

pondaison [põdɛzõ] *nf* egg-laying time

pondéral [põderal] *adj voir* **surcharge**

pondération [põderasjõ] *nf* **(a)** *(modération)* level-headedness **(b)** *Écon* weighting

pondéré, -e [põdere] *adj* **(a)** *(personne)* level-headed **(b)** *Écon* weighted

pondeuse [pɔ̃døz] *adj f & nf* (**poule**) p. layer

pondre [pɔ̃dr] *vt* (a) (*œuf*) to lay (b) *Fam* (*produire*) to turn out

poney [pɔnɛ] *nm* pony

pont [pɔ̃] *nm* (a) (*sur un cours d'eau*) bridge; **les Ponts et Chaussées** the Highways Department; *Fig* **faire un p. d'or à qn** to give sb a golden hello; **p. suspendu** suspension bridge (b) *Fig* (*congés*) long weekend; **le p. du premier mai** the May Day long weekend; **faire le p.** to make a long weekend of it (c) (*d'un navire*) deck; **sur le p.** on deck (d) (*lien*) **couper les ponts (avec qn)** to break off all relations (with sb); **p. aérien** airlift; *Ordinat* **p. routeur** routing node (e) *Ind* **p. roulant** travelling crane

pontage [pɔ̃taʒ] *nm Méd* bypass (operation)

ponte¹ [pɔ̃t] *nf* (*action*) (egg) laying; (*œufs*) eggs (laid)

ponte² *nm Fam* (**grand**) **p.** (*personnage important*) big shot

pontife [pɔ̃tif] *nm Rel* pontiff; **le souverain p.** the Supreme Pontiff

pontifiant, -e [pɔ̃tifjɑ̃, ɑ̃t] *adj Péj* pontificating

pontifical, -e, -aux, -ales [pɔ̃tifikal, -o] *adj* papal

pontifier [66] [pɔ̃tifje] *vi* to pontificate

pont-l'évêque [pɔ̃levɛk] *nm inv* Pont-l'Évêque (cheese)

pont-levis (*pl* **ponts-levis**) [pɔ̃ləvi] *nm* drawbridge

ponton [pɔ̃tɔ̃] *nm* pontoon

pop [pop] *adj inv & nf* pop

pop-corn [pɔpkɔrn] *nm inv* popcorn

pope [pop] *nm Rel* (Orthodox) priest

popeline [poplin] *nf* poplin

popote [pɔpɔt] *nf* (a) *Fam* (*cuisine*) cooking; **faire la p.** to do the cooking (b) *Mil* officers' mess
2 *adj inv Fam* stay-at-home

popotin [pɔpɔtɛ̃] *nm Fam Br* bum, *Am* butt

populace [pɔpylas] *nf* rabble, mob

populaire [pɔpylɛr] *adj* (a) (*du peuple, qui plaît*) popular (b) (*langue, expression*) vernacular (c) (*ouvrier*) working-class; **les classes populaires** the working classes

populariser [pɔpylarize] *vt* to popularize

popularité [pɔpylarite] *nf* popularity

population [pɔpylasjɔ̃] *nf* population; **p. active** working population

populeux, -euse [pɔpylø, -øz] *adj* crowded

populisme [pɔpylism] *nm* populism

populo [pɔpylo] *nm Fam* (*foule*) crowd (of people)

porc [pɔr] *nm* (a) (*animal*) pig, *Am* hog; *Fig* (*homme grossier*) pig (b) (*viande*) pork (c) (*cuir*) pigskin

porcelaine [pɔrsəlɛn] *nf* (*matière*) porcelain, china; (*objet*) piece of porcelain

porcelet [pɔrsəlɛ] *nm* piglet

porc-épic (*pl* **porcs-épics**) [pɔrkepik] *nm* porcupine

porche [pɔrʃ] *nm* porch

porcherie [pɔrʃəri] *nf aussi Fig Br* pigsty, *Am* pigpen

porcin, -e [pɔrsɛ̃, -in] **1** *adj* pig; *Péj* (*visage, yeux*) piggy
2 *nmpl* **porcins** pigs, *Am* hogs

pore [pɔr] *nm* pore

poreux, -euse [pɔrø, -øz] *adj* porous

porno [pɔrno] *adj & nm Fam* porn

pornographie [pɔrnɔgrafi] *nf* pornography

pornographique [pɔrnɔgrafik] *adj* pornographic

port¹ [pɔr] *nm* (a) (*pour bateaux*) harbour; (*plus important*) port; *Fig* **arriver à bon p.** to arrive safe and sound; **p. d'attache** home port; *Fig* home base; **p. de commerce** commercial port; **p. de pêche** fishing port; **p. de plaisance** marina (b) *Ordinat* port; **p. de communication** comms port, communications port; **p. d'entrée/sortie** input/output port; **p. d'E/S** I/O port; **p. d'extension** expansion port; **p. modem** modem port; **p. parallèle** parallel port; **p. série** serial port; **p. souris** mouse port

port² *nm* (a) (*fait de transporter*) carrying; **p. d'armes** carrying of firearms (b) (*fait de revêtir*) wearing; **le p. du casque est obligatoire** (*sur panneau*) safety helmets must be worn (c) (*de marchandises*) carriage; (*de paquets, de lettres, de télégrammes*) delivery; **p. et emballage** postage and packing; **p. franc** (*de marchandises*) carriage paid; **p. payé** (*de magazine*) postage paid (d) (*allure*) bearing; **un gracieux p. de tête** a graceful manner of holding one's head

portabilité [pɔrtabilite] *nf Ordinat* portability

portable [pɔrtabl] **1** *adj* (a) (*ordinateur, machine à écrire*) portable (b) (*vêtement*) wearable
2 *nm* (*ordinateur*) laptop, portable

portage [pɔrtaʒ] *nm Can* portage

portager [45] [pɔrtaʒe] *vi Can* to portage

portail [pɔrtaj] *nm* portal

portant, -e [pɔrtɑ̃, -ɑ̃t] *adj* **être bien/mal p.** to be in good/poor health

portatif, -ive [pɔrtatif, -iv] *adj* portable

Port-au-Prince [pɔroprɛ̃s] *n* Port-au-Prince

porte [pɔrt] *nf* (a) (*de maison, de placard, de véhicule*) door; **à ma p.** on my doorstep; **de p. à p.** door to door; **p. entre deux portes** briefly; **mettre qn à la p.** to throw sb out; (*d'un emploi*) to fire sb; **trouver p. close** to find nobody in; *Fam* **ce n'est pas la p. à côté** it's hardly just around the corner; **c'est la p. ouverte à...** it's leaving the door wide open to...; (*voiture*) **deux/quatre/cinq portes** two-/four-/five-door car; **p. cochère** carriage entrance; **p. de derrière** back; *Fig* **p. d'entrée** front door; **p. tournante, p. à tambour** revolving door; **p. vitrée** glass door (c) (*d'une ville*) gate; **aux portes du désert** at the gateway to the desert; **p. (d'embarquement)** (*dans un aéroport*) (boarding) gate (c) (*en ski*) gate

porté, -e [pɔrte] *adj* (*enclin*) **être p. à faire qch** to be inclined to do sth; *Fam* **être p. sur la bouteille** to be fond of the bottle; *Fam* **être p. sur la chose** to have a one-track mind

porte-à-faux [pɔrtafo] **en porte-à-faux** *adv* overhanging; *Fig* **être en p.** to be awkwardly placed

porte-à-porte [pɔrtapɔrt] *nm* door-to-door selling; **faire du p.** (*pour vendre*) to sell from door to door; (*faire des enquêtes*) to go from door to door

porte-avions [pɔrtavjɔ̃] *nm inv* aircraft carrier

porte-bagages [pɔrtbagaʒ] *nm inv* (*de bicyclette*) carrier; (*de train*) luggage rack

porte-bébé (*pl* **porte-bébés**) [pɔrtbebe] *nm* baby carrier

porte-bonheur [pɔrtbɔnœr] *nm inv* (lucky) charm

porte-bouteilles [pɔrtbutɛj] *nm inv* (*pour stocker*) wine rack; (*pour porter*) bottle-carrier

porte-cartes [pɔrtkart] *nm inv* (*portefeuille*) card-holder

porte-cigarettes [pɔrtsigarɛt] *nm inv* cigarette case

porte-clefs, porte-clés [pɔrtəklɛ] nm inv key ring

porte-documents [pɔrtdɔkymɑ̃] nm inv briefcase

porte-drapeau (pl **porte-drapeaux** ou **porte-drapeau**) [pɔrtdrapo] nm aussi Fig standard bearer

portée [pɔrte] nf (a) (petits) litter; (d'une truie) farrow (b) (amplitude) (d'un fusil, d'un émetteur, de la voix) range; Fig (d'un traité) scope; **à p. de (la) main** within reach, to hand; **à p. de (la) voix** within earshot; **à la p. de toutes les bourses** within everyone's means; **c'est à ma p.** (objet) it's within my reach; Fig (livre) I can understand it; **hors de ma p.** (objet) beyond my reach; Fig (livre) beyond me; **hors de p.** out of reach (c) Fig (impact) (de paroles, d'une décision) significance (d) Mus stave

portefaix [pɔrtəfɛ] nm porter

porte-fenêtre [pl **portes-fenêtres**] [pɔrtfənɛtr] nf French window

portefeuille [pɔrtəfœj] nm (a) (pour l'argent) wallet, Am billfold; **faire un lit en p.** to make an apple-pie bed; **jupe p.** wrapover skirt (b) Fin & Pol portfolio; **p. d'actions/de titres** share/securities portfolio

porte-jarretelles [pɔrtʒartɛl] nm inv Br suspender or Am garter belt

porte-malheur [pɔrtmalœr] nm inv jinx

portemanteau, -x [pɔrtmɑ̃to] nm (au mur) coat rack; (sur pied) coat stand

portemine [pɔrtəmin] nm propelling pencil

porte-monnaie [pɔrtmɔnɛ] nm inv purse; **p. électronique** electronic purse

porte-parapluies [pɔrtparaplɥi] nm inv umbrella stand

porte-parole [pɔrtparɔl] nm inv spokesperson, spokesman, f spokeswoman

porte-plume [pɔrtəplym] nm inv penholder

porter [pɔrte] 1 vt (a) (soutenir) to carry; **mes jambes ne me portent plus** my legs won't carry me any further; **je ne le porte pas dans mon cœur** he's not exactly my favourite person

(b) (emporter) to take; (amener) to bring

(c) (vêtement, chapeau, lunettes) to wear; (signature, date) to bear; (prénom, nom) to have; **p. une moustache/la barbe** to have a moustache/a beard; **p. les cheveux courts/longs** to wear one's hair short/long, to have short/long hair; **p. le nom de qn** to be named after sb; **p. le titre de...** (livre, film) to be entitled...

(d) (produire) (fruits) to bear

(e) (diriger) **p. un coup à qn** to strike sb; **p. la main à son front** to hold one's hand to one's forehead; **p. son attention sur qch** to turn one's attention to sth, to give sth one's attention; **p. une affaire devant les tribunaux** to bring a matter to court; **p. qch à la connaissance de qn** to bring sth to sb's attention

(f) (inscrire) to enter; **se faire p. malade** to report sick

(g) (inciter) **tout (me) porte à croire que...** everything leads me to believe that...

(h) (à un niveau plus élevé) **p. la température à 100°** to raise the temperature to 100°; **portez le liquide à ébullition** bring the liquid to the boil; **cela portera à 100 francs le prix du billet** that will bring the price of the ticket up to 100 francs

2 vi (a) (cogner) **p. sur/contre qch** to hit sth

(b) (atteindre son objectif) (coup) to strike home, to hit its target; (voix) to carry

3 **porter sur** vt ind (a) (avoir pour sujet) to be about

(b) Fam **p. sur les nerfs à qn** to get on sb's nerves

4 **se porter** vpr (a) (physiquement) **se p. bien** to be well; **je ne m'en porte pas plus mal** I'm none the worse for it; Hum **moins je le vois, mieux je me porte** the less I see him, the better I feel

(b) (devoir être porté) to be worn; (être à la mode) to be fashionable

(c) (se présenter comme) **se p. candidat** to Br stand or Am run as a candidate; **se p. caution** to stand surety

(d) (aller) **se p. au secours de qn** to go to sb's assistance

(e) **se p. sur** (sujet: regard, choix) to fall on

porte-savon (pl **porte-savons** ou **porte-savon**) [pɔrtsavɔ̃] nm soapdish

porte-serviettes [pɔrtsɛrvjɛt] nm inv towel rail

porteur, -euse [pɔrtœr, -øz] 1 nm,f (a) (d'un message, de nouvelles) bearer; **par p.** by messenger (b) (de gare, d'aéroport) porter; **p. d'eau** water carrier (c) Méd carrier; **p. sain** = carrier who doesn't have the symptoms of the disease (d) (détenteur) holder; (d'un chèque) bearer; **payable au p.** payable to bearer

2 adj (a) Él **fréquence/onde porteuse** carrier frequency/wave (b) (marché, créneau) growth

porte-voix [pɔrtavwa] nm inv megaphone; (électrique) Br loudhailer, Am bullhorn; **mettre ses mains en p.** to cup one's hands round one's mouth

portier [pɔrtje] nm porter, doorkeeper; (dans un hôtel) commissionaire; **p. de nuit** night porter

portière [pɔrtjɛr] nf (d'une voiture, d'un train) door

portillon [pɔrtijɔ̃] nm gate; (d'un passage à niveau) side gate; **p. (automatique)** (de gare, de métro) gate, barrier

portion [pɔrsjɔ̃] nf portion; **être réduit à la p. congrue** to get the smallest share

portique [pɔrtik] nm (a) (colonnes) portico (b) (pour agrès) (cross)beam

Porto [pɔrto] n Oporto

porto [pɔrto] nm port

portoricain, -e [pɔrtɔrikɛ̃, -ɛn] 1 adj Puerto Rican 2 nm,f P. Puerto Rican

Porto Rico [pɔrtoriko] n Puerto Rico

portrait [pɔrtrɛ] nm (a) (peinture, dessin, photo) portrait; **le p.** (genre) portrait painting, portraiture; **faire le p. de qn** to do a portrait of sb; Fig **c'est le p. vivant de son père**, **c'est tout le p. de son père** he's the spitting image of his father; Fam **il s'est fait abîmer** ou **arranger le p.** someone's made a real mess of his face; Fam **se faire tirer le p.** to have one's photo taken (b) (description) description; **faire le p. de qn/qch** to paint a picture of sb/sth (c) Ordinat **mode portrait** portrait mode

portraitiste [pɔrtrɛtist] nmf portrait painter, portraitist

portrait-robot (pl **portraits-robots**) [pɔrtrɛrɔbo] nm Photofit® (picture), identikit picture; Fig profile

portuaire [pɔrtɥɛr] adj port, harbour

portugais, -e [pɔrtygɛ, -ɛz] 1 adj Portuguese 2 nm,f P. Portuguese 3 nm (langue) Portuguese 4 nf **portugaise** (a) (huître) Portuguese oyster (b) Fam (oreille) **avoir les portugaises ensablées** to be as deaf as a post

Portugal [pɔrtygal] nm le P. Portugal

pose [poz] nf (a) (de rideaux, de papier peint) putting up, hanging; (d'une vitre) putting in; (de moquette, de câbles) laying; (d'appareils) installation; (d'une bombe) planting; Méd (d'un stérilet) putting in; (de ventouses) application (b) (pour photo, portrait) pose; **prendre la p.** to pose; **garder la p.** to hold the pose; Péj **prendre des poses** to pose (c) Phot exposure; **pellicule de 24 poses** 24-exposure film

posé, -e [poze] adj (réfléchi) composed, calm

posément [pozemã] adv calmly

poser [poze] **1** vt (a) (mettre) to put down; **p. qch sur/sous qch** to put sth on/under sth; Fig **p. son regard sur qn/qch** to look at sb/sth
(b) (formuler) (question) to ask; (hypothèse) to put forward; (principe) to lay down; **p. une question à qn** to ask sb a question; **p. un problème à qn** to pose a problem for sb; **p. sa candidature** (aux élections) to put oneself forward (as a candidate), Br to stand (as a candidate); (à un poste) to apply
(c) (rideaux, papier peint) to put up, to hang; (vitre) to put in; (moquette, câble) to lay; (appareil) to install; (bombe) to plant; Méd **p. qch à qn** (stérilet) to put sth in sb; (ventouses) to apply sth to sb
(d) Math (opération, équation) to set out; **je pose deux et je retiens un** put down two and carry one
2 vi (pour une photo, pour un tableau) to pose; Péj **p. pour la galerie** to play to the gallery
3 se poser vpr (a) (oiseau, avion) to land; Fig **se p. sur** (sujet: regard) to rest on
(b) (question, problème) to arise, to come up
(c) (à soi-même) **se p. des questions** to ask oneself questions; (avoir des doutes) to have one's doubts
(d) Fam **comme bricoleur/cuisinier, il se pose un peu là!** some handyman/cook, I don't think!; **comme enquiquineur, il se pose là!** he's a real pain in the neck!
(e) (se prétendre) **se p. en réformateur/redresseur de torts** to set oneself up as a reformer/a righter of wrongs

poseur, -euse [pozœr, -øz] nm,f (a) (de câbles, de carrelage) layer; **p. d'affiches** billsticker, billposter; **la police recherche les poseurs de bombes** the police are hunting the people who planted the bombs (b) Péj (pédant) show-off, poseur

positif, -ive [pozitif, -iv] adj positive; **il est p.** (à l'Alcotest, au contrôle antidopage) his test result is positive

position [pozisjã] nf (a) (emplacement) position; **être en première/deuxième p.** (dans une course) to be in first/second place; (sur une liste) to be first/second; **arriver en première/deuxième p.** to come first/second (b) (attitude, en danse) position; **être/se mettre en p.** to be in/get into position; **en p. debout/assise** in a standing/sitting position (c) (opinion) position (sur on); **prendre p.** to take a stand; **rester sur ses positions** to stand one's ground (d) (situation) position; **être en p. de faire qch** to be in a position to do sth; **p. sociale** social position

positionner [pozisjone] **1** vt to position
2 se positionner vpr to position oneself

positivement [pozitivmã] adv positively

posologie [pozolɔʒi] nf Méd dosage

possédé, -e [posede] **1** adj (du démon) possessed
2 nm,f person possessed; **hurler comme un p.** to scream like one possessed

posséder [34] [posede] vt (a) (biens matériels) to possess, to own; (talent, qualité) to possess, to have (b) (sujet) to have a thorough knowledge of; (langue, technique) to have mastered (c) (sujet: démon, passion) to possess (d) Fam (tromper) to take in; **se faire p.** to be taken in (e) Litt (femme) to possess

possesseur [posesœr] nm owner; (d'un titre) holder

possessif, -ive [posesif, -iv] adj & nm possessive

possession [posesjã] nf (a) (fait d'avoir) ownership, possession; (d'un titre) holding; **avoir qch en sa p.** to have sth in one's possession; **être en p. de qch** to be in possession of sth; **prendre p. de qch** to take possession of sth (b) (bien, territoire) possession (c) (par le démon) possession (d) (maîtrise) **être en p. de toutes ses facultés** to be in full possession of one's faculties; **être en pleine p. de ses moyens** to be at the peak of one's powers

possibilité [posibilite] nf (a) (éventualité) possibility (b) (moyen, occasion) opportunity, chance; **avoir la p. de faire qch** to have the opportunity or the chance of doing sth (c) **possibilités** (intellectuelles) potential; (financières) means (d) Ordinat **possibilités d'extension** upgradeability

possible [posibl] **1** adj (a) (faisable, vraisemblable) possible; **il leur est p. de vous héberger** it's possible for them to put you up; **il est p. qu'il soit mort** it's possible that he's dead, he might be dead; **aussitôt que p., dès que p.** as soon as possible; Fam **pas p.!** I don't believe it!; **si p.** if possible (b) (comme superlatif) **elle nous en parle le moins/plus p.** she talks to us about it as little/much as possible; **le moins/plus souvent p.** as infrequently/frequently as possible; **le moins/plus de détails p.** as few/many details as possible; **la boîte la plus grande p.** the largest box possible; **tous les détails possibles (et imaginables)** every possible detail (c) Fam (supportable) **pas p.** (personne, situation) impossible; **ça n'est plus p.!** I've had enough!
2 nm **faire tout son p. (pour faire qch)** to do everything one possibly can (to do sth)

postal, -e, -aux, -ales [postal, -o] adj (tarif, services) postal; (train, wagon) mail

postdater [postdate] vt to postdate

poste¹ [post] nf (a) (service) mail, Br post; **la P.** the postal service; **mettre qch à la p.** to mail or Br post sth; **par la p.** by mail, Br by post; **p. aérienne** airmail (b) (lieu) (bureau de) **p.** post office; **p. restante** Br poste restante, Am general delivery

poste² [post] nm (a) (fonction) position, post; **p. à pourvoir** vacancy (b) (appareil) **p. (de radio/télévision)** radio/television (set); Rad **p. émetteur** (équipement) transmitter (c) (local) **p. (de police)** station; **p. d'aiguillage** signal box; **p. d'essence** Br petrol or Am gas station; Ordinat **p. de travail** workstation (d) (d'un soldat) **être à son p.** to be at one's post; **p. de pilotage** cockpit (e) (d'un standard) extension (f) (comptable) entry, item

poster¹ [poste] **1** vt (sentinelle, hommes, troupes) to post, to station
2 se poster vpr to take up a position, to station oneself

poster² [poste] vt (courrier) to mail, Br to post

poster³ [poster] nm poster

postérieur, -e [posterjœr] **1** adj (a) (dans le temps) later, subsequent; **p. à** after (b) (de derrière) (pattes) back, hind; Anat posterior
2 nm Hum (derrière) posterior

postérieurement [posterjœrmã] adv later, subsequently; **p. à** after

postérité [posterite] nf posterity; **passer à la p.** (personne) to go down in history; (œuvre, mot) to be handed down to posterity

postface [postfas] nf postscript

posthume [postym] adj posthumous

postiche [postiʃ] **1** adj false
2 nm hairpiece

postier, -ère [pɔstje, -ɛr] *nm,f* postal worker

postillon [pɔstijɔ̃] *nm* (a) *Hist (cocher)* postilion (b) *postillons (salive)* shower of spit; **envoyer des postillons** to splutter

postillonner [pɔstijɔne] *vi* to splutter

postindustriel, -elle [pɔstɛ̃dystrijɛl] *adj* post-industrial

postmoderne [pɔstmɔdɛrn] *adj* post-modernist

postopératoire [pɔstɔperatwar] *adj Méd* post-operative

post-scriptum [pɔstskriptɔm] *nm inv* postscript

postsynchroniser [pɔstsɛ̃krɔnize] *vt Cin* to dub

postulant, -e [pɔstylɑ̃, -ɑ̃t] *nm,f (à un emploi)* applicant, candidate (**à** for)

postulat [pɔstyla] *nm* postulate

postuler [pɔstyle] *vi* **p. à** *ou* **pour un emploi** to apply for a job

posture [pɔstyr] *nf* (a) *(attitude)* posture (b) *(situation)* **être en fâcheuse p.** to be in an awkward situation

pot [po] *nm* (a) *(récipient, contenu)* pot; *(en verre)* jar; **p. à eau/à lait** water/milk jug; *Fam* **le p.** *(pour enfant)* the potty; **mettre en p.** *(plante)* to pot; *Fam* **quel p. de colle!** he sticks to you like glue!; **découvrir le p. aux roses** to find out what's been going on; **petit p.** *(pour bébé)* jar of baby food; **p. de chambre** chamber pot; **p. de fleurs** *(récipient)* flowerpot; *(plante)* pot of flowers; *Fam* **c'est un vrai p. de peinture!** *(femme)* she wears make-up an inch thick! (b) *Fam (chance)* **avoir du p.** to be lucky; **manque de p.,...** unfortunately,... (c) *(tuyau)* **p. (d'échappement)** *Br* exhaust (pipe), *Am* tail pipe; **p. catalytique** catalytic converter

potable [pɔtabl] *adj* (a) *(que l'on peut boire)* drinkable; **eau p./non p.** drinking/non-drinking water (b) *Fam (correct)* passable

potache [pɔtaʃ] *nm Fam* schoolboy

potage [pɔtaʒ] *nm* soup; **p. aux légumes** vegetable soup

potager, -ère [pɔtaʒe, -ɛr] **1** *adj voir* **jardin, plante**
2 *nm* vegetable *or* kitchen garden

potasser [pɔtase] *vt Fam (matière)* to bone up on, *Br* to swot up; *(examen)* to bone up for, *Br* to swot up for

potassium [pɔtasjɔm] *nm Chim* potassium

pot-au-feu [pɔtofø] *nm inv* = boiled beef with vegetables

pot-de-vin *(pl* **pots-de-vin)** [podvɛ̃] *nm* bribe

pote [pɔt] *nm Fam* pal

poteau, -x [pɔto] *nm* (a) *(piquet)* post; *(de but)* (goal)post; *Fam* **poteaux** *(jambes)* legs like tree-trunks; **p. (d'exécution)** execution stake; **p. électrique** electricity pylon; **p. indicateur** signpost; **p. télégraphique** telegraph pole (b) *Fam (ami)* pal

potée [pɔte] *nf* = boiled beef or pork with vegetables

potelé, -e [pɔtle] *adj* chubby, plump

potence [pɔtɑ̃s] *nf* (a) *(gibet)* gallows *(singulier)* (b) *(pièce de charpente)* bracket

potentiel, -elle [pɔtɑ̃sjɛl] *adj & nm* potential

potentiellement [pɔtɑ̃sjɛlmɑ̃] *adv* potentially

poterie [pɔtri] *nf* (a) *(art)* pottery; **faire de la p.** to make pottery (b) *(objet)* piece of pottery; *(objets)* pottery

potiche [pɔtiʃ] *nf* (a) *(vase)* oriental vase (b) *Fig* figurehead

potier, -ère [pɔtje, -ɛr] *nm,f* potter

potin [pɔtɛ̃] *nm Fam* (a) *potins (ragots)* gossip (b) *(bruit)* row; **faire du p.** to kick up a row

potion [pɔsjɔ̃] *nf* potion

potiron [pɔtirɔ̃] *nm* pumpkin

pot-pourri *(pl* **pots-pourris)** [popuri] *nm (chanson)* medley; *(fleurs séchées)* potpourri

pou, -x [pu] *nm* louse; *Fam* **chercher des poux dans la tête à qn** to try and pick a quarrel with sb

poubelle [pubɛl] *nf Br* (dust)bin, *Am* garbage can; **jeter** *ou* **mettre qch à la p.** to throw sth out; **faire les poubelles** to scrounge in *Br* dustbins *or Am* garbage cans

pouce [pus] *nm* (a) *(doigt)* thumb; *(gros orteil)* big toe; **p.!** *(dans un jeu)* truce!; *Fig* **manger sur le p.** to grab something to eat (b) *(mesure)* inch; **ne pas bouger d'un p.** not to move an inch (c) *Can* **faire du p.** *(faire du stop)* to hitch(hike)

Poucet [puse] *npr* **le Petit P.** Tom Thumb

poudre [pudr] *nf* (a) *(poussière)* powder; **réduire qch en p.** to reduce sth to powder; *Fig* **jeter de la p. aux yeux à qn** to try and dazzle sb; **p. compacte/libre** *(maquillage)* pressed/loose powder; **p. à éternuer** sneezing powder; **p. à laver** washing powder; **p. à récurer** scouring powder; *Vieilli* **p. de riz** face powder (b) *(explosif)* (gun)powder

poudrer [pudre] **1** *vt* to powder; **une femme poudrée** a woman with a powdered face
2 se poudrer *vpr* to powder one's face

poudrerie [pudrəri] *nf* (a) *(fabrique de poudre)* (gun)powder factory (b) *Can (neige)* drifting snow

poudreux, -euse [pudrø, -øz] **1** *adj* powdery; **neige poudreuse** powder snow
2 *nf* **poudreuse** powder snow

poudrier [pudrije] *nm* (*poudre)* compact

poudrière [pudrijɛr] *nf (entrepôt)* powder magazine; *Fig* powder keg

pouf [puf] **1** *exclam (chute)* thud!
2 *nm* (a) *(meuble)* pouf (b) *Belg* **à p.** *(à crédit)* on tick; **taper à p.** *(deviner)* to make a wild guess

pouffer [pufe] *vi* **p. (de rire)** to burst out laughing

pouffiasse [pufjas] *nf Vulg* bitch

pouilleux, -euse [pujø, -øz] **1** *adj (personne)* filthy; *(quartier, maison)* squalid
2 *nm,f* down-and-out

poulailler [pulaje] *nm* (a) *(basse-cour)* hen house (b) *(au théâtre)* **le p.** the gods

poulain [pulɛ̃] *nm* foal; *Fig* protégé

poulamon [pulamɔ̃] *nm Can* tomcod

poularde [pulard] *nf* fattened pullet

poulbot [pulbo] *nm Vieilli* street urchin of Montmartre

poule¹ [pul] *nf* (a) *(animal)* hen; *Culin* (boiling) fowl; *Fig* **la p. aux œufs d'or** the goose that lays the golden eggs; **quand les poules auront des dents** when pigs fly; **p. d'eau** moorhen; **p. faisane** hen pheasant; *Fig* **p. mouillée** wimp; **p. au pot** boiled chicken (b) *(terme d'affection)* **ma (petite) p.** darling (c) *Fam Péj (femme légère)* floozie; *(maîtresse)* mistress

poule² *nf (compétition)* tournament; *(groupe)* group

poulet [pulɛ] *nm* (a) *(animal)* chicken; **p. d'élevage** battery-reared chicken; **p. fermier** free-range chicken; **p. de grain** corn-fed chicken; **p. rôti** roast chicken (b) *(terme d'affection)* **mon (petit) p.** darling (c) *Fam (policier)* cop

poulette [pulɛt] *nf* (a) *(jeune poule)* pullet (b) *(terme d'affection)* **ma p.** darling

pouliche [pulif] *nf* filly

poulie [puli] *nf* pulley

poulpe [pulp] *nm* octopus

pouls [pu] *nm* pulse; **tâter le p. à qn** to feel sb's pulse; **prendre le p. à qn** to take sb's pulse

poumon [pumɔ̃] *nm* lung; **p. d'acier** iron lung; **respirer à pleins poumons** to breathe deeply

poupe [pup] *nf Naut* stern, poop

poupée [pupe] *nf* (a) *(jouet)* doll; **jouer à la p.** to play with dolls; **p. mannequin** Barbie doll®; **poupées russes** Russian dolls (b) *Fam (jolie fille)* doll (c) *(pansement)* finger bandage

poupin, -e [pupɛ̃, -in] *adj (personne)* chubby-cheeked; **visage p.** baby face

poupon [pupɔ̃] *nm* (a) *(bébé)* tiny baby (b) *(jouet)* baby doll

pouponner [pupone] *vi* to play the doting mother/father

pour [pur] 1 *prép* (a) *(indique le but, la destination)* for; **tiens, c'est p. toi** look, it's for you; **livres p. enfants** children's books; **p. faire qch** (in order) to do sth; **p. ne pas être en retard** so as not to be late; **p. bien faire** to do things properly; **p. que** + *subjunctive* so that, in order that; **j'épargne p. quand je serai vieux** I'm saving for when I'm old; **p. affaires** on business; **je viens p. la machine à laver** I've come about the washing machine; **c'est p. cela qu'il est venu** that's why he came, that's the reason he came; **p. quoi faire?** what for?; **tout ça p. rien!** all that for nothing!; *Fam* **c'est fait p.** that's what it's there for
(b) *(indique la direction)* for; **partir p. l'Espagne** to leave for Spain; **le train p. Paris** the Paris train, the train to *or* for Paris
(c) *(dans le temps)* for; **j'en ai p. une heure** it'll take me an hour, I'll be an hour; **il sera ici p. midi** he'll be here by midday
(d) *(contre)* for; **il me l'a vendu p. trois fois rien** he sold it to me for next to nothing; **donnez-moi p. 100 francs d'essence** give me 100 francs' worth of petrol
(e) *(en faveur de)* for, in favour of; **je suis p.** I'm (all) for it, I'm in favour of it
(f) *(à la place de)* for
(g) *(comme)* for; **j'avais p. ambition de...** my ambition was to...; **laisser qn p. mort** to leave sb for dead
(h) *(quant à, par rapport à)* for; **il est grand p. son âge** he's tall for his age; **p. ce qui est de...** as regards..., with regard to...; **p. moi, c'est absurde** in my opinion it's ridiculous, I think it's ridiculous
(i) *(indique le résultat)* **être trop faible p. marcher** to be too weak to walk; **cette situation n'était pas p. lui déplaire** the situation was rather to his liking
(j) *(à cause de)* for; **on l'apprécie p. sa gentillesse** people like her because she's so kind; **p. avoir désobéi** for having disobeyed, for disobeying
(k) *Litt (indique la concession)* **p. être célèbre, il n'en est pas moins modeste** although famous, he's nonetheless modest
(l) *(locutions)* **être p. beaucoup dans qch** to have a lot to do with sth; **je n'y suis p. rien!** it's got nothing to do with me!; *Fam* **être p. faire qch** *(être sur le point de)* to be about to do sth; *Fam* **p. une surprise, c'est une surprise!** that's a surprise and a half!; **perdre p. perdre, autant que tu...** if you're going to lose anyway, you might as well...

2 *nm inv* **le p. et le contre** the pros and cons

pourboire [purbwar] *nm* tip; **5 francs/10% de p.** a 5-franc/10% tip; **être payé au p.** to be paid in tips

pourceau, -x [purso] *nm Litt* swine

pourcentage [pursɑ̃taʒ] *nm* percentage; **être payé au p.** to be paid on a commission basis

pourchasser [purʃase] *vt* to pursue

pourfendre [purfɑ̃dr] *vt Hum (injustices, hypocrisie)* to combat

pourlécher [84] [purleʃe] **se pourlécher** *vpr* **se p. (les babines)** to lick one's lips

pourparlers [purparle] *nmpl* talks, negotiations; **entrer/être en p. (avec)** to enter into/be having talks (with)

pourpre [purpr] 1 *adj & nm* crimson
2 *nf (teinte naturelle)* purple (dye)

pourquoi [purkwa] 1 *adv & conj* why; **c'est p....** that's why...; **p. pas?** why not?
2 *nm inv (raison)* **le p. de** the reason for; **le p. et le comment** the whys and wherefores

pourrais *etc voir* **pouvoir**

pourri, -e [puri] 1 *adj* (a) *(bois, dent)* rotten; *(chair)* putrid; *(fruit, œufs)* bad (b) *Fam (corrompu)* corrupt (c) *Fam (déplaisant)* rotten (d) *Fam* **être p. de fric** to be stinking rich
2 *nm* (a) *(d'un fruit)* bad part; **sentir le p.** to smell rotten (b) *très Fam (personne)* bastard

pourrir [purir] 1 *vi (bois, dent)* to rot; *(corps)* to putrefy; *(aliments)* to go bad; *Fig* **p. en prison** to rot in prison
2 *vt* (a) *(gâter)* to rot (b) *Fam (enfant)* to spoil

pourriture [purityr] *nf* (a) *(décomposition)* rot (b) *Fam (corruption)* corruption (c) *très Fam (personne)* bastard

poursuite [pursɥit] *nf* (a) *(chasse)* pursuit; **se lancer à la p. de qn/qch** to set off in pursuit of sb/sth; **être à la p. de qch** *(bonheur, paix)* to be in pursuit of sth (b) *(continuation)* continuation (c) *Jur* **poursuites (judiciaires)** (legal) proceedings; *(en droit pénal)* prosecution; **engager des poursuites contre qn** to start proceedings against sb; *(en droit pénal)* to prosecute sb (d) *(sport cycliste)* pursuit

poursuivant, -e [pursɥivɑ̃, -ɑ̃t] *nm,f* pursuer

poursuivre [65] [pursɥivr] 1 *vt* (a) *(pourchasser)* to pursue; *(sujet: idée, crainte)* to haunt; *(sujet: malchance)* to dog (b) *(idéal, rêve, but)* to pursue (c) *(harceler)* to pester (de with); *(sujet: créancier)* to hound; **p. qn de ses assiduités** to force one's attentions on sb (d) *Jur* **p. qn (en justice)** to bring proceedings against sb; *(en droit pénal)* to prosecute sb (e) *(continuer)* to continue, to go on with; **poursuivre** *(histoire, exposé)* go on
2 **se poursuivre** *vpr (continuer)* to continue, to go on

pourtant [purtɑ̃] *adv* yet; **tout avait p. bien commencé** yet it all started so well; **je ne peux p. pas l'empêcher de venir** still, I can't stop him from coming; **ça n'est p. pas compliqué!** it's hardly complicated!

pourtour [purtur] *nm* circumference, perimeter

pourvoi [purvwa] *nm Jur* appeal; **p. en cassation** appeal to a higher court

pourvoir [73b] [purvwar] 1 *vt* **p. qn de qch** to provide sb with sth; **p. qch de qch** to equip *or* fit sth with sth
2 **pourvoir à** *vt ind (besoins)* to provide *or* cater for
3 **se pourvoir** *vpr* (a) *(se munir)* **se p. de qch** to provide oneself with sth (b) *Jur* **se p. en cassation** to take one's case to the Court of Appeal

pourvoyeur, -euse [purvwajœr, -øz] *nm,f* supplier

pourvu¹ [purvy] **pourvu que** *conj* (a) *(condition)* p. que tu y sois provided *(that)* *or* so long as you're there (b) *(souhait)* p. qu'il le fasse! let's just hope he does it!

pourvu², -e *voir* **pourvoir**

pousse [pus] *nf* (a) *(des feuilles, des cheveux)* growth (b) *(bourgeon)* shoot; **p. de bambou** bamboo shoot

poussé, -e [puse] *adj* *(en profondeur)* thorough

pousse-café [puskafe] *nm inv* (glass of) liqueur *(after coffee)*

poussée [puse] *nf* (a) *(pression)* pressure; *(d'un liquide)* upthrust; **la p. de la foule** the pushing and shoving of the crowd (b) *(croissance)* growth; *(de boutons, d'herpès)* eruption; **p. de fièvre** sudden rise in temperature; **p. démographique** sudden population increase; **faire une p. de croissance** to shoot up (c) *Fig (des prix)* upsurge (de in)

pousse-pousse [puspus] *nm inv* rickshaw

pousser [puse] **1** *vt* (a) *(soumettre à une force)* to push; *(sujet: vent) (embarcation)* to drive; **p. qn du coude** to nudge sb with one's elbow; *Fam* **à la va comme je te pousse** slipshod; *Fam* **faut pas p. Mémé** *ou* **Mémère dans les orties!** don't push your luck!
 (b) *(inciter)* **p. qn à faire qch** *(sujet: faim, jalousie)* to drive sb to do sth; *(sujet: personne)* to urge sb to do sth; **p. qn à qch** to drive sb to sth; **poussé par la curiosité** prompted by curiosity
 (c) *(continuer)* **p. trop loin une plaisanterie** to take a joke too far; **il a poussé la générosité jusqu'à l'héberger** he was so generous that he even put him up
 (d) *(émettre)* **p. un cri** to shout, to give a shout; **p. des cris** to shout; **p. un soupir** to sigh, to heave a sigh; **p. un gémissement** to groan; *Fam* **p. la chansonnette** to sing a song
 2 *vi* (a) *(exercer une pression)* to push; *(aux toilettes)* to strain; *(en accouchant)* to push; *Fam* **faut pas p.!** don't push your luck!
 (b) *(continuer)* **p. jusqu'au bois** to push on as far as the wood
 (c) *(plante, cheveux, ongles)* to grow; *(bourgeon)* to sprout; *(dents)* to come through; *Fam (enfant)* to shoot up; **se laisser p. la barbe** to grow a beard
 3 se pousser *vpr (pour faire de la place)* to move over *or* up

poussette [puset] *nf (pour enfants) Br* pushchair, *Am* stroller

poussière [pusjer] *nf* dust; **une p.** a speck of dust; *Fam* **faire la p.** *ou* **les poussières** to do the dusting, to dust; *Fig* **tomber en p.** to crumble to dust; *Fig* **mordre la p.** to bite the dust; *Fam* **10 francs et des poussières** 10 and a bit francs

poussiéreux, -euse [pusjerø, -øz] *adj* dusty; *Fig* stuffy

poussif, -ive [pusif, -iv] *adj (moteur, personne)* wheezy

poussin, -e [pusɛ̃, -in] **1** *nm* chick; *Fam* **mon p.** pet
 2 *nm,f Sp* junior (9 years old)

poutre [putr] *nf (en bois)* beam; *(en métal)* girder; **p. apparente** exposed beam; **p. maîtresse** main beam/girder

poutrelle [putrɛl] *nf* girder

pouvoir¹ [puvwar] *nm* (a) *(puissance)* power; **prendre**

le p. to assume power; **être au p.** to be in power; **p. absolu** absolute power; **p. exécutif** executive power; **p. judiciaire** judicial power; **p. législatif** legislative power; **les pouvoirs publics** the authorities (b) *(attributions)* power; **il n'est pas en mon p. de...** it is not within my power to... (c) **p. d'achat** purchasing power

pouvoir² [57] **1** *vt* (a) *(être capable de)* can, to be able to; **p. faire qch** to be able to do sth; **si je peux** if I can, if I'm able to; **je ne peux pas** I can't, I'm unable to; **comment a-t-il pu dire cela?** how could he say that?; **on n'y peut rien** it can't be helped, there's nothing that can be done about it; **on ne peut plus/moins aimable** extremely friendly/unfriendly; **il n'en peut plus** *(de fatigue)* he's exhausted; *(d'exaspération, d'impatience)* he can't take any more; **dès que je pourrai** as soon as I can; **où peut-il bien être?** where can he be?; **nous ne pouvons rien pour vous** we can't do anything for you
 (b) *(avoir le droit, la permission de)* can, to be allowed; **vous pouvez partir** you can go; **puis-je entrer?** can I come in?
 (c) *(être possible)* **la porte a pu se fermer toute seule** the door might have *or* could have closed on its own; **tout le monde peut se tromper** anyone can make a mistake; **elle peut bien s'excuser, je ne lui pardonnerai pas** she can apologize all she likes, but I won't forgive her; *Fam* **qu'est-ce que ça peut te faire?** what's that got to do with you?
 2 *v impersonnel* **cela se peut/se pourrait (bien)** it's quite possible; **il se peut qu'il vienne** he may *or* might come

PPCM [pepeseɛm] *nm Math (abrév* **plus petit commun multiple)** LCM

PQ [peky] *nm* (a) *Can Pol (abrév* **Parti Québécois)** PQ (b) *Fam (papier hygiénique)* toilet paper, *Br* loo paper

pragmatique [pragmatik] *adj* pragmatic

pragois, -e [pragwa, -az] **1** *adj* of Prague
 2 *nm,f* P. person from Prague

Prague [prag] *n* Prague

praire [prɛr] *nf* clam

prairie [preri] *nf* meadow; *Géog* **la P.** the Prairies

praline [pralin] *nf* praline

praliné, -e [praline] *adj (chocolat)* praline-filled; *(glace)* praline-flavoured

praticable [pratikabl] *adj* (a) *(route)* passable, negotiable; *(terrain)* playable (b) *(réalisable)* practicable

praticien, -enne [pratisjɛ̃, -ɛn] *nm,f (médecin)* (medical) practitioner

pratiquant, -e [pratikɑ̃, -ɑ̃t] **1** *adj* practising
 2 *nm,f* practising Christian/Jew/Muslim/*etc*

pratique [pratik] **1** *adj (méthode, personne)* practical; *(outil)* handy; *(date, heure, jour)* convenient; **avoir l'esprit p.** to have a practical turn of mind
 2 *nf* (a) *(application)* practice; **mettre qch en p.** to put sth into practice; **dans la p.** in practice (b) *(expérience)* (practical) experience; **avoir une longue p. de qch** to have had a lot of (practical) experience of sth (c) *(d'un sport)* playing; **la p. du yoga** doing yoga (d) *(procédé, coutume)* practice

pratiquement [pratikmɑ̃] *adv* (a) *(concrètement)* in practice (b) *(presque)* practically

pratiquer [pratike] **1** vt (a) (religion) to practise; (activité) to take part in; (langue) to use; (sport) to play; **p. la natation** to swim; **les prix pratiqués ici** the prices being asked here (b) (faire) (ouverture) to make; (opération chirurgicale) to carry out
2 vi (a) (médecin, avocat) to practise (b) (être religieux) to practise one's religion; **il est catholique mais il ne pratique pas** he's a Catholic but he doesn't go to church
3 se pratiquer vpr (sport) to be played; (coutume) to be practised

pré [pre] nm meadow

préadolescent, -e [preadɔlesã, -ãt] nm,f pre-adolescent

préalable [prealabl] **1** adj previous, prior (**à** to); (accord) prior; (formalités) preliminary
2 nm (condition) prerequisite, precondition; **au p.** first, beforehand

préalablement [prealabləmã] adv first, beforehand; **p. à...** prior to...

préambule [preãbyl] nm preamble (**de** to); **sans p., elle annonça...** without any warning, she announced...

PréAO [preao] nf Ordinat (abrév **présentation assistée par ordinateur**) computer-assisted presentation

préau, -x [preo] nm (de cour d'école) covered area; (salle) hall

préavis [preavi] nm (advance) notice; **un p. de trois mois** three months' notice; **p. de grève** strike notice; **déposer un p. de grève** to give notice of strike action; **p. de licenciement** notice (of dismissal)

précaire [preker] adj (position) precarious; (santé) delicate; **être en équilibre p.** to be precariously balanced

précambrien, -enne [prekãbrijɛ̃, -ɛn] Géol **1** adj Precambrian
2 nm **le P.** the Pre-Cambrian period

précarité [prekarite] nf precariousness

précaution [prekosjɔ̃] nf (a) (mesure) precaution; **par (mesure de) p.** as a precaution; **prendre des ou ses précautions** to take precautions; Prov **deux précautions valent mieux qu'une** better safe than sorry (b) (prudence) caution, care; **pour plus de p.** to be on the safe side

précautionneux, -euse [prekosjonø, -øz] adj careful

précédemment [presedamã] adv previously, before

précédent, -e [presedã, -ãt] **1** adj previous
2 nm precedent; **sans p.** unprecedented, without precedent

précéder [34] [presede] **1** vt to precede; **je l'ai précédé de dix minutes** I got there ten minutes before he did
2 vi **la page qui précède** the preceding or previous page; **dans les jours qui précèdent** in the preceding days; **ce qui précède** the foregoing

précepte [presɛpt] nm precept

précepteur, -trice [preseptœr, -tris] nm,f (private) tutor

préchauffage [preʃofaʒ] nm preheating

préchauffer [preʃofe] vt to preheat

prêcher [preʃe] **1** vt (a) (enseigner) to preach (**à** to) (b) (prôner) to advocate; Hum **p. la bonne parole** to spread the good word
2 vi (prononcer un sermon) to preach; Fig **p. dans le désert** to be a voice crying in the wilderness; Fig **p. pour sa paroisse** to look after one's own interests

prêchi-prêcha [preʃipreʃa] nm inv Fam Péj preachifying

précieusement [presjøzmã] adv **garder ou conserver qch p.** to keep sth safe

précieux, -euse [presjø, -øz] adj (a) (coûteux) precious (b) (conseil, temps) valuable (**à** to) (c) (style, personne) precious, affected

préciosité [presjozite] nf Litt affectation, preciosity

précipice [presipis] nm chasm, abyss; (d'une falaise, d'un ravin) precipice; Fig abyss; Fig **être au bord du p.** to be on the edge of an abyss

précipitamment [presipitamã] adv hurriedly, hastily; **entrer/sortir p.** to rush or dash in/out

précipitation [presipitasjɔ̃] nf (a) (hâte) haste (b) Chim precipitation (c) **précipitations** (pluies) precipitation

précipité, -e [presipite] **1** adj hasty, hurried
2 nm Chim precipitate

précipiter [presipite] **1** vt (a) (entraîner) to throw down, to hurl down; Fig to plunge; **p. qn dans le vide** to hurl sb over the edge (b) (hâter) to speed up; (événements) to precipitate; (la mort de quelqu'un) to hasten; **il ne faut rien p.** we mustn't rush things (c) Chim to precipitate
2 vi Chim to precipitate
3 se précipiter vpr (a) (se hâter) to rush, to hurry (b) (s'accélérer) **les événements se sont précipités** things started happening quickly (c) (se jeter) to rush (**sur/vers** at/towards)

précis, -e [presi, -iz] **1** adj precise, exact; **à deux heures précises** at two o'clock precisely or exactly; **penser à quelque chose de p.** to have something specific in mind
2 nm précis, summary; (livre) handbook; **p. d'histoire de France** short history of France

précisément [presizemã] adv precisely, exactly

préciser [presize] **1** vt (a) (déterminer) (date) to specify (b) (clarifier) (pensée) to clarify; **je tiens à p. que...** I wish to make it clear that...; **pourriez-vous p.?** could you be more specific?
2 se préciser vpr to become clear(er); (idée) to take shape

précision [presizjɔ̃] nf (a) (d'une information, d'une description) accuracy; (de mouvements) preciseness, precision; **avec p.** precisely (b) (détail) **une p.** a precise detail; **donner ou apporter des précisions sur qch** to give precise details about sth; **demander des précisions sur qch** to ask for further information about sth

précoce [prekɔs] adj (enfant) precocious; (fruit, été) early; (sénilité, calvitie) premature

précocité [prekɔsite] nf precociousness; (d'un fruit, d'une saison) earliness

précolombien, -enne [prekɔlɔ̃bjɛ̃, -ɛn] adj pre-Columbian

préconçu, -e [prekɔ̃sy] adj preconceived

préconiser [prekɔnize] vt to advocate; (remède) to recommend

précuit, -e [prekɥi, -it] adj precooked

précurseur [prekyrsœr] **1** nm precursor, forerunner
2 adj m **signe p.** forwarning

prédateur [predatœr] *nm* predator

prédécesseur [predesesœr] *nm* predecessor

prédécoupé, -e [predekupe] *adj* precut

prédestination [predestinasjɔ̃] *nf* predestination

prédestiné, -e [predestine] *adj* predestined (**à qch/à faire qch** for sth/to do sth)

prédestiner [predestine] *vt* to predestine (**à qch/à faire qch** for sth/to do sth)

prédicat [predika] *nm Gram* predicate

prédicateur, -trice [predikatœr, -tris] *nm,f* preacher

prédiction [prediksjɔ̃] *nf* prediction

prédilection [predileksjɔ̃] *nf* predilection, partiality; **de p.** favourite; **avoir une p. pour qch** to be partial to sth, to have a predilection for sth

prédire [27b] *vt* to predict; **p. qch à qn** to predict sth for sb

prédisposer [predispoze] *vt* to predispose (**à** to)

prédisposition [predispozisjɔ̃] *nf* predisposition (**à** to)

prédominant, -e [predominã, -ãt] *adj* predominant

prédominer [predomine] *vi* to predominate

préélectoral, -e, -aux, -ales [preelektoral, -o] *adj* pre-electoral, pre-election

préemballé, -e [preãbale] *adj* prepacked

prééminence [preeminãs] *nf* pre-eminence

prééminent, -e [preeminã, -ãt] *adj* pre-eminent

préempter [preãpte] *vt Jur* to pre-empt

préemption [preãpsjɔ̃] *nf Jur* pre-emption

préenregistré, -e [preãrʒistre] *adj* prerecorded

préétablir [preetablir] *vt* to pre-establish

préexistant, -e [preegzistã, -ãt] *adj* pre-existing

préexister [preegziste] *vi* to pre-exist; **p. à qch** to pre-exist sth

préfabrication [prefabrikasjɔ̃] *nf* prefabrication

préfabriqué, -e [prefabrike] **1** *adj* prefabricated
2 *nm* prefabricated material; **c'est du p.** it's prefabricated

préface [prefas] *nf* preface, foreword (**à** *ou* **de** to)

préfacer [16] [prefase] *vt* to preface

préfectoral, -e, -aux, -ales [prefektoral, -o] *adj* = relating to a "préfecture" or "préfet"

préfecture [prefektyr] *nf* prefecture; *(ville)* = administrative centre of a "département"; **la P. de police** police headquarters

préférable [preferabl] *adj* preferable (**à** to); **il serait p. de le revoir** *ou* **que nous le revoyions** it would be preferable to see him again

préféré, -e [prefere] *adj & nm,f* favourite

préférence [preferãs] *nf* preference; **de p.** preferably; **de p. à** in preference to

préférentiel, -elle [preferãsjɛl] *adj* preferential

préférer [34] [prefere] *vt* to prefer (**à** to); **je préférerais du thé** I'd prefer tea, I'd rather have tea; **je préférerais que vous veniez** I'd prefer it if you came, I'd rather you came; **p. faire qch** to prefer to do sth

préfet [prefɛ] *nm* prefect *(administrative head of a "département")*; **p. de police** = chief commissioner of police

préfigurer [prefigyre] *vt* to prefigure, to foreshadow

préfixe [prefiks] *nm* prefix

pré-formaté, -e *(mpl* **pré-formatés,** *fpl* **pré-formatées)** [preformate] *adj Ordinat* pre-formatted

préhension [preãsjɔ̃] *nf* gripping

préhistoire [preistwar] *nf* prehistory

préhistorique [preistorik] *adj* prehistoric

pré-impression [preɛ̃presjɔ̃] *nf Typ* pre-press

préindustriel, -elle [preɛ̃dystrijel] *adj* pre-industrial

préinscription [preɛ̃skripsjɔ̃] *nf* pre-check-in

préjudice [preʒydis] *nm (à une cause)* prejudice, detriment; *(à une personne)* harm, wrong; *Jur* tort; **subir un p. matériel** to sustain damage; *(de sécrétions)* to suffer mental distress; **porter p. à qn** to do sb harm; **au p. de qch** to the detriment of sth

préjugé [preʒyʒe] *nm* prejudice, bias (**contre** against); **avoir un p. contre qn/qch** to be prejudiced *or* biased against sb/sth

prélasser [prelase] **se prélasser** *vpr* to lounge

prélat [prela] *nm* prelate

prélavage [prelavaʒ] *nm* pre-wash

prélèvement [prelɛvmã] *nm* **(a)** *(en argent)* deduction (**sur** from); **faire un p. sur un compte** to debit an account; **p. automatique** direct debit; **prélèvements obligatoires** = tax and social security contributions **(b)** *(extraction) (d'un organe)* removal; *(de sécrétions)* taking a sample; *(d'un échantillon)* taking; **faire un p. de sang** *ou* **sanguin à qn** to take a blood sample from sb **(c)** *(partie prélevée) (de sécrétions)* swab; *(de sang)* sample

prélever [46] [prelve] *vt* **(a)** *(argent)* to deduct (**sur** from); *(impôt)* to levy **(b)** *(organe)* to remove; *(sécrétions, échantillon)* to take; **p. du sang à qn** to take a blood sample from sb

préliminaire [preliminer] **1** *adj* preliminary
2 *nmpl* **préliminaires** preliminaries

prélude [prelyd] *nm Mus & Fig* prelude (**de** *ou* **à** to)

prématuré, -e [prematyre] **1** *adj* premature; **être p. de six semaines** to be six weeks premature
2 *nm,f* premature baby

prématurément [prematyremã] *adv* prematurely

préméditation [premeditasjɔ̃] *nf* premeditation; **meurtre avec p.** premeditated murder

préméditer [premedite] *vt* to premeditate

prémenstruel, -elle [premãstryel] *adj* premenstrual

premier, -ère [prəmje, -ɛr] **1** *adj (à) (initial, dominant)* first; **les trois premières années** the first three years; **la première marche** the bottom stair; **le p. rang** the front row; **prendre la première place** *(dans une course)* to take the lead; **le p. venu** the first person who comes along; **les premiers arrivés** the first to arrive; **je suis le p. concerné** I'm the one most affected; **en p.** in the first place, firstly; **le p. de l'an** New Year's Day
(b) *(original)* primary, original
2 *nm,f* **(a)** *(dans un classement)* first; **arriver le p.** to arrive first; **être le p. de sa classe** to be top of one's class; **être le p. à faire qch** to be (the) first to do sth; *voir aussi* **cinquième**
(b) *(acteur)* **jeune p.** (young) romantic lead; *Fig* **avoir des airs de jeune p.** to look like a film star
3 *nm (date)* **le p. janvier** the first of January, January the first; **le p. de l'an** New Year's Day
4 *nf* **première (a)** *(d'une pièce)* first *or* opening night; *(d'un film)* première
(b) *(classe) Br* ≃ lower sixth, *Am* ≃ eleventh grade
(c) *(de train, d'avion)* first class; **voyager en première** to travel first-class
(d) *(vitesse)* first (gear)
(e) *(de chaussure)* insole

(f) *Fam* **de première** *(de très bonne qualité)* first-rate, first-class

premièrement [prəmjɛrmɑ̃] *adv* first, in the first place

prémisse [premis] *nf* premise

prémolaire [premɔlɛr] *nf* premolar

prémonition [premɔnisjɔ̃] *nf* premonition

prémonitoire [premɔnitwar] *adj* premonitory

prémunir [premynir] **se prémunir** *vpr* **se p. contre qch** to be on one's guard against sth

prenant, -e [prənɑ̃, -ɑ̃t] *adj (livre, spectacle)* fascinating; *(travail)* time-consuming

prénatal, -e, -als, -ales [prenatal] *adj* antenatal, prenatal

prendre [58] [prɑ̃dr] **1** *vt* (a) *(saisir)* to take; **p. qch dans un tiroir** to take sth out of a drawer; **prends-le par la poignée** take hold of it by the handle; **c'est à p. ou à laisser** take it or leave it; *Fam* **il faut savoir le p.** you have to know how to handle him; *Fam* **c'est toujours ça de pris** that's something at least; *Fam* **qu'est-ce qu'on va p.!** we're in for it!
(b) *(enlever)* to take (away); **p. qch à qn** to take sth (away) from sb; **cela m'a pris du temps/deux heures** it took me a while/two hours; **p. 100 francs de l'heure** to take 100 francs an hour
(c) *(s'emparer de) (personne, gibier)* to catch; *(ville, région)* to take, to capture; **se laisser p.** to let oneself be or get caught; *Fig* to let oneself be taken in; *Prov* **tel est pris qui croyait l'.** it's a case of the biter bit
(d) *(aller chercher)* to collect, to pick up; **attends, je vais p. mon parapluie** wait till I get my umbrella
(e) *(acheter)* to get; *(chambre, studio)* to take; **cette robe me plaît, je la prends** I like this dress, I'll take it
(f) *(bonne, assistant)* to take on; *(pensionnaire)* to take in; *(travail)* to take; **être pris** *(élève, candidat)* to be accepted; *(acteur)* to get the part
(g) *(repas, boisson, bain)* to have; *(médicament)* to take
(h) *(moyen de transport)* to take
(i) *(apparence)* to take on, to assume; *(attitude)* to take; *(accent)* to pick up
(j) **p. l'eau** *(bateau)* to be leaking, to be letting in water
(k) *(personne)* **p. qn comme exemple** to take sb as an example; **p. qn/qch pour** to take sb/sth for
(l) *Fam (arriver)* **qu'est-ce qui lui prend?** what's come over him? **ça te prend souvent?** do you get like that often?

2 *vi* (a) *(ciment, flan)* to set
(b) *(plante)* to take (root)
(c) *(feu)* to catch
(d) *(réussir) (vaccin)* to take effect; *(mode)* to catch on; *Fam* **avec moi, ça ne prend pas!** you can't fool me!
(e) *(tourner)* **p. à gauche/droite** to go left/right
(f) **p. sur soi** to restrain or contain oneself

3 se prendre *vpr* (a) *(s'accrocher)* **se p. dans une porte/à un clou** to get caught in the door/on a nail
(b) *(se considérer)* **se p. pour un héros** to consider oneself a hero; **pour qui vous prenez-vous?** who do you think you are?
(c) *(locutions)* **s'en p. à qn/qch** to take it out on sb/sth; **ne t'en prends qu'à toi-même** you've only got yourself to blame; **s'y p. bien avec qn** to know how to handle sb; **s'y p. mal avec qn** not to handle sb the right way; **vous vous y prenez mal** you're going about it the wrong way; **s'y p. à deux fois pour faire qch** to take two attempts to do sth

preneur, -euse [prənœr, -øz] *nm,f* (a) *(acheteur)* buyer,

purchaser; **trouver p.** to find a buyer; **je suis p.!** I'm interested! (b) **p. d'otages** hostage taker; **p. de son** sound engineer

prenne *etc voir* **prendre**

prénom [prenɔ̃] *nm* *Br* first *or* *Am* given name; *(de chrétiens)* Christian name

prénommé, -e [prenɔme] *adj* **le p. Victor** the man/boy called Victor

prénommer [prenɔme] **1** *vt* to call, to name
2 se prénommer *vpr* **il se prénomme Adam** his *Br* first *or* *Am* given name is Adam

prénuptial, -e, -aux, -ales [prenypsjal, -o] *adj* premarital; **examen p.** premarital medical check-up

préoccupant, -e [preɔkypɑ̃, -ɑ̃t] *adj* worrying

préoccupation [preɔkypasjɔ̃] *nf* concern, preoccupation; **j'ai d'autres préoccupations** I have other things to worry about

préoccupé, -e [preɔkype] *adj* worried

préoccuper [preɔkype] *vt* to worry; **être préoccupé par qch** to be worried about sth; **sa santé me préoccupe** I'm worried about his health
2 se préoccuper *vpr* **se p. de qn/qch** to concern oneself with sb/sth

prépa [prepa] *nf* *Fam* *Scol* preparatory class *(for the entrance exam to the 'grandes écoles')* ; **faire une p., être en p.** to be studying for the entrance exam to the grandes écoles

préparateur, -trice [preparatœr, -tris] *nm,f* laboratory assistant; **p. en pharmacie** pharmacist's *or* *Br* chemist's assistant

préparatifs [preparatif] *nmpl* preparations (**de** for)

préparation [preparasjɔ̃] *nf* preparation (**à** for); **faire une p. militaire** = to do an officer training course in preparation for military service; **faire une p. aux grandes écoles** to prepare for the entrance exam to the grandes écoles

préparatoire [preparatwar] *adj* preparatory

préparer [prepare] **1** *vt* (a) *(discours, repas, plat)* to prepare; *(réunion, soirée, vacances)* to make preparations for, to arrange; *(ordonnance)* to make up; **plats tout préparés** ready-cooked meals; *Fig* **je suis sûr qu'il nous prépare quelque chose** I'm sure he's up to something (b) *(personne)* **p. qn à qch** to prepare sb for sth; *(entraîner)* to train sb for sth (c) *(examen)* to prepare for, to study for
2 se préparer *vpr* (a) *(être imminent)* to be in the offing
(b) *(s'apprêter)* **se p. à qch/à faire qch** to prepare for sth/to do sth (c) *(se faire)* **se p. qch** *(boisson, plat)* to make oneself sth; **tu te prépares bien des désillusions** you're in for a big disappointment

prépayé, -e [prepeje] *adj* prepaid

prépondérant, -e [prepɔ̃derɑ̃, -ɑ̃t] *adj* predominant

préposé, -e [prepoze] *nm,f (employé)* employee; *(dans un vestiaire)* attendant; **p. (des postes)** *Br* postman, *f* postwoman, *Am* mailman, *f* mailwoman

préposer [prepoze] *vt* **p. qn à qch** to appoint sb to sth

préposition [prepozisjɔ̃] *nf* *Gram* preposition

prépuce [prepys] *nm* *Anat* foreskin, *Spéc* prepuce

préraphaélite [prerafaelit] *adj* & *nm* Pre-Raphaelite

préretraite [prerətrɛt] *nf* early retirement; *(pension)* early retirement pension; **partir en p.** to take early retirement

prérogative [pre rɔgativ] *nf* prerogative

près [prɛ] *adv* **(a)** *(dans l'espace)* near, close; *(dans le temps)* close; **de p.** closely; **voir qch de p.** to see sth close up; **à quelques détails p.** except for a few details; **la longueur, à 5 centimètres p.** the length, to within 5 centimetres; **à deux minutes p., je ratais le train** two minutes later and I would have missed the train; **je n'en suis pas à 10 francs p.** 10 francs more or less doesn't matter; **à peu de chose(s) p.** more or less
(b) p. de *(dans l'espace)* near (to), close to; *(dans le temps)* close to; *(environ)* nearly, almost; **p. de là** nearby, close by; **p. de chez eux** near (to) *or* close to where they live; *Fam* **être p. de ses sous** to be tight-fisted; *Hum* **nous ne sommes pas p. de le revoir** we won't see him again in a hurry
(c) à peu p. *(pas tout à fait)* nearly, almost; *(approximativement)* about, approximately; **il est à peu p. certain que...** it is fairly certain that...

présage [preza ʒ] *nm* omen, sign; **mauvais p.** bad omen

présager [45] [preza ʒe] *vt* **(a)** *(annoncer)* to presage; **cela ne présage rien de bon** it doesn't bode well **(b)** *(prévoir)* to predict; **ces gros nuages noirs laissent p. un orage** those big black clouds are a sure sign of a storm

pré-salé *(pl* **prés-salés)** [presale] *nm (mouton)* salt-meadow sheep; *(viande)* salt-meadow lamb

presbyte [prɛsbit] *adj* long-sighted

presbytère [prɛsbitɛr] *nm* presbytery

presbytérien, -enne [prɛsbiterjɛ̃, -ɛn] *adj & nm,f* Presbyterian

presbytie [prɛsbisi] *nf* long-sightedness

préscolaire [preskɔlɛr] *adj* preschool

prescription [prɛskripsjɔ̃] *nf* **(a)** *Jur* **après cinquante ans, il y a p.** the statute of limitations runs out after fifty years **(b)** *(ordonnance)* prescription **(c)** *(instruction)* rule, regulation

prescrire [30] [prɛskrir] *vt (médicament)* to prescribe; **à la date prescrite** on the date specified

préséance [preseɑ̃s] *nf* precedence, priority **(sur** over)

présélection [preselɛksjɔ̃] *nf* preselection; *(de candidats)* short-listing

présélectionner [preselɛksjɔne] *vt* to preselect; *(candidats)* to short-list

présence [prezɑ̃s] *nf* **(a)** *(dans un lieu)* presence; *(à l'école)* attendance; **il ignore votre p.** he doesn't know you're here; **avoir de la p.** *(acteur)* to have great presence; **les parties en p.** the parties present; **en p. de toute la famille** in front of the whole family; **en p. du virus** when the virus is present **(b) avoir la p. d'esprit de faire qch** to have the presence of mind to do sth

présent¹, -e [prezɑ̃, -ɑ̃t] **1** *adj* **(a)** *(physiquement)* present; **les personnes présentes** those present; **Jacques Martelin, ici p., vous le dira** Jacques Martelin, who is here with us, will tell you; **Tardieu? – p.!** Tardieu? – here! *or* present! **(b)** *(situation, moment)* present; **vivre dans l'instant p.** to live in the present
2 *nm* **(a)** *Gram* present (tense); **le p. du subjonctif/de l'indicatif** the present subjunctive/indicative; **au p.** in the present **(b)** *(moment présent)* present; **vivre dans le p.** to live in the present **(c) à p.** now, at present, (just) now; **jusqu'à p.** up to now, until now; **jusqu'à p., je n'ai pas reçu de nouvelles** I've not received any news as yet; **dès à p.** from now on; **à p. que...** now that...
3 *nf* **par la présente** *(par cette lettre)* hereby

présent² *nm Litt (cadeau)* present, gift; **faire p. de qch à qn** to present sth to sb

présentable [prezɑ̃tabl] *adj* presentable

présentateur, -trice [prezɑ̃tatœr, -tris] *nm,f* presenter; *(d'un spectacle télévisé)* compère; **p. de journal télévisé** newscaster, newsreader

présentation [prezɑ̃tasjɔ̃] *nf* **(a)** *(de faits, d'un billet)* presentation; **10% de réduction sur p. de la carte** 10% discount on presentation of this card **(b)** *(apparence)* *(d'une personne)* appearance; *(d'un document)* presentation, layout; **recherche hôtesses, excellente p.** *(petite annonce)* hostesses required, must have smart appearance; *Ordinat* **p. assistée par ordinateur** computer-aided presentation **(c)** *(dans un groupe)* introduction (à to); **faire les présentations** to make the introductions **(d)** *(d'un film)* showing, presentation; **p. de mode** fashion show

présenter [prezɑ̃te] **1** *vt* **(a)** *(montrer)* to show, to present; *(symptôme)* to present; *(facture)* to submit **(b)** *(par écrit)* to present **(c)** *(oralement)* *(arguments)* to set out; *(spectacle)* to present, to host; **p. ses condoléances à qn** to offer sb one's condolences **(d)** *(projet de loi)* to bring in, to introduce; **p. sa candidature à un poste** to apply for a job **(e)** *(personne)* **p. qn à qn** to introduce sb to sb; **je vous présente Marie** this is Marie
2 *vi Fam* **bien/mal p.** to look/not to look good
3 se présenter *vpr* **(a)** *(occasion, cas)* to arise, to present itself; **ça se présente bien** things are looking promising **(b)** *(à un poste)* to apply (à for); **se p. à un examen** to take *or Br* sit an examination; **se p. aux élections** to be a candidate *at or Br* stand at the elections **(c)** *(arriver)* to turn up; **présentez-vous au commissariat à huit heures** be at the police station at eight o'clock; **se p. chez qn** to call on sb **(d)** *(dire son nom)* to introduce oneself (à to) **(e) le bébé se présente par la tête** the baby is presenting normally

présentoir [prezɑ̃twar] *nm* display unit

préservatif [prezɛrvatif] *nm* condom; **p. féminin** female condom

préservation [prezɛrvasjɔ̃] *nf* preservation, protection

préserver [prezɛrve] **1** *vt* to preserve, to protect **(de** from); **le ciel m'en préserve!** heaven forbid!
2 se préserver *vpr* to protect oneself (**de** from)

présidence [prezidɑ̃s] *nf* **(a)** *(d'un état)* presidency **(b)** *(d'un club)* chairmanship

président, -e [prezidɑ̃, -ɑ̃t] *nm,f* **(a)** *(d'un état)* president; **le p. de la République** the President of the Republic **(b)** *(d'une assemblée, d'un club)* chairman, *f* chairwoman; **P. du conseil d'administration** Chairman of the Board; **p.-directeur général** *Br* chairman and managing director, *Am* chief executive officer **(c)** *(magistrat)* presiding judge; **p. du jury** foreman of the jury

présidentiel, -elle [prezidɑ̃sjɛl] **1** *adj* presidential
2 *nfpl* **présidentielles** presidential elections

présider [prezide] **1** *vt* **(a)** *(conseil)* to preside over; *(réunion)* to chair **(b)** *(banquet)* to be the guest of honour at
2 présider à *vt ind Litt* **p. aux destinées de...** to preside over the destinies of...

présomption [prezɔ̃psjɔ̃] *nf* presumption

présomptueux, -euse [prezɔ̃ptɥø, -øz] *adj* presumptuous

presque [prɛsk] *adv* (a) *(à peu près)* almost, nearly; p. jamais/rien scarcely or hardly ever/anything; je ne dors p. pas I hardly or scarcely get any sleep; rien ou p. scarcely anything (b) *(devant un nom)* la p. totalité de son œuvre nearly or almost all of his work

presqu'île [prɛskil] *nf* peninsula

pressant, -e [prɛsɑ̃, -ɑ̃t] *adj (besoin)* pressing, urgent; *(demande, vendeur)* insistent; *Fam Euph* avoir un besoin p. to need to go *(to the toilet)*

presse [prɛs] *nf* (a) *(ensemble des journaux)* press; travailler dans la p. to work in journalism; je l'ai lu dans la p. I read it in the papers; *Fig* avoir bonne/ mauvaise p. (auprès de) to be well/badly thought of (by); la p. écrite the print media, the press; la p. à scandale, la p. à sensation the popular press, the tabloids (b) *Tech* press (c) *(pour imprimer)* (printing) press; mettre qch sous p. to send sth to press

pressé, -e [prɛse] *adj* (a) *(personne)* in a hurry or rush; p. de faire qch in a hurry to do sth; être p. par le temps to be pushed for time; d'un pas p. hurriedly; on n'est pas p. there's no rush (b) *(urgent)* urgent; aller ou parer au plus p. to deal with the most urgent thing(s) first

presse-agrumes [prɛsagrym] *nm inv* juice extractor, juicer

presse-ail [prɛsaj] *nm inv* garlic press

presse-citron [prɛsitrɔ̃] *nm inv* lemon squeezer

pressentiment [prɛsɑ̃timɑ̃] *nm* presentiment; *(d'un malheur)* foreboding; j'ai le p. que... I've a (funny) feeling that...

pressentir [64a] [prɛsɑ̃tir] *vt* (a) *(deviner)* to have a premonition of, to sense; *(malheur)* to have a foreboding of (b) p. qn (pour qch) to sound sb out (about sth)

presse-papiers [prɛspapje] *nm inv* paperweight; *Ordinat* clipboard

presse-purée [prɛspyre] *nm inv* potato masher

presser [prɛse] 1 *vt* (a) *(agrume, éponge)* to squeeze; *(raisin, pommes)* to press; p. qn contre son cœur to clasp sb in one's arms, to hug sb (b) *(sonnette, bouton)* to press, to push (c) *(harceler)* p. qn de questions to ply or bombard sb with questions; p. qn de faire qch to urge sb to do sth (d) *(faire se hâter) (personne)* to hurry (up); *(travail, mouvement)* to speed up; le p. ou l'allure to speed up, to quicken one's pace

2 *vi* le temps presse there isn't much time (left); rien ne presse there's no hurry or rush; allons, pressons! come on, let's get a move on!

3 se presser *vpr* (a) *(se dépêcher)* to hurry (up); se p. de faire qch to hurry to do sth; faire qch sans se p. to take one's time doing sth (b) *(se serrer)* se p. contre to press (oneself) against; se p. autour de to crowd or cluster around

pressing [prɛsiŋ] *nm* dry cleaner's

pression [prɛsjɔ̃] *nf* (a) *Tech* pressure; mettre qch sous p. to pressurize sth; sous p. *(récipient)* pressurized; *Fig* être sous p. to be under pressure; p. atmosphérique atmospheric pressure; zone de hautes/basses pressions area of high/low pressure (b) *(action de presser)* pressure; d'une simple p. du doigt at the touch of a button (c) *Fig (influence)* pressure; faire p. sur qn to put pressure on sb, to pressurize sb; subir des pressions to be under pressure (d) *(bouton) Br* press stud, *Am* snap fastener (e) bière (à la) p. draught beer; une p., s'il vous plaît *Br* ≃ a half pint of lager, please, *Am* ≃ a beer, please

pressoir [prɛswar] *nm* (a) *(instrument)* press (b) *(lieu)* press house, press room

pressurer [prɛsyre] *vt (exploiter)* to squeeze

pressurisation [prɛsyrizasjɔ̃] *nf* pressurization

prestance [prɛstɑ̃s] *nf* presence; avoir de la p. to have (great) presence

prestataire [prɛstater] 1 *nmf* (a) *(bénéficiaire)* person receiving benefits (b) *(fournisseur)* p. de service service provider

2 *nm Ordinat* p. d'accès access provider

prestation [prɛstasjɔ̃] *nf* (a) *(allocation)* benefit; prestations familiales family benefits; prestations sociales social security benefits (b) *(services fournis)* services (c) *(fait de fournir)* provision; p. de service provision of a service (d) *(d'un comédien)* performance (e) p. de serment taking the oath

preste [prɛst] *adj* nimble

prestement [prɛstəmɑ̃] *adv* promptly

prestidigitateur, -trice [prɛstidiʒitatœr, -tris] *nm,f* conjurer, magician

prestidigitation [prɛstidiʒitasjɔ̃] *nf* conjuring, magic

prestige [prɛstiʒ] *nm* prestige; de p. *(voiture, hôtel)* luxury; *(réalisation)* prestige; le p. de l'uniforme the glamour of the uniform

prestigieux, -euse [prɛstiʒjø, -øz] *adj* prestigious

présumer [prezyme] 1 *vt (supposer)* to presume, to assume; p. qn innocent to presume sb (to be) innocent

2 présumer de *vt ind* trop p. de soi to be overconfident; p. de ses forces to overestimate one's strength

présupposer [presypoze] *vt* to presuppose

présure [prezyr] *nf* rennet

prêt¹, -e [prɛ, prɛt] *adj* ready; être p. à tout to be prepared to do anything; être p. à faire qch to be ready to do sth

prêt² *nm (action)* lending; *(somme)* loan

prêt-à-porter [prɛtaporte] *nm* (a) *(vêtements)* ready-to-wear clothes (b) *(secteur)* ready-to-wear (clothing business)

prétendant, -e [pretɑ̃dɑ̃, -ɑ̃t] 1 *nm,f* (a) *(à un poste)* applicant, candidate (à for); *(à un bien, à un titre)* claimant (à to); *(au trône)* pretender (à to)

2 *nm (d'une femme)* suitor

prétendre [pretɑ̃dr] 1 *vt (déclarer)* to maintain, to claim; on prétend que... people say that..., it is said that...; à ce qu'il prétend according to him; il ne prétend pas être artiste he doesn't claim or pretend to be an artist; on le prétend fou they say he's mad

2 prétendre à *vt ind* to lay claim to; p. à la victoire to aim to win

3 se prétendre *vpr* to claim to be

prétendu, -e [pretɑ̃dy] *adj (coupable, voleur)* alleged; *(progrès, égalité, héros)* so-called

prétendument [pretɑ̃dymɑ̃] *adv* supposedly

prête-nom *(pl* prête-noms*)* [prɛtnɔ̃] *nm Fig* figurehead

prétentieux, -euse [pretɑ̃sjø, -øz] 1 *adj* pretentious

2 *nm,f* pretentious person

prétention [pretɑ̃sjɔ̃] *nf* (a) *(vanité)* pretentiousness, pretension; sans p. *(repas, maison, personne)* unpretentious (b) *(revendication, ambition)* pretension, claim (à to); avoir la p. de faire qch to have the pretension to be able to do sth; quelles sont vos prétentions? *(salaire demandé)* what sort of salary are you looking for?

prêter [prete] **1** vt (a) (temporairement) to lend, Am to loan; **p. qch à qn** to lend sth to sb, to lend sb sth; **p. sur gages** to lend against security; Prov **on ne prête qu'aux riches** people don't lend money to those who really need it; Fig people are judged according to their reputation (b) (donner) **p. son appui** ou **son concours à qn** to give sb one's support; **p. assistance** ou **secours à qn** to lend or give assistance to sb; **p. main-forte à qn** to lend or give sb a hand; **p. l'oreille (à)** to listen or lend an ear (to); **p. attention à qch** to pay attention to sth; **p. serment** to take an oath; **p. le flanc à la critique** to lay oneself open to criticism (c) (attribuer) **p. qch à qn** (propos, intentions) to attribute or ascribe sth to sb

2 prêter à vt ind **p. à confusion** to give rise to confusion; **cela prête à rire** that's laughable

3 se prêter vpr (a) (consentir) **se p. à** to lend oneself to (b) (convenir) **se p. à** to lend itself to; **la situation ne s'y prête pas** the situation isn't ideal

prétérit [preterit] nm preterite (tense); **au p.** in the preterite

prêteur, -euse [pretœr, -øz] **1** nm,f lender; **p. sur gages** pawnbroker

2 adj ready or willing to lend things; **je ne suis pas p.** I don't like lending things

prétexte [pretekst] nm pretext, excuse; **sous p. de faire qch** on the pretext of doing sth; **sous p. que...** on the pretext that...; **sous aucun p.** on no account, under no circumstances

prétexter [pretekste] vt to give as a pretext or an excuse; **il a prétexté qu'il était malade** he gave the excuse that he was ill; **p. la fatigue** to plead tiredness

Pretoria [pretɔrja] n Pretoria

prêtre [pretr] nm priest

prêtresse [pretres] nf priestess

prêtrise [pretriz] nf priesthood

preuve [prœv] nf (a) (pour démontrer) piece of evidence; **il nous faut des preuves** we need proof or evidence; **faire la p. de qch** to prove sth; **avoir la p. que/de...** to have proof that/of...; **faire p. d'intelligence/de courage** to show intelligence/courage; **faire ses preuves** (personne) to prove oneself, to show one's ability; (technique) to be tried and tested; **jusqu'à p. du contraire** until there's proof to the contrary; Fam **elle ne m'aime pas: la p., elle ne m'écrit jamais** I know she doesn't like me because she never writes to me; **j'en veux pour p....** the proof of it is...; **p. d'achat** proof of purchase (b) Jur evidence (c) (témoignage) **une p. d'amour/d'amitié** a token of love/friendship (d) Math **faire la p. d'une opération** to prove or test the validity of a mathematical operation; **faire la p. par neuf** to cast out nines

prévaloir [69] [prevalwar] **1** vi to prevail (**sur** over); **faire p. son opinion** to win acceptance for one's opinion

2 se prévaloir vpr **se p. de qch** (profiter de) to take advantage of sth; (s'enorgueillir) to pride oneself on sth

prévenant, -e [prevnã, -ãt] adj (personne) kind (**envers** ou **avec** to), considerate (**envers** ou **avec** towards); (geste) thoughtful (**envers** ou **avec** towards)

prévenir [70] [prevnir] vt (a) (informer) to inform, to let know (**de** about or of); (mettre en garde) to warn; **tu es prévenu!** you've been warned!; **partir sans p.** to leave without telling anyone or without warning (b) (empêcher) (maladie) to prevent, to guard against; (danger, accident) to avert; Prov **mieux vaut p. que guérir** prevention is better than cure (c) (devancer) (désir) to anticipate; (objection) to forestall

préventif, -ive [prevãtif, -iv] adj preventive; Jur **détention préventive** custody; **être en détention préventive** to be remanded in custody

prévention [prevãsjɔ̃] nf (a) (pour empêcher) prevention; **p. routière** road safety (b) Jur custody; **mettre qn en p.** to remand sb in custody

prévenu, -e [prevny] nm,f defendant, accused

prévisible [previzibl] adj foreseeable

prévision [previzjɔ̃] nf forecast; (activité) forecasting; **en p. de qch** in expectation or anticipation of sth; **prévisions budgétaires** budget projections or forecasts; **prévisions météorologiques** weather forecast

prévisionnel, -elle [previzjɔnɛl] adj (coûts) estimated; (budget) projected; (analyse) preliminary

prévoir [73c] [prevwar] vt (a) (météo) to forecast; (réaction, difficultés, retards) to expect, to anticipate; **on ne peut pas tout p.** you can't think of everything (b) (programmer) (sortie, vacances) to plan; **la réunion est prévue pour demain** the meeting is scheduled for tomorrow; **il faudra des vêtements de pluie** we'll have to take waterproof clothes; **qu'est-ce que tu as prévu pour le dessert?** what are you planning to have for dessert?; **comme prévu** as planned; **cela s'est passé comme prévu** it went according to plan; **plus tôt/tard que prévu** sooner/later than expected; **cela n'était pas prévu au programme** that wasn't on the agenda

prévoyance [prevwajɑ̃s] nf foresight, forethought

prévoyant, -e [prevwajɑ̃, -ɑ̃t] adj far-sighted

prie-Dieu [pridjø] nm inv prie-dieu, prayer stool

prier [66] [prije] **1** vi to pray (**pour** for)

2 vt (a) (dieu) to pray to (b) (supplier) to beg; **il ne s'est pas fait p. pour venir** he didn't need much persuading to come; **allez, viens, arrête de te faire p.!** come on, stop being so difficult!; **sans se faire p.** without hesitation (c) (demander à) **p. qn de faire qch** to ask sb to do sth; **je te prie de te dépêcher!** please hurry up!; **taisez-vous, je vous prie!** please be quiet!; **je te prie de croire qu'elle a été surprise!** she was surprised, believe you me!; **je vous en prie!** (faites-le) please do!, of course!; (taisez-vous) stop it!; (il n'y a pas de quoi) you're welcome!

prière [prijɛr] nf (a) Rel prayer; **faire** ou **dire sa p.** to say one's prayers (b) (demande) request; **p. de ne pas fumer** (sur écriteau) no smoking; **p. de fermer la porte** (sur écriteau) please close the door

prieuré [prijœre] nm priory

primaire [primɛr] **1** adj (a) (école, couleur, secteur, ère) primary (b) Péj (personne) simple-minded; (réaction, racisme) narrow-minded

2 nm (a) Scol primary education; **être en p.** to be at primary school (b) Géol Primary era (c) Écon primary sector

primate [primat] nm Zool primate

primauté [primote] nf primacy

prime¹ [prim] adj (a) **de p. abord** at first sight; Litt **dès sa p. jeunesse** since her early youth (b) Math **B p.** B prime

prime² nf (d'assurance) premium; (allocation) grant; (sur salaire) bonus; **et vous aurez droit à un stylo en p.** and you will receive a free pen; Fig **en p.** into the bargain; **p. d'ancienneté** long-service award; **p. d'assurance** insurance premium; **p. de licenciement** severance allowance; **p. de transport** transport allowance

primer¹ [prime] **1** vt (avoir la priorité sur) to take precedence over

2 vi to come first; **p. sur** to take precedence over

primer² vt (attribuer un prix à) to award a prize to; **primé** (taureau) prize(winning); (roman, film) prizewinning, award-winning

primeur [primœr] nf (**a**) **primeurs** (fruits et légumes) (early) fruit and vegetables; **marchand de primeurs** greengrocer (selling early produce) (**b**) (exclusivité) **avoir la p. d'une nouvelle** to be the first to hear a piece of news

primevère [primver] nf primrose

primitif, -ive [primitif, -iv] **1** adj primitive; (originel) original

2 nm (artiste) primitive

primo [primo] adv first(ly), in the first place

primordial, -e, -aux, -ales [primɔrdjal, -o] adj essential, primordial

prince [prɛ̃s] nm prince; **comme un p.** (traité, élevé, habillé) like a prince; **être** ou **se montrer bon p.** to be very decent; **le p. charmant** Prince Charming

prince-de-galles [prɛ̃sdəgal] adj inv Prince of Wales check

princesse [prɛ̃ses] nf princess

princier, -ère [prɛ̃sje, -er] adj princely

principal, -e, -aux, -ales [prɛ̃sipal, -o] **1** adj aussi Gram main; (question, raison, but) main, principal; (rôle, acteur) leading

2 nm (**a**) (ce qui compte le plus) **le p.** the main thing, the most important thing (**b**) (d'une école) Br headmaster, f headmistress, Am principal

principalement [prɛ̃sipalmɑ̃] adv mainly, principally

principauté [prɛ̃sipote] nf principality

principe [prɛ̃sip] nm principle; **un accord de p.** an agreement in principle; **partir du p. que...** to assume that...; **c'est une question de p.** it's a matter of principle; **avoir pour p. de...** to make it a matter of principle to...; **avoir des principes** to have (high) principles; **en p.** in principle, theoretically; **par p.** on principle

printanier, -ère [prɛ̃tanje, -er] adj spring

printemps [prɛ̃tɑ̃] nm spring; **au p.** in (the) spring(time); **une journée de p.** a spring day; Fig **ses vingt-six p.** her twenty-six summers

prioritaire [prijoriter] adj (that has) priority; **être p.** to have priority; (en voiture) to have the right of way

priorité [prijorite] nf (**a**) (précédence) priority; **donner la p. à qn/qch** to give sb/sth priority; **leur dossier sera traité en p.** their file will get priority treatment; **avoir la p. sur** to have priority over (**b**) Aut right of way, priority; **avoir p.** to have the right of way; **accorder** ou **laisser la p. à une voiture** Br to give way or Am to yield to a car; **refuser la p.** to refuse to give way; **p. à droite** (sur panneau) = give way to vehicles coming from the right

pris, -e [pri, priz] **1** pp voir **prendre**

2 adj (**a**) (siège) occupied, taken; **avoir les mains prises** to have one's hands full (**b**) (personne) busy; **je suis déjà p. ce jour-là** I've already got something on that day (**c**) (saisi) **p. de peur** seized with fear; **p. de panique** panic-stricken; **p. de remords** racked with guilt (**d**) (gelé) frozen (over) (**e**) (encombré) **avoir le nez p.** to have a blocked nose; **avoir la gorge prise** to have a sore throat (**f**) **avoir la taille bien prise** to have a trim waist

prise [priz] nf (**a**) (d'une ville, de prisonniers) taking, capture; (à la pêche) catch; (de drogue) seize

(**b**) Él **p.** (de courant ou électrique) (femelle) Br socket, Am outlet; (mâle) plug; **p. multiple** adaptor; Ordinat **p. péritel** scart connector; **p. de terre** Br earth or Am ground (connection)

(**c**) Cin, Phot & TV **p. de son** sound recording; **p. de vue** (cliché) shot; (de tournage) take; (action) shooting

(**d**) Tech **en p.** in gear, engaged; Fig **en p. (directe) sur** ou **avec qch** in touch with sth

(**e**) (de judo, de lutte) hold; (pour se retenir) hold; (plus ferme) grasp, grip; (pour le pied) foothold; Fig **avoir p. sur** to have a hold on or over sb; **lâcher p.** to lose one's grip; Fig to give up; **donner p. aux reproches/critiques** to lay oneself open to reproach/criticism; **être aux prises avec des difficultés** to be grappling with difficulties; **être aux prises avec qn** to be at odds with sb

(**f**) (locutions) Fam **p. de bec** row, squabble; **p. en charge** (par un taxi) (d'un passager) picking up; (somme) minimum charge; (par la Sécurité sociale) (guaranteed) reimbursement; **p. de conscience** awareness, realization; **p. de contact** initial contact or meeting; **p. de notes** note-taking; **p. d'otages** hostage-taking; **p. de position** stance; **p. de pouvoir** (political) takeover; **faire une p. de sang à qn** to take a blood sample from sb

priser¹ [prize] **1** vt **p. du tabac** to take snuff

2 vi to take snuff

priser² vt Litt (estimer) to prize, to value

prisme [prism] nm prism

prison [prizɔ̃] nf (**a**) (lieu de détention) prison, jail; **mettre qn en prison** to put sb in prison; **faire de la p.** to serve a prison sentence (**b**) (peine) imprisonment; **cinq ans de p.** five years' imprisonment

prisonnier, -ère [prizonje, -er] **1** nm,f prisoner; **faire qn p.** to take sb prisoner; **p. de droit commun** common criminal; **p. de guerre** prisoner of war, POW; **p. politique** political prisoner

2 adj imprisoned, in prison; **ils sont encore prisonniers sous les décombres** they are still trapped in the rubble; **être p. de** to be a prisoner of; Fig to be a slave to

privation [privasjɔ̃] nf (**a**) (action de priver) deprivation (**b**) **privations** (manque) hardship, privation; **s'imposer des privations** to deprive oneself, to go without

privatisation [privatizasjɔ̃] nf privatization

privatiser [privatize] vt to privatize

privautés [privote] nfpl (undue) familiarity; **prendre** ou **se permettre des p. avec qn** to be over-familiar with sb

privé, -e [prive] **1** adj private; **à titre p.** in a private capacity

2 nm (**a**) (secteur) **le p.** the private sector; Scol the private education system; **mes enfants sont dans le p.** my children go to a private school (**b**) (intimité) **dans le p.** privately; **connaître qn dans le p.** to know sb personally; **en p.** in private (**c**) Fam (détective) private eye

priver [prive] **1** vt **p. qn de qch** to deprive sb of sth; **p. qn de sorties** not to allow sb to go out; **être privé de dessert** to go without pudding; **ça ne le prive pas du tout de ne plus fumer** he doesn't find it a hardship not to smoke any more

2 **se priver** vpr to do or go without; **se p. de** to do or go without; (plaisir) to deprive oneself of, to deny oneself; **ne pas se p. de faire qch** not to hesitate to do sth

privilège [privilɛʒ] nm privilege

privilégié, -e [privileʒje] **1** adj (personne, site) privileged; (conditions) privileged, favourable; (relations) special
2 nm,f privileged person; **les privilégiés** the privileged

privilégier [66] [privileʒje] vt (personne, groupe) to privilege; (facteur, aspect) to prioritize

prix [pri] nm (a) (coût) price; **à tout p.** at all costs, at any price; **à aucun p.** not at any price, on no account; **se vendre à p. d'or** to fetch huge prices; **acheter qch à p. d'or** to pay a (small) fortune for sth; **payer qch au p. fort** to pay a high price for sth; **faire un p. à qn** to give sb a good deal; **je vous fais un p. d'ami** I'll let you have it cheap; **y mettre le p.** to pay a high price; **la santé/le bonheur, ça n'a pas de p.** you can't put a price on health/happiness; **mettre à p. la tête de qn** to put a price on sb's head; **c'est mon dernier p.** that's my final offer; **votre p. sera le mien** name your price; **au p. coûtant** at cost price; **p. de revient** cost price; **p. de vente** selling price (b) (importance) **attacher beaucoup de p. ou un grand p. à qch** to set great store by sth (c) (récompense) prize; **p. de consolation** consolation prize; **le p. Goncourt** ≃ prestigious French literary prize; **le p. Nobel** (récompense) Nobel Prize; (personne) Nobel Br prizewinner or Am laureate; **le p. Nobel de la Paix** (récompense) the Nobel Peace Prize

pro [pro] nmf Fam pro

probabilité [probabilite] nf probability, likelihood; **selon toute p.** in all probability or likelihood; Math **calcul des probabilités** theory of probability

probable [probabl] adj probable, likely; **il est p. qu'elle viendra** she'll probably come; **peu p.** improbable, unlikely; **il est peu p. qu'elle vienne** she's not likely or she's unlikely to come

probablement [probablmɑ̃] adv probably

probant, -e [probɑ̃, -ɑ̃t] adj convincing, conclusive

probité [probite] nf probity, integrity

problématique [problematik] **1** adj problematic(al)
2 nf set of problems

problème [problɛm] nm problem; **c'est tout un p.!** it's such a problem!; **peau/cheveux à problèmes** problem skin/hair; **avoir des problèmes familiaux/d'argent** to have family/money problems

procédé [prosede] nm (a) (façon de faire) method; **échange de bons procédés** exchange of friendly services (b) (technique) process; **p. de fabrication** manufacturing process; Péj **ça sent le p.** it seems rather artificial

procéder [34] [prosede] **1** vi (a) (agir) to proceed, to act; **p. par ordre** to do things in order; **p. avec méthode** to proceed methodically; **p. par élimination** to follow a process of elimination (b) Formel **p. de** (venir de) to arise out of, to originate in
2 procéder à vt ind (recherches, arrestation, vérification) to carry out; (élections) to hold

procédure [prosedyr] nf (a) (méthode) procedure (b) Jur proceedings; **engager une p.** to take proceedings (c) Ordinat procedure; **p. de chargement** loading procedure

procédurier, -ère [prosedyrje, -ɛr] adj quibbling

procès [prosɛ] nm Jur (legal) proceedings; (civil) lawsuit; (criminel) (criminal) trial; **engager un p.** to take legal action; **faire ou intenter un p. à qn** to take proceedings against sb; **être en p. avec qn** to be involved in legal proceedings with sb; **gagner/perdre son p.** to win/lose one's case; **faire un p. d'intention à qn** to accuse sb on the basis of assumptions not facts; **faire le p. de qn/qch**

(critiquer) to attack sb/sth; Fig **sans autre forme de p.** without (any) further ceremony, without further ado

processeur [prosesœr] nm Ordinat processor; **p. central** central processing unit, CPU; **p. de données** data processor

procession [prosesjɔ̃] nf procession

processus [prosesys] nm process

procès-verbal [prosevɛrbal] (pl **procès-verbaux** [prosevɛrbo]) nm (a) Jur policeman's report (about an offence); (amende) fine (b) (rapport) (official) report; (d'une réunion) minutes; (d'un témoignage) record

prochain, -e [prɔʃɛ̃, -ɛn] **1** adj (qui suit) next; **ce sera pour une prochaine fois** Br another time, perhaps, Am let's have a rain check; **à la prochaine (fois)!** see you (soon)!; Fam **je descends à la prochaine** I'm getting off at the next stop (b) (imminent) imminent; **dans un avenir p.** in the near or not too distant future; **un jour p.** one day soon
2 nm (semblable) **aimer son p.** to love one's neighbour

prochainement [prɔʃɛnmɑ̃] adv shortly, soon; **p. sur vos écrans** coming soon to a cinema near you

proche [prɔʃ] **1** adj (a) (dans l'espace) near, close; **p. de qch** close to or near sth (b) (dans l'avenir) near, imminent; **dans un avenir p.** in the near or not too distant future; **la fin est p.** the end is nigh (c) (récent) recent (d) (semblable, intime) close (de to); **ils sont proches parents** they are closely related (e) **de p. en p.** gradually, step by step
2 nm close relative or relation

Proche-Orient [prɔʃɔrjɑ̃] nm **le P.** the Middle East

proclamation [proklamasjɔ̃] nf proclamation

proclamer [proklame] vt to proclaim; (résultats de scrutin) to declare

procréation [prokreasjɔ̃] nf procreation

procréer [24] [prokree] vi to procreate

procuration [prokyrasjɔ̃] nf proxy, power of attorney; **par p.** by proxy, Spéc per pro(curationem); Fig **vivre par p.** to live by proxy

procurer [prokyre] **1** vt **p. qch à qn** (sujet: personne) to get sth for sb; (sujet: chose) to bring sb sth
2 se procurer vpr to get (hold of), to obtain

procureur [prokyrœr] nm Jur procurator, proxy; **p. général/de la République** (système anglais) ≃ public prosecutor; (système écossais) ≃ procurator fiscal; (système américain) ≃ district attorney

prodigalité [prodigalite] nf extravagance, prodigality

prodige [prodiʒ] **1** nm wonder, marvel; (personne) prodigy; **faire des prodiges** to work wonders; **tenir du p.** to be extraordinary, to be something of a miracle
2 adj **enfant p.** child prodigy

prodigieusement [prodiʒjøzmɑ̃] adv prodigiously

prodigieux, -euse [prodiʒjø, -øz] adj prodigious, extraordinary

prodigue [prodig] adj (dépensier) wasteful, spendthrift; (généreux) lavish, unsparing (de in or with)

prodiguer [prodige] vt **p. qch à qn** to lavish sth on sb; **p. des conseils à qn** to pour out advice to sb

producteur, -trice [prodyktœr, -tris] **1** adj **pays p. de blé/pétrole** wheat-growing/oil-producing country
2 nm,f producer

productif, -ive [prodyktif, -iv] adj productive

production [prɔdyksjɔ̃] *nf* (a) *Ind & Cin* production; *(d'électricité)* production, generation (b) *(produit)* product; *Cin* production; *(d'une usine)* output; **p. littéraire** literary output

productivité [prɔdyktivite] *nf* productivity

produire [18] [prɔdɥir] **1** *vt* (a) *(marchandise, émission, gaz)* to produce; *(chaleur, électricité, odeur)* to generate, to produce (b) *(résultat, effet)* to produce, to bring about; *(irritation, sensation)* to cause
2 se produire *vpr* (a) *(événement)* to happen (b) *(acteur)* to appear

produit [prɔdɥi] *nm* (a) *(marchandise)* product; **produits agricoles** agricultural *or* farm produce; **p. de beauté** beauty product; **p. chimique** chemical; **p. de consommation** consumer product; **p. d'entretien** (household) cleaning product; **p. fini** finished product; **p. intérieur brut** gross domestic product; **p. de luxe** luxury product; **p. manufacturé** manufactured product; **produits ménagers** (household) cleaning products; **p. national brut** gross national product (b) *(profit)* yield; **p. d'une vente** proceeds of a sale; **le p. de dix années de travail** the result of ten years' work; **vivre du p. de la terre** to live off the land (c) *Math (d'une multiplication)* product (d) *(création)* **c'est le p. de son imagination** it's the product of his imagination

proéminent, -e [prɔeminɑ̃, -ɑ̃t] *adj* prominent

prof [prɔf] *nmf Fam* teacher

profanateur, -trice [prɔfanatœr, -tris] *nm,f (de tombes)* desecrator

profanation [prɔfanasjɔ̃] *nf* desecration, violation

profane [prɔfan] **1** *adj* non-religious, secular; *Fig* **être p. en la matière** to know nothing about the subject
2 *nmf (non-initié)* layman, *f* laywoman

profaner [prɔfane] *vt (église)* to desecrate; *(tombe)* to desecrate, to violate; *(souvenir, mémoire)* to defile

proférer [34] [prɔfere] *vt* to utter

professer [prɔfese] *vt* to profess

professeur [prɔfesœr] *nm* teacher; *(à l'université)* professor; **p. principal** *Br* class *or* form teacher, *Am* homeroom teacher

profession [prɔfesjɔ̃] *nf* (a) *(métier)* profession, occupation; *(d'artisans)* trade; **de p.** *(musicien)* professional; *(menuisier)* by trade; **p. libérale** profession; **sans p.** *(dans un questionnaire)* not working; **je suis sans p.** I don't work (b) *(déclaration)* **faire p. de qch** to profess sth; **p. de foi** profession of faith

professionnalisation [prɔfesjɔnalizasjɔ̃] *nf* professionalization

professionnalisme [prɔfesjɔnalism] *nm* professionalism

professionnel, -elle [prɔfesjɔnɛl] **1** *adj (attitude, sportif)* professional; *(enseignement)* vocational; *(maladie)* occupational
2 *nm,f* professional

professionnellement [prɔfesjɔnɛlmɑ̃] *adv* professionally

professoral, -e, -aux, -ales [prɔfesɔral, -o] *adj* professorial

professorat [prɔfesɔra] *nm* teaching profession *(especially in higher education)*

profil [prɔfil] *nm aussi Fig* profile; **dessiner qn de p.** to draw sb in profile; **se mettre de p.** to turn one's face *(so it is in profile)*; *Fig* **adopter un p. bas** to adopt a low profile; **p. de poste** job description; **avoir le p. de l'emploi** to fit the job description

profilé, -e [prɔfile] *adj* streamlined

profiler [prɔfile] **se profiler** *vpr* to stand out (in profile), to be outlined *(sur ou contre* against); *(problèmes)* to emerge, to loom; *(solution)* to emerge; *(événement)* to be in the offing

profit [prɔfi] *nm* (a) *(avantage)* profit, benefit; **mettre qch à p.** to put sth to good use; **tirer p. de qch** to take advantage of sth; **ce manteau m'a fait du p.** this coat has served me well; **au p. des pauvres** in aid of the poor; **concert donné au p. des orphelins** benefit concert for orphans; **perdre des voix au p. de qn** to lose votes to sb (b) *(gain)* profit; **il n'y a pas de petits profits** every little helps

profitable [prɔfitabl] *adj* profitable

profiter [prɔfite] **1 profiter de** *vt ind* to take advantage of; **je profite d'un moment de calme pour vous dire que...** I'm using these few moments of peace and quiet to tell you that...; **p. de la vie/de sa jeunesse** to make the most of life/one's youth
2 profiter à *vt ind* to be of benefit to, to benefit; **ses vacances lui ont bien profité** his holiday has done him a lot of good
3 *vi Fam (enfant, plante)* to thrive

profiteur, -euse [prɔfitœr, -øz] *nm,f Péj* profiteer

profond, -e [prɔfɔ̃, -ɔ̃d] **1** *adj* (a) *(trou, lac, voix)* deep; *(décolleté)* plunging; *(forêt)* dense, thick; *(sommeil)* deep; sound (b) *(cause)* underlying (c) *(paroles)* profound; *(haine, silence, dégoût)* profound, deep; *(soupir)* heavy
2 *adv* deep
3 *nm* **au plus p. de mon cœur** in my heart of hearts, deep down; **au plus p. de la nuit** at dead of night

profondément [prɔfɔ̃demɑ̃] *adv* (choqué, déçu, ému) deeply, profoundly; *(aimer, mépriser)* deeply; *(dormir)* soundly; *(creuser)* deep; **p. endormi** sound *or* fast asleep; **j'en suis p. convaincu** I'm quite convinced of it

profondeur [prɔfɔ̃dœr] *nf* (a) *(de l'eau, d'un trou)* depth; **faire 10 mètres de p.** to be 10 metres deep; **en p.** *(étude, analyse)* in-depth; *Phot* **p. de champ** depth of field (b) *(d'un sentiment)* depth; *(d'un texte)* profoundness, profundity

profusion [prɔfyzjɔ̃] *nf* profusion, abundance; **à p.** in profusion

progéniture [prɔʒenityr] *nf* progeny, offspring

progiciel [prɔʒisjɛl] *nm Ordinat* software package; **p. de communication** comms package

prognathe [prɔgnat] *adj (visage)* undershot, underhung, *Spéc* prognathous

programmable [prɔgramabl] *adj* programmable

programmateur, -trice [prɔgramatœr, -tris] **1** *nm,f Rad & TV* programme planner
2 *nm Tech* automatic control (device); *Ordinat* programmer

programmation [prɔgramasjɔ̃] *nf* (a) *TV & Rad* programme planning (b) *Ordinat* programming

programme [prɔgram] *nm* (a) *(émissions, œuvres)* programme; *(brochure)* *(de télévision)* TV guide; *(de cinéma)* cinema guide; *(au concert, au théâtre)* programme (b) *(d'activités)* programme (c) *Scol* curriculum; *(d'un cours)* syllabus; **les auteurs au** *ou* **du p.** the set books (d) *(d'un parti politique)* manifesto; **p. électoral** *(election)* platform; *Fig* **c'est tout un p.!** that'll be interesting! (e) *Ordinat* program; **p. d'amorçage** boot program; **p. d'arrière-plan** background program; **p. d'auto-test** self-test program; **p. de configuration** configuration program; **p. de conversion** conversion program; **p. détecteur de virus** virus detection program; **p. éditeur de liens** link program, linker; **p. d'évaluation de performance** benchmark program; **p. de formatage** formatter

programmer [prɔgrame] *vt* (a) *Ordinat* to program (b) *TV & Rad* to schedule (c) *(vacances, changements)* to plan

programmeur, -euse [prɔgramœr, -øz] *nm,f Ordinat* programmer

progrès [prɔgrɛ] *nm* progress; **faire des p.** to make progress; **être en p.** to be making progress; *Fam* **il y a du** *ou* **un p.** there's been an improvement

progresser [prɔgrese] *vi* (a) *(avancer)* *(armée)* to advance, to progress; *(marcheur)* to make progress (b) *(épidémie, incendie)* to spread; *(chômage, délinquance)* to rise, to increase (c) *(faire des progrès)* to make progress

progressif, -ive [prɔgresif, -iv] *adj* progressive; *(changement)* gradual

progression [prɔgresjɔ̃] *nf* (a) *(avance)* *(d'une armée)* advance, progress; *(de marcheurs)* progress (b) *(d'un incendie, d'une épidémie)* spread; *(de la délinquance, du chômage)* rise, increase; **être en p.** *(secteur économique)* to be growing or expanding; *(maladie)* to be spreading; *(chômage, criminalité)* to be rising, to be on the increase

progressiste [prɔgresist] *adj & nmf* progressive

progressivement [prɔgresivmã] *adv* progressively

prohiber [prɔibe] *vt* to prohibit, to forbid

prohibitif, -ive [prɔibitif, -iv] *adj* prohibitive

prohibition [prɔibisjɔ̃] *nf* prohibition; *Hist* **la P.** Prohibition

proie [prwa] *nf* prey; **être la p. de qn** to fall prey or victim to sb; **être en p. à** *(remords, doute)* to be racked or tormented by; *(hallucinations)* to suffer from; **lâcher la p. pour l'ombre** to go chasing after rainbows

projecteur [prɔʒɛktœr] *nm* (a) *Cin & Phot* projector (b) *(dans un stade, sur un monument)* floodlight; *Th* spotlight; *Fig* **sous les projecteurs de l'actualité** in the limelight

projectile [prɔʒɛktil] *nm* missile

projection [prɔʒɛksjɔ̃] *nf* (a) *(lancer)* projection; *(d'un liquide, de boue)* splashing; *(de graisse)* spattering; *(de cendres, de roches)* spewing out; **des projections de boue** splashes of mud (b) *Cin* projection; *(séance)* screening, showing; **p. de diapositives** slide show; **p. privée** private screening

projectionniste [prɔʒɛksjɔnist] *nmf* projectionist

projet [prɔʒɛ] *nm* *(intention)* plan; *(étude)* project; **faire des projets** to make plans; **p. de loi** bill; **en p.** at the planning stage; **c'est resté à l'état de p.** it never got off the ground

projeter [42] [prɔʒte] **1** *vt* (a) *(lancer)* to project; *(graisse)*

to spatter; *(liquide, boue)* to splash; *(cendres, roches)* to spew out; **être projeté au sol** to be hurled to the ground (b) *(prévoir)* to plan; **p. de faire qch** to plan to do sth (c) *(film)* to show, to screen (d) *(faire apparaître)* *(ombre)* to cast, to throw; *(image)* to project (e) *Psy* to project **(sur** onto)

2 se projeter *vpr (ombre)* to be cast

prolétaire [prɔletɛr] *adj & nmf* proletarian

prolétariat [prɔletarja] *nm* proletariat

prolétarien, -enne [prɔletarjɛ̃, -ɛn] *adj* proletarian

prolifération [prɔliferasjɔ̃] *nf* proliferation

proliférer [34] [prɔlifere] *vi* to proliferate

prolifique [prɔlifik] *adj* prolific

prolixe [prɔliks] *adj* wordy, verbose

prolo [prɔlo] *Fam* **1** *adj* plebby

2 *nmf* pleb, prole

prologue [prɔlɔg] *nm* prologue **(de** to)

prolongation [prɔlɔ̃gasjɔ̃] *nf* *(de discussions)* prolongation; *(d'un congé, d'un séjour)* extension; **jouer les prolongations** *(au football)* to play extra time *or Am* overtime

prolongé, -e [prɔlɔ̃ʒe] *adj* *(absence, séjour)* prolonged, lengthy; *(effort)* prolonged, sustained; *(week-end)* long; **pas d'utilisation prolongée sans avis médical** *(sur un médicament)* ≃ if symptoms persist, consult your doctor

prolongement [prɔlɔ̃ʒmã] *nm* (a) *(d'une rue)* continuation; *(d'un mur, d'une voie de chemin de fer)* extension; **être dans le p. de qch** *(meuble)* to be flush with sth; *(rue)* to be a continuation of sth (b) **prolongements** *(d'une action)* repercussions

prolonger [45] [prɔlɔ̃ʒe] **1** *vt* *(vie, débat, repas)* to prolong; *(séjour, absence)* to prolong, to extend; *(mur, route, voie ferrée)* to extend

2 se prolonger *vpr (séjour, absence)* to be prolonged or extended; *(réunion)* to go on; *(rue)* to continue, to extend

promenade [prɔmnad] *nf* (a) *(marche)* walk; *(courte)* stroll; **faire une p.** to go for a walk/stroll; **faire une p. en voiture** to go for a drive; **faire une p. à bicyclette** to go for a bike ride; **faire une p. à cheval** to go (horse)riding; **l'heure de la p.** *(d'un détenu)* exercise time (b) *(avenue)* promenade

promener [46] [prɔmne] **1** *vt* (a) *(personne, chien)* to take for a walk; *Fig* **p. qn de musée en musée** to take sb from museum to museum; *Fam* **cela te promènera un peu** it'll get you out a bit (b) *(passer)* **p. sa main/son regard sur qch** to run one's hand/one's eyes over sth

2 se promener *vpr* to go for a walk; **aller se p.** to go for a walk; *Ordinat* **se p. dans** *(texte)* to scroll through

promeneur, -euse [prɔmnœr, -øz] *nm,f* walker

promesse [prɔmɛs] *nf* promise; **faire une p. à qn** to make sb a promise; **p. de Gascon** empty promise; **p. d'achat/de vente** undertaking to buy/to sell

prometteur, -euse [prɔmetœr, -øz] *adj* promising

promettre [47] [prɔmɛtr] **1** *vt* (a) *(s'engager à)* to promise; **p. qch à qn** to promise sb sth; **je ne peux rien te p.** I can't promise (you) anything; **tu me le promets?** (do you) promise?; **je te promets de le faire** I promise you I'll do it; **je le ferai, c'est promis** I'll do it, I promise; **p. monts et merveilles à qn** to promise sb the earth *or* the moon (b) *(être prometteur)* **la soirée promet d'être amusante** it promises to be an amusing evening; *Fam* **ça ne promet rien de bon** it doesn't look good

2 *vi (projet, enfant)* to be promising; *Fam Ironique* **ça promet!** that's promising!

3 se promettre *vpr* **se p. qch** *(à soi-même)* to promise oneself sth; *(l'un l'autre)* to promise each other sth; **se p. de faire qch** *(à soi-même)* to resolve to do sth; **ils se sont promis de ne jamais se quitter** they promised each other they'd never part

promis, -e [promi, -iz] **1** *adj* promised
2 *nm,f Vieilli* betrothed

promiscuité [promiskчite] *nf* overcrowding; **vivre dans la p.** to live in crowded accommodation

promo [promo] *nf Fam* promo; **en p.** on special offer

promontoire [promɔ̃twar] *nm* promontory, headland

promoteur, -trice [promotœr, -tris] *nm,f* **(a) (immobilier)** property developer **(b)** *(créateur)* originator **(de** of**)**

promotion [promosjɔ̃] *nf* **(a)** *(avancement)* promotion; **p. à l'ancienneté** promotion by seniority; **p. interne** internal promotion; **p. sociale** upward mobility **(b)** *(d'une école) Br* year, *Am* class; **premier de sa p.** first in one's *Br* year or *Am* class **(c)** *(dans le commerce)* promotion; **faire la p. de qch** to promote sth; **la p. de la semaine** this week's special offer; **en p.** on special offer

promotionnel, -elle [promosjɔnɛl] *adj (article)* promotional; *(tarif)* special; **vente promotionnelle** special offer

promouvoir [31a] [promuvwar] *vt aussi Fig* to promote; **être promu chef du personnel** to be promoted to personnel manager

prompt, -e [prɔ̃, prɔ̃t] *adj (réaction)* prompt; **p. à faire qch** quick to do sth; **p. à la riposte** quick with a riposte

promptement [prɔ̃tmɑ̃, prɔ̃ptəmɑ̃] *adv Litt* promptly

promptitude [prɔ̃tityd] *nf Litt (d'une réaction)* promptness

promu, -e *voir* **promouvoir**

promulgation [promylgasjɔ̃] *nf* promulgation

promulguer [promylge] *vt* to promulgate

prôner [prone] *vt* to advocate

pronom [prɔnɔ̃] *nm Gram* pronoun; **p. personnel/ indéfini/interrogatif** personal/indefinite/interrogative pronoun

pronominal, -e, -aux, -ales [prɔnɔminal, -o] *adj Gram* pronominal

prononcé, -e [prɔnɔ̃se] **1** *adj* pronounced, strong
2 *nm Jur* **le p. du jugement** the verdict

prononcer [16] [prɔnɔ̃se] **1** *vt* **a)** *(articuler)* to pronounce; **mal p. un mot** to mispronounce a word **(b)** *(dire) (mot)* to utter; *(discours)* to deliver; *(sentence, divorce)* to pronounce
2 se prononcer *vpr* **(a)** *(être articulé)* to be pronounced; **ça s'écrit comme ça se prononce** it's written as it's pronounced **(b)** *(s'exprimer)* to give one's opinion; *(juge)* to give a verdict; **se p. pour** *ou* **en faveur de qn/qch** to express one's support for sb/sth; **se p. contre qn/qch** to express one's opposition to sb/sth; **50 pour cent ne se prononcent pas** *(dans un sondage)* 50 per cent are undecided

prononciation [prɔnɔ̃sjasjɔ̃] *nf* pronunciation; **elle a une bonne/mauvaise p.** her pronunciation is good/ bad

pronostic [prɔnɔstik] *nm* forecast; *(d'un médecin)* prognosis

propagande [prɔpagɑ̃d] *nf* propaganda; **faire de la p. pour qn/qch** to put out propaganda for sb/sth; *(pour une élection)* to campaign for sb/sth

propagation [prɔpagasjɔ̃] *nf* spreading

propager [45] [prɔpaʒe] **1** *vt* to spread
2 se propager *vpr* **(a)** *(épidémie, nouvelle, idée)* to spread **(b)** *(lumière, son)* to be propagated

propane [prɔpan] *nm Chim* propane

propension [prɔpɑ̃sjɔ̃] *nf* propensity (à for); **p. à faire qch** propensity to do sth

prophète [prɔfɛt] *nm* prophet; **p. de malheur** prophet of doom; *Prov* **nul n'est p. en son pays** no man is a prophet in his own country

prophétie [prɔfesi] *nf* prophecy

prophétique [prɔfetik] *adj* prophetic

prophylactique [prɔfilaktik] *adj* prophylactic

propice [prɔpis] *adj* **le moment p.** the right moment; **p. à qch** good for sth; **un endroit p. au repos** a restful spot; **un endroit p. aux rencontres** a good place to meet people

proportion [prɔpɔrsjɔ̃] *nf* proportion; **respecter les proportions** to get the proportions right; **en p. de qch** in proportion to sth; **hors de (toute) p.** out of (all) proportion to; **toutes proportions gardées** relatively speaking

proportionné, -e [prɔpɔrsjɔne] *adj* **(a)** *(bâti)* **bien-/ mal p.** well-/badly-proportioned **(b)** *(lié)* **être p. à** to be proportionate to

proportionnel, -elle [prɔpɔrsjɔnɛl] **1** *adj* proportional (à to); **inversement p. à qch** inversely proportional to sth
2 *nf* **proportionnelle** *Pol* proportional representation

proportionnellement [prɔpɔrsjɔnɛlmɑ̃] *adv* proportionally (à to)

propos [prɔpo] *nm* **(a)** *(sujet)* **à p. de qn/qch** about sb/ sth; **à ce p.,...** talking of which...; **à tout p.** constantly; **à p., avez-vous lu ce livre?** by the way, have you read this book?; **c'est à quel p.?** what's it about?; **arriver fort à p.** to arrive at just the right moment; **juger à p. de faire qch** to think it right to do sth; **hors de p.** *(remarque)* inappropriate **(b)** *(intention)* purpose, intention; **de p. délibéré** deliberately, on purpose **(c)** *(parole)* **des p.** talk, words; **tenir des p. étonnants** to say some surprising things

proposer [prɔpoze] **1** *vt (suggérer)* to suggest, to propose; *(offrir)* to offer; *(amendement, loi)* to table; **p. qch à qn** to suggest or propose sth to sb; *(argent, travail)* to offer sb sth; **je vous en propose 6000 francs/un bon prix** I'll give you 6,000 francs/a good price for it; **voilà ce que je vous propose** this is what I suggest; **le cinéma Le César vous propose cette semaine...** Le César will be showing the following films this week...; **je leur ai proposé de venir avec moi** I suggested (to them) that they should come with me; **elle m'a proposé de m'aider** she offered to help me; **je propose qu'on y aille demain** I suggest going tomorrow
2 se proposer *vpr* **(a)** *(être volontaire)* to offer one's services; **se p. pour faire qch** to offer to do sth **(b)** **se p. de faire qch** *(en avoir l'intention)* to propose to do sth

proposition [prɔpozisjɔ̃] *nf* **(a)** *(suggestion)* suggestion, proposal; *(offre)* offer; **faire une p.** to make a suggestion or proposal (to sb); **faire des propositions à une femme** to proposition a woman; **sur la p. de qn** at sb's suggestion; **p. de loi** bill **(b)** *Phil & Math* proposition **(c)** *Gram* clause

propre [prɔpr] **1** *adj* **(a)** *(impeccable) (personne, linge, maison)* clean; *(bébé)* potty-trained; *(copie d'élève)* neat; **n'utilise pas la serviette des autres, ce n'est pas p.!** don't use other people's towels, it's not hygienic!; **p. comme un sou neuf** spick and span; *Fam* **nous voilà propres!** now we're in a mess!
(b) *(à soi own)*; **voir qch de ses propres yeux** to see sth with one's own eyes; **ce sont là ses propres paroles** these are his very words
(c) *(particulier)* **être p. à qn/qch** to be characteristic of or peculiar to sb/sth
(d) *(adapté)* **être p. à qch** to be suitable for sth
(e) *(littéral)* **au sens p.** in the literal sense, literally
2 *nm* **(a)** *(caractéristique)* characteristic feature
(b) **appartenir en p. à qn** to be sb's sole property
(c) *(sens propre)* **au p.** literally
(d) **recopier qch au p.** to make a clean copy of sth
(e) **sentir le p.** to smell clean
(f) *Fam* **c'est du p.!** that's a fine way to carry on!

propre-à-rien *(pl* **propres-à-rien)** [prɔprarjɛ̃] *nmf* good-for-nothing

proprement [prɔprəmɑ̃] *adv* **(a)** *(avec propreté)* cleanly; *(vêtu)* tidily; **manger p.** to eat without making a mess **(b)** *(strictement)* strictly; **c'est un problème p. urbain** it's strictly an inner-city problem **(c)** **à p. parler** strictly speaking; **voilà la bibliothèque p. dite** there's the actual library **(d)** *Fam* **(vraiment) c'est p. scandaleux!** it's an absolute disgrace!

propreté [prɔprəte] *nf (hygiène)* cleanliness; *(des vêtements, de la vaisselle, d'une maison)* cleanness; *(d'un travail)* neatness

propriétaire [prɔprijetɛr] *nmf* **(a)** *(d'une voiture, d'une propriété, d'un hôtel)* owner; **devenir** *ou* **se rendre p. de qch** to become the owner of sth; **être p.** to be a landowner; *(de maison)* to be a home owner; **p. foncier** landowner **(b)** *(d'une location)* landlord, *f* landlady

propriété [prɔprijete] *nf* **(a)** *(fait de posséder)* ownership; **p. littéraire** copyright; **p. foncière** property ownership **(b)** *(chose ou terrain possédé)* property; **p. privée** private property **(c)** *(caractéristique)* property

proprio [prɔprijo] *nmf Fam* landlord, *f* landlady

propulser [prɔpylse] **1** *vt* to propel
2 se propulser *vpr Fam* **se p. en tête du peloton** to shoot to the front of the pack

propulsion [prɔpylsjɔ̃] *nf* propulsion; **sous-marin à p. nucléaire** nuclear-powered submarine

prorata [prɔrata] *nm inv* proportion; **au p. de qch** in proportion to sth

prorogation [prɔrɔgasjɔ̃] *nf (de contrat, de bail)* extension

proroger [45] [prɔrɔʒe] *vt (contrat, bail)* to extend; *(échéance)* to defer

prosaïque [prozaik] *adj* prosaic

proscrire [30] [prɔskrir] *vt* to ban, to proscribe

proscrit, -e [prɔskri, -it] **1** *adj* banned, proscribed
2 *nm,f Litt (banni)* exile

prose [proz] *nf* prose; **en p.** *(écrire)* in prose; *(texte, poème)* prose

prosélytisme [prozelitism] *nm* proselytism; **faire du p.** to proselytize

prosodie [prozɔdi] *nf* prosody

prospecter [prɔspɛkte] *vt* **(a)** *(terrain)* to prospect **(b)** *(client)* to canvass; *(marché)* to explore

prospecteur, -trice [prɔspɛktœr, -tris] *nm,f* **(a)** *(de terrain)* prospector **(b)** *(de clients)* canvasser

prospection [prɔspɛksjɔ̃] *nf* **(a)** *(de terrain)* prospecting; **faire de la p.** to prospect **(b)** *(de clients)* canvassing; **faire de la p.** to explore the market; **p. téléphonique** telephone canvassing

prospectus [prɔspɛktys] *nm* leaflet

prospère [prɔspɛr] *adj* prosperous; *(santé)* glowing

prospérer [34] [prɔspere] *vi* to prosper

prospérité [prɔsperite] *nf* prosperity; **en période de p.** in times of prosperity

prostate [prɔstat] *nf Anat* prostate (gland)

prosterner [prɔstɛrne] **se prosterner** *vpr (saluer)* to prostrate oneself *(devant* before); *Fig (s'abaisser)* to grovel, to kowtow *(devant* to)

prostitué, -e [prɔstitɥe] *nm,f (homme)* male prostitute; *(femme)* prostitute

prostituer [prɔstitɥe] **1** *vt* to prostitute
2 se prostituer *vpr* to prostitute oneself

prostitution [prɔstitɥsjɔ̃] *nf* prostitution

prostré, -e [prɔstre] *adj* prostrate

protagoniste [prɔtagɔnist] *nmf* protagonist

protecteur, -trice [prɔtɛktœr, -tris] **1** *adj (qui protège)* protective *(avec* towards); *Péj (ton)* patronizing
2 *nm,f* **(a)** *(d'une personne)* protector; *(d'une prostituée)* pimp **(b)** *(des arts)* patron

protection [prɔtɛksjɔ̃] *nf* protection *(contre* from *or* against); **de p.** *(écran, visière, vernis)* protective; **sous la p. de la police** under police protection; **p. de l'environnement** protection of the environment; **p. sociale** social welfare system; *Ordinat* **p. d'accès logique** logical access protection; **p. contre l'écriture** write-protection; **p. contre la copie** copy protection; **p. de fichiers** file protection; **p. par mot de passe** password protection

protectionnisme [prɔtɛksjɔnism] *nm Écon* protectionism

protectorat [prɔtɛktɔra] *nm* protectorate

protégé, -e [prɔteʒe] **1** *adj* protected; *Ordinat* **p. contre la copie** copy-protected
2 *nm,f* protégé, *f* protégée

protège-cahier *(pl* **protège-cahiers)** [prɔtɛʒkaje] *nm* exercise book cover

protège-dents [prɔtɛʒdɑ̃] *nm inv* gum shield

protéger [59] [prɔteʒe] **1** *vt* to protect *(contre/de* against/from); **ça protège bien** it gives good protection; **que Dieu vous protège!** God keep you!; *Ordinat* **p. contre l'écriture** *ou* **en écriture** to write-protect
2 se protéger *vpr* to protect oneself *(contre/de* against/from)

protège-slip *(pl* **protège-slips)** [prɔtɛʒslip] *nm* panty-liner

protéine [prɔtein] *nf* protein

protestant, -e [prɔtɛstɑ̃, -ɑ̃t] *adj & nm,f* Protestant

protestantisme [prɔtɛstɑ̃tism] *nm* Protestantism

protestataire [prɔtɛstatɛr] *nmf* protester

protestation [prɔtɛstasjɔ̃] *nf* **(a)** *(plainte)* protest; **émettre des protestations** to voice one's protest; **en signe de p.** as a protest **(b)** **des protestations d'amitié** protestations of friendship

protester [prɔtɛste] **1** *vi* to protest *(contre* against); **p. auprès de qn** to protest to sb
2 protester de *vt ind (innocence, bonne foi)* to protest

prothèse [prɔtɛz] *nf* prosthesis; **p. auditive** hearing aid; **p. dentaire** *(complète)* false teeth, dentures; *(partielle)* bridge

protocole [prɔtɔkɔl] *nm* (a) *(usages)* protocol (b) **p. d'accord** protocol of agreement (c) *Ordinat* protocol; **p. de téléchargement** download protocol; **p. de transmission** transmission protocol

proton [prɔtɔ̃] *nm* proton

prototype [prɔtɔtip] *nm* prototype

protozoaire [prɔtɔzɔɛr] *nm* protozoan; **les proto-zoaires** the Protozoa

protubérance [prɔtyberɑ̃s] *nf* protuberance

protubérant, -e [prɔtyberɑ̃, -ɑ̃t] *adj* protuberant

proue [pru] *nf* bows, prow

prouesse [prués] *nf* feat; **faire des prouesses pour obtenir qch** to work wonders to get sth

prouver [pruve] 1 *vt* (a) *(établir comme vrai)* to prove; **p. qch à qn** to prove sth to sb; **p. qch par A plus B** to prove sth in a logical fashion; **cela reste à p.** it still has to be proved (b) *(être la preuve de)* to prove, to show **(que** that)
2 **se prouver** *vpr* **se p. qch** *(à soi-même)* to prove sth to oneself

provenance [prɔvnɑ̃s] *nf* origin; **marchandises de p. italienne** goods of Italian origin; **en p. de Bordeaux** from Bordeaux

provençal, -e, -aux, -ales [prɔvɑ̃sal, -o] 1 *adj* Provençal
2 *nm,f* P. person from Provence
3 *nm (langue)* Provençal

Provence [prɔvɑ̃s] *nf* **la P.** Provence

provenir [70] [prɔvnir] *vi* **p. de** to come from; *(difficultés)* to arise from

proverbe [prɔvɛrb] *nm* proverb

proverbial, -e, -aux, -ales [prɔvɛrbjal, -o] *adj* proverbial

providence [prɔvidɑ̃s] *nf* (a) *(sort)* providence; **cette auberge est la p. des marcheurs** this inn is a haven for walkers (b) **la P.** Providence

providentiel, -elle [prɔvidɑ̃sjɛl] *adj* providential

province [prɔvɛ̃s] 1 *nf* (a) *(région)* province; *Can* **les Provinces Maritimes** the Maritime Provinces (b) **la p.** the provinces; **de p.** provincial; **en p.** in the provinces; **arriver de sa p.** to be new in town
2 *adj inv Fam Péj* provincial

provincial, -e, -aux, -ales [prɔvɛ̃sjal, -o] *adj & nm,f* provincial

proviseur [prɔvizœr] *nm Br* headmaster, *f* headmistress, *Am* principal

provision [prɔvizjɔ̃] *nf* (a) *(réserve)* stock, supply; **provisions** *(nourriture)* shopping; **faire des provisions ou faire p. de qch** to stock up on sth (b) *(de compte bancaire)* credit; *(acompte)* deposit

provisionnel, -elle [prɔvizjɔnɛl] *adj voir* **tiers**

provisoire [prɔvizwar] *adj* temporary; **à titre p.** temporarily

provisoirement [prɔvizwarmɑ̃] *adv* temporarily, provisionally

provocant, -e [prɔvɔkɑ̃, -ɑ̃t] *adj* provocative

provocateur, -trice [prɔvɔkatœr, -tris] 1 *adj* provocative; **agent p.** agent provocateur
2 *nm,f* troublemaker

provocation [prɔvɔkasjɔ̃] *nf* provocation; **il l'a dit par p.** he said it to be provocative

provoquer [prɔvɔke] *vt* (a) *(personne)* to provoke (b) *(réaction)* to provoke; *(incendie, mort, malaise)* to cause; *(jalousie, colère)* to arouse; **p. l'accouchement** to induce labour

proxénète [prɔksenɛt] *nmf* pimp

proxénétisme [prɔksenetism] *nm* pimping

proximité [prɔksimite] *nf* closeness, proximity; **à p.** close by; **à p. de qch** close to sth

prude [pryd] 1 *adj* prudish
2 *nf* prude

prudemment [prydamɑ̃] *adv* carefully, cautiously

prudence [prydɑ̃s] *nf* care, caution; **par (mesure de) p.** as a precaution; *Prov* **p. est mère de sûreté** discretion is the better part of valour

prudent, -e [prydɑ̃, -ɑ̃t] *adj (personne)* careful, cautious; *(décision)* wise, sensible

prud'homme [prydɔm] *nm Jur* member of an industrial tribunal; **conseil des prud'hommes** industrial tribunal

prune [pryn] 1 *nf (fruit)* plum; *(liqueur)* plum brandy; *Fam* **pour des prunes** for nothing
2 *adj inv* plum-coloured

pruneau, -x [pryno] *nm* (a) *(fruit)* prune (b) *Fam (balle)* slug

prunelle [prynɛl] *nf (pupille)* pupil; *Fig* **j'y tiens comme à la p. de mes yeux** it's the apple of my eye

prunier [prynje] *nm* plum tree; *Fam* **secouer qn comme un p.** to shake sb like a rag doll

prurit [pryrit] *nm Méd* pruritus

Prusse [prys] *nf voir* **bleu**

PS [pɛɛs] *nm* (a) *(abrév* **Parti socialiste)** Socialist Party (b) *(abrév* **post-scriptum)** PS

psalmodier [66] [psalmɔdje] 1 *vt* to chant; *Fig* to drone out
2 *vi* to chant; *Fig* to drone on

psaume [psom] *nm* psalm

pseudo- [psœdo] *préf* pseudo-; **un p.-intellectuel** a pseudo-intellectual

pseudonyme [psœdɔnim] *nm (pour un écrivain)* pen name, pseudonym; *(pour la scène)* stage name

psy [psi] *nmf Fam (médecin)* shrink

psychanalyse [psikanaliz] *nf* psychoanalysis; **faire une p.** to be in psychoanalysis

psychanalyser [psikanalize] *vt* to psychoanalyse; **se faire p.** to be psychoanalysed

psychanalyste [psikanalist] *nmf* psychoanalyst

psyché [psiʃe] *nf (miroir)* cheval glass

psychédélique [psikedelik] *adj* psychedelic

psychiatre [psikjatr] *nmf* psychiatrist

psychiatrie [psikjatri] *nf* psychiatry

psychiatrique [psikjatrik] *adj* psychiatric

psychique [psiʃik] *adj* psychic

psychisme [psiʃism] *nm* psyche

psychodrame [psikodram] *nm* role-playing, *Spéc* psychodrama

psychologie [psikɔlɔʒi] *nf* psychology; **comprendre la p. de qn** to understand the way sb's mind works

psychologique [psikɔlɔʒik] *adj* psychological

psychologiquement [psikɔlɔʒikmɑ̃] *adv* psychologically

psychologue [psikɔlɔg] 1 *nmf* psychologist; *Fig* être fin p. to be a good psychologist
2 *adj* être p. to be a good psychologist

psychopathe [psikɔpat] *nmf* psychopath

psychose [psikoz] *nf* psychosis; **p. maniaco-dépressive** manic depression; *Fig* **la p. de la maladie** an obsessive fear of illness

psychosomatique [psikɔsɔmatik] *adj* psychosomatic

psychothérapeute [psikoterapøt] *nmf* psychotherapist

psychothérapie [psikoterapi] *nf* psychotherapy; **p. de groupe** group therapy

psychotique [psikɔtik] *adj & nmf* psychotic

PTT [petete] *nfpl* (*abrév* **Postes, Télécommunications et Télédiffusion**) *Anciennement* ≃ Post Office and Telecommunications Service

pu *voir* **pouvoir**

puant, -e [pɥɑ̃, -ɑ̃t] *adj* stinking; *Fig* cocky

puanteur [pɥɑ̃tœr] *nf* stink, stench

pub [pyb] *nf Fam* (a) (*secteur*) advertising (b) (*message*) ad

pubère [pyber] *adj* pubescent

puberté [pyberte] *nf* puberty

pubis [pybis] *nm Anat* pubis; (*os*) pubic bone

public, -ique [pyblik] 1 *adj* public
2 *nm* (*d'un spectacle*) audience; **en p.** in public; (*émission*) before a live audience; **le grand p.** the general public

publication [pyblikasjɔ̃] *nf* (a) (*d'un ouvrage, d'une nouvelle*) publication; **p. assistée par ordinateur** desktop publishing (b) (*ouvrage*) publication

publiciste [pyblisist] *nmf Fam* advertising executive

publicitaire [pyblisiter] 1 *adj* advertising
2 *nmf* advertising executive

publicité [pyblisite] *nf* (a) (*secteur*) advertising; **être dans la p.** to be in advertising; **faire de la p. pour qch** to advertise sth; *Fig* **faire de la p. à qn** to give publicity for sb; **p. comparative** comparative advertising; **p. mensongère** misleading advertising (b) (*message*) advertisement, advert; **une pleine page de p.** a full-page advertisement

publier [66] [pyblije] *vt* to publish; (*communiqué*) to issue

Publiphone® [pyblifɔn] *nm* card phone

publiquement [pyblikmɑ̃] *adv* publicly

puce [pys] *nf* (a) (*insecte*) flea; **le marché aux puces, les puces** the flea market; *Fig* **mettre la p. à l'oreille à qn** to make sb suspicious; *Fam* **secouer les puces à qn** to give sb a good telling off; *Fam* **être excité comme une p.** to be jumping up and down with excitement (b) *Ordinat* (micro)chip; **p. mémoire** memory chip; **p. de reconnaissance vocale** voice recognition chip

puceau, -x [pyso] *nm & adj m Fam* virgin

pucelle [pysɛl] *nf & adj f* virgin

puceron [pysrɔ̃] *nm* greenfly

pudeur [pydœr] *nf* modesty; **avec p.** modestly; **sans p.** boldly; **par p.** out of a sense of decency; **avoir la p. de faire qch** to have the decency to do sth

pudibond, -e [pydibɔ̃, -ɔ̃d] *adj* prudish

pudique [pydik] *adj* modest

puer [pɥe] 1 *vi* to stink; **il pue des pieds** his feet stink
2 *vt* to stink of

puéricultrice [pɥerikyltris] *nf* nursery nurse

puériculture [pɥerikyltyr] *nf* child care

puéril, -e [pɥeril] *adj* childish, puerile

pugilat [pyʒila] *nm* brawl

pugnace [pygnas] *adj Litt* pugnacious

puis [pɥi] *adv* then; **et p.** (*ensuite*) and then; (*d'ailleurs*) and besides; **et p. c'est tout!** and that's all there is to it!; **et p. après?** (*et ensuite?*) then what?; *Fam* (*et alors?*) so what?

puisatier [pɥizatje] *nm* well digger

puiser [pɥize] *vt* (*eau, carte*) to draw (à from); *Fig* (*inspiration, idées*) to draw (dans/chez from); **p. dans ses réserves** to draw on one's reserves; **p. dans la caisse** to have one's hand in the till

puisque [pɥiskə] *conj* since, as; **p. c'est comme ça** if that's the way it is; **p. je te dis que je l'ai vu!** I'm telling you I saw him/it!; **tu en es bien sûr? – mais p. je te le dis!** are you really sure? – I've said it, haven't I?

puissamment [pɥisamɑ̃] *adv* powerfully

puissance [pɥisɑ̃s] *nf* power; **p. de feu** fire power; **les grandes puissances** the great powers; *Math* **élever un nombre à la p. trois/quatre** to raise a number to the third/fourth power; **dix (à la) p. quatre** ten to the power of four; **en p.** (*meurtrier*) potential

puissant, -ante [pɥisɑ̃, -ɑ̃t] *adj* powerful

puisse *etc voir* **pouvoir**

puits [pɥi] *nm* (a) (*pour l'eau*) well; **p. de pétrole** oil well; *Fig* **c'est un p. de science** he's/she's a fount of knowledge (b) (*de mine*) shaft, pit

pull [pyl] *nm Fam* sweater, *Br* jumper

pull-over (*pl* **pull-overs**) [pylɔvœr] *nm* sweater, *Br* jumper

pulluler [pylyle] *vi* (a) (*se reproduire*) to proliferate (b) (*exister en profusion*) to abound

pulmonaire [pylmɔner] *adj* pulmonary

pulpe [pylp] *nf* (a) (*de fruit*) pulp; **yaourt à la p. de fruits** yoghurt with real fruit (b) (*des doigts, des orteils*) pad; (*des dents*) pulp

pulpeux, -euse [pylpø, -øz] *adj* fleshy; (*femme*) curvaceous

pulsar [pylsar] *nm Astron* pulsar

pulsation [pylsasjɔ̃] *nf* (*de cœur*) beat; (*pulsations*) beating

pulsion [pylsjɔ̃] *nf* impulse; **pulsions sexuelles** sexual urges; **p. de mort** death wish

pulvérisateur [pylverizatœr] *nm* spray

pulvérisation [pylverizasjɔ̃] *nf* (*de liquides*) spraying

pulvériser [pylverize] *vt* (a) (*réduire en poudre*) to pulverize; *Fam* (*voiture*) to smash up (b) (*vaporiser*) to spray (c) *Fam* (*record*) to smash

puma [pyma] *nm* puma

punaise [pynez] *nf* (a) (*insecte*) bug; *Fam* **oh p.!** good grief! (b) (*pour accrocher*) *Br* drawing pin, *Am* thumbtack

punaiser [pyneze] *vt Fam* to pin up; **p. qch à qch** to pin sth to sth

punch¹ [pɔ̃ʃ] *nm* (*boisson*) punch

punch² [pœnʃ] *nm* punch; *Fig* (*de personne*) drive

punching-ball (*pl* **punching-balls**) [pœnʃiŋbol] *nm* punchball

punir [pynir] *vt* (*personne, crime*) to punish; **p. qn de mort** to punish sb with death; **p. qn d'un crime** to punish sb for a crime; **me voilà puni de ma gourmandise!** it serves me right for being greedy!

punitif, -ive [pynitif, -iv] *adj* punitive

punition [pynisjɔ̃] *nf* punishment; **p. corporelle** corporal punishment

punk [pœnk] *adj inv & nmf* punk

pupille¹ [pypij] *nmf* (*orphelin*) ward; **pupilles de la Nation** war orphans

pupille² *nf* (*de l'œil*) pupil

pupitre [pypitr] *nm* (a) (*d'écolier*) desk; (*d'orateur*) lectern; (*de musicien*) music stand (b) *Ordinat* **p. (de commande)** console (desk); **p. de visualisation** visual display unit

pupitreur, -euse [pypitrœr, -øz] *nm,f Ordinat* console operator

pur, -e [pyr] *adj* (a) (*or, air*) pure; (*ciel*) clear; (*whisky, gin*) straight, neat; **pure laine** pure wool; **biscuits p. beurre** all butter biscuits (b) (*recherche, mathématiques, théorie*) pure; **un communiste p. et dur** a hard-line Communist; **la vérité pure et simple** the plain and simple truth; **du vol p. et simple** sheer robbery; **c'est de la folie pure** it's sheer madness (c) (*lignes*) clean; (*visage*) clean-cut

purée [pyre] **1** *nf* purée; **p. (de pommes de terre)** mashed potatoes; *Fam* Fig **p. de pois** peasouper
2 *exclam Fam* (*colère*) hell!; (*surprise*) wow!

purement [pyrmɑ̃] *adv* purely; **p. et simplement** purely and simply

pureté [pyrte] *nf* purity; (*du ciel*) clearness; (*de lignes*) cleanness

purgatoire [pyrgatwar] *nm* purgatory

purge [pyrʒ] *nf* (a) (*pour raisons médicales*) purge (b) (*à des fins politiques*) purge (c) (*de freins, de radiateur*) bleeding

purger [45] [pyrʒe] *vt* (a) (*patient*) to purge (b) (*freins, radiateur*) to bleed (c) (*peine*) to serve

purifiant, -e [pyrifjɑ̃, -ɑ̃t] *adj* purifying

purificateur, -trice [pyrifikatœr, -tris] *adj* purifying

purification [pyrifikasjɔ̃] *nf* purification; **p. ethnique** ethnic cleansing

purifier [66] [pyrifje] **1** *vt aussi Fig* to purify; (*sang, teint*) to cleanse
2 se purifier *vpr* to be purified

purin [pyrɛ̃] *nm* liquid manure

puriste [pyrist] *nmf* purist

puritain, -e [pyritɛ̃, -ɛn] **1** *nm,f* puritan; *Hist* Puritan
2 *adj* puritanical; *Hist* Puritan

puritanisme [pyritanism] *nm* puritanism; *Hist* Puritanism

pur-sang [pyrsɑ̃] *nm inv* thoroughbred

purulent, -e [pyrylɑ̃, -ɑ̃t] *adj* suppurating

pus [py] *nm* pus

pusillanime [pyzilanim] *adj Litt* pusillanimous

pustule [pystyl] *nf* pustule

putain [pytɛ̃] *Vulg* **1** *nf* (a) (*prostituée*) whore (b) **une p. de machine/cravate** a fucking machine/tie
2 *exclam* fuck!

pute [pyt] *nf Vulg* whore; **fils de p.** son of a bitch

putois [pytwa] *nm* polecat; *Fam* **crier comme un p.** to scream blue murder

putréfaction [pytrefaksjɔ̃] *nf* putrefaction; **matière en p.** putrefying matter

putréfier [66] [pytrefje] **1** *vt* to putrefy
2 se putréfier *vpr* to putrefy

putrescent, -e [pytresɑ̃, -ɑ̃t] *adj* putrescent

putride [pytrid] *adj* putrid

putsch [putʃ] *nm* putsch

putschiste [putʃist] **1** *adj* putsch
2 *nmf* putschist

puzzle [pœzl] *nm* jigsaw (puzzle); *Fig* puzzle

P.-V. [peve] *nm Fam* (*abrév* **procès-verbal**) (parking) ticket

PVC [pevese] *nm* (*abrév* **polychlorure de vinyle**) PVC; **siège en P.** PVC seat

PVD [pevede] *nm* (*abrév* **pays en voie de développement**) developing country

pygmée [pigme] *nmf* pygmy

pyjama [piʒama] *nm* pyjamas; **un p.** a pair of pyjamas

pylône [pilon] *nm* pylon; (*pour fils télégraphiques*) mast

pyramidal, -e, -aux, -ales [piramidal, -o] *adj* pyramid-shaped

pyramide [piramid] *nf* pyramid; **p. des âges** population pyramid; **structure en p.** pyramid-like structure

pyrénéen, -enne [pirenéɛ̃, -ɛn] **1** *adj* Pyrenean
2 *nm,f* P. Pyrenean
3 *nm* (*chien*) Pyrenean mountain dog

Pyrénées [pirene] *nfpl* **les P.** the Pyrenees

Pyrex® [pireks] *nm* Pyrex®; **plat en P.** Pyrex® dish

pyrogravure [pirogravyr] *nf* poker work, pyrography; (*gravure*) pyrograph

pyrolyse [piroliz] *nf* pyrolysis; **four à p.** self-cleaning oven

pyromane [piroman] *nmf* arsonist; *Psy* pyromaniac

pyromanie [piromani] *nf* pyromania

pyrotechnique [piroteknik] *adj* pyrotechnic

python [pitɔ̃] *nm* python

Q

Q, q [ky] *nm inv* Q, q

Qatar [katar] *nm* le Q. Qatar

QCM [kyseem] *nm inv* (*abrév* **questionnaire à choix multiple**) multiple-choice questionnaire

QG [kyʒe] *nm inv* (*abrév* **quartier général**) HQ

QI [kyi] *nm inv* (*abrév* **quotient intellectuel**) IQ

quadra [kwadra] *nmf Fam* fortysomething

quadragénaire [kwadraʒener] **1** *adj* être q. to be in one's forties
  2 *nmf* person in his/her forties

quadrangulaire [kwadrɑ̃gyler] *adj* quadrangular

quadrature [kwadratyr] *nf* quadrature; **c'est la q. du cercle** it's like trying to square the circle

quadriceps [kwadriseps] *nm* quadriceps

quadrilatère [kwadrilater] *nm* quadrilateral

quadrillage [kadrijaʒ] *nm* (**a**) (*par la police*) tight surveillance (**b**) (*d'un tissu*) check pattern; (*sur une carte*) grid

quadrille [kadrij] *nm* quadrille

quadrillé, -e [kadrije] *adj* (*papier*) squared

quadriller [kadrije] *vt* (**a**) (*quartier, ville, région*) to put under tight surveillance (**b**) (*papier*) to mark into squares

quadrimoteur [kwadrimotœr, kwadrimotœr] **1** *adj* four-engined
  2 *nm* four-engined plane

quadriparti, -e [kwadriparti], **quadripartite** [kwadripartit] *adj* (*traité*) quadripartite; (*conférence, commission*) (*entre partis*) four-party; (*entre pays*) four-power

quadriphonie [kwadrifoni] *nf* quadraphony

quadrupède [kwadryped, kadryped] *adj & nm* quadruped

quadruple [kwadrypl, kadrypl] **1** *adj* quadruple, fourfold; *Mus* **q. croche** *Br* hemidemisemiquaver, *Am* sixty-fourth note
  2 *nm* **le q. (de)** (*quantité, prix*) four times as much (as); (*nombre*) four times as many (as); **douze est le q. de trois** twelve is four times three

quadrupler [kwadryple, kadryple] *vt & vi* to quadruple, to increase fourfold

quadruplés, -ées [kwadryple, kadryple] *nm,f pl* quadruplets

quai [ke] *nm* (**a**) (*de gare, de métro*) platform (**b**) (*d'un port*) quay; **se mettre à q.** to berth (**c**) (*d'une rivière, d'un fleuve*) embankment; **le Q. des Orfèvres** Police Headquarters (*in Paris*); **le Q. d'Orsay** the French Foreign Office

qualificatif, -ive [kalifikatif, -iv] **1** *adj Gram* (*adjectif*) qualifying
  2 *nm* term

qualification [kalifikasjɔ̃] *nf* (**a**) (*formation*) qualification (**b**) (*d'une équipe, d'un sportif*) qualification (**c**) (*désignation*) description

qualifié, -e [kalifje] *adj* (**a**) (*compétent*) qualified (**pour faire qch** to do sth) (**b**) (*délit, vol*) aggravated

qualifier [66] [kalifje] **1** *vt* (**a**) (*appeler*) to describe (**de** as) (**b**) (*autoriser*) **q. qn pour qch/pour faire qch** to qualify sb for sth/to do sth
  2 se qualifier *vpr* (*sportif, équipe*) to qualify (**pour** for)

qualitatif, -ive [kalitatif, -iv] *adj* qualitative

qualité [kalite] *nf* (**a**) (*d'un produit*) quality; **de q.** quality; **de bonne/mauvaise q.** of good/poor quality; *Ordinat* **q. brouillon, q. listing rapide, q. listing** draft quality; *Ordinat* **q. courrier** (near) letter quality; **la q. de la vie** the quality of life (**b**) (*d'une personne*) quality; **elle n'a pas que des qualités** she isn't all good (**c**) (*occupation*) occupation; (*fonction*) capacity; **en q. de** in my/her/*etc* capacity as

quand [kɑ̃] **1** *conj* (**a**) (*lorsque*) when; **je lui en parlerai q. je le verrai** I'll mention it to him when I see him; *Fam* **q. je pense que le voyage devait être annulé!** when I think that they were going to cancel the trip! (**b**) (*alors que*) when
  2 *adv* when; **q. viendra-t-il?** when will he come?; **demande-lui q. il va partir** ask him when he's going to leave; **à q. le mariage?** when's the wedding?; **de q. est ce journal?** what's the date of this paper?; **pour q. est la réunion?** when is the meeting?

quant [kɑ̃] **quant à** *prép* as for

quant-à-soi [kɑ̃taswa] *nm* **rester sur** *ou* **se tenir sur son q.** to keep oneself to oneself

quantième [kɑ̃tjem] *nm* day of the month

quantifiable [kɑ̃tifjabl] *adj* quantifiable

quantifier [66] [kɑ̃tifje] *vt* to quantify

quantitatif, -ive [kɑ̃titatif, -iv] *adj* quantitative

quantitativement [kɑ̃titativmɑ̃] *adv* quantitatively

quantité [kɑ̃tite] *nf* quantity; **en grande/petite q.** in large/small quantities; **en q.** in abundance; **q. de gens/réponses** a great many people/replies

quarantaine [karɑ̃ten] *nf* (**a**) (*environ quarante*) **une q. (de)** about forty, forty or so (**b**) (*âge*) **avoir la q.** to be about forty; **approcher de la q.** to be getting on for forty (**c**) (*isolement*) quarantine; **mettre qn en q.** to put sb in quarantine; *Fig* to send sb to Coventry

quarante [karɑ̃t] *adj & nm inv* forty; *Fam* **se ficher de qch comme de l'an q.** not to give two hoots about sth; *voir aussi* **trois**

quarante-cinq tours [karɑ̃tsɛ̃tur] *nm inv* single, 45

quarantième [karɑ̃tjem] *nmf, nm & adj* fortieth; *voir aussi* **cinquième**

quart¹ [kar] *adj* le q. monde *(dans les pays riches)* the underclass

quart² *nm* (a) *(fraction)* quarter; **un q. de siècle/de beurre** a quarter (of a) century/kilo of butter; **un q. d'heure** a quarter of an hour; *Fam* **passer un mauvais q. d'heure** to have a bad time of it; **deux heures et q.** (a) quarter past *or* Am after two; **deux heures moins le q.** (a) quarter to *or* Am of two; **il est moins le q.** it's (a) quarter to; **démarrer** *ou* **partir au q. de tour** *(voiture)* to start first time; *(personne)* to fly off the handle; **q. de cercle** quadrant; **q. de finale** quarter final; **q. de soupir** *Br* semiquaver *or* Am sixteenth rest (b) *(bouteille, pichet)* quarter litre (c) *(veille sur un bateau)* watch; **être de q.** to be on watch

quarte [kart] *nf Mus* fourth

quarté [karte] *nm* = system of betting on four horses in the same race

quartette [kwartɛt] *nm* jazz quartet

quartier [kartje] *nm* (a) *(d'une ville)* district, area; **les beaux quartiers** the fashionable districts; **les quartiers nord de la ville** the north side of the town; **de q., du q.** local (b) *(morceau)* *(d'une orange)* segment; *(d'une pomme)* piece (c) *(de la lune)* quarter (d) *(de viande)* quarter (e) *(en héraldique)* quarter; **avoir quatre quartiers de noblesse** to belong to the established nobility (f) *(locutions)* **avoir q. libre** to be off duty; **ne pas faire de q.** to give no quarter

quartz [kwarts] *nm* quartz; **horloge/montre à q.** quartz clock/watch

quasi [kazi] *adv* almost, nearly

quasi- [kazi] *préf* **la q.-totalité des membres** almost all the members

quasiment [kazimā] *adv* almost, nearly; **je n'ai q. rien senti** I hardly felt a thing

quaternaire [kwatɛrnɛr] *Géol* **1** *adj* Quaternary **2** *nm* Quaternary era

quatorze [katɔrz] *adj & nm inv* fourteen; *voir aussi* **trois**

quatorzième [katɔrzjɛm] *nmf, nm & adj* fourteenth; *voir aussi* **cinquième**

quatrain [katrɛ̃] *nm* quatrain

quatre [katr] *adj & nm inv* four; **aux q. coins du monde** throughout the world; **monter l'escalier q. à q.** to rush up the stairs; *Fig* **se mettre en q. pour qn/pour faire qch** to bend over backwards for sb/to do sth; *voir aussi* **trois**

quatre-quarts [katkar, katrɔkar] *nm inv* pound cake

quatre-quatre [katkatr] *nm inv ou nf inv* four-wheel drive

quatre-saisons [katsɛzɔ̃, katrasɛzɔ̃] *nfpl* **marchand des q.** fruit-and-vegetable merchant *(with outdoor stall)*

quatre-vingt [katrəvɛ̃] *voir* **quatre-vingts**

quatre-vingt-dix [katrəvɛ̃dis] *adj & nm inv* ninety; *voir aussi* **trois**

quatre-vingt-dixième [katrəvɛ̃dizjɛm] *adj, nmf & nm* ninetieth; *voir aussi* **cinquième**

quatre-vingtième [katrəvɛ̃tjɛm] *adj, nmf & nm* eightieth; *voir aussi* **cinquième**

quatre-vingts [katrəvɛ̃] *adj & nm inv* eighty; **quatre-vingt-deux** eighty-two; **page quatre-vingt** page eighty; *voir aussi* **trois**

quatrième [katrijɛm] **1** *adj & nmf* fourth **2** *nf* (a) *(classe)* *Br* ≃ third form, *Am* ≃ ninth grade (b) *(vitesse)* fourth (gear); *voir aussi* **cinquième**

quatrièmement [katrijɛmmā] *adv* fourthly

quatuor [kwatɥɔr] *nm* quartet; **q. à cordes** string quartet

que¹ [k(ə)]

> En anglais, le pronom relatif objet (voir (a)) peut être omis.

pron relatif (a) *(objet)* *(personne)* that, whom; *(chose)* that, which; **l'homme q. vous voyez** the man (that) you see; **la tarte q. j'ai fait cuire** the tart (that) I baked; **c'est le meilleur q. nous ayons** it is the best (that) we have (b) *(attribut)* **il mourut en brave soldat qu'il était** he died like the brave soldier he was (c) *(dans le temps)* **il y a trois mois q. j'habite Paris** I've been living in Paris for three months; **un jour q. j'étais de service** one day when I was on duty

que² *pron interrogatif* what; **q. voulez-vous?** what do you want?; **il ne savait q. penser** he didn't know what to think

que³ *adv exclamatif* **qu'elle est intelligente!** she's so intelligent!; **q. de monde!** what a lot of people!

que⁴

> La conjonction "that" peut être omise après les verbes d'opinion, ainsi que "say", "know", etc : **je sais que c'est possible** I know (that) it's possible.

conj (a) *(complétif)* that; **je pense qu'il a raison** I think (that) he's right; **je veux qu'il vienne** I want him to come; **c'est q. je ne le savais pas** I just didn't know (b) *(exprime le souhait)* **qu'elle entre!** let her come in! (c) *(exprime l'hypothèse)* **q. la machine chauffe, et il y aura un accident** let the machine get hot and there will be an accident; **qu'il essaie encore une fois!** just let him try again! (d) *(dans une alternative)* **q. tu le veuilles ou non** whether you like it or not (e) *(relie deux conditionnels)* **il me le dirait lui-même q. je ne le croirais pas** he could tell me himself and I still wouldn't believe it (f) *(afin que, pour que)* **approchez qu'on vous entende** come closer so (that) we can hear you (g) *(pour ne pas répéter une autre conjonction)* **quand tu iras mieux et q. tu voudras sortir** when you're better and you want to go out; **si ça te plaît et q. tu veux l'acheter...** if you like it and you want to buy it... (h) *(dans les comparaisons)* **plus/moins grand q. moi** bigger/smaller than me; **aussi grand q. moi** as big as me (i) **ne... q.** only; **il n'a qu'une jambe** he's only got one leg; **il ne me reste plus q. 20 francs** I've only got 20 francs left (j) *Fam* **ah! q. non!** surely not!; **il va au cercle – qu'il dit!** he goes to the club – so he says!

Québec [kebɛk] **1** *nm (province)* **le Q.** Quebec **2** *n (ville)* Quebec

québécisme [kebesism] *nm* = word or expression peculiar to Quebec French

québécois, -e [kebeka, -az] **1** *adj* of Quebec **2** *nm, f* Q. Quebecker **3** *nm (langue)* Quebec French

quel, quelle [kɛl] **1** *adj interrogatif (personne)* which; *(chose)* what; **q. homme?** which man?; **quelle heure est-il?** what time is it?, what's the time?; **q. genre d'homme est-ce?** what sort of a man is he?; **si tu savais à q. point il y tient** if you knew how fond he is of it; **à q. film faites-vous référence?** which or what film are you referring to?; **quelles sont ses raisons?**

what are his reasons?; *Litt* **q. est cet homme?** who is this man?

2 *adj exclamatif* **q. homme!** what a man!; **quelle surprise!** what a surprise!; **quelle bêtise de sa part!** how stupid of him!

3 *adj relatif* **q. que soit le coupable** whoever the culprit may be; **q. que soit le résultat** whatever the result may be; **q. que soit l'endroit où...** no matter where...

4 *pron interrogatif* which (one)

quelconque [kɛlkɔ̃k] **1** *adj indéfini* **donne-moi un livre q.** give me any book; **sous un prétexte q.** on some pretext or other

2 *adj (insignifiant)* ordinary

quelle [kɛl] *voir* **quel**

quelque [kɛlk] **1** *adj indéfini* some; **quelques** some, a few; **il y a quelques jours** a few days ago; **et quelque(s)** or so; **cent et quelques mètres** a hundred metres plus; **q....** que + *subjunctive* whatever; **sous q. prétexte que ce soit** on whatever pretext; **de q. côté que vous regardiez** whichever way you look

2 *adv* some, about; **q. dix ans** some or about ten years; **les q. 1000 francs qu'il m'a prêtés** the 1,000 francs or so that he lent me

quelque chose [kɛlkəʃoz] *pron indéfini* something; **avez-vous q. à dire?** do you have anything or something to say?; **est-ce que je peux te dire q.?** can I tell you something?; **q. d'autre/de neuf** something else/new; **cela m'a fait q.** it touched me; **ça te ferait vraiment q. si je m'en allais?** would it really matter to you if I went away?; *Fam* **ah, mais c'est q., ça!** that's a bit much!; *Fam* **un petit q.** *(cadeau)* a little something

quelquefois [kɛlkəfwa] *adv* sometimes

quelque part [kɛlkəpar] *adv* somewhere; *(dans les questions, les hypothèses)* anywhere; **q. où tu n'es jamais allé** somewhere you've never been before; *Fam* **je lui ai donné un coup de pied q.** I kicked him where it hurts

quelques-uns, quelques-unes [kɛlkəzœ̃, -yn] *pron indéfini* some, a few (**de** of)

quelqu'un [kɛlkœ̃] *pron indéfini* **(a)** *(une personne)* someone, somebody; *(dans les questions, les hypothèses)* anyone, anybody; **q. de trop** one too many; **q. d'important** someone important; **c'est q. de bien** he's a decent person **(b)** *(personne importante)* somebody

quémander [kemɑ̃de] *vt* to beg for (**à** from)

qu'en-dira-t-on [kɑ̃diratɔ̃] *nm* **le q.** gossip

quenelle [kənɛl] *nf* quenelle

quenotte [kənɔt] *nf Fam* tooth

quenouille [kənuj] *nf (pour filer)* distaff

quéquette [kekɛt] *nf Fam* willy

querelle [kərɛl] *nf* quarrel; **chercher q. à qn** to try to pick a quarrel with sb; **q. de clocher** petty dispute

quereller [kərele] **se quereller** *vpr* to quarrel (**avec** with)

querelleur, -euse [kərɛlœr, -øz] *adj* quarrelsome

quérir [kerir] *vt Litt* **aller q. qn/qch** to go and fetch sb/sth

qu'est-ce que [kɛskə] **1** *pron interrogatif* what; **q. vous voulez?** what do you want?; **q. c'est que ça?** what's that?; *Fam* **q. tu avais besoin d'aller lui dire ça?** what did you have to go and tell him that for?

2 *pron exclamatif* **qu'est-ce qu'il fait beau!** what lovely weather!; **qu'est-ce qu'il fait chaud!** it's so hot!; **qu'est-ce qu'on a rigolé!** we had such a good laugh!;

q. tu as changé! how you've changed!; **q. j'ai mangé!** I've eaten so much!

qu'est-ce qui [kɛski] *pron interrogatif* what

question [kɛstjɔ̃] *nf* **(a)** *(interrogation)* question (**sur** about); **q. de confiance** vote of confidence; **q. piège** trick question; **q. subsidiaire** tie-break **(b)** *(affaire)* question, matter; **le dossier en q.** the file in question; **remettre qch en q.** to call sth into question; **une q. d'argent/de temps/d'habitude** a question or matter of money/of time/of habit; **c'est une q. de vie ou de mort** it's a matter of life or death; **il est q. qu'ils déménagent** there's some talk of them moving; **il n'en est pas q.** it's out of the question; **là n'est pas la q.** it's not a question of that; *Fam* **pas q.!** no way!, no chance!; *Fam* **q. argent, ça va** moneywise or as far as money goes, things are OK

questionnaire [kɛstjɔnɛr] *nm* questionnaire; **q. à choix multiple** multiple-choice questionnaire

questionner [kɛstjɔne] *vt* to question (**sur** about)

quête [kɛt] *nf* **(a)** *(recherche)* quest, search (**de** for); **se mettre en q. de qn/qch** to go in search of sb/sth **(b)** *(collecte)* collection; **faire la q.** *(à l'église)* to take the collection

quêter [kete] **1** *vt* to seek

2 *vi* to collect money (**pour** for)

quêteux, -euse [ketø, -øz] *nm,f Can* beggar

quetsche [kwɛtʃ] *nf* **(a)** *(prune)* dark-red plum **(b)** *(eau-de-vie)* plum brandy

queue [kø] *nf* **(a)** *(d'animal)* tail; **n'avoir ni q. ni tête** to have neither rhyme nor reason; **faire une q. de poisson à qn** to cut (in) in front of sb; **finir en q. de poisson** *(pièce de théâtre, projet)* to end up in the air **(b)** *(d'une casserole)* handle; *(d'une comète, d'un cerf-volant)* tail; *(d'un fruit, d'une fleur)* stalk; *(d'une note de musique)* stem **(c)** *(d'une procession)* rear; **de q.** *(voiture, wagon)* rear; **être en q. de peloton** to be at the back of the bunch; **être en q. de classement** to be bottom of the table **(d)** *(file) Br* queue, *Am* line; **à la q. leu leu** in single file; **faire la q.** *Br* to queue (up), *Am* to stand in line **(e)** *(pour le billard)* cue **(f)** *Vulg (pénis)* cock

queue-de-cheval *(pl* **queues-de-cheval)** [kødʃəval] *nf* ponytail

queue-de-pie *(pl* **queues-de-pie)** [kødpi] *nf Fam* tails

qui¹ [ki]

En anglais, le pronom relatif objet peut être omis lorsque la préposition qui l'introduit est rejetée en fin de phrase: **l'amie avec qui j'ai passé mes vacances** the friend (who) I spent my holidays with.

---

pron relatif **(a)** *(personne)* who, that; *(animal, chose)* which, that; **vous q. êtes du pays, pourriez-vous me dire si...** you being from the country, could you tell me if...; **je le vois q. vient** I can see him coming **(b)** *(ce qui)* **q. plus est** what's more; **voilà q. me plaît** that's what I like **(c)** *(après une préposition)* who, whom; **voilà l'homme à q. je pensais** there's the man (who) I was thinking about; **il cherche quelqu'un avec q. jouer** he's looking for someone to play with; **c'est à q. finira le premier** everyone's trying to be the first to finish **(d)** **q. que vous soyez** whoever you are; **je défie q. que ce soit de le prouver** I challenge anyone to prove it

qui² *pron interrogatif* who; *(complément d'objet ou après une préposition)* who, whom; **q. a dit cela?** who said that?; **savez-vous q. a dit cela?** do you know who said that?; **à q. est-ce?** whose is it?; **de q. parlez-vous?** who are you talking about?; **de q. êtes-vous le fils?** whose son are you?; **q. d'autre?** who else?; *Fam* **q. ça?** who's that?; *Fam* **il est là – q. donc?** he's here – who?

quiche [kiʃ] *nf* quiche; **q. lorraine** quiche lorraine

quiconque [kikɔ̃k] *pron indéfini (sujet)* whoever, anyone who; *(complément)* anyone, anybody; **q. désobéira sera puni** anyone who disobeys will be punished; **sans l'aide de q.** without anyone's help

quidam [kidam] *nm* fellow

quiétude [kjetyd] *nf Litt* peace; **en toute q.** *(sans être dérangé)* without being disturbed; *(sans souci)* with an easy mind

quignon [kiɲɔ̃] *nm* hunk

quille¹ [kij] *nf* (a) *(jeu)* skittles (b) *Fam* **la q.** *(fin du service militaire)* discharge, *Br* demob (c) *Fam* **quilles** *(jambes)* pins

quille² *nf (d'un bateau)* keel

quilleur, -euse [kijœr, -øz] *nm,f Can* skittle player

quincaillerie [kɛ̃kɑjri] *nf* (a) *(magasin)* hardware shop, *Br* ironmonger's (b) *(ustensiles)* hardware (c) *Fam (bijoux voyants)* cheap jewellery

quincaillier, -ère [kɛ̃kɑje, -ɛr] *nm,f* hardware dealer, *Br* ironmonger

quinconce [kɛ̃kɔ̃s] **en quinconce** *adv* in staggered rows

quinine [kinin] *nf* quinine

quinquagénaire [kɛ̃kaʒenɛr] **1** *adj* **être q.** to be in one's fifties
2 *nmf* person in his/her fifties

quinquennal, -e, -aux, -ales [kɛ̃kenal, -o] *adj (plan)* five-year; *(exposition, élection)* five-yearly

quinquennat [kɛ̃kena] *nm* five-year term

quintal, -aux [kɛ̃tal, -o] *nm* quintal (= 100 kg)

quinte [kɛ̃t] *nf* (a) *(accès)* **q. de toux** coughing fit (b) *Mus* fifth

quintessence [kɛ̃tesɑ̃s] *nf* quintessence

quintette [kɛ̃tɛt, kɥɛtɛt] *nm* quintet

quintuple [kɛ̃typl] **1** *adj* quintuple, fivefold
2 *nm* **le q. (de)** *(quantité, prix)* five times as much (as); *(nombre)* five times as many (as); **quinze est le q. de trois** fifteen is five times three

quintupler [kɛ̃typle] *vt & vi* to quintuple, to increase fivefold

quintuplés, -ées [kɛ̃typle] *nm,f pl* quintuplets

quinzaine [kɛ̃zɛn] *nf* (a) *(environ quinze)* **une q. (de)** about fifteen, fifteen or so (b) *(deux semaines)* two weeks, *Br* fortnight; *Com* = sale lasting two weeks

quinze [kɛ̃z] **1** *adj inv* fifteen; **q. jours** two weeks, *Br* a fortnight
2 *nm inv* fifteen; **demain en q.** two weeks or *Br* a fortnight tomorrow; **les Quinze** *(de l'Europe)* the member countries of the EU; *voir aussi* **trois**

quinzième [kɛ̃zjɛm] *nmf, nm & adj* fifteenth; *voir aussi* **cinquième**

quiproquo [kiprɔko] *nm* mix-up

quittance [kitɑ̃s] *nf* receipt; **q. de loyer** rent receipt

quitte [kit] *adj* (a) *(libéré)* **nous sommes quittes** we're quits (b) *(locutions)* **en être q. pour qch** to get off with sth; **q. ou double** double or quits; **q. à faire qch** even if it means doing sth

quitter [kite] **1** *vt* (a) *(personne, lieu)* to leave; *(chambre d'hôtel)* to vacate; **q. la route** *(par accident)* to go off the road; *(délibérément)* to turn off the road; **un ami très cher vient de nous q.** we have just lost a very dear friend; *Ordinat* **q. le système** to quit (the system) (b) *(fonctions, poste)* to leave (c) *(vêtement)* to take off (d) *(au téléphone)* **ne quittez pas** hold the line (e) **ne pas q. qn/qch des yeux** to keep one's eye on sb/sth
2 se quitter *vpr* to part; **ils ne se quittent plus** they are inseparable

qui-vive [kiviv] *nm* **être** *ou* **se tenir sur le q.** to be on the alert

quoi¹ [kwa] *pron relatif* (a) what; **ce à q. je m'oppose** what I object to; **après q.** after which; **sur q.** whereupon; **avoir de q. vivre** to have enough to live on; **avez-vous de q. écrire?** do you have something to write with?; **il n'y a pas de q. être fier** that's nothing to be proud of; **il y a de q. se mettre en colère!** it's enough to make you really angry!; **je suis en colère – il y a de q.** I'm angry – you've every right to be; **il n'y a pas de q.** *(après des remerciements)* don't mention it, not at all (b) **q. que tu dises** whatever you say; **q. qu'il advienne** whatever happens; **q. qu'il en soit** be that as it may

quoi² *pron interrogatif* what; **q. d'autre?** what else?; **q. de neuf?** what's new?; **q. de plus simple?** what could be simpler?; **je ne sais q. penser** I don't know what to think; **à q. pensez-vous?** what are you thinking about?; **de q. parlez-vous?** what are you talking about?; **à q. bon?** what's the use?; *Fam* **tu es sourd ou q.?** are you deaf or what?; *Fam* **q.?** *(pardon?)* what?

quoi³ *exclam* what!; **et q. encore!** whatever next!; *Fam* **enfin, c'était nul, q.!** it was crap, basically!

quoique [kwak] *conj* (al)though; **q. je le sache déjà** (al)though I already know

quolibet [kɔlibɛ] *nm* gibe, jeer

quorum [kwɔrɔm] *nm* quorum; **atteindre le q.** to have a quorum

quota [kɔta] *nm* quota

quote-part *(pl* **quotes-parts)** [kɔtpar] *nf* share

quotidien, -enne [kɔtidjɛ̃, -ɛn] **1** *adj* daily
2 *nm* (a) *(journal)* daily (paper); **grand q.** national daily (paper) (b) *(routine)* daily life; **au q.** on a day-to-day basis

quotidiennement [kɔtidjɛnmɑ̃] *adv* daily

quotient [kɔsjɑ̃] *nm* quotient; **q. intellectuel** intelligence quotient

R

R, r [ɛr] *nm inv* R, r

rab [rab] *nm Fam (nourriture)* extra; **faire du r.** *(au travail)* to put in a bit of overtime; **en r.** left over

rabâchage [rabɑʃaʒ] *nm* tedious repetition

rabâcher [rabɑʃe] **1** *vi* to say the same thing over and over again
 2 *vt (conseils, recommandations)* to keep on repeating; *(leçon)* to repeat parrot-fashion

rabais [rabɛ] *nm* discount, reduction; **faire un r. à qn (sur qch)** to give sb a discount (on sth); *Fig* **au r.** *(travail)* badly paid

rabaisser [rabese] **1** *vt* **(a)** *(prétentions)* to moderate **(b)** *(personne, valeur, talents)* to belittle
 2 se rabaisser *vpr* to belittle oneself

Rabat [raba] *n* Rabat

rabat [raba] *nm* **(a)** *(de sac à main, d'enveloppe)* flap **(b)** *(de costume officiel)* bands

rabat-joie [rabaʒwa] **1** *adj inv* **être r.** to be a killjoy
 2 *nm inv* killjoy

rabattable [rabatabl] *adj (siège, dossier)* fold-down

rabatteur, -euse [rabatœr, -øz] *nm,f* **(a)** *(à la chasse)* beater **(b)** *Fig* tout

rabattre [11] [rabatr] **1** *vt* **(a)** *(col)* to turn down **(b)** *(couvercle)* to close; *(strapontin)* *(en se levant)* to fold up; *(pour s'asseoir)* to fold down **(c)** *(gibier, foule)* to drive **(vers** towards**) (d)** *(somme)* to deduct **(de** from**) (e)** *(prétentions)* to moderate
 2 se rabattre *vpr* **(a)** *(strapontin)* to fold down **(b)** *(véhicule)* to pull back in **(c)** *(foule)* **se r. vers qch** to veer off towards sth **(d)** *(avoir recours)* **se r. sur qn/qch** to fall back on sb/sth

rabbin [rabɛ̃] *nm* rabbi

rabibocher [rabibɔʃe] *Fam* **1** *vt* to patch things up between
 2 se rabibocher *vpr* to patch things up **(avec** with**)**

rabiot [rabjo] = **rab**

râble [rɑbl] *nm (de lièvre, lapin)* back; **r. de lièvre** *(plat)* saddle of hare

râblé, -e [rɑble] *adj* stocky

rabot [rabo] *nm* plane

raboter [rabote] *vt* to plane

raboteuse [rabotøz] *nf* planing machine

raboteux, -euse [rabotø, -øz] *adj* uneven

rabougri, -e [rabugri] *adj (plante, personne)* stunted

rabougrir [rabugrir] **se rabougrir** *vpr* to shrivel up

rabrouer [rabrue] *vt* to snub

racaille [rakaj] *nf (voyous)* scum; *Vieilli (populace)* rabble

raccommodage [rakɔmɔdaʒ] *nm (de vêtements)* mending; *(de bas, de chaussettes)* darning; **faire du r.** to do some mending/darning

raccommoder [rakɔmɔde] **1** *vt* **(a)** *(vêtement)* to mend; *(bas, chaussette)* to darn **(b)** *Fam (personnes)* to patch things up between
 2 se raccommoder *vpr Fam* to patch things up **(avec** with**)**

raccompagner [rakɔ̃paɲe] *vt* to take back

raccord [rakɔr] *nm* **(a)** *(de papier peint)* join; *(de peinture)* touch-up **(b)** *(pièce d'assemblage)* connection **(c)** *Cin* continuity; *(plan)* link

raccordement [rakɔrdəmɑ̃] *nm* **(a)** *(lien)* link, connection **(b)** *Ordinat* link

raccorder [rakɔrde] **1** *vt* **(a)** *(relier)* *(canalisations, bâtiments, routes)* to link up, to connect **(à** to**)**; *Ordinat* to connect **(b)** *(bande magnétique)* to splice
 2 se raccorder *vpr* to link up; *Ordinat* **se r. à** to link up to

raccourci [rakursi] *nm* short cut; **en r.** *(en bref)* in brief; *(en miniature)* in miniature; *Ordinat* **r. clavier** keyboard shortcut

raccourcir [rakursir] **1** *vt* to shorten **(de** by**)**
 2 *vi* to get shorter

raccrocher [rakrɔʃe] **1** *vt* to hang up again; **r. l'appareil** *ou* **le téléphone** to hang up
 2 *vi (au téléphone)* to hang up, to put the phone down; **r. au nez de qn** to hang up on sb, to put the phone down on sb **(b)** *Fam (sportif)* to retire
 3 se raccrocher *vpr* **se r. à qch** to catch hold of sth; *Fig (espérance)* to cling to sth

race [ras] *nf* **(a)** *(ethnie)* race; **la r. blanche/noire** the white/black race; **la r. humaine** the human race. **(b)** *(animale)* breed; **de r.** *(chien)* pedigree; *(cheval)* thoroughbred

racé, -e [rase] *adj (animal)* pure-bred; *(cheval, voiture)* thoroughbred; *(personne)* noble-looking

rachat [raʃa] *nm* **(a)** *(d'une voiture, d'un appartement)* repurchase, buying back **(b)** *(d'une société)* buy-out **(c)** *(d'un péché)* atonement

racheter [39] [raʃte] **1** *vt* **(a)** *(acheter davantage de)* to buy some more **(b)** *(remplacer)* to buy another **(à** for**) (c)** *(compagnie)* to buy out **(d)** *(après une vente)* to buy back **(à** from**) (e)** *(faute, prisonnier)* to pay a ransom for **(f)** *(faute, faiblesse)* to make up for; *(péché)* to atone for; *(honneur, réputation)* to retrieve
 2 se racheter *vpr* to make amends, to redeem oneself

rachitique [raʃitik] *adj (malade)* suffering from rickets; *(très maigre)* scrawny

rachitisme [raʃitism] *nm* rickets *(singulier)*

racial, -e, -aux, -ales [rasjal, -o] *adj* racial

racine [rasin] *nf* root; **prendre r.** *(plante, personne)* to take root; **r. carrée/cubique** square/cube root

racisme [rasism] *nm* racism

raciste [rasist] *adj & nmf* racist

racket [raket] *nm Fam* racket

racketter [rakɛte] *vt Fam (personne)* to extort money from; **se faire r.** to pay protection money

raclage [raklaʒ] *nm* scraping

raclée [rakle] *nf Fam* thrashing; **prendre une r.** to get a thrashing

raclement [rakləmɑ̃] *nm* scraping (noise)

racler [rakle] **1** *vt* to scrape; *(peinture, boue)* to scrape off; *Fig* **r. les fonds de tiroirs** to scrape some money together; *Fam* **r. la gorge ou le gosier** *(vin)* to be rough on the throat

2 se racler *vpr* **se r. la gorge** to clear one's throat

raclette [raklɛt] *nf* (a) *(plat)* raclette *(Swiss dish consisting of potatoes covered in melted cheese)* (b) *(outil)* scraper

racloir [raklwar] *nm* scraper

racolage [rakolaʒ] *nm* *(d'une prostituée)* soliciting; *(d'un publicitaire)* touting for business; **faire du r.** *(prostituée)* to solicit; *(publicitaire)* to tout for business

racoler [rakole] **1** *vt (sujet: prostituée)* to solicit; *(sujet: commerçant)* to tout for

2 *vi (prostituée)* to solicit; *(commerçant)* to tout for business

racoleur, -euse [rakolœr, -øz] **1** *adj (publicité, affiche)* eye-catching

2 *nm,f (politicien)* = canvasser who attempts to recruit party members using unscrupulous means; *(commerçant)* tout

3 *nf* racoleuse streetwalker

racontable [rakɔ̃tabl] *adj* relatable

racontar [rakɔ̃tar] *nm* piece of gossip; **racontars** gossip

raconter [rakɔ̃te] **1** *vt* (a) *(histoire, mensonge)* to tell; *(événement)* to tell about; **r. qch à qn** *(histoire)* to tell sb sth; *(événement)* to tell sb about sth (b) *(dire)* to say; **qu'est-ce qu'il raconte?** what's he talking about?; **alors, qu'est-ce que tu racontes (de beau ou de neuf)?** so what's new?

2 se raconter *vpr* (a) *(parler de soi)* to talk about oneself (b) *(être raconté)* to be talked about

racornir [rakɔrnir] **1** *vt* (a) *(durcir)* to harden (b) *(ratatiner)* to shrivel

2 se racornir *vpr* (a) *(durcir)* to harden (b) *(se ratatiner)* to shrivel

radar [radar] *nm* radar; *Fam* **être ou avancer au r.** to be on automatic pilot

rade [rad] *nf* harbour; **en r. de Toulon** off Toulon; *Fam* **laisser en r.** *(personne)* to leave in the lurch; *(projet)* to jettison; *Fam* **être en r.** *(personne)* to be stranded

radeau, -x [rado] *nm* raft; **r. pneumatique** inflatable raft; **r. de sauvetage** life raft

radial, -e, -aux, -ales [radjal, -o] *adj voir* **carcasse**

radiateur [radjatœr] *nm* radiator; **r. électrique** electric heater

radiation¹ [radjasjɔ̃] *nf (sur une liste)* striking off

radiation² *nf (d'une onde)* radiation

radical, -e, -aux, -ales [radikal, -o] **1** *adj* radical; **c'est r. (contre)** *(médicament, méthode)* it works like magic (on)

2 *nm (d'un mot)* stem

radicalement [radikalmɑ̃] *adv* radically

radicaliser [radikalize] **1** *vt* to radicalize

2 se radicaliser *vpr* to become more radical

radier [66] [radje] *vt* to strike off **(de** from)

radiesthésiste [radjɛstezist] *nmf* diviner

radieux, -euse [radjø, -øz] *adj (soleil, personne)* radiant; *(temps)* glorious

radin, -e [radɛ̃, -in] *Fam* **1** *adj* stingy

2 *nm,f* skinflint

radiner [radine] **se radiner** *vpr Fam* to roll up; **tu te radines?** are you coming or not?

radio [radjo] **1** *nf* (a) *(poste)* radio; *(station)* radio station; **à la r.** on the radio; **faire de la r.** to be *or* work as a radio presenter; **r. libre** independent radio station; **r. locale** local radio station (b) *(radiotéléphonie)* radio (c) *Méd* X-ray; **passer une r.** to have an X-ray

2 *nm (opérateur)* radio operator

3 *adj inv* radio

radioactif, -ive [radjoaktif, -iv] *adj* radioactive

radioactivité [radjoaktivite] *nf* radioactivity

radioamateur [radjoamatœr] *nm* radio ham

radiocassette [radjokasɛt] *nf* radio cassette player

radiodiffuser [radjodifyze] *vt* to broadcast

radiodiffusion [radjodifyzjɔ̃] *nf* broadcasting

radiographie [radjografi] *nf* (a) *(technique)* radiography (b) *(cliché)* X-ray

radiographier [66] [radjografje] *vt* to X-ray

radioguidé, -e [radjogide] *adj* radio-controlled; *(missile)* guided

radiologie [radjolɔʒi] *nf* radiology

radiologique [radjolɔʒik] *adj* radiological

radiologue [radjolɔg], **radiologiste** [radjolɔʒist] *nmf (médecin)* radiologist; *(technicien)* radiographer

radiophonique [radjofɔnik] *adj (de radio)* radio; *(bon pour la radio)* good for radio

radioreportage [radjorəpɔrtaʒ] *nm (activité)* radio reporting; *(émission)* radio report

radioreporter [radjorəpɔrter] *nmf* radio reporter

radio-réveil *(pl* **radios-réveils)** [radjorevɛj] *nm* radio-alarm (clock)

radioscopie [radjoskɔpi] *nf* radioscopy

radioscopique [radjoskɔpik] *adj (examen)* X-ray

radio-taxi *(pl* **radio-taxis)** [radjotaksi] *nm* radio taxi

radiotélescope [radjotelɛskɔp] *nm* radio telescope

radiotélévisé, -e [radjotelevize] *adj* broadcast on both radio and television

radiothérapie [radjoterapi] *nf* radiotherapy

radis [radi] *nm* radish; *Fam* **ne plus avoir un r.** not to have a bean; **r. noir** black radish

radium [radjɔm] *nm* radium

radius [radjys] *nm* radius

radotage [radotaʒ] *nm (rabâchage)* going on and on; *(divagations)* rambling

radoter [radote] **1** *vi (rabâcher)* to go on and on; *(divaguer)* to ramble on

2 *vt Fam* to go on and on about

radoteur, -euse [radotœr, -øz] *nm,f* rambling old fool

radoub [radu] *nm* **bassin de r.** dry dock

radoucir [radusir] **1** vt (a) (temps) to make milder (b) (personne) to calm down; (caractère) to soften
2 se radoucir vpr (a) (temps) to become milder (b) (personne) to calm down

radoucissement [radusismã] nm (a) (de la température) milder spell (b) (d'une personne) calming down

rafale [rafal] nf (a) (de vent, de pluie) gust; **par** ou **en rafales** in gusts (b) (de coups de feu) burst

raffermir [rafermir] **1** vt (a) (peau, muscles) to firm up (b) (autorité, courage) to strengthen
2 se raffermir vpr (a) (muscles, peau) to firm up (b) (gouvernement) (devenir plus intransigeant) to take a stronger line; (devenir plus fort) to become stronger; (autorité) to strengthen

raffermissement [rafermismã] nm (a) (des muscles, de la peau) firming up (b) (de l'autorité, du pouvoir) strengthening

raffinage [rafinaʒ] nm refining

raffiné, -e [rafine] adj refined

raffinement [rafinmã] nm refinement

raffiner [rafine] **1** vt to refine
2 raffiner sur vt ind to be overparticular about

raffinerie [rafinri] nf refinery

raffoler [rafole] **raffoler de** vt ind Fam **r. de qch** to be mad about sth

raffut [rafy] nm Fam (bruit) din, racket; **faire du r.** (bruit) to make a din; (scandale) to set tongues wagging; (pour protester) to kick up a fuss

rafiot [rafjo] nm Péj old tub

rafistolage [rafistolaʒ] nm Fam patching up

rafistoler [rafistole] vt Fam to patch up

rafle [rafl] nf raid

rafler [rafle] vt Fam to swipe

rafraîchir [rafreʃir] **1** vt (a) (rendre frais) (aliment, boisson) to chill; (pièce) to air; (atmosphère) to cool (b) (raviver) (couleur, maquillage, peintures) to freshen up; (appartement) to brighten up; Fam **r. la mémoire à qn** to refresh sb's memory
2 vi to cool down
3 se rafraîchir vpr (a) (temps) to turn cooler (b) (se mouiller le visage) to freshen up (c) Fam (boire) to have a cold drink

rafraîchissant, -e [rafreʃisã, -ãt] adj refreshing

rafraîchissement [rafreʃismã] nm (a) (de la température, d'une boisson) cooling (b) (boisson) cold drink; **rafraîchissements** refreshments (c) Ordinat refresh

rafting [raftiŋ] nm rafting

ragaillardir [ragajardir] Fam **1** vt to buck up
2 se ragaillardir vpr to buck up

rage [raʒ] nf (a) (maladie) rabies (b) (colère) rage; **faire r.** (tempête) to rage; **avoir la r. au cœur** to be seething with rage; **ivre** ou **fou de r.** furious; **mettre qn en r.** to enrage sb; **r. de dents** raging toothache (c) (passion) passion (**de qch** for sth); **avoir la r. du jeu** to have a passion for gambling

rageant, -e [raʒã, -ãt] adj Fam infuriating

rager [45] [raʒe] vi Fam to fume; **faire r. qn** to make sb mad

rageur, -euse [raʒœr, -øz] adj (ton, voix) furious

rageusement [raʒøzmã] adv furiously

raglan [raglã] nm raglan coat

ragot [rago] nm Fam piece of gossip; **ragots** gossip

ragoût [ragu] nm stew; **en r.** stewed

ragoûtant, -e [ragutã, -ãt] adj **peu** ou **pas r.** (plat) unappetizing; (personne) unsavoury

rai [re] nm (de lumière) ray

raï [raj] nm inv = North African popular music influenced by rock music

raid [red] nm raid; **r. aérien** air raid

raide [red] **1** adj (a) (membre, articulation) stiff; (cheveux) straight; (câble) taut (b) (escalier, pente) steep (c) (personne, démarche) stiff; **r. comme un piquet** as stiff as a ramrod (d) (caractère) inflexible; (manières) stiff (e) Fam (difficile à croire) far-fetched (f) Fam (osé) risqué (g) Fam (fort) (alcool) rough
2 adv (a) (de façon abrupte) steeply (b) (brutalement) **tomber r.** to fall to the ground; **tomber r. mort** to drop dead

raideur [redœr] nf (a) (d'un membre, d'une articulation, d'un mouvement) stiffness; **avoir une r. dans le cou/à l'épaule** to have a stiff neck/shoulder (b) (d'une personne) stiffness (c) (de caractère) inflexibility (d) (d'une pente) steepness

raidillon [redijõ] nm (chemin) steep path; (partie de route) steep rise

raidir [redir] **1** vt (bras, jambes) to brace; (corde, câble) to tauten; (tissu) to stiffen
2 se raidir vpr (a) (membres, articulations) to stiffen; (câble) to tauten (b) (personne) to tense up

raidissement [redismã] nm (a) (d'une matière, des muscles) stiffening; (d'une corde) tautening (b) (montée de la tension) **r. des rapports internationaux** increase of tension in international relations; **le r. des ouvriers face à la direction** the tougher line taken by the workers with the management

raie¹ [re] nf (a) (motif) stripe (b) (dans les cheveux) Br parting, Am part (c) (des fesses) cleft

raie² nf (poisson) skate

raifort [refor] nm horseradish

rail [roj] nm (a) (sur une voie de chemin de fer) rail; Fig **remettre qn sur les rails** to get sb back on the rails (b) **le r.** (les chemins de fer) rail (c) **r. de sécurité** crash barrier (d) (couloir) (aérien, maritime) lane

railler [roje] vt to mock

raillerie [rojri] nf gibe

railleur, -euse [rojœr, -øz] **1** adj mocking
2 nm,f scoffer

rainette [renet] nf (a) (grenouille) tree frog (b) (pomme) pippin

rainure [renyr] nf groove

raisin [rezε̃] nm grapes; **raisins de Corinthe** currants; **raisins secs** raisins; **raisins de Smyrne** sultanas

raison [rezõ] nf (a) (cause) reason (**de** for); **être absent pour r. de santé** to be absent for health reasons; **à plus forte r.** all the more so; **r. de plus (pour faire qch)** all the more reason (to do sth); **la r. pour laquelle il est venu** the reason (why) he came; **la r. d'État** reasons of State; **r. d'être** raison d'être; **r. de vivre** reason for living
(b) (entendement) reason; **recouvrer la r.** to come to one's senses; **perdre la r.** to take leave of one's senses; **entendre r.** to listen to reason; **de r.** (âge) of reason; (mariage) of convenience
(c) (satisfaction) satisfaction; **avoir r. de qn/qch** to get the better of sb/sth
(d) (proportion) **à r. de** at the rate of

(e) *(désignation)* r. sociale company name **(f)** *(locutions)* avoir r. (de faire qch) to be right (to do sth); donner r. à qn *(personne)* to admit that sb is right; *(événement)* to prove sb right; se faire une r. to accept the inevitable, to resign oneself; comme de r. as one might expect; plus que de r. more than is reasonable

raisonnable [rɛzɔnabl] *adj* reasonable

raisonnablement [rɛzɔnabləmɑ̃] *adv* (a) *(avec bon sens)* reasonably (b) *(modérément)* in moderation

raisonné, -e [rɛzɔne] *adj (argumentation, choix)* reasoned

raisonnement [rɛzɔnmɑ̃] *nm* (a) *(argumentation)* argument; *(faculté)* reasoning; tenir un r. to use an argument; r. par l'absurde reductio ad absurdum

raisonner [rɛzɔne] 1 *vt (personne)* to reason with 2 *vi* (a) *(penser)* to reason *(sur* about); *Fam* r. comme une pantoufle to talk through one's hat (b) *(discuter)* to argue *(avec* with) 3 se raisonner *vpr (personne)* to see reason

raisonneur, -euse [rɛzɔnœr, -øz] 1 *adj* reasoning; *Péj* argumentative 2 *nm,f Péj* arguer

rajeunir [raʒœnir] 1 *vt* (a) *(faire paraître plus jeune)* to make sb look younger; *(faire se sentir plus jeune)* to make sb feel younger (b) *(donner un âge moins élevé à)* r. qn to underestimate how old sb is; r. qn de trois ans to take three years off sb's age (c) *(robe, veste)* to update (d) *(organisation, bureau)* to modernize; *(équipe)* to bring new blood into 2 *vi (physiquement)* to look younger; *(moralement)* to seem younger; il a rajeuni de dix ans he looks ten years younger; ça ne nous rajeunit pas! we're showing our age! 3 se rajeunir *vpr (se prétendre plus jeune)* to make oneself out to be younger than one is

rajeunissant, -e [raʒœnisɑ̃, -ɑ̃t] *adj* rejuvenating

rajeunissement [raʒœnismɑ̃] *nm* (a) *(après un traitement)* rejuvenation (b) *(de la population, d'un secteur professionnel)* decrease in age

rajout [raʒu] *nm* addition

rajouter [raʒute] *vt* to add; *Fam* en r. to exaggerate

rajuster [raʒyste] 1 *vt (vêtement)* to adjust, to straighten 2 se rajuster *vpr* to tidy oneself up

râle [rɑl] *nm (bruit aux poumons)* rale; *(d'un agonisant)* death rattle

ralenti, -e [ralɑ̃ti] 1 *adj* slow 2 *nm* (a) *(régime du moteur)* idling speed; au r. *(vivre, fonctionner)* at a slower pace; tourner au r. *(moteur, usine) Br* to tick over, *Am* to turn over (b) *Cin* slow motion; au r. in slow motion

ralentir [ralɑ̃tir] *vt & vi* to slow down

ralentissement [ralɑ̃tismɑ̃] *nm* slowing down; *(embouteillage)* hold-up

ralentisseur [ralɑ̃tisœr] *nm (dos d'âne)* speed bump

râler [rɑle] *vi* (a) *Fam (protester)* to moan (b) *(mourant)* to give a death rattle

râleur, -euse [rɑlœr, -øz] *Fam* 1 *adj* moaning 2 *nm,f* moaner

ralliement [ralimɑ̃] *nm* rallying

rallier [66] [ralje] 1 *vt* (a) *(regagner) (lieu)* to return to (b) *(gagner à sa cause)* to win over (à to) (c) *(réunir) (adhérents)* to rally; r. tous les suffrages to win general approval (d) *(regrouper) (troupes)* to rally 2 se rallier *vpr* se r. à *(avis)* to come round to; *(parti)* to join; *(cause)* to rally to

rallonge [ralɔ̃ʒ] *nf* (a) *(de table)* extension (b) *(électrique)* extension (lead) (c) *Fam (d'argent)* extra money; *(de temps)* extra time

rallonger [45] [ralɔ̃ʒe] 1 *vt (vêtement)* to lengthen; *(période, route)* to extend (de by) 2 *vi* to get longer

rallumer [ralyme] 1 *vt* (a) *(appareil électrique, lumière)* to switch on again (b) *(feu, cigarette)* to light again; *(querelle, colère, espoir)* to rekindle 2 se rallumer *vpr (lumière, appareil électrique)* to come back on (b) *(feu, guerre, dispute)* to flare up again; *(espoir)* to rekindle

rallye [rali] *nm* (a) *(épreuve sportive)* (car) rally (b) *(soirée)* = dance attended by young people from rich families looking for a husband or wife

RAM [ram] *nf Ordinat* RAM

ramadan [ramadɑ̃] *nm* Ramadan; faire le r. to observe Ramadan

ramage [ramaʒ] *nm* (a) *(chant des oiseaux)* song (b) ramages *(motif)* leafy design

ramassage [ramasaʒ] *nm* (a) *(de fruits, de noix)* gathering (b) *(d'ordures, de vêtements, de vieux journaux)* collection; car de r. scolaire school bus

ramassé, -e [ramase] *adj* (a) *(trapu) (personne)* stocky (b) *(style)* compact

ramasse-miettes [ramasmjɛt] *nm inv* table tidy *(small brush and pan for clearing crumbs off the table)*

ramasser [ramase] 1 *vt* (a) *(prendre par terre) (objet, personne)* to pick up; *(fruits, noix, coquillages)* to gather; *(champignons)* to pick; *(pommes de terre)* to dig up; *Fam* se faire r. par la police to get picked up by the police (b) *(copies, affaires, informations)* to collect; *(cartes)* to pick up; r. ses forces to gather one's strength (c) *(enfants, ouvriers, courrier)* to pick up, to collect (d) *Fam (gifle)* to get; *(procès-verbal)* to pick up 2 se ramasser *vpr (après une chute)* to pick oneself up (b) *(se pelotonner)* to curl up (c) *Fam (échouer)* to come a cropper

ramassette [ramasɛt] *nf Belg* dustpan

ramasseur, -euse [ramasœr, -øz] *nm,f* (a) *(de champignons)* picker; *(de fruits)* gatherer (b) *(au tennis)* r. de balles ball boy, f ball girl

ramassis [ramasi] *nm Péj (de choses)* jumble; *(de gens)* bunch; *(d'idées)* hotchpotch; un r. de mensonges a tissue of lies

rambarde [rɑ̃bard] *nf* (guard)rail

ramdam [ramdam] *nm Fam* racket; faire du r. to make a heck of a racket

rame¹ [ram] *nf (pour plantes grimpantes)* stick

rame² *nf (aviron)* oar

rame³ *nf* (a) *(de papier)* ream (b) *(de wagons)* train; r. (de métro) *(Br* underground or *Am* subway) train

rameau, -x [ramo] *nm* (a) *(d'arbre)* branch (b) les Rameaux Palm Sunday

ramener [46] [ramne] **1** vt (a) (amener) to bring back; (raccompagner) to take back; **r. qn en voiture** to give sb a lift back; **r. qn à la vie** to bring sb back to life; **r. qn à la raison** to bring sb back to his/her senses (b) Fam (rapporter, revenir avec) to bring back; **r. tout à soi** to bring everything back to oneself (c) (remettre) (couverture, châle) to pull up (sur over) (d) (rétablir) (ordre, paix) to restore (e) (réduire) **r. qch à qch** to reduce sth to sth (f) Fam **r. sa fraise, la r.** to show off
2 se ramener vpr (a) (se réduire) **se r. à** to boil down to (b) Fam (arriver) to roll up

ramequin [ramkɛ̃] nm ramekin

ramer [rame] vi (a) (pagayer) to row (b) Fam (peiner) to sweat blood

rameur, -euse [ramœr, -øz] nm,f rower

ramier [ramje] adj m voir **pigeon**

ramification [ramifikasjɔ̃] nf (d'une plante) ramification; (d'une famille, d'une science) branch; **ramifications** (d'une société, d'une affaire) ramifications

ramifier [66] [ramifje] **se ramifier** vpr to branch out (en into)

ramolli, -e [ramoli] adj Fam (mentalement) soft-headed

ramollir [ramolir] **1** vt (substance) to soften; Fam **r. qn** (intellectuellement) to make sb soft in the head
2 se ramollir vpr (substance) to soften; Fam (personne) (moralement) to have no get-up-and-go

ramollissement [ramolismã] nm softening

ramonage [ramonaʒ] nm chimney sweeping

ramoner [ramone] vt (cheminée) to sweep

ramoneur [ramonœr] nm (chimney) sweep

rampant, -e [rãpã, -ãt] adj (a) (plante) creeping; (animal) crawling; Péj (personne, caractère) grovelling (b) **personnel r.** (de l'aviation) ground crew (c) (inflation) rampant

rampe [rãp] nf (a) (d'escalier) banister, handrail (b) (plan incliné) slope, incline; **r. d'accès** (d'un pont) access ramp; (d'une autoroute) Br slip road, Am ramp; **r. de lancement** launching ramp (c) (rebond d'une scène de théâtre) footlights

ramper [rãpe] vi (animal, enfant, soldat) to crawl; Péj **r. devant qn** to grovel to sb

ramure [ramyr] nf (a) (d'un arbre) branches (b) (d'un cerf) antlers

rancard [rãkar] nm Fam (rendez-vous) meeting; (amoureux) date

rancarder [rãkarde] très Fam **1** vt **r. qn sur qch** to tip sb off about sth
2 se rancarder vpr to find out (sur about)

rancart [rãkar] nm Fam **mettre qch au r.** to chuck sth out; **mettre qn au r.** to put sb on the rubbish heap

rance [rãs] **1** adj rancid
2 nm **goût de r.** rancid taste

ranch [rãtʃ] nm ranch

rancir [rãsir] vi to go rancid

rancœur [rãkœr] nf resentment, rancour; **avoir de la r. pour** ou **contre qn** to feel resentment towards sb

rançon [rãsɔ̃] nf ransom; Fig **la r. de la gloire** the price of fame

rançonner [rãsone] vt **r. qn** to hold sb to ransom

rancune [rãkyn] nf spite; **garder r. à qn, avoir de la r. contre qn** to have a grudge against sb, to bear sb a grudge; **sans r.!** no hard feelings!

rancunier, -ère [rãkynje, -ɛr] **1** adj spiteful
2 nm,f spiteful person

randonnée [rãdone] nf (a) (marche à pied) **r. (pédestre)** hike; (activité) hiking, rambling; (en montagne) hill-walking (b) (en voiture) drive; (à vélo) ride (c) (excursion à ski) ski-mountaineering

randonneur, -euse [rãdonœr, -øz] nm,f (à pied) hiker, rambler

rang [rã] nm (a) (d'arbres, de sièges) row; **se mettre en r. (par deux/trois)** to line up (in twos/threes); Hum **en r. d'oignons** in a neat row; **en rangs serrés** in serried ranks; Fig **se mettre sur les rangs** to put oneself in the running (b) (position sociale) station; (de militaire) rank; **de haut r.** high-ranking (c) (classement) rank; **par r. de taille** in order of size (d) Can (chemin) concession road

rangé, -e [rãʒe] adj (a) (maison, chambre) tidy (b) (personne) steady

rangée [rãʒe] nf row

rangement [rãʒmã] nm (a) (action) tidying up; **faire du r.** to do some tidying up; **faire du r. dans ses affaires** to tidy up one's things (b) (placard) **rangements** storage space (c) Ordinat storage

ranger [45] [rãʒe] **1** vt (a) (pièce, maison) to tidy (up) (b) (affaires, vêtements) to put away (c) (mettre) to put (d) (classer) to rank (parmi among); **r. par ordre alphabétique, taille)** to arrange by (e) (véhicule, vélo) to park (f) (soldats, élèves) to line up (g) Ordinat **r. en mémoire** to store
2 se ranger vpr (a) (se disposer) to line up (b) (s'écarter) (piéton) to stand aside; (véhicule) to pull over (c) (prendre position pour) **se r. du côté de qn** to side with sb, to take sb's side; **se r. à l'opinion de qn** to come round to sb's opinion (d) (se mettre) to go (e) Fam (s'assagir) to settle down; **se r. des voitures** to settle down

ranimer [ranime] **1** vt (a) (personne) (après un évanouissement) to bring round; (après un arrêt cardiaque) to resuscitate (b) (feu) to rekindle (c) (sentiment, souvenir, espoir) to reawaken; (débat) to revive
2 se ranimer vpr (a) (personne) to come round (b) (feu) to flicker into life

rap [rap] nm **le r.** rap

rapace [rapas] **1** nm bird of prey
2 adj (a) (oiseau) predatory (b) (personne) grasping

rapacité [rapasite] nf rapaciousness

rapatrié, -e [rapatrije] **1** adj repatriated
2 nm,f repatriate

rapatriement [rapatrimã] nm repatriation

rapatrier [66] [rapatrije] vt to repatriate

râpe [rap] nf (a) (de cuisine) grater; **r. à fromage** cheese grater (b) (lime) rasp

râpé, -e [rape] **1** adj (a) (fromage, carotte) grated (b) (vêtement) threadbare (c) Fam (raté) **c'est r.!** we've had it!
2 nm (fromage) grated cheese

râper [rape] vt (a) (carotte, fromage) to grate (b) (racler) **ce vin râpe la gorge** this wine's rough on the throat (c) (limer) to rasp

rapetasser [raptase] vt Fam (vêtement) to patch up

rapetisser [raptise] **1** vt (a) (rendre plus petit) to make smaller (b) (dévaluer) to belittle (c) (faire paraître plus petit) to make look smaller
2 vi (vêtement, personne) to shrink

râpeux, -euse [rapø, -øz] adj (langue) rough; (vin) harsh

raphia [rafja] *nm* raffia

rapiat, -e [rapja, -at] *Fam* **1** *adj (avare)* stingy **2** *nm,f* skinflint

rapide [rapid] **1** *adj* **(a)** *(coureur, voiture, itinéraire)* fast; *(pouls, progrès)* rapid; **r. comme l'éclair** as quick as lightning; **r. comme une flèche** as swift as an arrow **(b)** *(courant)* swift-flowing **(c)** *(prompt) (personne, esprit, intelligence)* quick **(d)** *(fait en peu de temps) (lecture, décision)* quick **(e)** *(pente)* steep **2** *nm* **(a)** *(train)* express (train) **(b)** *(dans un fleuve)* rapid

rapidement [rapidmã] *adv* quickly, rapidly

rapidité [rapidite] *nf* **(a)** *(d'actions, d'une décision, d'une réponse)* speed; **r. d'esprit** quickness of mind **(b)** *Ordinat* **r. d'impression** print speed; **r. de traitement** processing speed

rapiécer [16/34] [rapjese] *vt* to patch

rapine [rapin] *nf Litt* pillage

raplapla [raplapla] *adj inv Fam* **(a)** *(pneu, coussin)* flat as a pancake **(b)** *(personne)* washed out

rappel [rapel] *nm* **(a)** *(d'un événement, d'une promesse)* reminder; **r. de couleurs** repeat of colours; **r. à l'ordre** *(à un membre d'une assemblée)* call to order; *(d'un employé)* warning; **le r. des titres (de l'actualité)** the headlines; **dernier r.** *(de facture)* final demand **(b)** *(d'un ambassadeur, de réservistes)* recall **(c)** *(d'un salaire)* back pay **(d)** *(de vaccin)* booster; **faire un r.** to have a booster **(e)** *(au théâtre)* curtain call; *(à un concert)* encore **(f)** *(en alpinisme)* abseiling; **faire une descente** *ou* **descendre en r., faire du r.** to abseil down **(g)** *Ordinat (de texte)* restore

rappeler [42] [raple, raple] **1** *vt* **(a)** *(appeler) (personne)* to call back; *(chien)* to call off **(b)** *(au téléphone) (sujet: personne appelée)* to call back; *(sujet: personne qui appelle)* to call again; **r. dix fois** to call ten times **(c)** *(faire revenir) (personne)* to call back; *(ambassadeur)* to recall; **r. qn à l'ordre** *(membre d'une association)* to call sb to order; *(employé)* to warn sb **(d)** *(acteur, chanteur)* to call back **(e)** *(faire penser à)* **r. qn/qch à qn** to remind sb of sb/sth; **cela ne me rappelle rien** it doesn't ring a bell **(f)** *(remettre en mémoire)* **r. qch à qn** to remind sb of sth; **rappelez-moi votre nom** what was your name again?; **r. qn au bon souvenir de qn** to remember sb to sb **2 se rappeler** *vpr* **(a)** **se r. qn/qch** *(se souvenir de)* to remember sb/sth; **rappelle-toi que...** don't forget that... **(b)** *Fam (au téléphone)* **on se rappelle la semaine prochaine** we'll talk again next week

rappeur, -euse [rapœr, -øz] *nm,f* rapper

rappliquer [raplike] *vi Fam* to roll up

rapport [rapɔr] *nm* **(a)** *(relation)* **rapports** relations, relationship; **avoir de bons/mauvais rapports avec qn** to be on good/bad terms with sb; **entretenir de bons rapports avec qn** to stay on friendly terms with sb; **mettre qn en r. avec qn** to put sb in touch with sb; **être en r. avec qn** to be in touch with sb; **r. de forces** battle of wills **(b)** *(lien)* connection, link **(avec** with**)**; **avoir un r. avec qch** to have something to do with sth; **n'avoir aucun r. avec qch** to have nothing to do with sth; **faire le r.** to make the connection; **être sans r. avec qch** to be unconnected with sth; **en r. avec** *(lié à)* in keeping with; **par r. à qch** *(en comparaison)* compared with sth **(c)** *(aspect)* **sous ce r.** in this respect; **bien sous tous rapports** nice in every respect

(d) *(proportion)* ratio, proportion; **en r. avec** in proportion to; **d'un bon r. qualité-prix** good value for money **(e)** *(compte rendu)* report; **faire** *ou* **rédiger un r. sur qch** to draw up a report on sth; **r. annuel** annual report; **r. commercial** market report **(f)** *(profit)* return, yield; **d'un bon r.** profitable; **d'un mauvais r.** unprofitable **(g)** **rapports** *(relations sexuelles)* (sexual) intercourse; **avoir des rapports avec qn** to have sex with sb

rapporter [rapɔrte] **1** *vt* **(a)** *(apporter avec soi)* to bring back; **r. qch à qn** to bring sb sth back **(b)** *(rendre)* to bring back (à to); *(remporter)* to take back (à to) **(c)** *(ajouter) (poche, pièce)* to sew on **(d)** *(raconter)* to report; **on rapporte que...** it is reported that... **(e)** *(produire) (bénéfice, intérêt)* to yield; **r. de l'argent** to be profitable; **r. qch à qn** *(financièrement)* to bring sb in sth; *Fig (moralement)* to bring sb sth **(f)** *Péj (répéter)* to report (à to) **(g)** *(sujet: chien)* to retrieve; **rapporte!** fetch! **2 se rapporter** *vpr* **(a)** **se r. à qch** *(concerner)* to relate to sth **(b)** *(se remettre)* **s'en r. à qn/qch** to rely on sb/sth

rapporteur, -euse [rapɔrtœr, -øz] **1** *adj Péj* sneaky **2** *nm,f Péj* telltale, sneak **3** *nm* **(a)** *(d'une commission)* reporter **(b)** *(instrument)* protractor

rapproché, -e [raproʃe] *adj (dans l'espace, dans le temps)* close; *(yeux)* close-set; **des maisons très rapprochées** houses very close together; **des rendez-vous très rapprochés (dans le temps)** appointments very close to each other

rapprochement [raproʃmã] *nm* **(a)** *(rapport) (de faits, d'idées)* connection; **faire le r. (entre deux choses)** to make a connection (between two things) **(b)** *(de deux objets)* bringing together **(c)** *(réconciliation) (entre personnes)* reconciliation; *(entre pays)* rapprochement

rapprocher [raproʃe] **1** *vt* **(a)** *(mettre plus près) (deux ou plusieurs objets)* to move closer together; *(objet)* to move closer **(de** to**)**; **ça te rapprochera (de chez toi)** that'll get you a bit closer (to home) **(b)** *(réunir)* to join **(c)** *(séances)* to group closer together **(d)** *(unir) (personnes)* to bring together **(e)** *(lier) (idées, textes)* to compare **(de** with**)** **2 se rapprocher** *vpr* **(a)** *(aller plus près)* to get closer **(de** to**)**; **se r. de la vérité** to get close to the truth **(b)** *(devenir proche)* to get closer **(de** to**)**; *(après une brouille)* to become reconciled **(de** with**)** **(c)** **se r. de qn/qch** *(ressembler à)* to be similar to sb/sth

rapsodie [rapsɔdi] *nf* rhapsody

rapt [rapt] *nm* abduction

raquer [rake] *vt très Fam* to fork out

raquette [raket] *nf* **(a)** *(de tennis, de badminton, de squash)* racket **(b)** *(de ping-pong)* bat **(c)** *(pour marcher dans la neige)* snowshoe

rare [rar] *adj* **(a)** *(peu commun, peu fréquent)* rare; **c'est rare qu'il pleuve ici** it rarely rains here; **cela n'a rien de r.** it's quite common **(b)** *(peu nombreux, peu abondant)* être r. to be scarce; **c'est une des rares personnes que je connaisse à...** he's one of the few people I know to... **(c)** *(exceptionnel)* rare **(d)** *(clairsemé) (végétation)* sparse; **avoir le cheveu r.** to have thinning hair **(e)** **tu te fais r.** we've hardly seen you lately

raréfaction [rarefaksjɔ̃] *nf* **(a)** *(d'une denrée, de l'argent)* growing scarcity **(b)** *(de l'air)* rarefaction

raréfier [66] [rarefje] **se raréfier** *vpr* **(a)** *(denrée, argent)* to become scarce **(b)** *(air)* to become rarefied

rarement [rarmã] *adv* rarely, seldom

rareté [rarte] *nf* (a) (*de denrées, de main-d'œuvre*) scarcity; (*de visites*) infrequency; (*d'un phénomène, d'un mot, d'une maladie*) rareness (b) (*objet rare*) rarity

RAS [eraes] *Fam* (*abrév* **rien à signaler**) everything OK

ras, -e [ra, raz] **1** *adj* (a) (*cheveux*) close-cropped; (*barbe*) short; (*tapis*) short-pile (b) (*entier*) (*mesure*) full; **deux cuillerées rases** two level spoonfuls (c) (*locutions*) à **r. bord** to the brim; **en rase campagne** in the open country
2 *nm* (a) (*bord*) **à ou au r. de** level with; **voler au r. du sol/de l'eau** to fly close to the ground/water; *Fam Fig* **aux r. des pâquerettes** lowbrow (b) **r. du cou** (*pullover*) crew-neck sweater
3 *adv* short; *Fam* **en avoir le r. le bol** to have had it up to here

rasade [razad] *nf* glassful

rasage [raza3] *nm* shaving

rasant, -e [razɑ̃, -ɑ̃t] *adj* (a) *Fam* (*personne, discours, film*) boring (b) (*lumière*) low-angled; (*tir*) grazing

rascasse [raskas] *nf* scorpion fish

rasé, -e [raze] *adj* shaven; **r. de près** close-shaven

rase-mottes [razmɔt] *nm inv Fam* **faire du ou voler en r.** to hedgehop

raser [raze] **1** *vt* (a) (*visage, personne*) to shave; (*moustache, barbe, cheveux*) to shave off (b) (*passer très près de*) (*sol, eau*) to skim; (*filet, trottoir*) to graze; **r. les murs** to hug the walls (c) (*détruire*) (*bâtiment, ville*) to raze to the ground (d) *Fam* (*ennuyer*) to bore
2 *se raser vpr* (a) (*se couper la barbe*) to shave, to have a shave; **se r. les jambes** to shave one's legs (b) *Fam* (*s'ennuyer*) to be bored

raseur, -euse [razœr, -øz] *nm,f Fam* bore

rasibus [razibys] *adv Fam* **la balle est passée r.** the bullet whizzed past really close

ras-le-bol [ralbɔl] *Fam* **1** *nm inv* discontent; *Fam* **en avoir r. (de)** to be fed up (with)
2 *exclam* enough's enough!

rasoir [razwar] **1** *nm* razor; **r. électrique** electric razor *or* shaver
2 *adj inv Fam* boring

rassasier [66] [rasazje] **1** *vt* (*faim, curiosité*) to satisfy; **r. qn** to satisfy sb's hunger
2 *se rassasier vpr* **se r. de qch** to get one's fill of sth

rassemblement [rasɑ̃bləmɑ̃] *nm* (a) (*attroupement*) gathering (b) (*de documents, d'objets*) collecting, gathering (c) (*union politique*) union (d) *Mil* fall in, parade; **sonner le r.** to sound the assembly

rassembler [rasɑ̃ble] **1** *vt* (a) (*personnes, choses, documents*) to gather (together) (b) (*courage, forces*) to muster, to summon up; **r. ses idées** to collect one's thoughts; **r. ses esprits** to collect oneself
2 *se rassembler vpr* (*manifestants*) to gather, to assemble; (*famille*) to get together

rasseoir [10a] [raswar] **se rasseoir** *vpr* to sit down again

rasséréner [34] [raserene] **1** *vt* **r. qn** to put sb's mind at rest
2 *se rasséréner vpr* to calm down

rassir [rasir] *vi* to go stale

rassis, -e [rasi, -iz] *adj* (a) (*pain*) stale (b) *Litt* (*personne, esprit*) calm

rassurant, -e [rasyrɑ̃, -ɑ̃t] *adj* reassuring

rassuré, -e [rasyre] *adj* at ease; **me voilà r.!** that's a relief!

rassurer [rasyre] **1** *vt* to reassure; **ah, tu me rassures!** well, that's a relief!
2 *se rassurer vpr* to reassure oneself; **rassurez-vous** rest assured

rasta [rasta] *adj inv & nmf* Rasta

rat [ra] **1** *nm* (a) (*animal*) rat; **r. d'égout** sewer rat; *Fam* **être fait comme un r.** to be caught like a rat in a trap; **petit r.** (**de l'Opéra**) ballet pupil; **mon petit r.** darling; *Fam* **r. de bibliothèque** bookworm; **r. d'hôtel** hotel thief (b) *Can* (*sournois*) tricky customer
2 *adj Can* (a) (*avare*) stingy (b) *Can* (*sournois*) wily, sly

ratage [rata3] *nm Fam* botch-up

ratatiné, -e [ratatine] *adj* (a) (*fruit*) shrivelled (b) (*vieillard*) wizened (c) *Fam* (*véhicule*) smashed-up

ratatiner [ratatine] **1** *vt Fam* (a) (*voiture*) to smash up (b) (*équipe*) to thrash
2 *se ratatiner vpr* (a) (*fruit*) to shrivel up (b) (*vieillard*) to become wizened

ratatouille [ratatuj] *nf* ratatouille

rate[1] [rat] *nf* (*organe*) spleen

rate[2] *nf* (*animal*) female rat

raté, -e [rate] **1** *nm,f* loser
2 *nm* misfiring; *Fig* hitch; **avoir des ratés** to misfire

râteau, -x [rato] *nm* rake

râtelier [ratəlje] *nm* (a) (*pour le fourrage*) rack; *Fig* **manger à tous les râteliers** to have a finger in every pie (b) (*à outils, à armes*) rack (c) *Fam* (*dentier*) (set of) false teeth

rater [rate] **1** *vt* (a) (*examen*) to fail; (*vie, plat*) to make a mess of; **c'est raté** it hasn't worked; *Fig* **r. son coup** to make a mess of things (b) (*train, avion, personne, occasion*) to miss; **tu n'as pas raté grand-chose** you didn't miss much (c) *Fam* (*locutions*) **ne pas r. qn** to let sb have it; **elle n'en rate pas une** she's always putting her foot in it
2 *vi* (*examen*) to fail; **faire r. qch** to ruin sth; **j'étais sûr qu'elle allait oublier, et ça n'a pas raté** I was sure she was going to forget, and right enough she did
3 *se rater vpr Fam* (*ne pas se rencontrer*) to miss each other

ratiboiser [ratibwaze] *vt Fam* to clean out

ratier [ratje] *nm* (*chien*) ratter

ratière [ratjɛr] *nf* rat trap

ratification [ratifikasjɔ̃] *nf* ratification

ratifier [66] [ratifje] *vt* (*traité, acte*) to ratify; (*décision*) to confirm

ratio [rasjo] *nm* ratio

ration [rasjɔ̃] *nf* (*de pain, de nourriture*) ration; *Fig* (*de critiques, de difficultés*) share; **r. alimentaire** food ration

rationaliser [rasjonalize] *vt* to rationalize

rationnel, -elle [rasjonɛl] *adj* rational

rationnellement [rasjonɛlmɑ̃] *adv* rationally

rationnement [rasjonmɑ̃] *nm* rationing

rationner [rasjone] **1** *vt* to ration
2 *se rationner vpr* to ration oneself

ratissage [ratisa3] *nm* (a) (*allée, sol*) raking (b) *Fam* (*par la police*) combing

ratisser [ratise] **1** *vt* (a) (*allée, sol*) to rake; (*feuilles*) to rake up (b) *Fam* (*quartier*) to comb (c) *Fam* (*personne*) to clean out; **se faire r.** (*au jeu*) to be cleaned out
2 *vi* **r. large** to cast one's net wide

raton [ratɔ̃] *nm* (a) *(animal)* young rat; **r. laveur** raccoon (b) *Fam (Maghrébin)* = racist term used to refer to a North African Arab

ratonnade [ratɔnad] *nf* = racist attack on North African Arabs

ratoureux, -euse [raturø, -øz] *Can* 1 *adj* wily, devious
2 *nm,f* shady customer

RATP [ɛratepe] *nf* (*abrév* **Régie autonome des transports parisiens**) = Parisian transport authority

rattachement [rataʃmɑ̃] *nm* (d'une région) uniting (à with)

rattacher [rataʃe] 1 *vt* (a) *(attacher de nouveau) (lacets, chien, objet)* to tie up again (à to); *(cheveux)* to put up again; **r. qch sur qch** to tie sth onto sth again (b) *(région)* to unite (à with) (c) **être rattaché à** *(faire partie de)* to be attached to (d) *(lier)* **c'était la seule chose qui nous rattachait l'un à l'autre** it was the only thing that bound us together; **c'est tout ce qui le rattache à la vie** it's the only thing keeping him alive
2 **se rattacher** *vpr* **se r. à qch** to be linked to sth

rattrapage [ratrapaʒ] *nm* **être admis au r., être admis à passer les épreuves de r.** = to be allowed to sit further oral examinations to gain a pass mark in the baccalauréat; **cours de r.** remedial class

rattraper [ratrape] 1 *vt* (a) *(prisonnier, chien)* to recapture; **se faire r. par la police** to get caught by the police (b) *(objet ou personne qui tombe)* to catch (c) *(rejoindre) (personne, voiture)* to catch up with (d) *(regagner)* **r. le temps perdu** to make up for lost time; **r. son retard** to catch up; **avoir du sommeil à r.** to have to catch up on some sleep (e) *(rétablir) (erreur)* to correct; *(situation)* to salvage
2 **se rattraper** *vpr* (a) *(se retenir)* to catch oneself in time; **se r. à qch** to catch hold of sth (b) *(se reprendre)* to stop oneself (c) *(se faire pardonner)* to make up for it (d) *(compenser son retard)* to catch up

rature [ratyr] *nf* crossing-out, deletion; **faire une r.** to make a deletion

raturer [ratyre] *vt (mot)* to cross out, to delete

rauque [rok] *adj (cri)* raucous; *(voix) (enrouée)* hoarse; *(voilée)* husky

ravagé, -e [ravaʒe] *adj* (a) *(visage)* ravaged, haggard (b) *Fam (fou)* nuts

ravager [45] [ravaʒe] *vt* to ravage, to devastate

ravages [ravaʒ] *nmpl (du feu, de la tempête)* devastation; *(d'une guerre, d'une maladie)* ravages; **faire des r.** to wreak havoc; *Fig (mode)* to be all the rage; *(jeune femme)* to break hearts

ravageur, -euse [ravaʒœr, -øz] *adj* devastating

ravalement [ravalmɑ̃] *nm* cleaning

ravaler [ravale] 1 *vt* (a) *(façade)* to clean (b) *(avaler de nouveau) (salive)* to swallow; *Fig* **faire r. ses paroles à qn** to make sb eat his/her words (c) *(cacher) (sanglot, larmes)* to choke back; *(colère, indignation, reproches)* to stifle (d) *(abaisser)* **r. qn à** to lower sb to
2 **se ravaler** *vpr* to lower oneself; *Fam* **se r. la façade** to put on the warpaint

ravaudage [ravodaʒ] *nm (de vêtements)* mending, repairing

ravauder [ravode] *vt (vêtements)* to mend, to repair

rave¹ [rav] *nf (radis)* radish; *(navet)* turnip

rave² [rɛv] *nf Fam (soirée)* rave

ravi, -e [ravi] *adj* delighted (**de** with); **je suis r. de vous voir** I'm delighted to see you; **je suis r. que ça te plaise** I'm delighted you like it; **r. de vous connaître** pleased to meet you

ravier [ravje] *nm* hors d'œuvres dish

ravigotant, -e [ravigotɑ̃, -ɑ̃t] *adj Fam* invigorating

ravigote [ravigɔt] *nf* = highly seasoned oil-and-vinegar dressing with herbs and capers

ravigoter [ravigote] *vt Fam* **r. qn** to put new life into sb

ravin [ravɛ̃] *nm* ravine

ravine [ravin] *nf* gully

raviné, -e [ravine] *adj (visage)* deeply lined

ravinement [ravinmɑ̃] *nm* gullying

raviner [ravine] *vt* to gully

ravioli [ravjɔli] *nm* piece of ravioli; **des raviolis** ravioli

ravir [ravir] *vt* (a) *(plaire)* to delight; **à r.** *(jouer, chanter)* delightfully; **belle à r.** ravishingly beautiful; **aller à r.** to suit sb beautifully (b) *Litt* **r. qch à qn** to rob sb of sth

raviser [ravize] **se raviser** *vpr* to change one's mind

ravissant, -e [ravisɑ̃, -ɑ̃t] *adj* delightful

ravissement [ravismɑ̃] *nm* (a) *(enchantement)* rapture, ecstasy; **avec r.** *(écouter, contempler)* with great delight (b) *Litt (d'une femme)* ravishing

ravisseur, -euse [ravisœr, -øz] *nm,f* abductor

ravitaillement [ravitajmɑ̃] *nm (action)* supplying (**en** with); *(marchandises)* supplies; **r. (en carburant)** refuelling

ravitailler [ravitaje] 1 *vt (personne, groupe)* to supply; *(véhicule)* to refuel
2 **se ravitailler** *vpr* to get in supplies; **se r. (en carburant)** to refuel

raviver [ravive] *vt* (a) *(feu)* to rekindle (b) *(couleur)* to brighten up (c) *(colère, souvenir, querelle)* to rekindle; *(douleur)* to revive

ravoir [ravwar] *vt* (a) *(avoir de nouveau)* to have back (b) *Fam (nettoyer)* to get clean

rayé, -e [reje] *adj* (a) *(tissu)* striped (b) *(disque, parquet, carrosserie de voiture)* scratched (c) *(canon de fusil)* rifled

rayer [53] [reje] *vt* (a) *(verre, carrosserie de voiture, disque)* to scratch (b) *(mention, mot)* to cross out; **r. qn du barreau** to strike sb off; **r. qn/le nom de qn d'une liste** to cross sb/sb's name off a list

rayon¹ [rejɔ̃] *nm* (a) *(faisceau) (de lumière)* ray, beam; **r. laser** laser beam; **r. de soleil** sunbeam; *Fig* **être le r. de soleil de qn** to be sb's ray of sunshine; **rayons X** X-rays (b) *(d'un cercle)* radius; **dans un r. de 2 kilomètres (autour de)** within a radius of 2 kilometres (of); **r. d'action** range (c) *(de roue)* spoke

rayon² *nm* (a) *(dans un magasin)* department; *Fig* **c'est mon r.** that's my department (b) *(d'une étagère)* shelf; *Fam Fig* **en connaître un r. (sur qch)** to be well clued up (about sth) (c) **r. de miel** honeycomb

rayonnage [rejonaʒ] *nm* shelving, shelves

rayonnant, -e [rejɔnɑ̃, -ɑ̃t] *adj (de chaleur, lumière)* radiant; *Fig (visage)* beaming; **r. de bonheur** radiant with happiness; **r. de santé** glowing with health

rayonne [rejɔn] *nf* rayon

rayonnement [rejɔnmɑ̃] *nm* (a) *(du soleil)* radiance (b) *(influence)* influence

rayonner [rɛjɔne] vi (a) (soleil, visage) to beam; **r. de joie** to beam with joy (b) (voyager) to travel around (from a central base) (c) (se propager) to spread its influence (d) (avenues, douleur) to radiate

rayure [rɛjyr] nf (a) (motif) stripe; **tissu à rayures** striped material (b) (sur miroir, sur carrosserie) scratch (c) (d'un canon de fusil) groove

raz de marée [radmare] nm inv tidal wave; Fig r. électoral landslide

razzia [razja] nf raid; Fam **faire une r. sur qch** to raid sth

RD [ɛrde] nf (abrév **route départementale**) secondary road

RDA [ɛrdea] nf Anciennement (abrév **République démocratique allemande**) GDR

rdc (abrév **rez-de-chaussée**) Br ground or Am first floor

RDS [ɛrdeɛs] nm (abrév **Remboursement de la Dette Sociale**) = contribution paid by every tax-payer towards the social security deficit

ré [re] nm inv (note) D; (chantée) re

réabonnement [reabɔnmɑ̃] nm subscription renewal

réabonner [reabɔne] **1** vt **r. qn** to renew sb's subscription (à to)
2 se réabonner vpr to renew one's subscription (à to)

réac [reak] adj & nmf Fam Péj reactionary

réaccoutumer [reakutyme] **1** vt to reaccustom (à to)
2 se réaccoutumer vpr se **r. à qch** to become reaccustomed to sth

réacteur [reaktœr] nm (a) (moteur) jet engine (b) **r. nucléaire** nuclear reactor

réaction [reaksjɔ̃] nf (a) (attitude) reaction; **n'avoir aucune r.** not to react; **il eut une r. de peur/de colère** his reaction was one of fear/anger; **faire qch par r.** to do sth as a reaction; **en r. à qch** in reaction to sth; **rester sans r.** not to react; **r. en chaîne** chain reaction (b) (d'un organe, du corps) reaction; **r. cutanée** skin reaction

réactionnaire [reaksjɔner] adj & nmf Péj reactionary

réactiver [reaktive] vt (feu, négociations, sentiments) to revive

réactualisation [reaktɥalizasjɔ̃] nf updating

réactualiser [reaktɥalize] vt to update

réadaptation [readaptasjɔ̃] nf rehabilitation

réadapter [readapte] **1** vt to rehabilitate
2 se réadapter vpr to readjust

réaffirmer [reafirme] vt to reaffirm

réagir [reaʒir] vi to react (à/contre to/against); **r. sur qch** to affect sth

réajuster [reaʒyste] = **rajuster**

réalisable [realizabl] adj (a) (projet, proposition) feasible; (rêve) attainable (b) (avoirs) realizable

réalisateur, -trice [realizatœr, -tris] nm,f (d'un film, d'un feuilleton) director; (d'une émission de radio ou de télévision) producer

réalisation [realizasjɔ̃] nf (a) (d'un projet) realization; (d'un rêve) fulfilment (b) (d'un film, d'un feuilleton) direction; (d'une émission de radio ou de télévision) production (c) (d'une œuvre d'art) creation

réaliser [realize] **1** vt (a) (comprendre) to realize (que that) (b) (ambition, projet) to realize; (rêve) to fulfil (c) (œuvre d'art) to create (d) (film, feuilleton) to direct; (émission de radio ou de télévision) to produce (e) (bénéfices) to make; **r. un chiffre d'affaires de 10 millions de francs** to have a turnover of 10 million francs
2 se réaliser vpr (a) (prédiction, rêve) to come true (b) (personne) to fulfil oneself

réalisme [realism] nm realism; **faire preuve de r.** to be realistic; **avec r.** realistically

réaliste [realist] **1** adj (personne, description, portrait) realistic
2 nmf realist

réalité [realite] nf reality; **c'est une r.** it's a reality; **en r.** in reality; Ordinat **r. virtuelle** virtual reality

réamorcer [16] [reamɔrse] Ordinat **1** vt to reboot
2 se réamorcer vpr to reboot

réanimation [reanimasjɔ̃] nf resuscitation; **service de r.** intensive care unit; **en r.** in intensive care

réanimer [reanime] vt to resuscitate

réapparaître [20] [reaparɛtr] vi to reappear; (douleur) to come back, to recur

réapparition [reaparisjɔ̃] nf reappearance; (d'une douleur) recurrence

réapprovisionner [reaprɔvizjɔne] **1** vt (magasin) to restock (en with); (personne) to resupply (en with)
2 se réapprovisionner vpr to stock up again (en with)

réargenter [rearʒɑ̃te] vt to resilver

réarmement [rearməmɑ̃] nm rearmament

réarmer [rearme] **1** vt (a) (région, pays) to rearm (b) (arme à feu) to recock; (appareil photo) to reset
2 vi (pays, région) to rearm

réassortir [reasɔrtir] **1** vt (magasin) to restock
2 se réassortir vpr to restock

rebaptiser [rəbatize] vt (rue) to rename

rébarbatif, -ive [rebarbatif, -iv] adj (a) (sujet, tâche) daunting; (style) off-putting (b) (visage, mine) forbidding

rebâtir [rəbatir] vt to rebuild

rebattre [11] [rəbatr] vt **r. les oreilles à qn de qch** to go on to sb about sth

rebattu, -e [rəbaty] adj (histoire, sujet) hackneyed

rebelle [rəbɛl] **1** adj (a) (personne, esprit) rebellious; (camp, armée, troupes) rebel; **r. à toute discipline** unamenable to discipline (b) (mèches, boucle) unruly (c) (fièvre) stubborn; **r. aux antibiotiques** resistant to antibiotics
2 nmf rebel

rebeller [rəbele] **se rebeller** vpr to rebel (contre against)

rébellion [rebeljɔ̃] nf rebellion

rebelote [rəbəlɔt] exclam Fam not again!

rebiffer [rəbife] **se rebiffer** vpr Fam to hit back (contre at)

rebiquer [rəbike] vi Fam (mèche) to stick up

reblochon [rəblɔʃɔ̃] nm Reblochon (type of cheese from Savoie)

reboisement [rəbwazmɑ̃] nm reafforestation

reboiser [rəbwaze] vt to reafforest

rebond [rəbɔ̃] nm (d'un ballon) bounce

rebondi, -e [rəbɔ̃di] adj (joues, personne) chubby

rebondir [rǝbɔ̃dir] vi (a) *(ballon)* to bounce; **r. contre** *ou* **sur qch** to bounce off sth (b) *Fig (affaire, crise)* to be revived; **faire r. la discussion** to get the discussion going again (c) *Can (chèque)* to bounce

rebondissement [rǝbɔ̃dismɑ̃] nm (a) *(d'un ballon)* bounce (b) *Fig (d'une affaire)* revival

rebord [rǝbɔr] nm *(d'une table, d'un puits)* edge; *(de fenêtre)* sill

reboucher [rǝbuʃe] vt (a) *(bouteille)* to recork; *(tube)* to put the top back on (b) *(trou)* to fill in again

rebours [rǝbur] **à rebours** adv the wrong way; *Fig* the wrong way round

rebouteux, -euse [rǝbutø, -øz] nm,f *Fam* bonesetter

reboutonner [rǝbutɔne] **1** vt to button up again
2 se reboutonner vpr to do oneself up again

rebrousse-poil [rǝbruspwal] **à rebrousse-poil** adv the wrong way; **prendre qn à r.** to rub sb up the wrong way

rebrousser [rǝbruse] vt **r. chemin** to turn back

rebuffade [rǝbyfad] nf rebuff; **essuyer une r.** to meet with a rebuff

rébus [rebys] nm rebus

rebut [rǝby] nm **(article de) r.** reject; **mettre qch au r.** to throw sth out

rebutant, -e [rǝbytɑ̃, -ɑ̃t] adj *(tâche, manière, personne)* off-putting

rebuter [rǝbyte] vt (a) *(décourager)* to put off (b) *(déplaire)* to disgust

récalcitrant, -e [rekalsitrɑ̃, -ɑ̃t] adj *&* nm,f recalcitrant

recaler [rǝkale] vt *Fam* to fail; **être recalé, se faire r.** to fail

récapitulatif, -ive [rekapitylatif, -iv] **1** adj recapitulatory
2 nm recapitulation

récapitulation [rekapitylasjɔ̃] nf recapitulation; **faire la r. de qch** to recapitulate sth

récapituler [rekapityle] vt *&* vi to recapitulate

recaser [rǝkaze] *Fam* **1** vt (a) *(retrouver un emploi à)* to find a new job for (b) *(retrouver un logement à)* to rehouse
2 se recaser vpr (a) *(retrouver un emploi)* to find a new job (b) *(se remarier)* to get hitched again

recel [rǝsɛl] nm receiving stolen goods

receler [39] [rǝsǝle] vt (a) *(biens volés)* to receive; *(criminel)* to harbour (b) *Litt (renfermer) (secret, trésor)* to conceal

receleur, -euse [rǝsǝlœr, -øz] nm,f receiver

récemment [resamɑ̃] adv recently

recensement [rǝsɑ̃smɑ̃] nm *(d'objets)* inventory; *(de la population)* census

recenser [rǝsɑ̃se] vt *(objets)* to make an inventory of; *(habitants)* to take a census of

récent, -e [resɑ̃, -ɑ̃t] adj recent

recentrer [rǝsɑ̃tre] vt (a) *(parti politique)* to reorientate (b) *(balle)* to centre again

récépissé [resepise] nm receipt

réceptacle [reseptakl] nm (a) *(d'objets)* receptacle (b) *(de personnes)* gathering place (b) *Ordinat* **r. pour extension** extension slot

récepteur, -trice [reseptœr, -tris] **1** adj receiving
2 nm (a) *(de téléphone)* receiver (b) *Ordinat* **r. de données** data receiver

réceptif, -ive [reseptif, -iv] adj receptive (**à** to)

réception [resɛpsjɔ̃] nf (a) *(accueil)* reception; **faire une bonne/mauvaise r. à qn** to give sb a good/poor reception (b) *(d'une lettre, d'une commande, de biens)* receipt; **à payer à la r.** cash on delivery; **r. des travaux** acceptance of work (c) *(soirée)* reception (d) *(dans un hôtel)* reception (desk) (e) *(une radio)* reception (f) *(d'un gymnaste)* landing; *(d'un joueur de football)* control

réceptionner [resɛpsjɔne] vt (a) *(marchandises livrées)* to take delivery of (b) *(ballon)* to take

réceptionniste [resɛpsjɔnist] nmf receptionist

récessif, -ive [resesif, -iv] adj recessive

récession [resɛsjɔ̃] nf recession

recette [rǝsɛt] nf (a) *(pour plat) &* *Fig* recipe (**de** for) (b) *(bureau)* tax office (c) *(gain)* recettes takings; **recettes fiscales** tax revenue; **faire r.** to be a success

recevable [rǝsǝvabl] adj *(excuse, témoignage)* admissible

receveur, -euse [rǝsǝvœr, -øz] nm,f (a) *(fonctionnaire)* **r. des contributions** tax collector; **r. des Postes** postmaster, f postmistress (b) *(de bus)* (bus) conductor, f (bus) conductress

recevoir [60] [rǝsǝvwar] **1** vt (a) *(lettre, coup de téléphone, fleurs)* to receive, to get (**de** from); **r. la visite de qn** to have a visit from sb; **r. des nouvelles de qn** to hear from sb; **je n'ai de conseils à r. de personne!** I don't need advice from anybody!; **nous avons bien reçu votre lettre** we are in receipt of your letter (b) *(blâme, gifle, coup, balle)* to get; *Fam* **qu'est-ce que j'ai reçu!** I really got it! (c) *(amis, invités)* to receive, to welcome; **être mal/bien reçu** to get a poor/good reception; **r. qn à dîner** to have sb (round) to dinner; **aimer r.** to enjoy entertaining; **savoir r.** to be a good host/hostess; **ils reçoivent très peu** they don't do much entertaining (d) *(clients)* to see; **le docteur ne reçoit que sur rendez-vous** the doctor will see patients by appointment only (e) *(proposition, projet)* to receive (f) *(élève, candidat)* to admit; **être reçu à l'Académie française** to be admitted to the Académie française; **être reçu à un examen** to pass an exam (g) *(pluie, soleil, lumière)* to get; **r. des radiations** to be exposed to radiation, to receive a dose of radiation (h) *(chaîne)* to get; *(station de radio)* to pick up, to receive (i) *(communion, absolution)* to receive
2 se recevoir vpr *(gymnaste)* to land

rechange [rǝʃɑ̃ʒ] **de rechange** adj spare; *Fig* alternative

rechaper [rǝʃape] vt *(pneu)* to retread; **pneu rechapé** retread

réchapper [reʃape] vi **r. de qch** to survive sth

recharge [rǝʃarʒ] nf (a) *(de stylo, de briquet)* refill; **r. d'encre** ink refill (b) *(action) (d'une batterie)* recharging

rechargeable [rǝʃarʒabl] adj *(briquet, vaporisateur)* refillable; *(pile)* rechargeable

recharger [45] [rǝʃarʒe] **1** vt (a) *(batterie, pile)* to recharge; *Fam* **r. ses batteries** to recharge one's batteries (b) *(camion, arme, appareil photo)* to reload (c) *(stylo, briquet, vaporisateur)* to refill
2 se recharger vpr *Ordinat* to reload

réchaud [reʃo] nm *(portable)* stove; **r. à gaz** gas ring

réchauffé, -e [reʃofe] **1** adj (a) *(plat)* reheated, warmed-up (b) *(plaisanterie)* stale
2 nm **c'est du r.** *(plaisanterie)* that's a stale joke; *(nouvelles, politique)* that's old hat

réchauffement [reʃofmã] *nm* warming up; **le r. de la planète** *ou* **de l'atmosphère** global warming

réchauffer [reʃofe] **1** *vt* (a) *(plat)* to reheat, to warm up (b) *(personne)* to warm up (c) *Fig* to rekindle; *(cœur)* to warm
  2 se réchauffer *vpr* (a) *(temps)* to get warmer (b) *(personne)* to get warm; **se r. les pieds/les mains** to warm one's feet/one's hands

rechausser [raʃose] **se rechausser** *vpr* to put one's shoes on again

rêche [rɛʃ] *adj* rough

recherche [raʃɛrʃ] *nf* (a) *(prospection, quête)* search *(de* for); *(de la célébrité, du pouvoir)* quest *(de* for), pursuit *(de* of); **être à la r. de** to be in search of (b) **recherches** *(par la police) (pour retrouver une personne disparue)* search, hunt; **faire des recherches** to make inquiries (c) *(scientifique)* research *(sur* into); **faire de la r.** to do research; **faire des recherches sur qch** to do research into sth (d) *(raffinement)* elegance; **avec r.** elegantly; **sans r.** *(style)* straightforward (e) *Ordinat* find, search; **r. et remplacement** search and replace; **r. et remplacement global** global search and replace

recherché, -e [raʃɛrʃe] *adj* (a) *(demandé) (objet)* sought-after (b) *(apprécié) (personne)* in demand (c) *(raffiné)* elegant; *(plat)* exquisite (d) *(criminel)* wanted

rechercher [raʃɛrʃe] *vt* (a) *(chercher) (personne, objet, solution)* to look for, to search for; *(emploi)* to look for; *(sens, mot)* to look up; *(faveurs, honneurs)* to seek (b) *Ordinat* **r. qch** to search *or* do a search for sth; **r. et remplacer** to search and replace; **r. vers le bas/haut** to search forwards/backwards

rechigner [raʃiɲe] *vi* *Fam* **r. à qch** to balk at sth; **faire qch en rechignant** to do sth with bad grace; **faire qch sans r.** to do sth without (making) a fuss

rechute [raʃyt] *nf* relapse; **faire une r.** to have a relapse

rechuter [raʃyte] *vi* to have a relapse

récidive [residiv] *nf* (a) *(d'un délinquant)* repeat offence (b) *(d'une maladie)* recurrence

récidiver [residive] *vi* (a) *(délinquant)* to reoffend; *Fig* to do it again (b) *(maladie)* to recur

récidiviste [residivist] *nmf* repeat offender

récif [resif] *nm* reef; **r. de corail** *ou* **corallien** coral reef

récipient [resipjã] *nm* container

réciproque [resiprɔk] **1** *adj* *(sentiments)* mutual; *(bénéfices, accord, concessions)* reciprocal; **elle ne veut plus me voir, et c'est r.** she doesn't want to see me again, and the feeling's mutual
  2 *nf* **la r.** the reverse

réciproquement [resiprɔkmã] *adv* mutually; **et r.** and vice versa

récit [resi] *nm* story; **faire le r. de qch** to give an account of sth

récital, -als [resital] *nm* recital

récitant, -e [resitã, -ãt] *nm,f* narrator

récitation [resitasjɔ̃] *nf* recitation

réciter [resite] *vt* to recite

réclamation [reklamasjɔ̃] *nf* complaint; **faire une r.** to make a complaint; **le service des réclamations, les réclamations** the complaints department

réclame [reklam] *nf* (a) *(publicité)* advertising; **faire de la r. pour qch** to advertise sth (b) *(annonce)* advertisement (c) *(promotion)* **en r.** on special offer

réclamer [reklame] **1** *vt* (a) *(demander)* to ask for; *(droit, allocation)* to claim; **la fillette réclame ses parents** the little girl is calling for her parents (b) *(exiger)* to demand; **r. des dommages et intérêts** to claim damages (c) *(nécessiter)* to require
  2 se réclamer *vpr* **se r. de qn** *(se recommander)* to mention sb's name; **se r. de qch** *(d'un parti, d'une idéologie)* to identify with sth

reclasser [rəklase] *vt* (a) *(fichiers)* to reclassify (b) *(chômeur)* to find a new job for (c) *(personnel, salaires)* to regrade

reclus, -e [rəkly, -yz] **1** *adj* cloistered
  2 *nm,f* recluse

réclusion [reklyzjɔ̃] *nf* *(peine)* imprisonment; **r. à perpétuité** life imprisonment

recoiffer [rəkwafe] **se recoiffer** *vpr* (a) *(arranger ses cheveux)* to redo one's hair (b) *(remettre son chapeau)* to put one's hat back on

recoin [rəkwɛ̃] *nm* *(d'un lieu)* nook; *(de la mémoire)* recess

reçois, reçoit, reçoive *etc voir* **recevoir**

recoller [rəkɔle] *vt* *(objet cassé)* to stick back together; *(timbre)* to stick back on; *(enveloppe)* to stick back down; *Fam* **r. les morceaux** to patch things up

récoltant, -e [rekɔltã, -ãt] **1** *adj* **apiculteur r.** honey producer; **viticulteur r.** = winegrower who harvests his own grapes
  2 *nm,f* **mis en bouteille chez le r.** estate-bottled

récolte [rekɔlt] *nf* (a) *(action)* harvesting; **faire la r.** to harvest the crops (b) *(résultat)* harvest (c) *(d'informations)* crop

récolter [rekɔlte] *vt* *(cultures)* to harvest; *Fig (renseignements, documents)* to collect

recommandable [rəkɔmãdabl] *adj* *(personne, lieu)* reputable; **peu r.** *(personne, lieu)* disreputable

recommandation [rəkɔmãdasjɔ̃] *nf* *(appui, conseil)* recommendation

recommandé, -e [rəkɔmãde] **1** *adj* (a) *(lettre)* registered (b) *(conseillé)* recommended; **ce n'est pas très r.** it's not very advisable
  2 *nm* **en r.** registered

recommander [rəkɔmãde] **1** *vt* (a) *(lieu, produit, personne)* to recommend *(à* to) (b) *(conseiller)* to advise; **r. à qn de faire qch** to advise sb to do sth; **r. la prudence à qn** to advise sb to be cautious (c) *(lettre, paquet)* to register
  2 se recommander *vpr* (a) *(demander de l'aide)* **se r. à qn** to commend oneself to sb (b) **se r. de qn** *(pour un emploi)* to give sb's name as a reference

recommencement [rəkɔmãsmã] *nm* renewal; **la vie est un éternel** *ou* **perpétuel r.** life is a constant succession of new beginnings

recommencer [16] [rəkɔmãse] **1** *vt* to start *or* begin again
  2 *vi* to start *or* begin again; **ne recommencez pas!** don't do it again!
  3 recommencer à *vt ind* **r. à faire qch** to start *or* begin to do sth again

récompense [rekɔ̃pãs] *nf* reward; *(prix)* award; **1000 francs de r.** 1,000 francs reward; **en r. (de)** as a reward (for)

récompenser [rekɔ̃pãse] *vt* to reward *(de* for); **ce film a été récompensé à Cannes** this film won an award at Cannes

recomposer [rəkɔ̃poze] *vt* *(numéro de téléphone)* to redial

recompter [rəkɔ̃te] vt to count again

réconciliation [rekɔ̃siljasjɔ̃] nf reconciliation

réconcilier [66] [rekɔ̃silje] 1 vt to reconcile (avec with); **r. qn avec la vie** to renew sb's appetite for life
  2 se réconcilier vpr to make it up (avec with)

reconductible [rəkɔ̃dyktibl] adj (contrat, bail) renewable

reconduction [rəkɔ̃dyksjɔ̃] nf (a) (d'un bail, d'un contrat) renewal; **r. tacite** (d'un accord) tacit renewal (b) (d'un budget, d'une politique, d'une grève) continuation

reconduire [18] [rəkɔ̃dɥir] vt (a) (personne) to take sb back; **r. qn (à la porte)** to show sb out; **r. qn à la frontière** to escort sb back to the border (b) (bail, contrat) to renew (c) (budget, politique, grève) to continue

réconfort [rekɔ̃fɔr] nm comfort

réconfortant, -e [rekɔ̃fɔrtɑ̃, -ɑ̃t] adj comforting

réconforter [rekɔ̃fɔrte] vt to comfort; **cela me réconforte de le savoir** I'm glad to know it

reconnaissable [rəkɔnɛsabl] adj recognizable (à by or from); **r. entre tous** unmistakable

reconnaissance [rəkɔnɛsɑ̃s] nf (a) (action de reconnaître) recognition; **en r. de qch** in recognition of sth (b) (d'un droit, d'un gouvernement) recognition; **r. de dette** IOU (c) (gratitude) gratitude (pour for); **avec r.** gratefully (d) Mil reconnaissance; **partir en r.** to go off on reconnaissance; Fam Fig to go and reconnoitre (e) Ordinat **r. de l'écriture manuscrite** handwriting recognition; **r. optique des caractères** optical character recognition, OCR; **r. de la parole, r. vocale** speech recognition

reconnaissant, -e [rəkɔnɛsɑ̃, -ɑ̃t] adj grateful; **être r. à qn de qch** to be grateful to sb for sth; **je vous serais r. de ne plus en parler** I'd be grateful if you didn't mention it again

reconnaître [20] [rəkɔnɛtr] 1 vt (a) (identifier) to recognize (à by or from); **je te reconnais bien là!** that's just like you! (b) (admettre) (vérité, droit, gouvernement) to recognize; (enfant) to acknowledge; **r. qn pour chef** to recognize sb as leader (c) (avouer) (erreur, faute) to acknowledge (d) (accorder) **je lui reconnais des qualités** I recognize her qualities (e) (position, terrain) to reconnoitre
  2 se reconnaître vpr (a) (soi-même) to recognize oneself (b) (l'un l'autre) to recognize each other (c) (s'avouer) **se r. vaincu/coupable** to acknowledge defeat/one's guilt (d) (se retrouver) to find one's way around; **je ne me reconnais plus** I can't find my way around any more (e) (être identifiable) **le mâle se reconnaît à...** the male can be recognized by...

reconnu, -e [rəkɔny] adj recognized

reconquérir [7] [rəkɔ̃kerir] vt (estime, amitié) to win back; (territoire) to reconquer

reconquête [rəkɔ̃kɛt] nf reconquest

reconsidérer [34] [rəkɔ̃sidere] vt to reconsider

reconstituant, -e [rəkɔ̃stitɥɑ̃, -ɑ̃t] adj & nm tonic

reconstituer [rəkɔ̃stitɥe] vt (a) (reformer) (armée, gouvernement) to reconstitute; (société, parti) to revive; (fortune, forces) to build up again (b) (rétablir) (objet archéologique, faits) to piece together; (bâtiment, quartier) to restore (c) (avec simulation) (crime) to reconstruct

reconstitution [rəkɔ̃stitysjɔ̃] nf (d'un crime, d'une bataille) reconstruction; **r. historique** historical reconstruction

reconstruction [rəkɔ̃stryksjɔ̃] nf reconstruction, rebuilding

reconstruire [rəkɔ̃strɥir] vt to reconstruct, to rebuild

reconversion [rəkɔ̃vɛrsjɔ̃] nf (a) (d'une usine) conversion; **r. économique** economic restructuring (b) (d'une personne) retraining

reconvertir [rəkɔ̃vɛrtir] 1 vt (a) (entreprise) to convert (b) (personne) to retrain
  2 se reconvertir vpr (personne) to retrain; **se r. dans qch** to retrain for a new career in sth

recopier [66] [rəkɔpje] vt (a) (faire un double de) to recopy (b) (mettre au propre) to copy out

record [rəkɔr] 1 nm (chiffre, vitesse) record
  2 nm record; **détenir le r. (de qch)** to hold the record (for sth); **battre le r. (de qch)** to break the record (for sth)

recordman [rəkɔrdman] (pl recordmen [rəkɔrdmɛn]) nm (men's) record holder

recordwoman [rəkɔrdwuman] (pl recordwomen [rəkɔrdwumɛn]) nf (women's) record holder

recoucher [rəkuʃe] 1 vt (personne) to put to bed again
  2 se recoucher vpr to go back to bed

recoudre [21] [rəkudr] vt (bouton) to sew back on; (déchirure, plaie) to sew or stitch up; Fam (personne) to stitch up

recoupement [rəkupmɑ̃] nm crosscheck; **faire le r.** to crosscheck; **par r.** by crosschecking

recouper [rəkupe] 1 vt (a) (couper à nouveau) (vêtement) to recut; **r. du pain** to cut some more bread; **r. une tranche de gâteau** to cut another slice of cake (b) (faire coïncider) to confirm; **r. des témoignages** to crosscheck testimony
  2 se recouper vpr (témoignages) to tally

recourbé, -e [rəkurbe] adj (bec) curved; (nez) hooked

recourber [rəkurbe] 1 vt to bend
  2 se recourber vpr to bend

recourir [22] [rəkurir] 1 vt (épreuve sportive) to run again
  2 vi (courir de nouveau) to run again
  3 recourir à vt ind (a) (personne) to turn to (b) (moyen, violence) to resort to

recours [rəkur] nm (a) (personne, chose) recourse; **en dernier r.** as a last resort; **avoir r. à qn** to turn to sb; **avoir r. à qch** to resort to sth (b) Jur **r. en cassation** appeal; Can **r. collectif** class action; **r. en grâce** petition for reprieve

recouvrement [rəkuvrəmɑ̃] nm (de dettes, d'une facture) recovery; (de l'impôt) collection

recouvrer [rəkuvre] vt (a) (biens, argent, santé) to recover; (forces, liberté, vue) to regain; (courage, enthousiasme) to get back (b) (percevoir) (dettes) to recover; (impôts) to collect

recouvrir [52] [rəkuvrir] vt (a) (couvrir de nouveau) (cahier, toit) to re-cover; (enfant) to cover up again (b) (couvrir complètement) to cover (de with) (c) (tapisser) to cover (de with) (d) (inclure) to cover

recracher [rəkraʃe] vt to spit out

récré [rekre] nf Fam Br break, Am recess; (pour les plus jeunes) playtime

récréatif, -ive [rekreatif, -iv] adj (activité) entertaining; (lecture) light

récréation [rekreasjɔ̃] nf (a) (à l'école) Br break, Am recess; (pour les plus jeunes) playtime (b) (détente) recreation

recréer [24] [rəkree] vt to re-create

récrier [66] [rekrije] **se récrier** *vpr (mécontents)* to protest (**contre** about)

récrimination [rekriminasjɔ̃] *nf* recrimination

récriminer [rekrimine] *vi* to make recriminations (**contre** against)

récrire [30] [rekrir] = **réécrire**

récriture [rekrityr] = **réécriture**

recroquevillé, -e [rəkrɔkvije] *adj* huddled up

recroqueviller [rəkrɔkvije] **se recroqueviller** *vpr (personne)* to huddle up; *(papier, feuille morte)* to shrivel up

recru, -e [rəkry] *Litt* **r. (de fatigue)** exhausted

recrudescence [rəkrydesɑ̃s] *nf* renewed outbreak

recrue [rəkry] *nf* recruit; **faire une nouvelle r.** to gain a new recruit

recrutement [rəkrytmɑ̃] *nm* recruitment

recruter [rəkryte] **1** *vt* to recruit; **r. par concours** to recruit by competition
2 se recruter *vpr* to be recruited (**parmi** from)

rectal, -e, -aux, -ales [rɛktal, -o] *adj* rectal

rectangle [rɛktɑ̃gl] *nm* rectangle

rectangulaire [rɛktɑ̃gylɛr] *adj* rectangular

recteur [rɛktœr] *nm (d'une académie) Br* director *or Am* commissioner of education

rectificatif, -ive [rɛktifikatif, -iv] **1** *adj (lettre)* of amendment; *(texte, facture)* amended
2 *nm* correction

rectification [rɛktifikasjɔ̃] *nf (d'un texte, d'un calcul, d'une erreur)* correction; *(d'une compte, d'une courbe)* adjustment; *(d'un alignement)* straightening; **faire ou apporter une r.** to make a correction

rectifier [66] [rɛktifje] *vt* (a) *(texte, calcul, erreur)* to correct; *(prix, compte, courbe)* to adjust; *(alignement)* to straighten; **r. le tir** to adjust the range; *Fig* to take a slightly different tack (b) *Fam (tuer)* to bump off

rectiligne [rɛktilin] *adj (mouvement, figure)* rectilinear; *(avenue)* straight

rectitude [rɛktityd] *nf (d'un jugement, d'un raisonnement)* soundness

recto [rɛkto] *nm* front, *Spéc* recto; **r. verso** on both sides

rectorat [rɛktɔra] *nm* ≃ *Br* local education authority, *Am* board of education

rectum [rɛktɔm] *nm* rectum

reçu¹, -e *voir* **recevoir**

reçu², -e [rəsy] **1** *nm* receipt
2 *nm,f (à un examen)* successful candidate

recueil [rəkœj] *nm (de poèmes, de chansons, de recettes)* collection; *(de lois)* body; **r. de morceaux choisis** anthology

recueillement [rəkœjmɑ̃] *nm* meditation; **avec r.** meditatively

recueilli, -e [rəkœji] *adj* meditative

recueillir [5] [rəkœjir] **1** *vt* (a) *(argent, renseignements)* to collect (b) *(votes)* to win; *Fig* **r. le fruit de qch** to reap the fruit of sth (c) *(personne, animal)* to take in (d) *(miel)* to gather (e) *Jur* **r. un héritage** to inherit
2 se recueillir *vpr* to meditate; **se r. pour prier** to gather one's thoughts before praying

recuire [18] [rəkɥir] *vt (plat)* to cook longer

recul [rəkyl] *nm* (a) *(mouvement) (d'un glacier, d'une armée)* retreat; *(d'un canon)* recoil; **avoir un mouvement de r.** to recoil (b) *(déclin)* decline (c) *(baisse)* decline (**de in**) (d) *(espace nécessaire)* room to move back (e) *Fig (distance)* **considérer qch avec du r.** to consider sth with detachment; **manquer de r.** to be too closely involved; **prendre du r.** to stand back from things

reculade [rəkylad] *nf (d'une armée)* retreat; *Fig & Péj* climbdown

reculé, -e [rəkyle] *adj (endroit, époque)* remote

reculer [rəkyle] **1** *vi* (a) *(aller en arrière) (personne)* to move back; *(automobiliste, voiture)* to reverse; *(troupes)* to retreat; *(glacier, eaux)* to recede; **faire r. la foule** to move the crowd back (b) *(régresser) (épidémie)* to lose ground; *(chômage)* to decline; *Fig* **faire r. la maladie** to bring the disease under control (c) *(renoncer)* to retreat (**devant** in the face of); **il ne recule devant rien** nothing daunts him; **faire r. qn** to put sb off; **il est trop tard pour r.** it's too late to pull out; **c'est à r. pour mieux sauter** it's just putting off the evil day
2 *vt* (a) *(meuble)* to move back; *(voiture)* to reverse (b) *(paiement, décision)* to postpone

reculons [rəkylɔ̃] **à reculons** *adv* backwards

récupérable [rekyperabl] *adj (déchets)* salvageable; **les heures supplémentaires sont récupérables** additional time off may be taken in lieu

récupération [rekyperasjɔ̃] *nf* (a) *(d'une somme d'argent, d'un objet)* recovery; **la r. des heures supplémentaires** time off in lieu; **temps de r.** *(d'un sportif)* recovery time (b) *(de déchets)* salvage (c) *(d'un parti, d'une pensée)* exploitation

récupérer [34] [rekypere] *vt* (a) *(objet prêté ou pendu)* to get back, to recover; *Ordinat (fichier, données)* to retrieve (b) *(passer prendre) (personne, affaires, objet)* to collect; *(bagages)* to retrieve, to reclaim (c) *(retrouver) (forces)* to recover (d) *(recycler)* to salvage (e) *(détourner à son profit) (mouvement, idée)* to exploit (f) **r. des heures supplémentaires** to take time off in lieu

récurer [rekyre] *vt* to scour; **poudre/tampon à r.** scouring powder/pad

récurrent, -e [rekyrɑ̃, -ɑ̃t] *adj* recurring; *Ordinat* **processus r.** recursive process

récusable [rekyzabl] *adj (témoignage)* impugnable

récuser [rekyze] **1** *vt* to challenge
2 se récuser *vpr* to decline to give an opinion

recyclable [rəsiklabl] *adj* recyclable

recyclage [rəsiklaʒ] *nm* (a) *(de matériaux)* recycling (b) *(d'une personne)* retraining

recycler [rəsikle] **1** *vt* (a) *(matériaux)* to recycle (b) *(personne)* to retrain
2 se recycler *vpr (personne)* to retrain

rédacteur, -trice [redaktœr, -tris] *nm,f (d'un journal, d'un dictionnaire)* editor; **r. en chef** editor in chief

rédaction [redaksjɔ̃] *nf* (a) *(d'un texte)* writing (b) *(poste)* editorship; *(personnel)* editorial staff; *(département)* editorial department; *(salle de)* **r.** editorial office (c) *Scol* essay, composition

rédactionnel, -elle [redaksjɔnɛl] *adj* editorial

reddition [redisjɔ̃] *nf* surrender

redécouvrir [52] [rədekuvrir] *vt (auteur, œuvre)* to rediscover

redéfinir [rədefinir] *vt Ordinat (touche)* to redefine

redemander [rədəmɑ̃de] *vt* (*a*) (*en reposant une question*) to ask again; r. de l'aide à qn to ask sb again for help (b) (*pour en avoir plus*) r. du pain/des timbres to ask for more bread/stamps; r. un litre/un kilo de qch to ask for another litre/kilo of sth; des gens comme ça, on en redemande there aren't enough people like that in the world; *Ironique* il en redemande he's still asking for it (c) (*pour récupérer*) r. qch to ask for sth back

redémarrer [rademare] *vi* (*voiture*) to start again; (*économie, ventes*) to take off again; *Ordinat* to reboot; faire r. une voiture to start a car again

rédemption [redɑ̃psjɔ̃] *nf* redemption

redéploiement [rədeplwamɑ̃] *nm* redeployment

redescendre [rədesɑ̃dr, rədɛ-] **1** *vi* (*en s'approchant*) to come back down; (*en s'éloignant*) to go back down; r. de voiture to get back out of the car
  2 *vt* (*a*) (*apporter*) to bring back down; (*emporter*) to take back down (b) (*escalier, rivière*) to go/come back down

redevable [rədəvabl] *adj* être r. de qch à qn to be indebted to sb for sth; je vous suis r. de 100 francs I owe you 100 francs

redevance [rədəvɑ̃s] *nf* (*pour la télévision*) licence fee

redevenir [70] [rədəvənir] *vi* to become again; r. silencieux to fall silent again; r. normal to get back to normal

rédhibitoire [redibitwar] *adj* (*prix*) prohibitive; (*conditions, salaire*) unacceptable

rediffuser [rədifyze] *vt* (*émission*) to repeat; (*film*) to show again

rediffusion [rədifyzjɔ̃] *nf* (*d'une émission*) repeat; (*d'un film*) rerun

rédiger [45] [rediʒe] *vt* (*contrat*) to draw up; (*article, lettre*) to write; (*ordonnance*) to write out; savoir r. to write well; être bien/mal rédigé to be well/badly written

redingote [rədɛ̃gɔt] *nf* (*a*) (*manteau cintré*) fitted coat (b) (*manteau à basques*) frock coat

redire [27a] [rədir] **1** *vt* (*a*) (*répéter*) to say again, to repeat; pourrais-tu lui r. que...? could you tell him again that...?; on ne le redira jamais assez it can never be said often enough (b) (*révéler*) to repeat (à to)
  2 *vi* (*a*) *vt ind* avoir *ou* trouver à r. à qch to find fault with sth; il n'y a rien à r. à cela there's nothing wrong with that

redite [rədit] *nf* (useless) repetition

redondance [rədɔ̃dɑ̃s] *nf aussi Ordinat* redundancy; redondances redundancy

redondant, -e [rədɔ̃dɑ̃, -ɑ̃t] *adj* redundant

redonner [rədɔne] *vt* (*a*) (*donner davantage de*) redonne-lui de la soupe give him some more soup (b) (*rendre*) to give back; r. de l'appétit/du courage à qn to restore sb's appetite/courage; r. envie à qn de faire qch to make sb want to do sth again; r. des forces à qn to give sb back his/her strength (c) (*donner de nouveau*) to give again

redorer [rədɔre] *vt* to regild; *Fig* r. son blason to restore one's reputation

redoublant, -e [rədublɑ̃, -ɑ̃t] *nm,f* (*élève*) pupil repeating a year

redoublé, -e [rəduble] *adj* frapper à coups redoublés to knock harder

redoublement [rədubləmɑ̃] *nm* (*a*) (*de douleur, de joie, de prudence*) increase (b) (*d'une syllabe*) reduplication (c) *Scol* = repeating of a year; le professeur principal décidera des redoublements the head teacher will decide who will have to repeat the year

redoubler [rəduble] **1** *vt* (*a*) (*douleur, joie, prudence*) to increase; (*efforts*) to redouble (b) *Scol* r. une classe to repeat a year
  2 *vi* (*a*) *Scol* to repeat a year (b) (*sentiment*) to intensify
  3 redoubler de *vt ind* r. de violence (*orage, vent*) to become more and more severe; r. d'efforts to redouble one's efforts; r. de prudence/d'attention/de douceur to be twice as cautious/attentive/gentle

redoutable [rədutabl] *adj* (*adversaire, arme*) formidable; (*maladie*) dreadful

redouter [rədute] *vt* to dread; r. de faire qch to dread doing sth; je redoute qu'il ne soit déjà trop tard I'm afraid it's already too late

redoux [rədu] *nm* milder weather

redressement [rədrɛsmɑ̃] *nm* (*a*) (*économique, financier*) recovery (b) (*correction*) r. fiscal tax adjustment

redresser [rədrese] **1** *vt* (*a*) (*objet penché*) to put up straight; r. la tête to hold up one's head; (*la lever*) to raise one's head (b) (*rectifier*) (*erreur, situation*) to rectify; (*économie, entreprise*) to put back on its feet (c) (*bois courbé, tôle cabossée*) to straighten (out)
  2 *vi* (*automobiliste*) to straighten up
  3 se redresser *vpr* (*a*) (*personne*) to straighten up (b) (*économie, pays, ventes*) to recover

redresseur [rədrɛsœr] *nm* r. de torts righter of wrongs

réducteur, -trice [redyktœr, -tris] *adj* (*simpliste*) simplistic

réduction [redyksjɔ̃] *nf* (*a*) (*des prix, des dépenses, de la production*) reduction (de in) (b) (*rabais*) reduction; faire une r. de 600 francs (à qn) to give (sb) a reduction of 600 francs (c) (*reproduction*) small reproduction (d) (*d'une fracture*) setting

réduire [18] [redɥir] **1** *vt* (*a*) (*diminuer*) to reduce (de by); (*texte*) to shorten, to cut; réduit de moitié half size (b) (*transformer*) r. qch en qch to reduce sth to sth (c) (*contraindre*) r. qn à qch (*misère, désespoir*) to reduce sb to sth; en être réduit à faire qch to be reduced to doing sth (d) (*fracture*) to set (e) (*photographie, dessin*) to reduce
  2 *vi* (*sauce*) to reduce; faire r. qch to reduce sth
  3 se réduire *vpr* (*a*) se r. à (*se ramener à*) to come down to (b) se r. en (*se transformer en*) to be reduced to

réduit [redɥi] *nm* (*pièce*) small room

rééchelonnement [reeʃəlɔnmɑ̃] *nm* rescheduling

rééchelonner [reeʃəlɔne] *vt* to reschedule

réécrire [30] [reekrir] *vt* to rewrite

réécriture [reekrityr] *nf* rewriting

rééditer [reedite] *vt* (*a*) (*ouvrage*) to reissue (b) (*fait*) to repeat

réédition [reedisjɔ̃] *nf* (*a*) (*d'un ouvrage*) reissue (b) (*d'un fait*) repeat

rééducation [reedykasjɔ̃] *nf* (*a*) (*d'une partie du corps*) re-education; (*d'un handicapé, d'un accidenté*) rehabilitation; faire de la r. (*chez un kinésithérapeute*) to have physiotherapy (b) (*de délinquants*) rehabilitation

rééduquer [reedyke] *vt* (*handicapé, accidenté, délinquant*) to rehabilitate; (*partie du corps*) to re-educate

réel, -elle [reɛl] **1** *adj* real
  2 *nm* (*a*) (*nombre*) real number (b) le r. (*la réalité*) reality

réélection [reeleksjɔ̃] *nf* re-election

réélire [44] [reelir] *vt* to re-elect

réellement [reelmɑ̃] *adv* really

réembaucher [reɑ̃boʃe] *vt* to take on again

rééquilibrage [reekilibraʒ] *nm (de pneus)* balancing; *Fig* le r. du budget balancing the budget again

rééquilibrer [reekilibre] *vt (pneus)* to balance; *Fig (budget)* to balance again

réessayer [53] [reeseje] **1** *vt* to try again; *(vêtement)* to try on again
2 *vi* to try again

réévaluer [reevalɥe] *vt (monnaie)* to revalue; *(prix)* to reassess

réexamen [reegzamɛ̃] *nm* re-examination; *(d'une décision)* reconsideration

réexaminer [reegzamine] *vt* to re-examine; *(décision)* to reconsider

réexpédier [66] [reekspedje] *vt (a) (à une autre adresse)* to send on, to forward *(b) (à l'expéditeur)* to send back, to return

réexpédition [reekspedisjɔ̃] *nf (a) (à une autre adresse)* forwarding *(b) (à l'expéditeur)* return

refaire [36] [rəfɛr] **1** *vt (a) (faire à nouveau) (travail)* to do again, to redo; *(voyage)* to make again; **r. du riz** to make some more rice; **r. ses lacets** to tie one's laces again; *Hum* **ton éducation est à r.** where were you brought up?; **et si c'était à r.?** and if you had to do it again?; **r. le monde** to put the world to rights; **r. sa vie** to make a new life for oneself *(b) (remettre en état) (pièce, appartement)* to do up; **la peinture de qch** to repaint sth; **r. la moquette de qch** to recarpet sth; **r. qch à neuf** *(moteur)* to recondition sth; *(appartement)* to renovate sth completely *(c) Fam (duper)* to take in; **je me suis fait r. de 100 francs** I was done out of 100 francs
2 se refaire *vpr (a) (se changer)* to change the way one is; **on ne se refait pas** you can't change the way you are *(b) (se rétablir)* **se r. une santé** to recover *(c) Fam (financièrement)* to recoup one's losses *(d) (s'habituer)* **se r. à qch** to get used to sth again

réfection [refɛksjɔ̃] *nf* repair

réfectoire [refɛktwar] *nm* refectory, dining hall

référence [referɑ̃s] *nf (a) (renvoi)* reference (à to); **faire r. à qch** to refer to sth; **en r. à** with reference to *(b) (sur une lettre, sur un document)* reference; **r. à rappeler** please quote reference *(c) (d'employeur)* **références** references

référencer [16] [referɑ̃se] *vt Ordinat* to reference

référendum [referɛ̃dɔm] *nm* referendum; **faire un r.** to hold a referendum

référer [34] [refere] **1 référer à** *vt ind* **en r. à qn** to refer the matter to sb
2 se référer *vpr* **se r. à qch** to refer to sth; **se r. à un auteur** to refer to an author

refermer [rəfɛrme] **1** *vt* to shut or close again
2 se refermer *vpr (porte)* to close or shut again; *(fleur, blessure)* to close up

refiler [rəfile] *vt Fam* **r. qch à qn** *(pour s'en débarrasser)* to palm sth off on sb; *(maladie)* to give sb sth

réfléchi, -e [refleʃi] *adj (a) (personne)* thoughtful *(b) (action, opinion)* considered; **c'est tout r.** I've made up my mind; **tout bien r.** all things considered *(c) (verbe, pronom)* reflexive

réfléchir [refleʃir] **1** *vt (a) (image, lumière, son)* to reflect *(b)* **r. que** to realize that
2 *vi* to think (**à** ou **sur** about); **je réfléchis** I'm thinking; *(avant de décider)* I'm thinking about it; **sans r.** without thinking
3 se réfléchir *vpr* to be reflected

réfléchissant, -e [refleʃisɑ̃, -ɑ̃t] *adj* reflective

réflecteur, -trice [reflɛktœr, -tris] *adj* reflecting

reflet [rəflɛ] *nm (a) (dans un miroir, dans l'eau)* reflection; *(d'un tissu)* sheen; *(de la lune)* glint; **reflets** *(de cheveux)* highlights *(b) Fig (image)* reflection; **être le r. de qn** to be exactly like sb; **être le r. d'une époque** to symbolize an era

refléter [34] [rəflete] **1** *vt aussi Fig* to reflect
2 se refléter *vpr aussi Fig* to be reflected

refleurir [rəflœrir] **1** *vi* to flower again; *Fig* to flourish again
2 *vt (tombe)* to put fresh flowers on

réflexe [reflɛks] **1** *adj* reflex
2 *nm* reflex; **avoir de bons réflexes** to have good reflexes; **devenir un r.** to become automatic; **avoir le r. de faire qch** to do sth instinctively; **r. conditionné** conditioned reflex

réflexion [reflɛksjɔ̃] *nf (a) (d'une image, de la lumière, du son)* reflection *(b) (pensée)* reflection, thought; **r. faite, à la r.** on reflection, on second thoughts *(c) (remarque)* remark; **faire une r. à qn** to make a remark to sb

refluer [rəflɥe] *vi (liquide)* to flow back; *(marée)* to ebb; *(foule)* to surge back

reflux [rəfly] *nm (de la marée)* ebb; *(d'une foule)* backward surge

refondre [rəfɔ̃dr] *vt (ouvrage)* to revise

refonte [rəfɔ̃t] *nf (d'un ouvrage)* revision

reformater [rəfɔrmate] *vt Ordinat (page, disque)* to reformat

réformateur, -trice [reformatœr, -tris] **1** *adj* reforming
2 *nm,f* reformer

réforme [reform] *nf* reform; *Hist* **la R.** the Reformation

réformé, -e [reforme] **1** *adj (protestant)* Protestant
2 *nm,f (recrue)* recruit rejected as unfit; *(soldat)* soldier discharged as unfit

reformer [rəfɔrme] **1** *vt* to re-form; **r. les rangs** to fall into line again
2 se reformer *vpr* to re-form

réformer [reforme] *vt (a) (abus, loi)* to reform *(b) (recrue)* to reject as unfit; *(soldat)* to discharge as unfit

réformisme [reformism] *nm* reformism

réformiste [reformist] *adj & nmf* reformist

reformuler [rəfɔrmyle] *vt* to reformulate

refoulé, -e [rəfule] *adj* repressed

refouler [rəfule] **1** *vt (a) (faire reculer) (foule)* to drive or force back; *(étranger)* to turn away *(b) (sentiments, colère, souvenir)* to repress; *(larmes)* to hold back
2 vi l'évier refoule the water's coming up through the plughole in the sink

réfractaire [refraktɛr] *adj (a) (rebelle)* insubordinate; **r. à** *(loi, conseils, proposition)* unwilling to accept *(b) (brique, argile)* fireproof *(c) (prêtre)* non-juring

réfraction [refraksjɔ̃] *nf* refraction

refrain [rəfrɛ̃] *nm (d'une chanson)* chorus, refrain; *Fam* **c'est toujours le même r.** it's always the same old story

refréner [rəfrene], **réfréner** [refrene] [34] *vt* to curb

réfrigérant, -e [refriʒerɑ̃, -ɑ̃t] *adj* (a) *(appareil, produit)* refrigerating (b) *Fam (accueil, personne)* frosty

réfrigérateur [refriʒeratœr] *nm* refrigerator

réfrigération [refriʒerasjɔ̃] *nf* refrigeration

réfrigéré, -e [refriʒere] *adj* (a) *(wagon)* refrigerated (b) *Fam (personne)* frozen

réfrigérer [34] [refriʒere] *vt (aliment, boisson)* to refrigerate

refroidir [rafrwadir] **1** *vt* (a) *(eau)* to cool (down) (b) *Fig (amitié)* to cool; *(enthousiasme)* to dampen; *Fam* **sa réaction m'a refroidi** her reaction dampened my enthusiasm (c) *très Fam (tuer)* to bump off
2 *vi* (a) *(devenir froid)* to get cold; *(devenir moins chaud)* to cool down; **laisser r. qch** *(volontairement)* to let sth cool down; *(par négligence)* to let sth get cold (b) *(temps)* to get colder
3 se refroidir *vpr* (a) *(temps)* to get colder (b) *Fig (amitié, relations)* to cool (c) *(prendre froid)* to catch a chill

refroidissement [rafrwadismɑ̃] *nm* (a) *(de la température)* drop in temperature; *(de l'eau)* cooling (b) *(indisposition)* chill (c) *Fig (dans une amitié, dans des relations)* cooling off

refuge [rafyʒ] **1** *nm* (a) *(lieu)* & *Fig* refuge; **trouver/ chercher r.** *(auprès de qn)* to find/seek refuge (with sb) (b) *(en montagne)* (mountain) hut (c) *(sur la route)* traffic island
2 *adj* **valeur r.** safe investment

réfugié, -e [refyʒje] *nm,f* refugee

réfugier [66] [refyʒje] **se réfugier** *vpr* to take refuge (dans in)

refus [rafy] *nm (d'une invitation, d'une offre)* refusal; *(d'une proposition, d'un candidat, d'un manuscrit)* rejection; **essuyer un r.** to meet with a refusal; **opposer un r. à qn/qch** to turn sb/sth down; *Fam* **ce n'est pas de r.** I won't say no; **r. de priorité** *(infraction)* failure *Br* to give way or *Am* to yield

refuser [rafyze] **1** *vt* (a) *(offre, invitation, demande)* to refuse, to turn down; *(proposition, marchandises, manuscrit)* to reject; **r. qch à qn** to refuse sb sth (b) *(clients, spectateurs)* to turn away (c) *(candidat)* **être refusé** to fail
2 *vi* to refuse; **r. de faire qch** to refuse to do sth
3 se refuser (a) *(être rejeté)* **une offre pareille, ça ne se refuse pas** you can't refuse an offer like that (b) **se r. qch** *(se priver de)* to deny oneself sth; **ne rien se r.** not to stint oneself (c) *(résister)* **se r. à l'évidence** to shut one's eyes to the facts; **se r. à tout commentaire** to refuse to comment; **se r. à faire qch** to refuse to do sth

réfuter [refyte] *vt* to refute

regagner [rəgaɲe] *vt* (a) *(confiance, affection, estime)* to regain, to get back (b) *(argent perdu)* to win back; **r. le temps perdu** to make up for lost time (c) *(terrain)* **r. du terrain** *(reprendre l'avantage)* to make up lost ground (d) *(endroit)* to get back to; **r. son foyer** to get back home

regain [rəgɛ̃] *nm (d'intérêt, d'activité)* renewal; **un r. d'espoir** renewed hope

régal, -als [regal] *nm* treat

régalade [regalad] *nf* **boire à la r.** to drink without letting the bottle touch one's lips

régaler [regale] **1** *vt* **r. qn** to give sb a delicious meal
2 *vi Fam* **c'est moi qui régale** (it's) my treat
3 se régaler *vpr* **je me régale** *(en mangeant)* I'm really enjoying it; *(je m'amuse)* I'm having a great time

regard [rəgar] *nm* (a) *(coup d'œil)* look; **porter son r. sur qn/qch** to look at sb/sth; **jeter** *ou* **lancer un r. à qn** to glance at sb; **jeter un r. à** *ou* **sur qch** to glance at sth; **lancer un r. furieux à qn** to glare at sb; **chercher qn/ qch du r.** to look round for sb/sth; **interroger qn du r.** to give sb a questioning look; **soustraire qn/qch aux regards (b)** to keep sb/sth hidden (from sb); **attirer le r.** to attract attention; **sous les regards de la foule** while the crowd looked on; *Fig* **porter un nouveau r./ un r. critique sur qch** to take a fresh look/a critical look at sth (b) *(expression)* look (c) *(ouverture) (d'une porte)* peephole; *(d'un égout)* manhole (d) *(locutions)* **au r. de la loi** in the eyes of the law; **en r.** *(en face)* opposite

regardant, -e [rəgardɑ̃, -ɑ̃t] *adj* (a) *Fam (avare)* careful with money (b) *(exigeant)* particular *(sur* about)

regarder [rəgarde] **1** *vt* (a) *(personne, objet)* to look at; *(émission, film)* to watch; **r. qn droit dans les yeux** to look sb in the eye; **r. qn fixement** to stare at sb; **r. qn faire qch** to watch sb do sth; **regarde où tu marches!** watch where you're going!; *Fam* **non, mais tu ne m'as pas regardé!** what do you take me for? (b) *(considérer)* to regard, to consider *(comme* as); **r. qch en face** to face up to sth; **r. les choses telles qu'elles sont** to see things as they are (c) *(concerner)* to concern; **cela ne regarde que moi** that's nobody's business but mine; **cela ne vous regarde pas** that's none of your business
2 *vi* (a) *(observer)* to look; **r. autour de soi/en bas/en arrière** to look round/down/back; **r. par** *ou* **à la fenêtre** *(du dedans)* to look out of the window; *(du dehors)* to look in through the window (b) *(être orienté)* **r. sur** *ou* **vers** *(jardin, rue)* to look onto
3 regarder à *vt ind* to pay attention to; **r. à la dépense** to be careful with one's money; **y r. à deux fois avant de faire qch** to think twice before doing sth; **y r. de près** to look at it closely
4 se regarder *vpr* (a) *(soi-même)* to look at oneself; *Fam* **elle ne s'est pas regardée!** she can talk! (b) *(l'un l'autre)* to look at each other; **se r. dans les yeux** to look into each other's eyes (c) *(se faire face)* to face each other

regarnir [rəgarnir] *vt (garde-manger, étagères)* to restock

régate [regat] *nf* regatta

régence [reʒɑ̃s] **1** *adj inv* **style R.** Regency style
2 *nf* regency; *Hist* **la R.** the Regency

régénération [reʒenerasjɔ̃] *nf* (a) *(d'une cellule, de la peau)* regeneration (b) *Ordinat* **r. de l'écran** screen refresh

régénérer [34] [reʒenere] **1** *vt* to regenerate
2 se régénérer *vpr* to regenerate

régent, -e [reʒɑ̃, -ɑ̃t] *nm,f* (a) *(chef du gouvernement)* regent (b) *Belg Scol* (secondary) schoolteacher

régenter [reʒɑ̃te] *vt* **vouloir tout r.** to want to run the whole show

reggae [rege] **1** *adj inv* reggae **2** *nm* **le r.** reggae

régie [reʒi] *nf* (a) *(entreprise publique)* state-controlled company (b) *Cin* & *TV (organisation)* production management (c) *TV (local)* control room

regimber [rəʒɛ̃be] *vi (personne)* to balk *(contre* at); **il est inutile de r.** it's no use protesting

régime [reʒim] *nm* (a) **r. (alimentaire)** diet; **être au r.** to be on a diet; **faire** *ou* **suivre un r.** to diet; **se mettre au r.** to go on a diet; **r. amincissant** slimming diet (b) *(forme de gouvernement)* government, regime (c) *(pénitentiaire, hospitalier)* system; *(de retraite)* scheme; **r. matrimonial** marriage settlement; **r. de Sécurité sociale** = division of social security system applying to some professional groups (d) *(d'un moteur)* speed; **r. de**

croisière cruising speed; *Fig* **à ce r.** at this rate (**e**) (*d'une rivière, d'un fleuve*) rate of flow (**f**) (*de bananes, de dattes*) bunch

régiment [reʒimā] *nm* (*unité militaire*) regiment; *Fig* (*d'admirateurs, de créanciers*) host; *Fam* **il y en a pour un r.** there's enough for a whole army

région [reʒjɔ̃] *nf* area, region; **la r. parisienne** the Paris area or region; **la R.** = administrative area comprising several "départements"

régional, -e, -aux, -ales [reʒjɔnal, -o] *adj* regional

régionalisme [reʒjɔnalism] *nm* regionalism

régir [reʒir] *vt* (**a**) (*déterminer*) to govern (**b**) (*domaine*) to manage

régisseur [reʒisœr] *nm* (**a**) (*d'un domaine*) manager (**b**) *Cin & TV* assistant production manager; *Th* stage manager

registre [reʒistr] *nm* (**a**) (*livre*) register; (*de comptabilité*) account book; **r. du commerce** trade register; **r. de l'état civil** register of births, marriages and deaths (**b**) (*d'une voix, d'un instrument*) register (**c**) *Ordinat* register; **r. d'accès mémoire** memory access register (**d**) (*d'une œuvre*) style

réglable [reglabl] *adj* adjustable

réglage [reglaʒ] *nm* (**a**) (*d'un siège, d'un appareil*) adjustment; **r. automatique** automatic control (**b**) (*d'une radio, d'une télévision*) tuning; **r. du contraste** contrast control

règle [regl] *nf* (**a**) (*de conduite, de grammaire*) rule; *Fig* **la r. du jeu** the rules of the game; **en r.** (*passeport, papiers*) in order; **en r. générale** as a general rule; **dans** *ou* **selon les règles de l'art** according to the book, by a golden rule; **r. de trois** rule of three (**b**) (*pour tracer des lignes*) ruler (**c**) *Ordinat* (*sur écran*) ruler line (**d**) **règles** (*menstruation*) period; **avoir ses règles** to have one's period

réglé, -e [regle] *adj* (**a**) (*papier*) ruled (**b**) (*organisé*) well-ordered (**c**) (*résolu*) **c'est r.** it's settled (**d**) (*jeune fille*) who has started having periods

règlement [regləmā] *nm* (**a**) (*résolution*) settlement; **en cours de r.** being settled; **r. à l'amiable** amicable settlement; **r. de comptes** settling of scores (**b**) (*paiement*) payment; **pour r. de tout compte** in full settlement (**c**) (*règle*) regulations; **r. intérieur** (*d'une école*) school rules; (*d'un bureau*) company rules; **c'est le r.** that's the rule

réglementaire [regləmāter] *adj* (*tenue*) regulation; **faire qch dans le temps r.** to do sth in the time allowed

réglementation [regləmātasjɔ̃] *nf* (**a**) (*action*) regulation (**b**) (*ensemble de lois*) regulations; **la r. du travail** labour legislation

réglementer [regləmāte] *vt* to regulate

régler [regle] **1** *vt* (**a**) (*mécanisme, appareil, image*) to adjust; (*radio, moteur*) to tune (**b**) (*journée, emploi du temps*) to plan (**c**) **r. qch sur qch** (*conduite*) to model sth on sth; (*pas*) to adjust sth to sth (**d**) (*résoudre*) (*question, dispute*) to settle; **r. ses affaires** to put one's affairs in order; **r. qch à l'amiable** to settle sth out of court (**e**) (*payer*) (*facture*) to settle, to pay; (*employé, commerçant, loyer*) to pay; (*achats*) to pay for
2 *vi* to pay
3 se régler *vpr* (**a**) **se r. sur qn** to model oneself on sb (**b**) (*se conclure*) to be settled

réglette [reglet] *nf* small ruler; *Ordinat* **r. de clavier** key strip

réglisse [reglis] *nf* liquorice

réglo [reglo] *adj inv Fam* on the level

régnant, -e [renā, -āt] *adj* (*prince, famille*) reigning; (*idéologie, opinion*) prevailing

règne [reɲ] *nm* (**a**) (*d'un souverain*) reign; *Fig* (*de l'argent, de la technologie*) rule (**b**) (*végétal, animal*) kingdom

régner [reɲe] *vi* (**a**) (*souverain*) to reign, to rule (**sur** over); **r. en maître sur qch** to reign supreme over sth (**b**) (*exister, prévaloir*) to prevail; (*silence, atmosphère*) to reign; **faire r. la paix/l'ordre** to keep the peace/law and order; *Ironique* **la confiance règne!** there's confidence for you!

regonfler [rəgɔ̃fle] *vt* (*ballon, pneu*) to blow up again, to reinflate

regorger [rəgɔrʒe] *vi* **r. de qch** to be overflowing with sth; **r. de monde** to be packed with people

régresser [regrese] *vi* (**a**) (*criminalité, idéologie, production*) to decline (**b**) (*personne*) to regress

régression [regresjɔ̃] *nf* (**a**) (*de la criminalité, d'une idéologie, de la production*) decline; **être en r.** to be on the decline (**b**) (*d'une personne*) regression; **être en r.** to be regressing

regret [rəgre] *nm* regret (**de** for); **avoir des regrets** to have regrets; **à r.** with regret; **j'ai le r.** *ou* **je suis au r. de vous annoncer que...** I regret to tell you that...; **à mon (grand) r.** (much) to my regret

regrettable [rəgretabl] *adj* regrettable

regretter [rəgrete] *vt* (*avoir des remords sur*) to regret; **je ne regrette rien** I have no regrets; **il me ferait presque r. ma gentillesse** I'm almost sorry I was so kind to him; **r. de faire qch** to regret to do sth; **r. d'avoir fait qch** to regret having done sth; **r. que** + *subjunctive* to be sorry that; **il est à r. que...** it is to be regretted that...; **je regrette!** I'm sorry! (**b**) (*personne, endroit*) to miss; **r. sa jeunesse/son enfance** to wish one was young/a child again

regroupement [rəgrupmā] *nm* (**a**) (*action*) grouping; (*d'animaux, d'enfants*) round-up; (*de sociétés*) amalgamation; *Mil* regrouping; **r. familial** keeping immigrant families together (**b**) (*groupe*) grouping

regrouper [rəgrupe] **1** *vt* (**a**) (*personnes, objets*) to gather together; (*animaux, enfants*) to round up (**b**) (*sociétés*) to amalgamate
2 se regrouper *vpr* (**a**) (*personnes*) to gather together (**b**) (*sociétés*) to amalgamate

régularisation [regylarizasjɔ̃] *nf* (**a**) (*d'une situation*) regularization; (*d'un compte*) adjustment (**b**) (*d'un fleuve, d'un fonctionnement, de la circulation*) regulation

régulariser [regylarize] *vt* (**a**) (*situation*) to regularize; (*compte*) to adjust; **ils ont régularisé la situation** (*ils se sont mariés*) they made it official (**b**) (*fleuve, fonctionnement, circulation*) to regulate

régularité [regylarite] *nf* (**a**) (*exactitude*) regularity (**b**) (*constance*) steadiness (**c**) (*d'une décision, d'une situation*) legality

régulateur, -trice [regylatœr, -tris] **1** *adj* regulating
2 *nm* regulator

régulation [regylasjɔ̃] *nf* control; **r. des naissances** birth control

régulier, -ère [regylje, -er] **1** *adj* (**a**) (*à intervalles fixes*) regular (**b**) (*constant*) steady; (*travail, résultats*) consistent (**c**) (*écriture, ligne, couche*) even; (*traits du visage*) regular (**d**) (*légal*) (*situation*) legitimate; **être en situation régulière** to have one's papers in order (**e**) *Gram* regular (**f**) *Fam* (*honnête*) on the level (**g**) (*clergé*) regular
2 *nf* **régulière** *Fam Hum* (*femme*) steady

régulièrement [regyljɛrmɑ̃] *adv* (a) *(à intervalles fixes)* regularly (b) *(avec constance)* steadily (c) *(réparti, étalé)* evenly (d) *(selon la loi)* legitimately

régurgiter [regyrʒite] *vt (nourriture)* to regurgitate

réhabilitation [reabilitasjɔ̃] *nf* rehabilitation

réhabiliter [reabilite] **1** *vt* (a) *(délinquant)* to rehabilitate (b) *(personne accusée)* to clear (c) *(bâtiment, quartier)* to renovate
2 se réhabiliter *vpr* to rehabilitate oneself

réhabituer [reabitɥe] **1** *vt* **r. qn à qch/à faire qch** to get sb used to sth/to doing sth again
2 se réhabituer *vpr* **se r. à qch/à faire qch** to get used to sth/to doing sth again

rehausser [roose] *vt* (a) *(mur, bâtiment)* to make higher (b) *(couleur, teint)* to set off; *(détail)* to accentuate

réimplanter [reɛ̃plɑ̃te] **1** *vt* to relocate
2 se réimplanter *vpr* to relocate

réimpression [reɛ̃presjɔ̃] *nf* reprinting; **en cours de r.** *(ouvrage)* being reprinted

réimprimer [reɛ̃prime] *vt* to reprint

rein [rɛ̃] *nm* (a) *(organe)* kidney; **r. artificiel** kidney or dialysis machine (b) **reins** *(bas du dos)* lower back; **la chute** *ou* **le creux des reins** the small of the back; **avoir mal aux reins** to have a pain in the small of one's back; *Fig* **avoir les reins solides** to be tough; *(financièrement)* to have money behind one

réincarnation [reɛ̃karnasjɔ̃] *nf* reincarnation

réincarner [reɛ̃karne] **se réincarner** *vpr* to be reincarnated **(en** as)

reine [rɛn] *nf* (a) *(souveraine, épouse d'un roi)* queen; **un port** *ou* **un maintien de r.** a queenly bearing; **la r. Anne** Queen Anne; **la r. mère** the Queen Mother (b) *(femme)* **r. de beauté** beauty queen; **la r. du bal** the belle of the ball (c) *(abeille)* queen (bee) (d) **la petite r.** *(cyclisme)* cycling

reine-claude (*pl* **reines-claudes**) [rɛnklod] *nf* greengage

reinette [rɛnɛt] *nf* pippin; **r. grise** russet

réinitialiser [reinisjalize] *vt Ordinat* to reset; *(mémoire)* to reinitialize

réinscription [reɛ̃skripsjɔ̃] *nf* reregistration

réinscrire [reɛ̃skrir] **1** *vt* to reregister **(à** for)
2 se réinscrire *vpr* to reregister **(à** for)

réinsérer [reɛ̃sere] **1** *vt* (a) *(personne)* to reintegrate **(dans** into) (b) *Ordinat (bloc)* to reinsert
2 se réinsérer *vpr* to reintegrate **(dans** into)

réinsertion [reɛ̃sɛrsjɔ̃] *nf* reintegration; **r. sociale** rehabilitation

réintégrer [reɛ̃tegre] *vt* (a) *(fonctionnaire)* **r. qn (dans ses fonctions)** to reinstate sb (b) *(lieu)* **r. son domicile** to return to one's home

réintroduire [reɛ̃trɔdɥir] *vt* to reintroduce

réitérer [reitere] *vt (demande, promesse, question)* to repeat, to reiterate; *(démarche)* to repeat

rejaillir [rəʒajir] *vi* to spurt out; *Fig* **r. sur qn** *(scandale)* to reflect on sb

rejet [rəʒɛ] *nm* (a) *(de produits chimiques)* discharge (b) *(d'une proposition, d'une personne, d'une greffe)* rejection (c) *(en poésie)* enjambment

rejeter [42] [rəʒte] *vt* (a) *(relancer)* to throw back (b) *(candidature, offre, greffe)* to reject; *(témoignage)* to disallow; *(réclamation, accusation)* to dismiss; *(projet de loi)* to throw out (c) *(personne)* to reject (d) *(repousser)* **r. ses cheveux en arrière** to toss one's hair back; **r. la tête en arrière** to throw one's head back; **r. un mot en fin de phrase** to put a word at the end of a sentence (e) *(déchets, gaz toxiques)* to discharge; *(nourriture)* to regurgitate; *(épaves)* to cast up (f) *(blâme, responsabilité)* to shift **(sur** on)

rejeton [rəʒtɔ̃] *nm Fam Hum (enfant)* kid

rejoindre [43] [rəʒwɛ̃dr] **1** *vt* (a) *(personne)* *(pour un rendez-vous)* to meet; *(rattraper)* to catch up (with) (b) *(aboutir sur) (rue, rivière)* to join (up with) (c) *(atteindre) (lieu)* to reach; *(régiment, poste)* to return to (d) *(concorder avec)* to coincide with
2 se rejoindre *vpr* (a) *(amis)* to meet up (b) *(rivières, routes, lignes)* to join up (c) *(propos, idées)* to coincide

rejouer [rəʒwe] *vt (match, point)* to replay; *(morceau de musique)* to play again; *(pièce de théâtre)* to do again

réjoui, -e [reʒwi] *adj* joyful

réjouir [reʒwir] **1** *vt (personne)* to delight
2 se réjouir *vpr* to be delighted **(de** at); **se r. que** + *subjunctive* to be delighted that; **se r. de faire qch** to be delighted to be doing sth

réjouissance [reʒwisɑ̃s] *nf* rejoicing; **en signe de r.** to mark the occasion; **réjouissances** festivities

réjouissant, -e [reʒwisɑ̃, -ɑ̃t] *adj* delightful

relâche [rəlɑʃ] *nf* (a) *(arrêt)* **sans r.** without a break (b) *(au théâtre)* **il y a r. ce soir** there is no performance this evening; **faire r.** to be closed; **r.** *(sur panneau)* closed

relâché, -e [rəlɑʃe] *adj (mœurs, conduite)* lax

relâchement [rəlɑʃmɑ̃] *nm* (a) *(des muscles)* relaxing; *(d'une corde)* slackening (b) *(de la discipline)* relaxation; *(des mœurs)* laxness; *(des efforts)* let-up; *(de l'attention)* wavering

relâcher [rəlɑʃe] **1** *vt* (a) *(muscles)* to relax; *(corde, étreinte)* to loosen (b) *(discipline)* to relax; *(efforts)* to let up; **r. son attention** to let one's attention waver (c) *(prisonnier)* to release, to let go
2 se relâcher *vpr* (a) *(muscles)* to relax; *(corde)* to slacken; *(étreinte)* to loosen (b) *(discipline, mœurs)* to become lax; *(élève, employé)* to slack off; *(attention)* to waver

relais [rəlɛ] *nm* (a) *(épreuve sportive)* **(course de) r.** relay (race); **r. 4 x 100 mètres** 4 x 100-metre relay (b) *(relève)* **passer le r. à qn** to hand over to sb; **prendre le r.** (de) to take over (from) (c) *(intermédiaire)* intermediary (d) *(auberge)* coaching inn; **r. gastronomique** gourmet restaurant (e) *(dispositif émetteur)* relay

relance [rəlɑ̃s] *nf* (a) *(de l'économie, de la production)* revival (b) *(au jeu)* raise

relancer [16] [rəlɑ̃se] *vt* (a) *(lancer de nouveau)* to throw again; *(rendre)* to throw back (b) *(économie, ventes, production)* to boost (c) *(moteur)* to restart; *Ordinat (programme)* to rerun; *(logiciel)* to restart (d) *(client)* to follow up

relater [rəlate] *vt Litt (raconter)* to relate

relatif, -ive [rəlatif, -iv] **1** *adj* relative; **r. à** relating to
2 *nm (pronom)* relative pronoun
3 *nf* **relative** *(proposition)* relative clause

relation [rəlasjɔ̃] nf (a) (rapports entre personnes) relationship; **être en r. avec qn** to be in touch with sb; **mettre qn en r. (avec qn)** to put sb in touch (with sb); **avoir de bonnes/mauvaises relations avec qn** to be on good/bad terms with sb; **r. (amoureuse)** (love) affair; **relations extérieures** foreign affairs; **relations publiques** public relations; **relations sexuelles** (sexual) intercourse (b) (lien) (entre des phénomènes, des faits) relationship, connection; **être sans r. avec qch** to bear no relation to sth; **en r. avec...** in relation to...; **r. de cause à effet** cause-and-effect relationship (c) (connaissance) acquaintance; **avoir des relations** to have contacts; **une r. de travail** a colleague (d) (récit) account

relationnel, -elle [rəlasjɔnɛl] adj relational; Ordinat **base de données relationnelles** relational database

relativement [rəlativmɑ̃] adv (a) (assez) relatively (b) **r. à** (par rapport à) compared to

relativiser [rəlativize] vt to put into perspective; **il faut r.** you have to put things into perspective

relativisme [rəlativism] nm relativism

relativité [rəlativite] nf relativity

relax [rəlaks] adj Fam laid-back

relaxant, -e [rəlaksɑ̃, -ɑ̃t] adj relaxing

relaxation [rəlaksasjɔ̃] nf relaxation; **faire de la r.** to do relaxation exercises

relaxer [rəlakse] 1 vt (a) (détendre) to relax (b) (prisonnier) to release
2 se relaxer vpr to relax

relayer [53] [rəleje] 1 vt (personne) to take over from
2 se relayer vpr (a) (se remplacer) to take turns; **se r. pour faire qch** to take turns doing sth; **on se relaie toutes les trois heures** we change over every three hours (b) (coureurs) to take over from each other

relecture [rələktyr] nf (a) (d'épreuves) proofreading (b) (d'un livre, d'un texte) rereading

reléguer [34] [rəlege] vt to relegate (à/en to); Fig **r. qch au second plan** to push sth into the background

relent [rəlɑ̃] nm (a) (odeur) stench (b) (de scandale) whiff

relevable [rəlvabl] adj (dossier, appuie-tête) adjustable; (accoudoir) folding

relevé, -e [rəlve] 1 adj (a) (style) lofty (b) (sauce, plat) spicy, highly seasoned
2 nm (d'un compteur) reading; **r. de compte** bank statement; **r. d'identité bancaire** = document giving details of one's bank account

relève [rəlɛv] nf relief; **assurer ou prendre la r. (de qn)** to take over (from sb)

relèvement [rəlɛvmɑ̃] nm (a) (d'une économie, d'un pays) recovery (b) (des salaires, des tarifs, d'un impôt) raising

relever [46] [rəlve] 1 vt (a) (objet renversé) to pick up; (personne) to help back up; **r. la tête** to look up; Fig to stand up for oneself (b) (économie, pays) to revive (c) (col) to turn up; (manches, bas de pantalon) to roll up, to turn up; (voilette, jupe) to lift up; (cheveux) to put up (d) (augmenter) to raise (e) (contradiction, erreur) to pick out; (traces, empreinte) to find (f) (prêter attention à) **r. l'allusion** to pick up on the hint; **je n'ai pas relevé** I let it go (g) (adresse, coordonnées) to take down; (compteur) to read; (copies) to collect; **r. le gaz** to read the gas meter (h) (défi) to accept (i) (sauce, plat) to spice up (j) (remplacer) (troupes, sentinelle) to relieve (k) (libérer) **r. qn de ses fonctions** to relieve sb of his/her duties
2 relever de vt ind (a) (dépendre de) (personne, autorité) to

be answerable to; **r. de l'article 7** to come under article 7; **cette affaire relève de la justice** this is a matter for the courts; **son cas relève de la folie** he's well and truly insane (b) (se remettre de) to be recovering from
3 se relever vpr (a) (après une chute) to get up (b) (accoudoir, siège) to lift up (c) (se remettre) **se r. de qch** to get over sth, to recover from sth

relief [rəljɛf] nm (a) (d'un paysage, d'une médaille) relief; **en r.** in relief; Fig **mettre qch en r.** (idées, qualité) to bring sth out; (beauté) to set sth off; (avantage) to highlight; **sans r.** (paysage, style) flat (b) Litt **reliefs** (d'un repas) remains; Fig (de la gloire) shreds (c) Ordinat highlight; **mettre qch en r.** to highlight sth

relier [66] [rəlje] 1 vt (a) (mettre en contact) to connect, to link (à to) (b) (idées, faits) to link together (c) (livre) to bind
2 se relier vpr Ordinat to link up

relieur, -euse [rəljœr, -øz] nm,f (book)binder

religieusement [rəliʒjøzmɑ̃] adv (a) (selon la religion) religiously; **se marier r.** to get married in church (b) (avec révérence) reverently (c) (scrupuleusement) religiously

religieux, -euse [rəliʒjø, -øz] 1 adj religious; (mariage) church; Fig (silence) respectful
2 nm (moine) monk
3 nf religieuse (a) (sœur) nun (b) (gâteau) cream puff

religion [rəliʒjɔ̃] nf religion; **entrer en r.** to join a religious order

reliquaire [rəlikɛr] nm reliquary

reliquat [rəlika] nm (d'argent) remainder; **r. de caisse** cash balance; **r. de compte** account balance

relique [rəlik] nf relic

relire [44] [rəlir] 1 vt (a) (livre, auteur, notes) to reread (b) (épreuves) to proofread
2 se relire vpr to read (over) what one has written

reliure [rəljyr] nf (a) (activité, art) bookbinding (b) (couverture) binding

reloger [45] [rələʒe] vt to rehouse

reluire [18] [rəlɥir] vi (parquet, meuble, métal) to shine, to gleam; **faire r. qch** to polish sth (up)

reluisant, -e [rəlɥizɑ̃, -ɑ̃t] adj (a) (parquet, meuble, métal) shining, gleaming (b) Fig **ce qu'il a fait n'est pas très r.** what he did doesn't reflect very well on him

reluquer [rəlyke] vt Fam to eye up

remâcher [rəmɑʃe] vt (colère, échec) to brood over

remake [rimɛk] nm remake

remaniement [rəmanimɑ̃] nm (a) (d'un texte) revision (b) **r. ministériel** cabinet reshuffle

remanier [66] [rəmanje] vt (a) (texte) to revise (b) (ministère) to reshuffle

remariage [rəmarjaʒ] nm remarriage

remarier [66] [rəmarje] **se remarier** vpr to remarry; **se r. avec qn** to remarry sb

remarquable [rəmarkabl] adj remarkable (par for)

remarquablement [rəmarkabləmɑ̃] adv remarkably

remarque [rəmark] nf (a) (orale) remark; **faire une r.** to make a remark (b) (écrite) comment

remarqué, -e [rəmarke] adj (entrée, absence) conspicuous; (intervention) that attracted attention

remarquer [rəmarke] 1 vt (a) (observer) to notice; **faire r. qch à qn** to point sth out to sb; **je vous ferai r. que...** I'd like to point out that...; **se faire r.** to attract attention; Fam **remarque, il n'est pas le seul** he's not the only one, mind you (b) (dire) to remark, to observe
2 se remarquer vpr (tache, cicatrice) to show

remballer [rɑ̃bale] *vt* (*marchandises*) to repack; *Fig* (*compliment*) to keep to oneself

rembarrer [rɑ̃bare] *vt Fam* to snub

remblai [rɑ̃blɛ] *nm* embankment

remblayer [53] [rɑ̃bleje] *vt* (*route, voie ferrée*) to bank (up)

rembobiner [rɑ̃bɔbine] **1** *vt* to rewind
2 se rembobiner *vpr* to rewind

rembourrage [rɑ̃buraʒ] *nm* (*action, matériau*) stuffing

rembourrer [rɑ̃bure] *vt* to stuff

remboursable [rɑ̃bursabl] *adj* (*emprunt*) repayable; (*frais*) refundable

remboursement [rɑ̃bursəmɑ̃] *nm* (*d'un emprunt*) repayment; (*de frais*) refund

rembourser [rɑ̃burse] *vt* (**a**) (*frais, achat*) to refund; (*emprunt, dettes*) to pay back; **ce médicament est remboursé à 70%** 70% of the cost of this medicine will be refunded (**b**) (*personne*) to pay back; **r. qn de qch** to reimburse sb for sth; **se faire r.** to get a refund; *Fam* **remboursez!** (*au théâtre*) give us our money back!

rembrunir [rɑ̃brynir] **se rembrunir** *vpr* (*visage, personne*) to become sullen

remède [rəmɛd] *nm* remedy, cure (**contre** for); **r. de bonne femme** old wives' remedy; **r. de cheval** kill-or-cure remedy

remédier [66] [rəmedje] **remédier à** *vt ind* (*erreur, situation*) to remedy; (*inconvénient*) to make up for

remembrement [rəmɑ̃brəmɑ̃] *nm* (*de terres*) grouping of land

remémorer [rəmemɔre] **se remémorer** *vpr* to remember

remerciement [rəmɛrsimɑ̃] *nm* **lettre de r.** thank-you letter; **remerciements** thanks; (*dans un livre*) acknowledgements

remercier [66] [rəmɛrsje] *vt* (**a**) (*dire merci à*) to thank (**de** *ou* **pour** for); **r. qn d'avoir fait qch** to thank sb for doing sth; (*non,*) **je vous remercie** no, thank you (**b**) *Euph* (*congédier*) to ask to leave

remettre [47] [rəmɛtr] **1** *vt* (**a**) (*placer*) **r. qch à qn** (*lettre, télégramme, colis*) to deliver sth to sb; (*rapport*) to submit sth to sb; (*démission*) to hand sth in to sb; (*rançon*) to hand sth over to sb; **r. qn à la justice** to turn sb over to the police; **r. son sort entre les mains de qn** to put one's fate in sb's hands
(**b**) (*retarder*) to postpone (**à** to *ou* till); **r. qch à plus tard** to put sth off till later
(**c**) (*replacer*) to put back; **r. qch à sa place** *ou* **en place** to put sth back in its place; **r. qch en cause** *ou* **en question** to call sth into question; **r. qn en liberté** to set sb free
(**d**) (*reconnaître*) **je ne vous remets pas** I can't place you
(**e**) (*dans un état antérieur*) **r. une montre à l'heure** to set a watch to the right time; **r. qch à zéro** to reset sth to zero; **r. qch en marche** (*moteur, machine*) to restart sth; **r. qch en ordre** (*dossiers, maison*) to tidy sth (up)
(**f**) (*rétablir la santé de*) to make better
(**g**) (*manteau, chapeau*) to put back on
(**h**) (*chauffage, télévision*) to turn on again; (*disque, chanson*) to put on again
(**i**) (*ajouter*) (*sel, eau*) to add (**dans** to)
(**j**) *Fam* (*recommencer*) **on remet ça?** how about another (one)?; **tu ne vas pas r. ça!** you're not going to start that again, are you?
2 se remettre *vpr* (**a**) (*dans un endroit, dans un état*) **se r. debout** to get up again; **se r. au lit** to go back to bed; **se**

r. **en cause** *ou* **en question** to question oneself; **le temps s'est remis au beau** the weather has brightened up again
(**b**) (*recommencer*) **se r. à qch/à faire qch** to start sth/doing sth again; **se r. au français/au tennis** to take up French/tennis again
(**c**) (*après une maladie, un choc*) to recover (**de** from); *Fig* **voyons, remettez-vous!** come on, pull yourself together!
(**d**) (*faire confiance*) **je m'en remets à vous** I'll leave it to you, it's up to you
(**e**) (*se placer*) **se r. entre les mains de qn** to place oneself in sb's hands
(**f**) *Fam* (*renouer*) **se r. ensemble** to get back together again

réminiscence [reminisɑ̃s] *nf* (*souvenir imprécis*) vague recollection

remise [rəmiz] *nf* (**a**) (*dans son lieu ou son état d'origine*) **r. en état** (*d'une maison*) restoration; **r. à neuf** (*d'une machine*) reconditioning; **r. en question** *ou* **cause** questioning (**b**) (*d'une lettre*) delivery (**à** to); (*d'une rançon*) handing over (**à** to); **r. des prix** prizegiving (**c**) (*réduction*) **r. de peine** reduction of sentence (**d**) (*rabais*) discount; **faire une r. à qn** to give sb a discount (**e**) (*apprentis*) shed (**f**) *Ordinat* **r. à blanc** (*d'une disquette*) reformatting; **r. en forme** (*de texte*) reformatting

remiser [rəmize] *vt* to put away

rémission [remisjɔ̃] *nf* (**a**) (*d'un péché*) remission; *Fig* **sans r.** (*travailler*) unremittingly; (*punir*) mercilessly (**b**) (*d'une maladie*) remission

remmener [46] [rɑ̃mne] *vt* to take back; **r. qn en voiture** to drive sb back

remodeler [39] [rəmɔdle] *vt* (**a**) (*refaçonner*) to remodel (**b**) (*réorganiser*) to restructure

remontant [rəmɔ̃tɑ̃] *nm* tonic

remontée [rəmɔ̃te] *nf* (**a**) (*d'une pente*) ascent (**b**) (*dans un classement sportif*) recovery (**c**) (*des eaux*) rising (**d**) (*pour skieurs*) **r. mécanique** ski lift

remonte-pente (*pl* **remonte-pentes**) [rəmɔ̃tpɑ̃t] *nm* ski-tow

remonter [rəmɔ̃te] **1** *vt* (**a**) (*pente, escalier*) (*en s'éloignant*) to go up again, to climb back up; (*en s'approchant*) to come up again, to climb back up; **r. la rue** to go/come up the street; **r. la rivière** to go upstream (**b**) (*hausser*) (*étagère, poster*) to move up; (*pantalon, jupe*) to hitch up; (*manche, chaussettes*) to pull up; (*fermeture éclair*) to do up; (*vitre de voiture*) to wind up (**c**) (*porter en haut*) to take/bring up (**d**) (*horloge, montre*) to wind (up) (**e**) (*revigorer*) (*personne*) to cheer up (**f**) (*pièces d'une machine*) to reassemble
2 *vi* (**a**) (*dans l'espace*) (*personne*) to go/come back up; (*marée*) to flow; (*baromètre*) to rise again; (*route, ruelle*) to climb again; (*jupe*) to ride up; **r. en voiture** to get back in one's car; *Fig* **r. dans les sondages** to improve one's position in the polls (**b**) (*dans le temps*) to go back (**à** to); **ça remonte à loin** (*tradition*) it goes back a long way; (*épisode*) it was a long time ago (**c**) (*actions, monnaie, température*) to go up again, to rise again
3 se remonter *vpr* (*moralement*) to cheer up; (*physiquement*) to recover one's strength

remontoir [rəmɔ̃twar] *nm* winder

remontrance [rəmɔ̃trɑ̃s] *nf* remonstrance; **faire des remontrances à qn** to remonstrate with sb

remontrer [rəmɔ̃tre] **1** *vt* **en r. à qn** to show one knows better than sb
2 se remontrer *vpr* to show oneself again

remords [rəmɔr] *nm* remorse; **avoir du** *ou* **des r.** to feel remorse; **je n'ai aucun r.!** I'm not the slightest bit sorry!

remorque [rəmɔrk] *nf* **(a)** *(véhicule)* trailer **(b) prendre qch en r.** to take sth in tow; *Fig* **être à la r.** to lag behind

remorquer [rəmɔrke] *vt (voiture, bateau)* to tow; *(train)* to pull

remorqueur [rəmɔrkœr] *nm* tug(boat)

rémoulade [remulad] *nf Culin* **(sauce) r. remoulade** (sauce) *(mayonnaise sauce with mustard and herbs)*

rémouleur [remulœr] *nm* knife grinder

remous [rəmu] *nm (d'une rivière)* eddy; *(d'un bateau)* wash; *Fig (de la foule)* ripple; *Fig* **provoquer** *ou* **faire des r.** to cause a stir

rempailler [rɑ̃paje] *vt* to reseat

rempart [rɑ̃par] *nm* rampart; **remparts** walls; **faire un r. de son corps à qn** to shield sb with one's body

rempiler [rɑ̃pile] *vi Fam Hum* to sign up again

remplaçable [rɑ̃plasabl] *adj* replaceable

remplaçant, -e [rɑ̃plasɑ̃, -ɑ̃t] *nm,f (personne)* replacement; *(d'un médecin)* locum (tenens); *(d'un enseignant)* Br supply teacher, Am substitute teacher

remplacement [rɑ̃plasmɑ̃] *nm* replacement; **en r. de qn/qch** in place of sb/sth; **faire des remplacements** *(professeur)* to work as Br a supply teacher *or* Am a substitute teacher

remplacer [16] [rɑ̃plase] *vt* **(a)** *(être à la place de)* to take the place of, to replace; *(professionnellement)* to stand in for; **se faire r.** to get somebody to stand in *or* cover for one **(b)** *(substituer)* to replace **(par** with)

remplir [rɑ̃plir] **1** *vt* **(a)** *(récipient)* to fill (**de** with); *(espace, trou)* to fill (in); *Fig (journée, vie)* to take up; **r. qn de joie/colère** to fill sb with joy/anger **(b)** *(formulaire)* to fill in *or* out; *(chèque)* to write, to make out; *(page)* to fill **(c)** *(promesse, rôle, contrat)* to fulfil; *(devoirs, tâche)* to carry out **2 se remplir** *vpr* to fill up (**de** with); *Fig* **se r. les poches** to line one's pockets

remplissage [rɑ̃plisaʒ] *nm* **(a)** *(d'un tonneau, d'un réservoir)* filling (up); *(d'un trou, d'une espace)* filling (in) **(b)** *Péj* **faire du r.** *(dans un texte)* to pad

remplumer [rɑ̃plyme] **se remplumer** *vpr Fam* **(a)** *(financièrement)* to be in funds again **(b)** *(grossir)* to put some weight back on

rempocher [rɑ̃pɔʃe] *vt* to put back in one's pocket

remporter [rɑ̃pɔrte] *vt* **(a)** *(reprendre)* to take back *or* away **(b)** *(gagner)* *(prix, victoire)* to win; *(succès)* to achieve; *Fig* **r. tous les suffrages** to meet with universal approval

rempoter [rɑ̃pɔte] *vt* to repot

remuant, -e [rəmɥɑ̃, -ɑ̃t] *adj* hyperactive

remue-ménage [rəmɥmenaʒ] *nm inv* commotion

remuer [rəmɥe] **1** *vt* **(a)** *(partie du corps)* to move around; *(lèvres)* to move; **r. la queue** *(chien)* to wag its tail; **r. les oreilles** *(chien)* to waggle its ears **(b)** *(mobilier, objets)* to move, to shift **(c)** *(sauce, café)* to stir; *(salade)* to toss; *(terre)* to turn over; *Fig (vieux souvenirs, passé)* to rake up; **r. ciel et terre pour faire qch** to move heaven and earth to do sth **(d)** *(émouvoir)* to move **2** *vi (personne)* to move; *(queue)* to wag; **arrête de r.!** don't fidget!, keep still!

3 se remuer *vpr* **(a)** *(bouger)* to move **(b)** *Fam (être actif)* to have plenty of get-up-and-go; **remue-toi un peu!** get up off your backside!

rémunérateur, -trice [remyneratœr, -tris] *adj (travail)* remunerative; *(placement)* interest-bearing

rémunération [remynerasjɔ̃] *nf* remuneration (**de** for); *(salaire)* pay

rémunérer [34] [remynere] *vt (personne)* to pay; *(travail, services)* to pay for

renâcler [rənɑkle] *vi (personne)* to balk (**à faire** at doing); **il a accepté en renâclant** he accepted grudgingly

renaissance [rənesɑ̃s] *nf* **(a)** *(d'une personne)* rebirth **(b)** *(des lettres, des arts)* renaissance; **la R.** the Renaissance

renaître [50a] [rənɛtr] *vi* **(a)** *(personne)* to be born again; **r. de ses cendres** to rise again from its ashes **(b)** *(industrie, arts, espoir)* to revive; *Litt (printemps, plantes)* to return; *(nature)* to reawaken; **faire r. la confiance** to restore confidence

rénal, -e, -aux, -ales [renal, -o] *adj* renal

renard [rənar] *nm* **(a)** *(animal)* fox; *Fig* **c'est un vieux r.** he's a sly old fox **(b)** *(fourrure)* fox (fur)

renardeau, -x [rənardo] *nm* fox cub

rencard, rencart [rɑ̃kar] = **rancard**

renchérir [rɑ̃ʃerir] *vi* **(a)** *(prix, loyers, marchandises)* to go up **(b)** *(dire ou faire plus)* to go one better (**sur** than)

rencontre [rɑ̃kɔ̃tr] *nf* **(a)** *(de personnes)* meeting; *(de routes, de cours d'eau)* junction; **faire la r. de qn** to meet sb; **faire de mauvaises rencontres** to meet the wrong kind of people; **aller à la r. de qn** to go to meet sb **(b)** *(d'athlétisme)* meeting; *(match)* game, Br match

rencontrer [rɑ̃kɔ̃tre] **1** *vt* **(a)** *(personne)* to meet; **r. qn par hasard** to bump into *or* run into sb **(b)** *(trouver)* to come across; *(opposition, difficulté)* to encounter, to come up against

2 se rencontrer *vpr* **(a)** *(gens, rivières)* to meet **(b)** *Hum (être d'accord)* **les grands esprits se rencontrent** great minds think alike

rendement [rɑ̃dmɑ̃] *nm* **(a)** *(d'une terre, d'un impôt)* yield; *(d'un investissement)* return, yield **(b)** *(de travailleurs, d'une usine, d'une machine)* output; *(d'un ordinateur)* throughput; **travailler à plein r.** *(usine)* to work at full capacity

rendez-vous [rɑ̃devu] *nm inv* **(a)** *(rencontre)* appointment; *(amoureux)* date; **donner r. à qn** to arrange to meet sb; **prendre r. avec qn/chez le médecin** to make an appointment with sb/with the doctor **(b)** *(endroit)* meeting place

rendormir [29] [rɑ̃dɔrmir] **se rendormir** *vpr* to fall asleep again

rendre [rɑ̃dr] **1** *vt* **(a)** *(objet emprunté)* to give back, to return (**à** to); *(achat)* to take back (**à** to); *(copies, cadeau)* to give back (**à** to); *(otages)* to hand back (**à** to); **r. sa liberté à qn** to set sb free

(b) *(rembourser)* to pay back

(c) *(en retour)* **je lui ai rendu son compliment/son invitation** I returned his compliment/his invitation; **r. la monnaie à qn** to give sb his/her change; *Fig* **r. à qn la monnaie de sa pièce** to get even with sb; **r. les armes** *(soldats)* to surrender; *Fig* **r. qn aveugle/sourd** to make sb go blind/deaf; *Fig* **l'amour l'a rendu aveugle** he was blinded by love

(d) *(faire devenir)* to make; **r. qn triste** to make sb sad; **r. qn fou** to drive so mad; **r. qn aveugle/sourd** to make sb go blind/deaf; *Fig* **l'amour l'a rendu aveugle** he was blinded by love

2 *vi* **(a)** *(terre)* to be productive; *(placement)* to yield

(b) *(vomir)* to vomit

3 se rendre *vpr* **(a)** *(aller)* **se r. à** to go to; **se r. chez qn** to call on sb **(b)** *(se soumettre)* to give oneself up **(c)** *(devenir)* **se r. malade/utile** to make oneself ill/useful **(d)** *(locutions)* **se r. compte de qch/que...** to realize sth/that...; *Fam* **tu te rends compte!** who'd have believed it!; **se r. à la raison** to see reason

rendu, -e [rɑ̃dy] *adj* **(a)** *(arrivé)* **être r.** to have arrived **(b)** *Vieilli (fatigué)* tired out

rêne [rɛn] *nf* rein

renégat, -e [renega, -at] *nm,f* renegade

renfermé, -e [rɑ̃fɛrme] **1** *adj (personne)* withdrawn **2** *nm* **odeur de r.** musty smell; **sentir le r.** to smell musty

renfermer [rɑ̃fɛrme] **1** *vt (contenir)* to contain **2 se renfermer** *vpr* to withdraw into oneself

renflé, -e [rɑ̃fle] *adj* bulging

renflement [rɑ̃fləmɑ̃] *nm* bulge

renflouer [rɑ̃flue] *vt (bateau échoué)* to refloat **(b)** *(entreprise, personne)* to bail out

renfoncement [rɑ̃fɔ̃smɑ̃] *nm* recess

renforcement [rɑ̃fɔrsəmɑ̃] *nm (d'une poutre, d'une armée, d'une équipe)* strengthening, reinforcement; *(de la sécurité)* tightening up

renforcer [16] [rɑ̃fɔrse] **1** *vt* **(a)** *(poutre, armée, équipe)* to strengthen, to reinforce; *(sécurité)* to tighten up **(b)** *(couleur, éclairage)* to intensify **(c)** *(crainte)* to heighten; *(impression, convictions)* to strengthen; **r. qn dans une opinion** to confirm sb in an opinion **2 se renforcer** *vpr (tendance, impression, convictions)* to grow

renfort [rɑ̃fɔr] *nm* **renforts** reinforcements; *Fig* **demander du r.** to ask for help; **à grand r. de qch** with the help of lots of sth

renfrogné, -e [rɑ̃frɔɲe] *adj* scowling

renfrogner [rɑ̃frɔɲe] **se renfrogner** *vpr* to scowl

rengager [45] [rɑ̃ɡaʒe] **1** *vt (personnel)* to take on again; *(combat)* to renew; *(conversation, partie, débat)* to pick up again **2 se rengager** *vpr Mil* to re-enlist

rengaine [rɑ̃gɛn] *nf* tune; *Fam Fig* **c'est toujours la même r.** it's (always) the same old story

rengainer [rɑ̃gɛne] *vt (épée)* to sheathe; *Fig (compliment)* to keep to oneself

rengorger [45] [rɑ̃gɔrʒe] **se rengorger** *vpr* to strut

reniement [rənimɑ̃] *nm (d'une foi)* denial; *(d'idées, d'une action)* repudiation

renier [66] [rənje] **1** *vt (fils, racines)* to disown; *(foi)* to deny; *(action, idées)* to repudiate **2 se renier** *vpr* to repudiate one's opinions

reniflement [rəniflɑ̃mɑ̃] *nm* **(a)** *(action)* sniffing **(b)** *(bruit)* sniff

renifler [rənifle] **1** *vi* to sniff **2** *vt (fleur)* to sniff (at); *(tabac à priser)* to sniff (up); *Fig (bonne affaire, embrouille)* to sniff out

renne [rɛn] *nm* reindeer

renom [rənɔ̃] *nm* renown; **de r.** famous, renowned; **de grand r.** extremely famous

renommé, -e [rənɔme] *adj* renowned, famous (**pour** for)

renommée [rənɔme] *nf* fame, renown

renommer [rənɔme] *vt Ordinat (fichier)* to rename

renoncement [rənɔ̃smɑ̃] *nm* renunciation (**à** of)

renoncer [16] [rənɔ̃se] **renoncer à** *vt ind (droit, projet, activité)* to give up, to abandon; *(vacances, voyage)* to sacrifice, to forego; **r. à faire qch** to give up doing sth; *(avant d'avoir commencé)* to give up the idea of doing sth

renonciation [rənɔ̃sjasjɔ̃] *nf* renunciation (**à** of)

renoncule [rənɔ̃kyl] *nf* buttercup

renouer [rənwe] **1** *vt* **(a)** *(ruban, lacet)* to tie (up) again; *(cravate)* to do up again **(b)** *(conversation, relations)* to resume; *(amitié)* to renew **2 renouer avec** *vt ind* **r. avec qn** to take up with sb again; **r. avec qch** *(tradition)* to revive sth; *(habitude)* to go back to sth

renouveau, -x [rənuvo] *nm* revival

renouvelable [rənuvlabl] *adj (contrat, énergie)* renewable; *(expérience)* repeatable

renouveler [42] [rənuvle] **1** *vt* **(a)** *(stock, équipement)* to renew, to replace; *(eau)* to change **(b)** *(passeport, abonnement, demande)* to renew; *(expérience)* to repeat **(c)** *(style)* to change **2 se renouveler** *vpr* **(a)** *(cellule)* to be renewed **(b)** *(se produire de nouveau)* to recur, to happen again **(c)** *(changer)* to change; **un artiste/auteur qui ne se renouvelle pas** an artist/author whose style never changes

renouvellement [rənuvɛlmɑ̃] *nm* **(a)** *(de stock, d'équipement)* replacement, renewal **(b)** *(d'un style)* change **(c)** *(d'un traité, d'un contrat)* renewal

rénovateur, -trice [renɔvatœr, -tris] **1** *adj* reforming **2** *nm,f* reformer

rénovation [renɔvasjɔ̃] *nf* **(a)** *(d'un bâtiment, du mobilier)* renovation; **en (cours de) r.** undergoing renovation **(b)** *(d'une institution)* updating, reform

rénover [renɔve] *vt* **(a)** *(bâtiment, mobilier)* to renovate **(b)** *(institution)* to update, to reform

renseigné, -e [rɑ̃seɲe] *adj* **bien/mal r.** well-/ill-informed

renseignement [rɑ̃sɛɲmɑ̃] *nm* **(a)** *(précision)* piece of information; **renseignements** information; **pour tout r....** for information...; **prendre des renseignements sur qn/qch** to make enquiries about sb/sth; **aller aux renseignements** to go and make enquiries **(b)** *Tél* **les renseignements (téléphoniques)** *Br* directory enquiries, *Am* information **(c)** **les renseignements généraux** = police branch concerned with political security

renseigner [rɑ̃seɲe] **1** *vt* **r. qn (sur qch)** to give sb some information (about sth), to inform sb (about sth) **2 se renseigner** *vpr* to make enquiries; *(sur un point précis)* to find out (**sur** about)

rentabiliser [rɑ̃tabilize] *vt* to make profitable

rentabilité [rɑ̃tabilite] *nf* profitability

rentable [rɑ̃tabl] *adj* profitable

rente [rɑ̃t] *nf* **(a)** *(revenu)* **rentes** private income **(b)** *(pension)* annuity, pension; **r. viagère** life annuity **(c)** *(emprunt d'État)* government loan

rentier, -ère [rɑ̃tje, -ɛr] *nm,f* person of private means

rentré, -e [rɑ̃tre] *adj* **(a)** *(yeux)* sunken **(b)** *(colère)* suppressed

rentrée [rɑ̃tre] nf (a) (retour) return; **la r. (des classes)** the start of the new school year; **r. parlementaire** reopening of Parliament; **la r. sociale** the return to work (b) (d'argent) **attendre une r. d'argent** to expect some money

rentrer [rɑ̃tre] 1 vi (a) (aux être) (a) (entrer de nouveau) (en s'éloignant) to go in again; (en s'approchant) to come in again; (entrer) to go/come in, to enter; **rentre!** come in! (b) (à la maison) to go/come back home, to return home; **r. de vacances/de Paris** to come back from holiday/from Paris; **r. en France/à Paris** to return to France/to Paris; **r. dans son pays** to go back to one's own country; **r. tard/tôt** to come or get home late/early; **en rentrant chez moi** on my way home; **en rentrant de l'école** on my/his/etc way home from school (c) (reprendre ses occupations (école) to re-open; (élève, professeur) to go back (d) (tenir (objets) to go in, to fit (in); **je ne rentre plus dans mon pantalon!** I can't get into my trousers! (e) (pénétrer) to get in; **r. dans qch** to get into sth (f) (être inclus) **r. dans une catégorie** to fall into a category (g) (argent) to come in (h) (recouvrer) **r. dans ses frais** to recover one's expenses (i) **r. dans** (sujet: voiture) to crash into; (sujet: piéton) to bang into; Fam Fig **elle m'est rentrée dedans** ou **dans le chou** she laid into me

2 vt (aux avoir) (a) (linge, troupeau) (en venant) to bring in; (en allant) to take in (b) (introduire, mettre) to put in; **r. qch dans qch** to put sth into sth (c) (train d'atterrissage) to retract, to raise; **r. ses griffes** (chat) to retract its claws; Fig **r. ses larmes** to hold back one's tears; **r. le ventre** to pull one's stomach in (d) (colère, larmes) to stifle

renversant, -e [rɑ̃vɛrsɑ̃, -ɑ̃t] adj Fam astounding

renverse [rɑ̃vɛrs] **à la renverse** adv partir ou tomber **à la r.** to fall backwards; Fig **j'ai failli tomber à la r.** you could have knocked me over with a feather

renversé [rɑ̃vɛrse] 1 adj (a) (à l'envers) (image) reversed (b) (tombé) overturned (c) Fam (stupéfait) staggered

renversement [rɑ̃vɛrsəmɑ̃] nm (a) (d'une tendance, des rôles) reversal; (d'opinions) (dramatic) shift; **r. de situation** reversal of the situation (b) (d'un gouvernement) overthrow

renverser [rɑ̃vɛrse] 1 vt (a) (tendance, rôles) to reverse; (ordre) to invert; Fig **r. la vapeur** to do a U-turn; **r. la situation** to reverse the situation (b) (pencher en arrière) **r. la tête** to tilt one's head back (c) (faire tomber) to knock over; (liquide) to spill; **se faire r. par une voiture** to be knocked down by a car (d) (gouvernement) to overthrow (e) Fam (stupéfier) to stagger

2 se renverser vpr (a) (récipient) to fall over; (véhicule) to overturn (b) (personne) **se r. en arrière** to lean back

renvoi [rɑ̃vwa] nm (a) (de lettres, de marchandises, de colis) return, sending back (b) (d'employés) dismissal, Br sacking; (d'un élève) expulsion (c) (ajournement) postponement; Jur adjournment (d) (dans un texte) cross-reference (e) Jur (devant une autre juridiction) transfer (devant) (f) (éructation) burp, belch; **avoir des renvois** to burp, to belch

renvoyer [33] [rɑ̃vwaje] vt (a) (au point de départ) (personne) to send back; (cadeau, lettre) to send back, to return; (ballon) to throw back; (balle de tennis) to return (b) (employé) to dismiss, Br to sack; (élève) to expel; (visiteur) to send away (c) (son) to echo; (chaleur, lumière) to reflect (d) (ajourner) to postpone; Jur to adjourn (e) (lecteur) to refer (à to); Ordinat to cross-refer (f) Jur (devant une autre juridiction) to transfer (devant à)

réorganisation [reɔrganizasjɔ̃] nf reorganization

réorganiser [reɔrganize] 1 vt to reorganize

2 se réorganiser vpr to get reorganized

réorienter [reɔrjɑ̃te] vt to reorientate

réouverture [reuvɛrtyr] nf reopening

repaire [rəpɛr] nm (d'animaux) den, lair; (de malfrats) haunt

repaître [50c] [rəpɛtr] Littr 1 vt **r. ses yeux de qch** to feast one's eyes on sth

2 se repaître vpr (a) (manger à satiété) to eat one's fill (b) Fig **se r. de qch** to revel in sth

répandre [repɑ̃dr] 1 vt (a) (renverser) (accidentellement) to spill; (volontairement) to spread (b) (émettre) (lumière) to shed; (odeur, chaleur) to give off (c) (larmes, sang) to shed (d) (rumeur, terreur, doctrine) to spread

2 se répandre vpr (a) (liquide) to spill (b) (odeur, chaleur) to spread (c) (rumeur, opinion, pratique) to become widespread (d) (foule, touristes) to spill (dans into) (e) **se r. en excuses** to apologize profusely

répandu, -e [repɑ̃dy] adj (commun) widespread

réparable [reparabl] adj (a) (chaussure, machine) repairable (b) (erreur) which can be put right; (perte financière) which can be made up

reparaître [20] [rəparɛtr] vi to reappear

réparateur, -trice [reparatœr, -tris] 1 adj (sommeil) refreshing

2 nm,f repairman, f repairwoman

réparation [reparasjɔ̃] nf (a) (action) repairing, mending; (résultat) repair; **faire des réparations** to do repairs (b) (dédommagement) reparation; **demander r. (de qch)** to seek redress (for sth)

réparer [repare] vt (a) (toit, appareil, chaussures) to repair, to mend; (déchirure, accroc) to mend (b) (faute) to make amends for; (erreur) to put right, to rectify; (dommage) to make good

reparler [rəparle] vi to speak again; **r. à qn** to speak to sb again; **elle ne lui a pas reparlé depuis** she hasn't spoken to him since; **r. de qch** to speak about sth again; **on en reparlera** we'll talk about it later

repartie, répartie [reparti] nf retort; **avoir l'esprit de r.**, **avoir de la r.** to be good at repartee

repartir [64a] [rəpartir] vi (voyageur, train) to set off again (pour to); (machine) to start (up) again; Fam **c'est reparti, ils ont encore mis la musique à fond!** they're at it again, they've put their music on full blast!; Fam **c'est reparti comme en quarante!** here we go!

répartir [repartir] 1 vt (tâches, argent, vivres) to divide (entre between); (responsabilités) to allocate (entre between); (frais) to share (entre between) (b) (dans le temps) to spread (out) (sur over) (c) (classifier) to divide (en into) (d) (poids, charge) to distribute

2 se répartir vpr (a) (se diviser) to split up (en into) (b) (se classer) to be divided (en into) (c) **se r. qch** to divide sth up

répartition [repartisjɔ̃] nf (a) (de la population, du poids) distribution (b) (des tâches, d'argent, de vivres) distribution (entre between); (des dépenses, des responsabilités) allocation (entre to) (c) (dans le temps) spreading (sur over)

repas [rəpa] nm meal; **prendre un r.** to have a meal; **r. d'affaires** business lunch/dinner; **r. chaud/froid** hot/cold meal; **r. de noce** wedding breakfast

repassage [rəpasaʒ] nm ironing; **faire du r.** to do some ironing

repasser [rəpase] **1** vi (a) (passer à nouveau) (aller) to go by again, to pass by again; (venir) to come by again, to pass by again; (retourner) to go/come back; **r. chez qn** to drop in on sb again (b) (film) to be on again

2 vt (a) (vêtement) to iron (b) (montagne, frontière) to go across again (c) (cassette, disque) to play again; (film) to show again (d) (leçon) to go over; **r. qch dans son esprit** to go over sth in one's mind (e) (examen) to resit (f) **r. qch à qn** (donner à nouveau) to give sb sth again (g) (au téléphone) **je vous le repasse** I'll put you back through to him

repêchage [rəpeʃaʒ] nm (a) (d'un véhicule, d'un noyé) fishing out (b) (d'un candidat) **épreuve de r.** resit; **être reçu au r.** to pass on the resit

repêcher [rəpeʃe] vt (a) (retirer de l'eau) to fish out (b) (candidat) to let through

repeindre [54] [rəpɛ̃dr] vt to repaint

repenser [rəpɑ̃se] **1** vt (concept) to rethink
2 repenser à vt ind to think again about; **quand j'y repense** when I think back

repenti, -e [rəpɑ̃ti] adj repentant, penitent

repentir¹ [rəpɑ̃tir] nm (remords) regret

repentir² [64a] **se repentir** vpr to repent; **se r. de qch/d'avoir fait qch** to repent sth/doing sth; Fig to regret sth/doing sth

repérage [rəperaʒ] nm (a) Ordinat marking, flagging (b) (d'un lieu de tournage) recce

répercussion [rəperkysjɔ̃] nf (a) (du son) reverberation (b) (conséquence) repercussion (**sur** on)

répercuter [rəperkyte] **1** vt (a) (son, lumière) to reflect (b) (ordre, augmentation) to pass (**sur** on to)
2 se répercuter vpr (son, lumière) to be reflected (b) (avoir des conséquences) **se r. sur** to have repercussions on

repère [rəper] nm (a) (point de référence) mark; (pour s'orienter) landmark; aussi Fig **point de r.** reference point (b) (dans le temps) reference point (c) Ordinat marker, flag

repérer [34] [rəpere] **1** vt (a) (marquer) (terrain) to mark out (b) (trouver) (défaut, endroit) to locate; (lieu de tournage) to recce (c) Fam (apercevoir) to spot; **se faire r.** to attract attention
2 se repérer vpr to get one's bearings, to find one's place about

répertoire [rəpertwar] nm (a) (liste) index, list (b) (carnet) notebook with alphabetical index; **r. à onglets** thumb index (c) Ordinat directory; **r. central** ou **principal** main directory; **r. racine** root directory (d) (d'un théâtre, d'un artiste) repertoire

répertorier [rəpertɔrje] vt to list

répéter [34] [repete] **1** vt (a) (redire, refaire) to repeat (b) (pièce de théâtre, rôle) to rehearse
2 vi (acteur) to rehearse
3 se répéter vpr (personne) to repeat oneself; (événement) to recur, to happen again; **l'histoire se répète** history repeats itself

répétitif, -ive [repetitif, -iv] adj repetitive

répétition [repetisjɔ̃] nf (a) (d'un mot, d'une action, d'un événement) repetition; **fusil à r.** repeating rifle; **avoir des rhumes à r.** to have one cold after another (b) (d'une pièce de théâtre) rehearsal; **r. générale** dress rehearsal (c) Ordinat **fonction de r.** repeat function

repeuplement [rəpœpləmɑ̃] nm (d'un pays) repopulation; (d'un étang) restocking; (d'une forêt) replanting

repeupler [rəpœple] **1** vt (pays) to repopulate; (étang) to restock; (forêt) to replant
2 se repeupler vpr (pays) to be repopulated; (étang) to be restocked; (forêt) to be replanted

repiquage [rəpikaʒ] nm (a) (de plants) pricking out, planting out (b) (d'un disque, d'une cassette) taping

repiquer [rəpike] **1** vt (a) (plants) to prick out, to plant out (b) (disque, cassette) to record (c) Fam (reprendre) to catch again
2 vi Fam **il y a repiqué** he's been at it again

répit [repi] nm respite, breathing space; **sans r.** (travailler) without a break, continuously

replacer [16] [rəplase] **1** vt (remettre à sa place) to put back
2 se replacer vpr (trouver un emploi) to find (oneself) a new job

replanter [rəplɑ̃te] vt to replant

replâtrer [rəplɑtre] vt (a) (mur) to replaster (b) Péj patch up

replet, -ète [rəplɛ, -ɛt] adj (personne) podgy; (visage) chubby

repli [rəpli] nm (a) (d'une armée) retreat, withdrawal (b) (de la monnaie, des prix) fall (c) (d'un vêtement, de la peau, d'un terrain) fold; (d'une rivière) bend

replier [66] [rəplije] **1** vt (a) (objet) to fold up; (lame de couteau) to fold away; (jambes) to tuck up; (ailes) to fold (b) (troupes) to withdraw
2 se replier vpr (a) (objet) to fold up; Fig **se r. sur soi-même** to withdraw into oneself (b) (troupes) to retreat, to withdraw

réplique [replik] nf (a) (réponse) retort, rejoinder; **sans r.** unanswerable (b) (d'un acteur) line(s); **donner la r. à qn** to play opposite sb (c) (copie) replica; (sosie) double

répliquer [replike] **1** vt **r. que** to reply that; **je lui ai répliqué que...** I replied that...
2 vi to reply; (avec impertinence) to answer back; **r. à qn** to answer sb back

replonger [45] [rəplɔ̃ʒe] **1** vt aussi Fig to plunge back (**dans** into)
2 vi (a) (plonger à nouveau) to dive in again; Fig **r. dans l'alcoolisme** to fall back into alcoholism (b) Fam (délinquant) to reoffend
3 se replonger vpr **se r. dans qch** to immerse oneself in sth again

répondant [repɔ̃dɑ̃] nm Fam **avoir du r.** to have plenty of money stashed away

répondeur [repɔ̃dœr] nm **r.** (**automatique** ou **téléphonique**) (telephone) answering machine, answerphone

répondre [repɔ̃dr] **1** vt to answer, to reply; **je n'ai rien répondu** I made no reply
2 répondre à vt ind (a) (personne, lettre, question) to answer, to reply to; (salut) to return; (accusation) to answer; **elle n'a pas encore répondu** she hasn't answered yet; **r. par un sourire** to answer with a smile; Mil **r. à l'appel** to answer the roll (b) (téléphone, porte) to answer; **laisse, je vais r.!** leave it, I'll get it!; **ça ne répond pas** there's no answer (c) (amour) to return (d) (besoin, critères) to meet; **ne pas r. à l'attente de qn** to fall short of sb's expectations (e) **les freins ne répondent plus** the brakes aren't responding any more
3 répondre de vt ind to answer for; **j'en réponds** I guarantee it; **je ne réponds de rien** I'm promising nothing
4 se répondre vpr (personnes) to answer each other

réponse [repɔs] *nf* (a) *(à une question, à une lettre)* answer, reply (à to); *(à une offre d'emploi)* reply (à to); *Fig (solution)* answer (à to); **avoir r. à tout** to have an answer for everything (b) *(réaction)* response (c) *Ordinat* answering; **r. automatique** unattended answering; **temps de r.** response time

report [rapɔr] *nm* (a) *(de notes, de corrections)* transfer (sur to) (b) *(d'un rendez-vous)* postponement (c) *(en comptabilité)* carrying forward (d) *(dans une élection)* **r. de voix** (sur transfer (to)

reportage [rapɔrtaʒ] *nm* (a) *(article, émission)* report (b) *(activité)* reporting

reporter¹ [rapɔrtɛr] *nm* reporter; **r.-cameraman** film reporter; **r.-photographe** photojournalist

reporter² [rapɔrte] **1** *vt* (a) *(objet)* to take back, to return (b) *(affection)* to transfer (sur to) (c) *(différer)* **r. qch à plus tard** to postpone sth or put sth off until later (d) *(en comptabilité)* to carry forward (e) *(notes, corrections)* to transfer (sur to) (f) *(dans une élection)* **r. sa voix sur qn** to transfer one's vote to sb
  2 se reporter *vpr* (a) *(se référer)* **se r. à** *(document)* to refer to (b) **se r. sur** *(sujet: colère, affection)* to be transferred to

repos [rapo] *nm* (a) *(détente)* rest; **un mois de r.** a month's rest; **prendre du r.** to rest; **le r. éternel** eternal rest (b) *(tranquillité)* peace; **ce n'est pas de tout r.!** it's not exactly restful! (c) *Mil* **r.!** (stand) at ease!

reposant, -e [rapozɑ̃, -ɑ̃t] *adj* restful, relaxing

reposé, -e [rapoze] *adj* rested, refreshed

repose-pied [rapozpje] *nm inv* footrest

reposer [rapoze] **1** *vt* (a) *(remettre)* to put back (down), to replace (b) *(appuyer)* **r. sa tête contre** *ou* **sur qch** to lean one's head against *or* on sth (c) *(détendre) (jambes, esprit)* to rest; **ça te reposera** it'll be a rest for him; **une couleur qui repose les yeux** a colour that is restful to the eyes (d) *(question)* to ask again; *(problème)* to bring up again (e) *Mil* **reposez arme!** order arms!
  2 *vi* (a) *(s'appuyer)* **r. sur** to rest on; *Fig (être basé sur)* to be based on; *(dépendre de)* to depend on (b) *(liquide)* to settle; *(pâte à tarte)* to rest (c) *(personne décédée)* to lie; **qu'il repose en paix** may he rest in peace
  3 se reposer *vpr* (a) *(se relaxer)* to rest; **se r. les yeux/ les jambes** to rest one's eyes/legs (b) *(question, problème)* to crop up again (c) **se r. sur qn/qch** *(s'en remettre à)* to rely on sb/sth

repose-tête [rapoztɛt] *nm inv* headrest

repoussant, -e [rapusɑ̃, -ɑ̃t] *adj* repulsive

repousser [rapuse] **1** *vt* (a) *(écarter)* to push aside *or* away; *(en arrière)* to push back (b) *(ennemi, attaque, avances)* to repel; *(offre, idée)* to reject, to turn down; *(prétendant)* to rebuff (c) *(rendez-vous, réunion)* to postpone, to put off (à until)
  2 *vi (arbre, plante)* to shoot up again; *(cheveux, herbe, feuilles)* to grow again

repoussoir [rapuswar] *nm (femme)* ugly woman; **servir de r. à qn** to serve as a foil to sb

répréhensible [repreɑ̃sibl] *adj* reprehensible

reprendre [58] [raprɑ̃dr] **1** *vt* (a) *(ville, territoire, fugitif)* to recapture (à from) (b) *(se resservir de)* **r. du pain/vin** to take *or* have some more bread/wine; **vous reprendrez bien un peu de thé?** would you like some more tea? (c) *(rechercher) (personne)* to pick up again (d) *(récupérer) (objet)* to take back; **r. sa place** *(s'asseoir)* to return to one's seat; *Com* **les articles en solde ne sont ni repris ni échangés** ≃ sale goods are not returnable (e)

(surprendre) **r. qn à faire qch** to catch sb doing sth again; **on ne m'y reprendra plus!** I won't be caught again! (f) *(conversation, fonctions, lutte)* to resume, to take up again; *(négociations, relations)* to re-open, to resume; **r. le travail** to return *or* go back to work; **r. connaissance** to regain consciousness; **r. la parole** to speak again; **"oui, mais...", reprit-il** "yes, but...", he continued; *Fam* **ça le reprend!** he's off again! (g) *(répéter)* to repeat; *(refrain)* to take up (h) *(retoucher) (vêtement)* to alter (i) *(corriger)* to correct
  2 *vi* (a) *(recommencer) (cours)* to start again; *(pourparlers, hostilités)* to resume, to re-open (b) *(prendre de la vigueur) (affaires)* to recover, to pick up; *(plante)* to pick up
  3 se reprendre *vpr* (a) *(se ressaisir)* to pull oneself together (b) *(se corriger)* to correct oneself (c) *(recommencer)* **s'y r. à plusieurs fois pour faire qch** to make several attempts at doing sth

repreneur [raprənœr] *nm* purchaser, buyer

représailles [raprezaj] *nfpl* reprisals, retaliation; **en r.** in retaliation, as a reprisal

représentant, -e [raprezɑ̃tɑ̃, -ɑ̃t] *nm,f* representative; **r. de commerce** sales representative

représentatif, -ive [raprezɑ̃tatif, -iv] *adj* representative (de of)

représentation [raprezɑ̃tasjɔ̃] *nf* (a) *(de la réalité, d'un concept)* representation (b) *(spectacle)* performance (c) *(métier)* commercial travelling (d) *Pol* **r. proportionnelle** proportional representation

représentativité [raprezɑ̃tativite] *nf* representativeness

représenter [raprezɑ̃te] **1** *vt* (a) *(candidat, papiers)* to present again (b) *(figurer)* to represent, to depict; **r. qn sous les traits de** to depict sb as (c) *(être le porte-parole de)* to represent (d) *(constituer, équivaloir à)* to represent; **r. qch pour qn** to represent sth for sb
  2 se représenter *vpr* (a) *(occasion)* to arise again (b) *(s'imaginer)* to imagine (c) **se r. à** *(examen)* to retake *or Br* resit; *(poste)* to apply for again; **se r. aux élections** *Br* to stand *or Am* to run for election again

répressif, -ive [represif, -iv] *adj* repressive

répression [represjɔ̃] *nf* repression; *(d'une émeute, d'un abus)* suppression

réprimande [reprimɑ̃d] *nf* reprimand, rebuke; **faire des réprimandes à qn** to reprimand *or* rebuke sb

réprimander [reprimɑ̃de] *vt* to reprimand, to rebuke

réprimer [reprime] *vt* (a) *(retenir)* to repress, to suppress (b) *(crime, révolte)* to suppress

repris [rapri] *nm* **r. de justice** ex-prisoner

reprise [rapriz] *nf* (a) *(d'un débat, des hostilités)* resumption; *(des négociations)* re-opening, resumption (b) *(des affaires)* recovery; **les grévistes ont voté la r. du travail** the strikers have voted to go back to work; **r. économique** economic recovery (c) *(d'une émission télévisée)* repeat (d) *(d'un moteur)* pick-up, acceleration (e) **à plusieurs/trois reprises** several/three times (f) *(raccommodage)* **faire une r.** à qch to mend sth (g) *(somme payée à un locataire)* = money paid for fixtures and fittings *(paid to outgoing tenant)*; *(rachat d'un objet d'occasion)* part exchange, trade-in

repriser [raprize] *vt* to mend

réprobateur, -trice [reprɔbatœr, -tris] *adj* reproving

réprobation [reprɔbasjɔ̃] *nf* reproof

reproche [rəprɔʃ] *nm* (a) *(remontrance)* reproach; **faire des reproches à qn (sur qch)** to reproach sb (for sth); **sans r.** *(vie, personne)* beyond reproach, blameless (b) *(critique)* criticism

reprocher [rəprɔʃe] **1** *vt* **r. qch à qn** to blame *or* reproach sb for sth; **r. à qn de faire qch** to blame *or* reproach sb for doing sth; **je ne vous reproche rien** I'm not blaming you for anything; **qu'est-ce que vous reprochez à ce livre?** what have you got against the book?
2 se reprocher *vpr* **se r. qch** to blame *or* reproach oneself for sth; **tu n'as rien à te r.** you've nothing to blame yourself for

reproducteur, -trice [rəprɔdyktœr, -tris] *adj* reproductive

reproduction [rəprɔdyksjɔ̃] *nf* (a) *(sexuelle)* reproduction (b) *(d'un document, d'une image, du son)* reproduction, reproducing; *(copie)* reproduction

reproduire [18] [rəprɔdɥir] **1** *vt* (a) *(son, image, document)* to reproduce; **nous reproduisons ici l'article du Monde** we reprint here the article from Le Monde (b) *(acte)* to repeat
2 se reproduire *vpr* (a) *(sexuellement)* to reproduce (b) *(événement)* to recur, to happen again

reprogrammable [rəprɔgramabl] *adj Ordinat (touche)* reprogrammable

reprogrammer [rəprɔgrame] *vt Ordinat* to reprogram

réprouver [repruve] *vt* to condemn

reptation [rɛptasjɔ̃] *nf* crawling

reptile [rɛptil] *nm* reptile

repu, -e [rəpy] **1** *pp voir* **repaître**
2 *adj* pleasantly full

républicain, -e [repyblikɛ̃, -ɛn] *adj & nm,f* republican

république [repyblik] *nf* republic; **r. bananière** banana republic; **la R. centrafricaine** the Central African Republic; *Anciennement* **la R. démocratique allemande** the German Democratic Republic; **la R. dominicaine** the Dominican Republic; *Anciennement* **la R. fédérale d'Allemagne** the Federal Republic of Germany; **la R. Tchèque** the Czech Republic

répudiation [repydjasjɔ̃] *nf* repudiation

répudier [66] [repydje] *vt* to repudiate

répugnance [repyɲɑ̃s] *nf* (a) *(aversion)* repugnance, loathing **(pour** for); **avoir de la r. pour qn/qch** to loathe sb/sth (b) *(appréhension)* reluctance **(à faire qch** to do sth)

répugnant, -e [repyɲɑ̃, -ɑ̃t] *adj* repulsive

répugner [repyɲe] *vi* (a) *(appréhender)* **r. à faire qch** to be reluctant to do sth (b) *(être répugnant)* **r. à qn** to be repugnant to sb, to repel sb

répulsion [repylsjɔ̃] *nf* repulsion

réputation [repytasjɔ̃] *nf* reputation; **avoir (une) bonne/mauvaise r.** to have a good/bad reputation; **sa r. de chirurgien** his reputation as a surgeon; **connaître qn de r.** to know sb by reputation; **avoir la r. d'être franc** to have a reputation for being frank

réputé, -e [repyte] *adj* well-known, renowned **(pour** for); **être r. intelligent** to be reputed to be intelligent

requérir [7] [rəkerir] *vt* (a) *(solliciter) (faveur)* to ask for, to seek; *(présence, aide)* to request (b) *(nécessiter) (explication, soin, patience)* to require, to call for (c) *Jur (sentence)* to demand, to call for

requête [rəkɛt] *nf* (a) *(demande)* request; *Ordinat* query; **adresser une r. à qn** to make a request to sb (b) *Jur* petition

requiem [rekɥijem] *nm inv* requiem

requiers, requiert *voir* **requérir**

requin [rəkɛ̃] *nm* shark

requinquer [rəkɛ̃ke] *Fam* **1** *vt* to perk up
2 se requinquer *vpr* to perk up

requis, -e [rəki, -iz] **1** *pp voir* **requérir**
2 *adj* requisite, required; **les conditions requises** the requirements

réquisition [rekizisjɔ̃] *nf* (a) *(de vivres, de véhicules)* requisitioning, commandeering (b) *Jur (plaidoirie)* prosecution address

réquisitionner [rekizisjone] *vt* to requisition, to commander

réquisitoire [rekizitwar] *nm Jur* prosecution address; *Fig* indictment **(contre** of)

RER [ɛrəɛr] *nm* **(abrév Réseau express régional)** = express rail network serving Paris and its suburbs

RESA [reza] *nf* **(abrév réservation)** = TGV seat reservation ticket

rescapé, -e [rɛskape] **1** *adj* surviving
2 *nm,f* survivor

rescousse [rɛskus] *nf* **aller/venir à la r. de qn** to go/come to sb's rescue; **appeler qn à la r,** to call on sb for help

réseau, -x [rezo] *nm* (a) *(de routes, de voies ferrées, de rivières)* network, system; **r. autoroutier** *Br* motorway *or Am* freeway network; **r. ferroviaire** rail network (b) *Fig (de relations)* network, circle (c) *Ordinat* network; **mise en r.** networking; **r. de télématique** *ou* **de communication de données** datacomms network; **r. de données** data network; **r. local** local area network, LAN; **grand r.** wide area network, WAN; **r. numérique à intégration de services** integrated services digital network; **r. à valeur ajoutée** value-added network, VAN

réséda [rezeda] *nm* reseda

réservation [rezɛrvasjɔ̃] *nf* reservation, booking; **faire une r.** to make a reservation

réserve [rezɛrv] *nf* (a) *(restriction)* reservation; **émettre des réserves (sur qch)** to voice reservations (about sth); **sous r. de qch** subject to sth; **sans r.** *(éloges, admiration)* unqualified (b) *(discrétion)* reserve; **sortir de sa r.** to come out of one's shell (c) *(de vivres, d'équipement, d'argent)* reserve; **en r.** in reserve (d) *Mil* reserve (e) *(de chasse, de pêche)* reserve; *Can* **r. faunique** wildlife reserve; **r. indienne** (Native American) reservation; **r. naturelle** nature reserve (f) *(de magasin)* storeroom; *(de bibliothèque, de musée)* reserve collection

réservé, -e [rezɛrve] *adj* (a) *(chambre, siège)* reserved, booked (b) *(consacré)* **être r. à qn/qch** to be reserved for sb/sth (c) *(personne, attitude)* reserved

réserver [rezɛrve] **1** *vt* (a) *(chambre, place)* to reserve, to book; **vous avez réservé?** do you have a reservation? (b) *(mettre de côté)* to set aside, to put by (c) *(prévoir)* **r. le meilleur pour la fin** to save the best till last (d) *Fig* **r. son jugement** to reserve judgement; **r. une surprise à qn** to have a surprise in store for sb; **r. un bon accueil à qn** to welcome sb with open arms; **ce que le sort nous réserve** what fate has in store for us
2 se réserver *vpr* (a) *(garder pour soi)* **se r. qch** to keep sth for oneself; **se r. le droit de faire qch** to reserve the right to do sth (b) **se r. pour qch** to save oneself for sth

réserviste [rezɛrvist] nm Mil reservist

réservoir [rezɛrvwar] nm (a) (bassin) reservoir (b) (cuve) tank; r. d'essence Br petrol or Am gas tank

résidence [rezidɑ̃s] nf (a) (demeure) residence; r. principale main residence; r. secondaire second home (b) (habitations de standing) Br block of luxury flats, Am luxury apartment building (c) Jur en r. surveillée under house arrest (d) (séjour) residence

résident, -e [rezidɑ̃, -ɑ̃t] 1 adj (a) (personne) resident (b) Ordinat r. en mémoire memory-resident
2 nm,f (a) (habitant) resident (b) (étranger) foreign resident; les résidents français en Grande-Bretagne French nationals resident in Great Britain

résidentiel, -elle [rezidɑ̃sjɛl] adj residential

résider [rezide] vi (a) (personne) to reside (b) (consister) to lie (dans in)

résidu [rezidy] nm (reste) residue; résidus (déchets) waste

résiduel, -elle [rezidɥɛl] adj residual

résignation [reziɲasjɔ̃] nf resignation

résigné, -e [reziɲe] adj resigned (à to)

résigner [reziɲe] se résigner vpr to resign oneself (à to); se r. à faire qch to resign oneself to doing sth

résiliable [reziljabl] adj (contrat) which may be terminated

résiliation [reziljasjɔ̃] nf (d'un contrat) termination

résilier [66] [rezilje] vt (accord, contrat) to terminate

résille [rezij] nf hairnet

résine [rezin] nf resin

résiné [rezine] adj m & nm (vin) r. retsina

résineux, -euse [rezinø, -øz] 1 adj (a) (bois, odeur) resinous (b) (arbre, forêt) coniferous
2 nm conifer

résistance [rezistɑ̃s] nf (a) (action) resistance (à to); n'offrir aucune r. to put up or offer no resistance; opposer une r. à qn/qch to resist sb/sth; r. passive passive resistance (b) Hist la R. the Resistance (c) (endurance) stamina (d) Él resistance (e) (conducteur) (d'un appareil) element (f) (d'un matériau) resistance

résistant, -e [rezistɑ̃, -ɑ̃t] 1 adj (matériau) tough; (plante) hardy; c'est quelqu'un de très r. he has a lot of stamina
2 nm,f (combattant) freedom fighter; (pendant la Résistance) member of the Resistance

résister [reziste] résister à vt ind (a) (attaque, agresseur) to resist (b) (tentation, influence, personne) to resist; je n'ai pas pu r., je les ai achetées I couldn't resist, I bought them (c) (supporter) (douleur, pression, froid) to withstand; (mauvais traitement) to stand up to; (maladie, épidémie, fatigue) to overcome (d) (s'opposer à) to stand up to

résolu, -e [rezɔly] 1 pp voir résoudre
2 adj (personne) determined, resolute; être r. à faire qch to be determined to do sth

résolument [rezɔlymɑ̃] adv resolutely

résolution [rezɔlysjɔ̃] nf (a) (décision) resolution; prendre la r. de faire qch to make a resolution to do sth; prendre des résolutions to make resolutions (b) (d'un problème) solving (c) (détermination) determination, resolve (d) (d'un écran) resolution

résolvais etc voir résoudre

résonance [rezɔnɑ̃s] nf aussi Tech resonance; Fig (écho) echo

résonner [rezɔne] vi (a) (retentir) to resound (b) (faire un écho) to echo

résorber [rezɔrbe] 1 vt (a) (surplus, déficit) to absorb; (chômage) to bring down; (dettes) to clear (b) (sang, pus) to resorb
2 se résorber vpr (a) (surplus, déficit) to be absorbed; (chômage) to be brought down (b) (sang, pus) to be resorbed

résorption [rezɔrpsjɔ̃] nf (d'un surplus, d'un déficit) absorption; (du chômage) bringing down

résoudre [3b] [rezudr] 1 vt (a) (difficulté, conflit, crise) to resolve; (équation, énigme, problème) to solve (b) (décider) r. de faire qch to resolve to do sth (c) (décomposer) r. qch en qch to resolve sth into sth
2 se résoudre vpr se r. à faire qch to resolve to do sth; je ne peux pas me r. à la quitter I can't bring myself to leave her

respect [rɛspɛ] nm respect (pour for); avoir du r. pour qn to have respect for sb; manquer de r. envers qn to show sb a lack of respect; tenir qn en r. to keep sb at a distance; sauf le r. que je vous dois, sauf votre r. with all due respect; respects (hommages) respects

respectabilité [rɛspɛktabilite] nf respectability

respectable [rɛspɛktabl] adj respectable

respecter [rɛspɛkte] 1 vt to respect; faire r. la loi to enforce the law; se faire r. to command respect; r. la priorité (en voiture) to give way
2 se respecter vpr (a) (soi-même) to respect oneself; comme tout homme qui se respecte like any self-respecting man (b) (l'un l'autre) to respect each other

respectif, -ive [rɛspɛktif, -iv] adj respective

respectivement [rɛspɛktivmɑ̃] adv respectively

respectueusement [rɛspɛktɥøzmɑ̃] adv respectfully

respectueux, -euse [rɛspɛktɥø, -øz] adj respectful (de/envers of/to)

respirable [rɛspirabl] adj breathable; Fig l'atmosphère n'était plus r. the atmosphere had become oppressive

respirateur [rɛspiratœr] nm respirator

respiration [rɛspirasjɔ̃] nf breathing; reprendre sa r. to pause for breath; retenir sa r. to hold one's breath; r. artificielle artificial respiration

respiratoire [rɛspiratwar] adj (organe) respiratory; (appareil, exercice, problème) breathing

respirer [rɛspire] 1 vi (a) (personne, plante) to breathe (b) Fig (être soulagé) je respire! I can breathe again! (c) Fig (se reposer) to have a break
2 vt (a) (inhaler) to breathe (in) (b) (exprimer) r. la santé to be glowing with health; il ne respire pas l'intelligence he doesn't exactly radiate intelligence

resplendir [rɛsplɑ̃dir] vi (a) (briller) to shine (b) (personne) to be radiant; r. de joie/santé to radiate joy/health

resplendissant, -e [rɛsplɑ̃disɑ̃, -ɑ̃t] adj (personne, beauté) radiant; r. de joie/santé radiant with joy/health; il a une mine resplendissante he looks wonderfully well

responsabiliser [rɛspɔ̃sabilize] vt r. qn to give sb a sense of responsibility

responsabilité [rɛspɔ̃sabilite] nf (morale) responsibility; (légale) liability (de for); accepter une r. to take on or accept a responsibility; avoir la r. de qn/qch to be responsible for sb/sth; décliner toute r. to accept no liability; avoir un poste à responsabilités to have a responsible job; r. civile public liability; r. limitée limited liability; r. au tiers third-party liability

responsable [rɛspɔ̃sabl] **1** *adj* (a) *(moralement)* responsible (**de** for); *(légalement)* liable (**de** for) (b) *(mûr)* responsible

2 *nmf* (a) *(auteur, coupable)* person responsible (**de** for); **qui est le r. de cette plaisanterie?** who's (the person) responsible for this prank? (b) *(personne qui a la responsabilité)* person in charge; **r.** *(dirigeant élu)* official

resquiller [rɛskije] *vi (au théâtre, au concert)* to sneak in without paying; *(dans un bus, dans le métro)* to dodge paying one's fare

resquilleur, -euse [rɛskijœr, -øz] *nm,f (au théâtre, au cinéma)* = person who sneaks in without paying; *(dans un bus, dans le métro)* fare-dodger

ressac [rəsak] *nm* undertow

ressaisir [rəsezir] **se ressaisir** *vpr* to pull oneself together

ressasser [rəsase] *vt* (a) *(mentalement)* to brood over (b) *(répéter)* to keep coming out with

ressemblance [rəsãblãs] *nf (entre personnes)* resemblance, likeness; *(entre choses)* similarity

ressemblant, -e [rəsãblã, -ãt] *adj (portrait)* lifelike

ressembler [rəsãble] **1 ressembler à** *vt ind* (a) *(personne)* to resemble, to be like; **à quoi ressemble-t-elle?** what does she look like? (b) *Fig (chose)* **cela ne ressemble à rien** it doesn't look like anything; **cela ne lui ressemble pas** that's not like her

2 se ressembler *vpr* to be alike, to resemble each other; **ils se ressemblent comme des frères** you'd take them for brothers; **se r. comme deux gouttes d'eau** to be as like as two peas in a pod; **les jours se suivent et ne se ressemblent pas** day follows day and you never know what to expect; *Prov* **qui se ressemble s'assemble** birds of a feather flock together

ressemeler [42] [rəsəmle] *vt* to resole

ressentiment [rəsãtimã] *nm* resentment **(de/contre** at/against)

ressentir [64a] [rəsãtir] **1** *vt* to feel

2 se ressentir *vpr* **se r. de qch** *(personne, pays)* to feel the effects of sth; *(travail)* to show the effects of sth

resserrement [rəsɛrmã] *nm (d'une amitié, de liens)* strengthening

resserrer [rəsere] **1** *vt* (a) *(nœud, ceinture, écrou)* to tighten (b) *Fig (amitié, liens)* to strengthen

2 se resserrer *vpr* (a) *(vallée, route)* to narrow (b) *(nœud)* to tighten (c) *Fig (liens)* to strengthen

resservir [63] [rəservir] **1** *vt (plat)* to serve up again; **r. qn** to give sb another helping

2 *vi* to be used again (**à** for)

3 se resservir *vpr* **se r. de qch** *(plat)* to take another helping of sth; *(objet)* to use sth again

ressort [rəsɔr] *nm* (a) *(pièce)* spring (b) *(force morale)* resilience; **avoir du r.** to be resilient (c) *(motivation)* motive (d) **être du r. de qn** to be sb's responsibility (e) **en dernier r.** *Jur* without appeal; *Fig* as a last resort

ressortir¹ [rəsɔrtir] **1** *vi (aux être)* (a) *(personne) (en s'éloignant)* to go back out; *(en s'approchant)* to come back out (b) *(se détacher)* to stand out; **faire r.** *(couleur)* to bring out; *(regard, yeux, fait)* to highlight

2 *vt (aux avoir)* (a) *(parapluie, vêtements)* to get out again (b) *Fig (histoire)* to trot out again

3 *v impersonnel (aux être)* **il ressort de ceci que... il** emerges from this that...

ressortir² **ressortir à** *vt ind* (a) *(être de la compétence de)* to come under the jurisdiction of (b) *Litt (dépendre de)* to come within the province of

ressortissant, -e [rəsɔrtisã, -ãt] *nm,f* national

ressouder [rəsude] **1** *vt* to resolder; *Fig* to re-establish

2 se ressouder *vpr (os, fracture)* to knit

ressource [rəsurs] *nf* (a) *(moyen)* possibility; **je n'ai d'autre r. que de...** the only course of action open to me is to...; **avoir de la r.** to be resourceful; **en dernière r.** as a last resort (b) **ressources** *(argent, moyens d'action)* resources; **être sans ressources** to be without means; **ressources humaines** human resources (c) *(d'une nation)* **ressources** resources

ressourcer [16] [rəsurse] **se ressourcer** *vpr* *Fam* to get back in touch with one's inner self

ressusciter [rəsysite] **1** *vt (un mort)* to raise from the dead; *Fig* **ça ne va pas le r.** it won't bring him back (b) *Fig (querelle, mode)* to revive

2 *vi* to rise from the dead; **j'ai l'impression de r.** I feel like a new person

restant, -e [rɛstã, -ãt] **1** *adj* remaining

2 *nm* remainder, rest

restaurant [rɛstɔrã] *nm* restaurant; **aller au r.** to eat out; **r. d'entreprise** staff canteen; **r. universitaire** university refectory

restaurateur, -trice [rɛstɔratœr, -tris] *nm,f* (a) *(de tableaux)* restorer (b) *(de restaurant)* restaurateur, restaurant owner

restauration [rɛstɔrasjɔ̃] *nf* (a) *(de tableaux, de bâtiments)* restoration (b) *(métier)* catering; **r. rapide** fast food (c) *Hist* **la R.** the Restoration *(return to power of the Bourbon dynasty 1814–1830)* (d) *Ordinat* restore (e) *Suisse (restaurant)* restaurant

restaurer [rɛstɔre] **1** *vt* (a) *(rétablir, réparer)* to restore (b) *Ordinat* to restore (c) *Litt (faire manger)* **r. qn** to give sb something to eat

2 se restaurer *vpr* to have something to eat

reste [rɛst] *nm* (a) *(de travail, d'argent, de vin)* rest, remainder; **le r. du temps** the rest of the time; **le r.** *(des gens)* the rest; **il y avait un r. de beurre/lait** there was a bit of butter/milk left (over) (b) **restes** *(d'un repas)* leftovers (c) *(ossements)* **restes** remains (d) *(locutions)* **du** *ou* **au r.** besides; **pour le r.** as for the rest; **avoir qch de r.** to have sth to spare; **pour ne pas être en r.** *(pour ne pas avoir de dette)* so as not to be indebted; *(pour ne pas être surpassé)* so as not to be outdone; **partir sans demander son r.** to leave without further ado; *Fam* **avoir de beaux restes** to still have one's looks

rester [rɛste] *(aux être)* **1** *vi* (a) *(subsister)* to remain, to be left; **les 5 francs qui restent** the remaining 5 francs, the 5 francs left; **c'est tout ce qui me reste** that's all I have left; **le nom lui est resté** the name stayed with him (b) *(demeurer)* to stay, to remain; **restez où vous êtes** stay where you are; **r. assis** to stay seated; **r. au lit** to stay in bed; **r. (à) dîner** to stay to dinner; **r. sur place** to stay put; *Fam* **j'y suis, j'y reste** here I am and here I stay; *Fam* **y r.** *(mourir)* to kick the bucket; **que cela reste entre nous** this is strictly between ourselves; **r. sur une impression** to be left with an impression; **cela m'est resté sur l'estomac** *(plat)* it's lying heavy on my stomach; *Fig* it still rankles with me; **en r. là** to stop there; **r. dans les mémoires** to live on in people's memories; **le plus dur reste à faire** the hardest part is still to be done

2 *v impersonnel* **il me reste 5 francs** I've got 5 francs left; **il ne me reste qu'à vous remercier** it only remains for me to thank you; **il reste beaucoup de choses à faire** there are still a lot of things to be done; **il reste que... the**

fact remains that...; **il n'en reste pas moins que...** it is nevertheless the case that...; **(il) reste à savoir si c'est vrai** it remains to be seen whether it's true

restituer [restitye] *vt* (**a**) *(reconstituer) (inscription, texte)* to restore; *(passé, ambiance)* to recreate (**b**) *(rendre) (objets volés)* to restore, to return; *(argent, prêt)* to repay, to pay back (**c**) *(son)* to reproduce

restitution [restitysjɔ̃] *nf* (**a**) *(reconstitution) (d'un texte)* restoration; *(d'une ambiance, du passé)* recreation (**b**) *(d'objets volés)* return; *(d'argent, d'un prêt)* repayment (**c**) *(du son)* reproduction

Restoroute® [restorut] *nm Br* motorway *or Am* freeway restaurant

restreindre [54] [restrɛ̃dr] **1** *vt* to restrict (à to)
2 se restreindre *vpr* (**a**) *(réduire ses dépenses)* to cut down (**b**) *(domaine, recherche)* to become more restricted

restreint, -e [restrɛ̃, -ɛ̃t] *adj (production, vocabulaire)* restricted (à to); *(espace, service)* limited

restrictif, -ive [restriktif, -iv] *adj* restrictive

restriction [restriksjɔ̃] *nf* (**a**) *(diminution)* restriction (**b**) *(réserve)* reservation; **faire des restrictions** to express some reservations; **sans r.** *(accord)* unconditional; *(approuver)* unreservedly (**c**) *Ordinat* **r. d'accès** access restriction (**d**) **restrictions** *(mesures de rationnement)* restrictions

restructuration [rastryktyrasjɔ̃] *nf* restructuring

restructurer [rastryktyre] *vt* to restructure

résultant, -e [rezyltɑ̃, -ɑ̃t] **1** *adj* resulting
2 *nf* **résultante** consequence, result

résultat [rezylta] *nm* result; **sans r.** to no effect; *Fam* **r.:** **il a été licencié** the upshot was he was dismissed; **donner des résultats** to produce results; **résultats d'exercice** *ou* **d'exploitation** trading results

résulter [rezylte] **1** *vi* **r. de qch** to result from sth
2 *v impersonnel* **il en résulte que...** the result of this is that...

résumé [rezyme] *nm* (**a**) *(d'un texte)* summary, résumé; **faire le r. de qch** *(d'un texte)* to give a summary of sth; *(d'une histoire, d'une situation)* to sum sth up; **en r.** *(en bref)* in short (**b**) *(livre)* study guide

résumer [rezyme] **1** *vt (article, idées)* to summarize; *(situation, histoire)* to sum up
2 se résumer *vpr* (**a**) *(personne)* to sum up (**b**) *(se réduire)* **se r. à qch** to come down to sth

résurgence [rezyrʒɑ̃s] *nf* resurgence

resurgir [rasyrʒir] *vi* to reappear suddenly

résurrection [rezyrɛksjɔ̃] *nf aussi Fig* resurrection

rétabli, -e [retabli] *adj (après maladie)* recovered

rétablir [retablir] **1** *vt (téléphone, eau, gaz)* to restore (**b**) *(guérir)* to restore to health (**c**) *(faits, vérité)* to re-establish (**d**) *(ordre, relations, réputation)* to restore (**e**) *(réhabiliter)* **r. qn (dans ses fonctions)** to reinstate sb; **r. qn dans ses droits** to restore sb's rights
2 se rétablir *vpr* (**a**) *(malade)* to recover (**b**) *(silence, calme)* to return; *(situation)* to return to normal

rétablissement [retablismɑ̃] *nm* (**a**) *(de l'ordre, de la paix, d'une dynastie)* restoration (**b**) *(des communications, des relations)* restoration (**c**) *(d'un employé)* reinstatement (**d**) *(d'un malade)* recovery

rétamé, -e [retame] *adj Fam (fatigué)* whacked

rétamer [retame] *vt* (**a**) *(casserole)* to retin (**b**) *(miroir)* to resilver (**c**) *Fam (au jeu)* to clean out; **se faire r.** *(se faire battre)* to get hammered

retaper [rɔtape] **1** *vt* (**a**) *Fam (vieille maison, voiture)* to do up (**b**) *Fam (lit)* to straighten (**c**) *Fam* **r. qn** to buck sb up
2 se retaper *vpr Fam (convalescent)* to get back on one's feet

retard [rɔtar] *nm* (**a**) *(dans le temps)* delay; *(d'une personne attendue)* lateness; **je vous prie d'excuser mon r.** please excuse me for being late; **être en r.** to be late; *(sur un programme)* to be behind; **sans r.** without delay; **avoir du r.** to be late; **avoir une heure de r.** to be an hour late; **prendre du r.** *(personne)* to fall behind; *(train)* to be running late; **r. de paiement** late payment (**b**) *(dans un développement)* backwardness; **pays en r. sur les autres** country lagging behind the others; **être en r. pour son âge** to be backward for one's age; **en r. sur son temps** behind the times; **r. mental** backwardness (**c**) *(d'un véhicule)* **r. à l'allumage** retarded ignition

retardataire [rɔtardatɛr] **1** *nmf* latecomer
2 *adj* **un élève r.** a pupil who arrives late

retardé, -e [rɔtarde] *adj* (**a**) *(départ, arrivée)* late (**b**) *(mentalement) (enfant)* backward

retardement [rɔtardəmɑ̃] *nm* **à r.** *(bombe)* time; *(longtemps après)* belatedly

retarder [rɔtarde] **1** *vt* (**a**) *(faire arriver en retard)* to delay; **r. qn dans ses études** to hold sb back in his/her studies (**b**) *(différer)* to delay; **r. qch d'une heure/d'une semaine** to put sth back an hour/a week (**c**) *(montre, horloge)* to put back (**de** by)
2 *vi* (**a**) *(horloge)* to be slow; **ma montre retarde/je retarde de dix minutes** my watch is/I'm ten minutes slow (**b**) **r. sur son temps** *ou* **son époque** to be behind the times (**c**) *Fam (ne pas être au courant)* to be behind the times

retendre [rɔtɑ̃dr] *vt (cordes)* to retighten

retenir [70] [rɔtənir] **1** *vt* (**a**) *(faire rester) (personne)* to keep, to detain; **r. qn prisonnier/en otage** to keep *or* hold sb prisoner/hostage; **je ne vous retiens pas** I won't hold you back; **r. qn à dîner** to have sb stay for dinner; **r. qn par le bras** to hold sb back by the arm; **r. l'attention de qn** *(candidature, proposition)* to catch sb's attention (**b**) *(conserver) (eau, chaleur)* to retain (**c**) *(retirer) (argent)* to withhold; *(cotisation, impôt)* to deduct (**sur** from); **retenu à la source** deducted at source (**d**) *(se souvenir de) (leçon, nom)* to remember; **je le retiens, ton ami!** I won't forget your friend in a hurry! (**e**) *(réserver) (place, chambre, table)* to reserve, to book (**f**) *(accepter) (projet, suggestion)* to adopt; **votre candidature n'a pas été retenue** your application was unsuccessful (**g**) *(contenir) (colère)* to contain; *(larmes)* to hold back; *(cri)* to stifle; *(respiration, souffle)* to hold (**h**) *(garder en arrière) (personne, foule, chien)* to hold back, to restrain (**i**) *(empêcher)* **r. qn de faire qch** to restrain sb from doing sth, to hold sb back from doing sth; **qu'est-ce qui te retient de le lui dire?** what's stopping you telling her?; **qu'est-ce qui vous retient?** what's holding you back?
2 se retenir *vpr* (**a**) *(s'accrocher)* to hold on (à to) (**b**) *(se contenir)* to restrain oneself; **se r. de faire qch** to stop oneself (from) doing sth

rétention [retɑ̃sjɔ̃] *nf* retention; **faire de la r. d'information** to withhold information

retentir [rɔtɑ̃tir] *vi* (**a**) *(Klaxon*®*, alarme)* to sound; *(tonnerre, canon)* to rumble; *(coup de feu, cri)* to ring out; **l'explosion retentit dans toute la ville** the explosion was heard right across the city (**b**) *(lieu)* **r. de** to resound *or* echo with (**c**) *Fig* **r. sur** to have an impact on

retentissant, -e [rɔtɑ̃tisɑ̃, -ɑ̃t] *adj* (**a**) *(voix)* ringing (**b**) *(succès, échec)* resounding; *(scandale)* sensational

retentissement [rətɑ̃tismɑ̃] *nm (d'un événement)* impact; **avoir un r. sur qch** to have an impact on sth

retenue [rətəny] *nf (a) (d'une somme)* deduction; **r. sur salaire** wage deduction; *(mensuel)* salary deduction **(b)** *(dans un calcul)* carry over; **n'oublie pas la r.** don't forget to carry over **(c)** *Scol* detention **(d)** *(discrétion)* restraint **(e)** *(barrage)* dam

réticence [retisɑ̃s] *nf* hesitation, unwillingness; **sans r.** unhesitatingly

réticent, -e [retisɑ̃, -ɑ̃t] *adj (hésitant)* hesitant, unwilling

rétif, -ive [retif, -iv] *adj (cheval)* stubborn; *(personne)* recalcitrant

rétine [retin] *nf* retina

retiré, -e [rətiʁe] *adj (a) (lieu, vie)* secluded; **vivre r. du monde** to lead a secluded life **(b) être r. des affaires** to be retired from business

retirer [rətiʁe] **1** *vt (a) (faire sortir)* to take out; *(objet coincé)* to get out; *(bouchon, épine)* to pull out **(de** of); **r. un enfant d'une école** to remove a child from a school; **r. qch de la circulation** to withdraw sth from circulation; **r. qch du marché** to take sth off the market; **r. les mains de ses poches** to take one's hands out of one's pockets **(b)** *(argent)* to withdraw **(de** from), to take out **(de** of); *(bagages, billet)* to collect **(de** from), to pick up **(de** from) **(c)** *(obtenir)* **r. un profit de qch** to make a profit out of sth; **r. du plaisir de qch** to get pleasure from sth **(d)** *(ôter)* *(gants, lunettes, vêtement)* to take off, to remove **(e)** *(confisquer)* to take away **(à** from); **r. son permis de conduire à qn** to ban sb from driving **(f)** *(ramener en arrière)* *(main)* to remove **(g)** *(ne pas maintenir)* *(offre, plainte, candidature)* to withdraw; **je retire ce que j'ai dit** I take back what I said

2 se retirer *vpr (a) (s'en aller)* *(personne)* to withdraw; *(foule)* to move back; **vous pouvez vous r.** you may go **(b)** *(eaux, mer)* to recede; *(marée)* to ebb **(c)** **se r. d'une association/élection** to withdraw from a partnership/ an election; **se r. des affaires** to retire from business

retombées [rətɔ̃be] *nfpl (a) (répercussions)* repercussions; **avoir des retombées sur qch** to have repercussions on sth **(b)** *(déchets)* **retombées radioactives** radioactive fallout

retomber [rətɔ̃be] *vi (aux être) (a) (tomber de nouveau)* to fall again; **r. dans son fauteuil** to fall back into one's armchair; **laisser r. ses bras** to drop one's arms **(b)** *(après un saut, après avoir été en l'air)* *(personne, ballon)* to land; **r. sur ses pattes** *(chat)* to land on its feet; *Fig* **r. sur ses pieds** ou *Fam* **ses pattes** to land on one's feet **(c)** *(retourner)* **r. dans l'oubli** to sink back into obscurity; **r. dans le désespoir/le chaos** to fall back into despair/ chaos; **r. en enfance** to lapse into one's second childhood **(d)** *(redevenir)* **r. malade** to fall ill again **(e)** *(rencontrer)* **r. sur qch** to come across sth again; *Fam* **r. sur qn** to bump into sb again **(f)** *(se répercuter)* **r. sur qn** *(blâme, responsabilité)* to fall on sb; *Fam* **ça va me r. dessus** I'm going to take the rap for it **(g)** *(baisser)* *(enthousiasme, intérêt, attention)* to fall off **(h)** *(cheveux, rideaux)* to hang (down) **(sur** over)

rétorquer [retɔʁke] *vt* to retort

retors, -e [rətɔʁ, -ɔʁs] *adj (personne)* crafty, wily

rétorsion [retɔʁsjɔ̃] *nf* retaliation

retouche [rətuʃ] *nf (a) (sur photo)* touching up; *TV, Cin & Ordinat* **r. d'image(s)** image editing or retouching **(b)** *(d'un texte, d'un vêtement)* alteration

retoucher [rətuʃe] *vt (a) (texte, vêtement)* to alter **(b)** *(photo)* to touch up

retour [rətuʁ] **1** *nm (a) (d'une personne, d'une saison)* return **(à** to); **être de r.** *(de)* to be back (again) (from); **de r. chez moi** back home; **à mon r.** on my return; **en r.** *(de)* in return (for); **payer qn de r.** to repay sb in kind; **par r.** *(du courrier)* by return (of post); **par un juste r. des choses** as is/was only right and proper; *Fam* **être sur la r.** to be past one's prime; **r. à l'envoyeur** return to sender; **r. de manivelle** backfire kick; *Fig* **il y a eu un r. de manivelle** it backfired **(b)** *(trajet)* return journey **(c)** *(changement)* *(de fortune)* reversal; **r. d'âge** change of life **(d)** *Ordinat* **r. d'information** feedback; **r. ligne** line feed; **r. chariot obligatoire** hard carriage return **(e)** *(sur clavier)* return; **r. arrière** backspace; **r. de chariot** carriage return

2 *adj inv (match, touche)* return

retournement [rətuʁnəmɑ̃] *nm (de situation)* turnaround ou (de in), reversal (de of)

retourner [rətuʁne] **1** *vt (aux avoir) (a) (gant, vêtement)* to turn inside out; *(poche)* to turn out; *Fam* **r. sa veste** to change sides; *Fig* **r. le couteau dans la plaie** to twist the knife, to rub it in **(b)** *(terre, matelas, crêpe)* to turn (over); *(carte)* to turn over ou up; *Fig* *(idée, projet)* to turn over **(c)** *Fam (bouleverser)* *(personne)* to shake **(d)** *(renverser)* *(situation)* to reverse **(e)** *(rendre)* *(livre, lettre, compliment)* to return **(à** to) **(f)** *Fig (utiliser)* **r. un argument contre qn** to turn an argument against sb

2 *vi (aux être)* to go back, to return **(à** to)

3 *v impersonnel Fam* **voilà de quoi il retourne** that's what it's all about

4 se retourner *vpr (a) (dormeur, voiture)* to turn over; **il doit se r. dans sa tombe** he must be turning in his grave **(b)** *Fig (s'organiser)* to get one's head together **(c)** *(tourner la tête)* to turn round; **partir sans se r.** to leave without looking back **(d) se r. contre qn** *(personne)* to turn against sb; *(action, ambition)* to backfire on sb **(e)** *(aller)* **s'en r. quelque part** to return somewhere

retracer [rətʁase] *vt (événement, vie)* to recount

rétractation [retʁaktasjɔ̃] *nf* retraction

rétracter¹ [retʁakte] **1** *vt (griffes, antennes)* to retract **2 se rétracter** *vpr (muscle)* to retract

rétracter² **1** *vt (paroles)* to retract, to withdraw **2 se rétracter** *vpr (se dédire)* to retract

rétraction [retʁaksjɔ̃] *nf* retraction

retrait [rətʁɛ] *nm (a) (d'un permis)* withdrawal; **r. du permis de conduire** driving ban **(b)** *(d'une candidature)* withdrawal **(c)** *(fait de récupérer)* **r. des bagages** baggage reclaim **(d)** *(d'argent)* withdrawal; **r. d'espèces** cash withdrawal **(e)** *(des eaux)* receding **(f)** *(en typographie)* indent; **mettre en r.** to indent **(g) en r.** *(étagère)* recessed; *(maison)* set back; *Fig* **être/rester en r.** *(personne)* to be/stay in the background

retraite [rətʁɛt] *nf (a) (de la vie active)* retirement; **être à la r.** to be retired; **prendre sa r.** to retire; **être mis à la r.** to be retired; **r. anticipée** early retirement **(b)** *(pension)* (retirement) pension; **r. complémentaire** supplementary pension **(c)** *(procession)* **r. aux flambeaux** torchlight procession **(d)** *(refuge)* retreat; *(de voleurs)* hideout **(e)** *(expérience religieuse)* retreat; **faire une r.** to go into retreat **(f)** *Mil* retreat

retraité, -e [rətʁete] **1** *adj* retired **2** *nm,f* pensioner

retraitement [rətʁetmɑ̃] *nm* reprocessing

retraiter [rətʁete] *vt* to reprocess

retranchement [rətrɑ̃ʃmɑ̃] *nm* entrenchment; *Fig* **forcer qn dans ses (derniers) retranchements** to drive sb to the wall

retrancher [rətrɑ̃ʃe] 1 *vt* (a) *(soustraire) (chiffre)* to take away (**de** from); **r. qch sur une somme** to deduct sth from a sum of money (**de**) *(ôter) (passage, nom)* to remove (**de** from)

2 **se retrancher** *vpr (troupes)* to dig in; *Fig* **se r. dans le silence** to take refuge in silence; **se r. derrière qn/qch** to hide behind sb/sth

retransmettre [47] [rətrɑ̃smɛtr] *vt* to broadcast

retransmission [rətrɑ̃smisjɔ̃] *nf* broadcast

retravailler [rətravaje] 1 *vt (discours, texte, pas de danse)* to work on again

2 *vi* (a) *(reprendre le travail)* to go back to work (b) *(retrouver du travail)* to work again

rétréci, -e [retresi] *adj* (a) **un pull r.** a pullover that has shrunk (b) *(route)* narrow

rétrécir [retresir] 1 *vt (vêtement)* to take in

2 *vi (vêtement, tissu)* to shrink

3 **se rétrécir** *vpr (route)* to narrow

rétrécissement [retresismɑ̃] *nm* (a) *(action) (de route)* narrowing; *(de vêtement, de tissu)* shrinking (b) *(partie étroite) (de tuyau, de route)* narrowing

rétribuer [retribɥe] *vt (employé)* to pay; *(travail)* to pay for

rétribution [retribysjɔ̃] *nf* payment, remuneration

rétro [retro] 1 *adv* **s'habiller r.** to wear retro clothes; **meublé r.** furnished in retro style

2 *adj inv* retro

3 *nm* (a) *(style)* retro (b) *Fam (rétroviseur)* rear-view mirror

rétroactif, -ive [retroaktif, -iv] *adj* retroactive

rétroactivement [retroaktivmɑ̃] *adv* retroactively

rétroactivité [retroaktivite] *nf* retroactivity

rétrocéder [34] [retrosede] *vt (revendre)* to resell

rétrograde [retrograd] *adj (idée, mesure, politique)* reactionary

rétrograder [retrograde] 1 *vt (fonctionnaire)* to demote

2 *vi (conducteur)* to change down; **r. de troisième en seconde** to change down from third to second

rétroprojecteur [retroprɔʒɛktœr] *nm* overhead projector

rétrospectif, -ive [retrospektif, -iv] 1 *adj* retrospective

2 *nf* **rétrospective** retrospective

rétrospectivement [retrospektivmɑ̃] *adv* retrospectively, in retrospect

retroussé, -e [rətruse] *adj (manches)* rolled-up; *(nez)* snub, turned-up

retrousser [rətruse] *vt* (a) *(manches, pantalon)* to roll up; *(babines)* to curl up (b) *(jupe)* to tuck up

retrouvailles [rətruvaj] *nfpl* reunion

retrouver [rətruve] 1 *vt* (a) *(personne disparue, objet perdu)* to find again; *(adresse, nom)* to find; **r. son chemin** to find one's way again; **je ne retrouverai jamais une occasion pareille** I'll never have another opportunity like it (b) *(recouvrer) (santé, forces, enthousiasme)* to recover; *(voix, appétit)* to get back (c) *(reconnaître)* **r. qch chez qn** to recognize sth in sb; **r. qn dans qch** to recognize sb in sth (d) *(rencontrer) (thème, image, motif)* to come across (**dans** in) (e) *(rejoindre) (amis, parents)* to meet, to see; *(lieu)* to get back to

2 **se retrouver** *vpr* (a) *(être)* to find oneself; **se r. à la rue/sans un sou** to find oneself homeless/penniless (b)

(trouver son chemin) to find one's way (**dans** round); *Fig* **je ne m'y retrouve plus!** I'm completely lost! (c) *Fam (financièrement)* **s'y r.** to get one's money back (d) *(se rencontrer)* to meet; *Fig* **on se retrouvera!** I'll get even with you; **comme on se retrouve!** fancy meeting you! (e) *(soi-même)* to find oneself again (f) *(se reconnaître)* **se r. en qn** to recognize oneself in sb

rétroviseur [retrovizœr] *nm* rear-view mirror

réunification [reynifikasjɔ̃] *nf* reunification

réunifier [66] [reynifje] *vt* to reunify

Réunion [reynjɔ̃] *nf* **la R.** Réunion

réunion [reynjɔ̃] *nf* (a) *(de faits)* gathering (together); *(d'ensembles mathématiques, de pays)* union; *(d'entreprises)* merging (b) *(assemblée)* meeting; **être en r.** to be in a meeting; **r. de famille** family gathering

réunionnais, -e [reynjɔnɛ, -ɛz] 1 *adj* of Réunion

2 *nm,f* **R.** = person from Réunion

réunir [reynir] 1 *vt (rassembler) (objets)* to put together; *(faits, documents)* to gather together; *(fonds)* to raise (b) *(amis, famille)* to get together; *(après une rupture, une séparation)* to reunite (c) *(qualités, avantages)* to have, to possess (d) **r. qch à qch** to join sth to sth

2 **se réunir** *vpr* (a) *(personnes)* to meet, to get together; **se r. autour de qn/qch** to gather round sb/sth (b) *(routes)* to meet (c) *(entreprises)* to merge; *(États)* to unite

réussi, -e [reysi] *adj* successful; *Ironique* **c'est r.!** well done!

réussir [reysir] 1 *vt* (a) *(bien faire)* to make a success of; *(au rugby) (essai)* to score; **son soufflé était très réussi** her soufflé was a great success (b) *(examen)* to pass

2 *vi* (a) *(démarche, projet)* to be successful (b) *(personne)* to do well, to be successful

3 **réussir à** *vi ind* (a) **r. à un examen** to pass an exam; **r. à faire qch** to manage to do sth (b) **r. à qn** *(climat, plat)* to agree with sb; **tout lui réussit** he's successful in everything he does; **les réunions de famille ne me réussissent pas** family gatherings aren't for me

réussite [reysit] *nf* (a) *(succès)* success; **fêter sa r. à un examen** to celebrate passing an exam; **la r. sociale** social success (b) *(aux cartes) Br* patience, *Am* solitaire; **faire une r.** to play patience

réutiliser [reytilize] *vt* to reuse

revaloir [69] [rəvalwar] *vt* **je te revaudrai ça** *(je me vengerai)* I'll get you back for this!; *(je te rendrai service)* I'll do the same for you some time

revalorisation [rəvalɔrizasjɔ̃] *nf* (a) *(d'une monnaie)* revaluation; *(des salaires, des retraites)* upgrading (b) *(d'une image, d'une profession)* upgrading

revaloriser [rəvalɔrize] *vt* (a) *(monnaie)* to revalue; *(salaire, retraite)* to upgrade (b) *(image, profession)* to upgrade

revanchard, -e [rəvɑ̃ʃar, -ard] *adj & nm,f Péj* revanchist

revanche [rəvɑ̃ʃ] *nf* (a) *(vengeance)* revenge; **prendre sa r. (sur qn)** to get one's revenge (on sb) (b) *(d'un match, d'un jeu)* return game (c) *(locutions)* **en r.** on the other hand; **à charge de r.** on condition that I do the same for you

rêvasser [revase] *vi* to daydream

rêve [rɛv] *nm* (a) *(du dormeur)* dream; **faire un r.** to (have a) dream; **faites de beaux rêves!** sweet dreams! (b) *(idéal)* dream; **de r.** *(voiture, maison)* dream; *(silhouette)* gorgeous

rêvé, -e [reve] *adj* perfect, ideal

revêche [rəvɛʃ] *adj* bad-tempered

réveil [revɛj] nm (a) (d'une personne) waking, awakening; **à mon r., au r.** on waking (b) (d'un volcan) renewed rumblings; (de la nature, des nationalismes) reawakening (c) (pendule) alarm (clock)

réveille-matin [revɛjmatɛ̃] nm inv alarm clock

réveiller [revɛje] 1 vt (a) (personne endormie) to wake (up), to awaken; Fig **r. les consciences** to stir people's consciences (b) (raviver) (douleur) to revive
2 **se réveiller** vpr (a) (personne endormie) to wake (up), to awake; (personne dans le coma) to regain consciousness; Fig (peuple) to wake up (b) (douleur) to come back (c) (nature) to reawaken

réveillon [revɛjɔ̃] nm (repas) midnight supper; (soirée) midnight party (after midnight mass on Christmas Eve or New Year's Eve)

réveillonner [revɛjɔne] vi to see in Christmas/the New Year (with a midnight supper and party)

révélateur, -trice [revelatœr, -tris] 1 adj (signe, attitude, remarque) revealing
2 nm (a) (indice) sign (b) Phot developer

révélation [revelasjɔ̃] nf (a) (action) (d'un secret, d'intentions) revelation, disclosure; **faire des révélations** to disclose important information (b) (découverte fondamentale) revelation (c) (personne) discovery (d) (divine) revelation

révéler [revele] 1 vt (a) (dévoiler) to reveal (b) (témoigner de) to show
2 **se révéler** vpr (a) (personne) to reveal oneself or one's character; (talent, génie) to be revealed, to reveal itself (b) **se r. intelligent/exact** to turn out to be intelligent/correct; **il s'est révélé un bon ami** he proved to be a good friend

revenant, -e [rəvnɑ̃, -ɑ̃t] nm,f (a) (fantôme) ghost (b) Fam **tiens, un r.!** hello, stranger!

revendeur, -euse [rəvɑ̃dœr, -øz] nm,f retailer; (d'articles d'occasion) secondhand dealer

revendicatif, -ive [rəvɑ̃dikatif, -iv] adj (mouvement) protest

revendication [rəvɑ̃dikasjɔ̃] nf demand, claim

revendiquer [rəvɑ̃dike] vt (a) (demander) to claim, to demand; (droits) to assert; (territoire, succession) to lay claim to; **r. le droit de faire qch** to claim the right to do sth (b) (assumer) (responsabilité) to claim; (attentat) to claim responsibility for

revendre [rəvɑ̃dr] vt (a) (après achat) to resell; Fig **avoir du temps/de l'énergie à r.** to have time/energy to spare (b) (vendre de nouveau) to sell again

revenez-y [rəvnezi] nm inv Fam **avoir un goût de r.** to be very morish

revenir [70] [rəvnir] vi (a) (retourner, rentrer) to come back, to return; **r. à Paris/en France** to come back to Paris/France; **r. de Paris** to come back from Paris; Fig **r. de loin** (avoir failli mourir) to have been at death's door; **je reviens tout de suite** I'll be back in a minute; **quand l'été reviendra** when it's summer again (b) **r. dans qch** (refrain, image) to crop up in sth (c) **ses propos me sont revenus** what he said got back to me (d) **r. à la mémoire à qn** to come back to sb; **ça me revient maintenant!** it's come back to me!; **les forces me sont revenues** I got my strength back; Fam **j'en suis revenu, de l'informatique!** I'm finished with computers!; **je n'en reviens pas!** I can't get over it! (f) Fam **il a une tête qui ne me revient pas** I don't like the look of him (g) **faire r. qch** to brown sth (h) **r. cher** to work out expensive

2 **revenir à** vt ind (a) (coûter) **r. à 100 francs par personne** to work out at 100 francs each; **ça me revient à 200 francs par mois** it costs me 200 francs a month (b) (équivaloir à) **cela revient à dire que...** that amounts to saying that...
3 **revenir sur** vt ind (a) (sujet) to get back to (b) (aveux) to retract; (promesse, décision) to go back on
4 v impersonnel **il me revient encore 100 francs** I still have 100 francs owing to me; **il lui revient de le faire** it's up to him/her to do it
5 **s'en revenir** vpr Litt to return, to make one's way back

revente [rəvɑ̃t] nf resale

revenu [rəvany, rəvny] nm (d'une personne) income; (de l'État) revenue

rêver [reve] 1 vt to dream (that)...; **r. que...** to dream (that)...
2 vi (a) (dormeur) to dream; Fig **on croit r.!** we must be dreaming! (b) (rêvasser) to daydream
3 **rêver à** vt ind to dream of
4 **rêver de** vt ind (voir en rêve) to dream of; Fig **j'en rêve la nuit** I dream about it at night (b) (souhaiter) to dream of; **r. de faire qch** to dream of doing sth

réverbération [reverberasjɔ̃] nf (de la lumière, de la chaleur) reflection; (du son) reverberation, echo

réverbère [reverber] nm street lamp

réverbérer [34] [reverbere] vt (chaleur, lumière) to reflect, to throw back; (son) to reverberate

reverdir [rəverdir] vi to grow green again

révérence [reverɑ̃s] nf (a) (salut) (d'une femme) curtsey; **faire la r. à qn** to curtsey to sb; Fig **tirer sa r.** to leave (b) (respect) reverence (envers ou pour for)

révérend, -e [reverɑ̃, -ɑ̃d] 1 adj reverend
2 nm reverend

révérer [34] [revere] vt to revere

rêverie [revri] nf (activité, moment) daydream, reverie

revers [rəver] nm (a) (de pièce) reverse side, back; (de la main) back; **prendre l'ennemi à r.** (par l'arrière) to attack the enemy from the rear; (par le côté) to attack the enemy from the side; Fig **c'est le r. de la médaille** that's the other side of the coin (b) (de veste) lapel; (de pantalon) Br turn-up or Am cuff (c) (échec) **r. de fortune** reversal of fortune, setback (d) (au tennis) backhand (stroke)

reverser [rəverse] vt (a) (somme) to transfer (à ou sur to) (b) (liquide) to pour out again

réversible [reversibl] adj reversible

revêtement [rəvɛtmɑ̃] nm (enduit) coating; (de sol, d'un mur intérieur) covering; (d'un mur extérieur) facing; (pour canalisation, pour câble) sheathing; (de la chaussée) surface (material)

revêtir [71] [rəvetir] vt (a) (habiller) **r. qn de qch** to dress sb in sth (b) (endosser) (vêtement) to don (c) (enduire) to coat; (sol) to cover; (mur extérieur) to face; (chaussée) to surface (d) Fig (caractère, aspect, forme) to assume, to take on (e) **pièce revêtue d'une signature** document bearing a signature

rêveur, -euse [revœr, -øz] 1 adj dreamy; **laisser qn r.** to leave sb baffled
2 nm,f dreamer

rêveusement [revøzmɑ̃] adv dreamily

revient [rəvjɛ̃] nm voir **prix**

revigorant, -e [rəvigorɑ̃, -ɑ̃t] adj (vent, bain) invigorating; (boisson) reviving

revigorer [rəvigore] vt (vent, bain) to invigorate; (boisson) to revive

revirement [rəvirmɑ̃] *nm* (*de sentiments, d'opinion*) complete change, about-turn

réviser [revize] *vt* (a) (*texte, loi*) to revise; (*contrat, procès, politique*) to review (b) (*leçon, programme*) to revise (c) (*voiture, moteur*) to service (d) *Ordinat* (*texte, document*) to edit

révision [revizjɔ̃] *nf* (a) (*d'un texte, d'une loi*) revision; (*d'un contrat, d'un procès, d'une politique*) review; **r. des salaires** salary review (b) (*d'une leçon, d'un programme*) Br revision, Am review; **faire des révisions** to revise (c) (*d'une voiture, d'un moteur*) service (d) *Ordinat* edit

révisionnisme [revizjɔnism] *nm* revisionism

revisser [rəvise] *vt* to screw back again

revitalisant, -e [rəvitalizɑ̃, -ɑ̃t] *adj* revitalizing

revitaliser [rəvitalize] *vt* to revitalize

revivre [72] [rəvivr] **1** *vt* (*passé, expérience*) to relive **2** *vi* (a) (*recouvrer son énergie*) to come alive again; **se sentir r.** to feel alive again; **faire r. qn** to bring sb back to life (b) **r. dans qn/qch** to live on in sb/sth; **faire r. qch** (*coutume, tradition*) to revive sth; (*village*) to bring sth back to life

révocable [revɔkabl] *adj* (*fonctionnaire*) removable; (*testament*) revocable

révocation [revɔkasjɔ̃] *nf* (*d'un fonctionnaire*) removal; (*d'un testament*) revocation

revoici [rəvwasi] *prép Fam* **me r.!** here I am again!; **le r. au travail** he's back at work

revoilà [rəvwala] = **revoici**

revoir[1] [rəvwar] **au revoir 1** *exclam* goodbye **2** *nm inv* goodbye

revoir[2] [73a] **1** *vt* (a) (*rencontrer*) (*personne*) to see or meet again (b) (*leçon*) to revise; (*comptes, texte*) to go over again (c) (*se représenter mentalement*) to see again **2 se revoir** *vpr* (a) (*se rencontrer*) to see each other again, to meet again (b) (*soi-même*) to see oneself again

révoltant, -e [revɔltɑ̃, -ɑ̃t] *adj* appalling, revolting

révolte [revɔlt] *nf* revolt; **en r.** (**contre**) in revolt (against)

révolté, -e [revɔlte] *adj* (a) (*indigné*) outraged, appalled (**de**) (b) (*en révolte*) rebellious

révolter [revɔlte] **1** *vt* to outrage, to appal; **ça me révolte d'entendre ça!** I'm appalled to hear that! **2 se révolter** *vpr* to revolt, to rebel (**contre** *ou* **devant** against)

révolu, -e [revɔly] *adj* (*jours, époque*) past, bygone; **avoir quarante ans révolus** to be over forty years of age

révolution [revɔlysjɔ̃] *nf* revolution; **faire la r.** to cause a revolution; *Fig* **être en r.** to be up in arms; *Hist* **la R.** the French Revolution

révolutionnaire [revɔlysjɔner] *adj & nmf* revolutionary

révolutionner [revɔlysjɔne] *vt* (a) (*transformer*) (*industrie, théorie*) to revolutionize (b) *Fam* (*mettre en émoi*) (*village*) to cause a stir in

revolver [revɔlver] *nm* revolver

révoquer [revɔke] *vt* (a) (*fonctionnaire*) to remove from office (b) (*décret, contrat, testament*) to revoke

revue [rəvy] *nf* (a) (*examen*) review; **passer qch en r.** (*problèmes, possibilités*) to review sth; **r. de presse** (*de l'actualité*) review of the papers; (*sur un sujet particulier*) press review (b) (*magazine*) magazine; (*scientifique, littéraire*) review, journal (c) (*spectacle*) revue

révulsé, -e [revylse] *adj* (*yeux*) rolled back; (*personne*) disgusted

révulser [revylse] **1** *vt* (*dégoûter*) to disgust **2 se révulser** *vpr* (*yeux*) to roll back

Reykjavik [rekjavik] *n* Reykjavik

rez-de-chaussée [redʃose] *nm inv Br* ground floor, *Am* first floor; **au r.** on the *Br* ground *or Am* first floor

rez-de-jardin [redʒardɛ̃] *nm inv* garden level

RF [eref] *nf* (*abrév* **République française**) = written abbreviation seen on official documents, government buildings etc

RFA [erefa] *nf Anciennement* (*abrév* **République fédérale d'Allemagne**) FRG

RG [erʒe] *nmpl* (*abrév* **Renseignements généraux**) = police branch concerned with political security

rhabiller [rabije] **1** *vt* (*personne*) to dress sb again **2 se rhabiller** *vpr* (*remettre ses vêtements*) to get dressed again; *Fam* **il peut aller se r.** he might as well give up and go home

rhapsodie [rapsɔdi] *nf* rhapsody

Rhénanie [renani] *nf* **la R.** the Rhineland

Rhésus [rezys] *nm* Rhesus factor; **R. positif/négatif** Rhesus positive/negative

rhétorique [retɔrik] **1** *adj* (*effet*) rhetorical **2** *nf* rhetoric

Rhin [rɛ̃] *nm* **le R.** the Rhine

rhinocéros [rinɔserɔs] *nm* rhinoceros

rhino-pharyngite (*pl* **rhino-pharyngites**) [rinofarɛ̃ʒit] *nf* inflammation of the nose and throat, *Spéc* rhinopharyngitis

Rhodes [rɔd] *n* Rhodes

rhododendron [rɔdɔdɛ̃drɔ̃] *nm* rhododendron

Rhône [ron] *nm* **le R.** the Rhone

rhubarbe [rybarb] *nf* rhubarb

rhum [rɔm] *nm* rum

rhumatisant, -e [rymatizɑ̃, -ɑ̃t] *adj & nm,f* rheumatic

rhumatismal, -e, -aux, -ales [rymatismal, -o] *adj* rheumatic

rhumatisme [rymatism] *nm* rheumatism; **avoir des rhumatismes** to have rheumatism; **r. articulaire** rheumatoid arthritis; **r. articulaire aigu** rheumatic fever

rhumatologie [rymatɔlɔʒi] *nf* rheumatology

rhumatologue [rymatɔlɔg] *nmf* rheumatologist

rhume [rym] *nm* cold; **attraper un r.** to catch a cold; **r. de cerveau** head cold; **r. des foins** hay fever

riant, -e [rijɑ̃, -ɑ̃t] *adj* (a) (*visage*) smiling, cheerful; (*yeux*) laughing, merry (b) (*paysage, campagne*) cheerful, sunny

RIB [rib] *nm* (*abrév* **relevé d'identité bancaire**) = document showing details of one's bank account

ribambelle [ribɑ̃bɛl] *nf* (*de personnes*) string, crowd

ricanement [rikanmɑ̃] *nm* sneer, snigger

ricaner [rikane] *vi* to sneer, to snigger

richard, -e [riʃar, -ard] *nm,f Péj* moneybags

riche [riʃ] **1** *adj* (a) (*personne, pays*) rich, wealthy (b) (*cuisine, aliment*) rich (c) (*vocabulaire*) extensive; (*style*) elaborate; (*description*) detailed (d) (*luxueux*) (*demeure*) luxurious; (*étoffe*) rich; (*vêtement*) sumptuous (e) *Fam* **c'est une r. idée** that's a fabulous idea (f) **r. en qch** rich in sth; **la journée a été r. en événements** it's been an action-packed day (g) **r. de** (*espérances*) full of; **livre/expérience r. d'enseignements** very instructive book/experience **2** *nmf* rich person; **les riches** the rich

richement [riʃmɑ̃] adv richly

richesse [riʃɛs] nf (a) (d'une personne, d'un pays) wealth; **c'est le tableau qui fait la r. de notre musée** this painting is the prize item in our museum's collection; **richesses** (biens) riches, wealth; **Fam voilà toutes mes richesses** this is everything I've got (b) (luxe) (d'une demeure) luxuriousness; (de vêtements) sumptuousness (c) **richesses** (ressources) resources (d) (du sol, d'un gisement) richness; (de la végétation) lushness (e) (de l'imagination) vividness, liveliness; (d'un style) elaborateness; (du vocabulaire) richness; (d'une description) detailed nature

richissime [riʃisim] adj extremely wealthy

ricin [risɛ̃] nm voir **huile**

ricocher [rikɔʃe] vi (projectile) to ricochet (sur off); (sur l'eau) to bounce (sur off)

ricochet [rikɔʃɛ] nm (projectile) ricochet; (sur l'eau) bounce; **faire des ricochets** (pour s'amuser) to skim pebbles; Fig **par r.** indirectly

ric-rac [rikrak] adv Fam (a) (de justesse) **réussir un examen r.** to scrape through an exam (b) **être r.** (financièrement) to be a bit strapped for cash

rictus [riktys] nm grimace

ride [rid] nf (a) (sur le visage) wrinkle, line; Fam **ne pas prendre une r.** not to age (b) (sur l'eau) ripple

ridé, -e [ride] adj wrinkled

rideau, -x [rido] nm (a) (dans une pièce) Br curtain, Am drape; **r. de fer** (de boutique) metal shutter; (en Europe) Iron Curtain (b) (de théâtre) curtain (c) (écran) (d'arbres) screen, curtain; (de feu, de fumée) wall; (de pluie) curtain

rider [ride] 1 vt (a) (front) to wrinkle, to line; (peau) to wrinkle, to shrivel (b) (eau, sable) to ripple
2 se rider vpr (a) (front, peau) to become wrinkled or lined (b) (eau) to ripple

ridicule [ridikyl] 1 adj ridiculous, ludicrous; (prix) ridiculously low; **se rendre r.** to make a fool of oneself
2 nm (a) (absurdité) ridiculousness (b) (dérision) ridicule; **tourner qn/qch en r.** to ridicule sb/sth; **se couvrir de r.** to make a complete fool of oneself

ridiculement [ridikylmɑ̃] adv ridiculously, ludicrously

ridiculiser [ridikylize] 1 vt to ridicule, to make fun of
2 se ridiculiser vpr to make oneself look ridiculous, to make a fool of oneself

rien [rjɛ̃] 1 pron (a) (avec ne) nothing; **r. ne l'affecte** nothing affects him; **r. de ce que j'ai proposé ne leur a plu** they didn't like anything I suggested; **r. ne va plus!** (au casino) no more bets!; **ne... r.** nothing, not anything; **je n'ai r. à faire** I've got nothing to do; **il n'a r. mangé** he hasn't eaten a thing; **personne n'osa r. dire** nobody dared say anything; **il n'y a r. de nouveau** there's nothing new, there isn't anything new; **ce n'est r.** it's nothing; **comme si de r. n'était** as if nothing had happened; **elle ne ressemble en r. à sa sœur** she's nothing like her sister; Litt **il n'en est r.** such is not the case; **il n'a r. d'un don Juan** he's no Casanova; Fam **r. de r.** nothing at all
(b) (sans ne) **qu'avez-vous fait? – r. /presque r.** what did you do? – nothing/hardly anything; **de r.** (je vous en prie) you're welcome; don't mention it; **pour r.** (gratuitement) for nothing; **pourquoi demandez-vous cela? – pour r.** why do you ask? – no reason; **un petit problème de r. du tout** a trivial little problem; **quinze à r.** (au tennis) fifteen love
(c) (quelque chose) anything; **y a-t-il r. de plus triste?** is there anything more depressing?; **sans r. faire** without doing anything; **sans nous gêner en r.** without

troubling us at all or in the slightest
(d) (locutions) **r. que** just, only; **je frémis r. que d'y songer** just thinking about it makes me shudder; **r. que la vérité** nothing but the truth; **élever quatre enfants, ce n'est pas r.!** raising four children is quite an achievement
2 nm (a) (bagatelle) **un r. l'habille** she looks good in anything; **s'énerver pour un r.** to get annoyed over nothing; **il court un kilomètre comme un r.** he can run a kilometre just like that
(b) **un r. long/bête** (un peu) a bit long/stupid; **un r. de** (un petit peu de) a little; **en un r. de temps** in no time at all

rieur, -euse [rijœr, -øz] adj (air, visage) cheerful, bright; (yeux) laughing, merry

Riga [riga] n Riga

rigide [riʒid] adj (a) (matériau) rigid; (couverture de livre) hard (b) Fig (personne, règlement, système) rigid, inflexible

rigidité [riʒidite] nf (a) (d'un matériau) rigidity; Fig (d'une personne, d'un règlement, d'un système) rigidity, inflexibility; **r. cadavérique** rigor mortis

rigolade [rigɔlad] nf Fam (a) (amusement) fun (b) **c'était de la r.** (c'était facile) it was a walkover; **ça n'est pas de la r.** (c'est sérieux) it's no joke; **prendre qch à la r.** to treat sth as a joke

rigolard, -e [rigɔlar, -ard] adj Fam (air) grinning

rigole [rigɔl] nf (petit fossé) channel; (filet d'eau) rivulet

rigoler [rigɔle] vi Fam (a) (rire) to laugh (b) (s'amuser) to have a laugh (c) (plaisanter) to joke (avec about); Fig **il ne faut pas r. avec le fisc** you shouldn't mess about with the tax man

rigolo, -ote [rigɔlo, -ɔt] Fam 1 adj funny
2 nm,f (plaisantin) scream, hoot; Péj (fumiste) clown

rigorisme [rigɔrism] nm strictness

rigoriste [rigɔrist] 1 adj strict, rigorous
2 nmf strict moralist

rigoureusement [rigurøzmɑ̃] adv (a) (strictement) (interdit) strictly; (exact) absolutely; (contraire) rigorously (b) (scrupuleusement) **suivre r. les consignes** to follow the instructions to the letter (c) (sévèrement) severely

rigoureux, -euse [rigurø, -øz] adj (a) (dur) (punition, mesures, conditions) severe, harsh; (hiver) hard; (climat) harsh (b) (strict) (neutralité) strict; (analyse) rigorous; **être r. dans qch** (personne) to be rigorous in sth

rigueur [rigœr] nf (a) (dureté) harshness, severity; (de la loi) rigour (b) (austérité) austerity (c) (exactitude) (d'une analyse) rigour; **manquer de r.** (style, personne) to be sloppy (d) (locutions) **à la r.** (si nécessaire) if need be; **être de r.** to be compulsory; **tenir r. à qn de qch** to hold sth against sb

rillettes [rijɛt] nfpl potted meat (made from pork, rabbit, goose etc)

rime [rim] nf rhyme; **sans r. ni raison** without rhyme or reason

rimer [rime] vi (a) (mot) to rhyme (avec with) (b) Fig **ne r. à rien** not to make any sense

Rimmel® [rimɛl] nm mascara

rinçage [rɛ̃saʒ] nm (a) (action) rinsing (b) (pour les cheveux) tint, rinse

rince-doigts [rɛ̃sdwa] nm inv finger bowl

rincée [rɛ̃se] nf (a) Fam (averse) downpour (b) Fam (volée de coups) walloping

rincer [16] [rɛ̃se] **1** vt (vêtements, vaisselle, cheveux) to rinse; (verre, tasse) to rinse (out)

2 se rincer vpr (à l'eau douce) to rinse oneself; **se r. la bouche** to rinse out one's mouth; *Fam* **se r. l'œil** to get an eyeful

ring [riŋ] nm ring; **le r.** (la boxe) boxing

ringard, -e [rɛ̃gar, -ard] *Fam* **1** adj (a) (démodé) untrendy, unhip (b) (de mauvais goût) tacky

2 nm,f square

Rio de Janeiro [rijodadʒanero] n Rio de Janeiro

ripaille [ripaj] nf *Fam* **faire r.** to have a blow-out

riposte [ripɔst] nf (a) (en boxe, en escrime) riposte (b) (réponse) riposte, retort (c) (représailles) counterattack

riposter [ripɔste] **1** vt **il m'a riposté que...** he retorted that...

2 vi (a) (en boxe, en escrime) to riposte (b) (user de représailles) to counterattack

3 riposter à vt ind (attaque, injures) to counter

ripou (pl **ripoux** ou **ripous**) [ripu] *Fam* **1** adj (policier) bent

2 nm bent cop

riquiqui [rikiki] adj inv (tout petit) teeny-weeny; (portion, cadeau) stingy, mean; (maillot de bain) skimpy

rire¹ [rir] nm laughter, laughing

rire² [61] [rir] **1** vi (a) (personne) to laugh; **r. comme un bossu**, *Fam* **r. comme une baleine** to laugh like a drain; **r. jaune** to force a laugh; **r. aux éclats** to roar with laughter; **r. aux larmes** to cry with laughter; **r. tout bas** to laugh to oneself (b) (s'amuser) to have fun, to have a laugh; **pour r.** for a joke; **vous voulez r.!** you're joking!; **laissez-moi r.!** don't make me laugh!

2 rire de vt ind (se moquer de) (personne, remarques, situation) to laugh at; *Litt* **je ris de leurs insultes** I'm impervious to their insults; **il vaut mieux en r.** you have to laugh

3 se rire vpr *Litt* **se r. de** (se moquer de) to laugh at; (se jouer de) to make light of

ris¹ [ri] nm (sur une voile) reef

ris² nm **r. de veau** calf's sweetbread

risée [rize] nf (a) (moquerie, derision; **s'exposer à la r. publique** to expose oneself to public scorn (b) **être la r. de** to be the laughing stock of

risette [rizɛt] nf *Fam* little smile; **fais des risettes à ton papa!** smile for daddy!, give daddy a smile!

risible [rizibl] adj laughable, ridiculous

risque [risk] nm risk; **prendre un r./des risques** to take a risk/risks; **courir le r. de faire qch** to risk doing sth; **c'est un r. à courir** it's a risk I/we/etc have to take; **avoir le goût du r.** to like taking risks; **les risques du métier** occupational hazards; **faire qch à ses risques et périls** to do sth at one's own risk; **au r. de sa vie** at the risk of her life; **au r. de faire qch** at the risk of doing sth

risqué, -e [riske] adj (a) (dangereux) risky (b) (osé) risqué

risquer [riske] **1** vt (a) (mettre en danger) (vie, réputation) to risk; **qu'est-ce que tu risques?** what have you got to lose?; **r. sa tête** to put one's head on the block; **r. le tout pour le tout** to go for broke (b) **r. un œil** to peep out; **r. une question** to venture a question

2 risquer de vt ind **il risque de se faire renvoyer** he's in danger of being sacked; **ça risque de durer longtemps** that may well last for a long time; *Fam* **il risque de gagner** he stands a good chance of winning; *Fam* **il ne risque pas de te le dire** fat chance of him

telling you

3 se risquer vpr to take risks/a risk; **se r. à faire qch** to venture to do sth; **je ne m'y risquerais pas** I wouldn't risk it

risque-tout [riskatu] nmf inv daredevil

rissoler [risole] vt & vi to brown

ristourne [risturn] nf discount; **faire une r. à qn** to give sb a discount

rital, -e, -als, -ales [rital] nm,f *Fam* (Italien) wop, *Br* Eyetie, = racist term used to refer to an Italian

rite [rit] nm (a) (religieux) rite; **r. de passage** ou **initiatique** rite of passage (b) *Fig* (cérémonie, habitude) ritual

ritournelle [riturnɛl] nf (phrase musicale) ritornello; *Fam* **c'est toujours la même r.** it's always the same old story

rituel, -elle [rituɛl] **1** adj ritual

2 nm ritual; **r. d'initiation** initiation rites

rituellement [rituɛlmã] adv invariably

rivage [rivaʒ] nm shore

rival, -e, -aux, -ales [rival, -o] **1** adj rival

2 nm,f rival; **sans r.** unrivalled

rivaliser [rivalize] vi **r. avec qn** to compete with sb; **r. de qch avec qn** to try to outdo sb in sth

rivalité [rivalite] nf rivalry

rive [riv] nf (a) (de rivière) bank; (de lac, de mer) shore (b) **la r. gauche/droite** (à Paris) the Left/Right Bank

river [rive] vt (a) (fixer) to rivet; *Fig* **être rivé à qch** to be glued to sth; **avoir les yeux rivés sur qn/qch** not to be able to take one's eyes off sb/sth (b) (goupille, clou) to clinch; *Fam* **r. son clou à qn** to shut sb up

riverain, -e [rivrɛ̃, -ɛn] **1** adj (propriété) (le long d'une rivière) riverside, waterside; (autour d'un lac) lakeside, waterside

2 nm,f (a) (près d'une rivière) owner of a riverside property; (près d'un lac) owner of a lakeside property (b) (d'une rue) resident; **interdit sauf aux riverains** (sur panneau) ≃ no entry except for access

rivet [rive] nm rivet

rivetage [rivtaʒ] nm riveting

riveter [42] [rivte] vt to rivet

riveteuse [rivtøz] nf riveting machine

rivière [rivjer] nf (a) (cours d'eau) river (b) (de lave, de boue) river (c) **r. de diamants** diamond necklace, *Spéc* diamond rivière

rixe [riks] nf brawl

riz [ri] nm rice; **r. cantonais** Cantonese rice; **r. créole** boiled rice; **r. au lait** rice pudding; **r. pilaf** pilaf or pilau rice

riziculture [rizikyltyr] nf rice growing

rizière [rizjer] nf rice field, paddy field

RMI [eremi] nm (abrév **revenu minimum d'insertion**) *Br* ≃ income support, *Am* ≃ Welfare

RMiste [eremist] nmf *Br* ≃ person on income support, *Am* ≃ person on Welfare

RN [eren] nf (abrév **route nationale**) = designation of major road

RNIS [erenies] nm *Ordinat* (abrév **réseau numérique à intégration de services**) ISDN

robe [rɔb] nf (a) (de femme) dress; **r. de grossesse** maternity dress; **r. d'intérieur** housecoat; **r. de mariée** wedding dress; **r. du soir** evening gown (b) **r. de chambre** Br dressing gown, Am robe; **pommes de terre en r. de chambre** ou **des champs** jacket potatoes (c) (d'avocat, de juge) robe, gown (d) (habit religieux) robe (e) (pelage) (de cheval) coat (f) (du vin) colour

robinet [rɔbinɛ] nm Br tap, Am faucet

robinetterie [rɔbinɛtri] nf plumbing

robineux [rɔbinø] nm Can Fam Br tramp, Am hobo

robot [rɔbo] nm robot; **r. ménager** food processor

robotique [rɔbɔtik] 1 adj robotic
2 nf robotics (singulier)

robotisation [rɔbɔtizasjɔ̃] nf automation, robotization

robotiser [rɔbɔtize] vt to automate, to robotize

robuste [rɔbyst] adj (personne) robust; (bras, jambe) sturdy; (appétit) healthy; (plante) hardy; **être d'une santé r.** to have a healthy constitution

robustesse [rɔbystɛs] nf (d'une personne) robustness; (d'une plante) hardiness; (d'un véhicule) sturdiness

roc [rɔk] nm rock

rocade [rɔkad] nf (route) bypass

rocaille [rɔkaj] 1 nf (a) (terrain) stony ground (b) (jardin) rockery
2 adj inv (style) rocaille

rocailleux, -euse [rɔkajø, -øz] adj (a) (pierreux) stony, rocky (b) Fig (voix) harsh, rough

roche [rɔʃ] nf rock

rocher [rɔʃe] nm (a) (masse de pierre) rock; (escarpé) crag; **le R. = Monaco; le r. de Gibraltar** the Rock of Gibraltar (b) (paroi) rock face (c) **r. (au chocolat)** chocolate (containing nuts)

rocheux, -euse [rɔʃø, -øz] adj (paysage, région) rocky; **la paroi rocheuse** the rock face; **les (montagnes) Rocheuses** the Rocky Mountains

rock [rɔk] 1 adj inv (concert, groupe, chanteur) rock
2 nm inv le r. rock; **danser le r.** to jive

rocker [rɔkœr] nm, **rockeur, -euse** [rɔkœr, -øz] nm,f (musicien) rock musician; (fan) rock fan

rocking-chair [rɔkiŋtʃɛr] (pl rocking-chairs) [rɔkiŋtʃɛr] nm rocking chair

rock'n roll [rɔkɛnrɔl] nm le r. rock and roll

rococo [rɔkoko] 1 adj inv (a) (meuble, style) rococo (b) (démodé) old-fashioned
2 nm rococo

rodage [rɔdaʒ] nm (d'une voiture) running in; **en r.** (sur panneau) running in

rodéo [rodeo] nm (avec des chevaux) rodeo; Fig (bagarre) free-for-all

roder [rɔde] vt (moteur, voiture) to run in; Fig (entreprise, spectacle) to get into its stride; (équipe, structure) to break in; **être rodé** (entreprise, spectacle) to be into its stride; (employé) to have got the hang of things

rôder [rode] vi to be on the prowl

rôdeur, -euse [rodœr, -øz] nm,f prowler

rogne [rɔɲ] nf Fam bad temper; **être en r.** (contre) to be cross (with); **mettre qn en r.** to make sb cross; **se mettre** ou **Fam se ficher en r.** to get mad

rogner [rɔɲe] 1 vt (a) (griffes, ongles) to clip, to trim; Fig (économies) to eat away at; **r. les ailes à qn** to clip sb's wings (b) (retrancher) **r. qch à qn** to gradually take sth away from sb (c) Ordinat (image) to crop
2 rogner sur vt ind **r. sur qch** to cut down on sth

rognon [rɔɲɔ̃] nm kidney

rognures [rɔɲyr] nfpl (de cuir, de métal) trimmings, parings

rogue [rɔg] adj arrogant, haughty

roi [rwa] nm (a) (souverain) king; **tirer les rois** = to celebrate Twelfth Night by eating a cake containing a small charm. The person finding the charm in their piece of cake is given a paper crown to wear; **les Rois mages** the Three Wise Men; **le R.-Soleil** the Sun King; Fig (le plus grand) (des animaux) king; **c'est le r. des imbéciles** he's a prize idiot; très Fam **c'est le r. des cons** he's a complete arsehole (c) (aux cartes, aux échecs) king
2 adj inv **bleu r.** royal blue

roitelet [rwatlɛ] nm (oiseau) wren

rôle [rol] nm (a) (d'une pièce de théâtre) part, role; Fig **avoir le beau r.** to have the easy job; **premier r.** leading role; **r.-titre** title role (b) (fonction) (du médecin, d'un organe, d'une activité) role, function (dans in); **jouer un r. de premier plan** to play a key role; **jouer un r. secondaire** to play second fiddle

ROM [rɔm] nf Ordinat ROM

romain, -e[1] [rɔmɛ̃, -ɛn] 1 adj Roman
2 nm,f R. Roman
3 nm (caractère d'imprimerie) roman

romaine[2] [rɔmɛn] nf (salade) Br cos lettuce, Am romaine; Fig **être bon comme la r.** to be extremely kind

roman[1] [rɔmɑ̃] nm (a) (en prose) novel; **le nouveau r.** the anti-novel, the nouveau roman; **r. d'amour** love story, romance; Fam **r. à l'eau de rose** soppy love story, soppy romance; **r. noir** thriller; **r. policier** detective novel (b) (poème) romance (c) Fig **c'est du r.** (c'est invraisemblable) it's just a fairy tale; Fig **c'est tout un r.** (c'est incroyable) it's quite a tale

roman[2], -e [rɔmɑ̃, -an] 1 adj (a) (langue) Romance (b) Archit Romanesque
2 nm (a) (langue) Romance (b) Archit Romanesque style

romance [rɔmɑ̃s] nf (chanson) sentimental song or ballad

romancer [16] [rɔmɑ̃se] vt (événement, histoire) to romanticize; (biographie) to fictionalize

romanche [rɔmɑ̃ʃ] adj & nm Romansch

romancier, -ère [rɔmɑ̃sje, -ɛr] nm,f novelist

romand, -e [rɔmɑ̃, -ɑ̃d] 1 adj (Suisse) French-speaking
2 nm,f R. French-speaking Swiss person

romanesque [rɔmanɛsk] adj (a) (personne, aventure) romantic (b) (technique) novelistic

roman-feuilleton (pl romans-feuilletons) [rɔmɑ̃fœjtɔ̃] nm serial

roman-fleuve (pl romans-fleuves) [rɔmɑ̃flœv] nm saga

romanichel, -elle [rɔmaniʃɛl] nm,f (Tsigane) gypsy

roman-photo (pl romans-photos) [rɔmɑ̃foto] nm photo-story

romantique [rɔmɑ̃tik] 1 adj (a) (peinture, littérature, artiste) Romantic (b) (personne, idées, film) romantic
2 nmf (a) (artiste, auteur) Romantic(ist) (b) (personne) romantic

romantisme [rɔmɑ̃tism] nm (a) (courant artistique) Romanticism (b) (attitude, sensibilité) romanticism

romarin [rɔmarɛ̃] nm rosemary

rombière [rɔ̃bjɛr] nf Fam old biddy

Rome [rɔm] n Rome

rompre [rɔ̃pr] 1 vt (a) (casser) to break; **r. ses digues** (fleuve) to burst its banks (b) (négociations, fiançailles, relations) to break off; (contrat, charme, monotonie) to break; (équilibre) to upset (c) (locutions) **applaudir à tout r.** to applaud wildly; **r. les rangs** to fall out
2 vi (a) (casser) to break (b) (se séparer) to split up (avec with); **r. avec sa famille** to break off relations with one's family (c) **r. avec la tradition** to break with tradition
3 **se rompre** vpr (se casser) to break; **son cœur battait à se r.** his heart was pounding; Fig **se r. le cou** to break one's neck

rompu, -e [rɔ̃py] adj (a) (exténué) **être r. (de fatigue)** to be worn out (b) (expérimenté) **r. à qch** used to sth

romsteck [rɔmstɛk] nm rump steak

ronce [rɔ̃s] nf (a) (arbuste) bramble (bush), blackberry bush (b) (dans le bois) **r. de noyer** burr walnut

ronchon, -onne [rɔ̃ʃɔ̃, -ɔn] Fam 1 adj grouchy, grumpy
2 nm,f grumbler, grouser

ronchonnement [rɔ̃ʃɔnmɑ̃] nm Fam grumbling, grousing

ronchonner [rɔ̃ʃɔne] vi Fam to grumble, to grouse

roncier [rɔ̃sje] nm, **roncière** [rɔ̃sjɛr] nf thick bramble bush

rond, -e [rɔ̃, rɔ̃d] 1 adj (a) (balle, table, nappe) round; (ventre) rounded; (poitrine) full; (personne, joues, silhouette) plump; **avoir le dos r.** to be round-shouldered (b) (plein) (voix) full (c) (chiffre, compte) round (d) **être r. en affaires** to be straightforward where business is concerned (e) Fam (ivre) plastered; **r. comme une queue de pelle** rat-arsed
2 adv tout r. (exactement) exactly
3 nm (a) (figure) circle; **en r.** in a circle; Fam **faire des ronds de jambe** to bow and scrape; Fam **en rester comme deux ronds de flan** to be absolutely staggered; **r. de serviette** napkin ring (b) Fam (sou) **il n'a pas un r.** he hasn't got a penny

rond-de-cuir (pl ronds-de-cuir) [rɔ̃dkɥir] nm Fam Péj pen-pusher

ronde [rɔ̃d] nf (a) (danse) round (dance); (chanson) round, roundelay (b) (de gardien, de vigile) round(s); (de policier) beat; **faire une/sa r.** (gardien, vigile) to patrol; (policier) to be on the beat (c) Mus (note) Br semibreve, Am whole note (d) **à la r.** (autour) around; **à 10 kilomètres à la r.** within a radius of 10 kilometres

rondeau, -x [rɔ̃do] nm rondo

rondelet, -ette [rɔ̃dlɛ, -ɛt] adj (a) (personne) plump, chubby (b) (somme) tidy

rondelle [rɔ̃dɛl] nf (a) (de citron, de saucisson) slice; **couper qch en rondelles** to slice sth (b) Can **r.** (de hockey) puck (c) (d'écrou) washer

rondement [rɔ̃dmɑ̃] adv (a) (avec entrain) briskly, promptly; **mener qch r.** to make short work of sth (b) (franchement) bluntly, frankly

rondeur [rɔ̃dœr] nf (a) (d'un corps) roundness; (des joues) plumpness (b) **rondeurs** (d'une femme) curves (c) (amabilité) **avec r.** bluntly, frankly

rondin [rɔ̃dɛ̃] nm log

rondo [rɔ̃do] nm rondo

rondouillard, -e [rɔ̃dujar, -ard] adj Fam (personne) plump, chubby

---

rond-point (pl ronds-points) [rɔ̃pwɛ̃] nm (sens giratoire) Br roundabout, Am traffic circle

ronéotyper [rɔneotipe] vt to roneo

ronflant, -e [rɔ̃flɑ̃, -ɑ̃t] adj Péj high-flown, high-sounding

ronflement [rɔ̃fləmɑ̃] nm (a) (d'une personne) snoring (b) (d'un moteur, d'une machine) whirring, purring

ronfler [rɔ̃fle] vi (a) (dormeur) to snore (b) (moteur) to whirr, to purr; (poêle) to purr

ronfleur, -euse [rɔ̃flœr, -øz] nm,f (personne) snorer

ronger [45] [rɔ̃ʒe] 1 vt (a) (bois) to gnaw (at), to nibble (at); (os) to gnaw (on); **rongé par les vers** worm-eaten (b) (acide, rouille) to eat away or into; (falaise) to erode (c) (tourmenter) **être rongé de chagrin** to be tormented with grief; **être rongé de remords/par la jalousie/par l'anxiété** to be eaten up with remorse/jealousy/anxiety; **être rongé par la maladie** to be wasted by illness (d) Fig **r. son frein** to champ at the bit
2 **se ronger** vpr **se r. les ongles** to bite one's nails

rongeur, -euse [rɔ̃ʒœr, -øz] 1 adj (mammifère) rodent-like
2 nm rodent

ronron [rɔ̃rɔ̃], **ronronnement** [rɔ̃rɔnmɑ̃] nm (a) (d'un chat) purr (b) (d'un moteur) purr, whirr; (d'un avion, d'une voix) drone; (d'une machine) whirr (c) (routine) humdrum routine

ronronner [rɔ̃rɔne] vi (a) (chat) to purr (b) (moteur) to purr, to whirr; (avion) to drone (c) (machine) to whirr

roquefort [rɔkfɔr] nm Roquefort

roquet [rɔkɛ] nm Péj (chien) yap

roquette¹ [rɔkɛt] nf (salade) rocket

roquette² nf (projectile) rocket; **r. antichar** anti-tank rocket

rorqual, -als [rɔrkwal] nm rorqual, finback whale

rosace [rozas] nf (a) (vitrail) rose window (b) (au plafond) ceiling rose (c) (de guitare) rosette

rosaire [rozɛr] nm rosary; **dire ou réciter son r.** to say the rosary

rosâtre [rozatr] adj pinkish

rosbif [rɔzbif] nm (a) (viande, rôtie) roast beef; (à rôtir) roasting beef (b) Fam (Britannique) Brit, = racist term used to refer to a British person

rose [roz] 1 adj pink; Fig **tout n'est pas r.** it's not all rosy; **r. bonbon** candy pink; **r. thé** tea rose; **vieux r.** old rose
2 nf (a) (fleur) rose; **frais comme une r.** fresh as a daisy; Fam **ne pas sentir la r.** to be a bit whiffy; **r. trémière** hollyhock (b) **r. des sables** desert rose; **r. des vents** compass card
3 nm pink; **voir la vie ou tout en r.** to see everything through rose-coloured glasses

rosé, -e [roze] 1 adj pinkish
2 nm (vin) rosé

roseau, -x [rozo] nm reed

rosée [roze] nf dew

roseraie [rozrɛ] nf rose garden

rosette [rozɛt] nf (a) (nœud) bow; (ornement) rosette (b) (insigne) rosette (especially of the Legion of Honour)

rosier [rozje] nm rose-tree, rosebush

rosière [rozjɛr] nf Vieilli = village maiden awarded a wreath of roses for her virtuous conduct

rosir [rozir] 1 vt to turn pink
2 vi to go or turn pink

rosse [ʀɔs] *Péj* **1** *adj Fam (personne, conduite, remarque)* rotten

2 *nf* (a) *(cheval)* hack (b) *Fam (homme)* swine; *(femme)* bitch

rossée [ʀɔse] *nf Fam* beating, walloping

rosser [ʀɔse] *vt Fam* **r. qn** to beat sb up, to give sb a good hiding; **se faire r.** to get a hiding

rossignol [ʀɔsiɲɔl] *nm* (a) *(oiseau)* nightingale (b) *Fam (objet)* white elephant

rot [ʀo] *nm Fam* belch, burp; *(de bébé)* burp; **faire un r.** *(adulte)* to belch, to burp; *(bébé)* to burp

rotatif, -ive [ʀɔtatif, -iv] **1** *adj (pompe, moteur)* rotary
2 *nf* rotative rotary press

rotation [ʀɔtasjɔ̃] *nf* rotation; *(du stock, de fonds)* turnover

roter [ʀɔte] *vi Fam* to belch, to burp

rôti, -e [ʀoti] **1** *adj* roast
2 *nm (viande)* joint, roast; **r. de porc** *(cuit)* roast pork; *(non cuit)* joint of pork

rotin¹ [ʀɔtɛ̃] *nm* rattan; **chaise en r.** cane *or* rattan chair

rotin² [ʀɔtɛ̃] *nm Fam Vieilli (sou)* **il n'a plus un r.** he's stone-broke

rôtir [ʀotiʀ] **1** *vt (viande)* to roast
2 *vi* (a) *(viande)* to roast (b) **r. au soleil** to bask in the sun
3 **se rôtir** *vpr* **se r. au soleil** to bask in the sun

rôtisserie [ʀotisʀi] *nf* (a) *(boutique du rôtisseur)* = shop selling roast meat (b) *(restaurant)* grillroom, steakhouse

rôtissoire [ʀotiswaʀ] *nf (rotating)* spit, rotisserie

rotonde [ʀɔtɔ̃d] *nf* rotunda

rotor [ʀɔtɔʀ] *nm* rotor

rotule [ʀɔtyl] *nf* kneecap; *Fam* **être sur les rotules** to be dead beat

roturier, -ère [ʀɔtyʀje, -ɛʀ] **1** *adj* common
2 *nm,f* commoner

rouage [ʀwaʒ] *nm* (a) *(d'un mécanisme)* works (b) *Fig (d'une administration, d'une organisation)* workings

roublard, -e [ʀublaʀ, -aʀd] *Fam* **1** *adj (personne, air)* wily, cunning
2 *nm,f* wily *or* cunning devil

roublardise [ʀublaʀdiz] *nf Fam* (a) *(caractère)* cunning, wiliness (b) *(acte)* crafty *or* cunning trick

rouble [ʀubl] *nm* rouble

roucoulade [ʀukulad] *nf (d'oiseaux)* cooing; *Fam* **roucoulades** *(d'amoureux)* billing and cooing

roucoulement [ʀukulmɑ̃] *nm (d'un pigeon)* cooing; *Fig (d'amoureux)* billing and cooing

roucouler [ʀukule] **1** *vi (pigeon)* to coo; *Fig (amoureux)* to bill and coo
2 *vt (mots doux, promesses)* to coo

roue [ʀu] *nf* (a) *(d'un véhicule)* wheel; **être la cinquième r. du carrosse** *Br* to be a spare part, *Am* to be the fifth wheel; **faire la r.** *(oiseau)* to spread its tail; *Fig & Péj* to strut, to swagger; **un deux roues** a two-wheeled vehicle; **r. libre** freewheel; **descendre en r. libre** to freewheel downhill; **r. de secours** spare wheel (b) *(figure de gymnastique)* cartwheel

roué, -e [ʀwe] *Litt* **1** *adj* cunning, sly
2 *nm,f* cunning person

rouer [ʀwe] *vt* **r. qn de coups** to beat sb black and blue

rouerie [ʀuʀi] *nf (acte)* cunning *or* sly trick **(envers** played on)

rouet [ʀwɛ] *nm* spinning wheel

rouge [ʀuʒ] **1** *adj* (a) *(tissu, objet, joue, vin)* red; **r. cerise** cherry-red; **r. sang** blood-red (b) *(personne)* **r. de colère/ d'émotion** red in the face with anger/emotion; **être r. de honte** to blush with shame; **être r. comme une écrevisse** to be as red as a lobster; **être r. comme une tomate** *ou* **une pivoine** to be as red as a beetroot (c) *(chauffé) (fer)* red-hot
2 *adv* **se fâcher tout r.** to lose one's temper completely; **voir r.** to see red
3 *nm* (a) *(couleur)* red; **peindre/teindre qch en r.** to paint/dye sth red; **le r. lui monte aux joues** he's/she's going red in the face (b) *(chaleur extrême)* **porter** *ou* **chauffer qch au r.** to heat sth until it is red-hot (c) *(cosmétique)* **r. à lèvres** lipstick; **se mettre du r.** to put some *or* one's lipstick on (d) *Fam* **passer au r.** *(signal d'arrêt)* to turn or go red (e) *(vin)* red wine; *Fam* **gros r.** plonk (f) *Fam Fig* **être dans le r.** *(financièrement)* to be in the red
4 *nmf (communiste)* Red

rougeâtre [ʀuʒɑtʀ] *adj* reddish

rougeaud, -e [ʀuʒo, -od] **1** *adj* red-faced
2 *nm,f* red-faced person

rouge-gorge *(pl* rouges-gorges) [ʀuʒgɔʀʒ] *nm* robin

rougeoiement [ʀuʒwamɑ̃] *nm* red glow

rougeole [ʀuʒɔl] *nf* measles *(singulier)*; **avoir la r.** to have measles

rougeoyant, -e [ʀuʒwajɑ̃, -ɑ̃t] *adj* glowing (red)

rougeoyer [32] [ʀuʒwaje] *vi* to turn red

rouget [ʀuʒɛ] *nm* red mullet

rougeur [ʀuʒœʀ] *nf* (a) *(due à la chaleur, à l'émotion)* flush; *(due à la honte, à la gêne)* blush (b) *(tache)* blotch (c) *(couleur)* redness

rougir [ʀuʒiʀ] **1** *vt* (a) *(ciel, feuilles)* to turn red (b) *(visage)* to redden
2 *vi* (a) *(ciel, feuilles)* to turn red (b) *(personne)* to turn red; *(de honte, gêne)* to blush, to go red; *Fig (avoir honte)* to be ashamed; **r. jusqu'aux oreilles** to blush to the roots of one's hair; **r. de colère/d'émotion** to flush with anger/ emotion

rougissant, -e [ʀuʒisɑ̃, -ɑ̃t] *adj (personne, visage)* blushing

rouille [ʀuj] **1** *adj inv* rust(-coloured)
2 *nf* (a) *(sur le fer)* rust (b) *(sauce)* = spicy sauce made with garlic and chillis, traditionally served with fish soup

rouillé, -e [ʀuje] *adj* (a) *(métal, clef)* rusty, rusted (b) *Fig (personne)* rusty

rouiller [ʀuje] **1** *vt (métal, clef)* to rust, to make rusty
2 *vi (métal, clef)* to rust, to go rusty
3 **se rouiller** *vpr* (a) *(métal, clef)* to rust, to get rusty (b) *Fig (personne) (physiquement)* to get stiff; *(intellectuellement) (langue, connaissances)* to get rusty

roulade [ʀulad] *nf* (a) *(en gymnastique)* **r. avant/arrière** forward/backward roll; **faire des roulades** to do rolls (b) *(vocalise)* roulade (c) *(charcuterie)* rolled and stuffed meat

roulant, -e [ʀulɑ̃, -ɑ̃t] *adj* (a) *(porte)* sliding; *(pont)* travelling (b) *(capital)* working (c) *Fam (drôle) (personne, blague, histoire)* comical

roulé, -e [ʀule] **1** *adj* (a) *(journal, carte, tapis)* rolled(-up); *(charcuterie)* rolled (b) *Fam (femme)* **être bien roulée** to be curvy
2 *nm (gâteau)* Swiss roll

rouleau, -x [rulo] *nm* (a) *(bande) (de papier, de Scotch®, de pellicule)* roll; *Fam* **être au bout du r.** to be at the end of one's tether (b) *(objet circulaire) (pour peindre)* roller; **r. compresseur** steamroller; **r. à pâtisserie** rolling pin; **r. de printemps** spring roll (c) *(vague)* billow, roller (d) *(bigoudi)* roller (e) *(saut en hauteur)* **r. dorsal** Fosbury flop; **r. ventral** western roll

roulé-boulé (*pl* **roulés-boulés**) [rulebule] *nm* roll *(executed tucked up in a ball)*

roulement [rulmɑ̃] *nm* (a) *(d'une balle)* rolling (b) *(bruit)* **un r. de tonnerre** a roll or rumble of thunder; **des roulements de tambour** drum rolls (c) *(alternance)* rotation; **par r.** in rotation (d) *(pièce)* bearing; **r. à billes** ball bearing (e) *Fin (de fonds)* circulation; *(de capitaux)* turnover

rouler [rule] **1** *vt* (a) *(pierre, tonneau)* to roll (along) (b) *(tapis, papier, manches)* to roll up; *(cigarette)* to roll (c) *(yeux)* to roll (d) *(balancer)* **r. les épaules** to roll one's shoulders; **r. les hanches** to swing one's hips (e) *Fam (duper)* to do (de out of); **se faire r.** to be done (f) *(locutions)* **r. les r** to roll one's r's; *très Fam* **r. une pelle** *ou* **un palot** *ou* **un patin à qn** to give sb a French kiss

2 *vi* (a) *(balle)* to roll; **faire r. qch sur le sol** to roll sth along the ground (b) *(dégringoler) (personne)* to roll, to tumble (c) *(dans une voiture, dans un train)* to go, to travel; **on a beaucoup roulé** we drove for a long time; **ça roule bien ce matin** there are no traffic problems this morning; **à quelle vitesse rouliez-vous?** what speed were you doing? (d) *Fam* **ça roule** everything's fine (e) *Fig* **r. sur l'or** to be rolling in money (f) *(conversation)* **r. sur qch** to be about sth (g) *(tonnerre)* to roll, to rumble; *(tambour)* to roll (h) *(navire)* to roll

3 se rouler *vpr* (a) *(sur soi-même)* **se r. par terre** to roll about on the floor; *(dehors)* to roll about on the ground (b) **se r. une cigarette** to roll a cigarette; *Fam* **se r. les pouces**, **se les r.** to twiddle one's thumbs

roulette [rulɛt] *nf* (a) *(de meuble)* castor; **à roulettes** *(meuble)* on castors; *Fam* **marcher** *ou* **aller comme sur des roulettes** to go like clockwork (b) *Fam (de dentiste)* drill (c) *(au jeu)* roulette; **r. russe** Russian roulette

roulis [ruli] *nm* roll

roulotte [rulɔt] *nf (de bohémiens)* caravan

roulure [rulyr] *nf très Fam* whore

roumain, -e [rumɛ̃, -ɛn] **1** *adj* Romanian

2 *nm,f* **R.** Romanian

3 *nm (langue)* Romanian

Roumanie [rumani] *nf* **la R.** Romania

round [rawnd, rund] *nm* round

roupie [rupi] *nf* rupee

roupiller [rupije] *vi Fam* to sleep, *Br* to kip

roupillon [rupijɔ̃] *nm Fam* snooze; **piquer un r.** to have a snooze

rouquin, -e [rukɛ̃, -in] *Fam* **1** *adj (personne)* red-haired

2 *nm,f* redhead

rouspéter [34] [ruspete] *vi Fam* to moan and groan, to grumble (**contre** about)

rouspéteur, -euse [ruspetœr, -øz] *Fam* **1** *adj* grumpy

2 *nm,f* moan, grumbler

rousse [rus] *voir* **roux**

roussette [rusɛt] *nf* (a) *(poisson)* spotted dogfish (b) *(chauve-souris)* flying fox (c) *(grenouille)* common frog

rousseur [rusœr] *nf (couleur)* redness

roussi [rusi] *nm* **ça sent le r.** there's a smell of burning; *Fig* I smell trouble

roussir [rusir] **1** *vt* (a) *(rendre roux)* to turn brown (b) *(brûler)* to scorch, to singe

2 *vi (feuilles, arbres)* to turn brown

routage [rutaʒ] *nm (d'imprimés)* sorting and mailing

routard, -e [rutar, -ard] *nm,f Fam* backpacker

route [rut] *nf* (a) *(voie)* road; **prendre la r. de Paris** to take the Paris road; **r. à double voie** *ou* **à deux voies** *Br* dual carriageway, *Am* divided highway; **par la r.** by road; **r. départementale** secondary road, *Br* B-road; **r. nationale** main road, *Br* A-road, *Am* highway (b) *(itinéraire)* route, way; **montrer la r. à qn** to show sb the way; **c'est sur ma r.** it's on my way; **r. des vins** wine trail (c) *(trajet)* **après trois heures de r.** after three hours on the road; **se mettre en r.** *(personne)* to set off; **en r.!** let's be off!; *Fam Hum* **en r., mauvaise troupe!** come on, you lot!; **bonne r.!** have a good trip! (d) *Fig (chemin)* path (e) *(marche)* **mettre qch en r.** *(moteur)* to start sth up; *(projet, travaux)* to get sth under way; **avoir qch en r.** to be working on sth; *Fam* **ils ont un bébé en r.** they've got a baby on the way

routeur [rutœr] *nm Ordinat* router

routier, -ère [rutje, -ɛr] **1** *adj* road

2 *nm* (a) *(conducteur)* *Br* long-distance lorry driver, *Am* truck driver (b) *(restaurant)* *Br* transport cafe, *Am* truck stop

routine [rutin] *nf* (a) *(habitude)* routine; **s'enliser dans/ sortir de la r.** to get into/out of a rut (b) *Ordinat* **r. d'édition/de logiciel** edit/software routine

routinier, -ère [rutinje, -ɛr] *adj (tâches, travail)* routine; **être r.** to be set in one's ways

rouvrir [52] [ruvrir] **1** *vt* to reopen

2 se rouvrir *vpr* to reopen, to open again

roux, rousse [ru, rus] **1** *adj (feuilles)* russet, reddish-brown; *(cheveux)* red; *(personne)* red-haired; *(sucre)* brown

2 *nm,f (personne)* red-haired person, redhead

3 *nm* (a) *(couleur)* russet, reddish-brown (b) *(préparation culinaire)* roux

royal, -e, -aux, -ales [rwajal, -o] *adj (palais, visite)* royal (b) *(cadeau)* magnificent; *(pourboire)* huge (c) *(indifférence)* utter; *Fam* **ficher une paix royale à qn** to leave sb in complete peace

royalement [rwajalmɑ̃] *adv* (a) *(payé)* royally (b) *Fam* **je m'en fiche** *ou* **moque r.** I couldn't care less

royalisme [rwajalism] *nm* royalism

royaliste [rwajalist] **1** *adj* royalist; *Fig* **être plus r. que le roi** to overdo it

2 *nmf* royalist

royalties [rwajalti] *nfpl* royalties

royaume [rwajom] *nm* kingdom; *Fig* realm

Royaume-Uni [rwajomyni] *nm* **le R.** the United Kingdom

royauté [rwajote] *nf (monarchie)* monarchy; *(dignité)* kingship

RPR [ɛrpeɛr] *nm Pol (abrév* **Rassemblement pour la République***)* = right-wing political party

RSVP *(abrév* **répondez s'il vous plaît***)* RSVP

ruade [rɥad] *nf (d'un cheval)* lashing out, kick

Ruanda = **Rwanda**

ruandais, -e [rɥɑ̃dɛ, -ɛz] = **rwandais**

ruban [rybɑ̃] *nm* ribbon; **r. adhésif** adhesive *or* sticky tape; **r. encreur** *(de machine à écrire)* typewriter ribbon; *Ordinat* **r. perforé** punchtape

rubéole [rybeɔl] *nf* German measles *(singulier)*, rubella

rubicond, -e [rybikɔ̃, -ɔd] *adj (teint)* florid, rubicund

rubis [rybi] *nm* (a) *(pierre précieuse)* ruby; *Fig* payer r. sur l'ongle to pay cash on the nail (b) *(de montre, d'horloge)* jewel

rubrique [rybrik] *nf* (a) *(articles)* column (b) *(catégorie)* heading; r. nécrologique obituary section

ruche [ryʃ] *nf* (a) *(abri)* beehive (b) *(essaim)* hive; *Fig (ville, école)* hive of activity

rucher [ryʃe] *nm* apiary

rude [ryd] *adj* (a) *(fruste)* rough, uncouth (b) *(sévère) (personne, voix)* harsh (c) *(peau, tissu)* rough (d) *(hiver, climat)* severe, harsh (e) *(tâche, métier)* tough

rudement [rydmã] *adv* (a) *(répondre)* harshly; être r. éprouvé to be severely tested (b) *(frapper, heurter)* hard (c) *Fam (très)* really

rudesse [rydɛs] *nf* harshness; avec r. harshly

rudimentaire [rydimãtɛr] *adj* rudimentary

rudiments [rydimã] *nmpl (d'une matière)* rudiments; avoir des r. de chinois to speak basic Chinese

rudoyer [32] [rydwaje] *vt* to treat harshly

rue [ry] *nf* street; être/se retrouver à la r. to be/find oneself out on the street; mettre/jeter qn à la r. to put/throw sb out on the street; r. piétonnière *ou* piétonne pedestrian precinct; r. principale main street; la grande r. the main street

ruée [rɥe] *nf* rush; la r. vers l'or the gold rush

ruelle [rɥɛl] *nf* lane, alley(way)

ruer [rɥe] 1 *vi (cheval)* to kick; *Fig* r. dans les brancards to rebel
   2 se ruer *vpr* se r. sur qn to rush at sb; se r. sur qch to make a rush for sth; les invités se sont rués sur le buffet the guests made a dash for the buffet

rugby [rygbi] *nm* rugby; r. à treize/quinze Rugby League/Union

rugbyman [rygbiman] *(pl* rugbymen [rygbimɛn]) *nm* rugby player

rugir [ryʒir] 1 *vi* (a) *(fauve)* to roar (b) *(personne)* to roar (de with) (c) *(vent, tempête)* to howl
   2 *vt* to roar

rugissement [ryʒismã] *nm* (a) *(d'un fauve)* roar; des rugissements roaring (b) *(d'une personne)* roar; pousser des rugissements de colère to roar with anger (c) *(du vent, d'une tempête)* howling

rugosité [rygozite] *nf* roughness; rugosités rough patches

rugueux, -euse [rygø, -øz] *adj* rough

ruine [rɥin] *nf* (a) *(écroulement) (d'un édifice)* en r. in ruins, ruined; tomber en ruine(s) to go to ruin (b) *ruines (décombres)* ruins (c) *Fig (d'une personne, d'une société)* ruin, downfall; aller *ou* courir à la r. to be on the road to ruin (d) *(vieille maison)* ruin (e) *Fam* c'est la r.! *(c'est coûteux)* it's outrageously expensive!

ruiner [rɥine] 1 *vt* to ruin; *(espoirs)* to ruin, to dash
   2 se ruiner *vpr (perdre son argent)* to ruin *or* bankrupt oneself; *(dépenser beaucoup d'argent)* to spend a fortune

ruineux, -euse [rɥinø, -øz] *adj* ruinously expensive; ce n'est pas r. it won't ruin you/us/etc

ruisseau, -x [rɥiso] *nm* (a) *(cours d'eau)* brook, stream (b) *Fig (de sang, de lave)* stream; *(de larmes)* flood (c) *(caniveau)* gutter

ruisselant, -e [rɥislã, -ãt] *adj* dripping (de with)

ruisseler [42] [rɥisle] *vi* (a) *(liquide)* to stream, to run (b) *(surface)* to drip, to stream (de with); le front ruisselant de sueur with one's forehead dripping with sweat; ses joues ruisselaient de larmes tears were streaming down his cheeks

ruissellement [rɥislmã] *nm* streaming, running

rumba [rumba] *nf* rumba

rumeur [rymœr] *nf* (a) *(bruit confus)* distant murmur; *(de la circulation, d'une ville)* hum; *(de voix)* murmur (b) *(nouvelle)* rumour

ruminant [ryminã] *nm* ruminant

rumination [ryminasjõ] *nf* rumination, ruminating

ruminer [rymine] 1 *vt (herbe)* to chew; *Fig (idée, projet)* to mull over
   2 *vi* to ruminate, to chew the cud; *Fig* to brood

rumsteck [rɔmstɛk] *nm* rump steak

rupestre [rypɛstr] *adj* (a) *peinture* r. rock painting; *(dans une caverne)* cave painting (b) *(plante)* rock

rupin, -e [rypɛ̃, -in] *Fam* 1 *adj (riche) (personne)* loaded
   2 *nm,f* c'est un r. he's loaded; les rupins the rich

rupture [ryptyr] *nf* (a) *(d'une corde, d'une poutre)* breaking; *(d'un barrage)* bursting; *(d'un tendon)* rupture (b) *(interruption) (de négociations)* breaking off (de of), breakdown (de in); être en r. avec qn/qch to be at odds with sb/sth; être en r. avec la tradition to be in a break with tradition; être en r. de stock to be out of stock (c) *(annulation) (de fiançailles)* breaking off; *(de contrat)* breach (d) *(entre amoureux)* break-up

rural, -e, -aux, -ales [ryral, -o] 1 *adj (région, vie)* rural; *(chemin)* country
   2 *nm,f* country person

ruse [ryz] *nf* (a) *(procédé)* ruse, trick; r. de guerre stratagem (of war); *Fig* dodge (b) *(calcul)* faire qch par la r. to do sth by trickery

rusé, -e [ryze] *adj* cunning, crafty

ruser [ryze] *vi* to use trickery or cunning

russe [rys] 1 *adj* Russian
   2 *nmf* R. Russian
   3 *nm (langue)* Russian

Russie [rysi] *nf* la R. Russia

rustaud, -e [rysto, -od] 1 *adj* uncouth
   2 *nm,f Br* country bumpkin, *Am* hick

Rustine® [rystin] *nf* repair patch *(for mending inner tube of bicycle)*

rustique [rystik] *adj* (a) *(manières, vie)* rustic; *(meuble)* rustic-style (b) *(plante)* hardy

rustre [rystr] 1 *adj* uncouth
   2 *nm* boor, lout

rut [ryt] *nm (de mâle)* rut(ting); *(de femelle)* heat; en r. *(mâle)* rutting; *(femelle)* in heat

rutabaga [rytabaga] *nm Br* swede, *Am* rutabaga

rutilant, -e [rytilã, -ãt] *adj* gleaming

rutiler [rytile] *vi* to gleam

Rwanda [rwãda] *nm* le R. Rwanda

rwandais, -e [rwãdɛ, -ez] 1 *adj* Rwandan
   2 *nm,f* R. Rwandan

rythme [ritm] *nm* (**a**) *(succession)* rhythm; *(allure)* pace; **manquer de r.** *(film)* to be a bit slow; **au r. de** at the rate of; **r. cardiaque/respiratoire** heart/breathing rate (**b**) *(en musique)* rhythm; **en r.** in time; **marquer le r.** to beat time; **suivre le r.** to follow the beat; *Fig* to keep up; **avoir le sens du r.** to have a sense of rhythm; **avoir le r. dans la peau** to have rhythm in one's blood (**c**) *(d'une phrase)* rhythm

rythmé, -e [ritme] *adj* rhythmic(al)
rythmer [ritme] *vt* to give rhythm to
rythmique [ritmik] **1** *adj* rhythmic(al)
2 *nf (en poésie)* rhythmics *(singulier)*

S

S, s [ɛs] nm inv S, s; **faire des s** to zigzag; **en S** (crochet) S-shaped; (route) zigzagging

S (a) (abrév **sud**) S (b) (abrév **seconde(s)**) sec

s' [s] voir **se**

SA [ɛsa] nf (abrév **société anonyme**) plc

sa [sa] voir **son¹**

sabbat [saba] nm Sabbath

sabbatique [sabatik] adj (repos, année, congé) sabbatical; **prendre un an de congé s.** to take a year's sabbatical

sable [sabl] **1** nm sand; Fam **être sur le s.** (sans travail) to be out of work; (sans argent) to be down and out; Fam **mettre qn sur le s.** to ruin sb; **sables mouvants** quicksands
2 adj inv sand-coloured

sablé, -e [sable] **1** adj voir **pâte**
2 nm shortbread Br biscuit or Am cookie

sabler [sable] vt (a) (chemin) to sand; (route) to grit (b) (bâtiment) to sandblast (c) Fam **s. le champagne** to break open a bottle of champagne

sableuse [sabløz] nf sandblaster

sableux, -euse [sablø, -øz] adj sandy

sablier [sablije] nm hourglass

sablonneux, -euse [sablonø, -øz] adj sandy

sabord [sabor] nm = type of square porthole; Fam Vieilli **mille sabords!** shiver me timbers!

saborder [saborde] **1** vt (navire) to scuttle; Fig (entreprise) to scupper
2 se saborder vpr to scuttle one's ship

sabot [sabo] nm (a) (de cheval) hoof; Fam **ça ne se trouve pas sous le s. d'un cheval** it doesn't grow on trees (b) (chaussure) clog; Fam **je te vois venir avec tes gros sabots** I can see what you're after (c) **s. de Denver** wheel clamp; **mettre un s. de Denver à une voiture** to (wheel-)clamp a car

sabotage [sabotaʒ] nm sabotage; (acte) act of sabotage

saboter [sabote] vt (voiture, entreprise, plan de paix) to sabotage; (travail) to make a mess of

saboteur, -euse [sabotœr, -øz] nm,f saboteur

sabre [sabr] nm sabre; **au clair** with drawn sword

sabrer [sabre] vt (a) **une cicatrice lui sabrait la joue** there was the gash of a scar on his cheek (b) Fam (raccourcir) to slash (c) Fam (critiquer) to slate (d) Fam **se faire s.** (étudiant) to flunk; **il s'est fait s. par le prof** the teacher flunked him

sac¹ [sak] nm (a) (contenant, contenu) bag (**de** of); (grand et en toile) sack (**de** of); **s. de sable** sandbag; Fam **un s. de nœuds** a muddle; **partir s. au dos** to set off with one's rucksack on one's back; Fam **vider son s.** to get it off one's chest; Fam **je les mets dans le même s.** they're as bad as each other; Fam **l'affaire est dans le s.** it's in the bag; **s. de couchage** sleeping bag; **s. à dos** rucksack, backpack; **s. à main** handbag; Fam **s. d'os** bag of bones; **s. à ouvrage** work bag; **s. poubelle** Br bin liner, Am garbage bag; **s. à provisions** shopping bag; Fam **s. à vin** drunk; **s. de voyage** travel or overnight bag (b) très Fam (somme) 10 francs; **10 sacs** 100 francs

sac² [sak] nm (pillage) sacking; **mettre une ville à s.** to sack a town

saccade [sakad] nf jerk, jolt; **par saccades** in fits and starts

saccadé, -e [sakade] adj jerky

saccage [sakaʒ] nm havoc; **se livrer à un s. de** to wreak havoc in

saccager [45] [sakaʒe] vt (a) (piller) (ville) to sack; (maison) to ransack (b) (dévaster) (ville, maison) to wreak havoc in; **la récolte fut saccagée par l'orage** the crops were devastated by the storm

saccharose [sakaroz] nm Chim saccharose

sacerdoce [saserdos] nm priesthood; Fig vocation

sacerdotal, -e, -aux, -ales [saserdɔtal, -o] adj priestly

sachant, sache etc voir **savoir**

sachet [saʃe] nm sachet; **s. de thé** teabag; **thé en sachets** teabags

sacoche [sakɔʃ] nf (a) (de vélo) saddlebag (b) (besace) bag (c) Belg & Can handbag, Am purse

sacquer [sake] Fam **1** vt (a) (renvoyer) to fire, Br to sack; **se faire s.** to be fired (b) (noter sévèrement) to give a bad mark to; **se faire s. par un prof** to get a bad mark from a teacher (c) (supporter) **je ne peux pas le s.** I can't stand him
2 vi (professeur) to be a tough marker

sacre [sakr] nm (d'un roi) coronation; (d'un évêque) consecration; Fig rite

sacré, -e [sakre] **1** adj (a) Rel & Fig sacred (b) Fam (maudit) damn, Br bloody; **s. Paul, qu'est-ce qu'on ferait sans lui!** good old Paul, what would we do without him?
2 nm **le s.** the sacred

sacrement [sakramɑ̃] nm sacrament; **le saint S.** the Blessed Sacrament; **recevoir les derniers sacrements** to receive the last rites

sacrément [sakremɑ̃] adv Fam damn, Br bloody

sacrer [sakre] **1** vt (roi) to crown; (évêque) to consecrate; **s. qn roi** to crown sb king; Fig **il a été sacré champion de France en 1995** he won the French championship in 1995
2 vi Can to swear

sacrifice [sakrifis] nm sacrifice; **offrir qn/qch en s.** to offer sb/sth up as a sacrifice; **faire le s. de sa vie** to sacrifice one's life; Fig **faire des sacrifices (pour)** to make sacrifices (for)

sacrifier [66] [sakrifje] **1** vt aussi Fig to sacrifice (à to); **sacrifié** (prix) rock-bottom; (article) at a rock-bottom price
2 vi **s. à la mode** to be a slave to fashion
3 se sacrifier vpr to sacrifice oneself (**pour** for); Fam **allez, je me sacrifie, je vais les chercher à la gare!** right, I'll be the martyr and pick them up from the station!

sacrilège [sakrilɛʒ] **1** adj sacrilegious
2 nmf (personne) sacrilegious person
3 nm (acte) sacrilege

sacristie [sakristi] nf sacristy, vestry

sacro-saint, -e [sakrosɛ̃, -ɛ̃t] (mpl **sacro-saints**, fpl **sacro-saintes**) [sakrosɛ̃, -ɛ̃t] adj aussi Ironique sacrosanct

sadique [sadik] **1** adj sadistic
2 nmf sadist

sadisme [sadism] nm sadism

sadomaso [sadɔmazo] adj inv Fam SM

sadomasochisme [sadɔmazɔʃism] nm sadomasochism

sadomasochiste [sadɔmazɔʃist] **1** adj sadomasochistic
2 nmf sadomasochist

safari [safari] nm safari; **en s.** on safari; **s.-photo** photographic safari

safran [safrɑ̃] **1** nm (plante, épice) saffron
2 adj inv (jaune) **s.** saffron (yellow)

saga [saga] nf aussi Fig saga

sagace [sagas] adj shrewd, astute

sagacité [sagasite] nf shrewdness, astuteness; **avec s.** shrewdly, astutely

sage [saʒ] **1** adj (a) (avisé) (personne, décision) wise, sensible (b) (calme) (enfant, animal) good, well-behaved; **s. comme une image** as good as gold (c) (chaste) (personne) good; (tenue, robe) sober
2 nm wise man; **un vieux s.** a wise old man

sage-femme [saʒfam] (pl **sages-femmes**) [saʒfam] nf midwife

sagement [saʒmɑ̃] adv (a) (raisonnablement) wisely, sensibly (b) (tranquillement) quietly

sagesse [saʒɛs] nf (a) (intelligence) wisdom, good sense; **avoir la s. de faire qch** to be wise or sensible enough to do sth; **plein de s.** very sensible; Fig **la voix de la s.** the voice of reason (b) (calme) good behaviour

Sagittaire [saʒitɛr] nm Astron & Astrol **le S.** Sagittarius; **être S.** to be (a) Sagittarius

sagouin [sagwɛ̃] nm Fam (personne) slob

Sahara [saara] nm **le S.** the Sahara (Desert)

saharienne [saarjɛn] nf safari jacket

Sahel [sael] nm **le S.** the Sahel

saignant, -e [seɲɑ̃, -ɑ̃t] adj (a) (blessure) bleeding (b) (viande) rare

saignée [seɲe] nf blood-letting; Fig drain; **faire une s. à qn** to bleed sb

saignement [seɲəmɑ̃] nm bleeding; **s. de nez** nosebleed

saigner [seɲe] **1** vi (personne, blessure) to bleed; **je saigne du nez** my nose is bleeding, I've got a nosebleed; Fig & Litt **mon cœur saigne** my heart bleeds
2 vt (poulet, personne) to bleed; Fig **s. qn à blanc** to bleed sb dry
3 se saigner vpr Fig **se s. aux quatre veines** to bleed oneself dry

saillant, -e [sajɑ̃, -ɑ̃t] adj (qui dépasse) projecting; (pommettes) prominent; (muscles) bulging; Fig (trait) salient

saillie [saji] nf (a) (partie en avant) projection; **faire s.** to project, to jut out (b) (par un mâle) covering

saillir [67] [sajir] **1** vt (femelle) to cover
2 vi (s'avancer) to project, to jut out (**sur** over)

sain, -e [sɛ̃, sɛn] adj healthy; (fruit, gestion) sound; (lectures) wholesome; **s. de corps et d'esprit** sound in body and mind; **s. et sauf** safe and sound

sainement [sɛnmɑ̃] adv (a) (vivre) healthily (b) (juger) sensibly

saint, -e [sɛ̃, sɛt] **1** adj (lieu) holy; (personne, vie) saintly; **s. patron** patron saint; **s. Pierre** St Peter; **sainte Catherine** St Catherine; Fam **avoir une sainte horreur de qch** to have a holy horror of sth; Fam **ne rien faire de toute la sainte journée** to do nothing the whole blessed day
2 nm, f aussi Fig saint; **ne savoir plus à quel s. se vouer** not to know which way to turn; Hum **il vaut mieux s'adresser à Dieu qu'à ses saints** it's best to go right to the top
3 nm **le S. des Saints** the Holy of Holies

saint-bernard [sɛ̃bɛrnar] nm inv (chien) St Bernard

Saint-Cyr [sɛ̃sir] n Saint-Cyr military academy

Sainte-Lucie [sɛ̃tlysi] n St Lucia

sainte-nitouche [sɛ̃tnituʃ] (pl **saintes-nitouches**) [sɛ̃tnituʃ] nf little hypocrite; **avec ses airs de s.** looking as if butter wouldn't melt in her mouth

Saint-Esprit [sɛ̃tɛspri] nm **le S.** the Holy Ghost or Spirit; Hum **par l'opération du S.** by magic

sainteté [sɛ̃tate] nf (d'une personne) saintliness; (de la loi, d'un serment) sanctity; (d'un lieu) holiness; **sa S. (le pape)** His Holiness (the Pope)

saint-frusquin [sɛ̃fryskɛ̃] nm Fam **tout le s.** the whole caboodle; **il s'est pointé avec tout son s.** he turned up with all his gear

saint-glinglin [sɛ̃glɛ̃glɛ̃] à la **saint-glinglin** adv Fam **on sera payés à la s.** we'll be paid when pigs fly; **repoussé à la s.** postponed till whenever

saint-honoré [sɛ̃tɔnɔre] nm inv Saint-Honoré (choux pastry ring filled with confectioner's custard)

Saint-Jean [sɛ̃ʒɑ̃] nf (a) **la S.** Midsummer Day (b) Can **la Saint-Jean-Baptiste** Saint-Jean-Baptiste Day (24 July)

Saint-Laurent [sɛ̃lɔrɑ̃] nm **le S.** the St Lawrence (River); **la Voie maritime du S.** the St Lawrence Seaway

Saint-Marin [sɛ̃marɛ̃] n San Marino

saint-nectaire [sɛ̃nɛktɛr] nm inv = type of firm cheese

Saint-Père [sɛ̃pɛr] nm **le S.** the Holy Father

Saint-Pétersbourg [sɛ̃petɛrsbur] n St Petersburg

Saint-Pierre-et-Miquelon [sɛ̃pjeremiklɔ̃] n St Pierre and Miquelon

Saint-Siège [sɛ̃sjɛʒ] nm **le S.** the Holy See

Saint-Sylvestre [sɛ̃silvɛstr] nf **la S.** New Year's Eve

sais voir **savoir**

saisie [sezi] *nf (de biens)* seizure; *Ordinat* **s. de données** data capture, keyboarding; *Ordinat* **s. automatique/ manuelle** automatic/manual input

saisine [sezin] *nf Jur* referral to a court

saisir [sezir] **1** *vt* **(a)** *(attraper) (personne, objet)* to take hold of; *(brusquement)* to grab; **s. l'occasion (de faire qch)** to seize or grasp the opportunity (to do sth); **j'ai été saisi par le froid** the cold really hit me **(b)** *(comprendre) (signification, nuance)* to grasp, to get; *(nom)* to catch; to get **(c)** *Ordinat (données)* to key **(d)** *Jur (biens)* to seize **(e)** *Jur* **s. un tribunal d'une affaire** to refer a matter to a court **(f)** *(viande)* to seal
2 *vi (comprendre)* to get it
3 se saisir *vpr* **se s. de qn/qch** to take hold of sb/sth; *(brusquement)* to grab sb/sth

saisissant, -e [sezisã, -ãt] *adj (froid)* biting; *(ressemblance)* striking; *(scène)* gripping

saisissement [sezismã] *nm* **(a)** *(sensation de froid)* sudden chill **(b)** *(émotion)* shock

saison [sezõ] *nf* season; **en cette s.** at this time of year; **en toute s.** all (the) year round; **faire une bonne/ mauvaise s.** *(équipe)* to have a good/bad season; **être de s.** *(fruits)* to be in season; **des fraises! mais ce n'est pas la s.!** strawberries! but it isn't the season for them!; **un temps de s.** seasonal weather; **la belle s.** the summer months; **la haute/basse s.** the high/low season; **la morte s.** the off season; **la s. des amours** the mating season; **la s. des pluies** the rainy season

saisonnier, -ère [sezɔnje, -ɛr] **1** *adj* seasonal
2 *nm,f* seasonal worker

sait *voir* **savoir**

saké [sake] *nm* sake

salade [salad] *nf* **(a)** *(plante)* lettuce **(b)** *(plat)* salad; **s. composée** mixed salad; **s. de fruits** fruit salad; **s. niçoise** salade niçoise; **s. de tomates/de riz** tomato/ rice salad; **s. verte** green salad; **haricots verts en s.** green bean salad **(c)** *Fam (désordre)* mess **(d)** *Fam* **salades** *(mensonges)* whoppers

saladier [saladje] *nm* salad bowl

salaire [saler] *nm* **(a)** *(mensuel)* salary; *(hebdomadaire, journalier)* wages; *Prov* **toute peine mérite s.** the labourer is worthy of his hire; **s. minimum interprofessionnel de croissance** guaranteed minimum wage **(b)** *(récompense)* reward **(de fear)** *(de)* **le s. de la peur** the wages of fear

salaison [salezõ] *nf (action)* salting; **des salaisons** salted meats

salamalecs [salamalɛk] *nmpl Fam* bowing and scraping

salamandre [salamãdr] *nf* salamander

salami [salami] *nm* salami

salant [salã] *adj m voir* **marais**

salarial, -e, -aux, -ales [salarjal, -o] *adj* wage; *(mensuel)* salary

salarié, -e [salarje] **1** *adj* **(a)** *(travailleur) (payé mensuellement)* salaried; *(payé hebdomadairement)* wage-earning **(b)** *(travail)* paid
2 *nm,f (payé mensuellement)* salaried employee; *(payé hebdomadairement)* wage-earner; **salariés** *(d'une société)* employees

salaud [salo] *Vulg* **1** *nm* bastard
2 *adj* **c'était vraiment s. de faire ça** that was a really shitty thing to do; **t'as vraiment été s.!** you were a real shit!

sale [sal] **1** *adj* **(a)** *(peu soigné)* dirty **(b)** *Fam (grave) (maladie, situation)* nasty; *(affaire)* dirty; **avoir une s. tête ou gueule** *(antipathique)* to look really nasty; *(malade)* to look awful; **faire un s. coup à qn** to play a dirty trick on sb; **s. bête** horrible beast; **s. boulot** rotten job; **faire le s. boulot** to do the dirty work; **s. gosse** little brat; **s. temps** filthy weather; **s. type** nasty character
2 *nm Fam* **mettre une chemise au s.** to put a dirty shirt in the wash

salé, -e [sale] **1** *adj* **(a)** *(conservé au sel)* salt; *(additionné de sel)* salted; *(au goût)* salty **(b)** *Fig (histoire, plaisanterie)* spicy **(c)** *Fam (condamnation)* stiff; *(addition)* steep
2 *nm* **le s.** savoury food; **petit s.** salt pork

salement [salmã] *adv* **(a)** *(manger, boire)* in a disgusting manner **(b)** *Fam (blessé, touché)* really badly; **je suis s. emmerdé** I'm in a real mess

saler [sale] *vt* to salt

saleté [salte] *nf* **(a)** *(manque de soin)* dirtiness; *(crasse)* dirt; **faire des saletés** to make a mess **(b)** *(objet)* trash, junk; **manger des saletés** to eat junk food **(c)** *(acte obscène, remarque)* obscenity **(d)** *Fam (personne)* bastard

salière [saljer] *nf* salt cellar

saligaud [saligo] *nm Fam (ignoble individu)* bastard

salin, -e [salɛ̃, -in] **1** *adj* saline
2 *nm (marais salant)* salt marsh

salir [salir] **1** *vt* to make dirty, to dirty; *Fig* **s. le nom/la mémoire de qn** to sully sb's name/memory
2 se salir *vpr* to get dirty; *Fig* **se s. les mains** to get one's hands dirty

salissant, -e [salisã, -ãt] *adj* **(a)** *(travail)* dirty, messy **(b)** *(tissu, vêtement)* easily soiled; *(couleur)* that shows the dirt

salissure [salisyr] *nf* dirty mark

salivaire [saliver] *adj (glande)* salivary

salive [saliv] *nf* saliva

saliver [salive] *vi* to salivate; *Fig* **s. devant qch** to drool at the sight of sth

salle [sal] *nf* **(a)** *(pièce)* room; **s. d'armes** *(pour l'escrime)* fencing hall; *(pour les armes)* armoury; **s. d'attente** waiting room; **s. de bain(s)** bathroom; *Ordinat* **s. blanche** clean room; **s. des coffres** vaults; **s. commune** common room; **s. d'embarquement** *(d'un aéroport)* departure lounge; **s. d'exposition** showroom; *(pour une foire)* exhibition hall; **s. des fêtes** community hall; *(d'un village)* village hall; **s. de garde** *(d'hôpital)* staff room; *(de caserne)* guardroom; **s. des machines** *(d'un navire)* engine-room; **s. à manger** dining room; *(meubles)* dining-room suite; **s. d'opération** operating *Br* theatre *or Am* room; **s. des pas perdus** *(dans une gare)* concourse; **s. des professeurs** staff room; **s. de réunion** meeting room; **s. du trône** throneroom; **s. des ventes** saleroom **(b)** *(pour le cinéma, pour le théâtre)* auditorium; **toute la s. applaudit** the whole audience applauded; **les salles obscures** *Br* the cinema, *Am* the movies

salmonelle [salmɔnɛl] *nf* salmonella

salmonellose [salmɔneloz] *nf* salmonella poisoning

Salomon [salɔmõ] *voir* **île**

salon [salɔ̃] nm (a) (pièce) living room, Br lounge; (dans un bateau) saloon; (dans un train) saloon car; Can s. de barbier barber's; s. de coiffure hairdressing salon; s. d'essayage fitting room; s. de thé tea room (b) (meubles) suite (c) (exposition) exhibition; le S. des Arts ménagers ≃ the Ideal Home Exhibition; le S. de l'Automobile ou de l'Auto the Motor Show; le S. du Livre the Book Fair; le S. nautique the Boat Show (d) (littéraire) salon; tenir s. to hold a salon

salopard [salɔpar] nm Vulg bastard

salope [salɔp] nf Vulg (femme méprisable) bitch; (homme méprisable) bastard

saloperie [salɔpri] nf Fam (a) (camelote) trash, junk (b) (coup bas) dirty trick (c) dire des saloperies sur qn to bitch about sb

salopette [salɔpet] nf Br dungarees, Am overalls

salpêtre [salpetr] nm saltpetre

salsa [salsa] nf salsa

salsifis [salsifi] nm salsify

saltimbanque [saltɛ̃bãk] nm travelling acrobat

salto [salto] nm somersault

salubre [salybr] adj healthy

salubrité [salybrite] nf healthiness; la s. publique public health

saluer [salɥe] 1 vt (en arrivant) to greet; (en partant) to take one's leave of; (s'incliner devant) to bow to; (sujet: soldat) to salute; s. qn d'une inclination de la tête to nod to sb; il est passé sans me s. he walked past me without saying hello; saluez-le de ma part give him my regards; Rel je vous salue, Marie hail Mary
2 se saluer vpr (en arrivant) to greet each other; (en partant) to take leave of each other

salut [saly] 1 nm (a) (salutation) greeting; faire un s. à qn (en se découvrant) to raise one's hat to sb; (en inclinant la tête) to nod to sb (b) (de soldat) salute; faire le s. militaire to give a salute (c) (sauvegarde) rescue; Rel salvation
2 exclam Fam s.! (en arrivant) hi!; (en partant) bye!

salutaire [salyter] adj (décision, mesure) salutary; (remède) beneficial; être s. à qn to do sb good

salutation [salytasjɔ̃] nf greeting

Salvador [salvador] nm le S. El Salvador

salvadorien, -enne [salvadɔrjɛ̃, -ɛn] 1 adj Salvadorean
2 nm,f S. Salvadorean

salve [salv] nf salvo, volley

Samaritain [samaritɛ̃] nm le bon S. the good Samaritan

samba [sãba] nf samba

samedi [samdi] nm Saturday; le S. saint Easter Saturday; s. prochain/dernier next/last Saturday; s. matin Saturday morning; s. soir Saturday night or evening; dans la nuit de s. à dimanche on Saturday night; s. 11 mai 1997 Saturday 11 May 1997; nous sommes s. aujourd'hui today's Saturday; je commence s. I'm starting on Saturday; il vient le s./ tous les samedis he comes on Saturdays/every Saturday; un s. sur deux every second or other Saturday; s. en huit/quinze a week/fortnight on Saturday; passer tout son s. à faire qch to spend one's whole Saturday doing sth

Samoa [samoa] nfpl les S. occidentales Western Samoa

samouraï [samuraj] nm samurai

samovar [samovar] nm samovar

SAMU [samy] nm (abrév Service d'aide médicale d'urgence) ambulance service; appeler le S. to call an ambulance

sanatorium [sanatɔrjɔm] nm sanatorium

sanctifier [66] [sãktifje] vt (a) (rendre saint) to sanctify (b) (révérer) que Ton nom soit sanctifié hallowed be Thy name

sanction [sãksjɔ̃] nf (punition) sanction; Fig (désavantage) price; s. pénale penalty; sanctions économiques economic sanctions; prendre une s. contre qn to take action against sb

sanctionner [sãksjɔne] vt (a) (punir) to punish (b) (approuver) to sanction; sanctionné par l'usage sanctioned by custom

sanctuaire [sãktɥer] nm aussi Fig sanctuary

sandale [sãdal] nf sandal

sandalette [sãdalet] nf (light) sandal

sandre [sãdr] nm pikeperch

sandwich [pl sandwichs ou sandwiches] [sãdwitʃ] nm sandwich; s. au jambon ham sandwich; Fam pris en s. (entre) sandwiched (between)

San Francisco [sãfrãsisko] n San Francisco

sang [sã] nm blood; animaux à s. chaud/froid warm-/cold-blooded animals; Fig avoir le s. bleu to have blue blood; Fig avoir le s. chaud to be hot-blooded; Fig avoir qch dans le s. to have sth in one's blood; Fam avoir du s. de navet to be spineless; Fam se faire du mauvais s. to get all worked up; Fam se ronger les sangs, se faire un s. d'encre to worry oneself sick; le s. lui monta au visage the blood rushed to his face; mon s. n'a fait qu'un tour (de peur) my heart missed a beat; (de colère) I saw red; très Fam bon s. (de bonsoir)!, bon s. de bon Dieu! damn and blast it!

sang-froid [sãfrwa] nm inv composure, calm; garder son s. to keep calm, to keep one's head; perdre son s. to lose one's head, to lose one's composure; tuer qn de s. to kill sb in cold blood

sanglant, -e [sãglã, -ãt] adj bloody; Fig (offensant) scathing

sangle [sãgl] nf strap; (de selle) girth

sangler [sãgle] vt to put straps on; (cheval) to girth

sanglier [sãglije] nm (wild) boar

sanglot [sãglo] nm sob

sangloter [sãglɔte] vi to sob

sangria [sãgrija] nf sangria

sangsue [sãsy] nf (animal, personne) leech

sanguin, -e [sãgɛ̃, -in] adj (tempérament) fiery; (teint, visage) ruddy

sanguinaire [sãginer] adj (a) (homme) bloodthirsty (b) (combat) bloody

sanitaire [saniter] 1 adj (a) (personnel) medical; (mesures) health (b) (installation) sanitary
2 nmpl les sanitaires (toilettes) the toilet; (salle de bains et W.-C.) the bathroom and toilet

sans [sã] 1 prép (a) (indique l'absence, la privation, l'exclusion) without; s. parler without speaking; non s. difficulté not without difficulty (b) (indique la condition) but for; s. vous, je ne l'aurais jamais fait but for you, I'd never have done it; s. cela, s. quoi otherwise; Fam sois sage, s. ça tu seras puni! be good or else you'll be punished!

2 *adv Fam* without it/them; **faire s.** to do without

3 *conj* **s. que nous le sachions** without our knowing

sans-abri [sãzabri] *nmf inv* homeless person; **les s.** the homeless

San Salvador [sãsalvador] *n* San Salvador

sans-cœur [sãkœr] *nmf inv Fam* heartless person

sans-culotte (*pl* **sans-culottes**) [sãkylɔt] *nm Hist* sansculotte (*person with extreme republican sympathies during the French Revolution*)

sans-emploi [sãzãplwa] *nmf inv* unemployed person; **les s.** the unemployed

sans-faute [sãfot] *nm inv* (*de compétition hippique*) clear round; **faire un s.** (*cheval*) to have a clear round; *Fig* (*personne*) not to put a foot wrong

sans-gêne [sãʒɛn] **1** *adj inv* ill-mannered

2 *nm* lack of manners

sans-le-sou [sãləsu] *nmf inv Fam* penniless person

sans-logis [sãlɔʒi] *nmf* homeless person; **les s.** the homeless

sans-papiers [sãpapje] *nmf* illegal immigrant

sans-patrie [sãpatri] *nmf inv* stateless person

santé [sãte] *nf* health; **être en bonne s.** to be in good health; **avoir une bonne/mauvaise s.** to be healthy/unhealthy; **c'est bon/mauvais pour la s.** it's good/bad for your health; **boire à la s. de qn** to drink sb's health; **(à votre) s.!** cheers!, good health!; *Suisse Fam* **s.!** (*quand on éternue*) bless you!; **la s. publique** public health

santiag [sãtjag] *nf Fam* cowboy boot

santon [sãtõ] *nm* Christmas crib figure

São Tomé et Príncipe [saotomeeprẽsip] *n* São Tomé e Príncipe

saoudien, -enne [saudjẽ, -ɛn] **1** *adj* Saudi (Arabian)

2 *nm,f* **S.** Saudi (Arabian)

saoul [su], **saouler** [sule] = **soûl, soûler**

sape [sap] *nf* (a) (*tranchée*) sap; *Fig* **travail de s.** undermining (b) *Fam* **sapes** (*vêtements*) gear

saper [sape] **1** *vt* (a) *aussi Fig* to undermine; **s. le moral à qn** to sap sb's morale (b) *Fam* (*habiller*) to dress; **être bien sapé** to be all dolled up

2 se saper *vpr Fam* to dress

sapeur-pompier (*pl* **sapeurs-pompiers**) [sapœrpõpje] *nm* fireman; **les sapeurs-pompiers** (*service*) the fire *Br* brigade or *Am* department

saphir [safir] *nm* sapphire

sapin [sapẽ] *nm* (a) (*arbre*) fir (tree) (b) *Fam* **ça sent le s.** that sounds as if you're heading for an early grave; **il sent le s.** he's done for (c) *Can* **se faire passer un s.** (*se faire avoir*) to be taken for a ride

sapristi [sapristi] *exclam Fam Vieilli ou Hum* good heavens!

saquer [sake] = **sacquer**

sarabande [sarabãd] *nf* (*danse, air*) saraband; *Fam* (*tapage*) racket

Sarajevo [sarajevo] *n* Sarajevo

sarbacane [sarbakan] *nf* blowpipe; (*jouet*) peashooter

sarcasme [sarkasm] *nm* sarcasm; (*remarque*) sarcastic remark

sarcastique [sarkastik] *adj* sarcastic

sarcler [sarkle] *vt* (*jardin*) to weed; (*sol*) to hoe; (*champ*) to clean

sarclette [sarklɛt] *nf* hoe

sarcloir [sarklwar] *nm* hoe

sarcome [sarkom] *nm Méd* sarcoma; **s. de Kaposi** Kaposi's sarcoma

sarcophage [sarkofaʒ] *nm* sarcophagus

Sardaigne [sardɛɲ] *nf* la S. Sardinia

sarde [sard] **1** *adj* Sardinian

2 *nmf* **S.** Sardinian

3 *nm* (*langue*) Sardinian

sardine [sardin] *nf* sardine; **sardines à l'huile/à la tomate** sardines in oil/in tomato sauce; *Fam* **serrés comme des sardines** packed together like sardines

sardonique [sardɔnik] *adj* sardonic

Sargasses [sargas] *voir* **mer**

SARL [ɛsaerɛl] *nf* (*abrév* **société à responsabilité limitée**) limited (liability) company

sarment [sarmã] *nm* (*tige*) bine; (*de vigne*) vine shoot

saroual, -als [sarwal], **sarouel** [sarwɛl] *nm* = baggy trousers worn by North Africans

sarrasin, -e [sarazɛ̃, -in] **1** *adj Hist* Saracen

2 *nm,f Hist* **S.** Saracen

3 *nm* (*plante*) buckwheat

sarriette [sarjɛt] *nf* savory

sas [sɑs] *nm* (*pièce étanche*) airlock

Satan [satã] *npr* Satan

satané, -e [satane] *adj Fam* confounded

satanique [satanik] *adj* satanic; *Fig* (*cruauté, sourire*) fiendish

satellite [satelit] *nm* **1** (a) (*corps céleste, engin*) satellite; **émission retransmise par s.** satellite broadcast; **télévision par s.** satellite television; **s.-espion** spy satellite; **s. géostationnaire** geostationary satellite; **s. de télécommunications** telecommunications satellite; **s. de télédiffusion** broadcast satellite (b) *Pol* satellite

2 *adj* **pays s.** satellite state

satiété [sasjete] *nf* **manger/boire à s.** to eat/drink one's fill

satin [satẽ] *nm* satin

satiné, -e [satine] **1** *adj* (*tissu*) satiny; (*papier*) glazed; (*peau*) satin-smooth; **peinture satinée** silk-finish paint

2 *nm* satin finish; (*de la peau*) satin smoothness

satire [satir] *nf* satire; **faire la s. de qch** to satirize sth

satirique [satirik] *adj* satirical

satiriste [satirist] *nmf* satirist

satisfaction [satisfaksjõ] *nf* satisfaction; **à la s. générale** to everyone's satisfaction; **donner s. à qn** to give sb satisfaction; **obtenir s.** to obtain satisfaction

satisfaire [36] [satisfɛr] **1** *vt* to satisfy

2 satisfaire à *vt ind* (*demande, condition, besoins*) to satisfy; (*règlement, normes de sécurité*) to comply with; (*obligation*) to fulfil

3 se satisfaire *vpr* **s. de qch** to be satisfied with sth; **se s. de peu** to be content with very little; *Péj* to be easily satisfied

satisfaisant, -e [satisfəzã, -ãt] *adj* (*acceptable*) satisfactory; (*qui contente*) satisfying

satisfait, -e [satisfɛ, -ɛt] *adj* (a) (*heureux*) satisfied (**de** with); *Ironique* **vous voilà s.!** well, you asked for it!; **s. ou remboursé** (*dans une publicité*) satisfaction or your money back (b) (*suffisant*) satisfied

satisfecit [satisfesit] *nm inv Litt* **décerner un s. à qn** to congratulate sb on a job well done

saturation [satyrasjɔ̃] *nf aussi Fig* saturation; *(du réseau routier)* gridlock; *aussi Fig* **arriver à s.** to reach saturation point; *Ordinat (disquette)* to become full

saturer [satyre] **1** *vt* to saturate (**de** with); **les appels ont saturé le standard** the calls have jammed the switchboard
2 *vi Fam* **je sature** I've had it up to here

Saturne [satyrn] *npr (dieu, planète)* Saturn

satyre [satir] *nm* (a) *(demi-dieu)* satyr (b) *Fam (obsédé sexuel)* sex maniac

sauce [sos] *nf* (a) *(accompagnement)* sauce; **s. aux champignons** mushroom sauce; **s. de soja** soy sauce; **s. tomate** tomato sauce; *Fam Fig* **allonger la s.** to pad it out; *Fam* **mettre qch à toutes les sauces** to use sth in every way imaginable; *Fam* **à quelle s. sera-t-il mangé?** what'll be in store for him? (b) *Fam (pluie)* **prendre la s.** to get soaked

saucée [sose] *nf Fam (pluie)* downpour; **recevoir une s.** to get soaked

saucer [16] [sose] *vt* (a) *(assiette)* to mop up the sauce from (b) *Fam* **se faire s.** to get soaked

saucier [sosje] *nm* sauce cook

saucière [sosjɛr] *nf* sauce boat

sauciflard [sosiflar] *nm Fam* (slicing) sausage

saucisse [sosis] *nf* sausage; **s. de Francfort** frankfurter; **s. sèche** salami-type sausages; **s. de Strasbourg/Toulouse** = type of beef/pork sausage

saucisson [sosisɔ̃] *nm* (slicing) sausage; **s. à l'ail** garlic sausage; *Hum* **s. à pattes** sausage dog; **s. pur porc** 100% pork sausage

saucissonné, -e [sosisone] *adj Fam* trussed up

sauf¹, sauve [sof, sov] *adj (personne)* safe, unharmed; **avoir la vie sauve** to escape with one's life; **laisser la vie sauve à qn** to spare sb's life; **l'honneur est s.** honour is saved

sauf² *prép* except (for), apart from; **s. imprévu** unless anything unforeseen happens; **s. erreur de ma part** if I'm not mistaken; **s. votre respect** with all due respect; **s. s'il pleut** unless it rains; *Fam* **s. que** except that

sauf-conduit *(pl sauf-conduits)* [sofkɔ̃dɥi] *nm* safe conduct

sauge [soʒ] *nf* sage

saugrenu, -e [sogrəny] *adj* preposterous

saule [sol] *nm* willow; **s. pleureur** weeping willow

saumâtre [somatr] *adj (goût, eau)* brackish; *Fig* bitter

saumon [somɔ̃] **1** *nm* salmon; **s. fumé** smoked salmon
2 *adj inv (rose)* **s.** salmon-pink

saumoné, -e [somone] *adj voir* **truite**

saumure [somyr] *nf* brine

sauna [sona] *nm* sauna

saupoudrer [sopudre] *vt* to sprinkle (**de** with)

saupoudreuse [sopudrøz] *nf* dredger

saur [sor] *adj m voir* **hareng**

saurai, saurais *etc voir* **savoir**

saurien [sorjɛ̃] *nm* saurian

saut [so] *nm (bond)* jump, leap; **faire un s.** to jump, to leap; *Fig* **faire un s. à Paris/chez le boulanger/en ville** to pop or *Br* nip over to Paris/round to the baker's/into town; *Fig* **faire un s. de plusieurs années** to skip several years; **au s. du lit** first thing in the morning; **s. de l'ange** *Br* swallow dive, *Am* swan dive; **s. à l'élastique** bungee jumping; **s. en hauteur** high jump; **s. en longueur** long jump; **s. en parachute** parachute jump; *(activité)* parachute jumping; **faire du s. en parachute** to go parachute jumping; **s. à la perche** pole vaulting; **s. périlleux** somersault; **s. en** *ou* **à skis** ski jump; *(activité)* ski jumping; **faire du s. à skis** to go ski jumping

saute [sot] *nf* **sautes de température** sudden changes in temperature; **sautes d'humeur** mood swings

sauté, -e [sote] **1** *adj* sautéed, sauté
2 *nm* **s. de lapin** sauté of rabbit

saute-mouton [sotmutɔ̃] *nm inv* leapfrog; **jouer à s.** to play leapfrog

sauter [sote] **1** *vt* (a) *(fossé, barrière)* to jump (over), to leap over; *Fig* **s. le pas** to take the plunge (b) *(omettre) (page, ligne, repas)* to skip; *(maille)* to drop; **s. une classe** to skip a year (c) *Vulg (coucher avec)* to screw; **se faire s. par qn** to screw sb
2 *vi* (a) *(bondir)* to jump, to leap; **s. sur un pied** to hop; **s. à pieds joints** to jump with one's feet together; **s. à la perche** to pole-vault; **s. à la corde** *Br* to skip, *Am* to jump rope; **s. en parachute** to do a parachute jump; **s. à la gorge de qn** to go for sb; *(chien)* to fly at sb's throat; **s. au cou de qn** to fling one's arms round sb's neck; **s. aux yeux** to be obvious; **s. au plafond** *(bouchon)* to hit the ceiling; *Fig (de surprise)* to jump out of one's skin; *(d'indignation)* to hit the roof; **s. de joie** to jump for joy; *aussi Fam Fig* **s. sur qn** to pounce on sb; **faire s. un enfant sur ses genoux** to bounce a child on one's knees; **s. sur l'occasion** to jump at the opportunity; *Fig* **s. du coq à l'âne** to jump from one subject to another; **nous allons s. directement à la page 5** we're going to jump straight to page 5; *Fam* **et que ça saute!** and make it snappy! (b) *(exploser)* to blow up; *(bouton)* to come off; *(fusible)* to blow; *Fig (gouvernement)* to fall; **faire s.** *(rocher)* to blast; *(pont, mine)* to blow up; *(serrure)* to force; *Fig (gouvernement)* to bring down; *(personne)* to fire, *Br* to sack; *Fam* **faire s. la banque** to break the bank (c) *Culin* **faire s.** to sauté

sauterelle [sotrɛl] *nf* grasshopper; *(nuisible)* locust

sauterie [sotri] *nf Vieilli ou Hum* hop

sauteur, -euse [sotœr, -øz] **1** *adj* jumping
2 *nm,f* jumper; **s. en hauteur** high-jumper; **s. en longueur** long-jumper; **s. à la perche** pole-vaulter

sautillement [sotijmɑ̃] *nm* hopping about

sautiller [sotije] *vi* to hop about; **s. d'un pied sur l'autre** to hop from one foot to the other; **avancer en sautillant** to hop along

sautoir [sotwar] *nm* (a) *(collier)* chain; **s. de perles** string of pearls (b) *(de stade)* jumping area

sauvage [sovaʒ] **1** *adj* (a) *(plante, animal)* wild; **redevenir s.** *(animal apprivoisé)* to go back to the wild; **à l'état s.** wild (b) *(peuple, tribu)* savage, primitive (c) *(violent) (personne, agression)* savage (d) *(peu sociable)* unsociable (e) *(non autorisé)* unauthorized; **immigration s.** illegal immigration
2 *nmf* (a) *Vieilli (indigène)* savage; *Fam Hum* **on n'est pas des sauvages!** we're not savages!; *Fam Hum* **bande de sauvages!** you bunch of savages! (b) *(brute)* savage (c) *(solitaire)* recluse

sauvagement [sovaʒmɑ̃] *adv* savagely

sauvageon, -onne [sovaʒɔ̃, -ɔn] *nm,f (enfant)* little savage

sauvagerie [sovaʒri] *nf* (a) *(cruauté)* savagery (b) *(insociabilité)* unsociability

sauvegarde [sovgard] *nf* **(a)** *(protection)* safeguard (contre against) **(b)** *Ordinat* saving, backup; **faire la s. d'un fichier** to save a file; **s. externe** off-line backup; **s. en ligne** on-line backup; **copie de s.** backup (copy)

sauvegarder [sovgarde] *vt* **(a)** *(protéger)* to safeguard (contre against) **(b)** *Ordinat (fichier)* to save, to back up; **s. un fichier sur disque** to save a file to disk

sauver [sove] **1** *vt* **(a)** *(personne)* to save, to rescue (de from); *(âme)* to save; **s. la vie à qn** to save sb's life; **le malade est sauvé** the patient is out of danger **(b)** *(navire, marchandises)* to salvage; **s. les apparences** to keep up appearances; *Fam Fig* **s. les meubles** to salvage something from the wreckage
2 *vi* **sauve qui peut!** every man for himself!
3 se sauver *vpr* **(a)** *(s'échapper)* to escape (de from) **(b)** *(s'enfuir)* to run away; *Fam* **sauve-toi, tu vas être en retard** be off, you'll be late **(c)** *(lait)* to boil over

sauvetage [sovtaʒ] *nm* **(a)** *(d'un accidenté)* rescue **(b)** *(d'un navire, de marchandises)* salvage; *(d'une entreprise)* rescue

sauveteur [sovtœr] *nm* rescuer

sauvette [sovɛt] **à la sauvette** *adv (pour ne pas être vu)* on the sly; *(à la hâte)* in a hurry; **vendre à la s.** *(illégalement)* to peddle illegally on the streets; **marchand à la s.** illegal street vendor

sauveur [sovœr] *nm* saviour

savamment [savamɑ̃] *adv* **(a)** *(avec érudition)* learnedly **(b)** *(habilement)* cleverly, skilfully

savane [savan] *nf* savanna

savant, -e [savɑ̃, -ɑ̃t] **1** *adj* **(a)** *(érudit)* learned **(b)** *(habile)* clever, skilful **(c)** *(animal)* performing
2 *nm (scientifique)* scientist; *(érudit)* scholar

savate [savat] *nf (a) Fam (pantoufle)* slipper; **traîner la s.** *(être pauvre)* to be down at heel **(b)** *Fam* **comme une s.** atrociously **(c)** *Sp* kick boxing

saveur [savœr] *nf (a) (d'un vin, d'un aliment)* flavour **(b)** *Fig (d'une remarque, d'un récit)* savour

Savoie [savwa] *nf* **la S.** Savoy

savoir¹ [savwar] *nm* knowledge, learning

savoir² [62] **1** *vt* **(a)** *(avoir connaissance de)* to know; **s. qch par cœur** to know sth by heart; **je n'en sais rien** I don't know; **je ne sais trop rien** I'm not very sure; **en s. trop** to know too much; **qu'est-ce j'en sais?** what do I know?; **va s.!** who knows?; **je ne veux pas le s.** I don't want to know; **il n'a rien voulu s.** he didn't want to know; **reste à s. si...** it remains to be seen whether...; **je crois s. qu'il est ici** I understand he's here; **faire s. qch à qn** to tell sb sth, to let sb know about sth; **je le sais par ma sœur** I heard about it from my sister; **à s.** that is (to say), namely; **pas que je sache** not that I know of; **à ce que je sache**, for anything that I know as far as I know; **on ne sait jamais** you never know **(b)** *(être conscient de)* to know; **sans le s.** without realizing; **sachez que...** be advised that..., please note that... **(c)** *(connaître)* **qui tu sais** you know who; **je ne le savais pas si jaloux** I didn't know he was so jealous **(d)** *(être capable de)* **s. faire qch** to be able to do sth, to know how to do sth; **savez-vous nager/conduire?** can you swim/drive?; **je ne saurais vous le dire** I really couldn't tell you
2 se savoir *vpr* **(a)** *(se répandre)* **ça se saura vite** it'll soon get out **(b)** *(avoir conscience d'être)* **il se savait perdu/surveillé** he knew he was doomed/being watched

savoir-faire [savwarfɛr] *nm* expertise, know-how

savoir-vivre [savwarvivr] *nm* good manners; **manquer de s.** to have no manners

savon [savɔ̃] *nm* soap; **s. à barbe** shaving soap; **s. de Marseille** household soap; *Fam* **passer un s. à qn** to give sb a telling-off

savonner [savɔne] **1** *vt (mains, vêtement)* to soap; *(en faisant mousser)* to lather
2 se savonner *vpr* to soap oneself; **se s. les mains** to soap one's hands

savonnette [savɔnɛt] *nf* bar of soap

savonneux, -euse [savɔnø, -øz] *adj* soapy

savourer [savure] *vt aussi Fig* to savour

savoureux, -euse [savurø, -øz] *adj (plat)* tasty; *(vin)* full-flavoured; *Fig (récit, détails)* spicy

savoyard, -e [savwajar, -ard] **1** *adj* Savoyard
2 *nm,f* S. Savoyard

saxo [sakso] *nm Fam (instrument)* sax; *(musicien)* sax player

saxon, -onne [saksɔ̃, -ɔn] **1** *adj* Saxon
2 *nm,f* S. Saxon

saxophone [saksɔfɔn] *nm* saxophone

saxophoniste [saksɔfɔnist] *nmf* saxophonist

saynète [sɛnɛt] *nf (petite pièce)* sketch

sbire [sbir] *nm Péj* henchman

scabreux, -euse [skabrø, -øz] *adj* obscene

scalp [skalp] *nm (chevelure)* scalp

scalpel [skalpɛl] *nm* scalpel

scalper [skalpe] *vt* to scalp

scandale [skɑ̃dal] *nm* scandal; **faire s.** *(affaire)* to cause a scandal; **faire un s.** *(personne)* to make a scene; **au grand s. de** much to the indignation of; **c'est un s.!** it's a scandal!

scandaleux, -euse [skɑ̃dalø, -øz] *adj* scandalous, outrageous

scandaliser [skɑ̃dalize] **1** *vt* to scandalize, to shock
2 se scandaliser *vpr* to be scandalized or shocked (de by)

scander [skɑ̃de] *vt (slogan)* to chant; *(vers)* to scan

scandinave [skɑ̃dinav] **1** *adj* Scandinavian
2 *nmf* S. Scandinavian

Scandinavie [skɑ̃dinavi] *nf* **la S.** Scandinavia

scanner¹ [skanɛr] *nm* scanner; **on lui a fait un s.** he was given a scan

scanner² [skane] *vt Ordinat* to scan

scanneur [skanœr] *nm Ordinat & TV* scanner; **s. à main** handheld scanner; **s. à plat** flatbed scanner

scaphandre [skafɑ̃dr] *nm (a) (de plongeur)* diving suit **(b)** *(d'astronaute)* space suit

scaphandrier [skafɑ̃drije] *nm* diver

scarabée [skarabe] *nm* beetle

scarlatine [skarlatin] *nf* scarlet fever; **avoir la s.** to have scarlet fever

scarole [skarɔl] *nf* endive

scatologique [skatɔlɔʒik] *adj* scatological

sceau, -x [so] *nm* seal; *Fig* **le s. du génie** the mark of genius; **sous le s. du secret** under the seal of secrecy

scélérat, -e [selera, -at] *Litt* **1** *adj* villainous
2 *nm,f* villain

scellé, -e [sele] **1** *adj* sealed
2 *nm* seal; **apposer/lever les scellés** to put on/remove the seals

sceller [sele] vt (a) (apposer un sceau sur) & Fig to seal (b) Constr to embed

scénario [senarjo] nm script, screenplay

scénariste [senarist] nmf scriptwriter

scène [sɛn] nf (a) (plateau) stage; **la s.** (le métier d'acteur) the stage; **mettre en s.** (pièce de théâtre) to stage; (film) to direct; **entrer en s.** (acteur) to come on; Fig to appear on the scene; **sortir de s.** to go off; **quitter la s.** to retire from the stage; Fig **la s. politique/internationale** the political/international scene; **occuper le devant de la s.** to hold centre stage (b) (d'une pièce de théâtre, d'un film) scene (c) (action) action; **la s. se passe au Moyen Age** the action takes place in the Middle Ages (d) (événement) scene; **des scènes de panique** scenes of panic (e) Fam (dispute) scene; **il m'a fait une s.** he made a scene; **s. de ménage** domestic squabble (f) (peinture) **une s. de chasse** a hunting scene

scénique [senik] adj theatrical

scepticisme [sɛptisism] nm scepticism

sceptique [sɛptik] 1 adj sceptical
2 nmf sceptic

sceptre [sɛptr] nm sceptre

schéma [ʃema] nm (a) (dessin) diagram (b) (résumé) outline (c) Ordinat **s. de clavier** keyboard map

schématique [ʃematik] adj schematic; Péj over-simplified

schématiquement [ʃematikmã] adv (à l'aide d'un schéma) schematically; (en gros) in outline

schématiser [ʃematize] vt to schematize; Péj to over-simplify

schisme [ʃism] nm schism

schiste [ʃist] nm schist, shale

schizophrène [skizofrɛn] adj & nmf schizophrenic

schizophrénie [skizofreni] nf schizophrenia

schlinguer [ʃlɛ̃ge] vi très Fam to stink

schnaps [ʃnaps] nm schnapps

schnock, schnoque [ʃnɔk] nm Fam **un vieux s.** an old git

schuss [ʃus] nm schuss; **descendre la piste en s.** ou **tout s.** to schuss down the slope

sciatique [sjatik] 1 adj sciatic
2 nf sciatica

scie [si] nf (a) (outil) saw; **s. circulaire** circular saw; **s. mécanique** ou **à main** hand saw; **s. à métaux** hacksaw (b) **s. musicale** musical saw

sciemment [sjamã] adv knowingly

science [sjãs] nf(a) (savoir) science; Fig **je n'ai pas la s. infuse** I can't be expected to know everything (b) (domaine spécifique) science; **sciences économiques** economics; **sciences exactes** exact sciences; **sciences expérimentales** experimental science; **sciences humaines** ≃ social sciences; **sciences naturelles** natural science; **Sciences Po** = higher education establishment for students wishing to enter the Civil Service, the media etc

science-fiction [sjãsfiksjɔ̃] nf science fiction; Fig & Hum **c'est de la s.!** it's unreal!

scientifique [sjãtifik] 1 adj scientific
2 nmf scientist

scientifiquement [sjãtifikmã] adv scientifically

scier [66] [sje] vt (a) (bois, métal) to saw; (pour enlever) (branche) to saw off (b) Fam (étonner) to dumbfound

scierie [siri] nf sawmill

scieur [sjœr] nm sawyer

scinder [sɛ̃de] 1 vt to split up (en into)
2 se scinder vpr to split up (en into)

scintillement [sɛ̃tijmã] nm (de bijou, de lumière, des yeux) sparkling; (d'étoile) twinkling

scintiller [sɛ̃tije] vi (bijou, lumière, yeux) to sparkle; (étoile) to twinkle

scission [sisjɔ̃] nf split; **faire s.** to split away

sciure [sjyr] nf sawdust

sclérose [skleroz] nf sclerosis; Fig ossification; **s. en plaques** multiple sclerosis

scléroser [skleroze] 1 vt Méd to sclerose
2 se scléroser vpr Méd to sclerose; Fig to become fossilized

scolaire [skolɛr] adj (a) (résultats, réussite) academic; (réforme, organisation, vie) school (b) Péj (esprit, mentalité) bookish

scolarisation [skolarizasjɔ̃] nf education

scolariser [skolarize] vt to send to school; **enfant scolarisé** child attending school

scolarité [skolarite] nf schooling; **prolonger la s.** to raise the school-leaving age

scoliose [skoljoz] nf curvature of the spine

scoop [skup] nm scoop

scooter [skuter] nm (motor) scooter; **s. des mers** jet ski

scorbut [skorbyt] nm scurvy

score [skor] nm score; (en politique) result

scories [skori] nfpl (dans l'industrie) slag; (d'éruption volcanique) scoria

scorpion [skorpjɔ̃] nm (a) (animal) scorpion (b) Astron & Astrol **le S.** Scorpio; **être S.** to be (a) Scorpio

Scotch® [skotʃ] nm (ruban adhésif) Br sellotape®, Am scotch tape®

scotch [skotʃ] nm (boisson) scotch

scotcher [skotʃe] vt Br to sellotape, Am to scotch-tape

scout [skut] Scout

scoutisme [skutism] nm (activité) scouting; (mouvement) scout movement

scribe [skrib] nm (a) Péj pen-pusher (b) Hist scribe

scribouillard, -e [skribujar, -ard] nm,f Fam Péj pen-pusher

script [skript] nm (a) (écriture) printing; **écrire en s.** to print (b) Cin (film) script

scripte [skript] nmf Cin (homme) continuity man; (femme) continuity girl

scrupule [skrypyl] nm scruple; **sans scrupules** (personne) unscrupulous; (agir) unscrupulously

scrupuleusement [skrypyløzmã] adv scrupulously

scrupuleux, -euse [skrypylø, -øz] adj scrupulous; **peu s.** unscrupulous

scrutateur, -trice [skrytatœr, -tris] 1 adj Litt (esprit, regard) searching
2 nm,f (d'un scrutin) teller

scruter [skryte] vt to scrutinize; (horizon, paysage) to scan

scrutin [skrytɛ̃] nm (a) (élection) poll; **s. secret** secret vote (b) (vote) ballot (c) (système) voting system; **s. majoritaire** first-past-the-post system; **s. proportionnel** voting by proportional representation; **s. uninominal** voting for a single candidate

sculpter [skylte] vt to sculpt; *(dans du bois)* to carve *(dans* out of)

sculpteur [skyltœr] nm sculptor; **s. sur bois** woodcarver

sculptural, -e, -aux, -ales [skyltyral, -o] adj *(art)* sculptural; *(silhouette, beauté)* statuesque

sculpture [skyltyr] nf *(œuvre, art)* sculpture; **s. sur bois** woodcarving; **faire de la s.** to sculpt

SDF [esdeef] nmf *(abrév* **sans domicile fixe)** person of no fixed abode; *(sans abri)* homeless person; **les S.** *(sans abri)* the homeless

SDN [esdeen] nf *(abrév* **Société des Nations)** la S. the League of Nations

se [sə]

> s' is used before a word beginning with a vowel or h mute.

pron personnel **(a)** *(soi) (homme)* himself; *(femme)* herself; *(chose)* itself; *(indéfini)* oneself; *(pluriel)* themselves; **on se flatter** to flatter oneself; **il se rase** he is shaving; *Fam* **on s'est blessés** we hurt ourselves
(b) *(à soi) (homme)* to himself; *(femme)* to herself; *(chose)* to itself; *(indéfini)* to oneself; *(pluriel)* to themselves; **elle s'est coupé le doigt** she has cut her finger; *Fam* **on va s'acheter une voiture** we're going to buy (ourselves) a car
(c) *(réciproque) (objet direct)* each other; *(objet indirect)* to each other; **se nuire (l'un à l'autre)** to hurt each other; **ils se sont quittés en bons termes** they parted on good terms
(d) *(passif)* **ça se mange froid** you eat it cold; **les couteaux se rangent dans ce tiroir** the knives go in this drawer

séance [seɑ̃s] nf **(a)** *(réunion)* session, meeting; **tenir s.** to be in session **(b)** *(de travail, d'entraînement)* session; **s. de photo** photo session; **s. de pose** sitting **(c)** *Cin & Th* performance; *Cin* **s. privée** private showing **(d)** **s. tenante** straight away, at once

séant, -e [seɑ̃, -ɑ̃t] **1** adj *Litt (convenable)* fitting
2 nm *Litt ou Hum* **se mettre sur son s.** to sit up

seau, -x [so] nm bucket; *(contenu)* bucket(ful); *Fam* **il pleut à seaux** it's pouring down; **s. à champagne** champagne bucket; **s. à charbon** coal scuttle; **s. à glace** ice bucket

sébacé, -e [sebase] adj sebaceous

sébum [sebɔm] nm sebum

sec, sèche [sɛk, sɛʃ] **1** adj **(a)** *(temps, saison, sol, peau, bois)* dry; *(morue, fruit)* dried; **à pied s.** without getting one's feet wet; **avoir la gorge sèche** *(avoir soif)* to be dry **(b)** *(vin, cidre)* dry **(c)** *(maigre) (personne)* lean; **être s. comme un coup de trique** *(austère) (personne)* hard; *(réponse, ton, voix)* sharp; **avoir le cœur s.** to be hard-hearted **(e)** *(non appuyé) (coup)* sharp **(f)** *(sans rien ajouter)* **boire qch s.** to drink sth neat
2 adv **(a)** *(beaucoup) (frapper, pleuvoir)* hard; *(boire)* heavily; **démarrer s.** to shoot off **(b)** *Fam* **aussi s.** right away
3 nm **(a)** **tenir au s.** *(sur une étiquette)* keep in a dry place **(b)** **être à s.** *(source, puits, rivière)* to be dry; *Fam (sans argent)* to be broke

sécable [sekabl] adj divisible

sécateur [sekatœr] nm pruning shears, *Br* secateurs

sécession [sesesjɔ̃] nf secession; **faire s. (de)** to secede (from)

séchage [seʃaʒ] nm drying

sèche [sɛʃ] **1** nf *Fam Br* fag, *Am* butt
2 adj *voir* **sec**

sèche-cheveux [sɛʃʃəvø] nm inv hairdryer

sèche-linge [sɛʃlɛ̃ʒ] nm inv *(appareil)* tumble-drier; *(armoire)* airing cupboard

sèche-mains [sɛʃmɛ̃] nm inv hand-drier

sèchement [sɛʃmã] adv *(parler, répondre)* curtly

sécher [34] [seʃe] **1** vt to dry; *Fam* **s. un cours** to skip a class
2 vi **(a)** *(vêtement, cheveux)* to dry; **mettre du linge à s.** to put clothes out to dry **(b)** *Fam (ne pouvoir répondre)* to be stumped
3 se sécher vpr to dry oneself; **se s. les cheveux/les mains** to dry one's hair/hands

sécheresse [seʃrɛs, seʃrɛs] nf **(a)** *(absence de pluie)* drought **(b)** *(de l'air, du sol, de la peau)* dryness **(c)** *(des manières, du ton)* curtness; *(du cœur)* hardness; *(du style)* dryness

séchoir [seʃwar] nm **(a)** *(appareil)* drier; **s. (à cheveux)** hairdryer **(b)** *(dispositif pliant)* **s. (à linge)** clothes-horse

second, -e [səɡɔ̃, -ɔ̃d] **1** adj second; *(rôle)* supporting, minor
2 nm **(a)** *(assistant)* assistant; *Mil* second-in-command; *Naut* first mate; *(de duelliste)* second **(b)** *(étage) Br* second *or Am* third floor
3 nm,f second; **je préfère le s.** I prefer the second one; *voir aussi* **cinquième**

secondaire [səɡɔ̃dɛr] **1** adj **(a)** *Scol* secondary; **établissement d'enseignement s.** secondary school **(b)** *(pas essentiel)* secondary; *(personnage, rôle) Th* minor; *Fig* secondary; **c'est s.** it's of secondary importance **(c)** *Écon & Géol* secondary
2 nm *Géol* secondary era; *Écon* secondary sector

seconde [səɡɔ̃d] nf **(a)** *(unité de temps)* second; *(attendez)* **une s.!** just a second!; **pendant une fraction de s.** for a fraction of a second **(b)** *(vitesse)* second *(gear)* **(c)** *(dans les transports)* second class; **voyager en s.** to travel second-class **(d)** *(classe) Br* ≃ fifth form, *Am* ≃ tenth grade **(e)** *Mus* second

seconder [səɡɔ̃de] vt to assist

secouer [səkwe] **1** vt **(a)** *(arbre, tête, bouteille)* to shake; *(coussin, oreiller)* to plump up; *(vêtements, tapis)* to shake out; *(sujet: vent, vagues)* to buffet; **nous avons été secoués pendant la traversée** we were shaken about during the crossing; *Fam* **s. les puces à qn** *(réprimander)* to tell sb off **(b)** *(sujet: choc, maladie, nouvelles)* to shake (up) **(c)** *(se débarrasser de) (poussière, joug)* to shake off
2 se secouer vpr **(a)** *(s'agiter)* to shake oneself **(b)** *(agir)* to snap out of it

secourable [səkurabl] adj helpful

secourir [22] [səkurir] vt to help, to assist

secourisme [səkurism] nm first aid

secouriste [səkurist] nmf first-aid worker

secours [səkur] nm **(a)** *(aide)* help; *(financier, matériel)* aid; *Mil (renforts)* relief; **appel au s.** call for help; **au s.!** help!; **premiers s.** first aid; **porter s. à qn** to give sb help; **demander du s.** to ask for help; **aller au s. de qn** to go to sb's assistance; **cela m'a été d'un grand s.** it's been a great help to me **(b)** **de s.** *(trousse, poste)* first-aid; *(sortie, éclairage)* emergency; *(roue)* spare; *Ordinat (copie, fichier)* backup

secousse [səkus] nf jolt, jerk; **par secousses** *(avancer)* jerkily; **s. (sismique)** *(earth)* tremor

secret¹, -ète [sǝkrɛ, -ɛt] *adj* (a) *(non divulgué)* secret (b) *(personne)* reticent

secret² *nm* (a) *(confidence, mystère)* secret; **garder un s.** to keep a secret; **mettre qn dans le s.** to let sb in on the secret; **être dans le s.** to be in on the secret; **ne pas avoir de secrets pour qn** *(discipline)* to hold no secrets for sb; **ce n'est un s. pour personne** it's no secret; **le s. du bonheur/de la réussite** the secret of happiness/of success; **secrets d'alcôve** pillow talk; **s. d'État** state secret; **s. de fabrication** trade secret; **s. de Polichinelle** open secret; **emporter un s. dans la tombe** to take a secret to the grave (b) *(discrétion)* secrecy; **dans le plus grand s.** in the strictest secrecy; **en s.** *(en cachette)* in secret; **s. bancaire** banking secrecy; **s. professionnel** professional secrecy (c) **mettre qn au s.** *(l'enfermer)* to put sb in solitary confinement

secrétaire [sǝkretɛr] **1** *nmf* secretary; **s. d'ambassade** secretary; **s. de direction** personal assistant; **s. d'État** Secretary of State; **s. général** secretary general; *Com* company secretary; **s. médicale** medical secretary; **s. particulier** private secretary; **s. de rédaction** sub-editor **2** *nm (meuble)* writing desk

secrétariat [sǝkretarja] *nm* (a) *(fonction)* secretaryship (b) *(bureau)* secretary's office; *(d'un organisme international)* secretariat (c) *(métier)* secretarial work (d) *Pol* **s. d'État** ministry

secrètement [sǝkrɛtmã] *adv* secretly

sécréter [34] [sekrete] *vt* to secrete; *Fig (ennui)* to exude

sécrétion [sekresjɔ̃] *nf* secretion

sectaire [sɛktɛr] *adj & nmf* sectarian

sectarisme [sɛktarism] *nm* sectarianism

secte [sɛkt] *nf* sect

secteur [sɛktœr] *nm* (a) *(zone)* area, district; *Fam* **changer de s.** to move somewhere else (b) *Él* mains; **branché sur le s.** (c) *Écon* sector; **le s. privé/public** the private/public sector; **s. primaire/secondaire/tertiaire** primary/secondary/tertiary sector; *Fam* **ce n'est pas mon s.** that's not my line (c) *Math & Ordinat* sector; *Ordinat* **s. d'initialisation** boot sector

section [sɛksjɔ̃] *nf* (a) *(division) (d'un livre, d'un bâtiment, d'une autoroute)* section; *(d'une ligne d'autobus)* stage; *(d'un parti politique, d'un syndicat)* branch (b) *(de l'infanterie)* platoon; *(de l'artillerie)* section (c) *(coupe)* section; **ça fait 5 centimètres de s.** the diameter of the section is 5 centimetres (d) *Scol* = one of the groups into which baccalaureat students are divided, depending on their chosen area of specialization

sectionner [sɛksjone] *vt* (a) *(couper)* to sever (b) *(fractionner) (service, circonscription)* to divide into sections

sectoriel, -elle [sɛktɔrjɛl] *adj* sectorial

sécu [seky] *nf Fam (abrév* **Sécurité sociale**) *Br* Social Security, *Am* Welfare

séculaire [sekylɛr] *adj* (a) *(très ancien)* centuries-old (b) *(qui existe depuis un siècle)* a hundred years old (c) *(qui a lieu tous les cent ans)* centennial

séculier, -ère [sekylje, -ɛr] *adj* secular

secundo [sǝgɔdo] *adv* secondly

sécurisant, -e [sekyrizɑ̃, -ɑ̃t] *adj* reassuring

sécuriser [sekyrize] *vt* to reassure

sécurité [sekyrite] *nf* (a) *(ordre, stabilité)* security; **être/ se sentir en s.** to be/feel secure; **s. de l'emploi** job

security; **s. nationale/internationale** national/ international security (b) *(absence de danger)* safety; **s. routière** road safety; **S. Routière** = French road safety organization (c) *(dispositif)* safety catch; **porte munie d'une s.-enfants** door with a childproof lock (d) **S. sociale** *Br* Social Security, *Am* Welfare

sédatif, -ive [sedatif, -iv] *adj & nm* sedative

sédentaire [sedɑ̃tɛr] *adj* (a) *(vie, travail, travailleur)* sedentary; *(population)* settled (b) *(casanier)* stay-at-home

sédentariser [sedɑ̃tarize] **1** *vt (population)* to settle **2 se sédentariser** *vpr* to settle

sédiment [sedimɑ̃] *nm* sediment

sédimentaire [sedimɑ̃tɛr] *adj* sedimentary

sédimentation [sedimɑ̃tasjɔ̃] *nf* sedimentation

séditieux, -euse [sedisjø, -øz] **1** *adj* seditious **2** *nm,f* insurgent

sédition [sedisjɔ̃] *nf* sedition

séducteur, -trice [sedyktœr, -tris] **1** *nm,f* seducer, *f* seductress **2** *adj* seductive

séduction [sedyksjɔ̃] *nf* (a) *(physique)* seduction; *(par le charme)* charming (b) *(moyen de séduire)* attraction; **pouvoir de s.** power of attraction

séduire [18] [sedɥir] *vt* (a) *(charmer) (sujet: personne)* to charm; *(sujet: projet, proposition)* to appeal to (b) *(sexuellement)* to seduce

séduisant, -e [sedɥizɑ̃, -ɑ̃t] *adj* attractive

séfarade [sefarad] **1** *adj* Sephardic **2** *nmf* Sephardic Jew

segment [sɛgmɑ̃] *nm* segment

segmenter [sɛgmɑ̃te] *vt aussi Ordinat* to segment

ségrégation [segregasjɔ̃] *nf* segregation

ségrégationniste [segregasjɔnist] *adj & nmf* segregationist

seiche [sɛʃ] *nf* cuttlefish; **os de s.** cuttlebone

seigle [sɛgl] *nm* rye

seigneur [sɛɲœr] *nm* (a) *Hist* lord; **à tout s. tout honneur** honour where honour is due; **en grand s.** in grand style (b) *Rel* **le S.** the Lord

seigneurial, -e, -aux, -ales [sɛɲœrjal, -o] *adj (droits, domaine)* seigniorial

sein [sɛ̃] *nm (de femme)* breast; *Litt (poitrine)* bosom; **serrer ou presser qn sur son s.** to press sb to one's bosom; **donner le s. à un enfant, nourrir un enfant au s.** to breast-feed a child; **au s. de** within

Seine [sɛn] *nf* **la S.** the Seine

séisme [seism] *nm* earthquake; *Fig & Litt* upheaval

seize [sɛz] *adj & nm inv* sixteen; *voir aussi* **trois**

seizième [sɛzjɛm] *nmf, adj & adj* sixteenth; *voir aussi* **cinquième**

séjour [seʒur] *nm* (a) *(période)* stay; **s. linguistique** language-learning trip (b) *(pièce)* **(salle de) s.** living room (c) *Litt (lieu)* abode

séjourner [seʒurne] *vi* to stay

sel [sɛl] *nm* (a) *(substance)* salt; **gros s.** coarse salt; **s. fin** fine salt; **sels de bain** bath salts; **sels (à respirer)** (smelling) salts (b) *Fig (esprit)* piquancy

sélect, -e [selɛkt] *adj Fam (soirée, clientèle)* select

sélectif, -ive [selɛktif, -iv] *adj* selective; *Ordinat* **en mode s.** in veto mode

sélection [seleksjɔ̃] nf selection

sélectionné, -e [seleksjɔne] 1 adj selected 2 nm,f (sportif) selected competitor; (d'une équipe) selected player

sélectionner [seleksjɔne] vt to select

sélectionneur, -euse [seleksjɔnœr, -øz] nm,f selector

self [self] nm Fam self-service restaurant

self-service (pl self-services) [selfservis] nm (restaurant) self-service restaurant; (magasin) self-service shop

selle [sel] nf (a) (de cheval, bicyclette, moto) saddle; se mettre en s. to mount; monter sans s. to ride bareback (b) selles (matières fécales) stools, Br motions; aller à la s. to have a bowel movement (c) Culin s. de mouton/d'agneau saddle of mutton/lamb

seller [sele] vt to saddle

sellette [selet] nf Fam mettre qn/être sur la s. to put sb/to be in the hot seat

selon [səlɔ̃] prép (a) (d'après) according to; s. moi in my opinion (b) (conformément à) in accordance with; s. toute vraisemblance in all probability (c) (en fonction de) varier s. les cas/les saisons to vary from case to case/season to season; Fam c'est s. it all depends; s. que depending on whether

semailles [səmaj] nfpl (a) (action) sowing; (temps des) s. sowing time (b) (graines) seeds

semaine [səmɛn] nf (a) (sept jours) week; vivre à la petite s. to live from day to day; jour de s. weekday; en s. during the week, on weekdays; la s. sainte Holy Week (b) (salaire) week's pay; (argent de poche) week's pocket money (c) Mil (tour de service) week's duty; être de s. to be on duty for the week; officier de s. duty officer for the week

semainier [səmenje] nm (agenda) desk diary

sémantique [semātik] 1 adj semantic 2 nf semantics (singulier)

sémaphore [semafɔr] nm Rail semaphore signal; Naut signal station

semblable [sāblabl] 1 adj (a) (pareil) similar; s. à qch similar to sth, like sth; je n'ai rien dit de s. I said nothing of the sort (b) (tel) de semblables projets/propos such plans/remarks, plans/remarks like that 2 nm (être humain) fellow man; vous et vos semblables you and your kind

semblant [sāblā] nm (a) (apparence) un s. de a semblance of (b) faire s. to pretend; faire s. de faire qch to pretend to do sth; en faisant s. de rien without making it obvious

sembler [sāble] 1 vi to seem 2 v impersonnel il semble que... it seems that...; il me/leur semble que... it seems to me/them that...; me semble-t-il it seems to me; il me semble avoir entendu son nom I've a feeling I've heard his name; il me semble idiot d'attendre encore plus longtemps it seems stupid to me to wait any longer; faites comme bon vous semble ou semblera do as you think best; il le fera si bon lui semble he'll do it if he thinks fit

semé, -e [səme] adj s. de strewn with; (fleurs) dotted with; (étoiles) studded with; (citations) sprinkled with; s. d'embûches full of traps

semelle [səmel] nf sole; s. (intérieure) insole; s. de caoutchouc/de cuir rubber/leather sole; ne pas avancer d'une s. to make no progress whatsoever; il ne reculera pas d'une s. he won't give an inch; ne pas quitter qn d'une s. to be always at sb's heels; c'est de la s.! it's like shoe leather!

semence [səmɑ̃s] nf (graine) seed; (sperme) semen

semer [46] [səme] vt (a) (graines) to sow (b) (discorde, confusion, panique, doute) to sow, to spread; Prov qui sème le vent récolte la tempête he who sows the wind shall reap the whirlwind (c) Fam (distancer) to shake off (d) Fam (perdre) to lose

semestre [səmestr] nm half-year, six-month period; Scol & Univ term

semestriel, -elle [səmestrijel] adj half-yearly, six-monthly

semi-automatique [səmiɔtɔmatik] adj semi-automatic

semi-liberté [səmiliberte] nf Jur partial release

sémillant, -e [semijā, -āt] adj (personne) spirited; (regard) bright

séminaire [seminer] nm (a) (colloque) seminar (b) Rel seminary

séminariste [seminarist] nm Rel seminarist

sémiologie [semjɔlɔʒi] nf semiology

sémiotique [semjɔtik] 1 adj semiotic 2 nf semiotics (singulier)

semi-précieux, -euse (mpl semi-précieux, fpl semi-précieuses) [səmipresjø, -øz] adj semi-precious

semi-remorque (pl semi-remorques) [səmirəmɔrk] nm (poids lourd) Br articulated lorry, Am trailer truck

semis [səmi] nm (a) (action) sowing (b) (terrain) seedbed (c) (jeune plante) seedling

sémite [semit] 1 adj Semitic 2 nmf S. Semite

sémitique [semitik] adj Semitic

semoir [səmwar] nm (a) (sac) seed bag (b) (machine) seeder

semonce [səmɔ̃s] nf (remontrance) reprimand; aussi Fig coup de s. warning shot

semoule [səmul] nf semolina

sempiternel, -elle [sāpiternel] adj never-ending, endless

sénat [sena] nm senate

sénateur [senatœr] nm senator

sénatorial, -e, -aux, -ales [senatɔrjal, -o] adj senatorial

Sénégal [senegal] nm le S. Senegal

sénégalais, -e [senegale, -ez] 1 adj Senegalese 2 nm,f S. Senegalese; les S. the Senegalese

sénile [senil] adj senile

sénilité [senilite] nf senility

senior [senjɔr] adj & nmf Sp senior (above the age of 20)

sens¹ voir **sentir**

sens² [sās] nm (a) (de la perception) sense; les cinq s. the five senses; le sixième s. the sixth sense (b) les s. (sensualité) the senses; plaisir des s. sensual pleasure (c) (jugement) sense; avoir le s. de l'humour/du ridicule to have a sense of humour/of the ridiculous; avoir le s. des affaires/de l'orientation to have good business sense/a good sense of direction; s. commun common sense; **s. moral** moral sense; **s. pratique** practical sense; **bon s.** common sense; **un homme de bon s.** a sensible man

(d) *(avis)* **à mon s.** to my mind

(e) *(signification)* *(d'un mot)* meaning, sense; **au s. propre/figuré** in the literal/figurative sense, literally/figuratively; **cela n'a aucun s.** it doesn't make (any) sense; **en ce s. que…** in the sense that…

(f) *(direction)* direction; **tenir qch dans le mauvais s.** to hold sth the wrong way round; **en s. inverse** in the opposite direction; **dans le s. des aiguilles d'une montre** clockwise; **dans le s. inverse des aiguilles d'une montre** *Br* anticlockwise, *Am* counterclockwise; **dans le s. du courant** with the current; **dans le s. de la longueur** lengthwise, lengthways; **dans le s. de la largeur** widthwise, across; **s. dessus dessous** *(en désordre)* upside down; **s. devant derrière** back to front, the wrong way round; **dans les deux s.** both ways; *Fig* **ces mesures vont dans le bon s.** these measures are heading the right way; *Ordinat* **s. de déroulement** flow direction; **s. giratoire** *Br* roundabout, *Am* traffic circle; **s. interdit** *(sur panneau)* no entry; **s. unique** *(sur panneau)* one way

sensas(s) [sɑ̃sas] *adj Fam* fantastic, great

sensation [sɑ̃sasjɔ̃] *nf* **(a)** *(perception physique)* sensation **(b)** *(impression)* feeling; **avoir la s. que…** to have a or the feeling that… **(c)** *(scandale)* **faire s.** to create a sensation

sensationnel, -elle [sɑ̃sasjɔnɛl] *adj* **(a)** *(à sensation)* sensational **(b)** *Fam (fantastique)* fantastic, great

sensé, -e [sɑ̃se] *adj* sensible

sensibilisation [sɑ̃sibilizasjɔ̃] *nf* **(a)** **s. de l'opinion (à qch)** increasing public awareness (of sth) **(b)** *Phot & Méd* sensitization

sensibiliser [sɑ̃sibilize] *vt* **(a)** *(rendre conscient)* **s. qn à qch** to increase sb's awareness of sth; **s. l'opinion (à qch)** to increase public awareness (of sth) **(b)** *Phot & Méd* to sensitize

sensibilité [sɑ̃sibilite] *nf* sensitivity; **avoir une s. à fleur de peau** to be hypersensitive

sensible [sɑ̃sibl] *adj* **(a)** *(émotif)* sensitive **(b)** *(réceptif)* **être s. à qch** to be sensitive to sth; *(influence)* to be susceptible to sth **(c)** *(douloureux)* sensitive **(d)** *(appréciable)* noticeable, appreciable; **de manière s.** noticeably **(e)** *(balance, thermomètre, plaque)* sensitive; **s. à la lumière** light-sensitive

sensiblement [sɑ̃sibləmɑ̃] *adv* **(a)** *(notablement)* noticeably, appreciably **(b)** *(à peu près)* roughly, more or less

sensiblerie [sɑ̃sibləri] *nf* sentimentality

sensoriel, -elle [sɑ̃sɔrjɛl] *adj* sensory

sensualité [sɑ̃sɥalite] *nf* sensuality

sensuel, -elle [sɑ̃sɥɛl] *adj* sensual

sent *voir* **sentir**

sentence [sɑ̃tɑ̃s] *nf* **(a)** *(jugement)* sentence **(b)** *(maxime)* maxim

sentencieux, -euse [sɑ̃tɑ̃sjø, -øz] *adj* sententious

senteur [sɑ̃tœr] *nf* scent; *(dans un parfum)* note

senti, -e [sɑ̃ti] *adj* **bien s.** appropriate

sentier [sɑ̃tje] *nm* path; *Fig* **sortir des sentiers battus** to go off the beaten track; **sur le s. de la guerre** on the warpath

sentiment [sɑ̃timɑ̃] *nm* feeling; **prendre qn par les sentiments** to appeal to sb's feelings; *Fam* **ça partait d'un bon s.** it was well meant; **en affaires, je ne fais pas de s.** I don't let sentiment interfere with business; **avoir le s. que…** to have a or the feeling that…; **j'avais le s. de m'être trompé** I had the feeling I'd made a mistake

sentimental, -e, -aux, -ales [sɑ̃timɑ̃tal, -o] **1** *adj* *(personne, chanson, valeur)* sentimental; **vie sentimentale** love life

2 *nmf* sentimental person

sentimentalisme [sɑ̃timɑ̃talism] *nm* sentimentalism; **faire du s.** to be sentimental

sentinelle [sɑ̃tinɛl] *nf* sentry

sentir [64a] [sɑ̃tir] **1** *vt* **(a)** *(douleur, sensation tactile)* to feel; *Fam* **Fig je ne sens plus mes jambes/mes pieds** *(de froid)* I can't feel my legs/my feet; *(de fatigue)* my legs/my feet are killing me

(b) *(être conscient de) (danger)* to sense; **s. que…** to have a or the feeling that…; **faire s. à qn que…** to make sb feel that…; **se faire s.** to make itself felt; *Fig* **on sent l'influence de Wagner** one can detect Wagner's influence

(c) *(parfum, fleur)* to smell; **faire s. qch à qn** to let sb smell sth

(d) *(avoir l'odeur de)* to smell of; **ça sent le brûlé** there's a smell of burning; **ça sent bon le pain frais** there's a delicious smell of fresh bread; *Fig & Péj* **ce livre sent l'effort** this book is very laboured; **s. le soufre** to smack of subversiveness

(e) *Fam (supporter)* **je ne peux pas le s.** I can't stand him

2 *vi* **(a)** *(avoir comme odeur)* **s. bon/mauvais** to smell good/bad; **s. fort** to have a strong smell

(b) *Fam (puer)* to smell; **s. des pieds** to have smelly feet

3 **se sentir** *vpr* **(a)** *(être perceptible)* **cela se sent** you can tell

(b) *(suivi d'un adjectif ou d'un infinitif)* **se s. revivre** to feel oneself coming alive again; **se s. bien/fatigué** to feel well/tired; *Fam* **tu ne te sens pas bien, non?** have you taken leave of your senses?; **se s. capable de faire qch** to feel capable of doing sth

(c) *(avoir)* **se s. le courage de faire qch** to feel up to doing sth

(d) *Fam (se contrôler)* **il ne se sent plus!** he's too big for his boots!

(e) *Fam (se supporter)* **ils ne peuvent pas se s.** they can't stand each other

seoir [10a] [swar] *Litt* **1** *vi* **s. à** to suit

2 *v impersonnel* **il lui sied mal de…** it ill becomes him to…

Séoul [seul] *n* Seoul

séparable [separabl] *adj* separable (**de** from)

séparation [separasjɔ̃] *nf* **(a)** *(de personnes, d'objets)* separation (**de** from); *Ordinat* **s. automatique des pages** automatic pagination **(b)** *(cloison)* partition, division **(c)** *Jur* **s. de biens** = marriage settlement under which husband and wife administer their separate properties

séparatisme [separatism] *nm* separatism

séparatiste [separatist] *adj & nmf* separatist

séparé, -e [separe] *adj* **(a)** *(notions, chambres)* separate **(b)** *(personnes)* separated (**de** from); **nous vivons séparés** we live apart

séparément [separemɑ̃] *adv* separately

séparer [separe] **1** vt **(a)** (éloigner) to separate (de from) **(b)** (partager) to divide (en into) **(c)** (opposer) to divide; **tout les sépare** they are poles apart

2 se séparer vpr **(a)** (époux) to separate (de from), to split up (de with) **(b)** (foule, assemblée) to break up **(c)** (se défaire) **se s. de qch** to part with sth; **se s. de qn** (employé) to let sb go **(d)** (rivière, route) to divide (en into); **c'est ici que nos chemins se séparent** this is where we go our separate ways

sept [set] adj & nm inv seven; voir aussi **trois**

septante [septɑ̃t] adj inv Belg & Suisse seventy; voir aussi **trois**

septembre [septɑ̃br] nm September; voir aussi **janvier**

septennat [septena] nm (seven-year) term

septentrional, -e, -aux, -ales [septɑ̃trijɔnal, -o] adj northern

septicémie [septisemi] nf blood poisoning, septicaemia

septième [setjεm] nmf, nm & adj seventh; voir aussi **cinquième**

septique [septik] adj septic

septuagénaire [septɥaʒenεr] adj & nmf septuagenarian

sépulcre [sepylkr] nm sepulchre

sépulture [sepyltyr] nf Litt **(a)** (inhumation) burial **(b)** (lieu) burial place

séquelles [sekεl] nfpl (d'une maladie, d'un accident) after-effects; (d'une guerre, d'une catastrophe) aftermath

séquence [sekɑ̃s] nf **(a)** (d'objets, de mots) sequence; Ordinat **s. de caractères** character string, sequence of characters **(b)** (de film) sequence **(c)** (de cartes) run

séquestre [sekεstr] nm (action) sequestration; **mettre qch sous s.** to sequester sth

séquestrer [sekεstre] vt **(a)** (personne) **s. qn** to keep sb locked up **(b)** (biens) to sequester

séquoia [sekɔja] nm sequoia

sera, serai, serais etc voir **être**

sérail [seraj] nm seraglio; Fig inner circle

serbe [sεrb] **1** adj Serb, Serbian
2 nmf **S.** Serb, Serbian

Serbie [sεrbi] nf la S. Serbia

serbo-croate (pl **serbo-croates**) [sεrbokrɔat] **1** adj Serbo-Croat, Serbo-Croatian
2 nm (langue) Serbo-Croat

Sercq [sεrk] n Sark

serein, -e [sarε̃, -εn] adj (personne, visage, esprit) serene; (ciel, nuit) clear

sereinement [sarεnmɑ̃] adv calmly

sérénade [serenad] nf **(a)** Mus serenade; **donner la s. à qn** to serenade sb **(b)** Fam (tapage) racket

sérénité [serenite] nf serenity; **avec s.** serenely

serf, serve [sεrf, sεrv] nm, f Hist serf

sergent [sεrʒɑ̃] nm sergeant

sergent-chef (pl **sergents-chefs**) [sεrʒɑ̃ʃεf] nm staff sergeant

série [seri] nf **(a)** (suite, collection) series; (d'échantillons) range; (de casseroles) set; **des démissions en s.** a series of resignations **(b)** Rad & TV series **(c)** Ind **production en s.** mass production; **voiture de s.** standard car **(d)** (dans un classement) group; Sp heat; **(film de) B.** B B film **(e)** (locutions) **s. noire** (suite de catastrophes) series or catalogue of disasters; **(roman de) s. noire** crime thriller

sérieusement [serjøzmɑ̃] adv seriously; **parlez-vous s.?** are you serious?

sérieux, -euse [serjø, -øz] **1** adj **(a)** (personne, lecture) serious; **d'un air s.** seriously; **ce n'est pas s.!** you're not serious!; Fam **s. comme un pape** as solemn as a judge **(b)** (offre, acheteur) serious, genuine; (information, entreprise) reliable; (employé) conscientious **(c)** (important) (problèmes, ennuis) serious; (progrès) good

2 nm **(a)** (application) conscientiousness; **avec s.** conscientiously **(b)** (gravité) **garder son s.** to keep a straight face; **prendre qn/qch au s.** to take sb/sth seriously; **se prendre au s.** to take oneself seriously

sérigraphie [serigrafi] nf silk-screen printing

serin [sarε̃] nm (oiseau) canary

seriner [sarine] vt Fam **s. qch à qn** to go on and on at sb about sth; **s. à qn que...** to keep telling sb that...

seringue [sarε̃g] nf syringe

serment [sεrmɑ̃] nm **(a)** (parole solennelle) oath; **prêter s.** to take an oath; **sous s.** on oath **(b)** (promesse) pledge; (d'amoureux) vow; **faire le s. de faire qch** to swear or vow to do sth

sermon [sεrmɔ̃] nm **(a)** Rel sermon **(b)** Fam (remontrance) lecture, sermon

sermonner [sεrmɔne] vt Fam to lecture

séronégatif, -ive [seronegatif, -iv] **1** adj HIV negative
2 nm, f person who is HIV negative

séropositif, -ive [seropozitif, -iv] **1** adj HIV positive
2 nm, f person who is HIV positive

serpe [sεrp] nf billhook

serpent [sεrpɑ̃] nm **(a)** (reptile) snake; **s. à sonnette** rattlesnake **(b)** Écon **le s. monétaire européen** the European currency snake

serpenter [sεrpɑ̃te] vi to wind

serpentin [sεrpɑ̃tε̃] nm (cotillon) streamer

serpillière [sεrpijεr] nf floorcloth; **passer la s. dans la cuisine** to clean the kitchen floor

serpolet [sεrpɔlε] nm wild thyme

serre [sεr] nf **(a)** (local) greenhouse **(b)** **serres** (d'oiseau de proie) claws, talons

serré, -e [sεre] **1** adj **(a)** (chaussures, vêtement) tight; (personnes) packed together; (écriture) cramped; (rangs) serried; (dents) clenched; (lèvres) pressed tightly together **(b)** (emploi du temps, budget) tight; (surveillance, lutte, score) close **(c)** (café) strong

2 adv **écrire s.** to have cramped handwriting; Fig **jouer s.** to play a tight game

serre-livres [sεrlivr] nm inv book-end

serrement [sεrmɑ̃] nm **avoir un s. de cœur** to feel a pang

serrer [sεre] **1** vt **(a)** (tenir) to grip; **s. la main à qn** to shake hands with sb, to shake sb's hand; **s. qn dans ses bras** to hug sb; **s. qn/qch contre soi** to hold sb/sth tightly to one; Fig **s. le cœur à qn** to wring sb's heart **(b)** (sujet: vêtement, chaussures) to be too tight for **(c)** (nœud, écrou, ceinture) to tighten; (joint) to clamp; (poings) to clench; **s. les dents** to clench one's teeth; Fig to grit one's teeth; Fam Fig **s. les fesses** to be scared stiff **(d)** (rapprocher) to put close together; **s. les rangs** to close ranks **(e)** (ranger) to put away **(f)** (raser) (trottoir) to hug; **s. qn de près** to follow sb closely; **évite de s. la voiture de devant** don't drive too close to the car in front

2 vi **serrez à droite/gauche** (sur panneau) keep to the right/left

3 se serrer *vpr* (a) *(se rapprocher)* to squeeze up; **se s. contre qn** to snuggle up to sb (b) *Fig* **ma gorge se serra** I had a lump in my throat (c) *(pour se saluer)* **se s. la main** to shake hands

serre-tête [sɛʀtɛt] *nm inv* headband

serrure [seʀyʀ] *nf* lock

serrurerie [seʀyʀʀi] *nf (métier)* locksmith's trade

serrurier [seʀyʀje] *nm* locksmith

sers, sert *etc voir* **servir**

sertir [sɛʀtiʀ] *vt (pierre précieuse)* to set

sérum [seʀɔm] *nm* serum; **s. physiologique** saline solution

servage [sɛʀvaʒ] *nm* serfdom; *Fig* bondage

servante [sɛʀvɑ̃t] *nf (maid)* servant

serve [sɛʀv] *voir* **serf**

serveur, -euse [sɛʀvœʀ, -øz] **1** *nm,f* (a) *(dans un bar)* barman, *f* barmaid; *(dans un restaurant)* waiter, *f* waitress (b) *(au tennis)* server
2 *nm Ordinat* server; **s. de fichiers** file server; **s. de réseau** network server; **s. télématique** bulletin board (system)

serviable [sɛʀvjabl] *adj* obliging, helpful

service [sɛʀvis] *nm* (a) *(pour un client, pour un maître)* service; *Écon* **services** services; **faire le s.** *(à table)* to serve; **être au s. de qn** to be in sb's service; **à votre s.** at your service; **s. compris/non compris** service included/not included; **premier/deuxième s.** *(au restaurant)* first/second sitting; **s. après-vente** *(dépannage)* after-sales service
(b) *Mil* **s. militaire** *ou* **national** military service; **faire son s.** to do one's military service; **bon pour le s.** fit for service
(c) *(au tennis)* service; **au s., Martin** Martin to serve
(d) *(travail)* duty; **être de s.** to be on duty; **prendre/quitter son s.** to go on/off duty; *Fam* **le crétin de s.** the inevitable or obligatory idiot
(e) *(département)* department; **s. d'ordre** *(surveillance)* crowd control; *(personnes)* = police, security staff etc in charge of crowd control; **s. du personnel** personnel department; **s. public** public utility; **s. de renseignements** military intelligence department; *Ordinat* **s. télématique** bulletin board service
(f) *(d'une machine)* **en s.** in service; **mettre qch en s.** to bring sth into service
(g) *(de transports en commun)* service; **assurer le s. entre** to provide a service between
(h) *(aide)* favour; **rendre (un) s. à qn** *(personne)* to do sb a favour; *(objet)* to be of use to sb; **rendre un mauvais s. à qn** to do sb a bad turn
(i) *(de vaisselle)* set

serviette [sɛʀvjɛt] *nf* (a) *(en tissu)* s. (b) *(de table)* serviette, napkin; **s. (de toilette)** towel; **s. de plage** beach towel (b) *(sac)* briefcase (c) **s. hygiénique** sanitary *Br* towel *or Am* napkin

serviette-éponge *(pl* **serviettes-éponges)** [sɛʀ-vjetepɔ̃ʒ] *nf* terry towel

servile [sɛʀvil] *adj* servile; *(imitation, traduction)* slavish

servilement [sɛʀvilmɑ̃] *adv* servilely; *(imiter, traduire)* slavishly

servir [63] [sɛʀviʀ] **1** *vt* (a) *(client, convive, nourriture)* to serve; **tout le monde est servi?** *(à table)* has everybody been served?; **s. frais** *(sur étiquette)* serve chilled; **s. à boire à qn** to give sb a drink; *Ironique* **côté ennuis, je suis servi!** I've got more than my share of worries! (b) *(favoriser)* *(personne)* to serve; *(intérêts)* to further (c) *(au tennis)* to serve (d) *(aux cartes)* **à vous de s.** it's your deal
2 *vi (dans une administration)* to serve **(sous** under)
3 servir à *vt ind* (a) *(être utile à)* to be of use to; **ça peut toujours s.** it might still come in useful (b) *(être utilisé pour)* **s. à qch/à faire qch** to be used for sth/for doing sth; **ne s. à rien** to be useless; **ne pas s. à grand-chose** not to be much use; **à quoi ça sert?** *(objet)* what's that used for?; *(démarche)* what's the use of that?
4 servir de *vt ind (faire fonction de) (objet)* to serve as, to be used as; *(personne)* to act as; **ça me sert de porte-crayons** I use it as a pencil-holder
5 *v impersonnel Litt* **il ne sert à rien de pleurer** there's no point in crying
6 se servir *vpr* (a) *(prendre)* to help oneself; **je me suis déjà servie deux fois** I've already had two helpings; **se s. des pâtes/du poulet** to help oneself to pasta/to chicken (b) *(plat, vin)* to be served; **le champagne se sert frappé** champagne should be served chilled (c) **se s. de qch/qn** *(utiliser)* to use sb/sth (d) *(s'approvisionner)* **se s. chez...** to shop at...

serviteur [sɛʀvitœʀ] *nm* servant

servitude [sɛʀvityd] *nf* (a) *(asservissement)* servitude (b) *(contrainte)* constraint

ses [se] *voir* **son**[1]

sésame [sezam] *nm* (a) *(plante)* sesame (b) *Fig* **s., ouvre-toi!** open sesame!

session [sesjɔ̃] *nf* (a) *(d'une assemblée, d'un tribunal)* session, sitting (b) *(période d'examens)* *(exam)* session; **s. de rattrapage** repeat exams, *Br* resits

set [sɛt] *nm* (a) *(au tennis)* set (b) **s. de table** *(napperon)* table mat

setter [setɛʀ] *nm* setter; **s. irlandais** Irish setter

seuil [sœj] *nm* (a) *(entrée)* doorway threshold; **sur le s.** in the doorway (b) *Fig* threshold; *Litt* **au s. de...** on the threshold of...; **s. de rentabilité** break-even point

seul, -e [sœl] **1** *adj* (a) *(unique)* only; **une seule personne** *(et pas plus)* a single person; *(parmi d'autres)* only one person; **comme un s. homme** as one man; **il suffit d'une seule fois** once is enough; **la seule pensée de sa venue** the mere thought of him coming (b) *(isolé)* alone; **se sentir s.** to feel lonely or alone; **être s. au monde** to be alone in the world; **parler s. à s. à qn** to speak to sb in private; **faire qch tout s.** to do sth (by) oneself *or* on one's own; **parler tout s.** to talk to oneself; **cela va s.** it's plain sailing, it's straightforward; **ça descend tout s.** *(boisson)* it just slides down (c) *(seulement)* only alone; **s. un miracle...** only a miracle...
2 *nm,f* **le s.** the only one; **un s.** *(personne, objet)* only one

seulement [sœlmɑ̃] *adv* only; **je te demande s. un peu de patience** I'm just asking you to be a bit patient; **non s...., mais en plus...** not only..., but also...; *Fam* **essaie s.!** just you try!

sève [sɛv] *nf* (a) *(d'une plante)* sap (b) *Fig (de la jeunesse)* vitality

sévère [sevɛʀ] *adj* severe; *(principe, règle)* strict; **être s. envers** *ou* **avec qn** to be hard on sb

sévèrement [sevɛʀmɑ̃] *adv* severely; *(de façon stricte)* strictly

sévérité [severite] nf severity; *(d'une discipline, d'une éducation)* strictness

sévices [sevis] nmpl ill-treatment

Séville [sevij] n Seville

sévir [sevir] vi (a) *(agir avec rigueur)* to act ruthlessly; **s. contre qn/qch** to deal ruthlessly with sb/sth (b) *(épidémie, guerre)* to rage; *(malfaiteurs)* to operate; **la crise qui sévit actuellement** the present crisis

sevrage [səvraʒ] nm *(d'un enfant)* weaning; *(d'un drogué, d'un alcoolique)* withdrawal

sevrer [səvre] vt (a) *(enfant)* to wean; *(drogué)* to get off drugs; *(alcoolique)* to get off drink; *Litt (priver)* **s. qn de qch** to deprive sb of sth

sexagénaire [segzaʒener, seksaʒener] nmf person in his/her sixties

sex-appeal [seksapil] nm *Fam* sex appeal

sexe [seks] nm (a) *(genre)* sex; *Hum* **le beau s.** the fair sex; **le s. faible** the weaker sex; **le s. fort** the stronger sex (b) *(organes sexuels)* genitals (c) *(sexualité)* sex

sexisme [seksism] nm sexism

sexiste [seksist] adj & nmf sexist

sexologue [seksɔlɔg] nmf sexologist

sex-shop *(pl* sex-shops) [seksʃɔp] nm sex shop

sextant [sekstã] nm sextant

sextuor [sekstɥɔr] nm sextet

sextuplé, -e [sekstyple] nm,f sextuplet

sexualité [seksyalite] nf sexuality

sexué, -e [seksɥe] adj *(plante, animal)* sexed; *(reproduction)* sexual

sexuel, -elle [seksɥel] adj *(rapport)* sexual; *(vie, acte, organe)* sex

sexuellement [seksɥelmã] adv sexually

sexy [seksi] adj inv *Fam* sexy

seyant, -e [sejã, -ãt] adj becoming

Seychelles [seʃel] nfpl **les S.** the Seychelles

SFIO [esefio] nf *(abrév* **Section française de l'Internationale ouvrière)** = French Socialist Party 1905-1969

shaker [ʃɛkœr] nm cocktail shaker

shakespearien, -enne [ʃɛkspirjɛ̃, -en] adj Shakespearean

shampoing [ʃãpwɛ̃] nm shampoo; **faire un s. à qn** to shampoo sb's hair; **to give sb a shampoo**

shampouiner [ʃãpwine] vt to shampoo

shampouineur, -euse [ʃãpwinœr, -øz] 1 nm,f shampooer
2 nf **shampouineuse (à moquettes)** *(machine)* carpet shampooer

shérif [ʃerif] nm sheriff

shetland [ʃetlãd] 1 nfpl **les (îles) S.** the Shetland Islands, the Shetlands
2 nm (a) *(laine)* Shetland wool; *(pull)* Shetland jumper (b) *(poney)* Shetland pony

shinto [ʃinto] nm, **shintoïsme** [ʃintoism] nm Shinto, Shintoism

shoot [ʃut] nm shot

shooter [ʃute] 1 vi *(au football)* to shoot
2 se shooter *vpr Fam (se droguer)* to shoot up; **se s. à l'héroïne** to shoot (up) heroin

shopping [ʃɔpiŋ] nm shopping; **faire du s.** to go shopping

short [ʃɔrt] nm (pair of) shorts

show [ʃo] nm show

show-business [ʃobiznes] nm show business

si¹ [si] adv (a) *(tellement)* so; **un si bon dîner** such a good dinner; **il n'est pas si bête (que ça)** he's not that stupid; **il était si nerveux qu'il a tout oublié** he was so nervous (that) he forgot everything (b) *(indique la concession)* si... **que** + subjunctive however...; **si jeune qu'il soit** however young he may be; **si habile soit-il** however capable (he may be) (c) *(oui)* yes; **je crois que si** I think so; **mais si, je l'ai vue** I DID see her; **tu ne sais pas? – si,** si you don't know? – yes, I do (d) **si bien que...** *(indique le résultat)* so that...

si² 1 conj (a) *(exprime l'hypothèse, la condition)* if; **qui le fera si ce n'est moi?** who'll do it if I don't?; **un des plus grands, si ce n'est le plus grand** one of the biggest, if not the biggest; **si ce n'est que...** *(sauf que)* apart from the fact that...; **et quand bien même...** *(+ conditional)* and what if she finds out?; **si on faisait une partie de bridge?** what about a game of bridge?; **oui, si on veut** yes, if you like; **si seulement...** if only...; **si tant est que...** + subjunctive if... (b) *(combien)* how; **pensez si j'étais furieux!** imagine how angry I was! (c) *(dans les questions indirectes)* if, whether; *Fam* **si je connais Paris?** do I know Paris?; *Fam* **si c'est pas malheureux (de voir ça)!** isn't it just dreadful (to see that)!
2 nm inv **tes si et tes mais** your ifs and buts

si³ nm inv *(note)* B; *(chantée)* ti

siamois, -e [sjamwa, -az] 1 adj **frères s.** Siamese twins; **sœurs siamoises** Siamese twins
2 nm *(chat)* Siamese (cat)

Sibérie [siberi] nf **la S.** Siberia

sibérien, -enne [siberjɛ̃, -en] 1 adj Siberian
2 nm,f **S.** Siberian

sibyllin, -e [sibilɛ̃, -in] adj *(énigmatique)* cryptic, enigmatic

SICAV [sikav] nf inv *Fin (abrév* **société d'investissement à capital variable)** (a) *(organisme)* Br ≃ unit trust, Am ≃ mutual fund (b) *(titre)* share in a Br unit trust or Am mutual fund

Sicile [sisil] nf **la S.** Sicily

sicilien, -enne [sisiljɛ̃, -en] 1 adj Sicilian
2 nm,f **S.** Sicilian

sida [sida] nm *(abrév* **syndrome immunodéficitaire acquis)** AIDS; **avoir le s.** to have AIDS

side-car *(pl* side-cars) [sajdkar, sidkar] nm sidecar

sidéen, -enne [sideɛ̃, -en] 1 adj suffering from AIDS
2 nm,f AIDS sufferer

sidéral, -e, -aux, -ales [sideral, -o] adj sidereal

sidérant, -e [siderã, -ãt] adj *Fam* staggering

sidérer [34] [sidere] vt *Fam* to stagger

sidérurgie [sideryrʒi] nf (a) *(technique)* iron and steel metallurgy (b) *(industrie)* iron and steel industry

sidérurgique [sideryrʒik] adj *(industrie, usine)* iron and steel

sidérurgiste [sideryrʒist] nmf iron and steel worker

siècle [sjɛkl] nm (a) *(cent ans)* century; **au vingtième s.** in the twentieth century; **avoir un s.** to be a hundred years old; *Fam* **ça fait des siècles que j'attends** I've been waiting for ages (b) *(époque)* age; **le s. des Lumières** the Age of Enlightenment; **il est de son s.** he's a man of his times

sied *voir* **seoir**

siège [sjɛʒ] nm (a) (meuble) seat; **s. avant/arrière** front/back seat; **s. pliant** folding chair; **s. pour enfant** (en voiture) child seat (b) (d'une société, d'un organisme) headquarters; **s. administratif** administrative headquarters; **s. social** head office (c) (lieu d'origine) seat (d) Mil siege; **faire le s. de** to lay siege to; **lever le s.** to raise the siege; Fam (partir) to make tracks (e) Pol seat (f) Méd **accouchement par le s.** breech delivery; **se présenter par le s.** to be in the breech position

siéger [59] [sjeʒe] vi (a) (tribunal, assemblée) to sit (b) (se trouver) **c'est là que siège le mal** that's the root of the problem

sien, -enne [sjɛ̃, sjɛn] **1** pron possessif **le sien** m, **la sienne** f, **les siens** mpl, **les siennes** fpl (possesseur masculin) his; (possesseur féminin) hers; (en insistant) his/her own; **il te prête le s.** you can borrow his; **elle n'en a pas besoin, elle a le s.** she doesn't need it, she has her own; **on doit acheter la sienne** you must buy your own; **chacun doit apporter le s.** everyone must bring their own; **chaque pays a le s.** each country has its own

2 nm **il faut qu'il y mette du s.** he should do his share

3 nmpl **les siens** (sa famille) his/her family

4 nfpl Fam **il a encore fait des siennes** he's been up to his old tricks again

Sierra Leone [sjeraleɔn] nf **la S.** Sierra Leone

sieste [sjɛst] nf siesta, nap; **faire la s.** to have a nap

sifflant, -e [siflɑ̃, -ɑ̃t] adj (respiration, toux) wheezing

sifflement [sifləmɑ̃] nm (d'une personne, du vent) whistling; (d'un serpent, de la vapeur) hissing; (d'un asthmatique) wheezing; **sifflements d'oreilles** ringing in the ears

siffler [sifle] **1** vi (a) (air) to whistle (b) (chien, personne) to whistle at (c) (acteur, pièce) to boo (d) Fam (verre, bouteille) to knock back

2 vi (a) (personne, merle, bouilloire) to whistle (serpent) to hiss (b) (avec un sifflet) to blow one's whistle

sifflet [siflɛ] nm (a) (instrument) whistle; Fam **couper le s. à qn** to shut sb up (b) (au théâtre) **sifflets** booing, boos

siffleux [siflø] nm Can groundhog, woodchuck

siffloter [siflɔte] vt & vi to whistle to oneself

sigle [sigl] nm (acronyme) acronym; (suite d'initiales) abbreviation

signal, -aux [sinal, -o] nm (a) (signe) signal; **faire un s.** to signal; **envoyer** ou **lancer un s.** to send a signal; **au s., levez-vous** when the signal is given, stand up; **s. lumineux** indicator light, warning light (b) (panneau) sign (c) (dispositif sonore) **s. d'alarme** alarm (signal); **s. d'alerte** warning (signal); Tél **s. d'appel** call(ing) signal; **s. de détresse** distress signal; **s. sonore** warning sound (d) Ordinat **s. d'avertissement de réception** acknowledge; **s. horodateur** time and date signal; **s. d'invitation à transmettre** proceed-to-send signal

signalement [sinalmɑ̃] nm description, particulars

signaler [sinale] **1** vt (a) (faire remarquer) to point out (à to); **s. à qn que...** to point out to sb that... (b) (rapporter) to report (à to); **rien à s.** nothing to report (c) (par un panneau) to signpost (d) Ordinat (manquer) to flag up

2 se signaler vpr to distinguish oneself (par by); **se s. à l'attention de qn** to catch sb's eye

signalétique [sinaletik] adj **fiche s.** personal details card; **plaque s.** identification plate

signalisation [sinalizasjɔ̃] nf (signaux routiers) signs and markings; (signaux ferroviaires) signals; (de piste d'atterrissage) lights and markings; **s. routière** road signs

signaliser [sinalize] vt (route) to signpost and mark; (voie ferrée) to install signals on; (piste d'atterrissage) to install lights and markings on

signataire [sinater] nmf signatory

signature [sinatyr] nf (a) (griffe) signature; **présenter qch à la s.** to present sth for signature (b) (acte) signing

signe [sin] nm (a) (indice) sign; **il n'a pas donné s. de vie** there's been no sign of him; **il n'y a aucun s. de vie dans la maison** there's no sign of life at the house; **en s. de désapprobation/solidarité** as a sign of disapproval/solidarity; **s. avant-coureur** forerunner; **donner des signes d'usure** to show signs of wear (b) (symbole) sign, symbol; **s. moins/plus/égale** minus/plus/equals sign; **signes de ponctuation** punctuation marks (c) Astrol **s. du zodiaque** sign of the zodiac; **être né sous le s. du Capricorne** to be born under the sign of Capricorn; Fig **le sommet a eu lieu sous le s. de la réconciliation** the summit was held in a spirit of reconciliation (d) (trait distinctif) mark; **signes particuliers** distinguishing marks (e) (geste) sign, gesture; **faire un s. à qn** to gesture to sb; **parler par signes** to use sign language; **faire s. à qn** (de la main) to signal to sb; (le contacter) to get in touch with sb; **faire s. à qn de faire qch** to signal to sb to do sth; **faire s. que oui** (de la tête) to nod (one's head); **faire s. que non** (de la tête) to shake one's head; (du doigt) to shake one's finger; **faire un s. de la main** (à qn) to wave (at sb); **faire un s. de tête** (à qn) to nod (to sb) (f) Rel **s. de croix** sign of the cross; **faire le s. de croix** to make the sign of the cross

signer [sine] **1** vt (contrat, lettre, tableau) to sign; Fam Fig **ça c'est signé!** no prizes for guessing who did that!

2 vi to sign; **s. de son nom** to sign one's name

3 se signer vpr to cross oneself

signet [sinɛ] nm bookmark

significatif, -ive [sinifikatif, -iv] adj significant; **s. de qch** indicative of sth

signification [sinifikasjɔ̃] nf (a) (d'un mot, d'un symbole) meaning, sense; (d'un fait) significance (b) Jur (d'un jugement) notification

signifier [66] [sinifje] vt (a) (vouloir dire) to mean; **qu'est-ce que ça signifie?** (indignation) what's the meaning of this? (b) (notifier) (intentions) to make known (à to); **s. son congé à qn** (sujet: propriétaire, employeur) to give sb notice; **s. qch à qn** to inform or notify sb of sth

silence [silɑ̃s] nm (a) (absence de bruit) silence; **un s. de mort** a deadly silence; **rompre le s.** to break the silence; **garder le s. (sur)** to keep silent (about); **faire qch en s.** to do sth in silence; **passer qch sous s.** not to mention sth (b) Mus rest

silencieusement [silɑ̃sjøzmɑ̃] adv silently

silencieux, -euse [silɑ̃sjø, -øz] **1** adj silent; (qui ne fait pas beaucoup de bruit) quiet

2 nm (d'un véhicule) Br silencer, Am muffler; (d'une arme) silencer

silex [silɛks] nm flint

silhouette [silwɛt] nf (a) (du corps) figure (b) (d'un objet) silhouette, outline

silice [silis] nf silica

silicium [silisjɔm] nm Chim silicon

silicone [silikɔn] nf silicone

sillage [sijaʒ] nm (d'un navire) wake; Fig **marcher dans le s. de qn** to follow in sb's wake

sillon [sijɔ̃] nm (a) (d'un champ) furrow (b) (de disque) groove

sillonner [sijɔne] *vt (parcourir)* to criss-cross

silo [silo] *nm* silo

simagrées [simagre] *nfpl* airs and graces; **faire des s.** to make a fuss

simiesque [simjesk] *adj* monkey-like, ape-like

similaire [similer] *adj* similar (à to)

similarité [similarite] *nf* similarity

simili [simili] *nm Fam (imitation)* imitation

similicuir [similikɥir] *nm* imitation leather

similitude [similityd] *nf* similarity

simple [sɛ̃pl] **1** *adj (a) (sans prétentions)* simple **(b)** *(facile)* simple, easy; **c'est s. comme bonjour** it's as easy as pie **(c)** *(crédule)* simple; **s. d'esprit** simple-minded **(d)** *(pur)* **c'est une s. question de temps** it's simply a matter of time **(e)** *(ordinaire)* ordinary; **s. soldat** private (soldier) **(f)** *(composé d'un élément) (nœud)* single; **cornet s.** *(de glace)* cone with one scoop; *Ordinat* **s. densité** single density

2 *nm* **(a)** *(au tennis)* singles (match) **(b)** *(somme, quantité)* **varier du s. au double** to vary by twice as much **(c)** *(personne)* **un s. d'esprit** a simpleton

simplement [sɛ̃pləmɑ̃] *adv* simply; **le plus s. du monde** as if it was the most natural thing in the world; **prendre les choses s.** to take things as they come

simplet, -ette [sɛ̃plɛ, -ɛt] *adj (personne)* simple; *(idée, explication)* simplistic

simplicité [sɛ̃plisite] *nf* simplicity; **recevoir qn en toute s.** to entertain sb very simply; **d'une s. enfantine** childishly simple

simplificateur, -trice [sɛ̃plifikatœr, -tris] *adj* simplifying

simplification [sɛ̃plifikasjɔ̃] *nf* simplification

simplifier [66] [sɛ̃plifje] *vt aussi Math* to simplify; **ça me simplifiera l'existence** it'll make my life easier

simpliste [sɛ̃plist] *adj Péj* simplistic

simulacre [simylakr] *nm* **(a)** *(représentation)* reconstruction **(b)** *(parodie)* **s. de combat/négociations** sham fight/negotiations; **ce fut un s. de procès** the trial was a farce

simulateur, -trice [simylatœr, -tris] **1** *nm,f (d'un sentiment)* pretender; *(d'une maladie)* malingerer

2 *nm Tech* simulator

simulation [simylasjɔ̃] *nf* **(a)** *(action)* feigning **(b)** *(d'un vol, d'un phénomène)* & *Ordinat* simulation

simulé, -e [simyle] *adj (a) (sentiment, maladie)* feigned; *(combat)* sham **(b)** *(vol, phénomène)* simulated

simuler [simyle] *vt* **(a)** *(sentiment, maladie, folie)* to feign **(b)** *(vol, phénomène)* to simulate

simultané, -e [simyltane] *adj* simultaneous

simultanéité [simyltaneite] *nf* simultaneousness, simultaneity

simultanément [simyltanemɑ̃] *adv* simultaneously

sincère [sɛ̃ser] *adj* sincere

sincèrement [sɛ̃sermɑ̃] *adv* sincerely; **s., je trouve que...** frankly, I think...

sincérité [sɛ̃serite] *nf* sincerity; **en toute s.** in all sincerity

sinécure [sinekyr] *nf* sinecure; *Fam* **ce n'est pas une s.** it's not exactly a rest cure

sine die [sinedje] *adv* sine die

sine qua non [sinekwanɔn] *adj inv* **une condition s.** a prerequisite

Singapour [sɛ̃gapur] *n* Singapore

singapourien, -enne [sɛ̃gapurjɛ̃, -ɛn] **1** *adj* Singaporean

2 *nm,f* **S.** Singaporean

singe [sɛ̃ʒ] *nm* monkey; **grand s.** ape; **malin/adroit comme un s.** as crafty/clever as a monkey; **faire le s.** to clown around

singer [45] [sɛ̃ʒe] *vt (personne)* to ape, to mimic; *(sentiment)* to feign

singeries [sɛ̃ʒri] *nfpl (grimaces, gestes)* antics; **faire des singeries** to clown around

singulariser [sɛ̃gylarize] **1** *vt* **s. qn (de)** to set sb apart (from), to make sb stand out (from)

2 se singulariser *vpr* to draw attention to oneself; **il se singularise par sa façon de parler** the way he speaks makes him stand out

singularité [sɛ̃gylarite] *nf* peculiarity

singulier, -ère [sɛ̃gylje, -ɛr] **1** *adj (a) Gram* singular **(b)** *(combat)* single **(c)** *(remarquable)* remarkable; *(étrange)* peculiar, odd

2 *nm Gram* singular; **au s.** in the singular

singulièrement [sɛ̃gyljɛrmɑ̃] *adv* **(a)** *(étrangement)* oddly **(b)** *(en particulier)* especially, particularly **(c)** *(beaucoup)* remarkably, extremely

sinistre [sinistr] **1** *adj* **(a)** *(effrayant)* sinister; *(à faire froid dans le dos)* spooky **(b)** *(déprimant) (paysage)* bleak; *(soirée, repas)* dismal, grim **(c)** **un s. imbécile** an awful idiot

2 *nm* **(a)** *(catastrophe)* disaster **(b)** *Jur (dommage)* damage

sinistré, -e [sinistre] **1** *adj (population)* stricken; *(bâtiment)* damaged; *(région, zone)* disaster

2 *nm,f* disaster victim

sinistrose [sinistroz] *nf Fam* pessimism, gloom

sinologue [sinɔlɔg] *nmf* sinologist

sinon [sinɔ̃] *conj* **(a)** *(autrement)* otherwise, or else **(b)** *(excepté)* except **(c)** *(si ce n'est)* if not

sinueux, -euse [sinɥø, -øz] *adj (ligne)* sinuous; *(chemin, courant)* winding, meandering; *Fig (raisonnement)* tortuous

sinuosité [sinɥozite] *nf (d'un chemin, d'une rivière)* bend; *Fig* **les sinuosités d'un raisonnement** the twists and turns of an argument

sinus¹ [sinys] *nm Anat* sinus

sinus² *nm Math* sine

sinusite [sinyzit] *nf* sinusitis

sionisme [sjɔnism] *nm* Zionism

sioniste [sjɔnist] *adj* & *nmf* Zionist

sioux [sju] **1** *adj* Sioux

2 *nm,f* **S.** Sioux

siphon [sifɔ̃] *nm* **(a)** *(tube)* siphon **(b)** *(bouteille)* (soda) siphon **(c)** *(d'un évier, d'une canalisation)* U-bend, trap

siphonné, -e [sifɔne] *adj Fam (fou)* crackers, crazy

siphonner [sifɔne] *vt* to siphon

sire [sir] *nm* **S.** *(à un souverain)* Sire; *Péj* **un triste s.** an unsavoury character

sirène [siren] *nf* **(a)** *(personnage fantastique)* mermaid, siren; *Fig (femme)* siren **(b)** *(dispositif sonore)* siren

sirop [siro] *nm* syrup; **s. de fraise/menthe** strawberry/mint cordial; **s. contre la toux** cough mixture *or* syrup

siroter [sirɔte] *vt Fam* to sip

sirupeux, -euse [sirypø, -øz] *adj* syrupy; *(musique)* slushy

sismique [sismik] *adj* seismic

sismographe [sismɔgraf] *nm* seismograph

sismologie [sismɔlɔʒi] *nf* seismology

sitar [sitar] *nm* sitar

sitcom [sitkom] *nm ou nf* sitcom

site [sit] *nm* (a) *(emplacement)* site (b) *(pittoresque)* beauty spot; **s. classé** conservation area; **s. historique/archéologique** historic/archaeological site; **s. touristique** place of interest, tourist attraction

sitôt [sito] *adv* **elle le fera s. ses devoirs finis** she'll do it as soon as she's finished her homework; **s. dit, s. fait** no sooner said than done; **s. que** as soon as; **s. après** immediately after; **on ne le reverra pas de s.** we won't see him again in a hurry

situation [sitɥasjɔ̃] *nf* (a) *(d'une ville, d'un bâtiment)* position, location (b) *(circonstances)* situation; **être en s. de faire qch** to be in a position to do sth; **mettre qn en s.** to give sb experience of a real-life situation; **l'homme de la s.** the right man for the job; **s. de famille** marital status (c) *(emploi)* job, position (d) *Fin (de compte)* balance

situé, -e [sitɥe] *adj* situated

situer [sitɥe] **1** *vt* (a) *(placer)* to situate (b) *(trouver)* to locate (c) *(dans le temps)* to set; **je situe l'action au milieu du XIXᵉ siècle** I'd say the action takes place in the middle of the 19th century (d) *Fig (catégoriser)* to categorize
2 se situer *vpr* (a) *(être)* to be; **se s. à droite** to be right-wing (b) *(avoir lieu)* to take place

six [sis] *adj & nm inv* six; *voir aussi* **trois**

sixième [sizjɛm] **1** *adj, nmf & nm* sixth; *voir aussi* **cinquième**
2 *nf Scol (enseignement secondaire)* Br ≃ first form, Am ≃ sixth grade

sixièmement [sizjɛmmɑ̃] *adv* in the sixth place, sixthly

six-quatre-deux [siskatdø] **à la six-quatre-deux** *adv Fam* in a slapdash way

sixte [sikst] *nf Mus* sixth

Skaï® [skaj] *nm* imitation leather

skate [skɛt], **skateboard** [skɛtbord] *nm* skateboard; **faire du s.** to skateboard

sketch *(pl* **sketches** [skɛtʃ]) *nm* sketch

ski [ski] *nm* (a) *(matériel)* ski (b) *(activité)* skiing; **faire du s.** to ski; **s. alpin/de fond** downhill/cross-country skiing; **s. nautique** water skiing

skiable [skjabl] *adj voir* **domaine**

skier [66] [skje] *vi* to ski

skieur, -euse [skjœr, -øz] *nm,f* skier

skin [skin], **skinhead** [skinɛd] *nm* skinhead

skipper [skipœr] *nm* skipper

slalom [slalom] *nm* slalom; *Fig* **faire du s. (entre)** to dodge in and out (between); **s. géant** giant slalom; **s. spécial** special slalom

slalomer [slalɔme] *vi* to slalom; *Fig* to dodge in and out (entre between)

slalomeur, -euse [slalɔmœr, -øz] *nm,f* slalom skier

slave [slav] **1** *adj* Slav, Slavonic
2 *nmf* S. Slav
3 *nm (langue)* Slavonic

slip [slip] *nm (d'homme)* briefs, underpants; *(de femme)* pants, briefs; **s. de bain** *(d'homme)* swimming trunks; *(de femme)* bikini bottom

slogan [slɔgɑ̃] *nm* slogan

slovaque [slɔvak] **1** *adj* Slovak
2 *nmf* S. Slovak
3 *nm (langue)* Slovak

Slovaquie [slovaki] *nf* **la S.** Slovakia

slovène [slɔvɛn] **1** *adj* Slovene
2 *nmf* S. Slovene
3 *nm (langue)* Slovene

Slovénie [slɔveni] *nf* **la S.** Slovenia

slow [slo] *nm* slow dance

smala(h) [smala] *nf Fam (famille)* tribe

smash [smaʃ] *nm* smash; **faire un s.** to smash the ball

smasher [smaʃe] **1** *vt* to smash
2 *vi* to smash the ball

SME [ɛsɛmœ] *nm (abrév* **Système monétaire européen)** EMS

SMIC [smik] *nm (abrév* **salaire minimum interprofessionnel de croissance)** guaranteed minimum wage

smicard, -e [smikar, -ard] *nm,f Fam* minimum wage earner

smoking [smokiŋ] *nm* dinner *or* evening suit

snack [snak], **snack-bar** *(pl* **snack-bars** [snakbar]) *nm* snack bar

SNCF [ɛsɛnseɛf] *nf (abrév* **Société nationale des chemins de fer français)** = French national railway company

sniffer [snife] *vt Fam (drogue)* to sniff

snob [snɔb] **1** *adj* snobbish
2 *nmf* snob

snober [snɔbe] *vt* to snub

snobinard, -e [snɔbinar, -ard] *Fam Péj* **1** *adj* stuck-up
2 *nmf* stuck-up type

snobisme [snɔbism] *nm* snobbery, snobbishness

sobre [sɔbr] *adj* (a) *(personne) (qui n'a pas bu)* sober; *(qui boit ou mange peu)* abstemious (b) *(repas, vie)* simple (c) *(style, lignes, discours)* sober

sobrement [sɔbrəmɑ̃] *adv (s'exprimer, s'habiller)* soberly

sobriété [sɔbrijete] *nf* (a) *(tempérance)* temperance, sobriety (b) *(d'un repas, d'une vie)* simplicity (c) *(d'un style, de lignes, d'un discours)* sobriety; **s'exprimer avec s.** to speak soberly

sobriquet [sɔbrikɛ] *nm* nickname

sociabilité [sɔsjabilite] *nf* sociability

sociable [sɔsjabl] *adj* sociable

social, -e, -aux, -ales [sɔsjal, -o] **1** *adj (ordre, politique, réforme)* social
2 *nm* **le s.** social issues

social-démocrate, sociale-démocrate *(mpl* **sociaux-démocrates,** *fpl* **sociales-démocrates)** [sɔsjaldemokrat, sɔsjodemokrat] *adj & nmf* social democrat

social-démocratie *(pl* **social-démocraties)** [sɔsjaldemokrasi] *nf* social democracy

socialement [sɔsjalmɑ̃] *adv* socially

socialisation [sɔsjalizasjɔ̃] *nf* socialization

socialiser [sɔsjalize] *vt* to socialize

socialisme [sɔsjalism] *nm* socialism

socialiste [sɔsjalist] *adj & nmf* socialist

sociétaire [sɔsjeter] *nmf* (a) *(membre)* member (b) *(actionnaire)* shareholder

société [sɔsjete] *nf* (a) *(communauté)* society; **en s.** in society; **s. de consommation** consumer society; **la haute** *(b)* *(association)* society, association; *(sportive)* club; *Hist* **la S. des Nations** the League of Nations; **la S. protectrice des animaux** *Br* ≃ the RSPCA, *Am* ≃ the ASPCA (c) *(compagnie)* company, firm; **s. par actions** *Br* joint-stock company, *Am* incorporated company; **s. anonyme** *Br* public limited company, *Am* corporation; **s. en participation** joint venture; **s. à responsabilité limitée** limited (liability) company (d) *(présence)* company

socioculturel, -elle [sɔsjokyltyrɛl] *adj* social and cultural

socio-économique (*pl* **socio-économiques**) [sɔsjoekɔnɔmik] *adj* socioeconomic

sociolinguistique [sɔsjolɛ̃ɡɥistik] **1** *adj* sociolinguistic **2** *nf* sociolinguistics *(singulier)*

sociologie [sɔsjɔlɔʒi] *nf* sociology

sociologique [sɔsjɔlɔʒik] *adj* sociological

sociologiquement [sɔsjɔlɔʒikmɑ̃] *adv* sociologically

sociologue [sɔsjɔlɔg] *nmf* sociologist

socioprofessionnel, -elle [sɔsjoprofesjɔnɛl] *adj* socioprofessional

socle [sɔkl] *nm* (de statue, de colonne) plinth, pedestal; (de vase, de pendule, d'appareil) base; *Ordinat* **s. orientable** *ou* **pivotant** *(d'un moniteur)* swivel base

socquette [sɔkɛt] *nf* ankle sock

Socrate [sɔkrat] *npr* Socrates

soda [sɔda] *nm Br* fizzy drink, *Am* soda (pop)

sodium [sɔdjɔm] *nm* sodium

sodomie [sɔdɔmi] *nf* sodomy, buggery

sodomiser [sɔdɔmize] *vt* to sodomize, to bugger

sœur [sœr] *nf* (a) *(parente)* sister; *Fam* **et ta s.!** get lost!; **s. de lait** foster sister (b) *Rel* nun, sister

sœurette [sœrɛt] *nf Fam* little sister

sofa [sɔfa] *nm* sofa, settee

Sofia [sɔfja] *n* Sofia

SOFRES [sɔfrɛs] *nf* (abrév **Société française d'enquêtes par sondage**) = French opinion poll company

software [sɔftwɛr] *nm Ordinat* software

soi [swa] *pron personnel* **s.** (a) *(personne indéfinie)* oneself; *(homme)* himself; *(femme)* herself; **chez s.** at home; **il faut regarder devant s.** you must keep looking in front of you; **revenir à soi** to regain consciousness (b) *(chose, concept)* **en s.** in itself, per se

soi-disant [swadizɑ̃] **1** *adj inv* so-called **2** *adv* supposedly

soie [swa] *nf* (a) *(étoffe)* silk; **s. grège/naturelle** raw/ natural silk (b) *(de sanglier, de porc)* bristle

soierie [swari] *nf* (a) *(tissu)* silk (b) *(commerce)* silk trade

soif [swaf] *nf aussi Fig* thirst; **avoir s.** to be thirsty; **donner s. à qn** to make sb thirsty; **boire jusqu'à plus s.** to drink one's fill; *Fig* **s. de qch/de faire qch** thirst for sth/to do sth

soignant, -e [swaɲɑ̃, -ɑ̃t] *adj* **personnel s.** nursing staff; **équipe soignante** team of nursing staff

soigné, -e [swaɲe] *adj* (a) *(travail)* careful; *(style)* polished (b) *(personne, apparence)* neat, tidy; *(mains, ongles, jardin)* well-kept (c) *Fam (addition)* shockingly high

soigner [swaɲe] **1** *vt* (a) *(maladie)* to treat (b) *(malade)* *(sujet: médecin)* to treat; *(sujet: parent, infirmière)* to look after, to take care of; *Fam Fig* **il faut te faire s.!** you need your head examined! (c) *(apparence, invités, image)* to look after, to take care of; *(travail, présentation)* to take care over **2 se soigner** *vpr* (a) *(personne) (médicalement)* to treat oneself; *(faire attention à soi)* to take care of oneself, to look after oneself (b) *(maladie)* **ça se soigne très bien** it's easily treated

soigneur [swaɲœr] *nm* trainer; *(en boxe)* second

soigneusement [swaɲøzmɑ̃] *adv* carefully

soigneux, -euse [swaɲø, -øz] *adj* (a) *(attentif)* careful (de with) (b) *(méticuleux)* tidy, neat

soi-même [swamɛm] *pron personnel* oneself; *Prov* **on n'est jamais si bien servi que par s.** if you want something done, do it yourself

soin [swɛ̃] *nm* (a) *(attention)* care; **avec s.** carefully, with care; **sans s.** *(travail, exécution)* careless; *(travailler, exécuter)* carelessly; **aux bons soins de** *(sur une lettre)* care of.., c/o..; **avoir** *ou* **prendre s. de qn/qch** to look after *or* take care of sb/sth; **prendre s. de faire qch** to take care to do sth; **confier à qn le s. de faire qch** to entrust sb with the task of doing sth; **laisser à qn le s. de faire qch** to leave it to sb to do sth; **les soins du ménage** housekeeping (b) *(traitement)* **soins** care, attention; **soins de beauté** beauty care; **être aux petits soins pour** *ou* **avec qn** to wait on sb hand and foot (c) *(traitement médical)* **premiers soins, soins d'urgence** first aid; **soins à domicile** home care *or* nursing; **soins intensifs** intensive care; **soins médicaux** medical care; **soins palliatifs** palliative care

soir [swar] *nm* evening; **ce s.** this evening, tonight; **à ce s.!** see you tonight!; **à dix heures du s.** at ten o'clock in the evening *or* at night; **le jeudi 2 au s.** on the evening of Thursday 2nd; **tous les lundis s.** every Monday evening; **faire qch le s.** to do sth in the evening; **être du s.** to be a night owl

soirée [sware] *nf* (a) *(soir)* evening; **dans la s.** in (the course of) the evening; **en fin de s.** towards the end of the evening (b) *(fête)* party; **s. dansante** dance (c) *Th & Cin* evening performance; **le film passe en s.** there is an evening performance of the film

sois, sois¹ *etc voir* **être**

soit² **1** [swat] *adv* all right **2** [swa] *conj* (a) *(suppose)* **s. un point P** given a point P (b) *(c'est-à-dire)* that is to say; (c) **s...., s....** either... or...; **s. l'un, s. l'autre** (either) one or the other

soixantaine [swasɑ̃tɛn] *nf* (a) *(environ soixante)* **une s.** (de) about sixty, sixty or so (b) *(âge)* **avoir la s.** to be around sixty; **approcher de la s.** to be getting on for sixty

soixante [swasɑ̃t] *adj & nm inv* sixty; **s. et onze** seventy-one; *voir aussi* **trois**

soixante-dix [swasɑ̃tdis] *adj inv & nm* seventy; *voir aussi* **trois**

soixante-dixième [swasɑ̃tdizjɛm] *nmf, nm & adj* seventieth; *voir aussi* **cinquième**

soixante-huitard, -e [swasɑ̃tɥitar, -ard] *nm,f* = person involved in the events of May 1968

soixantième [swasɑ̃tjɛm] *nmf, nm & adj* sixtieth; *voir aussi* **cinquième**

soja [sɔʒa] *nm* soya

sol¹ [sɔl] *nm* (a) *(surface) (dehors)* ground; *(à l'intérieur)* floor; **au s.** at ground level (b) *(territoire)* soil (c) *(matière)* soil

sol² *nm inv (note)* G; *(chantée)* sol

sol-air [sɔlɛr] *adj inv (missile)* ground-to-air

solaire [sɔlɛr] *adj (système, chauffage, four)* solar; *(lotion, crème)* sun

solarium [sɔlarjɔm] *nm* (a) *(établissement)* solarium (b) *(terrasse)* sun terrace

soldat [sɔlda] *nm (personne)* soldier; **s. de deuxième classe** private; **s. de première classe** *Br* lance-corporal, *Am* private first class; **le S. inconnu** the Unknown Soldier (b) *(jouet)* (toy) soldier; **s. de plomb** tin soldier

solde¹ [sɔld] *nf (rémunération)* pay; *Péj* **à la s. de qn** in sb's pay

solde² *nm* (a) *(de compte)* balance; **pour s. (de tout compte)** in (full or final) settlement (b) *(rabais)* **acheter qch en s.** to buy sth in the sale; **vendre qch en s.** to sell sth off; **c'était en s.** it was in the sale; **des soldes** *(articles)* sale goods; **faire les soldes** *(acheteur)* to go round the sales; **faire des soldes** *(magasin)* to have a sale

solder [sɔlde] **1** *vt* (a) *(compte)* to close (b) *(article)* to sell off, to clear
2 se solder *vpr* **se s. par qch** *Fin* to show sth; *Fig (résultat, échec)* to end in sth

soldeur, -euse [sɔldœr, -øz] *nm, f* discount trader

sole [sɔl] *nf (poisson)* sole

soleil [sɔlɛj] *nm* (a) *(astre)* sun; **s. de minuit** midnight sun (b) *(lumière, chaleur)* sun, sunshine; **il y a ou il fait du s.** the sun's shining, it's sunny; *Fig* **se faire une place au s.** to find a place in the sun; *Fig* **avoir des biens au s.** to own property

solennel, -elle [sɔlanɛl] *adj* (a) *(occasion, cérémonie)* formal; *(serment, déclaration)* solemn (b) *Péj* pompous

solennellement [sɔlanɛlmɑ̃] *adv (officiellement)* formally; *(gravement)* solemnly

solennité [sɔlanite] *nf* (a) *(d'une occasion, d'une cérémonie)* formality; *(d'un serment, d'une déclaration)* solemnity (b) *Péj* pomposity

Solex® [sɔlɛks] *nm* moped

solfège [sɔlfɛʒ] *nm* (a) *(théorie)* rudiments of music (b) *(recueil)* music primer

solfier [66] [sɔlfje] *vt* to sol-fa

solidaire [sɔlidɛr] *adj* (a) *(personne)* **être s. de qn** to stand by sb, to support sb; **se sentir s. de qn** to feel a sense of solidarity with sb (b) *(pièces)* interdependent; **roue s. d'une autre** wheel integral with another

solidairement [sɔlidɛrmɑ̃] *adv* jointly

solidariser [sɔlidarize] **se solidariser** *vpr* to show solidarity (**avec** with)

solidarité [sɔlidarite] *nf (entre personnes)* solidarity

solide [sɔlid] **1** *adj* (a) *(résistant) (mur, meuble)* solid; *(tissu)* strong; *(personne)* sturdy; **s. sur ses jambes** steady on one's feet; **être s. comme un chêne** *ou* **un roc** to be hale and hearty (b) *(amitié, relation, liens)* strong (c) *(éducation, argumentation)* sound; *Fig* **ça ne repose sur rien de s.** there's no sound basis for that (d) *(repas)* solid; *(appétit)* healthy (e) *(position, affaire)* sound, strong (f) *(non liquide)* solid
2 *nm* (a) *(corps)* solid (b) *Fam* **c'est du s.!** *(meuble)* that's pretty solid!; *(vêtement)* it's indestructible!

solidement [sɔlidmɑ̃] *adv (construit)* solidly; *(attaché, implanté)* firmly

solidifier [66] [sɔlidifje] **1** *vt* to solidify
2 se solidifier *vpr* to solidify

solidité [sɔlidite] *nf* (a) *(d'un objet)* solidity; *(d'un matériau)* strength; **être d'une s. à toute épreuve** to be able to stand up to anything (b) *(d'un jugement)* soundness (c) *(d'une amitié)* strength

soliloque [sɔlilɔk] *nm* soliloquy

soliste [sɔlist] *nmf* soloist

solitaire [sɔlitɛr] **1** *adj* (a) *(personne) (par choix)* solitary; *(involontairement)* lonely; **passer des vacances solitaires** to spend one's holidays on one's own (b) *(arbre, maison)* solitary, lone
2 *nmf (personne)* loner; **en s.** on one's own, alone
3 *nm* (a) *(jeu)* solitaire (b) *(diamant)* solitaire

solitairement [sɔlitɛrmɑ̃] *adv* on one's own, alone

solitude [sɔlityd] *nf* (a) *(retraite)* solitude; *(involontaire)* loneliness; **aimer la s.** to like being alone (b) *(d'un lieu)* loneliness

solive [sɔliv] *nf Constr* joist

sollicitation [sɔlisitasjɔ̃] *nf* request

solliciter [sɔlisite] *vt* (a) *(entretien, audience)* to request; *(emploi)* to apply for (b) *(personne)* **s. qn (pour faire qch)** to appeal to sb (to do sth); **être sollicité de toutes parts** to be very much in demand (c) *(attention, regards)* to attract; *(curiosité)* to arouse

sollicitude [sɔlisityd] *nf* solicitude, concern *(pour* for)

solo [sɔlo] **1** *adj inv* solo
2 *nm* solo; **jouer en s.** to play solo

sol-sol [sɔlsɔl] *adj inv (missile)* ground-to-ground

solstice [sɔlstis] *nm* solstice; **s. d'été/d'hiver** summer/winter solstice

soluble [sɔlybl] *adj* (a) *(produit)* soluble; *(café)* instant (b) *(problème)* solvable

solution [sɔlysjɔ̃] *nf* (a) *(de problème, de situation, d'équation)* solution, answer (**de** to); **s. de facilité** easy way out (b) *(liquide)* solution

solutionner [sɔlysjɔne] *vt Fam* to solve

solvabilité [sɔlvabilite] *nf* solvency

solvable [sɔlvabl] *adj* solvent

solvant [sɔlvɑ̃] *nm* solvent

somali, -e [sɔmali] **1** *adj* Somali
2 *nm, f* S. Somali
3 *nm (langue)* Somali

Somalie [sɔmali] *nf* **la S.** Somalia

somalien, -enne [sɔmaljɛ̃, -ɛn] **1** *adj* Somalian
2 *nm, f* S. Somalian

somatique [sɔmatik] *adj* somatic

somatiser [sɔmatize] *vt* to react psychosomatically to

sombre [sɔ̃br] *adj* (a) *(couleur)* dark (b) *(forêt, pièce)* dark; *(ciel)* dull; **il fait s.** *(temps)* it's dull; *(pièce)* it's dark (c) *(visage, pensées, caractère)* gloomy, sombre (d) *(sinistre)* **une s. histoire de...** a sordid tale of... (e) *Fam* **un s. imbécile** a total fool

sombrement [sɔ̃brəmɑ̃] *adv (tristement)* gloomily, sombrely

sombrer [sɔ̃bre] *vi* (a) *(navire)* to sink; *(empire)* to founder; *(affaire)* to fail (b) *(personne)* **s. dans la déprime/la misère** to sink into depression/destitution

sombrero [sɔ̃brero] *nm* sombrero

sommaire [sɔmɛr] **1** adj (a) (récit) brief (b) (rudimentaire) (examen) hasty; (connaissances, repas, étude) basic; (jugement, exécution) summary; **faire une toilette s.** to have a quick wash

2 nm (table des matières) contents; **et au s. de l'émission de ce soir...** coming up in tonight's programme...

sommairement [sɔmɛrmɑ̃] adv (a) (expliquer, raconter) briefly (b) (de façon rudimentaire) (meublé) basically; (juger) summarily

sommation [sɔmasjɔ̃] nf (a) Jur (injonction) demand (b) Mil warning

somme¹ [sɔm] nf voir **bête**

somme² [sɔm] nf (a) (d'une addition) sum, total; **faire la s.** de to add up (b) (quantité) (d'objets) number; (de travail, d'efforts) amount (c) (argent) s. (d'argent) sum (of money); **pour la s. de 500 francs** for 500 francs; **dépenser des sommes folles** to spend vast sums of money; **c'est une s.!** that's a lot of money! (d) (locutions) **en s.** (tout compte fait) on the whole; (en bref) in short; **s. toute** when all's said and done

somme³ [sɔm] nm nap, snooze; **faire un (petit) s.** to have or take a nap or a snooze

sommeil [sɔmɛj] nm (a) (repos) sleep; **avoir s.** to be or feel sleepy; **dormir d'un s. de plomb** to sleep like a log; **avoir le s. léger/profond** to be a light/heavy sleeper; **chercher le s.** to try to sleep; **tomber de s.** to be dead on one's feet; **Fig le s. éternel** eternal rest (b) **en s.** (projet) (lying) dormant; Fig **laisser qch en s.** to put sth on hold

sommeiller [sɔmeje] vi (a) (personne) to doze (b) Fig to lie dormant

sommelier [sɔməlje] nm wine waiter

sommer [sɔme] vt **s. qn de faire qch** to charge sb to do sth

sommes voir **être**

sommet [sɔmɛ] nm (a) (de montagne) top, summit; (d'arbre, de toit) top; (de vague) crest; (de la tête) crown (b) Fig (de hiérarchie) top; (du pouvoir, de la gloire) height (c) (rencontre politique) summit; **conférence/rencontre au s.** summit conference/meeting (d) (d'angle) vertex

sommier [sɔmje] nm base; **s. à ressorts/lattes** sprung/slatted base

sommité [sɔmite] nf leading figure or light

somnambule [sɔmnɑ̃byl] **1** adj **être s.** to be a sleepwalker, to walk in one's sleep

2 nmf sleepwalker

somnambulisme [sɔmnɑ̃bylism] nm sleepwalking

somnifère [sɔmnifɛr] nm (substance) sedative; (cachet) sleeping pill

somnolence [sɔmnɔlɑ̃s] nf sleepiness, drowsiness; **peut provoquer un état de s.** (sur notice) may cause drowsiness

somnolent, -e [sɔmnɔlɑ̃, -ɑ̃t] adj sleepy, drowsy

somnoler [sɔmnɔle] vi to doze

somptuaire [sɔ̃ptɥɛr] adj extravagant

somptueusement [sɔ̃ptɥøzmɑ̃] adv sumptuously

somptueux, -euse [sɔ̃ptɥø, -øz] adj sumptuous

somptuosité [sɔ̃ptɥozite] nf sumptuousness

son¹, sa, ses [sɔ̃, sa, se]

> **sa** becomes **son** before a word beginning with a vowel or mute h.

adj possessif (possesseur masculin) his; (possesseur féminin) her; (d'animal, de chose, de pays) its; (possesseur indéfini) one's; **un de ses amis** one of his/her friends, a friend of his/hers; **chacun a pris s. sac** everyone took their bag; **perdre s. temps** to waste one's time; Fam **elle a eu s. vendredi** she got Friday off

son² nm (de voix, d'instrument) & Cin sound; Fig **n'entendre qu'un s. de cloche** to hear only one side of the story; (spectacle) **s. et lumière** son et lumière

son³ nm (de grains) bran

sonar [sɔnar] nm sonar

sonate [sɔnat] nf sonata; **s. pour violon** violin sonata

sondage [sɔ̃daʒ] nm (a) (de population) poll, survey; **faire un s.** to carry out a poll or a survey; **s. d'opinion** opinion poll; **s. par téléphone** telephone poll or survey (b) (de terrain) boring, drilling

sonde [sɔ̃d] nf (a) (de bateau) sounding line (b) (de pompe, de puits) sounding rod (c) Météo & Av **s. aérienne** sounding balloon; **s. spatiale** space probe (d) Méd (pour examiner) probe; (pour intervenir) tube (e) (de terrain) borer, drill

sondé, -e [sɔ̃de] nm,f respondent

sonder [sɔ̃de] vt (a) (fond) to sound; Fig (mystère) to fathom (b) Météo (atmosphère) to probe (c) (terrain) to bore, to drill; Fig **s. le terrain** to see how the land lies (d) (personne, opinion, intentions) to sound out (e) Méd (blessure) to probe; (patient) to sound

sondeur, -euse [sɔ̃dœr, -øz] **1** nm (appareil) sounder

2 nm,f (d'opinions) pollster

songe [sɔ̃ʒ] nm Litt dream; **en s.** in a dream; **faire un s.** to have a dream

songer [45] [sɔ̃ʒe] **1 songer à** vt ind (a) (penser à, se souvenir de) to think about (b) (envisager) to consider; **il ne faut pas y s.** that's quite out of the question; **s. à faire qch** to think of doing sth

2 vt **s. que** to think that

songerie [sɔ̃ʒri] nf Litt reverie

songeur, -euse [sɔ̃ʒœr, -øz] adj (a) (rêveur) dreamy (b) (pensif) pensive, thoughtful

sonnant, -e [sɔnɑ̃, -ɑ̃t] adj **arriver à dix heures sonnantes** to arrive on the stroke of ten or at ten o'clock sharp

sonné, -e [sɔne] adj (a) (accompli) **avoir quarante ans bien sonnés** to be well over forty (b) Fam (étourdi) groggy (c) Fam (fou) mad

sonner [sɔne] **1** vi (a) (horloge) to strike; (cloches, téléphone) to ring; (réveil) to go off; **faire s. son réveil (à six heures)** to set one's alarm (for six o'clock); **s. creux** (mur) to sound hollow; Fig to ring hollow; Fig **s. faux** not to ring true; Fig **s. bien/mal** to sound good/bad (b) (heure) **deux heures sonnèrent** the clock struck six; Fig **son heure ou sa dernière heure a sonné** his/her last hour has come (c) (à la porte) **on a sonné** that was the bell, there's someone at the door; **s. chez qn** to ring sb's bell; **s. avant d'entrer** (sur panneau) ring before entering (d) (jouer) **s. du clairon/de la trompette** to sound the bugle/the trumpet

2 vt (a) (cloche) to ring; Fam **s. les cloches à qn** to tell sb off; **se faire s. les cloches** to get a good telling-off (b) (heure) to strike; (messe, repas) to ring the bell for (c) (domestique, infirmière) to ring for; Fam **on ne t'a pas sonné!** nobody asked you! (c) Fam (assommer) to knock out

sonnerie [sɔnri] nf (a) (son) (de cloches, du téléphone) ringing; (de clairon, de trompette) call (b) (sonnette) bell

sonnet [sɔnɛ] nm sonnet

sonnette [sɔnɛt] nf bell; **s. d'alarme** alarm bell; aussi Fig **tirer la s. d'alarme** to sound the alarm

sono [sɔno] nf Fam PA system

sonore [sɔnɔr] **1** adj (a) (effet) sound; (pollution) noise (b) (voix) ringing; (rire) resounding; (salle) echoing (c) Ling (consonne) voiced
2 Ling voiced consonant

sonorisation [sɔnɔrizasjɔ̃] nf (a) (de film) addition of the soundtrack (de to) (b) (de salle) fitting of a PA system (de to) (c) (équipement) PA system, public address system

sonoriser [sɔnɔrize] vt (a) (film) to add the soundtrack to (b) (salle) to fit with a PA system

sonorité [sɔnɔrite] nf tone

sont voir **être**

sophisme [sɔfism] nm sophism

sophistication [sɔfistikasjɔ̃] nf sophistication

sophistiqué, -e [sɔfistike] adj sophisticated

soporifique [sɔpɔrifik] adj aussi Fig soporific

soprano [sɔprano] **1** nm (saxophone) soprano
2 nmf (personne) soprano
3 nm Ling (voice)

sorbet [sɔrbɛ] nm sorbet

sorbetière [sɔrbətjɛr] nf ice-cream maker

sorbier [sɔrbje] nm sorb (tree), service (tree)

sorcellerie [sɔrsɛlri] nf witchcraft, sorcery

sorcier [sɔrsje] **1** adj Fam **ce n'est pas s.** it's simple enough
2 nm sorcerer, wizard

sorcière [sɔrsjɛr] nf sorceress, witch; Fam Péj **vieille s.** old witch

sordide [sɔrdid] adj (a) (pièce, quartier) squalid (b) (crime, détails, avarice) sordid

sorgho [sɔrgo] nm sorghum

Sorlingues [sɔrlɛ̃g] nfpl **les S.** the Scilly Isles

sornettes [sɔrnɛt] nfpl twaddle, rubbish

sors, sort etc voir **sortir**

sort² [sɔr] nm (a) (condition) lot; Fam **faire un s. à qch** (bouteille, plat) to polish sth off (b) (destin) fate (c) (hasard) chance; **tirer au s.** to draw lots; **le s. en est jeté** the die is cast (d) (magique) spell; **jeter un s. à qn** to cast a spell on sb; **conjurer le mauvais s.** to ward off bad luck

sortable [sɔrtabl] adj Fam **tu n'es pas s.!** I can't take you anywhere!

sortant, -e [sɔrtɑ̃, -ɑ̃t] adj (numéro de loterie) winning; (élu) outgoing

sorte [sɔrt] nf (a) (genre) sort, kind; **toutes sortes de choses/gens, des choses/gens de toutes sortes** all sorts or kinds of things/people; **un homme de la s.** a man of that kind; **une s. de...** a sort or kind of...; **je n'ai rien dit/fait de la s.** I said/did no such thing, I said/did nothing of the sort (b) (manière) **de la s.** in that way; **en quelque s.** as it were, in a way, in a sense; **de s. que je puisse...** so that I can...; **de s. qu'il est arrivé en retard** with the result that he arrived late; **de s. à faire qch** so as to do sth; **faire en s. que** + subjunctive to see to it that; **fais en s. d'être à l'heure** see to it that you're on time

sortie [sɔrti] nf (a) (fait de sortir d'un lieu) **c'était ma première s. depuis...** it was my first time out since...; **à sa s. de l'hôpital/de prison** when he/she came out of

hospital/prison; **à la s. de l'école/du travail** after school/work; **à la s. des bureaux** when the offices come out
(b) (issue) exit, way out; **à la s. de la gare** at the station exit; **s. d'autoroute** motorway exit; **s. de secours** emergency exit
(c) (d'un livre, d'un journal) publication; (d'un disque) release; (d'un modèle) launch; (d'un film, d'un disque) release
(d) (de liquide, d'air) outflow
(e) (dispositif) outlet
(f) (de marchandises) export
(g) (dépense) **sorties** outgoings
(h) (excursion) trip, outing; **priver qn de s.** to stop sb from going out; **s. en mer** short sea trip; **jour de s.** day out; **ce soir je suis de s.** I'm going out tonight; **désolé, mais elle est de s.** sorry, but she's out
(i) Mil sortie
(j) Fam (emportement) outburst
(k) Ordinat exit; (information) output; **s. d'imprimante** printer output; **dispositif de s.** output device; **signal de s.** output signal; **s. écran** screen output; **s. imprimante** printout; **s. imprimée** printed output; **s. parallèle** parallel output; **s. série** serial output

sortie-de-bain (pl **sorties-de-bain**) [sɔrtidbɛ̃] nf bathrobe

sortilège [sɔrtilɛʒ] nm spell

sortir¹ [64a] [sɔrtir] **1** vt (aux avoir) (a) (enfant, chien) to take out; (voiture) to get out; **s. qn de** (situation) to get sb out of
(b) (objet) to take out (de of); **et si tu sortais ton bon whisky?** how about getting out your good whisky?
(c) (mettre sur le marché) (livre, journal) to bring out, to publish; (film, disque) to bring out, to release
(d) Fam (dire) to come out with
(e) Fam (expulser) to throw out; (vaincre) to knock out
2 vi (aux être) (a) (aller) to go out (de of); (venir) to come out (de of); (partir) to leave; (s'extraire, finir de travailler) to get out (de of); **s. en courant/en boitant** to run/limp out; **est-ce que je peux s.?** (en classe) may I be excused?; **sortez (d'ici)!** get out (of here)!; **s. de table** to leave the table; **je sors d'une mauvaise grippe** I'm just getting over a bad dose of flu; **il est sorti discrédité de ce scandale** he came out of this scandal with his reputation in ruins; **cela ne doit pas s. d'ici** (secret) it mustn't go any further; Fam **d'où sors-tu?** (d'où viens-tu?) where did you spring from?; (tu n'es pas au courant) what planet have you been on?; **cela m'est sorti de la tête** it's gone right out of my head; **il ne sortira pas grand-chose de tout cela** nothing much will come of all this
(b) (pour s'amuser) to go out; **s. avec qn** to go out with sb; Fig **il faut s. un peu!** (pour être au courant) what planet have you been on?
(c) (livre, journal) to come out, to be published; (film, disque) to come out, to be released
(d) (être issu) **s. de** (famille, milieu) to come from; **elle sort d'Harvard** she was at Harvard
(e) (numéro de loto, sujet d'examen) to come up
(f) (apparaître) (fleur) to come out; (dent) to come through; **les yeux lui sortaient de la tête** his eyes were popping out of his head
(g) Ordinat (d'un système) to exit
3 se sortir vpr **se s. de** (situation) to get out of; **s'en s.** (d'un travail) to manage; (d'une difficulté) to get through it; (malade) to pull through

sortir² nm **au s. du cinéma** on coming out of the cinema; **au s. de l'école** after school; **au s. de l'hiver** at the end of winter

SOS [esoes] *nm* SOS; **lancer un S. (à)** to send (out) an SOS (to); **S. Amitié** = helpline for people in need of emotional support; **S. femmes battues** = helpline for female victims of domestic violence; **S. médecins** emergency medical service; **S.-Racisme** = anti-racist movement

sosie [sozi] *nm* lookalike, double; **c'est un s. de Brando** he's a Brando lookalike; **c'est le s. de mon frère** he's my brother's double

sot, sotte [so, sot] **1** *adj* stupid, foolish; **il n'y a pas de sot métier** there's no such thing as a worthless profession
2 *nm,f* fool

sottement [sɔtmɑ̃] *adv* stupidly, foolishly

sottise [sotiz] *nf* (a) *(stupidité)* stupidity, foolishness (b) *(action)* stupid act; **faire des sottises** to do stupid things; **faire une s.** to do something stupid (c) *(parole)* stupid remark; **dire des sottises** to say stupid things; **dire une s.** to say something stupid

sottisier [sotizje] *nm* collection of howlers

sou [su] *nm* (a) *(argent)* **être sans le s.** to be penniless; **il est toujours en train de compter ses sous** he's always counting every penny; **avoir des sous** to have money; **c'est une affaire de gros sous** there's big money involved; **être près de ses sous** to be a penny-pincher; *Fig* **n'avoir pas (pour) un s. de courage/bon sens** not to have an ounce of courage/common sense (b) *(pièce)* **un s. est un s.** every penny counts (c) *(ancienne monnaie)* **sou** (d) *Can (cent)* **cent**

soubassement [subasmɑ̃] *nm (de construction)* base

soubresaut [subrəso] *nm (de véhicule)* jolt; *(de personne)* jerk

soubrette [subrɛt] *nf* maid

souche [suʃ] *nf* (a) *(d'arbre)* stump; *Fam* **rester (planté) comme une s.** to be rooted to the spot; **dormir comme une s.** to sleep like a log (b) *(de famille)* founder; **faire s.** to found a line (c) *(de virus)* strain (d) *(de chèques, de tickets)* counterfoil, stub (e) *(de langue)* root

souci¹ [susi] *nm* (a) *(inquiétude)* worry, anxiety; **avoir des soucis** to have worries; **se faire du s. (pour)** to worry (about); **donner du s. à qn** to worry sb; **c'est le dernier** *ou* **le cadet de mes soucis** that's the least of my worries (b) *(soin)* concern (de for); **avoir le s. de plaire** to be anxious to please

souci² *nm (fleur)* marigold

soucier [66] [susje] **se soucier** *vpr* **se s. de** to worry about; **ne se s. de rien** not to worry about anything; *Fam* **se s. de qch comme de l'an quarante** *ou* **de sa première chemise** not to give a damn about sth

soucieux, -euse [susjø, -øz] *adj* (a) *(attentif)* anxious, concerned (de about); **être s. de faire qch** to be anxious to do sth; **peu s. de qch** unconcerned about sth (b) *(inquiet)* worried

soucoupe [sukup] *nf* saucer; **s. volante** flying saucer

soudain, -e [sudɛ̃, -ɛn] **1** *adj* sudden, all of a sudden
2 *adj* sudden

soudainement [sudɛnmɑ̃] *adv* suddenly

soudaineté [sudɛnte] *nf* suddenness

Soudan [sudɑ̃] *nm* **le S.** the Sudan

soudanais, -e [sudanɛ, -ɛz] **1** *adj* Sudanese
2 *nm,f* **S.** Sudanese; **les S.** the Sudanese

soudard [sudar] *nm Fam* brutish soldier

soude [sud] *nf* soda; **s. caustique** caustic soda

souder [sude] **1** *vt* (a) *(par alliage)* to solder; *(par soudure autogène)* to weld (b) *(os fracturé)* to knit (c) *Fig (groupes, personnes)* to unite
2 se souder *vpr* (a) *(os)* to knit (together) (b) *Fig (groupe)* to unite

soudeur, -euse [sudœr, -øz] *nm,f (avec soudure par alliage)* solderer; *(avec soudure autogène)* welder

soudoyer [32] [sudwaje] *vt* to bribe

soudure [sudyr] *nf* (a) *(opération) (par alliage)* soldering; *(autogène)* welding (b) *(résultat) (par alliage)* soldered joint; *(autogène)* weld (c) *(d'os)* knitting (d) *Fig* **faire la s.** to make ends meet

soufflage [suflaʒ] *nm (du verre)* blowing

souffle [sufl] *nm* (a) *(d'air, de vent)* breath, puff (b) *(respiration)* breathing; **avoir du s.** to have stamina; **retenir son s.** to hold one's breath; **manquer de s.** to be short-winded; **avoir le s. court** to be short of breath; **à bout de s.** out of breath; *Fig* **couper le s. à qn** to take sb's breath away (c) *(d'une explosion)* blast (d) *(d'hélices)* slipstream, wash (e) *Méd* murmur; **s. au cœur** heart murmur (f) *(force créatrice)* inspiration (g) *(impulsion)* **donner un nouveau s. à qch** to give sth a new lease of life

soufflé, -e [sufle] **1** *adj* (a) *Culin* soufflé (b) *Fam (ahuri)* flabbergasted, staggered
2 *nm* soufflé; **s. au fromage/au chocolat** cheese/chocolate soufflé

souffler [sufle] **1** *vt* (a) *(fumée, poussière)* to blow; *(bougie)* to blow out (b) *(dire)* to whisper (à to); **s. une réplique à un acteur** to prompt an actor; **quelqu'un a dû lui s. l'idée** someone must have given him the idea; **ne pas s. mot (de qch)** not to breathe a word (about sth); **on ne souffle pas!** no prompting! (c) *Fam (prendre)* to pinch (à from); **se faire s. qch** to have sth pinched (d) *(détruire)* to blast (e) *Fam (ahurir)* to stagger (f) *(verre)* to blow (g) *(aux dames)* to huff; **s. n'est pas jouer** huffing doesn't count as a go
2 *vi* (a) *(expirer)* to blow; **s. dans ses doigts** to blow on one's fingers; **s. dans une trompette** to blow a trumpet (b) *(se reposer)* **laisser s. qn** to give sb time to catch his/her breath (c) *(haleter)* to pant, to puff; *Fam* **s. comme un bœuf** to puff and pant (d) *(vent)* to blow; *Fig* **un vent de révolte soufflait sur le pays** there was a spirit of revolt in the country

soufflerie [sufləri] *nf* (a) *(d'orgue, de forge)* bellows (b) *(de climatiseur)* blower

soufflet [suflɛ] *nm* (a) *(de forge)* bellows (b) *Rail (couloir)* concertina vestibule (c) *(en couture)* gusset (d) *(d'orgue)* swell (e) *Litt (gifle)* slap (in the face)

souffleter [42] [sufləte] *vt Litt* **s. qn** to slap sb's face

souffleur, -euse [suflœr, -øz] **1 s. de verre** glass blower
2 *nm,f (au théâtre)* prompter
3 *nf* **souffleuse** *Can* snowblower

souffrance [sufrɑ̃s] *nf* (a) *(douleur)* suffering (b) **en s.** *(travail)* pending

souffrant, -e [sufrɑ̃, -ɑ̃t] *adj (indisposé)* unwell, poorly

souffre-douleur [sufrədulœr] *nm inv* object of abuse

souffreteux, -euse [sufrətø, -øz] *adj* sickly

souffrir [52] [sufrir] **1** vi to suffer (**de** from); **faire s. qn** (physiquement) to hurt sb; (moralement) to make sb suffer; **je souffre de la voir malade** it upsets me to see her ill

2 vt (**a**) (physiquement) **s. le martyre** to go through agony; **faire s. le martyre à qn** to put sb through agony (**b**) (supporter) **je ne peux pas la s.** I can't stand her; **je ne peux pas s. qu'on vienne me déranger** I can't stand being disturbed; **il ne souffre pas la contradiction** he can't stand being contradicted; Litt **souffrez que je fasse une critique** permit me to make a criticism (**c**) Litt (admettre) **situation qui ne souffre aucun retard** situation that admits of no delay

3 se souffrir vpr Fam **ils ne peuvent pas se s.** they can't stand each other

soufre [sufr] nm sulphur

souhait [swɛ] nm wish; **faire un s.** to make a wish; **à s.** (à merveille) perfectly; **doré/ensoleillé à s.** beautifully golden/sunny; **à vos souhaits!** bless you!

souhaitable [swetabl] adj desirable; **il serait s. que tu lui parles** it is desirable that you should talk to him

souhaiter [swete] vt to wish for; **s. qch à qn** to wish sb sth; **s. faire qch** to hope to do sth; **s. à qn de faire qch** to hope that sb does sth; **s. que** + subjunctive to hope that; **je vous souhaite une bonne année/un joyeux anniversaire** best wishes for a happy New Year/a happy birthday; Ironique **je te souhaite bien du plaisir!** have fun!

souiller [suje] vt Litt (**a**) (vêtements) to soil, to dirty (**de** with) (**b**) (réputation, mémoire) to tarnish

souillon [sujɔ̃] nf Litt slut, sloven

souillure [sujyr] nf Litt (**a**) (sur un vêtement) stain (**b**) Fig (morale) blot, blemish

souk [suk] nm (**a**) (marché) souk (**b**) Fam (lieu en désordre) shambles (singulier)

soul [sul] adj inv & nf soul

soûl, -e [su, sul] **1** adj drunk

2 nm **tout son s.** to one's heart's content

soulagement [sulaʒmɑ̃] nm relief (**pour** to)

soulager [45] [sulaʒe] **1** vt (douleur) to ease, to relieve; (esprit, chagrin) to soothe; (personne) to relieve; **ce médicament vous soulagera** this medicine will make you feel better; **donne-moi un de tes sacs, ça te soulagera** give me one of your bags, that will take some of the weight off you; Fam **s. qn de son portefeuille** to relieve sb of his/her wallet

2 se soulager vpr (**a**) (en parlant) to ease one's mind (**b**) Fam (satisfaire un besoin naturel) to relieve oneself

soûlant, -e [sulɑ̃, -ɑ̃t] adj Fam exhausting

soûlard, -e [sular, -ard], **soûlaud, -e** [sulo, -od] nm,f Fam drunkard

soûler [sule] Fam **1** vt (**a**) (enivrer) **s. qn** to make sb drunk; Fig (sujet: parfum, succès, idées) to go to sb's head (**b**) (ennuyer) **arrête, tu me soûles!** stop, you're giving me a headache!

2 se soûler vpr to get drunk; Fig **se s. de paroles** to like the sound of one's own voice

soulèvement [sulɛvmɑ̃] nm (**a**) (de terrain) rising (**b**) (révolte) uprising

soulever [46] [sulve] **1** vt (**a**) (charge, personne, couvercle) to lift (up); (rideau) to raise (**b**) (agiter) (poussière) to raise, to throw up; Fig **s. le cœur à qn** to make sb feel sick (**c**) (doutes, question, objection) to raise (**d**) (population) to stir up (**e**) (passion, enthousiasme, indignation) to excite, to arouse; **s. un tollé** to raise an outcry

2 se soulever vpr (**a**) (s'élever) to rise (**b**) (se lever) (personne) to raise oneself, to lift oneself up (**c**) (se révolter) to rise up

soulier [sulje] nm shoe; Fam Fig **être dans ses petits souliers** to feel awkward

souligner [suliɲe] vt (**a**) (mot, passage) to underline (**b**) (yeux, taille) to emphasize (**c**) Fig (mettre en valeur) to emphasize

soumettre [47] [sumɛtr] **1** vt (**a**) (population, pays, passions) to subdue (**b**) (rapport, demande, projet) to submit (**à** to) (**c**) **s. qn à** (examen) to subject sb to; (épreuve) to put sb through; (traitement) to put sb on; **être soumis à des règles strictes** to be bound by strict rules; **s. les revenus à l'impôt** to make income liable to tax

2 se soumettre vpr (obéir) to submit; **se s. à** (autorité) to submit to; (volonté) to comply with; (loi, décision) to abide by

soumis, -e [sumi, -iz] adj (docile) submissive, obedient (**à** to)

soumission [sumisjɔ̃] nf (**a**) (à une loi, à une autorité) submission (**à** to) (**b**) (docilité) submissiveness, obedience (**à** to)

soupape [supap] nf valve; **s. de sécurité** safety valve

soupçon [supsɔ̃] nm (**a**) (suspicion) suspicion; **avoir des soupçons sur qn** to have (one's) suspicions about sb; **être au-dessus** ou **à l'abri de tout s.** to be above all suspicion (**b**) (faible quantité) (de vinaigre, de fard) dash, hint; (de fièvre, de fard, d'ironie) touch; (de vin) drop

soupçonner [supsɔne] vt to suspect; **s. qn de qch/de faire qch** to suspect sb of sth/of doing sth; **je soupçonne qu'il le sait** I suspect that he knows

soupçonneux, -euse [supsɔnø, -øz] adj suspicious

soupe [sup] nf (**a**) (plat) soup; Fam **à la s.!** grub's up!; Fam **être s. au lait** to flare up easily (**b**) **s. populaire** soup kitchen

soupente [supɑ̃t] nf (sous un toit) loft; (sous un escalier) Br cupboard, Am closet

souper¹ [supe] nm (**a**) (dîner) dinner (**b**) (après le spectacle) supper

souper² vi (**a**) (dîner) to have dinner (**b**) (après le spectacle) to have supper (**c**) Fam Fig (être excédé) **avoir soupé de qn/qch** to be fed up with sb/sth

soupeser [46] [supze] vt (objet) to feel the weight of, to weigh in one's hand; Fig (problème, argument) to weigh up

soupière [supjɛr] nf soup tureen

soupir [supir] nm (**a**) (souffle) sigh; **pousser un s.** to let out or give a sigh; **rendre le dernier s.** to breathe one's last; **un gros s.** a heavy or deep sigh (**b**) Mus Br crotchet or Am quarter rest

soupirail, -aux [supiraj, -o] nm cellar window

soupirant [supirɑ̃] nm Hum suitor, admirer

soupirer [supire] **1** vt to sigh

2 vi to sigh; **en soupirant** with a sigh

3 soupirer après vt ind Litt to long for, to yearn for

souple [supl] adj (**a**) (branche) flexible; (corps, danseur) supple; (reliure) limp; (cuir) soft, supple (**b**) Fig (système, loi, personne) flexible; (esprit) adaptable

souplesse [suplɛs] nf (a) (de branche) flexibility; (de corps, de danseur) suppleness; **en s.** (démarrer) smoothly (b) Fig (de système, de loi, de personne) flexibility

source [surs] nf (a) (d'eau) spring; **s. d'eau minérale** mineral spring; **s. thermale** hot spring (b) (de rivière) source; **prendre sa s.** to rise (c) (de chaleur, d'énergie) source (d) Fig (du mal, de richesse, d'informations) source; **tenir qch de bonne s.** to have sth on good authority or from a reliable source; **apprendre qch de s. sûre** to learn sth from a reliable source; **s. de revenus** source of revenue (e) Ordinat **s. de données** data source; **code s.** source code

sourcier [sursje] nm water diviner

sourcil [sursil] nm eyebrow

sourciller [sursije] vi **ne pas s.** not to bat an eyelid or turn a hair; **sans s.** without batting an eyelid, without turning a hair

sourcilleux, -euse [sursijø, -øz] adj fussy, finicky

sourd, -e [sur, surd] **1** adj (a) (personne) deaf; **devenir s.** to go deaf; Fig **rester s. à qch** to turn a deaf ear to sth, to be deaf to sth; **s. de naissance** deaf from birth; **s. d'une oreille** deaf in one ear; Fam **s. comme un pot** deaf as a post (b) (douleur, bruit) dull; (voix) hollow; (désir, lutte) secret; (hostilité) veiled; (consonne) voiceless
2 nmf (personne) deaf person; **les sourds** the deaf, deaf people; **comme un s.** (crier) at the top of one's voice; (frapper, taper) wildly
3 nf **sourde** Ling voiceless consonant

sourdine [surdin] nf mute; (d'un piano) practice pedal; **en s.** (violons) muted; (en secret) on the quiet; Fam Fig **mets-la en s.!** put a sock in it!

sourdingue [surdɛ̃g] Fam **1** adj cloth-eared
2 nmf cloth-ears

sourd-muet, sourde-muette (mpl **sourds-muets,** fpl **sourdes-muettes**) [surmɥɛ, surdmɥɛt] **1** adj deaf-and-dumb
2 nm,f deaf mute

souriant, -e [surjɑ̃, -ɑ̃t] adj smiling

souriceau, -x [suriso] nm young mouse

souricière [surisjɛr] nf mousetrap; Fig trap

sourire [61] [surir] **1** vi (a) (personne) to smile (à at); Ironique **ça fait s.** it makes you laugh (b) (être favorable) **la chance lui sourit** fortune smiles on him; **tout lui sourit** everything goes right for her
2 nm smile; **le s. aux lèvres** with a smile on one's lips; **faire un s. à qn** to give sb a smile; **avoir le s.** to have a smile on one's face; **garder le s.** to keep smiling; **retrouver le s.** to be smiling again

souris [suri] nf (a) (animal) mouse; **s. blanche** white mouse (b) Ordinat mouse; **s. à trois boutons** three-button mouse; **s. à infrarouge** infrared mouse; **s. optique** optical mouse; **s. sans fil** cordless mouse; **s. tactile** touchpad mouse (c) Fam (femme) Br bird, Am dame (d) (de gigot) knuckle end

sournois, -e [surnwa, -az] **1** adj sly
2 nm,f sly person

sournoisement [surnwazmɑ̃] adv slyly

sournoiserie [surnwazri] nf slyness

sous [su] prép (a) (position) under(neath); **s. terre** underground; **nager s. l'eau** to swim underwater; **lettre s. enveloppe** letter in an envelope; **s. la pluie in** the rain; **s. les tropiques** in the tropics; **s. les yeux de qn** before sb's eyes; **s. cet angle** from that angle; **chercher un mot s. la lettre S** to look up a word under the letter S (b) (à l'époque de) (monarque, président) under; **s. la IIIe République** during the Third Republic (c) (d'ici) within; **s. peu** shortly, before long (d) (locutions) **connu s. le nom de...** known as...; **être s. antibiotiques** to be on antibiotics; **opérer s. anesthésie** to operate under anaesthetic; **s. le poids de qch** under the weight of sth; **travailler s. les ordres de qn** to work under sb; **s. certaines conditions** on certain conditions; **s. peine de mort** on or under pain of death

sous-alimentation [suzalimɑ̃tasjɔ̃] nf malnutrition, undernourishment

sous-alimenté, -e (mpl **sous-alimentés,** fpl **sous-alimentées**) [suzalimɑ̃te] adj malnourished, undernourished

sous-bois [subwa] nm inv undergrowth

sous-chef (pl **sous-chefs**) [suʃɛf] nm second-in-command

sous-continent (pl **sous-continents**) [suk3tinɑ̃] nm subcontinent

sous-couche (pl **sous-couches**) [sukuʃ] nf undercoat

souscripteur, -trice [suskriptœr, -tris] nm,f (d'un emprunt) subscriber (de to); (d'une police d'assurance) policy holder

souscription [suskripsjɔ̃] nf (à un emprunt) subscription (à to); **la s. d'une police d'assurance** taking out an insurance policy

souscrire [30] [suskrir] **1** vt (police d'assurance) to take out
2 souscrire à vt ind aussi Fig to subscribe to

sous-culture (pl **sous-cultures**) [sukyltyr] nf subculture

sous-cutané, -e (mpl **sous-cutanés,** fpl **sous-cutanées**) [sukytane] adj subcutaneous

sous-développé, -e (mpl **sous-développés,** fpl **sous-développées**) [sudevlope] adj (pays) underdeveloped

sous-développement [sudevlopmɑ̃] nm underdevelopment

sous-directeur, -trice (mpl **sous-directeurs,** fpl **sous-directrices**) [sudirɛktœr, -tris] nm,f (dans une entreprise) assistant manager, f assistant manageress

sous-division nf subdivision

sous-emploi [suzɑ̃plwa] nm underemployment

sous-employé, -e (mpl **sous-employés,** fpl **sous-employées**) [suzɑ̃plwaje] adj underemployed

sous-ensemble (pl **sous-ensembles**) [suzɑ̃sɑ̃bl] nm subset

sous-entendre [suzɑ̃tɑ̃dr] vt to imply

sous-entendu (pl **sous-entendus**) [suzɑ̃tɑ̃dy] nm insinuation

sous-équipé, -e (mpl **sous-équipés,** fpl **sous-équipées**) [suzekipe] adj underequipped

sous-estimer [suzɛstime] vt to underestimate

sous-évaluer [suzevalɥe] vt to undervalue

sous-exposer [suzɛkspoze] vt to underexpose

sous-fifre (pl **sous-fifres**) [sufifr] nm Fam underling

sous-homme (pl **sous-hommes**) [suzɔm] nm subhuman

sous-jacent, -e (*mpl* **sous-jacents**, *fpl* **sous-jacentes**) [suʒasɑ̃, -ɑ̃t] *adj* underlying

Sous-le-Vent [sulvɑ̃] *n* **les îles S.** the Leeward Islands

sous-lieutenant (*pl* **sous-lieutenants**) [suljøtnɑ̃] *nm* (a) (*dans l'armée de terre*) second lieutenant (b) (*dans la marine*) sub-lieutenant (c) (*dans l'armée de l'air*) Br pilot officer, Am second lieutenant

sous-locataire (*pl* **sous-locataires**) [suləkatɛr] *nmf* subtenant

sous-location (*pl* **sous-locations**) [suləkasjɔ̃] *nf* (a) (*par le locataire*) subletting (b) (*par le sous-locataire*) subrenting

sous-louer [sulwe] *vt* (a) (*sujet: locataire*) to sublet (b) (*sujet: sous-locataire*) to subrent

sous-main [sumɛ̃] *nm inv* desk blotter; Fig **en s.** secretly

sous-marin, -e (*mpl* **sous-marins**, *fpl* **sous-marines**) [sumarɛ̃, -in] 1 *adj* underwater
2 *nm* submarine; **s. nucléaire** nuclear(-powered) submarine

sous-marinier (*pl* **sous-mariniers**) [sumarinje] *nm* submariner

sous-multiple (*pl* **sous-multiples**) [sumyltipl] *nm* Math submultiple (**de** of)

sous-nappe (*pl* **sous-nappes**) [sunap] *nf* undercloth

sous-officier (*pl* **sous-officiers**) [suzɔfisje] *nm* non-commissioned officer

sous-payer [53] [supeje] *vt* to underpay

sous-peuplé, -e (*mpl* **sous-peuplés**, *fpl* **sous-peuplées**) [supœple] *adj* underpopulated

sous-préfecture (*pl* **sous-préfectures**) [suprefɛktyr] *nf* subprefecture

sous-préfet (*pl* **sous-préfets**) [suprefɛ] *nm* subprefect

sous-production (*pl* **sous-productions**) [suprɔdyksjɔ̃] *nf* under-production

sous-produit (*pl* **sous-produits**) [suprɔdɥi] *nm* by-product; Fig poor imitation

sous-prolétaire (*pl* **sous-prolétaires**) [suprɔletɛr] *nmf* member of the underclass

sous-prolétariat (*pl* **sous-prolétariats**) [suprɔletarja] *nm* underclass

sous-pull (*pl* **sous-pulls**) [supyl] *nm* thin sweater

sous-répertoire (*pl* **sous-répertoires**) [surepɛrtwar] *nm Ordinat* subdirectory

sous-secrétaire (*pl* **sous-secrétaires**) [susəkretɛr] *nmf* **s. d'État** Under-Secretary of State

soussigné, -e [susiɲe] *adj & nm,f* undersigned; **je, s. Éric Blanc, donne mon autorisation à...** I, the undersigned Éric Blanc, hereby authorize...

sous-sol (*pl* **sous-sols**) [susɔl] *nm* (a) (*d'une maison*) basement (b) Géol subsoil

sous-tasse (*pl* **sous-tasses**) [sutas] *nf* saucer

sous-tendre [sutɑ̃dr] *vt* (*théorie*) to underlie

sous-titrage (*pl* **sous-titrages**) [sutitraʒ] *nm Cin* subtitling

sous-titre (*pl* **sous-titres**) [sutitr] *nm* (*de livre, de film*) subtitle

sous-titrer [sutitre] *vt Cin* to subtitle; **film sous-titré en anglais** film with English subtitles

sous-total (*pl* **sous-totaux**) [sutɔtal, -o] *nm* subtotal

soustraction [sustraksjɔ̃] *nf* subtraction

soustraire [28] [sustrɛr] 1 *vt* (a) (*enlever*) **s. qch à qn** to take sth away or remove sth from sb; **s. qn au danger/à l'influence de qn** to protect or shield sb from danger/from sb's influence (b) (*chiffre, somme*) to subtract (**de** from)
2 **se soustraire** *vpr* **se s. à** (*influence, regard*) to avoid, to elude; (*obligation*) to shirk

sous-traitance [sutrɛtɑ̃s] *nf* subcontracting; **travaux effectués en s.** subcontracted work

sous-traitant, -e [sutrɛtɑ̃, -ɑ̃t] 1 *adj* subcontracting
2 *nm* subcontractor

sous-traiter [sutrɛte] *vt* to subcontract

sous-verre [suvɛr] *nm inv* (*cadre*) glass mount; (*photo, image*) = photograph or picture mounted under glass

sous-vêtement [suvɛtmɑ̃] *nm* undergarment; **sous-vêtements** underwear

soutane [sutan] *nf* cassock

soute [sut] *nf* (*de bateau*) store; (*d'avion*) hold; **s. à bagages** (*d'avion*) baggage hold

soutenable [sutnabl] *adj* (a) (*supportable*) bearable (b) (*défendable*) tenable

soutenance [sutnɑ̃s] *nf Univ* viva (voce)

soutènement [sutɛnmɑ̃] *nm voir* **mur**

souteneur [sutnœr] *nm* pimp

soutenir [70] [sutnir] 1 *vt* (a) (*maintenir*) to support, to hold up (b) (*aider*) to support (c) (*opinion, théorie*) to maintain, to uphold; **s. que...** to maintain that... (d) Univ (*thèse*) to defend (e) (*conversation, vitesse, rythme*) to keep up, to maintain (f) (*résister à*) (*regard*) to hold; **s. la comparaison** to bear comparison
2 **se soutenir** *vpr* (*personnes*) to support each other; **se s. moralement** to give each other moral support

soutenu, -e [sutny] *adj* (a) (*attention, effort, intérêt*) sustained; (*rythme*) steady (b) (*style, langage*) formal, elevated (c) (*couleur*) deep

souterrain, -e [sutɛrɛ̃, -ɛn] 1 *adj* (a) (*eau, explosion*) underground; (*économie*) black (b) Fig (*manœuvres*) secret
2 *nm* underground passage

soutien [sutjɛ̃] *nm* (a) (*aide*) support; **apporter son s. à qn/qch** to give sb/sth one's support (b) (*personne, groupe*) support; **s. de famille** breadwinner

soutien-gorge (*pl* **soutiens-gorge**) [sutjɛ̃gɔrʒ] *nm* bra; **s. à armatures/d'allaitement** underwired/nursing bra

soutirer [sutire] *vt* (a) (*vin*) to rack, to decant (b) **s. qch à qn** (*argent, information*) to extract sth from sb

souvenance [suvnɑ̃s] *nf* **avoir s. de qch** to recollect sth

souvenir [suvnir] 1 *nm* (a) (*réminiscence*) memory; **en s. de** in memory of; **en s. du passé** for old times' sake; **garder un bon/mauvais s. de qch** to have good/bad memories of sth; **souvenirs d'enfance** childhood memories (b) (*objet*) memento; (*touristique*) souvenir
2 *v impersonnel* Litt **il me souvient que...** I recall that...
3 **se souvenir** *vpr* **se s. de** to remember; **se s. que** to remember that; **je ne me souviens de rien** I can't remember anything

souvent [suvɑ̃] *adv* often; **le plus s.** usually, more often than not; **plus s. qu'à son tour** far too often

souverain, -e [suvrɛ̃, -ɛn] 1 *adj* (*puissance, état, remède*) sovereign; (*bonheur, mépris*) supreme
2 *nm,f* sovereign

souverainement [suvrɛnmɑ̃] adv (intelligent, doué) supremely; (agacer, déplaire) intensely

souveraineté [suvrɛnte] nf sovereignty

soviétique [sɔvjetik] Anciennement **1** adj Soviet **2** nmf S. Soviet (citizen)

soyeux, -euse [swajø, -øz] **1** adj silky **2** nm silk merchant

soyez, soyons etc voir **être**

SPA [espea] nf (abrév **Société protectrice des animaux**) Br ≃ RSPCA, Am ≃ ASPCA

spacieusement [spasjøzmɑ̃] adv être logé s. to have spacious accommodation

spacieux, -euse [spasjø, -øz] adj spacious

spaghetti [spageti] nm piece of spaghetti; **des spaghettis** spaghetti

sparadrap [sparadra] nm Br sticking plaster, Am adhesive tape

spartiate [sparsjat] **1** adj Spartan; Fig **à la s.** in a spartan way **2** nfpl **spartiates** Roman sandals

spasme [spasm] nm spasm

spasmodique [spasmɔdik] adj spasmodic

spasmophilie [spasmɔfili] nf spasmophilia

spatial, -e, -aux, -ales [spasjal, -o] adj (a) (de l'espace) spatial (b) (de l'espace interplanétaire) space

spatio-temporel, -elle (mpl **spatio-temporels**, fpl **spatio-temporelles**) [spasjɔtɑ̃pɔrel] adj spatiotemporal

spatule [spatyl] nf (a) (de cuisinier, de peintre) spatula (b) (de ski) tip (c) (oiseau) spoonbill

speaker, speakerine [spikœr, spikrin] nm,f announcer

spécial, -e, -aux, -ales [spesjal, -o] adj (a) (particulier, extraordinaire) special (b) (bizarre) peculiar, odd

spécialement [spesjalmɑ̃] adv (particulièrement) especially, particularly; (exprès) specially

spécialisation [spesjalizasjɔ̃] nf specialization

spécialisé, -e [spesjalize] adj (travail, enseignement) specialized; (ouvrier) semi-skilled; (école, hôpital) special

spécialiser [spesjalize] **se spécialiser** vpr to specialize (**dans** ou **en** in)

spécialiste [spesjalist] nmf specialist (**de/en** in)

spécialité [spesjalite] nf Br speciality, Am specialty; **s. maison** speciality of the house

spécieux, -euse [spesjø, -øz] adj Litt specious

spécification [spesifikasjɔ̃] nf specification

spécificité [spesifisite] nf specificity

spécifier [spesifje] vt to specify

spécifique [spesifik] adj specific

spécifiquement [spesifikmɑ̃] adv specifically

spécimen [spesimen] nm (a) (modèle) specimen (b) (livre, fascicule) specimen copy

spectacle [spektakl] nm (a) (représentation) show; **le s.** (industrie) show business; **film à grand s.** epic (film); **s. de variétés** variety show (b) (vue) sight; **se donner en s.** to make an exhibition or a spectacle of oneself

spectaculaire [spektakyler] adj spectacular

spectateur, -trice [spektatœr, -tris] nm,f (a) (d'un événement sportif) spectator; (d'un spectacle) member of the audience; **spectateurs** (au spectacle) audience (b) (témoin) witness

spectre [spektr] nm (a) (fantôme) ghost, phantom; Fig (de la guerre, de la misère) spectre (b) Phys spectrum

spéculateur, trice [spekylatœr, -tris] nm,f speculator

spéculation [spekylasjɔ̃] nf speculation

spéculer [spekyle] vi (a) (intellectuellement) to speculate (**sur** on or about) (b) (à la Bourse) to speculate (**sur** in); Fig **s. sur qch** to count or bank on sth

speech (pl **speeches**) [spitʃ] nm Fam speech; **faire un s.** to make a speech; **faire un s. à qn sur qch** to give sb a speech about sth

speedé, -e [spide] adj Fam (hyperactif) hyped up, hyper

speeder [spide] vi Fam to get a move on

spéléologie [speleɔlɔʒi] nf (a) (exploration) Br potholing, Am spelunking (b) (science) speleology

spéléologue [speleɔlɔg] nmf (a) (explorateur) Br potholer, Am spelunker (b) (spécialiste) speleologist

spencer [spɛsœr] nm short jacket

spermatozoïde [spermatozɔid] nm spermatozoon

sperme [sperm] nm sperm, semen

sphère [sfer] nf (a) (boule) sphere (b) (d'activité, d'influence) sphere; **les hautes sphères de la politique** the higher realms of politics

sphérique [sferik] adj spherical

sphinx [sfɛks] nm (a) (monstre fabuleux) sphinx (b) (insecte) hawk or sphinx moth

spirale [spiral] nf spiral; **en s.** (s'élever) in a spiral; (escalier, coquillage) spiral

spiritisme [spiritism] nm spiritualism

spiritualité [spiritɥalite] nf spirituality

spirituel, -elle [spirituel] adj (a) (pouvoir, vie) spiritual (b) (fin) witty; Ironique **que c'est s.!** very witty!

spirituellement [spiritɥelmɑ̃] adv (a) (moralement) spiritually (b) (finement) wittily

spiritueux [spiritɥø] nm spirit

spleen [splin] nm Litt spleen, melancholy; **avoir le s.** to be melancholic

splendeur [splɑ̃dœr] nf splendour; **c'est une s.** it's splendid

splendide [splɑ̃did] adj splendid; (soleil) brilliant; (œuvre d'art, personne) magnificent

splendidement [splɑ̃didmɑ̃] adv splendidly

spolier [spɔlje] vt to despoil (**de** of)

spongieux, -euse [spɔ̃ʒjø, -øz] adj spongy

sponsor [spɔ̃sɔr] nm sponsor

sponsoriser [spɔ̃sɔrize] vt to sponsor

spontané, -e [spɔ̃tane] adj spontaneous

spontanéité [spɔ̃taneite] nf spontaneity

spontanément [spɔ̃tanemɑ̃] adv spontaneously

sporadique [spɔradik] adj sporadic

spore [spɔr] nf spore

sport [spɔr] **1** nm (a) (activité) sport; **de s.** (chaussures, terrain, voiture) sports; **faire du s.** to do sport; **s. de combat** combat sport; **s. d'équipe/individuel** team/individual sport; **sports d'hiver** winter sports; **aller aux sports d'hiver** to go skiing; **sports nautiques** water sports (b) Fam (locutions) **il va y avoir du s.!** there's going to be some fun!; **c'est du s.** it's a tough job **2** adj inv (vêtement) casual

sportif, -ive [spɔrtif, -iv] **1** adj (a) (résultats, journal, club) sports (b) (fair-play) sporting (c) (dynamique) sporty **2** nm,f sportsman, f sportswoman

sportivité [spɔʀtivite] *nf* sportsmanship

spot [spɔt] *nm* (a) *(projecteur)* spot, spotlight (b) *(à la télé, à la radio)* **s. publicitaire** commercial, advert

spoutnik [sputnik] *nm* sputnik

spray [sprɛ] *nm* spray, aerosol

sprint [sprint] *nm (accélération finale)* (final) sprint; *(course)* sprint; *Fam* **piquer un s.** to sprint

sprinter[1] [sprintœr] *nm* sprinter

sprinter[2] [sprinte] *vi* to sprint

squale [skwal] *nm* shark

square [skwar] *nm* public garden

squash [skwaʃ] *nm* squash

squat [skwat] *nm* squat

squatter[1] [skwatœr] *nm* squatter

squatter[2] [skwate] *vt* to squat in

squelette [skəlɛt] *nm* (a) *(d'être humain, d'animal)* skeleton; **c'est un vrai s.** he's/she's a bag of bones; **c'est un s. ambulant** he's/she's a walking skeleton (b) *Fig (de roman, de bâtiment)* skeleton, framework

squelettique [skəlɛtik] *adj* (a) *(personne, partie du corps)* skeleton-like (b) *(personnel, armée)* skeleton

Sri Lanka [srilãka] *nm* le S. Sri Lanka

sri lankais, -e [srilãke, -ɛz] **1** *adj* Sri Lankan
2 *nm,f* S. Sri Lankan

SRPJ [ɛsɛrpeʒi] *nm (abrév* **Service régional de la police judiciaire)** = regional crime unit

stabilisateur, -trice [stabilizatœr, -tris] **1** *adj* stabilizing
2 *nm (de vélo)* stabilizer

stabilisation [stabilizasjõ] *nf* stabilization

stabiliser [stabilize] **1** *vt* to stabilize
2 se stabiliser *vpr* to stabilize; *(personne)* to settle down

stabilité [stabilite] *nf* stability

stable [stabl] *adj* stable

stade [stad] *nm* (a) *(sportif)* stadium (b) *(étape)* stage; **en être au s.** embryonnaire to be at an embryonic stage

stage [staʒ] *nm (professionnel)* training course; **faire un s. de tennis/de voile** to have tennis/sailing lessons; *(vacances)* to go on a tennis/sailing holiday; **être en s.** to be on a training course; **s. de formation** training course

stagiaire [staʒjɛr] *adj & nmf* trainee

stagnant, -e [stagnã, -ãt] *adj* stagnant

stagnation [stagnasjõ] *nf* stagnation

stagner [stagne] *vi* to stagnate

stalactite [stalaktit] *nf* stalactite

stalagmite [stalagmit] *nf* stalagmite

stalinien, -enne [stalinjɛ̃, -ɛn] *adj & nm,f* Stalinist

stalle [stal] *nf (dans une écurie, une église)* stall

stand [stãd] *nm* (a) *(d'exposition)* stand; *(de foire)* stall; **s. de tir** rifle range (b) *(de course automobile)* **s. (de ravitaillement)** pit

standard [stãdar] **1** *adj inv* standard
2 *nm* (a) *(norme)* standard (b) **s. (téléphonique)** switchboard

standardisation [stãdardizasjõ] *nf* standardization

standardiser [stãdardize] *vt* to standardize

standardiste [stãdardist] *nmf* (switchboard) operator

standing [stãdiŋ] *nm* (social) standing; **de grand s.** *(appartement)* luxury; *(quartier)* select

staphylocoque [stafilokɔk] *nm* staphylococcus

star [star] *nf* star

starlette [starlɛt] *nf* starlet

starter [starter] *nm* (a) *(de voiture)* choke (b) *(dans une course)* starter

starting-block *(pl* **starting-blocks)** [startiŋblɔk] *nm* starting block

station [stasjõ] *nf* (a) *(de métro)* station; *(de train)* halt; *(de bus)* stop; **s. de taxis** *Br* taxi rank, *Am* taxi stand (b) *(ville, village)* **s. balnéaire** seaside resort; **s. de ski** ski resort; **s. de sports d'hiver** winter sports resort; **s. thermale** spa town (c) *(établissement)* station; **s. d'essence** *Br* petrol or *Am* gas station; **s. de lavage** car wash; **s. spatiale** space station (d) *(position)* **s. debout** standing position (e) **s. radio** radio station (f) *Ordinat (d'un réseau)* station, node; **s. d'accueil** docking station; **s. individuelle** standalone workstation; **s. de travail** workstation

stationnaire [stasjoner] *adj (satellite)* stationary; *(baromètre)* steady; *(état d'un malade)* stable

stationnement [stasjonmã] *nm* (a) *(de voitures)* parking; **en s.** parked; **s. alterné semi-mensuel** = system in which parking is permitted on one side of the street only for alternating periods of two weeks; **s. interdit** *(sur panneau)* no parking; **s. gênant** *(sur panneau)* ≃ restricted parking (b) *Can (parking)* car park, *Am* parking lot

stationner [stasjone] *vi* to park; **défense de s.** *(sur panneau)* no parking

station-service *(pl* **stations-service)** [stasjõservis] *nf* service station, *Br* petrol or *Am* gas station

statique [statik] **1** *adj* static
2 *nf* statics *(singulier)*

statisticien, -enne [statistisjɛ̃, -ɛn] *nm,f* statistician

statistique [statistik] **1** *adj* statistical
2 *nf* (a) *(donnée)* statistic (b) *(science)* statistics *(singulier)*

statistiquement [statistikmã] *adv* statistically

statuaire [statɥɛr] *adj & nf* statuary

statue [staty] *nf* statue

statuer [statɥe] *vi* **s. sur** *vt ind* to give a ruling on

statuette [statɥɛt] *nf* statuette

statu quo [statykwo] *nm* status quo

stature [statyr] *nf* stature

statut [staty] *nm* (a) *(position)* status; **s. juridique** *ou* **légal** legal status; **s. social** social status (b) **statuts** *(d'une société, d'une association)* statutes

statutaire [statyter] *adj* statutory

St *(abrév* **Saint)** St

Ste *(abrév* **Sainte)** St

Sté *(abrév* **Société)** Co

steak [stɛk] *nm* steak; **s. frites** steak and chips; **un s. haché** a beefburger; **du s. haché** *Br* mince, *Am* ground beef; **s. au poivre** pepper steak; **s. tartare** steak tartare *(raw minced beef served with a raw egg)*

stèle [stɛl] *nf* stele

stellaire [steler] *adj* stellar

stencil [stɛnsil] *nm* stencil

sténo [steno] **1** *nf (abrév* **sténographie)** shorthand; **prendre qch en s.** to take sth down in shorthand
2 *nmf (abrév* **sténographe)** stenographer

sténodactylo [stenodaktilo] **1** *nf* shorthand typing
2 *nmf* shorthand typist

sténodactylographie [stenodaktilografi] *nf* shorthand typing

sténographe [stenɔgraf] *nmf* stenographer

sténographie [stenɔgrafi] *nf* shorthand

sténographier [stenɔgrafje] *vt* to take down in shorthand

sténographique [stenɔgrafik] *adj* shorthand

stentor [stɑ̃tɔr] *nm voir* **voix**

steppe [step] *nf* steppe

stéréo [stereo] **1** *adj inv* stereo
2 *nf* stereo; **en s.** in stereo

stéréophonie [stereɔfɔni] *nf* stereophony

stéréophonique [stereɔfɔnik] *adj* stereophonic

stéréotype [stereɔtip] *nm* stereotype

stéréotypé, -e [stereɔtipe] *adj* stereotyped

stérile [steril] *adj* (a) *(personne, animal)* sterile; *(mariage)* childless; *(terre)* barren **(b)** *(discussion, efforts)* futile **(c)** *(instrument, chambre)* sterile

stérilet [sterile] *nm* coil, IUD

stérilisation [sterilizasjɔ̃] *nf* sterilization

stériliser [sterilize] *vt* to sterilize

stérilité [sterilite] *nf* (a) *(d'une personne, d'un animal)* sterility; *(de la terre)* barrenness **(b)** *(d'une discussion, d'efforts)* futility

sterling [sterliŋ] *adj inv voir* **livre²**

sterne [stern] *nf* tern

sternum [sternɔm] *nm* breastbone, *Spéc* sternum

stéthoscope [stetɔskɔp] *nm* stethoscope

steward [stjuwart, stiwart] *nm* steward

stick [stik] *nm* *(de colle, pour les lèvres)* stick; **déodorant en s.** stick deodorant

stigmate [stigmat] *nm* (a) *(trace)* mark **(b)** *Rel* stigmates stigmata

stigmatiser [stigmatize] *vt* *(dénoncer)* to condemn

stimulant, -e [stimylɑ̃, -ɑ̃t] **1** *adj* stimulating; *(résultats)* encouraging
2 *nm* (a) *(remède)* stimulant **(b)** *Fig* stimulus, incentive

stimulateur [stimylatœr] *nm* **s. cardiaque** pacemaker

stimulation [stimylasjɔ̃] *nf* stimulation

stimuler [stimyle] *vt* to stimulate

stipuler [stipyle] *vt* to stipulate

stock [stɔk] *nm* stock; **en s.** in stock

stockage [stɔkaʒ] *nm* (a) *(de marchandises)* stocking **(b)** *Ordinat* storage; **s. en mémoire tampon** buffering

stock-car *(pl* **stock-cars)** [stɔkkar] *nm* *(voiture)* stock car; *(sport)* stock-car racing

stocker [stɔke] *vt* (a) *(marchandises)* to stock **(b)** *Ordinat* to store

Stockholm [stɔkɔlm] *n* Stockholm

stoïcisme [stɔisism] *nm* (a) *(attitude)* stoicism **(b)** *(doctrine philosophique)* Stoicism

stoïque [stɔik] *adj* stoical

stoïquement [stɔikmɑ̃] *adv* stoically

stomatologie [stɔmatɔlɔʒi] *nf* stomatology

stop [stɔp] **1** *exclam* stop!; *(dans un télégramme)* stop; **savoir dire s.** to know when to say stop
2 *nm* (a) *(panneau)* stop sign **(b)** *(d'un véhicule)* brake light **(c)** *Fam* *(auto-stop)* hitching, hitchhiking; **faire du s.** to hitch, to hitchhike

stopper [stɔpe] *vt & vi (arrêter)* to stop

store [stɔr] *nm* (a) *(de fenêtre)* blind; **s. vénitien** Venetian blind **(b)** *(de magasin)* awning

strabisme [strabism] *nm* squint

stradivarius [stradivarjys] *nm* Stradivarius

strangulation [strɑ̃gylasjɔ̃] *nf* strangulation

strapontin [strapɔ̃tɛ̃] *nm* *(siège)* folding seat, tip-up seat

Strasbourg [strazbur] *n* Strasbourg

strasbourgeois, -e [strazburʒwa, -waz] **1** *adj* of Strasbourg
2 *nm,f* S. person from Strasbourg

strass [stras] *nm* paste; **en s.** paste

stratagème [strataʒɛm] *nm* stratagem

strate [strat] *nf* stratum

stratège [strateʒ] *nm* strategist

stratégie [strateʒi] *nf* strategy

stratégique [strateʒik] *adj* strategic

stratification [stratifikasjɔ̃] *nf* stratification

stratifié, -e [stratifje] *adj* (a) *(roche)* stratified **(b)** *(bois)* laminated

stratosphère [stratɔsfɛr] *nf* stratosphere

streptocoque [streptɔkɔk] *nm* streptococcus

stress [stres] *nm* stress

stressant, -e [stresɑ̃, -ɑ̃t] *adj* stressful

stresser [strese] **1** *vt* to put under stress; **être stressé** to be stressed
2 *vi Fam* to get stressed

Stretch® [stretʃ] *nm* stretch material

strict, -e [strikt] *adj* (a) *(obligation, principes)* strict; **au sens s.** in the strict sense of the word; **le s. minimum** the bare minimum; **le s. nécessaire** the bare essentials; **c'est la stricte vérité** that's the absolute truth; **c'est son droit le plus s.** it's her absolute right **(b)** *(personne)* strict *(sur about)* **(c)** *(costume, coupe de cheveux)* severe

strictement [striktəmɑ̃] *adv* (a) *(rigoureusement)* strictly; **je ne comprends s. rien** I don't understand a single thing **(b)** *(habillé)* severely

stricto sensu [striktosɛ̃sy] *adv* strictly speaking

strident, -e [stridɑ̃, -ɑ̃t] *adj* strident, shrill

strie [stri] *nf* groove

strié, -e [strije] *adj* grooved

string [striŋ] *nm* G-string

strip-tease *(pl* **strip-teases)** [striptiz] *nm* striptease

strip-teaseuse *(pl* **strip-teaseuses)** [striptizøz] *nf* stripper, striptease artist

stroboscope [strɔbɔskɔp] *nm* strobe, stroboscope

strophe [strɔf] *nf* stanza, verse

structural, -e, -aux, -ales [stryktyral, -o] *adj* structural

structuralement [stryktyralmɑ̃] *adv* structurally

structuralisme [stryktyralism] *nm* structuralism

structuraliste [stryktyralist] *adj & nmf* structuralist

structure [stryktyr] *nf* (a) *(disposition)* structure **(b)** *(organisation)* structure; **s. d'accueil** reception facilities **(c)** *Ordinat* **s. en anneau** ring structure; **s. en arbre** tree structure; **s. de bloc** block structure

structuré, -e [stryktyre] *adj* (a) *(ensemble, langage)* structured **(b)** *Ordinat* **fichier non s.** flat file

structurel, -elle [stryktyrɛl] *adj* structural

structurer [stryktyre] *vt* to structure

strychnine [striknin] *nf* strychnine

stuc [styk] *nm* stucco

studieusement [stydjøzmɑ̃] *adv* studiously

studieux, -euse [stydjø, -øz] *adj (personne)* studious; *(vacances)* study

studio [stydjo] *nm* (a) *(pour travailler)* studio; **s. de cinéma** *Br* film studio, *Am* movie studio; **tourné en s.** filmed in the studio; **s. d'enregistrement** recording studio (b) *(logement)* *Br* studio flat, *Am* studio apartment

stupéfaction [stypefaksjɔ̃] *nf* amazement, astonishment

stupéfait, -e [stypefɛ, -ɛt] *adj* amazed, astounded

stupéfiant, -e [stypefjɑ̃, -ɑ̃t] **1** *adj* amazing, astounding
2 *nm* drug, narcotic

stupéfier [stypefje] *vt* to amaze, to astound

stupeur [stypœr] *nf* amazement, astonishment

stupide [stypid] *adj* stupid

stupidement [stypidmɑ̃] *adv* stupidly

stupidité [stypidite] *nf* (a) *(caractère)* stupidity (b) *(remarque)* stupid remark; **dire des stupidités** to say stupid things

style [stil] *nm* style; **de s.** *(meuble)* period; **s. Louis XIII/Régence** Louis XIII-/Regency-style; **avoir du s.** to have style, to be stylish; *Fam* **ça serait bien son s.!** that would be just his style!; **s. de vie** lifestyle; *Gram* **s. direct/indirect** direct/indirect speech

stylé, -e [stile] *adj (domestique)* trained

stylet [stilɛ] *nm* (a) *(poignard)* stiletto (b) *Ordinat* **s. lumineux** light pen

styliser [stilize] *vt* to stylize

stylisme [stilism] *nm* designing

styliste [stilist] *nmf* designer

stylistique [stilistik] **1** *adj* stylistic
2 *nf* stylistics *(singulier)*

stylo [stilo] *nm* pen; **s. à encre** *ou* **à plume** fountain pen; **s. (à) bille** ballpoint (pen), *Br* biro®

stylo-feutre *(pl* stylos-feutres*)* [stiloføtr] *nm* felt-tip (pen)

su¹ *voir* savoir

su² [sy] *nm* **au vu et au su de tout le monde** quite openly

suave [sɥav] *adj* (a) *(parfum, mélodie)* sweet (b) *(ton, manières)* suave, smooth

suavité [sɥavite] *nf* (a) *(d'un parfum, d'une mélodie)* sweetness (b) *(des manières)* suavity

subalterne [sybaltɛrn] **1** *adj (officier, position)* subordinate, minor; *(employé)* junior
2 *nmf* subordinate

subconscient, -e [sybkɔ̃sjɑ̃, -ɑ̃t] *adj & nm* subconscious

subdiviser [sybdivize] **1** *vt* to subdivide (en into)
2 se subdiviser *vpr* to be subdivided (en into)

subdivision [sybdivizjɔ̃] *nf* subdivision

subir [sybir] *vt* (a) *(violence, conséquences)* to suffer; *(défaite, pertes)* to suffer, to sustain; *(influence)* to be under; **faire s. qch à qn** to subject sb to sth (b) *(examen, opération, changement)* to undergo (c) *Fam (personne)* to put up with

subit, -e [sybi, -it] *adj* sudden

subitement [sybitmɑ̃] *adv* suddenly, all of a sudden

subjectif, -ive [sybʒɛktif, -iv] *adj* subjective

subjectivement [sybʒɛktivmɑ̃] *adv* subjectively

subjectivité [sybʒɛktivite] *nf* subjectivity

subjonctif, -ive [sybʒɔ̃ktif, -iv] *Gram* **1** *adj* subjunctive
2 *nm* subjunctive; **au s.** in the subjunctive

subjuguer [sybʒyge] *vt (séduire)* to captivate

sublimation [syblimasjɔ̃] *nf* sublimation

sublime [syblim] **1** *adj* sublime
2 *nm* **le s.** the sublime

sublimement [syblimmɑ̃] *adv* sublimely

sublimer [syblime] *vt* to sublimate

subliminal, -e, -aux, -ales [sybliminal, -o] *adj* subliminal

submerger [sybmɛrʒe] *vt* to submerge; **submergé de travail** snowed under with work

submersible [sybmɛrsibl] **1** *adj* submersible
2 *nm* submarine

subodorer [sybodɔre] *vt* *Fam (danger, complot)* to scent

subordination [sybɔrdinasjɔ̃] *nf* subordination

subordonné, -e [sybɔrdone] **1** *adj* *Gram (proposition)* subordinate
2 *nm,f (personne)* subordinate
3 *nf* **subordonnée** *Gram* subordinate clause

subordonner [sybɔrdone] *vt* (a) *(dans une hiérarchie)* **être subordonné à qn** to be subordinate to sb (b) *(faire passer après)* **s. qch à qch** to accord less importance to sth than to sth (c) *(faire dépendre)* **être subordonné à qch** to be dependent on sth

subornation [sybɔrnasjɔ̃] *nf* *Jur* subornation

suborner [sybɔrne] *vt* (a) *Jur (témoin)* to suborn, to bribe (b) *Litt (séduire)* to seduce

subrepticement [sybrɛptismɑ̃] *adv* surreptitiously

subséquent, -e [sypsekɑ̃, -ɑ̃t] *adj* subsequent

subside [sybzid] *nm* subsidy, grant

subsidiaire [sybzidjɛr] *adj* subsidiary

subsistance [sybzistɑ̃s] *nf* subsistence; **pourvoir à la s. de sa famille** to keep or support one's family

subsistant, -e [sybzistɑ̃, -ɑ̃t] *adj* remaining

subsister [sybziste] *vi* (a) *(chose)* to remain (b) *(personne)* to subsist

substance [sypstɑ̃s] *nf* substance; **en s.** in substance

substantiel, -elle [sypstɑ̃sjɛl] *adj* substantial

substantiellement [sypstɑ̃sjɛlmɑ̃] *adv* substantially

substantif, -ive [sypstɑ̃tif, -iv] *Gram* **1** *adj* substantive
2 *nm* noun, substantive

substantiver [sypstɑ̃tive] *vt* to use as a noun *or* substantively

substituer [sypstitɥe] **1** *vt* **s. qn/qch à** to substitute sb/sth for
2 se substituer *vpr* **se s. à** to substitute for, to take the place of

substitut [sypstity] *nm* (a) *Jur* deputy public prosecutor (b) *(remplacement)* substitute

substitution [sypstitysjɔ̃] *nf* substitution

substrat [sypstra] *nm* *Géol* substratum

subterfuge [sypterfyʒ] *nm* subterfuge; **user de subterfuges** to resort to subterfuge

subtil, -e [syptil] *adj* subtle

subtilement [syptilmɑ̃] *adv* subtly

subtiliser [syptilize] *vt* to make off with; **on lui a subtilisé son portefeuille** someone's made off with his wallet

subtilité [syptilite] *nf* subtlety

subtropical, -e, -aux, -ales [syptrɔpikal, -o] *adj* subtropical

subvenir [sybvənir] **subvenir à** *vt ind* to meet

subvention [sybvɑ̃sjɔ̃] *nf* subsidy, grant

subventionner [sybvɑ̃sjɔne] *vt* to subsidize

subversif, -ive [sybvɛrsif, -iv] *adj* subversive

subversion [sybvɛrsjɔ̃] *nf* subversion

suc [syk] *nm* (a) *(de fruit, de viande)* juice (b) *Fig & Litt* essence

succédané [syksedane] *nm* substitute *(de* for)

succéder [syksede] **1 succéder à** *vt ind* (a) *(personne)* to succeed, to take over from (b) *(phénomène)* **la résignation succéda à la colère** anger gave way to resignation
2 se succéder *vpr* to follow one another

succès [syksɛ] *nm* (a) success; **avoir du s. (auprès de qn)** to be successful (with sb); **avoir un s. fou (auprès de qn)** to be a big hit (with sb); **faire le s. de qn** to make sb's name; **avec s.** successfully; **sans s.** unsuccessfully; **à s.** successful (b) *(pièce, chanson)* hit, success

successeur [syksescer] *nm* successor *(de* to)

successif, -ive [syksesif, -iv] *adj* successive

succession [syksesjɔ̃] *nf* (a) *(suite)* succession (b) *(remplacement)* succession (à to); **prendre la s. de qn** to succeed sb, to take over from sb (c) *Jur (par héritage)* succession; *(biens)* inheritance

successivement [syksesivmɑ̃] *adv* successively

succinct, -e [syksɛ̃, -ɛ̃t] *adj* succinct

succinctement [syksɛ̃tmɑ̃] *adv* succinctly

succion [sysjɔ̃, syksjɔ̃] *nf* suction

succomber [sykɔ̃be] *vi* to succumb (à to); **s. sous le nombre** to yield to greater numbers

succulent, -e [sykylɑ̃, -ɑ̃t] *adj (nourriture)* succulent

succursale [sykyrsal] *nf* branch

sucer [syse] *vt* to suck

sucette [sysɛt] *nf* (a) *(confiserie)* lollipop (b) *(tétine) Br* dummy, *Am* pacifier

suçon [sysɔ̃] *nm Fam Br* lovebite, *Am* hickey

suçoter [sysɔte] *vt* to suck (at)

sucre [sykr] *nm* (a) *(aliment, morceau)* sugar; *Fig* **être tout s. tout miel** to be all sweetness and light; **s. candi** candy sugar; **s. de canne** cane sugar; **s. cristallisé** granulated sugar; **s. glace** *Br* icing or *Am* confectioner's sugar; **s. en morceaux/en poudre** lump/caster sugar; **s. roux** brown sugar; **s. semoule** caster sugar (b) **s. d'orge** *(substance)* barley sugar; *(bâton)* stick of barley sugar

sucré, -e [sykre] *adj* (a) *(naturellement)* sweet; *(additionné de sucre)* sweetened (b) *Fig (paroles, sourire)* sugary

sucrer [sykre] **1** *vt* (a) *(boisson)* to sugar; *(mets)* to sweeten; *Fam Fig* **s. les fraises** *(trembler)* to shake; *(être gâteux)* to be an old dodderer (b) *Fam (supprimer) (passage, émission)* to cut; **on lui a sucré sa prime** he has been deprived of his bonus
2 *vi (miel, aspartame)* to sweeten
3 se sucrer *vpr Fam* (a) *(prendre du sucre)* to help oneself to sugar (b) *(s'enrichir)* to line one's pockets

sucrerie [sykrəri] *nf* (a) *(usine)* sugar refinery (b) *(friandise)* **sucreries** sweet things

Sucrette® [sykrɛt] *nf* (artificial) sweetener

sucrier, -ère [sykrije, -ɛr] **1** *adj* sugar
2 *nm* (a) *(récipient)* sugar bowl; *(verseur)* sugar shaker (b) *(fabricant)* sugar manufacturer

sud [syd] **1** *nm* south; **le vent du s.** the south wind; **dans le S. de l'Angleterre** in the South of England; **au s.** in the south; **au s. de** (to the) south of; **vers le s.** south, southward
2 *adj inv* southern

sud-africain, -e (*mpl* sud-africains, *fpl* sud-africaines) [sydafrikɛ̃, -ɛn] **1** *adj* South African
2 *nm,f* S. South African

sud-américain, -e (*mpl* sud-américains, *fpl* sud-américaines) [sydamerikɛ̃, -ɛn] **1** *adj* South American
2 *nm,f* S. South American

sud-coréen, -enne (*mpl* sud-coréens, *fpl* sud-coréennes) [sudkoreɛ̃, -ɛn] **1** *adj* South Korean
2 *nm,f* S. South Korean

sud-est [sydɛst] **1** *nm* south-east; **le S. asiatique** South-east Asia
2 *adj inv* south-east

sudiste [sydist] *adj & nmf Hist* Confederate

sud-ouest [sydwɛst] *nm & adj inv* south-west

Suède [sɥɛd] *nf* **la S.** Sweden

suédine [sɥedin] *nf* suedette

suédois, -e [sɥedwa, -az] **1** *adj* Swedish
2 *nm,f* S. Swede
3 *nm (langue)* Swedish

suée [sɥe] *nf Fam* sweat; **prendre une s.** to work up a sweat

suer [sɥe] **1** *vi* (a) *(personne)* to sweat; **s. à grosses gouttes** to be pouring with sweat; *Fam* **faire s. qn** *(embêter)* to bug sb; *Fam* **se faire s.** to be bored stiff (b) *(mur)* to ooze (c) *Fig (travailler)* to labour, to sweat
2 *vt (ennui, hypocrisie)* to ooze; **s. sang et eau** to sweat blood and tears

sueur [sɥœr] *nf* sweat; **être en s.** to be sweating or in a sweat; **avoir des sueurs froides** to be in a cold sweat; **à la s. de son front** by the sweat of one's brow

suffire [syfir] **1** *vi* to be enough, to be sufficient *(à/pour* for); **ça suffit!** that's enough!, that'll do!
2 *v impersonnel* **il suffit d'appuyer sur le bouton** you just have to press the button; **il suffit que je sorte deux minutes pour que le téléphone sonne** I only have to go out for two minutes for the phone to start ringing; **il a suffi de quelques mots pour le persuader** a few words were enough to persuade him
3 se suffire *vpr* **se s. (à soi-même)** to be self-sufficient

suffisamment [syfizamɑ̃] *adv* sufficiently, enough; **s. de** sufficient, enough

suffisance [syfizɑ̃s] *nf* self-importance

suffisant, -e [syfizɑ̃, -ɑ̃t] *adj* (a) *(satisfaisant)* sufficient, enough (b) *(vaniteux)* self-important, conceited

suffixe [syfiks] *nm Gram & Ordinat* suffix

suffocant, -e [syfokɑ̃, -ɑ̃t] *adj* (a) *(chaleur)* suffocating, stifling (b) *Fig (nouvelle, réponse)* staggering, astounding

suffocation [syfokasjɔ̃] *nf* suffocation

suffoquer [syfoke] **1** *vt* (a) *(sujet: odeur, fumée, chaleur)* to suffocate (b) *Fig (sujet: nouvelles)* to stagger, to astound
2 *vi* to suffocate, to choke; *Fig* **s. de colère/d'indignation** to choke with anger/indignation

suffrage [syfraʒ] *nm (voix)* vote; *(système)* suffrage; **s. direct/indirect** direct/indirect suffrage; **s. universel** universal suffrage

suffragette [syfraʒɛt] *nf* suffragette

suggérer [syg3ere] *vt* (**a**) *(proposer)* to suggest (à to); s. de faire qch to suggest doing sth; s. à qn de faire qch to suggest to sb that he/she should do sth (**b**) *(faire penser à)* to evoke

suggestif, -ive [syg3estif, -iv] *adj* (**a**) *(ton, musique)* evocative (**b**) *(plaisanterie, geste)* suggestive

suggestion [syg3estjɔ̃] *nf* suggestion

suicidaire [sɥisidɛr] **1** *adj* suicidal
  2 *nmf* suicidal person

suicide [sɥisid] *nm* suicide

suicidé, -e [sɥiside] **1** *adj* who has committed suicide
  2 *nm,f* suicide

suicider [sɥiside] **se suicider** *vpr* to commit suicide

suie [sɥi] *nf* soot

suif [sɥif] *nm* tallow

suintant, -e [sɥɛ̃tɑ̃, -ɑ̃t-] *adj* *(rocher, mur)* oozing, dripping; *(plaie)* weeping

suintement [sɥɛ̃tmɑ̃] *nm* *(de rochers, de mur)* oozing, dripping; *(de plaie)* weeping

suinter [sɥɛ̃te] *vi* *(rocher, mur)* to ooze, to drip; *(plaie)* to weep; *(liquide)* to ooze

suis *voir* **être, suivre**

Suisse [sɥis] *nf* la S. Switzerland; la S. alémanique/ romande German-speaking/French-speaking Switzerland

suisse [sɥis] **1** *adj* Swiss
  2 *nmf* S. Swiss (person); les Suisses the Swiss
  3 *nm* *(employé d'église)* verger; Fam Fig **manger/boire qch en s.** to eat/drink without sharing it

Suissesse [sɥisɛs] *nf* Swiss (woman)

suit *voir* **suivre**

suite [sɥit] *nf* (**a**) *(reste)* rest (de of); faire s. à qch to follow on from sth; **s. à votre lettre du 11 March** further to your letter of 10th March; **donner s.** à *(demande, lettre)* to follow up; *(commande)* to deal with; *(décision)* to give effect to; **prendre la s. de** *(personne)* to take over from; *(affaires)* to take over; **à la s. (les uns des autres)** one after the other; **à la s. de cette discussion** following this discussion (**b**) *(de roman, de film)* sequel; *(nouvel épisode)* continuation; **s. à la page 30** continued on page 30; **s. et fin** concluded; **la s. au prochain numéro** continued in the next issue (**c**) *(cohérence)* coherence; **sans s.** *(paroles, pensées)* incoherent; *(parler)* incoherently; **avoir de la s. dans les idées** to be very single-minded (**d**) *(escorte)* *(d'un président)* suite; *(d'un monarque)* retinue (**e**) *(série)* series (**f**) *Math* series (**g**) *Mus* suite (**h**) *(conséquence)* consequence; **suites** *(de maladie)* aftereffects; **mourir des suites d'une blessure** to die as the result of an injury; **par s.** consequently; **par s. de qch** as a result of sth (**i**) *(appartement)* suite (**j**) *(locutions)* **de s.** in a row; **et ainsi de s.** and so on; **tout de s.**, Fam **de s.** right away, immediately; **par la s.** afterwards

suivant¹ [sɥivɑ̃] **1** *prép* (**a**) *(direction)* along (**b**) *(selon)* according to (**c**) *(conformément à)* s. son habitude as is/ was his habit
  2 *conj* s. que according to whether

suivant², -e [sɥivɑ̃, -ɑ̃t] **1** *adj* (**a**) *(page, jour)* next, following; **voir page 6 et suivantes** see page 6 and following; **notre méthode est la suivante** our method is as follows (**b**) *(personne)* next
  2 *nm,f* *(prochain)* le s., la suivante the next (one); au s.! next!
  3 *nf* suivante *(personnage de théâtre)* attendant

suiveur [sɥivœr] *nm* (**a**) *(personne sans initiative)* follower (de of) (**b**) *(dans une course cycliste)* les suiveurs = officials and back-up squads following a cycle race

suivi, -e [sɥivi] **1** *adj* (**a**) *(discours, raisonnement)* coherent (**b**) *(correspondance)* regular; *(travail, effort, qualité)* consistent (**c**) *(émission, feuilleton)* popular
  2 *nm* follow-up; **assurer le s. de qch** to follow sth through

suivre [sɥivr] **1** *vt* (**a**) *(aller derrière)* to follow; **nous sommes suivis** we're being followed; **partez, je vous suis** you go, I'll follow (on); **s. qn des yeux** *ou* **du regard** to follow sb with one's eyes (**b**) *(se placer après)* to follow, to come after (**c**) *(longer)* to go along, to follow (**d**) *(accompagner)* to go with, to accompany (**e**) *(ligne de conduite, conseil, intuition)* to follow; **s. son idée** to do things one's own way (**f**) *(comprendre)* to follow; **là je ne le suis plus** she's lost me there (**g**) *(faire attention à, observer)* *(propos, démonstration)* to follow; *(malade, élève)* to monitor the progress of; **suivez bien ce que je vais dire** pay attention to what I'm about to say; **c'est une affaire à s.** it's worth keeping an eye on (**h**) *(mode, traitement, régime)* to follow; **le mouvement** to follow the crowd; **s. l'exemple de qn** to follow sb's example; **voici la marche à s.** this is what you have to do (**i**) *(assister à)* *(série de concerts, de conférences)* to attend; *(cours)* to follow
  2 *vi* (**a**) *(venir après)* to follow; **le reste du repas suit** the rest of the meal is coming; **les personnes dont les noms suivent** the following people; **faire s. une lettre** to forward a letter; **(prière de) faire s.** *(sur une enveloppe)* please forward; **faire s. ses bagages** to have one's luggage sent on; **à s.** *(à la fin d'un feuilleton)* to be continued (**b**) *(comprendre)* to follow; *(faire attention)* to pay attention (**c**) *(classe)* to keep up (**d**) *Fig (progresser au même rythme)* *(salaire)* to keep up
  3 se suivre *vpr* to follow each other

sujet¹, -ette [syʒɛ, -ɛt] **1** *adj* **être s. à qch** *(maladie)* to be subject *or* prone to sth; **être s. à caution** to be unconfirmed; **être s. à faire qch** to be apt *or* liable to do sth
  2 *nm,f* *(d'un monarque)* subject

sujet² *nm* (**a**) *(cause)* cause (de for); **s. de querelle** *ou* **dispute** cause for dispute; **avoir s. de se plaindre** to have cause for complaint (**b**) *(thème)* subject, topic; **changer de s.** to change the subject; **au s. de qn/qch** about sb/sth; **elle ne m'a rien dit à ce s.** she said nothing to me about it; **à ce s., je voulais vous dire que...** talking of which, I meant to tell you (that)... (**c**) *Gram & Ling* subject (**d**) *(individu)* individual; *Scol* **brillant s.** brilliant pupil (**e**) *(d'une expérience)* subject

sujétion [syʒesjɔ̃] *nf Litt* (**a**) *(servitude)* subjection (à to) (**b**) *(contrainte)* constraint

sulfate [sylfat] *nm* sulphate

sulfater [sylfate] *vt Agr & Ind* to sulphate

sulfure [sylfyr] *nm* sulphide

sulfureux, -euse [sylfyrø, -øz] *adj* (**a**) *(substance)* sulphurous; *(eau, source)* sulphur (**b**) *Fig (écrits, discours)* subversive

sulfurique [sylfyrik] *adj* sulphuric

sulfurisé, -e [sylfyrize] *adj (papier)* greaseproof

sulky [sylki] *nm* sulky

sultan [syltã] *nm* sultan

sultanat [syltana] *nm* sultanate

sultane [syltan] *nf (épouse d'un sultan)* sultana, sultaness

summum [sɔmɔm] *nm* **le s. de** the height of

sumo [symo] *nm* sumo (wrestling)

sunnite [synit] *adj & nmf* Sunni

super- [syper] *préf Fam* very, *Br* dead, *Am* real

super [syper] **1** *adj inv & exclam Fam* great, terrific

2 *nm Br* four-star (petrol), *Am* premium gas; **s. sans plomb** *Br* four-star or *Am* premium unleaded

superbe [syperb] **1** *adj* (a) *(lieu, temps, spectacle)* superb, magnificent (b) *(personne)* beautiful

2 *nf Litt* pride, haughtiness

superbement [syperbəmã] *adv* superbly, magnificently

supercarburant [syperkarbyrã] *nm Br* four-star petrol, *Am* premium gasoline

supercherie [syperʃəri] *nf* deception, hoax

supérette [syperɛt] *nf* mini-market, small supermarket

superfétatoire [syperfetatwar] *adj Litt* superfluous

superficialité [syperfisjalite] *nf* superficiality

superficie [syperfisi] *nf* (a) *(étendue)* (surface) area (b) *(surface)* surface

superficiel, -elle [syperfisjɛl] *adj* superficial

superficiellement [syperfisjɛlmã] *adv* superficially

superflu, -e [syperfly] **1** *adj* superfluous

2 *nm* **le s.** the superfluous

supergrand [sypergrã] *nm* superpower

super-huit [syperqit] *adj inv & nm inv Cin* super-eight

supérieur, -e [syperjœr] **1** *adj* (a) *(plus haut)* upper; **on a dû évacuer les étages supérieurs** the upper floors had to be evacuated; **elle est à l'étage s.** she's on the floor above (b) *(plus grand)* superior (à/en to/in); **s. à la moyenne** above average (c) *(intelligence, esprit)* superior (d) *(dans une hiérarchie) (rang, grade)* higher; *(cadre)* senior; **passer dans la classe supérieure** to go up into the class above (e) *(manières, ton)* superior, condescending

2 *nm,f aussi Rel* superior

supérieurement [syperjœrmã] *adv* exceptionally

supériorité [syperjorite] *nf* superiority

superlatif, -ive [syperlatif, -iv] *adj & nm* superlative

supermarché [sypermarʃe] *nm* supermarket

supernova [sypernova] *(pl* **supernovæ** [sypernove]*) nf* supernova

superpétrolier [syperpetrolje] *nm* supertanker

superposable [syperpozabl] *adj (caisses)* stacking; *(images)* superimposable

superposé, -e [syperpoze] *adj (images)* superimposed

superposer [syperpoze] **1** *vt (caisses)* to stack; *(images)* to superimpose (à on); *Ordinat* **s. une écriture** to overwrite

2 se superposer *vpr (caisses, chaises)* to stack, to be stackable; *(images)* to be superimposed

superposition [syperpozisjɔ̃] *nf (de caisses, de chaises)* stacking; *(d'images)* superimposition; *Ordinat* **mode de s. d'écriture** overwrite mode

superproduction [syperprɔdyksjɔ̃] *nf* big-budget film

superpuissance [syperpɥisãs] *nf* superpower

supersonique [sypersɔnik] *adj* supersonic

superstar [syperstar] *nf* superstar

superstitieux, -euse [syperstisjø, -øz] *adj* superstitious

superstition [syperstisjɔ̃] *nf* superstition

supertanker [sypertãkœr] *nm* supertanker

superviser [sypervize] *vt* to supervise; *Ordinat* to control

superviseur [sypervizœr] *nm* supervisor; *Ordinat* **s. d'alimentation** power supply controller

supervision [sypervizjɔ̃] *nf* supervision

supplanter [syplãte] *vt* to supplant, to supersede

suppléance [sypleãs] *nf Br* supply or *Am* substitute post

suppléant, -e [sypleã, -ãt] **1** *adj (fonctionnaire)* acting, temporary; *(juge)* surrogate

2 *nm,f* substitute, replacement (**de** for)

suppléer [syplee] **1** *vt* (a) *(personne)* to stand in for, to replace; **se faire s.** to be replaced (b) *Litt (manque)* to supply, to make up (for)

2 suppléer à *vt ind* to make up for, to compensate for

supplément [syplemã] *nm* (a) *(surcroît)* **un s. de** *(information, travail)* additional, extra; **en s.** extra (b) *(de prix)* extra or additional charge; *(de billet de train)* supplement (c) *(livre, magazine)* supplement (d) *(de plat)* extra portion

supplémentaire [syplemãter] *adj* additional, extra

suppliant, -e [syplijã, -ãt] *adj* imploring, pleading

supplication [syplikasjɔ̃] *nf* entreaty, plea

supplice [syplis] *nm* (a) *(torture)* torture (b) *(tourment, douleur)* torture, agony; **être au s.** to be in agony; **mettre qn au s.** to torture sb

supplicié, -e [syplisje] *nm,f* victim of torture

supplier [syplije] *vt* **s. qn de faire qch** to implore or beg sb to do sth; **je vous en supplie!** I beg you!

supplique [syplik] *nf* petition

support [sypor] *nm* (a) *(étai)* support (b) *(d'outils, de lampe)* stand (c) *Fig (de communication)* medium; **s. audiovisuel** audio-visual aid; **s. publicitaire** publicity or advertising medium; **s. visuel** visual aid (d) *Ordinat* **s. d'affichage** display medium; **s. de sortie** output medium; **s. de souris** mouse support; **s. de stockage** storage medium

supportable [syportabl] *adj* (a) *(douleur)* bearable; *(comportement)* tolerable (b) *(acceptable)* reasonable

supporter¹ [syporter] *nm* supporter

supporter² [syporte] **1** *vt* (a) *(résister à) (sujet: matériau, plante)* to withstand; **je supporte bien la chaleur** I can take the heat; **il ne supporterait pas le voyage** the journey would kill him; **je ne supporte pas l'aspirine/ l'alcool** I can't take aspirin/alcohol (b) *(tolérer) (personne, situation)* to put up with; **je ne la supporte pas** I can't stand her; **il ne supporte pas qu'on le contredise** he can't stand or bear being contradicted (c) *(assumer) (conséquence, coût)* to bear (d) *(soutenir) (plafond, structure)* to support

2 se supporter *vpr (l'un l'autre)* to stand each other; **ils ne se supportent plus** they can't stand each other any more

supposé, -e [sypoze] *adj (voleur)* alleged; *(auteur)* supposed

supposer [sypoze] *vt* (a) *(imaginer)* to suppose, to assume (**que** that); **à s. que... +** *subjunctive* suppose or supposing that...; **on suppose que...** it's thought that...; **être supposé faire qch** to be supposed to do sth (b) *(impliquer)* to imply (**que** that)

supposition [sypozisjɔ̃] *nf* supposition, assumption

suppositoire [sypozitwar] *nm* suppository

suppôt [sypo] *nm* henchman; **s. de Satan** fiend

suppression [sypresjɔ̃] nf (a) (de loi, d'impôt) abolition; (de train) cancellation; (de crédits, d'emploi, de service) axing (b) (de mot, de phrase) deletion (c) Jur (de document) suppression

supprimer [syprime] **1** vt (a) (loi, impôt) to abolish; (autobus, train) to cancel; (financement, crédits) to withdraw; (emploi, service) to axe; (mot, phrase) to delete (b) Jur (document) to suppress (c) (sucre, sel) to cut out (de from) (d) (ôter) **s. qch à qn** to take sth away from sb (e) (tuer) to do away with
2 se supprimer vpr to do away with oneself

suppurer [sypyre] vi to suppurate

supputation [sypytasjɔ̃] nf calculation

supputer [sypyte] vt to calculate

supranational, -e, -aux, -ales [sypranasjɔnal, -o] adj supranational

supranationalité [sypranasjɔnalite] nf supranationality

suprématie [sypremasi] nf supremacy

suprême [syprem] **1** adj (a) (effort, bonheur) supreme (b) (dernier) final, last
2 nm Culin **s. de volaille** chicken supreme

suprêmement [sypremmɑ̃] adv supremely

sur¹ [syr] prép (a) (dessus) on; (avec mouvement) on, onto; **s. la photo** in the picture; **regarder s. la carte** to look at the map; **la clef est s. la porte** the key's in the door; aussi Fig **les uns s. les autres** on top of each other
(b) (au-dessus de) over, above; **un pont s. une rivière** a bridge over or across a river
(c) (vers) towards; **fenêtre qui donne s. le jardin** window which looks onto the garden; **la police a tiré s. la foule** the police fired at the crowd; **s. la droite/gauche** on or to the right/left
(d) (à propos de) on, about; **savoir qch s. qn** to know sth about sb
(e) (parmi) out of; **7 s. 10** 7 out of 10; **une fois s. deux** every other time; **une femme s. deux** one in two women
(f) (mesure) by; **10 mètres s. 2** 10 metres by 2; **virages s. 2 kilomètres** (sur un panneau) bends for 2 kilometres
(g) (avec) vivre **s. ses économies** to live on or off one's savings; **s. des paroles de Prévert/une musique des Beatles** to words by Prévert/Beatles music; **ne me parle pas s. ce ton!** don't talk to me in that tone of voice!

sur², -e [syr] adj (fruit) sour

sur- [syr] préf over-

sûr, -e [syr] adj (a) (lieu) safe; **peu s.** unsafe (b) (digne de confiance) (personne, mémoire) trustworthy, reliable; (ami) true; (information, entreprise, goût) reliable (c) (certain) sure, certain (de of); **je suis s. de l'avoir dit** I'm sure I told you; **s. de soi** self-assured; **être s. et certain (de qch)** to be absolutely certain (of sth)
2 nm **le plus s. serait de...** the safest thing would be to...

surabondance [syrabɔ̃dɑ̃s] nf overabundance; **une s. de richesses/de détails** a wealth of riches/details

surabondant, -e [syrabɔ̃dɑ̃, -ɑ̃t] adj overabundant

surabonder [syrabɔ̃de] vi to be overabundant

suractivé, -e [syraktive] adj superactivated

surajouter [syraʒute] **1** vt to add (on)
2 se surajouter vpr to be added (on)

suralimentation [syralimɑ̃tasjɔ̃] nf (de personne) overfeeding; (de malade) feeding up

suralimenter [syralimɑ̃te] vt (personne) to overfeed; (malade) to feed up

suranné, -e [syrane] adj outdated, old-fashioned

surarmement [syrarməmɑ̃] nm excessive arms build-up

surbooker [syrbuke] vt to overbook

surcapacité [syrkapasite] nf overcapacity

surcharge [syrʃarʒ] nf (a) (poids) (de bagages) excess weight; (de véhicule) excess load; **prendre des passagers en s.** to take on excess passengers; **rouler en s.** to drive an overloaded vehicle; Méd **s. pondérale** excess weight (b) (action) (de véhicule) overloading (c) (d'accumulateur électrique) overcharge (d) Fig **une s. de travail** excess work (e) (à payer) surcharge (f) (correction) correction

surcharger [syrʃarʒe] vt (a) (véhicule, cheval, estomac) to overload; **s. qn de travail** to overload sb with work (b) (accumulateur électrique) to overcharge (c) (épreuves, texte) to write over with corrections

surchauffe [syrʃof] nf overheating

surchauffer [syrʃofe] vt & vi to overheat

surchoix [syrʃwa] adj inv top-quality

surclasser [syrklase] vt to outclass

surconsommation [syrkɔ̃sɔmasjɔ̃] nf overconsumption

surcroît [syrkrwa] nm **un s. de travail/dépenses** extra work/expenditure; **par s., de s.** in addition, moreover

surdéveloppé, -e [syrdevlɔpe] adj overdeveloped

surdéveloppement [syrdevlɔpmɑ̃] nm overdevelopment

surdité [syrdite] nf deafness

surdose [syrdoz] nf overdose

surdoué, -e [syrdwe] **1** adj gifted
2 nm,f gifted child

sureau, -x [syro] nm elder (tree)

sureffectif [syrefektif] nm overmanning; **en s.** surplus

surélevé, -e [syrelve] adj (a) (voie ferrée) elevated (b) (arche, rez-de-chaussée) raised

surélever [syrelve] vt to heighten, to raise

sûrement [syrmɑ̃] adv (a) (probablement) probably (b) (absolument) **s.!** certainly!; **s. pas!** certainly not! (c) (sans risque) safely

suremploi [syrɑ̃plwa] nm overemployment

surenchère [syrɑ̃ʃɛr] nf (dans une vente) higher bid; Fig **faire de la s.** to try to outdo one's rivals

surenchérir [syrɑ̃ʃerir] vi to bid higher; **s. sur qn** to outbid sb; Fig to go one further than sb

surencombré, -e [syrɑ̃kɔ̃bre] adj congested (de with)

surendetté, -e [syrɑ̃dete] adj overindebted

surendettement [syrɑ̃dɛtmɑ̃] nm overindebtedness

surentraîner [syrɑ̃trene] vt to overtrain

suréquipement [syrekipmɑ̃] nm overequipment

suréquiper [syrekipe] vt to overequip

surestimer [syrɛstime] **1** vt (a) (importance, capacité, personne) to overestimate (b) (œuvre d'art) to overvalue
2 se surestimer vpr to overestimate oneself

sûreté [syrte] nf (a) (absence de danger) safety; **être en s.** to be safe; **mettre qch en s.** to put sth in a safe place; **pour plus de s.** to be on the safe side; **de s.** (rasoir, épingle) safety (b) (du goût, du jugement) soundness (c) (d'un pays) security; **la s. de l'État** national security

surévaluation [syrevalɥasjɔ̃] nf overvaluation

surévaluer [syrevalɥe] vt (objet, antiquité) to overvalue; (efficacité, capacités) to overestimate

surexcitation [syrɛksitasjɔ̃] nf overexcitement

surexciter [syrɛksite] vt to overexcite

surexploiter [syrɛksplwate] vt to overexploit

surexposer [syrɛkspoze] vt to overexpose

surexposition [syrɛkspozisjɔ̃] nf overexposure

surf [sœrf] nm surfing; **faire du s.** to go surfing, to surf

surface [syrfas] nf (a) (partie extérieure) surface; **en s.** on the surface; Fig superficially; **remonter à la s.** to rise to the surface, to surface; **faire s.** (remonter, se réveiller) to surface (b) (étendue) (surface) area; **grande s.** hypermarket; **s. de réparation** (au football) penalty area; **s. au sol** floor area; **s. utile** floor space; **s. de vente** sales area (c) Ordinat **s. d'affichage** display area; **s. d'enregistrement** read-write surface

surfait, -e [syrfɛ, -ɛt] adj overrated

surfer [sœrfe] vi to surf

surfeur, -euse [sœrfœr, -øz] nm,f surfer

surfiler [syrfile] vt (vêtement) to overcast, to oversew

surfin, -e [syrfɛ̃, -in] adj superfine

surgelé, -e [syrʒəle] **1** adj frozen
2 nmpl **surgelés** frozen foods

surgeler [syrʒəle] vt to freeze

surgénérateur [syrʒeneratœr] nm breeder reactor

surgir [syrʒir] vi (personne) to appear suddenly; (difficulté) to crop up

surhomme [syrɔm] nm superman

surhumain, -e [syrymɛ̃, -ɛn] adj superhuman

surimposer [syrɛ̃poze] vt to overtax

surimposition [syrɛ̃pozisjɔ̃] nf overtaxation

surimpression [syrɛ̃presjɔ̃] nf (a) (d'images) superimposition; **en s.** superimposed (b) Ordinat overprinting, overstrike

Surinam(e) [syrinam] nm le S. Surinam

surinfection [syrɛ̃fɛksjɔ̃] nf secondary infection

surinformation [syrɛ̃fɔrmasjɔ̃] nf overinformation

surinformé, -e [syrɛ̃fɔrme] adj overinformed

sur-le-champ [syrləʃɑ̃] adv at once, immediately

surlendemain [syrlɑ̃dmɛ̃] nm **le s.** two days later; **le s. de leur départ** two days after they left

surligner [syrliɲe] vt to highlight

surligneur [syrliɲœr] nm highlighter (pen)

surlouer [syrlwe] vt to overbook

surmenage [syrmənaʒ] nm overwork; **s. intellectuel** mental strain

surmené, -e [syrməne] adj overworked

surmener [syrməne] **1** vt to overwork
2 se surmener vpr to overdo it

surmonter [syrmɔ̃te] **1** vt (a) (être placé sur) to surmount (b) Fig (obstacle, difficulté) to overcome
2 se surmonter vpr to control oneself

surnager [syrnaʒe] vi to float (on the surface)

surnaturel, -elle [syrnatyrɛl] **1** adj supernatural
2 le s. the supernatural

surnom [syrnɔ̃] nm nickname

surnombre [syrnɔ̃br] nm **il y avait trois passagers en s.** there were three passengers too many; **les exemplaires/passagers en s.** the excess copies/passengers

surnommer [syrnɔme] vt to nickname

surpasser [syrpase] **1** vt (rival) to surpass, to outdo
2 se surpasser vpr to surpass or excel oneself

surpayer [syrpeje] vt (personne) to overpay; (activité) to pay too much for

surpeuplé, -e [syrpœple] adj (pays, région) overpopulated; (plage) overcrowded

surpeuplement [syrpœpləmɑ̃] nm (de pays, de région) overpopulation; (de plage) overcrowding

surplace [syrplas] nm **faire du s.** (cycliste) to balance; Fig (automobiliste) to crawl along; (dans une carrière, dans des négociations) to make no headway

surplomb [syrplɔ̃] nm overhang; **en s.** overhanging

surplomber [syrplɔ̃be] vt to overhang

surplus [syrply] nm surplus; **le s. de marchandises** the surplus goods, the goods that are left (over)

surpopulation [syrpɔpylasjɔ̃] nf overpopulation

surprenant, -e [syrprənɑ̃, -ɑ̃t] adj surprising; **et, chose surprenante,...** and surprisingly,...

surprendre [syrprɑ̃dr] **1** vt (a) (prendre par surprise) to surprise; **s. qn en train de faire qch** to catch sb doing sth; **être surpris par la pluie** to be caught in the rain (b) (découvrir) (conversation) to overhear; (regard) to catch (c) (étonner) to surprise; **cela me surprendrait qu'il revienne ou s'il revenait** I'd be surprised if he came back
2 se surprendre vpr **se s. à faire qch** to find oneself doing sth

surpris, -e [syrpri, -iz] adj surprised; **être s. de qch/de faire qch** to be surprised at sth/to do sth

surprise [syrpriz] nf surprise; **à sa grande s.** to her great surprise, much to her surprise; **à la s. générale** to everyone's surprise; **sans s.** (expédition, voyage) uneventful; **prendre qn par s.** to take sb by surprise

surprise-partie [pl surprises-parties] [syrprizparti] nf Vieilli party

surproduction [syrprɔdyksjɔ̃] nf overproduction

surréalisme [syrrealism] nm surrealism

surréaliste [syrrealist] adj & nmf surrealist

sursaut [syrso] nm (a) (mouvement) start, jump; **en s.** with a start (b) (regain) (d'énergie) burst

sursauter [syrsote] vi to start, to jump; **faire s. qn** to make sb jump, to startle sb

surseoir [syrswar] **surseoir à** vt ind (jugement) to suspend; **s. à l'exécution d'un condamné** to reprieve a condemned man

sursis [syrsi] nm (a) (d'exécution) & Fig reprieve; **un an de prison avec s.** a one-year suspended sentence (b) (de conscrit) deferment of call-up

sursitaire [syrsiter] **1** adj (conscrit) provisionally exempted
2 nm provisionally exempted conscript

surtaxe [syrtaks] nf (de lettre) surcharge

surtout [syrtu] adv (a) (particulièrement) particularly, especially; Fam **s. que...** especially as... (b) (avant tout) above all; **s. pas!** certainly not!

surveillance [syrvejɑ̃s] *nf (de travail, d'élèves)* supervision; *(par la police, par un gardien)* surveillance, observation; *(de malade, de phénomène)* watch; **être sous s.** to be under surveillance; **s. médicale** medical supervision

surveillant, -e [syrvejɑ̃, -ɑ̃t] *nm,f* **(a)** *(d'une prison)* guard, Br warder **(b)** *(d'un hôpital)* supervisor **(c)** *Scol (pendant les examens)* invigilator; *(chargé de la discipline)* supervisor

surveiller [syrveje] **1** *vt* **(a)** *(contrôler) (travail, élèves)* to supervise; *(température, cuisson)* to keep a watch on; *(examen)* to invigilate **(b)** *(prendre soin de)* to watch (over) **(c)** *(situation)* to keep an eye on; **s. son langage** to watch or mind one's language; **s. sa ligne** to watch one's figure
2 se surveiller *vpr* to keep a watch on oneself

survenir [syrvənir] *vi (événements)* to occur; *(crise, difficulté)* to arise

survêt [syrvɛt] *nm Fam* = **survêtement**

survêtement [syrvɛtmɑ̃] *nm* tracksuit

survie [syrvi] *nf* survival

survivance [syrvivɑ̃s] *nf (vestige)* survival, relic

survivant, -e [syrvivɑ̃, -ɑ̃t] **1** *adj* surviving
2 *nm,f* survivor

survivre [syrvivr] **survivre à** *vt ind (personne)* to survive, to outlive; *(période, théorie)* to outlive; *(accident, maladie)* to survive

survol [syrvɔl] *nm* **(a)** **le s. d'un lieu** flying over a place **(b)** *Fig (de problème, de question)* cursory glance (**de** at)

survoler [syrvɔle] *vt* **(a)** *(lieu)* to fly over **(b)** *Fig (problème, question)* to skim over

survolté, -e [syrvɔlte] *adj Fam (personne)* overexcited; *(ambiance)* highly charged

sus [sys, sy] **1** *exclam* **s. à l'ennemi!** at them!
2 *adv* **en s.** in addition; **en s. de** in addition to, over and above

susceptibilité [syseptibilite] *nf* touchiness, sensitivity; **ménager la s. de qn** to tread carefully where sb is concerned

susceptible [syseptibl] *adj* **(a)** *(ombrageux)* touchy, sensitive **(b)** **s. de** *(interprétations, critiques)* open to; **être s. de faire qch** to be liable *or* likely to do sth

susciter [sysite] *vt (ennuis, problèmes)* to cause, to create; *(étonnement)* to cause; *(hostilité, intérêt)* to arouse; *(admiration, commentaires)* to attract

susdit, -e [sysdi, -it] *adj* aforesaid, above-mentioned

susmentionné, -e [sysmɑ̃sjɔne] *adj* above-mentioned, aforesaid

susnommé, -e [sysnɔme] *adj & nm,f* above-named

suspect, -e [syspɛ(kt), -ɛkt] **1** *adj (personne, action)* suspicious, suspect; *(idées, preuve, aliment)* suspect; **s. de qch** suspected of sth
2 *nm,f* suspect

suspecter [syspɛkte] *vt (personne)* to suspect (**de** of); *(sincérité)* to suspect, to question

suspendre [syspɑ̃dr] **1** *vt* **(a)** *(vêtements, tableau, hamac)* to hang (up); **s. qch au mur/au plafond** to hang sth on the wall/from the ceiling **(b)** *(interrompre)* to suspend; *(séance)* to adjourn **(c)** *(démettre de ses fonctions)* to suspend
2 se suspendre *vpr* to hang (**à** from)

suspendu, -e [syspɑ̃dy] *adj* **(a)** *(pendu)* hanging; **s. au mur/au plafond** hanging on the wall/from the ceiling; *Fig* **être s. aux lèvres de qn** to be hanging on sb's every word **(b)** *(interrompu)* suspended; *(séance)* adjourned

suspens [syspɑ̃] **en suspens** *adv* **(a)** *(en l'air)* suspended **(b)** *(en attente)* outstanding

suspense [syspɛns] *nm* suspense

suspension [syspɑ̃sjɔ̃] *nf* **(a)** *(de négociations, d'un travail)* suspension; *(d'une séance)* adjournment **(b)** *(retrait)* **s. du permis de conduire** driving ban **(c)** *(mise à pied)* suspension **(d)** *(de voiture)* suspension

suspicieux, -euse [syspisjø, -øz] *adj* suspicious

suspicion [syspisjɔ̃] *nf* suspicion

sustenter [systɑ̃te] **se sustenter** *vpr Hum* to take sustenance

susurrer [sysyre] *vt & vi* to whisper, to murmur

suture [sytyr] *nf* suture; **point de s.** stitch

suzerain, -e [syzrɛ̃, -ɛn] *nm,f* suzerain

svastika [svastika] *nm* swastika

svelte [svɛlt] *adj* slender

sveltesse [svɛltɛs] *nf* slenderness

SVP [ɛsvepe] *(abrév* **s'il vous plaît)** please

swahili, -e [swaili] **1** *adj* Swahili
2 *nm (langue)* Swahili

Swaziland [swazilɑ̃d] *nm* **le S.** Swaziland

sweat-shirt [swit∫œrt, swɛt∫œrt] *(pl* **sweat-shirts)** *nm* sweatshirt

swing [swiŋ] *nm* swing

swinguer [swiŋɡe] *vi* to swing

sycomore [sikɔmɔr] *nm* sycamore (tree)

syllabe [silab] *nf* syllable

syllabique [silabik] *adj* syllabic

sylphide [silfid] *nf* sylph

sylvestre [silvɛstr] *adj* woodland

sylviculture [silvikyltyr] *nf* forestry

symbiose [sɛ̃bjoz] *nf* symbiosis; *Fig* **en s. avec qn/qch** in harmony with sb/sth

symbole [sɛ̃bɔl] *nm* symbol

symbolique [sɛ̃bɔlik] **1** *adj* symbolic; *(paiement, geste)* token
2 *nf (système de symboles)* system of symbols

symboliquement [sɛ̃bɔlikmɑ̃] *adv* symbolically

symboliser [sɛ̃bɔlize] *vt* to symbolize

symbolisme [sɛ̃bɔlism] *nm* symbolism

symétrie [simetri] *nf* symmetry

symétrique [simetrik] *adj* symmetrical

symétriquement [simetrikmɑ̃] *adv* symmetrically

sympa [sɛ̃pa] *adj Fam* nice

sympathie [sɛ̃pati] *nf (a) (affinité)* liking; **avoir *ou* éprouver de la s. pour qn** to like sb; **inspirer la s.** to be likable **(b)** *(compassion, condoléances)* sympathy

sympathique [sɛ̃patik] *adj* **(a)** *(agréable)* nice **(b)** *Anat* sympathetic

sympathisant, -e [sɛ̃patizɑ̃, -ɑ̃t] *nm,f* sympathizer

sympathiser [sɛ̃patize] *vi* to get on well (**avec** with)

symphonie [sɛ̃fɔni] *nf* symphony

symphonique [sɛ̃fɔnik] *adj (forme, poème)* symphonic; *(orchestre)* symphony

symposium [sɛ̃pozjɔm] *nm* symposium

symptomatique [sɛ̃ptɔmatik] *adj* symptomatic (**de** of)

symptôme [sɛ̃ptom] *nm* symptom

synagogue [sinaɡɔɡ] *nf* synagogue

synchrone [sɛ̃krɔn] *adj* synchronous (**avec** with)

synchronisation [sɛ̃krɔnizasjɔ̃] *nf* synchronization

synchroniser [sɛ̃krɔnize] *vt* to synchronize (avec with)

synclinal, -e, -aux, -ales [sɛ̃klinal, -o] *adj* synclinal

syncope [sɛ̃kɔp] *nf* (a) *(perte de connaissance)* blackout; **tomber en s.** to black out; *Fam* **elle a failli avoir une s.** she nearly fainted (b) *Mus* syncopation

syncopé, -e [sɛ̃kɔpe] *adj Mus* syncopated

syndic [sɛ̃dik] *nm* **s. (de copropriété)** property manager

syndical, -e, -aux, -ales [sɛ̃dikal, -o] *adj* (*Br* trade or *Am* labor) union

syndicaliser [sɛ̃dikalize] = **syndiquer**

syndicalisme [sɛ̃dikalism] *nm* (a) *(mouvement) Br* trade or *Am* labor unionism (b) *(activité)* **faire du s.** to be involved in union activities

syndicaliste [sɛ̃dikalist] 1 *adj Br* (trade) union, *Am* (labor) union
2 *nmf Br* trade or *Am* labor unionist

syndicat [sɛ̃dika] *nm* (a) *(de travailleurs)* (*Br* trade or *Am* labor) union (b) *(d'employeurs, de producteurs)* association; **s. patronal** employers' association (c) **s. d'initiative** tourist (information) office

syndiqué, -e [sɛ̃dike] 1 *adj* belonging to a (*Br* trade or *Am* labor) union; **être s.** to belong to a (*Br* trade or *Am* labor) union
2 *nm,f* (*Br* trade or *Am* labor) union member

syndiquer [sɛ̃dike] 1 *vt* to unionize
2 **se syndiquer** *vpr* (a) *(se constituer en syndicat)* to form a (*Br* trade or *Am* labor) union (b) *(adhérer à un syndicat)* to join a (*Br* trade or *Am* labor) union

syndrome [sɛ̃drom] *nm* syndrome

synergie [sinɛrʒi] *nf* synergy

synode [sinɔd] *nm* synod

synonyme [sinɔnim] 1 *adj* synonymous (**de** with)
2 *nm* synonym

synopsis [sinɔpsis] *nm Cin* synopsis

synovial, -e, -aux, -ales [sinɔvjal, -o] *adj* synovial

syntagme [sɛ̃tagm] *nm* phrase

syntaxe [sɛ̃taks] *nf Gram & Ordinat* syntax

syntaxique [sɛ̃taksik] *adj* (a) *Gram* syntactic (b) *Ordinat* syntax

synthèse [sɛ̃tɛz] *nf* (a) *(exposé)* summary; **faire la s.** (**de qch**) to summarize (sth) (b) *(opération chimique)* synthesis; **de s.** synthetic

synthétique [sɛ̃tetik] 1 *adj* (a) *(présentation)* all-encompassing; *(bilan)* summary (b) *(tissu, fibres)* synthetic, man-made
2 *nm* synthetic material

synthétiser [sɛ̃tetize] *vt* to synthesize

synthétiseur [sɛ̃tetizœr] *nm* synthesizer

syphilis [sifilis] *nf* syphilis

syphilitique [sifilitik] *adj & nmf* syphilitic

Syrie [siri] *nf* la S. Syria

syrien, -enne [sirjɛ̃, -ɛn] 1 *adj* Syrian
2 *nm,f* S. Syrian

systématique [sistematik] 1 *adj* *(automatique, méthodique)* systematic; **il est toujours en retard, c'est s.** he's consistently late

systématiquement [sistematikmɑ̃] *adv* systematically

systématiser [sistematize] *vt* to systematize

système [sistɛm] *nm* system; *Fam* **il me tape** *ou* **porte sur le s.** he gets on my nerves; **s. D** resourcefulness; *Ordinat* **s. d'exploitation** operating system; *Ordinat* **s. de gestion de bases de données** database management system; **s. nerveux** nervous system; **s. solaire** solar system

T

T, t [te] *nm inv* T; *en* T T-shaped; **disposer qch en T** to arrange sth in a T-shape

t' [t] *voir* **te, tu**

ta [ta] *voir* **ton¹**

tabac¹ [taba] **1** *nm* (a) *(plante, produit)* tobacco; *Fig* **du même t.** of the same ilk; **t. blond** Virginia tobacco; **t. brun** dark tobacco; **t. à chiquer** chewing tobacco; **t. à priser** snuff (b) *(boutique)* **(bureau de) t.** *Br* tobacconist's (shop), *Am* tobacco store (which also sells stamps, phonecards and lottery tickets)
2 *adj inv* buff

tabac² *nm* **coup de t.** *(tempête)* squall; *Fam* **passer qn à t.** to beat sb up; *Fam* **faire un t.** to be a big hit

tabagie [tabaʒi] *nf* (a) *Fam* **c'est une vraie t. ici** you can't see a thing for the smoke in here (b) *Can (bureau de tabac) Br* tobacconist's (shop), *Am* tobacco store

tabagisme [tabaʒism] *nm* smoking

tabasser [tabase] *vt Fam* **t. qn** to beat sb up; **se faire t.** to be or get beaten up

tabatière [tabatjɛr] *nf* (a) *(boîte)* snuffbox (b) *(lucarne)* skylight

tabernacle [tabɛrnakl] *nm* tabernacle

table [tabl] *nf* (a) *(meuble)* table; **mettre** *ou* **dresser la t.** to lay or set the table; **être à t.** to be at the table; **se mettre** *ou* **passer à t.** to sit down at the table; *Fam Fig* **se mettre à t.** *(avouer)* to spill the beans; **à t.!** food's ready!; *Fig* **faire t. rase de qch** to make a clean sweep of sth; **t. basse** coffee table; **t. de billard** billiard table; **t. de chevet** bedside table; **t. de cuisson** hob; **t. à dessin** drawing board; **faire t. d'hôte** = to provide a meal where all paying guests eat at the same table; **t. de jeu** card table; **t. à langer** changing table; **t. de nuit** bedside table; **t. d'opération** operating table; **t. d'orientation** orientation or panoramic table; **t. à repasser** ironing board; **t. ronde** *(conférence)* round table; **t. roulante** trolley (b) *(restaurant)* **les meilleures tables de Paris** the finest restaurants in Paris (c) *(écrit)* table; **Tables de la Loi** Tables of the Law; **t. des matières** (table of) contents; **t. de multiplication** multiplication table (d) *(console)* **mettre qn sur t. d'écoute** to tap sb's phone; **il est sur t. d'écoute** his phone is being tapped; **t. de mixage** mixing desk (e) *(d'un instrument à cordes)* **t. d'harmonie** sounding board (f) *Ordinat* **t. à digitaliser** digitizing tab; **t. des fichiers** file allocation table, FAT; **t. traçante** plotter

tableau, -x [tablo] *nm* (a) *(panneau, support)* board; **t. (noir)** (black)board; **t. d'affichage** *Br* notice or *Am* bulletin board; **t. de bord** dashboard; *(d'un avion)* instrument panel; *Ordinat* control panel (b) *(œuvre d'art)* painting, picture; **t. de maître** old master (c) *Fig & Hum (scène)* scene; **faire un joli/charmant t.** to make a pretty/charming sight or scene; *Fig* **pour compléter le t.,...** to crown it all,... (d) *(au théâtre)* scene; **t. vivant** tableau (vivant) (e) *(liste)* list, table; *(graphique)* chart; **t. de chasse** *(de chasseur, d'aviateur)* bag; *Fig (conquêtes)* list of conquests (f) *Ordinat* spreadsheet (g) *(locutions)* **gagner sur les deux/sur tous les tableaux** to win on both/all counts

tablée [table] *nf (personnes à table)* table

tabler [table] **tabler sur** *vt ind* to count or bank on

tablette [tablɛt] *nf* (a) *(d'une étagère)* shelf; *(dans un avion)* table; **t. arrière** *(d'une voiture)* back shelf (b) *(de chocolat)* bar; *(de chewing-gum)* stick

tableur [tablœr] *nm Ordinat* spreadsheet; **t. de graphiques** graphics spreadsheet

tablier [tablije] *nm* (a) *(vêtement)* apron; *(d'écolier)* smock; *Fig* **rendre son t.** to hand in one's notice (b) *(de cheminée)* hood (c) *(de pont)* roadway

tabloïd(e) [tabloid] *adj & nm* tabloid

tabou, -e [tabu] *adj & nm* taboo

taboulé [tabule] *nm* tabbouleh

tabouret [taburɛ] *nm* stool; **t. de bar/de piano** bar/piano stool

tabulateur [tabylatœr] *nm* tab key, tabulator

tabulation [tabylasjɔ̃] *nf* tab

tac [tak] *nm* **du tac au tac** *adv* like a shot

tache [taʃ] *nf* (a) *(de boue, de sang, d'huile)* stain; *(de peinture, de couleur, de lumière)* splash; **tu as fait une t. à ta chemise** you've got a stain on your shirt; *Fig* **faire t. à** to stick out like a sore thumb; **t. d'encre** inkstain; *Fig* **faire t. d'huile** to spread (b) *(sur la peau)* mark; **t. de rousseur** freckle; **t. de vin** strawberry mark (c) *Fig (atteinte)* blot, stain; **sans t.** *(réputation)* spotless

taché, -e [taʃe] *adj* stained; **t. d'encre/de sang** ink-/blood-stained

tâche [taʃ] *nf* task, job; **être à la t.** to be on piecework; *Ordinat* **t. d'arrière-plan** *ou* **de fond** background task or job

tacher [taʃe] **1** *vt* (a) *(vêtement)* to stain (b) *(réputation)* to sully, to tarnish
2 *vi* to stain
3 **se tacher** *vpr (personne)* to stain one's clothes; *(tissu, vêtement)* to stain

tâcher [taʃe] **1** *vt* **tâchez que cela ne se reproduise plus** make sure it doesn't happen again
2 **tâcher de** *vt ind* to try to

tâcheron [taʃrɔ̃] *nm Péj* drudge

tacheté, -e [taʃte] *adj* speckled **(de** with); **chat noir t. de blanc** black cat with white markings

tacheter [taʃte] *vt* to spot, to speckle

tachycardie [takikardi] *nf* tachycardia

tachymètre [takimɛtr] *nm* tachometer; *Aut* speed-ometer

tacite [tasit] *adj* tacit

tacitement [tasitmɑ̃] *adv* tacitly

taciturne [tasityrn] *adj* taciturn

tacot [tako] *nm Fam Péj* jalopy, *Br* banger

tact [takt] *nm* tact; **avoir du t.** to be tactful; **plein de t.** very tactful; **manquer de t.** to be tactless

tacticien, -enne [taktisjɛ̃, -ɛn] *nm,f* tactician

tactile [taktil] *adj* tactile

tactique [taktik] **1** *adj* tactical
2 *nf* tactics

tadjik [tadʒik] **1** *adj* Tadjik
2 *nmf* T. Tadjik

Tadjikistan [tadʒikistɑ̃] *nm* **le T.** Tadjikistan

taffetas [tafta] *nm* taffeta

tag [tag] *nm* tag (*piece of graffiti*)

Tage [taʒ] *nm* **le T.** the Tagus

tagliatelle [taljatɛl] *nf* piece *or* strand of tagliatelle; **des tagliatelles** tagliatelle

taguer [tage] *vt* to cover in graffiti

tagueur, -euse [tagœr, -øz] *nm,f* tagger (*graffiti artist*)

Tahiti [taiti] *n* Tahiti

tahitien, -enne [taisjɛ̃, -ɛn] **1** *adj* Tahitian
2 *nm,f* T. Tahitian
3 *nm* (*langue*) Tahitian

taie [tɛ] *nf* **(a)** (*enveloppe*) **t. (d'oreiller)** pillowcase, pillowslip **(b)** (*sur l'œil*) leucoma

taïga [taiga] *nf* taiga

taillader [tajade] *vt* to slash, to gash

taille [taj] *nf* **(a)** (*dimensions*) size; **une pêche de la t. d'un melon** a peach the size of a melon; **quelle t. faites-vous?** what size are you?, what size do you take?; **la t. en dessus/dessous** the next size up/down; **t. unique** one size **(b)** (*hauteur*) height; **de petite t.** short; *Fig* **être de t. à faire qch** to be capable of doing sth; **trouver un adversaire à sa t.** to meet one's match **(c)** (*importance*) **de t.** (*erreur, mensonge*) big **(d)** (*partie du corps, sur un vêtement*) waist; **avoir la t. fine** to have a slim waist; **avoir une t. de guêpe** to be wasp-waisted **(e)** (*action*) (*de pierre*) cutting; (*d'un arbre*) pruning; (*d'une haie*) trimming **(f)** *Ordinat* **t. de champ** field size; **t. de disque dur** hard disk size; **t. de mémoire** memory size **(g)** *Hist* (*impôt*) tallage

taillé, -e [taje] *adj* **être t. pour faire qch** to be cut out to do sth

taille-crayon (*pl* **taille-crayon** *ou* **taille-crayons**) [tajkrɛjɔ̃] *nm* pencil sharpener

tailler [taje] **1** *vt* **(a)** (*pierre, diamant*) to cut; (*arbre, vigne*) to prune; (*haie, barbe*) to trim; (*crayon*) to sharpen; **t. une armée en pièces** to cut an army to pieces **(b)** (*vêtement*) to cut out
2 se tailler *vpr* **(a)** (*se couper*) **se t. la barbe** to trim one's beard **(b)** (*se faire*) **se t. un chemin à travers qch** to carve one's way through sth **(c)** (*s'attribuer*) **se t. un beau succès** to be very successful; **se t. un empire** to carve out an empire for oneself **(d)** *Fam* (*partir*) to beat it

tailleur [tajœr] *nm* **(a)** (*couturier*) tailor **(b)** (*ensemble pour femme*) suit **(c)** **s'asseoir en t.** to sit cross-legged

tailleur-pantalon (*pl* **tailleurs-pantalons**) [tajœr-pɑ̃talɔ̃] *nm Br* trouser *or* Am pant suit

taillis [taji] *nm* copse, coppice

tain [tɛ̃] *nm* silvering; **glace** *ou* **miroir sans t.** two-way mirror

taire [tɛr] **1** *vt* (*affaire, secret*) to say nothing about, not to mention; (*vérité*) to hide; **une personne dont je tairai le nom** a person who shall remain nameless
2 se taire *vpr* **(a)** (*être silencieux*) to be quiet *or* silent; (*cesser de parler*) to stop talking, to fall silent; (*décider de ne rien dire*) to keep quiet *or* silent; **tais-toi!** be quiet!; **faire t. qn** to make sb be quiet; (*adversaire, critique*) to silence; **tu as perdu une occasion de te t.** you should have kept your mouth shut **(b)** (*bruit*) to stop

taisais, taise *etc voir* **taire**

Taiwan [tajwan] *n* Taiwan

taiwanais, -e [tajwanɛ, -ɛz] **1** *adj* Taiwanese
2 *nm,f* T. Taiwanese

tajine [taʒin] *nm* tajine

talc [talk] *nm* talcum powder, talc

talé, -e [tale] *adj* bruised

talent [talɑ̃] *nm* **(a)** (*don*) talent; **son t. de pianiste** his talent as a pianist; **homme/musicien de t.** talented man/musician; **avoir du t.** to be talented **(b)** (*artiste*) **un jeune t.** a talented newcomer

talentueusement [talɑ̃tɥøzmɑ̃] *adv* with talent

talentueux, -euse [talɑ̃tɥø, -øz] *adj* talented

talion [taljɔ̃] *nm voir* **loi**

talisman [talismɑ̃] *nm* talisman

talkie-walkie (*pl* **talkies-walkies**) [tokiwoki] *nm* walkie-talkie

Tallinn [talin] *n* Tallin

Talmud [talmyd] *nm* **le T.** the Talmud

taloche [talɔʃ] *nf Fam* (*gifle*) clout

talon [talɔ̃] *nm* **(a)** (*du pied, de chaussure, de bas*) heel; *Fig* **être sur les talons de qn** to be on sb's heels; **t. d'Achille** Achilles' heel; **talons aiguilles** stiletto heels; (*chaussures*) stilettos; **talons hauts** high heels; **talons plats** flat heels **(b)** (*de chèque*) stub, counterfoil **(c)** (*aux cartes*) stock

talonner [talone] **1** *vt* **(a)** (*suivre*) **t. qn** to follow on sb's heels **(b)** (*cheval*) to spur on
2 *vi* (*au rugby*) to heel

talonnette [talonɛt] *nf* (*dans une chaussure*) heel pad

talonneur [talonœr] *nm* hooker

talquer [talke] *vt* to put talcum powder on

talus [taly] *nm* **(a)** (*terrain en pente*) slope **(b)** (*d'une voie ferrée, d'un canal*) embankment

tamanoir [tamanwar] *nm* great anteater

tamaris [tamaris] *nm* tamarisk

tambouille [tɑ̃buj] *nf Fam* (*cuisine*) cooking; **faire la t.** to do the cooking **(b)** (*nourriture*) grub

tambour [tɑ̃bur] *nm* **(a)** (*instrument de musique*) drum; **sans t. ni trompette** quietly, without any fuss; **faire qch t. battant** to do sth briskly **(b)** (*personne*) drummer **(c)** (*d'une machine à laver*) drum; **t. de frein** brake drum **(d)** (*à broder*) (*embroidery*) hoop, tambour

tambourin [tɑ̃burɛ̃] *nm* (*instrument plat*) tambourine; (*tambour*) tambourine

tambouriner [tɑ̃burine] **1** *vi* to drum
2 *vt* to drum out

tamis [tami] *nm* (*pour la farine*) sieve; (*pour le sable*) sifter; **passer au t.** (*farine*) to sieve; (*sable*) to sift

Tamise [tamiz] *nf* **la T.** the Thames

tamisé, -e [tamize] *adj* (*lumière*) subdued

tamiser [tamize] vt (farine) to sieve; (sable) to sift

tamoul, -e [tamul] **1** adj Tamil
2 nm,f T. Tamil
3 nm (langue) Tamil

tampon [tɑ̃pɔ̃] **1** nm (a) (de coton) pad; **t. hygiénique** ou **périodique** tampon (b) (cachet, instrument) stamp; (de la poste) postmark; **t. dateur** date stamp; **t. encreur** ink pad (c) (pour nettoyer) pad; **t. à récurer** scourer, scouring pad (d) (bouchon) plug, stopper (e) (à l'extrémité des wagons) & Fig buffer
2 adj inv État/zone t. buffer state/zone

tamponner [tɑ̃pɔne] **1** vt (a) (document) to stamp; (lettre) to postmark (b) (plaie) to dab (c) (heurter) to crash into
2 se tamponner vpr (a) (se heurter) to crash into each other (b) (s'essuyer) **t. le front** to mop one's brow; **se t. les yeux** to dab one's eyes; Fam **s'en t. (le coquillard)** not to give a damn

tamponneuse [tɑ̃pɔnøz] adj f voir **auto**

tam-tam (pl **tam-tams**) [tamtam] nm (tambour africain) tom-tom

tancer [tɑ̃se] vt Litt to berate, to scold

tanche [tɑ̃ʃ] nf tench

tandem [tɑ̃dɛm] nm (a) (bicyclette) tandem (b) (groupe de deux personnes) duo; **travailler en t.** to work in tandem

tandis [tɑ̃di, tɑ̃dis] **tandis que** conj (a) (marque l'opposition) while, whereas (b) (marque la simultanéité) while

tangage [tɑ̃gaʒ] nm (d'un bateau) pitching

tangent, -e [tɑ̃ʒɑ̃, -ɑ̃t] **1** adj Math tangential (à to); Fig c'était t. it was touch and go, it was a near thing
2 nf **tangente** Math tangent (à to); Fam **prendre la tangente** (partir) to slip away

tangible [tɑ̃ʒibl] adj tangible

tango [tɑ̃go] nm (danse, musique) tango; **danser le t.** to tango, to dance the tango

tanguer [tɑ̃ge] vi (bateau) to pitch; **tout tanguait autour de moi** everything was spinning around me

tanière [tanjɛr] nf (a) (d'animal) den, lair (b) (retraite) retreat

tanin [tanɛ̃] nm tannin

tank [tɑ̃k] nm tank

tanker [tɑ̃kœr] nm tanker

tannant, -e [tanɑ̃, -ɑ̃t] adj Fam (ennuyeux) annoying

tanné, -e [tane] adj (hâlé) weather-beaten

tanner [tane] vt (a) (peaux) to tan (b) (Fam harceler) to pester

tannerie [tanri] nf (établissement) tannery; (industrie) tanning

tanneur [tanœr] nm tanner

tannin [tanɛ̃] nm = **tanin**

tant [tɑ̃] adv (a) (tellement, à tel point) so much; **t. de** (quantité) so much; (nombre) so many **j'ai t. mangé que j'ai vomi** I ate so much I was sick; **pas que ça** (quantité) not that much; (nombre) not that many; **t. il est vrai que...** since it is the case that...
(b) (dans des comparaisons) **t. que** as much as; **t. pour vous que pour moi** for you as much as for me; **n'aimer rien t. que...** to like nothing more than...
(c) (substitué à un chiffre, à une date) **t. pour cent** so much per cent; **votre lettre du t.** your letter of such and such a date
(d) **t. que** (aussi longtemps que) as long as; (pendant que) while; **t. que vous y êtes** while you're at it

(e) (locutions) **t. bien que mal** somehow or other; **t. et si bien que** so much so that; **t. s'en faut** far from it; **s'il était un t. soit peu intelligent** if he was at all intelligent; **t. qu'à faire, autant en acheter deux** you/we/etc might as well buy two; **en t. que** (comme) as; **t. mieux!** so much the better!; **t. mieux pour toi!** good for you!; **t. pis!** too bad!; **t. pis pour toi!** too bad (for you)!

tante [tɑ̃t] nf (a) (parente) aunt (b) très Fam (homosexuel) queer, = offensive term used to refer to a male homosexual

tantine [tɑ̃tin] nf Fam auntie, aunty

tantinet [tɑ̃tinɛ] nm Fam **un t.** a tiny bit

tantôt [tɑ̃to] adv (a) (parfois) **t...., t....** sometimes..., sometimes... (b) (cet après-midi) this afternoon

Tanzanie [tɑ̃zani] nf la T. Tanzania

tanzanien, -enne [tɑ̃zanjɛ̃, -ɛn] **1** adj Tanzanian
2 nm,f T. Tanzanian

taoïsme [taoism] nm Taoism

taon [tɑ̃] nm gadfly, horsefly

tapage [tapaʒ] nm (a) (bruit) din, row; **faire du t.** to kick up a din or row; **t. nocturne** breach of the peace (at night) (b) (publicité) fuss; **faire du t. autour de qch** to make a fuss about sth

tapageur, -euse [tapaʒœr, -øz] adj (a) (enfant) rowdy (b) (vêtements, couleur) loud, flashy; (publicité) blatant (c) (liaison) scandalous

tapant, -e [tapɑ̃, -ɑ̃t] adj **à sept/dix heures t.** ou **tapantes** at seven/ten o'clock sharp

tape [tap] nf (pour punir) tap; (affectueuse) pat

tapé, -e [tape] adj Fam (fou) barking (mad)

tape-à-l'œil [tapalœj] Fam **1** adj inv gaudy, flashy
2 nm **c'est du t.** it's just show

tapecul [tapky] nm Fam (véhicule) rattletrap

taper [tape] **1** vt (a) (frapper) to hit; (affectueusement) to pat; (table) to bang (b) (dactylographier) **t. qch (à la machine)** to type sth (c) Ordinat to key; **tapez entrée ou retour** select enter or return (d) Fam (emprunter de l'argent à) to cadge money off; **t. qn de 10 francs** to cadge 10 francs off sb
2 vi (a) (frapper) to knock; (avec le poing) to bang; **t. à la porte** to knock on the door; **t. du pied** to stamp one's foot; **t. du poing sur qch** to bang on sth; **t. dans un ballon** to kick a ball around; Fam **t. dans l'œil à qn** to take sb's fancy; **t. sur qn** to hit sb; Fig (critiquer) to knock sb (b) (soleil) to beat down; Fam **ça tape** it's scorching (c) (dactylographier) **t. (à la machine)** to type
3 se taper vpr (a) (se cogner) **se t. la tête/le coude** to bang one's head/elbow; Fig **c'est à se t. la tête contre les murs** it's enough to drive you up the wall (b) Fam (repas, boisson) to have; **je me taperais bien une bière** I could murder a beer (c) Fam (corvée) to get landed with (d) très Fam (coucher avec) to screw (e) Fam (se moquer) **ses histoires de fesses, je m'en tape!** I couldn't care less about his sex life!

tapette [tapɛt] nf (a) (pour tapis) carpet beater; (contre les mouches) fly swatter (b) (piège) **t. (à souris)** mousetrap (c) (petite tape) tap (d) très Fam (homosexuel) queer, = offensive term used to refer to a male homosexual

tapeur, -euse [tapœr, -øz] nm,f Fam scrounger, sponger

tapin [tapɛ̃] nm très Fam **faire le t.** Br to be on the game, Am to work the streets

tapinois [tapinwa] **en tapinois** adv stealthily

tapioca [tapjɔka] *nm* tapioca

tapir¹ [tapir] *nm* tapir

tapir² **se tapir** *vpr* (*se blottir*) to crouch; (*se cacher*) to hide

tapis [tapi] *nm* (a) (*de sol*) carpet; (*de petite taille*) rug; *Fig* **mettre qch sur le t.** to bring sth up for discussion; **t. roulant** (*de marchandises, pour bagages*) conveyor belt; (*pour piétons*) moving walkway, travelator; **t. de salle de bain** bath mat; **t. de sol** earth mat; *Ordinat* **t. de souris** mouse mat *or* pad (b) (*en boxe*) canvas; **aller au t.** to go down; **envoyer qn au t.** to floor sb

tapis-brosse [*pl* tapis-brosses] [tapibrɔs] *nm* doormat

tapisser [tapise] *vt* (a) (*pièce, appartement*) to paper, to wallpaper; (*fauteuil, canapé*) to upholster (b) (*couvrir*) **être tapissé de** (*sujet: mur*) to be covered with; (*sujet: sol*) to be carpeted with (c) (*paroi d'un organe*) to line

tapisserie [tapisri] *nf* (a) (*broderie*) tapestry work; **faire de la t.** to do tapestry work (b) (*tenture*) tapestry; *Fig* **faire t.** to be a wallflower (c) (*papier peint*) wallpaper

tapissier, -ère [tapisje, -ɛr] *nm, f* (*tisseur*) tapestry maker (b) (*de meubles*) upholsterer

tapotement [tapɔtmɑ̃] *nm* tapping

tapoter [tapɔte] **1** *vt* to tap; (*joue, main*) to pat **2** *vi* **t. sur qch** to tap on sth

tapuscrit [tapyskri] *nm* typescript

taquet [takɛ] *nm* (a) (*de machine à écrire*) stop; *Ordinat* **t. de tabulation** tab stop (b) (*butée*) stop

taquin, -e [takɛ̃, -in] *adj* teasing

taquiner [takine] *vt* (*faire enrager*) to tease

taquinerie [takinri] *nf* **ce n'est qu'une t.** I'm/he's/*etc* only teasing; **j'en ai assez de ses taquineries** I've had enough of her teasing

tarabiscoté, -e [tarabiskɔte] *adj* over-elaborate

tarabuster [tarabyste] *vt* (a) (*harceler*) to pester (b) (*préoccuper*) to bother

tarama [tarama] *nm* taramasalata

taratata [taratata] *exclam Fam* rubbish!

tarauder [tarode] *vt* (a) (*acier*) to tap (b) (*obséder*) to gnaw at

tard [tar] **1** *adv* late; **plus t.** later (on); **au plus t.** at the latest; **t. dans la nuit** late at night; **pas plus t. qu'hier** only yesterday **2** *nm* **sur le t.** late in life

tarder [tarde] **1** *vi* to delay; **pourquoi tarde-t-elle?** why is she taking so long?; **il ne devrait pas t.** he shouldn't be long; **tu vas recevoir une gifle, cela ne va pas t.** you're going to get smacked before long; **sans t.** without delay; **t. à faire qch** to take a long time to do sth **2** *v impersonnel* **il me tarde de partir/qu'elle parte** I can't wait to leave/for her to leave

tardif, -ive [tardif, -iv] *adj* (*regrets, excuse*) belated; (*heure, récolte*) late

tardivement [tardivmɑ̃] *adv* (*prendre des mesures, s'excuser*) belatedly; (*rentrer, arriver*) late; (*se marier*) late in life

tare [tar] *nf* (a) (*défaut*) defect; *Hum* **ça n'est pas une t.!** it's not a crime! (b) (*pour calculer le poids net*) tare

taré, -e [tare] *adj* (a) (*anormal*) retarded (b) *Fam* (*fou*) crazy

tarentule [tarɑ̃tyl] *nf* tarantula

targette [tarʒɛt] *nf* bolt

targuer [targe] **se targuer** *vpr* **se t. de qch/de faire qch** to pride oneself on sth/on doing sth

tarif [tarif] *nm* (a) (*tableau des prix*) price list, *Br* tariff (b) (*prix*) rate; (*d'un billet d'avion, de train*) fare; **quels sont vos tarifs?** how much do you charge?; **payer plein t.** (*pour passagers*) to pay full fare; (*pour marchandises*) to pay the full rate; **faire un t. réduit pour les étudiants** to offer a student discount; **t. douanier** customs rate; **tarifs postaux** postal rates

tarifaire [tarifɛr] *adj* (*lois*) tariff

tarifer [tarife] *vt* to price

tarification [tarifikasjɔ̃] *nf* pricing

tarin [tarɛ̃] *nm Fam* (*nez*) *Br* hooter, *Am* snoot

tarir [tarir] **1** *vt* (*source, rivière*) to dry up; (*larmes*) to dry; (*créativité, inspiration*) to cause to dry up **2** *vi* (a) (*eau, source*) to dry up (b) *Fig* (*conversation, inspiration*) to dry up; **il ne tarit pas sur le sujet** he never stops talking *or* shuts up about it; **ne pas t. d'éloges sur qn/qch** to be forever praising sb/sth **3** **se tarir** *vpr* to dry up

tarissement [tarismɑ̃] *nm* drying up

tarot [taro] *nm* tarot; **jouer aux tarots** to play tarot

tartan [tartɑ̃] *nm* tartan

tartare [tartar] **1** *adj* (*sauce, steak*) tartare **2** *nmf* **T.** Tartar **3** *nm* (*steak*) steak tartare (*raw minced beef served with a raw egg*)

tarte [tart] **1** *nf* (a) (*salée ou sucrée*) *Br* tart, *Am* (open) pie; *Fam* **ce n'est pas de la t.** it's no easy matter; **t. à la crème** (*au cinéma*) custard pie; *Fig* cliché; **t. aux pommes** apple *Br* tart *or Am* pie; **t. Tatin** Tatin (*caramelized apples covered in shortcrust pastry and turned out upside down*) (b) *Fam* (*gifle*) slap **2** *adj Fam* (*ridicule*) naff (b) (*stupide*) thick

tartelette [tartəlɛt] *nf* tartlet

Tartempion [tartɑ̃pjɔ̃] *nm Fam* so-and-so

tartignole [tartiɲɔl] *adj Fam* naff

tartine [tartin] *nf* (a) (*tranche de pain*) slice of bread and butter; **t. de confiture** slice of bread and jam; **faire des tartines** to butter (some) bread (b) *Fam* (*texte*) screed; **en mettre des tartines** to write reams

tartiner [tartine] *vt* (a) (*beurre, pain*) to spread (b) *Fam* (*texte*) to churn out

tartre [tartr] *nm* (a) (*des dents, du vin*) tartar (b) (*dans une chaudière, dans une bouilloire*) fur, scale

tas [ta] *nm* (a) (*amas*) pile, heap; **mettre qch en t.** to pile sth up (b) *Fam* (*grand nombre*) **un t. de, des t. de** loads of (c) (*locutions*) **apprendre qch sur le t.** to learn sth on the job; *Fam* **dans le t. il y en aura bien un qui t'ira** you'll find one to suit you out of all that lot; *Fam* **tirer dans le t.** to fire at random

Tasmanie [tasmani] *nf la* **T.** Tasmania

tasse [tas] *nf* cup; **t. à café/thé** coffee/tea cup; **t. de café/thé** cup of coffee/tea; *Fig* **boire la t.** (*en nageant*) to get a mouthful of water

tassé, -e [tase] *adj* (a) (*serré*) crammed, squashed (b) *Fam* **bien t.** (*fort*) (*café*) strong; (*alcool*) stiff; (*dans un grand verre*) large; **il a 50 ans bien tassés** he's 50 if he's a day

tasseau, -x [taso] *nm* batten

tassement [tasmɑ̃] *nm* (a) (*de terre, de neige*) packing down; **t. de vertèbres** spinal compression (b) (*de fondations*) settling (c) (*déclin*) slowdown (de in)

tasser [tase] **1** vt (a) *(objets, personnes)* to cram, to pack (dans into) (b) *(terre, neige)* to pack down
2 se tasser vpr (a) *(fondations)* to settle (b) *(personne)* to shrink (c) **se t. dans qch** *(se serrer dans qch)* to squeeze into sth (d) *Fam* **ça se tassera** *(ça s'arrangera)* things will settle down

taste-vin [tastvɛ̃] nm inv wine taster

tata [tata] nf Fam auntie, aunty

tatami [tatami] nm tatami

tâter [tate] **1** vt (a) *(toucher)* to feel (b) Fig **t. le terrain** to see how the land lies
2 tâter de vt ind *(métier)* to try one's hand at; *(prison)* to have a taste of
3 se tâter vpr *(hésiter)* to be in two minds

tâte-vin [tatvɛ̃] nm = **taste-vin**

tatie [tati] nf Fam auntie, aunty

tatillon, -onne [tatijɔ̃, -ɔn] adj finicky

tâtonnements [tɑtɔnmɑ̃] nmpl (a) *(dans le noir)* groping (b) Fig *(essai)* trial and error; *(de la science, de la recherche)* tentative progress

tâtonner [tɑtɔne] vi (a) *(dans le noir)* to grope about (b) Fig *(chercher)* to proceed by trial and error

tâtons [tatɔ̃] **à tâtons** adv entrer/sortir à t. to feel one's way in/out

tatou [tatu] nm armadillo

tatouage [tatwaʒ] nm *(action)* tattooing; *(motif)* tattoo

tatouer [tatwe] vt **se faire t.** to get a tattoo

tatoueur [tatwœr] nm tattoo artist

taudis [todi] nm slum; Fig dump

taulard, -e [tolar, -ard] nm,f Fam jailbird

taule [tol] nf Fam Br nick, Am can; **faire de la t.** to do time

taulier, -ère [tolje, -ɛr] nm,f Fam *(propriétaire)* (hotel) owner; *(gérant)* (hotel) manager

taupe [top] nf (a) *(animal)* mole (b) Fam *(espion)* mole (c) Fam Péj **vieille t.** old hag

taupinière [topinjɛr] nf molehill

taureau, -x [toro] nm (a) *(animal)* bull; Fam **prendre le t. par les cornes** to take the bull by the horns (b) Astron & Astrol **T.** Taurus; **être T.** to be (a) Taurus

tauromachie [tɔromaʃi] nf bullfighting

tautologie [totɔlɔʒi] nf tautology

tautologique [totɔlɔʒik] adj tautological

taux [to] nm (a) *(montant)* *(des salaires, des impôts)* rate (b) *(pourcentage)* rate; *(d'alcool, de cholestérol)* level; **à t. fixe** fixed-rate; **t. de change** exchange rate; **t. de croissance** growth rate; **t. d'écoute** ratings; **t. d'épargne** savings rate; **t. d'inflation** rate of inflation; **t. d'intérêt** interest rate (c) Ordinat ratio, rate

tavelé, -e [tavle] adj marked

tavelure [tavlyr] nf mark

taverne [tavɛrn] nf (a) *(restaurant)* restaurant (b) Can beer parlour, tavern

tavernier, -ère [tavɛrnje, -ɛr] nm,f innkeeper

taxation [taksasjɔ̃] nf taxation

taxe [taks] nf tax; **toutes taxes comprises** inclusive of tax; **t. d'aéroport** airport tax; **t. d'apprentissage** = tax paid by businesses to fund training programmes; **t. d'habitation** local tax; **t. professionnelle** = tax paid by companies and self-employed people; **t. sur la valeur ajoutée** value added tax

taxer [takse] vt (a) *(imposer)* to tax (b) *(accuser)* **t. qn de négligence** to accuse sb of negligence (c) Fam *(soutirer)* **t. qch à qn** to cadge sth off sb

taxi [taksi] nm (a) *(voiture)* taxi, cab; **prendre un t.** to take a taxi (b) Fam *(chauffeur)* taxi driver, cabby

taxidermiste [taksidɛrmist] nmf taxidermist

taximètre [taksimɛtr] nm meter

Taxiphone® [taksifɔn] nm pay phone

Tbilissi [tbilisi] n Tbilisi

Tchad [tʃad] nm **le T.** Chad

tchadien, -enne [tʃadjɛ̃, -ɛn] **1** adj Chadian
2 nm,f **T.** Chadian

tchador [tʃadɔr] nm chador

tchécoslovaque [tʃekɔslɔvak] Anciennement **1** adj Czechoslovakian
2 nm,f **T.** Czechoslovak

Tchécoslovaquie [tʃekɔslɔvaki] nf Anciennement **la T.** Czechoslovakia

tchèque [tʃɛk] **1** adj Czech
2 nm,f **T.** Czech
3 nm *(langue)* Czech

tchétchène [tʃetʃɛn] **1** adj Chechen
2 nm,f **T.** Chechen

Tchétchénie [tʃetʃeni] nf **la T.** Chechnya

tchin-tchin [tʃintʃin] exclam Fam cheers!

TD [tede] nm *(abrév* **travaux dirigés***)* tutorial

te [tə]

t' is used before a word beginning with a vowel or h mute.

pron personnel (a) *(objet direct)* you; **te voilà** there you are (b) *(objet indirect)* to you; **j'ai vu qu'elle t'a serré la main** I saw her shake your hand; **ils t'ont lancé des cailloux?** did they throw stones at you? (c) *(dans les réfléchis)* yourself; **va te doucher** go and have a shower (d) *(dans les pronominaux)* **tu t'es trompée** you made a mistake

té [te] nm *(règle)* T-square; **en té** T-shaped

technicien, -enne [tɛknisjɛ̃, -ɛn] nm,f technician

technicité [tɛknisite] nf technical nature

technico-commercial, -e, -aux, -ales [tɛkniko-kɔmɛrsjal, -jo] **1** adj *(service)* technical sales; **agent t.** sales engineer
2 nm,f sales engineer

Technicolor® [tɛknikɔlɔr] nm Technicolor®

technique [tɛknik] **1** adj technical
2 nf (a) *(d'un artiste, d'un spécialiste)* technique; **avec lui, j'ai ma t.** I have my own way of dealing with him; **t. de vente** sales technique
3 nm **le t.** *(enseignement)* technical training

techniquement [tɛknikmɑ̃] adv technically

techno [tɛkno] adj inv & nf techno

technocrate [tɛknokrat] nmf technocrat

technocratie [tɛknokrasi] nf technocracy

technologie [tɛknolɔʒi] nf technology; **de haute t.** high-tech

technologique [tɛknolɔʒik] adj technological

teck [tɛk] nm teak

teckel [tɛkɛl] nm dachshund

tectonique [tɛktɔnik] **1** adj tectonic
2 nf tectonics *(singulier)*; **t. des plaques** plate tectonics

Te Deum [tedeɔm] nm inv Te Deum

teenager [tinedʒœr] nmf teenager

tee-shirt (*pl* **tee-shirts**) [tiʃœrt] *nm* T-shirt, tee-shirt

Téflon® [teflɔ̃] *nm* Teflon®

tégument [tegymɑ̃] *nm* integument

Téhéran [teerɑ̃] *n* Tehran

teignais, teigne *etc voir* **teindre**

teigne [tɛɲ] *nf* (a) (*maladie*) ringworm (b) *Fam* (*homme*) rat; (*femme*) cow

teigneux, -euse [tɛɲø, -øz] *adj Fam* (*personne*) nasty

teindre [tɛ̃dr] **1** *vt* (*vêtement, cheveux*) to dye; **t. qch en rouge** to dye sth red
  2 se teindre *vpr* (a) (*se colorer*) **se t. les cheveux (en blond)** to dye one's hair (blond) (b) *Litt* **se t. de** (*se mêler de*) to be tinged with

teint, -e *voir* **teindre**

teint [tɛ̃] *nm* (a) (*du visage*) complexion; **t. de rose** rosy complexion (b) (*d'un tissu*) colour; **tissu bon** *ou* **grand t.** colourfast material; *Fig* **bon t.** (*catholique, communiste*) staunch, dyed-in-the-wool

teinte [tɛ̃t] *nf* (a) (*couleur*) shade, tint (b) *Fig* (*nuance*) tinge

teinter [tɛ̃te] **1** *vt* (*colorer*) to tint; (*bois, meuble*) to stain (b) *Fig* (*nuancer*) **teinté de** tinged with
  2 se teinter *vpr* **se t. de** to become tinged with

teinture [tɛ̃tyr] *nf* (a) (*produit*) dye (b) (*action*) dyeing (c) (*préparation pharmaceutique*) tincture; **t. d'iode** tincture of iodine

teinturerie [tɛ̃tyrri] *nf* (*pressing*) dry cleaner's

teinturier, -ère [tɛ̃tyrje, -ɛr] *nm,f* dry cleaner

tek [tɛk] = **teak**

tel, telle [tɛl] **1** *adj* (a) (*semblable*) such; **un t. homme** such a man; **une telle conduite** such behaviour; **de telles choses** such things; **t. père, t. fils** like father like son; **rien de t. qu'un bon chocolat chaud** there's nothing like a nice cup of hot chocolate; **à t. ou t. endroit** in such and such a place; **il n'a rien dit de t.** he said nothing of the kind; **sa bonté est telle que...** she's so kind that...
  (b) (*comme*) **t. que** such as, like; **voir les choses telles qu'elles sont** to see things as they are; **t. que je le connais, il ne sera pas d'accord** knowing him, he won't agree; *Litt* **t. une bête furieuse** like an enraged animal
  (c) (*locutions*) **à t. point que** to such an extent that; **de telle sorte que...** so that..., in such a way that...; **elle me l'a dit t. quel** *ou Fam* **t. que** she told me just like that
  2 *pron indéfini* **t. ou t. vous dira que...** some people will tell you that...
  3 *pron démonstratif* such; **t. est mon désir** such is my wish
  4 *nm,f* **un t., une telle** so-and-so

télé [tele] *nf Fam* (a) (*appareil*) TV, *Br* telly (b) (*organisme*) **la t.** TV; **travailler à la t.** to work in TV

téléachat [teleaʃa] *nm* teleshopping

télécabine [telekabin] *nf* cable car

Télécarte® [telekart] *nf* phone card

télécommande [telekɔmɑ̃d] *nf* remote control

télécommander [telekɔmɑ̃de] *vt* (a) (*appareil*) to operate by remote control (b) *Fig* (*complot, soulèvement*) to mastermind from a distance

télécommunications [telekɔmynikasjɔ̃] *nfpl* **les t.** telecommunications

téléconférence [telekɔ̃ferɑ̃s] *nf* teleconference

télécopie [telekɔpi] *nf* fax

télécopieur [telekɔpjœr] *nm* fax (machine)

télédiffuser [teledifyze] *vt* to televise

télédiffusion [teledifyzjɔ̃] *nf* televising

télé-enseignement [teleɑ̃sɛɲmɑ̃] *nm* distance learning

téléfilm [telefilm] *nm* film made for television, TV movie

télégénique [teleʒenik] *adj* telegenic

télégramme [telegram] *nm* telegram

télégraphe [telegraf] *nm* telegraph

télégraphier [telegrafje] *vt* to cable, to wire

télégraphique [telegrafik] *adj* (*fil, poteau*) telegraph; **en style t.** in telegraphic style

télégraphiste [telegrafist] *nmf* (a) (*technicien*) telegraphist (b) (*porteur*) telegraph messenger

téléguidage [telegidaʒ] *nm* remote control

téléguidé, -e [telegide] *adj* remote-controlled

téléguider [telegide] *vt* (a) (*voiture, missile*) to operate by remote control (b) *Fig* (*complot, soulèvement*) to mastermind from a distance

télématique [telematik] **1** *adj* telematic
  2 *nf* telematics (*singulier*)

téléobjectif [teleɔbʒɛktif] *nm* telephoto lens

télépaiement [telepemɑ̃] *nm* telepayment

télépathe [telepat] **1** *adj* telepathic
  2 *nmf* telepathist

télépathie [telepati] *nf* telepathy

télépathique [telepatik] *adj* telepathic

téléphérique [teleferik] *nm* cable car

téléphone [telefɔn] *nm* (a) (*appareil, système*) phone, telephone; **avoir le t.** to be on the phone, to have a phone; **être au t.** to be on the phone; **un coup de t.** a phone call; *Fam* **par le t. arabe** on the grapevine; **t. cellulaire** cellular phone; **t. mobile** mobile (phone); **t. portatif** portable phone; **t. public** public phone; *Pol* **t. rouge** hot line; **t. sans fil** cordless phone; **t. de voiture** car phone (b) (*numéro*) phone number

téléphoner [telefɔne] **1** *vi* (a) (*nouvelle*) to phone, to telephone (**à** to) (b) *Fam* **c'était téléphoné** you could see it coming
  2 *vi* to phone, to telephone; **t. à qn** to phone sb
  3 se téléphoner *vpr* to phone each other

téléphonique [telefɔnik] *adj* telephone

téléphoniste [telefɔnist] *nmf* (telephone) operator, *Br* telephonist

téléprompteur [teleprɔ̃ptœr] *nm* Teleprompter®, *Br* Autocue®

téléprospecteur, -trice [teleprɔspɛktœr, -tris] *nm,f* telemarketer

téléprospection [teleprɔspɛksjɔ̃] *nf* telemarketing

téléreportage [teler(ə)pɔrtaʒ] *nm* (*activité*) television reporting; (*document*) television report

télescopage [teleskɔpaʒ] *nm* (*de trains*) telescoping; **télescopages en série** (*de véhicules*) pile-up

télescope [teleskɔp] *nm* telescope

télescoper [teleskɔpe] **1** *vt* (*véhicules, trains*) to crash into
  2 se télescoper *vpr* (a) (*véhicules, trains*) to concertina (b) (*souvenirs, images*) to intermingle

télescopique [teleskɔpik] *adj* telescopic

télescripteur [teleskriptœr] *nm* teleprinter

télésiège [telesjɛʒ] *nm* chair lift

téléski [teleski] *nm* ski tow

téléspectateur, -trice [telespektatœr, -tris] *nm,f* (television) viewer

télésurveillance [telesyrvejɑ̃s] *nf* electronic surveillance

Télétexte® [teletɛkst] *nm* teletext

télétravail [teletravaj] *nm* teleworking

télévisé, -e [televize] *adj* televised

téléviseur [televizœr] *nm* television (set)

télévision [televizjɔ̃] *nf* (a) (organisme, technique, émissions) television; **à la t.** on television; **travailler à la t.** to work in television; **t. par câble** cable television; **t. commerciale** commercial television; **t. haute définition** high-definition television; **(poste)** television (set); **regarder la t.** to watch television; **t. en couleur, t. couleur** colour television

télévisuel, -elle [televizɥɛl] *adj* television

télex [telɛks] *nm* telex

télexer [telɛkse] *vt* to telex

tellement [tɛlmã] *adv* (a) (si) so; **c'était t. intéressant que...** it was so interesting that...; **ce n'est pas t. beau** it's not all that beautiful (b) (tant) so much; **t. de** (nombre) so many; (quantité) so much; **elle a t. grandi** she's grown so much; **je n'ai pas t. aimé** I didn't like it that much; **je n'ai plus t. envie d'y aller** I'm no longer that keen on going; **il a t. crié que...** he shouted so much that...; *Fam* **je vais craquer t. il m'énerve** he annoys me so much I'm going to crack up

tellurique [telyrik] *adj* (courants) telluric; **secousse t.** earth tremor

téméraire [temerɛr] *adj* reckless

témérité [temerite] *nf* recklessness

témoignage [temwaɲaʒ] *nm* (a) *Jur* evidence, testimony; **porter t.** (en faveur de/contre qn) to give evidence (on behalf of/against sb); **faux t.** perjury (b) (compte rendu) report, account (c) (démonstration) **en t. d'amitié** as a token of friendship

témoigner [temwaɲe] **1** *vt* (a) (attester) **t. que** to testify that (b) (sentiments, gratitude) to show (à to)

2 *vi* to testify, to give evidence (**en faveur de/contre** on behalf of/against)

3 témoigner de *vt ind* (a) (montrer) to show (b) (se porter garant de) to testify to

témoin [temwɛ̃] **1** *nm* (a) (d'un événement, d'un mariage) witness; **être t. de qch** to witness sth, to be a witness to sth; **prendre qn à t.** to call sb to witness; **Dieu m'est t. que...** as God is my witness...; **t. à charge** witness for the prosecution; **t. oculaire** eyewitness (b) (dans un duel) second (c) (preuve) **t. les coups que j'ai reçus** witness the blows I received (d) (dans un relais) baton (e) *Rel* **T. de Jéhovah** Jehovah's Witness

2 *adj inv* (animal, plante) control; **appartement t.** *Br* show flat, *Am* model apartment

tempe [tãp] *nf* temple

tempérament [tãperamã] *nm* (a) (caractère) disposition; *Fam* **avoir du t.** (avoir du caractère) to have character (b) **acheter qch à t.** to buy sth *Br* on hire purchase or *Am* on the installment plan

tempérance [tãperãs] *nf* moderation, temperance

température [tãperatyr] *nf* temperature; **avoir de la t.** to have a (high) temperature; *Fig* **prendre la t. de qch** to gauge the temperature of sth

tempéré, -e [tãpere] *adj* (climat) temperate

tempérer [tãpere] *vt* (enthousiasme, passion) to moderate

tempête [tãpɛt] *nf* storm; *Fig* **une t. d'applaudissements** thunderous applause; *Fig* **une t. dans un verre d'eau** a storm in a *Br* teacup or *Am* teapot; **t. de neige** snowstorm, blizzard; **t. de sable** sandstorm

tempêter [tãpete] *vi* to storm, to rage

tempétueux, -euse [tãpetɥø, -øz] *adj Litt* stormy

temple [tãpl] *nm aussi Fig* temple; (protestant) church

tempo [tɛpo, tɛmpo] *nm* tempo

temporaire [tãporɛr] *adj* temporary

temporairement [tãporɛrmã] *adv* temporarily

temporel, -elle [tãporɛl] *adj* (a) (qui concerne le temps) temporal (b) (terrestre) temporal, worldly

temporellement [tãporɛlmã] *adv* temporally

temporisateur, -trice [tãporizatœr, -tris] *adj* (stratégie) delaying

temporiser [tãporize] *vi* to play for time, to stall

temps [tã] *nm* (a) (durée) time; **avoir le t. de faire qch** to have (the) time to do sth; **avoir tout le t.** to have plenty of time; **prendre le t. de faire qch** to take the time to do sth; **prendre son t.** to take one's time; **ça prend du t.** it takes time; **ça a pris un certain t.** it took quite a while; **donner** ou **laisser le t. à qn de faire qch** to give sb the time to do sth; *Fig* **en deux t. trois mouvements** in two ticks; **avec le t.** in or with time, with time; **combien de t. faut-il pour y aller?** how long does it take to get there?; *Prov* **le t., c'est de l'argent** time is money; *Ordinat* **base de t.** time base; *Ordinat* **t. d'adressage** address speed

(b) (moment) time; **en t. de crise** in a crisis; **en t. de guerre/paix** in wartime/peacetime; **de t. en t., de t. à autre** from time to time; **en même t.** (que) at the same time (as); **pendant ce t.** meanwhile, in the meantime; **il y a peu de t.** not long ago, a little while ago; **peu de t. après** shortly after; **d'ici quelque t.** soon, shortly; **tout le t.** all the time; **les premiers t.** at the beginning; **ces t.-ci** these days; **ces derniers t.** this last while; **il y est resté quelque t.** he stayed there for a while; **ça n'a qu'un t.** it won't last forever; **les t. forts de l'actualité** the main points of the news; **t. libre** free time; **t. mort** lull; (au basket-ball) time out

(c) (époque) time, days; **de mon t.** in my day or time; **du t. de ma jeunesse** in my younger days; **de tout t.** from time immemorial; **dans le t.** in the old days; **en ce t.-là** at that time, then; **par les t. qui courent** these days; **être de son t., vivre avec son t.** to move with the times; **être en avance sur son t.** to be ahead of one's time; **le bon vieux t.** the good old days; **les t. sont durs** times are hard

(d) (heure) **faire qch à t.** to do sth in time; **en t. voulu** ou **utile** in due course; **il est t. qu'elle descende** it's time she came down; **il n'est plus t.** it's too late; **le paquet est enfin arrivé, mais il était t.!** the parcel's finally arrived and about time too!

(e) (occasion) **il y a un t. pour tout** there's a time for everything; **chaque chose en son t.** all in good time

(f) (météo) weather; **par tous les t.** in all weathers; **quel t. fait-il?** what's the weather like?

(g) *Gram* tense

(h) *Mus* beat

(i) (d'un athlète) time

tenable [tanabl] *adj* (situation) bearable

tenace [tanas] *adj* (a) (personne) stubborn, tenacious (b) (préjugé, volonté) stubborn; (odeur, douleur, souvenir) lingering; (habitude) deep-rooted (c) (colle) strong

ténacité [tenasite] *nf* (*d'une personne*) stubbornness, tenacity; **avec t.** stubbornly; (*travailler*) doggedly **(b)** (*d'un préjugé*) stubbornness; (*d'une odeur, d'une douleur, d'un souvenir*) lingering nature; (*d'une habitude*) deep-rootedness

tenailler [tənaje] *vt Littt* to torture; **tenaillé par la faim** ravenously hungry; **tenaillé par la douleur** gripped with pain

tenailles [tənaj] *nfpl* pincers

tenancier, -ère [tənɑ̃sje, -ɛr] *nm,f* (*d'un bar, d'une maison de jeu*) manager, *f* manageress

tenant, -e [tənɑ̃, -ɑ̃t] **1** *adj voir* **séance**

2 *nm* **(a)** (*partisan*) champion, defender **(b)** **le t. du titre** the title holder **(c)** (*locutions*) **d'un seul t.** in one piece; **les tenants et les aboutissants** (*d'une affaire*) the ins and outs

tendance [tɑ̃dɑ̃s] *nf* **(a)** (*d'une personne*) tendency; **avoir t. à faire qch** to have a tendency to do sth; **avoir une t. à qch** to have a tendency to sth **(b)** (*de l'économie, du marché, d'une mode*) trend

tendancieusement [tɑ̃dɑ̃sjøzmɑ̃] *adv* tendentiously

tendancieux, -euse [tɑ̃dɑ̃sjø, -øz] *adj* tendentious

tendeur [tɑ̃dœr] *nm* (*pour bagages*) elastic strap

tendinite [tɑ̃dinit] *nf* tendinitis

tendon [tɑ̃dɔ̃] *nm* tendon; **t. d'Achille** Achilles tendon

tendre¹ [tɑ̃dr] **1** *adj* **(a)** (*bois, pierre, métal*) soft; (*viande, légume*) tender **(b)** (*couleur*) delicate, soft **(c)** (*personne, geste, cœur*) tender; **ne pas être t. (pour** *ou* **avec qn)** to be hard (on sb) **(d)** **l'âge t.** early childhood; **depuis ma plus t. enfance** since my earliest childhood

2 *nmf* (*personne*) softhearted person

tendre² **1** *vt* **(a)** (*corde*) to tighten; (*toile*) to stretch; (*muscle*) to tense; (*arc*) to bend **(b)** (*voile, filet*) to spread; (*papier peint, tapisserie*) to hang; **une pièce tendue de velours rouge** a room whose walls are covered in red velvet **(c)** (*piège*) to set (à for) **(d)** (*main, bras, jambe*) to stretch out, to hold out (à to); **les bras tendus** with outstretched arms; *Fig* **t. la main à qn** (*l'aider*) to offer sb a hand; *Fig* **t. l'oreille** to prick up one's ears

2 *vi* **t. vers zéro** to tend towards zero

3 tendre à *vt ind* **(a)** (*avoir pour but*) (*idéal*) to aim for **(b)** (*avoir tendance à*) **t. à faire qch** to tend to do sth **(c)** **t. à sa fin** to come to an end

4 se tendre *vpr* (*cordage*) to become taut; *Fig* (*relations, situation*) to become strained

tendrement [tɑ̃drəmɑ̃] *adv* tenderly, lovingly

tendresse [tɑ̃drɛs] *nf* **(a)** (*affection*) tenderness, affection; **avoir de la t. pour qn** to feel affection for sb; **avec t.** tenderly, affectionately **(b)** **tendresses** (*démonstrations*) expressions of affection

tendron [tɑ̃drɔ̃] *nm* **(a)** (*de veau*) flank **(b)** *Fam* (*jeune fille*) slip of a girl

tendu, -e [tɑ̃dy] *adj* **(a)** (*corde, toile*) taut, tight **(b)** (*main*) outstretched **(c)** (*relations, visage*) strained; (*personne, atmosphère, situation*) tense

ténèbres [tenɛbr] *nfpl* **les t.** the darkness

ténébreux, -euse [tenebrø, -øz] **1** *adj Littt* **(a)** (*obscur*) (*forêt*) dark, gloomy **(b)** (*mystérieux*) (*affaire*) murky; (*style*) obscure **(c)** (*personne*) melancholic

2 *nm* **beau t.** tall dark handsome man

teneur [tənœr] *nf* **(a)** (*d'un document, d'un discours*) content; (*d'un contrat*) terms **(b)** (*quantité*) content; **t. en eau/or** water/gold content

tenir [70] [tənir] **1** *vt* **(a)** (*à la main, sur ses genoux*) to hold; **t. qn par le cou/les épaules** to have one's arm round

sb's neck/shoulders; *Fig* **je tiens mon homme/la solution** I've got my man/the answer; *Fam* **t. un bon rhume** to have a stinking cold; *Fam* **qu'est-ce qu'il tient!** (*il est idiot*) what a pillock!; **tenez!** (*c'est pour vous*) here (you are)!; **tiens, voilà Paul!** oh, there's Paul!; *Prov* **un tiens vaut mieux que deux tu l'auras** a bird in the hand is worth two in the bush

(b) (*dans une position*) to hold; (*dans un état*) to keep; **t. sa droite** (*en voiture*) to keep to the right

(c) (*boutique, hôtel*) to run; (*caisse*) to be in charge of

(d) (*rôle*) to have

(e) (*parole, promesse*) to keep

(f) (*maîtriser*) (*enfants, cheval*) to control; **t. sa langue** to hold one's tongue

(g) (*résister à*) *Fam* **t. l'alcool** to hold one's drink; **t. la route** (*voiture*) to hold the road

(h) (*avoir*) **t. qch de qn** (*caractéristique*) to get sth from sb; **je tiens la nouvelle de ma mère** I got the news from my mother

(i) (*considérer*) **t. qn pour responsable** to hold sb responsible; **t. qch pour vrai** to consider sth to be true

2 *vi* **(a)** (*nœud, corde*) to hold; (*construction*) to stay up; (*autocollant, pansement*) to stay on; (*personne*) to last; *Fam* **il ne tient plus sur ses jambes** *ou* **debout** (*fatigué*) he's ready to drop, he's dead on his feet; (*ivre*) he can hardly stand; **t. debout** (*argument*) to stand up; **t. bon** (*personne*) to hold out; **je n'y tiens plus** I can't stand it any longer

(b) (*durer*) to last; **mon offre/le pari tient toujours** my offer/the bet still stands; **ça tient toujours pour dimanche?** is it still on for Sunday?

(c) (*être contenu*) to fit; **on tient à dix autour de cette table** this table seats ten; **ma conclusion tiendra en trois mots** my conclusion can be summed up in three words

2 *vimpersonnel* **il ne tient qu'à vous que cela se fasse** it depends entirely on you whether it gets done; **s'il ne tenait qu'à moi,...** if it was just up to me,...; **qu'à cela ne tienne** that's not a problem

3 tenir à *vt ind* **(a)** (*liberté, amitié*) to value; (*ami*) to care about; (*objet*) to be attached to; **t. à faire qch** to be anxious *or* keen to do sth; **je tiens à ce que tout soit rangé** I want everything to be tidy; **si vous y tenez** if you insist

(b) (*provenir de*) to be the result of, to be due to

4 tenir de *vt ind* (*ressembler à*) (*personne*) to take after; *Fam* **entre son oncle et son père, il a de qui t.!** it's not surprising when you consider his uncle and his father!; **cela tient du miracle** it's something of a miracle

5 se tenir *vpr* **(a)** (*rester*) (*debout*) to stand; (*assis*) to sit; **se t. debout** to be standing, to stand; **se t. tranquille** to keep quiet

(b) (*se comporter*) **bien se t.** to behave (oneself); *Fig* **il n'a qu'à bien se t.!** he'd better watch his step!; **se t. mal à table** to have no table manners

(c) (*s'accrocher*) to hold on (à to); **tenez-vous bien!** hold tight!; *Fig* **et alors, tiens-toi bien,...!** and would you believe it,...!; **se t. par la main** to hold hands; **ils se tenaient par la taille** they had their arms round each other's waist

(d) (*avoir lieu*) to be held, to take place

(e) (*être plausible*) to hang together

(f) **s'en t. à** (*généralités, sujet, budget*) to keep to; (*décision, consignes*) to abide by; **il ne s'en tint pas là** he didn't stop there; **je ne sais pas à quoi m'en t.** I don't know where I stand

(g) (*locutions*) **tiens-le-toi pour dit!** I'm telling you for the last time!

tennis [tenis] **1** *nm* (**a**) *(sport)* tennis; **t. de table** table tennis (**b**) *(court)* tennis court
2 *nm ou nf (chaussure)* tennis shoe

tennisman [tenisman] *(pl* **tennismen** [tenismɛn]) *nm* tennis player

ténor [tenɔr] **1** *adj (saxophone)* tenor
2 *nm* (**a**) *(voix, chanteur)* tenor (**b**) *Fig* **un t. de la politique** an influential figure in politics

tenseur [tɑ̃sœr] **1** *adj* **muscle t.** tensor
2 *nm* tensor

tension [tɑ̃sjɔ̃] *nf* (**a**) *(raideur, désaccord)* tension; **être sous t.** to be tense; **mettre qn sous t.** to put sb under stress; **t. nerveuse** nervous tension (**b**) **t. (artérielle)** blood pressure; **avoir de la t.** to have high blood pressure; **prendre la t. de qn** to take sb's blood pressure (**c**) *(électrique)* voltage, tension; **basse/haute t.** low/high voltage or tension

tentaculaire [tɑ̃takylɛr] *adj (ville)* sprawling; *(société, organisme)* octopus-like

tentacule [tɑ̃takyl] *nm* tentacle

tentant, -e [tɑ̃tɑ̃, -ɑ̃t] *adj* tempting

tentateur, -trice [tɑ̃tatœr, -tris] **1** *adj* tempting
2 *nm* tempter; *Rel* **le T.** the Tempter
3 *nf* **tentatrice** temptress

tentation [tɑ̃tasjɔ̃] *nf* temptation

tentative [tɑ̃tativ] *nf* attempt; **t. d'assassinat** attempted murder; **t. d'évasion** attempt to escape; **t. de suicide** suicide attempt

tente [tɑ̃t] *nf* (**a**) *(de camping)* tent; **coucher sous la t.** to sleep under canvas; **t. igloo** igloo tent (**b**) *Méd* **t. à oxygène** oxygen tent

tenter [tɑ̃te] *vt* (**a**) *(mettre à l'épreuve)* **t. sa chance** to try one's luck; *Fam* **t. le coup** to have a go; **t. le tout pour le tout** to go for broke (**b**) *(séduire)* to tempt; **être tenté de faire qch** to be tempted to do sth; **se laisser t.** to let oneself be tempted; **j'ai envie de me laisser t.** *(accepter)* I'm tempted to say yes; *(faire quelque chose)* I'm tempted to do it (**c**) *(essayer)* to try, to attempt; **t. de faire qch** to try or attempt to do sth

tenture [tɑ̃tyr] *nf (tapisserie)* hanging

tenu, -e [təny] *adj* (**a**) **bien/mal t.** *(maison, jardin)* well/poorly kept (**b**) *(contraint)* **être t. de faire qch** to be obliged to do sth; **être t. à qch** to be bound by sth (**c**) *(note)* held

ténu, -e [teny] *adj* (**a**) *(fil)* fine; *(nuance)* subtle; *(lien)* tenuous (**b**) *(voix)* thin

tenue [təny] *nf* (**a**) *(habillement)* outfit; *(militaire)* dress; **en t. légère** *(en vêtements d'été)* in light clothing; *Fam* **en petite t.** scantily dressed; **t. de combat** battledress; **t. de soirée** evening dress (**b**) *(bonne conduite)* good behaviour; **un peu de t.!** mind your manners!; **manquer de t.** to lack manners (**c**) *(maintien)* posture (**d**) *(niveau)* standard (**e**) *(d'une maison)* running (**f**) **t. de route** *(d'un véhicule)* road-holding

tequila [tekila] *nf* tequila

ter [tɛr] *adj* **5 t.** ≃ 5B

tercet [tɛrsɛ] *nm* tercet

térébenthine [terebɑ̃tin] *nf* turpentine

Tergal® [tɛrgal] *nm Br* Terylene®, *Am* Dacron®

tergiversations [tɛrʒiversasjɔ̃] *nfpl* equivocation

tergiverser [tɛrʒiverse] *vi* to equivocate

---

terme¹ [tɛrm] *nm* (**a**) *(fin)* end; **toucher à son t.** *(projet)* to be nearing completion; *(période)* to be drawing to a close; **mettre un t. à qch** to put an end to sth; **mener qch à bon t.** to bring sth to a successful conclusion (**b**) *(date limite)* time (limit); **à court/long t.** *(projet, prévisions)* short-/long-term; **à court/long t.,...** in the short/long term,... (**c**) *(d'une femme enceinte)* **être à t.** to have reached term; **avant t.** *(accoucher)* prematurely; *(accouchement)* premature (**d**) *(loyer)* rent; *(date de paiement du loyer)* rent day

terme² *nm (mot)* term; **en d'autres termes** in other words (**b**) *(relations)* **être en bons/mauvais termes avec qn** to be on good/bad terms with sb (**c**) **termes** *(d'un contrat)* terms

terminaison [tɛrminɛzɔ̃] *nf* (**a**) *(d'un mot)* ending (**b**) *Anat* **t. nerveuse** nerve ending

terminal, -e, -aux, -ales [tɛrminal, -o] **1** *adj (de la fin)* final; *Méd (phase)* terminal; **être en phase terminale** *(malade)* to be terminally ill
2 *nm* (**a**) *(dans un aéroport)* terminal (**b**) *Ordinat* terminal, VDU
3 *nf Scol* **terminale** *Br* ≃ upper sixth, *Am* ≃ twelfth grade, senior year

terminer [tɛrmine] **1** *vt (discours, lettre, repas)* to end, to finish *(par* with); *(travail)* to finish, to complete; **t. en avec qch** to put an end to sth
2 se terminer *vpr (saison)* to come to a close; *(soirée, concert, vacances)* to end *(par* with); *(rue)* to end; **se t. en** *(mot)* to end in

terminologie [tɛrminɔlɔʒi] *nf* terminology

terminus [tɛrminys] *nm* terminus

termite [tɛrmit] *nm* termite

terne [tɛrn] *adj* dull

ternir [tɛrnir] **1** *vt (meuble)* to fade; *(miroir, métal, réputation)* to tarnish
2 se ternir *vpr (meuble)* to fade; *(miroir, métal, réputation)* to become tarnished

terrain [tɛrɛ̃] *nm* (**a**) *(parcelle)* piece or plot of land (**b**) *(espace au sol, relief)* ground; **tout t.** *(véhicule)* all-terrain (**c**) *(terre)* soil (**d**) *(destiné à une activité)* (de football, de rugby) pitch, field; *(de golf)* course; **t. d'atterrissage** landing strip; **t. d'aviation** airfield; **t. à bâtir** development site; **t. de camping** campsite; *Fig* **t. d'entente** common ground; **t. de jeu** *(pour les sports)* *Br* playing field, *Am* athletic field; *(pour les enfants)* playground; **t. de sport** sports ground; **t. vague** waste ground (**e**) *Méd* **présenter un t. favorable à qch** to be prone to sth (**f**) *(locutions)* **être sur son t.** to be on familiar ground; **sur le t.** *(apprendre)* in the field; **perdre/céder du t.** to lose/give ground; **préparer le t.** to pave the way

terrasse [tɛras] *nf* (**a**) *(d'un café, d'un restaurant)* *Br* pavement or *Am* sidewalk area; **en t.** outside; **prix des consommations en t.** price of drinks served outside (**b**) *(de maison, d'appartement)* terrace; *(toit en)* **t.** terrace (roof) (**c**) *(levée de terre)* terrace; **en terrasses** *(jardin)* terraced; *(culture)* terrace

terrassement [tɛrasmɑ̃] *nm* (**a**) *(action)* excavation (**b**) *(remblai)* earthwork

terrasser [tɛrase] *vt (sujet: adversaire)* to floor; *(sujet: émotion, fatigue, nouvelle)* to overwhelm; *(sujet: maladie)* to lay low

terrassier [tɛrasje] *nm* labourer

terre [tɛr] *nf* (a) *(monde)* world; *Fig* **t. à t.** down-to-earth; *Fig* **revenir sur t.** to come down to earth; *Fig* **avoir les pieds sur t.** to have one's feet on the ground (b) *(planète)* **la T.** (the) Earth (c) *(sol)* ground; *(étendue)* land; **à t., par t.** on the ground; **tomber par t.** to fall down; **faire tomber qch par t.** to drop sth; **sous t.** underground; **basses terres** lowlands; **hautes terres** highlands (d) *Él Br* earth, *Am* ground; **relier** *ou* **raccorder à la t.** *Br* to earth, *Am* to ground (e) *(opposé à la mer)* land; **t. ferme** terra firma (f) *(matière)* soil, earth; **cultiver la t.** to cultivate the soil; **t. battue** mud; *(de court de tennis)* clay; **t. de Sienne** sienna (g) *(propriété)* **une t.** a piece of land; **terres** land (h) *(territoire)* land, country; **terres australes** southern lands; **la t.** Adélie Adélie Land; **la T. de Feu** Tierra del Fuego; **la T. promise** the Promised Land; **la T. sainte** the Holy Land (i) *(élément)* earth (j) *(argile)* clay; **cruche de** *ou* **en t.** earthenware jug; **t. cuite** terracotta; **une t. cuite** a piece of terracotta

terreau, -x [tɛro] *nm* compost

Terre-Neuve [tɛrnœv] *n* Newfoundland

terre-neuve [tɛrnœv] *nm inv* Newfoundland (dog)

terre-plein *(pl* **terre-pleins)** [tɛrplɛ̃] *nm (plate-forme)* platform; **t. central** *(sur route)* *Br* central reservation, *Am* median strip

terrer [tɛre] **se terrer** *vpr aussi Fig* to go to earth

terrestre [tɛrɛstr] *adj* (a) *(plante)* ground; *(animal)* land; *(transports)* surface (b) *(magnétisme, attraction)* of the earth (c) *(matériel)* worldly

terreur [tɛrœr] *nf* (a) *(effroi)* terror; **vivre dans la t.** to live in terror (b) *(emploi de la violence)* terror (c) *Fig (personne)* terror; **jouer les terreurs** to play the tough guy

terreux, -euse [tɛrø, -øz] *adj* (a) *(odeur)* earthy (b) *(mains)* muddy (c) *(teint, ciel, couleur)* muddy

terrible [tɛribl] *adj* (a) *(affreux, remarquable)* terrible (b) *Fam (formidable)* terrific, great; **pas t.** nothing special

terriblement [tɛribləmɑ̃] *adv* terribly

terrien, -enne [tɛrjɛ̃, -ɛn] **1** *adj* (a) **propriétaire t.** landowner (b) *(famille, vertu)* rural (c) *(de la Terre)* Earth **2** *nm,f (habitant de la Terre)* earthling

terrier[1] [tɛrje] *nm (d'un lapin)* burrow, hole; *(d'une taupe)* hole; *(d'un renard)* earth

terrier[2] *nm (chien)* terrier

terrifiant, -e [tɛrifjɑ̃, -ɑ̃t] *adj* terrifying

terrifier [tɛrifje] *vt* to terrify

terril [tɛril] *nm* slag heap

terrine [tɛrin] *nf* terrine

territoire [tɛritwar] *nm* (a) *(d'un État, d'un animal)* territory; **t. d'outre-mer** overseas territory; *Can* **Territoires du Nord-Ouest** Northwest Territories (b) *(de juge, d'évêque)* jurisdiction; *(de commune, d'arrondissement)* area

territorial, -e, -aux, -ales [tɛritɔrjal, -o] *adj* territorial

territorialité [tɛritɔrjalite] *nf* territoriality

terroir [tɛrwar] *nm* soil; **du t.** *(produit, accent, expression)* local

terrorisant, -e [tɛrɔrizɑ̃, -ɑ̃t] *adj* terrifying

terroriser [tɛrɔrize] *vt (sujet: personne)* to terrorize; *(sujet: expérience, souvenir)* to terrify

terrorisme [tɛrɔrism] *nm* terrorism

terroriste [tɛrɔrist] *adj & nmf* terrorist

tertiaire [tɛrsjɛr] **1** *adj* tertiary **2** *nm* (a) *(secteur économique)* service sector (b) *Géol* Tertiary era

tertio [tɛrsjo] *adv* thirdly

tertre [tɛrtr] *nm* hillock, mound

tes [te] *voir* **ton**[1]

tessiture [tesityr] *nf Mus* range

tesson [tesɔ̃] *nm* shard; **t. de bouteille** piece of broken bottle

test [tɛst] **1** *adj inv* test; *(période)* trial **2** *nm* test; **t. de grossesse** pregnancy test

Testament [tɛstamɑ̃] *nm* **l'Ancien/le Nouveau T.** the Old/the New Testament

testament [tɛstamɑ̃] *nm (dernières volontés)* will; *Fig* legacy; **ceci est mon t.** this is my last will and testament

testamentaire [tɛstamɑ̃tɛr] *adj voir* **exécuteur**

tester [tɛste] *vt (élève, produit)* to test

testicule [tɛstikyl] *nm* testicle

testostérone [tɛstosteron] *nf* testosterone

tétanie [tetani] *nf* spasms, *Spéc* tetany; **avoir une crise de t.** to go into spasms

tétanique [tetanik] **1** *adj* tetanic **2** *nmf* tetanus sufferer

tétaniser [tetanize] *vt (muscle)* to cause spasms in; *Fig* **tétanisé de peur** paralysed with fear

tétanos [tetanos] *nm* tetanus

têtard [tɛtar] *nm* tadpole

tête [tɛt] *nf* (a) *(d'une personne, d'un animal)* head; **cent cinquante têtes de bétail** a hundred and fifty head of cattle; **j'ai la t. qui tourne** my head is spinning; **tenir t. à qn** to stand up to sb; *Fam* **j'en ai par-dessus la t.** I've had it up to here; *Fam* **avoir la t. près du bonnet** to have a short fuse; *Fig* **t. marcher la t. haute** to walk with one's head held high; **la t. la première** head first; *Fig* **foncer t. baissée** to jump in head first; **de la t. aux pieds** from head to foot; **la t. nue** bare-headed; *Fam* **100 francs par t. de pipe** 100 francs a head; **t. de mort** death's head (b) *(visage)* face; **faire une drôle de t.** to look odd, to make an odd face; **avoir une drôle de t.** to look odd, to have an odd face; **faire la t.** to be in a huff (c) *(personne)* **une t. rousse/blonde** a redhead/blonde; **nos chères têtes blondes** *(enfants)* our little ones; **t. brûlée** hothead; *Fam* **c'est une t. à claques** he/she has a face you just want to slap; *Fam* **t. de cochon** pig-headed person; *Fam* **c'est une t. de lard** *ou* **mule** he/she's pig-headed; **t. de linotte** bird-brain; **t. de Turc** target; **forte t.** strong-minded person; *Fam* **grosse t.** highbrow; *Fam* **avoir la grosse t.** to have a big head, to be big-headed (d) *(esprit)* mind; *(cerveau)* brains; **des idées plein la t.** full of ideas; **avoir qch en t.** to have sth in one's head; **ne pas avoir de t.** to be very forgetful; **avoir toute sa t.** to be all there; **perdre la t.** to lose it; **faire qch à t. reposée** to do sth at one's leisure; **où ai-je la t.!** what am I thinking of!; **être t. en l'air** to have one's head in the clouds; **ne rien avoir dans la t.** to be empty-headed; **avoir la t. dure** to be pig-headed; **mettre qch dans la t. de qn** to put sth in sb's head; **se mettre en t. de faire qch** to get it into one's head to do sth; **se mettre dans la t. que** to get it into one's head that; **en faire à sa t.** to do exactly as one pleases; **avoir une idée derrière la t.** to have an ulterior motive; **de t.** *(calculer, additionner)* in one's head (e) *(cheveux)* hair (f) *(d'une liste)* top; *(de chapitre)* heading; **t. d'affiche** top of the bill

(g) *(d'ail)* head; *(d'un arbre)* top; *(du fémur)* head **(h)** *(d'une procession, d'un cortège)* head; *(d'un train)* front; le **wagon de t.** the front carriage; **prendre la t.** *(dans une course, dans un jeu)* to take the lead; **prendre la t. d'une entreprise** to take over as the head of a company; **être à la t. de qch** *(entreprise, fortune)* to be at the head of sth; *(protestation, révolte)* to be the leader of sth; **arriver en t.** to come in first; **être en t.** to be in the lead; **t. de lit** bed head; **t. de pont** bridgehead; **t. de série** *(au tennis)* seed **(i)** *(appareil)* **t. chercheuse** homing device; *Ordinat* **t. d'écriture** writing or write head; *Ordinat* **t. de lecture** read(ing) head; **t. à palpeur** sensor head

tête-à-queue [tɛtakø] *nm inv* spin; **faire un t.** to spin round

tête-à-tête [tɛtatɛt] *nm inv* *(rendez-vous)* tête-à-tête; **en t.** in private; **en t. avec** alone with

tête-bêche [tɛtbɛʃ] *adv (dormir)* head to foot

tête-de-nègre [tɛtdənɛgr] *adj inv & nm inv* dark brown

tétée [tete] *nf* feed; **donner la t. à un enfant** to feed a child

téter [tete] *vt* **(a)** *(lait)* to suck; **t. sa mère** to feed **(b)** *(cigare, pipe, stylo)* to suck on

tétine [tetin] *nf* **(a)** *(d'un biberon)* teat **(b)** *(sucette)* Br dummy, Am pacifier

téton [tetɔ̃] *nm* **(a)** *Fam (sein de femme)* tit **(b)** *(d'une pièce détachée)* lug

tétraèdre [tetraɛdr] **1** *adj* tetrahedral
2 *nm* tetrahedron

tétralogie [tetralɔʒi] *nf* tetralogy

tétraplégie [tetrapleʒi] *nf* quadriplegia

tétraplégique [tetrapleʒik] *adj & nmf* quadriplegic

tétras [tetra] *nm* grouse

têtu, -e [tety] **1** *adj* stubborn, obstinate; *Fam* **t. comme une mule** as stubborn as a mule
2 *nm,f* stubborn *or* obstinate person

teuf-teuf *(pl* teufs-teufs*)* [tœftœf] *Fam* **1** *nf (voiture)* old banger **2** *nm (bruit)* chug-chug

teuton, -onne [tøtɔ̃, -ɔn] **1** *adj* Teutonic
2 *nm,f* T. Teuton

texan, -e [tɛksɑ̃, -an] **1** *adj* Texan
2 *nm,f* T. Texan

texte [tɛkst] *nm* **(a)** *(d'un livre, d'un dépliant)* text; **t. publicitaire** advertising copy; **lire un auteur dans le t.** to read an author in the original; **textes choisis (de)** selected passages *(from)* **(b)** *(d'un opéra)* libretto; *(d'une chanson)* words; *(d'un acteur)* lines; *(d'une pièce de théâtre)* script

textile [tɛkstil] **1** *adj* textile
2 *nm* **(a)** *(fibre)* textile **(b)** *(industrie)* le **t.** the textile industry, textiles

texto [tɛksto] *adv Fam* word for word; **t.!** those were his/her/*etc* very words!

textuel, -elle [tɛkstɥɛl] *adj* **(a)** *(analyse)* textual **(b)** *(traduction)* word-for-word, literal; *Fam* **t.!** those were his/her/*etc* very words!

textuellement [tɛkstɥɛlmɑ̃] *adv* word for word, literally

texture [tɛkstyr] *nf (d'une substance, du sol)* texture

TF 1 [teɛfœ̃] *nf (abrév* **Télévision Française 1)** = French commercial television channel

TGV [teʒeve] *nm (abrév* **train à grande vitesse)** high-speed train

thaï, thaïe [taj] **1** *adj* Thai
2 *nm,f* T. Thai
3 *nm (langue)* Thai

thaïlandais, -e [tailɑ̃dɛ, -ɛz] **1** *adj* Thai
2 *nm,f* T. Thai

Thaïlande [tailɑ̃d] *nf* la T. Thailand

thalassothérapie [talasoterapi] *nf* seawater therapy

thé [te] *nm* **(a)** *(boisson)* tea; **t. au citron** tea with lemon; **t. glacé** iced tea; **t. à la menthe** mint tea; **t. nature/au lait** tea without milk/with milk; **t. en sachets** tea bags **(b)** *(goûter)* tea; **t. dansant** tea dance

théâtral, -e, -aux, -ales [teɑtral, -o] *adj* **(a)** *(œuvre, production)* theatrical; *(effet)* dramatic; *(représentation)* stage **(b)** *Péj (artificiel)* melodramatic

théâtre [teɑtr] *nm* **(a)** *(édifice, salle)* theatre; **t. de marionnettes** puppet theatre; **t. de verdure** open-air theatre **(b)** *(art, métier)* theatre; **c'est un homme de t.** he works in theatre; **faire du t.** *(professionnellement)* to be an actor/actress; *(en amateur)* to do some acting; **adapté pour le t.** adapted for the stage **(c)** *(œuvres) (d'un auteur)* plays; *(genre)* theatre; **t. de boulevard** light comedies **(d)** *Fig (attitude artificielle)* **c'est du t.** it's an act **(e)** *(d'un crime, d'un accident)* scene

théière [tejɛr] *nf* teapot

théine [tein] *nf* theine

thématique [tematik] **1** *adj* thematic
2 *nf* themes

thème [tɛm] *nm* **(a)** *(d'un discours, d'une œuvre, d'un morceau de musique)* theme **(b)** *(traduction)* prose **(c)** *(d'un verbe, d'un nom)* stem **(d)** *Astrol* **t. (astral)** birth chart

théocratie [teɔkrasi] *nf* theocracy

théocratique [teɔkratik] *adj* theocratic

théologie [teɔlɔʒi] *nf* theology

théologien, -enne [teɔlɔʒjɛ̃, -ɛn] *nm,f* theologian

théologique [teɔlɔʒik] *adj* theological

théorème [teɔrɛm] *nm* theorem

théoricien, -enne [teɔrisjɛ̃, -ɛn] *nm,f* theoretician, theorist

théorie [teɔri] *nf* theory; **en t.** in theory

théorique [teɔrik] *adj* theoretical

théoriquement [teɔrikmɑ̃] *adv* theoretically

thérapeute [terapøt] *nmf* therapist

thérapeutique [terapøtik] **1** *adj* therapeutic
2 *nf* **(a)** *(science)* therapeutics *(singulier)* **(b)** *(traitement)* therapy

thérapie [terapi] *nf* therapy; **t. de groupe** group therapy

thermal, -e, -aux, -ales [tɛrmal, -o] *adj* thermal

thermalisme [tɛrmalism] *nm* hydrotherapy

thermes [tɛrm] *nmpl* **(a)** *(établissement de soins)* thermal baths **(b)** *(chez les Anciens)* thermae, public baths

thermique [tɛrmik] *adj* thermal

thermoélectrique [tɛrmoelɛktrik] *adj* thermoelectric

thermomètre [tɛrmomɛtr] *nm* thermometer; *Fig (de l'opinion, d'une tendance)* barometer; **t. médical** clinical thermometer

thermonucléaire [tɛrmonykleɛr] *adj* thermonuclear

Thermos® [tɛrmos] *nm ou nf* **(bouteille)** T. Thermos® *(Br* flask *or Am* bottle)

thermostat [tɛrmosta] *nm* thermostat

thésard, -e [tezar, -ard] *nm,f* PhD student

thésaurisation [tezorizasjɔ̃] *nf* hoarding

thésauriser [tezorize] *vt & vi* to hoard

thesaurus [tezorys] *nm* thesaurus

thèse [tɛz] *nf* (a) *(proposition intellectuelle)* thesis; **roman/littérature à t.** novel/literature of ideas (b) *Univ* thesis *(submitted for doctorate)*

thon [tɔ̃] *nm* tuna; **t. blanc** longfin tuna ; **t. au naturel/à l'huile** tuna in brine/in oil

thoracique [torasik] *adj* thoracic

thorax [toraks] *nm* thorax

thriller [srilœr] *nm* thriller

thrombose [trɔ̃boz] *nf* thrombosis

thune [tyn] *nf très Fam* dosh; **ne pas avoir une t.** to be totally skint

thuya [tyja] *nm* thuja

thym [tɛ̃] *nm* thyme

thyroïde [tiroid] *adj & nf* thyroid

thyroïdien, -enne [tiroidjɛ̃, -ɛn] *adj* thyroid

tiare [tjar] *nf* tiara

Tibet [tibɛ] *nm* le T. Tibet

tibétain, -e [tibetɛ̃, -ɛn] **1** *adj* Tibetan
2 *nm,f* T. Tibetan
3 *nm (langue)* Tibetan

tibia [tibja] *nm* shinbone, *Spéc* tibia

Tibre [tibr] *nm* le T. the Tiber

tic [tik] *nm* (a) *(convulsion involontaire)* tic, twitch; **t. nerveux** nervous tic or twitch (b) *(manie)* habit, mannerism; **t. de langage** verbal mannerism

ticket [tikɛ] *nm* ticket; *Fam Fig* **avoir un t. avec qn** to have made a hit with sb; **t. de caisse** receipt; **t. modérateur** = portion of the cost of treatment paid by the patient; **t. de quai** platform ticket; **t. de rationnement** ration coupon

ticket-repas *(pl* tickets-repas*)* [tikɛrəpɑ] *nm Br* luncheon voucher, *Am* meal ticket

ticket-restaurant *(pl* tickets-restaurant*)* [tikɛrɛstɔrɑ̃] *nm Br* luncheon voucher, *Am* meal ticket

tic-tac [tiktak] *nm inv (d'une horloge)* tick-tock, ticking

tie-break [tajbrɛk] *nm* tie break

tiédasse [tjedas] *adj Péj* lukewarm, tepid

tiède [tjɛd] **1** *adv* il fait t. it's mild
2 *adj (a) (vent)* mild; *(bain, boisson)* tepid, lukewarm (b) *Péj (peu enthousiaste)* half-hearted

tiédeur [tjedœr] *nf* (a) *(du vent)* mildness; *(de l'eau)* tepidness (b) *Péj (manque d'enthousiasme)* half-heartedness

tiédir [tjedir] **1** *vt (réchauffer)* to warm (up); *(refroidir)* to cool (down)
2 *vi (devenir plus chaud)* to warm up; *(devenir moins chaud)* to cool down (b) *Fig (amitié, passion)* to cool off

tien, -enne [tjɛ̃, tjɛn] **1** *pron possessif* le t., la tienne, les tiens, les tiennes yours; *(en insistant)* your own; **tu me prêtes le t.?** can I borrow yours?; **tu n'en as pas besoin, tu as le t.** you don't need it, you've got your own; *Fam* **à la tienne!** cheers!
2 *nm* il faut que tu y mettes du t. you should really do your share
3 *nmpl* les tiens *(ta famille)* your family
4 *nfpl Fam* tu as encore fait des tiennes! you've been up to your old tricks again!

tiendrais, tienne, tiens *etc voir* **tenir**

tierce [tjɛrs] **1** *adj voir* **tiers**
2 *nf* (a) *Mus* third (b) *(aux cartes)* tierce

tiercé [tjɛrse] *nm* = forecast of the first three horses in a race; **jouer au t.** to bet on the horses; **le t. gagnant** the winning combination

tiers, tierce [tjɛr, tjɛrs] **1** *adj* third; **le t. état** the third estate; **une tierce personne** a third party
2 *nm* (a) *(fraction)* third; **t. payant** = system of direct payment for medical treatment by the insurer; **t. provisionnel** interim tax payment (= *approximately one third of previous year's tax)* (b) *(personne)* third party

tiers-monde *(pl* tiers-mondes*)* [tjɛrmɔ̃d] *nm* le t. the Third World

tifs [tif] *nmpl Fam* hair

TIG [tiʒ] *nm (abrév* travail d'intérêt général*)* community service

tige [tiʒ] *nf* (a) *(d'une plante)* stem, stalk; **rosier sur t.** standard rose (b) *(d'une chaussure)* upper (c) *(en métal)* rod (d) *Fam (cigarette)* Br fag, *Am* butt

tignasse [tiɲas] *nf Fam* mop (of hair)

Tigre [tigr] *nm* le T. the Tigris

tigre [tigr] *nm* tiger; **t. du Bengale** Bengal tiger

tigré, -e [tigre] *adj (rayé)* striped

tigresse [tigrɛs] *nf* tigress

tilde [tild] *nm* tilde

tilleul [tijœl] *nm* (a) *(arbre)* lime (tree) (b) *(infusion)* lime-blossom tea

tilt [tilt] *nm* faire t. (au billard électrique) to signal the end of the game; *Fig* ça a fait t. the penny dropped

timbale [tɛ̃bal] *nf* (a) *(gobelet)* (metal) drinking cup; *Fig* **décrocher la t.** to hit the jackpot (b) *(tambour)* kettledrum; **les timbales** *(dans un orchestre)* the timpani (c) *(moule, plat)* timbale

timbre [tɛ̃br] *nm* (a) *(vignette)* stamp; **t. de collection** collector's stamp; **t. fiscal** excise or tax stamp (b) *(instrument encreur, marque)* stamp; **t. dateur** date stamp (c) *(sonnette)* bell; **t. de bicyclette** bicycle bell (d) *(d'une voix, d'un instrument)* timbre, tone; **voix sans t.** toneless voice (e) *(pour traitement médical)* patch; **t. tuberculinique** TB patch

timbré, -e [tɛ̃bre] *adj* (a) *(document, enveloppe)* stamped (b) *Fam (fou)* mad

timbre-poste *(pl* timbres-poste*)* [tɛ̃brəpɔst] *nm* (postage) stamp

timbrer [tɛ̃bre] *vt* (a) *(lettre, paquet)* to put a stamp/stamps on (b) *(passeport, document)* to stamp

timide [timid] **1** *adj* (a) *(personne, sourire, voix)* shy (b) *(critique, protestation, tentative)* timid
2 *nmf* shy person; **c'est un grand t.** he's very shy

timidement [timidmɑ̃] *adv* (a) *(sourire, parler)* shyly (b) *(critiquer, protester)* timidly

timidité [timidite] *nf* (a) *(d'une personne)* shyness (b) *(d'une critique, d'une protestation)* timidity

timing [tajmiŋ] *nm* timing

timoré, -e [timore] *adj* timorous, fearful

tintamarre [tɛ̃tamar] *nm Fam* din, racket; **faire du t.** to make a din or racket

tintement [tɛ̃tmɑ̃] *nm (de clochettes)* tinkling; *(de pièces de monnaie)* jingling; **t. d'oreilles** ringing in the ears

tinter [tɛ̃te] *vi* (a) *(clochettes)* to tinkle; *(pièces de monnaie)* to jingle (b) *(oreilles)* to ring

tintin [tɛ̃tɛ̃] *exclam Fam* no way José!; **faire t.** to go without

tintouin [tɛ̃twɛ̃] nm Fam (a) (bruit) din, racket (b) (souci) trouble

tipi [tipi] nm tepee

tique [tik] nf tick

tiquer [tike] vi Fam (personne) to wince; **il n'a pas tiqué** he didn't bat an eyelid

TIR [tir] nm (abrév **transports internationaux routiers**) TIR

tir [tir] nm (a) (activité) shooting; **t. à l'arc** archery; **faire du t. à l'arc** to do archery; **t. à la carabine** rifle shooting (b) (coup de feu) shot (c) (à la pétanque) throw; **t. (au but)** (au football) shot (at goal) (d) (stand) rifle range; **t. (forain)** shooting gallery

tirade [tirad] nf Th monologue; Fig tirade

tirage [tiraʒ] nm (a) (impression) printing (b) (nombre d'exemplaires) (d'un journal) circulation; (d'un livre) print run; **édition à t. limité** limited edition (c) (d'une cheminée) draught (d) (de loterie) draw (de for); **t. au sort** drawing lots; **procéder à un t. au sort** to draw lots

tiraillement [tirajmɑ̃] nm (a) (crampe) **tiraillements d'estomac** stomach cramps (b) (conflit) **tiraillements (entre)** conflict (between)

tirailler [tiraje] **1** vt (a) (tirer sur) to pull at, to tug at (b) (écarteler) **être tiraillé entre** to be torn between
2 vi (avec une arme) to shoot wildly (b) (peau) **j'ai la peau qui tiraille** my skin feels tight

tirailleur [tirajœr] nm (soldat éclaireur) skirmisher

Tirana [tirana] n Tirana

tirant [tirɑ̃] nm (a) (de botte) boot strap (b) **t. d'eau** draught (volume of water)

tire [tir] nf (a) très Fam (voiture) car (b) Can (confiserie) molasses toffee, Am molasses candy, taffy

tiré, -e [tire] **1** adj (a) (traits) drawn; **avoir les traits tirés** to look drawn (b) (cheveux) scraped back
2 nf Fam **tirée** (trajet) long haul

tire-au-flanc [tiroflɑ̃] nm inv Fam shirker, Br skiver

tire-bouchon (pl tire-bouchons) [tirbuʃ5] nm corkscrew; **en t.** (queue) curly

tire-bouchonner [tirbuʃɔne] vi (chaussettes) to be at half-mast; (pantalon) to be crumpled

tire-d'aile [tirdɛl] **à tire-d'aile** adv **s'envoler à t.** to fly swiftly away; Fig **partir ou s'éloigner à t.** to fly off

tire-fesses [tirfɛs] nm inv Fam T-bar

tire-jus [tirʒy] nm inv très Fam snot rag

tire-lait [tirlɛ] nm inv breast pump

tire-larigot [tirlarigo] **à tire-larigot** adv Fam to one's heart's content

tirelire [tirlir] nf Br moneybox, Am coin bank; Fig **casser sa t.** to break into one's piggy bank

tirer [tire] **1** vt (a) (vers soi) to pull; (chaussettes) to pull up; **t. qch vers le haut/bas** to pull sth up/down; **t. qn par la manche** to pull at sb's sleeve; **t. qn par le bras** to pull sb by the arm; **t. les cheveux à qn** to pull sb's hair (b) (rideaux) to draw; (store) to pull down; (verrou) (fermer) to shoot; (ouvrir) to draw
(c) (extraire) **t. qch de qch** to pull sth out of sth; **t. de l'eau d'un puits** to draw water from a well; **une citation tirée d'un texte** a quotation taken from a text; **t. qn d'embarras** to get sb out of a tight spot; **t. qn de son lit** to drag sb out of bed; **t. son origine de qch** to have its origin in sth; **t. une conclusion de qch** to draw a conclusion from sth; **t. une leçon de qch** to learn a lesson from sth

(d) (tendre) (tissu, fil) to pull tight; Fig **t. les ficelles** to pull the strings
(e) (carte) to draw; **t. les cartes** (cartomancienne) to read the cards; **t. qch au sort** to draw lots for sth; **tirer qn au sort** to draw lots to choose sb
(f) (tracer) (trait) to draw; (plan) to draw up
(g) (imprimer) to print; Fam Hum **se faire t. le portrait** to have one's photograph taken
(h) (chèque) to draw (sur on)
(i) (coup de feu, balle) to fire; (flèche) to shoot; (feu d'artifice) to let off; **t. un coup de revolver (sur)** to fire a gun (at)
(j) (locutions) très Fam **plus qu'un mois à t.!** just one more month to get through!; **je te tire mon chapeau!** I take my hat off to you!

2 vi (a) (exercer une traction) to pull; **t. sur qch** (corde) to pull on sth; (pull) to pull sth down; (par tic) to pull at
(b) (personne armée, arme) to shoot; **t. à la carabine** to shoot with a rifle; **t. sur qn/qch** to shoot sb/sth; **t. dans le dos à qn** to shoot sb in the back
(c) (peau) to feel tight
(d) (être imprimé) **t. à 100 000 exemplaires** to have a circulation of 100,000
(e) (cheminée) to draw
(f) (à la pétanque) to throw; (au football) to shoot
(g) (aspirer) **t. sur une cigarette/pipe** to puff on a cigarette/pipe
(h) (locutions) **ça ne tire pas à conséquence** it's of no consequence; **t. à sa fin** (période, provision) to be drawing to a close; (réserves, économies) to be running out; Fam **t. au flanc** to shirk, Br to skive

3 tirer sur vt ind (se rapprocher de) (couleur) to verge on

4 se tirer vpr (a) (se sortir) **se t. de qch** to get out of sth; **s'en t.** (d'une maladie, d'un accident) to pull through; (financièrement) to make it; **s'en t. avec qch** to get away with sth
(b) Fam (partir) to make tracks

tiret [tirɛ] nm dash

tirette [tirɛt] nf (a) (d'un bureau) pull-out shelf; (d'une table) leaf (b) (de distributeur) pull handle (c) Belg (fermeture Éclair) Br zip, Am zipper

tireur, -euse [tirœr, -øz] **1** nm,f gunman; **t. d'élite** marksman, f markswoman; **c'est un bon t.** he's a good shot
2 nf **tireuse de cartes** fortune teller

tiroir [tirwar] nm drawer; Fig **à tiroirs** (roman) = containing individual episodes within the main storyline

tiroir-caisse (pl tiroirs-caisses) [tirwarkɛs] nm till, cash register

tisane [tizan] nf herbal tea

tison [tiz5] nm (fire)brand

tisonner [tizɔne] vt to poke

tisonnier [tizɔnje] nm poker

tissage [tisaʒ] nm (a) (activité) weaving; **t. à la main/mécanique** hand-loom/power-loom weaving (b) (établissement industriel) cloth mill

tisser [tise] **1** vt (a) (textile, liens, intrigue) to weave (b) (sujet: araignée) to spin
2 se tisser vpr (liens, intrigue) to be woven

tisserand, -e [tisrɑ̃, -ɑ̃d] nm,f weaver

tissu [tisy] nm (a) (étoffe) material, cloth; Fig (urbain, social) fabric; **t. d'ameublement** furnishing fabric (b) Fig (de mensonges, d'incohérences) tissue (c) Biol tissue

tissu-éponge (pl tissus-éponges) [tisyepɔ̃ʒ] nm (terry) towelling

titan [titɑ̃] nm Titan; **travail de t.** Herculean task

titane [titan] *nm* titanium

titi [titi] *nm Fam* cheeky urchin

titiller [titije] *vt* to titillate

titrage [titraʒ] *nm* (**a**) *(de film)* titling (**b**) *(d'un alcool)* determination of the strength

titre [titr] *nm* (**a**) *(de livre, de chanson, de film)* title (**b**) *(de chapitre, de page)* heading; **les gros titres** the headlines; **faire les gros titres** to hit the headlines (**c**) *(d'une personne)* title; **en t.** *(titulaire)* permanent; *(attitré)* official (**d**) *(qualité de champion)* title (**e**) *(diplôme)* qualification (**f**) *(certificat)* **t. de propriété** title deed; **t. de transport** ticket (**g**) *Fin* security (**h**) *(d'un alcool)* strength; *(de l'or, d'une monnaie)* fineness; *(d'un alliage)* grade (**i**) *(locutions)* **à ce t.** *(pour cette raison)* therefore; *(en cette qualité)* as such; **à quel t.?** *(de quel droit)* on what grounds?; **au même t. que** in the same way as; **à t. gratuit** free of charge; **à t. d'exemple** by way of example

titré, -e [titre] *adj (personne)* titled

titrer [titre] *vt* (**a**) *(livre, film)* to title (**b**) *(alcool)* to determine the strength of

tituber [titybe] *vi* to stagger (**de with**)

titulaire [titylɛr] **1** *adj* (**a**) *(dans l'administration)* with a permanent contract; *(professeur d'université)* with tenure (**b**) *(détenteur)* **être t. de qch** to be the holder of sth
2 *nmf (détenteur)* holder

titularisation [titylarizasjɔ̃] *nf* granting of permanent contract; *(à l'université)* granting of tenure

titulariser [titylarize] *vt* to give a permanent contract to; *(professeur d'université)* to give tenure to

TNT [teɛnte] *nm (abrév* **trinitrotoluène***)* TNT

toast [tost] *nm* (**a**) *(de pain)* piece *or* slice of toast; **t. beurré** piece *or* slice of buttered toast; **des toasts** toast (**b**) *(hommage)* toast; **porter un t. à qn** to drink a toast to sb

toboggan [tɔbɔgã] *nm* (**a**) *(de terrain de jeu)* slide; *(dans une piscine)* flume; **faire du t.** to play on the slide (**b**) *(pour marchandises)* chute (**c**) *(viaduc) Br* flyover, *Am* overpass (**d**) *Can (traîneau)* toboggan; **faire du t.** to go tobogganing

toc [tok] **1** *exclam* **t. t.!** knock knock!; *Fig* **et t.!** so there!
2 *adj inv Fam (faux)* fake; *(de mauvais goût)* tacky
3 *nm Fam* **bijoux en t.** fake jewellery; **c'est du t.** it's fake

toccata [tɔkata] *nf Mus* toccata

tocsin [tɔksɛ̃] *nm* alarm bell

toge [tɔʒ] *nf* (**a**) *(de magistrat, d'avocat)* gown (**b**) *(romaine)* toga

Togo [togo] *nm* **le T.** Togo

togolais, -e [tɔgɔlɛ, -ɛz] **1** *adj* Togolese
2 *nm, f* **T.** Togolese

tohu-bohu [tɔyboy] *nm (désordre)* confusion; *(bruit)* hubbub

toi [twa] *pron personnel* (**a**) *(sujet)* you; **t., ne m'énerve pas!** don't annoy me!; **t., tu aurais certainement cédé** YOU would probably have given in (**b**) *(objet direct)* you; **et t., il t'a salué?** and what about you, did he say hello to you? (**c**) *(avec préposition)* you; **je ne te le prêterai pas, à t.** I won't lend it to YOU; **c'est à t., tout ça?** is that all yours?; **tu auras ta chambre à t.** you'll have your own room; **Fam une copine à t.** a friend of yours; **tu ne penses qu'à t.** you think only of yourself (**d**) *(dans les comparaisons)* you; **je n'en sais pas plus que t.** I don't know any more about it than you (do)

toile [twal] *nf* (**a**) *(tissu)* cloth; **t. d'araignée** cobweb, spider's web; **t. cirée** oilcloth; **t. de fond** backdrop; *Fig* **en t. de fond** as a backdrop; **t. (de lin)** linen; **un pantalon en t.** linen trousers; **t. à matelas** ticking; **t. de tente** canvas (**b**) *(tableau)* painting, canvas (**c**) *Fam (film)* **se faire une t.** to go to the *Br* pictures *or Am* movies

toilettage [twaletaʒ] *nm* (**a**) *(d'un chien)* grooming (**b**) *(d'un texte)* tidying up

toilette [twalɛt] *nf* (**a**) *(action de se laver)* washing; **faire sa t.** to have a wash (**b**) **toilettes** *(W.-C.) Br* toilet, *Am* rest room; *(publiques)* public convenience; **toilettes pour dames** ladies' *Br* toilet *or Am* room; **toilettes pour hommes** *Br* gents' toilet, *Am* men's room (**c**) *(vêtements)* outfit; **porter bien la t.** to look good in formal clothes

toiletter [twalete] *vt* (**a**) *(chien)* to groom (**b**) *(texte)* to tidy up

toi-même [twamɛm] *pron personnel* yourself; *Fam* **menteur! – t.!** liar! – liar yourself!

toise [twaz] *nf* height gauge

toiser [twaze] **1** *vt* to look up and down
2 se toiser *vpr* to look each other up and down

toison [twazɔ̃] *nf* (**a**) *(de mouton)* fleece; **la T. d'or** the Golden Fleece (**b**) *(chevelure)* mane (of hair)

toit [twa] *nm* roof; *Fig* **être sans t.** not to have a roof over one's head; **accueillir qn sous son t.** to take sb in; **t. de chaume** thatched roof; **t. ouvrant** sun roof

toiture [twatyr] *nf* roofing, roof

Tokyo [tɔkjo] *n* Tokyo

tôle¹ [tol] *nf* (**a**) *(matériau)* sheet metal; **t. ondulée** corrugated iron (**b**) *(feuille)* metal sheet

tôle² = taule

tolérable [tɔlerabl] *adj* tolerable; **votre comportement n'est pas t.** your behaviour is intolerable

tolérance [tɔlerãs] *nf* tolerance; *(concession)* concession

tolérant, -e [tɔlerã, -ãt] *adj* tolerant

tolérer [tɔlere] **1** *vt* to tolerate; **je ne tolère pas qu'on me parle sur ce ton!** I won't tolerate being spoken to like that!
2 se tolérer *vpr* to tolerate each other

tôlier [tolje] *nm* **= taulier**

tollé [tɔle] *nm* outcry; **t. général** public outcry

TOM [tɔm] *nm (abrév* **territoire d'outre-mer***)* overseas territory

tomahawk [tɔmaok] *nm* tomahawk

tomate [tɔmat] *nf* tomato

tombal, -e, -als *ou* **-aux, -ales** [tɔ̃bal, -o] *adj voir* **pierre**

tombant, -e [tɔ̃bã, -ãt] *adj (épaules)* sloping; *(oreilles)* floppy

tombe [tɔ̃b] *nf* (**a**) *(sépulture)* grave; *(avec un monument)* tomb; **emporter un secret dans la t.** to take a secret to the grave; **suivre qn dans la t.** to follow sb to the grave (**b**) *(pierre tombale)* gravestone, tombstone

tombeau, -x [tɔ̃bo] *nm* tomb; *Fig* **à t. ouvert** at breakneck speed

tombée [tɔ̃be] *nf* **la t. du jour** *ou* **de la nuit** nightfall

tomber [tɔ̃be] **1** *vi (aux être)* **(a)** *(personne, objet)* to fall (down); *(précipitations, feuilles)* to fall; **t. de qch** *(chaise, échelle)* to fall off sth; *(arbre)* to fall out of sth; **t. dans un piège** to fall into a trap; *Fam Fig* **tu es tombé sur la tête?** were you dropped on your head?; **faire t. qn/qch** to knock sb/sth over; **laisser t.** *(objet)* to drop; *Fam* **laisser t. qn** to let sb down; *Fam* **laisse t., c'est inutile** forget it, it's pointless; **t. à l'eau** *(personne, objet)* to fall in (the water); *(projet)* to fall through; *Fig* **il faut être tombé bien bas** you have to have sunk pretty low; **t. de haut** to come back to earth with a bump **(b)** *(gouvernement, ville)* to fall **(c)** *(nouvelle)* to come through **(d)** *(mourir)* to fall; *Fam* **t. comme des mouches** to be dropping like flies **(e)** *(vent, prix, fièvre)* to drop; *(conversation)* to flag; *(enthousiasme)* to wane **(f)** *(nuit)* to fall **(g)** *(devenir brusquement)* **t. amoureux de qn** to fall in love with sb; *Fam* **t. enceinte** to get pregnant **(h)** *(date, événement)* to fall **(i)** *(pendre) (draperie, vêtement)* to hang; **ses cheveux lui tombent jusqu'aux reins** her hair hangs right down her back **(j)** *(locutions)* **t. bien** to come at just the right time; **t. mal** to come at the wrong time; **je suis bien/mal tombé** *(chanceux/malchanceux)* I was lucky/unlucky; **ça tombe sous le sens** it stands to reason; **t. sur qn** *(l'agresser)* to pitch into sb; *(le rencontrer par hasard)* to bump into sb; **t. sur qch** to come across sth; **il fallait que ça tombe sur moi!** it had to happen to me!

2 *vt Fam (aux avoir)* **(a)** *(séduire)* to pull **(b)** *(enlever)* **t. la veste** to take off one's jacket

tombereau, -x [tɔ̃bro] *nm* **(a)** *(charrette)* tip-cart **(b)** *(contenu)* cartload

tombeur [tɔ̃bœr] *nm Fam* womanizer, ladykiller

tombola [tɔ̃bɔla] *nf* raffle

tome [tɔm] *nm (volume)* volume

tomme [tɔm] *nf =* cheese made in Savoie

ton¹, ta, tes [tɔ̃, ta, te]

> ta becomes **ton** before a word beginning with a vowel or mute h.

adj possessif your; **t. chien** your dog; **ta voiture** your car; **t. ami/amie** your friend; **tes enfants** your children; **t. père et ta mère** your mother and father; **un de tes amis** one of your friends, a friend of yours; *Fam* **tu as eu t. vendredi** you got Friday off

ton² *nm* **(a)** *(qualité de voix)* tone; **hausser/baisser le t.** to raise/lower one's voice; **sur le t. de la plaisanterie** in a joking tone of voice **(b)** *(goût)* **il est de bon t. de le faire** it's good form to do it **(c)** *(gamme)* key; *(intervalle musical)* tone; **donner le t.** to give the pitch; *Fig* to set the tone **(d)** *Ling* tone; **langue à tons** tonal language **(e)** *(teinte)* shade, tone; *Ordinat* **tons de gris** shades of grey

tonal, -e, -als, -ales [tɔnal] *adj Mus* tonal

tonalité [tɔnalite] *nf* **(a)** *(au téléphone) Br* dialling *or Am* dial tone **(b)** *(d'un morceau de musique)* key; *Fig (d'une œuvre)* tone

tondeuse [tɔ̃døz] *nf* **(a)** *(de jardin)* **t. (à gazon)** (lawn) mower **(b)** *(de coiffeur)* clippers

tondre [tɔ̃dr] *vt* **(a)** *(herbe)* to mow; *(mouton)* to shear; **se faire t.** *(très court)* to have one's hair cropped; *(complètement)* to have all one's hair shaved off **(b)** *Fam (dépouiller)* to fleece

toner [tɔnɛr] *nm* toner

tong [tɔ̃g] *nf Br* flip-flop, *Am* thong

Tonga [tɔ̃ga] *nfpl* **les (îles)** T. Tonga

tonicité [tɔnisite] *nf* **(a)** *(des muscles)* tone **(b)** *(de l'air, du climat)* bracing effect

tonifiant, -e [tɔnifjɑ̃, -ɑ̃t] *adj (air, marche)* bracing

tonifier [tɔnifje] *vt (peau, muscles)* to tone up; *(esprit)* to stimulate

tonique [tɔnik] **1** *adj* **(a)** *(climat, vent)* bracing, invigorating **(b)** *(boisson, remède)* tonic **(c)** *(personne)* energetic, dynamic **(d)** *(accent)* tonic; *(syllabe)* accented **2** *nm* **(a)** *(remède)* tonic **(b)** *(lotion)* toner **3** *nf Mus* tonic, keynote

tonitruant, -e [tɔnitryɑ̃, -ɑ̃t] *adj (voix, bruit)* thundering

tonnage [tɔnaʒ] *nm* tonnage

tonnant, -e [tɔnɑ̃, -ɑ̃t] *adj (voix)* thundering

tonne [tɔn] *nf* metric ton, tonne; *Fam Fig* **des tonnes de qch** tons of sth; *Fam* **en faire des tonnes** to go overboard

tonneau, -x [tɔno] *nm* **(a)** *(récipient)* barrel, cask; *Fig* **du même t.** of the same type **(b)** *(en voiture)* roll; **faire un t.** to roll over

tonnelier [tɔnəlje] *nm* cooper

tonnelle [tɔnɛl] *nf (charmille)* arbour, bower

tonner [tɔne] **1** *vi (canons)* to thunder **(b)** *(fulminer)* to thunder **(contre** against) **2** *v impersonnel* **il tonne** it's thundering

tonnerre [tɔnɛr] *nm* thunder; **un t. d'applaudissements** thunderous applause; *Fam Fig* **du t.** terrific

tonsure [tɔ̃syr] *nf* tonsure

tonte [tɔ̃t] *nf (des moutons)* shearing; *(du gazon)* mowing

tonton [tɔ̃tɔ̃] *nm Fam* uncle

tonus [tɔnys] *nm* **(a)** *Fig (dynamisme)* energy, dynamism **(b)** *(d'un muscle)* tone

top [tɔp] *nm* **(a)** *(signal sonore)* beep; **au quatrième t. il sera midi** at the fourth stroke it will be twelve o'clock **(b)** *Fam* **être au t. niveau** *(sportif)* to be at one's peak; **c'est le t.!** it's the business!

topaze [tɔpaz] *nf* topaz

toper [tɔpe] *vi Fam* **tope(-là)!** put it there!

topinambour [tɔpinɑ̃bur] *nm* Jerusalem artichoke

topo [tɔpo] *nm Fam (discours)* lecture; *(exposé)* rundown; *Fig* **c'est toujours le même t.** it's always the same old story

topographie [tɔpɔgrafi] *nf* topography

topographique [tɔpɔgrafik] *adj* topographical

toponymie [tɔpɔnimi] *nf* toponymy

top secret [tɔpsəkrɛ] *adj inv* top secret

toquade [tɔkad] *nf Fam (pour une personne)* crush **(pour** on); *(pour un lieu, pour un objet)* craze **(pour** for)

toque [tɔk] *nf (de fourrure)* fur hat; *(de jockey)* cap; *(de cuisinier)* hat

toqué, -e [tɔke] *Fam* **1** *adj* crazy **(de** about) **2** *nm,f* nutcase

toquer [tɔke] **se toquer** *vpr Fam* **se t. de qn** to go crazy over sb

Torah [tɔra] *nf* **la T.** the Torah

torche [tɔrʃ] *nf* torch; **t. électrique** *Br* (electric) torch, *Am* flashlight

torcher [tɔrʃe] *Fam* **1** *vt* (a) *(fesses, enfant)* to wipe (b) *(travail)* to botch (c) *(bouteille)* to polish off
 2 se torcher *vpr* to wipe one's backside

torchis [tɔrʃi] *nm* cob *(for building)*

torchon [tɔrʃɔ̃] *nm* (a) *(de cuisine)* dish *or* tea towel; *Fam* **le t. brûle** they're at each other's throats; *Fig* **il ne faut pas mélanger les torchons et les serviettes** they're in a different league (b) *Fam (texte peu soigné)* mess (c) *Fam (journal)* rag

tordant, -e [tɔrdɑ̃, -ɑ̃t] *adj Fam* hilarious

tord-boyaux [tɔrbwajo] *nm Fam* rotgut

tordre [tɔrdr] **1** *vt (barre de fer, métal)* to bend; *(fil de fer)* to twist; *(linge)* to wring; **t. le cou à qn** to wring sb's neck; **t. le bras à qn** to twist sb's arm
 2 se tordre *vpr* **se t. les mains** to wring one's hands; **se t. la cheville** to twist one's ankle; **se t. de douleur** to writhe in pain; *Fam* **se t. (de rire)** to kill oneself (laughing)

tordu, -e [tɔrdy] **1** *adj* (a) *(objet)* twisted (b) *Fam (dérangé)* **être t.** to be a bit of a maniac; **avoir l'esprit t.** to have a warped mind
 2 *nm,f Fam* maniac

toréador [tɔreadɔr] *nm* bullfighter, toreador

toréer [tɔree] *vi* to fight *(in the bullring)*

torero [tɔrero] *nm* bullfighter

torgnole [tɔrɲɔl] *nf très Fam* clout

tornade [tɔrnad] *nf* tornado; **comme une t.** like a whirlwind

Toronto [tɔrɔ̃to] *n* Toronto

torpeur [tɔrpœr] *nf* torpor

torpillage [tɔrpijaʒ] *nm* torpedoing

torpille [tɔrpij] *nf* (a) *(engin militaire)* torpedo (b) *(poisson)* torpedo, electric ray

torpiller [tɔrpije] *vt aussi Fig* to torpedo

torpilleur [tɔrpijœr] *nm* torpedo boat

torréfaction [tɔrefaksjɔ̃] *nf* roasting

torréfier [tɔrefje] *vt* to roast

torrent [tɔrɑ̃] *nm (cours d'eau)* torrent; *Fig (de larmes, de lumière)* flood; *(d'injures)* torrent; *(de questions)* barrage; **pleuvoir à torrents** to pour down

torrentiel, -elle [tɔrɑ̃sjɛl] *adj* torrential

torride [tɔrid] *adj* torrid

tors, -e [tɔr, tɔrs] *adj* twisted

torsade [tɔrsad] *nf* (a) *(point de tricot)* cable; **pull à torsades** cable(-knit) jumper (b) *(de cheveux)* twist, coil

torsadé, -e [tɔrsade] *adj (pull)* cable(-knit)

torsader [tɔrsade] *vt* to twist

torse [tɔrs] *nm* chest; **t. nu** stripped to the waist

torsion [tɔrsjɔ̃] *nf* twisting

tort [tɔr] *nm* (a) *(faute)* fault; **avoir tous les torts** to be entirely to blame; **c'est un t. de l'avoir fait** it was a mistake to do it; **avoir t. (de faire qch)** to be wrong *(to do sth)*; **tu n'as pas t.** you're quite right; **donner t. à qn** *(personne)* to blame sb; *(résultat, preuve)* to prove sb wrong; **être en t.** *ou* **dans son t.** to be in the wrong (b) *(dommage)* wrong; **faire du t. à qn** to harm sb; *(désavantager)* to penalize sb (c) *(locutions)* **à t.** wrongly; **à t. ou à raison** rightly or wrongly; **à t. et à travers** *(dépenser)* recklessly; *(parler)* wildly

torticolis [tɔrtikɔli] *nm* stiff neck; **avoir le** *ou* **un t.** to have a stiff neck

tortillard [tɔrtijar] *nm Fam* local train

tortiller [tɔrtije] **1** *vt (papier, ruban, cheveux)* to twist; *(moustache)* to twirl
 2 *vi Fam* **il n'y a pas à t.** there are no two ways about it
 3 se tortiller *vpr (personne)* to wriggle

tortillon [tɔrtijɔ̃] *nm (de papier)* twist

tortionnaire [tɔrsjɔnɛr] *nmf* torturer

tortue [tɔrty] *nf* (a) *(reptile)* tortoise; **t. d'eau douce** terrapin; **t. de mer** turtle (b) *Fig (personne lente)* Br slowcoach, *Am* slowpoke

tortueusement [tɔrtɥøzmɑ̃] *adv (hypocritement)* deviously

tortueux, -euse [tɔrtɥø, -øz] *adj* (a) *(sinueux)* winding, tortuous (b) *(attitude, esprit)* devious; *(langage)* tortuous

torture [tɔrtyr] *nf aussi Fig* torture; *Fig* **mettre qn à la t.** to torture sb

torturer [tɔrtyre] **1** *vt aussi Fig* to torture
 2 se torturer *vpr* to torture oneself; **se t. l'esprit** to rack one's brains

torve [tɔrv] *adj* menacing

toscan, -e [tɔskɑ̃, -an] **1** *adj* Tuscan
 2 *nm,f* T. Tuscan
 3 *nm (langue)* Tuscan

Toscane [tɔskan] *nf* la T. Tuscany

tôt [to] *adv* (a) *(bientôt, vite)* soon, early; **nous n'étions pas plus t. rentrés que...** no sooner had we returned than...; **au plus t.** at the earliest; *Fam* **ce n'est pas trop t.!** and about time too!; **elle a eu t. fait de changer d'avis** she soon changed her mind; **t. ou tard** sooner or later (b) *(de bonne heure)* early

total, -e, -aux, -ales [tɔtal, -o] **1** *adj* total
 2 *nm* total; **faire le t.** to work out the total; **au t.** in all, in total; *(tout compte fait)* all in all; *Fam* **t., ils se sont fâchés** the upshot was that they fell out

totalement [tɔtalmɑ̃] *adv* totally

totaliser [tɔtalize] *vt* (a) *(additionner)* to total, to add up (b) *(avoir au total)* to have a total of

totalitaire [tɔtalitɛr] *adj* totalitarian

totalitarisme [tɔtalitarism] *nm* totalitarianism

totalité [tɔtalite] *nf* **la t. de** all of; **payer qch en t.** to pay sth in full

totem [tɔtɛm] *nm (mât)* totem pole

touareg [twarɛg] **1** *adj* Tuareg
 2 *nmf* T. Tuareg
 3 *nm (langue)* Tuareg

toubib [tubib] *nm Fam* doctor

toucan [tukɑ̃] *nm* toucan

touchant, -e [tuʃɑ̃, -ɑ̃t] *adj* touching

touche [tuʃ] *nf* (a) *(d'un piano, d'un clavier)* key; *Ordinat* **t. alt** alt *(key)* (b) *(tache de couleur)* touch; **mettre la t. finale à qch** to put the finishing touches to sth (c) *(style)* touch (d) *(en escrime)* hit; *(à la pêche)* bite; *Fam* **avoir une t. avec qn** to make a hit with sb; *Fam* **faire une t.** to make a hit (e) *(remise en jeu)* throw-in; *(par les avants au rugby)* line-out; **sortir en t.** to go into touch; *aussi Fig* **rester sur la t.** to stay on the sidelines (f) *Fam (allure)* look; **avoir une drôle de t.** to look weird (g) *(de violon)* finger board; *(de guitare)* fret

touche-à-tout [tuʃatu] *nmf inv Fam* (a) *(enfant)* **c'est un t.** he's into everything (b) *(qui a plusieurs occupations)* dabbler

toucher¹ [tuʃe] *nm* (a) *(sens)* **le t.** touch; **au t.** to the touch (b) *(d'un pianiste)* touch

toucher² 1 vt (a) (être en contact avec) to touch; (cible, adversaire) to hit; **je touche du bois!** touch wood!; Fam **pas touché!** hands off! (b) (blesser) to hit (à in) (c) (émouvoir) to touch, to move (d) (concerner) to concern, to affect (e) (port) to put in at; **t. le fond** (navire) to touch bottom; Fig (moralement) to hit rock bottom; **t. terre** (bateau) to reach dry land (f) (argent, intérêt, paie) to get; (chèque) to cash; **t. le tiercé** to win the tiercé (g) (jouxter) to adjoin (h) (dire) **t. un mot à qn** (de qch) to have a word with sb (about sth)

2 **toucher à** vt ind (a) (prendre, modifier) to touch; Fig **avec son air de ne pas y t.** looking as if butter wouldn't melt in his mouth (b) (problème, question) to touch on (approcher de) **t. au but** to be nearing one's goal; **t. à sa fin** to be nearing its end (d) (concerner) to concern

3 **se toucher** vpr (être en contact) to touch; (maisons) to adjoin

touer [twe] vt Can to tow

touffe [tuf] nf tuft

touffu, -e [tufy] adj (a) (bois, végétation) dense; (barbe, cheveux) bushy (b) Fig (livre) dense

touiller [tuje] vt Fam to stir; (salade) to toss

toujours [tuʒur] adv (a) (exprime la continuité, la répétition) always; **t. plus nombreux** more and more numerous; **un ami de t.** a lifelong friend; **pour t.** for ever; **depuis t.** always (b) (encore) still; **cherchez t.** keep looking; **alors, il est rentré? - t. pas** he's back then? - not yet (c) (quoi qu'il en soit) **t. est-il que...** the fact remains that...; **elle peut t. attendre!** she'll have a long wait!; **c'est t. ça** (de pris) at least it's something

toulousain, -e [tuluzɛ̃, -en] 1 adj of Toulouse
2 nm,f T. person from Toulouse

Toulouse [tuluz] n Toulouse

toundra [tundra] nf tundra

toupet [tupɛ] nm Fam (audace) cheek, nerve; **avoir du t., ne pas manquer de t.** to have a cheek or a nerve (b) (de cheveux) tuft of hair, Br quiff

toupie [tupi] nf (a) (jouet) (spinning) top (b) Fam (femme) **vieille t.** old trout

tour¹ [tur] nf (a) (construction) tower; **t. de contrôle** control tower; **la T. Eiffel** the Eiffel Tower (b) (immeuble) Br tower block, Am high-rise (c) (aux échecs) rook, castle (d) Ordinat tower

tour² nm (a) (circonférence) circumference; **t. de cou/de taille** collar/waist size or measurement; **avoir 75 cm de t. de taille** to have a waist measurement of 75 cm; **perdre 5 cm de t. de taille** to lose 5 cm round the waist; **t. de tête** hat size
(b) (mouvement circulaire) **faire le t.** (de qch) to go round (sth); **faire faire à qn le t. du propriétaire** to show sb round (a house); Fig **faire le t. de qch** (situation, problème) to review sth; Fam **faire le t. du cadran** to sleep for twelve hours; **faire un t. d'horizon** to review matters; **faire le t. du monde** to go round the world; **t. d'honneur** lap of honour; **t. de piste** lap
(c) (de potier) whee
(d) (tournure) (d'une situation) turn; **prendre un certain t.** to take a certain turn; **t. d'esprit** turn of mind; **t. de phrase** turn of phrase
(e) (rotation) turn; **donner un t. de clé** to turn the key; **à t. de bras** (frapper) with all one's might; Fig (distribuer) in huge quantities; **se faire un t. de reins** to strain one's back
(f) (promenade à pied) stroll; (à bicyclette, en voiture) ride; **faire un t.** to go for a stroll/ride

(g) (alternance) turn; **à qui le t.?** whose turn is it?; **chacun (à) son t.** each in turn; **t. à t.** in turn; **à t. de rôle** in turn
(h) Pol **t. (de scrutin)** ballot
(i) (mauvais coup) trick; **jouer un t. à qn** to play a trick on sb; **jouer un t. de cochon à qn** to play a dirty trick on sb; **cela te jouera des tours** you'll live to regret it
(j) (de prestidigitateur) trick; **t. de force** feat; Fam **en un t.** in no time at all; **t. de passe-passe** trick (using sleight of hand)

Touraine [turen] nf la T. Touraine

tourbe [turb] nf peat

tourbeux, -euse [turbø, -øz] adj peaty

tourbillon [turbijɔ̃] nm (a) (de vent) whirlwind; (de poussière, de fumée) swirl; (de neige) flurry (b) (d'eau) whirlpool (c) Fig (de la vie, d'activité) whirl

tourbillonnant, -e [turbijɔnɑ̃, -ɑ̃t] adj whirling

tourbillonner [turbijɔne] vi aussi Fig to whirl

tourelle [turel] nf turret

tourisme [turism] nm tourism; **faire du t.** to do some touring

touriste [turist] 1 adj (classe) tourist
2 nmf tourist; Fig & Péj **faire qch en t.** to play at doing sth

touristique [turistik] adj tourist; (route) scenic

tourment [turmɑ̃] nm Litt torment

tourmente [turmɑ̃t] nf (a) Litt (tempête) storm (b) (agitation politique) upheaval

tourmenté, -e [turmɑ̃te] adj (a) (paysage) wild (b) (mer, vie, période) turbulent (c) (visage, personne, âme) tortured

tourmenter [turmɑ̃te] 1 vt to torment
2 **se tourmenter** vpr to worry

tournage [turnaʒ] nm (d'un film) shooting, filming; **sur le t.** on shoot

tournant, -e [turnɑ̃, -ɑ̃t] adj (a) (fauteuil, siège) swivel; (pont) swing (b) (grève) rotating
2 nm (a) (de route, de rivière) bend (b) Fig (changement) turning point (de in)

tourné, -e [turne] adj (a) (formulé) **bien/mal t.** well/ badly phrased (b) (disposé) **avoir l'esprit mal t.** to have a dirty mind

tournebouler [turnəbule] vt Fam to upset

tournebroche [turnəbrɔʃ] nm spit

tourne-disque (pl tourne-disques) [turnədisk] nm record player

tournedos [turnədo] nm tournedos, fillet steak

tournée [turne] nf (a) (du facteur, d'un inspecteur) round; **faire sa t.** to do one's rounds; **faire la t. de** (magasins, musées) to go round; **faire sa t. électorale** to go on one's election tour; **faire la t. des grands-ducs** to go out on the town (b) (théâtrale, musicale) tour; **en t.** on tour (c) Fam (consommations) round

tournemain [turnəmɛ̃] **en un tournemain** adv Litt in an instant

tourner [turne] 1 vt (a) (clé, tête, yeux) to turn; **t. et retourner qch entre ses mains** to turn sth over and over in one's hands; Fig **t. et retourner qch (dans tous les sens)** to go over and over an idea (in one's mind); **t. le dos à qn/qch** (action) to turn one's back on sb/sth; (position) to have one's back to sb/sth; **t. les talons** (partir) to turn on one's heel; **t. la tête à qn** (succès, vin) to go to sb's head; (personne) to turn sb's head

(b) *(page)* to turn (over)

(c) *(remuer)* to stir; *(salade)* to toss

(d) *(film, documentaire, scène)* to shoot, to film

(e) *(attention, pensées)* to turn **(vers** to)

(f) *(changer)* **t. qn/qch en ridicule** to make fun of sb/sth

(g) *(contourner) (coin de la rue)* to turn, to go round; *(obstacle, difficulté, loi)* to get round

(h) *(confectionner) (pièce détachée)* to turn on a lathe; *(pot)* to throw; *Fig (phrase)* to turn; *(compliment)* to word

2 vi (a) *(clé, roue, aiguille, planète)* to turn; *(porte)* to swing; *(toupie)* to spin; **l'heure tourne** time is getting on; **t. de l'œil** to pass out

(b) *(se déplacer en rond)* to go round; *aussi Fig* **t. en rond** to go round in circles; *Fam* **il y a quelque chose qui ne tourne pas rond** there's something not right somewhere; *Fam* **il ne tourne pas rond en ce moment** he's not quite himself at the moment; *Fig* **t. autour de qch** *(avoir pour centre)* to centre on sth; *(par convoitise)* to hover round sth; *(valoir environ)* to be in the region of sth; *Fig* **t. autour du pot** to beat about the bush

(c) *(entreprise, moteur)* to run

(d) *(obliquer)* to turn; **tournez à gauche** turn left

(e) *(changer) (vent)* to shift (à to); *(chance)* to turn

(f) *(lait)* to turn, to go off

(g) *(avoir telle issue)* **t. court** to end abruptly; **bien/mal t.** *(personne)* to turn out well/badly; **ça va mal t.** it's going to go wrong; **t. à l'aigre** to turn sour

(h) *(dans un film)* to act

3 se tourner *vpr* to turn **(vers** towards); *Fig* **se t. vers qn/qch** to turn to sb/sth; *Fam* **se t. les pouces** to twiddle one's thumbs

tournesol [turnəsɔl] *nm* sunflower

tourneur, -euse [turnœr, -øz] *nm,f (ouvrier)* turner

tournevis [turnəvis] *nm* screwdriver; **t. cruciforme** Phillips® screwdriver

tournicoter [turnikɔte] *vi Fam* to wander round and round

tourniquet [turnike] *nm* **(a)** *(barrière)* turnstile **(b)** *(porte à tambour)* revolving door **(c)** *(présentoir)* revolving stand **(d)** *(arroseur)* sprinkler

tournis [turni] *nm Fam* **avoir le t.** to feel dizzy; **donner le t. à qn** to make sb dizzy

tournoi [turnwa] *nm* tournament

tournoiement [turnwamɑ̃] *nm (des oiseaux)* wheeling; *(des feuilles mortes)* swirl

tournoyer [turnwaje] *vi (oiseaux)* to wheel; *(des feuilles mortes)* to swirl (round); **faire t. qch** to twirl sth

tournure [turnyr] *nf* **(a)** *(des événements)* turn; **prendre une mauvaise t.** to take a turn for the worse **(b)** *(forme)* **prendre t.** to take shape; **t. d'esprit** turn of mind; **t. (de phrase)** turn of phrase

tour-opérateur *(pl* **tour-opérateurs)** [turɔperatœr] *nm* tour operator

tourte [turt] *nf* pie

tourteau, -x [turto] *nm (crustacé)* edible crab

tourtereau, -x [turtəro] *nm* young turtledove; *Fig* **tourtereaux** *(amoureux)* lovebirds

tourterelle [turtərɛl] *nf* turtledove

tourtière [turtjɛr] *nf* **(a)** *(pour tourte)* pie dish **(b)** *Can =* (minced) pork pie

tous [tu, tus] *voir* **tout**

Toussaint [tusɛ̃] *nf* **la T.** All Saints' Day

tousser [tuse] *vi* to cough; *Fig (moteur)* to splutter

toussotement [tusɔtmɑ̃] *nm* slight cough

toussoter [tusɔte] *vi (avoir une toux)* to have a slight cough; *(pour attirer l'attention)* to give a slight cough

tout, toute *(pl* **tous, toutes)** [tu, tut]

when **tous** is a pronoun as in **3 (b)**, it is pronounced [tus].

1 *adj (entier)* **t. l'univers** the whole universe; **t. mon argent** all my money; **toute la journée** the whole day; **je ne l'ai pas vu de toute la journée** I haven't seen him all day; **le T.-Paris** anyone who's anyone in Paris

2 *adj indéfini* **(a)** *(n'importe quel)* any; **t. élève en retard sera puni** any pupil arriving late will be punished; **à t. moment** at any time; **t. autre que vous** anybody but you

(b) *(chaque)* every; **tous les élèves de la classe** every pupil *or* all the pupils in the class; **toutes nos chambres ont l'air conditionné** all our rooms have air-conditioning; **tous les deux jours** every second day, every other day; **ils se retournèrent t. deux** they both turned round

(c) *(emploi intensif)* **à la toute dernière minute** at the very last minute; **de toute beauté** magnificent; **donner toute satisfaction à qn** to give sb complete *or* full satisfaction; **pour toute réponse, il éclata en sanglots** his only answer was to burst into tears; **je suis t. à toi** I'm all yours

3 *pron indéfini* **(a)** *(au singulier)* everything; **elle a t. de son père** she's her father's daughter; **il a t. du fonctionnaire** he's the typical civil servant; **être t. pour qn** to mean everything to sb; **manger de t.** to eat everything *or* anything; **elle fera t. pour t'ennuyer** she'll do anything to annoy you; **t. ce qu'il y a d'intéressant dans ce film, c'est...** the only interesting thing in this film is...; **ce sera t.?** *(dans un magasin)* will that be all *or* everything?; **elle est jolie/gentille comme t.** she's really pretty/nice; **tu n'y vas pas et c'est t.!** you're not going and that's that!; *Fam* **...et t. et t.!** ...and all that sort of stuff

(b) *(au pluriel)* all; **ils sont tous partis** they all left

4 *adv* **(a)** *(très)* very; **t. près** very close

(b) *(complètement)* **être t. en blanc** to be (dressed) all in white; **être t. en sueur** to be pouring with sweat; **t. autrement** quite differently; **être t. à qch** to be engrossed in sth; **t. enfant, il...** as a very young child, he...

(c) *(suivi d'un gérondif)* **t. en conduisant/écrivant** while driving/writing

(d) **t. ignorant/secrétaire que je suis** *ou* **sois...** I may be ignorant/just a secretary, but...

(e) *(expressions)* **être t. fait** *(complètement)* quite, completely; *(exactement)* exactly; **pas du t.** not at all; **t. à l'heure** *(dans le futur)* in a little while, shortly; *(dans le passé)* a little while ago; **à t. à l'heure!** see you later!; **t. de suite** right away, immediately; **à t. de suite** see you in a minute

5 *nm* **le t.** *(l'ensemble)* the whole; **le t., c'est de se concentrer** the most important thing is to concentrate

tout-à-l'égout [tutalegu] *nm inv* mains drainage

toutefois [tutfwa] *adv* however

toute-puissance [tutpɥisɑ̃s] *nf* absolute power

tout-fou *(pl* **tout-fous)** [tufu] *adj m Fam* bonkers

toutou [tutu] *nm Fam* doggie

tout-petit *(pl* **tout-petits)** [tupəti] *nm* tot, toddler

tout-puissant, toute-puissante *(mpl* **tout-puissants,** *fpl* **toutes-puissantes)** [tupɥisɑ̃, -ɑ̃t] **1** *adj* all-powerful

2 *nm* **le T.** the Almighty

tout-terrain (*pl* **tout-terrains**) [tuterɛ̃] *adj* (*véhicule*) all-terrain, off-road; (*vélo*) mountain

tout-venant [tuvənɑ̃] *nm* **le t.** (*gens*) ordinary people; (*choses*) ordinary things

toux [tu] *nf* cough; **t. sèche/grasse** dry/loose cough

toxicité [tɔksisite] *nf* toxicity

toxico [tɔksiko] *nmf Fam* addict

toxicologie [tɔksikɔlɔʒi] *nf* toxicology

toxicomane [tɔksikɔman] **1** *adj* addicted to drugs **2** *nmf* drug addict

toxicomanie [tɔksikɔmani] *nf* drug addiction

toxine [tɔksin] *nf* toxin

toxique [tɔksik] *adj* toxic, poisonous; (*gaz*) poison

toxoplasmose [tɔksoplasmoz] *nf* toxoplasmosis

TP [tepe] *nmpl* (*abrév* **travaux pratiques**) practical work

TPI [tepei] *nm* (*abrév* **Tribunal pénal international**) International Court of Justice

trac¹ [trak] *nm* nerves; (*au théâtre*) stage fright; **avoir le t.** to be nervous; (*acteur*) to have stage fright

trac² **tout à trac** *adv Vieilli* out of the blue

tracas [traka] *nm* worry, trouble

tracasser [trakase] **1** *vt* to worry, to bother **2 se tracasser** *vpr* to worry (**pour** about)

tracasserie [trakasri] *nf* worry; **les tracasseries administratives** red tape

tracassier, -ère [trakasje, -ɛr] *adj* nitpicking

trace [tras] *nf* (**a**) (*d'animal, d'une personne, de pneus*) tracks; **être sur la t. de qn/qch** to be on the track of sb/sth; **disparaître sans laisser de t.** to disappear without trace; **perdre la t. de qn** to lose track of sb; *Fig* **marcher sur** *ou* **suivre les traces de qn** to follow in sb's footsteps; **t. directe** (*en ski*) direct descent (**b**) (*tache*) mark; **des traces de gras** greasy marks; **des traces de doigts** finger marks; **des traces de pas** footprints; *Fig* **laisser des traces chez qn** (*traumatisme*) to leave its mark on sb; *aussi Fig* **effacer toute t. de qch** to cover up all traces of sth (**c**) (*petite quantité, vestige*) trace

tracé [trase] *nm* (**a**) (*plan*) layout; **faire le t. de qch** to plan the layout of sth (**b**) (*d'une côte*) line

tracer [trase] **1** *vt* (**a**) (*ligne, plan*) to draw; *Math* (*courbe, graphique*) to plot; (*lettre*) to write; *Fig* **t. les grandes lignes de qch** to give the general outline of sth (**route, chemin*) to mark out; *Fig* **son chemin est tout tracé** his path is all mapped out for him **2** *vi Fam* (*aller vite*) to bomb along

traceur [trasœr] *nm Ordinat* **t. (de courbes)** plotter; **t. à tambour** drum plotter

trachée-artère (*pl* **trachées-artères**) [traʃeartɛr] *nf* windpipe, *Spéc* trachea

trachéite [trakeit] *nf* throat infection

tract [trakt] *nm* leaflet

tractations [traktasjɔ̃] *nfpl* dealings, negotiations

tracter [trakte] *vt* to tow

tracteur [traktœr] *nm* tractor

traction [traksjɔ̃] *nf* (**a**) (*en gymnastique*) (*à la barre, aux anneaux*) pull-up; (*au sol*) *Br* press-up, *Am* push-up (**b**) (*véhicule*) traction; **t. avant/arrière** front-wheel/rear-wheel drive (**c**) (*action*) traction, pulling

tradition [tradisjɔ̃] *nf* tradition; **dans la plus pure t. française** in true French tradition

traditionalisme [tradisjɔnalism] *nm* traditionalism

traditionaliste [tradisjɔnalist] *adj & nmf* traditionalist

traditionnel, -elle [tradisjɔnɛl] *adj* (**a**) (*fondé sur la tradition*) traditional (**b**) (*habituel*) usual

traditionnellement [tradisjɔnɛlmɑ̃] *adv* traditionally

traducteur, -trice [tradyktœr, -tris] **1** *nm,f* translator **2** *nm Ordinat* translator

traduction [tradyksjɔ̃] *nf* (*action, texte*) translation (**de/en** from/into); **t. automatique/simultanée** machine/simultaneous translation; **t. assistée par ordinateur** computer-assisted translation

traduire [tradɥir] **1** *vt* (**a**) (*texte, terme*) to translate (**de/en** from/into); *Fig* (*sentiment*) to express (**b**) **t. qn en justice** to bring sb before the courts **2** *vi* to translate (**de/en** from/into) **3 se traduire** *vpr* (*terme*) to be translated; *Fig* **se t. par qch** (*se manifester par*) to be expressed by sth; (*avoir pour résultat*) to result in

traduisible [tradɥizibl] *adj* translatable

trafic [trafik] *nm* (**a**) (*de véhicules*) traffic; **t. aérien** air traffic (**b**) (*de marchandises*) traffic; **t. de drogue** drug trafficking

traficoter [trafikɔte] *Fam* **1** *vi* to be on the fiddle **2** *vt* (*vin*) to doctor; (*comptes*) to fiddle (**b**) (*manigancer*) **je me demande ce qu'il traficote** I wonder what he's up to

trafiquant, -e [trafikɑ̃, -ɑ̃t] *nm,f Péj* trafficker; **t. d'armes** arms dealer; **t. de drogue** drug trafficker

trafiquer [trafike] *vt Fam* (**a**) (*moteur*) to tinker with; (*freins, compteur*) to tamper with; (*vin*) to doctor; (*comptes*) to fiddle (**b**) (*manigancer*) **qu'est-ce qu'il trafique?** what's he up to?

tragédie [traʒedi] *nf* tragedy; *Fam Fig* **ce n'est pas une t.!** it's not the end of the world!

tragédien, -enne [traʒedjɛ̃, -ɛn] *nm,f* tragic actor, *f* tragic actress

tragi-comédie (*pl* **tragi-comédies**) [traʒikɔmedi] *nf* tragi-comedy

tragi-comique (*pl* **tragi-comiques**) [traʒikɔmik] *adj* tragi-comic

tragique [traʒik] **1** *adj* tragic **2** *nm* (*d'un événement*) tragedy; *Fig* **prendre qch au t.** to make a big thing out of sth (**b**) (*genre*) **le t.** tragedy (**c**) (*auteur*) tragic author

trahir [trair] *vt* (**a**) (*personne, pays*) to betray (*secret*) to betray, to give away (**b**) (*gêne, ignorance*) to betray (**d**) (*sujet: jambes, forces*) to fail **2 se trahir** *vpr* to give oneself away

trahison [traizɔ̃] *nf* (*d'une personne, d'un pays*) betrayal; *Jur* treason; **haute t.** high treason

train [trɛ̃] *nm* (**a**) (*moyen de transport, véhicule*) train; **voyager en** *ou* **par le t.** to travel by train; **être dans un t.** to be on a train; *Fig* **prendre le t. en marche** to jump *or* climb on the bandwagon; **t. autocouchette(s)** car-sleeper train; **t. de banlieue** commuter train; **t. corail** express train; **t. électrique** electric train; **t. express** express train; **t. à grande vitesse** high-speed train; **t. de marchandises** *Br* goods *or Am* freight train (**b**) (*de réformes*) series (**c**) (*derrière*) (*de chien*) rump; *Fam* (*d'une personne*) backside, rear (**d**) (*allure*) pace; **au t. où vont les choses** at the rate things are going; **à ce t.-là** at this rate; **aller bon t.** to go at a good pace; **rouler à un t. d'enfer** to go hell for leather (**e**) **t. d'atterrissage** (*d'un avion*) landing gear, undercarriage (**f**) (*locutions*) **en t.** (*projet, affaire*) under way; **mettre qch en t.** to get sth

traînailler [trenaje] = **traînasser**

traînant, -e [trenã, -ãt] *adj* **(a)** *(robe)* trailing **(b)** *(voix)* drawling; *(démarche, pas)* dragging

traînard, -e [trenar, -ard] *nm,f (promeneur)* straggler; *(travailleur)* dawdler

traînasser [trenase] *vi* Fam **(a)** *(errer)* to hang around **(b)** *(être lent)* to dawdle

train-couchettes [trēkuʃɛt] *nm inv* sleeper

traîne [tren] *nf* **(a)** *(d'une robe)* train **(b)** *(à la pêche)* drag net **(c)** *Can* **t. sauvage** toboggan **(d)** Fam **être à la t.** to lag behind

traîneau, -x [treno] *nm (tiré par des chevaux)* sleigh; *(tiré par des chiens)* Br sledge, Am sled

traînée [trene] *nf* **(a)** *(trace)* trail; **se répandre comme une t. de poudre** to spread like wildfire **(b)** Fam Péj *(femme)* tart

traîne-misère [trenmizɛr] *nmf inv* Fam down-and-out

traîner [trene] **1** *vt* **(a)** *(tirer) (objet, corps)* to drag; *(wagon)* to pull **(b)** Fig **t. un rhume** to have a nagging cold **(c)** Péj *(vieilles affaires)* to drag around; **t. qn au théâtre** to drag sb along to the theatre **(d)** *(locutions)* **t. les pieds** to drag one's feet; Fam **t. ses guêtres** ou **bottes** to hang around
2 *vi* **(a)** **t. par terre** *(jupe)* to trail on the ground **(b)** *(rester en arrière)* to lag behind **(c)** *(errer)* to hang around **(d)** *(virus)* to go around **(e)** *(affaires, livres, vêtements)* to lie around; **laisser t. qch** to leave sth lying around **(f)** *(être lent) (personne)* to dawdle; *(conversation, intrigue)* to drag; **t. en longueur** to drag on; **ça ne traîne pas avec vous!** you don't hang about!
3 se traîner *vpr* **(a)** *(sur le sol)* to crawl; Fig *(être fatigué)* to feel like a wet rag; *(aller à contrecœur)* to drag oneself along **(b)** *(journée, soirée)* to drag on

training [trenin] *nm (survêtement)* tracksuit

train-train [trētrē] *nm* Fam routine; **le t. quotidien** the daily grind

traire [trer] *vt* **(a)** *(vache, chèvre)* to milk **(b)** *(lait)* to draw

trait [tre] *nm* **(a)** *(ligne)* line; **d'un t. de plume** with a stroke of the pen; Fig **c'est sa sœur t. pour t.** she is her sister to a T; Fig **tirer un t. sur qch** to draw a line under sth; **t. d'union** hyphen; Fig **link (b)** *(du visage)* features; **des traits réguliers/fins** regular/fine features; **avoir les traits tirés** to look drawn **(c)** *(caractéristique)* feature, trait; **les grands traits de qch** the main features of sth; **t. de caractère** character trait **(d)** Fig **t. d'esprit** flash of wit; **t. de génie** stroke of genius **(e)** *(de lumière)* shaft **(f)** *(locutions)* **avoir t. à qch** to be connected with sth, to relate to sth; **boire qch à longs traits** to gulp sth down; **boire/lire qch d'un (seul) t.** to drink/read sth in one go

traitable [tretabl] *adj (sujet)* manageable

traitant, -e [tretã, -ãt] *adj (shampoing, crème)* medicated

traite [tret] *nf* **(a)** Fin draft, bill; **t. bancaire** bank draft **(b)** *(des nègres)* milking **(c)** *(trafic)* **la t. des Blanches** the white slave trade; **la t. des Noirs** the slave trade **(d)** *(locutions)* **(tout) d'une t., d'une seule t.** in one go

traité [trete] *nm* **(a)** *(ouvrage)* treatise **(de** *ou* **sur** on) **(b)** *(accord)* treaty

traitement [tretmã] *nm* **(a)** *(de personne, de maladie)* treatment; **t. de choc** shock treatment; **t. de faveur** preferential treatment **(b)** *(de matières premières)* processing; *(de l'eau)* treatment **(c)** *(rémunération)* salary **(d)** *Ordinat* processing; **données en t., capacité** ou **débit de t.** throughput; **t. à distance** teleprocessing; **t. des données** data processing, DP; **t. électronique de l'information** electronic data processing, EDP; **t. d'images** image processing; **t. de l'information** ou **des informations** data processing, DP; **t. par lots** batch processing; **t. en temps réel** real time processing; **t. de texte** word processing, WP; *(logiciel)* word processor, word processing software; **t. de texte à balises** word processing with embedded visible commands; **t. vectoriel** vector processing

traiter [trete] **1** *vt* **(a)** *(se conduire envers)* to treat; **t. qn en ami/frère** to treat sb like a friend/a brother **(b)** *(qualifier)* **t. qn de lâche/de menteur** to call sb a coward/a liar **(c)** *(patient, maladie)* to treat **(d)** *(matières premières, minerai)* to process; *(eau, bois, cultures)* to treat **(e)** *Ordinat (informations)* to process; **données non traitées** raw data **(f)** *(marché)* to negotiate; *(affaire)* to handle; **t. avec qn** to deal with sb **(g)** *(sujet, question, demande)* to deal with
2 traiter de *vt ind (sujet, problème)* to deal with
3 se traiter *vpr* **(a)** *(l'un l'autre)* **se t. d'imbéciles/lâches** to call each other idiots/cowards **(b)** *(être guéri)* **cette maladie se traite très bien maintenant** this disease responds very well to treatment now

traiteur [tretœr] *nm* caterer; **chez le t.** at the deli

traître, -esse [tretr, tretrɛs] **1** *adj (personne, visage)* treacherous; *(soleil, vin)* deceptively strong; **pas un t. mot** not a single word
2 *nm,f* traitor, f traitress; **être t. à sa patrie** to be a traitor to one's country; **en t.** treacherously

traîtreusement [tretrøzmã] *adv* treacherously

traîtrise [tretriz] *nf* **(a)** *(caractère)* treachery **(b)** *(action)* act of treachery

trajectoire [traʒɛktwar] *nf* path, trajectory

trajet [traʒɛ] *nm* **(a)** *(voyage)* journey; **faire le t. en voiture** to do the journey by car; **deux heures de t.** a two-hour journey **(b)** *(distance)* distance **(c)** *(itinéraire)* route

tralala [tralala] *nm inv* Fam **faire des tralalas** to make a great fuss; **... et tout le t.** ... etcetera, etcetera

tram [tram] = **tramway**

trame [tram] *nf (d'un tissu)* weft; Fig *(d'un récit)* framework

tramer [trame] **1** *vt (complot)* to hatch; **t. quelque chose** to be plotting something
2 se tramer *vpr* **il se trame quelque chose** there's something afoot

tramontane [tramõtan] *nf* tramontana

trampoline [trãpolin] *nm* **(a)** *(appareil)* trampoline **(b)** *(sport)* trampolining; **faire du t.** to do trampolining

tramway [tramwe] *nm* Br tram, Am streetcar

tranchant, -e [trãʃã, -ãt] **1** *adj* **(a)** *(outil, épée, bord)* sharp **(b)** Fig *(ton, personne)* curt
2 *nm (d'une lame)* cutting edge; *(de la main)* edge; Fig **à double t.** double-edged

tranche [trɑ̃ʃ] *nf* (**a**) *(de pain, de melon, de viande)* slice; **t. napolitaine** Neapolitan ice cream (**b**) *(d'un livre)* edge; **doré sur t.** gilt-edged (**c**) *(partie) (de paiement)* instalment; *(de revenus)* group; *(d'imposition)* band, bracket; **t. d'âge** age bracket; **t. horaire** (time) slot; **t. de vie** slice of life (**d**) *Fam* **s'en payer une t.** to have the time of one's life

tranché, -e [trɑ̃ʃe] *(opinion)* clear-cut

tranchée [trɑ̃ʃe] *nf* trench

trancher [trɑ̃ʃe] **1** *vt* (**a**) *(cordage, câble)* to cut; *(gorge)* to slit, to cut; **t. la tête à qn** to cut off sb's head; **la machine lui a tranché le doigt** the machine severed his finger (**b**) *(question, différend)* to settle

2 *vi* (**a**) *(décider)* to decide; *Fig* **t. dans le vif** to take drastic action (**b**) *(couleurs)* to contrast (**sur** with)

tranquille [trɑ̃kil] *adj* (**a**) *(paisible)* quiet; *(mer)* calm; *(sommeil)* peaceful; **laisser qn t.** to leave sb alone (**b**) *(rassuré)* **se sentir t.** to feel at peace; **vous pouvez dormir t.** you can rest easy; **soyez t.** don't worry; **je ne suis pas t.** I'm feeling uneasy; **avoir l'esprit t.** to have peace of mind

tranquillement [trɑ̃kilmɑ̃] *adv* *(calmement)* calmly; *(doucement)* quietly; *(dormir)* peacefully; *(partir)* with one's mind at rest

tranquillisant, -e [trɑ̃kilizɑ̃, -ɑ̃t] **1** *adj* (**a**) *(nouvelles, paroles)* reassuring; *(effet)* soothing (**b**) *(médicament)* tranquillizing

2 *nm* tranquillizer

tranquilliser [trɑ̃kilize] **1** *vt* to reassure

2 se tranquilliser *vpr* to set one's mind at rest

tranquillité [trɑ̃kilite] *nf* *(calme)* quietness; *(de la mer)* calmness; *(du sommeil)* peacefulness; **avoir besoin de t.** to need peace and quiet; **en toute t.** (without being disturbed; *(sans être dérangé)* without being disturbed; *(sans souci)* with an easy mind; **t. d'esprit** peace of mind

transaction [trɑ̃zaksjɔ̃] *nf* (**a**) *(opération)* transaction (**b**) *Jur* compromise

transactionnel, -elle [trɑ̃zaksjɔnɛl] *adj* (**a**) *Jur* *(solution)* compromise (**b**) *Psy* *(analyse)* transactional

transalpin, -e [trɑ̃zalpɛ̃, -in] *adj* transalpine

transat [trɑ̃zat] **1** *nm* *Fam* deckchair

2 *nf* transatlantic race

transatlantique [trɑ̃zatlɑ̃tik] **1** *adj* transatlantic

2 *nm* (**a**) *(paquebot)* transatlantic liner (**b**) *(chaise longue)* deckchair

transbahuter [trɑ̃sbayte] *vt* *Fam* to cart, to lug

transbordement [trɑ̃sbɔrdəmɑ̃] *nm* transfer; *Naut* transhipment

transcendant, -e [trɑ̃sɑ̃dɑ̃, -ɑ̃t] *adj* transcendent; *Fam* **ce n'est pas t.** it's nothing special

transcendantal, -e, -aux, -ales [trɑ̃sɑ̃dɑ̃tal, -o] *adj* transcendental

transcender [trɑ̃sɑ̃de] **1** *vt* to transcend

2 se transcender *vpr* to surpass oneself

transcontinental, -e, -aux, -ales [trɑ̃skɔ̃tinɑ̃tal, -o] *adj* transcontinental

transcription [trɑ̃skripsjɔ̃] *nf* (**a**) *(action)* transcription; *(dans un autre alphabet)* transliteration; **t. phonétique** phonetic transcription; **t. génétique** genetic transcription (**b**) *(texte)* transcript

transcrire [trɑ̃skrir] *vt* to transcribe; *(dans un autre alphabet)* to transliterate

transcutané, -e [trɑ̃skytane] *adj* transcutaneous

transe [trɑ̃s] *nf* trance; **être en t.** to be in a trance; *Fig* to be beside oneself

transept [trɑ̃sɛpt] *nm* transept

transférer [trɑ̃sfere] *vt* to transfer

transfert [trɑ̃sfɛr] *nm* transfer; *Psy* transference; *Tél* **t. d'appels** call transfer; *Ordinat* **t. de données** data transfer; *Ordinat* **t. électronique de fonds** electronic funds transfer, EFT

transfigurer [trɑ̃sfigyre] *vt* to transfigure

transformable [trɑ̃sfɔrmabl] *adj* convertible

transformateur [trɑ̃sfɔrmatœr] *nm* transformer

transformation [trɑ̃sfɔrmasjɔ̃] *nf* (**a**) *(changement)* transformation; *(d'un local)* conversion (**b**) *(de matières premières)* processing (**c**) *(au rugby)* conversion; **faire une t.** to convert

transformer [trɑ̃sfɔrme] **1** *vt* (**a**) *(changer)* to transform; *(local, maison)* to convert; **t. qn/qch en qch** to turn sb/sth into sth (**b**) *(matières premières)* to process (**c**) *(au rugby)* *(essai)* to convert

2 se transformer *vpr* to change; **se t. en qch** to turn into sth

transfuge [trɑ̃sfyʒ] *nmf* defector

transfuser [trɑ̃sfyze] *vt* *(sang)* to transfuse; *Fam* **t. qn** to give sb a transfusion

transfusion [trɑ̃sfyzjɔ̃] *nf* **t. (sanguine)** (blood) transfusion; **faire une t. à qn** to give sb a transfusion

transgresser [trɑ̃sgrese] *vt* *(règlement, loi)* to infringe; *(ordres)* to disobey

transgression [trɑ̃sgrɛsjɔ̃] *nf* *(du règlement, de la loi)* infringement; *(d'ordres)* disobeying

transhumance [trɑ̃zymɑ̃s] *nf* = the moving of livestock to different pastures according to the season

transhumer [trɑ̃zyme] *vt & vi* = to move to different pastures according to the season

transi, -e [trɑ̃zi] *adj* (**a**) *(paralysé)* **t. (de peur)** paralysed with fear; **t. (de froid)** chilled to the bone (**b**) *Fam (amoureux)* bashful

transiger [trɑ̃ziʒe] *vi* to compromise (**sur** on); **t. avec sa conscience** to compromise one's principles

transistor [trɑ̃zistɔr] *nm* (**a**) *Él (dispositif)* transistor (**b**) *(poste de radio)* transistor (radio)

transit [trɑ̃zit] *nm* (**a**) *(de passagers, de marchandises)* transit; **en t.** in transit (**b**) *(intestinal)* transit; **facilite le t. intestinal** *(sur paquet)* keeps you regular

transiter [trɑ̃zite] **1** *vt* *(marchandises)* to forward

2 *vi* *(marchandises, voyageurs)* to pass in transit (**par** through)

transitif, -ive [trɑ̃zitif, -iv] *adj* *Gram* transitive

transition [trɑ̃zisjɔ̃] *nf* transition; **assurer la t.** to ensure a smooth transition; **sans t.** abruptly

transitivement [trɑ̃zitivmɑ̃] *adv* transitively

transitivité [trɑ̃zitivite] *nf* transitivity

transitoire [trɑ̃zitwar] *adj* transitional

translation [trɑ̃slasjɔ̃] *nf* *Math* translation

translucide [trɑ̃slysid] *adj* translucent

transmanche [trɑ̃zmɑ̃ʃ] *adj inv* cross-Channel

transmetteur [trɑ̃smetœr] *nm* *Ordinat & Biol* transmitter

transmettre [trāsmetr] **1** vt (a) (lumière, chaleur, énergie) to transmit (b) (maladie, virus) to pass on, to transmit (à to) (c) (recette, don) to hand on (à to); (tradition, objet) to hand down (à to); (pouvoir) to hand over (à to) (d) (message, ordre, amitiés) to pass on (à to) (e) TV & Rad (information) to transmit; (émission) to broadcast (f) Jur (propriété, droit) to transfer; (actions) to assign; **t. ses pouvoirs à qn** to hand over to sb

2 se transmettre vpr (a) (maladie, virus) to be passed on (b) (recette, don) to be handed on; (tradition, objet) to be handed down

transmissible [trāsmisibl] adj (a) (maladie) transmissible; **maladie sexuellement t.** sexually transmitted disease (b) (droit, fortune) transferable

transmission [trāsmisjɔ̃] nf (a) (de la chaleur, de la lumière, d'une maladie, d'un virus) transmission; (d'un message, d'un ordre) passing on; (d'une tradition) handing down; **t. de pensée** thought transference (b) TV & Rad (d'une image, d'un message) transmission; (d'une émission) broadcasting (c) Ordinat transmission; **t. de données** data transmission or transfer; **t. par modem** modem transmission; **t. de paquets** packet transmission (d) Jur (d'une propriété, d'un droit) transfer, transference; (d'actions) assignment (e) Mil **les transmissions** the signals

transocéanien, -enne [trāzɔseanjɛ̃, -ɛn], **transocéanique** [trāzɔseanik] adj transoceanic

transparaître [trāsparetr] vi to show (through)

transparence [trāsparɑ̃s] nf (a) (d'un tissu, d'une allusion, d'un parti politique) transparency; **voir qch par t.** to see sth shining through (b) Cin back projection

transparent, -e [trāsparɑ̃, -ɑ̃t] **1** adj aussi Fig transparent
2 nm transparency

transpercer [trāsperse] vt (sujet: lame, flèche, balle) to pierce; (sujet: froid, vent, pluie) to go right through

transpiration [trāspirasjɔ̃] nf (a) (sueur) sweat, perspiration (b) (action) sweating, perspiration

transpirer [trāspire] vi (a) (personne) to sweat, to perspire; **t. des pieds/des aisselles** to have sweaty feet/armpits; **t. à grosses gouttes** to drip with sweat (b) Fig (secret, nouvelles) to leak out (c) Fam **t. sur** (travailler à) to sweat over

transplant [trāsplɑ̃] nm Méd transplant

transplantation [trāsplɑ̃tasjɔ̃] nf (a) (d'arbres, de personnes) transplantation (b) (d'organes) transplant; **t. cardiaque/rénale** heart/kidney transplant

transplanté, -e [trāsplɑ̃te] adj (organe) transplanted; **malade t.** transplant patient

transplanter [trāsplɑ̃te] vt to transplant

transport [trāspor] nm (a) (de marchandises, de passagers) transport; **les transports** transport; **les transports aériens** air transport; **les transports en commun** public transport; **t. fluvial** inland waterway transport (b) Jur (de biens, de droits) transfer (c) Litt (émotion) rapture; (de joie) transports; (de colère) outbursts

transportable [trāsportabl] adj (marchandises) transportable; (blessé) able to be moved

transporter [trāsporte] vt (a) (passagers, troupes, marchandises) to transport, to carry; **t. qn à l'hôpital** to take sb to hospital (b) (sujet: film, roman) to transport (c) Litt (ravir) to transport; **t. qn de joie** to make sb rapturous

transporteur [trāsportœr] nm carrier; **t. routier** road haulier

transposer [trāspoze] vt (a) (mots, morceau de musique) to transpose (b) **t. un roman à l'écran/à la scène** to adapt a novel for the screen/for the stage

transposition [trāspozisjɔ̃] nf (a) (mot, morceau de musique) transposition (b) **t. à l'écran/à la scène** screen/stage adaptation

transsexuel, -elle [trāsseksɥel] adj & nmf transsexual

Transsibérien [trāssiberjɛ̃] nm **le T.** the Trans-Siberian Railway

transvaser [trāsvaze] vt to pour, to transfer; (vin) to decant

transversal, -e, -aux, -ales [trāsversal, -o] adj (vallée) transverse; (rue) cross; **coupe transversale** cross-section

transversalement [trāsversalmɑ̃] adv crosswise

trapèze [trapez] nm (a) (forme géométrique) Br trapezium, Am trapezoid (b) (appareil de gymnastique) trapeze; **faire du t.** to perform on the trapeze

trapéziste [trapezist] nmf trapeze artist

trappage [trapaʒ] nm Can trapping

trappe [trap] nf (a) (dans le plancher) trap door (b) (piège) trap

trappeur [trapœr] nm trapper

trapu, -e [trapy] adj (a) (homme, cheval) thickset, stocky; (bâtiment) squat (b) Fam (élève, professeur) brainy (c) Fam (problème) tough

traquenard [traknar] nm trap

traquer [trake] vt (gibier, criminel) to hunt; (vedette) to hound

traumatisant, -e [tromatizɑ̃, -ɑ̃t] adj traumatizing

traumatiser [tromatize] vt to traumatize

traumatisme [tromatism] nm traumatism, trauma; **t. crânien** severe head injury

travail, -aux [travaj, -o] nm (a) (activité) work; (de l'imagination, de la mémoire) working; **se mettre au t.** to get (down) to work; **allons, au t.!** come on, let's get (down) to work!; **cesser le t.** to stop work; **à t. égal, salaire égal** equal pay for equal work (b) (emploi) work, job; **chercher du t.** to look for work or a job; **être sans t.** not to have a job, to be out of work; **t. à mi-temps/à plein temps** part-time/full-time work; **t. de bureau** office work; **les travaux des champs** work in the fields; Univ **travaux dirigés** tutorial; **travaux forcés** hard labour; Jur **t. d'intérêt général** community service; **t. manuel** manual labour; Scol **travaux manuels** arts and crafts; **travaux ménagers** housework; **t. de nuit** night work; Scol & Univ **travaux pratiques** practical work (c) (tâche) (piece of) work, job; **un t. bien/mal fait** a good/bad piece of work; **faire de petits travaux** to do odd jobs; **c'est du beau t.** it's a fine piece of work; Fam & Ironique **c'est du beau t.!** that was clever! (d) (lieu de travail) work (e) Ordinat job; **t. multitâche** multitasking; **t. en réseau** networking (f) (devoir) work (g) **travaux** (réparations) work; **le magasin est en travaux** there's work being done on the shop; **attention travaux** (sur panneau) roadworks ahead (h) (de l'accouchement) labour (i) (façonnage) **le t. du bois** woodwork; **le t. du fer** ironwork; **le t. de l'ivoire/de pierres précieuses** the shaping of ivory/precious stones

travaillé, -e [travaje] *adj* (a) *(fer, bois, pierre)* worked (b) *(style)* elaborate (c) *(tourmenté)* **être t. par qch** to be tormented by sth

travailler [travaje] **1** *vt* (a) *(matière, pâte)* to work (b) *(sujet, rôle, style)* to work on; *(texte, auteur)* to study; *(morceau de musique, technique)* to practise (c) *(inquiéter)* to torment

2 *vi* (a) *(personne)* to work; **t. à la pièce** to do piecework; **t. dans qch** to work in sth; **faire t. son argent** to make one's money work for one; **faire t. son imagination** to use one's imagination; *Fam* **t. du chapeau** to have a screw loose (b) *(s'entraîner) (sportif)* to train; *(musicien)* to practise (c) *(câble)* to strain; *(bois)* to warp; *(murs)* to crack; *(vin)* to ferment (d) *(agir)* **t. pour/contre qn** to be on sb's side/against sb

3 travailler à *vt ind (roman, documentaire)* to work on; **t. à la perte de qn** to try to ruin sb

travailleur, -euse [travajœr, -øz] **1** *adj* hard-working **2** *nm, f* worker; **t. manuel/intellectuel** manual/non-manual worker **t. indépendant** self-employed worker

travailliste [travajist] *Pol* **1** *nmf* member of the Labour Party
2 *adj (parti)* Labour

travée [trave] *nf* (a) *(de sièges)* row (b) *Archit* bay

traveller's check, traveller's cheque [travlœrʃek] *nm Br* traveller's cheque, *Am* traveler's check

travelling [travliŋ] *nm Cin (déplacement)* tracking; *(plan)* tracking shot; **faire un t.** to do a tracking shot; **t. avant/arrière** track in/out

travelo [travlo] *nm Fam* transvestite

travers [traver] *nm* (a) *(défaut)* failing (b) *(largeur)* breadth; *Culin* **t. de porc** spare ribs (c) *(locutions)* **à t. qch, au t. de qch** through sth; **à t. les siècles** down the centuries; **à t. le monde** throughout the world; **voir à t. qch** to see through sth; **passer au t. de qch** to go through sth; **marcher de t.** not to walk in a straight line; *Fig* **aller de t.** to go wrong; **être de t.** *(chapeau, tableau)* to be crooked; **prendre qch de t.** to take sth the wrong way; **regarder qn de t.** to look sideways at sb; **comprendre qch de t.** to misunderstand sth; **en t.** crosswise; **en t. de qch** across sth; **se mettre en t. de qch** to get in the way of sth

traverse [travers] *nf (sur une voie ferrée) Br* sleeper, *Am* tie

traversée [traverse] *nf (d'un cours d'eau)* crossing; *(d'une ville, d'une forêt)* going through; *Fig* **t. du désert** time in the wilderness

traverser [traverse] *vt* (a) *(rue, pont, cours d'eau)* to cross; *(ville, pays, forêt)* to go through; *Fig* **t. l'esprit à qn** *(idée, doute)* to cross sb's mind (b) *(tissu, mur)* to go (right) through (c) *(crise, période)* to go through; **t. les siècles** to come down through the ages

traversier [traversje] *nm Can (bac)* ferry

traversin [traversɛ̃] *nm* bolster

travesti [travesti] *nm* transvestite

travestir [travestir] **1** *vt* (a) *(personne)* to dress up (*en* as) (b) *(vérité, faits, pensée)* to distort
2 se travestir *vpr* (a) *(se déguiser)* to put on fancy dress (b) *(s'habiller en femme)* to put on drag

traviole [travjol] *nf* **de traviole** *adv Fam* **marcher de t.** to be staggering all over the place; **être de t.** to be lopsided

trayeuse [trejøz] *nf* milking machine

trébucher [trebyʃe] *vi* to trip, to stumble *(sur/contre* over/against); **faire t. qn** to trip sb up

trèfle [trefl] *nm* (a) *(plante)* clover; **t. à quatre feuilles** four-leaf clover (b) *(carte)* club; *(couleur)* clubs

tréfonds [tref5] *nm Litt* **au t. de son cœur** in one's heart of hearts; **au t. de son âme** in the depths of one's soul

treillage [trejaʒ] *nm (clôture)* trellis fencing

treille [trej] *nf* (a) *(tonnelle)* vine arbour (b) *(vigne)* climbing vine

treillis [treji] *nm* (a) *(treillage)* trellis; **t. métallique** wire mesh (b) *(tissu)* canvas (c) *(uniforme militaire)* combat uniform

treize [trez] **1** *adj inv* thirteen; *Fam* **en avoir t. à la douzaine** to have more than one knows what to do with
2 *nm inv* thirteen; *voir aussi* **trois**

treizième [trezjem] *adj, nmf & nm* thirteenth; *voir aussi* **cinquième**

trekking [trekiŋ] *nm* trek

tréma [trema] *nm* diaeresis; **e/i t.** e/i diaeresis

tremblant, -e [trɑ̃blɑ̃, -ɑ̃t] *adj (genoux, main)* trembling, shaky; **être t. de peur** to be trembling *or* shaking with fear; **être t. de froid/fièvre** to be shivering with cold/fever (b) *(voix)* quavering

tremble [trɑ̃bl] *nm* aspen

tremblement [trɑ̃bləmɑ̃] *nm* (a) *(du corps, de la main)* trembling, shaking; *(de fièvre)* shudder; **être pris de tremblements** to start to shake; *Fam* **et tout le t.** etcetera etcetera (b) *(de la voix)* quavering (c) **t. de terre** earthquake

trembler [trɑ̃ble] *vi* (a) *(main, genoux)* to shake, to tremble; *(lèvres)* to tremble; **t. de colère** to tremble *or* shake with anger; **t. de froid** to shiver with cold; **t. comme une feuille** to shake like a leaf (b) *(voix)* to quaver (c) *(terre, bâtiment)* to shake; *(feuilles)* to quiver; *(flamme)* to flicker; **faire t. les vitres** to make the windows shake *or* rattle; **faire t. un bâtiment** to rock *or* shake a building (d) *(avoir peur)* to tremble; **t. de tout son corps** to tremble all over; **t. devant qn** to be terrified of sb; **t. pour qn** to tremble for sb

tremblotant, -e [trɑ̃blɔtɑ̃, -ɑ̃t] *adj (personne, corps)* trembling; *(voix)* tremulous; *(lumière)* flickering

tremblote [trɑ̃blɔt] *nf Fam* **avoir la t.** to be shaky; *(de peur)* to have the jitters; *(de froid)* to have the shivers

tremblotement [trɑ̃blɔtmɑ̃] *nm (des mains)* trembling, shaking; *(de la voix)* quavering; *(de la lumière)* flickering

trembloter [trɑ̃blɔte] *vi (personne, mains)* to tremble *or* shake slightly; *(voix)* to quaver; *(lumière)* to flicker

trémière [tremjɛr] *adj f voir* **rose**

trémolo [tremolo] *nm* tremolo; *Fig* **avec des trémolos dans la voix** with a tremor in one's voice

trémousser [tremuse] **se trémousser** *vpr* to jig about; **se t. sur sa chaise** to wriggle about on one's chair

trempage [trɑ̃paʒ] *nm* soaking

trempe [trɑ̃p] *nf* (a) *(force de caractère)* calibre; **une femme de sa t.** a woman of her calibre (b) *Fam (volée de coups)* hiding

trempé, -e [trɑ̃pe] *adj* (a) *(personne, vêtement)* soaked; **t. de sueur** *(personne)* dripping with sweat; *(vêtement)* saturated with sweat (b) *(acier, verre)* hardened; *Fig* **bien t.** *(caractère)* sturdy

tremper [trɑ̃pe] **1** *vt* **(a)** *(mouiller)* to soak; **se faire t. (par la pluie)** to get soaked **(b)** *(plonger)* to dip **(dans** in**); t. les lèvres** to take a small sip **(c)** *(acier)* to quench

2 *vi* **(a) faire t. qch, mettre qch à t.** *(linge)* to soak sth **(b)** *Fig (se compromettre)* **t. dans qch** to be mixed up in sth

3 se tremper *vpr (se baigner)* to have a quick dip; **se t. les pieds dans l'eau** to go for a paddle

trempette [trɑ̃pet] *nf Fam* **faire t.** to have a quick dip

tremplin [trɑ̃plɛ̃] *nm (pour sauteur, pour plongeur) & Fig* springboard; *(pour skieur)* ski jump

trench-coat *(pl* **trench-coats)** [trɛnʃkot] *nm* trench coat

trentaine [trɑ̃ten] *nf* **(a)** *(nombre)* **une t. (de)** about thirty **(b)** *(âge)* **avoir la t.** to be about thirty; **approcher de la t.** to be getting on for thirty

trente [trɑ̃t] **1** *adj inv* thirty; *(au tennis)* **t. à** thirty all

2 *nm inv* thirty; *Fig* **être sur son t. et un** to be dressed up to the nines; *voir aussi* **trois**

trente-six [trɑ̃tsis] **1** *adj inv* thirty-six; *Fam (beaucoup)* umpteen; *Fig* **voir t. chandelles** *(après un coup sur la tête)* to see stars

2 *nm inv* thirty-six; *Fig* **tous les t. du mois** once in a blue moon; *voir aussi* **trois**

trente-sixième [trɑ̃tsizjɛm] *adj Fam Fig* **être au t. dessous** to be really down in the dumps; *voir aussi* **cinquième**

trente-trois tours [trɑ̃ttrwatur] *nm inv* LP

trentième [trɑ̃tjɛm] *nmf, nn & adj* thirtieth; *voir aussi* **cinquième**

trépanation [trepanasjɔ̃] *nf* trepanning

trépaner [trepane] *vt* to trepan

trépas [trepa] *nm Litt* death; **passer de vie à t.** to depart this life

trépasser [trepase] *vi Litt* to depart this life

trépidant, -e [trepidɑ̃, -ɑ̃t] *adj (vie, activité)* hectic

trépidation [trepidasjɔ̃] *nf (d'une machine, d'un moteur)* vibration

trépied [trepje] *nm* **(a)** *(d'appareil photo)* tripod **(b)** *(tabouret)* three-legged stool

trépignement [trepiɲmɑ̃] *nm* stamping (of feet)

trépigner [trepiɲe] *vi* to stamp (one's feet); **t. de colère/d'impatience** to jump up and down with rage/impatience

très [trɛ] *adv* very; **avoir t. faim/chaud/froid** to be very hungry/hot/cold; **avoir t. envie de faire qch** to really want to do sth; **t. estimé** highly respected; **t. aimé** much liked; **t. peu utilisé** very rarely used

trésor [trezɔr] *nm* **(a)** *(objets précieux)* treasure; *Fam* **mon t.** darling; *Fig* **des trésors de patience/générosité** boundless patience/generosity; **t. de guerre** war chest **(b)** *(dans une église)* relics and ornaments **(c) le T. (public)** ≃ the Treasury

trésorerie [trezɔrri] *nf* **(a)** *(bureau)* accounts department **(b)** *(ressources)* funds, finances

trésorier, -ère [trezɔrje, -ɛr] *nm,f* treasurer

tressaillement [tresajmɑ̃] *nm (de surprise, de peur)* jump, start; *(de plaisir)* quiver; *(de douleur)* wince

tressaillir [tresajir] *vi (de surprise, de peur)* to jump, to start; *(de plaisir)* to quiver; *(de douleur)* to wince

tressautement [tresotmɑ̃] *nm (secousse)* jolt

tressauter [tresote] *vi (être secoué)* to jolt about

tresse [tres] *nf* **(a)** *(de cheveux) Br* plait, *Am* braid; **se faire des tresses** to *Br* plait *or Am* braid one's hair **(b)** *(de fil)* braid

tresser [trese] *vt (cheveux) Br* to plait, *Am* to braid; *(paille, osier)* to plait; *(panier, guirlande)* to weave; *Fig* **t. des couronnes à qn** to sing sb's praises

tréteau, -x [treto] *nm* trestle

treuil [trœj] *nm* winch, windlass

trêve [trɛv] *nf* **(a)** *(amnistie)* truce **(b)** *Fig (pause, arrêt)* respite, rest; *Fam* **t. de plaisanteries!** joking apart; **sans t.** unremittingly; *Fam* **t. des confiseurs** = truce over Christmas and New Year between opposing political parties

Trèves [trɛv] *n* Trier

tri [tri] *nm* **(a)** *(d'objets, d'idées)* sorting out; *(de lettres)* sorting; *(de candidats)* selection; **faire le t. dans qch** to sort sth out; **il va falloir faire le t.** we'll have to sort through them; **faire du t. dans ses vêtements/papiers** to sort through one's clothes/papers; **t. postal** mail sorting **(b)** *Ordinat* sort; **effectuer un t.** to do a sort; **t. alphabétique** alphabetic sort

triage [trijaʒ] *nm* sorting out; *(de lettres)* sorting

trial [trijal] *nm* motorbike trials

triangle [trijɑ̃ɡl] *nm* triangle; **t. des Bermudes** Bermuda Triangle; **le T. d'or** the Golden Triangle

triangulaire [trijɑ̃ɡylɛr] *adj* triangular

triathlon [triatlɔ̃] *nm* triathlon

tribal, -e, -aux, -ales [tribal, -o] *adj* tribal

tribord [tribɔr] *nm* starboard; **t.** on the starboard side

tribu [triby] *nf* tribe

tribulations [tribylasjɔ̃] *nfpl* tribulations, troubles

tribun [tribɛ̃] *nm* **(a)** *(magistrat romain)* tribune **(b)** *(orateur)* popular orator

tribunal, -aux [tribynal, -o] *nm (bâtiment) Br* court, *Am* courthouse; *(magistrats)* court; **porter une affaire devant les tribunaux** to take a case to court; **t. administratif** = court which deals with civil law; **t. de commerce** trade tribunal; **t. pour enfants** juvenile court; **t. de grande instance** ≃ Crown Court, *Scot* High Court; **t. d'instance** ≃ magistrates' court, *Scot* district court; **t. militaire** military tribunal

tribune [tribyn] *nf* **(a)** *(d'orateur)* rostrum, platform **(b)** *(débat)* forum; **t. libre** *(dans un journal)* opinion column **(c) les tribunes** *(dans un stade)* the stand; **t. d'honneur** grandstand; **t. de la presse** press gallery

tribut [triby] *nm* tribute; **le pays a payé un lourd t. à la guerre** the war cost the country dearly

tributaire [tribytɛr] *adj (dépendant)* **être t. de** to be dependent on **(b)** *(cours d'eau)* tributary

tricentenaire [trisɑ̃tnɛr] **1** *adj* three hundred years old

2 *nm* tercentenary, tricentennial

triceps [trisɛps] *nm* triceps

triche [triʃ] *nf Fam* cheating

tricher [triʃe] *vi* to cheat; **t. sur qch** to lie about sth; **t. aux cartes/à un examen** to cheat at cards/in an exam

tricherie [triʃri] *nf* cheating

tricheur, -euse [triʃœr, -øz] *nm,f* cheat

trichloréthylène [triklɔretilɛn] *nm* trichlorethylene

tricolore [trikɔlɔr] **1** *adj* **(a)** *(à trois couleurs)* three-coloured **(b)** *(de la France)* French

2 *nmpl* **les tricolores** the French team

tricorne [trikɔrn] *nm* three-cornered hat, tricorn

tricot [triko] *nm* (a) *(activité)* knitting; **faire du t.** to do some knitting (b) *(ouvrage)* knitting (c) *(chandail)* sweater, jumper; **t. de corps** *Br* vest, *Am* undershirt (d) *(tissu)* knitted fabric

tricoter [trikɔte] **1** *vt* to knit; **tricoté (à la) main** hand-knitted

2 *vi* to knit; **t. à la main/à la machine** to hand-knit/machine-knit

tricycle [trisikl] *nm* tricycle; **faire du t.** to go tricycling

trident [tridɑ̃] *nm* (a) *(dans la mythologie)* trident (b) *(fourche)* three-pronged fork

tridimensionnel, -elle [tridimɑ̃sjɔnɛl] *adj* three-dimensional

triennal, -e, -aux, -ales [trienal, -o] *adj (élection, révision)* three-yearly, triennial; *(bail)* three-year

trier [trije] *vt* (a) *(lettres)* to sort; *(vêtements, informations)* to sort or go through; *(fruits, lentilles)* to pick over; **t. qn/qch sur le volet** to hand-pick sb/sth (b) *Ordinat* to sort; **t. par ordre alphabétique** to sort in alphabetical order

trifouiller [trifuje] *vi Fam* **qu'est-ce que tu trifouilles?** what are you up to?; **t. dans qch** to rummage around in sth

triglycéride [trigliserid] *nf* triglyceride

trigonométrie [trigɔnɔmetri] *nf* trigonometry

trigonométrique [trigɔnɔmetrik] *adj* trigonometric

trilatéral, -e, -aux, -ales [trilateral, -o] *adj* trilateral

trilingue [trilɛ̃g] *adj* trilingual

trille [trij] *nm* trill

trilogie [trilɔʒi] *nf* trilogy

trimaran [trimarɑ̃] *nm* trimaran

trimbal(l)er [trɛ̃bale] *Fam* **1** *vt (paquets)* to lug or cart around; *(enfants)* to trail around

2 se trimbal(l)er *vpr* to trail about; **elle se trimbal(l)e partout avec sa marmaille** she trails her kids around with her everywhere she goes

trimer [trime] *vi Fam* to slave away; **faire t. qn** to keep sb hard at it

trimestre [trimɛstr] *nm* quarter; *Scol & Univ Br* term, *Am* trimester

trimestriel, -elle [trimɛstrijɛl] *adj* quarterly

tringle [trɛ̃gl] *nf* rod; **t. à rideau** curtain rod

trinité [trinite] *nf (groupe de trois éléments)* trinity; *Rel* **la (sainte) T.** the (Holy) Trinity; **la T.** *(fête)* Trinity Sunday

Trinité-et-Tobago [triniteetɔbago] *n* Trinidad and Tobago

trinquer [trɛ̃ke] *vi* (a) *(porter un toast)* to clink glasses; **t. à qn/qch** to drink to sb/sth; **t. à la santé de qn** to drink a toast to sb (b) *Fam (souffrir)* to be the one who suffers

trio [trijo] *nm* (a) *(groupe de trois personnes)* threesome, trio (b) *(en musique)* trio

triolet [trijɔlɛ] *nm Mus* triplet

triomphal, -e, -aux, -ales [trijɔ̃fal, -o] *adj* triumphant

triomphalement [trijɔ̃falmɑ̃] *adv* triumphantly

triomphalisme [trijɔ̃falism] *nm* crowing; **sans faire de t....** while I don't want to crow,...

triomphant, -e [trijɔ̃fɑ̃, -ɑ̃t] *adj* triumphant; **d'un ton t.** triumphantly

triomphe [trijɔ̃f] *nm* triumph (sur over); **faire un t. à qn** to give sb an ovation; **porter qn en t.** to carry sb on one's shoulders

triompher [trijɔ̃fe] **1** *vi* (a) *(gagner)* to triumph; *Fig (vérité)* to prevail (b) *(exulter)* to crow

2 triompher de *vt ind* to triumph over

trip [trip] *nm Fam (d'un drogué)* trip; **faire un t.** to trip; **être dans un t. écolo** to be on an environmental kick

triparti, -e [triparti], **tripartite** [tripartit] *adj* tripartite

tripatouillage [tripatujaʒ] *nm Fam (de textes, de comptes)* tampering with; *(de statistiques)* massaging

tripatouiller [tripatuje] *vt Fam (a) (textes, comptes)* to tamper with; *(statistiques)* to massage (b) *(cheveux)* to play or fiddle with; *(bouton)* to pick at

tripe [trip] *nf* (a) **tripes** *(d'un animal)* entrails; *Fam (d'une personne)* guts; *Fam* **prendre qn aux tripes** to get sb by the guts (b) **tripes** *(plat)* tripe (c) *Fam Fig* **avoir la t. républicaine** to be a republican through and through

triperie [tripri] *nf (boutique)* tripe shop

tripette [tripɛt] *nf Fam* **ça ne vaut pas t.** it's not worth a damn

triphasé, -e [trifaze] *Él adj* three-phase

triphtongue [triftɔ̃g] *nf* triphthong

tripier, -ère [tripje, -ɛr] *nm,f* tripe butcher

triple [tripl] **1** *adj* (a) *(à trois éléments)* triple; **en t. exemplaire** in triplicate; **t. croche** *Br* demisemiquaver, *Am* thirty-second note (b) *(trois fois plus grand)* triple, treble (c) *(emploi intensif)* **t. buse** prize idiot; **au t. galop** at breakneck speed

2 *nm* **le t. (de)** *(quantité, prix)* three times as much (as); *(nombre)* three times as many (as); **douze est le t. de quatre** twelve is three times four

triplé, -e [triple] **1** *nm,f* triplet

2 *nm (triple succès)* triple victory; *(pari)* = bet on the first three horses in a race

triplement [tripləmɑ̃] *adv* trebly, triply

tripler [triple] **1** *vt (somme, quantité)* to treble, to triple; **t. une classe** to repeat a year twice

2 *vi* to treble, to triple

Tripoli [tripɔli] *n* Tripoli

triporteur [tripɔrtœr] *nm* delivery tricycle

tripot [tripo] *nm* gambling den

tripotée [tripɔte] *nf très Fam (a) (défaite)* hammering (b) *(grand nombre)* **une t. de** loads of

tripoter [tripɔte] *vt Fam (a) (objet, appareil, cheveux)* to play with, to fiddle with; *(boutons, plaie)* to touch (b) *(personne)* to feel up, to grope

triptyque [triptik] *nm* triptych

trique [trik] *nf* cudgel; *Fam* **mener qn à la t.** to rule sb with a rod of iron

trisomie [trizɔmi] *nf Méd* **t., t. 21** Down's syndrome

trisomique [trizɔmik] *adj* with Down's syndrome; **être t.** to have Down's syndrome

triste [trist] *adj* (a) *(malheureux)* sad (b) *(sinistre)* dreary, depressing; *Fam* **c'était pas t.!** *(soirée)* it was a night and a half!; *Fam* **il est pas t., son frère!** his brother's quite a character! (c) *(pénible)* sad; *(époque)* grim; **dans un t. état** in a sorry state; **c'est la t. réalité** that's the sad or harsh reality (d) *Péj* sad

tristement [tristəmɑ̃] *adv* sadly; **t. célèbre** notorious

tristesse [tristɛs] *nf* (a) *(d'une personne, d'un événement)* sadness; **c'est avec t. que je vous annonce...** I am sorry to have to tell you... (b) *(aspect sinistre)* dreariness

tristounet, -ette [tristune, -ɛt] *adj Fam* gloomy

triton [tritɔ̃] *nm* (a) *(amphibien)* newt (b) *(mollusque)* triton, trumpet shell (c) *(personnage mythologique)* Triton

triturer [trityre] 1 *vt* (a) *(broyer)* to grind (b) *Fam (tripoter)* to fiddle with
   2 **se triturer** *vpr Fam* **se t. la cervelle** *ou* **les méninges** to rack one's brains

triumvirat [trijɔmvira] *nm* triumvirate

trivial, -e, -aux, -ales [trivjal, -o] *adj* (a) *(vulgaire)* vulgar, coarse (b) *(commun)* banal

trivialité [trivjalite] *nf* (a) *(vulgarité)* vulgarity, coarseness (b) *(expression)* vulgar or coarse expression (c) *(banalité)* banality

troc [trɔk] *nm* (a) *(échange)* exchange (b) *(système économique)* barter; **faire du t.** to barter

troène [trɔɛn] *nm* privet

troglodyte [trɔglɔdit] *nm (personne)* cave dweller, *Spéc* troglodyte

trogne [trɔɲ] *nf Fam* face

trognon [trɔɲɔ̃] 1 *nm (de pomme)* core
   2 *adj inv Fam (mignon)* sweet

Troie [trwa] *n* Troy

troïka [trɔika] *nf* troika

trois [trwa] 1 *adj inv* three; **le t. août** *Br* (on) the third of August, *Am* (on) August third; **à t. heures** at three o'clock; **page t.** page three; **Henri T.** Henry the Third; **nous étions t.** there were three of us; **les t. quarts du temps** most of the time; **couper/partager qch en t.** to cut/divide sth into three; **t. par t.** three by three; **(hôtel) t. étoiles** three-star hotel; **en t. dimensions** in 3-D
   2 *nm inv* three

trois-huit [trwaɥit] *nm inv* **faire les t.** = to work three alternating eight-hour shifts

troisième [trwazjɛm] 1 *adj, nmf & n* third; **le t. âge** senior citizens, *Am* golden agers
   2 *nf* (a) *Scol Br* fourth year of secondary school, *Am* eighth grade (b) *(vitesse)* third (gear); *voir aussi* **cinquième**

troisièmement [trwazjɛmmɔ̃] *adv* thirdly

trois-mâts [trwamɑ] *nm inv* three-master

trois-pièces [trwapjɛs] *nm inv* (a) *(appartement)* three-room *Br* flat or *Am* apartment; **t. cuisine** *Br* three-room flat with kitchen, *Am* three and a half (b) *(costume)* three-piece suit

trois-quarts [trwakar] *nm inv* (a) *(manteau)* three-quarter-length coat (b) *(au rugby)* three-quarter

trolley [trɔlɛ], **trolleybus** [trɔlɛbys] *nm* trolleybus

trombe [trɔ̃b] *nf* waterspout; **il pleut des trombes** it's pouring down; **sous des trombes d'eau** in the torrential rain; *Fam Fig* **passer/partir en t.** to tear past/off

trombine [trɔ̃bin] *nf Fam* face

trombone [trɔ̃bɔn] *nm* (a) *(agrafe)* paper clip (b) *(instrument)* trombone; **t. à coulisse/à pistons** slide/valve trombone (c) *(instrumentiste)* trombone player, trombonist

trompe [trɔ̃p] *nf* (a) *(d'éléphant)* trunk; *(d'insecte)* proboscis (b) *(instrument à vent)* horn *Anat* **t. d'Eustache/de Fallope** Eustachian/Fallopian tube

trompe-l'œil [trɔ̃plœj] *nm inv (décor)* trompe l'œil; **en t.** trompe l'œil

tromper [trɔ̃pe] 1 *vt* (a) *(abuser)* to fool (**sur** about) (b) *(être infidèle à)* to be unfaithful to (c) *(vigilance, surveillance)* to elude, to escape (d) *Fig* **s. son ennui** to relieve the boredom; **t. sa faim** to stave off one's hunger
   2 **se tromper** *vpr (faire une erreur)* to make a mistake; *(avoir tort)* to be mistaken; **se t. dans les dates/proportions** to get the dates/the proportions wrong; **se t. de numéro** *(au téléphone)* to dial the wrong number; **se t. d'heure/de jour** to get the time/day wrong

tromperie [trɔ̃pri] *nf* deceit, deception

trompeter [trɔ̃pəte] *vt (nouvelles)* to shout from the rooftops

trompette [trɔ̃pɛt] *nf* trumpet; *Fig* **avoir le nez en t.** to have a turned-up nose; **t. bouchée** muted trumpet

trompette-de-la-mort [trɔ̃pɛtdəlamɔr] (*pl* **trompettes-de-la-mort**) *nf* horn of plenty

trompettiste [trɔ̃petist] *nmf* trumpet player, trumpeter

trompeur, -euse [trɔ̃pœr, -øz] *adj* (a) *(volontairement)* deceitful (b) *(symptôme, apparences)* deceptive; *(publicité)* misleading

tronc [trɔ̃] *nm* (a) *(d'un arbre, d'un corps)* trunk; *Fig* **t. commun** core syllabus (b) *(dans une église)* poor box

tronche [trɔ̃ʃ] *nf Fam (tête)* nut; *(visage)* mug; **faire la t.** to sulk

tronçon [trɔ̃sɔ̃] *nm* piece; *(de route)* section

tronçonner [trɔ̃sɔne] *vt* to cut into sections

tronçonneuse [trɔ̃sɔnøz] *nf* chain saw

trône [tron] *nm aussi Fam Fig* throne

trôner [trone] *vi* (a) *Hum (personne)* to sit on one's throne (b) *(objet)* to have pride of place

tronquer [trɔ̃ke] *vt (mot, scène)* to shorten

trop [tro] *adv* (a) *(avec un adjectif ou un adverbe)* too; **ça va? – pas t. mal** how are things? – not too bad; *Fam* **il est vraiment t.!** he's too much!
   (b) *(avec un verbe)* too much; **il n'y tient pas t.** he's not too bothered; **je ne sais pas t.** I'm not too sure; **ça te plaît? – pas t.** do you like it? – not much; **on ne saurait t. le répéter** it can't be repeated too often
   (c) *(quantité)* too much; *(nombre)* too many; **t. de** *(quantité)* too much; *(nombre)* too many; **nous sommes t.** there are too many of us; **il y a deux assiettes de** *ou* **en t.** there are two plates too many; **payer 500 francs de t.** *ou* **en t.** to pay 500 francs too much; **c'est une fois de t.** that's once too often; **se sentir de t.** to feel in the way; **t., c'est t.!** enough is enough!; **c'en est t.!** this really is too much!

trophée [trofe] *nm* trophy

tropical, -e, -aux, -ales [trɔpikal, -o] *adj* tropical

tropique [trɔpik] *nm* (a) *(parallèle)* tropic; **le T. du Cancer/du Capricorne** the tropic of Cancer/of Capricorn (b) **les tropiques** *(région)* the tropics; **sous les tropiques** in the tropics

trop-perçu (*pl* **trop-perçus**) [trɔpɛrsy] *nm* overpayment

trop-plein (*pl* **trop-pleins**) [trɔplɛ̃] *nm* (a) *(excédent)* overflow (b) *(dispositif d'évacuation)* overflow pipe

troquer [trɔke] *vt* **t. qch contre qch** to exchange sth for sth

troquet [trɔke] *nm Fam* small café

trot [tro] *nm* trot; **aller au t.** to trot; *Fam Fig* **allez-y, et au t.!** go on, and be quick about it!; **t. attelé** harness race

trotskiste, trotskyste [trotskist] *adj & nmf* Trotskyist

trotte [trot] *nf Fam (distance)* **il y a une bonne t. d'ici à chez elle** it's a fair distance from here to her house

trotter [trote] *vi* (a) *(cheval)* to trot (b) *(personne)* to trot about (c) *Fig* **cet air me trotte dans la tête depuis hier** I haven't been able to get that tune out of my head since yesterday; **cette idée me trottait dans la tête** the idea was running through my head

trotteur [trotœr] *nm* (a) *(cheval)* trotter (b) *(chaussure)* flat shoe

trotteuse [trotøz] *nf (de montre)* second hand

trottiner [trotine] *vi (personne)* to trot about

trottinette [trotinet] *nf* scooter; **faire de la t.** to ride one's scooter

trottoir [trotwar] *nm Br* pavement, *Am* sidewalk; *Fam* **faire le t.** to walk the streets (*of prostitute*); **t. roulant** *Br* travelator, *Am* moving sidewalk

trou [tru] *nm* (a) *(ouverture)* hole; *(d'aiguille)* eye; *Fig* **faire son t.** to find one's niche; **t. d'air** air pocket; *aussi Fig Vulg* **t. du cul** *Br* arsehole, *Am* asshole; **t. noir** black hole; *Fig* **je suis tombé de l'échelle, et après c'est le t. noir** I fell off the ladder, and after that it's all a blank; **t. de serrure** keyhole; **t. de souris** mouse hole (b) *(dans un emploi du temps, dans ses connaissances)* gap; **j'ai un t. de cinq à sept** I'm free between five and seven; **avoir un t. (de mémoire)** to have a memory lapse (c) *(déficit)* hole, dent; *Fam* **le t. de la sécu** the Social Security deficit (d) *Fam Péj (lieu reculé)* hole; **il n'est jamais sorti de son t.** he has never been out of his own backyard (e) *Fam (prison)* nick (f) **faire le t. normand** = to drink a glass of Calvados between courses to aid digestion

troubadour [trubadur] *nm* troubadour

troublant, -e [trublã, -ãt] *adj* (a) *(déconcertant)* disconcerting (b) *(sensuel)* provocative

trouble[1] [trubl] **1** *adj* (a) *(liquide)* cloudy; *(lumière)* dim; *(image, photo)* blurred (b) *(comportement, affaire)* shady; *(période)* murky
2 *adv* **voir t.** to have blurred vision

trouble[2] *nm* (a) *(désordre)* confusion, disorder; **semer ou jeter le t. dans l'esprit de qn** to confuse sb (b) *(émoi)* agitation (c) **troubles** *(révolte)* unrest (d) **troubles** *(maladie)* disorder; **troubles de la vision/respiratoires** eye/respiratory disorder; **troubles de la personnalité** personality disorder

trouble-fête [trublfɛt] *nm inv Br* spoilsport, *Am* party-pooper; **jouer les t.** *Br* to be a spoilsport, *Am* to be a party-pooper

troubler [truble] **1** *vt* (a) *(eau)* to make cloudy; *Fig (esprit)* to cloud; **t. la vue à qn** to blur sb's eyes (b) *(sommeil, silence)* to disturb; *(bonheur)* to spoil; **t. l'ordre public** to disturb the peace (c) *(mettre en émoi)* to make flustered; *(rendre perplexe)* to confuse
2 se troubler *vpr* (a) *(liquide)* to get cloudy; *(vue)* to become blurred (b) *(se déconcerter)* to become flustered; **sans se t.** unperturbed

trouée [true] *nf (dans une haie, dans un mur)* gap, opening; **une t. de ciel bleu** a patch of blue sky

trouer [true] **1** *vt* to make a hole in
2 se trouer *vpr* **mes chaussures se sont trouées au bout d'une semaine** there was a hole in my shoes after a week

troufion [trufjɔ̃] *nm Fam Br* soldier, *Am* grunt

trouillard, -e [trujar, -ard] *Fam* **1** *adj* yellow-bellied, chicken
2 *nm,f* yellow-belly, chicken

trouille [truj] *nf Fam* fear; **avoir la t.** to be scared stiff

trouillomètre [trujomɛtr] *nm Fam* **avoir le t. à zéro** to be scared stiff

troupe [trup] *nf* (a) *(groupe)* troop, band; **t. de théâtre** company, troupe (b) *(de soldats)* troop; **troupes** *(armée)* troops, forces

troupeau, -x [trupo] *nm (de bétail, d'éléphants)* herd; *(de moutons)* flock; *(d'oies)* gaggle; *(de gens)* herd

trousse [trus] *nf* (a) *(étui)* kit; **t. d'écolier** pencil case; **t. de secours** first-aid kit; **t. de toilette** toilet bag (b) *(locutions)* **être aux trousses de qn** to be hot on sb's heels; **avoir qn aux trousses** to have sb hot on one's heels

trousseau, -x [truso] *nm* (a) *(de clés)* bunch (b) *(de mariée)* trousseau (c) *(de pensionnaire)* clothes

trousser [truse] *vt* (a) *Culin (volaille)* to truss (b) **bien troussé** *(compliment)* well-turned (c) *Vieilli (retrousser)* to turn up

trouvaille [truvaj] *nf* (a) *(chose trouvée)* find (b) *(bonne idée)* brainwave

trouver [truve] **1** *vt* (a) *(en cherchant)* to find; *(procédé, vaccin)* to discover; **je ne trouve pas mes clefs** I can't find my keys; **aller t. qn** to go and see sb; **t. quelque chose à redire** to be sure to have something to say; **t. le sommeil** to get to sleep; **exemple bien trouvé** well-chosen example; **je me demande où il est allé t.** ça I wonder where he got that idea from; *Ironique* **tu as trouvé ça tout seul?** did you think of that all on your own?
(b) *(par hasard)* to find, to come across; **t. porte close** to find nobody home; *Fig* **il va t. à qui parler!** he'll have me/him/*etc* to reckon with!; *Fig* **t. son maître** to meet one's match; **t. la mort** to meet one's death
(c) *(juger)* to find; *(penser)* to think; **je trouve ça idiot** I think it's stupid; **qu'est-ce qu'elle lui trouve?** what does she see in him?; **je trouve que...** I think (that)...; **t. le temps long** to feel that the time is dragging
2 se trouver *vpr* (a) *(dans une situation, un lieu)* to be
(b) *(être disponible)* **ça se trouve dans les supermarchés** you can find *or* get it in supermarkets
(c) *(se sentir)* to feel; **je me trouve bien ici** I like it here; **se t. beau/gros** to think one is good-looking/fat; **se t. mal** to feel faint
(d) *(arriver)* **il se trouve que...** as it happens...; *Fam* **si ça se trouve** maybe

trouvère [truvɛr] *nm* trouvère

truand [tryɑ̃] *nm Fam* crook

truander [tryɑ̃de] *Fam* **1** *vt* to rip off; **se faire t.** to get ripped off
2 *vi (à un examen)* to cheat (**à** in)

trublion [tryblijɔ̃] *nm* troublemaker

truc [tryk] *nm Fam* (a) *Fam (chose)* thing; **j'ai un t. à faire/à te dire** I've something to do/to tell you (b) *(astuce)* trick; **connaître les trucs du métier** to know the tricks of the trade (c) *(personne)* **T.** what's-his-name, *f* what's-her-name (d) *(domaine)* **c'est vraiment son t.** he's really into it; **ce n'est pas son t.** it's not his thing

trucage [trykaʒ] *nm* (a) *(dans un film)* special effect (b) *(d'une photographie)* faking; *(d'un match, d'une élection)* rigging; *(de comptes)* fiddling

truchement [tryʃmɑ̃] *nm* **par le t. de...** through...

trucider [tryside] *vt Fam Hum* to bump off

trucmuche [trykmyʃ] *nm Fam* (a) *(chose)* thingy (b) T. *(personne)* what's-his-name, *f* what's-her-name

truculence [trykylɑ̃s] *nf (d'un récit, d'un style)* colourfulness; *(d'une personne)* flamboyance

truculent, -e [trykylɑ̃, -ɑ̃t] *adj (récit, style)* colourful; *(personne)* flamboyant

truelle [tryɛl] *nf* trowel

truffe [tryf] *nf* (a) *(champignon, au chocolat)* truffle (b) *(de chien)* nose

truffer [tryfe] *vt* (a) *(plat)* to garnish with truffles (b) *Fig (remplir)* **être truffé de** *(citations, balles)* to be peppered with; *(fautes)* to be riddled with

truie [trɥi] *nf* sow

truite [trɥit] *nf* trout; **t. arc-en-ciel/saumonée** rainbow/salmon trout

truquage [trykaʒ] = **trucage**

truquer [tryke] *vt* (a) *(photographie)* to fake; *(match, élection)* to rig; *(comptes)* to fiddle; *(dés)* to load (b) *(scène)* to use special effects in

trust [trœst] *nm* trust

truster [trœste] *vt aussi Fam* to monopolize

tsar [tsar, dzar] *nm* tsar, czar

tsé-tsé [tsetse] *nf inv voir* **mouche**

TSF [teesɛf] *nf (abrév* **télégraphie sans fil***) Vieilli (procédé)* wireless telegraphy; *(poste)* wireless

t-shirt *(pl* **t-shirts***)* [tiʃœrt] = **tee-shirt**

tsigane [tsigan] = **tzigane**

TSVP *(abrév* **tournez s'il vous plaît***)* PTO

TTC [tetese] *(abrév* **toutes taxes comprises***)* inclusive of tax

tu, -e *voir* **taire**

tu [ty] *pron personnel* you; *Fam* **t'as déjà fini?** have you already finished?; **être à tu et à toi avec qn** to be on first-name terms with sb; **dire tu à qn** to address sb as 'tu'

Tuamotu [twamotu] *nfpl* **les T.** the Tuamotu Archipelago

tuant, -e [tɥɑ̃, -ɑ̃t] *adj Fam* (a) *(fatigant)* exhausting (b) *(insupportable)* exasperating

tuba [tyba] *nm* (a) *(instrument de musique)* tuba (b) *(de plongée)* snorkel

tube [tyb] *nm* (a) *(tuyau)* tube; *Fam Fig* **à pleins tubes** at full blast; **t. digestif** digestive tract; **t. à essai** test tube (b) *(chanson)* hit (c) *(emballage)* tube; **t. de rouge à lèvres** lipstick

tubercule [tyberkyl] *nm (plante)* tuber

tuberculeux, -euse [tyberkylø, -øz] **1** *adj* with tuberculosis; **être t.** to have tuberculosis
 2 *nm,f* person with tuberculosis

tuberculose [tyberkyloz] *nf* tuberculosis; **avoir la t.** to have tuberculosis

tubéreuse [tyberøz] *nf* tuberose

tubulaire [tybylɛr] *adj* tubular

TUC [tyk] *nm (abrév* **travaux d'utilité collective***)* = community work project for unemployed young people

tuer [tɥe] **1** *vt* (a) *(être vivant)* to kill; **t. qn d'un coup de revolver/de couteau** to shoot/stab sb to death; **c'est le chagrin qui l'a tué** he died of grief; *Fig t.* **le temps** to kill time (b) *Fam (épuiser)* **tous ces déplacements m'ont tué** all that travelling was a killer; **ces escaliers/ces enfants me tuent** these stairs/these children will be the death of me (c) *Fam (sidérer)* **ça me tue!** it kills me!
 2 se tuer *vpr* (a) *(se suicider)* to kill oneself (b) *(dans un accident)* to die, to be killed (c) *(l'un l'autre)* to kill one another (d) *Fig* **se t. au travail** *ou* **à la tâche** to work oneself to death; **se t. à faire qch** to wear oneself out doing sth

tuerie [tyri] *nf* slaughter

tue-tête [tytɛt] **à tue-tête** *adv* at the top of one's voice

tueur, -euse [tɥœr, -øz] **1** *adj* killer
 2 *nm,f* killer; **t. à gages** hired killer

tuile [tɥil] *nf* (a) *(de toit)* tile (b) **t. aux amandes** = type of thin almond biscuit (c) *Fam (problème)* **il m'arrive une t.** I'm in a bit of a mess

tulipe [tylip] *nf (fleur)* tulip

tulle [tyl] *nm* (a) *(tissu)* tulle (b) *Méd* **t. gras** = dressing used for burns

tuméfié, -e [tymefje] *adj* swollen

tuméfier [tymefje] *vt* to cause to swell

tumeur [tymœr] *nf* tumour; **t. au cerveau** brain tumour

tumoral, -e, -aux, -ales [tymoral, -o] *adj* tumorous, tumoral

tumulte [tymylt] *nm (de la foule)* commotion; *(des passions)* turmoil

tumultueux, -euse [tymyltɥø, -øz] *adj (réunion)* noisy, tumultuous; *(vie, période)* tumultuous; *(relation)* stormy

tuner [tynœr, tynɛr] *nm* tuner

tungstène [tœksten] *nm* tungsten

tunique [tynik] *nf* tunic

Tunis [tynis] *n* Tunis

Tunisie [tynizi] *nf* **la T.** Tunisia

tunisien, -enne [tynizjɛ̃, -en] **1** *adj* Tunisian
 2 *nm,f* **T.** Tunisian

tunisois, -e [tynizwa, -az] **1** *adj* of Tunis
 2 *nm,f* **T.** person from Tunis

tunnel [tynɛl] *nm* tunnel; **le t. sous la Manche** the Channel Tunnel

tuque [tyk] *nf Can* bobble hat

turban [tyrbɑ̃] *nm* turban

turbin [tyrbɛ̃] *nm Fam (travail)* grind; **aller au t.** to go off to the daily grind

turbine [tyrbin] *nf* turbine

turbiner [tyrbine] *vi Fam (travailler)* to slog (away)

turbo [tyrbo] **1** *adj* turbocharged
 2 *nm* turbo

turboréacteur [tyrboreaktœr] *nm* turbojet (engine)

turbot [tyrbo] *nm* turbot

turbulence [tyrbylɑ̃s] *nf* (a) **turbulences** *(dans l'atmosphère)* turbulence (b) *(d'un enfant)* boisterousness

turbulent, -e [tyrbylɑ̃, -ɑ̃t] *adj (enfant, classe)* boisterous

turc, turque [tyrk] **1** *adj* Turkish
 2 *nm,f* **T.** Turk
 3 *nm (langue)* Turkish

turf [tœrf, tyrf] *nm (activité)* racing

turfiste [tœrfist, tyrfist] *nmf* racegoer

turkmène [tyrkmen] **1** *adj* Turkoman
2 *nmf* T. Turkoman
3 *nm (langue)* Turkmen

Turkménistan [tyrkmenistã] *nm* **le** T. Turkmenistan

turlupiner [tyrlypine] *vt Fam* to bother

turluter [tyrlyte] *vi Can Fam* to trill, to sing tra-la-la

turpitude [tyrpityd] *nf* **(a)** *(d'une conduite)* vileness, turpitude **(b)** *(action)* vile act

turque [tyrk] *voir* **turc**

Turquie [tyrki] *nf* **la** T. Turkey

turquoise [tyrkwaz] *nf, nm inv & adj inv* turquoise

tutelle [tytɛl] *nf* **(a)** *Jur* guardianship; *Pol* **territoires sous** t. trust territories **(b)** *(protection)* protection

tuteur, -trice [tytœr, -tris] **1** *nm,f* guardian; **t. légal** legal guardian
2 *nm (pour plante)* support

tutoiement [tytwamã] *nm* = use of the familiar "tu" instead of the more formal "vous"; **le t. est de rigueur** everybody calls each other "tu"

tutoyer [tytwaje] **1** *vt* **t. qn** = to address sb as "tu"
2 se tutoyer *vpr* = to address each other as "tu"

tutti quanti [tutikwãti] *adv* et t. etcetera, etcetera

tutu [tyty] *nm* tutu

tuyau, -x [tɥijo] *nm* **(a)** *(canalisation)* pipe; *(de cheminée)* flue; *(flexible)* tube; **t. d'arrosage** garden hose; **t. d'échappement** exhaust (pipe); **t. d'incendie** fire hose; **t. de poêle** stove pipe **(b)** *Fam (conseil)* tip; *(information)* tip-off

tuyauter [tɥijote] *vt Fam (conseiller)* to give a tip to (**sur** about); *(informer)* to tip off (**sur** about)

tuyauterie [tɥijotri] *nf* piping, pipes

TV [teve] *nf (abrév* **télévision***)* TV

TVA [tevea] *nf (abrév* **taxe à la valeur ajoutée***)* VAT

tweed [twid] *nm* tweed

twin-set (*pl* **twin-sets**) [twinset] *nm* twinset

tympan [tɛ̃pã] *nm* **(a)** *Anat* eardrum **(b)** *Archit* tympanum

type [tip] **1** *adj* typical; **lettre t.** standard letter
2 *nm* **(a)** *(genre)* type **(b)** *(personnification)* **le t. même de** the classic example of **(c)** *(apparence)* **avoir le t. latin/ nordique** to have Latin/Nordic looks **(d)** *Fam (homme)* guy, *Br* bloke

typé, -e [tipe] *adj* **il est italien – oui, et il est très t.** he's Italian – yes, he looks typically Italian

typhoïde [tifoid] **1** *adj (fièvre)* typhoid
2 *nf* typhoid (fever)

typhon [tifɔ̃] *nm* typhoon

typhus [tifys] *nm* typhus (fever)

typique [tipik] *adj* typical

typiquement [tipikmã] *adv* typically

typographe [tipɔgraf] *nmf* typographer

typographie [tipɔgrafi] *nf* typography, letterpress printing

typographique [tipɔgrafik] *adj* typographic

tyran [tirã] *nm* tyrant

tyrannie [tirani] *nf* tyranny

tyrannique [tiranik] *adj* tyrannical

tyranniser [tiranize] *vt (population)* to tyrannize; *(famille, collègue)* to bully

tzar [tsar, dzar] **= tsar**

tzigane [tsigan, dzigan] **1** *adj* gypsy
2 *nmf* T. gypsy

U

U, u [y] *nm inv* U, u; **en U** U-shaped; **tables disposées en U** tables arranged in a horseshoe (shape)

ubac [ybak] *nm* = shady side of an Alpine mountain, *Spéc* ubac

ubiquité [ybikɥite] *nf* ubiquity; **avoir le don d'u.** to have the ability to be in several places at the same time

UDF [ydeɛf] *nf (abrév* **Union pour la démocratie française)** = right-of-centre French political party

UE *nf (abrév* **Union européenne)** EU

UEO [yəo] *nf (abrév* **Union de l'Europe occidentale)** WEU

UFR [yefɛʁ] *nf (abrév* **unité de formation et de recherche)** = department *(in university)*

UHF [yaʃɛf] *Rad (abrév* **ultra-haute fréquence)** UHF

UHT [yaʃte] *(abrév* **ultra-haute température)** UHT

Ukraine [ykʁɛn] *nf* **l'U.** the Ukraine

ukrainien, -enne [ykʁɛnjɛ̃, -jɛn] **1** *adj* Ukrainian
2 *nm,f* U. Ukrainian
3 *nm (langue)* Ukranian

ukulélé [jukulele] *nm* ukelele

ulcération [ylseʁasjɔ̃] *nf* ulceration

ulcère [ylsɛʁ] *nm* ulcer; **avoir un u. à l'estomac** to have a stomach ulcer

ulcéré, -e [ylseʁe] *adj* **(a)** *Méd* ulcerated **(b)** *Fig (en colère)* seething

ulcérer [ylseʁe] **1** *vt* **(a)** *Méd* to ulcerate **(b)** *Fig (mettre en colère)* **u. qn** to make sb seethe
2 s'ulcérer *vpr Méd* to ulcerate

ULM [yɛlɛm] *nm inv Av (abrév* **ultraléger motorisé)** microlight

ultérieur, -e [ylteʁjœʁ] *adj* later, subsequent (**à** to)

ultérieurement [ylteʁjœʁmɑ̃] *adv* later (on), subsequently

ultimatum [yltimatɔm] *nm* ultimatum; **adresser un u. à qn** to give sb an ultimatum

ultime [yltim] *adj* last; *(préparatifs)* final

ultra- [yltʁa] *préf* ultra-

ultra-confidentiel, -elle [yltʁakɔ̃fidɑ̃sjɛl] *adj* top-secret

ultra-conservateur, -trice [yltʁakɔ̃sɛʁvatœʁ] *adj Pol* ultra-conservative

ultramoderne [yltʁamɔdɛʁn] *adj* high-tech

ultrarapide [yltʁaʁapid] *adj* ultrafast

ultrasensible [yltʁasɑ̃sibl] *adj* ultra-sensitive

ultrason [yltʁasɔ̃] *nm Phys* ultrasound; **ultrasons** ultrasonic waves

ultraviolet, -ette [yltʁavjɔlɛ, -ɛt] *adj & nm* ultraviolet

ululer [ylyle] *vi* to ululate

Ulysse [ylis] *npr* Ulysses

un, une [œ̃, yn] **1** *adj* one; **il est une heure** it's one o'clock; **page un** page one; **un jour** one day; **un, deux, trois, partez!** one, two, three, go!
2 *pron indéfini* one; **un de mes amis** one of my friends, a friend of mine; **un de ces jours** one of these days; **en voilà une qui sait ce qu'elle veut!** there's somebody who knows what she wants!; **il n'y en a pas un qui parle anglais** not one of them speaks English; *Fam* **être menteur/hypocrite comme pas un** to be a dreadful liar/hypocrite; **(l')** **un de nous, (l')** **un d'entre nous** one of us
3 *art indéfini (pl des)* **(a)** *(en général)* a; *(devant une voyelle ou un h muet)* an; **un jour/une pomme/une heure** a day/ an apple/an hour; **cela tombe un mardi** it falls on a Tuesday; **il y a des agrafes dans le tiroir** there are (some) staples in the drawer; **est-ce qu'il te reste des agrafes?** do you have any staples left?; **il y a des jours où...** there are days when..., some days... **(b)** *(intensif)* **il y a un de ces mondes en ville!** the town is so busy!; **il est d'une bêtise!** he's so stupid!; **il a fait une de ces têtes!** you should have seen his face!; **tu m'as fait une peur!** you gave me such a fright!
4 *nm (chiffre)* one
5 *nf* **(a)** *(première page)* **la une** the front page; **faire la une** *(d'un journal)* the front page; **faire la une** *(d'un magazine)* to appear on the front cover; *(d'un journal)* to appear on the front page **(b)** **il n'a fait ni une ni deux** he didn't hesitate for a moment

unanime [ynanim] *adj* unanimous

unanimité [ynanimite] *nf* unanimity; **à l'u.** unanimously; **faire l'u.** to be accepted unanimously

underground [œ̃ndœʁgʁawnd] *adj inv & nm inv* underground

une [yn] *voir* **un**

UNEF [ynɛf] *nf (abrév* **Union nationale des étudiants de France)** = French union of students, ≃ *Br* NUS

Unesco [ynɛsko] *nf* Unesco

Unetelle *voir* **Untel**

uni, -e [yni] *adj* **(a)** *(famille, couple)* close **(b)** *(sans irrégularité) (sol, surface)* smooth, level **(c)** *(couleur)* plain; *(tissu, vêtement)* self-coloured

Unicef [ynisɛf] *nm ou nf (abrév* **United Nations International Children's Emergency Fund)** **l'U.** Unicef

unicellulaire [yniselylɛʁ] *adj* unicellular

unidimensionnel, -elle [ynidimɑ̃sjɔnɛl] *adj* one-dimensional

unidirectionnel, -elle [ynidiʁɛksjɔnɛl] *adj* unidirectional

unificateur, -trice [ynifikatœʁ, -tʁis] *adj* unifying

unification [ynifikasjɔ̃] *nf* unification

unifier [ynifje] *vt* (a) *(parti politique, pays)* to unify (b) *(tarifs, poids et mesures)* to standardize

uniforme [yniform] **1** *adj (opinions, expression)* uniform; *(vie)* unchanging; *(allure, surface)* even; *(mouvement)* regular **2** *nm* uniform

uniformément [yniformemɑ̃] *adv* uniformly, evenly

uniformisation [yniformizasjɔ̃] *nf* standardization

uniformiser [yniformize] *vt* to standardize

uniformité [yniformite] *nf* (a) *(monotonie)* monotony (b) *(de couleurs, de teintes)* uniformity

unijambiste [yniʒãbist] **1** *adj* one-legged **2** *nmf* one-legged person

unilatéral, -e, -aux, -ales [ynilateral, -o] *adj (décision, désarmement)* unilateral; *(contrat, accord)* one-sided

unilingue [ynilɛ̃g] *adj* unilingual, monolingual

uninominal, -aux [yninominal, -o] *adj voir* **scrutin**

union [ynjɔ̃] *nf* (a) *(entre personnes)* closeness, unity; **vivre en parfaite u. avec qn** to live in perfect harmony with sb (b) *(association) (de partis, de consommateurs)* union, association; **u. douanière/économique/monétaire** customs/economic/monetary union; **l'U. européenne** the European Union; *Anciennement* **l'U. soviétique** the Soviet Union (c) *(mariage)* marriage; **u. libre** cohabitation; **vivre en u. libre** to cohabit

unique [ynik] *adj* (a) *(seul)* only; *(parti, prix)* single; *(occasion, cas)* unique; **être u. en son genre** to be one of a kind; **u. au monde** unlike anything else in the world; **c'est son seul et u. défaut** it's his one and only fault (b) *(incomparable)* unique (c) *Fam (très drôle)* priceless

uniquement [ynikmã] *adv* just, only

unir [ynir] **1** *vt* (a) *(relier)* (personnes, territoires) to unite; *(qualités)* to combine (à with) (b) *(réunir)* **l'amitié qui nous unit** the friendship that unites us (c) *(marier)* to join in marriage (d) *(sol, surface)* to smooth, to level **2 s'unir** *vpr* (a) *(s'associer)* to join together, to unite; **s'u. à qn** to join forces with sb (b) *(se marier)* to become joined in marriage

unisexe [yniseks] *adj* unisex

unisson [ynisɔ̃] *nm* unison; **à l'u.** in unison

unitaire [yniter] *adj (système)* unitary; *(prix)* unit

unité [ynite] *nf* (a) *(pour mesurer)* unit; **u. de longueur/de poids** unit of measurement/weight (b) *(élément simple)* unit; **10 francs l'u.** 10 francs each; *Com* **prix à l'u.** unit price; **vendu à l'u.** sold singly; **chiffre des unités** units figure; **u. de production** production unit; *Univ* **u. de valeur** credit (c) *(cohésion) (d'une nation, d'une association)* unity; *(du style)* consistency (d) *Ordinat* unit; *(de disque)* drive; **u. de bande** tape unit; **u. centrale** central processing unit; **u. de disque/logique** disk/logical drive

univers [yniver] *nm* (a) *(espace)* universe (b) *Fig (milieu)* world

universaliser [yniversalize] *vt* to universalize

universalité [yniversalite] *nf* universality

universel, -elle [yniversel] *adj* universal; *(savoir)* all-embracing

universellement [yniverselmã] *adv* universally

universitaire [yniversiter] **1** *adj (ville, études)* university **2** *nmf* academic

université [yniversite] *nf* university; **aller à l'u.** to go to university; **u. d'été** summer school; *Pol* **party conference (for young members)**; **u. du troisième âge** = classes for senior citizens

Untel, Unetelle [œ̃tel, yntel] *nm,f* what's-his-name, f what's-her-name; **M./Mme U.** Mr/Mrs So-and-So

uppercut [yperkyt] *nm* uppercut

uranium [yranjom] *nm* uranium; **u. enrichi** enriched uranium

Uranus [yranys] *npr (dieu, planète)* Uranus

urbain, -e [yrbɛ̃, -ɛn] *adj* (a) *(développement, milieu, transport)* urban (b) *Litt (poli)* urbane

urbanisation [yrbanizasjɔ̃] *nf* urbanization

urbaniser [yrbanize] *vt* to urbanize

urbanisme [yrbanism] *nm* town planning, urban development

urbaniste [yrbanist] **1** *adj* urban **2** *nmf* town planner

urbanité [yrbanite] *nf Litt* urbanity

urbi et orbi [yrbietorbi] *adv* urbi et orbi; *Fig* far and wide

urée [yre] *nf* urea

urètre [yretr] *nm* urethra

urgence [yrʒɑ̃s] *nf* (a) *(caractère pressé)* urgency; **en cas d'u.** in an emergency; **d'u.** urgently; **être opéré d'u.** to have an emergency operation; **il y a u.** it's a matter of urgency (b) *(à l'hôpital)* emergency; **les urgences** *(service) Br* casualty, accident and emergency, *Am* the emergency room

urgent, -e [yrʒã, -ãt] *adj* urgent; **il est u. de le faire** it must be done urgently

urger [yrʒe] *vi Fam* **ça urge** it's urgent

urinaire [yriner] *adj* urinary

urine [yrin] *nf* urine

uriner [yrine] *vi* to urinate

urinoir [yrinwar] *nm* (public) urinal

urique [yrik] *adj (acide)* uric

urne [yrn] *nf* (a) *(pour voter)* ballot box; **aller aux urnes** to go to the polls (b) *(vase)* urn

uro-génital, -e [mpl uro-génitaux, fpl uro-génitales] [yroʒenital, -o] *adj* urogenital

urologie [yroloʒi] *nf* urology

urologue [yrolog] *nmf* urologist

URSS [yeres, yrs] *nf Anciennement (abrév* **Union des républiques socialistes soviétiques)** **l'U.** the USSR

URSSAF [yrsaf] *nf (abrév* **Union de recouvrement des cotisations de Sécurité sociale et d'Allocations familiales)** = organization which collects social security and family allowance payments

urticaire [yrtiker] *nf* nettle rash, *Spéc* urticaria; **avoir une crise d'u.** to come out in nettle rash; *Fam* **donner de l'u. à qn** to set sb's teeth on edge

Uruguay [yrygwɛ] *nm* **l'U.** Uruguay

uruguayen, -enne [yrygwejɛ̃, -ɛn] **1** *adj* Uruguayan **2** *nm,f* **U.** Uruguayan

us [ys] *nmpl* **les us et coutumes** the habits and customs

usage [yzaʒ] *nm* (a) *(utilisation)* use; **faire u. de qch** to use sth; **faire bon u. de qch** to put sth to good use; **avoir l'u. de qch** to have the use of sth; **à u. externe/interne** *(médicament)* for external/internal use; **à l'u. des écoles/des étudiants** for use in schools/by students; **à usages multiples** multi-purpose; **hors d'u.** out of order; *Jur* **u. de faux** use of forged documents (b) *(d'un terme, d'une expression)* usage; **entrer dans l'u.** *(mot)* to come into common use; **le bon u.** correct usage (c) *(des vêtements)* **faire de l'u.** to wear well; **ce manteau vous fera de l'u.** you'll get a lot of wear out of this coat (d) *(coutume)* custom, practice; **c'est l'u.** it's the done thing; **comme il est d'u. en France** as is customary in France; **il est d'u. de** it's customary to

usagé, -e [yzaʒe] *adj (vêtement, livre)* worn; *(ticket)* used

usager [yzaʒe] *nm* user

usant, -e [yzã, -ãt] *adj Fam* (a) *(vie, travail)* exhausting, wearing (b) *(personne)* tiresome

usé, -e [yze] *adj* (a) *(vêtements)* worn, worn-out; **u. jusqu'à la corde** threadbare (b) *(eaux)* waste (c) *(sujet, plaisanterie)* tired, stale (d) *(épuisé)* worn-out

user [yze] 1 *vt* (a) *(consommer) (énergie, électricité)* to use (b) *(abîmer) (vêtements, chaussures)* to wear out; *Fig (résistance)* to break down; **u. qch jusqu'à la corde** to wear sth until it's threadbare (c) *(épuiser) (personne)* to wear down

2 **user de** *vi ind (patience, violence, ruse)* to use; *(droit)* to exercise; **u. de douceur avec qn** to handle sb gently; **u. de son influence pour faire qch** to use one's influence to do sth

3 **s'user** *vpr* (a) *(tissu, pneus, semelles)* to wear out; *(talons)* to wear down (b) *Fig (personne)* **s'u. à faire qch** to wear oneself out doing sth

usinage [yzinaʒ] *nm* machining

usine [yzin] *nf* factory, plant

usiner [yzine] *vt (façonner)* to machine

usité, -e [yzite] *adj (mot)* in common use; **très u.** very common; **peu u.** little used

ustensile [ystãsil] *nm* implement, tool; **u. de cuisine** kitchen utensil

usuel, -elle [yzɥɛl] *adj* everyday; *(dénomination)* common

usufruit [yzyfrɥi] *nm Jur* usufruct

usuraire [yzyrɛr] *adj* usurious

usure¹ [yzyr] *nf (intérêt, délit)* usury

usure² *nf (de pneu)* wear; *(du sol, de roches)* wearing away; **résister à l'u.** to wear well; *Fam* **avoir qn à l'u.** to wear sb down

usurier, -ère [yzyrje, -ɛr] *nm,f* usurer

usurpateur, -trice [yzyrpatœr, -tris] *nm,f* usurper

usurpation [yzyrpasjõ] *nf (d'un titre, de droits, du pouvoir)* usurpation

usurper [yzyrpe] *vt (titre, droits)* to usurp **(sur** from)

ut [yt] *nm inv (note)* C

utérin, -e [yterɛ̃, -in] *adj* uterine

utérus [yterys] *nm* uterus, womb

utile [ytil] *adj* useful **(à** to); **en quoi puis-je vous être u.?** what can I do for you?; **vous nous avez été bien u.** you've been very helpful to us; **se rendre u.** to make oneself useful; **en temps u.** in due course

utilement [ytilmã] *adv* usefully; **il m'a u. renseigné** he gave me useful information

utilisable [ytilizabl] *adj* usable; **facilement u.** easy to use

utilisateur, -trice [ytilizatœr, -tris] *nm,f* user

utilisation [ytilizasjõ] *nf* use

utiliser [ytilize] *vt* (a) *(se servir de)* to use (b) *Péj (personne)* to use (c) *Ordinat* to run

utilitaire [ytiliter] 1 *adj* (a) utilitarian; *(véhicule)* commercial (b) *Ordinat* utility

2 *nm Ordinat* utility; **u. de conversion** conversion utility

utilitarisme [ytilitarism] *nm* utilitarianism

utilité [ytilite] *nf (fonction)* usefulness; **être d'une grande u. (à qn)** to be very useful (to sb)

utopie [ytopi] *nf* utopia

utopique [ytopik] *adj* utopian

utopiste [ytopist] *nmf* Utopian

UV¹ [yve] *nf inv Univ (abrév* **unité de valeur***)* credit

UV² *nm inv (abrév* **ultraviolet***)* UV

V

V, v [ve] *nm inv* (a) *(lettre)* V, v; *Fam* **à la vitesse grand V** at a rate of knots (b) *(abrév* **voir)** see

va *voir* **aller**

vacance [vakɑ̃s] *nf* (a) *(d'un poste)* vacancy; **pendant la v. du pouvoir** while there is no one officially in power (b) **vacances** *(d'écoliers, de travailleurs) Br* holiday(s), *Am* vacation; **un jour de vacances** a day's holiday; **prendre des vacances** to take a holiday; **être en vacances** to be on holiday; **partir en vacances** to go away on holiday; *Fam* **faire des vacances à qn** to give sb a break; **vacances de neige** winter sports holiday; **vacances de Noël/Pâques** Christmas/Easter holidays; **vacances scolaires** school holidays; *Scol* **les grandes vacances** the summer holidays

vacancier, -ère [vakɑ̃sje, -ɛr] *nm,f Br* holidaymaker, *Am* vacationer

vacant, -e [vakɑ̃, -ɑ̃t] *adj* vacant

vacarme [vakarm] *nm* uproar, din; **faire du v.** to make an uproar

vacataire [vakatɛr] *nmf* short-term worker

vacation [vakasjɔ̃] *nf* (a) *(de juge, d'expert)* sitting, session (b) *(rémunération)* fees

vaccin [vaksɛ̃] *nm* vaccine

vaccination [vaksinasjɔ̃] *nf* vaccination, inoculation

vacciner [vaksine] *vt* to vaccinate, to inoculate (**contre** against); **se faire v. (contre)** to get vaccinated (against); *Fam* **je suis vacciné!** I've learnt my lesson!; *Fam* **je suis majeur et vacciné!** I'm a big boy now!

vache [vaʃ] **1** *nf* (a) *(animal)* cow; **v. à lait** dairy cow; *Fig* milch cow; **v. laitière** dairy cow; *Fam* **manger de la v. enragée** to have a hard time of it; *Fam* **parler français comme une v. espagnole** to speak rotten French (b) *Fam (homme)* swine; *(femme)* cow (c) *(cuir)* cowhide (d) *Fam (interjection)* **la v., qu'est-ce qu'il fait froid!** God, it's so cold!

2 *adj Fam* rotten, nasty; **être v. avec qn** to be rotten to sb

vachement [vaʃmɑ̃] *adv Fam (très) Br* dead, *Am* real; *(beaucoup)* a hell of a lot

vacher, -ère [vaʃe, -ɛr] *nm,f* cowherd, f cowgirl

vacherie [vaʃri] *nf Fam (action)* dirty trick; *(remarque)* nasty remark

vacherin [vaʃrɛ̃] *nm* (a) *(fromage)* = type of soft cheese (b) *(dessert)* = meringue with cream, ice cream and fruit

vachette [vaʃɛt] *nf* (a) *(petite vache)* small cow; *(jeune vache)* calf (b) *(cuir)* calfskin

vacillant, -e [vasijɑ̃, -ɑ̃t] *adj* (a) *(flamme)* flickering; *(démarche)* staggering (b) *(santé, mémoire)* failing

vacillation [vasijasjɔ̃] *nf,* **vacillement** [vasijmɑ̃] *nm* *(d'une flamme)* flickering

vaciller [vasije] *vi* (a) *(chanceler)* to be unsteady, to sway; **v. sur ses jambes** to stagger; **tout vacillait autour de moi** everything was swimming around me (b) *(flamme)* to flicker (c) *(mémoire, raison)* to fail

va-comme-je-te-pousse [vakɔmʃtəpus] **à la va-comme-je-te-pousse** *adv Fam* any old how

vacuité [vakɥite] *nf* vacuity

vadrouille [vadruj] *nf* (a) *Fam (balade)* ramble, saunter; **partir** *ou* **aller en v.** to roam about (b) *Can* mop

vadrouiller [vadruje] *vi Fam* to roam about

va-et-vient [vaevjɛ̃] *nm inv* (a) *(mouvement)* backward and forward movement; **faire le v. (entre)** *(personne)* to go back and forth (between) (b) *(circulation) (de personnes)* comings and goings (c) *(dispositif électrique)* two-way wiring (system)

vagabond, -e [vagabɔ̃, -ɔ̃d] **1** *adj* (a) *(vie)* wandering, roving (b) *Fig (pensées)* wandering, roaming; **avoir l'humeur vagabonde** to be in a restless mood

2 *nm,f* vagrant, tramp

vagabondage [vagabɔ̃daʒ] *nm* vagrancy

vagabonder [vagabɔ̃de] *vi (personne)* to wander, to roam; *Fig (pensées, imagination)* to wander, to stray

vagin [vaʒɛ̃] *nm* vagina

vaginal, -e, -aux, -ales [vaʒinal, -o] *adj* vaginal

vagir [vaʒir] *vi (nouveau-né)* to cry

vagissement [vaʒismɑ̃] *nm (de nouveau-né)* cry, wail

vague¹ [vag] *nf* (a) *(d'eau)* wave; **faire des vagues** to make waves; **arriver par vagues** to come in waves; *aussi Fig* **v. de fond** ground swell (b) *(ondulations) (de chevelure, de dunes)* wave (c) *(courant artistique)* **nouvelle v.** new wave (d) *(d'enthousiasme, de tendresse)* wave, surge; **v. de chaleur** heat wave; **v. de froid** cold spell (e) *(afflux) (d'immigrants)* influx

vague² **1** *adj* (a) *(impression, geste, souvenir)* vague; *(forme)* indistinct; **regarder qn d'un air v.** to look vacantly at sb; **rester v. sur qch** to be vague about sth (b) *(avant le nom)* **quelque v.** some writer or other

2 *nm* (a) *(imprécision)* vagueness; **rester dans le v.** to be vague; **avoir du v. à l'âme** to be melancholy (b) *(vide)* **regard perdu dans le v.** faraway look

vaguelette [vaglɛt] *nf* wavelet

vaguement [vagmɑ̃] *adv* vaguely

vahiné [vaine] *nf* Tahitian woman

vaillamment [vajamɑ̃] *adv* valiantly

vaillance [vajɑ̃s] *nf* valour, courage

vaillant, -e [vajɑ̃, -ɑ̃t] *adj* (a) *(courageux)* valiant, courageous; *(cœur)* stout (b) *(en forme)* **être v.** to be in good health

vaille, vailles *voir* **valoir**

vain, -e [vɛ̃, vɛn] *adj* (a) *(sans résultat) (démarche, entreprise)* futile; *(efforts)* vain; **en v.** in vain (b) *(vide de sens) (paroles, promesse)* empty; *(espoirs, regrets)* vain (c) *Litt (personne)* vain

vaincre [vɛ̃kr] *vt* (a) *(adversaire)* to defeat; *(en sport)* to beat (b) *Fig (maladie, difficulté)* to overcome

vaincu, -e [vɛ̃ky] **1** *adj* beaten, defeated; **s'avouer v.** to admit defeat
2 *nm,f* defeated man, *f* defeated woman

vainement [vɛnmã] *adv* in vain

vainqueur [vɛ̃kœr] **1** *nm* (a) *(dans une compétition sportive)* winner (b) *(d'une bataille, d'une lutte)* victor
2 *adj m (personne)* conquering, victorious

vairon[1] [vɛrõ] *adj* **avoir les yeux vairons** to have different-coloured eyes

vairon[2] *nm (poisson)* minnow

vais *voir* **aller**

vaisseau, -x [veso] *nm* (a) **v. (sanguin)** blood vessel (b) **v. spatial** spaceship (c) *(d'une église)* nave (d) *Litt* ship, vessel; **v. de guerre** warship

vaisselier [vesalje] *nm (meuble)* dresser

vaisselle [vesel] *nf* dishes, crockery; **faire** *ou* **laver la v.** to do the washing-up, to do the dishes

val [val] *nm* valley

valable [valabl] *adj* (a) *(ticket, raison, excuse)* valid; **ce qui est v. pour l'un est v. pour l'autre** what goes for one goes for the other (b) *(compétent) (interlocuteur)* authorized (c) *(de qualité) (roman)* good; *(idée)* valid

valdinguer [valdɛ̃ge] *vi Fam* **aller v. contre/sur qch** to go flying against/onto sth; **envoyer v. qch** to send sth flying

Valence [valɑ̃s] *n* (a) *(en Espagne)* Valencia (b) *(en France)* Valence

valériane [valerjan] *nf* valerian

valet [valɛ] *nm* (a) *(au jeu de cartes)* jack, knave (b) *(domestique)* **v. (de chambre)** valet; **v. de ferme** farmhand; **v. de pied** footman (c) *(meuble)* **v. de nuit** valet

valétudinaire [valetydinɛr] *adj & nmf* valetudinarian

valeur [valœr] *nf* (a) *(prix)* value, worth; **avoir de la v.** to be valuable; **de peu de v./de grande v.** of little/of great value; **d'une v. de 200 francs** worth 200 francs; **prendre de la v.** to increase in value; **v. d'achat** purchase value; **v. ajoutée** added value; **v. en Bourse** stock market value; **v. marchande** market value; **valeurs mobilières** stocks and shares; **v. nominale** nominal value (b) *(qualité, mérite)* value; **de v.** *(livre, œuvre)* of considerable merit; **homme de v.** *(de mérite)* man of merit; **avoir v. légale** to be legally binding; **attacher de la v. à qch** to value sth; **mettre en v.** to show to advantage; *(teint, yeux)* to bring out; *(mot)* to emphasize; **se mettre en v.** to show oneself off to advantage; **prendre toute sa v.** *(terme, expression)* to take on its full meaning (c) *(titre)* security (d) *(d'une note)* time, length; *(d'une carte)* value (e) *(équivalent) (d'une mesure)* equivalent (f) *(morale)* **valeurs** values (g) *Litt (courage)* valour

valeureux, -euse [valørø, -øz] *adj Litt* gallant

validation [validasjõ] *nf (d'un titre de transport)* validation; *(d'un document)* authentication

valide [valid] *adj* (a) *(contrat)* valid (b) *(personne) (en bonne santé)* fit; *(non blessé)* uninjured

valider [valide] *vt* (a) *(élection, mariage)* to validate; *(document)* to authenticate; **v. un titre de transport** *(dans une machine)* to stamp a ticket (b) *Ordinat (option)* to confirm; *(cellule, case)* to select

validité [validite] *nf (d'un contrat, d'un passeport)* validity

valise [valiz] *nf* (a) *(bagage)* suitcase; *aussi Fig* **faire ses valises** to pack one's bags (b) *(courrier)* **la v. diplomatique** the diplomatic *Br* bag *or Am* pouch (c) *Fam (sous les yeux)* bag

vallée [vale] *nf* valley; *Litt* **une v. de larmes** a vale of tears

vallon [valõ] *nm* small valley

vallonné, -e [valɔne] *adj (région)* undulating, hilly

vallonnement [valɔnmã] *nm* undulation

valoche [valɔʃ] *nf Fam* case, bag

valoir [69] [valwar] **1** *vi* (a) *(avoir comme valeur)* to be worth; **v. cher** *(objet en vente)* to be expensive; *(objet précieux)* to be worth a lot; *Fig* **ne pas v. cher** *(personne)* not to be up to much; **ne rien v.** *(objet)* to be worthless; *(idée)* to be useless; **ce climat ne vous vaut rien** this climate doesn't suit you; **il ne vaut pas mieux que son frère** he's no better than his brother; **ça vaut mieux comme ça** it's better that way
(b) *(avoir un intérêt)* **et ça vaut pour tout le monde** and that goes for everyone; **faire v. qch** *(opinions, droits)* to assert sth

2 *vt* (a) *(équivaloir à)* to be equivalent to; **une livre vaut environ huit francs** one pound is worth around eight francs; **ça ne vaut pas ce qui m'est arrivé l'autre jour** that's nothing to what happened to me the other day; **rien ne vaut un bon petit déjeuner** there's nothing like a good breakfast
(b) *(rapporter)* **v. qch à qn** *(punition)* to earn sb sth; *(soucis, ennuis)* to bring sb sth; **qu'est-ce qui me vaut cet honneur?** to what do I owe this honour?

3 *v impersonnel* **il vaut/vaudrait mieux faire qch** it's/it would be better to do sth; **il vaut mieux que vous restiez** you'd better stay, it would be better if you stayed; *Prov* **mieux vaut tard que jamais** better late than never
4 se valoir *vpr* **tous les métiers se valent** one job is as good as another; *(péjoratif)* they're as bad as each other; *(admiratif)* they're as good as each other

valorisant, -e [valɔrizã, -ãt] *adj* gratifying

valorisation [valɔrizasjõ] *nf* (a) *(augmentation de la valeur)* increase in value (b) *(développement)* development

valoriser [valɔrize] *vt (bien, monnaie)* to increase the value of; *(région)* to develop; *(personne)* to boost the self-esteem of

valse [vals] *nf* (a) *(morceau de musique, air de danse)* waltz (b) **la v. des ministres** frequent cabinet reshuffles

valse-hésitation *(pl* **valses-hésitations)** [valsezitasjõ] *nf Fam* pussyfooting, shilly-shallying

valser [valse] *vi* to waltz; **faire v. qn** to waltz with sb; *Fig* **faire v. les millions** to spend money like water; *Fam* **envoyer v. qn/qch** to send sb/sth flying

valseur, -euse [valsœr, -øz] *nm,f* waltzer

valu, -e *voir* **valoir**

valve [valv] *nf* valve

vamp [vãp] *nf Fam* vamp

vampire [vãpir] *nm* (a) *(suceur de sang)* vampire (b) *Fig (parasite)* bloodsucker

vampiriser [vãpirize] *vt Fam* to dominate psychologically

van[1] [vã] *nm (fourgon à chevaux)* horse box

van² [van] *nm (camionnette)* van

Vancouver [vãkuver] *n* Vancouver

vandale [vãdal] *nmf* vandal

vandaliser [vãdalize] *vt* to vandalize

vandalisme [vãdalism] *nm* vandalism

vanille [vanij] *nf* vanilla

vanillé, -e [vanije] *adj* vanilla-flavoured

vanité [vanite] *nf* (a) *(suffisance)* vanity; **tirer v. de qch** to pride oneself on sth (b) *Litt (insignifiance)* futility, emptiness

vaniteux, -euse [vanitø, -øz] **1** *adj* vain **2** *nm,f* vain person

vanne¹ [van] *nf (de canalisation, d'écluse)* sluice gate, floodgate; **ouvrir/fermer les vannes** to open/to close the floodgates

vanne² *nf Fam (remarque blessante)* dig, jibe; **envoyer une v. à qn** to have a dig at sb

vanné, -e [vane] *adj Fam* **être v.** to be dead beat

vanneau, -x [vano] *nm (oiseau)* lapwing, peewit

vanner [vane] *vt* (a) *Fam (fatiguer)* to wear out, to exhaust (b) *(grain)* to winnow

vannerie [vanri] *nf* (a) *(activité)* basket making, basketry (b) *(objets)* basketwork, wickerwork

vannier [vanje] *nm* basket worker or maker

vantard, -e [vãtar, -ard] **1** *adj* bragging, boastful **2** *nm,f* braggart, boaster

vantardise [vãtardiz] *nf (caractère)* bragging, boastfulness; *(parole)* boast

vanter [vãte] **1** *vt* to praise, to speak highly of **2 se vanter** *vpr* to boast, to brag (**de** about)

Vanuatu [vanwatu] *n* Vanuatu

va-nu-pieds [vanypje] *nmf inv* tramp, beggar

vapes [vap] *nfpl Fam* **être dans les v.** to be all woozy; **tomber dans les v.** to pass out

vapeur¹ [vapœr] *nf* (a) *(d'eau bouillante)* v. **(d'eau)** steam; **cuire qch à la v.** to steam sth; **à toute v.** full steam ahead; *Fig* at full speed (b) *(gaz)* **vapeurs** *(d'alcool, d'essence)* fumes (c) *Méd* **avoir des vapeurs** to have a fit of the vapours

vapeur² *nm (bateau)* steamer, steamship

vaporeux, -euse [vaporø, -øz] *adj* (a) *(atmosphère)* steamy (b) *(robe)* flimsy

vaporisateur [vaporizatœr] *nm (de parfum)* spray, atomizer; *(pour plantes)* spray

vaporiser [vaporize] **1** *vt* (a) *(pulvériser)* to spray (b) *(transformer en vapeur)* to vaporize **2 se vaporiser** *vpr* to vaporize

vaquer [vake] **1** *vi (parlement, tribunal)* to be on vacation **2 vaquer à** *vt ind* **v. à qch** to attend to sth; **v. à ses affaires** *ou* **occupations** to go about one's business

varappe [varap] *nf* rock climbing; **faire de la v.** to go rock climbing

varapper [varape] *vi* to go rock climbing

varappeur, -euse [varapœr, -øz] *nm,f* rock climber

vareuse [varøz] *nf* (a) *(de marin)* pea jacket (b) *(d'uniforme)* tunic (c) *(veste large)* loose-fitting jacket

variable [varjabl] **1** *adj* (a) *(temps, humeur)* changeable; *(vitesse)* varying (b) *(différent)* varied; **être v.** to vary **2** *nf* variable; *Ordinat* **v. de mémoire** memory variable

variante [varjãt] *nf* variant, variation

variation [varjasjɔ̃] *nf* (a) *(écart)* change (**de** in); **les variations de la température** the variations in the temperature (b) *Mus* variation

varice [varis] *nf* varicose vein

varicelle [varisel] *nf* chickenpox, *Spéc* varicella; **avoir la v.** to have chickenpox

varié, -e [varje] *adj (alimentation, paysage, travail)* varied; *(vocabulaire)* wide

varier [varje] **1** *vt (alimentation, occupations)* to vary; *Ironique* **pour v. les plaisirs** by way of a pleasant change **2** *vi* to vary, to change; **les opinions varient sur ce point** opinions differ on this point; **il n'a jamais varié sur ce point** he's never changed his mind about it

variété [varjete] **1** *nf* variety **2** *nfpl* **TV variétés** variety show; **chanteur de variétés** middle-of-the-road singer

variole [varjol] *nf* smallpox; **avoir la v.** to have smallpox

Varsovie [varsovi] *n* Warsaw

vas *voir* **aller**

vasculaire [vaskyler] *adj* vascular

vase¹ [vaz] *nm* vase; *Fig* **vivre en v. clos** to live in isolation; **vases communicants** communicating vessels

vase² *nf* mud, silt

vasectomie [vazektomi] *nf* vasectomy

vaseline [vazlin] *nf* Vaseline®, petroleum jelly

vaseux, -euse [vazø, -øz] *adj* (a) *Fam (mal en point)* off-colour (b) *(peu clair) (idée)* woolly; *(explication)* confused (c) *(plaisanterie)* unsavoury (d) *(rivière)* muddy, silty

vasistas [vazistas] *nm* fanlight

vasoconstricteur, -trice [vazokɔ̃striktœr, -tris] *adj & nm* vasoconstrictor

vasodilatateur, -trice [vazodilatatœr, -tris] *adj & nm* vasodilator

vasomoteur, -trice [vazomotœr, -tris] *adj (nerf)* vasomotor

vasouillard, -e [vazujar, -ard] *adj Fam (idée)* confused, muddled; **se sentir v.** to feel a bit under the weather

vasouiller [vazuje] *vi Fam* to flounder

vassal, -e, -aux, -ales [vasal, -o] *nm,f* vassal

vaste [vast] *adj* (a) vast, immense (b) *Fam (plaisanterie)* big, great; **c'est une v. fumisterie** it's a complete farce

Vatican [vatikã] *nm* **le V.** the Vatican; **la cité du V.** the Vatican City

va-tout [vatu] *nm inv* **jouer son v.** to stake one's all

vaudeville [vodvil] *nm Th* light farce; **tourner au v.** to become farcical

vaudou [vodu] *adj & nm* voodoo

vaudrai, vaudras *etc voir* **valoir**

vau-l'eau [volo] **à vau-l'eau** *adv* **aller à v.** to fall through

vaurien, -enne [vorjɛ̃, -ɛn] *nm,f* (a) *(brigand)* good-for-nothing (b) *(enfant)* rascal

vaut *voir* **valoir**

vautour [votur] *nm* vulture

vautrer [votre] **se vautrer** *vpr* (a) *(cochon)* to wallow (**dans** in) (b) *(personne)* to sprawl (**dans** in); *Fig* **se v. dans la débauche** to wallow in vice

vauvert [vover] *voir* **diable**

va-vite [vavit] **à la va-vite** *adv* in a rush

vaux *voir* **valoir**

VDQS [vedekyes] *nm (abrév* **vin délimité de qualité supérieure)** = label certifying that wine is of good quality

veau, -x [vo] *nm* (a) *(animal)* calf (b) *(viande)* veal (c) *(cuir)* calfskin (d) *Fam (personne lente)* lump (e) *Fam (voiture)* car with poor acceleration

vecteur [vɛktœr] *nm* (a) *Math* vector (b) *(d'information, de progrès)* vehicle

vectoriel, -elle [vɛktɔrjɛl] *adj* vectorial; *Ordinat* **police vectorielle** outline font

vécu, -e [veky] **1** *pp voir* **vivre**
2 *adj (expérience)* real-life
3 *nm* real-life experience

vedettariat [vədetarja] *nm* stardom

vedette [vədet] *nf* (a) *(acteur)* star; **v. de la chanson** singing star; **v. de cinéma** film star; **avoir la v., être en v.** *(dans un spectacle)* to top the bill; *(dans un film)* to be the main star (b) *Fig (de la politique)* leading light (c) *(bateau à moteur) (de plaisancier)* launch; *(de police)* patrol boat

végétal, -e, -aux, -ales [veʒetal, -o] **1** *adj (huile)* vegetable
2 *nm* vegetable, plant

végétarien, -enne [veʒetarjɛ̃, -ɛn] *adj & nm,f* vegetarian

végétatif, -ive [veʒetatif, -iv] *adj (appareil)* vegetative; *Fig & Péj (existence)* vegetable-like

végétation [veʒetasjɔ̃] *nf* (a) *(flore)* vegetation (b) *Méd* **végétations (adénoïdes)** adenoids

végéter [veʒete] *vi Péj (personne)* to vegetate

véhémence [veemɑ̃s] *nf Litt* vehemence; **avec v.** vehemently

véhément, -e [veemɑ̃, -ɑ̃t] *adj Litt* vehement, violent

véhicule [veikyl] *nm* (a) *(moyen de transport)* vehicle; **v. utilitaire** commercial vehicle (b) *(support) (du son, de la lumière)* vehicle

véhiculer [veikyle] *vt* (a) *(transporter)* to transport, to convey (b) *(transmettre)* to convey

veille [vɛj] *nf* (a) *(jour qui précède)* **la v.** the previous day, the day before; **à la v. de la réunion** the day before the meeting; **la v. au soir** the previous evening, the evening before; **la v. de Noël** Christmas Eve; *Fig* **être à la v. de qch/de faire qch** to be on the verge of sth/ of doing sth (b) *(éveil)* wakefulness; **entre la v. et le sommeil** between waking and sleeping; **après deux jours de v.** after staying up for two nights (c) *(garde)* (night) watch; **prendre la v.** to take one's turn on watch (d) *Ordinat* standby mode; **en v.** in standby mode

veillée [veje] *nf* (a) *(soirée)* evening; **v. au coin du feu** evening spent round the fire; **v. d'armes** knightly vigil (b) *(d'un mort)* watch, vigil

veiller [veje] **1** *vt (malade)* to sit up with; **v. un mort** to keep vigil over a dead body
2 *vi* to stay up
3 veiller à *vt ind* **v. à qch** to see to sth; **v. aux intérêts de qn** to look after sb's interests; **v. à ce que qn fasse qch** to make sure *or* see to it that sb does sth; *Fig* **v. au grain** to keep an eye open for trouble
4 veiller sur *vt ind* **v. sur qn** to take care of sb

veilleur [vejœr] *nm* **v. de nuit** night watchman

veilleuse [vejøz] *nf* (a) *(lampe)* night light; *(sur une télévision, sur un magnétoscope)* standby; *Fig* **mettre qch en v.** *(projet, problème)* to put sth on the back burner; *Fam* **la mettre en v.** to put a sock in it (b) *(d'un chauffe-eau, d'un réchaud)* pilot light (c) **veilleuses** *(d'une automobile)* sidelights

veinard, -e [venar, -ard] *Fam* **1** *adj* lucky
2 *nm,f* lucky devil

veine [vɛn] *nf* (a) *Anat* vein; **v. cave** vena cava (b) *Fam (chance)* luck; **avoir de la v.** to be lucky; *Fam* **avoir une v. de cocu** to have the luck of the devil (c) *(dans le marbre, le bois)* vein (d) *(filon) (de minerai)* vein; *(de charbon)* seam (e) *(inspiration)* vein; **en v. de plaisanterie** in humorous vein; **être en v. de générosité** to be in a generous mood

veiné, -e [vene] *adj (marbre, bois)* grained

veineux, -euse [venø, -øz] *adj (système, circulation)* venous

veinule [venyl] *nf* venule

Velcro® [vɛlkro] *nm (tissu)* Velcro®; *(fermeture)* Velcro® fastening

vêler [vele] *vi* to calve

vélin [velɛ̃] *nm* vellum

véliplanchiste [veliplɑ̃ʃist] *nmf* windsurfer

velléitaire [veleiter] **1** *adj* indecisive
2 *nmf* indecisive person

velléités [veleite] *nfpl* vague desire; **avoir des v. de faire qch** to toy with the idea of doing sth

vélo [velo] *nm* bike; **aller au bureau en v.** to cycle to the office, to go to the office on one's bike; **faire du v.** *(comme activité)* to go cycling; **est-ce que tu sais faire du v.?** can you ride a bike?; **v. d'appartement** exercise bike; **v. de course** racing cycle; **v. tout-terrain** mountain bike

vélocité [velosite] *nf* speed, swiftness

vélodrome [velodrom] *nm* velodrome

vélomoteur [velomotœr] *nm* moped

velours [vəlur] *nm (tissu)* velvet; **veste/rideaux en v.** velvet jacket/curtains; **v. côtelé** *ou* **à côtes** corduroy (b) *Fig* **faire des yeux de v. à qn** to make eyes at sb

velouté, -e [vəlute] **1** *adj* velvety
2 *nm* (a) *(texture)* velvetiness (b) *(soupe)* cream soup; **v. d'asperges** cream of asparagus soup

velouteux, -euse [vəlutø, -øz] *adj* velvety

Velpeau® [vɛlpo] *voir* **bande**

velu, -e [vəly] *adj* hairy

Vélux® [velyks] *nm* = window built into a sloping roof

venaison [vənɛzɔ̃] *nf* venison

vénal, -e, -aux, -ales [venal, -o] *adj* (a) *Péj (intéressé)* venal, mercenary (b) *(valeur)* market

venant [vənɑ̃] *nm* **à tout v., à tous venants** to all comers, to all and sundry

vendable [vɑ̃dabl] *adj* saleable, sellable; **facilement/difficilement v.** easy/difficult to sell

vendange [vɑ̃dɑ̃ʒ] *nf* (a) **vendanges** *(période)* grape-harvesting time (b) *(récolte)* grape harvest; **faire la v.** *ou* **les vendanges** to harvest *or* pick the grapes (c) *(raisin récolté)* grapes (harvested); **une bonne v.** a good vintage

vendanger [vɑ̃dɑ̃ʒe] **1** *vi* to harvest the grapes **2** *vt (vigne)* to pick the grapes from

vendangeur, -euse [vɑ̃dɑ̃ʒœr, -øz] *nm,f* grape picker

vendetta [vɑ̃deta] *nf* vendetta

vendeur, -euse [vãdœr, -øz] **1** *adj* **être v.** to be willing to sell

2 *nm,f* (*dans un magasin*) *Br* (shop) assistant, *Am* (sales)clerk; (*non professionnel*) seller; **v. ambulant** travelling salesman; **v. de journaux** newspaper seller or vendor

vendre [vãdr] **1** *vt* **a** (*article, produit*) to sell; **v. qch 50 francs** to sell sth for 50 francs; **v. qch à qn** to sell sb sth, to sell sth to sb; **à v.** (*sur panneau*) for sale; *Fig* **v. son âme au diable** to sell one's soul to the devil **(b)** (*trahir*) (*personne*) to sell out; (*secret*) to sell; **v. la mèche** to spill the beans

2 se vendre *vpr* **(a)** (*produit, article*) to be sold; **cela se vend comme des petits pains** it's selling like hot cakes **(b)** (*soi-même*) to sell oneself

vendredi [vãdrədi] *nm* Friday; **le v. saint** Good Friday; *voir aussi* **samedi**

vendu, -e [vãdy] **1** *adj* (*corrompu*) bribed

2 *nm,f* traitor

vénéneux, -euse [venenø, -øz] *adj* poisonous

vénérable [venerabl] *adj* venerable

vénération [venerasjõ] *nf* veneration; **avoir de la v. pour qn** to hold sb in veneration

vénérer [venere] *vt* to venerate

vénérien, -enne [venerjɛ̃, -ɛn] *adj* venereal

Venezuela [venezɥela] *nm* **le V.** Venezuela

vénézuélien, -enne [venezɥeljɛ̃, -ɛn] **1** *adj* Venezuelan

2 *nm,f* **V.** Venezuelan

vengeance [vãʒãs] *nf* revenge, vengeance; **la v. est un plat qui se mange froid** revenge is a dish best eaten cold

venger [vãʒe] **1** *vt* to avenge; **v. qn de qch** to avenge sb for sth

2 se venger *vpr* to get one's revenge; **se v. sur qn (de qch)** to get one's revenge on sb (for sth); *Fam* **pas la peine de te v. sur moi!** there's no point in taking it out on me!

vengeur, -eresse [vãʒœr, -ʒrɛs] *Litt* **1** *adj* vengeful

2 *nm,f* avenger

véniel, -elle [venjɛl] *adj* (*péché*) venial

venimeux, -euse [vənimø, -øz] *adj aussi Fig* venomous

venin [vənɛ̃] *nm aussi Fig* venom

venir [70] [vənir] (*aux être*) **1** *vi* **(a)** (*arriver*) to come (de from); **il vient passer quelques jours** he's coming to spend a few days; **viens me voir** come and see me; **d'où venez-vous?** where do you come from?; **je viens!** I'm coming!; **v. vers qn** to come up to sb; **vous y viendrez!** you'll come round to it, you'll change your mind; **dans les mois/années qui viennent** in the coming months/years; **le moment est venu de nous en aller** it's time we left; **le jour viendra où...** the day will come when...; **ton tour viendra** your turn will come, you'll get your turn; **l'eau leur venait aux genoux** the water came up to their knees

(b) (*tirer son origine*) to come (de from); **la maison lui vient de sa mère** he/she inherited the house from his/her mother

(c) **v. à qch/à faire qch** to come to sth/to do sth; **j'en suis venu à me demander si...** I began to wonder whether...; **où voulez-vous en v.?** what are you getting at?; **en v. aux mains** to come to blows

(d) **venir de faire qch** to have just done sth; **je viens de le lui dire** I've just told him; **je venais de terminer** I'd just finished

2 *v impersonnel* **s'il venait à pleuvoir** if it happened to rain; **il m'est venu une idée intéressante** an interesting idea occurred to me

3 s'en venir *vpr Litt* to come along

Venise [vaniz] *n* Venice

vénitien, -enne [venisjɛ̃, -ɛn] **1** *adj* Venetian

2 *nm,f* **V.** Venetian

vent [vã] *nm* **(a)** (*air*) wind; **les cheveux au v.** with one's hair streaming in the wind; **quel bon v. vous amène?** to what do I/we owe the pleasure?; *Fig* **avoir le v. en poupe** to have the wind in one's sails; *Fig* **avoir du v. dans les voiles** to be three sheets to the wind; **avoir v. de qch** to get wind of sth; **ce n'est que du v.** it's just hot air; *Fam* **être dans le v.** to be with it; **contre vents et marées** come hell or high water; *Ironique* **bon v.!** good riddance! **(b)** (*flatulence*) wind; **avoir des vents** to have wind

vente [vãt] *nf* (*transaction*) sale; (*activité*) selling; **en v.** (*par un particulier*) for sale; (*dans les magasins*) on sale; **en v. libre** available over the counter; **mettre qch en v.** to put sth up for sale; **v. de charité** charity sale; **v. par correspondance** mail order (selling); **v. à crédit** credit sale; **v. au détail** retailing; **v. aux enchères** (sale by) auction; **v. en gros** wholesaling; **v. à tempérament** *Br* hire purchase, *Am* installment plan

venter [vãte] *v impersonnel* **il vente** it's windy

venteux, -euse [vãtø, -øz] *adj* windy

ventilateur [vãtilatœr] *nm* **(a)** (*pour aérer*) fan **(b)** *Ordinat* **v. de refroidissement** cooling fan **(c)** (*d'une automobile*) blower

ventilation [vãtilasjõ] *nf* **(a)** (*aération*) ventilation **(b)** (*des dépenses*) breakdown

ventiler [vãtile] *vt* **(a)** (*aérer*) to ventilate **(b)** (*dépenses*) to break down

ventouse [vãtuz] *nf* **(a)** (*pour fixer*) suction grip; (*pour déboucher*) plunger; **faire v.** to adhere by suction **(b)** (*en verre*) cupping glass; **poser des ventouses à qn** to cup sb

ventral, -e, -aux, -ales [vãtral, -o] *adj* ventral

ventre [vãtr] *nm* **(a)** (*estomac*) stomach; **avoir le v. plein/vide** to have a full/an empty stomach; **avoir du v.** to have a paunch; **v. à terre** at full speed, flat out; **avoir mal au v.** to have a sore stomach; *Fig* **ça fait mal au v. de voir ça** it makes me sick to see that; *Fig* **ça me ferait mal au v.!** it would kill me!; **ne rien avoir dans le v.** to have no guts **(b)** (*utérus*) womb **(c)** (*d'une bouteille*) bulge

ventricule [vãtrikyl] *nm* ventricle

ventriloque [vãtrilɔk] *nmf* ventriloquist

ventru, -e [vãtry] *adj* **(a)** (*gros*) potbellied **(b)** (*colonne*) bulbous

venu, -e [vəny] **1** *adj* **bien v.** appropriate; **mal v.** inappropriate

2 *nm,f* **le premier v.** (*n'importe qui*) anybody; **un nouveau v.** a newcomer

3 *nf* **venue** (*d'une personne, du printemps*) coming; **dès sa venue au monde** since he/she came into the world

Vénus [venys] *npr* (*déesse, planète*) Venus

vêpres [vɛpr] *nfpl* vespers

ver [vɛr] *nm* **(a)** (*dans la terre*) worm; (*dans un fruit*) grub; *Fig* **tirer les vers du nez à qn** to drag it out of sb; **v. luisant** glow-worm; **v. à soie** silkworm; **v. de terre** earthworm; *Méd* **v. solitaire** tapeworm; **avoir le v. solitaire** to have a tapeworm

véracité [verasite] *nf* truthfulness

véranda [verɑ̃da] nf veranda(h)

verbal, -e, -aux, -ales [vɛrbal, -o] adj verbal

verbalement [vɛrbalmɑ̃] adv verbally

verbaliser [vɛrbalize] 1 vt (exprimer) to verbalize 2 vi (policier) to record the details of an offence

verbe [vɛrb] nm Gram verb; **v. à particule** (en anglais) phrasal verb

verbeux, -euse [vɛrbø, -øz] adj verbose

verbiage [vɛrbjaʒ] nm verbiage

verdâtre [vɛrdɑtr] adj greenish

verdeur [vɛrdœr] nf (a) (d'un fruit, d'un vin) tartness (b) (du langage) crudeness (c) (vitalité) vigour, vitality

verdict [vɛrdikt] nm verdict; **prononcer ou rendre un v.** to return a verdict

verdir [vɛrdir] 1 vt to turn green 2 vi to turn green; Fig **v. de jalousie/de peur** to go or turn green with envy/white with fear

verdoyant, -e [vɛrdwajɑ̃, ɑ̃t] adj green

verdoyer [vɛrdwaje] vi Litt to be green

verdure [vɛrdyr] nf (a) (couleur) greenness (b) (végétation) greenery (c) (légumes verts) greens

véreux, -euse [verø, -øz] adj (a) (fruit) wormy, maggoty (b) Péj (affaires, financier) shady, dubious

verge [vɛrʒ] nf (a) (pénis) penis (b) (baguette) cane (c) Can (mesure) yard

verger [vɛrʒe] nm orchard

vergetures [vɛrʒətyr] nfpl stretch marks

verglacé, -e [vɛrglase] adj icy

verglas [vɛrgla] nm Br (black) ice, Am glaze

vergogne [vɛrgɔɲ] **sans vergogne** 1 adj shameless 2 adv shamelessly

véridique [veridik] adj truthful

vérifiable [verifjabl] adj verifiable

vérificateur, -trice [verifikatœr, -tris] 1 nm,f (personne) inspector, examiner; **v. de comptes** auditor 2 nm Ordinat **v. orthographique** spellchecker

vérification [verifikasjɔ̃] nf (a) (d'un travail, des votes) checking; **v. de comptes** ou **d'écritures** audit(ing) of accounts (b) Ordinat **v. antivirale** antivirus check; **v. orthographique** spellcheck

vérifier [verifje] 1 vt to check; (comptes) to audit; **il doit être là, je vais** v. he must be there, I'll check 2 **se vérifier** vpr to prove correct

véritable [veritabl] adj (a) (histoire, ami) true; (nom, or, cuir) real (b) (en intensif) real

véritablement [veritabləmɑ̃] adv really

vérité [verite] nf (a) (d'une déclaration) truth; **dire la v.** to tell the truth; **c'est la v.** it's true, it's a fact; **à la v.** to tell the truth; **en v.** really, actually; **dire à qn ses quatre vérités** to tell sb a few home truths (b) (d'un personnage, d'une description) trueness to life (c) (sincérité) **un accent de v.** a ring of truth

verlan [vɛrlɑ̃] nm back slang

vermeil, -eille [vɛrmɛj] 1 adj bright red 2 nm silver gilt

vermicelle [vɛrmisɛl] nm vermicelli

vermifuge [vɛrmifyʒ] nm vermifuge

vermillon [vɛrmijɔ̃] adj inv & nm vermilion

vermine [vɛrmin] nf (a) (insectes) vermin; **couvert** ou **grouillant de v.** crawling with vermin (b) Péj (racaille) la v. vermin

vermisseau, -x [vɛrmiso] nm small worm; Fig (personne) worm

vermoulu, -e [vɛrmuly] adj worm-eaten

vermouth [vɛrmut] nm vermouth

vernaculaire [vɛrnakylɛr] adj **langue v.** vernacular

verni, -e [vɛrni] adj (a) (meuble, bois, parquet) varnished; (chaussures) patent (leather); (ongles) varnished, painted (b) Fam (chanceux) lucky

vernir [vɛrnir] vt to varnish

vernis [vɛrni] nm (a) (pour le bois) varnish; **v. à ongles** nail varnish or polish; **se mettre du v. à ongles** to varnish or paint one's nails (b) Fig **un v. de culture** a smattering of knowledge

vernissage [vɛrnisaʒ] nm (a) (du bois) varnishing (b) (d'une exposition) opening, private viewing

vérole [verɔl] nf Vieilli syphilis; **la petite v.** smallpox

verra, verrai etc voir **voir**

verre [vɛr] nm (a) (matière) glass; **sous v.** under glass; **gravure sous v.** glass-mounted engraving; **v. blanc** glass; **v. dépoli/feuilleté** frosted/laminated glass (b) (récipient) glass; **v. à dents** tooth glass; **v. doseur** ou **gradué** ≃ measuring jug; **v. à eau** large wine glass; **v. à pied** stemmed glass; **v. à vin** wineglass; **v. à whisky** whisky glass (c) (contenu) glass(ful) (d) (boisson) drink; **boire** ou **prendre un v.** to have a drink (e) (de lunettes) lens; **verres de contact** contact lenses; **v. à double foyer** bifocals; **verres teintés** ou **fumés** tinted lenses

verrerie [vɛrri] nf (a) (fabrication) glass-making (b) (atelier) glassworks (c) (marchandise) glassware

verrier [vɛrje] nm (artisan) glass-maker

verrière [vɛrjɛr] nf (a) (toit) glass roof; (paroi) glass wall (b) (pièce) conservatory

verroterie [vɛrɔtri] nf glass jewellery

verrou [vɛru] nm bolt; **mettre** ou **tirer le v.** to bolt the door; Fig **sous les verrous** behind bars, inside

verrouillage [vɛrujaʒ] nm (a) (d'une porte) bolting; (à clé) locking (b) (d'un mécanisme) locking; **v. central** central locking (c) Ordinat **v. des fichiers** file lock; **v. en lecture seule** read-only lock; **v. en majuscule(s)** caps lock

verrouiller [vɛruje] vt (a) (porte) to bolt; (à clé) to lock; (prisonnier) to lock up (b) (quartier) to close off, to seal off (c) Ordinat (capitales) to lock on; **verrouillé en majuscule(s)** (clavier) with caps lock on

verrue [vɛry] nf wart; **v. plantaire** verruca

vers¹ [vɛr] nm (poétique) line; **faire des v.** to write verse or poetry; **v. blancs** blank verse; **v. libres** free verse

vers² prép (a) (dans la direction de) towards (b) (aux alentours de) (dans le temps) about; (dans l'espace) near; **v. la fin** towards the end; Fam **v. les trois heures** about or around 3 o'clock

versant [vɛrsɑ̃] nm slope, side

versatile [vɛrsatil] adj changeable, fickle

versatilité [vɛrsatilite] nf changeability, fickleness

verse [vɛrs] à **verse** adv **il pleut à v.** it's pouring (down); **la pluie tombait à v.** the rain was coming down in torrents

versé, -e [vɛrse] adj **être v. dans qch** to be well-versed in sth

Verseau [vɛrso] nm Astron & Astrol **le V.** Aquarius; **être V.** to be (an) Aquarius or an Aquarian

versement [vɛrsəmɑ̃] nm payment

verser [vɛrse] **1** vt (a) *(liquide)* to pour (out) **(dans** into); **v. à boire à qn** to pour sb a drink, to pour a drink for sb **(b)** *(larmes, sang)* to shed **(c)** *(argent)* to pay; **v. de l'argent sur son compte** to pay *or* deposit money into one's account **(d)** *Jur (document)* to add **(à** to)
2 vi *(véhicule)* to overturn
3 verser dans vt ind to lapse into

verset [vɛrse] nm verse

verseur, -euse [vɛrsœr, -øz] **1** adj voir **bec**
2 nf **verseuse** jug, pot *(for coffee machine)*

versification [vɛrsifikasjɔ̃] nf versification

version [vɛrsjɔ̃] nf (a) *(d'un événement, d'un texte)* version **(b)** *(traduction)* translation; **v. anglaise/espagnole** *(à l'école)* translation from English/Spanish **(c)** *Cin* **en v. originale** in the original language; **en v. française** dubbed *(into French)* **(d)** *Ordinat* **v. bêta** beta version

verso [vɛrso] nm back; **voir au v.** see over(leaf)

vert, -e [vɛr, vɛrt] **1** adj (a) *(couleur)* green; *Fig* **v. de peur** white with fear; *Fig* **v. de jalousie** green with envy; *Fig* **avoir la main verte** to have *Br* green fingers *or Am* a green thumb **(b)** *(jeune) (bois)* green; *(fruit)* unripe; *(vin)* too young **(c)** *(écologique)* green **(d)** *(vieillard)* sprightly **(e)** *(histoire, propos)* spicy **(f)** *(réprimande)* sharp
2 nm (a) *(couleur)* green; **passer au v.** *(signal d'arrêt)* to go *or* turn green; **v. amande** almond green; **v. bouteille** bottle green; **v. d'eau** sea green; **v. émeraude** emerald green; **v. olive** olive green; **v. pomme** apple green **(b)** *Fam* **se mettre au v.** to go to the country **(c)** *Pol* **les Verts** ≃ The Green Party
3 nfpl **vertes** *Fam* **en dire de vertes** to tell spicy stories; **il en a vu des vertes et des pas mûres** he's been through a lot

vert-de-gris [vɛrdəgri] **1** nm inv verdigris
2 adj grey-green

vertébral, -e, -aux, -ales [vɛrtebral, -o] adj vertebral

vertèbre [vɛrtɛbr] nf vertebra

vertébré, -e [vɛrtebre] adj & nm vertebrate

vertement [vɛrtəmɑ̃] adv sharply

vertical, -e, -aux, -ales [vɛrtikal, -o] **1** adj vertical; **en position verticale** *(objet)* in a vertical position, upright
2 nf **verticale** à la **verticale** vertically

verticalement [vɛrtikalmɑ̃] adv vertically; *(dans les mots croisés)* down

vertige [vɛrtiʒ] nm (a) *(au-dessus du vide)* vertigo; **avoir le v.** *(toujours)* to suffer from vertigo; *(ponctuellement)* to feel dizzy; **donner le v. à qn** *(vide)* to make sb dizzy; *Fig* to make sb's head spin **(b)** *(étourdissement)* dizziness, giddiness; **avoir des vertiges** to have dizzy spells

vertigineusement [vɛrtiʒinøzmɑ̃] adv **grimper v.** to rocket; **chuter v.** to plummet

vertigineux, -euse [vɛrtiʒinø, -øz] adj *(hauteur)* dizzy; *(vitesse)* breakneck; *(somme, hausse des prix)* staggering

vertu [vɛrty] nf (a) *(propriété)* property **(b)** *(qualité morale)* virtue **(c)** *Litt (chasteté)* virtue; **femme de petite v.** woman of easy virtue **(d)** **en v. de qch** *(principe, loi)* in accordance with sth; **en v. des pouvoirs qui me sont conférés** by virtue of the powers bestowed upon me; **en v. de quoi est-il intervenu?** what gave him the right to intervene?

vertueux, -euse [vɛrtɥø, -øz] adj virtuous; *(intention)* honourable

verve [vɛrv] nf verve; **être en v.** to be on top form

verveine [vɛrvɛn] nf (a) *(plante)* verbena **(b)** *(tisane)* verbena tea

vésicule [vezikyl] nf vesicle; **v. biliaire** gall bladder

vespasienne [vɛspazjɛn] nf street urinal

vespéral, -e, -aux, -ales [vɛsperal, -o] adj *Litt* evening

vessie [vesi] nf bladder; *Fig* **prendre des vessies pour des lanternes** to believe that the moon is made of green cheese

veste [vɛst] nf jacket; **v. droite/croisée** single-/double-breasted jacket; *Fam Fig* **prendre une v.** to come a cropper

vestiaire [vɛstjɛr] nm (a) *(d'un théâtre)* cloakroom; *(d'un stade)* changing room, locker room **(b)** **récupérer son v.** to collect one's things from the cloakroom

vestibule [vɛstibyl] nm *(entrance)* hall

vestiges [vɛstiʒ] nmpl (a) *(ruines)* remains **(b)** *(traces)* relics

vestimentaire [vɛstimɑ̃tɛr] adj *(dépenses)* clothing

veston [vɛstɔ̃] nm jacket

Vésuve [vezyv] nm **le V.** Vesuvius

vêtement [vɛtmɑ̃] nm garment, article of clothing; **vêtements** clothes, clothing; **vêtements de travail** work clothes

vétéran [veterɑ̃] nm veteran

vétérinaire [veterinɛr] **1** adj veterinary
2 nmf vet; *(sur une plaque)* veterinary surgeon

vétille [vetij] nf trifle, triviality

vêtir [vetir] *Litt* **1** vt *(personne)* to clothe, to dress **(de** in)
2 **se vêtir** vpr to dress (oneself) **(de** in)

vétiver [vetivɛr] nm vetiver

veto [veto] nm veto; **opposer son v. à qch** to veto sth; **droit de v.** right of veto

vêtu, -e [vety] adj dressed **(de** in)

vétuste [vetyst] adj dilapidated

vétusté [vetyste] nf dilapidation

veuf, veuve [vœf, vœv] **1** adj **être v.** to be a widower; **être veuve** to be a widow
2 nm f widower, f widow

veuille etc voir **vouloir**

veule [vøl] adj *Litt (personne)* effete

veulerie [vølri] nf *Litt* effeteness

veut voir **vouloir**

veuvage [vœvaʒ] nm *(d'homme)* widowhood; *(de femme)* widowhood

veux voir **vouloir**

vexant, -e [vɛksɑ̃, -ɑ̃t] adj (a) *(blessant)* hurtful **(b)** *(contrariant)* annoying

vexation [vɛksasjɔ̃] nf humiliation

vexatoire [vɛksatwar] adj humiliating

vexer [vɛkse] **1** vt to hurt, to upset; *Fam* **être vexé comme un pou** to be extremely upset
2 **se vexer** vpr to get upset **(de** at)

VF [veɛf] nf *(abrév* **version française)** **en VF** dubbed *(into French)*

via [vja] prép via

viabiliser [vjabilize] vt to service

viabilité¹ [vjabilite] *nf (d'un nouveau-né, d'un projet)* viability

viabilité² *nf (d'un chemin)* practicability

viable [vjabl] *adj* viable

viaduc [vjadyk] *nm* viaduct

viager, -ère [vjaʒe, -er] **1** *adj* life
2 *nm* life annuity; **mettre qch en v.** to sell sth in return for a life annuity

viande [vjɑ̃d] *nf* meat; **v. blanche/rouge** white/red meat; **v. hachée** *Br* mince, *Am* ground meat

viander [vjɑ̃de] **se viander** *vpr très Fam* to get smashed up

vibrant, -e [vibrɑ̃, -ɑ̃t] *adj (discours, hommage)* rousing, stirring

vibraphone [vibrafɔn] *nm* vibraphone

vibration [vibrasjɔ̃] *nf* vibration

vibrato [vibrato] *nm* vibrato

vibrer [vibre] *vi* **(a)** *(objet)* to vibrate **(b)** *(personne)* to be stirred; **sa voix vibrait de colère** his/her voice was shaking with anger; **faire v. qn** to stir sb

vibromasseur [vibromasœr] *nm* vibrator

vicaire [viker] *nm (dans la religion catholique)* assistant priest; *(dans la religion anglicane)* curate

vice [vis] *nm* **(a)** *(défaut moral)* vice **(b)** *(défectuosité)* defect; **v. caché** hidden or latent defect; **v. de fabrication** manufacturing defect; *Jur* **v. de forme** legal flaw **(c)** *(débauche)* vice; *Fig* **mais c'est du v.!** it's an obsession!

vice-amiral [visamiral] *(pl* **vice-amiraux** [visamiro]*)* *nm* vice admiral

vice-consul *(pl* **vice-consuls** [viskɔ̃syl]*)* *nm* vice consul

vice-présidence *(mpl* **vice-présidences** [visprezidɑ̃s]*)* *nf (d'état, d'organisation)* vice-presidency; *(d'entreprise)* vice-chairmanship

vice-président, -e *(mpl* **vice-présidents** [visprezidɑ̃]*, fpl* **vice-présidentes** [visprezidɑ̃t]*)* *nmf (d'état, d'organisation)* vice-president; *(d'entreprise)* vice-chairman

vice versa [visversa] *adv* vice versa

vichy [viʃi] *nm (tissu)* gingham

vicié, -e [visje] *adj* **(a)** *(air)* polluted **(b)** *Jur* invalidated

vicieux, -euse [visjø, -jøz] *adj* **(a)** *(pervers)* depraved **(b)** *(perfide)* underhand **(c)** *(chien)* vicious

vicissitudes [visisityd] *nfpl* vicissitudes

vicomte [vikɔ̃t] *nm* viscount

vicomtesse [vikɔ̃tes] *nf* viscountess

victime [viktim] *nf* victim; *(d'un accident)* casualty; **être v. d'un attentat/d'une agression** to be the victim of an assassination attempt/of an attack; **être la v. d'une illusion/d'un malentendu** to labour under an illusion/a misconception

victoire [viktwar] *nf* victory; *(en sport)* win, victory; **chanter** *ou* **crier v.** to claim victory

victorien, -enne [viktɔrjɛ̃, -en] *adj* Victorian

victorieusement [viktɔrjøzmɑ̃] *adv* victoriously

victorieux, -euse [viktɔrjø, -øz] *adj* victorious; *(air, sourire)* triumphant

victuailles [viktɥaj] *nfpl* provisions

vidange [vidɑ̃ʒ] *nf (d'un moteur)* oil change; **faire la v.** to change the oil **(b)** *(d'une fosse septique)* draining, emptying

vidanger [vidɑ̃ʒe] *vt* **(a)** *(huile)* to change; *(moteur)* to change the oil in **(b)** *(fosse septique)* to drain, to empty

vide [vid] **1** *adj* empty; *(regard)* blank; **v. de sens** devoid of meaning, meaningless
2 *nm Phys* vacuum; *(espace)* empty space, gap; *Fig (dans un emploi du temps)* gap; **rouler à v.** *(bus)* to have no passengers; **emballé sous v.** vacuum-packed; **faire le v.** to create a vacuum; *Fig (se ressourcer)* to switch off; *Fig* **faire le v. dans son esprit** to clear one's mind; **regarder dans le v.** to stare into space; **c'est comme si je parlais dans le v.** it's like talking to a brick wall; **avoir peur du v.** to be afraid of or to have no head for heights; **il y a un v. juridique concernant cela** there's nothing in the law to cover that; **v. sanitaire** crawl space

vidé, -e [vide] *adj Fam (épuisé)* dead beat

vidéo [video] **1** *adj inv* video
2 *nf* video; *Ordinat* **v. inversée** reverse video

vidéocassette [videokaset] *nf* video cassette

vidéo-clip [videoklip] *nm* video

vidéoconférence [videokɔ̃ferɑ̃s] *nf* videoconference; *(concept)* videoconferencing

vidéodisque [videodisk] *nm* videodisk

vide-ordures [vidɔrdyr] *nm inv Br* rubbish or *Am* garbage chute

vidéothèque [videotek] *nf* video library

vide-poches [vidpɔʃ] *nm inv* **(a)** *(de voiture) (dans le tableau de bord)* storage tray; *(dans la porte)* door pocket **(b)** *(de maison)* tidy

vide-pomme *(pl* **vide-pommes** [vidpɔm]*)* *nm* apple corer

vider [vide] **1** *vt* **(a)** *(enlever le contenu de)* to empty **(de** of); *Fam Fig* **v. son sac** to get it off one's chest; *Fig* **v. son cœur** to pour out one's feelings **(b)** *Fam (épuiser)* to wear out **(c)** *Fam (expulser)* to chuck out; **se faire v.** to be chucked out **(d)** **v. les lieux** to vacate the premises **(e)** *(poisson)* to gut; *(volaille)* to draw **(f)** *Ordinat* **v. l'écran** to clear the screen; **v. la corbeille** to empty the wastebasket or *Am* the trash
2 se vider *vpr* to empty; **se v. de son sang** to bleed to death

videur, -euse [vidœr, -øz] *nm,f* bouncer

vie [vi] *nf* **(a)** *(d'êtres vivants)* life; **être en v.** to be alive; **être entre la v. et la mort** to be fighting for one's life; **donner la v. à un enfant** to give birth to a child; **avoir la v. dure** *(mauvaise herbe, parasite)* to be hard to kill off; *(superstitions, préjugés)* to die hard; **entre eux, c'est à la v., à la mort** they'd die for each other; **être plein de v.** to be full of life; **sans v.** lifeless **(b)** *(animation)* life; **donner de la v. à qch** to liven sth up **(c)** *(durée d'existence)* life, lifetime; **pour la v.** for life; **une (seule) fois dans la v.** once in a lifetime **(d)** *(biographie)* life story; *Fam* **raconter sa v. à qn** to tell sb one's life story **(e)** *(façon de vivre)* life; **c'est la v. de château!** this is the life! **v. nocturne** nightlife; *Fam Vieilli* **faire la v.** to live it up **(f)** *(subsistance)* **la v. est très chère dans ces pays** the cost of living is very high in these countries

vieil [vjɛj] *voir* **vieux**

vieillard [vjejar] *nm* old man

vieille [vjɛj] **1** *adj f voir* **vieux**
2 *nf (poisson)* wrasse

vieillerie [vjejri] *nf (objet)* old thing

vieillesse [vjejes] *nf* old age

vieilli, -e [vjeji] *adj* **(a)** *(mot, style)* old-fashioned, dated **(b)** *(personne)* aged

vieillir [vjejir] **1** *vi* (a) *(personne)* to get old, to age (b) *(mot, film, chanson)* to be dated (c) *(fromage, vin)* to mature

2 *vt (personne) (par l'apparence)* to age; **v. qn (de deux ans)** to make sb out to be (two years) older than he/she is **3 se vieillir** *vpr* (a) *(par l'apparence)* to make oneself look older (b) *(se dire plus âgé)* to pretend to be older than one is

vieillissant, -e [vjejisã, -ãt] *adj (personne)* ageing; *(institution, style)* which is becoming outdated

vieillissement [vjejismã] *nm* (a) *(d'une personne, de la population)* ageing; **retarder le v. de la peau** to delay the ageing process (b) *(d'un fromage, d'un vin)* maturing

vieillot, -otte [vjejo, -ɔt] *adj* old-fashioned

vielle [vjɛl] *nf* hurdy-gurdy

Vienne [vjɛn] *n* Vienna

vienne, viens *etc voir* **venir**

viennois, -e [vjenwa, -az] **1** *adj* Viennese; **un pain v.** a Vienna loaf
2 *nm,f* V. Viennese

vierge [vjɛrʒ] **1** *adj* (a) *(personne)* **être v.** to be a virgin; **une fille v.** a virgin (b) *(sol, huile)* virgin (c) *(page, cassette)* blank; *(casier judiciaire)* clean (d) *Ordinat (ligne, espace)* blank; *(disquette)* blank, unformatted
2 *nf* (a) *(personne)* virgin; **la (Sainte)** V. the Blessed Virgin (Mary) (b) *Astron & Astrol* **la** V. Virgo; **être** V. to be (a) Virgo

Viêt Nam [vjetnam] *nm* **le** V. Vietnam

vietnamien, -enne [vjetnamjɛ̃, -ɛn] **1** *adj* Vietnamese
2 *nm,f* V. Vietnamese
3 *nm (langue)* Vietnamese

vieux, vieille [vjø, vjɛj]

vieil is used before masculine singular nouns beginning with a vowel or h mute.

1 *adj* old; **plus/moins v. que qn** older/younger than sb; **v. comme le monde** as old as the hills; **être v. jeu** to be old-fashioned
2 *nm,f* (a) *(personne)* old man, *f* old woman; **les v.** old people, the elderly; *Fam* **un v. de la vieille** one of the old brigade (b) *Fam* **il a pris un coup de v.** he's failed (c) *Fam (parent)* **mes v.** my folks; **mon v.** my old man; **ma vieille** my old woman (d) *Fam (ami)* **mon v.** mate, pal; **ma vieille** old girl

vif, vive [vif, viv] **1** *adj* (a) *(personne, discussion)* lively (b) *(imagination)* vivid; *(intelligence)* sharp; *(mouvement)* quick; *Euph* **il n'est pas très v.** he's not very bright (c) *(vent, douleur)* sharp (d) *(couleur)* bright (e) *(satisfaction, intérêt)* great; *(félicitations)* warm (f) **dire qch à qn de vive voix** to tell sb sth personally
2 *nm* (a) *Jur* living person (b) *(à la pêche)* live bait (c) *(locutions)* **à v.** open; **avoir les nerfs à v.** to be on edge; **entrer dans le v. du sujet** to get to the heart of the matter; **une photo prise sur le v.** a natural or unposed photo

vif-argent [vifarʒã] *nm* quicksilver; *Fig (personne)* live wire

vigie [viʒi] *nf* (a) *(matelot)* lookout; **être de v.** to be on the lookout (b) *(poste) (sur un bateau)* lookout post; *(sur un train)* observation box

vigilance [viʒilãs] *nf* vigilance

vigilant, -e [viʒilã, -ãt] *adj* vigilant

vigile [viʒil] *nm* (night) watchman

vigne [viɲ] *nf* (a) *(petit arbre)* vine (b) *(vignoble)* vineyard (c) **v. vierge** Virginia creeper

vigneron, -onne [viɲarõ, -ɔn] *nm,f* wine grower

vignette [viɲɛt] *nf* (a) *(pharmaceutique)* label *(showing details of medication and which has to be attached to the 'feuille de maladie' in order to qualify for reimbursement by the Social Security)* (b) **la v.** *(automobile)* the (road) tax disc (c) *(motif)* vignette

vignoble [viɲɔbl] *nm* vineyard; **le v. français/californien** the French/Californian vineyards

vigoureusement [vigurøzmã] *adv* vigorously

vigoureux, -euse [vigurø, -øz] *adj (personne, animal)* vigorous; *(plante, arbre)* sturdy; *(résistance)* strong

vigueur [vigœr] *nf* (a) *(d'une personne, d'un animal, d'un style)* vigour; *(d'une plante, d'un arbre)* sturdiness (b) **en v.** *(décret)* in force; **entrer en v.** to come into force

VIH [veiaʃ] *nm (abrév* **virus de l'immunodéficience humaine)** HIV

viking [vikiŋ] **1** *adj* Viking
2 *nmf* V. Viking

vil, -e [vil] *adj* (a) *Litt (personne, motif)* vile (b) *(bas)* **à v. prix** at a very low price

vilain, -e [vilɛ̃, -ɛn] **1** *adj* (a) *(laid)* ugly (b) *(déplaisant)* nasty (c) *(pas sage)* naughty
2 *nm,f* **oh, le v./la vilaine!** *(à un enfant)* you naughty boy/girl!
3 *nm* *Fam* **il va y avoir du v.** there's going to be trouble (b) *Hist* villein

vilebrequin [vilbrəkɛ̃] *nm* (a) *(outil)* brace (b) *(dans un moteur)* crankshaft

vilenie [vileni] *nf Litt* (a) *(caractère)* vileness (b) *(action)* vile deed

villa [villa] *nf* villa

village [vilaʒ] *nm* village; **v. de pêcheurs** fishing village; **v. de vacances, v.-vacances** holiday village

villageois, -e [vilaʒwa, -az] *nm,f* villager

ville [vil] *nf* town; *(de grande taille)* city; **grande v.** city; **en v.** in (the) town; *(au centre ville)* Br in the town/city centre, *Am* downtown; **aller en v.** to go into town; **habiter à la v.** to live in a town *(as opposed to the country)*; **v. basse/haute** lower/upper part of town; **v. champignon** boom town; **v. d'eaux** spa (town); **v. nouvelle** new town

ville-dortoir *(pl* **villes-dortoirs)** [vildɔrtwar] *nf* dormitory town

villégiature [vileʒjatyr] *nf Br* holiday, *Am* vacation; **lieu de v.** *Br* holiday resort, *Am* resort

Vilnius [vilnjys] *n* Vilnius

vin [vɛ̃] *nm* (a) *(boisson)* wine; **avoir le v. gai/triste** to be/not to be a happy drunk; **grand v.** vintage wine; **v. d'appellation contrôlée** wine of guaranteed vintage; **v. blanc/rouge/rosé** white/red/rosé wine; **v. cuit** = type of mulled wine; **v. mousseux** sparkling wine; **v. de pays** regional wine; **v. de table** *ou* **ordinaire** table wine (b) **v. d'honneur** reception *(where wine is served)*

vinaigre [vinegr] *nm* vinegar; *Fam* **tourner au v.** to turn sour; **v. blanc** distilled vinegar; **v. à l'estragon** tarragon vinegar

vinaigrette [vinegret] *nf* vinaigrette, French dressing

vinasse [vinas] *nf Fam* cheap wine, *Br* plonk

vindicatif, -ive [vɛ̃dikatif, -iv] *adj* vindictive

vindicte [vɛ̃dikt] *nf* **désigner qn à la v. publique** to expose sb to public condemnation

vineux, -euse [vinø, -øz] *adj* (a) *(goût, odeur)* winy (b) *(couleur)* wine(-coloured)

vingt [vɛ̃] 1 *adj inv* twenty; **v.-quatre heures sur v.-quatre** round the clock, twenty-four hours a day

2 *nm inv* twenty; *voir aussi* **trois**

vingtaine [vɛ̃tɛn] *nf* **une v. (de)** about twenty, twenty or so

vingtième [vɛ̃tjɛm] *adj, nmf & nm* twentieth; *voir aussi* **cinquième**

vinicole [vinikɔl] *adj (région)* wine-growing

vinyle [vinil] *nm* vinyl

viol [vjɔl] *nm* (a) *(crime sexuel)* rape (b) *(d'un sanctuaire)* violation

violacé, -e [vjɔlase] *adj* purplish-blue

violation [vjɔlasjɔ̃] *nf* (a) *(de la loi, de règles)* violation (b) *(d'une sépulture)* desecration; **v. de domicile** illegal entry

viole [vjɔl] *nf* viol

violemment [vjɔlamɑ̃] *adv* violently

violence [vjɔlɑ̃s] *nf (physique)* violence; *(verbale)* fierceness; *(d'un sentiment)* intensity; **se faire v.** to force oneself

violent, -e [vjɔlɑ̃, -ɑ̃t] *adj (personne, douleur, quartier)* violent; *(vent, paroles)* fierce; *(odeur)* pungent; *(effort)* strenuous; **mort violente** violent death

violenter [vjɔlɑ̃te] *vt (femme)* to assault

violer [vjɔle] *vt* (a) *(personne)* to rape (b) *(trêve, loi)* to violate, to break; *(traité, confiance)* to break; *(secret)* to divulge (c) *(sépulture)* to desecrate

violet, -ette [vjɔlɛ, -ɛt] 1 *adj* purple

2 *nm (couleur)* purple

3 *nf* **violette** *(fleur)* violet

violeur [vjɔlœr] *nm* rapist

violon [vjɔlɔ̃] *nm* (a) *(instrument)* violin; *Fam* **accordez vos violons** make sure you get your stories straight; **v. d'Ingres** hobby (b) *(musicien)* violin (player); **premier v.** *(dans un orchestre)* first violin, *Br* leader, *Am* concertmaster (c) *Fam (prison)* **le v.** the cells, the lockup

violoncelle [vjɔlɔ̃sɛl] *nm* cello

violoncelliste [vjɔlɔ̃selist] *nmf* cellist

violoniste [vjɔlɔnist] *nmf* violinist, violin player

vipère [viper] *nf* adder, viper; *Fig (personne)* viper

virage [viraʒ] *nm* (a) *(mouvement)* turn (b) *(d'une route)* bend; **la route fait des virages** there are bends in the road; **prendre un v.** to take a bend; **v. sans visibilité** blind corner (c) *Fig (changement)* change of direction

viral, -e, -aux, -ales [viral, -o] *adj* viral

virée [vire] *nf Fam (en voiture)* run, drive; *(dans les bars) Br* pub crawl, *Am* bar hop; **faire une v.** *(en voiture)* to go for a run or a drive; *(dans les bars) Br* to go on a pub crawl, *Am* to bar hop

virement [virmɑ̃] *nm* (a) *(de banque)* transfer; **v. automatique** automatic transfer; **v. bancaire/interbancaire** bank/interbank transfer; **v. postal** post office transfer (b) *Naut* **v. de bord** tacking

virer [vire] 1 *vt* a *(somme)* to transfer (**sur** to) (b) *Fam (personne, objet)* to chuck out; **se faire v.** to get chucked out

2 *vi* (a) *(véhicule)* to turn; **v. de bord** *(voilier)* to tack (b) *(couleur)* to change; **le parfum a viré** the perfume smells off

3 virer à *vt ind* **v. à l'orange/au vert** to turn orange/green

4 se virer *vpr Fam* **vire-toi de là!** shift (yourself)!

virevolte [virvɔlt] *nf* (a) *(d'un danseur)* spin (b) *(changement brusque)* U-turn, about-turn

virevolter [virvɔlte] *vi (danseur)* to spin round

virginal, -e, -aux, -ales [virʒinal, -o] *adj* virginal

Virginie [virʒini] *nf* la V. Virginia; **la V.-occidentale** West Virginia

virginité [virʒinite] *nf* virginity

virgule [virgyl] *nf* (a) *(signe de ponctuation)* comma; *Fig* **ne pas changer une v. à qch** not to make a single alteration to sth (b) *(entre deux chiffres)* decimal point; **trois v. cinq** three point five; *Ordinat* **v. fixe** fixed point; *Ordinat* **v. flottante** floating point

viril, -e [viril] *adj* (a) *(propre à l'homme)* male; *(sexuellement)* virile (b) *(énergique) (action)* manly; *(allure, démarche)* masculine

virilité [virilite] *nf* virility

virologie [virɔlɔʒi] *nf* virology

virtualité [virtɥalite] *nf* potentiality

virtuel, -elle [virtɥɛl] *adj (potentiel, image)* virtual

virtuellement [virtɥɛlmɑ̃] *adv* virtually

virtuose [virtɥoz] *nmf* virtuoso

virtuosité [virtɥozite] *nf* virtuosity

virulence [virylɑ̃s] *nf* virulence

virulent, -e [virylɑ̃, -ɑ̃t] *adj* virulent

virus [virys] *nm Méd & Ordinat* virus

vis¹ *voir* **vivre, voir**

vis² [vis] *nf* screw; *Fig* **serrer la v. à qn** to crackdown on sb

visa [viza] *nm* (a) *(pour passeport)* visa; **v. d'entrée/de sortie** entry/exit visa (b) *(d'un film)* **v. de censure** certificate; **v. d'exploitation** exploitation licence

visage [vizaʒ] *nm* face; **elle a changé de v.** her face or expression changed; **à deux visages** two-faced; **à v. découvert** openly; **sous un autre** *ou* **nouveau v.** in a new light; **v. pâle** paleface

visagiste [vizaʒist] *nmf* **coiffeur-v.** hair stylist

vis-à-vis [vizavi] 1 *prép* **v. de** *(en face de)* opposite *or* facing; *(envers)* towards; *(en comparaison de)* compared with, next to

2 *nm* (a) *(personne)* person opposite; **mon v.** the person opposite me; **il n'y a pas de v.** there's nothing opposite (b) *(meuble)* vis-à-vis

viscéral, -e, -aux, -ales [viseral, -o] *adj Anat* visceral; *Fig (haine)* deep-seated; *(peur)* gut-wrenching; *(réaction)* gut

viscères [viser] *nmpl* viscera, internal organs

viscose [viskoz] *nf* viscose

viscosité [viskozite] *nf (de liquide)* viscosity; *(de surface)* stickiness

visée [vize] *nf* (a) *(action)* aiming (b) *Fig* **visées** *(intentions)* aims; **avoir des visées sur qn/qch** to have designs on sb/sth

viser¹ [vize] 1 *vt* a *(cible)* to aim at; *Fig (poste)* to set one's sights on (b) *Fig* **ces paroles te visent** these remarks are aimed at you; **qui visais-tu par cette remarque?** who was your remark aimed at?; **je me suis senti visé** I felt the remark was aimed at me (c) *Fam (regarder)* **vise un peu la fille!** get a load of her!

2 *vi* to aim, to take aim; *Fig* **v. haut** to aim high; **v. juste** to aim straight; *Fig* to hit the bull's-eye

3 viser à *vt ind* **v. à qch** to aim at sth; **v. à faire qch** to aim to do sth

viser² *vt (passeport)* to visa; *(document)* to stamp

viseur [vizœr] nm (d'un appareil photo) viewfinder; (d'une arme) sight

visibilité [vizibilite] nf visibility

visible [vizibl] adj (a) (signe, changement) visible (b) (clair) obvious; **il est v. que...** it's obvious that... (c) Fam **je ne suis pas v.** I'm not receiving visitors

visiblement [viziblemɑ̃] adv visibly

visière [vizjer] nf (a) (d'une casquette) peak (b) (d'un casque) visor (c) (pour protéger les yeux) eyeshade

visioconférence [vizjokɔ̃ferɑ̃s] nf videoconference; (concept) videoconferencing

vision [vizjɔ̃] nf (a) (sens) sight (b) (point de vue) view (c) (d'un créateur) vision (d) (hallucination) vision; **avoir des visions** to have visions, to see things

visionnaire [vizjoner] adj & nmf visionary

visionner [vizjone] vt (film) to view

visionneuse [vizjonøz] nf viewer

visite [vizit] nf (a) (à une personne, d'un lieu touristique) visit; **faire une v.** ou **rendre v. à qn** to visit sb, to pay sb a visit; **recevoir la v. de qn** to have a visit from sb; **v. officielle** official visit (b) Fam (personne) visitor; **avoir de la v.** (un visiteur) to have a visitor; (plusieurs visiteurs) to have visitors (c) (d'un médecin) visites (à domicile) (house) calls (d) (inspection) (d'un bâtiment, d'un navire) inspection, examination (e) **v. médicale** medical examination

visiter [vizite] **1** vt (a) (lieu touristique) to visit; (maison à vendre) to view; **faire v. qch à qn** to show sb round sth (b) (inspecter) (bâtiment) to inspect, to examine (c) (patient) to visit; (client) to call on
2 se visiter vpr to be open to visitors; **le musée se visite en deux heures** it takes two hours to go round the museum

visiteur, -euse [vizitœr, -øz] nm,f (a) (touriste, invité) visitor (b) (représentant) **v. médical** medical representative (c) **v. de prison** prison visitor

vison [vizɔ̃] nm mink; Fam (manteau) mink coat

visqueux, -euse [viskø, -øz] adj (a) (surface) sticky (b) (substance) viscous (c) Péj (personne, manière) slimy

visser [vise] **1** vt (a) (à quelque chose) to screw down; (ensemble) to screw together; **être vissé à qch** to be screwed to sth; **un chapeau vissé sur la tête** with a hat clamped on his/her head; Fam **être vissé sur sa chaise** to be glued to one's chair (b) (couvercle) to screw on
2 se visser vpr (à quelque chose) to screw on; (ensemble) to screw together

visualisation [vizɥalizasjɔ̃] nf visualization; Ordinat **console** ou **unité** ou **écran de v.** (visual) display unit; Ordinat **v. de la page à l'écran** page preview

visualiser [vizɥalize] vt (a) (imaginer) to visualize (b) (rendre visible) to make visible; Ordinat to display

visuel, -elle [vizɥɛl] **1** adj visual
2 nm Ordinat visual display unit, VDU

visuellement [vizɥɛlmɑ̃] adv visually

vit voir **vivre**, **voir**

vital, -e, -aux, -ales [vital, -o] adj vital

vitalité [vitalite] nf vitality

vitamine [vitamin] nf vitamin; **la v. E** vitamin E

vitaminé, -e [vitamine] adj with added vitamins, vitamin-enriched

vite [vit] adv (a) (rapidement) quickly, fast; **v.!** quick!, quickly!; **plus v.!** faster!; **ça ne va pas v.** it's slow work; Fam **et plus v. que cela!** now then, get a move on!; **au plus v.** as quickly as possible; Fig **parler trop v.** to speak too soon; **c'est v. dit** it's easy to say; Fam **faire qch v. fait (bien fait)** to do sth in no time (b) (sous peu) soon; **avoir v. fait de faire qch** to be quick to do sth

vitesse [vites] nf (a) (rapidité) speed; **prendre de la v.** to pick up or gather speed; Fam **prendre qn de v.** to beat sb to it; **à quelle v. allait-il?** how fast was he going?, what speed was he going at?; **une Europe à deux vitesses** a two-speed Europe; **à toute v.** at top speed; **à une v. folle** (rouler) at breakneck speed; Fam **en v.** quickly; **v. de croisière** cruising speed; Fig **trouver sa v. de croisière** to get into the swing of things (b) (d'un moteur) gear; **changer de v.** to change gear; **passer en deuxième/troisième v.** to go into second/third (gear); Fam Fig **en quatrième v.** at top speed (c) Ordinat **v. d'affichage** display speed; **v. de calcul** processing or computing speed; **v. d'écriture** write speed; **v. d'exécution** execution speed; **v. d'impression** print speed; **v. du processeur** processor speed; **v. de traitement** processing speed

viticole [vitikɔl] adj (région) wine-growing

viticulteur, -trice [vitikyltœr, -tris] nm,f wine grower

viticulture [vitikyltyr] nf wine growing

vitrage [vitraʒ] nm (vitres) windows

vitrail, -aux [vitraj, -o] nm stained-glass window

vitre [vitr] nf (a) (window (pane)) (plaque de verre) pane (of glass); (de voiture, de train) window; **faire les vitres** to clean the windows

vitré, -e [vitre] adj (porte) glazed

vitrer [vitre] vt to glaze

vitreux, -euse [vitrø, -øz] adj (yeux, regard) glazed, glassy

vitrier [vitrije] nm glazier

vitrification [vitrifikasjɔ̃] nf (a) (du sable) vitrification (b) (du parquet) varnishing, sealing

vitrifier [vitrifje] vt (a) (sable) to vitrify (b) (parquet) to varnish, to seal

vitrine [vitrin] nf (a) (de magasin) (shop) window; Fig showcase (b) (armoire) display cabinet

vitriol [vitrijɔl] nm vitriol; Fig **au v.** vitriolic

vitupérer [vitypere] **vitupérer contre** vt ind to protest about

vivable [vivabl] adj Fam (maison) livable in; (situation) tolerable; **il n'est pas v.** he's impossible to live with

vivace [vivas] adj (a) (plante) perennial (b) (croyance, tradition, sentiment) deep-rooted; (souvenir) vivid

vivacité [vivasite] nf (a) (d'une personne, d'une discussion) liveliness, vivacity; (d'une imagination) vividness; (d'une intelligence) sharpness; (d'un mouvement) quickness; **v. d'esprit** quick-wittedness (b) (de couleur) brightness (c) (de paroles) hastiness

vivant, -e [vivɑ̃, -ɑ̃t] **1** adj (a) (en vie) alive (b) (être, organisme) living (c) (rue, conversation, enfant) lively (d) Fig (souvenir) vivid; Hum **j'en suis la preuve vivante** I'm the living proof
2 nm (a) **les vivants** the living (b) **de son v.** in one's lifetime; **du v. de qn** in sb's lifetime

vivats [viva] nmpl cheers

vive[1] [viv] adj voir **vif**

vive[2] nf (poisson) weever

vive³ *exclam* **v. le roi!** long live the King!; **v. la télévision!** God bless television!

vivement [vivmã] *adv* (a) *(rapidement)* quickly (b) *(en colère)* sharply (c) *(éclairé, coloré)* brightly (d) *(remercier)* warmly; *(regretter)* deeply; **s'intéresser v. à qch** to take a keen interest in sth; **être v. ému** to be deeply moved (e) *(marque l'impatience)* **v. les vacances!** roll on the holidays!; **v. qu'il parte!** I'll be glad when he's gone!

viveur [vivœr] *nm* fast liver

vivier [vivje] *nm* (a) *(à l'air libre)* fish pond; *(aquarium)* fish tank; *Fig* breeding ground (**de** for)

vivifiant, -e [vivifjã, -ãt] *adj (air, climat)* invigorating, bracing

vivifier [vivifje] *vt* to invigorate

vivipare [vivipar] *adj* viviparous

vivisection [vivisɛksjɔ̃] *nf* vivisection

vivoter [vivote] *vi* (a) *(personne)* to struggle to get by (b) *(entreprise, usine)* to struggle along

vivre [vivr] **1** *vi* (a) *(être en vie)* to live, to be alive; **v. vieux** to live to a ripe old age; *Prov* **qui vivra verra** time will tell (b) *(mener une certaine existence)* to live; **avoir beaucoup vécu** to have seen life; **être facile/difficile à v.** to be easy/difficult to live with *or* to get on with; **se laisser v.** to take life as it comes; **il fait bon v. ici** life is pleasant here; *Fam* **je vais t'apprendre à v.!** I'll teach you some manners! (c) *(économiquement)* to live; **travailler pour v.** to work for a living; **faire v. sa famille** to support *or* keep one's family; **v. de qch** to live on sth; *Fig* **v. d'amour et d'eau fraîche** to live on fresh air

2 *vt* (a) **v. sa vie** to live one's own life (b) *(événements, guerre)* to live through; *(moments difficiles, expérience)* to go through

vivres [vivr] *nmpl* provisions, supplies; *Fig* **couper les v. à qn** to cut off sb's allowance

vivrier, -ère [vivrije, -ɛr] *adj* **cultures vivrières** food crops

vlan, v'lan [vlã] *exclam* bang!, wham!

vlimeux [vlimø] *nm Can très Fam* (a) *(chanceux)* lucky devil (b) *(intrigant)* crafty devil

VO [veo] *nf (abrév* **version originale) en VO** in the original language

vocabulaire [vɔkabylɛr] *nm* (a) *(d'une science)* glossary; *(d'une langue)* vocabulary (b) *(d'une personne)* vocabulary

vocal, -e, -aux, -ales [vɔkal, -o] *adj* vocal

vocalise [vɔkaliz] *nf* voice exercise; **faire des vocalises** to do voice exercises

vocation [vɔkasjɔ̃] *nf* (a) *(d'une personne)* vocation, calling (b) *(d'un pays, d'une institution)* role, mission; **région à v. agricole/industrielle** agricultural/industrial region

vociférations [vɔsiferasjɔ̃] *nfpl* shouting

vociférer [vɔsifere] **1** *vt* to shout (**contre** at)
2 *vi* to shout (**contre** about)

vodka [vɔdka] *nf* vodka

vœu, -x [vø] *nm* (a) *(souhait)* wish; **faire un v.** to make a wish; **faire le v. que** + *subjunctive* to pray that (b) *(promesse)* vow; **faire le v. de faire qch** to vow to do sth (c) *Rel* **faire v. de pauvreté/silence** to take a vow of poverty/silence; **prononcer ses vœux** to take one's vows (d) *(au moment d'une fête)* **tous mes/nos vœux,**

avec mes/nos meilleurs vœux best wishes, with all good wishes; **tous mes vœux de bonheur** best wishes for your future happiness; **vœux de Bonne** *ou* **de Nouvelle Année** New Year's greetings

vogue [vɔg] *nf* fashion, vogue; **en v.** fashionable, in vogue

voguer [vɔge] *vi Litt* to sail

voici [vwasi] *prép* (a) *(pour présenter, pour montrer)* here is/are; **v. Paul** here's Paul; **v. mes neveux** *(en les présentant)* these are my nephews; *(ils arrivent)* here are my nephews; **nous v. à Paris/installés** here we are in Paris/all settled in; **la v. qui vient** here she comes; **la pendule que v.** this clock; **v. ce dont il s'agit** this is what it's all about; **v. ce qu'il m'a dit** this is what he told me; **v. pourquoi** this is why; **tu voulais des fruits, eh bien, en v.** you wanted some fruit, well here you are (b) *(il y a)* **v. trois ans** three years ago; **v. dix ans que je la connais** I've known her for ten years now

voie [vwa] *nf* (a) *(route)* road; **route à quatre voies** four-lane road; **les voies de communication** the road and rail links; **v. express** *ou* **rapide** *Br* motorway, *Am* expressway; **v. publique** public highway; **v. sans issue** dead end
(b) **par la v. des airs** by air; **par v. de terre/de mer** by land/sea
(c) *(pour train)* track; **v. ferrée** *Br* railway *or Am* railroad line; *Fam* **mettre qn sur une v. de garage** to put sb on the sidelines
(d) *Ordinat* **v. d'accès** path; **v. d'entrée** input channel; **v. de transmission de données** data link
(e) *Fig (chemin)* way; **mettre qn sur la v.** to put sb on the right track; **être sur la bonne v.** to be on the right track; **par la v. diplomatique/hiérarchique** through diplomatic/official channels; **la v. est libre** the coast's clear
(f) **en v. d'achèvement** nearing completion; **en v. de construction** under construction; **un pays en v. de développement** a developing country; **être en v. de disparition** *(animal)* to be a dying breed *or* dying out; **être en v. de guérison** to be on the road to recovery
(g) *Jur* **v. de fait** assault and battery
(h) *Anat* passage, duct; **les voies digestives** the digestive tract; **par v. buccale** orally
(i) **v. d'eau** leak
(j) **la V. lactée** the Milky Way

voilà [vwala] *prép* (a) *(pour présenter, pour montrer)* there is/are; **v. Paul** there's Paul; **v. mes neveux** *(en les présentant)* these are my nephews; *(ils arrivent)* there are my nephews; **nous v. à Paris/installés** here we are in Paris/all settled in; **la v. qui vient** here she comes; **la pendule que v.** that clock; **v. ce que j'avais à dire** that's what I wanted to say; **v. ce qu'il m'a dit** that's what he told me; **tu voulais des fruits, eh bien, en v.** you wanted some fruit, well there you go; **v. pourquoi** that's why; **en v. assez** that's enough; **en v. une idée!** what an idea!; **v. tout** that's all; **nous v. bien!** what are we going to do now?; **et v.!** there you go! (b) *(il y a)* **v. trois ans** three years ago; **v. dix ans que je la connais** I've known him for ten years now

voilage [vwalaʒ] *nm (tissu)* net; **voilages** *(rideaux)* net curtains

voile¹ [vwal] *nf (de bateau)* sail; *(activité)* sailing; **faire de la v.** to sail; **toutes voiles dehors** in full sail; *Fam* **marcher à v. et à vapeur** to be AC/DC

549

voile² nm (a) (de femme) veil; **prendre le v.** (religieuse) to take the veil (b) (devant les yeux) film, mist; **un v. de fumée/de brouillard** a veil of smoke/fog; Fam **jeter un v. sur qch** to draw a veil over sth; Méd **avoir un v. au poumon** to have a shadow on one's lung (c) Anat **v. du palais** soft palate, velum

voilé, -e [vwale] adj (a) (femme) veiled (b) (lumière) (par le brouillard) hazy; (par les nuages) dim; (photo) fogged; **le ciel est v.** it's hazy (c) (voix) husky; **des yeux voilés de larmes** eyes blurred with tears (d) (allusion) veiled; **en termes voilés** in veiled terms (e) (roue, tige) buckled

voiler [vwale] **1** vt (a) (femme) to veil; (statue) to cover; Fig (trouble, émotion) to hide, to conceal (b) (lumière) to dim; (ciel, soleil) to cover; (photo) to fog (c) (roue, tige) to buckle

2 se voiler vpr (a) (personne) to wear a veil; Fig **se v. la face** to hide or bury one's head in the sand (b) (voix) to become husky (c) (ciel) to cloud over; (soleil) to become hazy; (yeux) to mist over (d) (roue, tige) to buckle

voilette [vwalɛt] nf (hat) veil

voilier [vwalje] nm (bateau à voiles) sailing boat; (bateau de plaisance) yacht; **faire du v.** to go yachting

voilure [vwalyr] nf (a) (d'un bateau) sails (b) (d'un avion) wings

voir [73a] [vwar] **1** vt (a) (distinguer) to see; **v. page 23/ci-après** see page 23/below; **je l'ai vu de mes propres yeux, je l'ai vu comme je te vois** I saw it with my own eyes; **je le vois qui arrive** I can see him coming; **je l'ai vu tomber/courir** I saw him fall/running; **faire v. qch à qn** to show sth to sb, to show sb sth; **faites v.!** let me see (it), let's have a look!; **laisser v. son ignorance/ émotion** to show one's ignorance/emotion (b) (rendre visite à, fréquenter) to visit; **aller/venir v. qn** to go/come and see sb (c) (comprendre, constater) to see; **à ce que je vois** from what I can see; **voyez vous-même!** see for yourself!; **on voit bien que...** you can see (that)...; **on verra bien** we'll see; **c'est ce que nous verrons!** we'll see about that!; Fam **vu?** understood?, OK? (d) (considérer) to see; **nous verrons demain** we'll see tomorrow (e) (imaginer, envisager) to see; **je ne le vois pas marié** I can't imagine him married; **elle voit en lui un père/un ami** she sees him as a father figure/a friend; **sa façon de v. les choses** his way of looking at things; **se faire bien/ mal v. de qn** to get into sb's good/bad books; **être bien/ mal vu** to be well/badly thought of; **c'est plutôt mal vu dans ce milieu** it's rather frowned upon in these circles (f) Fam (pour renforcer) **essayez v.** just try; (menace) just you try it; **voyons v.** let's see, let's have a look (g) (locutions) Fam **on aura tout vu!** we've seen it all now!; Fam **c'est tout vu, tu n'y vas pas!** you're not going and that's that!; **il faut le v. pour le croire** you have to see it to believe it; **j'aimerais (bien) t'y v.!** I'd like to see you try! Fam **en faire v. à qn** to give sb a hard time; **voyez-vous** (pour insister) you see; Fam **je ne peux pas le v.** I can't stand the sight of him; **file, je t'ai assez vu!** off you go, I've had enough of you!; **il n'a rien à v. là-dedans** ou **à y v.** he's got nothing to do with it; **ça n'a rien à voir!** (dans une discussion) that's beside the point, that's got nothing to do with it!; **voyons!** (indique la désapprobation) come on!; Fam **va t'en là-bas si j'y suis!** on your bike!; très Fam **va te faire v.!** piss off!

2 vi to see; **(y) v. bien/mal** to have good/poor eyesight; **on n'y voit rien** you can't see a thing; Fig **v. grand** to think big

3 voir à vt ind **il va v. à nous loger** he'll see that we have somewhere to stay; Fam **il faudrait v. à vous dépêcher!** you'd better get a move on!

4 se voir vpr (a) (objet, phénomène) to be seen; **la cathédrale se voit de loin** you can see the cathedral from miles away; **cela ne se voit pas tous les jours** it's not something you see every day; **ça se voit que j'ai pleuré?** can you tell I've been crying? (b) (soi-même) to see oneself; **elle ne se voit pas du tout avec des enfants** she just can't see herself with children (c) (avec un adjectif, un infinitif) **se v. forcé de faire qch** to find oneself forced to do sth; **se v. refuser qch** to find oneself refused sth (d) (l'un l'autre) (se distinguer, se rencontrer) to see each other

voire [vwar] adv indeed

voirie [vwari] nf = local council department responsible for road maintenance and refuse collection

voisin, -e [vwazɛ̃, -in] **1** adj (a) (personne, pays, ville) neighbouring; (chambre) next (de to); **les pays voisins de la France** the countries bordering on France; **deux maisons voisines** two houses next to each other (b) (semblable) similar (de to)

2 nmf neighbour; **v. de palier** next-door neighbour; **mon v. de table** the person sitting next to me (at the table)

voisinage [vwazinaʒ] nm (a) (proximité) proximity, closeness (b) (ensemble des voisins) neighbourhood (c) (alentours) vicinity; **dans le v.** in the vicinity (d) **entretenir des relations de bon v. avec qn** to be on neighbourly terms with sb

voisiner [vwazine] vi **v. avec qch** to be side by side with sth

voiture [vwatyr] nf (a) (automobile) car; **en v.** by car; **v. de course** racing car; **v. de fonction** company car; **v. de location** rental or Br hired car; **v. d'occasion** used or second-hand car; **v. de sport** sports car; **v. de tourisme** private or touring car; **petite v.** (jouet) toy car (b) (wagon) Br coach, Am car; **en v.!** all aboard!; **v. fumeurs** smoker; **v. non-fumeurs** non-smoker (c) (carriole) (pour passagers) carriage; (pour marchandises) cart; **v. à bras** barrow, handcart (d) **v. d'enfant** Br pram, Am baby carriage

voix [vwa] nf (a) (d'une personne) voice; **à v. haute, à haute v.** aloud; **à v. basse** in a low voice; **élever la v.** to speak up; (se mettre en colère) to raise one's voice; **rester sans v.** to remain speechless; Cin **v. off** voice-over; **une v. de stentor** a booming voice (b) Fig (de la raison) voice; (du sang) call (c) Mus (partie vocale) voice; **chanter à trois v.** to sing in three parts; **être en v.** to be in good voice; **v. de basse/de ténor** bass/tenor voice; **v. de fausset** falsetto (voice); **v. de tête** head voice (d) (d'électeur) vote; **donner sa v. à qn** to vote for sb; **élu à la majorité des v.** elected by a majority; **mettre une question aux v.** to put a question to the vote (e) Gram (voice); **à la v. active/ passive** in the active/passive voice

vol¹ [vɔl] nm (a) (d'un oiseau, d'un avion) flight; **à trois heures de v. de Paris** three hours' flying time from Paris; **prendre son v.** to fly off; **en plein v.** mid-flight; **à v. d'oiseau** as the crow flies; **de haut v.** (escroc) big-time; (discipline) high-flying; **v. charter** charter flight; **v. intérieur** domestic or internal flight; **v. de nuit** night flight; **v. plané** glide; Fam Fig **faire un v. plané** to go flying (b) (nuée d'oiseaux) flock, flight

vol² nm (délit) theft, stealing; Fam **c'est du v.!** it's a rip-off!, it's daylight robbery!; **v. avec effraction** breaking and entering; **v. à l'étalage** shoplifting; **v. à main armée** armed robbery; **v. à la tire** pickpocketing

volage [vɔlaʒ] adj fickle, flighty

volaille [vɔlaj] *nf (oiseau)* fowl; **la v.** poultry

volant, -e [vɔlɑ̃, -ɑ̃t] **1** *adj* (a) *(qui vole)* flying; **personnel v.** flight crew (b) **gardien de but v.** rush goalkeeper
2 *nm* (a) *(d'une automobile)* (steering) wheel; **prendre le v.** to take the wheel; **je te recommande la prudence au v.** take care when driving (b) *(de badminton)* shuttlecock (c) *(d'une robe)* flounce (d) *(de carnet)* tear-off portion

volatil, -e[1] [vɔlatil] *adj* volatile

volatile[2] [vɔlatil] *nm aussi Hum* winged creature

volatiliser [vɔlatilize] **se volatiliser** *vpr* to vanish into thin air

vol-au-vent [vɔlovɑ̃] *nm inv* vol-au-vent

volcan [vɔlkɑ̃] *nm* volcano; *Fig (personne)* spitfire; *(situation)* volcano

volcanique [vɔlkanik] *adj (roche)* volcanic; *Fig (tempérament)* fiery

volcanologue [vɔlkanɔlɔg] *nmf* vulcanologist

volée [vɔle] *nf* (a) *(d'oiseaux)* flock, flight; *Fig (d'enfants)* swarm (b) *(au football, au tennis)* volley; **attraper une balle à la v.** to catch a ball in midair (c) *(de flèches)* flight; *Fam (de coups)* shower; *Fam* **recevoir une v.** to get a good thrashing (d) **sonner à toute v.** to ring out

voler[1] [vɔle] *vi (oiseau, avion)* to fly; **faire v. un cerf-volant** to fly a kite; *Fig* **v. de ses propres ailes** to stand on one's own two feet, to fend for oneself; *Fig* **v. au secours de qn** to go to sb's assistance

voler[2] *vt* (a) *(objet, argent)* to steal (**à** from); **se faire v. qch** to have sth stolen; *Fig* **il ne l'a pas volé** *(il le mérite)* he's earned it; *(c'est bien fait pour lui)* it serves him right; *Prov* **qui vole un œuf vole un bœuf** there's no such thing as a petty thief (b) *(personne)* to rob; *(léser)* to swindle, to cheat

volet [vɔlɛ] *nm* (a) *(de fenêtre, de magasin)* shutter (b) *(d'un dépliant)* page; *(d'un formulaire)* section; *Fig (d'un plan)* stage

voleter [42] [vɔlte] *vi* to flutter

voleur, -euse [vɔlœr, -øz] **1** *nm,f* thief; **au v.!** stop thief!
2 *adj (personne)* thieving; **être v.** to be a thief

Volga [vɔlga] *nf* **la V.** the Volga

volière [vɔljɛr] *nf* aviary

volley [vɔlɛ] *nm Fam* volleyball

volley-ball [vɔlɛbɔl] *nm* volleyball

volleyeur, -euse [vɔlɛjœr, -øz] *nm,f* (a) *(joueur de volley-ball)* volleyball player (b) *(au tennis)* volley player

volontaire [vɔlɔ̃tɛr] **1** *adj* (a) *(action, omission)* deliberate; *(travail)* voluntary (b) *(enfant)* wilful; *(menton, front)* determined
2 *nmf* volunteer

volontairement [vɔlɔ̃tɛrmɑ̃] *adv* (a) *(spontanément)* voluntarily (b) *(délibérément)* deliberately

volontariat [vɔlɔ̃tarja] *nm* (a) voluntary work (b) *(dans l'armée)* = voluntary service in the armed forces

volontarisme [vɔlɔ̃tarism] *nm* voluntarism

volontariste [vɔlɔ̃tarist] *adj* voluntarist

volonté [vɔlɔ̃te] *nf* (a) *(faculté)* will; **la v. de vaincre/de puissance** the will to win/for power; **de sa propre v.** of one's own accord; **avec la meilleure v. du monde** with the best will in the world; **à v.** at will; **vin à v.** *(dans un restaurant)* unlimited wine (b) *(détermination)* willpower; **avoir de la v.** to have willpower (c) **bonne v.** willingness; **mauvaise v.** unwillingness; **mettre de la mauvaise v. à faire qch** to do sth with bad grace

(d) *(souhait)* wish; **ses dernières volontés** his last wishes

volontiers [vɔlɔ̃tje] *adv (avec plaisir)* willingly, gladly; **v.!** I'd be glad to! (b) **être v. pessimiste/bavard** to be naturally pessimistic/chatty

volt [vɔlt] *nm* volt

voltage [vɔltaʒ] *nm* voltage

volte-face [vɔltəfas] *nf inv Br* about-turn, *Am* about-face; *Fig* U-turn; **faire v.** to turn round; *Fig* to do a U-turn

voltige [vɔltiʒ] *nf* (a) *(sur un cheval)* acrobatics on horseback; *(sur un trapèze)* acrobatics; **haute v.** flying tapeze acrobatics (b) *(acrobatie aérienne)* aerobatics

voltiger [vɔltiʒe] *vi* (a) *(sur un cheval)* to perform on horseback; *(sur un trapèze)* to perform on the trapeze (b) *(feuilles)* to flutter

volubile [vɔlybil] *adj* voluble

volubilité [vɔlybilite] *nf* volubility

volume [vɔlym] *nm* (a) *(livre)* volume (b) *(d'un solide, d'un fluide, des ventes)* volume (c) *(du son, de la voix)* volume; **baisser/monter le v.** to turn the volume down/up; **v. sonore** noise level

volumineux, -euse [vɔlyminø, -øz] *adj* voluminous, bulky

volupté [vɔlypte] *nf* sensual pleasure

voluptueusement [vɔlyptɥøzmɑ̃] *adv* voluptuously

voluptueux, -euse [vɔlyptɥø, -øz] *adj* voluptuous

volute [vɔlyt] *nf* (a) *(de fumée)* curl, wreath (b) *Archit* helix

vomi [vɔmi] *nm* vomit

vomir [vɔmir] **1** *vt* (a) *(aliment)* to vomit, to bring up (b) *(fumée, flammes)* to vomit, to belch forth; *Fig (injures)* to spew out (c) *Fig (détester)* to loathe
2 *vi* to be sick, to vomit; **avoir envie de v.** to feel sick

vomissement [vɔmismɑ̃] *nm (action)* vomiting; **avoir des vomissements** to vomit

vomitif, -ive [vɔmitif, -iv] *adj & nm* emetic

vont *voir* **aller**

vorace [vɔras] *adj* voracious

voracement [vɔrasmɑ̃] *adv* voraciously

voracité [vɔrasite] *nf* voracity

vortex [vɔrtɛks] *nm* vortex

vos [vo] *voir* **votre**

Vosges [voʒ] *nfpl* **les V.** the Vosges

votant, -e [vɔtɑ̃, -ɑ̃t] *nm,f* voter

vote [vɔt] *nm* (a) *(pour une élection)* vote; *(action)* voting; **v. à bulletin secret** secret ballot; **v. à main levée** vote by a show of hands; **v. par procuration** proxy vote; **v. de protestation** protest vote (b) *(d'une loi)* passing; **v. de confiance** vote of confidence

voter [vɔte] **1** *vi* to vote (**pour/contre** for/against); **v. à bulletin secret** to vote in a secret ballot; **v. à main levée** to vote by a show of hands; **v. par procuration** to vote by proxy
2 *vt* (a) *(loi)* to pass (b) *(crédit)* to vote

votre [vɔtr] *(pl* **vos** [vo]) *adj possessif* your; **v. chien** your dog; **vos enfants** your children; **v. père et v. mère** *(à une personne)* your mother and father; *(à plusieurs personnes)* your mothers and fathers; **un de vos amis** one of your friends, a friend of yours; *Fam* **vous avez v. vendredi** you've got Friday off

vôtre [votr] **1** *pron possessif* **le v., la v., les vôtres** yours; *(en insistant)* your own; **vous me prêtez le v.?** can I borrow yours?; **vous n'en avez pas besoin, vous avez le v.** you don't need it, you've got your own; *Fam* **à la v.!** cheers!

2 *nm* **il faut que vous y mettiez du v.** you should do your share

3 *nmpl* **les vôtres** *(votre famille)* your family; **je serai des vôtres ce soir** I'll be joining you tonight

voudra, voudrai *etc voir* **vouloir**

vouer [vwe] **1** *vt* (a) *(jurer)* to vow (à to) (b) *(consacrer)* to devote (à to) (c) **voué à l'échec** doomed to failure

2 se vouer *vpr* **se v. à qch** to devote oneself to sth

vouloir[1] [74] **1** *vt* (a) *(désirer)* to want; **rentrons, voulez-vous?** let's go in, shall we?; **si vous voulez** if you like; **faites comme vous voudrez** do what you like, do as you please; **que veut-tu que je fasse?** what do you want me to do?; **le mauvais sort voulut que...** as bad luck would have it,...; **v. faire qch** to want to do sth; **quand j'ai voulu l'embrasser** when I tried to kiss him; **faire qch sans le v.** to do sth unintentionally; **le moteur ne veut pas démarrer** the engine won't start; **j'aurais tant voulu la voir** I would really have liked to see her; *(pourquoi le cherchez-vous?)* what do you want from him?; *(pourquoi me cherchez-vous?)* what do you want him for?; **ne pas v. de qn/qch** not to want sb/sth; **je ne veux pas de ça chez moi** I won't have that in my house; **en v.** *(être accrocheur)* to be very determined; **en v. à qn** *(de qch/d'avoir fait qch)* to bear sb a grudge (for sth/for doing sth); **ils en veulent à mon argent** they're after my money

(b) *(dans les formules de politesse)* **veuillez vous asseoir** please sit down; **voulez-vous faire moins de bruit!** will you please make less noise!

(c) *(exiger)* **la coutume veut que...** + *subjunctive* custom dictates that...; **le règlement veut que...** + *subjunctive* the rules state that...

(d) *(locutions)* **je veux bien** *(volontiers)* with pleasure; *(j'admets)* granted, fair enough; **c'est comme ça, que veux-tu** that's the way it is, what can you do?; *Fam* **en veux-tu, en voilà** galore; **tu l'auras voulu!** if that's the way you want it!; **v. dire** to mean; *Fam* **je veux!** *(absolument)* absolutely!

2 se vouloir *vpr* **(a)** *(vouloir être)* **elle se veut différente** she likes to think she's different; **il se voulait rassurant** he was trying to be reassuring

(b) **s'en v. (de qch/de faire qch)** to be annoyed with oneself (about sth/for doing sth)

vouloir[2] [vulwar] *nm* will; **bon v.** goodwill; **mauvais v.** ill will

voulu, -e [vuly] **1** *pp voir* **vouloir**

2 *adj* (a) *(requis)* required (b) *(délibéré)* deliberate, intentional

vous [vu] *pron personnel* (a) *(sujet)* you; **v. deux/tous** both/all of you; **v. autres les intellectuels** you intellectuals; **v., v. auriez certainement refusé** you would probably have refused (b) *(objet direct)* you; **et v., on v. a servis?** and what about you, have you been served? (c) *(objet indirect)* you; **vous a-t-elle serré la main?** did she shake your hand?; **elle v. a jeté un regard furieux** she glared at you (d) *(réfléchi)* *(singulier)* yourself; *(pluriel)* yourselves; **taisez-v.!** be quiet! (e) *(réciproque)* each other (f) *(avec préposition)* you; **v. ne pensez qu'à v.** you think only of yourself; **je v. le montre, à v.?** shall I show it to you?; **cet argent n'est pas à v.** this money isn't yours; **v. aurez une chambre à**

v. you'll have your own room; *Fam* **une connaissance à v.** an acquaintance of yours (g) *(dans les comparaisons)* you; **elle est aussi surprise que v.** she's as surprised as you (are) (h) *(remplace 'on')* you

vous-même [vumɛm] *pron personnel* yourself

vous-mêmes [vumɛm] *pron personnel* yourselves

voûte [vut] *nf* (a) *(arche)* arch; **la v. céleste** the vault or canopy of heaven; **v. d'ogive** vault (b) *Anat* **v. du palais** roof of the mouth; **v. plantaire** arch (of the foot)

voûté, -e [vute] *adj* bent; **avoir le dos v.** to have a stoop

voûter [vute] **se voûter** *vpr* to become bent, to begin to stoop

vouvoiement [vuvwamɑ̃] *nm* = use of the formal "vous" instead of the more familiar "tu"; **le v. est de rigueur** everybody calls each other "vous"

vouvoyer [vuvwaje] **1** *vt* **v. qn** = to address sb as "vous"

2 se vouvoyer *vpr* = to address each other as "vous"

voyage [vwajaʒ] *nm* trip, journey; **être en v.** to be away; **partir en v.** to go on a trip; **bon v.!** have a good trip!; **v. d'affaires** business trip; **v. d'agrément** pleasure trip; **v. de noces** honeymoon; **v. organisé** package holiday *or* tour

voyager [vwajaʒe] *vi* to travel

voyageur, -euse [vwajaʒœr, -øz] *nm,f* traveller; *(passager)* passenger; **v. de commerce** commercial traveller, travelling salesman

voyagiste [vwajaʒist] *nmf* tour operator

voyais *etc voir* **voir**

voyance [vwajɑ̃s] *nf* clairvoyance

voyant, -e [vwajɑ̃, -ɑ̃t] **1** *adj* *(de mauvais goût)* loud, garish

2 *nm,f* *(extralucide)* clairvoyant

3 *nm* **v. (lumineux)** warning light; **v. d'huile/d'essence** oil/petrol indicator light

voyelle [vwajɛl] *nf* vowel

voyeur, -euse [vwajœr, -øz] *nm,f* voyeur, *f* voyeuse

voyeurisme [vwajœrism] *nm* voyeurism

voyez, voyons *etc voir* **voir**

voyou [vwaju] *nm* lout, hooligan

VPC [vepese] *nf (abrév* **vente par correspondance**) mail order (selling)

vrac [vrak] **en vrac** *adv* (a) *(sans emballage)* loose (b) *(en désordre)* higgledy-piggledy, in a jumble

vrai, -e [vrɛ] **1** *adj* (a) *(indéniable)* true; **c'est v.!** that's true!, that's right!; *Fam* **elle est gentille, pas v.?** she's nice, isn't she?; *Fam* **c'est pas v.!** you're joking! (b) *(véritable)* real; *(tableau, antiquité)* genuine; **il a été un v. père pour moi** he was like a father to me

2 *nm* **être dans le v.** to be right; **à v. dire, à dire v.** as a matter of fact, to tell the truth; *Fam* **pour de v.** for real

vraiment [vrɛmɑ̃] *adv* really

vraisemblable [vrɛsɑ̃blabl] *adj* probable, likely; *(crédible)* believable, credible; **il est v. qu'il sera là demain** he'll probably be there tomorrow

vraisemblablement [vrɛsɑ̃blabləmɑ̃] *adv* probably

vraisemblance [vrɛsɑ̃blɑ̃s] *nf* probability, likelihood; *(crédibilité)* credibility; **selon toute v.** in all probability

vrille [vrij] *nf* (a) *(de la vigne)* tendril (b) *(outil)* gimlet (c) *(en avion)* spin; **descendre en v.** to spin down

vrillé, -e [vrije] *adj* *(corde)* twisted

vriller [vrije] **1** *vt* to bore into

2 *vi* **(a)** *(avion)* to spin **(b)** *(corde)* to twist

vrombir [vrɔ̃bir] *vi* to hum

vrombissement [vrɔ̃bismɑ̃] *nm* hum, humming

VRP [veɛrpe] *nm* (*abrév* **voyageur représentant placier**) sales rep

VTT [vetete] *nm* (*abrév* **vélo tout terrain**) mountain bike

vu¹, -e [vy] **1** *pp voir* **voir**

2 *adj* **faire qch ni vu ni connu** to do sth without being seen

vu² **1** *prép* in view of; **vu que** seeing that

2 *nm* **au vu et au su de tout le monde** openly

vue [vy] *nf* **(a)** *(faculté de voir)* sight, eyesight; **perdre la v.** to lose one's sight; **avoir une bonne/mauvaise v.** to have good/bad eyesight **(b)** *(regard)* **connaître qn de v.** to know sb by sight; **hors de v.** out of sight; **hors de ma v.!** (get) out of my sight!; **une personnalité en v.** a prominent personality; **mettre qch en v.** to display sth prominently; **à v. d'œil** before one's eyes, visibly; *Fam* **à v. de nez** at a rough guess; *Fam* **en mettre plein la v. à qn** to dazzle sb **(c)** **seconde v.** second sight **(d)** *(opinion)* view; **c'est une v. de l'esprit** that's a very theoretical point of view **(e)** *(panorama)* view; **chambre avec v.** room with a view; *Fig* **v. d'ensemble** overall view **(f)** *(locutions)* **à la v. de qn/qch** at the sight of sb/sth; **à première v.** at first sight; **à v.** *(tirer)* on sight; *(voler)* visually; **avoir qch en v.** to have sth in mind; **en v. de qch/de faire qch** with a view to sth/to doing sth; **avoir des vues sur qn/qch** to have designs on sb/sth

vulgaire [vylgɛr] *adj* **(a)** *(grossier)* vulgar **(b)** *(courant)* common **(c)** *(quelconque)* ordinary, common

vulgairement [vylgɛrmɑ̃] *adv* **(a)** *(grossièrement)* vulgarly **(b)** *(communément)* commonly

vulgarisation [vylgarizasjɔ̃] *nf* popularization

vulgariser [vylgarize] *vt* to popularize

vulgarité [vylgarite] *nf* vulgarity

vulnérabilité [vylnerabilite] *nf* vulnerability

vulnérable [vylnerabl] *adj* vulnerable

vulve [vylv] *nf* vulva

W, w [dubləve] *nm inv* W, w

wagon [vagɔ̃] *nm* **(a)** *(de passagers)* *Br* carriage, *Am* car; *(de marchandises)* *Br* wagon, *Am* car; **w. à bagages** *Br* luggage van, *Am* baggage car; **w. à bestiaux** *Br* cattle truck, *Am* stock car; **w. frigorifique** refrigerated van; **w. de marchandises** *Br* goods wagon, *Am* freight car **(b)** *(contenu)* *Br* wagonload, *Am* carload (**de** of)

wagon-citerne (*pl* **wagons-citernes**) [vagɔ̃sitɛrn] *nm* tank *Br* wagon *or Am* car

wagon-lit (*pl* **wagons-lits**) [vagɔ̃li] *nm* sleeping car, sleeper

wagon-restaurant (*pl* **wagons-restaurants**) [vagɔ̃rɛstorɑ̃] *nm* dining *or* restaurant car

Walkman® [wokman] *nm* Walkman®

Wallis-et-Futuna [walisefutuna] *n* Wallis and Futuna Islands

wallon, -onne [walɔ̃, -ɔn] **1** *adj* Walloon

2 *nm,f* **W.** Walloon

3 *nm (langue)* Walloon

Wallonie [waloni] *nf* **la W.** = the south and south-east regions of Belgium, where French and Walloon are spoken

wapiti [wapiti] *nm* wapiti, American elk

Washington [waʃintɔn, waʃiŋtɔn] *n* Washington

water-polo [waterpolo] *nm* water polo

watt [wat] *nm* watt

W.-C. [vese, dubləvese] *nmpl* toilet

week-end (*pl* **week-ends**) [wikend] *nm* weekend; **partir en w.** to go away for the weekend

western [wɛstɛrn] *nm* western

whisky [wiski] *nm (écossais)* whisky; *(irlandais, américain)* whiskey

white-spirit [wajtspirit] *nm* white spirit

wysiwyg [wiziwig] *adj & nm Ordinat* WYSIWYG

X, x [iks] *nm inv* (a) *(lettre)* X, x (b) *(nombre ou personne inconnus)* X, x; **Monsieur X** Mr X; **x fois** umpteen times; **dans x années** in x number of years (c) *Fam* **Univ l'X =** "grande école" specializing in technology (d) *Cin* **film classé X** adults-only film

xénophobe [gsenɔfɔb] **1** *adj* xenophobic
2 *nmf* xenophobe

xénophobie [gsenɔfɔbi] *nf* xenophobia
xérès [gzeres, kseres] *nm (vin)* sherry
xylophone [ksilɔfɔn, gzilɔfɔn] *nm* xylophone
xylophoniste [gzilɔfɔnist] *nmf* xylophone player

Y, y¹ [igrek] *nm inv* Y, y

y² [i] **1** *adv* there; **n'y être pour personne** not to be in for anyone; **vous n'y êtes pas du tout** you're way off the mark; **pendant que tu y es, tu pourrais m'apporter...** while you're at it, you could bring me...
2 *pron* **j'y pense** I'm thinking about it; **il y croit** he believes in it/them; **elle s'y intéresse** she's interested in it/them; **elle y compte** she's counting on it; **je n'y suis pour rien** I've got nothing to do with it

yacht [jɔt] *nm* yacht
yachting [jɔtiŋ] *nm* yachting; **faire du y.** to go yachting
yaourt [jaurt] *nm* yoghurt; **y. maigre** low-fat yoghurt; **y. nature/aux fruits** plain *or* natural/fruit yoghurt
yaourtière [jaurtjer] *nf* yoghurt maker
Yémen [jemen] *nm* **le Y.** Yemen
yéménite [jemenit] **1** *adj* Yemeni
2 *nmf* **Y.** Yemeni
yen [jen] *nm* yen
yeux [jø] *voir* **œil**
yé-yé [jeje] *adj inv Vieilli (chanteur, groupe)* 60s style pop; *(mode)* 60s

yiddish [jidiʃ] *adj inv & nm* Yiddish
yoga [jɔga] *nm* yoga; **faire du y.** to do yoga
yoghourt [jogurt] **= yaourt**
yogi [jɔgi] *nm* yogi
yogourt [jogurt] **= yaourt**
Yom Kippour [jɔmkipur] *nm* Yom Kippur
yorkshire [jɔrkʃir], **yorkshire-terrier** *(pl* **yorkshire-terriers)** [jɔrkʃœrtɛrje] *nm* Yorkshire terrier
yougoslave [jugoslav] **1** *adj* Yugoslav, Yugoslavian
2 *nmf* **Y.** Yugoslav, Yugoslavian
Yougoslavie [jugoslavi] *nf* **la Y.** Yugoslavia; **l'ex-Y.** the former Yugoslavia
youpi [jupi] *exclam* yippee!
youyou [juju] *nm* dinghy
Yo-Yo® [jojo] *nm inv* yo-yo
yuan [juan] *nm* yuan
yucca [juka] *nm* yucca
Yukon [jukɔ̃] *nm* **le Y.** the Yukon

Z

Z, z [zɛd] *nm inv* Z, z

ZAC [zak] *nf* (*abrév* **zone d'aménagement concerté**) = area developed by the state and subsequently sold to the public or private sectors

ZAD [zad] *nf* (*abrév* **zone d'aménagement différé**) = area which the state has the priority to build on or sell

Zagreb [zagrɛb] *n* Zagreb

Zaïre [zair] *nm* le Z. Zaire

zaïrois, -e [zairwa, -az] **1** *adj* Zairean
  2 *nm,f* Z. Zairean

Zambie [zɑ̃bi] *nf* la Z. Zambia

zambien, -enne [zɑ̃bjɛ̃, -ɛn] **1** *adj* Zambian
  2 *nm,f* Z. Zambian

Zanzibar [zɑ̃zibar] *n* Zanzibar

zapper [zape] *vi* to zap, to channel-hop

zapping [zapiŋ] *nm* zapping, channel-hopping; **faire du z.** to zap, to channel-hop

zébré, -e [zebre] *adj* striped (**de** with)

zèbre [zɛbr] *nm* zebra; *Fam* **un drôle de z.** a strange character

zébrure [zebryr] *nf* streak; (*d'un zèbre, d'un tigre*) stripe; *Fig* (*cicatrice*) weal

zébu [zeby] *nm* zebu

zélateur, -trice [zelatœr, -tris] *nm,f* zealot

zélé, -e [zele] *adj* zealous

zèle [zɛl] *nm* zeal; **faire du z.** to be overzealous

zen [zɛn] *adj inv & nm* Zen

zénith [zenit] *nm* zenith; *aussi Fig* **être à son z.** to be at one's zenith

ZEP [zɛp] *nf* (*abrév* **zone d'éducation prioritaire**) = area targeted for special help in education

zéphyr [zefir] *nm* (*vent*) zephyr

zéro [zero] **1** *nm* (a) (*chiffre*) zero, *Br* nought; (*dans un numéro de téléphone*) *Br* o [əʊ], *Am* zero (b) (*note*) zero (c) *Fam* (*personne*) loser (d) (*au football*) **trois à z.** three nil; (*au tennis*) **trois sets à z.** three sets to love (e) (*dans une graduation*) zero; *Fam* **avoir le moral à z.** to be feeling really down; **repartir à z.** to go back to square one
  2 *adj* **z. degré Celsius** zero degrees Celsius; **z. faute** no mistakes; **z. heure** twelve (midnight)

zeste [zɛst] *nm* zest; **un z. de citron** a piece of lemon zest

zézaiement [zezemɑ̃] *nm* lisp

zézayer [zezeje] *vi* to lisp

ZI [zedi] *nf* (*abrév* **zone industrielle**) industrial estate

zibeline [ziblin] *nf* sable

zieuter [zjøte] = **zyeuter**

zigoto [zigoto] *nm Fam* **c'est un drôle de z.** he's quite a character; **faire le z.** to clown around

zigouiller [ziguje] *vt Fam* to do in

zigzag [zigzag] *nm* zigzag; **en z.** (*chemin*) zigzag; (*éclair*) forked; **faire des zigzags** (*route*) to zigzag; (*personne ivre*) to zigzag along; **marcher en z.** to walk in a zigzag

zigzaguer [zigzage] *vi* (*route*) to zigzag; (*personne ivre*) to zigzag along

Zimbabwe [zimbabwe] *nm* le Z. Zimbabwe

zimbabwéen, -enne [zimbabweɛ̃, -ɛn] **1** *adj* Zimbabwean
  2 *nm,f* Z. Zimbabwean

zinc [zɛ̃g] *nm* (a) (*métal*) zinc (b) *Fam* (*comptoir*) counter, bar (c) *Fam* (*avion*) plane

zinzin [zɛ̃zɛ̃] *Fam* **1** *adj* off one's rocker
  2 *nm* (*truc*) thingummy, whatsit

Zip® [zip] *nm Br* zip, *Am* zipper

zizanie [zizani] *nf* discord; **semer la z.** to sow discord

zizi [zizi] *nm* (*langage enfantin*) *Br* willy, *Am* peter

zloty [zloti] *nm* zloty

zodiaque [zodjak] *nm* le z. the zodiac

zombie [zɔ̃bi] *nm Fam* zombie

zona [zona] *nm* shingles (*singulier*); **avoir un z.** to have shingles

zonard, -e [zonar, -ard] *nm,f Fam* (*marginal*) dropout

zone [zon] *nf* (a) (*espace*) zone; **z. dangereuse** danger zone; **z. fumeurs/non-fumeurs** smoking/no-smoking area; **z. de haute pression** area of high pressure; **z. interdite** prohibited *or* restricted area; *Hist* **z. libre** French zone; *Hist* **z. occupée** occupied zone; **z. tempérée** temperate zone (b) *Péj* **de seconde z.** second-rate (c) *Fam Péj* **la z.** (*bidonville*) the slums; *Fig* **c'est la z.!** it's a dump! (c) *Ordinat* **z. de dialogue** dialogue box; **z. d'état** status box; **z. tampon** (*en mémoire*) (memory) buffer; **z. de travail** work area

zoner [zone] *vi Fam* to hang about

zoo [zo, zoo] *nm* zoo

zoologie [zoɔlɔʒi] *nf* zoology

zoologique [zoɔlɔʒik] *adj* zoological

zoologiste [zoɔlɔʒist], **zoologue** [zoɔlɔg] *nmf* zoologist

zoom [zum] *nm* (a) (*effet*) zoom (b) (*objectif*) zoom (lens)

zou [zu] *exclam Fam* **allez z.!** off you go!

zouave [zwav] *nm* (*soldat*) Zouave; *Fam* (*pitre*) fool; *Fam* **faire le z.** to play the fool

zoulou, -e [zulu] **1** *adj* Zulu
  2 *nm,f* Z. Zulu

zozoter [zozɔte] *vi Fam* to lisp

ZUP [zyp] *nf* (*abrév* **zone à urbaniser en priorité**) priority development area

Zurich [zyrik] *n* Zurich

zut [zyt] *exclam Fam* blast!; **et puis z.!** what the heck!

zyeuter [zjøte] *vt Fam* (*regarder*) (*discrètement*) to have a look *or Br* a dekko at; (*avec insistance*) to eye up

zygomatique [zigomatik] *adj* zygomatic